2023–2024 Edition

International Income Taxation

Code and Regulations
Selected Sections

As of May 15, 2023

Coordinating Editor

ROBERT J. PERONI
Fondren Foundation Centennial Chair
for Faculty Excellence and Professor of Law,
University of Texas

Contributing Editors

KAREN B. BROWN
Theodore Rinehart Professor of Business Law,
George Washington University

DIANE M. RING
Professor of Law and
Dr. Thomas F. Carney Distinguished Scholar,
Boston College Law School

Wolters Kluwer

Editorial Staff

Production .... Diana Roozeboom

ISBN 978-0-8080-5914-1

2700 Lake Cook Road
Riverwoods, IL 60015
800 344 3734
ShopTax.WoltersKluwer.com/en

Printed in the United States of America

FSC
MIX
FSC® C103993

Preface

This volume represents an effort to collect the principal Code sections relating to the United States taxation of the income from international trade and investment, both inbound and outbound. Also included are most of the significant final, temporary, and proposed regulations associated with these Code sections. The volume is intended to serve as a convenient reference tool for lawyers, accountants, teachers, students, and others who work in this area. The volume reflects the state of the law and regulations as of May 15, 2023. Suggestions from users as to additions and deletions that would increase the usefulness of the volume would be greatly appreciated. Please send any suggested changes to Professor Peroni at rperoni@law.utexas.edu.

This work, by request, is also available in electronic format to purchasers of this print title. Access is subject to the License Agreement set forth on the following page. Email your request, along with proof of purchase, to: CCHChannelSales@wolterskluwer.com.

Robert J. Peroni

Karen B. Brown

Diane M. Ring

May 2023

LICENSE AGREEMENT FOR ELECTRONIC FILES TO ACCOMPANY

International Income Taxation Code & Regulations Selected Sections

Contents

CHAINED CONSUMER PRICE INDEX ADJUSTMENTS FOR 2023

Certain dollar amounts stated in the Internal Revenue Code are adjusted for inflation each year, based on changes in the Chained Consumer Price Index for all-urban consumers (C-CPI), published by the United States Department of Labor. The following revenue procedure contains the inflation adjustments for the Section 1 tax rates (including the maximum capital gains rates) included in this volume, for taxable years starting in 2023. The other inflation adjustments relevant to this volume are set forth in the Caution lines preceding the pertinent Code Sections.

Revenue Procedure 2022-38, 2022-45 I.R.B. 445

* * *

SECTION 1. PURPOSE

This revenue procedure sets forth inflation-adjusted items for 2023 for various Code provisions as in effect on October 18, 2022. The inflation adjusted items for the Code sections set forth in section 3 of this revenue procedure are generally determined by reference to § 1(f) of the Code. * * *

* * *

SECTION 3. 2023 ADJUSTED ITEMS

.01 *Tax Rate Tables*. For taxable years beginning in 2023, the tax rate tables under § 1 are as follows:

TABLE 1 - Section 1(j)(2)(A) - Married Individuals Filing Joint Returns and Surviving Spouses

If Taxable Income Is:	*The Tax Is:*
Not over $22,000	10% of the taxable income
Over $22,000 but not over $89,450	$2,200 plus 12% of the excess over $22,000
Over $89,450 but not over $190,750	$10,294 plus 22% of the excess over $89,450
Over $190,750 but not over $364,200	$32,580 plus 24% of the excess over $190,750
Over $364,200 but not over $462,500	$74,208 plus 32% of the excess over $364,200
Over $462,500 but not over $693,750	$105,664 plus 35% of the excess over $462,500
Over $693,750	$186,601.50 plus 37% of the excess over $693,750

TABLE 2 - Section 1(j)(2)(B) – Heads of Households

If Taxable Income Is:	*The Tax Is:*
Not over $15,700	10% of the taxable income
Over $15,700 but not over $59,850	$1,570 plus 12% of the excess over $15,700
Over $59,850 but not over $95,350	$6,868 plus 22% of the excess over $59,850
Over $95,350 but not over $182,100	$14,678 plus 24% of the excess over $95,350
Over $182,100 but not over $231,250	$35,498 plus 32% of the excess over $182,100
Over $231,250 but not over $578,100	$51,226 plus 35% of the excess over $231,250
Over $578,100	$172,623.50 plus 37% of the excess over $578,100

TABLE 3 - Section 1(j)(2)(C) – Unmarried Individuals (other than Surviving Spouses and Heads of Households)

If Taxable Income Is:	*The Tax Is:*
Not over $11,000	10% of the taxable income
Over $11,000 but not over $44,725	$1,100 plus 12% of the excess over $11,000
Over $44,725 but not over $95,375	$5,147 plus 22% of the excess over $44,725
Over $95,375 but not over $182,100	$16,290 plus 24% of the excess over $95,375
Over $182,100 but not over $231,250	$37,104 plus 32% of the excess over $182,100
Over $231,250 but not over $578,125	$52,832 plus 35% of the excess over $231,250
Over $578,125	$174,238.25 plus 37% of the excess over $578,125

TABLE 4 - Section 1(j)(2)(D) – Married Individuals Filing Separate Returns

If Taxable Income Is:	*The Tax Is:*
Not over $11,000	10% of the taxable income
Over $11,000 but not over $44,725	$1,100 plus 12% of the excess over $11,000
Over $44,725 but not over $95,375	$5,147 plus 22% of the excess over $44,725
Over $95,375 but not over $182,100	$16,290 plus 24% of the excess over $95,375
Over $182,100 but not over $231,250	$37,104 plus 32% of the excess over $182,100
Over $231,250 but not over $346,875	$52,832 plus 35% of the excess over $231,250
Over $346,875	$93,300.75 plus 37% of the excess over $346,875

TABLE 5 - Section 1(j)(2)(E) – Estates and Trusts

If Taxable Income Is:	*The Tax Is:*
Not over $2,900	10% of the taxable income
Over $2,900 but not over $10,550	$290 plus 24% of the excess over $2,900
Over $10,550 but not over $14,450	$2,126 plus 35% of the excess over $10,550
Over $14,450	$3,491 plus 37% of the excess over $14,450

* * *

.03 *Maximum Capital Gains Rate (§ 1(h), § 1(j)(5))*. For taxable years beginning in 2023, the maximum zero rate amounts and maximum 15 percent rate amounts under § 1(j)(5)(B) are as follows:

Filing Status	*Maximum Zero Rate Amount*	*Maximum 15% Rate Amount*
Married Individuals Filing Joint Returns and Surviving Spouse	$89,250	$553,850
Married Individuals Filing Separate Returns	$44,625	$276,900
Heads of Household	$59,750	$523,050
All Other Individuals	$44,625	$492,300
Estates and Trusts	$3,000	$14,650

* * *

.11 *Exemption Amounts for Alternative Minimum Tax*. For taxable years beginning in 2023, the exemption amounts under § 55(d)(1) are:

Joint Returns or Surviving Spouses	$126,500
Unmarried Individuals (other than Surviving Spouses)	$81,300
Married Individuals Filing Separate Returns	$63,250
Estates and Trusts	$28,400

For taxable years beginning in 2023, under § 55(b)(1), the excess taxable income above which the 28 percent tax rate applies is:

Married Individuals Filing Separate Returns	$110,350
All Other Taxpayers	$220,700

For taxable years beginning in 2023, the amounts used under § 55(d)(2) to determine the phaseout of the exemption amounts are:

	Threshold Phaseout amount	*Complete Phaseout amount*
Joint Returns or Surviving Spouses	$1,156,300	$1,662,300
Unmarried Individuals (other than Surviving Spouses)	$578,150	$903,350
Married Individuals Filing Separate Returns	$578,150	$831,150
Estates and Trusts	$94,600	$208,200

* * *

SECTION 4. EFFECTIVE DATE

.01 *General Rule*. Except as provided in section 4.02 of this revenue procedure, this revenue procedure applies to taxable years beginning in 2023.

.02 *Calendar Year Rule*. This revenue procedure applies to transactions or events occurring in calendar year 2023 for purposes of section[] * * * 3.37 (expatriation to avoid taxes) * * *.

* * *

Internal Revenue Code

INTERNAL REVENUE CODE OF 1986

SUBTITLE A—INCOME TAXES

CHAPTER 1—NORMAL TAXES AND SURTAXES

SUBCHAPTER A—DETERMINATION OF TAX LIABILITY

PART I—TAX ON INDIVIDUALS

»»→ Caution: As provided in Sections 1(f) and (j)(3), the income brackets set forth in Sections 1(a) and (j)(2) are adjusted for taxable years beginning after 2018 to reflect the increases in the Chained Consumer Price Index. As provided in Section 1(j)(5)(C), the dollar amounts set forth in Section 1(j)(5)(B) are adjusted for taxable years after 2018 to reflect increases in the Chained Consumer Price Index. The adjusted amounts that apply to taxable years beginning in 2023 are provided at page vii.

[Sec. 1]

SECTION 1. TAX IMPOSED.

[Sec. 1(a)]

(a) MARRIED INDIVIDUALS FILING JOINT RETURNS AND SURVIVING SPOUSES.—There is hereby imposed on the taxable income of—

(1) every married individual (as defined in section 7703) who makes a single return jointly with his spouse under section 6013, and

(2) every surviving spouse (as defined in section 2(a)),

a tax determined in accordance with the following table:

If taxable income is:	*The tax is:*
Not over $36,900	*15% of taxable income.*
Over $36,900 but not over $89,150	*$5,535, plus 28% of the excess over $36,900.*
Over $89,150 but not over $140,000	*$20,165, plus 31% of the excess over $89,150.*
Over $140,000 but not over $250,000	*$35,928.50, plus 36% of the excess over $140,000.*
Over $250,000	*$75,528.50, plus 39.6% of the excess over $250,000.*

[Sec. 1(b)]

(b) HEADS OF HOUSEHOLDS.—There is hereby imposed on the taxable income of every head of a household (as defined in section 2(b)) a tax determined in accordance with the following table:

If taxable income is:	*The tax is:*
Not over $29,600	*15% of taxable income.*
Over $29,600 but not over $76,400	*$4,440, plus 28% of the excess over $29,600.*
Over $76,400 but not over $127,500	*$17,544, plus 31% of the excess over $76,400.*
Over $127,500 but not over $250,000	*$33,385, plus 36% of the excess over $127,500.*
Over $250,000	*$77,485, plus 39.6% of the excess over $250,000.*

[Sec. 1(c)]

(c) UNMARRIED INDIVIDUALS (OTHER THAN SURVIVING SPOUSES AND HEADS OF HOUSEHOLDS).—There is hereby imposed on the taxable income of every individual (other than a surviving spouse as defined in section 2(a) or the head of a household as defined in section 2(b)) who is not a married individual (as defined in section 7703) a tax determined in accordance with the following table:

If taxable income is:	*The tax is:*
Not over $22,100	*15% of taxable income.*
Over $22,100 but not over $53,500	*$3,315, plus 28% of the excess over $22,100.*
Over $53,500 but not over $115,000	*$12,107, plus 31% of the excess over $53,500.*
Over $115,000 but not over $250,000	*$31,172, plus 36% of the excess over $115,000.*
Over $250,000	*$79,772, plus 39.6% of the excess over $250,000.*

[Sec. 1(d)]

(d) MARRIED INDIVIDUALS FILING SEPARATE RETURNS.—There is hereby imposed on the taxable income of every married individual (as defined in section 7703) who does not make a single return jointly with his spouse under section 6013, a tax determined in accordance with the following table:

If taxable income is:	*The tax is:*
Not over $18,450	*15% of taxable income.*
Over $18,450 but not over $44,575	*$2,767.50, plus 28% of the excess over $18,450.*
Over $44,575 but not over $70,000	*$10,082.50, plus 31% of the excess over $44,575.*
Over $70,000 but not over $125,000	*$17,964.25, plus 36% of the excess over $70,000.*
Over $125,000	*$37,764.25, plus 39.6% of the excess over $125,000.*

[Sec. 1(e)]

(e) ESTATES AND TRUSTS.—There is hereby imposed on the taxable income of—

(1) every estate, and

(2) every trust,

taxable under this subsection a tax determined in accordance with the following table:

If taxable income is:	*The tax is:*
Not over $1,500	*15% of taxable income.*
Over $1,500 but not over $3,500	*$225, plus 28% of the excess over $1,500.*
Over $3,500 but not over $5,500	*$785, plus 31% of the excess over $3,500.*
Over $5,500 but not over $7,500	*$1,405, plus 36% of the excess over $5,500.*
Over $7,500	*$2,125, plus 39.6% of the excess over $7,500.*

[Sec. 1(f)]

(f) PHASEOUT OF MARRIAGE PENALTY IN 15-PERCENT BRACKET; ADJUSTMENTS IN TAX TABLES SO THAT INFLATION WILL NOT RESULT IN TAX INCREASES.—

(1) IN GENERAL.—Not later than December 15 of 1993, and each subsequent calendar year, the Secretary shall prescribe tables which shall apply in lieu of the tables contained in subsections (a), (b), (c), (d), and (e) with respect to taxable years beginning in the succeeding calendar year.

(2) METHOD OF PRESCRIBING TABLES.—The table which under paragraph (1) is to apply in lieu of the table contained in subsection (a), (b), (c), (d), or (e), as the case may be, with respect to taxable years beginning in any calendar year shall be prescribed—

(A) except as provided in paragraph (8), by increasing the minimum and maximum dollar amounts for each bracket for which a tax is imposed under such table by the cost-of-living adjustment for such calendar year, determined—

(i) except as provided in clause (ii), by substituting "1992" for "2016" in paragraph (3)(A)(ii), and

(ii) in the case of adjustments to the dollar amounts at which the 36 percent rate bracket begins or at which the 39.6 percent rate bracket begins, by substituting "1993" for "2016" in paragraph (3)(A)(ii),

(B) by not changing the rate applicable to any rate bracket as adjusted under subparagraph (A), and

(C) by adjusting the amounts setting forth the tax to the extent necessary to reflect the adjustments in the rate brackets.

(3) COST-OF-LIVING ADJUSTMENT.—For purposes of this subsection—

(A) IN GENERAL.—The cost-of-living adjustment for any calendar year is the percentage (if any) by which—

(i) the C-CPI-U for the preceding calendar year, exceeds

(ii) the CPI for calendar year 2016, multiplied by the amount determined under subparagraph (B).

(B) AMOUNT DETERMINED.—The amount determined under this clause is the amount obtained by dividing—

(i) the C-CPI-U for calendar year 2016, by

(ii) the CPI for calendar year 2016.

(C) SPECIAL RULE FOR ADJUSTMENTS WITH A BASE YEAR AFTER 2016.—For purposes of any provision of this title which provides for the substitution of a year after 2016 for "2016" in subparagraph (A)(ii), subparagraph (A) shall be applied by substituting "the C-CPI-U for calendar year 2016" for "the CPI for calendar year 2016" and all that follows in clause (ii) thereof.

(4) CPI FOR ANY CALENDAR YEAR.—For purposes of paragraph (3), the CPI for any calendar year is the average of the Consumer Price Index as of the close of the 12-month period ending on August 31 of such calendar year.

(5) CONSUMER PRICE INDEX.—For purposes of paragraph (4), the term "Consumer Price Index" means the last Consumer Price Index for all-urban consumers published by the Department of Labor. For purposes of the preceding sentence, the revision of the Consumer Price Index which is most consistent with the Consumer Price Index for calendar year 1986 shall be used.

(6) C-CPI-U.—For purposes of this subsection—

(A) IN GENERAL.—The term "C-CPI-U" means the Chained Consumer Price Index for All Urban Consumers (as published by the Bureau of Labor Statistics of the Department of Labor). The values of the Chained Consumer Price Index for All Urban Consumers taken into account for purposes of determining the cost-of-living adjustment for any calendar year under this subsection shall be the latest values so published as of the date on which such Bureau publishes the initial value of the Chained Consumer Price Index for All Urban Consumers for the month of August for the preceding calendar year.

(B) DETERMINATION FOR CALENDAR YEAR.—The C-CPI-U for any calendar year is the average of the C-CPI-U as of the close of the 12-month period ending on August 31 of such calendar year.

(7) ROUNDING.—

(A) IN GENERAL.—If any increase determined under paragraph (2)(A), section 63(c)(4), section 68(b)(2) or section 151(d)(4) is not a multiple of $50, such increase shall be rounded to the next lowest multiple of $50.

(B) TABLE FOR MARRIED INDIVIDUALS FILING SEPARATELY.—In the case of a married individual filing a separate return, subparagraph (A) (other than with respect to sections 63(c)(4) and 151(d)(4)(A)) shall be applied by substituting "$25" for "$50" each place it appears.

(8) ELIMINATION OF MARRIAGE PENALTY IN 15-PERCENT BRACKET.—With respect to taxable years beginning after December 31, 2003, in prescribing the tables under paragraph (1)—

(A) the maximum taxable income in the 15-percent rate bracket in the table contained in subsection (a) (and the minimum taxable income in the next higher taxable income bracket in such table) shall be 200 percent of the maximum taxable income in the 15-percent rate bracket in the table contained in subsection (c) (after any other adjustment under this subsection), and

(B) the comparable taxable income amounts in the table contained in subsection (d) shall be 1/2 of the amounts determined under subparagraph (A).

***

[Sec. 1(h)]

(h) MAXIMUM CAPITAL GAINS RATE.—

(1) IN GENERAL.—If a taxpayer has a net capital gain for any taxable year, the tax imposed by this section for such taxable year shall not exceed the sum of—

(A) a tax computed at the rates and in the same manner as if this subsection had not been enacted on the greater of—

(i) taxable income reduced by the net capital gain, or

(ii) the lesser of—

(I) the amount of taxable income taxed at a rate below 25 percent; or

(II) taxable income reduced by the adjusted net capital gain;

(B) 0 percent of so much of the adjusted net capital gain (or, if less, taxable income) as does not exceed the excess (if any) of—

(i) the amount of taxable income which would (without regard to this paragraph) be taxed at a rate below 25 percent, over

(ii) the taxable income reduced by the adjusted net capital gain;

(C) 15 percent of the lesser of—

(i) so much of the adjusted net capital gain (or, if less, taxable income) as exceeds the amount on which a tax is determined under subparagraph (B), or

(ii) the excess of—

(I) the amount of taxable income which would (without regard to this paragraph) be taxed at a rate below 39.6 percent, over

(II) the sum of the amounts on which a tax is determined under subparagraphs (A) and (B),

(D) 20 percent of the adjusted net capital gain (or, if less, taxable income) in excess of the sum of the amounts on which tax is determined under subparagraphs (B) and (C),

(E) 25 percent of the excess (if any) of—

(i) the unrecaptured section 1250 gain (or, if less, the net capital gain (determined without regard to paragraph (11))), over

(ii) the excess (if any) of—

(I) the sum of the amount on which tax is determined under subparagraph (A) plus the net capital gain, over

(II) taxable income; and

(F) 28 percent of the amount of taxable income in excess of the sum of the amounts on which tax is determined under the preceding subparagraphs of this paragraph.

(2) NET CAPITAL GAIN TAKEN INTO ACCOUNT AS INVESTMENT INCOME.—For purposes of this subsection, the net capital gain for any taxable year shall be reduced (but not below zero) by the amount which the taxpayer takes into account as investment income under section 163(d)(4)(B)(iii).

(3) ADJUSTED NET CAPITAL GAIN.—For purposes of this subsection, the term "adjusted net capital gain" means the sum of—

(A) net capital gain (determined without regard to paragraph (11)) reduced (but not below zero) by the sum of—

(i) unrecaptured section 1250 gain, and

(ii) 28-percent rate gain, plus

(B) qualified dividend income (as defined in paragraph (11)).

(4) 28-PERCENT RATE GAIN.—For purposes of this subsection, the term "28-percent rate gain" means the excess (if any) of—

(A) the sum of—

(i) collectibles gain; and

(ii) section 1202 gain, over

(B) the sum of—

(i) collectibles loss;

(ii) the net short-term capital loss, and

(iii) the amount of long-term capital loss carried under section 1212(b)(1)(B) to the taxable year.

(5) COLLECTIBLES GAIN AND LOSS.—For purposes of this subsection—

(A) IN GENERAL.—The terms "collectibles gain" and "collectibles loss" mean gain or loss (respectively) from the sale or exchange of a collectible (as defined in section 408(m) without regard to paragraph (3) thereof) which is a capital asset held for more than 1 year but only to the extent such gain is taken into account in computing gross income and such loss is taken into account in computing taxable income.

(B) PARTNERSHIPS, ETC.—For purposes of subparagraph (A), any gain from the sale of an interest in a partnership, S corporation, or trust which is attributable to unrealized appreciation in the value of collectibles shall be treated as gain from the sale or exchange of a collectible. Rules similar to the rules of section 751 shall apply for purposes of the preceding sentence.

(6) UNRECAPTURED SECTION 1250 GAIN.—For purposes of this subsection—

(A) IN GENERAL.—The term "unrecaptured section 1250 gain" means the excess (if any) of—

(i) the amount of long-term capital gain (not otherwise treated as ordinary income) which would be treated as ordinary income if section 1250(b)(1) included all depreciation and the applicable percentage under section 1250(a) were 100 percent, over

(ii) the excess (if any) of—

(I) the amount described in paragraph (4)(B); over

(II) the amount described in paragraph (4)(A).

(B) LIMITATION WITH RESPECT TO SECTION 1231 PROPERTY.—The amount described in subparagraph (A)(i) from sales, exchanges, and conversions described in section 1231(a)(3)(A) for any taxable year shall not exceed the net section 1231 gain (as defined in section 1231(c)(3)) for such year.

(7) SECTION 1202 GAIN.—For purposes of this subsection, the term "section 1202 gain" means the excess of—

(A) the gain which would be excluded from gross income under section 1202 but for the percentage limitation in section 1202(a), over

(B) the gain excluded from gross income under section 1202.

(8) COORDINATION WITH RECAPTURE OF NET ORDINARY LOSSES UNDER SECTION 1231.—If any amount is treated as ordinary income under section 1231(c), such amount shall be allocated among the separate categories of net section 1231 gain (as defined in section 1231(c)(3)) in such manner as the Secretary may by forms or regulations prescribe.

(9) REGULATIONS.—The Secretary may prescribe such regulations as are appropriate (including regulations requiring reporting) to apply this subsection in the case of sales and exchanges by pass-thru entities and of interests in such entities.

(10) PASS-THRU ENTITY DEFINED.—For purposes of this subsection, the term "pass-thru entity" means—

(A) a regulated investment company;

(B) a real estate investment trust;

(C) an S corporation;

(D) a partnership;

(E) an estate or trust;

(F) a common trust fund; and

(G) a qualified electing fund (as defined in section 1295).

(11) DIVIDENDS TAXED AS NET CAPITAL GAIN.—

(A) IN GENERAL.—For purposes of this subsection, the term "net capital gain" means net capital gain (determined without regard to this paragraph) increased by qualified dividend income.

(B) QUALIFIED DIVIDEND INCOME.—For purposes of this paragraph—

(i) IN GENERAL.—The term "qualified dividend income" means dividends received during the taxable year from—

(I) domestic corporations, and

(II) qualified foreign corporations.

(ii) CERTAIN DIVIDENDS EXCLUDED.—Such term shall not include—

(I) any dividend from a corporation which for the taxable year of the corporation in which the distribution is made, or the preceding taxable year, is a corporation exempt from tax under section 501 or 521,

(II) any amount allowed as a deduction under section 591 (relating to deduction for dividends paid by mutual savings banks, etc.), and

(III) any dividend described in section 404(k).

***

(C) QUALIFIED FOREIGN CORPORATIONS.—

(i) IN GENERAL.—Except as otherwise provided in this paragraph, the term "qualified foreign corporation" means any foreign corporation if—

(I) such corporation is incorporated in a possession of the United States, or

(II) such corporation is eligible for benefits of a comprehensive income tax treaty with the United States which the Secretary determines is satisfactory for purposes of this paragraph and which includes an exchange of information program.

(ii) DIVIDENDS ON STOCK READILY TRADABLE ON UNITED STATES SECURITIES MARKET.—A foreign corporation not otherwise treated as a qualified foreign corporation under clause (i) shall be so treated with respect to any dividend paid by such corporation if the stock with respect to which such dividend is paid is readily tradable on an established securities market in the United States.

(iii) EXCLUSION OF DIVIDENDS OF CERTAIN FOREIGN CORPORATIONS.—Such term shall not include—

(I) any foreign corporation which for the taxable year of the corporation in which the dividend was paid, or the preceding taxable year, is a passive foreign investment company (as defined in section 1297), and

(II) any corporation which first becomes a surrogate foreign corporation (as defined in section 7874(a)(2)(B)) after the date of the enactment of this subclause, other than a foreign corporation which is treated as a domestic corporation under section 7874(b).

(iv) COORDINATION WITH FOREIGN TAX CREDIT LIMITATION.—Rules similar to the rules of section 904(b)(2)(B) shall apply with respect to the dividend rate differential under this paragraph.

***

[Sec. 1(i)]

(i) RATE REDUCTIONS AFTER 2000.—

(1) 10-PERCENT RATE BRACKET.—

(A) IN GENERAL.—In the case of taxable years beginning after December 31, 2000—

(i) the rate of tax under subsections (a), (b), (c), and (d) on taxable income not over the initial bracket amount shall be 10 percent, and

(ii) the 15 percent rate of tax shall apply only to taxable income over the initial bracket amount but not over the maximum dollar amount for the 15-percent rate bracket.

(B) INITIAL BRACKET AMOUNT.—For purposes of this paragraph, the initial bracket amount is—

(i) $14,000 in the case of subsection (a),

(ii) $10,000 in the case of subsection (b), and

(iii) 1/2 the amount applicable under clause (i) (after adjustment, if any, under subparagraph (C)) in the case of subsections (c) and (d).

(C) INFLATION ADJUSTMENT.—In prescribing the tables under subsection (f) which apply with respect to taxable years beginning in calendar years after 2003—

(i) the cost-of-living adjustment shall be determined under subsection (f)(3) by substituting "2002" for "2016" in subparagraph (A)(ii) thereof, and

(ii) the adjustments under clause (i) shall not apply to the amount referred to in subparagraph (B)(iii).

If any amount after adjustment under the preceding sentence is not a multiple of $50, such amount shall be rounded to the next lowest multiple of $50.

(2) 25-, 28-, AND 33-PERCENT RATE BRACKETS.—The tables under subsections (a), (b), (c), (d), and (e) shall be applied—

(A) by substituting "25%" for "28%" each place it appears (before the application of subparagraph (B)),

(B) by substituting "28%" for "31%" each place it appears, and

(C) by substituting "33%" for "36%" each place it appears.

(3) MODIFICATIONS TO INCOME TAX BRACKETS FOR HIGH-INCOME TAXPAYERS.—

(A) 35-PERCENT RATE BRACKET.—In the case of taxable years beginning after December 31, 2012—

(i) the rate of tax under subsections (a), (b), (c), and (d) on a taxpayer's taxable income in the highest rate bracket shall be 35 percent to the extent such income does not exceed an amount equal to the excess of—

(I) the applicable threshold, over

(II) the dollar amount at which such bracket begins, and

(ii) the 39.6 percent rate of tax under such subsections shall apply only to the taxpayer's taxable income in such bracket in excess of the amount to which clause (i) applies.

(B) APPLICABLE THRESHOLD.—For purposes of this paragraph, the term "applicable threshold" means—

(i) $450,000 in the case of subsection (a),

(ii) $425,000 in the case of subsection (b),

(iii) $400,000 in the case of subsection (c), and

(iv) 1/2 the amount applicable under clause (i) (after adjustment, if any, under subparagraph (C)) in the case of subsection (d).

(C) INFLATION ADJUSTMENT.—For purposes of this paragraph, with respect to taxable years beginning in calendar years after 2013, each of the dollar amounts under clauses (i), (ii), and (iii) of subparagraph (B) shall be adjusted in the same manner as under paragraph (1)(C)(i), except that subsection (f)(3)(A)(ii) shall be applied by substituting "2012" for "2016".

(4) ADJUSTMENT OF TABLES.—The Secretary shall adjust the tables prescribed under subsection (f) to carry out this subsection.

[Sec. 1(j)]

(j) MODIFICATIONS FOR TAXABLE YEARS 2018 THROUGH 2025.—

(1) IN GENERAL.—In the case of a taxable year beginning after December 31, 2017, and before January 1, 2026—

(A) subsection (i) shall not apply, and

(B) this section (other than subsection (i)) shall be applied as provided in paragraphs (2) through (6).

(2) RATE TABLES.—

(A) MARRIED INDIVIDUALS FILING JOINT RETURNS AND SURVIVING SPOUSES.—The following table shall be applied in lieu of the table contained in subsection (a):

If taxable income is:	The tax is:
Not over $19,050	10% of taxable income.
Over $19,050 but not over $77,400	$1,905, plus 12% of the excess over $19,050.
Over $77,400 but not over $165,000	$8,907, plus 22% of the excess over $77,400.
Over $165,000 but not over $315,000	$28,179, plus 24% of the excess over $165,000.
Over $315,000 but not over $400,000	$64,179, plus 32% of the excess over $315,000.
Over $400,000 but not over $600,000	$91,379, plus 35% of the excess over $400,000.
Over $600,000	$161,379 plus 37% of the excess over $600,000.

(B) HEADS OF HOUSEHOLDS.—The following table shall be applied in lieu of the table contained in subsection (b):

If taxable income is:	The tax is:
Not over $13,600	10% of taxable income.
Over $13,600 but not over $51,800	$1,360, plus 12% of the excess over $13,600.
Over $51,800 but not over $82,500	$5,944, plus 22% of the excess over $51,800.
Over $82,500 but not over $157,500	$12,698, plus 24% of the excess over $82,500.
Over $157,500 but not over $200,000	$30,698, plus 32% of the excess over $157,500.
Over $200,000 but not over $500,000	$44,298, plus 35% of the excess over $200,000.
Over $500,000	$149,298, plus 37% of the excess over $500,000.

(C) UNMARRIED INDIVIDUALS OTHER THAN SURVIVING SPOUSES AND HEADS OF HOUSEHOLDS.—The following table shall be applied in lieu of the table contained in subsection (c):

If taxable income is:	The tax is:
Not over $9,525	10% of taxable income.
Over $9,525 but not over $38,700	$952.50, plus 12% of the excess over $9,525.
Over $38,700 but not over $82,500	$4,453.50, plus 22% of the excess over $38,700.
Over $82,500 but not over $157,500	$14,089.50, plus 24% of the excess over $82,500.
Over $157,500 but not over $200,000	$32,089.50, plus 32% of the excess over $157,500.
Over $200,000 but not over $500,000	$45,689.50, plus 35% of the excess over $200,000.
Over $500,000	$150,689.50, plus 37% of the excess over $500,000.

(D) MARRIED INDIVIDUALS FILING SEPARATE RETURNS.—The following table shall be applied in lieu of the table contained in subsection (d):

If taxable income is:	The tax is:
Not over $9,525	10% of taxable income.
Over $9,525 but not over $38,700	$952.50, plus 12% of the excess over $9,525.
Over $38,700 but not over $82,500	$4,453.50, plus 22% of the excess over $38,700.
Over $82,500 but not over $157,500	$14,089.50, plus 24% of the excess over $82,500.
Over $157,500 but not over $200,000	$32,089.50, plus 32% of the excess over $157,500.
Over $200,000 but not over $300,000	$45,689.50, plus 35% of the excess over $200,000.
Over $300,000	$80,689.50, plus 37% of the excess over $300,000.

(E) ESTATES AND TRUSTS.—The following table shall be applied in lieu of the table contained in subsection (e):

If taxable income is:	The tax is:
Not over $2,550	10% of taxable income.
Over $2,550 but not over $9,150	$255, plus 24% of the excess over $2,550.
Over $9,150 but not over $12,500	$1,839, plus 35% of the excess over $9,150.
Over $12,500	$3,011.50, plus 37% of the excess over $12,500.

(F) REFERENCES TO RATE TABLES.—Any reference in this title to a rate of tax under subsection (c) shall be treated as a reference to the corresponding rate bracket under subparagraph (C) of this paragraph, except that the reference in section 3402(q)(1) to the third lowest rate of tax applicable under subsection (c) shall be treated as a reference to the fourth lowest rate of tax under subparagraph (C).

(3) ADJUSTMENTS.—

(A) NO ADJUSTMENT IN 2018.—The tables contained in paragraph (2) shall apply without adjustment for taxable years beginning after December 31, 2017, and before January 1, 2019.

(B) SUBSEQUENT YEARS.—For taxable years beginning after December 31, 2018, the Secretary shall prescribe tables which shall apply in lieu of the tables contained in paragraph (2) in the same manner as under paragraphs (1) and (2) of subsection (f) (applied without regard to clauses (i) and (ii) of subsection (f)(2)(A)), except that in prescribing such tables—

(i) subsection (f)(3) shall be applied by substituting "calendar year 2017" for "calendar year 2016" in subparagraph (A)(ii) thereof,

(ii) subsection (f)(7)(B) shall apply to any unmarried individual other than a surviving spouse or head of household, and

(iii) subsection (f)(8) shall not apply.

(4) [Stricken.]

(5) APPLICATION OF CURRENT INCOME TAX BRACKETS TO CAPITAL GAINS BRACKETS.—

(A) IN GENERAL.—Section 1(h)(1) shall be applied—

(i) by substituting "below the maximum zero rate amount" for "which would (without regard to this paragraph) be taxed at a rate below 25 percent" in subparagraph (B)(i), and

(ii) by substituting "below the maximum 15-percent rate amount" for "which would (without regard to this paragraph) be taxed at a rate below 39.6 percent" in subparagraph (C)(ii)(I).

(B) MAXIMUM AMOUNTS DEFINED.—For purposes of applying section 1(h) with the modifications described in subparagraph (A)—

(i) MAXIMUM ZERO RATE AMOUNT.—The maximum zero rate amount shall be—

(I) in the case of a joint return or surviving spouse, $77,200,

(II) in the case of an individual who is a head of household (as defined in section 2(b)), $51,700,

(III) in the case of any other individual (other than an estate or trust), an amount equal to 1/2 of the amount in effect for the taxable year under subclause (I), and

(IV) in the case of an estate or trust, $2,600.

(ii) MAXIMUM 15-PERCENT RATE AMOUNT.—The maximum 15-percent rate amount shall be—

(I) in the case of a joint return or surviving spouse, $479,000 (1/2 such amount in the case of a married individual filing a separate return),

(II) in the case of an individual who is the head of a household (as defined in section 2(b)), $452,400,

(III) in the case of any other individual (other than an estate or trust), $425,800, and

(IV) in the case of an estate or trust, $12,700.

(C) INFLATION ADJUSTMENT.—In the case of any taxable year beginning after 2018, each of the dollar amounts in clauses (i) and (ii) of subparagraph (B) shall be increased by an amount equal to—

(i) such dollar amount, multiplied by

(ii) the cost-of-living adjustment determined under subsection (f)(3) for the calendar year in which the taxable year begins, determined by substituting "calendar year 2017" for "calendar year 2016" in subparagraph (A)(ii) thereof.

If any increase under this subparagraph is not a multiple of $50, such increase shall be rounded to the next lowest multiple of $50.

(6) SECTION 15 NOT TO APPLY.—Section 15 shall not apply to any change in a rate of tax by reason of this subsection.

[Sec. 2]

SEC. 2. DEFINITIONS AND SPECIAL RULES.

* * *

[Sec. 2(d)]

(d) NONRESIDENT ALIENS.—In the case of a nonresident alien individual, the taxes imposed by sections 1 and 55 [relating to the alternative minimum tax] shall apply only as provided by section 871 or 877.

* * *

PART II—TAX ON CORPORATIONS

[Sec. 11]

SEC. 11. TAX IMPOSED.

[Sec. 11(a)]

(a) CORPORATIONS IN GENERAL.—A tax is hereby imposed for each taxable year on the taxable income of every corporation.

[Sec. 11(b)]

(b) AMOUNT OF TAX.—The amount of the tax imposed by subsection (a) shall be 21 percent of taxable income.

[Sec. 11(c)]

(c) EXCEPTIONS.—Subsection (a) shall not apply to a corporation subject to a tax imposed by—

(1) section 594 (relating to mutual savings banks conducting life insurance business),

(2) subchapter L (sec. 801 and following, relating to insurance companies), or

(3) subchapter M (sec. 851 and following, relating to regulated investment companies and real estate investment trusts).

[Sec. 11(d)]

(d) FOREIGN CORPORATIONS.—In the case of a foreign corporation, the taxes imposed by subsection (a) and section 55 shall apply only as provided by section 882.

PART IV—CREDITS AGAINST TAX

Subpart B—Foreign Tax Credit, Etc.

[Sec. 27]

SEC. 27. TAXES OF FOREIGN COUNTRIES AND POSSESSIONS OF THE UNITED STATES.

The amount of taxes imposed by foreign countries and possessions of the United States shall be allowed as a credit against the tax imposed by this chapter to the extent provided in section 901.

Subpart C—Refundable Credits

[Sec. 33]

SEC. 33. TAX WITHHELD AT SOURCE ON NONRESIDENT ALIENS AND FOREIGN CORPORATIONS.

There shall be allowed as a credit against the tax imposed by this subtitle the amount of tax withheld at source under subchapter A of chapter 3 (relating to withholding of tax on nonresident aliens and on foreign corporations).

Subpart D—Business Related Credits

[Sec. 41]

SEC. 41. CREDIT FOR INCREASING RESEARCH ACTIVITIES.

* * *

[Sec. 41(d)]

(d) QUALIFIED RESEARCH DEFINED.—For purposes of this section—

* * *

(4) ACTIVITIES FOR WHICH CREDIT NOT ALLOWED.—The term "qualified research" shall not include any of the following:

* * *

(F) FOREIGN RESEARCH.—Any research conducted outside the United States, the Commonwealth of Puerto Rico, or any possession of the United States.

* * *

Subpart G—Credit Against Regular Tax for Prior Year Minimum Tax Liability

[Sec. 53]

SEC. 53. CREDIT FOR PRIOR YEAR MINIMUM TAX LIABILITY.

[Sec. 53(a)]

(a) ALLOWANCE OF CREDIT.—There shall be allowed as a credit against the tax imposed by this chapter for any taxable year an amount equal to the minimum tax credit for such taxable year.

[Sec. 53(b)]

(b) MINIMUM TAX CREDIT.—For purposes of subsection (a), the minimum tax credit for any taxable year is the excess (if any) of—

(1) the adjusted net minimum tax imposed for all prior taxable years beginning after 1986, over

(2) the amount allowable as a credit under subsection (a) for such prior taxable years.

[Sec. 53(c)]

(c) LIMITATION.—The credit allowable under subsection (a) for any taxable year shall not exceed the excess (if any) of—

(1) The regular tax liability of the taxpayer for such taxable year reduced by the sum of the credits allowable under subparts A, B, D, E, and F of this part, over

(2) the tentative minimum tax for the taxable year.

[Sec. 53(d)]

(d) DEFINITIONS.—For purposes of this section—

(1) NET MINIMUM TAX.—

(A) IN GENERAL.—The term "net minimum tax" means the tax imposed by section 55.

(B) CREDIT NOT ALLOWED FOR EXCLUSION PREFERENCES.—

(i) ADJUSTED NET MINIMUM TAX.—The adjusted net minimum tax for any taxable year is—

(I) the amount of the net minimum tax for such taxable year, reduced by

(II) the amount which would be the net minimum tax for such taxable year if the only adjustments and items of tax preference taken into account were those specified in clause (ii).

(ii) SPECIFIED ITEMS.—The following are specified in this clause—

(I) the adjustments provided for in subsection (b)(1) of section 56, and

(II) the items of tax preference described in paragraphs (1), (5), and (7) of section 57(a).

(iii) CREDIT ALLOWABLE FOR EXCLUSION PREFERENCES OF CORPORATIONS.—In the case of a corporation—

(I) the preceding provisions of this subparagraph shall not apply, and

(II) the adjusted net minimum tax for any taxable year is the amount of the net minimum tax for such year.

(2) TENTATIVE MINIMUM TAX.—The term "tentative minimum tax" has the meaning given to such term by section 55(b).

[Sec. 53(e)]

(e) APPLICATION TO APPLICABLE CORPORATIONS.—In the case of a corporation—

(1) subsection (b)(1) shall be applied by substituting "the net minimum tax for all prior taxable years beginning after 2022" for "the adjusted net minimum tax imposed for all prior taxable years beginning after 1986", and

(2) the amount determined under subsection (c)(1) shall be increased by the amount of tax imposed under section 59A for the taxable year.

PART VI—ALTERNATIVE MINIMUM TAX

»→ ***Caution: As provided in Section 55(d)(4)(B), certain dollar amounts set forth in Section 55(d)(4)(A) are adjusted for taxable years after 2018 to reflect increases in the Chained Consumer Price Index. The dollar amounts applicable to taxable years beginning in 2023 are provided in the material beginning at page vii.***

[Sec. 55]

SEC. 55. ALTERNATIVE MINIMUM TAX IMPOSED.

(a) GENERAL RULE.—There is hereby imposed (in addition to any other tax imposed by this subtitle) a tax equal to the excess (if any) of—

(1) the tentative minimum tax for the taxable year, over

(2) the regular tax for the taxable year plus, in the case of an applicable corporation, the tax imposed by section 59A.

[Sec. 55(b)]

(b) TENTATIVE MINIMUM TAX.—For purposes of this part—

(1) NONCORPORATE TAXPAYERS.—In the case of a taxpayer other than a corporation—

(A) IN GENERAL.—The tentative minimum tax for the taxable year is the sum of—

(i) 26 percent of so much of the taxable excess as does not exceed $175,000, plus

(ii) 28 percent of so much of the taxable excess as exceeds $175,000.

The amount determined under the preceding sentence shall be reduced by the alternative minimum tax foreign tax credit for the taxable year.

(B) TAXABLE EXCESS.—For purposes of this subsection, the term "taxable excess" means so much of the alternative minimum taxable income for the taxable year as exceeds the exemption amount.

(C) MARRIED INDIVIDUAL FILING SEPARATE RETURN.—In the case of a married individual filing a separate return, subparagraph (A) shall be applied by substituting 50 percent of the dollar amount otherwise applicable under clause (i) and clause (ii) thereof. For purposes of the preceding sentence, marital status shall be determined under section 7703.

(D) ALTERNATIVE MINIMUM TAXABLE INCOME.—The term "alternative minimum taxable income" means the taxable income of the taxpayer for the taxable year—

(i) determined with the adjustments provided in section 56 and section 58, and

(ii) increased by the amount of the items of tax preference described in section 57.

If a taxpayer is subject to the regular tax, such taxpayer shall be subject to the tax imposed by this section (and, if the regular tax is determined by reference to an amount other than taxable income, such amount shall be treated as the taxable income of such taxpayer for purposes of the preceding sentence).

(2) CORPORATIONS.—

(A) APPLICABLE CORPORATIONS.—In the case of an applicable corporation, the tentative minimum tax for the taxable year shall be the excess of—

(i) 15 percent of the adjusted financial statement income for the taxable year (as determined under section 56A), over

(ii) the corporate AMT foreign tax credit for the taxable year.

(B) OTHER CORPORATIONS.—In the case of any corporation which is not an applicable corporation, the tentative minimum tax for the taxable year shall be zero.

(3) MAXIMUM RATE OF TAX ON NET CAPITAL GAIN OF NONCORPORATE TAXPAYERS.—The amount determined under the first sentence of paragraph (1)(A) shall not exceed the sum of—

(A) the amount determined under such first sentence computed at the rates and in the same manner as if this paragraph had not been enacted on the taxable excess reduced by the lesser of—

(i) the net capital gain; or

(ii) the sum of—

(I) the adjusted net capital gain, plus

(II) the unrecaptured section 1250 gain, plus

(B) 0 percent of so much of the adjusted net capital gain (or, if less, taxable excess) as does not exceed an amount equal to the excess described in section 1(h)(1)(B), plus

(C) 15 percent of the lesser of—

(i) so much of the adjusted net capital gain (or, if less, taxable excess) as exceeds the amount on which tax is determined under subparagraph (B), or

(ii) the excess described in section 1(h)(1)(C)(ii), plus

(D) 20 percent of the adjusted net capital gain (or, if less, taxable excess) in excess of the sum of the amounts on which tax is determined under subparagraphs (B) and (C), plus

(E) 25 percent of the amount of taxable excess in excess of the sum of the amounts on which tax is determined under the preceding subparagraphs of this paragraph.

Terms used in this paragraph which are also used in section 1(h) shall have the respective meanings given such terms by section 1(h) but computed with the adjustments under this part.

[Sec. 55(c)]

(c) REGULAR TAX.—

(1) IN GENERAL.—For purposes of this section, the term "regular tax" means the regular tax liability for the taxable year (as defined in section 26(b)) reduced by the foreign tax credit allowable under section 27(a). Such term shall not include any increase in tax under section 45(e)(11)(C), 49(b) or 50(a) or subsection (j) or (k) of section 42.

(2) COORDINATION WITH INCOME AVERAGING FOR FARMERS AND FISHERMEN.—Solely for purposes of this section, section 1301 (relating to averaging of farm and fishing income) shall not apply in computing the regular tax liability.

(3) CROSS REFERENCES.—

For provisions providing that certain credits are not allowable against the tax imposed by this section, see sections 30C(d)(2) and 38(c).

[Sec. 55(d)]

(d) EXEMPTION AMOUNT.—For purposes of this section—

(1) EXEMPTION AMOUNT FOR TAXPAYERS OTHER THAN CORPORATIONS.—In the case of a taxpayer other than a corporation, the term "exemption amount" means—

(A) $78,750 in the case of—

(i) a joint return, or

(ii) a surviving spouse,

(B) $50,600 in the case of an individual who—

(i) is not a married individual, and

(ii) is not a surviving spouse,

(C) 50 percent of the dollar amount applicable under subparagraph (A) in the case of a married individual who files a separate return, and

(D) $22,500 in the case of an estate or trust.

For purposes of this paragraph, the term "surviving spouse" has the meaning given to such term by section 2(a), and marital status shall be determined under section 7703.

(2) PHASE-OUT OF EXEMPTION AMOUNT.—The exemption amount of any taxpayers shall be reduced (but not below zero) by an amount equal to 25 percent of the amount by which the alternative minimum taxable income of the taxpayer exceeds—

(A) $150,000 in the case of a taxpayer described in paragraph (1)(A),

(B) $112,500 in the case of a taxpayer described in paragraph (1)(B), and

(C) 50 percent of the dollar amount applicable under subparagraph (A) in the case of a taxpayer described in subparagraph (C) or (D) of paragraph (1).

In the case of a taxpayer described in paragraph (1)(C), alternative minimum taxable income shall be increased by the lesser of (i) 25 percent of the excess of alternative minimum taxable income (determined without regard to this sentence) over the minimum amount of such income (as so determined) for which the exemption amount under paragraph (1)(C) is zero, or (ii) such exemption amount (determined without regard to this paragraph).

(3) INFLATION ADJUSTMENT.—

(A) IN GENERAL.—In the case of any taxable year beginning in a calendar year after 2012, the amounts described in subparagraph (B) shall each be increased by an amount equal to—

(i) such dollar amount, multiplied by

(ii) the cost-of-living adjustment determined under section 1(f)(3) for the calendar year in which the taxable year begins, determined by substituting "calendar year 2011" for "calendar year 2016" in subparagraph (A)(ii) thereof.

(B) AMOUNTS DESCRIBED.—The amounts described in this subparagraph are—

(i) each of the dollar amounts contained in subsection (b)(1)(A),

(ii) each of the dollar amounts contained in subparagraphs (A), (B), and (D) of paragraph (1), and

(iii) each of the dollar amounts in subparagraphs (A) and (B) of paragraph (2).

(C) ROUNDING.—Any increased amount determined under subparagraph (A) shall be rounded to the nearest multiple of $100.

(4) SPECIAL RULE FOR TAXABLE YEARS BEGINNING AFTER 2017 AND BEFORE 2026.—

(A) IN GENERAL.—In the case of any taxable year beginning after December 31, 2017, and before January 1, 2026—

(i) paragraph (1) shall be applied—

(I) by substituting "$109,400" for "$78,750" in subparagraph (A), and

(II) by substituting "$70,300" for "$50,600" in subparagraph (B),

(ii) paragraph (2) shall be applied—

(I) by substituting "$1,000,000" for "$150,000" in subparagraph (A),

(II) by substituting "50 percent of the dollar amount applicable under subparagraph (A)" for "$112,500" in subparagraph (B), and

(III) in the case of a taxpayer described in paragraph (1)(D), without regard to the substitution under subclause (I), and

(iii) subsection (j) of section 59 shall not apply.

(B) INFLATION ADJUSTMENT.—

(i) IN GENERAL.—In the case of any taxable year beginning in a calendar year after 2018, the amounts described in clause (ii) shall each be increased by an amount equal to—

(I) such dollar amount, multiplied by

(II) the cost-of-living adjustment determined under section 1(f)(3) for the calendar year in which the taxable year begins, determined by substituting "calendar year 2017" for "calendar year 2016" in subparagraph (A)(ii) thereof.

(ii) AMOUNTS DESCRIBED.—The amounts described in this clause are the $109,400 amount in subparagraph (A)(i)(I), the $70,300 amount in subparagraph (A)(i)(II), and the $1,000,000 amount in subparagraph (A)(ii)(I).

(iii) ROUNDING.—Any increased amount determined under clause (i) shall be rounded to the nearest multiple of $100.

(iv) COORDINATION WITH CURRENT ADJUSTMENTS.—In the case of any taxable year to which subparagraph (A) applies, no adjustment shall be made under paragraph (3) to any of the numbers which are substituted under subparagraph (A) and adjusted under this subparagraph.

[Sec. 56A]

SEC. 56A. ADJUSTED FINANCIAL STATEMENT INCOME.

[Sec. 56A(a)]

(a) IN GENERAL.—For purposes of this part, the term "adjusted financial statement income" means, with respect to any corporation for any taxable year, the net income or loss of the taxpayer set forth on the taxpayer's applicable financial statement for such taxable year, adjusted as provided in this section.

[Sec. 56A(b)]

(b) APPLICABLE FINANCIAL STATEMENT.—For purposes of this section, the term "applicable financial statement" means, with respect to any taxable year, an applicable financial statement (as defined in section 451(b)(3) or as specified by the Secretary in regulations or other guidance) which covers such taxable year.

[Sec. 56A(c)]

(c) GENERAL ADJUSTMENTS.—

(1) STATEMENTS COVERING DIFFERENT TAXABLE YEARS.—Appropriate adjustments shall be made in adjusted financial statement income in any case in which an applicable financial statement covers a period other than the taxable year.

(2) SPECIAL RULES FOR RELATED ENTITIES.—

(A) CONSOLIDATED FINANCIAL STATEMENTS.—If the financial results of a taxpayer are reported on the applicable financial statement for a group of entities, rules similar to the rules of section 451(b)(5) shall apply.

(B) CONSOLIDATED RETURNS.—Except as provided in regulations prescribed by the Secretary, if the taxpayer is part of an affiliated group of corporations filing a consolidated return for any taxable year, adjusted financial statement income for such group for such taxable year shall take into account items on the group's applicable financial statement which are properly allocable to members of such group.

(C) TREATMENT OF DIVIDENDS AND OTHER AMOUNTS.—In the case of any corporation which is not included on a consolidated return with the taxpayer, adjusted financial statement income of the taxpayer with respect to such other corporation shall be determined by only taking into account the dividends received from such other corporation (reduced to the extent provided by the Secretary in regulations or other guidance) and other amounts which are includible in gross income or deductible as a loss under this chapter (other than amounts required to be included under sections 951 and 951A or such other amounts as provided by the Secretary) with respect to such other corporation.

(D) TREATMENT OF PARTNERSHIPS.—

(i) IN GENERAL.—Except as provided by the Secretary, if the taxpayer is a partner in a partnership, adjusted financial statement income of the taxpayer with respect to such partnership shall be adjusted to only take into account the taxpayer's distributive share of adjusted financial statement income of such partnership.

(ii) ADJUSTED FINANCIAL STATEMENT INCOME OF PARTNERSHIPS.—For the purposes of this part, the adjusted financial statement income of a partnership shall be the partnership's net income or loss set forth on such partnership's applicable financial statement (adjusted under rules similar to the rules of this section).

(3) ADJUSTMENTS TO TAKE INTO ACCOUNT CERTAIN ITEMS OF FOREIGN INCOME.—

(A) IN GENERAL.—If, for any taxable year, a taxpayer is a United States shareholder of one or more controlled foreign corporations, the adjusted financial statement income of such taxpayer with respect to such controlled foreign corporation (as determined under paragraph (2)(C)) shall be adjusted to also take into account such taxpayer's pro rata share (determined under rules similar to the rules under section 951(a)(2)) of items taken into account in computing the net income or loss set forth on the applicable financial statement (as adjusted under rules similar to those that apply in determining adjusted financial statement income) of each such controlled foreign corporation with respect to which such taxpayer is a United States shareholder.

(B) NEGATIVE ADJUSTMENTS.—In any case in which the adjustment determined under subparagraph (A) would result in a negative adjustment for such taxable year—

(i) no adjustment shall be made under this paragraph for such taxable year, and

(ii) the amount of the adjustment determined under this paragraph for the succeeding taxable year (determined without regard to this paragraph) shall be reduced by an amount equal to the negative adjustment for such taxable year.

(4) EFFECTIVELY CONNECTED INCOME.—In the case of a foreign corporation, to determine adjusted financial statement income, the principles of section 882 shall apply.

(5) ADJUSTMENTS FOR CERTAIN TAXES.—Adjusted financial statement income shall be appropriately adjusted to disregard any Federal income taxes, or income, war profits, or excess profits taxes (within the meaning of section 901) with respect to a foreign country or possession of the United States, which are taken into account on the taxpayer's applicable financial statement. To the extent provided by the Secretary, the preceding sentence shall not apply to income, war profits, or excess profits taxes (within the meaning of section 901) that are imposed by a foreign country or possession of the United States and taken into account on the taxpayer's applicable financial statement if the taxpayer does not choose to have the benefits of subpart A of part III of subchapter N for the taxable year. The Secretary shall prescribe such regulations or other guidance as may be necessary and appropriate to provide for the proper treatment of current and deferred taxes for purposes of this paragraph, including the time at which such taxes are properly taken into account.

(6) ADJUSTMENT WITH RESPECT TO DISREGARDED ENTITIES.—Adjusted financial statement income shall be adjusted to take into account any adjusted financial statement income of a disregarded entity owned by the taxpayer.

* * *

(11) ADJUSTMENT WITH RESPECT TO DEFINED BENEFIT PENSIONS.—

(A) IN GENERAL.—Except as otherwise provided in rules prescribed by the Secretary in regulations or other guidance, adjusted financial statement income shall be—

(i) adjusted to disregard any amount of income, cost, or expense that would otherwise be included on the applicable financial statement in connection with any covered benefit plan,

(ii) increased by any amount of income in connection with any such covered benefit plan that is included in the gross income of the corporation under any other provision of this chapter, and

(iii) reduced by deductions allowed under any other provision of this chapter with respect to any such covered benefit plan.

(B) COVERED BENEFIT PLAN.—For purposes of this paragraph, the term "covered benefit plan" means—

(i) a defined benefit plan (other than a multiemployer plan described in section 414(f)) if the trust which is part of such plan is an employees' trust described in section 401(a) which is exempt from tax under section 501(a),

(ii) any qualified foreign plan (as defined in section 404A(e)), or

(iii) any other defined benefit plan which provides post-employment benefits other than pension benefits.

* * *

(13) DEPRECIATION.—Adjusted financial statement income shall be—

(A) reduced by depreciation deductions allowed under section 167 with respect to property to which section 168 applies to the extent of the amount allowed as deductions in computing taxable income for the taxable year, and

(B) appropriately adjusted—

(i) to disregard any amount of depreciation expense that is taken into account on the taxpayer's applicable financial statement with respect to such property, and

(ii) to take into account any other item specified by the Secretary in order to provide that such property is accounted for in the same manner as it is accounted for under this chapter.

* * *

(15) SECRETARIAL AUTHORITY TO ADJUST ITEMS.—The Secretary shall issue regulations or other guidance to provide for such adjustments to adjusted financial statement income as the Secretary determines necessary to carry out the purposes of this section, including adjustments—

(A) to prevent the omission or duplication of any item, and

(B) to carry out the principles of part II of subchapter C of this chapter (relating to corporate liquidations), part III of subchapter C of this chapter (relating to corporate organizations and reorganizations), and part II of subchapter K of this chapter (relating to partnership contributions and distributions).

[Sec. 56A(d)]

(d) DEDUCTION FOR FINANCIAL STATEMENT NET OPERATING LOSS.—

(1) IN GENERAL.—Adjusted financial statement income (determined after application of subsection (c) and without regard to this subsection) shall be reduced by an amount equal to the lesser of—

(A) the aggregate amount of financial statement net operating loss carryovers to the taxable year, or

(B) 80 percent of adjusted financial statement income computed without regard to the deduction allowable under this subsection.

(2) FINANCIAL STATEMENT NET OPERATING LOSS CARRYOVER.—A financial statement net operating loss for any taxable year shall be a financial statement net operating loss carryover to each taxable year following the taxable year of the loss. The portion of such loss which shall be carried to subsequent taxable years shall be the amount of such loss remaining (if any) after the application of paragraph (1).

(3) FINANCIAL STATEMENT NET OPERATING LOSS DEFINED.—For purposes of this subsection, the term "financial statement net operating loss" means the amount of the net loss (if any) set forth on the corporation's applicable financial statement (determined after application of subsection (c) and without regard to this subsection) for taxable years ending after December 31, 2019.

[Sec. 56A(e)]

(e) REGULATIONS AND OTHER GUIDANCE.—The Secretary shall provide for such regulations and other guidance as necessary to carry out the purposes of this section, including regulations and other guidance relating to the effect of the rules of this section on partnerships with income taken into account by an applicable corporation.

[Sec. 59]

SEC. 59. OTHER DEFINITIONS AND SPECIAL RULES.

[Sec. 59(a)]

(a) ALTERNATIVE MINIMUM TAX FOREIGN TAX CREDIT.—For purposes of this part—

(1) IN GENERAL.—The alternative minimum tax foreign tax credit for any taxable year shall be the credit which would be determined under section 27 for such taxable year if—

(A) the pre-credit tentative minimum tax were the tax against which such credit was taken for purposes of section 904 for the taxable year and all prior taxable years beginning after December 31, 1986,

(B) section 904 were applied on the basis of alternative minimum taxable income instead of taxable income, and

(C) the determination of whether any income is high-taxed income for purposes of section 904(d)(2) were made on the basis of the applicable rate specified in section 55(b)(1) in lieu of the highest rate of tax specified in section 1.

(2) PRE-CREDIT TENTATIVE MINIMUM TAX.—For purposes of this subsection, the term "pre-credit tentative minimum tax" means the amount determined under the first sentence of section 55(b)(1)(A).

(3) ELECTION TO USE SIMPLIFIED SECTION 904 LIMITATION.—

(A) IN GENERAL.—In determining the alternative minimum tax foreign tax credit for any taxable year to which an election under this paragraph applies—

(i) subparagraph (B) of paragraph (1) shall not apply, and

(ii) the limitation of section 904 shall be based on the proportion which—

(I) the taxpayer's taxable income (as determined for purposes of the regular tax) from sources without the United States (but not in excess of the taxpayer's entire alternative minimum taxable income), bears to

(II) the taxpayer's entire alternative minimum taxable income for the taxable year.

(B) ELECTION.—

(i) IN GENERAL.—An election under this paragraph may be made only for the taxpayer's first taxable year which begins after December 31, 1997, and for which the taxpayer claims an alternative minimum tax foreign tax credit.

(ii) ELECTION REVOCABLE ONLY WITH CONSENT.—An election under this paragraph, once made, shall apply to the taxable year for which made and all subsequent taxable years unless revoked with the consent of the Secretary.

* * *

[Sec. 59(k)]

(k) APPLICABLE CORPORATION.—For purposes of this part—

(1) APPLICABLE CORPORATION DEFINED.—

(A) IN GENERAL.—The term "applicable corporation" means, with respect to any taxable year, any corporation (other than an S corporation, a regulated investment company, or a real estate investment trust) which meets the average annual adjusted financial statement income test of subparagraph (B) for one or more taxable years which—

(i) are prior to such taxable year, and

(ii) end after December 31, 2021.

(B) AVERAGE ANNUAL ADJUSTED FINANCIAL STATEMENT INCOME TEST.—For purposes of this subsection—

(i) a corporation meets the average annual adjusted financial statement income test for a taxable year if the average annual adjusted financial statement income of such corporation (determined without regard to section 56A(d)) for the 3-taxable-year period ending with such taxable year exceeds $1,000,000,000, and

(ii) in the case of a corporation described in paragraph (2), such corporation meets the average annual adjusted financial statement income test for a taxable year if—

(I) the corporation meets the requirements of clause (i) for such taxable year (determined after the application of paragraph (2)), and

(II) the average annual adjusted financial statement income of such corporation (determined without regard to the application of paragraph (2) and without regard to section 56A(d)) for the 3-taxable-year-period ending with such taxable year is $100,000,000 or more.

(C) EXCEPTION.—Notwithstanding subparagraph (A), the term "applicable corporation" shall not include any corporation which otherwise meets the requirements of subparagraph (A) if—

(i) such corporation—

(I) has a change in ownership, or

(II) has a specified number (to be determined by the Secretary and which shall, as appropriate, take into account the facts and circumstances of the taxpayer) of consecutive taxable years, including the most recent taxable year, in which the corporation does not meet the average annual adjusted financial statement income test of subparagraph (B), and

(ii) the Secretary determines that it would not be appropriate to continue to treat such corporation as an applicable corporation.

The preceding sentence shall not apply to any corporation if, after the Secretary makes the determination described in clause (ii), such corporation meets the average annual adjusted financial statement income test of subparagraph (B) for any taxable year beginning after the first taxable year for which such determination applies.

(D) SPECIAL RULES FOR DETERMINING APPLICABLE CORPORATION STATUS.—Solely for purposes of determining whether a corporation is an applicable corporation under this paragraph, all adjusted financial statement income of persons treated as a single employer with such corporation under subsection (a) or (b) of section 52 shall be treated as adjusted financial statement income of such corporation, and adjusted financial statement income of such corporation shall be determined without regard to paragraphs (2)(D)(i) and (11) of section 56A(c).

(E) OTHER SPECIAL RULES.—

(i) CORPORATIONS IN EXISTENCE FOR LESS THAN 3 YEARS.—If the corporation was in existence for less than 3-taxable years, subparagraph (B) shall be applied on the basis of the period during which such corporation was in existence.

(ii) SHORT TAXABLE YEARS.—Adjusted financial statement income for any taxable year of less than 12 months shall be annualized by multiplying the adjusted financial statement income for the short period by 12 and dividing the result by the number of months in the short period.

(iii) TREATMENT OF PREDECESSORS.—Any reference in this subparagraph to a corporation shall include a reference to any predecessor of such corporation.

(2) SPECIAL RULE FOR FOREIGN-PARENTED MULTINATIONAL GROUPS.—

(A) IN GENERAL.—If a corporation is a member of a foreign-parented multinational group for any taxable year, then, solely for purposes of determining whether such corporation meets the average annual adjusted financial statement income test under paragraph (1)(B)(ii)(I) for such taxable year, the adjusted financial statement income of such corporation for such taxable year shall include the adjusted financial statement income of all members of such group. Solely for purposes of this subparagraph, adjusted financial statement income shall be determined without regard to paragraphs (2)(D)(i), (3), (4), and (11) of section 56A(c).

(B) FOREIGN-PARENTED MULTINATIONAL GROUP.—For purposes of subparagraph (A), the term "foreign- parented multinational group" means, with respect to any taxable year, two or more entities if—

(i) at least one entity is a domestic corporation and another entity is a foreign corporation,

(ii) such entities are included in the same applicable financial statement with respect to such year, and

(iii) either—

(I) the common parent of such entities is a foreign corporation, or

(II) if there is no common parent, the entities are treated as having a common parent which is a foreign corporation under subparagraph (D).

(C) FOREIGN CORPORATIONS ENGAGED IN A TRADE OR BUSINESS WITHIN THE UNITED STATES.—For purposes of this paragraph, if a foreign corporation is engaged in a trade or business within the United States, such trade or business shall be treated as a separate domestic corporation that is wholly owned by the foreign corporation.

(D) OTHER RULES.—The Secretary shall, applying the principles of this section, prescribe rules for the application of this paragraph, including rules for the determination of—

(i) the entities (if any) which are to be to be treated under subparagraph (B)(iii)(II) as having a common parent which is a foreign corporation,

(ii) the entities to be included in a foreign-parented multinational group, and

(iii) the common parent of a foreign-parented multinational group.

(3) REGULATIONS OR OTHER GUIDANCE.—The Secretary shall provide regulations or other guidance for the purposes of carrying out this subsection, including regulations or other guidance—

(A) providing a simplified method for determining whether a corporation meets the requirements of paragraph (1), and

(B) addressing the application of this subsection to a corporation that experiences a change in ownership.

***

[Sec. 59(l)]

(l) CORPORATE AMT FOREIGN TAX CREDIT.—

(1) IN GENERAL.—For purposes of this part, if an applicable corporation chooses to have the benefits of subpart A of part III of subchapter N for any taxable year, the corporate AMT foreign tax credit for the taxable year of the applicable corporation is an amount equal to [the] sum of—

(A) the lesser of—

(i) the aggregate of the applicable corporation's pro rata share (as determined under section 56A(c)(3)) of the amount of income, war profits, and excess profits taxes (within the meaning of section 901) imposed by any foreign country or possession of the United States which are—

(I) taken into account on the applicable financial statement of each controlled foreign corporation with respect to which the applicable corporation is a United States shareholder, and

(II) paid or accrued (for Federal income tax purposes) by each such controlled foreign corporation, or

(ii) the product of the amount of the adjustment under section 56A(c)(3) and the percentage specified in section 55(b)(2)(A)(i), and

(B) in the case of an applicable corporation that is a domestic corporation, the amount of income, war profits, and excess profits taxes (within the meaning of section 901) imposed by any foreign country or possession of the United States to the extent such taxes are—

(i) taken into account on the applicable corporation's applicable financial statement, and

(ii) paid or accrued (for Federal income tax purposes) by the applicable corporation.

(2) CARRYOVER OF EXCESS TAX PAID.—For any taxable year for which an applicable corporation chooses to have the benefits of subpart A of part III of subchapter N, the excess of the amount described in paragraph (1)(A)(i) over the amount described in paragraph (1)(A)(ii) shall increase the amount described in paragraph (1)(A)(i) in any of the first 5 succeeding taxable years to the extent not taken into account in a prior taxable year.

(3) REGULATIONS OR OTHER GUIDANCE.—The Secretary shall provide for such regulations or other guidance as is necessary to carry out the purposes of this subsection.

PART VII—BASE EROSION AND ANTI-ABUSE TAX

[Sec. 59A]

SEC. 59A. TAX ON BASE EROSION PAYMENTS OF TAXPAYERS WITH SUBSTANTIAL GROSS RECEIPTS.

[Sec. 59A(a)]

(a) IMPOSITION OF TAX.—There is hereby imposed on each applicable taxpayer for any taxable year a tax equal to the base erosion minimum tax amount for the taxable year. Such tax shall be in addition to any other tax imposed by this subtitle.

[Sec. 59A(b)]

(b) BASE EROSION MINIMUM TAX AMOUNT.—For purposes of this section—

(1) IN GENERAL.—Except as provided in paragraphs (2) and (3), the term "base erosion minimum tax amount" means, with respect to any applicable taxpayer for any taxable year, the excess (if any) of—

(A) an amount equal to 10 percent (5 percent in the case of taxable years beginning in calendar year 2018) of the modified taxable income of such taxpayer for the taxable year, over

(B) an amount equal to the regular tax liability (as defined in section 26(b)) of the taxpayer for the taxable year, reduced (but not below zero) by the excess (if any) of—

(i) the credits allowed under this chapter against such regular tax liability, over

(ii) the sum of—

(I) the credit allowed under section 38 for the taxable year which is properly allocable to the research credit determined under section 41(a), plus

(II) the portion of the applicable section 38 credits not in excess of 80 percent of the lesser of the amount of such credits or the base erosion minimum tax amount (determined without regard to this subclause).

(2) MODIFICATIONS FOR TAXABLE YEARS BEGINNING AFTER 2025.—In the case of any taxable year beginning after December 31, 2025, paragraph (1) shall be applied—

(A) by substituting "12.5 percent" for "10 percent" in subparagraph (A) thereof, and

(B) by reducing (but not below zero) the regular tax liability (as defined in section 26(b)) for purposes of subparagraph (B) thereof by the aggregate amount of the credits allowed under this chapter against such regular tax liability rather than the excess described in such subparagraph.

(3) INCREASED RATE FOR CERTAIN BANKS AND SECURITIES DEALERS.—

(A) IN GENERAL.—In the case of a taxpayer described in subparagraph (B) who is an applicable taxpayer for any taxable year, the percentage otherwise in effect under paragraphs (1)(A) and (2)(A) shall each be increased by one percentage point.

(B) TAXPAYER DESCRIBED.—A taxpayer is described in this subparagraph if such taxpayer is a member of an affiliated group (as defined in section 1504(a)(1)) which includes—

(i) a bank (as defined in section 581), or

(ii) a registered securities dealer under section 15(a) of the Securities Exchange Act of 1934.

(4) APPLICABLE SECTION 38 CREDITS.—For purposes of paragraph (1)(B)(ii)(II), the term "applicable section 38 credits" means the credit allowed under section 38 for the taxable year which is properly allocable to—

(A) the low-income housing credit determined under section 42(a),

(B) the renewable electricity production credit determined under section 45(a), and

(C) the investment credit determined under section 46, but only to the extent properly allocable to the energy credit determined under section 48.

[Sec. 59A(c)]

(c) MODIFIED TAXABLE INCOME.—For purposes of this section—

(1) IN GENERAL.—The term "modified taxable income" means the taxable income of the taxpayer computed under this chapter for the taxable year, determined without regard to—

(A) any base erosion tax benefit with respect to any base erosion payment, or

(B) the base erosion percentage of any net operating loss deduction allowed under section 172 for the taxable year.

(2) BASE EROSION TAX BENEFIT.—

(A) IN GENERAL.—The term "base erosion tax benefit" means—

(i) any deduction described in subsection (d)(1) which is allowed under this chapter for the taxable year with respect to any base erosion payment,

(ii) in the case of a base erosion payment described in subsection (d)(2), any deduction allowed under this chapter for the taxable year for depreciation (or amortization in lieu of depreciation) with respect to the property acquired with such payment,

(iii) in the case of a base erosion payment described in subsection (d)(3)—

(I) any reduction under section 803(a)(1)(B) in the gross amount of premiums and other consideration on insurance and annuity contracts for premiums and other consideration arising out of indemnity insurance, and

(II) any deduction under section 832(b)(4)(A) from the amount of gross premiums written on insurance contracts during the taxable year for premiums paid for reinsurance, and

(iv) in the case of a base erosion payment described in subsection (d)(4), any reduction in gross receipts with respect to such payment in computing gross income of the taxpayer for the taxable year for purposes of this chapter.

(B) TAX BENEFITS DISREGARDED IF TAX WITHHELD ON BASE EROSION PAYMENT.—

(i) IN GENERAL.—Except as provided in clause (ii), any base erosion tax benefit attributable to any base erosion payment—

(I) on which tax is imposed by section 871 or 881, and

(II) with respect to which tax has been deducted and withheld under section 1441 or 1442,

shall not be taken into account in computing modified taxable income under paragraph (1)(A) or the base erosion percentage under paragraph (4).

(ii) EXCEPTION.—The amount not taken into account in computing modified taxable income by reason of clause (i) shall be reduced under rules similar to the rules under section 163(j)(5)(B) (as in effect before the date of the enactment of the Tax Cuts and Jobs Act).

(3) SPECIAL RULES FOR DETERMINING INTEREST FOR WHICH DEDUCTION ALLOWED.—For purposes of applying paragraph (1), in the case of a taxpayer to which section 163(j) applies for the taxable year, the reduction in the amount of interest for which a deduction is allowed by reason of such subsection shall be treated as allocable first to interest paid or accrued to persons who are not related parties with respect to the taxpayer and then to such related parties.

(4) BASE EROSION PERCENTAGE.—For purposes of paragraph (1)(B)—

(A) IN GENERAL.—The term "base erosion percentage" means, for any taxable year, the percentage determined by dividing—

(i) the aggregate amount of base erosion tax benefits of the taxpayer for the taxable year, by

(ii) the sum of—

(I) the aggregate amount of the deductions (including deductions described in clauses (i) and (ii) of paragraph (2)(A)) allowable to the taxpayer under this chapter for the taxable year, plus

(II) the base erosion tax benefits described in clauses (iii) and (iv) of paragraph (2)(A) allowable to the taxpayer for the taxable year.

(B) CERTAIN ITEMS NOT TAKEN INTO ACCOUNT.—The amount under subparagraph (A)(ii) shall be determined by not taking into account—

(i) any deduction allowed under section 172, 245A, or 250 for the taxable year,

(ii) any deduction for amounts paid or accrued for services to which the exception under subsection (d)(5) applies, and

(iii) any deduction for qualified derivative payments which are not treated as a base erosion payment by reason of subsection (h).

[Sec. 59A(d)]

(d) BASE EROSION PAYMENT.—For purposes of this section—

(1) IN GENERAL.—The term "base erosion payment" means any amount paid or accrued by the taxpayer to a foreign person which is a related party of the taxpayer and with respect to which a deduction is allowable under this chapter.

(2) PURCHASE OF DEPRECIABLE PROPERTY.—Such term shall also include any amount paid or accrued by the taxpayer to a foreign person which is a related party of the taxpayer in connection with the acquisition by the taxpayer from such person of property of a character subject to the allowance for depreciation (or amortization in lieu of depreciation).

(3) REINSURANCE PAYMENTS.—Such term shall also include any premium or other consideration paid or accrued by the taxpayer to a foreign person which is a related party of the taxpayer for any reinsurance payments which are taken into account under sections 803(a)(1)(B) or 832(b)(4)(A).

(4) CERTAIN PAYMENTS TO EXPATRIATED ENTITIES.—

(A) IN GENERAL.—Such term shall also include any amount paid or accrued by the taxpayer with respect to a person described in subparagraph (B) which results in a reduction of the gross receipts of the taxpayer.

(B) PERSON DESCRIBED.—A person is described in this subparagraph if such person is a—

(i) surrogate foreign corporation which is a related party of the taxpayer, but only if such person first became a surrogate foreign corporation after November 9, 2017, or

(ii) foreign person which is a member of the same expanded affiliated group as the surrogate foreign corporation.

(C) DEFINITIONS.—For purposes of this paragraph—

(i) SURROGATE FOREIGN CORPORATION.—The term "surrogate foreign corporation" has the meaning given such term by section 7874(a)(2)(B) but does not include a foreign corporation treated as a domestic corporation under section 7874(b).

(ii) EXPANDED AFFILIATED GROUP.—The term "expanded affiliated group" has the meaning given such term by section 7874(c)(1).

(5) EXCEPTION FOR CERTAIN AMOUNTS WITH RESPECT TO SERVICES.—Paragraph (1) shall not apply to any amount paid or accrued by a taxpayer for services if—

(A) such services are services which meet the requirements for eligibility for use of the services cost method under section 482 (determined without regard to the requirement that the services not contribute significantly to fundamental risks of business success or failure), and

(B) such amount constitutes the total services cost with no markup component.

[Sec. 59A(e)]

(e) APPLICABLE TAXPAYER.—For purposes of this section—

(1) IN GENERAL.—The term "applicable taxpayer" means, with respect to any taxable year, a taxpayer—

(A) which is a corporation other than a regulated investment company, a real estate investment trust, or an S corporation,

(B) the average annual gross receipts of which for the 3-taxable-year period ending with the preceding taxable year are at least $500,000,000, and

(C) the base erosion percentage (as determined under subsection (c)(4)) of which for the taxable year is 3 percent (2 percent in the case of a taxpayer described in subsection (b)(3)(B)) or higher.

(2) GROSS RECEIPTS.—

(A) SPECIAL RULE FOR FOREIGN PERSONS.—In the case of a foreign person the gross receipts of which are taken into account for purposes of paragraph (1)(B), only gross receipts which are taken into account in determining income which is effectively connected with the conduct of a trade or business within the United States shall be taken into account. In the case of a taxpayer which is a foreign person, the preceding sentence shall not apply to the gross receipts of any United States person which are aggregated with the taxpayer's gross receipts by reason of paragraph (3).

(B) OTHER RULES MADE APPLICABLE.—Rules similar to the rules of subparagraphs (B), (C), and (D) of section 448(c)(3) shall apply in determining gross receipts for purposes of this section.

(3) AGGREGATION RULES.—All persons treated as a single employer under subsection (a) of section 52 shall be treated as 1 person for purposes of this subsection and subsection (c)(4), except that in applying section 1563 for purposes of section 52, the exception for foreign corporations under section 1563(b)(2)(C) shall be disregarded.

[Sec. 59A(f)]

(f) FOREIGN PERSON.—For purposes of this section, the term "foreign person" has the meaning given such term by section 6038A(c)(3).

[Sec. 59A(g)]

(g) RELATED PARTY.—For purposes of this section—

(1) IN GENERAL.—The term "related party" means, with respect to any applicable taxpayer—

(A) any 25-percent owner of the taxpayer,

(B) any person who is related (within the meaning of section 267(b) or 707(b)(1)) to the taxpayer or any 25-percent owner of the taxpayer, and

(C) any other person who is related (within the meaning of section 482) to the taxpayer.

(2) 25-PERCENT OWNER.—The term "25-percent owner" means, with respect to any corporation, any person who owns at least 25 percent of—

(A) the total voting power of all classes of stock of a corporation entitled to vote, or

(B) the total value of all classes of stock of such corporation.

(3) SECTION 318 TO APPLY.—Section 318 shall apply for purposes of paragraphs (1) and (2), except that—

(A) "10 percent" shall be substituted for "50 percent" in section 318(a)(2)(C), and

(B) subparagraphs (A), (B), and (C) of section 318(a)(3) shall not be applied so as to consider a United States person as owning stock which is owned by a person who is not a United States person.

[Sec. 59A(h)]

(h) EXCEPTION FOR CERTAIN PAYMENTS MADE IN THE ORDINARY COURSE OF TRADE OR BUSINESS.—For purposes of this section—

(1) IN GENERAL.—Except as provided in paragraph (3), any qualified derivative payment shall not be treated as a base erosion payment.

(2) QUALIFIED DERIVATIVE PAYMENT.—

(A) IN GENERAL.—The term "qualified derivative payment" means any payment made by a taxpayer pursuant to a derivative with respect to which the taxpayer—

(i) recognizes gain or loss as if such derivative were sold for its fair market value on the last business day of the taxable year (and such additional times as required by this title or the taxpayer's method of accounting),

(ii) treats any gain or loss so recognized as ordinary, and

(iii) treats the character of all items of income, deduction, gain, or loss with respect to a payment pursuant to the derivative as ordinary.

(B) REPORTING REQUIREMENT.—No payments shall be treated as qualified derivative payments under subparagraph (A) for any taxable year unless the taxpayer includes in the information required to be reported under section 6038B(b)(2) with respect to such taxable year such information as is necessary to identify the payments to be so treated and such other information as the Secretary determines necessary to carry out the provisions of this subsection.

(3) EXCEPTIONS FOR PAYMENTS OTHERWISE TREATED AS BASE EROSION PAYMENTS.—This subsection shall not apply to any qualified derivative payment if—

(A) the payment would be treated as a base erosion payment if it were not made pursuant to a derivative, including any interest, royalty, or service payment, or

(B) in the case of a contract which has derivative and nonderivative components, the payment is properly allocable to the nonderivative component.

(4) DERIVATIVE DEFINED.—For purposes of this subsection—

(A) IN GENERAL.—The term "derivative" means any contract (including any option, forward contract, futures contract, short position, swap, or similar contract) the value of which, or any payment or other transfer with respect to which, is (directly or indirectly) determined by reference to one or more of the following:

(i) Any share of stock in a corporation.

(ii) Any evidence of indebtedness.

(iii) Any commodity which is actively traded.

(iv) Any currency.

(v) Any rate, price, amount, index, formula, or algorithm.

Such term shall not include any item described in clauses (i) through (v).

(B) TREATMENT OF AMERICAN DEPOSITORY RECEIPTS AND SIMILAR INSTRUMENTS.—Except as otherwise provided by the Secretary, for purposes of this part, American depository receipts (and similar instruments) with respect to shares of stock in foreign corporations shall be treated as shares of stock in such foreign corporations.

(C) EXCEPTION FOR CERTAIN CONTRACTS.—Such term shall not include any insurance, annuity, or endowment contract issued by an insurance company to which subchapter L applies (or issued by any foreign corporation to which such subchapter would apply if such foreign corporation were a domestic corporation).

[Sec. 59A(i)]

(i) REGULATIONS.—The Secretary shall prescribe such regulations or other guidance as may be necessary or appropriate to carry out the provisions of this section, including regulations—

(1) providing for such adjustments to the application of this section as are necessary to prevent the avoidance of the purposes of this section, including through—

(A) the use of unrelated persons, conduit transactions, or other intermediaries, or

(B) transactions or arrangements designed, in whole or in part—

(i) to characterize payments otherwise subject to this section as payments not subject to this section, or

(ii) to substitute payments not subject to this section for payments otherwise subject to this section and

(2) for the application of subsection (g), including rules to prevent the avoidance of the exceptions under subsection (g)(3).

SUBCHAPTER B—COMPUTATION OF TAXABLE INCOME

PART I—DEFINITION OF GROSS INCOME, ADJUSTED GROSS INCOME, TAXABLE INCOME, ETC.

[Sec. 61]

SEC. 61. GROSS INCOME DEFINED.

[Sec. 61(a)]

(a) GENERAL DEFINITION.—Except as otherwise provided in this subtitle, gross income means all income from whatever source derived, including (but not limited to) the following items:

(1) Compensation for services, including fees, commissions, fringe benefits, and similar items;

(2) Gross income derived from business;

(3) Gains derived from dealings in property;

(4) Interest;

(5) Rents;

(6) Royalties;

(7) Dividends;

(8) Annuities;

(9) Income from life insurance and endowment contracts;

(10) Pensions;

(11) Income from discharge of indebtedness;

(12) Distributive share of partnership gross income;

(13) Income in respect of a decedent; and

(14) Income from an interest in an estate or trust.

***

[Sec. 63]

SEC. 63. TAXABLE INCOME DEFINED.

[Sec. 63(a)]

(a) IN GENERAL.—Except as provided in subsection (b), for purposes of this subtitle, the term "taxable income" means gross income minus the deductions allowed by this chapter (other than the standard deduction).

***

[Sec. 63(c)]

(c) STANDARD DEDUCTION.—For purposes of this subtitle—

***

(6) CERTAIN INDIVIDUALS, ETC., NOT ELIGIBLE FOR STANDARD DEDUCTION.—In the case of—

(A) a married individual filing a separate return where either spouse itemizes deductions,

(B) a nonresident alien individual,

(C) an individual making a return under section 443(a)(1) for a period of less than 12 months on account of a change in his annual accounting period, or

(D) an estate or trust, common trust fund, or partnership,

the standard deduction shall be zero.

***

PART II—ITEMS SPECIFICALLY INCLUDED IN GROSS INCOME

[Sec. 78]

SEC. 78. GROSS UP FOR DEEMED PAID FOREIGN TAX CREDIT.

If a domestic corporation chooses to have the benefits of subpart A of part III of subchapter N (relating to foreign tax credit) for any taxable year, an amount equal to the taxes deemed to be paid by such corporation under subsections (a), (b), and (d) of section 960 (determined without regard to the phrase "80 percent of" in subsection (d)(1) thereof) for such taxable year shall be treated for purposes of this title (other than sections 245 and 245A) as a dividend received by such domestic corporation from the foreign corporation.

[Sec. 91]

SEC. 91. CERTAIN FOREIGN BRANCH LOSSES TRANSFERRED TO SPECIFIED 10-PERCENT OWNED FOREIGN CORPORATIONS.

[Sec. 91(a)]

(a) IN GENERAL.—If a domestic corporation transfers substantially all of the assets of a foreign branch (within the meaning of section 367(a)(3)(C), as in effect before the date of the enactment of the Tax Cuts and Jobs Act) to a specified 10-percent owned foreign corporation (as defined in section 245A) with respect to which it is a United States shareholder after such transfer, such domestic corporation shall include in gross income for the taxable year which includes such transfer an amount equal to the transferred loss amount with respect to such transfer.

[Sec. 91(b)]

(b) TRANSFERRED LOSS AMOUNT.—For purposes of this section, the term "transferred loss amount" means, with respect to any transfer of substantially all of the assets of a foreign branch, the excess (if any) of—

(1) the sum of losses—

(A) which were incurred by the foreign branch after December 31, 2017, and before the transfer, and

(B) with respect to which a deduction was allowed to the taxpayer, over

(2) the sum of—

(A) any taxable income of such branch for a taxable year after the taxable year in which the loss was incurred and through the close of the taxable year of the transfer, and

(B) any amount which is recognized under section 904(f)(3) on account of the transfer.

[Sec. 91(c)]

(c) REDUCTION FOR RECOGNIZED GAINS.—The transferred loss amount shall be reduced (but not below zero) by the amount of gain recognized by the taxpayer on account of the transfer (other than amounts taken into account under subsection (b)(2)(B)).

[Sec. 91(d)]

(d) SOURCE OF INCOME.—Amounts included in gross income under this section shall be treated as derived from sources within the United States.

[Sec. 91(e)]

(e) BASIS ADJUSTMENTS.—Consistent with such regulations or other guidance as the Secretary shall prescribe, proper adjustments shall be made in the adjusted basis of the taxpayer's stock in the specified 10-percent owned foreign corporation to which the transfer is made, and in the transferee's adjusted basis in the property transferred, to reflect amounts included in gross income under this section.

PART III—ITEMS SPECIFICALLY EXCLUDED FROM GROSS INCOME

[Sec. 119]

SEC. 119. MEALS OR LODGING FURNISHED FOR THE CONVENIENCE OF THE EMPLOYER.

[Sec. 119(a)]

(a) MEALS AND LODGING FURNISHED TO EMPLOYEE, HIS SPOUSE, AND HIS DEPENDENTS, PURSUANT TO EMPLOYMENT.—There shall be excluded from gross income of an employee the value of any meals or lodging furnished to him, his spouse, or any of his dependents by or on behalf of his employer for the convenience of the employer, but only if—

(1) in the case of meals, the meals are furnished on the business premises of the employer, or

(2) in the case of lodging, the employee is required to accept such lodging on the business premises of his employer as a condition of his employment.

***

[Sec. 119(c)]

(c) EMPLOYEES LIVING IN CERTAIN CAMPS.—

(1) IN GENERAL.—In the case of an individual who is furnished lodging in a camp located in a foreign country by or on behalf of his employer, such camp shall be considered to be part of the business premises of the employer.

(2) CAMP.—For purposes of this section, a camp constitutes lodging which is—

(A) provided by or on behalf of the employer for the convenience of the employer because the place at which such individual renders services is in a remote area where satisfactory housing is not available on the open market,

(B) located, as near as practicable, in the vicinity of the place at which such individual renders services, and

(C) furnished in a common area (or enclave) which is not available to the public and which normally accommodates 10 or more employees.

***

PART IV—TAX EXEMPTION REQUIREMENTS FOR STATE AND LOCAL BONDS

Subpart B—Requirements Applicable to All State and Local Bonds

[Sec. 149]

SEC. 149. BONDS MUST BE REGISTERED TO BE TAX EXEMPT; OTHER REQUIREMENTS.

[Sec. 149(a)]

(a) BONDS MUST BE REGISTERED TO BE TAX EXEMPT.—

***

(3) SPECIAL RULES.—

(A) BOOK ENTRIES PERMITTED.—For purposes of paragraph (1), a book entry bond shall be treated as in registered form if the right to the principal of, and stated interest on, such bond may be transferred only through a book entry consistent with regulations prescribed by the Secretary.

(B) NOMINEES.—The Secretary shall prescribe such regulations as may be necessary to carry out the purpose of paragraph (1) where there is a nominee or chain of nominees.

***

PART VI—ITEMIZED DEDUCTIONS FOR INDIVIDUALS AND CORPORATIONS

[Sec. 162]

SEC. 162. TRADE OR BUSINESS EXPENSES.

[Sec. 162(a)]

(a) IN GENERAL.—There shall be allowed as a deduction all the ordinary and necessary expenses paid or incurred during the taxable year in carrying on any trade or business, including—

***

(2) traveling expenses (including amounts expended for meals and lodging other than amounts which are lavish or extravagant under the circumstances) while away from home in the pursuit of a trade or business; and

***

[Sec. 162(c)]

(c) ILLEGAL BRIBES, KICKBACKS, AND OTHER PAYMENTS.—

(1) ILLEGAL PAYMENTS TO GOVERNMENT OFFICIALS OR EMPLOYEES.—No deduction shall be allowed under subsection (a) for any payment made, directly or indirectly, to an official or employee of any government, or of any agency or instrumentality of any government, if the payment constitutes an illegal bribe or kickback or, if the payment is to an official or employee of a foreign government, the payment is unlawful under the Foreign Corrupt Practices Act of 1977. The burden of proof in respect of the issue, for the purposes of this paragraph, as to whether a payment constitutes an illegal bribe or kickback (or is unlawful under the Foreign Corrupt Practices Act of 1977) shall be upon the Secretary to the same extent as he bears the burden of proof under section 7454 (concerning the burden of proof when the issue relates to fraud).

***

[Sec. 162(f)]

(f) FINES, PENALTIES, AND OTHER AMOUNTS.—

(1) IN GENERAL.—Except as provided in the following paragraphs of this subsection, no deduction otherwise allowable shall be allowed under this chapter for any amount paid or incurred (whether by suit, agreement, or otherwise) to, or at the direction of, a government or governmental entity in relation to the violation of any law or the investigation or inquiry by such government or entity into the potential violation of any law.

(2) EXCEPTION FOR AMOUNTS CONSTITUTING RESTITUTION OR PAID TO COME INTO COMPLIANCE WITH LAW.—

(A) IN GENERAL.—Paragraph (1) shall not apply to any amount that—

(i) the taxpayer establishes.—

(I) constitutes restitution (including remediation of property) for damage or harm which was or may be caused by the violation of any law or the potential violation of any law, or

(II) is paid to come into compliance with any law which was violated or otherwise involved in the investigation or inquiry described in paragraph (1),

(ii) is identified as restitution or as an amount paid to come into compliance with such law, as the case may be, in the court order or settlement agreement, and

(iii) in the case of any amount of restitution for failure to pay any tax imposed under this title in the same manner as if such amount were such tax, would have been allowed as a deduction under this chapter if it had been timely paid.

The identification under clause (ii) alone shall not be sufficient to make the establishment required under clause (i).

(B) LIMITATION.—Subparagraph (A) shall not apply to any amount paid or incurred as reimbursement to the government or entity for the costs of any investigation or litigation.

(3) EXCEPTION FOR AMOUNTS PAID OR INCURRED AS THE RESULT OF CERTAIN COURT ORDERS.—Paragraph (1) shall not apply to any amount paid or incurred by reason of any order of a court in a suit in which no government or governmental entity is a party.

(4) EXCEPTION FOR TAXES DUE.—Paragraph (1) shall not apply to any amount paid or incurred as taxes due.

(5) TREATMENT OF CERTAIN NONGOVERNMENTAL REGULATORY ENTITIES.—For purposes of this subsection, the following nongovernmental entities shall be treated as governmental entities:

(A) Any nongovernmental entity which exercises self-regulatory powers (including imposing sanctions) in connection with a qualified board or exchange (as defined in section 1256(g)(7)).

(B) To the extent provided in regulations, any nongovernmental entity which exercises self-regulatory powers (including imposing sanctions) as part of performing an essential governmental function.

***

[Sec. 162(j)]

(j) CERTAIN FOREIGN ADVERTISING EXPENSES.—

(1) IN GENERAL.—No deduction shall be allowed under subsection (a) for any expenses of an advertisement carried by a foreign broadcast undertaking and directed primarily to a market in the United States. This paragraph shall apply only to foreign broadcast undertakings located in a country which denies a similar deduction for the cost of advertising directed primarily to a market in the foreign country when placed with a United States broadcast undertaking.

(2) BROADCAST UNDERTAKING.—For purposes of paragraph (1), the term "broadcast undertaking" includes (but is not limited to) radio and television stations.

***

[Sec. 163]

SEC. 163. INTEREST.

***

[Sec. 163(e)]

(e) ORIGINAL ISSUE DISCOUNT.—

(1) IN GENERAL.—The portion of the original issue discount with respect to any debt instrument which is allowable as a deduction to the issuer for any taxable year shall be equal to the aggregate daily portions of the original issue discount for days during such taxable year.

(2) DEFINITIONS AND SPECIAL RULES.—For purposes of this subsection—

(A) DEBT INSTRUMENT.—The term "debt instrument" has the meaning given such term by section 1275(a)(1).

(B) DAILY PORTIONS.—The daily portion of the original issue discount for any day shall be determined under section 1272(a) (without regard to paragraph (7) thereof and without regard to section 1273(a)(3)).

(C) SHORT-TERM OBLIGATIONS.—In the case of an obligor of a short-term obligation (as defined in section 1283(a)(1)(A)) who uses the cash receipts and disbursements method of accounting, the original issue discount (and any other interest payable) on such obligation shall be deductible only when paid.

(3) SPECIAL RULE FOR ORIGINAL ISSUE DISCOUNT ON OBLIGATION HELD BY RELATED FOREIGN PERSON.—

(A) IN GENERAL.—If any debt instrument having original issue discount is held by a related foreign person, any portion of such original issue discount shall not be allowable as a deduction to the issuer until paid. The preceding sentence shall not apply to the extent that the original issue discount is effectively connected with the conduct by such foreign related person of a trade or business within the United States unless such original issue discount is exempt from taxation (or is subject to a reduced rate of tax) pursuant to a treaty obligation of the United States.

(B) SPECIAL RULE FOR CERTAIN FOREIGN ENTITIES.—

(i) IN GENERAL.—In the case of any debt instrument having original issue discount which is held by a related foreign person which is a controlled foreign corporation (as defined in section 957) or a passive foreign investment company (as defined in section 1297), a deduction shall be allowable to the issuer with respect to such original issue discount for any taxable year before the taxable year in which paid only to the extent such original issue discount is includible (determined without regard to properly allocable deductions and qualified deficits under section 952(c)(1)(B)) during such prior taxable year in the gross income of a United States person who owns (within the meaning of section 958(a)) stock in such corporation.

(ii) SECRETARIAL AUTHORITY.—The Secretary may by regulation exempt transactions from the application of clause (i), including any transaction which is entered into by a payor in the ordinary course of a trade or business in which the payor is predominantly engaged.

(C) RELATED FOREIGN PERSON.—For purposes of subparagraph (A), the term "related foreign person" means any person—

(i) who is not a United States person, and

(ii) who is related (within the meaning of section 267(b)) to the issuer.

(4) EXCEPTION.—This subsection shall not apply to any debt instrument described in section 1272(a)(2)(D) (relating to loans between natural persons).

(5) SPECIAL RULES FOR ORIGINAL ISSUE DISCOUNT ON CERTAIN HIGH YIELD OBLIGATIONS.—

(A) IN GENERAL.—In the case of an applicable high yield discount obligation issued by a corporation—

(i) no deduction shall be allowed under this chapter for the disqualified portion of the original issue discount on such obligation, and

(ii) the remainder of such original issue discount shall not be allowable as a deduction until paid.

For purposes of this paragraph, rules similar to the rules of subsection (i)(3)(B) shall apply in determining the amount of the original issue discount and when the original issue discount is paid.

(B) DISQUALIFIED PORTION TREATED AS STOCK DISTRIBUTION FOR PURPOSES OF DIVIDEND RECEIVED DEDUCTION.—

(i) IN GENERAL.—Solely for purposes of sections 243, 245, 246, and 246A, the dividend equivalent portion of any amount includible in gross income of a corporation under section 1272(a) in respect of an applicable high yield discount obligation shall be treated as a dividend received by such corporation from the corporation issuing such obligation.

(ii) DIVIDEND EQUIVALENT PORTION.—For purposes of clause (i), the dividend equivalent portion of any amount includible in gross income under section 1272(a) in respect of an applicable high yield discount obligation is the portion of the amount so includible—

(I) which is attributable to the disqualified portion of the original issue discount on such obligation, and

(II) which would have been treated as a dividend if it had been a distribution made by the issuing corporation with respect to stock in such corporation.

(C) DISQUALIFIED PORTION.—

(i) IN GENERAL.—For purposes of this paragraph, the disqualified portion of the original issue discount on any applicable high yield discount obligation is the lesser of—

(I) the amount of such original issue discount, or

(II) the portion of the total return on such obligation which bears the same ratio to such total return as the disqualified yield on such obligation bears to the yield to maturity on such obligation.

(ii) DEFINITIONS.—For purposes of clause (i), the term "disqualified yield" means the excess of the yield to maturity on the obligation over the sum referred to in subsection (i)(1)(B) plus 1 percentage point, and the term "total return" is the amount which would have been the original issue discount on the obligation if interest described in the parenthetical in section 1273(a)(2) were included in the stated redemption price at maturity.

(D) EXCEPTION FOR S CORPORATIONS.—This paragraph shall not apply to any obligation issued by any corporation for any period for which such corporation is an S corporation.

(E) EFFECT ON EARNINGS AND PROFITS.—This paragraph shall not apply for purposes of determining earnings and profits; except that, for purposes of determining the dividend equivalent portion of any amount includible in gross income under section 1272(a) in respect of an applicable high yield discount obligation, no reduction shall be made for any amount attributable to the disqualified portion of any original issue discount on such obligation.

(F) SUSPENSION OF APPLICATION OF PARAGRAPH.—

(i) TEMPORARY SUSPENSION.—This paragraph shall not apply to any applicable high yield discount obligation issued during the period beginning on September 1, 2008, and ending on December 31, 2009, in exchange (including an exchange resulting from a modification of the debt instrument) for an obligation which is not an applicable high yield discount obligation and the issuer (or obligor) of which is the same as the issuer (or obligor) of such applicable high yield discount obligation. The preceding sentence shall not apply to any obligation the interest on which is interest described in section 871(h)(4) (without regard to subparagraph (D) thereof) or to any obligation issued to a related person (within the meaning of section 108(e)(4)).

(ii) SUCCESSIVE APPLICATION.—Any obligation to which clause (i) applies shall not be treated as an applicable high yield discount obligation for purposes of applying this subparagraph to any other obligation issued in exchange for such obligation.

(iii) SECRETARIAL AUTHORITY TO SUSPEND APPLICATION.—The Secretary may apply this paragraph with respect to debt instruments issued in periods following the period described in clause (i) if the Secretary determines that such application is appropriate in light of distressed conditions in the debt capital markets.

(G) CROSS REFERENCE.—

For definition of applicable high yield discount obligation, see subsection (i).

(6) CROSS REFERENCES.—

For provision relating to deduction of original issue discount on tax-exempt obligation, see section 1288.

For special rules in the case of the borrower under certain loans for personal use, see section 1275(b).

[Sec. 163(f)]

(f) DENIAL OF DEDUCTION FOR INTEREST ON CERTAIN OBLIGATIONS NOT IN REGISTERED FORM.—

(1) IN GENERAL.—Nothing in subsection (a) or in any other provision of law shall be construed to provide a deduction for interest on any registration-required obligation unless such obligation is in registered form.

(2) REGISTRATION-REQUIRED OBLIGATION.—For purposes of this section—

(A) IN GENERAL.—The term "registration-required obligation" means any obligation (including any obligation issued by a governmental entity) other than an obligation which—

(i) is issued by a natural person,

(ii) is not of a type offered to the public, or

(iii) has a maturity (at issue) of not more than 1 year.

(B) AUTHORITY TO INCLUDE OTHER OBLIGATIONS.—Clauses (ii) and (iii) of subparagraph (A) shall not apply to any obligation if—

(i) such obligation is of a type which the Secretary has determined by regulations to be used frequently in avoiding Federal taxes, and

(ii) such obligation is issued after the date on which the regulations referred to in clause (i) take effect.

(3) BOOK ENTRIES PERMITTED, ETC.—For purposes of this subsection, rules similar to the rules of section 149(a)(3) shall apply, except that a dematerialized book entry system or other book entry system specified by the Secretary shall be treated as a book entry system described in such section.

* * *

[Sec. 163(i)]

(i) APPLICABLE HIGH YIELD DISCOUNT OBLIGATION.—

(1) IN GENERAL.—For purposes of this section, the term "applicable high yield discount obligation" means any debt instrument if—

(A) the maturity date of such instrument is more than 5 years from the date of issue,

(B) the yield to maturity on such instrument equals or exceeds the sum of—

(i) the applicable Federal rate in effect under section 1274(d) for the calendar month in which the obligation is issued, plus

(ii) 5 percentage points, and

(C) such instrument has significant original issue discount.

For purposes of subparagraph (B)(i), the Secretary may by regulation (i) permit a rate to be used with respect to any debt instrument which is higher than the applicable Federal rate if the taxpayer establishes to the satisfaction of the Secretary that such higher rate is based on the same principles as the applicable Federal rate and is appropriate for the term of the instrument, or (ii) permit, on a temporary basis, a rate to be used with respect to any debt instrument which is higher than the applicable Federal rate if the Secretary determines that such rate is appropriate in light of distressed conditions in the debt capital markets.

(2) SIGNIFICANT ORIGINAL ISSUE DISCOUNT.—For purposes of paragraph (1)(C), a debt instrument shall be treated as having significant original issue discount if—

(A) the aggregate amount which would be includible in gross income with respect to such instrument for periods before the close of any accrual period (as defined in section 1272(a)(5)) ending after the date 5 years after the date of issue, exceeds—

(B) the sum of—

(i) the aggregate amount of interest to be paid under the instrument before the close of such accrual period, and

(ii) the product of the issue price of such instrument (as defined in sections 1273(b) and 1274(a)) and its yield to maturity.

(3) SPECIAL RULES.—For purposes of determining whether a debt instrument is an applicable high yield discount obligation—

(A) any payment under the instrument shall be assumed to be made on the last day permitted under the instrument, and

(B) any payment to be made in the form of another obligation of the issuer (or a related person within the meaning of section 453(f)(1) shall be assumed to be made when such obligation is required to be paid in cash or in property other than such obligation).

Except for purposes of paragraph (1)(B), any reference to an obligation in subparagraph (B) of this paragraph shall be treated as including a reference to stock.

(4) DEBT INSTRUMENT.—For purposes of this subsection, the term "debt instrument" means any instrument which is a debt instrument as defined in section 1275(a).

(5) REGULATIONS.—The Secretary shall prescribe such regulations as may be appropriate to carry out the purposes of this subsection and subsection (e)(5), including—

(A) regulations providing for modifications to the provisions of this subsection and subsection (e)(5) in the case of varying rates of interest, put or call options, indefinite maturities, contingent payments, assumptions of debt instruments, conversion rights, or other circumstances where such modifications are appropriate to carry out the purposes of this subsection and subsection (e)(5), and

(B) regulations to prevent avoidance of the purposes of this subsection and subsection (e)(5) through the use of issuers other than C corporations, agreements to borrow amounts due under the debt instrument, or other arrangements.

[Sec. 163(j)]

(j) LIMITATION ON BUSINESS INTEREST.—

(1) IN GENERAL.—The amount allowed as a deduction under this chapter for any taxable year for business interest shall not exceed the sum of—

(A) the business interest income of such taxpayer for such taxable year,

(B) 30 percent of the adjusted taxable income of such taxpayer for such taxable year, plus

(C) the floor plan financing interest of such taxpayer for such taxable year.

The amount determined under subparagraph (B) shall not be less than zero.

(2) CARRYFORWARD OF DISALLOWED BUSINESS INTEREST.—The amount of any business interest not allowed as a deduction for any taxable year by reason of paragraph (1) shall be treated as business interest paid or accrued in the succeeding taxable year.

(3) EXEMPTION FOR CERTAIN SMALL BUSINESSES.—In the case of any taxpayer (other than a tax shelter prohibited from using the cash receipts and disbursements method of accounting under section 448(a)(3)) which meets the gross receipts test of section 448(c) for any taxable year, paragraph (1) shall not apply to such taxpayer for such taxable year. In the case of any taxpayer which is not a corporation or a partnership, the gross receipts test of section 448(c) shall be applied in the same manner as if such taxpayer were a corporation or partnership.

(4) APPLICATION TO PARTNERSHIPS, ETC.—

(A) IN GENERAL.—In the case of any partnership—

(i) this subsection shall be applied at the partnership level and any deduction for business interest shall be taken into account in determining the non-separately stated taxable income or loss of the partnership, and

(ii) the adjusted taxable income of each partner of such partnership—

(I) shall be determined without regard to such partner's distributive share of any items of income, gain, deduction, or loss of such partnership, and

(II) shall be increased by such partner's distributive share of such partnership's excess taxable income.

For purposes of clause (ii)(II), a partner's distributive share of partnership excess taxable income shall be determined in the same manner as the partner's distributive share of nonseparately stated taxable income or loss of the partnership.

(B) SPECIAL RULES FOR CARRYFORWARDS.—

(i) IN GENERAL.—The amount of any business interest not allowed as a deduction to a partnership for any taxable year by reason of paragraph (1) for any taxable year—

(I) shall not be treated under paragraph (2) as business interest paid or accrued by the partnership in the succeeding taxable year, and

(II) shall, subject to clause (ii), be treated as excess business interest which is allocated to each partner in the same manner as the non-separately stated taxable income or loss of the partnership.

(ii) TREATMENT OF EXCESS BUSINESS INTEREST ALLOCATED TO PARTNERS.—If a partner is allocated any excess business interest from a partnership under clause (i) for any taxable year—

(I) such excess business interest shall be treated as business interest paid or accrued by the partner in the next succeeding taxable year in which the partner is allocated excess taxable income from such partnership, but only to the extent of such excess taxable income, and

(II) any portion of such excess business interest remaining after the application of subclause (I) shall, subject to the limitations of subclause (I), be treated as business interest paid or accrued in succeeding taxable years.

For purposes of applying this paragraph, excess taxable income allocated to a partner from a partnership for any taxable year shall not be taken into account under paragraph (1)(A) with respect to any business interest other than excess business interest from the partnership until all such excess business interest for such taxable year and all preceding taxable years has been treated as paid or accrued under clause (ii).

(iii) BASIS ADJUSTMENTS.—

(I) IN GENERAL.—The adjusted basis of a partner in a partnership interest shall be reduced (but not below zero) by the amount of excess business interest allocated to the partner under clause (i)(II).

(II) SPECIAL RULE FOR DISPOSITIONS.—If a partner disposes of a partnership interest, the adjusted basis of the partner in the partnership interest shall be increased immediately before the disposition by the amount of the excess (if any) of the amount of the basis reduction under subclause (I) over the portion of any excess business interest allocated to the partner under clause (i)(II) which has previously been treated under clause (ii) as business interest paid or accrued by the partner. The preceding sentence shall also apply to transfers of the partnership interest (including by reason of death) in a transaction in which gain is not recognized in whole or in part. No deduction shall be allowed to the transferor or transferee under this chapter for any excess business interest resulting in a basis increase under this subclause.

(C) EXCESS TAXABLE INCOME.—The term "excess taxable income" means, with respect to any partnership, the amount which bears the same ratio to the partnership's adjusted taxable income as—

(i) the excess (if any) of—

(I) the amount determined for the partnership under paragraph (1)(B), over

(II) the amount (if any) by which the business interest of the partnership, reduced by the floor plan financing interest, exceeds the business interest income of the partnership, bears to

(ii) the amount determined for the partnership under paragraph (1)(B).

(D) APPLICATION TO S CORPORATIONS.—Rules similar to the rules of subparagraphs (A) and (C) shall apply with respect to any S corporation and its shareholders.

(5) BUSINESS INTEREST.—For purposes of this subsection, the term "business interest" means any interest paid or accrued on indebtedness properly allocable to a trade or business. Such term shall not include investment interest (within the meaning of subsection (d)).

(6) BUSINESS INTEREST INCOME.—For purposes of this subsection, the term "business interest income" means the amount of interest includible in the gross income of the taxpayer for the taxable year which is properly allocable to a trade or business. Such term shall not include investment income (within the meaning of subsection (d)).

(7) TRADE OR BUSINESS.—For purposes of this subsection—

(A) IN GENERAL.—The term "trade or business" shall not include—

(i) the trade or business of performing services as an employee,

(ii) any electing real property trade or business,

(iii) any electing farming business, or

(iv) the trade or business of the furnishing or sale of—

(I) electrical energy, water, or sewage disposal services,

(II) gas or steam through a local distribution system, or

(III) transportation of gas or steam by pipeline,

if the rates for such furnishing or sale, as the case may be, have been established or approved by a State or political subdivision thereof, by any agency or instrumentality of the United States, by a public service or public utility commission or other similar body of any State or political subdivision thereof, or by the governing or ratemaking body of an electric cooperative.

(B) ELECTING REAL PROPERTY TRADE OR BUSINESS.—For purposes of this paragraph, the term "electing real property trade or business" means any trade or business which is described in section 469(c)(7)(C) and which makes an election under this subparagraph. Any such election shall be made at such time and in such manner as the Secretary shall prescribe, and, once made, shall be irrevocable.

(C) ELECTING FARMING BUSINESS.—For purposes of this paragraph, the term "electing farming business" means—

(i) a farming business (as defined in section 263A(e)(4)) which makes an election under this subparagraph, or

(ii) any trade or business of a specified agricultural or horticultural cooperative (as defined in section 199A(g)(2)) with respect to which the cooperative makes an election under this subparagraph.

Any such election shall be made at such time and in such manner as the Secretary shall prescribe, and, once made, shall be irrevocable.

(8) ADJUSTED TAXABLE INCOME.—For purposes of this subsection, the term "adjusted taxable income" means the taxable income of the taxpayer—

(A) computed without regard to—

(i) any item of income, gain, deduction, or loss which is not properly allocable to a trade or business,

(ii) any business interest or business interest income,

(iii) the amount of any net operating loss deduction under section 172,

(iv) the amount of any deduction allowed under section 199A, and

(v) in the case of taxable years beginning before January 1, 2022, any deduction allowable for depreciation, amortization, or depletion, and

(B) computed with such other adjustments as provided by the Secretary.

(9) FLOOR PLAN FINANCING INTEREST DEFINED.—For purposes of this subsection—

(A) IN GENERAL.—The term "floor plan financing interest" means interest paid or accrued on floor plan financing indebtedness.

(B) FLOOR PLAN FINANCING INDEBTEDNESS.—The term "floor plan financing indebtedness" means indebtedness—

(i) used to finance the acquisition of motor vehicles held for sale or lease, and

(ii) secured by the inventory so acquired.

(C) MOTOR VEHICLE.—The term "motor vehicle" means a motor vehicle that is any of the following:

(i) Any self-propelled vehicle designed for transporting persons or property on a public street, highway, or road.

(ii) A boat.

(iii) Farm machinery or equipment.

(10) SPECIAL RULE FOR TAXABLE YEARS BEGINNING IN 2019 AND 2020.—

(A) IN GENERAL.—

(i) IN GENERAL.—Except as provided in clause (ii) or (iii), in the case of any taxable year beginning in 2019 or 2020, paragraph (1)(B) shall be applied by substituting "50 percent" for "30 percent".

(ii) SPECIAL RULE FOR PARTNERSHIPS.—In the case of a partnership—

(I) clause (i) shall not apply to any taxable year beginning in 2019, but

(II) unless a partner elects not to have this subclause apply, in the case of any excess business interest of the partnership for any taxable year beginning in 2019 which is allocated to the partner under paragraph (4)(B)(i)(II)—

(aa) 50 percent of such excess business interest shall be treated as business interest which, notwithstanding paragraph (4)(B)(ii), is paid or accrued by the partner in the partner's first taxable year beginning in 2020 and which is not subject to the limits of paragraph (1), and

(bb) 50 percent of such excess business interest shall be subject to the limitations of paragraph (4)(B)(ii) in the same manner as any other excess business interest so allocated.

(iii) ELECTION OUT.—A taxpayer may elect, at such time and in such manner as the Secretary may prescribe, not to have clause (i) apply to any taxable year. Such an election, once made, may be revoked only with the consent of the Secretary. In the case of a partnership, any such election shall be made by the partnership and may be made only for taxable years beginning in 2020.

(B) ELECTION TO USE 2019 ADJUSTED TAXABLE INCOME FOR TAXABLE YEARS BEGINNING IN 2020.—

(i) IN GENERAL.—Subject to clause (ii), in the case of any taxable year beginning in 2020, the taxpayer may elect to apply this subsection by substituting the adjusted taxable income of the taxpayer for the last taxable year beginning in 2019 for the adjusted taxable income for such taxable year. In the case of a partnership, any such election shall be made by the partnership.

(ii) SPECIAL RULE FOR SHORT TAXABLE YEARS.—If an election is made under clause (i) for a taxable year which is a short taxable year, the adjusted taxable income for the taxpayer's last taxable year beginning in 2019 which is substituted under clause (i) shall be equal to the amount which bears the same ratio to such adjusted taxable income determined without regard to this clause as the number of months in the short taxable year bears to 12.

(11) CROSS REFERENCES.—

(A) For requirement that an electing real property trade or business use the alternative depreciation system, see section 168(g)(1)(F).

(B) For requirement that an electing farming business use the alternative depreciation system, see section 168(g)(1)(G).

* * *

[Sec. 164]

SEC. 164. TAXES.

[Sec. 164(a)]

(a) GENERAL RULE.—Except as otherwise provided in this section, the following taxes shall be allowed as a deduction for the taxable year within which paid or accrued:

(1) State and local, and foreign, real property taxes.

(2) State and local personal property taxes.

(3) State and local, and foreign, income, war profits, and excess profits taxes.

(4) The GST tax imposed on income distributions.

In addition, there shall be allowed as a deduction State and local, and foreign, taxes not described in the preceding sentence which are paid or accrued within the taxable year in carrying on a trade or business or an activity described in section 212 (relating to expenses for production of income). Notwithstanding the preceding sentence, any tax (not described in the first sentence of this subsection) which is paid or accrued by the taxpayer in connection with an acquisition or disposition of property shall be treated as part of the cost of the acquired property or, in the case of a disposition, as a reduction in the amount realized on the disposition.

[Sec. 164(b)]

(b) DEFINITIONS AND SPECIAL RULES.—For purposes of this section—

(1) PERSONAL PROPERTY TAXES.—The term "personal property tax" means an ad valorem tax which is imposed on an annual basis in respect of personal property.

(2) STATE OR LOCAL TAXES.—A State or local tax includes only a tax imposed by a State, a possession of the United States, or a political subdivision of any of the foregoing, or by the District of Columbia.

(3) FOREIGN TAXES.—A foreign tax includes only a tax imposed by the authority of a foreign country.

* * *

(6) LIMITATION ON INDIVIDUAL DEDUCTIONS FOR TAXABLE YEARS 2018 THROUGH 2025.—In the case of an individual and a taxable year beginning after December 31, 2017, and before January 1, 2026—

(A) foreign real property taxes shall not be taken into account under subsection (a)(1), and

(B) the aggregate amount of taxes taken into account under paragraphs (1), (2), and (3) of subsection (a) and paragraph (5) of this subsection for any taxable year shall not exceed $10,000 ($5,000 in the case of a married individual filing a separate return).

The preceding sentence shall not apply to any foreign taxes described in subsection (a)(3) or to any taxes described in paragraph (1) and (2) of subsection (a) which are paid or accrued in carrying on a trade or business or an activity described in section 212. For purposes of subparagraph (B), an amount paid in a taxable year beginning before January 1, 2018, with respect to a State or local income tax imposed for a taxable year beginning after December 31, 2017, shall be treated as paid on the last day of the taxable year for which such tax is so imposed.

* * *

[Sec. 165]

SEC. 165. LOSSES.

[Sec. 165(a)]

(a) GENERAL RULE.—There shall be allowed as a deduction any loss sustained during the taxable year and not compensated for by insurance or otherwise.

* * *

[Sec. 165(c)]

(c) LIMITATION ON LOSSES OF INDIVIDUALS.—In the case of an individual, the deduction under subsection (a) shall be limited to—

(1) losses incurred in a trade or business;

(2) losses incurred in any transaction entered into for profit, though not connected with a trade or business; and

(3) except as provided in subsection (h) [relating to casualty gains and losses], losses of property not connected with a trade or business or a transaction entered into for profit, if such losses arise from fire, storm, shipwreck, or other casualty, or from theft.

* * *

[Sec. 165(g)]

(g) WORTHLESS SECURITIES.—

(1) GENERAL RULE.—If any security which is a capital asset becomes worthless during the taxable year, the loss resulting therefrom shall, for purposes of this subtitle, be treated as a loss from the sale or exchange, on the last day of the taxable year, of a capital asset.

(2) SECURITY DEFINED.—For purposes of this subsection, the term "security" means—

(A) a share of stock in a corporation;

(B) a right to subscribe for, or to receive, a share of stock in a corporation; or

(C) a bond, debenture, note, or certificate, or other evidence of indebtedness, issued by a corporation or by a government or political subdivision thereof, with interest coupons or in registered form.

* * *

[Sec. 165(j)]

(j) DENIAL OF DEDUCTION FOR LOSSES ON CERTAIN OBLIGATIONS NOT IN REGISTERED FORM.—

(1) IN GENERAL.—Nothing in subsection (a) or in any other provision of law shall be construed to provide a deduction for any loss sustained on any registration-required obligation unless such obligation is in registered form (or the issuance of such obligation was subject to tax under section 4701).

(2) DEFINITIONS.—For purposes of this subsection—

(A) REGISTRATION-REQUIRED OBLIGATION.—The term "registration-required obligation" has the meaning given to such term by section 163(f)(2).

(B) REGISTERED FORM.—The term "registered form" has the same meaning as when used in section 163(f).

(3) EXCEPTIONS.—The Secretary may, by regulations, provide that this subsection and section 1287 shall not apply with respect to obligations held by any person if—

(A) such person holds such obligations in connection with a trade or business outside the United States,

(B) such person holds such obligations as a broker dealer (registered under Federal or State law) for sale to customers in the ordinary course of his trade or business,

(C) such person complies with reporting requirements with respect to ownership, transfers, and payments as the Secretary may require, or

(D) such person promptly surrenders the obligation to the issuer for the issuance of a new obligation in registered form,

but only if such obligations are held under arrangements provided in regulations or otherwise which are designed to assure that such obligations are not delivered to any United States person other than a person described in subparagraph (A), (B), or (C).

* * *

[Sec. 166]

SEC. 166. BAD DEBTS.

[Sec. 166(a)]

(a) GENERAL RULE.—

(1) WHOLLY WORTHLESS DEBTS.—There shall be allowed as a deduction any debt which becomes worthless within the taxable year.

(2) PARTIALLY WORTHLESS DEBTS.—When satisfied that a debt is recoverable only in part, the Secretary may allow such debt, in an amount not in excess of the part charged off within the taxable year, as a deduction.

[Sec. 166(b)]

(b) AMOUNT OF DEDUCTION.—For purposes of subsection (a), the basis for determining the amount of the deduction for any bad debt shall be the adjusted basis provided in section 1011 for determining the loss from the sale or other disposition of property.

[Sec. 166(c)—Stricken]

[Sec. 166(d)]

(d) NONBUSINESS DEBTS.—

(1) GENERAL RULE.—In the case of a taxpayer other than a corporation—

(A) subsection (a) shall not apply to any nonbusiness debt; and

(B) where any nonbusiness debt becomes worthless within the taxable year, the loss resulting therefrom shall be considered a loss from the sale or exchange, during the taxable year, of a capital asset held for not more than 1 year.

(2) NONBUSINESS DEBT DEFINED.—For purposes of paragraph (1), the term "nonbusiness debt" means a debt other than—

(A) a debt created or acquired (as the case may be) in connection with a trade or business of the taxpayer; or

(B) a debt the loss from the worthlessness of which is incurred in the taxpayer's trade or business.

[Sec. 166(e)]

(e) WORTHLESS SECURITIES.—This section shall not apply to a debt which is evidenced by a security as defined in section 165(g)(2)(C).

* * *

[Sec. 168]

SEC. 168. ACCELERATED COST RECOVERY SYSTEM.

* * *

[Sec. 168(g)]

(g) ALTERNATIVE DEPRECIATION SYSTEM FOR CERTAIN PROPERTY.—

(1) IN GENERAL.—In the case of—

(A) any tangible property which during the taxable year is used predominantly outside the United States,

(B) any tax-exempt use property,

(C) any tax-exempt bond financed property,

(D) any imported property covered by an Executive order under paragraph (6),

(E) any property to which an election under paragraph (7) applies,

(F) any property described in paragraph (8), and

(G) any property with a recovery period of 10 years or more which is held by an electing farming business (as defined in section 163(j)(7)(C)),

the depreciation deduction provided by section 167(a) shall be determined under the alternative depreciation system.

* * *

(4) EXCEPTION FOR CERTAIN PROPERTY USED OUTSIDE UNITED STATES.—Subparagraph (A) of paragraph (1) shall not apply to—

(A) any aircraft which is registered by the Administrator of the Federal Aviation Agency and which is operated to and from the United States or is operated under contract with the United States;

(B) rolling stock which is used within and without the United States and which is—

(i) of a rail carrier subject to part A of subtitle IV of title 49, or

(ii) of a United States person (other than a corporation described in clause (i)) but only if the rolling stock is not leased to one or more foreign persons for periods aggregating more than 12 months in any 24-month period;

(C) any vessel documented under the laws of the United States which is operated in the foreign or domestic commerce of the United States;

(D) any motor vehicle of a United States person (as defined in section 7701(a)(30)) which is operated to and from the United States;

(E) any container of a United States person which is used in the transportation of property to and from the United States;

(F) any property (other than a vessel or an aircraft) of a United States person which is used for the purpose of exploring for, developing, removing, or transporting resources from the outer Continental Shelf (within the meaning of section 2 of the Outer Continental Shelf Lands Act, as amended and supplemented; (43 U.S.C. 1331));

(G) any property which is owned by a domestic corporation or by a United States citizen (other than a citizen entitled to the benefits of section 931 or 933) and which is used predominantly in a possession of the United States by such a corporation or such a citizen, or by a corporation created or organized in, or under the law of, a possession of the United States;

(H) any communications satellite (as defined in section 103(3) of the Communications Satellite Act of 1962, 47 U.S.C. 702(3)), or any interest therein, of a United States person;

(I) any cable, or any interest therein, of a domestic corporation engaged in furnishing telephone service to which section 168(i)(10)(C) applies (or of a wholly owned domestic subsidiary of such a corporation), if such cable is part of a submarine cable system which constitutes part of a communication link exclusively between the United States and one or more foreign countries;

(J) any property (other than a vessel or an aircraft) of a United States person which is used in international or territorial waters within the northern portion of the Western Hemisphere for the purpose of exploring for, developing, removing, or transporting resources from ocean waters or deposits under such waters;

(K) any property described in section 48(l)(3)(A)(ix) (as in effect on the day before the date of the enactment of the Revenue Reconciliation Act of 1990) which is owned by a United States person and which is used in international or territorial waters to generate energy for use in the United States; and

(L) any satellite (not described in subparagraph (H)) or other spacecraft (or any interest therein) held by a United States person if such satellite or other spacecraft was launched from within the United States.

For purposes of subparagraph (J), the term "northern portion of the Western Hemisphere" means the area lying west of the 30th meridian west of Greenwich, east of the international dateline, and north of the Equator, but not including any foreign country which is a country of South America.

* * *

»»→ Caution: Code Sec. 174, below, prior to amendment by P.L. 115-97, applies to amounts paid or incurred in tax years beginning on or before December 31, 2021.

[Sec. 174]

SEC. 174. RESEARCH AND EXPERIMENTAL EXPENDITURES.

[Sec. 174(a)]

(a) TREATMENT AS EXPENSES.—

(1) IN GENERAL.—A taxpayer may treat research or experimental expenditures which are paid or incurred by him during the taxable year in connection with his trade or business as expenses which are not chargeable to capital account. The expenditures so treated shall be allowed as a deduction.

(2) WHEN METHOD MAY BE ADOPTED.—

(A) WITHOUT CONSENT.—A taxpayer may, without the consent of the Secretary, adopt the method provided in this subsection for his first taxable year for which expenditures described in paragraph (1) are paid or incurred.

(B) WITH CONSENT.—A taxpayer may, with the consent of the Secretary, adopt at any time the method provided in this subsection.

(3) SCOPE.—The method adopted under this subsection shall apply to all expenditures described in paragraph (1). The method adopted shall be adhered to in computing taxable income for the taxable year and for all subsequent taxable years unless, with the approval of the Secretary, a change to a different method is authorized with respect to part or all of such expenditures.

[Sec. 174(b)]

(b) AMORTIZATION OF CERTAIN RESEARCH AND EXPERIMENTAL EXPENDITURES.—

(1) IN GENERAL.—At the election of the taxpayer, made in accordance with regulations prescribed by the Secretary, research or experimental expenditures which are—

(A) paid or incurred by the taxpayer in connection with his trade or business,

(B) not treated as expenses under subsection (a), and

(C) chargeable to capital account but not chargeable to property of a character which is subject to the allowance under section 167 (relating to allowance for depreciation, etc.) or section 611 (relating to allowance for depletion),

may be treated as deferred expenses. In computing taxable income, such deferred expenses shall be allowed as a deduction ratably over such period of not less than 60 months as may be selected by the taxpayer (beginning with the month in which the taxpayer first realizes benefits from such expenditures). Such deferred expenses are expenditures properly chargeable to capital account for purposes of section 1016(a)(1) (relating to adjustments to basis of property).

(2) TIME FOR AND SCOPE OF ELECTION.—The election provided by paragraph (1) may be made for any taxable year, but only if made not later than the time prescribed by law for filing the return for such taxable year (including extensions thereof). The method so elected, and the period selected by the taxpayer, shall be adhered to in computing taxable income for the taxable year for which the election is made and for all subsequent taxable years unless, with the approval of the Secretary, a change to a different method (or to a different period) is authorized with respect to part or all of such expenditures. The election shall not apply to any expenditure paid or incurred during any taxable year before the taxable year for which the taxpayer makes the election.

[Sec. 174(c)]

(c) LAND AND OTHER PROPERTY.—This section shall not apply to any expenditure for the acquisition or improvement of land, or for the acquisition or improvement of property to be used in connection with the research or experimentation and of a character which is subject to the allowance under section 167 (relating to allowance for depreciation, etc.) or section 611 (relating to allowance for depletion); but for purposes of this section allowances under section 167, and allowances under section 611, shall be considered as expenditures.

[Sec. 174(d)]

(d) EXPLORATION EXPENDITURES.—This section shall not apply to any expenditure paid or incurred for the purpose of ascertaining the existence, location, extent, or quality of any deposit of ore or other mineral (including oil and gas).

[Sec. 174(e)]

(e) ONLY REASONABLE RESEARCH EXPENDITURES ELIGIBLE.—This section shall apply to a research or experimental expenditure only to the extent that the amount thereof is reasonable under the circumstances.

[Sec. 174(f)]

(f) CROSS REFERENCES.—

(1) For adjustments to basis of property for amounts allowed as deductions as deferred expenses under subsection (b), see section 1016(a)(14).

(2) For election of 10-year amortization of expenditures allowable as a deduction under subsection (a), see section 59(e).

»»→ Caution: Code Sec. 174, below, as amended by P.L. 115-97, applies to amounts paid or incurred in tax years beginning after December 31, 2021.

[Sec. 174]

SEC. 174. AMORTIZATION OF RESEARCH AND EXPERIMENTAL EXPENDITURES.

[Sec. 174(a)]

(a) IN GENERAL.—In the case of a taxpayer's specified research or experimental expenditures for any taxable year—

(1) except as provided in paragraph (2), no deduction shall be allowed for such expenditures, and

(2) the taxpayer shall—

(A) charge such expenditures to capital account, and

(B) be allowed an amortization deduction of such expenditures ratably over the 5-year period (15-year period in the case of any specified research or experimental expenditures which are attributable to foreign research (within the meaning of section 41(d)(4)(F))) beginning with the midpoint of the taxable year in which such expenditures are paid or incurred.

[Sec. 174(b)]

(b) SPECIFIED RESEARCH OR EXPERIMENTAL EXPENDITURES.—For purposes of this section, the term "specified research or experimental expenditures" means, with respect to any taxable year, research or experimental expenditures which are paid or incurred by the taxpayer during such taxable year in connection with the taxpayer's trade or business.

[Sec. 174(c)]

(c) SPECIAL RULES.—

(1) LAND AND OTHER PROPERTY.—This section shall not apply to any expenditure for the acquisition or improvement of land, or for the acquisition or improvement of property to be used in connection with the research or experimentation and of a character which is subject to the allowance under section 167 (relating to allowance for depreciation, etc.) or section 611 (relating to allowance for depletion); but for purposes of this section allowances under section 167, and allowances under section 611, shall be considered as expenditures.

(2) EXPLORATION EXPENDITURES.—This section shall not apply to any expenditure paid or incurred for the purpose of ascertaining the existence, location, extent, or quality of any deposit of ore or other mineral (including oil and gas).

(3) SOFTWARE DEVELOPMENT.—For purposes of this section, any amount paid or incurred in connection with the development of any software shall be treated as a research or experimental expenditure.

[Sec. 174(d)]

(d) TREATMENT UPON DISPOSITION, RETIREMENT, OR ABANDONMENT.—If any property with respect to which specified research or experimental expenditures are paid or incurred is disposed, retired, or abandoned during the period during which such expenditures are allowed as an amortization deduction under this section, no deduction shall be allowed with respect to such expenditures on account of such disposition, retirement, or abandonment and such amortization deduction shall continue with respect to such expenditures.

[Sec. 176]

SEC. 176. PAYMENTS WITH RESPECT TO EMPLOYEES OF CERTAIN FOREIGN CORPORATIONS.

In the case of a domestic corporation, there shall be allowed as a deduction amounts (to the extent not compensated for) paid or incurred pursuant to an agreement entered into under section 3121(l) with respect to services performed by United States citizens employed by foreign subsidiary corporations. Any reimbursement of any amount previously allowed as a deduction under this section shall be included in gross income for the taxable year in which received.

[Sec. 197]

SEC. 197. AMORTIZATION OF GOODWILL AND CERTAIN OTHER INTANGIBLES.

[Sec. 197(a)]

(a) GENERAL RULE.—A taxpayer shall be entitled to an amortization deduction with respect to any amortizable section 197 intangible. The amount of such deduction shall be determined by amortizing the adjusted basis (for purposes of determining gain) of such intangible ratably over the 15-year period beginning with the month in which such intangible was acquired.

[Sec. 197(b)]

(b) NO OTHER DEPRECIATION OR AMORTIZATION DEDUCTION ALLOWABLE.—Except as provided in subsection (a), no depreciation or amortization deduction shall be allowable with respect to any amortizable section 197 intangible.

[Sec. 197(c)]

(c) AMORTIZABLE SECTION 197 INTANGIBLE.—For purposes of this section—

(1) IN GENERAL.—Except as otherwise provided in this section, the term "amortizable section 197 intangible" means any section 197 intangible—

(A) which is acquired by the taxpayer after the date of the enactment of this section, and

(B) which is held in connection with the conduct of a trade or business or an activity described in section 212.

(2) EXCLUSION OF SELF-CREATED INTANGIBLES, ETC.—The term "amortizable section 197 intangible" shall not include any section 197 intangible—

(A) which is not described in subparagraph (D), (E), or (F) of subsection (d)(1), and

(B) which is created by the taxpayer.

This paragraph shall not apply if the intangible is created in connection with a transaction (or series of related transactions) involving the acquisition of assets constituting a trade or business or substantial portion thereof.

(3) ANTI-CHURNING RULES.—

For exclusion of intangibles acquired in certain transactions, see subsection (f)(9).

[Sec. 197(d)]

(d) SECTION 197 INTANGIBLE.—For purposes of this section—

(1) IN GENERAL.—Except as otherwise provided in this section, the term "section 197 intangible" means—

(A) goodwill,

(B) going concern value,

(C) any of the following intangible items:

(i) workforce in place including its composition and terms and conditions (contractual or otherwise) of its employment,

(ii) business books and records, operating systems, or any other information base (including lists or other information with respect to current or prospective customers),

(iii) any patent, copyright, formula, process, design, pattern, knowhow, format, or other similar item,

(iv) any customer-based intangible,

(v) any supplier-based intangible, and

(vi) any other similar item,

(D) any license, permit, or other right granted by a governmental unit or an agency or instrumentality thereof,

(E) any covenant not to compete (or other arrangement to the extent such arrangement has substantially the same effect as a covenant not to compete) entered into in connection with an acquisition (directly or indirectly) of an interest in a trade or business or substantial portion thereof, and

(F) any franchise, trademark, or trade name.

(2) CUSTOMER-BASED INTANGIBLE.—

(A) IN GENERAL.—The term "customer-based intangible" means—

(i) composition of market,

(ii) market share, and

(iii) any other value resulting from future provision of goods or services pursuant to relationships (contractual or otherwise) in the ordinary course of business with customers.

(B) SPECIAL RULE FOR FINANCIAL INSTITUTIONS.—In the case of a financial institution, the term "customer-based intangible" includes deposit base and similar items.

(3) SUPPLIER-BASED INTANGIBLE.—The term "supplier-based intangible" means any value resulting from future acquisitions of goods or services pursuant to relationships (contractual or otherwise) in the ordinary course of business with suppliers of goods or services to be used or sold by the taxpayer.

[Sec. 197(e)]

(e) EXCEPTIONS.—For purposes of this section, the term "section 197 intangible" shall not include any of the following:

(1) FINANCIAL INTERESTS.—Any interest—

(A) in a corporation, partnership, trust, or estate, or

(B) under an existing futures contract, foreign currency contract, notional principal contract, or other similar financial contract.

(2) LAND.—Any interest in land.

(3) COMPUTER SOFTWARE.—

(A) IN GENERAL.—Any—

(i) computer software which is readily available for purchase by the general public, is subject to a nonexclusive license, and has not been substantially modified, and

(ii) other computer software which is not acquired in a transaction (or series of related transactions) involving the acquisition of assets constituting a trade or business or substantial portion thereof.

(B) COMPUTER SOFTWARE DEFINED.—For purposes of subparagraph (A), the term "computer software" means any program designed to cause a computer to perform a desired function. Such term shall not include any data base or similar item unless the data base or item is in the public domain and is incidental to the operation of otherwise qualifying computer software.

(4) CERTAIN INTERESTS OR RIGHTS ACQUIRED SEPARATELY.—Any of the following not acquired in a transaction (or series of related transactions) involving the acquisition of assets constituting a trade business or substantial portion thereof:

(A) Any interest in a film, sound recording, video tape, book, or similar property.

(B) Any right to receive tangible property or services under a contract or granted by a governmental unit or agency or instrumentality thereof.

(C) Any interest in a patent or copyright.

(D) To the extent provided in regulations, any right under a contract (or granted by a governmental unit or an agency or instrumentality thereof) if such right—

(i) has a fixed duration of less than 15 years, or

(ii) is fixed as to amount and, without regard to this section, would be recoverable under a method similar to the unit-of-production method.

(5) INTERESTS UNDER LEASES AND DEBT INSTRUMENTS.—Any interest under—

(A) an existing lease of tangible property, or

(B) except as provided in subsection (d)(2)(B), any existing indebtedness.

(6) MORTGAGE SERVICING.—Any right to service indebtedness which is secured by residential real property unless such right is acquired in a transaction (or series of related transactions) involving the acquisition of assests (other than rights described in this paragraph) constituting a trade or business or substantial portion thereof.

(7) CERTAIN TRANSACTION COSTS.—Any fees for professional services, and any transaction costs, incurred by parties to a transaction with respect to which any portion of the gain or loss is not recognized under part III of subchapter C.

[Sec. 197(f)]

(f) SPECIAL RULES.—

* * *

(3) TREATMENT OF AMOUNTS PAID PURSUANT TO COVENANTS NOT TO COMPETE, ETC.—Any amount paid or incurred pursuant to a covenant or arrangement referred to in subsection (d)(1)(E) shall be treated as an amount chargeable to capital account.

(4) TREATMENT OF FRANCHISES, ETC.—

(A) FRANCHISE.—The term "franchise" has the meaning given to such term by section 1253(b)(1).

(B) TREATMENT OF RENEWALS.—Any renewal of a franchise, trademark, or trade name (or of a license, a permit, or other right referred to in subsection (d)(1)(D)) shall be treated as an acquisition. The preceding sentence shall only apply with respect to costs incurred in connection with such renewal.

(C) CERTAIN AMOUNTS NOT TAKEN INTO ACCOUNT.—Any amount to which section 1253(d)(1) applies shall not be taken into account under this section.

* * *

(7) TREATMENT AS DEPRECIABLE.—For purposes of this chapter, any amortizable section 197 intangible shall be treated as property which is of a character subject to the allowance for depreciation provided in section 167.

* * *

[Sec. 199A]

SEC. 199A. QUALIFIED BUSINESS INCOME.

[Sec. 199A(a)]

(a) ALLOWANCE OF DEDUCTION.—In the case of a taxpayer other than a corporation, there shall be allowed as a deduction for any taxable year an amount equal to the lesser of—

(1) the combined qualified business income amount of the taxpayer, or

(2) an amount equal to 20 percent of the excess (if any) of—

(A) the taxable income of the taxpayer for the taxable year, over

(B) the net capital gain (as defined in section 1(h)) of the taxpayer for such taxable year.

[Sec. 199A(b)]

(b) COMBINED QUALIFIED BUSINESS INCOME AMOUNT.—For purposes of this section—

(1) IN GENERAL.—The term "combined qualified business income amount" means, with respect to any taxable year, an amount equal to—

(A) the sum of the amounts determined under paragraph (2) for each qualified trade or business carried on by the taxpayer, plus

(B) 20 percent of the aggregate amount of the qualified REIT dividends and qualified publicly traded partnership income of the taxpayer for the taxable year.

(2) DETERMINATION OF DEDUCTIBLE AMOUNT FOR EACH TRADE OR BUSINESS.—The amount determined under this paragraph with respect to any qualified trade or business is the lesser of—

(A) 20 percent of the taxpayer's qualified business income with respect to the qualified trade or business, or

(B) the greater of—

(i) 50 percent of the W–2 wages with respect to the qualified trade or business, or

(ii) the sum of 25 percent of the W–2 wages with respect to the qualified trade or business, plus 2.5 percent of the unadjusted basis immediately after acquisition of all qualified property.

(3) MODIFICATIONS TO LIMIT BASED ON TAXABLE INCOME.—

(A) EXCEPTION FROM LIMIT.—In the case of any taxpayer whose taxable income for the taxable year does not exceed the threshold amount, paragraph (2) shall be applied without regard to subparagraph (B).

(B) PHASE-IN OF LIMIT FOR CERTAIN TAXPAYERS.—

(i) IN GENERAL.—If—

(I) the taxable income of a taxpayer for any taxable year exceeds the threshold amount, but does not exceed the sum of the threshold amount plus $50,000 ($100,000 in the case of a joint return), and

(II) the amount determined under paragraph (2)(B) (determined without regard to this subparagraph) with respect to any qualified trade or business carried on by the taxpayer is less than the amount determined under paragraph (2)(A) with respect [to] such trade or business,

then paragraph (2) shall be applied with respect to such trade or business without regard to subparagraph (B) thereof and by reducing the amount determined under subparagraph (A) thereof by the amount determined under clause (ii).

(ii) AMOUNT OF REDUCTION.—The amount determined under this subparagraph is the amount which bears the same ratio to the excess amount as—

(I) the amount by which the taxpayer's taxable income for the taxable year exceeds the threshold amount, bears to

(II) $50,000 ($100,000 in the case of a joint return).

(iii) EXCESS AMOUNT.—For purposes of clause (ii), the excess amount is the excess of—

(I) the amount determined under paragraph (2)(A) (determined without regard to this paragraph), over

(II) the amount determined under paragraph (2)(B) (determined without regard to this paragraph).

(4) WAGES, ETC.—

(A) IN GENERAL.—The term "W–2 wages" means, with respect to any person for any taxable year of such person, the amounts described in paragraphs (3) and (8) of section 6051(a) paid by such person with respect to employment of employees by such person during the calendar year ending during such taxable year.

(B) LIMITATION TO WAGES ATTRIBUTABLE TO QUALIFIED BUSINESS INCOME.—Such term shall not include any amount which is not properly allocable to qualified business income for purposes of subsection (c)(1).

(C) RETURN REQUIREMENT.—Such term shall not include any amount which is not properly included in a return filed with the Social Security Administration on or before the 60th day after the due date (including extensions) for such return.

(5) ACQUISITIONS, DISPOSITIONS, AND SHORT TAXABLE YEARS.—The Secretary shall provide for the application of this subsection in cases of a short taxable year or where the taxpayer acquires, or disposes of, the major portion of a trade or business or the major portion of a separate unit of a trade or business during the taxable year.

(6) QUALIFIED PROPERTY.—For purposes of this section:

(A) IN GENERAL.—The term "qualified property" means, with respect to any qualified trade or business for a taxable year, tangible property of a character subject to the allowance for depreciation under section 167—

(i) which is held by, and available for use in, the qualified trade or business at the close of the taxable year,

(ii) which is used at any point during the taxable year in the production of qualified business income, and

(iii) the depreciable period for which has not ended before the close of the taxable year.

(B) DEPRECIABLE PERIOD.—The term "depreciable period" means, with respect to qualified property of a taxpayer, the period beginning on the date the property was first placed in service by the taxpayer and ending on the later of—

(i) the date that is 10 years after such date, or

(ii) the last day of the last full year in the applicable recovery period that would apply to the property under section 168 (determined without regard to subsection (g) thereof).

(7) SPECIAL RULE WITH RESPECT TO INCOME RECEIVED FROM COOPERATIVES.—In the case of any qualified trade or business of a patron of a specified agricultural or horticultural cooperative, the amount determined under paragraph (2) with respect to such trade or business shall be reduced by the lesser of—

(A) 9 percent of so much of the qualified business income with respect to such trade or business as is properly allocable to qualified payments received from such cooperative, or

(B) 50 percent of so much of the W-2 wages with respect to such trade or business as are so allocable.

[Sec. 199A(c)]

(c) QUALIFIED BUSINESS INCOME.—For purposes of this section—

(1) IN GENERAL.—The term "qualified business income" means, for any taxable year, the net amount of qualified items of income, gain, deduction, and loss with respect to any qualified trade or business of the taxpayer. Such term shall not include any qualified REIT dividends or qualified publicly traded partnership income.

(2) CARRYOVER OF LOSSES.—If the net amount of qualified income, gain, deduction, and loss with respect to qualified trades or businesses of the taxpayer for any taxable year is less than zero, such amount shall be treated as a loss from a qualified trade or business in the succeeding taxable year.

(3) QUALIFIED ITEMS OF INCOME, GAIN, DEDUCTION, AND LOSS.—For purposes of this subsection—

(A) IN GENERAL.—The term "qualified items of income, gain, deduction, and loss" means items of income, gain, deduction, and loss to the extent such items are—

(i) effectively connected with the conduct of a trade or business within the United States (within the meaning of section 864(c), determined by substituting "qualified trade or business (within the meaning of section 199A)" for "nonresident alien individual or a foreign corporation" or for "a foreign corporation" each place it appears), and

(ii) included or allowed in determining taxable income for the taxable year.

(B) EXCEPTIONS.—The following items shall not be taken into account as a qualified item of income, gain, deduction, or loss:

(i) Any item of short-term capital gain, short-term capital loss, long-term capital gain, or long-term capital loss.

(ii) Any dividend, income equivalent to a dividend, or payment in lieu of dividends described in section 954(c)(1)(G). Any amount described in section 1385(a)(1) shall not be treated as described in this clause.

(iii) Any interest income other than interest income which is properly allocable to a trade or business.

(iv) Any item of gain or loss described in subparagraph (C) or (D) of section 954(c)(1) (applied by substituting "qualified trade or business" for "controlled foreign corporation").

(v) Any item of income, gain, deduction, or loss taken into account under section 954(c)(1)(F) (determined without regard to clause (ii) thereof and other than items attributable to notional principal contracts entered into in transactions qualifying under section 1221(a)(7)).

(vi) Any amount received from an annuity which is not received in connection with the trade or business.

(vii) Any item of deduction or loss properly allocable to an amount described in any of the preceding clauses.

(4) TREATMENT OF REASONABLE COMPENSATION AND GUARANTEED PAYMENTS.—Qualified business income shall not include—

(A) reasonable compensation paid to the taxpayer by any qualified trade or business of the taxpayer for services rendered with respect to the trade or business,

(B) any guaranteed payment described in section 707(c) paid to a partner for services rendered with respect to the trade or business, and

(C) to the extent provided in regulations, any payment described in section 707(a) to a partner for services rendered with respect to the trade or business.

[Sec. 199A(d)]

(d) QUALIFIED TRADE OR BUSINESS.—For purposes of this section—

(1) IN GENERAL.—The term "qualified trade or business" means any trade or business other than—

(A) a specified service trade or business, or

(B) the trade or business of performing services as an employee.

(2) SPECIFIED SERVICE TRADE OR BUSINESS.—The term "specified service trade or business" means any trade or business—

(A) which is described in section 1202(e)(3)(A) (applied without regard to the words "engineering, architecture,") or which would be so described if the term "employees or owners" were substituted for "employees" therein, or

(B) which involves the performance of services that consist of investing and investment management, trading, or dealing in securities (as defined in section 475(c)(2)), partnership interests, or commodities (as defined in section 475(e)(2)).

(3) EXCEPTION FOR SPECIFIED SERVICE BUSINESSES BASED ON TAXPAYER'S INCOME.—

(A) IN GENERAL.—If, for any taxable year, the taxable income of any taxpayer is less than the sum of the threshold amount plus $50,000 ($100,000 in the case of a joint return), then—

(i) any specified service trade or business of the taxpayer shall not fail to be treated as a qualified trade or business due to paragraph (1)(A), but

(ii) only the applicable percentage of qualified items of income, gain, deduction, or loss, and the W–2 wages and the unadjusted basis immediately after acquisition of qualified property, of the taxpayer allocable to such specified service trade or business shall be taken into account in computing the qualified business income, W–2 wages, and the unadjusted basis immediately after acquisition of qualified property of the taxpayer for the taxable year for purposes of applying this section.

(B) APPLICABLE PERCENTAGE.—For purposes of subparagraph (A), the term "applicable percentage" means, with respect to any taxable year, 100 percent reduced (not below zero) by the percentage equal to the ratio of—

(i) the taxable income of the taxpayer for the taxable year in excess of the threshold amount, bears to

(ii) $50,000 ($100,000 in the case of a joint return).

[Sec. 199A(e)]

(e) OTHER DEFINITIONS.—For purposes of this section—

(1) TAXABLE INCOME.—Except as otherwise provided in subsection (g)(2)(B), taxable income shall be computed without regard to any deduction allowable under this section.

»»→ Caution: Pursuant to Section 199A(e)(2)(B), for taxable years beginning in 2023, the inflation-adjusted threshold amounts under Section 199A(e)(2) are $364,200 for married filing joint returns, $182,100 for married filing separate returns, and $182,100 for all other returns, as provided in Rev. Proc. 2022-38, 2022-45 I.R.B. 445.

(2) THRESHOLD AMOUNT.—

(A) IN GENERAL.—The term "threshold amount" means $157,500 (200 percent of such amount in the case of a joint return).

(B) INFLATION ADJUSTMENT.—In the case of any taxable year beginning after 2018, the dollar amount in subparagraph (A) shall be increased by an amount equal to—

(i) such dollar amount, multiplied by

(ii) the cost-of-living adjustment determined under section 1(f)(3) for the calendar year in which the taxable year begins, determined by substituting "calendar year 2017" for "calendar year 2016" in subparagraph (A)(ii) thereof.

The amount of any increase under the preceding sentence shall be rounded as provided in section 1(f)(7).

(3) QUALIFIED REIT DIVIDEND.—The term "qualified REIT dividend" means any dividend from a real estate investment trust received during the taxable year which—

(A) is not a capital gain dividend, as defined in section 857(b)(3), and

(B) is not qualified dividend income, as defined in section 1(h)(11).

(4) QUALIFIED PUBLICLY TRADED PARTNERSHIP INCOME.—The term "qualified publicly traded partnership income" means, with respect to any qualified trade or business of a taxpayer, the sum of—

(A) the net amount of such taxpayer's allocable share of each qualified item of income, gain, deduction, and loss (as defined in subsection (c)(3) and determined after the application of subsection (c)(4)) from a publicly traded partnership (as defined in section 7704(a)) which is not treated as a corporation under section 7704(c), plus

(B) any gain recognized by such taxpayer upon disposition of its interest in such partnership to the extent such gain is treated as an amount realized from the sale or exchange of property other than a capital asset under section 751(a).

[Sec. 199A(f)]

(f) SPECIAL RULES.—

(1) APPLICATION TO PARTNERSHIPS AND S CORPORATIONS.—

(A) IN GENERAL.—In the case of a partnership or S corporation—

(i) this section shall be applied at the partner or shareholder level,

(ii) each partner or shareholder shall take into account such person's allocable share of each qualified item of income, gain, deduction, and loss, and

(iii) each partner or shareholder shall be treated for purposes of subsection (b) as having W–2 wages and unadjusted basis immediately after acquisition of qualified property for the taxable year in an amount equal to such person's allocable share of the W–2 wages and the unadjusted basis immediately after acquisition of qualified property of the partnership or S corporation for the taxable year (as determined under regulations prescribed by the Secretary).

For purposes of clause (iii), a partner's or shareholder's allocable share of W–2 wages shall be determined in the same manner as the partner's or shareholder's allocable share of wage expenses. For purposes of such clause, partner's or shareholder's allocable share of the unadjusted basis immediately after acquisition of qualified property shall be determined in the same manner as the partner's or shareholder's allocable share of depreciation. For purposes of this subparagraph, in the case of an S corporation, an allocable share shall be the shareholder's pro rata share of an item.

(B) APPLICATION TO TRUSTS AND ESTATES.—Rules similar to the rules under section 199(d)(1)(B)(i) (as in effect on December 1, 2017) for the apportionment of W–2 wages shall apply to the apportionment of W–2 wages and the apportionment of unadjusted basis immediately after acquisition of qualified property under this section.

(C) TREATMENT OF TRADES OR BUSINESS IN PUERTO RICO.—

(i) IN GENERAL.—In the case of any taxpayer with qualified business income from sources within the commonwealth of Puerto Rico, if all such income is taxable under section 1 for such taxable year, then for purposes of determining the qualified business income of such taxpayer for such taxable year, the term "United States" shall include the Commonwealth of Puerto Rico.

(ii) SPECIAL RULE FOR APPLYING LIMIT.—In the case of any taxpayer described in clause (i), the determination of W–2 wages of such taxpayer with respect to any qualified trade or business conducted in Puerto Rico shall be made without regard to any exclusion under section 3401(a)(8) for remuneration paid for services in Puerto Rico.

(2) COORDINATION WITH MINIMUM TAX.—For purposes of determining alternative minimum taxable income under section 55, qualified business income shall be determined without regard to any adjustments under sections 56 through 59.

(3) DEDUCTION LIMITED TO INCOME TAXES.—The deduction under subsection (a) shall only be allowed for purposes of this chapter.

(4) REGULATIONS.—The Secretary shall prescribe such regulations as are necessary to carry out the purposes of this section, including regulations—

(A) for requiring or restricting the allocation of items and wages under this section and such reporting requirements as the Secretary determines appropriate, and

(B) for the application of this section in the case of tiered entities.

* * *

[Sec. 199A(h)]

(h) ANTI-ABUSE RULES.—The Secretary shall—

(1) apply rules similar to the rules under section 179(d)(2) in order to prevent the manipulation of the depreciable period of qualified property using transactions between related parties, and

(2) prescribe rules for determining the unadjusted basis immediately after acquisition of qualified property acquired in like-kind exchanges or involuntary conversions.

[Sec. 199A(i)]

(i) TERMINATION.—This section shall not apply to taxable years beginning after December 31, 2025.

PART VIII—SPECIAL DEDUCTIONS FOR CORPORATIONS

[Sec. 243]

SEC. 243. DIVIDENDS RECEIVED BY CORPORATIONS.

[Sec. 243(a)]

(a) GENERAL RULE.—In the case of a corporation, there shall be allowed as a deduction an amount equal to the following percentages of the amount received as dividends from a domestic corporation which is subject to taxation under this chapter:

(1) 50 percent, in the case of dividends other than dividends described in paragraph (2) or (3);

(2) 100 percent, in the case of dividends received by a small business investment company operating under the Small Business Investment Act of 1958 (15 U.S.C. 661 and following); and

(3) 100 percent, in the case of qualifying dividends (as defined in subsection (b)(1)).

[Sec. 243(b)]

(b) QUALIFYING DIVIDENDS.—

(1) IN GENERAL.—For purposes of this section, the term "qualifying dividend" means any dividend received by a corporation—

(A) if at the close of the day on which such dividend is received, such corporation is a member of the same affiliated group as the corporation distributing such dividend, and

(B) if such dividend is distributed out of the earnings and profits of a taxable year of the distributing corporation which ends after December 31, 1963, and on each day of which the distributing corporation and the corporation receiving the dividend were members of such affiliated group.

(2) AFFILIATED GROUP.—For purposes of this subsection:

(A) IN GENERAL.—The term "affiliated group" has the meaning given such term by section 1504(a), except that for such purposes sections 1504(b)(2) and 1504(c) shall not apply.

(B) GROUP MUST BE CONSISTENT IN FOREIGN TAX TREATMENT.—The requirements of paragraph (1)(A) shall not be treated as being met with respect to any dividend received by a corporation if, for any taxable year which includes the day on which such dividend is received—

(i) 1 or more members of the affiliated group referred to in paragraph (1)(A) choose to any extent to take the benefits of section 901, and

(ii) 1 or more other members of such group claim to any extent a deduction for taxes otherwise creditable under section 901.

[Sec. 243(c)]

(c) INCREASED PERCENTAGE FOR DIVIDENDS FROM 20-PERCENT OWNED CORPORATIONS.—

(1) IN GENERAL.—In the case of any dividend received from a 20-percent owned corporation, subsection (a)(1) shall be applied by substituting "65 percent" for "50 percent".

(2) 20-PERCENT OWNED CORPORATION.—For purposes of this section, the term "20-percent owned corporation" means any corporation if 20 percent or more of the stock of such corporation (by vote and value) is owned by the taxpayer. For purposes of the preceding sentence, stock described in section 1504(a)(4) shall not be taken into account.

***

[Sec. 243(e)]

(e) CERTAIN DIVIDENDS FROM FOREIGN CORPORATIONS.—For purposes of subsection (a) and for purposes of section 245, any dividend from a foreign corporation from earnings and profits accumulated by a domestic corporation during a period with respect to which such domestic corporation was subject to taxation under this chapter (or corresponding provisions of prior law) shall be treated as a dividend from a domestic corporation which is subject to taxation under this chapter.

[Sec. 245]

SEC. 245. DIVIDENDS RECEIVED FROM CERTAIN FOREIGN CORPORATIONS.

[Sec. 245(a)]

(a) DIVIDENDS FROM 10-PERCENT OWNED FOREIGN CORPORATIONS.—

(1) IN GENERAL.—In the case of dividends received by a corporation from a qualified 10-percent owned foreign corporation, there shall be allowed as a deduction an amount equal to the percent (specified in section 243 for the taxable year) of the U.S.-source portion of such dividends.

(2) QUALIFIED 10-PERCENT OWNED FOREIGN CORPORATION.—For purposes of this subsection, the term "qualified 10-percent owned foreign corporation" means any foreign corporation (other than a passive foreign investment company) if at least 10 percent of the stock of such corporation (by vote and value) is owned by the taxpayer.

(3) U.S.-SOURCE PORTION.—For purposes of this subsection, the U.S.-source portion of any dividend is an amount which bears the same ratio to such dividends as—

(A) the post-1986 undistributed U.S. earnings, bears to

(B) the total post-1986 undistributed earnings.

(4) POST-1986 UNDISTRIBUTED EARNINGS.—The term "post-1986 undistributed earnings" means the amount of the earnings and profits of the foreign corporation (computed in accordance with sections 964(a) and 986) accumulated in taxable years beginning after December 31, 1986—

(A) as of the close of the taxable year of the foreign corporation in which the dividend is distributed, and

(B) without diminution by reason of dividends distributed during such taxable year.

(5) POST-1986 UNDISTRIBUTED U.S. EARNINGS.—For purposes of this subsection, the term "post-1986 undistributed U.S. earnings" means the portion of the post-1986 undistributed earnings which is attributable to—

(A) income of the qualified 10-percent owned foreign corporation which is effectively connected with the conduct of a trade or business within the United States and subject to tax under this chapter, or

(B) any dividend received (directly or through a wholly owned foreign corporation) from a domestic corporation at least 80 percent of the stock of which (by vote and value) is owned (directly or through such wholly owned foreign corporation) by the qualified 10-percent owned foreign corporation.

(6) SPECIAL RULE.—If the 1st day on which the requirements of paragraph (2) are met with respect to any foreign corporation is in a taxable year of such corporation beginning after December 31, 1986, the post-1986 undistributed earnings and the post-1986 undistributed U.S. earnings of such corporation shall be determined by only taking into account periods beginning on and after the 1st day of the 1st taxable year in which such requirements are met.

(7) COORDINATION WITH SUBSECTION (b).—Earnings and profits of any qualified 10-percent owned foreign corporation for any taxable year shall not be taken into account under this subsection if the deduction provided by subsection (b) would be allowable with respect to dividends paid out of such earnings and profits.

(8) DISALLOWANCE OF FOREIGN TAX CREDIT.—No credit shall be allowed under section 901 for any taxes paid or accrued (or treated as paid or accrued) with respect to the United States-source portion of any dividend received by a corporation from a qualified 10-percent-owned foreign corporation.

(9) COORDINATION WITH SECTION 904.—For purposes of section 904, the U.S.-source portion of any dividend received by a corporation from a qualified 10-percent owned foreign corporation shall be treated as from sources in the United States.

(10) COORDINATION WITH TREATIES.—If—

(A) any portion of a dividend received by a corporation from a qualified 10-percent-owned foreign corporation would be treated as from sources in the United States under paragraph (9),

(B) under a treaty obligation of the United States (applied without regard to this subsection), such portion would be treated as arising from sources outside the United States, and

(C) the taxpayer chooses the benefits of this paragraph,

this subsection shall not apply to such dividend (but subsections (a), (b), and (c) of section 904 and sections 907 and 960 shall be applied separately with respect to such portion of such dividend).

(11) COORDINATION WITH SECTION 1248.—For purposes of this subsection, the term "dividend" does not include any amount treated as a dividend under section 1248.

(12) DIVIDENDS DERIVED FROM RICS AND REITS INELIGIBLE FOR DEDUCTION.—Regulated investment companies and real estate investment trusts shall not be treated as domestic corporations for purposes of paragraph (5)(B).

[Sec. 245(b)]

(b) CERTAIN DIVIDENDS RECEIVED FROM WHOLLY OWNED FOREIGN SUBSIDIARIES.—

(1) IN GENERAL.—In the case of dividends described in paragraph (2) received from a foreign corporation by a domestic corporation which, for its taxable year in which such dividends are received, owns (directly or indirectly) all of the outstanding stock of such foreign corporation, there shall be allowed as a deduction (in lieu of the deduction provided by subsection (a)) an amount equal to 100 percent of such dividends.

(2) ELIGIBLE DIVIDENDS.—Paragraph (1) shall apply only to dividends which are paid out of the earnings and profits of a foreign corporation for a taxable year during which—

(A) all of its outstanding stock is owned (directly or indirectly) by the domestic corporation to which such dividends are paid; and

(B) all of its gross income from all sources is effectively connected with the conduct of a trade or business within the United States.

***

[Sec. 245A]

SEC. 245A. DEDUCTION FOR FOREIGN SOURCE-PORTION OF DIVIDENDS RECEIVED BY DOMESTIC CORPORATIONS FROM SPECIFIED 10-PERCENT OWNED FOREIGN CORPORATIONS.

[Sec. 245A(a)]

(a) IN GENERAL.—In the case of any dividend received from a specified 10-percent owned foreign corporation by a domestic corporation which is a United States shareholder with respect to such foreign corporation, there shall be allowed as a deduction an amount equal to the foreign-source portion of such dividend.

[Sec. 245A(b)]

(b) SPECIFIED 10-PERCENT OWNED FOREIGN CORPORATION.—For purposes of this section—

(1) IN GENERAL.—The term "specified 10-percent owned foreign corporation" means any foreign corporation with respect to which any domestic corporation is a United States shareholder with respect to such corporation.

(2) EXCLUSION OF PASSIVE FOREIGN INVESTMENT COMPANIES.—Such term shall not include any corporation which is a passive foreign investment company (as defined in section 1297) with respect to the shareholder and which is not a controlled foreign corporation.

[Sec. 245A(c)]

(c) FOREIGN-SOURCE PORTION.—For purposes of this section—

(1) IN GENERAL.—The foreign-source portion of any dividend from a specified 10-percent owned foreign corporation is an amount which bears the same ratio to such dividend as—

(A) the undistributed foreign earnings of the specified 10-percent owned foreign corporation, bears to

(B) the total undistributed earnings of such foreign corporation.

(2) UNDISTRIBUTED EARNINGS.—The term "undistributed earnings" means the amount of the earnings and profits of the specified 10-percent owned foreign corporation (computed in accordance with sections 964(a) and 986)—

(A) as of the close of the taxable year of the specified 10-percent owned foreign corporation in which the dividend is distributed, and

(B) without diminution by reason of dividends distributed during such taxable year.

(3) UNDISTRIBUTED FOREIGN EARNINGS.—The term "undistributed foreign earnings" means the portion of the undistributed earnings which is attributable to neither—

(A) income described in subparagraph (A) of section 245(a)(5), nor

(B) dividends described in subparagraph (B) of such section (determined without regard to section 245(a)(12)).

[Sec. 245A(d)]

(d) DISALLOWANCE OF FOREIGN TAX CREDIT, ETC.—

(1) IN GENERAL.—No credit shall be allowed under section 901 for any taxes paid or accrued (or treated as paid or accrued) with respect to any dividend for which a deduction is allowed under this section.

(2) DENIAL OF DEDUCTION.—No deduction shall be allowed under this chapter for any tax for which credit is not allowable under section 901 by reason of paragraph (1) (determined by treating the taxpayer as having elected the benefits of subpart A of part III of subchapter N).

[Sec. 245A(e)]

(e) SPECIAL RULES FOR HYBRID DIVIDENDS.—

(1) IN GENERAL.—Subsection (a) shall not apply to any dividend received by a United States shareholder from a controlled foreign corporation if the dividend is a hybrid dividend.

(2) HYBRID DIVIDENDS OF TIERED CORPORATIONS.—If a controlled foreign corporation with respect to which a domestic corporation is a United States shareholder receives a hybrid dividend from any other controlled foreign corporation with respect to which such domestic corporation is also a United States shareholder, then, notwithstanding any other provision of this title—

(A) the hybrid dividend shall be treated for purposes of section 951(a)(1)(A) as subpart F income of the receiving controlled foreign corporation for the taxable year of the controlled foreign corporation in which the dividend was received, and

(B) the United States shareholder shall include in gross income an amount equal to the shareholder's pro rata share (determined in the same manner as under section 951(a)(2)) of the subpart F income described in subparagraph (A).

(3) DENIAL OF FOREIGN TAX CREDIT, ETC.—The rules of subsection (d) shall apply to any hybrid dividend received by, or any amount included under paragraph (2) in the gross income of, a United States shareholder.

(4) HYBRID DIVIDEND.—The term "hybrid dividend" means an amount received from a controlled foreign corporation—

(A) for which a deduction would be allowed under subsection (a) but for this subsection, and

(B) for which the controlled foreign corporation received a deduction (or other tax benefit) with respect to any income, war profits, or excess profits taxes imposed by any foreign country or possession of the United States.

[Sec. 245A(f)]

(f) SPECIAL RULE FOR PURGING DISTRIBUTIONS OF PASSIVE FOREIGN INVESTMENT COMPANIES.—Any amount which is treated as a dividend under section 1291(d)(2)(B) shall not be treated as a dividend for purposes of this section.

[Sec. 245A(g)]

(g) REGULATIONS.—The Secretary shall prescribe such regulations or other guidance as may be necessary or appropriate to carry out the provisions of this section, including regulations for the treatment of United States shareholders owning stock of a specified 10 percent owned foreign corporation through a partnership.

[Sec. 246]

SEC. 246. RULES APPLYING TO DEDUCTIONS FOR DIVIDENDS RECEIVED.

* * *

[Sec. 246(c)]

(c) EXCLUSION OF CERTAIN DIVIDENDS.—

(1) IN GENERAL.—No deduction shall be allowed under section 243[,] 245, or 245A, in respect of any dividend on any share of stock—

(A) which is held by the taxpayer for 45 days or less during the 91-day period beginning on the date which is 45 days before the date on which such share becomes ex-dividend with respect to such dividend, or

(B) to the extent that the taxpayer is under an obligation (whether pursuant to a short sale or otherwise) to make related payments with respect to positions in substantially similar or related property.

* * *

(5) SPECIAL RULES FOR FOREIGN SOURCE PORTION OF DIVIDENDS RECEIVED FROM SPECIFIED 10-PERCENT OWNED FOREIGN CORPORATIONS.—

(A) 1-YEAR HOLDING PERIOD REQUIREMENT.—For purposes of section 245A—

(i) paragraph (1)(A) shall be applied—

(I) by substituting "365 days" for "45 days" each place it appears, and

(II) by substituting "731-day period" for "91-day period", and

(ii) paragraph (2) shall not apply.

(B) STATUS MUST BE MAINTAINED DURING HOLDING PERIOD.—For purposes of applying paragraph (1) with respect to section 245A, the taxpayer shall be treated as holding the stock referred to in paragraph (1) for any period only if—

(i) the specified 10-percent owned foreign corporation referred to in section 245A(a) is a specified 10-percent owned foreign corporation at all times during such period, and

(ii) the taxpayer is a United States shareholder with respect to such specified 10-percent owned foreign corporation at all times during such period.

[Sec. 246(d)]

(d) DIVIDENDS FROM A DISC OR FORMER DISC.—No deduction shall be allowed under section 243 in respect of a dividend from a corporation which is a DISC or former DISC (as defined in section 992(a)) to the extent such dividend is paid out of the corporation's accumulated DISC income or previously taxed income, or is a deemed distribution pursuant to section 995(b)(1).

[Sec. 250]

SEC. 250. FOREIGN-DERIVED INTANGIBLE INCOME AND GLOBAL INTANGIBLE LOW-TAXED INCOME.

[Sec. 250(a)]

(a) ALLOWANCE OF DEDUCTION.—

(1) IN GENERAL.—In the case of a domestic corporation for any taxable year, there shall be allowed as a deduction an amount equal to the sum of—

(A) 37.5 percent of the foreign-derived intangible income of such domestic corporation for such taxable year, plus

(B) 50 percent of—

(i) the global intangible low-taxed income amount (if any) which is included in the gross income of such domestic corporation under section 951A for such taxable year, and

(ii) the amount treated as a dividend received by such corporation under section 78 which is attributable to the amount described in clause (i).

(2) LIMITATION BASED ON TAXABLE INCOME.—

(A) IN GENERAL.—If, for any taxable year—

(i) the sum of the foreign-derived intangible income and the global intangible low-taxed income amount otherwise taken into account by the domestic corporation under paragraph (1), exceeds

(ii) the taxable income of the domestic corporation (determined without regard to this section),

then the amount of the foreign-derived intangible income and the global intangible low-taxed income amount so taken into account shall be reduced as provided in subparagraph (B).

(B) REDUCTION.—For purposes of subparagraph (A)—

(i) foreign-derived intangible income shall be reduced by an amount which bears the same ratio to the excess described in subparagraph (A) as such foreign-derived intangible income bears to the sum described in subparagraph (A)(i), and

(ii) the global intangible low-taxed income amount shall be reduced by the remainder of such excess.

(3) REDUCTION IN DEDUCTION FOR TAXABLE YEARS AFTER 2025.—In the case of any taxable year beginning after December 31, 2025, paragraph (1) shall be applied by substituting—

(A) "21.875 percent" for "37.5 percent" in subparagraph (A), and

(B) "37.5 percent" for "50 percent" in subparagraph (B).

[Sec. 250(b)]

(b) FOREIGN-DERIVED INTANGIBLE INCOME.—For purposes of this section—

(1) IN GENERAL.—The foreign-derived intangible income of any domestic corporation is the amount which bears the same ratio to the deemed intangible income of such corporation as—

(A) the foreign-derived deduction eligible income of such corporation, bears to

(B) the deduction eligible income of such corporation.

(2) DEEMED INTANGIBLE INCOME.—For purposes of this subsection—

(A) IN GENERAL.—The term "deemed intangible income" means the excess (if any) of—

(i) the deduction eligible income of the domestic corporation, over

(ii) the deemed tangible income return of the corporation.

(B) DEEMED TANGIBLE INCOME RETURN.—The term "deemed tangible income return" means, with respect to any corporation, an amount equal to 10 percent of the corporation's qualified business asset investment (as defined in section 951A(d), determined by substituting "deduction eligible income" for "tested income" in paragraph (2) thereof and without regard to whether the corporation is a controlled foreign corporation).

(3) DEDUCTION ELIGIBLE INCOME.—

(A) IN GENERAL.—The term "deduction eligible income" means, with respect to any domestic corporation, the excess (if any) of—

(i) gross income of such corporation determined without regard to—

(I) any amount included in the gross income of such corporation under section 951(a)(1),

(II) the global intangible low-taxed income included in the gross income of such corporation under section 951A,

(III) any financial services income (as defined in section 904(d)(2)(D)) of such corporation,

(IV) any dividend received from a corporation which is a controlled foreign corporation of such domestic corporation,

(V) any domestic oil and gas extraction income of such corporation, and

(VI) any foreign branch income (as defined in section 904(d)(2)(J)), over

(ii) the deductions (including taxes) properly allocable to such gross income.

(B) DOMESTIC OIL AND GAS EXTRACTION INCOME.—For purposes of subparagraph (A), the term "domestic oil and gas extraction income" means income described in section 907(c)(1), determined by substituting "within the United States" for "without the United States".

(4) Foreign-derived deduction eligible income.—The term "foreign-derived deduction eligible income" means, with respect to any taxpayer for any taxable year, any deduction eligible income of such taxpayer which is derived in connection with—

(A) property—

(i) which is sold by the taxpayer to any person who is not a United States person, and

(ii) which the taxpayer establishes to the satisfaction of the Secretary is for a foreign use, or

(B) services provided by the taxpayer which the taxpayer establishes to the satisfaction of the Secretary are provided to any person, or with respect to property, not located within the United States.

(5) Rules relating to foreign use property or services.—For purposes of this subsection—

(A) Foreign use.—The term "foreign use" means any use, consumption, or disposition which is not within the United States.

(B) Property or services provided to domestic intermediaries.—

(i) Property.—If a taxpayer sells property to another person (other than a related party) for further manufacture or other modification within the United States, such property shall not be treated as sold for a foreign use even if such other person subsequently uses such property for a foreign use.

(ii) Services.—If a taxpayer provides services to another person (other than a related party) located within the United States, such services shall not be treated as described in paragraph (4)(B) even if such other person uses such services in providing services which are so described.

(C) Special rules with respect to related party transactions.—

(i) Sales to related parties.—If property is sold to a related party who is not a United States person, such sale shall not be treated as for a foreign use unless—

(I) such property is ultimately sold by a related party, or used by a related party in connection with property which is sold or the provision of services, to another person who is an unrelated party who is not a United States person, and

(II) the taxpayer establishes to the satisfaction of the Secretary that such property is for a foreign use.

For purposes of this clause, a sale of property shall be treated as a sale of each of the components thereof.

(ii) Service provided to related parties.—If a service is provided to a related party who is not located in the United States, such service shall not be treated described in subparagraph (A)(ii) unless the taxpayer established to the satisfaction of the Secretary that such service is not substantially similar to services provided by such related party to persons located within the United States.

(D) Related party.—For purposes of this paragraph, the term "related party" means any member of an affiliated group as defined in section 1504(a), determined—

(i) by substituting "more than 50 percent" for "at least 80 percent" each place it appears, and

(ii) without regard to paragraphs (2) and (3) of section 1504(b).

Any person (other than a corporation) shall be treated as a member of such group if such person is controlled by members of such group (including any entity treated as a member of such group by reason of this sentence) or controls any such member. For purposes of the preceding sentence, control shall be determined under the rules of section 954(d)(3).

(E) Sold.—For purposes of this subsection, the terms "sold", "sells", and "sale" shall include any lease, license, exchange, or other disposition.

[Sec. 250(c)]

(c) Regulations.—The Secretary shall prescribe such regulations or other guidance as may be necessary or appropriate to carry out the provisions of this section.

PART IX—ITEMS NOT DEDUCTIBLE

[Sec. 263]

SEC. 263. CAPITAL EXPENDITURES.

[Sec. 263(a)]

(a) General Rule.—No deduction shall be allowed for—

(1) Any amount paid out for new buildings or for permanent improvements or betterments made to increase the value of any property or estate. This paragraph shall not apply to—

(A) expenditures for the development of mines or deposits deductible under section 616,

(B) research and experimental expenditures deductible under section 174,

(C) soil and water conservation expenditures deductible under section 175,

(D) expenditures by farmers for fertilizer, etc., deductible under section 180,

(E) expenditures for removal of architectural and transportation barriers to the handicapped and elderly which the taxpayer elects to deduct under section 190,

(F) expenditures for tertiary injectants with respect to which a deduction is allowed under section 193,

(G) expenditures for which a deduction is allowed under section 179,

(H) expenditures for which a deduction is allowed under section 179B,

(I) expenditures for which a deduction is allowed under section 179C,

(J) expenditures for which a deduction is allowed under section 179D, or

(K) expenditures for which a deduction is allowed under section 179E.

(2) Any amount expended in restoring property or in making good the exhaustion thereof for which an allowance is or has been made.

[Sec. 263(c)]

(c) Intangible Drilling and Development Costs in the Case of Oil and Gas Wells and Geothermal Wells.—Notwithstanding subsection (a), and except as provided in subsection (i), regulations shall be prescribed by the Secretary under this subtitle corresponding to the regulations which granted the option to deduct as expenses intangible drilling and development costs in the case of oil and gas wells and which were recognized and approved by the Congress in House Concurrent Resolution 50, Seventy-ninth Congress. Such regulations shall also grant the option to deduct as expenses intangible drilling and development costs in the case of wells drilled for any geothermal deposit (as defined in section 613(e)(2)) to the same extent and in the same manner as such expenses are deductible in the case of oil and gas wells. This subsection shall not apply with respect to any costs to which any deduction is allowed under section 59(e) or 291.

* * *

[Sec. 263(i)]

(i) Special Rules for Intangible Drilling and Development Costs Incurred Outside the United States.—In the case of intangible drilling and development costs paid or incurred with respect to an oil, gas, or geothermal well located outside the United States—

(1) subsection (c) shall not apply, and

(2) such costs shall—

(A) at the election of the taxpayer, be included in adjusted basis for purposes of computing the amount of any deduction allowable under section 611 (determined without regard to section 613), or

(B) if subparagraph (A) does not apply, be allowed as a deduction ratably over the 10-taxable year period beginning with the taxable year in which such costs were paid or incurred.

This subsection shall not apply to costs paid or incurred with respect to a nonproductive well.

[Sec. 267]

SEC. 267. LOSSES, EXPENSES, AND INTEREST WITH RESPECT TO TRANSACTIONS BETWEEN RELATED TAXPAYERS.

[Sec. 267(a)]

(a) IN GENERAL.—

(1) DEDUCTION FOR LOSSES DISALLOWED.—No deduction shall be allowed in respect of any loss from the sale or exchange of property, directly or indirectly, between persons specified in any of the paragraphs of subsection (b). The preceding sentence shall not apply to any loss of the distributing corporation (or the distributee) in the case of a distribution in complete liquidation.

(2) MATCHING OF DEDUCTION AND PAYEE INCOME ITEM IN THE CASE OF EXPENSES AND INTEREST.—If—

(A) by reason of the method of accounting of the person to whom the payment is to be made, the amount thereof is not (unless paid) includible in the gross income of such person, and

(B) at the close of the taxable year of the taxpayer for which (but for this paragraph) the amount would be deductible under this chapter, both the taxpayer and the person to whom the payment is to be made are persons specified in any of the paragraphs of subsection (b),

then any deduction allowable under this chapter in respect of such amount shall be allowable as of the day as of which such amount is includible in the gross income of the person to whom the payment is made (or, if later, as of the day on which it would be so allowable but for this paragraph). For purposes of this paragraph, in the case of a personal service corporation (within the meaning of section 441(i)(2)), such corporation and any employee-owner (within the meaning of section 269A(b)(2), as modified by section 441(i)(2)) shall be treated as persons specified in subsection (b).

(3) PAYMENTS TO FOREIGN PERSONS

(A) IN GENERAL.—The Secretary shall by regulations apply the matching principle of paragraph (2) in cases in which the person to whom the payment is to be made is not a United States person.

(B) SPECIAL RULE FOR CERTAIN FOREIGN ENTITIES.—

(i) IN GENERAL.—Notwithstanding subparagraph (A), in the case of any item payable to a controlled foreign corporation (as defined in section 957) or a passive foreign investment company (as defined in section 1297), a deduction shall be allowable to the payor with respect to such amount for any taxable year before the taxable year in which paid only to the extent that an amount attributable to such item is includible (determined without regard to properly allocable deductions and qualified deficits under section 952(c)(1)(B)) during such prior taxable year in the gross income of a United States person who owns (within the meaning of section 958(a)) stock in such corporation.

(ii) SECRETARIAL AUTHORITY.—The Secretary may by regulation exempt transactions from the application of clause (i), including any transaction which is entered into by a payor in the ordinary course of a trade or business in which the payor is predominantly engaged and in which the payment of the accrued amounts occurs within $8^1/_2$ months after accrual or within such other period as the Secretary may prescribe.

[Sec. 267(b)]

(b) RELATIONSHIPS.—The persons referred to in subsection (a) are:

(1) Members of a family, as defined in subsection (c)(4);

(2) An individual and a corporation more than 50 percent in value of the outstanding stock of which is owned, directly or indirectly, by or for such individual;

(3) Two corporations which are members of the same controlled group (as defined in subsection (f));

(4) A grantor and a fiduciary of any trust;

(5) A fiduciary of a trust and a fiduciary of another trust, if the same person is a grantor of both trusts;

(6) A fiduciary of a trust and a beneficiary of such trust;

(7) A fiduciary of a trust and a beneficiary of another trust, if the same person is a grantor of both trusts;

(8) A fiduciary of a trust and a corporation more than 50 percent in value of the outstanding stock of which is owned, directly or indirectly, by or for the trust or by or for a person who is a grantor of the trust;

(9) A person and an organization to which section 501 (relating to certain educational and charitable organizations which are exempt from tax) applies and which is controlled directly or indirectly by such person or (if such person is an individual) by members of the family of such individual;

(10) A corporation and a partnership if the same persons own—

(A) more than 50 percent in value of the outstanding stock of the corporation, and

(B) more than 50 percent of the capital interest, or the profits interest, in the partnership;

(11) An S corporation and another S corporation if the same persons own more than 50 percent in value of the outstanding stock of each corporation;

(12) An S corporation and a C corporation, if the same persons own more than 50 percent in value of the outstanding stock of each corporation; or

(13) Except in the case of a sale or exchange in satisfaction of a pecuniary bequest, an executor of an estate and a beneficiary of such estate.

[Sec. 267(c)]

(c) CONSTRUCTIVE OWNERSHIP OF STOCK.—For purposes of determining, in applying subsection (b), the ownership of stock—

(1) Stock owned, directly or indirectly, by or for a corporation, partnership, estate, or trust shall be considered as being owned proportionately by or for its shareholders, partners, or beneficiaries;

(2) An individual shall be considered as owning the stock owned, directly or indirectly, by or for his family;

(3) An individual owning (otherwise than by the application of paragraph (2)) any stock in a corporation shall be considered as owning the stock owned, directly or indirectly, by or for his partner;

(4) The family of an individual shall include only his brothers and sisters (whether by the whole or half blood), spouse, ancestors, and lineal descendants; and

(5) Stock constructively owned by a person by reason of the application of paragraph (1) shall, for the purpose of applying paragraph (1), (2), or (3), be treated as actually owned by such person, but stock constructively owned by an individual by reason of the application of paragraph (2) or (3) shall not be treated as owned by him for the purpose of again applying either of such paragraphs in order to make another the constructive owner of such stock.

[Sec. 267(d)]

(d) AMOUNT OF GAIN WHERE LOSS PREVIOUSLY DISALLOWED.—(1) IN GENERAL.—If—

(A) in the case of a sale or exchange of property to the taxpayer a loss sustained by the transferor is not allowable to the transferor as a deduction by reason of subsection (a)(1), and

(B) the taxpayer sells or otherwise disposes of such property (or of other property the basis of which in the taxpayer's hands is determined directly or indirectly by reference to such property) at a gain,

then such gain shall be recognized only to the extent that it exceeds so much of such loss as is properly allocable to the property sold or otherwise disposed of by the taxpayer.

(2) EXCEPTION FOR WASH SALES.—Paragraph (1) shall not apply if the loss sustained by the transferor is not allowable to the transferor as a deduction by reason of section 1091 (relating to wash sales).

(3) EXCEPTION FOR TRANSFERS FROM TAX INDIFFERENT PARTIES.—Paragraph (1) shall not apply to the extent any loss sustained by the transferor (if allowed) would not be taken into account in determining a tax imposed under section 1 or 11 or a tax computed as provided by either of such sections.

[Sec. 267(e)]

(e) SPECIAL RULES FOR PASS-THRU ENTITIES.—

(1) IN GENERAL.—In the case of any amount paid or incurred by, to, or on behalf of, a pass-thru entity, for purposes of applying subsection (a)(2)—

(A) such entity,

(B) in the case of—

(i) a partnership, any person who owns (directly or indirectly) any capital interest or profits interest of such partnership, or

(ii) an S corporation, any person who owns (directly or indirectly) any of the stock of such corporation,

(C) any person who owns (directly or indirectly) any capital interests or profits interest of a partnership in which such entity owns (directly or indirectly) any capital interest or profits interest, and

(D) any person related (within the meaning of subsection (b) of this section or section 707(b)(1)) to a person described in subparagraph (B) or (C),

shall be treated as persons specified in a paragraph of subsection (b). Subparagraph (C) shall apply to a transaction only if such transaction is related either to the operations of the partnership described in such subparagraph or to an interest in such partnership.

(2) PASS-THRU ENTITY.—For purposes of this section, the term "pass-thru entity" means—

(A) a partnership, and

(B) an S corporation.

(3) CONSTRUCTIVE OWNERSHIP IN THE CASE OF PARTNERSHIPS.—For purposes of determining ownership of a capital interest or profits interest of a partnership, the principles of subsection (c) shall apply, except that—

(A) paragraph (3) of subsection (c) shall not apply, and

(B) interests owned (directly or indirectly) by or for a C corporation shall be considered as owned by or for any shareholder only if such shareholder owns (directly or indirectly) 5 percent or more in value of the stock of such corporation.

(4) SUBSECTION (a)(2) NOT TO APPLY TO CERTAIN GUARANTEED PAYMENTS OF PARTNERSHIPS.—In the case of any amount paid or incurred by a partnership, subsection (a)(2) shall not apply to the extent that section 707(c) applies to such amount.

(5) EXCEPTION FOR CERTAIN EXPENSES AND INTEREST OF PARTNERSHIPS OWNING LOW-INCOME HOUSING.—

(A) IN GENERAL.—This subsection shall not apply with respect to qualified expenses and interest paid or incurred by a partnership owning low-income housing to—

(i) any qualified 5-percent or less partner of such partnership, or

(ii) any person related (within the meaning of subsection (b) of this section or section 707(b)(1)) to any qualified 5-percent or less partner of such partnership.

(B) QUALIFIED 5-PERCENT OR LESS PARTNER.—For purposes of this paragraph, the term "qualified 5-percent or less partner" means any partner who has (directly or indirectly) an interest of 5 percent or less in the aggregate capital and profits interests of the partnership but only if—

(i) such partner owned the low-income housing at all times during the 2-year period ending on the date such housing was transferred to the partnership, or

(ii) such partnership acquired the low-income housing pursuant to a purchase, assignment, or other transfer from the Department of Housing and Urban Development or any State or local housing authority.

For purposes of the preceding sentence, a partner shall be treated as holding any interest in the partnership which is held (directly or indirectly) by any person related (within the meaning of subsection (b) of this section or section 707(b)(1)) to such partner.

(C) QUALIFIED EXPENSES AND INTEREST.—For purpose of this paragraph, the term "qualified expenses and interest" means any expense or interest incurred by the partnership with respect to low-income housing held by the partnership but—

(i) only if the amount of such expense or interest (as the case may be) is unconditionally required to be paid by the partnership not later than 10 years after the date such amount was incurred, and

(ii) in the case of such interest, only if such interest is incurred at an annual rate not in excess of 12 percent.

(D) LOW-INCOME HOUSING.—For purposes of this paragraph, the term "low-income housing" means—

(i) any interest in property described in clause (i), (ii), or (iv) of section 1250(a)(1)(B), and

(ii) any interest in a partnership owning such property.

(6) CROSS REFERENCE.—

For additional rules relating to partnerships, see section 707(b).

[Sec. 267(f)]

(f) CONTROLLED GROUP DEFINED; SPECIAL RULES APPLICABLE TO CONTROLLED GROUPS.—

(1) CONTROLLED GROUP DEFINED.—For purposes of this section, the term "controlled group" has the meaning given to such term by section 1563(a), except that—

(A) "more than 50 percent" shall be substituted for "at least 80 percent" each place it appears in section 1563(a), and

(B) the determination shall be made without regard to subsections (a)(4) and (e)(3)(C) of section 1563.

(2) DEFERRAL (RATHER THAN DENIAL) OF LOSS FROM SALE OR EXCHANGE BETWEEN MEMBERS.—In the case of any loss from the sale or exchange of property which is between members of the same controlled group and to which subsection (a)(1) applies (determined without regard to this paragraph but with regard to paragraph (3))—

(A) subsections (a)(1) and (d) shall not apply to such loss, but

(B) such loss shall be deferred until the property is transferred outside such controlled group and there would be recognition of loss under consolidated return principles or until such other time as may be prescribed in regulations.

(3) LOSS DEFERRAL RULES NOT TO APPLY IN CERTAIN CASES.—

(A) TRANSFER TO DISC.—For purposes of applying subsection (a)(1), the term "controlled group" shall not include a DISC.

(B) CERTAIN SALES OF INVENTORY.—Except to the extent provided in regulations prescribed by the Secretary, subsection (a)(1) shall not apply to the sale or exchange of property between members of the same controlled group (or persons described in subsection (b)(10)) if—

(i) such property in the hands of the transferor is property described in section 1221(a)(1),

(ii) such sale or exchange is in the ordinary course of the transferor's trade or business,

(iii) such property in the hands of the transferee is property described in section 1221(a)(1), and

(iv) the transferee or the transferor is a foreign corporation.

(C) CERTAIN FOREIGN CURRENCY LOSSES.—To the extent povided in regulations, subsection (a)(1) shall not apply to any loss sustained by a member of a controlled group on the repayment of a loan made to another member of such group if such loan is payable in a foreign currency or is denominated in such a currency and such loss is attributable to a reduction in value of such foreign currency.

* * *

(4) DETERMINATION OF RELATIONSHIP RESULTING IN DISALLOWANCE OF LOSS, FOR PURPOSES OF OTHER PROVISIONS.—For purposes of any other section of this title which refers to a relationship which would result in a disallowance of losses under this section, deferral under paragraph (2) shall be treated as disallowance.

* * *

[Sec. 267A]

SEC. 267A. CERTAIN RELATED PARTY AMOUNTS PAID OR ACCRUED IN HYBRID TRANSACTIONS OR WITH HYBRID ENTITIES.

[Sec. 267A(a)]

(a) IN GENERAL.—No deduction shall be allowed under this chapter for any disqualified related party amount paid or accrued pursuant to a hybrid transaction or by, or to, a hybrid entity.

[Sec. 267A(b)]

(b) DISQUALIFIED RELATED PARTY AMOUNT.—For purposes of this section—

(1) DISQUALIFIED RELATED PARTY AMOUNT.—The term "disqualified related party amount" means any interest or royalty paid or accrued to a related party to the extent that—

(A) such amount is not included in the income of such related party under the tax law of the country of which such related party is a resident for tax purposes or is subject to tax, or

(B) such related party is allowed a deduction with respect to such amount under the tax law of such country.

Such term shall not include any payment to the extent such payment is included in the gross income of a United States shareholder under section 951(a).

(2) RELATED PARTY.—The term "related party" means a related person as defined in section 954(d)(3), except that such section shall be applied with respect to the person making the payment described in paragraph (1) in lieu of the controlled foreign corporation otherwise referred to in such section.

[Sec. 267A(c)]

(c) HYBRID TRANSACTION.—For purposes of this section, the term "hybrid transaction" means any transaction, series of transactions, agreement, or instrument one or more payments with respect to which are treated as interest or royalties for purposes of this chapter and which are not so treated for purposes [of] the tax law of the foreign country of which the recipient of such payment is resident for tax purposes or is subject to tax.

[Sec. 267A(d)]

(d) HYBRID ENTITY.—For purposes of this section, the term "hybrid entity" means any entity which is either—

(1) treated as fiscally transparent for purposes of this chapter but not so treated for purposes of the tax law of the foreign country of which the entity is resident for tax purposes or is subject to tax, or

(2) treated as fiscally transparent for purposes of such tax law but not so treated for purposes of this chapter.

[Sec. 267A(e)]

(e) REGULATIONS.—The Secretary shall issue such regulations or other guidance as may be necessary or appropriate to carry out the purposes of this section, including regulations or other guidance providing for—

(1) rules for treating certain conduit arrangements which involve a hybrid transaction or a hybrid entity as subject to subsection (a),

(2) rules for the application of this section to branches or domestic entities,

(3) rules for treating certain structured transactions as subject to subsection (a),

(4) rules for treating a tax preference as an exclusion from income for purposes of applying subsection (b)(1) if such tax preference has the effect of reducing the generally applicable statutory rate by 25 percent or more,

(5) rules for treating the entire amount of interest or royalty paid or accrued to a related party as a disqualified related party amount if such amount is subject to a participation exemption system or other system which provides for the exclusion or deduction of a substantial portion of such amount,

(6) rules for determining the tax residence of a foreign entity if the entity is otherwise considered a resident of more than one country or of no country,

(7) exceptions from subsection (a) with respect to—

(A) cases in which the disqualified related party amount is taxed under the laws of a foreign country other than the country of which the related party is a resident for tax purposes, and

(B) other cases which the Secretary determines do not present a risk of eroding the Federal tax base,

(8) requirements for record keeping and information reporting in addition to any requirements imposed by section 6038A.

[Sec. 269]

SEC. 269. ACQUISITIONS MADE TO EVADE OR AVOID INCOME TAX.

[Sec. 269(a)]

(a) IN GENERAL.—If—

(1) any person or persons acquire, directly or indirectly, control of a corporation, or

(2) any corporation acquires, directly or indirectly, property of another corporation, not controlled, directly or indirectly, immediately before such acquisition, by such acquiring corporation or its stockholders, the basis of which property, in the hands of the acquiring corporation, is determined by reference to the basis in the hands of the transferor corporation,

and the principal purpose for which such acquisition was made is evasion or avoidance of Federal income tax by securing the benefit of a deduction, credit, or other allowance which such person or corporation would not otherwise enjoy, then the Secretary may disallow such deduction, credit, or other allowance. For purposes of paragraphs (1) and (2), control means the ownership of stock possessing at least 50 percent of the total combined voting power of all classes of stock entitled to vote or at least 50 percent of the total value of shares of all classes of stock of the corporation.

[Sec. 269(b)]

(b) CERTAIN LIQUIDATIONS AFTER QUALIFIED STOCK PURCHASES.—

(1) IN GENERAL.—If—

(A) there is a qualified stock purchase by a corporation of another corporation,

(B) an election is not made under section 338 with respect to such purchase,

(C) the acquired corporation is liquidated pursuant to a plan of liquidation adopted not more than 2 years after the acquisition date, and

(D) the principal purpose for such liquidation is the evasion or avoidance of Federal income tax by securing the benefit of a deduction, credit, or other allowance which the acquiring corporation would not otherwise enjoy,

then the Secretary may disallow such deduction, credit, or other allowance.

(2) MEANING OF TERMS.—For purposes of paragraph (1), the terms "qualified stock purchase" and "acquisition date" have the same respective meanings as when used in section 338.

[Sec. 269(c)]

(c) POWER OF SECRETARY TO ALLOW DEDUCTION, ETC., IN PART.—In any case to which subsection (a) or (b) applies the Secretary is authorized—

(1) to allow as a deduction, credit, or allowance any part of any amount disallowed by such subsection, if he determines that such allowance will not result in the evasion or avoidance of Federal income tax for which the acquisition was made; or

(2) to distribute, apportion, or allocate gross income, and distribute, apportion, or allocate the deductions, credits, or allowances the benefit of which was sought to be secured, between or among the corporations, or properties, or parts thereof, involved, and to allow such deductions, credits, or allowances so distributed, apportioned, or allocated, but to give effect to such allowance only to such extent as he determines will not result in the evasion or avoidance of Federal income tax for which the acquisition was made; or

(3) to exercise his powers in part under paragraph (1) and in part under paragraph (2).

[Sec. 269B]

SEC. 269B. STAPLED ENTITIES.

[Sec. 269B(a)]

(a) GENERAL RULE.—Except as otherwise provided by regulations, for purposes of this title—

(1) if a domestic corporation and a foreign corporation are stapled entities, the foreign corporation shall be treated as a domestic corporation,

(2) in applying section 1563, stock in a second corporation which constitutes a stapled interest with respect to stock of a first corporation shall be treated as owned by such first corporation, and

(3) in applying subchapter M for purposes of determining whether any stapled entity is a regulated investment company or a real estate investment trust, all entities which are stapled entities with respect to each other shall be treated as 1 entity.

[Sec. 269B(b)]

(b) SECRETARY TO PRESCRIBE REGULATIONS.—The Secretary shall prescribe such regulations as may be necessary to prevent avoidance or evasion of Federal income tax through the use of stapled entities. Such regulations may include (but shall not be limited to) regulations providing the extent to which 1 of such entities shall be treated as owning the other entity (to the extent of the stapled interest) and regulations providing that any tax imposed on the foreign corporation referred to in subsection (a)(1) may, if not paid by such corporation, be collected from the domestic corporation referred to in such subsection or the shareholders of such foreign corporation.

[Sec. 269B(c)]

(c) DEFINITIONS.—For purposes of this section—

(1) ENTITY.—The term "entity" means any corporation, partnership, trust, association, estate, or other form of carrying on a business or activity.

(2) STAPLED ENTITIES.—The term "stapled entities" means any group of 2 or more entities if more than 50 percent in value of the beneficial ownership in each of such entities consists of stapled interests.

(3) STAPLED INTERESTS.—Two or more interests are stapled interests if, by reason of form of ownership, restrictions on transfer, or other terms or conditions, in connection with the transfer of 1 of such interests the other such interests are also transferred or required to be transferred.

[Sec. 269B(d)]

(d) SPECIAL RULE FOR TREATIES.—Nothing in section 894 or 7852(d) or in any other provision of law shall be construed as permitting an exemption, by reason of any treaty obligation of the United States heretofore or hereafter entered into, from the provisions of this section.

[Sec. 269B(e)]

(e) SUBSECTION (a)(1) NOT TO APPLY IN CERTAIN CASES.—

(1) IN GENERAL.—Subsection (a)(1) shall not apply if it is established to the satisfaction of the Secretary that the domestic corporation and the foreign corporation referred to in such subsection are foreign owned.

(2) FOREIGN OWNED.—For purposes of paragraph (1), a corporation is foreign owned if less than 50 percent of—

(A) the total combined voting power of all classes of stock of such corporation entitled to vote, and

(B) the total value of the stock of the corporation,

is held directly (or indirectly through applying paragraphs (2) and (3) of section 958(a) and paragraph (4) of section 318(a)) by United States persons (as defined in section 7701(a)(30)).

[Sec. 274]

SEC. 274. DISALLOWANCE OF CERTAIN ENTERTAINMENT, ETC., EXPENSES.

***

[Sec. 274(c)]

(c) CERTAIN FOREIGN TRAVEL.—

(1) IN GENERAL.—In the case of any individual who travels outside the United States away from home in pursuit of a trade or business or in pursuit of an activity described in section 212, no deduction shall be allowed under section 162 or section 212 for that portion of the expenses of such travel otherwise allowable under such section which, under regulations prescribed by the Secretary, is not allocable to such trade or business or to such activity.

(2) EXCEPTION.—Paragraph (1) shall not apply to the expenses of any travel outside the United States away from home if—

(A) such travel does not exceed one week, or

(B) the portion of the time of travel outside the United States away from home which is not attributable to the pursuit of the taxpayer's trade or business or an activity described in section 212 is less than 25 percent of the total time on such travel.

(3) DOMESTIC TRAVEL EXCLUDED.—For purposes of this subsection, travel outside the United States does not include any travel from one point in the United States to another point in the United States.

***

[Sec. 274(h)]

(h) ATTENDANCE AT CONVENTIONS, ETC.—

(1) IN GENERAL.—In the case of any individual who attends a convention, seminar, or similar meeting which is held outside the North American area, no deduction shall be allowed under section 162 for expenses allocable to such meeting unless the taxpayer establishes that the meeting is directly related to the active conduct of his trade or business and that, after taking into account in the manner provided by regulations prescribed by the Secretary—

(A) the purpose of such meeting and the activities taking place at such meeting,

(B) the purposes and activities of the sponsoring organizations or groups,

(C) the residences of the active members of the sponsoring organization and the places at which other meetings of the sponsoring organization or groups have been held or will be held, and

(D) such other relevant factors as the taxpayer may present,

it is as reasonable for the meeting to be held outside the North American area as within the North American area.

(2) CONVENTIONS ON CRUISE SHIPS.—In the case of any individual who attends a convention, seminar, or other meeting which is held on any cruise ship, no deduction shall be allowed under section 162 for expenses allocable to such meeting, unless the taxpayer meets the requirements of paragraph (5) and establishes that the meeting is directly related to the active conduct of his trade or business and that—

(A) the cruise ship is a vessel registered in the United States; and

(B) all ports of call of such cruise ship are located in the United States or in possessions of the United States.

With respect to cruises beginning in any calendar year, not more than $2,000 of the expenses attributable to an individual attending one or more meetings may be taken into account under section 162 by reason of the preceding sentence.

(3) DEFINITIONS.—For purposes of this subsection—

(A) NORTH AMERICAN AREA.—The term "North American area" means the United States, its possessions, and the Trust Territory of the Pacific Islands, and Canada and Mexico.

(B) CRUISE SHIP.—The term "cruise ship" means any vessel sailing within or without the territorial waters of the United States.

(4) SUBSECTION TO APPLY TO EMPLOYER AS WELL AS TO TRAVELER.—

(A) Except as provided in subparagraph (B), this subsection shall apply to deductions otherwise allowable under section 162 to any person, whether or not such person is the individual attending the convention, seminar, or similar meeting.

(B) This subsection shall not deny a deduction to any person other than the individual attending the convention, seminar, or similar meeting with respect to any amount paid by such person to or on behalf of such individual if includible in the gross income of such individual. The preceding sentence shall not apply if the amount is required to be included in any information return filed by such person under part III of subchapter A of chapter 61 and is not so included.

(5) REPORTING REQUIREMENTS.—No deduction shall be allowed under section 162 for expenses allocable to attendance at a convention, seminar, or similar meeting on any cruise ship unless the taxpayer claiming the deduction attaches to the return of tax on which the deduction is claimed—

(A) a written statement signed by the individual attending the meeting which includes—

(i) information with respect to the total days of the trip, excluding the days of transportation to and from the cruise ship port, and the number of hours of each day of the trip which such individual devoted to scheduled business activities,

(ii) a program of the scheduled business activities of the meeting, and

(iii) such other information as may be required in regulations prescribed by the Secretary; and

(B) a written statement signed by an officer of the organization or group sponsoring the meeting which includes—

(i) a schedule of business activities of each day of the meeting,

(ii) the number of hours which the individual attending the meeting attended such scheduled business activities, and

(iii) such other information as may be required in regulations prescribed by the Secretary.

(6) TREATMENT OF CONVENTIONS IN CERTAIN CARIBBEAN COUNTRIES.—

(A) IN GENERAL.—For purposes of this subsection, the term "North American area" includes, with respect to any convention, seminar, or similar meeting, any beneficiary country if (as of the time such meeting begins)—

(i) there is in effect a bilateral or multilateral agreement described in subparagraph (C) between such country and the United States providing for the exchange of information between the United States and such country, and

(ii) there is not in effect a finding by the Secretary that the tax laws of such country discriminate against conventions held in the United States.

(B) BENEFICIARY COUNTRY.—For purposes of this paragraph, the term "beneficiary country" has the meaning given to such term by section 212(a)(1)(A) of the Caribbean Basin Economic Recovery Act; except that such term shall include Bermuda.

(C) AUTHORITY TO CONCLUDE EXCHANGE OF INFORMATION AGREEMENTS.—

(i) IN GENERAL.—The Secretary is authorized to negotiate and conclude an agreement for the exchange of information with any beneficiary country. Except as provided in clause (ii), an exchange of information agreement shall provide for the exchange of such information (not limited to information concerning nationals or residents of the United States or the beneficiary country) as may be necessary or appropriate to carry out and enforce the tax laws of the United States and the beneficiary country (whether criminal or civil proceedings), including information which may otherwise be subject to nondisclosure provisions of the local law of the beneficiary country such as provisions respecting bank secrecy and bearer shares. The exchange of information agreement shall be terminable by either country on reasonable notice and shall provide that information received by either country will be disclosed only to persons or authorities (including courts and administrative bodies) involved in the administration or oversight of, or in the determination of appeals in respect of, taxes of the United States or the beneficiary country and will be used by such persons or authorities only for such purposes.

(ii) NONDISCLOSURE OF QUALIFIED CONFIDENTIAL INFORMATION SOUGHT FOR CIVIL TAX PURPOSES.—An exchange of information agreement need not provide for the exchange of qualified confidential information which is sought only for civil tax purposes if—

(I) the Secretary of the Treasury, after making all reasonable efforts to negotiate an agreement which includes the exchange of such information, determines that such an agreement cannot be negotiated but that the agreement which was negotiated will significantly assist in the administration and enforcement of the tax laws of the United States, and

(II) the President determines that the agreement as negotiated is in the national security interest of the United States.

(iii) QUALIFIED CONFIDENTIAL INFORMATION DEFINED.—For purposes of this subparagraph, the term "qualified confidential information" means information which is subject to the nondisclosure provisions of any local law of the beneficiary country regarding bank secrecy or ownership of bearer shares.

(iv) CIVIL TAX PURPOSES.—For purposes of this subparagraph, the determination of whether information is sought only for civil tax purposes shall be made by the requesting party.

(D) COORDINATION WITH OTHER PROVISIONS.—Any exchange of information agreement negotiated under subparagraph (C) shall be treated as an income tax convention for purposes of section 6103(k)(4). The Secretary may exercise his authority under subchapter A of chapter 78 to carry out any obligation of the United States under an agreement referred to in subparagraph (C).

(E) DETERMINATIONS PUBLISHED IN THE FEDERAL REGISTER.—The following shall be published in the Federal Register—

(i) any determination by the President under subparagraph (C)(ii) (including the reasons for such determination),

(ii) any determination by the Secretary under subparagraph (C)(ii) (including the reasons for such determination), and

(iii) any finding by the Secretary under subparagraph (A)(ii) (and any termination thereof).

(7) SEMINARS, ETC. FOR SECTION 212 PURPOSES.—No deduction shall be allowed under section 212 for expenses allocable to a convention, seminar, or similar meeting.

* * *

[Sec. 275]

SEC. 275. CERTAIN TAXES.

[Sec. 275(a)]

(a) GENERAL RULE.—No deduction shall be allowed for the following taxes:

* * *

(4) Income, war profits, and excess profits taxes imposed by the authority of any foreign country or possession of the United States if the taxpayer chooses to take to any extent the benefits of section 901.

* * *

SUBCHAPTER C—CORPORATE DISTRIBUTIONS AND ADJUSTMENTS

PART I—DISTRIBUTIONS BY CORPORATIONS

Subpart A—Effects on Recipients

[Sec. 301]

SEC. 301. DISTRIBUTIONS OF PROPERTY.

[Sec. 301(a)]

(a) IN GENERAL.—Except as otherwise provided in this chapter, a distribution of property (as defined in section 317(a)) made by a corporation to a shareholder with respect to its stock shall be treated in the manner provided in subsection (c).

[Sec. 301(b)]

(b) AMOUNT DISTRIBUTED.—

(1) GENERAL RULE.—For purposes of this section, the amount of any distribution shall be the amount of money received, plus the fair market value of the other property received.

(2) REDUCTION FOR LIABILITIES.—The amount of any distribution determined under paragraph (1) shall be reduced (but not below zero) by—

(A) the amount of any liability of the corporation assumed by the shareholder in connection with the distribution, and

(B) the amount of any liability to which the property received by the shareholder is subject immediately before, and immediately after, the distribution.

(3) DETERMINATION OF FAIR MARKET VALUE.—For purposes of this section, fair market value shall be determined as of the date of the distribution.

[Sec. 301(c)]

(c) AMOUNT TAXABLE.—In the case of a distribution to which subsection (a) applies—

(1) AMOUNT CONSTITUTING DIVIDEND.—That portion of the distribution which is a dividend (as defined in section 316) shall be included in gross income.

(2) AMOUNT APPLIED AGAINST BASIS.—That portion of the distribution which is not a dividend shall be applied against and reduce the adjusted basis of the stock.

(3) AMOUNT IN EXCESS OF BASIS.—

(A) IN GENERAL.—Except as provided in subparagraph (B), that portion of the distribution which is not a dividend, to the extent that it exceeds the adjusted basis of the stock, shall be treated as gain from the sale or exchange of property.

(B) DISTRIBUTIONS OUT OF INCREASE IN VALUE ACCRUED BEFORE MARCH 1, 1913.—That portion of the distribution which is not a dividend, to the extent that it exceeds the adjusted basis of the stock and to the extent that it is out of increase in value accrued before March 1, 1913, shall be exempt from tax.

[Sec. 301(d)]

(d) BASIS.—The basis of property received in a distribution to which subsection (a) applies shall be the fair market value of such property.

[Sec. 301(e)]

(e) SPECIAL RULE FOR CERTAIN DISTRIBUTIONS RECEIVED BY 20 PERCENT CORPORATE SHAREHOLDER.—

(1) IN GENERAL.—Except to the extent otherwise provided in regulations, solely for purposes of determining the taxable income of any 20 percent corporate shareholder (and its adjusted basis in the stock of the distributing corporation), section 312 shall be applied with respect to the distributing corporation as if it did not contain subsections (k) and (n) thereof.

(2) 20 PERCENT CORPORATE SHAREHOLDER.—For purposes of this subsection, the term "20 percent corporate shareholder" means, with respect to any distribution, any corporation which owns (directly or through the application of section 318)—

(A) stock in the corporation making the distribution possessing at least 20 percent of the total combined voting power of all classes of stock entitled to vote, or

(B) at least 20 percent of the total value of all stock of the distributing corporation (except nonvoting stock which is limited and preferred as to dividends),

but only if, but for this subsection, the distributee corporation would be entitled to a deduction under section 243, or 245 with respect to such distribution.

(3) APPLICATION OF SECTION 312(n)(7) NOT AFFECTED.—The reference in paragraph (1) to subsection (n) of section 312 shall be treated as not including a reference to paragraph (7) of such subsection.

(4) REGULATIONS.—The Secretary shall prescribe such regulations as may be necessary or appropriate to carry out the purposes of this subsection.

* * *

[Sec. 302]

SEC. 302. DISTRIBUTIONS IN REDEMPTION OF STOCK.

[Sec. 302(a)]

(a) GENERAL RULE.—If a corporation redeems its stock (within the meaning of section 317 (b)), and if paragraph (1), (2), (3), (4), or (5) of subsection (b) applies, such redemption shall be treated as a distribution in part or full payment in exchange for the stock.

[Sec. 302(b)]

(b) REDEMPTIONS TREATED AS EXCHANGES.—

(1) REDEMPTIONS NOT EQUIVALENT TO DIVIDENDS.—Subsection (a) shall apply if the redemption is not essentially equivalent to a dividend.

(2) SUBSTANTIALLY DISPROPORTIONATE REDEMPTION OF STOCK.—

(A) IN GENERAL.—Subsection (a) shall apply if the distribution is substantially disproportionate with respect to the shareholder.

(B) LIMITATION.—This paragraph shall not apply unless immediately after the redemption the shareholder owns less than 50 percent of the total combined voting power of all classes of stock entitled to vote.

(C) DEFINITIONS.—For purposes of this paragraph, the distribution is substantially disproportionate if—

(i) the ratio which the voting stock of the corporation owned by the shareholder immediately after the redemption bears to all of the voting stock of the corporation at such time,

is less than 80 percent of—

(ii) the ratio which the voting stock of the corporation owned by the shareholder immediately before the redemption bears to all of the voting stock of the corporation at such time.

For purposes of this paragraph, no distribution shall be treated as substantially disproportionate unless the shareholder's ownership of the common stock of the corporation (whether voting or nonvoting) after and before redemption also meets the 80 percent requirement of the preceding sentence. For purposes of the preceding sentence, if there is more than one class of common stock, the determinations shall be made by reference to fair market value.

(D) SERIES OF REDEMPTIONS.—This paragraph shall not apply to any redemption made pursuant to a plan the purpose or effect of which is a series of redemptions resulting in a distribution which (in the aggregate) is not substantially disproportionate with respect to the shareholder.

(3) TERMINATION OF SHAREHOLDER'S INTEREST.—Subsection (a) shall apply if the redemption is in complete redemption of all of the stock of the corporation owned by the shareholder.

(4) REDEMPTION FROM NONCORPORATE SHAREHOLDER IN PARTIAL LIQUIDATION.—Subsection (a) shall apply to a distribution if such distribution is—

(A) in redemption of stock held by a shareholder who is not a corporation, and

(B) in partial liquidation of the distributing corporation.

* * *

(6) APPLICATION OF PARAGRAPHS.—In determining whether a redemption meets the requirements of paragraph (1), the fact that such redemption fails to meet the requirements of paragraph (2), (3), or (4) shall not be taken into account. If a redemption meets the requirements of paragraph (3) and also the requirements of paragraph (1), (2), or (4), then so much of subsection (c) (2) as would (but for this sentence) apply in respect of the acquisition of an interest in the corporation within the 10-year period beginning on the date of the distribution shall not apply.

[Sec. 302(c)]

(c) CONSTRUCTIVE OWNERSHIP OF STOCK.—

(1) IN GENERAL.—Except as provided in paragraph (2) of this subsection, section 318(a) shall apply in determining the ownership of stock for purposes of this section.

(2) FOR DETERMINING TERMINATION OF INTEREST.—

(A) In the case of a distribution described in subsection (b)(3), section 318(a)(1) shall not apply if—

(i) immediately after the distribution the distributee has no interest in the corporation (including an interest as officer, director, or employee), other than an interest as a creditor,

(ii) the distributee does not acquire any such interest (other than stock acquired by bequest or inheritance) within 10 years from the date of such distribution, and

(iii) the distributee, at such time and in such manner as the Secretary by regulations prescribes, files an agreement to notify the Secretary of any acquisition described in clause (ii) and to retain such records as may be necessary for the application of this paragraph.

If the distributee acquires such an interest in the corporation (other than by bequest or inheritance) within 10 years from the date of the distribution, then the periods of limitation provided in sections 6501 and 6502 on the making of an assessment and the collection by levy or a proceeding in court shall, with respect to any deficiency (including interest and additions to the tax) resulting from such acquisition, include one year immediately following the date on which the distributee (in accordance with regulations prescribed by the Secretary) notifies the Secretary of such acquisition; and such assessment and collection may be made notwithstanding any provision of law or rule of law which otherwise would prevent such assessment and collection.

(B) Subparagraph (A) of this paragraph shall not apply if—

(i) any portion of the stock redeemed was acquired, directly or indirectly, within the 10-year period ending on the date of the distribution by the distributee from a person the ownership of whose stock would (at the time of distribution) be attributable to the distributee under section 318(a), or

(ii) any person owns (at the time of the distribution) stock the ownership of which is attributable to the distributee under section 318(a) and such person acquired any stock in the corporation, directly or indirectly, from the distributee within the 10-year period ending on the date of the distribution, unless such stock so acquired from the distributee is redeemed in the same transaction.

The preceding sentence shall not apply if the acquisition (or, in the case of clause (ii), the disposition) by the distributee did not have as one of its principal purposes the avoidance of Federal income tax.

(C) SPECIAL RULE FOR WAIVERS BY ENTITIES.—

(i) IN GENERAL.—Subparagraph (A) shall not apply to a distribution to any entity unless—

(I) such entity and each related person meet the requirements of clauses (i), (ii), and (iii) of subparagraph (A), and

(II) each related person agrees to be jointly and severally liable for any deficiency (including interest and additions to tax) resulting from an acquisition described in clause (ii) of subparagraph (A).

In any case to which the preceding sentence applies, the second sentence of subparagraph (A) and subparagraph (B)(ii) shall be applied by substituting "distributee or any related person" for "distributee" each place it appears.

(ii) DEFINITIONS.—For purposes of this subparagraph—

(I) the term "entity" means a partnership, estate, trust, or corporation; and

(II) the term "related person" means any person to whom ownership of stock in the corporation is (at the time of the distribution) attributable under section 318(a)(1) if such stock is further attributable to the entity under section 318(a)(3).

[Sec. 302(d)]

(d) REDEMPTIONS TREATED AS DISTRIBUTIONS OF PROPERTY.—Except as otherwise provided in this subchapter, if a corporation redeems its stock (within the meaning of section 317(b)), and if subsection (a) of this section does not apply, such redemption shall be treated as a distribution of property to which section 301 applies.

[Sec. 302(e)]

(e) PARTIAL LIQUIDATION DEFINED.—

(1) IN GENERAL.—For purposes of subsection (b)(4), a distribution shall be treated as in partial liquidation of a corporation if—

(A) the distribution is not essentially equivalent to a dividend (determined at the corporate level rather than at the shareholder level), and

(B) the distribution is pursuant to a plan and occurs within the taxable year in which the plan is adopted or within the succeeding taxable year.

(2) TERMINATION OF BUSINESS.—The distributions which meet the requirements of paragraph (1)(A) shall include (but shall not be limited to) a distribution which meets the requirements of subparagraphs (A) and (B) of this paragraph:

(A) The distribution is attributable to the distributing corporation's ceasing to conduct, or consists of the assets of, a qualified trade or business.

(B) Immediately after the distribution, the distributing corporation is actively engaged in the conduct of a qualified trade or business.

(3) QUALIFIED TRADE OR BUSINESS.—For purposes of paragraph (2), the term "qualified trade or business" means any trade or business which—

(A) was actively conducted throughout the 5-year period ending on the date of the redemption, and

(B) was not acquired by the corporation within such period in a transaction in which gain or loss was recognized in whole or in part.

(4) REDEMPTION MAY BE PRO RATA.—Whether or not a redemption meets the requirements of subparagraphs (A) and (B) of paragraph (2) shall be determined without regard to whether or not the redemption is pro rata with respect to all of the shareholders of the corporation.

(5) TREATMENT OF CERTAIN PASS-THRU ENTITIES.—For purposes of determining under subsection (b)(4) whether any stock is held by a shareholder who is not a corporation, any stock held by a partnership, estate, or trust shall be treated as if it were actually held proportionately by its partners or beneficiaries.

***

[Sec. 304]

SEC. 304. REDEMPTION THROUGH USE OF RELATED CORPORATIONS.

[Sec. 304(a)]

(a) TREATMENT OF CERTAIN STOCK PURCHASES.—

(1) ACQUISITION BY RELATED CORPORATION (OTHER THAN SUBSIDIARY).—For purposes of sections 302 and 303, if—

(A) one or more persons are in control of each of two corporations, and

(B) in return for property, one of the corporations acquires stock in the other corporation from the person (or persons) so in control,

then (unless paragraph (2) applies) such property shall be treated as a distribution in redemption of the stock of the corporation acquiring such stock. To the extent that such distribution is treated as a distribution to which section 301 applies, the transferor and the acquiring corporation shall be treated in the same manner as if the transferor had transferred the stock so acquired to the acquiring corporation in exchange for stock of the acquiring corporation in a transaction to which section 351(a) applies, and then the acquiring corporation had redeemed the stock it was treated as issuing in such transaction.

(2) ACQUISITION BY SUBSIDIARY.—For purposes of sections 302 and 303, if—

(A) in return for property, one corporation acquires from a shareholder of another corporation stock in such other corporation, and

(B) the issuing corporation controls the acquiring corporation,

then such property shall be treated as a distribution in redemption of the stock of the issuing corporation.

[Sec. 304(b)]

(b) SPECIAL RULES FOR APPLICATION OF SUBSECTION (a).—

(1) RULE FOR DETERMINATIONS UNDER SECTION 302(b).—In the case of any acquisition of stock to which subsection (a) of this section applies, determinations as to whether the acquisition is, by reason of section 302(b), to be treated as a distribution in part or full payment in exchange for the stock shall be made by reference to the stock of the issuing corporation. In applying section 318(a) (relating to constructive ownership of stock) with respect to section 302(b) for purposes of this paragraph, sections 318(a)(2)(C) and 318(a)(3)(C) shall be applied without regard to the 50 percent limitation contained therein.

(2) AMOUNT CONSTITUTING DIVIDEND.—In the case of any acquisition of stock to which subsection (a) applies, the determination of the amount which is a dividend (and the source thereof) shall be made as if the property were distributed—

(A) by the acquiring corporation to the extent of its earnings and profits, and

(B) then by the issuing corporation to the extent of its earnings and profits.

(3) COORDINATION WITH SECTION 351.—

(A) PROPERTY TREATED AS RECEIVED IN REDEMPTION.—Except as otherwise provided in this paragraph, subsection (a) (and not section 351 and not so much of sections 357 and 358 as relates to section 351) shall apply to any property received in a distribution described in subsection (a).

(B) CERTAIN ASSUMPTIONS OF LIABILITY, ETC.—

(i) IN GENERAL.—In the case of an acquisition described in section 351, subsection (a) shall not apply to any liability—

(I) assumed by the acquiring corporation, or

(II) to which the stock is subject,

if such liability was incurred by the transferor to acquire the stock. For purposes of the preceding sentence, the term "stock" means stock referred to in paragraph (1)(B) or (2)(A) of subsection (a).

(ii) EXTENSION OF OBLIGATIONS, ETC.—For purposes of clause (i), an extension, renewal, or refinancing of a libility which meets the requirements of clause (i) shall be treated as meeting such requirements.

(iii) CLAUSE (i) DOES NOT APPLY TO STOCK ACQUIRED FROM RELATED PERSON EXCEPT WHERE COMPLETE TERMINATION.—Clause (i) shall apply only to stock acquired by the transferor from a person—

(I) none of whose stock is attributable to the transferor under section 318(a) (other than paragraph (4) thereof), or

(II) who satisfies rules similar to the rules of section 302(c)(2) with respect to both the acquiring and the issuing corporations (determined as if such person were a distributee of each such corporation).

(C) DISTRIBUTIONS INCIDENT TO FORMATION OF BANK HOLDING COMPANIES.—If—

(i) pursuant to a plan, control of a bank is acquired and within 2 years after the date on which such control is acquired, stock constituting control of such bank is transferred to a BHC in connection with its formation,

(ii) incident to the formation of the BHC there is a distribution of property described in subsection (a), and

(iii) the shareholders of the BHC who receive distributions of such property do not have control of such BHC,

then, subsection (a) shall not apply to any securities received by a qualified minority shareholder incident to the formation of such BHC. For purposes of this subparagraph, any assumption of (or acquisition of stock subject to) a liability under subparagraph (B) shall not be treated as a distribution of property.

(D) DEFINITIONS.—For purposes of subparagraph (C) and this subparagraph—

(i) QUALIFIED MINORITY SHAREHOLDER.—The term "qualified minority shareholder" means any shareholder who owns less than 10 percent (in value) of the stock of the BHC. For purposes of the preceding sentence, the rules of paragraph (3) of subsection (c) shall apply.

(ii) BHC.—The term "BHC" means a bank holding company (within the meaning of section 2(a) of the Bank Holding Company Act of 1956).

(4) TREATMENT OF CERTAIN INTRAGROUP TRANSACTIONS.—

(A) IN GENERAL.—In the case of any transfer described in subsection (a) of stock from 1 member of an affiliated group to another member of such group, proper adjustments shall be made to—

(i) the adjusted basis of any intragroup stock, and

(ii) the earnings and profits of any member of such group,

to the extent necessary to carry out the purposes of this section.

(B) DEFINITIONS.—For purposes of this paragraph—

(i) AFFILIATED GROUP.—The term "affiliated group" has the meaning given such term by section 1504(a).

(ii) INTRAGROUP STOCK.—The term "intragroup stock" means any stock which—

(I) is in a corporation which is a member of an affiliated group, and

(II) is held by another member of such group.

(5) ACQUISITIONS BY FOREIGN CORPORATIONS.—

(A) IN GENERAL.—In the case of any acquisition to which subsection (a) applies in which the acquiring corporation is a foreign corporation, the only earnings and profits taken into account under paragraph (2)(A) shall be those earnings and profits—

(i) which are attributable (under regulations prescribed by the Secretary) to stock of the acquiring corporation owned (within the meaning of section 958(a)) by a corporation or individual which is—

(I) a United States shareholder (within the meaning of section 951(b)) of the acquiring corporation, and

(II) the transferor or a person who bears a relationship to the transferor described in section 267(b) or 707(b), and

(ii) which were accumulated during the period or periods such stock was owned by such person while the acquiring corporation was a controlled foreign corporation.

(B) SPECIAL RULE IN CASE OF FOREIGN ACQUIRING CORPORATION.—In the case of any acquisition to which subsection (a) applies in which the acquiring corporation is a foreign corporation, no earnings and profits shall be taken into account under paragraph (2)(A) (and subparagraph (A) shall not apply) if more than 50 percent of the dividends arising from such acquisition (determined without regard to this subparagraph) would neither—

(i) be subject to tax under this chapter for the taxable year in which the dividends arise, nor

(ii) be includible in the earnings and profits of a controlled foreign corporation (as defined in section 957 and without regard to section 953(c)).

(C) REGULATIONS.—The Secretary shall prescribe such regulations as are appropriate to carry out the purposes of this paragraph.

(6) AVOIDANCE OF MULTIPLE INCLUSIONS, ETC.—In the case of any acquisition to which subsection (a) applies in which the acquiring corporation or the issuing corporation is a foreign corporation, the Secretary shall prescribe such regulations as are appropriate in order to

eliminate a multiple inclusion of any item in income by reason of this subpart and to provide appropriate basis adjustments (including modifications to the application of sections 959 and 961).

[Sec. 304(c)]

(c) CONTROL.—

(1) IN GENERAL.—For purposes of this section, control means the ownership of stock possessing at least 50 percent of the total combined voting power of all classes of stock entitled to vote, or at least 50 percent of the total value of shares of all classes of stock. If a person (or persons) is in control (within the meaning of the preceding sentence) of a corporation which in turn owns at least 50 percent of the total combined voting power of all stock entitled to vote of another corporation, or owns at least 50 percent of the total value of the shares of all classes of stock of another corporation, then such person (or persons) shall be treated as in control of such other corporation.

(2) STOCK ACQUIRED IN THE TRANSACTION.—For purposes of subsection (a)(1)—

(A) GENERAL RULE.—Where 1 or more persons in control of the issuing corporation transfer stock of such corporation in exchange for stock of the acquiring corporation, the stock of the acquiring corporation received shall be taken into account in determining whether such person or persons are in control of the acquiring corporation.

(B) DEFINITION OF CONTROL GROUP.—Where 2 or more persons in control of the issuing corporation transfer stock of such corporation to acquiring corporation and, after the transfer, the transferors are in control of the acquiring corporation, the person or persons in control of each corporation shall include each of the persons who so transfer stock.

(3) CONSTRUCTIVE OWNERSHIP.—

(A) IN GENERAL.—Section 318(a) (relating to constructive ownership of stock) shall apply for purposes of determining control under this section.

(B) MODIFICATION OF 50-PERCENT LIMITATIONS IN SECTION 318.—For purposes of subparagraph (A)—

(i) paragraph (2)(C) of section 318(a) shall be applied by substituting "5 percent" for "50 percent", and

(ii) paragraph (3)(C) of section 318(a) shall be applied—

(I) by substituting "5 percent" for "50 percent", and

(II) in any case where such paragraph would not apply but for subclause (I), by considering a corporation as owning the stock (other than stock in such corporation) owned by or for any shareholder of such corporation in that proportion which the value of the stock which such shareholder owned in such corporation bears to the value of all stock in such corporation.

Subpart B—Effects on Corporation

[Sec. 311]

SEC. 311. TAXABILITY OF CORPORATION ON DISTRIBUTION.

[Sec. 311(a)]

(a) GENERAL RULE.—Except as provided in subsection (b), no gain or loss shall be recognized to a corporation on the distribution (not in complete liquidation) with respect to its stock of—

(1) its stock (or rights to acquire its stock), or

(2) property.

[Sec. 311(b)]

(b) DISTRIBUTIONS OF APPRECIATED PROPERTY.—

(1) IN GENERAL.—If—

(A) a corporation distributes property (other than an obligation of such corporation) to a shareholder in a distribution to which subpart A applies, and

(B) the fair market value of such property exceeds its adjusted basis (in the hands of the distributing corporation),

then gain shall be recognized to the distributing corporation as if such property were sold to the distributee at its fair market value.

(2) TREATMENT OF LIABILITIES.—Rules similar to the rules of section 336(b) shall apply for purposes of this subsection.

(3) SPECIAL RULE FOR CERTAIN DISTRIBUTIONS OF PARTNERSHIP OR TRUST INTERESTS.—If the property distributed consists of an interest in a partnership or trust, the Secretary may by regulations provide that the amount of the gain recognized under paragraph (1) shall be computed without regard to any loss attributable to property contributed to the partnership or trust for the principal purpose of recognizing such loss on the distribution.

[Sec. 312]

SEC. 312. EFFECT ON EARNINGS AND PROFITS.

* * *

[Sec. 312(k)]

(k) EFFECT OF DEPRECIATION ON EARNINGS AND PROFITS.—

(1) GENERAL RULE.—For purposes of computing the earnings and profits of a corporation for any taxable year beginning after June 30, 1972, the allowance for depreciation (and amortization, if any) shall be deemed to be the amount which would be allowable for such year if the straight line method of depreciation had been used for each taxable year beginning after June 30, 1972.

(2) EXCEPTION.—If for any taxable year a method of depreciation was used by the taxpayer which the Secretary has determined results in a reasonable allowance under section 167(a) and which is the unit-of-production method or other method not expressed in a term of years, then the adjustment to earnings and profits for depreciation for such year shall be determined under the method so used (in lieu of the straight line method).

(3) EXCEPTION FOR TANGIBLE PROPERTY.—

(A) IN GENERAL.—Except as provided in subparagraph (B), in the case of tangible property to which section 168 applies, the adjustment to earnings and profits for depreciation for any taxable year shall be determined under the alternative depreciation system (within the meaning of section 168(g)(2)).

(B) TREATMENT OF AMOUNTS DEDUCTIBLE UNDER SECTION 179, 179B, 179C, 179D, or 179E.—

(i) IN GENERAL.—For purposes of computing the earnings and profits of a corporation, except as provided in clause (ii), any amount deductible under section 179, 179B, 179C, 179D, or 179E shall be allowed as a deduction ratably over the period of 5 taxable years (beginning with the taxable year for which such amount is deductible under section 179, 179B, 179C, 179D, or 179E, as the case may be).

(ii) SPECIAL RULE.—In the case of a corporation that is a real estate investment trust, any amount deductible under section 179D shall be allowed in the year in which the property giving rise to such deduction is placed in service (or, in the case of energy efficient building retrofit property, the year in which the qualifying final certification is made).

(4) CERTAIN FOREIGN CORPORATIONS.—The provisions of paragraph (1) shall not apply in computing the earnings and profits of a foreign corporation for any taxable year for which less than 20 percent of the gross income from all sources of such corporation is derived from sources within the United States.

***

Subpart C—Definitions; Constructive Ownership of Stock

[Sec. 316]

SEC. 316. DIVIDEND DEFINED.

[Sec. 316(a)]

(a) GENERAL RULE.—For purposes of this subtitle, the term "dividend" means any distribution of property made by a corporation to its shareholders—

(1) out of its earnings and profits accumulated after February 28, 1913, or

(2) out of its earnings and profits of the taxable year (computed as of the close of the taxable year without diminution by reason of any distributions made during the taxable year), without regard to the amount of the earnings and profits at the time the distribution was made.

Except as otherwise provided in this subtitle, every distribution is made out of earnings and profits to the extent thereof, and from the most recently accumulated earnings and profits. To the extent that any distribution is, under any provision of this subchapter, treated as a distribution of property to which section 301 applies, such distribution shall be treated as a distribution of property for purposes of this subsection.

[Sec. 316(b)]

(b) SPECIAL RULES.—

(1) CERTAIN INSURANCE COMPANY DIVIDENDS.—The definition in subsection (a) shall not apply to the term "dividend" as used in subchapter L in any case where the reference is to dividends of insurance companies paid to policyholders as such.

(2) DISTRIBUTIONS BY PERSONAL HOLDING COMPANIES.—

(A) In the case of a corporation which—

(i) under the law applicable to the taxable year in which the distribution is made, is a personal holding company (as defined in section 542), or

(ii) for the taxable year in respect of which the distribution is made under section 563(b) (relating to dividends paid after the close of the taxable year), or section 547 (relating to deficiency dividends), or the corresponding provisions of prior law, is a personal holding company under the law applicable to such taxable year,

the term "dividend" also means any distribution of property (whether or not a dividend as defined in subsection (a)) made by the corporation to its shareholders, to the extent of its undistributed personal holding company income (determined under section 545 without regard to distributions under this paragraph) for such year.

(B) For purposes of subparagraph (A), the term "distribution of property" includes a distribution in complete liquidation occurring within 24 months after the adoption of a plan of liquidation, but—

(i) only to the extent of the amounts distributed to distributees other than corporate shareholders, and

(ii) only to the extent that the corporation designates such amounts as a dividend distribution and duly notifies such distributees of such designation, under regulations prescribed by the Secretary, but

(iii) not in excess of the sum of such distributees' allocable share of the undistributed personal holding company income for such year, computed without regard to this subparagraph or section 562(b).

***

[Sec. 317]

SEC. 317. OTHER DEFINITIONS.

[Sec. 317(a)]

(a) PROPERTY.—For purposes of this part, the term "property" means money, securities, and any other property; except that such term does not include stock in the corporation making the distribution (or rights to acquire such stock).

***

[Sec. 318]

SEC. 318. CONSTRUCTIVE OWNERSHIP OF STOCK.

[Sec. 318(a)]

(a) GENERAL RULE.—For purposes of those provisions of this subchapter to which the rules contained in this section are expressly made applicable—

(1) MEMBERS OF FAMILY.—

(A) IN GENERAL.—An individual shall be considered as owning the stock owned, directly or indirectly, by or for—

(i) his spouse (other than a spouse who is legally separated from the individual under a decree of divorce or separate maintenance), and

(ii) his children, grandchildren, and parents.

(B) EFFECT OF ADOPTION.—For purposes of subparagraph (A) (ii), a legally adopted child of an individual shall be treated as a child of such individual by blood.

(2) ATTRIBUTION FROM PARTNERSHIPS, ESTATES, TRUSTS, AND CORPORATIONS.—

(A) FROM PARTNERSHIPS AND ESTATES.—Stock owned, directly or indirectly, by or for a partnership or estate shall be considered as owned proportionately by its partners or beneficiaries.

(B) FROM TRUSTS.—

(i) Stock owned, directly or indirectly, by or for a trust (other than an employees' trust described in section 401(a) which is exempt from tax under section 501(a)) shall be considered as owned by its beneficiaries in proportion to the actuarial interest of such beneficiaries in such trust.

(ii) Stock owned, directly or indirectly, by or for any portion of a trust of which a person is considered the owner under subpart E of part I of subchapter J (relating to grantors and others treated as substantial owners) shall be considered as owned by such person.

(C) FROM CORPORATIONS.—If 50 percent or more in value of the stock in a corporation is owned, directly or indirectly, by or for any person, such person shall be considered as owning the stock owned, directly or indirectly, by or for such corporation, in that proportion which the value of the stock which such person so owns bears to the value of all the stock in such corporation.

(3) ATTRIBUTION TO PARTNERSHIPS, ESTATES, TRUSTS, AND CORPORATIONS.—

(A) TO PARTNERSHIPS AND ESTATES.—Stock owned, directly or indirectly, by or for a partner or a beneficiary of an estate shall be considered as owned by the partnership or estate.

(B) TO TRUSTS.—

(i) Stock owned, directly or indirectly, by or for a beneficiary of a trust (other than an employees' trust described in section 401(a) which is exempt from tax under section 501 (a)) shall be considered as owned by the trust, unless such beneficiary's interest in the trust is a remote contingent interest. For purposes of this clause, a contingent interest of a beneficiary in a trust shall be considered remote if, under the maximum exercise of discretion by the trustee in favor of such beneficiary, the value of such interest, computed actuarially, is 5 percent or less of the value of the trust property.

(ii) Stock owned, directly or indirectly, by or for a person who is considered the owner of any portion of a trust under subpart E of part I of subchapter J (relating to grantors and others treated as substantial owners) shall be considered as owned by the trust.

(C) TO CORPORATIONS.—If 50 percent or more in value of the stock in a corporation is owned, directly or indirectly, by or for any person, such corporation shall be considered as owning the stock owned, directly or indirectly, by or for such person.

(4) OPTIONS.—If any person has an option to acquire stock, such stock shall be considered as owned by such person. For purposes of this paragraph, an option to acquire such an option, and each one of a series of such options, shall be considered as an option to acquire such stock.

(5) OPERATING RULES.—

(A) IN GENERAL.—Except as provided in subparagraphs (B) and (C), stock constructively owned by a person by reason of the application of paragraph (1), (2), (3), or (4), shall, for purposes of applying paragraphs (1), (2), (3), and (4), be considered as actually owned by such person.

(B) MEMBERS OF FAMILY.—Stock constructively owned by an individual by reason of the application of paragraph (1) shall not be considered as owned by him for purposes of again applying paragraph (1) in order to make another the constructive owner of such stock.

(C) PARTNERSHIPS, ESTATES, TRUSTS, AND CORPORATIONS.—Stock constructively owned by a partnership, estate, trust, or corporation by reason of the application of paragraph (3) shall not be considered as owned by it for purposes of applying paragraph (2) in order to make another the constructive owner of such stock.

(D) OPTION RULE IN LIEU OF FAMILY RULE.—For purposes of this paragraph, if stock may be considered as owned by an individual under paragraph (1) or (4), it shall be considered as owned by him under paragraph (4).

(E) S CORPORATION TREATED AS PARTNERSHIP.—For purposes of this subsection—

(i) an S corporation shall be treated as a partnership, and

(ii) any shareholder of the S corporation shall be treated as a partner of such partnership.

The preceding sentence shall not apply for purposes of determining whether stock in the S corporation is constructively owned by any person.

***

PART II—CORPORATE LIQUIDATIONS

Subpart A—Effects on Recipients

[Sec. 331]

SEC. 331. GAIN OR LOSS TO SHAREHOLDER IN CORPORATE LIQUIDATIONS.

[Sec. 331(a)]

(a) DISTRIBUTIONS IN COMPLETE LIQUIDATION TREATED AS EXCHANGES.—Amounts received by a shareholder in a distribution in complete liquidation of a corporation shall be treated as in full payment in exchange for the stock.

[Sec. 331(b)]

(b) NONAPPLICATION OF SECTION 301.—Section 301 (relating to effects on shareholder of distributions of property) shall not apply to any distribution of property (other than a distribution referred to in paragraph (2)(B) of section 316(b)), in complete liquidation.

***

[Sec. 332]

SEC. 332. COMPLETE LIQUIDATIONS OF SUBSIDIARIES.

[Sec. 332(a)]

(a) GENERAL RULE.—No gain or loss shall be recognized on the receipt by a corporation of property distributed in complete liquidation of another corporation.

[Sec. 332(b)]

(b) LIQUIDATIONS TO WHICH SECTION APPLIES.—For purposes of this section, a distribution shall be considered to be in complete liquidation only if—

(1) the corporation receiving such property was, on the date of the adoption of the plan of liquidation, and has continued to be at all times until the receipt of the property, the owner of stock (in such other corporation) meeting the requirements of section 1504(a)(2); and either

(2) the distribution is by such other corporation in complete cancellation or redemption of all its stock, and the transfer of all the property occurs within the taxable year; in such case the adoption by the shareholders of the resolution under which is authorized the distribution of all the assets of such corporation in complete cancellation or redemption of all its stock shall be considered an adoption of a plan of liquidation, even though no time for the completion of the transfer of the property is specified in such resolution; or

(3) such distribution is one of a series of distributions by such other corporation in complete cancellation or redemption of all its stock in accordance with a plan of liquidation under which the transfer of all the property under the liquidation is to be completed within 3 years from the close of the taxable year during which is made the first of the series of distributions under the plan, except that if such transfer is not completed within such period, or if the taxpayer does not continue qualified under paragraph (1) until the completion of such transfer, no distribution under the plan shall be considered a distribution in complete liquidation.

If such transfer of all the property does not occur within the taxable year, the Secretary may require of the taxpayer such bond, or waiver of the statute of limitations on assessment and collection, or both, as he may deem necessary to insure, if the transfer of the property is not completed within such 3-year period, or if the taxpayer does not continue qualified under paragraph (1) until the completion of such transfer, the assessment and collection of all income taxes then imposed by law for such taxable year or subsequent taxable years, to the extent attributable to property so received. A distribution otherwise constituting a distribution in complete liquidation within the meaning of this subsection shall not be considered as not constituting such a distribution merely because it does not constitute a distribution or liquidation within the meaning of the corporate law under which the distribution is made; and for purposes of this subsection a transfer of property of such other corporation to the taxpayer shall not be considered as not constituting a distribution (or one of a series of distributions) in complete cancellation or redemption of all the stock of such other corporation, merely because the carrying out of the plan involves (A) the transfer under the plan to the taxpayer by such other corporation of property, not attributable to shares owned by the taxpayer, on an exchange described in section 361, and (B) the complete cancellation or redemption under the plan, as a result of exchanges described in section 354, of the shares not owned by the taxpayer.

[Sec. 332(c)]

(c) DEDUCTIBLE LIQUIDATING DISTRIBUTIONS OF REGULATED INVESTMENT COMPANIES AND REAL ESTATE INVESTMENT TRUSTS.—If a corporation receives a distribution from a regulated investment company or a real estate investment trust which is considered under subsection (b) as being in complete liquidation of such company or trust, then, notwithstanding any other provision of this chapter, such corporation shall recognize and treat as a dividend from such company or trust an amount equal to the deduction for dividends paid allowable to such company or trust by reason of such distribution.

[Sec. 332(d)]

(d) RECOGNITION OF GAIN ON LIQUIDATION OF CERTAIN HOLDING COMPANIES.—

(1) IN GENERAL.—In the case of any distribution to a foreign corporation in complete liquidation of an applicable holding company—

(A) subsection (a) and section 331 shall not apply to such distribution, and

(B) such distribution shall be treated as a distribution of property to which section 301 applies.

(2) APPLICABLE HOLDING COMPANY.—For purposes of this subsection:

(A) IN GENERAL.—The term "applicable holding company" means any domestic corporation—

(i) which is a common parent of an affiliated group,

(ii) stock of which is directly owned by the distributee foreign corporation,

(iii) substantially all of the assets of which consist of stock in other members of such affiliated group, and

(iv) which has not been in existence at all times during the 5 years immediately preceding the date of the liquidation.

(B) AFFILIATED GROUP.—For purposes of this subsection, the term "affiliated group" has the meaning given such term by section 1504(a) (without regard to paragraph (2) of section 1504(b)).

(3) COORDINATION WITH SUBPART F.—If the distributee of a distribution described in paragraph (1) is a controlled foreign corporation (as defined in section 957), then notwithstanding paragraph (1) or subsection (a), such distribution shall be treated as a distribution to which section 331 applies.

(4) REGULATIONS.—The Secretary shall provide such regulations as appropriate to prevent the abuse of this subsection, including regulations which provide, for the purposes of clause (iv) of paragraph (2)(A), that a corporation is not in existence for any period unless it is engaged in the active conduct of a trade or business or owns a significant ownership interest in another corporation so engaged.

[Sec. 334]

SEC. 334. BASIS OF PROPERTY RECEIVED IN LIQUIDATIONS.

[Sec. 334(a)]

(a) GENERAL RULE.—If property is received in a distribution in complete liquidation, and if gain or loss is recognized on receipt of such property, then the basis of the property in the hands of the distributee shall be the fair market value of such property at the time of the distribution.

[Sec. 334(b)]

(b) LIQUIDATION OF SUBSIDIARY.—

(1) IN GENERAL.—If property is received by a corporate distributee in a distribution in a complete liquidation to which section 332 applies (or in a transfer described in section 337(b)(1)), the basis of such property in the hands of such distributee shall be the same as it would be in the hands of the transferor; except that, in the hands of such distributee—

(A) the basis of such property shall be the fair market value of the property at the time of the distribution in any case in which gain or loss is recognized by the liquidating corporation with respect to such property, and

(B) the basis of any property described in section 362(e)(1)(B) shall be the fair market value of the property at the time of the distribution in any case in which such distributee's aggregate adjusted basis of such property would (but for this subparagraph) exceed the fair market value of such property immediately after such liquidation.

(2) CORPORATE DISTRIBUTEE.—For purposes of this subsection, the term "corporate distributee" means only the corporation which meets the stock ownership requirements specified in section 332(b).

Subpart B—Effects on Corporation

[Sec. 336]

SEC. 336. GAIN OR LOSS RECOGNIZED ON PROPERTY DISTRIBUTED IN COMPLETE LIQUIDATION.

[Sec. 336(a)]

(a) GENERAL RULE.—Except as otherwise provided in this section or section 337, gain or loss shall be recognized to a liquidating corporation on the distribution of property in complete liquidation as if such property were sold to the distributee at its fair market value.

[Sec. 336(b)]

(b) TREATMENT OF LIABILITIES.—If any property distributed in the liquidation is subject to a liability or the shareholder assumes a liability of the liquidating corporation in connection with the distribution, for purposes of subsection (a) and section 337, the fair market value of such property shall be treated as not less than the amount of such liability.

[Sec. 336(c)]

(c) EXCEPTION FOR LIQUIDATIONS WHICH ARE PART OF A REORGANIZATION.—For provision providing that this subpart does not apply to distributions in pursuance of a plan of reorganization, see section 361(c)(4).

[Sec. 336(d)]

(d) LIMITATIONS ON RECOGNITION OF LOSS.—

(1) NO LOSS RECOGNIZED IN CERTAIN DISTRIBUTIONS TO RELATED PERSONS.—

(A) IN GENERAL.—No loss shall be recognized to a liquidating corporation on the distribution of any property to a related person (within the meaning of section 267) if—

(i) such distribution is not pro rata, or

(ii) such property is disqualified property.

(B) DISQUALIFIED PROPERTY.—For purposes of subparagraph (A), the term "disqualified property" means any property which is acquired by the liquidating corporation in a transaction to which section 351 applied, or as a contribution to capital, during the 5-year period ending on the date of the distribution. Such term includes any property if the adjusted basis of such property is determined (in whole or in part) by reference to the adjusted basis of property described in the preceding sentence.

(2) SPECIAL RULE FOR CERTAIN PROPERTY ACQUIRED IN CERTAIN CARRYOVER BASIS TRANSACTIONS.—

(A) IN GENERAL.—For purposes of determining the amount of loss recognized by any liquidating corporation on any sale, exchange, or distribution of property described in subparagraph (B), the adjusted basis of such property shall be reduced (but not below zero) by the excess (if any) of—

(i) the adjusted basis of such property immediately after its acquisition by such corporation, over

(ii) the fair market value of such property as of such time.

(B) DESCRIPTION OF PROPERTY.—

(i) IN GENERAL.—For purposes of subparagraph (A), property is described in this subparagraph if—

(I) such property is acquired by the liquidating corporation in a transaction to which section 351 applied or as a contribution to capital, and

(II) the acquisition of such property by the liquidating corporation was part of a plan a principal purpose of which was to recognize loss by the liquidating corporation with respect to such property in connection with the liquidation.

Other property shall be treated as so described if the adjusted basis of such other property is determined (in whole or in part) by reference to the adjusted basis of property described in the preceding sentence.

(ii) CERTAIN ACQUISITIONS TREATED AS PART OF PLAN.—For purposes of clause (i), any property described in clause (i)(I) acquired by the liquidated corporation after the date 2 years before the date of the adoption of the plan of complete liquidation shall, except as provided in regulations, be treated as acquired as part of a plan described in clause (i)(II).

(C) RECAPTURE IN LIEU OF DISALLOWANCE.—The Secretary may prescribe regulations under which, in lieu of disallowing a loss under subparagraph (A) for a prior taxable year, the gross income of the liquidating corporation for the taxable year in which the plan of complete liquidation is adopted shall be increased by the amount of the disallowed loss.

(3) SPECIAL RULE IN CASE OF LIQUIDATION TO WHICH SECTION 332 APPLIES.—In the case of any liquidation to which section 332 applies, no loss shall be recognized to the liquidating corporation on any distribution in such liquidation. The preceding sentence shall apply to any distribution to the 80-percent distributee only if subsection (a) or (b)(1) of section 337 applies to such distribution.

[Sec. 336(e)]

(e) CERTAIN STOCK SALES AND DISTRIBUTIONS MAY BE TREATED AS ASSET TRANSFERS.—Under regulations prescribed by the Secretary, if—

(1) a corporation owns stock in another corporation meeting the requirements of section 1504(a)(2), and

(2) such corporation sells, exchanges, or distributes all of such stock,

an election may be made to treat such sale, exchange, or distribution as a disposition of all of the assets of such other corporation, and no gain or loss shall be recognized on the sale, exchange, or distribution of such stock.

[Sec. 337]

SEC. 337. NONRECOGNITION FOR PROPERTY DISTRIBUTED TO PARENT IN COMPLETE LIQUIDATION OF SUBSIDIARY.

[Sec. 337(a)]

(a) IN GENERAL.—No gain or loss shall be recognized to the liquidating corporation on the distribution to the 80-percent distributee of any property in a complete liquidation to which section 332 applies.

[Sec. 337(b)]

(b) TREATMENT OF INDEBTEDNESS OF SUBSIDIARY, ETC.—

(1) INDEBTEDNESS OF SUBSIDIARY TO PARENT.—If—

(A) a corporation is liquidated in a liquidation to which section 332 applies, and

(B) on the date of the adoption of the plan of liquidation, such corporation was indebted to the 80-percent distributee,

for purposes of this section and section 336, any transfer of property to the 80-percent distributee in satisfaction of such indebtedness shall be treated as a distribution to such distributee in such liquidation.

(2) TREATMENT OF TAX-EXEMPT DISTRIBUTEE.—

(A) IN GENERAL.—Except as provided in subparagraph (B), paragraph (1) and subsection (a) shall not apply where the 80-percent distributee is an organization (other than a cooperative described in section 521) which is exempt from the tax imposed by this chapter.

(B) EXCEPTION WHERE PROPERTY WILL BE USED IN UNRELATED BUSINESS.—

(i) IN GENERAL.—Subparagraph (A) shall not apply to any distribution of property to an organization described in section 511(a)(2) if, immediately after such distribution, such organization uses such property in an activity the income from which is subject to tax under 511(a).

(ii) LATER DISPOSITION OR CHANGE IN USE.—If any property to which clause (i) applied is disposed of by the organization acquiring such property, notwithstanding any other provision of law, any gain (not in excess of the amount not recognized by reason of clause (i)) shall be included in such organization's unrelated business taxable income. For purposes of the preceding sentence, if such property ceases to be used in an activity referred to in clause (i), such organization shall be treated as having disposed of such property on the date of such cessation.

[Sec. 337(c)]

(c) 80-PERCENT DISTRIBUTEE.—For purposes of this section, the term "80-percent distributee" means only the corporation which meets the 80-percent stock ownership requirements specified in section 332(b). For purposes of this section, the determination of whether any corporation is an 80-percent distributee shall be made without regard to any consolidated return regulation.

[Sec. 337(d)]

(d) REGULATIONS.—The Secretary shall prescribe such regulations as may be necessary or appropriate to carry out the purposes of the amendments made by subtitle D of title VI of the Tax Reform Act of 1986, including—

(1) regulations to ensure that such purposes may not be circumvented through the use of any provision of law or regulations (including the consolidated return regulations and part III of this subchapter) or through the use of a regulated investment company, real estate investment trust, or tax exempt entity, and

(2) regulations providing for appropriate coordination of the provisions of this section with the provisions of this title relating to taxation of foreign corporations and their shareholders.

[Sec. 338]

SEC. 338. CERTAIN STOCK PURCHASES TREATED AS ASSET ACQUISITIONS.

[Sec. 338(a)]

(a) GENERAL RULE.—For purposes of this subtitle, if a purchasing corporation makes an election under this section (or is treated under subsection (e) as having made such an election), then, in the case of any qualified stock purchase, the target corporation—

(1) shall be treated as having sold all of its assets at the close of the acquisition date at fair market value in a single transaction, and

(2) shall be treated as a new corporation which purchased all of the assets referred to in paragraph (1) as of the beginning of the day after the acquisition date.

[Sec. 338(b)]

(b) BASIS OF ASSETS AFTER DEEMED PURCHASE.—

(1) IN GENERAL.—For purposes of subsection (a), the assets of the target corporation shall be treated as purchased for an amount equal to the sum of—

(A) the grossed-up basis of the purchasing corporation's recently purchased stock, and

(B) the basis of the purchasing corporation's nonrecently purchased stock.

(2) ADJUSTMENT FOR LIABILITIES AND OTHER RELEVANT ITEMS.—The amount described in paragraph (1) shall be adjusted under regulations prescribed by the Secretary for liabilities of the target corporation and other relevant items.

(3) ELECTION TO STEP-UP THE BASIS OF CERTAIN TARGET STOCK.—

(A) IN GENERAL.—Under regulations prescribed by the Secretary, the basis of the purchasing corporation's nonrecently purchased stock shall be the basis amount determined under subparagraph (B) of this paragraph if the purchasing corporation makes an election to recognize gain as if such stock were sold on the acquisition date for an amount equal to the basis amount determined under subparagraph (B).

(B) DETERMINATION OF BASIS AMOUNT.—For purposes of subparagraph (A), the basis amount determined under this subparagraph shall be an amount equal to the grossed-up basis determined under subparagraph (A) of paragraph (1) multiplied by a fraction—

(i) the numerator of which is the percentage of stock (by value) in the target corporation attributable to the purchasing corporation's nonrecently purchased stock, and

(ii) the denominator of which is 100 percent minus the percentage referred to in clause (i).

(4) GROSSED-UP BASIS.—For purposes of paragraph (1), the grossed-up basis shall be an amount equal to the basis of the corporation's recently purchased stock, multiplied by a fraction—

(A) the numerator of which is 100 percent, minus the percentage of stock (by value) in the target corporation attributable to the purchasing corporation's nonrecently purchased stock, and

(B) the denominator of which is the percentage of stock (by value) in the target corporation attributable to the purchasing corporation's recently purchased stock.

(5) ALLOCATION AMONG ASSETS.—The amount determined under paragraphs (1) and (2) shall be allocated among the assets of the target corporation under regulations prescribed by the Secretary.

(6) DEFINITIONS OF RECENTLY PURCHASED STOCK AND NONRECENTLY PURCHASED STOCK.—For purposes of this subsection—

(A) RECENTLY PURCHASED STOCK.—The term "recently purchased stock" means any stock in the target corporation which is held by the purchasing corporation on the acquisition date and which was purchased by such corporation during the 12-month acquisition period.

(B) NONRECENTLY PURCHASED STOCK.—The term "nonrecently purchased stock" means any stock in the target corporation which is held by the purchasing corporation on the acquisition date and which is not recently purchased stock.

[Sec. 338(d)]

(d) PURCHASING CORPORATION; TARGET CORPORATION; QUALIFIED STOCK PURCHASE.—For purposes of this section—

(1) PURCHASING CORPORATION.—The term "purchasing corporation" means any corporation which makes a qualified stock purchase of stock of another corporation.

(2) TARGET CORPORATION.—The term "target corporation" means any corporation the stock of which is acquired by another corporation in a qualified stock purchase.

(3) QUALIFIED STOCK PURCHASE.—The term "qualified stock purchase" means any transaction or series of transactions in which stock (meeting the requirements of section 1504(a)(2)) of 1 corporation is acquired by another corporation by purchase during the 12-month acquisition period.

[Sec. 338(e)]

(e) DEEMED ELECTION WHERE PURCHASING CORPORATION ACQUIRES ASSET OF TARGET CORPORATION.—

(1) IN GENERAL.—A purchasing corporation shall be treated as having made an election under this section with respect to any target corporation if, at any time during the consistency period, it acquires any asset of the target corporation (or a target affiliate).

(2) EXCEPTIONS.—Paragraph (1) shall not apply with respect to any acquisition by the purchasing corporation if—

(A) such acquisition is pursuant to a sale by the target corporation (or the target affiliate) in the ordinary course of its trade or business,

(B) the basis of the property acquired is determined (wholly) by reference to the adjusted basis of such property in the hands of the person from whom acquired,

(C) such acquisition was before September 1, 1982, or

(D) such acquisition is described in regulations prescribed by the Secretary and meets such conditions as such regulations may provide.

(3) ANTI-AVOIDANCE RULE.—Whenever necessary to carry out the purpose of this subsection and subsection (f), the Secretary may treat stock acquisitions which are pursuant to a plan and which meet the requirements of section 1504(a)(2) as qualified stock purchases.

[Sec. 338(f)]

(f) CONSISTENCY REQUIRED FOR ALL STOCK ACQUISITIONS FROM SAME AFFILIATED GROUP.—If a purchasing corporation makes qualified stock purchases with respect to the target corporation and 1 or more target affiliates during any consistency period, then (except as otherwise provided in subsection (e))—

(1) any election under this section with respect to the first such purchase shall apply to each other such purchase, and

(2) no election may be made under this section with respect to the second or subsequent such purchase if such an election was not made with respect to the first such purchase.

[Sec. 338(g)]

(g) ELECTION.—

(1) WHEN MADE.—Except as otherwise provided in regulations, an election under this section shall be made not later than the 15th day of the 9th month, beginning after the month in which the acquisition date occurs.

(2) MANNER.—An election by the purchasing corporation under this section shall be made in such manner as the Secretary shall by regulations prescribe.

(3) ELECTION IRREVOCABLE.—An election by a purchasing corporation under this section, once made, shall be irrevocable.

[Sec. 338(h)]

(h) DEFINITIONS AND SPECIAL RULES.—For purposes of this section—

(1) 12-MONTH ACQUISITION PERIOD.—The term "12-month acquisition period" means the 12-month period beginning with the date of the first acquisition by purchase of stock included in a qualified stock purchase (or, if any of such stock was acquired in an acquisition which is a purchase by reason of subparagraph (C) of paragraph (3), the date on which the acquiring corporation is first considered under section 318(a) (other than paragraph (4) thereof) as owning stock owned by the corporation from which such acquisition was made).

(2) ACQUISITION DATE.—The term "acquisition date" means, with respect to any corporation, the first day on which there is a qualified stock purchase with respect to the stock of such corporation.

(3) PURCHASE.—

(A) IN GENERAL.—The term "purchase" means any acquisition of stock, but only if—

(i) the basis of the stock in the hands of the purchasing corporation is not determined (I) in whole or in part by reference to the adjusted basis of such stock in the hands of the person from whom acquired, or (II) under section 1014(a) (relating to property acquired from a decedent),

(ii) the stock is not acquired in an exchange to which section 351, 354, 355, or 356 applies and is not acquired in any other transaction described in regulations in which the transferor does not recognize the entire amount of the gain or loss realized on the transaction, and

(iii) the stock is not acquired from a person the ownership of whose stock would, under section 318(a) (other than paragraph (4) thereof), be attributed to the person acquiring such stock.

(B) DEEMED PURCHASE UNDER SUBSECTION (a).—The term "purchase" includes any deemed purchase under subsection (a)(2). The acquisition date for a corporation which is deemed purchased under subsection (a)(2) shall be determined under regulations prescribed by the Secretary.

(C) CERTAIN STOCK ACQUISITIONS FROM RELATED CORPORATIONS.—

(i) IN GENERAL.—Clause (iii) of subparagraph (A) shall not apply to an acquisition of stock from a related corporation if at least 50 percent in value of the stock of such related corporation was acquired by purchase (within the meaning of subparagraphs (A) and (B)).

(ii) CERTAIN DISTRIBUTIONS.—Clause (i) of subparagraph (A) shall not apply to an acquisition of stock described in clause (i) of this subparagraph if the corporation acquiring such stock—

(I) made a qualified stock purchase of stock of the related corporation, and

(II) made an election under this section (or is treated under subsection (e) as having made such an election) with respect to such qualified stock purchase.

(iii) RELATED CORPORATION DEFINED.—For purposes of this subparagraph, a corporation is a related corporation if stock owned by such corporation is treated (under section 318(a) other than paragraph (4) thereof) as owned by the corporation acquiring the stock.

(4) CONSISTENCY PERIOD.—

(A) IN GENERAL.—Except as provided in subparagraph (B), the term "consistency period" means the period consisting of—

(i) the 1-year period before the beginning of the 12-month acquisition period for the target corporation,

(ii) such acquisition period (up to and including the acquisition date), and

(iii) the 1-year period beginning on the day after the acquisition date.

(B) EXTENSION WHERE THERE IS PLAN.—The period referred to in subparagraph (A) shall also include any period during which the Secretary determines that there was in effect a plan to make a qualified stock purchase plus 1 or more other qualified stock purchases (or asset acquisitions described in subsection (e)) with respect to the target corporation or any target affiliate.

(5) AFFILIATED GROUP.—The term "affiliated group" has the meaning given to such term by section 1504(a) (determined without regard to the exceptions contained in section 1504(b)).

(6) TARGET AFFILIATE.—

(A) IN GENERAL.—A corporation shall be treated as a target affiliate of the target corporation if each of such corporations was, at any time during so much of the consistency period as ends on the acquisition date of the target corporation, a member of an affiliated group which had the same common parent.

(B) CERTAIN FOREIGN CORPORATIONS, ETC.—Except as otherwise provided in regulations (and subject to such conditions as may be provided in regulations)—

(i) the term "target affiliate" does not include a foreign corporation or a DISC, and

(ii) stock held by a target affiliate in a foreign corporation or a domestic corporation which is a DISC or described in section 1248(e) shall be excluded from the operation of this section.

(7) [Stricken]

(8) ACQUISITIONS BY AFFILIATED GROUP TREATED AS MADE BY 1 CORPORATION.—Except as provided in regulations prescribed by the Secretary, stock and asset acquisitions made by members of the same affiliated group shall be treated as made by 1 corporation.

(9) TARGET NOT TREATED AS MEMBER OF AFFILIATED GROUP.—Except as otherwise provided in paragraph (10) or in regulations prescribed under this paragraph, the target corporation shall not be treated as a member of an affiliated group with respect to the sale described in subsection (a)(1).

(10) ELECTIVE RECOGNITION OF GAIN OR LOSS BY TARGET CORPORATION, TOGETHER WITH NONRECOGNITION OF GAIN OR LOSS ON STOCK SOLD BY SELLING CONSOLIDATED GROUP.—

(A) IN GENERAL.—Under regulations prescribed by the Secretary, an election may be made under which if—

(i) the target corporation was, before the transaction, a member of the selling consolidated group, and

(ii) the target corporation recognizes gain or loss with respect to the transaction as if it sold all of its assets in a single transaction,

then the target corporation shall be treated as a member of the selling consolidated group with respect to such sale, and (to the extent provided in regulations) no gain or loss will be recognized on stock sold or exchanged in the transaction by members of the selling consolidated group.

(B) SELLING CONSOLIDATED GROUP.—For purposes of subparagraph (A), the term "selling consolidated group" means any group of corporations which (for the taxable period which includes the transaction)—

(i) includes the target corporation, and

(ii) files a consolidated return.

To the extent provided in regulations, such term also includes any affiliated group of corporations which includes the target corporation (whether or not such group files a consolidated return).

(C) INFORMATION REQUIRED TO BE FURNISHED TO THE SECRETARY.—Under regulations, where an election is made under subparagraph (A), the purchasing corporation and the common parent of the selling consolidated group shall, at such times and in such manner as may be provided in regulations, furnish to the Secretary the following information:

(i) The amount allocated under subsection (b)(5) to goodwill or going concern value.

(ii) Any modification of the amount described in clause (i).

(iii) Any other information as the Secretary deems necessary to carry out the provisions of this paragraph.

(11) ELECTIVE FORMULA FOR DETERMINING FAIR MARKET VALUE.—For purposes of subsection (a)(1), fair market value may be determined on the basis of a formula provided in regulations prescribed by the Secretary which takes into account liabilities and other relevant items.

(12) [Stricken]

(13) TAX ON DEEMED SALE NOT TAKEN INTO ACCOUNT FOR ESTIMATED TAX PURPOSES.—For purposes of section 6655, tax attributable to the sale described in subsection (a)(1) shall not be taken into account. The preceding sentence shall not apply with respect to a qualified stock purchase for which an election is made under paragraph (10).

(14) [Stricken.]

(15) COMBINED DEEMED SALE RETURN.—Under regulations prescribed by the Secretary, a combined deemed sale return may be filed by all target corporations acquired by a purchasing corporation on the same acquisition date if such target corporations were members of the same selling consolidated group (as defined in subparagraph (B) of paragraph (10)).

(16) COORDINATION WITH FOREIGN TAX CREDIT PROVISIONS.—Except as provided in regulations, this section shall not apply for purposes of determining the source or character of any item for purposes of subpart A of part III of subchapter N of this chapter (relating to foreign tax credit). The preceding sentence shall not apply to any gain to the extent such gain is includible in gross income as a dividend under section 1248 (determined without regard to any deemed sale under this section by a foreign corporation).

[Sec. 338(i)]

(i) REGULATIONS.—The Secretary shall prescribe such regulations as may be necessary or appropriate to carry out the purposes of this section, including—

(1) regulations to ensure that the purpose of this section to require consistency of treatment of stock and asset sales and purchases may not be circumvented through the use of any provision of law or regulations (including the consolidated return regulations) and

(2) regulations providing for the coordination of the provisions of this section with the provision of this title relating to foreign corporations and their shareholders.

Subpart D—Definition and Special Rule

[Sec. 346]

SEC. 346. DEFINITION AND SPECIAL RULE.

[Sec. 346(a)]

(a) COMPLETE LIQUIDATION.—For purposes of this subchapter, a distribution shall be treated as in complete liquidation of a corporation if the distribution is one of a series of distributions in redemption of all of the stock of the corporation pursuant to a plan.

***

PART III—CORPORATE ORGANIZATIONS AND REORGANIZATIONS

Subpart A—Corporate Organizations

[Sec. 351]

SEC. 351. TRANSFER TO CORPORATION CONTROLLED BY TRANSFEROR.

[Sec. 351(a)]

(a) GENERAL RULE.—No gain or loss shall be recognized if property is transferred to a corporation by one or more persons solely in exchange for stock in such corporation and immediately after the exchange such person or persons are in control (as defined in section 368(c)) of the corporation.

[Sec. 351(b)]

(b) RECEIPT OF PROPERTY.—If subsection (a) would apply to an exchange but for the fact that there is received, in addition to the stock permitted to be received under subsection (a), other property or money, then—

(1) gain (if any) to such recipient shall be recognized, but not in excess of—

(A) the amount of money received, plus

(B) the fair market value of such other property received; and

(2) no loss to such recipient shall be recognized.

[Sec. 351(c)]

(c) SPECIAL RULES WHERE DISTRIBUTION TO SHAREHOLDERS.—

(1) IN GENERAL.—In determining control for purposes of this section, the fact that any corporate transferor distributes part or all of the stock in the corporation which it receives in the exchange to its shareholders shall not be taken into account.

(2) SPECIAL RULE FOR SECTION 355.—If the requirements of section 355 (or so much of section 356 as relates to section 355) are met with respect to a distribution described in paragraph (1), then, solely for purposes of determining the tax treatment of the transfers of property to the controlled corporation by the distributing corporation, the fact that the shareholders of the distributing corporation dispose of part or all of the distributed stock, or the fact that the corporation whose stock was distributed issues additional stock, shall not be taken into account in determining control for purposes of this section.

[Sec. 351(d)]

(d) SERVICES, CERTAIN INDEBTEDNESS, AND ACCRUED INTEREST NOT TREATED AS PROPERTY.—For purposes of this section, stock issued for—

(1) services,

(2) indebtedness of the transferee corporation which is not evidenced by a security, or

(3) interest on indebtedness of the transferee corporation which accrued on or after the beginning of the transferor's holding period for the debt,

shall not be considered as issued in return for property.

[Sec. 351(e)]

(e) EXCEPTIONS.—This section shall not apply to—

(1) TRANSFER OF PROPERTY TO AN INVESTMENT COMPANY.—A transfer of property to an investment company. For purposes of the preceding sentence, the determination of whether a company is an investment company shall be made—

(A) by taking into account all stock and securities held by the company, and

(B) by treating as stock and securities—

(i) money,

(ii) stocks and other equity interests in a corporation, evidences of indebtedness, options, forward or futures contracts, notional principal contracts and derivatives,

(iii) any foreign currency,

(iv) any interest in a real estate investment trust, a common trust fund, a regulated investment company, a publicly-traded partnership (as defined in section 7704(b)) or any other equity interest (other than in a corporation) which pursuant to its terms or any other arrangement is readily convertible into, or exchangeable for, any asset described in any preceding clause, this clause or clause (v) or (viii),

(v) except to the extent provided in regulations prescribed by the Secretary, any interest in a precious metal, unless such metal is used or held in the active conduct of a trade or business after the contribution,

(vi) except as otherwise provided in regulations prescribed by the Secretary, interests in any entity if substantially all of the assets of such entity consist (directly or indirectly) of any assets described in any preceding clause or clause (viii),

(vii) to the extent provided in regulations prescribed by the Secretary, any interest in any entity not described in clause (vi), but only to the extent of the value of such interest that is attributable to assets listed in clauses (i) through (v) or clause (viii), or

(viii) any other asset specified in regulations prescribed by the Secretary.

The Secretary may prescribe regulations that, under appropriate circumstances, treat any asset described in clauses (i) through (v) as not so listed.

(2) TITLE 11 OR SIMILAR CASE.—A transfer of property of a debtor pursuant to a plan while the debtor is under the jurisdiction of a court in a title 11 or similar case (within the meaning of section 368(a)(3)(A)), to the extent that the stock received in the exchange is used to satisfy the indebtedness of such debtor.

[Sec. 351(f)]

(f) TREATMENT OF CONTROLLED CORPORATION.—If—

(1) property is transferred to a corporation (hereinafter in this subsection referred to as the "controlled corporation") in an exchange with respect to which gain or loss is not recognized (in whole or in part) to the transferor under this section, and

(2) such exchange is not in pursuance of a plan of reorganization,

section 311 shall apply to any transfer in such exchange by the controlled corporation in the same manner as if such transfer were a distribution to which subpart A of part I applies.

[Sec. 351(g)]

(g) NONQUALIFIED PREFERRED STOCK NOT TREATED AS STOCK.—

(1) IN GENERAL.—In the case of a person who transfers property to a corporation and receives nonqualified preferred stock—

(A) subsection (a) shall not apply to such transferor, and

(B) if (and only if) the transferor receives stock other than nonqualified preferred stock—

(i) subsection (b) shall apply to such transferor; and

(ii) such nonqualified preferred stock shall be treated as other property for purposes of applying subsection (b).

(2) NONQUALIFIED PREFERRED STOCK.—For purposes of paragraph (1)—

(A) IN GENERAL.—The term "nonqualified preferred stock" means preferred stock if—

(i) the holder of such stock has the right to require the issuer or a related person to redeem or purchase the stock,

(ii) the issuer or a related person is required to redeem or purchase such stock,

(iii) the issuer or a related person has the right to redeem or purchase the stock and, as of the issue date, it is more likely than not that such right will be exercised, or

(iv) the dividend rate on such stock varies in whole or in part (directly or indirectly) with reference to interest rates, commodity prices, or other similar indices.

(B) LIMITATIONS.—Clauses (i), (ii), and (iii) of subparagraph (A) shall apply only if the right or obligation referred to therein may be exercised within the 20-year period beginning on the issue date of such stock and such right or obligation is not subject to a contingency which, as of the issue date, makes remote the likelihood of the redemption or purchase.

(C) EXCEPTIONS FOR CERTAIN RIGHTS OR OBLIGATIONS.—

(i) IN GENERAL.—A right or obligation shall not be treated as described in clause (i), (ii), or (iii) of subparagraph (A) if—

(I) it may be exercised only upon the death, disability, or mental incompetency of the holder, or

(II) in the case of a right or obligation to redeem or purchase stock transferred in connection with the performance of services for the issuer or a related person (and which represents reasonable compensation), it may be exercised only upon the holder's separation from service from the issuer or a related person.

(ii) EXCEPTION.—Clause (i)(I) shall not apply if the stock relinquished in the exchange, or the stock acquired in the exchange is in—

(I) a corporation if any class of stock in such corporation or a related party is readily tradable on an established securities market or otherwise, or

(II) any other corporation if such exchange is part of a transaction or series of transactions in which such corporation is to become a corporation described in subclause (I).

(3) DEFINITIONS.—For purposes of this subsection—

(A) PREFERRED STOCK.—The term "preferred stock" means stock which is limited and preferred as to dividends and does not participate in corporate growth to any significant extent. Stock shall not be treated as participating in corporate growth to any significant extent unless there is a real and meaningful likelihood of the shareholder actually participating in the earnings and growth of the corporation. If there is not a real and meaningful likelihood that dividends beyond any limitation or preference will actually be paid, the possibility of such payments will be disregarded in determining whether stock is limited and preferred as to dividends.

(B) RELATED PERSON.—A person shall be treated as related to another person if they bear a relationship to such other person described in section 267(b) or 707(b).

(4) REGULATIONS.—The Secretary may prescribe such regulations as may be necessary or appropriate to carry out the purposes of this subsection and sections 354(a)(2)(C), 355(a)(3)(D), and 356(e). The Secretary may also prescribe regulations, consistent with the treatment under this subsection and such sections, for the treatment of nonqualified preferred stock under other provisions of this title.

[Sec. 351(h)]

(h) CROSS REFERENCES.—

(1) For special rule where another party to the exchange assumes a liability, see section 357.

(2) For the basis of stock or property received in an exchange to which this section applies, see sections 358 and 362.

(3) For special rule in the case of an exchange described in this section but which results in a gift, see section 2501 and following.

(4) For special rule in the case of an exchange described in this section but which has the effect of the payment of compensation by the corporation or by a transferor, see section 61(a)(1).

(5) For coordination of this section with section 304, see section 304(b)(3).

Subpart B—Effects on Shareholders and Security Holders

[Sec. 354]

SEC. 354. EXCHANGES OF STOCK AND SECURITIES IN CERTAIN REORGANIZATIONS.

[Sec. 354(a)]

(a) GENERAL RULE.—

(1) IN GENERAL.—No gain or loss shall be recognized if stock or securities in a corporation a party to a reorganization are, in pursuance of the plan of reorganization, exchanged solely for stock or securities in such corporation or in another corporation a party to the reorganization.

(2) LIMITATIONS.—

(A) EXCESS PRINCIPAL AMOUNT.—Paragraph (1) shall not apply if—

(i) the principal amount of any such securities received exceeds the principal amount of any such securities surrendered, or

(ii) any such securities are received and no such securities are surrendered.

(B) PROPERTY ATTRIBUTABLE TO ACCRUED INTEREST.—Neither paragraph (1) nor so much of section 356 as relates to paragraph (1) shall apply to the extent that any stock (including nonqualified preferred stock, as defined in section 351(g)(2)), securities, or other property received is attributable to interest which has accrued on securities on or after the beginning of the holder's holding period.

(C) NONQUALIFIED PREFERRED STOCK.—

(i) IN GENERAL.—Nonqualified preferred stock (as defined in section 351(g)(2)) received in exchange for stock other than nonqualified preferred stock (as so defined) shall not be treated as stock or securities.

(ii) RECAPITALIZATIONS OF FAMILY-OWNED CORPORATIONS.—

(I) IN GENERAL.—Clause (i) shall not apply in the case of a recapitalization under section 368(a)(1)(E) of a family-owned corporation.

(II) FAMILY-OWNED CORPORATION.—For purposes of this clause, except as provided in regulations, the term "family-owned corporation" means any corporation which is described in clause (i) of section 447(d)(2)(C) throughout the 8-year period beginning on the date which is 5 years before the date of the recapitalization. For purposes of the preceding sentence, stock shall not be treated as owned by a family member during any period described in section 355(d)(6)(B).

(III) EXTENSION OF STATUTE OF LIMITATIONS.—The statutory period for the assessment of any deficiency attributable to a corporation failing to be a family-owned corporation shall not expire before the expiration of 3 years after the date the Secretary is notified by the corporation (in such manner as the Secretary may prescribe) of such failure, and such deficiency may be assessed before the expiration of such 3-year period notwithstanding the provisions of any other law or rule of law which would otherwise prevent such assessment.

(3) CROSS REFERENCES.—

(A) For treatment of the exchange if any property is received which is not permitted to be received under this subsection (including nonqualified preferred stock and an excess principal amount of securities received over securities surrendered, but not including property to which paragraph (2)(B) applies), see section 356.

(B) For treatment of accrued interest in the case of an exchange described in paragraph (2)(B), see section 61.

[Sec. 354(b)]

(b) EXCEPTION.—

(1) IN GENERAL.—Subsection (a) shall not apply to an exchange in pursuance of a plan of reorganization within the meaning of subparagraph (D) or (G) of section 368(a)(1), unless—

(A) the corporation to which the assets are transferred acquires substantially all of the assets of the transferor of such assets; and

(B) the stock, securities, and other properties received by such transferor, as well as the other properties of such transferor, are distributed in pursuance of the plan of reorganization.

(2) CROSS REFERENCE.—

For special rules for certain exchanges in pursuance of plans of reorganization within the meaning of subparagraph (D) or (G) of section 368(a)(1), see section 355.

* * *

[Sec. 355]

SEC. 355. DISTRIBUTION OF STOCK AND SECURITIES OF A CONTROLLED CORPORATION.

[Sec. 355(a)]

(a) EFFECT ON DISTRIBUTEES.—

(1) GENERAL RULE.—If—

(A) a corporation (referred to in this section as the "distributing corporation")

(i) distributes to a shareholder, with respect to its stock, or

(ii) distributes to a security holder, in exchange for its securities, solely stock or securities of a corporation (referred to in this section as "controlled corporation") which it controls immediately before the distribution,

(B) the transaction was not used principally as a device for the distribution of the earnings and profits of the distributing corporation or the controlled corporation or both (but the mere fact that subsequent to the distribution stock or securities in one or more of such corporations are sold or exchanged by all or some of the distributees (other than pursuant to an arrangement negotiated or agreed upon prior to such distribution) shall not be construed to mean that the transaction was used principally as such a device),

(C) the requirements of subsection (b) (relating to active businesses) are satisfied, and

(D) as part of the distribution, the distributing corporation distributes—

(i) all of the stock and securities in the controlled corporation held by it immediately before the distribution, or

(ii) an amount of stock in the controlled corporation constituting control within the meaning of section 368 (c), and it is established to the satisfaction of the Secretary that the retention by the distributing corporation of stock (or stock and securities) in the controlled corporation was not in pursuance of a plan having as one of its principal purposes the avoidance of Federal income tax,

then no gain or loss shall be recognized to (and no amount shall be includible in the income of) such shareholder or security holder on the receipt of such stock or securities.

(2) NON PRO RATA DISTRIBUTIONS, ETC.—Paragraph (1) shall be applied without regard to the following:

(A) whether or not the distribution is pro rata with respect to all of the shareholders of the distributing corporation,

(B) whether or not the shareholder surrenders stock in the distributing corporation, and

(C) whether or not the distribution is in pursuance of a plan of reorganization (within the meaning of section 368(a)(1)(D)).

(3) LIMITATIONS.—

(A) EXCESS PRINCIPAL AMOUNT.—Paragraph (1) shall not apply if—

(i) the principal amount of the securities in the controlled corporation which are received exceeds the principal amount of the securities which are surrendered in connection with such distribution, or

(ii) securities in the controlled corporation are received and no securities are surrendered in connection with such distribution.

(B) STOCK ACQUIRED IN TAXABLE TRANSACTIONS WITHIN 5 YEARS TREATED AS BOOT.—For purposes of this section (other than paragraph (1)(D) of this subsection) and so much of section 356 as relates to this section, stock of a controlled corporation acquired by the distributing corporation by reason of any transaction—

(i) which occurs within 5 years of the distribution of such stock, and

(ii) in which gain or loss was recognized in whole or in part,

shall not be treated as stock of such controlled corporation, but as other property.

(C) PROPERTY ATTRIBUTABLE TO ACCRUED INTEREST.—Neither paragraph (1) nor so much of section 356 as relates to paragraph (1) shall apply to the extent that any stock (including nonqualified preferred stock, as defined in section 351(g)(2)), securities, or other property received is attributable to interest which has accrued on securities on or after the beginning of the holder's holding period.

(D) NONQUALIFIED PREFERRED STOCK.—Nonqualified preferred stock (as defined in section 351(g)(2)) received in a distribution with respect to stock other than nonqualified preferred stock (as so defined) shall not be treated as stock or securities.

(4) CROSS REFERENCES.—

(A) For treatment of the exchange if any property is received which is not permitted to be received under this subsection (including nonqualified preferred stock and an excess principal amount of securities received over securities surrendered, but not including property to which paragraph (3)(C) applies), see section 356.

(B) For treatment of accrued interest in the case of an exchange described in paragraph (3)(C), see section 61.

[Sec. 355(b)]

(b) REQUIREMENTS AS TO ACTIVE BUSINESS.—

(1) IN GENERAL.—Subsection (a) shall apply only if either—

(A) the distributing corporation, and the controlled corporation (or, if stock of more than one controlled corporation is distributed, each of such corporations), is engaged immediately after the distribution in the active conduct of a trade or business, or

(B) immediately before the distribution, the distributing corporation had no assets other than stock or securities in the controlled corporations and each of the controlled corporations is engaged immediately after the distribution in the active conduct of a trade or business.

(2) DEFINITION.—For purposes of paragraph (1), a corporation shall be treated as engaged in the active conduct of a trade or business if and only if—

(A) it is engaged in the active conduct of a trade or business,

(B) such trade or business has been actively conducted throughout the 5-year period ending on the date of the distribution,

(C) such trade or business was not acquired within the period described in subparagraph (B) in a transaction in which gain or loss was recognized in whole or in part, and

(D) control of a corporation which (at the time of acquisition of control) was conducting such trade or business—

(i) was not acquired by any distributee corporation directly (or through 1 or more corporations, whether through the distributing corporation or otherwise) within the period described in subparagraph (B) and was not acquired by the distributing corporation directly (or through 1 or more corporations) within such period, or

(ii) was so acquired by any such corporation within such period, but, in each case in which such control was so acquired, it was so acquired, only by reason of transactions in which gain or loss was not recognized in whole or in part, or only by reason of such transactions combined with acquisitions before the beginning of such period.

For purposes of subparagraph (D), all distributee corporations which are members of the same affiliated group (as defined in section 1504(a) without regard to section 1504(b)) shall be treated as 1 distributee corporation.

(3) SPECIAL RULES FOR DETERMINING ACTIVE CONDUCT IN THE CASE OF AFFILIATED GROUPS.—

(A) IN GENERAL.—For purposes of determining whether a corporation meets the requirements of paragraph (2)(A), all members of such corporation's separate affiliated group shall be treated as one corporation.

(B) SEPARATE AFFILIATED GROUP.—For purposes of this paragraph, the term "separate affiliated group" means, with respect to any corporation, the affiliated group which would be determined under section 1504(a) if such corporation were the common parent and section 1504(b) did not apply.

(C) TREATMENT OF TRADE OR BUSINESS CONDUCTED BY ACQUIRED MEMBER.—If a corporation became a member of a separate affiliated group as a result of one or more transactions in which gain or loss was recognized in whole or in part, any trade or business conducted by such corporation (at the time that such corporation became such a member) shall be treated for purposes of paragraph (2) as acquired in a transaction in which gain or loss was recognized in whole or in part.

(D) REGULATIONS.—The Secretary shall prescribe such regulations as are necessary or appropriate to carry out the purposes of this paragraph, including regulations which provide for the proper application of subparagraphs (B), (C), and (D) of paragraph (2), and modify the application of subsection (a)(3)(B), in connection with the application of this paragraph.

[Sec. 355(c)]

(c) TAXABILITY OF CORPORATION ON DISTRIBUTION.—

(1) IN GENERAL.—Except as provided in paragraph (2), no gain or loss shall be recognized to a corporation on any distribution to which this section (or so much of section 356 as relates to this section) applies and which is not in pursuance of a plan of reorganization.

(2) DISTRIBUTION OF APPRECIATED PROPERTY.—

(A) IN GENERAL.—If—

(i) in a distribution referred to in paragraph (1), the corporation distributes property other than qualified property, and

(ii) the fair market value of such property exceeds its adjusted basis (in the hands of the distributing corporation),

then gain shall be recognized to the distributing corporation as if such property were sold to the distributee at its fair market value.

(B) QUALIFIED PROPERTY.—For purposes of subparagraph (A), the term "qualified property" means any stock or securities in the controlled corporation.

(C) TREATMENT OF LIABILITIES.—If any property distributed in the distribution referred to in paragraph (1) is subject to a liability or the shareholder assumes a liability of the distributing corporation in connection with the distribution, then, for purposes of subparagraph (A), the fair market value of such property shall be treated as not less than the amount of such liability.

(3) COORDINATION WITH SECTIONS 311 AND 336(A).—Sections 311 and 336(a) shall not apply to any distribution referred to in paragraph (1).

[Sec. 355(d)]

(d) RECOGNITION OF GAIN ON CERTAIN DISTRIBUTIONS OF STOCK OR SECURITIES IN CONTROLLED CORPORATION.—

(1) IN GENERAL.—In the case of a disqualified distribution, any stock or securities in the controlled corporation shall not be treated as qualified property for purposes of subsection (c)(2) of this section or section 361(c)(2).

(2) DISQUALIFIED DISTRIBUTION.—For purposes of this subsection, the term "disqualified distribution" means any distribution to which this section (or so much of section 356 as relates to this section) applies if, immediately after the distribution—

(A) any person holds disqualified stock in the distributing corporation which constitutes a 50-percent or greater interest in such corporation, or

(B) any person holds disqualified stock in the controlled corporation (or, if stock of more than 1 controlled corporation is distributed, in any controlled corporation) which constitutes a 50-percent or greater interest in such corporation.

(3) DISQUALIFIED STOCK.—For purposes of this subsection, the term "disqualified stock" means—

(A) any stock in the distributing corporation acquired by purchase during the 5-year period ending on the date of the distribution, and

(B) any stock in any controlled corporation—

(i) acquired by purchase during the 5-year period ending on the date of the distribution, or

(ii) received in the distribution to the extent attributable to distributions on—

(I) stock described in subparagraph (A), or

(II) any securities in the distributing corporation acquired by purchase during the 5-year period ending on the date of the distribution.

(4) 50-PERCENT OR GREATER INTEREST.—For purposes of this subsection, the term "50-percent or greater interest" means stock possessing at least 50 percent of the total combined voting power of all classes of stock entitled to vote or at least 50 percent of the total value of shares of all classes of stock.

(5) PURCHASE.—For purposes of this subsection—

(A) IN GENERAL.—Except as otherwise provided in this paragraph, the term "purchase" means any acquisition but only if—

(i) the basis of the property acquired in the hands of the acquirer is not determined (I) in whole or in part by reference to the adjusted basis of such property in the hands of the person from whom acquired, or (II) under section 1014(a), and

(ii) the property is not acquired in an exchange to which section 351, 354, 355, or 356 applies.

(B) CERTAIN SECTION 351 EXCHANGES TREATED AS PURCHASES.—The term "purchase" includes any acquisition of property in an exchange to which section 351 applies to the extent such property is acquired in exchange for—

(i) any cash or cash item,

(ii) any marketable stock or security, or

(iii) any debt of the transferor.

(C) CARRYOVER BASIS TRANSACTIONS.—If—

(i) any person acquires property from another person who acquired such property by purchase (as determined under this paragraph with regard to this subparagraph), and

(ii) the adjusted basis of such property in the hands of such acquirer is determined in whole or in part by reference to the adjusted basis of such property in the hands of such other person,

such acquirer shall be treated as having acquired such property by purchase on the date it was so acquired by such other person.

(6) SPECIAL RULE WHERE SUBSTANTIAL DIMINUTION OF RISK.—

(A) IN GENERAL.—If this paragraph applies to any stock or securities for any period, the running of any 5-year period set forth in subparagraph (A) or (B) of paragraph (3) (whichever applies) shall be suspended during such period.

(B) PROPERTY TO WHICH SUSPENSION APPLIES.—This paragraph applies to any stock or securities for any period during which the holder's risk of loss with respect to such stock or securities, or with respect to any portion of the activities of the corporation, is (directly or indirectly) substantially diminished by—

(i) an option,

(ii) a short sale,

(iii) any special class of stock, or

(iv) any other device or transaction.

(7) AGGREGATION RULES.—

(A) IN GENERAL.—For purposes of this subsection, a person and all persons related to such person (within the meaning of section 267(b) or 707(b)(1)) shall be treated as one person.

(B) PERSONS ACTING PURSUANT TO PLANS OR ARRANGEMENTS.—If two or more persons act pursuant to a plan or arrangement with respect to acquisitions of stock or securities in the distributing corporation or controlled corporation, such persons shall be treated as one person for purposes of this subsection.

(8) ATTRIBUTION FROM ENTITIES.—

(A) IN GENERAL.—Paragraph (2) of section 318(a) shall apply in determining whether a person holds stock or securities in any corporation (determined by substituting "10 percent" for "50 percent" in subparagraph (C) of such paragraph (2) and by treating any reference to stock as including a reference to securities).

(B) DEEMED PURCHASE RULE.—If—

(i) any person acquires by purchase an interest in any entity, and

(ii) such person is treated under subparagraph (A) as holding any stock or securities by reason of holding such interest,

such stock or securities shall be treated as acquired by purchase by such person on the later of the date of the purchase of the interest in such entity or the date such stock or securities are acquired by purchase by such entity.

(9) REGULATIONS.—The Secretary shall prescribe such regulations as may be necessary to carry out the purposes of this subsection, including—

(A) regulations to prevent the avoidance of the purposes of this subsection through the use of related persons, intermediaries, pass-thru entities, options, or other arrangements, and

(B) regulations modifying the definition of the term "purchase".

[Sec. 355(e)]

(e) RECOGNITION OF GAIN ON CERTAIN DISTRIBUTIONS OF STOCK OR SECURITIES IN CONNECTION WITH ACQUISITIONS.—

(1) GENERAL RULE.—If there is a distribution to which this subsection applies, any stock or securities in the controlled corporation shall not be treated as qualified property for purposes of subsection (c)(2) of this section or section 361(c)(2).

(2) DISTRIBUTIONS TO WHICH SUBSECTION APPLIES.—

(A) IN GENERAL.—This subsection shall apply to any distribution—

(i) to which this section (or so much of section 356 as relates to this section) applies, and

(ii) which is part of a plan (or series of related transactions) pursuant to which 1 or more persons acquire directly or indirectly stock representing a 50-percent or greater interest in the distributing corporation or any controlled corporation.

(B) PLAN PRESUMED TO EXIST IN CERTAIN CASES.—If 1 or more persons acquire directly or indirectly stock representing a 50-percent or greater interest in the distributing corporation or any controlled corporation during the 4-year period beginning on the date which is 2 years before the date of the distribution, such acquisition shall be treated as pursuant to a plan described in subparagraph (A)(ii) unless it is established that the distribution and the acquisition are not pursuant to a plan or series of related transactions.

(C) CERTAIN PLANS DISREGARDED.—A plan (or series of related transactions) shall not be treated as described in subparagraph (A)(ii) if, immediately after the completion of such plan or transactions, the distributing corporation and all controlled corporations are members of a single affiliated group (as defined in section 1504 without regard to subsection (b) thereof).

(D) COORDINATION WITH SUBSECTION (d).—This subsection shall not apply to any distribution to which subsection (d) applies.

(3) SPECIAL RULES RELATING TO ACQUISITIONS.—

(A) CERTAIN ACQUISITIONS NOT TAKEN INTO ACCOUNT.—Except as provided in regulations, the following acquisitions shall not be taken into account in applying paragraph (2)(A)(ii):

(i) The acquisition of stock in any controlled corporation by the distributing corporation.

(ii) The acquisition by a person of stock in any controlled corporation by reason of holding stock or securities in the distributing corporation.

(iii) The acquisition by a person of stock in any successor corporation of the distributing corporation or any controlled corporation by reason of holding stock or securities in such distributing or controlled corporation.

(iv) The acquisition of stock in the distributing corporation or any controlled corporation to the extent that the percentage of stock owned directly or indirectly in such corporation by each person owning stock in such corporation immediately before the acquisition does not decrease.

This subparagraph shall not apply to any acquisition if the stock held before the acquisition was acquired pursuant to a plan (or series of related transactions) described in paragraph (2)(A)(ii).

(B) ASSET ACQUISITIONS.—Except as provided in regulations, for purposes of this subsection, if the assets of the distributing corporation or any controlled corporation are acquired by a successor corporation in a transaction described in subparagraph (A), (C), or (D) of section 368(a)(1) or any other transaction specified in regulations by the Secretary, the shareholders (immediately before the acquisition) of the corporation acquiring such assets shall be treated as acquiring stock in the corporation from which the assets were acquired.

(4) DEFINITION AND SPECIAL RULES.—For purposes of this subsection—

(A) 50-PERCENT OR GREATER INTEREST.—The term "50-percent or greater interest" has the meaning given such term by subsection (d)(4).

(B) DISTRIBUTIONS IN TITLE 11 OR SIMILAR CASE.—Paragraph (1) shall not apply to any distribution made in a title 11 or similar case (as defined in section 368(a)(3)).

(C) AGGREGATION AND ATTRIBUTION RULES.—

(i) AGGREGATION.—The rules of paragraph (7)(A) of subsection (d) shall apply.

(ii) ATTRIBUTION.—Section 318(a)(2) shall apply in determining whether a person holds stock or securities in any corporation. Except as provided in regulations, section 318(a)(2)(C) shall be applied without regard to the phrase "50 percent or more in value" for purposes of the preceding sentence.

(D) SUCCESSORS AND PREDECESSORS.—For purposes of this subsection, any reference to a controlled corporation or a distributing corporation shall include a reference to any predecessor or successor of such corporation.

(E) STATUTE OF LIMITATIONS.—If there is a distribution to which paragraph (1) applies—

(i) the statutory period for the assessment of any deficiency attributable to any part of the gain recognized under this subsection by reason of such distribution shall not expire before the expiration of 3 years from the date the Secretary is notified by the taxpayer (in such manner as the Secretary may by regulations prescribe) that such distribution occurred, and

(ii) such deficiency may be assessed before the expiration of such 3-year period notwithstanding the provisions of any other law or rule of law which would otherwise prevent such assessment.

(5) REGULATIONS.—The Secretary shall prescribe such regulations as may be necessary to carry out the purposes of this subsection, including regulations—

(A) providing for the application of this subsection where there is more than 1 controlled corporation,

(B) treating 2 or more distributions as 1 distribution where necessary to prevent the avoidance of such purposes, and

(C) providing for the application of rules similar to the rules of subsection (d)(6) where appropriate for purposes of paragraph (2)(B).

[Sec. 355(f)]

(f) SECTION NOT TO APPLY TO CERTAIN INTRAGROUP DISTRIBUTIONS.—Except as provided in regulations, this section (or so much of section 356 as relates to this section) shall not apply to the distribution of stock from 1 member of an affiliated group (as defined in section 1504(a)) to another member of such group if such distribution is part of a plan (or series of related transactions) described in subsection (e)(2)(A)(ii) (determined after the application of subsection (e)).

[Sec. 355(g)]

(g) SECTION NOT TO APPLY TO DISTRIBUTIONS INVOLVING DISQUALIFIED INVESTMENT CORPORATIONS.—

(1) IN GENERAL.—This section (and so much of section 356 as relates to this section) shall not apply to any distribution which is part of a transaction if—

(A) either the distributing corporation or controlled corporation is, immediately after the transaction, a disqualified investment corporation, and

(B) any person holds, immediately after the transaction, a 50-percent or greater interest in any disqualified investment corporation, but only if such person did not hold such an interest in such corporation immediately before the transaction.

(2) DISQUALIFIED INVESTMENT CORPORATION.—For purposes of this subsection—

(A) IN GENERAL.—The term "disqualified investment corporation" means any distributing or controlled corporation if the fair market value of the investment assets of the corporation is—

(i) in the case of distributions after the end of the 1-year period beginning on the date of the enactment of this subsection [May 17, 2006], $^{2}/_{3}$ or more of the fair market value of all assets of the corporation, and

(ii) in the case of distributions during such 1-year period, $^{3}/_{4}$ or more of the fair market value of all assets of the corporation.

(B) INVESTMENT ASSETS.—

(i) IN GENERAL.—Except as otherwise provided in this subparagraph, the term "investment assets" means—

(I) cash,

(II) any stock or securities in a corporation,

(III) any interest in a partnership,

(IV) any debt instrument or other evidence of indebtedness,

(V) any option, forward or futures contract, notional principal contract, or derivative,

(VI) foreign currency, or

(VII) any similar asset.

(ii) EXCEPTION FOR ASSETS USED IN ACTIVE CONDUCT OF CERTAIN FINANCIAL TRADES OR BUSINESSES.—Such term shall not include any asset which is held for use in the active and regular conduct of—

(I) a lending or finance business (within the meaning of section 954(h)(4)),

(II) a banking business through a bank (as defined in section 581), a domestic building and loan association (within the meaning of section 7701(a)(19)), or any similar institution specified by the Secretary, or

(III) an insurance business if the conduct of the business is licensed, authorized, or regulated by an applicable insurance regulatory body.

This clause shall only apply with respect to any business if substantially all of the income of the business is derived from persons who are not related (within the meaning of section 267(b) or 707(b)(1)) to the person conducting the business.

(iii) EXCEPTION FOR SECURITIES MARKED TO MARKET.—Such term shall not include any security (as defined in section 475(c)(2)) which is held by a dealer in securities and to which section 475(a) applies.

(iv) STOCK OR SECURITIES IN A 20-PERCENT CONTROLLED ENTITY.—

(I) IN GENERAL.—Such term shall not include any stock and securities in, or any asset described in subclause (IV) or (V) of clause (i) issued by, a corporation which is a 20-percent controlled entity with respect to the distributing or controlled corporation.

(II) LOOK-THRU RULE.—The distributing or controlled corporation shall, for purposes of applying this subsection, be treated as owning its ratable share of the assets of any 20-percent controlled entity.

(III) 20-PERCENT CONTROLLED ENTITY.—For purposes of this clause, the term "20-percent controlled entity" means, with respect to any distributing or controlled corporation, any corporation with respect to which the distributing or controlled corporation owns directly or indirectly stock meeting the requirements of section 1504(a)(2), except that such section shall be applied by substituting "20 percent" for "80 percent" and without regard to stock described in section 1504(a)(4).

(v) INTERESTS IN CERTAIN PARTNERSHIPS.—

(I) IN GENERAL.—Such term shall not include any interest in a partnership, or any debt instrument or other evidence of indebtedness, issued by the partnership, if 1 or more of the trades or businesses of the partnership are (or, without regard to the 5-year requirement under subsection (b)(2)(B), would be) taken into account by the distributing or controlled corporation, as the case may be, in determining whether the requirements of subsection (b) are met with respect to the distribution.

(II) LOOK-THRU RULE.—The distributing or controlled corporation shall, for purposes of applying this subsection, be treated as owning its ratable share of the assets of any partnership described in subclause (I).

(3) 50-PERCENT OR GREATER INTEREST.—For purposes of this subsection—

(A) IN GENERAL.—The term "50-percent or greater interest" has the meaning given such term by subsection (d)(4).

(B) ATTRIBUTION RULES.—The rules of section 318 shall apply for purposes of determining ownership of stock for purposes of this paragraph.

(4) TRANSACTION.—For purposes of this subsection, the term "transaction" includes a series of transactions.

(5) REGULATIONS.—The Secretary shall prescribe such regulations as may be necessary to carry out, or prevent the avoidance of, the purposes of this subsection, including regulations—

(A) to carry out, or prevent the avoidance of, the purposes of this subsection in cases involving—

(i) the use of related persons, intermediaries, pass-thru entities, options, or other arrangements, and

(ii) the treatment of assets unrelated to the trade or business of a corporation as investment assets if, prior to the distribution, investment assets were used to acquire such unrelated assets,

(B) which in appropriate cases exclude from the application of this subsection a distribution which does not have the character of a redemption which would be treated as a sale or exchange under section 302, and

(C) which modify the application of the attribution rules applied for purposes of this subsection.

[Sec. 355(h)]

(h) RESTRICTION ON DISTRIBUTIONS INVOLVING REAL ESTATE INVESTMENT TRUSTS.—

(1) IN GENERAL.—This section (and so much of section 356 as relates to this section) shall not apply to any distribution if either the distributing corporation or controlled corporation is a real estate investment trust.

(2) EXCEPTIONS FOR CERTAIN DISTRIBUTIONS.—

(A) DISTRIBUTIONS OF A REAL ESTATE INVESTMENT TRUST BY ANOTHER REAL ESTATE INVESTMENT TRUST.—Paragraph (1) shall not apply to any distribution if, immediately after the distribution, the distributing corporation and the controlled corporation are both real estate investment trusts.

(B) DISTRIBUTIONS OF CERTAIN TAXABLE REIT SUBSIDIARIES.—Paragraph (1) shall not apply to any distribution if—

(i) the distributing corporation has been a real estate investment trust at all times during the 3-year period ending on the date of such distribution,

(ii) the controlled corporation has been a taxable REIT subsidiary (as defined in section 856(l)) of the distributing corporation at all times during such period, and

(iii) the distributing corporation had control (as defined in section 368(c) applied by taking into account stock owned directly or indirectly, including through one or more corporations or partnerships, by the distributing corporation) of the controlled corporation at all times during such period.

A controlled corporation will be treated as meeting the requirements of clauses (ii) and (iii) if the stock of such corporation was distributed by a taxable REIT subsidiary in a transaction to which this section (or so much of section 356 as relates to this section) applies and the assets of such corporation consist solely of the stock or assets held by one or more taxable REIT subsidiaries of the distributing corporation meeting the requirements of clauses (ii) and (iii). For purposes of clause (iii), control of a partnership means ownership of at least 80 percent of the profits interest and at least 80 percent of the capital interests.

[Sec. 356]

SEC. 356. RECEIPT OF ADDITIONAL CONSIDERATION.

[Sec. 356(a)]

(a) GAIN ON EXCHANGES.—

(1) RECOGNITION OF GAIN.—If—

(A) section 354 or 355 would apply to an exchange but for the fact that

(B) the property received in the exchange consists not only of property permitted by section 354 or 355 to be received without the recognition of gain but also of other property or money,

then the gain, if any, to the recipient shall be recognized, but in an amount not in excess of the sum of such money and the fair market value of such other property.

(2) TREATMENT AS DIVIDEND.—If an exchange is described in paragraph (1) but has the effect of the distribution of a dividend (determined with the application of section 318(a)), then there shall be treated as a dividend to each distributee such an amount of the gain recognized under paragraph (1) as is not in excess of his ratable share of the undistributed earnings and profits of the corporation accumulated after February 28, 1913. The remainder, if any, of the gain recognized under paragraph (1) shall be treated as gain from the exchange of property.

[Sec. 356(b)]

(b) ADDITIONAL CONSIDERATION RECEIVED IN CERTAIN DISTRIBUTIONS.—If—

(1) section 355 would apply to a distribution but for the fact that

(2) the property received in the distribution consists not only of property permitted by section 355 to be received without the recognition of gain, but also of other property or money,

then an amount equal to the sum of such money and the fair market value of such other property shall be treated as a distribution of property to which section 301 applies.

[Sec. 356(c)]

(c) LOSS.—If—

(1) section 354 would apply to an exchange, or section 355 would apply to an exchange or distribution, but for the fact that

(2) the property received in the exchange or distribution consists not only of property permitted by section 354 or 355 to be received without the recognition of gain or loss, but also of other property or money,

then no loss from the exchange or distribution shall be recognized.

[Sec. 356(d)]

(d) SECURITIES AS OTHER PROPERTY.—For purposes of this section—

(1) IN GENERAL.—Except as provided in paragraph (2), the term "other property" includes securities.

(2) EXCEPTIONS.—

(A) SECURITIES WITH RESPECT TO WHICH NONRECOGNITION OF GAIN WOULD BE PERMITTED.—The term "other property" does not include securities to the extent that, under section 354 or 355, such securities would be permitted to be received without the recognition of gain.

(B) GREATER PRINCIPAL AMOUNT IN SECTION 354 EXCHANGE.—If—

(i) in an exchange described in section 354 (other than subsection (c) thereof), securities of a corporation a party to the reorganization are surrendered and securities of any corporation a party to the reorganization are received, and

(ii) the principal amount of such securities received exceeds the principal amount of such securities surrendered,

then, with respect to such securities received, the term "other property" means only the fair market value of such excess. For purposes of this subparagraph and subparagraph (C), if no securities are surrendered, the excess shall be the entire principal amount of the securities received.

(C) GREATER PRINCIPAL AMOUNT IN SECTION 355 TRANSACTION.—If, in an exchange or distribution described in section 355, the principal amount of the securities in the controlled corporation which are received exceeds the principal amount of the securities in the distributing corporation which are surrendered, then, with respect to such securities received, the term "other property" means only the fair market value of such excess.

[Sec. 356(e)]

(e) NONQUALIFIED PREFERRED STOCK TREATED AS OTHER PROPERTY.—For purposes of this section—

(1) IN GENERAL.—Except as provided in paragraph (2), the term "other property" includes nonqualified preferred stock (as defined in section 351(g)(2)).

(2) EXCEPTION.—The term "other property" does not include nonqualified preferred stock (as so defined) to the extent that, under section 354 or 355, such preferred stock would be permitted to be received without the recognition of gain.

[Sec. 356(f)]

(f) EXCHANGES FOR SECTION 306 STOCK.—Notwithstanding any other provision of this section, to the extent that any of the other property (or money) is received in exchange for section 306 stock, an amount equal to the fair market value of such other property (or the amount of such money) shall be treated as a distribution of property to which section 301 applies.

[Sec. 356(g)]

(g) TRANSACTIONS INVOLVING GIFT OR COMPENSATION.—

For special rules for a transaction described in section 354, 355, or this section, but which—

(1) results in a gift, see section 2501 and following, or

(2) has the effect of the payment of compensation, see section 61(a)(1).

[Sec. 357]

SEC. 357. ASSUMPTION OF LIABILITY.

[Sec. 357(a)]

(a) GENERAL RULE.—Except as provided in subsections (b) and (c), if—

(1) the taxpayer receives property which would be permitted to be received under section 351 or 361 without the recognition of gain if it were the sole consideration, and

(2) as part of the consideration, another party to the exchange assumes a liability of the taxpayer,

then such assumption shall not be treated as money or other property, and shall not prevent the exchange from being within the provisions of section 351 or 361, as the case may be.

[Sec. 357(b)]

(b) TAX AVOIDANCE PURPOSE.—

(1) IN GENERAL.—If, taking into consideration the nature of the liability and the circumstances in the light of which the arrangement for the assumption was made, it appears that the principal purpose of the taxpayer with respect to the assumption described in subsection (a)—

(A) was a purpose to avoid Federal income tax on the exchange, or

(B) if not such purpose, was not a bona fide business purpose,

then such assumption (in the total amount of the liability assumed pursuant to such exchange) shall, for purposes of section 351 or 361 (as the case may be), be considered as money received by the taxpayer on the exchange.

(2) BURDEN OF PROOF.—In any suit or proceeding where the burden is on the taxpayer to prove such assumption is not to be treated as money received by the taxpayer, such burden shall not be considered as sustained unless the taxpayer sustains such burden by the clear preponderance of the evidence.

[Sec. 357(c)]

(c) LIABILITIES IN EXCESS OF BASIS.—

(1) IN GENERAL.—In the case of an exchange—

(A) to which section 351 applies, or

(B) to which section 361 applies by reason of a plan of reorganization within the meaning of section 368(a)(1)(D) with respect to which stock or securities of the corporation to which the assets are transferred are distributed in a transaction which qualifies under section 355,

if the sum of the amount of the liabilities assumed exceeds the total of the adjusted basis of the property transferred pursuant to such exchange, then such excess shall be considered as a gain from the sale or exchange of a capital asset or of property which is not a capital asset, as the case may be.

(2) EXCEPTIONS.—Paragraph (1) shall not apply to any exchange—

(A) to which subsection (b)(1) of this section applies, or

(B) which is pursuant to a plan of reorganization within the meaning of section 368(a)(1)(G) where no former shareholder of the transferor corporation receives any consideration for his stock.

(3) CERTAIN LIABILITIES EXCLUDED.—

(A) IN GENERAL.—If a taxpayer transfers, in an exchange to which section 351 applies, a liability the payment of which either—

(i) would give rise to a deduction, or

(ii) would be described in section 736(a),

then, for purposes of paragraph (1), the amount of such liability shall be excluded in determining the amount of liabilities assumed.

(B) EXCEPTION.—Subparagraph (A) shall not apply to any liability to the extent that the incurrence of the liability resulted in the creation of, or an increase in, the basis of any property.

[Sec. 357(d)]

(d) DETERMINATION OF AMOUNT OF LIABILITY ASSUMED.—

(1) IN GENERAL.—For purposes of this section, section 358(d), section 358(h), section 361(b)(3), section 362(d), section 368(a)(1)(C), and section 368(a)(2)(B), except as provided in regulations—

(A) a recourse liability (or portion thereof) shall be treated as having been assumed if, as determined on the basis of all facts and circumstances, the transferee has agreed to, and is expected to, satisfy such liability (or portion), whether or not the transferor has been relieved of such liability; and

(B) except to the extent provided in paragraph (2), a nonrecourse liability shall be treated as having been assumed by the transferee of any asset subject to such liability.

(2) EXCEPTION FOR NONRECOURSE LIABILITY.—The amount of the nonrecourse liability treated as described in paragraph (1)(B) shall be reduced by the lesser of—

(A) the amount of such liability which an owner of other assets not transferred to the transferee and also subject to such liability has agreed with the transferee to, and is expected to, satisfy, or

(B) the fair market value of such other assets (determined without regard to section 7701(g)).

(3) REGULATIONS.—The Secretary shall prescribe such regulations as may be necessary to carry out the purposes of this subsection and section 362(d). The Secretary may also prescribe regulations which provide that the manner in which a liability is treated as assumed under this subsection is applied, where appropriate, elsewhere in this title.

[Sec. 358]

SEC. 358. BASIS TO DISTRIBUTEES.

[Sec. 358(a)]

(a) GENERAL RULE.—In the case of an exchange to which section 351, 354, 355, 356, or 361 applies—

(1) NONRECOGNITION PROPERTY.—The basis of the property permitted to be received under such section without the recognition of gain or loss shall be the same as that of the property exchanged—

(A) decreased by—

(i) the fair market value of any other property (except money) received by the taxpayer,

(ii) the amount of any money received by the taxpayer, and

(iii) the amount of loss to the taxpayer which was recognized on such exchange, and

(B) increased by—

(i) the amount which was treated as a dividend, and

(ii) the amount of gain to the taxpayer which was recognized on such exchange (not including any portion of such gain which was treated as a dividend).

(2) OTHER PROPERTY.—The basis of any other property (except money) received by the taxpayer shall be its fair market value.

[Sec. 358(b)]

(b) ALLOCATION OF BASIS.—

(1) IN GENERAL.—Under regulations prescribed by the Secretary, the basis determined under subsection (a) (1) shall be allocated among the properties permitted to be received without the recognition of gain or loss.

(2) SPECIAL RULE FOR SECTION 355.—In the case of an exchange to which section 355 (or so much of section 356 as relates to section 355) applies, then in making the allocation under paragraph (1) of this subsection, there shall be taken into account not only the property so permitted to be received without the recognition of gain or loss, but also the stock or securities (if any) of the distributing corporation which are retained, and the allocation of basis shall be made among all such properties.

[Sec. 358(c)]

(c) SECTION 355 TRANSACTIONS WHICH ARE NOT EXCHANGES.—For purposes of this section, a distribution to which section 355 (or so much of section 356 as relates to section 355) applies shall be treated as an exchange, and for such purposes the stock and securities of the distributing corporation which are retained shall be treated as surrendered, and received back, in the exchange.

[Sec. 358(d)]

(d) ASSUMPTION OF LIABILITY.—

(1) IN GENERAL.—Where, as part of the consideration to the taxpayer, another party to the exchange assumed a liability of the taxpayer, such assumption shall, for purposes of this section, be treated as money received by the taxpayer on the exchange.

(2) EXCEPTION.—Paragraph (1) shall not apply to the amount of any liability excluded under section 357(c)(3).

[Sec. 358(e)]

(e) EXCEPTION.—This section shall not apply to property acquired by a corporation by the exchange of its stock or securities (or the stock or securities of a corporation which is in control of the acquiring corporation) as consideration in whole or in part for the transfer of the property to it.

[Sec. 358(f)]

(f) DEFINITION OF NONRECOGNITION PROPERTY IN CASE OF SECTION 361 EXCHANGE.—For purposes of this section, the property permitted to be received under section 361 without the recognition of gain or loss shall be treated as consisting only of stock or securities in another corporation a party to the reorganization.

[Sec. 358(g)]

(g) ADJUSTMENTS IN INTRAGROUP TRANSACTIONS INVOLVING SECTION 355.—In the case of a distribution to which section 355 (or so much of section 356 as relates to section 355) applies and which involves the distribution of stock from 1 member of an affiliated group (as defined in section 1504(a) without regard to subsection (b) thereof) to another member of such group, the Secretary may, notwithstanding any other provision of this section, provide adjustments to the adjusted basis of any stock which—

(1) is in a corporation which is a member of such group, and

(2) is held by another member of such group, to appropriately reflect the proper treatment of such distribution.

[Sec. 358(h)]

(h) SPECIAL RULES FOR ASSUMPTION OF LIABILITIES TO WHICH SUBSECTION (D) DOES NOT APPLY.—

(1) IN GENERAL.—If, after application of the other provisions of this section to an exchange or series of exchanges, the basis of property to which subsection (a)(1) applies exceeds the fair market value of such property, then such basis shall be reduced (but not below such fair market value) by the amount (determined as of the date of the exchange) of any liability—

(A) which is assumed by another person as part of the exchange, and

(B) with respect to which subsection (d)(1) does not apply to the assumption.

(2) EXCEPTIONS.—Except as provided by the Secretary, paragraph (1) shall not apply to any liability if—

(A) the trade or business with which the liability is associated is transferred to the person assuming the liability as part of the exchange, or

(B) substantially all of the assets with which the liability is associated are transferred to the person assuming the liability as part of the exchange.

(3) LIABILITY.—For purposes of this subsection, the term "liability" shall include any fixed or contingent obligation to make payment, without regard to whether the obligation is otherwise taken into account for purposes of this title.

Subpart C—Effects on Corporations

[Sec. 361]

SEC. 361. NONRECOGNITION OF GAIN OR LOSS TO CORPORATIONS; TREATMENT OF DISTRIBUTIONS.

[Sec. 361(a)]

(a) GENERAL RULE.—No gain or loss shall be recognized to a corporation if such corporation is a party to a reorganization and exchanges property, in pursuance of the plan of reorganization, solely for stock or securities in another corporation a party to the reorganization.

[Sec. 361(b)]

(b) EXCHANGES NOT SOLELY IN KIND.—

(1) GAIN.—If subsection (a) would apply to an exchange but for the fact that the property received in exchange consists not only of stock or securities permitted by subsection (a) to be received without the recognition of gain, but also of other property or money, then—

(A) PROPERTY DISTRIBUTED.—If the corporation receiving such other property or money distributes it in pursuance of the plan of reorganization, no gain to the corporation shall be recognized from the exchange, but

(B) PROPERTY NOT DISTRIBUTED.—If the corporation receiving such other property or money does not distribute it in pursuance of the plan of reorganization, the gain, if any, to the corporation shall be recognized.

The amount of gain recognized under subparagraph (B) shall not exceed the sum of the money and the fair market value of the other property so received which is not so distributed.

(2) LOSS.—If subsection (a) would apply to an exchange but for the fact that the property received in exchange consists not only of property permitted by subsection (a) to be received without the recognition of gain or loss, but also of other property or money, then no loss from the exchange shall be recognized.

(3) TREATMENT OF TRANSFERS TO CREDITORS.—For purposes of paragraph (1), any transfer of the other property or money received in the exchange by the corporation to its creditors in connection with the reorganization shall be treated as a distribution in pursuance of the plan of reorganization. The Secretary may prescribe such regulations as may be necessary to prevent avoidance of tax through abuse of the preceding sentence or subsection (c)(3). In the case of a reorganization described in section 368(a)(1)(D) with respect to which stock or securities of the corporation to which the assets are transferred are distributed in a transaction which qualifies under section 355, this paragraph shall apply only to the extent that the sum of the money and the fair market value of other property transferred to such creditors does not exceed the adjusted bases of such assets transferred (reduced by the amount of the liabilities assumed (within the meaning of section 357(c))).

[Sec. 361(c)]

(c) TREATMENT OF DISTRIBUTIONS.—

(1) IN GENERAL.—Except as provided in paragraph (2), no gain or loss shall be recognized to a corporation a party to a reorganization on the distribution to its shareholders of property in pursuance of the plan of reorganization.

(2) DISTRIBUTIONS OF APPRECIATED PROPERTY.—

(A) IN GENERAL.—If—

(i) in a distribution referred to in paragraph (1), the corporation distributes property other than qualified property, and

(ii) the fair market value of such property exceeds its adjusted basis (in the hands of the distributing corporation),

then gain shall be recognized to the distributing corporation as if such property were sold to the distributee at its fair market value.

(B) QUALIFIED PROPERTY.—For purposes of this subsection, the term "qualified property" means—

(i) any stock in (or right to acquire stock in) the distributing corporation or obligation of the distributing corporation, or

(ii) any stock in (or right to acquire stock in) another corporation which is a party to the reorganization or obligation of another corporation which is such a party if such stock (or right) or obligation is received by the distributing corporation in the exchange.

(C) TREATMENT OF LIABILITIES.—If any property distributed in the distribution referred to in paragraph (1) is subject to a liability or the shareholder assumes a liability of the distributing corporation in connection with the distribution, then, for purposes of subparagraph (A), the fair market value of such property shall be treated as not less than the amount of such liability.

(3) TREATMENT OF CERTAIN TRANSFERS TO CREDITORS.—For purposes of this subsection, any transfer of qualified property by the corporation to its creditors in connection with the reorganization shall be treated as a distribution to its shareholders pursuant to the plan of reorganization.

(4) COORDINATION WITH OTHER PROVISIONS.—Section 311 and subpart B of part II of this subchapter shall not apply to any distribution referred to in paragraph (1).

(5) CROSS REFERENCE.—

For provision providing for recognition of gain in certain distributions, see section 355(d).

[Sec. 362]

SEC. 362. BASIS TO CORPORATIONS.

[Sec. 362(a)]

(a) PROPERTY ACQUIRED BY ISSUANCE OF STOCK OR AS PAID-IN SURPLUS.—If property was acquired by a corporation—

(1) in connection with a transaction to which section 351 (relating to transfer of property to corporation controlled by transferor) applies, or

(2) as paid-in surplus or as a contribution to capital,

then the basis shall be the same as it would be in the hands of the transferor, increased in the amount of gain recognized to the transferor on such transfer.

[Sec. 362(b)]

(b) TRANSFERS TO CORPORATIONS.—If property was acquired by a corporation in connection with a reorganization to which this part applies, then the basis shall be the same as it would be in the hands of the transferor, increased in the amount of gain recognized to the transferor on such transfer. This subsection shall not apply if the property acquired consists of stock or securities in a corporation a party to the reorganization, unless acquired by the exchange of stock or securities of the transferee (or of a corporation which is in control of the transferee) as the consideration in whole or in part for the transfer.

[Sec. 362(c)]

(c) SPECIAL RULE FOR CERTAIN CONTRIBUTIONS TO CAPITAL.—

(1) PROPERTY OTHER THAN MONEY.—Notwithstanding subsection (a)(2), if property other than money—

(A) is acquired by a corporation as a contribution to capital, and

(B) is not contributed by a shareholder as such,

then the basis of such property shall be zero.

(2) MONEY.—Notwithstanding subsection (a)(2), if money—

(A) is received by a corporation as a contribution to capital, and

(B) is not contributed by a shareholder as such,

then the basis of any property acquired with such money during the 12-month period beginning on the day the contribution is received shall be reduced by the amount of such contribution. The excess (if any) of the amount of such contribution over the amount of the reduction under the preceding sentence shall be applied to the reduction (as of the last day of the period specified in the preceding sentence) of the basis of any other property held by the taxpayer. The particular properties to which the reductions required by this paragraph shall be allocated shall be determined under regulations prescribed by the Secretary.

[Sec. 362(d)]

(d) LIMITATION ON BASIS INCREASE ATTRIBUTABLE TO ASSUMPTION OF LIABILITY.—

(1) IN GENERAL.—In no event shall the basis of any property be increased under subsection (a) or (b) above the fair market value of such property (determined without regard to section 7701(g)) by reason of any gain recognized to the transferor as a result of the assumption of a liability.

(2) TREATMENT OF GAIN NOT SUBJECT TO TAX.—Except as provided in regulations, if—

(A) gain is recognized to the transferor as a result of an assumption of a nonrecourse liability by a transferee which is also secured by assets not transferred to such transferee; and

(B) no person is subject to tax under this title on such gain,

then, for purposes of determining basis under subsections (a) and (b), the amount of gain recognized by the transferor as a result of the assumption of the liability shall be determined as if the liability assumed by the transferee equaled such transferee's ratable portion of such liability determined on the basis of the relative fair market values (determined without regard to section 7701(g)) of all of the assets subject to such liability.

[Sec. 362(e)]

(e) LIMITATIONS ON BUILT-IN LOSSES.—

(1) LIMITATION ON IMPORTATION OF BUILT-IN LOSSES.—

(A) IN GENERAL.—If in any transaction described in subsection (a) or (b) there would (but for this subsection) be an importation of a net built-in loss, the basis of each property described in subparagraph (B) which is acquired in such transaction shall (notwithstanding subsections (a) and (b)) be its fair market value immediately after such transaction.

(B) PROPERTY DESCRIBED.—For purposes of subparagraph (A), property is described in this subparagraph if—

(i) gain or loss with respect to such property is not subject to tax under this subtitle in the hands of the transferor immediately before the transfer, and

(ii) gain or loss with respect to such property is subject to such tax in the hands of the transferee immediately after such transfer.

In any case in which the transferor is a partnership, the preceding sentence shall be applied by treating each partner in such partnership as holding such partner's proportionate share of the property of such partnership.

(C) IMPORTATION OF NET BUILT-IN LOSS.—For purposes of subparagraph (A), there is an importation of a net built-in loss in a transaction if the transferee's aggregate adjusted bases of property described in subparagraph (B) which is transferred in such transaction would (but for this paragraph) exceed the fair market value of such property immediately after such transaction.

(2) LIMITATION ON TRANSFER OF BUILT-IN LOSSES IN SECTION 351 TRANSACTIONS.—

(A) IN GENERAL.—If—

(i) property is transferred by a transferor in any transaction which is described in subsection (a) and which is not described in paragraph (1) of this subsection, and

(ii) the transferee's aggregate adjusted bases of such property so transferred would (but for this paragraph) exceed the fair market value of such property immediately after such transaction,

then, notwithstanding subsection (a), the transferee's aggregate adjusted bases of the property so transferred shall not exceed the fair market value of such property immediately after such transaction.

(B) ALLOCATION OF BASIS REDUCTION.—The aggregate reduction in basis by reason of subparagraph (A) shall be allocated among the property so transferred in proportion to their respective built-in losses immediately before the transaction.

(C) ELECTION TO APPLY LIMITATION TO TRANSFEROR'S STOCK BASIS.—

(i) IN GENERAL.—If the transferor and transferee of a transaction described in subparagraph (A) both elect the application of this subparagraph—

(I) subparagraph (A) shall not apply, and

(II) the transferor's basis in the stock received for property to which subparagraph (A) does not apply by reason of the election shall not exceed its fair market value immediately after the transfer.

(ii) ELECTION.—Any election under clause (i) shall be made at such time and in such form and manner as the Secretary may prescribe, and, once made, shall be irrevocable.

Subpart D—Special Rule; Definitions

[Sec. 367]

SEC. 367. FOREIGN CORPORATIONS.

[Sec. 367(a)]

(a) TRANSFERS OF PROPERTY FROM THE UNITED STATES.—

(1) GENERAL RULE.—If, in connection with any exchange described in section 332, 351, 354, 356, or 361, a United States person transfers property to a foreign corporation, such foreign corporation shall not, for purposes of determining the extent to which gain shall be recognized on such transfer, be considered to be a corporation.

(2) EXCEPTION FOR CERTAIN STOCK OR SECURITIES.—Except to the extent provided in regulations, paragraph (1) shall not apply to the transfer of stock or securities of a foreign corporation which is a party to the exchange or a party to the reorganization.

(3) SPECIAL RULE FOR TRANSFER OF PARTNERSHIP INTERESTS.—Except as provided in regulations prescribed by the Secretary, a transfer by a United States person of an interest in a partnership to a foreign corporation in an exchange described in paragraph (1) shall, for purposes of this subsection, be treated as a transfer to such corporation of such person's pro rata share of the assets of the partnership.

(4) PARAGRAPH (2) NOT TO APPLY TO CERTAIN SECTION 361 TRANSACTIONS.—Paragraph (2) shall not apply in the case of an exchange described in subsection (a) or (b) of section 361. Subject to such basis adjustments and such other conditions as shall be provided in regulations, the preceding sentence shall not apply if the transferor corporation is controlled (within the meaning of section 368(c)) by 5 or fewer domestic corporations. For purposes of the preceding sentence, all members of the same affiliated group (within the meaning of section 1504) shall be treated as 1 corporation.

(5) SECRETARY MAY EXEMPT CERTAIN TRANSACTIONS FROM APPLICATION OF THIS SUBSECTION.—Paragraph (1) shall not apply to the transfer of any property which the Secretary, in order to carry out the purposes of this subsection, designates by regulation.

[Sec. 367(b)]

(b) OTHER TRANSFERS.—

(1) EFFECT OF SECTION TO BE DETERMINED UNDER REGULATIONS.—In the case of any exchange described in section 332, 351, 354, 355, 356, or 361 in connection with which there is no transfer of property described in subsection (a)(1), a foreign corporation shall be considered to be a

corporation except to the extent provided in regulations prescribed by the Secretary which are necessary or appropriate to prevent the avoidance of Federal income taxes.

(2) REGULATIONS RELATING TO SALE OR EXCHANGE OF STOCK IN FOREIGN CORPORATIONS.—The regulations prescribed pursuant to paragraph (1) shall include (but shall not be limited to) regulations dealing with the sale or exchange of stock or securities in a foreign corporation by a United States person, including regulations providing—

(A) the circumstances under which—

(i) gain shall be recognized currently, or amounts included in gross income currently as a dividend, or both, or

(ii) gain or other amounts may be deferred for inclusion in the gross income of a shareholder (or his successor in interest) at a later date, and

(B) the extent to which adjustments shall be made to earnings and profits, basis of stock or securities, and basis of assets.

[Sec. 367(c)]

(c) TRANSACTIONS TO BE TREATED AS EXCHANGES.—

(1) SECTION 355 DISTRIBUTION.—For purposes of this section, any distribution described in section 355 (or so much of section 356 as relates to section 355) shall be treated as an exchange whether or not it is an exchange.

(2) CONTRIBUTION OF CAPITAL TO CONTROLLED CORPORATIONS.—For purposes of this chapter, any transfer of property to a foreign corporation as a contribution to the capital of such corporation by one or more persons who, immediately after the transfer, own (within the meaning of section 318) stock possessing at least 80 percent of the total combined voting power of all classes of stock of such corporation entitled to vote shall be treated as an exchange of such property for stock of the foreign corporation equal in value to the fair market value of the property transferred.

[Sec. 367(d)]

(d) SPECIAL RULES RELATING TO TRANSFERS OF INTANGIBLES.—

(1) IN GENERAL.—Except as provided in regulations prescribed by the Secretary, if a United States person transfers any intangible property to a foreign corporation in an exchange described in section 351 or 361—

(A) subsection (a) shall not apply to the transfer of such property, and

(B) the provisions of this subsection shall apply to such transfer.

(2) TRANSFER OF INTANGIBLES TREATED AS TRANSFER PURSUANT TO SALE OF CONTINGENT PAYMENTS.—

(A) IN GENERAL.—If paragraph (1) applies to any transfer, the United States person transferring such property shall be treated as—

(i) having sold such property in exchange for payments which are contingent upon the productivity, use, or disposition of such property, and

(ii) receiving amounts which reasonably reflect the amounts which would have been received—

(I) annually in the form of such payments over the useful life of such property, or

(II) in the case of a disposition following such transfer (whether direct or indirect), at the time of the disposition.

The amounts taken into account under clause (ii) shall be commensurate with the income attributable to the intangible.

(B) EFFECT ON EARNINGS AND PROFITS.—For purposes of this chapter, the earnings and profits of a foreign corporation to which the intangible property was transferred shall be reduced by the amount required to be included in the income of the transferor of the intangible property under subparagraph (A)(ii).

(C) AMOUNTS RECEIVED TREATED AS ORDINARY INCOME.—For purposes of this chapter, any amount included in gross income by reason of this subsection shall be treated as ordinary income. For purposes of applying section 904(d), any such amount shall be treated in the same manner as if such amount were a royalty.

(D) REGULATORY AUTHORITY.—For purposes of the last sentence of subparagraph (A), the Secretary shall require—

(i) the valuation of transfers of intangible property, including intangible property transferred with other property or services, on an aggregate basis, or

(ii) the valuation of such a transfer on the basis of the realistic alternatives to such a transfer,

if the Secretary determines that such basis is the most reliable means of valuation of such transfers.

(3) REGULATIONS RELATING TO TRANSFERS OF INTANGIBLES TO PARTNERSHIPS.—The Secretary may provide by regulations that the rules of paragraph (2) also apply to the transfer of intangible property by a United States person to a partnership in circumstances consistent with the purposes of this subsection.

(4) INTANGIBLE PROPERTY.—For purposes of this subsection, the term "intangible property" means any—

(A) patent, invention, formula, process, design, pattern, or know-how,

(B) copyright, literary, musical, or artistic composition,

(C) trademark, trade name, or brand name,

(D) franchise, license, or contract,

(E) method, program, system, procedure, campaign, survey, study, forecast, estimate, customer list, or technical data,

(F) goodwill, going concern value, or workforce in place (including its composition and terms and conditions (contractual or otherwise) of its employment), or

(G) other item the value or potential value of which is not attributable to tangible property or the services of any individual.

[Sec. 367(e)]

(e) TREATMENT OF DISTRIBUTIONS DESCRIBED IN SECTION 355 OR LIQUIDATIONS UNDER SECTION 332.—

(1) DISTRIBUTIONS DESCRIBED IN SECTION 355.—In the case of any distribution described in section 355 (or so much of section 356 as relates to section 355) by a domestic corporation to a person who is not a United States person, to the extent provided in regulations, gain shall be recognized under principles similar to the principles of this section.

(2) LIQUIDATIONS UNDER SECTION 332.—In the case of any liquidation to which section 332 applies, except as provided in regulations, subsections (a) and (b)(1) of section 337 shall not apply where the 80-percent distributee (as defined in section 337(c)) is a foreign corporation.

[Sec. 367(f)]

(f) OTHER TRANSFERS.—To the extent provided in regulations, if a United States person transfers property to a foreign corporation as paid-in surplus or as a contribution to capital (in a transaction not otherwise described in this section), such transfer shall be treated as a sale or exchange for an amount equal to the fair market value of the property transferred, and the transferor shall recognize as gain the excess of—

(1) the fair market value of the property so transferred, over

(2) the adjusted basis (for purposes of determining gain) of such property in the hands of the transferor.

[Sec. 368]

SEC. 368. DEFINITIONS RELATING TO CORPORATE REORGANIZATIONS.

[Sec. 368(a)]

(a) REORGANIZATION.—

(1) IN GENERAL.—For purposes of parts I and II and this part, the term "reorganization" means—

(A) a statutory merger or consolidation;

(B) the acquisition by one corporation, in exchange solely for all or a part of its voting stock (or in exchange solely for all or a part of the voting stock of a corporation which is in control of the acquiring corporation), of stock of another corporation if, immediately after the acquisition, the acquiring corporation has control of such other corporation (whether or not such acquiring corporation had control immediately before the acquisition);

(C) the acquisition by one corporation, in exchange solely for all or a part of its voting stock (or in exchange solely for all or a part of the voting stock of a corporation which is in control of the acquiring corporation), of substantially all of the properties of another corporation, but in determining whether the exchange is solely for stock the assumption by the acquiring corporation of a liability of the other shall be disregarded;

(D) a transfer by a corporation of all or a part of its assets to another corporation if immediately after the transfer the transferor, or one or more of its shareholders (including persons who were shareholders immediately before the transfer), or any combination thereof, is in control of the corporation to which the assets are transferred; but only if, in pursuance of the plan, stock or securities of the corporation to which the assets are transferred are distributed in a transaction which qualifies under section 354, 355, or 356;

(E) a recapitalization;

(F) a mere change in identity, form, or place of organization of one corporation, however effected; or

(G) a transfer by a corporation of all or part of its assets to another corporation in a title 11 or similar case; but only if, in pursuance of the plan, stock or securities of the corporation to which the assets are transferred are distributed in a transaction which qualifies under section 354, 355, or 356.

(2) SPECIAL RULES RELATING TO PARAGRAPH (1).—

(A) REORGANIZATIONS DESCRIBED IN BOTH PARAGRAPH (1)(C) AND PARAGRAPH (1)(D).—If a transaction is described in both paragraph (1)(C) and paragraph (1)(D), then, for purposes of this subchapter (other than for purposes of subparagraph (C)), such transaction shall be treated as described only in paragraph (1)(D).

(B) ADDITIONAL CONSIDERATION IN CERTAIN PARAGRAPH (1)(C) CASES.—If—

(i) one corporation acquires substantially all of the properties of another corporation,

(ii) the acquisition would qualify under paragraph (1)(C) but for the fact that the acquiring corporation exchanges money or other property in addition to voting stock, and

(iii) the acquiring corporation acquires, solely for voting stock described in paragraph (1)(C), property of the other corporation having a fair market value which is at least 80 percent of the fair market value of all of the property of the other corporation,

then such acquisition shall (subject to subparagraph (A) of this paragraph) be treated as qualifying under paragraph (1)(C). Solely for the purpose of determining whether clause (iii) of the preceding sentence applies, the amount of any liability assumed by the acquiring corporation shall be treated as money paid for the property.

(C) TRANSFERS OF ASSETS OR STOCK TO SUBSIDIARIES IN CERTAIN PARAGRAPH (1)(A), (1)(B), (1)(C), AND (1)(G) CASES.—A transaction otherwise qualifying under paragraph (1)(A), (1)(B), or (1)(C) shall not be disqualified by reason of the fact that part or all of the assets or stock which were acquired in the transaction are transferred to a corporation controlled by the corporation acquiring such assets or stock. A similar rule shall apply to a transaction otherwise qualifying under paragraph (1)(G) where the requirements of subparagraphs (A) and (B) of section 354(b)(1) are met with respect to the acquisition of the assets.

(D) USE OF STOCK OF CONTROLLING CORPORATION IN PARAGRAPH (1)(A) AND (1)(G) CASES.—The acquisition by one corporation, in exchange for stock of a corporation (referred to in this subparagraph as "controlling corporation") which is in control of the acquiring corporation, of substantially all of the properties of another corporation shall not disqualify a transaction under paragraph (1)(A) or (1)(G) if—

(i) no stock of the acquiring corporation is used in the transaction, and

(ii) in the case of a transaction under paragraph (1)(A), such transaction would have qualified under paragraph (1)(A) had the merger been into the controlling corporation.

(E) STATUTORY MERGER USING VOTING STOCK OF CORPORATION CONTROLLING MERGED CORPORATION.—A transaction otherwise qualifying under paragraph (1)(A) shall not be disqualified by reason of the fact that stock of a corporation (referred to in this subparagraph as the "controlling corporation") which before the merger was in control of the merged corporation is used in the transaction, if—

(i) after the transaction, the corporation surviving the merger holds substantially all of its properties and of the properties of the merged corporation (other than stock of the controlling corporation distributed in the transaction); and

(ii) in the transaction, former shareholders of the surviving corporation exchanged, for an amount of voting stock of the controlling corporation, an amount of stock in the surviving corporation which constitutes control of such corporation.

(F) CERTAIN TRANSACTIONS INVOLVING 2 OR MORE INVESTMENT COMPANIES.—

(i) If immediately before a transaction described in paragraph (1) (other than subparagraph (E) thereof), 2 or more parties to the transaction were investment companies, then the transaction shall not be considered to be a reorganization with respect to any such investment company (and its shareholders and security holders) unless it was a regulated investment company, a real estate investment trust, or a corporation which meets the requirements of clause (ii).

(ii) A corporation meets the requirements of this clause if not more than 25 percent of the value of its total assets is invested in the stock and securities of any one issuer and not more than 50 percent of the value of its total assets is invested in the stock and securities of 5 or fewer issuers. For purposes of this clause, all members of a controlled group of corporations (within the meaning of section 1563(a)) shall be treated as one issuer. For purposes of this clause, a person holding stock in a regulated investment company, a real estate investment trust, or an investment company which meets the requirements of this clause shall, except as provided in regulations, be treated as holding its proportionate share of the assets held by such company or trust.

(iii) For purposes of this subparagraph the term "investment company" means a regulated investment company, a real estate investment trust, or a corporation 50 percent or more of the value of whose total assets are stock and securities and 80 percent or more of the value of whose total assets are assets held for investment. In making the 50-percent and 80-percent determinations under the preceding sentence, stock and securities in any subsidiary corporation shall be disregarded and the parent corporation shall be deemed to own its ratable share of the subsidiary's assets, and a corporation shall be considered a subsidiary if the parent owns 50 percent or more of the combined voting power of all classes of stock entitled to vote, or 50 percent or more of the total value of shares of all classes of stock outstanding.

(iv) For purposes of this subparagraph, in determining total assets there shall be excluded cash and cash items (including receivables), Government securities, and, under regulations prescribed by the Secretary, assets acquired (through incurring indebtedness or otherwise) for purposes of meeting the requirements of clause (ii) or ceasing to be an investment company.

(v) This subparagraph shall not apply if the stock of each investment company is owned substantially by the same persons in the same proportions.

(vi) If an investment company which does not meet the requirements of clause (ii) acquires assets of another corporation, clause (i) shall be applied to such investment company and its shareholders and security holders as though its assets had been acquired by such other corporation. If such investment company acquires stock of another corporation in a reorganization described in section 368(a)(1)(B), clause (i) shall be applied to the shareholders of such investment company as though they had exchanged with such other corporation all of their stock in such company for stock having a fair market value equal to the fair market value of their stock of such investment company immediately after the exchange. For purposes of section 1001, the deemed acquisition or exchange referred to in the two preceding sentences shall be treated as a sale or exchange of property by the corporation and by the shareholders and security holders to which clause (i) is applied.

(vii) For purposes of clauses (ii) and (iii), the term "securities" includes obligations of State and local governments, commodity futures contracts, shares of regulated investment companies and real estate investment trusts, and other investments constituting a security within the meaning of the Investment Company Act of 1940 (15 U.S.C. 80a-2(a)(36)).

(G) DISTRIBUTION REQUIREMENT FOR PARAGRAPH (1)(C).—

(i) IN GENERAL.—A transaction shall fail to meet the requirements of paragraph (1)(C) unless the acquired corporation distributes the stock, securities, and other properties it receives, as well as its other properties, in pursuance of the plan of reorganization. For purposes of the preceding sentence, if the acquired corporation is liquidated pursuant to the plan of reorganization, any distribution to its creditors in connection with such liquidation shall be treated as pursuant to the plan of reorganization.

(ii) EXCEPTION.—The Secretary may waive the application of clause (i) to any transaction subject to any conditions the Secretary may prescribe.

(H) SPECIAL RULES FOR DETERMINING WHETHER CERTAIN TRANSACTIONS ARE QUALIFIED UNDER PARAGRAPH (1)(D).—For purposes of determining whether a transaction qualifies under paragraph (1)(D)—

(i) in the case of a transaction with respect to which the requirements of subparagraphs (A) and (B) of section 354(b)(1) are met, the term "control" has the meaning given such term by section 304(c), and

(ii) in the case of a transaction with respect to which the requirements of section 355 (or so much of section 356 as relates to section 355) are met, the fact that the shareholders of the distributing corporation dispose of part or all of the distributed stock, or the fact that the corporation whose stock was distributed issues additional stock, shall not be taken into account.

(3) ADDITIONAL RULES RELATING TO TITLE 11 AND SIMILAR CASES.—

(A) TITLE 11 OR SIMILAR CASE DEFINED.—For purposes of this part, the term "title 11 or similar case" means—

(i) a case under title 11 of the United States Code, or

(ii) a receivership, foreclosure, or similar proceeding in a Federal or State court.

(B) TRANSFER OF ASSETS IN A TITLE 11 OR SIMILAR CASE.—In applying paragraph (1)(G), a transfer of the assets of a corporation shall be treated as made in a title 11 or similar case if and only if—

(i) any party to the reorganization is under the jurisdiction of the court in such case, and

(ii) the transfer is pursuant to a plan of reorganization approved by the court.

(C) REORGANIZATIONS QUALIFYING UNDER PARAGRAPH (1)(G) AND ANOTHER PROVISION.—If a transaction would (but for this subparagraph) qualify both—

(i) under subparagraph (G) of paragraph (1), and

(ii) under any other subparagraph of paragraph (1) or under section 332 or 351,

then, for purposes of this subchapter (other than section 357(c)(1)), such transaction shall be treated as qualifying only under subparagraph (G) of paragraph (1).

(D) AGENCY RECEIVERSHIP PROCEEDINGS WHICH INVOLVE FINANCIAL INSTITUTIONS.—For purposes of subparagraphs (A) and (B), in the case of a receivership, foreclosure, or similar proceeding before a Federal or State agency involving a financial institution referred to in section 581 or 591, the agency shall be treated as a court.

(E) APPLICATION OF PARAGRAPH (2)(E)(ii).—In the case of a title 11 or similar case, the requirement of clause (ii) of paragraph (2)(E) shall be treated as met if—

(i) no former shareholder of the surviving corporation received any consideration for his stock, and

(ii) the former creditors of the surviving corporation exchanged, for an amount of voting stock of the controlling corporation, debt of the surviving corporation which had a fair market value equal to 80 percent or more of the total fair market value of the debt of the surviving corporation.

[Sec. 368(b)]

(b) PARTY TO A REORGANIZATION.—For purposes of this part, the term "a party to a reorganization" includes—

(1) a corporation resulting from a reorganization, and

(2) both corporations, in the case of a reorganization resulting from the acquisition by one corporation of stock or properties of another.

In the case of a reorganization qualifying under paragraph (1)(B) or (1)(C) of subsection (a), if the stock exchanged for the stock or properties is stock of a corporation which is in control of the acquiring corporation, the term "a party to a reorganization" includes the corporation so controlling the acquiring corporation. In the case of a reorganization qualifying under paragraph (1)(A), (1)(B), (1)(C), or (1)(G) of subsection (a) by reason of paragraph (2)(C) of subsection (a), the term "a party to a reorganization" includes the corporation controlling the corporation to which the acquired assets or stock are transferred. In the case of a reorganization qualifying under paragraph (1)(A) or (1)(G) of subsection (a) by reason of paragraph (2)(D) of that subsection, the term "a party to a reorganization" includes the controlling corporation referred to in such paragraph (2)(D). In the case of a reorganization qualifying under subsection (a)(1)(A) by reason of subsection (a)(2)(E), the term "party to a reorganization" includes the controlling corporation referred to in subsection (a)(2)(E).

[Sec. 368(c)]

(c) CONTROL DEFINED.—For purposes of part I (other than section 304), part II, this part, and part V, the term "control" means the ownership of stock possessing at least 80 percent of the total combined voting power of all classes of stock entitled to vote and at least 80 percent of the total number of shares of all other classes of stock of the corporation.

PART VI—TREATMENT OF CERTAIN CORPORATE INTERESTS AS STOCK OR INDEBTEDNESS

[Sec. 385]

SEC. 385. TREATMENT OF CERTAIN INTERESTS IN CORPORATIONS AS STOCK OR INDEBTEDNESS.

[Sec. 385(a)]

(a) AUTHORITY TO PRESCRIBE REGULATIONS.—The Secretary is authorized to prescribe such regulations as may be necessary or appropriate to determine whether an interest in a corporation is to be treated for purposes of this title as stock or indebtedness (or as in part stock and in part indebtedness).

[Sec. 385(b)]

(b) FACTORS.—The regulations prescribed under this section shall set forth factors which are to be taken into account in determining with respect to a particular factual situation whether a debtor-creditor relationship exists or a corporation-shareholder relationship exists. The factors so set forth in the regulations may include among other factors:

(1) whether there is a written unconditional promise to pay on demand or on a specified date a sum certain in money in return for an adequate consideration in money or money's worth, and to pay a fixed rate of interest,

(2) whether there is subordination to or preference over any indebtedness of the corporation,

(3) the ratio of debt to equity of the corporation,

(4) whether there is convertibility into the stock of the corporation, and

(5) the relationship between holdings of stock in the corporation and holdings of the interest in question.

[Sec. 385(c)]

(c) EFFECT OF CLASSIFICATION BY ISSUER.—

(1) IN GENERAL.—The characterization (as of the time of issuance) by the issuer as to whether an interest in a corporation is stock or indebtedness shall be binding on such issuer and on all holders of such interest (but shall not be binding on the Secretary).

(2) NOTIFICATION OF INCONSISTENT TREATMENT.—Except as provided in regulations, paragraph (1) shall not apply to any holder of an interest if such holder on his return discloses that he is treating such interest in a manner inconsistent with the characterization referred to in paragraph (1).

(3) REGULATIONS.—The Secretary is authorized to require such information as the Secretary determines to be necessary to carry out the provisions of this subsection.

SUBCHAPTER E—ACCOUNTING PERIODS AND METHODS OF ACCOUNTING

PART I—ACCOUNTING PERIODS

[Sec. 441]

SEC. 441. PERIOD FOR COMPUTATION OF TAXABLE INCOME.

* * *

[Sec. 441(h)]

(h) TAXABLE YEAR OF DISC'S.—

(1) IN GENERAL.—For purposes of this subtitle, the taxable year of any DISC shall be the taxable year of that shareholder (or group of shareholders with the same 12-month taxable year) who has the highest percentage of voting power.

(2) SPECIAL RULE WHERE MORE THAN ONE SHAREHOLDER (OR GROUP) HAS HIGHEST PERCENTAGE.—If 2 or more shareholders (or groups) have the highest percentage of voting power under paragraph (1), the taxable year of the DISC shall be the same 12-month period as that of any such shareholder (or group).

(3) SUBSEQUENT CHANGES OF OWNERSHIP.—The Secretary shall prescribe regulations under which paragraphs (1) and (2) shall apply to a change of ownership of a corporation after the taxable year of the corporation has been determined under paragraph (1) or (2) only if such change is a substantial change of ownership.

(4) VOTING POWER DETERMINED.—For purposes of this subsection, voting power shall be determined on the basis of total combined voting power of all classes of stock of the corporation entitled to vote.

PART II—METHODS OF ACCOUNTING

Subpart B—Taxable Year for Which Items of Gross Income Included

[Sec. 457A]

SEC. 457A. NONQUALIFIED DEFERRED COMPENSATION FROM CERTAIN TAX INDIFFERENT PARTIES.

[Sec. 457A(a)]

(a) IN GENERAL.—Any compensation which is deferred under a nonqualified deferred compensation plan of a nonqualified entity shall be includible in gross income when there is no substantial risk of forfeiture of the rights to such compensation.

[Sec. 457A(b)]

(b) NONQUALIFIED ENTITY.—For purposes of this section, the term "nonqualified entity" means—

(1) any foreign corporation unless substantially all of its income is—

(A) effectively connected with the conduct of a trade or business in the United States, or

(B) subject to a comprehensive foreign income tax, and

(2) any partnership unless substantially all of its income is allocated to persons other than—

(A) foreign persons with respect to whom such income is not subject to a comprehensive foreign income tax, and

(B) organizations which are exempt from tax under this title.

[Sec. 457A(c)]

(c) DETERMINABILITY OF AMOUNTS OF COMPENSATION.—

(1) IN GENERAL.—If the amount of any compensation is not determinable at the time that such compensation is otherwise includible in gross income under subsection (a)—

(A) such amount shall be so includible in gross income when determinable, and

(B) the tax imposed under this chapter for the taxable year in which such compensation is includible in gross income shall be increased by the sum of—

(i) the amount of interest determined under paragraph (2), and

(ii) an amount equal to 20 percent of the amount of such compensation.

(2) INTEREST.—For purposes of paragraph (1)(B)(i), the interest determined under this paragraph for any taxable year is the amount of interest at the underpayment rate under section 6621 plus 1 percentage point on the underpayments that would have occurred had the deferred compensation been includible in gross income for the taxable year in which first deferred or, if later, the first taxable year in which such deferred compensation is not subject to a substantial risk of forfeiture.

[Sec. 457A(d)]

(d) OTHER DEFINITIONS AND SPECIAL RULES.—For purposes of this section—

(1) SUBSTANTIAL RISK OF FORFEITURE.—

(A) IN GENERAL.—The rights of a person to compensation shall be treated as subject to a substantial risk of forfeiture only if such person's rights to such compensation are conditioned upon the future performance of substantial services by any individual.

(B) EXCEPTION FOR COMPENSATION BASED ON GAIN RECOGNIZED ON AN INVESTMENT ASSET.—

(i) IN GENERAL.—To the extent provided in regulations prescribed by the Secretary, if compensation is determined solely by reference to the amount of gain recognized on the disposition of an investment asset, such compensation shall be treated as subject to a substantial risk of forfeiture until the date of such disposition.

(ii) INVESTMENT ASSET.—For purposes of clause (i), the term "investment asset" means any single asset (other than an investment fund or similar entity)—

(I) acquired directly by an investment fund or similar entity,

(II) with respect to which such entity does not (nor does any person related to such entity) participate in the active management of such asset (or if such asset is an interest in an entity, in the active management of the activities of such entity), and

(III) substantially all of any gain on the disposition of which (other than such deferred compensation) is allocated to investors in such entity.

(iii) COORDINATION WITH SPECIAL RULE.—Paragraph (3)(B) shall not apply to any compensation to which clause (i) applies.

(2) COMPREHENSIVE FOREIGN INCOME TAX.—The term "comprehensive foreign income tax" means, with respect to any foreign person, the income tax of a foreign country if—

(A) such person is eligible for the benefits of a comprehensive income tax treaty between such foreign country and the United States, or

(B) such person demonstrates to the satisfaction of the Secretary that such foreign country has a comprehensive income tax.

(3) NONQUALIFIED DEFERRED COMPENSATION PLAN.—

(A) IN GENERAL.—The term "nonqualified deferred compensation plan" has the meaning given such term under section 409A(d), except that such term shall include any plan that provides a right to compensation based on the appreciation in value of a specified number of equity units of the service recipient.

(B) EXCEPTION.—Compensation shall not be treated as deferred for purposes of this section if the service provider receives payment of such compensation not later than 12 months after the end of the taxable year of the service recipient during which the right to the payment of such compensation is no longer subject to a substantial risk of forfeiture.

(4) EXCEPTION FOR CERTAIN COMPENSATION WITH RESPECT TO EFFECTIVELY CONNECTED INCOME.—In the case of a foreign corporation with income which is taxable under section 882, this section shall not apply to compensation which, had such compensation been paid in cash on the date that such compensation ceased to be subject to a substantial risk of forfeiture, would have been deductible by such foreign corporation against such income.

(5) APPLICATION OF RULES.—Rules similar to the rules of paragraphs (5) and (6) of section 409A(d) shall apply.

[Sec. 457A(e)]

(e) REGULATIONS.—The Secretary shall prescribe such regulations as may be necessary or appropriate to carry out the purposes of this section, including regulations disregarding a substantial risk of forfeiture in cases where necessary to carry out the purposes of this section.

Subpart C—Taxable Year for Which Deductions Taken

[Sec. 461]

SEC. 461. GENERAL RULE FOR TAXABLE YEAR OF DEDUCTION.

* * *

[Sec. 461(l)]

(l) LIMITATION ON EXCESS BUSINESS LOSSES OF NONCORPORATE TAXPAYERS.—

Caution: Code Sec. 461(l)(1), below, prior to amendment by P.L. 117-2 and P.L. 117-169, applies to tax years beginning on or before December 31, 2025.

(1) LIMITATION.—In the case of a taxpayer other than a corporation—

(A) for any taxable year beginning after December 31, 2017, and before January 1, 2026, subsection (j) (relating to limitation on excess farm losses of certain taxpayers) shall not apply, and

(B) for any taxable year beginning after December 31, 2020, and before January 1, 2026, any excess business loss of the taxpayer for the taxable year shall not be allowed.

Caution: Code Sec. 461(l)(1), below, as amended by P.L. 117-2, but prior to amendment by P.L. 117-169, applies to tax years beginning after December 31, 2025, and on or before December 31, 2026.

(1) LIMITATION.—In the case of a taxpayer other than a corporation—

(A) for any taxable year beginning after December 31, 2017, and before January 1, 2027, subsection (j) (relating to limitation on excess farm losses of certain taxpayers) shall not apply, and

(B) for any taxable year beginning after December 31, 2020, and before January 1, 2027, any excess business loss of the taxpayer for the taxable year shall not be allowed.

Caution: Code Sec. 461(l)(1), below, as amended by P.L. 117-169, applies to tax years beginning after December 31, 2026.

(1) LIMITATION.—In the case of a taxpayer other than a corporation—

(A) for any taxable year beginning after December 31, 2017, and before January 1, 2029, subsection (j) (relating to limitation on excess farm losses of certain taxpayers) shall not apply, and

(B) for any taxable year beginning after December 31, 2020, and before January 1, 2029, any excess business loss of the taxpayer for the taxable year shall not be allowed.

(2) DISALLOWED LOSS CARRYOVER.—Any loss which is disallowed under paragraph (1) shall be treated as a net operating loss for the taxable year for purposes of determining any net operating loss carryover under section 172(b) for subsequent taxable years.

Caution: Pursuant to Section 461(l)(3)(C), the $250,000 amount in Section 461(l)(3)(A)(ii)(II) is adjusted for taxable years beginning after 2018 to reflect changes in the Chained Consumer Price Index. The adjusted amount that applies for taxable years beginning in 2023 is $289,000 ($578,000 for joint returns), as provided in Rev. Proc. 2022-38, 2022-45 I.R.B. 445.

(3) EXCESS BUSINESS LOSS.—For purposes of this subsection—

(A) IN GENERAL.—The term "excess business loss" means the excess (if any) of—

(i) the aggregate deductions of the taxpayer for the taxable year which are attributable to trades or businesses of such taxpayer (determined without regard to whether or not such deductions are disallowed for such taxable year under paragraph (1) and without regard to any deduction allowable under section 172 or 199A, over

(ii) the sum of—

(I) the aggregate gross income or gain of such taxpayer for the taxable year which is attributable to such trades or businesses, plus

(II) $250,000 (200 percent of such amount in the case of a joint return).

Such excess shall be determined without regard to any deductions, gross income, or gains attributable to any trade or business of performing services as an employee.

(B) TREATMENT OF CAPITAL GAINS AND LOSSES.—

(i) LOSSES.—Deductions for losses from sales or exchanges of capital assets shall not be taken into account under subparagraph (A)(i).

(ii) GAINS.—The amount of gains from sales or exchanges of capital assets taken into account under subparagraph (A)(ii) shall not exceed the lesser of—

(I) the capital gain net income determined by taking into account only gains and losses attributable to a trade or business, or

(II) the capital gain net income.

(C) ADJUSTMENT FOR INFLATION.—In the case of any taxable year beginning after December 31, 2018, the $250,000 amount in subparagraph (A)(ii)(II) shall be increased by an amount equal to—

(i) such dollar amount, multiplied by

(ii) the cost-of-living adjustment determined under section 1(f)(3) for the calendar year in which the taxable year begins, determined by substituting "2017" for "2016" in subparagraph (A)(ii) thereof.

If any amount as increased under the preceding sentence is not a multiple of $1,000, such amount shall be rounded to the nearest multiple of $1,000.

(4) APPLICATION OF SUBSECTION IN CASE OF PARTNERSHIPS AND S CORPORATIONS.—In the case of a partnership or S corporation—

(A) this subsection shall be applied at the partner or shareholder level, and

(B) each partner's or shareholder's allocable share of the items of income, gain, deduction, or loss of the partnership or S corporation for any taxable year from trades or businesses attributable to the partnership or S corporation shall be taken into account by the partner or shareholder in applying this subsection to the taxable year of such partner or shareholder with or within which the taxable year of the partnership or S corporation ends.

For purposes of this paragraph, in the case of an S corporation, an allocable share shall be the shareholder's pro rata share of an item.

(5) ADDITIONAL REPORTING.—The Secretary shall prescribe such additional reporting requirements as the Secretary determines necessary to carry out the purposes of this subsection.

(6) COORDINATION WITH SECTION 469.—This subsection shall be applied after the application of section 469.

Subpart D—Inventories

[Sec. 475]

SEC. 475. MARK TO MARKET ACCOUNTING METHOD FOR DEALERS IN SECURITIES.

* * *

[Sec. 475(c)]

(c) DEFINITIONS.—For purposes of this section—

(1) DEALER IN SECURITIES DEFINED.—The term "dealer in securities" means a taxpayer who—

(A) regularly purchases securities from or sells securities to customers in the ordinary course of a trade or business; or

(B) regularly offers to enter into, assume, offset, assign or otherwise terminate positions in securities with customers in the ordinary course of a trade or business.

(2) SECURITY DEFINED.—The term "security" means any—

(A) share of stock in a corporation;

(B) partnership or beneficial ownership interest in a widely held or publicly traded partnership or trust;

(C) note, bond, debenture, or other evidence of indebtedness;

(D) interest rate, currency, or equity notional principal contract;

(E) evidence of an interest in, or a derivative financial instrument in, any security described in subparagraph (A), (B), (C), or (D), or any currency, including any option, forward contract, short position, and any similar financial instrument in such a security or currency; and

(F) position which—

(i) is not a security described in subparagraph (A), (B), (C), (D), or (E),

(ii) is a hedge with respect to such a security, and

(iii) is clearly identified in the dealer's records as being described in this subparagraph before the close of the day on which it was acquired or entered into (or such other time as the Secretary may by regulations prescribe).

Subparagraph (E) shall not include any contract to which section 1256(a) applies.

* * *

PART III—ADJUSTMENTS

[Sec. 482]

SEC. 482. ALLOCATION OF INCOME AND DEDUCTIONS AMONG TAXPAYERS.

In any case of two or more organizations, trades, or businesses (whether or not incorporated, whether or not organized in the United States, and whether or not affiliated) owned or controlled directly or indirectly by the same interests, the Secretary may distribute, apportion, or allocate gross income, deductions, credits, or allowances between or among such organizations, trades, or businesses, if he determines that such distribution, apportionment, or allocation is necessary in order to prevent evasion of taxes or clearly to reflect the income of any of such organizations, trades, or businesses. In the case of any transfer (or license) of intangible property (within the meaning of section 367(d)(4)), the income with respect to such transfer or license shall be commensurate with the income attributable to the intangible. For purposes of this section, the Secretary shall require the valuation of transfers of intangible property (including intangible property transferred with other property or services) on an aggregate basis or the valuation of such a transfer on the basis of the realistic alternatives to such a transfer, if the Secretary determines that such basis is the most reliable means of valuation of such transfers.

[Sec. 483]

SEC. 483. INTEREST ON CERTAIN DEFERRED PAYMENTS.

[Sec. 483(a)]

(a) AMOUNT CONSTITUTING INTEREST.—For purposes of this title, in the case of any payment—

(1) under any contract for the sale or exchange of any property, and

(2) to which this section applies,

there shall be treated as interest that portion of the total unstated interest under such contract which, as determined in a manner consistent with the method of computing interest under section 1272(a), is properly allocable to such payment.

[Sec. 483(b)]

(b) TOTAL UNSTATED INTEREST.—For purposes of this section, the term "total unstated interest" means, with respect to a contract for the sale or exchange of property, an amount equal to the excess of—

(1) the sum of the payments to which this section applies which are due under the contract, over

(2) the sum of the present values of such payments and the present values of any interest payments due under the contract.

For purposes of the preceding sentence, the present value of a payment shall be determined under the rules of section 1274(b)(2) using a discount rate equal to the applicable Federal rate determined under section 1274(d).

[Sec. 483(c)]

(c) PAYMENTS TO WHICH SUBSECTION (a) APPLIES.—

(1) IN GENERAL.—Except as provided in subsection (d), this section shall apply to any payment on account of the sale or exchange of property which constitutes part or all of the sales price and which is due more than 6 months after the date of such sale or exchange under a contract—

(A) under which some or all of the payments are due more than 1 year after the date of such sale or exchange, and

(B) under which there is total unstated interest.

(2) TREATMENT OF OTHER DEBT INSTRUMENTS.—For purposes of this section, a debt instrument of the purchaser which is given in consideration for the sale or exchange of property shall not be treated as a payment, and any payment due under such debt instrument shall be treated as due under the contract for the sale or exchange.

(3) DEBT INSTRUMENT DEFINED.—For purposes of this subsection, the term "debt instrument" has the meaning given such term by section 1275(a)(1).

[Sec. 483(d)]

(d) EXCEPTIONS AND LIMITATIONS.—

(1) COORDINATION WITH ORIGINAL ISSUE DISCOUNT RULES.—This section shall not apply to any debt instrument for which an issue price is determined under section 1273(b) (other than paragraph (4) thereof) or section 1274.

(2) SALES PRICES OF $3,000 OR LESS.—This section shall not apply to any payment on account of the sale or exchange of property if it can be determined at the time of such sale or exchange that the sales price cannot exceed $3,000.

(3) CARRYING CHARGES.—In the case of the purchaser, the tax treatment of amounts paid on account of the sale or exchange of property shall be made without regard to this section if any such amounts are treated under section 163(b) as if they included interest.

(4) CERTAIN SALES OF PATENTS.—In the case of any transfer described in section 1235(a) (relating to sale or exchange of patents), this section shall not apply to any amount contingent on the productivity, use, or disposition of the property transferred.

[Sec. 483(e)]

(e) MAXIMUM RATE OF INTEREST ON CERTAIN TRANSFERS OF LAND BETWEEN RELATED PARTIES.—

(1) IN GENERAL.—In the case of any qualified sale, the discount rate used in determining the total unstated interest rate under subsection (b) shall not exceed 6 percent, compounded semiannually.

(2) QUALIFIED SALE.—For purposes of this subsection, the term "qualified sale" means any sale or exchange of land by an individual to a member of such individual's family (within the meaning of section 267(c)(4)).

(3) $500,000 LIMITATION.—Paragraph (1) shall not apply to any qualified sale between individuals made during any calendar year to the extent that the sales price for such sale (when added to the aggregate sale price for prior qualified sales between such individuals during the calendar year) exceeds $500,000.

(4) NONRESIDENT ALIEN INDIVIDUALS.—Paragraph (1) shall not apply to any sale or exchange if any party to such sale or exchange is a nonresident alien individual.

[Sec. 483(f)]

(f) REGULATIONS.—The Secretary shall prescribe such regulations as may be necessary or appropriate to carry out the purposes of this section including regulations providing for the application of this section in the case of—

(1) any contract for the sale or exchange of property under which the liability for, or the amount or due date of, a payment cannot be determined at the time of the sale or exchange, or

(2) any change in the liability for, or the amount or due date of, any payment (including interest) under a contract for the sale or exchange of property.

[Sec. 483(g)]

(g) CROSS REFERENCES.—

(1) For treatment of assumptions, see section 1274(c)(4).

(2) For special rules for certain transactions where stated principal amount does not exceed $2,800,000, see section 1274A.

(3) For special rules in the case of the borrower under certain loans for personal use, see section 1275(b).

SUBCHAPTER G—CORPORATIONS USED TO AVOID INCOME TAX ON SHAREHOLDERS

PART I—CORPORATIONS IMPROPERLY ACCUMULATING SURPLUS

[Sec. 531]

SEC. 531. IMPOSITION OF ACCUMULATED EARNINGS TAX.

In addition to other taxes imposed by this chapter, there is hereby imposed for each taxable year on the accumulated taxable income (as defined in section 535) of each corporation described in section 532, an accumulated earnings tax equal to 20 percent of the accumulated taxable income.

[Sec. 532]

SEC. 532. CORPORATIONS SUBJECT TO ACCUMULATED EARNINGS TAX.

[Sec. 532(a)]

(a) GENERAL RULE.—The accumulated earnings tax imposed by section 531 shall apply to every corporation (other than those described in subsection (b)) formed or availed of for the purpose of avoiding the income tax with respect to its shareholders or the shareholders of any other corporation, by permitting earnings and profits to accumulate instead of being divided or distributed.

[Sec. 532(b)]

(b) EXCEPTIONS.—The accumulated earnings tax imposed by section 531 shall not apply to—

(1) a personal holding company (as defined in section 542),

(2) a corporation exempt from tax under subchapter F (section 501 and following), or

(3) a passive foreign investment company (as defined in section 1297).

[Sec. 532(c)]

(c) APPLICATION DETERMINED WITHOUT REGARD TO NUMBER OF SHAREHOLDERS.—The application of this part to a corporation shall be determined without regard to the number of shareholders of such corporation.

[Sec. 533]

SEC. 533. EVIDENCE OF PURPOSE TO AVOID INCOME TAX.

[Sec. 533(a)]

(a) UNREASONABLE ACCUMULATION DETERMINATIVE OF PURPOSE.—For purposes of section 532, the fact that the earnings and profits of a corporation are permitted to accumulate beyond the reasonable needs of the business shall be determinative of the purpose to avoid the income tax with respect to shareholders, unless the corporation by the preponderance of the evidence shall prove to the contrary.

[Sec. 533(b)]

(b) HOLDING OR INVESTMENT COMPANY.—The fact that any corporation is a mere holding or investment company shall be prima facie evidence of the purpose to avoid the income tax with respect to shareholders.

[Sec. 534]

SEC. 534. BURDEN OF PROOF.

[Sec. 534(a)]

(a) GENERAL RULE.—In any proceeding before the Tax Court involving a notice of deficiency based in whole or in part on the allegation that all or any part of the earnings and profits have been permitted to accumulate beyond the reasonable needs of the business, the burden of proof with respect to such allegation shall—

(1) if notification has not been sent in accordance with subsection (b), be on the Secretary, or

(2) if the taxpayer has submitted the statement described in subsection (c), be on the Secretary with respect to the grounds set forth in such statement in accordance with the provisions of such subsection.

[Sec. 534(b)]

(b) NOTIFICATION BY SECRETARY.—Before mailing the notice of deficiency referred to in subsection (a), the Secretary may send by certified mail or registered mail a notification informing the taxpayer that the proposed notice of deficiency includes an amount with respect to the accumulated earnings tax imposed by section 531.

[Sec. 534(c)]

(c) STATEMENT BY TAXPAYER.—Within such time (but not less than 30 days) after the mailing of the notification described in subsection (b) as the Secretary may prescribe by regulations, the taxpayer may submit a statement of the grounds (together with facts sufficient to show the basis thereof) on which the taxpayer relies to establish that all or any part of the earnings and profits have not been permitted to accumulate beyond the reasonable needs of the business.

[Sec. 534(d)]

(d) JEOPARDY ASSESSMENT.—If pursuant to section 6861 (a) a jeopardy assessment is made before the mailing of the notice of deficiency referred to in subsection (a), for purposes of this section such notice of deficiency shall, to the extent that it informs the taxpayer that such deficiency includes the accumulated earnings tax imposed by section 531, constitute the notification described in subsection (b), and in that event the statement described in subsection (c) may be included in the taxpayer's petition to the Tax Court.

[Sec. 535]

SEC. 535. ACCUMULATED TAXABLE INCOME.

[Sec. 535(a)]

(a) DEFINITION.—For purposes of this subtitle, the term "accumulated taxable income" means the taxable income, adjusted in the manner provided in subsection (b), minus the sum of the dividends paid deduction (as defined in section 561) and the accumulated earnings credit (as defined in subsection (c)).

[Sec. 535(b)]

(b) ADJUSTMENTS TO TAXABLE INCOME.—For purposes of subsection (a), taxable income shall be adjusted as follows:

(1) TAXES.—There shall be allowed as a deduction Federal income and excess profits taxes and income, war profits, and excess profits taxes of foreign countries and possessions of the United States (to the extent not allowable as a deduction under section 275(a)(4)), accrued during the taxable year or deemed to be paid by a domestic corporation under section 960 for the taxable year, but not including the accumulated earnings tax imposed by section 531 or the personal holding company tax imposed by section 541.

(2) CHARITABLE CONTRIBUTIONS.—The deduction for charitable contributions provided under section 170 shall be allowed without regard to section 170(b)(2).

(3) SPECIAL DEDUCTIONS DISALLOWED.—The special deductions for corporations provided in part VIII (except section 248) of subchapter B (section 241 and following, relating to the deduction for dividends received by corporations, etc.) shall not be allowed.

(4) NET OPERATING LOSS.—The net operating loss deduction provided in section 172 shall not be allowed.

(5) CAPITAL LOSSES.—

(A) IN GENERAL.—Except as provided in subparagraph (B), there shall be allowed as a deduction an amount equal to the net capital loss for the taxable year (determined without regard to paragraph (7)(A)).

(B) RECAPTURE OF PREVIOUS DEDUCTIONS FOR CAPITAL GAINS.—The aggregate amount allowable as a deduction under subparagraph (A) for any taxable year shall be reduced by the lesser of—

(i) the nonrecaptured capital gains deductions, or

(ii) the amount of the accumulated earnings and profits of the corporation as of the close of the preceding taxable year.

(C) NONRECAPTURED CAPITAL GAINS DEDUCTIONS.—For purposes of subparagraph (B), the term "nonrecaptured capital gains deductions" means the excess of—

(i) the aggregate amount allowable as a deduction under paragraph (6) for preceding taxable years beginning after July 18, 1984, over

(ii) the aggregate of the reductions under subparagraph (B) for preceding taxable years.

(6) NET CAPITAL GAINS.—

(A) IN GENERAL.—There shall be allowed as a deduction—

(i) the net capital gain for the taxable year (determined with the application of paragraph (7)), reduced by

(ii) the taxes attributable to such net capital gain.

(B) ATTRIBUTABLE TAXES.—For purposes of subparagraph (A), the taxes attributable to the net capital gain shall be an amount equal to the difference between—

(i) the taxes imposed by this subtitle (except the tax imposed by this part) for the taxable year, and

(ii) such taxes computed for such year without including in taxable income the net capital gain for the taxable year (determined without the application of paragraph (7)).

(7) CAPITAL LOSS CARRYOVERS.—

(A) UNLIMITED CARRYFORWARD.—The net capital loss for any taxable year shall be treated as a short-term capital loss in the next taxable year.

(B) SECTION 1212 INAPPLICABLE.—No allowance shall be made for the capital loss carryback or carryforward provided in section 1212.

(8) SPECIAL RULES FOR MERE HOLDING OR INVESTMENT COMPANIES.—In the case of a mere holding or investment company—

(A) CAPITAL LOSS DEDUCTION, ETC., NOT ALLOWED.—Paragraphs (5) and (7)(A) shall not apply.

(B) DEDUCTION FOR CERTAIN OFFSETS.—There shall be allowed as a deduction the net short-term capital gain for the taxable year to the extent such gain does not exceed the amount of any capital loss carryover to such taxable year under section 1212 (determined without regard to paragraph (7)(B)).

(C) EARNINGS AND PROFITS.—For purposes of subchapter C, the accumulated earnings and profits at any time shall not be less than they would be if this subsection had applied to the computation of earnings and profits for all taxable years beginning after July 18, 1984.

(9) SPECIAL RULE FOR CAPITAL GAINS AND LOSSES OF FOREIGN CORPORATIONS.—In the case of a foreign corporation, paragraph (6) shall be applied by taking into account only gains and losses which are effectively connected with the conduct of a trade or business within the United States and are not exempt from tax under treaty.

(10) CONTROLLED FOREIGN CORPORATIONS.—There shall be allowed as a deduction the amount of the corporation's income for the taxable year which is included in the gross income of a United States shareholder under section 951(a). In the case of any corporation the accumulated taxable income of which would (but for this sentence) be determined without allowance of any deductions, the deduction under this paragraph shall be allowed and shall be appropriately adjusted to take into account any deductions which reduced such inclusion.

[Sec. 535(c)]

(c) ACCUMULATED EARNINGS CREDIT.—

(1) GENERAL RULE.—For purposes of subsection (a), in the case of a corporation other than a mere holding or investment company the accumulated earnings credit is (A) an amount equal to such part of the earnings and profits for the taxable year as are retained for the reasonable needs of the business, minus (B) the deduction allowed by subsection (b)(6). For purposes of this paragraph, the amount of the earnings and profits for the taxable year which are retained is the amount by which the earnings and profits for the taxable year exceed the dividends paid deduction (as defined in section 561) for such year.

(2) MINIMUM CREDIT.—

(A) IN GENERAL.—The credit allowable under paragraph (1) shall in no case be less than the amount by which $250,000 exceeds the accumulated earnings and profits of the corporation at the close of the preceding taxable year.

(B) CERTAIN SERVICE CORPORATIONS.—In the case of a corporation the principal function of which is the performance of services in the field of health, law, engineering, architecture, accounting, actuarial science, performing arts, or consulting, subparagraph (A) shall be applied by substituting "$150,000" for "$250,000".

(3) HOLDING AND INVESTMENT COMPANIES.—In the case of a corporation which is a mere holding or investment company, the accumulated earnings credit is the amount (if any) by which $250,000 exceeds the accumulated earnings and profits of the corporation at the close of the preceding taxable year.

(4) ACCUMULATED EARNINGS AND PROFITS.—For purposes of paragraphs (2) and (3), the accumulated earnings and profits at the close of the preceding taxable year shall be reduced by the dividends which under section 563(a) (relating to dividends paid after the close of the taxable year) are considered as paid during such taxable year.

(5) CROSS REFERENCE.—For limitation on credit provided in paragraph (2) or (3) in the case of certain controlled corporations, see section 1561.

[Sec. 535(d)]

(d) INCOME DISTRIBUTED TO UNITED STATES-OWNED FOREIGN CORPORATION RETAINS UNITED STATES CONNECTION.—

(1) IN GENERAL.—For purposes of this part, if 10 percent or more of the earnings and profits of any foreign corporation for any taxable year—

(A) is derived from sources within the United States, or

(B) is effectively connected with the conduct of a trade or business within the United States,

any distribution out of such earnings and profits (and any interest payment) received (directly or through 1 or more other entities) by a United States-owned foreign corporation shall be treated as derived by such corporation from sources within the United States.

(2) UNITED STATES-OWNED FOREIGN CORPORATION.—The term "United States-owned foreign corporation" has the meaning given to such term by section 904(h)(6).

[Sec. 536]

SEC. 536. INCOME NOT PLACED ON ANNUAL BASIS.

Section 443(b) (relating to computation of tax on change of annual accounting period) shall not apply in the computation of the accumulated earnings tax imposed by section 531.

[Sec. 537]

SEC. 537. REASONABLE NEEDS OF THE BUSINESS.

[Sec. 537(a)]

(a) GENERAL RULE.—For purposes of this part, the term "reasonable needs of the business" includes—

(1) the reasonably anticipated needs of the business,

(2) the section 303 redemption needs of the business, and

(3) the excess business holdings redemption needs of the business.

[Sec. 537(b)]

(b) SPECIAL RULES.—For purposes of subsection (a)—

(1) SECTION 303 REDEMPTION NEEDS.—The term "section 303 redemption needs" means, with respect to the taxable year of the corporation in which a shareholder of the corporation died or any taxable year thereafter, the amount needed (or reasonably anticipated to be needed) to make a redemption of stock included in the gross estate of the decedent (but not in excess of the maximum amount of stock to which section 303(a) may apply).

(2) EXCESS BUSINESS HOLDINGS REDEMPTION NEEDS.—The term "excess business holdings redemption needs" means the amount needed (or reasonably anticipated to be needed) to redeem from a private foundation stock which—

(A) such foundation held on May 26, 1969 (or which was received by such foundation pursuant to a will or irrevocable trust to which section 4943(c)(5) applies), and

(B) constituted excess business holdings on May 26, 1969, or would have constituted excess business holdings as of such date if there were taken into account (i) stock received pursuant to a will or trust described in subparagraph (A), and (ii) the reduction in the total outstanding stock of the corporation which would have resulted solely from the redemption of stock held by the private foundation.

(3) OBLIGATIONS INCURRED TO MAKE REDEMPTIONS.—In applying paragraphs (1) and (2), the discharge of any obligation incurred to make a redemption described in such paragraphs shall be treated as the making of such redemption.

(4) PRODUCT LIABILITY LOSS RESERVES.—The accumulation of reasonable amounts for the payment of reasonably anticipated product liability losses (as defined in section 172(f)) (as in effect before the date of enactment of the Tax Cuts and Jobs Act), as determined under regulations prescribed by the Secretary, shall be treated as accumulated for the reasonably anticipated needs of the business.

(5) NO INFERENCE AS TO PRIOR TAXABLE YEARS.—The application of this part to any taxable year before the first taxable year specified in paragraph (1) shall be made without regard to the fact that distributions in redemption coming within the terms of such paragraphs were subsequently made.

PART II—PERSONAL HOLDING COMPANIES

[Sec. 541]

SEC. 541. IMPOSITION OF PERSONAL HOLDING COMPANY TAX.

In addition to other taxes imposed by this chapter, there is hereby imposed for each taxable year on the undistributed personal holding company income (as defined in section 545) of every personal holding company (as defined in section 542) a personal holding company tax equal to 20 percent of the undistributed personal holding company income.

[Sec. 542]

SEC. 542. DEFINITION OF PERSONAL HOLDING COMPANY.

[Sec. 542(a)]

(a) GENERAL RULE.—For purposes of this subtitle, the term "personal holding company" means any corporation (other than a corporation described in subsection (c)) if—

(1) ADJUSTED ORDINARY GROSS INCOME REQUIREMENT.—At least 60 percent of its adjusted ordinary gross income (as defined in section 543(b)(2)) for the taxable year is personal holding company income (as defined in section 543(a)), and

(2) STOCK OWNERSHIP REQUIREMENT.—At any time during the last half of the taxable year more than 50 percent in value of its outstanding stock is owned, directly or indirectly, by or for not more than 5 individuals. For purposes of this paragraph, an organization described in section 401(a), 501(c)(17), or 509(a) or a portion of a trust permanently set aside or to be used exclusively for the purposes described in section 642(c) or a corresponding provision of a prior income tax law shall be considered an individual.

[Sec. 542(b)]

(b) CORPORATIONS FILING CONSOLIDATED RETURNS.—

(1) GENERAL RULE.—In the case of an affiliated group of corporations filing or required to file a consolidated return under section 1501 for any taxable year, the adjusted ordinary gross income requirement of subsection (a) (1) of this section shall, except as provided in paragraphs (2)

and (3), be applied for such year with respect to the consolidated adjusted ordinary gross income and the consolidated personal holding company income of the affiliated group. No member of such an affiliated group shall be considered to meet such adjusted ordinary gross income requirement unless the affiliated group meets such requirement.

(2) INELIGIBLE AFFILIATED GROUP.—Paragraph (1) shall not apply to an affiliated group of corporations if—

(A) any member of the affiliated group of corporations (including the common parent corporation) derived 10 percent or more of its adjusted ordinary gross income for the taxable year from sources outside the affiliated group, and

(B) 80 percent or more of the amount described in subparagraph (A) consists of personal holding company income (as defined in section 543).

For purposes of this paragraph, section 543 shall be applied as if the amount described in subparagraph (A) were the adjusted ordinary gross income of the corporation.

(3) EXCLUDED CORPORATIONS.—Paragraph (1) shall not apply to an affiliated group of corporations if any member of the affiliated group (including the common parent corporation) is a corporation excluded from the definition of personal holding company under subsection (c).

(4) CERTAIN DIVIDEND INCOME RECEIVED BY A COMMON PARENT.—In applying paragraph (2) (A) and (B), personal holding company income and adjusted ordinary gross income shall not include dividends received by a common parent corporation from another corporation if—

(A) the common parent corporation owns, directly or indirectly, more than 50 percent of the outstanding voting stock of such other corporation, and

(B) such other corporation is not a personal holding company for the taxable year in which the dividends are paid.

(5) CERTAIN DIVIDEND INCOME RECEIVED FROM A NONINCLUDIBLE LIFE INSURANCE COMPANY.—In the case of an affiliated group of corporations filing or required to file a consolidated return under section 1501 for any taxable year, there shall be excluded from consolidated personal holding company income and consolidated adjusted ordinary gross income for purposes of this part dividends received by a member of the affiliated group from a life insurance company taxable under section 801 that is not a member of the affiliated group solely by reason of the application of paragraph (2) of subsection (b) of section 1504.

[Sec. 542(c)]

(c) EXCEPTIONS.—The term "personal holding company" as defined in subsection (a) does not include—

(1) a corporation exempt from tax under subchapter F (sec. 501 and following);

(2) a bank as defined in section 581, or a domestic building and loan association within the meaning of section 7701(a)(19);

(3) a life insurance company;

(4) a surety company;

(5) a foreign corporation;

(6) a lending or finance company if—

(A) 60 percent or more of its ordinary gross income (as defined in section 543(b)(1)) is derived directly from the active and regular conduct of a lending or finance business;

(B) the personal holding company income for the taxable year (computed without regard to income described in subsection (d)(3) and income derived directly from the active and regular conduct of a lending or finance business, and computed by including as personal holding company income the entire amount of the gross income from rents, royalties, produced film rents, and compensation for use of corporate property by shareholders) is not more than 20 percent of the ordinary gross income;

(C) the sum of the deductions which are directly allocable to the active and regular conduct of its lending or finance business equals or exceeds the sum of—

(i) 15 percent of so much of the ordinary gross income derived therefrom as does not exceed $500,000, plus

(ii) 5 percent of so much of the ordinary gross income derived therefrom as exceeds $500,000; and

(D) the loans to a person who is a shareholder in such company during the taxable year by or for whom 10 percent or more in value of its outstanding stock is owned directly or indirectly (including, in the case of an individual, stock owned by members of his family as defined in section 544(a)(2)), outstanding at any time during such year do not exceed $5,000 in principal amount;

(7) a small business investment company which is licensed by the Small Business Administration and operating under the Small Business Investment Act of 1958 (15 U.S.C. 661 and following) and which is actively engaged in the business of providing funds to small business concerns under that Act. This paragraph shall not apply if any shareholder of the small business investment company owns at any time during the taxable year directly or indirectly (including, in the case of an individual, ownership by the members of his family as defined in section 544(a)(2)) a 5 per centum or more proprietary interest in a small business concern to which funds are provided by the investment company or 5 per centum or more in value of the outstanding stock of such concern; and

(8) a corporation which is subject to the jurisdiction of the court in a title 11 or similar case (within the meaning of section 368(a)(3)(A)) unless a major purpose of instituting or continuing such case is the avoidance of the tax imposed by section 541.

[Sec. 542(d)]

(d) SPECIAL RULES FOR APPLYING SUBSECTION (c)(6).—

(1) LENDING OR FINANCE BUSINESS DEFINED.—

(A) IN GENERAL.—Except as provided in subparagraph (B), for purposes of subsection (c)(6), the term "lending or finance business" means a business of—

(i) making loans,

(ii) purchasing or discounting accounts receivable, notes, or installment obligations,

(iii) rendering services or making facilities available in connection with activities described in clauses (i) and (ii) carried on by the corporation rendering services or making facilities available, or

(iv) rendering services or making facilities available to another corporation which is engaged in the lending or finance business (within the meaning of this paragraph), if such services or facilities are related to the lending or finance business (within such meaning) of such other corporation and such other corporation and the corporation rendering services or making facilities available are members of the same affiliated group (as defined in section 1504).

(B) EXCEPTIONS.—For purposes of subparagraph (A), the term "lending or finance business" does not include the business of—

(i) making loans, or purchasing or discounting accounts receivable, notes, or installment obligations, if (at the time of the loan, purchase, or discount) the remaining maturity exceeds 144 months; unless—

(I) the loans, notes, or installment obligations are evidenced or secured by contracts of conditional sale, chattel mortgages, or chattel lease agreements arising out of the sale of goods or services in the course of the borrower's or transferor's trade or business, or

(II) the loans, notes, or installment obligations are made or acquired by the taxpayer and meet the requirements of subparagraph (C), or

(ii) making loans evidenced by, or purchasing, certificates of indebtedness issued in a series, under a trust indenture, and in registered form or with interest coupons attached.

For purposes of clause (i), the remaining maturity shall be treated as including any period for which there may be a renewal or extension under the terms of an option exercisable by the borrower.

(C) INDEFINITE MATURITY CREDIT TRANSACTIONS.—For purposes of subparagraph (B)(i), a loan, note, or installment obligation meets the requirements of this subparagraph if it is made under an agreement—

(i) under which the creditor agrees to make loans or advances (not in excess of an agreed upon maximum amount) from time to time to or for the account of the debtor upon request, and

(ii) under which the debtor may repay the loan or advance in full or in installments.

(2) BUSINESS DEDUCTIONS.—For purposes of subsection (c)(6)(C), the deductions which may be taken into account shall include only—

(A) deductions which are allowable only by reason of section 162 or section 404, except there shall not be included any such deduction in respect of compensation for personal services rendered by shareholders (including members of the shareholder's family as described in section 544(a)(2)), and

(B) deductions allowable under section 167, and deductions allowable under section 164 for real property taxes, but in either case only to the extent that the property with respect to which such deductions are allowable is used directly in the active and regular conduct of the lending or finance business.

(3) INCOME RECEIVED FROM CERTAIN AFFILIATED CORPORATIONS.—For purposes of subsection (c)(6)(B), in the case of a lending or finance company which meets the requirements of subsection (c)(6)(A), there shall not be treated as personal holding company income the lawful income received from a corporation which meets the requirements of subsection (c)(6) and which is a member of the same affiliated group (as defined in section 1504) of which such company is a member.

[Sec. 543]

SEC. 543. PERSONAL HOLDING COMPANY INCOME.

[Sec. 543(a)]

(a) GENERAL RULE.—For purposes of this subtitle, the term "personal holding company income" means the portion of the adjusted ordinary gross income which consists of:

(1) DIVIDENDS, ETC.—Dividends, interest, royalties (other than mineral, oil, or gas royalties or copyright royalties), and annuities. This paragraph shall not apply to—

(A) interest constituting rent (as defined in subsection (b)(3)),

(B) interest on amounts set aside in a reserve fund under chapter 533 or 535 of title 46, United States Code,

(C) dividends received by a United States shareholder (as defined in section 951(b)) from a controlled foreign corporation (as defined in section 957(a)),

(D) active business computer software royalties (within the meaning of subsection (d)), and

(E) interest received by a broker or dealer (within the meaning of section 3(a)(4) or (5) of the Securities and Exchange Act of 1934) in connection with—

(i) any securities or money market instruments held as property described in section 1221(a)(1),

(ii) margin accounts, or

(iii) any financing for a customer secured by securities or money market instruments.

(2) RENTS.—The adjusted income from rents; except that such adjusted income shall not be included if—

(A) such adjusted income constitutes 50 percent or more of the adjusted ordinary gross income, and

(B) the sum of—

(i) the dividends paid during the taxable year (determined under section 562),

(ii) the dividends considered as paid on the last day of the taxable year under section 563(c) (as limited by the second sentence of section 563(b)), and

(iii) the consent dividends for the taxable year (determined under section 565),

equals or exceeds the amount, if any, by which the personal holding company income for the taxable year (computed without regard to this paragraph and paragraph (6), and computed by including as personal holding company income copyright royalties and the adjusted income from mineral, oil, and gas royalties) exceeds 10 percent of the ordinary gross income.

(3) MINERAL, OIL, AND GAS ROYALTIES.—The adjusted income from mineral, oil, and gas royalties; except that such adjusted income shall not be included if—

(A) such adjusted income constitutes 50 percent or more of the adjusted ordinary gross income,

(B) the personal holding company income for the taxable year (computed without regard to this paragraph, and computed by including as personal holding company income copyright royalties and the adjusted income from rents) is not more than 10 percent of the ordinary gross income, and

(C) the sum of the deductions which are allowable under section 162 (relating to trade or business expenses) other than—

(i) deductions for compensation for personal services rendered by the shareholders, and

(ii) deductions which are specifically allowable under sections other than section 162,

equals or exceeds 15 percent of the adjusted ordinary gross income.

(4) COPYRIGHT ROYALTIES.—Copyright royalties; except that copyright royalties shall not be included if—

(A) such royalties (exclusive of royalties received for the use of, or right to use, copyrights or interests in copyrights on works created in whole, or in part, by any shareholder) constitute 50 percent or more of the ordinary gross income,

(B) the personal holding company income for the taxable year computed—

(i) without regard to copyright royalties, other than royalties received for the use of, or right to use, copyrights or interests in copyrights in works created in whole, or in part, by any shareholder owning more than 10 percent of the total outstanding capital stock of the corporation,

(ii) without regard to dividends from any corporation in which the taxpayer owns at least 50 percent of all classes of stock entitled to vote and at least 50 percent of the total value of all classes of stock and which corporation meets the requirements of this subparagraph and subparagraphs (A) and (C), and

(iii) by including as personal holding company income the adjusted income from rents and the adjusted income from mineral, oil, and gas royalties,

is not more than 10 percent of the ordinary gross income, and

(C) the sum of the deductions which are properly allocable to such royalties and which are allowable under section 162, other than—

(i) deductions for compensation for personal services rendered by the shareholders,

(ii) deductions for royalties paid or accrued, and

(iii) deductions which are specifically allowable under sections other than section 162, equals or exceeds 25 percent of the amount by which the ordinary gross income exceeds the sum of the royalties paid or accrued and the amounts allowable as deductions under section 167 (relating to depreciation) with respect to copyright royalties.

For purposes of this subsection, the term "copyright royalties" means compensation, however designated, for the use of, or the right to use, copyrights in works protected by copyright issued under title 17 of the United States Code and to which copyright protection is also extended by the laws of any country other than the United States of America by virtue of any international treaty, convention, or agreement, or interests in any such copyrighted works, and includes payments from any person for performing rights in any such copyrighted work and payments (other than produced film rents as defined in paragraph (5)(B)) received for the use of, or right to use, films. For purposes of this paragraph, the term "shareholder" shall include any person who owns stock within the meaning of section 544. This paragraph shall not apply to active business computer software royalties.

(5) PRODUCED FILM RENTS.—

(A) Produced film rents; except that such rents shall not be included if such rents constitute 50 percent or more of the ordinary gross income.

(B) For purposes of this section, the term "produced film rents" means payments received with respect to an interest in a film for the use of, or right to use, such film, but only to the extent that such interest was acquired before substantial completion of production of such film. In the case of a producer who actively participates in the production of the film, such term includes an interest in the proceeds or profits from the film, but only to the extent such interest is attributable to such active participation.

(6) USE OF CORPORATE PROPERTY BY SHAREHOLDER.—

(A) Amounts received as compensation (however designated and from whomever received) for the use of, or the right to use, tangible property of the corporation in any case where, at any time during the taxable year, 25 percent or more in value of the outstanding stock of the corporation is owned, directly or indirectly, by or for an individual entitled to the use of the property (whether such right is obtained directly from the corporation or by means of a sublease or other arrangement).

(B) Subparagraph (A) shall apply only to a corporation which has personal holding company income in excess of 10 percent of its ordinary gross income.

(C) For purposes of the limitation in subparagraph (B), personal holding company income shall be computed—

(i) without regard to subparagraph (A) or paragraph (2),

(ii) by excluding amounts received as compensation for the use of (or right to use) intangible property (other than mineral, oil, or gas royalties or copyright royalties) if a substantial part of the tangible property used in connection with such intangible property is owned by the corporation and all such tangible and intangible property is used in the active conduct of a trade or business by an individual or individuals described in subparagraph (A), and

(iii) by including copyright royalties and adjusted income from mineral, oil, and gas royalties.

(7) PERSONAL SERVICE CONTRACTS.—

(A) Amounts received under a contract under which the corporation is to furnish personal services; if some person other than the corporation has the right to designate (by name or by description) the individual who is to perform the services, or if the individual who is to perform the services is designated (by name or by description) in the contract; and

(B) amounts received from the sale or other disposition of such a contract.

This paragraph shall apply with respect to amounts received for services under a particular contract only if at some time during the taxable year 25 percent or more in value of the outstanding stock of the corporation is owned, directly or indirectly, by or for the individual who has performed, is to perform, or may be designated (by name or by description) as the one to perform, such services.

(8) ESTATES AND TRUSTS.—Amounts includible in computing the taxable income of the corporation under part I of subchapter J (sec. 641 and following, relating to estates, trusts, and beneficiaries).

[Sec. 543(b)]

(b) DEFINITIONS.—For purposes of this part—

(1) ORDINARY GROSS INCOME.—The term "ordinary gross income" means the gross income determined by excluding—

(A) all gains from the sale or other disposition of capital assets, and

(B) all gains (other than those referred to in subparagraph (A)) from the sale or other disposition of property described in section 1231(b).

(2) ADJUSTED ORDINARY GROSS INCOME.—The term "adjusted ordinary gross income" means the ordinary gross income adjusted as follows:

(A) RENTS.—From the gross income from rents (as defined in the second sentence of paragraph (3) of this subsection) subtract the amount allowable as deductions for—

(i) exhaustion, wear and tear, obsolescence, and amortization of property other than tangible personal property which is not customarily retained by any one lessee for more than three years,

(ii) property taxes,

(iii) interest, and

(iv) rent,

to the extent allocable, under regulations prescribed by the Secretary, to such gross income from rents. The amount subtracted under this subparagraph shall not exceed such gross income from rents.

(B) MINERAL ROYALTIES, ETC.—From the gross income from mineral, oil, and gas royalties described in paragraph (4), and from the gross income from working interests in an oil or gas well, subtract the amount allowable as deductions for—

(i) exhaustion, wear and tear, obsolescence, amortization, and depletion,

(ii) property and severance taxes,

(iii) interest, and

(iv) rent,

to the extent allocable, under regulations prescribed by the Secretary, to such gross income from royalties or such gross income from working interests in oil or gas wells. The amount subtracted under this subparagraph with respect to royalties shall not exceed the gross income from such royalties, and the amount subtracted under this subparagraph with respect to working interests shall not exceed the gross income from such working interests.

(C) INTEREST.—There shall be excluded—

(i) interest received on a direct obligation of the United States held for sale to customers in the ordinary course of trade or business by a regular dealer who is making a primary market in such obligations, and

(ii) interest on a condemnation award, a judgment, and a tax refund.

(D) CERTAIN EXCLUDED RENTS.—From the gross income consisting of compensation described in subparagraph (D) of paragraph (3) subtract the amount allowable as deductions for the items described in clauses (i), (ii), (iii), and (iv) of subparagraph (A) to the extent allocable, under regulations prescribed by the Secretary, to such gross income. The amount subtracted under this subparagraph shall not exceed such gross income.

(3) ADJUSTED INCOME FROM RENTS.—The term "adjusted income from rents" means the gross income from rents, reduced by the amount subtracted under paragraph (2)(A) of this subsection. For purposes of the preceding sentence, the term "rents" means compensation, however designated, for the use of, or right to use, property, and the interest on debts owed to the corporation, to the extent such debts represent the price for which real property held primarily for sale to customers in the ordinary course of its trade or business was sold or exchanged by the corporation; but such term does not include—

(A) amounts constituting personal holding company income under subsection (a)(6),

(B) copyright royalties (as defined in subsection (a)(4)),

(C) produced film rents (as defined in subsection (a)(5)(B)),

(D) compensation, however designated, for the use of, or the right to use, any tangible personal property manufactured or produced by the taxpayer, if during the taxable year the taxpayer is engaged in substantial manufacturing or production of tangible personal property of the same type, or

(E) active business computer software royalties (as defined in subsection (d)).

(4) ADJUSTED INCOME FROM MINERAL, OIL, AND GAS ROYALTIES.—The term "adjusted income from mineral, oil, and gas royalties" means the gross income from mineral, oil, and gas royalties (including production payments and overriding royalties), reduced by the amount subtracted under paragraph (2)(B) of this subsection in respect of such royalties.

[Sec. 543(c)]

(c) GROSS INCOME OF INSURANCE COMPANIES OTHER THAN LIFE INSURANCE COMPANY.—In the case of an insurance company other than a life insurance company, the term "gross income" as used in this part means the gross income, as defined in section 832(b)(1), increased by the amount of losses incurred, as defined in section 832(b)(5), and the amount of expenses incurred, as defined in section 832(b)(6), and decreased by the amount deductible under section 832(c)(7) (relating to tax-free interest).

[Sec. 543(d)]

(d) ACTIVE BUSINESS COMPUTER SOFTWARE ROYALTIES.—

(1) IN GENERAL.—For purposes of this section, the term "active business computer software royalties" means any royalties—

(A) received by any corporation during the taxable year in connection with the licensing of computer software, and

(B) with respect to which the requirements of paragraphs (2), (3), (4), and (5) are met.

(2) ROYALTIES MUST BE RECEIVED BY CORPORATION ACTIVELY ENGAGED IN COMPUTER SOFTWARE BUSINESS.—The requirements of this paragraph are met if the royalties described in paragraph (1)—

(A) are received by a corporation engaged in the active conduct of the trade or business of developing, manufacturing, or producing computer software, and

(B) are attributable to computer software which—

(i) is developed, manufactured, or produced by such corporation (or its predecessor) in connection with the trade or business described in subparagraph (A), or

(ii) is directly related to such trade or business.

(3) ROYALTIES MUST CONSTITUTE AT LEAST 50 PERCENT OF INCOME.—The requirements of this paragraph are met if the royalties described in paragraph (1) constitute at least 50 percent of the ordinary gross income of the corporation for the taxable year.

(4) DEDUCTIONS UNDER SECTIONS 162 AND 174 RELATING TO ROYALTIES MUST EQUAL OR EXCEED 25 PERCENT OF ORDINARY GROSS INCOME.—

(A) IN GENERAL.—The requirements of this paragraph are met if—

(i) the sum of the deductions allowable to the corporation under sections 162, 174, and 195 for the taxable year which are properly allocable to the trade or business described in paragraph (2) equals or exceeds 25 percent of the ordinary gross income of such corporation for such taxable year, or

(ii) the average of such deductions for the 5-taxable year period ending with such taxable year equals or exceeds 25 percent of the average ordinary gross income of such corporation for such period.

If a corporation has not been in existence during the 5-taxable year period described in clause (ii), then the period of existence of such corporation shall be substituted for such 5-taxable year period.

(B) DEDUCTIONS ALLOWABLE UNDER SECTION 162.—For purposes of subparagraph (A), a deduction shall not be treated as allowable under section 162 if it is specifically allowable under another section.

(C) LIMITATION ON ALLOWABLE DEDUCTIONS.—For purposes of subparagraph (A), no deduction shall be taken into account with respect to compensation for personal services rendered by the 5 individual shareholders holding the largest percentage (by value) of the outstanding stock of the corporation. For purposes of the preceding sentence—

(i) individuals holding less than 5 percent (by value) of the stock of such corporation shall not be taken into account, and

(ii) stock deemed to be owned by a shareholder solely by attribution from a partner under section 544(a)(2) shall be disregarded.

(5) DIVIDENDS MUST EQUAL OR EXCEED EXCESS OF PERSONAL HOLDING COMPANY INCOME OVER 10 PERCENT OF ORDINARY GROSS INCOME.—

(A) IN GENERAL.—The requirements of this paragraph are met if the sum of—

(i) the dividends paid during the taxable year (determined under section 562),

(ii) the dividends considered as paid on the last day of the taxable year under section 563(c) (as limited by the second sentence of section 563(b)), and

(iii) the consent dividends for the taxable year (determined under section 565),

equals or exceeds the amount, if any, by which the personal holding company income for the taxable year exceeds 10 percent of the ordinary gross income of such corporation for such taxable year.

(B) COMPUTATION OF PERSONAL HOLDING COMPANY INCOME.—For purposes of this paragraph, personal holding company income shall be computed—

(i) without regard to amounts described in subsection (a)(1)(C),

(ii) without regard to interest income during any taxable year—

(I) which is in the 5-taxable year period beginning with the later of the 1st taxable year of the corporation or the 1st taxable year in which the corporation conducted the trade or business described in paragraph (2)(A), and

(II) during which the corporation meets the requirements of paragraphs (2), (3), and (4), and

(iii) by including adjusted income from rents and adjusted income from mineral, oil, and gas royalties (within the meaning of paragraphs (2) and (3) of subsection (a)).

(6) SPECIAL RULES FOR AFFILIATED GROUP MEMBERS.—

(A) IN GENERAL.—In any case in which—

(i) the taxpayer receives royalties in connection with the licensing of computer software, and

(ii) another corporation which is a member of the same affiliated group as the taxpayer meets the requirements of paragraphs (2), (3), (4), and (5) with respect to such computer software,

the taxpayer shall be treated as having met such requirements.

(B) AFFILIATED GROUP.—For purposes of this paragraph, the term "affiliated group" has the meaning given such term by section 1504(a).

[Sec. 544]

SEC. 544. RULES FOR DETERMINING STOCK OWNERSHIP.

[Sec. 544(a)]

(a) CONSTRUCTIVE OWNERSHIP.—For purposes of determining whether a corporation is a personal holding company, insofar as such determination is based on stock ownership under section 542(a)(2), section 543(a)(7), section 543(a)(6) or section 543(a)(4)—

(1) STOCK NOT OWNED BY INDIVIDUAL.—Stock owned, directly or indirectly, by or for a corporation, partnership, estate, or trust shall be considered as being owned proportionately by its shareholders, partners, or beneficiaries.

(2) FAMILY AND PARTNERSHIP OWNERSHIP.—An individual shall be considered as owning the stock owned, directly or indirectly, by or for his family or by or for his partner. For purposes of this paragraph, the family of an individual includes only his brothers and sisters (whether by the whole or half blood), spouse, ancestors, and lineal descendants.

(3) OPTIONS.—If any person has an option to acquire stock, such stock shall be considered as owned by such person. For purposes of this paragraph, an option to acquire such an option, and each one of a series of such options, shall be considered as an option to acquire such stock.

(4) APPLICATION OF FAMILY-PARTNERSHIP AND OPTION RULES.—Paragraphs (2) and (3) shall be applied—

(A) for purposes of the stock ownership requirement provided in section 542(a)(2), if, but only if, the effect is to make the corporation a personal holding company;

(B) for purposes of section 543(a)(7) (relating to personal service contracts), of section 543(a)(6) (relating to the use of property by shareholders), or of section 543(a)(4) (relating to copyright royalties), if, but only if, the effect is to make the amounts therein referred to includible under such paragraph as personal holding company income.

(5) CONSTRUCTIVE OWNERSHIP AS ACTUAL OWNERSHIP.—Stock constructively owned by a person by reason of the application of paragraph (1) or (3) shall, for purposes of applying paragraph (1) or (2), be treated as actually owned by such person; but stock constructively owned by an individual by reason of the application of paragraph (2) shall not be treated as owned by him for purposes of again applying such paragraph in order to make another the constructive owner of such stock.

(6) OPTION RULE IN LIEU OF FAMILY AND PARTNERSHIP RULE.—If stock may be considered as owned by an individual under either paragraph (2) or (3) it shall be considered as owned by him under paragraph (3).

[Sec. 544(b)]

(b) CONVERTIBLE SECURITIES.—Outstanding securities convertible into stock (whether or not convertible during the taxable year) shall be considered as outstanding stock—

(1) for purposes of the stock ownership requirement provided in section 542(a)(2), but only if the effect of the inclusion of all such securities is to make the corporation a personal holding company;

(2) for purposes of section 543(a)(7) (relating to personal service contracts), but only if the effect of the inclusion of all such securities is to make the amounts therein referred to includible under such paragraph as personal holding company income;

(3) for purposes of section 543(a)(6) (relating to the use of property by shareholders), but only if the effect of the inclusion of all such securities is to make the amounts therein referred to includible under such paragraph as personal holding company income; and

(4) for purposes of section 543(a)(4) (relating to copyright royalties), but only if the effect of the inclusion of all such securities is to make the amounts therein referred to includible under such paragraph as personal holding company income.

The requirement in paragraphs (1), (2), (3), and (4) that all convertible securities must be included if any are to be included shall be subject to the exception that, where some of the outstanding securities are convertible only after a later date than in the case of others, the class having the earlier conversion date may be included although the others are not included, but no convertible securities shall be included unless all outstanding securities having a prior conversion date are also included.

[Sec. 545]

SEC. 545. UNDISTRIBUTED PERSONAL HOLDING COMPANY INCOME.

[Sec. 545(a)]

(a) DEFINITION.—For purposes of this part, the term "undistributed personal holding company income" means the taxable income of a personal holding company adjusted in the manner provided in subsections (b), (c), and (d), minus the dividends paid deduction as defined in section 561. In the case of a personal holding company which is a foreign corporation, not more than 10 percent in value of the outstanding stock of which is owned (within the meaning of section 958(a)) during the last half of the taxable year by United States persons, the term "undistributed personal holding company income" means the amount determined by multiplying the undistributed personal holding company income (determined without regard to this sentence) by the percentage in value of its outstanding stock which is the greatest percentage in value of its outstanding stock so owned by United States persons on any one day during such period.

[Sec. 545(b)]

(b) ADJUSTMENTS TO TAXABLE INCOME.—For the purposes of subsection (a), the taxable income shall be adjusted as follows:

(1) TAXES.—There shall be allowed as a deduction Federal income and excess profits taxes and income, war profits and excess profits taxes of foreign countries and possessions of the United States (to the extent not allowable as a deduction under section 275(a)(4)), accrued during the taxable year or deemed to be paid by a domestic corporation under section 960 for the taxable year, but not including the accumulated earnings tax imposed by section 531 or the personal holding company tax imposed by section 541.

(2) CHARITABLE CONTRIBUTIONS.—The deduction for charitable contributions provided under section 170 shall be allowed, but in computing such deduction the limitations in section 170(b)(1)(A), (B), (D), and (E) shall apply, and section 170(b)(2) and (d)(1) shall not apply. For purposes of this paragraph, the term "contribution base" when used in section 170(b)(1) means the taxable income computed with the adjustments (other than the 10-percent limitation) provided in section 170(b)(2) and (d)(1) and without deduction of the amount disallowed under paragraph (6) of this subsection.

(3) SPECIAL DEDUCTIONS DISALLOWED.—The special deductions for corporations provided in part VIII (except section 248) of subchapter B (section 241 and following, relating to the deduction for dividends received by corporations, etc.) shall not be allowed.

(4) NET OPERATING LOSS.—The net operating loss deduction provided in section 172 shall not be allowed, but there shall be allowed as a deduction the amount of the net operating loss (as defined in section 172 (c)) for the preceding taxable year computed without the deductions provided in part VIII (except section 248) of subchapter B.

(5) NET CAPITAL GAINS.—There shall be allowed as a deduction the net capital gain for the taxable year, minus the taxes imposed by this subtitle attributable to such excess. The taxes attributable to such net capital gain shall be an amount equal to the difference between—

(A) the taxes imposed by this subtitle (except the tax imposed by this part) for such year, and

(B) such taxes computed for such year without including such net capital gain in taxable income.

(6) EXPENSES AND DEPRECIATION APPLICABLE TO PROPERTY OF THE TAXPAYER.—The aggregate of the deductions allowed under section 162 (relating to trade or business expenses) and section 167 (relating to depreciation), which are allocable to the operation and maintenance of property owned or operated by the corporation, shall be allowed only in an amount equal to the rent or other compensation received for the use of, or the right to use, the property, unless it is established (under regulations prescribed by the Secretary) to the satisfaction of the Secretary—

(A) that the rent or other compensation received was the highest obtainable, or, if none was received, that none was obtainable;

(B) that the property was held in the course of a business carried on bona fide for profit; and

(C) either that there was reasonable expectation that the operation of the property would result in a profit, or that the property was necessary to the conduct of the business.

(7) SPECIAL RULE FOR CAPITAL GAINS AND LOSSES OF FOREIGN CORPORATIONS.—In the case of a foreign corporation, paragraph (5) shall be applied by taking into account only gains and losses which are effectively connected with the conduct of a trade or business within the United States and are not exempt from tax under treaty.

[Sec. 545(c)]

(c) CERTAIN FOREIGN CORPORATIONS.—In the case of a foreign corporation all of the outstanding stock of which during the last half of the taxable year is owned by nonresident alien individuals (whether directly or indirectly through foreign estates, foreign trusts, foreign partnerships, or other foreign corporations), the taxable income for purposes of subsection (a) shall be the income which constitutes personal holding company income under section 543(a)(7), reduced by the deductions attributable to such income, and adjusted, with respect to such income, in the manner provided in subsection (b).

[Sec. 546]

SEC. 546. INCOME NOT PLACED ON ANNUAL BASIS.

Section 443(b) (relating to computation of tax on change of annual accounting period) shall not apply in the computation of the personal holding company tax imposed by section 541.

[Sec. 547]

SEC. 547. DEDUCTION FOR DEFICIENCY DIVIDENDS.

[Sec. 547(a)]

(a) GENERAL RULE.—If a determination (as defined in subsection (c)) with respect to a taxpayer establishes liability for personal holding company tax imposed by section 541 (or by a corresponding provision of a prior income tax law) for any taxable year, a deduction shall be allowed to the taxpayer for the amount of deficiency dividends (as defined in subsection (d)) for the purpose of determining the personal holding company tax for such year, but not for the purpose of determining interest, additional amounts, or assessable penalties computed with respect to such personal holding company tax.

[Sec. 547(b)]

(b) RULES FOR APPLICATION OF SECTION.—

(1) ALLOWANCE OF DEDUCTION.—The deficiency dividend deduction shall be allowed as of the date the claim for the deficiency dividend deduction is filed.

(2) CREDIT OR REFUND.—If the allowance of a deficiency dividend deduction results in an overpayment of personal holding company tax for any taxable year, credit or refund with respect to such overpayment shall be made as if on the date of the determination 2 years remained before the expiration of the period of limitation on the filing of claim for refund for the taxable year to which the overpayment relates. No interest shall be allowed on a credit or refund arising from the application of this section.

[Sec. 547(c)]

(c) DETERMINATION.—For purposes of this section, the term "determination" means—

(1) a decision by the Tax Court or a judgment, decree, or other order by any court of competent jurisdiction, which has become final;

(2) a closing agreement made under section 7121; or

(3) under regulations prescribed by the Secretary, an agreement signed by the Secretary and by, or on behalf of, the taxpayer relating to the liability of such taxpayer for personal holding company tax.

[Sec. 547(d)]

(d) DEFICIENCY DIVIDENDS.—

(1) DEFINITION.—For purposes of this section, the term "deficiency dividends" means the amount of the dividends paid by the corporation on or after the date of the determination and before filing claim under subsection (e), which would have been includible in the computation of the deduction for dividends paid under section 561 for the taxable year with respect to which the liability for personal holding company tax exists, if distributed during such taxable year. No dividends shall be considered as deficiency dividends for purposes of subsection (a) unless distributed within 90 days after the determination.

(2) EFFECT ON DIVIDENDS PAID DEDUCTION.—

(A) FOR TAXABLE YEAR IN WHICH PAID.—Deficiency dividends paid in any taxable year (to the extent of the portion thereof taken into account under subsection (a) in determining personal holding company tax) shall not be included in the amount of dividends paid for such year for purposes of computing the dividends paid deduction for such year and succeeding years.

(B) FOR PRIOR TAXABLE YEAR.—Deficiency dividends paid in any taxable year (to the extent of the portion thereof taken into account under subsection (a) in determining personal holding company tax) shall not be allowed for purposes of section 563 (b) in the computation of the dividends paid deduction for the taxable year preceding the taxable year in which paid.

[Sec. 547(e)]

(e) CLAIM REQUIRED.—No deficiency dividend deduction shall be allowed under subsection (a) unless (under regulations prescribed by the Secretary) claim therefor is filed within 120 days after the determination.

[Sec. 547(f)]

(f) SUSPENSION OF STATUTE OF LIMITATIONS AND STAY OF COLLECTION.—

(1) SUSPENSION OF RUNNING OF STATUTE.—If the corporation files a claim, as provided in subsection (e), the running of the statute of limitations provided in section 6501 on the making of assessments, and the bringing of distraint or a proceeding in court for collection, in respect of the deficiency and all interest, additional amounts, or assessable penalties, shall be suspended for a period of 2 years after the date of the determination.

(2) STAY OF COLLECTION.—In the case of any deficiency with respect to the tax imposed by section 541 established by a determination under this section—

(A) the collection of the deficiency and all interest, additional amounts, and assessable penalties shall, except in cases of jeopardy, be stayed until the expiration of 120 days after the date of the determination, and

(B) if claim for deficiency dividend deduction is filed under subsection (e), the collection of such part of the deficiency as is not reduced by the deduction for deficiency dividends provided in subsection (a) shall be stayed until the date the claim is disallowed (in whole or in part), and if disallowed in part collection shall be made only with respect to the part disallowed.

No distraint or proceeding in court shall be begun for the collection of an amount the collection of which is stayed under subparagraph (A) or (B) during the period for which the collection of such amount is stayed.

[Sec. 547(g)]

(g) DEDUCTION DENIED IN CASE OF FRAUD, ETC.—No deficiency dividend deduction shall be allowed under subsection (a) if the determination contains a finding that any part of the deficiency is due to fraud with intent to evade tax, or to wilful failure to file an income tax return within the time prescribed by law or prescribed by the Secretary in pursuance of law.

PART IV—DEDUCTION FOR DIVIDENDS PAID

[Sec. 561]

SEC. 561. DEFINITION OF DEDUCTION FOR DIVIDENDS PAID.

[Sec. 561(a)]

(a) GENERAL RULE.—The deduction for dividends paid shall be the sum of—

(1) the dividends paid during the taxable year,

(2) the consent dividends for the taxable year (determined under section 565), and

(3) in the case of a personal holding company, the dividend carryover described in section 564.

[Sec. 561(b)]

(b) SPECIAL RULES APPLICABLE.—In determining the deduction for dividends paid, the rules provided in section 562 (relating to rules applicable in determining dividends eligible for dividends paid deduction) and section 563 (relating to dividends paid after the close of the taxable year) shall be applicable.

[Sec. 562]

SEC. 562. RULES APPLICABLE IN DETERMINING DIVIDENDS ELIGIBLE FOR DIVIDENDS PAID DEDUCTION.

[Sec. 562(a)]

(a) GENERAL RULE.—For purposes of this part, the term "dividend" shall, except as otherwise provided in this section, include only dividends described in section 316 (relating to definition of dividends for purposes of corporate distributions).

[Sec. 562(b)]

(b) DISTRIBUTIONS IN LIQUIDATION.—

(1) Except in the case of a personal holding company described in section 542—

(A) in the case of amounts distributed in liquidation, the part of such distribution which is properly chargeable to earnings and profits accumulated after February 28, 1913, shall be treated as a dividend for purposes of computing the dividends paid deduction, and

(B) in the case of a complete liquidation occurring within 24 months after the adoption of a plan of liquidation, any distribution within such period pursuant to such plan shall, to the extent of the earnings and profits (computed without regard to capital losses) of the corporation for the taxable year in which such distribution is made, be treated as a dividend for purposes of computing the dividends paid deduction.

For purposes of subparagraph (A), a liquidation includes a redemption of stock to which section 302 applies. Except to the extent provided in regulations, the preceding sentence shall not apply in the case of any mere holding or investment company which is not a regulated investment company.

(2) In the case of a complete liquidation of a personal holding company occurring within 24 months after the adoption of a plan of liquidation, the amount of any distribution within such period pursuant to such plan shall be treated as a dividend for purposes of computing the dividends paid deduction, to the extent that such amount is distributed to corporate distributees and represents such corporate distributees' allocable share of the undistributed personal holding company income for the taxable year of such distribution computed without regard to this paragraph and without regard to subparagraph (B) of section 316(b)(2).

[Sec. 562(c)]

(c) PREFERENTIAL DIVIDENDS.—

(1) IN GENERAL.—Except in the case of a publicly offered regulated investment company (as defined in section 67(c)(2)(B)) or a publicly offered REIT, the amount of any distribution shall not be considered as a dividend for purposes of computing the dividends paid deduction, unless such distribution is pro rata, with no preference to any share of stock as compared with other shares of the same class, and with no preference to one class of stock as compared with another class except to the extent that the former is entitled (without reference to waivers of their rights by shareholders) to such preference. In the case of a distribution by a regulated investment company (other than a publicly offered regulated investment company (as so defined)) to a shareholder who made an initial investment of at least $10,000,000 in such company, such distribution shall not be treated as not being pro rata or as being preferential solely by reason of an increase in the distribution by reason of reductions in administrative expenses of the company.

(2) PUBLICLY OFFERED REIT.—For purposes of this subsection, the term "publicly offered REIT" means a real estate investment trust which is required to file annual and periodic reports with the Securities and Exchange Commission under the Securities Exchange Act of 1934.

[Sec. 562(d)]

(d) DISTRIBUTIONS BY A MEMBER OF AN AFFILIATED GROUP.—In the case where a corporation which is a member of an affiliated group of corporations filing or required to file a consolidated return for a taxable year is required to file a separate personal holding company schedule for such taxable year, a distribution by such corporation to another member of the affiliated group shall be considered as a dividend for purposes of computing the dividends paid deduction if such distribution would constitute a dividend under the other provisions of this section to a recipient which is not a member of an affiliated group.

[Sec. 562(e)]

(e) SPECIAL RULES FOR REAL ESTATE INVESTMENT TRUSTS.—

(1) DETERMINATION OF EARNINGS AND PROFITS FOR PURPOSES OF DIVIDENDS PAID DEDUCTION.—In the case of a real estate investment trust, in determining the amount of dividends under section 316 for purposes of computing the dividends paid deduction—

(A) the earnings and profits of such trust for any taxable year (but not its accumulated earnings) shall be increased by the amount of gain (if any) on the sale or exchange of real property which is taken into account in determining the taxable income of such trust for such taxable year (and not otherwise taken into account in determining such earnings and profits), and

(B) section 857(d)(1) shall be applied without regard to subparagraph (B) thereof.

(2) AUTHORITY TO PROVIDE ALTERNATIVE REMEDIES FOR CERTAIN FAILURES.—In the case of a failure of a distribution by a real estate investment trust to comply with the requirements of subsection (c), the Secretary may provide an appropriate remedy to cure such failure in lieu of not considering the distribution to be a dividend for purposes of computing the dividends paid deduction if—

(A) the Secretary determines that such failure is inadvertent or is due to reasonable cause and not due to willful neglect, or

(B) such failure is of a type of failure which the Secretary has identified for purposes of this paragraph as being described in subparagraph (A).

[Sec. 563]

SEC. 563. RULES RELATING TO DIVIDENDS PAID AFTER CLOSE OF TAXABLE YEAR.

[Sec. 563(a)]

(a) ACCUMULATED EARNINGS TAX.—In the determination of the dividends paid deduction for purposes of the accumulated earnings tax imposed by section 531, a dividend paid after the close of any taxable year and on or before the 15th day of the fourth month following the close of such taxable year shall be considered as paid during such taxable year.

[Sec. 563(b)]

(b) PERSONAL HOLDING COMPANY TAX.—In the determination of the dividends paid deduction for purposes of the personal holding company tax imposed by section 541, a dividend paid after the close of any taxable year and on or before the 15th day of the fourth month following the close of such taxable year shall, to the extent the taxpayer elects in its return for the taxable year, be considered as paid during such taxable year. The amount allowed as a dividend by reason of the application of this subsection with respect to any taxable year shall not exceed either—

(1) The undistributed personal holding company income of the corporation for the taxable year, computed without regard to this subsection, or

(2) 20 percent of the sum of the dividends paid during the taxable year, computed without regard to this subsection.

[Sec. 563(c)]

(c) DIVIDENDS CONSIDERED AS PAID ON LAST DAY OF TAXABLE YEAR.—For the purpose of applying section 562(a), with respect to distributions under subsection (a) or (b) of this section, a distribution made after the close of a taxable year and on or before the 15th day of the fourth month following the close of the taxable year shall be considered as made on the last day of such taxable year.

[Sec. 564]

SEC. 564. DIVIDEND CARRYOVER.

[Sec. 564(a)]

(a) GENERAL RULE.—For purposes of computing the dividends paid deduction under section 561, in the case of a personal holding company the dividend carryover for any taxable year shall be the dividend carryover to such taxable year, computed as provided in subsection (b), from the two preceding taxable years.

[Sec. 564(b)]

(b) COMPUTATION OF DIVIDEND CARRYOVER.—The dividend carryover to the taxable year shall be determined as follows:

(1) For each of the 2 preceding taxable years there shall be determined the taxable income computed with the adjustments provided in section 545 (whether or not the taxpayer was a personal holding company for either of such preceding taxable years), and there shall also be determined for each such year the deduction for dividends paid during such year as provided in section 561 (but determined without regard to the dividend carryover to such year).

(2) There shall be determined for each such taxable year whether there is an excess of such taxable income over such deduction for dividends paid or an excess of such deduction for dividends paid over such taxable income, and the amount of each such excess.

(3) If there is an excess of such deductions for dividends paid over such taxable income for the first preceding taxable year, such excess shall be allowed as a dividend carryover to the taxable year.

(4) If there is an excess of such deduction for dividends paid over such taxable income for the second preceding taxable year, such excess shall be reduced by the amount determined in paragraph (5), and the remainder of such excess shall be allowed as a dividend carryover to the taxable year.

(5) The amount of the reduction specified in paragraph (4) shall be the amount of the excess of the taxable income, if any, for the first preceding taxable year over such deduction for dividends paid, if any, for the first preceding taxable year.

[Sec. 565]

SEC. 565. CONSENT DIVIDENDS.

[Sec. 565(a)]

(a) GENERAL RULE.—If any person owns consent stock (as defined in subsection (f)(1)) in a corporation on the last day of the taxable year of such corporation, and such person agrees, in a consent filed with the return of such corporation in accordance with regulations prescribed by the Secretary, to treat as a dividend the amount specified in such consent, the amount so specified shall, except as provided in subsection (b), constitute a consent dividend for purposes of section 561 (relating to the deduction for dividends paid).

[Sec. 565(b)]

(b) LIMITATIONS.—A consent dividend shall not include—

(1) an amount specified in a consent which, if distributed in money, would constitute, or be part of, a distribution which would be disqualified for purposes of the dividends paid deduction under section 562(c) (relating to preferential dividends), or

(2) an amount specified in a consent which would not constitute a dividend (as defined in section 316) if the total amounts specified in consents filed by the corporation had been distributed in money to shareholders on the last day of the taxable year of such corporation.

[Sec. 565(c)]

(c) EFFECT OF CONSENT.—The amount of a consent dividend shall be considered, for purposes of this title—

(1) as distributed in money by the corporation to the shareholder on the last day of the taxable year of the corporation, and

(2) as contributed to the capital of the corporation by the shareholder on such day.

[Sec. 565(d)]

(d) CONSENT DIVIDENDS AND OTHER DISTRIBUTIONS.—If a distribution by a corporation consists in part of money or other property, the entire amount specified in the consents and the amount of such money or other property shall be considered together for purposes of applying this title.

[Sec. 565(e)]

(e) NONRESIDENT ALIENS AND FOREIGN CORPORATIONS.—In the case of a consent dividend which, if paid in money would be subject to the provisions of section 1441 (relating to withholding of tax on nonresident aliens) or section 1442 (relating to withholding of tax on foreign corporations), this section shall not apply unless the consent is accompanied by money, or such other medium of payment as the Secretary may by regulations authorize, in an amount equal to the amount that would be required to be deducted and withheld under sections 1441 or 1442 if the consent dividend had been, on the last day of the taxable year of the corporation, paid to the shareholder in money as a dividend. The amount accompanying the consent shall be credited against the tax imposed by this subtitle on the shareholder.

[Sec. 565(f)]

(f) DEFINITIONS.—

(1) CONSENT STOCK.—Consent stock, for purposes of this section, means the class or classes of stock entitled, after the payment of preferred dividends, to a share in the distribution (other than in complete or partial liquidation) within the taxable year of all the remaining earnings and profits, which share constitutes the same proportion of such distribution regardless of the amount of such distribution.

(2) PREFERRED DIVIDENDS.—Preferred dividends, for purposes of this section, means a distribution (other than in complete or partial liquidation), limited in amount, which must be made on any class of stock before a further distribution (other than in complete or partial liquidation) of earnings and profits may be made within the taxable year.

PART III—SALES AND EXCHANGES

[Sec. 631]

SEC. 631. GAIN OR LOSS IN THE CASE OF TIMBER, COAL, OR DOMESTIC IRON ORE.

* * *

[Sec. 631(b)]

(b) DISPOSAL OF TIMBER.—In the case of the disposal of timber held for more than 1 year before such disposal, by the owner thereof under any form or type of contract by virtue of which such owner either retains an economic interest in such timber or makes an outright sale of such timber, the difference between the amount realized from the disposal of such timber and the adjusted depletion basis thereof, shall be considered as though it were a gain or loss, as the case may be, on the sale of such timber. In determining the gross income, the adjusted gross income, or the taxable income of the lessee, the deductions allowable with respect to rents and royalties shall be determined without regard to the provisions of this subsection. In the case of disposal of timber with a retained economic interest, the date of disposal of such timber shall be deemed to be the date such timber is cut, but if payment is made to the owner under the contract before such timber is cut the owner may elect to treat the date of such payment as the date of disposal of such timber. For purposes of this subsection, the term "owner" means any person who owns an interest in such timber, including a sublessor and a holder of a contract to cut timber.

[Sec. 631(c)]

(c) DISPOSAL OF COAL OR DOMESTIC IRON ORE WITH A RETAINED ECONOMIC INTEREST.—In the case of the disposal of coal (including lignite), or iron ore mined in the United States, held for more than 1 year before such disposal, by the owner thereof under any form of contract by virtue of which such owner retains an economic interest in such coal or iron ore, the difference between the amount realized from the disposal of such coal or iron ore and the adjusted depletion basis thereof plus the deductions disallowed for the taxable year under section 272 shall be considered as though it were a gain or loss, as the case may be, on the sale of such coal or iron ore. If for the taxable year of such gain or loss the maximum rate of tax imposed by this chapter on any net capital gain is less than such maximum rate for ordinary income, such owner shall not be entitled to the allowance for percentage depletion provided in section 613 with respect to such coal or iron ore. This subsection shall not apply to income realized by any owner as a co-adventurer, partner, or principal in the mining of such coal or iron ore, and the word "owner" means any person who owns an economic interest in coal or iron ore in place, including a sublessor. The date of disposal of such coal or iron ore shall be deemed to be the date such coal or iron ore is mined. In determining the gross income, the adjusted gross income, or the taxable income of the lessee, the deductions allowable with respect to rents and royalties shall be determined without regard to the provisions of this subsection. This subsection shall have no application, for purposes of applying subchapter G, relating to corporations used to avoid income tax on shareholders (including the determinations of the amount of the deductions under section 535(b)(6) or section 545(b)(5)). This subsection shall not apply to any disposal of iron ore or coal—

(1) to a person whose relationship to the person disposing of such iron ore or coal would result in the disallowance of losses under section 267 or 707(b), or

(2) to a person owned or controlled directly or indirectly by the same interests which own or control the person disposing of such iron ore or coal.

PART V—CONTINENTAL SHELF AREAS

[Sec. 638]

SEC. 638. CONTINENTAL SHELF AREAS.

For purposes of applying the provisions of this chapter (including sections 861(a)(3) and 862(a)(3) in the case of the performance of personal services) with respect to mines, oil and gas wells, and other natural deposits—

(1) the term "United States" when used in a geographical sense includes the seabed and subsoil of those submarine areas which are adjacent to the territorial waters of the United States and over which the United States has exclusive rights, in accordance with international law, with respect to the exploration and exploitation of natural resources; and

(2) the terms "foreign country" and "possession of the United States" when used in a geographical sense include the seabed and subsoil of those submarine areas which are adjacent to the territorial waters of the foreign country or such possession and over which the foreign country (or the United States in case of such possession) has exclusive rights, in accordance with international law, with respect to the exploration and exploitation of natural resources, but this paragraph shall apply in the case of a foreign country only if it exercises, directly or indirectly, taxing jurisdiction with respect to such exploration or exploitation.

No foreign country shall, by reason of the application of this section, be treated as a country contiguous to the United States.

SUBCHAPTER J—ESTATES, TRUSTS, BENEFICIARIES, AND DECEDENTS

PART I—ESTATES, TRUSTS, AND BENEFICIARIES

Subpart E—Grantors and Others Treated as Substantial Owners

[Sec. 679]

SEC. 679. FOREIGN TRUSTS HAVING ONE OR MORE UNITED STATES BENEFICIARIES.

[Sec. 679(a)]

(a) TRANSFEROR TREATED AS OWNER.—

(1) IN GENERAL.—A United States person who directly or indirectly transfers property to a foreign trust (other than a trust described in section 6048(a)(3)(B)(ii)) shall be treated as the owner for his taxable year of the portion of such trust attributable to such property if for such year there is a United States beneficiary of any portion of such trust.

(2) EXCEPTIONS.—Paragraph (1) shall not apply—

(A) TRANSFERS BY REASON OF DEATH.—To any transfer by reason of the death of the transferor.

(B) TRANSFERS AT FAIR MARKET VALUE.—To any transfer of property to a trust in exchange for consideration of at least the fair market value of the transferred property. For purposes of the preceding sentence, consideration other than cash shall be taken into account at its fair market value.

(3) CERTAIN OBLIGATIONS NOT TAKEN INTO ACCOUNT UNDER FAIR MARKET VALUE EXCEPTION.—

(A) IN GENERAL.—In determining whether paragraph (2)(B) applies to any transfer by a person described in clause (ii) or (iii) of subparagraph (C), there shall not be taken into account—

(i) except as provided in regulations, any obligation of a person described in subparagraph (C), and

(ii) to the extent provided in regulations, any obligation which is guaranteed by a person described in subparagraph (C).

(B) TREATMENT OF PRINCIPAL PAYMENTS ON OBLIGATION.—Principal payments by the trust on any obligation referred to in subparagraph (A) shall be taken into account on and after the date of the payment in determining the portion of the trust attributable to the property transferred.

(C) PERSONS DESCRIBED.—The persons described in this subparagraph are—

(i) the trust,

(ii) any grantor, owner, or beneficiary of the trust, and

(iii) any person who is related (within the meaning of section 643(i)(2)(B)) to any grantor, owner, or beneficiary of the trust.

(4) SPECIAL RULES APPLICABLE TO FOREIGN GRANTOR WHO LATER BECOMES A UNITED STATES PERSON.—

(A) IN GENERAL.—If a nonresident alien individual has a residency starting date within 5 years after directly or indirectly transferring property to a foreign trust, this section and section 6048 shall be applied as if such individual transferred to such trust on the residency starting date an amount equal to the portion of such trust attributable to the property transferred by such individual to such trust in such transfer.

(B) TREATMENT OF UNDISTRIBUTED INCOME.—For purposes of this section, undistributed net income for periods before such individual's residency starting date shall be taken into account in determining the portion of the trust which is attributable to property transferred by such individual to such trust but shall not otherwise be taken into account.

(C) RESIDENCY STARTING DATE.—For purposes of this paragraph, an individual's residency starting date is the residency starting date determined under section 7701(b)(2)(A).

(5) OUTBOUND TRUST MIGRATIONS.—If—

(A) an individual who is a citizen or resident of the United States transferred property to a trust which was not a foreign trust, and

(B) such trust becomes a foreign trust while such individual is alive,

then this section and section 6048 shall be applied as if such individual transferred to such trust on the date such trust becomes a foreign trust an amount equal to the portion of such trust attributable to the property previously transferred by such individual to such trust. A rule similar to the rule of paragraph (4)(B) shall apply for purposes of this paragraph.

[Sec. 679(b)]

(b) TRUSTS ACQUIRING UNITED STATES BENEFICIARIES.—If—

(1) subsection (a) applies to a trust for the transferor's taxable year, and

(2) subsection (a) would have applied to the trust for his immediately preceding taxable year but for the fact that for such preceding taxable year there was no United States beneficiary for any portion of the trust,

then, for purposes of this subtitle, the transferor shall be treated as having income for the taxable year (in addition to his other income for such year) equal to the undistributed net income (at the close of such immediately preceding taxable year) attributable to the portion of the trust referred to in subsection (a).

[Sec. 679(c)]

(c) TRUSTS TREATED AS HAVING A UNITED STATES BENEFICIARY.—

(1) IN GENERAL.—For purposes of this section, a trust shall be treated as having a United States beneficiary for the taxable year unless—

(A) under the terms of the trust, no part of the income or corpus of the trust may be paid or accumulated during the taxable year to or for the benefit of a United States person, and

(B) if the trust were terminated at any time during the taxable year, no part of the income or corpus of such trust could be paid to or for the benefit of a United States person.

For purposes of subparagraph (A), an amount shall be treated as accumulated for the benefit of a United States person even if the United States person's interest in the trust is contingent on a future event.

(2) ATTRIBUTION OF OWNERSHIP.—For purposes of paragraph (1), an amount shall be treated as paid or accumulated to or for the benefit of a United States person if such amount is paid to or accumulated for a foreign corporation, foreign partnership, or foreign trust or estate, and—

(A) in the case of a foreign corporation, such corporation is a controlled foreign corporation (as defined in section 957(a)),

(B) in the case of a foreign partnership, a United States person is a partner of such partnership, or

(C) in the case of a foreign trust or estate, such trust or estate has a United States beneficiary (within the meaning of paragraph (1)).

(3) CERTAIN UNITED STATES BENEFICIARIES DISREGARDED.—A beneficiary shall not be treated as a United States person in applying this section with respect to any transfer of property to foreign trust if such beneficiary first became a United States person more than 5 years after the date of such transfer.

(4) SPECIAL RULE IN CASE OF DISCRETION TO IDENTIFY BENEFICIARIES.—For purposes of paragraph (1)(A), if any person has the discretion (by authority given in the trust agreement, by power of appointment, or otherwise) of making a distribution from the trust to, or for the benefit of, any person, such trust shall be treated as having a beneficiary who is a United States person unless—

(A) the terms of the trust specifically identify the class of persons to whom such distributions may be made, and

(B) none of those persons are United States persons during the taxable year.

(5) CERTAIN AGREEMENTS AND UNDERSTANDINGS TREATED AS TERMS OF THE TRUST.—For purposes of paragraph (1)(A), if any United States person who directly or indirectly transfers property to the trust is directly or indirectly involved in any agreement or understanding (whether written, oral, or otherwise) that may result in the income or corpus of the trust being paid or accumulated to or for the benefit of a United States person, such agreement or understanding shall be treated as a term of the trust.

(6) UNCOMPENSATED USE OF TRUST PROPERTY TREATED AS A PAYMENT.—For purposes of this subsection, a loan of cash or marketable securities (or the use of any other trust property) directly or indirectly to or by any United States person (whether or not a beneficiary under the terms of the trust) shall be treated as paid or accumulated for the benefit of a United States person. The preceding sentence shall not apply to the extent that the United States person repays the loan at a market rate of interest (or pays the fair market value of the use of such property) within a reasonable period of time.

(d) PRESUMPTION THAT FOREIGN TRUST HAS UNITED STATES BENEFICIARY.—If a United States person directly or indirectly transfers property to a foreign trust (other than a trust described in section 6048(a)(3)(B)(ii)), the Secretary may treat such trust as having a United States beneficiary for purposes of applying this section to such transfer unless such person—

(1) submits such information to the Secretary as the Secretary may require with respect to such transfer, and

(2) demonstrates to the satisfaction of the Secretary that such trust satisfies the requirements of subparagraphs (A) and (B) of subsection (c)(1).

(e) REGULATIONS.—The Secretary shall prescribe such regulations as may be necessary or appropriate to carry out the purposes of this section.

Subpart F—Miscellaneous

[Sec. 684]

SEC. 684. RECOGNITION OF GAIN ON CERTAIN TRANSFERS TO CERTAIN FOREIGN TRUSTS AND ESTATES.

[Sec. 684(a)]

(a) IN GENERAL.—Except as provided in regulations, in the case of any transfer of property by a United States person to a foreign estate or trust, for purposes of this subtitle, such transfer shall be treated as a sale or exchange for an amount equal to the fair market value of the property transferred, and the transferor shall recognize as gain the excess of—

(1) the fair market value of the property so transferred, over

(2) the adjusted basis (for purposes of determining gain) of such property in the hands of the transferor.

[Sec. 684(b)]

(b) EXCEPTION.—Subsection (a) shall not apply to a transfer to a trust by a United States person to the extent that any person is treated as the owner of such trust under section 671.

[Sec. 684(c)]

(c) TREATMENT OF TRUSTS WHICH BECOME FOREIGN TRUSTS.—If a trust which is not a foreign trust becomes a foreign trust, such trust shall be treated for purposes of this section as having transferred, immediately before becoming a foreign trust, all of its assets to a foreign trust.

SUBCHAPTER K—PARTNERS AND PARTNERSHIPS

PART I—DETERMINATION OF TAX LIABILITY

[Sec. 701]

SEC. 701. PARTNERS, NOT PARTNERSHIP, SUBJECT TO TAX.

A partnership as such shall not be subject to the income tax imposed by this chapter. Persons carrying on business as partners shall be liable for income tax only in their separate or individual capacities.

[Sec. 702]

SEC. 702. INCOME AND CREDITS OF PARTNER.

[Sec. 702(a)]

(a) GENERAL RULE.—In determining his income tax, each partner shall take into account separately his distributive share of the partnership's—

(1) gains and losses from sales or exchanges of capital assets held for not more than 1 year,

(2) gains and losses from sales or exchanges of capital assets held for more than 1 year,

(3) gains and losses from sales or exchanges of property described in section 1231 (relating to certain property used in a trade or business and involuntary conversions),

(4) charitable contributions (as defined in section 170(c)),

(5) dividends with respect to which section 1(h)(11) or part VIII of subchapter B applies,

(6) taxes, described in section 901, paid or accrued to foreign countries and to possessions of the United States,

(7) other items of income, gain, loss, deduction, or credit, to the extent provided by regulations prescribed by the Secretary, and

(8) taxable income or loss, exclusive of items requiring separate computation under other paragraphs of this subsection.

[Sec. 702(b)]

(b) CHARACTER OF ITEMS CONSTITUTING DISTRIBUTIVE SHARE.—The character of any item of income, gain, loss, deduction, or credit included in a partner's distributive share under paragraphs (1) through (7) of subsection (a) shall be determined as if such item were realized directly from the source from which realized by the partnership, or incurred in the same manner as incurred by the partnership.

* * *

[Sec. 703]

SEC. 703. PARTNERSHIP COMPUTATIONS.

[Sec. 703(a)]

(a) INCOME AND DEDUCTIONS.—The taxable income of a partnership shall be computed in the same manner as in the case of an individual except that—

(1) the items described in section 702(a) shall be separately stated, and

(2) the following deductions shall not be allowed to the partnership:

* * *

(B) the deduction for taxes provided in section 164(a) with respect to taxes, described in section 901, paid or accrued to foreign countries and to possessions of the United States,

* * *

[Sec. 703(b)]

(b) ELECTIONS OF THE PARTNERSHIP.—Any election affecting the computation of taxable income derived from a partnership shall be made by the partnership, except that any election under—

* * *

(3) section 901 (relating to taxes of foreign countries and possessions of the United States),

shall be made by each partner separately.

[Sec. 704]

SEC. 704. PARTNER'S DISTRIBUTIVE SHARE.

[Sec. 704(a)]

(a) EFFECT OF PARTNERSHIP AGREEMENT.—A partner's distributive share of income, gain, loss, deduction, or credit shall, except as otherwise provided in this chapter, be determined by the partnership agreement.

[Sec. 704(b)]

(b) DETERMINATION OF DISTRIBUTIVE SHARE.—A partner's distributive share of income, gain, loss, deduction, or credit (or item thereof) shall be determined in accordance with the partner's interest in the partnership (determined by taking into account all facts and circumstances), if—

(1) the partnership agreement does not provide as to the partner's distributive share of income, gain, loss, deduction, or credit (or item thereof), or

(2) the allocation to a partner under the agreement of income, gain, loss, deduction, or credit (or item thereof) does not have substantial economic effect.

* * *

[Sec. 706]

SEC. 706. TAXABLE YEARS OF PARTNER AND PARTNERSHIP.

[Sec. 706(a)]

(a) YEAR IN WHICH PARTNERSHIP INCOME IS INCLUDIBLE.—In computing the taxable income of a partner for a taxable year, the inclusions required by section 702 and section 707(c) with respect to a partnership shall be based on the income, gain, loss, deduction, or credit of the partnership for any taxable year of the partnership ending within or with the taxable year of the partner.

[Sec. 706(b)]

(b) TAXABLE YEAR.—

(1) PARTNERSHIP'S TAXABLE YEAR.—

(A) PARTNERSHIP TREATED AS TAXPAYER.—The taxable year of a partnership shall be determined as though the partnership were a taxpayer.

(B) TAXABLE YEAR DETERMINED BY REFERENCE TO PARTNERS.—Except as provided in subparagraph (C), a partnership shall not have a taxable year other than—

(i) the majority interest taxable year (as defined in paragraph (4)),

(ii) if there is no taxable year described in clause (i), the taxable year of all the principal partners of the partnership, or

(iii) if there is no taxable year described in clause (i) or (ii), the calendar year unless the Secretary by regulations prescribes another period.

(C) BUSINESS PURPOSE.—A partnership may have a taxable year not described in subparagraph (B) if it establishes, to the satisfaction of the Secretary, a business purpose therefor. For purposes of this subparagraph, any deferral of income to partners shall not be treated as a business purpose.

(2) PARTNER'S TAXABLE YEAR.—A partner may not change to a taxable year other than that of a partnership in which he is a principal partner unless he establishes, to the satisfaction of the Secretary, a business purpose therefor.

(3) PRINCIPAL PARTNER.—For the purpose of this subsection, a principal partner is a partner having an interest of 5 percent or more in partnership profits or capital.

(4) MAJORITY INTEREST TAXABLE YEAR; LIMITATION ON REQUIRED CHANGES.—

(A) MAJORITY INTEREST TAXABLE YEAR DEFINED.—For purposes of paragraph (1)(B)(i)—

(i) IN GENERAL.—The term "majority interest taxable year" means the taxable year (if any) which, on each testing day, constituted the taxable year of 1 or more partners having (on such day) an aggregate interest in partnership profits and capital of more than 50 percent.

(ii) TESTING DAYS.—The testing days shall be—

(I) the 1st day of the partnership taxable year (determined without regard to clause (i)), or

(II) the days during such representative period as the Secretary may prescribe.

(B) FURTHER CHANGE NOT REQUIRED FOR 3 YEARS.—Except as provided in regulations necessary to prevent the avoidance of this section, if, by reason of paragraph (1)(B)(i), the taxable year of a partnership is changed, such partnership shall not be required to change to another taxable year for either of the 2 taxable years following the year of change.

* * *

[Sec. 707]

SEC. 707. TRANSACTIONS BETWEEN PARTNER AND PARTNERSHIP.

* * *

[Sec. 707(b)]

(b) CERTAIN SALES OR EXCHANGES OF PROPERTY WITH RESPECT TO CONTROLLED PARTNERSHIPS.—

(1) LOSSES DISALLOWED.—No deduction shall be allowed in respect of losses from sales or exchanges of property (other than an interest in the partnership), directly or indirectly, between—

(A) a partnership and a person owning, directly or indirectly, more than 50 percent of the capital interest, or the profits interest, in such partnership, or

(B) two partnerships in which the same persons own, directly or indirectly, more than 50 percent of the capital interests or profits interests.

In the case of a subsequent sale or exchange by a transferee described in this paragraph, section 267(d) shall be applicable as if the loss were disallowed under section 267(a)(1). For purposes of section 267(a)(2), partnerships described in subparagraph (B) of this paragraph shall be treated as persons specified in section 267(b).

***

PART II—CONTRIBUTIONS, DISTRIBUTIONS, AND TRANSFERS

Subpart A—Contributions to a Partnership

[Sec. 721]

SEC. 721. NONRECOGNITION OF GAIN OR LOSS ON CONTRIBUTION.

***

[Sec. 721(c)]

(c) REGULATIONS RELATING TO CERTAIN TRANSFERS TO PARTNERSHIPS.—The Secretary may provide by regulations that subsection (a) shall not apply to gain realized on the transfer of property to a partnership if such gain, when recognized, will be includible in the gross income of a person other than a United States person.

***

SUBCHAPTER N—TAX BASED ON INCOME FROM SOURCES WITHIN OR WITHOUT THE UNITED STATES

PART I—DETERMINATION OF SOURCES OF INCOME

[Sec. 861]

SEC. 861. INCOME FROM SOURCES WITHIN THE UNITED STATES.

[Sec. 861(a)]

(a) GROSS INCOME FROM SOURCES WITHIN UNITED STATES.—The following items of gross income shall be treated as income from sources within the United States:

(1) INTEREST.—Interest from the United States or the District of Columbia, and interest on bonds, notes, or other interest-bearing obligations of noncorporate residents or domestic corporations, not including—

(A) interest—

(i) on deposits with a foreign branch of a domestic corporation or a domestic partnership if such branch is engaged in the commercial banking business, and

(ii) on amounts satisfying the requirements of subparagraph (B) of section 871(i)(3) which are paid by a foreign branch of a domestic corporation or a domestic partnership, and

(B) in the case of a foreign partnership, which is predominantly engaged in the active conduct of a trade or business outside the United States, any interest not paid by a trade or business engaged in by the partnership in the United States and not allocable to income which is effectively connected (or treated as effectively connected) with the conduct of a trade or business in the United States.

(2) DIVIDENDS.—The amount received as dividends—

(A) from a domestic corporation, or

(B) from a foreign corporation unless less than 25 percent of the gross income from all sources of such foreign corporation for the 3-year period ending with the close of its taxable year preceding the declaration of such dividends (or for such part of such period as the corporation has been in existence) was effectively connected (or treated as effectively connected other than income described in section 884(d)(2)) with the conduct of a trade or business within the United States; but only in an amount which bears the same ratio to such dividends as the gross income of the corporation for such period which was effectively connected (or treated as effectively connected other than income described in section 884(d)(2)) with the conduct of a trade or business within the United States bears to its gross income from all sources; but dividends (other than dividends for which a deduction is allowable under section 245(b)) from a foreign corporation shall, for purposes of subpart A of part III (relating to foreign tax credit), be treated as income from sources without the United States to the extent (and only to the extent) exceeding the amount which is 100/50th of the amount of the deduction allowable under section 245 in respect of such dividends, or

(C) from a foreign corporation to the extent that such amount is required by section 243(e) (relating to certain dividends from foreign corporations) to be treated as dividends from a domestic corporation which is subject to taxation under this chapter, and to such extent subparagraph (B) shall not apply to such amount, or

(D) from a DISC or former DISC (as defined in section 992(a)) except to the extent attributable (as determined under regulations prescribed by the Secretary) to qualified export receipts described in section 993(a)(1) (other than interest and gains described in section 995(b)(1)).

In the case of any dividend from a 20-percent owned corporation (as defined in section 243(c)(2)), subparagraph (B) shall be applied by substituting "100/65th" for "100/50th".

(3) PERSONAL SERVICES.—Compensation for labor or personal services performed in the United States; except that compensation for labor or services performed in the United States shall not be deemed to be income from sources within the United States if—

(A) the labor or services are performed by a nonresident alien individual temporarily present in the United States for a period or periods not exceeding a total of 90 days during the taxable year,

(B) such compensation does not exceed $3,000 in the aggregate, and

(C) the compensation is for labor or services performed as an employee of or under a contract with—

(i) a nonresident alien, foreign partnership, or foreign corporation, not engaged in trade or business within the United States, or

(ii) an individual who is a citizen or resident of the United States, a domestic partnership, or a domestic corporation, if such labor or services are performed for an office or place of business maintained in a foreign country or in a possession of the United States by such individual, partnership, or corporation.

In addition, compensation for labor or services performed in the United States shall not be deemed to be income from sources within the United States if the labor or services are performed by a nonresident alien individual in connection with the individual's temporary presence in the United States as a regular member of the crew of a foreign vessel engaged in transportation between the United States and a foreign country or a possession of the United States.

(4) RENTALS AND ROYALTIES.—Rentals or royalties from property located in the United States or from any interest in such property, including rentals or royalties for the use of or for the privilege of using in the United States patents, copyrights, secret processes and formulas, good will, trade-marks, trade brands, franchises, and other like property.

(5) DISPOSITION OF UNITED STATES REAL PROPERTY INTEREST.—Gains, profits, and income from the disposition of a United States real property interest (as defined in section 897(c)).

(6) SALE OR EXCHANGE OF INVENTORY PROPERTY.—Gains, profits, and income derived from the purchase of inventory property (within the meaning of section 865(i)(1)) without the United States (other than within a possession of the United States) and its sale or exchange within the United States.

(7) Amounts received as underwriting income (as defined in section 832(b)(3)) derived from the issuing (or reinsuring) of any insurance or annuity contract—

(A) in connection with property in, liability arising out of an activity in, or in connection with the lives or health of residents of, the United States, or

(B) in connection with risks not described in subparagraph (A) as a result of any arrangement whereby another corporation receives a substantially equal amount of premiums or other consideration in respect to issuing (or reinsuring) any insurance or annuity contract in connection with property in, liability arising out of activity in, or in connection with the lives or health of residents of, the United States.

(8) SOCIAL SECURITY BENEFITS.—Any social security benefit (as defined in section 86(d)).

(9) GUARANTEES.—Amounts received, directly or indirectly, from—

(A) a noncorporate resident or domestic corporation for the provision of a guarantee of any indebtedness of such resident or corporation, or

(B) any foreign person for the provision of a guarantee of any indebtedness of such person, if such amount is connected with income which is effectively connected (or treated as effectively connected) with the conduct of a trade or business in the United States.

[Sec. 861(b)]

(b) TAXABLE INCOME FROM SOURCES WITHIN UNITED STATES.—From the items of gross income specified in subsection (a) as being income from sources within the United States there shall be deducted the expenses, losses, and other deductions properly apportioned or allocated thereto and a ratable part of any expenses, losses, or other deductions which cannot definitely be allocated to some item or class of gross income. The remainder, if any, shall be included in full as taxable income from sources within the United States. In the case of an individual who does not itemize deductions, an amount equal to the standard deduction shall be considered a deduction which cannot definitely be allocated to some item or class of gross income.

[Sec. 861(c)]

(c) SPECIAL RULE FOR APPLICATION OF SUBSECTION (a)(2)(B).—For purposes of subsection (a)(2)(B), if the foreign corporation has no gross income from any source for the 3-year period (or part thereof) specified, the requirements of such subsection shall be applied with respect to the taxable year of such corporation in which the payment of the dividend is made.

[Sec. 861(d)]

(d) INCOME FROM CERTAIN RAILROAD ROLLING STOCK TREATED AS INCOME FROM SOURCES WITHIN THE UNITED STATES.

(1) GENERAL RULE.—For purposes of subsection (a) and section 862(a), if—

(A) a taxpayer leases railroad rolling stock which is section 1245 property (as defined in section 1245(a)(3)) to a domestic common carrier by railroad or a corporation which is controlled, directly or indirectly, by one or more such common carriers, and

(B) the use under such lease is expected to be use within the United States,

all amounts includible in gross income by the taxpayer with respect to such railroad rolling stock (including gain from sale or other disposition of such railroad rolling stock) shall be treated as income from sources within the United States. The requirements of subparagraph (B) of the preceding sentence shall be treated as satisfied if the only expected use outside the United States is use by a person (whether or not a United States person) in Canada or Mexico on a temporary basis which is not expected to exceed a total of 90 days in any taxable year.

(2) PARAGRAPH (1) NOT TO APPLY WHERE LESSOR IS A MEMBER OF CONTROLLED GROUP WHICH INCLUDES A RAILROAD.—Paragraph (1) shall not apply to a lease between two members of the same controlled group of corporations (as defined in section 1563) if any member of such group is a domestic common carrier by railroad or a switching or terminal company all of whose stock is owned by one or more domestic common carriers by railroad.

(3) DENIAL OF FOREIGN TAX CREDIT.—No credit shall be allowed under section 901 for any payments to foreign countries with respect to any amount received by the taxpayer with respect to railroad rolling stock which is subject to paragraph (1).

[Sec. 861(e)]

(e) CROSS REFERENCE.—

For treatment of interest paid by the branch of a foreign corporation, see section 884(f).

[Sec. 862]

SEC. 862. INCOME FROM SOURCES WITHOUT THE UNITED STATES.

[Sec. 862(a)]

(a) GROSS INCOME FROM SOURCES WITHOUT UNITED STATES.—The following items of gross income shall be treated as income from sources without the United States:

(1) interest other than that derived from sources within the United States as provided in section 861(a)(1);

(2) dividends other than those derived from sources within the United States as provided in section 861(a)(2);

(3) compensation for labor or personal services performed without the United States;

(4) rentals or royalties from property located without the United States or from any interest in such property, including rentals or royalties for the use of or for the privilege of using without the United States patents, copyrights, secret processes and formulas, good will, trade-marks, trade brands, franchises, and other like properties;

(5) gains, profits, and income from the sale or exchange of real property located without the United States;

(6) gains, profits, and income derived from the purchase of inventory property (within the meaning of section 865(i)(1)) within the United States and its sale or exchange without the United States;

(7) underwriting income other than that derived from sources within the United States as provided in section 861(a)(7);

(8) gains, profits, and income from the disposition of a United States real property interest (as defined in section 897(c)) when the real property is located in the Virgin Islands; and

(9) amounts received, directly or indirectly, from a foreign person for the provision of a guarantee of indebtedness of such person other than amounts which are derived from sources within the United States as provided in section 861(a)(9).

[Sec. 862(b)]

(b) TAXABLE INCOME FROM SOURCES WITHOUT UNITED STATES.—From the items of gross income specified in subsection (a) there shall be deducted the expenses, losses, and other deductions properly apportioned or allocated thereto, and a ratable part of any expenses, losses, or other deductions which cannot definitely be allocated to some item or class of gross income. The remainder, if any, shall be treated in full as taxable income from sources without the United States. In the case of an individual who does not itemize deductions, an amount equal to the standard deduction shall be considered a deduction which cannot definitely be allocated to some item or class of gross income.

[Sec. 863]

SEC. 863. SPECIAL RULES FOR DETERMINING SOURCE.

[Sec. 863(a)]

(a) ALLOCATION UNDER REGULATIONS.—Items of gross income, expenses, losses, and deductions, other than those specified in sections 861 (a) and 862 (a), shall be allocated or apportioned to sources within or without the United States, under regulations prescribed by the Secretary. Where items of gross income are separately allocated to sources within the United States, there shall be deducted (for the purpose of computing the taxable income therefrom) the expenses, losses, and other deductions properly apportioned or allocated thereto and a ratable part of other expenses, losses, or other deductions which cannot definitely be allocated to some item or class of gross income. The remainder, if any, shall be included in full as taxable income from sources within the United States.

[Sec. 863(b)]

(b) INCOME PARTLY FROM WITHIN AND PARTLY FROM WITHOUT THE UNITED STATES.—In the case of gross income derived from sources partly within and partly without the United States, the taxable income may first be computed by deducting the expenses, losses, or other deductions apportioned or allocated thereto and a ratable part of any expenses, losses, or other deductions which cannot definitely be allocated to some item or class of gross income; and the portion of such taxable income attributable to sources within the United States may be determined by processes or formulas of general apportionment prescribed by the Secretary. Gains, profits, and income—

(1) from services rendered partly within and partly without the United States,

(2) from the sale or exchange of inventory property (within the meaning of section 865(i)(1)) produced (in whole or in part) by the taxpayer within and sold or exchanged without the United States, or produced (in whole or in part) by the taxpayer without and sold or exchanged within the United States, or

(3) derived from the purchase of inventory property (within the meaning of section 865(i)(1)) within a possession of the United States and its sale or exchange within the United States,

shall be treated as derived partly from sources within and partly from sources without the United States. Gains, profits, and income from the sale or exchange of inventory property described in paragraph (2) shall be allocated and apportioned between sources within and without the United States solely on the basis of the production activities with respect to the property.

[Sec. 863(c)]

(c) SOURCE RULE FOR CERTAIN TRANSPORTATION INCOME.—

(1) TRANSPORTATION BEGINNING AND ENDING IN THE UNITED STATES.—All transportation income attributable to transportation which begins and ends in the United States shall be treated as derived from sources within the United States.

(2) OTHER TRANSPORTATION HAVING UNITED STATES CONNECTION.—

(A) IN GENERAL.—50 percent of all transportation income attributable to transportation which—

(i) is not described in paragraph (1), and

(ii) begins or ends in the United States,

shall be treated as from sources in the United States.

(B) SPECIAL RULE FOR PERSONAL SERVICE INCOME.—Subparagraph (A) shall not apply to any transportation income which is income derived from personal services performed by the taxpayer, unless such income is attributable to transportation which—

(i) begins in the United States and ends in a possession of the United States, or

(ii) begins in a possession of the United States and ends in the United States.

In the case of transportation income derived from, or in connection with, a vessel, this subparagraph shall only apply if the taxpayer is a citizen or resident alien.

(3) TRANSPORTATION INCOME.—For purposes of this subsection, the term "transportation income" means any income derived from, or in connection with—

(A) the use (or hiring or leasing for use) of a vessel or aircraft, or

(B) the performance of services directly related to the use of a vessel or aircraft.

For purposes of the preceding sentence, the term "vessel or aircraft" includes any container used in connection with a vessel or aircraft.

[Sec. 863(d)]

(d) SOURCE RULES FOR SPACE AND CERTAIN OCEAN ACTIVITIES.—

(1) IN GENERAL.—Except as provided in regulations, any income derived from a space or ocean activity—

(A) if derived by a United States person, shall be sourced in the United States, and

(B) if derived by a person other than a United States person, shall be sourced outside the United States.

(2) SPACE OR OCEAN ACTIVITY.—For purposes of paragraph (1)—

(A) IN GENERAL.—The term "space or ocean activity" means—

(i) any activity conducted in space, and

(ii) any activity conducted on or under water not within the jurisdiction (as recognized by the United States) of a foreign country, possession of the United States, or the United States.

Such term includes any activity conducted in Antarctica.

(B) EXCEPTION FOR CERTAIN ACTIVITIES.—The term "space or ocean activity" shall not include—

(i) any activity giving rise to transportation income (as defined in section 863(c)),

(ii) any activity giving rise to international communications income (as defined in subsection (e)(2)), and

(iii) any activity with respect to mines, oil and gas wells, or other natural deposits to the extent within the United States or any foreign country or possession of the United States (as defined in section 638).

For purposes of applying section 638, the jurisdiction of any foreign country shall not include any jurisdiction not recognized by the United States.

[Sec. 863(e)]

(e) INTERNATIONAL COMMUNICATIONS INCOME.—

(1) SOURCE RULES.—

(A) UNITED STATES PERSONS.—In the case of any United States person, 50 percent of any international communications income shall be sourced in the United States and 50 percent of such income shall be sourced outside the United States.

(B) FOREIGN PERSONS.—

(i) IN GENERAL.—Except as provided in regulations or clause (ii), in the case of any person other than a United States person, any international communications income shall be sourced outside the United States.

(ii) SPECIAL RULE FOR INCOME ATTRIBUTABLE TO OFFICE OR FIXED PLACE OF BUSINESS IN THE UNITED STATES.—In the case of any person (other than a United States person) who maintains an office or other fixed place of business in the United States, any international communications income attributable to such office or other fixed place of business shall be sourced in the United States.

(2) DEFINITION.—For purposes of this section, the term "international communications income" includes all income derived from the transmission of communications or data from the United States to any foreign country (or possession of the United States) or from any foreign country (or possession of the United States) to the United States.

[Sec. 864]

SEC. 864. DEFINITIONS AND SPECIAL RULES.

[Sec. 864(a)]

(a) PRODUCED.—For purposes of this part, the term "produced" includes created, fabricated, manufactured, extracted, processed, cured, or aged.

[Sec. 864(b)]

(b) TRADE OR BUSINESS WITHIN THE UNITED STATES.—For purposes of this part, part II, and chapter 3, the term "trade or business within the United States" includes the performance of personal services within the United States at any time within the taxable year, but does not include—

(1) PERFORMANCE OF PERSONAL SERVICES FOR FOREIGN EMPLOYER.—The performance of personal services—

(A) for a nonresident alien individual, foreign partnership, or foreign corporation, not engaged in trade or business within the United States, or

(B) for an office or place of business maintained in a foreign country or in a possession of the United States by an individual who is a citizen or resident of the United States or by a domestic partnership or a domestic corporation,

by a nonresident alien individual temporarily present in the United States for a period or periods not exceeding a total of 90 days during the taxable year and whose compensation for such services does not exceed in the aggregate $3,000.

(2) TRADING IN SECURITIES OR COMMODITIES.—

(A) STOCKS AND SECURITIES.—

(i) IN GENERAL.—Trading in stocks or securities through a resident broker, commission agent, custodian, or other independent agent.

(ii) TRADING FOR TAXPAYER'S OWN ACCOUNT.—Trading in stocks or securities for the taxpayer's own account, whether by the taxpayer or his employees or through a resident broker, commission agent, custodian, or other agent, and whether or not any such employee or agent has discretionary authority to make decisions in effecting the transactions. This clause shall not apply in the case of a dealer in stocks or securities.

(B) COMMODITIES.—

(i) IN GENERAL.—Trading in commodities through a resident broker, commission agent, custodian, or other independent agent.

(ii) TRADING FOR TAXPAYER'S OWN ACCOUNT.—Trading in commodities for the taxpayer's own account, whether by the taxpayer or his employees or through a resident broker, commission agent, custodian, or other agent, and whether or not any such employee or agent has discretionary authority to make decisions in effecting the transactions. This clause shall not apply in the case of a dealer in commodities.

(iii) LIMITATION.—Clauses (i) and (ii) shall apply only if the commodities are of a kind customarily dealt in on an organized commodity exchange and if the transaction is of a kind customarily consummated at such place.

(C) LIMITATION.—Subparagraphs (A)(i) and (B)(i) shall apply only if, at no time during the taxable year, the taxpayer has an office or other fixed place of business in the United States through which or by the direction of which the transactions in stocks or securities, or in commodities, as the case may be, are effected.

[Sec. 864(c)]

(c) EFFECTIVELY CONNECTED INCOME, ETC.—

(1) GENERAL RULE.—For purposes of this title—

(A) In the case of a nonresident alien individual or a foreign corporation engaged in trade or business within the United States during the taxable year, the rules set forth in paragraphs (2), (3), (4), (6), (7), and (8) shall apply in determining the income, gain, or loss which shall be treated as effectively connected with the conduct of a trade or business within the United States.

(B) Except as provided in paragraph (6)[,] (7), or (8) or in section 871(d) or sections 882(d) and (e), in the case of a nonresident alien individual or a foreign corporation not engaged in trade or business within the United States during the taxable year, no income, gain, or loss shall be treated as effectively connected with the conduct of a trade or business within the United States.

(2) PERIODICAL, ETC., INCOME FROM SOURCES WITHIN UNITED STATES—FACTORS.—In determining whether income from sources within the United States of the types described in section 871(a)(1), section 871(h), section 881(a), or section 881(c), or whether gain or loss from sources within the United States from the sale or exchange of capital assets, is effectively connected with the conduct of a trade or business within the United States, the factors taken into account shall include whether—

(A) the income, gain, or loss is derived from assets used in or held for use in the conduct of such trade or business, or

(B) the activities of such trade or business were a material factor in the realization of the income, gain, or loss.

In determining whether an asset is used in or held for use in the conduct of such trade or business or whether the activities of such trade or business were a material factor in realizing an item of income, gain, or loss, due regard shall be given to whether or not such asset or such income, gain, or loss was accounted for through such trade or business.

(3) OTHER INCOME FROM SOURCES WITHIN UNITED STATES.—All income, gain, or loss from sources within the United States (other than income, gain, or loss to which paragraph (2) applies) shall be treated as effectively connected with the conduct of a trade or business within the United States.

(4) INCOME FROM SOURCES WITHOUT UNITED STATES.—

(A) Except as provided in subparagraphs (B) and (C), no income, gain, or loss from sources without the United States shall be treated as effectively connected with the conduct of a trade or business within the United States.

(B) Income, gain, or loss from sources without the United States shall be treated as effectively connected with the conduct of a trade or business within the United States by a nonresident alien individual or a foreign corporation if such person has an office or other fixed place of business within the United States to which such income, gain, or loss is attributable and such income, gain, or loss

(i) consists of rents or royalties for the use of or for the privilege of using intangible property described in section 862(a)(4) derived in the active conduct of such trade or business;

(ii) consists of dividends, interest, or amounts received for the provision of guarantees of indebtedness, and either is derived in the active conduct of a banking, financing, or similar business within the United States or is received by a corporation the principal business of which is trading in stocks or securities for its own account; or

(iii) is derived from the sale or exchange (outside the United States) through such office or other fixed place of business of personal property described in section 1221(a)(1), except that this clause shall not apply if the property is sold or exchanged for use, consumption, or disposition outside the United States and an office or other fixed place of business of the taxpayer in a foreign country participated materially in such sale.

Any income or gain which is equivalent to any item of income or gain described in clause (i), (ii), or (iii) shall be treated in the same manner as such item for purposes of this subparagraph.

(C) In the case of a foreign corporation taxable under part I or part II of subchapter L, any income from sources without the United States which is attributable to its United States business shall be treated as effectively connected with the conduct of a trade or business within the United States.

(D) No income from sources without the United States shall be treated as effectively connected with the conduct of a trade or business within the United States if it either—

(i) consists of dividends, interest, or royalties paid by a foreign corporation in which the taxpayer owns (within the meaning of section 958(a)), or is considered as owning (by applying the ownership rules of section 958(b)), more than 50 percent of the total combined voting power of all classes of stock entitled to vote, or

(ii) is subpart F income within the meaning of section 952(a).

(5) RULES FOR APPLICATION OF PARAGRAPH (4)(B).—For purposes of subparagraph (B) of paragraph (4)—

(A) in determining whether a nonresident alien individual or a foreign corporation has an office or other fixed place of business, an office or other fixed place of business of an agent shall be disregarded unless such agent (i) has the authority to negotiate and conclude contracts in the name of the nonresident alien individual or foreign corporation and regularly exercises that authority or has a stock of merchandise from which he regularly fills orders on behalf of such individual or foreign corporation, and (ii) is not a general commission agent, broker, or other agent of independent status acting in the ordinary course of his business,

(B) income, gain, or loss shall not be considered as attributable to an office or other fixed place of business within the United States unless such office or fixed place of business is a material factor in the production of such income, gain, or loss and such office or fixed place of business regularly carries on activities of the type from which such income, gain, or loss is derived, and

(C) the income, gain, or loss which shall be attributable to an office or other fixed place of business within the United States shall be the income, gain, or loss properly allocable thereto, but, in the case of a sale or exchange described in clause (iii) of such subparagraph, the income which shall be treated as attributable to an office or other fixed place of business within the United States shall not exceed the income which would be derived from sources within the United States if the sale or exchange were made in the United States.

(6) TREATMENT OF CERTAIN DEFERRED PAYMENTS, ETC.—For purposes of this title, in the case of any income or gain of a nonresident alien individual or a foreign corporation which—

(A) is taken into account for any taxable year, but

(B) is attributable to a sale or exchange of property or the performance of services (or any other transaction) in any other taxable year,

the determination of whether such income or gain is taxable under section 871(b) or 882 (as the case may be) shall be made as if such income or gain were taken into account in such other taxable year and without regard to the requirement that the taxpayer be engaged in a trade or business within the United States during the taxable year referred to in subparagraph (A).

(7) TREATMENT OF CERTAIN PROPERTY TRANSACTIONS.—For purposes of this title, if—

(A) any property ceases to be used or held for use in connection with the conduct of a trade or business within the United States, and

(B) such property is disposed of within 10 years after such cessation,

the determination of whether any income or gain attributable to such disposition is taxable under section 871(b) or 882 (as the case may be) shall be made as if such sale or exchange occurred immediately before such cessation and without regard to the requirement that the taxpayer be engaged in a trade or business within the United States during the taxable year for which such income or gain is taken into account.

(8) GAIN OR LOSS OF FOREIGN PERSONS FROM SALE OR EXCHANGE OF CERTAIN PARTNERSHIP INTERESTS.—

(A) IN GENERAL.—Notwithstanding any other provision of this subtitle, if a nonresident alien individual or foreign corporation owns, directly or indirectly, an interest in a partnership which is engaged in any trade or business within the United States, gain or loss on the sale or exchange of all (or any portion of) such interest shall be treated as effectively connected with the conduct of such trade or business to the extent such gain or loss does not exceed the amount determined under subparagraph (B).

(B) AMOUNT TREATED AS EFFECTIVELY CONNECTED.—The amount determined under this subparagraph with respect to any partnership interest sold or exchanged—

(i) in the case of any gain on the sale or exchange of the partnership interest, is—

(I) the portion of the partner's distributive share of the amount of gain which would have been effectively connected with the conduct of a trade or business within the United States if the partnership had sold all of its assets at their fair market value as of the date of the sale or exchange of such interest, or

(II) zero if no gain on such deemed sale would have been so effectively connected, and

(ii) in the case of any loss on the sale or exchange of the partnership interest, is—

(I) the portion of the partner's distributive share of the amount of loss on the deemed sale described in clause (i)(I) which would have been so effectively connected, or

(II) zero if no loss on such deemed sale would be [sic] have been so effectively connected.

For purposes of this subparagraph, a partner's distributive share of gain or loss on the deemed sale shall be determined in the same manner as such partner's distributive share of the non-separately stated taxable income or loss of such partnership.

(C) COORDINATION WITH UNITED STATES REAL PROPERTY INTERESTS.—If a partnership described in subparagraph (A) holds any United States real property interest (as defined in section 897(c)) at the time of the sale or exchange of the partnership interest, then the gain or loss treated as effectively connected income under subparagraph (A) shall be reduced by the amount so treated with respect to such United States real property interest under section 897.

(D) SALE OR EXCHANGE.—For purposes of this paragraph, the term "sale or exchange" means any sale, exchange, or other disposition.

(E) SECRETARIAL AUTHORITY.—The Secretary shall prescribe such regulations or other guidance as the Secretary determines appropriate for the application of this paragraph, including with respect to exchanges described in section 332, 351, 354, 355, 356, or 361.

[Sec. 864(d)]

(d) TREATMENT OF RELATED PERSON FACTORING INCOME.—

(1) IN GENERAL.—For purposes of the provisions set forth in paragraph (2), if any person acquires (directly or indirectly) a trade or service receivable from a related person, any income of such person from the trade or service receivable so acquired shall be treated as if it were interest on a loan to the obligor under the receivable.

(2) PROVISIONS TO WHICH PARAGRAPH (1) APPLIES.—The provisions set forth in this paragraph are as follows:

(A) Section 904 (relating to limitation on foreign tax credit).

(B) Subpart F of part III of this subchapter (relating to controlled foreign corporations).

(3) TRADE OR SERVICE RECEIVABLE.—For purposes of this subsection, the term "trade or service receivable" means any account receivable or evidence of indebtedness arising out of—

(A) the disposition by a related person of property described in section 1221(a)(1), or

(B) the performance of services by a related person.

(4) RELATED PERSON.—For purposes of this subsection, the term "related person" means—

(A) any person who is a related person (within the meaning of section 267(b)), and

(B) any United States shareholder (as defined in section 951(b)) and any person who is a related person (within the meaning of section 267(b)) to such a shareholder.

(5) CERTAIN PROVISIONS NOT TO APPLY.—The following provisions shall not apply to any amount treated as interest under paragraph (1) or (6):

(A) Section 904(d)(2)(B)(iii)(I) (relating to exceptions for export financing interest).

(B) Subparagraph (A) of section 954(b)(3) (relating to exception where foreign base company income is less than 5 percent or $1,000,000).

(C) Subparagraph (B) of section 954(c)(2) (relating to certain export financing).

(D) Clause (i) of section 954(c)(3)(A) (relating to certain income received from related persons).

(6) SPECIAL RULE FOR CERTAIN INCOME FROM LOANS OF A CONTROLLED FOREIGN CORPORATION.—Any income of a controlled foreign corporation (within the meaning of section 957(a)) from a loan to a person for the purpose of financing—

(A) the purchase of property described in section 1221(a)(1) of a related person, or

(B) the payment for the performance of services by a related person,

shall be treated as interest described in paragraph (1).

(7) EXCEPTION FOR CERTAIN RELATED PERSONS DOING BUSINESS IN SAME FOREIGN COUNTRY.—Paragraph (1) shall not apply to any trade or service receivable acquired by any person from a related person if—

(A) the person acquiring such receivable and such related person are created or organized under the laws of the same foreign country and such related person has a substantial part of its assets used in its trade or business located in such same foreign country, and

(B) such related person would not have derived any foreign base company income (as defined in section 954(a), determined without regard to section 954(b)(3)(A)), or any income effectively connected with the conduct of a trade or business within the United States, from such receivable if it had been collected by such related person.

(8) REGULATIONS.—The Secretary shall prescribe such regulations as may be necessary to prevent the avoidance of the provisions of this subsection or section 956(c)(3).

[Sec. 864(e)]

(e) RULES FOR ALLOCATING INTEREST, ETC.—For purposes of this subchapter—

(1) TREATMENT OF AFFILIATED GROUPS.—The taxable income of each member of an affiliated group shall be determined by allocating and apportioning interest expense of each member as if all members of such group were a single corporation.

(2) GROSS INCOME AND FAIR MARKET VALUE METHODS MAY NOT BE USED FOR INTEREST.—All allocations and apportionments of interest expense shall be determined using the adjusted bases of assets rather than on the basis of the fair market value of the assets or gross income.

(3) TAX-EXEMPT ASSETS NOT TAKEN INTO ACCOUNT.—For purposes of allocating and apportioning any deductible expense, any tax-exempt asset (and any income from such an asset) shall not be taken into account. A similar rule shall apply in the case of the portion of any dividend (other than a qualifying dividend as defined in section 243(b)) equal to the deduction allowable under section 243 or 245(a)with respect to such dividend and in the case of a like portion of any stock the dividends on which would be so deductible and would not be qualifying dividends (as so defined).

(4) BASIS OF STOCK IN NONAFFILIATED 10-PERCENT OWNED CORPORATIONS ADJUSTED FOR EARNINGS AND PROFITS CHANGES.—

(A) IN GENERAL.—For purposes of allocating and apportioning expenses on the basis of assets, the adjusted basis of any stock in a nonaffiliated 10-percent owned corporation shall be—

(i) increased by the amount of the earnings and profits of such corporation attributable to such stock and accumulated during the period the taxpayer held such stock, or

(ii) reduced (but not below zero) by any deficit in earnings and profits of such corporation attributable to such stock for such period.

(B) NONAFFILIATED 10-PERCENT OWNED CORPORATION.—For purposes of this paragraph, the term "nonaffiliated 10-percent owned corporation" means any corporation if—

(i) such corporation is not included in the taxpayer's affiliated group, and

(ii) members of such affiliated group own 10 percent or more of the total combined voting power of all classes of stock of such corporation entitled to vote.

(C) EARNINGS AND PROFITS OF LOWER TIER CORPORATIONS TAKEN INTO ACCOUNT.—

(i) IN GENERAL.—If, by reason of holding stock in a nonaffiliated 10-percent owned corporation, the taxpayer is treated under clause (iii) as owning stock in another corporation with respect to which the stock ownership requirements of clause (ii) are met, the adjustment under subparagraph (A) shall include an adjustment for the amount of the earnings and profits (or deficit therein) of such other corporation which are attributable to the stock the taxpayer is so treated as owning and to the period during which the taxpayer is treated as owning such stock.

(ii) STOCK OWNERSHIP REQUIREMENTS.—The stock ownership requirements of this clause are met with respect to any corporation if members of the taxpayer's affiliated group own (directly or through the application of clause (iii)) 10 percent or more of the total combined voting power of all classes of stock of such corporation entitled to vote.

(iii) STOCK OWNED THROUGH ENTITIES.—For purposes of this subparagraph, stock owned (directly or indirectly) by a corporation, partnership, or trust shall be treated as being owned proportionately by its shareholders, partners, or beneficiaries. Stock considered to be owned by a person by reason of the application of the preceding sentence, shall, for purposes of applying such sentence, be treated as actually owned by such person.

(D) COORDINATION WITH SUBPART F, ETC.—For purposes of this paragraph, proper adjustment shall be made to the earnings and profits of any corporation to take into account any earnings and profits included in gross income under section 951 or under any other provision of this title and reflected in the adjusted basis of the stock.

(5) AFFILIATED GROUP.—For purposes of this subsection—

(A) IN GENERAL.—Except as provided in subparagraph (B), the term "affiliated group" has the meaning given such term by section 1504. Notwithstanding the preceding sentence, a foreign corporation shall be treated as a member of the affiliated group if—

(i) more than 50 percent of the gross income of such foreign corporation for the taxable year is effectively connected with the conduct of a trade or business within the United States, and

(ii) at least 80 percent of either the vote or value of all outstanding stock of such foreign corporation is owned directly or indirectly by members of the affiliated group (determined with regard to this sentence).

(B) TREATMENT OF CERTAIN FINANCIAL INSTITUTIONS.—For purposes of subparagraph (A), any corporation described in subparagraph (C) shall be treated as an includible corporation for purposes of section 1504 only for purposes of applying such section separately to corporations so described. This subparagraph shall not apply for purposes of paragraph (6).

(C) DESCRIPTION.—A corporation is described in this subparagraph if—

(i) such corporation is a financial institution described in section 581 or 591,

(ii) the business of such financial institution is predominantly with persons other than related persons (within the meaning of subsection (d)(4)) or their customers, and

(iii) such financial institution is required by State or Federal law to be operated separately from any other entity which is not such an institution.

(D) TREATMENT OF BANK HOLDING COMPANIES.—To the extent provided in regulations—

(i) a bank holding company (within the meaning of section 2(a) of the Bank Holding Company Act of 1956), and

(ii) any subsidiary of a financial institution described in section 581 or 591 or of any bank holding company if such subsidiary is predominantly engaged (directly or indirectly) in the active conduct of a banking, financing, or similar business,

shall be treated as a corporation described in subparagraph (C).

(6) ALLOCATION AND APPORTIONMENT OF OTHER EXPENSES.—Expenses other than interest which are not directly allocable or apportioned to any specific income producing activity shall be allocated and apportioned as if all members of the affiliated group were a single corporation.

(7) REGULATIONS.—The Secretary shall prescribe such regulations as may be necessary or appropriate to carry out the purposes of this section, including regulations providing—

(A) for the resourcing of income of any member of an affiliated group or modifications to the consolidated return regulations to the extent such resourcing or modification is necessary to carry out the purposes of this section,

(B) for direct allocation of interest expense incurred to carry out an integrated financial transaction to any interest (or interest-type income) derived from such transaction and in other circumstances where such allocation would be appropriate to carry out the purposes of this subsection,

(C) for the apportionment of expenses allocated to foreign source income among the members of the affiliated group and various categories of income described in section 904(d)(1),

(D) for direct allocation of interest expense in the case of indebtedness resulting in a disallowance under section 246A,

(E) for appropriate adjustments in the application of paragraph (3) in the case of an insurance company,

(F) preventing assets or interest expense from being taken into account more than once, and

(G) that this subsection shall not apply for purposes of any provision of this subchapter to the extent the Secretary determines that the application of this subsection for such purposes would not be appropriate.

[Sec. 864(f)—Stricken]

[Sec. 865]

SEC. 865. SOURCE RULES FOR PERSONAL PROPERTY SALES.

[Sec. 865(a)]

(a) GENERAL RULE.—Except as otherwise provided in this section, income from the sale of personal property—

(1) by a United States resident shall be sourced in the United States, or

(2) by a nonresident shall be sourced outside the United States.

[Sec. 865(b)]

(b) EXCEPTION FOR INVENTORY PROPERTY.—In the case of income derived from the sale of inventory property—

(1) this section shall not apply, and

(2) such income shall be sourced under the rules of sections 861(a)(6), 862(a)(6), and 863.

Notwithstanding the preceding sentence, any income from the sale of any unprocessed timber which is a softwood and was cut from an area in the United States shall be sourced in the United States and the rules of sections 862(a)(6) and 863(b) shall not apply to any such income. For purposes of the preceding sentence, the term "unprocessed timber" means any log, cant, or similar form of timber.

[Sec. 865(c)]

(c) EXCEPTION FOR DEPRECIABLE PERSONAL PROPERTY.—

(1) IN GENERAL.—Gain (not in excess of the depreciation adjustments) from the sale of depreciable personal property shall be allocated between sources in the United States and sources outside the United States—

(A) by treating the same proportion of such gain as sourced in the United States as the United States depreciation adjustments with respect to such property bear to the total depreciation adjustments, and

(B) by treating the remaining portion of such gain as sourced outside the United States.

(2) GAIN IN EXCESS OF DEPRECIATION.—Gain (in excess of the depreciation adjustments) from the sale of depreciable personal property shall be sourced as if such property were inventory property.

(3) UNITED STATES DEPRECIATION ADJUSTMENTS.—For purposes of this subsection—

(A) IN GENERAL.—The term "United States depreciation adjustments" means the portion of the depreciation adjustments to the adjusted basis of the property which are attributable to the depreciation deductions allowable in computing taxable income from sources in the United States.

(B) SPECIAL RULE FOR CERTAIN PROPERTY.—Except in the case of property of a kind described in section 168(g)(4), if, for any taxable year—

(i) such property is used predominantly in the United States, or

(ii) such property is used predominantly outside the United States,

all of the depreciation deductions allowable for such year shall be treated as having been allocated to income from sources in the United States (or, where clause (ii) applies, from sources outside the United States).

(4) OTHER DEFINITIONS.—For purposes of this subsection—

(A) DEPRECIABLE PERSONAL PROPERTY.—The term "depreciable personal property" means any personal property if the adjusted basis of such property includes depreciation adjustments.

(B) DEPRECIATION ADJUSTMENTS.—The term "depreciation adjustments" means adjustments reflected in the adjusted basis of any property on account of depreciation deductions (whether allowed with respect to such property or other property and whether allowed to the taxpayer or to any other person).

(C) DEPRECIATION DEDUCTIONS.—The term "depreciation deductions" means any deductions for depreciation or amortization or any other deduction allowable under any provision of this chapter which treats an otherwise capital expenditure as a deductible expense.

[Sec. 865(d)]

(d) EXCEPTION FOR INTANGIBLES.—

(1) IN GENERAL.—In the case of any sale of an intangible—

(A) this section shall apply only to the extent the payments in consideration of such sale are not contingent on the productivity, use, or disposition of the intangible, and

(B) to the extent such payments are so contingent, the source of such payments shall be determined under this part in the same manner as if such payments were royalties.

(2) INTANGIBLE.—For purposes of paragraph (1), the term "intangible" means any patent, copyright, secret process or formula, goodwill, trademark, trade brand, franchise, or other like property.

(3) SPECIAL RULE IN THE CASE OF GOODWILL.—To the extent this section applies to the sale of goodwill, payments in consideration of such sale shall be treated as from sources in the country in which such goodwill was generated.

(4) COORDINATION WITH SUBSECTION (c).—

(A) GAIN NOT IN EXCESS OF DEPRECIATION ADJUSTMENTS SOURCED UNDER SUBSECTION (c).—Notwithstanding paragraph (1), any gain from the sale of an intangible shall be sourced under subsection (c) to the extent such gain does not exceed the depreciation adjustments with respect to such intangible.

(B) SUBSECTION (c)(2) NOT TO APPLY TO INTANGIBLES.—Paragraph (2) of subsection (c) shall not apply to any gain from the sale of an intangible.

[Sec. 865(e)]

(e) SPECIAL RULES FOR SALES THROUGH OFFICES OR FIXED PLACES OF BUSINESS.—

(1) SALES BY RESIDENTS.—

(A) IN GENERAL.—In the case of income not sourced under subsection (b), (c), (d)(1)(B) or (3), or (f), if a United States resident maintains an office or other fixed place of business in a foreign country, income from sales of personal property attributable to such office or other fixed place of business shall be sourced outside the United States.

(B) TAX MUST BE IMPOSED.—Subparagraph (A) shall not apply unless an income tax equal to at least 10 percent of the income from the sale is actually paid to a foreign country with respect to such income.

(2) SALES BY NONRESIDENTS.—

(A) IN GENERAL.—Notwithstanding any other provisions of this part, if a nonresident maintains an office or other fixed place of business in the United States, income from any sale of personal property (including inventory property) attributable to such office or other fixed place of business shall be sourced in the United States. The preceding sentence shall not apply for purposes of section 971 (defining export trade corporation).

(B) EXCEPTION.—Subparagraph (A) shall not apply to any sale of inventory property which is sold for use, disposition, or consumption outside the United States if an office or other fixed place of business of the taxpayer in a foreign country materially participated in the sale.

(3) SALES ATTRIBUTABLE TO AN OFFICE OR OTHER FIXED PLACE OF BUSINESS.—The principles of section 864(c)(5) shall apply in determining whether a taxpayer has an office or other fixed place of business and whether a sale is attributable to such an office or other fixed place of business.

[Sec. 865(f)]

(f) STOCK OF AFFILIATES.—If—

(1) a United States resident sells stock in an affiliate which is a foreign corporation,

(2) such sale occurs in a foreign country in which such affiliate is engaged in the active conduct of a trade or business, and

(3) more than 50 percent of the gross income of such affiliate for the 3-year period ending with the close of such affiliate's taxable year immediately preceding the year in which the sale occurred was derived from the active conduct of a trade or business in such foreign country,

any gain from such sale shall be sourced outside the United States. For purposes of paragraphs (2) and (3), the United States resident may elect to treat an affiliate and all other corporations which are wholly owned (directly or indirectly) by the affiliate as one corporation.

[Sec. 865(g)]

(g) UNITED STATES RESIDENT; NONRESIDENT.—For purposes of this section—

(1) IN GENERAL.—Except as otherwise provided in this subsection—

(A) UNITED STATES RESIDENT.—The term "United States resident" means—

(i) any individual who—

(I) is a United States citizen or a resident alien and does not have a tax home (as defined in section 911(d)(3)) in a foreign country, or

(II) is a nonresident alien and has a tax home (as so defined) in the United States, and

(ii) any corporation, trust, or estate which is a United States person (as defined in section 7701(a)(30)).

(B) NONRESIDENT.—The term "nonresident" means any person other than a United States resident.

(2) SPECIAL RULES FOR UNITED STATES CITIZENS AND RESIDENT ALIENS.—For purposes of this section, a United States citizen or resident alien shall not be treated as a nonresident with respect to any sale of personal property unless an income tax equal to a least 10 percent of the gain derived from such sale is actually paid to a foreign country with respect to that gain.

(3) SPECIAL RULE FOR CERTAIN STOCK SALES BY RESIDENTS OF PUERTO RICO.—Paragraph (2) shall not apply to the sale by an individual who was a bona fide resident of Puerto Rico during the entire taxable year of stock in a corporation if—

(A) such corporation is engaged in the active conduct of a trade or business in Puerto Rico, and

(B) more than 50 percent of its gross income for the 3-year period ending with the close of such corporation's taxable year immediately preceding the year in which such sale occurred was derived from the active conduct of a trade or business in Puerto Rico.

For purposes of the preceding sentence, the taxpayer may elect to treat a corporation and all other corporations which are wholly owned (directly or indirectly) by such corporation as one corporation.

[Sec. 865(h)]

(h) TREATMENT OF GAINS FROM SALE OF CERTAIN STOCK OR INTANGIBLES AND FROM CERTAIN LIQUIDATIONS.—

(1) IN GENERAL.—In the case of gain to which this subsection applies—

(A) such gain shall be sourced outside the United States, but

(B) subsections (a), (b), and (c) of section 904 and sections 907 and 960 shall be applied separately with respect to such gain.

(2) GAIN TO WHICH SUBSECTION APPLIES.—This subsection shall apply to—

(A) GAIN FROM SALE OF CERTAIN STOCK OR INTANGIBLES.—Any gain—

(i) which is from the sale of stock in a foreign corporation or an intangible (as defined in subsection (d)(2)) and which would otherwise be sourced in the United States under this section,

(ii) which, under a treaty obligation of the United States (applied without regard to this section), would be sourced outside the United States, and

(iii) with respect to which the taxpayer chooses the benefits of this subsection.

(B) GAIN FROM LIQUIDATION IN POSSESSION.—Any gain which is derived from the receipt of any distribution in liquidation of a corporation—

(i) which is organized in a possession of the United States, and

(ii) more than 50 percent of the gross income of which during the 3-taxable year period ending with the close of the taxable year immediately preceding the taxable year in which the distribution is received from the active conduct of a trade or business in such possession.

[Sec. 865(i)]

(i) OTHER DEFINITIONS.—For purposes of this section—

(1) INVENTORY PROPERTY.—The term "inventory property" means personal property described in paragraph (1) of section 1221(a).

(2) SALE INCLUDES EXCHANGE.—The term "sale" includes an exchange or any other disposition.

(3) TREATMENT OF POSSESSIONS.—Any possession of the United States shall be treated as a foreign country.

(4) AFFILIATE.—The term "affiliate" means a member of the same affiliated group (within the meaning of section 1504(a) without regard to section 1504(b)).

(5) TREATMENT OF PARTNERSHIPS.—In the case of a partnership, except as provided in regulations, this section shall be applied at the partner level.

[Sec. 865(j)]

(j) REGULATIONS.—The Secretary shall prescribe such regulations as may be necessary or appropriate to carry out the purpose of this section, including regulations—

(1) relating to the treatment of losses from sales of personal property,

(2) applying the rules of this section to income derived from trading in futures contracts, forward contracts, options contracts, and other instruments, and

(3) providing that, subject to such conditions (which may include provisions comparable to section 877) as may be provided in such regulations, subsections (e)(1)(B) and (g)(2) shall not apply for purposes of sections 931 and 933.

[Sec. 865(k)]

(k) CROSS REFERENCES.—

(1) For provisions relating to the characterization as dividends for source purposes of gains from the sale of stock in certain foreign corporations, see section 1248.

(2) For sourcing of income from certain foreign currency transactions, see section 988.

PART II—NONRESIDENT ALIENS AND FOREIGN CORPORATIONS

Subpart A—Nonresident Alien Individuals

[Sec. 871]

SEC. 871. TAX ON NONRESIDENT ALIEN INDIVIDUALS.

[Sec. 871(a)]

(a) INCOME NOT CONNECTED WITH UNITED STATES BUSINESS—30 PERCENT TAX.—

(1) INCOME OTHER THAN CAPITAL GAINS.—Except as provided in subsection (h), there is hereby imposed for each taxable year a tax of 30 percent of the amount received from sources within the United States by a nonresident alien individual as—

(A) interest (other than original issue discount as defined in section 1273), dividends, rents, salaries, wages, premiums, annuities, compensations, remunerations, emoluments, and other fixed or determinable annual or periodical gains, profits, and income,

(B) gains described in subsection (b) or (c) of section 631,

(C) in the case of—

(i) a sale or exchange of an original issue discount obligation, the amount of the original issue discount accruing while such obligation was held by the nonresident alien individual (to the extent such discount was not theretofore taken into account under clause (ii)), and

(ii) a payment on an original issue discount obligation, an amount equal to the original issue discount accruing while such obligation was held by the nonresident alien individual (except that such original issue discount shall be taken into account under this clause only to the extent such discount was not theretofore taken into account under this clause and only to the extent that the tax thereon does not exceed the payment less the tax imposed by subparagraph (A) thereon), and

(D) gains from the sale or exchange after October 4, 1966, of patents, copyrights, secret processes and formulas, good will, trademarks, trade brands, franchises, and other like property, or of any interest in any such property, to the extent such gains are from payments which are contingent on the productivity, use, or disposition of the property or interest sold or exchanged,

but only to the extent the amount so received is not effectively connected with the conduct of a trade or business within the United States.

(2) CAPITAL GAINS OF ALIENS PRESENT IN THE UNITED STATES 183 DAYS OR MORE.—In the case of a nonresident alien individual present in the United States for a period or periods aggregating 183 days or more during the taxable year, there is hereby imposed for such year a tax of 30 percent of the amount by which his gains, derived from sources within the United States, from the sale or exchange at any time during such year of capital assets exceed his losses, allocable to sources within the United States, from the sale or exchange at any time during such year of capital assets. For purposes of this paragraph, gains and losses shall be taken into account only if, and to the extent that, they would be recognized and taken into account if such gains and losses were effectively connected with the conduct of a trade or business within the United States, except that such gains and losses shall be determined without regard to section 1202 and such losses shall be determined without the benefits of the capital loss carryover provided in section 1212. Any gain or loss which is taken into account in determining the tax under paragraph (1) or subsection (b) shall not be taken into account in determining the tax under this paragraph. For purposes of the 183-day requirement of this paragraph, a nonresident alien individual not engaged in trade or business within the United States who has not established a taxable year for any prior period shall be treated as having a taxable year which is the calendar year.

(3) TAXATION OF SOCIAL SECURITY BENEFITS.—For purposes of this section and section 1441—

(A) 85 percent of any social security benefit (as defined in section 86(d)) shall be included in gross income (notwithstanding section 207 of the Social Security Act), and

(B) section 86 shall not apply.

[Sec. 871(b)]

(b) INCOME CONNECTED WITH UNITED STATES BUSINESS—GRADUATED RATE OF TAX.—

(1) IMPOSITION OF TAX.—A nonresident alien individual engaged in trade or business within the United States during the taxable year shall be taxable as provided in section 1 or 55 on his taxable income which is effectively connected with the conduct of a trade or business within the United States.

(2) DETERMINATION OF TAXABLE INCOME.—In determining taxable income for purposes of paragraph (1), gross income includes only gross income which is effectively connected with the conduct of a trade or business within the United States.

[Sec. 871(c)]

(c) PARTICIPANTS IN CERTAIN EXCHANGE OR TRAINING PROGRAMS.—For purposes of this section, a nonresident alien individual who (without regard to this subsection) is not engaged in trade or business within the United States and who is temporarily present in the United States as a nonimmigrant under subparagraph (F), (J), (M), or (Q) of section 101(a)(15) of the Immigration and Nationality Act, as amended (8 U.S.C. 1101(a)(15)(F), (J), (M), or (Q)), shall be treated as a nonresident alien individual engaged in trade or business within the United States, and any income described in the second sentence of section 1441(b) which is received by such individual shall, to the extent derived from sources within the United States, be treated as effectively connected with the conduct of a trade or business within the United States.

[Sec. 871(d)]

(d) ELECTION TO TREAT REAL PROPERTY INCOME AS INCOME CONNECTED WITH UNITED STATES BUSINESS.—

(1) IN GENERAL.—A nonresident alien individual who during the taxable year derives any income—

(A) from real property held for the production of income and located in the United States, or from any interest in such real property, including (i) gains from the sale or exchange of such real property or an interest therein, (ii) rents or royalties from mines, wells, or other natural deposits, and (iii) gains described in section 631(b) or (c), and

(B) which, but for this subsection, would not be treated as income which is effectively connected with the conduct of a trade or business within the United States,

may elect for such taxable year to treat all such income as income which is effectively connected with the conduct of a trade or business within the United States. In such case, such income shall be taxable as provided in subsection (b)(1) whether or not such individual is engaged in trade or business within the United States during the taxable year. An election under this paragraph for any taxable year shall remain in effect for all subsequent taxable years, except that it may be revoked with the consent of the Secretary with respect to any taxable year.

(2) ELECTION AFTER REVOCATION.—If an election has been made under paragraph (1) and such election has been revoked, a new election may not be made under such paragraph for any taxable year before the 5th taxable year which begins after the first taxable year for which such revocation is effective, unless the Secretary consents to such new election.

(3) FORM AND TIME OF ELECTION AND REVOCATION.—An election under paragraph (1), and any revocation of such an election, may be made only in such manner and at such time as the Secretary may by regulations prescribe.

* * *

[Sec. 871(g)]

(g) SPECIAL RULES FOR ORIGINAL ISSUE DISCOUNT.—For purposes of this section and section 881—

(1) ORIGINAL ISSUE DISCOUNT OBLIGATION.—

(A) IN GENERAL.—Except as provided in subparagraph (B), the term "original issue discount obligation" means any bond or other evidence of indebtedness having original issue discount (within the meaning of section 1273).

(B) EXCEPTIONS.—The term "original issue discount obligation" shall not include—

(i) CERTAIN SHORT-TERM OBLIGATIONS.—Any obligation payable 183 days or less from the date of original issue (without regard to the period held by the taxpayer).

(ii) TAX-EXEMPT OBLIGATIONS.—Any obligation the interest on which is exempt from tax under section 103 or under any other provision of law without regard to the identity of the holder.

(2) DETERMINATION OF PORTION OF ORIGINAL ISSUE DISCOUNT ACCRUING DURING ANY PERIOD.—The determination of the amount of the original issue discount which accrues during any period shall be made under the rules of section 1272 (or the corresponding provisions of prior law) without regard to any exception for short-term obligations.

(3) SOURCE OF ORIGINAL ISSUE DISCOUNT.—Except to the extent provided in regulations prescribed by the Secretary, the determination of whether any amount described in subsection (a)(1)(C) is from sources within the United States shall be made at the time of the payment (or sale or exchange) as if such payment (or sale or exchange) involved the payment of interest.

(4) STRIPPED BONDS.—The provisions of section 1286 (relating to the treatment of stripped bonds and stripped coupons as obligations with original issue discount) shall apply for purposes of this section.

[Sec. 871(h)]

(h) REPEAL OF TAX ON INTEREST OF NONRESIDENT ALIEN INDIVIDUALS RECEIVED FROM CERTAIN PORTFOLIO DEBT INVESTMENTS.—

(1) IN GENERAL.—In the case of any portfolio interest received by a nonresident individual from sources within the United States, no tax shall be imposed under paragraph (1)(A) or (1)(C) of subsection (a).

(2) PORTFOLIO INTEREST.—For purposes of this subsection, the term "portfolio interest" means any interest (including original issue discount) which—

(A) would be subject to tax under subsection (a) but for this subsection, and

(B) is paid on an obligation—

(i) which is in registered form, and

(ii) with respect to which—

(I) the United States person who would otherwise be required to deduct and withhold tax from such interest under section 1441(a) receives a statement (which meets the requirements of paragraph (5)) that the beneficial owner of the obligation is not a United States person, or

(II) the Secretary has determined that such a statement is not required in order to carry out the purposes of this subsection.

(3) PORTFOLIO INTEREST NOT TO INCLUDE INTEREST RECEIVED BY 10-PERCENT SHAREHOLDERS.—For purposes of this subsection—

(A) IN GENERAL.—The term "portfolio interest" shall not include any interest described in paragraph (2) which is received by a 10-percent shareholder.

(B) 10-PERCENT SHAREHOLDER.—The term "10-percent shareholder" means—

(i) in the case of an obligation issued by a corporation, any person who owns 10 percent or more of the total combined voting power of all classes of stock of such corporation entitled to vote, or

(ii) in the case of an obligation issued by a partnership, any person who owns 10 percent or more of the capital or profits interest in such partnership.

(C) ATTRIBUTION RULES.—For purposes of determining ownership of stock under subparagraph (B)(i) the rules of section 318(a) shall apply, except that—

(i) section 318(a)(2)(C) shall be applied without regard to the 50-percent limitation therein,

(ii) section 318(a)(3)(C) shall be applied—

(I) without regard to the 50-percent limitation therein; and

(II) in any case where such section would not apply but for subclause (I), by considering a corporation as owning the stock (other than stock in such corporation) which is owned by or for any shareholder of such corporation in that proportion which the value of the stock which such shareholder owns in such corporation bears to the value of all stock in such corporation, and

(iii) any stock which a person is treated as owning after application of section 318(a)(4) shall not, for purposes of applying paragraphs (2) and (3) of section 318(a), be treated as actually owned by such person.

Under regulations prescribed by the Secretary, rules similar to the rules of the preceding sentence shall be applied in determining the ownership of the capital or profits interest in a partnership for purposes of subparagraph (B)(ii).

(4) PORTFOLIO INTEREST NOT TO INCLUDE CERTAIN CONTINGENT INTEREST.—For purposes of this subsection—

(A) IN GENERAL.—Except as otherwise provided in this paragraph, the term "portfolio interest" shall not include—

(i) any interest if the amount of such interest is determined by reference to—

(I) any receipts, sales or other cash flow of the debtor or a related person,

(II) any income or profits of the debtor or a related person,

(III) any change in value of any property of the debtor or a related person, or

(IV) any dividend, partnership distributions, or similar payments made by the debtor or a related person, or

(ii) any other type of contingent interest that is identified by the Secretary by regulation, where a denial of the portfolio interest exemption is necessary or appropriate to prevent avoidance of Federal income tax.

(B) RELATED PERSON.—The term "related person" means any person who is related to the debtor within the meaning of section 267(b) or 707(b)(1), or who is a party to any arrangement undertaken for a purpose of avoiding the application of this paragraph.

(C) EXCEPTIONS.—Subparagraph (A)(i) shall not apply to—

(i) any amount of interest solely by reason of the fact that the timing of any interest or principal payment is subject to a contingency,

(ii) any amount of interest solely by reason of the fact that the interest is paid with respect to nonrecourse or limited recourse indebtedness,

(iii) any amount of interest all or substantially all of which is determined by reference to any other amount of interest not described in subparagraph (A) (or by reference to the principal amount of indebtedness on which such other interest is paid),

(iv) any amount of interest solely by reason of the fact that the debtor or a related person enters into a hedging transaction to manage the risk of interest rate or currency fluctuations with respect to such interest,

(v) any amount of interest determined by reference to—

(I) changes in the value of property (including stock) that is actively traded (within the meaning of section 1092(d)) other than property described in section 897(c)(1) or (g),

(II) the yield on property described in subclause (I), other than a debt instrument that pays interest described in subparagraph (A), or stock or other property that represents a beneficial interest in the debtor or a related person, or

(III) changes in any index of the value of property described in subclause (I) or of the yield on property described in subclause (II), and

(vi) any other type of interest identified by the Secretary by regulation.

(D) EXCEPTION FOR CERTAIN EXISTING INDEBTEDNESS.—Subparagraph (A) shall not apply to any interest paid or accrued with respect to any indebtedness with a fixed term—

(i) which was issued on or before April 7, 1993, or

(ii) which was issued after such date pursuant to a written binding contract in effect on such date and at all times thereafter before such indebtedness was issued.

(5) CERTAIN STATEMENTS.—A statement with respect to any obligation meets the requirements of this paragraph if such statement is made by—

(A) the beneficial owner of such obligation, or

(B) a securities clearing organization, a bank, or other financial institution that holds customers' securities in the ordinary course of its trade or business.

The preceding sentence shall not apply to any statement with respect to payment of interest on any obligation by any person if, at least one month before such payment, the Secretary has published a determination that any statement from such person (or any class including such person) does not meet the requirements of this paragraph.

(6) SECRETARY MAY PROVIDE SUBSECTION NOT TO APPLY IN CASES OF INADEQUATE INFORMATION EXCHANGE.—

(A) IN GENERAL.—If the Secretary determines that the exchange of information between the United States and a foreign country is inadequate to prevent evasion of the United States income tax by United States persons, the Secretary may provide in writing (and publish a statement) that the provisions of this subsection shall not apply to payments of interest to any person within such foreign country (or payments addressed to, or for the account of, persons within such foreign country) during the period—

(i) beginning on the date specified by the Secretary, and

(ii) ending on the date that the Secretary determines that the exchange of information between the United States and the foreign country is adequate to prevent the evasion of United States income tax by United States persons.

(B) EXCEPTION FOR CERTAIN OBLIGATIONS.—Subparagraph (A) shall not apply to the payment of interest on any obligation which is issued on or before the date of the publication of the Secretary's determination under such subparagraph.

(7) REGISTERED FORM.—For purposes of this subsection, the term "registered form" has the same meaning given such term by section 163(f).

[Sec. 871(i)]

(i) TAX NOT TO APPLY TO CERTAIN INTEREST AND DIVIDENDS.—

(1) IN GENERAL.—No tax shall be imposed under paragraph (1)(A) or (1)(C) of subsection (a) on any amount described in paragraph (2).

(2) AMOUNTS TO WHICH PARAGRAPH (1) APPLIES.—The amounts described in this paragraph are as follows:

(A) Interest on deposits, if such interest is not effectively connected with the conduct of a trade or business within the United States.

(B) The active foreign business percentage of—

(i) any dividend paid by an existing 80/20 company, and

(ii) any interest paid by an existing 80/20 company.

(C) Income derived by a foreign central bank of issue from bankers' acceptances.

(D) Dividends paid by a foreign corporation which are treated under section 861(a)(2)(B) as income from sources within the United States.

(3) DEPOSITS.—For purposes of paragraph (2), the term "deposit" means amounts which are—

(A) deposits with persons carrying on the banking business,

(B) deposits or withdrawable accounts with savings institutions chartered and supervised as savings and loan or similar associations under Federal or State law, but only to the extent that amounts paid or credited on such deposits or accounts are deductible under section 591 (determined without regard to sections 265 and 291) in computing the taxable income of such institutions, and

(C) amounts held by an insurance company under an agreement to pay interest thereon.

[Sec. 871(j)]

(j) EXEMPTION FOR CERTAIN GAMBLING WINNINGS.—No tax shall be imposed under paragraph (1)(A) of subsection (a) on the proceeds from a wager placed in any of the following games: blackjack, baccarat, craps, roulette, or big-6 wheel. The preceding sentence shall not apply in any case where the Secretary determines by regulation that the collection of the tax is administratively feasible.

* * *

[Sec. 871(l)]

(l) RULES RELATING TO EXISTING 80/20 COMPANIES .—For purposes of this subsection and subsection (i)(2)(B)—

(1) EXISTING 80/20 COMPANY.—

(A) IN GENERAL .—The term "existing 80/20 company" means any corporation if—

(i) such corporation met the 80-percent foreign business requirements of section 861(c)(1) (as in effect before the date of the enactment of this subsection) for such corporation's last taxable year beginning before January 1, 2011,

(ii) such corporation meets the 80-percent foreign business requirements of subparagraph (B) with respect to each taxable year after the taxable year referred to in clause (i), and

(iii) there has not been an addition of a substantial line of business with respect to such corporation after the date of the enactment of this subsection.

(B) FOREIGN BUSINESS REQUIREMENTS.—

(i) IN GENERAL .—Except as provided in clause (iv), a corporation meets the 80-percent foreign business requirements of this subparagraph if it is shown to the satisfaction of the Secretary that at least 80 percent of the gross income from all sources of such corporation for the testing period is active foreign business income.

(ii) ACTIVE FOREIGN BUSINESS INCOME .—For purposes of clause (i), the term "active foreign business income" means gross income which—

(I) is derived from sources outside the United States (as determined under this subchapter), and

(II) is attributable to the active conduct of a trade or business in a foreign country or possession of the United States.

(iii) TESTING PERIOD .—For purposes of this subsection, the term "testing period" means the 3-year period ending with the close of the taxable year of the corporation preceding the payment (or such part of such period as may be applicable). If the corporation has no gross income for such 3-year period (or part thereof), the testing period shall be the taxable year in which the payment is made.

(iv) TRANSITION RULE .—In the case of a taxable year for which the testing period includes 1 or more taxable years beginning before January 1, 2011—

(I) a corporation meets the 80-percent foreign business requirements of this subparagraph if and only if the weighted average of—

(aa) the percentage of the corporation's gross income from all sources that is active foreign business income (as defined in subparagraph (B) of section 861(c)(1) (as in effect before the date of the enactment of this subsection)) for the portion of the testing period that includes taxable years beginning before January 1, 2011, and

(bb) the percentage of the corporation's gross income from all sources that is active foreign business income (as defined in clause (ii) of this subparagraph) for the portion of the testing period, if any, that includes taxable years beginning on or after January 1, 2011,

is at least 80 percent, and

(II) the active foreign business percentage for such taxable year shall equal the weighted average percentage determined under subclause (I).

(2) ACTIVE FOREIGN BUSINESS PERCENTAGE .—Except as provided in paragraph (1)(B)(iv), the term "active foreign business percentage" means, with respect to any existing 80/20 company, the percentage which—

(A) the active foreign business income of such company for the testing period, is of

(B) the gross income of such company for the testing period from all sources.

(3) AGGREGATION RULES .—For purposes of applying paragraph (1) (other than subparagraphs (A)(i) and (B)(iv) thereof) and paragraph (2)—

(A) IN GENERAL .—The corporation referred to in paragraph (1)(A) and all of such corporation's subsidiaries shall be treated as one corporation.

(B) SUBSIDIARIES .—For purposes of subparagraph (A), the term "subsidiary" means any corporation in which the corporation referred to in subparagraph (A) owns (directly or indirectly) stock meeting the requirements of section 1504(a)(2) (determined by substituting "50 percent" for "80 percent" each place it appears and without regard to section 1504(b)(3)).

(4) REGULATIONS .—The Secretary may issue such regulations or other guidance as is necessary or appropriate to carry out the purposes of this section, including regulations or other guidance which provide for the proper application of the aggregation rules described in paragraph (3).

[Sec. 871(m)]

(m) TREATMENT OF DIVIDEND EQUIVALENT PAYMENTS.—

(1) IN GENERAL .—For purposes of subsection (a), sections 881 and 4948(a), and chapters 3 and 4, a dividend equivalent shall be treated as a dividend from sources within the United States.

(2) DIVIDEND EQUIVALENT .—For purposes of this subsection, the term "dividend equivalent" means—

(A) any substitute dividend made pursuant to a securities lending or a sale-repurchase transaction that (directly or indirectly) is contingent upon, or determined by reference to, the payment of a dividend from sources within the United States,

(B) any payment made pursuant to a specified notional principal contract that (directly or indirectly) is contingent upon, or determined by reference to, the payment of a dividend from sources within the United States, and

(C) any other payment determined by the Secretary to be substantially similar to a payment described in subparagraph (A) or (B).

(3) SPECIFIED NOTIONAL PRINCIPAL CONTRACT .—For purposes of this subsection, the term "specified notional principal contract" means—

(A) any notional principal contract if—

(i) in connection with entering into such contract, any long party to the contract transfers the underlying security to any short party to the contract,

(ii) in connection with the termination of such contract, any short party to the contract transfers the underlying security to any long party to the contract,

(iii) the underlying security is not readily tradable on an established securities market,

(iv) in connection with entering into such contract, the underlying security is posted as collateral by any short party to the contract with any long party to the contract, or

(v) such contract is identified by the Secretary as a specified notional principal contract,

(B) in the case of payments made after the date which is 2 years after the date of the enactment of this subsection, any notional principal contract unless the Secretary determines that such contract is of a type which does not have the potential for tax avoidance.

(4) DEFINITIONS .—For purposes of paragraph (3)(A)—

(A) LONG PARTY .—The term "long party" means, with respect to any underlying security of any notional principal contract, any party to the contract which is entitled to receive any payment pursuant to such contract which is contingent upon, or determined by reference to, the payment of a dividend from sources within the United States with respect to such underlying security.

(B) SHORT PARTY .—The term "short party" means, with respect to any underlying security of any notional principal contract, any party to the contract which is not a long party with respect to such underlying security.

(C) UNDERLYING SECURITY .—The term "underlying security" means, with respect to any notional principal contract, the security with respect to which the dividend referred to in paragraph (2)(B) is paid. For purposes of this paragraph, any index or fixed basket of securities shall be treated as a single security.

(5) PAYMENTS DETERMINED ON GROSS BASIS .—For purposes of this subsection, the term "payment" includes any gross amount which is used in computing any net amount which is transferred to or from the taxpayer.

(6) PREVENTION OF OVER-WITHHOLDING .—In the case of any chain of dividend equivalents one or more of which is subject to tax under subsection (a) or section 881, the Secretary may reduce such tax, but only to the extent that the taxpayer can establish that such tax has been paid with respect to another dividend equivalent in such chain, or is not otherwise due, or as the Secretary determines is appropriate to address the role of financial intermediaries in such chain. For purposes of this paragraph, a dividend shall be treated as a dividend equivalent.

(7) COORDINATION WITH CHAPTERS 3 AND 4 .—For purposes of chapters 3 and 4, each person that is a party to any contract or other arrangement that provides for the payment of a dividend equivalent shall be treated as having control of such payment.

[Sec. 871(n)]

(n) CROSS REFERENCES.—

(1) For tax treatment of certain amounts distributed by the United States to nonresident alien individuals, see section 402(e)(2).

(2) For taxation of nonresident alien individuals who are expatriate United States citizens, see section 877.

(3) For doubling of tax on citizens of certain foreign countries, see section 891.

(4) For adjustment of tax in case of nationals or residents of certain foreign countries, see section 896.

(5) For withholding of tax at source on nonresident alien individuals, see section 1441.

(6) For election to treat married nonresident alien individual as resident of United States in certain cases, see subsections (g) and (h) of section 6013.

(7) For special tax treatment of gain or loss from the disposition by a nonresident alien individual of a United States real property interest, see section 897.

[Sec. 872]

SEC. 872. GROSS INCOME.

[Sec. 872(a)]

(a) GENERAL RULE.—In the case of a nonresident alien individual, except where the context clearly indicates otherwise, gross income includes only—

(1) gross income which is derived from sources within the United States and which is not effectively connected with the conduct of a trade or business within the United States, and

(2) gross income which is effectively connected with the conduct of a trade or business within the United States.

[Sec. 872(b)]

(b) EXCLUSIONS.—The following items shall not be included in gross income of a nonresident alien individual, and shall be exempt from taxation under this subtitle:

(1) SHIPS OPERATED BY CERTAIN NONRESIDENTS.—Gross income derived by an individual resident of a foreign country from the international operation of a ship or ships if such foreign country grants an equivalent exemption to individual residents of the United States.

(2) AIRCRAFT OPERATION BY CERTAIN NONRESIDENTS.—Gross income derived by an individual resident of a foreign country from the international operation of aircraft if such foreign country grants an equivalent exemption to individual residents of the United States.

(3) COMPENSATION OF PARTICIPANTS IN CERTAIN EXCHANGE OR TRAINING PROGRAMS.—Compensation paid by a foreign employer to a nonresident alien individual for the period he is temporarily present in the United States as a nonimmigrant under subparagraph (F), (J), or (Q) of section 101(a)(15) of the Immigration and Nationality Act, as amended. For purposes of this paragraph, the term "foreign employer" means—

(A) a nonresident alien individual, foreign partnership, or foreign corporation, or

(B) an office or place of business maintained in a foreign country or in a possession of the United States by a domestic corporation, a domestic partnership, or an individual who is a citizen or resident of the United States.

(4) CERTAIN BOND INCOME OF RESIDENTS OF THE RYUKYU ISLANDS OR THE TRUST TERRITORY OF THE PACIFIC ISLANDS.—Income derived by a nonresident alien individual from a series E or series H United States savings bond, if such individual acquired such bond while a resident of the Ryukyu Islands or the Trust Territory of the Pacific Islands.

(5) INCOME DERIVED FROM WAGERING TRANSACTIONS IN CERTAIN PARIMUTUEL POOLS.—Gross income derived by a nonresident alien individual from a legal wagering transaction initiated outside the United States in a parimutuel pool with respect to a live horse race or dog race in the United States.

(6) CERTAIN RENTAL INCOME.—Income to which paragraphs (1) and (2) apply shall include income which is derived from the rental on a full or bareboat basis of a ship or ships or aircraft, as the case may be.

(7) APPLICATION TO DIFFERENT TYPES OF TRANSPORTATION.—The Secretary may provide that this subsection be applied separately with respect to income from different types of transportation.

(8) TREATMENT OF POSSESSIONS.—To the extent provided in regulations, a possession of the United States shall be treated as a foreign country for purposes of this subsection.

[Sec. 873]

SEC. 873. DEDUCTIONS.

[Sec. 873(a)]

(a) GENERAL RULE.—In the case of a nonresident alien individual, the deductions shall be allowed only for purposes of section 871(b) and (except as provided by subsection (b)) only if and to the extent that they are connected with income which is effectively connected with the conduct of a trade or business within the United States; and the proper apportionment and allocation of the deductions for this purpose shall be determined as provided in regulations prescribed by the Secretary.

[Sec. 873(b)]

(b) EXCEPTIONS.—The following deductions shall be allowed whether or not they are connected with income which is effectively connected with the conduct of a trade or business within the United States:

(1) LOSSES.—The deduction allowed by section 165 for casualty or theft losses described in paragraph (2) or (3) of section 165(c), but only if the loss is of property located within the United States.

(2) CHARITABLE CONTRIBUTIONS.—The deduction for charitable contributions and gifts allowed by section 170.

(3) PERSONAL EXEMPTION.—The deduction for personal exemptions allowed by section 151, except that only one exemption shall be allowed under section 151 unless the taxpayer is a resident of a contiguous country or is a national of the United States.

* * *

[Sec. 874]

SEC. 874. ALLOWANCE OF DEDUCTIONS AND CREDITS.

[Sec. 874(a)]

(a) RETURN PREREQUISITE TO ALLOWANCE.—A nonresident alien individual shall receive the benefit of the deductions and credits allowed to him in this subtitle only by filing or causing to be filed with the Secretary a true and accurate return, in the manner prescribed in subtitle F (sec. 6001 and following, relating to procedure and administration), including therein all the information which the Secretary may deem necessary for the calculation of such deductions and credits. This subsection shall not be construed to deny the credits provided by sections 31 and 33 for tax withheld at source or the credit provided by section 34 for certain uses of gasoline and special fuels.

[Sec. 874(b)]

(b) TAX WITHHELD AT SOURCE.—The benefit of the deduction for exemptions under section 151 may, in the discretion of the Secretary, and under regulations prescribed by the Secretary, be received by a nonresident alien individual entitled thereto, by filing a claim therefor with the withholding agent.

[Sec. 874(c)]

(c) FOREIGN TAX CREDIT.—Except as provided in section 906, a nonresident alien individual shall not be allowed the credits against the tax for taxes of foreign countries and possessions of the United States allowed by section 901.

[Sec. 875]

SEC. 875. PARTNERSHIPS; BENEFICIARIES OF ESTATES AND TRUSTS.

For purposes of this subtitle—

(1) a nonresident alien individual or foreign corporation shall be considered as being engaged in a trade or business within the United States if the partnership of which such individual or corporation is a member is so engaged, and

(2) a nonresident alien individual or foreign corporation which is a beneficiary of an estate or trust which is engaged in any trade or business within the United States shall be treated as being engaged in such trade or business within the United States.

[Sec. 876]

SEC. 876. ALIEN RESIDENTS OF PUERTO RICO, GUAM, AMERICAN SAMOA, OR THE NORTHERN MARIANA ISLANDS.

[Sec. 876(a)]

(a) GENERAL RULE.—This subpart shall not apply to any alien individual who is a bona fide resident of Puerto Rico, Guam, American Samoa, or the Northern Mariana Islands during the entire taxable year and such alien shall be subject to the tax imposed by section 1.

[Sec. 876(b)]

(b) CROSS REFERENCES.—

For exclusion from gross income of income derived from sources within—

(1) Guam, American Samoa, and the Northern Mariana Islands, see section 931, and

(2) Puerto Rico, see section 933.

[Sec. 877]

SEC. 877. EXPATRIATION TO AVOID TAX.

[Sec. 877(a)]

(a) TREATMENT OF EXPATRIATES.—

(1) IN GENERAL.—Every nonresident alien individual to whom this section applies and who, within the 10-year period immediately preceding the close of the taxable year, lost United States citizenship shall be taxable for such taxable year in the manner provided in subsection (b) if the tax imposed pursuant to such subsection (after any reduction in such tax under the last sentence of such subsection) exceeds the tax which, without regard to this section, is imposed pursuant to section 871.

»»→ Caution: Pursuant to Section 877(a), the $124,000 amount in Section 877(a)(2)(A) is adjusted for calendar years beginning after 2004 to reflect increases in the Chained Consumer Price Index. The adjusted amount that applies for calendar year 2023 is $190,000, as provided in Rev. Proc. 2022-38, 2022-45 I.R.B. 445.

(2) INDIVIDUALS SUBJECT TO THIS SECTION.—This section shall apply to any individual if—

(A) the average annual net income tax (as defined in section 38(c)(1)) of such individual for the period of 5 taxable years ending before the date of the loss of United States citizenship is greater than $124,000,

(B) the net worth of the individual as of such date is $2,000,000 or more, or

(C) such individual fails to certify under penalty of perjury that he has met the requirements of this title for the 5 preceding taxable years or fails to submit such evidence of such compliance as the Secretary may require.

In the case of the loss of United States citizenship in any calendar year after 2004, such $124,000 amount shall be increased by an amount equal to such dollar amount multiplied by the cost-of-living adjustment determined under section 1(f)(3)for such calendar year by substituting "2003" for "1992" in subparagraph (B) thereof. Any increase under the preceding sentence shall be rounded to the nearest multiple of $1,000.

[Sec. 877(b)]

(b) ALTERNATIVE TAX.—A nonresident alien individual described in subsection (a) shall be taxable for the taxable year as provided in section 1 or 55, except that—

(1) the gross income shall include only the gross income described in section 872(a) (as modified by subsection (d) of this section), and

(2) the deductions shall be allowed if and to the extent that they are connected with the gross income included under this section, except that the capital loss carryover provided by section 1212(b) shall not be allowed; and the proper allocation and apportionment of the deductions for this purpose shall be determined as provided under regulations prescribed by the Secretary.

For purposes of paragraph (2), the deductions allowed by section 873(b) shall be allowed; and the deduction (for losses not connected with the trade or business if incurred in transactions entered into for profit) allowed by section 165(c)(2) shall be allowed, but only if the profit, if such transaction had resulted in a profit, would be included in gross income under this section. The tax imposed solely by reason of this section shall be reduced (but not below zero) by the amount of any income, war profits, and excess profits taxes (within the meaning of section 903) paid to any foreign country or possession of the United States on any income of the taxpayer on which tax is imposed solely by reason of this section.

[Sec. 877(c)]

(c) EXCEPTIONS.—

(1) IN GENERAL.—Subparagraphs (A) and (B) of subsection (a)(2) shall not apply to an individual described in paragraph (2) or (3).

(2) DUAL CITIZENS.—

(A) IN GENERAL.—An individual is described in this paragraph if—

(i) the individual became at birth a citizen of the United States and a citizen of another country and continues to be a citizen of such other country, and

(ii) the individual has had no substantial contacts with the United States.

(B) SUBSTANTIAL CONTACTS.—An individual shall be treated as having no substantial contacts with the United States only if the individual—

(i) was never a resident of the United States (as defined in section 7701(b)),

(ii) has never held a United States passport, and

(iii) was not present in the United States for more than 30 days during any calendar year which is 1 of the 10 calendar years preceding the individual's loss of United States citizenship.

(3) CERTAIN MINORS.—An individual is described in this paragraph if—

(A) the individual became at birth a citizen of the United States,

(B) neither parent of such individual was a citizen of the United States at the time of such birth,

(C) the individual's loss of United States citizenship occurs before such individual attains age 18$^1/_2$, and

(D) the individual was not present in the United States for more than 30 days during any calendar year which is 1 of the 10 calendar years preceding the individual's loss of United States citizenship.

[Sec. 877(d)]

(d) SPECIAL RULES FOR SOURCE, ETC.—For purposes of subsection (b)—

(1) SOURCE RULES.—The following items of gross income shall be treated as income from sources within the United States:

(A) SALE OF PROPERTY.—Gains on the sale or exchange of property (other than stock or debt obligations) located in the United States.

(B) STOCK OR DEBT OBLIGATIONS.—Gains on the sale or exchange of stock issued by a domestic corporation or debt obligations of United States persons or of the United States, a State or political subdivision thereof, or the District of Columbia.

(C) INCOME OR GAIN DERIVED FROM CONTROLLED FOREIGN CORPORATION.—Any income or gain derived from stock in a foreign corporation but only—

(i) if the individual losing United States citizenship owned (within the meaning of section 958(a)), or is considered as owning (by applying the ownership rules of section 958(b)), at any time during the 2-year period ending on the date of the loss of United States citizenship, more than 50 percent of—

(I) the total combined voting power of all classes of stock entitled to vote of such corporation, or

(II) the total value of the stock of such corporation, and

(ii) to the extent such income or gain does not exceed the earnings and profits attributable to such stock which were earned or accumulated before the loss of citizenship and during periods that the ownership requirements of clause (i) are met.

(2) GAIN RECOGNITION ON CERTAIN EXCHANGES.—

(A) IN GENERAL.—In the case of any exchange of property to which this paragraph applies, notwithstanding any other provision of this title, such property shall be treated as sold for its fair market value on the date of such exchange, and any gain shall be recognized for the taxable year which includes such date.

(B) EXCHANGES TO WHICH PARAGRAPH APPLIES.—This paragraph shall apply to any exchange during the 10-year period beginning on the date the individual loses United States citizenship if—

(i) gain would not (but for this paragraph) be recognized on such exchange in whole or in part for purposes of this subtitle,

(ii) income derived from such property was from sources within the United States (or, if no income was so derived, would have been from such sources), and

(iii) income derived from the property acquired in the exchange would be from sources outside the United States.

(C) EXCEPTION.—Subparagraph (A) shall not apply if the individual enters into an agreement with the Secretary which specifies that any income or gain derived from the property acquired in the exchange (or any other property which has a basis determined in whole or part by reference to such property) during such 10-year period shall be treated as from sources within the United States. If the property transferred in the exchange is disposed of by the person acquiring such property, such agreement shall terminate and any gain which was not recognized by reason of such agreement shall be recognized as of the date of such disposition.

(D) SECRETARY MAY EXTEND PERIOD.—To the extent provided in regulations prescribed by the Secretary, subparagraph (B) shall be applied by substituting the 15-year period beginning 5 years before the loss of United States citizenship for the 10-year period referred to therein. In the case of any exchange occurring during such 5 years, any gain recognized under this subparagraph shall be recognized immediately after such loss of citizenship.

(E) SECRETARY MAY REQUIRE RECOGNITION OF GAIN IN CERTAIN CASES.—To the extent provided in regulations prescribed by the Secretary—

(i) the removal of appreciated tangible personal property from the United States, and

(ii) any other occurrence which (without recognition of gain) results in a change in the source of the income or gain from property from sources within the United States to sources outside the United States,

shall be treated as an exchange to which this paragraph applies.

(3) SUBSTANTIAL DIMINISHING OF RISKS OF OWNERSHIP.—For purposes of determining whether this section applies to any gain on the sale or exchange of any property, the running of the 10-year period described in subsection (a) and the period applicable under paragraph (2) shall be suspended for any period during which the individual's risk of loss with respect to the property is substantially diminished by—

(A) the holding of a put with respect to such property (or similar property),

(B) the holding by another person of a right to acquire the property, or

(C) a short sale or any other transaction.

(4) TREATMENT OF PROPERTY CONTRIBUTED TO CONTROLLED FOREIGN CORPORATIONS.—

(A) IN GENERAL.—If—

(i) an individual losing United States citizenship contributes property during the 10-year period beginning on the date the individual loses United States citizenship to any corporation which, at the time of the contribution, is described in subparagraph (B), and

(ii) income derived from such property immediately before such contribution was from sources within the United States (or, if no income was so derived, would have been from such sources),

any income or gain on such property (or any other property which has a basis determined in whole or part by reference to such property) received or accrued by the corporation shall be treated as received or accrued directly by such individual and not by such corporation. The preceding sentence shall not apply to the extent the property has been treated under subparagraph (C) as having been sold by such corporation.

(B) CORPORATION DESCRIBED.—A corporation is described in this subparagraph with respect to an individual if, were such individual a United States citizen—

(i) such corporation would be a controlled foreign corporation (as defined in section 957), and

(ii) such individual would be a United States shareholder (as defined in section 951(b)) with respect to such corporation.

(C) DISPOSITION OF STOCK IN CORPORATION.—If stock in the corporation referred to in subparagraph (A) (or any other stock which has a basis determined in whole or part by reference to such stock) is disposed of during the 10-year period referred to in subsection (a) and while the property referred to in subparagraph (A) is held by such corporation, a pro rata share of such property (determined on the basis of the value of such stock) shall be treated as sold by the corporation immediately before such disposition.

(D) ANTI-ABUSE RULES.—The Secretary shall prescribe such regulations as may be necessary to prevent the avoidance of the purposes of this paragraph, including where—

(i) the property is sold to the corporation, and

(ii) the property taken into account under subparagraph (A) is sold by the corporation.

(E) INFORMATION REPORTING.—The Secretary shall require such information reporting as is necessary to carry out the purposes of this paragraph.

[Sec. 877(e)]

(e) COMPARABLE TREATMENT OF LAWFUL PERMANENT RESIDENTS WHO CEASE TO BE TAXED AS RESIDENTS.—

(1) IN GENERAL.—Any long-term resident of the United States who ceases to be a lawful permanent resident of the United States (within the meaning of section 7701(b)(6)) shall be treated for purposes of this section and sections 2107, 2501, and 6039G in the same manner as if such resident were a citizen of the United States who lost United States citizenship on the date of such cessation or commencement.

(2) LONG-TERM RESIDENT.—For purposes of this subsection, the term "long-term resident" means any individual (other than a citizen of the United States) who is a lawful permanent resident of the United States in at least 8 taxable years during the period of 15 taxable years ending with the taxable year during which the event described in paragraph (1) occurs. For purposes of the preceding sentence, an individual shall not be treated as a lawful permanent resident for any taxable year if such individual is treated as a resident of a foreign country for the taxable year under the provisions of a tax treaty between the United States and the foreign country and does not waive the benefits of such treaty applicable to residents of the foreign country.

(3) SPECIAL RULES.—

(A) EXCEPTIONS NOT TO APPLY.—Subsection (c) shall not apply to an individual who is treated as provided in paragraph (1).

(B) STEP-UP IN BASIS.—Solely for purposes of determining any tax imposed by reason of this subsection, property which was held by the long-term resident on the date the individual first became a resident of the United States shall be treated as having a basis on such date of not less than the fair market value of such property on such date. The preceding sentence shall not apply if the individual elects not to have such sentence apply. Such an election, once made, shall be irrevocable.

(4) AUTHORITY TO EXEMPT INDIVIDUALS.—This subsection shall not apply to an individual who is described in a category of individuals prescribed by regulation by the Secretary.

(5) REGULATIONS.—The Secretary shall prescribe such regulations as may be appropriate to carry out this subsection, including regulations providing for the application of this subsection in cases where an alien individual becomes a resident of the United States during the 10-year period after being treated as provided in paragraph (1).

[Sec. 877(f)]

(f) BURDEN OF PROOF.—If the Secretary establishes that it is reasonable to believe that an individual's loss of United States citizenship would, but for this section, result in a substantial reduction for the taxable year in the taxes on his probable income for such year, the burden of proving for such taxable year that such loss of citizenship did not have for one of its principal purposes the avoidance of taxes under this subtitle or subtitle B shall be on such individual.

[Sec. 877(g)]

(g) PHYSICAL PRESENCE.—

(1) IN GENERAL.—This section shall not apply to any individual to whom this section would otherwise apply for any taxable year during the 10-year period referred to in subsection (a) in which such individual is physically present in the United States at any time on more than 30 days in the calendar year ending in such taxable year, and such individual shall be treated for purposes of this title as a citizen or resident of the United States, as the case may be, for such taxable year.

(2) EXCEPTION.—

(A) IN GENERAL.—In the case of an individual described in any of the following subparagraphs of this paragraph, a day of physical presence in the United States shall be disregarded if the individual is performing services in the United States on such day for an employer. The preceding sentence shall not apply if—

(i) such employer is related (within the meaning of section 267 and 707) to such individual, or

(ii) such employer fails to meet such requirements as the Secretary may prescribe by regulations to prevent the avoidance of the purposes of this paragraph.

Not more than 30 days during any calendar year may be disregarded under this subparagraph.

(B) INDIVIDUALS WITH TIES TO OTHER COUNTRIES.—An individual is described in this subparagraph if—

(i) the individual becomes (not later than the close of a reasonable period after loss of United States citizenship or termination of residency) a citizen or resident of the country in which—

(I) such individual was born,

(II) if such individual is married, such individual's spouse was born, or

(III) either of such individual's parents were born, and

(ii) the individual becomes fully liable for income tax in such country.

(C) MINIMAL PRIOR PHYSICAL PRESENCE IN THE UNITED STATES.—An individual is described in this subparagraph if, for each year in the 10-year period ending on the date of loss of United States citizenship or termination of residency, the individual was physically present in the United States for 30 days or less. The rule of section 7701(b)(3)(D) shall apply for purposes of this subparagraph.

→ Caution: This termination provision applies to any individual whose expatriation date is on or after June 17, 2008 (the date of enactment of the Heroes Earnings Assistance and Relief Tax Act of 2008 (P.L. 110-245)).

[Sec. 877(h)]

(h) TERMINATION.—This section shall not apply to any individual whose expatriation date (as defined in section 877A(g)(3)) is on or after the date of the enactment of this subsection.

[Sec. 877A]

SEC. 877A. TAX RESPONSIBILITIES OF EXPATRIATION.

[Sec. 877A(a)]

(a) GENERAL RULES.—For purposes of this subtitle—

(1) MARK TO MARKET.—All property of a covered expatriate shall be treated as sold on the day before the expatriation date for its fair market value.

(2) RECOGNITION OF GAIN OR LOSS.—In the case of any sale under paragraph (1)—

(A) notwithstanding any other provision of this title, any gain arising from such sale shall be taken into account for the taxable year of the sale, and

(B) any loss arising from such sale shall be taken into account for the taxable year of the sale to the extent otherwise provided by this title, except that section 1091 shall not apply to any such loss.

Proper adjustment shall be made in the amount of any gain or loss subsequently realized for gain or loss taken into account under the preceding sentence, determined without regard to paragraph (3).

(3) EXCLUSION FOR CERTAIN GAIN.—

→ Caution: Pursuant to Section 877A(a)(3)(B), the $600,000 exclusion amount in Section 877A(a)(3)(A) is adjusted for taxable years beginning in a calendar year after 2008 to reflect increases in the Chained Consumer Price Index. The adjusted amount that applies for taxable years beginning in 2023 is $821,000, as provided in Rev. Proc. 2022-38, 2022-45 I.R.B. 445.

(A) IN GENERAL.—The amount which would (but for this paragraph) be includible in the gross income of any individual by reason of paragraph (1) shall be reduced (but not below zero) by $600,000.

(B) ADJUSTMENT FOR INFLATION.—

(i) IN GENERAL.—In the case of any taxable year beginning in a calendar year after 2008, the dollar amount in subparagraph (A) shall be increased by an amount equal to—

(I) such dollar amount, multiplied by

(II) the cost-of-living adjustment determined under section 1(f)(3) for the calendar year in which the taxable year begins, by substituting "calendar year 2007" for "calendar year 2016" in subparagraph (A)(ii) thereof.

(ii) ROUNDING.—If any amount as adjusted under clause (i) is not a multiple of $1,000, such amount shall be rounded to the nearest multiple of $1,000.

[Sec. 877A(b)]

(b) ELECTION TO DEFER TAX.—

(1) IN GENERAL.—If the taxpayer elects the application of this subsection with respect to any property treated as sold by reason of subsection (a), the time for payment of the additional tax attributable to such property shall be extended until the due date of the return for the

taxable year in which such property is disposed of (or, in the case of property disposed of in a transaction in which gain is not recognized in whole or in part, until such other date as the Secretary may prescribe).

(2) DETERMINATION OF TAX WITH RESPECT TO PROPERTY.—For purposes of paragraph (1), the additional tax attributable to any property is an amount which bears the same ratio to the additional tax imposed by this chapter for the taxable year solely by reason of subsection (a) as the gain taken into account under subsection (a) with respect to such property bears to the total gain taken into account under subsection (a) with respect to all property to which subsection (a) applies.

(3) TERMINATION OF EXTENSION.—The due date for payment of tax may not be extended under this subsection later than the due date for the return of tax imposed by this chapter for the taxable year which includes the date of death of the expatriate (or, if earlier, the time that the security provided with respect to the property fails to meet the requirements of paragraph (4), unless the taxpayer corrects such failure within the time specified by the Secretary).

(4) SECURITY.—

(A) IN GENERAL.—No election may be made under paragraph (1) with respect to any property unless adequate security is provided with respect to such property.

(B) ADEQUATE SECURITY.—For purposes of subparagraph (A), security with respect to any property shall be treated as adequate security if—

(i) it is a bond which is furnished to, and accepted by, the Secretary, which is conditioned on the payment of tax (and interest thereon), and which meets the requirements of section 6325, or

(ii) it is another form of security for such payment (including letters of credit) that meets such requirements as the Secretary may prescribe.

(5) WAIVER OF CERTAIN RIGHTS.—No election may be made under paragraph (1) unless the taxpayer makes an irrevocable waiver of any right under any treaty of the United States which would preclude assessment or collection of any tax imposed by reason of this section.

(6) ELECTIONS.—An election under paragraph (1) shall only apply to property described in the election and, once made, is irrevocable.

(7) INTEREST.—For purposes of section 6601, the last date for the payment of tax shall be determined without regard to the election under this subsection.

[Sec. 877A(c)]

(c) EXCEPTION FOR CERTAIN PROPERTY.—Subsection (a) shall not apply to—

(1) any deferred compensation item (as defined in subsection (d)(4)),

(2) any specified tax deferred account (as defined in subsection (e)(2)), and

(3) any interest in a nongrantor trust (as defined in subsection (f)(3)).

[Sec. 877A(d)]

(d) TREATMENT OF DEFERRED COMPENSATION ITEMS.—

(1) WITHHOLDING ON ELIGIBLE DEFERRED COMPENSATION ITEMS.—

(A) IN GENERAL.—In the case of any eligible deferred compensation item, the payor shall deduct and withhold from any taxable payment to a covered expatriate with respect to such item a tax equal to 30 percent thereof.

(B) TAXABLE PAYMENT.—For purposes of subparagraph (A), the term "taxable payment" means with respect to a covered expatriate any payment to the extent it would be includible in the gross income of the covered expatriate if such expatriate continued to be subject to tax as a citizen or resident of the United States. A deferred compensation item shall be taken into account as a payment under the preceding sentence when such item would be so includible.

(2) OTHER DEFERRED COMPENSATION ITEMS.—In the case of any deferred compensation item which is not an eligible deferred compensation item—

(A)(i) with respect to any deferred compensation item to which clause (ii) does not apply, an amount equal to the present value of the covered expatriate's accrued benefit shall be treated as having been received by such individual on the day before the expatriation date as a distribution under the plan, and

(ii) with respect to any deferred compensation item referred to in paragraph (4)(D), the rights of the covered expatriate to such item shall be treated as becoming transferable and not subject to a substantial risk of forfeiture on the day before the expatriation date,

(B) no early distribution tax shall apply by reason of such treatment, and

(C) appropriate adjustments shall be made to subsequent distributions from the plan to reflect such treatment.

(3) ELIGIBLE DEFERRED COMPENSATION ITEMS.—For purposes of this subsection, the term "eligible deferred compensation item" means any deferred compensation item with respect to which—

(A) the payor of such item is—

(i) a United States person, or

(ii) a person who is not a United States person but who elects to be treated as a United States person for purposes of paragraph (1) and meets such requirements as the Secretary may provide to ensure that the payor will meet the requirements of paragraph (1), and

(B) the covered expatriate—

(i) notifies the payor of his status as a covered expatriate, and

(ii) makes an irrevocable waiver of any right to claim any reduction under any treaty with the United States in withholding on such item.

(4) DEFERRED COMPENSATION ITEM.—For purposes of this subsection, the term "deferred compensation item" means—

(A) any interest in a plan or arrangement described in section 219(g)(5),

(B) any interest in a foreign pension plan or similar retirement arrangement or program,

(C) any item of deferred compensation, and

(D) any property, or right to property, which the individual is entitled to receive in connection with the performance of services to the extent not previously taken into account under section 83 or in accordance with section 83.

(5) EXCEPTION.—Paragraphs (1) and (2) shall not apply to any deferred compensation item to the extent attributable to services performed outside the United States while the covered expatriate was not a citizen or resident of the United States.

(6) SPECIAL RULES.—

(A) APPLICATION OF WITHHOLDING RULES.—Rules similar to the rules of subchapter B of chapter 3 shall apply for purposes of this subsection.

(B) APPLICATION OF TAX.—Any item subject to the withholding tax imposed under paragraph (1) shall be subject to tax under section 871.

(C) COORDINATION WITH OTHER WITHHOLDING REQUIREMENTS.—Any item subject to withholding under paragraph (1) shall not be subject to withholding under section 1441 or chapter 24.

[Sec. 877A(e)]

(e) TREATMENT OF SPECIFIED TAX DEFERRED ACCOUNTS.—

(1) ACCOUNT TREATED AS DISTRIBUTED.—In the case of any interest in a specified tax deferred account held by a covered expatriate on the day before the expatriation date—

(A) the covered expatriate shall be treated as receiving a distribution of his entire interest in such account on the day before the expatriation date,

(B) no early distribution tax shall apply by reason of such treatment, and

(C) appropriate adjustments shall be made to subsequent distributions from the account to reflect such treatment.

(2) SPECIFIED TAX DEFERRED ACCOUNT.—For purposes of paragraph (1), the term "specified tax deferred account" means an individual retirement plan (as defined in section 7701(a)(37)) other than any arrangement described in subsection (k) or (p) of section 408, a qualified tuition program (as defined in section 529), a qualified ABLE program (as defined in section 529A), a Coverdell education savings account (as defined in section 530), a health savings account (as defined in section 223), and an Archer MSA (as defined in section 220).

[Sec. 877A(f)]

(f) SPECIAL RULES FOR NONGRANTOR TRUSTS.—

(1) IN GENERAL.—In the case of a distribution (directly or indirectly) of any property from a nongrantor trust to a covered expatriate—

(A) the trustee shall deduct and withhold from such distribution an amount equal to 30 percent of the taxable portion of the distribution, and

(B) if the fair market value of such property exceeds its adjusted basis in the hands of the trust, gain shall be recognized to the trust as if such property were sold to the expatriate at its fair market value.

(2) TAXABLE PORTION.—For purposes of this subsection, the term "taxable portion" means, with respect to any distribution, that portion of the distribution which would be includible in the gross income of the covered expatriate if such expatriate continued to be subject to tax as a citizen or resident of the United States.

(3) NONGRANTOR TRUST.—For purposes of this subsection, the term "nongrantor trust" means the portion of any trust that the individual is not considered the owner of under subpart E of part I of subchapter J. The determination under the preceding sentence shall be made immediately before the expatriation date.

(4) SPECIAL RULES RELATING TO WITHHOLDING.—For purposes of this subsection—

(A) rules similar to the rules of subsection (d)(6) shall apply, and

(B) the covered expatriate shall be treated as having waived any right to claim any reduction under any treaty with the United States in withholding on any distribution to which paragraph (1)(A) applies unless the covered expatriate agrees to such other treatment as the Secretary determines appropriate.

(5) APPLICATION.—This subsection shall apply to a nongrantor trust only if the covered expatriate was a beneficiary of the trust on the day before the expatriation date.

[Sec. 877A(g)]

(g) DEFINITIONS AND SPECIAL RULES RELATING TO EXPATRIATION.—For purposes of this section—

(1) COVERED EXPATRIATE.—

(A) IN GENERAL.—The term "covered expatriate" means an expatriate who meets the requirements of subparagraph (A), (B), or (C) of section 877(a)(2).

(B) EXCEPTIONS.—An individual shall not be treated as meeting the requirements of subparagraph (A) or (B) of section 877(a)(2) if—

(i) the individual—

(I) became at birth a citizen of the United States and a citizen of another country and, as of the expatriation date, continues to be a citizen of, and is taxed as a resident of, such other country, and

(II) has been a resident of the United States (as defined in section 7701(b)(1)(A)(ii)) for not more than 10 taxable years during the 15-taxable year period ending with the taxable year during which the expatriation date occurs, or

(ii)(I) the individual's relinquishment of United States citizenship occurs before such individual attains age 18½, and

(II) the individual has been a resident of the United States (as so defined) for not more than 10 taxable years before the date of relinquishment.

(C) COVERED EXPATRIATES ALSO SUBJECT TO TAX AS CITIZENS OR RESIDENTS.—In the case of any covered expatriate who is subject to tax as a citizen or resident of the United States for any period beginning after the expatriation date, such individual shall not be treated as a covered expatriate during such period for purposes of subsections (d)(1) and (f) and section 2801.

(2) EXPATRIATE.—The term "expatriate" means—

(A) any United States citizen who relinquishes his citizenship, and

(B) any long-term resident of the United States who ceases to be a lawful permanent resident of the United States (within the meaning of section 7701(b)(6)).

(3) EXPATRIATION DATE.—The term "expatriation date" means—

(A) the date an individual relinquishes United States citizenship, or

(B) in the case of a long-term resident of the United States, the date on which the individual ceases to be a lawful permanent resident of the United States (within the meaning of section 7701(b)(6)).

(4) RELINQUISHMENT OF CITIZENSHIP.—A citizen shall be treated as relinquishing his United States citizenship on the earliest of—

(A) the date the individual renounces his United States nationality before a diplomatic or consular officer of the United States pursuant to paragraph (5) of section 349(a) of the Immigration and Nationality Act (8 U.S.C. 1481(a)(5)),

(B) the date the individual furnishes to the United States Department of State a signed statement of voluntary relinquishment of United States nationality confirming the performance of an act of expatriation specified in paragraph (1), (2), (3), or (4) of section 349(a) of the Immigration and Nationality Act (8 U.S.C. 1481(a)(1)-(4)),

(C) the date the United States Department of State issues to the individual a certificate of loss of nationality, or

(D) the date a court of the United States cancels a naturalized citizen's certificate of naturalization.

Subparagraph (A) or (B) shall not apply to any individual unless the renunciation or voluntary relinquishment is subsequently approved by the issuance to the individual of a certificate of loss of nationality by the United States Department of State.

(5) LONG-TERM RESIDENT.—The term "long-term resident" has the meaning given to such term by section 877(e)(2).

(6) EARLY DISTRIBUTION TAX.—The term "early distribution tax" means any increase in tax imposed under section 72(t), 220(f)(4), 223(f)(4), 409A(a)(1)(B), 529(c)(6), 529A(c)(3), or 530(d)(4).

[Sec. 877A(h)]

(h) OTHER RULES.—

(1) TERMINATION OF DEFERRALS, ETC.—In the case of any covered expatriate, notwithstanding any other provision of this title—

(A) any time period for acquiring property which would result in the reduction in the amount of gain recognized with respect to property disposed of by the taxpayer shall terminate on the day before the expatriation date, and

(B) any extension of time for payment of tax shall cease to apply on the day before the expatriation date and the unpaid portion of such tax shall be due and payable at the time and in the manner prescribed by the Secretary.

(2) STEP-UP IN BASIS.—Solely for purposes of determining any tax imposed by reason of subsection (a), property which was held by an individual on the date the individual first became a resident of the United States (within the meaning of section 7701(b)) shall be treated as having a basis on such date of not less than the fair market value of such property on such date. The preceding sentence shall not apply if the individual elects not to have such sentence apply. Such an election, once made, shall be irrevocable.

(3) COORDINATION WITH SECTION 684.—If the expatriation of any individual would result in the recognition of gain under section 684, this section shall be applied after the application of section 684.

[Sec. 877A(i)]

(i) REGULATIONS.—The Secretary shall prescribe such regulations as may be necessary or appropriate to carry out the purposes of this section.

[Sec. 878]

SEC. 878. FOREIGN EDUCATIONAL, CHARITABLE, AND CERTAIN OTHER EXEMPT ORGANIZATIONS.

For special provisions relating to foreign educational, charitable, and other exempt organizations, see sections 512(a) and 4948.

[Sec. 879]

SEC. 879. TAX TREATMENT OF CERTAIN COMMUNITY INCOME IN THE CASE OF NONRESIDENT ALIEN INDIVIDUALS.

[Sec. 879(a)]

(a) GENERAL RULE.—In the case of a married couple 1 or both of whom are nonresident alien individuals and who have community income for the taxable year, such community income shall be treated as follows:

(1) Earned income (within the meaning of section 911(d)(2)), other than trade or business income and a partner's distributive share of partnership income, shall be treated as the income of the spouse who rendered the personal services,

(2) Trade or business income, and a partner's distributive share of partnership income, shall be treated as provided in section 1402(a)(5),

(3) Community income not described in paragraph (1) or (2) which is derived from the separate property (as determined under the applicable community property law) of one spouse shall be treated as the income of such spouse, and

(4) All other such community income shall be treated as provided in the applicable community property law.

[Sec. 879(b)]

(b) EXCEPTION WHERE ELECTION UNDER SECTION 6013(g) IS IN EFFECT.—Subsection (a) shall not apply for any taxable year for which an election under subsection (g) or (h) of section 6013 (relating to election to treat nonresident alien individual as resident of the United States) is in effect.

[Sec. 879(c)]

(c) DEFINITIONS AND SPECIAL RULES.—For purposes of this section—

(1) COMMUNITY INCOME.—The term "community income" means income which, under applicable community property laws, is treated as community income.

(2) COMMUNITY PROPERTY LAWS.—The term "community property laws" means the community property laws of a State, a foreign country, or a possession of the United States.

(3) DETERMINATION OF MARITAL STATUS.—The determination of marital status shall be made under section 7703(a).

Subpart B—Foreign Corporations

[Sec. 881]

SEC. 881. TAX ON INCOME OF FOREIGN CORPORATIONS NOT CONNECTED WITH UNITED STATES BUSINESS.

[Sec. 881(a)]

(a) IMPOSITION OF TAX.—Except as provided in subsection (c), there is hereby imposed for each taxable year a tax of 30 percent of the amount received from sources within the United States by a foreign corporation as—

(1) interest (other than original issue discount as defined in section 1273), dividends, rents, salaries, wages, premiums, annuities, compensations, remunerations, emoluments, and other fixed or determinable annual or periodical gains, profits, and income,

(2) gains described in section 631(b) or (c),

(3) in the case of—

(A) a sale or exchange of an original issue discount obligation, the amount of the original issue discount accruing while such obligation was held by the foreign corporation (to the extent such discount was not theretofore taken into account under subparagraph (B)), and

(B) a payment on an original issue discount obligation, an amount equal to the original issue discount accruing while such obligation was held by the foreign corporation (except that such original issue discount shall be taken into account under this subparagraph only to the extent such discount was not theretofore taken into account under this subparagraph and only to the extent that the tax thereon does not exceed the payment less the tax imposed by paragraph (1) thereon), and

(4) gains from the sale or exchange after October 4, 1966, of patents, copyrights, secret processes and formulas, good will, trademarks, trade brands, franchises, and other like property, or of any interest in any such property, to the extent such gains are from payments which are contingent on the productivity, use, or disposition of the property or interest sold or exchanged,

but only to the extent the amount so received is not effectively connected with the conduct of a trade or business within the United States.

[Sec. 881(b)]

(b) EXCEPTION FOR CERTAIN POSSESSIONS.—

(1) GUAM, AMERICAN SAMOA, THE NORTHERN MARIANA ISLANDS, AND THE VIRGIN ISLANDS.—For purposes of this section and section 884, a corporation created or organized in Guam, American Samoa, the Northern Mariana Islands, or the Virgin Islands or under the law of any such possession shall not be treated as a foreign corporation for any taxable year if—

(A) at all times during such taxable year less than 25 percent in value of the stock of such corporation is beneficially owned (directly or indirectly) by foreign persons,

(B) at least 65 percent of the gross income of such corporation is shown to the satisfaction of the Secretary to be effectively connected with the conduct of a trade or business in such a possession or the United States for the 3-year period ending with the close of the taxable year of such corporation (or for such part of such period as the corporation or any predecessor had been in existence), and

(C) no substantial part of the income of such corporation is used (directly or indirectly) to satisfy obligations to persons who are not bona fide residents of such a possession or the United States.

(2) COMMONWEALTH OF PUERTO RICO.—

(A) IN GENERAL.—If dividends are received during a taxable year by a corporation—

(i) created or organized in, or under the law of, the Commonwealth of Puerto Rico, and

(ii) with respect to which the requirements of subparagraphs (A), (B), and (C) of paragraph (1) are met for the taxable year, subsection (a) shall be applied for such taxable year by substituting "10 percent" for "30 percent".

(B) APPLICABILITY.—If, on or after the date of the enactment of this paragraph, an increase in the rate of the Commonwealth of Puerto Rico's withholding tax which is generally applicable to dividends paid to United States corporations not engaged in a trade or business in the Commonwealth to a rate greater than 10 percent takes effect, this paragraph shall not apply to dividends received on or after the effective date of the increase.

(3) DEFINITIONS.—

(A) FOREIGN PERSON.—For purposes of paragraph (1), the term "foreign person" means any person other than—

(i) a United States person, or

(ii) a person who would be a United States person if references to the United States in section 7701 included references to a possession of the United States.

(B) INDIRECT OWNERSHIP RULES.—For purposes of paragraph (1), the rules of section 318(a)(2) shall apply except that "5 percent" shall be substituted for "50 percent" in subparagraph (C) thereof.

[Sec. 881(c)]

(c) REPEAL OF TAX ON INTEREST OF FOREIGN CORPORATIONS RECEIVED FROM CERTAIN PORTFOLIO DEBT INVESTMENTS.—

(1) IN GENERAL.—In the case of any portfolio interest received by a foreign corporation from sources within the United States, no tax shall be imposed under paragraph (1) or (3) of subsection (a).

(2) PORTFOLIO INTEREST.—For purposes of this subsection, the term "portfolio interest" means any interest (including original issue discount) which—

(A) would be subject to tax under subsection (a) but for this subsection, and

(B) is paid on an obligation—

(i) which is in registered form, and

(ii) with respect to which—

(I) the person who would otherwise be required to deduct and withhold tax from such interest under section 1442(a) receives a statement which meets the requirements of section 871(h)(5) that the beneficial owner of the obligation is not a United States person, or

(II) the Secretary has determined that such a statement is not required in order to carry out the purposes of this subsection.

(3) PORTFOLIO INTEREST SHALL NOT INCLUDE INTEREST RECEIVED BY CERTAIN PERSONS.—For purposes of this subsection, the term "portfolio interest" shall not include any portfolio interest which—

(A) except in the case of interest paid on an obligation of the United States, is received by a bank on an extension of credit made pursuant to a loan agreement entered into in the ordinary course of its trade or business,

(B) is received by a 10-percent shareholder (within the meaning of section 871(h)(3)(B)), or

(C) is received by a controlled foreign corporation from a related person (within the meaning of section 864(d)(4)).

(4) PORTFOLIO INTEREST NOT TO INCLUDE CERTAIN CONTINGENT INTEREST.—For purposes of this subsection, the term "portfolio interest" shall not include any interest which is treated as not being portfolio interest under the rules of section 871(h)(4).

(5) SPECIAL RULES FOR CONTROLLED FOREIGN CORPORATIONS.—

(A) IN GENERAL.—In the case of any portfolio interest received by a controlled foreign corporation, the following provisions shall not apply:

(i) Subparagraph (A) of section 954(b)(3) (relating to exception where foreign base company income is less than 5 percent or $1,000,000).

(ii) Paragraph (4) of section 954(b) (relating to exception for certain income subject to high foreign taxes).

(iii) Clause (i) of section 954(c)(3)(A) (relating to certain income received from related persons).

(B) CONTROLLED FOREIGN CORPORATION.—For purposes of this subsection, the term "controlled foreign corporation" has the meaning given to such term by section 957(a).

(6) SECRETARY MAY CEASE APPLICATION OF THIS SUBSECTION.—Under rules similar to the rules of section 871(h)(6), the Secretary may provide that this subsection shall not apply to payments of interest described in section 871(h)(6).

(7) REGISTERED FORM.—For purposes of this subsection, the term "registered form" has the meaning give such term by section 163(*f*).

[Sec. 881(d)]

(d) TAX NOT TO APPLY TO CERTAIN INTEREST AND DIVIDENDS.—No tax shall be imposed under paragraph (1) or (3) of subsection (a) on any amount described in section 871(i)(2).

[Sec. 881(e)]

(e) TAX NOT TO APPLY TO CERTAIN DIVIDENDS OF REGULATED INVESTMENT COMPANIES.—

(1) INTEREST-RELATED DIVIDENDS.—

(A) IN GENERAL.—Except as provided in subparagraph (B), no tax shall be imposed under paragraph (1) of subsection (a) on any interest-related dividend (as defined in section 871(k)(1)) received from a regulated investment company.

(B) EXCEPTION.—Subparagraph (A) shall not apply—

(i) to any dividend referred to in section 871(k)(1)(B), and

(ii) to any interest-related dividend received by a controlled foreign corporation (within the meaning of section 957(a)) to the extent such dividend is attributable to interest received by the regulated investment company from a person who is a related person (within the meaning of section 864(d)(4)) with respect to such controlled foreign corporation.

(C) TREATMENT OF DIVIDENDS RECEIVED BY CONTROLLED FOREIGN CORPORATIONS.—The rules of subsection (c)(5)(A) shall apply to any interest-related dividend received by a controlled foreign corporation (within the meaning of section 957(a)) to the extent such dividend is attributable to interest received by the regulated investment company which is described in clause (ii) of section 871(k)(1)(E) (and not described in clause (i) or (iii) of such section).

(2) SHORT-TERM CAPITAL GAIN DIVIDENDS.—No tax shall be imposed under paragraph (1) of subsection (a) on any short-term capital gain dividend (as defined in section 871(k)(2)) received from a regulated investment company.

[Sec. 881(f)]

(f) CROSS REFERENCE.—

For doubling of tax on corporations of certain foreign countries, see section 891.

For special rules for original issue discount, see section 871(g).

[Sec. 882]

SEC. 882. TAX ON INCOME OF FOREIGN CORPORATIONS CONNECTED WITH UNITED STATES BUSINESS.

[Sec. 882(a)]

(a) IMPOSITION OF TAX.—

(1) IN GENERAL.—A foreign corporation engaged in trade or business within the United States during the taxable year shall be taxable as provided in section 11, 55, or 59A, on its taxable income which is effectively connected with the conduct of a trade or business within the United States.

(2) DETERMINATION OF TAXABLE INCOME.—In determining taxable income for purposes of paragraph (1), gross income includes only gross income which is effectively connected with the conduct of a trade or business within the United States.

(3) For special tax treatment of gain or loss from the disposition by a foreign corporation of a United States real property interest, see section 897.

[Sec. 882(b)]

(b) GROSS INCOME.—In the case of a foreign corporation, except where the context clearly indicates otherwise, gross income includes only—

(1) gross income which is derived from sources within the United States and which is not effectively connected with the conduct of a trade or business within the United States, and

(2) gross income which is effectively connected with the conduct of a trade or business within the United States.

[Sec. 882(c)]

(c) ALLOWANCE OF DEDUCTIONS AND CREDITS.—

(1) ALLOCATION OF DEDUCTIONS.—

(A) GENERAL RULE.—In the case of a foreign corporation, the deductions shall be allowed only for purposes of subsection (a) and (except as provided by subparagraph (B)) only if and to the extent that they are connected with income which is effectively connected with the conduct of a trade or business within the United States; and the proper apportionment and allocation of the deductions for this purpose shall be determined as provided in regulations prescribed by the Secretary.

(B) CHARITABLE CONTRIBUTIONS.—The deduction for charitable contributions and gifts provided by section 170 shall be allowed whether or not connected with income which is effectively connected with the conduct of a trade or business within the United States.

(2) DEDUCTIONS AND CREDITS ALLOWED ONLY IF RETURN FILED.—A foreign corporation shall receive the benefit of the deductions and credits allowed to it in this subtitle only by filing or causing to be filed with the Secretary a true and accurate return, in the manner prescribed in subtitle F, including therein all the information which the Secretary may deem necessary for the calculation of such deductions and credits. The preceding sentence shall not apply for purposes of the tax imposed by section 541 (relating to personal holding company tax), and shall not be construed to deny the credit provided by section 33 for tax withheld at source or the credit provided by section 34 for certain uses of gasoline.

(3) FOREIGN TAX CREDIT.—Except as provided by section 906, foreign corporations shall not be allowed the credit against the tax for taxes of foreign countries and possessions of the United States allowed by section 901.

(4) CROSS REFERENCE.—

For rule that certain foreign taxes are not to be taken into account in determining deduction or credit, see section 906(b)(1).

[Sec. 882(d)]

(d) ELECTION TO TREAT REAL PROPERTY INCOME AS INCOME CONNECTED WITH UNITED STATES BUSINESS.—

(1) IN GENERAL.—A foreign corporation which during the taxable year derives any income—

(A) from real property located in the United States, or from any interest in such real property, including (i) gains from the sale or exchange of real property or an interest therein, (ii) rents or royalties from mines, wells, or other natural deposits, and (iii) gains described in section 631(b) or (c), and

(B) which, but for this subsection, would not be treated as income effectively connected with the conduct of a trade or business within the United States,

may elect for such taxable year to treat all such income as income which is effectively connected with the conduct of a trade or business within the United States. In such case, such income shall be taxable as provided in subsection (a)(1) whether or not such corporation is engaged in trade or business within the United States during the taxable year. An election under this paragraph for any taxable year shall remain in effect for all subsequent taxable years, except that it may be revoked with the consent of the Secretary with respect to any taxable year.

(2) ELECTION AFTER REVOCATION, ETC.—Paragraphs (2) and (3) of section 871(d) shall apply in respect of elections under this subsection in the same manner and to the same extent as they apply in respect of elections under section 871(d).

[Sec. 882(e)]

(e) INTEREST ON UNITED STATES OBLIGATIONS RECEIVED BY BANKS ORGANIZED IN POSSESSIONS.—In the case of a corporation created or organized in, or under the law of, a possession of the United States which is carrying on the banking business in a possession of the United States, interest on obligations of the United States which is not portfolio interest (as defined in section 881(c)(2)) shall—

(1) for purposes of this subpart, be treated as income which is effectively connected with the conduct of a trade or business within the United States, and

(2) shall be taxable as provided in subsection (a)(1) whether or not such corporation is engaged in trade or business within the United States during the taxable year.

[Sec. 882(f)]

(f) RETURNS OF TAX BY AGENT.—If any foreign corporation has no office or place of business in the United States but has an agent in the United States, the return required under section 6012 shall be made by the agent.

[Sec. 883]

SEC. 883. EXCLUSIONS FROM GROSS INCOME.

[Sec. 883(a)]

(a) INCOME OF FOREIGN CORPORATIONS FROM SHIPS AND AIRCRAFT.—The following items shall not be included in gross income of a foreign corporation, and shall be exempt from taxation under this subtitle:

(1) SHIPS OPERATED BY CERTAIN FOREIGN CORPORATIONS.—Gross income derived by a corporation organized in a foreign country from the international operation of a ship or ships if such foreign country grants an equivalent exemption to corporations organized in the United States.

(2) AIRCRAFT OPERATED BY CERTAIN FOREIGN CORPORATIONS.—Gross income derived by a corporation organized in a foreign country from the international operation of aircraft if such foreign country grants an equivalent exemption to corporations organized in the United States.

(3) RAILROAD ROLLING STOCK OF FOREIGN CORPORATIONS.—Earnings derived from payments by a common carrier for the use on a temporary basis (not expected to exceed a total of 90 days in any taxable year) of railroad rolling stock owned by a corporation of a foreign country which grants an equivalent exemption to corporations organized in the United States.

(4) SPECIAL RULES.—The rules of paragraphs (6), (7), and (8) of section 872(b) shall apply for purposes of this subsection.

(5) SPECIAL RULE FOR COUNTRIES WHICH TAX ON RESIDENCE BASIS.—For purposes of this subsection, there shall not be taken into account any failure of a foreign country to grant an exemption to a corporation organized in the United States if such corporation is subject to tax by such foreign country on a residence basis pursuant to provisions of foreign law which meets such standards (if any) as the Secretary may prescribe.

[Sec. 883(b)]

(b) EARNINGS DERIVED FROM COMMUNICATIONS SATELLITE SYSTEM.—The earnings derived from the ownership or operation of a communications satellite system by a foreign entity designated by a foreign government to participate in such ownership or operation shall be exempt from taxation under this subtitle, if the United States, through its designated entity, participates in such system pursuant to the Communications Satellite Act of 1962 (47 U.S.C. 701 and following).

[Sec. 883(c)]

(c) TREATMENT OF CERTAIN FOREIGN CORPORATIONS.—

(1) IN GENERAL.—Paragraphs (1) or (2) of subsection (a) (as the case may be) shall not apply to any foreign corporation if 50 percent or more of the value of the stock of such corporation is owned by individuals who are not residents of such foreign country or another foreign country meeting the requirements of such paragraph.

(2) TREATMENT OF CONTROLLED FOREIGN CORPORATIONS.—Paragraph (1) shall not apply to any foreign corporation which is a controlled foreign corporation (as defined in section 957(a)).

(3) SPECIAL RULES FOR PUBLICLY TRADED CORPORATIONS.—

(A) EXCEPTION.—Paragraph (1) shall not apply to any corporation which is organized in a foreign country meeting the requirements of paragraph (1) or (2) of subsection (a) (as the case may be) and the stock of which is primarily and regularly traded on an established securities market in such foreign country, another foreign country meeting the requirements of such paragraph, or the United States.

(B) TREATMENT OF STOCK OWNED BY PUBLICLY TRADED CORPORATION.—Any stock in another corporation which is owned (directly or indirectly) by a corporation meeting the requirements of subparagraph (A) shall be treated as owned by individuals who are residents of the foreign country in which the corporation meeting the requirements of subparagraph (A) is organized.

(4) STOCK OWNERSHIP THROUGH ENTITIES.—For purposes of paragraph (1), stock owned (directly or indirectly) by or for a corporation, partnership, trust, or estate shall be treated as being owned proportionately by its shareholders, partners, or beneficiaries. Stock considered to be owned by a person by reason of the application of the preceding sentence shall, for purposes of applying such sentence, be treated as actually owned by such person.

[Sec. 884]

SEC. 884. BRANCH PROFITS TAX.

[Sec. 884(a)]

(a) IMPOSITION OF TAX.—In addition to the tax imposed by section 882 for any taxable year, there is hereby imposed on any foreign corporation a tax equal to 30 percent of the dividend equivalent amount for the taxable year.

[Sec. 884(b)]

(b) DIVIDEND EQUIVALENT AMOUNT.—For purposes of subsection (a), the term "dividend equivalent amount" means the foreign corporation's effectively connected earnings and profits for the taxable year adjusted as provided in this subsection:

(1) REDUCTION FOR INCREASE IN U.S. NET EQUITY.—If—

(A) the U.S. net equity of the foreign corporation as of the close of the taxable year, exceeds

(B) the U.S. net equity of the foreign corporation as of the close of the preceding taxable year,

the effectively connected earnings and profits for the taxable year shall be reduced (but not below zero) by the amount of such excess.

(2) INCREASE FOR DECREASE IN NET EQUITY.—

(A) IN GENERAL.—If—

(i) the U.S. net equity of the foreign corporation as of the close of the preceding taxable year, exceeds

(ii) the U.S. net equity of the foreign corporation as of the close of the taxable year,

the effectively connected earnings and profits for the taxable year shall be increased by the amount of such excess.

(B) LIMITATION.—

(i) IN GENERAL.—The increase under subparagraph (A) for any taxable year shall not exceed the accumulated effectively connected earnings and profits as of the close of the preceding taxable year.

(ii) ACCUMULATED EFFECTIVELY CONNECTED EARNINGS AND PROFITS.—For purposes of clause (i), the term "accumulated effectively connected earnings and profits" means the excess of—

(I) the aggregate effectively connected earnings and profits for preceding taxable years beginning after December 31, 1986, over

(II) the aggregate dividend equivalent amounts determined for such preceding taxable years.

[Sec. 884(c)]

(c) U.S. NET EQUITY.—For purposes of this section—

(1) IN GENERAL.—The term "U.S. net equity" means—

(A) U.S. assets, reduced (including below zero) by

(B) U.S. liabilities.

(2) U.S. ASSETS AND U.S. LIABILITIES.—For purposes of paragraph (1)—

(A) U.S. ASSETS.—The term "U.S. assets" means the money and aggregate adjusted bases of property of the foreign corporation treated as connected with the conduct of a trade or business in the United States under regulations prescribed by the Secretary. For purposes of the preceding sentence, the adjusted basis of any property shall be its adjusted basis for purposes of computing earnings and profits.

(B) U.S. LIABILITIES.—The term "U.S. liabilities" means the liabilities of the foreign corporation treated as connected with the conduct of a trade or business in the United States under regulations prescribed by the Secretary.

(C) REGULATIONS TO BE CONSISTENT WITH ALLOCATION OF DEDUCTIONS.—The regulations prescribed under subparagraphs (A) and (B) shall be consistent with the allocation of deductions under section 882(c)(1).

[Sec. 884(d)]

(d) EFFECTIVELY CONNECTED EARNINGS AND PROFITS.—For purposes of this section—

(1) IN GENERAL.—The term "effectively connected earnings and profits" means earnings and profits (without diminution by reason of any distributions made during the taxable year) which are attributable to income which is effectively connected (or treated as effectively connected) with the conduct of a trade or business within the United States.

(2) EXCEPTION FOR CERTAIN INCOME.—The term "effectively connected earnings and profits" shall not include any earnings and profits attributable to—

(A) income not includible in gross income under paragraph (1) or (2) of section 883(a),

(B) income treated as effectively connected with the conduct of a trade or business within the United States under section 921(d) or 926(b) (as in effect before their repeal by the FSC Repeal and Extraterritorial Income Exclusion Act of 2000),

(C) gain on the disposition of a United States real property interest described in section 897(c)(1)(A)(ii),

(D) income treated as effectively connected with the conduct of a trade or business within the United States under section 953(c)(3)(C), or

(E) income treated as effectively connected with the conduct of a trade or business within the United States under section 882(e).

Property and liabilities of the foreign corporation treated as connected with such income under regulations prescribed by the Secretary shall not be taken into account in determining the U.S. assets or U.S. liabilities of the foreign corporation.

[Sec. 884(e)]

(e) COORDINATION WITH INCOME TAX TREATIES; ETC.—

(1) LIMITATION ON TREATY EXEMPTION.—No treaty between the United States and a foreign country shall exempt any foreign corporation from the tax imposed by subsection (a) (or reduce the amount thereof) unless—

(A) such treaty is an income tax treaty, and

(B) such foreign corporation is a qualified resident of such foreign country.

(2) TREATY MODIFICATIONS.—If a foreign corporation is a qualified resident of a foreign country with which the United States has an income tax treaty—

(A) the rate of tax under subsection (a) shall be the rate of tax specified in such treaty—

(i) on branch profits if so specified, or

(ii) if not so specified, on dividends paid by a domestic corporation to a corporation resident in such country which wholly owns such domestic corporation, and

(B) any other limitations under such treaty on the tax imposed by subsection (a) shall apply.

(3) COORDINATION WITH WITHHOLDING TAX.—

(A) IN GENERAL.—If a foreign corporation is subject to the tax imposed by subsection (a) for any taxable year (determined after the application of any treaty), no tax shall be imposed by section 871(a), 881(a), 1441, or 1442 on any dividends paid by such corporation out of its earnings and profits for such taxable year.

(B) LIMITATION ON CERTAIN TREATY BENEFITS.—If—

(i) any dividend described in section 861(a)(2)(B) is received by a foreign corporation, and

(ii) subparagraph (A) does not apply to such dividend,

rules similar to the rules of subparagraphs (A) and (B) of subsection (f)(3) shall apply to such dividend.

(4) QUALIFIED RESIDENT.—For purposes of this subsection—

(A) IN GENERAL.—Except as otherwise provided in this paragraph, the term "qualified resident" means, with respect to any foreign country, any foreign corporation which is a resident of such foreign country unless—

(i) 50 percent or more (by value) of the stock of such foreign corporation is owned (within the meaning of section 883(c)(4)) by individuals who are not residents of such foreign country and who are not United States citizens or resident aliens, or

(ii) 50 percent or more of its income is used (directly or indirectly) to meet liabilities to persons who are not residents of such foreign country or citizens or residents of the United States.

(B) SPECIAL RULE FOR PUBLICLY TRADED CORPORATIONS.—A foreign corporation which is a resident of a foreign country shall be treated as a qualified resident of such foreign country if—

(i) the stock of such corporation is primarily and regularly traded on an established securities market in such foreign country, or

(ii) such corporation is wholly owned (either directly or indirectly) by another foreign corporation which is organized in such foreign country and the stock of which is so traded.

(C) CORPORATIONS OWNED BY PUBLICLY TRADED DOMESTIC CORPORATIONS.—A foreign corporation which is a resident of a foreign country shall be treated as a qualified resident of such foreign country if—

(i) such corporation is wholly owned (directly or indirectly) by a domestic corporation, and

(ii) the stock of such domestic corporation is primarily and regularly traded on an established securities market in the United States.

(D) SECRETARIAL AUTHORITY.—The Secretary may, in his sole discretion, treat a foreign corporation as being a qualified resident of a foreign country if such corporation establishes to the satisfaction of the Secretary that such corporation meets such requirements as the Secretary may establish to ensure that individuals who are not residents of such foreign country do not use the treaty between such foreign country and the United States in a manner inconsistent with the purposes of this subsection.

(5) EXCEPTION FOR INTERNATIONAL ORGANIZATIONS.—This section shall not apply to an international organization (as defined in section 7701(a)(18)).

[Sec. 884(f)]

(f) TREATMENT OF INTEREST ALLOCABLE TO EFFECTIVELY CONNECTED INCOME.—

(1) IN GENERAL.—In the case of a foreign corporation engaged in a trade or business in the United States (or having gross income treated as effectively connected with the conduct of a trade or business in the United States), for purposes of this subtitle—

(A) any interest paid by such trade or business in the United States shall be treated as if it were paid by a domestic corporation, and

(B) to the extent that the allocable interest exceeds the interest described in subparagraph (A), such foreign corporation shall be liable for tax under section 881(a) in the same manner as if such excess were interest paid to such foreign corporation by a wholly owned domestic corporation on the last day of such foreign corporation's taxable year.

To the extent provided in regulations, subparagraph (A) shall not apply to interest in excess of the amounts reasonably expected to be allocable interest.

(2) ALLOCABLE INTEREST.—For purposes of this subsection, the term "allocable interest" means any interest which is allocable to income which is effectively connected (or treated as effectively connected) with the conduct of a trade or business in the United States.

(3) COORDINATION WITH TREATIES.—

(A) PAYOR MUST BE QUALIFIED RESIDENT.—In the case of any interest described in paragraph (1) which is paid or accrued by a foreign corporation, no benefit under any treaty between the United States and the foreign country of which such corporation is a resident shall apply unless—

(i) such treaty is an income tax treaty, and

(ii) such foreign corporation is a qualified resident of such foreign country.

(B) RECIPIENT MUST BE QUALIFIED RESIDENT.—In the case of any interest described in paragraph (1) which is received or accrued by any corporation, no benefit under any treaty between the United States and the foreign country of which such corporation is a resident shall apply unless—

(i) such treaty is an income treaty, and

(ii) such foreign corporation is a qualified resident of such foreign country.

[Sec. 884(g)]

(g) REGULATIONS.—The Secretary shall prescribe such regulations as may be necessary or appropriate to carry out the purposes of this section, including regulations providing for appropriate adjustments in the determination of the dividend equivalent amount in connection with the distribution to shareholders or transfer to a controlled corporation of the taxpayer's U.S. assets and other adjustments in such determination as are necessary or appropriate to carry out the purposes of this section.

Subpart C—Tax on Gross Transportation Income

[Sec. 887]

SEC. 887. IMPOSITION OF TAX ON GROSS TRANSPORTATION INCOME OF NONRESIDENT ALIENS AND FOREIGN CORPORATIONS.

[Sec. 887(a)]

(a) IMPOSITION OF TAX.—In the case of any nonresident alien individual or foreign corporation, there is hereby imposed for each taxable year a tax equal to 4 percent of such individual's or corporation's United States source gross transportation income for such taxable year.

[Sec. 887(b)]

(b) UNITED STATES SOURCE GROSS TRANSPORTATION INCOME.—

(1) IN GENERAL.—Except as provided in paragraphs (2) and (3), the term "United States source gross transportation income" means any gross income which is transportation income (as defined in section 863(c)(3)) to the extent such income is treated as from sources in the United States under section 863(c)(2). To the extent provided in regulations, such term does not include any income of a kind to which an exemption under paragraph (1) or (2) of section 883(a) would not apply.

(2) EXCEPTION FOR CERTAIN INCOME EFFECTIVELY CONNECTED WITH BUSINESS IN THE UNITED STATES.—The term "United States source gross transportation income" shall not include any income taxable under section 871(b) or 882.

(3) EXCEPTION FOR CERTAIN INCOME TAXABLE IN POSSESSIONS.—The term "United States source gross transportation income" does not include any income taxable in a possession of the United States under the provisions of this title as made applicable in such possession.

(4) DETERMINATION OF EFFECTIVELY CONNECTED INCOME.—For purposes of this chapter, United States source gross transportation income of any taxpayer shall not be treated as effectively connected with the conduct of a trade or business in the United States unless—

(A) the taxpayer has a fixed place of business in the United States involved in the earning of United States source gross transportation income, and

(B) substantially all of the United States source gross transportation income (determined without regard to paragraph (2)) of the taxpayer is attributable to regularly scheduled transportation (or, in the case of income from the leasing of a vessel or aircraft, is attributable to a fixed place of business in the United States).

[Sec. 887(c)]

(c) COORDINATION WITH OTHER PROVISIONS.—Any income taxable under this section shall not be taxable under section 871, 881, or 882.

Subpart D—Miscellaneous Provisions

[Sec. 891]

SEC. 891. DOUBLING OF RATES OF TAX ON CITIZENS AND CORPORATIONS OF CERTAIN FOREIGN COUNTRIES.

Whenever the President finds that, under the laws of any foreign country, citizens or corporations of the United States are being subjected to discriminatory or extraterritorial taxes, the President shall so proclaim and the rates of tax imposed by sections 1, 3, 11, 801, 831, 852, 871, and 881 shall, for the taxable year during which such proclamation is made and for each taxable year thereafter, be doubled in the case of each citizen and corporation of such foreign country; but the tax at such doubled rate shall be considered as imposed by such sections as the case may be. In no case shall this section operate to increase the taxes imposed by such sections (computed without regard to this section) to an amount in excess of 80 percent of the taxable income of the taxpayer (computed without regard to the deductions allowable under section 151 and under part VIII of subchapter B). Whenever the President finds that the laws of any foreign country with respect to which the President has made a proclamation under the preceding provisions of this section have been modified so that discriminatory and extraterritorial taxes applicable to citizens and corporations of the United States have been removed, he shall so proclaim, and the provisions of this section providing for doubled rates of tax shall not apply to any citizen or corporation of such foreign country with respect to any taxable year beginning after such proclamation is made.

[Sec. 892]

SEC. 892. INCOME OF FOREIGN GOVERNMENTS AND OF INTERNATIONAL ORGANIZATIONS.

[Sec. 892(a)]

(a) FOREIGN GOVERNMENTS.—

(1) IN GENERAL.—The income of foreign governments received from—

(A) investments in the United States in—

(i) stock, bonds, or other domestic securities owned by such foreign governments, or

(ii) financial instruments held in the execution of governmental financial or monetary policy, or

(B) interest on deposits in banks in the United States of moneys belonging to such foreign governments,

shall not be included in gross income and shall be exempt from taxation under this subtitle.

(2) INCOME RECEIVED DIRECTLY OR INDIRECTLY FROM COMMERCIAL ACTIVITIES.—

(A) IN GENERAL.—Paragraph (1) shall not apply to any income—

(i) derived from the conduct of any commercial activity (whether within or outside the United States),

(ii) received by a controlled commercial entity or received (directly or indirectly) from a controlled commercial entity, or

(iii) derived from the disposition of any interest in a controlled commercial entity.

(B) CONTROLLED COMMERCIAL ENTITY.—For purposes of subparagraph (A), the term "controlled commercial entity" means any entity engaged in commercial activities (whether within or outside the United States) if the government—

(i) holds (directly or indirectly) any interest in such entity which (by value or voting interest) is 50 percent or more of the total of such interests in such entity, or

(ii) holds (directly or indirectly) any other interest in such entity which provides the foreign government with effective control of such entity.

For purposes of the preceding sentence, a central bank of issue shall be treated as a controlled commercial entity only if engaged in commercial activities within the United States.

(3) TREATMENT AS RESIDENT.—For purposes of this title, a foreign government shall be treated as a corporate resident of its country. A foreign government shall be so treated for purposes of any income tax treaty obligation of the United States if such government grants equivalent treatment to the Government of the United States.

[Sec. 892(b)]

(b) INTERNATIONAL ORGANIZATIONS.—The income of international organizations received from investments in the United States in stocks, bonds, or other domestic securities owned by such international organizations, or from interest on deposits in banks in the United States of moneys belonging to such international organizations, or from any other source within the United States, shall not be included in gross income and shall be exempt from taxation under this subtitle.

[Sec. 892(c)]

(c) REGULATIONS.—The Secretary shall prescribe such regulations as may be necessary or appropriate to carry out the purposes of this section.

[Sec. 893]

SEC. 893. COMPENSATION OF EMPLOYEES OF FOREIGN GOVERNMENTS OR INTERNATIONAL ORGANIZATIONS.

[Sec. 893(a)]

(a) RULE FOR EXCLUSION.—Wages, fees, or salary of any employee of a foreign government or of an international organization (including a consular or other officer, or a nondiplomatic representative), received as compensation for official services to such government or international organization shall not be included in gross income and shall be exempt from taxation under this subtitle if—

(1) such employee is not a citizen of the United States, or is a citizen of the Republic of the Philippines (whether or not a citizen of the United States); and

(2) in the case of an employee of a foreign government, the services are of a character similar to those performed by employees of the Government of the United States in foreign countries; and

(3) in the case of an employee of a foreign government, the foreign government grants an equivalent exemption to employees of the Government of the United States performing similar services in such foreign country.

[Sec. 893(b)]

(b) CERTIFICATE BY SECRETARY OF STATE.—The Secretary of State shall certify to the Secretary of the Treasury the names of the foreign countries which grant an equivalent exemption to the employees of the Government of the United States performing services in such foreign countries, and the character of the services performed by employees of the Government of the United States in foreign countries.

[Sec. 893(c)]

(c) LIMITATION ON EXCLUSION.—Subsection (a) shall not apply to—

(1) any employee of a controlled commercial entity (as defined in section 892(a)(2)(B)), or

(2) any employee of a foreign government whose services are primarily in connection with a commercial activity (whether within or outside the United States) of the foreign government.

[Sec. 894]

SEC. 894. INCOME AFFECTED BY TREATY.

[Sec. 894(a)]

(a) TREATY PROVISIONS.—

(1) IN GENERAL.—The provisions of this title shall be applied to any taxpayer with due regard to any treaty obligation of the United States which applies to such taxpayer.

(2) CROSS REFERENCE.—

For relationship between treaties and this title, see section 7852(d).

[Sec. 894(b)]

(b) PERMANENT ESTABLISHMENT IN UNITED STATES.—For purposes of applying any exemption from, or reduction of, any tax provided by any treaty to which the United States is a party with respect to income which is not effectively connected with the conduct of a trade or business within the United States, a nonresident alien individual or a foreign corporation shall be deemed not to have a permanent establishment in the United States at any time during the taxable year. This subsection shall not apply in respect of the tax computed under section 877(b).

[Sec. 894(c)]

(c) DENIAL OF TREATY BENEFITS FOR CERTAIN PAYMENTS THROUGH HYBRID ENTITIES.—

(1) APPLICATION TO CERTAIN PAYMENTS.—A foreign person shall not be entitled under any income tax treaty of the United States with a foreign country to any reduced rate of any withholding tax imposed by this title on an item of income derived through an entity which is treated as a partnership (or is otherwise treated as fiscally transparent) for purposes of this title if—

(A) such item is not treated for purposes of the taxation laws of such foreign country as an item of income of such person,

(B) the treaty does not contain a provision addressing the applicability of the treaty in the case of an item of income derived through a partnership, and

(C) the foreign country does not impose tax on a distribution of such item of income from such entity to such person.

(2) REGULATIONS.—The Secretary shall prescribe such regulations as may be necessary or appropriate to determine the extent to which a taxpayer to which paragraph (1) does not apply shall not be entitled to benefits under any income tax treaty of the United States with respect to any payment received by, or income attributable to any activities of, an entity organized in any jurisdiction (including the United States) that is treated as a partnership or is otherwise treated as fiscally transparent for purposes of this title (including a common investment trust under section 584, a grantor trust, or an entity that is disregarded for purposes of this title) and is treated as fiscally nontransparent for purposes of the tax laws of the jurisdiction of residence of the taxpayer.

[Sec. 895]

SEC. 895. INCOME DERIVED BY A FOREIGN CENTRAL BANK OF ISSUE FROM OBLIGATIONS OF THE UNITED STATES OR FROM BANK DEPOSITS.

Income derived by a foreign central bank of issue from obligations of the United States or of any agency or instrumentality thereof (including beneficial interests, participations, and other instruments issued under section 302(c) of the Federal National Mortgage Association Charter Act (12 U. S. C. 1717)) which are owned by such foreign central bank of issue, or derived from interest on deposits with persons carrying on the banking business, shall not be included in gross income and shall be exempt from taxation under this subtitle unless such obligations or deposits are held for, or used in connection with, the conduct of commercial banking functions or other commercial activities. For purposes of the preceding sentence the Bank for International Settlements shall be treated as a foreign central bank of issue.

[Sec. 896]

SEC. 896. ADJUSTMENT OF TAX ON NATIONALS, RESIDENTS, AND CORPORATIONS OF CERTAIN FOREIGN COUNTRIES.

[Sec. 896(a)]

(a) IMPOSITION OF MORE BURDENSOME TAXES BY FOREIGN COUNTRY.—Whenever the President finds that—

(1) under the laws of any foreign country, considering the tax system of such foreign country, citizens of the United States not residents of such foreign country or domestic corporations are being subjected to more burdensome taxes, on any item of income received by such citizens or corporations from sources within such foreign country, than taxes imposed by the provisions of this subtitle on similar income derived from sources within the United States by residents or corporations of such foreign country,

(2) such foreign country, when requested by the United States to do so, has not acted to revise or reduce such taxes so that they are no more burdensome than taxes imposed by the provisions of this subtitle on similar income derived from sources within the United States by residents or corporations of such foreign country, and

(3) it is in the public interest to apply pre-1967 tax provisions in accordance with the provisions of this subsection to residents or corporations of such foreign country,

the President shall proclaim that the tax on such similar income derived from sources within the United States by residents or corporations of such foreign country shall, for taxable years beginning after such proclamation, be determined under this subtitle without regard to amendments made to this subchapter and chapter 3 on or after the date of enactment of this section.

[Sec. 896(b)]

(b) IMPOSITION OF DISCRIMINATORY TAXES BY FOREIGN COUNTRY.—Whenever the President finds that—

(1) under the laws of any foreign country, citizens of the United States or domestic corporations (or any class of such citizens or corporations) are, with respect to any item of income, being subjected to a higher effective rate of tax than are nationals, residents, or corporations of such foreign country (or a similar class of such nationals, residents, or corporations) under similar circumstances;

(2) such foreign country, when requested by the United States to do so, has not acted to eliminate such higher effective rate of tax; and

(3) it is in the public interest to adjust, in accordance with the provisions of this subsection, the effective rate of tax imposed by this subtitle on similar income of nationals, residents, or corporations of such foreign country (or such similar class of such nationals, residents, or corporations),

the President shall proclaim that the tax on similar income of nationals, residents, or corporations of such foreign country (or such similar class of such nationals, residents, or corporations) shall, for taxable years beginning after such proclamation, be adjusted so as to cause the effective rate of tax imposed by this subtitle on such similar income to be substantially equal to the effective rate of tax imposed by such foreign country on such item of income of citizens of the United States or domestic corporations (or such class of citizens or corporations). In implementing a proclamation made under this subsection, the effective rate of tax imposed by this subtitle on an item of income may be adjusted by the disallowance, in whole or in part, of any deduction, credit, or exemption which would otherwise be allowed with respect to that item of income or by increasing the rate of tax otherwise applicable to that item of income.

[Sec. 896(c)]

(c) ALLEVIATION OF MORE BURDENSOME OR DISCRIMINATORY TAXES.—Whenever the President finds that—

(1) the laws of any foreign country with respect to which the President has made a proclamation under subsection (a) have been modified so that citizens of the United States not residents of such foreign country or domestic corporations are no longer subject to more burdensome taxes on the item of income derived by such citizens or corporations from sources within such foreign country, or

(2) the laws of any foreign country with respect to which the President has made a proclamation under subsection (b) have been modified so that citizens of the United States or domestic corporations (or any class of such citizens or corporations) are no longer subject to a higher effective rate of tax on the item of income,

he shall proclaim that the tax imposed by this subtitle on the similar income of nationals, residents, or corporations of such foreign country shall, for any taxable year beginning after such proclamation, be determined under this subtitle without regard to such subsection.

[Sec. 896(d)]

(d) NOTIFICATION OF CONGRESS REQUIRED.—No proclamation shall be issued by the President pursuant to this section unless, at least 30 days prior to such proclamation, he has notified the Senate and the House of Representatives of his intention to issue such proclamation.

[Sec. 896(e)]

(e) IMPLEMENTATION BY REGULATIONS.—The Secretary shall prescribe such regulations as he deems necessary or appropriate to implement this section.

[Sec. 897]

SEC. 897. DISPOSITION OF INVESTMENT IN UNITED STATES REAL PROPERTY.

[Sec. 897(a)]

(a) GENERAL RULE.—

(1) TREATMENT AS EFFECTIVELY CONNECTED WITH UNITED STATES TRADE OR BUSINESS.—For purposes of this title, gain or loss of a nonresident alien individual or a foreign corporation from the disposition of a United States real property interest shall be taken into account—

(A) in the case of a nonresident alien individual, under section 871(b)(1), or

(B) in the case of a foreign corporation, under section 882(a)(1),

as if the taxpayer were engaged in a trade or business within the United States during the taxable year and as if such gain or loss were effectively connected with such trade or business.

(2) MINIMUM TAX ON NONRESIDENT ALIEN INDIVIDUALS.—

(A) IN GENERAL.—In the case of any nonresident alien individual, the taxable excess for purposes of section 55(b)(1) shall not be less than the lesser of—

(i) the individual's alternative minimum taxable income (as defined in section 55(b)(1)(D)) for the taxable year, or

(ii) the individual's net United States real property gain for the taxable year.

(B) NET UNITED STATES REAL PROPERTY GAIN.—For purposes of subparagraph (A), the term "net United States real property gain" means the excess of—

(i) the aggregate of the gains for the taxable year from dispositions of United States real property interests, over

(ii) the aggregate of the losses for the taxable year from dispositions of such interests.

[Sec. 897(b)]

(b) LIMITATION ON LOSSES OF INDIVIDUALS.—In the case of an individual, a loss shall be taken into account under subsection (a) only to the extent such loss would be taken into account under section 165(c) (determined without regard to subsection (a) of this section).

[Sec. 897(c)]

(c) UNITED STATES REAL PROPERTY INTEREST.—For purposes of this section—

(1) UNITED STATES REAL PROPERTY INTEREST.—

(A) IN GENERAL.—Except as provided in subparagraph (B) or subsection (k), the term "United States real property interest" means—

(i) an interest in real property (including an interest in a mine, well, or other natural deposit) located in the United States or the Virgin Islands, and

(ii) any interest (other than an interest solely as a creditor) in any domestic corporation unless the taxpayer establishes (at such time and in such manner as the Secretary by regulations prescribes) that such corporation was at no time a United States real property holding corporation during the shorter of—

(I) the period after June 18, 1980, during which the taxpayer held such interest, or

(II) the 5-year period ending on the date of the disposition of such interest.

(B) EXCLUSION FOR INTEREST IN CERTAIN CORPORATIONS.—The term "United States real property interest" does not include any interest in a corporation if—

(i) as of the date of the disposition of such interest, such corporation did not hold any United States real property interests,

(ii) all of the United States real property interests held by such corporation at any time during the shorter of the periods described in subparagraph (A)(ii)—

(I) were disposed of in transactions in which the full amount of the gain (if any) was recognized, or

(II) ceased to be United States real property interests by reason of the application of this subparagraph to 1 or more other corporations, and

(iii) neither such corporation nor any predecessor of such corporation was a regulated investment company or a real estate investment trust at any time during the shorter of the periods described in subparagraph (A)(ii).

(2) UNITED STATES REAL PROPERTY HOLDING CORPORATION.—The term "United States real property holding corporation" means any corporation if—

(A) the fair market value of its United States real property interests equals or exceeds 50 percent of

(B) the fair market value of—

(i) its United States real property interests,

(ii) its interests in real property located outside the United States, plus

(iii) any other of its assets which are used or held for use in a trade or business.

(3) EXCEPTION FOR STOCK REGULARLY TRADED ON ESTABLISHED SECURITIES MARKETS.—If any class of stock of a corporation is regularly traded on an established securities market, stock of such class shall be treated as a United States real property interest only in the case of a person who, at some time during the shorter of the periods described in paragraph (1)(A)(ii), held more than 5 percent of such class of stock.

(4) INTERESTS HELD BY FOREIGN CORPORATIONS AND BY PARTNERSHIPS, TRUSTS, AND ESTATES.—For purpose of determining whether any corporation is a United States real property holding corporation—

(A) FOREIGN CORPORATIONS.—Paragraph (1)(A)(ii) shall be applied by substituting "any corporation (whether foreign or domestic)" for "any domestic corporation".

(B) ASSETS HELD BY PARTNERSHIPS, ETC.—Under regulations prescribed by the Secretary, assets held by a partnership, trust, or estate shall be treated as held proportionately by its partners or beneficiaries. Any asset treated as held by a partner or beneficiary by reason of this subparagraph which is used or held for use by the partnership, trust, or estate in a trade or business shall be treated as so used or held by the partner or beneficiary. Any asset treated as held by a partner or beneficiary by reason of this subparagraph shall be so treated for purposes of applying this subparagraph successively to partnerships, trusts, or estates which are above the first partnership, trust, or estate in a chain thereof.

(5) TREATMENT OF CONTROLLING INTERESTS.—

(A) IN GENERAL.—Under regulations, for purposes of determining whether any corporation is a United States real property holding corporation, if any corporation (hereinafter in this paragraph referred to as the "first corporation") holds a controlling interest in a second corporation—

(i) the stock which the first corporation holds in the second corporation shall not be taken into account,

(ii) the first corporation shall be treated as holding a portion of each asset of the second corporation equal to the percentage of the fair market value of the stock of the second corporation represented by the stock held by the first corporation, and

(iii) any asset treated as held by the first corporation by reason of clause (ii) which is used or held for use by the second corporation in a trade or business shall be treated as so used or held by the first corporation.

Any asset treated as held by the first corporation by reason of the preceding sentence shall be so treated for purposes of applying the preceding sentence successively to corporations which are above the first corporation in a chain of corporations.

(B) CONTROLLING INTEREST.—For purposes of subparagraph (A), the term "controlling interest" means 50 percent or more of the fair market value of all classes of stock of a corporation.

(6) OTHER SPECIAL RULES.—

(A) INTEREST IN REAL PROPERTY.—The term "interest in real property" includes fee ownership and co-ownership of land or improvements thereon, leaseholds of land or improvements thereon, options to acquire land or improvements thereon, and options to acquire leaseholds of land or improvements thereon.

(B) REAL PROPERTY INCLUDES ASSOCIATED PERSONAL PROPERTY.—The term "real property" includes movable walls, furnishings, and other personal property associated with the use of the real property.

(C) CONSTRUCTIVE OWNERSHIP RULES.—For purposes of determining under paragraph (3) whether any person holds more than 5 percent of any class of stock and of determining under paragraph (5) whether a person holds a controlling interest in any corporation, section 318(a) shall apply (except that paragraphs (2)(C) and (3)(C) of section 318(a) shall be applied by substituting "5 percent" for "50 percent").

[Sec. 897(d)]

(d) TREATMENT OF DISTRIBUTIONS BY FOREIGN CORPORATIONS.—

(1) IN GENERAL.—Except to the extent otherwise provided in regulations, notwithstanding any other provision of this chapter, gain shall be recognized by a foreign corporation on the distribution (including a distribution in liquidation or redemption) of a United States real property interest in an amount equal to the excess of the fair market value of such interest (as of the time of the distribution) over its adjusted basis.

(2) EXCEPTIONS.—Gain shall not be recognized under paragraph (1)—

(A) if—

(i) at the time of the receipt of the distributed property, the distributee would be subject to taxation under this chapter on a subsequent disposition of the distributed property, and

(ii) the basis of the distributed property in the hands of the distributee is no greater than the adjusted basis of such property before the distribution, increased by the amount of gain (if any) recognized by the distributing corporation, or

(B) if such nonrecognition is provided in regulations prescribed by the Secretary under subsection (e)(2).

[Sec. 897(e)]

(e) COORDINATION WITH NONRECOGNITION PROVISIONS.—

(1) IN GENERAL.—Except to the extent otherwise provided in subsection (d) and paragraph (2) of this subsection, any nonrecognition provision shall apply for purposes of this section to a transaction only in the case of an exchange of a United States real property interest for an interest the sale of which would be subject to taxation under this chapter.

(2) REGULATIONS.—The Secretary shall prescribe regulations (which are necessary or appropriate to prevent the avoidance of Federal income taxes) providing—

(A) the extent to which nonrecognition provisions shall, and shall not, apply for purposes of this section, and

(B) the extent to which—

(i) transfers of property in reorganization, and

(ii) changes in interests in, or distributions from, a partnership, trust, or estate,

shall be treated as sales of property at fair market value.

(3) NONRECOGNITION PROVISION DEFINED.—For purposes of this subsection, the term "nonrecognition provision" means any provision of this title for not recognizing gain or loss.

[Sec. 897(f)—Stricken]

[Sec. 897(g)]

(g) SPECIAL RULE FOR SALES OF INTEREST IN PARTNERSHIPS, TRUSTS, AND ESTATES.—Under regulations prescribed by the Secretary, the amount of any money, and the fair market value of any property, received by a nonresident alien individual or foreign corporation in exchange for all or part of its interest in a partnership, trust, or estate shall, to the extent attributable to United States real property interests, be considered as an amount received from the sale or exchange in the United States of such property.

[Sec. 897(h)]

(h) SPECIAL RULES FOR CERTAIN INVESTMENT ENTITIES.—For purposes of this section—

(1) LOOK-THROUGH OF DISTRIBUTIONS.—Any distribution by a qualified investment entity to a nonresident alien individual, a foreign corporation, or other qualified investment entity shall, to the extent attributable to gain from sales or exchanges by the qualified investment entity of United States real property interests, be treated as gain recognized by such nonresident alien individual, foreign corporation, or other qualified investment entity from the sale or exchange of a United States real property interest. Notwithstanding the preceding sentence, any distribution by a qualified investment entity to a nonresident alien individual or a foreign corporation with respect to any class of stock which is regularly traded on an established securities market located in the United States shall not be treated as gain recognized from the sale or exchange of a United States real property interest if such individual or corporation did not own more than 5 percent of such class of stock at any time during the 1-year period ending on the date of such distribution.

(2) SALE OF STOCK IN DOMESTICALLY CONTROLLED ENTITY NOT TAXED.—The term "United States real property interest" does not include any interest in a domestically controlled qualified investment entity.

(3) DISTRIBUTIONS BY DOMESTICALLY CONTROLLED QUALIFIED INVESTMENT ENTITIES.—In the case of a domestically controlled qualified investment entity, rules similar to the rules of subsection (d) shall apply to the foreign ownership percentage of any gain.

(4) DEFINITIONS AND SPECIAL RULES.—

(A) QUALIFIED INVESTMENT ENTITY.—The term "qualified investment entity" means—

(i) any real estate investment trust, and

(ii) any regulated investment company which is a United States real property holding corporation or which would be a United States real property holding corporation if the exceptions provided in subsections (c)(3) and (h)(2) did not apply to interests in any real estate investment trust and for purposes of determining whether a real estate investment trust is a domestically controlled qualified investment entity under this subsection or regulated investment company.

(B) DOMESTICALLY CONTROLLED.—The term "domestically controlled qualified investment entity" means any qualified investment entity in which at all times during the testing period less than 50 percent in value of the stock was held directly or indirectly by foreign persons.

(C) FOREIGN OWNERSHIP PERCENTAGE.—The term "foreign ownership percentage" means that percentage of the stock of the qualified investment entity which was held (directly or indirectly) by foreign persons at the time during the testing period during which the direct and indirect ownership of stock by foreign persons was greatest.

(D) TESTING PERIOD.—The term "testing period" means whichever of the following periods is the shortest:

(i) the period beginning on June 19, 1980, and ending on the date of the disposition or of the distribution, as the case may be,

(ii) the 5-year period ending on the date of the disposition or of the distribution, as the case may be, or

(iii) the period during which the qualified investment entity was in existence.

(E) SPECIAL OWNERSHIP RULES.—For purposes of determining the holder of stock under subparagraphs (B) and (C)—

(i) in the case of any class of stock of the qualified investment entity which is regularly traded on an established securities market in the United States, a person holding less than 5 percent of such class of stock at all times during the testing period shall be treated as a United States person unless the qualified investment entity has actual knowledge that such person is not a United States person,

(ii) any stock in the qualified investment entity held by another qualified investment entity—

(I) any class of stock of which is regularly traded on an established securities market, or

(II) which is a regulated investment company which issues redeemable securities (within the meaning of section 2 of the Investment Company Act of 1940),

shall be treated as held by a foreign person, except that if such other qualified investment entity is domestically controlled (determined after application of this subparagraph), such stock shall be treated as held by a United States person, and

(iii) any stock in the qualified investment entity held by any other qualified investment entity not described in subclause (I) or (II) of clause (ii) shall only be treated as held by a United States person in proportion to the stock of such other qualified investment entity which is (or is treated under clause (ii) or (iii) as) held by a United States person.

(5) TREATMENT OF CERTAIN WASH SALE TRANSACTIONS.—

(A) IN GENERAL.—If an interest in a domestically controlled qualified investment entity is disposed of in an applicable wash sale transaction, the taxpayer shall, for purposes of this section, be treated as having gain from the sale or exchange of a United States real property interest in an amount equal to the portion of the distribution described in subparagraph (B) with respect to such interest which, but for the disposition, would have been treated by the taxpayer as gain from the sale or exchange of a United States real property interest under paragraph (1).

(B) APPLICABLE WASH SALES TRANSACTION.—For purposes of this paragraph—

(i) IN GENERAL.—The term "applicable wash sales transaction" means any transaction (or series of transactions) under which a nonresident alien individual, foreign corporation, or qualified investment entity—

(I) disposes of an interest in a domestically controlled qualified investment entity during the 30-day period preceding the ex-dividend date of a distribution which is to be made with respect to the interest and any portion of which, but for the disposition, would have been treated by the taxpayer as gain from the sale or exchange of a United States real property interest under paragraph (1), and

(II) acquires, or enters into a contract or option to acquire, a substantially identical interest in such entity during the 61-day period beginning with the 1st day of the 30-day period described in subclause (I).

For purposes of subclause (II), a nonresident alien individual, foreign corporation, or qualified investment entity shall be treated as having acquired any interest acquired by a person related (within the meaning of section 267(b) or 707(b)(1)) to the individual, corporation, or entity, and any interest which such person has entered into any contract or option to acquire.

(ii) APPLICATION TO SUBSTITUTE DIVIDEND AND SIMILAR PAYMENTS.—Subparagraph (A) shall apply to—

(I) any substitute dividend payment (within the meaning of section 861), or

(II) any other similar payment specified in regulations which the Secretary determines necessary to prevent avoidance of the purposes of this paragraph.

The portion of any such payment treated by the taxpayer as gain from the sale or exchange of a United States real property interest under subparagraph (A) by reason of this clause shall be equal to the portion of the distribution such payment is in lieu of which would have been so treated but for the transaction giving rise to such payment.

(iii) EXCEPTION WHERE DISTRIBUTION ACTUALLY RECEIVED.—A transaction shall not be treated as an applicable wash sales transaction if the nonresident alien individual, foreign corporation, or qualified investment entity receives the distribution described in clause (i)(I) with respect to either the interest which was disposed of, or acquired, in the transaction.

(iv) EXCEPTION FOR CERTAIN PUBLICLY TRADED STOCK.—A transaction shall not be treated as an applicable wash sales transaction if it involves the disposition of any class of stock in a qualified investment entity which is regularly traded on an established securities market within the United States but only if the nonresident alien individual, foreign corporation, or qualified investment entity did not own more than 5 percent of such class of stock at any time during the 1-year period ending on the date of the distribution described in clause (i)(I).

[Sec. 897(i)]

(i) ELECTION BY FOREIGN CORPORATION TO BE TREATED AS DOMESTIC CORPORATION.—

(1) IN GENERAL.—If—

(A) a foreign corporation holds a United States real property interest, and

(B) under any treaty obligation of the United States the foreign corporation is entitled to nondiscriminatory treatment with respect to that interest,

then such foreign corporation may make an election to be treated as a domestic corporation for purposes of this section, section 1445, and section 6039C.

(2) REVOCATION ONLY WITH CONSENT.—Any election under paragraph (1), once made, may be revoked only with the consent of the Secretary.

(3) MAKING OF ELECTION.—An election under paragraph (1) may be made only—

(A) if all of the owners of all classes of interests (other than interests solely as a creditor) in the foreign corporation at the time of the election consent to the making of the election and agree that gain, if any, from the disposition of such interest after June 18, 1980, which would be taken into account under subsection (a) shall be taxable notwithstanding any provision to the contrary in a treaty to which the United States is a party, and

(B) subject to such other conditions as the Secretary may prescribe by regulations with respect to the corporation or its shareholders.

In the case of a class of interest (other than an interest solely as a creditor) which is regularly traded on an established securities market, the consent described in subparagraph (A) need only be made by any person if such person held more than 5 percent of such class of interest at some time during the shorter of the periods described in subsection (c)(1)(A)(ii). The constructive ownership rules of subsection (c)(6)(C) shall apply in determining whether a person held more than 5 percent of a class of interest.

(4) EXCLUSIVE METHOD OF CLAIMING NONDISCRIMINATION.—The election provided by paragraph (1) shall be the exclusive remedy for any person claiming discriminatory treatment with respect to this section, section 1445, and section 6039C.

[Sec. 897(j)]

(j) CERTAIN CONTRIBUTIONS TO CAPITAL.—Except to the extent otherwise provided in regulations, gain shall be recognized by a nonresident alien individual or foreign corporation on the transfer of a United States real property interest to a foreign corporation if the transfer is made as paid in surplus or as a contribution to capital, in the amount of the excess of—

(1) the fair market value of such property transferred, over

(2) the sum of—

(A) the adjusted basis of such property in the hands of the transferor, plus

(B) the amount of gain, if any, recognized to the transferor under any other provision at the time of the transfer.

[Sec. 897(k)]

(k) SPECIAL RULES RELATING TO REAL ESTATE INVESTMENT TRUSTS.—

(1) INCREASE IN PERCENTAGE OWNERSHIP FOR EXCEPTIONS FOR PERSONS HOLDING PUBLICLY TRADED STOCK.—

(A) DISPOSITIONS.—In the case of any disposition of stock in a real estate investment trust, paragraphs (3) and (6)(C) of subsection (c) shall each be applied by substituting "more than 10 percent" for "more than 5 percent".

(B) DISTRIBUTIONS.—In the case of any distribution from a real estate investment trust, subsection (h)(1) shall be applied by substituting "10 percent" for "5 percent".

(2) STOCK HELD BY QUALIFIED SHAREHOLDERS NOT TREATED AS UNITED STATES REAL PROPERTY INTEREST.—

(A) IN GENERAL.—Except as provided in subparagraph (B)—

(i) stock of a real estate investment trust which is held directly (or indirectly through 1 or more partnerships) by a qualified shareholder shall not be treated as a United States real property interest, and

(ii) notwithstanding subsection (h)(1), any distribution to a qualified shareholder shall not be treated as gain recognized from the sale or exchange of a United States real property interest to the extent the stock of the real estate investment trust held by such qualified shareholder is not treated as a United States real property interest under clause (i).

(B) EXCEPTION.—In the case of a qualified shareholder with one or more applicable investors—

(i) subparagraph (A)(i) shall not apply to the applicable percentage of the stock of the real estate investment trust held by the qualified shareholder, and

(ii) the applicable percentage of the amounts realized by the qualified shareholder with respect to any disposition of stock in the real estate investment trust or with respect to any distribution from the real estate investment trust attributable to gain from sales or exchanges of a United States real property interest shall be treated as amounts realized from the disposition of United States real property interests.

(C) SPECIAL RULE FOR CERTAIN DISTRIBUTIONS TREATED AS SALE OR EXCHANGE.—If a distribution by a real estate investment trust is treated as a sale or exchange of stock under section 301(c)(3), 302, or 331 with respect to a qualified shareholder—

(i) in the case of an applicable investor, subparagraph (B) shall apply with respect to such distribution, and

(ii) in the case of any other person, such distribution shall be treated under section 857(b)(3)(F) as a dividend from a real estate investment trust notwithstanding any other provision of this title.

(D) APPLICABLE INVESTOR.—For purposes of this subsection, the term "applicable investor" means, with respect to any qualified shareholder holding stock in a real estate investment trust, a person (other than a qualified shareholder) which—

(i) holds an interest (other than an interest solely as a creditor) in such qualified shareholder, and

(ii) holds more than 10 percent of the stock of such real estate investment trust (whether or not by reason of the person's ownership interest in the qualified shareholder).

(E) CONSTRUCTIVE OWNERSHIP RULES.—For purposes of subparagraphs (B)(i) and (D), the constructive ownership rules under subsection (c)(6)(C) shall apply.

(F) APPLICABLE PERCENTAGE.—For purposes of subparagraph (B), the term "applicable percentage" means the percentage of the value of the interests (other than interests held solely as a creditor) in the qualified shareholder held by applicable investors.

(3) QUALIFIED SHAREHOLDER.—For purposes of this subsection—

(A) IN GENERAL.—The term "qualified shareholder" means a foreign person which—

(i)(I) is eligible for benefits of a comprehensive income tax treaty with the United States which includes an exchange of information program and the principal class of interests of which is listed and regularly traded on 1 or more recognized stock exchanges (as defined in such comprehensive income tax treaty), or

(II) is a foreign partnership that is created or organized under foreign law as a limited partnership in a jurisdiction that has an agreement for the exchange of information with respect to taxes with the United States and has a class of limited partnership units which is regularly traded on the New York Stock Exchange or Nasdaq Stock Market and such class of limited partnership units value is greater than 50 percent of the value of all the partnership units,

(ii) is a qualified collective investment vehicle, and

(iii) maintains records on the identity of each person who, at any time during the foreign person's taxable year, holds directly 5 percent or more of the class of interest described in subclause (I) or (II) of clause (i), as the case may be.

(B) QUALIFIED COLLECTIVE INVESTMENT VEHICLE.—For purposes of this subsection, the term "qualified collective investment vehicle" means a foreign person—

(i) which—

(I) is eligible for benefits under the comprehensive income tax treaty described in subparagraph (A)(i)(I), but only if the dividends article of such treaty imposes conditions on the benefits allowable in the case of dividends paid by a real estate investment trust, and

(II) is eligible under such treaty for a reduced rate of withholding with respect to ordinary dividends paid by a real estate investment trust even if such person holds more than 10 percent of the stock of such real estate investment trust,

(ii) which—

(I) is a publicly traded partnership (as defined in section 7704(b)) to which subsection (a) of section 7704 does not apply,

(II) is a withholding foreign partnership for purposes of chapters 3, 4, and 61, and

(III) if such foreign partnership were a domestic corporation, would be a United States real property holding corporation (determined without regard to paragraph (1)) at any time during the 5-year period ending on the date of disposition of, or distribution with respect to, such partnership's interests in a real estate investment trust, or

(iii) which is designated as a qualified collective investment vehicle by the Secretary and is either—

(I) fiscally transparent within the meaning of section 894, or

(II) required to include dividends in its gross income, but entitled to a deduction for distributions to persons holding interests (other than interests solely as a creditor) in such foreign person.

(4) PARTNERSHIP ALLOCATIONS.—

(A) IN GENERAL.—For the purposes of this subsection, in the case of an applicable investor who is a nonresident alien individual or a foreign corporation and is a partner in a partnership that is a qualified shareholder, if such partner's proportionate share of USRPI gain for the taxable year exceeds such partner's distributive share of USRPI gain for the taxable year, then

(i) such partner's distributive share of the amount of gain taken into account under subsection (a)(1) by the partner for the taxable year (determined without regard to this paragraph) shall be increased by the amount of such excess, and

(ii) such partner's distributive share of items of income or gain for the taxable year that are not treated as gain taken into account under subsection (a)(1) (determined without regard to this paragraph) shall be decreased (but not below zero) by the amount of such excess.

(B) USRPI GAIN.—For the purposes of this paragraph, the term "USRPI gain" means the excess (if any) of—

(i) the sum of—

(I) any gain recognized from the disposition of a United States real property interest, and

(II) any distribution by a real estate investment trust that is treated as gain recognized from the sale or exchange of a United States real property interest, over

(ii) any loss recognized from the disposition of a United States real property interest.

(C) PROPORTIONATE SHARE OF USRPI GAIN.—For purposes of this paragraph, an applicable investor's proportionate share of USRPI gain shall be determined on the basis of such investor's share of partnership items of income or gain (excluding gain allocated under section 704(c)), whichever results in the largest proportionate share. If the investor's share of partnership items of income or gain (excluding gain allocated under section 704(c)) may vary during the period such investor is a partner in the partnership, such share shall be the highest share such investor may receive.

[Sec. 897(l)]

(l) EXCEPTION FOR QUALIFIED FOREIGN PENSION FUNDS.—

(1) IN GENERAL.—For purposes of this section, a qualified foreign pension fund shall not be treated as a nonresident alien individual or a foreign corporation. For purposes of the preceding sentence, an entity all the interests of which are held by a qualified foreign pension fund shall be treated as such a fund.

(2) QUALIFIED FOREIGN PENSION FUND.—For purposes of this subsection, the term "qualified foreign pension fund" means any trust, corporation, or other organization or arrangement—

(A) which is created or organized under the law of a country other than the United States,

(B) which is established—

(i) by such country (or one or more political subdivisions thereof) to provide retirement or pension benefits to participants or beneficiaries that are current or former employees (including self-employed individuals) or persons designated by such employees, as a result of services rendered by such employees to their employers, or

(ii) by one or more employers to provide retirement or pension benefits to participants or beneficiaries that are current or former employees (including self-employed individuals) or persons designated by such employees in consideration for services rendered by such employees to such employers,

(C) which does not have a single participant or beneficiary with a right to more than five percent of its assets or income,

(D) which is subject to government regulation and with respect to which annual information about its beneficiaries is provided, or is otherwise available, to the relevant tax authorities in the country in which it is established or operates, and

(E) with respect to which, under the laws of the country in which it is established or operates—

(i) contributions to such trust, corporation, organization, or arrangement which would otherwise be subject to tax under such laws are deductible or excluded from the gross income of such entity or arrangement or taxed at a reduced rate, or

(ii) taxation of any investment income of such trust, corporation, organization or arrangement is deferred, or such income is excluded from the gross income of such entity or arrangement or is taxed at a reduced rate.

(3) REGULATIONS.—The Secretary shall prescribe such regulations as may be necessary or appropriate to carry out the purposes of this subsection.

[Sec. 898]

SEC. 898. TAXABLE YEAR OF CERTAIN FOREIGN CORPORATIONS.

[Sec. 898(a)]

(a) GENERAL RULE.—For purposes of this title, the taxable year of any specified foreign corporation shall be the required year determined under subsection (c).

[Sec. 898(b)]

(b) SPECIFIED FOREIGN CORPORATION.—For purposes of this section—

(1) IN GENERAL.—The term "specified foreign corporation" means any foreign corporation—

(A) which is treated as a controlled foreign corporation for any purpose under subpart F of part III of this subchapter, and

(B) with respect to which the ownership requirements of paragraph (2) are met.

(2) OWNERSHIP REQUIREMENTS.—

(A) IN GENERAL.—The ownership requirements of this paragraph are met with respect to any foreign corporation if a United States shareholder owns, on each testing day, more than 50 percent of—

(i) the total voting power of all classes of stock of such corporation entitled to vote, or

(ii) the total value of all classes of stock of such corporation.

(B) OWNERSHIP.—For purposes of subparagraph (A), the rules of subsections (a) and (b) of section 958 shall apply in determining ownership.

(3) UNITED STATES SHAREHOLDER.—The term "United States shareholder" has the meaning given to such term by section 951(b), except that, in the case of a foreign corporation having related person insurance income (as defined in section 953(c)(2)), the Secretary may treat any person as a United States shareholder for purposes of this section if such person is treated as a United States shareholder under section 953(c)(1).

[Sec. 898(c)]

(c) DETERMINATION OF REQUIRED YEAR.—

(1) IN GENERAL.—The required year is—

(A) the majority U.S. shareholder year, or

(B) if there is no majority U.S. shareholder year, the taxable year prescribed under regulations.

(2) 1-MONTH DEFERRAL ALLOWED.—A specified foreign corporation may elect, in lieu of the taxable year under paragraph (1)(A), a taxable year beginning 1 month earlier than the majority U.S. shareholder year.

(3) MAJORITY U.S. SHAREHOLDER YEAR.—

(A) IN GENERAL.—For purposes of this subsection, the term "majority U.S. shareholder year" means the taxable year (if any) which, on each testing day, constituted the taxable year of—

(i) each United States shareholder described in subsection (b)(2)(A), and

(ii) each United States shareholder not described in clause (i) whose stock was treated as owned under subsection (b)(2)(B) by any shareholder described in such clause.

(B) TESTING DAY.—The testing days shall be—

(i) the first day of the corporation's taxable year (determined without regard to this section), or

(ii) the days during such representative period as the Secretary may prescribe.

PART III—INCOME FROM SOURCES WITHOUT THE UNITED STATES

Subpart A—Foreign Tax Credit

[Sec. 901]

SEC. 901. TAXES OF FOREIGN COUNTRIES AND OF POSSESSIONS OF UNITED STATES.

[Sec. 901(a)]

(a) ALLOWANCE OF CREDIT.—If the taxpayer chooses to have the benefits of this subpart, the tax imposed by this chapter shall, subject to the limitation of section 904, be credited with the amounts provided in the applicable paragraph of subsection (b) plus, in the case of a corporation, the taxes deemed to have been paid under section 960. Such choice for any taxable year may be made or changed at any time before the expiration of the period prescribed for making a claim for credit or refund of the tax imposed by this chapter for such taxable year. The credit shall not be allowed against any tax treated as a tax not imposed by this chapter under section 26(b).

[Sec. 901(b)]

(b) AMOUNT ALLOWED.—Subject to the limitation of section 904, the following amounts shall be allowed as the credit under subsection (a):

(1) CITIZENS AND DOMESTIC CORPORATIONS.—In the case of a citizen of the United States and of a domestic corporation, the amount of any income, war profits, and excess profits taxes paid or accrued during the taxable year to any foreign country or to any possession of the United States; and

(2) RESIDENT OF THE UNITED STATES OR PUERTO RICO.—In the case of a resident of the United States and in the case of an individual who is a bona fide resident of Puerto Rico during the entire taxable year, the amount of any such taxes paid or accrued during the taxable year to any possession of the United States; and

(3) ALIEN RESIDENT OF THE UNITED STATES OR PUERTO RICO.—In the case of an alien resident of the United States and in the case of an alien individual who is a bona fide resident of Puerto Rico during the entire taxable year, the amount of any such taxes paid or accrued during the taxable year to any foreign country; and

(4) NONRESIDENT ALIEN INDIVIDUALS AND FOREIGN CORPORATIONS.—In the case of any nonresident alien individual not described in section 876 and in the case of any foreign corporation, the amount determined pursuant to section 906; and

(5) PARTNERSHIPS AND ESTATES.—In the case of any person described in paragraph (1), (2), (3), or (4), who is a member of a partnership or a beneficiary of an estate or trust, the amount of his proportionate share of the taxes (described in such paragraph) of the partnership or the estate or trust paid or accrued during the taxable year to a foreign country or to any possession of the United States, as the case may be. Under rules or regulations prescribed by the Secretary, in the case of any foreign trust of which the settlor or another person would be treated as owner of any portion of the trust under subpart E but for section 672(f), [the term "taxes imposed on the trust" includes] the allocable amount of any income, war profits, and excess profits taxes imposed by any foreign country or possession of the United States on the settlor or such other person in respect of trust income.

[Sec. 901(c)]

(c) SIMILAR CREDIT REQUIRED FOR CERTAIN ALIEN RESIDENTS.—Whenever the President finds that—

(1) a foreign country, in imposing income, war profits, and excess profits taxes, does not allow to citizens of the United States residing in such foreign country a credit for any such taxes paid or accrued to the United States or any foreign country, as the case may be, similar to the credit allowed under subsection (b)(3),

(2) such foreign country, when requested by the United States to do so, has not acted to provide such a similar credit to citizens of the United States residing in such foreign country, and

(3) it is in the public interest to allow the credit under subsection (b)(3) to citizens or subjects of such foreign country only if it allows such a similar credit to citizens of the United States residing in such foreign country,

the President shall proclaim that, for taxable years beginning while the proclamation remains in effect, the credit under subsection (b)(3) shall be allowed to citizens or subjects of such foreign country only if such foreign country, in imposing income, war profits, and excess profits taxes, allows to citizens of the United States residing in such foreign country such a similar credit.

[Sec. 901(d)]

(d) TREATMENT OF DIVIDENDS FROM A DISC OR FORMER DISC.—For purposes of this subpart, dividends from a DISC or former DISC (as defined in section 992(a)) shall be treated as dividends from a foreign corporation to the extent such dividends are treated under part I as income from sources without the United States.

[Sec. 901(e)]

(e) FOREIGN TAXES ON MINERAL INCOME.—

(1) REDUCTION IN AMOUNT ALLOWED.—Notwithstanding subsection (b), the amount of any income, war profits, and excess profits taxes paid or accrued during the taxable year to any foreign country or possession of the United States with respect to foreign mineral income from sources within such country or possession which would (but for this paragraph) be allowed under such subsection shall be reduced by the amount (if any) by which—

(A) the amount of such taxes (or, if smaller, the amount of the tax which would be computed under this chapter with respect to such income determined without the deduction allowed under section 613), exceeds

(B) the amount of the tax computed under this chapter with respect to such income.

(2) FOREIGN MINERAL INCOME DEFINED.—For purposes of paragraph (1), the term "foreign mineral income" means income derived from the extraction of minerals from mines, wells, or other natural deposits, the processing of such minerals into their primary products, and the transportation, distribution, or sale of such minerals or primary products. Such term includes, but is not limited to that portion of the taxpayer's distributive share of the income of partnerships attributable to foreign mineral income.

[Sec. 901(f)]

(f) CERTAIN PAYMENTS FOR OIL OR GAS NOT CONSIDERED AS TAXES.—Notwithstanding subsection (b) and section 960, the amount of any income, or profits, and excess profits taxes paid or accrued during the taxable year to any foreign country in connection with the purchase and sale of oil or gas extracted in such country is not to be considered as tax for purposes of section 275(a) and this section if—

(1) the taxpayer has no economic interest in the oil or gas to which section 611(a) applies, and

(2) either such purchase or sale is at a price which differs from the fair market value for such oil or gas at the time of such purchase or sale.

[Sec. 901(g)]

(g) CERTAIN TAXES PAID WITH RESPECT TO DISTRIBUTIONS FROM POSSESSIONS CORPORATIONS.—

(1) IN GENERAL.—For purposes of this chapter, any tax of a foreign country or possession of the United States which is paid or accrued with respect to any distribution from a corporation—

(A) to the extent that such distribution is attributable to periods during which such corporation is a possessions corporation, and

(B) (i) if a dividends received deduction is allowable with respect to such distribution under part VIII of subchapter B, or

(ii) to the extent that such distribution is received in connection with a liquidation or other transaction with respect to which gain or loss is not recognized,

shall not be treated as income, war profits, or excess profits taxes paid or accrued to a foreign country or possession of the United States, and no deduction shall be allowed under this title with respect to any amount so paid or accrued.

(2) POSSESSIONS CORPORATION.—For purposes of paragraph (1), a corporation shall be treated as a possessions corporation for any period during which an election under section 936 (as in effect on the day before the date of the enactment of the Tax Technical Corrections Act of 2018) applied to such corporation, during which section 931 (as in effect on the day before the date of the enactment of the Tax Reform Act of 1976) applied to such corporation, or during which section 957(c) (as in effect on the day before the date of the enactment of the Tax Reform Act of 1986) applied to such corporation.

[Sec. 901(h)—Stricken]

[Sec. 901(i)]

(i) TAXES USED TO PROVIDE SUBSIDIES.—Any income, war profits, or excess profits tax shall not be treated as a tax for purposes of this title to the extent—

(1) the amount of such tax is used (directly or indirectly) by the country imposing such tax to provide a subsidy by any means to the taxpayer, a related person (within the meaning of section 482), or any party to the transaction or to a related transaction, and

(2) such subsidy is determined (directly or indirectly) by reference to the amount of such tax, or the base used to compute the amount of such tax.

[Sec. 901(j)]

(j) DENIAL OF FOREIGN TAX CREDIT, ETC., WITH RESPECT TO CERTAIN FOREIGN COUNTRIES.—

(1) IN GENERAL.—Notwithstanding any other provision of this part—

(A) no credit shall be allowed under subsection (a) for any income, war profits, or excess profits taxes paid or accrued (or deemed paid under section 960) to any country if such taxes are with respect to income attributable to a period during which this subsection applies to such country, and

(B) subsections (a), (b), and (c) of section 904 and section 960 shall be applied separately with respect to income attributable to such a period from sources within such country.

(2) COUNTRIES TO WHICH SUBSECTION APPLIES.—

(A) IN GENERAL.—This subsection shall apply to any foreign country—

(i) the government of which the United States does not recognize, unless such government is otherwise eligible to purchase defense articles or services under the Arms Export Control Act,

(ii) with respect to which the United States has severed diplomatic relations,

(iii) with respect to which the United States has not severed diplomatic relations but does not conduct such relations, or

(iv) which the Secretary of State has, pursuant to section 6(j) of the Export Administration Act of 1979, as amended, designated as a foreign country which repeatedly provides support for acts of international terrorisms.

(B) PERIOD FOR WHICH SUBSECTION APPLIES.—This subsection shall apply to any foreign country described in subparagraph (A) during the period—

(i) beginning on the later of—

(I) January 1, 1987, or

(II) 6 months after such country becomes a country described in subparagraph (A), and

(ii) ending on the date the Secretary of State certifies to the Secretary of the Treasury that such country is no longer described in subparagraph (A).

(3) TAXES ALLOWED AS A DEDUCTION, ETC.—Sections 275 and 78 shall not apply to any tax which is not allowable as a credit under subsection (a) by reason of this subsection.

(4) REGULATIONS.—The Secretary shall prescribe such regulations as may be necessary or appropriate to carry out the purposes of this subsection, including regulations which treat income paid through 1 or more entities as derived from a foreign country to which this subsection applies if such income was, without regard to such entities, derived from such country.

(5) WAIVER OF DENIAL.—

(A) IN GENERAL.—Paragraph (1) shall not apply with respect to taxes paid or accrued to a country if the President—

(i) determines that a waiver of the application of such paragraph is in the national interest of the United States and will expand trade and investment opportunities for United States companies in such country; and

(ii) reports such waiver under subparagraph (B).

(B) REPORT.—Not less than 30 days before the date on which a waiver is granted under this paragraph, the President shall report to Congress—

(i) the intention to grant such waiver; and

(ii) the reason for the determination under subparagraph (A)(i).

[Sec. 901(k)]

(k) MINIMUM HOLDING PERIOD FOR CERTAIN TAXES ON DIVIDENDS.—

(1) WITHHOLDING TAXES.—

(A) IN GENERAL.—In no event shall a credit be allowed under subsection (a) for any withholding tax on a dividend with respect to stock in a corporation if—

(i) such stock is held by the recipient of the dividend for 15 days or less during the 31-day period beginning on the date which is 15 days before the date on which such share becomes ex-dividend with respect to such dividend, or

(ii) to the extent that the recipient of the dividend is under an obligation (whether pursuant to a short sale or otherwise) to make related payments with respect to positions in substantially similar or related property.

(B) WITHHOLDING TAX.—For purposes of this paragraph, the term "withholding tax" includes any tax determined on a gross basis; but does not include any tax which is in the nature of a prepayment of a tax imposed on a net basis.

(2) DEEMED PAID TAXES.—In the case of income, war profits, or excess profits taxes deemed paid under section 853 or 960 through a chain of ownership of stock in 1 or more corporations, no credit shall be allowed under subsection (a) for such taxes if—

(A) any stock of any corporation in such chain (the ownership of which is required to obtain credit under subsection (a) for such taxes) is held for less than the period described in paragraph (1)(A)(i), or

(B) the corporation holding the stock is under an obligation referred to in paragraph (1)(A)(ii).

(3) 45-DAY RULE IN THE CASE OF CERTAIN PREFERENCE DIVIDENDS.—In the case of stock having preference in dividends and dividends with respect to such stock which are attributable to a period or periods aggregating in excess of 366 days, paragraph (1)(A)(i) shall be applied—

(A) by substituting "45 days" for "15 days" each place it appears, and

(B) by substituting "91-day period" for "31-day period".

(4) EXCEPTION FOR CERTAIN TAXES PAID BY SECURITIES DEALERS.—

(A) IN GENERAL.—Paragraphs (1) and (2) shall not apply to any qualified tax with respect to any security held in the active conduct in a foreign country of a business as a securities dealer of any person—

(i) who is registered as a securities broker or dealer under section 15(a) of the Securities Exchange Act of 1934,

(ii) who is registered as a Government securities broker or dealer under section 15C(a) of such Act, or

(iii) who is licensed or authorized in such foreign country to conduct securities activities in such country and is subject to bona fide regulation by a securities regulating authority of such country.

(B) QUALIFIED TAX.—For purposes of subparagraph (A), the term "qualified tax" means a tax paid to a foreign country (other than the foreign country referred to in subparagraph (A)) if—

(i) the dividend to which such tax is attributable is subject to taxation on a net basis by the country referred to in subparagraph (A), and

(ii) such country allows a credit against its net basis tax for the full amount of the tax paid to such other foreign country.

(C) REGULATIONS.—The Secretary may prescribe such regulations as may be appropriate to carry out this paragraph, including regulations to prevent the abuse of the exception provided by this paragraph and to treat other taxes as qualified taxes.

(5) CERTAIN RULES TO APPLY.—For purposes of this subsection, the rules of paragraphs (3) and (4) of section 246(c) shall apply.

(6) TREATMENT OF BONA FIDE SALES.—If a person's holding period is reduced by reason of the application of the rules of section 246(c)(4) to any contract for the bona fide sale of stock, the determination of whether such person's holding period meets the requirements of paragraph (2) with respect to taxes deemed paid under section 960 shall be made as of the date such contract is entered into.

(7) TAXES ALLOWED AS DEDUCTION, ETC.—Sections 275 and 78 shall not apply to any tax which is not allowable as a credit under subsection (a) by reason of this subsection.

[Sec. 901(l)]

(l) MINIMUM HOLDING PERIOD FOR WITHHOLDING TAXES ON GAIN AND INCOME OTHER THAN DIVIDENDS ETC.—

(1) IN GENERAL.—In no event shall a credit be allowed under subsection (a) for any withholding tax (as defined in subsection (k)) on any item of income or gain with respect to any property if—

(A) such property is held by the recipient of the item for 15 days or less during the 31-day period beginning on the date which is 15 days before the date on which the right to receive payment of such item arises, or

(B) to the extent that the recipient of the item is under an obligation (whether pursuant to a short sale or otherwise) to make related payments with respect to positions in substantially similar or related property.

This paragraph shall not apply to any dividend to which subsection (k) applies.

(2) EXCEPTION FOR TAXES PAID BY DEALERS.—

(A) IN GENERAL.—Paragraph (1) shall not apply to any qualified tax with respect to any property held in the active conduct in a foreign country of a business as a dealer in such property.

(B) QUALIFIED TAX.—For purposes of subparagraph (A), the term "qualified tax" means a tax paid to a foreign country (other than the foreign country referred to in subparagraph (A)) if—

(i) the item to which such tax is attributable is subject to taxation on a net basis by the country referred to in subparagraph (A), and

(ii) such country allows a credit against its net basis tax for the full amount of the tax paid to such other foreign country.

(C) DEALER.—For purposes of subparagraph (A), the term "dealer" means—

(i) with respect to a security, any person to whom paragraphs (1) and (2) of subsection (k) would not apply by reason of paragraph (4) thereof, and

(ii) with respect to any other property, any person with respect to whom such property is described in section 1221(a)(1).

(D) REGULATIONS.—The Secretary may prescribe such regulations as may be appropriate to carry out this paragraph, including regulations to prevent the abuse of the exception provided by this paragraph and to treat other taxes as qualified taxes.

(3) EXCEPTIONS.—The Secretary may by regulation provide that paragraph (1) shall not apply to property where the Secretary determines that the application of paragraph (1) to such property is not necessary to carry out the purposes of this subsection.

(4) CERTAIN RULES TO APPLY.—Rules similar to the rules of paragraphs (5), (6), and (7) of subsection (k) shall apply for purposes of this subsection.

(5) DETERMINATION OF HOLDING PERIOD.—Holding periods shall be determined for purposes of this subsection without regard to section 1235 or any similar rule.

[Sec. 901(m)]

(m) DENIAL OF FOREIGN TAX CREDIT WITH RESPECT TO FOREIGN INCOME NOT SUBJECT TO UNITED STATES TAXATION BY REASON OF COVERED ASSET ACQUISITIONS.—

(1) IN GENERAL .—In the case of a covered asset acquisition, the disqualified portion of any foreign income tax determined with respect to the income or gain attributable to the relevant foreign assets—

(A) shall not be taken into account in determining the credit allowed under subsection (a), and

(B) in the case of a foreign income tax paid by a foreign corporation, shall not be taken into account for purposes of section 960.

(2) COVERED ASSET ACQUISITION .—For purposes of this section, the term "covered asset acquisition" means—

(A) a qualified stock purchase (as defined in section 338(d)(3)) to which section 338(a) applies,

(B) any transaction which—

(i) is treated as an acquisition of assets for purposes of this chapter, and

(ii) is treated as the acquisition of stock of a corporation (or is disregarded) for purposes of the foreign income taxes of the relevant jurisdiction,

(C) any acquisition of an interest in a partnership which has an election in effect under section 754, and

(D) to the extent provided by the Secretary, any other similar transaction.

(3) DISQUALIFIED PORTION .—For purposes of this section—

(A) IN GENERAL .—The term "disqualified portion" means, with respect to any covered asset acquisition, for any taxable year, the ratio (expressed as a percentage) of—

(i) the aggregate basis differences (but not below zero) allocable to such taxable year under subparagraph (B) with respect to all relevant foreign assets, divided by

(ii) the income on which the foreign income tax referred to in paragraph (1) is determined (or, if the taxpayer fails to substantiate such income to the satisfaction of the Secretary, such income shall be determined by dividing the amount of such foreign income tax by the highest marginal tax rate applicable to such income in the relevant jurisdiction).

(B) ALLOCATION OF BASIS DIFFERENCE .—For purposes of subparagraph (A)(i)—

(i) IN GENERAL .—The basis difference with respect to any relevant foreign asset shall be allocated to taxable years using the applicable cost recovery method under this chapter.

(ii) SPECIAL RULE FOR DISPOSITION OF ASSETS .—Except as otherwise provided by the Secretary, in the case of the disposition of any relevant foreign asset—

(I) the basis difference allocated to the taxable year which includes the date of such disposition shall be the excess of the basis difference with respect to such asset over the aggregate basis difference with respect to such asset which has been allocated under clause (i) to all prior taxable years, and

(II) no basis difference with respect to such asset shall be allocated under clause (i) to any taxable year thereafter.

(C) BASIS DIFFERENCE.—

(i) IN GENERAL .—The term "basis difference" means, with respect to any relevant foreign asset, the excess of—

(I) the adjusted basis of such asset immediately after the covered asset acquisition, over

(II) the adjusted basis of such asset immediately before the covered asset acquisition.

(ii) BUILT-IN LOSS ASSETS .—In the case of a relevant foreign asset with respect to which the amount described in clause (i)(II) exceeds the amount described in clause (i)(I), such excess shall be taken into account under this subsection as a basis difference of a negative amount.

(iii) SPECIAL RULE FOR SECTION 338 ELECTIONS .—In the case of a covered asset acquisition described in paragraph (2)(A), the covered asset acquisition shall be treated for purposes of this subparagraph as occurring at the close of the acquisition date (as defined in section 338(h)(2)).

(4) RELEVANT FOREIGN ASSETS .—For purposes of this section, the term "relevant foreign asset" means, with respect to any covered asset acquisition, any asset (including any goodwill, going concern value, or other intangible) with respect to such acquisition if income, deduction, gain, or loss attributable to such asset is taken into account in determining the foreign income tax referred to in paragraph (1)

(5) FOREIGN INCOME TAX .—For purposes of this section, the term "foreign income tax" means any income, war profits, or excess profits tax paid or accrued to any foreign country or to any possession of the United States.

(6) TAXES ALLOWED AS A DEDUCTION, ETC .— Sections 275 and 78 shall not apply to any tax which is not allowable as a credit under subsection (a) by reason of this subsection.

(7) REGULATIONS .—The Secretary may issue such regulations or other guidance as is necessary or appropriate to carry out the purposes of this subsection, including to exempt from the application of this subsection certain covered asset acquisitions, and relevant foreign assets with respect to which the basis difference is de minimis.

[Sec. 901(n)]

(n) CROSS REFERENCE.—

(1) For deductions of income, war profits, and excess profits taxes paid to a foreign country or a possession of the United States, see sections 164 and 275.

(2) For right of each partner to make election under this section, see section 703(b).

(3) For right of estate or trust to the credit for taxes imposed by foreign countries and possessions of the United States under this section, see section 642(a).

(4) For reduction of credit for failure of a United States person to furnish certain information with respect to a foreign corporation or partnership controlled by him, see section 6038.

Caution: Section 902 was repealed by P.L. 115-97, effective for taxable years of foreign corporations starting after 2017, and to taxable years of United States shareholders in which or with which such taxable years of foreign corporations end.

[Sec. 902—Stricken]

SEC. 902. DEEMED PAID CREDIT WHERE DOMESTIC CORPORATION OWNS 10 PERCENT OR MORE OF VOTING STOCK OF FOREIGN CORPORATION.

[Sec. 902(a)]

(a) TAXES PAID BY FOREIGN CORPORATION TREATED AS PAID BY DOMESTIC CORPORATION.—For purposes of this subpart, a domestic corporation which owns 10 percent or more of the voting stock of a foreign corporation from which it receives dividends in any taxable year shall be deemed to have paid the same proportion of such foreign corporation's post-1986 foreign income taxes as—

(1) the amount of such dividends (determined without regard to section 78), bears to

(2) such foreign corporation's post-1986 undistributed earnings.

[Sec. 902(b)]

(b) DEEMED TAXES INCREASED IN CASE OF CERTAIN LOWER TIER CORPORATIONS.—

(1) IN GENERAL.—If—

(A) any foreign corporation is a member of a qualified group, and

(B) such foreign corporation owns 10 percent or more of the voting stock of another member of such group from which it receives dividends in any taxable year,

such foreign corporation shall be deemed to have paid the same proportion of such other member's post-1986 foreign income taxes as would be determined under subsection (a) if such foreign corporation were a domestic corporation.

(2) QUALIFIED GROUP.—For purposes of paragraph (1), the term "qualified group" means—

(A) the foreign corporation described in subsection (a), and

(B) any other foreign corporation if—

(i) the domestic corporation owns at least 5 percent of the voting stock of such other foreign corporation indirectly through a chain of foreign corporations connected through stock ownership of at least 10 percent of their voting stock,

(ii) the foreign corporation described in subsection (a) is the first tier corporation in such chain, and

(iii) such other corporation is not below the sixth tier in such chain.

The term "qualified group" shall not include any foreign corporation below the third tier in the chain referred to in clause (i) unless such foreign corporation is a controlled foreign corporation (as defined in section 957) and the domestic corporation is a United States shareholder (as defined in section 951(b)) in such foreign corporation. Paragraph (1) shall apply to those taxes paid by a member of the qualified group below the third tier only with respect to periods during which it was a controlled foreign corporation.

[Sec. 902(c)]

(c) DEFINITIONS AND SPECIAL RULES.—For purposes of this section—

(1) POST-1986 UNDISTRIBUTED EARNINGS.—The term "post-1986 undistributed earnings" means the amount of the earnings and profits of the foreign corporation (computed in accordance with sections 964(a) and 986) accumulated in taxable years beginning after December 31, 1986—

(A) as of the close of the taxable year of the foreign corporation in which the dividend is distributed, and

(B) without diminution by reason of dividends distributed during such taxable year.

(2) POST-1986 FOREIGN INCOME TAXES.—The term "post-1986 foreign income taxes" means the sum of—

(A) the foreign income taxes with respect to the taxable year of the foreign corporation in which the dividend is distributed, and

(B) the foreign income taxes with respect to prior taxable years beginning after December 31, 1986, to the extent such foreign taxes were not attributable to dividends distributed by the foreign corporation in prior taxable years.

(3) SPECIAL RULE WHERE FOREIGN CORPORATION FIRST QUALIFIES AFTER DECEMBER 31, 1986.—

(A) IN GENERAL.—If the 1st day on which the requirements of subparagraph (B) are met with respect to any foreign corporation is in a taxable year of such corporation beginning after December 31, 1986, the post-1986 undistributed earnings and the post-1986 foreign income taxes of such foreign corporation shall be determined by taking into account only periods beginning on and after the 1st day of the 1st taxable year in which such ownership are met.

(B) REQUIREMENTS.—The requirements of this subparagraph are met with respect to any foreign corporation if—

(i) 10 percent of more of the voting stock of such foreign corporation is owned by a domestic corporation, or

(ii) the requirements of subsection (b)(2) are met with respect to such foreign corporation.

(4) FOREIGN INCOME TAXES.—

(A) IN GENERAL.—The term "foreign income taxes" means any income, war profits, or excess profits taxes paid by the foreign corporation to any foreign country or possession of the United States.

(B) TREATMENT OF DEEMED TAXES.—Except for purposes of determining the amount of the post-1986 foreign income taxes of a sixth tier foreign corporation referred to in subsection (b)(2), the term "foreign income taxes" includes any such taxes deemed to be paid by the foreign corporation under this section.

(5) ACCOUNTING PERIODS.—In the case of a foreign corporation the income, war profits, and excess profits taxes of which are determined on the basis of an accounting period of less than 1 year, the word "year" as used in this subsection shall be construed to mean such accounting period.

(6) TREATMENT OF DISTRIBUTIONS FROM EARNINGS BEFORE 1987.—

(A) IN GENERAL.—In the case of any dividend paid by a foreign corporation out of accumulated profits (as defined in this section as in effect on the day before the date of the enactment of the Tax Reform Act of 1986) for taxable years beginning before the 1st taxable year taken into account in determining the post-1986 undistributed earnings of such corporation—

(i) this section (as amended by the Tax Reform Act of 1986) shall not apply, but

(ii) this section (as in effect on the day before the date of the enactment of such Act) shall apply.

(B) DIVIDENDS PAID FIRST OUT OF POST-1986 EARNINGS.—Any dividend in a taxable year beginning after December 31, 1986, shall be treated as made out of post-1986 undistributed earnings to the extent thereof.

(7) CONSTRUCTIVE OWNERSHIP THROUGH PARTNERSHIPS.—Stock owned, directly or indirectly, by or for a partnership shall be considered as being owned proportionately by its partners. Stock considered to be owned by a person by reason of the preceding sentence shall, for purposes of applying such sentence, be treated as actually owned by such person. The Secretary may prescribe such regulations as may be necessary to carry out the purposes of this paragraph, including rules to account for special partnership allocations of dividends, credits, and other incidents of ownership of stock in determining proportionate ownership.

(8) REGULATIONS.—The Secretary shall provide such regulations as may be necessary or appropriate to carry out the provisions of this section and section 960, including provisions which provide for the separate application of this section and section 960 to reflect the separate application of section 904 to separate types of income and loss.

[Sec. 902(d)]

(d) CROSS REFERENCES.—

(1) For inclusion in gross income of an amount equal to taxes deemed paid under subsection (a), see section 78.

(2) For application of subsections (a) and (b) with respect to taxes deemed paid in a prior taxable year by a United States shareholder with respect to a controlled foreign corporation, see section 960.

(3) For reduction of credit with respect to dividends paid out of post-1986 undistributed earnings for years for which certain information is not furnished, see section 6038.

[Sec. 903]

SEC. 903. CREDIT FOR TAXES IN LIEU OF INCOME, ETC., TAXES.

For purposes of this part and of sections 164(a) and 275(a), the term "income, war profits, and excess profits taxes" shall include a tax paid in lieu of a tax on income, war profits, or excess profits otherwise generally imposed by any foreign country or by any possession of the United States.

[Sec. 904]

SEC. 904. LIMITATION ON CREDIT.

[Sec. 904(a)]

(a) LIMITATION.—The total amount of the credit taken under section 901(a) shall not exceed the same proportion of the tax against which such credit is taken which the taxpayer's taxable income from sources without the United States (but not in excess of the taxpayer's entire taxable income) bears to his entire taxable income for the same taxable year.

[Sec. 904(b)]

(b) TAXABLE INCOME FOR PURPOSE OF COMPUTING LIMITATION.—

(1) PERSONAL EXEMPTIONS.—For purposes of subsection (a), the taxable income in the case of an individual, estate, or trust shall be computed without any deduction for personal exemptions under section 151 or 642(b).

(2) CAPITAL GAINS.—For purposes of this section—

(A) IN GENERAL.—Taxable income from sources outside the United States shall include gain from the sale or exchange of capital assets only to the extent of foreign source capital gain net income.

(B) SPECIAL RULES WHERE CAPITAL GAIN RATE DIFFERENTIAL.—In the case of any taxable year for which there is a capital gain rate differential—

(i) in lieu of applying subparagraph (A), the taxable income from sources outside the United States shall include gain from the sale or exchange of capital assets only in an amount equal to foreign source capital gain net income reduced by the rate differential portion of foreign source net capital gain,

(ii) the entire taxable income shall include gain from the sale or exchange of capital assets only in an amount equal to capital gain net income reduced by the rate differential portion of net capital gain, and

(iii) for purposes of determining taxable income from sources outside the United States, any net capital loss (and any amount which is a short-term capital loss under section 1212(a)) from sources outside the United States to the extent taken into account in determining capital gain net income for the taxable year shall be reduced by an amount equal to the rate differential portion of the excess of the net capital gain from sources within the United States over net capital gain.

(C) COORDINATION WITH CAPITAL GAINS RATES.—The Secretary may by regulations modify the application of this paragraph and paragraph (3) to the extent necessary to properly reflect any capital gain rate differential under section 1(h) and the computation of net capital gain.

(3) DEFINITIONS.—For purposes of this subsection—

(A) FOREIGN SOURCE CAPITAL GAIN NET INCOME.—The term "foreign source capital gain net income" means the lesser of—

(i) capital gain net income from sources without the United States, or

(ii) capital gain net income.

(B) FOREIGN SOURCE NET CAPITAL GAIN.—The term "foreign source net capital gain" means the lesser of—

(i) net capital gain from sources without the United States, or

(ii) net capital gain.

(C) SECTION 1231 GAINS.—The term "gain from the sale or exchange of capital assets" includes any gain so treated under section 1231.

(D) CAPITAL GAIN RATE DIFFERENTIAL.—There is a capital gain rate differential for any year if subsection (h) of section 1 applies to such taxable year.

(E) RATE DIFFERENTIAL PORTION.—The rate differential portion of foreign source net capital gain, net capital gain, or the excess of net capital gain from sources within the United States over net capital gain, as the case may be, is the same proportion of such amount as—

(i) the excess of—

(I) the highest rate of tax set forth in subsection (a), (b), (c), (d), or (e) of section 1 (whichever applies), over

(II) the alternative rate of tax determined under section 1(h), bears to

(ii) that rate referred to in subclause (I).

(4) TREATMENT OF DIVIDENDS FOR WHICH DEDUCTION IS ALLOWED UNDER SECTION 245A.—For purposes of subsection (a), in the case of a domestic corporation which is a United States shareholder with respect to a specified 10-percent owned foreign corporation, such shareholder's taxable income from sources without the United States (and entire taxable income) shall be determined without regard to—

(A) the foreign-source portion of any dividend received from such foreign corporation, and

(B) any deductions properly allocable or apportioned to—

(i) income (other than amounts includible under section 951(a)(1) or 951A(a)) with respect to stock of such specified 10-percent owned foreign corporation, or

(ii) such stock to the extent income with respect to such stock is other than amounts includible under section 951(a)(1) or 951A(a).

Any term which is used in section 245A and in this paragraph shall have the same meaning for purposes of this paragraph as when used in such section.

[Sec. 904(c)]

(c) CARRYBACK AND CARRYOVER OF EXCESS TAX PAID.—Any amount by which all taxes paid or accrued to foreign countries or possessions of the United States for any taxable year for which the taxpayer chooses to have the benefits of this subpart exceed the limitation under subsection (a) shall be deemed taxes paid or accrued to foreign countries or possessions of the United States in the first preceding taxable year, and in any of the first 10 succeeding taxable years, in that order and to the extent not deemed taxes paid or accrued in a prior taxable year, in the amount by which the limitation under subsection (a) for such preceding or succeeding taxable year exceeds the sum of the taxes paid or accrued to foreign countries or possessions of the United States for such preceding or succeeding taxable year and the amount of the taxes for any taxable year earlier than the current taxable year which shall be deemed to have been paid or accrued in such preceding or subsequent taxable year (whether or not the taxpayer chooses to have the benefits of this subpart with respect to such earlier taxable year). Such amount deemed paid or accrued in any year may be availed of only as a tax credit and not as a deduction and only if the taxpayer for such year chooses to have the benefits of this subpart as to taxes paid or accrued for that year to foreign countries or possessions of the United States. This subsection shall not apply to taxes paid or accrued with respect to amounts described in subsection (d)(1)(A).

[Sec. 904(d)]

(d) SEPARATE APPLICATION OF SECTION WITH RESPECT TO CERTAIN CATEGORIES OF INCOME.—

(1) IN GENERAL.—The provisions of subsections (a), (b), and (c) and sections 902, 907, and 960 shall be applied separately with respect to—

(A) any amount includible in gross income under section 951A (other than passive category income),

(B) foreign branch income,

(C) passive category income, and

(D) general category income.

(2) DEFINITIONS AND SPECIAL RULES.—For purposes of this subsection—

(A) CATEGORIES.—

(i) PASSIVE CATEGORY INCOME.—The term "passive category income" means passive income and specified passive category income.

(ii) GENERAL CATEGORY INCOME.—The term "general category income" means income other than income described in paragraph (1)(A), foreign branch income, and passive category income.

(B) PASSIVE INCOME.—

(i) IN GENERAL.—Except as otherwise provided in this subparagraph, the term "passive income" means any income received or accrued by any person which is of a kind which would be foreign personal holding company income (as defined in section 954(c)).

(ii) CERTAIN AMOUNTS INCLUDED.—Except as provided in clause (iii), subparagraph (E)(ii), or paragraph (3)(H), the term "passive income" includes any amount includible in gross income under section 1293 (relating to certain passive foreign investment companies).

(iii) EXCEPTIONS.—The term "passive income" shall not include—

(I) any export financing interest, and

(II) any high-taxed income.

(iv) CLARIFICATION OF APPLICATION OF SECTION 864(d)(6).—In determining whether any income is of a kind which would be foreign personal holding company income, the rules of section 864(d)(6) shall apply only in the case of income of a controlled foreign corporation.

(v) SPECIFIED PASSIVE CATEGORY INCOME.—The term "specified passive category income" means—

(I) dividends from a DISC or former DISC (as defined in section 992(a)) to the extent such dividends are treated as income from sources without the United States, and

(II) distributions from a former FSC (as defined in section 922) out of earnings and profits attributable to foreign trade income (within the meaning of section 923(b)) or interest or carrying charges (as defined in section 927(d)(1)) derived from a transaction which results in foreign trade income (as defined in section 923(b)).

Any reference in subclause (II) to section 922, 923, or 927 shall be treated as a reference to such section as in effect before its repeal by the FSC Repeal and Extraterritorial Income Exclusion Act of 2000.

(C) TREATMENT OF FINANCIAL SERVICES INCOME AND COMPANIES.—

(i) IN GENERAL.—Financial services income shall be treated as general category income in the case of—

(I) a member of a financial services group,

(II) any other person if such person is predominantly engaged in the active conduct of a banking, insurance, financing, or similar business.

(ii) FINANCIAL SERVICES GROUP.—The term "financial services group" means any affiliated group (as defined in section 1504(a) without regard to paragraphs (2) and (3) of section 1504(b)) which is predominantly engaged in the active conduct of a banking, insurance, financing, or similar business. In determining whether such a group is so engaged, there shall be taken into account only the income of members of the group that are—

(I) United States corporations, or

(II) controlled foreign corporations in which such United States corporations own, directly or indirectly, at least 80 percent of the total voting power and value of the stock.

(iii) PASS-THRU ENTITIES.—The Secretary shall by regulation specify for purposes of this subparagraph the treatment of financial services income received or accrued by partnerships and by other pass-thru entities which are not members of a financial services group.

(D) FINANCIAL SERVICES INCOME.—

(i) IN GENERAL.—Except as otherwise provided in this subparagraph, the term "financial services income" means any income which is received or accrued by any person predominantly engaged in the active conduct of a banking, insurance, financing, or similar business, and which is—

(I) described in clause (ii), or

(II) passive income (determined without regard to subparagraph (B)(iii)(II)).

(ii) GENERAL DESCRIPTION OF FINANCIAL SERVICES INCOME.—Income is described in this clause if such income is—

(I) derived in the active conduct of a banking, financing, or similar business,

(II) derived from the investment by an insurance company of its unearned premiums or reserves ordinary and necessary for the proper conduct of its insurance business, or

(III) of a kind which would be insurance income as defined in section 953(a) determined without regard to those provisions of paragraph (1)(A) of such section which limit insurance income to income from countries other than the country in which the corporation was created or organized.

(E) NONCONTROLLED SECTION 902 CORPORATION.—

(i) NONCONTROLLED 10-PERCENT OWNED FOREIGN CORPORATION.—The term "noncontrolled 10-percent owned foreign corporation" means any foreign corporation which is—

(I) a specified 10-percent owned foreign corporation (as defined in section 245A(b)), or

(II) a passive foreign investment company (as defined in section 1297(a)) with respect to which the taxpayer meets the stock ownership requirements of section 902(a) (or, for purposes of applying paragraphs (3) and (4), the requirements of section 902(b)).

A controlled foreign corporation shall not be treated as a noncontrolled 10-percent owned foreign corporation with respect to any distribution out of its earnings and profits for periods during which it was a controlled foreign corporation. Any reference to section 902 in this clause shall be treated as a reference to such section as in effect before its repeal.

(ii) TREATMENT OF INCLUSIONS UNDER SECTION 1293.—If any foreign corporation is a noncontrolled 10-percent owned foreign corporation with respect to the taxpayer, any inclusion under section 1293 with respect to such corporation shall be treated as a dividend from such corporation.

(F) HIGH-TAXED INCOME.—The term "high-taxed income" means any income which (but for this subparagraph) would be passive income if the sum of—

(i) the foreign income taxes paid or accrued by the taxpayer with respect to such income, and

(ii) the foreign income taxes deemed paid by the taxpayer with respect to such income under section 902 or 960,

exceeds the highest rate of tax specified in section 1 or 11 (whichever applies) multiplied by the amount of such income (determined with regard to section 78). For purposes of the preceding sentence, the term "foreign income taxes" means any income, war profits, or excess profits tax imposed by any foreign country or possession of the United States.

(G) EXPORT FINANCING INTEREST.—For purposes of this paragraph, the term "export financing interest" means any interest derived from financing the sale (or other disposition) for use or consumption outside the United States of any property—

(i) which is manufactured, produced, grown, or extracted in the United States by the taxpayer or a related person, and

(ii) not more than 50 percent of the fair market value of which is attributable to products imported into the United States.

For purposes of clause (ii), the fair market value of any property imported into the United States shall be its appraised value, as determined by the Secretary under section 402 of the Tariff Act of 1930 (19 U.S.C. 1401a) in connection with its importation.

(H) TREATMENT OF INCOME TAX BASE DIFFERENCES.—

(i) IN GENERAL.—In the case of taxable years beginning after December 31, 2006, tax imposed under the law of a foreign country or possession of the United States on an amount which does not constitute income under United States tax principles shall be treated as imposed on income described in paragraph (1)(B) [(1)(D)].

(ii) SPECIAL RULE FOR YEARS BEFORE 2007.—

(I) IN GENERAL.—In the case of taxes paid or accrued in taxable years beginning after December 31, 2004, and before January 1, 2007, a taxpayer may elect to treat tax imposed under the law of a foreign country or possession of the United States on an amount which does not constitute income under United States tax principles as tax imposed on income described in subparagraph (C) or (I) of paragraph (1).

(II) ELECTION IRREVOCABLE.—Any such election shall apply to the taxable year for which made and all subsequent taxable years described in subclause (I) unless revoked with the consent of the Secretary.

(I) RELATED PERSON.—For purposes of this paragraph, the term "related person" has the meaning given such term by section 954(d)(3), except that such section shall be applied by substituting "the person with respect to whom the determination is being made" for "controlled foreign corporation" each place it appears.

(J) FOREIGN BRANCH INCOME.—

(i) IN GENERAL.—The term "foreign branch income" means the business profits of such United States person which are attributable to 1 or more qualified business units (as defined in section 989(a)) in 1 or more foreign countries. For purposes of the preceding sentence, the amount of business profits attributable to a qualified business unit shall be determined under rules established by the Secretary.

(ii) EXCEPTION.—Such term shall not include any income which is passive category income.

(K) TRANSITIONAL RULES FOR 2007 CHANGES.—For purposes of paragraph (1)—

(i) taxes carried from any taxable year beginning before January 1, 2007, to any taxable year beginning on or after such date, with respect to any item of income, shall be treated as described in the subparagraph of paragraph (1) in which such income would be described were such taxes paid or accrued in a taxable year beginning on or after such date, and

(ii) the Secretary may by regulations provide for the allocation of any carryback of taxes with respect to income from a taxable year beginning on or after January 1, 2007, to a taxable year beginning before such date for purposes of allocating such income among the separate categories in effect for the taxable year to which carried.

(3) LOOK-THRU IN CASE OF CONTROLLED FOREIGN CORPORATIONS.—

(A) IN GENERAL.—Except as otherwise provided in this paragraph, dividends, interest, rents, and royalties received or accrued by the taxpayer from a controlled foreign corporation in which the taxpayer is a United States shareholder shall not be treated as passive category income.

(B) SUBPART F INCLUSIONS.—Any amount included in gross income under section 951(a)(1)(A) shall be treated as passive category income to the extent the amount so included is attributable to passive category income.

(C) INTEREST, RENTS, AND ROYALTIES.—Any interest, rent, or royalty which is received or accrued from a controlled foreign corporation in which the taxpayer is a United States shareholder shall be treated as passive category income to the extent it is properly allocable (under regulations prescribed by the Secretary) to passive category income of the controlled foreign corporation.

(D) DIVIDENDS.—Any dividend paid out of the earnings and profits of any controlled foreign corporation in which the taxpayer is a United States shareholder shall be treated as passive category income in proportion to the ratio of—

(i) the portion of the earnings and profits attributable to passive category income, to

(ii) the total amount of earnings and profits.

(E) LOOK-THRU APPLIES ONLY WHERE SUBPART F APPLIES.—If a controlled foreign corporation meets the requirements of section 954(b)(3)(A) (relating to de minimis rule) for any taxable year, for purposes of this paragraph, none of its foreign base company income (as defined in section 954(a) without regard to section 954(b)(5)) and none of its gross insurance income (as defined in section 954(b)(3)(C)) for such taxable year shall be treated as passive category income, except that this sentence shall not apply to any income which (without regard to this sentence) would be treated as financial services income. Solely for purposes of applying subparagraph (D), passive income of a controlled foreign corporation shall not be treated as passive category income if the requirements of section 954(b)(4) are met with respect to such income.

(F) COORDINATION WITH HIGH-TAXED INCOME PROVISIONS.—

(i) In determining whether any income of a controlled foreign corporation is passive category income, subclause (II) of paragraph (2)(B)(iii) shall not apply.

(ii) Any income of the taxpayer which is treated as passive category income under this paragraph shall be so treated notwithstanding any provision of paragraph (2); except that the determination of whether any amount is high-taxed income shall be made after the application of this paragraph.

(G) DIVIDEND.—For purposes of this paragraph, the term "dividend" includes any amount included in gross income in section 951(a)(1)(B). Any amount included in gross income under section 78 to the extent attributable to amounts included in gross income in section 951(a)(1)(A) shall not be treated as a dividend but shall be treated as included in gross income under section 951(a)(1)(A).

(H) LOOK-THRU APPLIES TO PASSIVE FOREIGN INVESTMENT COMPANY INCLUSION.—If—

(i) a passive foreign investment company is a controlled foreign corporation, and

(ii) the taxpayer is a United States shareholder in such controlled foreign corporation,

any amount included in gross income under section 1293 shall be treated as income in a separate category to the extent such amount is attributable to income in such category.

(4) LOOK-THRU APPLIES TO DIVIDENDS FROM NONCONTROLLED 10-PERCENT OWNED FOREIGN CORPORATIONS.—

(A) IN GENERAL.—For purposes of this subsection, any dividend from a noncontrolled 10-percent owned foreign corporation with respect to the taxpayer shall be treated as income described in a subparagraph of paragraph (1) in proportion to the ratio of—

(i) the portion of earnings and profits attributable to income described in such subparagraph, to

(ii) the total amount of earnings and profits.

(B) EARNINGS AND PROFITS OF CONTROLLED FOREIGN CORPORATIONS.—In the case of any distribution from a controlled foreign corporation to a United States shareholder, rules similar to the rules of subparagraph (A) shall apply in determining the extent to which earnings and profits of the controlled foreign corporation which are attributable to dividends received from a noncontrolled 10-percent owned foreign corporation may be treated as income in a separate category.

(C) SPECIAL RULES.—For purposes of this paragraph—

(i) EARNINGS AND PROFITS.—

(I) IN GENERAL.—The rules of section 316 shall apply.

(II) REGULATIONS.—The Secretary may prescribe regulations regarding the treatment of distributions out of earnings and profits for periods before the taxpayer's acquisition of the stock to which the distributions relate.

(ii) INADEQUATE SUBSTANTIATION.—If the Secretary determines that the proper subparagraph of paragraph (1) in which a dividend is described has not been substantiated, such dividend shall be treated as income described in paragraph (1)(A).

(iii) COORDINATION WITH HIGH-TAXED INCOME PROVISIONS.—Rules similar to the rules of paragraph (3)(F) shall apply for purposes of this paragraph.

(iv) LOOK-THRU WITH RESPECT TO CARRYOVER OF CREDIT.—Rules similar to subparagraph (A) also shall apply to any carryforward under subsection (c) from a taxable year beginning before January 1, 2003, of tax allocable to a dividend from a noncontrolled 10-percent owned foreign corporation with respect to the taxpayer. The Secretary may by regulations provide for the allocation of any carryback of tax allocable to a dividend from a noncontrolled 10-percent owned foreign corporation from a taxable year beginning on or after January 1, 2003, to a taxable year beginning before such date for purposes of allocating such dividend among the separate categories in effect for the taxable year to which carried.

(5) CONTROLLED FOREIGN CORPORATION; UNITED STATES SHAREHOLDER.—For purposes of this subsection—

(A) CONTROLLED FOREIGN CORPORATION.—The term "controlled foreign corporation" has the meaning given such term by section 957 (taking into account section 953(c)).

(B) UNITED STATES SHAREHOLDER.—The term "United States shareholder" has the meaning given such term by section 951(b) (taking into account section 953(c)).

(6) SEPARATE APPLICATION TO ITEMS RESOURCED UNDER TREATIES.—

(A) IN GENERAL.—If—

(i) without regard to any treaty obligation of the United States, any item of income would be treated as derived from sources within the United States,

(ii) under a treaty obligation of the United States, such item would be treated as arising from sources outside the United States, and

(iii) the taxpayer chooses the benefits of such treaty obligation,

subsections (a), (b), and (c) of this section and sections 907 and 960 shall be applied separately with respect to each such item.

(B) COORDINATION WITH OTHER PROVISIONS.—This paragraph shall not apply to any item of income to which subsection (h)(10) or section 865(h) applies.

(C) REGULATIONS.—The Secretary may issue such regulations or other guidance as is necessary or appropriate to carry out the purposes of this paragraph, including regulations or other guidance which provides that related items of income may be aggregated for purposes of this paragraph.

(7) REGULATIONS.—The Secretary shall prescribe such regulations as may be necessary or appropriate for the purposes of this subsection, including regulations—

(A) for the application of paragraph (3) and subsection (f)(5) in the case of income paid (or loans made) through 1 or more entities or between 2 or more chains of entities,

(B) preventing the manipulation of the character of income the effect of which is to avoid the purposes of this subsection, and

(C) providing that rules similar to the rules of paragraph (3)(C) shall apply to interest, rents, and royalties received or accrued from entities which would be controlled foreign corporations if they were foreign corporations.

[Sec. 904(e)—Stricken]

[Sec. 904(f)]

(f) RECAPTURE OF OVERALL FOREIGN LOSS.—

(1) GENERAL RULE.—For purposes of this subpart, in the case of any taxpayer who sustains an overall foreign loss for any taxable year, that portion of the taxpayer's taxable income from sources without the United States for each succeeding taxable year which is equal to the lesser of—

(A) the amount of such loss (to the extent not used under this paragraph in prior taxable years), or

(B) 50 percent (or such larger percent as the taxpayer may choose) of the taxpayer's taxable income from sources without the United States for such succeeding taxable year,

shall be treated as income from sources within the United States (and not as income from sources without the United States).

(2) OVERALL FOREIGN LOSS DEFINED.—For purposes of this subsection, the term "overall foreign loss" means the amount by which the gross income for the taxable year from sources without the United States (whether or not the taxpayer chooses the benefits of this subpart for such taxable year) for such year is exceeded by the sum of the deductions properly apportioned or allocated thereto, except that there shall not be taken into account—

(A) any net operating loss deduction allowable for such year under section 172(a), and

(B) any—

(i) foreign expropriation loss for such year, as defined in section 172(h) (as in effect on the day before the date of the enactment of the Revenue Reconciliation Act of 1990), or

(ii) loss for such year which arises from fire, storm, shipwreck, or other casualty, or from theft,

to the extent such loss is not compensated for by insurance or otherwise.

(3) DISPOSITIONS.—

(A) IN GENERAL.—For purposes of this chapter, if property which has been used predominantly without the United States in a trade or business is disposed of during any taxable year—

(i) the taxpayer, notwithstanding any other provision of this chapter (other than paragraph (1)), shall be deemed to have received and recognized taxable income from sources without the United States in the taxable year of the disposition, by reason of such disposition, in an amount equal to the lesser of the excess of the fair market value of such property over the taxpayer's adjusted basis in such property or the remaining amount of the overall foreign losses which were not used under paragraph (1) for such taxable year or any prior taxable year, and

(ii) paragraph (1) shall be applied with respect to such income by substituting "100 percent" for "50 percent".

In determining for purposes of this subparagraph whether the predominant use of any property has been without the United States, there shall be taken into account use during the 3-year period ending on the date of the disposition (or, if shorter, the period during which the property has been used in the trade or business).

(B) DISPOSITION DEFINED AND SPECIAL RULES.—

(i) For purposes of this subsection, the term "disposition" includes a sale, exchange, distribution, or gift of property whether or not gain or loss is recognized on the transfer.

(ii) Any taxable income recognized solely by reason of subparagraph (A) shall have the same characterization it would have had if the taxpayer had sold or exchanged the property.

(iii) The Secretary shall prescribe such regulations as he may deem necessary to provide for adjustments to the basis of property to reflect taxable income recognized solely by reason of subparagraph (A).

(C) EXCEPTIONS.—Notwithstanding subparagraph (B), the term "disposition" does not include—

(i) a disposition of property which is not a material factor in the realization of income by the taxpayer, or

(ii) a disposition of property to a domestic corporation in a distribution or transfer described in section 381(a).

(D) APPLICATION TO CERTAIN DISPOSITIONS OF STOCK IN CONTROLLED FOREIGN CORPORATION.—

(i) IN GENERAL.—This paragraph shall apply to an applicable disposition in the same manner as if it were a disposition of property described in subparagraph (A), except that the exception contained in subparagraph (C)(i) shall not apply.

(ii) APPLICABLE DISPOSITION.—For purposes of clause (i), the term "applicable disposition" means any disposition of any share of stock in a controlled foreign corporation in a transaction or series of transactions if, immediately before such transaction or series of transactions, the taxpayer owned more than 50 percent (by vote or value) of the stock of the controlled foreign corporation. Such term shall not include a disposition described in clause (iii) or (iv), except that clause (i) shall apply to any gain recognized on any such disposition.

(iii) EXCEPTION FOR CERTAIN EXCHANGES WHERE OWNERSHIP PERCENTAGE RETAINED.—A disposition shall not be treated as an applicable disposition under clause (ii) if it is part of a transaction or series of transactions—

(I) to which section 351 or 721 applies, or under which the transferor receives stock in a foreign corporation in exchange for the stock in the controlled foreign corporation and the stock received is exchanged basis property (as defined in section 7701(a)(44)), and

(II) immediately after which, the transferor owns (by vote or value) at least the same percentage of stock in the controlled foreign corporation (or, if the controlled foreign corporation is not in existence after such transaction or series of transactions, in another foreign corporation stock in which was received by the transferor in exchange for stock in the controlled foreign corporation) as the percentage of stock in the controlled foreign corporation which the taxpayer owned immediately before such transaction or series of transactions.

(iv) EXCEPTION FOR CERTAIN ASSET ACQUISITIONS.—A disposition shall not be treated as an applicable disposition under clause (ii) if it is part of a transaction or series of transactions in which the taxpayer (or any member of an affiliated group of corporations filing a consolidated return under section 1501 which includes the taxpayer) acquires the assets of a controlled foreign corporation in exchange for the shares of the controlled foreign corporation in a liquidation described in section 332 or a reorganization described in section 368(a)(1).

(v) CONTROLLED FOREIGN CORPORATION.—For purposes of this subparagraph, the term "controlled foreign corporation" has the meaning given such term by section 957.

(vi) STOCK OWNERSHIP.—For purposes of this subparagraph, ownership of stock shall be determined under the rules of subsections (a) and (b) of section 958.

(4) ACCUMULATION DISTRIBUTIONS OF FOREIGN TRUST.—For purposes of this chapter, in the case of amounts of income from sources without the United States which are treated under section 666 (without regard to subsections (b) and (c) thereof if the taxpayer chose to take a deduction with respect to the amounts described in such subsections under section 667(d)(1)(B)) as having been distributed by a foreign trust in a preceding taxable year, that portion of such amounts equal to the amount of any overall foreign loss sustained by the beneficiary in a year prior to the taxable year of the beneficiary in which such distribution is received from the trust shall be treated as income from sources within the United States (and not income from sources without the United States) to the extent that such loss was not used under this subsection in prior taxable years, or in the current taxable year, against other income of the beneficiary.

(5) TREATMENT OF SEPARATE LIMITATION LOSSES.—

(A) IN GENERAL.—The amount of the separate limitation losses for any taxable year shall reduce income from sources within the United States for such taxable year only to the extent the aggregate amount of such losses exceeds the aggregate amount of the separate limitation incomes for such taxable year.

(B) ALLOCATION OF LOSSES.—The separate limitation losses for any taxable year (to the extent such losses do not exceed the separate limitation incomes for such year) shall be allocated among (and operate to reduce) such incomes on a proportionate basis.

(C) RECHARACTERIZATION OF SUBSEQUENT INCOME.—If—

(i) a separate limitation loss from any income category (hereinafter in this subparagraph referred to as "the loss category") was allocated to income from any other category under subparagraph (B), and

(ii) the loss category has income for a subsequent taxable year,

such income (to the extent it does not exceed the aggregate separate limitation losses from the loss category not previously recharacterized under this subparagraph) shall be recharacterized as income from such other category in proportion to the prior reductions under subparagraph (B) in such other category not previously taken into account under this subparagraph. Nothing in the preceding sentence shall be construed as recharacterizing any tax.

(D) SPECIAL RULES FOR LOSSES FROM SOURCES IN THE UNITED STATES.—Any loss from sources in the United States for any taxable year (to the extent such loss does not exceed the separate limitation incomes from such year) shall be allocated among (and operate to reduce) such incomes on a proportionate basis. This subparagraph shall be applied after subparagraph (B).

(E) DEFINITIONS.—For purposes of this paragraph—

(i) INCOME CATEGORY.—The term "income category" means each separate category of income described in subsection (d)(1).

(ii) SEPARATE LIMITATION INCOME.—The term "separate limitation income" means, with respect to any income category, the taxable income from sources outside the United States, separately computed for such category.

(iii) SEPARATE LIMITATION LOSS.—The term "separate limitation loss" means, with respect to any income category, the loss from such category determined under the principles of section 907(c)(4)(B).

(F) DISPOSITIONS.—If any separate limitation loss for any taxable year is allocated against any separate limitation income for such taxable year, except to the extent provided in regulations, rules similar to the rules of paragraph (3) shall apply to any disposition of property if gain from such disposition would be in the income category with respect to which there was such separate limitation loss.

[Sec. 904(g)]

(g) RECHARACTERIZATION OF OVERALL DOMESTIC LOSS.—

(1) GENERAL RULE.—For purposes of this subpart and section 936, in the case of any taxpayer who sustains an overall domestic loss for any taxable year beginning after December 31, 2006, that portion of the taxpayer's taxable income from sources within the United States for each succeeding taxable year which is equal to the lesser of—

(A) the amount of such loss (to the extent not used under this paragraph in prior taxable years), or

(B) 50 percent of the taxpayer's taxable income from sources within the United States for such succeeding taxable year,

shall be treated as income from sources without the United States (and not as income from sources within the United States).

(2) OVERALL DOMESTIC LOSS.—For purposes of this subsection—

(A) IN GENERAL.—The term "overall domestic loss" means—

(i) with respect to any qualified taxable year, the domestic loss for such taxable year to the extent such loss offsets taxable income from sources without the United States for the taxable year or for any preceding qualified taxable year by reason of a carryback, and

(ii) with respect to any other taxable year, the domestic loss for such taxable year to the extent such loss offsets taxable income from sources without the United States for any preceding qualified taxable year by reason of a carryback.

(B) DOMESTIC LOSS.—For purposes of subparagraph (A), the term "domestic loss" means the amount by which the gross income for the taxable year from sources within the United States is exceeded by the sum of the deductions properly apportioned or allocated thereto (determined without regard to any carryback from a subsequent taxable year).

(C) QUALIFIED TAXABLE YEAR.—For purposes of subparagraph (A), the term "qualified taxable year" means any taxable year for which the taxpayer chose the benefits of this subpart.

(3) CHARACTERIZATION OF SUBSEQUENT INCOME.—

(A) IN GENERAL.—Any income from sources within the United States that is treated as income from sources without the United States under paragraph (1) shall be allocated among and increase the income categories in proportion to the loss from sources within the United States previously allocated to those income categories.

(B) INCOME CATEGORY.—For purposes of this paragraph, the term "income category" has the meaning given such term by subsection (f)(5)(E)(i).

(4) COORDINATION WITH SUBSECTION (f).—The Secretary shall prescribe such regulations as may be necessary to coordinate the provisions of this subsection with the provisions of subsection (f).

(5) ELECTION TO INCREASE PERCENTAGE OF TAXABLE INCOME TREATED AS FOREIGN SOURCE.—

(A) IN GENERAL.—If any pre-2018 unused overall domestic loss is taken into account under paragraph (1) for any applicable taxable year, the taxpayer may elect to have such paragraph applied to such loss by substituting a percentage greater than 50 percent (but not greater than 100 percent) for 50 percent in subparagraph (B) thereof.

(B) PRE-2018 UNUSED OVERALL DOMESTIC LOSS.—For purposes of this paragraph, the term "pre-2018 unused overall domestic loss" means any overall domestic loss which—

(i) arises in a qualified taxable year beginning before January 1, 2018, and

(ii) has not been used under paragraph (1) for any taxable year beginning before such date.

(C) APPLICABLE TAXABLE YEAR.—For purposes of this paragraph, the term "applicable taxable year" means any taxable year of the taxpayer beginning after December 31, 2017, and before January 1, 2028.

[Sec. 904(h)]

(h) SOURCE RULES IN CASE OF UNITED STATES-OWNED FOREIGN CORPORATIONS.—

(1) IN GENERAL.—The following amounts which are derived from a United States-owned foreign corporation and which would be treated as derived from sources outside the United States without regard to this subsection shall, for purposes of this section, be treated as derived from sources within the United States to the extent provided in this subsection:

(A) Any amount included in gross income under—

(i) section 951(a) (relating to amounts included in gross income of United States shareholders), or

(ii) section 1293 (relating to current taxation of income from qualified funds).

(B) Interest.

(C) Dividends.

(2) SUBPART F AND PASSIVE FOREIGN INVESTMENT COMPANY INCLUSIONS.—Any amount described in subparagraph (A) of paragraph (1) shall be treated as derived from sources within the United States to the extent such amount is attributable to income of the United States-owned foreign corporation from sources within the United States.

(3) CERTAIN INTEREST ALLOCABLE TO UNITED STATES SOURCE INCOME.—Any interest which—

(A) is paid or accrued by a United States-owned foreign corporation during any taxable year,

(B) is paid or accrued to a United States shareholder (as defined in section 951(b)) or a related person (within the meaning of section 267(b)) to such a shareholder, and

(C) is properly allocable (under regulations prescribed by the Secretary) to income of such foreign corporation for the taxable year from sources within the United States,

shall be treated as derived from sources within the United States.

(4) DIVIDENDS.—

(A) IN GENERAL.—The United States source ratio of any dividend paid or accrued by a United States-owned foreign corporation shall be treated as derived from sources within the United States.

(B) UNITED STATES SOURCE RATIO.—For purposes of subparagraph (A), the term "United States source ratio" means, with respect to any dividend paid out of the earnings and profits for any taxable year, a fraction—

(i) the numerator of which is the portion of the earnings and profits for such taxable year from sources within the United States, and

(ii) the denominator of which is the total amount of earnings and profits for such taxable year.

(5) EXCEPTION WHERE UNITED STATES-OWNED FOREIGN CORPORATION HAS SMALL AMOUNT OF UNITED STATES SOURCE INCOME.—Paragraph (3) shall not apply to interest paid or accrued during any taxable year (and paragraph (4) shall not apply to any dividends paid out of the earnings and profits for such taxable year) if—

(A) the United States-owned foreign corporation has earnings and profits for such taxable year, and

(B) less than 10 percent of such earnings and profits is attributable to sources within the United States.

For purposes of the preceding sentence, earnings and profits shall be determined without any reduction for interest described in paragraph (3) (determined without regard to subparagraph (C) thereof).

(6) UNITED STATES-OWNED FOREIGN CORPORATION.—For purposes of this subsection, the term "United States-owned foreign corporation" means any foreign corporation if 50 percent or more of—

(A) the total combined voting power of all classes of stock of such corporation entitled to vote, or

(B) the total value of the stock of such corporation,

is held directly (or indirectly through applying paragraphs (2) and (3) of section 958(a) and paragraph (4) of section 318(a)) by United States persons (as defined in section 7701(a)(30)).

(7) DIVIDEND.—For purposes of this subsection, the term "dividend" includes any gain treated as a dividend under section 1248.

(8) COORDINATION WITH SUBSECTION (f).—This subsection shall be applied before subsection (f).

(9) TREATMENT OF CERTAIN DOMESTIC CORPORATIONS.—In the case of any dividend treated as not from sources within the United States under section 861(a)(2)(A), the corporation paying such dividend shall be treated for purposes of this subsection as a United States-owned foreign corporation.

(10) COORDINATION WITH TREATIES.—

(A) IN GENERAL.—If—

(i) any amount derived from a United States-owned foreign corporation would be treated as derived from sources within the United States under this subsection by reason of an item of income of such United States-owned foreign corporation,

(ii) under a treaty obligation of the United States (applied without regard to this subsection and by treating any amount included in gross income under section 951(a)(1) as a dividend), such amount would be treated as arising from sources outside the United States, and

(iii) the taxpayer chooses the benefits of this paragraph,

this subsection shall not apply to such amount to the extent attributable to such item of income (but subsections (a), (b), and (c) of this section and sections 907 and 960 shall be applied separately with respect to such amount to the extent so attributable).

(B) SPECIAL RULE.—Amounts included in gross income under section 951(a)(1) shall be treated as a dividend under subparagraph (A)(ii) only if dividends paid by each corporation (the stock in which is taken into account in determining whether the shareholder is a United States shareholder in the United States-owned foreign corporation), if paid to the United States shareholder, would be treated under a treaty obligation of the United States as arising from sources outside the United States (applied without regard to this subsection).

(11) REGULATIONS.—The Secretary shall prescribe such regulations as may be necessary or appropriate for purposes of this subsection, including—

(A) regulations for the application of this subsection in the case of interest or dividend payments through 1 or more entities, and

(B) regulations providing that this subsection shall apply to interest paid or accrued to any person (whether or not a United States shareholder).

[Sec. 904(i)]

(i) LIMITATION ON USE OF DECONSOLIDATION TO AVOID FOREIGN TAX CREDIT LIMITATIONS.—If 2 or more domestic corporations would be members of the same affiliated group if—

(1) section 1504(b) were applied without regard to the exceptions contained therein, and

(2) the constructive ownership rules of section 1563(e) applied for purposes of section 1504(a),

the Secretary may by regulations provide for resourcing the income of any of such corporations or for modifications to the consolidated return regulations to the extent that such resourcing or modifications are necessary to prevent the avoidance of the provisions of this subpart.

[Sec. 904(j)]

(j) CERTAIN INDIVIDUALS EXEMPT.—

(1) IN GENERAL.—In the case of an individual to whom this subsection applies for any taxable year—

(A) the limitation of subsection (a) shall not apply,

(B) no taxes paid or accrued by the individual during such taxable year may be deemed paid or accrued under subsection (c) in any other taxable year, and

(C) no taxes paid or accrued by the individual during any other taxable year may be deemed paid or accrued under subsection (c) in such taxable year.

(2) INDIVIDUALS TO WHOM SUBSECTION APPLIES.—This subsection shall apply to an individual for any taxable year if—

(A) the entire amount of such individual's gross income for the taxable year from sources without the United States consists of qualified passive income,

(B) the amount of the creditable foreign taxes paid or accrued by the individual during the taxable year does not exceed $300 ($600 in the case of a joint return), and

(C) such individual elects to have this subsection apply for the taxable year.

(3) DEFINITIONS.—For purposes of this subsection—

(A) QUALIFIED PASSIVE INCOME.—The term "qualified passive income" means any item of gross income if—

(i) such item of income is passive income (as defined in subsection (d)(2)(B) without regard to clause (iii) thereof), and

(ii) such item of income is shown on a payee statement furnished to the individual.

(B) CREDITABLE FOREIGN TAXES.—The term "creditable foreign taxes" means any taxes for which a credit is allowable under section 901; except that such term shall not include any tax unless such tax is shown on a payee statement furnished to such individual.

(C) PAYEE STATEMENT.—The term "payee statement" has the meaning given to such term by section 6724(d)(2).

(D) ESTATES AND TRUSTS NOT ELIGIBLE.—This subsection shall not apply to any estate or trust.

[Sec. 904(k)]

(k) CROSS REFERENCES.—For increase of limitation under subsection (a) for taxes paid with respect to amounts received which were included in the gross income of the taxpayer for a prior taxable year as a United States shareholder with respect to a controlled foreign corporation, see section 960(c).

[Sec. 905]

SEC. 905. APPLICABLE RULES.

[Sec. 905(a)]

(a) YEAR IN WHICH CREDIT TAKEN.—The credits provided in this subpart may, at the option of the taxpayer and irrespective of the method of accounting employed in keeping his books, be taken in the year in which the taxes of the foreign country or the possession of the United States accrued, subject, however, to the conditions prescribed in subsection (c). If the taxpayer elects to take such credits in the year in which the taxes of the foreign country or the possession of the United States accrued, the credits for all subsequent years shall be taken on the same basis, and no portion of any such taxes shall be allowed as a deduction in the same or any succeeding year.

[Sec. 905(b)]

(b) PROOF OF CREDITS.—The credits provided in this subpart shall be allowed only if the taxpayer establishes to the satisfaction of the Secretary—

(1) the total amount of income derived from sources without the United States, determined as provided in part I,

(2) the amount of income derived from each country, the tax paid or accrued to which is claimed as a credit under this subpart, such amount to be determined under regulations prescribed by the Secretary, and

(3) all other information necessary for the verification and computation of such credits.

[Sec. 905(c)]

(c) ADJUSTMENTS TO ACCRUED TAXES.—

(1) IN GENERAL.—If—

(A) accrued taxes when paid differ from the amounts claimed as credits by the taxpayer,

(B) accrued taxes are not paid before the date 2 years after the close of the taxable year to which such taxes relate, or

(C) any tax paid is refunded in whole or in part,

the taxpayer shall notify the Secretary, who shall redetermine the amount of the tax for the year or years affected.

(2) SPECIAL RULE FOR TAXES NOT PAID WITHIN 2 YEARS.—

(A) IN GENERAL.—Except as provided in subparagraph (B), in making the redetermination under paragraph (1), no credit shall be allowed for accrued taxes not paid before the date referred to in subparagraph (B) of paragraph (1).

(B) TAXES SUBSEQUENTLY PAID.—Any such taxes if subsequently paid—

(i) shall be taken into account for the taxable year to which such taxes relate, and

(ii) shall be translated as provided in section 986(a)(2)(A).

(3) ADJUSTMENTS.—The amount of tax (if any) due on any redetermination under paragraph (1) shall be paid by the taxpayer on notice and demand by the Secretary, and the amount of tax overpaid (if any) shall be credited or refunded to the taxpayer in accordance with subchapter B of chapter 66 (section 6511 et seq.).

(4) BOND REQUIREMENTS.—In the case of any tax accrued but not paid, the Secretary, as a condition precedent to the allowance of the credit provided in this subpart, may require the taxpayer to give a bond, with sureties satisfactory to and approved by the Secretary, in such sum as the Secretary may require, conditioned on the payment by the taxpayer of any amount of tax found due on any such redetermination. Any such bond shall contain such further conditions as the Secretary may require.

(5) OTHER SPECIAL RULES.—In any redetermination under paragraph (1) by the Secretary of the amount of tax due from the taxpayer for the year or years affected by a refund, the amount of the taxes refunded for which credit has been allowed under this section shall be reduced by the amount of any tax described in section 901 imposed by the foreign country or possession of the United States with respect to such refund; but no credit under this subpart, or deduction under section 164, shall be allowed for any taxable year with respect to any such tax imposed on the refund. No interest shall be assessed or collected on any amount of tax due on any redetermination by the Secretary, resulting from a refund to the taxpayer, for any period before the receipt of such refund, except to the extent interest was paid by the foreign country or possession of the United States on such refund for such period.

[Sec. 906]

SEC. 906. NONRESIDENT ALIEN INDIVIDUALS AND FOREIGN CORPORATIONS.

[Sec. 906(a)]

(a) ALLOWANCE OF CREDIT.—A nonresident alien individual or a foreign corporation engaged in trade or business within the United States during the taxable year shall be allowed a credit under section 901 for the amount of any income, war profits, and excess profits taxes paid or accrued during the taxable year to any foreign country or possession of the United States with respect to income effectively connected with the conduct of a trade or business within the United States.

[Sec. 906(b)]

(b) SPECIAL RULES.—

(1) For purposes of subsection (a) and for purposes of determining the deductions allowable under sections 873(a) and 882(c), in determining the amount of any tax paid or accrued to any foreign country or possession there shall not be taken into account any amount of tax to the extent the tax so paid or accrued is imposed with respect to income from sources within the United States which would not be taxed by such foreign country or possession but for the fact that—

(A) in the case of a nonresident alien individual, such individual is a citizen or resident of such foreign country or possession, or

(B) in the case of a foreign corporation, such corporation was created or organized under the law of such foreign country or possession or is domiciled for tax purposes in such country or possession.

(2) For purposes of subsection (a), in applying section 904 the taxpayer's taxable income shall be treated as consisting only of the taxable income effectively connected with the taxpayer's conduct of a trade or business within the United States.

(3) The credit allowed pursuant to subsection (a) shall not be allowed against any tax imposed by section 871(a) (relating to income of nonresident alien individual not connected with United States business) or 881 (relating to income of foreign corporations not connected with United States business).

(4) [Stricken.]

(5) [Stricken.]

(6) No credit shall be allowed under this section against the tax imposed by section 884.

[Sec. 907]

SEC. 907. SPECIAL RULES IN CASE OF FOREIGN OIL AND GAS INCOME.

[Sec. 907(a)]

(a) REDUCTION IN AMOUNT ALLOWED AS FOREIGN TAX UNDER SECTION 901.—In applying section 901, the amount of any oil and gas taxes paid or accrued (or deemed to have been paid) during the taxable year which would (but for this subsection) be taken into account for purposes of section 901 shall be reduced by the amount (if any) by which the amount of such taxes exceeds the product of—

(1) the amount of the foreign oil and gas income for the taxable year,

(2) multiplied by—

(A) in the case of a corporation, the percentage which is equal to the highest rate of tax specified under section 11(b), or

(B) in the case of an individual, a fraction the numerator of which is the tax against which the credit under section 901(a) is taken and the denominator of which is the taxpayer's entire taxable income.

[Sec. 907(b)]

(b) COMBINED FOREIGN OIL AND GAS INCOME; FOREIGN OIL AND GAS TAXES.—For purposes of this section—

(1) COMBINED FOREIGN OIL AND GAS INCOME.—The term "combined foreign oil and gas income" means, with respect to any taxable year, the sum of—

(A) foreign oil and gas extraction income, and

(B) foreign oil related income.

(2) FOREIGN OIL AND GAS TAXES.—The term "foreign oil and gas taxes" means, with respect to any taxable year, the sum of—

(A) oil and gas extraction taxes, and

(B) any income, war profits, and excess profits taxes paid or accrued (or deemed to have been paid or accrued under section 960) during the taxable year with respect to foreign oil related income (determined without regard to subsection (c)(4)) or loss which would be taken into account for purposes of section 901 without regard to this section.

[Sec. 907(c)]

(c) FOREIGN INCOME DEFINITIONS AND SPECIAL RULES.—For purposes of this section—

(1) FOREIGN OIL AND GAS EXTRACTION INCOME.—The term "foreign oil and gas extraction income" means the taxable income derived from sources without the United States and its possessions from—

(A) the extraction (by the taxpayer or any other person) of minerals from oil or gas wells, or

(B) the sale or exchange of assets used by the taxpayer in the trade or business described in subparagraph (A).

Such term does not include any dividend or interest income which is passive income (as defined in section 904(d)(2)(A)).

(2) FOREIGN OIL RELATED INCOME.—The term "foreign oil related income" means the taxable income derived from sources outside the United States and its possessions from—

(A) the processing of minerals extracted (by the taxpayer or by any other person) from oil or gas wells into their primary products,

(B) the transportation of such minerals or primary products,

(C) the distribution or sale of such minerals or primary products,

(D) the disposition of assets used by the taxpayer in the trade or business described in subparagraph (A), (B), or (C), or

(E) the performance of any other related service.

Such term does not include any dividend or interest income which is passive income (as defined in section 904(d)(2)(A)).

(3) DIVIDENDS, INTEREST, PARTNERSHIP DISTRIBUTION, ETC.—The term "foreign oil and gas extraction income" and the term "foreign oil related income" include—

(A) interest, to the extent the category of income of such interest is determined under section 904(d)(3),

(B) amounts with respect to which taxes are deemed paid under section 960, and

(C) the taxpayer's distributive share of the income of partnerships,

to the extent such dividends, interest, amounts, or distributive share is attributable to foreign oil and gas extraction income, or to foreign oil related income, as the case may be; except that interest described in subparagraph (A) shall not be taken into account in computing foreign oil and gas extraction income but shall be taken into account in computing foreign oil-related income.

(4) RECAPTURE OF FOREIGN OIL AND GAS LOSSES BY RECHARACTERIZING LATER COMBINED FOREIGN OIL AND GAS INCOME.—

(A) IN GENERAL.—The combined foreign oil and gas income of a taxpayer for a taxable year (determined without regard to this paragraph) shall be reduced—

(i) first by the amount determined under subparagraph (B), and

(ii) then by the amount determined under subparagraph (C).

The aggregate amount of such reductions shall be treated as income (from sources without the United States) which is not combined foreign oil and gas income.

(B) REDUCTION FOR PRE-2009 FOREIGN OIL EXTRACTION LOSSES.—The reduction under this paragraph shall be equal to the lesser of—

(i) the foreign oil and gas extraction income of the taxpayer for the taxable year (determined without regard to this paragraph), or

(ii) the excess of—

(I) the aggregate amount of foreign oil extraction losses for preceding taxable years beginning after December 31, 1982, and before January 1, 2009, over

(II) so much of such aggregate amount as was recharacterized under this paragraph (as in effect before and after the date of the enactment of the Energy Improvement and Extension Act of 2008) for preceding taxable years beginning after December 31, 1982.

(C) REDUCTION FOR POST-2008 FOREIGN OIL AND GAS LOSSES.—The reduction under this paragraph shall be equal to the lesser of—

(i) the combined foreign oil and gas income of the taxpayer for the taxable year (determined without regard to this paragraph), reduced by an amount equal to the reduction under subparagraph (A) for the taxable year, or

(ii) the excess of—

(I) the aggregate amount of foreign oil and gas losses for preceding taxable years beginning after December 31, 2008, over

(II) so much of such aggregate amount as was recharacterized under this paragraph for preceding taxable years beginning after December 31, 2008.

(D) FOREIGN OIL AND GAS LOSS DEFINED.—

(i) IN GENERAL.—For purposes of this paragraph, the term "foreign oil and gas loss" means the amount by which—

(I) the gross income for the taxable year from sources without the United States and its possessions (whether or not the taxpayer chooses the benefits of this subpart for such taxable year) taken into account in determining the combined foreign oil and gas income for such year, is exceeded by

(II) the sum of the deductions properly apportioned or allocated thereto.

(ii) NET OPERATING LOSS DEDUCTION NOT TAKEN INTO ACCOUNT.—For purposes of clause (i), the net operating loss deduction allowable for the taxable year under section 172(a) shall not be taken into account.

(iii) EXPROPRIATION AND CASUALTY LOSSES NOT TAKEN INTO ACCOUNT.—For purposes of clause (i), there shall not be taken into account—

(I) any foreign expropriation loss (as defined in section 172(h) (as in effect on the day before the date of the enactment of the Revenue Reconciliation Act of 1990)) for the taxable year, or

(II) any loss for the taxable year which arises from fire, storm, shipwreck, or other casualty, or from theft,

to the extent such loss is not compensated for by insurance or otherwise.

(iv) FOREIGN OIL EXTRACTION LOSS.—For purposes of subparagraph (B)(ii)(I), foreign oil extraction losses shall be determined under this paragraph as in effect on the day before the date of the enactment of the Energy Improvement and Extension Act of 2008.

(5) OIL AND GAS EXTRACTION TAXES.—The term "oil and gas extraction taxes" means any income, war profits, and excess profits tax paid or accrued (or deemed to have been paid under section 960) during the taxable year with respect to foreign oil and gas extraction income (determined without regard to paragraph (4)) or loss which would be taken into account for purposes of section 901 without regard to this section.

[Sec. 907(d)]

(d) DISREGARD OF CERTAIN POSTED PRICES, ETC.—For purposes of this chapter, in determining the amount of taxable income in the case of foreign oil and gas extraction income, if the oil or gas is disposed of, or is acquired other than from the government of a foreign country, at a posted price (or other pricing arrangement) which differs from the fair market value for such oil or gas, such fair market value shall be used in lieu of such posted price (or other pricing arrangement).

[Sec. 907(e)—Stricken]

[Sec. 907(f)]

(f) CARRYBACK AND CARRYOVER OF DISALLOWED CREDITS.—

(1) IN GENERAL.—If the amount of the foreign oil and gas taxes paid or accrued during any taxable year exceeds the limitation provided by subsection (a) for such taxable year (hereinafter in this subsection referred to as the "unused credit year"), such excess shall be deemed to be foreign oil and gas taxes paid or accrued in the first preceding taxable year and in any of the first 10 succeeding taxable years, in that order and to the extent not deemed tax paid or accrued in a prior taxable year by reason of the limitation imposed by paragraph (2). Such amount deemed paid or accrued in any taxable year may be availed of only as a tax credit and not as a deduction and only if the taxpayer for such year chooses to have the benefits of this subpart as to taxes paid or accrued for that year to foreign countries or possessions.

(2) LIMITATION.—The amount of the unused foreign oil and gas taxes which under paragraph (1) may be deemed paid or accrued in any preceding or succeeding taxable year shall not exceed the lesser of—

(A) the amount by which the limitation provided by subsection (a) for such taxable year exceeds the sum of—

(i) the foreign oil and gas taxes paid or accrued during such taxable year, plus

(ii) the amounts of the foreign oil and gas taxes which by reason of this subsection are deemed paid or accrued in such taxable year and are attributable to taxable years preceding the unused credit year; or

(B) the amount by which the limitation provided by section 904 for such taxable year exceeds the sum of—

(i) the taxes paid or accrued (or deemed to have been paid under section 960) to all foreign countries and possessions of the United States during such taxable year,

(ii) the amount of such taxes which were deemed paid or accrued in such taxable year under section 904(c) and which are attributable to taxable years preceding the unused credit year, plus

(iii) the amount of the foreign oil and gas taxes which by reason of this subsection are deemed paid or accrued in such taxable year and are attributable to taxable years preceding the unused credit year.

(3) SPECIAL RULES.—

(A) In the case of any taxable year which is an unused credit year under this subsection and which is an unused credit year under section 904(c), the provisions of this subsection shall be applied before section 904(c).

(B) For purposes of determining the amount of taxes paid or accrued in any taxable year which may be deemed paid or accrued in a preceding or succeeding taxable year under section 904(c), any tax deemed paid or accrued in such preceding or succeeding taxable year under this subsection shall be considered to be tax paid or accrued in such preceding or succeeding taxable year.

(4) TRANSITION RULES FOR PRE-2009 AND 2009 DISALLOWED CREDITS.—

(A) PRE-2009 CREDITS.—In the case of any unused credit year beginning before January 1, 2009, this subsection, as in effect on the day before the date of the enactment of the Energy Improvement and Extension Act of 2008, shall apply to unused oil and gas extraction taxes carried from such unused credit year to a taxable year beginning after December 31, 2008.

(B) 2009 CREDITS.—In the case of any unused credit year beginning in 2009, the amendments made to this subsection by the Energy Improvement and Extension Act of 2008 shall be treated as being in effect for any preceding year beginning before January 1, 2009, solely for purposes of determining how much of the unused foreign oil and gas taxes for such unused credit year may be deemed paid or accrued in such preceding year.

[Sec. 908]

SEC. 908. REDUCTION OF CREDIT FOR PARTICIPATION IN OR COOPERATION WITH AN INTERNATIONAL BOYCOTT.

[Sec. 908(a)]

(a) IN GENERAL.—If a person, or a member of a controlled group (within the meaning of section 993(a)(3)) which includes such person, participates in or cooperates with an international boycott during the taxable year (within the meaning of section 999(b)), the amount of the credit allowable under section 901 to such person, or under section 960 to United States shareholders of such person, for foreign taxes paid during the taxable year shall be reduced by an amount equal to the product of—

(1) the amount of the credit which, but for this section, would be allowed under section 901 for the taxable year, multiplied by

(2) the international boycott factor (determined under section 999).

[Sec. 908(b)]

(b) APPLICATION WITH SECTIONS 275(a)(4) and 78.—Section 275(a)(4) and section 78 shall not apply to any amount of taxes denied credit under subsection (a).

[Sec. 909]

SEC. 909. SUSPENSION OF TAXES AND CREDITS UNTIL RELATED INCOME TAKEN INTO ACCOUNT.

[Sec. 909(a)]

(a) IN GENERAL.—If there is a foreign tax credit splitting event with respect to a foreign income tax paid or accrued by the taxpayer, such tax shall not be taken into account for purposes of this title before the taxable year in which the related income is taken into account under this chapter by the taxpayer.

[Sec. 909(b)]

(b) SPECIAL RULES WITH RESPECT TO SPECIFIED 10-PERCENT OWNED FOREIGN CORPORATIONS.—If there is a foreign tax credit splitting event with respect to a foreign income tax paid or accrued by a specified 10-percent owned foreign corporation (as defined in section 245A(b) without regard to paragraph (2) thereof), such tax shall not be taken into account—

(1) for purposes of section 960, or

(2) for purposes of determining earnings and profits under section 964(a),

before the taxable year in which the related income is taken into account under this chapter by such specified 10-percent owned foreign corporation or a domestic corporation which is a United States shareholder with respect to such specified 10-percent owned foreign corporation.

[Sec. 909(c)]

(c) SPECIAL RULES.—For purposes of this section—

(1) APPLICATION TO PARTNERSHIPS, ETC.—In the case of a partnership, subsections (a) and (b) shall be applied at the partner level. Except as otherwise provided by the Secretary, a rule similar to the rule of the preceding sentence shall apply in the case of any S corporation or trust.

(2) TREATMENT OF FOREIGN TAXES AFTER SUSPENSION.—In the case of any foreign income tax not taken into account by reason of subsection (a) or (b), except as otherwise provided by the Secretary, such tax shall be so taken into account in the taxable year referred to in such subsection (other than for purposes of section 986(a)) as a foreign income tax paid or accrued in such taxable year.

[Sec. 909(d)]

(d) DEFINITIONS.—For purposes of this section—

(1) FOREIGN TAX CREDIT SPLITTING EVENT.—There is a foreign tax credit splitting event with respect to a foreign income tax if the related income is (or will be) taken into account under this chapter by a covered person.

(2) FOREIGN INCOME TAX.—The term "foreign income tax" means any income, war profits, or excess profits tax paid or accrued to any foreign country or to any possession of the United States.

(3) RELATED INCOME.—The term "related income" means, with respect to any portion of any foreign income tax, the income (or, as appropriate, earnings and profits) to which such portion of foreign income tax relates.

(4) COVERED PERSON.—The term "covered person" means, with respect to any person who pays or accrues a foreign income tax (hereafter in this paragraph referred to as the "payor")—

(A) any entity in which the payor holds, directly or indirectly, at least a 10 percent ownership interest (determined by vote or value),

(B) any person which holds, directly or indirectly, at least a 10 percent ownership interest (determined by vote or value) in the payor,

(C) any person which bears a relationship to the payor described in section 267(b) or 707(b), and

(D) any other person specified by the Secretary for purposes of this paragraph.

[Sec. 909(e)]

(e) REGULATIONS.—The Secretary may issue such regulations or other guidance as is necessary or appropriate to carry out the purposes of this section, including regulations or other guidance which provides—

(1) appropriate exceptions from the provisions of this section, and

(2) for the proper application of this section with respect to hybrid instruments.

Subpart B—Earned Income of Citizens or Residents of United States

[Sec. 911]

SEC. 911. CITIZENS OR RESIDENTS OF THE UNITED STATES LIVING ABROAD.

[Sec. 911(a)]

(a) EXCLUSION FROM GROSS INCOME.—At the election of a qualified individual (made separately with respect to paragraphs (1) and (2)), there shall be excluded from the gross income of such individual, and exempt from taxation under this subtitle, for any taxable year—

(1) the foreign earned income of such individual, and

(2) the housing cost amount of such individual.

[Sec. 911(b)]

(b) FOREIGN EARNED INCOME.—

(1) DEFINITION.—For purposes of this section—

(A) IN GENERAL.—The term "foreign earned income" with respect to any individual means the amount received by such individual from sources within a foreign country or countries which constitute earned income attributable to services performed by such individual during the period described in subparagraph (A) or (B) of subsection (d)(1), whichever is applicable.

(B) CERTAIN AMOUNTS NOT INCLUDED IN FOREIGN EARNED INCOME.—The foreign earned income for an individual shall not include amounts—

(i) received as a pension or annuity,

(ii) paid by the United States or an agency thereof to an employee of the United States or an agency thereof,

(iii) included in gross income by reason of section 402(b) (relating to taxability of beneficiary of nonexempt trust) or section 403(c) (relating to taxability of beneficiary under a nonqualified annuity), or

(iv) received after the close of the taxable year following the taxable year in which the services to which the amounts are attributable are performed.

(2) LIMITATION ON FOREIGN EARNED INCOME.—

(A) IN GENERAL.—The foreign earned income of an individual which may be excluded under subsection (a)(1) for any taxable year shall not exceed the amount of foreign earned income computed on a daily basis at an annual rate equal to the exclusion amount for the calendar year in which such taxable year begins.

(B) ATTRIBUTION TO YEAR IN WHICH SERVICES ARE PERFORMED.—For purposes of applying subparagraph (A), amounts received shall be considered received in the taxable year in which the services to which the amounts are attributable are performed.

(C) TREATMENT OF COMMUNITY INCOME.—In applying subparagraph (A) with respect to amounts received from services performed by a husband or wife which are community income under community property laws applicable to such income, the aggregate amount which may be excludable from the gross income of such husband and wife under subsection (a)(1) for any taxable year shall equal the amount which would be so excludable if such amounts did not constitute community income.

(D) EXCLUSION AMOUNT.—

→ Caution: Pursuant to Section 911(b)(2)(D)(ii), the $80,000 exclusion amount in Section 911(b)(2)(D)(i) is adjusted for taxable years beginning in a calendar year after 2005 to reflect increases in the Chained Consumer Price Index. The adjusted amount that applies for taxable years beginning in 2023 is $120,000, as provided in Rev. Proc. 2022-38, 2022-45 I.R.B. 445.

(i) IN GENERAL.—The exclusion amount for any calendar year is $80,000.

(ii) INFLATION ADJUSTMENT.—In the case of any taxable year beginning in a calendar year after 2005, the $80,000 amount in clause (i) shall be increased by an amount equal to the product of—

(I) such dollar amount, and

(II) the cost-of-living adjustment determined under section 1(f)(3) for the calendar year in which the taxable year begins, determined by substituting "2004" for "2016" in subparagraph (A)(ii) thereof.

If any increase determined under the preceding sentence is not a multiple of $100, such increase shall be rounded to the next lowest multiple of $100.

[Sec. 911(c)]

(c) HOUSING COST AMOUNT.—For purposes of this section—

(1) IN GENERAL.—The term "housing cost amount" means an amount equal to the excess of—

(A) the housing expenses of an individual for the taxable year to the extent such expenses do not exceed the amount determined under paragraph (2), over

(B) an amount equal to the product of—

(i) 16 percent of the amount (computed on a daily basis) in effect under subsection (b)(2)(D) for the calendar year in which such taxable year begins, multiplied by

(ii) the number of days of such taxable year within the applicable period described in subparagraph (A) or (B) of subsection (d)(1).

(2) LIMITATION.—

(A) IN GENERAL.—The amount determined under this paragraph is an amount equal to the product of—

(i) 30 percent (adjusted as may be provided under subparagraph (B)) of the amount (computed on a daily basis) in effect under subsection (b)(2)(D) for the calendar year in which the taxable year of the individual begins, multiplied by

(ii) the number of days of such taxable year within the applicable period described in subparagraph (A) or (B) of subsection (d)(1).

(B) REGULATIONS.—The Secretary may issue regulations or other guidance providing for the adjustment of the percentage under subparagraph (A)(i) on the basis of geographic differences in housing costs relative to housing costs in the United States.

(3) HOUSING EXPENSES.—

(A) IN GENERAL.—The term "housing expenses" means the reasonable expenses paid or incurred during the taxable year by or on behalf of an individual for housing for the individual (and, if they reside with him, for his spouse and dependents) in a foreign country. The term—

(i) includes expenses attributable to the housing (such as utilities and insurance), but

(ii) does not include interest and taxes of the kind deductible under section 163 or 164 or any amount allowable as a deduction under section 216(a).

Housing expenses shall not be treated as reasonable to the extent such expenses are lavish or extravagant under the circumstances.

(B) SECOND FOREIGN HOUSEHOLD.—

(i) IN GENERAL.—Except as provided in clause (ii), only housing expenses incurred with respect to that abode which bears the closest relationship to the tax home of the individual shall be taken into account under paragraph (1).

(ii) SEPARATE HOUSEHOLD FOR SPOUSE AND DEPENDENTS.—If an individual maintains a separate abode outside the United States for his spouse and dependents and they do not reside with him because of living conditions which are dangerous, unhealthful, or otherwise adverse, then—

(I) the words "if they reside with him" in subparagraph (A) shall be disregarded, and

(II) the housing expenses incurred with respect to such abode shall be taken into account under paragraph (1).

(4) SPECIAL RULES WHERE HOUSING EXPENSES NOT PROVIDED BY EMPLOYER.—

(A) IN GENERAL.—To the extent the housing cost amount of any individual for any taxable year is not attributable to employer provided amounts, such amount shall be treated as a deduction allowable in computing adjusted gross income to the extent of the limitation of subparagraph (B).

(B) LIMITATION.—For purposes of subparagraph (A), the limitation of this subparagraph is the excess of—

(i) the foreign earned income of the individual for the taxable year, over

(ii) the amount of such income excluded from gross income under subsection (a) for the taxable year.

(C) 1-YEAR CARRYOVER OF HOUSING AMOUNTS NOT ALLOWED BY REASON OF SUBPARAGRAPH (B).—

(i) IN GENERAL.—The amount not allowable as a deduction for any taxable year under subparagraph (A) by reason of the limitation of subparagraph (B) shall be treated as a deduction allowable in computing adjusted gross income for the succeeding taxable year (and only for the succeeding taxable year) to the extent of the limitation of clause (ii) for such succeeding taxable year.

(ii) LIMITATION.—For purposes of clause (i), the limitation of this clause for any taxable year is the excess of—

(I) the limitation of subparagraph (B) for such taxable year, over

(II) amounts treated as a deduction under subparagraph (A) for such taxable year.

(D) EMPLOYER PROVIDED AMOUNTS.—For purposes of this paragraph, the term "employer provided amounts" means any amount paid or incurred on behalf of the individual by the individual's employer which is foreign earned income included in the individual's gross income for the taxable year (without regard to this section).

(E) FOREIGN EARNED INCOME.—For purposes of this paragraph, an individual's foreign earned income for any taxable year shall be determined without regard to the limitation of subparagraph (A) of subsection (b)(2).

[Sec. 911(d)]

(d) DEFINITIONS AND SPECIAL RULES.—For purposes of this section—

(1) QUALIFIED INDIVIDUAL.—The term "qualified individual" means an individual whose tax home is in a foreign country and who is—

(A) a citizen of the United States and establishes to the satisfaction of the Secretary that he has been a bona fide resident of a foreign country or countries for an uninterrupted period which includes an entire taxable year, or

(B) a citizen or resident of the United States and who, during any period of 12 consecutive months, is present in a foreign country or countries during at least 330 full days in such period.

(2) EARNED INCOME.—

(A) IN GENERAL.—The term "earned income" means wages, salaries, or professional fees, and other amounts received as compensation for personal services actually rendered, but does not include that part of the compensation derived by the taxpayer for personal services rendered by him to a corporation which represents a distribution of earnings or profits rather than a reasonable allowance as compensation for the personal services actually rendered.

(B) TAXPAYER ENGAGED IN TRADE OR BUSINESS.—In the case of a taxpayer engaged in a trade or business in which both personal services and capital are material income-producing factors, under regulations prescribed by the Secretary, a reasonable allowance as compensation for the personal services rendered by the taxpayer, not in excess of 30 percent of his share of the net profits of such trade or business, shall be considered as earned income.

(3) TAX HOME.—The term "tax home" means, with respect to any individual, such individual's home for purposes of section 162(a)(2) (relating to traveling expenses while away from home). An individual shall not be treated as having a tax home in a foreign country for any period for which his abode is within the United States, unless such individual is serving in an area designated by the President of the United States by Executive order as a combat zone for purposes of section 112 in support of the Armed Forces of the United States.

(4) WAIVER OF PERIOD OF STAY IN FOREIGN COUNTRY.—Notwithstanding paragraph (1), an individual who—

(A) is a bona fide resident of, or is present in, a foreign country for any period,

(B) leaves such foreign country after August 31, 1978—

(i) during any period during which the Secretary determines, after consultation with the Secretary of State or his delegate, that individuals were required to leave such foreign country because of war, civil unrest, or similar adverse conditions in such foreign country which precluded the normal conduct of business by such individuals, and

(ii) before meeting the requirements of such paragraph (1), and

(C) establishes to the satisfaction of the Secretary that such individual could reasonably have been expected to have met such requirements but for the conditions referred to in clause (i) of subparagraph (B),

shall be treated as a qualified individual with respect to the period described in subparagraph (A) during which he was a bona fide resident of, or was present in, the foreign country, and in applying subsections (b)(2)(A), (c)(1)(B)(ii), and (c)(2)(A)(ii) with respect to such individual, only the days within such period shall be taken into account.

(5) TEST OF BONA FIDE RESIDENCE.—If—

(A) an individual who has earned income from sources within a foreign country submits a statement to the authorities of that country that he is not a resident of that country, and

(B) such individual is held not subject as a resident of that country to the income tax of that country by its authorities with respect to such earnings,

then such individual shall not be considered a bona fide resident of that country for purposes of paragraph (1)(A).

(6) DENIAL OF DOUBLE BENEFITS.—No deduction or exclusion from gross income under this subtitle or credit against the tax imposed by this chapter (including any credit or deduction for the amount of taxes paid or accrued to a foreign country or possession of the United States) shall be allowed to the extent such deduction, exclusion, or credit is properly allocable to or chargeable against amounts excluded from gross income under subsection (a).

(7) AGGREGATE BENEFIT CANNOT EXCEED FOREIGN EARNED INCOME.—The sum of the amount excluded under subsection (a) and the amount deducted under subsection (c)(4)(A) for the taxable year shall not exceed the individual's foreign earned income for such year.

(8) LIMITATION ON INCOME EARNED IN RESTRICTED COUNTRY.—

(A) IN GENERAL.—If travel (or any transaction in connection with such travel) with respect to any foreign country is subject to the regulations described in subparagraph (B) during any period—

(i) the term "foreign earned income" shall not include any income from sources within such country attributable to services performed during such period,

(ii) the term "housing expenses" shall not include any expenses allocable to such period for housing in such country or for housing of the spouse or dependents of the taxpayer in another country while the taxpayer is present in such country, and

(iii) an individual shall not be treated as a bona fide resident of, or as present in, a foreign country for any day during which such individual was present in such country during such period.

(B) REGULATIONS.—For purposes of this paragraph, regulations are described in this subparagraph if such regulations—

(i) have been adopted pursuant to the Trading With the Enemy Act (50 U.S.C. 4301 et seq.), or the International Emergency Economic Powers Act (50 U.S.C. 1701 et seq.), and

(ii) include provisions generally prohibiting citizens and residents of the United States from engaging in transactions related to travel to, from, or within a foreign country.

(C) EXCEPTION.—Subparagraph (A) shall not apply to any individual during any period in which such individual's activities are not in violation of the regulations described in subparagraph (B).

(9) REGULATIONS.—The Secretary shall prescribe such regulations as may be necessary or appropriate to carry out the purposes of this section, including regulations providing rules—

(A) for cases where a husband and wife each have earned income from sources outside the United States, and

(B) for married individuals filing separate returns.

[Sec. 911(e)]

(e) ELECTION.—

(1) IN GENERAL.—An election under subsection (a) shall apply to the taxable year for which made and to all subsequent taxable years unless revoked under paragraph (2).

(2) REVOCATION.—A taxpayer may revoke an election made under paragraph (1) for any taxable year after the taxable year for which such election was made. Except with the consent of the Secretary, any taxpayer who makes such a revocation for any taxable year may not make another election under this section for any subsequent taxable year before the 6th taxable year after the taxable year for which such revocation was made.

[Sec. 911(f)]

(f) DETERMINATION OF TAX LIABILITY.—

(1) IN GENERAL.—If, for any taxable year, any amount is excluded from gross income of a taxpayer under subsection (a), then, notwithstanding sections 1 and 55—

(A) if such taxpayer has taxable income for such taxable year, the tax imposed by section 1 for such taxable year shall be equal to the excess (if any) of—

(i) the tax which would be imposed by section 1 for such taxable year if the taxpayer's taxable income were increased by the amount excluded under subsection (a) for such taxable year, over

(ii) the tax which would be imposed by section 1 for such taxable year if the taxpayer's taxable income were equal to the amount excluded under subsection (a) for such taxable year, and

(B) if such taxpayer has a taxable excess (as defined in section 55(b)(1)(B)) for such taxable year, the amount determined under the first sentence of section 55(b)(1)(A) for such taxable year shall be equal to the excess (if any) of—

(i) the amount which would be determined under such sentence for such taxable year (subject to the limitation of section 55(b)(3)) if the taxpayer's taxable excess (as so defined) were increased by the amount excluded under subsection (a) for such taxable year, over

(ii) the amount which would be determined under such sentence for such taxable year if the taxpayer's taxable excess (as so defined) were equal to the amount excluded under subsection (a) for such taxable year.

For purposes of this paragraph, the amount excluded under subsection (a) shall be reduced by the aggregate amount of any deductions or exclusions disallowed under subsection (d)(6) with respect to such excluded amount.

(2) SPECIAL RULES.—

(A) REGULAR TAX.—In applying section 1(h) for purposes of determining the tax under paragraph (1)(A)(i) for any taxable year in which, without regard to this subsection, the taxpayer's net capital gain exceeds taxable income (hereafter in this subparagraph referred to as the capital gain excess)—

(i) the taxpayer's net capital gain (determined without regard to section 1(h)(11)) shall be reduced (but not below zero) by such capital gain excess,

(ii) the taxpayer's qualified dividend income shall be reduced by so much of such capital gain excess as exceeds the taxpayer's net capital gain (determined without regard to section 1(h)(11) and the reduction under clause (i)), and

(iii) adjusted net capital gain, unrecaptured section 1250 gain, and 28-percent rate gain shall each be determined after increasing the amount described in section 1(h)(4)(B) by such capital gain excess.

(B) ALTERNATIVE MINIMUM TAX.—In applying section 55(b)(3) for purposes of determining the tax under paragraph (1)(B)(i) for any taxable year in which, without regard to this subsection, the taxpayer's net capital gain exceeds the taxable excess (as defined in section 55(b)(1)(B))—

(i) the rules of subparagraph (A) shall apply, except that such subparagraph shall be applied by substituting "the taxable excess (as defined in section 55(b)(1)(B))" for "taxable income", and

(ii) the reference in section 55(b)(3)(B) to the excess described in section 1(h)(1)(B), and the reference in section 55(b)(3)(C)(ii) to the excess described in section 1(h)(1)(C)(ii), shall each be treated as a reference to each such excess as determined under the rules of subparagraph (A) for purposes of determining the tax under paragraph (1)(A)(i).

(C) DEFINITIONS.—Terms used in this paragraph which are also used in section 1(h) shall have the respective meanings given such terms by section 1(h), except that in applying subparagraph (B) the adjustments under part VI of subchapter A shall be taken into account.

[Sec. 911(g)]

(g) CROSS REFERENCES.—

For administrative and penal provisions relating to the exclusions provided for in this section, see sections 6001, 6011, 6012(c), and the other provisions of subtitle F.

[Sec. 912]

SEC. 912. EXEMPTION FOR CERTAIN ALLOWANCES.

The following items shall not be included in gross income, and shall be exempt from taxation under this subtitle:

(1) FOREIGN AREAS ALLOWANCES.—In the case of civilian officers and employees of the Government of the United States, amounts received as allowances or otherwise (but not amounts received as post differentials) under—

(A) chapter 9 of title I of the Foreign Service Act of 1980,

(B) section 4 of the Central Intelligence Agency Act of 1949, as amended (50 U.S.C. 3505),

(C) title II of the Overseas Differentials and Allowances Act, or

(D) subsection (e) or (f) of the first section of the Administrative Expenses Act of 1946, as amended, or section 22 of such Act.

(2) COST-OF-LIVING ALLOWANCES.—In the case of civilian officers or employees of the Government of the United States stationed outside the continental United States (other than Alaska), amounts (other than amounts received under title II of the Overseas Differentials and Allowances Act) received as cost-of-living allowances in accordance with regulations approved by the President (or in the case of judicial officers or employees of the United States, in accordance with rules similar to such regulations).

(3) PEACE CORPS ALLOWANCES.—In the case of an individual who is a volunteer or volunteer leader within the meaning of the Peace Corps Act and members of his family, amounts received as allowances under section 5 or 6 of the Peace Corps Act other than amounts received as—

(A) termination payments under section 5(c) or section 6(1) of such Act,

(B) leave allowances,

(C) if such individual is a volunteer leader training in the United States, allowances to members of his family, and

(D) such portion of living allowances as the President may determine under the Peace Corps Act as constituting basic compensation.

Subpart D—Possessions of the United States

[Sec. 931]

SEC. 931. INCOME FROM SOURCES WITHIN GUAM, AMERICAN SAMOA, OR THE NORTHERN MARIANA ISLANDS.

[Sec. 931(a)]

(a) GENERAL RULE.—In the case of an individual who is a bona fide resident of a specified possession during the entire taxable year, gross income shall not include—

(1) income derived from sources within any specified possession, and

(2) income effectively connected with the conduct of a trade or business by such individual within any specified possession.

[Sec. 931(b)]

(b) DEDUCTIONS, ETC. ALLOCABLE TO EXCLUDED AMOUNTS NOT ALLOWABLE.—An individual shall not be allowed—

(1) as a deduction from gross income any deductions (other than the deduction under section 151, relating to personal exemptions), or

(2) any credit,

properly allocable or chargeable against amounts excluded from gross income under this section.

[Sec. 931(c)]

(c) SPECIFIED POSSESSION.—For purposes of this section, the term "specified possession" means Guam, American Samoa, and the Northern Mariana Islands.

[Sec. 931(d)]

(d) EMPLOYEES OF THE UNITED STATES.—Amounts paid for services performed as an employee of the United States (or any agency thereof) shall be treated as not described in paragraph (1) or (2) of subsection (a).

[Sec. 932]

SEC. 932. COORDINATION OF UNITED STATES AND VIRGIN ISLANDS INCOME TAXES.

[Sec. 932(a)]

(a) TREATMENT OF UNITED STATES RESIDENTS.—

(1) APPLICATION OF SUBSECTION.—This subsection shall apply to an individual for the taxable year if—

(A) such individual—

(i) is a citizen or resident of the United States (other than a bona fide resident of the Virgin Islands during the entire taxable year), and

(ii) has income derived from sources within the Virgin Islands, or effectively connected with the conduct of a trade or business within such possession, for the taxable year, or

(B) such individual files a joint return for the taxable year with an individual described in subparagraph (A).

(2) FILING REQUIREMENT.—Each individual to whom this subsection applies for the taxable year shall file his income tax return for the taxable year with both the United States and the Virgin Islands.

(3) EXTENT OF INCOME TAX LIABILITY.—In the case of an individual to whom this subsection applies in a taxable year for purposes of so much of this title (other than this section and section 7654) as relates to the taxes imposed by this chapter, the United States shall be treated as including the Virgin Islands.

[Sec. 932(b)]

(b) PORTION OF UNITED STATES TAX LIABILITY PAYABLE TO THE VIRGIN ISLANDS.—

(1) IN GENERAL.—Each individual to whom subsection (a) applies for the taxable year shall pay the applicable percentage of the taxes imposed by this chapter for such taxable year (determined without regard to paragraph (3)) to the Virgin Islands.

(2) APPLICABLE PERCENTAGE.—

(A) IN GENERAL.—For purposes of paragraph (1), the term "applicable percentage" means the percentage which Virgin Islands adjusted gross income bears to adjusted gross income.

(B) VIRGIN ISLANDS ADJUSTED GROSS INCOME.—For purposes of subparagraph (A), the term "Virgin Islands adjusted gross income" means adjusted gross income determined by taking into account only income derived from sources within the Virgin Islands and deductions properly apportioned or allocable thereto.

(3) AMOUNTS PAID ALLOWED AS CREDIT.—There shall be allowed as a credit against the tax imposed by this chapter for the taxable year an amount equal to the taxes required to be paid to the Virgin Islands under paragraph (1) which are so paid.

[Sec. 932(c)]

(c) TREATMENT OF VIRGIN ISLANDS RESIDENTS.—

(1) APPLICATION OF SUBSECTION.—This subsection shall apply to an individual for the taxable year if—

(A) such individual is a bona fide resident of the Virgin Islands during the entire taxable year, or

(B) such individual files a joint return for the taxable year with an individual described in subparagraph (A).

(2) FILING REQUIREMENT.—Each individual to whom this subsection applies for the taxable year shall file an income tax return for the taxable year with the Virgin Islands.

(3) EXTENT OF INCOME TAX LIABILITY.—In the case of an individual to whom this subsection applies in a taxable year for purposes of so much of this title (other than this section and section 7654) as relates to the taxes imposed by this chapter, the Virgin Islands shall be treated as including the United States.

(4) RESIDENTS OF THE VIRGIN ISLANDS.—In the case of an individual—

(A) who is a bona fide resident of the Virgin Islands during the entire taxable year,

(B) who, on his return of income tax to the Virgin Islands, reports income from all sources and identifies the source of each item shown on such return, and

(C) who fully pays his tax liability referred to in section 934(a) to the Virgin Islands with respect to such income,

for purposes of calculating income tax liability to the United States, gross income shall not include any amount included in gross income on such return, and allocable deductions and credits shall not be taken into account.

[Sec. 932(d)]

(d) SPECIAL RULE FOR JOINT RETURNS.—In the case of a joint return, this section shall be applied on the basis of the residence of the spouse who has the greater adjusted gross income (determined without regard to community property laws) for the taxable year.

[Sec. 932(e)]

(e) SPECIAL RULE FOR APPLYING SECTION TO TAX IMPOSED IN VIRGIN ISLANDS.—In applying this section for purposes of determining income tax liability incurred to the Virgin Islands, the provisions of this section shall not be affected by the provisions of Federal law referred to in section 934(a).

[Sec. 933]

SEC. 933. INCOME FROM SOURCES WITHIN PUERTO RICO.

The following items shall not be included in gross income and shall be exempt from taxation under this subtitle:

(1) RESIDENT OF PUERTO RICO FOR ENTIRE TAXABLE YEAR.—In the case of an individual who is a bona fide resident of Puerto Rico during the entire taxable year, income derived from sources within Puerto Rico (except amounts received for services performed as an employee of the United States or any agency thereof); but such individual shall not be allowed as a deduction from his gross income any deductions (other than the deduction under section 151, relating to personal exemptions), or any credit, properly allocable to or chargeable against amounts excluded from gross income under this paragraph.

(2) TAXABLE YEAR OF CHANGE OF RESIDENCE FROM PUERTO RICO.—In the case of an individual citizen of the United States who has been a bona fide resident of Puerto Rico for a period of at least 2 years before the date on which he changes his residence from Puerto Rico, income derived from sources therein (except amounts received for services performed as an employee of the United States or any agency thereof) which is attributable to that part of such period of Puerto Rican residence before such date; but such individual shall not be allowed as a deduction from his gross income any deductions (other than the deduction for personal exemptions under section 151), or any credit, properly allocable to or chargeable against amounts excluded from gross income under this paragraph.

[Sec. 934]

SEC. 934. LIMITATION ON REDUCTION IN INCOME TAX LIABILITY INCURRED TO THE VIRGIN ISLANDS

[Sec. 934(a)]

(a) GENERAL RULE.—Tax liability incurred to the Virgin Islands pursuant to this subtitle, as made applicable in the Virgin Islands by the Act entitled "An Act making appropriations for the naval service for the fiscal year ending June 30, 1922, and for other purposes", approved July 12, 1921 (48 U. S. C. 1397), or pursuant to section 28(a) of the Revised Organic Act of the Virgin Islands, approved July 22, 1954 (48 U. S. C. 1642), shall not be reduced or remitted in any way, directly or indirectly, whether by grant, subsidy, or other similar payment, by any law enacted in the Virgin Islands, except to the extent provided in subsection (b).

[Sec. 934(b)]

(b) REDUCTIONS PERMITTED WITH RESPECT TO CERTAIN INCOME.—

(1) IN GENERAL.—Except as provided in paragraph (2), subsection (a) shall not apply with respect to so much of the tax liability referred to in subsection (a) as is attributable to income derived from sources within the Virgin Islands or income effectively connected with the conduct of a trade or business within the Virgin Islands.

(2) EXCEPTION FOR LIABILITY PAID BY CITIZENS OR RESIDENTS OF THE UNITED STATES.—Paragraph (1) shall not apply to any liability payable to the Virgin Islands under section 932(b).

(3) SPECIAL RULE FOR NON-UNITED STATES INCOME OF CERTAIN FOREIGN CORPORATIONS.—

(A) IN GENERAL.—In the case of a qualified foreign corporation, subsection (a) shall not apply with respect to so much of the tax liability referred to in subsection (a) as is attributable to income which is derived from sources outside the United States and which is not effectively connected with the conduct of a trade or business within the United States.

(B) QUALIFIED FOREIGN CORPORATION.—For purposes of subparagraph (A), the term "qualified foreign corporation" means any foreign corporation if less than 10 percent of—

(i) the total voting power of the stock of such corporation, and

(ii) the total value of the stock of such corporation,

is owned or treated as owned (within the meaning of section 958) by 1 or more United States persons.

(4) DETERMINATION OF INCOME SOURCE, ETC.—The determination as to whether income is derived from sources within the United States or is effectively connected with the conduct of a trade or business within the United States shall be made under regulations prescribed by the Secretary.

»»→ ***Caution: Code Sec. 935, below, has been repealed by the Tax Reform Act of 1986 but remains effective until an implementing agreement between the U.S. and Guam is entered into.***

[Sec. 935]

SEC. 935. COORDINATION OF UNITED STATES AND GUAM INDIVIDUAL INCOME TAXES.

[Sec. 935(a)]

(a) APPLICATION OF SECTION.—This section shall apply to any individual who, during the entire taxable year—

(1) is a bona fide resident of Guam,

(2) is a citizen of Guam but not otherwise a citizen of the United States,

(3) has income derived from Guam for the taxable year and is a citizen or resident of the United States, or

(4) files a joint return for the taxable year with an individual who satisfies paragraph (1), (2), or (3) for the taxable year.

[Sec. 935(b)]

(b) FILING REQUIREMENT.—

(1) IN GENERAL.—Each individual to whom this section applies for the taxable year shall file his income tax return for the taxable year—

(A) with the United States (other than a bona fide resident of Guam during the entire taxable year), if he is a resident of the United States,

(B) with Guam, if he is a bona fide resident of Guam, and

(C) if neither subparagraph (A) nor subparagraph (B) applies—

(i) with Guam, if he is a citizen of Guam but not otherwise a citizen of the United States, or

(ii) with the United States, if clause (i) does not apply.

(2) DETERMINATION DATE.—For purposes of this section, determinations of citizenship for the taxable year shall be made as of the close of the taxable year.

(3) SPECIAL RULE FOR JOINT RETURNS.—In the case of a joint return, this subsection shall be applied on the basis of the residence and citizenship of the spouse who has the greater adjusted gross income (determined without regard to community property laws) for the taxable year.

[Sec. 935(c)]

(c) EXTENT OF INCOME TAX LIABILITY.—In the case of any individual to whom this section applies for the taxable year—

(1) for purposes of so much of this title (other than this section and section 7654) as relates to the taxes imposed by this chapter, the United States shall be treated as including Guam,

(2) for purposes of the Guam territorial income tax, Guam shall be treated as including the United States, and

(3) such individual is hereby relieved of liability for income tax for such year to the jurisdiction (the United States or Guam) other than the jurisdiction with which he is required to file under subsection (b).

[Sec. 935(d)]

(d) SPECIAL RULES FOR ESTIMATED INCOME TAX.—If there is reason to believe that this section will apply to an individual for the taxable year, then—

(1) he shall file any declaration of estimated income tax (and all amendments thereto) with the jurisdiction with which he would be required to file a return for such year under subsection (b) if his taxable year closed on the date he is required to file such declaration.

(2) he is hereby relieved of any liability to file a declaration of estimated income tax (and amendments thereto) for such taxable year to the other jurisdiction, and

(3) his liability for underpayments of estimated income tax shall be to the jurisdiction with which he is required to file his return for the taxable year (determined under subsection (b)).

[Sec. 937]

SEC. 937. RESIDENCE AND SOURCE RULES INVOLVING POSSESSIONS.

[Sec. 937(a)]

(a) BONA FIDE RESIDENT.—For purposes of this subpart, section 865(g)(3), section 876, section 881(b), paragraphs (2) and (3) of section 901(b), section 957(c), section 3401(a)(8)(C), and section 7654(a), except as provided in regulations, the term "bona fide resident" means a person—

(1) who is present for at least 183 days during the taxable year in Guam, American Samoa, the Northern Mariana Islands, Puerto Rico, or the Virgin Islands, as the case may be, and

(2) who does not have a tax home (determined under the principles of section 911(d)(3) without regard to the second sentence thereof) outside such specified possession during the taxable year and does not have a closer connection (determined under the principles of section 7701(b)(3)(B)(ii)) to the United States or a foreign country than to such specified possession.

For purposes of paragraph (1), the determination as to whether a person is present for any day shall be made under the principles of section 7701(b).

[Sec. 937(b)]

(b) SOURCE RULES.—Except as provided in regulations, for purposes of this title—

(1) except as provided in paragraph (2), rules similar to the rules for determining whether income is income from sources within the United States or is effectively connected with the conduct of a trade or business within the United States shall apply for purposes of determining whether income is from sources within a possession specified in subsection (a)(1) or effectively connected with the conduct of a trade or business within any such possession, and

(2) any income treated as income from sources within the United States or as effectively connected with the conduct of a trade or business within the United States shall not be treated as income from sources within any such possession or as effectively connected with the conduct of a trade or business within any such possession.

[Sec. 937(c)]

(c) REPORTING REQUIREMENT.—

(1) IN GENERAL.—If, for any taxable year, an individual takes the position for United States income tax reporting purposes that the individual became, or ceases to be, a bona fide resident of a possession specified in subsection (a)(1), such individual shall file with the Secretary, at such time and in such manner as the Secretary may prescribe, notice of such position.

(2) TRANSITION RULE.—If, for any of an individual's 3 taxable years ending before the individual's first taxable year ending after the date of the enactment of this subsection, the individual took a position described in paragraph (1), the individual shall file with the Secretary, at such time and in such manner as the Secretary may prescribe, notice of such position.

Subpart F—Controlled Foreign Corporations

[Sec. 951]

SEC. 951. AMOUNTS INCLUDED IN GROSS INCOME OF UNITED STATES SHAREHOLDERS.

[Sec. 951(a)]

(a) AMOUNTS INCLUDED.

(1) IN GENERAL.—If a foreign corporation is a controlled foreign corporation at any time during any taxable year, every person who is a United States shareholder (as defined in subsection (b)) of such corporation and who owns (within the meaning of section 958(a)) stock in such corporation on the last day, in such year, on which such corporation is a controlled foreign corporation shall include in his gross income, for his taxable year in which or with which such taxable year of the corporation ends—

(A) his pro rata share (determined under paragraph (2)) of the corporation's subpart F income for such year, and

(B) the amount determined under section 956 with respect to such shareholder for such year (but only to the extent not excluded from gross income under section 959(a)(2)).

(2) PRO RATA SHARE OF SUBPART F INCOME.—The pro rata share referred to in paragraph (1)(A)(i) in the case of any United States shareholder is the amount—

(A) which would have been distributed with respect to the stock which such shareholder owns (within the meaning of section 958(a)) in such corporation if on the last day, in its taxable year, on which the corporation is a controlled foreign corporation it had distributed pro rata to its shareholders an amount (i) which bears the same ratio to its subpart F income for the taxable year, as (ii) the part of such year during which the corporation is a controlled foreign corporation bears to the entire year, reduced by

(B) the amount of distributions received by any other person during such year as a dividend with respect to such stock, but only to the extent of the dividend which would have been received if the distribution by the corporation had been the amount (i) which bears the same ratio to the subpart F income of such corporation for the taxable year, as (ii) the part of such year during which such shareholder did not own (within the meaning of section 958(a)) such stock bears to the entire year. For purposes of subparagraph (B), any gain included in the gross income of any person as a dividend under section 1248 shall be treated as a distribution received by such person with respect to the stock involved.

[Sec. 951(b)]

(b) UNITED STATES SHAREHOLDER DEFINED.—For purposes of this title, the term "United States shareholder" means, with respect to any foreign corporation, a United States person (as defined in section 957(c)) who owns (within the meaning of section 958(a)), or is considered as owning by applying the rules of ownership of section 958(b), 10 percent or more of the total combined voting power of all classes of stock entitled to vote of such foreign corporation, or 10 percent or more of the total value of shares of all classes of stock of such foreign corporation.

[Sec. 951(c)]

(c) COORDINATION WITH PASSIVE FOREIGN INVESTMENT COMPANY PROVISIONS.—If, but for this subsection, an amount would be included in the gross income of a United States shareholder for any taxable year both under subsection (a)(1)(A)(i) and under section 1293 (relating to current taxation of income from certain passive foreign investment companies), such amount shall be included in the gross income of such shareholder only under subsection (a)(1)(A).

[Sec. 951A]

SEC. 951A. GLOBAL INTANGIBLE LOW-TAXED INCOME INCLUDED IN GROSS INCOME OF UNITED STATES SHAREHOLDERS.

[Sec. 951A(a)]

(a) IN GENERAL.—Each person who is a United States shareholder of any controlled foreign corporation for any taxable year of such United States shareholder shall include in gross income such shareholder's global intangible low-taxed income for such taxable year.

[Sec. 951A(b)]

(b) GLOBAL INTANGIBLE LOW-TAXED INCOME.—For purposes of this section—

(1) IN GENERAL.—The term "global intangible low taxed income" means, with respect to any United States shareholder for any taxable year of such United States shareholder, the excess (if any) of—

(A) such shareholder's net CFC tested income for such taxable year, over

(B) such shareholder's net deemed tangible income return for such taxable year.

(2) NET DEEMED TANGIBLE INCOME RETURN.—The term "net deemed tangible income return" means, with respect to any United States shareholder for any taxable year, the excess of—

(A) 10 percent of the aggregate of such shareholder's pro rata share of the qualified business asset investment of each controlled foreign corporation with respect to which such shareholder is a United States shareholder for such taxable year (determined for each taxable year of each such controlled foreign corporation which ends in or with such taxable year of such United States shareholder), over

(B) the amount of interest expense taken into account under subsection (c)(2)(A)(ii) in determining the shareholder's net CFC tested income for the taxable year to the extent the interest income attributable to such expense is not taken into account in determining such shareholder's net CFC tested income.

[Sec. 951A(c)]

(c) NET CFC TESTED INCOME.—For purposes of this section—

(1) IN GENERAL.—The term "net CFC tested income" means, with respect to any United States shareholder for any taxable year of such United States shareholder, the excess (if any) of—

(A) the aggregate of such shareholder's pro rata share of the tested income of each controlled foreign corporation with respect to which such shareholder is a United States shareholder for such taxable year of such United States shareholder (determined for each taxable year of such controlled foreign corporation which ends in or with such taxable year of such United States shareholder), over

(B) the aggregate of such shareholder's pro rata share of the tested loss of each controlled foreign corporation with respect to which such shareholder is a United States shareholder for such taxable year of such United States shareholder (determined for each taxable year of such controlled foreign corporation which ends in or with such taxable year of such United States shareholder).

(2) TESTED INCOME; TESTED LOSS.—For purposes of this section—

(A) TESTED INCOME.—The term "tested income" means, with respect to any controlled foreign corporation for any taxable year of such controlled foreign corporation, the excess (if any) of—

(i) the gross income of such corporation determined without regard to—

(I) any item of income described in section 952(b),

(II) any gross income taken into account in determining the subpart F income of such corporation,

(III) any gross income excluded from the foreign base company income (as defined in section 954) and the insurance income (as defined in section 953) of such corporation by reason of section 954(b)(4),

(IV) any dividend received from a related person (as defined in section 954(d)(3)), and

(V) any foreign oil and gas extraction income (as defined in section 907(c)(1)) of such corporation, over

(ii) the deductions (including taxes) properly allocable to such gross income under rules similar to the rules of section 954(b)(5) (or to which such deductions would be allocable if there were such gross income).

(B) TESTED LOSS.—

(i) IN GENERAL.—The term "tested loss" means, with respect to any controlled foreign corporation for any taxable year of such controlled foreign corporation, the excess (if any) of the amount described in subparagraph (A)(ii) over the amount described in subparagraph (A)(i).

(ii) COORDINATION WITH SUBPART F TO DENY DOUBLE BENEFIT OF LOSSES.—Section 952(c)(1)(A) shall be applied by increasing the earnings and profits of the controlled foreign corporation by the tested loss of such corporation.

[Sec. 951A(d)]

(d) QUALIFIED BUSINESS ASSET INVESTMENT.—For purposes of this section—

(1) IN GENERAL.—The term "qualified business asset investment" means, with respect to any controlled foreign corporation for any taxable year, the average of such corporation's aggregate adjusted bases as of the close of each quarter of such taxable year in specified tangible property—

(A) used in a trade or business of the corporation, and

(B) of a type with respect to which a deduction is allowable under section 167.

(2) SPECIFIED TANGIBLE PROPERTY.—

(A) IN GENERAL.—The term "specified tangible property" means, except as provided in subparagraph (B), any tangible property used in the production of tested income.

(B) DUAL USE PROPERTY.—In the case of property used both in the production of tested income and income which is not tested income, such property shall be treated as specified tangible property in the same proportion that the gross income described in subsection (c)(1)(A) produced with respect to such property bears to the total gross income produced with respect to such property.

(3) DETERMINATION OF ADJUSTED BASIS.—For purposes of this subsection, notwithstanding any provision of this title (or any other provision of law) which is enacted after the date of the enactment of this section, the adjusted basis in any property shall be determined—

(A) by using the alternative depreciation system under section 168(g), and

(B) by allocating the depreciation deduction with respect to such property ratably to each day during the period in the taxable year to which such depreciation relates.

(3) [sic] PARTNERSHIP PROPERTY.—For purposes of this subsection, if a controlled foreign corporation holds an interest in a partnership at the close of such taxable year of the controlled foreign corporation, such controlled foreign corporation shall take into account under paragraph (1) the controlled foreign corporation's distributive share of the aggregate of the partnership's adjusted bases (determined as of such date in the hands of the partnership) in tangible property held by such partnership to the extent such property—

(A) is used in the trade or business of the partnership,

(B) is of a type with respect to which a deduction is allowable under section 167, and

(C) is used in the production of tested income (determined with respect to such controlled foreign corporation's distributive share of income with respect to such property).

For purposes of this paragraph, the controlled foreign corporation's distributive share of the adjusted basis of any property shall be the controlled foreign corporation's distributive share of income with respect to such property.

(4) REGULATIONS.—The Secretary shall issue such regulations or other guidance as the Secretary determines appropriate to prevent the avoidance of the purposes of this subsection, including regulations or other guidance which provide for the treatment of property if—

(A) such property is transferred, or held, temporarily, or

(B) the avoidance of the purposes of this paragraph is a factor in the transfer or holding of such property.

[Sec. 951A(e)]

(e) DETERMINATION OF PRO RATA SHARE, ETC.—For purposes of this section—

(1) IN GENERAL.—The pro rata shares referred to in subsections (b), (c)(1)(A), and (c)(1)(B), respectively, shall be determined under the rules of section 951(a)(2) in the same manner as such section applies to subpart F income and shall be taken into account in the taxable year of the United States shareholder in which or with which the taxable year of the controlled foreign corporation ends.

(2) TREATMENT AS UNITED STATES SHAREHOLDER.—A person shall be treated as a United States shareholder of a controlled foreign corporation for any taxable year of such person only if such person owns (within the meaning of section 958(a)) stock in such foreign corporation on the last day in the taxable year of such foreign corporation on which such foreign corporation is a controlled foreign corporation.

(3) TREATMENT AS CONTROLLED FOREIGN CORPORATION.—A foreign corporation shall be treated as a controlled foreign corporation for any taxable year if such foreign corporation is a controlled foreign corporation at any time during such taxable year.

[Sec. 951A(f)]

(f) TREATMENT AS SUBPART F INCOME FOR CERTAIN PURPOSES.—

(1) IN GENERAL.—

(A) APPLICATION.—Except as provided in subparagraph (B), any global intangible low-taxed income included in gross income under subsection (a) shall be treated in the same manner as an amount included under section 951(a)(1)(A) for purposes of applying sections 168(h)(2)(B), 535(b)(10), 851(b), 904(h)(1), 959, 961, 962, 993(a)(1)(E), 996(f)(1), 1248(b)(1), 1248(d)(1), 6501(e)(1)(C), 6654(d)(2)(D), and 6655(e)(4).

(B) EXCEPTION.—The Secretary shall provide rules for the application of subparagraph (A) to other provisions of this title in any case in which the determination of subpart F income is required to be made at the level of the controlled foreign corporation.

(2) ALLOCATION OF GLOBAL INTANGIBLE LOW-TAXED INCOME TO CONTROLLED FOREIGN CORPORATIONS.—For purposes of the sections referred to in paragraph (1), with respect to any controlled foreign corporation any pro rata amount from which is taken into account in determining the global intangible low-taxed income included in gross income of a United States shareholder under subsection (a), the portion of such global intangible low-taxed income which is treated as being with respect to such controlled foreign corporation is—

(A) in the case of a controlled foreign corporation with no tested income, zero, and

(B) in the case of a controlled foreign corporation with tested income, the portion of such global intangible low-taxed income which bears the same ratio to such global intangible low-taxed income as—

(i) such United States shareholder's pro rata amount of the tested income of such controlled foreign corporation, bears to

(ii) the aggregate amount described in subsection (c)(1)(A) with respect to such United States shareholder.

[Sec. 952]

SEC. 952. SUBPART F INCOME DEFINED.

[Sec. 952(a)]

(a) IN GENERAL.—For purposes of this subpart, the term "subpart F income" means, in the case of any controlled foreign corporation, the sum of—

(1) insurance income (as defined under section 953),

(2) the foreign base company income (as determined under section 954),

(3) an amount equal to the product of—

(A) the income of such corporation other than income which—

(i) is attributable to earnings and profits of the foreign corporation included in the gross income of a United States person under section 951 (other than by reason of this paragraph), or

(ii) is described in subsection (b),

multiplied by

(B) the international boycott factor (as determined under section 999),

(4) the sum of the amounts of any illegal bribes, kickbacks, or other payments (within the meaning of section 162(c)) paid by or on behalf of the corporation during the taxable year of the corporation directly or indirectly to an official, employee, or agent in fact of a government, and

(5) the income of such corporation derived from any foreign country during any period during which section 901(j) applies to such foreign country.

The payments referred to in paragraph (4) are payments which would be unlawful under the Foreign Corrupt Practices Act of 1977 if the payor were a United States person. For purposes of paragraph (5), the income described therein shall be reduced, under regulations prescribed by the Secretary, so as to take into account deductions (including taxes) properly allocable to such income.

[Sec. 952(b)]

(b) EXCLUSION OF UNITED STATES INCOME.—In the case of a controlled foreign corporation, subpart F income does not include any item of income from sources within the United States which is effectively connected with the conduct by such corporation of a trade or business within the United States unless such item is exempt from taxation (or is subject to a reduced rate of tax) pursuant to a treaty obligation of the United States. For purposes of this subsection, any exemption (or reduction) with respect to the tax imposed by section 884 shall not be taken into account.

[Sec. 952(c)]

(c) LIMITATION.—

(1) IN GENERAL.—

(A) SUBPART F INCOME LIMITED TO CURRENT EARNINGS AND PROFITS.—For purposes of subsection (a), the subpart F income of any controlled foreign corporation for any taxable year shall not exceed the earnings and profits of such corporation for such taxable year.

(B) CERTAIN PRIOR YEAR DEFICITS MAY BE TAKEN INTO ACCOUNT.—

(i) IN GENERAL.—The amount included in the gross income of any United States shareholder under section 951(a)(1)(A) for any taxable year and attributable to a qualified activity shall be reduced by the amount of such shareholder's pro rata share of any qualified deficit.

(ii) QUALIFIED DEFICIT.—The term "qualified deficit" means any deficit in earnings and profits of the controlled foreign corporation for any prior taxable year which began after December 31, 1986, and for which the controlled foreign corporation was a controlled foreign corporation; but only to the extent such deficit—

(I) is attributable to the same qualified activity as the activity giving rise to the income being offset, and

(II) has not previously been taken into account under this subparagraph.

In determining the deficit attributable to qualified activities described in subclause (II) or (III) of clause (iii), deficits in earnings and profits (to the extent not previously taken into account under this section) for taxable years beginning after 1962 and before 1987 also shall be taken into account. In the case of the qualified activity described in clause (iii)(I), the rule of the preceding sentence shall apply, except that "1982" shall be substituted for "1962".

(iii) QUALIFIED ACTIVITY.—For purposes of this paragraph, the term "qualified activity" means any activity giving rise to—

(I) foreign base company sales income,

(II) foreign base company services income,

(III) in the case of a qualified insurance company, insurance income or foreign personal holding company income, or

(IV) in the case of a qualified financial institution, foreign personal holding company income.

(iv) PRO RATA SHARE.—For purposes of this paragraph, the shareholder's pro rata share of any deficit for any prior taxable year shall be determined under rules similar to rules under section 951(a)(2) for whichever of the following yields the smaller share:

(I) the close of the taxable year, or

(II) the close of the taxable year in which the deficit arose.

(v) QUALIFIED INSURANCE COMPANY.—For purposes of this subparagraph, the term "qualified insurance company" means any controlled foreign corporation predominantly engaged in the active conduct of an insurance business in the taxable year and in the prior taxable years in which the deficit arose.

(vi) QUALIFIED FINANCIAL INSTITUTION.—For purposes of this paragraph, the term "qualified financial institution" means any controlled foreign corporation predominantly engaged in the active conduct of a banking, financing, or similar business in the taxable year and in the prior taxable year in which the deficit arose.

(vii) SPECIAL RULES FOR INSURANCE INCOME.—

(I) IN GENERAL.—An election may be made under this clause to have section 953(a) applied for purposes of this title without regard to the same country exception under paragraph (1)(A) thereof. Such election, once made, may be revoked only with the consent of the Secretary.

(II) SPECIAL RULES FOR AFFILIATED GROUPS.—In the case of an affiliated group of corporations (within the meaning of section 1504 but without regard to section 1504(b)(3) and by substituting "more than 50 percent" for "at least 80 percent" each place it appears), no election may be made under subclause (I) for any controlled foreign corporation unless such election is made for all other controlled foreign corporations who are members of such group and who were created or organized under the laws of the same country as such controlled foreign corporation. For purposes of clause (v), in determining whether any controlled corporation described in the preceding sentence is a qualified insurance company, all such corporations shall be treated as 1 corporation.

(C) CERTAIN DEFICITS OF MEMBER OF THE SAME CHAIN OF CORPORATIONS MAY BE TAKEN INTO ACCOUNT.—

(i) IN GENERAL.—A controlled foreign corporation may elect to reduce the amount of its subpart F income for any taxable year which is attributable to any qualified activity by the amount of any deficit in earnings and profits of a qualified chain member for a taxable year ending with (or within) the taxable year of such controlled foreign corporation to the extent such deficit is attributable to such activity. To the extent any deficit reduces subpart F income under the preceding sentence, such deficit shall not be taken into account under subparagraph (B).

(ii) QUALIFIED CHAIN MEMBER.—For purposes of this subparagraph, the term "qualified chain member" means, with respect to any controlled foreign corporation, any other corporation which is created or organized under the laws of the same foreign country as the controlled foreign corporation but only if—

(I) all the stock of such other corporation (other than directors' qualifying shares) is owned at all times during the taxable year in which the deficit arose (directly or through 1 or more corporations other than the common parent) by such controlled foreign corporation, or

(II) all the stock of such controlled foreign corporation (other than directors' qualifying shares) is owned at all times during the taxable year in which the deficit arose (directly or through 1 or more corporations other than the common parent) by such other corporation.

(iii) COORDINATION.—This subparagraph shall be applied after subparagraphs (A) and (B).

(2) RECHARACTERIZATION IN SUBSEQUENT TAXABLE YEARS.—If the subpart F income of any controlled foreign corporation for any taxable year was reduced by reason of paragraph (1)(A), any excess of the earnings and profits of such corporation for any subsequent taxable year over the subpart F income of such foreign corporation for such taxable year shall be recharacterized as subpart F income under rules similar to the rules applicable under section 904(f)(5).

(3) SPECIAL RULE FOR DETERMINING EARNINGS AND PROFITS.—For purposes of this subsection, earnings and profits of any controlled foreign corporation shall be determined without regard to paragraphs (4), (5), and (6) of section 312(n). Under regulations, the preceding sentence shall not apply to the extent it would increase earnings and profits by an amount which was previously distributed by the controlled foreign corporation.

[Sec. 953]

SEC. 953. INSURANCE INCOME.

[Sec. 953(a)]

(a) INSURANCE INCOME.—

(1) IN GENERAL.—For purposes of section 952(a)(1), the term "insurance income" means any income which—

(A) is attributable to the issuing (or reinsuring) of an insurance or annuity contract, and

(B) would (subject to the modifications provided by subsection (b)) be taxed under subchapter L of this chapter if such income were the income of a domestic insurance company.

(2) EXCEPTION.—Such term shall not include any exempt insurance income (as defined in subsection (e)).

[Sec. 953(b)]

(b) SPECIAL RULES.—For purposes of subsection (a)—

(1) The following provisions of subchapter L shall not apply:

(A) So much of section 805(a)(8) as relates to the deduction allowed under section 172.

(B) Section 832(c)(5) (relating to certain capital losses).

(2) The items referred to in—

(A) section 803(a)(1) (relating to gross amount of premiums and other considerations),

(B) section 803(a)(2) (relating to net decrease in reserves),

(C) section 805(a)(2) (relating to net increase [in] reserves), and

(D) section 832(b)(4) (relating to premiums earned on insurance contracts),

shall be taken into account only to the extent they are in respect of any reinsurance or the issuing of any insurance or annuity contract described in subsection (a)(1).

(3) Reserves for any insurance or annuity contract shall be determined in the same manner as under section 954(i).

(4) All items of income, expenses, losses, and deductions shall be properly allocated or apportioned under regulations prescribed by the Secretary.

[Sec. 953(c)]

(c) SPECIAL RULE FOR CERTAIN CAPTIVE INSURANCE COMPANIES.—

(1) IN GENERAL.—For purposes only of taking into account related person insurance income—

(A) the term "United States shareholder" means, with respect to any foreign corporation, a United States person (as defined in section 957(c)) who owns (within the meaning of section 958(a)) any stock of the foreign corporation,

(B) the term "controlled foreign corporation" has the meaning given to such term by section 957(a) determined by substituting "25 percent or more" for "more than 50 percent", and

(C) the pro rata share referred to in section 951(a)(1)(A) shall be determined under paragraph (5) of this subsection.

(2) RELATED PERSON INSURANCE INCOME.—For purposes of this subsection, the term "related person insurance income" means any insurance income (within the meaning of subsection (a)) attributable to a policy of insurance or reinsurance with respect to which the person (directly or indirectly) insured is a United States shareholder in the foreign corporation or a related person to such a shareholder.

(3) EXCEPTIONS.—

(A) CORPORATIONS NOT HELD BY INSUREDS.—Paragraph (1) shall not apply to any foreign corporation if at all times during the taxable year of such foreign corporation—

(i) less than 20 percent of the total combined voting power of all classes of stock of such corporation entitled to vote, and

(ii) less than 20 percent of the total value of such corporation,

is owned (directly or indirectly under the principles of section 883(c)(4)) by persons who are (directly or indirectly) insured under any policy of insurance or reinsurance issued by such corporation or who are related persons to any such person.

(B) DE MINIMIS EXCEPTION.—Paragraph (1) shall not apply to any foreign corporation for a taxable year of such corporation if the related person insurance income (determined on a gross basis) of such corporation for such taxable year is less than 20 percent of its insurance income (as so determined) for such taxable year determined without regard to those provisions of subsection (a)(1) which limit insurance income to income from countries other than the country in which the corporation was created or organized.

(C) ELECTION TO TREAT INCOME AS EFFECTIVELY CONNECTED.—Paragraph (1) shall not apply to any foreign corporation for any taxable year if—

(i) such corporation elects (at such time and in such manner as the Secretary may prescribe)—

(I) to treat its related person insurance income for such taxable year as income effectively connected with the conduct of a trade or business in the United States, and

(II) to waive all benefits (other than with respect to section 884) with respect to related person insurance income granted by the United States under any treaty between the United States and any foreign country, and

(ii) such corporation meets such requirements as the Secretary shall prescribe to ensure that the tax imposed by this chapter on such income is paid.

An election under this subparagraph made for any taxable year shall not be effective if the corporation (or any predecessor thereof) was a disqualified corporation for the taxable year for which the election was made or for any prior taxable year beginning after 1986.

(D) SPECIAL RULES FOR SUBPARAGRAPH (C).—

(i) PERIOD DURING WHICH ELECTION IN EFFECT.—

(I) IN GENERAL.—Except as provided in subclause (II), any election under subparagraph (C) shall apply to the taxable year for which made and all subsequent taxable years unless revoked with the consent of the Secretary.

(II) TERMINATION.—If a foreign corporation which made an election under subparagraph (C) for any taxable year is a disqualified corporation for any subsequent taxable year, such election shall not apply to any taxable year beginning after such subsequent taxable year.

(ii) EXEMPTION FROM TAX IMPOSED BY SECTION 4371.—The tax imposed by section 4371 shall not apply with respect to any related person insurance income treated as effectively connected with the conduct of a trade or business within the United States under subparagraph (C).

(E) DISQUALIFIED CORPORATION.—For purposes of this paragraph the term "disqualified corporation" means, with respect to any taxable year, any foreign corporation which is a controlled foreign corporation for an uninterrupted period of 30 days or more during such taxable year (determined without regard to this subsection) but only if a United States shareholder (determined without regard to this subsection) owns (within the meaning of section 958(a)) stock in such corporation at some time during such taxable year.

(4) TREATMENT OF MUTUAL INSURANCE COMPANIES.—In the case of a mutual insurance company—

(A) this subsection shall apply,

(B) policyholders of such company shall be treated as shareholders, and

(C) appropriate adjustments in the application of this subpart shall be made under regulations prescribed by the Secretary.

(5) DETERMINATION OF PRO RATA SHARE.—

(A) IN GENERAL.—The pro rata share determined under this paragraph for any United States shareholder is the lesser of—

(i) the amount which would be determined under paragraph (2) of section 951(a) if—

(I) only related person insurance income were taken into account,

(II) stock owned (within the meaning of section 958(a)) by United States shareholders on the last day of the taxable year were the only stock in the foreign corporation, and

(III) only distributions received by United States shareholders were taken into account under subparagraph (B) of such paragraph (2), or

(ii) the amount which would be determined under paragraph (2) of section 951(a) if the entire earnings and profits of the foreign corporation for the taxable year were subpart F income.

(B) COORDINATION WITH OTHER PROVISIONS.—The Secretary shall prescribe regulations providing for such modifications to the provisions of this subpart as may be necessary or appropriate by reason of subparagraph (A).

(6) RELATED PERSON.—For purposes of this subsection—

(A) IN GENERAL.—Except as provided in subparagraph (B), the term "related person" has the meaning given such term by section 954(d)(3).

(B) TREATMENT OF CERTAIN LIABILITY INSURANCE POLICIES.—In the case of any policy of insurance covering liability arising from services performed as a director, officer, or employee of a corporation or as a partner or employee of a partnership, the person performing such services and the entity for which such services are performed shall be treated as related persons.

(7) COORDINATION WITH SECTION 1248.—For purposes of section 1248, if any person is (or would be but for paragraph (3)) treated under paragraph (1) as a United States shareholder with respect to any foreign corporation which would be taxed under subchapter L if it were a domestic corporation and which is (or would be but for paragraph (3)) treated under paragraph (1) as a controlled foreign corporation—

(A) such person shall be treated as meeting the stock ownership requirements of section 1248(a)(2) with respect to such foreign corporation, and

(B) such foreign corporation shall be treated as a controlled foreign corporation.

(8) REGULATIONS.—The Secretary shall prescribe such regulations as may be necessary to carry out the purposes of this subsection, including—

(A) regulations preventing the avoidance of this subsection through cross insurance arrangements or otherwise, and

(B) regulations which may provide that a person will not be treated as a United States shareholder under paragraph (1) with respect to any foreign corporation if neither such person (nor any related person to such person) is (directly or indirectly) insured under any policy of insurance or reinsurance issued by such foreign corporation.

[Sec. 953(d)]

(d) ELECTION BY FOREIGN INSURANCE COMPANY TO BE TREATED AS DOMESTIC CORPORATION.—

(1) IN GENERAL.—If—

(A) a foreign corporation is a controlled foreign corporation (as defined in section 957(a) by substituting "25 percent or more" for "more than 50 percent" and by using the definition of United States shareholder under 953(c)(1)(A)),

(B) such foreign corporation would qualify under part I or II of subchapter L for the taxable year if it were a domestic corporation,

(C) such foreign corporation meets such requirements as the Secretary shall prescribe to ensure that the taxes imposed by this chapter on such foreign corporation are paid, and

(D) such foreign corporation makes an election to have this paragraph apply and waives all benefits to such corporation granted by the United States under any treaty,

for purposes of this title, such corporation shall be treated as a domestic corporation.

(2) PERIOD DURING WHICH ELECTION IS IN EFFECT.—

(A) IN GENERAL.—Except as provided in subparagraph (B), an election under paragraph (1) shall apply to the taxable year for which made and all subsequent taxable years unless revoked with the consent of the Secretary.

(B) TERMINATION.—If a corporation which made an election under paragraph (1) for any taxable year fails to meet the requirements of subparagraphs (A), (B), and (C), of paragraph (1) for any subsequent taxable year, such election shall not apply to any taxable year beginning after such subsequent taxable year.

(3) TREATMENT OF LOSSES.—If any corporation treated as a domestic corporation under this subsection is treated as a member of an affiliated group for purposes of chapter 6 (relating to consolidated returns), any loss of such corporation shall be treated as a dual consolidated loss for purposes of section 1503(d) without regard to paragraph (2)(B) thereof.

(4) EFFECT OF ELECTION.—

(A) IN GENERAL.—For purposes of section 367, any foreign corporation making an election under paragraph (1) shall be treated as transferring (as of the 1st day of the 1st taxable year to which such election applies) all of its assets to a domestic corporation in connection with an exchange to which section 354 applies.

(B) EXCEPTION FOR PRE-1988 EARNINGS AND PROFIT.—

(i) IN GENERAL.—Earnings and profits of the foreign corporation accumulated in taxable years beginning before January 1, 1988, shall not be included in the gross income of the persons holding stock in such corporation by reason of subparagraph (A).

(ii) TREATMENT OF DISTRIBUTIONS.—For purposes of this title, any distribution made by a corporation to which an election under paragraph (1) applies out of earnings and profits accumulated in taxable years beginning before January 1, 1988, shall be treated as a distribution made by a foreign corporation.

(iii) CERTAIN RULES TO CONTINUE TO APPLY TO PRE-1988 EARNINGS.—The provisions specified in clause (iv) shall be applied without regard to paragraph (1), except that, in the case of a corporation to which an election under paragraph (1) applies, only earnings and profits accumulated in taxable years beginning before January 1, 1988, shall be taken into account.

(iv) SPECIFIED PROVISIONS.—The provisions specified in this clause are:

(I) Section 1248 (relating to gain from certain sales or exchanges of stock in certain foreign corporations).

(II) Subpart F of part III of subchapter N to the extent such subpart relates to earnings invested in United States property.

(III) Section 884 to the extent the foreign corporation reinvested 1987 earnings and profits in United States assets.

(5) EFFECT OF TERMINATION.—For purposes of section 367, if—

(A) an election is made by a corporation under paragraph (1) for any taxable year, and

(B) such election ceases to apply for any subsequent taxable year,

such corporation shall be treated as a domestic corporation transferring (as of the 1st day of such subsequent taxable year) all of its property to a foreign corporation in connection with an exchange to which section 354 applies.

(6) ADDITIONAL TAX ON CORPORATION MAKING ELECTION.—

(A) IN GENERAL.—If a corporation makes an election under paragraph (1), the amount of tax imposed by this chapter for the 1st taxable year to which such election applies shall be increased by the amount determined under subparagraph (B).

(B) AMOUNT OF TAX.—The amount of tax determined under this paragraph shall be equal to the lesser of—

(i) $^{3}/_{4}$ of 1 percent of the aggregate amount of capital and accumulated surplus of the corporation as of December 31, 1987, or

(ii) $1,500,000.

[Sec. 953(e)]

(e) EXEMPT INSURANCE INCOME.—For purposes of this section—

(1) EXEMPT INSURANCE INCOME DEFINED.—

(A) IN GENERAL.—The term "exempt insurance income" means income derived by a qualifying insurance company which—

(i) is attributable to the issuing (or reinsuring) of an exempt contract by such company or a qualifying insurance company branch of such company, and

(ii) is treated as earned by such company or branch in its home country for purposes of such country's tax laws.

(B) EXCEPTION FOR CERTAIN ARRANGEMENTS.—Such term shall not include income attributable to the issuing (or reinsuring) of an exempt contract as the result of any arrangement whereby another corporation receives a substantially equal amount of premiums or other consideration in respect of issuing (or reinsuring) a contract which is not an exempt contract.

(C) DETERMINATIONS MADE SEPARATELY.—For purposes of this subsection and section 954(i), the exempt insurance income and exempt contracts of a qualifying insurance company or any qualifying insurance company branch of such company shall be determined separately for such company and each such branch by taking into account—

(i) in the case of the qualifying insurance company, only items of income, deduction, gain, or loss, and activities of such company not properly allocable or attributable to any qualifying insurance company branch of such company, and

(ii) in the case of a qualifying insurance company branch, only items of income, deduction, gain, or loss and activities properly allocable or attributable to such branch.

(2) EXEMPT CONTRACT.—

(A) IN GENERAL.—The term "exempt contract" means an insurance or annuity contract issued or reinsured by a qualifying insurance company or qualifying insurance company branch in connection with property in, liability arising out of activity in, or the lives or health of residents of, a country other than the United States.

(B) MINIMUM HOME COUNTRY INCOME REQUIRED.—

(i) IN GENERAL.—No contract of a qualifying insurance company or of a qualifying insurance company branch shall be treated as an exempt contract unless such company or branch derives more than 30 percent of its net written premiums from exempt contracts (determined without regard to this subparagraph)—

(I) which cover applicable home country risks, and

(II) with respect to which no policyholder, insured, annuitant, or beneficiary is a related person (as defined in section 954(d)(3)).

(ii) APPLICABLE HOME COUNTRY RISKS.—The term "applicable home country risks" means risks in connection with property in, liability arising out of activity in, or the lives or health of residents of, the home country of the qualifying insurance company or qualifying insurance company branch, as the case may be, issuing or reinsuring the contract covering the risks.

(C) SUBSTANTIAL ACTIVITY REQUIREMENTS FOR CROSS BORDER RISKS.—A contract issued by a qualifying insurance company or qualifying insurance company branch which covers risks other than applicable home country risks (as defined in subparagraph (B)(ii)) shall not be treated as an exempt contract unless such company or branch, as the case may be—

(i) conducts substantial activity with respect to an insurance business in its home country, and

(ii) performs in its home country substantially all of the activities necessary to give rise to the income generated by such contract.

(3) QUALIFYING INSURANCE COMPANY.—The term "qualifying insurance company" means any controlled foreign corporation which—

(A) is subject to regulation as an insurance (or reinsurance) company by its home country, and is licensed, authorized, or regulated by the applicable insurance regulatory body for its home country to sell insurance, reinsurance, or annuity contracts to persons other than related persons (within the meaning of section 954(d)(3)) in such home country,

(B) derives more than 50 percent of its aggregate net written premiums from the issuance or reinsurance by such controlled foreign corporation and each of its qualifying insurance company branches of contracts—

(i) covering applicable home country risks (as defined in paragraph (2)) of such corporation or branch, as the case may be, and

(ii) with respect to which no policyholder, insured, annuitant, or beneficiary is a related person (as defined in section 954(d)(3)),

except that in the case of a branch, such premiums shall only be taken into account to the extent such premiums are treated as earned by such branch in its home country for purposes of such country's tax laws, and

(C) is engaged in the insurance business and would be subject to tax under subchapter L if it were a domestic corporation.

(4) QUALIFYING INSURANCE COMPANY BRANCH.—The term "qualifying insurance company branch" means a qualified business unit (within the meaning of section 989(a)) of a controlled foreign corporation if—

(A) such unit is licensed, authorized, or regulated by the applicable insurance regulatory body for its home country to sell insurance, reinsurance, or annuity contracts to persons other than related persons (within the meaning of section 954(d)(3)) in such home country, and

(B) such controlled foreign corporation is a qualifying insurance company, determined under paragraph (3) as if such unit were a qualifying insurance company branch.

(5) LIFE INSURANCE OR ANNUITY CONTRACT.—For purposes of this section and section 954, the determination of whether a contract issued by a controlled foreign corporation or a qualified business unit (within the meaning of section 989(a)) is a life insurance contract or an annuity contract shall be made without regard to sections 72(s), 101(f), 817(h), and 7702 if—

(A) such contract is regulated as a life insurance or annuity contract by the corporation's or unit's home country, and

(B) no policyholder, insured, annuitant, or beneficiary with respect to the contract is a United States person.

(6) HOME COUNTRY.—For purposes of this subsection, except as provided in regulations—

(A) CONTROLLED FOREIGN CORPORATION.—The term "home country" means, with respect to a controlled foreign corporation, the country in which such corporation is created or organized.

(B) QUALIFIED BUSINESS UNIT.—The term "home country" means, with respect to a qualified business unit (as defined in section 989(a)), the country in which the principal office of such unit is located and in which such unit is licensed, authorized, or regulated by the applicable insurance regulatory body to sell insurance, reinsurance, or annuity contracts to persons other than related persons (as defined in section 954(d)(3)) in such country.

(7) ANTI-ABUSE RULES.—For purposes of applying this subsection and section 954(i)—

(A) the rules of section 954(h)(7) (other than subparagraph (B) thereof) shall apply,

(B) there shall be disregarded any item of income, gain, loss, or deduction of, or derived from, an entity which is not engaged in regular and continuous transactions with persons which are not related persons,

(C) there shall be disregarded any change in the method of computing reserves a principal purpose of which is the acceleration or deferral of any item in order to claim the benefits of this subsection or section 954(i),

(D) a contract of insurance or reinsurance shall not be treated as an exempt contract (and premiums from such contract shall not be taken into account for purposes of paragraph (2)(B) or (3)) if—

(i) any policyholder, insured, annuitant, or beneficiary is a resident of the United States and such contract was marketed to such resident and was written to cover a risk outside the United States, or

(ii) the contract covers risks located within and without the United States and the qualifying insurance company or qualifying insurance company branch does not maintain such contemporaneous records, and file such reports, with respect to such contract as the Secretary may require,

(E) the Secretary may prescribe rules for the allocation of contracts (and income from contracts) among 2 or more qualifying insurance company branches of a qualifying insurance company in order to clearly reflect the income of such branches, and

(F) premiums from a contract shall not be taken into account for purposes of paragraph (2)(B) or (3) if such contract reinsures a contract issued or reinsured by a related person (as defined in section 954(d)(3)).

For purposes of subparagraph (D), the determination of where risks are located shall be made under the principles of section 953.

(8) COORDINATION WITH SUBSECTION (c).—In determining insurance income for purposes of subsection (c), exempt insurance income shall not include income derived from exempt contracts which cover risks other than applicable home country risks.

(9) REGULATIONS.—The Secretary shall prescribe such regulations as may be necessary or appropriate to carry out the purposes of this subsection and section 954(i).

(10) CROSS REFERENCE.—

For income exempt from foreign personal holding company income, see section 954(i).

[Sec. 954]

SEC. 954. FOREIGN BASE COMPANY INCOME.

[Sec. 954(a)]

(a) FOREIGN BASE COMPANY INCOME.—For purposes of section 952(a)(2), the term "foreign base company income" means for any taxable year the sum of—

(1) the foreign personal holding company income for the taxable year (determined under subsection (c) and reduced as provided in subsection (b)(5)),

(2) the foreign base company sales income for the taxable year (determined under subsection (d) and reduced as provided in subsection (b)(5)), and

(3) the foreign base company services income for the taxable year (determined under subsection (e) and reduced as provided in subsection (b)(5)).

[Sec. 954(b)]

(b) EXCLUSIONS AND SPECIAL RULES.—

(1) [Stricken]

(2) [Stricken]

(3) DE MINIMIS, ETC., RULES.—For purposes of subsection (a) and section 953—

(A) DE MINIMIS RULE.—If the sum of foreign base company income (determined without regard to paragraph (5)) and the gross insurance income for the taxable year is less than the lesser of—

(i) 5 percent of gross income, or

(ii) $1,000,000,

no part of the gross income for the taxable year shall be treated as foreign base company income or insurance income.

(B) FOREIGN BASE COMPANY INCOME AND INSURANCE INCOME IN EXCESS OF 70 PERCENT OF GROSS INCOME.—If the sum of the foreign base company income (determined without regard to paragraph (5)) and the gross insurance income for the taxable year exceeds 70 percent of gross income, the entire gross income for the taxable year shall, subject to the provisions of paragraphs (4) and (5), be treated as foreign base company income or insurance income (whichever is appropriate).

(C) GROSS INSURANCE INCOME.—For purposes of subparagraphs (A) and (B), the term "gross insurance income" means any item of gross income taken into account in determining insurance income under section 953.

(4) EXCEPTION FOR CERTAIN INCOME SUBJECT TO HIGH FOREIGN TAXES.—For purposes of subsection (a) and section 953, foreign base company income and insurance income shall not include any item of income received by a controlled foreign corporation if the taxpayer establishes to the satisfaction of the Secretary that such income was subject to an effective rate of income tax imposed by a foreign country greater than 90 percent of the maximum rate of tax specified in section 11.

(5) DEDUCTIONS TO BE TAKEN INTO ACCOUNT.—For purposes of subsection (a), the foreign personal holding company income, the foreign base company sales income, and the foreign base company services income shall be reduced, under regulations prescribed by the Secretary, so as to take into account deductions (including taxes) properly allocable to such income. Except to the extent provided in regulations prescribed by the Secretary, any interest which is paid or accrued by the controlled foreign corporation to any United States shareholder in such corporation (or any controlled foreign corporation related to such a shareholder) shall be allocated first to foreign personal holding company income which is passive income (within the meaning of section 904(d)(2)) of such corporation to the extent thereof. The Secretary may, by regulations, provide that the preceding sentence shall apply also to interest paid or accrued to other persons.

[Sec. 954(c)]

(c) FOREIGN PERSONAL HOLDING COMPANY INCOME.—

(1) IN GENERAL.—For purposes of subsection (a)(1), the term "foreign personal holding company income" means the portion of the gross income which consists of:

(A) DIVIDENDS, ETC.—Dividends, interest, royalties, rents, and annuities.

(B) CERTAIN PROPERTY TRANSACTIONS.—The excess of gains over losses from the sale or exchange of property—

(i) which gives rise to income described in subparagraph (A) (after application of paragraph (2)(A)) other than property which gives rise to income not treated as foreign personal holding company income by reason of subsection (h) or (i) for the taxable year,

(ii) which is an interest in a trust, partnership, or REMIC, or

(iii) which does not give rise to any income.

Gains and losses from the sale or exchange of any property which, in the hands of the controlled foreign corporation, is properly described in section 1221(a)(1) shall not be taken into account under this subparagraph.

(C) COMMODITIES TRANSACTIONS.—The excess of gains over losses from transactions (including futures, forward, and similar transactions) in any commodities. This subparagraph shall not apply to gains or losses which—

(i) arise out of commodity hedging transactions (as defined in paragraph (5)(A)),

(ii) are active business gains or losses from the sale of commodities, but only if substantially all of the controlled foreign corporation's commodities are property described in paragraph (1), (2), or (8) of section 1221(a), or

(iii) are foreign currency gains or losses (as defined in section 988(b)) attributable to any section 988 transactions.

(D) FOREIGN CURRENCY GAINS.—The excess of foreign currency gains over foreign currency losses (as defined in section 988(b)) attributable to any section 988 transactions. This subparagraph shall not apply in the case of any transaction directly related to the business needs of the controlled foreign corporation.

(E) INCOME EQUIVALENT TO INTEREST.—Any income equivalent to interest, including income from commitment fees (or similar amounts) for loans actually made.

(F) INCOME FROM NOTIONAL PRINCIPAL CONTRACTS.—

(i) IN GENERAL.—Net income from notional principal contracts.

(ii) COORDINATION WITH OTHER CATEGORIES OF FOREIGN PERSONAL HOLDING COMPANY INCOME.—Any item of income, gain, deduction, or loss from a notional principal contract entered into for purposes of hedging any item described in any preceding subparagraph shall not be taken into account for purposes of this subparagraph but shall be taken into account under such other subparagraph.

(G) PAYMENTS IN LIEU OF DIVIDENDS.—Payments in lieu of dividends which are made pursuant to an agreement to which section 1058 applies.

(H) PERSONAL SERVICE CONTRACTS.—

(i) Amounts received under a contract under which the corporation is to furnish personal services if—

(I) some person other than the corporation has the right to designate (by name or by description) the individual who is to perform the services, or

(II) the individual who is to perform the services is designated (by name or by description) in the contract, and

(ii) amounts received from the sale or other disposition of such a contract.

This subparagraph shall apply with respect to amounts received for services under a particular contract only if at some time during the taxable year 25 percent or more in value of the outstanding stock of the corporation is owned, directly or indirectly, by or for the individual who has performed, is to perform, or may be designated (by name or by description) as the one to perform, such services.

(2) EXCEPTION FOR CERTAIN AMOUNTS.—

(A) RENTS AND ROYALTIES DERIVED IN ACTIVE BUSINESS.—Foreign personal holding company income shall not include rents and royalties which are derived in the active conduct of a trade or business and which are received from a person other than a related person (within the meaning of subsection (d)(3)). For purposes of the preceding sentence, rents derived from leasing an aircraft or vessel in foreign commerce shall not fail to be treated as derived in the active conduct of a trade or business if, as determined under regulations prescribed by the Secretary, the active leasing expenses are not less than 10 percent of the profit on the lease.

(B) CERTAIN EXPORT FINANCING.—Foreign personal holding company income shall not include any interest which is derived in the conduct of a banking business and which is export financing interest (as defined in section 904(d)(2)(G)).

(C) EXCEPTION FOR DEALERS.—Except as provided by regulations, in the case of a regular dealer in property which is property described in paragraph (1)(B), forward contracts, option contracts, or similar financial instruments (including notional principal contracts and all instruments referenced to commodities), there shall not be taken into account in computing foreign personal holding company income—

(i) any item of income, gain, deduction, or loss (other than any item described in subparagraph (A), (E), or (G) of paragraph (1)) from any transaction (including hedging transactions and transactions involving physical settlement) entered into in the ordinary course of such dealer's trade or business as such a dealer, and

(ii) if such dealer is a dealer in securities (within the meaning of section 475), any interest or dividend or equivalent amount described in subparagraph (E) or (G) of paragraph (1) from any transaction (including any hedging transaction or transaction described in section 956(c)(2)(I)) entered into in the ordinary course of such dealer's trade or business as such a dealer in securities, but only if the income from the transaction is attributable to activities of the dealer in the country under the laws of which the dealer is created or organized (or in the case of a qualified business unit described in section 989(a), is attributable to activities of the unit in the country in which the unit both maintains its principal office and conducts substantial business activity).

(3) CERTAIN INCOME RECEIVED FROM RELATED PERSONS.—

(A) IN GENERAL.—Except as provided in subparagraph (B), the term "foreign personal holding company income" does not include—

(i) dividends and interest received from a related person which (I) is a corporation created or organized under the laws of the same foreign country under the laws of which the controlled foreign corporation is created or organized, and (II) has a substantial part of its assets used in its trade or business located in such same foreign country, and

(ii) rents and royalties received from a corporation which is a related person for the use of, or the privilege of using, property within the country under the laws of which the controlled foreign corporation is created or organized.

To the extent provided in regulations, payments made by a partnership with 1 or more corporate partners shall be treated as made by such corporate partners in proportion to their respective interests in the partnership.

(B) EXCEPTION NOT TO APPLY TO ITEMS WHICH REDUCE SUBPART F INCOME.—Subparagraph (A) shall not apply in the case of any interest, rent, or royalty to the extent such interest, rent, or royalty reduces the payor's subpart F income or creates (or increases) a deficit which under section 952(c) may reduce the subpart F income of the payor or another controlled foreign corporation.

(C) EXCEPTION FOR CERTAIN DIVIDENDS.—Subparagraph (A)(i) shall not apply to any dividend with respect to any stock which is attributable to earnings and profits of the distributing corporation accumulated during any period during which the person receiving such dividend did not hold such stock either directly, or indirectly through a chain of one or more subsidiaries each of which meets the requirements of subparagraph (A)(i).

(4) LOOK-THRU RULE FOR CERTAIN PARTNERSHIP SALES.—

(A) IN GENERAL.—In the case of any sale by a controlled foreign corporation of an interest in a partnership with respect to which such corporation is a 25-percent owner, such corporation shall be treated for purposes of this subsection as selling the proportionate share of the assets of the partnership attributable to such interest. The Secretary shall prescribe such regulations as may be appropriate to prevent abuse of the purposes of this paragraph, including regulations providing for coordination of this paragraph with the provisions of subchapter K.

(B) 25-PERCENT OWNER.—For purposes of this paragraph, the term "25-percent owner" means a controlled foreign corporation which owns directly 25 percent or more of the capital or profits interest in a partnership. For purposes of the preceding sentence, if a controlled foreign corporation is a shareholder or partner of a corporation or partnership, the controlled foreign corporation shall be treated as owning directly its proportionate share of any such capital or profits interest held directly or indirectly by such corporation or partnership. If a controlled foreign corporation is treated as owning a capital or profits interest in a partnership under constructive ownership rules similar to the rules of section 958(b), the controlled foreign corporation shall be treated as owning such interest directly for purposes of this subparagraph.

(5) DEFINITION AND SPECIAL RULES RELATING TO COMMODITY TRANSACTIONS.—

(A) COMMODITY HEDGING TRANSACTIONS.—For purposes of paragraph (1)(C)(i), the term "commodity hedging transaction" means any transaction with respect to a commodity if such transaction—

(i) is a hedging transaction as defined in section 1221(b)(2), determined—

(I) without regard to subparagraph (A)(ii) thereof,

(II) by applying subparagraph (A)(i) thereof by substituting "ordinary property or property described in section 1231(b)" for "ordinary property", and

(III) by substituting "controlled foreign corporation" for "taxpayer" each place it appears, and

(ii) is clearly identified as such in accordance with section 1221(a)(7).

(B) TREATMENT OF DEALER ACTIVITIES UNDER PARAGRAPH (1)(C).—Commodities with respect to which gains and losses are not taken into account under paragraph (2)(C) in computing a controlled foreign corporation's foreign personal holding company income shall not be taken into account in applying the substantially all test under paragraph (1)(C)(ii) to such corporation.

(C) REGULATIONS.—The Secretary shall prescribe such regulations as are appropriate to carry out the purposes of paragraph (1)(C) in the case of transactions involving related parties.

(6) LOOK-THRU RULE FOR RELATED CONTROLLED FOREIGN CORPORATIONS.—

(A) IN GENERAL.—For purposes of this subsection, dividends, interest, rents, and royalties received or accrued from a controlled foreign corporation which is a related person shall not be treated as foreign personal holding company income to the extent attributable or properly allocable (determined under rules similar to the rules of subparagraphs (C) and (D) of section 904(d)(3)) to income of the related person which is neither subpart F income nor income treated as effectively connected with the conduct of a trade or business in the United States. For purposes of this subparagraph, interest shall include factoring income which is treated as income equivalent to interest for purposes of paragraph (1)(E). The Secretary shall prescribe such regulations as may be necessary or appropriate to carry out this paragraph, including such regulations as may be necessary or appropriate to prevent the abuse of the purposes of this paragraph.

(B) EXCEPTION.—Subparagraph (A) shall not apply in the case of any interest, rent, or royalty to the extent such interest, rent, or royalty creates (or increases) a deficit which under section 952(c) may reduce the subpart F income of the payor or another controlled foreign corporation.

(C) APPLICATION.—Subparagraph (A) shall apply to taxable years of foreign corporations beginning after December 31, 2005, and before January 1, 2026, and to taxable years of United States shareholders with or within which such taxable years of foreign corporations end.

[Sec. 954(d)]

(d) FOREIGN BASE COMPANY SALES INCOME.—

(1) IN GENERAL.—For purposes of subsection (a)(2), the term "foreign base company sales income" means income (whether in the form of profits, commissions, fees, or otherwise) derived in connection with the purchase of personal property from a related person and its sale to any person, the sale of personal property to any person on behalf of a related person, the purchase of personal property from any person and its sale to a related person, or the purchase of personal property from any person on behalf of a related person where—

(A) the property which is purchased (or in the case of property sold on behalf of a related person, the property which is sold) is manufactured, produced, grown, or extracted outside the country under the laws of which the controlled foreign corporation is created or organized, and

(B) the property is sold for use, consumption, or disposition outside such foreign country, or, in the case of property purchased on behalf of a related person, is purchased for use, consumption, or disposition outside such foreign country.

For purposes of this subsection, personal property does not include agricultural commodities which are not grown in the United States in commercially marketable quantities.

(2) CERTAIN BRANCH INCOME.—For purposes of determining foreign base company sales income in situations in which the carrying on of activities by a controlled foreign corporation through a branch or similar establishment outside the country of incorporation of the controlled foreign corporation has substantially the same effect as if such branch or similar establishment were a wholly owned subsidiary corporation deriving such income, under regulations prescribed by the Secretary the income attributable to the carrying on of such activities of such branch or similar establishment shall be treated as income derived by a wholly owned subsidiary of the controlled foreign corporation and shall constitute foreign base company sales income of the controlled foreign corporation.

(3) RELATED PERSON DEFINED.—For purposes of this section, a person is a related person with respect to a controlled foreign corporation, if—

(A) such person is an individual, corporation, partnership, trust, or estate which controls, or is controlled by, the controlled foreign corporation, or

(B) such person is a corporation, partnership, trust, or estate which is controlled by the same person or persons which control the controlled foreign corporation.

For purposes of the preceding sentence, control means, with respect to a corporation, the ownership, directly or indirectly, of stock possessing more than 50 percent of the total voting power of all classes of stock entitled to vote or of the total value of stock of such corporation. In the case of a partnership, trust, or estate, control means the ownership, directly or indirectly, more than 50 percent (by value) of the beneficial interests in such partnership, trust, or estate. For purposes of this paragraph, rules similar to the rules of section 958 shall apply.

(4) SPECIAL RULE FOR CERTAIN TIMBER PRODUCTS.—For purposes of subsection (a)(2), the term "foreign base company sales income" includes any income (whether in the form of profits, commissions, fees, or otherwise) derived in connection with—

(A) the sale of any unprocessed timber referred to in section 865(b), or

(B) the milling of any such timber outside the United States.

Subpart G shall not apply to any amount treated as subpart F income by reason of this paragraph.

[Sec. 954(e)]

(e) FOREIGN BASE COMPANY SERVICES INCOME.—

(1) IN GENERAL.—For purposes of subsection (a)(3), the term "foreign base company services income" means income (whether in the form of compensation, commissions, fees, or otherwise) derived in connection with the performance of technical, managerial, engineering, architectural, scientific, skilled, industrial, commercial, or like services which—

(A) are performed for or on behalf of any related person (within the meaning of subsection (d)(3)), and

(B) are performed outside the country under the laws of which the controlled foreign corporation is created or organized.

(2) EXCEPTION.—Paragraph (1) shall not apply to income derived in connection with the performance of services which are directly related to—

(A) the sale or exchange by the controlled foreign corporation of property manufactured, produced, grown, or extracted by it and which are performed before the time of the sale or exchange, or

(B) an offer or effort to sell or exchange such property.

Paragraph (1) shall also not apply to income which is exempt insurance income (as defined in section 953(e)) or which is not treated as foreign personal holding income by reason of subsection (c)(2)(C)(ii), (h), or (i).

[Sec. 954(f)—Stricken]

[Sec. 954(g)—Stricken]

[Sec. 954(h)]

(h) SPECIAL RULE FOR INCOME DERIVED IN THE ACTIVE CONDUCT OF BANKING, FINANCING, OR SIMILAR BUSINESSES.—

(1) IN GENERAL.—For purposes of subsection (c)(1), foreign personal holding company income shall not include qualified banking or financing income of an eligible controlled foreign corporation.

(2) ELIGIBLE CONTROLLED FOREIGN CORPORATION.—For purposes of this subsection—

(A) IN GENERAL.—The term "eligible controlled foreign corporation" means a controlled foreign corporation which—

(i) is predominantly engaged in the active conduct of a banking, financing, or similar business, and

(ii) conducts substantial activity with respect to such business.

(B) PREDOMINANTLY ENGAGED.—A controlled foreign corporation shall be treated as predominantly engaged in the active conduct of a banking, financing, or similar business if—

(i) more than 70 percent of the gross income of the controlled foreign corporation is derived directly from the active and regular conduct of a lending or finance business from transactions with customers which are not related persons,

(ii) it is engaged in the active conduct of a banking business and is an institution licensed to do business as a bank in the United States (or is any other corporation not so licensed which is specified by the Secretary in regulations), or

(iii) it is engaged in the active conduct of a securities business and is registered as a securities broker or dealer under section 15(a) of the Securities Exchange Act of 1934 or is registered as a Government securities broker or dealer under section 15C(a) of such Act (or is any other corporation not so registered which is specified by the Secretary in regulations).

(3) QUALIFIED BANKING OR FINANCING INCOME.—For purposes of this subsection—

(A) IN GENERAL.—The term "qualified banking or financing income" means income of an eligible controlled foreign corporation which—

(i) is derived in the active conduct of a banking, financing, or similar business by—

(I) such eligible controlled foreign corporation, or

(II) a qualified business unit of such eligible controlled foreign corporation,

(ii) is derived from one or more transactions—

(I) with customers located in a country other than the United States, and

(II) substantially all of the activities in connection with which are conducted directly by the corporation or unit in its home country, and

(iii) is treated as earned by such corporation or unit in its home country for purposes of such country's tax laws.

(B) LIMITATION ON NONBANKING AND NONSECURITIES BUSINESSES.—No income of an eligible controlled foreign corporation not described in clause (ii) or (iii) of paragraph (2)(B) (or of a qualified business unit of such corporation) shall be treated as qualified banking or financing income unless more than 30 percent of such corporation's or unit's gross income is derived directly from the active and regular conduct of a lending or finance business from transactions with customers which are not related persons and which are located within such corporation's or unit's home country.

(C) SUBSTANTIAL ACTIVITY REQUIREMENT FOR CROSS BORDER INCOME.—The term "qualified banking or financing income" shall not include income derived from 1 or more transactions with customers located in a country other than the home country of the eligible controlled foreign corporation or a qualified business unit of such corporation unless such corporation or unit conducts substantial activity with respect to a banking, financing, or similar business in its home country.

(D) DETERMINATIONS MADE SEPARATELY.—For purposes of this paragraph, the qualified banking or financing income of an eligible controlled foreign corporation and each qualified business unit of such corporation shall be determined separately for such corporation and each such unit by taking into account

(i) in the case of the eligible controlled foreign corporation, only items of income, deduction, gain, or loss and activities of such corporation not properly allocable or attributable to any qualified business unit of such corporation, and

(ii) in the case of a qualified business unit, only items of income, deduction, gain, or loss and activities properly allocable or attributable to such unit.

(E) DIRECT CONDUCT OF ACTIVITIES.—For purposes of subparagraph (A)(ii)(II), an activity shall be treated as conducted directly by an eligible controlled foreign corporation or qualified business unit in its home country if the activity is performed by employees of a related person and—

(i) the related person is an eligible controlled foreign corporation the home country of which is the same as the home country of the corporation or unit to which subparagraph (A)(ii)(II) is being applied,

(ii) the activity is performed in the home country of the related person, and

(iii) the related person is compensated on an arm's-length basis for the performance of the activity by its employees and such compensation is treated as earned by such person in its home country for purposes of the home country's tax laws.

(4) LENDING OR FINANCE BUSINESS.—For purposes of this subsection, the term "lending or finance business" means the business of—

(A) making loans,

(B) purchasing or discounting accounts receivable, notes, or installment obligations,

(C) engaging in leasing (including entering into leases and purchasing, servicing, and disposing of leases and leased assets),

(D) issuing letters of credit or providing guarantees,

(E) providing charge and credit card services, or

(F) rendering services or making facilities available in connection with activities described in subparagraphs (A) through (E) carried on by—

(i) the corporation (or qualified business unit) rendering services or making facilities available, or

(ii) another corporation (or qualified business unit of a corporation) which is a member of the same affiliated group (as defined in section 1504, but determined without regard to section 1504(b)(3)).

(5) OTHER DEFINITIONS.—For purposes of this subsection—

(A) CUSTOMER.—The term "customer" means, with respect to any controlled foreign corporation or qualified business unit, any person which has a customer relationship with such corporation or unit and which is acting in its capacity as such.

(B) HOME COUNTRY.—Except as provided in regulations—

(i) CONTROLLED FOREIGN CORPORATION.—The term "home country" means, with respect to any controlled foreign corporation, the country under the laws of which the corporation was created or organized.

(ii) QUALIFIED BUSINESS UNIT.—The term "home country" means, with respect to any qualified business unit, the country in which such unit maintains its principal office.

(C) LOCATED.—The determination of where a customer is located shall be made under rules prescribed by the Secretary.

(D) QUALIFIED BUSINESS UNIT.—The term "qualified business unit" has the meaning given such term by section 989(a).

(E) RELATED PERSON.—The term "related person" has the meaning given such term by subsection (d)(3).

(6) COORDINATION WITH EXCEPTION FOR DEALERS.—Paragraph (1) shall not apply to income described in subsection (c)(2)(C)(ii) of a dealer in securities (within the meaning of section 475) which is an eligible controlled foreign corporation described in paragraph (2)(B)(iii).

(7) ANTI-ABUSE RULES.—For purposes of applying this subsection and subsection (c)(2)(C)(ii)—

(A) there shall be disregarded any item of income, gain, loss, or deduction with respect to any transaction or series of transactions one of the principal purposes of which is qualifying income or gain for the exclusion under this section, including any transaction or series of transactions a principal purpose of which is the acceleration or deferral of any item in order to claim the benefits of such exclusion through the application of this subsection,

(B) there shall be disregarded any item of income, gain, loss, or deduction of an entity which is not engaged in regular and continuous transactions with customers which are not related persons,

(C) there shall be disregarded any item of income, gain, loss, or deduction with respect to any transaction or series of transactions utilizing, or doing business with—

(i) one or more entities in order to satisfy any home country requirement under this subsection, or

(ii) a special purpose entity or arrangement, including a securitization, financing, or similar entity or arrangement,

if one of the principal purposes of such transaction or series of transactions is qualifying income or gain for the exclusion under this subsection, and

(D) a related person, an officer, a director, or an employee with respect to any controlled foreign corporation (or qualified business unit) which would otherwise be treated as a customer of such corporation or unit with respect to any transaction shall not be so treated if a principal purpose of such transaction is to satisfy any requirement of this subsection.

(8) REGULATIONS.—The Secretary shall prescribe such regulations as may be necessary or appropriate to carry out the purposes of this subsection, subsection (c)(1)(B)(i), subsection (c)(2)(C)(ii), and the last sentence of subsection (e)(2).

[Sec. 954(i)]

(i) SPECIAL RULE FOR INCOME DERIVED IN THE ACTIVE CONDUCT OF INSURANCE BUSINESS.—

(1) IN GENERAL.—For purposes of subsection (c)(1), foreign personal holding company income shall not include qualified insurance income of a qualifying insurance company.

(2) QUALIFIED INSURANCE INCOME.—The term "qualified insurance income" means income of a qualifying insurance company which is—

(A) received from a person other than a related person (within the meaning of subsection (d)(3)) and derived from the investments made by a qualifying insurance company or a qualifying insurance company branch of its reserves allocable to exempt contracts or of 80 percent of its unearned premiums from exempt contracts (as both are determined in the manner prescribed under paragraph (4)), or

(B) received from a person other than a related person (within the meaning of subsection (d)(3)) and derived from investments made by a qualifying insurance company or a qualifying insurance company branch of an amount of its assets allocable to exempt contracts equal to—

(i) in the case of property, casualty, or health insurance contracts, one-third of its premiums earned on such insurance contracts during the taxable year (as defined in section 832(b)(4)), and

(ii) in the case of life insurance or annuity contracts, 10 percent of the reserves described in subparagraph (A) for such contracts.

(3) PRINCIPLES FOR DETERMINING INSURANCE INCOME.—Except as provided by the Secretary, for purposes of subparagraphs (A) and (B) of paragraph (2)—

(A) in the case of any contract which is a separate account-type contract (including any variable contract not meeting the requirements of section 817), income credited under such contract shall be allocable only to such contract, and

(B) income not allocable under subparagraph (A) shall be allocated ratably among contracts not described in subparagraph (A).

(4) METHODS FOR DETERMINING UNEARNED PREMIUMS AND RESERVES.—For purposes of paragraph (2)(A)—

(A) PROPERTY AND CASUALTY CONTRACTS.—The unearned premiums and reserves of a qualifying insurance company or a qualifying insurance company branch with respect to property, casualty, or health insurance contracts shall be determined using the same methods and interest rates which would be used if such company or branch were subject to tax under subchapter L, except that—

(i) the interest rate determined for the functional currency of the company or branch, and which, except as provided by the Secretary, is calculated in the same manner as the Federal mid-term rate under section 1274(d), shall be substituted for the applicable Federal interest rate, and

(ii) such company or branch shall use the appropriate foreign loss payment pattern.

(B) LIFE INSURANCE AND ANNUITY CONTRACTS.—

(i) IN GENERAL.—Except as provided in clause (ii), the amount of the reserve of a qualifying insurance company or qualifying insurance company branch for any life insurance or annuity contract shall be equal to the greater of—

(I) the net surrender value of such contract (as defined in section 807(e)(1)(A)), or

(II) the reserve determined under paragraph (5).

(ii) RULING REQUEST, ETC.—The amount of the reserve under clause (i) shall be the foreign statement reserve for the contract (less any catastrophe, deficiency, equalization, or similar reserves), if, pursuant to a ruling request submitted by the taxpayer or as provided in published guidance, the Secretary determines that the factors taken into account in determining the foreign statement reserve provide an appropriate means of measuring income.

(C) LIMITATION ON RESERVES.—In no event shall the reserve determined under this paragraph for any contract as of any time exceed the amount which would be taken into account with respect to such contract as of such time in determining foreign statement reserves (less any catastrophe, deficiency, equalization, or similar reserves).

(5) AMOUNT OF RESERVE.—The amount of the reserve determined under this paragraph with respect to any contract shall be determined in the same manner as it would be determined if the qualifying insurance company or qualifying insurance company branch were subject to tax under subchapter L, except that in applying such subchapter—

(A) the interest rate determined for the functional currency of the company or branch, and which, except as provided by the Secretary, is calculated in the same manner as the Federal mid-term rate under section 1274(d), shall be substituted for the applicable Federal interest rate,

(B) the highest assumed interest rate permitted to be used in determining foreign statement reserves shall apply, and

(C) tables for mortality and morbidity which reasonably reflect the current mortality and morbidity risks in the company's or branch's home country shall be substituted for the mortality and morbidity tables otherwise used for such subchapter.

The Secretary may provide that the interest rate and mortality and morbidity tables of a qualifying insurance company may be used for 1 or more of its qualifying insurance company branches when appropriate.

(6) DEFINITIONS.—For purposes of this subsection, any term used in this subsection which is also used in section 953(e) shall have the meaning given such term by section 953.

[Sec. 956]

SEC. 956. INVESTMENT OF EARNINGS IN UNITED STATES PROPERTY.

[Sec. 956(a)]

(a) GENERAL RULE.—In the case of any controlled foreign corporation, the amount determined under this section with respect to any United States shareholder for any taxable year is the lesser of—

(1) the excess (if any) of—

(A) such shareholder's pro rata share of the average of the amounts of United States property held (directly or indirectly) by the controlled foreign corporation as of the close of each quarter of such taxable year, over

(B) the amount of earnings and profits described in section 959(c)(1)(A) with respect to such shareholder, or

(2) such shareholder's pro rata share of the applicable earnings of such controlled foreign corporation.

The amount taken into account under paragraph (1) with respect to any property shall be its adjusted basis as determined for purposes of computing earnings and profits, reduced by any liability to which the property is subject.

[Sec. 956(b)]

(b) SPECIAL RULES.—

(1) APPLICABLE EARNINGS.—For purposes of this section, the term "applicable earnings" means, with respect to any controlled foreign corporation, the sum of—

(A) the amount (not including a deficit) referred to in section 316(a)(1) to the extent such amount was accumulated in prior taxable years, and

(B) the amount referred to in section 316(a)(2),

but reduced by distributions made during the taxable year and by earnings and profits described in section 959(c)(1).

(2) SPECIAL RULE FOR U.S. PROPERTY ACQUIRED BEFORE CORPORATION IS A CONTROLLED FOREIGN CORPORATION.—In applying subsection (a) to any taxable year, there shall be disregarded any item of United States property which was acquired by the controlled foreign corporation before the first day on which such corporation was treated as a controlled foreign corporation. The aggregate amount of property disregarded under the preceding sentence shall not exceed the portion of the applicable earnings of such controlled foreign corporation which were accumulated during periods before such first day.

(3) SPECIAL RULE WHERE CORPORATION CEASES TO BE CONTROLLED FOREIGN CORPORATION.—If any foreign corporation ceases to be a controlled foreign corporation during any taxable year—

(A) the determination of any United States shareholder's pro rata share shall be made on the basis of stock owned (within the meaning of section 958(a)) by such shareholder on the last day during the taxable year on which the foreign corporation is a controlled foreign corporation,

(B) the average referred to in subsection (a)(1)(A) for such taxable year shall be determined by only taking into account quarters ending on or before such last day, and

(C) in determining applicable earnings, the amount taken into account by reason of being described in paragraph (2) of section 316(a) shall be the portion of the amount so described which is allocable (on a pro rata basis) to the part of such year during which the corporation is a controlled foreign corporation.

[Sec. 956(c)]

(c) UNITED STATES PROPERTY DEFINED.—

(1) IN GENERAL.—For purposes of subsection (a), the term "United States property" means any property acquired after December 31, 1962, which is—

(A) tangible property located in the United States;

(B) stock of a domestic corporation;

(C) an obligation of a United States person; or

(D) any right to the use in the United States of—

(i) a patent or copyright,

(ii) an invention, model, or design (whether or not patented),

(iii) a secret formula or process, or

(iv) any other similar property right,

which is acquired or developed by the controlled foreign corporation for use in the United States.

(2) EXCEPTIONS.—For purposes of subsection (a), the term "United States property" does not include—

(A) obligations of the United States, money, or deposits with—

(i) any bank (as defined by section 2(c) of the Bank Holding Company Act of 1956 (12 U.S.C. 1841(c)), without regard to subparagraphs (C) and (G) of paragraph (2) of such section), or

(ii) any corporation not described in clause (i) with respect to which a bank holding company (as defined by section 2(a) of such Act) or financial holding company (as defined by section 2(p) of such Act) owns directly or indirectly more than 80 percent by vote or value of the stock of such corporation;

(B) property located in the United States which is purchased in the United States for export to, or use in, foreign countries;

(C) any obligation of a United States person arising in connection with the sale or processing of property if the amount of such obligation outstanding at no time during the taxable year exceeds the amount which would be ordinary and necessary to carry on the trade or business of both the other party to the sale or processing transaction and the United States person had the sale or processing transaction been made between unrelated persons;

(D) any aircraft, railroad rolling stock, vessel, motor vehicle, or container used in the transportation of persons or property in foreign commerce and used predominantly outside the United States;

(E) an amount of assets of an insurance company equivalent to the unearned premiums or reserves ordinary and necessary for the proper conduct of its insurance business attributable to contracts which are contracts described in section 953(e)(2);

(F) the stock or obligations of a domestic corporation which is neither a United States shareholder (as defined in section 951(b)) of the controlled foreign corporation, nor a domestic corporation, 25 percent or more of the total combined voting power of which, immediately after the acquisition of any stock in such domestic corporation by the controlled foreign corporation, is owned, or is considered as being owned, by such United States shareholders in the aggregate;

(G) any movable property (other than a vessel or aircraft) which is used for the purpose of exploring for, developing, removing, or transporting resources from ocean waters or under such waters when used on the Continental Shelf of the United States;

(H) an amount of assets of the controlled foreign corporation equal to the earnings and profits accumulated after December 31, 1962, and excluded from subpart F income under section 952(b);

(I) deposits of cash or securities made or received on commercial terms in the ordinary course of a United States or foreign person's business as a dealer in securities or in commodities, but only to the extent such deposits are made or received as collateral or margin for (i) a securities loan, notional principal contract, options contract, forward contract, or futures contract, or (ii) any other financial transaction in which the Secretary determines that it is customary to post collateral or margin;

(J) an obligation of a United States person to the extent the principal amount of the obligation does not exceed the fair market value of readily marketable securities sold or purchased pursuant to a sale and repurchase agreement or otherwise posted or received as collateral for the obligation in the ordinary course of its business by a United States or foreign person which is a dealer in securities or commodities;

(K) securities acquired and held by a controlled foreign corporation in the ordinary course of its business as a dealer in securities if—

(i) the dealer accounts for the securities as securities held primarily for sale to customers in the ordinary course of business, and

(ii) the dealer disposes of the securities (or such securities mature while held by the dealer) within a period consistent with the holding of securities for sale to customers in the ordinary course of business; and

(L) an obligation of a United States person which—

(i) is not a domestic corporation, and

(ii) is not—

(I) a United States shareholder (as defined in section 951(b)) of the controlled foreign corporation, or

(II) a partnership, estate, or trust in which the controlled foreign corporation, or any related person (as defined in section 954(d)(3)), is a partner, beneficiary, or trustee immediately after the acquisition of any obligation of such partnership, estate, or trust by the controlled foreign corporation.

For purposes of subparagraphs (I), (J), and (K), the term "dealer in securities" has the meaning given such term by section 475(c)(1), and the term "dealer in commodities" has the meaning given such term by section 475(e), except that such term shall include a futures commission merchant.

(3) CERTAIN TRADE OR SERVICE RECEIVABLES ACQUIRED FROM RELATED UNITED STATES PERSONS.—

(A) IN GENERAL.—Notwithstanding paragraph (2) (other than subparagraph (H) thereof), the term "United States property" includes any trade or service receivable if—

(i) such trade or service receivable is acquired (directly or indirectly) from a related person who is a United States person, and

(ii) the obligor under such receivable is a United States person.

(B) DEFINITIONS.—For purposes of this paragraph, the term "trade or service receivable" and "related person" have the respective meanings given to such terms by section 864(d).

[Sec. 956(d)]

(d) PLEDGES AND GUARANTEES.—For purposes of subsection (a), a controlled foreign corporation shall, under regulations prescribed by the Secretary, be considered as holding an obligation of a United States person if such controlled foreign corporation is a pledgor or guarantor of such obligation.

[Sec. 956(e)]

(e) REGULATIONS.—The Secretary shall prescribe such regulations as may be necessary to carry out the purposes of this section, including regulations to prevent the avoidance of the provisions of this section through reorganizations or otherwise.

[Sec. 957]

SEC. 957. CONTROLLED FOREIGN CORPORATIONS; UNITED STATES PERSONS.

[Sec. 957(a)]

(a) GENERAL RULE.—For purposes of this title, the term "controlled foreign corporation" means any foreign corporation if more than 50 percent of—

(1) the total combined voting power of all classes of stock of such corporation entitled to vote, or

(2) the total value of the stock of such corporation,

is owned (within the meaning of section 958(a)), or is considered as owned by applying the rules of ownership of section 958(b), by United States shareholders on any day during the taxable year of such foreign corporation.

[Sec. 957(b)]

(b) SPECIAL RULE FOR INSURANCE.—For purposes only of taking into account income described in section 953(a) (relating to insurance income), the term "controlled foreign corporation" includes not only a foreign corporation as defined by subsection (a) but also one of which more than 25 percent of the total combined voting power of all classes of stock (or more than 25 percent of the total value of the stock) is owned (within the meaning of section 958(a)), or is considered as owned by applying the rules of ownership of section 958(b), by United States shareholders on any day during the taxable year of such corporation, if the gross amount of premiums or other consideration in respect of the reinsurance or the issuing of insurance or annuity contracts not described in section 953(e)(2) exceeds 75 percent of the gross amount of all premiums or other consideration in respect of all risks.

[Sec. 957(c)]

(c) UNITED STATES PERSON.—For purposes of this subpart, the term "United States person" has the meaning assigned to it by section 7701(a)(30) except that—

(1) with respect to a corporation organized under the laws of the Commonwealth of Puerto Rico, such term does not include an individual who is a bona fide resident of Puerto Rico, if a dividend received by such individual during the taxable year from such corporation would, for purposes of section 933(1), be treated as income derived from sources within Puerto Rico, and

(2) with respect to a corporation organized under the laws of Guam, American Samoa, or the Northern Mariana Islands—

(A) 80 percent or more of the gross income of which for the 3-year period ending at the close of the taxable year (or for such part of such period as such corporation or any predecessor has been in existence) was derived from sources within such a possession or was effectively connected with the conduct of a trade or business in such a possession, and

(B) 50 percent or more of the gross income of which for such period (or part) was derived from the active conduct of a trade or business within such a possession,

such term does not include an individual who is a bona fide resident of Guam, American Samoa, or the Northern Mariana Islands.

For purposes of subparagraph (A) and (B) of paragraph (2), the determination as to whether income was derived from the active conduct of a trade or business within a possession shall be made under regulations prescribed by the Secretary.

[Sec. 958]

SEC. 958. RULES FOR DETERMINING STOCK OWNERSHIP.

[Sec. 958(a)]

(a) DIRECT AND INDIRECT OWNERSHIP.—

(1) GENERAL RULE.—For purposes of this subpart (other than section 960), stock owned means—

(A) stock owned directly, and

(B) stock owned with the application of paragraph (2).

(2) STOCK OWNERSHIP THROUGH FOREIGN ENTITIES.—For purposes of subparagraph (B) of paragraph (1), stock owned, directly or indirectly, by or for a foreign corporation, foreign partnership, or foreign trust or foreign estate (within the meaning of section 7701(a)(31)) shall be considered as being owned proportionately by its shareholders, partners, or beneficiaries. Stock considered to be owned by a person by reason of the application of the preceding sentence shall, for purposes of applying such sentence, be treated as actually owned by such person.

(3) SPECIAL RULE FOR MUTUAL INSURANCE COMPANIES.—For purposes of applying paragraph (1) in the case of a foreign mutual insurance company, the term "stock" shall include any certificate entitling the holder to voting power in the corporation.

[Sec. 958(b)]

(b) CONSTRUCTIVE OWNERSHIP.—For purposes of sections 951(b), 954(d)(3), 956(c)(2), and 957, section 318(a) (relating to constructive ownership of stock) shall apply to the extent that the effect is to treat any United States person as a United States shareholder within the meaning of section 951(b), to treat a person as a related person within the meaning of section 954(d)(3), to treat the stock of a domestic corporation as owned by a United States shareholder of the controlled foreign corporation for purposes of section 956(c)(2), or to treat a foreign corporation as a controlled foreign corporation under section 957, except that—

(1) In applying paragraph (1)(A) of section 318(a), stock owned by a nonresident alien individual (other than a foreign trust or foreign estate) shall not be considered as owned by a citizen or by a resident alien individual.

(2) In applying subparagraphs (A), (B), and (C) of section 318(a)(2), if a partnership, estate, trust, or corporation owns, directly or indirectly, more than 50 percent of the total combined voting power of all classes of stock entitled to vote of a corporation, it shall be considered as owning all the stock entitled to vote.

(3) In applying subparagraph (C) of section 318(a)(2), the phrase "10 percent" shall be substituted for the phrase "50 percent" used in subparagraph (C).

Paragraph (1) shall not apply for purposes of section 956(c)(2) to treat stock of a domestic corporation as not owned by a United States shareholder.

[Sec. 959]

SEC. 959. EXCLUSION FROM GROSS INCOME OF PREVIOUSLY TAXED EARNINGS AND PROFITS.

[Sec. 959(a)]

(a) EXCLUSION FROM GROSS INCOME OF UNITED STATES PERSONS.—For purposes of this chapter, the earnings and profits of a foreign corporation attributable to amounts which are, or have been, included in the gross income of a United States shareholder under section 951(a) shall not, when—

(1) such amounts are distributed to, or

(2) such amounts would, but for this subsection, be included under section 951(a)(1)(B) in the gross income of,

such shareholder (or any other United States person who acquires from any person any portion of the interest of such United States shareholder in such foreign corporation, but only to the extent of such portion, and subject to such proof of the identity of such interest as the Secretary may by regulations prescribe) directly, or indirectly through a chain of ownership described under section 958(a), be again included in the gross income of such United States shareholder (or of such other United States person). The rules of subsection (c) shall apply for purposes of paragraph (1) of this subsection and the rules of subsection (f) shall apply for purposes of paragraph (2) of this subsection.

[Sec. 959(b)]

(b) EXCLUSION FROM GROSS INCOME OF CERTAIN FOREIGN SUBSIDIARIES.—For purposes of section 951(a), the earnings and profits of a controlled foreign corporation attributable to amounts which are, or have been, included in the gross income of a United States shareholder under section 951(a), shall not, when distributed through a chain of ownership described under section 958(a), be also included in the gross income of another controlled foreign corporation in such chain for purposes of the application of section 951(a) to such other controlled foreign corporation with respect to such United States shareholder (or to any other United States shareholder who acquires from any person any portion of the interest of such United States shareholder in the controlled foreign corporation, but only to the extent of such portion, and subject to such proof of identity of such interest as the Secretary may prescribe by regulations).

[Sec. 959(c)]

(c) ALLOCATION OF DISTRIBUTIONS.—For purposes of subsections (a) and (b), section 316(a) shall be applied by applying paragraph (2) thereof, and then paragraph (1) thereof—

(1) first to the aggregate of—

(A) earnings and profits attributable to amounts included in gross income under section 951(a)(1)(B) (or which would have been included except for subsection (a)(2) of this section), and

(B) earnings and profits attributable to amounts included in gross income under section 951(a)(1)(C) (or which would have been included except for subsection (a)(3) of this section),

with any distribution being allocated between earnings and profits described in subparagraph (A) and earnings and profits described in subparagraph (B) proportionately on the basis of the respective amounts of such earnings and profits,

(2) then to earnings and profits attributable to amounts included in gross income under section 951(a)(1)(A) (but reduced by amounts not included under subparagraph (B) or (C) of section 951(a)(1) because of the exclusions in paragraphs (2) and (3) of subsection (a) of this section), and

(3) then to other earnings and profits.

References in this subsection to section 951(a)(1)(C) and subsection (a)(3) shall be treated as references to such provisions as in effect on the day before the date of the enactment of the Small Business Job Protection Act of 1996.

[Sec. 959(d)]

(d) DISTRIBUTIONS EXCLUDED FROM GROSS INCOME NOT TO BE TREATED AS DIVIDENDS.—Any distribution excluded from gross income under subsection (a) shall be treated, for purposes of this chapter, as a distribution which is not a dividend; except that such distributions shall immediately reduce earnings and profits.

[Sec. 959(e)]

(e) COORDINATION WITH AMOUNTS PREVIOUSLY TAXED UNDER SECTION 1248.—For purposes of this section and section 960(c), any amount included in the gross income of any person as a dividend by reason of subsection (a) or (f) of section 1248 shall be treated as an amount included in the gross income of such person (or, in any case to which section 1248(e) applies, of the domestic corporation referred to in section 1248(e)(2)) under section 951(a)(1)(A).

[Sec. 959(f)]

(f) ALLOCATION RULES FOR CERTAIN INCLUSIONS.—

(1) IN GENERAL.—For purposes of this section, amounts that would be included under subparagraph (B) of section 951(a)(1) (determined without regard to this section) shall be treated as attributable first to earnings described in subsection (c)(2), and then to earnings described in subsection (c)(3).

(2) TREATMENT OF DISTRIBUTIONS.—In applying this section, actual distributions shall be taken into account before amounts that would be included under section 951(a)(1)(B) (determined without regard to this section).

[Sec. 960]

SEC. 960. DEEMED PAID CREDIT FOR SUBPART F INCLUSIONS.

[Sec. 960(a)]

(a) IN GENERAL.—For purposes of subpart A of this part, if there is included in the gross income of a domestic corporation any item of income under section 951(a)(1) with respect to any controlled foreign corporation with respect to which such domestic corporation is a United States shareholder, such domestic corporation shall be deemed to have paid so much of such foreign corporation's foreign income taxes as are properly attributable to such item of income.

[Sec. 960(b)]

(b) SPECIAL RULES FOR DISTRIBUTIONS FROM PREVIOUSLY TAXED EARNINGS AND PROFITS.—For purposes of subpart A of this part—

(1) IN GENERAL.—If any portion of a distribution from a controlled foreign corporation to a domestic corporation which is a United States shareholder with respect to such controlled foreign corporation is excluded from gross income under section 959(a), such domestic corporation shall be deemed to have paid so much of such foreign corporation's foreign income taxes as—

(A) are properly attributable to such portion, and

(B) have not been deemed to have to [sic] been paid by such domestic corporation under this section for the taxable year or any prior taxable year.

(2) TIERED CONTROLLED FOREIGN CORPORATIONS.—If section 959(b) applies to any portion of a distribution from a controlled foreign corporation to another controlled foreign corporation, such controlled foreign corporation shall be deemed to have paid so much of such other controlled foreign corporation's foreign income taxes as—

(A) are properly attributable to such portion, and

(B) have not been deemed to have been paid by a domestic corporation under this section for the taxable year or any prior taxable year.

[Sec. 960(c)]

(c) SPECIAL RULES FOR FOREIGN TAX CREDIT IN YEAR OF RECEIPT OF PREVIOUSLY TAXED EARNINGS AND PROFITS.—

(1) INCREASE IN SECTION 904 LIMITATION.—In the case of any taxpayer who—

(A) either (i) chose to have the benefits of subpart A of this part for a taxable year beginning after September 30, 1993, in which he was required under section 951(a) to include any amount in his gross income, or (ii) did not pay or accrue for such taxable year any income, war profits, or excess profits taxes to any foreign country or to any possession of the United States,

(B) chooses to have the benefits of subpart A of this part for any taxable year in which he receives 1 or more distributions or amounts which are excludable from gross income under section 959(a) and which are attributable to amounts included in his gross income for taxable years referred to in subparagraph (A), and

(C) for the taxable year in which such distributions or amounts are received, pays, or is deemed to have paid, or accrues income, war profits, or excess profits taxes to a foreign country or to any possession of the United States with respect to such distributions or amounts,

the limitation under section 904 for the taxable year in which such distributions or amounts are received shall be increased by the lesser of the amount of such taxes paid, or deemed paid, or accrued with respect to such distributions or amounts or the amount in the excess limitation account as of the beginning of such taxable year.

(2) EXCESS LIMITATION ACCOUNT.—

(A) ESTABLISHMENT OF ACCOUNT.—Each taxpayer meeting the requirements of paragraph (1)(A) shall establish an excess limitation account. The opening balance of such account shall be zero.

(B) INCREASES IN ACCOUNT.—For each taxable year beginning after September 30, 1993, the taxpayer shall increase the amount in the excess limitation account by the excess (if any) of—

(i) the amount by which the limitation under section 904(a) for such taxable year was increased by reason of the total amount of the inclusions in gross income under section 951(a) for such taxable year, over

(ii) the amount of any income, war profits, and excess profits taxes paid, or deemed paid, or accrued to any foreign country or possession of the United States which were allowable as a credit under section 901 for such taxable year and which would not have been allowable but for the inclusions in gross income described in clause (i).

Proper reductions in the amount added to the account under the preceding sentence for any taxable year shall be made for any increase in the credit allowable under section 901 for such taxable year by reason of a carryback if such increase would not have been allowable but for the inclusions in gross income described in clause (i).

(C) DECREASES IN ACCOUNT.—For each taxable year beginning after September 30, 1993, for which the limitation under section 904 was increased under paragraph (1), the taxpayer shall reduce the amount in the excess limitation account by the amount of such increase.

(3) DISTRIBUTIONS OF INCOME PREVIOUSLY TAXED IN YEARS BEGINNING BEFORE OCTOBER 1, 1993.—If the taxpayer receives a distribution or amount in a taxable year beginning after September 30, 1993, which is excluded from gross income under section 959(a) and is attributable to any amount included in gross income under section 951(a) for a taxable year beginning before October 1, 1993, the limitation under section 904 for the taxable year in which such amount or distribution is received shall be increased by the amount determined under this subsection as in effect on the day before the date of the enactment of the Revenue Reconcilation Act of 1993.

(4) CASES IN WHICH TAXES NOT TO BE ALLOWED AS DEDUCTION.—In the case of any taxpayer who—

(A) chose to have the benefits of subpart A of this part for a taxable year in which he was required under section 951(a) to include in his gross income an amount in respect of a controlled foreign corporation, and

(B) does not choose to have the benefits of subpart A of this part for the taxable year in which he receives a distribution or amount which is excluded from gross income under section 959(a) and which is attributable to earnings and profits of the controlled foreign corporation which was included in his gross income for the taxable year referred to in subparagraph (A), no deduction shall be allowed under section 164 for the taxable year in which such distribution or amount is received for any income, war profits, or excess profits taxes paid or accrued to any foreign country or to any possession of the United States on or with respect to such distribution or amount.

(5) INSUFFICIENT TAXABLE INCOME.—If an increase in the limitation under this subsection exceeds the tax imposed by this chapter for such year, the amount of such excess shall be deemed an overpayment of tax for such year.

[Sec. 960(d)]

(d) DEEMED PAID CREDIT FOR TAXES PROPERLY ATTRIBUTABLE TO TESTED INCOME.—

(1) IN GENERAL.—For purposes of subpart A of this part, if any amount is includible in the gross income of a domestic corporation under section 951A, such domestic corporation shall be deemed to have paid foreign income taxes equal to 80 percent of the product of—

(A) such domestic corporation's inclusion percentage, multiplied by

(B) the aggregate tested foreign income taxes paid or accrued by controlled foreign corporations.

(2) INCLUSION PERCENTAGE.—For purposes of paragraph (1), the term "inclusion percentage" means, with respect to any domestic corporation, the ratio (expressed as a percentage) of—

(A) such corporation's global intangible low-taxed income (as defined in section 951A(b)), divided by

(B) the aggregate amount described in section 951A(c)(1)(A) with respect to such corporation.

(3) TESTED FOREIGN INCOME TAXES.—For purposes of paragraph (1), the term "tested foreign income taxes" means, with respect to any domestic corporation which is a United States shareholder of a controlled foreign corporation, the foreign income taxes paid or accrued by such foreign corporation which are properly attributable to the tested income of such foreign corporation taken into account by such domestic corporation under section 951A.

[Sec. 960(e)]

(e) FOREIGN INCOME TAXES.—The term "foreign income taxes" means any income, war profits, or excess profits taxes paid or accrued to any foreign country or possession of the United States.

[Sec. 960(f)]

(f) REGULATIONS.—The Secretary shall prescribe such regulations or other guidance as may be necessary or appropriate to carry out the provisions of this section.

[Sec. 961]

SEC. 961. ADJUSTMENTS TO BASIS OF STOCK IN CONTROLLED FOREIGN CORPORATIONS AND OF OTHER PROPERTY.

[Sec. 961(a)]

(a) INCREASE IN BASIS.—Under regulations prescribed by the Secretary, the basis of a United States shareholder's stock in a controlled foreign corporation, and the basis of property of a United States shareholder by reason of which he is considered under section 958(a)(2) as owning stock of a controlled foreign corporation, shall be increased by the amount required to be included in his gross income under section 951(a) with respect to such stock or with respect to such property, as the case may be, but only to the extent to which such amount was included in the gross income of such United States shareholder. In the case of a United States shareholder who has made an election under section 962 for the taxable year, the increase in basis provided by this subsection shall not exceed an amount equal to the amount of tax paid under this chapter with respect to the amounts required to be included in his gross income under section 951(a).

[Sec. 961(b)]

(b) REDUCTION IN BASIS.—

(1) IN GENERAL.—Under regulations prescribed by the Secretary, the adjusted basis of stock or other property with respect to which a United States shareholder or a United States person receives an amount which is excluded from gross income under section 959(a) shall be reduced by the amount so excluded. In the case of a United States shareholder who has made an election under section 962 for any prior taxable year, the reduction in basis provided by this paragraph shall not exceed an amount equal to the amount received which is excluded from gross income under section 959(a) after the application of section 962(d).

(2) AMOUNT IN EXCESS OF BASIS.—To the extent that an amount excluded from gross income under section 959(a) exceeds the adjusted basis of the stock or other property with respect to which it is received, the amount shall be treated as gain from the sale or exchange of property.

[Sec. 961(c)]

(c) BASIS ADJUSTMENTS IN STOCK HELD BY FOREIGN CORPORATIONS.—Under regulations prescribed by the Secretary, if a United States shareholder is treated under section 958(a)(2) as owning stock in a controlled foreign corporation which is owned by another controlled foreign corporation, then adjustments similar to the adjustments provided by subsections (a) and (b) shall be made to—

(1) the basis of such stock, and

(2) the basis of stock in any other controlled foreign corporation by reason of which the United States shareholder is considered under section 958(a)(2) as owning the stock described in paragraph (1),

but only for the purposes of determining the amount included under section 951 in the gross income of such United States shareholder (or any other United States shareholder who acquires from any person any portion of the interest of such United States shareholder by reason of which such shareholder was treated as owning such stock, but only to the extent of such portion, and subject to such proof of identity of such interest as the Secretary may prescribe by regulations). The preceding sentence shall not apply with respect to any stock to which a basis adjustment applies under subsection (a) or (b).

[Sec. 961(d)]

(d) BASIS IN SPECIFIED 10-PERCENT OWNED FOREIGN CORPORATION REDUCED BY NONTAXED PORTION OF DIVIDEND FOR PURPOSES OF DETERMINING LOSS.—If a domestic corporation received a dividend from a specified 10-percent owned foreign corporation (as defined in section 245A) in any taxable year, solely for purposes of determining loss on any disposition of stock of such foreign corporation in such taxable year or any subsequent taxable year, the basis of such domestic corporation in such stock shall be reduced (but not below zero) by the amount of any deduction allowable to such domestic corporation under section 245A with respect to such stock except to the extent such basis was reduced under section 1059 by reason of a dividend for which such a deduction was allowable.

[Sec. 962]

SEC. 962. ELECTION BY INDIVIDUALS TO BE SUBJECT TO TAX AT CORPORATE RATES.

[Sec. 962(a)]

(a) GENERAL RULE.—Under regulations prescribed by the Secretary, in the case of a United States shareholder who is an individual and who elects to have the provisions of this section apply for the taxable year—

(1) the tax imposed under this chapter on amounts which are included in his gross income under section 951(a) shall (in lieu of the tax determined under sections 1 and 55) be an amount equal to the tax which would be imposed under section 11 if such amounts were received by a domestic corporation, and

(2) for purposes of applying the provisions of section 960 (relating to foreign tax credit) such amounts shall be treated as if they were received by a domestic corporation.

[Sec. 962(b)]

(b) ELECTION.—An election to have the provisions of this section apply for any taxable year shall be made by a United States shareholder at such time and in such manner as the Secretary shall prescribe by regulations. An election made for any taxable year may not be revoked except with the consent of the Secretary

[Sec. 962(c)]

(c) PRO RATION OF EACH SECTION 11 BRACKET AMOUNT.—For purposes of applying subsection (a)(1), the amount in each taxable income bracket in the tax table in section 11(b) shall not exceed an amount which bears the same ratio to such bracket amount as the amount included in the gross income of the United States shareholder under section 951(a) for the taxable year bears to such shareholder's pro rata share of the earnings and profits for the taxable year of all controlled foreign corporations with respect to which such shareholder includes any amount in gross income under section 951(a).

[Sec. 962(d)]

(d) SPECIAL RULE FOR ACTUAL DISTRIBUTIONS.—The earnings and profits of a foreign corporation attributable to amounts which were included in the gross income of a United States shareholder under section 951(a) and with respect to which an election under this section applied shall, when such earnings and profits are distributed, notwithstanding the provisions of section 959(a)(1), be included in gross income to the extent that such earnings and profits so distributed exceed the amount of tax paid under this chapter on the amounts to which such election applied.

[Sec. 964]

SEC. 964. MISCELLANEOUS PROVISIONS.

[Sec. 964(a)]

(a) EARNINGS AND PROFITS.—Except as provided in section 312(k)(4), for purposes of this subpart the earnings and profits of any foreign corporation, and the deficit in earnings and profits of any foreign corporation, for any taxable year shall be determined according to rules substantially similar to those applicable to domestic corporations, under regulations prescribed by the Secretary. In determining such earnings and profits, or the deficit in such earnings and profits, the amount of any illegal bribe, kickback, or other payment (within the meaning of section 162(c)) shall not be taken into account to decrease such earnings and profits or to increase such deficit. The payments referred to in the preceding sentence are payments which would be unlawful under the Foreign Corrupt Practices Act of 1977 if the payor were a United States person.

[Sec. 964(b)]

(b) BLOCKED FOREIGN INCOME.—Under regulations prescribed by the Secretary, no part of the earnings and profits of a controlled foreign corporation for any taxable year shall be included in earnings and profits for purposes of sections 952 and 956, if it is established to the satisfaction of the Secretary that such part could not have been distributed by the controlled foreign corporation to United States shareholders who own (within the meaning of section 958(a)) stock of such controlled foreign corporation because of currency or other restrictions or limitations imposed under the laws of any foreign country.

[Sec. 964(c)]

(c) RECORDS AND ACCOUNTS OF UNITED STATES SHAREHOLDERS.—

(1) RECORDS AND ACCOUNTS TO BE MAINTAINED.—The Secretary may by regulations require each person who is, or has been, a United States shareholder of a controlled foreign corporation to maintain such records and accounts as may be prescribed by such regulations as necessary to carry out the provisions of this subpart and subpart G.

(2) TWO OR MORE PERSONS REQUIRED TO MAINTAIN OR FURNISH THE SAME RECORDS AND ACCOUNTS WITH RESPECT TO THE SAME FOREIGN CORPORATION.—Where, but for this paragraph, two or more United States persons would be required to maintain or furnish the same records and accounts as may by regulations be required under paragraph (1) with respect to the same controlled foreign corporation for the same period, the Secretary may by regulations provide that the maintenance or furnishing of such records and accounts by only one such person shall satisfy the requirements of paragraph (1) for such other persons.

[Sec. 964(d)]

(d) TREATMENT OF CERTAIN BRANCHES.—

(1) IN GENERAL.—For purposes of this chapter, section 6038, section 6046, and such other provisions as may be specified in regulations—

(A) a qualified insurance branch of a controlled foreign corporation shall be treated as a separate foreign corporation created under the laws of the foreign country with respect to which such branch qualifies under paragraph (2), and

(B) except as provided in regulations, any amount directly or indirectly transferred or credited from such branch to one or more other accounts of such controlled foreign corporation shall be treated as a dividend paid to such controlled foreign corporation.

(2) QUALIFIED INSURANCE BRANCH.—For purposes of paragraph (1), the term "qualified insurance branch" means any branch of a controlled foreign corporation which is licensed and predominantly engaged on a permanent basis in the active conduct of an insurance business in a foreign country if—

(A) separate books and accounts are maintained for such branch,

(B) the principal place of business of such branch is in such foreign country,

(C) such branch would be taxable under subchapter L if it were a separate domestic corporation, and

(D) an election under this paragraph applies to such branch.

An election under this paragraph shall apply to the taxable year for which made and all subsequent taxable years unless revoked with the consent of the Secretary.

(3) REGULATIONS.—The Secretary shall prescribe such regulations as may be necessary or appropriate to carry out the purposes of this subsection.

[Sec. 964(e)]

(e) GAIN ON CERTAIN STOCK SALES BY CONTROLLED FOREIGN CORPORATIONS TREATED AS DIVIDENDS.—

(1) IN GENERAL.—If a controlled foreign corporation sells or exchanges stock in any other foreign corporation, gain recognized on such sale or exchange shall be included in the gross income of such controlled foreign corporation as a dividend to the same extent that it would have been so included under section 1248(a) if such controlled foreign corporation were a United States person. For purposes of determining the amount which would have been so includible, the determination of whether such other foreign corporation was a controlled foreign corporation shall be made without regard to the preceding sentence.

(2) SAME COUNTRY EXCEPTION NOT APPLICABLE.—Clause (i) of section 954(c)(3)(A) shall not apply to any amount treated as a dividend by reason of paragraph (1).

(3) CLARIFICATION OF DEEMED SALES.—For purposes of this subsection, a controlled foreign corporation shall be treated as having sold or exchanged any stock if, under any provision of this subtitle, such controlled foreign corporation is treated as having gain from the sale or exchange of such stock.

(4) COORDINATION WITH DIVIDENDS RECEIVED DEDUCTION.—

(A) IN GENERAL.—If, for any taxable year of a controlled foreign corporation beginning after December 31, 2017, any amount is treated as a dividend under paragraph (1) by reason of a sale or exchange by the controlled foreign corporation of stock in another foreign corporation held for 1 year or more, then, notwithstanding any other provision of this title—

(i) the foreign-source portion of such dividend shall be treated for purposes of section 951(a)(1)(A) as subpart F income of the selling controlled foreign corporation for such taxable year,

(ii) a United States shareholder with respect to the selling controlled foreign corporation shall include in gross income for the taxable year of the shareholder with or within which such taxable year of the controlled foreign corporation ends an amount equal to the shareholder's pro rata share (determined in the same manner as under section 951(a)(2)) of the amount treated as subpart F income under clause (i), and

(iii) the deduction under section 245A(a) shall be allowable to the United States shareholder with respect to the subpart F income included in gross income under clause (ii) in the same manner as if such subpart F income were a dividend received by the shareholder from the selling controlled foreign corporation.

(B) APPLICATION OF BASIS OR SIMILAR ADJUSTMENT.—For purposes of this title, in the case of a sale or exchange by a controlled foreign corporation of stock in another foreign corporation in a taxable year of the selling controlled foreign corporation beginning after December 31, 2017, rules similar to the rules of section 961(d) shall apply.

(C) FOREIGN-SOURCE PORTION.—For purposes of this paragraph, the foreign-source portion of any amount treated as a dividend under paragraph (1) shall be determined in the same manner as under section 245A(c).

[Sec. 965]

SEC. 965. TREATMENT OF DEFERRED FOREIGN INCOME UPON TRANSITION TO PARTICIPATION EXEMPTION SYSTEM OF TAXATION.

[Sec. 965(a)]

(a) TREATMENT OF DEFERRED FOREIGN INCOME AS SUBPART F INCOME.—In the case of the last taxable year of a deferred foreign income corporation which begins before January 1, 2018, the subpart F income of such foreign corporation (as otherwise determined for such taxable year under section 952) shall be increased by the greater of—

(1) the accumulated post-1986 deferred foreign income of such corporation determined as of November 2, 2017, or

(2) the accumulated post-1986 deferred foreign income of such corporation determined as of December 31, 2017.

[Sec. 965(b)]

(b) REDUCTION IN AMOUNTS INCLUDED IN GROSS INCOME OF UNITED STATES SHAREHOLDERS OF SPECIFIED FOREIGN CORPORATIONS WITH DEFICITS IN EARNINGS AND PROFITS.—

(1) IN GENERAL.—In the case of a taxpayer which is a United States shareholder with respect to at least one deferred foreign income corporation and at least one E&P deficit foreign corporation, the amount which would (but for this subsection) be taken into account under section 951(a)(1) by reason of subsection (a) as such United States shareholder's pro rata share of the subpart F income of each deferred foreign income corporation shall be reduced by the amount of such United States shareholder's aggregate foreign E&P deficit which is allocated under paragraph (2) to such deferred foreign income corporation.

(2) ALLOCATION OF AGGREGATE FOREIGN E&P DEFICIT.—The aggregate foreign E&P deficit of any United States shareholder shall be allocated among the deferred foreign income corporations of such United States shareholder in an amount which bears the same proportion to such aggregate as—

(A) such United States shareholder's pro rata share of the accumulated post-1986 deferred foreign income of each such deferred foreign income corporation, bears to

(B) the aggregate of such United States shareholder's pro rata share of the accumulated post-1986 deferred foreign income of all deferred foreign income corporations of such United States shareholder.

(3) DEFINITIONS RELATED TO E&P DEFICITS.—For purposes of this subsection—

(A) AGGREGATE FOREIGN E&P DEFICIT.—

(i) IN GENERAL.—The term "aggregate foreign E&P deficit" means, with respect to any United States shareholder, the lesser of—

(I) the aggregate of such shareholder's pro rata shares of the specified E&P deficits of the E&P deficit foreign corporations of such shareholder, or

(II) the amount determined under paragraph (2)(B).

(ii) ALLOCATION OF DEFICIT.—If the amount described in clause (i)(II) is less than the amount described in clause (i)(I), then the shareholder shall designate, in such form and manner as the Secretary determines—

(I) the amount of the specified E&P deficit which is to be taken into account for each E&P deficit corporation with respect to the taxpayer, and

(II) in the case of an E&P deficit corporation which has a qualified deficit (as defined in section 952), the portion (if any) of the deficit taken into account under subclause (I) which is attributable to a qualified deficit, including the qualified activities to which such portion is attributable.

(B) E&P DEFICIT FOREIGN CORPORATION.—The term "E&P deficit foreign corporation" means, with respect to any taxpayer, any specified foreign corporation with respect to which such taxpayer is a United States shareholder, if, as of November 2, 2017—

(i) such specified foreign corporation has a deficit in post-1986 earnings and profits,

(ii) such corporation was a specified foreign corporation, and

(iii) such taxpayer was a United States shareholder of such corporation.

(C) SPECIFIED E&P DEFICIT.—The term "specified E&P deficit" means, with respect to any E&P deficit foreign corporation, the amount of the deficit referred to in subparagraph (B).

(4) TREATMENT OF EARNINGS AND PROFITS IN FUTURE YEARS.—

(A) REDUCED EARNINGS AND PROFITS TREATED AS PREVIOUSLY TAXED INCOME WHEN DISTRIBUTED.—For purposes of applying section 959 in any taxable year beginning with the taxable year described in subsection (a), with respect to any United States shareholder of a deferred foreign income corporation, an amount equal to such shareholder's reduction under paragraph (1) which is allocated to such deferred foreign income corporation under this subsection shall be treated as an amount which was included in the gross income of such United States shareholder under section 951(a).

(B) E&P DEFICITS.—For purposes of this title, with respect to any taxable year beginning with the taxable year described in subsection (a), a United States shareholder's pro rata share of the earnings and profits of any E&P deficit foreign corporation under this subsection shall be increased by the amount of the specified E&P deficit of such corporation taken into account by such shareholder under paragraph (1), and, for purposes of section 952, such increase shall be attributable to the same activity to which the deficit so taken into account was attributable.

(5) NETTING AMONG UNITED STATES SHAREHOLDERS IN SAME AFFILIATED GROUP.—

(A) IN GENERAL.—In the case of any affiliated group which includes at least one E&P net surplus shareholder and one E&P net deficit shareholder, the amount which would (but for this paragraph) be taken into account under section 951(a)(1) by reason of subsection (a) by each such E&P net surplus shareholder shall be reduced (but not below zero) by such shareholder's applicable share of the affiliated group's aggregate unused E&P deficit.

(B) E&P NET SURPLUS SHAREHOLDER.—For purposes of this paragraph, the term "E&P net surplus shareholder" means any United States shareholder which would (determined without regard to this paragraph) take into account an amount greater than zero under section 951(a)(1) by reason of subsection (a).

(C) E&P NET DEFICIT SHAREHOLDER.—For purposes of this paragraph, the term "E&P net deficit shareholder" means any United States shareholder if—

(i) the aggregate foreign E&P deficit with respect to such shareholder (as defined in paragraph (3)(A) without regard to clause (i)(II) thereof), exceeds

(ii) the amount which would (but for this subsection) be taken into account by such shareholder under section 951(a)(1) by reason of subsection (a).

(D) AGGREGATE UNUSED E&P DEFICIT.—For purposes of this paragraph—

(i) IN GENERAL.—The term "aggregate unused E&P deficit" means, with respect to any affiliated group, the lesser of—

(I) the sum of the excesses described in subparagraph (C), determined with respect to each E&P net deficit shareholder in such group, or

(II) the amount determined under subparagraph (E)(ii).

(ii) REDUCTION WITH RESPECT TO E&P NET DEFICIT SHAREHOLDERS WHICH ARE NOT WHOLLY OWNED BY THE AFFILIATED GROUP.—If the group ownership percentage of any E&P net deficit shareholder is less than 100 percent, the amount of the excess described in subparagraph (C) which is taken into account under clause (i)(I) with respect to such E&P net deficit shareholder shall be such group ownership percentage of such amount.

(E) APPLICABLE SHARE.—For purposes of this paragraph, the term "applicable share" means, with respect to any E&P net surplus shareholder in any affiliated group, the amount which bears the same proportion to such group's aggregate unused E&P deficit as—

(i) the product of—

(I) such shareholder's group ownership percentage, multiplied by

(II) the amount which would (but for this paragraph) be taken into account under section 951(a)(1) by reason of subsection (a) by such shareholder, bears to

(ii) the aggregate amount determined under clause (i) with respect to all E&P net surplus shareholders in such group.

(F) GROUP OWNERSHIP PERCENTAGE.—For purposes of this paragraph, the term "group ownership percentage" means, with respect to any United States shareholder in any affiliated group, the percentage of the value of the stock of such United States shareholder which is held by other includible corporations in such affiliated group. Notwithstanding the preceding sentence, the group ownership percentage of the common parent of the affiliated group is 100 percent. Any term used in this subparagraph which is also used in section 1504 shall have the same meaning as when used in such section.

[Sec. 965(c)]

(c) APPLICATION OF PARTICIPATION EXEMPTION TO INCLUDED INCOME.—

(1) IN GENERAL.—In the case of a United States shareholder of a deferred foreign income corporation, there shall be allowed as a deduction for the taxable year in which an amount is included in the gross income of such United States shareholder under section 951(a)(1) by reason of this section an amount equal to the sum of—

(A) the United States shareholder's 8 percent rate equivalent percentage of the excess (if any) of—

(i) the amount so included as gross income, over

(ii) the amount of such United States shareholder's aggregate foreign cash position, plus

(B) the United States shareholder's 15.5 percent rate equivalent percentage of so much of the amount described in subparagraph (A)(ii) as does not exceed the amount described in subparagraph (A)(i).

(2) 8 AND 15.5 PERCENT RATE EQUIVALENT PERCENTAGES.—For purposes of this subsection—

(A) 8 PERCENT RATE EQUIVALENT PERCENTAGE.—The term "8 percent rate equivalent percentage" means, with respect to any United States shareholder for any taxable year, the percentage which would result in the amount to which such percentage applies being subject to a 8 percent rate of tax determined by only taking into account a deduction equal to such percentage of such amount and the highest rate of tax specified in section 11 for such taxable year. In the case of any taxable year of a United States shareholder to which section 15 applies, the highest rate of tax under section 11 before the effective date of the change in rates and the highest rate of tax under section 11 after the effective date of such change shall each be taken into account under the preceding sentence in the same proportions as the portion of such taxable year which is before and after such effective date, respectively.

(B) 15.5 PERCENT RATE EQUIVALENT PERCENTAGE.—The term "15.5 percent rate equivalent percentage" means, with respect to any United States shareholder for any taxable year, the percentage determined under subparagraph (A) applied by substituting "15.5 percent rate of tax" for "8 percent rate of tax".

(3) AGGREGATE FOREIGN CASH POSITION.—For purposes of this subsection—

(A) IN GENERAL.—The term "aggregate foreign cash position" means, with respect to any United States shareholder, the greater of—

(i) the aggregate of such United States shareholder's pro rata share of the cash position of each specified foreign corporation of such United States shareholder determined as of the close of the last taxable year of such specified foreign corporation which begins before January 1, 2018, or

(ii) one half of the sum of—

(I) the aggregate described in clause (i) determined as of the close of the last taxable year of each such specified foreign corporation which ends before November 2, 2017, plus

(II) the aggregate described in clause (i) determined as of the close of the taxable year of each such specified foreign corporation which precedes the taxable year referred to in subclause (I).

(B) CASH POSITION.—For purposes of this paragraph, the cash position of any specified foreign corporation is the sum of—

(i) cash held by such foreign corporation,

(ii) the net accounts receivable of such foreign corporation, plus

(iii) the fair market value of the following assets held by such corporation:

(I) Personal property which is of a type that is actively traded and for which there is an established financial market.

(II) Commercial paper, certificates of deposit, the securities of the Federal government and of any State or foreign government.

(III) Any foreign currency.

(IV) Any obligation with a term of less than one year.

(V) Any asset which the Secretary identifies as being economically equivalent to any asset described in this subparagraph.

(C) NET ACCOUNTS RECEIVABLE.—For purposes of this paragraph, the term "net accounts receivable" means, with respect to any specified foreign corporation, the excess (if any) of—

(i) such corporation's accounts receivable, over

(ii) such corporation's accounts payable (determined consistent with the rules of section 461).

(D) PREVENTION OF DOUBLE COUNTING.—Cash positions of a specified foreign corporation described in clause (ii), (iii)(I), or (iii)(IV) of subparagraph (B) shall not be taken into account by a United States shareholder under subparagraph (A) to the extent that such United States shareholder demonstrates to the satisfaction of the Secretary that such amount is so taken into account by such United States shareholder with respect to another specified foreign corporation.

(E) CASH POSITIONS OF CERTAIN NON-CORPORATE ENTITIES TAKEN INTO ACCOUNT.—An entity (other than a corporation) shall be treated as a specified foreign corporation of a United States shareholder for purposes of determining such United States shareholder's aggregate foreign cash position if any interest in such entity is held by a specified foreign corporation of such United States shareholder (determined after application of this subparagraph) and such entity would be a specified foreign corporation of such United States shareholder if such entity were a foreign corporation.

(F) ANTI-ABUSE.—If the Secretary determines that a principal purpose of any transaction was to reduce the aggregate foreign cash position taken into account under this subsection, such transaction shall be disregarded for purposes of this subsection.

[Sec. 965(d)]

(d) DEFERRED FOREIGN INCOME CORPORATION; ACCUMULATED POST-1986 DEFERRED FOREIGN INCOME.—For purposes of this section—

(1) DEFERRED FOREIGN INCOME CORPORATION.—The term "deferred foreign income corporation" means, with respect to any United States shareholder, any specified foreign corporation of such United States shareholder which has accumulated post-1986 deferred foreign income (as of the date referred to in paragraph (1) or (2) of subsection (a)) greater than zero.

(2) ACCUMULATED POST-1986 DEFERRED FOREIGN INCOME.—The term "accumulated post-1986 deferred foreign income" means the post-1986 earnings and profits except to the extent such earnings—

(A) are attributable to income of the specified foreign corporation which is effectively connected with the conduct of a trade or business within the United States and subject to tax under this chapter, or

(B) in the case of a controlled foreign corporation, if distributed, would be excluded from the gross income of a United States shareholder under section 959.

To the extent provided in regulations or other guidance prescribed by the Secretary, in the case of any controlled foreign corporation which has shareholders which are not United States shareholders, accumulated post-1986 deferred foreign income shall be appropriately reduced by amounts which would be described in subparagraph (B) if such shareholders were United States shareholders.

(3) POST-1986 EARNINGS AND PROFITS.—The term "post-1986 earnings and profits" means the earnings and profits of the foreign corporation (computed in accordance with sections 964(a) and 986, and by only taking into account periods when the foreign corporation was a specified foreign corporation) accumulated in taxable years beginning after December 31, 1986, and determined—

(A) as of the date referred to in paragraph (1) or (2) of subsection (a), whichever is applicable with respect to such foreign corporation, and

(B) without diminution by reason of dividends distributed during the taxable year described in subsection (a) other than dividends distributed to another specified foreign corporation.

[Sec. 965(e)]

(e) SPECIFIED FOREIGN CORPORATION.—

(1) IN GENERAL.—For purposes of this section, the term "specified foreign corporation" means—

(A) any controlled foreign corporation, and

(B) any foreign corporation with respect to which one or more domestic corporations is a United States shareholder.

(2) APPLICATION TO CERTAIN FOREIGN CORPORATIONS.—For purposes of sections 951 and 961, a foreign corporation described in paragraph (1)(B) shall be treated as a controlled foreign corporation solely for purposes of taking into account the subpart F income of such corporation under subsection (a) (and for purposes of applying subsection (f)).

(3) EXCLUSION OF PASSIVE FOREIGN INVESTMENT COMPANIES.—Such term shall not include any corporation which is a passive foreign investment company (as defined in section 1297) with respect to the shareholder and which is not a controlled foreign corporation.

[Sec. 965(f)]

(f) DETERMINATIONS OF PRO RATA SHARE.—

(1) IN GENERAL.—For purposes of this section, the determination of any United States shareholder's pro rata share of any amount with respect to any specified foreign corporation shall be determined under rules similar to the rules of section 951(a)(2) by treating such amount in the same manner as subpart F income (and by treating such specified foreign corporation as a controlled foreign corporation).

(2) SPECIAL RULES.—The portion which is included in the income of a United States shareholder under section 951(a)(1) by reason of subsection (a) which is equal to the deduction allowed under subsection (c) by reason of such inclusion—

(A) shall be treated as income exempt from tax for purposes of sections 705(a)(1)(B) and 1367(a)(1)(A), and

(B) shall not be treated as income exempt from tax for purposes of determining whether an adjustment shall be made to an accumulated adjustment account under section 1368(e)(1)(A).

[Sec. 965(g)]

(g) DISALLOWANCE OF FOREIGN TAX CREDIT, ETC.—

(1) IN GENERAL.—No credit shall be allowed under section 901 for the applicable percentage of any taxes paid or accrued (or treated as paid or accrued) with respect to any amount for which a deduction is allowed under this section.

(2) APPLICABLE PERCENTAGE.—For purposes of this subsection, the term "applicable percentage" means the amount (expressed as a percentage) equal to the sum of—

(A) 0.771 multiplied by the ratio of—

(i) the excess to which subsection (c)(1)(A) applies, divided by

(ii) the sum of such excess plus the amount to which subsection (c)(1)(B) applies, plus

(B) 0.557 multiplied by the ratio of—

(i) the amount to which subsection (c)(1)(B) applies, divided by

(ii) the sum described in subparagraph (A)(ii).

(3) DENIAL OF DEDUCTION.—No deduction shall be allowed under this chapter for any tax for which credit is not allowable under section 901 by reason of paragraph (1) (determined by treating the taxpayer as having elected the benefits of subpart A of part III of subchapter N).

(4) COORDINATION WITH SECTION 78.—With respect to the taxes treated as paid or accrued by a domestic corporation with respect to amounts which are includible in gross income of such domestic corporation by reason of this section, section 78 shall apply only to so much of such taxes as bears the same proportion to the amount of such taxes as—

(A) the excess of—

(i) the amounts which are includible in gross income of such domestic corporation by reason of this section, over

(ii) the deduction allowable under subsection (c) with respect to such amounts, bears to

(B) such amounts.

[Sec. 965(h)]

(h) ELECTION TO PAY LIABILITY IN INSTALLMENTS.—

(1) IN GENERAL.—In the case of a United States shareholder of a deferred foreign income corporation, such United States shareholder may elect to pay the net tax liability under this section in 8 installments of the following amounts:

(A) 8 percent of the net tax liability in the case of each of the first 5 of such installments,

(B) 15 percent of the net tax liability in the case of the 6th such installment,

(C) 20 percent of the net tax liability in the case of the 7th such installment, and

(D) 25 percent of the net tax liability in the case of the 8th such installment.

(2) DATE FOR PAYMENT OF INSTALLMENTS.—If an election is made under paragraph (1), the first installment shall be paid on the due date (determined without regard to any extension of time for filing the return) for the return of tax for the taxable year described in subsection (a) and each succeeding installment shall be paid on the due date (as so determined) for the return of tax for the taxable year following the taxable year with respect to which the preceding installment was made.

(3) ACCELERATION OF PAYMENT.—If there is an addition to tax for failure to timely pay any installment required under this subsection, a liquidation or sale of substantially all the assets of the taxpayer (including in a title 11 or similar case), a cessation of business by the taxpayer, or any similar circumstance, then the unpaid portion of all remaining installments shall be due on the date of such event (or in the case of a title 11 or similar case, the day before the petition is filed). The preceding sentence shall not apply to the sale of substantially all the assets of a taxpayer to a buyer if such buyer enters into an agreement with the Secretary under which such buyer is liable for the remaining installments due under this subsection in the same manner as if such buyer were the taxpayer.

(4) PRORATION OF DEFICIENCY TO INSTALLMENTS.—If an election is made under paragraph (1) to pay the net tax liability under this section in installments and a deficiency has been assessed with respect to such net tax liability, the deficiency shall be prorated to the installments payable under paragraph (1). The part of the deficiency so prorated to any installment the date for payment of which has not arrived shall be collected at the same time as, and as a part of, such installment. The part of the deficiency so prorated to any installment the date for payment of which has arrived shall be paid upon notice and demand from the Secretary. This subsection shall not apply if the deficiency is due to negligence, to intentional disregard of rules and regulations, or to fraud with intent to evade tax.

(5) ELECTION.—Any election under paragraph (1) shall be made not later than the due date for the return of tax for the taxable year described in subsection (a) and shall be made in such manner as the Secretary shall provide.

(6) NET TAX LIABILITY UNDER THIS SECTION.—For purposes of this subsection—

(A) IN GENERAL.—The net tax liability under this section with respect to any United States shareholder is the excess (if any) of—

(i) such taxpayer's net income tax for the taxable year in which an amount is included in the gross income of such United States shareholder under section 951(a)(1) by reason of this section, over

(ii) such taxpayer's net income tax for such taxable year determined—

(I) without regard to this section, and

(II) without regard to any income or deduction properly attributable to a dividend received by such United States shareholder from any deferred foreign income corporation.

(B) NET INCOME TAX.—The term "net income tax" means the regular tax liability reduced by the credits allowed under subparts A, B, and D of part IV of subchapter A.

[Sec. 965(i)]

(i) SPECIAL RULES FOR S CORPORATION SHAREHOLDERS.—

(1) IN GENERAL.—In the case of any S corporation which is a United States shareholder of a deferred foreign income corporation, each shareholder of such S corporation may elect to defer payment of such shareholder's net tax liability under this section with respect to such S corporation until the shareholder's taxable year which includes the triggering event with respect to such liability. Any net tax liability payment of which is deferred under the preceding sentence shall be assessed on the return of tax as an addition to tax in the shareholder's taxable year which includes such triggering event.

(2) TRIGGERING EVENT.—

(A) IN GENERAL.—In the case of any shareholder's net tax liability under this section with respect to any S corporation, the triggering event with respect to such liability is whichever of the following occurs first:

(i) Such corporation ceases to be an S corporation (determined as of the first day of the first taxable year that such corporation is not an S corporation).

(ii) A liquidation or sale of substantially all the assets of such S corporation (including in a title 11 or similar case), a cessation of business by such S corporation, such S corporation ceases to exist, or any similar circumstance.

(iii) A transfer of any share of stock in such S corporation by the taxpayer (including by reason of death, or otherwise).

(B) PARTIAL TRANSFERS OF STOCK.—In the case of a transfer of less than all of the taxpayer's shares of stock in the S corporation, such transfer shall only be a triggering event with respect to so much of the taxpayer's net tax liability under this section with respect to such S corporation as is properly allocable to such stock.

(C) TRANSFER OF LIABILITY.—A transfer described in clause (iii) of subparagraph (A) shall not be treated as a triggering event if the transferee enters into an agreement with the Secretary under which such transferee is liable for net tax liability with respect to such stock in the same manner as if such transferee were the taxpayer.

(3) NET TAX LIABILITY.—A shareholder's net tax liability under this section with respect to any S corporation is the net tax liability under this section which would be determined under subsection (h)(6) if the only subpart F income taken into account by such shareholder by reason of this section were allocations from such S corporation.

(4) ELECTION TO PAY DEFERRED LIABILITY IN INSTALLMENTS.—In the case of a taxpayer which elects to defer payment under paragraph (1)—

(A) subsection (h) shall be applied separately with respect to the liability to which such election applies,

(B) an election under subsection (h) with respect to such liability shall be treated as timely made if made not later than the due date for the return of tax for the taxable year in which the triggering event with respect to such liability occurs,

(C) the first installment under subsection (h) with respect to such liability shall be paid not later than such due date (but determined without regard to any extension of time for filing the return), and

(D) if the triggering event with respect to any net tax liability is described in paragraph (2)(A)(ii), an election under subsection (h) with respect to such liability may be made only with the consent of the Secretary.

(5) JOINT AND SEVERAL LIABILITY OF S CORPORATION.—If any shareholder of an S corporation elects to defer payment under paragraph (1), such S corporation shall be jointly and severally liable for such payment and any penalty, addition to tax, or additional amount attributable thereto.

(6) EXTENSION OF LIMITATION ON COLLECTION.—Any limitation on the time period for the collection of a liability deferred under this subsection shall not be treated as beginning before the date of the triggering event with respect to such liability.

(7) ANNUAL REPORTING OF NET TAX LIABILITY.—

(A) IN GENERAL.—Any shareholder of an S corporation which makes an election under paragraph (1) shall report the amount of such shareholder's deferred net tax liability on such shareholder's return of tax for the taxable year for which such election is made and on the return of tax for each taxable year thereafter until such amount has been fully assessed on such returns.

(B) DEFERRED NET TAX LIABILITY.—For purposes of this paragraph, the term "deferred net tax liability" means, with respect to any taxable year, the amount of net tax liability payment of which has been deferred under paragraph (1) and which has not been assessed on a return of tax for any prior taxable year.

(C) FAILURE TO REPORT.—In the case of any failure to report any amount required to be reported under subparagraph (A) with respect to any taxable year before the due date for the return of tax for such taxable year, there shall be assessed on such return as an addition to tax 5 percent of such amount.

(8) ELECTION.—Any election under paragraph (1)—

(A) shall be made by the shareholder of the S corporation not later than the due date for such shareholder's return of tax for the taxable year which includes the close of the taxable year of such S corporation in which the amount described in subsection (a) is taken into account, and

(B) shall be made in such manner as the Secretary shall provide.

[Sec. 965(j)]

(j) REPORTING BY S CORPORATION.—Each S corporation which is a United States shareholder of a specified foreign corporation shall report in its return of tax under section 6037(a) the amount includible in its gross income for such taxable year by reason of this section and the amount of the deduction allowable by subsection (c). Any copy provided to a shareholder under section 6037(b) shall include a statement of such shareholder's pro rata share of such amounts.

[Sec. 965(k)]

(k) EXTENSION OF LIMITATION ON ASSESSMENT.—Notwithstanding section 6501, the limitation on the time period for the assessment of the net tax liability under this section (as defined in subsection (h)(6)) shall not expire before the date that is 6 years after the return for the taxable year described in such subsection was filed.

[Sec. 965(l)]

(l) RECAPTURE FOR EXPATRIATED ENTITIES.—

(1) IN GENERAL.—If a deduction is allowed under subsection (c) to a United States shareholder and such shareholder first becomes an expatriated entity at any time during the 10-year period beginning on the date of the enactment of the Tax Cuts and Jobs Act (with respect to a surrogate foreign corporation which first becomes a surrogate foreign corporation during such period), then—

(A) the tax imposed by this chapter shall be increased for the first taxable year in which such taxpayer becomes an expatriated entity by an amount equal to 35 percent of the amount of the deduction allowed under subsection (c), and

(B) no credits shall be allowed against the increase in tax under subparagraph (A).

(2) EXPATRIATED ENTITY.—For purposes of this subsection, the term "expatriated entity" has the same meaning given such term under section 7874(a)(2), except that such term shall not include an entity if the surrogate foreign corporation with respect to the entity is treated as a domestic corporation under section 7874(b).

(3) SURROGATE FOREIGN CORPORATION.—For purposes of this subsection, the term "surrogate foreign corporation" has the meaning given such term in section 7874(a)(2)(B).

[Sec. 965(m)]

(m) SPECIAL RULES FOR UNITED STATES SHAREHOLDERS WHICH ARE REAL ESTATE INVESTMENT TRUSTS.—

(1) IN GENERAL.—If a real estate investment trust is a United States shareholder in 1 or more deferred foreign income corporations—

(A) any amount required to be taken into account under section 951(a)(1) by reason of this section shall not be taken into account as gross income of the real estate investment trust for purposes of applying paragraphs (2) and (3) of section 856(c) to any taxable year for which such amount is taken into account under section 951(a)(1), and

(B) if the real estate investment trust elects the application of this subparagraph, notwithstanding subsection (a), any amount required to be taken into account under section 951(a)(1) by reason of this section shall, in lieu of the taxable year in which it would otherwise be included in gross income (for purposes of the computation of real estate investment trust taxable income under section 857(b)), be included in gross income as follows:

(i) 8 percent of such amount in the case of each of the taxable years in the 5-taxable year period beginning with the taxable year in which such amount would otherwise be included.

(ii) 15 percent of such amount in the case of the 1st taxable year following such period.

(iii) 20 percent of such amount in the case of the 2nd taxable year following such period.

(iv) 25 percent of such amount in the case of the 3rd taxable year following such period.

(2) RULES FOR TRUSTS ELECTING DEFERRED INCLUSION.—

(A) ELECTION.—Any election under paragraph (1)(B) shall be made not later than the due date for the first taxable year in the 5-taxable year period described in clause (i) of paragraph (1)(B) and shall be made in such manner as the Secretary shall provide.

(B) SPECIAL RULES.—If an election under paragraph (1)(B) is in effect with respect to any real estate investment trust, the following rules shall apply:

(i) APPLICATION OF PARTICIPATION EXEMPTION.—For purposes of subsection (c)(1)—

(I) the aggregate amount to which subparagraph (A) or (B) of subsection (c)(1) applies shall be determined without regard to the election,

(II) each such aggregate amount shall be allocated to each taxable year described in paragraph (1)(B) in the same proportion as the amount included in the gross income of such United States shareholder under section 951(a)(1) by reason of this section is allocated to each such taxable year.

(III) NO INSTALLMENT PAYMENTS.—The real estate investment trust may not make an election under subsection (g) for any taxable year described in paragraph (1)(B).

(ii) ACCELERATION OF INCLUSION.—If there is a liquidation or sale of substantially all the assets of the real estate investment trust (including in a title 11 or similar case), a cessation of business by such trust, or any similar circumstance, then any amount not yet included in gross income under paragraph (1)(B) shall be included in gross income as of the day before the date of the event and the unpaid portion of any tax liability with respect to such inclusion shall be due on the date of such event (or in the case of a title 11 or similar case, the day before the petition is filed).

[Sec. 965(n)]

(n) ELECTION NOT TO APPLY NET OPERATING LOSS DEDUCTION.—

(1) IN GENERAL.—If a United States shareholder of a deferred foreign income corporation elects the application of this subsection for the taxable year described in subsection (a), then the amount described in paragraph (2) shall not be taken into account—

(A) in determining the amount of the net operating loss deduction under section 172 of such shareholder for such taxable year, or

(B) in determining the amount of taxable income for such taxable year which may be reduced by net operating loss carryovers or carrybacks to such taxable year under section 172.

(2) AMOUNT DESCRIBED.—The amount described in this paragraph is the sum of—

(A) the amount required to be taken into account under section 951(a)(1) by reason of this section (determined after the application of subsection (c)), plus

(B) in the case of a domestic corporation which chooses to have the benefits of subpart A of part III of subchapter N for the taxable year, the taxes deemed to be paid by such corporation under subsections (a) and (b) of section 960 for such taxable year with respect to the amount described in subparagraph (A) which are treated as a dividends [sic] under section 78.

(3) ELECTION.—Any election under this subsection shall be made not later than the due date (including extensions) for filing the return of tax for the taxable year and shall be made in such manner as the Secretary shall prescribe.

[Sec. 965(o)]

(o) REGULATIONS.—The Secretary shall prescribe such regulations or other guidance as may be necessary or appropriate to carry out the provisions of this section, including—

(1) regulations or other guidance to provide appropriate basis adjustments, and

(2) regulations or other guidance to prevent the avoidance of the purposes of this section, including through a reduction in earnings and profits, through changes in entity classification or accounting methods, or otherwise.

Subpart G—Export Trade Corporations

[Sec. 970]

SEC. 970. REDUCTION OF SUBPART F INCOME OF EXPORT TRADE CORPORATIONS.

[Sec. 970(a)]

(a) EXPORT TRADE INCOME CONSTITUTING FOREIGN BASE COMPANY INCOME.—

(1) IN GENERAL.—In the case of a controlled foreign corporation (as defined in section 957) which for the taxable year is an export trade corporation, the subpart F income (determined without regard to this subpart) of such corporation for such year shall be reduced by an amount equal to so much of the export trade income (as defined in section 971(b)) of such corporation for such year as constitutes foreign base company income (as defined in section 954), but only to the extent that such amount does not exceed whichever of the following amounts is the lesser:

(A) an amount equal to $1^1/2$ times so much of the export promotion expenses (as defined in section 971(d)) of such corporation for such year as is properly allocable to the export trade income which constitutes foreign base company income of such corporation for such year, or

(B) an amount equal to 10 percent of so much of the gross receipts for such year (or, in the case of gross receipts arising from commissions, fees, or other compensation for its services, so much of the gross amount upon the basis of which such commissions, fees, or other compensation is computed) accruing to such export trade corporation from the sale, installation, operation, maintenance, or use of property in respect of which such corporation derives export trade income as is properly allocable to the export trade income which constitutes foreign base company income of such corporation for such year.

The allocations with respect to export trade income which constitutes foreign base company income under subparagraphs (A) and (B) shall be made under regulations prescribed by the Secretary.

(2) OVERALL LIMITATION.—The reduction under paragraph (1) for any taxable year shall not exceed an amount which bears the same ratio to the increase in the investments in export trade assets (as defined in section 971(c)) of such corporation for such year as the export trade income which constitutes foreign base company income of such corporation for such year bears to the entire export trade income of such corporation for such year.

[Sec. 970(b)—Stricken]

[Sec. 970(c)]

(c) INVESTMENTS IN EXPORT TRADE ASSETS.—

(1) AMOUNT OF INVESTMENTS.—For purposes of this section, the amount taken into account with respect to any export trade asset shall be its adjusted basis, reduced by any liability to which the asset is subject.

(2) INCREASE IN INVESTMENTS IN EXPORT TRADE ASSETS.—For purposes of subsection (a), the amount of increase in investments in export trade assets of any controlled foreign corporation for any taxable year is the amount by which—

(A) the amount of such investments at the close of the taxable year, exceeds

(B) the amount of such investments at the close of the preceding taxable year.

(3) DECREASE IN INVESTMENTS IN EXPORT TRADE ASSETS.—For purposes of subsection (b), the amount of decrease in investments in export trade assets of any controlled foreign corporation for any taxable year is the amount by which—

(A) the amount of such investments at the close of the preceding taxable year (reduced by an amount equal to the amount of net loss sustained during the taxable year with respect to export trade assets), exceeds

(B) the amount of such investments at the close of the taxable year.

(4) SPECIAL RULE.—A United States shareholder of an export trade corporation may, under regulations prescribed by the Secretary, make the determinations under paragraphs (2) and (3) as of the close of the 75th day after the close of the years referred to in such paragraphs in lieu

of on the last day of such years. A United States shareholder of an export trade corporation may, under regulations prescribed by the Secretary, make the determinations under paragraphs (2) and (3) with respect to export trade assets described in section 971(c)(3) as of the close of the years following the years referred to in such paragraphs, or as of the close of such longer period of time as such regulations may permit, in lieu of on the last day of such years and in lieu of on the day prescribed in the preceding sentence. Any election under this paragraph made with respect to any taxable year shall apply to such year and to all succeeding taxable years unless the Secretary consents to the revocation of such election.

[Sec. 971]

SEC. 971. DEFINITIONS.

[Sec. 971(a)]

(a) EXPORT TRADE CORPORATIONS.—For purposes of this subpart, the term "export trade corporation" means—

(1) IN GENERAL.—A controlled foreign corporation (as defined in section 957) which satisfies the following conditions:

(A) 90 percent or more of the gross income of such corporation for the 3-year period immediately preceding the close of the taxable year (or such part of such period subsequent to the effective date of this subpart during which the corporation was in existence) was derived from sources without the United States, and

(B) 75 percent or more of the gross income of such corporation for such period constituted gross income in respect of which such corporation derived export trade income.

(2) SPECIAL RULE.—If 50 percent or more of the gross income of a controlled foreign corporation in the period specified in subsection (a)(1)(A) is gross income in respect of which such corporation derived export trade income in respect of agricultural products grown in the United States, it may qualify as an export trade corporation although it does not meet the requirements of subsection (a)(1)(B).

(3) LIMITATION.—No controlled foreign corporation may qualify as an export trade corporation for any taxable year beginning after October 31, 1971, unless it qualified as an export trade corporation for any taxable year beginning before such date. If a corporation fails to qualify as an export trade corporation for a period of any 3 consecutive taxable years beginning after such date, it may not qualify as an export trade corporation for any taxable year beginning after such period.

[Sec. 971(b)]

(b) EXPORT TRADE INCOME.—For the purposes of this subpart the term "export trade income" means net income from—

(1) the sale to an unrelated person for use, consumption, or disposition outside the United States of export property (as defined in subsection (e)), or from commissions, fees, compensation, or other income from the performance of commercial, industrial, financial, technical, scientific, managerial, engineering, architectural, skilled, or other services in respect of such sales or in respect of the installation or maintenance of such export property;

(2) commissions, fees, compensation, or other income from commercial, industrial, financial, technical, scientific, managerial, engineering, architectural, skilled, or other services performed in connection with the use by an unrelated person outside the United States of patents, copyrights, secret processes and formulas, goodwill, trademarks, trade brands, franchises, and other like property acquired or developed and owned by the manufacturer, producer, grower, or extractor of export property in respect of which the export trade corporation earns export trade income under paragraph (1);

(3) commissions, fees, rentals, or other compensation or income attributable to the use of export property by an unrelated person or attributable to the use of export property in the rendition of technical, scientific, or engineering services to an unrelated person; and

(4) interest from export trade assets described in subsection (c)(4).

For purposes of paragraph (3), if a controlled foreign corporation receives income from an unrelated person attributable to the use of export property in the rendition of services to such unrelated person together with income attributable to the rendition of other services to such unrelated person, including personal services, the amount of such aggregate income which shall be considered to be attributable to the use of the export property shall (if such amount cannot be established by reference to transactions between unrelated persons) be that part of such aggregate income which the cost of the export property consumed in the rendition of such services (including a reasonable allowance for depreciation) bears to the total costs and expenses attributable to such aggregate income.

[Sec. 971(c)]

(c) EXPORT TRADE ASSETS.—For purposes of this subpart, the term "export trade assets" means—

(1) working capital reasonably necessary for the production of export trade income,

(2) inventory of export property held for use, consumption, or disposition outside the United States,

(3) facilities located outside the United States for the storage, handling, transportation, packaging, or servicing of export property, and

(4) evidences of indebtedness executed by persons, other than related persons, in connection with payment for purchases of export property for use, consumption, or disposition outside the United States, or in connection with the payment for services described in subsections (b)(2) and (3).

[Sec. 971(d)]

(d) EXPORT PROMOTION EXPENSES.—For purposes of this subpart, the term "export promotion expenses" means the following expenses paid or incurred in the receipt or production of export trade income—

(1) a reasonable allowance for salaries or other compensation for personal services actually rendered for such purpose,

(2) rentals or other payments for the use of property actually used for such purpose,

(3) a reasonable allowance for the exhaustion, wear and tear, or obsolescence of property actually used for such purpose, and

(4) any other ordinary and necessary expenses of the corporation to the extent reasonably allocable to the receipt or production of export trade income.

No expense incurred within the United States shall be treated as an export promotion expense within the meaning of the preceding sentence, unless at least 90 percent of each category of expenses described in such sentence is incurred outside the United States.

[Sec. 971(e)]

(e) EXPORT PROPERTY.—For purposes of this subpart, the term "export property" means any property or any interest in property manufactured, produced, grown, or extracted in the United States.

[Sec. 971(f)]

(f) UNRELATED PERSON.—For purposes of this subpart, the term "unrelated person" means a person other than a related person as defined in section 954(d)(3).

Subpart I—Admissibility of Documentation Maintained in Foreign Countries

[Sec. 982]

SEC. 982. ADMISSIBILITY OF DOCUMENTATION MAINTAINED IN FOREIGN COUNTRIES.

[Sec. 982(a)]

(a) GENERAL RULE.—If the taxpayer fails to substantially comply with any formal document request arising out of the examination of the tax treatment of any item (hereinafter in this section referred to as the "examined item") before the 90th day after the date of the mailing of such request on motion by the Secretary, any court having jurisdiction of a civil proceeding in which the tax treatment of the examined item is an issue shall prohibit the introduction by the taxpayer of any foreign-based documentation covered by such request.

[Sec. 982(b)]

(b) REASONABLE CAUSE EXCEPTION.—

(1) IN GENERAL.—Subsection (a) shall not apply with respect to any documentation if the taxpayer establishes that the failure to provide the documentation as requested by the Secretary is due to reasonable cause.

(2) FOREIGN NONDISCLOSURE LAW NOT REASONABLE CAUSE.—For purposes of paragraph (1), the fact that a foreign jurisdiction would impose a civil or criminal penalty on the taxpayer (or any other person) for disclosing the requested documentation is not reasonable cause.

[Sec. 982(c)]

(c) FORMAL DOCUMENT REQUEST.—For purposes of this section—

(1) FORMAL DOCUMENT REQUEST.—The term "formal document request" means any request (made after the normal request procedures have failed to produce the requested documentation) for the production of foreign-based documentation which is mailed by registered or certified mail to the taxpayer at his last known address and which sets forth—

(A) the time and place for the production of the documentation,

(B) a statement of the reason the documentation previously produced (if any) is not sufficient,

(C) a description of the documentation being sought, and

(D) the consequences to the taxpayer of the failure to produce the documentation described in subparagraph (C).

(2) PROCEEDING TO QUASH.—

(A) IN GENERAL.—Notwithstanding any other law or rule of law, any person to whom a formal document request is mailed shall have the right to begin a proceeding to quash such request not later than the 90th day after the day such request was mailed. In any such proceeding, the Secretary may seek to compel compliance with such request.

(B) JURISDICTION.—The United States district court for the district in which the person (to whom the formal document request is mailed) resides or is found shall have jurisdiction to hear any proceeding brought under subparagraph (A). An order denying the petition shall be deemed a final order which may be appealed.

(C) SUSPENSION OF 90-DAY PERIOD.—The running of the 90-day period referred to in subsection (a) shall be suspended during any period during which a proceeding brought under subparagraph (A) is pending.

[Sec. 982(d)]

(d) DEFINITIONS AND SPECIAL RULES.—For purposes of this section—

(1) FOREIGN-BASED DOCUMENTATION.—The term "foreign-based documentation" means any documentation which is outside the United States and which may be relevent or material to the tax treatment of the examined item.

(2) DOCUMENTATION.—The term "documentation" includes books and records.

(3) AUTHORITY TO EXTEND 90-DAY PERIOD.—The Secretary, and any court having jurisdiction over a proceeding under subsection (c)(2), may extend the 90-day period referred to in subsection (a).

[Sec. 982(e)]

(e) SUSPENSION OF STATUTE OF LIMITATIONS.—If any person takes any action as provided in subsection (c)(2), the running of any period of limitations under section 6501 (relating to the assessment and collection of tax) or under section 6531 (relating to criminal prosecutions) with respect to such person shall be suspended for the period during which the proceeding under such subsection, and appeals therein, are pending.

Subpart J—Foreign Currency Transactions

[Sec. 985]

SEC. 985. FUNCTIONAL CURRENCY.

[Sec. 985(a)]

(a) IN GENERAL.—Unless otherwise provided in regulations, all determinations under this subtitle shall be made in the taxpayer's functional currency.

[Sec. 985(b)]

(b) FUNCTIONAL CURRENCY.—

(1) IN GENERAL.—For purposes of this subtitle, the term "functional currency" means—

(A) except as provided in subparagraph (B), the dollar, or

(B) in the case of a qualified business unit, the currency of the economic environment in which a significant part of such unit's activities are conducted and which is used by such unit in keeping its books and records.

(2) FUNCTIONAL CURRENCY WHERE ACTIVITIES PRIMARILY CONDUCTED IN DOLLARS.—The functional currency of any qualified business unit shall be the dollar if activities of such unit are primarily conducted in dollars.

(3) ELECTION.—To the extent provided in regulations, the taxpayer may elect to use the dollar as the functional currency for any qualified business unit if—

(A) such unit keeps its books and records in dollars, or

(B) the taxpayer uses a method of accounting that approximates a separate transactions method.

Any such election shall apply to the taxable year for which made and all subsequent taxable years unless revoked with the consent of the Secretary.

(4) CHANGE IN FUNCTIONAL CURRENCY TREATED AS A CHANGE IN METHOD OF ACCOUNTING.—Any change in the functional currency shall be treated as a change in the taxpayer's method of accounting for purposes of section 481 under procedures to be established by the Secretary.

[Sec. 986]

SEC. 986. DETERMINATION OF FOREIGN TAXES AND FOREIGN CORPORATION'S EARNINGS AND PROFITS.

[Sec. 986(a)]

(a) FOREIGN INCOME TAXES.—

(1) TRANSLATION OF ACCRUED TAXES.—

(A) IN GENERAL.—For purposes of determining the amount of the foreign tax credit, in the case of a taxpayer who takes foreign income taxes into account when accrued, the amount of any foreign income taxes (and any adjustment thereto) shall be translated into dollars by using the average exchange rate for the taxable year to which such taxes relate.

(B) EXCEPTION FOR CERTAIN TAXES.—Subparagraph (A) shall not apply to any foreign income taxes—

(i) paid after the date 2 years after the close of the taxable year to which such taxes relate, or

(ii) paid before the beginning of the taxable year to which such taxes relate.

(C) EXCEPTION FOR INFLATIONARY CURRENCIES.—Subparagraph (A) shall not apply to any foreign income taxes the liability for which is denominated in any inflationary currency (as determined under regulations).

(D) ELECTIVE EXCEPTION FOR TAXES PAID OTHER THAN IN FUNCTIONAL CURRENCY.—

(i) IN GENERAL.—At the election of the taxpayer, subparagraph (A) shall not apply to any foreign income taxes the liability for which is denominated in any currency other than in the taxpayer's functional currency.

(ii) APPLICATION TO QUALIFIED BUSINESS UNITS.—An election under this subparagraph may apply to foreign income taxes attributable to a qualified business unit in accordance with regulations prescribed by the Secretary.

(iii) ELECTION.—Any such election shall apply to the taxable year for which made and all subsequent taxable years unless revoked with the consent of the Secretary.

(E) SPECIAL RULE FOR REGULATED INVESTMENT COMPANIES.—In the case of a regulated investment company which takes into account income on an accrual basis, subparagraphs (A) through (D) shall not apply and foreign income taxes paid or accrued with respect to such income shall be translated into dollars using the exchange rate as of the date the income accrues.

(F) CROSS REFERENCE.—

For adjustments where tax is not paid within 2 years, see section 905(c).

(2) TRANSLATION OF TAXES TO WHICH PARAGRAPH (1) DOES NOT APPLY.—For purposes of determining the amount of the foreign tax credit, in the case of any foreign income taxes to which subparagraph (A) or (E) of paragraph (1) does not apply—

(A) such taxes shall be translated into dollars using the exchange rates as of the time such taxes were paid to the foreign country or possession of the United States, and

(B) any adjustment to the amount of such taxes shall be translated into dollars using—

(i) except as provided in clause (ii), the exchange rate as of the time when such adjustment is paid to the foreign country or possession, or

(ii) in the case of any refund or credit of foreign income taxes, using the exchange rate as of the time of the original payment of such foreign income taxes.

(3) AUTHORITY TO PERMIT USE OF AVERAGE RATES.—To the extent prescribed in regulations, the average exchange rate for the period (specified in such regulations) during which the taxes or adjustment is paid may be used instead of the exchange rate as of the time of such payment.

(4) FOREIGN INCOME TAXES.—For purposes of this subsection, the term "foreign income taxes" means any income, war profits, or excess profits taxes paid or accrued to any foreign country or to any possession of the United States.

[Sec. 986(b)]

(b) EARNINGS AND PROFITS AND DISTRIBUTIONS.—For purposes of determining the tax under this subtitle—

(1) of any shareholder of any foreign corporation, the earnings and profits of such corporation shall be determined in the corporation's functional currency, and

(2) in the case of any United States person, the earnings and profits determined under paragraph (1) (when distributed, deemed distributed, or otherwise taken into account under this subtitle) shall (if necessary) be translated into dollars using the appropriate exchange rate.

[Sec. 986(c)]

(c) PREVIOUSLY TAXED EARNINGS AND PROFITS.—

(1) IN GENERAL.—Foreign currency gain or loss with respect to distributions of previously taxed earnings and profits (as described in section 959 or 1293(c)) attributable to movements in exchange rates between the times of deemed and actual distribution shall be recognized and treated as ordinary income or loss from the same source as the associated income inclusion.

(2) DISTRIBUTIONS THROUGH TIERS.—The Secretary shall prescribe regulations with respect to the treatment of distributions of previously taxed earnings and profits through tiers of foreign corporations.

[Sec. 987]

SEC. 987. BRANCH TRANSACTIONS.

In the case of any taxpayer having 1 or more qualified business units with a functional currency other than the dollar, taxable income of such taxpayer shall be determined—

(1) by computing the taxable income or loss separately for each such unit in its functional currency,

(2) by translating the income or loss separately computed under paragraph (1) at the appropriate exchange rate, and

(3) by making proper adjustments (as prescribed by the Secretary) for transfers of property between qualified business units of the taxpayer having different functional currencies, including—

(A) treating post-1986 remittances from each such unit as made on a pro rata basis out of post-1986 accumulated earnings, and

(B) treating gain or loss determined under this paragraph as ordinary income or loss, respectively, and sourcing such gain or loss by reference to the source of the income giving rise to post-1986 accumulated earnings.

[Sec. 988]

SEC. 988. TREATMENT OF CERTAIN FOREIGN CURRENCY TRANSACTIONS.

[Sec. 988(a)]

(a) GENERAL RULE.—Notwithstanding any other provisions of this chapter—

(1) TREATMENT AS ORDINARY INCOME OR LOSS.—

(A) IN GENERAL.—Except as otherwise provided in this section, any foreign currency gain or loss attributable to a section 988 transaction shall be computed separately and treated as ordinary income or loss (as the case may be).

(B) SPECIAL RULE FOR FORWARD CONTRACTS, ETC.—Except as provided in regulations, a taxpayer may elect to treat any foreign currency gain or loss attributable to a forward contract, a futures contract, or option described in subsection (c)(1)(B)(iii) which is a capital asset in the hands of the taxpayer and which is not a part of a straddle (within the meaning of section 1092(c), without regard to paragraph (4) thereof) as capital gain or loss (as the case may be) if the taxpayer makes such election and identifies such transaction before the close of the day on which such transaction is entered into (or such earlier time as the Secretary may prescribe).

(2) GAIN OR LOSS TREATED AS INTEREST FOR CERTAIN PURPOSES.—To the extent provided in regulations, any amount treated as ordinary income or loss under paragraph (1) shall be treated as interest income or expense (as the case may be).

(3) SOURCE.—

(A) IN GENERAL.—Except as otherwise provided in regulations, in the case of any amount treated as ordinary income or loss under paragraph (1) (without regard to paragraph (1)(B)), the source of such amount shall be determined by reference to the residence of the taxpayer or the qualified business unit of the taxpayer on whose books the asset, liability, or item of income or expense is properly reflected.

(B) RESIDENCE.—For purposes of this subpart—

(i) IN GENERAL.—The residence of any person shall be—

(I) in the case of an individual, the country in which such individual's tax home (as defined in section 911(d)(3)) is located,

(II) in the case of any corporation, partnership, trust, or estate which is a United States person (as defined in section 7701(a)(30)), the United States, and

(III) in the case of any corporation, partnership, trust, or estate which is not a United States person, a country other than the United States.

If an individual does not have a tax home (as so defined), the residence of such individual shall be the United States if such individual is a United States citizen or a resident alien and shall be a country other than the United States if such individual is not a United States citizen or a resident alien.

(ii) EXCEPTION.—In the case of a qualified business unit of any taxpayer (including an individual), the residence of such unit shall be the country in which the principal place of business of such qualified business unit is located.

(iii) SPECIAL RULE FOR PARTNERSHIPS.—To the extent provided in regulations, in the case of a partnership, the determination of residence shall be made at the partner level.

(C) SPECIAL RULE FOR CERTAIN RELATED PARTY LOANS.—Except to the extent provided in regulations, in the case of a loan by a United States person or a related person to a 10-percent owned foreign corporation which is denominated in a currency other than the dollar and bears interest at a rate at least 10 percentage points higher than the Federal mid-term rate (determined under section 1274(d)) at the time such loan is entered into, the following rules shall apply:

(i) For purposes of section 904 only, such loan shall be marked to market on an annual basis.

(ii) Any interest income earned with respect to such loan for the taxable year shall be treated as income from sources within the United States to the extent of any loss attributable to clause (i).

For purposes of this subparagraph, the term "related person" has the meaning given such term by section 954(d)(3), except that such section shall be applied by substituting "United States person" for "controlled foreign corporation" each place such term appears.

(D) 10-PERCENT OWNED FOREIGN CORPORATION.—The term "10-percent owned foreign corporation" means any foreign corporation in which the United States person owns directly or indirectly at least 10 percent of the voting stock.

[Sec. 988(b)]

(b) FOREIGN CURRENCY GAIN OR LOSS.—For purposes of this section—

(1) FOREIGN CURRENCY GAIN.—The term "foreign currency gain" means any gain from a section 988 transaction to the extent such gain does not exceed gain realized by reason of changes in exchange rates on or after the booking date and before the payment date.

(2) FOREIGN CURRENCY LOSS.—The term "foreign currency loss" means any loss from a section 988 transaction to the extent such loss does not exceed the loss realized by reason of changes in exchange rates on or after the booking date and before the payment date.

(3) SPECIAL RULE FOR CERTAIN CONTRACTS, ETC.—In the case of any section 988 transaction described in subsection (c)(1)(B)(iii), any gain or loss from such transaction shall be treated as foreign currency gain or loss (as the case may be).

[Sec. 988(c)]

(c) OTHER DEFINITIONS.—For purposes of this section—

(1) SECTION 988 TRANSACTION.—

(A) IN GENERAL.—The term "section 988 transaction" means any transaction described in subparagraph (B) if the amount which the taxpayer is entitled to receive (or is required to pay) by reason of such transaction—

(i) is denominated in terms of a nonfunctional currency, or

(ii) is determined by reference to the value of 1 or more nonfunctional currencies.

(B) DESCRIPTION OF TRANSACTIONS.—For purposes of subparagraph (A), the following transactions are described in this subparagraph:

(i) The acquisition of a debt instrument or becoming the obligor under a debt instrument.

(ii) Accruing (or otherwise taking into account) for purposes of this subtitle any item of expense or gross income or receipts which is to be paid or received after the date on which so accrued or taken into account.

(iii) Entering into or acquiring any forward contract, futures contract, option, or similar financial instrument.

The Secretary may prescribe regulations excluding from the application of clause (ii) any class of items the taking into account of which is not necessary to carry out the purposes of this section by reason of the small amounts or short periods involved, or otherwise.

(C) SPECIAL RULES FOR DISPOSITION OF NONFUNCTIONAL CURRENCY.—

(i) IN GENERAL.—In the case of any disposition of any nonfunctional currency—

(I) such disposition shall be treated as a section 988 transaction, and

(II) any gain or loss from such transaction shall be treated as foreign currency gain or loss (as the case may be).

(ii) NONFUNCTIONAL CURRENCY.—For purposes of this section, the term "nonfunctional currency" includes coin or currency, and nonfunctional currency denominated demand or time deposits or similar instruments issued by a bank or other financial institution.

(D) EXCEPTION FOR CERTAIN INSTRUMENTS MARKED TO MARKET.—

(i) IN GENERAL.—Clause (iii) of subparagraph (B) shall not apply to any regulated futures contract or nonequity option which would be marked to market under section 1256 if held on the last day of the taxable year.

(ii) ELECTION OUT.—

(I) IN GENERAL.—The taxpayer may elect to have clause (i) not apply to such taxpayer. Such an election shall apply to contracts held at any time during the taxable year for which such election is made or any succeeding taxable year unless such election is revoked with the consent of the Secretary.

(II) TIME FOR MAKING ELECTION.—Except as provided in regulations, an election under subclause (I) for any taxable year shall be made on or before the 1st day of such taxable year (or, if later, on or before the 1st day during such year on which the taxpayer holds a contract described in clause (i)).

(III) SPECIAL RULE FOR PARTNERSHIPS, ETC.—In the case of a partnership, an election under subclause (I) shall be made by each partner separately. A similar rule shall apply in the case of an S corporation.

(iii) TREATMENT OF CERTAIN PARTNERSHIPS.—This subparagraph shall not apply to any income or loss of a partnership for any taxable year if such partnership made an election under subparagraph (E)(iii)(V) for such year or any preceding year.

(E) SPECIAL RULES FOR CERTAIN FUNDS.—

(i) IN GENERAL.—In the case of a qualified fund, clause (iii) of subparagraph (B) shall not apply to any instrument which would be marked to market under section 1256 if held on the last day of the taxable year (determined after the application of clause (iv)).

(ii) SPECIAL RULE WHERE ELECTING PARTNERSHIP DOES NOT QUALIFY.—If any partnership made an election under clause (iii)(V) for any taxable year and such partnership has a net loss for such year or any succeeding year from instruments referred to in clause (i), the rules of clauses (i) and (iv) shall apply to any such loss year whether or not such partnership is a qualified fund for such year.

(iii) QUALIFIED FUND DEFINED.—For purposes of this subparagraph, the term "qualified fund" means any partnership if—

(I) at all times during the taxable year (and during each preceding taxable year to which an election under subclause (V) applied), such partnership has at least 20 partners and no single partner owns more than 20 percent of the interests in the capital or profits of the partnership,

(II) the principal activity of such partnership for such taxable year (and each such preceding taxable year) consists of buying and selling options, futures, or forwards with respect to commodities,

(III) at least 90 percent of the gross income of the partnership for the taxable year (and for each such preceding taxable year) consisted of income or gains described in subparagraph (A), (B), or (G) of section 7704(d)(1) or gain from the sale or disposition of capital assets held for the production of interest or dividends,

(IV) no more than a de minimis amount of the gross income of the partnership for the taxable year (and each such preceding taxable year) was derived from buying and selling commodities, and

(V) an election under this subclause applies to the taxable year.

An election under subclause (V) for any taxable year shall be made on or before the 1st day of such taxable year (or, if later, on or before the 1st day during such year on which the partnership holds an instrument referred to in clause (i)). Any such election shall apply to the taxable year for which made and all succeeding taxable years unless revoked with the consent of the Secretary.

(iv) TREATMENT OF CERTAIN CURRENCY CONTRACTS.—

(I) IN GENERAL.—Except as provided in regulations, in the case of a qualified fund, any bank forward contract, any foreign currency futures contract traded on a foreign exchange, or to the extent provided in regulations any similar instrument, which is not otherwise a section 1256 contract shall be treated as a section 1256 contract for purposes of section 1256.

(II) GAINS AND LOSSES TREATED AS SHORT-TERM.—In the case of any instrument treated as a section 1256 contract under subclause (I), subparagraph (A) of section 1256(a)(3) shall be applied by substituting "100 percent" for "40 percent" (and subparagraph (B) of such section shall not apply).

(v) SPECIAL RULES FOR CLAUSE (iii)(I).—

(I) CERTAIN GENERAL PARTNERS.—The interest of a general partner in the partnership shall not be treated as failing to meet the 20-percent ownership requirements of clause (iii)(I) for any taxable year of the partnership if, for the taxable year of the partner in which such partnership taxable year ends, such partner (and each corporation filing a consolidated return with such partner) had no ordinary income or loss from a section 988 transaction which is foreign currency gain or loss (as the case may be).

(II) TREATMENT OF INCENTIVE COMPENSATION.—For purposes of clause (iii)(I), any income allocable to a general partner as incentive compensation based on profits rather than capital shall not be taken into account in determining such partner's interest in the profits of the partnership.

(III) TREATMENT OF TAX-EXEMPT PARTNERS.—Except as provided in regulations, the interest of a partner in the partnership shall not be treated as failing to meet the 20-percent ownership requirements of clause (iii)(I) if none of the income of such partner from such partnership is subject to tax under this chapter (whether directly or through 1 or more pass-thru entities).

(IV) LOOK-THRU RULE.—In determining whether the requirements of clause (iii)(I) are met with respect to any partnership, except to the extent provided in regulations, any interest in such partnership held by another partnership shall be treated as held proportionately by the partners in such other partnership.

(vi) OTHER SPECIAL RULES.—For purposes of this subparagraph—

(I) RELATED PERSONS.—Interest in the partnership held by persons related to each other (within the meaning of sections 267(b) and 707(b)) shall be treated as held by 1 person.

(II) PREDECESSORS.—References to any partnership shall include a reference to any predecessor thereof.

(III) INADVERTENT TERMINATIONS.—Rules similar to the rules of section 7704(e) shall apply.

(IV) TREATMENT OF CERTAIN DEBT INSTRUMENTS.—For purposes of clause (iii)(IV), any debt instrument which is a section 988 transaction shall be treated as a commodity.

(2) BOOKING DATE.—The term "booking date" means—

(A) in the case of a transaction described in paragraph (1)(B)(i), the date of acquisition or on which the taxpayer becomes the obligor, or

(B) in the case of a transaction described in paragraph (1)(B)(ii), the date on which accrued or otherwise taken into account.

(3) PAYMENT DATE.—The term "payment date" means the date on which the payment is made or received.

(4) DEBT INSTRUMENT.—The term "debt instrument" means a bond, debenture, note, or certificate or other evidence of indebtedness. To the extent provided in regulations, such term shall include preferred stock.

(5) SPECIAL RULES WHERE TAXPAYER TAKES OR MAKES DELIVERY.—If the taxpayer takes or makes delivery in connection with any section 988 transaction described in paragraph (1)(B)(iii), any gain or loss (determined as if the taxpayer sold the contract, option, or instrument on the date on which he took or made delivery for its fair market value on such date) shall be recognized in the same manner as if such contract, option, or instrument were so sold.

[Sec. 988(d)]

(d) TREATMENT OF 988 HEDGING TRANSACTIONS.—

(1) IN GENERAL.—To the extent provided in regulations, if any section 988 transaction is part of a 988 hedging transaction, all transactions which are part of such 988 hedging transaction shall be integrated and treated as a single transaction or otherwise treated consistently for purposes of this subtitle. For purposes of the preceding sentence, the determination of whether any transaction is a section 988 transaction shall be determined without regard to whether such transaction would otherwise be marked-to-market under Section 475 or 1256 and such

term shall not include any transaction with respect to which an election is made under subsection (a)(1)(B). Sections 475, 1092, and 1256 shall not apply to a transaction covered by this subsection.

(2) 988 HEDGING TRANSACTION.—For purposes of paragraph (1), the term "988 hedging transaction" means any transaction—

(A) entered into by the taxpayer primarily—

(i) to manage risk of currency fluctuations with respect to property which is held or to be held by the taxpayer, or

(ii) to manage risk of currency fluctuations with respect to borrowings made or to be made, or obligations incurred or to be incurred, by the taxpayer, and

(B) identified by the Secretary or the taxpayer as being a 988 hedging transaction.

[Sec. 988(e)]

(e) APPLICATION TO INDIVIDUALS.—

(1) IN GENERAL.—The preceding provisions of this section shall not apply to any section 988 transaction entered into by an individual which is a personal transaction.

(2) EXCLUSION FOR CERTAIN PERSONAL TRANSACTIONS.—If—

(A) nonfunctional currency is disposed of by an individual in any transaction, and

(B) such transaction is a personal transaction,

no gain shall be recognized for purposes of this subtitle by reason of changes in exchange rates after such currency was acquired by such individual and before such disposition. The preceding sentence shall not apply if the gain which would otherwise be recognized on the transaction exceeds $200.

(3) PERSONAL TRANSACTIONS.—For purposes of this subsection, the term "personal transaction" means any transaction entered into by an individual, except that such term shall not include any transaction to the extent that expenses properly allocable to such transaction meet the requirements of—

(A) section 162 (other than traveling expenses described in subsection (a)(2) thereof), or

(B) section 212 (other than that part of section 212 dealing with expenses incurred in connection with taxes).

[Sec. 989]

SEC. 989. OTHER DEFINITIONS AND SPECIAL RULES.

[Sec. 989(a)]

(a) QUALIFIED BUSINESS UNIT.—For purposes of this subpart, the term "qualified business unit" means any separate and clearly identified unit of a trade or business of a taxpayer which maintains separate books and records.

[Sec. 989(b)]

(b) APPROPRIATE EXCHANGE RATE.—Except as provided in regulations, for purposes of this subpart, the term "appropriate exchange rate" means—

(1) in the case of an actual distribution of earnings and profits, the spot rate on the date such distribution is included in income,

(2) in the case of an actual or deemed sale or exchange of stock in a foreign corporation treated as a dividend under section 1248, the spot rate on the date the deemed dividend is included in income,

(3) in the case of any amounts included in income under section 951(a)(1)(A) or 1293(a), the averaged exchange rate for the taxable year of the foreign corporation, or

(4) in the case of any other qualified business unit of a taxpayer, the average exchange rate for the taxable year of such qualified business unit.

For purposes of the preceding sentence, any amount included in income under section 951(a)(1)(B) shall be treated as an actual distribution made on the last day of the taxable year for which such amount was so included.

[Sec. 989(c)]

(c) REGULATIONS.—The Secretary shall prescribe such regulations as may be necessary or appropriate to carry out the purposes of this subpart, including regulations—

(1) setting forth procedures to be followed by taxpayers with qualified business units using a net worth method of accounting before the enactment of this subpart,

(2) limiting the recognition of foreign currency loss on certain remittances from qualified business units,

(3) providing for the recharacterization of interest and principal payments with respect to obligations denominated in certain hyperinflationary currencies,

(4) providing for alternative adjustments to the application of section 905(c),

(5) providing for the appropriate treatment of related party transactions (including transactions between qualified business units of the same taxpayer), and

(6) setting forth procedures for determining the average exchange rate for any period.

PART IV—DOMESTIC INTERNATIONAL SALES CORPORATIONS

Subpart A—Treatment of Qualifying Corporations

[Sec. 991]

SEC. 991. TAXATION OF A DOMESTIC INTERNATIONAL SALES CORPORATION.

For purposes of the taxes imposed by this subtitle upon a DISC (as defined in section 992(a)), a DISC shall not be subject to the taxes imposed by this subtitle.

[Sec. 992]

SEC. 992. REQUIREMENTS OF A DOMESTIC INTERNATIONAL SALES CORPORATION.

[Sec. 992(a)]

(a) DEFINITION OF "DISC" AND "FORMER DISC".—

(1) DISC.—For purposes of this title, the term "DISC" means, with respect to any taxable year, a corporation which is incorporated under the laws of any State and satisfies the following conditions for the taxable year:

(A) 95 percent or more of the gross receipts (as defined in section 993(f)) of such corporation consist of qualified export receipts (as defined in section 993(a)),

(B) the adjusted basis of the qualified export assets (as defined in section 993(b)) of the corporation at the close of the taxable year equals or exceeds 95 percent of the sum of the adjusted basis of all assets of the corporation at the close of the taxable year,

(C) such corporation does not have more than one class of stock and the par or stated value of its outstanding stock is at least $2,500 on each day of the taxable year, and

(D) the corporation has made an election pursuant to subsection (b) to be treated as a DISC and such election is in effect for the taxable year.

(2) STATUS AS DISC AFTER HAVING FILED A RETURN AS A DISC.—The Secretary shall prescribe regulations setting forth the conditions under and the extent to which a corporation which has filed a return as a DISC for a taxable year shall be treated as a DISC for such taxable year for all purposes of this title, notwithstanding the fact that the corporation has failed to satisfy the conditions of paragraph (1).

(3) "FORMER DISC".—For purposes of this title, the term "former DISC" means, with respect to any taxable year, a corporation which is not a DISC for such year but was a DISC in a preceding taxable year and at the beginning of the taxable year has undistributed previously taxed income or accumulated DISC income.

[Sec. 992(b)]

(b) ELECTION.—

(1) ELECTION.—

(A) An election by a corporation to be treated as a DISC shall be made by such corporation for a taxable year at any time during the 90-day period immediately preceding the beginning of the taxable year, except that the Secretary may give his consent to the making of an election at such other times as he may designate.

(B) Such election shall be made in such manner as the Secretary shall prescribe and shall be valid only if all persons who are shareholders in such corporation on the first day of the first taxable year for which such election is effective consent to such election.

(2) EFFECT OF ELECTION.—If a corporation makes an election under paragraph (1), then the provisions of this part shall apply to such corporation for the taxable year of the corporation for which made and for all succeeding taxable years and shall apply to each person who at any time is a shareholder of such corporation for all periods on or after the first day of the first taxable year of the corporation for which the election is effective.

(3) TERMINATION OF ELECTION.—

(A) REVOCATION.—An election under this subsection made by any corporation may be terminated by revocation of such election for any taxable year of the corporation after the first taxable year of the corporation for which the election is effective. A termination under this paragraph shall be effective with respect to such election—

(i) for the taxable year in which made, if made at any time during the first 90 days of such taxable year, or

(ii) for the taxable year following the taxable year in which made, if made after the close of such 90 days,

and for all succeeding taxable years of the corporation. Such termination shall be made in such manner as the Secretary shall prescribe by regulations.

(B) CONTINUED FAILURE TO BE DISC.—If a corporation is not a DISC for each of any 5 consecutive taxable years of the corporation for which an election under this subsection is effective, the election shall be terminated and not be in effect for any taxable year of the corporation after such 5th year.

[Sec. 992(c)]

(c) DISTRIBUTIONS TO MEET QUALIFICATION REQUIREMENTS.—

(1) IN GENERAL.—Subject to the conditions provided by paragraph (2), a corporation which for a taxable year does not satisfy a condition specified in paragraph (1)(A) (relating to gross receipts) or (1)(B) (relating to assets) of subsection (a) shall nevertheless be deemed to satisfy such condition for such year if it makes a pro rata distribution of property after the close of the taxable year to its shareholders (designated at the time of such distribution as a distribution to meet qualification requirements) with respect to their stock in an amount which is equal to—

(A) if the condition of subsection (a)(1)(A) is not satisfied, the portion of such corporation's taxable income attributable to its gross receipts which are not qualified export receipts for such year,

(B) if the condition of subsection (a)(1)(B) is not satisfied, the fair market value of those assets which are not qualified export assets on the last day of such taxable year, or

(C) if neither of such conditions is satisfied, the sum of the amounts required by subparagraphs (A) and (B).

(2) REASONABLE CAUSE FOR FAILURE.—The conditions under paragraph (1) shall be deemed satisfied in the case of a distribution made under such paragraph—

(A) if the failure to meet the requirements of subsection (a)(1)(A) or (B), and the failure to make such distribution prior to the date on which made, are due to reasonable cause; and

(B) the corporation pays, within the 30-day period beginning with the day on which such distribution is made, to the Secretary, if such corporation makes such distribution after the 15th day of the 9th month after the close of the taxable year, an amount determined by multiplying (i) the amount equal to $4^1/2$ percent of such distribution, by (ii) the number of its taxable years which begin after the taxable year with respect to which such distribution is made and before such distribution is made. For purposes of this title, any payment made pursuant to this paragraph shall be treated as interest.

(3) CERTAIN DISTRIBUTIONS MADE WITHIN $8^1/2$ MONTHS AFTER CLOSE OF TAXABLE YEAR DEEMED FOR REASONABLE CAUSE.—A distribution made on or before the 15th day of the 9th month after the close of the taxable year shall be deemed for reasonable cause for purposes of paragraph 2(A) if—

(A) at least 70 percent of the gross receipts of such corporation for such taxable year consist of qualified export receipts, and

(B) the adjusted basis of the qualified export assets held by the corporation on the last day of each month of the taxable year equals or exceeds 70 percent of the sum of the adjusted basis of all assets held by the corporation on such day.

[Sec. 992(d)]

(d) INELIGIBLE CORPORATIONS.—The following corporations shall not be eligible to be treated as a DISC—

(1) a corporation exempt from tax by reason of section 501,

(2) a personal holding company (as defined in section 542),

(3) a financial institution to which section 581 applies,

(4) an insurance company subject to the tax imposed by subchapter L,

(5) a regulated investment company (as defined in section 851(a)), or

(6) an S corporation.

[Sec. 992(e)]

(e) COORDINATION WITH PERSONAL HOLDING COMPANY PROVISIONS IN CASE OF CERTAIN PRODUCED FILM RENTS.—If—

(1) a corporation (hereinafter in this subsection referred to as "subsidiary") was established to take advantage of the provisions of this part, and

(2) a second corporation (hereinafter in this subsection referred to as "parent") throughout the taxable year owns directly at least 80 percent of the stock of the subsidiary,

then, for purposes of applying subsection (d)(2) and section 541 (relating to personal holding company tax) to the subsidiary for the taxable year, there shall be taken into account under section 543(a)(5) (relating to produced film rents) any interest in a film acquired by the parent and transferred to the subsidiary as if such interest were acquired by the subsidiary at the time it was acquired by the parent.

[Sec. 993]

SEC. 993. DEFINITIONS AND SPECIAL RULES.

[Sec. 993(a)]

(a) QUALIFIED EXPORT RECEIPTS.—

(1) GENERAL RULE.—For purposes of this part, except as provided by regulations under paragraph (2), the qualified export receipts of a corporation are—

(A) gross receipts from the sale, exchange, or other disposition of export property,

(B) gross receipts from the lease or rental of export property, which is used by the lessee of such property outside the United States,

(C) gross receipts for services which are related and subsidiary to any qualified sale, exchange, lease, rental, or other disposition of export property by such corporation,

(D) gross receipts from the sale, exchange, or other disposition of qualified export assets (other than export property),

(E) dividends (or amounts includible in gross income under section 951) with respect to stock of a related foreign export corporation (as defined in subsection (e)),

(F) interest on any obligation which is a qualified export asset,

(G) gross receipts for engineering or architectural services for construction projects located (or proposed for location) outside the United States, and

(H) gross receipts for the performance of managerial services in furtherance of the production of other qualified export receipts of a DISC.

(2) EXCLUDED RECEIPTS.—The Secretary may under regulations designate receipts from the sale, exchange, lease, rental, or other disposition of export property, and from services, as not being receipts described in paragraph (1) if he determines that such sale, exchange, lease, rental, or other disposition, or furnishing of services—

(A) is for ultimate use in the United States;

(B) is accomplished by a subsidy granted by the United States or any instrumentality thereof;

(C) is for use by the United States or any instrumentality thereof where the use of such export property or services is required by law or regulation.

For purposes of this part, the term "qualified export receipts" does not include receipts from a corporation which is a DISC for its taxable year in which the receipts arise and which is a member of a controlled group (as defined in paragraph (3)) which includes the recipient corporation.

(3) DEFINITION OF CONTROLLED GROUP.—For purposes of this part, the term "controlled group" has the meaning assigned to the term "controlled group of corporations" by section 1563(a), except that the phrase "more than 50 percent" shall be substituted for the phrase "at least 80 percent" each place it appears therein, and section 1563(b) shall not apply.

[Sec. 993(b)]

(b) QUALIFIED EXPORT ASSETS.—For purposes of this part, the qualified export assets of a corporation are—

(1) export property (as defined in subsection (c));

(2) assets used primarily in connection with the sale, lease, rental, storage, handling, transportation, packaging, assembly, or servicing of export property, or the performance of engineering or architectural services described in subparagraph (G) of subsection (a)(1) or managerial services in furtherance of the production of qualified export receipts described in subparagraphs (A), (B), (C), and (G) of subsection (a)(1);

(3) accounts receivable and evidences of indebtedness which arise by reason of transactions of such corporation or of another corporation which is a DISC and which is a member of a controlled group which includes such corporation described in subparagraph (A), (B), (C), (D), (G), or (H), of subsection (a)(1);

(4) money, bank deposits, and other similar temporary investments, which are reasonably necessary to meet the working capital requirements of such corporation;

(5) obligations arising in connection with a producer's loan (as defined in subsection (d));

(6) stock or securities of a related foreign export corporation (as defined in subsection (e));

(7) obligations issued, guaranteed, or insured, in whole or in part, by the Export-Import Bank of the United States or the Foreign Credit Insurance Association in those cases where such obligations are acquired from such Bank or Association or from the seller or purchaser of the goods or services with respect to which such obligations arose;

(8) obligations issued by a domestic corporation organized solely for the purpose of financing sales of export property pursuant to an agreement with the Export-Import Bank of the United States under which such corporation makes export loans guaranteed by such bank; and

(9) amounts (other than reasonable working capital) on deposit in the United States that are utilized during the period provided for in, and otherwise in accordance with, regulations prescribed by the Secretary to acquire other qualified export assets.

[Sec. 993(c)]

(c) EXPORT PROPERTY.—

(1) IN GENERAL.—For purposes of this part, the term "export property" means property—

(A) manufactured, produced, grown, or extracted in the United States by a person other than a DISC,

(B) held primarily for sale, lease, or rental, in the ordinary course of trade or business, by, or to, a DISC, for direct use, consumption, or disposition outside the United States, and

(C) not more than 50 percent of the fair market value of which is attributable to articles imported into the United States.

In applying subparagraph (C), the fair market value of any article imported into the United States shall be its appraised value, as determined by the Secretary under section 402 of the Tariff Act of 1930 (19 U.S.C. 1401a) in connection with its importation.

(2) EXCLUDED PROPERTY.—For purposes of this part, the term "export property" does not include—

(A) property leased or rented by a DISC for use by any member of a controlled group (as defined in subsection (a)(3)) which includes the DISC,

(B) patents, inventions, models, designs, formulas, or processes, whether or not patented, copyrights (other than films, tapes, records, or similar reproductions, for commercial or home use), good will, trademarks, trade brands, franchises, or other like property,

(C) products of a character with respect to which a deduction for depletion is allowable (including oil, gas, coal, or uranium products) under section 613 or 613A,

(D) products the export of which is prohibited or curtailed under section 7(a) of the Export Administration Act of 1979 to effectuate the policy set forth in paragraph (2)(C) of section 3 of such Act (relating to the protection of the domestic economy), or

(E) any unprocessed timber which is a softwood.

Subparagraph (C) shall not apply to any commodity or product at least 50 percent of the fair market value of which is attributable to manufacturing or processing, except that subparagraph (C) shall apply to any primary product from oil, gas, coal, or uranium. For purposes of the preceding sentence, the term "processing" does not include extracting or handling, packing, packaging, grading, storing, or transporting. For purposes of subparagraph (E), the term "unprocessed timber" means any log, cant, or similar form of timber.

(3) PROPERTY IN SHORT SUPPLY.—If the President determines that the supply of any property described in paragraph (1) is insufficient to meet the requirements of the domestic economy, he may by Executive order designate the property as in short supply. Any property so designated shall be treated as property not described in paragraph (1) during the period beginning with the date specified in the Executive order and ending with the date specified in an Executive order setting forth the President's determination that the property is no longer in short supply.

[Sec. 993(d)]

(d) PRODUCER'S LOANS.—

(1) IN GENERAL.—An obligation, subject to the rules provided in paragraphs (2) and (3), shall be treated as arising out of a producer's loan if—

(A) the loan, when added to the unpaid balance of all other producer's loans made by the DISC, does not exceed the accumulated DISC income at the beginning of the month in which the loan is made;

(B) the obligation is evidenced by a note (or other evidence of indebtedness) with a stated maturity date not more than 5 years from the date of the loan;

(C) the loan is made to a person engaged in the United States in the manufacturing, production, growing, or extraction of export property determined without regard to subparagraph (C) or (D) of subsection (c)(2), (referred to hereinafter as the "borrower"); and

(D) at the time of such loan it is designated as a producer's loan.

(2) LIMITATION.—An obligation shall be treated as arising out of a producer's loan only to the extent that such loan, when added to the unpaid balance of all other producer's loans to the borrower outstanding at the time such loan is made, does not exceed an amount determined by multiplying the sum of—

(A) the amount of the borrower's adjusted basis determined at the beginning of the borrower's taxable year in which the loan is made, in plant, machinery, and equipment, and supporting production facilities in the United States;

(B) the amount of the borrower's property held primarily for sale, lease, or rental, to customers in the ordinary course of trade or business, at the beginning of such taxable year; and

(C) the aggregate amount of the borrower's research and experimental expenditures (within the meaning of section 174) in the United States during all preceding taxable years beginning after December 31, 1971,

by the percentage which the borrower's receipts, during the 3 taxable years immediately preceding the taxable year (but not including any taxable year commencing prior to 1972) in which the loan is made, from the sale, lease, or rental outside the United States of property which would be export property (determined without regard to subparagraph (C) or (D) of subsection (c)(2)) if held by a DISC is of the gross receipts during such 3 taxable years from the sale, lease, or rental of property held by such borrower primarily for sale, lease, or rental to customers in the ordinary course of the trade or business of such borrower.

(3) INCREASED INVESTMENT REQUIREMENT.—An obligation shall be treated as arising out of a producer's loan in a taxable year only to the extent that such loan, when added to the unpaid balance of all other producer's loans to the borrower made during such taxable year, does not exceed an amount equal to—

(A) the amount by which the sum of the adjusted basis of assets described in paragraph (2)(A) and (B) on the last day of the taxable year in which the loan is made exceeds the sum of the adjusted basis of such assets on the first day of such taxable year; plus

(B) the aggregate amount of the borrower's research and experimental expenditures (within the meaning of section 174) in the United States during such taxable year.

(4) SPECIAL LIMITATION IN THE CASE OF DOMESTIC FILM MAKER.—

(A) IN GENERAL.—In the case of a borrower who is a domestic film maker and who incurs an obligation to a DISC for the making of a film, and such DISC is engaged in the trade or business of selling, leasing, or renting films which are export property, the limitation described in paragraph (2) may be determined (to the extent provided under regulations prescribed by the Secretary) on the basis of—

(i) the sum of the amounts described in subparagraphs (A), (B), and (C) thereof plus reasonable estimates of all such amounts to be incurred at any time by the borrower with respect to films which are commenced within the taxable year in which the loan is made, and

(ii) the percentage which, based on the experience of producers of similar films, the annual receipts of such producers from the sale, lease, or rental of such films outside the United States is of the annual gross receipts of such producers from the sale, lease, or rental of such films.

(B) DOMESTIC FILM MAKER.—For purposes of this paragraph, a borrower is a domestic film maker with respect to a film if—

(i) such borrower is a United States person within the meaning of section 7701(a)(30), except that with respect to a partnership, all of the partners must be United States persons, and with respect to a corporation, all of its officers and at least a majority of its directors must be United States persons;

(ii) such borrower is engaged in the trade or business of making the film with respect to which the loan is made;

(iii) the studio, if any, used or to be used for the taking of photographs and the recording of sound incorporated into such film is located in the United States;

(iv) the aggregate playing time of portions of such film photographed outside the United States does not or will not exceed 20 percent of the playing time of such film; and

(v) not less than 80 percent of the total amount paid or to be paid for services performed in the making of such film is paid or to be paid to persons who are United States persons at the time such services are performed or consists of amounts which are fully taxable by the United States.

(C) SPECIAL RULES FOR APPLICATION OF SUBPARAGRAPH (B)(v).—For purposes of clause (v) of subparagraph (B)—

(i) there shall not be taken into account any amount which is contingent upon receipts or profits of the film and which is fully taxable by the United States (within the meaning of clause (ii)); and

(ii) any amount paid or to be paid to a United States person, to a non-resident alien individual, or to a corporation which furnishes the services of an officer or employee to the borrower with respect to the making of a film, shall be treated as fully taxable by the United States only if the total amount received by such person, individual, officer, or employee for services performed in the making of such films is fully included in gross income for purposes of this chapter.

[Sec. 993(e)]

(e) RELATED FOREIGN EXPORT CORPORATION.—In determining whether a corporation (hereinafter in this subsection referred to as "the domestic corporation") is a DISC—

(1) FOREIGN INTERNATIONAL SALES CORPORATION.—A foreign corporation is a related foreign export corporation if—

(A) stock possessing more than 50 percent of the total combined voting power of all classes of stock entitled to vote is owned directly by the domestic corporation,

(B) 95 percent or more of such foreign corporation's gross receipts for its taxable year ending with or within the taxable year of the domestic corporation consists of qualified export receipts described in subparagraphs (A), (B), (C), and (D) of subsection (a)(1) and interest on any obligation described in paragraphs (3) and (4) of subsection (b), and

(C) the adjusted basis of the qualified export assets (described in paragraphs (1), (2), (3), and (4) of subsection (b)) held by such foreign corporation at the close of such taxable year equals or exceeds 95 percent of the sum of the adjusted basis of all assets held by it at the close of such taxable year.

(2) REAL PROPERTY HOLDING COMPANY.—A foreign corporation is a related foreign export corporation if—

(A) stock possessing more than 50 percent of the total combined voting power of all classes of stock entitled to vote is owned directly by the domestic corporation, and

(B) its exclusive function is to hold real property for the exclusive use (under a lease or otherwise) of the domestic corporation.

(3) ASSOCIATED FOREIGN CORPORATION.—A foreign corporation is a related foreign export corporation if—

(A) less than 10 percent of the total combined voting power of all classes of stock entitled to vote of such foreign corporation is owned (within the meaning of section 1563(d) and (e)) by the domestic corporation or by a controlled group of corporations (within the meaning of section 1563) of which the domestic corporation is a member, and

(B) the ownership of stock or securities in such foreign corporation by the domestic corporation is determined (under regulations prescribed by the Secretary) to be reasonably in furtherance of a transaction or transactions giving rise to qualified export receipts of the domestic corporation.

[Sec. 993(f)]

(f) GROSS RECEIPTS.—For purposes of this part, the term "gross receipts" means the total receipts from the sale, lease, or rental of property held primarily for sale, lease, or rental in the ordinary course of trade or business, and gross income from all other sources. In the case of commissions on the sale, lease, or rental of property, the amount taken into account for purposes of this part as gross receipts shall be the gross receipts on the sale, lease, or rental of the property on which such commissions arose.

[Sec. 993(g)]

(g) UNITED STATES DEFINED.—For purposes of this part, the term "United States" includes the Commonwealth of Puerto Rico and the possessions of the United States.

[Sec. 994]

SEC. 994. INTER-COMPANY PRICING RULES.

[Sec. 994(a)]

(a) IN GENERAL.—In the case of a sale of export property to a DISC by a person described in section 482, the taxable income of such DISC and such person shall be based upon a transfer price which would allow such DISC to derive taxable income attributable to such sale (regardless of the sales price actually charged) in an amount which does not exceed the greatest of—

(1) 4 percent of the qualified export receipts on the sale of such property by the DISC plus 10 percent of the export promotion expenses of such DISC attributable to such receipts.

(2) 50 percent of the combined taxable income of such DISC and such person which is attributable to the qualified export receipts on such property derived as the result of a sale by the DISC plus 10 percent of the export promotion expenses of such DISC attributable to such receipts, or

(3) taxable income based upon the sale price actually charged (but subject to the rules provided in section 482).

[Sec. 994(b)]

(b) RULES FOR COMMISSIONS, RENTALS, AND MARGINAL COSTING.—The Secretary shall prescribe regulations setting forth—

(1) rules which are consistent with the rules set forth in subsection (a) for the application of this section in the case of commissions, rentals, and other income, and

(2) rules for the allocation of expenditures in computing combined taxable income under subsection (a)(2) in those cases where a DISC is seeking to establish or maintain a market for export property.

[Sec. 994(c)]

(c) EXPORT PROMOTION EXPENSES.—For purposes of this section, the term "export promotion expenses" means those expenses incurred to advance the distribution or sale of export property for use, consumption, or distribution outside of the United States, but does not include income taxes. Such expenses shall also include freight expenses to the extent of 50 percent of the cost of shipping export property aboard airplanes owned and operated by United States persons or ships documented under the laws of the United States in those cases where law or regulations does not require that such property be shipped aboard such airplanes or ships.

Subpart B—Treatment of Distributions to Shareholders

[Sec. 995]

SEC. 995. TAXATION OF DISC INCOME TO SHAREHOLDERS.

[Sec. 995(a)]

(a) GENERAL RULE.—A shareholder of a DISC or former DISC shall be subject to taxation on the earnings and profits of a DISC as provided in this chapter, but subject to the modifications of this subpart.

[Sec. 995(b)]

(b) DEEMED DISTRIBUTIONS.—

(1) DISTRIBUTIONS IN QUALIFIED YEARS.—A shareholder of a DISC shall be treated as having received a distribution taxable as a dividend with respect to his stock in an amount which is equal to his pro rata share of the sum (or, if smaller, the earnings and profits for the taxable year) of—

(A) the gross interest derived during the taxable year from producer's loans,

(B) the gain recognized by the DISC during the taxable year on the sale or exchange of property, other than property which in the hands of the DISC is a qualified export asset, previously transferred to it in a transaction in which gain was not recognized in whole or in part, but only to the extent that the transferor's gain on the previous transfer was not recognized,

(C) the gain (other than the gain described in subparagraph (B)) recognized by the DISC during the taxable year on the sale or exchange of property (other than property which in the hands of the DISC is stock in trade or other property described in section 1221(a)(1)) previously transferred to it in a transaction in which gain was not recognized in whole or in part, but only to the extent that the transferor's gain on the previous transfer was not recognized and would have been treated as ordinary income if the property had been sold or exchanged rather than transferred to the DISC,

(D) 50 percent of the taxable income of the DISC for the taxable year attributable to military property.[,]

(E) the taxable income of the DISC attributable to qualified export receipts of the DISC for the taxable year which exceed $10,000,000,

(F) the sum of—

(i) in the case of a shareholder which is a C corporation, one-seventeenth of the excess of the taxable income of the DISC for the taxable year, before reduction for any distributions during the year, over the sum of the amounts deemed distributed for the taxable year under subparagraphs (A), (B), (C), (D), and (E),

(ii) an amount equal to $^{16}/_{17}$ of the excess referred to in clause (i) multiplied by the international boycott factor determined under section 999, and

(iii) any illegal bribe, kickback, or other payment (within the meaning of section 162(c)) paid by or on behalf of the DISC directly or indirectly to an official, employee, or agent in fact of a government, and

(G) the amount of foreign investment attributable to producer's loans (as defined in subsection (d)) of a DISC for the taxable year.

Distributions described in this paragraph shall be deemed to be received on the last day of the taxable year of the DISC in which the income was derived. In the case of a distribution described in subparagraph (G), earnings and profits for the taxable year shall include accumulated earnings and profits.

(2) DISTRIBUTIONS UPON DISQUALIFICATION.—

(A) A shareholder of a corporation which revoked its election to be treated as a DISC or failed to satisfy the conditions of section 992(a)(1) for a taxable year shall be deemed to have received (at the time specified in subparagraph (B)) a distribution taxable as a dividend equal to his pro rata share of the DISC income of such corporation accumulated during the immediately preceding consecutive taxable years for which the corporation was a DISC.

(B) Distributions described in subparagraph (A) shall be deemed to be received in equal installments on the last day of each of the 10 taxable years of the corporation following the year of the termination or disqualification described in subparagraph (A) (but in no case over more than twice the number of immediately preceding consecutive taxable years during which the corporation was a DISC).

(3) TAXABLE INCOME ATTRIBUTABLE TO MILITARY PROPERTY.—

(A) IN GENERAL.—For purposes of paragraph (1)(D), taxable income of a DISC for the taxable year attributable to military property shall be determined by only taking into account—

(i) the gross income of the DISC for the taxable year which is attributable to military property, and

(ii) the deductions which are properly apportioned or allocated to such income.

(B) MILITARY PROPERTY.—For purposes of subparagraph (A), the term "military property" means any property which is an arm, ammunition, or implement of war designated in the munitions list published pursuant to section 38 of the Arms Export Control Act (22 U.S.C. 2778).

(4) AGGREGATION OF QUALIFIED EXPORT RECEIPTS.—

(A) IN GENERAL.—For purposes of applying paragraph (1)(E), all DISC's which are members of the same controlled group shall be treated as a single corporation.

(B) ALLOCATION.—The dollar amount under paragraph (1)(E) shall be allocated among the DISC's which are members of the same controlled group in a manner provided in regulations prescribed by the Secretary.

[Sec. 995(c)]

(c) GAIN ON DISPOSITION OF STOCK IN A DISC.—

(1) IN GENERAL.—If—

(A) a shareholder disposes of stock in a DISC or former DISC any gain recognized on such disposition shall be included in gross income as a dividend to the extent provided in paragraph (2), or

(B) stock of a DISC or former DISC is disposed of in a transaction in which the separate corporate existence of the DISC or former DISC is terminated other than by a mere change in place of organization, however effected, any gain realized on the disposition of such stock in the transaction shall be recognized notwithstanding any other provision of this title to the extent provided in paragraph (2) and to the extent so recognized shall be included in gross income as a dividend.

(2) AMOUNT INCLUDED.—The amounts described in paragraph (1) shall be included in gross income as a dividend to the extent of the accumulated DISC income of the DISC or former DISC which is attributable to the stock disposed of and which was accumulated in taxable years of such corporation during the period or periods the stock disposed of was held by the shareholder which disposed of such stock.

[Sec. 995(d)]

(d) FOREIGN INVESTMENT ATTRIBUTABLE TO DISC EARNINGS.—For the purposes of this part—

(1) IN GENERAL.—The amount of foreign investment attributable to producer's loans of a DISC for a taxable year shall be the smallest of—

(A) the net increase in foreign assets by members of the controlled group (as defined in section 993(a)(3)) which includes the DISC,

(B) the actual foreign investment by domestic members of such group, or

(C) the amount of outstanding producer's loans by such DISC to members of such controlled group.

(2) NET INCREASE IN FOREIGN ASSETS.—The term "net increase in foreign assets" of a controlled group means the excess of—

(A) the amount incurred by such group to acquire assets (described in section 1231(b)) located outside the United States over,

(B) the sum of—

(i) the depreciation with respect to assets of such group located outside the United States;

(ii) the outstanding amount of stock or debt obligations of such group issued after December 31, 1971, to persons other than the United States persons or any member of such group;

(iii) one-half the earnings and profits of foreign members of such group and foreign branches of domestic members of such group;

(iv) one-half the royalties and fees paid by foreign members of such group to domestic members of such group; and

(v) the uncommitted transitional funds of the group as determined under paragraph (4).

For purposes of this paragraph, assets which are qualified export assets of a DISC (or would be qualified export assets if owned by a DISC) shall not be taken into account. Amounts described in this paragraph (other than in subparagraphs (B)(ii) and (v)) shall be taken into account only to the extent they are attributable to taxable years beginning after December 31, 1971.

(3) ACTUAL FOREIGN INVESTMENT.—The term "actual foreign investment" by domestic members of a controlled group means the sum of—

(A) contributions to capital of foreign members of the group by domestic members of the group after December 31, 1971,

(B) the outstanding amount of stock or debt obligations of foreign members of such group (other than normal trade indebtedness) issued after December 31, 1971, to domestic members of such group,

(C) amounts transferred by domestic members of the group after December 31, 1971, to foreign branches of such members, and

(D) one-half the earnings and profits of foreign members of such group and foreign branches of domestic members of such group for taxable years beginning after December 31, 1971.

As used in this subsection, the term "domestic member" means a domestic corporation which is a member of a controlled group (as defined in section 993(a)(3)), and the term "foreign member" means a foreign corporation which is a member of such a controlled group.

(4) UNCOMMITTED TRANSITIONAL FUNDS.—The uncommitted transitional funds of the group shall be an amount equal to the sum of—

(A) the excess of—

(i) the amount of stock or debt obligations of domestic members of such group outstanding on December 31, 1971, and issued on or after January 1, 1968, to persons other than United States persons or any members of such group, but only to the extent the taxpayer establishes that such amount constitutes a long-term borrowing for purposes of the foreign direct investment program, over

(ii) the net amount of actual foreign investment by domestic members of such group during the period that such stock or debt obligations have been outstanding; and

(B) the amount of liquid assets to the extent not included in subparagraph (A) held by foreign members of such group and foreign branches of domestic members of such group on October 31, 1971, in excess of their reasonable working capital needs on such date.

For purposes of this paragraph, the term "liquid assets" means money, bank deposits (not including time deposits), and indebtedness of 2 years or less to maturity on the date of acquisition; and the actual foreign investment shall be determined under paragraph (3) without regard to the date in subparagraph (A) of such paragraph and without regard to subparagraph (D) of such paragraph.

(5) SPECIAL RULE.—Under regulations prescribed by the Secretary the determinations under this subsection shall be made on a cumulative basis with proper adjustments for amounts previously taken into account.

[Sec. 995(e)]

(e) CERTAIN TRANSFERS OF DISC ASSETS.—If—

(1) a corporation owns, directly or indirectly, all of the stock of a subsidiary and a DISC,

(2) the subsidiary has been engaged in the active conduct of a trade or business (within the meaning of section 355(b)) throughout the 5-year period ending on the date of the transfer and continues to be so engaged thereafter, and

(3) during the taxable year of the subsidiary in which its stock is transferred and its preceding taxable year, such trade or business gives rise to qualified export receipts of the subsidiary and the DISC,

then, under such terms and conditions as the Secretary by regulations shall prescribe, transfers of assets, stock, or both, will be deemed to be a reorganization within the meaning of section 368, a transaction to which section 355 applies, an exchange of stock to which section 351 applies, or a combination thereof. The preceding sentence shall apply only to the extent that the transfer or transfers involved are for the purpose of preventing the separation of the ownership of the stock in the DISC from the ownership of the trade or business which (during the base period) produced the export gross receipts of the DISC.

[Sec. 995(f)]

(f) INTEREST ON DISC-RELATED DEFERRED TAX LIABILITY.—

(1) IN GENERAL.—A shareholder of a DISC shall pay for each taxable year interest in an amount equal to the product of—

(A) the shareholder's DISC-related deferred tax liability for such year, and

(B) the base period T-bill rate.

(2) SHAREHOLDER'S DISC-RELATED DEFERRED TAX LIABILITY.—For purposes of this subsection—

(A) IN GENERAL.—The term "shareholder's DISC-related deferred tax liability" means, with respect to any taxable year of a shareholder of a DISC, the excess of—

(i) the amount which would be the tax liability of the shareholder for the taxable year if the deferred DISC income of such shareholder for such taxable year were included in gross income as ordinary income, over

(ii) the actual amount of the tax liability of such shareholder for such taxable year.

Determinations under the preceding sentence shall be made without regard to carrybacks to such taxable year.

(B) ADJUSTMENTS FOR LOSSES, CREDITS, AND OTHER ITEMS.—The Secretary shall prescribe regulations which provide such adjustments—

(i) to the accounts of the DISC, and

(ii) to the amount of any carryover or carryback of the shareholder,

as may be necessary or appropriate in the case of net operating losses, credits, and carryovers, and carrybacks of losses and credits.

(C) TAX LIABILITY.—The term "tax liability" means the amount of the tax imposed by this chapter for the taxable year reduced by credits allowable against such tax (other than credits allowable under sections 31, 32, and 34).

(3) DEFERRED DISC INCOME.—For purposes of this subsection—

(A) IN GENERAL.—The term "deferred DISC income" means, with respect to any taxable year of a shareholder, the excess of—

(i) the shareholder's pro rata share of accumulated DISC income (for periods after 1984) of the DISC as of the close of the computation year, over

(ii) the amount of the distributions-in-excess-of-income for the taxable year of the DISC following the computation year.

(B) COMPUTATION YEAR.—For purposes of applying subparagraph (A) with respect to any taxable year of a shareholder, the computation year is the taxable year of the DISC which ends with (or within) the taxable year of the shareholder which precedes the taxable year of the shareholder for which the amount of deferred DISC income is being determined.

(C) DISTRIBUTIONS-IN-EXCESS-OF-INCOME.—For purposes of subparagraph (A), the term "distributions-in-excess-of-income" means, with respect to any taxable year of a DISC, the excess (if any) of—

(i) the amount of actual distributions to the shareholder out of accumulated DISC income, over

(ii) the shareholder's pro rata share of the DISC income for such taxable year.

(4) BASE PERIOD T-BILL RATE.—For purposes of this subsection, the term "base period T-bill rate" means the annual rate of interest determined by the Secretary to be equivalent to the average of the 1-year constant maturity Treasury yields, as published by the Board of Governors of the Federal Reserve System, for the 1-year period ending on September 30 of the calendar year ending with (or of the most recent calendar year ending before) the close of the taxable year of the shareholder.

(5) SHORT YEARS.—The Secretary shall prescribe such regulations as may be necessary for the application of this subsection to short years of the DISC, the shareholder, or both.

(6) PAYMENT AND ASSESSMENT AND COLLECTION OF INTEREST.—The interest accrued during any taxable year which a shareholder is required to pay under paragraph (1) shall be treated, for purposes of this title, as interest payable under section 6601 and shall be paid by the shareholder at the time the tax imposed by this chapter for such taxable year is required to be paid.

(7) DISC INCLUDES FORMER DISC.—For purposes of this subsection, the term "DISC" includes a former DISC.

[Sec. 995(g)]

(g) TREATMENT OF TAX-EXEMPT SHAREHOLDERS.—If any organization described in subsection (a)(2) or (b)(2) of section 511 (or any other person otherwise subject to tax under section 511) is a shareholder in a DISC—

(1) any amount deemed distributed to such shareholder under subsection (b),

(2) any actual distribution to such shareholder which under section 996 is treated as out of accumulated DISC income, and

(3) any gain which is treated as a dividend under subsection (c),

shall be treated as derived from the conduct of an unrelated trade or business (and the modifications of section 512(b) shall not apply). The rules of the preceding sentence shall apply also for purposes of determining any such shareholder's DISC-related deferred tax liability under subsection (f).

[Sec. 996]

SEC. 996. RULES FOR ALLOCATION IN THE CASE OF DISTRIBUTIONS AND LOSSES.

[Sec. 996(a)]

(a) RULES FOR ACTUAL DISTRIBUTIONS AND CERTAIN DEEMED DISTRIBUTIONS.—

(1) IN GENERAL.—Any actual distribution (other than a distribution described in paragraph (2) or to which section 995(c) applies) to a shareholder by a DISC (or former DISC) which is made out of earnings and profits shall be treated as made—

(A) first, out of previously taxed income, to the extent thereof,

(B) second, out of accumulated DISC income, to the extent thereof, and

(C) finally, out of other earnings and profits.

(2) QUALIFYING DISTRIBUTIONS.—Any actual distribution made pursuant to section 992(c) (relating to distributions to meet qualification requirements), and any deemed distribution pursuant to section 995(b)(1)(G) (relating to foreign investment attributable to producer's loans), shall be treated as made—

(A) first, out of accumulated DISC income, to the extent thereof,

(B) second, out of the earnings and profits described in paragraph (1)(C), to the extent thereof, and

(C) finally, out of previously taxed income.

In the case of any amount of any actual distribution to a C corporation made pursuant to section 992(c) which is required to satisfy the condition of section 992(a)(1)(A), the preceding sentence shall apply to $^{16}/_{17}$ths of such amount, and paragraph (1) shall apply to the remaining $^{1}/_{17}$th of such amount.

(3) EXCLUSION FROM GROSS INCOME.—Amounts distributed out of previously taxed income shall be excluded by the distributee from gross income except for gains described in subsection (e)(2), and shall reduce the amount of the previously taxed income.

[Sec. 996(b)]

(b) ORDERING RULES FOR LOSSES.—If for any taxable year a DISC, or a former DISC, incurs a deficit in earnings and profits, such deficit shall be chargeable—

(1) first, to earnings and profits described in subsection (a)(1)(C), to the extent thereof,

(2) second, to accumulated DISC income, to the extent thereof, and

(3) finally, to previously taxed income, except that a deficit in earnings and profits shall not be applied against accumulated DISC income which has been determined is to be deemed distributed to the shareholders (pursuant to section 995(b)(2)(A)) as a result of a revocation of election or other disqualification.

[Sec. 996(c)]

(c) PRIORITY OF DISTRIBUTIONS.—Any actual distribution made during a taxable year shall be treated as being made subsequent to any deemed distribution made during such year. Any actual distribution made pursuant to section 992(c) (relating to distributions to meet qualification requirements) shall be treated as being made before any other actual distributions during the taxable year.

[Sec. 996(d)]

(d) SUBSEQUENT EFFECT OF PREVIOUS DISPOSITION OF DISC STOCK.—

(1) SHAREHOLDER PREVIOUSLY TAXED INCOME ADJUSTMENT.—If—

(A) gain with respect to a share of stock of a DISC or former DISC is treated under section 995(c) as a dividend or as ordinary income, and

(B) any person subsequently receives an actual distribution made out of accumulated DISC income, or a deemed distribution made pursuant to section 995(b)(2), with respect to such share,

such person shall treat such distribution in the same manner as a distribution from previously taxed income to the extent that (i) the gain referred to in subparagraph (A), exceeds (ii) any other amounts with respect to such share which were treated under this paragraph as made from previously taxed income. In applying this paragraph with respect to a share of stock in a DISC or former DISC, gain on the acquisition of such share by the DISC or former DISC or gain on a transaction prior to such acquisition shall not be considered gain referred to in subparagraph (A).

(2) CORPORATE ADJUSTMENT UPON REDEMPTION.—If section 995(c) applies to a redemption of stock in a DISC or former DISC, the accumulated DISC income shall be reduced by an amount equal to the gain described in section 995(c) with respect to such stock which is (or has been) treated as ordinary income, except to the extent distributions with respect to such stock have been treated under paragraph (1).

[Sec. 996(e)]

(e) ADJUSTMENT TO BASIS.—

(1) ADDITIONS TO BASIS.—Amounts representing deemed distributions as provided in section 995(b) shall increase the basis of the stock with respect to which the distribution is made.

(2) REDUCTIONS OF BASIS.—The portion of an actual distribution made out of previously taxed income shall reduce the basis of the stock with respect to which it is made, and to the extent that it exceeds the adjusted basis of such stock, shall be treated as gain from the sale or exchange of property. In the case of stock includible in the gross estate of a decedent for which an election is made under section 2032 (relating to alternate valuation), this paragraph shall not apply to any distribution made after the date of the decedent's death and before the alternate valuation date provided by section 2032.

[Sec. 996(f)]

(f) DEFINITIONS OF DIVISIONS OF EARNINGS AND PROFITS.—For purposes of this part:

(1) DISC INCOME.—The earnings and profits derived by a corporation during a taxable year in which such corporation is a DISC, before reduction for any distributions during the year, but reduced by amounts deemed distributed under section 995(b)(1), shall constitute the DISC income for such year. The earnings and profits of a DISC for a taxable year include any amounts includible in such DISC's gross income pursuant to section 951(a) for such year. Accumulated DISC income shall be reduced by deemed distributions under section 995(b)(2).

(2) PREVIOUSLY TAXED INCOME.—Earnings and profits deemed distributed under section 995(b) for a taxable year shall constitute previously taxed income for such year.

(3) OTHER EARNINGS AND PROFITS.—The earnings and profits for a taxable year which are described in neither paragraph (1) nor (2) shall constitute the other earnings and profits for such year.

[Sec. 996(g)]

(g) EFFECTIVELY CONNECTED INCOME.—In the case of a shareholder who is a nonresident alien individual or a foreign corporation, trust, or estate, gains referred to in section 995(c) and all distributions out of accumulated DISC income including deemed distributions shall be treated as gains and distributions which are effectively connected with the conduct of a trade or business conducted through a permanent establishment of such shareholder within the United States and which are derived from sources within the United States.

[Sec. 997]

SEC. 997. SPECIAL SUBCHAPTER C RULES.

For purposes of applying the provisions of subchapter C of chapter 1, any distribution in property to a corporation by a DISC or former DISC which is made out of previously taxed income or accumulated DISC income shall—

(1) be treated as a distribution in the same amount as if such distribution of property were made to an individual, and

(2) have a basis, in the hands of the recipient corporation, equal to the amount determined under paragraph (1).

PART V—INTERNATIONAL BOYCOTT DETERMINATIONS

[Sec. 999]

SEC. 999. REPORTS BY TAXPAYERS; DETERMINATIONS.

[Sec. 999(a)]

(a) INTERNATIONAL BOYCOTT REPORTS BY TAXPAYERS.—

(1) REPORT REQUIRED.—If any person, or a member of a controlled group (within the meaning of section 993(a)(3)) which includes that person, has operations in, or related to—

(A) a country (or with the government, a company, or a national of a country) which is on the list maintained by the Secretary under paragraph (3), or

(B) any other country (or with the government, a company, or a national of that country) in which such person or such member had operations during the taxable year if such person (or, if such person is a foreign corporation, any United States shareholder of that corporation) knows or has reason to know that participation in or cooperation with an international boycott is required as a condition of doing business within such country or with such government, company, or national,

that person or shareholder (within the meaning of section 951(b)) shall report such operations to the Secretary at such time and in such manner as the Secretary prescribes, except that in the case of a foreign corporation such report shall be required only of a United States shareholder (within the meaning of such section) of such corporation.

(2) PARTICIPATION AND COOPERATION; REQUEST THEREFOR.—A taxpayer shall report whether he, a foreign corporation of which he is a United States shareholder, or any member of a controlled group which includes the taxpayer or such foreign corporation has participated in or cooperated with an international boycott at any time during the taxable year, or has been requested to participate in or cooperate with such a boycott, and, if so, the nature of any operation in connection with which there was participation in or cooperation with such boycott (or there was a request to participate or cooperate).

(3) LIST TO BE MAINTAINED.—The Secretary shall maintain and publish not less frequently than quarterly a current list of countries which require or may require participation in or cooperation with an international boycott (within the meaning of subsection (b)(3)).

[Sec. 999(b)]

(b) PARTICIPATION IN OR COOPERATION WITH AN INTERNATIONAL BOYCOTT.—

(1) GENERAL RULE.—If the person or a member of a controlled group (within the meaning of section 993(a)(3)) which includes the person participates in or cooperates with an international boycott in the taxable year, all operations of the taxpayer or such group in that country and in any other country which requires participation in or cooperation with the boycott as a condition of doing business within that country, or with the government, a company, or a national of that country, shall be treated as operations in connection with which such participation or cooperation occurred, except to the extent that the person can clearly demonstrate that a particular operation is a clearly separate and identifiable operation in connection with which there was no participation in or cooperation with an international boycott.

(2) SPECIAL RULE.—

(A) NONBOYCOTT OPERATIONS.—A clearly separate and identifiable operation of a person, or of a member of the controlled group (within the meaning of section 993(a)(3)) which includes that person, in or related to any country within the group of countries referred to in paragraph (1) shall not be treated as an operation in or related to a group of countries associated in carrying out an international boycott if the person can clearly demonstrate that he, or that such member, did not participate in or cooperate with the international boycott in connection with that operation.

(B) SEPARATE AND IDENTIFIABLE OPERATIONS.—A taxpayer may show that different operations within the same country, or operations in different countries, are clearly separate and identifiable operations.

(3) DEFINITION OF BOYCOTT PARTICIPATION AND COOPERATION.—For purposes of this section, a person participates in or cooperates with an international boycott if he agrees—

(A) as a condition of doing business directly or indirectly within a country or with the government, a company, or a national of a country—

(i) to refrain from doing business with or in a country which is the object of the boycott or with the government, companies, or nationals of that country;

(ii) to refrain from doing business with any United States person engaged in trade in a country which is the object of the boycott or with the government, companies, or nationals of that country;

(iii) to refrain from doing business with any company whose ownership or management is made up, all or in part, of individuals of a particular nationality, race, or religion, or to remove (or refrain from selecting) corporate directors who are individuals of a particular nationality, race, or religion; or

(iv) to refrain from employing individuals of a particular nationality, race, or religion; or

(B) as a condition of the sale of a product to the government, a company, or a national of a country, to refrain from shipping or insuring that product on a carrier owned, leased, or operated by a person who does not participate in or cooperate with an international boycott (within the meaning of subparagraph (A)).

(4) COMPLIANCE WITH CERTAIN LAWS.—This section shall not apply to any agreement by a person (or such member)—

(A) to meet requirements imposed by a foreign country with respect to an international boycott if United States law or regulations, or an Executive Order, sanctions participation in, or cooperation with, that international boycott,

(B) to comply with a prohibition on the importation of goods produced in whole or in part in any country which is the object of an international boycott, or

(C) to comply with a prohibition imposed by a country on the exportation of products obtained in such country to any country which is the object of an international boycott.

[Sec. 999(c)]

(c) INTERNATIONAL BOYCOTT FACTOR.—

(1) INTERNATIONAL BOYCOTT FACTOR.—For purposes of sections 908(a), 952(a)(3), and 995(b)(1)(F)(ii), the international boycott factor is a fraction, determined under regulations prescribed by the Secretary, the numerator of which reflects the world-wide operations of a person (or, in the case of a controlled group (within the meaning of section 993(a)(3)) which includes that person, of the group) which are operations in or related to a group of countries associated in carrying out an international boycott in or with which that person or a member of that controlled group has participated or cooperated in the taxable year, and the denominator of which reflects the world-wide operations of that person or group.

(2) SPECIFICALLY ATTRIBUTABLE TAXES AND INCOME.—If the taxpayer clearly demonstrates that the foreign taxes paid and income earned for the taxable year are attributable to specific operations, then, in lieu of applying the international boycott factor for such taxable year, the amount of the credit disallowed under section 908(a), the addition to subpart F income under section 952(a)(3), and the amount of deemed distribution under section 995(b)(1)(F)(ii) for the taxable year, if any, shall be the amount specifically attributable to the operations in which there was participation in or cooperation with an international boycott under section 999(b)(1).

(3) WORLD-WIDE OPERATIONS.—For purposes of this subsection, the term "world-wide operations" means operations in or related to countries other than the United States.

[Sec. 999(d)]

(d) DETERMINATION WITH RESPECT TO PARTICULAR OPERATIONS.—Upon a request made by the taxpayer, the Secretary shall issue a determination with respect to whether a particular operation of the person, or of a member of a controlled group which includes that person, constitutes participation in or cooperation with an international boycott. The Secretary may issue such a determination in advance of such operation in cases which are of such a nature that an advance determination is possible and appropriate under the circumstances. If the request is made before the operation is commenced, or before the end of a taxable year in which the operation is carried out, the Secretary may decline to issue such a determination before the close of the taxable year.

[Sec. 999(e)]

(e) PARTICIPATION OR COOPERATION BY RELATED PERSONS.—If a person controls (within the meaning of section 304(c)) a corporation—

(1) participation in or cooperation with an international boycott by such corporation shall be presumed to be such participation or cooperation by such person, and

(2) participation in or cooperation with such a boycott by such person shall be presumed to be such participation or cooperation by such corporation.

[Sec. 999(f)]

(f) WILLFUL FAILURE TO REPORT.—Any person (within the meaning of section 6671(b)) required to report under this section who willfully fails to make such report shall, in addition to other penalties provided by law, be fined not more than $25,000, imprisoned for not more than one year, or both.

SUBCHAPTER O—GAIN OR LOSS ON DISPOSITION OF PROPERTY

PART III—COMMON NONTAXABLE EXCHANGES

[Sec. 1031]

SEC. 1031. EXCHANGE OF REAL PROPERTY HELD FOR PRODUCTIVE USE OR INVESTMENT.

* * *

[Sec. 1031(h)]

(h) SPECIAL RULES FOR FOREIGN REAL PROPERTY.—Real property located in the United States and real property located outside the United States are not property of a like kind.

PART IV—SPECIAL RULES

[Sec. 1058]

SEC. 1058. TRANSFER OF SECURITIES UNDER CERTAIN AGREEMENTS.

[Sec. 1058(a)]

(a) GENERAL RULE.—In the case of a taxpayer who transfers securities (as defined in section 1236(c)) pursuant to an agreement which meets the requirements of subsection (b), no gain or loss shall be recognized on the exchange of such securities by the taxpayer for an obligation under such agreement, or on the exchange of rights under such agreement by that taxpayer for securities identical to the securities transferred by that taxpayer.

[Sec. 1058(b)]

(b) AGREEMENT REQUIREMENTS.—In order to meet the requirements of this subsection, an agreement shall—

(1) provide for the return to the transferor of securities identical to the securities transferred;

(2) require that payments shall be made to the transferor of amounts equivalent to all interest, dividends, and other distributions which the owner of the securities is entitled to receive during the period beginning with the transfer of the securities by the transferor and ending with the transfer of identical securities back to the transferor;

(3) not reduce the risk of loss or opportunity for gain of the transferor of the securities in the securities transferred; and

(4) meet such other requirements as the Secretary may by regulation prescribe.

[Sec. 1058(c)]

(c) BASIS.—Property acquired by a taxpayer described in subsection (a), in a transaction described in that subsection, shall have the same basis as the property transferred by that taxpayer.

[Sec. 1059A]

SEC. 1059A. LIMITATION ON TAXPAYER'S BASIS OR INVENTORY COST IN PROPERTY IMPORTED FROM RELATED PERSONS.

[Sec. 1059A(a)]

(a) IN GENERAL.—If any property is imported into the United States in a transaction (directly or indirectly) between related persons (within the meaning of section 482), the amount of any costs—

(1) which are taken into account in computing the basis or inventory cost of such property by the purchaser, and

(2) which are also taken into account in computing the customs value of such property,

shall not, for purposes of computing such basis or inventory cost for purposes of this chapter, be greater than the amount of such costs taken into account in computing such customs value.

[Sec. 1059A(b)]

(b) CUSTOMS VALUE; IMPORT.—For purposes of this section—

(1) CUSTOMS VALUE.—The term "customs value" means the value taken into account for purposes of determining the amount of any customs duties or any other duties which may be imposed on the importation of any property.

(2) IMPORT.—Except as provided in regulations, the term "import" means the entering, or withdrawal from warehouse, for consumption.

SUBCHAPTER P—CAPITAL GAINS AND LOSSES

PART III—GENERAL RULES FOR DETERMINING CAPITAL GAINS AND LOSSES

[Sec. 1221]

SEC. 1221. CAPITAL ASSET DEFINED.

[Sec. 1221(a)]

(a) IN GENERAL.—For purposes of this subtitle, the term "capital asset" means property held by the taxpayer (whether or not connected with his trade or business), but does not include—

(1) stock in trade of the taxpayer or other property of a kind which would properly be included in the inventory of the taxpayer if on hand at the close of the taxable year, or property held by the taxpayer primarily for sale to customers in the ordinary course of his trade or business;

(2) property, used in his trade or business, of a character which is subject to the allowance for depreciation provided in section 167, or real property used in his trade or business;

(3) a patent, invention, model or design (whether or not patented), a secret formula or process, a copyright, a literary, musical, or artistic composition, a letter or memorandum, or similar property, held by—

(A) a taxpayer whose personal efforts created such property,

(B) in the case of a letter, memorandum, or similar property, a taxpayer for whom such property was prepared or produced, or

(C) a taxpayer in whose hands the basis of such property is determined, for purposes of determining gain from a sale or exchange, in whole or part by reference to the basis of such property in the hands of a taxpayer described in subparagraph (A) or (B);

(4) accounts or notes receivable acquired in the ordinary course of trade or business for services rendered or from the sale of property described in paragraph (1);

(5) a publication of the United States Government (including the Congressional Record) which is received from the United States Government or any agency thereof, other than by purchase at the price at which it is offered for sale to the public, and which is held by—

(A) a taxpayer who so received such publication, or

(B) a taxpayer in whose hands the basis of such publication is determined, for purposes of determining gain from a sale or exchange, in whole or in part by reference to the basis of such publication in the hands of a taxpayer described in subparagraph (A);

(6) any commodities derivative financial instrument held by a commodities derivatives dealer, unless—

(A) it is established to the satisfaction of the Secretary that such instrument has no connection to the activities of such dealer as a dealer, and

(B) such instrument is clearly identified in such dealer's records as being described in subparagraph (A) before the close of the day on which it was acquired, originated, or entered into (or such other time as the Secretary may by regulations prescribe);

(7) any hedging transaction which is clearly identified as such before the close of the day on which it was acquired, originated, or entered into (or such other time as the Secretary may by regulations prescribe); or

(8) supplies of a type regularly used or consumed by the taxpayer in the ordinary course of a trade or business of the taxpayer.

[Sec. 1221(b)]

(b) DEFINITIONS AND SPECIAL RULES.—

(1) COMMODITIES DERIVATIVE FINANCIAL INSTRUMENTS.—For purposes of subsection (a)(6)—

(A) COMMODITIES DERIVATIVES DEALER.—The term "commodities derivatives dealer" means a person which regularly offers to enter into, assume, offset, assign, or terminate positions in commodities derivative financial instruments with customers in the ordinary course of a trade or business.

(B) COMMODITIES DERIVATIVE FINANCIAL INSTRUMENT.—

(i) IN GENERAL.—The term "commodities derivative financial instrument" means any contract or financial instrument with respect to commodities (other than a share of stock in a corporation, a beneficial interest in a partnership or trust, a note, bond, debenture, or other evidence of indebtedness, or a section 1256 contract (as defined in section 1256(b))), the value or settlement price of which is calculated by or determined by reference to a specified index.

(ii) SPECIFIED INDEX.—The term "specified index" means any one or more or any combination of—

(I) a fixed rate, price, or amount, or

(II) a variable rate, price, or amount,

which is based on any current, objectively determinable financial or economic information with respect to commodities which is not within the control of any of the parties to the contract or instrument and is not unique to any of the parties' circumstances.

(2) HEDGING TRANSACTION.—

(A) IN GENERAL.—For purposes of this section, the term "hedging transaction" means any transaction entered into by the taxpayer in the normal course of the taxpayer's trade or business primarily—

(i) to manage risk of price changes or currency fluctuations with respect to ordinary property which is held or to be held by the taxpayer,

(ii) to manage risk of interest rate or price changes or currency fluctuations with respect to borrowings made or to be made, or ordinary obligations incurred or to be incurred, by the taxpayer, or

(iii) to manage such other risks as the Secretary may prescribe in regulations.

(B) TREATMENT OF NONIDENTIFICATION OR IMPROPER IDENTIFICATION OF HEDGING TRANSACTIONS.—Notwithstanding subsection (a)(7), the Secretary shall prescribe regulations to properly characterize any income, gain, expense, or loss arising from a transaction—

(i) which is a hedging transaction but which was not identified as such in accordance with subsection (a)(7), or

(ii) which was so identified but is not a hedging transaction.

(3) SALE OR EXCHANGE OF SELF-CREATED MUSICAL WORKS.—At the election of the taxpayer, paragraphs (1) and (3) of subsection (a) shall not apply to musical compositions or copyrights in musical works sold or exchanged by a taxpayer described in subsection (a)(3).

(4) REGULATIONS.—The Secretary shall prescribe such regulations as are appropriate to carry out the purposes of paragraph (6) and (7) of subsection (a) in the case of transactions involving related parties.

[Sec. 1222]

SEC. 1222. OTHER TERMS RELATING TO CAPITAL GAINS AND LOSSES.

For purposes of this subtitle—

(1) SHORT-TERM CAPITAL GAIN.—The term "short-term capital gain" means gain from the sale or exchange of a capital asset held for not more than 1 year, if and to the extent such gain is taken into account in computing gross income.

(2) SHORT-TERM CAPITAL LOSS.—The term "short-term capital loss" means loss from the sale or exchange of a capital asset held for not more than 1 year, if and to the extent that such loss is taken into account in computing taxable income.

(3) LONG-TERM CAPITAL GAIN.—The term "long-term capital gain" means gain from the sale or exchange of a capital asset held for more than 1 year, if and to the extent such gain is taken into account in computing gross income.

(4) LONG-TERM CAPITAL LOSS.—The term "long-term capital loss" means loss from the sale or exchange of a capital asset held for more than 1 year, if and to the extent that such loss is taken into account in computing taxable income.

(5) NET SHORT-TERM CAPITAL GAIN.—The term "net short-term capital gain" means the excess of short-term capital gains for the taxable year over the short-term capital losses for such year.

(6) NET SHORT-TERM CAPITAL LOSS.—The term "net short-term capital loss" means the excess of short-term capital losses for the taxable year over the short-term capital gains for such year.

(7) NET LONG-TERM CAPITAL GAIN.—The term "net long-term capital gain" means the excess of long-term capital gains for the taxable year over the long-term capital losses for such year.

(8) NET LONG-TERM CAPITAL LOSS.—The term "net long-term capital loss" means the excess of long-term capital losses for the taxable year over the long-term capital gains for such year.

(9) CAPITAL GAIN NET INCOME.—The term "capital gain net income" means the excess of the gains from sales or exchanges of capital assets over the losses from such sales or exchanges.

(10) NET CAPITAL LOSS.—The term "net capital loss" means the excess of the losses from sales or exchanges of capital assets over the sum allowed under section 1211. In the case of a corporation, for the purpose of determining losses under this paragraph, amounts which are short-term capital losses under section 1212(a)(1) shall be excluded.

(11) NET CAPITAL GAIN.—The term "net capital gain" means the excess of the net long-term capital gain for the taxable year over the net short-term capital loss for such year.

PART IV—SPECIAL RULES FOR DETERMINING CAPITAL GAINS AND LOSSES

[Sec. 1231]

SEC. 1231. PROPERTY USED IN THE TRADE OR BUSINESS AND INVOLUNTARY CONVERSIONS.

[Sec. 1231(a)]

(a) GENERAL RULE.—

(1) GAINS EXCEED LOSSES.—If—

(A) the section 1231 gains for any taxable year, exceed

(B) the section 1231 losses for such taxable year,

such gains and losses shall be treated as long-term capital gains or long-term capital losses, as the case may be.

(2) GAINS DO NOT EXCEED LOSSES.—If—

(A) the section 1231 gains for any taxable year, do not exceed

(B) the section 1231 losses for such taxable year,

such gains and losses shall not be treated as gains and losses from sales or exchanges of capital assets.

(3) SECTION 1231 GAINS AND LOSSES.—For purposes of this subsection—

(A) SECTION 1231 GAIN.—The term "section 1231 gain" means—

(i) any recognized gain on the sale or exchange of property used in the trade or business, and

(ii) any recognized gain from the compulsory or involuntary conversion (as a result of destruction in whole or in part, theft or seizure, or an exercise of the power of requisition or condemnation or the threat or imminence thereof) into other property or money of—

(I) property used in the trade or business, or

(II) any capital asset which is held for more than 1 year and is held in connection with a trade or business or a transaction entered into for profit.

(B) SECTION 1231 LOSS.—The term "section 1231 loss" means any recognized loss from a sale or exchange or conversion described in subparagraph (A).

(4) SPECIAL RULES.—For purposes of this subsection—

(A) In determining under this subsection whether gains exceed losses—

(i) the section 1231 gains shall be included only if and to the extent taken into account in computing gross income, and

(ii) the section 1231 losses shall be included only if and to the extent taken into account in computing taxable income, except that section 1211 shall not apply.

(B) Losses (including losses not compensated for by insurance or otherwise) on the destruction, in whole or in part, theft or seizure, or requisition or condemnation of—

(i) property used in the trade or business, or

(ii) capital assets which are held for more than 1 year and are held in connection with a trade or business or a transaction entered into for profit,

shall be treated as losses from a compulsory or involuntary conversion.

(C) In the case of any involuntary conversion (subject to the provisions of this subsection but for this sentence) arising from fire, storm, shipwreck, or other casualty, or from theft, of any—

(i) property used in the trade or business, or

(ii) any capital asset which is held for more than 1 year and is held in connection with a trade or business or a transaction entered into for profit,

this subsection shall not apply to such conversion (whether resulting in gain or loss) if during the taxable year the recognized losses from such conversions exceed the recognized gains from such conversions.

[Sec. 1231(b)]

(b) DEFINITION OF PROPERTY USED IN THE TRADE OR BUSINESS.—For purposes of this section—

(1) GENERAL RULE.—The term "property used in the trade or business" means property used in the trade or business, of a character which is subject to the allowance for depreciation provided in section 167, held for more than 1 year, and real property used in the trade or business, held for more than 1 year, which is not—

(A) property of a kind which would properly be includible in the inventory of the taxpayer if on hand at the close of the taxable year,

(B) property held by the taxpayer primarily for sale to customers in the ordinary course of his trade or business,

(C) a patent, invention, model or design (whether or not patented), a secret formula or process, a copyright, a literary, musical, or artistic composition, a letter or memorandum, or similar property, held by a taxpayer described in paragraph (3) of section 1221(a), or

(D) a publication of the United States Government (including the Congressional Record) which is received from the United States Government, or any agency thereof, other than by purchase at the price at which it is offered for sale to the public, and which is held by a taxpayer described in paragraph (5) of section 1221(a).

(2) TIMBER, COAL, OR DOMESTIC IRON ORE.—Such term includes timber, coal, and iron ore with respect to which section 631 applies.

(3) LIVESTOCK.—Such term includes—

(A) cattle and horses, regardless of age, held by the taxpayer for draft, breeding, dairy, or sporting purposes, and held by him for 24 months or more from the date of acquisition, and

(B) other livestock, regardless of age, held by the taxpayer for draft, breeding, dairy, or sporting purposes, and held by him for 12 months or more from the date of acquisition.

Such term does not include poultry.

(4) UNHARVESTED CROP.—In the case of an unharvested crop on land used in the trade or business and held for more than 1 year, if the crop and the land are sold or exchanged (or compulsorily or involuntarily converted) at the same time and to the same person, the crop shall be considered as "property used in the trade or business."

***

[Sec. 1235]

SEC. 1235. SALE OR EXCHANGE OF PATENTS.

[Sec. 1235(a)]

(a) GENERAL.—A transfer (other than by gift, inheritance, or devise) of property consisting of all substantial rights to a patent, or an undivided interest therein which includes a part of all such rights, by any holder shall be considered the sale or exchange of a capital asset held for more than 1 year, regardless of whether or not payments in consideration of such transfer are—

(1) payable periodically over a period generally coterminous with the transferee's use of the patent, or

(2) contingent on the productivity, use, or disposition of the property transferred.

[Sec. 1235(b)]

(b) "HOLDER" DEFINED.—For purposes of this section, the term "holder" means—

(1) any individual whose efforts created such property, or

(2) any other individual who has acquired his interest in such property in exchange for consideration in money or money's worth paid to such creator prior to actual reduction to practice of the invention covered by the patent, if such individual is neither—

(A) the employer of such creator, nor

(B) related to such creator (within the meaning of subsection (c)).

[Sec. 1235(c)]

(c) RELATED PERSONS.—Subsection (a) shall not apply to any transfer, directly or indirectly, between persons specified within any one of the paragraphs of section 267(b) or persons described in section 707(b); except that, in applying section 267(b) and (c) and section 707(b) for purposes of this section—

(1) the phrase "25 percent or more" shall be substituted for the phrase "more than 50 percent" each place it appears in section 267(b) or 707(b), and

(2) paragraph (4) of section 267(c) shall be treated as providing that the family of an individual shall include only his spouse, ancestors, and lineal descendants.

[Sec. 1235(d)]

(d) CROSS REFERENCE.—

For special rule relating to nonresident aliens, see section 871(a).

[Sec. 1236]

SEC. 1236. DEALERS IN SECURITIES.

***

[Sec. 1236(c)]

(c) DEFINITION OF SECURITY.—For purposes of this section, the term "security" means any share of stock in any corporation, certificate of stock or interest in any corporation, note, bond, debenture, or evidence of indebtedness, or any evidence of an interest in or right to subscribe to or purchase any of the foregoing.

***

[Sec. 1239]

SEC. 1239. GAIN FROM SALE OF DEPRECIABLE PROPERTY BETWEEN CERTAIN RELATED TAXPAYERS.

[Sec. 1239(a)]

(a) TREATMENT OF GAIN AS ORDINARY INCOME.—In the case of a sale or exchange of property, directly or indirectly, between related persons, any gain recognized to the transferor shall be treated as ordinary income if such property is, in the hands of the transferee, of a character which is subject to the allowance for depreciation provided in section 167.

[Sec. 1239(b)]

(b) RELATED PERSONS.—For purposes of subsection (a), the term "related persons" means—

(1) a person and all entities which are controlled entities with respect to such person,

(2) a taxpayer and any trust in which such taxpayer (or his spouse) is a beneficiary, unless such beneficiary's interest in the trust is a remote contingent interest (within the meaning of section 318(a)(3)(B)(i)), and

(3) except in the case of a sale or exchange in satisfaction of a pecuniary bequest, an executor of an estate and a beneficiary of such estate.

[Sec. 1239(c)]

(c) CONTROLLED ENTITY DEFINED.—

(1) GENERAL RULE.—For purposes of this section, the term "controlled entity" means, with respect to any person—

(A) a corporation more than 50 percent of the value of the outstanding stock of which is owned (directly or indirectly) by or for such person,

(B) a partnership more than 50 percent of the capital interest or profits interest in which is owned (directly or indirectly) by or for such person, and

(C) any entity which is a related person to such person under paragraph (3), (10), (11), or (12) of section 267(b).

(2) CONSTRUCTIVE OWNERSHIP.—For purposes of this section, ownership shall be determined in accordance with rules similar to the rules under section 267(c) (other than paragraph (3) thereof).

* * *

[Sec. 1239(e)]

(e) PATENT APPLICATIONS TREATED AS DEPRECIABLE PROPERTY.—For purposes of this section, a patent application shall be treated as property which, in the hands of the transferee, is of a character which is subject to the allowance for depreciation provided in section 167.

[Sec. 1248]

SEC. 1248. GAIN FROM CERTAIN SALES OR EXCHANGES OF STOCK IN CERTAIN FOREIGN CORPORATIONS.

[Sec. 1248(a)]

(a) GENERAL RULE.—If—

(1) a United States person sells or exchanges stock in a foreign corporation, and

(2) such person owns, within the meaning of section 958(a), or is considered as owning by applying the rules of ownership of section 958(b), 10 percent or more of the total combined voting power of all classes of stock entitled to vote of such foreign corporation at any time during the 5-year period ending on the date of the sale or exchange when such foreign corporation was a controlled foreign corporation (as defined in section 957),

then the gain recognized on the sale or exchange of such stock shall be included in the gross income of such person as a dividend, to the extent of the earnings and profits of the foreign corporation attributable (under regulations prescribed by the Secretary) to such stock which were accumulated in taxable years of such foreign corporation beginning after December 31, 1962, and during the period or periods the stock sold or exchanged was held by such person while such foreign corporation was a controlled foreign corporation. For purposes of this section, a United States person shall be treated as having sold or exchanged any stock if, under any provision of this subtitle, such person is treated as realizing gain from the sale or exchange of such stock.

[Sec. 1248(b)]

(b) LIMITATION ON TAX APPLICABLE TO INDIVIDUALS.—In the case of an individual, if the stock sold or exchanged is a capital asset (within the meaning of section 1221) and has been held for more than 1 year, the tax attributable to an amount included in gross income as a dividend under subsection (a) shall not be greater than a tax equal to the sum of—

(1) a pro rata share of the excess of—

(A) the taxes that would have been paid by the foreign corporation with respect to its income had it been taxed under this chapter as a domestic corporation (but without allowance for deduction of, or credit for, taxes described in subparagraph (B)), for the period or periods the stock sold or exchanged was held by the United States person in taxable years beginning after December 31, 1962, while the foreign corporation was a controlled foreign corporation, adjusted for distributions and amounts previously included in gross income of a United States shareholder under section 951, over

(B) the income, war profits, or excess profits taxes paid by the foreign corporation with respect to such income; and

(2) an amount equal to the tax that would result by including in gross income, as gain from the sale or exchange of a capital asset held for more than 1 year, an amount equal to the excess of (A) the amount included in gross income as a dividend under subsection (a), over (B) the amount determined under paragraph (1).

[Sec. 1248(c)]

(c) DETERMINATION OF EARNINGS AND PROFITS.—

(1) IN GENERAL.—Except as provided in section 312(k)(4), for purposes of this section the earnings and profits of any foreign corporation for any taxable year shall be determined according to rules substantially similar to those applicable to domestic corporations, under regulations prescribed by the Secretary.

(2) EARNINGS AND PROFITS OF SUBSIDIARIES OF FOREIGN CORPORATIONS.—If—

(A) subsection (a) or (f) applies to a sale, exchange, or distribution by a United States person of stock of a foreign corporation and, by reason of the ownership of the stock sold or exchanged, such person owned within the meaning of section 958(a)(2) stock of any other foreign corporation; and

(B) such person owned, within the meaning of section 958(a), or was considered as owning by applying the rules of ownership of section 958(b), 10 percent or more of the total combined voting power of all classes of stock entitled to vote of such other foreign corporation at any time during the 5-year period ending on the date of the sale or exchange when such other foreign corporation was a controlled foreign corporation (as defined in section 957),

then, for purposes of this section, the earnings and profits of the foreign corporation the stock of which is sold or exchanged which are attributable to the stock sold or exchanged shall be deemed to include the earnings and profits of such other foreign corporation which—

(C) are attributable (under regulations prescribed by the Secretary) to the stock of such other foreign corporation which such person owned within the meaning of section 958(a)(2) (by reason of his ownership within the meaning of section 958(a)(1)(A) of the stock sold or exchanged) on the date of such sale or exchange (or on the date of any sale or exchange of the stock of such other foreign corporation occurring during the 5-year period ending on the date of the sale or exchange of the stock of such foreign corporation, to the extent not otherwise taken into account under this section but not in excess of the fair market value of the stock of such other foreign corporation sold or exchanged over the basis of such stock (for determining gain) in the hands of the transferor); and

(D) were accumulated in taxable years of such other corporation beginning after December 31, 1962, and during the period or periods—

(i) such other corporation was a controlled foreign corporation, and

(ii) such person owned within the meaning of section 958(a) the stock of such other foreign corporation.

[Sec. 1248(d)]

(d) EXCLUSIONS FROM EARNINGS AND PROFITS.—For purposes of this section, the following amounts shall be excluded, with respect to any United States person, from the earnings and profits of a foreign corporation.

(1) AMOUNTS INCLUDED IN GROSS INCOME UNDER SECTION 951.—Earnings and profits of the foreign corporation attributable to any amount previously included in the gross income of such person under section 951, with respect to the stock sold or exchanged, but only to the extent the inclusion of such amount did not result in an exclusion of an amount from gross income under section 959.

(2) [Stricken]

(3) LESS DEVELOPED COUNTRY CORPORATIONS UNDER PRIOR LAW.—Earnings and profits of a foreign corporation which were accumulated during any taxable year beginning before January 1, 1976, while such corporation was a less developed country corporation under section 902(d) as in effect before the enactment of the Tax Reduction Act of 1975.

(4) UNITED STATES INCOME.—Any item includible in gross income of the foreign corporation under this chapter—

(A) for any taxable year beginning before January 1, 1967, as income derived from sources within the United States of a foreign corporation engaged in trade or business within the United States, or

(B) for any taxable year beginning after December 31, 1966, as income effectively connected with the conduct by such corporation of a trade or business within the United States.

This paragraph shall not apply with respect to any item which is exempt from taxation (or is subject to a reduced rate of tax) pursuant to a treaty obligation of the United States.

(5) FOREIGN TRADE INCOME.—Earnings and profits of the foreign corporation attributable to foreign trade income of a FSC (as defined in section 922) other than foreign trade income which—

(A) is section 923(a)(2) non-exempt income (within the meaning of section 927(d)(6)), or

(B) would not (but for section 923(a)(4)) be treated as exempt foreign trade income.

For purposes of the preceding sentence, the terms "foreign trade income" and "exempt foreign trade income" have the respective meanings given such terms by section 923. Any reference in this paragraph to section 922, 923, or 927 shall be treated as a reference to such section as in effect before its repeal by the FSC Repeal and Extraterritorial Income Exclusion Act of 2000.

(6) AMOUNTS INCLUDED IN GROSS INCOME UNDER SECTION 1293.—Earnings and profits of the foreign corporation attributable to any amount previously included in the gross income of such person under section 1293 with respect to the stock sold or exchanged, but only to the extent the inclusion of such amount did not result in an exclusion of an amount under section 1293(c).

[Sec. 1248(e)]

(e) SALES OR EXCHANGES OF STOCK IN CERTAIN DOMESTIC CORPORATIONS.—Except as provided in regulations prescribed by the Secretary, if—

(1) a United States person sells or exchanges stock of a domestic corporation, and

(2) such domestic corporation was formed or availed of principally for the holding, directly or indirectly, of stock of one or more foreign corporations,

such sale or exchange shall, for purposes of this section, be treated as a sale or exchange of the stock of the foreign corporation or corporations held by the domestic corporation.

[Sec. 1248(f)]

(f) NONRECOGNITION TRANSACTIONS.—Except as provided in regulations prescribed by the Secretary—

(1) IN GENERAL.—If—

(A) a domestic corporation satisfies the stock ownership requirements of subsection (a)(2) with respect to a foreign corporation, and

(B) such domestic corporation distributes stock of such foreign corporation in a distribution to which section 311(a), 337, 355(c)(1), or 361(c)(1) applies,

then, notwithstanding any other provision of this subtitle, an amount equal to the excess of the fair market value of such stock over its adjusted basis in the hands of the domestic corporation shall be included in the gross income of the domestic corporation as a dividend to the extent of the earnings and profits of the foreign corporation attributable (under regulations prescribed by the Secretary) to such stock which were accumulated in taxable years of such foreign corporation beginning after December 31, 1962, and during the period or periods the stock was held by such domestic corporation while such foreign corporation was a controlled foreign corporation. For purposes of subsections (c)(2), (d), and (h), a distribution of stock to which this subsection applies shall be treated as a sale of stock to which subsection (a) applies.

(2) EXCEPTION FOR CERTAIN DISTRIBUTIONS.—In the case of any distribution of stock of a foreign corporation, paragraph (1) shall not apply if such distribution is to a domestic corporation—

(A) which is treated under this section as holding such stock for the period for which the stock was held by the distributing corporation, and

(B) which, immediately after the distribution, satisfies the stock ownership requirements of subsection (a)(2) with respect to such foreign corporation.

(3) APPLICATION TO CASES DESCRIBED IN SUBSECTION (e).—To the extent that earnings and profits are taken into account under this subsection, they shall be excluded and not taken into account for purposes of subsection (e).

[Sec. 1248(g)]

(g) EXCEPTIONS.—This section shall not apply to—

(1) distributions to which section 303 (relating to distributions in redemption of stock to pay death taxes) applies; or

(2) any amount to the extent that such amount is, under any other provision of this title, treated as—

(A) a dividend (other than an amount treated as a dividend under subsection (f)),

(B) ordinary income, or

(C) gain from the sale of an asset held for not more than 1 year.

[Sec. 1248(h)]

(h) TAXPAYER TO ESTABLISH EARNINGS AND PROFITS.—Unless the taxpayer establishes the amount of the earnings and profits of the foreign corporation to be taken into account under subsection (a) or (f), all gain from the sale or exchange shall be considered a dividend under subsection (a) or (f), and unless the taxpayer establishes the amount of foreign taxes to be taken into account under subsection (b), the limitation of such subsection shall not apply.

[Sec. 1248(i)]

(i) TREATMENT OF CERTAIN INDIRECT TRANSFERS.—

(1) IN GENERAL.—If any shareholder of a 10-percent corporate shareholder of a foreign corporation exchanges stock of the 10-percent corporate shareholder for stock of the foreign corporation, such 10-percent corporate shareholder shall recognize gain in the same manner as if the stock of the foreign corporation received in such exchange had been—

(A) issued to the 10-percent corporate shareholder, and

(B) then distributed by the 10-percent corporate shareholder to such shareholder in redemption or liquidation (whichever is appropriate).

The amount of gain recognized by such 10-percent corporate shareholder under the preceding sentence shall not exceed the amount treated as a dividend under this section.

(2) 10-PERCENT CORPORATE SHAREHOLDER DEFINED.—For purposes of this subsection, the term "10-percent corporate shareholder" means any domestic corporation which, as of the day before the exchange referred to in paragraph (1), satisfies the stock ownership requirements of subsection (a)(2) with respect to the foreign corporation.

[Sec. 1248(j)]

(j) COORDINATION WITH DIVIDENDS RECEIVED DEDUCTION.—In the case of the sale or exchange by a domestic corporation of stock in a foreign corporation held for 1 year or more, any amount received by the domestic corporation which is treated as a dividend by reason of this section shall be treated as a dividend for purposes of applying section 245A.

[Sec. 1248(k)]

(k) CROSS REFERENCE.—

For provision excluding amounts previously taxed under this section from gross income when subsequently distributed, see section 959(e).

[Sec. 1249]

SEC. 1249. GAIN FROM CERTAIN SALES OR EXCHANGES OF PATENTS, ETC., TO FOREIGN CORPORATIONS.

[Sec. 1249(a)]

(a) GENERAL RULE.—Gain from the sale or exchange of a patent, an invention, model, or design (whether or not patented), a copyright, a secret formula or process, or any other similar property right to any foreign corporation by any United States person (as defined in section 7701(a)(30)) which controls such foreign corporation shall, if such gain would (but for the provisions of this subsection) be gain from the sale or exchange of a capital asset or of property described in section 1231, be considered as ordinary income.

[Sec. 1249(b)]

(b) CONTROL.—For purposes of subsection (a), control means, with respect to any foreign corporation, the ownership, directly or indirectly, of stock possessing more than 50 percent of the total combined voting power of all classes of stock entitled to vote. For purposes of this subsection, the rules for determining ownership of stock prescribed by section 958 shall apply.

[Sec. 1253]

SEC. 1253. TRANSFERS OF FRANCHISES, TRADEMARKS, AND TRADE NAMES.

[Sec. 1253(a)]

(a) GENERAL RULE.—A transfer of a franchise, trademark, or trade name shall not be treated as a sale or exchange of a capital asset if the transferor retains any significant power, right, or continuing interest with respect to the subject matter of the franchise, trademark, or trade name.

[Sec. 1253(b)]

(b) DEFINITIONS.—For purposes of this section—

(1) FRANCHISE.—The term "franchise" includes an agreement which gives one of the parties to the agreement the right to distribute, sell, or provide goods, services, or facilities, within a specified area.

(2) SIGNIFICANT POWER, RIGHT, OR CONTINUING INTEREST.—The term "significant power, right, or continuing interest" includes, but is not limited to, the following rights with respect to the interest transferred:

(A) A right to disapprove any assignment of such interest, or any part thereof.

(B) A right to terminate at will.

(C) A right to prescribe the standards of quality of products used or sold, or of services furnished, and of the equipment and facilities used to promote such products or services.

(D) A right to require that the transferee sell or advertise only products or services of the transferor.

(E) A right to require that the transferee purchase substantially all of his supplies and equipment from the transferor.

(F) A right to payments contingent on the productivity, use, or disposition of the subject matter of the interest transferred, if such payments constitute a substantial element under the transfer agreement.

(3) TRANSFER.—The term "transfer" includes the renewal of a franchise, trademark, or trade name.

[Sec. 1253(c)]

(c) TREATMENT OF CONTINGENT PAYMENTS BY TRANSFEROR.—Amounts received or accrued on account of a transfer, sale, or other disposition of a franchise, trademark, or trade name which are contingent on the productivity, use, or disposition of the franchise, trademark, or trade name transferred shall be treated as amounts received or accrued from the sale or other disposition of property which is not a capital asset.

[Sec. 1253(d)]

(d) Treatment of Payments by Transferee.—

(1) Contingent serial payments.—

(A) In general.—Any amount described in subparagraph (B) which is paid or incurred during the taxable year on account of a transfer, sale, or other disposition of a franchise, trademark, or trade name shall be allowed as a deduction under section 162(a) (relating to trade or business expenses).

(B) Amounts to which paragraph applies.—An amount is described in this subparagraph if it—

(i) is contingent on the productivity, use, or disposition of the franchise, trademark, or trade name, and

(ii) is paid as part of a series of payments—

(I) which are payable not less frequently than annually throughout the entire term of the transfer agreement, and

(II) which are substantially equal in amount (or payable under a fixed formula).

(2) Other payments.—Any amount paid or incurred on account of a transfer, sale, or other disposition of a franchise, trademark, or trade name to which paragraph (1) does not apply shall be treated as an amount chargeable to capital account.

(3) Renewals, etc.—For purposes of determining the term of a transfer agreement under this section, there shall be taken into account all renewal options (and any other period for which the parties reasonably expect the agreement to be renewed).

PART V—SPECIAL RULES FOR BONDS AND OTHER DEBT INSTRUMENTS

Subpart A—Original Issue Discount

[Sec. 1271]

SEC. 1271. TREATMENT OF AMOUNTS RECEIVED ON RETIREMENT OR SALE OR EXCHANGE OF DEBT INSTRUMENTS.

[Sec. 1271(a)]

(a) General Rule.—For purposes of this title—

(1) Retirement.—Amounts received by the holder on retirement of any debt instrument shall be considered as amounts received in exchange therefor.

(2) Ordinary income on sale or exchange where intention to call before maturity.—

(A) In general.—If at the time of original issue there was an intention to call a debt instrument before maturity, any gain realized on the sale or exchange thereof which does not exceed an amount equal to—

(i) the original issue discount, reduced by

(ii) the portion of original issue discount previously includible in the gross income of any holder (without regard to section 1272(a)(7) (or the corresponding provisions of prior law)),

shall be treated as ordinary income.

(B) Exceptions.—This paragraph shall not apply to—

(i) any tax-exempt obligation, or

(ii) any holder who has purchased the debt instrument at a premium.

(3) Certain short-term government obligations.—

(A) In general.—On the sale or exchange of any short-term Government obligation, any gain realized which does not exceed an amount equal to the ratable share of the acquisition discount shall be treated as ordinary income.

(B) Short-term government obligation.—For purposes of this paragraph, the term "short-term Government obligation" means any obligation of the United States or any of its possessions, or of a State or any political subdivision thereof, or of the District of Columbia, which has a fixed maturity date not more than 1 year from the date of issue. Such term does not include any tax-exempt obligation.

(C) Acquisition discount.—For purposes of this paragraph, the term "acquisition discount" means the excess of the stated redemption price at maturity over the taxpayer's basis for the obligation.

(D) Ratable share.—For purposes of this paragraph, except as provided in subparagraph (E) the ratable share of the acquisition discount is an amount which bears the same ratio to such discount as—

(i) the number of days which the taxpayer held the obligation, bears to

(ii) the number of days after the date the taxpayer acquired the obligation and up to (and including) the date of its maturity.

(E) Election of accrual on basis of constant interest rate.—At the election of the taxpayer with respect to any obligation, the ratable share of the aquisition discount is the portion of the acquisition discount accruing while the taxpayer held the obligation determined (under regulations prescribed by the Secretary) on the basis of—

(i) the taxpayer's yield to maturity based on the taxpayer's cost of acquiring the obligation, and

(ii) compounding daily.

An election under this subparagraph, once made with respect to any obligation, shall be irrevocable.

(4) Certain short-term nongovernment obligations.—

(A) In general.—On the sale or exchange of any short-term nongovernment obligation, any gain realized which does not exceed an amount equal to the ratable share of the original issue discount shall be treated as ordinary income.

(B) Short-term nongovernment obligation.—For purposes of this paragraph, the term "short-term nongovernment obligation" means any obligation which—

(i) has a fixed maturity date not more than 1 year from the date of the issue, and

(ii) is not a short-term Government obligation (as defined in paragraph (3)(B) without regard to the last sentence thereof).

(C) Ratable share.—For purposes of this paragraph, except as provided in subparagraph (D), the ratable share of the original issue discount is an amount which bears the same ratio to such discount as—

(i) the number of days which the taxpayer held the obligation, bears to

(ii) the number of days after the date of original issue and up to (and including) the date of its maturity.

(D) Election of accrual on basis of constant interest rate.—At the election of the taxpayer with respect to any obligation, the ratable share of the original issue discount is the portion of the original issue discount accruing while the taxpayer held the obligation determined (under regulations prescribed by the Secretary) on the basis of—

(i) the yield to maturity based on the issue price of the obligation, and

(ii) compounding daily.

Any election under this subparagraph, once made with respect to any obligation, shall be irrevocable.

[Sec. 1271(b)]

(b) EXCEPTION FOR CERTAIN OBLIGATIONS.—

(1) IN GENERAL.—This section shall not apply to any obligation issued by a natural person before June 9, 1997.

(2) TERMINATION.—Paragraph (1) shall not apply to any obligation purchased (within the meaning of section 1272(d)(1)) after June 8, 1997.

* * *

[Sec. 1272]

SEC. 1272. CURRENT INCLUSION IN INCOME OF ORIGINAL ISSUE DISCOUNT.

[Sec. 1272(a)]

(a) ORIGINAL ISSUE DISCOUNT INCLUDED IN INCOME ON BASIS OF CONSTANT INTEREST RATE.—

(1) GENERAL RULE.—For purposes of this title, there shall be included in the gross income of the holder of any debt instrument having original issue discount an amount equal to the sum of the daily portions of the original issue discount for each day during the taxable year on which such holder held such debt instrument.

(2) EXCEPTIONS.—Paragraph (1) shall not apply to—

(A) TAX-EXEMPT OBLIGATIONS.—Any tax-exempt obligation.

(B) UNITED STATES SAVINGS BONDS.—Any United States savings bond.

(C) SHORT-TERM OBLIGATIONS.—Any debt instrument which has a fixed maturity date not more than 1 year from the date of issue.

(D) LOANS BETWEEN NATURAL PERSONS.—

(i) IN GENERAL.—Any loan made by a natural person to another natural person if—

(I) such loan is not made in the course of a trade or business of the lender, and

(II) the amount of such loan (when increased by the outstanding amount of prior loans by such natural person to such other natural person) does not exceed $10,000.

(ii) CLAUSE (i) NOT TO APPLY WHERE TAX AVOIDANCE A PRINCIPAL PURPOSE.—Clause (i) shall not apply if the loan has as 1 of its principal purposes the avoidance of any Federal tax.

(iii) TREATMENT OF HUSBAND AND WIFE.—For purposes of this subparagraph, a husband and wife shall be treated as 1 person. The preceding sentence shall not apply where the spouses lived apart at all times during the taxable year in which the loan is made.

(3) DETERMINATION OF DAILY PORTIONS.—For purposes of paragraph (1), the daily portion of the original issue discount on any debt instrument shall be determined by allocating to each day in any accrual period its ratable portion of the increase during such accrual period in the adjusted issue price of the debt instrument. For purposes of the preceding sentence, the increase in the adjusted issue price for any accrual period shall be an amount equal to the excess (if any) of—

(A) the product of—

(i) the adjusted issue price of the debt instrument at the beginning of such accrual period, and

(ii) the yield to maturity (determined on the basis of compounding at the close of each accrual period and properly adjusted for the length of the accrual period), over

(B) the sum of the amounts payable as interest on such debt instrument during such accrual period.

(4) ADJUSTED ISSUE PRICE.—For purposes of this subsection, the adjusted issue price of any debt instrument at the beginning of any accrual period is the sum of—

(A) the issue price of such debt instrument, plus

(B) the adjustments under this subsection to such issue price for all periods before the first day of such accrual period.

(5) ACCRUAL PERIOD.—Except as otherwise provided in regulations prescribed by the Secretary, the term "accrual period" means a 6-month period (or shorter period from the date of original issue of the debt instrument) which ends on a day in the calendar year corresponding to the maturity date of the debt instrument or the date 6 months before such maturity date.

(6) DETERMINATION OF DAILY PORTIONS WHERE PRINCIPAL SUBJECT TO ACCELERATION.—

(A) IN GENERAL.—In the case of any debt instrument to which this paragraph applies, the daily portion of the original issue discount shall be determined by allocating to each day in any accrual period its ratable portion of the excess (if any) of—

(i) the sum of (I) the present value determined under subparagraph (B) of all remaining payments under the debt instrument as of the close of such period, and (II) the payments during the accrual period of amounts included in the stated redemption price of the debt instrument, over

(ii) the adjusted issue price of such debt instrument at the beginning of such period.

(B) DETERMINATION OF PRESENT VALUE.—For purposes of subparagraph (A), the present value shall be determined on the basis of—

(i) the original yield to maturity (determined on the basis of compounding at the close of each accrual period and properly adjusted for the length of the accrual period),

(ii) events which have occurred before the close of the accrual period, and

(iii) a prepayment assumption determined in the manner prescribed by regulations.

(C) DEBT INSTRUMENTS TO WHICH PARAGRAPH APPLIES.—This paragraph applies to—

(i) any regular interest in a REMIC or qualified mortgage held by a REMIC,

(ii) any other debt instrument if payments under such debt instrument may be accelerated by reason of prepayments of other obligations securing such debt instrument (or, to the extent provided in regulations, by reason of other events), or

(iii) any pool of debt instruments the yield on which may be affected by reason of prepayments (or to the extent provided in regulations, by reason of other events).

To the extent provided in regulations prescribed by the Secretary, in the case of a small business engaged in the trade or business of selling tangible personal property at retail, clause (iii) shall not apply to debt instruments incurred in the ordinary course of such trade or business while held by such business.

(7) REDUCTION WHERE SUBSEQUENT HOLDER PAYS ACQUISITION PREMIUM.—

(A) REDUCTION.—For purposes of this subsection, in the case of any purchase after its original issue of a debt instrument to which this subsection applies, the daily portion for any day shall be reduced by an amount equal to the amount which would be the daily portion for such day (without regard to this paragraph) multiplied by the fraction determined under subparagraph (B).

(B) DETERMINATION OF FRACTION.—For purposes of subparagraph (A), the fraction determined under this subparagraph is a fraction—

(i) the numerator of which is the excess (if any) of—

(I) the cost of such debt instrument incurred by the purchaser, over

(II) the issue price of such debt instrument, increased by the portion of original issue discount previously includible in the gross income of any holder (computed without regard to this paragraph), and

(ii) the denominator of which is the sum of the daily portions for such debt instrument for all days after the date of such purchase and ending on the stated maturity date (computed without regard to this paragraph).

[Sec. 1272(b)]

(b) EXCEPTIONS.—This section shall not apply to any holder—

(1) who has purchased the debt instrument at a premium, or

(2) which is a life insurance company to which section 811(b) applies.

* * *

[Sec. 1273]

SEC. 1273. DETERMINATION OF AMOUNT OF ORIGINAL ISSUE DISCOUNT.

[Sec. 1273(a)]

(a) GENERAL RULE.—for purposes of this subpart—

(1) IN GENERAL.—The term "original issue discount" means the excess (if any) of—

(A) the stated redemption price at maturity, over

(B) the issue price.

(2) STATED REDEMPTION PRICE AT MATURITY.—The term "stated redemption price at maturity" means the amount fixed by the last modification of the purchase agreement and includes interest and other amounts payable at that time (other than any interest based on a fixed rate, and payable unconditionally at fixed periodic intervals of 1 year or less during the entire term of the debt instrument).

(3) 1/4 OF 1 PERCENT DE MINIMIS RULE.—If the original issue discount determined under paragraph (1) is less than—

(A) 1/4 of 1 percent of the stated redemption price at maturity, multiplied by

(B) the number of complete years to maturity,

then the original issue discount shall be treated as zero.

[Sec. 1273(b)]

(b) ISSUE PRICE.—For purposes of this subpart—

(1) PUBLICLY OFFERED DEBT INSTRUMENTS NOT ISSUED FOR PROPERTY.—In the case of any issue of debt instruments—

(A) publicly offered, and

(B) not issued for property,

the issue price is the initial offering price to the public (excluding bond houses and brokers) at which price a substantial amount of such debt instruments was sold.

(2) OTHER DEBT INSTRUMENTS NOT ISSUED FOR PROPERTY.—In the case of any isssue of debt instruments not issued for property and not publicly offered, the issue price of each such instrument is the price paid by the first buyer of such debt instrument.

(3) DEBT INSTRUMENTS ISSUED FOR PROPERTY WHERE THERE IS PUBLIC TRADING.—In the case of a debt instrument which is issued for property and which—

(A) is part of an issue a portion of which is traded on an established securities market, or

(B)(i) is issued for stock or securities which are traded on an established securities market, or

(ii) to the extent provided in regulations, is issued for property (other than stock or securities) of a kind regularly traded on an established market,

the issue price of such debt instrument shall be the fair market value of such property.

(4) OTHER CASES.—Except in any case—

(A) to which paragraph (1), (2), or (3) of this subsection applies, or

(B) to which section 1274 applies,

the issue price of a debt instrument which is issued for property shall be the stated redemption price at maturity.

(5) PROPERTY.—In applying this subsection, the term "property" includes services and the right to use property, but such term does not include money.

[Sec. 1273(c)]

(c) SPECIAL RULES FOR APPLYING SUBSECTION (b).—for purposes of subsection (b)—

(1) INITIAL OFFERING PRICE; PRICE PAID BY THE FIRST BUYER.—The terms "initial offering price" and "price paid by the first buyer" include the aggregate payments made by the purchaser under the purchase agreement, including modifications thereof.

(2) TREATMENT OF INVESTMENT UNITS.—In the case of any debt instrument and an option, security, or other property issued together as an investment unit—

(A) the issue price for such unit shall be determined in accordance with the rules of this subsection and subsection (b) as if it were a debt instrument,

(B) the issue price determined for such unit shall be allocated to each element of such unit on the basis of the relationship of the fair market value of such element to the fair market value of all elements in such unit, and

(C) the issue price of any debt instrument included in such unit shall be the portion of the issue price of the unit allocated to the debt instrument under subparagraph (B).

[Sec. 1274]

SEC. 1274. DETERMINATION OF ISSUE PRICE IN THE CASE OF CERTAIN DEBT INSTRUMENTS ISSUED FOR PROPERTY.

[Sec. 1274(a)]

(a) IN GENERAL.—In the case of any debt instrument to which this section applies, for purposes of this subpart, the issue price shall be—

(1) where there is adequate stated interest, the stated principal amount, or

(2) in any other case, the imputed principal amount.

[Sec. 1274(b)]

(b) IMPUTED PRINCIPAL AMOUNT.—For purposes of this section—

(1) IN GENERAL.—Except as provided in paragraph (3), the imputed principal amount of any debt instrument shall be equal to the sum of the present values of all payments due under such debt instrument.

(2) DETERMINATION OF PRESENT VALUE.—For purposes of paragraph (1), the present value of a payment shall be determined in the manner provided by regulations prescribed by the Secretary—

(A) as of the date of the sale or exchange, and

(B) by using a discount rate equal to the applicable Federal rate, compounded semiannually.

(3) FAIR MARKET VALUE RULE IN POTENTIALLY ABUSIVE SITUATIONS.—

(A) IN GENERAL.—In the case of any potentially abusive situation, the imputed principal amount of any debt instrument received in exchange for property shall be the fair market value of such property adjusted to take into account other consideration involved in the transaction.

(B) POTENTIALLY ABUSIVE SITUATION DEFINED.—For purposes of subparagraph (A), the term "potentially abusive situation" means—

(i) a tax shelter (as defined in section 6662(d)(2)(C)(ii)), and

(ii) any other situation which, by reason of—

(I) recent sales transactions,

(II) nonrecourse financing,

(III) financing with a term in excess of the economic life of the property, or

(IV) other circumstances,

is of a type which the Secretary specifies by regulations as having potential for tax avoidance.

[Sec. 1274(c)]

(c) DEBT INSTRUMENTS TO WHICH SECTION APPLIES.—

(1) IN GENERAL.—Except as otherwise provided in this subsection, this section shall apply to any debt instrument given in consideration for the sale or exchange of property if—

(A) the stated redemption price at maturity for such debt instrument exceeds—

(i) where there is adequate stated interest, the stated principal amount, or

(ii) in any other case, the imputed principal amount of such debt instrument determined under subsection (b), and

(B) some or all of the payments due under such debt instrument are due more than 6 months after the date of such sale or exchange.

(2) ADEQUATE STATED INTEREST.—For purposes of this section, there is adequate stated interest with respect to any debt instrument if the stated principal amount for such debt instrument is less than or equal to the imputed principal amount of such debt instrument determined under subsection (b).

(3) EXCEPTIONS.—This section shall not apply to—

(A) SALES FOR $1,000,000 OR LESS OF FARMS BY INDIVIDUALS OR SMALL BUSINESSES.—

(i) IN GENERAL.—Any debt instrument arising from the sale or exchange of a farm (within the meaning of section 6420(c)(2))—

(I) by an individual, estate, or testamentary trust,

(II) by a corporation which as of the date of the sale or exchange is a small business corporation (as defined in section 1244(c)(3)), or

(III) by a partnership which as of the date of the sale or exchange meets requirements similar to those of section 1244(c)(3).

(ii) $1,000,000 LIMITATION.—Clause (i) shall apply only if it can be determined at the time of the sale or exchange that the sales price cannot exceed $1,000,000. For purposes of the preceding sentence, all sales and exchanges which are part of the same transaction (or a series of related transactions) shall be treated as 1 sale or exchange.

(B) SALES OF PRINCIPAL RESIDENCES.—Any debt instrument arising from the sale or exchange by an individual of his principal residence (within the meaning of section 121).

(C) SALES INVOLVING TOTAL PAYMENTS OF $250,000 OR LESS.—

(i) IN GENERAL.—Any debt instrument arising from the sale or exchange of property if the sum of the following amounts does not exceed $250,000:

(I) the aggregate amount of the payments due under such debt instrument and all other debt instruments received as consideration for the sale or exchange, and

(II) the aggregate amount of any other consideration to be received for the sale or exchange.

(ii) CONSIDERATION OTHER THAN DEBT INSTRUMENT TAKEN INTO ACCOUNT AT FAIR MARKET VALUE.—For purposes of clause (i), any consideration (other than a debt instrument) shall be taken into account at its fair market value.

(iii) AGGREGATION OF TRANSACTIONS.—For purposes of this subparagraph, all sales and exchanges which are part of the same transaction (or a series of related transactions) shall be treated as 1 sale or exchange.

(D) DEBT INSTRUMENTS WHICH ARE PUBLICLY TRADED OR ISSUED FOR PUBLICLY TRADED PROPERTY.—Any debt instrument to which section 1273(b)(3) applies.

(E) CERTAIN SALES OF PATENTS.—In the case of any transfer described in section 1235(a) (relating to sale or exchange of patents), any amount contingent on the productivity, use, or disposition of the property transferred.

(F) SALES OR EXCHANGES TO WHICH SECTION 483(e) APPLIES.—Any debt instrument to the extent section 483(e) (relating to certain land transfers between related persons) applies to such instrument.

(4) EXCEPTION FOR ASSUMPTIONS.—If any person—

(A) in connection with the sale or exchange of property, assumes any debt instrument, or

(B) acquires any property subject to any debt instrument,

in determining whether this section or section 483 applies to such debt instrument, such assumption (or such acquisition) shall not be taken into account unless the terms and conditions of such debt instrument are modified (or the nature of the transaction is changed) in connection with the assumption (or acquisition).

[Sec. 1274(d)]

(d) DETERMINATION OF APPLICABLE FEDERAL RATE.—For purposes of this section—

(1) APPLICABLE FEDERAL RATE.—

(A) IN GENERAL.—

In the case of a debt instrument with a term of:	The applicable Federal rate is:
Not over 3 years	The Federal short-term rate.
Over 3 years but not over 9 years	The Federal mid-term rate.
Over 9 years	The Federal long-term rate.

(B) DETERMINATION OF RATES.—During each calendar month, the Secretary shall determine the Federal short-term rate, mid-term rate, and long-term rate which shall apply during the following calendar month.

(C) FEDERAL RATE FOR ANY CALENDAR MONTH.—For purposes of this paragraph—

(i) FEDERAL SHORT-TERM RATE.—The Federal short-term rate shall be the rate determined by the Secretary based on the average market yield (during any 1-month period selected by the Secretary and ending in the calendar month in which the determination is made) on outstanding marketable obligations of the United States with remaining periods to maturity of 3 years or less.

(ii) FEDERAL MID-TERM AND LONG-TERM RATES.—The Federal mid-term and long-term rate shall be determined in accordance with the principles of clause (i).

(D) LOWER RATE PERMITTED IN CERTAIN CASES.—The Secretary may by regulations permit a rate to be used with respect to any debt instrument which is lower than the applicable Federal rate if the taxpayer establishes to the satisfaction of the Secretary that such lower rate is based on the same principles as the applicable Federal rate and is appropriate for the term of such instrument.

(2) LOWEST 3-MONTH RATE APPLICABLE TO ANY SALE OR EXCHANGE.—

(A) IN GENERAL.—In the case of any sale or exchange, the applicable Federal rate shall be the lowest 3-month rate.

(B) LOWEST 3-MONTH RATE.—For purposes of subparagraph (A), the term "lowest 3-month rate" means the lowest of the applicable Federal rates in effect for any month in the 3-calendar-month period ending with the 1st calendar month in which there is a binding contract in writing for such sale or exchange.

(3) TERM OF DEBT INSTRUMENT.—In determining the term of a debt instrument for purposes of this subsection, under regulations prescribed by the Secretary, there shall be taken into account options to renew or extend.

[Sec. 1274(e)]

(e) 110 PERCENT RATE WHERE SALE-LEASEBACK INVOLVED.—

(1) IN GENERAL.—In the case of any debt instrument to which this subsection applies, the discount rate used under subsection (b)(2)(B) or section 483(b) shall be 110 percent of the applicable Federal rate, compounded semiannually.

(2) LOWER DISCOUNT RATES SHALL NOT APPLY.—Section 1274A shall not apply to any debt instrument to which this subsection applies.

(3) DEBT INSTRUMENTS TO WHICH THIS SUBSECTION APPLIES.—This subsection shall apply to any debt instrument given in consideration for the sale or exchange of any property if, pursuant to a plan, the transferor or any related person leases a portion of such property after such sale or exchange.

Subpart D—Miscellaneous Provisions

[Sec. 1287]

SEC. 1287. DENIAL OF CAPITAL GAIN TREATMENT FOR GAINS ON CERTAIN OBLIGATIONS NOT IN REGISTERED FORM.

[Sec. 1287(a)]

(a) IN GENERAL.—If any registration-required obligation is not in registered form, any gain on the sale or other disposition of such obligation shall be treated as ordinary income (unless the issuance of such obligation was subject to tax under section 4701).

[Sec. 1287(b)]

(b) DEFINITIONS.—For purposes of subsection (a)—

(1) REGISTRATION-REQUIRED OBLIGATION.—The term "registration-required obligation" has the meaning given to such term by section 163(f)(2).

(2) REGISTERED FORM.—the term "registered form" has the same meaning as when used in section 163(f).

PART VI—TREATMENT OF CERTAIN PASSIVE FOREIGN INVESTMENT COMPANIES

Subpart A—Interest on Tax Deferral

[Sec. 1291]

SEC. 1291. INTEREST ON TAX DEFERRAL.

[Sec. 1291(a)]

(a) TREATMENT OF DISTRIBUTIONS AND STOCK DISPOSITIONS.—

(1) DISTRIBUTIONS.—If a United States person receives an excess distribution in respect of stock in a passive foreign investment company, then—

(A) the amount of the excess distribution shall be allocated ratably to each day in the taxpayer's holding period for the stock,

(B) with respect to such excess distribution, the taxpayer's gross income for the current year shall include (as ordinary income) only the amounts allocated under subparagraph (A) to—

(i) the current year, or

(ii) any period in the taxpayer's holding period before the 1st day of the 1st taxable year of the company which begins after December 31, 1986, and for which it was a passive foreign investment company, and

(C) the tax imposed by this chapter for the current year shall be increased by the deferred tax amount (determined under subsection (c)).

(2) DISPOSITIONS.—If the taxpayer disposes of stock in a passive foreign investment company, then the rules of paragraph (1) shall apply to any gain recognized on such disposition in the same manner as if such gain were an excess distribution.

(3) DEFINITIONS.—For purposes of this section—

(A) HOLDING PERIOD.—The taxpayer's holding period shall be determined under section 1223; except that—

(i) for purposes of applying this section to an excess distribution, such holding period shall be treated as ending on the date of such distribution, and

(ii) if section 1296 applied to such stock with respect to the taxpayer for any prior taxable year, such holding period shall be treated as beginning on the first day of the first taxable year beginning after the last taxable year for which section 1296 so applied.

(B) CURRENT YEAR.—The term "current year" means the taxable year in which the excess distribution or disposition occurs.

[Sec. 1291(b)]

(b) EXCESS DISTRIBUTION.—

(1) IN GENERAL.—For purposes of this section, the term "excess distribution" means any distribution in respect of stock received during any taxable year to the extent such distribution does not exceed its ratable portion of the total excess distribution (if any) for such taxable year.

(2) TOTAL EXCESS DISTRIBUTION.—For purposes of this subsection—

(A) IN GENERAL.—The term "total excess distribution" means the excess (if any) of—

(i) the amount of the distributions in respect of the stock received by the taxpayer during the taxable year, over

(ii) 125 percent of the average amount received in respect of such stock by the taxpayer during the 3 preceding taxable years (or, if shorter, the portion of the taxpayer's holding period before the taxable year).

For purposes of clause (ii), any excess distribution received during such 3-year period shall be taken into account only to the extent it was included in gross income under subsection (a)(1)(B).

(B) NO EXCESS FOR 1ST YEAR.—The total excess distributions with respect to any stock shall be zero for the taxable year in which the taxpayer's holding period in such stock begins.

(3) ADJUSTMENTS.—Under regulations prescribed by the Secretary—

(A) determinations under this subsection shall be made on a share-by-share basis, except that shares with the same holding period may be aggregated,

(B) proper adjustments shall be made for stock splits and stock dividends,

(C) if the taxpayer does not hold the stock during the entire taxable year, distributions received during such year shall be annualized,

(D) if the taxpayer's holding period includes periods during which the stock was held by another person, distributions received by such other person shall be taken into account as if received by the taxpayer,

(E) if the distributions are received in a foreign currency, determinations under this subsection shall be made in such currency and the amount of any excess distribution determined in such currency shall be translated into dollars,

(F) proper adjustment shall be made for amounts not includible in gross income by reason of section 959(a) or 1293(c), and

(G) if a charitable deduction was allowable under section 642(c) to a trust for any distribution of its income, proper adjustments shall be made for the deduction so allowable to the extent allocable to distributions or gain in respect of stock in a passive foreign investment company.

[Sec. 1291(c)]

(c) DEFERRED TAX AMOUNT.—For purposes of this section—

(1) IN GENERAL.—The term "deferred tax amount" means, with respect to any distribution or disposition to which subsection (a) applies, an amount equal to the sum of—

(A) the aggregate increases in taxes described in paragraph (2), plus

(B) the aggregate amount of interest (determined in the manner provided under paragraph (3)) on such increases in tax.

Any increase in the tax imposed by this chapter for the current year under subsection (a) to the extent attributable to the amount referred to in subparagraph (B) shall be treated as interest paid under section 6601 on the due date for the current year.

(2) AGGREGATE INCREASES IN TAXES.—For purposes of paragraph (1)(A), the aggregate increases in taxes shall be determined by multiplying each amount allocated under subsection (a)(1)(A) to any taxable year (other than any taxable year referred to in subsection (a)(1)(B)) by the highest rate of tax in effect for such taxable year under section 1 or 11, whichever applies.

(3) COMPUTATION OF INTEREST.—

(A) IN GENERAL.—The amount of interest referred to in paragraph (1)(B) on any increase determined under paragraph (2) for any taxable year shall be determined for the period—

(i) beginning on the due date for such taxable year, and

(ii) ending on the due date for the taxable year with or within which the distribution or disposition occurs,

by using the rates and method applicable under section 6621 for underpayments of tax for such period.

(B) DUE DATE.—For purposes of this subsection, the term "due date" means the date prescribed by law (determined without regard to extensions) for filing the return of the tax imposed by this chapter for the taxable year.

[Sec. 1291(d)]

(d) COORDINATION WITH SUBPART B AND C.—

(1) IN GENERAL.—This section shall not apply with respect to any distribution paid by a passive foreign investment company, or any disposition of stock in a passive foreign investment company, if such company is a qualified electing fund with respect to the taxpayer for each of its taxable years—

(A) which begins after December 31, 1986, and for which such company is a passive foreign investment company, and

(B) which includes any portion of the taxpayer's holding period.

Except as provided in section 1296(j), this section also shall not apply if an election under section 1296(k) is in effect for the taxpayer's taxable year. In the case of stock which is marked to market under section 475 or any other provision of this chapter, this section shall not apply, except that rules similar to the rules of section 1296(j) shall apply.

(2) ELECTION TO RECOGNIZE GAIN WHERE COMPANY BECOMES QUALIFIED ELECTING FUND.—

(A) IN GENERAL.—If—

(i) a passive foreign investment company becomes a qualified electing fund with respect to the taxpayer for a taxable year which begins after December 31, 1986,

(ii) the taxpayer holds stock in such company on the first day of such taxable year, and

(iii) the taxpayer establishes to the satisfaction of the Secretary the fair market value of such stock on such first day,

the taxpayer may elect to recognize gain as if he sold such stock on such first day for such fair market value.

(B) ADDITIONAL ELECTION FOR SHAREHOLDER OF CONTROLLED FOREIGN CORPORATIONS.—

(i) IN GENERAL.—If—

(I) a passive foreign investment company becomes a qualified electing fund with respect to the taxpayer for a taxable year which begins after December 1, 1986,

(II) the taxpayer holds stock in such company on the first day of such taxable year, and

(III) such company is a controlled foreign corporation (as defined in section 957(a)),

the taxpayer may elect to include in gross income as a dividend received on such first day an amount equal to the portion of the post-1986 earnings and profits of such company attributable (under regulations prescribed by the Secretary) to the stock in such company held by the taxpayer on such first day. The amount treated as a dividend under the preceding sentence shall be treated as a excess distribution and shall be allocated under subsection (a)(1)(A) only to days during periods taken into account in determining the post-1986 earnings and profits so attributable.

(ii) POST-1986 EARNINGS AND PROFITS.—For purposes of clause (i), the term "post-1986 earnings and profits" means earnings and profits which were accumulated in taxable years of such company beginning after December 31, 1986, and during the period or periods the stock was held by the taxpayer while the company was a passive foreign investment company.

(iii) COORDINATION WITH SECTION 959(e).—For purposes of section 959(e), any amount included in gross income under this subparagraph shall be treated as included in gross income under section 1248(a).

(C) ADJUSTMENTS.—In the case of any stock to which subparagraph (A) or (B) applies.—

(i) the adjusted basis of such stock shall be increased by the gain recognized under subparagraph (A) or the amount treated as a dividend under subparagraph (B), as the case may be, and

(ii) the taxpayer's holding period in such stock shall be treated as beginning on the first day referred to in such subparagraph.

[Sec. 1291(e)]

(e) CERTAIN BASIS, ETC., RULES MADE APPLICABLE..—Except to the extent inconsistent with the regulations prescribed under subsection (f), rules similar to the rules of subsections (c), (d), and (e) of section 1246 (as in effect on the day before the date of the enactment of the American Jobs Creation Act of 2004) shall apply for purposes of this section; except that—

(1) the reduction under subsection (e) of such section shall be the excess of the basis determined under section 1014 over the adjusted basis of the stock immediately before the decedent's death, and

(2) such a reduction shall not apply in the case of a decedent who was a nonresident alien at all times during his holding period in the stock.

[Sec. 1291(f)]

(f) RECOGNITION OF GAIN.—To the extent provided in regulations, in the case of any transfer of stock in a passive foreign investment company where (but for this subsection) there is not full recognition of gain, the excess (if any) of—

(1) the fair market value of such stock, over

(2) its adjusted basis,

shall be treated as gain from the sale or exchange of such stock and shall be recognized notwithstanding any provision of law. Proper adjustment shall be made to the basis of any such stock for gain recognized under the preceding sentence.

[Sec. 1291(g)]

(g) COORDINATION WITH FOREIGN TAX CREDIT RULES.—

(1) IN GENERAL.—If there are creditable foreign taxes with respect to any distribution in respect of stock in a passive foreign investment company—

(A) the amount of such distribution shall be determined for purposes of this section with regard to section 78,

(B) the excess distribution taxes shall be allocated ratably to each day in the taxpayer's holding period for the stock, and

(C) to the extent—

(i) that such excess distribution taxes are allocated to a taxable year referred to in subsection (a)(1)(B), such taxes shall be taken into account under section 901 for the current year, and

(ii) that such excess distribution taxes are allocated to any other taxable year, such taxes shall reduce (subject to the principles of section 904(d) and not below zero) the increase in tax determined under subsection (c)(2) for such taxable year by reason of such distribution (but such taxes shall not be taken into account under section 901).

(2) DEFINITIONS.—For purposes of this subsection—

(A) CREDITABLE FOREIGN TAXES.—The term "creditable foreign taxes" means, with respect to any distribution, any withholding tax imposed with respect to such distribution, but only if the taxpayer chooses the benefits of section 901 and such taxes are creditable under section 901 (determined without regard to paragraph (1)(C)(ii)).

(B) EXCESS DISTRIBUTION TAXES.—The term "excess distribution taxes" means, with respect to any distribution, the portion of the creditable foreign taxes with respect to such distribution which is attributable (on a pro rata basis) to the portion of such distribution which is an excess distribution.

(C) SECTION 1248 GAIN.—The rules of this subsection also shall apply in the case of any gain which but for this section would be includible in gross income as a dividend under section 1248.

Subpart B—Treatment of Qualified Electing Funds

[Sec. 1293]

SEC. 1293. CURRENT TAXATION OF INCOME FROM QUALIFIED ELECTING FUNDS.

[Sec. 1293(a)]

(a) INCLUSION.—

(1) IN GENERAL.—Every United States person who owns (or is treated under section 1298(a) as owning) stock of a qualified electing fund at any time during the taxable year of such fund shall include in gross income—

(A) as ordinary income, such shareholder's pro rata share of the ordinary earnings of such fund for such year, and

(B) as long-term capital gain, such shareholder's pro rata share of the net capital gain of such fund for such year.

(2) YEAR OF INCLUSION.—The inclusion under paragraph (1) shall be for the taxable year of the shareholder in which or with which the taxable year of the fund ends.

[Sec. 1293(b)]

(b) PRO RATA SHARE.—The pro rata share referred to in subsection (a) in the case of any shareholder is the amount which would have been distributed with respect to the shareholder's stock if, on each day during the taxable year of the fund, the fund had distributed to each shareholder a pro rata share of that day's ratable share of the fund's ordinary earnings and net capital gain for such year. To the extent provided in regulations, if the fund establishes to the satisfaction of the Secretary that it uses a shorter period than the taxable year to determine shareholders' interests in the earnings of such fund, pro rata shares may be determined by using such shorter period.

[Sec. 1293(c)]

(c) PREVIOUSLY TAXED AMOUNTS DISTRIBUTED TAX FREE.—If the taxpayer establishes to the satisfaction of the Secretary that any amount distributed by a passive foreign investment company is paid out of earnings and profits of the company which were included under subsection (a) in the income of any United States person, such amount shall be treated, for purposes of this chapter, as a distribution which is not a dividend; except that such distribution shall immediately reduce earnings and profits. If the passive foreign investment company is a controlled foreign corporation (as defined in section 957(a)), the preceding sentence shall not apply to any United States shareholder (as defined in section 951(b)) in such corporation, and, in applying section 959 to any such shareholder, any inclusion under this section shall be treated as an inclusion under section 951(a)(1)(A).

[Sec. 1293(d)]

(d) BASIS ADJUSTMENTS.—The basis of taxpayer's stock in a passive foreign investment company shall be—

(1) increased by any amount which is included in the income of the taxpayer under subsection (a) with respect to such stock, and

(2) decreased by any amount distributed with respect to such stock which is not includible in the income of the taxpayer by reason of subsection (c).

A similar rule shall apply also in the case of any property if by reason of holding such property the taxpayer is treated under section 1298(a) as owning stock in a qualified electing fund.

[Sec. 1293(e)]

(e) ORDINARY EARNINGS.—For purposes of this section—

(1) ORDINARY EARNINGS.—The term "ordinary earnings" means the excess of the earnings and profits of the qualified electing fund for the taxable year over its net capital gain for such taxable year.

(2) LIMITATION ON NET CAPITAL GAIN.—A qualified electing fund's capital gain for any taxable year shall not exceed its earnings and profits for such taxable year.

(3) DETERMINATION OF EARNINGS AND PROFITS.—The earnings and profits of any qualified electing fund shall be determined without regard to paragraphs (4), (5), and (6) of section 312(n). Under regulations, the preceding sentence shall not apply to the extent it would increase earnings and profits by an amount which was previously distributed by the qualified electing fund.

[Sec. 1293(f)]

(f) FOREIGN TAX CREDIT ALLOWED IN THE CASE OF 10-PERCENT CORPORATE SHAREHOLDER.—For purposes of section 960—

(1) any amount included in the gross income under subsection (a) shall be treated as if it were included under section 951(a),

(2) any amount excluded from gross income under subsection (c) shall be treated in the same manner as amounts excluded from gross income under section 959, and

(3) a domestic corporation which owns (or is treated under section 1298(a) as owning) stock of a qualified electing fund shall be treated in the same manner as a United States shareholder of a controlled foreign corporation (and such qualified electing fund shall be treated in the same manner as such controlled foreign corporation) if such domestic corporation meets the stock ownership requirements of subsection (a) or (b) of section 902 (as in effect before its repeal) with respect to such qualified electing fund.

[Sec. 1293(g)]

(g) OTHER SPECIAL RULES.—

(1) EXCEPTION FOR CERTAIN INCOME.—For purposes of determining the amount included in the gross income of any person under this section, the ordinary earnings and net capital gain of a qualified electing fund shall not include any item of income received by such fund if—

(A) such fund is a controlled foreign corporation (as defined in section 957(a)) and such person is a United States shareholder (as defined in section 951(b)) in such fund, and

(B) such person establishes to the satisfaction of the Secretary that—

(i) such income was subject to an effective rate of income tax imposed by a foreign country greater than 90 percent of the maximum rate of tax specified in section 11, or

(ii) such income is—

(I) from sources within the United States,

(II) effectively connected with the conduct by the qualified electing fund of a trade or business in the United States, and

(III) not exempt from taxation (or subject to a reduced rate of tax) pursuant to a treaty obligation of the United States.

(2) PREVENTION OF DOUBLE INCLUSION.—The Secretary shall prescribe such adjustment to the provisions of this section as may be necessary to prevent the same item of income of a qualified electing fund from being included in the gross income of a United States person more than once.

[Sec. 1294]

SEC. 1294. ELECTION TO EXTEND TIME FOR PAYMENT OF TAX ON UNDISTRIBUTED EARNINGS.

[Sec. 1294(a)]

(a) EXTENSION ALLOWED BY ELECTION.—

(1) IN GENERAL.—At the election of the taxpayer, the time for payment of any undistributed PFIC earnings tax liability of the taxpayer for the taxable year shall be extended to the extent and subject to the limitations provided in this section.

(2) ELECTION NOT PERMITTED WHERE AMOUNTS OTHERWISE INCLUDIBLE UNDER SECTION 951.—The taxpayer may not make an election under paragraph (1) with respect to the undistributed PFIC earnings tax liability attributable to a qualified electing fund for the taxable year if any amount is includible in the gross income of the taxpayer under section 951 with respect to such fund for such taxable year.

[Sec. 1294(b)]

(b) DEFINITIONS.—For purposes of this section—

(1) UNDISTRIBUTED PFIC EARNINGS TAX LIABILITY.—The term "undistributed PFIC earnings tax liability" means, in the case of any taxpayer, the excess of—

(A) the tax imposed by this chapter for the taxable year, over

(B) the tax which would be imposed by this chapter for such year without regard to the inclusion in gross income under section 1293 of the undistributed earnings of a qualified electing fund.

(2) UNDISTRIBUTED EARNINGS.—The term "undistributed earnings" means, with respect to any qualified electing fund, the excess (if any) of—

(A) the amount includible in gross income by reason of section 1293(a) for the taxable year, over

(B) the amount not includible in gross income by reason of section 1293(c) for such taxable year.

[Sec. 1294(c)]

(c) TERMINATION OF EXTENSION.—

(1) DISTRIBUTIONS.—

(A) IN GENERAL.—If a distribution is not includible in gross income for the taxable year by reason of section 1293(c), then the extension under subsection (a) for payment of the undistributed PFIC earnings tax liability with respect to the earnings to which such distribution is attributable shall expire on the last date prescribed by law (determined without regard to extensions) for filing the return of tax for such taxable year.

(B) ORDERING RULE.—For purposes of subparagraph (A), a distribution shall be treated as made from the most recently accumulated earnings and profits.

(2) TRANSFERS, ETC.—If—

(A) stock in a passive foreign investment company is transferred during the taxable year, or

(B) a passive foreign investment company ceases to be a qualified electing fund, all extensions under subsection (a) for payment of undistributed PFIC earnings tax liability attributable to such stock (or, in the case of such a cessation, attributable to any stock in such company) which had not expired before the date of such transfer or cessation shall expire on the last date prescribed by law (determined without regard to extensions) for filing the return of tax for the taxable year in which such transfer or cessation occurs. To the extent provided in regulations, the preceding sentence shall not apply in the case of a transfer in a transaction with respect to which gain or loss is not recognized (in whole or in part), and the transferee in such transaction shall succeed to the treatment under this section of the transferor.

(3) JEOPARDY.—If the Secretary believes that collection of an amount to which an extension under this section relates is in jeopardy, the Secretary shall immediately terminate such extension with respect to such amount, and notice and demand shall be made by him for payment of such amount.

[Sec. 1294(d)]

(d) ELECTION.—The election under subsection (a) shall be made not later than the time prescribed by law (including extensions) for filing the return of tax imposed by this chapter for the taxable year.

[Sec. 1294(e)]

(e) AUTHORITY TO REQUIRE BOND.—Section 6165 shall apply to any extension under this section as though the Secretary were extending the time for payment of the tax.

[Sec. 1294(f)]

(f) TREATMENT OF LOANS TO SHAREHOLDER.—For purposes of this section and section 1293, any loan by a qualified electing fund (directly or indirectly) to a shareholder of such fund shall be treated as a distribution to such shareholder.

[Sec. 1294(g)]

(g) CROSS REFERENCE.—For provisions providing for interest for the period of the extension under this section, see section 6601.

[Sec. 1295]

SEC. 1295. QUALIFIED ELECTING FUND.

[Sec. 1295(a)]

(a) GENERAL RULE.—For purposes of this part, any passive foreign investment company shall be treated as a qualified electing fund with respect to the taxpayer if—

(1) an election by the taxpayer under subsection (b) applies to such company for the taxable year, and

(2) such company complies with such requirements as the Secretary may prescribe for purposes of—

(A) determining the ordinary earnings and net capital gain of such company, and

(B) otherwise carrying out the purposes of this subpart.

[Sec. 1295(b)]

(b) ELECTION.—

(1) IN GENERAL.—A taxpayer may make an election under this subsection with respect to any passive foreign investment company for any taxable year of the taxpayer. Such an election, once made with respect to any company, shall apply to all subsequent taxable years of the taxpayer with respect to such company unless revoked by the taxpayer with the consent of the Secretary.

(2) WHEN MADE.—An election under this subsection may be made for any taxable year at any time on or before the due date (determined with regard to extensions) for filing the return of the tax imposed by this chapter for such taxable year. To the extent provided in regulations, such an election may be made later than as required in the preceding sentence where the taxpayer fails to make a timely election because the taxpayer reasonably believed that the company was not a passive foreign investment company.

Subpart C—Election of Mark to Market for Marketable Stock

[Sec. 1296]

SEC. 1296. ELECTION OF MARK TO MARKET FOR MARKETABLE STOCK.

[Sec. 1296(a)]

(a) GENERAL RULE.—In the case of marketable stock in a passive foreign investment company which is owned (or treated under subsection (g) as owned) by a United States person at the close of any taxable year of such person, at the election of such person—

(1) If the fair market value of such stock as of the close of such taxable year exceeds its adjusted basis, such United States person shall include in gross income for such taxable year an amount equal to the amount of such excess.

(2) If the adjusted basis of such stock exceeds the fair market value of such stock as of the close of such taxable year, such United States person shall be allowed a deduction for such taxable year equal to the lesser of—

(A) the amount of such excess, or

(B) the unreversed inclusions with respect to such stock.

[Sec. 1296(b)]

(b) BASIS ADJUSTMENTS.—

(1) IN GENERAL.—The adjusted basis of stock in a passive foreign investment company—

(A) shall be increased by the amount included in the gross income of the United States person under subsection (a)(1) with respect to such stock, and

(B) shall be decreased by the amount allowed as a deduction to the United States person under subsection (a)(2) with respect to such stock.

(2) SPECIAL RULE FOR STOCK CONSTRUCTIVELY OWNED.—In the case of stock in a passive foreign investment company which the United States person is treated as owning under subsection (g)—

(A) the adjustments under paragraph (1) shall apply to such stock in the hands of the person actually holding such stock but only for purposes of determining the subsequent treatment under this chapter of the United States person with respect to such stock, and

(B) similar adjustments shall be made to the adjusted basis of the property by reason of which the United States person is treated as owning such stock.

[Sec. 1296(c)]

(c) CHARACTER AND SOURCE RULES.—

(1) ORDINARY TREATMENT.—

(A) GAIN.—Any amount included in gross income under subsection (a)(1), and any gain on the sale or other disposition of marketable stock in a passive foreign investment company (with respect to which an election under this section is in effect), shall be treated as ordinary income.

(B) LOSS.—Any—

(i) amount allowed as a deduction under subsection (a)(2), and

(ii) loss on the sale or other disposition of marketable stock in a passive foreign investment company (with respect to which an election under this section is in effect) to the extent that the amount of such loss does not exceed the unreversed inclusions with respect to such stock,

shall be treated as an ordinary loss. The amount so treated shall be treated as a deduction allowable in computing adjusted gross income.

(2) SOURCE.—The source of any amount included in gross income under subsection (a)(1) (or allowed as a deduction under subsection (a)(2)) shall be determined in the same manner as if such amount were gain or loss (as the case may be) from the sale of stock in the passive foreign investment company.

[Sec. 1296(d)]

(d) UNREVERSED INCLUSIONS.—For purposes of this section, the term "unreversed inclusions" means, with respect to any stock in a passive foreign investment company, the excess (if any) of—

(1) the amount included in gross income of the taxpayer under subsection (a)(1) with respect to such stock for prior taxable years, over

(2) the amount allowed as a deduction under subsection (a)(2) with respect to such stock for prior taxable years.

The amount referred to in paragraph (1) shall include any amount which would have been included in gross income under subsection (a)(1) with respect to such stock for any prior taxable year but for section 1291. In the case of a regulated investment company which elected to mark to market the stock held by such company as of the last day of the taxable year preceding such company's first taxable year for which such company elects the application of this section, the amount referred to in paragraph (1) shall include amounts included in gross income under such mark to market with respect to such stock for prior taxable years.

[Sec. 1296(e)]

(e) MARKETABLE STOCK.—For purposes of this section—

(1) IN GENERAL.—The term "marketable stock" means—

(A) any stock which is regularly traded on—

(i) a national securities exchange which is registered with the Securities and Exchange Commission or the national market system established pursuant to section 11A of the Securities and Exchange Act of 1934, or

(ii) any exchange or other market which the Secretary determines has rules adequate to carry out the purposes of this part,

(B) to the extent provided in regulations, stock in any foreign corporation which is comparable to a regulated investment company and which offers for sale or has outstanding any stock of which it is the issuer and which is redeemable at its net asset value, and

(C) to the extent provided in regulations, any option on stock described in subparagraph (A) or (B).

(2) SPECIAL RULE FOR REGULATED INVESTMENT COMPANIES.—In the case of any regulated investment company which is offering for sale or has outstanding any stock of which it is the issuer and which is redeemable at its net asset value, all stock in a passive foreign investment company which it owns directly or indirectly shall be treated as marketable stock for purposes of this section. Except as provided in regulations, similar treatment as marketable stock shall apply in the case of any other regulated investment company which publishes net asset valuations at least annually.

[Sec. 1296(f)]

(f) TREATMENT OF CONTROLLED FOREIGN CORPORATIONS WHICH ARE SHAREHOLDERS IN PASSIVE FOREIGN INVESTMENT COMPANIES.—In the case of a foreign corporation which is a controlled foreign corporation and which owns (or is treated under subsection (g) as owning) stock in a passive foreign investment company—

(1) this section (other than subsection (c)(2)) shall apply to such foreign corporation in the same manner as if such corporation were a United States person, and

(2) for purposes of subpart F of part III of subchapter N—

(A) any amount included in gross income under subsection (a)(1) shall be treated as foreign personal holding company income described in section 954(c)(1)(A), and

(B) any amount allowed as a deduction under subsection (a)(2) shall be treated as a deduction allocable to foreign personal holding company income so described.

[Sec. 1296(g)]

(g) STOCK OWNED THROUGH CERTAIN FOREIGN ENTITIES.—Except as provided in regulations—

(1) IN GENERAL.—For purposes of this section, stock owned, directly or indirectly, by or for a foreign partnership or foreign trust or foreign estate shall be considered as being owned proportionately by its partners or beneficiaries. Stock considered to be owned by a person by reason of the application of the preceding sentence shall, for purposes of applying such sentence, be treated as actually owned by such person.

(2) TREATMENT OF CERTAIN DISPOSITIONS.—In any case in which a United States person is treated as owning stock in a passive foreign investment company by reason of paragraph (1)—

(A) any disposition by the United States person or by any other person which results in the United States person being treated as no longer owning such stock, and

(B) any disposition by the person owning such stock,

shall be treated as a disposition by the United States person of the stock in the passive foreign investment company.

[Sec. 1296(h)]

(h) COORDINATION WITH SECTION 851(b).—For purposes of section 851(b)(2), any amount included in gross income under subsection (a) shall be treated as a dividend.

[Sec. 1296(i)]

(i) STOCK ACQUIRED FROM A DECEDENT.—In the case of stock of a passive foreign investment company which is acquired by bequest, devise, or inheritance (or by the decedent's estate) and with respect to which an election under this section was in effect as of the date of the decedent's death, notwithstanding section 1014, the basis of such stock in the hands of the person so acquiring it shall be the adjusted basis of such stock in the hands of the decedent immediately before his death (or, if lesser, the basis which would have been determined under section 1014 without regard to this subsection).

[Sec. 1296(j)]

(j) COORDINATION WITH SECTION 1291 FOR FIRST YEAR OF ELECTION.—

(1) TAXPAYERS OTHER THAN REGULATED INVESTMENT COMPANIES.—

(A) IN GENERAL.—If the taxpayer elects the application of this section with respect to any marketable stock in a corporation after the beginning of the taxpayer's holding period in such stock, and if the requirements of subparagraph (B) are not satisfied, section 1291 shall apply to—

(i) any distributions with respect to, or disposition of, such stock in the first taxable year of the taxpayer for which such election is made, and

(ii) any amount which, but for section 1291, would have been included in gross income under subsection (a) with respect to such stock for such taxable year in the same manner as if such amount were gain on the disposition of such stock.

(B) REQUIREMENTS.—The requirements of this subparagraph are met if, with respect to each of such corporation's taxable years for which such corporation was a passive foreign investment company and which begin after December 31, 1986, and included any portion of the taxpayer's holding period in such stock, such corporation was treated as a qualified electing fund under this part with respect to the taxpayer.

(2) SPECIAL RULES FOR REGULATED INVESTMENT COMPANIES.—

(A) IN GENERAL.—If a regulated investment company elects the application of this section with respect to any marketable stock in a corporation after the beginning of the taxpayer's holding period in such stock, then, with respect to such company's first taxable year for which such company elects the application of this section with respect to such stock—

(i) section 1291 shall not apply to such stock with respect to any distribution or disposition during, or amount included in gross income under this section for, such first taxable year, but

(ii) such regulated investment company's tax under this chapter for such first taxable year shall be increased by the aggregate amount of interest which would have been determined under section 1291(c)(3) if section 1291 were applied without regard to this subparagraph.

Clause (ii) shall not apply if for the preceding taxable year the company elected to mark to market the stock held by such company as of the last day of such preceding taxable year.

(B) DISALLOWANCE OF DEDUCTION.—No deduction shall be allowed to any regulated investment company for the increase in tax under subparagraph (A)(ii).

[Sec. 1296(k)]

(k) ELECTION.—This section shall apply to marketable stock in a passive foreign investment company which is held by a United States person only if such person elects to apply this section with respect to such stock. Such an election shall apply to the taxable year for which made and all subsequent taxable years unless—

(1) such stock ceases to be marketable stock, or

(2) the Secretary consents to the revocation of such election.

[Sec. 1296(l)]

(l) TRANSITION RULE FOR INDIVIDUALS BECOMING SUBJECT TO UNITED STATES TAX.—If any individual becomes a United States person in a taxable year beginning after December 31, 1997, solely for purposes of this section, the adjusted basis (before adjustments under subsection (b)) of any marketable stock in a passive foreign investment company owned by such individual on the first day of such taxable year shall be treated as being the greater of its fair market value on such first day or its adjusted basis on such first day.

Subpart D—General Provisions

[Sec. 1297]

SEC. 1297. PASSIVE FOREIGN INVESTMENT COMPANY.

[Sec. 1297(a)]

(a) IN GENERAL.—For purposes of this part, except as otherwise provided in this subpart, the term "passive foreign investment company" means any foreign corporation if—

(1) 75 percent of more of the gross income of such corporation for the taxable year is passive income, or

(2) the average percentage of assets (as determined in accordance with subsection (e)) held by such corporation during the taxable year which produce passive income or which are held for the production of passive income is at least 50 percent.

[Sec. 1297(b)]

(b) PASSIVE INCOME.—For purposes of this section—

(1) IN GENERAL.—Except as provided in paragraph (2), the term "passive income" means any income which is of a kind which would be foreign personal holding company income as defined in section 954(c).

(2) EXCEPTIONS.—Except as provided in regulations, the term "passive income" does not include any income—

(A) derived in the active conduct of a banking business by an institution licensed to do business as a bank in the United States (or, to the extent provided in regulations, by any other corporation),

(B) derived in the active conduct of an insurance business by a qualifying insurance corporation (as defined in subsection (f)),

(C) which is interest, a dividend, or a rent or royalty, which is received or accrued from a related person (within the meaning of section 954(d)(3)) to the extent such amount is properly allocable (under regulations prescribed by the Secretary) to income of such related person which is not passive income, or

(D) which is export trade income of an export trade corporation (as defined in section 971).

For purposes of subparagraph (C), the term "related person" has the meaning given such term by section 954(d)(3) determined by substituting "foreign corporation" for "controlled foreign corporation" each place it appears in section 954(d)(3).

[Sec. 1297(c)]

(c) LOOK-THRU IN THE CASE OF 25-PERCENT OWNED CORPORATIONS.—If a foreign corporation owns (directly or indirectly) at least 25 percent (by value) of the stock of another corporation, for purposes of determining whether such foreign corporation is a passive foreign investment company, such foreign corporation shall be treated as if it—

(1) held its proportionate share of the assets of such other corporation, and

(2) received directly its proportionate share of the income of such other corporation.

[Sec. 1297(d)]

(d) EXCEPTION FOR UNITED STATES SHAREHOLDERS OF CONTROLLED FOREIGN CORPORATIONS.—

(1) IN GENERAL.—For purposes of this part, a corporation shall not be treated with respect to a shareholder as a passive foreign investment company during the qualified portion of such shareholder's holding period with respect to stock in such corporation.

(2) QUALIFIED PORTION.—For purposes of this subsection, the term "qualified portion" means the portion of the shareholder's holding period—

(A) which is after December 31, 1997, and

(B) during which the shareholder is a United States shareholder (as defined in section 951(b)) of the corporation and the corporation is a controlled foreign corporation.

(3) NEW HOLDING PERIOD IF QUALIFIED PORTION ENDS.—

(A) IN GENERAL.—Except as provided in subparagraph (B), if the qualified portion of a shareholder's holding period with respect to any stock ends after December 31, 1997, solely for purposes of this part, the shareholder's holding period with respect to such stock shall be treated as beginning as of the first day following such period.

(B) EXCEPTION.—Subparagraph (A) shall not apply if such stock was, with respect to such shareholder, stock in a passive foreign investment company at any time before the qualified portion of the shareholder's holding period with respect to such stock and no election under section 1298(b)(1) is made.

(4) TREATMENT OF HOLDERS OF OPTIONS.—Paragraph (1) shall not apply to stock treated as owned by a person by reason of section 1298(a)(4) (relating to the treatment of a person that has an option to acquire stock as owning such stock) unless such person establishes that such stock is owned (within the meaning of section 958(a)) by a United States shareholder (as defined in section 951(b)) who is not exempt from tax under this chapter.

[Sec. 1297(e)]

(e) METHODS FOR MEASURING ASSETS.—

(1) DETERMINATION USING VALUE.—The determination under subsection (a)(2) shall be made on the basis of the value of the assets of a foreign corporation if—

(A) such corporation is a publicly traded corporation for the taxable year, or

(B) paragraph (2) does not apply to such corporation for the taxable year.

(2) DETERMINATION USING ADJUSTED BASES.—The determination under subsection (a)(2) shall be based on the adjusted bases (as determined for the purposes of computing earnings and profits) of the assets of a foreign corporation if such corporation is not described in paragraph (1)(A) and such corporation—

(A) is a controlled foreign corporation, or

(B) elects the application of this paragraph.

An election under subparagraph (B), once made, may be revoked only with the consent of the Secretary.

(3) PUBLICLY TRADED CORPORATION.—For purposes of this subsection, a foreign corporation shall be treated as a publicly traded corporation if the stock in the corporation is regularly traded on—

(A) a national securities exchange which is registered with the Securities and Exchange Commission or the national market system established pursuant to section 11A of the Securities and Exchange Act of 1934, or

(B) any exchange or other market which the Secretary determines has rules adequate to carry out the purposes of this subsection.

[Sec. 1297(f)]

(f) QUALIFYING INSURANCE CORPORATION.—For purposes of subsection (b)(2)(B)—

(1) IN GENERAL.—The term "qualifying insurance corporation" means, with respect to any taxable year, a foreign corporation—

(A) which would be subject to tax under subchapter L if such corporation were a domestic corporation, and

(B) the applicable insurance liabilities of which constitute more than 25 percent of its total assets, determined on the basis of such liabilities and assets as reported on the corporation's applicable financial statement for the last year ending with or within the taxable year.

(2) ALTERNATIVE FACTS AND CIRCUMSTANCES TEST FOR CERTAIN CORPORATIONS.—If a corporation fails to qualify as a qualified insurance corporation under paragraph (1) solely because the percentage determined under paragraph (1)(B) is 25 percent or less, a United States person that owns stock in such corporation may elect to treat such stock as stock of a qualifying insurance corporation if—

(A) the percentage so determined for the corporation is at least 10 percent, and

(B) under regulations provided by the Secretary, based on the applicable facts and circumstances—

(i) the corporation is predominantly engaged in an insurance business, and

(ii) such failure is due solely to runoff-related or rating-related circumstances involving such insurance business.

(3) APPLICABLE INSURANCE LIABILITIES.—For purposes of this subsection—

(A) IN GENERAL.—The term "applicable insurance liabilities" means, with respect to any life or property and casualty insurance business—

(i) loss and loss adjustment expenses, and

(ii) reserves (other than deficiency, contingency, or unearned premium reserves) for life and health insurance risks and life and health insurance claims with respect to contracts providing coverage for mortality or morbidity risks.

(B) LIMITATIONS ON AMOUNT OF LIABILITIES.—Any amount determined under clause (i) or (ii) of subparagraph (A) shall not exceed the lesser of such amount—

(i) as reported to the applicable insurance regulatory body in the applicable financial statement described in paragraph (4)(A) (or, if less, the amount required by applicable law or regulation), or

(ii) as determined under regulations prescribed by the Secretary.

(4) OTHER DEFINITIONS AND RULES.—For purposes of this subsection—

(A) APPLICABLE FINANCIAL STATEMENT.—The term "applicable financial statement" means a statement for financial reporting purposes which—

(i) is made on the basis of generally accepted accounting principles,

(ii) is made on the basis of international financial reporting standards, but only if there is no statement that meets the requirement of clause (i), or

(iii) except as otherwise provided by the Secretary in regulations, is the annual statement which is required to be filed with the applicable insurance regulatory body, but only if there is no statement which meets the requirements of clause (i) or (ii).

(B) APPLICABLE INSURANCE REGULATORY BODY.—The term "applicable insurance regulatory body" means, with respect to any insurance business, the entity established by law to license, authorize, or regulate such business and to which the statement described in subparagraph (A) is provided.

[Sec. 1298]

SEC. 1298. SPECIAL RULES.

[Sec. 1298(a)]

(a) ATTRIBUTION OF OWNERSHIP.—For purposes of this part—

(1) ATTRIBUTION TO UNITED STATES PERSONS.—This subsection—

(A) shall apply to the extent that the effect is to treat stock of a passive foreign investment company as owned by a United States person, and

(B) except to the extent provided in regulations, shall not apply to treat stock owned (or treated as owned under this subsection) by a United States person as owned by any other person.

(2) CORPORATIONS.—

(A) IN GENERAL.—If 50 percent or more in value of the stock of a corporation is owned, directly or indirectly, by or for any person, such person shall be considered as owning the stock owned directly or indirectly by or for such corporation in that proportion which the value of the stock which such person so owns bears to the value of all stock in the corporation.

(B) 50-PERCENT LIMITATION NOT TO APPLY TO PFIC.—For purposes of determining whether a shareholder of a passive foreign investment company is treated as owning stock owned directly or indirectly by or for such company, subparagraph (A) shall be applied without regard to the 50-percent limitation contained therein. Section 1297(d) shall not apply in determining whether a corporation is a passive foreign investment company for purposes of this subparagraph.

(3) PARTNERSHIPS, ETC.—Stock owned, directly or indirectly, by or for a partnership, estate, or trust shall be considered as being owned proportionately by its partners or beneficiaries.

(4) OPTIONS.—To the extent provided in regulations, if any person has an option to acquire stock, such stock shall be considered as owned by such person. For purposes of this paragraph, an option to acquire such an option, and each one of a series of such options, shall be considered as an option to acquire such stock.

(5) SUCCESSIVE APPLICATION.—Stock considered to be owned by a person by reason of the application of paragraph (2), (3), or (4) shall, for purposes of applying such paragraphs, be considered as actually owned by such person.

[Sec. 1298(b)]

(b) OTHER SPECIAL RULES.—For purposes of this part—

(1) TIME FOR DETERMINATION.—Stock held by a taxpayer shall be treated as stock in a passive foreign investment company if, at any time during the holding period of the taxpayer with respect to such stock, such corporation (or any predecessor) was a passive foreign investment company which was not a qualified electing fund. The preceding sentence shall not apply if the taxpayer elects to recognize gain (as of the last day of the last taxable year for which the company was a passive foreign investment company (determined without regard to the preceding sentence)) under rules similar to the rules of section 1291(d)(2).

(2) CERTAIN CORPORATIONS NOT TREATED AS PFIC'S DURING START-UP YEAR.—A corporation shall not be treated as a passive foreign investment company for the first taxable year such corporation has gross income (hereinafter in this paragraph referred to as the "start-up year") if—

(A) no predecessor of such corporation was a passive foreign investment company,

(B) it is established to the satisfaction of the Secretary that such corporation will not be a passive foreign investment company for either of the 1st 2 taxable years following the start-up year, and

(C) such corporation is not a passive foreign investment company for either of the 1st 2 taxable years following the start-up year.

(3) CERTAIN CORPORATIONS CHANGING BUSINESSES.—A corporation shall not be treated as a passive foreign investment company for any taxable year if—

(A) neither such corporation (nor any predecessor) was a passive foreign investment company for any prior taxable year,

(B) it is established to the satisfaction of the Secretary that—

(i) substantially all of the passive income of the corporation for the taxable year is attributable to proceeds from the disposition of 1 or more active trades or businesses, and

(ii) such corporation will not be a passive foreign investment company for either of the 1st 2 taxable years following such taxable year, and

(C) such corporation is not a passive foreign investment company for either of such 2 taxable years.

(4) SEPARATE INTERESTS TREATED AS SEPARATE CORPORATIONS.—Under regulations prescribed by the Secretary, where necessary to carry out the purposes of this part, separate classes of stock (or other interests) in a corporation shall be treated as interests in separate corporations.

(5) APPLICATION OF PART WHERE STOCK HELD BY OTHER ENTITY.—

(A) IN GENERAL.—Under regulations, in any case in which a United States person is treated as owning stock in a passive foreign investment company by reason of subsection (a)—

(i) any disposition by the United States person or the person owning such stock which results in the United States person being treated as no longer owning such stock, or

(ii) any distribution of property in respect of such stock to the person holding such stock,

shall be treated as a disposition by, or distribution to, the United States person with respect to the stock in the passive foreign investment company.

(B) AMOUNT TREATED IN SAME MANNER AS PREVIOUSLY TAXED INCOME.—Rules similar to the rules of section 959(b) shall apply to any amount described in subparagraph (A) and to any amount included in gross income under section 1293(a) (or which would have been so included but for section 951(c)) in respect of stock which the taxpayer is treated as owning under subsection (a).

(6) DISPOSITIONS.—Except as provided in regulations, if a taxpayer uses any stock in a passive foreign investment company as security for a loan, the taxpayer shall be treated as having disposed of such stock.

(7) TREATMENT OF CERTAIN FOREIGN CORPORATIONS OWNING STOCK IN 25-PERCENT OWNED DOMESTIC CORPORATION.—

(A) IN GENERAL.—If—

(i) a foreign corporation is subject to the tax imposed by section 531 (or waives any benefit under any treaty which would otherwise prevent the imposition of such tax), and

(ii) such foreign corporation owns at least 25 percent (by value) of the stock of a domestic corporation,

for purposes of determining whether such foreign corporation is a passive foreign investment company, any qualified stock held by such domestic corporation shall be treated as an asset which does not produce passive income (and is not held for the production of passive income) and any amount included in gross income with respect to such stock shall not be treated as passive income.

(B) QUALIFIED STOCK.—For purposes of subparagraph (A), the term "qualified stock" means any stock in a C corporation which is a domestic corporation and which is not a regulated investment company or real estate investment trust.

(8) TREATMENT OF CERTAIN SUBPART F INCLUSIONS.—Any amount included in gross income under section 951(a)(1)(B) shall be treated as a distribution received with respect to the stock.

[Sec. 1298(c)]

(c) TREATMENT OF STOCK HELD BY POOLED INCOME FUND.—If stock in a passive foreign investment company is owned (or treated as owned under subsection (a)) by a pooled income fund (as defined in section 642(c)(5)) and no portion of any gain from a disposition of such stock may be allocated to income under the terms of the governing instrument of such fund—

(1) section 1291 shall not apply to any gain on a disposition of such stock by such fund if (without regard to section 1291) a deduction would be allowable with respect to such gain under section 642(c)(3),

(2) section 1293 shall not apply with respect to such stock, and

(3) in determining whether section 1291 applies to any distribution in respect of such stock, subsection (d) of section 1291 shall not apply.

[Sec. 1298(d)]

(d) TREATMENT OF CERTAIN LEASED PROPERTY.—For purposes of this part—

(1) IN GENERAL.—Any tangible personal property with respect to which a foreign corporation is the lessee under a lease with a term of at least 12 months shall be treated as an asset actually held by such corporation.

(2) AMOUNT TAKEN INTO ACCOUNT.—

(A) IN GENERAL.—The amount taken into account under section 1297(a)(2) with respect to any asset to which paragraph (1) applies shall be the unamortized portion (as determined under regulations prescribed by the Secretary) of the present value of the payments under the lease for the use of such property.

(B) PRESENT VALUE.—For purposes of subparagraph (A), the present value of payments described in subparagraph (A) shall be determined in the manner provided in regulations prescribed by the Secretary—

(i) as of the beginning of the lease term, and

(ii) except as provided in such regulations, by using a discount rate equal to the applicable Federal rate determined under section 1274(d)—

(I) by substituting the lease term for the term of the debt instrument, and

(II) without regard to paragraph (2) or (3) thereof.

(3) EXCEPTIONS.—This subsection shall not apply in any case where—

(A) the lessor is a related person (as defined in section 954(d)(3)) with respect to the foreign corporation, or

(B) a principal purpose of leasing the property was to avoid the provisions of this part.

[Sec. 1298(e)]

(e) SPECIAL RULES FOR CERTAIN INTANGIBLES.—For purposes of this part—

(1) RESEARCH EXPENDITURES.—The adjusted basis of the total assets of a controlled foreign corporation shall be increased by the research or experimental expenditures (within the meaning of section 174) paid or incurred by such foreign corporation during the taxable year and the preceding 2 taxable years. Any expenditure otherwise taken into account under the preceding sentence shall be reduced by the amount of any reimbursement received by the controlled foreign corporation with respect to such expenditure.

(2) CERTAIN LICENSED INTANGIBLES.—

(A) IN GENERAL.—In the case of any intangible property (as defined in section 367(d)(4)) with respect to which a controlled foreign corporation is a licensee and which is used by such foreign corporation in the active conduct of a trade or business, the adjusted basis of the total assets of such foreign corporation shall be increased by an amount equal to 300 percent of the payments made during the taxable year by such foreign corporation for the use of such intangible property.

(B) EXCEPTIONS.—Subparagraph (A) shall not apply to—

(i) any payments to a foreign person if such foreign person is a related person (as defined in section 954(d)(3)) with respect to the controlled foreign corporation, and

(ii) any payments under a license if a principal purpose of entering into such license was to avoid the provisions of this part.

(3) CONTROLLED FOREIGN CORPORATION.—For purposes of this subsection, the term "controlled foreign corporation" has the meaning given such term by section 957(a).

[Sec. 1298(f)]

(f) REPORTING REQUIREMENT.—Except as otherwise provided by the Secretary, each United States person who is a shareholder of a passive foreign investment company shall file an annual report containing such information as the Secretary may require.

[Sec. 1298(g)]

(g) REGULATIONS.—The Secretary shall prescribe such regulations as may be necessary or appropriate to carry out the purposes of this part.

SUBCHAPTER Q—READJUSTMENT OF TAX BETWEEN YEARS AND SPECIAL LIMITATIONS

PART VII—RECOVERIES OF FOREIGN EXPROPRIATION LOSSES

[Sec. 1351]

SEC. 1351. TREATMENT OF RECOVERIES OF FOREIGN EXPROPRIATION LOSSES.

[Sec. 1351(a)]

(a) ELECTION.—

(1) IN GENERAL.—This section shall apply only to a recovery, by a domestic corporation subject to the tax imposed by section 11 or 801, of a foreign expropriation loss sustained by such corporation and only if such corporation was subject to the tax imposed by section 11 or 801, as the case may be, for the year of the loss and elects to have the provisions of this section apply with respect to such loss.

(2) TIME, MANNER, AND SCOPE.—An election under paragraph (1) shall be made at such time and in such manner as the Secretary may prescribe by regulations. An election made with respect to any foreign expropriation loss shall apply to all recoveries in respect of such loss.

[Sec. 1351(b)]

(b) DEFINITION OF FOREIGN EXPROPRIATION LOSS.—For purposes of this section, the term "foreign expropriation loss" means any loss sustained by reason of the expropriation, intervention, seizure, or similar taking of property by the government of any foreign country, any political subdivision thereof, or any agency or instrumentality of the foregoing. For purposes of the preceding sentence, a debt which becomes worthless shall, to the extent of any deduction allowed under section 166(a), be treated as a loss.

[Sec. 1351(c)]

(c) AMOUNT OF RECOVERY.—

(1) GENERAL RULE.—The amount of any recovery of a foreign expropriation loss is the amount of money and the fair market value of other property received in respect of such loss, determined as of the date of receipt.

(2) SPECIAL RULE FOR LIFE INSURANCE COMPANIES.—The amount of any recovery of a foreign expropriation loss includes, in the case of a life insurance company, the amount of decrease of any item taken into account under section 807(c), to the extent such decrease is attributable to the release, by reason of such loss, of its liabilities with respect to such item.

[Sec. 1351(d)]

(d) ADJUSTMENT FOR PRIOR TAX BENEFITS.—

(1) IN GENERAL.—That part of the amount of a recovery of a foreign expropriation loss to which this section applies which, when added to the aggregate of the amounts of previous recoveries with respect to such loss, does not exceed the allowable deductions in prior taxable years on account of such loss shall be excluded from gross income for the taxable year of the recovery for purposes of computing the tax under this subtitle; but there shall be added to, and assessed and collected as a part of, the tax under this subtitle for such taxable year an amount equal to the total increase in the tax under this subtitle for all taxable years which would result by decreasing, in an amount equal to such part of the recovery so excluded, the deductions allowable in the prior taxable years on account of such loss. For purposes of this paragraph, if the loss to which the recovery relates was taken into account as a loss from the sale or exchange of a capital asset, the amount of the loss shall be treated as an allowable deduction even though there were no gains against which to allow such loss.

(2) COMPUTATION.—The increase in the tax for each taxable year referred to in paragraph (1) shall be computed in accordance with regulations prescribed by the Secretary. Such regulations shall give effect to previous recoveries of any kind (including recoveries described in section 111, relating to recovery of tax benefit items) with respect to any prior taxable year, but shall otherwise treat the tax previously determined for any taxable year in accordance with the principles set forth in section 1314(a) (relating to correction of errors). Subject to the provisions of paragraph (3), all credits allowable against the tax for any taxable year, and all carryovers and carrybacks affected by so decreasing the allowable deductions, shall be taken into account in computing the increase in the tax.

(3) FOREIGN TAXES.—For purposes of this subsection, any choice made under subpart A of part III of subchapter N (relating to foreign tax credit) for any taxable year may be changed.

(4) SUBSTITUTION OF CURRENT TAX RATE.—For purposes of this subsection, the rates of tax specified in section 11(b) for the taxable year of the recovery shall be treated as having been in effect for all prior taxable years.

[Sec. 1351(e)]

(e) GAIN ON RECOVERY.—That part of the amount of a recovery of a foreign expropriation loss to which this section applies which is not excluded from gross income under subsection (d)(1) shall be considered for the taxable year of the recovery as gain on the involuntary conversion of property as a result of its destruction or seizure and shall be recognized or not recognized as provided in section 1033.

[Sec. 1351(f)]

(f) BASIS OF RECOVERED PROPERTY.—The basis of property (other than money) received as a recovery of a foreign expropriation loss to which this section applies shall be an amount equal to its fair market value on the date of receipt, reduced by such part of the gain under subsection (e) which is not recognized as provided in section 1033.

[Sec. 1351(g)]

(g) RESTORATION OF VALUE OF INVESTMENTS.—For purposes of this section, if the value of any interest in, or with respect to, property (including any interest represented by a security, as defined in section 165(g)(2))—

(1) which became worthless by reason of the expropriation, intervention, seizure, or similar taking of such property by the government of any foreign country, any political subdivision thereof, or any agency or instrumentality of the foregoing, and

(2) which was taken into account as a loss from the sale or exchange of a captial asset or with respect to which a deduction for a loss was allowed under section 165 or a deduction for a bad debt was allowed under section 166,

is restored in whole or in part by reason of any recovery of money or other property in respect of the property which became worthless, the value so restored shall be treated as property received as a recovery in respect of such loss or such bad debt.

[Sec. 1351(h)]

(h) SPECIAL RULE FOR EVIDENCES OF INDEBTEDNESS.—Bonds or other evidences of indebtedness received as a recovery of a foreign expropriation loss to which this section applies shall not be considered to have any original issue discount within the meaning of section 1273(a).

[Sec. 1351(i)]

(i) ADJUSTMENTS FOR SUCCEEDING YEARS.—For purposes of this subtitle, proper adjustment shall be made, under regulations prescribed by the Secretary, in—

(1) the credit under section 27 (relating to foreign tax credit),

(2) the credit under section 38 (relating to general business credit),

(3) the net operating loss deduction under section 172,

(4) the capital loss carryover under section 1212(a), and

(5) such other items as may be specified by such regulations,

for the taxable year of a recovery of a foreign expropriation loss to which this section applies, and for succeeding taxable years, to take into account items changed in making the computations under subsection (d) for taxable years prior to the taxable year of such recovery.

SUBCHAPTER R—ELECTION TO DETERMINE CORPORATE TAX ON CERTAIN INTERNATIONAL SHIPPING ACTIVITIES USING PER TON RATE

[Sec. 1352]

SEC. 1352. ALTERNATIVE TAX ON QUALIFYING SHIPPING ACTIVITIES.

In the case of an electing corporation, the tax imposed by section 11 shall be the amount equal to the sum of—

(1) the tax imposed by section 11 determined after the application of this subchapter, and

(2) a tax equal to—

(A) the highest rate of tax specified in section 11, multiplied by

(B) the notional shipping income for the taxable year.

[Sec. 1353]

SEC. 1353. NOTIONAL SHIPPING INCOME.

[Sec. 1353(a)]

(a) IN GENERAL.—For purposes of this subchapter, the notional shipping income of an electing corporation shall be the sum of the amounts determined under subsection (b) for each qualifying vessel operated by such electing corporation.

[Sec. 1353(b)]

(b) AMOUNTS.—

(1) IN GENERAL.—For purposes of subsection (a), the amount of notional shipping income of an electing corporation for each qualifying vessel for the taxable year shall equal the product of—

(A) the daily notional shipping income, and

(B) the number of days during the taxable year that the electing corporation operated such vessel as a qualifying vessel in United States foreign trade.

(2) TREATMENT OF VESSELS THE INCOME FROM WHICH IS NOT OTHERWISE SUBJECT TO TAX.—In the case of a qualifying vessel any of the income from which is not included in gross income by reason of section 883 or otherwise, the amount of notional shipping income from such vessel for the taxable year shall be the amount which bears the same ratio to such shipping income (determined without regard to this paragraph) as the gross income from the operation of such vessel in the United States foreign trade bears to the sum of such gross income and the income so excluded.

[Sec. 1353(c)]

(c) DAILY NOTIONAL SHIPPING INCOME.—For purposes of subsection (b), the daily notional shipping income from the operation of a qualifying vessel is—

(1) 40 cents for each 100 tons of so much of the net tonnage of the vessel as does not exceed 25,000 net tons, and

(2) 20 cents for each 100 tons of so much of the net tonnage of the vessel as exceeds 25,000 net tons.

[Sec. 1353(d)]

(d) MULTIPLE OPERATORS OF VESSEL.—If for any period 2 or more persons are operators of a qualifying vessel, the notional shipping income from the operation of such vessel for such period shall be allocated among such persons on the basis of their respective ownership, charter, and operating agreement interests in such vessel or on such other basis as the Secretary may prescribe by regulations.

[Sec. 1354]

SEC. 1354. ALTERNATIVE TAX ELECTION; REVOCATION; TERMINATION.

[Sec. 1354(a)]

(a) IN GENERAL.—A qualifying vessel operator may elect the application of this subchapter.

[Sec. 1354(b)]

(b) TIME AND MANNER; YEARS FOR WHICH EFFECTIVE.—An election under this subchapter—

(1) shall be made in such form as prescribed by the Secretary, and

(2) shall be effective for the taxable year for which made and all succeeding taxable years until terminated under subsection (d).

Such election may be effective for any taxable year only if made on or before the due date (including extensions) for filing the corporation's return for such taxable year.

[Sec. 1354(c)]

(c) CONSISTENT ELECTIONS BY MEMBERS OF CONTROLLED GROUPS.—An election under subsection (a) by a member of a controlled group shall apply to all qualifying vessel operators that are members of such group.

[Sec. 1354(d)]

(d) TERMINATION.—

(1) BY REVOCATION.—

(A) IN GENERAL.—An election under subsection (a) may be terminated by revocation.

(B) WHEN EFFECTIVE.—Except as provided in subparagraph (C)—

(i) a revocation made during the taxable year and on or before the 15th day of the 3d month thereof shall be effective on the 1st day of such taxable year, and

(ii) a revocation made during the taxable year but after such 15th day shall be effective on the 1st day of the following taxable year.

(C) REVOCATION MAY SPECIFY PROSPECTIVE DATE.—If the revocation specifies a date for revocation which is on or after the day on which the revocation is made, the revocation shall be effective for taxable years beginning on and after the date so specified.

(2) BY PERSON CEASING TO BE QUALIFYING VESSEL OPERATOR.—

(A) IN GENERAL.—An election under subsection (a) shall be terminated whenever (at any time on or after the 1st day of the 1st taxable year for which the corporation is an electing corporation) such corporation ceases to be a qualifying vessel operator.

(B) WHEN EFFECTIVE.—Any termination under this paragraph shall be effective on and after the date of cessation.

(C) ANNUALIZATION.—The Secretary shall prescribe such annualization and other rules as are appropriate in the case of a termination under this paragraph.

[Sec. 1354(e)]

(e) ELECTION AFTER TERMINATION.—If a qualifying vessel operator has made an election under subsection (a) and if such election has been terminated under subsection (d), such operator (and any successor operator) shall not be eligible to make an election under subsection (a) for any taxable year before its 5th taxable year which begins after the 1st taxable year for which such termination is effective, unless the Secretary consents to such election.

[Sec. 1355]

SEC. 1355. DEFINITIONS AND SPECIAL RULES.

[Sec. 1355(a)]

(a) DEFINITIONS.—For purposes of this subchapter—

(1) ELECTING CORPORATION.—The term "electing corporation" means any corporation for which an election is in effect under this subchapter.

(2) ELECTING GROUP; CONTROLLED GROUP.—

(A) ELECTING GROUP.—The term "electing group" means a controlled group of which one or more members is an electing corporation.

(B) CONTROLLED GROUP.—The term "controlled group" means any group which would be treated as a single employer under subsection (a) or (b) of section 52 if paragraphs (1) and (2) of section 52(a) did not apply.

(3) QUALIFYING VESSEL OPERATOR.—The term "qualifying vessel operator" means any corporation—

(A) who operates one or more qualifying vessels, and

(B) who meets the shipping activity requirement in subsection (c).

(4) QUALIFYING VESSEL.—The term "qualifying vessel" means a self-propelled (or a combination self-propelled and non-self-propelled) United States flag vessel of not less than 6,000 deadweight tons used exclusively in the United States foreign trade during the period that the election under this subchapter is in effect.

(5) UNITED STATES FLAG VESSEL.—The term "United States flag vessel" means any vessel documented under the laws of the United States.

(6) UNITED STATES DOMESTIC TRADE.—The term "United States domestic trade" means the transportation of goods or passengers between places in the United States.

(7) UNITED STATES FOREIGN TRADE.—The term "United States foreign trade" means the transportation of goods or passengers between a place in the United States and a foreign place or between foreign places.

[Sec. 1355(b)]

(b) OPERATING A VESSEL.—For purposes of this subchapter—

(1) IN GENERAL.—Except as provided in paragraph (2), a person is treated as operating any vessel during any period if—

(A)(i) such vessel is owned by, or chartered (including a time charter) to, the person, or

(ii) the person provides services for such vessel pursuant to an operating agreement, and

(B) such vessel is in use as a qualifying vessel during such period.

(2) BAREBOAT CHARTERS.—A person is treated as operating and using a vessel that it has chartered out on bareboat charter terms only if—

(A)(i) the vessel is temporarily surplus to the person's requirements and the term of the charter does not exceed 3 years, or

(ii) the vessel is bareboat chartered to a member of a controlled group which includes such person or to an unrelated person who subbareboats or time charters the vessel to such a member (including the owner of the vessel), and

(B) the vessel is used as a qualifying vessel by the person to whom ultimately chartered.

[Sec. 1355(c)]

(c) SHIPPING ACTIVITY REQUIREMENT.—For purposes of this section—

(1) IN GENERAL.—Except as otherwise provided in this subsection, a corporation meets the shipping activity requirement of this subsection for any taxable year only if the requirement of paragraph (4) is met for each of the 2 preceding taxable years.

(2) SPECIAL RULE FOR 1ST YEAR OF ELECTION.—A corporation meets the shipping activity requirement of this subsection for the first taxable year for which the election under section 1354(a) is in effect only if the requirement of paragraph (4) is met for the preceding taxable year.

(3) CONTROLLED GROUPS.—A corporation who is a member of a controlled group meets the shipping activity requirement of this subsection only if such requirement is met determined by treating all members of such group as 1 person.

(4) REQUIREMENT.—The requirement of this paragraph is met for any taxable year if, on average during such year, at least 25 percent of the aggregate tonnage of qualifying vessels used by the corporation were owned by such corporation or chartered to such corporation on bareboat charter terms.

[Sec. 1355(d)]

(d) ACTIVITIES CARRIED ON [BY] PARTNERSHIPS, ETC.—In applying this subchapter to a partner in a partnership—

(1) each partner shall be treated as operating vessels operated by the partnership,

(2) each partner shall be treated as conducting the activities conducted by the partnership, and

(3) the extent of a partner's ownership, charter, or operating agreement interest in any vessel operated by the partnership shall be determined on the basis of the partner's interest in the partnership.

A similar rule shall apply with respect to other pass-thru entities.

[Sec. 1355(e)]

(e) EFFECT OF TEMPORARILY CEASING TO OPERATE A QUALIFYING VESSEL.—

(1) IN GENERAL.—For purposes of subsections (b) and (c), an electing corporation shall be treated as continuing to use a qualifying vessel during any period of temporary cessation if the electing corporation gives timely notice to the Secretary stating—

(A) that it has temporarily ceased to operate the qualifying vessel, and

(B) its intention to resume operating the qualifying vessel.

(2) NOTICE.—Notice shall be deemed timely if given not later than the due date (including extensions) for the corporation's tax return for the taxable year in which the temporary cessation begins.

(3) PERIOD DISREGARD IN EFFECT.—The period of temporary cessation under paragraph (1) shall continue until the earlier of the date on which—

(A) the electing corporation abandons its intention to resume operation of the qualifying vessel, or

(B) the electing corporation resumes operation of the qualifying vessel.

[Sec. 1355(f)]

(f) EFFECT OF TEMPORARILY OPERATING A QUALIFYING VESSEL IN THE UNITED STATES DOMESTIC TRADE.—

(1) IN GENERAL.—For purposes of this subchapter, an electing corporation shall be treated as continuing to use a qualifying vessel in the United States foreign trade during any period of temporary use in the United States domestic trade if the electing corporation gives timely notice to the Secretary stating—

(A) that it temporarily operates or has operated in the United States domestic trade a qualifying vessel which had been used in the United States foreign trade, and

(B) its intention to resume operation of the vessel in the United States foreign trade.

(2) NOTICE.—Notice shall be deemed timely if given not later than the due date (including extensions) for the corporation's tax return for the taxable year in which the temporary cessation begins.

(3) PERIOD DISREGARD IN EFFECT.—The period of temporary use under paragraph (1) continues until the earlier of the date on which—

(A) the electing corporation abandons its intention to resume operations of the vessel in the United States foreign trade, or

(B) the electing corporation resumes operation of the vessel in the United States foreign trade.

(4) NO DISREGARD IF DOMESTIC TRADE USE EXCEEDS 30 DAYS.—Paragraph (1) shall not apply to any qualifying vessel which is operated in the United States domestic trade for more than 30 days during the taxable year.

[Sec. 1355(g)]

(g) GREAT LAKES DOMESTIC SHIPPING TO NOT DISQUALIFY VESSEL.—

(1) IN GENERAL.—If the electing corporation elects (at such time and in such manner as the Secretary may require) to apply this subsection for any taxable year to any qualifying vessel which is used in qualified zone domestic trade during the taxable year—

(A) solely for purposes of subsection (a)(4), such use shall be treated as use in United States foreign trade (and not as use in United States domestic trade), and

(B) subsection (f) shall not apply with respect to such vessel for such taxable year.

(2) EFFECT OF TEMPORARILY OPERATING VESSEL IN UNITED STATES DOMESTIC TRADE.—In the case of a qualifying vessel to which this subsection applies—

(A) IN GENERAL.—An electing corporation shall be treated as using such vessel in qualified zone domestic trade during any period of temporary use in the United States domestic trade (other than qualified zone domestic trade) if the electing corporation gives timely notice to the Secretary stating—

(i) that it temporarily operates or has operated in the United States domestic trade (other than qualified zone domestic trade) a qualifying vessel which had been used in the United States foreign trade or qualified zone domestic trade, and

(ii) its intention to resume operation of the vessel in the United States foreign trade or qualified zone domestic trade.

(B) NOTICE.—Notice shall be deemed timely if given not later than the due date (including extensions) for the corporation's tax return for the taxable year in which the temporary cessation begins.

(C) PERIOD DISREGARD IN EFFECT.—The period of temporary use under subparagraph (A) continues until the earlier of the date of which—

(i) the electing corporation abandons its intention to resume operations of the vessel in the United States foreign trade or qualified zone domestic trade, or

(ii) the electing corporation resumes operation of the vessel in the United States foreign trade or qualified zone domestic trade.

(D) NO DISREGARD IF DOMESTIC TRADE USE EXCEEDS 30 DAYS.—Subparagraph (A) shall not apply to any qualifying vessel which is operated in the United States domestic trade (other than qualified zone domestic trade) for more than 30 days during the taxable year.

(3) ALLOCATION OF INCOME AND DEDUCTIONS TO QUALIFYING SHIPPING ACTIVITIES.—In the case of a qualifying vessel to which this subsection applies, the Secretary shall prescribe rules for the proper allocation of income, expenses, losses, and deductions between the qualified shipping activities and the other activities of such vessel.

(4) QUALIFIED ZONE DOMESTIC TRADE.—For purposes of this subsection—

(A) IN GENERAL.—The term "qualified zone domestic trade" means the transportation of goods or passengers between places in the qualified zone if such transportation is in the United States domestic trade.

(B) QUALIFIED ZONE.—The term "qualified zone" means the Great Lakes Waterway and the St. Lawrence Seaway.

[Sec. 1355(h)]

(h) REGULATIONS.—The Secretary shall prescribe such regulations as may be necessary or appropriate to carry out the purposes of this section.

[Sec. 1356]

SEC. 1356. QUALIFYING SHIPPING ACTIVITIES.

[Sec. 1356(a)]

(a) QUALIFYING SHIPPING ACTIVITIES.—For purposes of this subchapter, the term "qualifying shipping activities" means—

(1) core qualifying activities,

(2) qualifying secondary activities, and

(3) qualifying incidental activities.

[Sec. 1356(b)]

(b) CORE QUALIFYING ACTIVITIES.—For purposes of this subchapter, the term "core qualifying activities" means activities in operating qualifying vessels in United States foreign trade.

[Sec. 1356(c)]

(c) QUALIFYING SECONDARY ACTIVITIES.—For purposes of this section—

(1) IN GENERAL.—The term "qualifying secondary activities" means secondary activities but only to the extent that, without regard to this subchapter, the gross income derived by such corporation from such activities does not exceed 20 percent of the gross income derived by the corporation from its core qualifying activities.

(2) SECONDARY ACTIVITIES.—The term "secondary activities" means—

(A) the active management or operation of vessels other than qualifying vessels in the United States foreign trade,

(B) the provision of vessel, barge, container, or cargo-related facilities or services to any person,

(C) other activities of the electing corporation and other members of its electing group that are an integral part of its business of operating qualifying vessels in United States foreign trade, including—

(i) ownership or operation of barges, containers, chassis, and other equipment that are the complement of, or used in connection with, a qualifying vessel in United States foreign trade,

(ii) the inland haulage of cargo shipped, or to be shipped, on qualifying vessels in United States foreign trade, and

(iii) the provision of terminal, maintenance, repair, logistical, or other vessel, barge, container, or cargo-related services that are an integral part of operating qualifying vessels in United States foreign trade, and

(D) such other activities as may be prescribed by the Secretary pursuant to regulations.

Such term shall not include any core qualifying activities.

[Sec. 1356(d)]

(d) QUALIFYING INCIDENTAL ACTIVITIES.—For purposes of this section, the term "qualified incidental activities" means shipping-related activities if—

(1) they are incidental to the corporation's core qualifying activities,

(2) they are not qualifying secondary activities, and

(3) without regard to this subchapter, the gross income derived by such corporation from such activities does not exceed 0.1 percent of the corporation's gross income from its core qualifying activities.

[Sec. 1356(e)]

(e) APPLICATION OF GROSS INCOME TESTS IN CASE OF ELECTING GROUP.—In the case of an electing group, subsections (c)(1) and (d)(3) shall be applied as if such group were 1 entity, and the limitations under such subsections shall be allocated among the corporations in such group.

[Sec. 1357]

SEC. 1357. ITEMS NOT SUBJECT TO REGULAR TAX; DEPRECIATION; INTEREST.

[Sec. 1357(a)]

(a) EXCLUSION FROM GROSS INCOME.—Gross income of an electing corporation shall not include its income from qualifying shipping activities.

[Sec. 1357(b)]

(b) ELECTING GROUP MEMBER.—Gross income of a corporation (other than an electing corporation) which is a member of an electing group shall not include its income from qualifying shipping activities conducted by such member.

[Sec. 1357(c)]

(c) DENIAL OF LOSSES, DEDUCTIONS, AND CREDITS.—

(1) GENERAL RULE.—Subject to paragraph (2), each item of loss, deduction (other than for interest expense), or credit of any taxpayer with respect to any activity the income from which is excluded from gross income under this section shall be disallowed.

(2) DEPRECIATION.—

(A) IN GENERAL.—Notwithstanding paragraph (1), the adjusted basis (for purposes of determining gain) of any qualifying vessel shall be determined as if the deduction for depreciation had been allowed.

(B) METHOD.—

(i) IN GENERAL.—Except as provided in clause (ii), the straight-line method of depreciation shall apply to qualifying vessels the income from operation of which is excluded from gross income under this section.

(ii) EXCEPTION.—Clause (i) shall not apply to any qualifying vessel which is subject to a charter entered into before the date of the enactment of this subchapter.

(3) INTEREST.—

(A) IN GENERAL.—Except as provided in subparagraph (B), the interest expense of an electing corporation shall be disallowed in the ratio that the fair market value of such corporation's qualifying vessels bears to the fair market value of such corporation's total assets.

(B) ELECTING GROUP.—In the case of a corporation which is a member of an electing group, the interest expense of such corporation shall be disallowed in the ratio that the fair market value of such corporation's qualifying vessels bears to the fair market value of the electing group['']s total assets.

[Sec. 1358]

SEC. 1358. ALLOCATION OF CREDITS, INCOME, AND DEDUCTIONS.

[Sec. 1358(a)]

(a) QUALIFYING SHIPPING ACTIVITIES.—For purposes of this chapter, the qualifying shipping activities of an electing corporation shall be treated as a separate trade or business activity distinct from all other activities conducted by such corporation.

[Sec. 1358(b)]

(b) EXCLUSION OF CREDITS OR DEDUCTIONS.—

(1) No deduction shall be allowed against the notional shipping income of an electing corporation, and no credit shall be allowed against the tax imposed by section 1352(2).

(2) No deduction shall be allowed for any net operating loss attributable to the qualifying shipping activities of any person to the extent that such loss is carried forward by such person from a taxable year preceding the first taxable year for which such person was an electing corporation.

[Sec. 1358(c)]

(c) TRANSACTIONS NOT AT ARM'S LENGTH.—Section 482 applies in accordance with this subsection to a transaction or series of transactions—

(1) as between an electing corporation and another person, or

(2) as between a person's qualifying shipping activities and other activities carried on by it.

[Sec. 1359]

SEC. 1359. DISPOSITION OF QUALIFYING VESSELS.

[Sec. 1359(a)]

(a) IN GENERAL.—If any qualifying vessel operator sells or disposes of any qualifying vessel in an otherwise taxable transaction, at the election of such operator, no gain shall be recognized if any replacement qualifying vessel is acquired during the period specified in subsection (b), except to the extent that the amount realized upon such sale or disposition exceeds the cost of the replacement qualifying vessel.

[Sec. 1359(b)]

(b) PERIOD WITHIN WHICH PROPERTY MUST BE REPLACED.—The period referred to in subsection (a) shall be the period beginning one year prior to the disposition of the qualifying vessel and ending—

(1) 3 years after the close of the first taxable year in which the gain is realized, or

(2) subject to such terms and conditions as may be specified by the Secretary, on such later date as the Secretary may designate on application by the taxpayer.

Such application shall be made at such time and in such manner as the Secretary may by regulations prescribe.

[Sec. 1359(c)]

(c) APPLICATION OF SECTION TO NONCORPORATE OPERATORS.—For purposes of this section, the term "qualifying vessel operator" includes any person who would be a qualifying vessel operator were such person a corporation.

[Sec. 1359(d)]

(d) TIME FOR ASSESSMENT OF DEFICIENCY ATTRIBUTABLE TO GAIN.—If a qualifying vessel operator has made the election provided in subsection (a), then—

(1) the statutory period for the assessment of any deficiency, for any taxable year in which any part of the gain is realized, attributable to such gain shall not expire prior to the expiration of 3 years from the date the Secretary is notified by such operator (in such manner as the Secretary may by regulations prescribe) of the replacement qualifying vessel or of an intention not to replace, and

(2) such deficiency may be assessed before the expiration of such 3-year period notwithstanding the provisions of section 6212(c) or the provisions of any other law or rule of law which would otherwise prevent such assessment.

[Sec. 1359(e)]

(e) BASIS OF REPLACEMENT QUALIFYING VESSEL.—In the case of any replacement qualifying vessel purchased by the qualifying vessel operator which resulted in the nonrecognition of any part of the gain realized as the result of a sale or other disposition of a qualifying vessel, the basis shall be the cost of the replacement qualifying vessel decreased in the amount of the gain not so recognized; and if the property purchased consists of more than one piece of property, the basis determined under this sentence shall be allocated to the purchased properties in proportion to their respective costs.

Subchapter S—Tax Treatment of S Corporations and Their Shareholders

PART III—SPECIAL RULES

[Sec. 1373]

SEC. 1373. FOREIGN INCOME.

[Sec. 1373(a)]

(a) S CORPORATION TREATED AS PARTNERSHIP, ETC.—For purposes of subparts A and F of part III, and part V, of subchapter N (relating to income from sources without the United States)—

(1) an S corporation shall be treated as a partnership, and

(2) the shareholders of such corporation shall be treated as partners of such partnership.

[Sec. 1373(b)]

(b) RECAPTURE OF OVERALL FOREIGN LOSS.—For purposes of section 904(f) (relating to recapture of overall foreign loss), the making or termination of an election to be treated as an S corporation shall be treated as a disposition of the business.

CHAPTER 2A—UNEARNED INCOME MEDICARE CONTRIBUTION

[Sec. 1411]

SEC. 1411. IMPOSITION OF TAX.

[Sec. 1411(a)]

(a) IN GENERAL.—Except as provided in subsection (e)—

(1) APPLICATION TO INDIVIDUALS.—In the case of an individual, there is hereby imposed (in addition to any other tax imposed by this subtitle) for each taxable year a tax equal to 3.8 percent of the lesser of—

(A) net investment income for such taxable year, or

(B) the excess (if any) of—

(i) the modified adjusted gross income for such taxable year, over

(ii) the threshold amount.

(2) APPLICATION TO ESTATES AND TRUSTS.—In the case of an estate or trust, there is hereby imposed (in addition to any other tax imposed by this subtitle) for each taxable year a tax of 3.8 percent of the lesser of—

(A) the undistributed net investment income for such taxable year, or

(B) the excess (if any) of

(i) the adjusted gross income (as defined in section 67(e)) for such taxable year, over

(ii) the dollar amount at which the highest tax bracket in section 1(e) begins for such taxable year.

[Sec. 1411(b)]

(b) THRESHOLD AMOUNT.—For purposes of this chapter, the term "threshold amount" means—

(1) in the case of a taxpayer making a joint return under section 6013 or a surviving spouse (as defined in section 2(a)), $250,000,

(2) in the case of a married taxpayer (as defined in section 7703) filing a separate return, 1/2 of the dollar amount determined under paragraph (1), and

(3) in any other case, $200,000.

[Sec. 1411(c)]

(c) NET INVESTMENT INCOME.—For purposes of this chapter—

(1) IN GENERAL.—The term "net investment income" means the excess (if any) of—

(A) the sum of—

(i) gross income from interest, dividends, annuities, royalties, and rents, other than such income which is derived in the ordinary course of a trade or business not described in paragraph (2),

(ii) other gross income derived from a trade or business described in paragraph (2), and

(iii) net gain (to the extent taken into account in computing taxable income) attributable to the disposition of property other than property held in a trade or business not described in paragraph (2), over

(B) the deductions allowed by this subtitle which are properly allocable to such gross income or net gain.

(2) TRADES AND BUSINESSES TO WHICH TAX APPLIES.—A trade or business is described in this paragraph if such trade or business is—

(A) a passive activity (within the meaning of section 469) with respect to the taxpayer, or

(B) a trade or business of trading in financial instruments or commodities (as defined in section 475(e)(2)).

(3) INCOME ON INVESTMENT OF WORKING CAPITAL SUBJECT TO TAX.—A rule similar to the rule of section 469(e)(1)(B) shall apply for purposes of this subsection.

(4) EXCEPTION FOR CERTAIN ACTIVE INTERESTS IN PARTNERSHIPS AND S CORPORATIONS.—In the case of a disposition of an interest in a partnership or S corporation—

(A) gain from such disposition shall be taken into account under clause (iii) of paragraph (1)(A) only to the extent of the net gain which would be so taken into account by the transferor if all property of the partnership or S corporation were sold for fair market value immediately before the disposition of such interest, and

(B) a rule similar to the rule of subparagraph (A) shall apply to a loss from such disposition.

(5) EXCEPTION FOR DISTRIBUTIONS FROM QUALIFIED PLANS.—The term "net investment income" shall not include any distribution from a plan or arrangement described in section 401(a), 403(a), 403(b), 408, 408A, or 457(b).

(6) SPECIAL RULE.—Net investment income shall not include any item taken into account in determining self-employment income for such taxable year on which a tax is imposed by section 1401(b).

[Sec. 1411(d)]

(d) MODIFIED ADJUSTED GROSS INCOME.—For purposes of this chapter, the term "modified adjusted gross income" means adjusted gross income increased by the excess of—

(1) the amount excluded from gross income under section 911(a)(1), over

(2) the amount of any deductions (taken into account in computing adjusted gross income) or exclusions disallowed under section 911(d)(6) with respect to the amounts described in paragraph (1).

[Sec. 1411(e)]

(e) NONAPPLICATION OF SECTION.—This section shall not apply to—

(1) a nonresident alien, or

(2) a trust all of the unexpired interests in which are devoted to one or more of the purposes described in section 170(c)(2)(B).

CHAPTER 3—WITHHOLDING OF TAX ON NONRESIDENT ALIENS AND FOREIGN CORPORATIONS

SUBCHAPTER A—NONRESIDENT ALIENS AND FOREIGN CORPORATIONS

[Sec. 1441]

SEC. 1441. WITHHOLDING OF TAX ON NONRESIDENT ALIENS.

[Sec. 1441(a)]

(a) GENERAL RULE.—Except as otherwise provided in subsection (c), all persons, in whatever capacity acting (including lessees or mortgagors of real or personal property, fiduciaries, employers, and all officers and employees of the United States) having the control, receipt, custody, disposal, or payment of any of the items of income specified in subsection (b) (to the extent that any of such items constitutes gross income from sources within the United States), of any nonresident alien individual or of any foreign partnership shall (except as otherwise provided in regulations prescribed by the Secretary under section 874) deduct and withhold from such items a tax equal to 30 percent thereof, except that in the case of any item of income specified in the second sentence of subsection (b), the tax shall be equal to 14 percent of such item.

[Sec. 1441(b)]

(b) INCOME ITEMS.—The items of income referred to in subsection (a) are interest (other than original issue discount as defined in section 1273), dividends, rent, salaries, wages, premiums, annuities, compensations, remunerations, emoluments, or other fixed or determinable annual or periodical gains, profits, and income, gains described in section 631(b) or (c), amounts subject to tax under section 871(a)(1)(C), and gains subject to tax under section 871(a)(1)(D). The items of income referred to in subsection (a) from which tax shall be deducted and withheld at the rate of 14 percent are amounts which are received by a nonresident alien individual who is temporarily present in the United States as a nonimmigrant under subparagraph (F), (J), (M), or (Q) of section 101(a)(15) of the Immigration and Nationality Act and which are—

(1) incident to a qualified scholarship to which section 117(a) applies, but only to the extent includible in gross income; or

(2) in the case of an individual who is not a candidate for a degree at an educational organization described in section 170(b)(1)(A)(ii), granted by—

(A) an organization described in section 501(c)(3) which is exempt from tax under section 501(a),

(B) a foreign government,

(C) an international organization, or a binational or multinational educational and cultural foundation or commission created or continued pursuant to the Mutual Educational and Cultural Exchange Act of 1961, or

(D) the United States, or an instrumentality or agency thereof, or a State, or a possession of the United States, or any political subdivision thereof, or the District of Columbia,

as a scholarship or fellowship for study, training, or research in the United States.

In the case of a nonresident alien individual who is a member of a domestic partnership, the items of income referred to in subsection (a) shall be treated as referring to items specified in this subsection included in his distributive share of the income of such partnership.

[Sec. 1441(c)]

(c) EXCEPTIONS.—

(1) INCOME CONNECTED WITH UNITED STATES BUSINESS.—No deduction or withholding under subsection (a) shall be required in the case of any item of income (other than compensation for personal services) which is effectively connected with the conduct of a trade or business within the United States and which is included in the gross income of the recipient under section 871(b)(2) for the taxable year.

(2) OWNER UNKNOWN.—The Secretary may authorize the tax under subsection (a) to be deducted and withheld from the interest upon any securities the owners of which are not known to the withholding agent.

(3) BONDS WITH EXTENDED MATURITY DATES.—The deduction and withholding in the case of interest on bonds, mortgages, or deeds of trust or other similar obligations of a corporation, within subsections (a), (b), and (c) of section 1451 (as in effect before its repeal by the Tax Reform Act of 1984) were it not for the fact that the maturity date of such obligations has been extended on or after January 1, 1934, and the liability assumed by the debtor exceeds 27$^1/_2$ percent of the interest, shall not exceed the rate of 27$^1/_2$ percent per annum.

(4) COMPENSATION OF CERTAIN ALIENS.—Under regulations prescribed by the Secretary, compensation for personal services may be exempted from deduction and withholding under subsection (a).

(5) SPECIAL ITEMS.—In the case of gains described in section 631(b) or (c), and gains subject to tax under section 871(a)(1)(D), the amount required to be deducted and withheld shall, if the amount of such gain is not known to the withholding agent, be such amount, not exceeding 30 percent of the amount payable, as may be necessary to assure that the tax deducted and withheld shall not be less than 30 percent of such gain.

(6) PER DIEM OF CERTAIN ALIENS.—No deduction or withholding under subsection (a) shall be required in the case of amounts of per diem for subsistence paid by the United States Government (directly or by contract) to any nonresident alien individual who is engaged in any program of training in the United States under the Mutual Security Act of 1954, as amended.

(7) CERTAIN ANNUITIES RECEIVED UNDER QUALIFIED PLANS.—No deduction or withholding under subsection (a) shall be required in the case of any amount received as an annuity if such amount is, under section 871(f), exempt from the tax imposed by section 871(a).

(8) ORIGINAL ISSUE DISCOUNT.—The Secretary may prescribe such regulations as may be necessary for the deduction and withholding of the tax on original issue discount subject to tax under section 871(a)(1)(C) including rules for the deduction and withholding of the tax on original issue discount from payments of interest.

(9) INTEREST INCOME FROM CERTAIN PORTFOLIO DEBT INVESTMENTS.—In the case of portfolio interest (within the meaning of 871(h)), no tax shall be required to be deducted and withheld from such interest unless the person required to deduct and withhold tax from such interest knows, or has reason to know, that such interest is not portfolio interest by reason of section 871(h)(3) or (4).

(10) EXCEPTION FOR CERTAIN INTEREST AND DIVIDENDS.—No tax shall be required to be deducted and withheld under subsection (a) from any amount described in section 871(i)(2).

(11) CERTAIN GAMBLING WINNINGS.—No tax shall be required to be deducted and withheld under subsection (a) from any amount exempt from the tax imposed by section 871(a)(1)(A) by reason of section 871(j).

(12) CERTAIN DIVIDENDS RECEIVED FROM REGULATED INVESTMENT COMPANIES.—

(A) IN GENERAL.—No tax shall be required to be deducted and withheld under subsection (a) from any amount exempt from the tax imposed by section 871(a)(1)(A) by reason of section 871(k).

(B) SPECIAL RULE.—For purposes of subparagraph (A), clause (i) of section 871(k)(1)(B) shall not apply to any dividend unless the regulated investment company knows that such dividend is a dividend referred to in such clause. A similar rule shall apply with respect to the exception contained in section 871(k)(2)(B).

[Sec. 1441(d)]

(d) EXEMPTION OF CERTAIN FOREIGN PARTNERSHIPS.—Subject to such terms and conditions as may be provided by regulations prescribed by the Secretary, subsection (a) shall not apply in the case of a foreign partnership engaged in trade or business within the United States if the Secretary determines that the requirements of subsection (a) impose an undue administrative burden and that the collection of the tax imposed by section 871(a) on the members of such partnership who are nonresident alien individuals will not be jeopardized by the exemption.

[Sec. 1441(e)]

(e) ALIEN RESIDENT OF PUERTO RICO.—For purposes of this section, the term "nonresident alien individual" includes an alien resident of Puerto Rico.

[Sec. 1441(f)]

(f) CONTINENTAL SHELF AREAS.—For sources of income derived from, or for services performed with respect to, the exploration or exploitation of natural resources on submarine areas adjacent to the territorial waters of the United States, see section 638.

[Sec. 1441(g)]

(g) CROSS REFERENCE.—

For provision treating 85 percent of social security benefits as subject to withholding under this section, see section 871(a)(3).

[Sec. 1442]

SEC. 1442. WITHHOLDING OF TAX ON FOREIGN CORPORATIONS.

[Sec. 1442(a)]

(a) GENERAL RULE.—In the case of foreign corporations subject to taxation under this subtitle, there shall be deducted and withheld at the source in the same manner and on the same items of income as is provided in section 1441 a tax equal to 30 percent thereof. For purposes of the preceding sentence, the references in section 1441(b) to sections 871(a)(1)(C) and (D) shall be treated as referring to sections 881(a)(3) and (4), the reference in section 1441(c)(1) to section 871(b)(2) shall be treated as referring to section 842 or section 882(a)(2), as the case may be, the reference in section 1441(c)(5) to section 871(a)(1)(D) shall be treated as referring to section 881(a)(4), the reference in section 1441(c)(8) to section 871(a)(1)(C) shall be treated as referring to section 881(a)(3), the references in section 1441(c)(9) to sections 871(h) and 871(h)(3) or (4) shall be treated as referring to sections 881(c) and 881(c)(3) or (4), the reference in section 1441(c)(10) to section 871(i)(2) shall be treated as referring to section 881(d), and the references in section 1441(c)(12) to sections 871(a) and 871(k) shall be treated as referring to sections 881(a) and 881(e) (except that for purposes of applying subparagraph (A) of section 1441(c)(12), as so modified, clause (ii) of section 881(e)(1)(B) shall not apply to any dividend unless the regulated investment company knows that such dividend is a dividend referred to in such clause).

[Sec. 1442(b)]

(b) EXEMPTION.—Subject to such terms and conditions as may be provided by regulations prescribed by the Secretary, subsection (a) shall not apply in the case of a foreign corporation engaged in trade or business within the United States if the Secretary determines that the requirements of subsection (a) impose an undue administrative burden and that the collection of the tax imposed by section 881 on such corporation will not be jeopardized by the exemption.

[Sec. 1442(c)]

(c) EXCEPTION FOR CERTAIN POSSESSIONS CORPORATIONS.—

(1) GUAM, AMERICAN SAMOA, THE NORTHERN MARIANA ISLANDS, AND THE VIRGIN ISLANDS.—For purposes of this section, the term "foreign corporation" does not include a corporation created or organized in Guam, American Samoa, the Northern Mariana Islands, or the Virgin Islands or under the law of any such possession if the requirements of subparagraphs (A), (B), and (C) of section 881(b)(1) are met with respect to such corporation.

(2) COMMONWEALTH OF PUERTO RICO.—

(A) IN GENERAL.—If dividends are received during a taxable year by a corporation—

(i) created or organized in, or under the law of, the Commonwealth of Puerto Rico, and

(ii) with respect to which the requirements of subparagraphs (A), (B), and (C) of section 881(b)(1) are met for the taxable year,

subsection (a) shall be applied for such taxable year by substituting "10 percent" for "30 percent".

(B) APPLICABILITY.—If, on or after the date of the enactment of this paragraph, an increase in the rate of the Commonwealth of Puerto Rico's withholding tax which is generally applicable to dividends paid to United States corporations not engaged in a trade or business in the Commonwealth to a rate greater than 10 percent takes effect, this paragraph shall not apply to dividends received on or after the effective date of the increase.

[Sec. 1444]

SEC. 1444. WITHHOLDING ON VIRGIN ISLANDS SOURCE INCOME.

For purposes of determining the withholding tax liability incurred in the Virgin Islands pursuant to this title (as made applicable to the Virgin Islands) with respect to amounts received from sources within the Virgin Islands by citizens and resident alien individuals of the United States, and corporations organized in the United States, the rate of withholding tax under sections 1441 and 1442 on income subject to tax under section 871(a)(1) or 881 shall not exceed the rate of tax on such income under section 871(a)(1) or 881, as the case may be.

[Sec. 1445]

SEC. 1445. WITHHOLDING OF TAX ON DISPOSITIONS OF UNITED STATES REAL PROPERTY INTERESTS.

[Sec. 1445(a)]

(a) GENERAL RULE.—Except as otherwise provided in this section, in the case of any disposition of a United States real property interest (as defined in section 897(c)) by a foreign person, the transferee shall be required to deduct and withhold a tax equal to 15 percent of the amount realized on the disposition.

[Sec. 1445(b)]

(b) EXEMPTIONS.—

(1) IN GENERAL.—No person shall be required to deduct and withhold any amount under subsection (a) with respect to a disposition if paragraph (2), (3), (4), (5), or (6) applies to the transaction.

(2) TRANSFEROR FURNISHES NONFOREIGN AFFIDAVIT.—Except as provided in paragraph (7), this paragraph applies to the disposition if the transferor furnishes to the transferee an affidavit by the transferor stating, under penalty of perjury, the transferor's United States taxpayer identification number and that the transferor is not a foreign person.

(3) NONPUBLICLY TRADED DOMESTIC CORPORATION FURNISHES AFFIDAVIT THAT INTEREST IN CORPORATION NOT UNITED STATES REAL PROPERTY INTERESTS.—Except as provided in paragraph (7), this paragraph applies in the case of a disposition of any interest in any domestic corporation if the domestic corporation furnishes to the transferee an affidavit by the domestic corporation stating, under penalty of perjury, that—

(A) the domestic corporation is not and has not been a United States real property holding corporation (as defined in section 897(c)(2)) during the applicable period specified in section 897(c)(1)(A)(ii),

(B) as of the date of the disposition, interests in such corporation are not United States real property interests by reason of section 897(c)(1)(B).

(4) TRANSFEREE RECEIVES QUALIFYING STATEMENT.—

(A) IN GENERAL.—This paragraph applies to the disposition if the transferee receives a qualifying statement at such time, in such manner, and subject to such terms and conditions as the Secretary may by regulations prescribe.

(B) QUALIFYING STATEMENT.—For purposes of subparagraph (A), the term "qualifying statement" means a statement by the Secretary that—

(i) the transferor either—

(I) has reached agreement with the Secretary (or such agreement has been reached by the transferee) for the payment of any tax imposed by section 871(b)(1) or 882(a)(1) on any gain recognized by the transferor on the disposition of the United States real property interest, or

(II) is exempt from any tax imposed by section 871(b)(1) or 882(a)(1) on any gain recognized by the transferor on the disposition of the United States real property interest, and

(ii) the transferor or transferee has satisfied any transferor's unsatisfied withholding liability or has provided adequate security to cover such liability.

(5) RESIDENCE WHERE AMOUNT REALIZED DOES NOT EXCEED $300,000.—This paragraph applies to the disposition if—

(A) the property is acquired by the transferee for use by him as a residence, and

(B) the amount realized for the property does not exceed $300,000.

(6) STOCK REGULARLY TRADED ON ESTABLISHED SECURITIES MARKET.—This paragraph applies if the disposition is of a share of a class of stock that is regularly traded on an established securities market.

(7) SPECIAL RULES FOR PARAGRAPHS (2), (3), AND (9).—Paragraph (2), (3), or (9) (as the case may be) shall not apply to any disposition—

(A) if—

(i) the transferee or qualified substitute has actual knowledge that the affidavit referred to in such paragraph, or the statement referred to in paragraph (9)(A)(ii), is false, or

(ii) the transferee or qualified substitute receives a notice (as described in subsection (d)) from a transferor's agent, transferee's agent, or qualified substitute that such affidavit or statement is false, or

(B) if the Secretary by regulations requires the transferee or qualified substitute to furnish a copy of such affidavit or statement to the Secretary and the transferee or qualified substitute fails to furnish a copy of such affidavit or statement to the Secretary at such time and in such manner as required by such regulations.

(8) APPLICABLE WASH SALES TRANSACTIONS.—No person shall be required to deduct and withhold any amount under subsection (a) with respect to a disposition which is treated as a disposition of a United States real property interest solely by reason of section 897(h)(5).

(9) ALTERNATIVE PROCEDURE FOR FURNISHING NONFOREIGN AFFIDAVIT.—For purposes of paragraphs (2) and (7)—

(A) IN GENERAL.—Paragraph (2) shall be treated as applying to a transaction if, in connection with a disposition of a United States real property interest—

(i) the affidavit specified in paragraph (2) is furnished to a qualified substitute, and

(ii) the qualified substitute furnishes a statement to the transferee stating, under penalty of perjury, that the qualified substitute has such affidavit in his possession.

(B) REGULATIONS.—The Secretary shall prescribe such regulations as may be necessary or appropriate to carry out this paragraph.

[Sec. 1445(c)]

(c) LIMITATIONS ON AMOUNT REQUIRED TO BE WITHHELD.—

(1) CANNOT EXCEED TRANSFEROR'S MAXIMUM TAX LIABILITY.—

(A) IN GENERAL.—The amount required to be withheld under this section with respect to any disposition shall not exceed the amount (if any) determined under subparagraph (B) as the transferor's maximum tax liability.

(B) REQUEST.—At the request of the transferor or transferee, the Secretary shall determine, with respect to any disposition, the transferor's maximum tax liability.

(C) REFUND OF EXCESS AMOUNTS WITHHELD.—Subject to such terms and conditions as the Secretary may by regulations prescribe, a transferor may seek and obtain a refund of any amounts withheld under this section in excess of the transferor's maximum tax liability.

(2) AUTHORITY OF SECRETARY TO PRESCRIBE REDUCED AMOUNT.—At the request of the transferor or transferee, the Secretary may prescribe a reduced amount to be withheld under this section if the Secretary determines that to substitute such reduced amount will not jeopardize the collection of the tax imposed by section 871(b)(1) or 882(a)(1).

(3) PROCEDURAL RULES.—

(A) REGULATIONS.—Request for—

(i) qualifying statements under subsection (b)(4),

(ii) determinations of transferor's maximum tax liability under paragraph (1), and

(iii) reductions under paragraph (2) in the amount required to be withheld,

shall be made at the time and manner, and shall include such information, as the Secretary shall prescribe by regulations.

(B) REQUESTS TO BE HANDLED WITHIN 90 DAYS.—The Secretary shall take action with respect to any request described in subparagraph (A) within 90 days after the Secretary receives the request.

(4) REDUCED RATE OF WITHHOLDING FOR RESIDENCE WHERE AMOUNT REALIZED DOES NOT EXCEED $1,000,000.—In the case of a disposition—

(A) of property which is acquired by the transferee for use by the transferee as a residence,

(B) with respect to which the amount realized for such property does not exceed $1,000,000, and

(C) to which subsection (b)(5) does not apply,

subsection (a) shall be applied by substituting "10 percent" for "15 percent".

[Sec. 1445(d)]

(d) LIABILITY OF TRANSFEROR'S AGENTS, TRANSFEREE'S AGENTS, OR QUALIFIED SUBSTITUTES.—

(1) NOTICE OF FALSE AFFIDAVIT; FOREIGN CORPORATIONS.—If—

(A) the transferor furnishes the transferee or qualified substitute an affidavit described in paragraph (2) of subsection (b) or a domestic corporation furnishes the transferee an affidavit described in paragraph (3) of subsection (b), and

(B) in the case of—

(i) any transferor's agent—

(I) such agent has actual knowledge that such affidavit is false, or

(II) in the case of an affidavit described in subsection (b)(2) furnished by a corporation, such corporation is a foreign corporation, or

(ii) any transferee's agent or qualified substitute, such agent or substitute has actual knowledge that such affidavit is false, such agent or qualified substitute shall so notify the transferee at such time and in such manner as the Secretary shall require by regulations.

(2) FAILURE TO FURNISH NOTICE.—

(A) IN GENERAL.—If any transferor's agent, transferee's agent, or qualified substitute is required by paragraph (1) to furnish notice, but fails to furnish such notice at such time or times and in such manner as may be required by regulations, such agent or substitute shall have the same duty to deduct and withhold that the transferee would have had if such agent or substitute had complied with paragraph (1).

(B) LIABILITY LIMITED TO AMOUNT OF COMPENSATION.—An agent's or substitute's liability under subparagraph (A) shall be limited to the amount of compensation the agent or substitute derives from the transaction.

(3) TRANSFEROR'S AGENT.—For purposes of this subsection, the term "transferor's agent" means any person who represents the transferor—

(A) in any negotiation with the transferee or any transferee's agent related to the transaction, or

(B) in settling the transaction.

(4) TRANSFEREE'S AGENT.—For purposes of this subsection, the term "transferee's agent" means any person who represents the transferee—

(A) in any negotiation with the transferor or any transferor's agent related to the transaction, or

(B) in settling the transaction.

(5) SETTLEMENT OFFICER NOT TREATED AS TRANSFEROR'S AGENT.—For purposes of this subsection, a person shall not be treated as a transferor's agent or transferee's agent with respect to any transaction merely because such person performs 1 or more of the following acts:

(A) The receipt and the disbursement of any portion of the consideration for the transaction.

(B) The recording of any document in connection with the transaction.

[Sec. 1445(e)]

(e) SPECIAL RULES RELATING TO DISTRIBUTIONS, ETC., BY CORPORATIONS, PARTNERSHIPS, TRUSTS, OR ESTATES.—

(1) CERTAIN DOMESTIC PARTNERSHIPS, TRUSTS, AND ESTATES.—In the case of any disposition of a United States real property interest as defined in section 897(c) (other than a disposition described in paragraph (4) or (5)) by a domestic partnership, domestic trust, or domestic estate, such partnership, the trustee or such trust, or the executor of such estate (as the case may be) shall be required to deduct and withhold under subsection (a) a tax equal to the highest rate of tax in effect for the taxable year under section 11(b) (or, to the extent provided in regulations, 20 percent) multiplied by the gain realized to the extent such gain—

(A) is allocable to a foreign person who is a partner or beneficiary of such partnership, trust, or estate, or

(B) is allocable to a portion of the trust treated as owned by a foreign person under subpart E of Part I of subchapter J.

(2) CERTAIN DISTRIBUTIONS BY FOREIGN CORPORATIONS.—In the case of any distribution by a foreign corporation on which gain is recognized under subsection (d) or (e) of section 897, the foreign corporation shall deduct and withhold under subsection (a) a tax equal to the highest rate of tax in effect for the taxable year under section 11(b) multiplied by the amount of gain recognized on such distribution under such subsection.

(3) DISTRIBUTIONS BY CERTAIN DOMESTIC CORPORATIONS TO FOREIGN SHAREHOLDERS.—If a domestic corporation which is or has been a United States real property holding corporation (as defined in section 897(c)(2)) during the applicable period specified in section 897(c)(1)(A)(ii) distributes property to a foreign person in a transaction to which section 302 or part II of subchapter C applies, such corporation shall deduct and withhold under subsection (a) a tax equal to 15 percent of the amount realized by the foreign shareholder. The preceding sentence shall not apply if, as of the date of the distribution, interests in such corporation are not United States real property interests by reason of section 897(c)(1)(B). Rules similar to the rules of the preceding provisions of this paragraph shall apply in the case of any distribution to which section 301 applies and which is not made out of the earnings and profits of such a domestic corporation.

(4) TAXABLE DISTRIBUTIONS BY DOMESTIC OR FOREIGN PARTNERSHIPS, TRUSTS, OR ESTATES.—A domestic or foreign partnership, the trustee of a domestic or foreign trust, or the executor of a domestic or foreign estate shall be required to deduct and withhold under subsection (a) a tax equal to 15 percent of the fair market value (as of the time of the taxable distribution) of any United States real property interest distributed to a partner of the partnership or a beneficiary of the trust or estate, as the case may be, who is a foreign person in a transaction which would constitute a taxable distribution under the regulations promulgated by the Secretary pursuant to section 897.

(5) RULES RELATING TO DISPOSITIONS OF INTEREST IN PARTNERSHIPS, TRUSTS, OR ESTATES.—To the extent provided in regulations, the transferee of a partnership interest or of a beneficial interest in a trust or estate shall be required to deduct and withhold under subsection (a) a tax equal to 15 percent of the amount realized on the disposition.

(6) DISTRIBUTIONS BY REGULATED INVESTMENT COMPANIES AND REAL ESTATE INVESTMENT TRUSTS.—If any portion of a distribution from a qualified investment entity (as defined in section 897(h)(4)) to a nonresident alien individual or a foreign corporation is treated under section 897(h)(1) as gain realized by such individual or corporation from the sale or exchange of a United States real property interest, the qualified investment entity shall deduct and withhold under subsection (a) a tax equal to the highest rate of tax in effect for the taxable year under section 11(b) (or, to the extent provided in regulations, 20 percent) multiplied by the amount so treated.

(7) REGULATIONS.—The Secretary shall prescribe such regulations as may be necessary to carry out the purposes of this subsection, including regulations providing for exceptions from provisions of this subsection and regulations for the application of this subsection in the case of payments through 1 or more entities.

[Sec. 1445(f)]

(f) DEFINITIONS.—For purposes of this section—.

(1) TRANSFEROR.—The term "transferor" means the person disposing of the United States real property interest.

(2) TRANSFEREE.—The term "transferee" means the person acquiring the United States real property interest.

(3) FOREIGN PERSON.—The term "foreign person" means any person other than—

(A) a United States person, and

(B) except as otherwise provided by the Secretary, an entity with respect to which section 897 does not apply by reason of subsection (l) thereof.

(4) TRANSFEROR'S MAXIMUM TAX LIABILITY.—The term "transferor's maximum tax liability" means, with respect to the disposition of any interest, the sum of—

(A) the maximum amount which the Secretary determines could be imposed as tax under section 871(b)(1) or 882(a)(1) by reason of the disposition, plus

(B) the amount the Secretary determines to be the transferor's unsatisfied withholding liability with respect to such interest.

(5) TRANSFEROR'S UNSATISFIED WITHHOLDING LIABILITY.—The term "transferor's unsatisfied withholding liability" means the withholding obligation imposed by this section on the transferor's acquisition of the United States real property interest or on the acquisition of a predecessor interest, to the extent such obligation has not been satisfied.

(6) QUALIFIED SUBSTITUTE.—The term "qualified substitute" means, with respect to a disposition of a United States real property interest—

(A) the person (including any attorney or title company) responsible for closing the transaction, other than the transferor's agent, and

(B) the transferee's agent.

[Sec. 1446]

SEC. 1446. WITHHOLDING OF TAX ON FOREIGN PARTNERS' SHARE OF EFFECTIVELY CONNECTED INCOME.

[Sec. 1446(a)]

(a) GENERAL RULE.—If—

(1) a partnership has effectively connected taxable income for any taxable year, and

(2) any portion of such income is allocable under section 704 to a foreign partner,

such partnership shall pay a withholding tax under this section at such time and in such manner as the Secretary shall by regulations prescribe.

[Sec. 1446(b)]

(b) AMOUNT OF WITHHOLDING TAX.—

(1) IN GENERAL.—The amount of the withholding tax payable by any partnership under subsection (a) shall be equal to the applicable percentage of the effectively connected taxable income of the partnership which is allocable under section 704 to foreign partners.

(2) APPLICABLE PERCENTAGE.—For purposes of paragraph (1), the term "applicable percentage" means—

(A) the highest rate of tax specified in section 1 in the case of the portion of the effectively connected taxable income which is allocable under section 704 to foreign partners who are not corporations, and

(B) the highest rate of tax specified in section 11(b) in the case of the portion of the effectively connected taxable income which is allocable under section 704 to foreign partners which are corporations.

[Sec. 1446(c)]

(c) EFFECTIVELY CONNECTED TAXABLE INCOME.—For purposes of this section, the term "effectively connected taxable income" means the taxable income of the partnership which is effectively connected (or treated as effectively connected) with the conduct of a trade or business in the United States computed with the following adjustments:

(1) Paragraph (1) [of] section 703(a) shall not apply.

(2) The partnership shall be allowed a deduction for depletion with respect to oil and gas wells but the amount of such deduction shall be determined without regard to sections 613 and 613A.

(3) There shall not be taken into account any item of income, gain, loss, or deduction to the extent allocable under section 704 to any partner who is not a foreign partner.

[Sec. 1446(d)]

(d) TREATMENT OF FOREIGN PARTNERS.—

(1) ALLOWANCE OF CREDIT.—Each foreign partner of a partnership shall be allowed a credit under section 33 for such partner's share of the withholding tax paid by the partnership under this section. Such credit shall be allowed for the partner's taxable year in which (or with which) the partnership taxable year (for which such tax was paid) ends.

(2) CREDIT TREATED AS DISTRIBUTED TO PARTNER.—Except as provided in regulations, a foreign partner's share of any withholding tax paid by the partnership under this section shall be treated as distributed to such partner by such partnership on the earlier of—

(A) the day on which such tax was paid by the partnership, or

(B) the last day of the partnership's taxable year for which such tax was paid.

[Sec. 1446(e)]

(e) FOREIGN PARTNER.—For purposes of this section, the term "foreign partner" means any partner who is not a United States person.

[Sec. 1446(f)]

(f) SPECIAL RULES FOR WITHHOLDING ON DISPOSITIONS OF PARTNERSHIP INTERESTS.—

(1) IN GENERAL.—Except as provided in this subsection, if any portion of the gain (if any) on any disposition of an interest in a partnership would be treated under section 864(c)(8) as effectively connected with the conduct of a trade or business within the United States, the transferee shall be required to deduct and withhold a tax equal to 10 percent of the amount realized on the disposition.

(2) EXCEPTION IF NONFOREIGN AFFIDAVIT FURNISHED.—

(A) IN GENERAL.—No person shall be required to deduct and withhold any amount under paragraph (1) with respect to any disposition if the transferor furnishes to the transferee an affidavit by the transferor stating, under penalty of perjury, the transferor's United States taxpayer identification number and that the transferor is not a foreign person.

(B) FALSE AFFIDAVIT.—Subparagraph (A) shall not apply to any disposition if—

(i) the transferee has actual knowledge that the affidavit is false, or the transferee receives a notice (as described in section 1445(d)) from a transferor's agent or transferee's agent that such affidavit or statement is false, or

(ii) the Secretary by regulations requires the transferee to furnish a copy of such affidavit or statement to the Secretary and the transferee fails to furnish a copy of such affidavit or statement to the Secretary at such time and in such manner as required by such regulations.

(C) RULES FOR AGENTS.—The rules of section 1445(d) shall apply to a transferor's agent or transferee's agent with respect to any affidavit described in subparagraph (A) in the same manner as such rules apply with respect to the disposition of a United States real property interest under such section.

(3) AUTHORITY OF SECRETARY TO PRESCRIBE REDUCED AMOUNT.—At the request of the transferor or transferee, the Secretary may prescribe a reduced amount to be withheld under this section if the Secretary determines that to substitute such reduced amount will not jeopardize the collection of the tax imposed under this title with respect to gain treated under section 864(c)(8) as effectively connected with the conduct of a trade or business with in [sic] the United States.

(4) PARTNERSHIP TO WITHHOLD AMOUNTS NOT WITHHELD BY THE TRANSFEREE.—If a transferee fails to withhold any amount required to be withheld under paragraph (1), the partnership shall be required to deduct and withhold from distributions to the transferee a tax in an amount equal to the amount the transferee failed to withhold (plus interest under this title on such amount).

(5) DEFINITIONS.—Any term used in this subsection which is also used under section 1445 shall have the same meaning as when used in such section.

(6) REGULATIONS.—The Secretary shall prescribe such regulations or other guidance as may be necessary to carry out the purposes of this subsection, including regulations providing for exceptions from the provisions of this subsection.

[Sec. 1446(g)]

(g) REGULATIONS.—The Secretary shall prescribe such regulations as may be necessary to carry out the purposes of this section, including—

(1) regulations providing for the application of this section in the case of publicly traded partnerships, and

(2) regulations providing—

(A) that, for purposes of section 6655, the withholding tax imposed under this section shall be treated as a tax imposed by section 11 and any partnership required to pay such tax shall be treated as a corporation, and

(B) appropriate adjustments in applying section 6655 with respect to such withholding tax.

SUBCHAPTER B—APPLICATION OF WITHHOLDING PROVISIONS

[Sec. 1461]

SEC. 1461. LIABILITY FOR WITHHELD TAX.

Every person required to deduct and withhold any tax under this chapter is hereby made liable for such tax and is hereby indemnified against the claims and demands of any person for the amount of any payments made in accordance with the provisions of this chapter.

[Sec. 1462]

SEC. 1462. WITHHELD TAX AS CREDIT TO RECIPIENT OF INCOME.

Income on which any tax is required to be withheld at the source under this chapter shall be included in the return of the recipient of such income, but any amount of tax so withheld shall be credited against the amount of income tax as computed in such return.

[Sec. 1463]

SEC. 1463. TAX PAID BY RECIPIENT OF INCOME.

If—

(1) any person, in violation of the provisions of this chapter, fails to deduct and withhold any tax under this chapter, and

(2) thereafter the tax against which such tax may be credited is paid,

the tax so required to be deducted and withheld shall not be collected from such person; but this section shall in no case relieve such person from liability for interest or any penalties or additions to the tax otherwise applicable in respect of such failure to deduct and withhold.

[Sec. 1464]

SEC. 1464. REFUNDS AND CREDITS WITH RESPECT TO WITHHELD TAX.

Where there has been an overpayment of tax under this chapter, any refund or credit made under chapter 65 shall be made to the withholding agent unless the amount of such tax was actually withheld by the withholding agent.

CHAPTER 4—TAXES TO ENFORCE REPORTING ON CERTAIN FOREIGN ACCOUNTS

[Sec. 1471]

SEC. 1471. WITHHOLDABLE PAYMENTS TO FOREIGN FINANCIAL INSTITUTIONS.

[Sec. 1471(a)]

(a) IN GENERAL.—In the case of any withholdable payment to a foreign financial institution which does not meet the requirements of subsection (b), the withholding agent with respect to such payment shall deduct and withhold from such payment a tax equal to 30 percent of the amount of such payment.

[Sec. 1471(b)]

(b) REPORTING REQUIREMENTS, ETC.—

(1) IN GENERAL.—The requirements of this subsection are met with respect to any foreign financial institution if an agreement is in effect between such institution and the Secretary under which such institution agrees—

(A) to obtain such information regarding each holder of each account maintained by such institution as is necessary to determine which (if any) of such accounts are United States accounts,

(B) to comply with such verification and due diligence procedures as the Secretary may require with respect to the identification of United States accounts,

(C) in the case of any United States account maintained by such institution, to report on an annual basis the information described in subsection (c) with respect to such account,

(D) to deduct and withhold a tax equal to 30 percent of—

(i) any passthru payment which is made by such institution to a recalcitrant account holder or another foreign financial institution which does not meet the requirements of this subsection, and

(ii) in the case of any passthru payment which is made by such institution to a foreign financial institution which has in effect an election under paragraph (3) with respect to such payment, so much of such payment as is allocable to accounts held by recalcitrant account holders or foreign financial institutions which do not meet the requirements of this subsection,

(E) to comply with requests by the Secretary for additional information with respect to any United States account maintained by such institution, and

(F) in any case in which any foreign law would (but for a waiver described in clause (i)) prevent the reporting of any information referred to in this subsection or subsection (c) with respect to any United States account maintained by such institution—

(i) to attempt to obtain a valid and effective waiver of such law from each holder of such account, and

(ii) if a waiver described in clause (i) is not obtained from each such holder within a reasonable period of time, to close such account.

Any agreement entered into under this subsection may be terminated by the Secretary upon a determination by the Secretary that the foreign financial institution is out of compliance with such agreement.

(2) FINANCIAL INSTITUTIONS DEEMED TO MEET REQUIREMENTS IN CERTAIN CASES.—A foreign financial institution may be treated by the Secretary as meeting the requirements of this subsection if—

(A) such institution—

(i) complies with such procedures as the Secretary may prescribe to ensure that such institution does not maintain United States accounts, and

(ii) meets such other requirements as the Secretary may prescribe with respect to accounts of other foreign financial institutions maintained by such institution, or

(B) such institution is a member of a class of institutions with respect to which the Secretary has determined that the application of this section is not necessary to carry out the purposes of this section.

(3) ELECTION TO BE WITHHELD UPON RATHER THAN WITHHOLD ON PAYMENTS TO RECALCITRANT ACCOUNT HOLDERS AND NONPARTICIPATING FOREIGN FINANCIAL INSTITUTIONS.—In the case of a foreign financial institution which meets the requirements of this subsection and such other requirements as the Secretary may provide and which elects the application of this paragraph—

(A) the requirements of paragraph (1)(D) shall not apply,

(B) the withholding tax imposed under subsection (a) shall apply with respect to any withholdable payment to such institution to the extent such payment is allocable to accounts held by recalcitrant account holders or foreign financial institutions which do not meet the requirements of this subsection, and

(C) the agreement described in paragraph (1) shall—

(i) require such institution to notify the withholding agent with respect to each such payment of the institution's election under this paragraph and such other information as may be necessary for the withholding agent to determine the appropriate amount to deduct and withhold from such payment, and

(ii) include a waiver of any right under any treaty of the United States with respect to any amount deducted and withheld pursuant to an election under this paragraph.

To the extent provided by the Secretary, the election under this paragraph may be made with respect to certain classes or types of accounts of the foreign financial institution.

[Sec. 1471(c)]

(c) INFORMATION REQUIRED TO BE REPORTED ON UNITED STATES ACCOUNTS.—

(1) IN GENERAL.—The agreement described in subsection (b) shall require the foreign financial institution to report the following with respect to each United States account maintained by such institution:

(A) The name, address, and TIN of each account holder which is a specified United States person and, in the case of any account holder which is a United States owned foreign entity, the name, address, and TIN of each substantial United States owner of such entity.

(B) The account number.

(C) The account balance or value (determined at such time and in such manner as the Secretary may provide).

(D) Except to the extent provided by the Secretary, the gross receipts and gross withdrawals or payments from the account (determined for such period and in such manner as the Secretary may provide).

(2) ELECTION TO BE SUBJECT TO SAME REPORTING AS UNITED STATES FINANCIAL INSTITUTIONS.—In the case of a foreign financial institution which elects the application of this paragraph—

(A) subparagraphs (C) and (D) of paragraph (1) shall not apply, and

(B) the agreement described in subsection (b) shall require such foreign financial institution to report such information with respect to each United States account maintained by such institution as such institution would be required to report under sections 6041, 6042, 6045, and 6049 if—

(i) such institution were a United States person, and

(ii) each holder of such account which is a specified United States person or United States owned foreign entity were a natural person and citizen of the United States.

An election under this paragraph shall be made at such time, in such manner, and subject to such conditions as the Secretary may provide.

(3) SEPARATE REQUIREMENTS FOR QUALIFIED INTERMEDIARIES.—In the case of a foreign financial institution which is treated as a qualified intermediary by the Secretary for purposes of section 1441 and the regulations issued thereunder, the requirements of this section shall be in addition to any reporting or other requirements imposed by the Secretary for purposes of such treatment.

[Sec. 1471(d)]

(d) DEFINITIONS.—For purposes of this section—

(1) UNITED STATES ACCOUNT.—

(A) IN GENERAL.—The term "United States account" means any financial account which is held by one or more specified United States persons or United States owned foreign entities.

(B) EXCEPTION FOR CERTAIN ACCOUNTS HELD BY INDIVIDUALS.—Unless the foreign financial institution elects to not have this subparagraph apply, such term shall not include any depository account maintained by such financial institution if—

(i) each holder of such account is a natural person, and

(ii) with respect to each holder of such account, the aggregate value of all depository accounts held (in whole or in part) by such holder and maintained by the same financial institution which maintains such account does not exceed $50,000.

To the extent provided by the Secretary, financial institutions which are members of the same expanded affiliated group shall be treated for purposes of clause (ii) as a single financial institution.

(C) ELIMINATION OF DUPLICATIVE REPORTING REQUIREMENTS.—Such term shall not include any financial account in a foreign financial institution if—

(i) such account is held by another financial institution which meets the requirements of subsection (b), or

(ii) the holder of such account is otherwise subject to information reporting requirements which the Secretary determines would make the reporting required by this section with respect to United States accounts duplicative.

(2) FINANCIAL ACCOUNT.—Except as otherwise provided by the Secretary, the term "financial account" means, with respect to any financial institution—

(A) any depository account maintained by such financial institution,

(B) any custodial account maintained by such financial institution, and

(C) any equity or debt interest in such financial institution (other than interests which are regularly traded on an established securities market).

Any equity or debt interest which constitutes a financial account under subparagraph (C) with respect to any financial institution shall be treated for purposes of this section as maintained by such financial institution.

(3) UNITED STATES OWNED FOREIGN ENTITY.—The term "United States owned foreign entity" means any foreign entity which has one or more substantial United States owners.

(4) FOREIGN FINANCIAL INSTITUTION.—The term "foreign financial institution" means any financial institution which is a foreign entity. Except as otherwise provided by the Secretary, such term shall not include a financial institution which is organized under the laws of any possession of the United States.

(5) FINANCIAL INSTITUTION.—Except as otherwise provided by the Secretary, the term "financial institution" means any entity that—

(A) accepts deposits in the ordinary course of a banking or similar business,

(B) as a substantial portion of its business, holds financial assets for the account of others, or

(C) is engaged (or holding itself out as being engaged) primarily in the business of investing, reinvesting, or trading in securities (as defined in section 475(c)(2) without regard to the last sentence thereof), partnership interests, commodities (as defined in section 475(e)(2)), or any interest (including a futures or forward contract or option) in such securities, partnership interests, or commodities.

(6) RECALCITRANT ACCOUNT HOLDER.—The term "recalcitrant account holder" means any account holder which—

(A) fails to comply with reasonable requests for the information referred to in subsection (b)(1)(A) or (c)(1)(A), or

(B) fails to provide a waiver described in subsection (b)(1)(F) upon request.

(7) PASSTHRU PAYMENT.—The term "passthru payment" means any withholdable payment or other payment to the extent attributable to a withholdable payment.

[Sec. 1471(e)]

(e) AFFILIATED GROUPS.—

(1) IN GENERAL.—The requirements of subsections (b) and (c)(1) shall apply—

(A) with respect to United States accounts maintained by the foreign financial institution, and

(B) except as otherwise provided by the Secretary, with respect to United States accounts maintained by each other foreign financial institution (other than any foreign financial institution which meets the requirements of subsection (b)) which is a member of the same expanded affiliated group as such foreign financial institution.

(2) EXPANDED AFFILIATED GROUP.—For purposes of this section, the term "expanded affiliated group" means an affiliated group as defined in section 1504(a), determined—

(A) by substituting "more than 50 percent" for "at least 80 percent" each place it appears, and

(B) without regard to paragraphs (2) and (3) of section 1504(b).

A partnership or any other entity (other than a corporation) shall be treated as a member of an expanded affiliated group if such entity is controlled (within the meaning of section 954(d)(3)) by members of such group (including any entity treated as a member of such group by reason of this sentence).

[Sec. 1471(f)]

(f) EXCEPTION FOR CERTAIN PAYMENTS.—Subsection (a) shall not apply to any payment to the extent that the beneficial owner of such payment is—

(1) any foreign government, any political subdivision of a foreign government, or any wholly owned agency or instrumentality of any one or more of the foregoing,

(2) any international organization or any wholly owned agency or instrumentality thereof,

(3) any foreign central bank of issue, or

(4) any other class of persons identified by the Secretary for purposes of this subsection as posing a low risk of tax evasion.

[Sec. 1472]

SEC. 1472. WITHHOLDABLE PAYMENTS TO OTHER FOREIGN ENTITIES.

[Sec. 1472(a)]

(a) IN GENERAL.—In the case of any withholdable payment to a non-financial foreign entity, if—

(1) the beneficial owner of such payment is such entity or any other non-financial foreign entity, and

(2) the requirements of subsection (b) are not met with respect to such beneficial owner,

then the withholding agent with respect to such payment shall deduct and withhold from such payment a tax equal to 30 percent of the amount of such payment.

[Sec. 1472(b)]

(b) REQUIREMENTS FOR WAIVER OF WITHHOLDING.—The requirements of this subsection are met with respect to the beneficial owner of a payment if—

(1) such beneficial owner or the payee provides the withholding agent with either—

(A) a certification that such beneficial owner does not have any substantial United States owners, or

(B) the name, address, and TIN of each substantial United States owner of such beneficial owner,

(2) the withholding agent does not know, or have reason to know, that any information provided under paragraph (1) is incorrect, and

(3) the withholding agent reports the information provided under paragraph (1)(B) to the Secretary in such manner as the Secretary may provide.

[Sec. 1472(c)]

(c) EXCEPTIONS.—Subsection (a) shall not apply to—

(1) except as otherwise provided by the Secretary, any payment beneficially owned by—

(A) any corporation the stock of which is regularly traded on an established securities market,

(B) any corporation which is a member of the same expanded affiliated group (as defined in section 1471(e)(2) without regard to the last sentence thereof) as a corporation described in subparagraph (A),

(C) any entity which is organized under the laws of a possession of the United States and which is wholly owned by one or more bona fide residents (as defined in section 937(a)) of such possession,

(D) any foreign government, any political subdivision of a foreign government, or any wholly owned agency or instrumentality of any one or more of the foregoing,

(E) any international organization or any wholly owned agency or instrumentality thereof,

(F) any foreign central bank of issue, or

(G) any other class of persons identified by the Secretary for purposes of this subsection, and

(2) any class of payments identified by the Secretary for purposes of this subsection as posing a low risk of tax evasion.

[Sec. 1472(d)]

(d) NON-FINANCIAL FOREIGN ENTITY.—For purposes of this section, the term "non-financial foreign entity" means any foreign entity which is not a financial institution (as defined in section 1471(d)(5)).

[Sec. 1473]

SEC. 1473. DEFINITIONS.

For purposes of this chapter—

(1) WITHHOLDABLE PAYMENT.—Except as otherwise provided by the Secretary—

(A) IN GENERAL.—The term "withholdable payment" means—

(i) any payment of interest (including any original issue discount), dividends, rents, salaries, wages, premiums, annuities, compensations, remunerations, emoluments, and other fixed or determinable annual or periodical gains, profits, and income, if such payment is from sources within the United States, and

(ii) any gross proceeds from the sale or other disposition of any property of a type which can produce interest or dividends from sources within the United States.

(B) EXCEPTION FOR INCOME CONNECTED WITH UNITED STATES BUSINESS.—Such term shall not include any item of income which is taken into account under section 871(b)(1) or 882(a)(1) for the taxable year.

(C) SPECIAL RULE FOR SOURCING INTEREST PAID BY FOREIGN BRANCHES OF DOMESTIC FINANCIAL INSTITUTIONS.—Subparagraph (B) of section 861(a)(1) shall not apply.

(2) SUBSTANTIAL UNITED STATES OWNER.—

(A) IN GENERAL.—The term "substantial United States owner" means—

(i) with respect to any corporation, any specified United States person which owns, directly or indirectly, more than 10 percent of the stock of such corporation (by vote or value),

(ii) with respect to any partnership, any specified United States person which owns, directly or indirectly, more than 10 percent of the profits interests or capital interests in such partnership, and

(iii) in the case of a trust—

(I) any specified United States person treated as an owner of any portion of such trust under subpart E of part I of subchapter J of chapter 1, and

(II) to the extent provided by the Secretary in regulations or other guidance, any specified United States person which holds, directly or indirectly, more than 10 percent of the beneficial interests of such trust.

(B) SPECIAL RULE FOR INVESTMENT VEHICLES.—In the case of any financial institution described in section 1471(d)(5)(C), clauses (i), (ii), and (iii) of subparagraph (A) shall be applied by substituting "0 percent" for "10 percent".

(3) SPECIFIED UNITED STATES PERSON.—Except as otherwise provided by the Secretary, the term "specified United States person" means any United States person other than—

(A) any corporation the stock of which is regularly traded on an established securities market,

(B) any corporation which is a member of the same expanded affiliated group (as defined in section 1471(e)(2) without regard to the last sentence thereof) as a corporation the stock of which is regularly traded on an established securities market,

(C) any organization exempt from taxation under section 501(a) or an individual retirement plan,

(D) the United States or any wholly owned agency or instrumentality thereof,

(E) any State, the District of Columbia, any possession of the United States, any political subdivision of any of the foregoing, or any wholly owned agency or instrumentality of any one or more of the foregoing,

(F) any bank (as defined in section 581),

(G) any real estate investment trust (as defined in section 856),

(H) any regulated investment company (as defined in section 851),

(I) any common trust fund (as defined in section 584(a)), and

(J) any trust which—

(i) is exempt from tax under section 664(c), or

(ii) is described in section 4947(a)(1).

(4) WITHHOLDING AGENT.—The term "withholding agent" means all persons, in whatever capacity acting, having the control, receipt, custody, disposal, or payment of any withholdable payment.

(5) FOREIGN ENTITY.—The term "foreign entity" means any entity which is not a United States person.

[Sec. 1474]

SEC. 1474. SPECIAL RULES.

[Sec. 1474(a)]

(a) LIABILITY FOR WITHHELD TAX.—Every person required to deduct and withhold any tax under this chapter is hereby made liable for such tax and is hereby indemnified against the claims and demands of any person for the amount of any payments made in accordance with the provisions of this chapter.

[Sec. 1474(b)]

(b) CREDITS AND REFUNDS.—

(1) IN GENERAL.—Except as provided in paragraph (2), the determination of whether any tax deducted and withheld under this chapter results in an overpayment by the beneficial owner of the payment to which such tax is attributable shall be made as if such tax had been deducted and withheld under subchapter A of chapter 3.

(2) SPECIAL RULE WHERE FOREIGN FINANCIAL INSTITUTION IS BENEFICIAL OWNER OF PAYMENT.—

(A) IN GENERAL.—In the case of any tax properly deducted and withheld under section 1471 from a specified financial institution payment—

(i) if the foreign financial institution referred to in subparagraph (B) with respect to such payment is entitled to a reduced rate of tax with respect to such payment by reason of any treaty obligation of the United States—

(I) the amount of any credit or refund with respect to such tax shall not exceed the amount of credit or refund attributable to such reduction in rate, and

(II) no interest shall be allowed or paid with respect to such credit or refund, and

(ii) if such foreign financial institution is not so entitled, no credit or refund shall be allowed or paid with respect to such tax.

(B) SPECIFIED FINANCIAL INSTITUTION PAYMENT.—The term "specified financial institution payment" means any payment if the beneficial owner of such payment is a foreign financial institution.

(3) REQUIREMENT TO IDENTIFY SUBSTANTIAL UNITED STATES OWNERS.—No credit or refund shall be allowed or paid with respect to any tax properly deducted and withheld under this chapter unless the beneficial owner of the payment provides the Secretary such information as the Secretary may require to determine whether such beneficial owner is a United States owned foreign entity (as defined in section 1471(d)(3)) and the identity of any substantial United States owners of such entity.

[Sec. 1474(c)]

(c) CONFIDENTIALITY OF INFORMATION.—

(1) IN GENERAL.—For purposes of this chapter, rules similar to the rules of section 3406(f) shall apply.

(2) DISCLOSURE OF LIST OF PARTICIPATING FOREIGN FINANCIAL INSTITUTIONS PERMITTED.—The identity of a foreign financial institution which meets the requirements of section 1471(b) shall not be treated as return information for purposes of section 6103.

[Sec. 1474(d)]

(d) COORDINATION WITH OTHER WITHHOLDING PROVISIONS.—The Secretary shall provide for the coordination of this chapter with other withholding provisions under this title, including providing for the proper crediting of amounts deducted and withheld under this chapter against amounts required to be deducted and withheld under such other provisions.

[Sec. 1474(e)]

(e) TREATMENT OF WITHHOLDING UNDER AGREEMENTS.—Any tax deducted and withheld pursuant to an agreement described in section 1471(b) shall be treated for purposes of this title as a tax deducted and withheld by a withholding agent under section 1471(a).

[Sec. 1474(f)]

(f) REGULATIONS.—The Secretary shall prescribe such regulations or other guidance as may be necessary or appropriate to carry out the purposes of, and prevent the avoidance of, this chapter.

CHAPTER 6—CONSOLIDATED RETURNS

SUBCHAPTER A—RETURNS AND PAYMENT OF TAX

[Sec. 1501]

SEC. 1501. PRIVILEGE TO FILE CONSOLIDATED RETURNS.

An affiliated group of corporations shall, subject to the provisions of this chapter, have the privilege of making a consolidated return with respect to the income tax imposed by chapter 1 for the taxable year in lieu of separate returns. The making of a consolidated return shall be upon the condition that all corporations which at any time during the taxable year have been members of the affiliated group consent to all the consolidated return regulations prescribed under section 1502 prior to the last day prescribed by law for the filing of such return. The making of a consolidated return shall be considered as such consent. In the case of a corporation which is a member of the affiliated group for a fractional part of the year, the consolidated return shall include the income of such corporation for such part of the year as it is a member of the affiliated group.

[Sec. 1502]

SEC. 1502. REGULATIONS.

The Secretary shall prescribe such regulations as he may deem necessary in order that the tax liability of any affiliated group of corporations making a consolidated return and of each corporation in the group, both during and after the period of affiliation, may be returned, determined, computed, assessed, collected, and adjusted, in such manner as clearly to reflect the income tax liability and the various factors necessary for the determination of such liability, and in order to prevent avoidance of such tax liability. In carrying out the preceding sentence, the Secretary may prescribe rules that are different from the provisions of chapter 1 that would apply if such corporations filed separate returns.

[Sec. 1503]

SEC. 1503. COMPUTATION AND PAYMENT OF TAX.

* * *

[Sec. 1503(d)[c]]

(d)[c] DUAL CONSOLIDATED LOSS.—

(1) IN GENERAL.—The dual consolidated loss for any taxable year of any corporation shall not be allowed to reduce the taxable income of any other member of the affiliated group for the taxable year or any other taxable year.

(2) DUAL CONSOLIDATED LOSS.—For purposes of this section—

(A) IN GENERAL.—Except as provided in subparagraph (B), the term "dual consolidated loss" means any net operating loss of a domestic corporation which is subject to an income tax of a foreign country on its income without regard to whether such income is from sources in or outside of such foreign country, or is subject to such a tax on a residence basis.

(B) SPECIAL RULE WHERE LOSS NOT USED UNDER FOREIGN LAW.—To the extent provided in regulations, the term "dual consolidated loss" shall not include any loss which, under the foreign income tax law, does not offset the income of any foreign corporation.

(3) TREATMENT OF LOSSES OF SEPARATE BUSINESS UNITS.—To the extent provided in regulations, any loss of a separate unit of a domestic corporation shall be subject to the limitations of this subsection in the same manner as if such unit were a wholly owned subsidiary of such corporation.

(4) INCOME ON ASSETS ACQUIRED AFTER THE LOSS.—The Secretary shall prescribe such regulations as may be necessary or appropriate to prevent the avoidance of the purposes of this subsection by contributing assets to the corporation with the dual consolidated loss after such loss was sustained.

***

[Sec. 1504]

SEC. 1504. DEFINITIONS.

[Sec. 1504(a)]

(a) AFFILIATED GROUP DEFINED.—For purposes of this subtitle—

(1) IN GENERAL.—The term "affiliated group" means—

(A) 1 or more chains of includible corporations connected through stock ownership with a common parent corporation which is an includible corporation, but only if—

(B)(i) the common parent owns directly stock meeting the requirements of paragraph (2) in at least 1 of the other includible corporations, and

(ii) stock meeting the requirements of paragraph (2) in each of the includible corporations (except the common parent) is owned directly by 1 or more of the other includible corporations.

(2) 80-PERCENT VOTING AND VALUE TEST.—The ownership of stock of any corporation meets the requirements of this paragraph if it—

(A) possesses at least 80 percent of the total voting power of the stock of such corporation, and

(B) has a value equal to at least 80 percent of the total value of the stock of such corporation.

(3) 5 YEARS MUST ELAPSE BEFORE RECONSOLIDATION.—

(A) IN GENERAL.—If—

(i) a corporation is included (or required to be included) in a consolidated return filed by an affiliated group, and

(ii) such corporation ceases to be a member of such group,

with respect to periods after such cessation, such corporation (and any successor of such corporation) may not be included in any consolidated return filed by the affiliated group (or by another affiliated group with the same common parent or a successor of such common parent) before the 61st month beginning after its first taxable year in which it ceased to be a member of such affiliated group.

(B) SECRETARY MAY WAIVE APPLICATION OF SUBPARAGRAPH (A).—The Secretary may waive the application of subparagraph (A) to any corporation for any period subject to such conditions as the Secretary may prescribe.

(4) STOCK NOT TO INCLUDE CERTAIN PREFERRED STOCK.—For purposes of this subsection, the term "stock" does not include any stock which—

(A) is not entitled to vote,

(B) is limited and preferred as to dividends and does not participate in corporate growth to any significant extent,

(C) has redemption and liquidation rights which do not exceed the issue price of such stock (except for a reasonable redemption or liquidation premium), and

(D) is not convertible into another class of stock.

(5) REGULATIONS.—The Secretary shall prescribe such regulations as may be necessary or appropriate to carry out the purposes of this subsection, including (but not limited to) regulations—

(A) which treat warrants, obligations convertible into stock, and other similar interests as stock, and stock as not stock,

(B) which treat options to acquire or sell stock as having been exercised,

(C) which provide that the requirements of paragraph (2)(B) shall be treated as met if the affiliated group, in reliance on a good faith determination of value, treated such requirements as met,

(D) which disregard an inadvertent ceasing to meet the requirements of paragraph (2)(B) by reason of changes in relative values of different classes of stock,

(E) which provide that transfers of stock within the group shall not be taken into account in determining whether a corporation ceases to be a member of an affiliated group, and

(F) which disregard changes in voting power to the extent such changes are disproportionate to related changes in value.

[Sec. 1504(b)]

(b) DEFINITION OF "INCLUDIBLE CORPORATION".—As used in this chapter, the term "includible corporation" means any corporation except—

(1) Corporations exempt from taxation under section 501.

(2) Insurance companies subject to taxation under section 801.

(3) Foreign corporations.

(4) Regulated investment companies and real estate investment trusts subject to tax under subchapter M of chapter 1.

(5) A DISC (as defined in section 992(a)(1)).

(6) An S corporation.

***

[Sec. 1504(d)]

(d) SUBSIDIARY FORMED TO COMPLY WITH FOREIGN LAW.—In the case of a domestic corporation owning or controlling, directly or indirectly, 100 percent of the capital stock (exclusive of directors' qualifying shares) of a corporation organized under the laws of a contiguous foreign country and maintained solely for the purpose of complying with the laws of such country as to title and operation of property, such foreign corporation may, at the option of the domestic corporation, be treated for the purpose of this subtitle as a domestic corporation.

***

SUBCHAPTER B—RELATED RULES

PART II—CERTAIN CONTROLLED CORPORATIONS

[Sec. 1563]

SEC. 1563. DEFINITIONS AND SPECIAL RULES.

[Sec. 1563(a)]

(a) CONTROLLED GROUP OF CORPORATIONS.—For purposes of this part, the term "controlled group of corporations" means any group of—

(1) PARENT-SUBSIDIARY CONTROLLED GROUP.—One or more chains of corporations connected through stock ownership with a common parent corporation if—

(A) stock possessing at least 80 percent of the total combined voting power of all classes of stock entitled to vote or at least 80 percent of the total value of shares of all classes of stock of each of the corporations, except the common parent corporation, is owned (within the meaning of subsection (d)(1)) by one or more of the other corporations; and

(B) the common parent corporation owns (within the meaning of subsection (d)(1)) stock possessing at least 80 percent of the total combined voting power of all classes of stock entitled to vote or at least 80 percent of the total value of shares of all classes of stock of at least one of the other corporations, excluding, in computing such voting power or value, stock owned directly by such other corporations.

(2) BROTHER-SISTER CONTROLLED GROUP.—Two or more corporations if 5 or fewer persons who are individuals, estates, or trusts own (within the meaning of subsection (d)(2)) stock possessing more than 50 percent of the total combined voting power of all classes of stock entitled to vote or more than 50 percent of the total value of shares of all classes of stock of each corporation, taking into account the stock ownership of each such person only to the extent such stock ownership is identical with respect to each such corporation.

(3) COMBINED GROUP.—Three or more corporations each of which is a member of a group of corporations described in paragraph (1) or (2), and one of which—

(A) is a common parent corporation included in a group of corporations described in paragraph (1), and also

(B) is included in a group of corporations described in paragraph (2).

* * *

SUBTITLE B—ESTATE AND GIFT TAXES

CHAPTER 11—ESTATE TAX

SUBCHAPTER B—ESTATES OF NONRESIDENTS NOT CITIZENS

[Sec. 2107]

SEC. 2107. EXPATRIATION TO AVOID TAX.

[Sec. 2107(a)]

(a) TREATMENT OF EXPATRIATES.—A tax computed in accordance with the table contained in section 2001 is hereby imposed on the transfer of the taxable estate, determined as provided in section 2106, of every decedent nonresident not a citizen of the United States if the date of death occurs during a taxable year with respect to which the decedent is subject to tax under section 877(b).

* * *

CHAPTER 12—GIFT TAX

SUBCHAPTER A—DETERMINATION OF TAX LIABILITY

[Sec. 2501]

SEC. 2501. IMPOSITION OF TAX.

[Sec. 2501(a)]

(a) TAXABLE TRANSFERS.—

(1) GENERAL RULE.—A tax, computed as provided in section 2502, is hereby imposed for each calendar year on the transfer of property by gift during such calendar year by any individual, resident or nonresident.

(2) TRANSFERS OF INTANGIBLE PROPERTY.—Except as provided in paragraph (3), paragraph (1) shall not apply to the transfer of intangible property by a nonresident not a citizen of the United States.

(3) EXCEPTION.—

(A) CERTAIN INDIVIDUALS.—Paragraph (2) shall not apply in the case of a donor to whom section 877(b) applies for the taxable year which includes the date of the transfer.

(B) CREDIT FOR FOREIGN GIFT TAXES.—The tax imposed by this section solely by reason of this paragraph shall be credited with the amount of any gift tax actually paid to any foreign country in respect of any gift which is taxable under this section solely by reason of this paragraph.

(4) TRANSFERS TO POLITICAL ORGANIZATIONS.—Paragraph (1) shall not apply to the transfer of money or other property to a political organization (within the meaning of section 527(e)(1)) for the use of such organization.

(5) TRANSFERS OF CERTAIN STOCK.—

(A) IN GENERAL.—In the case of a transfer of stock in a foreign corporation described in subparagraph (B) by a donor to whom section 877(b) applies for the taxable year which includes the date of the transfer—

(i) section 2511(a) shall be applied without regard to whether such stock is situated within the United States, and

(ii) the value of such stock for purposes of this chapter shall be its U.S.-asset value determined under subparagraph (C).

(B) FOREIGN CORPORATION DESCRIBED.—A foreign corporation is described in this subparagraph with respect to a donor if—

(i) the donor owned (within the meaning of section 958(a)) at the time of such transfer 10 percent or more of the total combined voting power of all classes of stock entitled to vote of the foreign corporation, and

(ii) such donor owned (within the meaning of section 958(a)), or is considered to have owned (by applying the ownership rules of section 958(b)), at the time of such transfer, more than 50 percent of—

(I) the total combined voting power of all classes of stock entitled to vote of such corporation, or

(II) the total value of the stock of such corporation.

(C) U.S.-ASSET VALUE.—For purposes of subparagraph (A), the U.S.-asset value of stock shall be the amount which bears the same ratio to the fair market value of such stock at the time of transfer as—

(i) the fair market value (at such time) of the assets owned by such foreign corporation and situated in the United States, bears to

(ii) the total fair market value (at such time) of all assets owned by such foreign corporation.

(6) TRANSFERS TO CERTAIN EXEMPT ORGANIZATIONS.—Paragraph (1) shall not apply to the transfer of money or other property to an organization described in paragraph (4), (5), or (6) of section 501(c) and exempt from tax under section 501(a), for the use of such organization.

* * *

CHAPTER 15—GIFTS AND BEQUESTS FROM EXPATRIATES

[Sec. 2801]

SEC. 2801. IMPOSITION OF TAX.

[Sec. 2801(a)]

(a) IN GENERAL.—If, during any calendar year, any United States citizen or resident receives any covered gift or bequest, there is hereby imposed a tax equal to the product of—

(1) the highest rate of tax specified in the table contained in section 2001(c) as in effect on the date of such receipt, and

(2) the value of such covered gift or bequest.

[Sec. 2801(b)]

(b) TAX TO BE PAID BY RECIPIENT.—The tax imposed by subsection (a) on any covered gift or bequest shall be paid by the person receiving such gift or bequest.

[Sec. 2801(c)]

(c) EXCEPTION FOR CERTAIN GIFTS.—Subsection (a) shall apply only to the extent that the value of covered gifts and bequests received by any person during the calendar year exceeds the dollar amount in effect under section 2503(b) for such calendar year.

[Sec. 2801(d)]

(d) TAX REDUCED BY FOREIGN GIFT OR ESTATE TAX.—The tax imposed by subsection (a) on any covered gift or bequest shall be reduced by the amount of any gift or estate tax paid to a foreign country with respect to such covered gift or bequest.

[Sec. 2801(e)]

(e) COVERED GIFT OR BEQUEST.—

(1) IN GENERAL.—For purposes of this chapter, the term "covered gift or bequest" means—

(A) any property acquired by gift directly or indirectly from an individual who, at the time of such acquisition, is a covered expatriate, and

(B) any property acquired directly or indirectly by reason of the death of an individual who, immediately before such death, was a covered expatriate.

(2) EXCEPTIONS FOR TRANSFERS OTHERWISE SUBJECT TO ESTATE OR GIFT TAX.—Such term shall not include—

(A) any property shown on a timely filed return of tax imposed by chapter 12 which is a taxable gift by the covered expatriate, and

(B) any property included in the gross estate of the covered expatriate for purposes of chapter 11 and shown on a timely filed return of tax imposed by chapter 11 of the estate of the covered expatriate.

(3) EXCEPTIONS FOR TRANSFERS TO SPOUSE OR CHARITY.—Such term shall not include any property with respect to which a deduction would be allowed under section 2055, 2056, 2522, or 2523, whichever is appropriate, if the decedent or donor were a United States person.

(4) TRANSFERS IN TRUST.—

(A) DOMESTIC TRUSTS.—In the case of a covered gift or bequest made to a domestic trust—

(i) subsection (a) shall apply in the same manner as if such trust were a United States citizen, and

(ii) the tax imposed by subsection (a) on such gift or bequest shall be paid by such trust.

(B) FOREIGN TRUSTS.—

(i) IN GENERAL.—In the case of a covered gift or bequest made to a foreign trust, subsection (a) shall apply to any distribution attributable to such gift or bequest from such trust (whether from income or corpus) to a United States citizen or resident in the same manner as if such distribution were a covered gift or bequest.

(ii) DEDUCTION FOR TAX PAID BY RECIPIENT.—There shall be allowed as a deduction under section 164 the amount of tax imposed by this section which is paid or accrued by a United States citizen or resident by reason of a distribution from a foreign trust, but only to the extent such tax is imposed on the portion of such distribution which is included in the gross income of such citizen or resident.

(iii) ELECTION TO BE TREATED AS DOMESTIC TRUST.—Solely for purposes of this section, a foreign trust may elect to be treated as a domestic trust. Such an election may be revoked with the consent of the Secretary.

[Sec. 2801(f)]

(f) COVERED EXPATRIATE.—For purposes of this section, the term "covered expatriate" has the meaning given to such term by section 877A(g)(1).

SUBTITLE C—EMPLOYMENT TAXES

CHAPTER 21—FEDERAL INSURANCE CONTRIBUTIONS ACT

SUBCHAPTER C—GENERAL PROVISIONS

[Sec. 3121]

SEC. 3121. DEFINITIONS.

* * *

[Sec. 3121(h)]

(h) AMERICAN EMPLOYER.—For purposes of this chapter, the term "American employer" means an employer which is—

(1) the United States or any instrumentality thereof,

(2) an individual who is a resident of the United States,

(3) a partnership, if two-thirds or more of the partners are residents of the United States,

(4) a trust, if all of the trustees are residents of the United States, or

(5) a corporation organized under the laws of the United States or of any State.

* * *

[Sec. 3121(l)]

(l) AGREEMENTS ENTERED INTO BY AMERICAN EMPLOYERS WITH RESPECT TO FOREIGN AFFILIATES.—

(1) AGREEMENT WITH RESPECT TO CERTAIN EMPLOYEES OF FOREIGN AFFILIATE.—The Secretary shall, at the American employer's request, enter into an agreement (in such manner and form as may be prescribed by the Secretary) with any American employer (as defined in subsection (h))

who desires to have the insurance system established by title II of the Social Security Act extended to service performed outside the United States in the employ of any 1 or more of such employer's foreign affiliates (as defined in paragraph (6)) by all employees who are citizens or residents of the United States, except that the agreement shall not apply to any service performed by, or remuneration paid to, an employee if such service or remuneration would be excluded from the term "employment" or "wages", as defined in this section, had the service been performed in the United States. Such agreement may be amended at any time so as to be made applicable, in the same manner and under the same conditions, with respect to any other foreign affiliate of such American employer. Such agreement shall be applicable with respect to citizens or residents of the United States who, on or after the effective date of the agreement, are employees of and perform services outside the United States for any foreign affiliate specified in the agreement. Such agreement shall provide—

(A) that the American employer shall pay to the Secretary, at such time or times as the Secretary may by regulations prescribe, amounts equivalent to the sum of the taxes which would be imposed by sections 3101 and 3111 (including amounts equivalent to the interest, additions to the taxes, additional amounts, and penalties which would be applicable) with respect to the remuneration which would be wages if the services covered by the agreement constituted employment as defined in this section; and

(B) that the American employer will comply with such regulations relating to payments and reports as the Secretary may prescribe to carry out the purposes of this subsection.

(2) EFFECTIVE PERIOD OF AGREEMENT.—An agreement entered into pursuant to paragraph (1) shall be in effect for the period beginning with the first day of the calendar quarter in which such agreement is entered into or the first day of the succeeding calendar quarter, as may be specified in the agreement; except that in case such agreement is amended to include the services performed for any other affiliate and such amendment is executed after the first month following the first calendar quarter for which the agreement is in effect, the agreement shall be in effect with respect to service performed for such other affiliate only after the calendar quarter in which such amendment is executed. Notwithstanding any other provision of this subsection, the period for which any such agreement is effective with respect to any foreign entity shall terminate at the end of any calendar quarter in which the foreign entity, at any time in such quarter, ceases to be a foreign affiliate as defined in paragraph (6).

(3) NO TERMINATION OF AGREEMENT.—No agreement under this subsection may be terminated, either in its entirety or with respect to any foreign affiliate, on or after June 15, 1989.

(4) DEPOSITS IN TRUST FUNDS.—For purposes of section 201 of the Social Security Act, relating to appropriations to the Federal Old-Age and Survivors Insurance Trust Fund and the Federal Disability Insurance Trust Fund, such remuneration—

(A) paid for services covered by an agreement entered into pursuant to paragraph (1) as would be wages if the services constituted employment, and

(B) as is reported to the Secretary pursuant to the provisions of such agreement or of the regulations issued under this subsection,

shall be considered wages subject to the taxes imposed by this chapter.

(5) OVERPAYMENTS AND UNDERPAYMENTS.—

(A) If more or less than the correct amount due under an agreement entered into pursuant to this subsection is paid with respect to any payment of remuneration, proper adjustments with respect to the amounts due under such agreement shall be made, without interest, in such manner and at such times as may be required by regulations prescribed by the Secretary.

(B) If an overpayment cannot be adjusted under subparagraph (A), the amount thereof shall be paid by the Secretary, through the Fiscal Service of the Treasury Department, but only if a claim for such overpayment is filed with the Secretary within two years from the time such overpayment was made.

(6) FOREIGN AFFILIATE DEFINED.—For purposes of this subsection and section 210(a) of the Social Security Act—

(A) IN GENERAL.—A foreign affiliate of an American employer is any foreign entity in which such American employer has not less than a 10-percent interest.

(B) DETERMINATION OF 10-PERCENT INTEREST.—For purposes of subparagraph (A), an American employer has a 10-percent interest in any entity if such employer has such an interest directly (or through one or more entities)—

(i) in the case of a corporation, in the voting stock thereof, and

(ii) in the case of any other entity, in the profits thereof.

(7) AMERICAN EMPLOYER AS SEPARATE ENTITY.—Each American employer which enters into an agreement pursuant to paragraph (1) of this subsection shall, for purposes of this subsection and section 6413(c)(2)(C), relating to special refunds in the case of employees of certain foreign entities, be considered an employer in its capacity as a party to such agreement separate and distinct from its identity as a person employing individuals on its own account.

(8) REGULATIONS.—Regulations of the Secretary to carry out the purposes of this subsection shall be designed to make the requirements imposed on American employers with respect to services covered by an agreement entered into pursuant to this subsection the same, so far as practicable, as those imposed upon employers pursuant to this title with respect to the taxes imposed by this chapter.

***

[Sec. 3121(z)]

(z) TREATMENT OF CERTAIN FOREIGN PERSONS AS AMERICAN EMPLOYERS.—

(1) IN GENERAL.—If any employee of a foreign person is performing services in connection with a contract between the United States Government (or any instrumentality thereof) and any member of any domestically controlled group of entities which includes such foreign person, such foreign person shall be treated for purposes of this chapter as an American employer with respect to such services performed by such employee.

(2) DOMESTICALLY CONTROLLED GROUP OF ENTITIES.—For purposes of this subsection—

(A) IN GENERAL.—The term "domestically controlled group of entities" means a controlled group of entities the common parent of which is a domestic corporation.

(B) CONTROLLED GROUP OF ENTITIES.—The term "controlled group of entities" means a controlled group of corporations as defined in section 1563(a)(1), except that—

(i) "more than 50 percent" shall be substituted for "at least 80 percent" each place it appears therein, and

(ii) the determination shall be made without regard to subsections (a)(4) and (b)(2) of section 1563.

A partnership or any other entity (other than a corporation) shall be treated as a member of a controlled group of entities if such entity is controlled (within the meaning of section 954(d)(3)) by members of such group (including any entity treated as a member of such group by reason of this sentence).

(3) LIABILITY OF COMMON PARENT.—In the case of a foreign person who is a member of any domestically controlled group of entities, the common parent of such group shall be jointly and severally liable for any tax under this chapter for which such foreign person is liable by reason of this subsection, and for any penalty imposed on such person by this title with respect to any failure to pay such tax or to file any return or statement with respect to such tax or wages subject to such tax. No deduction shall be allowed under this title for any liability imposed by the preceding sentence.

(4) PROVISIONS PREVENTING DOUBLE TAXATION.—

(A) AGREEMENTS.—Paragraph (1) shall not apply to any services which are covered by an agreement under subsection (l).

(B) EQUIVALENT FOREIGN TAXATION.—Paragraph (1) shall not apply to any services if the employer establishes to the satisfaction of the Secretary that the remuneration paid by such employer for such services is subject to a tax imposed by a foreign country which is substantially equivalent to the taxes imposed by this chapter.

(5) CROSS REFERENCE.—For relief from taxes in cases covered by certain international agreements, see sections 3101(c) and 3111(c).

CHAPTER 24—COLLECTION OF INCOME TAX AT SOURCE ON WAGES

SUBCHAPTER A—WITHHOLDING FROM WAGES

[Sec. 3401]

SEC. 3401. DEFINITIONS.

[Sec. 3401(a)]

(a) WAGES.—For purposes of this chapter, the term "wages" means all remuneration (other than fees paid to a public official) for services performed by an employee for his employer, including the cash value of all remuneration (including benefits) paid in any medium other than cash; except that such term shall not include remuneration paid—

* * *

(5) for services by a citizen or resident of the United States for a foreign government or an international organization,

(6) for such services, performed by a nonresident alien individual, as may be designated by regulations prescribed by the Secretary,

(7) [Stricken]

(8)(A) for services for an employer (other than the United States or any agency thereof)—

(i) performed by a citizen of the United States if, at the time of the payment of such remuneration, it is reasonable to believe that such remuneration will be excluded from gross income under section 911, or

(ii) performed in a foreign country or in a possession of the United States by such a citizen if, at the time of the payment of such remuneration, the employer is required by the law of any foreign country or possession of the United States to withhold income tax upon such remuneration,

(B) for services for an employer (other than the United States or any agency thereof) performed by a citizen of the United States within a possession of the United States (other than Puerto Rico), if it is reasonable to believe that at least 80 percent of the remuneration to be paid to the employee by such employer during the calendar year will be for such services,

(C) for services for an employer (other than the United States or any agency thereof) performed by a citizen of the United States within Puerto Rico, if it is reasonable to believe that during the entire calendar year the employee will be a bona fide resident of Puerto Rico, or

(D) for services for the United States (or any agency thereof) performed by a citizen of the United States within a possession of the United States to the extent the United States (or such agency) withholds taxes on such remuneration pursuant to an agreement with such possession,

* * *

[Sec. 3402]

SEC. 3402. INCOME TAX COLLECTED AT SOURCE.

* * *

[Sec. 3402(f)]

(f) WITHHOLDING ALLOWANCE.—

* * *

(6) EXEMPTION OF CERTAIN NONRESIDENT ALIENS.—Notwithstanding the provisions of paragraph (1), a nonresident alien individual (other than an individual described in section 3401(a)(6)(A) or (B)) shall be entitled to only one withholding exemption.

* * *

[Sec. 3406]

SEC. 3406. BACKUP WITHHOLDING.

[Sec. 3406(a)]

(a) REQUIREMENT TO DEDUCT AND WITHHOLD.—

(1) IN GENERAL.—In the case of any reportable payment, if—

(A) the payee fails to furnish his TIN to the payor in the manner required,

(B) the Secretary notifies the payor that the TIN furnished by the payee is incorrect,

(C) there has been a notified payee underreporting described in subsection (c), or

(D) there has been a payee certification failure described in subsection (d),

then the payor shall deduct and withhold from such payment a tax equal to the product of the fourth lowest rate of tax applicable under section 1(c) and such payment.

(2) SUBPARAGRAPHS (C) AND (D) OF PARAGRAPH (1) APPLY ONLY TO INTEREST AND DIVIDEND PAYMENTS.—Subparagraphs (C) and (D) of paragraph (1) shall apply only to reportable interest or dividend payments.

* * *

[Sec. 3406(g)]

(g) EXCEPTIONS.—

(1) PAYMENTS TO CERTAIN PAYEES.—Subsection (a) shall not apply to any payment made to—

(A) any organization or governmental unit described in subparagraph (B), (C), (D), (E), or (F) of section 6049(b)(4), or

(B) any other person specified in regulations.

(2) AMOUNTS FOR WHICH WITHHOLDING OTHERWISE REQUIRED.—Subsection (a) shall not apply to any amount for which withholding is otherwise required by this title.

(3) EXEMPTION WHILE WAITING FOR TIN.—The Secretary shall prescribe regulations for exemptions from the tax imposed by subsection (a) during the period during which a person is waiting for receipt of a TIN.

* * *

SUBTITLE D—MISCELLANEOUS EXCISE TAXES

CHAPTER 37—REPURCHASE OF CORPORATE STOCK

[Sec. 4501]

SEC. 4501. REPURCHASE OF CORPORATE STOCK.

[Sec. 4501(a)]

(a) GENERAL RULE.—There is hereby imposed on each covered corporation a tax equal to 1 percent of the fair market value of any stock of the corporation which is repurchased by such corporation during the taxable year.

[Sec. 4501(b)]

(b) COVERED CORPORATION.—For purposes of this section, the term "covered corporation" means any domestic corporation the stock of which is traded on an established securities market (within the meaning of section 7704(b)(1)).

[Sec. 4501(c)]

(c) REPURCHASE.—For purposes of this section—

(1) IN GENERAL.—The term "repurchase" means—

(A) a redemption within the meaning of section 317(b) with regard to the stock of a covered corporation, and

(B) any transaction determined by the Secretary to be economically similar to a transaction described in subparagraph (A).

(2) TREATMENT OF PURCHASES BY SPECIFIED AFFILIATES.—

(A) IN GENERAL.—The acquisition of stock of a covered corporation by a specified affiliate of such covered corporation, from a person who is not the covered corporation or a specified affiliate of such covered corporation, shall be treated as a repurchase of the stock of the covered corporation by such covered corporation.

(B) SPECIFIED AFFILIATE.—For purposes of this section, the term "specified affiliate" means, with respect to any corporation—

(i) any corporation more than 50 percent of the stock of which is owned (by vote or by value), directly or indirectly, by such corporation, and

(ii) any partnership more than 50 percent of the capital interests or profits interests of which is held, directly or indirectly, by such corporation.

(3) ADJUSTMENT.—The amount taken into account under subsection (a) with respect to any stock repurchased by a covered corporation shall be reduced by the fair market value of any stock issued by the covered corporation during the taxable year, including the fair market value of any stock issued or provided to employees of such covered corporation or employees of a specified affiliate of such covered corporation during the taxable year, whether or not such stock is issued or provided in response to the exercise of an option to purchase such stock.

[Sec. 4501(d)]

(d) SPECIAL RULES FOR ACQUISITION OF STOCK OF CERTAIN FOREIGN CORPORATIONS.—

(1) IN GENERAL.—In the case of an acquisition of stock of an applicable foreign corporation by a specified affiliate of such corporation (other than a foreign corporation or a foreign partnership (unless such partnership has a domestic entity as a direct or indirect partner)) from a person who is not the applicable foreign corporation or a specified affiliate of such applicable foreign corporation, for purposes of this section—

(A) such specified affiliate shall be treated as a covered corporation with respect to such acquisition,

(B) such acquisition shall be treated as a repurchase of stock of a covered corporation by such covered corporation, and

(C) the adjustment under subsection (c)(3) shall be determined only with respect to stock issued or provided by such specified affiliate to employees of the specified affiliate.

(2) SURROGATE FOREIGN CORPORATIONS.—In the case of a repurchase of stock of a covered surrogate foreign corporation by such covered surrogate foreign corporation, or an acquisition of stock of a covered surrogate foreign corporation by a specified affiliate of such corporation, for purposes of this section—

(A) the expatriated entity with respect to such covered surrogate foreign corporation shall be treated as a covered corporation with respect to such repurchase or acquisition,

(B) such repurchase or acquisition shall be treated as a repurchase of stock of a covered corporation by such covered corporation, and

(C) the adjustment under subsection (c)(3) shall be determined only with respect to stock issued or provided by such expatriated entity to employees of the expatriated entity.

(3) DEFINITIONS.—For purposes of this subsection—

(A) APPLICABLE FOREIGN CORPORATION.—The term "applicable foreign corporation" means any foreign corporation the stock of which is traded on an established securities market (within the meaning of section 7704(b)(1)).

(B) COVERED SURROGATE FOREIGN CORPORATION.—The term "covered surrogate foreign corporation" means any surrogate foreign corporation (as determined under section 7874(a)(2)(B) by substituting "September 20, 2021" for "March 4, 2003" each place it appears) the stock of which is traded on an established securities market (within the meaning of section 7704(b)(1)), but only with respect to taxable years which include any portion of the applicable period with respect to such corporation under section 7874(d)(1).

(C) EXPATRIATED ENTITY.—The term "expatriated entity" has the meaning given such term by section 7874(a)(2)(A).

[Sec. 4501(e)]

(e) EXCEPTIONS.—Subsection (a) shall not apply—

(1) to the extent that the repurchase is part of a reorganization (within the meaning of section 368(a)) and no gain or loss is recognized on such repurchase by the shareholder under chapter 1 by reason of such reorganization,

(2) in any case in which the stock repurchased is, or an amount of stock equal to the value of the stock repurchased is, contributed to an employer-sponsored retirement plan, employee stock ownership plan, or similar plan,

(3) in any case in which the total value of the stock repurchased during the taxable year does not exceed $1,000,000,

(4) under regulations prescribed by the Secretary, in cases in which the repurchase is by a dealer in securities in the ordinary course of business,

(5) to repurchases by a regulated investment company (as defined in section 851) or a real estate investment trust, or

(6) to the extent that the repurchase is treated as a dividend for purposes of this title.

[Sec. 4501(f)]

(f) REGULATIONS AND GUIDANCE.—The Secretary shall prescribe such regulations and other guidance as are necessary or appropriate to carry out, and to prevent the avoidance of, the purposes of this section, including regulations and other guidance—

(1) to prevent the abuse of the exceptions provided by subsection (e),

(2) to address special classes of stock and preferred stock, and

(3) for the application of the rules under subsection (d).

CHAPTER 39—REGISTRATION-REQUIRED OBLIGATIONS

[Sec. 4701]

SEC. 4701. TAX ON ISSUER OF REGISTRATION-REQUIRED OBLIGATION NOT IN REGISTERED FORM.

[Sec. 4701(a)]

(a) IMPOSITION OF TAX.—In the case of any person who issues a registration-required obligation which is not in registered form, there is hereby imposed on such person on the issuance of such obligation a tax in an amount equal to the product of—

(1) 1 percent of the principal amount of such obligation, multiplied by

(2) the number of calendar years (or portions thereof) during the period beginning on the date of issuance of such obligation and ending on the date of maturity.

[Sec. 4701(b)]

(b) DEFINITIONS.—For purposes of this section—

(1) REGISTRATION-REQUIRED OBLIGATION.—

(A) IN GENERAL.—The term "registration-required obligation" has the same meaning as when used in section 163(f), except that such term shall not include any obligation which—

(i) is required to be registered under section 149(a), or

(ii) is described in subparagraph (B).

(B) CERTAIN OBLIGATIONS NOT INCLUDED.—An obligation is described in this subparagraph if—

(i) there are arrangements reasonably designed to ensure that such obligation will be sold (or resold in connection with the original issue) only to a person who is not a United States person,

(ii) interest on such obligation is payable only outside the United States and its possessions, and

(iii) on the face of such obligation there is a statement that any United States person who holds such obligation will be subject to limitations under the United States income tax laws.

(2) REGISTERED FORM.—The term "registered form" has the same meaning as when used in section 163(f).

CHAPTER 45—PROVISIONS RELATING TO EXPATRIATED ENTITIES

[Sec. 4985]

SEC. 4985. STOCK COMPENSATION OF INSIDERS IN EXPATRIATED CORPORATIONS.

[Sec. 4985(a)]

(a) IMPOSITION OF TAX.—In the case of an individual who is a disqualified individual with respect to any expatriated corporation, there is hereby imposed on such person a tax equal to—

(1) the rate of tax specified in section 1(h)(1)(D), multiplied by

(2) the value (determined under subsection (b)) of the specified stock compensation held (directly or indirectly) by or for the benefit of such individual or a member of such individual's family (as defined in section 267) at any time during the 12-month period beginning on the date which is 6 months before the expatriation date.

[Sec. 4985(b)]

(b) VALUE.—For purposes of subsection (a)—

(1) IN GENERAL.—The value of specified stock compensation shall be—

(A) in the case of a stock option (or other similar right) or a stock appreciation right, the fair value of such option or right, and

(B) in any other case, the fair market value of such compensation.

(2) DATE FOR DETERMINING VALUE.—The determination of value shall be made—

(A) in the case of specified stock compensation held on the expatriation date, on such date,

(B) in the case of such compensation which is canceled during the 6 months before the expatriation date, on the day before such cancellation, and

(C) in the case of such compensation which is granted after the expatriation date, on the date such compensation is granted.

[Sec. 4985(c)]

(c) TAX TO APPLY ONLY IF SHAREHOLDER GAIN RECOGNIZED.—Subsection (a) shall apply to any disqualified individual with respect to an expatriated corporation only if gain (if any) on any stock in such corporation is recognized in whole or part by any shareholder by reason of the acquisition referred to in section 7874(a)(2)(B)(i) with respect to such corporation.

[Sec. 4985(d)]

(d) EXCEPTION WHERE GAIN RECOGNIZED ON COMPENSATION.—Subsection (a) shall not apply to—

(1) any stock option which is exercised on the expatriation date or during the 6-month period before such date and to the stock acquired in such exercise, if income is recognized under section 83 on or before the expatriation date with respect to the stock acquired pursuant to such exercise, and

(2) any other specified stock compensation which is exercised, sold, exchanged, distributed, cashed-out, or otherwise paid during such period in a transaction in which income, gain, or loss is recognized in full.

[Sec. 4985(e)]

(e) DEFINITIONS.—For purposes of this section—

(1) DISQUALIFIED INDIVIDUAL.—The term "disqualified individual" means, with respect to a corporation, any individual who, at any time during the 12-month period beginning on the date which is 6 months before the expatriation date—

(A) is subject to the requirements of section 16(a) of the Securities Exchange Act of 1934 with respect to such corporation or any member of the expanded affiliated group which includes such corporation, or

(B) would be subject to such requirements if such corporation or member were an issuer of equity securities referred to in such section.

(2) EXPATRIATED CORPORATION; EXPATRIATION DATE.—

(A) EXPATRIATED CORPORATION.—The term "expatriated corporation" means any corporation which is an expatriated entity (as defined in section 7874(a)(2)). Such term includes any predecessor or successor of such a corporation.

(B) EXPATRIATION DATE.—The term "expatriation date" means, with respect to a corporation, the date on which the corporation first becomes an expatriated corporation.

(3) SPECIFIED STOCK COMPENSATION.—

(A) IN GENERAL.—The term "specified stock compensation" means payment (or right to payment) granted by the expatriated corporation (or by any member of the expanded affiliated group which includes such corporation) to any person in connection with the performance of services by a disqualified individual for such corporation or member if the value of such payment or right is based on (or determined by reference to) the value (or change in value) of stock in such corporation (or any such member).

(B) EXCEPTIONS.—Such term shall not include—

(i) any option to which part II of subchapter D of chapter 1 applies, or

(ii) any payment or right to payment from a plan referred to in section 280G(b)(6).

(4) EXPANDED AFFILIATED GROUP.—The term "expanded affiliated group" means an affiliated group (as defined in section 1504(a) without regard to section 1504(b)(3)); except that section 1504(a) shall be applied by substituting "more than 50 percent" for "at least 80 percent" each place it appears.

[Sec. 4985(f)]

(f) SPECIAL RULES.—For purposes of this section—

(1) CANCELLATION OF RESTRICTION.—The cancellation of a restriction which by its terms will never lapse shall be treated as a grant.

(2) PAYMENT OR REIMBURSEMENT OF TAX BY CORPORATION TREATED AS SPECIFIED STOCK COMPENSATION.—Any payment of the tax imposed by this section directly or indirectly by the expatriated corporation or by any member of the expanded affiliated group which includes such corporation—

(A) shall be treated as specified stock compensation, and

(B) shall not be allowed as a deduction under any provision of chapter 1.

(3) CERTAIN RESTRICTIONS IGNORED.—Whether there is specified stock compensation, and the value thereof, shall be determined without regard to any restriction other than a restriction which by its terms will never lapse.

(4) PROPERTY TRANSFERS.—Any transfer of property shall be treated as a payment and any right to a transfer of property shall be treated as a right to a payment.

(5) OTHER ADMINISTRATIVE PROVISIONS.—For purposes of subtitle F, any tax imposed by this section shall be treated as a tax imposed by subtitle A.

[Sec. 4985(g)]

(g) REGULATIONS.—The Secretary shall prescribe such regulations as may be necessary or appropriate to carry out the purposes of this section.

SUBTITLE F—PROCEDURE AND ADMINISTRATION

CHAPTER 61—INFORMATION AND RETURNS

SUBCHAPTER A—RETURNS AND RECORDS

PART II—TAX RETURNS OR STATEMENTS

Subpart A—General Requirement

[Sec. 6011]

SEC. 6011. GENERAL REQUIREMENT OF RETURN, STATEMENT, OR LIST.

* * *

[Sec. 6011(c)]

(c) RETURNS, ETC., OF DISCS AND FORMER DISCS AND FORMER FSC'S.—

(1) RECORDS AND INFORMATION.—A DISC, former DISC, or former FSC (as defined in section 922 as in effect before its repeal by the FSC Repeal and Extraterritorial Income Exclusion Act of 2000) shall for the taxable year—

(A) furnish such information to persons who were shareholders at any time during such taxable year, and to the Secretary, and

(B) keep such records, as may be required by regulations prescribed by the Secretary.

(2) RETURNS.—A DISC shall file for the taxable year such returns as may be prescribed by the Secretary by forms or regulations.

* * *

[Sec. 6011(e)]

(e) REGULATIONS REQUIRING RETURNS ON MAGNETIC MEDIA, ETC.—

* * *

(4) SPECIAL RULE FOR RETURNS FILED BY FINANCIAL INSTITUTIONS WITH RESPECT TO WITHHOLDING ON FOREIGN TRANSFERS.—The numerical limitation under paragraph (2)(A) shall not apply to any return filed by a financial institution (as defined in section 1471(d)(5)) with respect to tax for which such institution is made liable under section 1461 or 1474(a).

* * *

[Sec. 6013]

SEC. 6013. JOINT RETURNS OF INCOME TAX BY HUSBAND AND WIFE.

* * *

[Sec. 6013(g)]

(g) ELECTION TO TREAT NONRESIDENT ALIEN INDIVIDUAL AS RESIDENT OF THE UNITED STATES.—

(1) IN GENERAL.—A nonresident alien individual with respect to whom this subsection is in effect for the taxable year shall be treated as a resident of the United States—

(A) for purposes of chapter 1 for all of such taxable year, and

(B) for purposes of chapter 24 (relating to wage withholding) for payments of wages made during such taxable year.

(2) INDIVIDUALS WITH RESPECT TO WHOM THIS SUBSECTION IS IN EFFECT.—This subsection shall be in effect with respect to any individual who, at the close of the taxable year for which an election under this subsection was made, was a nonresident alien individual married to a citizen or resident of the United States, if both of them made such election to have the benefits of this subsection apply to them.

(3) DURATION OF ELECTION.—An election under this subsection shall apply to the taxable year for which made and to all subsequent taxable years until terminated under paragraph (4) or (5); except that any such election shall not apply for any taxable year if neither spouse is a citizen or resident of the United States at any time during such year.

(4) TERMINATION OF ELECTION.—An election under this subsection shall terminate at the earliest of the following times:

(A) REVOCATION BY TAXPAYERS.—If either taxpayer revokes the election, as of the first taxable year for which the last day prescribed by law for filing the return of tax under chapter 1 has not yet occurred.

(B) DEATH.—In the case of the death of either spouse, as of the beginning of the first taxable year of the spouse who survives following the taxable year in which such death occurred; except that if the spouse who survives is a citizen or resident of the United States who is a surviving spouse entitled to the benefits of section 2, the time provided by this subparagraph shall be as of the close of the last taxable year for which such individual is entitled to the benefits of section 2.

(C) LEGAL SEPARATION.—In the case of the legal separation of the couple under a decree of divorce or of separate maintenance, as of the beginning of the taxable year in which such legal separation occurs.

(D) TERMINATION BY SECRETARY.—At the time provided in paragraph (5).

(5) TERMINATION BY SECRETARY.—The Secretary may terminate any election under this subsection for any taxable year if he determines that either spouse has failed—

(A) to keep such books and records,

(B) to grant such access to such books and records, or

(C) to supply such other information,

as may be reasonably necessary to ascertain the amount of liability for taxes under chapter 1 of either spouse for such taxable year.

(6) ONLY ONE ELECTION.—If any election under this subsection for any two individuals is terminated under paragraph (4) or (5) for any taxable year, such two individuals shall be ineligible to make an election under this subsection for any subsequent taxable year.

[Sec. 6013(h)]

(h) JOINT RETURN, ETC., FOR YEAR IN WHICH NONRESIDENT ALIEN BECOMES RESIDENT OF UNITED STATES.—

(1) IN GENERAL.—If—

(A) any individual is a nonresident alien individual at the beginning of any taxable year but is a resident of the United States at the close of such taxable year,

(B) at the close of such taxable year, such individual is married to a citizen or resident of the United States, and

(C) both individuals elect the benefits of this subsection at the time and in the manner prescribed by the Secretary by regulation,

then the individual referred to in subparagraph (A) shall be treated as a resident of the United States for purposes of chapter 1 for all of such taxable year, and for purposes of chapter 24 (relating to wage withholding) for payments of wages made during such taxable year.

(2) ONLY ONE ELECTION.—If any election under this subsection applies for any 2 individuals for any taxable year, such 2 individuals shall be ineligible to make an election under this subsection for any subsequent taxable year.

PART III—INFORMATION RETURNS

Subpart A—Information Concerning Persons Subject to Special Provisions

[Sec. 6031]

SEC. 6031. RETURN OF PARTNERSHIP INCOME.

[Sec. 6031(a)]

(a) GENERAL RULE.—Every partnership (as defined in section 761(a)) shall make a return for each taxable year, stating specifically the items of its gross income and the deductions allowable by subtitle A, and such other information for the purpose of carrying out the provisions of subtitle A as the Secretary may by forms and regulations prescribe, and shall include in the return the names and addresses of the individuals who would be entitled to share in the taxable income if distributed and the amount of the distributive share of each individual.

***

[Sec. 6031(e)]

(e) FOREIGN PARTNERSHIPS.—

(1) EXCEPTION FOR FOREIGN PARTNERSHIP.—Except as provided in paragraph (2), the preceding provisions of this section shall not apply to a foreign partnership.

(2) CERTAIN FOREIGN PARTNERSHIPS REQUIRED TO FILE RETURN.—Except as provided in regulations prescribed by the Secretary, this section shall apply to a foreign partnership for any taxable year if for such year, such partnership has—

(A) gross income derived from sources within the United States, or

(B) gross income which is effectively connected with the conduct of a trade or business within the United States.

The Secretary may provide simplified filing procedures for foreign partnerships to which this section applies.

***

[Sec. 6038]

SEC. 6038. INFORMATION WITH RESPECT TO CERTAIN FOREIGN CORPORATIONS.

[Sec. 6038(a)]

(a) REQUIREMENT.—

(1) IN GENERAL.—Every United States person shall furnish, with respect to any foreign business entity which such person controls, such information as the Secretary may prescribe relating to—

(A) the name, the principal place of business, and the nature of business of such entity, and the country under whose laws such entity is incorporated (or organized in the case of a partnership);

(B) in the case of a foreign corporation, its post-1986 undistributed earnings (as defined in section 902(c));

(C) a balance sheet for such entity listing assets, liabilities, and capital;

(D) transactions between such entity and—

(i) such person,

(ii) any corporation or partnership which such person controls, and

(iii) any United States person owning, at the time the transaction takes place—

(I) in the case of a foreign corporation, 10 percent or more of the value of any class of stock outstanding of such corporation, and

(II) in the case of a foreign partnership, at least a 10-percent interest in such partnership; and

(E)(i) in the case of a foreign corporation, a description of the various classes of stock outstanding, and a list showing the name and address of, and number of shares held by, each United States person who is a shareholder of record owning at any time during the annual accounting period 5 percent or more in value of any class of stock outstanding of such foreign corporation, and

(ii) information comparable to the information described in clause (i) in the case of a foreign partnership.

The Secretary may also require the furnishing of any other information which is similar or related in nature to that specified in the preceding sentence or which the Secretary determines to be appropriate to carry out the provisions of this title.

(2) PERIOD FOR WHICH INFORMATION IS TO BE FURNISHED, ETC.—The information required under paragraph (1) shall be furnished for the annual accounting period of the foreign business entity ending with or within the United States person's taxable year. The information so required shall be furnished at such time and in such manner as the Secretary shall prescribe.

(3) LIMITATION.—No information shall be required to be furnished under this subsection with respect to any foreign business entity for any annual accounting period unless the Secretary has prescribed the furnishing of such information on or before the first day of such annual accounting period.

(4) INFORMATION REQUIRED FROM CERTAIN SHAREHOLDERS IN CERTAIN CASES.—If any foreign corporation is treated as a controlled foreign corporation for any purpose under subpart F of part III of subchapter N of chapter 1, the Secretary may require any United States person treated as a United States shareholder of such corporation for any purpose under subpart F to furnish the information required under paragraph (1).

(5) INFORMATION REQUIRED FROM 10-PERCENT PARTNER OF CONTROLLED FOREIGN PARTNERSHIP.—In the case of a foreign partnership which is controlled by United States persons holding at least 10-percent interests (but not by any one United States person), the Secretary may require each United States person who holds a 10-percent interest in such partnership to furnish information relating to such partnership, including information relating to such partner's ownership interests in the partnership and allocations to such partner of partnership items.

[Sec. 6038(b)]

(b) DOLLAR PENALTY FOR FAILURE TO FURNISH INFORMATION.—

(1) IN GENERAL.—If any person fails to furnish, within the time prescribed under paragraph (2) of subsection (a), any information with respect to any foreign business entity required under paragraph (1) of subsection (a), such person shall pay a penalty of $10,000 for each annual accounting period with respect to which such failure exists.

(2) INCREASE IN PENALTY WHERE FAILURE CONTINUES AFTER NOTIFICATION.—If any failure described in paragraph (1) continues for more than 90 days after the day on which the Secretary mails notice of such failure to the United States person, such person shall pay a penalty (in addition to the amount required under paragraph (1)) of $10,000 for each 30-day period (or fraction thereof) during which such failure continues with respect to any annual accounting period after the expiration of such 90-day period. The increase in any penalty under this paragraph shall not exceed $50,000.

[Sec. 6038(c)]

(c) PENALTY OF REDUCING FOREIGN TAX CREDIT.—

(1) IN GENERAL.—If a United States person fails to furnish, within the time prescribed under paragraph (2) of subsection (a), any information with respect to any foreign business entity required under paragraph (1) of subsection (a), then—

(A) in applying section 901 (relating to taxes of foreign countries and possessions of the United States) to such United States person for the taxable year, the amount of taxes (other than taxes reduced under subparagraph (B)) paid or deemed paid (other than those deemed paid under section 904(c)) to any foreign country or possession of the United States for the taxable year shall be reduced by 10 percent, and

(B) in the case of a foreign business entity which is a foreign corporation, in applying section 960 to any such United States person which is a corporation (or to any person who acquires from any other person any portion of the interest of such other person in any such foreign corporation, but only to the extent of such portion) for any taxable year, the amount of taxes paid or deemed paid by each foreign corporation with respect to which such person is required to furnish information during the annual accounting period or periods with respect to which such information is required under paragraph (2) of subsection (a) shall be reduced by 10 percent.

If such failure continues 90 days or more after notice of such failure by the Secretary to the United States person, then the amount of the reduction under this paragraph shall be 10 percent plus an additional 5 percent for each 3-month period, or fraction thereof, during which such failure to furnish information continues after the expiration of such 90-day period.

(2) LIMITATION.—The amount of the reduction under paragraph (1) for each failure to furnish information with respect to a foreign business entity required under subsection (a)(1) shall not exceed whichever of the following amounts is the greater:

(A) $10,000, or

(B) the income of the foreign business entity for its annual accounting period with respect to which the failure occurs.

(3) COORDINATION WITH SUBSECTION (b).—The amount of the reduction which (but for this paragraph) would be made under paragraph (1) with respect to any annual accounting period shall be reduced by the amount of the penalty imposed by subsection (b) with respect to such period.

(4) SPECIAL RULES.—

(A) No taxes shall be reduced under this subsection more than once for the same failure.

(B) For purposes of this subsection and subsection (b), the time prescribed under paragraph (2) of subsection (a) to furnish information (and the beginning of the 90-day period after notice by the Secretary) shall be treated as being not earlier than the last day on which (as shown to the satisfaction of the Secretary) reasonable cause existed for failure to furnish such information.

[Sec. 6038(d)]

(d) TWO OR MORE PERSONS REQUIRED TO FURNISH INFORMATION WITH RESPECT TO SAME FOREIGN BUSINESS ENTITY.—Where, but for this subsection, two or more United States persons would be required to furnish information under subsection (a) with respect to the same foreign business entity for the same period, the Secretary may by regulations provide that such information shall be required only from one person. To the extent practicable, the determination of which person shall furnish the information shall be made on the basis of actual ownership of stock.

[Sec. 6038(e)]

(e) DEFINITIONS.—For purposes of this section—

(1) FOREIGN BUSINESS ENTITY.—The term "foreign business entity" means a foreign corporation and a foreign partnership.

(2) CONTROL OF CORPORATION.—A person is in control of a corporation if such person owns stock possessing more than 50 percent of the total combined voting power of all classes of stock entitled to vote, or more than 50 percent of the total value of shares of all classes of stock, of a corporation. If a person is in control (within the meaning of the preceding sentence) of a corporation which in turn owns more than 50 percent of the total combined voting power of all classes of stock entitled to vote of another corporation, or owns more than 50 percent of the total value of the shares of all classes of stock of another corporation, then such person shall be treated as in control of such other corporation. For purposes of this paragraph, the rules prescribed by section 318(a) for determining ownership of stock shall apply; except that—

(A) subparagraphs (A), (B), and (C) of section 318(a)(3) shall not be applied so as to consider a United States person as owning stock which is owned by a person who is not a United States person, and

(B) in applying subparagraph (C) of section 318(a)(2), the phrase "10 percent" shall be substituted for the phrase "50 percent" used in subparagraph (C).

(3) PARTNERSHIP-RELATED DEFINITIONS.—

(A) CONTROL.—A person is in control of a partnership if such person owns directly or indirectly more than a 50 percent interest in such partnership.

(B) 50-PERCENT INTEREST.—For purposes of subparagraph (A), a 50-percent interest in a partnership is—

(i) an interest equal to 50 percent of the capital interest, or 50 percent of the profits interest, in such partnership, or

(ii) to the extent provided in regulations, an interest to which 50 percent of the deductions or losses of such partnership are allocated.

For purposes of the preceding sentence, rules similar to the rules of section 267(c) (other than paragraph (3)) shall apply.

(C) 10-PERCENT INTEREST.—A 10-percent interest in a partnership is an interest which would be described in subparagraph (B) if "10 percent" were substituted for "50 percent" each place it appears.

(4) ANNUAL ACCOUNTING PERIOD.—The annual accounting period of a foreign business entity is the annual period on the basis of which such foreign business entity regularly computes its income in taxable year of such foreign business entity shall be treated as its annual accounting period.

[Sec. 6038(f)]

(f) CROSS REFERENCES.—

(1) For provisions relating to penalties for violations of this section, see section 7203.

(2) For definition of the term "United States person", see section 7701(a)(30).

[Sec. 6038A]

SEC. 6038A. INFORMATION WITH RESPECT TO CERTAIN FOREIGN-OWNED CORPORATIONS.

[Sec. 6038A(a)]

(a) REQUIREMENT.—If, at any time during a taxable year, a corporation (hereinafter in this section referred to as the "reporting corporation")—

(1) is a domestic corporation, and

(2) is 25-percent foreign-owned,

such corporation shall furnish, at such time and in such manner as the Secretary shall by regulations prescribe, the information described in subsection (b) and such corporation shall maintain (in the location, in the manner, and to the extent prescribed in regulations) such records as may be appropriate to determine the correct treatment of transactions with related parties as the Secretary shall by regulations prescribe (or shall cause another person to so maintain such records).

[Sec. 6038A(b)]

(b) REQUIRED INFORMATION.—

(1) IN GENERAL.—For purposes of subsection (a), the information described in this subsection is such information as the Secretary prescribes by regulations relating to—

(A) the name, principal place of business, nature of business, and country or countries in which organized or resident, of each person which—

(i) is a related party to the reporting corporation, and

(ii) had any transaction with the reporting corporation during its taxable year,

(B) the manner in which the reporting corporation is related to each person referred to in subparagraph (A), and

(C) transactions between the reporting corporation and each foreign person which is a related party to the reporting corporation.

(2) ADDITIONAL INFORMATION REGARDING BASE EROSION PAYMENTS.—For purposes of subsection (a) and section 6038C, if the reporting corporation or the foreign corporation to whom section 6038C applies is an applicable taxpayer, the information described in this subsection shall include—

(A) such information as the Secretary determines necessary to determine the base erosion minimum tax amount, base erosion payments, and base erosion tax benefits of the taxpayer for purposes of section 59A for the taxable year, and

(B) such other information as the Secretary determines necessary to carry out such section.

For purposes of this paragraph, any term used in this paragraph which is also used in section 59A shall have the same meaning as when used in such section.

[Sec. 6038A(c)]

(c) DEFINITIONS.—For purposes of this section—

(1) 25-PERCENT FOREIGN-OWNED.—A corporation is 25-percent foreign-owned if at least 25 percent of—

(A) the total voting power of all classes of stock of such corporation entitled to vote, or

(B) the total value of all classes of stock of such corporation,

is owned at any time during the taxable year by 1 foreign person (hereinafter in this section referred to as a "25-percent foreign shareholder").

(2) RELATED PARTY.—The term "related party" means—

(A) any 25-percent foreign shareholder of the reporting corporation,

(B) any person who is related (within the meaning of section 267(b) or 707(b)(1)) to the reporting corporation or to a 25-percent foreign shareholder of the reporting corporation, and

(C) any other person who is related (within the meaning of section 482) to the reporting corporation.

(3) FOREIGN PERSON.—The term "foreign person" means any person who is not a United States person. For purposes of the preceding sentence, the term "United States person" has the meaning given to such term by section 7701(a)(30), except that any individual who is a citizen of any possession of the United States (but not otherwise a citizen of the United States) and who is not a resident of the United States shall not be treated as a United States person.

(4) RECORDS.—The term "records" includes any books, papers, or other data.

(5) SECTION 318 TO APPLY.—Section 318 shall apply for purposes of paragraph (1) and (2), except that—

(A) "10 percent" shall be substituted for "50 percent" in section 318(a)(2)(C), and

(B) subparagraphs (A), (B), and (C) of section 318(a)(3) shall not be applied so as to consider a United States person as owning stock which is owned by a person who is not a United States person.

[Sec. 6038A(d)]

(d) PENALTY FOR FAILURE TO FURNISH INFORMATION OR MAINTAIN RECORDS.—

(1) IN GENERAL.—If a reporting corporation—

(A) fails to furnish (within the time prescribed by regulations) any information described in subsection (b), or

(B) fails to maintain (or cause another to maintain) records as required by subsection (a),

such corporation shall pay a penalty of $25,000 for each taxable year with respect to which such failure occurs.

(2) INCREASE IN PENALTY WHERE FAILURE CONTINUES AFTER NOTIFICATION.—If any failure described in paragraph (1) continues for more than 90 days after the day on which the Secretary mails notice of such failure to the reporting corporation, such corporation shall pay a penalty (in addition to the amount required under paragraph (1)) of $25,000 for each 30-day period (or fraction thereof) during which such failure continues after the expiration of such 90-day period.

(3) REASONABLE CAUSE.—For purposes of this subsection, the time prescribed by regulations to furnish information or maintain records (and the beginning of the 90-day period after notice by the Secretary) shall be treated as not earlier than the last day on which (as shown to the satisfaction of the Secretary) reasonable cause existed for failure to furnish the information or maintain the records.

[Sec. 6038A(e)]

(e) ENFORCEMENT OF REQUESTS FOR CERTAIN RECORDS.—

(1) AGREEMENT TO TREAT CORPORATION AS AGENT.—The rules of paragraph (3) shall apply to any transaction between the reporting corporation and any related party who is a foreign person unless such related party agrees (in such manner and at such time as the Secretary shall prescribe) to authorize the reporting corporation to act as such related party's limited agent solely for purposes of applying sections 7602, 7603, and 7604 with respect to any request by the Secretary to examine records or produce testimony related to any such transaction or with respect to any summons by the Secretary for such records or testimony. The appearance of persons or production of records by reason of the reporting corporation being such an agent shall not subject such persons or records to legal process for any purpose other than determining the correct treatment under this title of any transaction between the reporting corporation and such related party.

(2) RULES WHERE INFORMATION NOT FURNISHED.—If—

(A) for purposes of determining the correct treatment under this title of any transaction between the reporting corporation and a related party who is a foreign person, the Secretary issues a summons to such corporation to produce (either directly or as agent for such related party) any records or testimony,

(B) such summons is not quashed in a proceeding begun under paragraph (4) and is not determined to be invalid in a proceeding begun under section 7604(b) to enforce such summons, and

(C) the reporting corporation does not substantially comply in a timely manner with such summons and the Secretary has sent by certified or registered mail a notice to such reporting corporation that such reporting corporation has not so substantially complied,

the Secretary may apply the rules of paragraph (3) with respect to such transaction (whether or not the Secretary begins a proceeding to enforce such summons). If the reporting corporation fails to maintain (or cause another to maintain) records as required by subsection (a), and by reason of that failure, the summons is quashed in a proceeding described in subparagraph (B) or the reporting corporation is not able to provide the records requested in the summons, the Secretary may apply the rules of paragraph (3) with respect to any transaction to which the records relate.

(3) APPLICABLE RULES IN CASES OF NONCOMPLIANCE.—If the rules of this paragraph apply to any transaction—

(A) the amount of the deduction allowed under subtitle A for any amount paid or incurred by the reporting corporation to the related party in connection with such transaction, and

(B) the cost to the reporting corporation of any property acquired in such transaction from the related party (or transferred by such corporation in such transaction to the related party),

shall be the amount determined by the Secretary in the Secretary's sole discretion from the Secretary's own knowledge or from such information as the Secretary may obtain through testimony or otherwise.

(4) JUDICIAL PROCEEDINGS.—

(A) PROCEEDINGS TO QUASH.—Notwithstanding any law or rule of law, any reporting corporation to which the Secretary issues a summons referred to in paragraph (2)(A) shall have the right to begin a proceeding to quash such summons not later than the 90th day after such summons was issued. In any such proceeding, the Secretary may seek to compel compliance with such summons.

(B) REVIEW OF SECRETARIAL DETERMINATION OF NONCOMPLIANCE.—Notwithstanding any law or rule of law, any reporting corporation which has been notified by the Secretary that the Secretary has determined that such corporation has not substantially complied with a summons referred to in paragraph (2) shall have the right to begin a proceeding to review such determination not later than the 90th day after the day on which the notice referred to in paragraph (2)(C) was mailed. If such a proceeding is not begun on or before such 90th day, such determination by the Secretary shall be binding and shall not be reviewed by any court.

(C) JURISDICTION.—The United States district court for the district in which the person (to whom the summons is issued) resides or is found shall have jurisdiction to hear any proceeding brought under subparagraph (A) or (B). Any order or other determination in such a proceeding shall be treated as a final order which may be appealed.

(D) SUSPENSION OF STATUTE OF LIMITATIONS.—If the reporting corporation brings an action under subparagraph (A) or (B), the running of any period of limitations under section 6501 (relating to assessment and collection of tax) or under section 6531 (relating to criminal prosecutions) with respect to any affected taxable year shall be suspended for the period during which such proceeding, and appeals therein, are pending. In no event shall any such period expire before the 90th day after the day on which there is a final determination in such proceeding. For purposes of this subparagraph, the term "affected taxable year" means any taxable year if the determination of the amount of tax imposed for such taxable year is affected by the treatment of the transaction to which the summons relates.

[Sec. 6038A(f)]

(f) CROSS REFERENCE.—

For provisions relating to criminal penalties for violation of this section, see section 7203.

[Sec. 6038B]

SEC. 6038B. NOTICE OF CERTAIN TRANSFERS TO FOREIGN PERSONS.

[Sec. 6038B(a)]

(a) IN GENERAL.—Each United States person who—

(1) transfers property to—

(A) a foreign corporation in an exchange described in section 332, 351, 354, 355, 356, or 361, or

(B) a foreign partnership in a contribution described in section 721 or in any other contribution described in regulations prescribed by the Secretary, or

(2) makes a distribution described in section 336 to a person who is not a United States person,

shall furnish to the Secretary, at such time and in such manner as the Secretary shall by regulations prescribe, such information with respect to such exchange or distribution as the Secretary may require in such regulations.

[Sec. 6038B(b)]

(b) EXCEPTIONS FOR CERTAIN TRANSFERS TO FOREIGN PARTNERSHIPS; SPECIAL RULE.—

(1) EXCEPTIONS.—Subsection (a)(1)(B) shall apply to a transfer by a United States person to a foreign partnership only if—

(A) the United States person holds (immediately after the transfer) directly or indirectly at least a 10-percent interest (as defined in section 6046A(d)) in the partnership, or

(B) the value of the property transferred (when added to the value of the property transferred by such person or any related person to such partnership or a related partnership during the 12-month period ending on the date of the transfer) exceeds $100,000.

For purposes of the preceding sentence, the value of any transferred property is its fair market value at the time of its transfer.

(2) SPECIAL RULE.—If by reason of an adjustment under section 482 or otherwise, a contribution described in subsection (a)(1) is deemed to have been made, such contribution shall be treated for purposes of this section as having been made not earlier than the date specified by the Secretary.

[Sec. 6038B(c)]

(c) PENALTY FOR FAILURE TO FURNISH INFORMATION.—

(1) IN GENERAL.—If any United States person fails to furnish the information described in subsection (a) at the time and in the manner required by regulations, such person shall pay a penalty equal to 10 percent of the fair market value of the property at the time of the exchange (and, in the case of a contribution described in subsection (a)(1)(B), such person shall recognize gain as if the contributed property had been sold for such value at the time of such contribution).

(2) REASONABLE CAUSE EXCEPTION.—Paragraph (1) shall not apply to any failure if the United States person shows such failure is due to reasonable cause and not to willful neglect.

(3) LIMIT ON PENALTY.—The penalty under paragraph (1) with respect to any exchange shall not exceed $100,000 unless the failure with respect to such exchange was due to intentional disregard.

[Sec. 6038C]

SEC. 6038C. INFORMATION WITH RESPECT TO FOREIGN CORPORATIONS ENGAGED IN U.S. BUSINESS.

[Sec. 6038C(a)]

(a) REQUIREMENT.—If a foreign corporation (hereinafter in this section referred to as the "reporting corporation") is engaged in a trade or business within the United States at any time during a taxable year—

(1) such corporation shall furnish (at such time and in such manner as the Secretary shall by regulations prescribe) the information described in subsection (b), and

(2) such corporation shall maintain (at the location, in the manner, and to the extent prescribed in regulations) such records as may be appropriate to determine the liability of such corporation for tax under this title as the Secretary shall by regulations prescribe (or shall cause another person to so maintain such records).

[Sec. 6038C(b)]

(b) REQUIRED INFORMATION.—For purposes of subsection (a), the information described in this subsection is—

(1) the information described in section 6038A(b), and

(2) such other information as the Secretary may prescribe by regulations relating to any item not directly connected with a transaction for which information is required under paragraph (1).

[Sec. 6038C(c)]

(c) PENALTY FOR FAILURE TO FURNISH INFORMATION OR MAINTAIN RECORDS.—The provisions of subsection (d) of section 6038A shall apply to—

(1) any failure to furnish (within the time prescribed by regulations) any information described in subsection (b), and

(2) any failure to maintain (or cause another to maintain) records as required by subsection (a),

in the same manner as if such failure were a failure to comply with the provisions of section 6038A.

[Sec. 6038C(d)]

(d) ENFORCEMENT OF REQUESTS FOR CERTAIN RECORDS.—

(1) AGREEMENT TO TREAT CORPORATION AS AGENT.—The rules of paragraph (3) shall apply to any transaction between the reporting corporation and any related party who is a foreign person unless such related party agrees (in such manner and at such time as the Secretary shall prescribe) to authorize the reporting corporation to act as such related party's limited agent solely for purposes of applying sections 7602, 7603, and 7604 with respect to any request by the Secretary to examine records or produce testimony related to any such transaction or with respect to any summons by the Secretary for such records or testimony. The appearance of persons or production of records by reason of the reporting corporation being such an agent shall not subject such persons or records to legal process for any purpose other than determining the correct treatment under this title of any transaction between the reporting corporation and such related party.

(2) RULES WHERE INFORMATION NOT FURNISHED.—If—

(A) for purposes of determining the amount of the reporting corporation's liability for tax under this title, the Secretary issues a summons to such corporation to produce (either directly or as an agent for a related party who is a foreign person) any records or testimony,

(B) such summons is not quashed in a proceeding begun under paragraph (4) of section 6038A(e) (as made applicable by paragraph (4) of this subsection) and is not determined to be invalid in a proceeding begun under section 7604(b) to enforce such summons, and

(C) the reporting corporation does not substantially comply in a timely manner with such summons and the Secretary has sent by certified or registered mail a notice to such reporting corporation that such reporting corporation has not so substantially complied, the Secretary may apply the rules of paragraph (3) with respect to any transaction or item to which such summons relates (whether or not the Secretary begins a proceeding to enforce such summons). If the reporting corporation fails to maintain (or cause another to maintain) records as required by subsection (a), and by reason of that failure, the summons is quashed in a proceeding described in subparagraph (B) or the reporting corporation is not able to provide the records requested in the summons, the Secretary may apply the rules of paragraph (3) with respect to any transaction or item to which the records relate.

(3) APPLICABLE RULES.—If the rules of this paragraph apply to any transaction or item, the treatment of such transaction (or the amount and treatment of any such item) shall be determined by the Secretary in the Secretary's sole discretion from the Secretary's own knowledge or from such information as the Secretary may obtain through testimony or otherwise.

(4) JUDICIAL PROCEEDINGS.—The provisions of section 6038A(e)(4) shall apply with respect to any summons referred to in paragraph (2)(A); except that subparagraph (D) of such section shall be applied by substituting "transaction or item" for "transaction".

[Sec. 6038C(e)]

(e) DEFINITIONS.—For purposes of this section, the terms "related party", "foreign person", and "records" have the respective meanings given to such terms by section 6038A(c).

[Sec. 6038D]

SEC. 6038D. INFORMATION WITH RESPECT TO FOREIGN FINANCIAL ASSETS.

[Sec. 6038D(a)]

(a) IN GENERAL.—Any individual who, during any taxable year, holds any interest in a specified foreign financial asset shall attach to such person's return of tax imposed by subtitle A for such taxable year the information described in subsection (c) with respect to each such asset if the aggregate value of all such assets exceeds $50,000 (or such higher dollar amount as the Secretary may prescribe).

[Sec. 6038D(b)]

(b) SPECIFIED FOREIGN FINANCIAL ASSETS.—For purposes of this section, the term "specified foreign financial asset" means—

(1) any financial account (as defined in section 1471(d)(2)) maintained by a foreign financial institution (as defined in section 1471(d)(4)), and

(2) any of the following assets which are not held in an account maintained by a financial institution (as defined in section 1471(d)(5))—

(A) any stock or security issued by a person other than a United States person,

(B) any financial instrument or contract held for investment that has an issuer or counterparty which is other than a United States person, and

(C) any interest in a foreign entity (as defined in section 1473).

[Sec. 6038D(c)]

(c) REQUIRED INFORMATION.—The information described in this subsection with respect to any asset is:

(1) In the case of any account, the name and address of the financial institution in which such account is maintained and the number of such account.

(2) In the case of any stock or security, the name and address of the issuer and such information as is necessary to identify the class or issue of which such stock or security is a part.

(3) In the case of any other instrument, contract, or interest—

(A) such information as is necessary to identify such instrument, contract, or interest, and

(B) the names and addresses of all issuers and counterparties with respect to such instrument, contract, or interest.

(4) The maximum value of the asset during the taxable year.

[Sec. 6038D(d)]

(d) PENALTY FOR FAILURE TO DISCLOSE.—

(1) IN GENERAL.—If any individual fails to furnish the information described in subsection (c) with respect to any taxable year at the time and in the manner described in subsection (a), such person shall pay a penalty of $10,000.

(2) INCREASE IN PENALTY WHERE FAILURE CONTINUES AFTER NOTIFICATION.—If any failure described in paragraph (1) continues for more than 90 days after the day on which the Secretary mails notice of such failure to the individual, such individual shall pay a penalty (in addition to the penalties under paragraph (1)) of $10,000 for each 30-day period (or fraction thereof) during which such failure continues after the expiration of such 90-day period. The penalty imposed under this paragraph with respect to any failure shall not exceed $50,000.

[Sec. 6038D(e)]

(e) PRESUMPTION THAT VALUE OF SPECIFIED FOREIGN FINANCIAL ASSETS EXCEEDS DOLLAR THRESHOLD.—If—

(1) the Secretary determines that an individual has an interest in one or more specified foreign financial assets, and

(2) such individual does not provide sufficient information to demonstrate the aggregate value of such assets,

then the aggregate value of such assets shall be treated as being in excess of $50,000 (or such higher dollar amount as the Secretary prescribes for purposes of subsection (a)) for purposes of assessing the penalties imposed under this section.

[Sec. 6038D(f)]

(f) APPLICATION TO CERTAIN ENTITIES.—To the extent provided by the Secretary in regulations or other guidance, the provisions of this section shall apply to any domestic entity which is formed or availed of for purposes of holding, directly or indirectly, specified foreign financial assets, in the same manner as if such entity were an individual.

[Sec. 6038D(g)]

(g) REASONABLE CAUSE EXCEPTION.—No penalty shall be imposed by this section on any failure which is shown to be due to reasonable cause and not due to willful neglect. The fact that a foreign jurisdiction would impose a civil or criminal penalty on the taxpayer (or any other person) for disclosing the required information is not reasonable cause.

[Sec. 6038D(h)]

(h) REGULATIONS.—The Secretary shall prescribe such regulations or other guidance as may be necessary or appropriate to carry out the purposes of this section, including regulations or other guidance which provide appropriate exceptions from the application of this section in the case of—

(1) classes of assets identified by the Secretary, including any assets with respect to which the Secretary determines that disclosure under this section would be duplicative of other disclosures,

(2) nonresident aliens, and

(3) bona fide residents of any possession of the United States.

[Sec. 6039C]

SEC. 6039C. RETURNS WITH RESPECT TO FOREIGN PERSONS HOLDING DIRECT INVESTMENTS IN UNITED STATES REAL PROPERTY INTERESTS.

[Sec. 6039C(a)]

(a) GENERAL RULE.—To the extent provided in regulations, any foreign person holding direct investments in United States real property interests for the calendar year shall make a return setting forth—

(1) the name and address of such person,

(2) a description of all United States real property interests held by such person at any time during the calendar year, and

(3) such other information as the Secretary may by regulations prescribe.

[Sec. 6039C(b)]

(b) DEFINITION OF FOREIGN PERSONS HOLDING DIRECT INVESTMENTS IN UNITED STATES REAL PROPERTY INTERESTS.—For purposes of this section, a foreign person shall be treated as holding direct investments in United States real property interests during any calendar year if—

(1) such person did not engage in a trade or business in the United States at any time during such calendar year, and

(2) the fair market value of the United States real property interests held directly by such person at any time during such year equals or exceeds $50,000.

[Sec. 6039C(c)]

(c) DEFINITIONS AND SPECIAL RULES.—For purposes of this section—

(1) UNITED STATES REAL PROPERTY INTEREST.—The term "United States real property interest" has the meaning given to such term by section 897(c).

(2) FOREIGN PERSON.—The term "foreign person" means any person who is not a United States person.

(3) ATTRIBUTION OF OWNERSHIP.—For purposes of subsection (b)(2)—

(A) INTERESTS HELD BY PARTNERSHIPS, ETC.—United States real property interests held by a partnership, trust, or estate shall be treated as owned proportionately by its partners or beneficiaries.

(B) INTERESTS HELD BY FAMILY MEMBERS.—United States real property interests held by the spouse or any minor child of an individual shall be treated as owned by such individual.

(4) TIME AND MANNER OF FILING RETURN.—All returns required to be made under this section shall be made at such time and in such manner as the Secretary shall by regulations prescribe.

[Sec. 6039C(d)]

(d) SPECIAL RULE FOR UNITED STATES INTEREST AND VIRGIN ISLANDS INTEREST.—A nonresident alien individual or foreign corporation subject to tax under section 897(a) (and any person required to withhold tax under section 1445) shall pay any tax and file any return required by this title—

(1) to the United States, in the case of any interest in real property located in the United States and an interest (other than an interest solely as a creditor) in a domestic corporation (with respect to the United States) described in section 897(c)(1)(A)(ii), and

(2) to the Virgin Islands, in the case of any interest in real property located in the Virgin Islands and an interest (other than an interest solely as a creditor) in a domestic corporation (with respect to the Virgin Islands) described in section 897(c)(1)(A)(ii).

[Sec. 6039E]

SEC. 6039E. INFORMATION CONCERNING RESIDENT STATUS.

[Sec. 6039E(a)]

(a) GENERAL RULE.—Notwithstanding any other provision of law, any individual who—

(1) applies for a United States passport (or a renewal thereof), or

(2) applies to be lawfully accorded the privilege of residing permanently in the United States as an immigrant in accordance with the immigration laws,

shall include with any such application a statement which includes the information described in subsection (b).

[Sec. 6039E(b)]

(b) INFORMATION TO BE PROVIDED.—Information required under subsection (a) shall include—

(1) the taxpayer's TIN (if any),

(2) in the case of a passport applicant, any foreign country in which such individual is residing,

(3) in the case of an individual seeking permanent residence, information with respect to whether such individual is required to file a return of the tax imposed by chapter 1 for such individual's most recent 3 taxable years, and

(4) such other information as the Secretary may prescribe.

[Sec. 6039E(c)]

(c) PENALTY.—Any individual failing to provide a statement required under subsection (a) shall be subject to a penalty equal to $500 for each such failure, unless it is shown that such failure is due to reasonable cause and not to willful neglect.

[Sec. 6039E(d)]

(d) INFORMATION TO BE PROVIDED TO SECRETARY.—Notwithstanding any other provision of law, any agency of the United States which collects (or is required to collect) the statement under subsection (a) shall—

(1) provide any such statement to the Secretary, and

(2) provide to the Secretary the name (and any other identifying information) of any individual refusing to comply with the provisions of subsection (a).

Nothing in the preceding sentence shall be construed to require the disclosure of information which is subject to section 245A of the Immigration and Nationality Act (as in effect on the date of the enactment of this sentence).

[Sec. 6039E(e)]

(e) EXEMPTION.—The Secretary may by regulations exempt any class of individuals from the requirements of this section if he determines that applying this section to such individuals is not necessary to carry out the purposes of this section.

[Sec. 6039G]

SEC. 6039G. INFORMATION ON INDIVIDUALS LOSING UNITED STATES CITIZENSHIP.

[Sec. 6039G(a)]

(a) IN GENERAL.—Notwithstanding any other provision of law, any individual to whom section 877(b) or 877A applies for any taxable year shall provide a statement for such taxable year which includes the information described in subsection (b).

[Sec. 6039G(b)]

(b) INFORMATION TO BE PROVIDED.—Information required under subsection (a) shall include—

(1) the taxpayer's TIN,

(2) the mailing address of such individual's principal foreign residence,

(3) the foreign country in which such individual is residing,

(4) the foreign country of which such individual is a citizen,

(5) information detailing the income, assets, and liabilities of such individual,

(6) the number of days during any portion of which that the individual was physically present in the United States during the taxable year, and

(7) such other information as the Secretary may prescribe.

[Sec. 6039G(c)]

(c) PENALTY.—If—

(1) an individual is required to file a statement under subsection (a) for any taxable year, and

(2) fails to file such a statement with the Secretary on or before the date such statement is required to be filed or fails to include all the information required to be shown on the statement or includes incorrect information,

such individual shall pay a penalty of $10,000 unless it is shown that such failure is due to reasonable cause and not to willful neglect.

[Sec. 6039G(d)]

(d) INFORMATION TO BE PROVIDED TO SECRETARY.—Notwithstanding any other provision of law—

(1) any Federal agency or court which collects (or is required to collect) the statement under subsection (a) shall provide to the Secretary—

(A) a copy of any such statement, and

(B) the name (and any other identifying information) of any individual refusing to comply with the provisions of subsection (a),

(2) the Secretary of State shall provide to the Secretary a copy of each certificate as to the loss of American nationality under section 358 of the Immigration and Nationality Act which is approved by the Secretary of State, and

(3) the Federal agency primarily responsible for administering the immigration laws shall provide to the Secretary the name of each lawful permanent resident of the United States (within the meaning of section 7701(b)(6)) whose status as such has been revoked or has been administratively or judicially determined to have been abandoned.

Notwithstanding any other provision of law, not later than 30 days after the close of each calendar quarter, the Secretary shall publish in the Federal Register the name of each individual losing United States citizenship (within the meaning of section 877(a) or 877A) with respect to whom the Secretary receives information under the preceding sentence during such quarter.

Subpart B—Information Concerning Transactions With Other Persons

[Sec. 6041]

SEC. 6041. INFORMATION AT SOURCE.

[Sec. 6041(a)]

(a) PAYMENTS OF $600 OR MORE.—All persons engaged in a trade or business and making payment in the course of such trade or business to another person, of rent, salaries, wages, premiums, annuities, compensations, remunerations, emoluments, or other fixed or determinable gains, profits, and income (other than payments to which section 6042(a)(1), 6044(a)(1), 6047(e)[d], 6049(a), or 6050N(a) applies, and other than payments with respect to which a statement is required under the authority of section 6042(a)(2), 6044(a)(2), or 6045), of $600 or more in any taxable year, or, in the case of such payments made by the United States, the officers or employees of the United States having information as to such payments and required to make returns in regard thereto by the regulations hereinafter provided for, shall render a true and accurate return to the Secretary, under such regulations and in such form and manner and to such extent as may be prescribed by the Secretary, setting forth the amount of such gains, profits, and income, and the name and address of the recipient of such payment.

[Sec. 6041(b)]

(b) COLLECTION OF FOREIGN ITEMS.—In the case of collections of items (not payable in the United States) of interest upon the bonds of foreign countries and interest upon the bonds of and dividends from foreign corporations by any person undertaking as a matter of business or for profit the collection of foreign payments of such interest or dividends by means of coupons, checks, or bills of exchange, such person shall make a return according to the forms or regulations prescribed by the Secretary, setting forth the amount paid and the name and address of the recipient of each such payment.

[Sec. 6041(c)]

(c) RECIPIENT TO FURNISH NAME AND ADDRESS.—When necessary to make effective the provisions of this section, the name and address of the recipient of income shall be furnished upon demand of the person paying the income.

[Sec. 6041(d)]

(d) STATEMENTS TO BE FURNISHED TO PERSONS WITH RESPECT TO WHOM INFORMATION IS REQUIRED.—Every person required to make a return under subsection (a) shall furnish to each person with respect to whom such a return is required a written statement showing—

(1) the name, address, and phone number of the information contact of the person required to make such return, and

(2) the aggregate amount of payments to the person required to be shown on the return.

The written statement required under the preceding sentence shall be furnished to the person on or before January 31 of the year following the calendar year for which the return under subsection (a) was required to be made. To the extent provided in regulations prescribed by the Secretary, this subsection shall also apply to persons required to make returns under subsection (b).

[Sec. 6041(e)]

(e) SECTION DOES NOT APPLY TO CERTAIN TIPS.—This section shall not apply to tips with respect to which section 6053(a) (relating to reporting of tips) applies.

[Sec. 6041(f)]

(f) SECTION DOES NOT APPLY TO CERTAIN HEALTH ARRANGEMENTS.—This section shall not apply to any payment for medical care (as defined in section 213(d)) made under—

(1) a flexible spending arrangement (as defined in section 106(c)(2)), or

(2) a health reimbursement arrangement which is treated as employer-provided coverage under an accident or health plan for purposes of section 106.

[Sec. 6041(g)]

(g) NONQUALIFIED DEFERRED COMPENSATION.—Subsection (a) shall apply to—

(1) any deferrals for the year under a nonqualified deferred compensation plan (within the meaning of section 409A(d)), whether or not paid, except that this paragraph shall not apply to deferrals which are required to be reported under section 6051(a)(13) (without regard to any de minimis exception), and

(2) any amount includible under section 409A and which is not treated as wages under section 3401(a).

[Sec. 6042]

SEC. 6042. RETURNS REGARDING PAYMENTS OF DIVIDENDS AND CORPORATE EARNINGS AND PROFITS.

[Sec. 6042(a)]

(a) REQUIREMENT OF REPORTING.—

(1) IN GENERAL.—Every person—

(A) who makes payments of dividends aggregating $10 or more to any other person during any calendar year, or

(B) who receives payments of dividends as a nominee and who makes payments aggregating $10 or more during any calendar year to any other person with respect to the dividends so received,

shall make a return according to the forms or regulations prescribed by the Secretary, setting forth the aggregate amount of such payments and the name and address of the person to whom paid.

(2) RETURNS REQUIRED BY THE SECRETARY.—Every person who makes payments of dividends aggregating less than $10 to any other person during any calendar year shall, when required by the Secretary, make a return setting forth the aggregate amount of such payments, and the name and address of the person to whom paid.

[Sec. 6042(b)]

(b) DIVIDEND DEFINED.—

(1) GENERAL RULE.—For purposes of this section, the term "dividend" means—

(A) any distribution by a corporation which is a dividend (as defined in section 316); and

(B) any payment made by a stockbroker to any person as a substitute for a dividend (as so defined).

(2) EXCEPTIONS.—For purposes of this section, the term "dividend" does not include any distribution or payment—

(A) to the extent provided in regulations prescribed by the Secretary—

(i) by a foreign corporation, or

(ii) to a foreign corporation, a nonresident alien, or a partnership not engaged in a trade or business in the United States and composed in whole or in part of nonresident aliens, or

(B) except to the extent otherwise provided in regulations prescribed by the Secretary, to any person described in section 6049(b)(4).

(3) SPECIAL RULE.—If the person making any payment described in subsection (a)(1)(A) or (B) is unable to determine the portion of such payment which is a dividend or is paid with respect to a dividend, he shall, for purposes of subsection (a)(1), treat the entire amount of such payment as a dividend or as an amount paid with respect to a dividend.

* * *

[Sec. 6045]

SEC. 6045. RETURNS OF BROKERS.

[Sec. 6045(a)]

(a) GENERAL RULE.—Every person doing business as a broker shall, when required by the Secretary, make a return, in accordance with such regulations as the Secretary may prescribe, showing the name and address of each customer, with such details regarding gross proceeds and such other information as the Secretary may by forms or regulations require with respect to such business.

[Sec. 6045(b)]

(b) STATEMENTS TO BE FURNISHED TO CUSTOMERS.—Every person required to make a return under subsection (a) shall furnish to each customer whose name is required to be set forth in such return a written statement showing—

(1) the name, address and phone number of the information contact of the person required to make such return, and

(2) the information required to be shown on such return with respect to such customer.

The written statement required under the preceding sentence shall be furnished to the customer on or before February 15 of the year following the calendar year for which the return under subsection (a) was required to be made. In the case of a consolidated reporting statement (as defined in regulations) with respect to any customer, any statement which would otherwise be required to be furnished on or before January 31 of a calendar year with respect to any item reportable to the taxpayer shall instead be required to be furnished on or before February 15 of such calendar year if furnished with such consolidated reporting statement.

[Sec. 6045(c)]

(c) DEFINITIONS.—For purposes of this section—

(1) BROKER.—The term "broker" includes—

(A) a dealer,

⋙→ *Caution: Code Sec. 6045(c)(1)(B)-(C), below, prior to amendment by P.L. 117-58, applies to returns required to be filed, and statements required to be furnished, on or before December 31, 2023.*

(B) a barter exchange, and

(C) any other person who (for a consideration) regularly acts as a middleman with respect to property or services.

⋙→ *Caution: Code Sec. 6045(c)(1)(B)-(C), below, as amended by P.L. 117-58, applies to returns required to be filed, and statements required to be furnished, after December 31, 2023.*

(B) a barter exchange,

(C) any person who (for consideration) regularly acts as a middleman with respect to property or services, and

⋙→ *Caution: Code Sec. 6045(c)(1)(D), below, as added by P.L. 117-58, applies to returns required to be filed, and statements required to be furnished, after December 31, 2023.*

(D) any person who (for consideration) is responsible for regularly providing any service effectuating transfers of digital assets on behalf of another person.

A person shall not be treated as a broker with respect to activities consisting of managing a farm on behalf of another person.

(2) CUSTOMER.—The term "customer" means any person for whom the broker has transacted any business.

(3) BARTER EXCHANGE.—The term "barter exchange" means any organization of members providing property or services who jointly contract to trade or barter such property or services.

(4) PERSON.—The term "person" includes any governmental unit and any agency or instrumentality thereof.

[Sec. 6045(d)]

(d) STATEMENTS REQUIRED IN CASE OF CERTAIN SUBSTITUTE PAYMENTS.—If any broker—

(1) transfers securities of a customer for use in a short sale or similar transaction, and

(2) receives (on behalf of the customer) a payment in lieu of—

(A) a dividend,

(B) tax-exempt interest, or

(C) such other items as the Secretary may prescribe by regulations,

during the period such short sale or similar transaction is open, the broker shall furnish such customer a written statement (in the manner as the Secretary shall prescribe by regulations) identifying such payment as being in lieu of the dividend, tax-exempt interest, or such other item. The written statement required under the preceding sentence shall be furnished on or before February 15 of the year following the calendar year in which the payment was made. The Secretary may prescribe regulations which require the broker to make a return which includes the information contained in such written statement.

[Sec. 6045(e)]

(e) RETURN REQUIRED IN THE CASE OF REAL ESTATE TRANSACTIONS.—

(1) IN GENERAL.—In the case of a real estate transaction, the real estate reporting person shall file a return under subsection (a) and a statement under subsection (b) with respect to such transaction.

(2) REAL ESTATE REPORTING PERSON.—For purposes of this subsection, the term "real estate reporting person" means any of the following persons involved in a real estate transaction in the following order:

(A) the person (including any attorney or title company) responsible for closing the transaction,

(B) the mortgage lender,

(C) the seller's broker,

(D) the buyer's broker, or

(E) such other person designated in regulations prescribed by the Secretary.

Any person treated as a real estate reporting person under the preceding sentence shall be treated as a broker for purposes of subsection (c)(1).

(3) PROHIBITION OF SEPARATE CHARGE FOR FILING RETURN.—It shall be unlawful for any real estate reporting person to separately charge any customer for complying with any requirement of paragraph (1). Nothing in this paragraph shall be construed to prohibit the real estate reporting person from taking into account its cost of complying with such requirement in establishing its charge (other than a separate charge for complying with such requirement) to any customer for performing services in the case of a real estate transaction.

(4) ADDITIONAL INFORMATION REQUIRED.—In the case of a real estate transaction involving a residence, the real estate reporting person shall include the following information on the return under subsection (a) and on the statement under subsection (b):

(A) The portion of any real property tax which is treated as a tax imposed on the purchaser by reason of section 164(d)(1)(B).

(B) Whether or not the financing (if any) of the seller was federally-subsidized indebtedness (as defined in section 143(m)(3)).

(5) EXCEPTION FOR SALES OR EXCHANGES OF CERTAIN PRINCIPAL RESIDENCES.—

(A) IN GENERAL.—Paragraph (1) shall not apply to any sale or exchange of a residence for $250,000 or less if the person referred to in paragraph (2) receives written assurance in a form acceptable to the Secretary from the seller that—

(i) such residence is the principal residence (within the meaning of section 121) of the seller,

(ii) if the Secretary requires the inclusion on the return under subsection (a) of information as to whether there is federally subsidized mortgage financing assistance with respect to the mortgage on residences, that there is no such assistance with respect to the mortgage on such residence, and

(iii) the full amount of the gain on such sale or exchange is excludable from gross income under section 121.

If such assurance includes an assurance that the seller is married, the preceding sentence shall be applied by substituting "$500,000" for "$250,000". The Secretary may by regulation increase the dollar amounts under this subparagraph if the Secretary determines that such an increase will not materially reduce revenues to the Treasury.

(B) SELLER.—For purposes of this paragraph, the term "seller" includes the person relinquishing the residence in an exchange.

[Sec. 6045(f)]

(f) RETURN REQUIRED IN THE CASE OF PAYMENTS TO ATTORNEYS.—

(1) IN GENERAL.—Any person engaged in a trade or business and making a payment (in the course of such trade or business) to which this subsection applies shall file a return under subsection (a) and a statement under subsection (b) with respect to such payment.

(2) APPLICATION OF SUBSECTION.—

(A) IN GENERAL.—This subsection shall apply to any payment to an attorney in connection with legal services (whether or not such services are performed for the payor).

(B) EXCEPTION.—This subsection shall not apply to the portion of any payment which is required to be reported under section 6041(a) (or would be so required but for the dollar limitation contained therein) or section 6051.

[Sec. 6045(g)]

(g) ADDITIONAL INFORMATION REQUIRED IN THE CASE OF SECURITIES TRANSACTIONS, ETC.—

(1) IN GENERAL.—If a broker is otherwise required to make a return under subsection (a) with respect to the gross proceeds of the sale of a covered security, the broker shall include in such return the information described in paragraph (2).

(2) ADDITIONAL INFORMATION REQUIRED.—

(A) IN GENERAL.—The information required under paragraph (1) to be shown on a return with respect to a covered security of a customer shall include the customer's adjusted basis in such security and whether any gain or loss with respect to such security is long-term or short-term (within the meaning of section 1222).

(B) DETERMINATION OF ADJUSTED BASIS.—For purposes of subparagraph (A)—

(i) IN GENERAL.—The customer's adjusted basis shall be determined—

(I) in the case of any security (other than any stock for which an average basis method is permissible under section 1012), in accordance with the first-in first-out method unless the customer notifies the broker by means of making an adequate identification of the stock sold or transferred, and

(II) in the case of any stock for which an average basis method is permissible under section 1012, in accordance with the broker's default method unless the customer notifies the broker that he elects another acceptable method under section 1012 with respect to the account in which such stock is held.

(ii) EXCEPTION FOR WASH SALES.—Except as otherwise provided by the Secretary, the customer's adjusted basis shall be determined without regard to section 1091 (relating to loss from wash sales of stock or securities) unless the transactions occur in the same account with respect to identical securities.

(iii) TREATMENT OF UNCORRECTED DE MINIMIS ERRORS.—Except as otherwise provided by the Secretary, the customer's adjusted basis shall be determined by treating any incorrect dollar amount which is not required to be corrected by reason of section 6721(c)(3) or section 6722(c)(3) as the correct amount.

(3) COVERED SECURITY.—For purposes of this subsection—

(A) IN GENERAL.—The term "covered security" means any specified security acquired on or after the applicable date if such security—

(i) was acquired through a transaction in the account in which such security is held, or

(ii) was transferred to such account from an account in which such security was a covered security, but only if the broker received a statement under section 6045A with respect to the transfer.

(B) SPECIFIED SECURITY.—The term "specified security" means—

(i) any share of stock in a corporation,

(ii) any note, bond, debenture, or other evidence of indebtedness,

»» *Caution: Code Sec. 6045(g)(3)(B)(iii)-(iv), below, prior to amendment by P.L. 117-58, applies to returns required to be filed, and statements required to be furnished, on or before December 31, 2023.*

(iii) any commodity, or contract or derivative with respect to such commodity, if the Secretary determines that adjusted basis reporting is appropriate for purposes of this subsection, and

(iv) any other financial instrument with respect to which the Secretary determines that adjusted basis reporting is appropriate for purposes of this subsection.

»» *Caution: Code Sec. 6045(g)(3)(B)(iii)-(v), below, as amended by P.L. 117-58, applies to returns required to be filed, and statements required to be furnished, after December 31, 2023.*

(iii) any commodity, or contract or derivative with respect to such commodity, if the Secretary determines that adjusted basis reporting is appropriate for purposes of this subsection,

(iv) any digital asset, and

(v) any other financial instrument with respect to which the Secretary determines that adjusted basis reporting is appropriate for purposes of this subsection.

(C) APPLICABLE DATE.—The term "applicable date" means—

(i) January 1, 2011, in the case of any specified security which is stock in a corporation (other than any stock described in clause (ii)),

»» *Caution: Code Sec. 6045(g)(3)(C)(ii)-(iii), below, prior to amendment by P.L. 117-58, applies to returns required to be filed, and statements required to be furnished, on or before December 31, 2023.*

(ii) January 1, 2012, in the case of any stock for which an average basis method is permissible under section 1012, and

(iii) January 1, 2013, or such later date determined by the Secretary in the case of any other specified security.

»» *Caution: Code Sec. 6045(g)(3)(C)(ii)-(iv), below, as amended by P.L. 117-58, applies to returns required to be filed, and statements required to be furnished, after December 31, 2023.*

(ii) January 1, 2012, in the case of any stock for which an average basis method is permissible under section 1012,

(iii) January 1, 2023, in the case of any specified security which is a digital asset, and

(iv) January 1, 2013, or such later date determined by the Secretary in the case of any other specified security.

»» *Caution: Code Sec. 6045(g)(3)(D), below, as added by P.L. 117-58, applies to returns required to be filed, and statements required to be furnished, after December 31, 2023.*

(D) DIGITAL ASSET.—Except as otherwise provided by the Secretary, the term "digital asset" means any digital representation of value which is recorded on a cryptographically secured distributed ledger or any similar technology as specified by the Secretary.

(4) TREATMENT OF S CORPORATIONS.—In the case of the sale of a covered security acquired by an S corporation (other than a financial institution) after December 31, 2011, such S corporation shall be treated in the same manner as a partnership for purposes of this section.

(5) SPECIAL RULES FOR SHORT SALES.—In the case of a short sale, reporting under this section shall be made for the year in which such sale is closed.

(6) SPECIAL RULE FOR CERTAIN STOCK HELD IN CONNECTION WITH DIVIDEND REINVESTMENT PLAN.—For purposes of this subsection, stock acquired before January 1, 2012, in connection with a dividend reinvestment plan shall be treated as stock described in clause (ii) of paragraph (3)(C) (unless the broker with respect to such stock elects not to have this paragraph apply with respect to such stock).

[Sec. 6045(h)]

(h) APPLICATION TO OPTIONS ON SECURITIES.—

(1) EXERCISE OF OPTION.—For purposes of this section, if a covered security is acquired or disposed of pursuant to the exercise of an option that was granted or acquired in the same account as the covered security, the amount received with respect to the grant or paid with respect to the acquisition of such option shall be treated as an adjustment to gross proceeds or as an adjustment to basis, as the case may be.

(2) LAPSE OR CLOSING TRANSACTION.—In the case of the lapse (or closing transaction (as defined in section 1234(b)(2)(A))) of an option on a specified security or the exercise of a cash-settled option on a specified security, reporting under subsections (a) and (g) with respect to such option shall be made for the calendar year which includes the date of such lapse, closing transaction, or exercise.

(3) PROSPECTIVE APPLICATION.—Paragraphs (1) and (2) shall not apply to any option which is granted or acquired before January 1, 2013.

(4) DEFINITIONS.—For purposes of this subsection, the terms "covered security" and "specified security" shall have the meanings given such terms in subsection (g)(3).

[Sec. 6045A]

SEC. 6045A. INFORMATION REQUIRED IN CONNECTION WITH TRANSFERS OF COVERED SECURITIES TO BROKERS.

Caution: Code Sec. 6045A(a), below, prior to amendment by P.L. 117-58, applies to returns required to be filed, and statements required to be furnished, on or before December 31, 2023.

[Sec. 6045A(a)]

(a) FURNISHING OF INFORMATION.—Every applicable person which transfers to a broker (as defined in section 6045(c)(1)) a security which is a covered security (as defined in section 6045(g)(3)) in the hands of such applicable person shall furnish to such broker a written statement in such manner and setting forth such information as the Secretary may by regulations prescribe for purposes of enabling such broker to meet the requirements of section 6045(g).

Caution: Code Sec. 6045A(a), below, as amended by P.L. 117-58, applies to returns required to be filed, and statements required to be furnished, after December 31, 2023.

[Sec. 6045A(a)]

(a) FURNISHING OF INFORMATION.—Every applicable person which transfers to a broker (as defined in section 6045(c)(1)) a covered security (as defined in section 6045(g)(3)) in the hands of such applicable person shall furnish to such broker a written statement in such manner and setting forth such information as the Secretary may by regulations prescribe for purposes of enabling such broker to meet the requirements of section 6045(g).

[Sec. 6045A(b)]

(b) APPLICABLE PERSON.—For purposes of subsection (a), the term "applicable person" means—

(1) any broker (as defined in section 6045(c)(1)), and

(2) any other person as provided by the Secretary in regulations.

[Sec. 6045A(c)]

(c) TIME FOR FURNISHING STATEMENT.—Except as otherwise provided by the Secretary, any statement required by subsection (a) shall be furnished not later than 15 days after the date of the transfer described in such subsection.

Caution: Code Sec. 6045A(d), below, as added by P.L. 117-58, applies to returns required to be filed, and statements required to be furnished, after December 31, 2023.

[Sec. 6045A(d)]

(d) RETURN REQUIREMENT FOR CERTAIN TRANSFERS OF DIGITAL ASSETS NOT OTHERWISE SUBJECT TO REPORTING.—Any broker, with respect to any transfer (which is not part of a sale or exchange executed by such broker) during a calendar year of a covered security which is a digital asset from an account maintained by such broker to an account which is not maintained by, or an address not associated with, a person that such broker knows or has reason to know is also a broker, shall make a return for such calendar year, in such form as determined by the Secretary, showing the information otherwise required to be furnished with respect to transfers subject to subsection (a).

[Sec. 6046]

SEC. 6046. RETURNS AS TO ORGANIZATION OR REORGANIZATION OF FOREIGN CORPORATIONS AND AS TO ACQUISITIONS OF THEIR STOCK.

[Sec. 6046(a)]

(a) REQUIREMENT OF RETURN.—

(1) IN GENERAL.—A return complying with the requirements of subsection (b) shall be made by—

(A) each United States citizen or resident who becomes an officer or director of a foreign corporation if a United States person (as defined in section 7701(a)(30)) meets the stock ownership requirements of paragraph (2) with respect to such corporation,

(B) each United States person—

(i) who acquires stock which, when added to any stock owned on the date of such acquisition, meets the stock ownership requirements of paragraph (2) with respect to a foreign corporation, or

(ii) who acquires stock which, without regard to stock owned on the date of such acquisition, meets the stock ownership requirements of paragraph (2) with respect to a foreign corporation,

(C) each person (not described in subparagraph (B)) who is treated as a United States shareholder under section 953(c) with respect to a foreign corporation, and

(D) each person who becomes a United States person while meeting the stock ownership requirements of paragraph (2) with respect to stock of a foreign corporation.

In the case of a foreign corporation with respect to which any person is treated as a United States shareholder under section 953(c), subparagraph (A) shall be treated as including a reference to each United States person who is an officer or director of such corporation.

(2) STOCK OWNERSHIP REQUIREMENTS.—A person meets the stock ownership requirements of this paragraph with respect to any corporation if such person owns 10 percent or more of—

(A) the total combined voting power of all classes of stock of such corporation entitled to vote, or

(B) the total value of the stock of such corporation.

[Sec. 6046(b)]

(b) FORM AND CONTENTS OF RETURNS.—The returns required by subsection (a) shall be in such form and shall set forth, in respect of the foreign corporation, such information as the Secretary prescribes by forms or regulations as necessary for carrying out the provisions of the income tax laws, except that in the case of persons described only in subsection (a)(1)(A) the information required shall be limited to the names and addresses of persons described in subparagraph (B) or (C) of subsection (a)(1).

[Sec. 6046(c)]

(c) OWNERSHIP OF STOCK.—For purposes of subsection (a), stock owned directly or indirectly by a person (including, in the case of an individual, stock owned by members of his family) shall be taken into account. For purposes of the preceding sentence, the family of an individual shall be considered as including only his brothers and sisters (whether by the whole or half blood), spouse, ancestors, and lineal descendants.

[Sec. 6046(d)]

(d) TIME FOR FILING.—Any return required by subsection (a) shall be filed on or before the 90th day after the day on which, under any provision of subsection (a), the United States citizen, resident, or person becomes liable to file such return (or on or before such later day as the Secretary may by forms or regulations prescribe).

[Sec. 6046(e)]

(e) LIMITATION.—No information shall be required to be furnished under this section with respect to any foreign corporation unless such information was required to be furnished under regulations which have been in effect for at least 90 days before the date on which the United States citizen, resident, or person becomes liable to file a return required under subsection (a).

***

[Sec. 6046A]

SEC. 6046A. RETURNS AS TO INTERESTS IN FOREIGN PARTNERSHIPS.

[Sec. 6046A(a)]

(a) REQUIREMENT OF RETURN.—Any United States person, except to the extent otherwise provided by regulations—

(1) who acquires any interest in a foreign partnership,

(2) who disposes of any portion of his interest in a foreign partnership, or

(3) whose proportional interest in a foreign partnership changes substantially,

shall file a return. Paragraphs (1) and (2) shall apply to any acquisition or disposition only if the United States person directly or indirectly holds at least a 10-percent interest in such partnership either before or after such acquisition or disposition, and paragraph (3) shall apply to any change only if the change is equivalent to at least a 10-percent interest in such partnership.

[Sec. 6046A(b)]

(b) FORM AND CONTENTS OF RETURN.—Any return required by subsection (a) shall be in such form and set forth such information as the Secretary shall by regulations prescribe.

[Sec. 6046A(c)]

(c) TIME FOR FILING RETURN.—Any return required by subsection (a) shall be filed on or before the 90th day (or on or before such later day as the Secretary may by regulations prescribe) after the day on which the United States person becomes liable to file such return.

[Sec. 6046A(d)]

(d) 10-PERCENT INTEREST.—For purposes of subsection (a), a 10-percent interest in a partnership is an interest described in section 6038(e)(3)(C).

[Sec. 6046A(e)]

(e) CROSS REFERENCE.—

For provisions relating to penalties for violations of this section, see sections 6679 and 7203.

[Sec. 6048]

SEC. 6048. INFORMATION WITH RESPECT TO CERTAIN FOREIGN TRUSTS.

[Sec. 6048(a)]

(a) NOTICE OF CERTAIN EVENTS.—

(1) GENERAL RULE.—On or before the 90th day (or such later day as the Secretary may prescribe) after any reportable event, the responsible party shall provide written notice of such event to the Secretary in accordance with paragraph (2).

(2) CONTENTS OF NOTICE.—The notice required by paragraph (1) shall contain such information as the Secretary may prescribe, including—

(A) the amount of money or other property (if any) transferred to the trust in connection with the reportable event, and

(B) the identity of the trust and of each trustee and beneficiary (or class of beneficiaries) of the trust.

(3) REPORTABLE EVENT.—For purposes of this subsection—

(A) IN GENERAL.—The term "reportable event" means—

(i) the creation of any foreign trust by a United States person,

(ii) the transfer of any money or property (directly or indirectly) to a foreign trust by a United States person, including a transfer by reason of death, and

(iii) the death of a citizen or resident of the United States if—

(I) the decedent was treated as the owner of any portion of a foreign trust under the rules of subpart E of part I of subchapter J of chapter 1, or

(II) any portion of a foreign trust was included in the gross estate of the decedent.

(B) EXCEPTIONS.—

(i) FAIR MARKET VALUE SALES.—Subparagraph (A)(ii) shall not apply to any transfer of property to a trust in exchange for consideration of at least the fair market value of the transferred property. For purposes of the preceding sentence, consideration other than cash shall be taken into account at its fair market value and the rules of section 679(a)(3) shall apply.

(ii) DEFERRED COMPENSATION AND CHARITABLE TRUSTS.—Subparagraph (A) shall not apply with respect to a trust which is—

(I) described in section 402(b), 404(a)(4), or 404A, or

(II) determined by the Secretary to be described in section 501(c)(3).

(4) RESPONSIBLE PARTY.—For purposes of this subsection, the term "responsible party" means—

(A) the grantor in the case of the creation of an inter vivos trust,

(B) the transferor in the case of a reportable event described in paragraph (3)(A)(ii) other than a transfer by reason of death, and

(C) the executor of the decedent's estate in any other case.

[Sec. 6048(b)]

(b) UNITED STATES OWNER OF FOREIGN TRUST.—

(1) IN GENERAL.—If, at any time during any taxable year of a United States person, such person is treated as the owner of any portion of a foreign trust under the rules of subpart E of part I of subchapter J of chapter 1, such person shall submit such information as the Secretary may prescribe with respect to such trust for such year and shall be responsible to ensure that—

(A) such trust makes a return for such year which sets forth a full and complete accounting of all trust activities and operations for the year, the name of the United States agent for such trust, and such other information as the Secretary may prescribe, and

(B) such trust furnishes such information as the Secretary may prescribe to each United States person (i) who is treated as the owner of any portion of such trust or (ii) who receives (directly or indirectly) any distribution from the trust.

(2) TRUSTS NOT HAVING UNITED STATES AGENT.—

(A) IN GENERAL.—If the rules of this paragraph apply to any foreign trust, the determination of amounts required to be taken into account with respect to such trust by a United States person under the rules of subpart E of part I of subchapter J of chapter 1 shall be determined by the Secretary.

(B) UNITED STATES AGENT REQUIRED.—The rules of this paragraph shall apply to any foreign trust to which paragraph (1) applies unless such trust agrees (in such manner, subject to such conditions, and at such time as the Secretary shall prescribe) to authorize a United States person to act as such trust's limited agent solely for purposes of applying sections 7602, 7603, and7604 with respect to—

(i) any request by the Secretary to examine records or produce testimony related to the proper treatment of amounts required to be taken into account under the rules referred to in subparagraph (A), or

(ii) any summons by the Secretary for such records or testimony.

The appearance of persons or production of records by reason of a United States person being such an agent shall not subject such persons or records to legal process for any purpose other than determining the correct treatment under this title of the amounts required to be taken into account under the rules referred to in subparagraph (A). A foreign trust which appoints an [agent] described in this subparagraph shall not be considered to have an office or a permanent establishment in the United States, or to be engaged in a trade or business in the United States, solely because of the activities of such agent pursuant to this subsection.

(C) OTHER RULES TO APPLY.—Rules similar to the rules of paragraphs (2) and (4) of section 6038A(e) shall apply for purposes of this paragraph.

[Sec. 6048(c)]

(c) REPORTING BY UNITED STATES BENEFICIARIES OF FOREIGN TRUSTS.—

(1) IN GENERAL.—If any United States person receives (directly or indirectly) during any taxable year of such person any distribution from a foreign trust, such person shall make a return with respect to such trust for such year which includes—

(A) the name of such trust,

(B) the aggregate amount of the distributions so received from such trust during such taxable year, and

(C) such other information as the Secretary may prescribe.

(2) INCLUSION IN INCOME IF RECORDS NOT PROVIDED.—

(A) IN GENERAL.—If adequate records are not provided to the Secretary to determine the proper treatment of any distribution from a foreign trust, such distribution shall be treated as an accumulation distribution includible in the gross income of the distributee under chapter 1. To the extent provided in regulations, the preceding sentence shall not apply if the foreign trust elects to be subject to rules similar to the rules of subsection (b)(2)(B).

(B) APPLICATION OF ACCUMULATION DISTRIBUTION RULES.—For purposes of applying section 668 in a case to which subparagraph (A) applies, the applicable number of years for purposes of section 668(a) shall be 1/2 of the number of years the trust has been in existence.

[Sec. 6048(d)]

(d) SPECIAL RULES.—

(1) DETERMINATION OF WHETHER UNITED STATES PERSON MAKES TRANSFER OR RECEIVES DISTRIBUTION.—For purposes of this section, in determining whether a United States person makes a transfer to, or receives a distribution from, a foreign trust, the fact that a portion of such trust is treated as owned by another person under the rules of subpart E of part I of subchapter J of chapter 1 shall be disregarded.

(2) DOMESTIC TRUSTS WITH FOREIGN ACTIVITIES.—To the extent provided in regulations, a trust which is a United States person shall be treated as a foreign trust for purposes of this section and section 6677 if such trust has substantial activities, or holds substantial property, outside the United States.

(3) TIME AND MANNER OF FILING INFORMATION.—Any notice or return required under this section shall be made at such time and in such manner as the Secretary shall prescribe.

(4) MODIFICATION OF RETURN REQUIREMENTS.—The Secretary is authorized to suspend or modify any requirement of this section if the Secretary determines that the United States has no significant tax interest in obtaining the required information.

(5) UNITED STATES PERSON'S RETURN MUST BE CONSISTENT WITH TRUST RETURN OR SECRETARY NOTIFIED OF INCONSISTENCY.—Rules similar to the rules of section 6034A(c) shall apply to items reported by a trust under subsection (b)(1)(B) and to United States persons referred to in such subsection.

[Sec. 6049]

SEC. 6049. RETURNS REGARDING PAYMENTS OF INTEREST.

[Sec. 6049(a)]

(a) REQUIREMENT OF REPORTING.—Every person—

(1) who makes payments of interest (as defined in subsection (b)) aggregating $10 or more to any other person during any calendar year, or

(2) who receives payments of interest (as so defined) as a nominee and who makes payments aggregating $10 or more during any calendar year to any other person with respect to the interest so received,

shall make a return according to the forms or regulations prescribed by the Secretary, setting forth the aggregate amount of such payments and the name and address of the person to whom paid.

[Sec. 6049(b)]

(b) INTEREST DEFINED.—

(1) GENERAL RULE.—For purposes of subsection (a), the term "interest" means—

(A) interest on any obligation—

(i) issued in registered form, or

(ii) of a type offered to the public,

other than any obligation with a maturity (at issue) of not more than 1 year which is held by a corporation,

(B) interest on deposits with persons carrying on the banking business,

(C) amounts (whether or not designated as interest) paid by a mutual savings bank, savings and loan association, building and loan association, cooperative bank, homestead association, credit union, industrial loan association or bank, or similar organization, in respect of deposits, investment certificates, or withdrawable or repurchasable shares,

(D) interest on amounts held by an insurance company under an agreement to pay interest thereon,

(E) interest on deposits with brokers (as defined in section 6045(c)),

(F) interest paid on amounts held by investment companies (as defined in section 3 of the Investment Company Act of 1940 (15 U.S.C. 80a-3)) and on amounts invested in other pooled funds or trusts, and

(G) to the extent provided in regulations prescribed by the Secretary, any other interest (which is not described in paragraph (2)).

(2) EXCEPTIONS.—For purposes of subsection (a), the term "interest" does not include—

(A) interest on any obligation issued by a natural person,

(B) except to the extent otherwise provided in regulations—

(i) any amount paid to any person described in paragraph (4), or

(ii) any amount described in paragraph (5), and

(C) except to the extent otherwise provided in regulations, any amount not described in subparagraph (B) of this paragraph which is income from sources outside the United States or which is paid by—

(i) a foreign government or international organization or any agency or instrumentality thereof.

(ii) a foreign central bank of issue.

(iii) a foreign corporation not engaged in a trade or business in the United States,

(iv) a foreign corporation, the interest payments of which would be exempt from withholding under subchapter A of chapter 3 if paid to a person who is not a United States person, or

(v) a partnership not engaged in a trade or business in the United States and composed in whole of nonresident alien individuals and persons described in clause (i), (ii), or (iii).

(3) PAYMENTS BY UNITED STATES NOMINEES ETC., OF UNITED STATES PERSON.—If, within the United States, a United States person—

(A) collects interest (or otherwise acts as a middleman between the payor and payee) from a foreign person described in paragraph (2)(D) or collects interest from a United States person which is income from sources outside the United States for a second person who is a United States person, or

(B) makes payments of such interest to such second United States person,

notwithstanding paragraph (2)(D), such payment shall be subject to the requirements of subsection (a) with respect to such second United States person.

(4) PERSONS DESCRIBED IN THIS PARAGRAPH.—A person is described in this paragraph if such person is—

(A) a corporation,

(B) an organization exempt from taxation under section 501(a) or an individual retirement plan,

(C) the United States or any wholly owned agency or instrumentality thereof,

(D) a State, the District of Columbia, a possession of the United States, any political subdivision of any of the foregoing, or any wholly owned agency or instrumentality of any one or more of the foregoing,

(E) a foreign government, a political subdivision of a foreign government, or any wholly owned agency or instrumentality of any one or more of the foregoing,

(F) an international organization or any wholly owned agency or instrumentality thereof,

(G) a foreign central bank of issue,

(H) a dealer in securities or commodities required to register as such under the laws of the United States or a State, the District of Columbia, or a possession of the United States,

(I) a real estate investment trust (as defined in section 856),

(J) an entity registered at all times during the taxable year under the Investment Company Act of 1940,

(K) a common trust fund (as defined in section 584(a)), or

(L) any trust which—

(i) is exempt from tax under section 664(c), or

(ii) is described in section 4947(a)(1).

(5) AMOUNTS DESCRIBED IN THIS PARAGRAPH.—An amount is described in this paragraph if such amount—

(A) is subject to withholding under subchapter A of chapter 3 (relating to withholding of tax on nonresident aliens and foreign corporations) by the person paying such amount, or

(B) would be subject to withholding under subchapter A of chapter 3 by the person paying such amount but for the fact that—

(i) such amount is income from sources outside the United States,

(ii) the payor thereof is exempt from the application of section 1441(a) by reason of section 1441(c) or a tax treaty,

(iii) such amount is original issue discount (within the meaning of section 1273(a)), or

(iv) such amount is described in section 871(i)(2).

[Sec. 6049(c)]

(c) STATEMENTS TO BE FURNISHED TO PERSONS WITH RESPECT TO WHOM INFORMATION IS REQUIRED.—

(1) IN GENERAL.—Every person required to make a return under subsection (a) shall furnish to each person whose name is required to be set forth in such return a written statement showing—

(A) the name, address, and phone number of the information contact of the person required to make such return, and

(B) the aggregate amount of payments to, or the aggregate amount includible in the gross income of, the person required to be shown on the return.

(2) TIME AND FORM OF STATEMENT.—The written statement under paragraph (1)—

(A) shall be furnished (either in person or in a statement mailing by first-class mail which includes adequate notice that the statement is enclosed) to the person on or before January 31 of the year following the calendar year for which the return under subsection (a) was required to be made, and

(B) shall be in such form as the Secretary may prescribe by regulations.

[Sec. 6049(d)]

(d) DEFINITIONS AND SPECIAL RULES.—For purposes of this section—

(1) PERSON.—The term "person" includes any governmental unit and any agency or instrumentality thereof and any international organization and any agency or instrumentality thereof.

(2) OBLIGATION.—The term "obligation" includes bonds, debentures, notes, certificates, and other evidences of indebtedness.

(3) PAYMENTS BY GOVERNMENTAL UNITS.—In the case of payments made by any governmental unit or any agency or instrumentality thereof, the officer or employee having control of the payment of interest (or the person appropriately designated for purposes of this section) shall make the returns and statements required by this section.

(4) FINANCIAL INSTITUTIONS, BROKERS, ETC., COLLECTING INTEREST MAY BE SUBSTITUTED FOR PAYOR.—To the extent and in the manner provided by regulations, in the case of any obligation—

(A) a financial institution, broker, or other person specified in such regulations which collects interest on such obligation for the payee (or otherwise acts as a middleman between the payor and the payee) shall comply with the requirements of subsections (a) and (c), and

(B) no other person shall be required to comply with the requirements of subsections (a) and (c) with respect to any interest on such obligation for which reporting is required pursuant to subparagraph (A).

(5) INTEREST ON CERTAIN OBLIGATIONS MAY BE TREATED ON A TRANSACTIONAL BASIS.—

(A) IN GENERAL.—To the extent and in the manner provided in regulations, this section shall apply with respect to—

(i) any person described in paragraph (4)(A), and

(ii) in the case of any United States savings bonds, any Federal agency making payments thereon,

on any transactional basis rather than on an annual aggregation basis.

(B) SEPARATE RETURNS AND STATEMENTS.—If subparagraph (A) applies to interest on any obligation, the return under subsection (a) and the statement furnished under subsection (c) with respect to such transaction may be made separately, but any such statement shall be furnished to the payee at such time as the Secretary may prescribe by regulations but not later than January 31 of the next calendar year.

(C) STATEMENT TO PAYEE REQUIRED IN CASE OF TRANSACTIONS INVOLVING $10 OR MORE.—In the case of any transaction to which this paragraph applies which involves the payment of $10 or more of interest, a statement of the transaction may be provided to the payee of such interest in lieu of the statement required under subsection (c). Such statement shall be provided during January of the year following the year in which such payment is made.

(6) TREATMENT OF ORIGINAL ISSUE DISCOUNT.—

(A) IN GENERAL.—Original issue discount on any obligation shall be reported—

(i) as if paid at the time it is includible in gross income under section 1272 (except that for such purpose the amount reportable with respect to any subsequent holder shall be determined as if he were the original holder), and

(ii) if section 1272 does not apply to the obligation, at maturity (or, if earlier, on redemption).

In the case of any obligation not in registered form issued before January 1, 1983, clause (ii) and not clause (i) shall apply.

(B) ORIGINAL ISSUE DISCOUNT.—For purposes of this paragraph, the term "original issue discount" has the meaning given to such term by section 1273(a).

(7) INTERESTS IN REMIC'S AND CERTAIN OTHER DEBT INSTRUMENTS.—

(A) IN GENERAL.—For purposes of subsection (a), the term "interest" includes amounts includible in gross income with respect to regular interests in REMIC's (and such amounts shall be treated as paid when includible in gross income under section 860B(b)).

(B) REPORTING TO CORPORATIONS, ETC.—Except as otherwise provided in regulations, in the case of any interest described in subparagraph (A) of this paragraph and any other debt instrument to which section 1272(a)(6) applies, subsection (b)(4) of this section shall be applied without regard to subparagraphs (A), (H), (I), (J), (K), and (L)(i).

(C) ADDITIONAL INFORMATION.—Except as otherwise provided in regulations, any return or statement required to be filed or furnished under this section with respect to interest income described in subparagraph (A) and interest on any other debt instrument to which section 1272(a)(6) applies shall also provide information setting forth the adjusted issue price of the interest to which the return or statement relates at the beginning of each accrual period with respect to which interest income is required to be reported on such return or statement and information necessary to compute accrual of market discount.

(D) REGULATORY AUTHORITY.—The Secretary may prescribe such regulations as are necessary or appropriate to carry out the purposes of this subparagraph, including regulations which require more frequent or more detailed reporting.

(8) REPORTING OF CREDIT ON CLEAN RENEWABLE ENERGY BONDS.—

(A) IN GENERAL.—For purposes of subsection (a), the term "interest" includes amounts includible in gross income under section 54(g) and such amounts shall be treated as paid on the credit allowance date (as defined in section 54(b)(4).

(B) REPORTING TO CORPORATIONS, ETC.—Except as otherwise provided in regulations, in the case of any interest described in subparagraph (A), subsection (b)(4) shall be applied without regard to subparagraphs (A), (H), (I), (J), (K), and (L)(i) of such subsection.

(C) REGULATORY AUTHORITY.—The Secretary may prescribe such regulations as are necessary or appropriate to carry out the purposes of this paragraph, including regulations which require more frequent or more detailed reporting.

(9) REPORTING OF CREDIT ON QUALIFIED TAX CREDIT BONDS.—

(A) IN GENERAL.—For purposes of subsection (a), the term "interest" includes amounts includible in gross income under section 54A and such amounts shall be treated as paid on the credit allowance date (as defined in section 54A(e)(1)).

(B) REPORTING TO CORPORATIONS, ETC.—Except as otherwise provided in regulations, in the case of any interest described in subparagraph (A) of this paragraph, subsection (b)(4) of this section shall be applied without regard to subparagraphs (A), (H), (I), (J), (K), and (L)(i).

(C) REGULATORY AUTHORITY.—The Secretary may prescribe such regulations as are necessary or appropriate to carry out the purposes of this paragraph, including regulations which require more frequent or more detailed reporting.

[Sec. 6050I]

SEC. 6050I. RETURNS RELATING TO CASH RECEIVED IN TRADE OR BUSINESS, ETC.

[Sec. 6050I(a)]

(a) CASH RECEIPTS OF MORE THAN $10,000.—Any person—

(1) who is engaged in a trade or business, and

(2) who, in the course of such trade or business, receives more than $10,000 in cash in 1 transaction (or 2 or more related transactions),

shall make the return described in subsection (b) with respect to such transaction (or related transactions) at such time as the Secretary may by regulations prescribe.

[Sec. 6050I(b)]

(b) FORM AND MANNER OF RETURNS.—A return is described in this subsection if such return—

(1) is in such form as the Secretary may prescribe,

(2) contains—

(A) the name, address, and TIN of the person from whom the cash was received,

(B) the amount of cash received,

(C) the date and nature of the transaction, and

(D) such other information as the Secretary may prescribe.

[Sec. 6050I(c)]

(c) EXCEPTIONS.—

(1) CASH RECEIVED BY FINANCIAL INSTITUTIONS.—Subsection (a) shall not apply to—

(A) cash received in a transaction reported under title 31, United States Code, if the Secretary determines that reporting under this section would duplicate the reporting to the Treasury under title 31, United States Code, or

(B) cash received by any financial institution (as defined in subparagraphs (A), (B), (C), (D), (E), (F), (G), (J), (K), (R), and (S) of section 5312(a)(2) of title 31, United States Code).

(2) TRANSACTIONS OCCURRING OUTSIDE THE UNITED STATES.—Except to the extent provided in regulations prescribed by the Secretary, subsection (a) shall not apply to any transaction if the entire transaction occurs outside the United States.

[Sec. 6050I(d)]

(d) CASH INCLUDES FOREIGN CURRENCY AND CERTAIN MONETARY INSTRUMENTS.—For purposes of this section, the term "cash" includes—

(1) foreign currency,

(2) to the extent provided in regulations prescribed by the Secretary, any monetary instrument (whether or not in bearer form) with a face amount of not more than $10,000, and

»»→ ***Caution: Code Sec. 6050I(d)(3), below, as added by P.L. 117-58, applies to returns required to be filed, and statements required to be furnished, after December 31, 2023.***

(3) any digital asset (as defined in section 6045(g)(3)(D)).

Paragraph (2) shall not apply to any check drawn on the account of the writer in a financial institution referred to in subsection (c)(1)(B).

[Sec. 6050I(e)]

(e) STATEMENTS TO BE FURNISHED TO PERSONS WITH RESPECT TO WHOM INFORMATION IS REQUIRED.—Every person required to make a return under subsection (a) shall furnish to each person whose name is required to be set forth in such return a written statement showing—

(1) the name, address, and phone number of the information contact of the person required to make such return, and

(2) the aggregate amount of cash described in subsection (a) received by the person required to make such return.

The written statement required under the preceding sentence shall be furnished to the person on or before January 31 of the year following the calendar year for which the return under subsection (a) was required to be made.

[Sec. 6050I(f)]

(f) STRUCTURING TRANSACTIONS TO EVADE REPORTING REQUIREMENTS PROHIBITED.—

(1) IN GENERAL.—No person shall for the purpose of evading the return requirements of this section—

(A) cause or attempt to cause a trade or business to fail to file a return required under this section,

(B) cause or attempt to cause a trade or business to file a return required under this section that contains a material omission or misstatement of fact, or

(C) structure or assist in structuring, or attempt to structure or assist in structuring, any transaction with one or more trades or businesses.

(2) PENALTIES.—A person violating paragraph (1) of this subsection shall be subject to the same civil and criminal sanctions applicable to a person which fails to file or completes a false or incorrect return under this section.

[Sec. 6050I(g)]

(g) CASH RECEIVED BY CRIMINAL COURT CLERKS.—

(1) IN GENERAL.—Every clerk of a Federal or State criminal court who receives more than $10,000 in cash as bail for any individual charged with a specified criminal offense shall make a return described in paragraph (2) (at such time as the Secretary may by regulations prescribe) with respect to the receipt of such bail.

(2) RETURN.—A return is described in this paragraph if such return—

(A) is in such form as the Secretary may prescribe, and

(B) contains—

(i) the name, address, and TIN of—

(I) the individual charged with the specified criminal offense, and

(II) each person posting the bail (other than a person licensed as a bail bondsman),

(ii) the amount of cash received,

(iii) the date the cash was received, and

(iv) such other information as the Secretary may prescribe.

(3) SPECIFIED CRIMINAL OFFENSE.—For purposes of this subsection, the term "specified criminal offense" means—

(A) any Federal criminal offense involving a controlled substance,

(B) racketeering (as defined in section 1951, 1952, or 1955 of title 18, United States Code),

(C) money laundering (as defined in section 1956 or 1957 of such title), and

(D) any State criminal offense substantially similar to an offense described in subparagraph (A), (B), or (C).

(4) INFORMATION TO FEDERAL PROSECUTORS.—Each clerk required to include on a return under paragraph (1) the information described in paragraph (2)(B) with respect to an individual described in paragraph (2)(B)(i)(I) shall furnish (at such time as the Secretary may by regulations prescribe) a written statement showing such information to the United States Attorney for the jurisdiction in which such individual resides and the jurisdiction in which the specified criminal offense occurred.

(5) INFORMATION TO PAYORS OF BAIL.—Each clerk required to make a return under paragraph (1) shall furnish (at such time as the Secretary may by regulations prescribe) to each person whose name is required to be set forth in such return by reason of paragraph (2)(B)(i)(II) a written statement showing—

(A) the name and address of the clerk's office required to make the return, and

(B) the aggregate amount of cash described in paragraph (1) received by such clerk.

[Sec. 6050X]

SEC. 6050X. INFORMATION WITH RESPECT TO CERTAIN FINES, PENALTIES, AND OTHER AMOUNTS.

[Sec. 6050X(a)]

(a) REQUIREMENT OF REPORTING.—

(1) IN GENERAL.—The appropriate official of any government or any entity described in section 162(f)(5) which is involved in a suit or agreement described in paragraph (2) shall make a return in such form as determined by the Secretary setting forth—

(A) the amount required to be paid as a result of the suit or agreement to which paragraph (1) of section 162(f) applies,

(B) any amount required to be paid as a result of the suit or agreement which constitutes restitution or remediation of property, and

(C) any amount required to be paid as a result of the suit or agreement for the purpose of coming into compliance with any law which was violated or involved in the investigation or inquiry.

(2) SUIT OR AGREEMENT DESCRIBED.—

(A) IN GENERAL.—A suit or agreement is described in this paragraph if—

(i) it is—

(I) a suit with respect to a violation of any law over which the government or entity has authority and with respect to which there has been a court order, or

(II) an agreement which is entered into with respect to a violation of any law over which the government or entity has authority, or with respect to an investigation or inquiry by the government or entity into the potential violation of any law over which such government or entity has authority, and

(ii) the aggregate amount involved in all court orders and agreements with respect to the violation, investigation, or inquiry is $600 or more.

(B) ADJUSTMENT OF REPORTING THRESHOLD.—The Secretary shall adjust the $600 amount in subparagraph (A)(ii) as necessary in order to ensure the efficient administration of the internal revenue laws.

(3) TIME OF FILING.—The return required under this subsection shall be filed at the time the agreement is entered into, as determined by the Secretary.

[Sec. 6050X(b)]

(b) STATEMENTS TO BE FURNISHED TO INDIVIDUALS INVOLVED IN THE SETTLEMENT.—Every person required to make a return under subsection (a) shall furnish to each person who is a party to the suit or agreement a written statement showing—

(1) the name of the government or entity, and

(2) the information supplied to the Secretary under subsection (a)(1).

The written statement required under the preceding sentence shall be furnished to the person at the same time the government or entity provides the Secretary with the information required under subsection (a).

[Sec. 6050X(c)]

(c) APPROPRIATE OFFICIAL DEFINED.—For purposes of this section, the term "appropriate official" means the officer or employee having control of the suit, investigation, or inquiry or the person appropriately designated for purposes of this section.

PART V—TIME FOR FILING RETURNS AND OTHER DOCUMENTS

[Sec. 6072]

SEC. 6072. TIME FOR FILING INCOME TAX RETURNS.

[Sec. 6072(a)]

(a) GENERAL RULE.—In the case of returns under section 6012, 6013, or6017 (relating to income tax under subtitle A), returns made on the basis of the calendar year shall be filed on or before the 15th day of April following the close of the calendar year and returns made on the basis of a fiscal year shall be filed on or before the 15th day of the fourth month following the close of the fiscal year, except as otherwise provided in the following subsections of this section.

[Sec. 6072(b)]

(b) RETURNS OF PARTNERSHIPS AND S CORPORATIONS.—Returns of partnerships under section 6031 and returns of S coprorations unders sections 6012 and 6037 made on the basis of the calendar year shall be filed on or before the 15th day of March following the close of the calendar year, and such returns made on the basis of a fiscal year shall be filed on or before the 15th day of the third month following the close of the fiscal year. Returns required for a taxable year by section 6011(c)(2) (relating to returns of a DISC) shall be filed on or before the fifteenth day of the ninth month following the close of the taxable year.

[Sec. 6072(c)]

(c) RETURNS BY CERTAIN NONRESIDENT ALIEN INDIVIDUALS AND FOREIGN CORPORATIONS.—Returns made by nonresident alien individuals (other than those whose wages are subject to withholding under chapter 24) and foreign corporations (other than those having an office or place of business in the United States or a former FSC (as defined in section 922 as in effect before its repeal by the FSC Repeal and Extraterritorial Income Exclusion Act of 2000)) under section 6012 on the basis of a calendar year shall be filed on or before the 15th day of June following the close of the calendar year and such returns made on the basis of a fiscal year shall be filed on or before the 15th day of the 6th month following the close of the fiscal year.

***

SUBCHAPTER B—MISCELLANEOUS PROVISIONS

[Sec. 6103]

SEC. 6103. CONFIDENTIALITY AND DISCLOSURE OF RETURNS AND RETURN INFORMATION.

[Sec. 6103(a)]

(a) GENERAL RULE.—Returns and return information shall be confidential, and except as authorized by this title—

(1) no officer or employee of the United States,

(2) no officer or employee of any State, any local law enforcement agency receiving information under subsection (i)(1)(C) or (7)(A), any local child support enforcement agency, or any local agency administering a program listed in subsection (l)(7)(D) who has or had access to returns or return information under this section or section 6104(c), and

(3) no other person (or officer or employee thereof) who has or had access to returns or return information under subsection (c), subsection (e)(1)(D)(iii), paragraph (10), (13), (14), or (15) of subsection (k), paragraph (6), (10), (12), (13) (other than subparagraphs (D)(v) and (D)(vi) thereof), (16), (19), (20), or (21) of subsection (l), paragraph (2) or (4)(B) of subsection (m), or subsection (n),

shall disclose any return or return information obtained by him in any manner in connection with his service as such an officer or an employee or otherwise or under the provisions of this section. For purposes of this subsection, the term "officer or employee" includes a former officer or employee.

[Sec. 6103(b)]

(b) DEFINITIONS.—For purposes of this section—

(1) RETURN.—The term "return" means any tax or information return, declaration of estimated tax, or claim for refund required by, or provided for or permitted under, the provisions of this title which is filed with the Secretary by, on behalf of, or with respect to any person, and any amendment or supplement thereto, including supporting schedules, attachments, or lists which are supplemental to, or part of, the return so filed.

(2) RETURN INFORMATION.—The term "return information" means—

(A) a taxpayer's identity, the nature, source, or amount of his income, payments, receipts, deductions, exemptions, credits, assets, liabilities, net worth, tax liability, tax withheld, deficiencies, overassessments, or tax payments, whether the taxpayer's return was, is being, or will be examined or subject to other investigation or processing, or any other data, received by, recorded by, prepared by, furnished to, or collected by the Secretary with respect to a return or with respect to the determination of the existence, or possible existence, of liability (or the amount thereof) of any person under this title for any tax, penalty, interest, fine, forfeiture, or other imposition, or offense,

(B) any part of any written determination or any background file document relating to such written determination (as such terms are defined in section 6110(b)) which is not open to public inspection under section 6110,

(C) any advance pricing agreement entered into by a taxpayer and the Secretary and any background information related to such agreement or any application for an advance pricing agreement, and

(D) any agreement under section 7121, and any similar agreement, and any background information related to such an agreement or request for such an agreement,

but such term does not include data in a form which cannot be associated with, or otherwise identify, directly or indirectly, a particular taxpayer. Nothing in the preceding sentence, or in any other provision of law, shall be construed to require the disclosure of standards used or to be used for the selection of returns for examination, or data used or to be used for determining such standards, if the Secretary determines that such disclosure will seriously impair assessment, collection, or enforcement under the internal revenue laws.

***

[Sec. 6110]

SEC. 6110. PUBLIC INSPECTION OF WRITTEN DETERMINATIONS.

[Sec. 6110(a)]

(a) GENERAL RULE.—Except as otherwise provided in this section, the text of any written determination and any background file document relating to such written determination shall be open to public inspection at such place as the Secretary may by regulations prescribe.

[Sec. 6110(b)]

(b) DEFINITIONS.—For purposes of this section—

(1) WRITTEN DETERMINATION.—

(A) IN GENERAL.—The term "written determination" means a ruling, determination letter, technical advice memorandum, or Chief Counsel advice.

(B) EXCEPTIONS.—Such term shall not include any matter referred to in subparagraph (C) or (D) of section 6103(b)(2).

***

[Sec. 6111]

SEC. 6111. DISCLOSURE OF REPORTABLE TRANSACTIONS.

[Sec. 6111(a)]

(a) IN GENERAL.—Each material advisor with respect to any reportable transaction shall make a return (in such form as the Secretary may prescribe) setting forth—

(1) information identifying and describing the transaction,

(2) information describing any potential tax benefits expected to result from the transaction, and

(3) such other information as the Secretary may prescribe.

Such return shall be filed not later than the date specified by the Secretary.

[Sec. 6111(b)]

(b) DEFINITIONS.—For purposes of this section—

(1) MATERIAL ADVISOR.—

(A) IN GENERAL.—The term "material advisor" means any person—

(i) who provides any material aid, assistance, or advice with respect to organizing, managing, promoting, selling, implementing, insuring, or carrying out any reportable transaction, and

(ii) who directly or indirectly derives gross income in excess of the threshold amount (or such other amount as may be prescribed by the Secretary) for such aid, assistance, or advice.

(B) THRESHOLD AMOUNT.—For purposes of subparagraph (A), the threshold amount is—

(i) $50,000 in the case of a reportable transaction substantially all of the tax benefits from which are provided to natural persons, and

(ii) $250,000 in any other case.

(2) REPORTABLE TRANSACTION.—The term "reportable transaction" has the meaning given to such term by section 6707A(c).

[Sec. 6111(c)]

(c) REGULATIONS.—The Secretary may prescribe regulations which provide—

(1) that only 1 person shall be required to meet the requirements of subsection (a) in cases in which 2 or more persons would otherwise be required to meet such requirements,

(2) exemptions from the requirements of this section, and

(3) such rules as may be necessary or appropriate to carry out the purposes of this section.

[Sec. 6114]

SEC. 6114. TREATY-BASED RETURN POSITIONS.

[Sec. 6114(a)]

(a) IN GENERAL.—Each taxpayer who, with respect to any tax imposed by this title, takes the position that a treaty of the United States overrules (or otherwise modifies) an internal revenue law of the United States shall disclose (in such manner as the Secretary may prescribe) such position—

(1) on the return of tax for such tax (or any statement attached to such return), or

(2) if no return of tax is required to be filed, in such form as the Secretary may prescribe.

[Sec. 6114(b)]

(b) WAIVER AUTHORITY.—The Secretary may waive the requirements of subsection (a) with respect to classes of cases for which the Secretary determines that the waiver will not impede the assessment and collection of tax.

CHAPTER 62—TIME AND PLACE FOR PAYING TAX

SUBCHAPTER B—EXTENSIONS OF TIME FOR PAYMENT

[Sec. 6167]

SEC. 6167. EXTENSION OF TIME FOR PAYMENT OF TAX ATTRIBUTABLE TO RECOVERY OF FOREIGN EXPROPRIATION LOSSES.

[Sec. 6167(a)]

(a) EXTENSION ALLOWED BY ELECTION.—If—

(1) a corporation has a recovery of a foreign expropriation loss to which section 1351 applies, and

(2) the portion of the recovery received in money is less than 25 percent of the amount of such recovery (as defined in section 1351(c)) and is not greater than the tax attributable to such recovery,

the tax attributable to such recovery shall, at the election of the taxpayer, be payable in 10 equal installments on the 15th day of the fourth month of each of the taxable years following the taxable year of the recovery. Such election shall be made at such time and in such manner as the Secretary may prescribe by regulations. If an election is made under this subsection, the provisions of this subtitle shall apply as though the Secretary were extending the time for payment of such tax.

[Sec. 6167(b)]

(b) EXTENSION PERMITTED BY SECRETARY.—If a corporation has a recovery of a foreign expropriation loss to which section 1351 applies and if an election is not made under subsection (a), the Secretary may, upon finding that the payment of the tax attributable to such recovery at the time otherwise provided in this subtitle would result in undue hardship, extend the time for payment of such tax for a reasonable period or periods not in excess of 9 years from the date on which such tax is otherwise payable.

[Sec. 6167(c)]

(c) ACCELERATION OF PAYMENTS.—If—

(1) an election is made under subsection (a),

(2) during any taxable year before the tax attributable to such recovery is paid in full—

(A) any property (other than money) received on such recovery is sold or exchanged, or

(B) any property (other than money) received on any sale or exchange described in subparagraph (A) is sold or exchanged, and

(3) the amount of money received on such sale or exchange (reduced by the amount of the tax imposed under chapter 1 with respect to such sale or exchange), when added to the amount of money—

(A) received on such recovery, and

(B) received on previous sales or exchanges described in subparagraphs (A) and (B) of paragraph (2) (as so reduced),

exceeds the amount of money which may be received under subsection (a)(2),

an amount of the tax attributable to such recovery equal to such excess shall be payable on the 15th day of the fourth month of the taxable year following the taxable year in which such sale or exchange occurs. The amount of such tax so paid shall be treated, for purposes of this section, as a payment of the first unpaid installment or installments (or portion thereof) which become payable under subsection (a) following such taxable year.

[Sec. 6167(d)]

(d) PRORATION OF DEFICIENCY TO INSTALLMENTS.—If an election is made under subsection (a), and a deficiency attributable to the recovery of a foreign expropriation loss has been assessed, the deficiency shall be prorated to such installments. The part of the deficiency so prorated to any installment the date for payment of which has not arrived shall be collected at the same time as, and as part of, such installment. The part of the deficiency so prorated to any installment the date for payment of which has arrived shall be paid upon notice and demand from the Secretary. This subsection shall not apply if the deficiency is due to negligence, to intentional disregard of rules and regulations, or to fraud with intent to evade tax.

[Sec. 6167(e)]

(e) TIME FOR PAYMENT OF INTEREST.—If the time for payment for any amount of tax has been extended under this section, interest payable under section 6601 on any unpaid portion of such amount shall be paid annually at the same time as, and as part of, each installment payment of the tax. Interest, on that part of a deficiency prorated under this section to any installment the date for payment of which has not arrived, for the period before the date fixed for the last installment preceding the assessment of the deficiency, shall be paid upon notice and demand from the Secretary.

[Sec. 6167(f)]

(f) TAX ATTRIBUTABLE TO RECOVERY OF FOREIGN EXPROPRIATION LOSS.—For purposes of this section, the tax attributable to a recovery of a foreign expropriation loss is the sum of—

(1) the additional tax imposed by section 1351(d)(1) on such recovery, and

(2) the amount by which the tax imposed under subtitle A is increased by reason of the gain on such recovery which under section 1351(e) is considered as gain on the involuntary conversion of property.

[Sec. 6167(g)]

(g) FAILURE TO PAY INSTALLMENT.—If any installment under this section is not paid on or before the date fixed for its payment by this section (including any extension of time for the payment of such installment), the unpaid portion of the tax payable in installments shall be paid upon notice and demand from the Secretary.

* * *

CHAPTER 63—ASSESSMENT

SUBCHAPTER C—TREATMENT OF PARTNERSHIPS

PART II—PARTNERSHIP ADJUSTMENTS

[Sec. 6226]

SEC. 6226. ALTERNATIVE TO PAYMENT OF IMPUTED UNDERPAYMENT BY PARTNERSHIP.

***

[Sec. 6226(b)]

(b) ADJUSTMENTS TAKEN INTO ACCOUNT BY PARTNER.—

***

(4) TREATMENT OF PARTNERSHIPS AND S CORPORATIONS IN TIERED STRUCTURES.—

(A) IN GENERAL.—If a partner which receives a statement under subsection (a)(2) is a partnership or an S corporation, such partner shall, with respect to the partner's share of the adjustment—

(i) file with the Secretary a partnership adjustment tracking report which includes such information as the Secretary may require, and

(ii)(I) furnish statements under rules similar to the rules of subsection (a)(2), or

(II) if no such statements are furnished, compute and pay an imputed underpayment under rules similar to the rules of section 6225 (other than paragraphs (2), (7), and (9) of subsection (c) thereof).

(B) DUE DATE.—For purposes of subparagraph (A), with respect to a partner's share of the adjustment, the partnership adjustment tracking report shall be filed, and the imputed underpayment shall be paid or statements shall be furnished, not later than the due date for the return for the adjustment year of the audited partnership.

(C) PARTNERSHIP PAYMENT OF TAX IF ELECTED OUT OF SUBCHAPTER.—In the case of a partnership which has elected the application of section 6221(b) with respect to the taxable year of the partnership which includes the end of the reviewed year of the audited partnership, this paragraph shall apply notwithstanding such election.

(D) AUDITED PARTNERSHIP.—For purposes of this paragraph, the term "audited partnership" means, with respect to any partner described in subparagraph (A), the partnership in the chain of ownership originally electing the application of this section.

(E) TREATMENT OF TRUSTS.—The Secretary shall prescribe such rules as may be necessary with respect to trusts which receive a statement under subsection (a)(2).

***

CHAPTER 64—COLLECTION

SUBCHAPTER B—RECEIPT OF PAYMENT

[Sec. 6316]

SEC. 6316. PAYMENT BY FOREIGN CURRENCY.

The Secretary is authorized in his discretion to allow payment of taxes in the currency of a foreign country under such circumstances and subject to such conditions as the Secretary may by regulations prescribe.

CHAPTER 66—LIMITATIONS

SUBCHAPTER A—LIMITATIONS ON ASSESSMENT AND COLLECTION

[Sec. 6503]

SEC. 6503. SUSPENSION OF RUNNING OF PERIOD OF LIMITATION.

***

[Sec. 6503(c)]

(c) TAXPAYER OUTSIDE UNITED STATES.—The running of the period of limitations on collection after assessment prescribed in section 6502 shall be suspended for the period during which the taxpayer is outside the United States if such period of absence is for a continuous period of at least 6 months. If the preceding sentence applies and at the time of the taxpayer's return to the United States the period of limitations on collection after assessment prescribed in section 6502 would expire before the expiration of 6 months from the date of his return, such period shall not expire before the expiration of such 6 months.

***

[Sec. 6503(e)]

(e) EXTENSIONS OF TIME FOR PAYMENT OF TAX ATTRIBUTABLE TO RECOVERIES OF FOREIGN EXPROPRIATION LOSSES.—The running of the period of limitations for collection of the tax attributable to a recovery of a foreign expropriation loss (within the meaning of section 6167(f)) shall be suspended for the period of any extension of time for payment under subsection (a) or (b) of section 6167.

***

[Sec. 6503(i)]

(i) EXTENSION OF TIME FOR PAYMENT OF UNDISTRIBUTED PFIC EARNINGS TAX LIABILITY.—The running of any period of limitations for collection of any amount of undistributed PFIC earnings tax liability (as defined in section 1294(b)) shall be suspended for the period of any extension of time under section 1294 for payment of such amount.

***

SUBCHAPTER B—LIMITATIONS ON CREDIT OR REFUND

[Sec. 6511]

SEC. 6511. LIMITATIONS ON CREDIT OR REFUND.

***

[Sec. 6511(d)]

(d) SPECIAL RULES APPLICABLE TO INCOME TAXES.—

***

(3) SPECIAL RULES RELATING TO FOREIGN TAX CREDIT.—

(A) SPECIAL PERIOD OF LIMITATION WITH RESPECT TO FOREIGN TAXES PAID OR ACCRUED.—If the claim for credit or refund relates to an overpayment attributable to any taxes paid or accrued to any foreign country or to any possession of the United States for which credit is allowed against the tax imposed by subtitle A in accordance with the provisions of section 901 or the provisions of any treaty to which the United States is a party, in lieu of the 3-year period of limitation prescribed in subsection (a), the period shall be 10 years from the date prescribed by law for filing the return for the year in which such taxes were actually paid or accrued.

(B) EXCEPTION IN THE CASE OF FOREIGN TAXES PAID OR ACCRUED.—In the case of a claim described in subparagraph (A), the amount of the credit or refund may exceed the portion of the tax paid within the period provided in subsection (b) or (c), whichever is applicable, to the extent of the amount of the overpayment attributable to the allowance of a credit for the taxes described in subparagraph (A).

* * *

CHAPTER 68—ADDITIONS TO THE TAX, ADDITIONAL AMOUNTS, AND ASSESSABLE PENALTIES

SUBCHAPTER A—ADDITIONS TO THE TAX AND ADDITIONAL AMOUNTS

PART I—GENERAL PROVISIONS

[Sec. 6652]

SEC. 6652. FAILURE TO FILE CERTAIN INFORMATION RETURNS, REGISTRATION STATEMENTS, ETC.

* * *

[Sec. 6652(f)]

(f) RETURNS REQUIRED UNDER SECTION 6039C.—

(1) IN GENERAL.—In the case of each failure to make a return by section 6039C which contains the information required by such section on the date prescribed therefor (determined with regard to any extension of time for filing), unless it is shown that such failure is due to reasonable cause and not to willful neglect, the amount determined under paragraph (2) shall be paid (upon notice and demand by the Secretary and in the same manner as tax) by the person failing to make such return.

(2) AMOUNT OF PENALTY.—For purposes of paragraph (1), the amount determined under this paragraph with respect to any failure shall be $25 for each day during which such failure continues.

(3) LIMITATION.—The amount determined under paragraph (2) with respect to any person for failing to meet the requirements of section 6039C for any calendar year shall not exceed the lesser of—

(A) $25,000, or

(B) 5 percent of the aggregate of the fair market value of the United States real property interests owned by such person at any time during such year.

For purposes of the preceding sentence, fair market value shall be determined as of the end of the calendar year (or, in the case of any property disposed of during the calendar year, as of the date of such disposition).

* * *

PART II—ACCURACY AND FRAUD-RELATED PENALTIES

[Sec. 6662]

SEC. 6662. IMPOSITION OF ACCURACY-RELATED PENALTY ON UNDERPAYMENTS.

[Sec. 6662(a)]

(a) IMPOSITION OF PENALTY.—If this section applies to any portion of an underpayment of tax required to be shown on a return, there shall be added to the tax an amount equal to 20 percent of the portion of the underpayment to which this section applies.

[Sec. 6662(b)]

(b) PORTION OF UNDERPAYMENT TO WHICH SECTION APPLIES.—This section shall apply to the portion of any underpayment which is attributable to 1 or more of the following:

(1) Negligence or disregard of rules or regulations.

(2) Any substantial understatement of income tax.

(3) Any substantial valuation misstatement under chapter 1.

(4) Any substantial overstatement of pension liabilities.

(5) Any substantial estate or gift tax valuation understatement.

(6) Any disallowance of claimed tax benefits by reason of a transaction lacking economic substance (within the meaning of section 7701(o)) of failing to meet the requirements of any similar rule of law.

(7) Any undisclosed foreign financial asset understatement.

(8) Any inconsistent estate basis.

(9) Any overstatement of the deduction provided in section 170(p).

(10) Any disallowance of a deduction by reason of section 170(h)(7).

This section shall not apply to any portion of an underpayment on which a penalty is imposed under section 6663. Except as provided in paragraph (1) or (2)(B) of section 6662A(e), this section shall not apply to the portion of any underpayment which is attributable to a reportable transaction understatement on which a penalty is imposed under section 6662A.

[Sec. 6662(c)]

(c) NEGLIGENCE.—For purposes of this section, the term "negligence" includes any failure to make a reasonable attempt to comply with the provisions of this title, and the term "disregard" includes any careless, reckless, or intentional disregard.

[Sec. 6662(d)]

(d) SUBSTANTIAL UNDERSTATEMENT OF INCOME TAX.—

(1) SUBSTANTIAL UNDERSTATEMENT.—

(A) IN GENERAL.—For purposes of this section, there is a substantial understatement of income tax for any taxable year if the amount of the understatement for the taxable year exceeds the greater of—

(i) 10 percent of the tax required to be shown on the return for the taxable year, or

(ii) $5,000.

(B) SPECIAL RULE FOR CORPORATIONS.—In the case of a corporation other than an S corporation or a personal holding company (as defined in section 542), there is a substantial understatement of income tax for any taxable year if the amount of the understatement for the taxable year exceeds the lesser of—

(i) 10 percent of the tax required to be shown on the return for the taxable year (or, if greater, $10,000), or

(ii) $10,000,000.

(C) SPECIAL RULE FOR TAXPAYERS CLAIMING SECTION 199A DEDUCTION.—In the case of any taxpayer who claims any deduction allowed under section 199A for the taxable year, subparagraph (A) shall be applied by substituting "5 percent" for "10 percent".

(2) UNDERSTATEMENT.—

(A) IN GENERAL.—For purposes of paragraph (1), the term "understatement" means the excess of—

(i) the amount of the tax required to be shown on the return for the taxable year, over

(ii) the amount of the tax imposed which is shown on the return, reduced by any rebate (within the meaning of section 6211(b)(2)).

The excess under the preceding sentence shall be determined without regard to items to which section 6662A applies.

(B) REDUCTION FOR UNDERSTATEMENT DUE TO POSITION OF TAXPAYER OR DISCLOSED ITEM.—The amount of the understatement under subparagraph (A) shall be reduced by that portion of the understatement which is attributable to—

(i) the tax treatment of any item by the taxpayer if there is or was substantial authority for such treatment, or

(ii) any item if—

(I) the relevant facts affecting the item's tax treatment are adequately disclosed in the return or in a statement attached to the return, and

(II) there is a reasonable basis for the tax treatment of such item by the taxpayer.

For purposes of clause (ii)(II), in no event shall a corporation be treated as having a reasonable basis for its tax treatment of an item attributable to a multiple-party financing transaction if such treatment does not clearly reflect the income of the corporation.

(C) REDUCTION NOT TO APPLY TO TAX SHELTERS.—

(i) IN GENERAL.—Subparagraph (B) shall not apply to any item attributable to a tax shelter.

(ii) TAX SHELTER.—For purposes of clause (i), the term "tax shelter" means—

(I) a partnership or other entity,

(II) any investment plan or arrangement, or

(III) any other plan or arrangement,

if a significant purpose of such partnership, entity, plan, or arrangement is the avoidance or evasion of Federal income tax.

(3) SECRETARIAL LIST.—The Secretary may prescribe a list of positions which the Secretary believes do not meet 1 or more of the standards specified in paragraph (2)(B)(i), section 6664(d)(3), and section 6694(a)(1). Such list (and any revisions thereof) shall be published in the Federal Register or the Internal Revenue Bulletin.

[Sec. 6662(e)]

(e) SUBSTANTIAL VALUATION MISSTATEMENT UNDER CHAPTER 1.—

(1) IN GENERAL.—For purposes of this section, there is a substantial valuation misstatement under chapter 1 if—

(A) the value of any property (or the adjusted basis of any property) claimed on any return of tax imposed by chapter 1 is 150 percent or more of the amount determined to be the correct amount of such valuation or adjusted basis (as the case may be), or

(B)(i) the price for any property or services (or for the use of property) claimed on any such return in connection with any transaction between persons described in section 482 is 200 percent or more (or 50 percent or less) of the amount determined under section 482 to be the correct amount of such price, or

(ii) the net section 482 transfer price adjustment for the taxable year exceeds the lesser of $5,000,000 or 10 percent of the taxpayer's gross receipts.

(2) LIMITATION.—No penalty shall be imposed by reason of subsection (b)(3) unless the portion of the underpayment for the taxable year attributable to substantial valuation misstatements under chapter 1 exceeds $5,000 ($10,000 in the case of a corporation other than an S corporation or a personal holding company (as defined in section 542)).

(3) NET SECTION 482 TRANSFER PRICE ADJUSTMENT.—For purposes of this subsection—

(A) IN GENERAL.—The term "net section 482 transfer price adjustment" means, with respect to any taxable year, the net increase in taxable income for the taxable year (determined without regard to any amount carried to such taxable year from another taxable year) resulting from adjustments under section 482 in the price for any property or services (or for the use of property).

(B) CERTAIN ADJUSTMENTS EXCLUDED IN DETERMINING THRESHOLD.—For purposes of determining whether the threshold requirements of paragraph (1)(B)(ii) are met, the following shall be excluded:

(i) Any portion of the net increase in taxable income referred to in subparagraph (A) which is attributable to any redetermination of a price if—

(I) it is established that the taxpayer determined such price in accordance with a specific pricing method set forth in the regulations prescribed under section 482 and that the taxpayer's use of such method was reasonable,

(II) the taxpayer has documentation (which was in existence as of the time of filing the return) which sets forth the determination of such price in accordance with such a method and which establishes that the use of such method was reasonable, and

(III) the taxpayer provides such documentation to the Secretary within 30 days of a request for such documentation.

(ii) Any portion of the net increase in taxable income referred to in subparagraph (A) which is attributable to a redetermination of price where such price was not determined in accordance with such a specific pricing method if—

(I) the taxpayer establishes that none of such pricing methods was likely to result in a price that would clearly reflect income, the taxpayer used another pricing method to determine such price, and such other pricing method was likely to result in a price that would clearly reflect income,

(II) the taxpayer has documentation (which was in existence as of the time of filing the return) which sets forth the determination of such price in accordance with such other method and which establishes that the requirements of subclause (I) were satisfied, and

(III) the taxpayer provides such documentation to the Secretary within 30 days of a request for such documentation.

(iii) Any portion of such net increase which is attributable to any transaction solely between foreign corporations unless, in the case of any such corporations, the treatment of such transaction affects the determination of income from sources within the United States or taxable income effectively connected with the conduct of a trade or business within the United States.

(C) SPECIAL RULE.—If the regular tax (as defined in section 55(c)) imposed by chapter 1 on the taxpayer is determined by reference to an amount other than taxable income, such amount shall be treated as the taxable income of such taxpayer for purposes of this paragraph.

(D) COORDINATION WITH REASONABLE CAUSE EXCEPTION.—For purposes of section 6664(c) the taxpayer shall not be treated as having reasonable cause for any portion of an underpayment attributable to a net section 482 transfer price adjustment unless such taxpayer meets the requirements of clause (i), (ii), or (iii) of subparagraph (B) with respect to such portion.

* * *

[Sec. 6662(h)]

(h) INCREASE IN PENALTY IN CASE OF GROSS VALUATION MISSTATEMENTS.—

(1) IN GENERAL.—To the extent that a portion of the underpayment to which this section applies is attributable to one or more gross valuation misstatements, subsection (a) shall be applied with respect to such portion by substituting "40 percent" for "20 percent".

(2) GROSS VALUATION MISSTATEMENTS.—The term "gross valuation misstatements" means—

(A) any substantial valuation misstatement under chapter 1 as determined under subsection (e) by substituting—

(i) in paragraph (1)(A), "200 percent" for "150 percent",

(ii) in paragraph (1)(B)(i)—

(I) "400 percent" for "200 percent", and

(II) "25 percent" for "50 percent", and

(iii) in paragraph (1)(B)(ii)—

(I) "$20,000,000" for "$5,000,000", and

(II) "20 percent" for "10 percent".

(B) any substantial overstatement of pension liabilities as determined under subsection (f) by substituting "400 percent" for "200 percent",

(C) any substantial estate or gift tax valuation understatement as determined under subsection (g) by substituting "40 percent" for "65 percent", and

(D) Any disallowance of a deduction described in subsection (b)(10).

[Sec. 6662(i)]

(i) INCREASE IN PENALTY IN CASE OF NONDISCLOSED NONECONOMIC SUBSTANCE TRANSACTIONS.—

(1) IN GENERAL.—In the case of any portion of an underpayment which is attributable to one or more nondisclosed noneconomic substance transactions, subsection (a) shall be applied with respect to such portion by substituting "40 percent" for "20 percent".

(2) NONDISCLOSED NONECONOMIC SUBSTANCE TRANSACTIONS.—For purposes of this subsection, the term "nondisclosed noneconomic substance transaction" means any portion of a transaction described in subsection (b)(6) with respect to which the relevant facts affecting the tax treatment are not adequately disclosed in the return nor in a statement attached to the return.

(3) SPECIAL RULE FOR AMENDED RETURNS.—In no event shall any amendment or supplement to a return of tax be taken into account for purposes of this subsection if the amendment or supplement is filed after the earlier of the date the taxpayer is first contacted by the Secretary regarding the examination of the return or such other date as is specified by the Secretary.

[Sec. 6662(j)]

(j) UNDISCLOSED FOREIGN FINANCIAL ASSET UNDERSTATEMENT.—

(1) IN GENERAL.—For purposes of this section, the term "undisclosed foreign financial asset understatement" means, for any taxable year, the portion of the understatement for such taxable year which is attributable to any transaction involving an undisclosed foreign financial asset.

(2) UNDISCLOSED FOREIGN FINANCIAL ASSET.—For purposes of this subsection, the term "undisclosed foreign financial asset" means, with respect to any taxable year, any asset with respect to which information was required to be provided under section 6038, 6038B, 6038D, 6046A, or 6048 for such taxable year but was not provided by the taxpayer as required under the provisions of those sections.

(3) INCREASE IN PENALTY FOR UNDISCLOSED FOREIGN FINANCIAL ASSET UNDERSTATEMENTS.—In the case of any portion of an underpayment which is attributable to any undisclosed foreign financial asset understatement, subsection (a) shall be applied with respect to such portion by substituting "40 percent" for "20 percent".

[Sec. 6662(k)]

(k) INCONSISTENT ESTATE BASIS REPORTING.—For purposes of this section, the term "inconsistent estate basis" means any portion of an underpayment attributable to the failure to comply with section 1014(f).

[Sec. 6663]

SEC. 6663. IMPOSITION OF FRAUD PENALTY.

[Sec. 6663(a)]

(a) IMPOSITION OF PENALTY.—If any part of any underpayment of tax required to be shown on a return is due to fraud, there shall be added to the tax an amount equal to 75 percent of the portion of the underpayment which is attributable to fraud.

[Sec. 6663(b)]

(b) DETERMINATION OF PORTION ATTRIBUTABLE TO FRAUD.—If the Secretary establishes that any portion of an underpayment is attributable to fraud, the entire underpayment shall be treated as attributable to fraud, except with respect to any portion of the underpayment which the taxpayer establishes (by a preponderance of the evidence) is not attributable to fraud.

* * *

[Sec. 6664]

SEC 6664. DEFINITIONS AND SPECIAL RULES.

[Sec. 6664(a)]

(a) UNDERPAYMENT.—For purposes of this part, the term "underpayment" means the amount by which any tax imposed by this title exceeds the excess of—

(1) the sum of—

(A) the amount shown as the tax by the taxpayer on his return, plus

(B) amounts not so shown previously assessed (or collected without assessment), over

(2) the amount of rebates made.

For purposes of paragraph (2), the term "rebate" means so much of an abatement, credit, refund, or other repayment, as was made on the ground that tax imposed was less than the excess of the amount specified in paragraph (1) over the rebates previously made. A rule similar to the rule of section 6211(b)(4) shall apply for purposes of this subsection.

[Sec. 6664(b)]

(b) PENALTIES APPLICABLE ONLY WHERE RETURN FILED.—The penalties provided in this part shall apply only in cases where a return of tax is filed (other than a return prepared by the Secretary under the authority of section 6020(b)).

[Sec. 6664(c)]

(c) REASONABLE CAUSE EXCEPTION FOR UNDERPAYMENTS.—

(1) IN GENERAL.—No penalty shall be imposed under section 6662 or 6663 with respect to any portion of an underpayment if it is shown that there was a reasonable cause for such portion and that the taxpayer acted in good faith with respect to such portion.

(2) EXCEPTION.—Paragraph (1) shall not apply to any portion of an underpayment which is attributable to one or more transactions described in section 6662(b)(6) or to any disallowance of a deduction described in section 6662(b)(10).

(3) SPECIAL RULE FOR CERTAIN VALUATION OVERSTATEMENTS.—In the case of any underpayment attributable to a substantial or gross valuation over statement under chapter 1 with respect to charitable deduction property, paragraph (1) shall not apply. The preceding sentence shall not apply to a substantial valuation overstatement under chapter 1 if—

(A) the claimed value of the property was based on a qualified appraisal made by a qualified appraiser, and

(B) in addition to obtaining such appraisal, the taxpayer made a good faith investigation of the value of the contributed property.

(4) DEFINITIONS.—For purposes of this subsection—

(A) CHARITABLE DEDUCTION PROPERTY.—The term "charitable deduction property" means any property contributed by the taxpayer in a contribution for which a deduction was claimed under section 170. For purposes of paragraph (3), such term shall not include any securities for which (as of the date of the contribution) market quotations are readily available on an established securities market.

(B) QUALIFIED APPRAISAL.—The term "qualified appraisal" has the meaning given such term by section 170(f)(11)(E)(i).

(C) QUALIFIED APPRAISER.—The term "qualified appraiser" has the meaning given such term by section 170(f)(11)(E)(ii).

[Sec. 6664(d)]

(d) REASONABLE CAUSE EXCEPTION FOR REPORTABLE TRANSACTION UNDERSTATEMENTS.—

(1) IN GENERAL.—No penalty shall be imposed under section 6662A with respect to any portion of a reportable transaction understatement if it is shown that there was a reasonable cause for such portion and that the taxpayer acted in good faith with respect to such portion.

(2) EXCEPTION.—Paragraph (1) shall not apply to any portion of a reportable transaction understatement which is attributable to one or more transactions described in section 6662(b)(6).

(3) SPECIAL RULES.—Paragraph (1) shall not apply to any reportable transaction understatement unless—

(A) the relevant facts affecting the tax treatment of the item are adequately disclosed in accordance with the regulations prescribed under section 6011,

(B) there is or was substantial authority for such treatment, and

(C) the taxpayer reasonably believed that such treatment was more likely than not the proper treatment.

A taxpayer failing to adequately disclose in accordance with section 6011 shall be treated as meeting the requirements of subparagraph (A) if the penalty for such failure was rescinded under section 6707A(d).

(4) RULES RELATING TO REASONABLE BELIEF.—For purposes of paragraph (3)(C)—

(A) IN GENERAL.—A taxpayer shall be treated as having a reasonable belief with respect to the tax treatment of an item only if such belief—

(i) is based on the facts and law that exist at the time the return of tax which includes such tax treatment is filed, and

(ii) relates solely to the taxpayer's chances of success on the merits of such treatment and does not take into account the possibility that a return will not be audited, such treatment will not be raised on audit, or such treatment will be resolved through settlement if it is raised.

(B) CERTAIN OPINIONS MAY NOT BE RELIED UPON.—

(i) IN GENERAL.—An opinion of a tax advisor may not be relied upon to establish the reasonable belief of a taxpayer if—

(I) the tax advisor is described in clause (ii), or

(II) the opinion is described in clause (iii).

(ii) DISQUALIFIED TAX ADVISORS.—A tax advisor is described in this clause if the tax advisor—

(I) is a material advisor (within the meaning of section 6111(b)(1)) and participates in the organization, management, promotion, or sale of the transaction or is related (within the meaning of section 267(b) or 707(b)(1)) to any person who so participates,

(II) is compensated directly or indirectly by a material advisor with respect to the transaction,

(III) has a fee arrangement with respect to the transaction which is contingent on all or part of the intended tax benefits from the transaction being sustained, or

(IV) as determined under regulations prescribed by the Secretary, has a disqualifying financial interest with respect to the transaction.

(iii) DISQUALIFIED OPINIONS.—For purposes of clause (i), an opinion is disqualified if the opinion—

(I) is based on unreasonable factual or legal assumptions (including assumptions as to future events),

(II) unreasonably relies on representations, statements, findings, or agreements of the taxpayer or any other person,

(III) does not identify and consider all relevant facts, or

(IV) fails to meet any other requirement as the Secretary may prescribe.

SUBCHAPTER B—ASSESSABLE PENALTIES

PART I—GENERAL PROVISIONS

[Sec. 6672]

SEC. 6672. FAILURE TO COLLECT AND PAY OVER TAX, OR ATTEMPT TO EVADE OR DEFEAT TAX.

[Sec. 6672(a)]

(a) GENERAL RULE.—Any person required to collect, truthfully account for, and pay over any tax imposed by this title who willfully fails to collect such tax, or truthfully account for and pay over such tax, or willfully attempts in any manner to evade or defeat any such tax or the payment thereof, shall, in addition to other penalties provided by law, be liable to a penalty equal to the total amount of the tax evaded, or not collected, or not accounted for and paid over. No penalty shall be imposed under section 6653 or part II of subchapter A of chapter 68 for any offense to which this section is applicable.

* * *

[Sec. 6676]

SEC. 6676. ERRONEOUS CLAIM FOR REFUND OR CREDIT.

[Sec. 6676(a)]

(a) CIVIL PENALTY.—If a claim for refund or credit with respect to income tax is made for an excessive amount, unless it is shown that the claim for such excessive amount has a reasonable basis, the person making such claim shall be liable for a penalty in an amount equal to 20 percent of the excessive amount.

[Sec. 6676(b)]

(b) EXCESSIVE AMOUNT.—For purposes of this section, the term "excessive amount" means in the case of any person the amount by which the amount of the claim for refund or credit for any taxable year exceeds the amount of such claim allowable under this title for such taxable year.

[Sec. 6676(c)]

(c) NONECONOMIC SUBSTANCE TRANSACTIONS TREATED AS LACKING REASONABLE CAUSE.—For purposes of this section, any excessive amount which is attributable to any transaction described in section 6662(b)(6) shall not be treated as due to reasonable cause.

[Sec. 6676(d)]

(d) COORDINATION WITH OTHER PENALTIES.—This section shall not apply to any portion of the excessive amount of a claim for refund or credit which is subject to a penalty imposed under part II of subchapter A of chapter 68.

[Sec. 6677]

SEC. 6677. FAILURE TO FILE INFORMATION WITH RESPECT TO CERTAIN FOREIGN TRUSTS.

[Sec. 6677(a)]

(a) CIVIL PENALTY.—In addition to any criminal penalty provided by law, if any notice or return required to be filed by section 6048—

(1) is not filed on or before the time provided in such section, or

(2) does not include all the information required pursuant to such section or includes incorrect information,

the person required to file such notice or return shall pay a penalty equal to the greater of $10,000 or 35 percent of the gross reportable amount. If any failure described in the preceding sentence continues for more than 90 days after the day on which the Secretary mails notice of such failure to the person required to pay such penalty, such person shall pay a penalty (in addition to the amount determined under the preceding sentence) of $10,000 for each 30-day period (or fraction thereof) during which such failure continues after the expiration of such 90-day period. At such time as the gross reportable amount with respect to any failure can be determined by the Secretary, any subsequent penalty imposed under this subsection with respect to such failure shall be reduced as necessary to assure that the aggregate amount of such penalties do not exceed the gross reportable amount (and to the extent that such aggregate amount already exceeds the gross reportable amount the Secretary shall refund such excess to the taxpayer).

[Sec. 6677(b)]

(b) SPECIAL RULES FOR RETURNS UNDER SECTION 6048(b).—In the case of a return required under section 6048(b)—

(1) the United States person referred to in such section shall be liable for the penalty imposed by subsection (a), and

(2) subsection (a) shall be applied by substituting "5 percent" for "35 percent".

[Sec. 6677(c)]

(c) GROSS REPORTABLE AMOUNT.—For purposes of subsection (a), the term "gross reportable amount" means—

(1) the gross value of the property involved in the event (determined as of the date of the event) in the case of a failure relating to section 6048(a),

(2) the gross value of the portion of the trust's assets at the close of the year treated as owned by the United States person in the case of a failure relating to section 6048(b)(1), and

(3) the gross amount of the distributions in the case of a failure relating to section 6048(c).

[Sec. 6677(d)]

(d) REASONABLE CAUSE EXCEPTION.—No penalty shall be imposed by this section on any failure which is shown to be due to reasonable cause and not due to willful neglect. The fact that a foreign jurisdiction would impose a civil or criminal penalty on the taxpayer (or any other person) for disclosing the required information is not reasonable cause.

* * *

[Sec. 6679]

SEC. 6679. FAILURE TO FILE RETURNS, ETC., WITH RESPECT TO FOREIGN CORPORATIONS OR FOREIGN PARTNERSHIPS.

[Sec. 6679(a)]

(a) CIVIL PENALTY.—

(1) IN GENERAL.—In addition to any criminal penalty provided by law, any person required to file a return under section 6046 or 6046A who fails to file such return at the time provided in such section, or who files a return which does not show the information required pursuant to such section, shall pay a penalty of $10,000, unless it is shown that such failure is due to reasonable cause.

(2) INCREASE IN PENALTY WHERE FAILURE CONTINUES AFTER NOTIFICATION.—If any failure described in paragraph (1) continues for more than 90 days after the day on which the Secretary mails notice of such failure to the United States person, such person shall pay a penalty (in addition

to the amount required under paragraph (1)) of $10,000 for each 30-day period (or fraction thereof) during which such failure continues after the expiration of such 90-day period. The increase in any penalty under this paragraph shall not exceed $50,000.

***

[Sec. 6686]

SEC. 6686. FAILURE TO FILE RETURNS OR SUPPLY INFORMATION BY DISC OR FORMER FSC.

In addition to the penalty imposed by section 7203 (relating to willful failure to file return, supply information, or pay tax) any person required to supply information or to file a return under section 6011(c) who fails to supply such information or file such return at the time prescribed by the Secretary, or who files a return which does not show the information required, shall pay a penalty of $100 for each failure to supply information (but the total amount imposed on the delinquent person for all such failures during any calendar year shall not exceed $25,000) or a penalty of $1,000 for each failure to file a return, unless it is shown that such failure is due to reasonable cause.

[Sec. 6688]

SEC. 6688. ASSESSABLE PENALTIES WITH RESPECT TO INFORMATION REQUIRED TO BE FURNISHED UNDER SECTION 7654.

In addition to any criminal penalty provided by law, any person described in section 7654(a) who is required under section 937(c) or by regulations prescribed under section 7654 to furnish information and who fails to comply with such requirement at the time prescribed by such regulations, unless it is shown that such failure is due to reasonable cause and not to willful neglect, shall pay (upon notice and demand by the Secretary and in the same manner as tax) a penalty of $1,000 for each such failure.

[Sec. 6689]

SEC. 6689. FAILURE TO FILE NOTICE OF REDETERMINATION OF FOREIGN TAX.

[Sec. 6689(a)]

(a) CIVIL PENALTY.—If the taxpayer fails to notify the Secretary (on or before the date prescribed by regulations for giving such notice) of foreign tax redetermination, unless it is shown that such failure is due to reasonable cause and not due to willful neglect, there shall be added to the deficiency attributable to such redetermination an amount (not in excess of 25 percent of the deficiency) determined as follows—

(1) 5 percent of the deficiency if the failure is for not more than 1 month, with

(2) an additional 5 percent of the deficiency for each month (or fraction thereof) during which the failure continues.

[Sec. 6689(b)]

(b) FOREIGN TAX REDETERMINATION DEFINED.—For purposes of this section, the term "foreign tax redetermination" means any redetermination for which a notice is required under subsection (c) of section 905 or paragraph (2) of section 404A(g).

[Sec. 6707A]

SEC. 6707A. PENALTY FOR FAILURE TO INCLUDE REPORTABLE TRANSACTION INFORMATION WITH RETURN.

[Sec. 6707A(a)]

(a) IMPOSITION OF PENALTY.—Any person who fails to include on any return or statement any information with respect to a reportable transaction which is required under section 6011 to be included with such return or statement shall pay a penalty in the amount determined under subsection (b).

[Sec. 6707A(b)]

(b) AMOUNT OF PENALTY.—

(1) IN GENERAL.—Except as otherwise provided in this subsection, the amount of the penalty under subsection (a) with respect to any reportable transaction shall be 75 percent of the decrease in tax shown on the return as a result of such transaction (or which would have resulted from such transaction were respected for Federal tax purposes.

(2) MAXIMUM PENALTY.—The amount of the penalty under subsection (a) with respect to any reportable transaction shall not exceed—

(A) in the case of a listed transaction, $200,000 ($100,000 in the case of a natural person), or

(B) in the case of any other reportable transaction, $50,000 ($10,000 in the case of a natural person).

(3) MINIMUM PENALTY.—The amount of the penalty under subsection (a) with respect to any transaction shall not be less than $10,000 ($5,000 in the case of a natural person).

[Sec. 6707A(c)]

(c) DEFINITIONS.—For purposes of this section:

(1) REPORTABLE TRANSACTION.—The term "reportable transaction" means any transaction with respect to which information is required to be included with a return or statement because, as determined under regulations prescribed under section 6011, such transaction is of a type which the Secretary determines as having a potential for tax avoidance or evasion.

(2) LISTED TRANSACTION.—The term "listed transaction" means a reportable transaction which is the same as, or substantially similar to, a transaction specifically identified by the Secretary as a tax avoidance transaction for purposes of section 6011.

[Sec. 6707A(d)]

(d) AUTHORITY TO RESCIND PENALTY.—

(1) IN GENERAL.—The Commissioner of Internal Revenue may rescind all or any portion of any penalty imposed by this section with respect to any violation if—

(A) the violation is with respect to a reportable transaction other than a listed transaction, and

(B) rescinding the penalty would promote compliance with the requirements of this title and effective tax administration.

(2) NO JUDICIAL APPEAL.—Notwithstanding any other provision of law, any determination under this subsection may not be reviewed in any judicial proceeding.

(3) RECORDS.—If a penalty is rescinded under paragraph (1), the Commissioner shall place in the file in the Office of the Commissioner the opinion of the Commissioner with respect to the determination, including—

(A) a statement of the facts and circumstances relating to the violation,

(B) the reasons for the rescission, and

(C) the amount of the penalty rescinded.

[Sec. 6707A(e)]

(e) PENALTY REPORTED TO SEC.—In the case of a person—

(1) which is required to file periodic reports under section 13 or 15(d) of the Securities Exchange Act of 1934 or is required to be consolidated with another person for purposes of such reports, and

(2) which—

(A) is required to pay a penalty under this section with respect to a listed transaction,

(B) is required to pay a penalty under section 6662A with respect to any reportable transaction at a rate prescribed under section 6662A(c), or

(C) is required to pay a penalty under section 6662(h) with respect to any reportable transaction and would (but for section 6662A(e)(2)(B)) have been subject to penalty under section 6662A at a rate prescribed under section 6662A(c),

the requirement to pay such penalty shall be disclosed in such reports filed by such person for such periods as the Secretary shall specify. Failure to make a disclosure in accordance with the preceding sentence shall be treated as a failure to which the penalty under subsection (b)(2) applies.

[Sec. 6707A(f)]

(f) COORDINATION WITH OTHER PENALTIES.—The penalty imposed by this section shall be in addition to any other penalty imposed by this title.

[Sec. 6708]

SEC. 6708. FAILURE TO MAINTAIN LISTS OF ADVISEES WITH RESPECT TO REPORTABLE TRANSACTIONS.

[Sec. 6708(a)]

(a) IMPOSITION OF PENALTY.—

(1) IN GENERAL.—If any person who is required to maintain a list under section 6112(a) fails to make such list available upon written request to the Secretary in accordance with section 6112(b) within 20 business days after the date of such request, such person shall pay a penalty of $10,000 for each day of such failure after such 20th day.

(2) REASONABLE CAUSE EXCEPTION.—No penalty shall be imposed by paragraph (1) with respect to the failure on any day if such failure is due to reasonable cause.

[Sec. 6708(b)]

(b) PENALTY IN ADDITION TO OTHER PENALTIES.—The penalty imposed by this section shall be in addition to any other penalty provided by law.

[Sec. 6712]

SEC. 6712. FAILURE TO DISCLOSE TREATY-BASED RETURN POSITIONS.

[Sec. 6712(a)]

(a) GENERAL RULE.—If a taxpayer fails to meet the requirements of section 6114, there is hereby imposed a penalty equal to $1000 ($10,000 in the case of a C corporation) on each such failure.

[Sec. 6712(b)]

(b) AUTHORITY TO WAIVE.—The Secretary may waive all or any part of the penalty provided by this section on a showing by the taxpayer that there was reasonable cause for the failure and that the taxpayer acted in good faith.

[Sec. 6712(c)]

(c) PENALTY IN ADDITION TO OTHER PENALTIES.—The penalty imposed by this section shall be in addition to any other penalty imposed by law.

CHAPTER 70—JEOPARDY, RECEIVERSHIPS, ETC.

SUBCHAPTER A—JEOPARDY

PART I—TERMINATION OF TAXABLE YEAR

[Sec. 6851]

SEC. 6851. TERMINATION ASSESSMENTS OF INCOME TAX.

* * *

[Sec. 6851(d)]

(d) DEPARTURE OF ALIEN.—Subject to such exceptions as may, by regulations, be prescribed by the Secretary—

(1) No alien shall depart from the United States unless he first procures from the Secretary a certificate that he has complied with all the obligations imposed upon him by the income tax laws.

(2) Payment of taxes shall not be enforced by any proceedings under the provisions of this section prior to the expiration of the time otherwise allowed for paying such taxes if, in the case of an alien about to depart from the United States, the Secretary determines that the collection of the tax will not be jeopardized by the departure of the alien.

* * *

CHAPTER 75—CRIMES, OTHER OFFENSES, AND FORFEITURES

SUBCHAPTER A—CRIMES

PART I—GENERAL PROVISIONS

Caution: A larger fine may be imposed with respect to Code Sec. 7201 under 18 U.S.C. §3571.

[Sec. 7201]

SEC. 7201. ATTEMPT TO EVADE OR DEFEAT TAX.

Any person who willfully attempts in any manner to evade or defeat any tax imposed by this title or the payment thereof shall, in addition to other penalties provided by law, be guilty of a felony and, upon conviction thereof, shall be fined not more than $100,000 ($500,000 in the case of a corporation), or imprisoned not more than 5 years, or both, together with the costs of prosecution.

Caution: A larger fine may be imposed with respect to Code Sec. 7202 under 18 U.S.C. §3571.

[Sec. 7202]

SEC. 7202. WILLFUL FAILURE TO COLLECT OR PAY OVER TAX.

Any person required under this title to collect, account for, and pay over any tax imposed by this title who willfully fails to collect or truthfully account for and pay over such tax shall, in addition to other penalties provided by law, be guilty of a felony and, upon conviction thereof, shall be fined not more than $10,000, or imprisoned not more than 5 years, or both, together with the costs of prosecution.

⋙→ *Caution: A larger fine may be imposed with respect to Code Sec. 7203 under 18 U.S.C. §3571.*

[Sec. 7203]

SEC. 7203. WILLFUL FAILURE TO FILE RETURN, SUPPLY INFORMATION, OR PAY TAX.

Any person required under this title to pay any estimated tax or tax, or required by this title or by regulations made under authority thereof to make a return, keep any records, or supply any information, who willfully fails to pay such estimated tax or tax, make such return, keep such records, or supply such information, at the time or times required by law or regulations, shall, in addition to other penalties provided by law, be guilty of a misdemeanor and, upon conviction thereof, shall be fined not more than $25,000 ($100,000 in the case of a corporation), or imprisoned not more than 1 year, or both, together with the costs of prosecution. In the case of any person with respect to whom there is a failure to pay any estimated tax, this section shall not apply to such person with respect to such failure if there is no addition to tax under section 6654 or 6655 with respect to such failure. In the case of a willful violation of any provision of section 6050 I, the first sentence of this section shall be applied by substituting "felony" for "misdemeanor" and "5 years" for "1 year".

CHAPTER 78—DISCOVERY OF LIABILITY AND ENFORCEMENT OF TITLE

SUBCHAPTER D—POSSESSIONS

[Sec. 7651]

SEC. 7651. ADMINISTRATION AND COLLECTION OF TAXES IN POSSESSIONS.

Except as otherwise provided in this subchapter, and except as otherwise provided in section 28(a) of the Revised Organic Act of the Virgin Islands and section 30 of the Organic Act of Guam (relating to the covering of the proceeds of certain taxes into the treasuries of the Virgin Islands and Guam, respectively)—

(1) APPLICABILITY OF ADMINISTRATIVE PROVISIONS.—All provisions of the laws of the United States applicable to the assessment and collection of any tax imposed by this title or of any other liability arising under this title (including penalties) shall, in respect of such tax or liability, extend to and be applicable in any possession of the United States in the same manner and to the same extent as if such possession were a State, and as if the term "United States" when used in a geographical sense included such possession.

(2) TAX IMPOSED IN POSSESSION.—In the case of any tax which is imposed by this title in any possession of the United States—

(A) INTERNAL REVENUE COLLECTIONS.—Such tax shall be collected under the direction of the Secretary, and shall be paid into the Treasury of the United States as internal revenue collections; and

(B) APPLICABLE LAWS.—All provisions of the laws of the United States applicable to the administration, collection, and enforcement of such tax (including penalties) shall, in respect of such tax, extend to and be applicable in such possession of the United States in the same manner and to the same extent as if such possession were a State, and as if the term "United States" when used in a geographical sense included such possession.

(3) OTHER LAWS RELATING TO POSSESSIONS.—This section shall apply notwithstanding any other provision of law relating to any possession of the United States.

(4) VIRGIN ISLANDS.—

(A) For purposes of this section, the reference in section 28(a) of the Revised Organic Act of the Virgin Islands to "any tax specified in section 3811 of the Internal Revenue Code" shall be deemed to refer to any tax imposed by chapter 2 or by chapter 21.

(B) For purposes of this title, section 28(a) of the Revised Organic Act of the Virgin Islands shall be effective as if such section 28(a) had been enacted before the enactment of this title and such section 28(a) shall have no effect on the amount of income tax liability required to be paid by any person to the United States.

[Sec. 7654]

SEC. 7654. COORDINATION OF UNITED STATES AND CERTAIN POSSESSION INDIVIDUAL INCOME TAXES.

[Sec. 7654(a)]

(a) GENERAL RULE.—The net collection of taxes imposed by chapter 1 for each taxable year with respect to an individual to whom section 931 or 932(c) applies shall be covered into the Treasury of the specified possession of which such individual is a bona fide resident.

[Sec. 7654(b)]

(b) DEFINITION AND SPECIAL RULE.—For purposes of this section—

(1) NET COLLECTION.—In determining net collections for a taxable year, an appropriate adjustment shall be made for credits allowed against the tax liability and refunds made of income taxes for the taxable year.

(2) SPECIFIED POSSESSION.—The term "specified possession" means Guam, American Samoa, the Northern Mariana Islands, and the Virgin Islands.

[Sec. 7654(c)]

(c) TRANSFERS.—The transfers of funds between the United States and any specified possession required by this section shall be made not less frequently than annually.

[Sec. 7654(d)]

(d) FEDERAL PERSONNEL.—In addition to the amount determined under subsection (a), the United States shall pay to each specified possession at such times and in such manner as determined by the Secretary—

(1) the amount of the taxes deducted and withheld by the United States under chapter 24 with respect to compensation paid to members of the Armed Forces who are stationed in such possession but who have no income tax liability to such possession with respect to such compensation by reason of the Servicemembers Civil Relief Act (50 U.S.C. 3901 et seq.), and

(2) the amount of the taxes deducted and withheld under chapter 24 with respect to amounts paid for services performed as an employee of the United States (or any agency thereof) in a specified possession with respect to an individual unless section 931 or 932(c) applies.

[Sec. 7654(e)]

(e) REGULATIONS.—The Secretary shall prescribe such regulations as may be necessary to carry out the provisions of this section and sections 931 and 932, including regulations prohibiting the rebate of taxes covered over which are allocable to United States source income and prescribing the information which the individuals to whom such sections may apply shall furnish to the Secretary.

CHAPTER 79—DEFINITIONS

[Sec. 7701]

SEC. 7701. DEFINITIONS.

[Sec. 7701(a)]

(a) When used in this title, where not otherwise distinctly expressed or manifestly incompatible with the intent thereof—

(1) PERSON.—The term "person" shall be construed to mean and include an individual, a trust, estate, partnership, association, company or corporation.

(2) PARTNERSHIP AND PARTNER.—The term "partnership" includes a syndicate, group, pool, joint venture, or other unincorporated organization, through or by means of which any business, financial operation, or venture is carried on, and which is not, within the meaning of this title, a trust or estate or a corporation; and the term "partner" includes a member in such a syndicate, group, pool, joint venture, or organization.

(3) CORPORATION.—The term "corporation" includes associations, joint-stock companies, and insurance companies.

(4) DOMESTIC.—The term "domestic" when applied to a corporation or partnership means created or organized in the United States or under the law of the United States or of any State unless, in the case of a partnership, the Secretary provides otherwise by regulations.

(5) FOREIGN.—The term "foreign" when applied to a corporation or partnership means a corporation or partnership which is not domestic.

* * *

(9) UNITED STATES.—The term "United States" when used in a geographical sense includes only the States and the District of Columbia.

(10) STATE.—The term "State" shall be construed to include the District of Columbia, where such construction is necessary to carry out provisions of this title.

* * *

(18) INTERNATIONAL ORGANIZATION.—The term "international organization" means a public international organization entitled to enjoy privileges, exemptions, and immunities as an international organization under the International Organizations Immunities Act (22 U. S. C. 288-288f).

* * *

(23) TAXABLE YEAR.—The term "taxable year" means the calendar year, or the fiscal year ending during such calendar year, upon the basis of which the taxable income is computed under subtitle A. "Taxable year" means, in the case of a return made for a fractional part of a year under the provisions of subtitle A or under regulations prescribed by the Secretary, the period for which such return is made.

(24) FISCAL YEAR.—The term "fiscal year" means an accounting period of 12 months ending on the last day of any month other than December.

* * *

(30) UNITED STATES PERSON.—The term "United States person" means—

(A) a citizen or resident of the United States,

(B) a domestic partnership,

(C) a domestic corporation,

(D) any estate (other than a foreign estate, within the meaning of paragraph (31)), and

(E) any trust if—

(i) a court within the United States is able to exercise primary supervision over the administration of the trust, and

(ii) one or more United States persons have the authority to control all substantial decisions of the trust.

(31) FOREIGN ESTATE OR TRUST.—

(A) FOREIGN ESTATE.—The term "foreign estate" means an estate the income of which, from sources without the United States which is not effectively connected with the conduct of a trade or business within the United States, is not includible in gross income under subtitle A.

(B) FOREIGN TRUST.—The term "foreign trust" means any trust other than a trust described in subparagraph (E) of paragraph (30).

* * *

(39) PERSONS RESIDING OUTSIDE UNITED STATES.—If any citizen or resident of the United States does not reside in (and is not found in) any United States judicial district, such citizen or resident shall be treated as residing in the District of Columbia for purposes of any provision of this title relating to—

(A) jurisdiction of courts, or

(B) enforcement of summons.

* * *

(50) TERMINATION OF UNITED STATES CITIZENSHIP.—

(A) IN GENERAL.—An individual shall not cease to be treated as a United States citizen before the date on which the individual's citizenship is treated as relinquished under section 877A(g)(4).

(B) DUAL CITIZENS.—Under regulations prescribed by the Secretary, subparagraph (A) shall not apply to an individual who became at birth a citizen of the United States and a citizen of another country.

[Sec. 7701(b)]

(b) DEFINITION OF RESIDENT ALIEN AND NONRESIDENT ALIEN.—

(1) IN GENERAL.—For purposes of this title (other than subtitle B)—

(A) RESIDENT ALIEN.—An alien individual shall be treated as a resident of the United States with respect to any calendar year if (and only if) such individual meets the requirements of clause (i), (ii), or (iii):

(i) LAWFULLY ADMITTED FOR PERMANENT RESIDENCE.—Such individual is a lawful permanent resident of the United States at any time during such calendar year.

(ii) SUBSTANTIAL PRESENCE TEST.—Such individual meets the substantial presence test of paragraph (3).

(iii) FIRST YEAR ELECTION.—Such individual makes the election provided in paragraph (4).

(B) NONRESIDENT ALIEN.—An individual is a nonresident alien if such individual is neither a citizen of the United States nor a resident of the United States (within the meaning of subparagraph (A)).

(2) SPECIAL RULES FOR FIRST AND LAST YEAR OF RESIDENCY.—

(A) FIRST YEAR OF RESIDENCY.—

(i) IN GENERAL.—If an alien individual is a resident of the United States under paragraph (1)(A) with respect to any calendar year, but was not a resident of the United States at any time during the preceding calendar year, such alien individual shall be treated as a resident of the United States only for the portion of such calendar year which begins on the residency starting date.

(ii) RESIDENCY STARTING DATE FOR INDIVIDUALS LAWFULLY ADMITTED FOR PERMANENT RESIDENCE.—In the case of an individual who is a lawfully permanent resident of the United States at any time during the calendar year, but does not meet the substantial presence test of paragraph (3), the residency starting date shall be the first day in such calendar year on which he was present in the United States while a lawful permanent resident of the United States.

(iii) RESIDENCY STARTING DATE FOR INDIVIDUALS MEETING SUBSTANTIAL PRESENCE TEST.—In the case of an individual who meets the substantial presence test of paragraph (3) with respect to any calendar year, the residency starting date shall be the first day during such calendar year on which the individual is present in the United States.

(iv) RESIDENCY STARTING DATE FOR INDIVIDUALS MAKING FIRST YEAR ELECTION.—In the case of an individual who makes the election provided by paragraph (4) with respect to any calendar year, the residency starting date shall be the 1st day during such calendar year on which the individual is treated as a resident of the United States under that paragraph.

(B) LAST YEAR OF RESIDENCY.—An alien individual shall not be treated as a resident of the United States during a portion of any calendar year if—

(i) such portion is after the last day in such calendar year on which the individual was present in the United States (or, in the case of an individual described in paragraph (1)(A)(i), the last day on which he was so described),

(ii) during such portion the individual has a closer connection to a foreign country than to the United States, and

(iii) the individual is not a resident of the United States at any time during the next calendar year.

(C) CERTAIN NOMINAL PRESENCE DISREGARDED.—

(i) IN GENERAL.—For purposes of subparagraphs (A)(iii) and (B), an individual shall not be treated as present in the United States during any period for which the individual establishes that he has a closer connection to a foreign country than to the United States.

(ii) NOT MORE THAN 10 DAYS DISREGARDED.—Clause (i) shall not apply to more than 10 days on which the individual is present in the United States.

(3) SUBSTANTIAL PRESENCE TEST.—

(A) IN GENERAL.—Except as otherwise provided in this paragraph, an individual meets the substantial presence test of this paragraph with respect to any calendar year (hereinafter in this subsection referred to as the "current year") if—

(i) such individual was present in the United States on at least 31 days during the calendar year, and

(ii) the sum of the number of days on which such individual was present in the United States during the current year and the 2 preceding calendar years (when multiplied by the applicable multiplier determined under the following table) equals or exceeds 183 days:

In the case of days in:	The applicable multiplier is:
Current year	1
1st preceding year	1/3
2nd preceding year	1/6

(B) EXCEPTION WHERE INDIVIDUAL IS PRESENT IN THE UNITED STATES DURING LESS THAN ONE-HALF OF CURRENT YEAR AND CLOSER CONNECTION TO FOREIGN COUNTRY IS ESTABLISHED.—An individual shall not be treated as meeting the substantial presence test of this paragraph with respect to any current year if—

(i) such individual is present in the United States on fewer than 183 days during the current year, and

(ii) it is established that for the current year such individual has a tax home (as defined in section 911(d)(3) without regard to the second sentence thereof) in a foreign country and has a closer connection to such foreign country than to the United States.

(C) SUBPARAGRAPH (B) NOT TO APPLY IN CERTAIN CASES.—Subparagraph (B) shall not apply to any individual with respect to any current year if at any time during such year—

(i) such individual had an application for adjustment of status pending, or

(ii) such individual took other steps to apply for status as a lawful permanent resident of the United States.

(D) EXCEPTION FOR EXEMPT INDIVIDUALS OR FOR CERTAIN MEDICAL CONDITIONS.—An individual shall not be treated as being present in the United States on any day if—

(i) such individual is an exempt individual for such day, or

(ii) such individual was unable to leave the United States on such day because of a medical condition which arose while such individual was present in the United States.

(4) FIRST-YEAR ELECTION.—

(A) An alien individual shall be deemed to meet the requirements of this subparagraph if such individual—

(i) is not a resident of the United States under clause (i) or (ii) of paragraph (1)(A) with respect to a calendar year (hereinafter referred to as the "election year"),

(ii) was not a resident of the United States under paragraph (1)(A) with respect to the calendar year immediately preceding the election year,

(iii) is a resident of the United States under clause (ii) of paragraph (1)(A) with respect to the calendar year immediately following the election year, and

(iv) is both—

(I) present in the United States for a period of at least 31 consecutive days in the election year, and

(II) present in the United States during the period beginning with the first day of such 31-day period and ending with the last day of the election year (hereinafter referred to as the "testing period") for a number of days equal to or exceeding 75 percent of the number of days in the testing period (provided that an individual shall be treated for purposes of this subclause as present in the United States for a number of days during the testing period not exceeding 5 days in the aggregate, notwithstanding his absence from the United States on such days).

(B) An alien individual who meets the requirements of subparagraph (A) shall, if he so elects, be treated as a resident of the United States with respect to the election year.

(C) An alien individual who makes the election provided by subparagraph (B) shall be treated as a resident of the United States for the portion of the election year which begins on the 1st day of the earliest testing period during such year with respect to which the individual meets the requirements of clause (iv) of subparagraph (A).

(D) The rules of subparagraph (D)(i) of paragraph (3) shall apply for purposes of determining an individual's presence in the United States under this paragraph.

(E) An election under subparagraph (B) shall be made on the individual's tax return for the election year, provided that such election may not be made before the individual has met the substantial presence test of paragraph (3) with respect to the calendar year immediately following the election year.

(F) An election once made under subparagraph (B) remains in effect for the election year, unless revoked with the consent of the Secretary.

(5) EXEMPT INDIVIDUAL DEFINED.—For purposes of this subsection—

(A) IN GENERAL.—An individual is an exempt individual for any day if, for such day, such individual is—

(i) a foreign government-related individual,

(ii) a teacher or trainee,

(iii) a student, or

(iv) a professional athlete who is temporarily in the United States to compete in a sports event—

(I) which is organized for the primary purpose of benefiting an organization which is described in section 501(c)(3) and exempt from tax under section 501(a),

(II) all of the net proceeds of which are contributed to such organization, and,

(III) which utilizes volunteers for substantially all of the work performed in carrying out such event.

(B) FOREIGN GOVERNMENT-RELATED INDIVIDUAL.—The term "foreign government-related individual" means any individual temporarily present in the United States by reason of—

(i) diplomatic status, or a visa which the Secretary (after consultation with the Secretary of State) determines represents full-time diplomatic or consular status for purposes of this subsection,

(ii) being a full-time employee of an international organization, or

(iii) being a member of the immediate family of an individual described in clause (i) or (ii).

(C) TEACHER OR TRAINEE.—The term "teacher or trainee" means any individual—

(i) who is termporarily present in the United States under subparagraph (J) or (Q) of section 101(15) of the Immigration and Nationality Act (other than as a student), and

(ii) who substantially complies with the requirements for being so present.

(D) STUDENT.—The term "student" means any individual—

(i) who is temporarily present in the United States—

(I) under subparagraph (F) or (M) of section 101(15) of the Immigration and Nationality Act, or

(II) as a student under subparagraph (J) or (Q) of such section 101(15), and

(ii) who substantially complies with the requirements for being so present.

(E) SPECIAL RULES FOR TEACHERS, TRAINEES, AND STUDENTS.—

(i) LIMITATION ON TEACHERS AND TRAINEES.—An individual shall not be treated as an exempt individual by reason of clause (ii) of subparagraph (A) for the current year if, for any 2 calendar years during the preceding 6 calendar years, such person was an exempt person under clause (ii) or (iii) of subparagraph (A). In the case of an individual all of whose compensation is described in section 872(b)(3), the preceding sentence shall be applied by substituting "4 calendar years" for "2 calendar years".

(ii) LIMITATION ON STUDENTS.—For any calendar year after the 5th calendar year for which an individual was an exempt individual under clause (ii) or (iii) of subparagraph (A), such individual shall not be treated as an exempt individual by reason of clause (iii) of subparagraph (A), unless such individual establishes to the satisfaction of the Secretary that such individual does not intend to permanently reside in the United States and that such individual meets the requirements of subparagraph (D)(ii).

(6) LAWFUL PERMANENT RESIDENT.—For purposes of this subsection, an individual is a lawful permanent resident of the United States at any time if—

(A) such individual has the status of having been lawfully accorded the privilege of residing permanently in the United States as an immigrant in accordance with the immigration laws, and

(B) such status has not been revoked (and has not been administratively or judicially determined to have been abandoned).

An individual shall cease to be treated as a lawful permanent resident of the United States if such individual commences to be treated as a resident of a foreign country under the provisions of a tax treaty between the United States and the foreign country, does not waive the benefits of such treaty applicable to residents of the foreign country, and notifies the Secretary of the commencement of such treatment.

(7) PRESENCE IN THE UNITED STATES.—For purposes of this subsection—

(A) IN GENERAL.—Except as provided in subparagraph (B), (C), or (D) an individual shall be treated as present in the United States on any day if such individual is physically present in the United States at any time during such day.

(B) COMMUTERS FROM CANADA OR MEXICO.—If an individual regularly commutes to employment (or self-employment) in the United States from a place of residence in Canada or Mexico, such individual shall not be treated as present in the United States on any day during which he so commutes.

(C) TRANSIT BETWEEN 2 FOREIGN POINTS.—If an individual, who is in transit between 2 points outside the United States, is physically present in the United States for less than 24 hours, such individual shall not be treated as present in the United States on any day during such transit.

(D) CREW MEMBERS TEMPORARILY PRESENT.—An individual who is temporarily present in the United States on any day as a regular member of the crew of a foreign vessel engaged in transportation between the United States and a foreign country or a possession of the United States shall not be treated as present in the United States on such day unless such individual otherwise engages in any trade or business in the United States on such day.

(8) ANNUAL STATEMENTS.—The Secretary may prescribe regulations under which an individual who (but for subparagraph (B) or (D) of paragraph (3)) would meet the substantial presence test of paragraph (3) is required to submit an annual statement setting forth the basis on which such individual claims the benefits of subparagraph (B) or (D) of paragraph (3), as the case may be.

(9) TAXABLE YEAR.—

(A) IN GENERAL.—For purposes of this title, an alien individual who has not established a taxable year for any prior period shall be treated as having a taxable year which is the calendar year.

(B) FISCAL YEAR TAXPAYER.—If—

(i) an individual is treated under paragraph (1) as a resident of the United States for any calendar year, and

(ii) after the application of subparagraph (A), such individual has a taxable year other than a calendar year,

he shall be treated as a resident of the United States with respect to any portion of a taxable year which is within such calendar year.

(10) COORDINATION WITH SECTION 877.—If—

(A) an alien individual was treated as a resident of the United States during any period which includes at least 3 consecutive calendar years (hereinafter referred to as the "initial residency period"), and

(B) such individual ceases to be treated as a resident of the United States but subsequently becomes a resident of the United States before the close of the 3rd calendar year beginning after the close of the initial residency period,

such individual shall be taxable for the period after the close of the initial residency period and before the day on which he subsequently became a resident of the United States in the manner provided in section 877(b). The preceding sentence shall apply only if the tax imposed pursuant to section 877(b) exceeds the tax which, without regard to this paragraph, is imposed pursuant to section 871.

(11) REGULATIONS.—The Secretary shall prescribe such regulations as may be necessary or appropriate to carry out the purposes of this subsection.

***

[Sec. 7701(d)]

(d) COMMONWEALTH OF PUERTO RICO.—Where not otherwise distinctly expressed or manifestly incompatible with the intent thereof, references in this title to possessions of the United States shall be treated as also referring to the Commonwealth of Puerto Rico.

***

[Sec. 7701(l)]

(l) REGULATIONS RELATING TO CONDUIT ARRANGEMENTS.—The Secretary may prescribe regulations recharacterizing any multiple-party financing transaction as a transaction directly among any 2 or more of such parties where the Secretary determines that such recharacterization is appropriate to prevent avoidance of any tax imposed by this title.

***

[Sec. 7701(o)]

(o) CLARIFICATION OF ECONOMIC SUBSTANCE DOCTRINE.—

(1) APPLICATION OF DOCTRINE.—In the case of any transaction to which the economic substance doctrine is relevant, such transaction shall be treated as having economic substance only if—

(A) the transaction changes in a meaningful way (apart from Federal income tax effects) the taxpayer's economic position, and

(B) the taxpayer has a substantial purpose (apart from Federal income tax effects) for entering into such transaction.

(2) SPECIAL RULE WHERE TAXPAYER RELIES ON PROFIT POTENTIAL.—

(A) IN GENERAL.—The potential for profit of a transaction shall be taken into account in determining whether the requirements of subparagraphs (A) and (B) of paragraph (1) are met with respect to the transaction only if the present value of the reasonably expected pre-tax profit from the transaction is substantial in relation to the present value of the expected net tax benefits that would be allowed if the transaction were respected.

(B) TREATMENT OF FEES AND FOREIGN TAXES.—Fees and other transaction expenses shall be taken into account as expenses in determining pre-tax profit under subparagraph (A). The Secretary shall issue regulations requiring foreign taxes to be treated as expenses in determining pre-tax profit in appropriate cases.

(3) STATE AND LOCAL TAX BENEFITS.—For purposes of paragraph (1), any State or local income tax effect which is related to a Federal income tax effect shall be treated in the same manner as a Federal income tax effect.

(4) FINANCIAL ACCOUNTING BENEFITS.—For purposes of paragraph (1)(B), achieving a financial accounting benefit shall not be taken into account as a purpose for entering into a transaction if the origin of such financial accounting benefit is a reduction of Federal income tax.

(5) DEFINITIONS AND SPECIAL RULES.—For purposes of this subsection—

(A) ECONOMIC SUBSTANCE DOCTRINE.—The term "economic substance doctrine" means the common law doctrine under which tax benefits under subtitle A with respect to a transaction are not allowable if the transaction does not have economic substance or lacks a business purpose.

(B) EXCEPTION FOR PERSONAL TRANSACTIONS OF INDIVIDUALS.—In the case of an individual, paragraph (1) shall apply only to transactions entered into in connection with a trade or business or an activity engaged in for the production of income.

(C) DETERMINATION OF APPLICATION OF DOCTRINE NOT AFFECTED.—The determination of whether the economic substance doctrine is relevant to a transaction shall be made in the same manner as if this subsection had never been enacted.

(D) TRANSACTION.—The term "transaction" includes a series of transactions.

***

CHAPTER 80—GENERAL RULES

SUBCHAPTER B—EFFECTIVE DATE AND RELATED PROVISIONS

[Sec. 7852]

SEC. 7852. OTHER APPLICABLE RULES.

***

[Sec. 7852(d)]

(d) TREATY OBLIGATIONS.—

(1) IN GENERAL.—For purposes of determining the relationship between a provision of a treaty and any law of the United States affecting revenue, neither the treaty nor the law shall have preferential status by reason of its being a treaty or law.

(2) SAVINGS CLAUSE FOR 1954 TREATIES.—No provision of this title (as in effect without regard to any amendment thereto enacted after August 16, 1954) shall apply in any case where its application would be contrary to any treaty obligation of the United States in effect on August 16, 1954.

***

SUBCHAPTER C—PROVISIONS AFFECTING MORE THAN ONE SUBTITLE

[Sec. 7874]

SEC. 7874. RULES RELATING TO EXPATRIATED ENTITIES AND THEIR FOREIGN PARENTS.

[Sec. 7874(a)]

(a) TAX ON INVERSION GAIN OF EXPATRIATED ENTITIES.—

(1) IN GENERAL.—The taxable income of an expatriated entity for any taxable year which includes any portion of the applicable period shall in no event be less than the inversion gain of the entity for the taxable year.

(2) EXPATRIATED ENTITY.—For purposes of this subsection—

(A) IN GENERAL.—The term "expatriated entity" means—

(i) the domestic corporation or partnership referred to in subparagraph (B)(i) with respect to which a foreign corporation is a surrogate foreign corporation, and

(ii) any United States person who is related (within the meaning of section 267(b) or 707(b)(1)) to a domestic corporation or partnership described in clause (i).

(B) SURROGATE FOREIGN CORPORATION.—A foreign corporation shall be treated as a surrogate foreign corporation if, pursuant to a plan (or a series of related transactions)—

(i) the entity completes after March 4, 2003, the direct or indirect acquisition of substantially all of the properties held directly or indirectly by a domestic corporation or substantially all of the properties constituting a trade or business of a domestic partnership,

(ii) after the acquisition at least 60 percent of the stock (by vote or value) of the entity is held—

(I) in the case of an acquisition with respect to a domestic corporation, by former shareholders of the domestic corporation by reason of holding stock in the domestic corporation, or

(II) in the case of an acquisition with respect to a domestic partnership, by former partners of the domestic partnership by reason of holding a capital or profits interest in the domestic partnership, and

(iii) after the acquisition the expanded affiliated group which includes the entity does not have substantial business activities in the foreign country in which, or under the law of which, the entity is created or organized, when compared to the total business activities of such expanded affiliated group.

An entity otherwise described in clause (i) with respect to any domestic corporation or partnership trade or business shall be treated as not so described if, on or before March 4, 2003, such entity acquired directly or indirectly more than half of the properties held directly or indirectly by such corporation or more than half of the properties constituting such partnership trade or business, as the case may be.

(3) COORDINATION WITH SUBSECTION (b).—A corporation which is treated as a domestic corporation under subsection (b) shall not be treated as a surrogate foreign corporation for purposes of paragraph (2)(A).

[Sec. 7874(b)]

(b) INVERTED CORPORATIONS TREATED AS DOMESTIC CORPORATIONS.—Notwithstanding section 7701(a)(4), a foreign corporation shall be treated for purposes of this title as a domestic corporation if such corporation would be a surrogate foreign corporation if subsection (a)(2) were applied by substituting "80 percent" for "60 percent".

[Sec. 7874(c)]

(c) DEFINITIONS AND SPECIAL RULES.—

(1) EXPANDED AFFILIATED GROUP.—The term "expanded affiliated group" means an affiliated group as defined in section 1504(a) but without regard to section 1504(b)(3), except that section 1504(a) shall be applied by substituting "more than 50 percent" for "at least 80 percent" each place it appears.

(2) CERTAIN STOCK DISREGARDED.—There shall not be taken into account in determining ownership under subsection (a)(2)(B)(ii)—

(A) stock held by members of the expanded affiliated group which includes the foreign corporation, or

(B) stock of such foreign corporation which is sold in a public offering related to the acquisition described in subsection (a)(2)(B)(i).

(3) PLAN DEEMED IN CERTAIN CASES.—If a foreign corporation acquires directly or indirectly substantially all of the properties of a domestic corporation or partnership during the 4-year period beginning on the date which is 2 years before the ownership requirements of subsection (a)(2)(B)(ii) are met, such actions shall be treated as pursuant to a plan.

(4) CERTAIN TRANSFERS DISREGARDED.—The transfer of properties or liabilities (including by contribution or distribution) shall be disregarded if such transfers are part of a plan a principal purpose of which is to avoid the purposes of this section.

(5) SPECIAL RULE FOR RELATED PARTNERSHIPS.—For purposes of applying subsection (a)(2)(B)(ii) to the acquisition of a trade or business of a domestic partnership, except as provided in regulations, all partnerships which are under common control (within the meaning of section 482) shall be treated as 1 partnership.

(6) REGULATIONS.—The Secretary shall prescribe such regulations as may be appropriate to determine whether a corporation is a surrogate foreign corporation, including regulations—

(A) to treat warrants, options, contracts to acquire stock, convertible debt interests, and other similar interests as stock, and

(B) to treat stock as not stock.

[Sec. 7874(d)]

(d) OTHER DEFINITIONS.—For purposes of this section—

(1) APPLICABLE PERIOD.—The term "applicable period" means the period—

(A) beginning on the first date properties are acquired as part of the acquisition described in subsection (a)(2)(B)(i), and

(B) ending on the date which is 10 years after the last date properties are acquired as part of such acquisition.

(2) INVERSION GAIN.—The term "inversion gain" means the income or gain recognized by reason of the transfer during the applicable period of stock or other properties by an expatriated entity, and any income received or accrued during the applicable period by reason of a license of any property by an expatriated entity—

(A) as part of the acquisition described in subsection (a)(2)(B)(i), or

(B) after such acquisition if the transfer or license is to a foreign related person.

Subparagraph (B) shall not apply to property described in section 1221(a)(1) in the hands of the expatriated entity.

(3) FOREIGN RELATED PERSON.—The term "foreign related person" means, with respect to any expatriated entity, a foreign person which—

(A) is related (within the meaning of section 267(b) or 707(b)(1)) to such entity, or

(B) is under the same common control (within the meaning of section 482) as such entity.

[Sec. 7874(e)]

(e) SPECIAL RULES.—

(1) CREDITS NOT ALLOWED AGAINST TAX ON INVERSION GAIN.—Credits (other than the credit allowed by section 901) shall be allowed against the tax imposed by this chapter on an expatriated entity for any taxable year described in subsection (a) only to the extent such tax exceeds the product of—

(A) the amount of the inversion gain for the taxable year, and

(B) the highest rate of tax specified in section 11(b).

For purposes of determining the credit allowed by section 901, inversion gain shall be treated as from sources within the United States.

(2) SPECIAL RULES FOR PARTNERSHIPS.—In the case of an expatriated entity which is a partnership—

(A) subsection (a)(1) shall apply at the partner rather than the partnership level,

(B) the inversion gain of any partner for any taxable year shall be equal to the sum of—

(i) the partner's distributive share of inversion gain of the partnership for such taxable year, plus

(ii) gain recognized for the taxable year by the partner by reason of the transfer during the applicable period of any partnership interest of the partner in such partnership to the surrogate foreign corporation, and

(C) the highest rate of tax specified in the rate schedule applicable to the partner under this chapter shall be substituted for the rate of tax referred to in paragraph (1).

(3) COORDINATION WITH SECTION 172 AND MINIMUM TAX.—Rules similar to the rules of paragraphs (3) and (4) of section 860E(a) shall apply for purposes of subsection (a).

(4) STATUTE OF LIMITATIONS.—

(A) IN GENERAL.—The statutory period for the assessment of any deficiency attributable to the inversion gain of any taxpayer for any pre-inversion year shall not expire before the expiration of 3 years from the date the Secretary is notified by the taxpayer (in such manner as the Secretary may prescribe) of the acquisition described in subsection (a)(2)(B)(i) to which such gain relates and such deficiency may be assessed before the expiration of such 3-year period notwithstanding the provisions of any other law or rule of law which would otherwise prevent such assessment.

(B) PRE-INVERSION YEAR.—For purposes of subparagraph (A), the term "pre-inversion year" means any taxable year if—

(i) any portion of the applicable period is included in such taxable year, and

(ii) such year ends before the taxable year in which the acquisition described in subsection (a)(2)(B)(i) is completed.

[Sec. 7874(f)]

(f) SPECIAL RULE FOR TREATIES.—Nothing in section 894 or 7852(d) or in any other provision of law shall be construed as permitting an exemption, by reason of any treaty obligation of the United States heretofore or hereafter entered into, from the provisions of this section.

[Sec. 7874(g)]

(g) REGULATIONS.—The Secretary shall provide such regulations as are necessary to carry out this section, including regulations providing for such adjustments to the application of this section as are necessary to prevent the avoidance of the purposes of this section, including the avoidance of such purposes through—

(1) the use of related persons, pass-through or other noncorporate entities, or other intermediaries, or

(2) transactions designed to have persons cease to be (or not become) members of expanded affiliated groups or related persons.

Income Tax Regulations

Tax on Individuals

§1.1-1. Income tax on individuals.—

* * *

(b) *Citizens or residents of the United States liable to tax.*—In general, all citizens of the United States, wherever resident, and all resident alien individuals are liable to the income taxes imposed by the Code whether the income is received from sources within or without the United States. Pursuant to section 876, a nonresident alien individual who is a bona fide resident of a section 931 possession (as defined in §1.931-1(c)(1) of this chapter) or Puerto Rico during the entire taxable year is, except as provided in section 931 or 933 with respect to income from sources within such possessions, subject to taxation in the same manner as a resident alien individual. As to tax on nonresident alien individuals, see sections 871 and 877.

(c) *Who is a citizen.*—Every person born or naturalized in the United States and subject to its jurisdiction is a citizen. For other rules governing the acquisition of citizenship, see chapters 1 and 2 of title III of the Immigration and Nationality Act (8 U.S.C. 1401-1459). For rules governing loss of citizenship, see sections 349 to 357, inclusive, of such Act (8 U.S.C. 1481-1489), *Schneider v. Rusk,* (1964) 377 U.S. 163, and Rev. Rul. 70-506, C.B. 1970-2, 1. For rules pertaining to persons who are nationals but not citizens at birth, e.g., a person born in American Samoa, see section 308 of such Act (8 U.S.C. 1408). For special rules applicable to certain expatriates who have lost citizenship with a principal purpose of avoiding certain taxes, see section 877. A foreigner who has filed his declaration of intention of becoming a citizen but who has not yet been admitted to citizenship by a final order of a naturalization court is an alien.

(d) *Effective/applicability date.*—The second sentence of paragraph (b) of this section applies to taxable years ending after April 9, 2008. [Reg. § 1.1-1.]

□ [*T.D.* 6161, 2-3-56. *Amended by T.D.* 7117, 5-24-71, *T.D.* 7332, 12-20-74 *and T.D.* 9391, 4-4-2008.]

Tax on Corporations

§1.11-1. Tax on corporations.—(a) Every corporation, foreign or domestic, is liable to the tax imposed under section 11 except (1) corporations specifically excepted under such section from such tax: (2) corporations expressly exempt from all taxation under subtitle A of the Code (see section 501); and (3) corporations subject to tax under section 511(a). For taxable years beginning after December 31, 1966, foreign corporations engaged in trade or business in the United States shall be taxable under section 11 only on their taxable income which is effectively connected with the conduct of a trade or business in the United States (see section 882(a)(1)). For definition of the terms "corporations," "domestic," and "foreign," see section 7701(a)(3), (4), and (5), respectively. It is immaterial that a domestic corporation, and for taxable years beginning after December 31, 1966, a foreign corporation engaged in trade or business in the United States, which is subject to the tax imposed by section 11 may derive no income from sources within the United States. The tax imposed by section 11 is payable upon the basis of the returns rendered by the corporations liable thereto, except that in some cases a tax is to be paid at the source of the income. See subchapter A (sections 6001 and following), chapter 61 of the Code, and section 1442.

* * *

[Reg. § 1.11-1.]

□ [*T.D.* 6161, 2-3-56. *Amended by T.D.* 6237, 6-10-57; *T.D.* 6350, 1-6-59; *T.D.* 6407, 8-14-59; *T.D.* 6610, 8-30-62; *T.D.* 6681, 10-16-63, *T.D.* 7100, 3-19-71, *T.D.* 7181, 4-24-72, *T.D.* 7293, 11-27-73 *and T.D.* 7413, 3-25-76.]

Base Erosion and Anti-Abuse Tax

§1.59A-1. Base erosion and anti-abuse tax.—(a) *Purpose.*—This section and §§1.59A-2 through 1.59A-10 (collectively, the "section 59A regulations") provide rules under section 59A to determine the amount of the base erosion and anti-abuse tax. Paragraph (b) of this section provides definitions applicable to the section 59A regulations. Section 1.59A-2 provides rules regarding how to determine whether a taxpayer is an applicable taxpayer. Section 1.59A-3 provides rules regarding base erosion payments and base erosion tax benefits. Section 1.59A-4 provides rules for calculating modified taxable income. Section 1.59A-5 provides rules for calculating the base erosion minimum tax amount. Section 1.59A-6 provides rules relating to qualified derivative payments. Section 1.59A-7 provides rules regarding the application of section 59A to partnerships. Section 1.59A-8 is reserved for rules regarding the application of section 59A to certain expatriated entities. Section 1.59A-9 provides anti-abuse rules to prevent avoidance of section 59A. Finally, §1.59A-10 provides the applicability date for the section 59A regulations.

(b) *Definitions.*—For purposes of this section and §§1.59A-2 through 1.59A-10, the following terms have the meanings provided in this paragraph (b).

(1) *Aggregate group.*—The term *aggregate group* means the group of corporations determined by—

(i) Identifying a controlled group of corporations as defined in section 1563(a), except that the phrase "more than 50 percent" is substituted for "at least 80 percent" each place it appears in section 1563(a)(1) and the determination is made without regard to sections 1563(a)(4) and (e)(3)(C), and

(ii) Once the controlled group of corporations is determined, excluding foreign corporations except with regard to income that is, or is treated as, effectively connected with the conduct of a trade or business in the United States under an applicable provision of the Internal Revenue Code or regulations published under 26 CFR chapter I. Notwithstanding the foregoing, if a foreign corporation is subject to tax on a net basis pursuant to an applicable income tax treaty of the United States, it is excluded from the controlled group of corporations except with regard to income taken into account in determining its net taxable income.

(2) *Applicable section 38 credits.*—The term *applicable section 38 credits* means the credits allowed under section 38 for the taxable year that are properly allocable to—

(i) The low-income housing credit determined under section 42(a),

(ii) The renewable electricity production credit determined under section 45(a), and

(iii) The investment credit determined under section 46, but only to the extent properly allocable to the energy credit determined under section 48.

(3) *Applicable taxpayer.*—The term *applicable taxpayer* means a taxpayer that meets the requirements set forth in §1.59A-2(b).

(4) *Bank.*—The term *bank* has the meaning provided in section 581.

(5) *Base erosion and anti-abuse tax rate.*—The term *base erosion and anti-abuse tax rate* means the percentage that the taxpayer applies to its modified taxable income for the taxable year to calculate its base erosion minimum tax amount. See §1.59A-5(c) for the base erosion and anti-abuse tax rate applicable for the relevant taxable year.

(6) *Business interest expense.*—The term *business interest expense,* with respect to a taxpayer and a taxable year, has the meaning provided in §1.163(j)-1(b)(3).

(7) *Deduction.*—The term *deduction* means any deduction allowable under chapter 1 of subtitle A of the Internal Revenue Code.

(8) *Disallowed business interest expense carryforward.*—The term *disallowed business interest expense carryforward* has the meaning provided in §1.163(j)-1(b)(11).

(9) *Domestic related business interest expense.*—The term *domestic related business interest expense* for any taxable year is the taxpayer's business interest expense paid or accrued to a related party that is not a foreign related party.

(10) *Foreign person.*—The term *foreign person* means any person who is not a United States person. For purposes of the preceding sentence, a United States person has the meaning provided in section 7701(a)(30), except that any individual who is a citizen of any possession of the United States (but not otherwise a citizen of the United States) and who is not a resident of the United States is not a United States person. See § 1.59A-7(b) for rules applicable to partnerships.

(11) *Foreign related business interest expense.*—The term *foreign related business interest expense* for any taxable year is the taxpayer's business interest expense paid or accrued to a foreign related party.

(12) *Foreign related party.*—The term *foreign related party* means a foreign person, as defined in paragraph (b)(10) of this section, that is a related party, as defined in paragraph (b)(17) of this section, with respect to the taxpayer. In addition, for purposes of § 1.59A-3(b)(4)(v)(B) (relating to internal dealings under certain income tax treaties), a foreign related party also includes the foreign corporation's home office or a foreign branch of the foreign corporation. See § 1.59A-7(b), (c), and (f) for rules applicable to partnerships.

(13) *Gross receipts.*—The term *gross receipts* has the meaning provided in § 1.448-1T(f)(2)(iv).

(14) *Member of an aggregate group.*—The term *member of an aggregate group* means a corporation that is included in an aggregate group, as defined in paragraph (b)(1) of this section.

(15) *Registered securities dealer.*—The term *registered securities dealer* means any dealer as defined in section 3(a)(5) of the Securities Exchange Act of 1934 that is registered, or required to be registered, under section 15 of the Securities Exchange Act of 1934.

(16) *Regular tax liability.*—The term *regular tax liability* has the meaning provided in section 26(b).

(17) *Related party.*—(i) *In general.*—A *related party*, with respect to an applicable taxpayer, is—

(A) Any 25-percent owner of the taxpayer;

(B) Any person who is related (within the meaning of section 267(b) or 707(b)(1)) to the taxpayer or any 25-percent owner of the taxpayer; or

(C) A controlled taxpayer within the meaning of § 1.482-1(i)(5) together with, or with respect to, the taxpayer.

(ii) *25-percent owner.*—With respect to any corporation, a *25-percent owner* means any person who owns at least 25 percent of—

(A) The total voting power of all classes of stock of the corporation entitled to vote; or

(B) The total value of all classes of stock of the corporation.

(iii) *Application of section 318.*—Section 318 applies for purposes of paragraphs (b)(17)(i) and (ii) of this section, except that—

(A) "10 percent" is substituted for "50 percent" in section 318(a)(2)(C); and

(B) Section 318(a)(3)(A) through (C) are not applied so as to consider a United States person as owning stock that is owned by a person who is not a United States person.

(18) *TLAC long-term debt required amount.*—The term *TLAC long-term debt required amount* means the specified minimum amount of debt that is required pursuant to 12 CFR 252.162(a).

(19) *TLAC securities amount.*—The term *TLAC securities amount* is the sum of the adjusted issue prices (as determined for purposes of § 1.1275-1(b)) of all TLAC securities issued and outstanding by the taxpayer, without regard to whether interest thereunder would be a base erosion payment absent § 1.59A-3(b)(3)(v).

(20) *TLAC security.*—The term *TLAC security* means an eligible internal debt security, as defined in 12 CFR 252.161.

(21) *Unrelated business interest expense.*—The term *unrelated business interest expense* for any taxable year is the taxpayer's business interest expense paid or accrued to a party that is not a related party. [Reg. § 1.59A-1.]

☐ [*T.D.* 9885, 12-2-2019. *Amended by T.D.* 9910, 10-8-2020.]

§ 1.59A-2. Applicable taxpayer.—(a) *Scope.*—This section provides rules for determining whether a taxpayer is an applicable taxpayer. Paragraph (b) of this section defines an applicable taxpayer. Paragraph (c) of this section provides rules for determining whether a taxpayer is an applicable taxpayer by reference to the aggregate group of which the taxpayer is a member. Paragraph (d) of this section provides rules regarding the gross receipts test. Paragraph (e) of this section provides rules regarding the base erosion percentage test. Paragraph (f) of this section provides examples illustrating the rules of this section.

(b) *Applicable taxpayer.*—For purposes of section 59A, a taxpayer is an applicable taxpayer with respect to any taxable year if the taxpayer—

(1) Is a corporation, but not a regulated investment company, a real estate investment trust, or an S corporation;

(2) Satisfies the gross receipts test of paragraph (d) of this section; and

(3) Satisfies the base erosion percentage test of paragraph (e) of this section.

(c) *Aggregation rules.*—(1) *In general.*—Solely for purposes of this section and § 1.59A-4, a taxpayer that is a member of an aggregate group determines its gross receipts and its base erosion percentage on the basis of the aggregate group. For these purposes, transactions that occur between members of the taxpayer's aggregate group that were members of the aggregate group as of the time of the transaction are not taken into account. In the case of a foreign corporation that is a member of an aggregate group, only transactions that occur between members of the aggregate group and that relate to income effectively connected with, or treated as effectively connected with, the conduct of a trade or business in the United States are not taken into account for this purpose. In the case of a foreign corporation that is a member of an aggregate group and that is subject to tax on a net basis pursuant to an applicable income tax treaty of the United States, only transactions that occur between members of the aggregate group and that relate to income that is taken into account in determining its net taxable income are not taken into account for this purpose. For purposes of this paragraph (c)(1), each payment or accrual is treated as a separate transaction.

(2) *Aggregate group determined with respect to each taxpayer.*—(i) *In general.*—Solely for purposes of this section, an aggregate group is determined with respect to each taxpayer. As a result, the aggregate group of one taxpayer may be different than the aggregate group of another member of the taxpayer's aggregate group.

(ii) *Change in the composition of an aggregate group.*—A change in ownership of the taxpayer (for example, a sale of the taxpayer to a third party) does not cause the taxpayer to leave its own aggregate group. Instead, any members of the taxpayer's aggregate group before the change in ownership that are no longer members following the change in ownership are treated as having left the taxpayer's aggregate group, and any new members that become members of the taxpayer's aggregate group following the change in ownership are treated as having joined the taxpayer's aggregate group. A change in ownership of another member of the aggregate group of the taxpayer (for example, a sale of the member to a third party) may result in the member joining or leaving the aggregate group of the taxpayer. See paragraph (c)(4) of this section for the treatment of members joining or leaving the aggregate group of a taxpayer.

(3) *Taxable year of members of an aggregate group.*—Solely for purposes of this section, a taxpayer that is a member of an aggregate group measures the gross receipts and base erosion percentage of the aggregate group for a taxable year by reference to the taxpayer's gross receipts, base erosion tax benefits, and deductions for the taxable year and the gross receipts, base erosion tax benefits, and deductions of each member of the aggregate group for the taxable year of the member that ends with or within the taxpayer's taxable year.

(4) *Periods before and after a corporation is a member of an aggregate group.*—(i) *In general.*—Solely for purposes of this section, to determine the gross receipts and the base erosion percentage of the aggregate group of a taxpayer, the taxpayer takes into account only the portion of another corporation's taxable year during which the corporation is a member of the aggregate group of the taxpayer. The gross receipts, base erosion tax benefits, and deductions of a corporation that are properly included in the gross receipts and base erosion percentage of the aggregate group of a taxpayer are not reduced as a result of the member leaving the aggregate group of the taxpayer.

(ii) *Deemed taxable year-end.*—Solely for purposes of this paragraph (c), if a corporation leaves or joins the aggregate group of a taxpayer, the corporation is treated as ceasing to be a member of the aggregate group at the time of its taxable year-end, or becoming a member of the aggregate group immediately after the time of its taxable year-end, resulting from the transaction. For purposes of this paragraph (c), if a corporation joins or leaves an aggregate group in a transaction that does not result in the corporation having a taxable year-end, the corporation is treated as having a taxable year-end ("deemed taxable year-end") at the end of the day on which the transaction occurs.

(iii) *Items allocable to deemed taxable years before and after deemed taxable year-end.*—Solely for purposes of this paragraph (c), a corporation that has a deemed taxable year-end determines gross receipts, base erosion tax benefits, and deductions attributable to the deemed taxable year ending upon, or beginning immediately after, the deemed taxable year-end by either treating the corporation's books as closing ("deemed closing of the books") at the deemed taxable year-end or, in the case of items other than extraordinary items, allocating those items on a pro-rata basis without a closing of the books. Extraordinary items are allocated to the deemed taxable year ending upon, or beginning immediately after, the deemed taxable year-end based on the day that they are taken into account. For purposes of applying this paragraph (c)(4)(iii), extraordinary items that are attributable to a transaction that occurs during the portion of the corporation's day after the event resulting in the corporation joining or leaving the aggregate group are treated as taken into account at the beginning of the following day. Additionally, for purposes of applying this paragraph (c)(4)(iii), "extraordinary items" include the items enumerated in §1.1502-76(b)(2)(ii)(C) as well as any other payment not made in the ordinary course of business that would be treated as a base erosion payment.

(5) *Short taxable year.*—(i) *Short period of the taxpayer.*—(A) *In general.*—Solely for purposes of this section, if a taxpayer has a taxable year of fewer than 12 months (a short period), the gross receipts, base erosion tax benefits, and deductions of the taxpayer are annualized by multiplying the total amount for the short period by 365 and dividing the result by the number of days in the short period.

(B) *Determining the gross receipts and base erosion percentage of the aggregate group of a taxpayer for a short period.*—When a taxpayer has a taxable year that is a short period and a member of the taxpayer's aggregate group does not have a taxable year that ends with or within the taxpayer's taxable year as a result of the taxpayer's short period, the taxpayer must use a reasonable approach to determine the gross receipts and base erosion percentage of its aggregate group for the short period. A reasonable approach should neither over-count nor under-count the gross receipts, base erosion tax benefits, and deductions of the aggregate group of the taxpayer. A reasonable approach does not include an approach that does not take into account the gross receipts, base erosion tax benefits, or deductions of the member. The taxpayer must consistently apply the reasonable approach. Examples of a reasonable approach may include an approach that takes into account 12 months of gross receipts, base erosion tax benefits, and deductions of the member by reference to—

(1) The 12-month period ending on the last day of the short period;

(2) The member's taxable year that ends nearest to the last day of the short period or that begins nearest to the first day of the short period; or

(3) An average of the two taxable years of the member ending before and after the short period.

(ii) *Short period of a member of the taxpayer's aggregate group.*—(A) *Multiple taxable years of a member of the taxpayer's aggregate group comprised of more than 12 months.*—If a member of a taxpayer's aggregate group has more than one taxable year ending with or within the taxpayer's taxable year, and the member's taxable years ending with or within the taxpayer's taxable year are comprised of more than 12 months in total, then the aggregate group member's gross receipts, base erosion tax benefits, and deductions are annualized for purposes of determining the gross receipts and base erosion percentage of the taxpayer's aggregate group. The aggregate group member's gross receipts, base erosion tax benefits, and deductions are annualized by multiplying the total amount for the member's taxable years by 365 and dividing the result by the total number of days in the multiple taxable years.

(B) *Short period or periods of a member of the taxpayer's aggregate group comprised of fewer than 12 months from change in taxable year.*—If, as a result of a member of a taxpayer's aggregate group changing its taxable year-end (other than as a result of the application of §1.1502-76(a)), the member's taxable year or years ending with or within the taxpayer's taxable year are comprised of fewer than 12 months in total, then the aggregate group member's gross receipts, base erosion tax benefits, and deductions are annualized for purposes of determining the gross receipts and base erosion percentage of the taxpayer's aggregate group. The aggregate group member's gross receipts, base erosion tax benefits, and deductions are annualized by multiplying the total amount for the member's taxable year or years by 365 and dividing the result by the total number of days in the taxable year or years.

(iii) *Anti-abuse rule.*—If a taxpayer or a member of a taxpayer's aggregate group enters into a transaction (or series of transactions), plan, or arrangement with another corporation that is a member of the aggregate group or a foreign related party that has a principal purpose of changing the period taken into account under the gross receipts test or the base erosion percentage test to avoid applicable taxpayer status under paragraph (b) of this section, then the gross receipts test or base erosion percentage test, respectively, applies as if that transaction (or series of transactions), plan, or arrangement had not occurred.

(6) *Treatment of predecessors.*—(i) *In general.*—Solely for purposes of this section, in determining gross receipts under paragraph (d) of this section, any reference to a taxpayer includes a reference to any predecessor of the taxpayer. For this purpose, a predecessor is the distributor or transferor corporation in a transaction described in section 381(a) in which the taxpayer is the acquiring corporation. For purposes of determining the gross receipts of a predecessor that are taken into account by a taxpayer, the operating rules set forth in this paragraph (c) and in paragraph (d) of this section are applied to the same extent they were applied to the predecessor.

(ii) *No duplication.*—If the taxpayer or any member of its aggregate group is also a predecessor of the taxpayer or any member of its aggregate group, the gross receipts of each member are taken into account only once.

(7) *Partnerships.*—For the treatment of partnerships for purposes of determining gross receipts and base erosion tax benefits, see §1.59A-7(e)(2) and (d), respectively.

(8) *Transition rule for aggregate group members with different taxable years.*—If the taxpayer has a different taxable year than another member of the taxpayer's aggregate group (other member), and the other member is eligible for the exception in §1.59A-3(b)(3)(vi) (amounts paid or accrued in taxable years beginning before January 1, 2018) with respect to a taxable year ending with or within the taxpayer's taxable year ("excepted taxable year"), the excepted taxable year of the other member is not taken into account for purposes of paragraph (e) of this section. This rule applies solely for purposes of determining whether a taxpayer is an applicable taxpayer under this section.

(9) *Consolidated groups.*—For the treatment of consolidated groups for purposes of determining gross receipts and base erosion tax benefits, see §1.1502-59A(b).

(d) *Gross receipts test.*—(1) *Amount of gross receipts.*—A taxpayer, or the aggregate group of which the taxpayer is a member, satisfies the gross receipts test of this section if it has average annual gross receipts of at least $500,000,000 for the three-taxable-year period ending with the preceding taxable year.

(2) *Taxpayer not in existence for entire three-year period.*—If a taxpayer was not in existence for the entire three-year period referred to in paragraph (d)(1) of this section, the taxpayer determines a gross receipts average for the period that it was in existence (which includes gross receipts in the current year).

(3) *Gross receipts of foreign corporations.*—With respect to any foreign corporation, only gross receipts that are taken into account in determining income that is, or is treated as, effectively connected with the conduct of a trade or business within the United States are taken into account for purposes of paragraph (d)(1) of this section. In the case of a foreign corporation that is a member of an aggregate group and that is subject to tax on a net basis pursuant to an applicable income tax treaty of the United States, the foreign corpora-

tion includes only gross receipts that are attributable to transactions taken into account in determining its net taxable income.

(4) *Gross receipts of an insurance company.*—Solely for purposes of this section, for any corporation that is subject to tax under subchapter L or any corporation that would be subject to tax under subchapter L if that corporation were a domestic corporation, gross receipts are reduced by return premiums (within the meaning of section 803(a)(1)(B) and section 832(b)(4)(A)), but are not reduced by any reinsurance premiums paid or accrued.

(5) *Reductions in gross receipts.*—For purposes of this section, gross receipts for any taxable year are reduced by returns and allowances made during that taxable year.

(6) *Gross receipts of consolidated groups.*—For purposes of this section, the gross receipts of a consolidated group are determined by aggregating the gross receipts of all of the members of the consolidated group. See § 1.1502-59A(b).

(e) *Base erosion percentage test.*—(1) *In general.*—A taxpayer, or the aggregate group of which the taxpayer is a member, satisfies the base erosion percentage test if its base erosion percentage is three percent or higher.

(2) *Base erosion percentage test for banks and registered securities dealers.*—(i) *In general.*—A taxpayer that is a member of an affiliated group (as defined in section 1504(a)(1)) that includes a bank (as defined in § 1.59A-1(b)(4)) or a registered securities dealer (as defined in section § 1.59A-1(b)(15)) satisfies the base erosion percentage test if its base erosion percentage is two percent or higher.

(ii) *Aggregate groups.*—An aggregate group of which a taxpayer is a member and that includes a bank or a registered securities dealer that is a member of an affiliated group (as defined in section 1504(a)(1)) is subject to the base erosion percentage threshold described in paragraph (e)(2)(i) of this section.

(iii) *De minimis exception for banking and registered securities dealer activities.*—An aggregate group that includes a bank or a registered securities dealer that is a member of an affiliated group (as defined in section 1504(a)(1)) is not treated as including a bank or registered securities dealer for purposes of paragraph (e)(2)(i) of this section for a taxable year, if, for that taxable year, the total gross receipts of the aggregate group attributable to the bank or the registered securities dealer (or attributable to all of the banks and registered securities dealers in the group, if more than one) represent less than two percent of the total gross receipts of the aggregate group, as determined under paragraph (d) of this section. When there is no aggregate group, a consolidated group that includes a bank or a registered securities dealer is not treated as including a bank or registered securities dealer for purposes of paragraph (e)(2)(i) of this section for a taxable year, if, for that taxable year, the total gross receipts of the consolidated group attributable to the bank or the registered securities dealer (or attributable to all of the banks or registered securities dealers in the group, if more than one) represent less than two percent of the total gross receipts of the consolidated group, as determined under paragraph (d) of this section.

(3) *Computation of base erosion percentage.*—(i) *In general.*—The taxpayer's base erosion percentage for any taxable year is determined by dividing—

(A) The aggregate amount of the taxpayer's (or in the case of a taxpayer that is a member of an aggregate group, the aggregate group's) base erosion tax benefits (as defined in § 1.59A-3(c)(1)) for the taxable year, by

(B) The sum of—

(1) The aggregate amount of the deductions (including deductions for base erosion tax benefits described in § 1.59A-3(c)(1)(i) and base erosion tax benefits described in § 1.59A-3(c)(1)(ii)) allowable to the taxpayer (or in the case of a taxpayer that is a member of an aggregate group, any member of the aggregate group) under chapter 1 of Subtitle A for the taxable year;

(2) The base erosion tax benefits described in § 1.59A-3(c)(1)(iii) with respect to any premiums or other consideration paid or accrued by the taxpayer (or in the case of a taxpayer that is a member of an aggregate group, any member of the aggregate group) to a foreign related party for any reinsurance payment taken into account under sections 803(a)(1)(B) or 832(b)(4)(A) for the taxable year; and

(3) Any amount paid or accrued by the taxpayer (or in the case of a taxpayer that is a member of an aggregate group, any member of the aggregate group) resulting in a reduction of gross receipts described in § 1.59A-3(c)(1)(iv) for the taxable year.

(ii) *Certain items not taken into account in denominator.*—Except as provided in paragraph (e)(3)(viii) of this section, the amount under paragraph (e)(3)(i)(B) of this section is determined by not taking into account—

(A) Any deduction allowed under section 172, 245A, or 250 for the taxable year;

(B) Any deduction for amounts paid or accrued for services to which the exception described in § 1.59A-3(b)(3)(i) applies;

(C) Any deduction for qualified derivative payments that are not treated as base erosion payments by reason of § 1.59A-3(b)(3)(ii);

(D) Any exchange loss within the meaning of § 1.988-2 from a section 988 transaction as described in § 1.988-1(a)(1) that is not treated as a base erosion payment by reason of § 1.59A-3(b)(3)(iv);

(E) Any deduction for amounts paid or accrued to foreign related parties with respect to TLAC securities and foreign TLAC securities that are not treated as base erosion payments by reason of § 1.59A-3(b)(3)(v);

(F) Any reinsurance losses incurred and claims payments described in § 1.59A-3(b)(3)(ix); and

(G) Any deduction not allowed in determining taxable income for the taxable year.

(iii) *Effect of treaties on base erosion percentage determination.*—See § 1.59A-3(c)(2) and (3).

(iv) *Amounts paid or accrued between members of a consolidated group.*—See § 1.1502-59A(b).

(v) *Deductions and base erosion tax benefits from partnerships.*—See § 1.59A-7(b), (d), and (e).

(vi) *Mark-to-market positions.*—For any position with respect to which the taxpayer (or in the case of a taxpayer that is a member of an aggregate group, a member of the aggregate group) applies a mark-to-market method of accounting for U.S. federal income tax purposes, the taxpayer must determine its gain or loss with respect to that position for any taxable year by combining all items of income, gain, loss, or deduction arising with respect to the position during the taxable year, regardless of how each item arises (including from a payment, accrual, or mark) for purposes of paragraph (e)(3) of this section. See paragraph (f)(1) of this section (*Example 1*) for an illustration of this rule. For purposes of section 59A, a taxpayer computes its losses resulting from positions subject to a mark-to-market regime under the Internal Revenue Code based on a single mark for the taxable year on the earlier of the last business day of the taxpayer's taxable year and the disposition (whether by sale, offset, exercise, termination, expiration, maturity, or other means) of the position, regardless of how frequently a taxpayer marks to market for other purposes. See § 1.59A-3(b)(2)(iii) for the application of this rule for purposes of determining the amount of base erosion payments.

(vii) *Reinsurance losses incurred and claims payments.*—Except as provided in paragraph (e)(3)(ii)(F) of this section, amounts paid for losses incurred (as defined in section 832(b)(5)) and claims and benefits under section 805(a)(1) are taken into account for purposes of paragraph (e)(3)(i)(B)*(1)* of this section.

(viii) *Certain payments that qualify for the effectively connected income exception and another base erosion payment exception.*—Subject to paragraph (c) of this section (transactions that occur between members of the taxpayer's aggregate group), a payment that qualifies for the effectively connected income exception described in § 1.59A-3(b)(3)(iii) and either the service cost method exception described in § 1.59A-3(b)(3)(i), the qualified derivative payment exception described in § 1.59A-3(b)(3)(ii), or the TLAC exception described in § 1.59A-3(b)(3)(v) is not subject to paragraph (e)(3)(ii)(B), (C), or (E) of this section and those amounts are included in the denominator of the base erosion percentage if the foreign related party who received the payment is not a member of the aggregate group.

(f) *Examples.*—(1) *Example 1: Mark-to market.*—(i) *Facts.* (A) Foreign Parent (FP) is a foreign corporation that owns all of the stock of domestic corporation (DC). FP is a foreign related party of DC under § 1.59A-1(b)(12). DC is a registered securities dealer that does not hold any securities for investment. On January 1 of year 1, DC enters into two interest rate swaps for a term of two years, one with unrelated Customer A as the counterparty (position A) and one with unrelated Customer B as the counterparty (position B). Each of the swaps provides for semiannual periodic payments to be made or received on June 30 and December 31. No party makes any payment to any other party upon initiation of either of the swaps (that is, they are entered into at-the-money). DC is required to mark-to-market positions A and B for U.S. federal income tax purposes. DC is a calendar year taxpayer.

(B) For position A in year 1, DC makes a payment of $150x on June 30, and receives a payment of $50x on December 31. There are no other payments in year 1. On December 31, position A has a value to DC of $110x (that is, position A is in-the-money by $110x).

(C) For position B in year 1, DC receives a payment of $120x on June 30, and makes a payment of $30x on December 31. There are no other payments in year 1. On December 31, position B has a value to DC of ($130x) (that is, position B is out-of-the-money by $130x).

(ii) *Analysis.* (A) With respect to position A, based on the total amount of payments made and received in year 1, DC has a net deduction of $100x. In addition, DC has a mark-to-market gain of $110x. As described in paragraph (e)(3)(vi) of this section, the mark-to-market gain of $110x is combined with the net deduction of $100x resulting from the payments. Therefore, with respect to position A, DC has a gain of $10x, and thus has no deduction in year 1 for purposes of section 59A.

(B) With respect to position B, based on the total amount of payments made and received in year 1, DC has net income of $90x. In addition, DC has a mark-to-market loss of $130x. As described in paragraph (e)(3)(vi) of this section, the mark-to-market loss of $130x is combined with the net income of $90x resulting from the payments. Therefore, with respect to position B, DC has a loss of $40x, and thus has a $40x deduction in year 1 for purposes of section 59A.

(2) *Example 2: Member leaving an aggregate group.*—(i) *Facts.* Parent Corporation wholly owns Corporation 1 and Corporation 2. Each corporation is a domestic corporation and a calendar-year taxpayer that does not file a consolidated return. The aggregate group of Corporation 1 includes Parent Corporation and Corporation 2. At noon on June 30, Year 1, Parent Corporation sells the stock of Corporation 2 to Corporation 3, an unrelated domestic corporation, in exchange for cash consideration. Before the acquisition, Corporation 3 was not a member of an aggregate group. Corporation 2 and Corporation 3 do not file a consolidated return.

(ii) *Analysis.* (A) For purposes of section 59A, to determine the gross receipts and base erosion percentage of the aggregate group of Corporation 1 for calendar Year 1, Corporation 2 is treated as having a taxable year end at the end of the day on June 30, Year 1, as a result of the sale. Corporation 2 leaves the aggregate group of Corporation 1 and Parent Corporation at the end of the day on June 30, Year 1. The aggregate group of Corporation 1 takes into account only the gross receipts, base erosion tax benefits, and deductions of Corporation 2 allocable to the period from January 1 to the end of the day on June 30, Year 1, in accordance with paragraph (c)(4)(ii) and (iii) of this section. The same results apply to the aggregate group of Parent Corporation for calendar Year 1. See paragraph (d)(1) and (2) of this section for the periods taken into account in determining whether the taxpayer or its aggregate group satisfies the gross receipts test.

(B) For purposes of section 59A, to determine the gross receipts and base erosion percentage of the aggregate group of Corporation 2 for calendar Year 1, each of Parent Corporation, Corporation 1, and Corporation 3 are treated as having a taxable year-end at the end of the day on June 30, Year 1. Because Corporation 2 does not have a short taxable year, paragraph (c)(5)(i) of this section does not apply. The aggregate group of Corporation 2 takes into account the gross receipts, base erosion tax benefits, and deductions of Parent Corporation and Corporation 1 allocable to the period from January 1 to the end of the day on June 30, Year 1, and the gross receipts, base erosion tax benefits, and deductions of Corporation 3 allocable to the period from July 1 to December 31, Year 1 in accordance with paragraph (c)(4)(ii) and (iii) of this section. See paragraph (d)(1) and (2) of this section for the periods taken into account in determining whether the taxpayer or its aggregate group satisfies the gross receipts test. [Reg. § 1.59A-2.]

☐ [*T.D. 9885, 12-2-2019. Amended by T.D. 9910, 10-8-2020.*]

§ 1.59A-3. Base erosion payments and base erosion tax benefits.—(a) *Scope.*—This section provides definitions and related rules regarding base erosion payments and base erosion tax benefits. Paragraph (b) of this section provides definitions and rules regarding base erosion payments. Paragraph (c) of this section provides rules for determining the amount of base erosion tax benefits. Paragraph (d) of this section provides examples illustrating the rules described in this section.

(b) *Base erosion payments.*—(1) *In general.*—Except as provided in paragraph (b)(3) of this section, a *base erosion payment* means—

(i) Any amount paid or accrued by the taxpayer to a foreign related party of the taxpayer and with respect to which a deduction is allowable under chapter 1 of subtitle A of the Internal Revenue Code;

(ii) Any amount paid or accrued by the taxpayer to a foreign related party of the taxpayer in connection with the acquisition of property by the taxpayer from the foreign related party if the character of the property is subject to the allowance for depreciation (or amortization in lieu of depreciation);

(iii) Any premium or other consideration paid or accrued by the taxpayer to a foreign related party of the taxpayer for any reinsurance payments that are taken into account under section 803(a)(1)(B) or 832(b)(4)(A); or

(iv) Any amount paid or accrued by the taxpayer that results in a reduction of the gross receipts of the taxpayer if the amount paid or accrued is with respect to—

(A) A surrogate foreign corporation, as defined in section 59A(d)(4)(C)(i), that is a related party of the taxpayer (but only if the corporation first became a surrogate foreign corporation after November 9, 2017); or

(B) A foreign person that is a member of the same expanded affiliated group, as defined in section 59A(d)(4)(C)(ii), as the surrogate foreign corporation.

(2) *Operating rules.*—(i) *In general.*—The determination of the amount paid or accrued, and the identity of the payor and recipient of any amount paid or accrued, is made under general U.S. federal income tax law.

(ii) *Amounts paid or accrued in cash and other consideration.*—For purposes of paragraph (b)(1) of this section, an amount paid or accrued includes an amount paid or accrued using any form of consideration, including cash, property, stock, a partnership interest, or the assumption of a liability, including any exchange transaction. A distribution of property that is not part of an exchange (such as a distribution under section 301, without regard to whether section 301(c)(1), (c)(2), or (c)(3) applies), is not received with respect to an amount paid or accrued and does not give rise to a base erosion payment. In contrast, a redemption of stock by a corporation within the meaning of section 317(b) (such as a redemption described in section 302(a) or (d) or section 306(a)(2)), or a transaction in which there is an exchange for stock (such as a section 304 or section 331 transaction), is an amount paid or accrued by the shareholder to the corporation (or by the acquiring corporation to the transferor in a section 304 transaction), without regard to the treatment of such transaction for U.S. federal income tax purposes. See paragraph (b)(3)(viii) of this section for an exception for specified nonrecognition transactions (as defined in paragraph (b)(3)(viii)(A) of this section).

(iii) *Transactions providing for net payments.*—Except as otherwise provided in paragraph (b)(2)(iv) of this section or as permitted by the Internal Revenue Code or the regulations, the amount of any base erosion payment is determined on a gross basis, regardless of any contractual or legal right to make or receive payments on a net basis. For this purpose, a right to make or receive payments on a net basis permits the parties to a transaction or series of transactions to settle obligations by offsetting any amounts to be paid by one party against amounts owed by that party to the other party. For example, any premium or other consideration paid or accrued by a taxpayer to a foreign related party for any reinsurance payments is not reduced by or netted against other amounts owed to the taxpayer from the foreign related party or by reserve adjustments or other returns.

(iv) *Amounts paid or accrued with respect to mark-to-market position.*—For any transaction with respect to which the taxpayer applies the mark-to-market method of accounting for U.S. federal income tax purposes, the rules set forth in § 1.59A-2(e)(3)(vi) apply to determine the amount of the base erosion payment.

(v) *Coordination among categories of base erosion payments.*—A payment that does not satisfy the criteria of one category of base erosion payment may be a base erosion payment described in one of the other categories.

(vi) *Certain domestic passthrough entities.*—(A) *In general.*—If a taxpayer pays or accrues an amount that would be a base erosion payment except for the fact that the payment is made to a specified domestic passthrough, then the taxpayer will be treated as making a base erosion payment to each specified foreign related party for purposes of section 59A and §§1.59A-2 through 1.59A-10. This rule has no effect on the taxation of the specified domestic passthrough under subchapter J or subchapter M of the Code (as applicable).

(B) *Amount of base erosion payment.*—The amount of the base erosion payment is equal to the lesser of the amount paid or accrued by the taxpayer to or for the benefit of the specified domestic passthrough and the amount of the deduction allowed under section 561, 651, or 661 to the specified domestic passthrough with respect to amounts paid, credited, distributed, deemed distributed, or required to be distributed to a specified foreign related party.

(C) *Specified domestic passthrough.*—For purposes of this paragraph (b)(2)(vi), specified domestic passthrough means:

(1) A domestic trust that is not a grantor trust under subpart E of subchapter J of chapter 1 of the Code ("domestic trust") and which domestic trust is allowed a deduction under section 651 or section 661 with respect to amounts paid, credited, or required to be distributed to a specified foreign related party;

(2) A real estate investment trust (as defined in §1.856-1(a)) that pays, or is deemed to pay, a dividend to a specified foreign related party for which a deduction is allowed under section 561; or

(3) A regulated investment company (as defined in §1.851-1(a)) that pays, or is deemed to pay, a dividend to a specified foreign related party for which a deduction is allowed under section 561.

(D) *Specified foreign related party.*—For purposes of this paragraph (b)(2)(vi), specified foreign related party means, with respect to a specified domestic passthrough, any foreign related party of a taxpayer that is a direct or indirect beneficiary or shareholder of the specified domestic passthrough.

(vii) *Transfers of property to related taxpayers.*—If a taxpayer owns property of a character subject to the allowance for depreciation (or amortization in lieu of depreciation) with respect to which paragraph (c)(1)(ii) of this section applies, and the taxpayer sells, exchanges, or otherwise transfers the property to another taxpayer that is a member of an aggregate group that includes the taxpayer (taking into account §1.59A-7), any deduction for depreciation (or amortization in lieu of depreciation) by the transferee taxpayer remains subject to paragraph (c)(1)(ii) of this section to the same extent the amounts would have been so subject in the hands of the transferor. See paragraph (d)(7) of this section (*Example 7*) for an illustration of this rule.

(viii) *Reductions to determine gross income.*—For purposes of paragraphs (b)(1)(i) and (ii) of this section, any amount resulting in a reduction to determine gross income under section 61, including an amount properly treated as cost of goods sold under the Code, is not a base erosion payment.

(ix) *Losses recognized on the sale or transfer of property.*—If a taxpayer recognizes a loss on a sale or transfer of property to a foreign related party, the loss recognized with respect to the sale or transfer is not a deduction that would cause the payment to be treated as a base erosion payment under paragraph (b)(1)(i) of this section. However, if a taxpayer uses property to make a payment to a foreign related party and the payment otherwise meets the requirements of paragraph (b)(1) of this section, the amount of the payment that is treated as a base erosion payment equals the fair market value of the property at the time of the transfer.

(3) *Exceptions to base erosion payment.*—Paragraph (b)(1) of this section does not apply to the types of payments or accruals described in paragraphs (b)(3)(i) through (ix) of this section.

(i) *Certain services cost method amounts.*—(A) *In general.*—Amounts paid or accrued by a taxpayer to a foreign related party for services that meet the requirements in paragraph (b)(3)(i)(B) of this section, but only to the extent of the total services cost of those services. Thus, any amount paid or accrued to a foreign related party in excess of the total services cost of services eligible for the services cost method exception (the mark-up component) remains a base erosion payment. For this purpose, services are an activity as defined in §1.482-9(l)(2) performed by a foreign related party (the renderer) that provides a benefit as defined in §1.482-9(l)(3) to the taxpayer (the recipient).

(B) *Eligibility for the services cost method exception.*—To be eligible for the services cost method exception, all of the requirements of §1.482-9(b) must be satisfied, except that:

(1) The requirements of §1.482-9(b)(5) do not apply for purposes of determining eligibility for the service cost method exception in this section; and

(2) Adequate books and records must be maintained as described in paragraph (b)(3)(i)(C) of this section, instead of as described in §1.482-9(b)(6).

(C) *Adequate books and records.*—Permanent books of account and records must be maintained for as long as the costs with respect to the services are incurred by the renderer. The books and records must be adequate to permit verification by the Commissioner of the amount charged for the services and the total services costs incurred by the renderer, including a description of the services in question, identification of the renderer and the recipient of the services, calculation of the amount of profit mark-up (if any) paid for the services, and sufficient documentation to allow verification of the methods used to allocate and apportion the costs to the services in question in accordance with §1.482-9(k). For example, where a renderer incurs costs that are attributable to performing a service for the taxpayer that includes services eligible for the services cost method exception under this section (regardless of whether the taxpayer determined its payments for those services based on the services cost method) and another service that is not eligible for the services cost method exception, books and records must be maintained that show, among other things: the total amount of costs that are attributable to each of those services, the method chosen under §1.482-9(k) to apportion the costs between the service eligible for the services cost method under this section and the other service, and the application of that method in calculating the amount eligible for the services cost method exception. This paragraph (b)(3)(i)(C) does not affect the recordkeeping requirements imposed by any other provision, including §1.6001-1.

(D) *Total services cost.*—For purposes of this section, total services cost has the same meaning as total services costs in §1.482-9(j).

(ii) *Qualified derivative payments.*—Any qualified derivative payment as described in §1.59A-6.

(iii) *Effectively connected income.*—(A) *In general.*—Except as provided in paragraph (b)(3)(iii)(B) of this section, amounts paid or accrued to a foreign related party that are subject to U.S. federal income taxation as income that is, or is treated as, effectively connected with the conduct of a trade or business in the United States under an applicable provision of the Internal Revenue Code or regulations. Paragraph (b)(3)(iii) of this section applies only if the taxpayer receives a withholding certificate on which the foreign related party claims an exemption from withholding under section 1441 or 1442 because the amounts are effectively connected income.

(B) *Application to certain treaty residents.*—If a foreign related party determines its taxable income pursuant to the business profits provisions of an applicable income tax treaty, amounts paid or accrued to the foreign related party that are taken into account in determining its taxable income.

(C) *Application to partnerships.*—To the extent that paragraph (b)(3)(iii)(A) or (B) of this section would apply to a payment or accrual made directly by a taxpayer to a foreign related party, paragraph (b)(3)(iii)(A) or (B) of this section apply to an amount treated as paid or accrued by a taxpayer to a foreign related party under §1.59A-7(b) or (c) (generally applying aggregate principles to treat partnership transactions as partner level transactions for purposes of section 59A). The certification requirement in paragraph (b)(3)(iii)(A) of this section is met if the taxpayer receives a written statement from the foreign related party that is comparable to the certification provided in paragraph (b)(3)(iii)(A) of this section but based on the deemed transaction under §1.59A-7(b) or (c) and the extent to which paragraph (b)(3)(iii)(A) or (B) of this section would have applied to that deemed transaction. The taxpayer may rely on the written statement unless it has reason to know or actual knowledge that the statement is incorrect.

(iv) *Exchange loss on a section 988 transaction.*—Any exchange loss within the meaning of § 1.988-2 from a section 988 transaction described in § 1.988-1(a)(1) that is an allowable deduction and that results from a payment or accrual by the taxpayer to a foreign related party.

(v) *Amounts paid or accrued with respect to TLAC securities and foreign TLAC securities.*—(A) *In general.*—Except as provided in paragraph (b)(3)(v)(B) and (F) of this section, amounts paid or accrued to foreign related parties with respect to TLAC securities and foreign TLAC securities.

(B) *Limitation on exclusion for TLAC securities.*—The amount excluded under paragraph (b)(3)(v)(A) of this section is no greater than the product of the scaling ratio and amounts paid or accrued to foreign related parties with respect to TLAC securities for which a deduction is allowed.

(C) *Scaling ratio.*—For purposes of this paragraph (b)(3)(v), the scaling ratio for a taxable year of a taxpayer is a fraction the numerator of which is 115 percent of the average TLAC long-term debt required amount and the denominator of which is the average TLAC securities amount. The scaling ratio may in no event be greater than one.

(D) *Average TLAC securities amount.*—The average TLAC securities amount for a taxable year is the average of the TLAC securities amounts for the year, computed at regular time intervals in accordance with this paragraph. The TLAC securities amount used in calculating the average TLAC securities amount is computed on a monthly basis.

(E) *Average TLAC long-term debt required amount.*—The average TLAC longterm debt required amount for a taxable year is the average of the TLAC long-term debt required amounts, computed on a monthly basis.

(F) *Limitation on exclusion for foreign TLAC securities.*—*(1) In general.*—The amount excluded under paragraph (b)(3)(v)(A) of this section for foreign TLAC securities is limited to the extent that interest deducted by a U.S. trade or business or permanent establishment with respect to foreign TLAC securities exceeds the interest expense associated with the foreign TLAC long-term debt required amount, applying the scaling ratio principles set forth under paragraphs (b)(3)(v)(B) through (E) of this section.

(2) Foreign TLAC long-term debt required amount.—For purposes of paragraph (b)(3)(v) of this section, the term *foreign TLAC long-term debt required amount* means in the case of a trade or business or a permanent establishment in the United States, the lesser of—

(i) The specified minimum amount of debt, if any, required pursuant to a bank regulatory requirement imposed under the laws or regulations of a foreign country that are comparable to 12 CFR 252.160-167; or

(ii) The specified minimum amount of debt, if any, that would be required pursuant to 12 CFR 252.162(a) if the trade or business or permanent establishment were a U.S. person (as determined under Federal Reserve regulations).

(3) No specified minimum provided by local law.—For purposes of paragraph (b)(3)(v)(F)(2)(*ii*) of this section, if the bank regulatory requirements imposed under the laws or regulations of a foreign country do not specify a minimum amount, the limitation for purposes of paragraph (b)(3)(v)(F)(2) of this section is determined by reference solely to paragraph (b)(3)(v)(F)(2)(*ii*) of this section.

(4) Foreign TLAC security.—For purposes of paragraph (b)(3)(v) of this section, the term *foreign TLAC security* means an internal debt security issued under a bank regulatory requirement imposed under the laws or regulations of a foreign country that is comparable to 12 CFR 252.160-167. The laws or regulations of a foreign country are comparable to 12 CFR 252.160-167 if the requirement is imposed by a Financial Stability Board member state and those laws or regulations are substantially consistent with TLAC standards of the Financial Stability Board.

(vi) *Amounts paid or accrued in taxable years beginning before January 1, 2018.*—Any amount paid or accrued in taxable years beginning before January 1, 2018.

(vii) *Business interest carried forward from taxable years beginning before January 1, 2018.*—Any disallowed business interest described in section 163(j)(2) that is carried forward from a taxable year beginning before January 1, 2018.

(viii) *Specified nonrecognition transactions.*—(A) *In general.*—Subject to paragraph (b)(3)(viii)(B) and (C) of this section, any amount transferred to, or exchanged with, a foreign related party pursuant to a transaction to which sections 332, 351, 355, or 368 apply ("specified nonrecognition transaction"). See § 1.59A-9(b)(4) for anti-abuse rules.

(B) *Other property transferred to a foreign related party in a specified nonrecognition transaction.*—If a taxpayer transfers other property (as defined in paragraph (b)(3)(viii)(D) of this section) to a foreign related party pursuant to a specified nonrecognition transaction, the other property is treated as an amount paid or accrued to which paragraph (b)(3) of this section does not apply, regardless of whether gain is recognized on the transaction.

(C) *Other property received from a foreign related party in certain specified nonrecognition transactions.*—If, in a transaction described in section 351, 355, or 368, the taxpayer transfers property and receives other property (as defined in paragraph (b)(3)(viii)(D) of this section) from a foreign related party, the property transferred by the taxpayer is treated as an amount paid or accrued to which paragraph (b)(3) of this section does not apply, regardless of whether gain is recognized on the transaction.

(D) *Definition of other property.*—Solely for purposes of this paragraph (b)(3)(viii), the term *other property* has the meaning of the phrase "other property or money" as used in section 351(b), with respect to a transaction to which section 351 applies, and as used in sections 356(a)(1)(B) and 361(b), with respect to a transaction to which sections 355 or 368 apply, as applicable, including liabilities treated as money under section 357(b). However, the term *other property* does not include the sum of any money and the fair market value of any other property to which section 361(b)(3) applies. The term *other property* also includes liabilities that are assumed by the taxpayer in the specified nonrecognition transaction, but only to the extent of the amount of gain recognized under section 357(c).

(E) *Allocation of other property.*—Other property is treated as exchanged for property in a specified nonrecognition transaction in a manner consistent with U.S. federal income tax law. For purposes making the allocation under this paragraph (b)(3)(viii)(E), liabilities described in paragraph (b)(3)(viii)(D) of this section are treated as money received.

(ix) *Reinsurance losses incurred and claims payments.*—(A) *In general.*—Any amounts paid by a taxpayer subject to tax under subchapter L to a foreign related party that is a regulated insurance company under a reinsurance contract between the taxpayer and the regulated foreign insurance company for losses incurred (as defined in section 832(b)(5)) and claims and benefits under section 805(a)(1), to the extent that the amounts paid or accrued are properly allocable to amounts required to be paid by the regulated foreign insurance company (or indirectly through another regulated foreign insurance company), pursuant to an insurance, annuity, or reinsurance contract, to a person other than a related party. For purposes of this paragraph (b)(3)(ix), the determination of whether a contract is an insurance contract or an annuity contract is made without regard to sections 72(s), 101(f), 817(h), and 7702, provided that the contract is regulated as a life insurance or annuity contract in its jurisdiction of issuance and no policyholder, insured, annuitant or beneficiary with respect to the contract is a United States person.

(B) *Regulated foreign insurance company.*—The term regulated foreign insurance company means any foreign corporation which—

(1) Is subject to regulation as an insurance (or reinsurance) company by the country in which the corporation is created, organized, or maintains its registered office, and is licensed, authorized, or regulated by the applicable insurance regulatory body for that country to sell insurance, annuity, or reinsurance contracts to persons other than related parties in that country, and

(2) Would be subject to tax under subchapter L if it were a domestic corporation.

(4) *Rules for determining the amount of certain base erosion payments.*—The following rules apply in determining the amount that is a base erosion payment.

(i) *Interest expense allocable to a foreign corporation's effectively connected income.*—(A) *Methods described in § 1.882-5.*—A foreign corporation that has interest expense allocable under section 882(c) to income that is, or is treated as, effectively connected with the conduct of a trade or business within the United States applying the method described in § 1.882-5(b) through (d) or the method described in § 1.882-5(e) has base erosion payments under paragraph (b)(1)(i) of this section for the taxable year equal to the sum of—

(1) The interest expense on a liability described in § 1.882-5(a)(1)(ii)(A) or (B) (direct allocations) that is paid or accrued by the foreign corporation to a foreign related party;

(2) The interest expense on U.S.-booked liabilities, as described in § 1.882-5(d)(2), determined by taking into account paragraph (b)(4)(i)(B) of this section, that is paid or accrued by the foreign corporation to a foreign related party; and

(3) The interest expense on U.S.-connected liabilities, as described in § 1.882-5(d) or 1.882-5(e), in excess of interest expense on U.S.-booked liabilities as described in § 1.882-5(d)(2), if any (hereafter, excess U.S.-connected liabilities), multiplied by a fraction, the numerator of which is the foreign corporation's average worldwide interest expense due to a foreign related party, and the denominator of which is the foreign corporation's average total worldwide interest expense. The numerator and denominator of this fraction are determined by translating interest expense into the functional currency of the foreign corporation using any reasonable method, consistently applied. Any interest expense that is interest expense on a U.S.-booked liability or is subject to a direct allocation is excluded from both the numerator and the denominator of the fraction.

(B) *U.S.-booked liabilities determination.*—For purposes of paragraph (b)(4)(i)(A) of this section, the determination of the interest expense on U.S.-booked liabilities, as described in § 1.882-5(d)(2), is made without regard to whether the foreign corporation applies the method described in § 1.882-5(b) through (d) or the method described in § 1.882-5(e) for purposes of determining interest expense.

(C) *U.S.-booked liabilities in excess of U.S.-connected liabilities.*—For purposes of paragraph (b)(4)(i)(A)*(2)* of this section, if a foreign corporation has U.S.-booked liabilities, as described in § 1.882-5(d)(2), in excess of U.S.-connected liabilities, as described in § 1.882-5(d) or § 1.882-5(e), the foreign corporation applies the scaling ratio pro-rata to all interest expense on U.S.-booked liabilities consistent with § 1.882-5(d)(4) for purposes of determining the amount of allocable interest expense on U.S.-booked liabilities that is a base erosion payment. This paragraph (b)(4)(i)(C) applies without regard to whether the foreign corporation applies the method described in § 1.882-5(b) through (d) or the method described in § 1.882-5(e) for purposes of determining its interest expense.

(D) *Election to use financial statements.*—A foreign corporation may elect to calculate the fraction described in paragraph (b)(4)(i)(A)*(3)* of this section on the basis of its applicable financial statement rather than U.S. tax principles. For purposes of this section, an applicable financial statement has the meaning provided in section 451(b)(3). The applicable financial statement must be the applicable financial statement of the foreign corporation, not a consolidated applicable financial statement. A foreign corporation makes this election in accordance with the requirements of Form 8991 (or successor).

(E) *Coordination with certain tax treaties.*—*(1) In general.*—If a foreign corporation elects to determine its taxable income pursuant to business profits provisions of an income tax treaty rather than provisions of the Internal Revenue Code, or the regulations published under 26 CFR chapter I, for determining effectively connected income, and the foreign corporation does not apply § 1.882-5 to allocate interest expense to a permanent establishment, then paragraph (b)(4)(i)(A) through (D) of this section applies to determine the amount of hypothetical § 1.882-5 interest expense that is a base erosion payment under paragraph (b)(1) of this section. Interest expense allowed to the permanent establishment in excess of the hypothetical § 1.882-5 interest expense, if any, is treated as an amount paid or accrued by the permanent establishment to the foreign corporation's home office or to another branch of the foreign corporation and is a base erosion payment to the extent that the payment or accrual is described under paragraph (b)(1) of this section.

(2) Hypothetical § 1.882-5 interest expense defined.—The hypothetical § 1.882-5 interest expense is equal to the amount of interest expense that would have been allocable under section 882(c) to income that is, or is treated as, effectively connected with the conduct of a trade or business within the United States if the foreign corporation determined interest expense in accordance with section § 1.882-5. However, the hypothetical § 1.882-5 interest expense shall not exceed the amount of interest expense allowed to the permanent establishment.

(3) Consistency requirement.—For purposes of determining the amount described in paragraph (b)(4)(i)(E)*(2)* of this section and applying paragraph (b)(4)(i)(A) through (D) of this section, the elections of § 1.882-5 must be applied consistently and are subject to the rules and limitations of § 1.882-5, including limitations on the time period in which an election may be made or revoked. If a foreign corporation otherwise meets the requirements for making or revoking an election under § 1.882-5, then solely for purposes of this section, the foreign corporation is treated as making or revoking the election in accordance with the requirements of Form 8991 (or successor) and its instructions.

(F) *Coordination with exception for foreign TLAC securities.*—For purposes of paragraph (b)(4)(i)(A) of this section, amounts paid or accrued to a foreign related party with respect to securities that are eligible for the foreign TLAC exception in paragraph (b)(3)(v) of this section are not treated as paid to a foreign related party.

(ii) *Other deductions allowed with respect to effectively connected income.*—A deduction allowed under § 1.882-4 for an amount paid or accrued by a foreign corporation to a foreign related party (including a deduction for an amount apportioned in part to effectively connected income and in part to income that is not effectively connected income) is a base erosion payment under paragraph (b)(1) of this section.

(iii) *Depreciable property.*—Any amount paid or accrued by a foreign corporation to a foreign related party of the taxpayer in connection with the acquisition of property by the foreign corporation from the foreign related party if the character of the property is subject to the allowance for depreciation (or amortization in lieu of depreciation) is a base erosion payment to the extent the property so acquired is used, or held for use, in the conduct of a trade or business within the United States.

(iv) *Coordination with ECI exception.*—For purposes of paragraph (b)(4) of this section, amounts paid or accrued to a foreign related party treated as effectively connected income (or, in the case of a foreign related party that determines taxable income pursuant to the business profits provisions of an applicable income tax treaty, such amounts that are taken into account in determining taxable income) are not treated as paid to a foreign related party.

(v) *Coordination with certain tax treaties.*—(A) *Allocable expenses.*—Except as provided in paragraph (b)(4)(i)(E) of this section with respect to interest, if a foreign corporation determines its taxable income on a net basis pursuant to an applicable income tax treaty rather than provisions of the Internal Revenue Code, or the regulations published under 26 CFR chapter I, for determining effectively connected income, then the foreign corporation must determine whether each allowable deduction is a base erosion payment under paragraph (b)(1) of this section.

(B) *Internal dealings under certain income tax treaties.*—Except as provided in paragraph (b)(4)(i)(E) of this section with respect to interest, if, pursuant to the terms of an applicable income tax treaty, a foreign corporation determines the profits attributable to a permanent establishment based on the assets used, risks assumed, and functions performed by the permanent establishment, then any deduction attributable to any amount paid or accrued (or treated as paid or accrued) by the permanent establishment to the foreign corporation's home office or to another branch of the foreign corporation (an "internal dealing") is a base erosion payment to the extent that the payment or accrual is described under paragraph (b)(1) of this section.

(vi) *Business interest expense arising in taxable years beginning after December 31, 2017.*—Any disallowed business interest expense described in section 163(j)(2) that resulted from a payment or accrual to a foreign related party that first arose in a taxable year beginning after December 31, 2017, is treated as a base erosion payment under paragraph (b)(1)(i) of this section in the year that the business interest expense initially arose. See paragraph (c)(4) of this section for rules that apply when business interest expense is limited under section 163(j)(1) in order to determine whether the disallowed business interest is attributed to business interest expense paid to a person that is not a related party, a foreign related party, or a domestic related party.

(c) *Base erosion tax benefit.*—(1) *In general.*—Except as provided in paragraph (c)(2) of this section, a base erosion tax benefit means:

(i) In the case of a base erosion payment described in paragraph (b)(1)(i) of this section, any deduction that is allowed under chapter 1 of subtitle A of the Internal Revenue Code for the taxable year with respect to that base erosion payment;

(ii) In the case of a base erosion payment described in paragraph (b)(1)(ii) of this section, any deduction allowed under chapter 1 of subtitle A of the Internal Revenue Code for the taxable year for depreciation (or amortization in lieu of depreciation) with respect to the property acquired with that payment;

(iii) In the case of a base erosion payment described in paragraph (b)(1)(iii) of this section, any reduction under section 803(a)(1)(B) in the gross amount of premiums and other consideration on insurance and annuity contracts for premiums and other consideration arising out of indemnity reinsurance, or any deduction under section 832(b)(4)(A) from the amount of gross premiums written on insurance contracts during the taxable year for premiums paid for reinsurance; or

(iv) In the case of a base erosion payment described in paragraph (b)(1)(iv) of this section, any reduction in gross receipts with respect to the payment in computing gross income of the taxpayer for the taxable year for purposes of chapter 1 of subtitle A of the Internal Revenue Code.

(2) *Exception to base erosion tax benefit.*—(i) *In general.*—Except as provided in paragraph (c)(3) of this section, any base erosion tax benefit attributable to any base erosion payment is not taken into account as a base erosion tax benefit if tax is imposed on that payment under section 871 or 881, and the tax has been deducted and withheld under section 1441 or 1442. If a payment is taken into account for purposes of the fraction described in paragraph (b)(4)(i)(A)(*3*) of this section, and tax is imposed on the payment under section 871 or 881, and the tax has been deducted and withheld under section 1441 or 1442, the payment is treated as not paid or accrued to a foreign related party.

(ii) *Branch-level interest tax.*—Except as provided in paragraph (c)(3) of this section, any base erosion tax benefit of a foreign corporation attributable to any base erosion payment determined under paragraph (b)(4)(i)(A)(*3*) of this section or attributable to interest expense in excess of the hypothetical section 1.882-5 interest expense determined under paragraph (b)(4)(i)(E)(*1*) of this section is not taken into account as a base erosion tax benefit to the extent of the amount of excess interest, as defined in § 1.884-4(a)(2), if any, on which tax is imposed on the foreign corporation under section 884(f) and § 1.884-4, if the tax is properly reported on the foreign corporation's income tax return and paid in accordance with § 1.884-4(a)(2)(iv).

(3) *Effect of treaty on base erosion tax benefit.*—If any treaty between the United States and any foreign country reduces the rate of tax imposed by section 871 or 881, the amount of base erosion tax benefit that is not taken into account under paragraph (c)(2) of this section is equal to the amount of the base erosion tax benefit before the application of paragraph (c)(2) of this section multiplied by a fraction of—

(i) The rate of tax imposed under the treaty; over

(ii) The rate of tax imposed without regard to the treaty.

(4) *Application of section 163(j) to base erosion payments.*—(i) *Classification of payments or accruals of business interest expense based on the payee.*—The following rules apply for corporations and partnerships:

(A) *Classification of payments or accruals of business interest expense of a corporation.*—For purposes of this section, in the year that business interest expense of a corporation is paid or accrued the business interest expense is classified as foreign related business interest expense, domestic related business interest expense, or unrelated business interest expense.

(B) *Classification of payments or accruals of business interest expense by a partnership.*—For purposes of this section, in the year that business interest expense of a partnership is paid or accrued, the business interest expense that is allocated to a partner is classified separately with respect to each partner in the partnership as foreign related business interest expense, domestic related business interest expense, or unrelated business interest expense.

(C) *Classification of payments or accruals of business interest expense paid or accrued to a foreign related party that is subject to an exception.*—(*1*) *ECI exception.*—For purposes of paragraph (c)(4)(i)(A) and (B) of this section, business interest expense paid or accrued to a foreign related party to which the exception in paragraph (b)(3)(iii) of this section (effectively connected income) applies is classified as domestic related business interest expense.

(*2*) *TLAC interest and interest subject to withholding tax.*—For purposes of paragraph (c)(4)(i)(A) and (B) of this section, if the exception in paragraph (b)(3)(v) of this section (TLAC securities) or paragraph (c)(2) or (3) of this section (withholding tax) applies to business interest expense paid or accrued to a foreign related party, that business interest expense remains classified as foreign related business interest expense, and retains its classification as eligible for those exceptions, on a pro-rata basis with other foreign related business interest expense.

(ii) *Ordering rules for business interest expense that is limited under section 163(j)(1) to determine which classifications of business interest expense are deducted and which classifications of business interest expense are carried forward.*—(A) *In general.*—Section 163(j) and the regulations published under 26 CFR chapter I provide a limitation on the amount of business interest expense allowed as a deduction in a taxable year by a corporation or a partner in a partnership. In the case of a corporation with a disallowed business interest expense carryforward, the regulations under section 163(j) determine the ordering of the business interest expense deduction that is allowed on a year-by-year basis by reference first to business interest expense incurred in the current taxable year and then to disallowed business interest expense carryforwards from prior years. To determine the amount of base erosion tax benefit under paragraph (c)(1) of this section, this paragraph (c)(4)(ii) sets forth ordering rules that determine the amount of the deduction of business interest expense allowed under section 163(j) that is classified as paid or accrued to a foreign related party for purposes of paragraph (c)(1)(i) of this section. This paragraph (c)(4)(ii) also sets forth similar ordering rules that apply to disallowed business interest expense carryforwards for which a deduction is permitted under section 163(j) in a later year.

(B) *Ordering rules for treating business interest expense deduction and disallowed business interest expense carryforwards as foreign related business interest expense, domestic related business interest expense, and unrelated business interest expense.*—(*1*) *General ordering rule for allocating business interest expense deduction between classifications.*—For purposes of paragraph (c)(1) of this section, if a deduction for business interest expense is not subject to the limitation under section 163(j)(1) in a taxable year, the deduction is treated first as foreign related business interest expense and domestic related business interest expense (on a pro-rata basis), and second as unrelated business interest expense. The same principle applies to business interest expense of a partnership that is deductible at the partner level under § 1.163(j)-6(f).

(*2*) *Ordering of business interest expense incurred by a corporation.*—If a corporation's business interest expense deduction allowed for any taxable year is attributable to business interest expense paid or accrued in that taxable year and to disallowed business interest expense carryforwards from prior taxable years, the ordering of business interest expense deduction provided in paragraph (c)(4)(ii)(B)(*1*) of this section among the classifications described therein applies separately for the carryforward amount from each taxable year, following the ordering set forth in § 1.163(j)-5(b)(2). Corresponding adjustments to the classification of disallowed business interest expense carryforwards are made consistent with this year-by-year approach. For purposes of section 59A and this section, an acquiring corporation in a transaction described in section 381(a) will succeed to and take into account the classification of any disallowed business interest expense carryforward. See § 1.381(c)(20)-1.

(*3*) *Ordering of business interest expense incurred by a partnership and allocated to a corporate partner.*—For a corporate partner in a partnership that is allocated a business interest expense deduction under § 1.163(j)-6(f), the ordering rule provided in paragraph (c)(4)(ii)(B)(*1*) of this section applies separately to the corporate partner's allocated business interest expense deduction from the partnership; that deduction is not comingled with the business interest expense deduction addressed in paragraph (c)(4)(ii)(B)(*1*) or (*2*) of this section or the corporate partner's items from any other partnership. Similarly, when a corporate partner in a partnership is allocated excess business interest expense from a partnership under the rules set forth in § 1.163(j)-6(f) and the excess interest expense becomes deductible to the corporate partner, that partner applies the ordering rule provided in paragraph (c)(4)(ii)(B)(*1*) of this section separately to that excess interest expense on a year-by-year basis. Corresponding adjustments to the classification of disallowed business interest expense carryforwards are made consistent with this year-by-year and partnership-by-partnership approach.

(5) *Allowed deduction.*—Solely for purposes of paragraph (c)(1) of this section, all deductions (and any premium or other consideration paid or accrued by the taxpayer for any reinsurance payments that are taken into account under section 803(a)(1)(B) or 832(b)(4)(A)) that could be properly claimed by a taxpayer for the taxable year (determined after giving effect to the taxpayer's permissible method of accounting and to any election, such as the election under section 173 to capitalize circulation expenditures or the election under section 168(g)(7) to use the alternative depreciation system of depreciation) are treated as allowed deductions under chapter 1 of subtitle A of the Internal Revenue Code.

(6) *Election to waive allowed deductions.*—(i) *In general.*—If a taxpayer elects to waive certain deductions, in whole or in part, pursuant to this paragraph (c)(6)(i), the amount of allowed deductions as described in paragraph (c)(5) of this section is reduced by the amounts that are properly waived. In order to make the election or increase the amount of the deduction waived, the taxpayer must determine that it could satisfy the requirements of § 1.59A-2(b) absent the election to waive certain deductions. For rules applicable to partners and partnerships, see paragraph (c)(6)(iv) of this section. For rules addressing waiver of premium or other consideration paid or accrued by a taxpayer for any reinsurance payments that are taken into account under section 803(a)(1)(B) or 832(b)(4)(A), see paragraph (c)(6)(v) of this section.

(ii) *Time and manner for election to waive deduction.*—(A) *In general.*—A taxpayer may make the election described in paragraph (c)(6)(i) of this section on its original filed Federal income tax return. In addition, a taxpayer may elect to waive deductions or increase the amount of deductions waived pursuant to the election described in paragraph (c)(6)(i) of this section on an amended Federal income tax return filed within the later of three years from the date the original return was filed, taking into account section 6501(b)(1), for the taxable year for which the election is made or the period described in section 6501(c)(4), or during the course of an examination of the taxpayer's income tax return for the relevant taxable year pursuant to procedures prescribed by the Commissioner. However, a taxpayer may not decrease the amount of deductions waived by the election, or otherwise revoke the election that is described in paragraph (c)(6)(i) of this section on any amended Federal income tax return or during the course of an examination. To make the election, a taxpayer must complete the appropriate part of Form 8991, *Tax on Base Erosion Payments of Taxpayers With Substantial Gross Receipts* (or successor), including the information described in paragraph (c)(6)(ii)(B) of this section and any other information required by the form or instructions. A taxpayer makes the election described in paragraph (c)(6)(i) of this section on an annual basis, and the taxpayer does not need the consent of the Commissioner if the taxpayer chooses not to make the election for a subsequent taxable year. The election described in paragraph (c)(6)(i) of this section may not be made in any other manner than as described in this paragraph (c)(6)(ii) (for example, by filing an application for a change in accounting method).

(B) *Information required to make the election to waive allowed deductions.*—To make this election, a taxpayer must maintain contemporaneous documentation and provide information related to each deduction waived as required by applicable forms and instructions issued by the Commissioner, including—

(*1*) A description of the item or property to which the deduction relates, including sufficient information to identify that item or property on the taxpayer's books and records;

(*2*) The date on which, or period in which, the waived deduction was paid or accrued;

(*3*) The provision of the Internal Revenue Code (and regulations, as applicable) that allows the deduction for the item or property to which the election relates;

(*4*) The amount of the deduction that is claimed for the taxable year with respect to the item or property;

(*5*) The amount of the deduction being waived for the taxable year with respect to the item or property;

(*6*) A description of where the deduction is reflected (or would have been reflected) on the Federal income tax return (such as a line number); and

(*7*) The name, Taxpayer Identification Number (or, if the foreign person does not have a Taxpayer Identification Number, the foreign equivalent), and country of organization of the foreign related party that is or will be the recipient of the payment that generates the deduction.

(iii) *Effect of election to waive deduction.*—(A) *In general.*—(*1*) *Consistent treatment.*—Except as otherwise provided in this paragraph (c)(6)(iii), any deduction waived under paragraph (c)(6)(i) of this section is treated as having been waived for all purposes of the Internal Revenue Code and regulations.

(*2*) *No allocation and apportionment of waived deductions.*—The waiver of deductions described in paragraph (c)(6)(i) of this section is treated as occurring before the allocation and apportionment of deductions under § § 1.861-8 through 1.861-14T and 1.861-17 (such as for purposes of section 904).

(*3*) *Effect of waiver of deductions described in § § 1.861-10 and 1.861-10T.*—To the extent that any waived deduction is interest expense that would have been directly allocated under the rules of § 1.861-10 or 1.861-10T and would have resulted in the reduction of value of any assets for purposes of allocating other interest expense under § § 1.861-9 and 1.861-9T, the value of the assets is reduced to the same extent as if the taxpayer had not elected to waive the deduction.

(*4*) *Effect of the election to waive deductions on the stock basis of a consolidated group member.*—For purposes of § 1.1502-32, any deduction waived under paragraph (c)(6)(i) of this section is a noncapital, nondeductible expense under § 1.1502-32(b)(2)(iii).

(B) *Effect of the election to waive deductions disregarded for certain purposes.*—If a taxpayer makes the election to waive a deduction, in whole or in part, under paragraph (c)(6)(i) of this section, the election is disregarded for determining—

(*1*) The taxpayer's overall method of accounting, or the taxpayer's method of accounting for any item, under section 446;

(*2*) Whether a change in the taxpayer's overall plan of accounting or the taxpayer's treatment of a material item is a change in method of accounting under section 446(e) and § 1.446-1(e);

(*3*) The amount allowable under subtitle A of the Internal Revenue Code for depreciation or amortization for purposes of section 167(c) and section 1016(a)(2) or section 1016(a)(3) and any other adjustment to basis under section 1016(a);

(*4*) For purposes of applying the exclusive apportionment rule in § 1.861-17(b), the geographic source where the research and experimental activities which account for more than fifty percent of the amount of the deduction for research and experimentation was performed;

(*5*) The application of section 482;

(*6*) The amount of the taxpayer's earnings and profits; and

(*7*) Any other item as necessary to prevent a taxpayer from receiving the benefit of a waived deduction.

(C) *Not a method of accounting.*—The election described in paragraph (c)(6)(i) of this section is not a method of accounting under section 446.

(D) *Effect of the election in determining section 481(a) adjustments.*—A taxpayer making the election described in paragraph (c)(6)(i) of this section agrees that if the method of accounting for a waived deduction is changed, the amount of adjustment taken into account under section 481(a)(2) is determined without regard to the election described in paragraph (c)(6)(i) of this section. As a result, a waived deduction has no effect on the amount of a section 481(a) adjustment compared to what the adjustment would have been if the deduction had not been waived. See paragraph (d)(9) of this section (*Example 9*).

(iv) *Rules applicable to partners and partnerships.*—(A) *In general.*—Except as provided in paragraph (c)(6)(iv)(D) of this section, deductions allocated to a corporate partner by a partnership may only be waived by the partner and not by the partnership, and then only to the extent the partner otherwise qualifies for the waiver under paragraph (c)(6) of this section. For purposes of complying with the documentation requirements in paragraph (c)(6)(ii)(B) of this section, the partner is not required to report the information in paragraphs (c)(6)(ii)(B)(2) and (3) of this section, and in lieu of reporting the information in paragraphs (c)(6)(ii)(B)(*1*) of this section, the partner is required to report the partnership from which the item is allocated.

(B) *Rule for determining the adjusted basis of a partner's interest in a partnership.*—If a partner elects to waive a deduction or increases the amount of deduction waived with respect to deductions allocated to it by a partnership, the partner treats the waived amount as a nondeductible expenditure under section 705(a)(2)(B).

(C) *Rule for applying section 163(j).*—If a partner waives a deduction pursuant to paragraph (c)(6)(iv)(A) of this section that was taken into account by the partnership in determining the partnership's adjusted taxable income for purposes of section 163(j), then the increase in the partner's income resulting from the waiver is treated by the partner (but not the partnership) as a partner basis item (as defined in § 1.163(j)-6(b)(2)) for purposes of section 163(j).

(D) *Limited application of election to waive deductions with respect to adjustments made pursuant to audit procedures under sections 6221 through 6241.*—Except as provided in this paragraph (c)(6)(iv)(D), a partner is not permitted to waive any adjustment by the Secretary to any partnership-related items that is made pursuant to subchapter C of chapter 63. A partner in a partnership subject to subchapter C of chapter 63 may only make an election to waive any increase in a deduction due to an adjustment made under subchapter C of chapter 63 that the partner takes into account under section 6225(c)(2)(A), 6226, or 6227 in a manner consistent with paragraph (c)(6) of this section. If the partner makes an election under paragraph (c)(6)(i) of this section, the partner will compute its additional reporting year tax (as described in § 301.6226-3 of this chapter) or amount due under § 301.6225-2(d)(2)(ii)(A) of this chapter taking into account the rules in paragraph (c)(6) of this section with respect to the increase in the deduction that is waived.

(v) *Rule applicable to premium and other consideration paid or accrued by the taxpayer for any reinsurance payments that are taken into account under section 803(a)(1)(B) or 832(b)(4)(A).*—For purposes of paragraph (c)(6)(i) of this section, a taxpayer may elect to waive (or increase the amount waived of) any premium or other consideration paid or accrued by the taxpayer for any reinsurance payments that are taken into account under section 803(a)(1)(B) or 832(b)(4)(A) that would be a base erosion tax benefit within the meaning of section 59A(c)(2)(A)(iii), in accordance with the rules and principles of this paragraph (c)(6).

(d) *Examples.*—The following examples illustrate the application of this section. For purposes of all the examples, assume that the taxpayer is an applicable taxpayer and all payments apply to a taxable year beginning after December 31, 2017.

(1) *Example 1: Determining a base erosion payment*—(i) *Facts.* FP is a foreign corporation that owns all of the stock of FC, a foreign corporation, and DC, a domestic corporation. FP has a trade or business in the United States with effectively connected income (USTB). DC owns FDE, a foreign disregarded entity. DC pays interest to FDE and FC. FDE pays interest to USTB. All interest paid by DC to FC and by FDE to USTB is deductible by DC in the current year for regular income tax purposes. FDE also acquires depreciable property from FP during the taxable year. FP's income from the sale of the depreciable property is not effectively connected with the conduct of FP's trade or business in the United States. DC and FP (based only on the activities of USTB) are applicable taxpayers under § 1.59A-2(b).

(ii) *Analysis.* The payment of interest by DC to FC is a base erosion payment under paragraph (b)(1)(i) of this section because the payment is made to a foreign related party and the interest payment is deductible. The payment of interest by DC to FDE is not a base erosion payment because the transaction is not a payment to a foreign person and the transaction is not a deductible payment. With respect to the payment of interest by FDE to USTB, if FP's USTB treats the payment of interest by FDE to USTB as income that is effectively connected with the conduct of a trade or business in the United States pursuant to section 864 or as profits attributable to a U.S. permanent establishment of a tax treaty resident, and if DC receives a withholding certificate from FP with respect to the payment, then the exception in paragraph (b)(3)(iii) of this section applies. Accordingly, the payment from DC, through FDE, to USTB is not a base erosion payment even though the payment is to the USTB of FP, a foreign related party. The acquisition of depreciable property by DC, through FDE, from FP is a base erosion payment under paragraph (b)(1)(ii) of this section because there is a payment to a foreign related party in connection with the acquisition by the taxpayer of property of a character subject to the allowance for depreciation and the exception in paragraph (b)(3)(iii) of this section does not apply because FP's income from the sale of the depreciable property is not effectively connected with the conduct of FP's trade or business in the United States. See § 1.59A-2 for the application of the aggregation rule with respect to DC and FP's USTB.

(2) *Example 2: Interest allocable under § 1.882-5*—(i) *Facts.* FC, a foreign corporation, has income that is effectively connected with the conduct of a trade or business within the United States. FC determines its interest expense under the three-step process described in § 1.882-5(b) through (d) with a total interest expense of $125x. The total interest expense is comprised of interest expense of $100x on U.S.-booked liabilities ($60x paid to a foreign related party and $40x paid to unrelated persons) and $25x of interest on excess U.S.-connected liabilities. FC has average worldwide interest expense (not including interest expense on U.S.-booked liabilities) of $500x, of which $100x is interest expense paid to a foreign related party. FC is an applicable taxpayer with respect to its effectively connected income. Assume all of the interest expense is deductible in the current taxable year and that none of the interest is subject to the effectively connected income exception in paragraph (b)(3)(iii) of this section.

(ii) *Analysis.* Under paragraph (b)(4)(i) of this section, the total amount of interest expense determined under § 1.882-5 that is a base erosion payment is $65x ($60x + 5x). FC has $60x of interest on U.S.-booked liabilities that is paid to a foreign related party and that is treated as a base erosion payment under paragraph (b)(4)(i)(A)(*2*) of this section. Additionally, $5x of the $25x of interest expense on excess U.S.-connected liabilities is treated as a base erosion payment under paragraph (b)(4)(i)(A)(*3*) of this section ($25x * ($100x / $500x)).

(3) *Example 3: Interaction with section 163(j)*—(i) *Facts.* Foreign Parent (FP) is a foreign corporation that owns all of the stock of DC, a domestic corporation that is an applicable taxpayer. DC does not conduct a utility trade or business as described in section 163(j)(7)(A)(iv), an electing real property trade or business as described in section 163(j)(7)(B), or an electing farming business as described in section 163(j)(7)(C). In Year 1, DC has adjusted taxable income, as defined in section 163(j)(8), of $1000x and pays the following amounts of business interest expense: $420x that is paid to unrelated Bank, and $360x that is paid to FP. DC does not earn any business interest income or incur any floor plan financing interest expense in Year 1. None of the exceptions in paragraph (b)(3) of this section apply, and the interest is not subject to withholding.

(ii) *Analysis*—(A) *Classification of business interest.* In Year 1, DC is permitted to deduct only $300x of business interest expense under section 163(j)(1) ($1000x x 30%). Paragraph (c)(4)(ii)(B) of this section provides that for purposes of paragraph (c)(1) of this section the deduction is treated first as foreign related business interest expense and domestic related business interest expense (here, only FP); and second as unrelated business interest expense (Bank). As a result, the $300x of business interest expense that is permitted under section 163(j)(1) is treated entirely as the business interest paid to the related foreign party, FP. All of DC's $300x deductible interest is treated as an add-back to modified taxable income in the Year 1 taxable year for purposes of § 1.59A-4(b)(2)(i).

(B) *Ordering rules for disallowed business interest expense carryforward.* Under section 163(j)(2), the $480x of disallowed business interest ($420x + $360x - $300x) is carried forward to the subsequent year. Under paragraph (c)(4)(ii)(B)(*1*) and (2) of this section, the disallowed business interest carryforward is correspondingly treated first as unrelated business interest expense, and second pro-rata as foreign related business interest expense and domestic related business interest expense. As a result, $420x of the $480x disallowed business interest expense carryforward is treated first as business interest expense paid to Bank and the remaining $60x of the $480x disallowed business interest expense carryforward is treated as interest paid to FP and as an add-back to modified taxable income.

(4) *Example 4: Interaction with section 163(j); carryforward*—(i) *Facts.* The facts are the same as in paragraph (d)(3) of this section (the facts in *Example 3*), except that in addition, in Year 2, DC has adjusted taxable income of $250x, and pays the following amounts of business interest expense: $50x that is paid to unrelated Bank, and $45x that is paid to FP. DC does not earn any business interest income or incur any floor plan financing interest expense in Year 2. None of the exceptions in paragraph (b)(3) of this section apply.

(ii) *Analysis*—(A) *Classification of business interest.* In Year 2, for purposes of section 163(j)(1), DC is treated as having paid or accrued total business interest expense of $575x, consisting of $95x business interest expense actually paid in Year 2 and $480x of business interest expense that is carried forward from Year 1. DC is permitted to deduct $75x of business interest expense in Year 2 under the limitation in section 163(j)(1) ($250x x 30%). Section 1.163(j)-5(b)(2) provides that, for purposes of section 163(j), the allowable business interest expense is first attributed to amounts paid or accrued in the current year, and then attributed to amounts carried over from earlier years on a first-in-first-out basis from the earliest year. Accordingly, the $75x of deductible business interest expense is deducted entirely from the $95x business interest expense incurred in Year 2 for section 163(j) purposes. Because DC's business interest expense deduction is limited under section 163(j)(1) and because DC's total business interest expense is attributable to more than one taxable year, paragraph (c)(4)(ii)(B)(2) of this section provides that the ordering rule in paragraph (c)(4)(ii)(B)(*1*) of this section is applied separately to each annual amount of section 163(j) disallowed business interest expense carryforward. With respect to the Year 2 layer, which is deducted first, paragraph (c)(4)(ii)(B) of this section provides that, for purposes of paragraph (c)(1) of this section, the Year 2 $75x deduction is treated first as foreign related business interest expense and domestic related business interest expense (here, only FP, $45x); and second as unrelated business interest expense (Bank, $30x). Consequentially, all of the $45x deduction of business interest expense that was paid to FP in Year 2 is treated as a base erosion tax benefit and an add-back to modified taxable income for the Year 2 taxable year for purposes of § 1.59A-4(b)(2)(i).

(B) *Ordering rules for disallowed business interest expense carryforward.* The disallowed business interest expense carryforward of $20x from Year 2 is correspondingly treated first as business interest expense paid to Bank under paragraph (c)(4)(i) of this section. The disallowed business interest expense carryforward of $480x from the Year 1 layer that is also not allowed as a deduction in Year 2 remains treated as $420x paid to Bank and $60 paid to FP.

(5) *Example 5: Interaction with section 163(j); carryforward*—(i) *Facts.* The facts are the same as in paragraph (d)(4) of this section (the facts in *Example 4*), except that in addition, in Year 3, DC has adjusted taxable income of $4000x and pays no business interest expense. DC does not earn any business interest income or incur any floor plan financing interest expense in Year 3.

(ii) *Analysis.* In Year 3, DC is treated as having paid or accrued total business interest expense of $500x, consisting of $480x of business interest expense that is carried forward from Year 1 and $20x of business interest expense that is carried forward from Year 2 for purposes of section 163(j)(1). DC is permitted to deduct $1200x of business interest expense in Year 3 under the limitation in section 163(j)(1) ($4000x x 30%). For purposes of section 163(j), DC is treated as first deducting the business interest expense from Year 1 then the business interest expense from Year 2. See § 1.163(j)-5(b)(2). Because none of DC's $500x business interest expense is limited under section 163(j), the stacking rule in paragraph (c)(4)(ii) of this section for allowed and disallowed business interest expense does not apply. For purposes of § 1.59A-4(b)(2)(i), DC's add-back to modified taxable income is $60x determined by the classifications in paragraph (c)(4)(i)(A) of this section ($60x treated as paid to FP from Year 1).

(6) *Example 6: Interaction with section 163(j); partnership*—(i) *Facts.* The facts are the same as in paragraph (d)(4) of this section (the facts in *Example 4*), except that in addition, in Year 2, DC forms a domestic partnership (PRS) with Y, a domestic corporation that is not related to DC within the meaning of § 1.59A-1(b)(17). PRS does not conduct a utility trade or business as described in section 163(j)(7)(A)(iv), an electing real property trade or business as described in section 163(j)(7)(B) or an electing farming business as described in section 163(j)(7)(C) subject to section 163(j). PRS is not a small business described in section 163(j)(3). DC and Y are equal partners in partnership PRS. In Year 2, PRS has ATI of $100x and $48x of business interest expense. $12x of PRS's business interest expense is paid to Bank, and $36x of PRS's business interest expense is paid to FP. PRS allocates the items comprising its $100x of ATI $50x to DC and $50x to Y. PRS allocates its $48x of business interest expense $24x to DC and $24x to Y. DC classifies its $24x of business interest expense as $6x unrelated business interest expense (Bank) and $18x as foreign related business interest expense (FP) under paragraph (c)(4)(i)(B) of this section. Y classifies its $24x of business interest expense as entirely unrelated business interest expense of Y (Bank and FP) under paragraph (c)(4)(i)(B) of this section. None of the exceptions in paragraph (b)(3) of this section apply.

(ii) *Partnership level analysis.* In Year 2, PRS's section 163(j) limit is 30 percent of its ATI, or $30x ($100x x 30 percent). Thus, PRS has $30x of deductible business interest expense and $18x of excess business interest expense ($48x - $30x). The $30x of deductible business interest expense is includible in PRS's non-separately stated income or loss, and is not subject to further limitation under section 163(j) at the partners' level.

(iii) *Partner level allocations analysis.* Pursuant to § 1.163(j)-6(f)(2), DC and Y are each allocated $15x of deductible business interest expense and $9x of excess business interest expense. At the end of Year 2, DC and Y each have $9x of excess business interest expense from PRS, which under § 1.163(j)-6 is not treated as paid or accrued by the partner until such partner is allocated excess taxable income or excess business interest income from PRS in a succeeding year. Pursuant to § 1.163(j)-6(e), DC and Y, in computing their limit under section 163(j), do not increase any of their section 163(j) items by any of PRS's section 163(j) items.

(iv) *Partner level allocations for determining base erosion tax benefits.* The $15x of deductible business interest expense allocated to DC is treated first as foreign related business interest expense (FP) under paragraph (c)(4)(ii)(B) of this section. DC's excess business interest expense from PRS of $9x is classified first as the unrelated business interest expense with respect to Bank ($6x) and then as the remaining portion of the business interest expense paid to FP ($3x, or $18x - $15x). Under paragraph (c)(4)(ii)(B)(3) of this section, these classifications of the PRS items apply irrespective of the classifications of DC's own interest expense as set forth in paragraph (d)(4) of this section (*Example 4*).

(v) *Computation of modified taxable income.* For Year 2, DC is treated as having incurred base erosion tax benefits of $60x, consisting of the $15x base erosion tax benefit with respect to its interest in PRS that is computed in paragraph (d)(6)(iii) of this section (*Example 6*) and $45x that is computed in paragraph (d)(4) of this section (*Example 4*).

(7) *Example 7: Transfers of property to related taxpayers*—(i) *Facts.* FP is a foreign corporation that owns all of the stock of DC1 and DC2, both domestic corporations. DC1 and DC2 are both members of the same aggregate group but are not members of the same consolidated tax group under section 1502. In Year 1, FP sells depreciable property to DC1. On the first day of the Year 2 tax year, DC1 sells the depreciable property to DC2.

(ii) *Analysis*—(A) *Year 1.* The acquisition of depreciable property by DC1 from FP is a base erosion payment under paragraph (b)(1)(ii) of this section because there is a payment to a foreign related party in connection with the acquisition by the taxpayer of property of a character subject to the allowance for depreciation.

(B) *Year 2.* The acquisition of the depreciable property in Year 2 by DC2 is not itself a base erosion payment because DC2 did not acquire the property from a foreign related party. However, under paragraph (b)(2)(viii) of this section any depreciation expense taken by DC2 on the property acquired from DC1 is a base erosion payment and a base erosion tax benefit under paragraph (c)(1)(ii) of this section because the acquisition of the depreciable property was a base erosion payment by DC1 and the property was sold to a member of the aggregate group; therefore, the depreciation expense continues as a base erosion tax benefit to DC2 as it would have been to DC1 if it continued to own the property.

(8) *Example 8: Effect of election to waive deduction on method of accounting*—(i) *Facts.* DC, a domestic corporation, purchased and placed in service a depreciable asset (Asset A) from a foreign related party on the first day of its taxable year 1 for $100x. DC elects to use the alternative depreciation system under section 168(g) to depreciate all properties placed in service during taxable year 1. Asset A is not eligible for the additional first year depreciation deduction. Beginning in taxable year 1, DC depreciates Asset A under the alternative depreciation system using the straight-line depreciation method, a 5-year recovery period, and the half-year convention. This depreciation method, recovery period, and convention are permissible for Asset A under section 168(g). On its timely filed original Federal income tax return for taxable year 1, DC does not elect to waive any deductions and DC claims a depreciation deduction of $10x for Asset A. On its timely filed original Federal income tax return for taxable year 2, DC does not elect to waive any deductions and DC claims a depreciation deduction of $20x for Asset A. During taxable year 3, DC files an amended return for taxable year 1 to elect to waive the depreciation deduction for Asset A and reports in accordance with paragraph (c)(6)(ii) of this section with its amended return for taxable year 1 that the amount of the waived depreciation deduction for Asset A is $10x and the amount of the claimed depreciation deduction is $0x.

(ii) *Analysis.* Pursuant to paragraph (c)(6)(iii)(B)(*1*) of this section, DC's election to waive the depreciation deduction for Asset A for taxable year 1 is disregarded for determining DC's method of accounting for Asset A. Accordingly, after DC's election to waive the depreciation deduction for Asset A for taxable year 1, DC's method of accounting for depreciation for Asset A continues to be the straight-line depreciation method, a 5-year recovery period, and the half-year convention. Pursuant to paragraph (c)(6)(iii)(C) of this section, the election made by DC in taxable year 3 on its amended return for taxable year 1 is not a method of accounting.

(9) *Example 9: Change of accounting method when taxpayer has waived a deduction*—(i) *Facts.*DC, a domestic corporation, purchased and placed in service a depreciable asset (Asset B) from a foreign related party on the first day of its taxable year 1 for $100x. DC elects to use the alternative depreciation system under section 168(g) to depreciate all properties placed in service during taxable year 1. Asset B is not eligible for the additional first year depreciation deduction. Beginning in taxable year 1, DC depreciates Asset B under the alternative depreciation system using the straight-line depreciation method, a 10-year recovery period, and the half-year convention. Under this method of accounting, the depreciation deductions for Asset B are $5x for taxable year 1 and $10x for taxable year 2. However, for taxable years 1 and 2, DC elects to waive $3x and $6x, respectively, of the depreciation deductions for Asset B and reports the information required under paragraph (c)(6)(ii) of this section with its returns. In taxable year 3, DC realizes that the correct recovery period for Asset B is 5 years. If DC had used the correct recovery period for Asset B, the depreciation deductions for Asset B would have been $10x for taxable year 1 and $20x for taxable year 2. DC timely files a Form 3115 to change its method of accounting for Asset B from a 10-year recovery period to a 5-year recovery period, beginning with taxable year 3. DC was not under examination as of the date on which it timely filed this Form 3115.

(ii) *Analysis*—(A) *Computation of the section 481(a) adjustment.* In determining the net negative section 481(a) adjustment for this method change, DC compares the depreciation deductions under its present method of accounting to the depreciation deductions under its proposed method of accounting. Pursuant to paragraph (c)(6)(iii)(D) of this section, DC agreed that, by making the election to waive depreciation deductions for Asset B, DC will not take into account the fact that depreciation deductions for Asset B were waived under paragraph (c)(6)(i) of this section. Accordingly, DC's net negative section 481(a) adjustment for this method change is $15x, which is calculated by determining the difference between the depreciation deductions for Asset B for taxable years 1 and 2 under DC's present method of accounting ($15x) and the depreciation deductions that would have been allowable for Asset B for taxable years 1 and 2 under DC's proposed method of accounting ($30x).

(B) *Computation of basis adjustments.* Pursuant to paragraph (c)(6)(iii)(B)(3) of this section, DC's elections to waive the depreciation deductions for Asset B for taxable years 1 and 2 are disregarded for determining the amount allowable for depreciation for purposes of section 1016(a)(2). The amount allowable for depreciation of Asset B is determined based on the proper method of computing depreciation for Asset B. Accordingly, Asset B's adjusted basis at the end of taxable year 1 is $90x ($100x - $10x) and at the end of taxable year 2 is $70x ($90x - $20x). [Reg. § 1.59A-3.]

☐ [*T.D. 9885, 12-2-2019. Amended by T.D. 9910, 10-8-2020.*]

§ 1.59A-4. Modified taxable income.—(a) *Scope.*—Paragraph (b)(1) of this section provides rules for computing modified taxable income. Paragraph (b)(2) of this section provides rules addressing how base erosion tax benefits and net operating losses affect modified taxable income. Paragraph (b)(3) of this section provides a rule for a holder of a residual interest in a REMIC. Paragraph (c) of this section provides examples illustrating the rules described in this section.

(b) *Computation of modified taxable income.*—(1) *In general.*—The term *modified taxable income* means a taxpayer's taxable income, as defined in section 63(a), determined with the additions described in paragraph (b)(2) of this section. Notwithstanding the foregoing, the taxpayer's taxable income may not be reduced to an amount less than zero as a result of a net operating loss deduction allowed under section 172. See paragraphs (c)(1) and (2) of this section (*Examples 1* and 2).

(2) *Modifications to taxable income.*—The amounts described in this paragraph (b)(2) are added back to a taxpayer's taxable income to determine its modified taxable income.

(i) *Base erosion tax benefits.*—The amount of any base erosion tax benefit as defined in § 1.59A-3(c)(1).

(ii) *Certain net operating loss deductions.*—The base erosion percentage, as described in § 1.59A-2(e)(3), of any net operating loss deduction allowed to the taxpayer under section 172 for the taxable year. For purposes of determining modified taxable income, the net operating loss deduction allowed does not exceed taxable income before taking into account the net operating loss deduction. See paragraph (c)(1) and (2) of this section (*Examples 1* and 2). The base erosion percentage for the taxable year that the net operating loss arose is used to determine the addition under this paragraph (b)(2)(ii). For a net operating loss that arose in a taxable year beginning before January 1, 2018, the base erosion percentage for the taxable year is zero.

(3) *Rule for holders of a residual interest in a REMIC.*—For purposes of paragraph (b)(1) of this section, the limitation in section 860E(a)(1) is not taken into account in determining the taxable income amount that is used to compute modified taxable income for the taxable year.

(c) *Examples.*—The following examples illustrate the rules of paragraph (b) of this section.

(1) *Example 1: Current year loss*—(i) *Facts.* A domestic corporation (DC) is an applicable taxpayer that has a calendar taxable year. In 2020, DC has gross income of $100x, a deduction of $80x that is not a base erosion tax benefit, and a deduction of $70x that is a base erosion tax benefit. In addition, DC has a net operating loss carryforward to 2020 of $400x that arose in 2016.

(ii) *Analysis.* DC's starting point for computing modified taxable income is $(50x), computed as gross income of $100x, less a deduction of $80x (non-base erosion tax benefit) and a deduction of $70x (base erosion tax benefit). Under paragraph (b)(2)(ii) of this section, DC's starting point for computing modified taxable income does not take into account the $400x net operating loss carryforward because the allowable deductions for 2020, not counting the NOL deduction, exceed the gross income for 2020. DC's modified taxable income for 2020 is $20x, computed as $(50x) + $70x base erosion tax benefit.

(2) *Example 2: Net operating loss deduction*—(i) *Facts.* The facts are the same as in paragraph (c)(1)(i) of this section (the facts in *Example 1*), except that DC's gross income in 2020 is $500x.

(ii) *Analysis.* DC's starting point for computing modified taxable income is $0x, computed as gross income of $500x, less: a deduction of $80x (non-base erosion tax benefit), a deduction of $70x (base erosion tax benefit), and a net operating loss deduction of $350x (which is the amount of taxable income before taking into account the net operating loss deduction, as provided in paragraph (b)(2)(ii) of this section ($500x - $150x)). DC's modified taxable income for 2020 is $70x, computed as $0x + $70x base erosion tax benefit. DC's modified taxable income is not increased as a result of the $350x net operating loss deduction in 2020 because the base erosion percentage of the net operating loss that arose in 2016 is zero under paragraph (b)(2)(ii) of this section. [Reg. § 1.59A-4.]

☐ [*T.D. 9885, 12-2-2019.*]

§ 1.59A-5. Base erosion minimum tax amount.—(a) *Scope.*—Paragraph (b) of this section provides rules regarding the calculation of the base erosion minimum tax amount. Paragraph (c) of this section describes the base erosion and anti-abuse tax rate applicable to the taxable year.

(b) *Base erosion minimum tax amount.*—(1) *In general.*—For each taxable year, an applicable taxpayer must determine its base erosion minimum tax amount.

(2) *Calculation of base erosion minimum tax amount.*—With respect to any applicable taxpayer, the base erosion minimum tax amount for any taxable year is, the excess (if any) of—

(i) An amount equal to the base erosion and anti-abuse tax rate multiplied by the modified taxable income of the taxpayer for the taxable year, over

(ii) An amount equal to the regular tax liability as defined in § 1.59A-1(b)(16) of the taxpayer for the taxable year, reduced (but not below zero) by the excess (if any) of—

(A) The credits allowed under chapter 1 of subtitle A of the Code against regular tax liability over

(B) The sum of the credits described in paragraph (b)(3) of this section.

(3) *Credits that do not reduce regular tax liability.*—The sum of the following credits are used in paragraph (b)(2)(ii)(B) of this section to limit the amount by which the credits allowed under chapter 1 of subtitle A of the Internal Revenue Code reduce regular tax liability—

(i) *Taxable years beginning on or before December 31, 2025.*—For any taxable year beginning on or before December 31, 2025—

(A) The credit allowed under section 38 for the taxable year that is properly allocable to the research credit determined under section 41(a);

(B) The portion of the applicable section 38 credits not in excess of 80 percent of the lesser of the amount of those applicable section 38 credits or the base erosion minimum tax amount (determined without regard to this paragraph (b)(3)(i)(B)); and

(C) Any credits allowed under sections 33, 37, and 53.

(ii) *Taxable years beginning after December 31, 2025.*—For any taxable year beginning after December 31, 2025, any credits allowed under sections 33, 37, and 53.

(c) *Base erosion and anti-abuse tax rate.*—(1) *In general.*—For purposes of calculating the base erosion minimum tax amount, the base erosion and anti-abuse tax rate is—

(i) *Calendar year 2018.*—For taxable years beginning in calendar year 2018, five percent.

(ii) *Calendar years 2019 through 2025.*—For taxable years beginning after December 31, 2018, through taxable years beginning before January 1, 2026, 10 percent.

(iii) *Calendar years after 2025.*—For taxable years beginning after December 31, 2025, 12.5 percent.

(2) *Increased rate for banks and registered securities dealers.*—(i) *In general.*—In the case of a taxpayer that is a member of an affiliated group (as defined in section 1504(a)(1)) that includes a bank or a registered securities dealer, the percentage otherwise in effect under paragraph (c)(1) of this section is increased by one percentage point.

(ii) *De minimis exception to increased rate for banks and registered securities dealers.*—Paragraph (c)(2)(i) of this section does not apply to a taxpayer that is a member of an affiliated group (as defined in section 1504(a)(1)) that includes a bank or registered securities dealer if, in that taxable year, the total gross receipts of the affiliated group attributable to the bank or the registered securities dealer (or attributable to all of the banks and registered securities dealers in the group, if more than one) represent less than two percent of the total gross receipts of the affiliated group, as determined under § 1.59A-2(d).

(3) *Application of section 15 to tax rates in section 59A.*—(i) *New tax.*—Section 15 does not apply to any taxable year that includes January 1, 2018.

(ii) *Change in tax rate pursuant to section 59A(b)(1)(A).*—Section 15 does not apply to any taxable year that includes January 1, 2019.

(iii) *Change in rate pursuant to section 59A(b)(2).*—Section 15 applies to the change in tax rate pursuant to section 59A(b)(2)(A). [Reg. § 1.59A-5.]

☐ [*T.D. 9885, 12-2-2019.*]

§ 1.59A-6. Qualified derivative payment.—(a) *Scope.*—This section provides additional guidance regarding qualified derivative payments. Paragraph (b) of this section defines the term qualified derivative payment. Paragraph (c) of this section provides guidance on certain payments that are not treated as qualified derivative payments. Paragraph (d) defines the term derivative for purposes of section 59A. Paragraph (e) of this section provides examples illustrating the rules of this section.

(b) *Qualified derivative payment.*—(1) *In general.*—A *qualified derivative payment* means any payment made by a taxpayer to a foreign related party pursuant to a derivative with respect to which the taxpayer—

(i) Recognizes gain or loss as if the derivative were sold for its fair market value on the last business day of the taxable year (and any additional times as required by the Internal Revenue Code or the taxpayer's method of accounting);

(ii) Treats any gain or loss so recognized as ordinary; and

(iii) Treats the character of all items of income, deduction, gain, or loss with respect to a payment pursuant to the derivative as ordinary.

(2) *Reporting requirements.*—(i) *In general.*—No payment is a qualified derivative payment under paragraph (b)(1) of this section for any taxable year unless the taxpayer (whether or not the taxpayer is a reporting corporation as defined in § 1.6038A-1(c)) reports the information required in § 1.6038A-2(b)(7)(ix) for the taxable year. To report its qualified derivative payments, a taxpayer must include the payment in the aggregate amount of qualified derivative payments on Form 8991 (or successor).

(ii) *Failure to satisfy the reporting requirement.*—If a taxpayer fails to satisfy the reporting requirement described in paragraph (b)(2)(i) of this section with respect to any payments, those payments are not eligible for the qualified derivative payment exception described in § 1.59A-3(b)(3)(ii) and are base erosion payments unless an exception in § 1.59A-3(b)(3) otherwise applies. A taxpayer's failure to report a payment as a qualified derivative payment does not impact the eligibility of any other payment which the taxpayer properly reported under paragraph (b)(2)(i) of this section from being a qualified derivative payment.

(iii) *Reporting of aggregate amount of qualified derivative payments.*—The aggregate amount of qualified derivative payments is the sum of the amount described in paragraph (b)(3) of this section for each derivative. To the extent that the taxpayer is treated as receiving a payment, as determined in § 1.59A-2(e)(3)(vi), for the taxable year with respect to a derivative, the payment is not included in the aggregate qualified derivative payments.

(iv) *Transition period for qualified derivative payment reporting.*—Before paragraph (b)(2)(i) of this section is applicable, a taxpayer will be treated as satisfying the reporting requirement described section 59A(h)(2)(B) to the extent that the taxpayer reports the aggregate amount of qualified derivative payments on Form 8991 (or successor). *See* § 1.6038A-2(g) (applicability date for § 1.6038A-2(b)(7)(ix)). Until paragraph (b)(2)(i) of this section is applicable, paragraph (b)(2)(ii) of this section will not apply to a taxpayer who reports the aggregate amount of qualified derivative payments in good faith.

(3) *Amount of any qualified derivative payment.*—(i) *In general.*—The amount of any qualified derivative payment excluded from the denominator of the base erosion percentage as provided in § 1.59A-2(e)(3)(ii)(C) is determined as provided in § 1.59A-2(e)(3)(vi).

(ii) *Net qualified derivative payment that includes a payment that is a base erosion payment.*—Any net amount determined in paragraph (b)(3)(i) of this section must be reduced by any gross items that are treated as a base erosion payment pursuant to paragraph (c) of this section.

(c) *Exceptions for payments otherwise treated as base erosion payments.*—A payment does not constitute a qualified derivative payment if—

(1) The payment would be treated as a base erosion payment if it were not made pursuant to a derivative, including any interest, royalty, or service payment; or

(2) In the case of a contract that has derivative and nonderivative components, the payment is properly allocable to the nonderivative component.

(d) *Derivative defined.*—(1) *In general.*—For purposes of this section, the term *derivative* means any contract (including any option, forward contract, futures contract, short position, swap, or similar contract) the value of which, or any payment or other transfer with respect to which, is (directly or indirectly) determined by reference to one or more of the following:

(i) Any share of stock in a corporation;

(ii) Any evidence of indebtedness;

(iii) Any commodity that is actively traded;

(iv) Any currency; or

(v) Any rate, price, amount, index, formula, or algorithm.

(2) *Exceptions.*—The following contracts are not treated as derivatives for purposes of section 59A.

(i) *Direct interest.*—A derivative contract does not include a direct interest in any item described in paragraph (d)(1)(i) through (v) of this section.

(ii) *Insurance contracts.*—A derivative contract does not include any insurance, annuity, or endowment contract issued by an insurance company to which subchapter L applies (or issued by any foreign corporation to which the subchapter would apply if the foreign corporation were a domestic corporation).

(iii) *Securities lending and sale-repurchase transactions.*—(A) *Multi-step transactions treated as financing.*—For purposes of paragraph (d)(1) of this section, a derivative does not include any securities lending transaction, sale-repurchase transaction, or substantially similar transaction that is treated as a secured loan for federal tax purposes. Securities lending transaction and sale-repurchase transaction have the meanings provided in § 1.861-2(a)(7).

(B) *Special rule for payments associated with the cash collateral provided in a securities lending transaction or substantially similar transaction.*—For purposes of paragraph (d)(1) of this section, a derivative does not include the cash collateral component of a securities lending transaction (or the cash payments pursuant to a sale-repurchase transaction, or similar payments pursuant to a substantially similar transaction).

(C) *Anti-abuse exception for certain transactions that are the economic equivalent of substantially unsecured cash borrowing.*—For purposes of paragraph (d)(1) of this section, a derivative does not include any securities lending transaction or substantially similar transaction that is part of an arrangement that has been entered into with a principal purpose of avoiding the treatment of any payment with respect to that transaction as a base erosion payment and that provides the taxpayer with the economic equivalent of a substantially unsecured cash borrowing. The determination of whether the securities lending transaction or substantially similar transaction provides the taxpayer with the economic equivalent of a substantially unsecured cash borrowing takes into account arrangements that effectively serve as collateral due to the taxpayer's compliance with any U.S. regulatory requirements governing such transaction.

(3) *American depository receipts.*—For purposes of section 59A, American depository receipts (or any similar instruments) with respect to shares of stock in a foreign corporation are treated as shares of stock in that foreign corporation.

(e) *Examples.*—The following examples illustrate the rules of this section.

(1) *Example 1: Notional principal contract as QDP*—(i) *Facts.* Domestic Corporation (DC) is a dealer in securities within the meaning of section 475. On February 1, 2019, DC enters into a contract (Interest Rate Swap) with Foreign Parent (FP), a foreign related party, for a term of five years. Under the Interest Rate Swap, DC is obligated to make a payment to FP each month, beginning March 1, 2019, in an amount equal to a variable rate determined by reference to the prime rate, as determined on the first business day of the immediately preceding month, multiplied by a notional principal amount of $50x. Under the Interest Rate Swap, FP is obligated to make a payment to DC each month, beginning March 1, 2019, in an amount equal to 5% multiplied by the same notional principal amount. The Interest Rate Swap satisfies the definition of a notional principal contract under § 1.446-3(c). DC recognizes gain or loss on the Interest Rate Swap pursuant to section 475. DC reports the information required to be reported for the taxable year under § 1.6038A-2(b)(7)(ix).

(ii) *Analysis.* The Interest Rate Swap is a derivative as described in paragraph (d) of this section because it is a contract that references the prime rate and a fixed rate for determining the amount of payments. The exceptions described in paragraph (c) of this section do not apply to the Interest Rate Swap. Because DC recognizes ordinary gain or loss on the Interest Rate Swap pursuant to section 475(d)(3), it satisfies the condition in paragraph (b)(1)(ii) of this section. Because DC satisfies the requirement relating to the information required to be reported under paragraph (b)(2) of this section, any payment to FP with respect to the Interest Rate Swap will be a qualified derivative payment. Therefore, under § 1.59A-3(b)(3)(ii), the payments to FP are not base erosion payments.

(2) *Example 2: Securities lending anti-abuse rule*—(i) *Facts.* (A) Foreign Parent (FP) is a foreign corporation that owns all of the stock of domestic corporation (DC) and foreign corporation (FC). FP and FC are foreign related parties of DC under § 1.59A-1(b)(12) but not members of DC's aggregate group. On January 1 of year 1, with a principal purpose of providing financing to DC without DC making a base erosion payment to FC, FC lends 100x U.S. Treasury bills with a remaining maturity of 11 months (Securities A) to DC (Securities Lending Transaction 1) for a period of six months. Pursuant to the terms of Securities Lending Transaction 1, DC is obligated to make substitute payments to FC corresponding to the interest payments on Securities A. DC does not post cash collateral with respect to Securities Lending Transaction 1, and no other arrangements of FC or DC effectively serve as collateral under any U.S. regulatory requirements governing the transaction. Immediately thereafter, DC sells Securities A for cash.

(B) On June 30 of year 1, FC lends 100x U.S. Treasury bills with a remaining maturity of 11 months (Securities B) to DC (Securities Lending Transaction 2) for a period of six months. Pursuant to the terms of Securities Lending Transaction 2, DC is obligated to make substitute payments to FC corresponding to the interest payments on Securities B. Immediately thereafter, DC sells Securities B for cash and uses the cash to purchase U.S. Treasury bills with a remaining maturity equal to the Securities A bills that DC then transfers to FC in repayment of Securities Lending Transaction 1.

(ii) *Analysis.* Securities Lending Transaction 1 and Securities Lending Transaction 2 are not treated as derivatives for purposes of paragraph (d)(1) of this section because the transactions are part of an arrangement that has been entered into with a principal purpose of avoiding the treatment of any payment with respect to Securities Lending Transaction 1 and Securities Lending Transaction 2 as a base erosion payment and provides DC with the economic equivalent of a substantially unsecured cash borrowing by DC. As a result, pursuant to paragraph (d)(2)(iii)(C) of this section, the substitute payments made by DC to FC with respect to Securities A and Securities B are not eligible for the exception in § 1.59A-3(b)(3)(ii) (qualified derivative payment). [Reg. § 1.59A-6.]

☐ [*T.D.* 9885, 12-2-2019.]

§ 1.59A-7. Application of base erosion and anti-abuse tax to partnerships.—(a) *Scope.*—This section provides rules regarding how partnerships and their partners are treated for purposes of making certain determinations under section 59A, including whether there is a base erosion payment or base erosion tax benefit. All references to partnerships in this section include domestic and foreign partnerships. This section applies to payments to a partnership and payments from a partnership as well as transfers of partnership interests (as defined in paragraph (c)(3)(iv) of this section). The aggregate principle described in this section does not override the treatment of partnership items under any Code section other than section 59A. The aggregate principles provided in this section apply without regard to any tax avoidance purpose relating to a particular partnership. See § 1.701-2(e). Paragraph (b) of this section describes how the aggregate approach to partnerships applies for purposes of certain section 59A determinations. Paragraph (c) of this section provides rules for determining whether there is a base erosion payment with respect to a payment to or from a partnership. Paragraph (d) of this section provides rules for determining the base erosion tax benefits of a partner. Paragraph (e) of this section provides additional rules relating to the application of section 59A to partnerships. Paragraph (f) of this section provides a rule for determining whether a person is a foreign related party. Paragraph (g) of this section provides examples that illustrate the application of the rules of this section.

(b) *Application of section 59A to partnerships.*—The purpose of this section is to provide a set of operating rules for the application of section 59A to partnerships and partners in a manner consistent with the purposes of section 59A. Except for purposes of determining a partner's base erosion tax benefits under paragraph (d)(1) of this section and whether a taxpayer is a registered securities dealer under paragraph (e)(3) of this section, section 59A determinations are made at the partner level in the manner described in this section. The provisions of section 59A must be interpreted in a manner consistent with this approach. If a transaction is not specifically described in this section, whether the transaction gives rise to a base erosion payment or base erosion tax benefit is determined in accordance with the principles of this section and the purposes of section 59A.

(c) *Base erosion payment.*—For purposes of determining whether a taxpayer has made a base erosion payment as described in § 1.59A-3(b), the taxpayer must treat a payment to or from a partnership as made to or from each partner and the assets and liabilities of the partnership as assets and liabilities of each partner. This paragraph (c) provides specific rules for determining whether a partner has made or received a payment, including as a result of a partnership interest transfer (as defined in paragraph (c)(3)(iv) of this section).

(1) *Payments made by or to a partnership.*—For purposes of determining whether a payment or accrual by a partnership is a base erosion payment described in § 1.59A-3(b)(1)(i), any amount paid or accrued by the partnership (including any guaranteed payment described in section 707(c)) is treated as paid or accrued by each partner based on the partner's distributive share of the item of deduction with respect to that amount. For purposes of determining whether a payment or accrual to a partnership is a base erosion payment described in § 1.59A-3(b)(1)(i) or (iii), any amount paid or accrued to the partnership (including any guaranteed payment described in section 707(c)) is treated as paid or accrued to each partner based on

the partner's distributive share of the item of income with respect to that amount. See paragraph (e)(1) of this section to determine the partner's distributive share.

(2) *Transfers of certain property.*—When a partnership transfers property, each partner is treated as transferring its proportionate share of the property transferred for purposes of determining whether there is a base erosion payment described in § 1.59A-3(b)(1)(ii) or (iv). When a partnership acquires property, each partner is treated as acquiring its proportionate share of the property acquired for purposes of determining whether there is a base erosion payment described in § 1.59A-3(b)(1)(ii) or (iv). For purposes of this paragraph (c)(2), a transfer of property does not include a transfer of a partnership interest (as defined in paragraph (c)(3)(iv) of this section). See paragraph (c)(3) of this section for rules applicable to transfers of partnership interests. See paragraphs (g)(2)(v) and (vi) of this section (*Example 5* and *Example 6*) for examples illustrating the application of this paragraph (c)(2).

(3) *Transfers of a partnership interest.*—(i) *In general.*—A transfer of a partnership interest (as defined in paragraph (c)(3)(iv) of this section) is generally treated as a transfer by each partner in the partnership of its proportionate share of the partnership's assets to the extent of any change in its proportionate share of any partnership asset, as well as any assumption of associated liabilities by the partner. Paragraphs (c)(3)(ii) and (iii) of this section provide rules for applying the general rule to transfers of a partnership interest by a partner and issuances of a partnership interest by the partnership for contributed property, respectively. See paragraph (g)(2)(vii) of this section (*Example 7*) for an example illustrating the application of this paragraph (c)(3)(i).

(ii) *Transfers of a partnership interest by a partner.*—A transfer of a partnership interest (as defined in paragraph (c)(3)(iv) of this section) by a partner is treated as a transfer by the transferor to the recipient of the transferor's proportionate share of each of the partnership assets and an assumption by the recipient of the transferor's proportionate share of the partnership liabilities. If the partner's entire partnership interest is not transferred, only the proportionate share of each of the partnership assets and liabilities associated with the transferred partnership interest is treated as transferred and assumed. See paragraphs (g)(2)(iii), (iv), and (vi) of this section (*Example 3, Example 4,* and *Example 6*) for examples illustrating the application of this paragraph (c)(3)(ii).

(iii) *Certain issuances of a partnership interest by a partnership.*—If a partnership issues an interest in the partnership in exchange for a contribution of property to the partnership, the contributing partner is treated as exchanging a portion of the contributed property and assuming any liabilities associated with the transferred partnership interest for a portion of the partners' pre-contribution interests in the partnership's assets and the partners' assumption of any liabilities transferred to the partnership. For purposes of this paragraph (c)(3)(iii), a reference to the "partnership's assets" includes the assets contributed by the contributing partner and any other assets that are contributed to the partnership at the same time. Each partner whose proportionate share in a partnership asset (including the assets contributed to the partnership as part of the transaction) is reduced as a result of the transaction is treated as transferring the asset to the extent of the reduction, and each person who receives a proportionate share or an increased proportionate share in an asset as a result of the transaction is treated as receiving an asset to the extent of the increase, proportionately from the partners' reduced interests. For example, if a person contributes property to a partnership in which each of two existing partners has a 50 percent pro-rata interest in the partnership in exchange for a one-third pro-rata partnership interest, each of the pre-contribution partners is treated as transferring a one-third interest in their share of existing partnership assets to the contributing partner, and the contributing partner is treated as transferring a one-third interest in the contributed assets to each of the original partners. See paragraphs (g)(2)(i) and (ii) of this section (*Example 1* and *Example 2*) for additional examples illustrating the application of this paragraph (c)(3)(iii).

(iv) *Partnership interest transfers defined.*—For purposes of paragraphs (c)(3) and (4) of this section, a transfer of a partnership interest includes any issuance of a partnership interest by a partnership; any sale of a partnership interest; any increase or decrease in a partner's proportionate share of any partnership asset as a result of a contribution of property or services to a partnership, a distribution, or a redemption; or any other transfer of a proportionate share of any partnership asset (other than a transfer of a partnership asset that is not a partnership interest by the partnership to a person not acting in a partner capacity), whether by a partner or the partnership (including as a result of a deemed or actual sale or a capital shift).

(4) *Increased basis from a distribution.*—If a distribution of property from a partnership to a partner results in an increase in the tax basis of either the distributed property or other partnership property, such as under section 732(b) or 734(b), the increase in tax basis attributable to a foreign related party is treated as if it was newly purchased property acquired by the taxpayer (to the extent of its proportionate share) from the foreign related party that is placed in service when the distribution occurs. See § 1.734-1(e). This increased basis treated as newly purchased property is treated as acquired with a base erosion payment, unless an exception in § 1.59A-3(b) applies. For this purpose, in the case of a distribution to a foreign related party, the increased basis in the remaining partnership property that is treated as newly purchased property is entirely attributable to the foreign related party. In the case of a distribution to a taxpayer, the increased basis in the distributed property that is treated as newly purchased property is attributable to each foreign related party in proportion to the foreign related party's proportionate share of the asset immediately before the distribution. If the distribution is to a person other than a taxpayer or a foreign related party, there is no base erosion payment caused by the distribution under this paragraph (c)(4). See paragraphs (g)(2)(vii), (viii), and (ix) of this section (*Example 7, Example 8,* and *Example 9*) for examples illustrating the application of this paragraph (c)(4).

(5) *Operating rules applicable to base erosion payments.*—(i) *Single payment characterized as separate transactions.*—If a single transaction is partially characterized in one manner and partially characterized in another manner, each part of the transaction is separately analyzed. For example, if a contribution of property to a partnership is partially treated as a contribution and partially treated as a disguised sale, the contribution and sale are separately analyzed under paragraph (c) of this section.

(ii) *Ordering rule with respect to transfers of a partnership interest.*—If a partnership interest is transferred (within the meaning of paragraph (c)(3)(iv) of this section), paragraph (c)(3) of this section first applies to determine the assets deemed transferred by the transferor(s) to the transferee(s) and liabilities deemed assumed by the parties. Then, to the extent applicable (such as where a partnership makes a contribution in exchange for an interest in another partnership or when a partnership receives an interest in another partnership as a contribution to it), paragraph (c)(2) of this section applies for purposes of determining the proportionate share of the property received by the partners in a partnership. See paragraph (g)(2)(vi) of this section (*Example 6*) for an illustration of this rule.

(iii) *Consideration for base erosion payment or property resulting in base erosion tax benefits.*—When a partnership pays or receives property, services, or other consideration, each partner is deemed to pay or receive the property, services, or other consideration paid or received by the partnership for purposes of determining if there is a base erosion payment, except as otherwise provided in paragraph (c) of this section. See paragraphs (g)(2)(v) and (vi) of this section (*Example 5* and *Example 6*) for illustrations of this rule.

(iv) *Non-cash consideration.*—When both parties to a transaction use non-cash consideration, each party must separately apply paragraph (c) of this section to determine its base erosion payment with respect to each property. For example, if two partnerships, each with a domestic corporation and a foreign corporation as partners, all of whom are related, exchange depreciable property, each transfer of property would be separately analyzed to determine whether it is a base erosion payment.

(v) *Allocations of income in lieu of deductions.*—If a partnership adopts the curative method of making section 704(c) allocations under § 1.704-3(c), an allocation of income to the partner to whom any built-in gain or built-in loss would be allocable under section 704(c) (the 704(c) partner), in an amount necessary to offset the effect of the ceiling rule (as defined in § 1.704-3(b)(1)), in lieu of a deduction allocation to a partner other than the 704(c) partner (a non-704(c) partner), is treated as a deduction to the non-704(c) partner for purposes of section 59A in an amount equal to the income allocation. See paragraph (g)(2)(x) of this section (*Example 10*) for an example illustrating the application of this paragraph (c)(5)(v).

(d) *Base erosion tax benefit for partners.*—(1) *In general.*—A partner's distributive share of any deduction or reduction in gross receipts attributable to a base erosion payment (including as a result of sections 704(b) and (c), 707(a) and (c), 732(b) and (d), 734(b) and (d), 737, 743(b) and (d), and 751(b)) is the partner's base erosion tax benefit, subject to the exceptions in § 1.59A-3(c)(2). See paragraph (e)(1) of this section to determine the partner's distributive share for purposes of section 59A. A partner's base erosion tax benefit may be more than the partner's base erosion payment. For example, if a partnership makes a payment to a foreign related party of its domestic partner to acquire a depreciable asset, and the partnership specially allocates more depreciation deductions to a partner than its proportionate share of the asset, the partner's base erosion tax benefit includes the specially allocated depreciation deduction even if the total allocated deduction exceeds the partner's share of the base erosion payment made to acquire the asset. Base erosion tax benefits are determined separately for each asset, payment, or accrual, as applicable, and are not netted with other items. A taxpayer determines its base erosion tax benefits for non-partnership items pursuant to § 1.59A-3(c).

(2) *Exception for base erosion tax benefits of certain small partners.*—(i) *In general.*—For purposes of determining a partner's amount of base erosion tax benefits attributable to a base erosion payment made by a partnership, a partner does not take into account its distributive share of any base erosion tax benefits from the partnership for the taxable year if—

(A) The partner's interest in the partnership represents less than ten percent of the capital and profits of the partnership at all times during the taxable year;

(B) The partner is allocated less than ten percent of each partnership item of income, gain, loss, deduction, and credit for the taxable year; and

(C) The partner's interest in the partnership has a fair market value of less than $25 million on the last day of the partner's taxable year, determined using a reasonable method.

(ii) *Attribution.*—For purposes of paragraph (d)(2)(i) of this section, a partner's interest in a partnership or partnership item is determined by adding the interests of the partner and any related party of the partner (as determined under section 59A), taking into account any interest owned directly, indirectly, or through constructive ownership (applying the section 318 rules as modified by section 59A (except section 318(a)(3)(A) through (C) will also apply so as to consider a United States person as owning stock that is owned by a person who is not a United States person), but excluding any interest to the extent already taken into account).

(e) *Other rules for applying section 59A to partnerships.*—(1) *Partner's distributive share.*—For purposes of section 59A, each partner's distributive share of an item of income or deduction of the partnership is determined under sections 704(b) and (c) and takes into account amounts determined under other provisions of the Code, including but not limited to sections 707(a) and (c), 732(b) and (d), 734(b) and (d), 737, 743(b) and (d), and 751(b). *See* § 1.704-1(b)(1)(iii) regarding the application of section 482. These amounts are calculated separately for each payment or accrual on a property-by-property basis, including for purposes of section 704(c), and are not netted. For purposes of section 59A, a partner's distributive share of a reduction to determine gross income is equal to a proportionate amount of the partnership's reduction to determine gross income corresponding to the partner's share of the partnership gross receipts (as determined under paragraph (e)(2)(i) of this section) related to that reduction.

(2) *Gross receipts.*—(i) *In general.*—For purposes of section 59A, each partner in the partnership includes a share of partnership gross receipts in proportion to the partner's distributive share (as determined under sections 704(b) and (c)) of items of gross income that were taken into account by the partnership under section 703 or 704(c) (such as remedial or curative items under § 1.704-3(c) or (d)).

(ii) *Foreign corporation.*—See § 1.59A-2(d)(3) for gross receipts of foreign corporations.

(3) *Registered securities dealers.*—If a partnership, or a branch of the partnership, is a registered securities dealer, each partner is treated as a registered securities dealer unless the partner's interest in the registered securities dealer would satisfy the criteria for the exception in paragraph (d)(2) of this section. For purposes of applying the de minimis exception in § 1.59A-2(e)(2)(iii), a partner takes into account its distributive share of the relevant partnership items.

(4) *Application of sections 163(j) and 59A(c)(3) to partners.*—See § 1.59A-3(c)(4).

(5) *Tiered partnerships.*—In the case of one or more partnerships owning an interest in another partnership (or partnerships), the rules of this section apply successively to each partnership and its partners in the chain of ownership. Paragraphs (d)(2) and (f) of this section and the small partner exception in paragraph (e)(3) of this section apply only to a partner that is not itself a partnership.

(f) *Foreign related party.*—With respect to any person that owns an interest in a partnership, the related party determination in section 59A(g) applies at the partner level.

(g) *Examples.*—The following examples illustrate the application of this section.

(1) *Facts.*—The following facts are assumed for purposes of the examples.

(i) DC is a domestic corporation that is an applicable taxpayer for purposes section 59A.

(ii) FC is a foreign corporation that is a foreign related party with respect to DC.

(iii) UC is a domestic corporation that is not related to DC and FC.

(iv) Neither FC nor any partnership in the examples is (or is treated as) engaged in a U.S. trade or business or has a permanent establishment in the United States.

(v) All payments apply to a taxable year beginning after December 31, 2017.

(vi) Unless otherwise stated, all allocations are pro-rata and satisfy the requirements of section 704(b) and all the partners have equal interests in the partnership.

(vii) Unless otherwise stated, depreciable property acquired and placed in service by the partnership has a remaining recovery period of five years and is depreciated under the alternative depreciation system of section 168(g) using the straight line method. Solely for purposes of simplifying the calculations in these examples, assume the applicable convention rules in section 168(d) do not apply.

(viii) No exception under § 1.59A-3(b) or (c) applies to any amount paid or accrued.

(2) *Examples.*—(i) *Example 1: Contributions to a partnership on partnership formation*—(A) *Facts.* DC and FC form partnership PRS, with each contributing depreciable property that has a fair market value and tax basis of $100x, Property A and Property B, respectively. Therefore, the property contributed by FC, Property B, will generate $20x of annual section 704(b) and tax depreciation deductions for five years. The depreciation deductions will be allocated $10x to each of DC and FC each year. Before the transactions, for purposes of section 59A, DC is treated as owning a 100 percent interest in Property A and a zero percent interest in Property B, and FC is treated as owning a 100 percent interest in Property B and a zero percent interest in Property A. After the formation of PRS, for purposes of section 59A, DC and FC are each treated as owning a 50 percent proportionate share of each of Property A and Property B.

(B) *Analysis.* The treatment of contributions of property in exchange for an interest in a partnership is described in paragraph (c)(3)(iii) of this section. Under paragraph (c)(3)(iii) of this section, DC is treated as exchanging a 50 percent interest in Property A for a 50 percent proportionate share of Property B. Under § 1.59A-3(b)(1)(ii), the payment to acquire depreciable property, Property B, from FC is a base erosion payment. The base erosion tax benefit is the amount of depreciation allocated to DC with respect to Property B ($10x per year) and is not netted with any other partnership item pursuant to paragraph (d)(1) of this section.

(ii) *Example 2: Section 704(c) and remedial allocations*—(A) *Facts.* The facts are the same as in paragraph (g)(2)(i)(A) of this section (the facts in *Example 1*), except that Property B has a tax basis of $40x and PRS adopts the remedial method under § 1.704-3(d).

(B) *Analysis.* The analysis and results are the same as in paragraph (g)(2)(i)(B) of this section (the analysis in *Example 1*), except that annual tax depreciation is $8x ($40x/5) and annual remedial tax deduction allocation to DC is $2x (with $2x of remedial income to FC) for five years. Both the tax depreciation and the remedial tax allocation to DC are base erosion tax benefits to DC under paragraph (d)(1) of this section.

(iii) *Example 3: Sale of a partnership interest without a section 754 election*—(A) *Facts.* UC and FC are equal partners in partnership PRS, the only asset of which is Property A, a depreciable property with a fair market value of $200x and a tax basis of $120x. PRS does not have any section 704(c) assets. DC purchases 50 percent of FC's interest in PRS for $50x. Prior to the sale, for section 59A purposes, FC is treated as owning a 50 percent proportionate share of Property A and DC is treated as owning no interest in Property A. Following the sale, for section 59A purposes, DC is treated as owning a 25 percent proportionate share of Property A, all of which is treated as acquired from FC. The partnership does not have an election under section 754 in effect. Property A will generate $24x of annual tax and section 704(b) depreciation deductions for five years. The depreciation deductions will be allocated $12x to UC and $6x to both FC and DC each year.

(B) *Analysis.* The sale of a partnership interest by a partner is analyzed under paragraph (c)(3)(ii) of this section. Under section (c)(3)(ii) of this section, FC is treated as selling to DC 25 percent of Property A. Under §1.59A-3(b)(1)(ii), the payment to acquire depreciable property is a base erosion payment. Under paragraph (d)(1) of this section, the base erosion tax benefit is the amount of depreciation allocated to DC with respect to the base erosion payment, which would be the depreciation deductions allocated to DC with respect to Property A. DC's annual $6x depreciation deduction is its base erosion tax benefit with respect to the base erosion payment.

(iv) *Example 4: Sale of a partnership interest with section 754 election*—(A) *Facts.* The facts are the same as in paragraph (g)(2)(iii)(A) of this section (the facts in *Example 3*), except that the partnership has an election under section 754 in effect. As a result of the sale, there is a $20x positive adjustment to the tax basis in Property A with respect to DC under section 743(b) (DC's $50x basis in the PRS interest less DC's $30x share of PRS's tax basis in Property A). The section 743(b) step-up in tax basis is recovered over a depreciable recovery period of five years. Therefore, DC will be allocated a total of $10x in annual depreciation deductions for five years, comprised of $6x with respect to DC's proportionate share of PRS's common tax basis in Property A ($30x over 5 years) and $4x with respect to the section 743(b) adjustment ($20x over 5 years).

(B) *Analysis.* The analysis is the same as in paragraph (g)(2)(iii)(B) of this section (the analysis in *Example 3*); however, because section 743(b) increases the basis in Property A for DC by $20x, DC is allocated additional depreciation deductions of $4x per year as a result of the section 743(b) adjustment and has an annual base erosion tax benefit of $10x ($6x plus $4x) for five years under paragraph (d)(1) of this section.

(v) *Example 5: Purchase of depreciable property from a partnership*—(A) *Facts.* The facts are the same as in paragraph (d)(2)(iii)(A) of this section (the facts in *Example* 3), except that instead of DC purchasing an interest in the partnership, DC purchases Property A from the partnership for $200x.

(B) *Analysis.* DC must analyze whether the purchase of the depreciable property from the partnership is a base erosion payment under paragraph (c)(2) of this section. Under paragraph (c)(2) of this section, DC is treated as acquiring FC's proportionate share of Property A from FC. Because DC paid the partnership for the partnership's interest in Property A, under paragraph (c)(5)(iii) of this section, DC is treated as paying FC for FC's proportionate share of Property A. Under §1.59A-3(b)(1)(ii), the payment to FC to acquire depreciable property is a base erosion payment. DC's base erosion tax benefit is the amount of depreciation allocated to DC with respect to the base erosion payment, which in this case is the amount of depreciation deductions with respect to the property acquired with a base erosion payment, or the depreciation deductions from FC's (but not UC's) proportionate share of the asset. See §1.59A-7(d)(1).

(vi) *Example 6: Sale of a partnership interest to a second partnership*—(A) *Facts.* FC, UC1, and UC2 are equal partners in partnership PRS1. DC and UC3 are equal partners in partnership PRS2. UC1, UC2, and UC3 are not related to DC or FC. PRS1's sole asset is Property A, which is depreciable property with a fair market value and tax basis of $300x. FC sells its entire interest in PRS1 to PRS2 for $100. For section 59A purposes, FC's proportionate share of Property A prior to the sale is one-third. Following the sale, for section 59A purposes, PRS2's proportionate share of Property A is one-third and DC's proportionate share of Property A (through PRS2) is one-sixth (50 percent of one-third).

(B) *Analysis.* Under paragraph (c)(5)(ii) of this section (the ordering rule), FC's transfer of its interest in PRS1 is first analyzed under paragraph (c)(3) of this section to determine how the transfer of the partnership interest is treated. Then, paragraph (c)(2) of this section applies to analyze how the acquisition of property by PRS2 is treated. Under paragraph (c)(3)(ii) of this section, FC is deemed to transfer its proportionate share of PRS1's assets, which is one-third of Property A. Then, under paragraph (c)(2) of this section, DC is treated as acquiring its proportionate share of PRS2's proportionate share of Property A from FC, which is one-sixth (50 percent of one-third). Under paragraph (c)(5)(iii) of this section, DC is treated as paying for the property it is treated as acquiring from FC. Therefore, DC's deemed payment to FC to acquire depreciable property is a base erosion payment under §1.59A-3(b)(1)(ii). DC's base erosion tax benefit is equal to DC's distributive share of depreciation deductions that PRS2 allocates to DC attributable to Property A. See §1.59A-7(d)(1).

(vii) *Example 7: Distribution of cash by a partnership to a foreign related party*—(A) *Facts.* DC, FC, and UC are equal partners in a partnership, PRS, the assets of which consist of cash of $90x and a depreciable asset (Property A) with a fair market value of $180x and a tax basis of $60x. Each partner's interest in PRS has a fair market value of $90x ($270x/3) and a tax basis of $50x. Assume that all non-depreciable assets are capital assets, all depreciable assets are non-residential real property under section 168, and that no depreciation has been claimed prior to the transaction below. PRS has an election under section 754 in effect. PRS distributes the $90x of cash to FC in complete liquidation of its interest, resulting in gain to FC of $40x ($90x minus its tax basis in PRS of $50x) under section 731(a)(1) and an increase to the tax basis of Property A under section 734(b) of $40x. Prior to the distribution, for section 59A purposes, each partner had a one-third proportionate share of Property A. After the distribution, for section 59A purposes, the remaining partners each have a 50 percent proportionate share of Property A. Each partner's pro-rata allocation of depreciation deductions with respect to Property A is in proportion to each partner's proportionate share of Property A both before and after the distribution. Half of the depreciation deductions attributable to the $40x section 734(b) step-up will be allocated to DC. In addition, DC's proportionate share of Property A increased from one-third to one-half and therefore DC will be allocated depreciation deductions with respect to half of the original basis of $60x (or $30x) instead of one-third of $60x (or $20x).

(B) *Analysis.* Distributions of property that cause an increase in the tax basis of property that continues to be held by the partnership are analyzed under paragraph (c)(4) of this section. The $40x increase in the tax basis of Property A as a result of the distribution of cash to FC is treated as newly purchased property acquired from FC under paragraph (c)(4) of this section and therefore acquired with a base erosion payment under §1.59A-3(b)(1)(ii) to DC to the extent of DC's proportionate share. DC's base erosion tax benefit is the amount of DC's depreciation deductions attributable to that base erosion payment, which is DC's distributive share of the depreciation deductions with respect to the $40x increase in the tax basis of Property A. See §1.59A-7(d)(1). In addition, FC transferred a partnership interest to DC (as defined in paragraph (c)(3)(iv) of this section), which is analyzed under paragraph (c)(3)(i) of this section. Under paragraph (c)(3)(i) of this section, DC is deemed to acquire a one-sixth interest in Property A from FC (the increase in DC's proportionate share from one-third to one-half). DC's base erosion tax benefit from this additional one-sixth interest in Property A is the amount of DC's depreciation deductions attributable to this interest.

(viii) *Example 8: Distribution of property by a partnership to a taxpayer*—(A) *Facts.* The facts are the same as paragraph (g)(2)(vii)(A) of this section (the facts of *Example 7*), except that PRS's depreciable property consists of two assets, Property A having a fair market value of $90x and a tax basis of $60x and Property B having a fair market value of $90x and a tax basis of zero. Instead of distributing cash to FC, PRS distributes Property B to DC in liquidation of its interest, resulting in an increase in the basis of the distributed Property B to DC of $50x (from zero to $50x) under section 732(b) because DC's tax basis in the PRS interest was $50x. For section 59A purposes, prior to the distribution, each partner had a one-third proportionate share of Property B and after the distribution, the property is wholly owned by DC.

(B) *Analysis.* Distributions of property that cause an increase in the tax basis of property that is distributed to a taxpayer are analyzed under paragraph (c)(4) of this section. Under paragraph (c)(4) of this section, the $50x increase in tax basis is treated as newly purchased property that was acquired with a base erosion payment to the extent that the increase in tax basis is attributable to FC. Under paragraph (c)(4) of this section, the portion of the increase that is attributable to FC is the proportionate share of the Property B immediately before the distribution that was treated as owned by FC. Immediately before the distribution, FC had a one-third proportionate share of Property B. Accordingly, one-third of the $50x increase in the tax basis of Property B is treated as if it was newly purchased property acquired by DC from FC with a base erosion payment under §1.59A-3(b)(1)(ii). DC's base erosion tax benefit is the amount of DC's depreciation deductions with respect to the base erosion payment, which in this case is the depreciation deductions with respect to the one-third interest in the increased basis treated as newly purchased property deemed acquired from FC. See §1.59A-3(c)(1). In addition, PRS transferred Property B to DC, which is analyzed under paragraph (c)(2) of this section. Prior to the distribution, DC, FC, and UC each owned one-third of Property B. After the distribution, DC entirely owned Property B. Therefore, under paragraph (c)(2) of this section, DC is treated as acquiring one-third of Property B from FC. DC's depreciation deductions with respect to the one-third of Property B acquired from FC (without regard to the basis increase) is also a base erosion tax benefit.

(ix) *Example 9: Distribution of property by a partnership in liquidation of a foreign related party's interest*—(A) *Facts*. The facts are the same as paragraph (g)(2)(viii)(A) (the facts of *Example 8*), except that Property B is not distributed to DC and, instead, Property A is distributed to FC in liquidation of its interest, resulting in a tax basis in Property A of $50x in FC's hands under section 732(b) and a section 734(b) step-up in Property B of $10x (because Property A's tax basis was reduced from $60x to $50x), allocable to DC and UC. For section 59A purposes, prior to the distribution, each partner had a one-third proportionate share of Property B and after the distribution, DC and UC each have a one-half proportionate share of Property B.

(B) *Analysis*. Distributions of property that cause an increase in the tax basis of property that continues to be held by the partnership are analyzed under paragraph (c)(4) of this section. Under paragraph (c)(4) of this section, because the distribution of Property A to FC from PRS caused an increase in the tax basis of Property B, the entire $10x increase in tax basis is treated as newly purchased property that was acquired with a base erosion payment under § 1.59A-3(b)(1)(ii). DC's base erosion tax benefit is the amount of DC's depreciation deductions attributable to the base erosion payment, which is DC's distributive share of the depreciation deductions with respect to the $10x increase in the tax basis of Property B. See § 1.59A-7(d)(1). In addition, under paragraph (c)(3)(i) of this section, DC is deemed to acquire a one-sixth interest in Property B from FC (the increase in DC's proportionate share from one-third to one-half). While this increase is a base erosion payment under § 1.59A-3(b)(1)(ii), there is no base erosion tax benefit from this additional one-sixth interest in Property B because the tax basis in Property B (without regard to the basis) is zero and therefore the increase in DC's proportionate share does not result in any additional depreciation deductions.

(x) *Example 10: Section 704(c) and curative allocations*—(A) *Facts*. The facts are the same as in paragraph (d)(2)(ii)(A) of this section (the facts in *Example 2*), except that DC's property is not depreciable, PRS uses the traditional method with curative allocations under § 1.704-3(c), and the curative allocations are to be made from operating income. Also assume that the partnership has $20x of gross operating income in each year and a curative allocation of the operating income satisfies the "substantially the same effect" requirement of § 1.704-3(c)(3)(iii)(A).

(B) *Analysis*. The analysis and results are the same as in paragraph (d)(2)(i)(B) of this section (the analysis in *Example 1*), except that actual depreciation is $8x ($40x/5) per year and the ceiling rule shortfall under § 1.704-3(b)(1) of $2x per year is corrected with a curative allocation of income from DC to FC of $2x per year. Solely for U.S. federal income tax purposes, each year FC is allocated $12x of total operating income and DC is allocated $8x of operating income. Both the actual depreciation deduction to DC and the curative allocation of income from DC are base erosion tax benefits to DC under paragraphs (c)(5)(v) and (d)(1) of this section. [Reg. § 1.59A-7.]

☐ [*T.D.* 9885, 12-2-2019. *Amended by T.D.* 9910, 10-8-2020.]

§ 1.59A-8. [Reserved].

[Reg. § 1.59A-8.]

☐ [*T.D.* 9885, 12-2-2019.]

§ 1.59A-9. Anti-abuse and recharacterization rules.—(a) *Scope*.—This section provides rules for recharacterizing certain transactions according to their substance for purposes of applying section 59A and the section 59A regulations. Paragraph (b) of this section provides specific anti-abuse rules. Paragraph (c) of this section provides examples illustrating the rules of paragraph (b) of this section.

(b) *Anti-abuse rules*.—(1) *Transactions involving unrelated persons, conduits, or intermediaries*.—If a taxpayer pays or accrues an amount to one or more intermediaries (including an intermediary unrelated to the taxpayer) that would have been a base erosion payment if paid or accrued to a foreign related party, and one or more of the intermediaries makes (directly or indirectly) corresponding payments to or for the benefit of a foreign related party as part of a transaction (or series of transactions), plan, or arrangement that has as a principal purpose of avoiding a base erosion payment (or reducing the amount of a base erosion payment), the role of the intermediary or intermediaries is disregarded as a conduit, or the amount paid or accrued to the intermediary is treated as a base erosion payment, as appropriate.

(2) *Transactions to increase the amount of deductions taken into account in the denominator of the base erosion percentage computation*.—A transaction (or component of a transaction or series of transactions), plan, or arrangement that has a principal purpose of increasing the deductions taken into account for purposes of § 1.59A-2(e)(3)(i)(B) (the denominator of the base erosion percentage computation) is disregarded for purposes of § 1.59A-2(e)(3).

(3) *Transactions to avoid the application of rules applicable to banks and registered securities dealers*.—A transaction (or series of transactions), plan, or arrangement that occurs among related parties that has a principal purpose of avoiding the rules applicable to certain banks and registered securities dealers in § 1.59A-2(e)(2) (base erosion percentage test for banks and registered securities dealers) or § 1.59A-5(c)(2) (increased base erosion and anti-abuse tax rate for banks and registered securities dealers) is not taken into account for purposes of § 1.59A-2(e)(2) or § 1.59A-5(c)(2).

(4) *Nonrecognition transactions*.—If a transaction (or series of transactions), plan, or arrangement (the first transaction) increases the adjusted basis of property that the taxpayer acquires in a transaction (the second transaction) that qualifies for the specified nonrecognition transaction exception in § 1.59A-3(b)(3)(viii)(A) (or would qualify, but for this paragraph (b)(4)), and a principal purpose of the first transaction was to increase the taxpayer's depreciation or amortization deductions without increasing the taxpayer's base erosion tax benefits, then § 1.59A-3(b)(3)(viii)(A) does not apply to the property acquired in the second transaction to the extent of the increase in adjusted basis. For purposes of this paragraph (b)(4), if a transaction (or series of transactions), plan, or arrangement between related parties increases the adjusted basis of property within the six-month period before the taxpayer acquires the property, the transaction (or series of transactions), plan, or arrangement is deemed to have such a principal purpose.

(5) *Transactions involving derivatives on a partnership interest*.—If a taxpayer acquires a derivative on a partnership interest (or partnership assets) as part of a transaction (or series of transactions), plan, or arrangement that has as a principal purpose of avoiding a base erosion payment (or reducing the amount of a base erosion payment) and the partnership interest (or partnership assets) would have resulted in a base erosion payment had the taxpayer acquired that interest (or partnership asset) directly, then the taxpayer is treated as having a direct interest instead of a derivative interest for purposes of applying section 59A. This paragraph (b)(5), however, does not apply to a derivative, as defined in section 59A(h)(4)(A)(v), on a partnership asset to the extent the payment pursuant to the derivative qualifies for the exception for qualified derivative payments in § 1.59A-3(b)(3)(ii) and § 1.59A-6. A derivative interest in a partnership includes any contract (including any financial instrument) the value of which, or any payment or other transfer with respect to which, is (directly or indirectly) determined in whole or in part by reference to the partnership, including the amount of partnership distributions, the value of partnership assets, or the results of partnership operations.

(6) *Allocations to eliminate or reduce a base erosion payment*.—If a partnership receives (or accrues) an amount from a person not acting in a partner capacity (including a person who is not a partner) and allocates the income or loss with respect to that amount to its partners with a principal purpose of avoiding a base erosion payment (or reducing the amount of a base erosion payment), then the taxpayer transacting (directly or indirectly) with the partnership will determine its base erosion payment as if the allocations had not been made and the items of income or loss had been allocated proportionately. The preceding sentence applies only when the allocations, in combination with any related allocations, do not change the economic arrangement of the partners to the partnership.

(c) *Examples*.—The following examples illustrate the application of this section.

(1) *Facts*.—The following facts are assumed for purposes of the examples.

(i) DC is a domestic corporation that is an applicable taxpayer for purposes section 59A.

(ii) FP is a foreign corporation that owns all the stock of DC.

(iii) None of the foreign corporations have income that is, or is treated as, effectively connected with the conduct of a trade or business in the United States under an applicable provision of the Internal Revenue Code or regulations thereunder.

(iv) All payments occur in a taxable year beginning after December 31, 2017.

(2) *Example 1: Substitution of payments that are not base erosion payments for payments that otherwise would be base erosion payments through a conduit or intermediary*—(i) *Facts.* FP owns Property 1 with a fair market value of $95x, which FP intends to transfer to DC. A payment from DC to FP for Property 1 would be a base erosion payment. Corp A is a domestic corporation that is not a related party with respect to DC. As part of a plan with a principal purpose of avoiding a base erosion payment, FP enters into an arrangement with Corp A to transfer Property 1 to Corp A in exchange for $95x. Pursuant to the same plan, Corp A transfers Property 1 to DC in exchange for $100x. Property 1 is subject to the allowance for depreciation (or amortization in lieu of depreciation) in the hands of DC.

(ii) *Analysis.* The arrangement between FP, DC, and Corp A is deemed to result in a $95x base erosion payment under paragraph (b)(1) of this section because DC's payment to Corp A would have been a base erosion payment if paid to a foreign related party, and Corp A makes a corresponding payment to FP as part of the series of transactions that has as a principal purpose of avoiding a base erosion payment.

(3) *Example 2: Alternative transaction to base erosion payment*—(i) *Facts.* The facts are the same as in paragraph (c)(2)(i) of this section (the facts in *Example 1*), except that DC does not purchase Property 1 from FP or Corp A. Instead, DC purchases Property 2 from Corp B, a domestic corporation that is not a related party with respect to DC and that originally produced or acquired Property 2 for Corp B's own account. Property 2 is substantially similar to Property 1, and DC uses Property 2 in substantially the same manner that DC would have used Property 1.

(ii) *Analysis.* Paragraph (b)(1) of this section does not apply to the transaction between DC and Corp B because Corp B does not make a corresponding payment to or for the benefit of FP as part of a transaction, plan, or arrangement.

(4) *Example 3: Alternative financing source*—(i) *Facts.* On Date 1, FP loaned $200x to DC in exchange for Note A. DC pays or accrues interest annually on Note A, and the payment or accrual is a base erosion payment within the meaning of § 1.59A-3(b)(1)(i). On Date 2, DC borrows $200x from Bank, a corporation that is not a related party with respect to DC, in exchange for Note B. The terms of Note B are substantially similar to the terms of Note A. DC uses the proceeds from Note B to repay Note A.

(ii) *Analysis.* Paragraph (b)(1) of this section does not apply to the transaction between DC and Bank because Bank does not make a corresponding payment to or for the benefit of FP as part of the series of transactions.

(5) *Example 4: Alternative financing source that is a conduit*—(i) *Facts.* The facts are the same as in paragraph (c)(4)(i) of this section (the facts in *Example 3*) except that in addition, as part of the same plan or arrangement as the Note B transaction and with a principal purpose of avoiding a base erosion payment, FP deposits $250x with Bank. The difference between the interest rate paid by Bank to FP on FP's deposit and the interest rate paid by DC to Bank is less than one percentage point. The interest rate charged by Bank to DC would have differed absent the deposit by FP.

(ii) *Analysis.* The transactions between FP, DC, and Bank are deemed to result in a base erosion payment under paragraph (b)(1) of this section because DC's payment to Bank would have been a base erosion payment if paid to a foreign related party, and Bank makes a corresponding payment to FP as part of the series of transactions that has as a principal purpose of avoiding a base erosion payment. See Rev. Rul. 87-89, 1987-2 C.B. 195, Situation 3.

(6) *Example 5: Intermediary acquisition*—(i) *Facts.* FP owns all of the stock of DC1 and DC2, each domestic corporations. FP is a manufacturer of lawn equipment. DC1 is in the trade or business of renting equipment to unrelated third parties. DC2 is a dealer in property that capitalizes its purchases into inventory and recovers the amount through cost of goods sold. Before Date 1, in the ordinary course of DC1's business, DC1 acquired depreciable property from FP that DC1 in turn rented to unrelated third parties. DC1's purchases from FP were base erosion payments within the meaning of § 1.59A-3(b)(1)(ii). On Date 1, with a principal purpose of avoiding a base erosion payment, FP and DC2 reorganized their operations so that DC2 acquires the lawn equipment from FP and immediately thereafter, DC2 resells the lawn equipment to DC1.

(ii) *Analysis.* The transactions between FP, DC1, and DC2 are deemed to result in a base erosion payment under paragraph (b)(1) of this section because DC1's payment to DC2 would have been a base erosion payment if paid directly to FP, and DC2 makes a corresponding payment to FP as part of a series of transactions, plan, or arrangement that has a principal purpose of avoiding a base erosion payment from DC1 to FP.

(7) *Example 6: Offsetting transactions to increase the amount of deductions taken into account in the denominator of the base erosion percentage computation*—(i) *Facts.* With a principal purpose of increasing the deductions taken into account by DC for purposes of § 1.59A-2(e)(3)(i)(B), DC enters into a long position with respect to Asset with Financial Institution 1 and simultaneously enters into a short position with respect to Asset with Financial Institution 2. Financial Institution 1 and Financial Institution 2 are not related to DC and are not related to each other.

(ii) *Analysis.* Paragraph (b)(2) of this section applies to the transactions between DC and Financial Institution 1 and DC and Financial Institution 2. These transactions are not taken into account for purposes of § 1.59A-2(e)(3)(i)(B) because the transactions have a principal purpose of increasing the deductions taken into account for purposes of § 1.59A-2(e)(3)(i)(B).

(8) *Example 7: Ordinary course transactions that increase the amount of deductions taken into account in the denominator of the base erosion percentage computation*—(i) *Facts.* DC, a financial institution, enters into a long position with respect to stock in Corporation with Person 1 and later on the same day enters into a short position with respect to stock in Corporation with Person 2. Person 1 and Person 2 are not related to DC and are not related to each other. DC entered into the positions in the ordinary course of its business and did not have a principal purpose of increasing the deductions taken into account by DC for purposes of § 1.59A-2(e)(3)(i)(B).

(ii) *Analysis.* Paragraph (b)(2) of this section does not apply because the transactions between DC and Person 1 and Person 2 were not entered into with a principal purpose of increasing the deductions taken into account by DC for purposes of § 1.59A-2(e)(3)(i)(B).

(9) *Example 8: Transactions to avoid the application of rules applicable to banks and registered securities dealers*—(i) *Facts.* DC owns all of the stock of DC1 and Bank (an entity defined in section 581). DC, DC1, and Bank are members of an affiliated group of corporations within the meaning of section 1504(a) that elect to file a consolidated U.S. federal income tax return. With a principal purpose of avoiding the rules of § 1.59A-2(e)(2) or § 1.59A-5(c)(2), DC and DC1 form a new partnership (PRS). DC contributes all of its stock of Bank, and DC1 contributes cash, to PRS. DC, DC1, and Bank do not materially change their business operations following the formation of PRS.

(ii) *Analysis.* Paragraph (b)(3) of this section applies to transactions with respect to Bank because the transactions with respect to PRS were entered into with a principal purpose of avoiding the rules of § 1.59A-2(e)(2) or § 1.59A-5(c)(2). The contribution of Bank to a PRS is not taken into account, and Bank will be deemed to be part of the affiliated group including DC and DC1 for purposes of § 1.59A-2(e)(2) and § 1.59A-5(c)(2).

(10) *Example 9: Transactions that do not avoid the application of rules applicable to banks and registered securities dealers*—(i) *Facts.* The facts are the same as the facts of paragraph (c)(9)(i) of this section (the facts of Example 8), except that DC sells 90 percent of the stock of Bank to an unrelated party in exchange for cash.

(ii) *Analysis.* Paragraph (b)(3) of this section does not apply to DC's sale of the stock of Bank because the sale was not made with a principal purpose of avoiding the rules of § 1.59A-2(e)(2) or § 1.59A-5(c)(2). Bank will not be treated as part of the affiliated group including DC and DC1 for purposes of § 1.59A-2(e)(2) and § 1.59A-5(c)(2).

(11) *Example 10: Acquisition of depreciable property in a nonrecognition transaction*—(i) *Facts.* U, which is not a related party with respect to FP or DC, owns Property 1 with an adjusted basis of $50x and a fair market value of $100x. On Date 1, FP purchases property, including Property 1, from U in exchange for cash, and then FP contributes Property 1 to DC in an exchange described in section 351. Following the exchange, DC's basis in Property 1 is $100x.

(ii) *Analysis.* Paragraph (b)(4) of this section does not apply to DC's acquisition of Property 1 because the purchase of Property 1 from U (first transaction) did not have a principal purpose of increasing DC's adjusted basis of Property 1 without increasing DC's base erosion tax benefits. The transaction is economically equivalent to an alternative transaction under which FP contributed $100x to DC and then DC purchased Property 1 from U. Further, the second sentence of paragraph (b)(4) of this section (providing that certain transactions are deemed to have a principal purpose of increasing the adjusted basis of property acquired in a second transaction) does not apply because FP purchased Property 1 from an unrelated party.

(12) *Example 11: Transactions between related parties with a principal purpose of increasing the adjusted basis of property*—(i) *Facts.* The facts are the same as paragraph (c)(11)(i) of this section (the facts in *Example 10*), except that U is related to FP and DC.

(ii) *Analysis.* Paragraph (b)(4) of this section applies to DC's acquisition of Property 1 because the transaction that increased the adjusted basis of Property 1 (the purchase of Property 1 from U) was between related parties, and within six months DC acquired Property 1 from FP in a specified nonrecognition transaction. Accordingly, the purchase of property from U (first transaction) is deemed to have a principal purpose of increasing the adjusted basis of Property 1 that DC acquires in the second transaction – the contribution (a transaction that qualifies as a specified nonrecognition transaction in part and would wholly qualify but for the application of paragraph (b)(4) of this section). Accordingly, the exception in § 1.59A-3(b)(3)(viii)(A) for specified nonrecognition transactions does not apply to the contribution of Property 1 to DC to the extent of the increased adjusted basis from the first transaction ($50x), and DC's depreciation deductions with respect to Property 1 will be base erosion tax benefits to the extent of the $50x increase in adjusted basis in Property 1. [Reg. § 1.59A-9.]

☐ [*T.D. 9885, 12-2-2019 (corrected 2-18-2020). Amended by T.D. 9910,* 10-8-2020.]

§ 1.59A-10. Applicability date.—(a) *General applicability date.*—Sections 1.59A-1 through 1.59A-9, other than the provisions described in the first sentence of paragraph (b) of this section, apply to taxable years ending on or after December 17, 2018. However, taxpayers may apply these regulations in their entirety for taxable years beginning after December 31, 2017, and ending before December 17, 2018. In lieu of applying the regulations referred to in the first sentence of this paragraph, taxpayers may apply the provisions matching § § 1.59A-1 through 1.59A-9 from the Internal Revenue Bulletin (IRB) 2019-02 (*https://www.irs.gov/irb/2019-02_IRB*) in their entirety for all taxable years beginning after December 31, 2017 and ending on or before December 6, 2019.

(b) *Exception.*—Sections 1.59A-2(c)(2)(ii) and (c)(4) through (6), 1.59A-3(b)(3)(iii)(C), 1.59A-3(c)(5) and (6), and 1.59A-9(b)(4) apply to taxable years beginning on or after October 9, 2020, and § § 1.59A-7(c)(5)(v) and 1.59A-9(b)(5) and (6) apply to taxable years ending on or after December 2, 2019. Taxpayers may apply those regulations in their entirety for taxable years beginning after December 31, 2017, and before their applicability date, provided that, once applied, taxpayers must continue to apply them in their entirety for all subsequent taxable years. Alternatively, taxpayers may apply only § 1.59A-3(c)(5) and (6) for taxable years beginning after December 31, 2017, and before their applicability date, provided that, once applied, taxpayers must continue to apply § 1.59A-3(c)(5) and (6) in their entirety for all subsequent taxable years. [Reg. § 1.59A-10.]

☐ [*T.D. 9885, 12-2-2019. Amended by T.D. 9910, 10-8-2020.*]

Items Specifically Included in Gross Income

§ 1.78-1. Gross up for deemed paid foreign tax credit.—(a) *Taxes deemed paid by certain domestic corporations treated as a dividend.*—If a domestic corporation chooses to have the benefits of the foreign tax credit under section 901 for any taxable year, an amount that is equal to the U.S. dollar amount of foreign income taxes deemed to be paid by the corporation for the year under section 960 (in the case of section 960(d), determined without regard to the phrase "80 percent of" in section 960(d)(1)) is, to the extent provided by this section, treated as a dividend (*a section 78 dividend*) received by the domestic corporation from the foreign corporation. A section 78 dividend is treated as a dividend for all purposes of the Code, except that it is not treated as a dividend for purposes of section 245 or 245A, and does not increase the earnings and profits of the domestic corporation or decrease the earnings and profits of the foreign corporation. Any reduction under section 907(a) of the foreign income taxes deemed paid with respect to combined foreign oil and gas income does not affect the amount treated as a section 78 dividend. See § 1.907(a)-1(e)(3). Similarly, any reduction under section 901(e) of the foreign income taxes deemed paid with respect to foreign mineral income does not affect the amount treated as a section 78 dividend. See § 1.901-3(a)(2)(i), (b)(2)(i)(b), and (d) *Example 8.* Any reduction under section 6038(c)(1)(B) in the foreign taxes paid or accrued by a foreign corporation is taken into account in determining foreign taxes deemed paid and the amount treated as a section 78 dividend. See, for example, § 1.6038-2(k)(5) *Example 1.* To the extent provided in the Code, section 78 does not apply to any tax not allowed as a credit. See, for example, sections 901(j)(3), 901(k)(7), 901(l)(4), 901(m)(6), and 908(b). For rules on determining the source of a section 78 dividend in computing the limitation on the foreign tax credit under section 904, see § § 1.861-3(a)(3), 1.862-1(a)(1)(ii), and 1.904-5(m)(6). For rules on assigning a section 78 dividend to a separate category, see § 1.904-4.

(b) *Date on which section 78 dividend is received.*—A section 78 dividend is considered received by a domestic corporation on the date on which—

(1) The corporation includes in gross income under section 951(a)(1)(A) the amounts by reason of which there are deemed paid under section 960(a) the foreign income taxes that give rise to that section 78 dividend, notwithstanding that the foreign income taxes may be carried back or carried over to another taxable year and deemed to be paid or accrued in such other taxable year under section 904(c); or

(2) The corporation includes in gross income under section 951A(a) the amounts by reason of which there are deemed paid under section 960(d) the foreign income taxes that give rise to that section 78 dividend.

(c) *Applicability date.*—This section applies to taxable years of foreign corporations that begin after December 31, 2017, and to taxable years of United States shareholders in which or with which such taxable years of foreign corporations end. The second sentence of paragraph (a) of this section also applies to section 78 dividends that are received after December 31, 2017, by reason of taxes deemed paid under section 960(a) with respect to a taxable year of a foreign corporation beginning before January 1, 2018. [Reg. § 1.78-1.]

☐ [*T.D. 6805, 3-8-65. Amended by T.D. 7120, 6-3-71, T.D. 7481, 4-15-77, T.D. 7490, 6-10-77, T.D. 7649, 10-17-79, T.D. 7961, 6-20-84, T.D. 9849, 3-11-2019 and T.D. 9866, 6-14-2019.*]

Items Specifically Excluded from Gross Income

§ 5f.103-1. Obligations issued after December 31, 1982, required to be in registered form (Temporary).—

* * *

(c) *Registered form.*—(1) *General rule.*—An obligation issued after January 20, 1987, pursuant to a binding contract entered into after January 20, 1987, is in registered form if—

(i) The obligation is registered as to both principal and any stated interest with the issuer (or its agent) and transfer of the obligation may be effected only by surrender of the old instrument and either the reissuance by the issuer of the old instrument to the new holder or the issuance by the issuer of a new instrument to the new holder,

(ii) The right to the principal of, and stated interest on, the obligation may be transferred only through a book entry system maintained by the issuer (or its agent) (as described in paragraph (c)(2) of this section), or

(iii) The obligation is registered as to both principal and any stated interest with the issuer (or its agent) and may be transferred through both of the methods described in subdivisions (i) and (ii).

(2) *Special rule for registration of a book entry obligation.*—An obligation shall be considered transferable through a book entry system if the ownership of an interest in the obligation is required to be reflected in a book entry, whether or not physical securities are issued. A book entry is a record of ownership that identifies the owner of an interest in the obligation.

* * *

[Temporary Reg. § 5f.103-1.]

☐ [*T.D. 7852, 11-9-82. Amended by T.D.* 8111, 12-16-86.]

Itemized Deductions for Individuals and Corporations

§ 5f.163-1. Denial of interest deduction on certain obligations issued after December 31, 1982, unless issued in registered form (temporary).—(a) *Denial of deduction generally.*—Interest paid or accrued on a registration-required obligation (as defined in paragraph (b) of this section) shall not be allowed as a deduction under section 163 or any other provision of law unless such obligation is issued in registered form (as defined in § 5f.103-1(c)).

(b) *Registration-required obligation.*—For purposes of this section, the term "registration-required obligation" means any obligation except any one of the following:

(1) An obligation issued by a natural person.

(2) An obligation not of a type offered to the public. The determination as to whether an obligation is not of a type offered to the public shall be based on whether similar obligations are in fact publicly offered or traded.

(3) An obligation that has a maturity at the date of issue of not more than 1 year.

(4) An obligation issued before January 1, 1983. An obligation first issued before January 1, 1983, shall not be considered to have been issued on or after such date merely as a result of the existence of a right on the part of the holder of such obligation to convert such obligation from registered form into bearer form, or as a result of the exercise of such a right.

(5) An obligation described in subparagraph (1) of paragraph (c) (relating to certain obligations issued to foreign persons).

(d) *Effective date.*—The provisions of this section shall apply to obligations issued after December 31, 1982, unless issued on an exercise of a warrant for the conversion of a convertible obligation if such warrant or obligation was offered or sold outside the United States without registration under the Securities Act of 1933 and was issued before August 10, 1982.

(e) *Obligations first issued after December 31, 1982, where the right exists for the holder to convert such obligation from registered form into bearer form.*—[Reserved]

(f) *Examples.*—The application of this section may be illustrated by the following examples:

Example (1). All of the shares of Corporation X are owned by two individuals, A and B. X desires to sell all of its assets to Corporation Y, all of the shares of which are owned by individual C. Following the sale, Corporation X will be completely liquidated. As partial consideration for the Corporation X assets, Corporation Y delivers a promissory note to X, secured by a security interest and mortgage on the acquired assets. The note given by Y to X is not of a type offered to the public.

Example (2). Corporation 2 has a credit agreement with Bank M pursuant to which Corporation Z may borrow amounts not exceeding $10X upon delivery of Z's note to Bank M. The note Z delivers to M is not of a type offered to the public.

Example (3). Individuals D and E operate a retail business through partnership DE. D wishes to loan partnership DE $5X. DE's note evidencing the loan from D is not of a type offered to the public.

Example (4). Individual F owns one-third of the shares of Corporation W. F makes a cash advance to W. W's note evidencing F's cash advance is not of a type offered to the public.

Example (5). Closely-held Corporation R places its convertible debentures with 30 individuals who are United States persons. The offering is not required to be registered under the Securities Act of 1933. Similar debentures are publicly offered and traded. The obligations are not considered of a type not offered to the public.

Example (6). In 1980, Corporation V issued its bonds due in 1986 through an offering registered with the Securities and Exchange Commission. Although the bonds were initially issued in registered form, the terms of the bonds permit a holder, at his option, to convert a bond into bearer form at any time prior to maturity. Similarly, a person who holds a bond in bearer form may, at any time, have the bond converted into registered form.

(i) Assume G bought one of Corporation V's bonds upon the original issuance in 1980. In 1983, G requests that V convert the bond into bearer form. Except for the change from registered to bearer form, the terms of the bond are unchanged. The bond held by G is not considered issued after December 31, 1982, under § 5f.163-1(b)(4).

(ii) Assume H buys one of Corporation V's bonds in the secondary market in 1983. The bond H receives is in registered form, but H requests that V convert the obligation into bearer form. There is no other change in the terms of the instrument. The bond held by H is not considered issued after December 31, 1982, under § 5f.163-1(b)(4).

(iii) Assume the same facts as in (ii) except that in 1984 I purchases H's V Corporation bond, which is in bearer form. I requests V to convert the bond into registered form. There is no other change in the terms of the instrument. In 1985, I requests V to convert the bond bank into bearer form. Again, there is no other change in the terms of the instrument. The bond purchased by I is not considered issued after December 31, 1982, under § 5f.163-1(b)(4).

Example (7). Corporation U wishes to make a public offering of its debentures to United States persons. U issues a master note to Bank N. The terms of the note require that any person who acquires an interest in the note must have such interest reflected in a book entry. Bank N offers for sale interests in the Corporation U note. Ownership interests in the note are reflected on the books of Bank N. Corporation U's debenture is considered issued in registered form.

Example (8). Issuer S wishes to make a public offering of its debt obligations to United States persons. The obligations will have a maturity in excess of one year. On November 1, 1982, the closing on the debt offering occurs. At the closing, the net cash proceeds of the offering are delivered to S, and S delivers a master note to the underwriter of the offering. On January 2, 1983, S delivers the debt obligations to the purchasers, in definitive form and the master note is cancelled. The obligations are not registration-required because they are considered issued before January 1, 1983.

Example (9). In July 1983, Corporation T sells an issue of debt obligations maturing in 1985 to the public in the United States. Three of the obligations of the issue are issued to J in bearer form. The balance of the obligations of the issue are issued in registered form. The terms of the registered and bearer obligations are identical. The obligations issued to J are of a type offered to the public and are registration-required obligations. Since the three obligations are issued in bearer form, T is subject to the tax imposed under section 4701 with respect to the three bearer obligations. In addition, interest paid or accrued on the three bearer obligations is not deductible by T. Moreover, since the issuance of the three bearer obligations is subject to tax under section 4701, J is not prohibited from deducting losses on the obligations under section 165(j) or from treating gain on the obligations as capital gain under section 1232(d). The balance of the obligations in the issue do not give rise to liability for the tax under section 4701, and the deductibility of interest on such obligations is not affected by section 163(f).

Example (10). Broker K acquires a bond issued in 1980 by the United States Treasury through the Bureau of Public Debt. Broker K sells interests in the bond to the public after December 31, 1982. A purchaser may acquire an interest in any interest payment falling due under the bond or an interest in the principal of the bond. The bond is held by Custodian L for the benefit of the persons acquiring these interests. On receipt of interest and principal payments under the bond, Custodian L transfers the amount received to the person whose ownership interest corresponds to the bond component giving rise to the payment. Under section 1232B, each bond component is treated as an obligation issued with original issue discount equal to the excess of the stated redemption price at maturity over the purchase price of the bond component. The interests sold by K are obligations of a type offered to the public. Further, the interests are, in accordance with section 1232B, considered issued after December 31, 1982. Accordingly, the interests are registration-required obligations under § 5f.163-1(b). [Temporary Reg. § 5f.163-1.]

□ [*T.D. 7852, 11-9-82. Amended by T.D. 7965, 8-17-84.*]

§ 1.163-5. Denial of interest deduction on certain obligations issued after December 31, 1982, unless issued in registered form.—
(a) [Reserved]

(b) [Reserved]

(c) *Obligations issued to foreign persons after September 21, 1984.*—(1) *In general.*—A determination of whether an obligation satisfies each of the requirements of this paragraph shall be made on an obligation-by-obligation basis. An obligation issued directly (or through affiliated entities) in bearer form by, or guaranteed by, a United States Government-owned agency or a United States Government-sponsored enterprise, such as the Federal National Mortgage Association, the Federal Home Loan Banks, the Federal Loan Mortgage Corporation, the Farm Credit Administration, and the Student Loan Marketing Association, may not satisfy this paragraph (c). An obligation issued after September 21, 1984 is described in this paragraph if—

(i) There are arrangements reasonably designed to ensure that such obligation will be sold (or resold in connection with its original issuance) only to a person who is not a United States person or who is a United States person that is a financial institution (as defined in § 1.165-12 (c)(1)(v)) purchasing for its own account or for the account of a customer and that agrees to comply with the requirements of section 165 (j)(3)(A), (B), or (C) and the regulations thereunder, and

(ii) In the case of an obligation which is not in registered form—

(A) Interest on such obligation is payable only outside the United States and its possessions, and

(B) Unless the obligation is described in subparagraph (2)(i)(C) of this paragraph or is a temporary global security, the following statement in English either appears on the face of the obligation and on any interest coupons which may be detached therefrom or, if the obligation is evidenced by a book entry, appears in the book or record in which the book entry is made: "Any United States person who holds this obligation will be subject to limitations under the United States income tax laws, including the limitations provided in sections 165(j) and 1287(a) of the Internal Revenue Code." For purposes of this paragraph, the term "temporary global security" means a security which is held for the benefit of the purchasers of the obligations of the issuer and interests in which are exchangeable for securities in definitive registered or bearer form prior to its stated maturity.

(2) *Rules for the application of this paragraph.*—(i) *Arrangements reasonably designed to ensure sale to non-United States persons.*—An obligation will be considered to satisfy paragraph (c)(1)(i) of this section if the conditions of paragraph (c)(2)(i)(A), (B), (C) or (D) of this section are met in connection with the original issuance of the obligation. An exchange of one obligation for another is considered an original issuance if and only if the exchange constitutes a disposition of property for purposes of section 1001 of the Code. However, an exchange of one obligation for another will not be considered a new issuance if the obligation received is identical in all respects to the obligation surrendered in exchange therefor, except that the obligor of the obligation received need not be the same obligor as the obligor of the obligation surrendered. Obligations that meet the conditions of paragraph (c)(2)(i)(A), (B), (C) or (D) of this section may be issued in a single public offering. The preceding sentence does not apply to certificates of deposit issued under the conditions of paragraph (c)(2)(i)(C) of this section by a United States person or by a controlled foreign corporation within the meaning of section 957(a) that is engaged in the active conduct of a banking business within the meaning of section 954(c)(3)(B) as in effect prior to the Tax Reform Act of 1986, and the regulations thereunder. A temporary global security need not satisfy the conditions of paragraph (c)(2)(i)(A), (B) or (C) of this section, but must satisfy the applicable requirements of paragraph (c)(2)(i)(D) of this section.

(A) In connection with the original issuance of an obligation, the obligation is offered for sale or resale only outside of the United States and its possessions, is delivered only outside the United States and its possessions and is not registered under the Securities Act of 1933 because it is intended for distribution to persons who are not United States persons. An obligation will not be considered to be required to be registered under the Securities Act of 1933 if the issuer, in reliance on the written opinion of counsel received prior to the issuance thereof, determines in good faith that the obligation need not be registered under the Securities Act of 1933 for the reason that it is intended for distribution to persons who are not United States persons. Solely for purposes of this subdivision (i)(A), the term "United States person" has the same meaning as it has for purposes of determining whether an obligation is intended for distribution to persons under the Securities Act of 1933. Except as provided in paragraph (c)(3) of this section, this paragraph (c)(2)(i)(A) applies only to obligations issued on or before September 7, 1990.

(B) The obligation is registered under the Securities Act of 1933, is exempt from registration by reason of section 3 or section 4 of such Act, or does not qualify as a security under the Securities Act of 1933; all of the conditions set forth in paragraph (c)(2)(i)(B)(*1*), (*2*), (*3*), (*4*), and (*5*) of this section are met with respect to such obligations; and, except as provided in paragraph (c)(3) of this section, the obligation is issued on or before September 7, 1990.

(*1*) In connection with the original issuance of an obligation in bearer form, the obligation is offered for sale or resale only outside the United States and its possessions.

(*2*) The issuer does not, and each underwriter and each member of the selling group, if any, covenants that it will not, in connection with the original issuance of the obligation, offer to sell or resell the obligation in bearer form to any person inside the United States or to a United States person unless such United States person is a financial institution as defined in § 1.165-12(c)(v) purchasing for its own account or for the account of a customer, which financial institution, as a condition of the purchase, agrees to provide on delivery of the obligation (or on issuance, if the obligation is not in definitive form) the certificate required under paragraph (c)(2)(i)(B)(*4*).

(*3*) In connection with its sale or resale during the original issuance of the obligation in bearer form, each underwriter and each member of the selling group, if any, or the issuer, if there is no underwriter or selling group, sends a confirmation to the purchaser of the bearer obligation stating that the purchaser represents that it is not a United States person or, if it is a United States person, it is a financial institution as defined in § 1.165-12(c)(v) purchasing for its own account or for the account of a customer and that the financial institution will comply with the requirements of section 165(j)(3)(A), (B), or (C) and the regulations thereunder. The confirmation must also state that, if the purchaser is a dealer, it will send similar confirmations to whomever purchases from it.

(*4*) In connection with the original issuance of the obligation in bearer form it is delivered in definitive form (or issued, if the obligation is not in definitive form) to the person entitled to physical delivery thereof only outside the United States and its possessions and only upon presentation of a certificate signed by such person to the issuer, underwriter, or member of the selling group, which certificate states that the obligation is not being acquired by or on behalf of a United States person, or for offer to resell or for resale to a United States person or any person inside the United States, or, if a beneficial interest in the obligation is being acquired by a United States person, that such person is a financial institution as defined in § 1.165-12(c)(1)(v) or is acquiring through a financial institution and that the obligation is held by a financial institution that has agreed to comply with the requirements of section 165(j)(3)(A), (B), or (C) and the regulations thereunder and that is not purchasing for offer to resell or for resale inside the United States. When a certificate is provided by a clearing organization, it must be based on statements provided to it by its member organizations. A clearing organization is an entity which is in the business of holding obligations for member organizations and transferring obligations among such members by credit or debit to the account of a member without the necessity of physical delivery of the obligation. For purposes of paragraph (c)(2)(i)(B), the term "delivery" does not include the delivery of an obligation to an underwriter or member of the selling group, if any.

(*5*) The issuer, underwriter, or member of the selling group does not have actual knowledge that the certificate described in paragraph (c)(2)(i)(B)(*4*) of this section is false. The issuer, underwriter, or member of the selling group shall be deemed to have actual knowledge that the certificate described in paragraph (c)(2)(i)(B)(*4*) of this section is false if the issuer, underwriter, or member of the selling group has a United States address for the beneficial owner (other than a financial institution as defined in § 1.165-12(c)(v) that represents that it will comply with the requirements of section 165(j)(3)(A), (B), or (C) and the regulations thereunder) and does not have documentary evidence as described in § 1.6049-5(c)(1) that the beneficial owner is not a United States person.

(C) The obligation is issued only outside the United States and its possessions by an issuer that does not significantly engage in interstate commerce with respect to the issuance of such obligation either directly or through its agent, an underwriter, or a member of the selling group. In the case of an issuer that is a United States person, such issuer may only satisfy the test set forth in this paragraph (c)(2)(i)(C) if—

(*1*) It is engaged through a branch in the active conduct of a banking business, within the meaning of section 954(c)(3)(B) as in effect before the Tax Reform Act of 1986, and the regulations thereunder, outside the United States;

(*2*) The obligation is issued outside of the United States by the branch in connection with that trade or business;

(*3*) The obligation that is so issued is sold directly to the public and is not issued as a part of a larger issuance made by means of a public offering; and

(*4*) The issuer either maintains documentary evidence as described in subdivision (iii) of A-5 of 35a.9999-4T that the purchaser is not a United States person (provided that the issuer has no actual knowledge that the documentary evidence is false) or on delivery of the obligation the issuer receives a statement signed by the person entitled to physical delivery thereof and stating either that the obligation is not being acquired by or on behalf of a United States person or that, if a beneficial interest in the obligation is being acquired by a United States person, such person is a financial institution as defined in § 1.165-12(c)(v) or is acquiring through a financial institution and the obligation is held by a financial institution that has agreed to comply with the requirements of 165 (j)(3)(A), (B), or (C) and the regulations thereunder and that it is not purchasing for offer to resell or for resale inside the United States (provided that the issuer has no actual knowledge that the statement is false).

In addition, an issuer that is a controlled foreign corporation within the meaning of section 957(a) that is engaged in the active conduct of a banking business outside the United States within the meaning of section 954(c)(3)(B) as in effect before the Tax Reform Act of 1986, and the regulations thereunder, can only satisfy the provisions of this paragraph (c)(2)(i)(C), if it meets the requirements of this paragraph (c)(2)(i)(C)(2), (3) and (4).

(D) The obligation is issued after September 7, 1990, and all of the conditions set forth in this paragraph (c)(2)(i)(D) are met with respect to such obligation.

(1) Offers and sales.—(i) Issuer.—The issuer does not offer or sell the obligation during the restricted period to a person who is within the United States or its possessions or to a United States person.

(ii) Distributors.—(A) The distributor of the obligation does not offer or sell the obligation during the restricted period to a person who is within the United States or its possessions or to a United States person.

(B) The distributor of the obligation will be deemed to satisfy the requirements of paragraph (c)(2)(i)(D)(*1*)(*ii*)(*A*) of this section if the distributor of the obligation covenants that it will not offer or sell the obligation during the restricted period to a person who is within the United States or its possessions or to a United States person; and the distributor of the obligation has in effect, in connection with the offer and sale of the obligation during the restricted period, procedures reasonably designed to ensure that its employees or agents who are directly engaged in selling the obligation are aware that the obligation cannot be offered or sold during the restricted period to a person who is within the United States or its possessions or is a United States person.

(iii) Certain rules.—For purposes of paragraph (c)(2)(i)(D)(*1*)(*i*) and (*ii*) of this section:

(A) An offer or sale will be considered to be made to a person who is within the United States or its possessions if the offeror or seller of the obligation has an address within the United States or its possessions for the offeree or buyer of the obligation with respect to the offer or sale.

(B) An offer or sale of an obligation will not be treated as made to a person within the United States or its possessions or to a United States person if the person to whom the offer or sale is made is: An exempt distributor, as defined in paragraph (c)(2)(i)(D)(*5*) of this section; An international organization as defined in section 7701(a)(18) and the regulations thereunder, or a foreign central bank as defined in section 895 and the regulations thereunder, or the foreign branch of a United States financial institution as described in paragraph (c)(2)(i)(D)(*6*)(*i*) of this section.

Paragraph (c)(2)(i)(D)(*1*)(*iii*)(*B*) regarding an exempt distributor will only apply to an offer to the United States office of an exempt distributor, and paragraph (c)(2)(i)(D)(*1*)(*iii*)(*B*) regarding an international organization or foreign central bank will only apply to an offer to an international organization or foreign central bank, if such offer is made directly and specifically to the United States office, organization or bank.

(C) A sale of an obligation will not be treated as made to a person within the United States or its possessions or to a United States person if the person to whom the sale is made is a person described in paragraph (c)(2)(i)(D)(*6*)(*ii*) of this section.

(2) Delivery.—In connection with the sale of the obligation during the restricted period, neither the issuer nor any distributor delivers the obligation in definitive form within the United States or its possessions.

(3) Certification.—(i) In general.—On the earlier of the date of the first actual payment of interest by the issuer on the obligation or the date of delivery by the issuer of the obligation in definitive form, a certificate is provided to the issuer of the obligation stating that on such date:

(A) The obligation is owned by a person that is not a United States person;

(B) The obligation is owned by a United States person described in paragraph (c)(2)(i)(D)(*6*) of this section; or

(C) The obligation is owned by a financial institution for purposes of resale during the restricted period, and such financial institution certifies in addition that it has not acquired the obligation for purposes of resale directly or indirectly to a United States person or to a person within the United States or its possessions.

A certificate described in paragraph (c)(2)(i)(D)(*3*)(*i*)(*A*) or (*B*) of this section may not be given with respect to an obligation that is owned by a financial institution for purposes of resale during the restricted period. For purposes of paragraph (c)(2)(i)(D)(*2*) and (*3*) of this section, a temporary global security (as defined in § 1.163-5(c)(1)(ii)(B)) is not considered to be an obligation in definitive form. If the issuer does not make the obligation available for delivery in definitive form within a reasonable period of time after the end of the restricted period, then the obligation shall be treated as not satisfying the requirements of this paragraph (c)(2)(i)(D)(*3*). The certificate must be signed (or sent, as provided in paragraph (c)(2)(i)(D)(*3*)(*ii*) of this section) either by the owner of the obligation or by a financial institution or clearing organization through which the owner holds the obligation, directly or indirectly. For purposes of this paragraph (c)(2)(i)(D)(*3*), the term "financial institution" means a financial institution described in § 1.165-12(c)(1)(v). When a certificate is provided by a clearing organization, the certificate must be based on statements provided to it by its member organizations. The requirement of this paragraph (c)(1)(D)(*3*) shall be deemed not to be satisfied with respect to an obligation if the issuer knows or has reason to know that the certificate with respect to such obligation is false. The certificate must be retained by the issuer (and statements by member organizations must be retained by the clearing organization, in the case of certificates based on such statements) for a period of four calendar years following the year in which the certificate is received.

(ii) Electronic certification.—The certificate required by paragraph (c)(2)(i)(D)(*3*)(*i*) of this section (including a statement provided to a clearing organization by a member organization) may be provided electronically, but only if the person receiving such electronic certificate maintains adequate records, for the retention period described in paragraph (c)(2)(i)(D)(*3*)(*i*) of this section, establishing that such certificate was received in respect of the subject obligation, and only if there is a written agreement entered into prior to the time of certification (including the written membership rules of a clearing organization) to which the sender and recipient are subject, providing that the electronic certificate shall have the effect of a signed certificate described in paragraph (c)(2)(i)(D)(*3*)(*i*) of this section.

(iii) Exception for certain obligations.—This paragraph (c)(2)(i)(D)(*3*) shall not apply, and no certificate shall be required, in the case of an obligation that is sold during the restricted period and that satisfies all of the following requirements:

(A) The interest and principal with respect to the obligation are denominated only in the currency of a single foreign country.

(B) The interest and principal with respect to the obligation are payable only within that foreign country (according to rules similar to those set forth in § 1.163-5(c)(2)(v)).

(C) The obligation is offered and sold in accordance with practices and documentation customary in that foreign country.

(D) The distributor covenants to use reasonable efforts to sell the obligation within that foreign country.

(E) The obligation is not listed, or the subject of an application for listing, on an exchange located outside that foreign country.

(F) The Commissioner has designated that foreign country as a foreign country in which certification under paragraph (c)(2)(i)(D)(*3*)(*i*) of this section is not permissible.

(G) The issuance of the obligation is subject to guidelines or restrictions imposed by governmental, banking or securities authorities in that foreign country.

(H) More than 80 percent by value of the obligations included in the offering of which the obligation is a part are offered and sold to non-distributors by distributors maintaining an office located in that foreign country. Foreign currency denominated obligations that are convertible into U.S. dollar denominated obligations or that by their terms are linked to the U.S. dollar in a way which effectively converts the obligations to U.S. dollar denominated obligations do not satisfy the requirements of this paragraph (c)(2)(i)(D)(*3*)(*iii*). A foreign currency denominated obligation will not be treated as linked, by its terms, to the U.S. dollar solely because the obligation is the subject of a swap transaction.

(4) *Distributor.*—For purposes of this paragraph (c)(2)(i)(D), the term "distributor" means:

(*i*) a person that offers or sells the obligation during the restricted period pursuant to a written contract with the issuer;

(*ii*) any person that offers or sells the obligation during the restricted period pursuant to a written contract with a person described in paragraph (c)(2)(i)(D)(*4*)(*i*); and

(*iii*) any affiliate that acquires the obligation from another member of its affiliated group for the purpose of offering or selling the obligation during the restricted period, but only if the transferor member of the group is the issuer or a person described in paragraph (c)(2)(i)(D)(*4*)(*i*) or (*ii*) of this section. The terms "affiliate" and "affiliated group" have the same meanings as in section 1504(a) of the Code, but without regard to the exceptions contained in section 1504(b) and substituting "50 percent" for "80 percent" each time it appears.

For purposes of this paragraph (c)(2)(i)(D)(*4*), a written contract does not include a confirmation or other notice of the transaction.

(*5*) *Exempt distributor.*—For purposes of this paragraph (c)(2)(i)(D), the term "exempt distributor" means a distributor that covenants in its contract with the issuer or with a distributor described in paragraph (c)(2)(i)(D)(*4*)(*i*) that it is buying the obligation for the purpose of resale in connection with the original issuance of the obligation, and that if it retains the obligation for its own account, it will only do so in accordance with the requirements of paragraph (c)(2)(i)(D)(*6*) of this section. In the latter case, the covenant will constitute the certificate required under paragraph (c)(2)(i)(D)(*6*). The provisions of paragraph (c)(2)(i)(D)(*7*) governing the restricted period for unsold allotments or subscriptions shall apply to any obligation retained for investment by an exempt distributor.

(*6*) *Certain United States persons.*—A person is described in this paragraph (c)(2)(i)(D)(*6*) if the requirements of this paragraph are satisfied and the person is:

(*i*) The foreign branch of a United States financial institution purchasing for its own account or for resale, or

(*ii*) A United States person who acquired the obligation through the foreign branch of a United States financial institution and who, for purposes of the certification required in paragraph (c)(2)(i)(D)(*3*) of this section, holds the obligation through such financial institution on the date of certification.

For purposes of paragraph (c)(2)(i)(D)(*6*)(*ii*) of this section, a United States person will be considered to acquire and hold an obligation through the foreign branch of a United States financial institution if the United States person has an account with the United States office of a financial institution, and the transaction is executed by a foreign office of that financial institution, or by the foreign office of another financial institution acting on behalf of that financial institution. This paragraph (c)(2)(i)(D)(*6*) will apply, however, only if the United States financial institution (or the United States office of a foreign financial institution) holding the obligation provides a certificate to the issuer or distributor selling the obligation within a reasonable time stating that it agrees to comply with the requirements of section 165(j)(3)(A), (B), or (C) and the regulations thereunder. For purposes of this paragraph (c)(2)(i)(D)(*6*), the term "financial institution" means a financial institution as defined in § 1.165-12(c)(1)(v). As an alternative to the certification required above, a financial institution may provide a blanket certificate to the issuer or distributor selling the obligation stating that the financial institution will comply with the requirements of section 165(j)(3)(A), (B) or (C) and the regulations thereunder. A blanket certificate must be received by the issuer or the distributor in the year of the issuance of the obligation or in either of the preceding two calendar years, and must be retained by the issuer or distributor for at least four years after the end of the last calendar year to which it relates.

(*7*) *Restricted period.*—For purposes of this paragraph (c)(2)(i)(D), the restricted period with respect to an obligation begins on the earlier of the closing date (or the date on which the issuer receives the loan proceeds, if there is no closing with respect to the obligation), or the first date on which the obligation is offered to persons other than a distributor. The restricted period with respect to an obligation ends on the expiration of the forty day period beginning on the closing date (or the date on which the issuer receives the loan proceeds, if there is no closing with respect to the obligation). Notwithstanding the preceding sentence, any offer or sale of the obligation by the issuer or a distributor shall be deemed to be during the restricted period if the issuer or distributor holds the obligation as part of an unsold allotment or subscription.

(*8*) *Clearing organization.*—For purposes of this paragraph (c)(2)(i)(D), a "clearing organization" is an entity which is in the business of holding obligations for member organizations and transferring obligations among such members by credit or debit to the account of a member without the necessity of physical delivery of the obligation.

(ii) *Special rules.*—An obligation shall not be considered to be described in paragraph (c)(2)(i)(C) of this section if it is—

(A) Guaranteed by a United States shareholder of the issuer;

(B) Convertible into a debt or equity interest in a United States shareholder of the issuer; or

(C) Substantially identical to an obligation issued by a United States shareholder of the issuer.

For purposes of this paragraph (c)(2)(ii), the term "United States shareholder" is defined as it is defined in section 951(b) and the regulations thereunder. For purposes of this paragraph (c)(2)(ii)(C), obligations are substantially identical if the face amount, interest rate, term of the issue, due dates for payments, and maturity date of each is substantially identical to the other.

(iii) *Interstate commerce.*—For purposes of this paragraph, the term "interstate commerce" means trade or commerce in obligations or any transportation or communication relating thereto between any foreign country and the United States or its possessions.

(A) An issuer will not be considered to engage significantly in interstate commerce with respect to the issuance of an obligation if the only activities with respect to which the issuer uses the means or instrumentalities of interstate commerce are activities of a preparatory or auxiliary character that do not involve communication between a prospective purchaser and an issuer, its agent, an underwriter, or member of the selling group if either is inside the United States or its possessions. Activities of a preparatory or auxiliary character include, but are not limited to, the following activities:

(*1*) Establishment or participation in establishment of policies concerning the issuance of obligations and the allocation of funding by a United States shareholder with respect to obligations issued by a foreign corporation or by a United States office with respect to obligations issued by a foreign branch;

(*2*) Negotiation between the issuer and underwriters as to the terms and pricing of an issue;

(*3*) Transfer of funds to an office of an issuer in the United States or its possessions by a foreign branch or to a United States shareholder by a foreign corporation;

(*4*) Consultation by an issuer with accountants and lawyers or other financial advisors in the United States or its possessions regarding the issuance of an obligation;

(*5*) Document drafting and printing; and

(*6*) Provision of payment or delivery instructions to members of the selling group by an issuer's office or agent that is located in the United States or its possessions.

(B) Activities that will not be considered to be of a preparatory or auxiliary character include, but are not limited to, any of the following activities:

(*1*) Negotiation or communication between a prospective purchaser and an issuer, its agent, an underwriter, or a member of the selling group concerning the sale of an obligation if either is inside the United States or its possessions;

(*2*) Involvement of an issuer's office, its agent, an underwriter, or a member of the selling group in the United States or its possessions in the offer or sale of a particular obligation, either directly with the prospective purchaser, or through the issuer in a foreign country;

(*3*) Delivery of an obligation in the United States or its possessions; or

(*4*) Advertising or otherwise promoting an obligation in the United States or its possessions.

(C) The following examples illustrate the application of this subdivision (iii) of § 1.163-5(c)(2).

Example (1). Foreign corporation A, a corporation organized in and doing business in foreign country Z, and not a controlled foreign corporation within the meaning of section 957(a) that is engaged in the conduct of a banking business within the meaning of section 954(c)(3)(B) as in effect before the Tax Reform Act of 1986, issues its debentures outside the United States. The debentures are not guaranteed by a United States shareholder of A, nor are they convertible into a debt or equity interest of a United States shareholder of A, nor are they substantially identical to an obligation issued by a United States shareholder of A. A consults its accountants and lawyers in the United States for certain securities and tax advice regarding the debt offering. The underwriting and selling group in respect of A's offering is composed entirely of foreign securities firms, some of which are foreign subsidiaries of United States securities firms. A U.S. affiliate of the foreign underwriter communicates payment and delivery instruction to the selling group. All offering circulars for the offering are mailed and delivered outside the United States and its possessions. All debentures are delivered and paid for outside the United States and its possessions. No office located in the United States or in a United States possession is involved in the sale of debentures. Interest on the debentures is payable only outside the United States and its possessions. A is not significantly engaged in interstate commerce with respect to the offering.

Example (2). B, a United States bank, does business in foreign country X through a branch located in X. The branch is a staffed and operating unit engaged in the active conduct of a banking business consisting of one or more of the activities set forth in § 1.954-2(d)(2)(ii). As part of its ongoing business, the branch in X issues negotiable certificates of deposit with a maturity in excess of one year to customers upon request. The certificates of deposit are not guaranteed by a United States shareholder of B, nor are they convertible into a debt or equity interest of a United States shareholder of B, nor are they substantially identical to an obligation issued by a United States shareholder of B. Policies regarding the issuance of negotiable certificates of deposit and funding allocations for foreign branches are set in the United States at B's main office. Branch personnel decide whether to issue a negotiable certificate of deposit based on the guidelines established by the United States offices of B, but without communicating with the United States offices of B with respect to the issuance of a particular obligation. Negotiable certificates of deposits are delivered and paid for outside the United States and its possessions. Interest on the negotiable certificates of deposit is payable only outside the United States and its possessions. B maintains documentary evidence described in § 1.163-5(c)(2)(i)(C)(*4*). After the issuance of negotiable certificates of deposit by the foreign branch of B, the foreign branch sends the funds to a United States branch of B for use in domestic operations. B is not significantly engaged in interstate commerce with respect to the issuance of such obligation.

Example (3). The facts in Example (2) apply except that the foreign branch of B consulted, by telephone, the main office in the United States to request approval of the issuance of the certificate of deposit at a particular rate of interest. The main office granted permission to issue the negotiable certificate of deposit to the customer by a telex sent from the main office of B to the branch in X. B is significantly engaged in interstate commerce with respect to the issuance of the obligation as a result of the involvement of B's United States office in the issuance of the obligation.

Example (4). The facts in Example (2) apply with the additional fact that a customer contacted the foreign branch of B through a telex originating in the United States or its possessions. Subsequent to the telex, the foreign branch issued the negotiable certificate of deposit and recorded it on the books. B is significantly engaged in interstate commerce with respect to the issuance of the obligation as a result of its communication by telex with a customer in the United States.

(iv) *Possessions.*—For purposes of this section, the term "possessions" includes Puerto Rico, the U.S. Virgin Islands, Guam, American Samoa, Wake Island, and Northern Mariana Islands.

(v) *Interest payable outside of the United States.*—Interest will be considered payable only outside the United States and its possessions if payment of such interest can be made only upon presentation of a coupon, or upon making of any other demand for payment, outside of the United States and its possessions to the issuer or a paying agent. The fact that payment is made by a draft drawn on a United States bank account or by a wire or other electronic transfer from a United States account does not affect this result. Interest payments will be considered to be made within the United States if the payments are made by a transfer of funds into an account maintained by the payee in the United States or mailed to an address in the United States, if—

(A) The interest is paid on an obligation issued by either a United States person, a controlled foreign corporation as defined in section 957(a), or a foreign corporation if 50 percent or more of the gross income of the foreign corporation from all sources of the 3-year period ending with the close of its taxable year preceding the original issuance of the obligation (or for such part of the period that the foreign corporation has been in existence) was effectively connected with the conduct of a trade or business within the United States; and

(B) The interest is paid to a person other than—

(*1*) A person who may satisfy the requirements of section 165(j)(3)(A), (B), or (C) and the regulations thereunder; and

(*2*) A financial institution as a step in the clearance of funds and such interest is promptly credited to an account maintained outside the United States for such financial institution or for persons for which the financial institution has collected such interest. Interest is considered to be paid within the United States and its possessions if a coupon is presented, or a demand for payment is otherwise made, to the issuer or a paying agent (whether a United States or foreign person) in the United States and its possessions even if the funds paid are credited to an account maintained by the payee outside the United States and its possessions. Interest will be considered payable only outside the United States and its possessions notwithstanding that such interest may become payable at the office of the issuer or its United States paying agent under the following conditions: the issuer has appointed paying agents located outside the United States and its possessions with the reasonable expectation that such paying agents will be able to pay the interest in United States dollars, and the full amount of such payment at the offices of all such paying agents is illegal or effectively precluded because of the imposition of exchange controls or other similar restrictions on the full payment or receipt of interest in United States dollars. A lawsuit brought in the United States or its possessions for payment of the obligation or interest thereon as a result of a default shall not be considered to be a demand for payment. For purposes of this subdivision (v), interest includes original issue discount as defined in section 1273(a). Therefore, an amount equal to the original issue discount as defined in section 1273(a) is payable only outside the United States and its possessions. The amount of market discount as defined in section 1278(a) does not affect the amount of interest to be considered payable only outside the United States and its possessions.

(vi) *Rules relating to obligations issued after December 31, 1982 and on or before September 21, 1984.*—Whether an obligation originally issued after December 31, 1982 and on or before September 21, 1984, or an obligation originally issued after September 21, 1984 pursuant to the exercise of a warrant or the conversion of a convertible obligation, which warrant or obligation (including conversion privilege) was issued after December 31, 1982 and on or before September 21, 1984, is described in section 163(f)(2)(B) shall be determined under the rules provided in § 5f.163-1(c) as in effect prior to its removal. Notwithstanding the preceding sentence, an issuer will be considered to satisfy the requirements of section 163(f)(2)(B) with respect to an obligation issued after December 31, 1982 and on or before September 21, 1984 or after September 21, 1984 pursuant to the exercise of a warrant or the conversion of a convertible obligation, which warrant or obligation (including conversion privilege) was issued after December 31, 1982 and on or before September 21, 1984, if the issuer substantially complied with the proposed regulations provided in § 1.163-5(c), which were published in the Federal Register on September 2, 1983 (48 FR 39953) and superseded by temporary regulations published in the Federal Register on August 22, 1984 (49 FR 33228).

(3) *Effective date.*—(i) *In general.*—These regulations apply generally to obligations issued after January 20, 1987. A taxpayer may choose to apply the rules of § 1.163-5(c) with respect to an obligation issued after December 31, 1982 and on or before January 20, 1987. If this choice is made, the rules of § 1.163-5(c) will apply in lieu of § 1.163-5T(c) except that the legend requirement under § 1.163-5(c)(1)(ii)(B) does not apply with respect to a bearer obligation evidenced exclusively by a book entry and that the certification requirement under § 1.163-5T(c)(2)(i)(B)(*4*) applies in lieu of the certification under § 1.163-5(c)(2)(i)(B)(*4*).

(ii) *Special rules.*—If an obligation is originally issued after September 7, 1990 pursuant to the exercise of a warrant or the conversion of a convertible obligation, which warrant or obligation (including conversion privilege) was issued on or before May 10, 1990, then the issuer may choose to apply either the rules of § 1.163-5(c)(2)(i)(A) or § 1.163-5(c)(2)(i)(B), or the rules of § 1.163-5(c)(2)(i)(D). The issuer of an obligation may choose to apply either the rules of § 1.163-5(c)(2)(i)(A) or (B), or the rules of § 1.163-5(c)(2)(i)(D), to an obligation that is originally issued after May 10, 1990, and on or before September 7, 1990. However, any issuer choosing to apply the rules of § 1.163-5(c)(2)(i)(A) must apply the definition of United States person used for such purposes on December 31, 1989, and must obtain any certificates that would have been required under applicable law on December 31, 1989. [Reg. § 1.163-5.]

□ [*T.D.* 8110, 12-16-86. *Amended by* T.D. 8203, 5-19-88; *T.D.* 8300, 5-9-90 *and T.D.* 8734, 10-6-97 (T.D. 8804 extended the effective date of T.D. 8734 from January 1, 1999, to January 1, 2000; T.D. 8856 further delayed the effective date of T.D. 8734 until January 1, 2001).]

§1.163(j)-1. Definitions.—(a) *In general.*—The definitions provided in this section apply for purposes of the section 163(j) regulations. For purposes of the rules set forth in §§1.163(j)-2 through 1.163(j)-11, additional definitions for certain terms are provided in those sections.

(b) *Definitions.*—(1) *Adjusted taxable income.*—The term *adjusted taxable income* (ATI) means the tentative taxable income of the taxpayer for the taxable year, with the adjustments in this paragraph (b)(1).

(i) *Additions.*—The amounts of the following items that were included in the computation of the taxpayer's tentative taxable income (if any) are added to tentative taxable income to determine ATI—

(A) Any business interest expense, other than disallowed business interest expense carryforwards;

(B) Any net operating loss deduction under section 172;

(C) Any deduction under section 199A;

(D) Subject to paragraph (b)(1)(iii) of this section, for taxable years beginning before January 1, 2022, any depreciation under section 167, section 168, or section 168 of the Internal Revenue Code (Code) of 1954 (former section 168);

(E) Subject to paragraph (b)(1)(iii) of this section, for taxable years beginning before January 1, 2022, any amortization of intangibles (for example, under section 167 or 197) and other amortized expenditures (for example, under section 174(b), 195(b)(1)(B), 248, or 1245(a)(2)(C));

(F) Subject to paragraph (b)(1)(iii) of this section, for taxable years beginning before January 1, 2022, any depletion under section 611;

(G) Any deduction for a capital loss carryback or carryover; and

(H) Any deduction or loss that is not properly allocable to a non-excepted trade or business (for rules governing the allocation of items to an excepted trade or business, see §§1.163(j)-1(b)(44) and 1.163(j)-10).

(ii) *Subtractions.*—The amounts of the following items (if any) are subtracted from the taxpayer's tentative taxable income to determine ATI—

(A) Any business interest income that was included in the computation of the taxpayer's tentative taxable income;

(B) Any floor plan financing interest expense for the taxable year that was included in the computation of the taxpayer's tentative taxable income;

(C) With respect to the sale or other disposition of property, the greater of the allowed or allowable depreciation, amortization, or depletion of the property, as provided under section 1016(a)(2), for the taxpayer (or, if the taxpayer is a member of a consolidated group, the consolidated group) for the taxable years beginning after December 31, 2017, and before January 1, 2022, with respect to such property;

(D) With respect to the sale or other disposition of stock of a member of a consolidated group by another member, the investment adjustments under §1.1502-32 with respect to such stock that are attributable to deductions described in paragraph (b)(1)(ii)(C) of this section;

(E) With respect to the sale or other disposition of an interest in a partnership, the taxpayer's distributive share of deductions described in paragraph (b)(1)(ii)(C) of this section with respect to property held by the partnership at the time of such sale or other disposition to the extent such deductions were allowable under section 704(d);

(F) Any income or gain that is not properly allocable to a non-excepted trade or business (for rules governing the allocation of items to an excepted trade or business, see §§1.163(j)-1(b)(44) and 1.163(j)-10)) and that was included in the computation of the taxpayer's tentative taxable income; and

(G) An amount equal to the sum of any specified deemed inclusions that were included in the computation of the taxpayer's tentative taxable income, reduced by the portion of the deduction allowed under section 250(a) by reason of the specified deemed inclusions. For this purpose, a *specified deemed inclusion* is the inclusion of an amount by a United States shareholder (as defined in section 951(b)) in gross income under section 78, 951(a), or 951A(a) with respect to an applicable CFC (as defined in §1.163(j)-1(b)(2)) that is properly allocable to a non-excepted trade or business. Furthermore, a specified deemed inclusion includes any amounts included in a domestic partnership's gross income under section 951(a) or 951A(a) with respect to an applicable CFC to the extent such amounts are attributable to investment income of the partnership and are allocated to a domestic C corporation that is a direct (or indirect partner) and treated as properly allocable to a non-excepted trade or business of the domestic C corporation under §§1.163(j)-4(b)(3) and 1.163(j)-10. To determine the amount of a specified deemed inclusion described in this paragraph (b)(1)(ii)(G), the portion of a United States shareholder's inclusion under section 951A(a) treated as being with respect to an applicable CFC is determined under section 951A(f)(2) and §1.951A-6(b)(2).

(iii) *Depreciation, amortization, or depletion capitalized under section 263A.*—For purposes of paragraph (b)(1)(i) of this section, amounts of depreciation, amortization, or depletion that are capitalized under section 263A during the taxable year are deemed to be included in the computation of the taxpayer's tentative taxable income for such taxable year, regardless of the period in which the capitalized amount is recovered. See *Example 3* in §1.163(j)-2(h)(3).

(iv) *Application of §1.163(j)-1(b)(1)(ii)(C), (D), and (E).*—(A) *Sale or other disposition.*—*(1) In general.*—For purposes of paragraphs (b)(1)(ii)(C), (D), and (E) and paragraphs (b)(1)(iv)(B) and (E) of this section, except as otherwise provided in this paragraph (b)(1)(iv)(A), the term *sale or other disposition* does not include a transfer of an asset to an acquiring corporation in a transaction to which section 381(a) applies.

(2) Intercompany transactions.—For purposes of paragraphs (b)(1)(ii)(C) and (D) and paragraphs (b)(1)(iv)(B) and (b)(1)(iv)(E)(*1*) and (*2*) of this section, the term *sale or other disposition* excludes all intercompany transactions, within the meaning of §1.1502-13(b)(1)(i), to the extent necessary to achieve single-entity taxation of the consolidated group.

(3) Deconsolidations.—Notwithstanding any other rule in this paragraph (b)(1)(iv)(A), any transaction in which a member (S) leaves a consolidated group (selling group), including a section 381(a) transaction described in paragraph (b)(1)(iv)(A)(*1*) of this section, is treated as a taxable disposition of all S stock held by any member of the selling group for purposes of paragraphs (b)(1)(ii)(C) and (D) and paragraphs (b)(1)(iv)(B) and (b)(1)(iv)(E)(*1*) and (*2*) of this section, unless the transaction is described in §1.1502-13(j)(5)(i). Following S's deconsolidation, any subsequent sales or dispositions of S stock by the selling group do not trigger further adjustments under paragraphs (b)(1)(ii)(C) and (D) and paragraphs (b)(1)(iv)(B) and (b)(1)(iv)(E)(*1*) and (*2*) of this section. If a transaction is described in §1.1502-13(j)(5)(i), the transaction is not treated as a sale or other disposition for purposes of paragraphs (b)(1)(ii)(C) and (D) and paragraphs (b)(1)(iv)(B) and (b)(1)(iv)(E)(*1*) and (*2*) of this section. See also the successor rules in paragraph (b)(1)(iv)(C) of this section.

(4) Nonrecognition transactions.—The disposition of property, member stock (other than in a deconsolidation described in paragraph (b)(1)(iv)(A)(*3*) of this section), or partnership interests in a nonrecognition transaction, other than a section 381(a) transaction described in paragraph (b)(1)(iv)(A)(*1*) of this section, is treated as a taxable disposition of the property, member stock, or partnership interest disposed of for purposes of paragraph (b)(1)(iv)(E)(*1*)(*i*), (b)(1)(iv)(E)(*2*)(*i*), and (b)(1)(iv)(E)(*3*)(*i*) of this section, respectively. For example, if a taxpayer transfers property to a wholly owned, non-consolidated subsidiary, the transfer of the property is treated as a taxable disposition for purposes of paragraph (b)(1)(iv)(E)(*1*)(*i*) of this section notwithstanding the application of section 351.

(B) *Deductions by members of a consolidated group.*—*(1) In general.*—If paragraph (b)(1)(ii)(C), (D), or (E) of this section applies to adjust the tentative taxable income of a consolidated group, and if the consolidated group does not use the alternative computation method in paragraph (b)(1)(iv)(E) of this section, the amount of the adjustment under paragraph (b)(1)(ii)(C) of this section equals the greater of the allowed or allowable depreciation, amortization, or depletion of the property, as provided under section 1016(a)(2), for the consolidated group for the taxable years beginning after December 31, 2017, and before January 1, 2022, with respect to such property.

(2) *Application of the alternative computation method.*—If paragraph (b)(1)(ii)(C), paragraph (b)(1)(ii)(D), or paragraph (b)(1)(ii)(E) of this section applies to adjust the tentative taxable income of a consolidated group, and if the consolidated group uses the alternative computation method in paragraph (b)(1)(iv)(E) of this section, the amount of the adjustment computed under paragraph (b)(1)(iv)(E)(*1*)(*i*), paragraph (b)(1)(iv)(E)(*2*)(*i*), or paragraph (b)(1)(iv)(E)(*3*)(*i*) of this section must take into account the net gain that would be taken into account by the consolidated group, including from intercompany transactions, determined by treating the sale or other disposition as a taxable transaction (see paragraphs (b)(1)(iv)(A)(*3*) and (*4*) of this section regarding deconsolidations and certain nonrecognition transactions, respectively).

(C) *Successor rules.*—(*1*) *Successor assets.*—This paragraph (b)(1)(iv)(C)(*1*) applies if deductions described in paragraph (b)(1)(ii)(C) of this section are allowed or allowable to a consolidated group member (S) and either the depreciable property or S's stock is subsequently transferred to another member (S1) in an intercompany transaction in which the transferor receives S1 stock. If this paragraph (b)(1)(iv)(C)(*1*) applies, and if the transferor's basis in the S1 stock received in the intercompany transaction is determined, in whole or in part, by reference to its basis in the depreciable property or the S stock, the S1 stock received in the intercompany transaction is treated as a successor asset for purposes of paragraph (b)(1)(ii)(D) and (b)(1)(iv)(E)(*2*) of this section. Thus, except as otherwise provided in paragraph (b)(1)(iv)(D) of this section, the subsequent disposition of either the S1 stock or the S stock (or both) may require the application of the adjustment rules of paragraph (b)(1)(ii)(D) or paragraph (b)(1)(iv)(E)(*2*) of this section.

(*2*) *Successor entities.*—The acquiring corporation in a section 381(a) transaction to which the exception in paragraph (b)(1)(iv)(A)(*1*) of this section applies is treated as a successor to the distributor or transferor corporation for purposes of paragraphs (b)(1)(ii)(C) through (E) and (b)(1)(iv)(B) and (E) of this section. Therefore, for example, in applying paragraphs (b)(1)(ii)(C) through (E) and (b)(1)(iv)(B) and (E) of this section, the acquiring corporation is treated as succeeding to the allowed or allowable items of the distributor or transferor corporation. Similarly, the surviving group in a transaction described in § 1.1502-13(j)(5)(i) to which the exception in paragraph (b)(1)(iv)(A)(*3*) of this section applies is treated as a successor to the terminating group for purposes of paragraphs (b)(1)(ii)(C) through (E) and (b)(1)(iv)(B) and (E) of this section.

(D) *Anti-duplication rule.*—(*1*) *In general.*—The aggregate of the subtractions from tentative taxable income of a consolidated group under paragraphs (b)(1)(ii)(C) through (E) or paragraphs (b)(1)(iv)(E)(*1*) through (3) of this section with respect to an item of property (including with regard to dispositions of successor assets described in paragraph (b)(1)(iv)(C)(*1*) of this section) cannot exceed the aggregate amount of the consolidated group members' deductions described in paragraph (b)(1)(ii)(C) of this section with respect to such item of property. In addition, once an item of property is no longer held by any member of a consolidated group (whether or not an adjustment to the tentative taxable income of the group is made under paragraph (b)(1)(ii)(C) of this section with respect to the direct or indirect disposition of that property), no further adjustment to the group's tentative taxable income is made under paragraph (b)(1)(ii)(D) or paragraph (b)(1)(iv)(E)(*2*) of this section in relation to the same property with respect to any subsequent stock disposition.

(*2*) *Adjustments following deconsolidation.*—If a corporation (S) leaves a consolidated group (Group 1) in a transaction that requires an adjustment under paragraph (b)(1)(ii)(D) or paragraph (b)(1)(iv)(E)(*2*) of this section, no further adjustment is required under paragraph (b)(1)(ii)(C) or (E) or paragraph (b)(1)(iv)(E) of this section in a separate return year (as defined in § 1.1502-1(e)) of S with respect to depreciation, amortization, or depletion deductions allowed or allowable to Group 1. See paragraph (b)(1)(iv)(A) of this section for special rules regarding the meaning of the term "sale or other disposition" for purposes of the adjustments required under paragraphs (b)(1)(ii)(C) through (E) and paragraphs (b)(1)(iv)(B) and (E) of this section. For example, assume that S deconsolidates from Group 1 in a transaction not described in § 1.1502-13(j)(5)(i) after holding property for which depreciation, amortization, or depletion deductions were allowed or allowable in Group 1. On the deconsolidation, S and Group 1 would adjust tentative taxable income with regard to that property. See paragraphs (b)(1)(iv)(A)(3), (b)(1)(ii)(D), and (b)(1)(iv)(E)(2) of this section. If, following the deconsolidation, S sells the property referred to in the previous sentence, no subtraction from tentative taxable income is made under paragraph (b)(1)(ii)(C) or paragraph (b)(1)(iv)(E)(*1*) of this section during S's separate return year with regard to the amounts included in Group 1. See paragraphs (b)(1)(iv)(A)(*3*), (b)(1)(ii)(D), and (b)(1)(iv)(E)(*2*) of this section.

(E) *Alternative computation method.*—If paragraph (b)(1)(ii)(C), (D), or (E) of this section applies to adjust the tentative taxable income of a taxpayer, the taxpayer may compute the amount of the adjustments required by such paragraph using the formulas in paragraph (b)(1)(iv)(E)(*1*), (*2*), and (*3*) of this section, respectively, provided that the taxpayer applies such formulas to all dispositions for which an adjustment is required under paragraph (b)(1)(ii)(C), (D), or (E) of this section. For special rules regarding the treatment of deconsolidating transactions and nonrecognition transactions, see paragraph (b)(1)(iv)(A)(3) and (4) of this section, respectively. For special rules regarding the application of the formulas in paragraph (b)(1)(iv)(E)(*1*), (*2*), and (*3*) of this section by consolidated groups, see paragraph (b)(1)(iv)(B)(*2*) of this section.

(*1*) *Alternative computation method for property dispositions.*—With respect to the sale or other disposition of property, the lesser of:

(*i*) Any gain recognized on the sale or other disposition of such property by the taxpayer (or, if the taxpayer is a member of a consolidated group, the consolidated group); and

(*ii*) The greater of the allowed or allowable depreciation, amortization, or depletion of the property, as provided under section 1016(a)(2), for the taxpayer (or, if the taxpayer is a member of a consolidated group, the consolidated group) for the taxable years beginning after December 31, 2017, and before January 1, 2022, with respect to such property.

(*2*) *Alternative computation method for dispositions of member stock.*—With respect to the sale or other disposition by a member of a consolidated group of stock of another member for whom depreciation, amortization, or depletion was allowed or allowable with regard to an item of property (or stock of any successor to that member), the lesser of:

(*i*) Any gain recognized on the sale or other disposition of such stock; and

(*ii*) The investment adjustments under § 1.1502-32 with respect to such stock that are attributable to deductions described in paragraph (b)(1)(ii)(C) of this section. The investment adjustments referred to in this paragraph (b)(1)(iv)(E)(2)(ii) include investment adjustments replicated in stock of members that are successor entities.

(*3*) *Alternative computation method for dispositions of partnership interests.*—With respect to the sale or other disposition of an interest in a partnership, the lesser of:

(*i*) Any gain recognized on the sale or other disposition of such interest; and

(*ii*) The taxpayer's (or, if the taxpayer is a consolidated group, the consolidated group's) distributive share of deductions described in paragraph (b)(1)(ii)(C) of this section with respect to property held by the partnership at the time of such sale or other disposition to the extent such deductions were allowable under section 704(d).

(F) *Cap on negative adjustments.*—(*1*) *In general.*—A subtraction from (or negative adjustment to) tentative taxable income that is required under paragraph (b)(1)(ii)(C), (D), or (E) or paragraph (b)(1)(iv)(B) or (E) of this section is reduced to the extent the taxpayer establishes that the positive adjustments to tentative taxable income under paragraphs (b)(1)(i)(D) through (F) of this section in a prior taxable year did not result in an increase in the amount allowed as a deduction for business interest expense for such year. The extent to which the positive adjustments under paragraphs (b)(1)(i)(D) through (F) of this section resulted in an increase in the amount allowed as a deduction for business interest expense in a prior taxable year (such amount of positive adjustments, the *negative adjustment cap*) is determined after taking into account all other adjustments to tentative taxable income under paragraph (b)(1)(i) and (ii) of this section for that year, as established through books and records. The amount of the negative adjustment cap for a prior taxable year is reduced in future taxable years to the extent of negative adjustments under paragraphs (b)(1)(ii)(C) through (E) and paragraphs (b)(1)(iv)(B) and (E) of this section with respect to the prior taxable year.

(*2*) *Example.*—A is a calendar-year individual taxpayer engaged in a trade or business that is neither an excepted trade or business nor eligible for the small business exemption. A has no disallowed business interest expense carryforwards. In 2021, A has $100x of business interest expense, no business interest income or floor plan financing interest expense, and $400x of tentative taxable income. After taking into account the adjustments to tentative taxable income under paragraph (b)(1)(i) and (ii) of this section other than positive adjustments under paragraphs (b)(1)(i)(D) through (F) of this section, A has tentative taxable income of $450x. A increases its tentative taxable income by $30x (from $450x to $480x) under paragraph (b)(1)(i)(D) of this section to reflect $30x of depreciation deductions with respect to Asset Y in 2021. Thus, for 2021, A would have a section 163(j) limitation of $135x ($450x x 30 percent) without regard to adjustments under paragraphs (b)(1)(i)(D) through (F) of this section. After the application of paragraph (b)(1)(i)(D) of this section, A has a section 163(j) limitation of $144x ($480x x 30 percent). In 2022, A sells Asset Y at a gain of $50x. Under paragraph (b)(1)(iv)(F)(*1*) of this section, A is not required to reduce its tentative taxable income in 2022 under paragraph (b)(1)(ii)(C) through (E) or paragraph (b)(1)(iv)(E) of this section. As established by A, the $30x addition to tentative taxable income under paragraph (b)(1)(i)(D) of this section resulted in no increase in the amount allowed as a deduction for business interest expense in 2021.

(G) *Treatment of depreciation, amortization, or depletion capitalized under section 263A.*—Paragraphs (b)(1)(ii)(C) through (E) of this section and this paragraph (b)(1)(iv) apply with respect to the sale or other disposition of property to which paragraph (b)(1)(iii) of this section applies. For example, if a taxpayer with depreciable machinery capitalizes the depreciation into inventory under section 263A, paragraph (b)(1)(ii)(C) or paragraph (b)(1)(iv)(E) of this section (and, if the taxpayer is a consolidated group, paragraph (b)(1)(iv)(B) of this section) applies upon the disposition of the machinery, subject to the cap in paragraph (b)(1)(iv)(F) of this section. Similarly, the successor asset rules in paragraph (b)(1)(iv)(C)(*1*) of this section would apply if the depreciable machinery subsequently were transferred to another member (S1) in an intercompany transaction in which the transferor received S1 stock.

(v) *Other adjustments.*—ATI is computed with the other adjustments provided in §§1.163(j)-2 through 1.163(j)-11.

(vi) *Additional rules relating to adjusted taxable income in other sections.*—(A) For rules governing the ATI of C corporations, see §§1.163(j)-4(b)(2) and (3) and 1.163(j)-10(a)(2)(ii).

(B) For rules governing the ATI of RICs and REITs, see §1.163(j)-4(b)(4).

(C) For rules governing the ATI of tax-exempt corporations, see §1.163(j)-4(b)(5).

(D) For rules governing the ATI of consolidated groups, see §1.163(j)-4(d)(2)(iv) and (v).

(E) For rules governing the ATI of partnerships, see §1.163(j)-6(d).

(F) For rules governing the ATI of partners, see §§1.163(j)-6(e) and 1.163(j)-6(m)(1) and (2).

(G) For rules governing partnership basis adjustments affecting ATI, see §1.163(j)-6(h)(2).

(H) For rules governing the ATI of S corporations, see §1.163(j)-6(l)(3).

(I) For rules governing the ATI of S corporation shareholders, see §1.163(j)-6(l)(4).

(J) For rules governing the ATI of certain beneficiaries of trusts and estates, see §1.163(j)-2(f).

(vii) *ATI cannot be less than zero.*—If the ATI of a taxpayer would be less than zero, the ATI of the taxpayer is zero.

(viii) *Examples.*—The examples in this paragraph (b)(1)(viii) illustrate the application of paragraphs (b)(1)(ii), (iii), and (iv) of this section. Unless otherwise indicated, A, B, P, S, and T are calendar-year domestic C corporations; P is the parent of a consolidated group of which S and T are members; the exemption for certain small businesses in §1.163(j)-2(d) does not apply; no entity is engaged in an excepted trade or business; no entity has business interest income or floor plan financing interest expense; and all amounts of interest expense are deductible except for the potential application of section 163(j).

(A) *Example 1.*—(*1*) *Facts.* In 2021, A purchases a depreciable asset (Asset X) for $30x and fully depreciates Asset X under section 168(k). For the 2021 taxable year, A establishes that its ATI before adding back depreciation deductions with respect to Asset X under paragraph (b)(1)(i)(D) of this section is $130x, and that its ATI after adding back depreciation deductions with respect to Asset X under paragraph (b)(1)(i)(D) of this section is $160x. A incurs $45x of business interest expense in 2021. In 2024, A sells Asset X to an unrelated third party for $25x.

(*2*) *Analysis.* A's section 163(j) limitation for 2021 is $48x ($160x × 30 percent). Thus, all $45x of A's business interest expense incurred in 2021 is deductible in that year. Under paragraph (b)(1)(ii)(C) of this section, A must subtract $30x from its tentative taxable income in computing its ATI for its 2024 taxable year. Alternatively, under paragraph (b)(1)(iv)(E)(*1*) of this section, A must subtract $25x (the lesser of $30x or $25x ($25x - $0x)) from its tentative taxable income in computing its ATI for its 2024 taxable year. However, the negative adjustments under paragraphs (b)(1)(ii)(C) and (b)(1)(iv)(E)(*1*) of this section are both subject to the negative adjustment cap in paragraph (b)(1)(iv)(F) of this section. Under that paragraph, A's negative adjustment under either paragraph (b)(1)(ii)(C) or paragraph (b)(1)(iv)(E)(*1*) of this section is capped at $20x, or $150x (the amount of ATI that A needed in order to deduct all $45x of business interest expense in 2021) minus $130x (the amount of A's tentative taxable income in 2021 before adding back any amounts under paragraph (b)(1)(i)(D) through (F) of this section). As established by A, the additional $10x ($30x - $20x) of depreciation deductions that were added back to tentative taxable income in 2021 under paragraph (b)(1)(i)(D) of this section did not increase A's business interest expense deduction for that year.

(*3*) *Transfer of assets in a nonrecognition transaction to which section 381 applies.* The facts are the same as in paragraph (b)(1)(viii)(A)(*1*) of this section, except that, rather than sell Asset X to an unrelated third party in 2024, A merges with and into an unrelated third party in 2024 in a transaction described in section 368(a)(1)(A) in which no gain is recognized. As provided in paragraph (b)(1)(iv)(A)(*1*) of this section, the merger transaction is not treated as a "sale or other disposition" for purposes of paragraph (b)(1)(ii)(C) or paragraph (b)(1)(iv)(E)(*1*) of this section. Thus, no adjustment to tentative taxable income is required in 2024 under paragraph (b)(1)(ii)(C) or paragraph (b)(1)(iv)(E)(*1*) of this section.

(*4*) *Transfer of assets in a nonrecognition transaction to which section 351 applies.* The facts are the same as in paragraph (b)(1)(viii)(A)(*1*) of this section, except that, rather than sell Asset X to an unrelated third party in 2024, A transfers Asset X to B (A's wholly owned subsidiary) in 2024 in a transaction to which section 351 applies. The section 351 transaction is treated as a "sale or other disposition" for purposes of paragraphs (b)(1)(ii)(C) and (b)(1)(iv)(E)(*1*) of this section, and it is treated as a taxable disposition for purposes of paragraph (b)(1)(iv)(E)(*1*) of this section. See paragraph (b)(1)(iv)(A)(*1*) and (*4*) of this section. However, the negative adjustments under paragraphs (b)(1)(ii)(C) and (b)(1)(iv)(E)(*1*) of this section are both subject to the negative adjustment cap in paragraph (b)(1)(iv)(F) of this section. Thus, A must subtract $20x from its tentative taxable income in computing its ATI for its 2024 taxable year.

(B) *Example 2.*—(*1*) *Facts.* In 2021, S purchases a depreciable asset (Asset Y) for $30x and fully depreciates Asset Y under section 168(k). P reduces its basis in its S stock by $30x under §1.1502-32 to reflect S's depreciation deductions with respect to Asset Y. For the 2021 taxable year, the P group establishes that its ATI before adding back S's depreciation deductions with respect to Asset Y under paragraph (b)(1)(i)(D) of this section is $130x, and that its ATI after adding back S's depreciation deductions with respect to Asset Y under paragraph (b)(1)(i)(D) of this section is $160x. The P group incurs $45x of business interest expense in 2021. In 2024, P sells all of its S stock to an unrelated third party at a gain of $25x.

(*2*) *Analysis.* The P group's section 163(j) limitation for 2021 is $48x ($160x × 30 percent). Thus, all $45x of the P group's business interest expense incurred in 2021 is deductible in that year. Under paragraph (b)(1)(ii)(D) of this section, the P group must subtract $30x from its tentative taxable income in computing its ATI for its 2024 taxable year. Alternatively, under paragraph (b)(1)(iv)(E)(*2*) of this section, the P group must subtract $25x (the lesser of $30x or $25x) from its tentative taxable income in computing its ATI for its 2024 taxable year. However, the negative adjustments under paragraphs (b)(1)(ii)(D) and (b)(1)(iv)(E)(*2*) of this section are both subject to the negative adjustment cap in paragraph (b)(1)(iv)(F) of this section. Under that paragraph, the P group's negative adjustment under either paragraph (b)(1)(ii)(D) or paragraph (b)(1)(iv)(E)(*2*) of this section is capped at $20x, or $150x (the amount of ATI the P group needed in order to deduct all $45x of business interest expense in 2021) minus $130x (the amount of the P group's tentative taxable income in 2021 before adding back any amounts under paragraph (b)(1)(i)(D) through (F) of this section). As established by the P group, the additional $10x ($30x - $20x) of depreciation deductions that were added back to tentative taxable income in 2021 under paragraph (b)(1)(i)(D) of this section did not increase the P group's business interest expense deduction for that year.

(3) *Disposition of less than all member stock.* The facts are the same as in paragraph (b)(1)(viii)(B)(*1*) of this section, except that, in 2024, P sells half of its S stock to an unrelated third party. The results are the same as in paragraph (b)(1)(viii)(B)(*2*) of this section. See paragraph (b)(1)(iv)(A)(*3*) of this section. Thus, the P group must subtract $20x from its tentative taxable income in computing its ATI for its 2021 taxable year. No further adjustment under paragraphs (b)(1)(ii)(C) and (D) or paragraphs (b)(1)(iv)(E)(*1*) and (*2*) of this section is required if P subsequently sells its remaining S stock or if S subsequently disposes of Asset Y. See paragraphs (b)(1)(iv)(A)(*3*) and (b)(1)(iv)(D) of this section.

(4) *Intercompany transfer; disposition of successor assets*—(*i*) *Adjustments in 2024.* The facts are the same as in paragraph (b)(1)(viii)(B)(*1*) of this section, except that, rather than sell all of its S stock to an unrelated third party in 2024, P transfers all of its S stock to T in 2024 in a transaction to which section 351 applies and, in 2025, P sells all of its T stock to an unrelated third party at a gain of $40x. As provided in paragraph (b)(1)(iv)(A)(2) of this section, P's intercompany transfer of its S stock to T is not a "sale or other disposition" for purposes of paragraph (b)(1)(ii)(D) or paragraph (b)(1)(iv)(E)(2) of this section. Thus, no adjustment to tentative taxable income is required in 2024 under paragraph (b)(1)(ii)(D) or paragraph (b)(1)(iv)(E)(2) of this section.

(*ii*) *Adjustments in 2025.* Pursuant to paragraph (b)(1)(iv)(C)(*1*) of this section, P's stock in T is treated as a successor asset for purposes of paragraph (b)(1)(ii)(D) and (b)(1)(iv)(E)(2) of this section. Moreover, P's sale of its T stock causes both T and S to deconsolidate. Thus, under paragraph (b)(1)(iv)(A)(3) of this section, the transaction is treated as a taxable disposition of all of the T stock and all of the S stock held by all members of the P group. Under the anti-duplication rule in paragraph (b)(1)(iv)(D) of this section, the total amount of gain recognized for purposes of paragraph (b)(1)(iv)(E)(2)(*i*) of this section is $40x, the greater of the gain on the disposition of the T stock ($40x) or on the disposition of the S stock ($25x). However, the negative adjustments under paragraph (b)(1)(iv)(E)(2) of this section are subject to the negative adjustment cap in paragraph (b)(1)(iv)(F) of this section. Thus, the P group must subtract $20x from its tentative taxable income in computing its ATI for its 2025 taxable year.

(5) *Alternative computation and non-deconsolidating disposition of member stock.* The facts are the same as in paragraph (b)(1)(viii)(B)(*1*) of this section, except that, in 2024, P sells just ten percent of its S stock to an unrelated third party at a gain of $2.5x. Under paragraph (b)(1)(iv)(E)(2) of this section, the lesser of P's gain recognized on the sale of the S stock ($2.5x) and the investment adjustments under § 1.1502-32 with respect to the S stock P sold ($3x) is $2.5x, an amount less than the $20x limitation under paragraph (b)(1)(iv)(F) of this section. Thus, the P group must subtract $2.5x from its tentative taxable income in computing its ATI for its 2024 taxable year.

(6) *Non-deconsolidating disposition of member stock followed by asset disposition.* The facts are the same as in paragraph (b)(1)(viii)(B)(*5*) of this section, except that, in 2025, S sells Asset Y to an unrelated third party for a gain of $20x. Under paragraph (b)(1)(iv)(E)(*1*) of this section, the amount of the adjustment in 2025 is the lesser of two amounts. The first amount is the amount of S's gain recognized on the sale of Asset Y ($20x). See paragraph (b)(1)(iv)(E)(*1*)(*i*) of this section. The second amount is the amount of depreciation with respect to Asset Y (see paragraph (b)(1)(iv)(E)(*1*)(*ii*) of this section), reduced by the amount of depreciation previously taken into account in the computation under paragraph (b)(1)(iv)(E)(*2*)(*ii*) of this section ($30x - $3x, or $27x). See paragraph (b)(1)(iv)(D)(*1*) of this section. Thus, the amount of the adjustment under paragraphs (b)(1)(iv)(D) and (b)(1)(iv)(E)(*1*) of this section is $20x. In turn, this amount is subject to the negative adjustment cap under paragraph (b)(1)(iv)(F), which, after accounting for the negative adjustment on the earlier sale of S stock in 2024, is $17.5x ($20x - $2.5x). Accordingly, the P group must subtract $17.5x from its tentative taxable income in computing its ATI for its 2025 taxable year.

(C) *Example 3.*—(*1*) *Facts.* The facts are the same as in paragraph (b)(1)(viii)(B)(*1*) of this section, except that, in 2024, S sells Asset Y to an unrelated third party for $25x and, in 2025, P sells all of its S stock to an unrelated third party at a gain of $25x.

(2) *Analysis.* The results are the same as in paragraph (b)(1)(viii)(B)(2) of this section. Thus, the P group must subtract $20x from its tentative taxable income in computing its ATI for its 2024 taxable year. P's sale of all of its S stock in 2025 is a "sale or other disposition" for purposes of paragraph (b)(1)(ii)(D) and (b)(1)(iv)(E)(2) of this section. However, pursuant to paragraph (b)(1)(iv)(D)(*1*) of this section, no further adjustment to the P group's tentative taxable income is required in 2025 under paragraph (b)(1)(ii)(D) or paragraph (b)(1)(iv)(E)(2) of this section.

(3) *Disposition of S stock prior to S's asset disposition.* The facts are the same as in paragraph (b)(1)(viii)(C)(*1*) of this section, except that, in 2024, P sells all of its S stock to an unrelated third party at a gain of $25x and, in 2025, S sells Asset Y to an unrelated third party for $25x. The results are the same as in paragraph (b)(1)(viii)(B)(*2*) of this section. Thus, the P group must subtract $20x from its tentative taxable income in computing its ATI for its 2024 taxable year. Pursuant to paragraph (b)(1)(iv)(D)(*2*) of this section, no adjustment to the acquiring group's tentative taxable income is required in 2025 under paragraph (b)(1)(ii)(C) or paragraph (b)(1)(iv)(E)(*1*) of this section.

(4) *Deconsolidation of S in nonrecognition transaction.* The facts are the same as in paragraph (b)(1)(viii)(C)(*3*) of this section, except that, rather than sell all of its S stock to an unrelated third party, P causes S to merge with and into an unrelated third party in a transaction described in section 368(a)(1)(A). As provided in paragraph (b)(1)(iv)(A)(*3*) of this section, the merger transaction is treated as a taxable disposition of all of P's stock in S for purposes of paragraphs (b)(1)(ii)(D) and (b)(1)(iv)(E)(2) of this section because S leaves the P group. Thus, the results are the same as in paragraph (b)(1)(viii)(C)(*3*) of this section.

(D) *Example 4.*—(*1*) *Facts.* P wholly owns T, which wholly owns S. In 2021, S purchases a depreciable asset (Asset Z) for $30x and fully depreciates Asset Z under section 168(k). T reduces its basis in its S stock, and P reduces its basis in its T stock, by $30x under § 1.1502-32 to reflect S's depreciation deductions with respect to Asset Z. For the 2021 taxable year, the P group establishes that its ATI before adding back S's depreciation deductions with respect to Asset Z under paragraph (b)(1)(i)(D) of this section is $130x, and that its ATI after adding back S's depreciation deductions with respect to Asset Z under paragraph (b)(1)(i)(D) of this section is $160x. The P group incurs $45x of business interest expense in 2021. In 2024, T sells all of its S stock to an unrelated third party at a gain of $25x. In 2025, P sells all of its T stock to an unrelated third party at a gain of $40x.

(2) *Analysis.* The results are the same as in paragraph (b)(1)(viii)(3)(2) of this section. Thus, the P group must subtract $20x from its tentative taxable income in computing its ATI for its 2024 taxable year. Pursuant to paragraph (b)(1)(iv)(D)(1) of this section, no negative adjustment to the P group's tentative taxable income is required in 2025 under paragraph (b)(1)(ii)(D) or paragraph (b)(1)(iv)(E)(2) of this section.

(3) *Disposition of T stock in 2024.* The facts are the same as in paragraph (b)(1)(viii)(D)(*1*) of this section, except that, in 2024, P sells all of its T stock to another consolidated group at a gain of $40x and, in 2025, T sells all of its S stock to an unrelated party at a gain of $25x. Whereas the transaction described in paragraph (b)(1)(viii)(B)(*4*) of this section is treated as a taxable disposition of both the T stock and the S stock, only the actual disposition of the T stock in the transaction described in this paragraph (b)(1)(viii)(D)(*3*) is treated as a taxable disposition for purposes of paragraphs (b)(1)(ii)(D) and (b)(1)(iv)(E)(2) of this section. See paragraph (b)(1)(iv)(A)(*3*) of this section. However, the results are the same as in paragraph (b)(1)(viii)(B)(2) and (b)(1)(viii)(B)(*4*) of this section because of the negative adjustment cap in paragraph (b)(1)(iv)(F) of this section. Thus, the P group must subtract $20x from its tentative taxable income in computing its ATI for its 2024 taxable year. Pursuant to paragraph (b)(1)(iv)(D) of this section, no negative adjustment to the acquiring group's tentative taxable income is required in 2025 under paragraph (b)(1)(ii)(D) or paragraph (b)(1)(iv)(E)(*2*) of this section.

(E) *Example 5.*—(*1*) *Facts.* In 2021, A purchases Assets X and Y for $30x and $80x, respectively, and fully depreciates each asset under section 168(k). For the 2021 taxable year, A establishes that its ATI before adding back depreciation deductions with respect to Assets X and Y under paragraph (b)(1)(i)(D) of this section is $150x, and that its ATI after adding back depreciation deductions with respect to Assets X and Y under paragraph (b)(1)(i)(D) of this section is $260x. A incurs $75x of business interest expense in 2021. In 2024, A sells Assets X and Y to an unrelated third party for $40x and $90x, respectively.

(2) *Analysis.* A's section 163(j) limitation for 2021 is $78x ($260x × 30 percent). Thus, all $75x of A's business interest expense incurred in 2021 is deductible in that year. Under paragraph (b)(1)(ii)(C) of this section, A must subtract $110x ($30x + $80x) from its tentative taxable income in computing its ATI for its 2024 taxable

year. Alternatively, under paragraph (b)(1)(iv)(E)(*1*) of this section, A must subtract $30x with respect to Asset X (the lesser of $30x or $40x ($40x - $0x)), and $80x with respect to Asset Y (the lesser of $80x or $90x ($90x - $0x)), from its tentative taxable income in computing its ATI for its 2024 taxable year. However, the negative adjustments under paragraphs (b)(1)(ii)(C) and (b)(1)(iv)(E)(*1*) of this section are both subject to the negative adjustment cap in paragraph (b)(1)(iv)(F) of this section. Under that paragraph, A's negative adjustment in 2024 under either paragraph (b)(1)(ii)(C) ($110x) or paragraph (b)(1)(iv)(E)(*1*) (also $110x) of this section is limited to $100x. This amount equals $250x (the amount of ATI that A needed in order to deduct all $75x of business interest expense in 2021) minus $150x (the amount of A's tentative taxable income in 2021 before adding back any amounts under paragraph (b)(1)(i)(D) through (F) of this section). As established by A, the additional $10x ($110x - $100x) of depreciation deductions that were added back to tentative taxable income in 2021 under paragraph (b)(1)(i)(D) of this section did not increase A's business interest expense deduction for that year.

(*3*) *Sale of assets in different taxable years*. The facts are the same as in paragraph (b)(1)(viii)(E)(*1*) of this section, except that A sells Asset Y to an unrelated third party for $90x in 2025. Under paragraph (b)(1)(ii)(C) of this section, A must subtract $30x from its tentative taxable income in computing its ATI for its 2024 taxable year. Alternatively, under paragraph (b)(1)(iv)(E)(*1*) of this section, A must subtract $30x (the lesser of $30x or $40x ($40x - $0x)) from its tentative taxable income in computing its ATI for its 2024 taxable year. Because A's negative adjustment cap for its 2021 taxable year is $100x (see paragraph (b)(1)(viii)(E)(*2*) of this section), A's negative adjustment in 2024 of $30x is not reduced under paragraph (b)(1)(iv)(F) of this section. In 2025, A must subtract $80x from its tentative taxable income under paragraph (b)(1)(ii)(C) of this section in computing its ATI. Alternatively, under paragraph (b)(1)(iv)(E)(*1*) of this section, A must subtract $80x (the lesser of $80x or $90x ($90x - $0x)) from its tentative taxable income in computing its ATI for its 2025 taxable year. However, the negative adjustments under paragraphs (b)(1)(ii)(C) and (b)(1)(iv)(E)(*1*) of this section are both subject to the negative adjustment cap in paragraph (b)(1)(iv)(F) of this section. Moreover, A's negative adjustment cap for its 2021 taxable year is reduced from $100x to $70x to reflect A's $30x negative adjustment in 2024. See paragraph (b)(1)(iv)(F) of this section. Thus, A's negative adjustment for 2025 under either paragraph (b)(1)(ii)(C) or paragraph (b)(1)(iv)(E)(*1*) of this section is reduced from $80x to $70x. As established by A, the additional $10x ($110x - $100x) of depreciation deductions that were added back to tentative taxable income in 2021 under paragraph (b)(1)(i)(D) of this section did not increase A's business interest expense deduction for that year.

(2) *Applicable CFC*.—The term *applicable CFC* means a foreign corporation described in section 957, but only if the foreign corporation has at least one United States shareholder that owns, within the meaning of section 958(a), stock of the foreign corporation.

(3) *Business interest expense*.—(i) *In general*.—The term *business interest expense* means interest expense that is properly allocable to a non-excepted trade or business or that is floor plan financing interest expense. Business interest expense also includes disallowed business interest expense carryforwards (as defined in paragraph (b)(11) of this section). However, business interest expense does not include amounts of interest expense carried forward to the taxable year from a prior taxable year due to the application of section 465 or section 469, which apply after the application of section 163(j). For the treatment of investment interest, see section 163(d); and for the treatment of personal interest, see section 163(h).

(ii) *Special rules*.—For special rules for defining business interest expense in certain circumstances, see §§1.163(j)-3(b)(2) (regarding disallowed interest expense), 1.163(j)-4(b) (regarding C corporations) and 1.163(j)-4(d)(2)(iii) (regarding consolidated groups), 1.163(j)-1(b)(9)(regarding current-year business interest expense), and 1.163(j)-6(c) (regarding partnerships and S corporations).

(4) *Business interest income*.—(i) *In general*.—The term *business interest income* means interest income includible in the gross income of a taxpayer for the taxable year which is properly allocable to a non-excepted trade or business. For the treatment of investment income, see section 163(d).

(ii) *Special rules*.—For special rules defining business interest income in certain circumstances, see §§1.163(j)-4(b) (regarding C corporations), 1.163(j)-4(d)(2)(iii) (regarding consolidated groups), and 1.163(j)-6(c) (regarding partnerships and S corporations).

(5) *C corporation*.—The term *C corporation* has the meaning provided in section 1361(a)(2).

(6) *Cleared swap*.—The term *cleared swap* means a swap that is cleared by a derivatives clearing organization, as such term is defined in section 1a of the Commodity Exchange Act (7 U.S.C. 1a), or by a clearing agency, as such term is defined in section 3 of the Securities Exchange Act of 1934 (15 U.S.C. 78c), that is registered as a derivatives clearing organization under the Commodity Exchange Act or as a clearing agency under the Securities Exchange Act of 1934, respectively, if the derivatives clearing organization or clearing agency requires the parties to the swap to post and collect margin or collateral.

(7) *Consolidated group*.—The term *consolidated group* has the meaning provided in §1.1502-1(h).

(8) *Consolidated return year*.—The term *consolidated return year* has the meaning provided in §1.1502-1(d).

(9) *Current-year business interest expense*.—The term *current-year business interest expense* means business interest expense that would be deductible in the current taxable year without regard to section 163(j) and that is not a disallowed business interest expense carryforward from a prior taxable year.

(10) *Disallowed business interest expense*.—The term *disallowed business interest expense* means the amount of business interest expense for a taxable year in excess of the amount allowed as a deduction for the taxable year under section 163(j)(1) and §1.163(j)-2(b). For purposes of section 163(j) and the regulations in this part under section 163(j) of the Internal Revenue Code (Code) disallowed business interest expense is treated as "paid or accrued" in the taxable year in which the expense is deductible for Federal income tax purposes (without regard to section 163(j)) or in the taxable year in which a deduction for the business interest expense is permitted under section 163(j), as the context may require.

(11) *Disallowed business interest expense carryforward*.—The term *disallowed business interest expense carryforward* means any business interest expense described in §1.163(j)-2(c).

(12) *Disallowed disqualified interest*.—The term *disallowed disqualified interest* means interest expense, including carryforwards, for which a deduction was disallowed under old section 163(j) (as defined in paragraph (b)(27) of this section) in the taxpayer's last taxable year beginning before January 1, 2018, and that was carried forward pursuant to old section 163(j).

(13) *Electing farming business*.—The term *electing farming business* means a trade or business that makes an election as provided in §1.163(j)-9 or other published guidance and that is—

(i) A farming business, as defined in section 263A(e)(4) or §1.263A-4(a)(4);

(ii) Any trade or business of a specified agricultural or horticultural cooperative, as defined in section 199A(g)(4); or

(iii) Specifically designated by the Secretary in guidance published in the Federal Register or the Internal Revenue Bulletin (see §601.601(d) of this chapter) as a farming business for purposes of section 163(j).

(14) *Electing real property trade or business*.—The term *electing real property trade or business* means a trade or business that makes an election as provided in §1.163(j)-9 or other published guidance and that is—

(i) A real property trade or business described in section 469(c)(7)(C) and §1.469-9(b)(2); or

(ii) A REIT that qualifies for the safe harbor described in §1.163(j)-9(h); or

(iii) A trade or business specifically designated by the Secretary in guidance published in the Federal Register or the Internal Revenue Bulletin (see §601.601(d) of this chapter) as a real property trade or business for purposes of section 163(j).

(15) *Excepted regulated utility trade or business*.—(i) *In general*.—The term *excepted regulated utility trade or business* means:

(A) *Automatically excepted regulated utility trades or businesses*.—A trade or business—

(*1*) That furnishes or sells—

(*i*) Electrical energy, water, or sewage disposal services;

(*ii*) Gas or steam through a local distribution system; or

(*iii*) Transportation of gas or steam by pipeline; but only

(*2*) To the extent that the rates for the furnishing or sale of the items in paragraph (b)(15)(i)(A)(*1*) of this section—

(*i*) Have been established or approved by a State or political subdivision thereof, by any agency or instrumentality of the United States, or by a public service or public utility commission or other similar body of any State or political subdivision thereof and are determined on a cost of service and rate of return basis; or

(*ii*) Have been established or approved by the governing or ratemaking body of an electric cooperative; or

(B) *Electing regulated utility trades or businesses.*—A trade or business that makes a valid election under paragraph (b)(15)(iii) of this section; or

(C) *Designated excepted regulated utility trades or businesses.*—A trade or business that is specifically designated by the Secretary in guidance published in the Federal Register or the Internal Revenue Bulletin as an excepted regulated utility trade or business (see § 601.601(d) of this chapter) for section 163(j) purposes.

(ii) *Depreciation and excepted and non-excepted utility trades or businesses.*—(A) *Depreciation.*—Taxpayers engaged in an excepted trade or business described in paragraph (b)(15)(i) of this section cannot claim the additional first-year depreciation deduction under section 168(k) for any property that is primarily used in the excepted regulated utility trade or business.

(B) *Allocation of items.*—If a taxpayer is engaged in one or more excepted trades or businesses, as described in paragraph (b)(15)(i) of this section, and one or more non-excepted trades or businesses, the taxpayer must allocate items between the excepted and non-excepted utility trades or businesses. See § § 1.163(j)-1(b)(44) and 1.163(j)-10(c)(3)(iii)(C). Some trades or businesses with de minimis furnishing or sales of items described in paragraph (b)(15)(i)(A)(*1*) of this section that are not sold pursuant to rates that are determined on a cost of service and rate of return basis or established or approved by the governing or ratemaking body of an electric cooperative, and are not subject to an election in paragraph (b)(15)(iii), are treated as excepted trades or businesses. See § 1.163(j)-10(c)(3)(iii)(C)(*3*). For look-through rules applicable to certain CFCs that furnish or sell items described in paragraph (b)(15)(i)(A)(*1*) of this section that are not sold pursuant to rates that are determined on a cost of service and rate of return basis or established or approved by the governing or ratemaking body of an electric cooperative as described in paragraph (b)(15)(i)(A)(2) of this section, see § 1.163(j)-10(c)(5)(ii)(C).

(iii) *Election to be an excepted regulated utility trade or business.*—(A) *In general.*—A trade or business that is not an excepted regulated utility trade or business described in paragraph (b)(15)(i)(A) or (C) of this section and that furnishes or sells items described in paragraph (b)(15)(i)(A)(*1*) of this section is eligible to make an election to be an excepted regulated utility trade or business to the extent that the rates for furnishing or selling the items described in paragraph (b)(15)(i)(A)(*1*) of this section have been established or approved by a regulatory body described in paragraph (b)(15)(i)(A)(*2*)(i) of this section.

(B) *Scope and effect of election.*—*(1) In general.*—An election under paragraph (b)(15)(iii) of this section is made with respect to each eligible trade or business of the taxpayer and applies only to the trade or business for which the election is made. An election under paragraph (b)(15)(iii) of this section applies to the taxable year in which the election is made and to all subsequent taxable years.

(2) Irrevocability.—An election under paragraph (b)(15)(iii) of this section is irrevocable.

(C) *Time and manner of making election.*—*(1) In general.*—Subject to paragraph (b)(15)(iii)(C)(5) of this section, a taxpayer makes an election under paragraph (b)(15)(iii) by attaching an election statement to the taxpayer's timely filed original Federal income tax return, including extensions. A taxpayer may make elections for multiple trades or businesses on a single election statement.

(2) Election statement contents.—The election statement should be titled "Section 1.163(j)-1(b)(15)(iii) Election" and must contain the following information for each trade or business:

(*i*) The taxpayer's name;

(*ii*) The taxpayer's address;

(*iii*) The taxpayer's social security number (SSN) or employer identification number (EIN);

(*iv*) A description of the taxpayer's electing trade or business sufficient to demonstrate qualification for an election under this section, including the principal business activity code; and

(*v*) A statement that the taxpayer is making an election under section 1.163(j)-1(b)(15)(iii).

(3) Consolidated group's or partnership's trade or business.—The rules in § 1.163(j)-9(d)(3) and (4) apply with respect to an election under paragraph (b)(15)(iii) of this section for a consolidated group's or partnership's trade or business.

(4) Termination of election.—The rules in § 1.163(j)-9(e) apply to determine when an election under paragraph (b)(15)(iii) of this section terminates.

(5) Additional guidance.—The rules and procedures regarding the time and manner of making an election under paragraph (b)(15)(iii) of this section and the election statement contents in paragraph (b)(15)(iii)(C)(*2*) of this section may be modified through other guidance (see § § 601.601(d) and 601.602 of this chapter). Additional situations in which an election may terminate under paragraph (b)(15)(iii)(C)(*4*) of this section may be provided through guidance published in the Federal Register or in the Internal Revenue Bulletin (see § 601.601(d) of this chapter).

(16) *Excess business interest expense.*—For any partnership, the term *excess business interest expense* means the amount of disallowed business interest expense of the partnership for a taxable year under section § 1.163(j)-2(b). With respect to a partner, see § 1.163(j)-6(g) and (h).

(17) *Excess taxable income.*—With respect to any partnership or S corporation, the term *excess taxable income* means the amount which bears the same ratio to the partnership's ATI as—

(i) The excess (if any) of—

(A) The amount determined for the partnership or S corporation under section 163(j)(1)(B); over

(B) The amount (if any) by which the business interest expense of the partnership, reduced by the floor plan financing interest expense, exceeds the business interest income of the partnership or S corporation; bears to

(ii) The amount determined for the partnership or S corporation under section 163(j)(1)(B).

(18) *Floor plan financing indebtedness.*—The term floor plan financing indebtedness means indebtedness—

(i) Used to finance the acquisition of motor vehicles held for sale or lease; and

(ii) Secured by the motor vehicles so acquired.

(19) *Floor plan financing interest expense.*—The term *floor plan financing interest expense* means interest paid or accrued on floor plan financing indebtedness. For purposes of the section 163(j) regulations, all floor plan financing interest expense is treated as business interest expense. See paragraph (b)(3) of this section.

(20) *Group.*—The term *group* has the meaning provided in § 1.1502-1(a).

(21) *Intercompany transaction.*—The term *intercompany transaction* has the meaning provided in § 1.1502-13(b)(1)(i).

(22) *Interest.*—The term *interest* means any amount described in paragraph (b)(22)(i), (ii), (iii), or (iv) of this section.

(i) *In general.*—Interest is an amount paid, received, or accrued as compensation for the use or forbearance of money under the terms of an instrument or contractual arrangement, including a series of transactions, that is treated as a debt instrument for purposes of section 1275(a) and § 1.1275-1(d), and not treated as stock under § 1.385-3, or an amount that is treated as interest under other provisions of the Code or the Income Tax Regulations. Thus, interest includes, but is not limited to, the following:

(A) Original issue discount (OID), as adjusted by the holder for any acquisition premium or amortizable bond premium;

(B) Qualified stated interest, as adjusted by the holder for any amortizable bond premium or by the issuer for any bond issuance premium;

(C) Acquisition discount;

(D) Amounts treated as taxable OID under section 1286 (relating to stripped bonds and stripped coupons);

(E) Accrued market discount on a market discount bond to the extent includible in income by the holder under either section 1276(a) or 1278(b);

(F) OID includible in income by a holder that has made an election under § 1.1272-3 to treat all interest on a debt instrument as OID;

(G) OID on a synthetic debt instrument arising from an integrated transaction under § 1.1275-6;

(H) Repurchase premium to the extent deductible by the issuer under § 1.163-7(c) (determined without regard to section 163(j));

(I) Deferred payments treated as interest under section 483;

(J) Amounts treated as interest under a section 467 rental agreement;

(K) Amounts treated as interest under section 988;

(L) Forgone interest under section 7872;

(M) De minimis OID taken into account by the issuer;

(N) Amounts paid or received in connection with a sale-repurchase agreement treated as indebtedness under Federal tax principles; however, in the case of a sale-repurchase agreement relating to tax-exempt bonds, the amount is not tax-exempt interest;

(O) Redeemable ground rent treated as interest under section 163(c); and

(P) Amounts treated as interest under section 636.

(ii) *Swaps with significant nonperiodic payments.*—(A) *In general.*—Except as provided in paragraphs (b)(22)(ii)(B) and (C) of this section, a swap with significant nonperiodic payments is treated as two separate transactions consisting of an on-market, level payment swap and a loan. The loan must be accounted for by the parties to the contract independently of the swap. The time value component associated with the loan, determined in accordance with § 1.446-3(f)(2)(iii)(A), is recognized as interest expense to the payor and interest income to the recipient.

(B) *Exception for cleared swaps.*—Paragraph (b)(22)(ii)(A) of this section does not apply to a cleared swap (as defined in paragraph (b)(6) of this section).

(C) *Exception for non-cleared swaps subject to margin or collateral requirements.*—Paragraph (b)(22)(ii)(A) of this section does not apply to a non-cleared swap that requires the parties to meet the margin or collateral requirements of a federal regulator or that provides for margin or collateral requirements that are substantially similar to a cleared swap or a non-cleared swap subject to the margin or collateral requirements of a federal regulator. For purposes of this paragraph (b)(22)(ii)(C), the term *federal regulator* means the Securities and Exchange Commission (SEC), the Commodity Futures Trading Commission (CFTC), or a prudential regulator, as defined in section 1a(39) of the Commodity Exchange Act (7 U.S.C. 1a), as amended by section 721 of the Dodd-Frank Wall Street Reform and Consumer Protection Act of 2010, Public Law No. 111-203, 124 Stat. 1376, Title VII.

(iii) *Other amounts treated as interest.*—(A) *Treatment of premium.*—(*1*) *Issuer.*—If a debt instrument is issued at a premium within the meaning of § 1.163-13, any ordinary income under § 1.163-13(d)(4) is treated as interest income of the issuer.

(*2*) *Holder.*—If a taxable debt instrument is acquired at a premium within the meaning of § 1.171-1 and the holder elects to amortize the premium, any amount deductible as a bond premium deduction under section 171(a)(1) and § 1.171-2(a)(4)(i)(A) or (C) is treated as interest expense of the holder.

(B) *Treatment of ordinary income or loss on certain debt instruments.*—If an issuer of a contingent payment debt instrument subject to § 1.1275-4(b), a nonfunctional currency contingent payment debt instrument subject to § 1.988-6, or an inflation-indexed debt instrument subject to § 1.1275-7 recognizes ordinary income on the debt instrument in accordance with the rules in § 1.1275-4(b), § 1.988-6(b)(2), or § 1.1275-7(f), whichever is applicable, the ordinary income is treated as interest income of the issuer. If a holder of a contingent payment debt instrument subject to § 1.1275-4(b), a nonfunctional currency contingent payment debt instrument subject to § 1.988-6, or an inflation-indexed debt instrument subject to § 1.1275-7 recognizes an ordinary loss on the debt instrument in accordance with the rules in § 1.1275-4(b), § 1.988-6(b)(2), or § 1.1275-7(f), whichever is applicable, the ordinary loss is treated as interest expense of the holder.

(C) *Substitute interest payments.*—A substitute interest payment described in § 1.861-2(a)(7) is treated as interest expense to the payor only if the payment relates to a sale-repurchase agreement or a securities lending transaction that is not entered into by the payor in the ordinary course of the payor's business. A substitute interest payment described in § 1.861-2(a)(7) is treated as interest income to the recipient only if the payment relates to a sale-repurchase agreement or a securities lending transaction that is not entered into by the recipient in the ordinary course of the recipient's business; however, in the case of a sale-repurchase agreement or a securities lending transaction relating to tax-exempt bonds, the recipient of a substitute payment does not receive tax-exempt interest income. This paragraph (b)(22)(iii)(C) does not apply to an amount described in paragraph (b)(22)(i)(N) of this section.

(D) *Section 1258 gain.*—Any gain treated as ordinary gain under section 1258 is treated as interest income.

(E) *Factoring income.*—The excess of the amount that a taxpayer collects on a factored receivable (or realizes upon the sale or other disposition of the factored receivable) over the amount paid for the factored receivable by the taxpayer is treated as interest income. For purposes of this paragraph (b)(22)(iii)(E), the term *factored receivable* includes any account receivable or other evidence of indebtedness, whether or not issued at a discount and whether or not bearing stated interest, arising out of the disposition of property or the performance of services by any person, if such account receivable or evidence of indebtedness is acquired by a person other than the person who disposed of the property or provided the services that gave rise to the account receivable or evidence of indebtedness. This paragraph (b)(22)(iii)(E) does not apply to an amount described in paragraph (b)(22)(i)(C) or (E) of this section.

(F) *Section 163(j) interest dividends.*—(*1*) *In general.*—Except as otherwise provided in this paragraph (b)(22)(iii)(F), a section 163(j) interest dividend is treated as interest income.

(*2*) *Limitation on amount treated as interest income.*—A shareholder may not treat any part of a section 163(j) interest dividend as interest income to the extent the amount of the section 163(j) interest dividend exceeds the excess of the amount of the entire dividend that includes the section 163(j) interest dividend over the sum of the conduit amounts other than interest-related dividends under section 871(k)(1)(C) and section 163(j) interest dividends that affect the shareholder's treatment of that dividend.

(*3*) *Conduit amounts.*—For purposes of paragraph (b)(22)(iii)(F)(*2*) of this section, the term *conduit amounts* means, with respect to any category of income (including tax-exempt interest) earned by a RIC for a taxable year, the amounts identified by the RIC (generally in a designation or written report) in connection with dividends of the RIC for that taxable year that are subject to a limit determined by reference to that category of income. For example, a RIC's conduit amount with respect to its net capital gain is the amount of the RIC's capital gain dividends under section 852(b)(3)(C).

(*4*) *Holding period.*—Except as provided in paragraph (b)(22)(iii)(F)(*5*) of this section, no dividend is treated as interest income under paragraph (b)(22)(iii)(F)(*1*) of this section if the dividend is received with respect to a share of RIC stock—

(*i*) That is held by the shareholder for 180 days or less (taking into account the principles of section 246(c)(3) and (4)) during the 361-day period beginning on the date which is 180 days before the date on which the share becomes ex-dividend with respect to such dividend; or

(*ii*) To the extent that the shareholder is under an obligation (whether pursuant to a short sale or otherwise) to make related payments with respect to positions in substantially similar or related property.

(*5*) *Exception to holding period requirement for money market funds and certain regularly declared dividends.*—Paragraph (b)(22)(iii)(F)(*4*)(*i*) of this section does not apply to dividends distributed by any RIC regulated as a money market fund under 17 CFR 270.2a-7 (Rule 2a-7 under the 1940 Act) or to regular dividends paid by a RIC that declares section 163(j) interest dividends on a daily basis in an amount equal to at least 90 percent of its excess section 163(j) interest income, as defined in paragraph (b)(35)(iv)(E) of this section, and distributes such dividends on a monthly or more frequent basis.

(iv) *Anti-avoidance rules.*—(A) *Principal purpose to reduce interest expense.*—*(1) Treatment as interest expense.*—Any expense or loss economically equivalent to interest is treated as interest expense if a principal purpose of structuring the transaction(s) is to reduce an amount incurred by the taxpayer that otherwise would have been described in paragraph (b)(22)(i), (ii), or (iii) of this section. For this purpose, the fact that the taxpayer has a business purpose for obtaining the use of funds does not affect the determination of whether the manner in which the taxpayer structures the transaction(s) is with a principal purpose of reducing the taxpayer's interest expense. In addition, the fact that the taxpayer has obtained funds at a lower pre-tax cost based on the structure of the transaction(s) does not affect the determination of whether the manner in which the taxpayer structures the transaction(s) is with a principal purpose of reducing the taxpayer's interest expense. For purposes of this paragraph (b)(22)(iv)(A)*(1)*, any expense or loss is economically equivalent to interest to the extent that the expense or loss is—

(i) Deductible by the taxpayer;

(ii) Incurred by the taxpayer in a transaction or series of integrated or related transactions in which the taxpayer secures the use of funds for a period of time;

(iii) Substantially incurred in consideration of the time value of money; and

(iv) Not described in paragraph (b)(22)(i), (ii), or (iii) of this section.

(2) Corresponding treatment of amounts as interest income.—If a taxpayer knows that an expense or loss is treated by the payor as interest expense under paragraph (b)(22)(iv)(A)*(1)* of this section, the taxpayer provides the use of funds for a period of time in the transaction(s) subject to paragraph (b)(22)(iv)(A)*(1)* of this section, the taxpayer earns income or gain with respect to the transaction(s), and such income or gain is substantially earned in consideration of the time value of money provided by the taxpayer, such income or gain is treated as interest income to the extent of the expense or loss treated by the payor as interest expense under paragraph (b)(22)(iv)(A)*(1)* of this section.

(B) *Interest income artificially increased.*—Notwithstanding paragraphs (b)(22)(i) through (iii) of this section, any income realized by a taxpayer in a transaction or series of integrated or related transactions is not treated as interest income of the taxpayer if and to the extent that a principal purpose for structuring the transaction(s) is to artificially increase the taxpayer's business interest income. For this purpose, the fact that the taxpayer has a business purpose for holding interest generating assets does not affect the determination of whether the manner in which the taxpayer structures the transaction(s) is with a principal purpose of artificially increasing the taxpayer's business interest income.

(C) *Principal purpose.*—Whether a transaction or a series of integrated or related transactions is entered into with a principal purpose described in paragraph (b)(22)(iv)(A) or (B) of this section depends on all the facts and circumstances related to the transaction(s), except for those facts described in paragraph (b)(22)(iv)(A) or (B) of this section. A purpose may be a principal purpose even though it is outweighed by other purposes (taken together or separately). Factors to be taken into account in determining whether one of the taxpayer's principal purposes for entering into the transaction(s) include the taxpayer's normal borrowing rate in the taxpayer's functional currency, whether the taxpayer would enter into the transaction(s) in the ordinary course of the taxpayer's trade or business, whether the parties to the transaction(s) are related persons (within the meaning of section 267(b) or section 707(b)), whether there is a significant and bona fide business purpose for the structure of the transaction(s), whether the transactions are transitory, for example, due to a circular flow of cash or other property, and the substance of the transaction(s).

(D) *Coordination with anti-avoidance rule in §1.163(j)-2(j).*—The anti-avoidance rules in paragraphs (b)(22)(iv)(A) through (C) of this section, rather than the anti-avoidance rules in §1.163(j)-2(j), apply to determine whether an item is treated as interest expense or interest income.

(v) *Examples.*—The examples in this paragraph (b)(22)(v) illustrate the application of paragraph (b)(22)(iv) of this section. Unless otherwise indicated, A, B, C, D, and Bank are domestic C corporations that are publicly traded; the exemption for certain small businesses in §1.163(j)-2(d) does not apply; A is not engaged in an excepted trade or business; and all amounts of interest expense are deductible except for the potential application of section 163(j).

(A) *Example 1.*—*(1) Facts.* A is engaged in a manufacturing business and uses the calendar year as its annual accounting period. A's functional currency is the U.S. dollar and A conducts virtually all of its business in the U.S. dollar. A has no connection to Japan or the Japanese yen in the ordinary course of business. A projects that it will have business interest expense of $100x on an existing loan obligation with a stated principal amount of $2,000x (Loan 1) and no business interest income in its taxable year ending December 31, 2021. In early 2021, A enters into the following transactions, which A would not have entered into in the ordinary course of A's trade or business:

*(i)*A enters into a loan obligation in which A borrows Japanese yen from Bank in an amount equivalent to $2,000x with an interest rate of 1 percent (Loan 2) (at the time of the loan, the U.S. dollar equivalent interest rate on a loan of $2,000x is 5 percent);

*(ii)*A enters into a foreign currency swap transaction (FX Swap) with Bank with a notional principal amount of $2,000x under which A receives Japanese yen at 1 percent multiplied by the amount of Japanese yen borrowed from Bank (which for 2021 equals $20x) and pays U.S. dollars at 5 percent multiplied by a notional amount of $2,000x ($100x per year);

(iii) The FX Swap is not integrated with Loan 2 under §1.988-5; and

(iv) A enters into a spot transaction with Bank to convert the proceeds of Loan 2 into $2,000x U.S. dollars and A uses the U.S. dollars to repay Loan 1.

(2) Analysis. A principal purpose of A entering into the transactions with Bank was to try to reduce the amount incurred by A that otherwise would be interest expense; in effect, A sought to alter A's cost of borrowing by converting a substantial portion of its interest expense deductions on Loan 1 into section 165 deductions on the FX Swap ($100x interest expense related to Loan 1 compared to $20x interest expense related to Loan 2 and $80x section 165 deduction). A's functional currency is the U.S. dollar and A conducts virtually all of its business in the U.S. dollar. A has no connection to Japan or the Japanese yen and would not have entered into the transactions in the ordinary course of A's trade or business. The section 165 deductions related to the FX Swap were incurred by A in a series of transactions in which A secured the use of funds for a period of time and were substantially incurred in consideration of the time value of money. As a result, under paragraph (b)(22)(iv)(A)*(1)* of this section, for purposes of section 163(j), the $80x paid by A to Bank on the FX Swap is treated by A as interest expense.

(B) *Example 2.*—*(1) Facts.* A is engaged in a manufacturing business and uses the calendar year as its annual accounting period. A does not use gold in its manufacturing business. In 2021, A expects to borrow $1,000x for six months. In January 2021, A borrows from B two ounces of gold at a time when the spot price for gold is $500x per ounce. A agrees to return the two ounces of gold in six months. A sells the two ounces of gold to C for $1,000x. A then enters into a contract with D to purchase two ounces of gold six months in the future for $1,013x. In exchange for the use of $1,000x in cash for six months, A has sustained a loss of $13x in connection with these related transactions. A would not have entered into the gold transactions in the ordinary course of A's trade or business.

(2) Analysis. In a series of related transactions, A has obtained the use of $1,000x for six months and created a loss of $13x substantially incurred in consideration of the time value of money. A would not have entered into the gold transactions in the ordinary course of A's trade or business. A entered into the transactions with a principal purpose of structuring the transactions to reduce its interest expense (in effect, A sought to convert what otherwise would be interest expense into a loss through the transactions). As a result, under paragraph (b)(22)(iv)(A)(1) of this section, for purposes of section 163(j), the loss of $13x is treated by A as interest expense.

(C) *Example 3.*—*(1) Facts.* A is engaged in a manufacturing business and uses the calendar year as its annual accounting period. A's functional currency is the U.S. dollar and A conducts virtually all of its business in the U.S. dollar. A has no connection to Argentina or the Argentine peso as part of its ordinary course of business. As of January 1, 2021, A expects to have adjusted taxable income (as defined in paragraph (b)(1) of this section) of $200x in the taxable year ending December 31, 2021. A also projects that it will have business interest expense of $70x on an existing loan in 2021. A has cash equivalents of $100x on which A expects to earn $5x of business interest income. In early 2021, A enters into the following transactions, which A would not have entered into in the ordinary course of A's trade or business:

(*i*)A enters into a spot transaction with Bank to convert the $100x of cash equivalents into an amount in Argentine pesos equivalent to $100x and A uses the Argentine pesos to purchase an Argentine peso note (Note) issued by a subsidiary of Bank for the Argentine peso equivalent of $100x; the Note pays interest at a 10 percent rate; and

(*ii*) A enters into a foreign currency swap transaction (FX Swap) with Bank with a notional principal amount of $100x under which A pays Argentine pesos at 10 percent multiplied by the amount of Argentine peso principal amount on the Note (which for 2021 equals $10x) and receives U.S. dollars at 5 percent multiplied by a notional amount of $100x ($5x per year).

(2) *Analysis.* A principal purpose of A entering into the transactions was to increase the amount of business interest income received by A; in effect, A increased its business interest income by separately accounting for its net deduction of $5x per year on the FX Swap. A's functional currency is the U.S. dollar and A conducts virtually all of its business in the U.S. dollar. A has no connection to Argentina or the Argentine peso and would not have entered into the transactions in the ordinary course of A's trade or business. The FX Swap was incurred by A as a part of a transaction that A entered into with a principal purpose of artificially increasing its business interest income. As a result, under paragraph (b)(22)(iv)(B) of this section, for purposes of section 163(j), the $10x business interest income earned on the Note by A is reduced by $5x (the net $5x paid by A on the FX Swap).

(D) *Example 4.*—(1) *Facts.* A is wholly owned by FC, a foreign corporation organized in foreign country X. A uses the calendar year for its annual accounting period. FC has a better credit rating than A. A needs to borrow $2,000x in the taxable year ending December 31, 2021, to fund its business operations. A also projects that, if it borrows $2,000x on January 1, 2021, and pays a market rate of interest, it will have business interest expense of $100x in its taxable year ending December 31, 2021. In early 2021, A enters into the following transactions:

(*i*) A enters into a loan obligation in which A borrows $2,000x from Bank with an interest rate of 3 percent (Loan 1);

(*ii*) FC and Bank enter into a guarantee arrangement (Guarantee) under which FC agrees to guarantee Bank that Bank will be timely paid all of the amounts due on Loan 1; and

(*iii*) A enters into a guarantee fee agreement with FC (Guarantee Fee Agreement) under which A agrees to pay FC $40x in return for FC entering into the Guarantee, which was not an agreement that A would have entered into in the ordinary course of A's trade or business.

(2) *Analysis.* A principal purpose of A entering into the transactions was to reduce the amount incurred by A that otherwise would be interest expense; in effect, A sought to convert a substantial portion of its interest expense deductions on Loan 1 into section 162 deductions on the Guarantee Fee Agreement ($100x interest expense had A borrowed without the Guarantee compared to $60x interest expense related to Loan 1 and $40x section 162 deduction). A would not have entered into the Guarantee Fee Agreement in the ordinary course of A's trade or business. The $40x section 162 deductions related to the Guarantee Fee Agreement were incurred by A in a series of transactions in which A secured the use of funds for a period of time and were substantially incurred in consideration of the time value of money. As a result, under paragraph (b)(22)(iv)(A)(*1*) of this section, for purposes of section 163(j), the $40x paid by A to FC on the Guarantee Fee Agreement is treated by A as interest expense.

(E) *Example 5.*—(1) *Facts.* A, B, and C are equal partners in ABC partnership. ABC is considering acquiring an additional loan from a third-party lender to expand its business operations. However, ABC already has significant debt and interest expense. For the purpose of reducing the amount of additional interest expense ABC would have otherwise incurred by borrowing, A agrees to make an additional contribution to ABC for use in its business operations in exchange for a guaranteed payment for the use of capital under section 707(c).

(2) *Analysis.* The guaranteed payment is deductible by ABC, incurred by ABC in a transaction in which ABC secures the use of funds for a period of time, substantially incurred in consideration of the time value of money, and not described in paragraph (b)(22)(i), (ii), or (iii) of this section. As a result, the guaranteed payment to A is economically equivalent to the interest that ABC would have incurred on an additional loan from a third-party lender. A principal purpose of A making a contribution in exchange for a guaranteed payment for the use of capital was to reduce the amount incurred by ABC that otherwise would be interest expense. As a result, under paragraph (b)(22)(iv)(A)(*1*) of this section, for purposes of section 163(j), such guaranteed payment is treated as interest expense of ABC for purposes of section 163(j). In addition, under paragraph (b)(22)(iv)(A)(2) of this section, if A knows that the guaranteed payment is treated as interest expense of ABC, because A provides the use of funds for a period of time in a transaction subject to paragraph (b)(22)(iv)(A)(*1*) of this section, A earns income or gain with respect to the transaction, and such income or gain is substantially earned in consideration of the time value of money provided by A, the guaranteed payment is treated as interest income of A for purposes of section 163(j).

(23) *Interest expense.*—The term *interest expense* means interest that is paid or accrued, or treated as paid or accrued, for the taxable year.

(24) *Interest income.*—The term *interest income* means interest that is included in gross income for the taxable year.

(25) *Member.*—The term *member* has the meaning provided in § 1.1502-1(b).

(26) *Motor vehicle.*—The term *motor vehicle* means a motor vehicle as defined in section 163(j)(9)(C).

(27) *Old section 163(j).*—The term *old section 163(j)* means section 163(j) immediately prior to its amendment by Public Law No. 115-97, 131 Stat. 2054 (2017).

(28) *Ownership change.*—The term *ownership change* has the meaning provided in section 382 and the regulations in this part under section 382 of the Code.

(29) *Ownership date.*—The term *ownership date* has the meaning provided in section 382 and the regulations in this part under section 382 of the Code.

(30) *Real estate investment trust.*—The term *real estate investment trust* (REIT) has the meaning provided in section 856.

(31) *Real property.*—The term *real property* includes—

(i) Real property as defined in § 1.469-9(b)(2); and

(ii) Any direct or indirect right, including a license or other contractual right, to share in the appreciation in value of, or the gross or net proceeds or profits generated by, an interest in real property, including net proceeds or profits associated with tolls, rents or other similar fees.

(32) *Regulated investment company.*—The term *regulated investment company* (RIC) has the meaning provided in section 851.

(33) *Relevant foreign corporation.*—The term *relevant foreign corporation* means any foreign corporation whose classification is relevant under § 301.7701-3(d)(1) for a taxable year, other than solely pursuant to section 881 or 882.

(34) *S corporation.*—The term *S corporation* has the meaning provided in section 1361(a)(1).

(35) *Section 163(j) interest dividend.*—The term *section 163(j) interest dividend* means a dividend paid by a RIC for a taxable year for which section 852(b) applies to the RIC, to the extent described in paragraph (b)(35)(i) or (ii) of this section, as applicable.

(i) *In general.*—Except as provided in paragraph (b)(35)(ii) of this section, a section 163(j) interest dividend is any dividend, or part of a dividend, that is reported by the RIC as a section 163(j) interest dividend in written statements furnished to its shareholders.

(ii) *Reduction in the case of excess reported amounts.*—If the aggregate reported amount with respect to the RIC for the taxable year exceeds the excess section 163(j) interest income of the RIC for such taxable year, the section 163(j) interest dividend is—

(A) The reported section 163(j) interest dividend amount; reduced by

(B) The excess reported amount that is allocable to that reported section 163(j) interest dividend amount.

(iii) *Allocation of excess reported amount.*—(A) *In general.*—Except as provided in paragraph (b)(35)(iii)(B) of this section, the excess reported amount, if any, that is allocable to the reported section 163(j) interest dividend amount is that portion of the excess reported amount that bears the same ratio to the excess reported amount as the reported section 163(j) interest dividend amount bears to the aggregate reported amount.

(B) *Special rule for noncalendar year RICs.*—In the case of any taxable year that does not begin and end in the same calendar year, if the post-December reported amount equals or exceeds the excess reported amount for that taxable year, paragraph (b)(35)(iii)(A) of this section is applied by substituting "post-December reported amount" for "aggregate reported amount," and no excess reported amount is allocated to any dividend paid on or before December 31 of such taxable year.

(iv) *Definitions.*—The following definitions apply for purposes of this paragraph (b)(35):

(A) *Reported section 163(j) interest dividend amount.*—The term *reported section 163(j) interest dividend amount* means the amount of a dividend distribution reported to the RIC's shareholders under paragraph (b)(35)(i) of this section as a section 163(j) interest dividend.

(B) *Excess reported amount.*—The term *excess reported amount* means the excess of the aggregate reported amount over the RIC's excess section 163(j) interest income for the taxable year.

(C) *Aggregate reported amount.*—The term *aggregate reported amount* means the aggregate amount of dividends reported by the RIC under paragraph (b)(35)(i) of this section as section 163(j) interest dividends for the taxable year (including section 163(j) interest dividends paid after the close of the taxable year described in section 855).

(D) *Post-December reported amount.*—The term *post-December reported amount* means the aggregate reported amount determined by taking into account only dividends paid after December 31 of the taxable year.

(E) *Excess section 163(j) interest income.*—The term *excess section 163(j) interest income* means, with respect to a taxable year of a RIC, the excess of the RIC's business interest income for the taxable year over the sum of the RIC's business interest expense for the taxable year and the RIC's other deductions for the taxable year that are properly allocable to the RIC's business interest income.

(v) *Example.*—(A) *Facts.* X is a domestic C corporation that has elected to be a RIC. For its taxable year ending December 31, 2021, X has $100x of business interest income (all of which is qualified interest income for purposes of section 871(k)(1)(E)) and $10x of dividend income (all of which is qualified dividend income within the meaning of section 1(h)(11) and would be eligible for the dividends received deduction under section 243, determined as described in section 854(b)(3)). X has $10x of business interest expense and $20x of other deductions. X has no other items for the taxable year. On December 31, 2021, X pays a dividend of $80x to its shareholders, and reports, in written statements to its shareholders, $71.82x as a section 163(j) interest dividend; $10x as dividends that may be treated as qualified dividend income or as dividends eligible for the dividends received deduction; and $72.73x as interest-related dividends under section 871(k)(1)(C). Shareholder A, a domestic C corporation, meets the holding period requirements in paragraph (b)(22)(iii)(F)(4) of this section with respect to the stock of X, and receives a dividend of $8x from X on December 31, 2021.

(B) *Analysis.* X determines that $18.18x of other deductions are properly allocable to X's business interest income. X's excess section 163(j) interest income under paragraph (b)(35)(iv)(E) of this section is $71.82x ($100x business interest income − ($10x business interest expense + $18.18x other deductions allocated) = $71.82x). Thus, X may report up to $71.82x of its dividends paid on December 31, 2021, as section 163(j) interest dividends to its shareholders. X may also report up to $10x of its dividends paid on December 31, 2021, as dividends that may be treated as qualified dividend income or as dividends that are eligible for the dividends received deduction. X determines that $9.09x of interest expense and $18.18x of other deductions are properly allocable to X's qualified interest income. Therefore, X may report up to $72.73x of its dividends paid on December 31, 2021, as interest-related dividends under section 871(k)(1)(C) ($100x qualified interest income - $27.27x deductions allocated = $72.73x). A treats $1x of its $8x dividend as a dividend eligible for the dividends received deduction and no part of the dividend as an interest-related dividend under section 871(k)(1)(C). Therefore, under paragraph (b)(22)(iii)(F)(2) of this section, A may treat $7x of the section 163(j) interest dividend as interest income for purposes of section 163(j) ($8x dividend - $1x conduit amount = $7x limitation).

(36) *Section 163(j) limitation.*—The term *section 163(j) limitation* means the limit on the amount of business interest expense that a taxpayer may deduct in a taxable year under section 163(j) and § 1.163(j)-2(b).

(37) *Section 163(j) regulations.*—The term *section 163(j) regulations* means this section and §§ 1.163(j)-2 through 1.163(j)-11.

(38) *Separate return limitation year.*—The term *separate return limitation year* (SRLY) has the meaning provided in § 1.1502-1(f).

(39) *Separate return year.*—The term *separate return year* has the meaning provided in § 1.1502-1(e).

(40) *Separate tentative taxable income.*—The term *separate tentative taxable income* with respect to a taxpayer and a taxable year has the meaning provided in § 1.1502-12, but for this purpose computed without regard to the application of the section 163(j) limitation and with the addition of the adjustments made in paragraph (b)(43)(ii) of this section and § 1.163(j)-4(d)(2)(iv).

(41) *Tax-exempt corporation.*—The term *tax-exempt corporation* means any tax-exempt organization that is organized as a corporation.

(42) *Tax-exempt organization.*—The term *tax-exempt organization* means any entity subject to tax under section 511.

(43) *Tentative taxable income.*—(i) *In general.*—The term *tentative taxable income*, with respect to a taxpayer and a taxable year, generally is determined in the same manner as taxable income under section 63 but for this purpose computed without regard to the application of the section 163(j) limitation. Tentative taxable income is computed without regard to any disallowed business interest expense carryforwards.

(ii) [Reserved]

(iii) *Special rules for defining tentative taxable income.*—(A) For special rules defining the tentative taxable income of a RIC or REIT, see § 1.163(j)-4(b)(4)(ii).

(B) For special rules defining the tentative taxable income of consolidated groups, see § 1.163(j)-4(d)(2)(iv).

(C) For special rules defining the tentative taxable income of a partnership, see § 1.163(j)-6(d)(1).

(D) For special rules defining the tentative taxable income of an S corporation, see § 1.163(j)-6(l)(3).

(E) For special rules clarifying that tentative taxable income takes sections 461(l), 465, and 469 into account, see § 1.163(j)-3(b)(4).

(F) For special rules clarifying that tentative taxable income takes sections 461(l), 465, and 469 into account, see § 1.163(j)-3(b)(4).

(G) For special rules clarifying that tentative taxable income takes sections 461(l), 465, and 469 into account, see § 1.163(j)-3(b)(4).

(44) *Trade or business.*—(i) *In general.*—The term *trade or business* means a trade or business within the meaning of section 162.

(ii) *Excepted trade or business.*—The term *excepted trade or business* means the trade or business of performing services as an employee, an electing real property trade or business, an electing farming business, or an excepted regulated utility trade or business. For additional rules related to excepted trades or businesses, including elections made under section 163(j)(7)(B) and (C), see § 1.163(j)-9.

(iii) *Non-excepted trade or business.*—The term *non-excepted trade or business* means any trade or business that is not an excepted trade or business.

(45) *Unadjusted basis.*—The term *unadjusted basis* means the basis as determined under section 1012 or other applicable sections of chapter 1 of subtitle A of the Code, including subchapters O (relating to gain or loss on dispositions of property), C (relating to corporate distributions and adjustments), K (relating to partners and partnerships), and P (relating to capital gains and losses) of the Code. Unadjusted basis is determined without regard to any adjustments described in section 1016(a)(2) or (3), any adjustments for tax credits claimed by the taxpayer (for example, under section 50(c)), or any adjustments for any portion of the basis that the taxpayer has elected to treat as an expense (for example, under section 179, 179B, or 179C).

(46) *United States shareholder.*—The term *United States shareholder* has the meaning provided in section 951(b).

(c) *Applicability date.*—(1) *In general.*—Except as provided in paragraphs (c)(2), (3), and (4) of this section, this section applies to taxable years beginning on or after November 13, 2020. However, taxpayers and their related parties, within the meaning of sections 267(b) and 707(b)(1), may choose to apply the rules of this section to a taxable year beginning after December 31, 2017, and before November 13, 2020 so long as the taxpayers and their related parties consistently apply the rules of the section 163(j) regulations, and, if applicable, §§1.263A-9, 1.263A-15, 1.381(c)(20)-1, 1.382-1, 1.382-2, 1.382-5, 1.382-6, 1.383-0, 1.383-1, 1.469-9, 1.469-11, 1.704-1, 1.882-5, 1.1362-3, 1.1368-1, 1.1377-1, 1.1502-13, 1.1502-21, 1.1502-36, 1.1502-79, 1.1502-91 through 1.1502-99 (to the extent they effectuate the rules of §§1.382-2, 1.382-5, 1.382-6, and 1.383-1), and 1.1504-4, to that taxable year. Additionally, taxpayers and their related parties within the meaning of sections 267(b) and 707(b)(1), otherwise relying on the notice of proposed rulemaking that was published on December 28, 2018, in the Federal Register (83 FR 67490) in its entirety under §1.163(j)-1(c), may alternatively choose to follow §1.163(j)-1(b)(1)(iii), rather than proposed §1.163(j)-1(b)(1)(iii).

(2) *Anti-avoidance rules.*—The anti-avoidance rules in paragraph (b)(22)(iv) of this section apply to transactions entered into on or after September 14, 2020.

(3) *Swaps with significant nonperiodic payments.*—(i) *In general.*—Except as provided in paragraph (c)(3)(ii) of this section, the rules provided in paragraph (b)(22)(ii) of this section apply to notional principal contracts entered into on or after September 14, 2021. However, taxpayers may choose to apply the rules provided in paragraph (b)(22)(ii) of this section to notional principal contracts entered into before September 14, 2021.

(ii) *Anti-avoidance rule.*—The anti-avoidance rules in paragraph (b)(22)(iv) of this section (applied without regard to the references to paragraph (b)(22)(ii) of this section) apply to a notional principal contract entered into on or after September 14, 2020.

(4) *Paragraphs (b)(1)(iv)(A)(2) through (4), (B) through (G), (b)(22)(iii)(F), and (b)(35).*—Paragraphs (b)(1)(iv)(A)(2) through (4), (b)(1)(iv)(B) through (G), (b)(22)(iii)(F), and (b)(35) of this section apply to taxable years beginning on or after March 22, 2021. Taxpayers and their related parties, within the meaning of sections 267(b) (determined without regard to section 267(c)(3)) and 707(b)(1), may choose to apply the rules in paragraphs (b)(1)(iv)(A)(2) through (4), (b)(1)(iv) (B) through (G), (b)(22)(iii)(F), and (b)(35) of this section to a taxable year beginning after December 31, 2017, and before March 22, 2021, provided that those taxpayers and their related parties consistently apply all of the rules in the section 163(j) regulations contained in T.D. 9905, (§§1.163(j)-0 through 1.163(j)-11, effective November 13, 2020) as modified by T.D. 9943 (effective January 13, 2021), and, if applicable, §§1.263A-9, 1.263A-15, 1.381(c)(20)-1, 1.382-1, 1.382-2, 1.382-5, 1.382-6, 1.382-7, 1.383-0, 1.383-1, 1.469-9, 1.469-11, 1.704-1, 1.882-5, 1.1362-3, 1.1368-1, 1.1377-1, 1.1502-13, 1.1502-21, 1.1502-36, 1.1502-79, 1.1502-91 through 1.1502-99 (to the extent they effectuate the rules of §§1.382-2, 1.382-5, 1.382-6, and 1.383-1), and 1.1504-4 contained in T.D. 9905 as modified by T.D. 9943, to that taxable year and all subsequent taxable years. [Reg. §1.163(j)-1.]

☐ [*T.D. 9905, 9-3-2020. Amended by T.D. 9943, 1-13-2021.*]

§1.163(j)-2. Deduction for business interest expense limited.—(a) *Overview.*—This section provides general rules regarding the section 163(j) limitation. Paragraph (b) of this section provides rules regarding the basic computation of the section 163(j) limitation. Paragraph (c) of this section provides rules for disallowed business interest expense carryforwards. Paragraph (d) of this section provides rules regarding the small business exemption from the section 163(j) limitation. Paragraph (e) of this section that is part of provides rules regarding real estate mortgage investment conduits (REMICs). Paragraph (f) of this section provides rules regarding the calculation of ATI with respect to certain beneficiaries. Paragraph (g) of this section provides rules regarding tax-exempt organizations. Paragraph (h) of this section provides examples illustrating the application of this section. Paragraph (i) of this section is reserved. Paragraph (j) of this section provides an anti-avoidance rule.

(b) *General rule.*—(1) *In general.*—Except as otherwise provided in this section or in §§1.163(j)-3 through 1.163(j)-11, the amount allowed as a deduction for business interest expense for the taxable year cannot exceed the sum of—

(i) The taxpayer's business interest income for the taxable year;

(ii) 30 percent of the taxpayer's ATI for the taxable year, or zero if the taxpayer's ATI for the taxable year is less than zero; and

(iii) The taxpayer's floor plan financing interest expense for the taxable year.

(2) *50 percent ATI limitation for taxable years beginning in 2019 or 2020.*—(i) *In general.*—Except as otherwise provided in section 163(j)(10) and paragraph (b)(2) of this section, for any taxable year beginning in 2019 or 2020, paragraph (b)(1)(ii) of this section is applied by substituting 50 percent for 30 percent. The 50 percent ATI limitation does not apply to partnerships for taxable years beginning in 2019. Further, for a partnership taxable year beginning in 2020 for which an election out of section 163(j)(10)(A)(i) has not been made, §1.163(j)-6(f)(2)(xi) is applied by substituting two for ten-thirds when grossing up each partner's final ATI capacity excess amount.

(ii) *Election out of the 50 percent ATI limitation.*—A taxpayer may elect to not have paragraph (b)(2)(i) of this section apply for any taxable year beginning in 2019 or 2020. In the case of a partnership, the election must be made by the partnership and may be made only for taxable years beginning in 2020.

(3) *Election to use 2019 ATI in 2020.*—(i) *In general.*—Subject to paragraph (b)(3)(ii), a taxpayer may elect to use the taxpayer's ATI for the last taxable year beginning in 2019 (2019 ATI) as the ATI for any taxable year beginning in 2020.

(ii) *Short taxable years.*—If an election is made under paragraph (b)(3)(i) of this section for a taxable year beginning in 2020 that is a short taxable year, the ATI for such taxable year is equal to the amount that bears the same ratio to 2019 ATI as the number of months in the short taxable year bears to 12.

(iii) *Transactions to which section 381 applies.*—For purposes of the election described in paragraph (b)(3)(i) of this section, and subject to the limitation in paragraph (b)(3)(ii) of this section, the 2019 ATI of the acquiring corporation in a transaction to which section 381 applies equals the amount of the acquiring corporation's ATI for its last taxable year beginning in 2019.

(iv) *Consolidated groups.*—For purposes of the election described in paragraph (b)(3)(i) of this section, and subject to the limitation in paragraph (b)(3)(ii) of this section, the 2019 ATI of a consolidated group equals the amount of the consolidated group's ATI for its last taxable year beginning in 2019.

(4) *Time and manner of making or revoking the elections.*—The rules and procedures regarding the time and manner of making, or revoking, an election under paragraphs (b)(2) and (3) of this section are provided in Revenue Procedure 2020-22, 2020-18 I.R.B. 745, or in other guidance that may be issued (see §§601.601(d) and 601.602 of this chapter).

(c) *Disallowed business interest expense carryforward.*—(1) *In general.*—Any business interest expense disallowed under paragraph (b) of this section, or any disallowed disqualified interest that is properly allocable to a non-excepted trade or business under §1.163(j)-10, is carried forward to the succeeding taxable year as a disallowed business interest expense carryforward, and is therefore business interest expense that is subject to paragraph (b) of this section in such succeeding taxable year. Disallowed business interest expense carryforwards are not re-allocated between non-excepted and excepted trades or businesses in a succeeding taxable year. Instead, the carryforwards continue to be treated as allocable to a non-excepted trade or business. See § 1.163(j)-10(c)(4).

(2) *Coordination with small business exemption.*—If disallowed business interest expense is carried forward under the rules of paragraph (c)(1) of this section to a taxable year in which the small business exemption in paragraph (d) of this section applies to the taxpayer, then the general rule in paragraph (b) of this section does not apply to limit the deduction of the disallowed business interest expense carryforward of the taxpayer in that taxable year. See § 1.163(j)-6(m)(3) for rules applicable to the treatment of excess business interest expense from a partnership that is not subject to section 163(j) in a succeeding taxable year, and see § 1.163(j)-6(m)(4) for rules applicable to S corporations with disallowed business interest expense carryforwards that are not subject to section 163(j) in a succeeding taxable year.

(3) *Cross-references.*—(i) For special rules regarding disallowed business interest expense carryforwards for taxpayers that are C corporations, including members of a consolidated group, see § 1.163(j)-5.

(ii) For special rules regarding disallowed business interest expense carryforwards of S corporations, see § § 1.163(j)-5(b)(2) and 1.163(j)-6(l)(5).

(iii) For special rules regarding disallowed business interest expense carryforwards from partnerships, see § 1.163(j)-6.

(iv)-(v) [Reserved]

(d) *Small business exemption.*—(1) *Exemption.*—The general rule in paragraph (b) of this section does not apply to any taxpayer, other than a tax shelter as defined in section 448(d)(3), in any taxable year in which the taxpayer meets the gross receipts test of section 448(c) and the regulations in this part under section 448 of the Code for the taxable year. See § 1.163(j)-9(b) for elections available under section 163(j)(7)(B) and 163(j)(7)(C) for real property trades or businesses or farming businesses that also may be exempt small businesses. See § 1.163(j)-6(m) for rules applicable to partnerships and S corporations not subject to section 163(j).

(2) *Application of the gross receipts test.*—(i) *In general.*—In the case of any taxpayer that is not a corporation or a partnership, and except as provided in paragraphs (d)(2)(ii), (iii), and (iv) of this section, the gross receipts test of section 448(c) and the regulations in this part under section 448 of the Code are applied in the same manner as if such taxpayer were a corporation or partnership.

(ii) *Gross receipts of individuals.*—Except as provided in paragraph (d)(2)(iii) of this section (regarding partnership and S corporation interests), an individual taxpayer's gross receipts include all items specified as gross receipts in regulations under section 448(c), whether or not derived in the ordinary course of the taxpayer's trade or business. For purposes of section 163(j), an individual taxpayer's gross receipts do not include inherently personal amounts, including, but not limited to, personal injury awards or settlements with respect to an injury of the individual taxpayer, disability benefits, Social Security benefits received by the taxpayer during the taxable year, and wages received as an employee that are reported on Form W-2.

(iii) *Partners and S corporation shareholders.*—Except when the aggregation rules of section 448(c) apply, each partner in a partnership includes a share of partnership gross receipts in proportion to such partner's distributive share (as determined under section 704) of items of gross income that were taken into account by the partnership under section 703. Additionally, each shareholder in an S corporation includes a pro rata share of S corporation gross receipts.

(iv) *Tax-exempt organizations.*—For purposes of section 163(j), the gross receipts of a tax-exempt organization include only gross receipts taken into account in determining its unrelated business taxable income.

(3) *Determining a syndicate's loss amount.*—For purposes of section 163(j), losses allocated under section 1256(e)(3)(B) and § 1.448-1T(b)(3) are determined without regard to section 163(j). See also § 1.1256(e)-2(b).

(e) *REMICs.*—For the treatment of interest expense by a REMIC as defined in section 860D, see § 1.860C-2(b)(2)(ii).

(f) *Trusts.*—(i) *Calculation of ATI with respect to certain trusts and estates.*—The ATI of a trust or a decedent's estate taxable under section 641 is computed without regard to deductions under sections 642(c), 651, and 661.

(ii) *Calculation of ATI with respect to certain beneficiaries.*—The ATI of a beneficiary (including a tax-exempt beneficiary) of a trust or a decedent's estate is reduced by any income (including any distributable net income) received from the trust or estate by the beneficiary to the extent such income was necessary to permit a deduction under section 163(j)(1)(B) and § 1.163(j)-2(b) for any business interest expense of the trust or estate that was in excess of any business interest income of the trust or estate.

(g) *Tax-exempt organizations.*—Except as provided in paragraph (d) of this section, the section 163(j) limitation applies to tax-exempt organizations for purposes of computing their unrelated business taxable income under section 512. For rules on determining the gross receipts of a tax-exempt organization for purposes of the small business exemption, see paragraph (d)(2)(iv) of this section. For special rules applicable to tax-exempt beneficiaries of a trust or a decedent's estate, see § 1.163(j)-2(f). For special rules applicable to tax-exempt corporations, see § 1.163(j)-4. For special allocation rules applicable to tax-exempt organizations, see § 1.163(j)-10(a)(5).

(h) *Examples.*—The examples in this paragraph (h) illustrate the application of section 163(j) and the provisions of this section. Unless otherwise indicated, X and Y are domestic C corporations; C and D are U.S. resident individuals not subject to any foreign income tax; PRS is a domestic partnership with partners who are all individuals; all taxpayers use a calendar taxable year; the exemption for certain small businesses in section 163(j)(3) and paragraph (d) of this section does not apply; and the interest expense would be deductible but for section 163(j).

(1) *Example 1: Limitation on business interest expense deduction.*—(i) *Facts.* During its taxable year ending December 31, 2021, X has ATI of $100x. X has business interest expense of $50x, which includes $10x of floor plan financing interest expense, and business interest income of $20x.

(ii) *Analysis.* For the 2021 taxable year, X's section 163(j) limitation is $60x, which is the sum of its business interest income ($20x), plus 30 percent of its ATI ($100x x 30 percent = $30x), plus its floor plan financing interest expense ($10x). See § 1.163(j)-2(b). Because X's business interest expense ($50x) does not exceed X's section 163(j) limitation ($60x), X can deduct all $50x of its business interest expense for the 2021 taxable year.

(2) *Example 2: Carryforward of business interest expense.*—(i) *Facts.* The facts are the same as in *Example 1* in paragraph (h)(1)(i) of this section, except that X has $80x of business interest expense, which includes $10x of floor plan financing interest expense.

(ii) *Analysis.* As in *Example 1* in paragraph (h)(1)(ii) of this section, X's section 163(j) limitation is $60x. Because X's business interest expense ($80x) exceeds X's section 163(j) limitation ($60x), X may only deduct $60x of its business interest expense for the 2021 taxable year, and the remaining $20x of its business interest expense will be carried forward to the succeeding taxable year as a disallowed business interest expense carryforward. See § 1.163(j)-2(c).

(3) *Example 3: ATI computation.*—(i) *Facts.* During the 2020 taxable year, Y has tentative taxable income of $30x, which is determined without regard to the application of the section 163(j) limitation on business interest expense. Y's tentative taxable income includes the following: $20x of business interest income; $50x of business interest expense, which includes $10x of floor plan financing interest expense; $25x of net operating loss deduction under section 172; and $15x of depreciation under section 167, of which $10x is capitalized to inventory under section 263A. Of the $10x capitalized to inventory, only $7x is recovered through cost of goods sold during the 2020 taxable year and $3x remains in ending inventory at the end of the 2020 taxable year. The $3x of ending inventory is recovered through cost of goods sold during the 2021 taxable year. Y also has a disallowed business interest expense carryforward from the prior year of $8x.

(ii) *Analysis.* (A) For purposes of determining the section 163(j) limitation for 2020, Y's disallowed business interest expense carryforward is not taken into account in determining tentative taxable income or ATI. Y's ATI is $90x, calculated as follows:

Table 1 to paragraph (h)(3)(ii)(A)

Tentative taxable income:	$30x
Less:	
Floor plan financing interest	10x
Business interest income	*20x*
	0x

(B) Plus:

Table 2 to paragraph (h)(3)(ii)(B)

Business interest expense	$50x
Net operating loss deduction	25x
Depreciation	*15x*
ATI	$90x

(C)For Y's 2021 taxable year, the $3x of ending inventory that is recovered through cost of goods sold in 2021 is not added back to tentative taxable income (TTI) in determining ATI because it was already included as an addback in ATI in Y's 2020 taxable year. See § 1.163(j)-1(b)(1)(iii).

(4) *Example 4: Floor plan financing interest expense.*—(i) *Facts.* C is the sole proprietor of an automobile dealership that uses a cash method of accounting. In the 2021 taxable year, C paid $30x of interest on a loan that was obtained to purchase sedans for sale by the dealership. The indebtedness is secured by the sedans purchased with the loan proceeds. In addition, C paid $20x of interest on a loan, secured by the dealership's office equipment, which C obtained to purchase convertibles for sale by the dealership.

(ii) *Analysis.* For the purpose of calculating C's section 163(j) limitation, only the $30x of interest paid on the loan to purchase the sedans is floor plan financing interest expense. The $20x paid on the loan to purchase the convertibles is not floor plan financing interest expense for purposes of section 163(j) because the indebtedness was not secured by the inventory of convertibles. However, because under § 1.163(j)-10 the interest paid on the loan to purchase the convertibles is properly allocable to C's dealership trade or business, and because floor plan financing interest expense is also business interest expense, C has $50x of business interest expense for the 2021 taxable year.

(5) *Example 5: Interest not properly allocable to non-excepted trade or business.*—(i) *Facts.* The facts are the same as in *Example 4* in paragraph (h)(4)(i) of this section, except that the $20x of interest C pays is on acquisition indebtedness obtained to purchase C's personal residence and not to purchase convertibles for C's dealership trade or business.

(ii) *Analysis.* Because the $20x of interest expense is not properly allocable to a non-excepted trade or business, and therefore is not business interest expense, C's only business interest expense is the $30x that C pays on the loan used to purchase sedans for sale in C's dealership trade or business. C deducts the $20x of interest related to his residence under the rules of section 163(h), without regard to section 163(j).

(6) *Example 6: Small business exemption.*—(i) *Facts.* During the 2021 taxable year, D, the sole proprietor of a trade or business reported on Schedule C, has interest expense properly allocable to that trade or business. D does not conduct an electing real property trade or business or an electing farming business. D also earns gross income from providing services as an employee that is reported on a Form W-2. Under section 448(c) and the regulations in this part under section 448, D has average annual gross receipts of $21 million, including $1 million of wages in each of the three prior taxable years and $2 million of income from investments not related to a trade or business in each of the three prior taxable years. Also, in each of the three prior taxable years, D received $5 million in periodic payments of compensatory damages awarded in a personal injury lawsuit.

(ii) *Analysis.* Section 163(j) does not apply to D for the taxable year, because D qualifies for the small business exemption under § 1.163(j)-2(d). The wages that D receives as an employee and the compensatory damages that D received from D's personal injury lawsuit are not gross receipts, as provided in § 1.163(j)-2(d)(2)(ii). D may deduct all of its business interest expense for the 2021 taxable year without regard to section 163(j).

(7) *Example 7: Partnership with excess business interest expense qualifies for the small business exemption in a succeeding taxable year.*—(i) *Facts.* X and Y are equal partners in partnership PRS. In addition to being partners in PRS, X and Y each operate their own sole proprietorships. For the taxable year ending December 31, 2021, PRS is subject to section 163(j) and has excess business interest expense of $10x. For the taxable year ending December 31, 2022, PRS has $40x of business interest expense, and X and Y have $20x of business interest expense from their respective sole proprietorships. For the taxable year ending December 31, 2022, PRS and Y qualify for the small business exemption under § 1.163(j)-2(d), while X is subject to section 163(j) and has a section 163(j) limitation of $22x.

(ii)*Partnership-level analysis.* For the 2021 taxable year, PRS allocates the $10x of excess business interest expense equally to X and Y ($5x each). See § 1.163(j)-6(f)(2). For the 2022 taxable year, section 163(j) does not apply to PRS because PRS qualifies for the small business exemption. As a result, none of PRS's $40x of business interest expense for the 2022 taxable year is subject to the section 163(j) limitation at the partnership level.

(iii) *Partner-level analysis.* For the 2022 taxable year, each partner treats its $5x of excess business interest expense from PRS as paid or accrued in that year. See § 1.163(j)-6(m)(3). This amount becomes business interest expense that each partner must subject to its own section 163(j) limitation, if any. With this $5x, each partner has $25x of business interest expense for the 2022 taxable year ($20x from its sole proprietorship, plus $5x of excess business interest expense treated as paid or accrued in the 2020 taxable year). X deducts $22x of its business interest expense pursuant to its section 163(j) limitation and carries forward the remainder ($3x) as a disallowed business interest expense carryforward to the taxable year ending December 31, 2023. Y is not subject to section 163(j) because Y qualifies for the small business exemption. Y therefore deducts all $25x of its business interest expense for the 2022 taxable year.

(8) *Example 8: Aggregation of gross receipts.*—(i) *Facts.* X and Y are domestic C corporations under common control, within the meaning of section 52(a) and § 1.52-1(b). X's only trade or business is a farming business described in § 1.263A-4(a)(4). During the taxable year ending December 31, 2020, X has average annual gross receipts under section 448(c) of $6 million. During the same taxable year, Y has average annual gross receipts under section 448(c) of $21 million.

(ii) *Analysis.* Because X and Y are under common control, they must aggregate gross receipts for purposes of section 448(c) and the small business exemption in § 1.163(j)-2(d). See section 448(c)(2). Therefore, X and Y are both considered to have $27 million in average annual gross receipts for 2020. X and Y must separately apply section 163(j) to determine any limitation on the deduction for business interest expense. Assuming X otherwise meets the requirements in § 1.163(j)-9 in 2020, X may elect for its farming business to be an excepted trade or business.

(i) [Reserved]

(j) *Anti-avoidance rule.*—(1) *In general.*—Arrangements entered into with a principal purpose of avoiding the rules of section 163(j) or the section 163(j) regulations, including the use of multiple entities to avoid the gross receipts test of section 448(c), may be disregarded or recharacterized by the Commissioner of the IRS to the extent necessary to carry out the purposes of section 163(j).

(2) *Examples.*—The examples in this paragraph (j)(2) illustrate the application of this section.

(i) *Example 1.*—(A) *Facts.* Individual A operates an excepted trade or business (Business X) and a non-excepted trade or business (Business Y). With a principal purpose of avoiding the rules of section 163(j) or the regulations in this part under section 163(j) of the Code, A contributes Business X to newly-formed C corporation B in exchange for stock; A then causes B to borrow funds from a third party and distributes a portion of the borrowed funds to A for use in Business Y. B takes the position that its interest payments on the debt are not subject to the section 163(j) limitation because B is engaged solely in an excepted trade or business.

(B) *Analysis.* A has entered into an arrangement with a principal purpose of avoiding the rules of section 163(j) or the regulations in this part under section 163(j). Thus, under paragraph (j)(1) of this section, the Commissioner of the IRS may disregard or recharacterize this transaction to the extent necessary to carry out the purposes of section 163(j). In this case, payments of interest on the debt may be recharacterized as payments of interest properly allocable to a non-excepted trade or business subject to the section 163(j) limitation.

(ii) *Example 2.*—(A) *Facts.* Partnership UTP has two non-excepted trades or businesses. Business A has gross income of $1000x and gross deductions of $200x. Business B has gross income of $100x and gross deductions of $600x. With a principal purpose of avoiding the rules in section 163(j) or the regulations in this part under section 163(j), UTP and a partner of UTP form partnership LTP and UTP contributes Business B to LTP prior to borrowing funds. UTP takes the position that it does not take its share of LTP gross deductions into account when computing its ATI.

(B) *Analysis.* UTP has entered into an arrangement with a principal purpose of avoiding the rules of section 163(j) or the regulations in this part under section 163(j). Thus, under paragraph (j)(1) of this section, the Commissioner of the IRS may disregard or recharacterize this transaction to the extent necessary to carry out the purposes of section 163(j). In this case, UTP's share of gross deductions from LTP may be recharacterized as gross deductions incurred directly by UTP solely for purposes of computing UTP's ATI.

(k) *Applicability dates.*—(1) *In general.*—This section applies to taxable years beginning on or after November 13, 2020. However, taxpayers and their related parties, within the meaning of sections 267(b) and 707(b)(1), may choose to apply the rules of this section to a taxable year beginning after December 31, 2017, so long as the taxpayers and their related parties consistently apply the rules of the section 163(j) regulations, and, if applicable, §§1.263A-9, 1.263A-15, 1.381(c)(20)-1, 1.382-1, 1.382-2, 1.382-5, 1.382-6, 1.382-7, 1.383-0, 1.383-1, 1.469-9, 1.469-11, 1.704-1, 1.882-5, 1.1362-3, 1.1368-1, 1.1377-1, 1.1502-13, 1.1502-21, 1.1502-36, 1.1502-79, 1.1502-91 through 1.1502-99 (to the extent they effectuate the rules of §§1.382-2, 1.382-5, 1.382-6, and 1.383-1), and 1.1504-4, to that taxable year.

(2) *Paragraphs (b)(3)(iii), (b)(3)(iv), and (d)(3).*—Paragraphs (b)(3)(iii) and (iv) and (d)(3) of this section apply to taxable years beginning on or after March 22, 2021. However, taxpayers and their related parties, within the meaning of sections 267(b) (determined without regard to section 267(c)(3)) and 707(b)(1), may choose to apply the rules in paragraphs (b)(3)(iii), (b)(3)(iv), and (d)(3) of this section to a taxable year beginning after December 31, 2017, and before March 22, 2021, provided that those taxpayers and their related parties consistently apply all of the rules in paragraphs (b)(3)(iii) and (iv) of this section and the rules in the section 163(j) regulations contained in T.D. 9905 (§§1.163(j)-0 through 1.163(j)-11, effective November 13, 2020) as modified by T.D. 9943, (effective January 13, 2021), and, if applicable, §§1.263A-9, 1.263A-15, 1.381(c)(20)-1, 1.382-1, 1.382-2, 1.382-5, 1.382-6, 1.382-7, 1.383-0, 1.383-1, 1.469-9, 1.469-11, 1.704-1, 1.882-5, 1.1362-3, 1.1368-1, 1.1377-1, 1.1502-13, 1.1502-21, 1.1502-36, 1.1502-79, 1.1502-91 through 1.1502-99 (to the extent they effectuate the rules of §§1.382-2, 1.382-5, 1.382-6, and 1.383-1), and 1.1504-4 contained in T.D. 9905 as modified by T.D. 9943, for that taxable year and for each subsequent taxable year. [Reg. §1.163(j)-2.]

☐ [*T.D. 9905, 9-3-2020. Amended by T.D. 9943, 1-13-2021.*]

§1.163(j)-3. Relationship of the section 163(j) limitation to other provisions affecting interest.—

* * *

(b) *Coordination of section 163(j) with certain other provisions.*—

* * *

(2) *Disallowed interest provisions.*—For purposes of section 163(j), business interest expense does not include interest expense that is permanently disallowed as a deduction under another provision of the Code, such as in section 163(e)(5)(A)(i), (f), (l), or (m), or section 264(a), 265, 267A, or 279.

(3) *Deferred interest provisions.*—Other than sections 461(l), 465, and 469, Code provisions that defer the deductibility of interest expense, such as section 163(e)(3) and (e)(5)(A)(ii), 267(a)(2) and (3), 1277, or 1282, apply before the application of section 163(j).

* * *

[Reg. §1.163(j)-3.]

☐ [*T.D. 9905, 9-3-2020.*]

§1.163(j)-4. General rules applicable to C corporations (including REITs, RICs, and members of consolidated groups) and tax-exempt corporations.—

* * *

(b) *Characterization of items of income, gain, deduction, or loss.*—

* * *

(3) *Investment interest, investment income, investment expenses, and certain other tax items of a partnership with a C corporation partner.*—

* * *

(iv) *Treatment of deemed inclusions of a domestic partnership that are not allocable to any trade or business.*—If a United States shareholder that is a domestic partnership includes amounts in gross income under sections 951(a) or 951A(a) that are not properly allocable to a trade or business of the domestic partnership, then, notwithstanding paragraph (b)(3)(i) of this section, to the extent a C corporation partner, including an indirect partner in the case of tiered partnerships, takes such amounts into account as a distributive share in accordance with section 702 and §1.702-1(a)(8)(ii), the C corporation partner may not treat such amounts as properly allocable to a trade or business of the C corporation partner.

* * *

(c) *Effect on earnings and profits.*—(1) *In general.*—In the case of a taxpayer that is a domestic C corporation, except as otherwise provided in paragraph (c)(2) of this section, the disallowance and carryforward under §1.163(j)-2 (and §1.163(j)-5, in the case of a taxpayer that is a consolidated group member) of a deduction for business interest expense of the taxpayer or of a partnership in which the taxpayer is a partner does not affect whether or when the business interest expense reduces the taxpayer's earnings and profits. In the case of a foreign corporation, the disallowance and carryforward of a deduction for the corporation's business interest expense under §1.163(j)-2 does not affect whether and when such business interest expense reduces the corporation's earnings and profits. Thus, for example, if a United States person has elected under section 1295 to treat a passive foreign investment company (as defined in section 1297) (PFIC) as a qualified electing fund, then the disallowance and carryforward of a deduction for the PFIC's business interest expense under §1.163(j)-2 does not affect whether or when such business interest expense reduces the PFIC's earnings and profits.

* * *

[Reg. §1.163(j)-4.]

☐ [*T.D. 9905, 9-3-2020.*]

§1.163(j)-7. Application of the section 163(j) limitation to foreign corporations and United States shareholders.—(a) *Overview.*—This section provides rules for the application of section 163(j) to relevant foreign corporations and United States shareholders of relevant foreign corporations. Paragraph (b) of this section provides the general rule regarding the application of section 163(j) to a relevant foreign corporation. Paragraph (c) of this section provides rules for applying section 163(j) to CFC group members of a CFC group. Paragraph (d) of this section provides rules for determining a specified group and specified group members. Paragraph (e) of this section provides rules and procedures for treating a specified group member as a CFC group member and for determining a CFC group. Paragraph (f) of this section provides rules regarding the treatment of a CFC group member that has ECI. Paragraph (g) of this section provides rules concerning the computation of ATI of an applicable CFC. Paragraph (h) of this section provides a safe harbor that exempts certain standalone applicable CFCs and CFC groups from the application of section 163(j) for a taxable year. Paragraphs (i) and (j) of this section are reserved. Paragraph (k) of this section provides definitions that apply for purposes of this section (see also §1.163(j)-1 for additional definitions). Paragraph (l) of this section provides examples illustrating the application of this section.

(b) *General rule regarding the application of section 163(j) to relevant foreign corporations.*—Except as otherwise provided in this section, section 163(j) and the section 163(j) regulations apply to determine the deductibility of a relevant foreign corporation's business interest expense for purposes of computing its taxable income for U.S. income tax purposes (if any) in the same manner as those provisions apply to determine the deductibility of a domestic C corporation's business interest expense for purposes of computing its taxable income. See also §1.952-2. If a relevant foreign corporation is a direct or indirect partner in a partnership, see §1.163(j)-6 (concerning the application of section 163(j) to partnerships).

(c) *Application of section 163(j) to CFC group members of a CFC group.*—(1) *Scope.*—This paragraph (c) provides rules for applying section 163(j) to a CFC group and a CFC group member. Paragraph (c)(2) of this section provides rules for computing a single section 163(j) limitation for a specified period of a CFC group. Paragraph (c)(3) of this section provides rules for allocating a CFC group's section 163(j) limitation to CFC group members for specified taxable years. Paragraph (c)(4) of this section provides currency translation rules. Paragraph (c)(5) of this section provides special rules for specified periods beginning in 2019 or 2020.

(2) *Calculation of section 163(j) limitation for a CFC group for a specified period.*—(i) *In general.*—A single section 163(j) limitation is computed for a specified period of a CFC group. For purposes of applying section 163(j) and the section 163(j) regulations, the current-year business interest expense, disallowed business interest expense carryforwards, business interest income, floor plan financing interest expense, and ATI of a CFC group for a specified period equal the sums of each CFC group member's respective amounts for its specified taxable year with respect to the specified period. A CFC group member's current-year business interest expense, business interest income, floor plan financing interest expense, and ATI for a specified taxable year are generally determined on a separate-company basis. For purposes of determining the ATI of a CFC group, § 1.163(j)-1(b)(1)(vii) (providing that ATI cannot be less than zero) applies with respect to the ATI of the CFC group but not the ATI of any CFC group member.

(ii) *Certain transactions between CFC group members disregarded.*—Any transaction between CFC group members of a CFC group that is entered into with a principal purpose of affecting a CFC group or a CFC group member's section 163(j) limitation by increasing or decreasing a CFC group or a CFC group member's ATI or business interest income for a specified taxable year is disregarded for purposes of applying section 163(j) and the section 163(j) regulations.

(3) *Deduction of business interest expense.*—(i) *CFC group business interest expense.*—(A) *In general.*—The extent to which a CFC group member's current-year business interest expense and disallowed business interest expense carryforwards for a specified taxable year that ends with or within a specified period may be deducted under section 163(j) is determined under the rules and principles of § 1.163(j)-5(a)(2) and (b)(3)(ii), subject to the modifications described in paragraph (c)(3)(i)(B) of this section.

(B) *Modifications to relevant terms.*—For purposes of paragraph (c)(3)(i)(A) of this section, the rules and principles of § 1.163(j)-5(b)(3)(ii) are applied by—

(*1*) Replacing "§ 1.163(j)-4(d)(2)" in § 1.163(j)-5(a)(2)(ii) with "§ 1.163(j)-7(c)(2)(i)";

(*2*) Replacing the term "allocable share of the consolidated group's remaining section 163(j) limitation" with "allocable share of the CFC group's remaining section 163(j) limitation";

(*3*) Replacing the terms "consolidated group" and "group" with "CFC group";

(*4*) Replacing the term "consolidated group's remaining section 163(j) limitation" with "CFC group's remaining section 163(j) limitation";

(*5*) Replacing the term "consolidated return year" with "specified period";

(*6*) Replacing the term "current year" or "current-year" with "current specified period" or "specified taxable year with respect to the current specified period," as the context requires;

(*7*) Replacing the term "member" with "CFC group member"; and

(*8*) Replacing the term "taxable year" with "specified taxable year with respect to a specified period."

(ii) *Carryforwards treated as attributable to the same taxable year.*—For purposes of applying the principles of § 1.163(j)-5(b)(3)(ii), as required under paragraph (c)(3)(i) of this section, CFC group members' disallowed business interest expense carryforwards that arose in specified taxable years with respect to the same specified period are treated as disallowed business interest expense carryforwards from taxable years ending on the same date and are deducted on a pro rata basis, under the principles of § 1.163(j)-5(b)(3)(ii)(C)(3), pursuant to paragraph (c)(3)(i) of this section.

(iii) *Multiple specified taxable years of a CFC group member with respect to a specified period.*—If a CFC group member has more than one specified taxable year (each year, an *applicable specified taxable year*) with respect to a single specified period of a CFC group, then all the applicable specified taxable years are taken into account for purposes of applying the principles of § 1.163(j)-5(b)(3)(ii), as required under paragraph (c)(3)(i) of this section, with respect to the specified period. The portion of the section 163(j) limitation allocable to disallowed business interest expense carryforwards of the CFC group member that arose in taxable years before the first applicable specified taxable year is prorated among the applicable specified taxable years in proportion to the number of days in each applicable specified taxable year.

(iv) *Limitation on pre-group disallowed business interest expense carryforward.*—(A) *General rule.*—(*1*) *CFC group member pre-group disallowed business interest expense carryforward.*—This paragraph (c)(3)(iv) applies to pre-group disallowed business interest expense carryforwards of a CFC group member. The amount of the pre-group disallowed business interest expense carryforwards described in the preceding sentence that may be included in any CFC group member's business interest expense deduction for any specified taxable year under this paragraph (c)(3) may not exceed the aggregate section 163(j) limitation for all specified periods of the CFC group, determined by reference only to the CFC group member's items of income, gain, deduction, and loss, and reduced (including below zero) by the CFC group member's business interest expense (including disallowed business interest expense carryforwards) taken into account as a deduction by the CFC group member in all specified taxable years in which the CFC group member has continuously been a CFC group member of the CFC group *(cumulative section 163(j) pre-group carryforward limitation)*.

(*2*) *Subgrouping.*—In the case of a pre-group disallowed business interest expense carryforward, a pre-group subgroup is composed of the CFC group member with the pre-group disallowed business interest expense carryforward (the *loss member*) and each other CFC group member of the loss member's CFC group (the *current group*) that was a member of the CFC group in which the pre-group disallowed business interest expense carryforward arose and joined the specified group of the current group at the same time as the loss member. A CFC group member that is a member of a pre-group subgroup remains a member of the pre-group subgroup until its first taxable year during which it ceases to be a member of the same specified group as the loss member. For purposes of this paragraph (c), the rules and principles of § 1.163(j)-5(d)(1)(B) apply to a pre-group subgroup as if the pre-group subgroup were a SRLY subgroup.

(*3*) *Transition rule.*—Solely for purposes of paragraph (c)(3)(iv)(A)(*2*) of this section, a CFC group includes a group of applicable CFCs for which a CFC group election was made under guidance under section 163(j) published on December 28, 2018. Therefore, if the requirements of paragraph (c)(3)(iv)(A)(*2*) of this section are satisfied, a group of applicable CFCs described in the preceding sentence may be treated as a pre-group subgroup.

(B) *Deduction of pre-group disallowed business interest expense carryforwards.*—Notwithstanding paragraph (c)(3)(iv)(A)(*1*) of this section, pre-group disallowed business interest expense carryforwards are available for deduction by a CFC group member in its specified taxable year only to the extent the CFC group has remaining section 163(j) limitation for the specified period after the deduction of current-year business interest expense and disallowed business interest expense carryforwards from earlier taxable years that are permitted to be deducted in specified taxable years of CFC group members with respect to the specified period. See paragraph (c)(3)(i) of this section and § 1.163(j)-5(b)(3)(ii)(A). Pre-group disallowed business interest expense carryforwards are deducted on a pro rata basis (under the principles of paragraph (c)(3)(i) of this section and § 1.163(j)-5(b)(3)(ii)(C)(*4*)) with other disallowed business interest expense carryforwards from taxable years ending on the same date.

(4) *Currency translation.*—For purposes of applying this paragraph (c), items of a CFC group member are translated into a single currency for the CFC group and back to the functional currency of the CFC group member using the average exchange rate for the CFC group member's specified taxable year. The single currency for the CFC group may be the U.S. dollar or the functional currency of a plurality of the CFC group members.

(5) *Special rule for specified periods beginning in 2019 or 2020.*—(i) *50 percent ATI limitation applies to a specified period of a CFC group.*—In the case of a CFC group, § 1.163(j)-2(b)(2) (including the election under § 1.163(j)-2(b)(2)(ii)) applies to a specified period of the CFC group beginning in 2019 or 2020, rather than to a specified taxable year of a CFC group member. An election under § 1.163(j)-2(b)(2)(ii) for a specified period of a CFC group is not effective unless made by each designated U.S. person. Except as otherwise provided in this

paragraph (c)(5)(i), the election is made in accordance with Revenue Procedure 2020-22, 2020-18 I.R.B. 745. For purposes of applying §1.964-1(c), the election is treated as if made for each CFC group member.

(ii) *Election to use 2019 ATI applies to a specified period of a CFC group.*—(A) *In general.*—In the case of a CFC group, for purposes of applying paragraph (c)(2) of this section, an election under §1.163(j)-2(b)(3)(i) is made for a specified period of a CFC group beginning in 2020 and applies to the specified taxable years of each CFC group member with respect to such specified period, taking into account the application of paragraph (c)(5)(ii)(B) of this section. The election under §1.163(j)-2(b)(3)(i) does not apply to any specified taxable year of a CFC group member other than those described in the preceding sentence. An election under §1.163(j)-2(b)(3)(i) for a specified period of a CFC group is not effective unless made by each designated U.S. person. Except as otherwise provided in this paragraph (c)(5)(ii)(A), the election is made in accordance with Revenue Procedure 2020-22, 2020-18 I.R.B. 745. For purposes of applying §1.964-1(c), the election is treated as if made for each CFC group member.

(B) *Specified taxable years that do not begin in 2020.*—If a specified taxable year of a CFC group member with respect to the specified period described in paragraph (c)(5)(ii)(A) of this section begins in 2019, then, for purposes of applying paragraph (c)(2) of this section, §1.163(j)-2(b)(3) is applied to such specified taxable year by substituting "2018" for "2019" and "2019" for "2020." If a specified taxable year of a CFC group member with respect to the specified period described in paragraph (c)(5)(ii)(A) of this section begins in 2021, then, for purposes of applying paragraph (c)(2) of this section, §1.163(j)-2(b)(3) is applied to such specified taxable year by substituting "2020" for "2019" and "2021" for "2020."

(d) *Determination of a specified group and specified group members.*—(1) *Scope.*—This paragraph (d) provides rules for determining a specified group and specified group members. Paragraph (d)(2) of this section provides rules for determining a specified group. Paragraph (d)(3) of this section provides rules for determining specified group members.

(2) *Rules for determining a specified group.*—(i) *Definition of a specified group.*—Subject to paragraph (d)(2)(ii) of this section, the term *specified group* means one or more applicable CFCs or chains of applicable CFCs connected through stock ownership with a specified group parent (which is included in the specified group only if it is an applicable CFC), but only if—

(A) The specified group parent owns directly or indirectly stock meeting the requirements of section 1504(a)(2)(B) in at least one applicable CFC; and

(B) Stock meeting the requirements of section 1504(a)(2)(B) in each of the applicable CFCs (except the specified group parent) is owned directly or indirectly by one or more of the other applicable CFCs or the specified group parent.

(ii) *Indirect ownership.*—For purposes of applying paragraph (d)(2)(i) of this section, stock is owned indirectly only if it is owned under section 318(a)(2)(A) through a partnership or under section 318(a)(2)(A) or (B) through an estate or trust not described in section 7701(a)(30).

(iii) *Specified group parent.*—The term *specified group parent* means a qualified U.S. person or an applicable CFC.

(iv) *Qualified U.S. person.*—The term *qualified U.S. person* means a United States person described in section 7701(a)(30)(A) or (C). For purposes of this paragraph (d), members of a consolidated group that file (or that are required to file) a consolidated U.S. Federal income tax return are treated as a single qualified U.S person and individuals described in section 7701(a)(30)(A) whose filing status is married filing jointly are treated as a single qualified U.S. person.

(v) *Stock.*—For purposes of this paragraph (d)(2), the term *stock* has the same meaning as "stock" in section 1504 (without regard to §1.1504-4, except as provided in paragraph (d)(2)(vi) of this section) and all shares of stock within a single class are considered to have the same value. Thus, control premiums and minority and blockage discounts within a single class are not taken into account.

(vi) *Options treated as exercised.*—For purposes of this paragraph (d)(2), options that are reasonably certain to be exercised, as determined under §1.1504-4(g), are treated as exercised. For purposes of this paragraph (d)(2)(vi), options include call options, warrants, convertible obligations, put options, and any other instrument treated as an option under §1.1504-4(d), determined by replacing the term "a principal purpose of avoiding the application of section 1504 and this section" with "a principal purpose of avoiding the application of section 163(j)."

(vii) *When a specified group ceases to exist.*—The principles of §1.1502-75(d)(1), (d)(2)(i) and (ii), and (d)(3)(i) through (iv), apply for purposes of determining when a specified group ceases to exist. Solely for purposes of applying these principles, references to the common parent are treated as references to the specified group parent and each applicable CFC that is treated as a specified group member for a taxable year with respect to a specified period is treated as affiliated with the specified group parent from the beginning to the end of the specified period, without regard to the beginning or end of its taxable year.

(3) *Rules for determining a specified group member.*—If two or more applicable CFCs are included in a specified group on the last day of a taxable year of each applicable CFC that ends with or within a specified period, then each applicable CFC is a *specified group member* with respect to the specified period for its entire taxable year ending with or within the specified period. If only one applicable CFC is included in a specified group on the last day of its taxable year that ends with or within the specified period, it is not a specified group member. If an applicable CFC has multiple taxable years that end with or within a specified period, this paragraph (d)(3) is applied separately to each taxable year to determine if the applicable CFC is a specified group member for such taxable year.

(e) *Rules and procedures for treating a specified group as a CFC group.*—(1) *Scope.*—This paragraph (e) provides rules and procedures for treating a specified group member as a CFC group member and for determining a CFC group for purposes of applying section 163(j) and the section 163(j) regulations.

(2) *CFC group and CFC group member.*—(i) *CFC group.*—The term *CFC group* means, with respect to a specified period, all CFC group members for their specified taxable years.

(ii) *CFC group member.*—The term *CFC group member* means, with respect to a specified taxable year and a specified period, a specified group member of a specified group for which a CFC group election is in effect. However, notwithstanding the prior sentence, a specified group member is not treated as a CFC group member for a taxable year of the specified group member beginning before January 1, 2018.

(3) *Duration of a CFC group.*—A CFC group continues until the CFC group election is revoked, or there is no longer a specified period with respect to the specified group. A failure to provide the information described in paragraph (e)(6) of this section does not terminate a CFC group election.

(4) *Joining or leaving a CFC group.*—If an applicable CFC becomes a specified group member for a specified taxable year with respect to a specified period of a specified group for which a CFC group election is in effect, the CFC group election applies to the applicable CFC and the applicable CFC becomes a CFC group member. If an applicable CFC ceases to be a specified group member for a specified taxable year with respect to a specified period of a specified group for which a CFC group election is in effect, the CFC group election terminates solely with respect to the applicable CFC.

(5) *Manner of making or revoking a CFC group election.*—(i) *In general.*—An election is made or revoked under this paragraph (e)(5) *(CFC group election)* with respect to a specified period of a specified group. A CFC group election remains in effect for each specified period of the specified group until revoked. A CFC group election that is in effect with respect to a specified period of a specified group applies to each specified group member for its specified taxable year that ends with or within the specified period. The making or revoking of a CFC group election is not effective unless made or revoked by each designated U.S. person.

(ii) *Revocation by election.*—A CFC group election cannot be revoked with respect to any specified period beginning before 60 months following the last day of the specified period for which the election was made. Once a CFC group election has been revoked, a new CFC group election cannot be made with respect to any specified period beginning before 60 months following the last day of the specified period for which the election was revoked.

(iii) *Timing.*—A CFC group election must be made or revoked with respect to a specified period of a specified group no later than the due date (taking into account extensions, if any) of the original Federal income tax return for the taxable year of each designated U.S. person in which or with which the specified period ends.

(iv) *Election statement.*—To make or revoke a CFC group election for a specified period of a specified group, each designated U.S. person must attach a statement to its relevant Federal income tax or information return in accordance with publications, forms, instructions, or other guidance. The statement must include the name and taxpayer identification number of all designated U.S. persons, a statement that the CFC group election is being made or revoked, as applicable, the specified period for which the CFC group election is being made or revoked, and the name of each CFC group member and its specified taxable year with respect to the specified period. The statement must be filed in the manner prescribed in publications, forms, instructions, or other guidance.

(v) *Effect of prior CFC group election.*—A CFC group election is made solely pursuant to the provisions of this paragraph (e)(5), without regard to whether a CFC group election described in guidance under section 163(j) published on December 28, 2018, was in effect.

(6) *Annual information reporting.*—Each designated U.S. person must attach a statement to its relevant Federal income tax or information return for each taxable year in which a CFC group election is in effect that contains information concerning the computation of the CFC group's section 163(j) limitation and the application of paragraph (c)(3) of this section to the CFC group in accordance with publications, forms, instructions, or other guidance.

(f) *Treatment of a CFC group member that has ECI.*—(1) *In general.*—If a CFC group member has ECI in its specified taxable year, then for purposes of section 163(j) and the section 163(j) regulations—

(i) The items, disallowed business interest expense carryforwards, and other attributes of the CFC group member that are ECI are treated as items, disallowed business interest expense carryforwards, and attributes of a separate applicable CFC (such deemed corporation, an *ECI deemed corporation)* that has the same taxable year and shareholders as the applicable CFC; and

(ii) The ECI deemed corporation is not treated as a specified group member for the specified taxable year.

(2) [Reserved].

(g) *Rules concerning the computation of adjusted taxable income of a relevant foreign corporation.*—(1) *Tentative taxable income.*—For purposes of computing the tentative taxable income of a relevant foreign corporation for a taxable year, the relevant foreign corporation's gross income and allowable deductions are determined under the principles of § 1.952-2 or under the rules of section 882 for determining income that is, or deductions that are allocable to, effectively connected income, as applicable.

(2) *Treatment of certain dividends.*—For purposes of computing the ATI of a relevant foreign corporation for a taxable year, any dividend included in gross income that is received from a related person, within the meaning of section 954(d)(3), with respect to the distributee is subtracted from tentative taxable income.

(3) *Treatment of certain foreign income taxes.*—For purposes of computing the ATI of a relevant foreign corporation for a taxable year, no deduction is taken into account for any foreign income tax (as defined in § 1.960-1(b), but substituting the phrase "relevant foreign corporation" for the phrase "controlled foreign corporation").

(4) *Anti-abuse rule.*—(i) *In general.*—If a specified group member of a specified group or an applicable partnership *(specified lender)* includes an amount *(payment amount)* in income and such amount is attributable to business interest expense incurred by another specified group member or an applicable partnership of the specified group *(specified borrower)* during its taxable year, then the ATI of the specified borrower for the taxable year is increased by the ATI adjustment amount if—

(A) The business interest expense is incurred with a principal purpose of reducing the Federal income tax liability of any United States shareholder of a specified group member (including over other taxable years);

(B) Absent the application of this paragraph (g)(4), the effect of the specified borrower treating all or part of the payment amount as disallowed business interest expense would be to reduce the Federal income tax liability of any United States shareholder of a specified group member; and

(C) Either no CFC group election is in effect with respect to the specified group or the specified borrower is an applicable partnership.

(ii) *ATI adjustment amount.*—(A) *In general.*—For purposes of this paragraph (g)(4), the term *ATI adjustment amount* means, with respect to a specified borrower and a taxable year, the product of 3 1/3 and the lesser of the payment amount or the disallowed business interest expense, computed without regard to this paragraph (g)(4).

(B) *Special rule for taxable years or specified periods beginning in 2019 or 2020.*—For any taxable year of an applicable CFC or specified taxable year of a CFC group member with respect to a specified period for which the section 163(j) limitation is determined based, in part, on 50 percent of ATI, in accordance with § 1.163(j)-2(b)(2), paragraph (g)(4)(ii)(A) of this section is applied by substituting "2" for "3 1/3."

(iii) *Applicable partnership.*—For purposes of this paragraph (g)(4), the term *applicable partnership* means, with respect to a specified group, a partnership in which at least 80 percent of the interests in profits or capital is owned, directly or indirectly through one or more other partnerships, by specified group members of the specified group. For purposes of this paragraph (g)(4)(iii), a partner's interest in the profits of a partnership is determined in accordance with the rules and principles of § 1.706-1(b)(4)(ii) and a partner's interest in the capital of a partnership is determined in accordance with the rules and principles of § 1.706-1(b)(4)(iii).

(h) *Election to apply safe-harbor.*—(1) *In general.*—If an election to apply this paragraph (h)(1) *(safe-harbor election)* is in effect with respect to a taxable year of a stand-alone applicable CFC or a specified taxable year of a CFC group member, as applicable, then, for such year, no portion of the applicable CFC's business interest expense is disallowed under the section 163(j) limitation. This paragraph (h) does not apply to excess business interest expense, as described in § 1.163(j)-6(f)(2), until the taxable year in which it is treated as paid or accrued by an applicable CFC under § 1.163(j)-6(g)(2)(i). Furthermore, excess business interest expense is not taken into account for purposes of determining whether the safe-harbor election is available for a stand-alone applicable CFC or a CFC group until the taxable year in which it is treated as paid or accrued by an applicable CFC under § 1.163(j)-6(g)(2)(i).

(2) *Eligibility for safe-harbor election.*—(i) *Stand-alone applicable CFC.*—The safe-harbor election may be made for the taxable year of a stand-alone applicable CFC only if, for the taxable year, the business interest expense of the applicable CFC is less than or equal to either—

(A) The business interest income of the applicable CFC; or

(B) 30 percent of the lesser of the eligible amount or the qualified tentative taxable income of the applicable CFC.

(ii) *CFC group.*—The safe-harbor election may be made for the specified period of a CFC group only if, for the specified period, no CFC group member has any pre-group disallowed business interest expense carryforward and the business interest expense of the CFC group for the specified period is less than or equal to either—

(A) The business interest income of the CFC group; or

(B) 30 percent of the lesser of the eligible amount or the qualified tentative taxable income of the CFC group.

(iii) *Currency translation.*—For purposes of applying this paragraph (h), BII, BIE, and qualified tentative taxable income of a stand-alone applicable CFC or a CFC group must be determined using the U.S. dollar. If BII, BIE, or any items of income, gain, deduction, or loss that are taken into account in computing qualified tentative taxable income are maintained in a currency other than the U.S. dollar, then those items must be translated into the U.S. dollar using the average exchange rate for the taxable year or the specified taxable year, as applicable.

(3) *Eligible amount.*—(i) *Stand-alone applicable CFC.*—The *eligible amount* of a stand-alone applicable CFC for a taxable year is the sum of the amounts a domestic corporation would include in gross income under sections 951(a)(1)(A) and 951A(a), reduced by any deductions that would be allowed under section 245A (by reason of section 964(e)(4)) or section 250(a)(1)(B)(i), determined as if the domestic corporation has a taxable year that ends on the last date of the taxable year of the stand-alone applicable CFC, it wholly owns the stand-alone applicable CFC throughout the CFC's taxable year, it does not own any assets other than stock in the stand-alone applicable CFC, and it has no other items of income, gain, deduction, or loss.

(ii) *CFC group.*—The *eligible amount* of a CFC group for a specified period is the sum of the amounts a domestic corporation would include in gross income under sections 951(a)(1)(A) and 951A(a), reduced by any deductions that would be allowed under section 245A (by reason of section 964(e)(4)) or section 250(a)(1)(B)(i), determined as if the domestic corporation has a taxable year that is the specified period, it wholly owns each CFC group member throughout the CFC group member's specified taxable year, it does not own any assets other than stock in the CFC group members, and it has no other items of income, gain, deduction, or loss.

(iii) *Additional rules for determining an eligible amount.*—For purposes of paragraphs (h)(3)(i) and (ii) of this section, the amounts that would be included in gross income of a United States shareholder under sections 951(a)(1)(A) and 951A(a), and any corresponding deductions that would be allowed under section 245A (by reason of section 964(e)(4)) or section 250(a)(1)(B)(i), are determined by taking into account any elections that are made with respect to the applicable CFC(s), including under § 1.954-1(d)(5) (relating to the subpart F high-tax exception) and § 1.951A-2(c)(7)(viii) (relating to the GILTI high-tax exclusion). These amounts are also determined without regard to any section 163(j) limitation on business interest expense and without regard to any disallowed business interest expense carryovers. In addition, those amounts are determined by only taking in account items of the applicable CFC(s) that are properly allocable to a non-excepted trade or business under § 1.163(j)-10.

(4) *Qualified tentative taxable income.*—The term *qualified tentative taxable income* means, with respect to a taxable year of a stand-alone applicable CFC, the applicable CFC's tentative taxable income, and with respect to a specified period of a CFC group, the sum of each CFC group member's tentative taxable income for the specified taxable year; provided that for purposes of this paragraph (h)(4), tentative taxable income is determined by taking into account only items properly allocable to a non-excepted trade or business under § 1.163(j)-10.

(5) *Manner of making a safe-harbor election.*—(i) *In general.*—A safe-harbor election is an annual election made under this paragraph (h)(5) with respect to a taxable year of a stand-alone applicable CFC or with respect to a specified period of a CFC group. A safe-harbor election that is made with respect to a specified period of a CFC group is effective with respect to each CFC group member for its specified taxable year. A safe-harbor election is only effective if made by each designated U.S. person with respect to a stand-alone applicable CFC or a CFC group. A safe-harbor election is made with respect to a taxable year of a stand-alone applicable CFC, or a specified period of a CFC group, no later than the due date (taking into account extensions, if any) of the original Federal income tax return for the taxable year of each designated U.S. person, respectively, in which or with which the taxable year of the stand-alone applicable CFC ends or the specified period of the CFC group ends.

(ii) *Election statement.*—To make a safe-harbor election, each designated U.S. person must attach to its relevant Federal income tax return or information return a statement that includes the name and taxpayer identification number of all designated U.S. persons, a statement that a safe-harbor election is being made pursuant to § 1.163(j)-7(h) and a calculation that substantiates that the requirements for making the election are satisfied, and the taxable year of the stand-alone applicable CFC or the specified period of the CFC group, as applicable, for which the safe-harbor election is being made in accordance with publications, forms, instructions, or other guidance. In the case of a CFC group, the statement must also include the name of each CFC group member and its specified taxable year that ends with or within the specified period for which the safe-harbor election is being made. The statement must be filed in the manner prescribed in publications, forms, instructions, or other guidance.

(6) *Special rule for taxable years or specified periods beginning in 2019 or 2020.*—In the case of a stand-alone applicable CFC, for any taxable year beginning in 2019 or 2020, paragraph (h)(2)(i) of this section is applied by substituting "50 percent" for "30 percent." In the case of a CFC group, for any specified period beginning in 2019 or 2020, paragraph (h)(2)(ii)(A) of this section is applied by substituting "50 percent" for "30 percent."

(i)-(j) [Reserved]

(k) *Definitions.*—The following definitions apply for purposes of this section.

(1) *Applicable partnership.*—The term *applicable partnership* has the meaning provided in paragraph (g)(4)(iii) of this section.

(2) *Applicable specified taxable year.*—The term *applicable specified taxable year* has the meaning provided in paragraph (c)(3)(iii) of this section.

(3) *ATI adjustment amount.*—The term *ATI adjustment amount* has the meaning provided in paragraph (g)(4)(ii) of this section.

(4)-(5) [Reserved].

(6) *CFC group.*—The term *CFC group* has the meaning provided in paragraph (e)(2)(i) of this section.

(7) *CFC group election.*—The term *CFC group election* means the election described in paragraph (e)(5) of this section.

(8) *CFC group member.*—The term *CFC group member* has the meaning provided in paragraph (e)(2)(ii) of this section.

(9) [Reserved].

(10) *Cumulative section 163(j) pre-group carryforward limitation.*—The term *cumulative section 163(j) pre-group carryforward limitation* has the meaning provided in paragraph (c)(3)(iv)(A)(*1*) of this section.

(11) *Current group.*—The term *current group* has the meaning provided in paragraph (c)(3)(iv)(A)(*2*) of this section.

(12) *Designated U.S. person.*—The term *designated U.S. person* means—

(i) With respect to a stand-alone applicable CFC, each controlling domestic shareholder, as defined in § 1.964-1(c)(5)(i) of the applicable CFC; or

(ii) With respect to a specified group, the specified group parent, if the specified group parent is a qualified U.S. person, or each controlling domestic shareholder, as defined in § 1.964-1(c)(5)(i), of the specified group parent, if the specified group parent is an applicable CFC.

(13) *ECI deemed corporation.*—The term *ECI deemed corporation* has the meaning provided in paragraph (f)(1)(i) of this section.

(14) *Effectively connected income.*—The term *effectively connected income* (or *ECI*) means income or gain that is ECI, as defined in § 1.884-1(d)(1)(iii), and deduction or loss that is allocable to, ECI, as defined in § 1.884-1(d)(1)(iii).

(15) *Eligible amount.*—The term *eligible amount* has the meaning provided in paragraph (h)(3)(i) of this section.

(16) *Former group.*—The term *former group* has the meaning provided in paragraph (c)(3)(iv)(A)(*2*) of this section.

(17) *Loss member.*—The term *loss member* has the meaning provided in paragraph (c)(3)(iv)(A)(*2*) of this section.

(18) *Payment amount.*—The term *payment amount* has the meaning provided in paragraph (g)(4)(i) of this section.

(19) *Pre-group disallowed business interest expense carryforward.*—The term *pre-group disallowed business interest expense carryforward* means, with respect to a CFC group member and a specified taxable year, any disallowed business interest expense carryforward of the CFC group member that arose in a taxable year during which the CFC group member (or its predecessor) was not a CFC group member of the CFC group.

(20) *Qualified tentative taxable income.*—The term *qualified tentative taxable income* has the meaning provided in paragraph (h)(4) of this section.

(21) *Qualified U.S. person.*—The term *qualified U.S. person* has the meaning provided in paragraph (d)(2)(iv) of this section.

(22) *Relevant period.*—The term *relevant period* has the meaning provided in paragraph (c)(3)(iv)(A)(2) of this section.

(23) *Safe-harbor election.*—The term *safe-harbor election* has the meaning provided in paragraph (h)(1) of this section.

(24) *Specified borrower.*—The term *specified borrower* has the meaning provided in paragraph (g)(4)(i) of this section.

(25) *Specified group.*—The term *specified group* has the meaning provided in paragraph (d)(2)(i) of this section.

(26) *Specified group member.*—The term *specified group member* has the meaning provided in paragraph (d)(3) of this section.

(27) *Specified group parent.*—The term *specified group parent* has the meaning provided in paragraph (d)(2)(iii) of this section.

(28) *Specified lender.*—The term *specified lender* has the meaning provided in paragraph (g)(4)(i) of this section.

(29) *Specified period.*—(i) *In general.*—Except as otherwise provided in paragraph (k)(29)(ii) of this section, the term *specified period* means, with respect to a specified group—

(A) If the specified group parent is a qualified U.S. person, the period ending on the last day of the taxable year of the specified group parent and beginning on the first day after the last day of the specified group's immediately preceding specified period; or

(B) If the specified group parent is an applicable CFC, the period ending on the last day of the specified group parent's required year described in section 898(c)(1), without regard to section 898(c)(2), and beginning on the first day after the last day of the specified group's immediately preceding specified period.

(ii) *Short specified period.*—A specified period begins no earlier than the first date on which a specified group exists. A specified period ends on the date a specified group ceases to exist under paragraph (d)(2)(vii) of this section. If the last day of a specified period, as determined under paragraph (k)(29)(i) of this section, changes, and, but for this paragraph (k)(29)(ii), the change in the last day of the specified period would result in the specified period being longer than 12 months, the specified period ends on the date on which the specified period would have ended had the change not occurred.

(30) *Specified taxable year.*—The term *specified taxable year* means, with respect to an applicable CFC that is a specified group member of a specified group and a specified period, a taxable year of the applicable CFC that ends with or within the specified period.

(31) *Stand-alone applicable CFC.*—The term *stand-alone applicable CFC* means any applicable CFC that is not a specified group member.

(32) *Stock.*—The term *stock* has the meaning provided in paragraph (d)(2)(v) of this section.

(l) *Examples.*—The following examples illustrate the application of this section. For each example, unless otherwise stated, no exemptions from the application of section 163(j) are available, no foreign corporation has ECI, and all relevant taxable years and specified periods begin after December 31, 2020.

(1) *Example 1. Specified taxable years included in specified period of a specified group.*—(i) *Facts.* As of June 30, Year 1, USP, a domestic corporation, owns 60 percent of the common stock of FP, which owns all of the stock of FC1, FC2, and FC3. The remaining 40 percent of the common stock of FP is owned by an unrelated foreign corporation. FP has a single class of stock. FP acquired the stock of FC3 from an unrelated person on March 22, Year 1. The acquisition did not result in a change in FC3's taxable year or a close of its taxable year. USP's interest in FP and FP's interest in FC1 and FC2 has been the same for several years. USP has a taxable year ending June 30, Year 1, which is not a short taxable year. Each of FP, FC1, FC2, and FC3 are applicable CFCs. Pursuant to section 898(c)(2), FP and FC1 have taxable years ending May 31, Year 1. Pursuant to section 898(c)(1), FC2 and FC3 have taxable years ending June 30, Year 1.

(ii) *Analysis*—(A) *Determining a specified group and specified period of the specified group.* Pursuant to paragraph (d) of this section, FP, FC1, FC2, and FC3 are members of a specified group, and FP is the specified group parent. Because the specified group parent, FP, is an applicable CFC, the specified period of the specified group is the period ending on June 30, Year 1, which is the last day of FP's required year described in section 898(c)(1), without regard to section 898(c)(2), and beginning on July 1, Year 0, which is the first day following the last day of the specified group's immediately preceding specified period (June 30, Year 0). See paragraph (k)(29)(i)(B) of this section.

(B) *Determining the specified taxable years with respect to the specified period.* Pursuant to paragraph (d)(3) of this section, because each of FP and FC1 are included in the specified group on the last day of their taxable years ending May 31, Year 1, and such taxable years end with or within the specified period ending June 30, Year 1, FP and FC1 are specified group members with respect to the specified period ending June 30, Year 1, for their entire taxable years ending May 31, Year 1, and those taxable years are specified taxable years. Similarly, because each of FC2 and FC3 are included in the specified group on the last day of their taxable years ending June 30, Year 1, and such taxable years end with or within the specified period ending June 30, Year 1, FC2 and FC3 are specified group members with respect to the specified period ending June 30, Year 1, for their entire taxable years ending June 30, Year 1, and those taxable years are specified taxable years. The fact that FC3 was acquired on March 22, Year 1, does not prevent FC3 from being a specified group member with respect to the specified period for the portion of its specified taxable year before March 22, Year 1.

(2) *Example 2. CFC groups.*—(i) *Facts.* The facts are the same as in *Example 1* in paragraph (l)(1)(i) of this section except that, in addition, a CFC group election is in place with respect to the specified period ending June 30, Year 1.

(ii) *Analysis.* Because a CFC group election is in place for the specified period ending June 30, Year 1, pursuant to paragraph (e)(2)(ii) of this section, each specified group member is a CFC group member with respect to its specified taxable year ending with or within the specified period. Accordingly, FP, FC1, FC2, and FC3 are CFC group members with respect to the specified period ending June 30, Year 1, for their specified taxable years ending May 31, Year 1, and June 30, Year 1, respectively. Pursuant to paragraph (e)(2)(i) of this section, the CFC group for the specified period ending June 30, Year 1, consists of FP, FC1, FC2, and FC3 for their specified taxable years ending May 31, Year 1, and June 30, Year 1, respectively. Pursuant to paragraph (c)(2) of this section, a single section 163(j) limitation is computed for the specified period ending June 30, Year 1. That section 163(j) calculation will include FP and FC1's specified taxable years ending May 31, Year 1, and FC2 and FC3's specified taxable years ending June 30, Year 1.

(3) *Example 3. Application of anti-abuse rule.*—(i) *Facts.* USP, a domestic corporation, owns all of the stock of CFC1 and CFC2. Thus, USP is the specified group parent of a specified group, the specified group members of which are CFC1 and CFC2. USP has a calendar year taxable year. All specified group members also have a calendar year taxable year and a functional currency of the U.S. dollar. CFC1 is organized in, and a tax resident of, a jurisdiction that imposes no tax on certain types of income, including interest income. With respect to Year 1, USP expects to pay no residual U.S. tax on its income inclusion under section 951A(a) (GILTI inclusion amount) and expects to have unused foreign tax credits in the category described in section 904(d)(1)(A). A CFC group election is not in effect for Year 1. With a principal purpose of reducing USP's Federal income tax liability in subsequent taxable years, on January 1, Year 1, CFC1 loans $100x to CFC2. On December 31, Year 1, CFC2 pays interest of $10x to CFC1 and repays the principal of $100x. Absent the application of paragraph (g)(4)(i) of this section, all $10x of CFC2's interest expense would be disallowed business interest expense and, therefore, CFC2 would have $10x of disallowed business interest expense carryforward to Year 2. In Year 2, CFC2 disposes of one of its businesses at a substantial gain that gives rise to tested income (within the meaning of section 951A(c)(2)(A) and §1.951A-2(b)(1)). As a result of the gain being included in the ATI of CFC2, absent the application of paragraph (g)(4)(i) of this section, CFC2 would be allowed to deduct the entire $10x of disallowed business interest expense carryforward and therefore reduce the amount of its tested income. Also, USP would pay residual U.S. tax on its GILTI inclusion amount in Year 2, without regard to the application of paragraph (g)(4)(i) of this section.

(ii) *Analysis.* The $10x of business interest expense paid in Year 1 is a payment amount described in paragraph (g)(4)(i) of this section because it is between specified group members, CFC1 and CFC2. Furthermore, the requirements of paragraphs (g)(4)(i)(A), (B), and (C) of this section are satisfied because the $10x of business interest expense is incurred with a principal purpose of reducing USP's Federal income tax liability; absent the application of paragraph (g)(4)(i) of this section, the effect of CFC2 treating the $10x of business interest expense as disallowed business interest expense in Year 1 would be to reduce USP's Federal income tax liability in Year 2; and no CFC group election is in effect with respect to the specified group in Year 1. Because the requirements of paragraphs (g)(4)(i)(A), (B), and (C) of this section are satisfied, CFC2's ATI for Year 1 is increased by the ATI adjustment amount, or $33.33x, which is the amount equal to 3 1/3 multiplied by $10x (the lesser of the payment amount of $10x and the disallowed business interest expense of $10x). As a result, the $10x of business interest expense is not disallowed business interest expense of CFC2 in Year 1, and therefore does not give rise to a disallowed business interest expense carryforward to Year 2.

(m) *Applicability dates.*—(1) *General applicability date.*—Except as provided in paragraph (m)(2) of this section, this section applies for a taxable year of a foreign corporation beginning on or after November 13, 2020.

(2) *Exception.*—Paragraphs (a), (c)(1), (2)(i) and (ii), and (3) through (5), (d), (e), (f)(1), (g)(3) and (4), (h), and (k)(1) through (3), (6) through (8), and (10) through (32) of this section apply for a taxable year of a foreign corporation beginning on or after March 22, 2021.

(3) *Early application.*—(i) *Rules for paragraphs (b) and (g)(1) and (2) of this section.*—Taxpayers and their related parties, within the meaning of sections 267(b) (determined without regard to section 267(c)(3)) and 707(b)(1), may choose to apply the rules in paragraphs (b) and (g)(1) and (2) of this section for a taxable year beginning after December 31, 2017, and before November 13, 2020, provided that those taxpayers and their related parties consistently apply all of those rules and the rules described in paragraph (m)(4) of this section for that taxable year. If a taxpayer and its related parties apply the rules described in paragraph (m)(4) of this section, as contained in T.D. 9905 (§§1.163(j)-0 through 1.163(j)-11, effective November 13, 2020), they will be considered as applying the rules described in paragraph (m)(4) of this section for purposes of this paragraph (m)(3)(i).

(ii) *Rules for certain other paragraphs in this section.*—Taxpayers and their related parties, within the meaning of sections 267(b) (determined without regard to section 267(c)(3)) and 707(b)(1), may choose to apply the rules in paragraphs (a), (c)(1), (2)(i) and (ii), and (3) through (5), (d), (e), (f)(1), (g)(3) and (4), (h), and (k)(1) through (3), (6) through (8), and (10) through (32) of this section for a taxable year beginning after December 31, 2017, and before March 22, 2021, provided that those taxpayers and their related parties consistently apply all of those rules and the rules described in paragraph (m)(4) of this section for that taxable year and for each subsequent taxable year. If a taxpayer and its related parties apply the rules described in paragraph (m)(4) of this section, as contained in T.D. 9905 (§§1.163(j)-0 through 1.163(j)-11, effective November 13, 2020) as modified by T.D. 9943, (effective January 13, 2021), they will be considered as applying the rules described in paragraph (m)(4) of this section for purposes of this paragraph (m)(3)(ii).

(4) *Additional rules that must be applied consistently.*—The rules described in this paragraph (m)(4) are the section 163(j) regulations and, if applicable, §§1.263A-9, 1.263A-15, 1.381(c)(20)-1, 1.382-1, 1.382-2, 1.382-5, 1.382-6, 1.382-7, 1.383-0, 1.383-1, 1.469-9, 1.469-11, 1.704-1, 1.882-5, 1.1362-3, 1.1368-1, 1.1377-1, 1.1502-13, 1.1502-21, 1.1502-36, 1.1502-79, 1.1502-91 through 1.1502-99 (to the extent they effectuate the rules of §§1.382-2, 1.382-5, 1.382-6, and 1.383-1), and 1.1504-4.

(5) *Election for prior taxable years and specified periods.*—Notwithstanding paragraph (e)(5)(iii) or (h)(5)(i) of this section, in the case of a specified period of a specified group or a taxable year of a standalone applicable CFC that ends with or within a taxable year of a designated U.S. person ending before November 13, 2020, a CFC group election or a safe-harbor election may be made on an amended Federal income tax return filed on or before the due date (taking into account extensions, if any) of the original Federal income tax return for the first taxable year of each designated U.S. person ending on or after November 13, 2020. [Reg. §1.163(j)-7.]

□ [*T.D. 9905, 9-3-2020. Amended by T.D. 9943, 1-13-2021.*]

Proposed Regulation

§1.163(j)-8. Application of the section 163(j) limitation to foreign persons with effectively connected income.—(a) *Overview.*—This section provides rules concerning the application of section 163(j) to foreign persons with ECI. Paragraph (b) of this section modifies the application of section 163(j) for a specified foreign person with ECI. Paragraph (c) of this section sets forth rules for a specified foreign partner in a partnership with ECI. Paragraph (d) of this section allocates disallowed business interest expense for relevant foreign corporations with ECI. Paragraph (e) of this section provides rules concerning disallowed business interest expense. Paragraph (f) of this section coordinates the application of section 163(j) with §1.882-5 and the branch profits tax under section 884. Paragraph (g) of this section provides definitions that apply for purposes of this section. Paragraph (h) of this section illustrates the application of this section through examples.

(b) *Application to a specified foreign person with ECI.*—(1) *In general.*—If a taxpayer is a specified foreign person, then the taxpayer applies the modifications described in this paragraph (b), taking into account the application of paragraph (c) of this section.

(2) *Modification of adjusted taxable income.*—Adjusted taxable income for a specified foreign person for a taxable year means the specified foreign person's adjusted taxable income, as determined under §1.163(j)-1(b)(1), taking into account only items that are ECI.

(3) *Modification of business interest expense.*—Business interest expense for a specified foreign person means business interest expense described in §1.163(j)-1(b)(3) that is ECI, taking into account the application of paragraph (f)(1)(iii) of this section.

(4) *Modification of business interest income.*—The business interest income of a specified foreign person means business interest income described in §1.163(j)-1(b)(4) that is ECI.

(5) *Modification of floor plan financing interest expense.*—The floor plan financing interest expense of a specified foreign person means floor plan financing interest expense described §1.163(j)-1(b)(19) that is ECI.

(6) *Modification of allocation of interest expense and interest income that is allocable to a trade or business.*—For purposes of applying §1.163(j)-10(c) to a specified foreign person, only interest income and interest expense that are ECI and only assets that are U.S. assets, as defined in §1.884-1(d), are taken into account. If the specified foreign person is also a specified foreign partner, this paragraph (b)(6) does not apply to any trade or business of the partnership.

(c) *Rules for a specified foreign partner.*—(1) *Characterization of excess taxable income.*—(i) *In general.*—The portion of excess taxable income allocated to a specified foreign partner from a partnership pursuant to §1.163(j)-6(f)(2) that is ECI is equal to the specified foreign partner's allocation of excess taxable income from the partnership multiplied by its specified ATI ratio with respect to the partnership, and the remainder is not ECI.

(ii) *Specified ATI ratio.*—The term *specified ATI ratio* means the fraction described in this paragraph (c)(1)(ii). If the specified foreign partner's distributive share of ECI and distributive share of non-ECI are both positive, the numerator of this fraction is the specified foreign partner's distributive share of ECI and the denominator is the specified foreign partner's distributive share of partnership items of income, gain, deduction, and loss. If the specified foreign partner's distributive share of ECI is negative or zero and its distributive share of non-ECI is positive, this fraction is treated as zero. If the specified foreign partner's distributive share of non-ECI is negative or zero and its distributive share of ECI is positive, this fraction is treated as one. If the specified foreign partner's distributive share of ECI and distributive share of non-ECI are both negative, the numerator of this fraction is its distributive share of non-ECI and the denominator is its distributive share of partnership items of income, gain, deduction, and loss.

(iii) *Distributive share of ECI.*—The term *distributive share of ECI* means the net amount of the specified foreign partner's distributive share of partnership items of income, gain, deduction, and loss that are ECI.

(iv) *Distributive share of non-ECI.*—The term *distributive share of non-ECI* means the net amount of the specified foreign partner's distributive share of partnership items of income, gain, deduction, and loss that are not ECI.

(2) *Characterization of excess business interest expense.*—(i) *Allocable ECI excess BIE.*—The portion of excess business interest expense allocated to a specified foreign partner from a partnership pursuant to § 1.163(j)-6(f)(2) or paragraph (e)(2) of this section that is ECI (*allocable ECI excess BIE*) is equal to the excess, if any, of allocable ECI BIE over allocable ECI deductible BIE.

(ii) *Allocable non-ECI excess BIE.*—The portion of excess business interest expense allocated to a specified foreign partner from a partnership pursuant to § 1.163(j)-6(f)(2) or paragraph (e)(2) of this section that is not ECI (*allocable non-ECI excess BIE*) is equal to the excess, if any, of allocable non-ECI BIE over allocable non-ECI deductible BIE.

(3) *Characterization of deductible business interest expense.*—(i) *In general.*—The portion of deductible business interest expense, if any, that is allocated to a specified foreign partner from a partnership pursuant to § 1.163(j)-6(f)(2) that is ECI (*allocable ECI deductible BIE*) is equal to the sum of the amounts described in paragraphs (c)(3)(ii)(A)(*1*)(*i*) and (c)(3)(ii)(B)(*1*) of this section. The portion of deductible business interest expense, if any, that is allocated to a specified foreign partner from a partnership pursuant to § 1.163(j)-6(f)(2) that is not ECI (*allocable non-ECI deductible BIE*) is equal to the sum of the amounts described in paragraphs (c)(3)(ii)(A)(*1*)(*ii*) and (c)(3)(ii)(B)(*2*) of this section.

(ii) *Allocation between allocable ECI deductible BIE and allocable non-ECI deductible BIE.*—For purposes of paragraph (c)(3)(i) of this section—

(A) *Allocation to hypothetical deductible amounts.*—(*1*) *In general.*—Subject to paragraph (c)(3)(ii)(A)(*2*) of this section, deductible business interest expense that is allocated to the specified foreign partner from the partnership pursuant to § 1.163(j)-6(f)(2) is allocated pro rata to—

(*i*) Hypothetical partnership ECI deductible BIE; and

(*ii*) Hypothetical partnership non-ECI deductible BIE.

(*2*) *Limitation.*—The amount allocated to hypothetical partnership ECI deductible BIE in paragraph (c)(3)(ii)(A)(*1*)(*i*) of this section cannot exceed the lesser of hypothetical partnership ECI deductible BIE or allocable ECI BIE, and the amount allocated to hypothetical partnership non-ECI deductible BIE in paragraph (c)(3)(ii)(A)(*1*)(*ii*) of this section cannot exceed the lesser of hypothetical partnership non-ECI deductible BIE or allocable non-ECI BIE.

(B) *Allocation of remaining deductible amounts.*—Deductible business interest expense that is allocated to the specified foreign partner from the partnership pursuant to § 1.163(j)-6(f)(2) in excess of the amount allocated in paragraph (c)(3)(ii)(A) of this section, if any, is allocated pro rata to—

(*1*) Allocable ECI BIE, reduced by the amount described in paragraph (c)(3)(ii)(A)(*1*)(*i*) of this section; and

(*2*) Allocable non-ECI BIE, reduced by the amount described in paragraph (c)(3)(ii)(A)(*1*)(*ii*) of this section.

(iii) *Hypothetical partnership deductible business interest expense.*—(A) *Hypothetical partnership ECI deductible BIE.*—The term *hypothetical partnership ECI deductible BIE* means the deductible business interest expense of the partnership, as defined in § 1.163(j)-6(b)(5), determined by only taking into account the specified foreign partner's allocable share of items that are ECI (including by reason of paragraph (f)(1)(iii) of this section).

(B) *Hypothetical partnership non-ECI deductible BIE.*—The term *hypothetical partnership non-ECI deductible BIE* means the deductible business interest expense of the partnership, as defined in § 1.163(j)-6(b)(5), determined by only taking into account the specified foreign partner's allocable share of items that are not ECI (including by reason of paragraph (f)(1)(iii) of this section).

(4) *Characterization of excess business interest income.*—(i) *In general.*—The portion of excess business interest income allocated to a specified foreign partner from a partnership pursuant to § 1.163(j)-6(f)(2) that is ECI is equal to the specified foreign partner's allocation of excess business interest income from the partnership multiplied by its specified BII ratio with respect to the partnership, and the remainder is not ECI.

(ii) *Specified BII ratio.*—The term *specified BII ratio* means the ratio of the specified foreign partner's allocable ECI BII to allocable business interest income (determined under § 1.163(j)-6(f)(2)(ii)).

(iii) *Allocable ECI BII.*—The term *allocable ECI BII* means the specified foreign partner's allocable BII, as determined under § 1.163(j)-6(f)(2)(ii), computed by only taking into account income that is ECI.

(5) *Rules for determining ECI.*—Except as described in paragraph (f)(1) of this section, if the determination as to whether partnership items are ECI is made by a direct or indirect partner, rather than the partnership itself, then for purposes of this paragraph (c), the partnership must use a reasonable method to characterize such items as ECI or as not ECI.

(d) *Characterization of disallowed business interest expense by a relevant foreign corporation with ECI.*—(1) *Scope.*—A relevant foreign corporation that has ECI and disallowed business interest expense for a taxable year determines the portion of its disallowed business interest expense and deductible business interest expense that is characterized as ECI or as not ECI under this paragraph (d). A relevant foreign corporation that is a specified foreign partner also applies the rules in paragraph (c) of this section. See also § 1.163(j)-7(f) for rules regarding CFC group members with ECI.

(2) *Characterization of disallowed business interest expense.*—(i) *FC ECI disallowed BIE.*—For purposes of this section, the portion of disallowed business interest expense of a relevant foreign corporation that is ECI (*FC ECI disallowed BIE*) is equal to the excess, if any, of FC ECI BIE over FC ECI deductible BIE.

(ii) *FC non-ECI disallowed BIE.*—For purposes of this section, the portion of disallowed business interest expense of a relevant foreign corporation that is not ECI (*FC non-ECI disallowed BIE*) is equal to the excess, if any, of FC non-ECI BIE over FC non-ECI deductible BIE.

(3) *Characterization of deductible business interest expense.*—(i) *In general.*—The portion of deductible business interest expense, if any, that is ECI (*FC ECI deductible BIE*) is equal to the sum of the amounts described in paragraphs (d)(3)(ii)(A)(*1*)(*i*) and (d)(3)(ii)(*B*)(*1*) of this section. The portion of deductible business interest expense, if any, that is allocable to income that is not ECI (*FC non-ECI deductible BIE*) is equal to the sum of the amounts described in paragraphs (d)(3)(ii)(A)(*1*)(*ii*) and (d)(3)(ii)(*B*)(*2*) of this section.

(ii) *Allocation between FC ECI deductible BIE and FC non-ECI deductible BIE.*—For purposes of paragraph (d)(3)(i) of this section—

(A) *Allocation to hypothetical deductible amounts.*—(*1*) *In general.*—Subject to paragraph (d)(3)(ii)(A)(*2*) of this section, deductible business interest expense is allocated pro rata to—

(*i*) Hypothetical FC ECI deductible BIE; and

(*ii*) Hypothetical FC non-ECI deductible BIE.

(*2*) *Limitation.*—The amount allocated to hypothetical FC ECI deductible BIE in paragraph (d)(3)(ii)(A)(*1*)(*i*) of this section cannot exceed the lesser of hypothetical FC ECI deductible BIE or FC ECI BIE, and the amount allocated to hypothetical FC non-ECI deductible BIE in paragraph (d)(3)(ii)(A)(*1*)(*ii*) of this section cannot exceed the lesser of hypothetical FC non-ECI deductible BIE or FC non-ECI BIE.

(B) *Allocation of remaining deductible amounts.*—Deductible business interest expense in excess of the amount allocated in paragraph (d)(3)(ii)(A) of this section, if any, is allocated pro rata to—

(*1*) FC ECI BIE, reduced by the amount described in paragraph (d)(3)(ii)(A)(*1*)(*i*) of this section; and

(*2*) FC non-ECI BIE, reduced by the amount described in paragraph (d)(3)(ii)(A)(*1*)(*ii*) of this section.

(iii) *Hypothetical FC deductible business interest expense.*—(A) *Hypothetical FC ECI deductible BIE.*—The term *hypothetical FC ECI deductible BIE* means the deductible business interest expense of the relevant foreign corporation determined by only taking into account its items that are ECI.

(B) *Hypothetical FC non-ECI deductible BIE.*—The term *hypothetical FC non-ECI deductible BIE* means the deductible business interest expense of the relevant foreign corporation determined by only taking into account its items that are not ECI.

(e) *Rules regarding disallowed business interest expense.*—(1) *Retention of character in a succeeding taxable year.*—Disallowed business interest expense of a specified foreign person or a relevant foreign corporation for a taxable year (including excess business interest expense allocated to a specified foreign partner under § 1.163(j)-6(f)(2) or paragraph (e)(2) of this section) that is ECI or is not ECI retains its character as ECI or as not ECI in a succeeding taxable year.

(2) *Deemed allocation of excess business interest expense of a partnership to a specified foreign partner.*—For purposes of this paragraph (e) and paragraphs (c)(2), (g)(3), and (g)(7) of this section, a specified foreign partner's allocable share of business interest expense is deemed to include its allocable share of excess business interest expense of a partnership in which it is a direct or indirect partner. For purposes of this paragraph (e)(2), a specified foreign partner's allocable share of excess business interest expense of a partnership in which it is a direct or indirect partner is determined as if the excess business interest expense of the partnership were deductible in the taxable year in which the interest expense is first paid or accrued.

(3) *Ordering rule for conversion of excess business interest expense to business interest expense paid or accrued by a partner.*—A specified foreign partner's allocable share of excess business interest expense (determined under § 1.163(j)-6(f)(2) or paragraph (e)(2) of this section) is treated as business interest expense paid or accrued under § 1.163(j)-6(g)(2)(i) in the order of the taxable years in which the excess business interest expense arose, and pro rata between allocable ECI excess BIE and allocable non-ECI excess BIE that arose in the same taxable year. This paragraph (e)(3) applies before application of paragraph (b)(3) of this section.

(4) *Allocable ECI excess BIE and allocable non-ECI excess BIE retains its character when treated as business interest expense paid or accrued in a succeeding taxable year.*—If excess business interest expense of a partnership in which a specified foreign partner is a direct or indirect partner is treated as business interest expense paid or accrued by the specified foreign partner or a partnership in which it is a direct or indirect partner under § 1.163(j)-6(g)(2)(i), then allocable ECI excess BIE is treated as business interest expense allocable to ECI and allocable non-ECI excess BIE is treated as business interest expense allocable to income that is not ECI.

(f) *Coordination of the application of section 163(j) with § 1.882-5 and similar provisions and with the branch profits tax.*—(1) *Coordination of section 163(j) with § 1.882-5 and similar provisions.*—(i) *Ordering rule.*—A foreign corporation first determines its business interest expense allocable to ECI under § 1.882-5 or any other relevant provision (*§ 1.882-5 and similar provisions*) before applying section 163(j) to the foreign corporation. If a foreign corporation has a disallowed business interest expense carryforward from a taxable year, then none of that business interest expense is taken into account for purposes of determining business interest expense under § 1.882-5 and similar provisions in a succeeding taxable year.

(ii) *Treatment of excess business interest expense.*—For purposes of applying § 1.882-5 and similar provisions, the business interest expense of a specified foreign partner that is a direct or indirect partner in a partnership is determined without regard to the application of section 163(j) to the partnership. As a result, for purposes of applying § 1.882-5 and similar provisions, the specified foreign partner's share of business interest expense on liabilities of a partnership in which it is a direct or indirect partner is determined as if any excess business interest expense of the partnership (determined under § 1.163(j)-6(f)(2) or paragraph (e)(2) of this section) were deductible in the taxable year in which the business interest expense is first paid or accrued and not in a succeeding taxable year.

(iii) *Attribution of certain § 1.882-5 interest expense among the foreign corporation and its partnership interests.*—(A) *In general.*—If a foreign corporation is a specified foreign partner in one or more partnerships, then, for purposes of section 163(j) and the section 163(j) regulations, interest expense determined under § 1.882-5(b) through (d) or § 1.882-5(e) (*§ 1.882-5 three-step interest expense*) is treated as attributable to liabilities of the foreign corporation or the foreign corporation's share of liabilities of each partnership in accordance with paragraphs (f)(1)(iii)(B) and (f)(1)(iii)(C) of this section. Accordingly, the portion of the § 1.882-5 three-step interest expense attributable to liabilities of the foreign corporation described in this paragraph (f)(1)(iii) is subject to section 163(j) and the section 163(j) regulations at the level of the foreign corporation. The portion of the § 1.882-5 three-step interest expense interest attributable to liabilities of a partnership described in this paragraph (f)(1)(iii) is subject to section 163(j) and the section 163(j) regulations at the partnership-level. See § 1.163(j)-6. This paragraph (f)(1)(iii) merely characterizes interest expense of the foreign corporation and its partnership interests as ECI or not ECI. It does not change the amount of interest expense of the foreign corporation or its partnership interests.

(B) *Attribution of interest expense on U.S. booked liabilities.*—The § 1.882-5 three-step interest expense is treated as attributable, pro rata, to interest expense on U.S. booked liabilities of a foreign corporation, determined under § 1.882-5(d)(2)(ii)-(iii) or its interest expense on its share of U.S. booked liabilities of a partnership, determined under § 1.882-5(d)(2)(vii), as applicable, to the extent thereof (without regard to whether the foreign corporation uses the method described in § 1.882-5(b) through (d) or the method described in § 1.882-5(e) for purposes of determining § 1.882-5 interest expense).

(C) *Attribution of excess § 1.882-5 three-step interest expense.*—(*1*) *In general.*—The § 1.882-5 three-step interest expense in excess of interest expense attributable to U.S. booked liabilities described in § 1.882-5(d)(2), if any (*excess § 1.882-5 three-step interest expense*), is treated as attributable to liabilities of the foreign corporation or the foreign corporation's allocable share of liabilities of one or more partnerships, in accordance with paragraphs (f)(1)(iii)(C)(*2*) and (f)(1)(iii)(C)(*3*) of this section, subject to the limitation in paragraph (f)(1)(iii)(C)(*4*) of this section. For purposes of this paragraph (f)(1)(iii)(C), the term "U.S. assets" means U.S. assets described in § 1.882-5(b).

(*2*) *Attribution of excess § 1.882-5 three-step interest expense to the foreign corporation.*—Excess § 1.882-5 three-step interest expense is treated as attributable to interest expense on liabilities of the foreign corporation (and not its partnership interests) in proportion to its U.S. assets other than its partnership interests over all of its U.S. assets.

(*3*) *Attribution of excess § 1.882-5 three-step interest expense to partnerships.*—(*i*) *In general.*—Excess § 1.882-5 three-step interest expense is treated as attributable to interest expense on the foreign corporation's direct or indirect allocable share of liabilities of a partnership in proportion to the portion of the partnership interest that is treated as a U.S. asset under paragraph (f)(1)(iii)(C)(*3*)(*ii*) of this section over all of the foreign corporation's U.S. assets.

(*ii*) *Direct and indirect partnership interests.*—If a foreign corporation owns an interest in a partnership that does not own an interest in any other partnerships, the portion of the partnership interest that is a U.S. asset is determined under § 1.882-5(b). If a foreign corporation owns an interest in a partnership (the top-tier partnership) that owns an interest in one or more other partnerships, directly or indirectly (the lower-tier partnerships), the portion of the foreign corporation's direct or indirect interest in the top-tier partnership and lower-tier partnerships that is a U.S. asset is determined by re-attributing the portion of the top-tier partnership interest that is a U.S. asset, as determined under § 1.882-5(b), among the foreign corporation's direct interest in the top-tier partnership and indirect interests in each lower-tier partnership in proportion to their contribution to the portion of the foreign corporation's interest in the upper-tier partnership that is a U.S. asset. Each partnership interest's contribution is determined based on a reasonable method consistent with the method used to determine the portion of the top-tier partnership interest that is a U.S. asset under § 1.882-5(b).

(*4*) *Limitation on attribution of excess § 1.882-5 three-step interest expense.*—The portion of excess § 1.882-5 three-step interest expense attributable to a foreign corporation under paragraph (f)(1)(iii)(C)(*2*) of this section or to a partnership under paragraph (f)(1)(iii)(C)(*2*) or (f)(1)(iii)(C)(*3*) of this section, as applicable, is limited to interest on liabilities of the foreign corporation or the foreign corporation's allocable share of liabilities of the partnership, reduced by the sum of the amounts of interest expense on its U.S. booked liabilities described in § 1.882-5(d)(2) and interest expense on liabilities described in § 1.882-5(a)(1)(ii)(A) or (B) (regarding direct allocations of interest expense). The portion of any excess § 1.882-5 three-step interest expense that would be treated as attributable to the foreign corporation or a partnership interest, as applicable, but for this paragraph (f)(1)(iii)(C)(*4*) is re-attributable in accordance with the rules and principles of this paragraph (f)(1)(iii)(C). The portion of any excess § 1.882-5 three-step interest expense that cannot be re-attributed under the rules of (f)(1)(iii)(C)(*1*) through (*3*) of this section because of the application of the first sentence of this paragraph (f)(1)(iii)(C)(*4*) is attributable, first to interest on liabilities of the foreign corporation, and then, pro rata, to the foreign corporation's allocable share of interest on liabilities of its direct or indirect partnership interests, to the extent such attribution is not in excess of the limitation described in this paragraph (f)(1)(iii)(C)(*4*), and without regard to whether the foreign corporation or its partnership interests have U.S. assets.

(2) *Coordination with the branch profits tax.*—The disallowance and carryforward of business interest expense under § 1.163(j)-2(b) and (c) will not affect the computation of the U.S. net equity of a foreign corporation, as defined in § 1.884-1(c).

(g) *Definitions.*—The following definitions apply for purposes of this section.

(1) *§ 1.882-5 and similar provisions.*—The term *§ 1.882-5 and similar provisions* has the meaning provided in paragraph (f)(1)(i) of this section.

(2) *§ 1.882-5 three-step interest expense.*—The term *§ 1.882-5 three-step interest expense* has the meaning provided in paragraph (f)(1)(iii)(A) of this section.

(3) *Allocable ECI BIE.*—The term *allocable ECI BIE* means, with respect to a partnership, the specified foreign partner's allocable share of the partnership's business interest expense that is ECI, taking into account the application of paragraph (e)(2) of this section.

(4) *Allocable ECI BII.*—The term *allocable ECI BII* has the meaning provided in paragraph (c)(4)(ii) of this section.

(5) *Allocable ECI deductible BIE.*—The term *allocable ECI deductible BIE* has the meaning provided in paragraph (c)(3)(i) of this section.

(6) *Allocable ECI excess BIE.*—The term *allocable ECI excess BIE* has the meaning provided in paragraph (c)(2)(i) of this section.

(7) *Allocable non-ECI BIE.*—The term *allocable non-ECI BIE* means, with respect a partnership, the specified foreign partner's allocable share of the partnership's business interest expense that is not ECI, taking into account the application of paragraph (e)(2) of this section.

(8) *Allocable non-ECI deductible BIE.*—The term *allocable non-ECI deductible BIE* has the meaning provided in paragraph (c)(3)(i) of this section.

(9) *Allocable non-ECI excess BIE.*—The term *allocable non-ECI excess BIE* has the meaning provided in paragraph (c)(2)(ii) of this section.

(10) *Distributive share of ECI.*—The term *distributive share of ECI* has the meaning provided in paragraph (c)(1)(iii) of this section.

(11) *Distributive share of non-ECI.*—The term *distributive share of non-ECI* has the meaning provided in paragraph (c)(1)(iv) of this section.

(12) *Effectively connected income.*—The term *effectively connected income* (or *ECI*) means income or gain that is ECI, as defined in § 1.884-1(d)(1)(iii), and deduction or loss that is allocable to, ECI, as defined in § 1.884-1(d)(1)(iii).

(13) *Excess § 1.882-5 three-step interest expense.*—The term *excess § 1.882-5 three-step interest expense* has the meaning provided in paragraph (f)(1)(iii)(C)(*1*) of this section.

(14) *FC ECI BIE.*—The term *FC ECI BIE* means, with respect to a relevant foreign corporation and a taxable year, business interest expense that is ECI, determined without regard to the application of section 163(j) and the section 163(j) regulations except for the application of paragraph (f)(1)(iii) of this section.

(15) *FC ECI deductible BIE.*—The term *FC ECI deductible BIE* has the meaning provided in paragraph (d)(3)(i) of this section.

(16) *FC ECI disallowed BIE.*—The term *FC ECI disallowed BIE* has the meaning provided in paragraph (d)(2)(i) of this section.

(17) *FC non-ECI BIE.*—The term *FC non-ECI BIE* means, with respect to a relevant foreign corporation and a taxable year, business interest expense that is not ECI, determined without regard to the application of section 163(j) and the section 163(j) regulations except for the application of paragraph (f)(1)(iii) of this section.

(18) *FC non-ECI deductible BIE.*—The term *FC non-ECI deductible BIE* has the meaning provided in paragraph (d)(3)(i) of this section.

(19) *FC non-ECI disallowed BIE.*—The term *FC non-ECI disallowed BIE* has the meaning provided in paragraph (d)(2)(ii) of this section.

(20) *Hypothetical partnership ECI deductible BIE.*—The term *hypothetical partnership ECI deductible BIE* has the meaning provided in paragraph (c)(3)(iii)(A) of this section.

(21) *Hypothetical partnership non-ECI deductible BIE.*—The term *hypothetical partnership non-ECI deductible BIE* has the meaning provided in paragraph (c)(3)(iii)(B) of this section.

(22) *Hypothetical FC ECI deductible BIE.*—The term *hypothetical FC ECI deductible BIE* has the meaning provided in paragraph (d)(3)(iii)(A) of this section.

(23) *Hypothetical FC non-ECI deductible BIE.*—The term *hypothetical FC non-ECI deductible BIE* has the meaning provided in paragraph (d)(3)(iii)(B) of this section.

(24) *Specified ATI ratio.*—The term *specified ATI ratio* has the meaning provided in paragraph (c)(1)(ii) of this section.

(25) *Specified BII ratio.*—The term *specified BII ratio* has the meaning provided in paragraph (c)(4)(ii) of this section.

(26) *Specified foreign partner.*—The term *specified foreign partner* means, with respect to a partnership that has ECI, a direct or indirect partner that is a specified foreign person or a relevant foreign corporation.

(27) *Specified foreign person.*—The term *specified foreign person* means a nonresident alien individual, as defined in section 7701(b) and the regulations under section 7701(b), or a foreign corporation other than a relevant foreign corporation.

(28) *Successor.*—The term *successor* includes, with respect to a foreign corporation, the acquiring corporation in a transaction described in section 381(a) in which the foreign corporation is the distributor or transferor corporation.

(h) *Examples.*—The following examples illustrate the application of this section. For all examples, assume that all referenced interest expense is deductible but for the application of section 163(j), the small business exemption under § 1.163(j)-2(d) is not available, no entity is engaged in an excepted trade or business, no business interest expense is floor plan financing interest expense, all entities have the same taxable year, all entities use the U.S. dollar as their functional currency, no foreign corporation is a relevant foreign corporation, all relevant taxable years begin after December 31, 2020, and, for purposes of computing ATI, none of the adjustments described in § 1.163(j)-1(b) are relevant other than the adjustment for business interest expense.

(1) *Example 1. Limitation on business interest deduction of a foreign corporation.*—(i) *Facts.* FC, a foreign corporation, has $100x of gross income that is ECI. FC has $60x of other income which is not ECI. FC has total expenses of $100x, of which $50x is business interest expense. Assume that FC has $30x of § 1.882-5 three-step interest expense. Under section 882(c) and the regulations, FC has $40x of other expenses that are ECI, none of which are business interest expense. FC does not have any business interest income. All amounts described in this paragraph (h)(1)(i) are with respect to a single taxable year of FC.

(ii) *Analysis.* FC is a specified foreign person under paragraph (g)(27) of this section. The amount of FC's business interest expense that is disallowed for the taxable year is determined under § 1.163(j)-2(b) with respect to business interest expense described in paragraph (b)(3) of this section. Under paragraph (b)(3) of this section, FC has business interest expense of $30x. Under paragraph (b)(2) of this section, FC has ATI of $60x ($100x - $40x). Accordingly, FC's section 163(j) limitation is $18x ($60x x 30 percent). Because FC's business interest expense ($30x) that is ECI exceeds the section 163(j) limitation ($18x), FC may only deduct $18x of business interest expense. Under § 1.163(j)-2(c), the remaining $12x is disallowed business interest expense carryforward, and under paragraph (f)(1)(i) of this section, the $12x is not taken into account for purposes of applying § 1.882-5 in the succeeding taxable year.

(2) *Example 2. Use of a disallowed business interest expense carryforward.* (i) *Facts*. The facts are the same as in *Example 1* in paragraph (h)(1)(i) of this section except that for the taxable year FC has $300x of gross income that is all ECI. Furthermore, assume that for the taxable year FC has a disallowed business interest expense carryforward of $25x with respect to business interest expense described in paragraph (b)(3) of this section.

(ii) *Analysis*. Under paragraph (f)(1)(i) of this section, FC's $25x of disallowed business interest expense carryforward is not taken into account for purposes of determining FC's interest expense under § 1.882-5 for the taxable year. Therefore, FC has $30x of § 1.882-5 three-step interest expense. Under paragraph (b)(2) of this section, FC has ATI of $260x ($300x of gross income reduced by $40 of expenses other than business interest expense). Accordingly, FC's section 163(j) limitation is $78x ($260x x 30 percent). Because FC's business interest expense ($55x) does not exceed the section 163(j) limitation ($78x), FC may deduct all $55x of business interest expense.

(3) *Example 3. Foreign corporation is engaged in a U.S. trade or business and is also a specified foreign partner.*—(i) *Facts*. FC, a foreign corporation, owns a 50-percent interest in ABC, a partnership that has ECI. In addition to owning a 50-percent interest in ABC, FC conducts a separate business that is engaged in a trade or business in the United States, Business Y. Business Y produces $65x of taxable income before taking into account business interest expense and has U.S. assets with an adjusted basis of $300x, business interest expense of $15x on $160x of liabilities, and no business interest income. All of the liabilities of Business Y are U.S. booked liabilities for purposes of § 1.882-5(d). FC also has various foreign operations, some of which have U.S. dollar denominated debt. ABC has two lines of business, Business S and Business T. FC is allocated 50 percent of all items of income and expense of Business S and Business T. Business S produces $140x of taxable income before taking into account business interest expense, and Business T produces $80x of taxable income before taking into account business interest expense. Business S has business interest expense of $20x on $400x of liabilities and no business interest income. Business T has business interest expense of $10x on $150x of liabilities and no business interest income. With respect to FC, only Business S produces ECI. FC has an outside basis of $600x in the portion of its ABC partnership interest that is a U.S. asset for purposes of § 1.882-5(b), step 1. All of the liabilities of Business S are U.S. booked liabilities for purposes of § 1.882-5(d). FC computes its interest expense under the three-step method described in § 1.882-5(b) through (d) and for purposes of § 1.882-5(c), step 2, FC uses the fixed ratio of 50 percent described in § 1.882-5(c)(4) for taxpayers that are neither a bank nor an insurance company. Under § 1.882-5(d)(5)(ii), FC's interest rate on excess U.S. connected liabilities is 5 percent. For the taxable year, assume FC has total interest expense of $100x for purposes of § 1.882-5(a)(3). All amounts described in this paragraph (h)(3)(i) are with respect to a single taxable year of FC or ABC, as applicable.

(ii) *Analysis*—(A) *Application of § 1.882-5 to FC*. FC is a specified foreign person under paragraph (g)(27) of this section and a specified foreign partner under paragraph (g)(26) of this section. Under paragraph (f)(1) of this section, FC first determines its § 1.882-5 three-step interest expense and then applies section 163(j). Under § 1.882-5(b), step 1, FC has U.S. assets of $900x ($600x of basis in the portion of its ABC partnership interest that is a U.S. asset determined using the asset method described in § 1.884-1(d)(3)(ii) + $300x basis in U.S. assets of Business Y). Under § 1.882-5(c), step 2, applying the 50-percent fixed ratio described in § 1.882-5(c)(4), FC has U.S. connected liabilities of $450x ($900x x 50 percent). Under § 1.882-5(d), step 3, FC has U.S. booked liabilities of $360x ($200x attributable to its 50-percent share of Business S liabilities of ABC + $160x of Business Y liabilities) and interest on U.S. booked liabilities of $25x ($10x attributable to its 50-percent share of $20x interest expense of Business S + $15x of Business Y interest expense). FC has excess U.S. connected liabilities of $90x ($450x – $360x) and under § 1.882-5(d)(5) has interest expense on excess U.S. connected liabilities of $4.50x ($90x x 5 percent), which is excess § 1.882-5 three-step interest expense. FC's § 1.882-5 three-step interest expense is $29.50x ($25x + $4.50x).

(B) *Attribution of § 1.882-5 business interest expense between FC and ABC*. Under paragraph (f)(1)(iii) of this section, FC's § 1.882-5 three-step interest expense is attributable to interest on its liabilities or on its share of ABC liabilities. Under paragraph (f)(1)(iii)(B), FC's § 1.882-5 three-step interest expense of $29.50x is first attributable to $15 of interest expense on FC's (Business Y) U.S. booked liabilities and $10x of interest expense on FC's share of U.S. booked liabilities of ABC. Under paragraph (f)(1)(iii)(C)(2) of this section, of the excess § 1.882-5 three-step interest expense of $4.50x ($29.50x - $15x - $10x), 66.67 percent ($600x of basis in the portion of the ABC partnership interest that is a U.S. asset / $900x of total U.S. assets), or $3.00x, is attributable to interest expense on FC's share of liabilities of ABC and 33.33 percent ($300x U.S. assets other than partnership interests / $900x of total U.S. assets), or $1.50x, is attributable to interest expense on liabilities of FC. As a result, $16.50x of business interest expense ($15x + $1.50x) is attributed to FC and $13x of business interest expense ($10x + $3x) is attributed to ABC. The limitation under paragraph (f)(1)(iii)(C)(*4*) of this section does not change the result described in the preceding sentence. Specifically, under paragraph (f)(1)(iii)(C)(*4*) of this section, the amount attributed to ABC (tentatively, $3.00x) is limited to $5x (FC's 50-percent share of the $30x of business interest expense of ABC or $15x, reduced by FC's 50-percent share of the $20x of business interest expense on U.S. booked liabilities of Business S), and the amount attributed to FC (tentatively, $1.50x) is limited to $70x (FC's business interest expense of $100x, reduced by $15x of business interest expense on U.S. booked liabilities of Business Y and its $15x allocable share of ABC's business interest expense).

(C) *Application of the section 163(j) limitation to ABC*. Under § 1.163(j)-6(a), ABC computes a section 163(j) limitation at the partnership level. ABC has business interest expense of $30x ($20x from Business S and $10x from Business T). Under § 1.163(j)-6(d), ABC has ATI of $220x ($140 + $80). Under § 1.163(j)-2(b), ABC's section 163(j) limitation is $66x ($220x x 30 percent). Because ABC's business interest expense ($30x) does not exceed the section 163(j) limitation ($66x), all of ABC's business interest expense is deductible for the taxable year.

(D) *Excess taxable income of ABC*. Under § 1.163(j)-1(b)(15), ABC has excess taxable income of $120x ($220x x ($36x/$66x)). Under § 1.163(j)-6(f)(2), FC is allocated 50 percent of the $120x of ABC's excess taxable income or $60x of allocable excess taxable income. Under paragraph (c)(1) of this section, the amount of the allocable excess taxable income of $60x that is ECI is equal to FC's allocable excess taxable income multiplied by the specified ATI ratio. Under paragraph (c)(1)(iii) of this section, FC's distributive share of ECI of ABC is $57x (FC's 50-percent share of $140x (Business S income computed without regard to business interest expense) or $70x - $13x of business interest expense that is ECI). Under paragraph (c)(1)(iv) of this section, FC's distributive share of non-ECI of ABC is $38x (FC's 50-percent share of $80x (Business T income computed without regard to business interest expense) or $40x - $2x of business interest expense that is not ECI). FC's distributive share of partnership items of income, gain, deduction, and loss of ABC is $95x ($57x distributive share of ECI and $38x distributive share of non-ECI). Because both FC's distributive share of ECI and distributive share of non-ECI are positive, under paragraph (c)(1)(ii) of this section, the specified ATI ratio is 60 percent ($57x distributive share of ECI / $95x distributive share of partnership items of income, gain, deduction, and loss of ABC). As a result, the amount of FC's allocable excess taxable income from ABC that is ECI is $36x ($60 of allocable excess taxable income x 60 percent specified ATI ratio).

(E) *Application of section 163(j) to FC*. Under paragraph (b)(3) of this section, FC's business interest expense is $16.50x. Under § 1.163(j)-6(e)(1), FC's ATI is determined under § 1.163(j)-1(b)(1) without regard to FC's distributive share of any items of income, gain, deduction, or loss of ABC. Under paragraph (b)(2) of this section, FC's ATI is $101x ($65x of ECI from Business Y + $36x of allocable excess taxable income from ABC that is ECI). FC's section 163(j) limitation is $30.30x ($101x x 30 percent). Because FC's business interest expense ($16.50x) is less than FC's section 163(j) limitation ($30.30x) and all of its share of ABC's business interest expense that is allocable to ECI ($13x) is deductible, FC may deduct all $29.50x of § 1.882-5 three-step interest expense determined under paragraph (h)(3)(ii)(A) of this section.

(4) *Example 4. Specified foreign partner with excess business interest expense from a partnership.*—(i) *Facts*—(A) *In general*. FC, a foreign corporation, owns a 50-percent interest in ABC, a partnership that has ECI. In addition to owning a 50-percent interest in ABC, FC conducts a separate business that is engaged in a trade or business in the United States, Business Y. Business Y produces $56x of taxable income before taking into account business interest expense and has U.S. assets with an adjusted basis of $800x, business interest expense of $16x on $200x of liabilities, and no business interest income. All of

the liabilities of Business Y are U.S. booked liabilities for purposes of §1.882-5(d). FC also has various foreign operations, some of which have U.S. dollar denominated debt.

(B) *ABC Partnership.* ABC has two lines of business, Business S and Business T, and owns a 50-percent interest in DEF, a partnership. FC is allocated 50 percent of all items of income and expenses of Business S and Business T and ABC's allocable share of items from partnership DEF. Business S produces $80x of taxable income before taking into account business interest expense, and Business T produces $90x of taxable income before taking into account business interest expense. Business S has business interest expense of $30x on $500x of liabilities and no business interest income. Business T has business interest expense of $50x on $500x of liabilities and no business interest income. With respect to FC, only Business S produces ECI. All of the liabilities of Business S are U.S. booked liabilities for purposes of §1.882-5(d).

(C) *DEF Partnership.* DEF has two lines of business, Business U and Business V. ABC is allocated 50 percent of all items of income and expenses of Business U and Business V. Business U produces $100x of taxable income before taking into account business interest expense and Business V produces $140x of taxable income before taking into account business interest expense. Business U has business interest expense of $40x on $600x of liabilities and no business interest income. Business V has business interest expense of $60x on $600x of liabilities and no business interest income. With respect to FC, only Business U produces ECI. All of the liabilities of Business U are U.S. booked liabilities for purposes of §1.882-5(d).

(D) *Section 1.882-5.* FC has an outside basis of $600x in the portion of its ABC partnership interest that is a U.S. asset for purposes of §1.882-5(b), step 1, determined using the asset method described in §1.884-1(d)(3)(ii). For purposes of §1.884-1(d)(3)(ii), ABC has a total basis of $500 in assets that would be treated as U.S. assets if ABC were a foreign corporation, including a basis of $250x in the portion of its interest in DEF partnership interest that would be treated as a U.S. asset if ABC were a foreign corporation. FC computes its interest expense under the three-step method described in §1.882-5(b) through (d), and for purposes of §1.882-5(c), step 2, FC uses the fixed ratio of 50 percent described in §1.882-5(c)(4) for taxpayers that are neither a bank nor an insurance company. FC has total interest expense of $100x for purposes of §1.882-5(a)(3). Under §1.882-5(d)(5)(ii), FC's interest rate on excess U.S. connected liabilities is 6 percent. All amounts described in this paragraph (h)(4)(i) are with respect to a single taxable year of FC, ABC, or DEF, as applicable.

(ii) *Analysis—(A) Application of §1.882-5 to FC.* FC is a specified foreign person under paragraph (g)(27) of this section and a specified foreign partner under paragraph (g)(26) of this section. Under paragraph (f)(1) of this section, FC first determines its §1.882-5 three-step interest expense and then applies section 163(j). Under §1.882-5(b), step 1, FC has U.S. assets of $1400x ($600x of basis in the portion of its ABC partnership interest that is a U.S. asset + $800x basis in U.S. assets of Business Y). Under §1.882-5(c), step 2, applying the 50-percent fixed ratio described in §1.882-5(c)(4), FC has U.S. connected liabilities of $700x ($1400x x 50 percent). Under §1.882-5(d), step 3, FC has U.S. booked liabilities of $600x ($250x attributable to its 50-percent share of Business S liabilities of ABC + $150x attributable to its indirect 25-percent share of Business U liabilities of DEF + $200x of Business Y liabilities), and interest on U.S. booked liabilities of $41x ($15x attributable to its 50-percent share of $30x interest expense of Business S + $10x attributable to its 25-percent share of $40 interest expense of Business U + $16x of Business Y interest expense). FC has excess U.S. connected liabilities of $100x ($700x – $600x) and under §1.882-5(d)(5), interest expense on excess U.S. connected liabilities of $6x ($100x x 6 percent), which is excess §1.882-5 three-step interest expense. FC's §1.882-5 three-step interest expense is $47x ($41x + $6x).

(B) *Attribution of certain §1.882-5 business interest expense among FC, ABC, and DEF.* Under paragraph (f)(1)(iii) of this section, FC's §1.882-5 three-step interest expense is attributable to interest on its liabilities or on its share of ABC and DEF's liabilities. Under paragraph (f)(1)(iii)(B) of this section, FC's §1.882-5 three-step interest expense of $47x is first attributable to $16 of interest expense on FC's U.S. booked liabilities, $15x of interest expense on FC's share of U.S. booked liabilities of ABC, and $10x of interest expense on FC's share of U.S. booked liabilities of DEF. Under paragraph (f)(1)(iii)(C)(*2*) of this section, of the excess §1.882-5 three-step interest expense of $6x ($47x - $16x - $15x - $10x), 42.86 percent ($600x of basis in the portion of the ABC partnership interest that is a U.S. asset / $1400x of total U.S. assets) or $2.57x is attributable to interest expense on FC's share of liabilities of ABC (and its partnership interests), and 57.14 percent ($800x U.S. assets other than partnership interests / $1400x of total U.S. assets) or $3.43x is attributable to interest expense on liabilities of FC. Under paragraph (f)(1)(iii)(C)(*3*) of this section, of the $2.57x of business interest expense that is ECI and that is attributable to interest expense on FC's share of liabilities of ABC (and its partnership interests), 50 percent ($250x of basis in the portion of the DEF partnership interest that would be a U.S. asset if ABC were a foreign corporation / $500x total basis in assets that would be U.S. assets if ABC were a foreign corporation), or $1.29x, is attributable to interest expense on FC's share of liabilities of ABC and 50 percent ($250x of basis in assets other than partnership interests that would be U.S. assets if ABC were a foreign corporation / $500x of total basis in assets that would be U.S. assets if ABC were a foreign corporation), or $1.29x is attributable to interest expense on FC's share of liabilities of DEF. As a result, $19.43x ($16x + $3.43x) of business interest expense is attributed to FC, $16.29x ($15x + $1.29x) of business interest expense is attributed to ABC, and $11.29x ($10x + $1.29x) of business interest expense is attributed to DEF. The limitation under paragraph (f)(1)(iii)(C)(*4*) of this section does not change the result described in the preceding sentence. Specifically, under paragraph (f)(1)(iii)(C)(*4*) of this section, the amount attributed to FC (tentatively, $3.43x) is limited to $19x (FC's business interest expense of $100x, reduced by $16x of business interest expense on U.S. booked liabilities of Business Y, its $40x allocable share of ABC's business interest expense, and its $25 allocable share of DEF's business interest expense); the amount attributed to ABC (tentatively, $1.29x) is limited to $25x (FC's 50-percent share of the $80x of business interest expense of ABC, or $40x, reduced by FC's 50-percent share of the $30x of business interest expense on U.S. booked liabilities of Business S, or $15x); and the amount attributed to DEF (tentatively, $1.29x) is limited to $15x (FC's 25-percent share of the $100x of business interest expense of DEF, or $25x, reduced by FC's 25-percent share of the $40x of business interest expense on U.S. booked liabilities of Business U, or $10x).

(C) *Application of section 163(j) to DEF—(1) In general.* Under §1.163(j)-6(a), DEF computes a section 163(j) limitation at the partnership-level. DEF has business interest expense of $100x ($40x from Business U + $60x from Business V). Under §1.163(j)-6(d), DEF has ATI of $240x ($100x + $140x). Under §1.163(j)-2(b), DEF's section 163(j) limitation is $72x ($240x x 30 percent). Because DEF's business interest expense ($100x) exceeds the section 163(j) limitation ($72x), only $72x of DEF's business interest expense is deductible and $28x is disallowed under section 163(j). Pursuant to paragraph (e)(2) of this section, FC is allocated $7x of excess business interest expense (25 percent x $28x) and $18x of deductible business interest expense (25 percent x $72x).

(*2*) *Deductible business interest expense.* Under paragraph (c)(3) of this section, in order to determine the portion of FC's allocable deductible business interest expense ($18x) that is allocable ECI deductible BIE and the portion that is allocable non-ECI deductible BIE, the hypothetical partnership ECI deductible BIE and hypothetical partnership non-ECI deductible BIE must be determined. Under paragraph (c)(3)(iii)(A) of this section, FC's hypothetical partnership ECI deductible BIE with respect to DEF is $7.50x ($25x of FC's allocable share of ECI before taking into account interest expense x 30 percent). Under paragraph (c)(3)(iii)(B) of this section, FC's hypothetical partnership non-ECI deductible BIE with respect to DEF is $10.50x ($35x of FC's allocable share of income that is not ECI before taking into account interest expense x 30 percent). Under paragraph (c)(3)(i) of this section, allocable ECI deductible BIE is equal to the amounts described in paragraphs (c)(3)(ii)(A)(*1*)(*i*) and (c)(3)(ii)(*B*)(*1*) of this section and allocable non-ECI deductible BIE is equal to the amounts described in paragraphs (c)(3)(ii)(A)(*1*)(*ii*) and (c)(3)(ii)(*B*)(*2*) of this section. Under paragraph (c)(3)(ii)(A)(*1*) of this section, FC's allocable deductible business interest expense ($18x) is allocated pro rata between hypothetical partnership ECI deductible BIE ($7.50x) and hypothetical partnership non-ECI deductible BIE ($10.50x). However, the amount allocated to hypothetical partnership ECI deductible BIE cannot exceed the lesser of hypothetical partnership ECI deductible BIE ($7.50x) or allocable ECI BIE ($11.29x), and the amount allocated to hypothetical partnership non-ECI deductible BIE cannot exceed the lesser of hypothetical partnership non-ECI deductible BIE ($10.50x) or allocable non-ECI BIE (total allocable business interest expense of $25x reduced by allocable ECI BIE of $11.29x, or $13.71x). The portion of FC's allocable deductible business interest expense ($18x) from DEF that is allocable ECI deductible BIE is 41.67 percent ($7.50x of hypothetical partnership ECI deductible BIE / $18x of total hypothetical partnership deductible BIE), or $7.5x. The portion of FC's allocable deductible business interest expense from DEF ($18x) that is allocable non-ECI deductible BIE is 58.33 percent ($10.50x of hypothetical partnership ECI deductible BIE / $18x of total hypothetical partnership deductible BIE), or $10.50x. Because the full amount of FC's allocable deductible business interest expense

($18x) is allocable under paragraph (c)(3)(ii)(A)(*1*) of this section, no portion is allocated under paragraph (c)(3)(ii)(B) of this section.

(*3*) *Excess business interest expense.* Under paragraph (c)(2)(i) of this section, the portion of excess business interest expense allocated to FC from DEF pursuant to paragraph (e)(2) of this section ($7x) that is allocable ECI excess BIE is $3.79x ($11.29x of allocable ECI BIE - $7.50x allocable ECI deductible BIE). Under paragraph (c)(2)(ii) of this section, the portion of excess business interest expense allocated to FC from DEF pursuant to paragraph (e)(2) of this section ($7x) that is allocable non-ECI excess BIE is $3.21x ($13.71x of allocable non-ECI BIE - $10.50x allocable non-ECI deductible BIE).

(D) *Application of section 163(j) to ABC*—(*1*) *In general.* Under § 1.163(j)-6(a), ABC computes a section 163(j) limitation at the partnership-level. ABC has business interest expense of $80x ($30x from Business S + $50x from Business T). Under § 1.163(j)-6(d), ABC has ATI of $170x ($80x + $90x). Under § 1.163(j)-2(b), ABC's section 163(j) limitation is $51x ($170x x 30 percent). Because ABC's business interest expense ($80x) exceeds the section 163(j) limitation ($51x), ABC may only deduct $51x of business interest expense, and $29x is disallowed under section 163(j). Pursuant to § 1.163(j)-6(f)(2), FC is allocated $14.50x of excess business interest expense (50 percent x $29x) and $25.50x of deductible business interest expense (50 percent x $51x).

(*2*) *Deductible business interest expense.* Under paragraph (c)(3) of this section, in order to determine the portion of FC's allocable deductible business interest expense ($25.50x) that is allocable ECI deductible BIE and the portion that is allocable non-ECI deductible BIE, the hypothetical partnership ECI deductible BIE and hypothetical partnership non-ECI deductible BIE must be determined. Under paragraph (c)(3)(iii)(A) of this section, FC's hypothetical partnership ECI deductible BIE with respect to ABC is $12x ($40x of FC's allocable share of ECI before taking into account interest expense x 30 percent). Under paragraph (c)(3)(iii)(B) of this section, FC's hypothetical partnership non-ECI deductible BIE with respect to ABC is $13.50x ($45x of FC's allocable share of income that is not ECI before taking into account interest expense x 30 percent). Under paragraph (c)(3)(i) of this section, allocable ECI deductible BIE is equal to the amounts described in paragraphs (c)(3)(ii)(A)(*1*)(*i*) and (c)(3)(ii)(B)(*1*) of this section and allocable non-ECI deductible BIE is equal to the amounts described in paragraphs (c)(3)(ii)(A)(*1*)(*ii*) and (c)(3)(ii)(*B*)(*2*) of this section. Under paragraph (c)(3)(ii)(*A*)(*1*) of this section, FC's allocable deductible business interest expense ($25.50x) is allocated pro rata between hypothetical partnership ECI deductible BIE ($12x) and hypothetical partnership non-ECI deductible BIE ($13.50x). However, the amount allocated to hypothetical partnership ECI deductible BIE cannot exceed the lesser of hypothetical partnership ECI deductible BIE ($12x) or allocable ECI BIE ($16.29x), and the amount allocated to hypothetical partnership non-ECI deductible BIE cannot exceed the lesser of hypothetical partnership non-ECI deductible BIE ($13.50x) or allocable non-ECI BIE (total allocable business interest expense of $40x reduced by allocable ECI BIE of $16.29x, or $23.71x). The portion of FC's allocable deductible business interest expense from ABC ($25.50x) that is allocable ECI deductible BIE is 47.06 percent ($12x of hypothetical partnership ECI deductible BIE / $25.50x of total hypothetical partnership deductible BIE), or $12x. The portion of FC's allocable deductible business interest expense from ABC that is allocable non-ECI deductible BIE is 52.94 percent ($13.50x of hypothetical partnership ECI deductible BIE / $25.50x of total hypothetical partnership deductible BIE), or $13.50x. Because the full amount of FC's allocable deductible business interest expense ($25.50x) is allocable under paragraph (c)(3)(ii)(*A*)(*1*) of this section, no portion is allocated under paragraph (c)(3)(ii)(B) of this section.

(*3*) *Excess business interest expense.* Under paragraph (c)(2)(i) of this section, the portion of excess business interest expense allocated to FC from ABC pursuant to § 1.163(j)-6(f)(2)($14.50x) that is allocable ECI excess BIE is $4.29x ($16.29x of allocable ECI BIE - $12x allocable ECI deductible BIE). Under paragraph (c)(2)(ii) of this section, the portion of excess business interest expense allocated to FC from ABC pursuant to § 1.163(j)-6(f)(2) ($14.50x) that is allocable non-ECI excess BIE is $10.21x ($23.71x of allocable non-ECI BIE - $13.50x allocable non-ECI deductible BIE).

(E) *Application of section 163(j) to FC.* Under paragraph (b)(3) of this section, FC's business interest expense is $19.43x. Under § 1.163(j)-6(e)(1), FC's ATI is determined under § 1.163(j)-1(b)(1) without regard to FC's distributive share of any items of income, gain, deduction, or loss of ABC or DEF. Under paragraph (b)(2) of this section, FC's ATI is $56x ($56x of ECI of Business Y before taking into account interest expense). FC's section 163(j) limitation is $16.80x ($56x x 30 percent). Because the portion of FC's business interest expense determined under § 1.882-5 that is attributed to FC ($19.43x) exceeds the section 163(j) limitation ($16.80x), FC may only deduction $16.80x of business interest expense, and $2.63x is disallowed business interest expense carryforward. After taking into account FC's allocable share of deductible business interest expense, FC may deduct $36.30x ($16.80x from FC + $12x allocable ECI deductible BIE from ABC + $7.50x allocable ECI deductible BIE from DEF). FC also has $2.63x disallowed business interest expense carryforward characterized as ECI, $4.29x allocable ECI excess BIE from ABC, $10.21x allocable non-ECI excess BIE from ABC, and, under paragraph (e)(2) of this section, is deemed to have $3.79x allocable ECI excess BIE from DEF and $3.21x allocable non ECI excess BIE from DEF.

(i) [Reserved]

(j) *Applicability date.*—This section applies to taxable years beginning on or after **[DATE 60 DAYS AFTER DATE OF PUBLICATION OF THE FINAL RULE IN THE FEDERAL REGISTER]**. However, taxpayers and their related parties, within the meaning of sections 267(b) and 707(b)(1) may choose to apply this section in its entirety for a taxable year beginning after December 31, 2017, so long as the taxpayers and their related parties also apply § 1.163(j)-7(a), (c) through (f), (g)(3) and (4), and (h) through (k) for the taxable year. For a taxable year beginning before November 13, 2020, taxpayers and their related parties may not choose to apply this section unless they also apply § 1.163(j)-7(b) and (g)(1) and (2) in accordance with the second sentence of § 1.163(j)-7(m)(1). [Prop. Reg. § 1.163(j)-8.]

[Proposed 9-14-2020.]

§ 1.163(j)-10. Allocation of interest expense, interest income, and other items of expense and gross income to an excepted trade or business.—(a) *Overview.*—(1) *In general.*—(i) *Purposes.*—Except as provided in § 1.163(j)-6(m) or § 1.163(j)-9(h), this section provides the exclusive rules for allocating tax items that are properly allocable to a trade or business between excepted trades or businesses and non-excepted trades or businesses for purposes of section 163(j). The amount of a taxpayer's interest expense that is properly allocable to excepted trades or businesses is not subject to the section 163(j) limitation. The amount of a taxpayer's other items of income, gain, deduction, or loss, including interest income, that is properly allocable to excepted trades or businesses is excluded from the calculation of the taxpayer's section 163(j) limitation. See section 163(j)(6) and (j)(8)(A)(i); see also § 1.163(j)-1(b)(1)(i)(H), (b)(1)(ii)(F), and (b)(3). The general method of allocation set forth in paragraph (c) of this section is based on the approach that money is fungible and that interest expense is attributable to all activities and property, regardless of any specific purpose for incurring an obligation on which interest is paid. In no event may the amount of interest expense allocated under this section exceed the amount of interest paid or accrued, or treated as paid or accrued, by the taxpayer within the taxable year.

(ii) *Application of section.*—The amount of a taxpayer's tax items properly allocable to a trade or business, other than interest expense and interest income, that is properly allocable to excepted trades or businesses for purposes of section 163(j) is determined as set forth in paragraph (b) of this section. The amount of a taxpayer's interest expense and interest income that is properly allocable to excepted trades or businesses for purposes of section 163(j) generally is determined as set forth in paragraph (c) of this section, except as otherwise provided in paragraph (d) of this section. For purposes of this section, a taxpayer's activities are not treated as a separate trade or business to the extent those activities involve the provision of real property, goods, or services to a trade or business of the taxpayer (or, if the taxpayer is a member of a consolidated group, the consolidated group). For example, if a taxpayer engaged in a manufacturing trade or business has in-house legal personnel that provide legal services solely with respect to the taxpayer's manufacturing business, the taxpayer is not treated as also engaged in the trade or business of providing legal services. Similarly, if the taxpayer described in the previous sentence constructs or acquires real property solely for use by the taxpayer's manufacturing business, the taxpayer is not treated as also engaged in a real property trade or business.

(2) *Coordination with other rules.*—(i) *In general.*—The rules of this section apply after a taxpayer has determined whether any interest expense or interest income paid, received, or accrued is properly allocable to a trade or business. Similarly, the rules of this section apply to other tax items after a taxpayer has determined whether those items are properly allocable to a trade or business. For instance, a taxpayer must apply § 1.163-8T, if applicable, to determine which items of interest expense are investment interest under section 163(d) before applying the rules in paragraph (c) of this section to allocate interest expense between excepted and non-excepted trades or businesses. After determining whether its tax items are properly allocable to a trade or business, a taxpayer that is engaged in both excepted and non-excepted trades or businesses must apply the rules

of this section to determine the amount of interest expense that is business interest expense subject to the section 163(j) limitation and to determine which items are included or excluded in computing its section 163(j) limitation.

(ii) *Treatment of investment interest, investment income, investment expenses, and certain other tax items of a partnership with a C corporation or tax-exempt corporation as a partner.*—For rules governing the treatment of investment interest, investment income, investment expenses, and certain other separately stated tax items of a partnership with a C corporation or tax-exempt corporation as a partner, see §§1.163(j)-4(b)(3) and 1.163(j)-6(k).

(3) *Application of allocation rules to foreign corporations and foreign partnerships.*—The rules of this section apply to foreign corporations and foreign partnerships.

(4) *Application of allocation rules to members of a consolidated group.*—(i) *In general.*—As provided in §1.163(j)-4(d), the computations required by section 163(j) and the regulations in this part under section 163(j) of the Code generally are made for a consolidated group on a consolidated basis. In this regard, for purposes of applying the allocation rules of this section, all members of a consolidated group are treated as one corporation. Therefore, the rules of this section apply to the activities conducted by the group as if those activities were conducted by a single corporation. For example, the group (rather than a particular member) is treated as engaged in excepted or non-excepted trades or businesses. In the case of intercompany obligations, within the meaning of §1.1502-13(g)(2)(ii), for purposes of allocating asset basis between excepted and non-excepted trades or businesses, the obligation of the member borrower is not considered an asset of the creditor member. Similarly, intercompany transactions, within the meaning of §1.1502-13(b)(1)(i), are disregarded for purposes of this section, as are the resulting offsetting items, and property is allocated to a trade or business based on the activities of the group as if the members of the group were divisions of a single corporation. Further, stock of a group member that is owned by another member of the same group is not treated as an asset for purposes of this section, and the transfer of any amount of member stock to a non-member is treated by the group as a transfer of the member's assets proportionate to the amount of member stock transferred. Additionally, stock of a corporation that is not a group member is treated as owned by the group.

(ii) *Application of excepted business percentage to members of a consolidated group.*—After a consolidated group has determined the percentage of the group's interest expense allocable to excepted trades or businesses for the taxable year (and thus not subject to the section 163(j) limitation), this exempt percentage is applied to the interest paid or accrued by each member during the taxable year to any lender that is not a group member. Therefore, except to the extent paragraph (d) of this section (providing rules for certain qualified nonrecourse indebtedness) applies, an identical percentage of the interest paid or accrued by each member of the group to any lender that is not a group member is treated as allocable to excepted trades or businesses, regardless of whether any particular member actually engaged in an excepted trade or business.

(iii) *Basis in assets transferred in an intercompany transaction.*—For purposes of allocating interest expense and interest income under paragraph (c) of this section, the basis of property does not include any gain or loss realized with respect to the property by another member in an intercompany transaction, as defined in §1.1502-13(b), whether or not the gain or loss is deferred.

(5) *Tax-exempt organizations.*—For tax-exempt organizations, section 512 and the regulations in this part under section 512 of the Code determine the rules for allocating all income and expenses among multiple trades or businesses.

(6) *Application of allocation rules to disallowed disqualified interest.*—A taxpayer may apply the allocation rules of this section to disallowed disqualified interest by either:

(i) Applying the allocation rules of this section to all of the taxpayer's disallowed disqualified interest in the taxable year(s) in which the disallowed disqualified interest was paid or accrued (the historical approach); or

(ii) Treating all of the taxpayer's disallowed disqualified interest as if it were paid or accrued in the taxpayer's first taxable year beginning after December 31, 2017 (the effective date approach).

(7) *Examples.*—The following examples illustrate the principles of this paragraph (a).

(i) *Example 1: Items properly allocable to a trade or business.*—(A) *Facts.* Individual T operates Business X, a non-excepted trade or business, as a sole proprietor. In Year 1, T pays or accrues $40x of interest expense and receives $100x of gross income with respect to Business X that is not eligible for a section 199A deduction. T borrows money to buy a car for personal use, and T pays or accrues $20x of interest expense with respect to the car loan. T also invests in corporate bonds, and, in Year 1, T receives $50x of interest income on those bonds.

(B) *Analysis.* Under paragraphs (a)(1) and (2) of this section, T must determine which items of income and expense, including items of interest income and interest expense, are properly allocable to a trade or business. T's $100x of gross income and T's $40x of interest expense with respect to Business X are properly allocable to a trade or business. However, the interest expense on T's car loan is personal interest within the meaning of section 163(h)(2) rather than interest properly allocable to a trade or business. Similarly, T's interest income from corporate bonds is not properly allocable to a trade or business because it is interest from investment activity. See section 163(d)(4)(B).

(ii) *Example 2: Intercompany transaction.*—(A) *Facts.* S is a member of a consolidated group of which P is the common parent. P conducts an electing real property trade or business (Business X), and S conducts a non-excepted trade or business (Business Y). P leases Building V (which P owns) to S for use in Business Y.

(B) *Analysis.* Under paragraph (a)(4)(i) of this section, a consolidated group is treated as a single corporation for purposes of applying the allocation rules of this section, and the consolidated group (rather than a particular member of the group) is treated as engaged in excepted and non-excepted trades or businesses. Thus, intercompany transactions are disregarded for purposes of this section. As a result, the lease of Building V by P to S is disregarded. Moreover, because Building V is used in Business Y, basis in this asset is allocated to Business Y rather than Business X for purposes of these allocation rules, regardless of which member (P or S) owns the building.

(iii) *Example 3: Intercompany sale of natural gas.*—(A) *Facts.* S is a member of a consolidated group of which P is the common parent. S drills for natural gas and is not an excepted regulated utility trade or business. S sells most of its natural gas production to P, which produces electricity at its natural gas-fired power plants, and S sells the rest of its natural gas production to third parties at market rates. P is an excepted regulated utility trade or business to the extent that it is engaged in a trade or business described in §1.163(j)-1(b)(15)(i).

(B) *Analysis.* Intercompany transactions are disregarded for purposes of this section. As a result, the intercompany sales of natural gas by S to P are disregarded. Moreover, the assets of S and P are allocated between the excepted and non-excepted trades or businesses of the P group based on the assets used in each trade or business. Assets of S may be allocated to the P group's excepted trade or business to the extent those assets are used in the trade or business of the furnishing or sale of electrical energy. Likewise, assets of P may be allocated to the P group's non-excepted trade or business to the extent those assets are used in the trade or business of natural gas production.

(iv) *Example 4: Disallowed disqualified interest.*—(A) *Facts.* S is a member of a consolidated group of which P is the common parent. P and S are the only members of an affiliated group under old section 163(j)(6)(C). S operates a farm equipment leasing business (Business X) that is not an excepted trade or business. P is engaged in an electing farming business (Business Y). Entering its first taxable year beginning after December 31, 2017, the P group has disallowed disqualified interest of $120x, all of which the P group paid or accrued in earlier taxable years in which it only operated Business X. The P group also incurs $100x of interest expense during its 2018 taxable year, of which $25x (25 percent of $100x) is business interest expense properly allocable to Business X and $75x (75 percent of $100x) is properly allocable to Business Y under paragraph (c) of this section.

(B) *Analysis.* Under paragraph (a)(6) of this section, the P group may allocate disallowed disqualified interest to Business X and Business Y by either applying the allocation rules of this section in the taxable years in which the disallowed disqualified interest was paid or accrued (the historical approach) or by treating such interest as though it were paid or accrued in the P group's first taxable year beginning after December 31, 2017 (the effective date approach). Accordingly, if the P group chooses to rely on the historical approach, it allocates all $120x of disallowed disqualified interest to Business X (a non-excepted trade or business), and all $120x of disallowed disqualified interest is subject to the section 163(j) limitation. If, instead, the P group chooses to rely on the effective date approach, it allocates its $120x of disallowed disqualified interest in the same proportion as its $100x of business interest expense that was paid or accrued in its 2018 taxable year. Of the $120x of disallowed disqualified interest, $30x (25 percent of $120x) is allocated to Business X and $90x (75 percent of $120x) is allocated to Business Y. The $90x of disallowed disqualified interest that is properly allocable to Business Y (an excepted trade or business) is not subject to the section 163(j) limitation.

(b) *Allocation of tax items other than interest expense and interest income.*—(1) *In general.*—Except as otherwise provided in § 1.163(j)-6(m) or § 1.163(j)-9(h), for purposes of calculating ATI, tax items other than interest expense and interest income are allocated to a particular trade or business in the manner described in this paragraph (b). It is not necessary to allocate items under this paragraph (b) for purposes of calculating ATI if all of the taxpayer's items subject to allocation under this paragraph (b) are allocable to excepted trades or businesses, or if all of those items are allocable to non-excepted trades or businesses.

(2) *Gross income other than dividends and interest income.*—A taxpayer's gross income other than dividends and interest income is allocated to the trade or business that generated the gross income.

(3) *Dividends.*—(i) *Look-through rule.*—If a taxpayer receives a dividend, within the meaning of section 316, that is not investment income, within the meaning of section 163(d), and if the taxpayer satisfies the minimum ownership threshold in paragraph (c)(7) of this section, then, solely for purposes of allocating amounts received as a dividend during the taxable year to excepted or non-excepted trades or businesses under this paragraph (b), the dividend income is treated as allocable to excepted or non-excepted trades or businesses based upon the relative amounts of the payor corporation's adjusted basis in the assets used in its trades or businesses, determined pursuant to paragraph (c) of this section. If at least 90 percent of the payor corporation's adjusted basis in its assets during the taxable year, determined pursuant to paragraph (c) of this section, is allocable to either excepted trades or businesses or to non-excepted trades or businesses, all of the taxpayer's dividend income from the payor corporation for the taxable year is treated as allocable to either excepted or non-excepted trades or businesses, respectively.

(ii) *Inapplicability of the look-through rule.*—If a taxpayer receives a dividend that is not investment income, within the meaning of section 163(d), and if the taxpayer does not satisfy the minimum ownership threshold in paragraph (c)(7) of this section, then the taxpayer must treat the dividend as allocable to a non-excepted trade or business.

(4) *Gain or loss from the disposition of non-consolidated C corporation stock, partnership interests, or S corporation stock.*—(i) *Non-consolidated C corporations.*—(A) If a taxpayer recognizes gain or loss upon the disposition of stock in a non-consolidated C corporation that is not property held for investment, within the meaning of section 163(d)(5), and if the taxpayer looks through to the assets of the C corporation under paragraph (c)(5)(ii) of this section for the taxable year, then the taxpayer must allocate gain or loss from the disposition of stock to excepted or non-excepted trades or businesses based upon the relative amounts of the C corporation's adjusted basis in the assets used in its trades or businesses, determined pursuant to paragraph (c) of this section. If at least 90 percent of the C corporation's adjusted basis in its assets during the taxable year, determined pursuant to paragraph (c) of this section, is allocable to either excepted trades or businesses or to non-excepted trades or businesses, all of the taxpayer's gain or loss from the disposition is treated as allocable to either excepted or non-excepted trades or businesses, respectively.

(B) If a taxpayer recognizes gain or loss upon the disposition of stock in a non-consolidated C corporation that is not property held for investment, within the meaning of section 163(d)(5), and if the taxpayer does not look through to the assets of the C corporation under paragraph (c)(5)(ii) of this section for the taxable year, then the taxpayer must treat the gain or loss from the disposition of stock as allocable to a non-excepted trade or business.

(C) For rules governing the transfer of stock of a member of a consolidated group, see paragraph (a)(4)(i) of this section.

(ii) *Partnerships and S corporations.*—(A) If a taxpayer recognizes gain or loss upon the disposition of interests in a partnership or stock in an S corporation that owns—

(*1*) Non-excepted assets and excepted assets;

(*2*) Investment assets; or

(*3*) Both;

(B) The taxpayer determines a proportionate share of the amount properly allocable to a non-excepted trade or business in accordance with the allocation rules set forth in paragraph (c)(5)(ii)(A) or (c)(5)(ii)(B)(*3*) of this section, as appropriate, and includes such proportionate share of gain or loss in the taxpayer's ATI. However, if at least 90 percent of the partnership's or S corporation's adjusted basis in its assets during the taxable year, determined pursuant to paragraph (c) of this section, is allocable to either excepted trades or businesses or to non-excepted trades or businesses, all of the taxpayer's gain or loss from the disposition is treated as allocable to either excepted or non-excepted trades or businesses, respectively. This rule also applies to tiered passthrough entities by looking through each passthrough entity tier (for example, an S corporation that is the partner of the highest-tier partnership would look through each lower-tier partnership), subject to paragraph (c)(5)(ii)(D) of this section. With respect to a partner that is a C corporation or tax-exempt corporation, a partnership's investment assets are taken into account and treated as non-excepted trade or business assets. For purposes of this paragraph, a passthrough entity means a partnership, S corporation, or any other entity (domestic or foreign) that is not a corporation if all items of income and deduction of the entity are included in the income of its owners or beneficiaries.

(5) *Expenses, losses, and other deductions.*—(i) *Expenses, losses, and other deductions that are definitely related to a trade or business.*—Expenses (other than interest expense), losses, and other deductions (collectively, *deductions* for purposes of this paragraph (b)(5)) that are definitely related to a trade or business are allocable to the trade or business to which they relate. A deduction is considered definitely related to a trade or business if the item giving rise to the deduction is incurred as a result of, or incident to, an activity of the trade or business or in connection with property used in the trade or business (see § 1.861-8(b)(2)). If a deduction is definitely related to one or more excepted trades or businesses and one or more non-excepted trades or businesses, the deduction is apportioned between the excepted and non-excepted trades or businesses based upon the relative amounts of the taxpayer's adjusted basis in the assets used in those trades or businesses, as determined under paragraph (c) of this section.

(ii) *Other deductions.*—Deductions that are not described in paragraph (b)(5)(i) of this section are ratably apportioned based on the gross income of each trade or business.

(6) *Treatment of investment items and certain other items of a partnership with a C corporation partner.*—Any investment income, investment expense, or other item that a partnership receives, pays, or accrues and that is treated as properly allocable to a trade or business of a C corporation partner under § 1.163(j)-4(b)(3)(i) is treated as properly allocable to a non-excepted trade or business of the C corporation partner, except that any item with respect to property or activities for which an election has been made by the partnership under § 1.163(j)-9(b) is treated as properly allocable to an excepted trade or business. See, for example, an election for activities described in § 1.163(j)-9(b)(2)(ii) or an election under § 1.163(j)-9(h).

(7) *Examples: Allocation of income and expense.*—The following examples illustrate the principles of this paragraph (b):

(i) *Example 1: Allocation of income and expense between excepted and non-excepted trades or businesses.*—(A) *Facts.* T conducts an electing real property trade or business (Business Y), which is an excepted trade or business. T also operates a lumber yard (Business Z), which is a non-excepted trade or business. In Year 1, T receives $100x of gross rental income from real property leasing activities. T also pays or accrues $60x of expenses in connection with its real property leasing activities and $20x of legal services performed on behalf of both Business Y and Business Z. T receives $60x of gross income from lumber yard customers and pays or accrues $50x of expenses related to the lumber yard business. For purposes of expense allocations under paragraphs (b) and (c) of this section, T has $240x of adjusted basis in its Business Y assets and $80x of adjusted basis in its Business Z assets.

(B) *Analysis.* Under paragraph (b)(2) of this section, for Year 1, $100x of rental income is allocated to Business Y, and $60x of income from lumber yard customers is allocated to Business Z. Under paragraph (b)(5)(i) of this section, $60x of expenses paid or accrued in connection with real property leasing activities are allocated to Business Y, and $50x of expenses related to the lumber yard are allocated to Business Z. The $20x of remaining expenses for legal services performed on behalf of both Business Y and Business Z are allocated according to the relative amounts of T's basis in the assets used in each business. The total amount of T's basis in the assets used in Businesses Y and Z is $320x, of which 75 percent ($240x / $320x) is used in Business Y and 25 percent ($80x / $320x) is used in Business Z. Accordingly, $15x of the expenses for legal services are allocated to Business Y and $5x are allocated to Business Z.

(ii) *Example 2: Allocation of partnership items from investment activity.*—(A) *Facts.* U, a domestic C corporation, directly conducts an electing real property trade or business. U also has an interest in PRS, a partnership that holds real property for investment. PRS's investment in real property is not a trade or business under section 162 or a real property trade or business under section 469. During the taxable year, PRS sells some of its real property to third parties and allocates $80x of income to U from these sales. In addition, PRS incurs deductible expenses related to its investment in real property and allocates $9x of these deductible expenses to U.

(B) *Analysis.* Under paragraph (b)(6) of this section, any investment income or investment expense that a partnership receives, pays, or accrues and that is treated as properly allocable to a trade or business of a C corporation partner is treated as properly allocable to a non-excepted trade or business of the C corporation partner. Because PRS generates its income and expense from investment activity that is not a trade or business under section 162 or a real property trade or business under section 469, U's allocation of $80x of income and $9x of deductible expense from PRS is treated as properly allocable to a non-excepted trade or business.

(c) *Allocating interest expense and interest income that is properly allocable to a trade or business.*—(1) *General rule.*—(i) *In general.*—Except as otherwise provided in this section, § 1.163(j)-6(m), or § 1.163(j)-9(h), the amount of a taxpayer's interest expense and interest income that is properly allocable to a trade or business is allocated to the taxpayer's excepted or non-excepted trades or businesses for purposes of section 163(j) based upon the relative amounts of the taxpayer's adjusted basis in the assets, as determined under paragraph (c)(5) of this section, used in its excepted or non-excepted trades or businesses. The taxpayer must determine the adjusted basis in its assets as of the close of each determination date, as defined in paragraph (c)(6) of this section, in the taxable year and average those amounts to determine the relative amounts of asset basis for its excepted and non-excepted trades or businesses for that year. It is not necessary to allocate interest expense or interest income under this paragraph (c) for purposes of determining a taxpayer's business interest expense and business interest income if all of the taxpayer's interest income and expense is allocable to excepted trades or businesses (in which case the taxpayer is not subject to the section 163(j) limitation) or if all of the taxpayer's interest income and expense is allocable to non-excepted trades or businesses.

(ii) *De minimis exception.*—If at least 90 percent of the taxpayer's basis in its assets for the taxable year is allocable to either excepted or non-excepted trades or businesses pursuant to this paragraph (c), then all of the taxpayer's interest expense and interest income for that year that is properly allocable to a trade or business is treated as allocable to either excepted or non-excepted trades or businesses, respectively.

(2) *Example.*—The following example illustrates the principles of paragraph (c)(1) of this section:

(i) *Facts.* T is a calendar-year C corporation engaged in an electing real property trade or business, the business of selling wine, and the business of selling hand-carved wooden furniture. In Year 1, T has $100x of interest expense that is deductible except for the potential application of section 163(j). Based upon determinations made on the determination dates in Year 1, T's average adjusted basis in the assets used in the electing real property trade or business (an excepted trade or business) in Year 1 is $800x, and T's total average adjusted basis in the assets used in the other two businesses (which are non-excepted trades or businesses) in Year 1 is $200x.

(ii) *Analysis.* $80x (($800x / ($800x + $200x)) x $100x) of T's interest expense for Year 1 is allocable to T's electing real property trade or business and is not business interest expense subject to the section 163(j) limitation. The remaining $20x of T's interest expense is business interest expense for Year 1 that is subject to the section 163(j) limitation.

(3) *Asset used in more than one trade or business.*—(i) *General rule.*—If an asset is used in more than one trade or business during a determination period, as defined in paragraph (c)(6) of this section, the taxpayer's adjusted basis in the asset is allocated to each trade or business using the permissible methodology under this paragraph (c)(3) that most reasonably reflects the use of the asset in each trade or business during that determination period. An allocation methodology most reasonably reflects the use of the asset in each trade or business if it most properly reflects the proportionate benefit derived from the use of the asset in each trade or business. A taxpayer is not required to use the same allocation methodology for each type of asset used in a trade a business. Instead, a taxpayer may use different allocation methodologies for different types of assets used in a trade or business. If none of the permissible methodologies set forth in paragraph (c)(3)(ii) of this section reasonably reflects the use of the asset in each trade or business, the taxpayer's basis in the asset is not taken into account for purposes of this paragraph (c).

(ii) *Permissible methodologies for allocating asset basis between or among two or more trades or businesses.*—Subject to the special rules in paragraphs (c)(3)(iii) and (c)(5) of this section, a taxpayer's basis in an asset used in two or more trades or businesses during a determination period may be allocated to those trades or businesses based upon—

(A) The relative amounts of gross income that an asset generates, has generated, or may reasonably be expected to generate, within the meaning of § 1.861-9T(g)(3), with respect to the trades or businesses;

(B) If the asset is land or an inherently permanent structure, the relative amounts of physical space used by the trades or businesses; or

(C) If the trades or businesses generate the same unit of output, the relative amounts of output of those trades or businesses (for example, if an asset is used in two trades or businesses, one of which is an excepted regulated utility trade or business, and the other of which is a non-excepted regulated utility trade or business, the taxpayer may allocate basis in the asset based upon the relative amounts of kilowatt-hours generated by each trade or business).

(iii) *Special rules.*—(A) *Consistent allocation methodologies.*—*(1) In general.*—Except as otherwise provided in paragraph (c)(3)(iii)(A)(*2*) of this section, a taxpayer must maintain the same allocation methodology for a period of at least five taxable years.

(2) Consent to change allocation methodology.—If a taxpayer has used the same allocation methodology for at least five taxable years, the taxpayers may change its method of allocation under paragraphs (c)(3)(i) and (ii) of this section without the consent of the Commissioner. If a taxpayer has used the same allocation methodology for less than five taxable years, and if the taxpayer determines that a different allocation methodology properly reflects the proportionate benefit derived from the use of assets in its trades or businesses, the taxpayer may change its method of allocation under paragraphs (c)(3)(i) and (ii) of this section only with the consent of the Commissioner. To obtain consent, a taxpayer must submit a request for a letter ruling under the applicable administrative procedures, and consent will be granted only in extraordinary circumstances.

(B) *De minimis exception.*—If at least 90 percent of the taxpayer's basis in an asset would be allocated to either excepted trades or businesses or non-excepted trades or businesses during a determination period pursuant to this paragraph (c)(3), the taxpayer's entire basis in the asset for the determination period must be allocated to either excepted or non-excepted trades or businesses, respectively. This rule applies before the application of paragraph (c)(1)(ii) of this section.

(C) *Allocations of excepted regulated utility trades or businesses.*—*(1) In general.*—Except as provided in the de minimis rule in paragraph (c)(3)(iii)(C)(*3*) of this section, a taxpayer is engaged in an excepted regulated utility trade or business only to the extent that the taxpayer is engaged in an excepted regulated utility trade or business described in § 1.163(j)-1(b)(15)(i)(A), (B), or (C), and any remaining utility trade or business is a non-excepted trade or business. Thus, for example, electricity sold by a utility trade or business at rates not established or approved by an entity described in § 1.163(j)-1(b)(15)(i)(A)(*2*) and not subject to an election under § 1.163(j)-1(b)(15)(iii) must be treated as electricity sold by a non-excepted regulated utility trade or business. The taxpayer must allocate under this paragraph (c) the basis of assets used in the utility trade or business between its excepted and non-excepted trades or businesses.

(2) *Permissible method for allocating asset basis for utility trades or businesses.* In the case of a utility trade or business described in paragraph (c)(3)(iii)(C)(*1*) of this section, and except as provided in the de minimis rule in paragraph (c)(3)(iii)(C)(*3*) of this section, the method described in paragraph (c)(3)(ii)(C) of this section is the only permissible method under this paragraph (c)(3) for allocating the taxpayer's basis in assets used in both the excepted and non-excepted trades or businesses of selling or furnishing the items described in § 1.163(j)-1(b)(15)(i)(A)(1).

(3) *De minimis rule for excepted utility trades or businesses.*—If a taxpayer is engaged in a utility trade or business described in paragraph (c)(3)(iii)(C)(*1*) of this section, and if at least 90 percent of the items described in § 1.163(j)-1(b)(15)(i)(A)(*1*) are furnished or sold by trades or businesses described in § 1.163(j)-1(b)(15)(i)(A), (B) or (C), the taxpayer's entire trade or business is an excepted regulated utility trade or business, and paragraph (c)(3)(iii)(C)(2) of this section does not apply. This rule applies before the application of paragraph (c)(3)(iii)(B) of this section.

(4) *Example.*—The following example illustrates the principles of this paragraph (c)(3)(iii)(C):

(*i*) *Facts.* X, a C corporation, is engaged in the trade or business of generating electrical energy. During each determination period in the taxable year, 80 percent of the megawatt-hours generated in the electricity generation trade or business is sold at rates negotiated with the purchaser, and with respect to which X filed a schedule of rates with a public utility commission. The public utility commission has the authority to take action on the filed schedule of rates, but if no action is taken, the rules governing the public utility commission explicitly state that the public utility commission is deemed to have approved the rates. The public utility has taken no action with respect to the negotiated rate. The remaining 20 percent of the megawatt-hours is sold on the wholesale market at rates not established or subject to approval by a regulator described in § 1.163(j)-1(b)(15)(i)(A)(2). X has not made an election under § 1.163(j)-1(b)(15)(iii). None of the assets used in X's utility generation trade or business are used in any other trade or business.

(*ii*) *Analysis.* For purposes of section 163(j), under paragraph (c)(3)(iii)(C)(*1*) of this section, 80 percent of X's electricity generation business is an excepted regulated utility trade or business, because the rate for the sale of the electricity was subject to approval by a regulator described in § 1.163(j)-1(b)(15)(i)(A)(2). The remaining 20 percent of X's business is a non-excepted utility trade or business. Under paragraph (c)(3)(iii)(C)(2) of this section, X must allocate 80 percent of the basis of the assets used in its utility business to excepted trades or business and the remaining 20 percent of the basis in the assets to non-excepted trades or businesses.

(D) *Special allocation rule for real property trades or businesses subject to special anti-abuse rule.*—(*1*) *In general.*—In the case of a trade or business that leases real property subject to an arrangement described in § 1.163(j)-9(j)(1), including trades or businesses to which the look-through exception in § 1.163(j)-9(j)(2)(ii) applies, the taxpayer must allocate under this paragraph (c)(3) the basis of property used in both the excepted and non-excepted portions of its trade or business, as determined under § 1.163(j)-9(j)(3).

(*2*) *Allocation methodology for real property.*—For purposes of this paragraph (c)(3)(iii)(D), a taxpayer must allocate the basis of real property leased under an arrangement described in § 1.163(j)-9(j)(1) or (j)(2)(i) between the excepted and non-excepted portions of the real property trade or business based on the relative fair market rental value of the real property that is attributable to the excepted and non-excepted portions of the trade or business, respectively.

(*3*) *Example.*—The following example illustrates the principles of this paragraph (c)(3)(iii)(D):

(*i*) *Facts.* X and Y are domestic C corporations under common control within the meaning of section 267(b), but neither X nor Y are members of a consolidated group. The small business exemption in § 1.163(j)-2(d) does not apply to X or Y. X owns an office building and leases the entire building to Y. Y subleases 80 percent of the office building, measured by fair market rental value, to a related party. Y subleases the remaining 20 percent of the building to unrelated third parties. X also owns depreciable scaffolding equipment, which it uses to clean all of the building's windows as part of its leasing arrangement with Y.

(*ii*) *Analysis.* Under § 1.163(j)-9(j)(2)(ii), X is eligible to make an election for 20 percent of its business of leasing the office building to be an electing real property trade or business. Assuming X makes such an election, X must allocate the basis of assets used in both the excepted and non-excepted portions of its leasing trade or business under this paragraph (c). Under paragraph (c)(3)(iii)(D)(*2*) of this section, X must allocate the basis of the office building based on the relative fair market value attributable to the excepted and non-excepted portions of its leasing business. Therefore, X must allocate 20 percent of the basis of the building to the excepted portion of its leasing business, and it must allocate the remaining 80 percent of the building to the non-excepted portion of its leasing business. Under paragraph (c)(3)(iii)(D)(*2*) of this section, X may use one of the allocation methods described in paragraph (c)(3)(ii) of this section to allocate the basis of its scaffolding equipment between the excepted and non-excepted portions of its leasing trade or business.

(4) *Disallowed business interest expense carryforwards; floor plan financing interest expense.*—Disallowed business interest expense carryforwards (which were treated as allocable to a non-excepted trade or business in a prior taxable year) are not re-allocated between non-excepted and excepted trades or businesses in a succeeding taxable year. Instead, the carryforwards continue to be treated as allocable to a non-excepted trade or business. Floor plan financing interest expense also is not subject to allocation between excepted and non-excepted trades or businesses (see § 1.163(j)-1(b)(19)) and is always treated as allocable to non-excepted trades or businesses.

(5) *Additional rules relating to basis.*—(i) *Calculation of adjusted basis.*—(A) *Non-depreciable property other than land.*—Except as otherwise provided in paragraph (c)(5)(i)(E) of this section, for purposes of this section, the adjusted basis of an asset other than land with respect to which no deduction is allowable under section 167, former section 168, or section 197, as applicable, is the adjusted basis of the asset for determining gain or loss from the sale or other disposition of that asset as provided in § 1.1011-1. Self-created intangible assets are not taken into account for purposes of this paragraph (c).

(B) *Depreciable property other than inherently permanent structures.*—For purposes of this section, the adjusted basis of any tangible asset with respect to which a deduction is allowable under section 167, other than inherently permanent structures, is determined by using the alternative depreciation system under section 168(g) before any application of the additional first-year depreciation deduction (for example, under section 168(k) or (m)), and the adjusted basis of any tangible asset with respect to which a deduction is allowable under former section 168, other than inherently permanent structures, is determined by using the taxpayer's method of computing depreciation for the asset under former section 168. The depreciation deduction with respect to the property described in this paragraph (c)(5)(i)(B) is allocated ratably to each day during the period in the taxable year to which the depreciation relates. A change to the alternative depreciation system should be determined in a manner similar to that in § 1.168(i)-4(d)(4) or (d)(5)(ii)(B), as applicable.

(C) *Special rule for land and inherently permanent structures.*—Except as otherwise provided in paragraph (c)(5)(i)(E) of this section, for purposes of this section, the adjusted basis of any asset that is land, including nondepreciable improvements to land, or an inherently permanent structure is its unadjusted basis.

(D) *Depreciable or amortizable intangible property and depreciable income forecast method property.*—For purposes of this section, the adjusted basis of any intangible asset with respect to which a deduction is allowable under section 167 or 197, as applicable, is determined in accordance with section 167 or 197, as applicable, and the adjusted basis of any asset described in section 167(g)(6) for which a deduction is allowable under section 167 is determined in accordance with section 167(g). The adjusted basis of any intangible asset under this paragraph (c)(5)(i)(D) is determined before any application of the additional first-year depreciation deduction. The depreciation or amortization deduction with respect to the property described in this paragraph (c)(5)(i)(D) is allocated ratably to each day during the period in the taxable year to which the depreciation or amortization relates.

(E) *Assets not yet used in a trade or business.*—Assets that have been acquired or that are under development but that are not yet used in a trade or business are not taken into account for purposes of this paragraph (c). For example, construction works in progress (such as buildings, airplanes, or ships) are not taken into account for purposes of this paragraph (c). Similarly, land acquired by a taxpayer for construction of a building by the taxpayer to be used in a trade or business is not taken into account for purposes of under this paragraph (c) until the building is placed in service. This rule does not apply to interests in a partnership or stock in a corporation.

(F) *Trusts established to fund specific liabilities.*—Trusts required to fund specific liabilities (for example, pension trusts, and nuclear decommissioning funds (including, but not limited to, those funds for which an election is made under section 468A)) are not taken into account for purposes of this paragraph (c).

(G) *Inherently permanent structure.*—For purposes of this section, the term *inherently permanent structure* has the meaning provided in § 1.856-10(d)(2).

(ii) *Partnership interests; stock in non-consolidated C corporations.*—(A) *Partnership interests.*—*(1) Calculation of asset basis.*—For purposes of this section, a partner's interest in a partnership is treated as an asset of the partner. For these purposes, the partner's adjusted basis in a partnership interest is reduced, but not below zero, by the partner's share of partnership liabilities, as determined under section 752, and is further reduced as provided in paragraph (c)(5)(ii)(A)(*2*)(*iii*) of this section. If a partner elects or is required to apply the rules in this paragraph (c)(5)(ii)(A) to look through to a partnership's basis in the partnership's assets, the partner's basis in the partnership interest is adjusted to the extent of the partner's share of any adjustments to the basis of the partnership's assets required pursuant to the rules in paragraph (c)(5)(i) of this section.

(2) Allocation of asset basis—

(i) In general.—For purposes of determining the extent to which a partner's adjusted basis in its partnership interest is allocable to an excepted or non-excepted trade or business, the partner may look through to such partner's share of the partnership's basis in the partnership's assets, taking into account any adjustments under sections 734(b) and 743(b), and adjusted to the extent required under paragraph (d)(4) of this section, except as otherwise provided in paragraph (c)(5)(ii)(D) of this section. For purposes of the preceding sentence, such partner's share of partnership assets is determined using a reasonable method taking into account special allocations under section 704(b). Notwithstanding paragraph (c)(7) of this section, if a partner's direct and indirect interest in a partnership is greater than or equal to 80 percent of the partnership's capital or profits, the partner must apply the rules in this paragraph (c)(5)(ii)(A)(*2*) to look through to the partnership's basis in the partnership's assets. If a partner elects or is required to apply the rules in this paragraph (c)(5)(ii)(A)(*2*) to look through to a partnership's basis in the partnership's assets, the partner allocates the basis of its partnership interest between excepted and non-excepted trades or businesses based on the ratio in which the partner's share of the partnership's adjusted tax basis in its trade or business assets is allocated between excepted and non-excepted trade or business assets.

(ii) De minimis rule.—If, after applying paragraph (c)(5)(ii)(A)(*2*)(*iii*) of this section, at least 90 percent of a partner's share of a partnership's basis in its assets (including adjustments under sections 734(b) and 743(b)) is allocable to either excepted trades or businesses or non-excepted trades or businesses, without regard to assets not properly allocable to a trade or business, the partner's entire basis in its partnership interest is treated as allocable to either excepted or non-excepted trades or businesses, respectively. For purposes of the preceding sentence, such partner's share of partnership assets is determined using a reasonable method taking into account special allocations under section 704(b).

(iii) *Partnership assets not properly allocable to a trade or business.*—For purposes of applying paragraphs (c)(5)(ii)(A)(*2*)(*i*) and (*ii*) of this section to a partner that is a C corporation or tax-exempt corporation, such partner's share of a partnership's assets that are not properly allocable to a trade or business is treated as properly allocable to a non-excepted trade or business of such partner. However, if the partnership made an election under § 1.163(j)-9(b) or § 1.163(j)-9(h) with respect to an asset or activity, the assets (or assets related to such activities) are treated as properly allocable to an excepted trade or business of such partner. See, for example, an election under § 1.163(j)-9(h) for an asset or an election under § 1.163(j)-9(b) with respect to activities described in § 1.163(j)-9(b)(2)(ii). For a partner other than a C corporation or tax-exempt corporation, a partnership's assets that are not properly allocable to a trade or business are treated as neither excepted nor non-excepted trade or business assets; instead, such partner's adjusted basis in its partnership interest is decreased by that partner's share of the excess of the partnership's basis in those assets over the partnership's debt that is traced to such assets in accordance with § 1.163-8T, and it is increased by that partner's share of the excess of the partnership's debt that is traced to such assets in accordance with § 1.163-8T over the partnership's basis in those assets. For purposes of the preceding sentence, the partnership's asset basis in property not allocable to a trade or business is adjusted pursuant to the rules in paragraph (c)(5)(i) of this section. For purposes of this paragraph (c)(5)(ii)(A)(*2*)(*iii*), such partner's share of a partnership's assets is determined under a reasonable method taking into account special allocations under section 704(b).

(iv) Inapplicability of partnership look-through rule.—If a partner, other than a C corporation or a tax-exempt corporation, chooses not to look through to the partnership's basis in the partnership's assets under paragraph (c)(5)(ii)(A)(*2*)(*i*) of this section or is precluded by paragraph (c)(5)(ii)(D) of this section from applying such partnership look-through rule, the partner generally will treat its basis in the partnership interest as either an asset held for investment or a non-excepted trade or business asset as determined under section 163(d). If a partner that is a C corporation or a tax-exempt corporation chooses not to look through to the partnership's basis in the partnership's assets under paragraph (c)(5)(ii)(A)(*2*)(*i*) of this section or is precluded by paragraph (c)(5)(ii)(D) of this section from applying such partnership look-through rule, the taxpayer must treat its entire basis in the partnership interest as allocable to a non-excepted trade or business.

(B) *Stock in domestic non-consolidated corporations.*—*(1) In general.*—For purposes of this section, if a taxpayer owns stock in a domestic C corporation that is not a member of the taxpayer's consolidated group, or if the taxpayer owns stock in an S corporation, the stock is treated as an asset of the taxpayer.

(2) Domestic non-consolidated C corporations—

(i) Allocation of asset basis.—If a shareholder satisfies the minimum ownership threshold in paragraph (c)(7) of this section for stock in a domestic non-consolidated C corporation, and if dividends paid on such stock would not be included in the shareholder's investment income under section 163(d)(4)(B), then, for purposes of determining the extent to which the shareholder's basis in the stock is allocable to an excepted or non-excepted trade or business, the shareholder must look through to the corporation's basis in the corporation's assets, adjusted to the extent required under paragraph (d)(4) of this section, except as otherwise provided in paragraph (c)(5)(ii)(D) of this section. If a shareholder does not satisfy the minimum ownership threshold in paragraph (c)(7) of this section for stock in a domestic non-consolidated C corporation, but the shareholder's direct and indirect interest in such corporation is greater than or equal to 80 percent by value, and if dividends paid on such stock would not be included in the shareholder's investment income under section 163(d)(4)(B), then, for purposes of determining the extent to which the shareholder's basis in the stock is allocable to an excepted or non-excepted trade or business, the shareholder may look through to the corporation's basis in the corporation's assets, adjusted to the extent required under paragraph (d)(4) of this section, except as otherwise provided in paragraph (c)(5)(ii)(D) of this section. For purposes of the preceding sentence, indirect stock ownership is determined by applying the constructive ownership rules of section 318(a).

(ii) De minimis rule.—If at least 90 percent of the domestic non-consolidated C corporation's basis in the corporation's assets is allocable to either excepted trades or businesses or non-excepted trades or businesses, the shareholder's entire interest in the corporation's stock is treated as allocable to either excepted or non-excepted trades or businesses, respectively.

(iii) Inapplicability of corporate look-through rule.—If a shareholder other than a C corporation or a tax-exempt corporation is ineligible to look through or chooses not to look through to a corporation's basis in its assets under paragraph (c)(5)(ii)(B)(*2*)(*i*) of this section, the shareholder generally will treat its entire basis in the corporation's stock as an asset held for investment. If a shareholder that is a C corporation or a tax-exempt corporation is ineligible to look through or chooses not to look through to a corporation's basis in its assets under paragraph (c)(5)(ii)(B)(*2*)(*i*) of this section, the

shareholder must treat its entire basis in the corporation's stock as allocable to a non-excepted trade or business.

(iv) Use of inside basis for purposes of C corporation look-through rule.—This paragraph (c)(5)(ii)(B)(2)(*iv*) applies if a shareholder meets the requirements to look through the stock of a domestic non-consolidated C corporation under paragraph (c)(5)(ii)(B)(2)(*i*) of this section, determined without applying the constructive ownership rules of section 318(a). If this paragraph (c)(5)(ii)(B)(2)(*iv*) applies, then solely for purposes of allocating asset basis under paragraph (c)(5)(ii)(B)(2)(*i*) of this section, and except as otherwise provided in paragraph (c)(5)(ii)(D) of this section, the shareholder may look through to such shareholder's pro rata share of the C corporation's basis in its assets, taking into account the modifications in paragraph (c)(5)(i) of this section with respect to the C corporation's assets, and adjusted to the extent required under paragraph (d)(4) of this section (asset basis look-through approach). If a shareholder applies the asset basis look-through approach, it must do so for all domestic non-consolidated C corporations for which the shareholder is eligible to use this approach, and it must report its use of this approach on the information statement described in paragraph (c)(6)(iii) of this section. The shareholder also must continue to use the asset basis look-through approach in all future taxable years in which the shareholder is eligible to use this approach.

(3) S corporations.—(i) Calculation of asset basis.—For purposes of this section, a shareholder's share of stock in an S corporation is treated as an asset of the shareholder. Additionally, for these purposes, the shareholder's adjusted basis in a share of S corporation stock is adjusted to take into account the modifications in paragraph (c)(5)(i) of this section with respect to the assets of the S corporation (for example, a shareholder's adjusted basis in its S corporation stock is increased by the shareholder's share of depreciation with respect to an inherently permanent structure owned by the S corporation).

(ii) Allocation of asset basis.—For purposes of determining the extent to which a shareholder's basis in its stock of an S corporation is allocable to an excepted or non-excepted trade or business, the shareholder may look through to such shareholder's share of the S corporation's basis in the S corporation's assets, allocated on a pro rata basis, adjusted to the extent required under paragraph (d)(4) of this section, except as otherwise provided in paragraph (c)(5)(ii)(D) of this section. Notwithstanding paragraph (c)(7) of this section, if a shareholder's direct and indirect interest in an S corporation is greater than or equal to 80 percent of the S corporation's stock by vote and value, the shareholder must apply the rules in this paragraph (c)(5)(ii)(B)(*3*) to look through to the S corporation's basis in the S corporation's assets. For these purposes, indirect stock ownership is determined by applying the constructive ownership rules of section 318(a).

(iii) *De minimis rule.*—If at least 90 percent of a shareholder's share of an S corporation's basis in its assets is allocable to either excepted trades or businesses or non-excepted trades or businesses, the shareholder's entire basis in its S corporation stock is treated as allocable to either excepted or non-excepted trades or businesses, respectively.

(iv) *Inapplicability of S corporation look-through rule.*—If a shareholder chooses not to look through to the S corporation's basis in the S corporation's assets under paragraph (c)(5)(ii)(B)(*3*)(*ii*) of this section or is precluded by paragraph (c)(5)(ii)(D) of this section from applying such S corporation look-through rule, the shareholder will treat its basis in the S corporation stock as either an asset held for investment or a non-excepted trade or business asset as determined under section 163(d).

(C) *Stock in relevant foreign corporations.—(1) In general.*—The rules applicable to domestic non-consolidated C corporations in paragraph (c)(5)(ii)(B) of this section also apply to relevant foreign corporations (as defined in § 1.163(j)-1(b)(33)).

(2) Special rule for CFC utilities.—Solely for purposes of applying the rules in paragraph (c)(5)(ii)(B) of this section, a utility trade or business conducted by an applicable CFC is treated as an excepted regulated utility trade or business, but only to the extent that the applicable CFC sells or furnishes the items described in § 1.163(j)-1(b)(15)(i)(A)(*1*) pursuant to rates established or approved by an entity described in § 1.163(j)-1(b)(15)(i)(A)(2), a foreign government, a public service or public utility commission or other similar body of any foreign government, or the governing or ratemaking body of a foreign electric cooperative. For purposes of this paragraph (c)(5)(ii)(C)(*2*), the term *foreign government* means any foreign government, any political subdivision of a foreign government, or any wholly owned agency or instrumentality of any one of the foregoing within the meaning of § 1.1471-6(b).

(D) *Limitations on application of look-through rules.—(1) Inapplicability of look-through rule to partnerships or non-consolidated C corporations to which the small business exemption applies.*—A taxpayer may not apply the look-through rules in paragraphs (b)(3) and (c)(5)(ii)(A), (B), and (C) of this section to a partnership, S corporation, or non-consolidated C corporation that is eligible for the small business exemption under section 163(j)(3) and § 1.163(j)-2(d)(1), unless the partnership, S corporation, or non-consolidated C corporation elects under § 1.163(j)-9 for a trade or business to be an electing real property trade or business or an electing farming business.

(2) Limitation on application of look-through rule to C corporations.—Except as provided in § 1.163(j)-9(h)(4)(iii) and (iv) (for a REIT or a partnership making the election under § 1.163(j)-9(h)(1) or (7), respectively), for purposes of applying the look-through rules in paragraph (c)(5)(ii)(B) and (C) of this section to a non-consolidated C corporation (upper-tier entity), that upper-tier entity may not apply these look-through rules to a lower-tier non-consolidated C corporation if a principal purpose for borrowing funds at the upper-tier entity level or adding an upper-tier or lower-tier entity to the ownership structure is increasing the amount of the taxpayer's basis allocable to excepted trades or businesses. For example, P wholly and directly owns S1 (the upper-tier entity), which wholly and directly owns S2. Each of S1 and S2 is a non-consolidated C corporation to which the small business exemption does not apply, and S2 is engaged in an excepted trade or business. With a principal purpose of increasing the amount of basis allocable to its excepted trades or businesses, P has S1 (rather than S2) borrow funds from a third party. S1 may not look through the stock of S2 (and may not apply the asset basis look-through rule described in paragraph (c)(5)(ii)(B)(2)(iv) of this section) for purposes of P's allocation of its basis in its S1 stock between excepted and non-excepted trades or businesses; instead, S1 must treat its stock in S2 as an asset used in a non-excepted trade or business for that purpose. However, S1 may look through the stock of S2 for purposes of S1's allocation of its basis in its S2 stock between excepted and non-excepted trades or businesses.

(E) *Tiered entities.*—If a taxpayer applies the look-through rules of this paragraph (c)(5)(ii), the taxpayer must do so for all lower-tier entities with respect to which the taxpayer satisfies, directly or indirectly, the minimum ownership threshold in paragraph (c)(7) of this section, subject to the limitation in paragraph (c)(5)(ii)(D) of this section, beginning with the lowest-tier entity.

(iii) *Cash and cash equivalents and customer receivables.*—Except as otherwise provided in the last sentence of this paragraph (c)(5)(iii), a taxpayer's basis in its cash and cash equivalents and customer receivables is not taken into account for purposes of this paragraph (c). This rule also applies to a lower-tier entity if a taxpayer looks through to the assets of that entity under paragraph (c)(5)(ii) of this section. For purposes of this paragraph (c)(5)(iii), the term *cash and cash equivalents* includes cash, foreign currency, commercial paper, any interest in an investment company registered under the Investment Company Act of 1940 (1940 Act) and regulated as a money market fund under 17 CFR 270.2a-7 (Rule 2a-7 under the 1940 Act), any obligation of a government, and any derivative that is substantially secured by an obligation of a government, or any similar asset. For purposes of this paragraph (c)(5)(iii), a *derivative* is a derivative described in section 59A(h)(4)(A), without regard to section 59A(h)(4)(C). For purposes of this paragraph (c)(5)(iii), the term *government* means the United States or any agency or instrumentality of the United States; a State, a territory, a possession of the United States, the District of Columbia, or any political subdivision thereof within the meaning of section 103 and § 1.103-1; or any foreign government, any political subdivision of a foreign government, or any wholly owned agency or instrumentality of any one of the foregoing within the meaning of § 1.1471-6(b). This paragraph (c)(5)(iii) does not apply to an entity that qualifies as a financial services entity as described in § 1.904-4(e)(3).

(iv) *Deemed asset sale.*—Solely for purposes of determining the amount of basis allocable to excepted and non-excepted trades or businesses under this section, an election under section 336, 338, or 754, as applicable, is deemed to have been made for any acquisition of corporate stock or partnership interests with respect to which the taxpayer demonstrates, in the information statement required by paragraph (c)(6)(iii)(B) of this section, that the acquisition qualified for such an election and that, immediately before the acquisition, the acquired entity had a regulatory liability for deferred taxes recorded on its books with respect to property predominantly used in an excepted regulated utility trade or business. Any additional basis taken into account under this rule is reduced ratably over a 15-year period beginning with the month of the acquisition and is not subject to the anti-abuse rule in paragraph (c)(8) of this section.

(v) *Other adjustments.*—The Commissioner may make appropriate adjustments to prevent a taxpayer from intentionally and artificially increasing its basis in assets attributable to an excepted trade or business.

(6) *Determination dates; determination periods; reporting requirements.*—(i) *Determination dates and determination periods.*—(A) *Quarterly determination periods.*—For purposes of this section, and except as otherwise provided in paragraph (c)(6)(i)(B) of this section, the term *determination date* means the last day of each quarter of the taxpayer's taxable year (and the last day of the taxpayer's taxable year, if the taxpayer has a short taxable year), and the term *determination period* means the period beginning the day after one determination date and ending on the next determination date.

(B) *Annual determination periods.*—If a taxpayer satisfies the requirements of the last sentence of this paragraph (c)(6)(i)(B), the taxpayer may allocate asset basis for a taxable year based on the average of adjusted asset basis at the beginning of the year and the end of the year (annual determination method). For these purposes, the term *determination date* means the last day of the taxpayer's taxable year, and the term *determination period* has the same meaning as provided in paragraph (c)(6)(i)(A) of this section. A taxpayer may use the annual determination method for a taxable year only if the taxpayer demonstrates that its total adjusted basis (as determined under paragraph (c)(5) of this section) at the end of the year in its assets used in its excepted trades or businesses, as a percentage of the taxpayer's total adjusted basis at the end of such year in all of its assets used in a trade or business, does not differ by more than 20 percent from such percentage at the beginning of the year.

(ii) *Application of look-through rules.*—If a taxpayer that applies the look-through rules of paragraph (c)(5)(ii) of this section has a different taxable year than the partnership or non-consolidated C corporation to which the taxpayer is applying those rules, then, for purposes of this paragraph (c)(6), the taxpayer must use the most recent asset basis figures from the partnership or non-consolidated C corporation. For example, assume that PS1 is a partnership with a May 31 taxable year, and that C (a calendar-year C corporation that is ineligible to use the annual determination method for the taxable year) is a partner in PS1. PS1's determination dates are February 28, May 31, August 31, and November 30. In turn, C's determination dates are March 31, June 30, September 30, and December 31. If C looks through to PS1's basis in its assets under paragraph (c)(5)(ii) of this section, then, for purposes of determining the amount of C's asset basis that is attributable to its excepted and non-excepted businesses on March 31, C must use PS1's asset basis calculations for February 28.

(iii) *Reporting requirements.*—(A) *Books and records.*—A taxpayer must maintain books of account and other records and data as necessary to substantiate the taxpayer's use of an asset in an excepted trade or business and to substantiate any adjustments to asset basis for purposes of applying this paragraph (c). One indication that a particular asset is used in a particular trade or business is if the taxpayer maintains separate books and records for all of its excepted and non-excepted trades or businesses and can show the asset in the books and records of a particular excepted or non-excepted trade or business. For rules governing record retention, see § 1.6001-1.

(B) *Information statement.*—Except as otherwise provided in publications, forms, instructions, or other guidance, each taxpayer that is making an allocation under this paragraph (c), including any taxpayer that satisfies the de minimis rule in paragraph (c)(1)(ii) of this section, must prepare a statement titled "Section 163(j) Asset Basis Calculations" containing the information described in paragraphs (c)(6)(iii)(B)(*1*) through (*7*) of this section and must attach the statement to its timely filed Federal income tax return for the taxable year:

(*1*) The taxpayer's adjusted basis in the assets used in its excepted and non-excepted businesses, determined as set forth in this section, including detailed information for the different groups of assets identified in paragraphs (c)(5)(i) and (ii) and (d) of this section;

(*2*) The determination dates on which asset basis was measured during the taxable year;

(*3*) The names and taxpayer identification numbers (TINs) of all entities for which basis information is being provided, including partnerships and corporations if the taxpayer that owns an interest in a partnership or corporation looks through to the partnership's or corporation's basis in the partnership's or corporation's assets under paragraph (c)(5)(ii) of this section. If the taxpayer is a member of a consolidated group, the name and TIN of the agent for the group, as defined in § 1.1502-77, must be provided, but the taxpayer need not provide the names and TINs of all other consolidated group members;

(*4*) Asset basis information for corporations or partnerships if the taxpayer looks through to the corporation's or partnership's basis in the corporation's or partnership's assets under paragraph (c)(5)(ii) of this section;

(*5*) A summary of the method or methods used to determine asset basis in property used in both excepted and non-excepted businesses, as well as information regarding any deemed sale under paragraph (c)(5)(iv) of this section;

(*6*) Whether the taxpayer used the historical approach or the effective date approach for all of its disallowed disqualified interest; and

(*7*) If the taxpayer changed its methodology for allocating asset basis between or among two or more trades or businesses under paragraph (c)(3)(ii) of this section, a statement that the taxpayer has changed the allocation methodology and a description of the new methodology or, if the taxpayer is required to request consent for the allocation methodology change under paragraph (c)(3)(iii)(A)(*2*) of this section, a statement that the request has been or will be filed and a description of the methodology change.

(iv) *Failure to file statement.*—If a taxpayer fails to file the statement described in paragraph (c)(6)(iii) of this section or files a statement that does not comply with the requirements of paragraph (c)(6)(iii) of this section, the Commissioner may treat the taxpayer as if all of its interest expense is properly allocable to a non-excepted trade or business, unless the taxpayer shows that there was reasonable cause for failing to comply with, and the taxpayer acted in good faith with respect to, the requirements of paragraph (c)(6)(iii) of this section, taking into account all pertinent facts and circumstances.

(7) *Ownership threshold for look-through rules.*—(i) *Corporations.*—(A) *Asset basis.*—For purposes of this section, a shareholder must look through to the assets of a domestic non-consolidated C corporation or a relevant foreign corporation under paragraph (c)(5)(ii) of this section if the shareholder's direct and indirect interest in the corporation satisfies the ownership requirements of section 1504(a)(2). For purposes of this paragraph (c)(7)(i)(A), indirect stock ownership is determined by applying the constructive ownership rules of section 318(a). A shareholder may look through to the assets of an S corporation under paragraph (c)(5)(ii) of this section for purposes of allocating the shareholder's basis in its stock in the S corporation between excepted and non-excepted trades or businesses regardless of the shareholder's direct and indirect interest in the S corporation.

(B) *Dividends.*—A shareholder must look through to the activities of a domestic non-consolidated C corporation or a relevant foreign corporation under paragraph (b)(3) of this section if the shareholder's direct interest in the corporation satisfies the ownership requirements of section 1504(a)(2). A shareholder may look through to the activities of a domestic non-consolidated C corporation or an applicable CFC under paragraph (b)(3) of this section if the shareholder's direct interest in the corporation is greater than or equal to 80 percent by value. A shareholder may look through to the activities of an S corporation under paragraph (b)(3) of this section regardless of the shareholder's direct interest in the S corporation.

(ii) *Partnerships.*—A partner may look through to the assets of a partnership under paragraph (c)(5)(ii) of this section for purposes of allocating the partner's basis in its partnership interest between excepted and non-excepted trades or businesses regardless of the partner's direct and indirect interest in the partnership.

(iii) *Inapplicability of look-through rule.*—For circumstances in which a taxpayer that satisfies the ownership threshold in this paragraph (c)(7) may not apply the look-through rules in paragraphs (b)(3) and (c)(5)(ii) of this section, see paragraph (c)(5)(ii)(D) of this section.

(8) *Anti-abuse rule.*—If a principal purpose for the acquisition, disposition, or change in use of an asset was to artificially shift the amount of basis allocable to excepted or non-excepted trades or businesses on a determination date, the additional basis or change in use will not be taken into account for purposes of this section. For example, if an asset is used in a non-excepted trade or business for most of the taxable year, and if the taxpayer begins using the asset in an excepted trade or business towards the end of the year with a principal purpose of shifting the amount of basis in the asset that is allocable to the excepted trade or business, the change in use is disregarded for purposes of this section. A purpose may be a principal purpose even though it is outweighed by other purposes (taken together or separately). In determining whether a taxpayer has a principal purpose described in this paragraph (c)(8), factors to be considered include, for example, the following: the business purpose for the acquisition, disposition, or change in use; the length of time the asset was used in a trade or business; whether the asset was acquired from a related person; and whether the taxpayer's aggregate basis in its assets increased or decreased temporarily on or around a determination date. A principal purpose is presumed to be present in any case in which the acquisition, disposition, or change in use lacks a substantial business purpose and increases the taxpayer's basis in assets used in its excepted trades or businesses by more than 10 percent during the taxable year.

(d) *Direct allocations.*—(1) *In general.*—It is not necessary to allocate interest expense under this paragraph (d) if all of the taxpayer's interest expense is allocable to excepted trades or businesses or if all of the taxpayer's interest expense is allocable to non-excepted trades or businesses.

(2) *Qualified nonrecourse indebtedness.*—For purposes of this section, a taxpayer with qualified nonrecourse indebtedness must directly allocate interest expense from the indebtedness to the taxpayer's assets in the manner and to the extent provided in § 1.861-10T(b). For purposes of this paragraph (d)(2), the term *qualified nonrecourse indebtedness* has the meaning provided in § 1.861-10T(b), except that the term *cash flow from the property* (within the meaning of § 1.861-10T(b)(3)(i)) includes revenue derived from the sale or lease of inventory or similar property with respect to an excepted regulated utility trade or business or a non-excepted regulated utility trade or business.

(3) *Assets used in more than one trade or business.*—If an asset is used in more than one trade or business, the taxpayer must apply the rules in paragraph (c)(3) of this section to determine the extent to which interest that is directly allocated under this paragraph (d) is allocable to excepted or non-excepted trades or businesses.

(4) *Adjustments to basis of assets to account for direct allocations.*—In determining the amount of a taxpayer's basis in the assets used in its excepted and non-excepted trades or businesses for purposes of paragraph (c) of this section, adjustments must be made to reflect direct allocations under this paragraph (d). These adjustments consist of reductions in the taxpayer's basis in its assets for purposes of paragraph (c) of this section to reflect assets to which interest expense is directly allocated under this paragraph (d). The amount of the taxpayer's basis in these assets must be reduced, but not below zero, by the amount of qualified nonrecourse indebtedness secured by these assets. These adjustments must be made before the taxpayer averages the adjusted basis in its assets as determined on each determination date during the taxable year.

(5) *Example: Direct allocation of interest expense.*—(i) *Facts.* T conducts an electing real property trade or business (Business X) and operates a retail store that is a non-excepted trade or business (Business Y). In Year 1, T issues Note A to a third party in exchange for $1,000x for the purpose of acquiring Building B. Note A is qualified nonrecourse indebtedness (within the meaning of § 1.861-10T(b)) secured by Building B. T then uses those funds to acquire Building B for $1,200x, and T uses Building B in Business X. During Year 1, T pays $500x of interest, of which $100x is interest payments on Note A. For Year 1, T's basis in its assets used in Business X (as determined under paragraph (c) of this section) is $3,600x (excluding cash and cash equivalents), and T's basis in its assets used in Business Y (as determined under paragraph (c) of this section) is $800x (excluding cash and cash equivalents). Each of Business X and Business Y also has $100x of cash and cash equivalents.

(ii) *Analysis.* Because Note A is qualified nonrecourse indebtedness that is secured by Building B, in allocating interest expense between Businesses X and Y, T first must directly allocate the $100x of interest expense it paid with respect to Note A to Business X in accordance with paragraph (d)(2) of this section. Thereafter, T must allocate the remaining $400x of interest expense between Businesses X and Y under paragraph (c) of this section. After excluding $1,000x of T's basis in Building B to reflect the amount of Note A (see paragraph (d)(4) of this section), and without regard to T's $200x of cash and cash equivalents (see paragraph (c)(5)(iii) of this section), T's basis in its assets used in Businesses X and Y is $2,600x and $800x (76.5 percent and 23.5 percent), respectively. Thus, $306x of the remaining $400x of interest expense would be allocated to Business X, and $94x would be allocated to Business Y.

(e) *Examples.*—The examples in this paragraph (e) illustrate the principles of this section. For purposes of these examples, no taxpayer is eligible for the small business exemption under section 163(j)(3) and § 1.163(j)-2(d), no taxpayer has floor plan financing interest expense, and no taxpayer has qualified nonrecourse indebtedness within the meaning of § 1.861-10T(b).

(1) *Example 1: Interest allocation within a consolidated group.*—(i) *Facts.* S is a member of a consolidated group of which P is the common parent. P conducts an electing real property trade or business (Business X), and S conducts a non-excepted trade or business (Business Y). In Year 1, P pays or accrues (without regard to section 163(j)) $35x of interest expense and receives $10x of interest income, and S pays or accrues (without regard to section 163(j)) $115x of interest expense and receives $5x of interest income (for a total of $150x of interest expense and $15x of interest income). For purposes of this example, assume that, pursuant to paragraph (c) of this section, $30x of the P group's interest expense and $3x of the P group's interest income is allocable to Business X, and the remaining $120x of interest expense and $12x of interest income is allocable to Business Y.

(ii) *Analysis.* Under paragraph (a)(4) of this section, 20 percent of the P group's Year 1 interest expense ($30x / $150x) and interest income ($3x / $15x) is allocable to an excepted trade or business. Thus, $7x ($35x x 20 percent) of P's interest expense and $2x ($10x x 20 percent) of P's interest income is allocable to an excepted trade or business. The remaining $28x of P's interest expense is business interest expense subject to the section 163(j) limitation, and the remaining $8x of P's interest income is business interest income that increases the group's section 163(j) limitation. In turn, $23x ($115x x 20 percent) of S's interest expense and $1x ($5x x 20 percent) of S's interest income is allocable to an excepted trade or business. The remaining $92x of S's interest expense is business interest expense subject to the section 163(j) limitation, and the remaining $4x of S's interest income is business interest income that increases the group's section 163(j) limitation.

(2) *Example 2: Interest allocation within a consolidated group with assets used in more than one trade or business.*—(i) *Facts.* S is a member of a consolidated group of which P is the common parent. P conducts an electing real property trade or business (Business X), and S conducts a non-excepted trade or business (Business Y). In Year 1, P pays or accrues (without regard to section 163(j)) $50x of interest expense, and S pays or accrues $100x of interest expense (without regard to section 163(j)). P leases 40 percent of space in Building V (which P owns) to S for use in Business Y, and P leases the remaining 60 percent of space in Building V to third parties. For purposes of allocating interest expense under paragraph (c) of this section, the P group's basis in its assets (excluding Building V) used in Businesses X and Y is $180x and $620x, respectively. The P group's basis in Building V for purposes of allocating interest expense under paragraph (c) of this section is $200x.

(ii) *Analysis.* Under paragraph (c)(3)(ii) of this section, the P group's basis in Building V ($200x) is allocated to excepted and non-excepted trades or businesses in accordance with the use of space by Business Y (40 percent) and Business X (the remainder, or 60 percent). Accordingly, $120x of the basis in Building V is allocated to excepted trades or businesses (60 percent x $200x), and $80x is allocated to non-excepted trades or businesses (40 percent x $200x). After allocating the basis in Building V, the P group's total basis in the assets used in excepted and non-excepted trades or businesses is $300x and $700x, respectively. Under paragraphs (a)(4) and (c) of this section, 30 percent ($300x / $1,000x) of the P group's Year 1 interest expense is properly allocable to an excepted trade or business. Thus, $15x ($50x x 30 percent) of P's interest expense is properly allocable to an excepted trade or business, and the remaining $35x of P's interest expense is business interest expense subject to the section 163(j) limitation. In turn, $30x ($100x x 30 percent) of S's interest expense is properly allocable to an excepted trade or business, and the remaining $70x of S's interest expense is business interest expense subject to the section 163(j) limitation.

(3) *Example 3: Application of look-through rules.*—(i) *Facts.* A) Each of Corp A, Corp B, Corp C, and Corp D is a domestic calendar-year corporation that is not a member of a consolidated group. Corp A owns 100 percent of the stock of Corp C; the basis of Corp A's stock in Corp C is $500x. Corp C owns 10 percent of the interests in PS1 (a domestic partnership), and Corp B owns the remaining 90 percent. Corp C's basis in its PS1 interests is $25x; Corp B's basis in its PS1 interests is $225x. PS1 owns 100 percent of the stock of Corp D; the basis of PS1's stock in Corp D is $1,000x. Corp A and Corp B are owned by unrelated, non-overlapping shareholders.

(B) In 2021, Corp C was engaged solely in a non-excepted trade or business. That same year, PS1's only activity was holding Corp D stock. In turn, Corp D was engaged in both an electing farming business and a non-excepted trade or business. Under the allocation rules in paragraph (c) of this section, 50 percent of Corp D's asset basis in 2021 was allocable to the electing farming business, and the remaining 50 percent was allocable to the non-excepted trade or business.

(C) Corp A and Corp B each paid or accrued (without regard to section 163(j)) $150x of interest expense allocable to a trade or business. Corp A's trade or business was an excepted trade or business, and Corp B's trade or business was a non-excepted trade or business. Corp A's basis in the assets used in its trade or business was $100x, and Corp B's basis in the assets used in its trade or business was $112.5x.

(ii) *Analysis.* (A) As provided in paragraph (c)(5)(ii)(E) of this section, if a taxpayer applies the look-through rules of paragraph (c)(5)(ii) of this section, the taxpayer must begin with the lowest-tier entity to which it is eligible to apply the look-through rules. Corp A directly owns 100 percent of the stock of Corp C; thus, Corp A satisfies the 80 percent minimum ownership threshold with respect to Corp C. Corp A also owns 10 percent of the interests in PS1. There is no minimum ownership threshold for partnerships; thus, Corp A may apply the look-through rules to PS1. However, Corp A does not directly or indirectly own at least 80 percent of the stock of Corp D; thus, Corp A cannot look through its indirect interest in Corp D. In turn, Corp B directly owns 90 percent of the interests in PS1, and Corp B indirectly owns at least 80 percent of the stock of Corp D. Thus, Corp B must apply the look-through rules to PS1 and Corp D.

(B) From Corp A's perspective, PS1 is not engaged in a trade or business for purposes of section 163(j); instead, PS1 is merely holding its Corp D stock as an investment. Under paragraph (c)(5)(ii)(A)(2) of this section, if a partnership is not engaged in a trade or business, then its C corporation partner must treat its entire basis in the partnership interest as allocable to a non-excepted trade or business. Thus, for purposes of Corp A's application of the look-through rules, Corp C's entire basis in its PS1 interest ($25x) is allocable to a non-excepted trade or business. Corp C's basis in its other assets also is allocable to a non-excepted trade or business (the only trade or business in which Corp C is engaged). Thus, under paragraph (c) of this section, Corp A's $500x basis in its Corp C stock is allocable entirely to a non-excepted trade or business. Corp A's $100x basis in its other business assets is allocable to an excepted trade or business. Thus, 5/6 (or $125x) of Corp A's $150x of interest expense is properly allocable to a non-excepted trade or business and is business interest expense subject to the section 163(j) limitation, and the remaining $25x of Corp A's $150x of interest expense is allocable to an excepted trade or business and is not subject to the section 163(j) limitation.

(C) From Corp B's perspective, PS1 must look through its stock in Corp D to determine the extent to which PS1's basis in the stock is allocable to an excepted or non-excepted trade or business. Half of Corp D's basis in its assets is allocable to an excepted trade or business, and the other half is allocable to a non-excepted trade or business. Thus, from Corp B's perspective, $500x of PS1's basis in its Corp D stock (PS1's only asset) is allocable to an excepted trade or business, and the other half is allocable to a non-excepted trade or business. Corp B's basis in its PS1 interests is $225x. Applying the look-through rules to Corp B's PS1 interests, $112.5x of Corp B's basis in its PS1 interests is allocable to an excepted trade or business, and $112.5x of Corp B's basis in its PS1 interests is allocable to a non-excepted trade or business. Since Corp B's basis in the assets used in its non-excepted trade or business also was $112.5x, two-thirds of Corp B's interest expense ($100x) is properly allocable to a non-excepted trade or business and is business interest expense subject to the section 163(j) limitation, and one-third of Corp B's interest expense ($50x) is allocable to an excepted trade or business and is not subject to the section 163(j) limitation.

(4) *Example 4: Excepted and non-excepted trades or businesses in a consolidated group.*—(i) *Facts.* P is the common parent of a consolidated group of which A and B are the only other members. A conducts an electing real property trade or business (Business X), and B conducts a non-excepted trade or business (Business Y). In Year 1, A pays or accrues (without regard to section 163(j)) $50x of interest expense and earns $70x of gross income in the conduct of Business X, and B pays or accrues (without regard to section 163(j)) $100x of interest expense and earns $150x of gross income in the conduct of Business Y. B owns Building V, which it uses in Business Y. For purposes of allocating the P group's Year 1 business interest expense between excepted and non-excepted trades or businesses under paragraph (c) of this section, the P group's basis in its assets (other than Building V) used in Businesses X and Y is $180x and $620x, respectively, and the P group's basis in Building V is $200x. At the end of Year 1, B sells Building V to a third party and realizes a gain of $60x in addition to the $150x of gross income B earned that year from the conduct of Business Y.

(ii) *Analysis.* (A) Under paragraphs (a)(4) and (c) of this section, the P group's basis in its assets used in its trades or businesses is allocated between the P group's excepted trade or business (Business X) and its non-excepted trade or business (Business Y) as though these trades or businesses were conducted by a single corporation. Under paragraph (c) of this section, the P group's basis in its assets used in Businesses X and Y is $180x and $820x, respectively. Accordingly, 18 percent ($180x / $1,000x) of the P group's total interest expense ($150x) is properly allocable to an excepted trade or business ($27x), and the remaining 82 percent of the P group's total interest expense is business interest expense properly allocable to a non-excepted trade or business ($123x).

(B) To determine the P group's section 163(j) limitation, paragraph (a) of this section requires that certain items of income and deduction be allocated to the excepted and non-excepted trades or businesses of the P group as though these trades or businesses were conducted by a single corporation. In Year 1, the P group's excepted trade or business (Business X) has gross income of $70x, and the P group's non-excepted trade or business (Business Y) has gross income of $150x. Because Building V was used exclusively in Business Y, the $60x of gain from the sale of Building V in Year 1 is attributed to Business Y under paragraph (b)(2) of this section. The P group's section 163(j) limitation is $63x (30 percent x $210x), which allows the P group to deduct $63x of its $123x of business interest expense allocated to the P group's non-excepted trades or businesses. The group's $27x of interest expense that is allocable to excepted trades or businesses may be deducted without limitation under section 163(j).

(iii) *Intercompany transaction.* The facts are the same as in *Example 4* in paragraph (e)(4)(i) of this section, except that A owns Building V and leases it to B in Year 1 for $20x for use in Business Y, and A sells Building V to a third party for a $60 gain at the end of Year 1. Under paragraphs (a)(4) and (c) of this section, all members of the P group are treated as a single corporation. As a result, the P group's basis in its assets used in its trades or businesses is allocated between the P group's excepted trade or business (Business X) and its non-excepted trade or business (Business Y) as though these trades or businesses were conducted by a single corporation. A lease between two divisions of a single corporation would produce no rental income or expense. Thus, the $20x of rent paid by B to A does not affect the P group's ATI. Moreover, under paragraph (c) of this section, Building V is an asset used in the P group's non-excepted trade or business (Business Y). Accordingly, although A owns Building V, the basis in Building V is added to the P group's basis in assets used in Business Y for purposes of allocating interest expense under paragraph (c) of this section. In the same vein, when A sells Building V to a third party at a gain of $60x, the gain is included in the P group's ATI because Building V was used in a non-excepted trade or business of the P group (Business Y) prior to its sale.

(5) *Example 5: Captive activities.*—(i) *Facts.* S and T are members of a consolidated group of which P is the common parent. P conducts an electing real property trade or business (Business X), S conducts a non-excepted trade or business (Business Y), and T provides transportation services to Businesses X and Y but does not have any customers outside of the P group. For Year 1, T provides transportation services using a single bus with a basis of $120x.

(ii) *Analysis.* Under paragraph (a)(4) of this section, activities conducted by a consolidated group are treated as though those activities were conducted by a single corporation. Because the activities of T are limited to providing intercompany transportation services, T does not conduct a trade or business for purposes of section 163(j). Under paragraph (c)(3) of this section, business interest expense is allocated to excepted and non-excepted trades or businesses based on the relative basis of the assets used in those businesses. The basis in T's only asset, a bus, is therefore allocated between Business X and Business Y according to the use of T's bus by these businesses. Business X uses one-third of T's services, and Business Y uses two-thirds of T's services. Thus, $40x of the basis of T's bus is allocated to Business X, and $80x of the basis of T's bus is allocated to Business Y.

(6) *Example 6: Constructive ownership.*—(i) *Facts.* P, S, T, and U are domestic C corporations that are not members of a consolidated group. P directly owns 80 percent of the stock of each of S and T as measured by total voting power and value; an unrelated third party, X, owns the remaining 20 percent. In turn, S and T directly own 15 percent and 80 percent, respectively, of the stock of U as measured by total voting power and value; P directly owns the remaining 5 percent. P conducts both excepted and non-excepted trades or businesses. S and T conduct only non-excepted trades or businesses, and U conducts both excepted and non-excepted trades or businesses.

(ii) *Analysis.* Under paragraph (c)(7)(i)(A) of this section, a shareholder must look through to the assets of a domestic non-consolidated C corporation for purposes of allocating the shareholder's basis in its stock in the corporation between excepted and non-excepted trades or businesses if the shareholder's direct and indirect interest in the corporation satisfies the ownership requirements of section 1504(a)(2). For purposes of paragraph (c)(7)(i)(A) of this section, a shareholder's stock ownership is determined by applying the constructive ownership rules of section 318(a). P directly owns 80 percent of each of S and T as measured by total voting power and value; thus, P must look through to the assets of S and T when allocating the basis in its stock of S and T. P directly owns 5 percent of the stock of U as measured by total voting power and value, and P constructively owns the other 95 percent; thus, P also must look through to U's assets when allocating the basis in its U stock. S directly owns 15 percent of the stock of U, and S constructively owns only 5 percent through P; thus, S cannot look through to U's assets when allocating the basis in its U stock. T directly owns 80 percent of the stock of U, and T constructively owns an additional 5 percent; thus, T must look through to U's assets when allocating the basis in its U stock.

(iii) *Dividend.* The facts are the same as in paragraph (e)(6)(i) of this section, except that U distributes a $160x dividend pro rata to its shareholders. Thus, P receives $8x (5 percent of $160x) of the U dividend, S receives $24x (15 percent of $160x), and T receives $128x (80 percent of $160x). Under paragraph (c)(7)(i)(B) of this section, if a shareholder's direct interest in a corporation satisfies the ownership requirements of section 1504(a)(2), the shareholder must look through to the activities of a domestic non-consolidated C corporation in determining whether dividend income is from an excepted or non-excepted trade or business. The constructive ownership rules do not apply in allocating dividends under paragraph (c)(7)(i)(B) of this section. P directly owns 5 percent of the stock of U as measured by vote and value, and S directly owns 15 percent of the stock of U as measured by vote and value; thus, neither P nor S is required to apply the look-through rules in allocating its dividend income from U, and all such income is allocable to non-excepted trades or businesses. T directly owns 80 percent of the stock of U as measured by vote and value; thus, T must allocate its U dividend in accordance with the activities of U's excepted and non-excepted trades or businesses.

(7) *Example 7: Dispositions with a principal purpose of shifting basis.*—(i) *Facts.* U and V are members of a consolidated group of which P is the common parent. U conducts an electing farming business (Business F), and V conducts a farm equipment leasing business (Business L) that is a non-excepted trade or business. After the end of a farming season, the P group, with a principal purpose of shifting basis from Business L to Business F, has V sell to U all off-lease farming equipment that previously was leased out as part of Business L. Immediately before the start of the next season, U sells the farming equipment back to V for use in Business L.

(ii) *Analysis.* Under paragraph (c)(8) of this section, in the case of a disposition of assets undertaken with a principal purpose of artificially shifting the amount of basis allocable to excepted or non-excepted trades or businesses on a determination date, the additional basis or change in use will not be taken into account. Because V's sale of farming equipment to U for storage in Business F's facilities is undertaken with a principal purpose of shifting basis from Business L to Business F, the additional basis Business F receives from these transactions will not be taken into account for purposes of this section. Instead, the basis of the farming equipment will be allocated as though the farming equipment continued to be used in Business L.

(f) *Applicability dates.*—(1) *In general.*—This section applies to taxable years beginning on or after November 13, 2020. However, taxpayers and their related parties, within the meaning of sections 267(b) and 707(b)(1), may choose to apply the rules of this section to a taxable year beginning after December 31, 2017, so long as the taxpayers and their related parties consistently apply the rules of the section 163(j) regulations, and, if applicable, §§1.263A-9, 1.263A-15, 1.381(c)(20)-1, 1.382-1, 1.382-2, 1.382-5, 1.382 6, 1.382-7, 1.383-0, 1.383-1, 1.469-9, 1.469-11, 1.704-1, 1.882-5, 1.1362-3, 1.1368-1, 1.1377-1, 1.1502-13, 1.1502-21, 1.1502-36, 1.1502-79, 1.1502-91 through 1.1502-99 (to the extent they effectuate the rules of §§1.382-2, 1.382-5, 1.382-6, and 1.383-1), and 1.1504-4, to that taxable year. Accordingly, for purposes of §1.163(j)-10(c)(5), taxpayers make any change to the alternative depreciation system as of November 13, 2020, or if relying on the provisions of §1.163(j)-10 in regulation project REG-106089-18 (83 FR 67490), as of December 28, 2018.

(2) *Paragraph (c)(5)(ii)(D)(2).*—The rules contained in paragraph (c)(5)(ii)(D)(2) of this section apply for taxable years beginning on or after March 22, 2021. However, taxpayers may choose to apply the rules in paragraph (c)(5)(ii)(D)(2) of this section to a taxable year beginning after December 31, 2017, and before March 22, 2021, provided that those taxpayers and their related parties consistently apply all of the rules in the section 163(j) regulations as contained in T.D. 9905 (§§1.163(j)-0 through 1.163(j)-11, effective November 13, 2020) as modified by T.D. 9943, (effective January 13, 2021), and, if applicable, §§1.263A-9, 1.263A-15, 1.381(c)(20)-1, 1.382-1, 1.382-2, 1.382-5, 1.382-6, 1.383-0, 1.383-1, 1.469-9, 1.704-1, 1.882-5, 1.1362-3, 1.1368-1, 1.1377-1, 1.1502-13, 1.1502-21, 1.1502-79, 1.1502-91 through 1.1502-99 (to the extent they effectuate the rules of §§1.382-2, 1.382-5, 1.382-6, and 1.383-1), and 1.1504-4 contained in T.D. 9905 as modified by T.D. 9943, to that taxable year and each subsequent taxable year. [Reg. §1.163(j)-10.]

☐ [*T.D. 9905, 9-3-2020. Amended by T.D. 9943, 1-13-2021.*]

§1.164-1. Deduction for taxes.—(a) *In general.*—Only the following taxes shall be allowed as a deduction under this section for the taxable year within which paid or accrued, according to the method of accounting used in computing taxable income:

(1) State and local, and foreign, real property taxes.

(2) State and local personal property taxes.

(3) State and local, and foreign, income, war profits, and excess profits taxes.

(4) State and local general sales taxes.

(5) State and local taxes on the sale of gasoline, diesel fuel, and other motor fuels.

In addition, there shall be allowed as a deduction under this section State and local, and foreign, taxes not described in subparagraphs (1) through (5) of this paragraph which are paid or accrued within the taxable year in carrying on a trade or business or an activity described in section 212 (relating to expenses for production of income).

* * *

[Reg. §1.164-1.]

☐ [*T.D. 6256, 10-7-57. Amended by T.D. 6406, 8-14-59, T.D. 6780, 12-21-64 and T.D. 7577, 12-19-78.*]

§1.164-2. Deduction denied in case of certain taxes.—

* * *

(d) *Foreign income taxes.*—Except as provided in §1.901-1(c)(2) and (3), foreign income taxes, as defined in §1.901-2(a), paid or accrued (as the case may be, depending on the taxpayer's method of accounting for such taxes) in a taxable year, if the taxpayer chooses to take to any extent the benefits of section 901, relating to the credit for taxes of foreign countries and possessions of the United States, for taxes that are paid or accrued (according to the taxpayer's method of accounting for such taxes) in such taxable year.

* * *

(i) *Applicability dates.*—Paragraph (d) of this section applies to foreign taxes paid or accrued in taxable years beginning on or after December 28, 2021. [Reg. §1.164-2.]

☐ [*T.D. 6256, 10-7-57. Amended by T.D. 6780, 12-21-64, T.D. 7767, 2-3-81 and T.D. 9959, 12-28-2021.*]

§1.164-3. Definitions and special rules.—

* * *

(d) *Foreign taxes.*—The term "foreign tax" includes only a tax imposed by the authority of a foreign country. A tax imposed by a political subdivision of a foreign country is considered to be imposed by the authority of that foreign country.

* * *

[Reg. §1.164-3.]

☐ [*T.D. 6256, 10-7-57. Amended by T.D. 6780, 12-21-64 and T.D. 9907, 8-7-2020.*]

Special Deductions for Corporations

§1.243-3. Certain dividends from foreign corporations.—

* * *

(b) *Establishing separate earnings and profits accounts.*—A foreign corporation shall, for purposes of section 243(d), maintain a separate account for earnings and profits to which it succeeds which were accumulated by a domestic corporation, and such foreign corporation shall treat such earnings and profits as having been accumulated during the accounting periods in which earned by such domestic corporation. Such foreign corporation shall also maintain such a separate account for the earnings and profits, or deficit in earnings and profits, accumulated by it or accumulated by any other corporations to the earnings and profits of which it succeeds.

(c) *Effect of dividends on earnings and profits accounts.*—Dividends paid out of the accumulated earnings and profits (see section 316(a)(1)) of such foreign corporation shall be treated as having been paid out of the most recently accumulated earnings and profits of such corporation. A deficit in an earnings and profits account for any accounting period shall reduce the most recently accumulated earnings and profits for a prior accounting period in such account. If there are no accumulated earnings and profits in an earnings and profits account because of a deficit incurred in a prior accounting period, such deficit must be restored before earnings and profits can be accumulated in a subsequent accounting period. If a dividend is paid out of earnings and profits of a foreign corporation which maintains two or more accounts (established under the provisions of paragraph (b) of this section) with respect to two or more accounting periods ending on the same day, then the portion of such dividend considered as paid out of each account shall be the same proportion of the total dividend as the amount of earnings and profits in that account bears to the sum of the earnings and profits in all such accounts.

* * *

[Reg. §1.243-3.]

☐ [*T.D.* 6830, 6-22-65. *Amended by T.D.* 9194, 4-6-2005.]

§1.245-1. Dividends received from certain foreign corporations.—(a) *General rule.*—(1) A corporation is allowed a deduction under section 245(a) for dividends received from a foreign corporation (other than a foreign personal holding company as defined in section 552) which is subject to taxation under chapter 1 of the Code if, for an uninterrupted period of not less than 36 months ending with the close of the foreign corporation's taxable year in which the dividends are paid, (i) the foreign corporation is engaged in trade or business in the United States, and (ii) 50 percent or more of the foreign corporation's entire gross income is effectively connected with the conduct of a trade or business in the United States by that corporation. If the foreign corporation has been in existence less than 36 months as of the close of the taxable year in which the dividends are paid, then the applicable uninterrupted period to be taken into consideration in lieu of the uninterrupted period of 36 or more months is the entire period such corporation has been in existence as of the close of such taxable year. An uninterrupted period which satisfied the twofold requirement with respect to business activity and gross income may start at a date later than the date on which the foreign corporation first commenced an uninterrupted period of engaging in trade or business within the United States, but the applicable uninterrupted period is in any event the longest uninterrupted period which satisfies such twofold requirement. The deduction under section 245(a) is allowable to any corporation, whether foreign or domestic, receiving dividends from a distributing corporation which meets the requirements of that section.

(2) Any taxable year of a foreign corporation which falls within the uninterrupted period described in section 245(a)(2) shall not be taken into account in applying section 245(a)(2) and this paragraph if the 100 percent dividends received deduction would be allowable under paragraph (b) of this section, whether or not in fact allowed, with respect to any dividends payable, whether or not in fact paid, out of the earnings and profits of such foreign corporation for that taxable year. Thus, in such case the foreign corporation shall be treated as having no earnings and profits for that taxable year for purposes of determining the dividends received deduction allowance under section 245(a) and this paragraph. However, that taxable year may be taken into account for purposes of determining whether the foreign corporation meets the requirements of section 245(a) that, for the uninterrupted period specified therein, the foreign corporation is engaged in trade or business in the United States and meets the 50 percent gross income requirement.

(b) *Dividends from wholly owned foreign subsidiaries.*—(1) A domestic corporation is allowed a deduction under section 245(b) for any taxable year beginning after December 31, 1966, for dividends received from a foreign corporation (other than a foreign personal holding company as defined in section 552) which is subject to taxation under chapter 1 of the Code if—

(i) The domestic corporation owns either directly or indirectly all of the outstanding stock of the foreign corporation during the entire taxable year of the domestic corporation in which the dividends are received, and

(ii) The dividends are paid out of earnings and profits of a taxable year of the foreign corporation during which (*a*) the domestic corporation receiving the dividends owns directly or indirectly throughout such year all of the outstanding stock of the foreign corporation, and (*b*) all of the gross income of the foreign corporation from all sources is effectively connected for that year with the conduct of a trade or business in the United States by that corporation.

* * *

(c) *Rules of application.*—(1) Except as provided in section 246, the deduction provided by section 245 for any taxable year is the sum of the amounts computed under paragraphs (1) and (2) of section 245(a) plus, in the case of a domestic corporation for any taxable year beginning after December 31, 1966, the sum of the amounts computed under section 245(b)(2).

(2) To the extent that a dividend received from a foreign corporation is treated as a dividend from a domestic corporation in accordance with section 243(d) and §1.243-3, it shall not be treated as a dividend received from a foreign corporation for purposes of this section.

(3) For purposes of section 245(a) and (b), the amount of a distribution shall be determined under subparagraph (B) (without reference to subparagraph (C)) of section 301(b)(1).

(4) In determining from what year's earnings and profits a dividend is treated as having been distributed for purposes of this section, the principles of paragraph (a) of §1.316-2 shall apply. A dividend shall be considered to be distributed, first, out of the earnings and profits of the taxable year which includes the date the dividend is distributed, second, out of the earnings and profits accumulated for the immediately preceding taxable year, third, out of the earnings and profits accumulated for the second preceding taxable year, etc. A deficit in an earnings and profits account for any taxable year shall reduce the most recently accumulated earnings and profits for a prior year in such account. If there are no accumulated earnings and profits in an earnings and profits account because of a deficit incurred in a prior year, such deficit must be restored before earnings and profits can be accumulated in a subsequent accounting year. See also paragraph (c) of §1.243-3 and paragraph (a)(6) of §1.243-4.

(5) For purposes of this section the gross income of a foreign corporation for any period before its first taxable year beginning after December 31, 1966, which is from sources within the United States shall be treated as gross income which is effectively connected for that period with the conduct of a trade or business in the United States by that corporation.

(6) For the determination of the source of income and the income which is effectively connected with the conduct of a trade or business in the United States, see sections 861 through 864, and the regulations thereunder.

* * *

[Reg. §1.245-1.]

☐ [*T.D.* 6183, 6-13-56. *Amended by T.D.* 6752, 9-8-64, *T.D.* 6830, 6-22-65 *and T.D.* 7293, 11-27-73.]

§1.245A-1. [Reserved].

☐ [*T.D.* 9909, 8-21-2020.]

§1.245A-2. [Reserved].

☐ [*T.D.* 9909, 8-21-2020.]

§1.245A-3. [Reserved].

☐ [*T.D.* 9909, 8-21-2020.]

§1.245A-4. [Reserved].

☐ [*T.D.* 9909, 8-21-2020.]

§1.245A-5. Limitation of section 245A deduction and section 954(c)(6) exception.—(a) *Overview.*—This section provides rules that limit a deduction under section 245A(a) to the portion of a dividend that exceeds the ineligible amount of such dividend or the applicability of section 954(c)(6) when a portion of a dividend is paid out of an extraordinary disposition account or when an extraordinary reduction occurs. Paragraph (b) of this section provides rules regarding ineligible amounts. Paragraph (c) of this section provides rules for determining ineligible amounts attributable to an extraordinary disposition. Paragraph (d) of this section provides rules that limit the application of section 954(c)(6) when one or more section 245A shareholders of a lower-tier CFC have an extraordinary disposition account. Paragraph (e) of this section provides rules for determining ineligible amounts attributable to an extraordinary reduction. Paragraph (f) of this section provides rules that limit the application of section 954(c)(6) when a lower-tier CFC has an extraordinary reduction amount. Paragraph (g) of this section provides special rules for purposes of applying this section. Paragraph (h) of this section provides an anti-abuse rule. Paragraph (i) of this section provides definitions. Paragraph (j) of this section provides examples illustrating the application of this section. Paragraph (k) of this section provides the applicability date of this section.

(b) *Limitation of deduction under section 245A.*—(1) *In general.*—A section 245A shareholder is allowed a section 245A deduction for any dividend received from an SFC (provided all other applicable requirements are satisfied) only to the extent that the dividend exceeds the ineligible amount of the dividend. See paragraphs (j)(2), (4), and (5) of this section for examples illustrating the application of this paragraph (b)(1).

(2) *Definition of ineligible amount.*—The term *ineligible amount* means, with respect to a dividend received by a section 245A shareholder from an SFC, an amount equal to the sum of—

(i) 50 percent of the extraordinary disposition amount (as determined under paragraph (c) of this section); and

(ii) The extraordinary reduction amount (as determined under paragraph (e) of this section).

(c) *Rules for determining extraordinary disposition amount.*—(1) *Definition of extraordinary disposition amount.*—The term *extraordinary disposition amount* means the portion of a dividend received by a section 245A shareholder from an SFC that is paid out of the extraordinary disposition account with respect to the section 245A shareholder. See paragraph (j)(2) of this section for an example illustrating the application of this paragraph (c).

(2) *Determination of portion of dividend paid out of extraordinary disposition account.*—(i) *In general.*—For purposes of determining the portion of a dividend received by a section 245A shareholder from an SFC that is paid out of the extraordinary disposition account with respect to the section 245A shareholder, the following rules apply—

(A) The dividend is first considered paid out of non-extraordinary disposition E&P with respect to the section 245A shareholder; and

(B) The dividend is next considered paid out of the extraordinary disposition account to the extent of the section 245A shareholder's extraordinary disposition account balance.

(ii) *Definition of non-extraordinary disposition E&P.*—The term *non-extraordinary disposition E&P* means, with respect to a section 245A shareholder and an SFC, an amount of earnings and profits of the SFC equal to the excess, if any, of—

(A) The product of—

(1) The amount of the SFC's earnings and profits described in section 959(c)(3), determined as of the end of the SFC's taxable year (for purposes of paragraph (c)(2)(ii) of this section, without regard to distributions during the taxable year other than as provided in this paragraph (c)(2)(ii)(A)(1)), but, if during the taxable year the SFC pays more than one dividend, reduced (but not below zero) by the amounts of any dividends paid by the SFC earlier in the taxable year; and

(2) The percentage of the stock (by value) of the SFC that the section 245A shareholder owns directly or indirectly immediately before the distribution; over

(B) The balance of the section 245A shareholder's extraordinary disposition account with respect to the SFC, determined immediately before the distribution.

(3) *Definitions with respect to extraordinary disposition accounts.*—(i) *Extraordinary disposition account.*—(A) *In general.*—The term *extraordinary disposition account* means, with respect to a section 245A shareholder of an SFC, an account, the balance of which is equal to the product of the extraordinary disposition ownership percentage and the extraordinary disposition E&P, reduced (but not below zero) by the prior extraordinary disposition amount and as provided in §1.245A-7 or §1.245A-8, and adjusted under paragraph (c)(4) of this section, as applicable. An extraordinary disposition account is maintained in the same functional currency as the extraordinary disposition E&P.

(B) *Extraordinary disposition ownership percentage.*—The term *extraordinary disposition ownership percentage* means the percentage of stock (by value) of an SFC that a section 245A shareholder owns directly or indirectly at the beginning of the disqualified period or, if later, on the first day during the disqualified period on which the SFC is a CFC, regardless of whether the section 245A shareholder owns directly or indirectly such stock of the SFC on the date of an extraordinary disposition giving rise to extraordinary disposition E&P; if not, see paragraph (c)(4) of this section.

(C) *Extraordinary disposition E&P.*—The term *extraordinary disposition E&P* means an amount of earnings and profits of an SFC equal to the sum of the net gain recognized by the SFC with respect to specified property in each extraordinary disposition. In the case of an extraordinary disposition with respect to the SFC arising as a result of a disposition of specified property by a specified entity (other than a foreign corporation), an interest of which is owned directly or indirectly (through one or more other specified entities that are not foreign corporations) by the SFC, the net gain taken into account for purposes of the preceding sentence is the SFC's distributive share of the net gain recognized by the specified entity with respect to the specified property.

(D) *Prior extraordinary disposition amount.*—*(1) General rule.*—The term *prior extraordinary disposition amount* means, with respect to an SFC and a section 245A shareholder, the sum of the extraordinary disposition amount of each prior dividend received by the section 245A shareholder from the SFC by reason of paragraph (c)(1) of this section and 200 percent of the sum of the amounts included in the section 245A shareholder's gross income under section 951(a) by reason of paragraph (d) of this section (in the case in which the SFC is, or has been, a lower-tier CFC). A section 245A shareholder's prior extraordinary disposition amount also includes—

(i) A prior dividend received by the section 245A shareholder from the SFC to the extent not an extraordinary reduction amount and to the extent the dividend would have been an extraordinary disposition amount but for the failure of the dividend to qualify for the section 245A deduction by reason of one or more of the following: application of section 245A(e); the recipient domestic corporation does not satisfy the holding period requirement of section 246; or the recipient domestic corporation is not a United States shareholder with respect to the foreign corporation from whose earnings and profits the dividend is sourced;

(ii) The portion of a prior dividend (to the extent not a tiered extraordinary disposition amount by reason of paragraph (d) of this section) received by an upper-tier CFC from the SFC that by reason of section 245A(e) or being properly allocable to subpart F income of the SFC for the taxable year of the dividend pursuant to section 954(c)(6)(A) was included in the upper-tier CFC's foreign personal holding company income and was included in gross income by the section 245A shareholder under section 951(a) but would have been a tiered extraordinary disposition amount by reason of paragraph (d) of this section had paragraph (d) applied to the dividend;

(iii) If a prior dividend received by an upper-tier CFC from a lower-tier CFC gives rise to a tiered extraordinary disposition amount with respect to the section 245A shareholder by reason of paragraph (d) of this section, the qualified portion; and

(iv) 200 percent of an amount included in the gross income of a domestic corporation under section 951(a)(1)(B) with respect to a CFC for the taxable year of the domestic corporation in which or with which the CFC's taxable year ends, to the extent so included by reason of the application of this section to the hypotheti-

cal distribution described in §1.956-1(a)(2), or to the extent the amount would have been so included by reason of the application of this section to the hypothetical distribution but for the application of section 245A(e) or the holding period requirement in section 246 to the hypothetical distribution.

(2) *Definition of qualified portion.—(i) In general.*—The term *qualified portion* means, with respect to a tiered extraordinary disposition amount of a section 245A shareholder and a lower-tier CFC, 200 percent of the portion of the disqualified amount with respect to the tiered extraordinary disposition amount equal to the sum of the amounts included in gross income by each U.S. tax resident under section 951(a) in the taxable year in which the tiered extraordinary disposition amount arose with respect to the lower-tier CFC by reason of paragraph (d) of this section. For purposes of the preceding sentence, the reference to a U.S. tax resident does not include any section 245A shareholder with a tiered extraordinary disposition amount with respect to the lower-tier CFC.

(*ii*) *Determining a qualified portion if multiple section 245A shareholders have tiered extraordinary disposition amounts.* For the purposes of applying paragraph (c)(3)(i)(D)(2)(*i*) of this section, if more than one section 245A shareholder has a tiered extraordinary disposition amount with respect to a dividend received by an upper-tier CFC from a lower-tier CFC, then the qualified portion with respect to each section 245A shareholder is equal to the amount described in paragraph (c)(3)(i)(D)(2)(*i*) of this section, without regard to this paragraph (c)(3)(i)(D)(2)(*ii*), multiplied by a fraction, the numerator of which is the section 245A shareholder's tiered extraordinary disposition amount with respect to the lower-tier CFC and the denominator of which is the sum of the tiered extraordinary disposition amounts with respect to each section 245A shareholder and the lower-tier CFC.

(ii) *Extraordinary disposition.*—(A) *In general.*—Except as provided in paragraph (c)(3)(ii)(E) of this section, the term *extraordinary disposition* means, with respect to an SFC, any disposition of specified property by the SFC on a date on which it was a CFC and during the SFC's disqualified period to a related party if the disposition occurs outside of the ordinary course of the SFC's activities. An extraordinary disposition also includes a disposition during the disqualified period on a date on which the SFC is not a CFC if there is a plan, agreement, or understanding involving a section 245A shareholder to cause the SFC to recognize gain that would give rise to an extraordinary disposition if the SFC were a CFC.

(B) *Facts and circumstances.*—A determination as to whether a disposition is undertaken outside of the ordinary course of an SFC's activities is made on the basis of facts and circumstances, taking into account whether the transaction is consistent with the SFC's past activities, including with respect to quantity and frequency. In addition, a disposition of specified property by an SFC to a related party may be considered outside of the ordinary course of the SFC's activities notwithstanding that the SFC regularly disposes of property of the same type of, or similar to, the specified property to persons that are not related parties.

(C) *Per se rules.—(1) In general.*—Even if a disposition would otherwise be considered to be undertaken in the ordinary course of an SFC's activities under the requirements of paragraph (c)(3)(ii)(B) of this section, that disposition is treated as occurring outside of the ordinary course of an SFC's activities if the disposition is undertaken with a principal purpose of generating earnings and profits during the disqualified period or, except as provided in paragraph (c)(3)(ii)(C)(2) of this section, if the disposition is of intangible property, as defined in section 367(d)(4).

(2) Exception to the per se rule for certain property.—(i) Exception.—Paragraph (c)(3)(ii)(C)(*1*) of this section does not apply to a disposition of intangible property that is not described in section 367(d)(4)(C) or (F), provided that the property is transferred to a related person during the disqualified period with a reasonable expectation that the related person will resell the property to an unrelated customer within one year. Subject to paragraph (c)(3)(ii)(C)(2)(*ii*) of this section, a disposition of intangible property that satisfies the requirements of this paragraph (c)(3)(ii)(C)(2)(*i*) is determined to be within or without the ordinary course of an SFC's activities based on the test described in paragraph (c)(3)(ii)(B) of this section.

(ii) Facts and circumstances presumption for property described in section 367(d)(4)(A).—Notwithstanding paragraph (c)(3)(ii)(B) of this section, any disposition described in paragraph (c)(3)(ii)(C)(2)(*i*) of this section of a copyright right within the meaning of §1.861-18 or of intangible property described in section 367(d)(4)(A) is presumed to take place outside of the ordinary course of an SFC's activities for purposes of paragraph (c)(3)(ii)(A) of this section. The presumption in the preceding sentence may be rebutted only if the taxpayer can show that the facts and circumstances clearly establish that the disposition took place in the ordinary course of the SFC's activities.

(D) *Treatment of dispositions by certain specified entities.*—For purposes of paragraph (c)(3)(ii)(A) of this section, an extraordinary disposition with respect to an SFC includes a disposition by a specified entity other than a foreign corporation, provided that immediately before or immediately after the disposition the specified entity is a related party with respect to the SFC, the SFC directly or indirectly (through one or more other specified entities other than foreign corporations) owns an interest in the specified entity, and the disposition would have otherwise qualified as an extraordinary disposition had the specified entity been a foreign corporation.

(E) *De minimis exception to extraordinary disposition.*—If the sum of the net gain recognized by an SFC with respect to specified property in all dispositions otherwise described in paragraph (c)(3)(ii)(A) of this section does not exceed the lesser of $50 million or 5 percent of the gross value of all of the SFC's property held immediately before the beginning of its disqualified period, then no disposition of specified property by the SFC is an extraordinary disposition.

(iii) *Disqualified period.*—The term *disqualified period* means, with respect to an SFC that is a CFC on any day during the taxable year that includes January 1, 2018, the period beginning on January 1, 2018, and ending as of the close of the taxable year of the SFC, if any, that begins before January 1, 2018, and ends after December 31, 2017.

(iv) *Specified property.*—The term *specified property* means any property if gain recognized with respect to such property during the disqualified period is not described in section 951A(c)(2)(A)(i)(I) through (V). If only a portion of the gain recognized with respect to property during the disqualified period is gain that is not described in section 951A(c)(2)(A)(i)(I) through (V), then a portion of the property is treated as specified property in an amount that bears the same ratio to the value of the property as the amount of gain not described in section 951A(c)(2)(A)(i)(I) through (V) bears to the total amount of gain recognized with respect to such property during the disqualified period. Specified property is also property with respect to which a loss was recognized during the disqualified period if the loss is properly allocable to income not described in section 951A(c)(2)(A)(i)(I) through (V) under the principles of section 954(b)(5) (specified loss). If only a portion of the loss recognized with respect to property during the disqualified period is specified loss, then a portion of the property is treated as specified property in an amount that bears the same ratio to the value of the property as the amount of specified loss bears to the total amount of loss recognized with respect to such property during the disqualified period.

(4) *Successor rules for extraordinary disposition accounts.*—This paragraph (c)(4) applies with respect to an extraordinary disposition account upon certain direct or indirect transfers of stock of an SFC by a section 245A shareholder.

(i) *Another section 245A shareholder succeeds to all or portion of account.*—Except as provided in paragraph (c)(4)(vi) of this section, paragraphs (c)(4)(i)(A) through (D) of this section apply when a section 245A shareholder of an SFC (the *transferor*) transfers directly or indirectly a share of stock (or a portion of a share of stock) of the SFC that it owns directly or indirectly (the share or portion thereof, a *transferred share*).

(A) If immediately after the transfer (taking into account all transactions related to the transfer) another person is a section 245A shareholder of the SFC, then such other person's extraordinary disposition account with respect to the SFC is increased by the person's proportionate share of the amount allocated to the transferred share.

(B) For purposes of paragraph (c)(4)(i)(A) of this section, the amount allocated to a transferred share is equal to the product of—

(*1*) The balance of the transferor's extraordinary disposition account with respect to the SFC, determined after any reduction pursuant to paragraph (c)(3) of this section by reason of dividends and before the application of this paragraph (c)(4)(i)(B); and

(*2*) A fraction, the numerator of which is the value of the transferred share and the denominator of which is the value of all of the stock of the SFC that the transferor owns directly or indirectly immediately before the transfer.

(C) For purposes of paragraph (c)(4)(i)(A) of this section, a person's proportionate share of the amount allocated to a transferred share under paragraph (c)(4)(i)(B) of this section is equal to the product of—

(1) The amount allocated to the share; and

(2) The percentage of the share (by value) that the person owns directly or indirectly immediately after the transfer (taking into account all transactions related to the transfer).

(D) The transferor's extraordinary disposition account with respect to the SFC is decreased by the amount by which another person's extraordinary disposition account with respect to the SFC is increased pursuant to paragraph (c)(4)(i)(A) of this section.

(ii) *Certain section 381 transactions.*—(A) *In general.*—If assets of an SFC (the *acquired corporation*) are acquired by another SFC (the *acquiring corporation*) pursuant to a transaction described in section 381(a) in which the acquired corporation is the transferor corporation for purposes of section 381, then a section 245A shareholder's extraordinary disposition account with respect to the acquiring corporation is increased by the balance of its extraordinary disposition account with respect to the acquired corporation, determined after any reduction pursuant to paragraph (c)(3) of this section by reason of dividends and before the application of this paragraph (c)(4)(ii)(A).

(B) *Certain triangular asset reorganizations.*—If, in a transaction described in paragraph (c)(4)(ii)(A) of this section, the section 245A shareholder receives stock of a domestic corporation that controls (within the meaning of section 368(c)) the acquiring corporation, the domestic corporation's extraordinary disposition account with respect to the acquiring corporation is increased by the balance of the section 245A shareholder's extraordinary disposition account with respect to the acquired corporation, determined after any reduction pursuant to paragraph (c)(3) of this section by reason of dividends and before the application of this paragraph (c)(4)(ii)(B).

(iii) *Certain distributions involving section 355 or 356.*—In the case of a transaction involving a distribution under section 355 (or so much of section 356 as it relates to section 355) by an SFC (the *distributing corporation*) of stock of another SFC (the *controlled corporation*), a section 245A shareholder's extraordinary disposition account with respect to the distributing corporation is attributed to (and treated as) an extraordinary disposition account with respect to the controlled corporation in a manner similar to how earnings and profits of the distributing corporation and the controlled corporation are adjusted under §1.312-10. To the extent that a section 245A shareholder's extraordinary disposition account with respect to the distributing CFC is not so attributed to (and treated as) an extraordinary disposition account with respect to the controlled corporation, the extraordinary disposition account remains as an extraordinary disposition account with respect to the distributing corporation.

(iv) *Transfer of all of the stock of the SFC owned by a section 245A shareholder.*—(A) *In general.*—If, in a transaction described in paragraph (c) of this section, a section 245A shareholder of an SFC transfers directly or indirectly all of the stock of the SFC that it owns directly or indirectly, then, except as provided in paragraph (c)(4)(iv)(B) of this section, any remaining balance of the section 245A shareholder's extraordinary disposition account that is not allocated or attributed under paragraph (c) of this section is eliminated and therefore not taken into account by any person.

(B) *Related party retains the extraordinary distribution account.*—If any related party with respect to the section 245A shareholder described in paragraph (c)(4)(iv)(A) of this section is a section 245A shareholder with respect to the SFC immediately after the transfer (taking into account all transactions related to the transfer), then the remaining balance of the section 245A shareholder's extraordinary disposition account with respect to the SFC is added to the related party's extraordinary disposition account. If multiple related parties are section 245A shareholders of the SFC, then the remaining balance of the extraordinary disposition account is allocated between the related parties in proportion to the value of the stock of the SFC that they own directly or indirectly immediately after the transfer (taking into account all transactions related to the transfer).

(v) *Effect of section 338(g) election.*—(A) *In general.*—Except as provided in paragraph (c)(4)(v)(B) of this section, if an election under section 338(g) is made with respect to a qualified stock purchase (as defined in section 338(d)(3)) of stock of an SFC, then a section 245A shareholder's extraordinary disposition account with respect to the old target (as defined in §1.338-2(c)(17)) is not treated as (or attributed to) an extraordinary disposition account with respect to the new target (as defined in §1.338-2(c)(17)). Accordingly, the remaining balance of the old target's extraordinary disposition account is eliminated and is not thereafter taken into account by any person.

(B) *Special rules regarding carryover foreign target stock.*—If an election under section 338(g) is made with respect to a qualified stock purchase (as described in section 338(d)(3)) of stock of an SFC and there are one or more shares of carryover foreign target stock ("FT stock") (as described in §1.338-9(b)(3)(i)), then the following rules apply as to a section 245A shareholder of the new target that after the qualified stock purchase directly or indirectly owns carryover FT stock (such shareholder, the *carryover FT stock shareholder*):

(1) In a case in which before the qualified stock purchase the carryover FT stock shareholder directly or indirectly owned carryover FT stock, the carryover FT stock shareholder's extraordinary disposition account with respect to the old target, determined after any reduction pursuant to paragraph (c)(3) of this section by reason of dividends, is treated as its extraordinary disposition account with respect to the new target.

(2) In a case in which before the qualified stock purchase the carryover FT stock shareholder did not directly or indirectly own carryover FT stock, but the stock retains its character as carryover FT stock (taking into account §1.338-9(b)(3)(vi)), a ratable portion of each section 245A shareholder's extraordinary disposition account with respect to the old target, determined after any reduction pursuant to paragraph (c)(3) of this section by reason of dividends, is treated as the carryover FT stock shareholder's extraordinary disposition account with respect to the new target, based on the value of the carryover FT stock that the carryover FT stock shareholder owns directly or indirectly after the qualified stock purchase relative to the value of all of the stock of the new target.

(vi) *Certain transfers described in §1.1248-8(a)(1).*—(A) *In general.*—If a person transfers stock of an SFC with respect to which a section 245A shareholder has an extraordinary disposition account to a foreign acquiring corporation in a transaction described §1.1248-8(a)(1) (other than a transfer that is also described in §1.1248(f)-1(b)(2) or (3)) in which stock of a foreign corporation is received by the transferor, then, except in the case in which the transfer is also described in paragraph (c)(4)(ii) or (iii) of this section, the section 245A shareholder's extraordinary disposition account is not adjusted under this paragraph (c)(4).

(B) *Certain transfers described in §1.1248(f)-1(b).*—In the case of a transfer directly or indirectly of stock of an SFC by a section 245A shareholder described in §1.1248(f)-1(b)(2) or (3), but which does not result in an income inclusion, in whole or in part, by reason of §1.1248-2, the section 245A shareholder's extraordinary disposition account with respect to the SFC, determined after any reduction pursuant to paragraph (c)(3) of this section by reason of dividends and before the application of this paragraph (c)(4)(vi)(B), is allocated and adjusted in the same manner as under paragraph (c)(4)(i) of this section, except that, for purposes of applying paragraphs (c)(4)(i)(B) and (C) of this section, stock of the SFC that is owned directly or indirectly by persons who are not section 1248 shareholders (as defined in §1.1248(f)-1(c)(12)) is disregarded.

(vii) *Anti-abuse rule.*—Pursuant to paragraph (h) of this section, if a principal purpose of a transaction or series of transactions is to shift to another person, or to avoid, an amount of a section 245A shareholder's extraordinary disposition account with respect to an SFC or otherwise avoid the purposes of this section, then appropriate adjustments are made for purposes of this section, including disregarding the transaction or series of transactions. A principal purpose described in the preceding sentence is deemed to exist if stock of an SFC is directly or indirectly acquired by one of more section 245A shareholders within one year of a transaction or transactions to which paragraph (c)(4)(iv)(A) of this section would otherwise apply.

(d) *Limitation of amount eligible for section 954(c)(6) when there is an extraordinary disposition account with respect to a lower-tier CFC.*—(1) *In general.*—If an upper-tier CFC receives a dividend from a lower-tier CFC, then the dividend is eligible for the exception to foreign personal holding company income under section 954(c)(6) (provided all other applicable requirements are satisfied) with respect to the portion of the dividend that exceeds the disqualified amount. With respect to the portion of the dividend that does not exceed the disqualified amount, the exception to foreign personal holding company income under section 954(c)(6) is allowed (provided all other applicable requirements are satisfied) only for the amount equal to 50 percent of the portion of the dividend that does not exceed the disqualified amount. The disqualified amount is the quotient of the amounts described in paragraphs (d)(1)(i) and (ii) of this section.

(i) The sum of each section 245A shareholder's tiered extraordinary disposition amount with respect to the lower-tier CFC.

(ii) The percentage of stock of the upper-tier CFC (by value) owned, in the aggregate, by U.S. tax residents that include in gross income their pro rata share of the upper-tier CFC's subpart F income under section 951(a) on the last day of the upper-tier CFC's taxable year. If a U.S. tax resident is a direct or indirect partner in a domestic partnership that is a United States shareholder of the upper-tier CFC, the amount of stock owned by the U.S. tax resident for purposes of the preceding sentence is determined under the principles of paragraph (g)(3) of this section.

(2) *Definition of tiered extraordinary disposition amount.*—(i) *In general.*—The term *tiered extraordinary disposition amount* means, with respect to a dividend received by an upper-tier CFC from a lower-tier CFC and a section 245A shareholder, the portion of the dividend that would be an extraordinary disposition amount if the section 245A shareholder received as a dividend its pro rata share of the dividend from the lower-tier CFC. The preceding sentence does not apply to an amount treated as a dividend received by an upper-tier CFC from a lower-tier CFC by reason of section 964(e)(4) (in such case, see paragraphs (b)(1) and (g)(2) of this section).

(ii) *Section 245A shareholder's pro rata share of a dividend received by an upper-tier CFC.*—For the purposes of paragraph (d)(2)(i) of this section, a section 245A shareholder's pro rata share of the amount of a dividend received by an upper-tier CFC from a lower-tier CFC equals the amount by which the dividend would increase the section 245A shareholder's pro rata share of the upper-tier CFC's subpart F income under section 951(a)(2) and § 1.951-1(b) and (e) if the dividend were included in the upper-tier CFC's foreign personal holding company income under section 951(a)(1), determined without regard to section 952(c) and as if the upper-tier CFC had no deductions properly allocable to the dividend under section 954(b)(5).

(e) *Extraordinary reduction amount.*—(1) *In general.*—Except as provided in paragraph (e)(3) of this section, the term *extraordinary reduction amount* means, with respect to a dividend received by a controlling section 245A shareholder from a CFC during a taxable year of the CFC ending after December 31, 2017, in which an extraordinary reduction occurs with respect to the controlling section 245A shareholder's ownership of the CFC, the lesser of the amounts described in paragraph (e)(1)(i) or (ii) of this section. *See* paragraphs (j)(4) through (6) of this section for examples illustrating the application of this paragraph (e).

(i) The amount of the dividend.

(ii) The amount equal to the sum of the controlling section 245A shareholder's pre-reduction pro rata share of the CFC's subpart F income (as defined in section 952(a)) and tested income (as defined in section 951A(c)(2)(A)) for the taxable year, reduced, but not below zero, by the prior extraordinary reduction amount.

(2) *Rules regarding extraordinary reduction amounts.*—(i) *Extraordinary reduction.*—(A) *In general.*—Except as provided in paragraph (e)(2)(i)(C) of this section, an *extraordinary reduction* occurs, with respect to a controlling section 245A shareholder's ownership of a CFC during a taxable year of the CFC, if either of the conditions described in paragraph (e)(2)(i)(A)(*1*) or (2) of this section is satisfied. See paragraphs (j)(4) and (5) of this section for examples illustrating an extraordinary reduction.

(*1*) The condition of this paragraph (e)(2)(i)(A)(*1*) requires that during the taxable year, the controlling section 245A shareholder transfers directly or indirectly (other than by reason of a transfer occurring pursuant to an exchange described in section 368(a)(1)(E) or (F)), in the aggregate, more than 10 percent (by value) of the stock of the CFC that the section 245A shareholder owns directly or indirectly as of the beginning of the taxable year of the CFC, provided the stock transferred, in the aggregate, represents at least 5 percent (by value) of the outstanding stock of the CFC as of the beginning of the taxable year of the CFC; or

(*2*) The condition of this paragraph (e)(2)(i)(A)(*2*) requires that, as a result of one or more transactions occurring during the taxable year, the percentage of stock (by value) of the CFC that the controlling section 245A shareholder owns directly or indirectly as of the close of the last day of the taxable year of the CFC is less than 90 percent of the percentage of stock (by value) that the controlling section 245A shareholder owns directly or indirectly on either of the dates described in paragraphs (e)(2)(i)(B)(*1*) and (2) of this section (such percentage, the *initial percentage*), provided the difference between the initial percentage and percentage at the end of the year is at least five percentage points.

(B) *Dates for purposes of the initial percentage.*—For purposes of paragraph (e)(2)(i)(A)(*2*) of this section, the dates described in paragraphs (e)(2)(i)(B)(*1*) and (2) of this section are—

(*1*) The day of the taxable year on which the controlling section 245A shareholder owns directly or indirectly its highest percentage of stock (by value) of the CFC; and

(*2*) The day immediately before the first day on which stock was transferred directly or indirectly in the preceding taxable year in a transaction (or a series of transactions) occurring pursuant to a plan to reduce the percentage of stock (by value) of the CFC that the controlling section 245A shareholder owns directly or indirectly.

(C) *Transactions pursuant to which CFC's taxable year ends.*—A controlling section 245A shareholder's direct or indirect transfer of stock of a CFC that but for this paragraph (e)(2)(i)(C) would give rise to an extraordinary reduction under paragraph (e)(2)(i)(A) of this section does not give rise to an extraordinary reduction if the taxable year of the CFC ends immediately after the transfer, provided that the controlling section 245A shareholder directly or indirectly owns the stock on the last day of such year. Thus, for example, if a controlling section 245A shareholder exchanges all the stock of a CFC pursuant to a complete liquidation of the CFC, the exchange does not give rise to an extraordinary reduction.

(ii) *Rules for determining pre-reduction pro rata share.*—(A) *In general.*—Except as provided in paragraph (e)(2)(ii)(B) of this section, the term *pre-reduction pro rata share* means, with respect to a controlling section 245A shareholder and the subpart F income or tested income of a CFC, the controlling section 245A shareholder's pro rata share of the CFC's subpart F income or tested income under section 951(a)(2) and § 1.951-1(b) and (e) or section 951A(e)(1) and § 1.951A-1(d)(1), respectively, determined based on the controlling section 245A shareholder's direct or indirect ownership of stock of the CFC immediately before the extraordinary reduction (or, if the extraordinary reduction occurs by reason of multiple transactions, immediately before the first transaction) and without regard to section 951(a)(2)(B) and § 1.951-1(b)(1)(ii), but only to the extent that such subpart F income or tested income is not included in the controlling section 245A shareholder's pro rata share of the CFC's subpart F income or tested income under section 951(a)(2) and § 1.951-1(b) and (e) or section 951A(e)(1) and § 1.951A-1(d)(1), respectively.

(B) *Decrease in section 245A shareholder's pre-reduction pro rata share for amounts taken into account by U.S. tax resident.*—A controlling section 245A shareholder's pre-reduction pro rata share of subpart F income or tested income of a CFC for a taxable year is reduced by an amount equal to the sum of the amounts by which each U.S. tax resident's pro rata share of the subpart F income or tested income is increased as a result of a transfer directly or indirectly of stock of the CFC by the controlling section 245A shareholder or an issuance of stock by the CFC (such an amount with respect to a U.S. tax resident, a *specified amount*), in either case, during the taxable year in which the extraordinary reduction occurs. For purposes of this paragraph (e)(2)(ii)(B), if there are extraordinary reductions with respect to more than one controlling section 245A shareholder during the CFC's taxable year, then a U.S. tax resident's specified amount attributable to an acquisition of stock from the CFC is prorated with respect to each controlling section 245A shareholder based on its relative decrease in ownership of the CFC. See paragraph (j)(5) of this section for an example illustrating a decrease in a section 245A shareholder's pre-reduction pro rata share for amounts taken into account by a U.S. tax resident.

(C) *Prior extraordinary reduction amount.*—The term *prior extraordinary reduction amount* means, with respect to a CFC and section 245A shareholder and a taxable year of the CFC in which an extraordinary reduction occurs, the sum of the extraordinary reduction amount of each prior dividend received by the section 245A shareholder from the CFC during the taxable year. A section 245A shareholder's prior extraordinary reduction amount also includes—

(*1*) A prior dividend received by the section 245A shareholder from the CFC during the taxable year to the extent the dividend was not eligible for the section 245A deduction by reason of section 245A(e) or the holding period requirement of section 246 not being satisfied but would have been an extraordinary reduction amount had this paragraph (e) applied to the dividend;

(2) If the CFC is a lower-tier CFC for a portion of the taxable year during which the lower-tier CFC pays any dividend to an upper tier-CFC, the portion of a prior dividend received by an upper-tier CFC from the lower-tier CFC during the taxable year of the lower-tier CFC that, by reason of section 245A(e), was included in the upper-tier CFC's foreign personal holding company income and that by reason of section 951(a) was included in income of the section 245A shareholder, and that would have given rise to a tiered extraordinary reduction amount by reason of paragraph (f) of this section had paragraph (f) applied to the dividend of which the section 245A shareholder would have included a pro rata share of the tiered extraordinary reduction amount in income by reason of section 951(a); and

(3) If the CFC is a lower-tier CFC for a portion of the taxable year during which the lower-tier CFC pays any dividend to an upper-tier CFC, the sum of the portion of the tiered extraordinary reduction amount of each prior dividend received by an upper-tier CFC from the lower-tier CFC during the taxable year that is included in income of the section 245A shareholder by reason of section 951(a).

(3) *Exceptions*.—(i) *Elective exception to close CFC's taxable year*.—(A) *In general*.—For a taxable year of a CFC in which an extraordinary reduction occurs with respect to a controlling section 245A shareholder and for which, absent this paragraph (e)(3)(i), there would be an extraordinary reduction amount or tiered extraordinary reduction amount greater than zero, no amount is considered an extraordinary reduction amount or tiered extraordinary reduction amount with respect to the controlling section 245A shareholder if each controlling section 245A shareholder elects, and each U.S. tax resident described in paragraph (e)(3)(i)(C)(2) of this section agrees, pursuant to this paragraph (e)(3)(i), to close the CFC's taxable year for all purposes of the Internal Revenue Code (and, therefore, as to all shareholders of the CFC) as of the end of the date on which the extraordinary reduction occurs, or, if the extraordinary reduction occurs by reason of multiple transactions, as of the end of each date on which a transaction forming a part of the extraordinary reduction occurs. Because the determination as to whether there would be an extraordinary reduction amount or tiered extraordinary reduction amount greater than zero is made without regard to this paragraph (e)(3)(i), this determination is made without taking into account any elections that may be available, or other events that may occur, solely by reason of an election described in this paragraph (e)(3)(i), such as the application of section 954(b)(4) to a short taxable year created as a result of the election. If an election is made pursuant to this paragraph (e)(3)(i), all shareholders of the CFC that are a controlling section 245A shareholder or a U.S. tax resident described in paragraph (e)(3)(i)(C)(2) of this section must file their respective U.S. income tax and information returns consistently with the election. If each controlling section 245A shareholder elects to close the CFC's taxable year, that closing will be treated as a change in accounting period for purposes of the notice requirement in § 1.964-1(c)(3)(iii), treating any controlling section 245A shareholders as controlling domestic shareholders for this purpose. However, the notice described in § 1.964-1(c)(3)(iii) does not need to be provided to persons that are U.S. tax residents described in paragraph (e)(3)(i)(C) of this section. For purposes of applying this paragraph (e)(3)(i), a controlling section 245A shareholder that has an extraordinary reduction (or a transaction forming a part thereof) with respect to a CFC is treated as owning the same amount of stock it owned in the CFC immediately before the extraordinary reduction (or a transaction forming a part thereof) on the end of the date on which the extraordinary reduction occurs (or such transaction forming a part thereof occurs). To the extent that shares of a CFC are treated as owned by a controlling section 245A shareholder as of the close of the CFC's taxable year pursuant to the preceding sentence, such shares are treated as not being owned by any other person as of the close of the CFC's taxable year.

(B) *Allocation of foreign taxes*.—If an election is made pursuant to this paragraph (e)(3) to close a CFC's taxable year and the CFC's taxable year under foreign law (if any) does not close at the end of the date on which the CFC's taxable year closes as a result of the election, foreign taxes paid or accrued with respect to such foreign taxable year are allocated between the period of the foreign taxable year that ends with, and the period of the foreign taxable year that begins after, the date on which the CFC's taxable year closes as a result of the election. If there is more than one date on which the CFC's taxable year closes as a result of the election, foreign taxes paid or accrued with respect to the foreign taxable year are allocated to all such periods. The allocation is made based on the respective portions of the taxable income of the CFC (as determined under foreign law) for the foreign taxable year that are attributable under the principles of § 1.1502-76(b) to the periods during the foreign taxable year. Foreign taxes allocated to a period under this paragraph (e)(3)(i)(B) are treated as paid or accrued by the CFC as of the close of that period.

(C) *Time and manner of making election*.—*(1) Election by controlling section 245A shareholder*.—An election pursuant to this paragraph (e)(3) is made and effective if the statement described in paragraph (e)(3)(i)(D) of this section is timely filed (including extensions) by each controlling section 245A shareholder making the election with its original U.S. tax return for the taxable year in which the extraordinary reduction occurs. If a controlling section 245A shareholder is a member of a consolidated group (within the meaning of § 1.1502-1(h)) and participates in the extraordinary reduction, the agent for such group (within the meaning of § 1.1502-77(c)(1)) must file the election described in this paragraph (e)(3) on behalf of such member.

(2) Binding agreement.—Before the filing of the statement described in paragraph (e)(3)(i)(D) of this section, each controlling section 245A shareholder must enter into a written, binding agreement with each U.S. tax resident that on the end of the date on which the extraordinary reduction occurs (or, if the extraordinary reduction occurs by reason of multiple transactions, each U.S. tax resident that on the end of each date on which a transaction forming a part of the extraordinary reduction occurs) owns directly or indirectly, without regard to the final two sentences of paragraph (e)(3)(i)(A) of this section, stock of the CFC and is a United States shareholder with respect to the CFC. In the case of a U.S. tax resident that owns stock of the CFC indirectly through one or more partnerships, the partnership that directly owns the stock of the CFC may enter into the binding agreement on behalf of the U.S. tax resident partner provided that, before the due date of the partner's original Federal income tax return, including extensions, the partner delegated the authority to the partnership to enter into the binding agreement pursuant to a written partnership agreement (within the meaning of § 1.704-1(b)(2)(ii)(*h*)). The written, binding agreement must provide that each controlling section 245A shareholder will elect to close the taxable year of the CFC.

(3) Transition rule.—In the case of an extraordinary reduction occurring before August 27, 2020, the statement described in paragraph (e)(3)(i)(D) of this section is considered timely filed if it is attached by each controlling section 245A shareholder to an original or amended return for the taxable year in which the extraordinary reduction occurs. In the case of an amended return, the statement is considered timely filed only if it is filed with an amended return no later than February 23, 2021.

(D) *Form and content of statement*.—The statement required by paragraph (e)(3)(i)(C) of this section is to be titled "Elective Section 245A Year-Closing Statement." The statement must—

(1) Identify (by name and tax identification number, if any) each controlling section 245A shareholder, each U.S tax resident described in paragraph (e)(3)(i)(C) of this section, and the CFC;

(2) State the date of the extraordinary reduction (or, if the extraordinary reduction includes transactions on more than one date, the dates of all such transactions) to which the election applies;

(3) State the filing controlling section 245A shareholder's pro rata share of the subpart F income, tested income, and foreign taxes described in section 960 with respect to the stock of the CFC subject to the extraordinary reduction, and, if applicable, the amount of earnings and profits attributable to such stock within the meaning of section 1248, as of the date of the extraordinary reduction;

(4) State that each controlling section 245A shareholder and each U.S tax resident described in paragraph (e)(3)(i)(C) of this section have entered into a written, binding agreement to elect to close the CFC's taxable year in accordance with paragraph (e)(3)(i)(C) of this section; and

(5) Be filed in the manner, if any, prescribed by forms, publications, or other guidance published in the Internal Revenue Bulletin.

(E) *Consistency requirements*.—If multiple extraordinary reductions occur with respect to one or more controlling section 245A shareholders' ownership in a single CFC during one or more taxable years of the CFC, then to the extent those extraordinary reductions occur pursuant to a plan or series of related transactions, the election described in this paragraph (e)(3) section may be made only if it is made for all such extraordinary reductions with respect to the CFC for which there was an extraordinary reduction amount. Furthermore, if an extraordinary reduction occurs with respect to a controlling section 245A shareholders' ownership in one or more CFCs, then, to the extent those extraordinary reductions occur pursuant to a plan or series of related transactions, the election described in this paragraph (e)(3) may be made only if it is made for each extraordinary reduction for which there was an extraordinary reduction amount with respect to all of the CFCs that have the same or related (within the meaning of section 267(b) or 707(b)) controlling section 245A shareholders.

(ii) *De minimis subpart F income and tested income.*—For a taxable year of a CFC in which an extraordinary reduction occurs, no amount is considered an extraordinary reduction amount (or, with respect to a lower-tier CFC, a tiered extraordinary reduction amount under paragraph (f) of this section) with respect to a controlling section 245A shareholder of the CFC if the sum of the CFC's subpart F income and tested income (as defined in section 951A(c)(2)(A)) for the taxable year does not exceed the lesser of $50 million or 5 percent of the CFC's total income for the taxable year.

(f) *Limitation of amount eligible for section 954(c)(6) where extraordinary reduction occurs with respect to lower-tier CFCs.*—(1) *In general.*—If an extraordinary reduction occurs with respect to a lower-tier CFC and an upper-tier CFC receives a dividend from the lower-tier CFC in the taxable year in which the extraordinary reduction occurs, then the dividend is eligible for the exception to foreign personal holding company income under section 954(c)(6) (provided all other applicable requirements are satisfied) only with respect to the portion of the dividend that exceeds the tiered extraordinary reduction amount. The preceding sentence does not apply to an amount treated as a dividend received by an upper-tier CFC by reason of section 964(e)(4) (in this case, see paragraphs (b)(1) and (g)(2) of this section). See paragraph (j)(7) of this section for an example illustrating the application of this paragraph (f)(1).

(2) *Definition of tiered extraordinary reduction amount.*—The term *tiered extraordinary reduction amount* means, with respect to the portion of a dividend received by an upper-tier CFC from a lower-tier CFC during a taxable year of the lower-tier CFC, the amount of such dividend equal to the excess, if any, of—

(i) The product of—

(A) The sum of the amount of the subpart F income and tested income of the lower-tier CFC for the taxable year; and

(B) The percentage (by value) of stock of the lower-tier CFC owned (within the meaning of section 958(a)(2)) by the upper-tier CFC immediately before the extraordinary reduction (or the first transaction forming a part thereof); over

(ii) The following amounts—

(A) The sum of each U.S. tax resident's pro rata share of the lower-tier CFC's subpart F income and tested income under section 951(a) or 951A(a), respectively, that is attributable to shares of the lower-tier CFC owned (within the meaning of section 958(a)(2)) by the upper-tier CFC immediately prior to the extraordinary reduction (or the first transaction forming a part thereof), computed without the application of this paragraph (f);

(B) The sum of each prior tiered extraordinary reduction amount and sum of each amount included in an upper-tier CFC's subpart F income by reason of section 245A(e) with respect to prior dividends from the lower-tier CFC during the taxable year;

(C) The sum of each U.S. tax resident's pro rata share of an upper-tier CFC's subpart F income under section 951(a) and §1.951-1(e) that is attributable to dividends received from the lower-tier CFC in the taxable year of the extraordinary reduction that do not qualify for the exception to foreign personal holding company income under section 954(c)(6) because the dividends, or portions thereof, are properly allocable to subpart F income of the lower-tier CFC for the taxable year of the extraordinary reduction pursuant to section 954(c)(6)(A);

(D) The sum of the prior extraordinary reduction amounts (but, for this purpose, computed without regard to amounts described in paragraphs (e)(2)(ii)(C)(2) and (3) of this section) of each controlling section 245A shareholder with respect to shares of the lower-tier CFC that were owned by such controlling section 245A shareholder (including indirectly through a specified entity other than a foreign corporation) for a portion of the taxable year but are owned by an upper-tier CFC (including indirectly through a specified entity other than a foreign corporation) at the time of the distribution of the dividend; and

(E) The product of the amount described in paragraph (f)(2)(i)(B) of this section and the sum of the amounts of each U.S. tax resident's pro rata share of subpart F income and tested income for the taxable year under section 951(a) or 951A(a), respectively, attributable to shares of the lower-tier CFC directly or indirectly acquired by the U.S. tax resident from the lower-tier CFC during the taxable year.

(3) *Transition rule for computing tiered extraordinary reduction amount.*—Solely for purposes of applying this paragraph (f) in taxable years of a lower-tier CFC beginning on or after January 1, 2018, and ending before June 14, 2019, a tiered extraordinary reduction amount is determined by treating the lower-tier CFC's subpart F income for the taxable year as if it were neither subpart F income nor tested income.

(g) *Special rules.*—The rules in this paragraph (g) apply for purposes of this section.

(1) *Source of dividends.*—A dividend received by any person is considered received directly by such person from the foreign corporation whose earnings and profits give rise to the dividend. Therefore, for example, if a section 245A shareholder sells or exchanges stock of an upper-tier CFC and the gain recognized on the sale or exchange is included in the gross income of the section 245A shareholder as a dividend under section 1248(a), then, to the extent the dividend is attributable under section 1248(c)(2) to the earnings and profits of a lower-tier CFC owned, within the meaning of section 958(a)(2), by the section 245A shareholder through the upper-tier CFC, the dividend is considered received directly by the section 245A shareholder from the lower-tier CFC.

(2) *Certain section 964(e) inclusions treated as dividends.*—An amount included in the gross income of a section 245A shareholder under section 951(a)(1)(A) by reason of section 964(e)(4) is considered a dividend received by the section 245A shareholder directly from the foreign corporation whose earnings and profits give rise to the amount described in section 964(e)(1). Therefore, for example, if an upper-tier CFC sells or exchanges stock of a lower-tier CFC, and, as a result of the sale or exchange, a section 245A shareholder with respect to the upper-tier CFC includes an amount in gross income under section 951(a)(1)(A) by reason of section 964(e)(4), then the inclusion is treated as a dividend received directly by the section 245A shareholder from the lower-tier CFC whose earnings and profits give rise to the dividend, and the section 245A shareholder is not allowed a section 245A deduction for the dividend to the extent of the ineligible amount of such dividend.

(3) *Rules regarding stock ownership and stock transfers.*—(i) *Determining indirect ownership of stock of an SFC or a CFC.*—For purposes of this section, if a person owns an interest in, or stock of, a specified entity, including through a chain of ownership of one or more other specified entities, then the person is considered to own indirectly a pro rata share of stock of an SFC or a CFC owned by the specified entity. To determine a person's pro rata share of stock owned by a specified entity, the principles of section 958(a) apply without regard to whether the specified entity is foreign or domestic.

(ii) *Determining indirect transfers for stock owned indirectly.*—If, under paragraph (g)(3)(i) of this section, a person is considered to own indirectly stock of an SFC or CFC that is owned by a specified entity, then the following rules apply in determining if the person transfers stock of the SFC or CFC—

(A) To the extent the specified entity transfers stock that is considered owned indirectly by the person immediately before the transfer, the person is considered to transfer indirectly such stock;

(B) If the person transfers an interest in, or stock of, the specified entity, then the person is considered to transfer indirectly the stock of the SFC or CFC attributable to the interest in, or the stock of, the specified entity that is transferred; and

(C) In the case in which the person owns the specified entity through a chain of ownership of one or more other specified entities, if there is a transfer of an interest in, or stock of, another specified entity in the chain of ownership, then the person is considered to transfer indirectly the stock of the SFC or CFC attributable to the interest in, or the stock of, the other specified entity transferred.

(iii) *Definition of specified entity.*—The term *specified entity* means any partnership, trust (other than a trust treated as a corporation for U.S. income tax purposes), or estate (in each case, domestic or foreign), or any foreign corporation.

(4) *Coordination rules.*—(i) *General rule.*—A dividend is first subject to section 245A(e). To the extent the dividend is not a hybrid dividend or tiered hybrid dividend under section 245A(e), the dividend is subject to paragraph (e) or (f) of this section, as applicable, and then, to the extent the dividend is not subject to paragraph (e) or (f) of this section, it is subject to paragraph (c) or (d) of this section, as applicable.

(ii) *Coordination rule for paragraphs (c) and (d) and (e) and (f) of this section, respectively.*—If an SFC or CFC pays a dividend (or simultaneous dividends), a portion of which may be subject to paragraph (c) or (e) of this section and a portion of which may be subject to paragraph (d) or (f) of this section, the rules of this section apply by treating the portion of the dividend or dividends that may be subject to paragraph (c) or (e) of this section as if it occurred immediately before the portion of the dividend or dividends that may be subject to paragraph (d) or (f) of this section. For example, if a dividend arising under section 964(e)(4) occurs at the same time as a dividend that would be eligible for the exception to foreign personal holding company income under section 954(c)(6) but for the potential application of paragraph (d) this section, then the tiered extraordinary disposition amount with respect to the other dividend is determined as if the dividend arising under section 964(e)(4) occurs immediately before the other dividend.

(5) *Ordering rule for multiple dividends made by an SFC or a CFC during a taxable year.*—If an SFC or a CFC pays dividends on more than one date during its taxable year or at different times on the same date, this section applies based on the order in which the dividends are paid.

(6) *Partner's distributive share of a domestic partnership's pro rata share of subpart F income or tested income.*—If a section 245A shareholder or a U.S. tax resident is a direct or indirect partner in a domestic partnership that is a United States shareholder with respect to a CFC and includes in gross income its distributive share of the domestic partnership's inclusion under section 951(a) or 951A(a) with respect to the CFC then, solely for purposes of this section, a reference to the section 245A shareholder's or U.S. tax resident's pro rata share of the CFC's subpart F income or tested income included in gross income under section 951(a) or 951A(a), respectively, includes such person's distributive share of the domestic partnership's pro rata share of the CFC's subpart F income or tested income. A person is an indirect partner with respect to a domestic partnership if the person indirectly owns the domestic partnership through one or more specified entities (other than a foreign corporation).

(7) *Related domestic corporations treated as a single domestic corporation for certain purposes.*—For purposes of determining the extent that a dividend is an extraordinary disposition amount or a tiered extraordinary disposition amount, as well as for purposes of determining the extent to which an extraordinary disposition account is reduced by a prior extraordinary disposition amount, domestic corporations that are related parties are treated as a single domestic corporation. Thus, for example, if two domestic corporations are related parties and either or both of them are section 245A shareholders with respect to an SFC, then the extent to which a dividend received by either domestic corporation from the SFC is an extraordinary disposition amount is based on the sum of each domestic corporation's extraordinary disposition account with respect to the SFC. When, by reason of this paragraph (g)(7), the extent to which a dividend is an extraordinary disposition amount or tiered extraordinary disposition amount is determined based on the sum of two or more extraordinary disposition accounts, a pro rata amount in each extraordinary disposition account is considered to give rise to the extraordinary disposition amount or tiered extraordinary disposition amount, if any.

(h) *Anti-abuse rule.*—Appropriate adjustments are made pursuant to this section, including adjustments that would disregard a transaction or arrangement in whole or in part, to any amounts determined under (or subject to the application of) this section if a transaction or arrangement is engaged in with a principal purpose of avoiding the purposes of this section. For examples illustrating the application of this paragraph (h), see paragraphs (j)(8) through (10) of this section.

(i) *Definitions.*—The following definitions apply for purposes of this section.

(1) *Controlled foreign corporation.*—The term *controlled foreign corporation* (or CFC) has the meaning provided in section 957.

(2) *Controlling section 245A shareholder.*—The term *controlling section 245A shareholder* means, with respect to a CFC, any section 245A shareholder that owns directly or indirectly more than 50 percent (by vote or value) of the stock of the CFC. For purposes of determining whether a section 245A shareholder is a controlling section 245A shareholder with respect to a CFC, all stock of the CFC owned by a related party with respect to the section 245A shareholder or by other persons acting in concert with the section 245A shareholder to undertake an extraordinary reduction is considered owned by the section 245A shareholder. If section 964(e)(4) applies to a sale or exchange of a lower-tier CFC with respect to a controlling section 245A shareholder, all United States shareholders of the CFC are considered to act in concert with regard to the sale or exchange. In addition, if all persons selling stock in a CFC, held directly, sell such stock to the same buyer or buyers (or a related party with respect to the buyer or buyers) as part of the same plan, all sellers will be considered to act in concert with regard to the sale or exchange.

(3) *Disqualified amount.*—The term *disqualified amount* has the meaning set forth in paragraph (d)(1) of this section.

(4) *Disqualified period.*—The term *disqualified period* has the meaning set forth in paragraph (c)(3)(iii) of this section.

(5) *Extraordinary disposition.*—The term *extraordinary disposition* has the meaning set forth in paragraph (c)(3)(ii) of this section.

(6) *Extraordinary disposition account.*—The term *extraordinary disposition amount* has the meaning set forth in paragraph (c)(3)(i) of this section.

(7) *Extraordinary disposition amount.*—The term *extraordinary disposition amount* has the meaning set forth in paragraph (c)(1) of this section.

(8) *Extraordinary disposition E&P.*—The term *extraordinary disposition E&P* has the meaning set forth in paragraph (c)(3)(i)(C) of this section.

(9) *Extraordinary disposition ownership percentage.*—The term *extraordinary disposition ownership percentage* has the meaning set forth in paragraph (c)(3)(i)(B) of this section.

(10) *Extraordinary reduction.*—The term *extraordinary reduction* has the meaning set forth in paragraph (e)(2)(i)(A) of this section.

(11) *Extraordinary reduction amount.*—The term *extraordinary reduction amount* has the meaning set forth in paragraph (e)(1) of this section.

(12) *Ineligible amount.*—The term *ineligible amount* has the meaning set forth in paragraph (b)(2) of this section.

(13) *Lower-tier CFC.*—The term *lower-tier CFC* means a CFC whose stock is owned (within the meaning of section 958(a)(2)), in whole or in part, by another CFC.

(14) *Non-extraordinary disposition E&P.*—The term *non-extraordinary disposition E&P* has the meaning set forth in paragraph (c)(2)(ii) of this section.

(15) *Pre-reduction pro rata share.*—The term *pre-reduction pro rata share* has the meaning set forth in paragraph (e)(2)(ii) of this section.

(16) *Prior extraordinary disposition amount.*—The term *prior extraordinary disposition amount* has the meaning set forth in paragraph (c)(3)(i)(D) of this section.

(17) *Prior extraordinary reduction amount.*—The term *prior extraordinary reduction amount* has the meaning set forth in paragraph (e)(2)(ii)(C) of this section.

(18) *Qualified portion.*—The term *qualified portion* has the meaning set forth in paragraph (c)(3)(i)(D)(*2*)(*i*) of this section.

(19) *Related party.*—The term *related party* means, with respect to a person, another person bearing a relationship described in section 267(b) or 707(b) to the person, in which case such persons are *related.*

(20) *Section 245A deduction.*—The term *section 245A deduction* means, with respect to a dividend received by a section 245A share-

holder from an SFC, the amount of the deduction allowed to the section 245A shareholder by reason of the dividend.

(21) *Section 245A shareholder*.—The term *section 245A shareholder* means a domestic corporation that is a United States shareholder with respect to an SFC and that owns directly or indirectly stock of the SFC.

(22) *Specified 10-percent owned foreign corporation (SFC)*.—The term *specified 10-percent owned foreign corporation* (or *SFC*) has the meaning provided in section 245A(b)(1).

(23) *Specified entity*.—The term *specified entity* has the meaning set forth in paragraph (g)(3)(iii) of this section.

(24) *Specified property*.—The term *specified property* has the meaning set forth in paragraph (c)(3)(iv) of this section.

(25) *Tiered extraordinary disposition amount*.—The term *tiered extraordinary disposition amount* has the meaning set forth in paragraph (d)(2)(i) of this section.

(26) *Tiered extraordinary reduction amount*.—The term *tiered extraordinary reduction amount* has the meaning set forth in paragraph (f)(2) of this section.

(27) *United States shareholder*.—The term *United States shareholder* has the meaning provided in section 951(b).

(28) *Upper-tier CFC*.—The term *upper-tier CFC* means a CFC that owns (within the meaning of section 958(a)(2)) stock in another CFC.

(29) *U.S. tax resident*.—The term *U.S. tax resident* means a United States person described in section 7701(a)(30)(A) or (C).

(j) *Examples*.—The application of this section is illustrated by the examples in this paragraph (j).

(1) *Facts*.—Except as otherwise stated, the facts described in this paragraph (j)(1) are assumed for purposes of the examples.

(i) US1 and US2 are domestic corporations, each with a calendar taxable year, and are not related parties with respect to each other.

(ii) CFC1, CFC2, and CFC3 are foreign corporations that are SFCs and CFCs.

(iii) Each entity uses the U.S. dollar as its functional currency.

(iv) Year 2 begins on or after January 1, 2018 and has 365 days.

(v) Absent application of this section, dividends received by US1 and US2 from a CFC meet the requirements to qualify for the section 245A deduction, and dividends received by one CFC from another CFC qualify for the exception to foreign personal holding company income under section 954(c)(6).

(vi) The de minimis rules in paragraphs (c)(3)(ii)(E) and (e)(3)(ii) of this section do not apply.

(vii) Section 1059 is not relevant to the tax results described in the examples in this paragraph (j).

(2) *Example 1. Extraordinary disposition*.—(i) *Facts*. US1 and US2 own 60% and 40%, respectively, of the single class of stock of CFC1. CFC1 owns all of the single class of stock of CFC2. CFC1 and CFC2 use the taxable year ending November 30 as their taxable year. On November 1, 2018, CFC1 sells specified property to CFC2 in exchange for $200x of cash (the "Property Transfer"). The Property Transfer is outside of CFC1's ordinary course of activities. The transferred property has a basis of $100x in the hands of CFC1. CFC1 recognizes $100x of gain as a result of the Property Transfer ($200x - $100x). On December 1, 2018, CFC1 distributes $80x pro rata to US1 ($48x) and US2 ($32x), all of which is a dividend within the meaning of section 316 and treated as a distribution out of earnings described in section 959(c)(3). No other distributions are made by CFC1 to either US1 or US2 in CFC1's taxable year ending November 30, 2019. For its taxable year ending on November 30, 2019, CFC1 has $110x of earnings and profits described in section 959(c)(3), without regard to any distributions during the taxable year.

(ii) *Analysis*—(A) *Identification of extraordinary disposition*. Because CFC1 is a CFC and uses the taxable year ending on November 30, under paragraph (c)(3)(iii) of this section, it has a disqualified period beginning on January 1, 2018, and ending on November 30, 2018. In addition, under paragraph (c)(3)(ii) of this section, the Property Transfer is an extraordinary disposition because it: is a disposition of specified property by CFC1 on a date on which it was a CFC and during CFC1's disqualified period; is to CFC2, a related party with respect to CFC1; occurs outside of the ordinary course of CFC1's activities; and, is not subject to the de minimis rule in paragraph (c)(3)(ii)(E) of this section.

(B) *Determination of section 245A shareholders and their extraordinary disposition accounts*. Because CFC1 undertook an extraordinary disposition, under paragraph (c)(3)(i) of this section, a portion of CFC1's earnings and profits are extraordinary disposition E&P and, therefore, give rise to an extraordinary disposition account with respect to each of CFC1's section 245A shareholders. Under paragraph (i)(21) of this section, US1 and US2 are both section 245A shareholders with respect to CFC1. The amount of the extraordinary disposition account with respect to US1 is $60x, which is equal to the product of the extraordinary disposition E&P (the amount of the net gain recognized by CFC1 as a result of the Property Transfer ($100x)) and the extraordinary disposition ownership percentage (the percentage of the stock of CFC1 owned directly or indirectly by US1 on January 1, 2018 (60%)), reduced by the prior extraordinary disposition amount ($0). *See* paragraph (c)(3)(i) of this section. Similarly, the amount of the extraordinary disposition account with respect to US2 is $40x, which is equal to the product of the extraordinary disposition E&P (the net gain recognized by CFC1 as a result of the Property Transfer ($100x)) and extraordinary disposition ownership percentage (the percentage of the stock of CFC1 owned directly or indirectly by US2 on January 1, 2018 (40%)), reduced by the prior extraordinary disposition amount ($0).

(C) *Determination of extraordinary disposition amount with respect to US1*. The dividend of $48x paid to US1 on December 1, 2018, is an extraordinary disposition amount to the extent the dividend is paid out of the extraordinary disposition account with respect to US1. *See* paragraph (c)(1) of this section. Under paragraph (c)(2)(i) of this section, the dividend is first considered paid out of non-extraordinary disposition E&P with respect to US1, to the extent thereof. With respect to US1, $6x of CFC1's earnings and profits is non-extraordinary disposition E&P, calculated as the excess of $66x (the product of $110x of earnings and profits described in section 959(c)(3), without regard to the $80x distribution, and 60%) over $60x (the balance of US1's extraordinary disposition account with respect to CFC1, immediately before the distribution). *See* paragraph (c)(2)(ii) of this section. Thus, $6x of the dividend is considered paid out of non-extraordinary disposition E&P with respect to US1. Under paragraph (c)(2)(i)(B) of this section, the remaining $42x of the dividend is next considered paid out of US1's extraordinary disposition account with respect to CFC1, to the extent thereof. Accordingly, $42x of the dividend is considered paid out of the extraordinary disposition account with respect to CFC1 and gives rise to $42x of an extraordinary disposition amount. As a result, US1's prior extraordinary disposition amount is increased by $42x under paragraph (c)(3)(i)(D) of this section, and US1's extraordinary disposition account is reduced to $18x ($60x - $42x) under paragraph (c)(3)(i)(A) of this section.

(D) *Determination of extraordinary disposition amount with respect to US2*. The dividend of $32x paid to US2, on December 1, 2018, is an extraordinary disposition amount to the extent the dividend is paid out of extraordinary disposition E&P with respect to US2. *See* paragraph (c)(1) of this section. Under paragraph (c)(2)(i) of this section, the dividend is first considered paid out of non-extraordinary disposition E&P with respect to US2, to the extent thereof. With respect to US2, $4x of CFC1's earnings and profits is non-extraordinary disposition E&P, calculated as the excess of $44x (the product of $110x of earnings and profits described in section 959(c)(3), without regard to the $80x distribution, and 40%) over $40x (the balance of US2's extraordinary disposition account with respect to CFC1, immediately before the distribution). *See* paragraph (c)(2)(ii) of this section. Thus, $4x of the dividend is considered paid out of non-extraordinary disposition E&P with respect to US2. Under paragraph (c)(2)(i)(B) of this section, the remaining $28x of the dividend is next considered paid out of US2's extraordinary disposition account with respect to CFC1, to the extent thereof. Accordingly, $28x of the dividend is considered paid out of the extraordinary disposition account with respect to US2 and gives rise to $28x of an extraordinary disposition amount. As a result, US2's prior extraordinary disposition amount is increased by $28x under paragraph (c)(3)(i)(D) of this section, and US2's extraordinary disposition account is reduced to $12x ($40x - $28x) under paragraph (c)(3)(i)(A) of this section.

(E) *Determination of ineligible amount with respect to US1 and US2*. Under paragraph (b)(2) of this section, with respect to US1 and the dividend of $48x, the ineligible amount is $21x, the sum of 50 percent of the extraordinary disposition amount ($42x) and extraordinary reduction amount ($0). Therefore, with respect to the dividend received by US1 of $48x, $27x is eligible for a section 245A deduction. With respect to US2 and the dividend of $32x, the ineligible amount is $14x, the sum of 50% of the extraordinary disposition amount ($28x) and extraordinary reduction amount ($0). Therefore, with respect to the dividend received by US2 of $32x, $18x is eligible for a section 245A deduction.

(3) *Example 2. Application of section 954(c)(6) exception with extraordinary disposition account.*—(i) *Facts.* The facts are the same as in paragraph (j)(2)(i) of this section (the facts in *Example 1*) except that the Property Transfer is a sale by CFC2 to CFC1 instead of a sale by CFC1 to CFC2, the $80x distribution is by CFC2 to CFC1 in a separate transaction that is unrelated to the Property Transfer, and the description of the earnings and profits of CFC1 is applied to CFC2. Additionally, absent the application of this section, section 954(c)(6) would apply to the distribution by CFC2 to CFC1. Under section 951(a)(2) and § 1.951-1(b) and (e), US1's pro rata share of any subpart F income of CFC1 is 60% and US2's pro rata share of any subpart F income of CFC2 is 40%.

(ii) *Analysis*—(A) *Identification of extraordinary disposition.* The Property Transfer is an extraordinary disposition under the same analysis as provided in paragraph (j)(2)(ii)(A) of this section (the analysis in *Example 1*).

(B) *Determination of section 245A shareholders and their extraordinary disposition accounts.* Both US1 and US2 are section 245A shareholders with respect to CFC2, US1 has an extraordinary disposition account of $60x with respect to CFC2, and US2 has an extraordinary disposition account of $40x with respect to CFC2 under the same analysis as provided in paragraph (j)(2)(ii)(B) of this section (the analysis in *Example 1*).

(C) *Determination of tiered extraordinary disposition amount*—(*1*) *In general.* US1 and US2 each have a tiered extraordinary disposition amount with respect to the $80x dividend paid by CFC2 to CFC1 to the extent that US1 and US2 would have an extraordinary disposition amount if each had received as a dividend its pro rata share of the dividend from CFC2. *See* paragraph (d)(2)(i) of this section. Under paragraph (d)(2)(ii) of this section, US1's pro rata share of the dividend is $48x (60% x $80x), that is, the increase to US1's pro rata share of the subpart F income if the dividend were included in CFC1's foreign personal holding company income, without regard to section 952(c) and the allocation of expenses. Similarly, US2's pro rata share of the dividend is $32x (40% x $80x).

(*2*) *Determination of tiered extraordinary disposition amount with respect to US1.* The extraordinary disposition amount with respect to US1 is $42x, under the same analysis provided in paragraph (j)(2)(ii)(C) of this section (the analysis in *Example 1*). Accordingly, the tiered extraordinary disposition amount with respect to US1 is $42x.

(*3*) *Determination of extraordinary disposition amount with respect to US2.* The extraordinary disposition amount with respect to US2 is $28x, under the same analysis provided in paragraph (j)(2)(ii)(D) of this section (the analysis in *Example 1*). Accordingly, the tiered extraordinary disposition amount with respect to US2 is $28x.

(D) *Limitation of section 954(c)(6) exception.* The sum of US1 and US2's tiered extraordinary disposition amounts is $70x ($42x + $28x). The portion of the stock of CFC1 (by value) owned (within the meaning of section 958(a)) by U.S. tax residents on the last day of CFC1's taxable year is 100%. Under paragraph (d)(1) of this section, the disqualified amount with respect to the dividend is $70x ($70x/100%). Accordingly, the portion of the $80x dividend from CFC2 to CFC1 that is eligible for the exception to foreign personal holding company income under section 954(c)(6) is $45x, equal to the sum of $10x (the portion of the $80x dividend that exceeds the $70x disqualified amount) and $35x (50 percent of $70x, the portion of the dividend that does not exceed the disqualified amount). Under section 951(a)(2) and § 1.951-1(b) and (e), US1 includes $21x (60% x $35x) and US2 includes $14x (40% x $35x) in income under section 951(a).

(E) *Changes in extraordinary disposition account of US1.* Under paragraph (c)(3)(i)(D)(*1*) of this section, US1's prior extraordinary disposition amount with respect to CFC2 is increased by $42x, or 200% of $21x, the amount US1 included in income under section 951(a) with respect to CFC1. Under paragraph (c)(3)(i)(D)(*1*)(*iii*) of this section, US1 has no qualified portion because all of the owners of CFC2 are section 245A shareholders with a tiered extraordinary disposition amount with respect to CFC2. As a result, US1's extraordinary disposition account is reduced to $18x ($60x - $42x) under paragraph (c)(3)(i)(A) of this section.

(F) *Changes in extraordinary disposition account of US2.* Under paragraph (c)(3)(i)(D)(*1*) of this section, US2's prior extraordinary disposition amount with respect to CFC2 is increased by $28x, or 200% of $14x, the amount US2 included in income under section 951(a) with respect to CFC1. Under paragraph (c)(3)(i)(D)(*1*)(*iii*) of this section, US2 has no qualified portion because all of the owners of CFC2 are section 245A shareholders with a tiered extraordinary disposition amount with respect to CFC2. As a result, US2's extraordinary disposition account is reduced to $12x ($40x - $28x) under paragraph (c)(3)(i)(A) of this section.

(4) *Example 3. Extraordinary reduction.*—(i) *Facts.* At the beginning of CFC1's taxable year ending on December 31, Year 2, US1 owns all of the single class of stock of CFC1, and no person transferred any CFC1 stock directly or indirectly in Year 1 pursuant to a plan to reduce the percentage of stock (by value) of CFC1 owned by US1. Also as of the beginning of Year 2, CFC1 has no earnings and profits described in section 959(c)(1) or (2), and US1 does not have an extraordinary disposition account with respect to CFC1. As of the end of Year 2, CFC1 has $160x of tested income and no other income. CFC1 has $160x of earnings and profits for Year 2. On October 19, Year 2, US1 sells all of its CFC1 stock to US2 for $100x in a transaction (the "Stock Sale") in which US1 recognizes $90x of gain. Under section 1248(a), the entire $90x of gain is included in US1's gross income as a dividend and, pursuant to section 1248(j), the $90x is treated as a dividend for purposes of applying section 245A. At the end of Year 2, under section 951A, US2 takes into account $70x of tested income, calculated as $160x (100% of the $160x of tested income) less $90x, the amount described in section 951(a)(2)(B). The amount described in section 951(a)(2)(B) is the lesser of $90x, the amount of dividends received by US1 with respect to the transferred stock, and $128x, the amount of tested income attributable to the transferred stock ($160x) multiplied by 292/365 (the ratio of the number of days in Year 2 that US2 did not own the transferred stock to the total number of days in Year 2). US1 does not make an election pursuant to paragraph (e)(3)(i) of this section.

(ii) *Analysis*—(A) *Determination of controlling section 245A shareholder and extraordinary reduction of ownership.* Under paragraph (i)(2) of this section, US1 is a controlling section 245A shareholder with respect to CFC1. In addition, the Stock Sale results in an extraordinary reduction with respect to US1's ownership of CFC1. *See* paragraph (e)(2)(i) of this section. The extraordinary reduction occurs because during Year 2, US1 transferred 100% of the CFC1 stock it owned at the beginning of the year and such amount is more than 5% of the total value of the stock of CFC1 at the beginning of Year 2; it also occurs because on the last day of the year the percentage of stock (by value) of CFC1 that US1 owns directly or indirectly (0%) (the end of year percentage) is less than 90% of the stock (by value) of CFC1 that US1 owns directly or indirectly on the day of the taxable year when it owned the highest percentage of CFC1 stock by value (100%) (the initial percentage), no transactions occurred in the preceding year pursuant to a plan to reduce the percentage of CFC1 stock owned by US1, and the difference between the initial percentage and the end of year percentage (100 percentage points) is at least 5 percentage points.

(B) *Determination of extraordinary reduction amount.* Under paragraph (e)(1) of this section, the entire $90x dividend to US1 is an extraordinary reduction amount with respect to US1 because the dividend is at least equal to US1's pre-reduction pro rata share of CFC1's Year 2 tested income described in paragraph (e)(2)(ii)(A) of this section ($160x), reduced by the amount of tested income taken into account by US2, a U.S. tax resident, under paragraph (e)(2)(ii)(B) of this section ($70x).

(C) *Determination of ineligible amount.* Under paragraph (b)(2) of this section, with respect to US1 and the dividend of $90x, the ineligible amount is $90x, the sum of 50% of the extraordinary disposition amount ($0) and extraordinary reduction amount ($90x). Therefore, with respect to the dividend received of $90x, no portion is eligible for the dividends received deduction allowed under section 245A(a).

(iii) *Alternative facts – election to close CFC's taxable year.* The facts are the same as in paragraph (j)(4)(i) of this section (the facts of this *Example 3*), except that, pursuant to paragraph (e)(3)(i) of this section, US1 elects to close CFC1's Year 2 taxable year for all purposes of the Code as of the end of October 19, Year 2, the date on which the Stock Sale occurs; in addition, US1 and US2 enter into a written, binding agreement that US1 will elect to close CFC1's Year 2 taxable year. Accordingly, under section 951A(a), US1 takes into account 100% of CFC1's tested income for the taxable year beginning January 1, Year 2, and ending October 19, Year 2, and US2 takes into account 100% of CFC1's tested income for the taxable year beginning October 20, Year 2, and ending December 31, Year 2. Under paragraph (e)(3)(i)(A) of this section, no amount is considered an extraordinary reduction amount with respect to US1.

(5) *Example 4. Extraordinary reduction; decrease in section 245A shareholder's pre-reduction pro rata share for amounts taken into account by U.S. tax residents.*—(i) *Facts.* At the beginning of CFC1's taxable year ending December 31, Year 2, US1 owns all of the single class of stock

of CFC1, and no person transferred any CFC1 stock directly or indirectly in Year 1 pursuant to a plan to reduce the percentage of stock (by value) of CFC1 owned by US1. CFC1 generates $120x of subpart F income during its taxable year ending on December 31, Year 2. On October 1, Year 2, CFC1 distributes a $120x dividend to US1. On October 19, Year 2, US1 sells 100% of its stock of CFC1 to PRS, a domestic partnership, in a transaction in which no gain or loss is realized (the "Stock Sale"). A, an individual who is a citizen of the United States, and B, a foreign individual who is not a U.S. tax resident, each own 50% of the capital and profits interests of PRS. On December 1, Year 2, US2 and FP, a foreign corporation, contribute property to CFC1; in exchange, each of US2 and FP receives 25% of the stock of CFC1. PRS owns the remaining 50% of the stock of CFC1. US1 does not make an election pursuant to paragraph (e)(3)(i) of this section.

(ii) *Analysis—(A) Determination of controlling section 245A shareholder and extraordinary reduction.* Under paragraph (i)(2) of this section, US1 is a controlling section 245A shareholder with respect to CFC1. In addition, the Stock Sale results in an extraordinary reduction with respect to US1's ownership of CFC1. *See* paragraph (e)(2)(i) of this section. The extraordinary reduction occurs because during Year 2, US1 transferred 100% of the CFC1 stock it owns on the first day of Year 2, and that amount is more than 5% of the total value of the stock of CFC1 at the beginning of Year 2; it also occurs because on the last day of Year 2 the percentage of stock (by value) of CFC1 that US1 owns directly or indirectly (0%) (the end of year percentage) is less than 90% of the highest percentage of stock (by value) of CFC1 that US1 owns directly or indirectly on the day of the taxable year when it owned the highest percentage of CFC1 stock by value (100%) (the initial percentage), no transactions occurred in the preceding year pursuant to a plan to reduce the percentage of CFC1 stock owned by US1, and the difference between the initial percentage and the end of year percentage (100 percentage points) is at least 5 percentage points.

(B) *Determination of pre-reduction pro rata share.* Before the extraordinary reduction, US1 owned 100% of the stock of CFC1. Thus, under paragraph (e)(2)(ii)(A) of this section, the tentative amount of US1's pre-reduction pro rata share of CFC1's subpart F income is $120x. A and US2 are U.S. tax residents pursuant to paragraph (i)(29) of this section because they are United States persons described in section 7701(a)(30)(A) or (C). Thus, US1's pre-reduction pro rata share amount is subject to the reduction described in paragraph (e)(2)(ii)(B) of this section because U.S. tax residents directly or indirectly acquire stock of CFC1 from US1 or CFC1 during the taxable year in which the extraordinary reduction occurs. With respect to US1's pre-reduction pro rata share of CFC1's subpart F income, the reduction equals the amount of subpart F income of CFC1 taken into account under section 951(a) by these U.S. tax residents.

(C) *Determination of decrease in pre-reduction pro rata share for amounts taken into account by U.S. tax resident.* On December 31, Year 2, both PRS and US2 will be United States shareholders with respect to CFC1 and will include in gross income their pro rata share of CFC1's subpart F income under section 951(a). With respect to US2, this amount will be $30x, which is equal to 25% of CFC1's subpart F income for the taxable year. With respect to PRS, its pro rata share of $60x under section 951(a)(2)(A) (50% of $120x) will be reduced under section 951(a)(2)(B) by $48x. The section 951(a)(2)(B) reduction is equal to the lesser of the $120x dividend paid with respect to those shares to US1 or $48x (50% x $120x x 292/365, the period during the taxable year that PRS did not own CFC1 stock). Thus, PRS includes $12x in gross income pursuant to section 951(a). Of this amount, $6x is allocated to A (as a 50% partner of PRS) and, therefore, treated as taken into account by A under paragraphs (e)(2)(ii)(B) and (g)(6) of this section. Thus, A and US2 take into account a total of $36x of CFC1's subpart F income under section 951(a). This amount reduces US1's pre-reduction pro rata share of CFC1's subpart F income to $84x ($120x - $36x) under paragraph (e)(2)(ii)(B) of this section. CFC1 did not generate tested income during the taxable year and, therefore, no amount is taken into account under section 951A with respect to CFC1, and US1 has no pre-reduction pro rata share with respect to tested income of CFC1.

(D) *Determination of extraordinary reduction amount.* Under paragraph (e)(1) of this section, the extraordinary reduction amount equals $84x, which is the lesser of the amount of the dividend received by US1 from CFC1 during Year 2 ($120x) and the sum of US1's pre-reduction pro rata share of CFC1's subpart F income ($84x) and tested income ($0).

(E) *Determination of ineligible amount.* Under paragraph (b)(2) of this section, with respect to US1 and the dividend of $120x, the ineligible amount is $84x, the sum of 50% of the extraordinary disposition amount ($0) and extraordinary reduction amount ($84x). Therefore, with respect to the dividend received by US1 from CFC1, $36x ($120x - $84x) is eligible for a section 245A deduction.

(6) *Example 5. Controlling section 245A shareholder.*—(i) *Facts.* US1 and US2 own 30% and 25% of the stock of CFC1, respectively. FP, a foreign corporation that is not a CFC, owns all of the stock of US1 and US2. FP owns the remaining 45% of the stock of CFC1. On September 30, Year 2, US1 sells all of its stock of CFC1 to US3, a domestic corporation that is not a related party with respect to FP, US1, or US2. No person transferred any stock of CFC1 directly or indirectly in Year 1 pursuant to a plan to reduce the percentage of stock (by value) of CFC1 owned by US1.

(ii) *Analysis.* Under paragraph (i)(21) of this section, US1 is a section 245A shareholder with respect to CFC1, an SFC. Because US1 owns, together with US2 and FP (related persons with respect to US1), more than 50% of the stock of CFC1, US1 is a controlling section 245A shareholder of CFC1. The sale of US1's CFC1 stock results in an extraordinary reduction occurring with respect to US1's ownership of CFC1. The extraordinary reduction occurs because during Year 2, US1 transferred 100% of the stock of CFC1 that it owned at the beginning of the year and that amount is more than 5% of the total value of the stock of CFC1 at the beginning of Year 2. The extraordinary disposition also occurs because on the last day of the year the percentage of stock (by value) of CFC1 that US1 directly or indirectly owns (0%) (the end of year percentage) is less than 90% of the stock (by value) of CFC1 that US1 directly or indirectly owned on the day of the taxable year when it owned the highest percentage of CFC1 stock by value (30%) (the initial percentage), no transactions occurred in the preceding year pursuant to a plan to reduce the percentage of CFC1 stock owned by US1, and the difference between the initial percentage and end of year percentage (30 percentage points) is at least 5 percentage points.

(7) *Example 6. Limitation of section 954(c)(6) exception with respect to an extraordinary reduction.*—(i) *Facts.* At the beginning of CFC1 and CFC2's taxable year ending on December 31, Year 2, US1 and A, an individual who is a citizen of the United States, own 80% and 20% of the single class of stock of CFC1, respectively. CFC1 owns 100% of the stock of CFC2. Both US1 and A are United States shareholders with respect to CFC1 and CFC2, and US1 and A are not related parties with respect to each other. No person transferred CFC2 stock directly or indirectly in Year 2 pursuant to a plan to reduce the percentage of stock (by value) of CFC2 owned by US1, and US1 does not have an extraordinary disposition account with respect to CFC2. At the end of Year 2, and without regard to any distributions during Year 2, CFC2 had $150x of tested income and no other income, and CFC1 had no income or expenses. On June 30, Year 2, CFC2 distributed $150x as a dividend to CFC1, which would qualify for the exception from foreign personal holding company income under section 954(c)(6) but for the application of this section. On August 7, Year 2, CFC1 sells all of its CFC2 stock to US2 for $100x in a transaction (the "Stock Sale") in which CFC1 realizes no gain or loss. At the end of Year 2, under section 951A, US2 takes into account $60x of tested income, calculated as $150x (100% of the $150x of tested income) less $90x, the amount described in section 951(a)(2)(B). The amount described in section 951(a)(2)(B) is the lesser of $150x, the amount of dividends received by CFC1 during Year 2 with respect to the transferred stock, and $90x, the amount of tested income attributable to the transferred stock ($150x) multiplied by 219/365 (the ratio of the number of days in Year 2 that US2 did not own the transferred stock to the total number of days in Year 2). US1 does not make an election pursuant to paragraph (e)(3)(i) of this section.

(ii) *Analysis—(A) Determination of controlling section 245A shareholder and extraordinary reduction of ownership.* Under paragraph (i)(2) of this section, US1 is a controlling section 245A shareholder with respect to CFC2, but A is not. In addition, the Stock Sale results in an extraordinary reduction with respect to US1's ownership of CFC2. *See* paragraph (e)(2)(i) of this section. The extraordinary reduction occurs because during Year 2, US1 transferred indirectly 100% of the CFC2 stock it owned at the beginning of the year and such amount is more than 5% of the total value of the stock of CFC2 at the beginning of Year 2. The extraordinary disposition also occurs because on the last day of the year the percentage of stock (by value) of CFC2 that US1 owns directly or indirectly (0%) (the end of year percentage) is less than 90% of the stock (by value) of CFC2 that US1 owns directly or indirectly on the day of the taxable year when it owned the highest percentage of CFC2 stock by value (80%) (the initial percentage), no transactions occurred in the preceding year pursuant to a plan to reduce the percentage of CFC2 stock owned by US1, and the difference between the initial percentage and the end of year percentage (80 percentage points) is at least 5 percentage points. Because there is an extraordinary reduction with respect to CFC2 in Year 2 and CFC1 received a dividend from CFC2 in Year 2, under paragraph (f)(1) of this section, it is necessary to determine the limitation on the amount of the dividend eligible for the exception under section 954(c)(6).

(B) *Determination of tiered extraordinary reduction amount.* The limitation on the amount of the dividend eligible for the exception under section 954(c)(6) is based on the tiered extraordinary reduction amount. The sum of the amount of subpart F income and tested income of CFC2 for Year 2 is $150x, and immediately before the extraordinary reduction, CFC1 held 100% of the stock of CFC2. Additionally, US2 is a U.S. tax resident as defined in paragraph (i)(29) of this section because it is a United States person described in section 7701(a)(30)(A) or (C), and US2 has a pro rata share of $60x of tested income under section 951A with respect to CFC2. Accordingly, under paragraph (f)(2) of this section, the tiered extraordinary reduction amount is $90x (($150x x 100%) - $60x).

(C) *Limitation of section 954(c)(6) exception.* Under paragraph (f)(1) of this section, the portion of the $150x dividend from CFC2 to CFC1 that is eligible for the exception to foreign personal holding company income under section 954(c)(6) is $60x ($150x - $90x). To the extent that the $90x that does not qualify for the exception gives rise to additional subpart F income to CFC1, both US1 and A will take into account their pro rata share of that subpart F income under section 951(a)(2) and § 1.951-1(b) and (e).

(8) *Example 7. Application of anti-abuse rule to a prepayment of a royalty.*—(i) *Facts.* US1 owns 100% of the single class of stock of CFC1 and CFC2. CFC1 has a November 30 taxable year, and CFC2 has a calendar year taxable year. There is a license agreement between CFC1 and CFC2 pursuant to which CFC2 is obligated to pay annual royalties to CFC1 for the use of intangible property. As of November 1, 2018, the remaining term of the agreement is 10 years. On November 1, 2018, CFC1 receives from CFC2, and accrues into income, $100x of pre-paid royalties that are for the use of the intangible property for the subsequent 10 years. The form of the arrangement as a license, including the prepayment of the royalty, is respected for U.S. tax purposes; therefore CFC1's receipt of the $100x royalty prepayment does not constitute a disposition of the intangible property and is excluded from CFC1's subpart F income pursuant to section 954(c)(6). A principal purpose of CFC2 prepaying the royalty is for CFC1 to generate earnings and profits during the disqualified period that would not be subject to current U.S. tax yet may be eligible for the section 245A deduction and could, for example, be used to reduce the amount of gain recognized on a disposition of the stock of CFC1 that would be subject to U.S. tax by increasing the portion of such gain treated as a dividend.

(ii) *Analysis.* Because the royalty prepayment was carried out with a principal purpose of avoiding the purposes of this section, appropriate adjustments are required to be made under the anti-abuse rule in paragraph (h) of this section. CFC1 is a CFC that has a November 30 taxable year, so under paragraph (c)(3)(iii) of this section, CFC1 has a disqualified period beginning on January 1, 2018, and ending on November 30, 2018. In addition, even though the intangible property licensed by CFC1 to CFC2 is specified property, CFC2's prepayment of the royalty would not be treated as a disposition of the specified property by CFC1 and, therefore, would not constitute an extraordinary disposition (and thus would not give rise to extraordinary disposition E&P), absent the application of the anti-abuse rule of paragraph (h) of this section. Pursuant to paragraph (h) of this section, the earnings and profits of CFC1 generated as a result of the $100x of prepaid royalty are treated as extraordinary disposition E&P for purposes of this section and, therefore, US1 has an extraordinary disposition account with respect to CFC1 of $100x. In addition, the prepaid royalty gives rise to a disqualified payment (as defined in § 1.951A-2(c)(6)(ii)(A)) of $100x. As a result, § 1.245A-7(b) or § 1.245A-8(b), as applicable, applies to reduce the disqualified payment in the same manner as if the disqualified payment were disqualified basis, and § 1.245A-7(c) or § 1.245A-8(c), as applicable, applies to reduce the extraordinary disposition account in the same manner as if the deductions directly or indirectly related to the disqualified payment were deductions attributable to disqualified basis of an item of specified property that corresponds to the extraordinary disposition account.

(9) *Example 8. Application of anti-abuse rule to restructuring transaction.*—(i) *Facts.* FP, a foreign corporation with no United States shareholders, owns 100% of the single class of stock of US1. US1 owns 100% of the single class of stock of CFC1 that, in turn, owns 100% of the single class of stock of CFC2. CFC2 has $100x of extraordinary disposition E&P, and US1 has a $100x extraordinary disposition account with respect to CFC2. In Year 1, FP transfers property to CFC1 in exchange for newly issued stock of CFC1. After the transfer, FP and US1 own, respectively, 90% and 10% of the single class of stock of CFC1. In Year 3, CFC2 pays a $100x dividend to CFC1, and the dividend gives rise to a tiered extraordinary disposition amount with respect to US1 of $10x. US1 includes $10x in gross income under section 951(a) with respect to the tiered extraordinary disposition amount. The $10x tiered extraordinary disposition amount reduces US1's extraordinary disposition account from $100x to $90x. In Year 5, CFC1 redeems all of the stock of CFC1 held by US1 in exchange for $100x of cash. Under sections 302(d) and 301(c)(1), the redemption results in a $100x dividend to US1. Under section 959(a), $10x of the $100x dividend is not included in US1's gross income and, but for the application of paragraph (h) of this section, US1 would claim a section 245A deduction of $90x with respect to $90x of the dividend. The transfer of property from FP to CFC1 in exchange for stock of CFC1, the $100x dividend from CFC2 to CFC1, and CFC1's redemption of all of its stock held by US1 (together, the "Transaction") were undertaken with the principal purpose of avoiding the application of this section to distributions from CFC2. As a result of the redemption, CFC2 is wholly owned by FP through CFC1, and CFC2's earnings and profits can be distributed without incurring U.S. tax irrespective of the availability of the section 245A deduction or the exception under section 954(c)(6).

(ii) *Analysis.* Because the Transaction was carried out with a principal purpose of avoiding the purposes of this section, appropriate adjustments are required to be made under the anti-abuse rule in paragraph (h) of this section. Pursuant to paragraph (h) of this section, all $90x of the dividend included in US1's income in Year 5 is treated as an extraordinary disposition amount. Therefore, $45x of the dividend is treated as an ineligible amount for which US1 cannot claim a section 245A deduction pursuant to paragraph (b)(2)(i) of this section (that is, 50% of the extraordinary disposition amount) and, accordingly, US1 is only allowed a section 245A deduction of $45x ($90x dividend received, less the $45x ineligible amount) with respect to the $90x dividend from CFC1 that it included in income. In addition, US1's extraordinary disposition account with respect to CFC2 is reduced from $90x to zero pursuant to paragraph (c)(3)(i)(A) and (D) of this section.

(10) *Example 9. Application of anti-abuse rule to a related-party loan.*—(i) *Facts.* US1 owns 100% of the single class of stock of CFC1 and CFC2. US1 does not own stock of any other foreign corporation. US1 intends to repatriate $100x cash from CFC1 at the end of taxable year Y1. At the end of taxable year Y1, CFC1 has $100x of earnings and profits described in section 959(c)(3) (all of which is extraordinary disposition E&P) and $100x of cash, and US1 has an extraordinary disposition account balance with respect to CFC1 equal to $100x. In addition, at the end of taxable year Y1, CFC2 has $100x of earnings and profits described in section 959(c)(3). US1 does not have an extraordinary disposition account with respect to CFC2. Anticipating the application of this section to a distribution from CFC1, US1 instead causes CFC1 to loan $100x of cash to CFC2 during taxable year Y1 in exchange for a $100x note. The form of the transaction is respected as a loan for U.S. tax purposes. At the end of taxable Y1, CFC2 distributes $100x of cash to US1. The loan and distribution are part of a plan a principal purpose of which is to repatriate CFC1's $100x cash without triggering the application of this section.

(ii) *Analysis.* Because the loan from CFC1 to CFC2 and the subsequent distribution of cash were carried out with a principal purpose of avoiding the purposes of this section, appropriate adjustments are required to be made under the anti-abuse rule in paragraph (h) of this section. Pursuant to that rule, the distribution of $100x of cash is treated as a distribution out of US1's extraordinary disposition account with respect to CFC1. Accordingly, the $100x distribution is taxed as a dividend, and only $50x of the dividend received by US1 is eligible for the section 245A deduction pursuant to paragraph (b)(1) of this section. As a result of the distribution, the balance of US1's extraordinary disposition account with respect to CFC1 is reduced by $100x to zero pursuant to paragraph (c)(3)(i)(A) of this section.

(k) *Applicability date.*—(1) *In general.*—This section applies to taxable periods of a foreign corporation ending on or after June 14, 2019, and to taxable periods of section 245A shareholders in which or with which such taxable periods end. For taxable periods described in the previous sentence, this section (and not § 1.245A-5T) applies regardless of whether, but for this paragraph (k)(1), § 1.245A-5T would apply. See § 1.245A-5T as contained in 26 CFR part 1 edition revised as of April 1, 2020 for distributions occurring after December 31, 2017, as to which this section does not apply.

(2) *Early application of this section.*—Notwithstanding paragraph (k)(1) of this section, a taxpayer may choose to apply this section to taxable periods of a foreign corporation ending before June 14, 2019, and to taxable periods of section 245A shareholders in which or with which such taxable periods end, provided that the taxpayer and all persons bearing a relationship to the taxpayer described in section 267(b) or 707(b) apply this section in its entirety for all such taxable periods. [Reg. § 1.245A-5.]

□ [*T.D.* 9909, 8-21-2020 (*corrected* 11-12-2020). *Amended by T.D.* 9934, 11-25-2020]

§ 1.245A-6. Coordination of extraordinary disposition and disqualified basis rules.—(a) *Scope.*—This section and §§ 1.245A-7 through 1.245A-11coordinate the application of the extraordinary disposition rules of § 1.245A-5(c) and (d) and the disqualified basis rule of § 1.951A-2(c)(5). Section 1.245A-7 provides coordination rules for simple cases, and § 1.245A-8 provides coordination rules for complex cases. Section 1.245A-9 provides definitions and other rules, including rules of general applicability for purposes of this section and §§ 1.245A-7 through 1.245A-11. Section 1.245A-10 provides examples illustrating the application of this section and §§ 1.245A-7 through 1.245A-9. Section 1.245A-11 provides applicability dates.

(b) *Conditions to apply coordination rules for simple cases.*—For a taxable year of a section 245A shareholder for which the conditions described in paragraphs (b)(1) and (2) of this section are satisfied, the section 245A shareholder may apply the coordination rules of § 1.245A-7 (rules for simple cases) to an extraordinary disposition account of the section 245A shareholder with respect to an SFC and disqualified basis of an item of specified property that corresponds to the extraordinary disposition account (as determined pursuant to § 1.245A-9(b)(1)). If the conditions are not satisfied, then the coordination rules of § 1.245A-8 (rules for complex cases) apply beginning with the first day of the first taxable year of the section 245A shareholder for which the conditions are not satisfied and all taxable years thereafter. If the conditions are satisfied for a taxable year of the section 245A shareholder but the section 245A shareholder chooses not to apply the coordination rules of § 1.245A-7 for that taxable year, then the coordination rules of § 1.245A-8 apply to that taxable year (though, for a subsequent taxable year, the section 245A shareholder may apply the coordination rules of § 1.245A-7, provided that the conditions described in paragraphs (b)(1) and (2) of this section are satisfied for such subsequent taxable year and have been satisfied for all earlier taxable years). For purposes of applying paragraphs (b)(1) and (2) of this section, a reference to a section 245A shareholder, an SFC, or a CFC does not include a successor of the section 245A shareholder, the SFC, or the CFC, respectively.

(1) *Requirements related to the SFC.*—The condition of this paragraph (b)(1) is satisfied for a taxable year of the section 245A shareholder if the following requirements are satisfied:

(i) On January 1, 2018, the section 245A shareholder owns (within the meaning of section 958(a)) all of the stock (by vote and value) of the SFC.

(ii) On each day of the taxable year of the section 245A shareholder, the section 245A shareholder owns (within the meaning of section 958(a)) all of the stock (by vote and value) of the SFC.

(iii) On no day during the taxable year of the section 245A shareholder was the SFC a distributing or controlled corporation in a transaction described in a section 355, or did the SFC acquire the assets of a corporation as to which there is an extraordinary disposition account pursuant to a transaction described in section 381 (that is, taking into account the requirements of this paragraph (b)(1) and paragraph (b)(2) of this section, the section 245A shareholder's extraordinary disposition account with respect to the SFC has not been not been adjusted pursuant to the rules of § 1.245A-5(c)(4)).

(2) *Requirements related to an item of specified property that corresponds to an extraordinary disposition account and a CFC holding the item.*—The condition of this paragraph (b)(2) is satisfied for a taxable year of a section 245A shareholder if the following requirements are satisfied:

(i) For each item of specified property with disqualified basis that corresponds to the extraordinary disposition account, the item of specified property is held by a CFC immediately after the extraordinary disposition of the item of specified property.

(ii) For each CFC described in paragraph (b)(2)(i) of this section—

(A) All of the stock (by vote and value) of the CFC is owned (within the meaning of section 958(a)) by the section 245A shareholder and any domestic affiliates of the section 245A shareholder immediately after the extraordinary disposition described in paragraph (b)(2)(i) of this section;

(B) For each taxable year of the CFC that ends with or within the taxable year of the section 245A shareholder, there is no extraordinary disposition account with respect to the CFC, and the sum of the balance of the hybrid deduction accounts (as described in § 1.245A(e)-1(d)(1) with respect to shares of stock of the CFC is zero (determined as of the end of the taxable year of the CFC and taking into account any adjustments to the accounts for the taxable year); and

(C) On each day of each taxable year of the CFC that ends with or within the taxable year of the section 245A shareholder, and on each day of each taxable year of the CFC that begins with or within the taxable year of the section 245A shareholder—

(1) The CFC holds the item of specified property described in paragraph (b)(1)(i) of this section;

(2) The section 245A shareholder and any domestic affiliates own (within the meaning of section 958(a)) all of the stock (by vote and value) of the CFC;

(3) The CFC does not hold any item of specified property with disqualified basis other than an item of specified property that corresponds to the extraordinary disposition account;

(4) The CFC does not own an interest in a partnership, trust, or estate (directly or indirectly through one or more other partnerships, trusts, or estates) that holds an item of specified property with disqualified basis; and

(5) The CFC is not engaged in the conduct of a trade or business in the United States and therefore does not have ECTI, and the CFC does not have any deficit in earnings and profits subject to § 1.381(c)(2)-1(a)(5). [Reg. § 1.245A-6.]

□ [*T.D.* 9934, 11-25-2020.]

§ 1.245A-7. Coordination rules for simple cases.—(a) *Scope.*—This section applies for a taxable year of a section 245A shareholder for which the conditions of § 1.245A-6(b)(1) and (2) are satisfied and for which the section 245A shareholder chooses to apply this section (in lieu of § 1.245A-8).

(b) *Reduction of disqualified basis by reason of an extraordinary disposition amount or tiered extraordinary disposition amount.*—(1) *In general.*—If, for a taxable year of a section 245A shareholder, an extraordinary disposition account of the section 245A shareholder gives rise to one or more extraordinary disposition amounts or tiered extraordinary disposition amounts, then, with respect to an item of specified property that corresponds to the extraordinary disposition account, the disqualified basis of the item of specified property is, solely for purposes of § 1.951A-2(c)(5), reduced (but not below zero) by an amount (determined in the functional currency in which the extraordinary disposition account is maintained) equal to the product of—

(i) The sum of the extraordinary disposition amounts and the tiered extraordinary disposition amounts; and

(ii) A fraction, the numerator of which is the disqualified basis of the item of specified property, and the denominator of which is the sum of the disqualified basis of each item of specified property that corresponds to the extraordinary disposition account.

(2) *Timing rules regarding disqualified basis.*—See § 1.245A-9(b)(2) for timing rules regarding the determination of, and reduction to, disqualified basis of an item of specified property.

(3) *Special rule regarding prior extraordinary disposition amounts.*—For purposes of paragraph (b)(1) of this section, to the extent that an extraordinary disposition account of a section 245A shareholder is reduced under § 1.245A-5(c)(3)(i)(A) by reason of a prior extraordinary disposition amount described in § 1.245A-5(c)(3)(i)(D)*(1)*(*i*) through (*iv*), the extraordinary disposition account is considered to give rise to an extraordinary disposition amount or tiered extraordinary disposition amount (and the amount by which the account is reduced is treated as an extraordinary disposition amount or tiered extraordinary disposition amount).

(c) *Reduction of extraordinary disposition account by reason of the allocation and apportionment of deductions or losses attributable to disqualified basis.*—(1) *In general.*—If, for a taxable year of a CFC, the CFC holds one or more items of specified property that correspond to an extraordinary disposition account of a section 245A shareholder with respect to an SFC, then the extraordinary disposition account is reduced (but not below zero) by the lesser of the amounts described in paragraphs (c)(1)(i) and (ii) of this section (each determined in the functional currency of the CFC).

(i) The excess (if any) of the adjusted earnings of the CFC for the taxable year of the CFC, over the sum of the previously taxed earnings and profits accounts with respect to the CFC for purposes of section 959 (determined as of the end of the taxable year of the CFC and taking into account any adjustments to the accounts for the taxable year).

(ii) The balance of the section 245A shareholder's RGI account with respect to the CFC (determined as of the end of the taxable year of the CFC, but without regard to the application of paragraph (c)(4)(ii) of this section for the taxable year).

(2) *Timing of reduction to extraordinary disposition account.*—See § 1.245A-9(b)(3) for timing rules regarding the reduction to an extraordinary disposition account.

(3) *Adjusted earnings.*—The term *adjusted earnings* means, with respect to a CFC and a taxable year of the CFC, the earnings and profits of the CFC, determined as of the end of the CFC's taxable year (taking into account all distributions during the taxable year), and with the adjustments described in paragraphs (c)(3)(i) through (iii) of this section.

(i) The earnings and profits are increased by the amount of any deduction or loss that is or was allocated and apportioned to residual CFC gross income of the CFC solely by reason of § 1.951A-2(c)(5)(i).

(ii) The earnings and profits are decreased by the amount by which an RGI account with respect to the CFC has been decreased pursuant to paragraph (c)(4)(ii) of this section for a prior taxable year of the CFC.

(iii) The earnings and profits are determined without regard to income described in section 245(a)(5)(A) or dividends described in section 245(a)(5)(B) (determined without regard to section 245(a)(12)).

(4) *RGI account.*—For a taxable year of a CFC, the following rules apply to determine the balance of a section 245A shareholder's RGI account with respect to the CFC:

(i) The balance of the RGI account is increased by the sum of the amounts of deductions and losses of the CFC that, but for § 1.951A-2(c)(5)(i), would have decreased one or more categories of the CFC's positive subpart F income or the CFC's tested income, or increased or given rise to a tested loss or one or more qualified deficits of the CFC.

(ii) The balance of the RGI account is decreased to the extent that, by reason of the application of paragraph (c)(1) of this section with respect to the taxable year of the CFC, there is a reduction to the extraordinary disposition account of the section 245A shareholder. [Reg. § 1.245A-7.]

☐ [*T.D.* 9934, 11-25-2020.]

§ 1.245A-8. Coordination rules for complex cases.—(a) *Scope.*—This section applies beginning with the first day of the first taxable year of a section 245A shareholder for which § 1.245A-7 does not apply and for all taxable years thereafter, or for a taxable year of a section 245A shareholder for which the section 245A shareholder chooses not to apply § 1.245A-7.

(b) *Reduction of disqualified basis by reason of an extraordinary disposition amount or tiered extraordinary disposition amount.*—(1) *In general.*—If, for a taxable year of a section 245A shareholder, an extraordinary disposition account of the section 245A shareholder gives rise to one or more extraordinary disposition amounts or tiered extraordinary disposition amounts, then, with respect to an item of specified property that corresponds to the extraordinary disposition account and for which the ownership requirement of paragraph (b)(3)(i) of this section is satisfied for the taxable year of the section 245A shareholder, solely for purposes of § 1.951A-2(c)(5), the disqualified basis of the item of specified property is reduced (but not below zero) by an amount (determined in the functional currency in which the extraordinary disposition account is maintained) equal to the product of—

(i) The excess (if any) of—

(A) The sum of the extraordinary disposition amounts and the tiered extraordinary disposition amounts; over

(B) The basis benefit account with respect to the extraordinary disposition account (determined as of the end of the taxable year of the section 245A shareholder, and without regard to the application of paragraph (b)(4)(i)(B) of this section for the taxable year); and

(ii) A fraction, the numerator of which is the disqualified basis of the item of specified property, and the denominator of which is the sum of the disqualified basis of each item of specified property that corresponds to the extraordinary disposition account and for which the ownership requirement of paragraph (b)(3)(i) of this section is satisfied for the taxable year of the section 245A shareholder.

(2) *Timing rules regarding disqualified basis.*—See § 1.245A-9(b)(2) for timing rules regarding the determination of, and reduction to, disqualified basis of an item of specified property.

(3) *Ownership requirement with respect to an item of specified property.*—(i) *In general.*—For a taxable year of a section 245A shareholder, the ownership requirement of this paragraph (b)(3)(i) is satisfied with respect to an item of specified property if, on at least one day that falls within the taxable year, the item of specified property is held by—

(A) The section 245A shareholder;

(B) A person (other than the section 245A shareholder) that, on at least one day that falls within the section 245A shareholder's taxable year, is a related party with respect to the section 245A shareholder (such a person, a *qualified related party* with respect to the section 245A shareholder for the taxable year of the section 245A shareholder); or

(C) A specified entity at least 10 percent of the interests of which are, on at least one day that falls within the section 245A shareholder's taxable year, owned directly or indirectly through one or more other specified entities by the section 245A shareholder or a qualified related party.

(ii) *Rules for determining an interest in a specified entity.*—For purposes of paragraph (b)(3)(i)(C) of this section, the phrase *at least 10 percent of the interests* means—

(A) If the specified entity is a foreign corporation, at least 10 percent of the stock (by vote or value) of the foreign corporation;

(B) If the specified entity is a partnership, at least 10 percent of the interests in the capital or profits of the partnership; or

(C) If the specified entity is not a foreign corporation or a partnership, at least 10 percent of the value of the interests in the specified entity.

(4) *Basis benefit account.*—(i) *General rules.*—The term *basis benefit account* means, with respect to an extraordinary disposition account of a section 245A shareholder, an account of the section 245A shareholder (the initial balance of which is zero), adjusted pursuant to the rules of paragraphs (b)(4)(i)(A) and (B) of this section on the last day of each taxable year of the section 245A shareholder. The basis benefit account must be maintained in the same functional currency as the extraordinary disposition account.

(A) The balance of the basis benefit account is increased to the extent that a basis benefit amount with respect to an item of specified property that corresponds to the section 245A shareholder's extraordinary disposition account is assigned to the taxable year of the section 245A shareholder. However, if the extraordinary disposition ownership percentage applicable to the section 245A shareholder's extraordinary disposition account is less than 100 percent, then, the basis benefit account is instead increased by the amount equal to the basis benefit amount multiplied by the extraordinary disposition ownership percentage.

(B) The balance of the basis benefit account is decreased to the extent that, for a taxable year that includes the date on which the section 245A shareholder's taxable year ends, disqualified basis of an item of specified property would have been reduced pursuant to paragraph (b)(1) of this section but for an amount in the basis benefit account.

(ii) *Rules for determining a basis benefit amount.*—(A) *In general.*—The term *basis benefit amount* means, with respect to an item of specified property that has disqualified basis, the portion of disqualified basis that, for a taxable year, is directly (or indirectly through one or more specified entities that are not corporations) taken into account for U.S. tax purposes by a U.S. tax resident, a CFC described in § 1.267A-5(a)(17), or a specified foreign person and—

(*1*) Reduces the amount of the U.S. tax resident's taxable income, one or more categories of the CFC's positive subpart F income, the CFC's tested income, or the specified foreign person's ECTI, as applicable; or

(*2*) Prevents a decrease or offset of the amount of the CFC's tested loss or qualified deficits.

(B) *Rules for determining whether disqualified basis of an item of specified property is taken into account.*—For purposes of paragraph (b)(4)(ii)(A) of this section, disqualified basis of an item of specified property is taken into account for U.S. tax purposes without regard to whether the disqualified basis is reduced or eliminated under § 1.951A-3(h)(2)(ii)(B)(*1*).

(C) *Timing rules when disqualified basis gives rise to a deferred or disallowed loss.*—To the extent disqualified basis of an item of specified property gives rise to a deduction or loss during a taxable year that is deferred, then the determination of whether the item of deduction or loss gives rise to a basis benefit amount under paragraph (b)(4)(ii)(A) of this section is made when the item of deduction or loss is no longer deferred. In addition, to the extent disqualified basis of an item of specified property gives rise to a deduction or loss during a taxable year that is disallowed under section 267(a)(1), then a basis benefit amount is treated as occurring in the taxable year when and to the extent that gain is reduced pursuant to section 267(d), and provided that the gain is described in paragraph (b)(4)(ii)(A) of this section.

(iii) *Rules for assigning a basis benefit amount to a taxable year of a section 245A shareholder.*—(A) *In general.*—For purposes of applying paragraph (b)(4)(i)(A) of this section with respect to a section 245A shareholder, a basis benefit amount with respect to an item of specified property is assigned to a taxable year of the section 245A shareholder if—

(*1*) With respect to the item of specified property, the ownership requirement of paragraph (b)(3)(i) of this section is satisfied for the taxable year of the section 245A shareholder; and

(*2*) The basis benefit amount occurs during the taxable year of the section 245A shareholder, or a taxable year of a U.S. tax resident (other than the section 245A shareholder), a CFC described in § 1.267A-5(a)(17), or a specified foreign person, as applicable, that—

(*i*) Ends with or within the taxable year of the section 245A shareholder; or

(*ii*) Begins with or within the taxable year of the section 245A shareholder, but only in a case in which but for this paragraph (b)(4)(iii)(A)(*2*)(*ii*) the basis benefit amount would not be assigned to a taxable year of the section 245A shareholder.

(B) *Anti-duplication rule.*—For purposes of paragraph (b)(4)(i)(A) of this section, to the extent that disqualified basis of an item of specified property gives rise to a basis benefit amount that is assigned to a taxable year of a section 245A shareholder under paragraph (b)(4)(iii)(A) of this section, and thereafter such disqualified basis gives rise to an additional basis benefit amount, the additional basis benefit amount cannot be assigned to another taxable year of any section 245A shareholder. Thus, for example, if the entire amount of disqualified basis of an item of specified property gives rise to a basis benefit amount for a particular taxable year of a CFC and is assigned to a taxable year of a section 245A shareholder but, pursuant to § 1.951A-3(h)(2)(ii)(B)(*1*)(*ii*), the disqualified basis is not reduced or eliminated in such taxable year of the CFC (because, for example, the buyer is a CFC that is a related party) and, as a result, the disqualified basis thereafter gives rise to an additional basis benefit amount, then no portion of the additional basis benefit amount is assigned to a taxable year of any section 245A shareholder.

(iv) *Successor rules for basis benefit accounts.*—To the extent that an extraordinary disposition account of a section 245A shareholder is adjusted pursuant to § 1.245A-5(c)(4), a basis benefit account with respect to the extraordinary disposition account is adjusted in a similar manner.

(5) *Special rules regarding duplicate DQB of an item of exchanged basis property.*—(i) *Adjustments to certain rules in applying paragraph (b)(1) of this section.*—For purposes of paragraph (b)(1) of this section for a taxable year of a section 245A shareholder, the following rules apply with respect to duplicate DQB of an item of exchanged basis property:

(A) Duplicate DQB of the item of exchanged basis property with respect to an item of specified property to which the item of exchanged property relates is not taken into account for purposes of paragraph (b)(1) of this section if the disqualified basis of the item of specified property is taken into account for purposes of paragraph (b)(1) of this section. Thus, for example, if for a taxable year of a section 245A shareholder the ownership requirement of paragraph (b)(3) of this section is satisfied with respect to an item of specified property and an item of exchanged basis property that relates to the item of specified property, all of the disqualified basis of which is duplicate DQB with respect to the item of specified property, then only the disqualified basis of the item of specified property is taken into account for purposes of, and is subject to reduction under, paragraph (b)(1) of this section.

(B) If, pursuant to paragraph (b)(5)(i)(A) of this section, duplicate DQB of an item of exchanged basis property with respect to an item of specified property is not taken into account for purposes of paragraph (b)(1) of this section, then, solely for purposes of § 1.951A-2(c)(5), the duplicate DQB of the item of exchanged basis property is reduced (in the same manner as it would be if the disqualified basis were taken into account for purposes of paragraph (b)(1) of this section) by the product of the amounts described in paragraphs (b)(5)(i)(B)(*1*) and (*2*) of this section.

(*1*) The reduction, under paragraph (b)(1) of this section for the taxable year of the section 245A shareholder, to the disqualified basis of the item of specified property to which the item of exchanged basis property relates.

(*2*) A fraction, the numerator of which is the duplicate DQB of the item of exchanged basis property with respect to the item of specified property, and the denominator of which is the sum of the amounts of duplicate DQB with respect to the item of specified property of each item of exchanged basis property that relates to the item of specified property and for which the ownership requirement of paragraph (b)(3)(i) of this section is satisfied for the taxable year of the section 245A shareholder. For purposes of determining this fraction, duplicate DQB of an item of exchanged basis property is determined pursuant to the rules of paragraph (b)(2)(i) of this section (by replacing the term "paragraph (b)(1)" in that paragraph with the term "paragraph (b)(5)(i)(B)"). In addition, duplicate DQB of an item of exchanged basis property is excluded from the denominator of the fraction to the extent the duplicate DQB is attributable to duplicate DQB of another item of exchanged basis property that is included in the denominator of the fraction.

(ii) *Adjustments to certain rules in applying paragraph (b)(4) of this section.*—For purposes of paragraph (b)(4)(i)(A) of this section, to the extent that disqualified basis of an item of specified property gives rise to a basis benefit amount that is assigned to a taxable year of a section 245A shareholder under paragraph (b)(4)(iii)(A) of this section, and thereafter duplicate DQB attributable to such disqualified basis of the item of specified property gives rise to an additional basis benefit amount, the additional basis benefit amount cannot be assigned to another taxable year of any section 245A shareholder. Similarly, for purposes of paragraph (b)(4)(i)(A) of this section, to the extent that duplicate DQB attributable to disqualified basis of an item of specified property gives rise to a basis benefit amount that is assigned to a taxable year of a section 245A shareholder under paragraph (b)(4)(iii)(A) of this section, and thereafter such disqualified basis of the item of specified property (or duplicate DQB attributable to such disqualified basis of the item of specified property) gives rise to an additional basis benefit amount, the additional basis benefit amount cannot be assigned to another taxable year of any section 245A shareholder.

(6) *Special rule regarding prior extraordinary disposition amounts.*—For purposes of paragraph (b)(1) of this section, to the extent that an extraordinary disposition account of a section 245A shareholder is reduced under § 1.245A-5(c)(3)(i)(A) by reason of a prior extraordinary disposition amount described in § 1.245A-5(c)(3)(i)(D)(*1*)(*i*) through (*iv*), the extraordinary disposition account is considered to give rise to an extraordinary disposition amount or tiered extraordinary disposition amount (and the amount by which the account is reduced is treated as an extraordinary disposition amount or tiered extraordinary disposition amount).

(c) *Reduction of extraordinary disposition account by reason of the allocation and apportionment of deductions or losses attributable to disqualified basis.*—(1) *In general.*—For a taxable year of a CFC, if there is an RGI account with respect to the CFC that relates to an extraordinary disposition account of a section 245A shareholder with respect to an SFC, and the section 245A shareholder satisfies the ownership requirement of paragraph (c)(5) of this section for the taxable year of the CFC, then, subject to the limitations in paragraphs (c)(6) and (7) of this section, the extraordinary disposition account is reduced (but not below zero) by the lesser of the following amounts (each determined in the functional currency of the CFC)—

(i) The excess (if any) of—

(A) The product of—

(*1*) The adjusted earnings of the CFC for the taxable year of the CFC; and

(2) The percentage of stock of the CFC (by value) that, in aggregate, is owned directly or indirectly through one or more specified entities by the section 245A shareholder and any domestic affiliates on the last day of the taxable year of the CFC; over

(B) The sum of—

(1) The sum of the balance of the section 245A shareholder's and any domestic affiliates' previously taxed earnings and profits accounts with respect to the CFC for purposes of section 959 (determined as of the end of the taxable year of the CFC and taking into account any adjustments to the accounts for the taxable year);

(2) The sum of the balance of the hybrid deduction accounts (as described in § 1.245A(e)-1(d)(1)) with respect to shares of stock of the CFC that the section 245A shareholder and any domestic affiliates own (within the meaning of section 958(a), and determined by treating a domestic partnership as foreign) as of the end of the taxable year of the CFC and taking into account any adjustments to the accounts for the taxable year; and

(3) The sum of the balance of the section 245A shareholder's and any domestic affiliates' extraordinary disposition accounts with respect to the CFC (determined as of the end of the taxable year of the CFC and taking into account any adjustments to the accounts for the taxable year). However, if the section 245A shareholder or a domestic affiliate has an RGI account with respect to the CFC that relates to an extraordinary disposition account with respect to the CFC, then only the excess, if any, of the balance of the extraordinary disposition account over the balance of the RGI account that relates to the extraordinary disposition account (determined as of the end of the taxable year of the CFC, but without regard to the application of paragraph (c)(4)(i)(B) of this section for the taxable year) is taken into account for purposes of this paragraph (c)(1)(i)(B)(*3*). In addition, for purposes of this paragraph (c)(1)(i)(B)(*3*), an extraordinary disposition account that but for paragraph (e)(1) of this section would be with respect to the CFC for purposes of this section is treated as an extraordinary disposition account with respect to the CFC and thus is taken into account for purposes of this paragraph (c)(1)(i)(B)(3).

(ii) The balance of the RGI account with respect to the CFC that relates to the section 245A shareholder's extraordinary disposition account with respect to the SFC (determined as of the end of the taxable year of the CFC, but without regard to the application of paragraph (c)(4)(i)(B) of this section for the taxable year).

(2) *Timing of reduction to extraordinary disposition account.*—See § 1.245A-9(b)(3) for timing rules regarding the reduction to an extraordinary disposition account.

(3) *Adjusted earnings.*—The term *adjusted earnings* means, with respect to a CFC and a taxable year of the CFC, the earnings and profits of the CFC, determined as of the end of the CFC's taxable year (taking into account all distributions during the taxable year, and not taking into account any deficit in earnings and profits subject to § 1.381(c)(2)-1(a)(5)) and with the adjustments described in paragraphs (c)(3)(i) through (iv) of this section.

(i) The earnings and profits are increased by the amount of any deduction or loss that—

(A) Is or was attributable to disqualified basis of an item of specified property, but only to the extent that gain recognized on the extraordinary disposition of the item of specified property was included in the initial balance of an extraordinary disposition account;

(B) Is or was allocated and apportioned to residual CFC gross income of the CFC (or a predecessor) solely by reason of § 1.951A-2(c)(5)(i); and

(C) Does not or has not given rise to or increased a deficit in earnings and profits subject to § 1.381(c)(2)-1(a)(5), determined as of the end of the taxable year of the CFC.

(ii) The earnings and profits are decreased by the amount by which any RGI account with respect to the CFC has been decreased pursuant to paragraph (c)(4)(i)(B) of this section for a prior taxable year of the CFC.

(iii) The earnings and profits are determined without regard to earnings attributable to income described in section 245(a)(5)(A) or dividends described in section 245(a)(5)(B) (determined without regard to section 245(a)(12)).

(iv) The earnings and profits are decreased by the amount of any deduction or loss that, but for paragraph (c)(3)(i)(C) of this section, would be described in paragraph (c)(3)(i) of this section.

(4) *RGI account.*—(i) *In general.*—For a taxable year of a CFC, the following rules apply to determine the balance of a section 245A shareholder's RGI account that is with respect to the CFC and that relates to an extraordinary disposition account of the section 245A shareholder with respect to an SFC:

(A) The balance of the RGI account is increased by the product of the amounts described in paragraphs (c)(4)(i)(A)(*1*) and (*2*) of this section for a taxable year of the CFC.

(1) The sum of the amounts of deductions and losses of the CFC that—

(i) Are attributable to disqualified basis of one or more items of specified property that correspond to the extraordinary disposition account; and

(ii) But for § 1.951A-2(c)(5)(i), would have decreased one or more categories of the CFC's positive subpart F income, the CFC's tested income, or the CFC's ECTI, or increased or given rise to a tested loss or one or more qualified deficits of the CFC.

(2) The lesser of—

(i) A fraction (expressed as a percentage), the numerator of which is the sum of the portions of the CFC's subpart F income and tested income or tested loss (expressed as a positive number) taken into account under sections 951(a)(1)(A) and 951A(a) (as determined under the rules of §§ 1.951-1(b) and (e) and 1.951A-1(d)) by the section 245A shareholder and any domestic affiliates of the section 245A shareholder and the section 245A shareholder's and any domestic affiliates' pro rata shares of the CFC's qualified deficits (expressed as a positive number), and the denominator of which is the sum of the CFC's subpart F income, tested income or tested loss (expressed as a positive number), and qualified deficits (expressed as a positive number), but for purposes of this paragraph (c)(4)(i)(A)(*2*)(*i*) treating ECTI (expressed as a positive number) as if it were subpart F income; and

(ii) The extraordinary disposition ownership percentage applicable as to the section 245A shareholder's extraordinary disposition account.

(B) The balance of the RGI account is decreased to the extent that, by reason of the application of paragraph (c)(1) of this section with respect to the taxable year of the CFC, there is a reduction to the extraordinary disposition account of the section 245A shareholder.

(ii) *Successor rules for RGI accounts.*—To the extent that an extraordinary disposition account of a section 245A shareholder is adjusted pursuant to § 1.245A-5(c)(4), an RGI account of a CFC with respect to the extraordinary disposition account is adjusted in a similar manner.

(5) *Ownership requirement with respect to a CFC.*—For a taxable year of a CFC, a section 245A shareholder satisfies the ownership requirement of this paragraph (c)(5) if, on the last day of the CFC's taxable year, the section 245A shareholder or a domestic affiliate is a United States shareholder with respect to the CFC.

(6) *Allocation of reductions among multiple extraordinary disposition accounts.*—This paragraph (c)(6) applies if, by reason of the application of paragraph (c)(1) of this section with respect to a taxable year of a CFC (and but for the application of this paragraph (c)(6) and paragraph (c)(7) of this section), the sum of the reductions under paragraph (c)(1) of this section to two or more extraordinary disposition accounts of a section 245A shareholder or a domestic affiliate of the section 245A shareholder would exceed the amount described in paragraph (c)(1)(i)(A) of this section (the amount of such excess, the *excess amount*). When this paragraph (c)(6) applies, the reduction to each extraordinary disposition account described in the previous sentence is equal to the reduction that would occur but for this paragraph (c)(6) and paragraph (c)(7) of this section, less the product of the excess amount and a fraction, the numerator of which is the balance of the extraordinary disposition account, and the denominator of which is the sum of the balances of all of the extraordinary dispositions accounts described in the previous sentence. For purposes of determining this fraction, the balance of an extraordinary disposition account is determined as of the end of the taxable year of the section 245A shareholder or the domestic affiliate, as applicable, that includes the date on which the CFC's taxable year ends (and after the determination of any extraordinary disposition amounts or tiered extraordinary disposition amounts for the taxable year of the section 245A shareholder or the domestic affiliate, as applicable, and adjustments to the extraordinary disposition account for prior extraordinary disposition amounts).

(7) *Extraordinary disposition account not reduced below balance of basis benefit account.*—An extraordinary disposition account of a section 245A shareholder cannot be reduced pursuant to paragraph (c)(1) of this section below the balance of the basis benefit account

with respect to the extraordinary disposition account (determined when a reduction to the extraordinary disposition account would occur under paragraph (c)(1) of this section).

(d) *Special rules for determining when specified property corresponds to an extraordinary disposition account.*—(1) *Substituted property.*—(i) *Treatment as specified property that corresponds to an extraordinary disposition account.*—For purposes of this section, an item of substituted property is treated as an item of specified property that corresponds to an extraordinary disposition account to which the related item of specified property (that is, the item of specified property to which the item of substituted property relates, as described in paragraph (d)(1)(ii) of this section) corresponds. In addition, in a case in which an item of substituted property relates to an item of specified property that corresponds to a particular extraordinary disposition account and an item of specified property that corresponds to another extraordinary disposition account (such that, pursuant to this paragraph (d)(1)(i), the item of substituted property is treated as corresponding to multiple extraordinary disposition accounts), only the disqualified basis of the item of substituted property attributable to the first item of specified property is taken into account for purposes of applying this section as to the first extraordinary disposition account, and, similarly, only the disqualified basis of the item of substituted property attributable to the second item of specified property is taken into account for purposes of applying this section as to the second extraordinary disposition account.

(ii) *Definition of substituted property.*—The term *substituted property* means an item of property the disqualified basis of which is, pursuant to § 1.951A-3(h)(2)(ii)(B)(2)(*i*) or (*iii*), increased by reason of a reduction under § 1.951A-3(h)(2)(ii)(*B*)(*1*) in disqualified basis of an item of specified property. An item of substituted property relates to an item of specified property if the disqualified basis of the item of substituted property was increased by reason of a reduction in disqualified basis of the item of specified property.

(2) *Exchanged basis property.*—(i) *Treatment as specified property that corresponds to an extraordinary disposition account for certain purposes.*—For purposes of this section, an item of exchanged basis property is treated as an item of specified property that corresponds to an extraordinary disposition account to which the related item of specified property (that is, the item of specified property to which the item of exchanged basis property relates) corresponds.

(ii) *Definition of exchanged basis property.*—The term *exchanged basis property* means an item of property the disqualified basis of which, pursuant to § 1.951A-3(h)(2)(ii)(B)(2)(*ii*), includes disqualified basis of an item of specified property. An item of exchanged basis property relates to an item of specified property if the disqualified basis of the item of exchanged basis property includes disqualified basis of the item of specified property.

(iii) *Definition of duplicate DQB.*—(A) *In general.*—The term *duplicate DQB* means, with respect to an item of exchanged basis property and the item of specified property to which the exchanged basis property relates, the disqualified basis of the item of exchanged basis property that includes or is attributable to disqualified basis of the item of specified property.

(B) *Certain nonrecognition transfers involving stock or a partnership interest.*—To the extent that an item of exchanged basis property that is stock or an interest in a partnership *(lower-tier item)* includes disqualified basis of an item of specified property to which the lower-tier item relates *(contributed item)*, and another item of exchanged basis property that is stock or a partnership interest *(upper-tier item)* includes disqualified basis of the lower-tier item that is attributable to disqualified basis of the contributed item, the disqualified basis of the upper-tier item is attributable to disqualified basis of the contributed item and the upper-tier item is an item of exchanged basis property that relates to the contributed item. The principles of the preceding sentence apply each time disqualified basis of an item of exchanged basis property that is stock or an interest in a partnership is included in disqualified basis of another item of exchanged basis property that is stock or an interest in a partnership.

(C) *Multiple nonrecognition transfers of an item of specified property.*—To the extent that multiple items of exchanged basis property that are stock or interests in a partnership include disqualified basis of the same item of specified property *(contributed item)* to which the items of exchanged basis property relate, and the issuer of one of the items of exchanged basis property *(upper-tier successor item)* receives the other item of exchanged basis property *(lower-tier successor item)* in exchange for the contributed property, the disqualified basis of the upper-tier successor item is attributable to disqualified basis of the lower-tier successor item and the upper-tier successor item is an item of exchanged basis property that relates to the lower-tier successor item. The principles of the preceding sentence apply each time disqualified basis of an item of specified property to which an item of exchanged basis property that is stock or an interest in partnership relates is included in disqualified basis of another item of exchanged basis property that is stock or an interest in a partnership.

(e) *Special rules when extraordinary disposition accounts are adjusted pursuant to § 1.245A-5(c)(4).*—(1) *Extraordinary disposition account with respect to multiple SFCs.*—This paragraph (e)(1) applies if, pursuant to § 1.245A-5(c)(4)(ii) or (iii) (the transaction or transactions by reason of which § 1.245A-5(c)(4)(ii) or (iii) applies, the *adjustment transaction*), an extraordinary disposition account of a section 245A shareholder with respect to an SFC (such extraordinary disposition account, the *transferor ED account;* and such SFC, the *transferor SFC)* gives rise to an increase in the balance of an extraordinary disposition account with respect to another SFC (such extraordinary disposition account, the *transferee ED account;* such SFC, the *transferee SFC;* and such increase, the *adjustment amount*). When this paragraph (e)(1) applies, the following rules apply for purposes of this section:

(i) A ratable portion of the transferee ED account is treated as retaining its status as an extraordinary disposition account with respect to the transferor SFC and is not treated as an extraordinary disposition account with respect to the transferee SFC (the transferee ED account to such extent, the *deemed transferor ED account*), based on the adjustment amount relative to the balance of the transferee ED account (without regard to this paragraph (e)(1)) immediately after the adjustment transaction. Thus, for example, whether or not the transferor SFC is in existence immediately after the transaction, the items of specified property that correspond to the deemed transferor ED account are the same as the items of specified property that correspond to the transferor ED account. As an additional example, whether or not the transferor SFC is in existence immediately after the transaction the extraordinary disposition ownership percentage with respect to the deemed transferor ED account is the same as the extraordinary disposition ownership percentage with respect to the transferor ED account (except to the extent the extraordinary disposition ownership percentage is adjusted pursuant to the rules of paragraph (e)(2) of this section).

(ii) In the case of an amount (such as an extraordinary disposition amount or tiered extraordinary disposition amount) determined by reference to the transferee ED account (without regard to this paragraph (e)(1)), the portion of the amount that is considered attributable to the deemed transferor ED account (and not the transferee ED account) is equal to the product of such amount and a fraction, the numerator of which is the balance of the deemed transferor ED account, and the denominator of which is the balance of the transferee ED account (determined without regard to this paragraph (e)(1)). Thus, for example, if after an adjustment transaction the transferee ED account (without regard to this paragraph (e)(1)) gives rise to an extraordinary disposition amount, and if the fraction (expressed as a percentage) is 40, then, for purposes of this section, 40 percent of the extraordinary disposition amount is treated as attributable to the deemed transferor ED account and the remaining 60 percent of the extraordinary disposition amount is attributable to the transferee ED account, and the balance of each of the deemed transferor ED account and the transferee ED account is correspondingly reduced.

(2) *Extraordinary disposition accounts with respect to a single SFC.*—If an extraordinary disposition account of a section 245A shareholder with respect to an SFC is reduced by reason of § 1.245A-5(c)(4), then, except as provided in paragraph (e)(1) of this section, for purposes of this section, the extraordinary disposition ownership percentage as to the extraordinary disposition account (as well as the extraordinary disposition ownership percentage as to any extraordinary disposition account with respect to the SFC that is increased by reason of the reduction) is adjusted in a similar manner. [Reg. § 1.245A-8.]

☐ [*T.D.* 9934, 11-25-2020.]

§ 1.245A-9. Other rules and definitions.—(a) *In general.*—This section provides rules of general applicability for purposes of §§ 1.245A-6 through 1.245A-10, a transition rule to revoke an election to eliminate disqualified basis, and definitions.

(b) *Rules of general applicability.*—(1) *Correspondence.*—An item of specified property corresponds to a section 245A shareholder's extraordinary disposition account if gain was recognized on the extraordinary disposition of the item and the gain was taken into account in determining the initial balance of the account. See § 1.245A-8(d) for additional rules regarding when an item of property is treated as corresponding to an extraordinary disposition account in certain complex cases.

(2) *Timing rules related to disqualified basis for purposes of applying §§ 1.245A-7(b) and 1.245A-8(b).*—(i) *Determination of disqualified basis.*—For purposes of determining the fraction described in § 1.245A-7(b)(1)(ii) or § 1.245A-8(b)(1)(ii) when applying § 1.245A-7(b)(1) or § 1.245A-8(b)(1)(ii), respectively, for a taxable year of a section 245A shareholder, disqualified basis of an item of specified property is determined as of the beginning of the taxable year of the CFC that holds the item of specified property (in a case in which § 1.245A-7(b) applies) or the specified property owner (in a case in which § 1.245A-8(b) applies), in either case, that includes the date on which the section 245A shareholder's taxable year ends (and without regard to any reductions to the disqualified basis of the item of specified property pursuant to § 1.245A-7(b)(1) or § 1.245A-8(b)(1) for such taxable year of the CFC or the specified property owner, as applicable). However, if disqualified basis of the item of specified property arose as a result of an extraordinary disposition that occurred after the beginning of the taxable year of the CFC or the specified property owner described in the preceding sentence, then the disqualified basis of the item of specified property is determined as of the date on which the extraordinary disposition occurred (and without regard to any reductions to the disqualified basis of the item of specified property pursuant to paragraph (b)(1) of this section for such taxable year of the CFC or the specified property owner).

(ii) *Reduction to disqualified basis of an item of specified property.*—The reduction to disqualified basis of an item of specified property pursuant to § 1.245A-7(b)(1) or § 1.245A-8(b)(1) occurs on the date described in paragraph (b)(2)(i) of this section.

(iii) *Definition of specified property owner.*—For purposes of applying § 1.245A-8(b)(1) and paragraphs (b)(2)(i) and (ii) of this section for a taxable year of a section 245A shareholder, the term *specified property owner* means, with respect to an item of specified property, the person that, on at least one day of the taxable year of the person that includes the date on which the section 245A shareholder's taxable year ends, held the item of specified property. However, if, but for this sentence, there would be more than one specified property owner with respect to the item of specified property, then the specified property owner is the person that held the item of specified property on the earliest date that falls within the section 245A shareholder's taxable year.

(3) *Timing rules for reducing an extraordinary disposition account under §§ 1.245A-7(c) and 1.245A-8(c).*—For purposes of § 1.245A-7(c)(1) or § 1.245A-8(c)(1), as applicable, with respect to a taxable year of a CFC, the reduction to an extraordinary disposition account pursuant to § 1.245A-7(c)(1) or § 1.245A-8(c)(1) occurs as of the end of the taxable year of the section 245A shareholder that includes the date on which the CFC's taxable year ends (and after the determination of any extraordinary disposition amounts or tiered extraordinary amounts, adjustments to the extraordinary disposition account for prior extraordinary disposition amounts, and the application of § 1.245A-7(b) or § 1.245A-8(b), as applicable, each for the taxable year of the section 245A shareholder).

(4) *Currency translation.*—For purposes of applying §§ 1.245A-7(b) and 1.245A-8(b), the disqualified basis of (and, if applicable, a basis benefit amount with respect to) an item of specified property that corresponds to an extraordinary disposition account are translated (if necessary) into the functional currency in which the extraordinary disposition account is maintained, using the spot rate on the date the extraordinary disposition occurred. A reduction in disqualified basis of an item of specified property determined under § 1.245A-7(b)(1) or § 1.245A-8(b)(1) is translated (if necessary) into the functional currency in which the disqualified basis of the item of specified property is maintained, and a reduction in an extraordinary disposition account determined under § 1.245A-7(c) or § 1.245A-8(c) section is translated (if necessary) into the functional currency in which the extraordinary disposition account is maintained, in each case using the spot rate described in the preceding sentence.

(5) *Anti-avoidance rule.*—Appropriate adjustments are made pursuant to this paragraph (b)(5), including adjustments that would disregard a transaction or arrangement in whole or in part, to any amounts determined under (or subject to application of) this section if a transaction or arrangement is engaged in with a principal purpose of avoiding the purposes of §§ 1.245A-6 through 1.245A-10.

(c) *Transition rule to revoke election to eliminate disqualified basis.*—(1) *In general.*—This paragraph (c)(1) applies to an election that is filed, pursuant to § 1.951A-3(h)(2)(ii)(B)(3), to eliminate the disqualified basis of an item of specified property. An election to which this paragraph (c)(1) applies may be revoked if, on or before March 1, 2021—

(i) All controlling domestic shareholders (as defined in § 1.964-1(c)(5)) of the CFC (or, in the case of an election made by a partnership, the partnership) each attach a revocation statement (in the manner described in paragraph (c)(2) of this section) to an amended return, for the taxable year to which the election applies, that revokes the election (or, in the case of a partnership subject to subchapter C of chapter 63 of the Internal Revenue Code, requests administrative adjustment under section 6227); and

(ii) The controlling domestic shareholders (or the partnership) each file an amended tax return, for any other taxable years reflecting the election to eliminate the disqualified basis, that reflects the election having been revoked (or, in the case of a partnership subject to subchapter C of chapter 63, requests administrative adjustment under section 6227).

(2) *Revocation statement.*—Except as otherwise provided in publications, forms, instructions, or other guidance, a revocation statement attached by a person to an amended tax return must include the person's name, taxpayer identification number, and a statement that the revocation statement is filed pursuant to paragraph (c)(1) of this section to revoke an election pursuant to § 1.951A-3(h)(2)(ii)(B)(3). In addition, the revocation statement must be filed in the manner prescribed in publications, forms, instructions, or other guidance.

(d) *Definitions.*—In addition to the definitions in § 1.245A-5, the following definitions apply for purposes of §§ 1.245A-6 through 1.245A-11.

(1) The term *adjusted earnings* has the meaning provided in § 1.245A-7(c)(3) or § 1.245A-8(c)(3), as applicable.

(2) The term *basis benefit account* has the meaning provided in § 1.245A-8(b)(4)(i).

(3) The term *basis benefit amount* has the meaning provided in § 1.245A-8(b)(4)(ii).

(4) The term *disqualified basis* has the meaning provided in § 1.951A-3(h)(2)(ii).

(5) The term *domestic affiliate* means, with respect to a section 245A shareholder, a domestic corporation that is a related party with respect to the section 245A shareholder. *See also* § 1.245A-5(i)(19) (defining related party).

(6) The term *duplicate DQB* has the meaning provided in § 1.245A-8(d)(2)(iii).

(7) The term *ECTI* means, with respect to a taxable year of a specified foreign person, the taxable income (or loss) of the specified foreign person determined by taking into account only items of income and gain that are, or are treated as, effectively connected with the conduct of a trade or business in the United States (as described in § 1.882-4(a)(1)) and are not exempt from U.S. tax pursuant to a treaty obligation of the United States, and items of deduction and loss that are allocated and apportioned to such items of income and gain.

(8) The term *exchanged basis property* has the meaning provided in § 1.245A-8(d)(2)(ii).

(9) The term *qualified deficit* has the meaning provided in section 952(c)(1)(B)(ii).

(10) The term *qualified related party* has the meaning provided in § 1.245A-8(b)(3)(ii).

(11) The term *RGI account* means, with respect to a CFC and an extraordinary disposition account of a section 245A shareholder with respect to an SFC, an account of the section 245A shareholder with respect to an SFC (the initial balance of which is zero), adjusted at the end of each taxable year of the CFC pursuant to the rules of § 1.245A-7(c)(4) or § 1.245A-8(c)(4), as applicable. The RGI account must be maintained in the functional currency of the CFC.

(12) The term *specified foreign person* means a nonresident alien individual (as defined in section 7701(b) and the regulations under section 7701(b)) or a foreign corporation (including a CFC) that conducts, or is treated as conducting, a trade or business in the United States (as described in § 1.882-4(a)(1)).

(13) The term *specified property owner* has the meaning provided in § 1.245A-8(b)(2)(iii).

(14) The term *subpart F income* has the meaning provided in section 952(a).

(15) The term *substituted property* has the meaning provided in § 1.245A-8(d)(1)(ii).

(16) The term *tested income* has the meaning provided in section 951A(c)(2)(A).

(17) The term *tested loss* has the meaning provided in section 951A(c)(2)(B). [Reg. § 1.245A-9.]

☐ [*T.D. 9934, 11-25-2020.*]

§ 1.245A-10. Examples.—(a) *Scope.*—This section provides examples illustrating the application of § § 1.245A-6 through 1.245A-9.

(b) *Presumed facts.*—For purposes of the examples in the section, except as otherwise stated, the following facts are presumed:

(1) US1 and US2 are both domestic corporations that have calendar taxable years.

(2) CFC1, CFC2, CFC3, and CFC4 are all SFCs and CFCs that have taxable years ending November 30.

(3) Each entity uses the U.S. dollar as its functional currency.

(4) There are no items of deduction or loss attributable to an item of specified property.

(5) Absent the application of § 1.245A-5, any dividends received by US1 from CFC1 would meet the requirements to qualify for the section 245A deduction.

(6) All dispositions of items of specified property by an SFC during a disqualified period of the SFC to a related party give rise to an extraordinary disposition.

(7) None of the CFCs have a deficit subject to § 1.381(c)(2)-1(a)(5), and none of the CFCs are engaged in the conduct of a trade or business in the United States (and therefore none of the CFCs have ECTI).

(8) There is no previously taxed earnings and profits account with respect to any CFC for purposes of section 959. In addition, each hybrid deduction account with respect to a share of stock of a CFC has a zero balance at all times. Further, there is no extraordinary disposition account with respect to any CFC.

(9) Under § 1.245A-11(b), taxpayers choose to apply § § 1.245A-6 through 1.245A-11 to the relevant taxable years.

(c) *Examples.*—(1) *Example 1. Reduction of disqualified basis under rule for simple cases by reason of dividend paid out of extraordinary disposition account.*—(i) *Facts.* US1 owns 100% of the single class of stock of CFC1 and CFC2. On November 30, 2018, in a transaction that is an extraordinary disposition, CFC1 sells two items of specified property, Item 1 and Item 2, to CFC2 in exchange for $150x of cash (the "Disqualified Transfer"). Item 1 is sold for $90x and Item 2 is sold for $60x. Item 1 and Item 2 each has a basis of $0 in the hands of CFC1 immediately before the Disqualified Transfer, and therefore CFC1 recognizes $150x of gain as a result of the Disqualified Transfer ($150x - $0). After the Disqualified Transfer, CFC2's only assets are Item 1 and Item 2. On November 30, 2018, and thus during US1's taxable year ending December 31, 2018, CFC1 distributes $150x of cash to US1, and all of the distribution is characterized as a dividend under section 301(c)(1) and treated as a distribution out of earnings and profits described in section 959(c)(3). For CFC1's taxable year ending on November 30, 2018, CFC1 has $160x of earnings and profits described in section 959(c)(3), without regard to any distributions during the taxable year. CFC2 continues to hold Item 1 and Item 2. Lastly, because the conditions of § 1.245A-6(b)(1) and (2) are satisfied for US1's 2018 taxable year, US1 chooses to apply § 1.245A-7 (rules for simple cases) in lieu of § 1.245A-8 (rules for complex cases) for that taxable year.

(ii) *Analysis*—(A) *Application of § § 1.245A-5 and 1.951A-2 as a result of the Disqualified Transfer.* As a result of the Disqualified Transfer, under § 1.951A-2(c)(5), Item 1 has disqualified basis of $90x, and Item 2 has disqualified basis of $60x. In addition, as a result of the Disqualified Transfer, under § 1.245A-5(c)(3)(i)(A), US1 has an extraordinary disposition account with respect to CFC1 with an initial balance of $150x. Under § 1.245A-5(c)(2)(i), $10x of the dividend is considered paid out of non-extraordinary disposition E&P of CFC1 with respect to US1, and $140x of the dividend is considered paid out of US1's extraordinary disposition account with respect to CFC1 to the extent of the balance of the extraordinary disposition account ($150x). Thus, the dividend of $150x is an extraordinary disposition amount, within the meaning of § 1.245A-5(c)(1), to the extent of $140x. As a result, the balance of the extraordinary disposition account is reduced to $10x ($150x - $140x).

(B) *Correspondence requirement.* Under § 1.245A-9(b)(1), each of Item 1 and Item 2 corresponds to US1's extraordinary disposition account with respect to CFC1, because as a result of the Disqualified Transfer CFC1 recognized gain with respect to Item 1 and Item 2, and the gain was taken into account in determining the initial balance of US1's extraordinary disposition account with respect to CFC1.

(C) *Reduction of disqualified basis of Item 1.* Because Item 1 corresponds to US1's extraordinary disposition account, the disqualified basis of Item 1 is reduced pursuant to § 1.245A-7(b)(1) by reason of US1's $140x extraordinary disposition amount for US1's 2018 taxable year. Paragraphs (c)(2)(ii)(C)(*1*) through (*3*) of this section describe the determinations pursuant to § 1.245A-7(b)(1).

(*1*) To determine the reduction to the disqualified basis of Item 1, the disqualified basis of Item 1, as well as the disqualified basis of Item 2, must be determined as of the date described in § 1.245A-9(b)(2)(i) (and before the application of § 1.245A-7(b)(1)). *See* § 1.245A-7(b)(1)(ii). For each of Item 1 and Item 2, that date is December 1, 2018. December 1, 2018, is the first day of the taxable year of CFC2 (the CFC that holds Item 1 and Item 2) beginning on December 1, 2018, which is the taxable year of CFC2 that includes December 31, 2018, the date on which US1's 2018 taxable year ends. *See* § 1.245A-9(b)(2)(i).

(*2*) Pursuant to § 1.245A-7(b)(1), the disqualified basis of Item 1 is reduced by $84x, computed as the product of—

(*i*) $140x, the extraordinary disposition amount; and

(*ii*) A fraction, the numerator of which is $90x (the disqualified basis of Item 1 on December 1, 2018, and before the application of § 1.245A-7(b)(1)), and the denominator of which is $150x (the disqualified basis of Item 1, $90x, plus the disqualified basis of Item 2, $60x, in each case determined on December 1, 2018, and before the application of § 1.245A-7(b)(1)). *See* § 1.245A-7(b)(1).

(*3*) The $84x reduction to the disqualified basis of Item 1 occurs on December 1, 2018, the date on which the disqualified basis of Item 1 is determined for purposes of determining the reduction pursuant to § 1.245A-7(b)(1). *See* § 1.245A-9(b)(2)(ii).

(D) *Reduction of disqualified basis of Item 2.* For reasons similar to those described in paragraph (c)(2)(ii)(C) of this section, on December 1, 2018, the disqualified basis of Item 2 is reduced by $56x, the amount equal to the product of $140x, the extraordinary disposition amount, and a fraction, the numerator of which is $60x (the disqualified basis of Item 2 on December 1, 2018, and before the application of § 1.245A-7(b)(1)), and the denominator of which is $150x (the disqualified basis of Item 1, $90x, plus the disqualified basis of Item 2, $60x, in each case determined on December 1, 2018, and before the application of § 1.245A-7(b)(1)).

(2) *Example 2. Basis benefit amount and impact on reduction to disqualified basis under rule for complex cases.*—(i) *Facts.* The facts are the same as in paragraph (c)(1)(i) of this section *(Example 1)* (and the results are the same as in paragraph (c)(1)(ii)(A) of this section), except that, on December 1, 2018, CFC2 sells Item 1 for $90x of cash to an individual that is not a related party with respect to US1 or CFC2 (such transaction, the "Sale," and such individual, "Individual A"). At the time of the Sale, CFC2's basis in Item 1 is $90x (all of which is disqualified basis, as described in § 1.951A-3(h)(2)(ii)(A)). CFC2 takes into the account the disqualified basis of Item 1 for purposes of determining the amount of gain recognized on the Sale, which is $0 ($90x - $90x); but for the disqualified basis, CFC2 would have had $90x of gain that would have been taken into account in computing its tested income. As a result of the Sale, the condition of § 1.245A-6(b)(2) is not satisfied, because on at least one day of CFC2's taxable year beginning on December 1, 2018 (which begins within US1's 2018 taxable year) CFC2 does not hold Item 1. *See* § 1.245A-6(b)(2)(ii)(C)(*1*). US1 therefore applies § 1.245A-8 (rules for complex cases) for its 2018 taxable year. *See* § 1.245A-6(b).

(ii) *Analysis*—(A) *Ownership requirement.* With respect to each of Item 1 and Item 2, the ownership requirement of § 1.245A-8(b)(3)(i) is satisfied for US1's 2018 taxable year. This is because on at least one day that falls within US1's 2018 taxable year, each of Item 1 and Item 2 is held by CFC2, and US1 directly owns all of the stock of CFC2 throughout such taxable year (and thus, for purposes of applying § 1.245A-8(b)(3)(i), US1 owns at least 10% of the interests of CFC2 on at least one day that falls within such taxable year). *See* § 1.245A-8(b)(3).

(B) *Basis benefit amount with respect to Item 1 as a result of the Sale.* Under § 1.245A-8(b)(4)(i), US1 has a basis benefit account with respect to its extraordinary disposition account with respect to CFC1. As described in paragraphs (c)(2)(ii)(B)(*1*) through (3) of this section, the balance of the basis benefit account (which is initially zero) is, on December 31, 2018, increased by $90x, the basis benefit amount with respect to Item 1 and assigned to US1's 2018 taxable year.

(*1*) By reason of the Sale, for CFC2's taxable year beginning December 1, 2018, and ending November 30, 2019, the entire $90x of disqualified basis of Item 1 is taken into account for U.S. tax purposes by CFC2 and, as a result, reduces CFC2's tested income or increases CFC2's tested loss. Accordingly, for such taxable year, there is a $90x basis benefit amount with respect to Item 1. *See* § 1.245A-8(b)(4)(ii)(A). The result would be the same if the Sale were to a related person and thus, pursuant to § 1.951A-3(h)(2)(ii)(B)(*1*)(*ii*), no portion of the $90x of disqualified basis were eliminated or reduced by reason of the Sale. *See* § 1.245A-8(b)(4)(ii)(B).

(*2*) The $90x basis benefit amount with respect to Item 1 is assigned to US1's 2018 taxable year. This is because the ownership requirement of § 1.245A-8(b)(3)(i) is satisfied with respect to Item 1 for US1's 2018 taxable year, and the basis benefit amount occurs in CFC2's taxable year beginning December 1, 2018, a taxable year of CFC2 that begins within US1's 2018 taxable year (and, but for § 1.245A-8(b)(4)(iii)(A)(2)(*ii*), the basis benefit amount would not be assigned to a taxable year of US1, such as the taxable year of US1 beginning January 1, 2019, given that, as result of the Sale, the ownership requirement of § 1.245A-8(b)(3)(i) would not be satisfied with respect to Item 1 for such taxable year). *See* § 1.245A-8(b)(4)(iii)(A).

(*3*) On December 31, 2018 (the last day of US1's 2018 taxable year), US1's basis benefit account with respect to its extraordinary disposition account with respect to CFC1 is increased by $90x, the $90x basis benefit amount with respect to Item 1 and assigned to US1's 2018 taxable year. The basis benefit account is increased by such amount because Item 1 corresponds to US1's extraordinary disposition account with respect to CFC1, and the extraordinary disposition ownership percentage applicable to such extraordinary disposition account is 100. *See* § 1.245A-8(b)(4)(i)(A).

(C) *Basis benefit amount limitation on reduction to disqualified basis.* By reason of US1's $140x extraordinary disposition amount for US1's 2018 taxable year, the disqualified basis of Item 1 is reduced by $30x, and the disqualified basis of Item 2 is reduced by $20x, pursuant to § 1.245A-8(b)(1). *See* § 1.245A-8(b). Paragraphs (c)(2)(ii)(C)(*1*) through (*4*) of this section describe the determinations pursuant to § 1.245A-8(b)(1).

(*1*) For purposes of determining the reduction to the disqualified bases of Item 1 and Item 2, the disqualified bases of the Items are determined on December 1, 2018 (and before the application of § 1.245A-8(b)(1)). *See* § 1.245A-8(b)(1)(ii). The disqualified bases of the Items are determined on December 1, 2018, because that date is the first day of the taxable year of CFC2 beginning on December 1, 2018, which is the taxable year of CFC2 (the specified property owner of each of Item 1 and Item 2) that includes December 31, 2018, the date on which US1's 2018 taxable year ends. *See* § 1.245A-8(b)(2)(i). For purposes of applying §§ 1.245A-8(b)(1) and § 1.245A-9(b)(2) for US1's 2018 taxable year, CFC2 is the specified property owner of each of Item 1 and Item 2 because, on at least one day of CFC2's taxable year that includes the date on which US1's 2018 taxable year ends (that is, on at least one day of CFC2's taxable year beginning December 1, 2018), CFC2 held the Item. *See* § 1.245A-9(b)(2)(iii). CFC2 is the specified property owner of Item 1 even though Individual A also held Item 1 during Individual A's taxable year that includes the date on which US1's 2018 taxable year ends because CFC2 held Item 1 on an earlier date than Individual A. *See* § 1.245A-9(b)(2)(iii).

(*2*) Pursuant to § 1.245A-8(b)(1), the disqualified basis of Item 1 is reduced by $30x, computed as the product of—

(*i*) $50x, the excess of the extraordinary disposition amount ($140x) over the balance of the basis benefit account with respect to US1's extraordinary disposition with respect to CFC1 ($90x); and

(*ii*) A fraction, the numerator of which is $90x (the disqualified basis of Item 1 on December 1, 2018, and before the application of § 1.245A-8(b)(1)), and the denominator of which is $150x (the disqualified basis of Item 1, $90x, plus the disqualified basis of Item 2, $60x, in each case determined on December 1, 2018, and before the application of § 1.245A-8(b)(1)). *See* paragraph § 1.245A-8(b)(1).

(*3*) Pursuant to § 1.245A-8(b)(1), the disqualified basis of Item 2 is reduced by $20x, computed as the product of—

(*i*) $50x, the excess of the extraordinary disposition amount ($140x) over the balance of the basis benefit account with respect to US1's extraordinary disposition with respect to CFC1 ($90x); and

(*ii*) A fraction, the numerator of which is $60x (the disqualified basis of Item 2 on December 1, 2018, and before the application of paragraph (b)(1) of this section), and the denominator of which is $150x (the disqualified basis of Item 1, $90x, plus the disqualified basis of Item 2, $60x, in each case determined on December 1, 2018, and before the application of § 1.245A-8(b)(1)). *See* § 1.245A-8(b)(1).

(*4*) The $30x and $20x reductions to the disqualified bases of Item 1 and Item 2, respectively, occur on December 1, 2018, the date on which the disqualified bases of the Items are determined for purposes of determining the reductions pursuant to § 1.245A-8(b)(1). *See* § 1.245A-9(b)(2)(ii).

(D) *Reduction of basis benefit account.* The balance of the basis benefit account with respect to US1's extraordinary disposition account with respect to CFC1 is decreased by $90x, the amount by which, for CFC2's taxable year beginning December 1, 2018, the disqualified bases of Item 1 and Item 2 would have been reduced pursuant to § 1.245A-8(b)(1) but for the $90x balance of the basis benefit account. *See* § 1.245A-8(b)(4)(i)(B). The reduction to the balance of the basis benefit account occurs on December 31, 2018, and after the completion of all other computations pursuant to § 1.245A-8(b). *See* § 1.245A-8(b)(4)(i)(B).

(3) *Example 3. Reduction in balance of extraordinary disposition account under rules for simple cases by reason of allocation and apportionment of deductions to residual CFC gross income.*—(i) *Facts.* The facts are the same as in paragraph (c)(1)(i) of this section *(Example 1)* (and the results are the same as in paragraph (c)(1)(ii)(A) of this section), except that CFC1 does not make a distribution to US1. In addition, during CFC2's taxable year beginning December 1, 2018, and ending November 30, 2019, the disqualified basis of Item 1 gives rise to a $6x amortization deduction, and the disqualified basis of Item 2 gives rise to a $4x amortization deduction, and each of the amortization deductions is allocated and apportioned to residual CFC gross income of CFC2 solely by reason of § 1.951A-2(c)(5) (though, but for § 1.951A-2(c)(5), would have been allocated and apportioned to gross tested income of CFC2). Further, as of the end of CFC2's taxable year ending November 30, 2019, CFC2 has $15x of earnings and profits. Lastly, because the conditions of § 1.245A-6(b)(1) and (2) are satisfied for US1's 2018 taxable year, US1 chooses to apply § 1.245A-7 (rules for simple cases) in lieu of § 1.245A-8 (rules for complex cases) for that taxable year.

(ii) *Analysis.* Pursuant to § 1.245A-7(c)(1), US1's extraordinary disposition account with respect to CFC1 is reduced by the lesser of the amount described in § 1.245A-7(c)(1)(i) with respect to US1, and the RGI account of US1 with respect to CFC2 that relates to its extraordinary disposition account with respect to CFC1. *See* § 1.245A-7(c)(1). Paragraphs (c)(3)(ii)(A) through (D) of this section describe the determinations pursuant to § 1.245A-8(c)(1).

(A) *Computation of adjusted earnings of CFC2, and amount described in § 1.245A-7(c)(1)(i) with respect to US1.* To determine the amount described in § 1.245A-7(c)(1)(i) with respect to US1, the adjusted earnings of CFC2 must be computed for CFC2's taxable year ending November 30, 2019. *See* § 1.245A-7(c)(1)(i). Paragraphs (c)(3)(ii)(A)(*1*) and (*2*) of this section describe these determinations.

(*1*) The adjusted earnings of CFC2 for its taxable year ending November 30, 2019, is $25x, computed as $15x (CFC2's earnings and profits as of November 30, 2019, the last day of that taxable year), plus $10x (the sum of the $6x and $4x amortization deductions of CFC2 for that taxable year, which is the amount of all deductions or losses of CFC2 that is or was attributable to disqualified basis of items of specified property and allocated and apportioned to residual CFC gross income of CFC2 solely by reason of § 1.951A-2(c)(5)(i)). *See* § 1.245A-7(c)(3).

(*2*) For CFC2's taxable year ending November 30, 2019, the amount described in § 1.245A-7(c)(1)(i) with respect to US1 is $25x, computed as the excess of $25x (the adjusted earnings) over $0 (the sum of the balance of the previously taxed earnings and profits accounts with respect to CFC2).

(B) *Increase to balance of RGI account.* Under § 1.245A-9(d)(11), US1 has an RGI account with respect to CFC2 that relates to its extraordinary disposition account with respect to CFC1. On November 30, 2019 (the last day of CFC2's taxable year), the balance of the RGI account (which is initially zero) is increased by $10x, the sum of the $6x and $4x amortization deductions of CFC2 for its taxable year ending November 30, 2019. *See* § 1.245A-7(c)(4)(i). Each of the amortization deductions is taken into account for this purpose because, but for § 1.951A-2(c)(5)(i), the deduction would have decreased CFC2's tested income or increased or given rise to a tested loss of CFC2. *See* § 1.245A-7(c)(4)(i).

(C) *Reduction in balance of extraordinary disposition account.* Pursuant to § 1.245A-7(c)(1), US1's extraordinary disposition account with respect to CFC1 is reduced by $10x, the lesser of the amount described in § 1.245A-7(c)(1)(i) with respect to US1 for CFC2's taxable year ending November 30, 2019 ($25x), and the balance of US1's RGI account with respect to CFC2 that relates to its extraordinary disposition account with respect to CFC1 ($10x, determined as of November 30, 2019, but without regard to the application of § 1.245A-7(c)(4)(ii) for the taxable year of CFC2 ending on that date). *See* § 1.245A-7(c)(1). The $10x reduction in the balance of US1's extraordinary disposition account occurs on December 31, 2019, the last day of US1's taxable year that includes November 30, 2019 (the last day of CFC2's taxable year). *See* § 1.245A-9(c)(3).

(D) *Reduction in balance of RGI account*. On November 30, 2019 (the last day of CFC2's taxable year), the balance of US1's RGI account with respect to CFC2 that relates to its extraordinary disposition account with respect to CFC1 is decreased by $10x, the amount of the reduction, pursuant to § 1.245A-7(c)(1) section and by reason of the RGI account, to US1's extraordinary disposition account with respect to CFC1. *See* § 1.245A-7(c)(4)(ii). Therefore, following that reduction, the balance of the RGI account is zero ($10x - $10x).

(iii) *Alternative facts in which the reduction is limited by earnings and profits*. The facts are the same as in paragraph (c)(3)(i) of this section (*Example 3*), except that CFC2 has a $5x deficit in its earnings and profits as of the end of its taxable year ending November 30, 2019. In this case—

(A) The adjusted earnings of CFC2 for its taxable year ending November 30, 2019, is $5x, computed as -$5x (CFC2's deficit in earnings and profits as of November 30, 2019) plus $10x (the sum of the $6x and $4x amortization deductions of CFC2), *see* § 1.245A-7(c)(3);

(B) The amount described in § 1.245A-7(c)(1)(i) with respect to US1 for CFC's taxable year ending November 30, 2019, is $5x, computed as the excess of $5x (the adjusted earnings) over $0 (the sum of the balance of the previously taxed earnings and profits accounts with respect to CFC2), *see* § 1.245A-7(c)(1)(i);

(C) On December 31, 2019, US1's extraordinary disposition account with respect to CFC1 is reduced by $5x, the lesser of the amount described in § 1.245A-7(c)(1)(i) with respect to US1 for CFC2's taxable year ending November 30, 2019 ($5x), and the balance of US1's RGI account with respect to CFC2 that relates to its extraordinary disposition account with respect to CFC1 ($10x, determined as of November 30, 2019, but without regard to the application of § 1.245A-8(c)(4)(i)(B) for the taxable year of CFC2 ending on that date), *see* §§ 1.245A-7(c)(1) and 1.245A-9(c)(3); and

(D) On November 30, 2019 (the last day of CFC2's taxable year), the balance of US1's RGI account with respect to CFC2 is decreased by $5x (the amount of the reduction, pursuant to § 1.245A-7(c)(1) and by reason of the RGI account, to US1's extraordinary disposition account with respect to CFC1) and, therefore, following such reduction, the balance of the RGI account is $5x ($10x - $5x), *see* § 1.245A-7(c)(4)(ii).

(4) *Example 4. Reduction to extraordinary disposition accounts limited by § 1.245A-8(c)(6)*.—(i) *Facts*. The facts are the same as in paragraph (c)(3)(iii) of this section (*Example 3*, alternative facts in which the reduction is limited by earnings and profits) (and the results are the same as in paragraph (c)(1)(ii)(A) of this section), except that US1 also owns 100% of the stock of US2, which owns 100% of the stock of CFC3, and on November 30, 2018, in a transaction that was an extraordinary disposition, CFC3 sold an item of specified property ("Item 3") to CFC2 in exchange for $200x of cash. Item 3 had a basis of $0 in the hands of CFC3 immediately before the sale and, therefore, CFC3 recognized $200x of gain as a result of the sale ($200x - $0), Item 3 has $200x of disqualified basis under § 1.951A-2(c)(5), and US2 has an extraordinary disposition account with respect to CFC3 with an initial balance of $200x under § 1.245A-5(c)(3)(i)(A). Moreover, during CFC2's taxable year beginning December 1, 2018, and ending November 30, 2019, the disqualified basis of Item 3 gives rise to a $20x amortization deduction, which is allocated and apportioned to residual CFC gross income of CFC2 solely by reason of § 1.951A-2(c)(5) (though, but for § 1.951A-2(c)(5), would have been allocated and apportioned to gross tested income of CFC2). Further, as of the end of US1's 2018 taxable year, the balance of US1's basis benefit account with respect to its extraordinary disposition account with respect to CFC1 is $0; similarly, as of the end of US2's 2018 taxable year, the balance of US2's basis benefit account with respect to its extraordinary disposition account with respect to CFC2 is $0. Because CFC2 holds items of specified property that correspond to more than one extraordinary disposition account (that is, Item 1 and Item 2 correspond to US1's extraordinary disposition account with respect to CFC2, and Item 3 corresponds to US2's extraordinary disposition account with respect to CFC2), the condition of § 1.245A-6(b)(2) is not satisfied. *See* § 1.245A-6(b)(2)(ii)(C)(*3*). US1 and US2 therefore apply § 1.245A-8 (rules for complex cases) for their 2018 taxable years.

(ii) *Analysis*. Pursuant to § 1.245A-8(c)(1), US1's extraordinary disposition account with respect to CFC1 is, subject to the limitation in § 1.245A-8(c)(6), reduced by the lesser of the amount described in § 1.245A-8(c)(1)(i) with respect to US1, and the RGI account of US1 with respect to CFC2 that relates to its extraordinary disposition account with respect to CFC1. *See* § 1.245A-8(c)(1). Similarly, US2's extraordinary disposition account with respect to CFC3 is, subject to the limitation in § 1.245A-8(c)(6), reduced by the lesser of the amount described in § 1.245A-8(c)(1)(i) with respect to US2, and the RGI account of US2 with respect to CFC2 that relates to its extraordinary disposition account with respect to CFC3. *See* § 1.245A-8(c)(1). Paragraphs (c)(4)(ii)(A) through (F) of this section describe the determinations pursuant to § 1.245A-8(c)(1).

(A) *Ownership requirement*. Each of US1 and US2 satisfy the ownership requirement of § 1.245A-8(c)(5) for CFC2's taxable year ending November 30, 2019, because on the last day of that taxable year each is a United States shareholder with respect to CFC2. *See* § 1.245A-8(c)(5).

(B) *Computation of adjusted earnings of CFC2, and amount described in § 1.245A-8(c)(1)(i) with respect to US1 and US2*. The adjusted earnings of CFC2 for its taxable year ending November 30, 2019, is $25x, computed as -$5x (CFC2's deficit in earnings and profits as of November 30, 2019), plus $30x (the sum of the $6x, $4x, and $20x amortization deductions of CFC2). *See* § 1.245A-8(c)(3). For CFC2's taxable year ending November 30, 2019, the amount described in § 1.245A-8(c)(1)(i) with respect to US1 is $25x, computed as the excess of the product of $25x (the adjusted earnings) and 100% (the percentage of the stock of CFC2 that US1 and its domestic affiliate, US2, own), over $0 (the sum of the balance of certain previously taxed earnings and profits accounts and hybrid deduction accounts). *See* § 1.245A-8(c)(1)(i). Similarly, for CFC2's taxable year ending November 30, 2019, the amount described in § 1.245A-8(c)(1)(i) with respect to US2 is $25x, computed as the excess of the product of $25x (the adjusted earnings) and 100% (the percentage of the stock of CFC2 that US2 and its domestic affiliate, US1, own), over $0 (the sum of the balance of certain previously taxed earnings and profits accounts and hybrid deduction accounts). *See* § 1.245A-8(c)(1)(i).

(C) *Increase to balance of RGI account*. As described in paragraph (c)(3)(ii)(B) of this section, US1 has an RGI account with respect to CFC2 that relates to its extraordinary disposition account with respect to CFC1, and the balance of the RGI account is $10x on November 30, 2019 (the last day of CFC2's taxable year). Similarly, US2 has an RGI account with respect to CFC2 that relates to its extraordinary disposition account with respect to CFC3, and the balance of the RGI account is $20x on November 30, 2019 (reflecting a $20x increase to the balance of the account for the $20x amortization deduction of CFC2 for its taxable year ending November 30, 2019). *See* § 1.245A-8(c)(4)(i).

(D) *Reduction in balance of extraordinary disposition accounts but for § 1.245A-8(c)(6)*. But for the application of § 1.245A-8(c)(6), US1's extraordinary disposition account with respect to CFC2 would be reduced by $10x, which is the lesser of $25x, the amount described in § 1.245A-8(c)(1)(i) with respect to US1 for CFC2's taxable year ending November 30, 2019, and $10x, the balance of the RGI account of US1 with respect to CFC2 that relates to its extraordinary disposition account with respect to CFC1 (determined as of November 30, 2019, but without regard to the application of § 1.245A-8(c)(4)(i)(B) for the taxable year of CFC2 ending on that date). *See* § 1.245A-8(c)(1)(i) and (ii). Similarly, but for the application of § 1.245A-8(c)(6), US2's extraordinary disposition account with respect to CFC3 would be reduced by $20x, which is the lesser of $25x, the amount described in § 1.245A-8(c)(1)(i) with respect to US2 for CFC2's taxable year ending November 30, 2019, and $20x, the balance of the RGI account of US2 with respect to CFC2 that relates to its extraordinary disposition account with respect to CFC3 (determined as of November 30, 2019, but without regard to the application of § 1.245A-8(c)(4)(i)(B) for the taxable year of CFC2 ending on that date). *See* § 1.245A-8(c)(1)(i) and (ii).

(E) *Application of limitation of § 1.245A-8(c)(6)*. As described in paragraph (c)(4)(ii)(D) of this section, but for the application of § 1.245A-8(c)(6), there would be a total of $30x of reductions to US1's extraordinary disposition account with respect to CFC1, and US2's extraordinary disposition account with respect to CFC3, by reason of the application of § 1.245A-8(c)(1) with respect to CFC2's taxable year ending November 30, 2019. Because that $30x exceeds the amount described in § 1.245A-8(c)(1)(i) with respect to US1 and US2 ($25x)—

(*1*) US1's extraordinary disposition account with respect to CFC1 is reduced by $7.86x, computed as $10x (the reduction that would occur but for § 1.245A-8(c)(6)) less the product of $5x (the excess amount, computed as $30x, the total reductions that would occur but for the application of § 1.245A-8(c)(6), less $25x, the amount described in § 1.245A-8(c)(1)(i)) and a fraction, the numerator of which is $150x (the balance of US1's extraordinary disposition account with respect to CFC1) and the denominator of which is $350x ($150x, the balance of US1's extraordinary disposition account with respect to CFC1, plus $200x, the balance of US2's extraordinary disposition account with respect to CFC3), *see* § 1.245A-8(c)(6); and

(2) US2's extraordinary disposition account with respect to CFC3 is reduced by $17.14x, computed as $20x (the reduction that would occur but for § 1.245A-8(c)(6)) less the product of $5x (the excess amount, computed as $30x, the total reductions that would occur but for the application of § 1.245A-8(c)(6), less $25x, the amount described in § 1.245A-8(c)(1)(i)) and a fraction, the numerator of which is $200x (the balance of US2's extraordinary disposition account with respect to CFC3) and the denominator of which is $350x ($150x, the balance of US1's extraordinary disposition account with respect to CFC1, plus $200x, the balance of US2's extraordinary disposition account with respect to CFC3), *see* § 1.245A-8(c)(6) of this section.

(F) *Reduction in balance of RGI accounts.* On November 30, 2019 (the last day of CFC2's taxable year)—

(*1*) The balance of US1's RGI account with respect to CFC2 that relates to its extraordinary disposition account with respect to CFC1 is decreased by $7.86x (the amount of the reduction, pursuant to § 1.245A-8(c)(1) and by reason of the RGI account, to US1's extraordinary disposition account with respect to CFC1) and, thus, following that reduction, the balance of the RGI account is $2.14x ($10x - $7.86x), *see* § 1.245A-8(c)(4)(i)(B); and

(*2*) The balance of US2's RGI account with respect to CFC2 that relates to its extraordinary disposition account with respect to CFC3 is decreased by $17.14x (the amount of the reduction, pursuant to § 1.245A-8(c)(1) and by reason of the RGI account, to US2's extraordinary disposition account with respect to CFC3) and, thus, following that reduction, the balance of the RGI account is $2.86x ($20x - $17.14x), *see* § 1.245A-8(c)(4)(i)(B).

(5) *Example 5. Computation of duplicate DQB.*—(i) *Facts.* The facts are the same as in paragraph (c)(1)(i) of this section *(Example 1)* (and the results are the same as in paragraph (c)(1)(ii)(A) of this section), except that CFC1 does not make any distribution to US1, and on November 30, 2018, immediately after the Disqualified Transfer, CFC2 transfers Item 1 to newly-formed CFC3 solely in exchange for the sole share of stock of CFC3 (the contribution, "Contribution 1," and the share of stock of CFC3, the "CFC3 Share") and, immediately after Contribution 1, CFC3 transfers Item 1 to newly-formed CFC4 solely in exchange for the sole share of stock of CFC4 (the contribution, "Contribution 2," and the share of stock of CFC4, the "CFC4 Share"). Pursuant to section 358(a)(1), CFC2's basis in its share of stock of CFC3 is $90x, and CFC3's basis in its share of stock of CFC4 is $90x basis. As a result of Contribution 1, the condition of § 1.245A-6(b)(2) is not satisfied, because on at least one day of CFC2's taxable year ending on November 30, 2018 (which ends within US1's 2018 taxable year), CFC2 does not hold Item 1. *See* § 1.245A-6(b)(2)(ii)(C)(*1*). US1 therefore applies § 1.245A-8 (rules for complex cases) for its 2018 taxable year. *See* § 1.245A-6(b).

(ii) *Analysis*—(A) *Application of exchanged basis rule under section 951A to Contribution 1 and Contribution 2.* As a result of Contribution 1, pursuant to § 1.951A-3(h)(2)(ii)(B)(*2*)(*ii*), the disqualified basis of CFC3 Share includes the disqualified basis of Item 1 ($90x), and therefore the disqualified basis of CFC3 Share is $90x. Similarly, as a result of Contribution 2, pursuant to § 1.951A-3(h)(2)(ii)(B)(*2*)(*ii*), the disqualified basis of CFC4 Share also includes the disqualified basis of Item 1 ($90x), and therefore the disqualified basis of CFC4 Share is $90x.

(B) *Determination of duplicate DQB of CFC3 Share as a result of Contribution 1.* Because the disqualified basis of CFC3 Share includes the disqualified basis of Item 1, CFC3 Share is an item of exchanged basis property that relates to Item 1. *See* § 1.245A-8(d)(2)(ii). In addition, because CFC3 Share is an item of exchanged basis property that relates to Item 1 (which corresponds to US1's extraordinary disposition account with respect to CFC1), CFC3 Share is, for purposes of § 1.245A-8, treated as an item of specified property that corresponds to US1's extraordinary disposition account with respect to CFC1. *See* § 1.245A-8(d)(2)(i). Further, the duplicate DQB of CFC3 Share as to Item 1 is $90x, the portion of the disqualified basis of CFC3 Share that includes Item 1's disqualified basis of $90x. *See* § 1.245A-8(d)(2)(iii)(A).

(C) *Determination of duplicate DQB of CFC4 Share as a result of Contribution 2.* For reasons similar to those described in paragraph (c)(5)(ii)(B) of this section, CFC4 Share is an item of exchanged basis property that relates to Item 1, CFC4 is treated for purposes of § 1.245A-8 as an item of specified property that corresponds to US1's extraordinary disposition account with respect to CFC1, and the duplicate DQB of CFC4 Share as to Item 1 is $90x.

(D) *Determination of duplicate DQB of CFC3 Share as a result of Contribution 2.* Because the disqualified basis of CFC3 Share and the disqualified basis of CFC4 Share each includes $90x of the disqualified basis of Item 1 and CFC3 receives the CFC4 Share in Contribution 2, the $90x of disqualified basis of CFC3 Share is attributable to the $90x of disqualified basis of CFC4 Share, and CFC3 Share is an item of exchanged basis property that relates to CFC4 Share. *See* § 1.245A-8(d)(2)(i) and (d)(2)(iii)(C). In addition, the duplicate DQB of CFC3 Share as to CFC4 Share is $90x. *See* § 1.245A-8(d)(2)(iii)(A).

(E) *Application of duplicate basis rules in § 1.245A-8(b)(5).* For purposes of computing the fraction described in § 1.245A-8(b)(1)(ii), if US1's extraordinary disposition account with respect to CFC1 were to give rise to an extraordinary disposition amount or a tiered extraordinary disposition amount during US1's 2018 taxable year, then the duplicate DQB of CFC3 Share and the duplicate DQB of CFC4 Share would not be taken into account, because the disqualified basis of Item 1 (an item of specified property that corresponds to US1's extraordinary disposition account and as to which each of CFC3 Share and CFC4 share relates) would be taken into account. *See* § 1.245A-8(b)(1)(ii) and (b)(5)(i)(A). Accordingly, in such a case, for US1's 2018 taxable year, the numerator of the fraction described in § 1.245A-8(b)(1)(ii) would reflect only the disqualified basis of Item 1 or Item 2, as applicable, and the denominator would reflect only the sum of the disqualified basis of each of Item 1 and Item 2. *See* § 1.245A-8(b)(1)(ii) and (b)(5)(i)(A). Furthermore, to the extent there were to be a reduction under § 1.245A-8(b)(1) to the disqualified basis of Item 1, then the duplicate DQB of CFC4 Share would be reduced (but not below zero) by the product of the reduction to the disqualified basis of Item 1 and a fraction, the numerator of which would be $90x (the duplicate DQB of CFC4 Share), and the denominator of which would also be $90x (the duplicate DQB of CFC4 Share). *See* § 1.245A-8(b)(5)(i)(B). The $90x of duplicate DQB of CFC3 Share would be excluded from the denominator of the fraction described in the previous sentence because it is attributable to the $90x of duplicate DQB of CFC4 Share. *See* § 1.245A-8(b)(5)(i)(B)(*2*) (last sentence). For reasons similar to those described in this paragraph (c)(4)(ii)(E) with respect to the application of § 1.245A-8(b)(5)(i)(B) to CFC4 Share, the duplicate DQB of CFC3 Share would be reduced (but not below zero) by the product of the reduction to the disqualified basis of Item 1 and a fraction, the numerator of which would be $90x, and the denominator of which would also be $90x. [Reg. § 1.245A-10.]

☐ [*T.D. 9934, 11-25-2020.*]

§ 1.245A-11. Applicability dates.—(a) *In general.*—Sections 1.245A-6 through 1.245A-11 apply to taxable years of a foreign corporation beginning on or after December 1, 2020 and to taxable years of section 245A shareholders in which or with which such taxable years end.

(b) *Exception.*—Notwithstanding paragraph (a) of this section, a taxpayer may choose to apply §§ 1.245A-6 through 1.245A-11 for a taxable year of a foreign corporation beginning before December 1, 2020 and to a taxable year of a section 245A shareholder in which or with which such taxable year ends, provided that the taxpayer and all persons bearing a relationship to the taxpayer described in section 267(b) or 707(b) apply §§ 1.245A-6 through 1.245A-11, in their entirety, and § 1.6038-2(f)(18) for all such taxable years and any subsequent taxable years beginning before December 1, 2020. [Reg. § 1.245A-11.]

☐ [*T.D. 9934, 11-25-2020.*]

§ 1.245A(d)-1. Disallowance of foreign tax credit or deduction.—(a) *No foreign tax credit or deduction allowed under section 245A(d).*—(1) *Foreign income taxes paid or accrued by domestic corporations or successors.*—No credit under section 901 or deduction is allowed in any taxable year for:

(i) Foreign income taxes paid or accrued by a domestic corporation that are attributable to section 245A(d) income of the domestic corporation;

(ii) Foreign income taxes paid or accrued by a successor to a domestic corporation that are attributable to section 245A(d) income of the successor; and

(iii) Foreign income taxes paid or accrued by a domestic corporation that is a United States shareholder of a foreign corporation, other than a foreign corporation that is a passive foreign investment company (as defined in section 1297) with respect to the domestic corporation and that is not a controlled foreign corporation, that are attributable to non-inclusion income of the foreign corporation and are not otherwise disallowed under paragraph (a)(1)(i) or (ii) of this section.

(2) *Foreign income taxes paid or accrued by foreign corporations.*—No credit under section 901 or deduction is allowed in any taxable year for foreign income taxes paid or accrued by a foreign corporation that are attributable to section 245A(d) income, and such taxes are not eligible to be deemed paid under section 960 in any taxable year.

(3) *Effect of disallowance on earnings and profits.*—The disallowance of a credit or deduction for foreign income taxes under this paragraph (a) does not affect whether the foreign income taxes reduce earnings and profits of a corporation.

(b) *Attribution of foreign income taxes.*—(1) *Section 245A(d) income.*—Foreign income taxes are attributable to section 245A(d) income to the extent that the foreign income taxes are allocated and apportioned under § 1.861-20 to the section 245A(d) income group. For purposes of this paragraph (b)(1), § 1.861-20 is applied by treating the section 245A(d) income group in each section 904 category of a domestic corporation, successor, or foreign corporation as a statutory grouping and treating all other income, including the receipt of a distribution of previously taxed earnings and profits other than section 245A(d) PTEP, as income in the residual grouping. See § 1.861-20(d)(2) through (3) for rules regarding the allocation and apportionment of foreign income taxes to the statutory and residual groupings if the taxpayer does not realize, recognize, or take into account a corresponding U.S. item in the U.S. taxable year in which the foreign income taxes are paid or accrued. In the case of a foreign law distribution or foreign law disposition, a corresponding U.S. item is assigned to the statutory and residual groupings under § 1.861-20(d)(2)(ii)(B) and (C) without regard to the application of section 246(c), the holding periods described in sections 964(e)(4)(A) and 1248(j), and § 1.245A-5.

(2) *Non-inclusion income of a foreign corporation.*—(i) *Scope.*—This paragraph (b)(2) provides rules for attributing foreign income taxes paid or accrued by a domestic corporation that is a United States shareholder of a foreign corporation to non-inclusion income of the foreign corporation. It applies only in cases in which the foreign income taxes are allocated and apportioned under § 1.861-20 by reference to the characterization of the tax book value of stock, whether the stock is held directly or indirectly through a partnership or other passthrough entity, for purposes of allocating and apportioning the domestic corporation's interest expense, or by reference to the income of a foreign corporation that is a reverse hybrid or foreign law CFC.

(ii) *Foreign income taxes on a remittance, U.S. return of capital amount, or U.S. return of partnership basis amount.*—This paragraph (b)(2)(ii) applies to foreign income taxes paid or accrued by a domestic corporation that is a United States shareholder of a foreign corporation with respect to foreign taxable income that the domestic corporation includes by reason of a remittance, a distribution (including a foreign law distribution) that is a U.S. return of capital amount or U.S. return of partnership basis amount, or a disposition (including a foreign law disposition) that gives rise to a U.S. return of capital amount or a U.S. return of partnership basis amount. These foreign income taxes are attributable to non-inclusion income of the foreign corporation to the extent that they are allocated and apportioned to the domestic corporation's section 245A subgroup of general category stock, section 245A subgroup of passive category stock, or section 245A subgroup of U.S. source category stock in applying § 1.861-20 for purposes of section 904 as the operative section. For purposes of this paragraph (b)(2)(ii), § 1.861-20 is applied by treating the domestic corporation's section 245A subgroup of general category stock, section 245A subgroup of passive category stock, and section 245A subgroup of U.S. source category stock as the statutory groupings and treating the tax book value of the non-section 245A subgroup of stock for each separate category as tax book value in the residual grouping.

(iii) *Foreign income taxes on income of a reverse hybrid or a foreign law CFC.*—This paragraph (b)(2)(iii) applies to foreign income taxes paid or accrued by a domestic corporation, other than a regulated investment company (as defined in section 851), real estate investment trust (as defined in section 856), or S corporation (as defined in section 1361), that is a United States shareholder of a foreign corporation that is a reverse hybrid or foreign law CFC with respect to the foreign law pass-through income or foreign law inclusion regime income of the reverse hybrid or foreign law CFC, respectively. These taxes are attributable to the non-inclusion income of a reverse hybrid or foreign law CFC to the extent that they are allocated and apportioned to the non-inclusion income group under § 1.861-20. For purposes of this paragraph (b)(2)(iii), § 1.861-20 is applied by treating the non-inclusion income group in each section 904 category of the domestic corporation and the foreign corporation as a statutory grouping and treating all other income as income in the residual grouping.

(3) *Anti-avoidance rule.*—Foreign income taxes are treated as attributable to section 245A(d) income of a domestic corporation or foreign corporation, or non-inclusion income of a foreign corporation, if a transaction, series of related transactions, or arrangement is undertaken with a principal purpose of avoiding the purposes of section 245A(d) and this section with respect to such foreign income taxes, including, for example, by separating foreign income taxes from the income, or earnings and profits, to which such foreign income taxes relate or by making distributions (or causing inclusions) under foreign law in multiple years that give rise to foreign income taxes that are allocated and apportioned with reference to the same previously taxed earnings and profits. See paragraph (d)(4) of this section (*Example 3*).

(c) *Definitions.*—The following definitions apply for purposes of this section.

(1) *Corresponding U.S. item.*—The term *corresponding U.S. item* has the meaning set forth in § 1.861-20(b).

(2) *Foreign income tax.*—The term *foreign income tax* has the meaning set forth in § 1.901-2(a).

(3) *Foreign law CFC.*—The term *foreign law CFC* has the meaning set forth in § 1.861-20(b).

(4) *Foreign law disposition.*—The term *foreign law disposition* has the meaning set forth in § 1.861-20(b).

(5) *Foreign law distribution.*—The term *foreign law distribution* has the meaning set forth in § 1.861-20(b).

(6) *Foreign law inclusion regime.*—The term *foreign law inclusion regime* has the meaning set forth in § 1.861-20(b).

(7) *Foreign law inclusion regime income.*—The term *foreign law inclusion regime income* has the meaning set forth in § 1.861-20(b).

(8) *Foreign law pass-through income.*—The term *foreign law pass-through income* has the meaning set forth in § 1.861-20(b).

(9) *Foreign taxable income.*—The term *foreign taxable income* has the meaning set forth in § 1.861-20(b).

(10) *Gross included tested income.*—The term *gross included tested income* means, with respect to a foreign corporation that is described in paragraph (b)(2)(iii) of this section, an item of gross tested income multiplied by the inclusion percentage of a domestic corporation that is described in paragraph (b)(2)(iii) of this section for the domestic corporation's U.S. taxable year with or within which the foreign corporation's taxable year described in § 1.861-20(d)(3)(i)(C) or § 1.861-20(d)(3)(iii) ends.

(11) *Hybrid dividend.*—The term *hybrid dividend* has the meaning set forth in § 1.245A(e)-1(b)(2).

(12) *Inclusion percentage.*—The term *inclusion percentage* has the meaning set forth in § 1.960-1(b).

(13) *Non-inclusion income.*—The term *non-inclusion income* means the items of gross income of a foreign corporation other than the items that are described in § 1.960-1(d)(2)(ii)(B)(2) (items of income assigned to the subpart F income groups) and section 245(a)(5) (without regard to section 245(a)(12)), and other than gross included tested income.

(14) *Non-inclusion income group.*—The term *non-inclusion income group* means the income group within a section 904 category that consists of non-inclusion income.

(15) *Non-section 245A subgroup.*—The term *non-section 245A subgroup* means each non-section 245A subgroup determined under § 1.861-13(a)(5), applied as if the foreign corporation whose stock is being characterized were a controlled foreign corporation.

(16) *Pass-through entity.*—The term *pass-through entity* has the meaning set forth in § 1.904-5(a)(4).

(17) *Remittance.*—The term *remittance* has the meaning set forth in § 1.861-20(d)(3)(v)(E).

(18) *Reverse hybrid.*—The term *reverse hybrid* has the meaning set forth in § 1.861-20(b).

(19) *Section 245A subgroup.*—The term *section 245A subgroup* means each section 245A subgroup determined under § 1.861-13(a)(5), applied as if the foreign corporation whose stock is being characterized were a controlled foreign corporation.

(20) *Section 245A(d) income.*—With respect to a domestic corporation, the term *section 245A(d) income* means a dividend (including a section 1248 dividend and a dividend received indirectly through a pass-through entity) or an inclusion under section 951(a)(1)(A) for which a deduction under section 245A(a) is allowed, a distribution of section 245A(d) PTEP, a hybrid dividend, or an inclusion under section 245A(e)(2) and § 1.245A(e)-1(c)(1) by reason of a tiered hybrid dividend. With respect to a successor of a domestic corporation, the term *section 245A(d) income* means the receipt of a distribution of section 245A(d) PTEP. With respect to a foreign corporation, the term *section 245A(d) income* means an item of subpart F income that gave rise to a deduction under section 245A(a), a tiered hybrid dividend or a distribution of section 245A(d) PTEP. An item described in this paragraph (c)(20) that qualifies for the deduction under section 245A(a) is considered section 245A(d) income regardless of whether the domestic corporation claims the deduction on its return with respect to the item.

(21) *Section 245A(d) income group.*—The term *section 245A(d) income group* means an income group within a section 904 category that consists of section 245A(d) income.

(22) *Section 245A(d) PTEP.*—The term *section 245A(d) PTEP* means previously taxed earnings and profits described in § 1.960-3(c)(2)(v) or (ix) if such previously taxed earnings and profits arose either as a result of a dividend that gave rise to a deduction under section 245A(a), or as a result of a tiered hybrid dividend that, by reason of section 245A(e)(2) and § 1.245A(e)-1(c)(1), gave rise to an inclusion in the gross income of a United States shareholder. For purposes of this paragraph (c)(22), a dividend that qualifies for the deduction under section 245A(a) is considered to have given rise to a deduction under section 245A(a) regardless of whether the domestic corporation claims the deduction on its return with respect to the dividend.

(23) *Section 904 category.*—The term *section 904 category* has the meaning set forth in § 1.960-1(b).

(24) *Section 1248 dividend.*—The term *section 1248 dividend* means an amount of gain that is treated as a dividend under section 1248.

(25) *Successor.*—The term successor means a person, including an individual who is a citizen or resident of the United States, that acquires from any person any portion of the interest of a United States shareholder in a foreign corporation for purposes of section 959(a).

(26) *Tested income.*—The term *tested income* has the meaning set forth in § 1.960-1(b).

(27) *Tiered hybrid dividend.*—The term *tiered hybrid dividend* has the meaning set forth in § 1.245A(e)-1(c)(2).

(28) *U.S. capital gain amount.*—The term *U.S. capital gain amount* has the meaning set forth in § 1.861-20(b).

(29) *U.S. return of capital amount.*—The term *U.S. return of capital amount* has the meaning set forth in § 1.861-20(b).

(30) *U.S. return of partnership basis amount.*—The term *U.S. return of partnership basis amount* means, with respect to a partnership in which a domestic corporation is a partner, the portion of a distribution by the partnership to the domestic corporation, or the portion of the proceeds of a disposition of the domestic corporation's interest in the partnership, that exceeds the U.S. capital gain amount.

(d) *Examples.*—The following examples illustrate the application of this section.

(1) *Presumed facts.*—Except as otherwise provided, the following facts are presumed for purposes of the examples:

(i) USP is a domestic corporation;

(ii) CFC is a controlled foreign corporation organized in Country A, and is not a reverse hybrid or a foreign law CFC;

(iii) USP owns all of the outstanding stock of CFC;

(iv) USP would be allowed a deduction under section 245A(a) for dividends received from CFC;

(v) All parties have a U.S. dollar functional currency and a U.S. taxable year and foreign taxable year that correspond to the calendar year; and

(vi) References to income are to gross items of income, and no party has deductions for Country A tax purposes or deductions for Federal income tax purposes (other than foreign income tax expense).

(2) *Example 1: Distribution for foreign and Federal income tax purposes.*—(i) *Facts.* As of December 31, Year 1, CFC has $800x of section 951A PTEP (as defined in § 1.960-3(c)(2)(viii)) in a single annual PTEP account (as defined in § 1.960-3(c)(1)), and $500x of earnings and profits described in section 959(c)(3). On December 31, Year 1, CFC distributes $1,000x of cash to USP. For Country A tax purposes, the entire $1,000x distribution is a dividend and is therefore a foreign dividend amount (as defined in § 1.861-20(b)). Country A imposes a withholding tax on USP of $150x with respect to the $1,000x of foreign gross dividend income under Country A law. For Federal income tax purposes, USP includes in gross income $200x of the distribution as a dividend for which a deduction is allowable under section 245A(a). The remaining $800x of the distribution is a distribution of PTEP that is excluded from USP's gross income and not treated as a dividend under section 959(a) and (d), respectively. The entire $1,000x dividend is a U.S. dividend amount (as defined in § 1.861-20(b)).

(ii) *Analysis*—(A) *In general.* The rules of this section are applied by first determining the portion of the $150x Country A withholding tax that is attributable under paragraph (b)(1) of this section to the section 245A(d) income of USP, and then by determining the portion of the $150x Country A withholding tax that is described in paragraph (b)(2)(i) of this section and that is attributable under either paragraph (b)(2)(ii) or (b)(2)(iii) of this section to the non-inclusion income of CFC. No credit or deduction is allowed in any taxable year under paragraph (a)(1)(i) of this section for any portion of the $150x Country A withholding tax that is attributable to the section 245A(d) income of USP, or, under paragraph (a)(1)(iii) of this section, for any portion of that tax that is attributable to the non-inclusion income of CFC, to the extent the tax is not disallowed under paragraph (a)(1)(i) of this section.

(B) *Attribution of foreign income taxes to section 245A(d) income.* Under paragraph (b)(1) of this section, the $150x Country A withholding tax is attributable to the section 245A(d) income of USP to the extent that it is allocated and apportioned to the section 245A(d) income group (the statutory grouping) under § 1.861-20. Section 1.861-20(c) allocates and apportions foreign income tax to the statutory and residual groupings to which the items of foreign gross income that were included in the foreign tax base are assigned under § 1.861-20(d). Section 1.861-20(d)(3)(i) assigns foreign gross income that is a foreign dividend amount, to the extent of the U.S. dividend amount, to the statutory and residual groupings to which the U.S. dividend amount is assigned. The $1,000x foreign dividend amount is therefore assigned to the statutory and residual groupings to which the $1,000x U.S. dividend amount is assigned under Federal income tax law. The $1,000x U.S. dividend amount comprises a $200x dividend for which a deduction under section 245A(a) is allowed, which is an item of section 245A(d) income, and $800x of section 951A PTEP, the receipt of which is income in the residual grouping. Accordingly, $200x of the $1,000x of foreign gross dividend income is assigned to the section 245A(d) income group, and $800x is assigned to the residual grouping. Under § 1.861-20(f), $30x ($150x × $200x/$1,000x) of the $150x Country A withholding tax is apportioned to the section 245A(d) income group and is attributable to the section 245A(d) income of USP. The remaining $120x ($150x × $800x/$1,000x) of the tax is apportioned to the residual grouping.

(C) *Attribution of foreign income taxes to non-inclusion income.* Under paragraph (b)(2) of this section, the $150x Country A withholding tax may be attributed to non-inclusion income of CFC if the tax is allocated and apportioned under § 1.861-20 by reference to either the characterization of the tax book value of stock under § 1.861-9 or the income of a foreign corporation that is a reverse hybrid or foreign law CFC. CFC is neither a reverse hybrid nor a foreign law CFC. In addition, no portion of the $150x Country A withholding tax is allocated and apportioned under § 1.861-20 by reference to the characterization of the tax book value of CFC's stock. See § 1.861-20(d)(3)(i). Therefore, none of the tax is attributable to non-inclusion income of CFC.

(D) *Disallowance.* Under paragraph (a)(1)(i) of this section, no credit under section 901 or deduction is allowed in any taxable year to USP for the $30x portion of the Country A withholding tax that is attributable to section 245A(d) income of USP.

(3) *Example 2: Distribution for foreign law purposes.*—(i) *Facts.* As of December 31, Year 1, CFC has $800x of section 951A PTEP (as defined in § 1.960-3(c)(2)(viii)) in a single annual PTEP account (as defined in § 1.960-3(c)(1)), and $500x of earnings and profits described in section 959(c)(3). On December 31, Year 1, CFC distributes $1,000x of its stock to USP. For Country A tax purposes, the entire $1,000x stock distribution is treated as a dividend to USP and is therefore a foreign dividend amount (as defined in § 1.861-20(b)). Country A imposes a withholding tax on USP of $150x with respect to the $1,000x of foreign gross dividend income that USP includes under Country A law. For Federal income tax purposes, USP does not recognize gross income as a result of the stock distribution under section 305(a). The $1,000x stock distribution is therefore a foreign law distribution.

(ii) *Analysis*—(A) *In general.* The rules of this section are applied by first determining the portion of the $150x Country A withholding tax that is attributable under paragraph (b)(1) of this section to the section 245A(d) income of USP, and then by determining the portion of the $150x Country A withholding tax that is described in paragraph (b)(2)(i) of this section and that is attributable under either paragraph (b)(2)(ii) or (b)(2)(iii) of this section to the non-inclusion income of CFC. No credit or deduction is allowed in any taxable year under paragraph (a)(1)(i) of this section for any portion of the $150x Country A withholding tax that is attributable to the section 245A(d) income of USP or, under paragraph (a)(1)(iii) of this section, for any portion of that tax that is attributable to the non-inclusion income of CFC, to the extent the tax is not disallowed under paragraph (a)(1)(i) of this section.

(B) *Attribution of foreign income taxes to section 245A(d) income.* Under paragraph (b)(1) of this section, the $150x Country A withholding tax is attributable to the section 245A(d) income of USP to the extent that it is allocated and apportioned to the section 245A(d) income group (the statutory grouping) under § 1.861-20. Section 1.861-20(c) allocates and apportions foreign income tax to the statutory and residual groupings to which the items of foreign gross income that were included in the foreign tax base are assigned under § 1.861-20(d). In general, § 1.861-20(d) assigns foreign gross income to the statutory and residual groupings to which the corresponding U.S. item is assigned. If a taxpayer does not recognize a corresponding U.S. item in the year in which it pays or accrues foreign income tax with respect to foreign gross income that it includes by reason of a foreign law dividend, § 1.861-20(d)(2)(ii)(B) assigns the foreign dividend amount to the same statutory or residual groupings to which the foreign dividend amount would be assigned if a distribution were made for Federal income tax purposes in the amount of, and on the date of, the foreign law distribution. Further, § 1.861-20(d)(2)(ii)(B) computes the U.S. dividend amount (as defined in § 1.861-20(b)) as if the distribution occurred on the date the distribution occurs for foreign law purposes. Therefore, the foreign dividend amount is assigned to the same statutory and residual groupings to which it would be assigned if a $1,000x distribution occurred on December 31, Year 1 for Federal income tax purposes. If such a distribution occurred, it would result in a $200x dividend to USP for which a deduction would be allowed under section 245A(a). The remaining $800x of the distribution would be excluded from USP's gross income and not treated as a dividend under section 959(a) and (d), respectively. Under paragraphs (c)(20) and (b)(1) of this section, the $1,000x U.S. dividend amount comprises a $200x dividend for which a deduction under section 245A(a) would be allowed, which is an item of section 245A(d) income, and $800x of section 951A PTEP, which is income in the residual grouping. Accordingly, $200x of the $1,000x foreign gross dividend income is assigned to the section 245A(d) income group, and $800x is assigned to the residual grouping. Under § 1.861-20(f), $30x ($150x × $200x/ $1,000x) of the Country A foreign income tax is apportioned to the section 245A(d) income group and is attributable to the section 245A(d) income of USP. The remaining $120x ($150x × $800x/ $1,000x) of the tax is apportioned to the residual grouping.

(C) *Attribution of foreign income taxes to non-inclusion income.* Under paragraph (b)(2) of this section, the $150x Country A withholding tax may be attributed to non-inclusion income of CFC if the tax is allocated and apportioned under § 1.861-20 by reference to either the characterization of the tax book value of stock under § 1.861-9 or the income of a foreign corporation that is a reverse hybrid or foreign law CFC. CFC is neither a reverse hybrid nor a foreign law CFC. In addition, no portion of the $150x Country A withholding tax is allocated and apportioned under § 1.861-20 by reference to the characterization of the tax book value of CFC's stock. See § 1.861-20(d)(3)(i). Therefore, none of the tax is attributable to non-inclusion income of CFC.

(D) *Disallowance.* Under paragraph (a)(1)(i) of this section, no credit under section 901 or deduction is allowed in any taxable year to USP for the $30x portion of the Country A withholding tax that is attributable to section 245A(d) income of USP.

(4) *Example 3: Successive foreign law distributions subject to anti-avoidance rule.*—(i) *Facts.* For Year 1, CFC earns $500x of subpart F income that gives rise to a $500x gross income inclusion to USP under section 951(a), and income that creates $500x of earnings and profits described in section 959(c)(3). CFC earns no income in Years 2 through 4. As of January 1, Year 2, and through December 31, Year 4, CFC has $500x of earnings and profits described in section 959(c)(3) and $500x of section 951(a)(1)(A) PTEP (as defined in § 1.960-3(c)(2)(x)) in a single annual PTEP account (as defined in § 1.960-3(c)(1)). In each of Years 2 and 3, USP makes a consent dividend election under Country A law that, for Country A tax purposes, deems CFC to distribute to USP, and USP immediately to contribute to CFC, $500x on December 31 of each year. For Country A tax purposes, each deemed distribution is a dividend of $500x to USP, and each deemed contribution is a non-taxable contribution of $500x to the capital of CFC. Each $500x deemed distribution is therefore a foreign dividend amount (as defined in § 1.861-20(b)). Country A imposes $150x of withholding tax on USP in each of Years 2 and 3 with respect to the $500x of foreign gross dividend income that USP includes in income under Country A law. For Federal income tax purposes, the Country A deemed distributions in Years 2 and 3 are disregarded such that USP recognizes no income, and the deemed distributions are therefore foreign law distributions. On December 31, Year 4, CFC distributes $1,000x to USP, which for Country A tax purposes is treated as a return of contributed capital on which no withholding tax is imposed. For Federal income tax purposes, $500x of the $1,000x distribution is a dividend to USP for which a deduction under section 245A(a) is allowed; the remaining $500x of the distribution is a distribution of section 951(a)(1)(A) PTEP that is excluded from USP's gross income and not treated as a dividend under section 959(a) and (d), respectively. The entire $1,000x dividend is a U.S. dividend amount (as defined in § 1.861-20(b)). The Country A consent dividend elections in Years 2 and 3 are made with a principal purpose of avoiding the purposes of section 245A(d) and this section to disallow a credit or deduction for Country A withholding tax incurred with respect to USP's section 245A(d) income.

(ii) *Analysis*—(A) *In general.* The rules of this section are applied by first determining the portion of the $150x Country A withholding tax paid by USP in each of Years 2 and 3 that is attributable under paragraph (b)(1) of this section to the section 245A(d) income of USP, and then by determining the portion of the $150x Country A withholding tax paid by USP in each of Years 2 and 3 that is described in paragraph (b)(2)(i) of this section and that is attributable under either paragraph (b)(2)(ii) or (b)(2)(iii) of this section to the non-inclusion income of CFC. Finally, the anti-avoidance rule under paragraph (b)(3) of this section applies to treat any portion of the $150x Country A withholding tax paid by USP in each of Years 2 and 3 as attributable to section 245A(d) income of USP or non-inclusion income of CFC, if a transaction, series of related transactions, or arrangement is undertaken with a principal purpose of avoiding the purposes of section 245A(d) and this section. No credit or deduction is allowed in any taxable year under paragraph (a)(1)(i) of this section for any portion of the $150x Country A withholding tax paid by USP in each of Years 2 and 3 that is attributable to the section 245A(d) income of USP or, under paragraph (a)(1)(iii) of this section, for any portion of that tax that is attributable to the non-inclusion income of CFC, to the extent the tax is not disallowed under paragraph (a)(1)(i) of this section.

(B) *Attribution of foreign income taxes to section 245A(d) income.* Under paragraph (b)(1) of this section, the $150x Country A withholding tax paid by USP in each of Years 2 and 3 is attributable to the section 245A(d) income of USP to the extent that it is allocated and apportioned to the section 245A(d) income group (the statutory grouping) under § 1.861-20. Section 1.861-20(c) allocates and apportions foreign income tax to the statutory and residual groupings to which the items of foreign gross income that were included in the foreign tax base are assigned under § 1.861-20(d). In general, § 1.861-20(d) assigns foreign gross income to the statutory and residual groupings to which the corresponding U.S. item is assigned. If a taxpayer does not recognize a corresponding U.S. item in the year in which it pays or accrues foreign income tax with respect to foreign gross income that it includes by reason of a foreign law dividend, § 1.861-20(d)(2)(ii)(B) assigns the foreign dividend amount to the same statutory or residual groupings to which the foreign dividend amount would be assigned if a distribution were made for Federal income tax purposes in the amount of, and on the date of, the foreign law distribution. Therefore, the $500x foreign dividend amount in each of Years 2 and 3 is assigned to the same statutory and residual groupings to which it would be assigned if a $500x distribution occurred on December 31 of each of those years for Federal income tax purposes.

(1) Year 2 $500x deemed distribution. CFC made no distributions in Year 1 and earned no income and made no distributions in Year 2 for Federal income tax purposes. As of December 31, Year 2, CFC has $500x of earnings and profits described in section 959(c)(3) and $500x of section 951(a)(1)(A) PTEP. If CFC distributed $500x on that date, the distribution would be a distribution of section 951(a)(1)(A) PTEP. A distribution of previously taxed earnings and profits is a U.S. dividend amount. Section 1.861-20(d)(3)(i) assigns the foreign dividend amount, to the extent of the U.S. dividend amount, to the statutory and residual groupings to which the U.S. dividend amount is assigned. The receipt of a distribution of previously taxed earnings and profits is assigned to the residual grouping under paragraph (b)(1) of this section. Therefore, all $500x foreign dividend amount would be assigned to the residual grouping, and none of the $150x withholding tax paid or accrued by USP in Year 2 would be treated as attributable to section 245A(d) income of USP.

(2) Year 3 $500x deemed distribution. CFC made no distributions in Year 1 and earned no income and made no distributions in Year 2 or Year 3 for Federal income tax purposes. Consequently, as of December 31, Year 3, CFC has $500x of earnings and profits described in section 959(c)(3) and $500x of section 951(a)(1)(A) PTEP. If CFC distributed $500x on that date, the distribution would be a distribution of section 951(a)(1)(A) PTEP. For the reasons described in paragraph (d)(4)(ii)(B)(*1*) of this section, all $500x of the foreign dividend amount would be assigned to the residual grouping, and none of the $150x withholding tax paid or accrued by USP in Year 3 would be treated as attributable to section 245A(d) income of USP.

(3) Year 4 $1,000x distribution. The Year 4 $1,000x distribution is, for Country A purposes, a return of capital distribution that is not subject to withholding tax. For Federal income tax purposes, it comprises a $500x dividend for which a deduction under section 245A(a) is allowed, which is an item of section 245A(d) income of USP, and a $500x distribution of section 951(a)(1)(A) PTEP, the receipt of which is income in the residual grouping.

(C) *Attribution of foreign income taxes to non-inclusion income.* Under paragraph (b)(2) of this section, the $150x Country A withholding tax paid by USP in each of Years 2 and 3 may be attributed to non-inclusion income of CFC if the tax is allocated and apportioned under § 1.861-20 by reference to either the characterization of the tax book value of stock under § 1.861-9 or the income of a foreign corporation that is a reverse hybrid or foreign law CFC. CFC is neither a reverse hybrid nor a foreign law CFC. In addition, no portion of the Country A withholding tax is allocated and apportioned under § 1.861-20 by reference to the characterization of the tax book value of CFC's stock. See § 1.861-20(d)(3)(i). Therefore, none of the tax is attributable to non-inclusion income of CFC.

(D) *Attribution of foreign income taxes pursuant to anti-avoidance rule.* USP made two successive foreign law distributions in Years 2 and 3 that were subject to Country A withholding tax and that did not individually exceed, but together exceeded, the section 951(a)(1)(A) PTEP of CFC. The Country A withholding tax on each consent dividend is allocated to the residual grouping rather than to the statutory grouping of section 245A(d) income under §§ 1.861-20(d)(2)(ii) and 1.861-20(d)(3)(i). USP paid no Country A withholding tax on the Year 4 distribution as a result of the Country A consent dividends in Years 2 and 3. If CFC had distributed its earnings and profits in Year 4 without the prior consent dividends, the distribution would have been subject to withholding tax, a portion of which would have been attributable to the section 245A(d) income arising from the distribution. But for the application of the anti-avoidance rule in paragraph (b)(3) of this section, USP would avoid the disallowance under section 245A(d) with respect to this portion of the withholding tax. Because USP made foreign law distributions that caused withholding tax from multiple foreign law distributions to be associated with the same previously taxed earnings and profits with a principal purpose of avoiding the purposes of section 245A(d) and this section, the $150x Country A withholding tax paid by USP in each of Years 2 and 3 is treated as being attributable to section 245A(d) income of USP.

(E) *Disallowance.* Under paragraph (a)(1)(i) of this section, no credit under section 901 or deduction is allowed in any taxable year to USP for the $150x Country A withholding tax paid by USP in each of Years 2 and 3 that is attributable to section 245A(d) income of USP.

(5) *Example 4: Distribution that is in part a dividend and in part a return of capital.*—(i) *Facts.* CFC uses the modified gross income method to allocate and apportion its interest expense, and its stock has a tax book value of $10,000x. For Year 1, CFC earns $500x of income that is specified foreign source general category gross income as that term is defined in § 1.861-13(a)(1)(i)(A)(*9*) and is therefore neither tested income nor subpart F income of CFC. As of December 31, Year 1, CFC has $500x of earnings and profits described in section 959(c)(3). On that date, CFC distributes $1,000x of cash to USP. For Country A tax purposes, the entire $1,000x distribution is a dividend to USP and is therefore a foreign dividend amount (as defined in § 1.861-20(b)). Country A imposes a withholding tax on USP of $150x with respect to the $1,000x of foreign gross dividend income that USP includes under the law of Country A. For Federal income tax purposes, USP includes $500x of the distribution in its gross income as a dividend for which a $500x deduction is allowed to USP under section 245A(a); the remaining $500x of the distribution is applied against and reduces USP's basis in its CFC stock under section 301(c)(2). The portion of the distribution that is a $500x dividend is a U.S. dividend amount (as defined in § 1.861-20(b)). The remaining $500x of the distribution is a U.S. return of capital amount.

(ii) *Analysis*—(A) *In general.* The rules of this section are applied by first determining the portion of the $150x Country A withholding tax that is attributable under paragraph (b)(1) of this section to the section 245A(d) income of USP, and then by determining the portion of the $150x Country A withholding tax that is described in paragraph (b)(2)(i) of this section and that is attributable under either paragraph (b)(2)(ii) or (b)(2)(iii) of this section to the non-inclusion income of CFC. No credit or deduction is allowed under paragraph (a)(1)(i) of this section for any portion of the $150x Country A withholding tax that is attributable to the section 245A(d) income of USP or, under paragraph (a)(1)(iii) of this section, for any portion of that tax that is attributable to the non-inclusion income of CFC, to the extent the tax is not disallowed under paragraph (a)(1)(i) of this section.

(B) *Attribution of foreign income taxes to section 245A(d) income.* Under paragraph (b)(1) of this section, the $150x Country A withholding tax is attributable to the section 245A(d) income of USP to the extent that it is allocated and apportioned to the section 245A(d) income group (the statutory grouping) under § 1.861-20. Section 1.861-20(c) allocates and apportions foreign income tax to the statutory and residual groupings to which the items of foreign gross income that were included in the foreign tax base are assigned under § 1.861-20(d). Section 1.861-20(d)(3)(i) assigns foreign gross income that is a foreign dividend amount, to the extent of the U.S. dividend amount, to the statutory and residual groupings to which the U.S. dividend amount is assigned. Of the $1,000x foreign dividend amount, $500x is therefore assigned to the statutory and residual groupings to which the $500x U.S. dividend amount is assigned under Federal income tax law. The entire $500x U.S. dividend amount is a dividend for which a section 245A(a) deduction is allowed and is therefore section 245A(d) income that is assigned to the section 245A(d) income group. Accordingly, $500x of the foreign dividend amount is assigned to the section 245A(d) income group. Under § 1.861-20(f), $75x ($150x × $500x/$1,000x) of the Country A withholding tax is allocated to the section 245A(d) income group and so under paragraph (b)(1) of this section is attributable to the section 245A(d) income of USP.

(C) *Attribution of foreign income taxes to non-inclusion income.* The remaining $75x of the Country A withholding tax is described in paragraph (b)(2)(i) of this section because the $500x of foreign dividend amount that corresponds to the $500x U.S. return of capital amount is assigned, and the remaining withholding tax imposed on that foreign dividend amount is allocated and apportioned, by reference to the characterization of the tax book value of the stock of CFC. Under paragraph (b)(2)(ii) of this section, the remaining $75x Country A withholding tax is attributable to non-inclusion income of CFC to the extent that the tax is allocated and apportioned under § 1.861-20 to USP's section 245A subgroup of general category stock, section 245A subgroup of passive category stock, and section 245A subgroup of U.S. source category stock (the statutory groupings) for purposes of section 904 as the operative section. Under § 1.861-20(d)(3)(i), the $500x portion of the foreign dividend amount that corresponds to the $500x U.S. return of capital amount is assigned to the statutory and residual groupings to which $500x of earnings of CFC would be assigned if CFC recognized them in Year 1. Those earnings are deemed to arise in the statutory and residual groupings in the same proportions as the proportions of the tax book value of CFC's stock in the groupings for Year 1 for purposes of applying the asset method of expense allocation and apportionment under § 1.861-9. Under § 1.861-9, § 1.861-9T(f), and § 1.861-13, for purposes of section 904 as the operative section, all of the tax book value of the stock of CFC is assigned to USP's section 245A subgroup of general category stock because CFC uses the modified gross income method to allocate and apportion its interest expense and earns only specified foreign source general category gross income for Year 1. Under § 1.861-20(d)(3)(i), if CFC recognized $500x of earnings in Year 1 these earnings would be deemed to arise in the section 245A subgroup of general category stock. Accordingly, the remaining $500x of foreign dividend amount is assigned to USP's section 245A subgroup of general category stock. Under § 1.861-20(f), the remaining $75x of withholding tax is allocated to the section 245A subgroup and, under paragraph (b)(2)(ii) of this section, is attributable to the non-inclusion income of CFC.

(D) *Disallowance.* Under paragraph (a)(1)(i) of this section, no credit under section 901 or deduction is allowed in any taxable year to USP for the $75x portion of the Country A withholding tax that is attributable to section 245A(d) income of USP. Under paragraph (a)(1)(iii) of this section, no credit under section 901 or deduction is allowed in any taxable year to USP for the $75x portion of the Country A withholding tax that is attributable to non-inclusion income of CFC.

(6) *Example 5: Income of a reverse hybrid.*—(i) *Facts.* CFC is a reverse hybrid. In Year 1, CFC earns a $500x item of gain described in section 907(c)(1)(B) that is non-inclusion income. CFC also earns for Federal income tax purposes and Country A tax purposes a $1,000x item of royalty income, of which $500x is gross included tested income and $500x is non-inclusion income. USP includes the $500x item of foreign gain and the $1,000x item of foreign gross royalty income in its Country A taxable income, and the items are foreign law pass-through income. If CFC included these items under Country A tax law, its $1,000x of royalty income for Federal income tax purposes would be the corresponding U.S. item for the foreign gross royalty income, and its $500x of gain for Federal income tax purposes would be the corresponding U.S. item for the foreign gain. Country A imposes a $150x foreign income tax on USP with respect to $1,500x of foreign gross income.

(ii) *Analysis*—(A) *In general.* The rules of this section are applied by first determining the portion of the $150x Country A tax that is attributable under paragraph (b)(1) of this section to the section 245A(d) income of USP, and then by determining the portion of the $150x Country A tax that is described in paragraph (b)(2)(i) of this section and that is attributable under either paragraph (b)(2)(ii) or (iii) of this section to the non-inclusion income of CFC. No credit or deduction is allowed under paragraph (a)(1)(i) of this section for any portion of the $150x Country A tax that is attributable to the section 245A(d) income of USP or, under paragraph (a)(1)(iii) of this section, for any portion of that tax that is attributable to the non-inclusion income of CFC, to the extent the tax is not disallowed under paragraph (a)(1)(i) of this section.

(B) *Attribution of foreign income taxes to section 245A(d) income.* Under paragraph (b)(1) of this section, the $150x Country A tax is attributable to section 245A(d) income to the extent the tax is allocated and apportioned to the section 245A(d) income group (the statutory grouping) under § 1.861-20. Section 1.861-20(c) allocates and apportions foreign income tax to the statutory and residual groupings to which the items of foreign gross income that were included in the foreign tax base are assigned under § 1.861-20(d). In general, § 1.861-20(d) assigns foreign gross income to the statutory and residual groupings to which the corresponding U.S. item is assigned. Section 1.861-20(d)(3)(i)(C) assigns the foreign law pass-through income that USP includes by reason of its ownership of CFC to the statutory and residual groupings by treating USP's foreign law pass-through income as foreign gross income of CFC, and by treating CFC as paying the $150x of Country A tax in CFC's U.S. taxable year within which its foreign taxable year ends (Year 1). CFC is therefore treated as including a $1,000x foreign gross royalty item and a $500x foreign gross income item of gain and paying $150x of Country A tax in Year 1. These foreign gross income items are assigned to the statutory and residual groupings to which the corresponding U.S. items are assigned under Federal income tax law. No foreign gross income is assigned to the section 245A(d) income group because neither the corresponding U.S. item of royalty income nor the corresponding U.S. item of gain is assigned to the section 245A(d) income group. Therefore, none of USP's Country A tax is allocated to the section 245A(d) income group.

(C) *Attribution of foreign income taxes to non-inclusion income.* The $150x Country A tax is described in paragraph (b)(2) of this section because USP is a United States shareholder of CFC, CFC is a reverse hybrid, and § 1.861-20(d)(3)(i)(C) allocates and apportions the tax by reference to the income of CFC. Under paragraph (b)(2)(iii) of this section, the $150x Country A tax is attributable to the non-inclusion income of CFC to the extent that the foreign income taxes are allocated and apportioned to the non-inclusion income group under § 1.861-20. For the reasons described in paragraph (d)(6)(ii)(B) of this section, under § 1.861-20(d)(3)(i)(C) CFC is treated as including a $1,000x foreign gross royalty item and a $500x foreign gross income item of gain and paying $150x of Country A tax in Year 1. These foreign gross income items are assigned to the statutory and residual groupings to which the corresponding U.S. items are assigned under Federal income tax law. For Federal income tax purposes, the $500x item of gain and $500x of the $1,000x item of royalty income are items of non-inclusion income that are therefore assigned to the non-inclusion income group. The remaining $500x of the foreign gross royalty income item is assigned to the residual grouping. Under § 1.861-20(f), $100x ($150x × $1,000x/$1,500x) of the Country A tax is apportioned to the non-inclusion income group, and $50x ($150x × $500x/$1,500x) is apportioned to the residual grouping. Under paragraph (b)(2)(iii) of this section, the $100x of Country A tax that is apportioned to the non-inclusion income group under § 1.861-20(d)(3)(i)(C) is attributable to non-inclusion income of CFC.

(D) *Disallowance.* Under paragraph (a)(1)(iii) of this section, no credit under section 901 or deduction is allowed in any taxable year to USP for the $100x of Country A foreign income tax that is attributable to non-inclusion income of CFC.

(e) *Applicability date.*—This section applies to taxable years of a foreign corporation that begin after December 31, 2019, and end on or after November 2, 2020, and with respect to a United States person, taxable years in which or with which such taxable years of the foreign corporation end. [Reg. § 1.245A(d)-1.]

☐ [*T.D. 9959*, 12-28-2021 (*corrected* 7-26-2022).]

§ 1.245A(e)-1. Special rules for hybrid dividends.—(a) *Overview.*—This section provides rules for hybrid dividends. Paragraph (b) of this section disallows the deduction under section 245A(a) for a hybrid dividend received by a United States shareholder from a CFC. Paragraph (c) of this section provides a rule for hybrid dividends of tiered corporations. Paragraph (d) of this section sets forth rules regarding a hybrid deduction account. Paragraph (e) of this section provides an anti-avoidance rule. Paragraph (f) of this section provides definitions. Paragraph (g) of this section illustrates the application of the rules of this section through examples. Paragraph (h) of this section provides the applicability date.

(b) *Hybrid dividends received by United States shareholders.*—(1) *In general.*—If a United States shareholder receives a hybrid dividend, then—

(i) The United States shareholder is not allowed a deduction under section 245A(a) for the hybrid dividend; and

(ii) The rules of section 245A(d) and § 1.245A(d)-1 (disallowance of foreign tax credits and deductions) apply to the hybrid dividend. See paragraph (g)(1) of this section for an example illustrating the application of paragraph (b) of this section.

(2) *Definition of hybrid dividend.*—The term *hybrid dividend* means an amount received by a United States shareholder from a CFC for which, without regard to section 245A(e) and this section as well as § 1.245A-5, the United States shareholder would be allowed a deduction under section 245A(a), to the extent of the sum of the United States shareholder's hybrid deduction accounts (as described in paragraph (d) of this section) with respect to each share of stock of the CFC, determined at the close of the CFC's taxable year (or in accordance with paragraph (d)(5) of this section, as applicable). No other amount received by a United States shareholder from a CFC is a hybrid dividend for purposes of section 245A.

(3) *Special rule for certain dividends attributable to earnings of lower-tier foreign corporations.*—This paragraph (b)(3) applies if a domestic corporation directly or indirectly (as determined under the principles of § 1.245A-5(g)(3)(ii)) sells or exchanges stock of a foreign corporation and, pursuant to section 1248, the gain recognized on the sale or exchange is included in gross income as a dividend. In such a case, for purposes of this section—

(i) To the extent that earnings and profits of a lower-tier CFC gave rise to the dividend under section 1248(c)(2), those earnings and profits are treated as distributed as a dividend by the lower-tier CFC directly to the domestic corporation under the principles of § 1.1248-1(d); and

(ii) To the extent the domestic corporation indirectly owns (within the meaning of section 958(a)(2), and determined by treating a domestic partnership as foreign) shares of stock of the lower-tier CFC, the hybrid deduction accounts with respect to those shares are treated as the domestic corporation's hybrid deduction accounts with respect to stock of the lower-tier CFC. Thus, for example, if a domestic corporation sells or exchanges all the stock of an upper-tier CFC and under this paragraph (b)(3) there is considered to be a dividend paid directly by the lower-tier CFC to the domestic corporation, then the dividend is generally a hybrid dividend to the extent of the sum of the upper-tier CFC's hybrid deduction accounts with respect to stock of the lower-tier CFC.

(4) *Ordering rule.*—Amounts received by a United States shareholder from a CFC are subject to the rules of section 245A(e) and this section based on the order in which they are received. Thus, for example, if on different days during a CFC's taxable year a United States shareholder receives dividends from the CFC, then the rules of section 245A(e) and this section apply first to the dividend received on the earliest date (based on the sum of the United States shareholder's hybrid deduction accounts with respect to each share of stock of the CFC), and then to the dividend received on the next earliest date (based on the remaining sum).

(c) *Hybrid dividends of tiered corporations.*—(1) *In general.*—If a CFC (the *receiving CFC*) receives a tiered hybrid dividend from another CFC, and a domestic corporation is a United States shareholder with respect to both CFCs, then, notwithstanding any other provision of the Code—

(i) For purposes of section 951(a) as to the United States shareholder, the tiered hybrid dividend is treated for purposes of section 951(a)(1)(A) as subpart F income of the receiving CFC for the taxable year of the CFC in which the tiered hybrid dividend is received;

(ii) The United States shareholder includes in gross income an amount equal to its pro rata share (determined in the same manner as under section 951(a)(2)) of the subpart F income described in paragraph (c)(1)(i) of this section; and

(iii) The rules of section 245A(d) and § 1.245A(d)-1 (disallowance of foreign tax credit, including for taxes that would have been deemed paid under section 960(a) or (b), and deductions) apply to the amount included under paragraph (c)(1)(ii) of this section in the United States shareholder's gross income. See paragraph (g)(2) of this section for an example illustrating the application of paragraph (c) of this section.

(2) *Definition of tiered hybrid dividend.*—The term *tiered hybrid dividend* means an amount received by a receiving CFC from another CFC to the extent that the amount would be a hybrid dividend under paragraph (b)(2) of this section if, for purposes of section 245A and the regulations in this part under section 245A (except for section 245A(e)(2) and this paragraph (c)), the receiving CFC were a domestic corporation. A tiered hybrid dividend does not include an amount described in section 959(b). No other amount received by a receiving CFC from another CFC is a tiered hybrid dividend for purposes of section 245A.

(3) *Special rule for certain dividends attributable to earnings of lower-tier foreign corporations.*—This paragraph (c)(3) applies if a CFC directly or indirectly (as determined under the principles of § 1.245A-5(g)(3)(ii)) sells or exchanges stock of a foreign corporation and pursuant to section 964(e)(1) the gain recognized on the sale or exchange is included in gross income as a dividend. In such a case, the rules of paragraph (b)(3) of this section apply, by treating the CFC as the domestic corporation described in paragraph (b)(3) of this section and substituting the phrase "sections 964(e)(1) and 1248(c)(2)" for the phrase "section 1248(c)(2)" in paragraph (b)(3)(i) of this section.

(4) *Interaction with rules under section 964(e).*—To the extent a dividend described in section 964(e)(1) (gain on certain stock sales by CFCs treated as dividends) is a tiered hybrid dividend, the rules of section 964(e)(4) do not apply as to a domestic corporation that is a United States shareholder of both of the CFCs described in paragraph (c)(1) of this section and, therefore, such United States shareholder is not allowed a deduction under section 245A(a) for the amount included in gross income under paragraph (c)(1)(ii) of this section.

(d) *Hybrid deduction accounts.*—(1) *In general.*—A specified owner of a share of CFC stock must maintain a hybrid deduction account with respect to the share. The hybrid deduction account with respect to the share must reflect the amount of hybrid deductions of the CFC allocated to the share (as determined under paragraphs (d)(2) and (3) of this section), and must be maintained in accordance with the rules of paragraphs (d)(4) through (6) of this section.

(2) *Hybrid deductions.*—(i) *In general.*—The term *hybrid deduction* of a CFC means a deduction or other tax benefit (such as an exemption, exclusion, or credit, to the extent equivalent to a deduction) for which the requirements of paragraphs (d)(2)(i)(A) and (B) of this section are both satisfied.

(A) The deduction or other tax benefit is allowed to the CFC (or a person related to the CFC) under a relevant foreign tax law, regardless of whether the deduction or other tax benefit is used, or otherwise reduces tax, currently under the relevant foreign tax law.

(B) The deduction or other tax benefit relates to or results from an amount paid, accrued, or distributed with respect to an instrument issued by the CFC and treated as stock for U.S. tax purposes, or is a deduction allowed to the CFC with respect to equity. Examples of such a deduction or other tax benefit include an interest deduction, a dividends paid deduction, and a notional interest deduction (or similar deduction determined with respect to the CFC's equity). However, a deduction or other tax benefit relating to or resulting from a distribution by the CFC that is a dividend for purposes of the relevant foreign tax law is considered a hybrid deduction only to the extent it has the effect of causing the earnings that funded the distribution to not be included in income (determined under the principles of § 1.267A-3(a)) or otherwise subject to tax under such tax law. Thus, for example, upon a distribution by a CFC that is treated as a dividend for purposes of the CFC's tax law to a shareholder of the CFC, a dividends paid deduction allowed to the CFC under its tax law (or a refund to the shareholder, including through a credit, of tax paid by the CFC on the earnings that funded the distribution) pursuant to an integration or imputation system is not a hybrid deduction of the CFC to the extent that the shareholder, if a tax resident of the CFC's country, includes the distribution in income under the CFC's tax law or, if not a tax resident of the CFC's country, is subject to withholding tax (as defined in section 901(k)(1)(B)) on the distribution under the CFC's tax law. As an additional example, upon a distribution by a CFC to a shareholder of the CFC that is a tax resident of the CFC's country, a dividends received deduction allowed to the shareholder under the tax law of such foreign country pursuant to a regime intended to relieve double-taxation within the group is not a hybrid deduction of the CFC (though if the CFC were also allowed a deduction or other tax benefit for the distribution under such tax, such deduction or other tax benefit would be a hybrid deduction of the CFC). See paragraphs (g)(1) and (2) of this section for examples illustrating the application of paragraph (d) of this section.

(ii) *Coordination with foreign disallowance rules.*—The following special rules apply for purposes of determining whether a deduction or other tax benefit is allowed to a CFC (or a person related to the CFC) under a relevant foreign tax law:

(A) Whether the deduction or other tax benefit is allowed is determined without regard to a rule under the relevant foreign tax law that disallows or suspends deductions if a certain ratio or percentage is exceeded (for example, a thin capitalization rule that disallows interest deductions if debt to equity exceeds a certain ratio, or a rule similar to section 163(j) that disallows or suspends interest deductions if interest exceeds a certain percentage of income).

(B) Except as provided in this paragraph (d)(2)(ii)(B), whether the deduction or other tax benefit is allowed is determined without regard to hybrid mismatch rules, if any, under the relevant foreign tax law that may disallow such deduction or other tax benefit. However, whether the deduction or other tax benefit is allowed is determined with regard to hybrid mismatch rules under the relevant foreign tax law if the amount giving rise to the deduction or other tax benefit neither gives rise to a dividend for U.S. tax purposes nor, based on all the facts and circumstances, is reasonably expected to give rise to a dividend for U.S. tax purposes that will be paid within 12 months from the end of the taxable period for which the deduction or other tax benefit would be allowed but for the hybrid mismatch rules. For purposes of this paragraph (d)(2)(ii)(B), the term *hybrid mismatch rules* has the meaning provided in § 1.267A-5(b)(10).

(iii) *Anti-duplication rule.*—A deduction or other tax benefit allowed to a CFC (or a person related to the CFC) under a relevant foreign tax law for an amount paid, accrued, or distributed with respect to an instrument issued by the CFC is not a hybrid deduction to the extent that treating it as a hybrid deduction would have the effect of duplicating a hybrid deduction that is a deduction or other tax benefit allowed under such tax law for an amount paid, accrued, or distributed with respect to an instrument that is issued by a CFC at a higher tier and that has terms substantially similar to the terms of the first instrument. For example, if an upper tier CFC issues to a corporate United States shareholder a hybrid instrument (the "upper tier instrument"), a lower tier CFC issues to the upper tier CFC a hybrid instrument that has terms substantially similar to the terms of the upper tier instrument (the "mirror instrument"), the CFCs are tax residents of the same foreign country, and the upper tier CFC includes in income under its tax law (as determined under the principles of § 1.267A-3(a)) amounts accrued with respect to the mirror instrument, then a deduction allowed to the lower tier CFC under such foreign tax law for an amount accrued pursuant to the mirror instrument is not a hybrid deduction (but a deduction allowed to the upper tier CFC under the foreign tax law for an amount accrued with respect to the upper tier instrument is a hybrid deduction).

(iv) *Application limited to items allowed in taxable years ending on or after December 20, 2018; special rule for deductions with respect to equity.*—A deduction or other tax benefit, other than a deduction with respect to equity, allowed to a CFC (or a person related to the CFC) under a relevant foreign tax law is taken into account for purposes of this section only if it was allowed with respect to a taxable year under the relevant foreign tax law ending on or after December 20, 2018. A deduction with respect to equity allowed to a CFC under a relevant foreign tax law is taken into account for purposes of this section only if it was allowed with respect to a taxable year under the relevant foreign tax law beginning on or after December 20, 2018.

(3) *Allocating hybrid deductions to shares.*—A hybrid deduction is allocated to a share of stock of a CFC to the extent that the hybrid deduction (or amount equivalent to a deduction) relates to an amount paid, accrued, or distributed by the CFC with respect to the share. However, in the case of a hybrid deduction that is a deduction with respect to equity (such as a notional interest deduction), the deduction is allocated to a share of stock of a CFC based on the product of—

(i) The amount of the deduction allowed for all of the equity of the CFC; and

(ii) A fraction, the numerator of which is the value of the share and the denominator of which is the value of all of the stock of the CFC.

(4) *Maintenance of hybrid deduction accounts.*—(i) *In general.*—A specified owner's hybrid deduction account with respect to a share of stock of a CFC is, as of the close of the taxable year of the CFC, adjusted pursuant to the following rules.

(A) First, the account is increased by the amount of hybrid deductions of the CFC allocated to the share for the taxable year.

(B) Second, the account is decreased (but not below zero) pursuant to the rules of paragraphs (d)(4)(i)(B)(*1*) through (*3*) of this section, in the order set forth in this paragraph (d)(4)(i)(B).

(*1*) *Adjusted subpart F inclusions.*—(*i*) *In general.*—Subject to the limitation in paragraph (d)(4)(i)(B)(*1*)(*ii*) of this section, the account is reduced by an adjusted subpart F inclusion with respect to the share for the taxable year, as determined pursuant to the rules of paragraph (d)(4)(ii) of this section.

(*ii*) *Limitation.*—The reduction pursuant to paragraph (d)(4)(i)(B)(*1*)(*i*) of this section cannot exceed the hybrid deductions of the CFC allocated to the share for the taxable year multiplied by a fraction, the numerator of which is the sum of the items of gross income of the CFC that give rise to subpart F income (determined without regard to an amount treated as subpart F income by reason of section 964(e)(4)(A)(i), to the extent that a deduction under section 245A(a) is allowed for a portion of the amount included under section 964(e)(4)(A)(ii) in the gross income of a domestic corporation) of the CFC for the taxable year and the denominator of which is the sum of all the items of gross income of the CFC for the taxable year.

(*iii*) *Special rule allocating otherwise unused adjusted subpart F inclusions across accounts in certain cases.*—This paragraph (d)(4)(i)(B)(*1*)(*iii*) applies after each of the specified owner's hybrid deduction accounts with respect to its shares of stock of the CFC are adjusted pursuant to paragraph (d)(4)(i)(B)(*1*)(*i*) of this section but before the accounts are adjusted pursuant to paragraph (d)(4)(i)(B)(*2*) of this section, to the extent that one or more of the hybrid deduction accounts would have been reduced by an amount pursuant to paragraph (d)(4)(i)(B)(*1*)(*i*) of this section but for the limitation in paragraph (d)(4)(i)(B)(*1*)(*ii*) of this section (the aggregate of the amounts that would have been reduced but for the limitation, the *unused reduction amount*, and the accounts that would have been reduced by the unused reduction amount, the *unused reduction amount accounts*). When this paragraph (d)(4)(i)(B)(*1*)(*iii*) applies, the specified owner's hybrid deduction accounts other than the unused reduction amount accounts (if any) are ratably reduced by the lesser of the unused reduction amount and the difference of the following two amounts: the hybrid deductions of the CFC allocated to the specified owner's shares of stock of the CFC for the taxable year multiplied by the fraction described in paragraph (d)(4)(i)(B)(*1*)(*ii*) of this section; and the reductions pursuant to paragraph (d)(4)(i)(B)(*1*)(*i*) of this section with respect to the specified owner's shares of stock of the CFC.

(*2*) *Adjusted GILTI inclusions.*—(*i*) *In general.*—Subject to the limitation in paragraph (d)(4)(i)(B)(*2*)(*ii*) of this section, the account is reduced by an adjusted GILTI inclusion with respect to the share for the taxable year, as determined pursuant to the rules of paragraph (d)(4)(ii) of this section.

(*ii*) *Limitation.*—The reduction pursuant to paragraph (d)(4)(i)(B)(*2*)(*i*) of this section cannot exceed the hybrid deductions of the CFC allocated to the share for the taxable year multiplied by a fraction, the numerator of which is the sum of the items of gross tested income of the CFC for the taxable year and the denominator of which is the sum of all the items of gross income of the CFC for the taxable year.

(*iii*) *Special rule allocating otherwise unused adjusted GILTI inclusions across accounts in certain cases.*—This paragraph (d)(4)(i)(B)(*2*)(*iii*) applies after each of the specified owner's hybrid deduction accounts with respect to its shares of stock of the CFC are adjusted pursuant to paragraph (d)(4)(i)(B)(*2*)(*i*) of this section but before the accounts are adjusted pursuant to paragraph (d)(4)(i)(B)(*3*) of this section, to the extent that one or more of the hybrid deduction accounts would have been reduced by an amount pursuant to paragraph (d)(4)(i)(B)(*2*)(*i*) of this section but for the limitation in paragraph (d)(4)(i)(B)(*2*)(*ii*) of this section (the aggregate of the amounts that would have been reduced but for the limitation, the *unused reduction amount*, and the accounts that would have been reduced by the unused reduction amount, the *unused reduction amount accounts*). When this paragraph (d)(4)(i)(B)(*2*)(*iii*) applies, the specified owner's hybrid deduction accounts other than the unused reduction amount accounts (if any) are ratably reduced by the lesser of the unused reduction amount and the difference of the following two amounts: the hybrid deductions of the CFC allocated to the specified owner's shares of stock of the CFC for the taxable year multiplied by the fraction described in paragraph (d)(4)(i)(B)(*2*)(*ii*) of this section; and the reductions pursuant to paragraph (d)(4)(i)(B)(*2*)(*i*) of this section with respect to the specified owner's shares of stock of the CFC. *See* paragraph (g)(1)(v)(C) of this section for an illustration of the application of this paragraph (d)(4)(i)(B)(*2*)(*iii*).

(*3*) *Certain section 956 inclusions.*—The account is reduced by an amount included in the gross income of a domestic corporation under sections 951(a)(1)(B) and 956 with respect to the share for the taxable year of the domestic corporation in which or with which the CFC's taxable year ends, to the extent so included by reason of the application of section 245A(e) and this section to the hypothetical distribution described in § 1.956-1(a)(2).

(C) Third, the account is decreased by the amount of hybrid deductions in the account that gave rise to a hybrid dividend or tiered hybrid dividend during the taxable year. If the specified owner has more than one hybrid deduction account with respect to its stock of the CFC, then a pro rata amount in each hybrid deduction account is considered to have given rise to the hybrid dividend or tiered hybrid dividend, based on the amounts in the accounts before applying this paragraph (d)(4)(i)(C).

(ii) *Rules regarding adjusted subpart F and GILTI inclusions.*—(A) The term *adjusted subpart F inclusion* means, with respect to a share of stock of a CFC for a taxable year of the CFC, a domestic corporation's pro rata share of the CFC's subpart F income included in gross income under section 951(a)(1)(A) (determined without regard to an amount included in gross income by the domestic corporation by reason of section 964(e)(4)(A)(ii), to the extent a deduction under section 245A(a) is allowed for the amount) for the taxable year of the domestic corporation in which or with which the CFC's taxable year ends, to the extent attributable to the share (as determined under the principles of section 951(a)(2) and § 1.951-1(b) and (e)), adjusted (but not below zero) by—

(*1*) Adding to the amount the associated foreign income taxes with respect to the amount; and

(2) Subtracting from such sum the quotient of the associated foreign income taxes divided by the percentage described in section 11(b).

(B) The term *adjusted GILTI inclusion* means, with respect to a share of stock of a CFC for a taxable year of the CFC, a domestic corporation's GILTI inclusion amount (within the meaning of § 1.951A-1(c)(1)) for the U.S. shareholder inclusion year (within the meaning of § 1.951A-1(f)(7)), to the extent attributable to the share (as determined under paragraph (d)(4)(ii)(C) of this section), adjusted (but not below zero) by—

(1) Adding to the amount the associated foreign income taxes with respect to the amount;

(2) Multiplying such sum by the difference of 100 percent and the section 250(a)(1)(B)(i) deduction percentage; and

(3) Subtracting from such product the quotient of 80 percent of the associated foreign income taxes divided by the percentage described in section 11(b).

(C) A domestic corporation's GILTI inclusion amount for a U.S. shareholder inclusion year is attributable to a share of stock of the CFC based on a fraction—

(1) The numerator of which is the domestic corporation's pro rata share of the tested income of the CFC for the U.S. shareholder inclusion year, to the extent attributable to the share (as determined under the principles of § 1.951A-1(d)(2)); and

(2) The denominator of which is the aggregate of the each domestic corporation's pro rata share of the tested income of each tested income CFC (as defined in § 1.951A-2(b)(1)) for the U.S. shareholder inclusion year.

(D) The term *associated foreign income taxes* means—

(1) With respect to a domestic corporation's pro rata share of the subpart F income of the CFC included in gross income under section 951(a)(1)(A) and attributable to a share of stock of a CFC for a taxable year of the CFC, current year tax (as described in § 1.960-1(b)(4)) allocated and apportioned under § 1.960-1(d)(3)(ii) to the subpart F income groups (as described in § 1.960-1(b)(30)) of the CFC for the taxable year, to the extent allocated to the share under paragraph (d)(4)(ii)(E) of this section; and

(2) With respect to a domestic corporation's GILTI inclusion amount under section 951A attributable to a share of stock of a CFC for a taxable year of the CFC, the product of—

(i) Current year tax (as described in § 1.960-1(b)(4)) allocated and apportioned under § 1.960-1(d)(3)(ii) to the tested income groups (as described in § 1.960-1(b)(33)) of the CFC for the taxable year, to the extent allocated to the share under paragraph (d)(4)(ii)(F) of this section;

(ii) The domestic corporation's inclusion percentage (as described in § 1.960-2(c)(2)); and

(iii) The section 904 limitation fraction with respect to the domestic corporation for the U.S. shareholder inclusion year.

(E) Current year tax allocated and apportioned to a subpart F income group of a CFC for a taxable year is allocated to a share of stock of the CFC by multiplying the foreign income tax by a fraction—

(1) The numerator of which is the domestic corporation's pro rata share of the subpart F income of the CFC for the taxable year, to the extent attributable to the share (as determined under the principles of section 951(a)(2) and § 1.951-1(b) and (e)); and

(2) The denominator of which is the subpart F income of the CFC for the taxable year.

(F) Current year tax allocated and apportioned to a tested income group of a CFC for a taxable year is allocated to a share of stock of the CFC by multiplying the foreign income tax by a fraction—

(1) The numerator of which is the domestic corporation's pro rata share of tested income of the CFC for the taxable year, to the extent attributable to the share (as determined under the principles § 1.951A-1(d)(2)); and

(2) The denominator of which is the tested income of the CFC for the taxable year.

(G) The term *section 904 limitation fraction* means, with respect to a domestic corporation for a U.S. shareholder inclusion year, a fraction—

(1) The numerator of which is the amount of foreign tax credits for the U.S. shareholder inclusion year that, by reason of sections 901 and 960(d) and taking into account section 904, the domestic corporation is allowed for the separate category set forth in section 904(d)(1)(A) (amounts includible in gross income under section 951A); and

(2) The denominator of which is the amount of foreign tax credits for the U.S. shareholder inclusion year that, by reason of sections 901 and 960(d) and without regard to section 904, the domestic corporation would be allowed for the separate category set forth in section 904(d)(1)(A) (amounts includible in gross income under section 951A).

(H) The term *section 250(a)(1)(B)(i) deduction percentage* means, with respect to a domestic corporation for a U.S. shareholder inclusion year, a fraction—

(1) The numerator of which is the amount of the deduction under section 250 allowed to the domestic corporation for the U.S. shareholder inclusion year by reason of section 250(a)(1)(B)(i) (taking into account section 250(a)(2)(B)); and

(2) The denominator of which is the domestic corporation's GILTI inclusion amount for the U.S. shareholder inclusion year.

(iii) *Acquisition of account and certain other adjustments.*—(A) *In general.*—The following rules apply when a person (the *acquirer*) directly or indirectly through a partnership, trust, or estate acquires a share of stock of a CFC from another person (the *transferor*).

(1) In the case of an acquirer that is a specified owner of the share immediately after the acquisition, the transferor's hybrid deduction account, if any, with respect to the share becomes the hybrid deduction account of the acquirer.

(2) In the case of an acquirer that is not a specified owner of the share immediately after the acquisition, the transferor's hybrid deduction account, if any, is eliminated and accordingly is not thereafter taken into account by any person.

(B) *Additional rules.*—The following rules apply in addition to the rules of paragraph (d)(4)(iii)(A) of this section.

(1) Certain section 354 or 356 exchanges.—The following rules apply when a shareholder of a CFC (the CFC, the *target CFC;* the shareholder, the *exchanging shareholder*) exchanges stock of the target CFC for stock of another CFC (the *acquiring CFC*) pursuant to an exchange described in section 354 or 356 that occurs in connection with a transaction described in section 381(a)(2) in which the target CFC is the transferor corporation.

(i) In the case of an exchanging shareholder that is a specified owner of one or more shares of stock of the acquiring CFC immediately after the exchange, the exchanging shareholder's hybrid deduction accounts with respect to the shares of stock of the target CFC that it exchanges are attributed to the shares of stock of the acquiring CFC that it receives in the exchange.

(ii) In the case of an exchanging shareholder that is not a specified owner of one or more shares of stock of the acquiring CFC immediately after the exchange, the exchanging shareholder's hybrid deduction accounts with respect to its shares of stock of the target CFC are eliminated and accordingly are not thereafter taken into account by any person.

(2) Section 332 liquidations.—If a CFC is a distributor corporation in a transaction described in section 381(a)(1) (the *distributor CFC*) in which a controlled foreign corporation is the acquiring corporation (the *distributee CFC*), then each hybrid deduction account with respect to a share of stock of the distributee CFC is increased pro rata by the sum of the hybrid deduction accounts with respect to shares of stock of the distributor CFC.

(3) Recapitalizations.—If a shareholder of a CFC exchanges stock of the CFC pursuant to a reorganization described in section 368(a)(1)(E) or a transaction to which section 1036 applies, then the shareholder's hybrid deduction accounts with respect to the stock of the CFC that it exchanges are attributed to the shares of stock of the CFC that it receives in the exchange.

(4) Certain distributions involving section 355 or 356.—In the case of a transaction involving a distribution under section 355 (or so much of section 356 as it relates to section 355) by a CFC (the *distributing CFC*) of stock of another CFC (the *controlled CFC*), the balance of the hybrid deduction accounts with respect to stock of the distributing CFC is attributed to stock of the controlled CFC in a manner similar to how earnings and profits of the distributing CFC and controlled CFC are adjusted. To the extent the balance of the hybrid deduction accounts with respect to stock of the distributing CFC is not so attributed to stock of the controlled CFC, such balance remains as the balance of the hybrid deduction accounts with respect to stock of the distributing CFC.

(5) Effect of section 338(g) election.—*(i) In general.*—If an election under section 338(g) is made with respect to a qualified stock purchase (as described in section 338(d)(3)) of stock of a CFC, then a

hybrid deduction account with respect to a share of stock of the old target is not treated as (or attributed to) a hybrid deduction account with respect to a share of stock of the new target. Accordingly, immediately after the deemed asset sale described in § 1.338-1, the balance of a hybrid deduction account with respect to a share of stock of the new target is zero; the account must then be maintained in accordance with the rules of paragraph (d) of this section.

(ii) *Special rule regarding carryover FT stock.*—Paragraph (d)(4)(iii)(B)(5)(*i*) of this section does not apply as to a hybrid deduction account with respect to a share of carryover FT stock (as described in § 1.338-9(b)(3)(i)). A hybrid deduction account with respect to a share of carryover FT stock is attributed to the corresponding share of stock of the new target.

(5) *Determinations and adjustments made during year of transfer in certain cases.*—This paragraph (d)(5) applies if on a date other than the date that is the last day of the CFC's taxable year a United States shareholder of the CFC or an upper-tier CFC with respect to the CFC directly or indirectly (as determined under the principles of § 1.245A-5(g)(3)(ii)) transfers a share of stock of the CFC, and, during the taxable year, but on or before the transfer date, the United States shareholder or upper-tier CFC receives an amount from the CFC that is subject to the rules of section 245A(e) and this section. In such a case, the following rules apply:

(i) As to the United States shareholder or upper-tier CFC and the United States shareholder's or upper-tier CFC's hybrid deduction accounts with respect to each share of stock of the CFC (regardless of whether such share is transferred), the determinations and adjustments under this section that would otherwise be made at the close of the CFC's taxable year are made at the close of the date of the transfer. When making these determinations and adjustments at the close of the date of the transfer, each hybrid deduction account described in the previous sentence is pursuant to paragraph (d)(4)(ii)(A) of this section increased by a ratable portion (based on the number of days in the taxable year within the pre-transfer period to the total number of days in the taxable year) of the hybrid deductions of the CFC allocated to the share for the taxable year, and pursuant to paragraph (d)(4)(ii)(C) of this section decreased by the amount of hybrid deductions in the account that gave rise to a hybrid dividend or tiered hybrid dividend during the portion of the taxable year up to and including the transfer date. Thus, for example, if a United States shareholder of a CFC exchanges stock of the CFC in an exchange described in § 1.367(b)-4(b)(1)(i) and is required to include in income as a deemed dividend the section 1248 amount attributable to the stock exchanged, then: as of the close of the date of the exchange, each of the United States shareholder's hybrid deductions accounts with respect to a share of stock of the CFC is increased by a ratable portion of the hybrid deductions of the CFC allocated to the share for the taxable year (based on the number of days in the taxable year within the pre-transfer period to the total number of days in the taxable year); the deemed dividend is a hybrid dividend to the extent of the sum of the United States shareholder's hybrid deduction accounts with respect to each share of stock of the CFC; and, as the close of the date of the exchange, each of the accounts is decreased by the amount of hybrid deductions in the account that gave rise to a hybrid dividend during the portion of the taxable year up to and including the date of the exchange.

(ii) As to a hybrid deduction account described in paragraph (d)(5)(i) of this section, the adjustments to the account as of the close of the taxable year of the CFC must take into account the adjustments, if any, occurring with respect to the account pursuant to paragraph (d)(5)(i) of this section. Thus, for example, if an acquisition of a share of stock of a CFC occurs on a date other than the date that is the last day of the CFC's taxable year and pursuant to paragraph (d)(4)(iii)(A)(*1*) of this section the acquirer succeeds to the transferor's hybrid deduction account with respect to the share, then, as of the close of the taxable year of the CFC, the account is increased by a ratable portion of the hybrid deductions of the CFC allocated to the share for the taxable year (based on the number of days in the taxable year within the post-transfer period to the total number of days in the taxable year), and, decreased by the amount of hybrid deductions in the account that gave rise to a hybrid dividend or tiered hybrid dividend during the portion of the taxable year following the transfer date.

(6) *Effects of CFC functional currency.*—(i) *Maintenance of the hybrid deduction account.*—A hybrid deduction account with respect to a share of CFC stock must be maintained in the functional currency (within the meaning of section 985) of the CFC. Thus, for example, the amount of a hybrid deduction and the adjustments described in paragraphs (d)(4)(i)(A) and (B) of this section are determined based on the functional currency of the CFC. In addition, for purposes of this section, the amount of a deduction or other tax benefit allowed to a CFC (or a person related to the CFC) is determined taking into account foreign currency gain or loss recognized with respect to such deduction or other tax benefit under a provision of foreign tax law comparable to section 988 (treatment of certain foreign currency transactions).

(ii) *Determination of amount of hybrid dividend.*—This paragraph (d)(6)(ii) applies if a CFC's functional currency is other than the functional currency of a United States shareholder or upper-tier CFC that receives an amount from the CFC that is subject to the rules of section 245A(e) and this section. In such a case, the sum of the United States shareholder's or upper-tier CFC's hybrid deduction accounts with respect to each share of stock of the CFC is, for purposes of determining the extent that a dividend is a hybrid dividend or tiered hybrid dividend, translated into the functional currency of the United States shareholder or upper-tier CFC based on the spot rate (within the meaning of § 1.988-1(d)) as of the date of the dividend.

(e) *Anti-avoidance rule.*—Appropriate adjustments are made pursuant to this section, including adjustments that would disregard the transaction or arrangement, if a transaction or arrangement is undertaken with a principal purpose of avoiding the purposes of section 245A(e) and this section. For example, if a specified owner of a share of CFC stock transfers the share to another person, and a principal purpose of the transfer is to shift the hybrid deduction account with respect to the share to the other person or to cause the hybrid deduction account to be eliminated, then for purposes of this section the shifting or elimination of the hybrid deduction account is disregarded as to the transferor. As another example, if a transaction or arrangement is undertaken to affirmatively fail to satisfy the holding period requirement under section 246(c)(5) with a principal purpose of avoiding the tiered hybrid dividend rules described in paragraph (c) of this section, the transaction or arrangement is disregarded for purposes of this section. This paragraph (e) will not apply, however, to disregard (or make other adjustments with respect to) a transaction pursuant to which an instrument or arrangement that gives rise to hybrid deductions is eliminated or otherwise converted into another instrument or arrangement that does not give rise to hybrid deductions.

(f) *Definitions.*—The following definitions apply for purposes of this section.

(1) The term *controlled foreign corporation* (or *CFC*) has the meaning provided in section 957.

(2) The term *domestic corporation* means an entity classified as a domestic corporation under section 7701(a)(3) and (4) or otherwise treated as a domestic corporation by the Internal Revenue Code. However, for purposes of this section, a domestic corporation does not include a regulated investment company (as described in section 851), a real estate investment trust (as described in section 856), or an S corporation (as described in section 1361).

(3) The term *person* has the meaning provided in section 7701(a)(1).

(4) The term *related* has the meaning provided in this paragraph (f)(4). A person is related to a CFC if the person is a related person within the meaning of section 954(d)(3). *See also* § 1.954-1(f)(2)(iv)(B)(*1*) (neither section 318(a)(3), nor § 1.958-2(d) or the principles thereof, applies to attribute stock or other interests).

(5) The term *relevant foreign tax law* means, with respect to a CFC, any regime of any foreign country or possession of the United States that imposes an income, war profits, or excess profits tax with respect to income of the CFC, other than a foreign anti-deferral regime under which a person that owns an interest in the CFC is liable to tax. If a foreign country has an income tax treaty with the United States that applies to taxes imposed by a political subdivision or other local authority of that country, then the tax law of the political subdivision or other local authority is deemed to be a tax law of a foreign country. Thus, the term includes any regime of a foreign country or possession of the United States that imposes income, war profits, or excess profits tax under which—

(i) The CFC is liable to tax as a resident;

(ii) The CFC has a branch that gives rise to a taxable presence in the foreign country or possession of the United States; or

(iii) A person related to the CFC is liable to tax as a resident, provided that under such person's tax law the person is allowed a deduction for amounts paid or accrued by the CFC (because the CFC is fiscally transparent under the person's tax law).

(6) The term *specified owner* means, with respect to a share of stock of a CFC, a person for which the requirements of paragraphs (f)(6)(i) and (ii) of this section are satisfied.

(i) The person is a domestic corporation that is a United States shareholder of the CFC, or is an upper tier CFC that would be a United States shareholder of the CFC were the upper-tier CFC a domestic corporation (provided that, for purposes of sections 951 and 951A, a domestic corporation that is a United States shareholder of the upper-tier CFC owns (within the meaning of section 958(a), and determined by treating a domestic partnership as foreign) one or more shares of stock of the upper-tier CFC).

(ii) The person owns the share directly or indirectly through a partnership, trust, or estate. Thus, for example, if a domestic corporation directly owns all the shares of stock of an upper-tier CFC and the upper-tier CFC directly owns all the shares of stock of another CFC, the domestic corporation is the specified owner with respect to each share of stock of the upper-tier CFC and the upper-tier CFC is the specified owner with respect to each share of stock of the other CFC.

(7) The term *United States shareholder* has the meaning provided in section 951(b).

(g) *Examples.*—This paragraph (g) provides examples that illustrate the application of this section. For purposes of the examples in this paragraph (g), unless otherwise indicated, the following facts are presumed. US1 is a domestic corporation. FX and FZ are CFCs formed at the beginning of year 1, and the functional currency (within the meaning of section 985) of each of FX and FZ is the dollar. FX is a tax resident of Country X and FZ is a tax resident of Country Z. US1 is a United States shareholder with respect to FX and FZ. No distributed amounts are attributable to amounts which are, or have been, included in the gross income of a United States shareholder under section 951(a). All instruments are treated as stock for U.S. tax purposes. Only the tax law of the United States contains hybrid mismatch rules. No amounts are included in the gross income of US1 under section 951(a)(1)(A), 951A(a), or 951(a)(1)(B) and section 956.

(1) *Example 1. Hybrid dividend resulting from hybrid instrument.*—(i) *Facts.* US1 holds both shares of stock of FX, which have an equal value. One share is treated as indebtedness for Country X tax purposes ("Share A"), and the other is treated as equity for Country X tax purposes ("Share B"). During year 1, under Country X tax law, FX accrues $80x of interest to US1 with respect to Share A and is allowed a deduction for the amount (the "Hybrid Instrument Deduction"). During year 2, FX distributes $30x to US1 with respect to each of Share A and Share B. For U.S. tax purposes, each of the $30x distributions is treated as a dividend for which, without regard to section 245A(e) and this section as well as § 1.245A-5, US1 would be allowed a deduction under section 245A(a). For Country X tax purposes, the $30x distribution with respect to Share A represents a payment of interest for which a deduction was already allowed (and thus FX is not allowed an additional deduction for the amount), and the $30x distribution with respect to Share B is treated as a dividend (for which no deduction is allowed).

(ii) *Analysis.* The entire $30x of each dividend received by US1 from FX during year 2 is a hybrid dividend, because the sum of US1's hybrid deduction accounts with respect to each of its shares of FX stock at the end of year 2 ($80x) is at least equal to the amount of the dividends ($60x). *See* paragraph (b)(2) of this section. This is the case for the $30x dividend with respect to Share B even though there are no hybrid deductions allocated to Share B. *See* paragraph (b)(2) of this section. As a result, US1 is not allowed a deduction under section 245A(a) for the entire $60x of hybrid dividends and the rules of section 245A(d) and § 1.245A(d)-1 (disallowance of foreign tax credits and deductions) apply. *See* paragraph (b)(1) of this section. Paragraphs (g)(1)(ii)(A) through (D) of this section describe the determinations under this section.

(A) At the end of year 1, US1's hybrid deduction accounts with respect to Share A and Share B are $80x and $0, respectively, calculated as follows.

(*1*) The $80x Hybrid Instrument Deduction allowed to FX under Country X tax law (a relevant foreign tax law) is a hybrid deduction of FX, because the deduction is allowed to FX and relates to or results from an amount accrued with respect to an instrument issued by FX and treated as stock for U.S. tax purposes. *See* paragraph (d)(2)(i) of this section. Thus, FX's hybrid deductions for year 1 are $80x.

(*2*) The entire $80x Hybrid Instrument Deduction is allocated to Share A, because the deduction was accrued with respect to Share A. *See* paragraph (d)(3) of this section. As there are no additional hybrid deductions of FX for year 1, there are no additional hybrid deductions to allocate to either Share A or Share B. Thus, there are no hybrid deductions allocated to Share B.

(*3*) At the end of year 1, US1's hybrid deduction account with respect to Share A is increased by $80x (the amount of hybrid deductions allocated to Share A). *See* paragraph (d)(4)(i)(A) of this section. Because FX did not pay any dividends with respect to either Share A or Share B during year 1 (and therefore did not pay any hybrid dividends or tiered hybrid dividends), no further adjustments are made. *See* paragraph (d)(4)(i)(C) of this section. Therefore, at the end of year 1, US1's hybrid deduction accounts with respect to Share A and Share B are $80x and $0, respectively.

(B) At the end of year 2, and before the adjustments described in paragraph (d)(4)(i)(C) of this section, US1's hybrid deduction accounts with respect to Share A and Share B remain $80x and $0, respectively. This is because there are no hybrid deductions of FX for year 2. *See* paragraph (d)(4)(i)(A) of this section.

(C) Because at the end of year 2 (and before the adjustments described in paragraph (d)(4)(i)(C) of this section) the sum of US1's hybrid deduction accounts with respect to Share A and Share B ($80x, calculated as $80x plus $0) is at least equal to the aggregate $60x of year 2 dividends, the entire $60x dividend is a hybrid dividend. *See* paragraph (b)(2) of this section.

(D) At the end of year 2, US1's hybrid deduction account with respect to Share A is decreased by $60x, the amount of the hybrid deductions in the account that gave rise to a hybrid dividend or tiered hybrid dividend during year 2. *See* paragraph (d)(4)(i)(C) of this section. Because there are no hybrid deductions in the hybrid deduction account with respect to Share B, no adjustments with respect to that account are made under paragraph (d)(4)(i)(C) of this section. Therefore, at the end of year 2 and taking into account the adjustments under paragraph (d)(4)(i)(C) of this section, US1's hybrid deduction account with respect to Share A is $20x ($80x less $60x) and with respect to Share B is $0.

(iii) *Alternative facts – notional interest deductions.* The facts are the same as in paragraph (g)(1)(i) of this section, except that for each of year 1 and year 2 FX is allowed $10x of notional interest deductions with respect to its equity, Share B, under Country X tax law (the "NIDs"). In addition, during year 2, FX distributes $47.5x (rather than $30x) to US1 with respect to each of Share A and Share B. For U.S. tax purposes, each of the $47.5x distributions is treated as a dividend for which, without regard to section 245A(e) and this section as well as § 1.245A-5, US1 would be allowed a deduction under section 245A(a). For Country X tax purposes, the $47.5x distribution with respect to Share A represents a payment of interest for which a deduction was already allowed (and thus FX is not allowed an additional deduction for the amount), and the $47.5x distribution with respect to Share B is treated as a dividend (for which no deduction is allowed). The entire $47.5x of each dividend received by US1 from FX during year 2 is a hybrid dividend, because the sum of US1's hybrid deduction accounts with respect to each of its shares of FX stock at the end of year 2 ($80x plus $20x, or $100x) is at least equal to the amount of the dividends ($95x). *See* paragraph (b)(2) of this section. As a result, US1 is not allowed a deduction under section 245A(a) for the $95x hybrid dividend and the rules of section 245A(d) and § 1.245A(d)-1 (disallowance of foreign tax credits and deductions) apply. *See* paragraph (b)(1) of this section. Paragraphs (g)(1)(iii)(A) through (D) of this section describe the determinations under this section.

(A) The $10x of NIDs allowed to FX under Country X tax law in year 1 are hybrid deductions of FX for year 1. *See* paragraph (d)(2)(i) of this section. The $10x of NIDs is allocated equally to each of Share A and Share B, because the hybrid deduction is with respect to equity and the shares have an equal value. *See* paragraph (d)(3) of this section. Thus, $5x of the NIDs is allocated to each of Share A and Share B for year 1. For the reasons described in paragraph (g)(1)(ii)(A)(*2*) of this section, the entire $80x Hybrid Instrument Deduction is allocated to Share A. Therefore, at the end of year 1, US1's hybrid deduction accounts with respect to Share A and Share B are $85x and $5x, respectively.

(B) Similarly, the $10x of NIDs allowed to FX under Country X tax law in year 2 are hybrid deductions of FX for year 2, and $5x of the NIDs is allocated to each of Share A and Share B for year 2. *See* paragraphs (d)(2)(i) and (d)(3) of this section. Thus, at the end of year 2 (and before the adjustments described in paragraph (d)(4)(i)(C) of this section), US1's hybrid deduction account with respect to Share A is $90x ($85x plus $5x) and with respect to Share B is $10x ($5x plus $5x). *See* paragraph (d)(4)(i) of this section.

(C) Because at the end of year 2 (and before the adjustments described in paragraph (d)(4)(i)(C) of this section) the sum of US1's hybrid deduction accounts with respect to Share A and Share B ($100x, calculated as $90x plus $10x) is at least equal to the aggregate $95x of year 2 dividends, the entire $95x of dividends are hybrid dividends. *See* paragraph (b)(2) of this section.

(D) At the end of year 2, US1's hybrid deduction accounts with respect to Share A and Share B are decreased by the amount of hybrid deductions in the accounts that gave rise to a hybrid dividend or tiered hybrid dividend during year 2. *See* paragraph (d)(4)(i)(C) of this section. A total of $95x of hybrid deductions in the accounts gave rise to a hybrid dividend during year 2. For the hybrid deduction account with respect to Share A, $85.5x in the account is considered to have given rise to a hybrid deduction (calculated as $95x multiplied by $90x/$100x). *See* paragraph (d)(4)(i)(C) of this section. For the hybrid deduction account with respect to Share B, $9.5x in the account is considered to have given rise to a hybrid deduction (calculated as $95x multiplied by $10x/$100x). *See* paragraph (d)(4)(i)(C) of this section. Thus, following these adjustments, at the end of year 2, US1's hybrid deduction account with respect to Share A is $4.5x ($90x less $85.5x) and with respect to Share B is $0.5x ($10x less $9.5x).

(iv) *Alternative facts – deduction in branch country*—(A) *Facts.* The facts are the same as in paragraph (g)(1)(i) of this section, except that for Country X tax purposes Share A is treated as equity (and thus the Hybrid Instrument Deduction does not exist, and under Country X tax law FX is not allowed a deduction for the $30x distributed in year 2 with respect to Share A). However, FX has a branch in Country Z that gives rise to a taxable presence under Country Z tax law, and for Country Z tax purposes Share A is treated as indebtedness and Share B is treated as equity. Also, during year 1, for Country Z tax purposes, FX accrues $80x of interest to US1 with respect to Share A and is allowed an $80x interest deduction with respect to its Country Z branch income. Moreover, for Country Z tax purposes, the $30x distribution with respect to Share A in year 2 represents a payment of interest for which a deduction was already allowed (and thus FX is not allowed an additional deduction for the amount), and the $30x distribution with respect to Share B in year 2 is treated as a dividend (for which no deduction is allowed).

(B) *Analysis.* The $80x interest deduction allowed to FX under Country Z tax law (a relevant foreign tax law) with respect to its Country Z branch income is a hybrid deduction of FX for year 1. *See* paragraphs (d)(2)(i) and (f)(5) of this section. For reasons similar to those discussed in paragraph (g)(1)(ii) of this section, at the end of year 2 (and before the adjustments described in paragraph (d)(4)(i)(C) of this section), US1's hybrid deduction accounts with respect to Share A and Share B are $80x and $0, respectively, and the sum of the accounts is $80x. Accordingly, the entire $60x of the year 2 dividend is a hybrid dividend. *See* paragraph (b)(2) of this section. Further, for the reasons described in paragraph (g)(1)(ii)(D) of this section, at the end of year 2 and taking into account the adjustments under paragraph (d)(4)(i)(C) of this section, US1's hybrid deduction account with respect to Share A is $20x ($80x less $60x) and with respect to Share B is $0.

(v) *Alternative facts — account reduced by adjusted GILTI inclusion*—The facts are the same as in paragraph (g)(1)(i) of this section, except that for taxable year 1 FX has $130x of gross tested income and $10.5x of current year tax (as described in § 1.960-1(b)(4)) that is allocated and apportioned under § 1.960-1(d)(3)(ii) to the tested income groups of FX. US1's ability to credit the $10.5x of current year tax is not limited under section 904(a). In addition, FX has $119.5x of tested income ($130x of gross tested income, less the $10.5x of current year tax deductions properly allocable to the gross tested income). Further, of US1's pro rata share of the tested income ($119.5x), $80x is attributable to Share A and $39.5x is attributable to Share B (as determined under the principles of § 1.951A-1(d)(2)). Moreover, US1's net deemed tangible income return (as defined in § 1.951A-1(c)(3)) for taxable year 1 is $71.7x, and US1 does not own any stock of a CFC other than its stock of FX. Thus, US1's GILTI inclusion amount (within the meaning of § 1.951A-1(c)(1)) for taxable year 1, the U.S. shareholder inclusion year, is $47.8x (net CFC tested income of $119.5x, less net deemed tangible income return of $71.7x) and US1's inclusion percentage (as described in § 1.960-2(c)(2)) is 40 ($47.8x/$119.5x). The deduction allowed to US1 under section 250 by reason of section 250(a)(1)(B)(i) is not limited as a result of section 250(a)(2)(B). At the end of year 1, US1's hybrid deduction account with respect to Share A is: first, increased by $80x (the amount of hybrid deductions allocated to Share A); and second, decreased by $10x (the sum of the adjusted GILTI inclusion with respect to Share A, and the adjusted GILTI inclusion with respect to Share B that is allocated to the hybrid deduction account with respect to Share A) to $70x. *See* paragraphs (d)(4)(i)(A) and (B) of this section. In year 2, the entire $30x of each dividend received by US1 from FX during year 2 is a hybrid dividend, because the sum of US1's hybrid deduction accounts with respect to each of its shares of FX stock at the end of year 2 ($70x) is at least equal to the amount of the dividends ($60x). *See* paragraph (b)(2) of this section. At the end of year 2, US1's hybrid deduction account with respect to Share A is decreased by $60x (the amount of the hybrid deductions in the account that give rise to a hybrid dividend or tiered hybrid dividend during year 2) to $10x. *See* paragraph (d)(4)(i)(C) of this section. Paragraphs (g)(1)(v)(A) through (C) of this section describe the computations pursuant to paragraph (d)(4)(i)(B)(*2*) of this section.

(A) To determine the adjusted GILTI inclusion with respect to Share A for taxable year 1, it must be determined to what extent US1's $47.8x GILTI inclusion amount is attributable to Share A. *See* paragraph (d)(4)(ii)(B) of this section. Here, $32x of the inclusion is attributable to Share A, calculated as $47.8x multiplied by a fraction, the numerator of which is $80x (US1's pro rata share of the tested income of FX attributable to Share A) and denominator of which is $119.5x (US1's pro rata share of the tested income of FX, its only CFC). *See* paragraph (d)(4)(ii)(C) of this section. Next, the associated foreign income taxes with respect to the $32x GILTI inclusion amount attributable to Share A must be determined. *See* paragraphs (d)(4)(ii)(B) and (D) of this section. Such associated foreign income taxes are $2.8x, calculated as $10.5x (the current year tax allocated and apportioned to the tested income groups of FX) multiplied by a fraction, the numerator of which is $80x (US1's pro rata share of the tested income of FX attributable to Share A) and the denominator of which is $119.5x (the tested income of FX), multiplied by 40% (US1's inclusion percentage), multiplied by 1 (the section 904 limitation fraction with respect to US1's GILTI inclusion amount). *See* paragraphs (d)(4)(ii)(D), (F), and (G) of this section. Thus, pursuant to paragraph (d)(4)(ii)(B) of this section, the adjusted GILTI inclusion with respect to Share A is $6.7x, computed by—

(*1*) Adding $2.8x (the associated foreign income taxes with respect to the $32x GILTI inclusion attributable to Share A) to $32x, which is $34.8x;

(*2*) Multiplying $34.8x (the sum of the amounts in paragraph (g)(1)(v)(A)(*1*) of this section) by 50% (the difference of 100 percent and the section 250(a)(1)(B)(i) deduction percentage), which is $17.4x; and

(*3*) Subtracting $10.7x (calculated as $2.24x (80% of the $2.8x of associated foreign income taxes) divided by .21 (the percentage described in section 11(b)) from $17.4x (the product of the amounts in paragraph (g)(1)(v)(A)(*2*) of this section), which is $6.7x.

(B) Pursuant to computations similar to those discussed in paragraph (g)(1)(v)(A) of this section, the adjusted GILTI inclusion with respect to Share B is $3.3x. However, the hybrid deduction account with respect to Share B is not reduced by such $3.3x, because of the limitation in paragraph (d)(4)(i)(B)(*2*)(*ii*) of this section, which, with respect to Share B, limits the reduction pursuant to paragraph (d)(4)(i)(B)(*2*)(*i*) of this section to $0 (calculated as $0, the hybrid deductions allocated to the share for the taxable year, multiplied by 1, the fraction described in paragraph (d)(4)(i)(B)(*2*)(*ii*) of this section (computed as $130x, the sole item of gross tested income, divided by $130x, the sole item of gross income)). *See* paragraphs (d)(4)(i)(B)(*2*)(*i*) and (*ii*) of this section.

(C) US1's hybrid deduction account with respect to Share A is reduced by the entire $6.7x adjusted GILTI inclusion with respect to the share, as such $6.7x does not exceed the limit in paragraph (d)(4)(i)(B)(*2*)(*ii*) of this section ($80x, calculated as $80x, the hybrid deductions allocated to the share for the taxable year, multiplied by 1, the fraction described in paragraph (d)(4)(i)(B)(*2*)(*ii*) of this section). *See* paragraphs (d)(4)(i)(B)(*2*)(*i*) and (*ii*) of this section. In addition, the hybrid deduction account is reduced by another $3.3x, the amount of the adjusted GILTI inclusion with respect to Share B that is allocated to the hybrid deduction account with respect to Share A. *See* paragraph (d)(4)(i)(B)(*2*)(*iii*) of this section. As a result, pursuant to paragraph (d)(4)(i)(B)(*2*) of this section, US1's hybrid deduction account with respect to Share A is reduced by $10x ($6.7x plus $3.3x).

(2) *Example 2. Tiered hybrid dividend rule; tax benefit equivalent to a deduction.*—(i) *Facts.* US1 holds all the stock of FX, and FX holds all 100 shares of stock of FZ (the "FZ shares"), which have an equal value. The FZ shares are treated as equity for Country Z tax purposes. At the end of year 1, the sum of FX's hybrid deduction accounts with respect to each of its shares of FZ stock is $0. During year 2, FZ distributes $10x to FX with respect to each of the FZ shares, for a total of $1,000x. The $1,000x is treated as a dividend for U.S. and Country Z tax purposes, and is not deductible for Country Z tax purposes. If FX were a domestic corporation, then, without regard to section 245A(e) and this section as well as § 1.245A-5, FX would be allowed a deduction under section 245A(a) for the $1,000x. Under Country Z tax law, 75% of the corporate income tax paid by a Country Z corporation with respect to a dividend distribution is refunded to the corporation's shareholders (regardless of where such shareholders are tax residents) upon a dividend distribution by the corporation. The corporate tax rate in Country Z is 20%. With respect

to FZ's distributions, FX is allowed a refundable tax credit of $187.5x. The $187.5x refundable tax credit is calculated as $1,250x (the amount of pre-tax earnings that funded the distribution, determined as $1,000x (the amount of the distribution) divided by 0.8 (the percentage of pre-tax earnings that a Country Z corporation retains after paying Country Z corporate tax)) multiplied by 0.2 (the Country Z corporate tax rate) multiplied by 0.75 (the percentage of the Country Z tax credit). Under Country Z tax law, FX is not subject to Country Z withholding tax (or any other tax) with respect to the $1,000x dividend distribution.

(ii) *Analysis*. As described in paragraphs (g)(2)(ii)(A) and (B) of this section, the sum of FX's hybrid deduction accounts with respect to each of its shares of FZ stock at the end of year 2 is $937.5x and, as a result, $937.5x of the $1,000x of dividends received by FX from FZ during year 2 is a tiered hybrid dividend. *See* paragraphs (b)(2) and (c)(2) of this section. The $937.5x tiered hybrid dividend is treated for purposes of section 951(a)(1)(A) as subpart F income of FX and US1 must include in gross income its pro rata share of such subpart F income, which is $937.5x. *See* paragraph (c)(1) of this section. This is the case notwithstanding any other provision of the Code, including section 952(c) or section 954(c)(3) or (6). In addition, the rules of section 245A(d) and § 1.245A(d)-1 (disallowance of foreign tax credits and deductions) apply with respect to US1's inclusion. *See* paragraph (c)(1) of this section. Paragraphs (g)(2)(ii)(A) through (C) of this section describe the determinations under this section. The characterization of the FZ stock for Country X tax purposes (or for purposes of any other foreign tax law) does not affect this analysis.

(A) The $187.5x refundable tax credit allowed to FX under Country Z tax law (a relevant foreign tax law) is equivalent to a $937.5x deduction, calculated as $187.5x (the amount of the credit) divided by 0.2 (the Country Z corporate tax rate). The $937.5x is a hybrid deduction of FZ because it is allowed to FX (a person related to FZ), it relates to or results from amounts distributed with respect to instruments issued by FZ and treated as stock for U.S. tax purposes, and it has the effect of causing the earnings that funded the distributions to not be included in income under Country Z tax law. *See* paragraph (d)(2)(i) of this section. $9.375x of the hybrid deduction is allocated to each of the FZ shares, calculated as $937.5x (the amount of the hybrid deduction) multiplied by 1/100 (the value of each FZ share relative to the value of all the FZ shares). *See* paragraph (d)(3) of this section. The result would be the same if FX were instead a tax resident of Country Z (and not Country X), FX were allowed the $187.5x refundable tax credit under Country Z tax law, and under Country Z tax law FX were to not include the $1,000x in income (because, for example, Country Z tax law provides Country Z resident corporations a 100% exclusion or dividends received deduction with respect to dividends received from a resident corporation). *See* paragraph (d)(2)(i) of this section.

(B) At the end of year 2, and before the adjustments described in paragraph (d)(4)(i)(C) of this section, the sum of FX's hybrid deduction accounts with respect to each of its shares of FZ stock is $937.5x, calculated as $9.375x (the amount in each account) multiplied by 100 (the number of accounts). *See* paragraph (d)(4)(i) of this section. Accordingly, $937.5x of the $1,000x dividend received by FX from FZ during year 2 is a tiered hybrid dividend. *See* paragraphs (b)(2) and (c)(2) of this section.

(C) At the end of year 2, each of FX's hybrid deduction accounts with respect to its shares of FZ is decreased by the $9.375x in the account that gave rise to a hybrid dividend or tiered hybrid dividend during year 2. *See* paragraph (d)(4)(i)(C) of this section. Thus, following these adjustments, at the end of year 2, each of FX's hybrid deduction accounts with respect to its shares of FZ stock is $0, calculated as $9.375x (the amount in the account before the adjustments described in paragraph (d)(4)(i)(C) of this section) less $9.375x (the adjustment described in paragraph (d)(4)(i)(C) of this section with respect to the account).

(iii) *Alternative facts – imputation system that taxes shareholders*. The facts are the same as in paragraph (g)(2)(i) of this section, except that under Country Z tax law the $1,000x dividend to FX is subject to a 30% gross basis withholding tax, or $300x, and the $187.5x refundable tax credit is applied against and reduces the withholding tax to $112.5x. The $187.5x refundable tax credit provided to FX is not a hybrid deduction because FX was subject to Country Z withholding tax of $300x on the $1,000x dividend (such withholding tax being greater than the $187.5x credit). *See* paragraph (d)(2)(i) of this section. If instead FZ were allowed a $1,000x dividends paid deduction for the $1,000x dividend (and FX were not allowed the refundable tax credit) and the dividend were subject to 5% gross basis withholding tax (or $50x), then $750x of the dividends paid deduction would be a hybrid deduction, calculated as the excess of $1,000x (the dividends paid deduction) over $250x (the amount of income that under Country Z tax law would produce an amount of tax equal to the $50x of withholding tax, calculated as $50x, the amount of withholding tax, divided by 0.2, the Country Z corporate tax rate). *See* paragraph (d)(2)(i) of this section.

(h) *Applicability dates*.—(1) *In general*.—Except as provided in paragraph (h)(2) of this section, this section applies to distributions made after December 31, 2017, provided that such distributions occur during taxable years ending on or after December 20, 2018. However, taxpayers may apply this section in its entirety to distributions made after December 31, 2017 and occurring during taxable years ending before December 20, 2018. In lieu of applying the regulations in this section, taxpayers may apply the provisions matching this section from the Internal Revenue Bulletin (IRB) 2019-03 (https://www.irs.gov/pub/irs-irbs/irb19-03.pdf) in their entirety for all taxable years ending on or before April 8, 2020.

(2) *Special rules*.—Paragraphs (d)(4)(i)(B) and (d)(4)(ii) of this section (decrease of hybrid deduction accounts; rules regarding adjusted subpart F and GILTI inclusions) apply to taxable years ending on or after November 12, 2020. However, a taxpayer may choose to apply paragraphs (d)(4)(i)(B) and (d)(4)(ii) of this section to a taxable year ending before November 12, 2020, so long as the taxpayer consistently applies paragraphs (d)(4)(i)(B) and (d)(4)(ii) of this section to that taxable year and any subsequent taxable year ending before November 12, 2020. [Reg. § 1.245A(e)-1.]

☐ [*T.D. 9896, 4-7-2020. Amended by T.D. 9909, 8-21-2020, T.D. 9922, 11-2-2020 and T.D. 9959, 12-28-2021.*]

§ 1.250-1. Introduction.—(a) *Overview*.—Sections 1.250(a)-1 and 1.250(b)-1 through 1.250(b)-6 provide rules to determine a domestic corporation's section 250 deduction. Section 1.250(a)-1 provides rules to determine the amount of a domestic corporation's deduction for foreign-derived intangible income and global intangible low-taxed income. Section 1.250(b)-1 provides general rules and definitions regarding the computation of foreign-derived intangible income. Section 1.250(b)-2 provides rules for determining a domestic corporation's qualified business asset investment. Section 1.250(b)-3 provides general rules and definitions regarding the determination of gross foreign-derived deduction eligible income. Section 1.250(b)-4 provides rules regarding the determination of gross foreign-derived deduction eligible income from the sale of property. Section 1.250(b)-5 provides rules regarding the determination of gross foreign-derived deduction eligible income from the provision of a service. Section 1.250(b)-6 provides rules regarding the sale of property or provision of a service to a related party.

(b) *Applicability dates*.—Except as otherwise provided in this paragraph (b), §§ 1.250(a)-1 and §§ 1.250(b)-1 through 1.250(b)-6 apply to taxable years beginning on or after January 1, 2021. Section 1.250(b)-2(h) applies to taxable years ending on or after March 4, 2019. However, taxpayers may choose to apply §§ 1.250(a)-1 and 1.250(b)-1 through 1.250(b)-6 for taxable years beginning on or after January 1, 2018, and before January 1, 2021, provided they apply the regulations in their entirety (other than § 1.250(b)-3(f) and the applicable provisions in § 1.250(b)-4(d)(3) or § 1.250(b)-5(e)(4)), but once applied, taxpayers must apply the final regulations for all subsequent taxable years beginning before January 1, 2021. The last sentence in § 1.250(b)-2(e)(2) applies to taxable years beginning after December 31, 2017. [Reg. § 1.250-1.]

☐ [*T.D. 9901, 7-9-2020 (corrected 10-27-2020). Amended by T.D. 9956, 9-21-2021.*]

§ 1.250(a)-1. Deduction for foreign-derived intangible income (FDII) and global intangible low-taxed income (GILTI).—(a) *Scope*.—This section provides rules for determining the amount of a domestic corporation's deduction for foreign-derived intangible income (FDII) and global intangible low-taxed income (GILTI). Paragraph (b) of this section provides general rules for determining the amount of the deduction. Paragraph (c) of this section provides definitions relevant for determining the amount of the deduction. Paragraph (d) of this section provides reporting requirements for a domestic corporation claiming the deduction. Paragraph (e) of this section provides a rule for determining the amount of the deduction of a member of a consolidated group. Paragraph (f) of this section provides examples illustrating the application of this section.

(b) *Allowance of deduction*.—(1) *In general*.—A domestic corporation is allowed a deduction for any taxable year equal to the sum of—

(i) 37.5 percent of its foreign-derived intangible income for the year; and

(ii) 50 percent of—

(A) Its global intangible low-taxed income for the year; and

(B) The amount treated as a dividend received by the corporation under section 78 which is attributable to its GILTI for the year.

(2) *Taxable income limitation.*—In the case of a domestic corporation with a section 250(a)(2) amount for a taxable year, for purposes of applying paragraph (b)(1) of this section for the year—

(i) The corporation's FDII for the year (if any) is reduced (but not below zero) by an amount that bears the same ratio to the corporation's section 250(a)(2) amount that the corporation's FDII for the year bears to the sum of the corporation's FDII and GILTI for the year; and

(ii) The corporation's GILTI for the year (if any) is reduced (but not below zero) by the excess of the corporation's section 250(a)(2) amount over the amount of the reduction described in paragraph (b)(2)(i) of this section.

(3) *Reduction in deduction for taxable years after 2025.*—For any taxable year of a domestic corporation beginning after December 31, 2025, paragraph (b)(1) of this section applies by substituting—

(i) 21.875 percent for 37.5 percent in paragraph (b)(1)(i) of this section; and

(ii) 37.5 percent for 50 percent in paragraph (b)(1)(ii) of this section.

(4) *Treatment under section 4940.*—For purposes of section 4940(c)(3)(A), a deduction under section 250(a) is not treated as an ordinary and necessary expense paid or incurred for the production or collection of gross investment income.

(c) *Definitions.*—The following definitions apply for purposes of this section.

(1) *Domestic corporation.*—The term *domestic corporation* has the meaning set forth in section 7701(a), but does not include a regulated investment company (as defined in section 851), a real estate investment trust (as defined in section 856), or an S corporation (as defined in section 1361).

(2) *Foreign-derived intangible income (FDII).*—The term *foreign-derived intangible income* or *FDII* has the meaning set forth in § 1.250(b)-1(b).

(3) *Global intangible low-taxed income (GILTI).*—The term *global intangible low-taxed income* or *GILTI* means, with respect to a domestic corporation for a taxable year, the corporation's GILTI inclusion amount under § 1.951A-1(c) for the taxable year.

(4) *Section 250(a)(2) amount.*—The term *section 250(a)(2) amount* means, with respect to a domestic corporation for a taxable year, the excess (if any) of the sum of the corporation's FDII and GILTI (determined without regard to section 250(a)(2) and paragraph (b)(2) of this section), over the corporation's taxable income. For a corporation that is subject to the unrelated business income tax under section 511, taxable income is determined only by reference to that corporation's unrelated business taxable income defined under section 512.

(5) *Taxable income.*—(i) *In general.*—The term *taxable income* has the meaning set forth in section 63(a) determined without regard to the deduction allowed under section 250 and this section.

(ii) [Reserved]

(d) *Reporting requirement.*—Each domestic corporation (or individual making an election under section 962) that claims a deduction under section 250 for a taxable year must make an annual return on Form 8993, "Section 250 Deduction for Foreign-Derived Intangible Income (FDII) and Global Intangible Low-Taxed Income (GILTI)" (or any successor form) for such year, setting forth the information, in such form and manner, as Form 8993 (or any successor form) or its instructions prescribe. Returns on Form 8993 (or any successor form) for a taxable year must be filed with the domestic corporation's (or in the case of a section 962 election, the individual's) income tax return on or before the due date (taking into account extensions) for filing the corporation's (or in the case of a section 962 election, the individual's) income tax return.

(e) *Determination of deduction for consolidated groups.*—A member of a consolidated group (as defined in § 1.1502-1(h)) determines its deduction under section 250(a) and this section under the rules provided in § 1.1502-50(b).

(f) *Example: Application of the taxable income limitation.*—The following example illustrates the application of this section. For purposes of the example, it is assumed that DC is a domestic corporation that is not a member of a consolidated group and the taxable year of DC begins after 2017 and before 2026.

(1) *Facts.* For the taxable year, without regard to section 250(a)(2) and paragraph (b)(2) of this section, DC has FDII of $100x and GILTI of $300x. DC's taxable income (without regard to section 250(a) and this section) is $300x.

(2) *Analysis.* DC has a section 250(a)(2) amount of $100x, which is equal to the excess of the sum of DC's FDII and GILTI of $400x ($100x + $300x) over its taxable income of $300x. As a result, DC's FDII and GILTI are reduced, in the aggregate, by $100x under section 250(a)(2) and paragraph (b)(2) of this section for purposes of calculating DC's deduction allowed under section 250(a)(1) and paragraph (b)(1) of this section. DC's FDII is reduced by $25x, the amount that bears the same ratio to the section 250(a)(2) amount ($100x) as DC's FDII ($100x) bears to the sum of DC's FDII and GILTI ($400x). DC's GILTI is reduced by $75x, which is the remainder of the section 250(a)(2) amount ($100x - $25x). Therefore, for purposes of calculating its deduction under section 250(a)(1) and paragraph (b)(1) of this section, DC's FDII is $75x ($100x - $25x) and its GILTI is $225x ($300x - $75x). Accordingly, DC is allowed a deduction for the taxable year under section 250(a)(1) and paragraph (b)(1) of this section of $140.63x ($75x x 0.375 + $225x x 0.50). [Reg. § 1.250(a)-1.]

☐ [*T.D. 9901, 7-9-2020.*]

§ 1.250(b)-1. Computation of foreign-derived intangible income (FDII).—(a) *Scope.*—This section provides rules for computing FDII. Paragraph (b) of this section defines FDII. Paragraph (c) of this section provides definitions that are relevant for computing FDII. Paragraph (d) of this section provides rules for computing gross income and allocating and apportioning deductions for purposes of computing deduction eligible income (DEI) and foreign-derived deduction eligible income (FDDEI). Paragraph (e) of this section provides rules for computing the DEI and FDDEI of a domestic corporate partner. Paragraph (f) of this section provides a rule for computing the FDII of a member of a consolidated group. Paragraph (g) of this section provides a rule for computing the FDII of a tax-exempt corporation.

(b) *Definition of FDII.*—Subject to the provisions of this section, the term *FDII* means, with respect to a domestic corporation for a taxable year, the corporation's deemed intangible income for the year multiplied by the corporation's foreign-derived ratio for the year.

(c) *Definitions.*—This paragraph (c) provides definitions that apply for purposes of this section and §§ 1.250(b)-2 through 1.250(b)-6.

(1) *Controlled foreign corporation.*—The term *controlled foreign corporation* has the meaning set forth in section 957(a) and § 1.957-1(a).

(2) *Deduction eligible income.*—The term *deduction eligible income* or *DEI* means, with respect to a domestic corporation for a taxable year, the excess (if any) of the corporation's gross DEI for the year over the deductions properly allocable to gross DEI for the year, as determined under paragraph (d)(2) of this section.

(3) *Deemed intangible income.*—The term *deemed intangible income* means, with respect to a domestic corporation for a taxable year, the excess (if any) of the corporation's DEI for the year over the corporation's deemed tangible income return for the year.

(4) *Deemed tangible income return.*—The term *deemed tangible income return* means, with respect to a domestic corporation and a taxable year, 10 percent of the corporation's qualified business asset investment for the year.

(5) *Dividend.*—The term *dividend* has the meaning set forth in section 316, and includes any amount treated as a dividend under any other provision of subtitle A of the Internal Revenue Code or the regulations in this part (for example, under section 78, 356(a)(2), 367(b), or 1248).

(6) *Domestic corporation.*—The term *domestic corporation* has the meaning set forth in § 1.250(a)-1(c)(1).

(7) *Domestic oil and gas extraction income.*—The term *domestic oil and gas extraction income* means income described in section 907(c)(1), substituting "within the United States" for "without the United States." A taxpayer must use a consistent method to determine the

amount of its domestic oil and gas extraction income ("DOGEI") and its foreign oil and gas extraction income ("FOGEI") from the sale of oil or gas that has been transported or processed. For example, a taxpayer must use a consistent method to determine the amount of FOGEI from the sale of gasoline from foreign crude oil sources in computing the exclusion from gross tested income under § 1.951A-2(c)(1)(v) and the amount of DOGEI from the sale of gasoline from domestic crude oil sources in computing its section 250 deduction.

(8) *FDDEI sale*.—The term *FDDEI sale* has the meaning set forth in § 1.250(b)-4(b).

(9) *FDDEI service*.—The term *FDDEI service* has the meaning set forth in § 1.250(b)-5(b).

(10) *FDDEI transaction*.—The term *FDDEI transaction* means a FDDEI sale or a FDDEI service.

(11) *Foreign branch income*.—The term *foreign branch income* has the meaning set forth in section 904(d)(2)(J) and § 1.904-4(f)(2).

(12) *Foreign-derived deduction eligible income*.—The term *foreign-derived deduction eligible income* or *FDDEI* means, with respect to a domestic corporation for a taxable year, the excess (if any) of the corporation's gross FDDEI for the year, over the deductions properly allocable to gross FDDEI for the year, as determined under paragraph (d)(2) of this section.

(13) *Foreign-derived ratio*.—The term *foreign-derived ratio* means, with respect to a domestic corporation for a taxable year, the ratio (not to exceed one) of the corporation's FDDEI for the year to the corporation's DEI for the year. If a domestic corporation has no FDDEI for a taxable year, the corporation's foreign-derived ratio is zero for the taxable year.

(14) *Gross RDEI*.—The term *gross RDEI* means, with respect to a domestic corporation or a partnership for a taxable year, the portion of the corporation or partnership's gross DEI for the year that is not included in gross FDDEI.

(15) *Gross DEI*.—The term *gross DEI* means, with respect to a domestic corporation or a partnership for a taxable year, the gross income of the corporation or partnership for the year determined without regard to the following items of gross income—

(i) Amounts included in gross income under section 951(a)(1);

(ii) GILTI (as defined in § 1.250(a)-1(c)(3));

(iii) Financial services income (as defined in section 904(d)(2)(D) and § 1.904-4(e)(1)(ii));

(iv) Dividends received from a controlled foreign corporation with respect to which the corporation or partnership is a United States shareholder;

(v) Domestic oil and gas extraction income; and

(vi) Foreign branch income.

(16) *Gross FDDEI*.—The term *gross FDDEI* means, with respect to a domestic corporation or a partnership for a taxable year, the portion of the gross DEI of the corporation or partnership for the year which is derived from all of its FDDEI transactions.

(17) *Modified affiliated group*.—(i) *In general*.—The term *modified affiliated group* means an affiliated group as defined in section 1504(a) determined by substituting "more than 50 percent" for "at least 80 percent" each place it appears, and without regard to section 1504(b)(2) and (3).

(ii) *Special rule for noncorporate entities*.—Any person (other than a corporation) that is controlled by one or more members of a modified affiliated group (including one or more persons treated as a member or members of a modified affiliated group by reason of this paragraph (c)(17)(ii)) or that controls any such member is treated as a member of the modified affiliated group.

(iii) *Definition of control*.—For purposes of paragraph (c)(17)(ii) of this section, the term *control* has the meaning set forth in section 954(d)(3).

(18) *Qualified business asset investment*.—The term *qualified business asset investment* or *QBAI* has the meaning set forth in § 1.250(b)-2(b).

(19) *Related party*.—The term *related party* means, with respect to any person, any member of a modified affiliated group that includes such person.

(20) *United States shareholder*.—The term *United States shareholder* has the meaning set forth in section 951(b) and § 1.951-1(g).

(d) *Treatment of cost of goods sold and allocation and apportionment of deductions*.—(1) *Cost of goods sold for determining gross DEI and gross FDDEI*.—For purposes of determining the gross income included in gross DEI and gross FDDEI of a domestic corporation or a partnership, the cost of goods sold of the corporation or partnership is attributed to gross receipts with respect to gross DEI or gross FDDEI under any reasonable method that is applied consistently. Cost of goods sold must be attributed to gross receipts with respect to gross DEI or gross FDDEI regardless of whether certain costs included in cost of goods sold can be associated with activities undertaken in an earlier taxable year (including a year before the effective date of section 250). A domestic corporation or partnership may not segregate cost of goods sold with respect to a particular product into component costs and attribute those component costs disproportionately to gross receipts with respect to amounts excluded from gross DEI or gross FDDEI, as applicable.

(2) *Deductions properly allocable to gross DEI and gross FDDEI*.—(i) *In general*.—For purposes of determining a domestic corporation's deductions that are properly allocable to gross DEI and gross FDDEI, the corporation's deductions are allocated and apportioned to gross DEI and gross FDDEI under the rules of §§ 1.861-8 through 1.861-14T and 1.861-17 by treating section 250(b) as an operative section described in § 1.861-8(f). In allocating and apportioning deductions under §§ 1.861-8 through 1.861-14T and 1.861-17, gross FDDEI and gross RDEI are treated as separate statutory groupings. The deductions allocated and apportioned to gross DEI equal the sum of the deductions allocated and apportioned to gross FDDEI and gross RDEI. All items of gross income described in paragraphs (c)(15)(i) through (vi) of this section are in the residual grouping.

(ii) *Determination of deductions to allocate*.—For purposes of determining the deductions of a domestic corporation for a taxable year properly allocable to gross DEI and gross FDDEI, the deductions of the corporation for the taxable year are determined without regard to sections 163(j), 170(b)(2), 172, 246(b), and 250.

(3) *Examples*.—The following examples illustrate the application of this paragraph (d).

(i) *Assumed facts*.—The following facts are assumed for purposes of the examples—

(A) DC is a domestic corporation that is not a member of a consolidated group.

(B) All sales and services are provided to persons that are not related parties.

(C) All sales and services to foreign persons qualify as FDDEI transactions.

(ii) *Examples*—

(A) *Example 1: Allocation of deductions*.—(*1*) *Facts*. For a taxable year, DC manufactures products A and B in the United States. DC sells products A and B and provides services associated with products A and B to United States and foreign persons. DC's QBAI for the taxable year is $1,000x. DC has $300x of deductible interest expense allowed under section 163. DC has assets with a tax book value of $2,500x. The tax book value of DC's assets used to produce products A and B and services is split evenly between assets that produce gross FDDEI and assets that produce gross RDEI. DC has $840x of supportive deductions, as defined in § 1.861-8(b)(3), attributable to general and administrative expenses incurred for the purpose of generating the class of gross income that consists of gross DEI. DC apportions the $840x of deductions on the basis of gross income in accordance with § 1.861-8T(c)(1). For purposes of determining gross FDDEI and gross DEI under paragraph (d)(1) of this section, DC attributes $200x of cost of goods sold to Product A and $400x of cost of goods sold to Product B, and then attributes the cost of goods sold for each product ratably between the gross receipts of such product sold to foreign persons and the gross receipts of such product sold to United States persons. The manner in which DC attributes the cost of goods sold is a reasonable method. DC has no other items of income, loss, or deduction. For the taxable year, DC has the following income tax items relevant to the determination of its FDII:

Table 1 to paragraph (d)(3)(ii)(A)(1)				
	Product A	Product B	Services	Total
Gross receipts from U.S. persons	$200x	$800x	$100x	$1,100x
Gross receipts from foreign persons	$200x	$800x	$100x	$1,100x
Total gross receipts	$400x	$1,600x	$200x	$2,200x
Cost of goods sold for gross receipts from U.S. persons	$100x	$200x	$0	$300x
Cost of goods sold for gross receipts from foreign persons	$100x	$200x	$0	$300x
Total cost of goods sold	$200x	$400x	$0	$600x
Gross income	$200x	$1,200x	$200x	$1,600x
Tax book value of assets used to produce products/ services	$500x	$500x	$1,500x	$2,500x

(2) *Analysis—(i) Determination of gross FDDEI and gross RDEI.* Because DC does not have any income described in section 250(b)(3)(A)(i)(I) through (VI) and paragraphs (c)(15)(i) through (vi) of this section, none of its gross income is excluded from gross DEI. DC's gross DEI is $1,600x ($2,200x total gross receipts less $600x total cost of goods sold). DC's gross FDDEI is $800x ($1,100x of gross receipts from foreign persons minus attributable cost of goods sold of $300x).

(ii) *Determination of foreign-derived deduction eligible income.* To calculate its FDDEI, DC must determine the amount of its deductions that are allocated and apportioned to gross FDDEI and then subtract those amounts from gross FDDEI. DC's interest deduction of $300x is allocated and apportioned to gross FDDEI on the basis of the average total value of DC's assets in each grouping. DC has assets with a tax book value of $2,500x split evenly between assets that produce gross FDDEI and assets that produce gross RDEI. Accordingly, an interest expense deduction of $150x is apportioned to DC's gross FDDEI. With respect to DC's supportive deductions of $840x that are related to DC's gross DEI, DC apportions such deductions between gross FDDEI and gross RDEI on the basis of gross income. Accordingly, supportive deductions of $420x are apportioned to DC's gross FDDEI. Thus, DC's FDDEI is $230x, which is equal to its gross FDDEI of $800x less $150x of interest expense deduction and $420x of supportive deductions.

(iii) *Determination of deemed intangible income.* DC's deemed tangible income return is $100x, which is equal to 10 percent of its QBAI of $1,000x. DC's DEI is $460x, which is equal to its gross DEI of $1,600x less $300x of interest expense deductions and $840x of supportive deductions. Therefore, DC's deemed intangible income is $360x, which is equal to the excess of its DEI of $460x over its deemed tangible income return of $100x.

(iv) *Determination of foreign-derived intangible income.* DC's foreign-derived ratio is 50 percent, which is the ratio of DC's FDDEI of $230x to DC's DEI of $460x. Therefore, DC's FDII is $180x, which is equal to DC's deemed intangible income of $360x multiplied by its foreign-derived ratio of 50 percent.

(B) *Example 2: Allocation of deductions with respect to a partnership.—(1) Facts—(i) DC's operations.* DC is engaged in the production and sale of products consisting of two separate product groups in three-digit Standard Industrial Classification (SIC) Industry Groups, hereafter referred to as Group AAA and Group BBB. All of the gross income of DC is included in gross DEI. DC incurs $250x of research and experimental (R&E) expenditures in the United States that are deductible under section 174. None of the R&E is included in cost of goods sold. For purposes of determining gross FDDEI and gross DEI under paragraph (d)(1) of this section, DC attributes $210x of cost of goods sold to Group AAA products and $900x of cost of goods sold to Group BBB products, and then attributes the cost of goods sold with respect to each such product group ratably between the gross receipts with respect to such product group sold to foreign persons and the gross receipts with respect to such product group not sold to foreign persons. The manner in which DC attributes the cost of goods sold is a reasonable method. For the taxable year, DC has the following income tax items relevant to the determination of its FDII:

Table 2 to (d)(3)(ii)(B)(1)(i)			
	Group AAA Products	Group BBB Products	Total
Gross receipts from U.S. persons	$200x	$800x	$1,000x
Gross receipts from foreign persons	$100x	$400x	$500x
Total gross receipts	$300x	$1,200x	$1,500x
Cost of goods sold for gross receipts from U.S. persons	$140x	$600x	$740x
Cost of goods sold for gross receipts from foreign persons	$70x	$300x	$370x
Total cost of goods sold	$210x	$900x	$1,110x
Gross income	$90x	$300x	$390x
R&E deductions	$40x	$210x	$250x

(ii) *PRS's operations.* In addition to its own operations, DC is a partner in PRS, a partnership that also produces products described in SIC Group AAA. DC is allocated 50 percent of all income, gain, loss, and deductions of PRS. During the taxable year, PRS sells Group AAA products solely to foreign persons, and all of its gross income is included in gross DEI. PRS has $400 of gross receipts from sales of Group AAA products for the taxable year and incurs $100x of research and experimental (R&E) expenditures in the United States that are deductible under section 174. None of the R&E is included in cost of goods sold. For purposes of determining gross FDDEI and gross DEI under paragraph (d)(1) of this section, PRS attributes $200x of cost of goods sold to Group AAA products, and then attributes the cost of goods sold with respect to such product group ratably between the gross receipts with respect to such product group sold to foreign persons and the gross receipts with respect to such product group not sold to foreign persons. The manner in which PRS attributes the cost of goods sold is a reasonable method. DC's distributive share of PRS taxable items is $100x of gross income and $50x of R&E deductions, and DC's share of PRS's gross receipts from sales of Group AAA products for the taxable year is $200x under § 1.861-17(f)(3).

(iii) *Application of the sales method to allocate and apportion R&E.* DC applies the sales method to apportion its R&E deductions under § 1.861-17. Neither DC nor PRS licenses or sells its intangible property to controlled or uncontrolled corporations in a manner that necessitates including the sales by such corporations for purposes of apportioning DC's R&E deductions.

(2) *Analysis—(i) Determination of gross DEI and gross FDDEI.* Under paragraph (e)(1) of this section, DC's gross DEI, gross FDDEI, and deductions allocable to those amounts include its distributive share of gross DEI, gross FDDEI, and deductions of PRS. Thus, DC's gross DEI for the year is $490x ($390x attributable to DC and $100x attributable to DC's interest in PRS). DC's gross income from sales of Group AAA products to foreign persons is $30x ($100x of gross receipts minus attributable cost of goods sold of $70x). DC's gross income from sales of Group BBB products to foreign persons is $100x ($400x of gross receipts minus attributable cost of goods sold of $300x). DC's gross FDDEI for the year is $230x ($30x from DC's sale

of Group AAA products plus $100x from DC's sale of Group BBB products plus DC's distributive share of PRS's gross FDDEI of $100x).

(ii) *Allocation and apportionment of R&E deductions.* To determine FDDEI, DC must allocate and apportion its R&E expense of $300x ($250x incurred directly by DC and $50x incurred indirectly through DC's interest in PRS). In accordance with § 1.861-17, R&E expenses are first allocated to a class of gross income related to a three-digit SIC group code. DC's R&E expenses related to products in Group AAA are $90x ($40x incurred directly by DC and $50x incurred indirectly through DC's interest in PRS) and its expenses related to Group BBB are $210x. See paragraph (d)(2)(i) of this section. Accordingly, all R&E expense attributable to a particular SIC group code is apportioned on the basis of the amounts of sales within that SIC group code. Total sales within Group AAA were $500x ($300x directly by DC and $200x attributable to DC's interest in PRS), $300x of which were made to foreign persons ($100x directly by DC and $200x attributable to DC's interest in PRS). Therefore, the $90x of R&E expense related to Group AAA is apportioned $54x to gross FDDEI ($90x x $300x/$500x) and $36x to gross RDEI ($90x x $200x/ $500x). Total sales within Group BBB were $1,200x, $400x of which were made to foreign persons. Therefore, the $210x of R&E expense related to products in Group BBB is apportioned $70x to gross FDDEI ($210x x $400x/$1,200x) and $140x to gross RDEI ($210x x $800x/ $1,200x). Accordingly, DC's FDDEI for the tax year is $106x ($230x gross FDDEI minus $124x of R&E ($54x + $70x) allocated and apportioned to gross FDDEI).

(e) *Domestic corporate partners.*—(1) *In general.*—A domestic corporation's DEI and FDDEI for a taxable year are determined by taking into account the corporation's share of gross DEI, gross FDDEI, and deductions of any partnership (whether domestic or foreign) in which the corporation is a direct or indirect partner. For purposes of the preceding sentence, a domestic corporation's share of each such item of a partnership is determined in accordance with the corporation's distributive share of the underlying items of income, gain, deduction, and loss of the partnership that comprise such amounts. See § 1.250(b)-2(g) for rules on calculating the increase to a domestic corporation's QBAI by the corporation's share of partnership QBAI.

(2) *Reporting requirement for partnership with domestic corporate partners.*—A partnership that has one or more direct partners that are domestic corporations and that is required to file a return under section 6031 must furnish to each such partner on or with such partner's Schedule K-1 (Form 1065 or any successor form) by the due date (including extensions) for furnishing Schedule K-1 the partner's share of the partnership's gross DEI, gross FDDEI, deductions that are properly allocable to the partnership's gross DEI and gross FDDEI, and partnership QBAI (as determined under § 1.250(b)-2(g)) for each taxable year in which the partnership has gross DEI, gross FDDEI, deductions that are properly allocable to the partnership's gross DEI or gross FDDEI, or partnership specified tangible property (as defined in § 1.250(b)-2(g)(5)). In the case of tiered partnerships where one or more partners of an upper-tier partnership are domestic corporations, a lower-tier partnership must report the amount specified in this paragraph (e)(2) to the upper-tier partnership to allow reporting of such information to any partner that is a domestic corporation. To the extent that a partnership cannot determine the information described in the first sentence of this paragraph (e)(2), the partnership must instead furnish to each partner its share of the partnership's attributes that a partner needs to determine the partner's gross DEI, gross FDDEI, deductions that are properly allocable to the partner's gross DEI and gross FDDEI, and the partner's adjusted bases in partnership specified tangible property.

(3) *Examples.*—The following examples illustrate the application of this paragraph (e).

(i) *Assumed facts.*—The following facts are assumed for purposes of the examples—

(A) DC, a domestic corporation, is a partner in PRS, a partnership.

(B) FP and FP2 are foreign persons.

(C) FC is a foreign corporation.

(D) The allocations under PRS's partnership agreement satisfy the requirements of section 704.

(E) No partner of PRS is a related party of DC.

(F) DC, PRS, and FC all use the calendar year as their taxable year.

(G) PRS has no items of income, loss, or deduction for its taxable year, except the items of income described.

(ii) *Examples*—

(A) *Example 1: Sale by partnership to foreign person.*—(*1*) *Facts.* Under the terms of the partnership agreement, DC is allocated 50 percent of all income, gain, loss, and deductions of PRS. For the taxable year, PRS recognizes $20x of gross income on the sale of general property (as defined in § 1.250(b)-3(b)(10)) to FP, a foreign person (as determined under § 1.250(b)-4(c)), for a foreign use (as determined under § 1.250(b)-4(d)). The gross income recognized on the sale of property is not described in section 250(b)(3)(A)(I) through (VI) or paragraphs (c)(15)(i) through (vi) of this section.

(*2*) *Analysis.* PRS's sale of property to FP is a FDDEI sale as described in § 1.250(b)-4(b). Therefore, the gross income derived from the sale ($20x) is included in PRS's gross DEI and gross FDDEI, and DC's share of PRS's gross DEI and gross FDDEI ($10x) is included in DC's gross DEI and gross FDDEI for the taxable year.

(B) *Example 2: Sale by partnership to foreign person attributable to foreign branch.*—(*1*) *Facts.* The facts are the same as in paragraph (e)(3)(ii)(A)(*1*) of this section (the facts in *Example 1*), except the income from the sale of property to FP is attributable to a foreign branch of PRS.

(*2*) *Analysis.* PRS's sale of property to FP is excluded from PRS's gross DEI under section 250(b)(3)(A)(VI) and paragraph (c)(15)(vi) of this section. Accordingly, DC's share of PRS's gross income of $10x from the sale is not included in DC's gross DEI or gross FDDEI for the taxable year.

(C) *Example 3: Partnership with a loss in gross FDDEI.*—(*1*) *Facts.* The facts are the same as in paragraph (e)(3)(ii)(A)(*1*) of this section (the facts in *Example 1*), except that in the same taxable year, PRS also sells property to FP2, a foreign person (as determined under § 1.250(b)-4(c)), for a foreign use (as determined under § 1.250(b)-4(d)). After taking into account both sales, PRS has a gross loss of $30x.

(*2*) *Analysis.* Both the sale of property to FP and the sale of property to FP2 are FDDEI sales because each sale is described in § 1.250(b)-4(b). DC's share of PRS's gross loss ($15x) from the sales is included in DC's gross DEI and gross FDDEI.

(D) *Example 4: Sale by partnership to foreign related party of the partnership.*—(*1*) *Facts.* Under the terms of the partnership agreement, DC has 25 percent of the capital and profits interest in the partnership and is allocated 25 percent of all income, gain, loss, and deductions of PRS. PRS owns 100 percent of the single class of stock of FC. In the taxable year, PRS has $20x of gain on the sale of general property (as defined in § 1.250(b)-3(b)(10)) to FC, and FC makes a physical and material change to the property within the meaning of § 1.250(b)-4(d)(1)(iii)(B) outside the United States before selling the property to customers in the United States.

(*2*) *Analysis.* The sale of property by PRS to FC is described in § 1.250(b)-4(b) without regard to the application of § 1.250(b)-6, since the sale is to a foreign person (as determined under § 1.250(b)-4(c)) for a foreign use (as determined under § 1.250(b)-4(d)). However, FC is a foreign related party of PRS within the meaning of section 250(b)(5)(D) and § 1.250(b)-3(b)(6), because FC and PRS are members of a modified affiliated group within the meaning of paragraph (c)(17) of this section. Therefore, the sale by PRS to FC is a related party sale within the meaning of § 1.250(b)-6(b)(1). Under section 250(b)(5)(C)(i) and § 1.250(b)-6(c), because FC did not sell the property, or use the property in connection with other property sold or the provision of a service, to a foreign unrelated party before the property was subject to a domestic use, the sale by PRS to FC is not a FDDEI sale. See § 1.250(b)-6(c)(1). Accordingly, the gain from the sale ($20x) is included in PRS's gross DEI but not its gross FDDEI, and DC's share of PRS's gain ($5x) is included in DC's gross DEI but not gross FDDEI. This is the result notwithstanding that FC is not a related party of DC because FC and DC are not members of a modified affiliated group within the meaning of paragraph (c)(17) of this section.

(f) *Determination of FDII for consolidated groups.*—A member of a consolidated group (as defined in § 1.1502-1(h)) determines its FDII under the rules provided in § 1.1502-50.

(g) *Determination of FDII for tax-exempt corporations.*—The FDII of a corporation that is subject to the unrelated business income tax under section 511 is determined only by reference to that corporation's items of income, gain, deduction, or loss, and adjusted bases in property, that are taken into account in computing the corporation's unrelated business taxable income (as defined in section 512). For example, if a corporation that is subject to the unrelated business income tax under section 511 has tangible property used in the production of both unrelated business income and gross income that is not unrelated business income, only the portion of the basis of such property taken into account in computing the corporation's unrelated business taxable income is taken into account in determining the corporation's QBAI. Similarly, if a corporation that is subject to the unrelated business income tax under section 511 has tangible property that is used in both the production of gross DEI and the production of gross income that is not gross DEI, only the corporation's unrelated business income is taken into account in determining the corporation's dual use ratio with respect to such property under § 1.250(b)-2(d)(3). [Reg. § 1.250(b)-1.]

☐ [*T.D. 9901, 7-9-2020. Amended by T.D. 9959, 12-28-2021.*]

§ 1.250(b)-2. Qualified business asset investment (QBAI).—(a) *Scope.*—This section provides general rules for determining the qualified business asset investment of a domestic corporation for purposes of determining its deemed tangible income return under § 1.250(b)-1(c)(4). Paragraph (b) of this section defines qualified business asset investment (QBAI). Paragraph (c) of this section defines tangible property and specified tangible property. Paragraph (d) of this section provides rules for determining the portion of property that is specified tangible property when the property is used in the production of both gross DEI and gross income that is not gross DEI. Paragraph (e) of this section provides rules for determining the adjusted basis of specified tangible property. Paragraph (f) of this section provides rules for determining QBAI of a domestic corporation with a short taxable year. Paragraph (g) of this section provides rules for increasing the QBAI of a domestic corporation by reason of property owned through a partnership. Paragraph (h) of this section provides an anti-avoidance rule that disregards certain transfers when determining the QBAI of a domestic corporation.

(b) *Definition of qualified business asset investment.*—The term *qualified business asset investment (QBAI)* means the average of a domestic corporation's aggregate adjusted bases as of the close of each quarter of the domestic corporation's taxable year in specified tangible property that is used in a trade or business of the domestic corporation and is of a type with respect to which a deduction is allowable under section 167. In the case of partially depreciable property, only the depreciable portion of the property is of a type with respect to which a deduction is allowable under section 167.

(c) *Specified tangible property.*—(1) *In general.*—The term *specified tangible property* means, with respect to a domestic corporation for a taxable year, tangible property of the domestic corporation used in the production of gross DEI for the taxable year. For purposes of the preceding sentence, tangible property of a domestic corporation is used in the production of gross DEI for a taxable year if some or all of the depreciation or cost recovery allowance with respect to the tangible property is either allocated and apportioned to the gross DEI of the domestic corporation for the taxable year under § 1.250(b)-1(d)(2) or capitalized to inventory or other property held for sale, some or all of the gross income or loss from the sale of which is taken into account in determining DEI of the domestic corporation for the taxable year.

(2) *Tangible property.*—The term *tangible property* means property for which the depreciation deduction provided by section 167(a) is eligible to be determined under section 168 without regard to section 168(f)(1), (2), or (5), section 168(k)(2)(A)(i)(II), (IV), or (V), and the date placed in service.

(d) *Dual use property.*—(1) *In general.*—The amount of the adjusted basis in dual use property of a domestic corporation for a taxable year that is treated as adjusted basis in specified tangible property for the taxable year is the average of the domestic corporation's adjusted basis in the property multiplied by the dual use ratio with respect to the property for the taxable year.

(2) *Definition of dual use property.*—The term *dual use property* means, with respect to a domestic corporation and a taxable year, specified tangible property of the domestic corporation that is used in both the production of gross DEI and the production of gross income that is not gross DEI for the taxable year. For purposes of the preceding sentence, specified tangible property of a domestic corporation is used in the production of gross DEI and the production of gross income that is not gross DEI for a taxable year if less than all of the depreciation or cost recovery allowance with respect to the property is either allocated and apportioned to the gross DEI of the domestic corporation for the taxable year under § 1.250(b)-1(d)(2) or capitalized to inventory or other property held for sale, the gross income or loss from the sale of which is taken into account in determining the DEI of the domestic corporation for the taxable year.

(3) *Dual use ratio.*—The term *dual use ratio* means, with respect to dual use property, a domestic corporation, and a taxable year, a ratio (expressed as a percentage) calculated as—

(i) The sum of-

(A) The depreciation deduction or cost recovery allowance with respect to the property that is allocated and apportioned to the gross DEI of the domestic corporation for the taxable year under § 1.250(b)-1(d)(2); and

(B) The depreciation or cost recovery allowance with respect to the property that is capitalized to inventory or other property held for sale, the gross income or loss from the sale of which is taken into account in determining the DEI of the domestic corporation for the taxable year; divided by

(ii) The sum of—

(A) The total amount of the domestic corporation's depreciation deduction or cost recovery allowance with respect to the property for the taxable year; and

(B) The total amount of the domestic corporation's depreciation or cost recovery allowance with respect to the property capitalized to inventory or other property held for sale, the gross income or loss from the sale of which is taken into account in determining the income or loss of the domestic corporation for the taxable year.

(4) *Example.*—The following example illustrates the application of this paragraph (d).

(i) *Facts.* DC, a domestic corporation, owns a machine that produces both gross DEI and income that is not gross DEI. The average adjusted basis of the machine for the taxable year in the hands of DC is $4,000x. The depreciation with respect to the machine for the taxable year is $400x, $320x of which is capitalized to inventory of Product A, gross income or loss from the sale of which is taken into account in determining DC's gross DEI for the taxable year, and $80x of which is capitalized to inventory of Product B, gross income or loss from the sale of which is not taken into account in determining DC's gross DEI for the taxable year. DC also owns an office building for its administrative functions with an average adjusted basis for the taxable year of $10,000x. DC does not capitalize depreciation with respect to the office building to inventory or other property held for sale. DC's depreciation deduction with respect to the office building is $1,000x for the taxable year, $750x of which is allocated and apportioned to gross DEI under § 1.250(b)-1(d)(2), and $250x of which is allocated and apportioned to income other than gross DEI under § 1.250(b)-1(d)(2).

(ii) *Analysis*—(A) *Dual use property.* The machine and office building are property for which the depreciation deduction provided by section 167(a) is eligible to be determined under section 168 (without regard to section 168(f)(1), (2), or (5), section 168(k)(2)(A)(i)(II), (IV), or (V), and the date placed in service). Therefore, under paragraph (c)(2) of this section, the machine and office building are tangible property. Furthermore, because the machine and office building are used in the production of gross DEI for the taxable year within the meaning of paragraph (c)(1) of this section, the machine and office building are specified tangible property. Finally, because the machine and office building are used in both the production of gross DEI and the production of gross income that is not gross DEI for the taxable year within the meaning of paragraph (d)(2) of this section, the machine and office building are dual use property. Therefore, under paragraph (d)(1) of this section, the amount of DC's adjusted basis in the machine and office building that is treated as adjusted basis in specified tangible property for the taxable year is determined by multiplying DC's adjusted basis in the machine and office building by DC's dual use ratio with respect to the machine and office building determined under paragraph (d)(3) of this section.

(B) *Depreciation not capitalized to inventory.* Because none of the depreciation with respect to the office building is capitalized to inventory or other property held for sale, DC's dual use ratio with respect to the office building is determined entirely by reference to the depreciation deduction with respect to the office building. Therefore, under paragraph (d)(3) of this section, DC's dual use ratio with respect to the office building for Year 1 is 75 percent, which is DC's depreciation deduction with respect to the office building that is allocated and apportioned to gross DEI under § 1.250(b)-1(d)(2) for Year 1 ($750x), divided by the total amount of DC's depreciation deduction with respect to the office building for Year 1 ($1000x). Accordingly, under paragraph (d)(1) of this section, $7,500x ($10,000x x 0.75) of DC's average adjusted bases in the office building is taken into account under paragraph (b) of this section in determining DC's QBAI for the taxable year.

(C) *Depreciation capitalized to inventory*. Because all of the depreciation with respect to the machine is capitalized to inventory, DC's dual use ratio with respect to the machine is determined entirely by reference to the depreciation with respect to the machine that is capitalized to inventory and included in cost of goods sold. Therefore, under paragraph (d)(3) of this section, DC's dual use ratio with respect to the machine for the taxable year is 80 percent, which is DC's depreciation with respect to the machine that is capitalized to inventory of Product A, the gross income or loss from the sale of which is taken into account in determining DC's DEI for the taxable year ($320x), divided by DC's depreciation with respect to the machine that is capitalized to inventory, the gross income or loss from the sale of which is taken into account in determining DC's income for Year 1 ($400x). Accordingly, under paragraph (d)(1) of this section, $3,200x ($4,000x x 0.8) of DC's average adjusted basis in the machine is taken into account under paragraph (b) of this section in determining DC's QBAI for the taxable year.

(e) *Determination of adjusted basis of specified tangible property*.—(1) *In general*.—The adjusted basis in specified tangible property for purposes of this section is determined by using the cost capitalization methods of accounting used by the domestic corporation for purposes of determining the gross income and deductions of the domestic corporation and the alternative depreciation system under section 168(g), and by allocating the depreciation deduction with respect to such property for the domestic corporation's taxable year ratably to each day during the period in the taxable year to which such depreciation relates. For purposes of the preceding sentence, the period in the taxable year to which such depreciation relates is determined without regard to the applicable convention under section 168(d).

(2) *Effect of change in law*.—The adjusted basis in specified tangible property is determined without regard to any provision of law enacted after December 22, 2017, unless such later enacted law specifically and directly amends the definition of QBAI under section 250 or section 951A. For purposes of applying section 250(b)(2)(B) and this paragraph (e), the technical amendment to section 168(g) (to provide a recovery period of 20 years for qualified improvement property for purposes of the alternative depreciation system) enacted in section 2307(a) of the Coronavirus Aid, Relief, and Economic Security Act, Pub. L. 116-136 (2020) is treated as enacted on December 22, 2017.

(3) *Specified tangible property placed in service before enactment of section 250*.—The adjusted basis in specified tangible property placed in service before December 22, 2017, is determined using the alternative depreciation system under section 168(g), as if this system had applied from the date that the property was placed in service.

(f) *Special rules for short taxable years*.—(1) *In general*.—In the case of a domestic corporation that has a taxable year that is less than twelve months (a *short taxable year*), the rules for determining the QBAI of the domestic corporation under this section are modified as provided in paragraphs (f)(2) and (3) of this section with respect to the taxable year.

(2) *Determination of when the quarter closes*.—For purposes of determining when the quarter closes, in determining the QBAI of a domestic corporation for a short taxable year, the quarters of the domestic corporation for purposes of this section are the full quarters beginning and ending within the short taxable year (if any), determining quarter length as if the domestic corporation did not have a short taxable year, plus one or more short quarters (if any).

(3) *Reduction of qualified business asset investment*.—The QBAI of a domestic corporation for a short taxable year is the sum of—

(i) The sum of the domestic corporation's aggregate adjusted bases in specified tangible property as of the close of each full quarter (if any) in the domestic corporation's taxable year divided by four; plus

(ii) The domestic corporation's aggregate adjusted bases in specified tangible property as of the close of each short quarter (if any) in the domestic corporation's taxable year multiplied by the sum of the number of days in each short quarter divided by 365.

(4) *Example*.—The following example illustrates the application of this paragraph (f).

(i) *Facts*. A, an individual, owns all of the stock of DC, a domestic corporation. A owns DC from the beginning of the taxable year. On July 15 of the taxable year, A sells DC to USP, a domestic corporation that is unrelated to A. DC becomes a member of the consolidated group of which USP is the common parent and as a result, under § 1.1502-76(b)(2)(ii), DC's taxable year is treated as ending on July 15. USP and DC both use the calendar year as their taxable year. DC's aggregate adjusted bases in specified tangible property for the taxable year are $250x as of March 31, $300x as of June 30, $275x as of July 15, $500x as of September 30, and $450x as of December 31.

(ii) *Analysis*—(A) *Determination of short taxable years and quarters*. DC has two short taxable years during the year. The first short taxable year is from January 1 to July 15, with two full quarters (January 1 through March 31 and April 1 through June 30) and one short quarter (July 1 through July 15). The second taxable year is from July 16 to December 31, with one short quarter (July 16 through September 30) and one full quarter (October 1 through December 31).

(B) *Calculation of qualified business asset investment for the first short taxable year*. Under paragraph (f)(2) of this section, for the first short taxable year, DC has three quarter closes (March 31, June 30, and July 15). Under paragraph (f)(3) of this section, the QBAI of DC for the first short taxable year is $148.80x, the sum of $137.50x (($250x + $300x)/4) attributable to the two full quarters and $11.30x ($275x x 15/365) attributable to the short quarter.

(C) *Calculation of qualified business asset investment for the second short taxable year*. Under paragraph (f)(2) of this section, for the second short taxable year, DC has two quarter closes (September 30 and December 31). Under paragraph (f)(3) of this section, the QBAI of DC for the second short taxable year is $217.98x, the sum of $112.50x ($450x/4) attributable to the one full quarter and $105.48x ($500x x 77/365) attributable to the short quarter.

(g) *Partnership property*.—(1) *In general*.—If a domestic corporation holds an interest in one or more partnerships during a taxable year (including indirectly through one or more partnerships that are partners in a lower-tier partnership), the QBAI of the domestic corporation for the taxable year (determined without regard to this paragraph (g)(1)) is increased by the sum of the domestic corporation's partnership QBAI with respect to each partnership for the taxable year.

(2) *Determination of partnership QBAI*.—For purposes of paragraph (g)(1) of this section, the term *partnership QBAI* means, with respect to a partnership, a domestic corporation, and a taxable year, the sum of the domestic corporation's partner adjusted basis in each partnership specified tangible property of the partnership for each partnership taxable year that ends with or within the taxable year. If a partnership taxable year is less than twelve months, the principles of paragraph (f) of this section apply in determining a domestic corporation's partnership QBAI with respect to the partnership.

(3) *Determination of partner adjusted basis*.—(i) *In general*.—For purposes of paragraph (g)(2) of this section, the term *partner adjusted basis* means the amount described in paragraph (g)(3)(ii) of this section with respect to sole use partnership property or paragraph (g)(3)(iii) of this section with respect to dual use partnership property. The principles of section 706(d) apply to this determination.

(ii) *Sole use partnership property*.—(A) *In general*.—The amount described in this paragraph (g)(3)(ii), with respect to sole use partnership property, a partnership taxable year, and a domestic corporation, is the sum of the domestic corporation's proportionate share of the partnership adjusted basis in the sole use partnership property for the partnership taxable year and the domestic corporation's partner-specific QBAI basis in the sole use partnership property for the partnership taxable year.

(B) *Definition of sole use partnership property*.—The term *sole use partnership property* means, with respect to a partnership, a partnership taxable year, and a domestic corporation, partnership specified tangible property of the partnership that is used in the production of only gross DEI of the domestic corporation for the taxable year in which or with which the partnership taxable year ends. For purposes of the preceding sentence, partnership specified tangible property of a partnership is used in the production of only gross DEI for a taxable year if all the domestic corporation's distributive share of the partnership's depreciation deduction or cost recovery allowance with respect to the property (if any) for the partnership taxable year that ends with or within the taxable year is allocated and apportioned to the domestic corporation's gross DEI for the taxable year under § 1.250(b)-1(d)(2) and, if any of the partnership's depreciation or cost recovery allowance with respect to the property is capitalized to inventory or other property held for sale, all the domestic corporation's distributive share of the partnership's gross income or loss from the sale of such inventory or other property for the partnership taxable year that ends with or within the taxable year is taken into account in determining the DEI of the domestic corporation for the taxable year.

(iii) *Dual use partnership property.*—(A) *In general.*—The amount described in this paragraph (g)(3)(iii), with respect to dual use partnership property, a partnership taxable year, and a domestic corporation, is the sum of the domestic corporation's proportionate share of the partnership adjusted basis in the property for the partnership taxable year and the domestic corporation's partner-specific QBAI basis in the property for the partnership taxable year, multiplied by the domestic corporation's dual use ratio with respect to the property for the partnership taxable year determined under the principles of paragraph (d)(3) of this section, except that the ratio described in paragraph (d)(3) of this section is determined by reference to the domestic corporation's distributive share of the amounts described in paragraph (d)(3) of this section.

(B) *Definition of dual use partnership property.*—The term *dual use partnership property* means partnership specified tangible property other than sole use partnership property.

(4) *Determination of proportionate share of the partnership's adjusted basis in partnership specified tangible property.*—(i) *In general.*—For purposes of paragraph (g)(3) of this section, the domestic corporation's proportionate share of the partnership adjusted basis in partnership specified tangible property for a partnership taxable year is the partnership adjusted basis in the property multiplied by the domestic corporation's proportionate share ratio with respect to the property for the partnership taxable year. Solely for purposes of determining the proportionate share ratio under paragraph (g)(4)(ii) of this section, the partnership's calculation of, and a partner's distributive share of, any income, loss, depreciation, or cost recovery allowance is determined under section 704(b).

(ii) *Proportionate share ratio.*—The term *proportionate share ratio* means, with respect to a partnership, a partnership taxable year, and a domestic corporation, the ratio (expressed as a percentage) calculated as—

(A) The sum of—

(1) The domestic corporation's distributive share of the partnership's depreciation deduction or cost recovery allowance with respect to the property for the partnership taxable year; and

(2) The amount of the partnership's depreciation or cost recovery allowance with respect to the property that is capitalized to inventory or other property held for sale, the gross income or loss from the sale of which is taken into account in determining the domestic corporation's distributive share of the partnership's income or loss for the partnership taxable year; divided by

(B) The sum of—

(1) The total amount of the partnership's depreciation deduction or cost recovery allowance with respect to the property for the partnership taxable year; and

(2) The total amount of the partnership's depreciation or cost recovery allowance with respect to the property capitalized to inventory or other property held for sale, the gross income or loss from the sale of which is taken into account in determining the partnership's income or loss for the partnership taxable year.

(5) *Definition of partnership specified tangible property.*—The term *partnership specified tangible property* means, with respect to a domestic corporation, tangible property (as defined in paragraph (c)(2) of this section) of a partnership that is—

(i) Used in the trade or business of the partnership;

(ii) Of a type with respect to which a deduction is allowable under section 167; and

(iii) Used in the production of gross income included in the domestic corporation's gross DEI.

(6) *Determination of partnership adjusted basis.*—For purposes of this paragraph (g), the term *partnership adjusted basis* means, with respect to a partnership, partnership specified tangible property, and a partnership taxable year, the amount equal to the average of the partnership's adjusted basis in the partnership specified tangible property as of the close of each quarter in the partnership taxable year determined without regard to any adjustments under section 734(b) except for adjustments under section 734(b)(1)(B) or section 734(b)(2)(B) that are attributable to distributions of tangible property (as defined in paragraph (c)(2) of this section) and for adjustments under section 734(b)(1)(A) or 734(b)(2)(A). The principles of paragraphs (e) and (h) of this section apply for purposes of determining a partnership's adjusted basis in partnership specified tangible property and the proportionate share of the partnership's adjusted basis in partnership specified tangible property.

(7) *Determination of partner-specific QBAI basis.*—For purposes of this paragraph (g), the term *partner-specific QBAI basis* means, with respect to a domestic corporation, a partnership, and partnership specified tangible property, the amount that is equal to the average of the basis adjustment under section 743(b) that is allocated to the partnership specified tangible property of the partnership with respect to the domestic corporation as of the close of each quarter in the partnership taxable year. For this purpose, a negative basis adjustment under section 743(b) is expressed as a negative number. The principles of paragraphs (e) and (h) of this section apply for purposes of determining the partner-specific QBAI basis with respect to partnership specified tangible property.

(8) *Examples.*—The following examples illustrate the rules of this paragraph (g).

(i) *Assumed facts.*—Except as otherwise stated, the following facts are assumed for purposes of the examples:

(A) DC, DC1, DC2, and DC3 are domestic corporations.

(B) PRS is a partnership and its allocations satisfy the requirements of section 704.

(C) All properties are partnership specified tangible property.

(D) All persons use the calendar year as their taxable year.

(E) There is no partner-specific QBAI basis with respect to any property.

(ii) *Example 1: Sole use partnership property.*—(A) *Facts.* DC is a partner in PRS. PRS owns two properties, Asset A and Asset B. The average of PRS's adjusted basis as of the close of each quarter of PRS's taxable year in Asset A is $100x and in Asset B is $500x. In Year 1, PRS's section 704(b) depreciation deduction is $10x with respect to Asset A and $5x with respect to Asset B, and DC's section 704(b) distributive share of the depreciation deduction is $8x with respect to Asset A and $1x with respect to Asset B. None of the depreciation with respect to Asset A or Asset B is capitalized to inventory or other property held for sale. DC's entire distributive share of the depreciation deduction with respect to Asset A and Asset B is allocated and apportioned to DC's gross DEI for Year 1 under § 1.250(b)-1(d)(2).

(B) *Analysis*—*(1) Sole use partnership property.* Because all of DC's distributive share of the depreciation deduction with respect to Asset A and B is allocated and apportioned to gross DEI for Year 1, Asset A and Asset B are sole use partnership property within the meaning of paragraph (g)(3)(ii)(B) of this section. Therefore, under paragraph (g)(3)(ii)(A) of this section, DC's partner adjusted basis in Asset A and Asset B is equal to the sum of DC's proportionate share of PRS's partnership adjusted basis in Asset A and Asset B for Year 1 and DC's partner-specific QBAI basis in Asset A and Asset B for Year 1, respectively.

(2) Proportionate share. Under paragraph (g)(4)(i) of this section, DC's proportionate share of PRS's partnership adjusted basis in Asset A and Asset B is PRS's partnership adjusted basis in Asset A and Asset B for Year 1, multiplied by DC's proportionate share ratio with respect to Asset A and Asset B for Year 1, respectively. Because none of the depreciation with respect to Asset A or Asset B is capitalized to inventory or other property held for sale, DC's proportionate share ratio with respect to Asset A and Asset B is determined entirely by reference to the depreciation deduction with respect to Asset A and Asset B. Therefore, DC's proportionate share ratio with respect to Asset A for Year 1 is 80 percent, which is the ratio of DC's section 704(b) distributive share of PRS's section 704(b) depreciation deduction with respect to Asset A for Year 1 ($8x), divided by the total amount of PRS's section 704(b) depreciation deduction with respect to Asset A for Year 1 ($10x). DC's proportionate share ratio with respect to Asset B for Year 1 is 20 percent, which is the ratio of DC's section 704(b) distributive share of PRS's section 704(b) depreciation deduction with respect to Asset B for Year 1 ($1x), divided by the total amount of PRS's section 704(b) depreciation deduction with respect to Asset B for Year 1 ($5x). Accordingly, under paragraph (g)(4)(i) of this section, DC's proportionate share of PRS's partnership adjusted basis in Asset A is $80x ($100x x 0.8), and DC's proportionate share of PRS's partnership adjusted basis in Asset B is $100x ($500x x 0.2).

(3) *Partner adjusted basis.* Because DC has no partner-specific QBAI basis with respect to Asset A and Asset B, DC's partner adjusted basis in Asset A and Asset B is determined entirely by reference to its proportionate share of PRS's partnership adjusted basis in Asset A and Asset B. Therefore, under paragraph (g)(3)(ii)(A) of this section, DC's partner adjusted basis in Asset A is $80x, DC's proportionate share of PRS's partnership adjusted basis in Asset A, and DC's partner adjusted basis in Asset B is $100x, DC's proportionate share of PRS's partnership adjusted basis in Asset B.

(4) *Partnership QBAI.* Under paragraph (g)(2) of this section, DC's partnership QBAI with respect to PRS is $180x, the sum of DC's partner adjusted basis in Asset A ($80x) and DC's partner adjusted basis in Asset B ($100x). Accordingly, under paragraph (g)(1) of this section, DC increases its QBAI for Year 1 by $180x.

(iii) *Example 2: Dual use partnership property.*—(A) *Facts.* DC owns a 50 percent interest in PRS. All section 704(b) and tax items are identical and are allocated equally between DC and its other partner. PRS owns three properties, Asset C, Asset D, and Asset E. PRS sells two products, Product A and Product B. All of DC's distributive share of the gross income or loss from the sale of Product A is taken into account in determining DC's DEI, and none of DC's distributive share of the gross income or loss from the sale of Product B is taken into account in determining DC's DEI.

(1) *Asset C.* The average of PRS's adjusted basis as of the close of each quarter of PRS's taxable year in Asset C is $100x. In Year 1, PRS's depreciation is $10x with respect to Asset C, none of which is capitalized to inventory or other property held for sale. DC's distributive share of the depreciation deduction with respect to Asset C is $5x ($10x x 0.5), $3x of which is allocated and apportioned to DC's gross DEI under § 1.250(b)-1(d)(2).

(2) *Asset D.* The average of PRS's adjusted basis as of the close of each quarter of PRS's taxable year in Asset D is $500x. In Year 1, PRS's depreciation is $50x with respect to Asset D, $10x of which is capitalized to inventory of Product A and $40x is capitalized to inventory of Product B. None of the $10x depreciation with respect to Asset D capitalized to inventory of Product A is capitalized to ending inventory. However, of the $40x capitalized to inventory of Product B, $10x is capitalized to ending inventory. Therefore, the amount of depreciation with respect to Asset D capitalized to inventory of Product A that is taken into account in determining DC's distributive share of the income or loss of PRS for Year 1 is $5x ($10x x 0.5), and the amount of depreciation with respect to Asset D capitalized to inventory of Product B that is taken into account in determining DC's distributive share of the income or loss of PRS for Year 1 is $15x ($30x x 0.5).

(3) *Asset E.* The average of PRS's adjusted basis as of the close of each quarter of PRS's taxable year in Asset E is $600x. In Year 1, PRS's depreciation is $60x with respect to Asset E. Of the $60x depreciation with respect to Asset E, $20x is allowed as a deduction, $24x is capitalized to inventory of Product A, and $16x is capitalized to inventory of Product B. DC's distributive share of the depreciation deduction with respect to Asset E is $10x ($20x x 0.5), $8x of which is allocated and apportioned to DC's gross DEI under § 1.250(b)-1(d)(2). None of the $24x depreciation with respect to Asset E capitalized to inventory of Product A is capitalized to ending inventory. However, of the $16x depreciation with respect to Asset E capitalized to inventory of Product B, $10x is capitalized to ending inventory. Therefore, the amount of depreciation with respect to Asset E capitalized to inventory of Product A that is taken into account in determining DC's distributive share of the income or loss of PRS for Year 1 is $12x ($24x x 0.5), and the amount of depreciation with respect to Asset E capitalized to inventory of Product B that is taken into account in determining DC's distributive share of the income or loss of PRS for Year 1 is $3x ($6x x 0.5).

(B) *Analysis.* Because Asset C, Asset D, and Asset E are not used in the production of only gross DEI in Year 1 within the meaning of paragraph (g)(3)(ii)(B) of this section, Asset C, Asset D, and Asset E are dual use partnership property within the meaning of paragraph (g)(3)(iii)(B) of this section. Therefore, under paragraph (g)(3)(iii)(A) of this section, DC's partner adjusted basis in Asset C, Asset D, and Asset E is the sum of DC's proportionate share of PRS's partnership adjusted basis in Asset C, Asset D, and Asset E, respectively, for Year 1, and DC's partner-specific QBAI basis in Asset C, Asset D, and Asset E, respectively, for Year 1, multiplied by DC's dual use ratio with respect to Asset C, Asset D, and Asset E, respectively, for Year 1, determined under the principles of paragraph (d)(3) of this section, except that the ratio described in paragraph (d)(3) of this section is determined by reference to DC's distributive share of the amounts described in paragraph (d)(3) of this section.

(1) *Asset C—(i) Proportionate share.* Under paragraph (g)(4)(i) of this section, DC's proportionate share of PRS's partnership adjusted basis in Asset C is PRS's partnership adjusted basis in Asset C for Year 1, multiplied by DC's proportionate share ratio with respect to Asset C for Year 1. Because none of the depreciation with respect to Asset C is capitalized to inventory or other property held for sale, DC's proportionate share ratio with respect to Asset C is determined entirely by reference to the depreciation deduction with respect to Asset C. Therefore, DC's proportionate share ratio with respect to Asset C is 50 percent, which is the ratio calculated as the amount of DC's section 704(b) distributive share of PRS's section 704(b) depreciation deduction with respect to Asset C for Year 1 ($5x), divided by the total amount of PRS's section 704(b) depreciation deduction with respect to Asset C for Year 1 ($10x). Accordingly, under paragraph (g)(4)(i) of this section, DC's proportionate share of PRS's partnership adjusted basis in Asset C is $50x ($100x x 0.5).

(ii) *Dual use ratio.* Because none of the depreciation with respect to Asset C is capitalized to inventory or other property held for sale, DC's dual use ratio with respect to Asset C is determined entirely by reference to the depreciation deduction with respect to Asset C. Therefore, DC's dual use ratio with respect to Asset C is 60 percent, which is the ratio calculated as the amount of DC's distributive share of PRS's depreciation deduction with respect to Asset C that is allocated and apportioned to DC's gross DEI under § 1.250(b)-1(d)(2) for Year 1 ($3x), divided by the total amount of DC's distributive share of PRS's depreciation deduction with respect to Asset C for Year 1 ($5x).

(iii) *Partner adjusted basis.* Because DC has no partner-specific QBAI basis with respect to Asset C, DC's partner adjusted basis in Asset C is determined entirely by reference to DC's proportionate share of PRS's partnership adjusted basis in Asset C, multiplied by DC's dual use ratio with respect to Asset C. Under paragraph (g)(3)(iii)(A) of this section, DC's partner adjusted basis in Asset C is $30x, DC's proportionate share of PRS's partnership adjusted basis in Asset C for Year 1 ($50x), multiplied by DC's dual use ratio with respect to Asset C for Year 1 (60 percent).

(2) *Asset D—(i) Proportionate share.* Under paragraph (g)(4)(i) of this section, DC's proportionate share of PRS's partnership adjusted basis in Asset D is PRS's partnership adjusted basis in Asset D for Year 1, multiplied by DC's proportionate share ratio with respect to Asset D for Year 1. Because all of the depreciation with respect to Asset D is capitalized to inventory, DC's proportionate share ratio with respect to Asset D is determined entirely by reference to the depreciation with respect to Asset D that is capitalized to inventory and included in cost of goods sold. Therefore, DC's proportionate share ratio with respect to Asset D is 50 percent, which is the ratio calculated as the amount of PRS's section 704(b) depreciation with respect to Asset D capitalized to Product A and Product B that is taken into account in determining DC's section 704(b) distributive share of PRS's income or loss for Year 1 ($20x), divided by the total amount of PRS's section 704(b) depreciation with respect to Asset D capitalized to Product A and Product B that is taken into account in determining PRS's section 704(b) income or loss for Year 1 ($40x). Accordingly, under paragraph (g)(4)(i) of this section, DC's proportionate share of PRS's partnership adjusted basis in Asset D is $250x ($500x x 0.5).

(ii) *Dual use ratio.* Because all of the depreciation with respect to Asset D is capitalized to inventory, DC's dual use ratio with respect to Asset D is determined entirely by reference to the depreciation with respect to Asset D that is capitalized to inventory and included in cost of goods sold. Therefore, DC's dual use ratio with respect to Asset D is 25 percent, which is the ratio calculated as the amount of depreciation with respect to Asset D capitalized to inventory of Product A and Product B that is taken into account in determining DC's DEI for Year 1 ($5x), divided by the total amount of depreciation with respect to Asset D capitalized to inventory of Product A and Product B that is taken into account in determining DC's income or loss for Year 1 ($20x).

(iii) *Partner adjusted basis.* Because DC has no partner-specific QBAI basis with respect to Asset D, DC's partner adjusted basis in Asset D is determined entirely by reference to DC's proportionate share of PRS's partnership adjusted basis in Asset D, multiplied by DC's dual use ratio with respect to Asset D. Under paragraph (g)(3)(iii)(A) of this section, DC's partner adjusted basis in Asset D is $62.50x, DC's proportionate share of PRS's partnership adjusted basis in Asset D for Year 1 ($250x), multiplied by DC's dual use ratio with respect to Asset D for Year 1 (25 percent).

(3) *Asset E—(i) Proportionate share.* Under paragraph (g)(4)(i) of this section, DC's proportionate share of PRS's partnership adjusted basis in Asset E is PRS's partnership adjusted basis in Asset E for Year 1, multiplied by DC's proportionate share ratio with respect to

Asset E for Year 1. Because the depreciation with respect to Asset E is partly deducted and partly capitalized to inventory, DC's proportionate share ratio with respect to Asset E is determined by reference to both the depreciation that is deducted and the depreciation that is capitalized to inventory and included in cost of goods sold. Therefore, DC's proportionate share ratio with respect to Asset E is 50 percent, which is the ratio calculated as the sum ($25x) of the amount of DC's section 704(b) distributive share of PRS's section 704(b) depreciation deduction with respect to Asset E for Year 1 ($10x) and the amount of PRS's section 704(b) depreciation with respect to Asset E capitalized to inventory of Product A and Product B that is taken into account in determining DC's section 704(b) distributive share of PRS's income or loss for Year 1 ($15x), divided by the sum ($50x) of the total amount of PRS's section 704(b) depreciation deduction with respect to Asset E for Year 1 ($20x) and the total amount of PRS's section 704(b) depreciation with respect to Asset E capitalized to inventory of Product A and Product B that is taken into account in determining PRS's section 704(b) income or loss for Year 1 ($30x). Accordingly, under paragraph (g)(4)(i) of this section, DC's proportionate share of PRS's partnership adjusted basis in Asset E is $300x ($600x x 0.5).

(ii) *Dual use ratio*. Because the depreciation with respect to Asset E is partly deducted and partly capitalized to inventory, DC's dual use ratio with respect to Asset E is determined by reference to the depreciation that is deducted and the depreciation that is capitalized to inventory and included in cost of goods sold. Therefore, DC's dual use ratio with respect to Asset E is 80 percent, which is the ratio calculated as the sum ($20x) of the amount of DC's distributive share of PRS's depreciation deduction with respect to Asset E that is allocated and apportioned to DC's gross DEI under § 1.250(b)-1(d)(2) for Year 1 ($8x) and the amount of depreciation with respect to Asset E capitalized to inventory of Product A and Product B that is taken into account in determining DC's DEI for Year 1 ($12x), divided by the sum ($25x) of the total amount of DC's distributive share of PRS's depreciation deduction with respect to Asset E for Year 1 ($10x) and the total amount of depreciation with respect to Asset E capitalized to inventory of Product A and Product B that is taken into account in determining DC's income or loss for Year 1 ($15x).

(iii) *Partner adjusted basis*. Because DC has no partner-specific QBAI basis with respect to Asset E, DC's partner adjusted basis in Asset E is determined entirely by reference to DC's proportionate share of PRS's partnership adjusted basis in Asset E, multiplied by DC's dual use ratio with respect to Asset E. Under paragraph (g)(3)(iii)(A) of this section, DC's partner adjusted basis in Asset E is $240x, DC's proportionate share of PRS's partnership adjusted basis in Asset E for Year 1 ($300x), multiplied by DC's dual use ratio with respect to Asset E for Year 1 (80 percent).

(4) *Partnership QBAI*. Under paragraph (g)(2) of this section, DC's partnership QBAI with respect to PRS is $332.50x, the sum of DC's partner adjusted basis in Asset C ($30x), DC's partner adjusted basis in Asset D ($62.50x), and DC's partner adjusted basis in Asset E ($240x). Accordingly, under paragraph (g)(1) of this section, DC increases its QBAI for Year 1 by $332.50x.

(iv) *Example 3: Sole use partnership specified tangible property; section 743(b) adjustments*.—(A) *Facts*. The facts are the same as in paragraph (g)(8)(ii)(A) of this section (the facts in *Example 1*), except that there is an average of $40x positive adjustment to the adjusted basis in Asset A as of the close of each quarter of PRS's taxable year with respect to DC under section 743(b) and an average of $20x negative adjustment to the adjusted basis in Asset B as of the close of each quarter of PRS's taxable year with respect to DC under section 743(b).

(B) *Analysis*. Under paragraph (g)(3)(ii)(A) of this section, DC's partner adjusted basis in Asset A is $120x, which is the sum of $80x (DC's proportionate share of PRS's partnership adjusted basis in Asset A as illustrated in paragraph (g)(8)(ii)(B)(2) of this section (the analysis in *Example 1*)) and $40x (DC's partner-specific QBAI basis in Asset A). Under paragraph (g)(3)(ii)(A) of this section, DC's partner adjusted basis in Asset B is $80x, the sum of $100x (DC's proportionate share of the partnership adjusted basis in the property as illustrated in paragraph (g)(8)(ii)(B)(2) of this section (the analysis in *Example 1*)) and (-$20x) (DC's partner-specific QBAI basis in Asset B). Therefore, under paragraph (g)(2) of this section, DC's partnership QBAI with respect to PRS is $200x ($120x + $80x). Accordingly, under paragraph (g)(1) of this section, DC increases its QBAI for Year 1 by $200x.

(v) *Example 4: Sale of partnership interest before close of taxable year*.—(A) *Facts*. DC1 owns a 50 percent interest in PRS on January 1 of Year 1. PRS does not have an election under section 754 in effect. On July 1 of Year 1, DC1 sells its entire interest in PRS to DC2. PRS owns Asset G. The average of PRS's adjusted basis as of the close of each quarter of PRS's taxable year in Asset G is $100x. DC1's section 704(b) distributive share of the depreciation deduction with respect to Asset G is 25 percent with respect to PRS's entire year. DC2's section 704(b) distributive share of the depreciation deduction with respect to Asset G is also 25 percent with respect to PRS's entire year. Both DC1's and DC2's entire distributive shares of the depreciation deduction with respect to Asset G are allocated and apportioned under § 1.250(b)-1(d)(2) to DC1's and DC2's gross DEI, respectively, for Year 1. PRS's allocations satisfy section 706(d).

(B) *Analysis*—*(1) DC1*. Because DC1 owns an interest in PRS during DC1's taxable year and receives a distributive share of partnership items of the partnership under section 706(d), DC1 has partnership QBAI with respect to PRS in the amount determined under paragraph (g)(2) of this section. Under paragraph (g)(3)(i) of this section, DC1's partner adjusted basis in Asset G is $25x, the product of $100x (the partnership's adjusted basis in the property) and 25 percent (DC1's section 704(b) distributive share of depreciation deduction with respect to Asset G). Therefore, DC1's partnership QBAI with respect to PRS is $25x. Accordingly, under paragraph (g)(1) of this section, DC1 increases its QBAI by $25x for Year 1.

(2) DC2. DC2's partner adjusted basis in Asset G is also $25x, the product of $100x (the partnership's adjusted basis in the property) and 25 percent (DC2's section 704(b) distributive share of depreciation deduction with respect to Asset G). Therefore, DC2's partnership QBAI with respect to PRS is $25x. Accordingly, under paragraph (g)(1) of this section, DC2 increases its QBAI by $25x for Year 1.

(vi) *Example 5: Partnership adjusted basis; distribution of property in liquidation of partnership interest*.—(A) *Facts*. DC1, DC2, and DC3 are equal partners in PRS, a partnership. DC1 and DC2 each has an adjusted basis of $100x in its partnership interest. DC3 has an adjusted basis of $50x in its partnership interest. PRS has a section 754 election in effect. PRS owns Asset H with a fair market value of $50x and an adjusted basis of $0, Asset I with a fair market value of $100x and an adjusted basis of $100x, and Asset J with a fair market value of $150x and an adjusted basis of $150x. Asset H and Asset J are tangible property, but Asset I is not tangible property. PRS distributes Asset I to DC3 in liquidation of DC3's interest in PRS. None of DC1, DC2, DC3, or PRS recognizes gain on the distribution. Under section 732(b), DC3's adjusted basis in Asset I is $50x. PRS's adjusted basis in Asset H is increased by $50x to $50x under section 734(b)(1)(B), which is the amount by which PRS's adjusted basis in Asset I immediately before the distribution exceeds DC3's adjusted basis in Asset I.

(B) *Analysis*. Under paragraph (g)(6) of this section, PRS's adjusted basis in Asset H is determined without regard to any adjustments under section 734(b) except for adjustments under section 734(b)(1)(B) or section 734(b)(2)(B) that are attributable to distributions of tangible property and for adjustments under section 734(b)(1)(A) or 734(b)(2)(A). The adjustment to the adjusted basis in Asset H is under section 734(b)(1)(B) and is attributable to the distribution of Asset I, which is not tangible property. Accordingly, for purposes of applying paragraph (g)(1) of this section, PRS's adjusted basis in Asset H is $0.

(h) *Anti-avoidance rule for certain transfers of property*.—(1) *In general*.—If, with a principal purpose of decreasing the amount of its deemed tangible income return, a domestic corporation transfers specified tangible property (*transferred property*) to a specified related party of the domestic corporation and, within the disqualified period, the domestic corporation or an FDII-eligible related party of the domestic corporation leases the same or substantially similar property from any specified related party, then, solely for purposes of determining the QBAI of the domestic corporation under paragraph (b) of this section, the domestic corporation is treated as owning the transferred property from the later of the beginning of the term of the lease or date of the transfer of the property until the earlier of the end of the term of the lease or the end of the recovery period of the property.

(2) *Rule for structured arrangements*.—For purposes of paragraph (h)(1) of this section, a transfer of specified tangible property to a person that is not a related party or lease of property from a person that is not a related party is treated as a transfer to or lease from a specified related party if the transfer or lease is pursuant to a structured arrangement. A structured arrangement exists only if either paragraph (h)(2)(i) or (ii) of this section is satisfied.

(i) The reduction in the domestic corporation's deemed tangible income return is priced into the terms of the arrangement with the transferee.

(ii) Based on all the facts and circumstances, the reduction in the domestic corporation's deemed tangible income return is a principal purpose of the arrangement. Facts and circumstances that indicate the reduction in the domestic corporation's deemed tangible income return is a principal purpose of the arrangement include—

(A) Marketing the arrangement as tax-advantaged where some or all of the tax advantage derives from the reduction in the domestic corporation's deemed tangible income return;

(B) Primarily marketing the arrangement to domestic corporations which earn FDDEI;

(C) Features that alter the terms of the arrangement, including the return, in the event the reduction in the domestic corporation's deemed tangible income return is no longer relevant; or

(D) A below-market return absent the tax effects or benefits resulting from the reduction in the domestic corporation's deemed tangible income return.

(3) *Per se rules for certain transactions*.—For purposes of paragraph (h)(1) of this section, a transfer of property by a domestic corporation to a specified related party (including a party deemed to be a specified related party under paragraph (h)(2) of this section) followed by a lease of the same or substantially similar property by the domestic corporation or an FDII-eligible related party from a specified related party (including a party deemed to be a specified related party under paragraph (h)(2) of this section) is treated per se as occurring pursuant to a principal purpose of decreasing the amount of the domestic corporation's deemed tangible income return if both the transfer and the lease occur within a six-month period.

(4) *Definitions related to anti-avoidance rule*.—The following definitions apply for purpose of this paragraph (h).

(i) *Disqualified period*.—The term *disqualified period* means, with respect to a transfer, the period beginning one year before the date of the transfer and ending the earlier of the end of the remaining recovery period (under the system described in section 951A(d)(3)(A)) of the property or one year after the date of the transfer.

(ii) *FDII-eligible related party*.—The term *FDII-eligible related party* means, with respect to a domestic corporation, a member of the same consolidated group as the domestic corporation or a partnership with respect to which at least 80 percent of the interests in partnership capital and profits are owned, directly or indirectly, by the domestic corporation or one or more members of the consolidated group that includes the domestic corporation.

(iii) *Specified related party*.—The term *specified related party* means, with respect to a domestic corporation, a related party other than an FDII-eligible related party.

(iv) *Transfer*.—The term *transfer* means any disposition, exchange, contribution, or distribution of property, and includes an indirect transfer. For example, a transfer of an interest in a partnership is treated as a transfer of the assets of the partnership. In addition, if paragraph (h)(1) of this section applies to treat a domestic corporation as owning specified tangible property by reason of a lease of property, the termination or lapse of the lease of the property is treated as a transfer of the specified tangible property by the domestic corporation to the lessor.

(5) *Transactions occurring before March 4, 2019*.—Paragraph (h)(1) of this section does not apply to a transfer of property that occurs before March 4, 2019.

(6) *Examples*.—The following examples illustrate the application of this paragraph (h).

(i) *Example 1: Sale-leaseback with a related party*.—(A) *Facts*. DC, a domestic corporation, owns Asset A, which is specified tangible property. DC also owns all the single class of stock of DS, a domestic corporation, and FS1 and FS2, each a controlled foreign corporation. DC and DS are members of the same consolidated group. On January 1, Year 1, DC sells Asset A to FS1. At the time of the sale, Asset A had a remaining recovery period of 10 years under the alternative depreciation system. On February 1, Year 1, FS2 leases Asset B, which is substantially similar to Asset A, to DS for a five-year term ending on January 31, Year 6.

(B) *Analysis*. Because DC transfers specified tangible property (Asset A), to a specified related party of DC (FS1), and, within a six month period (January 1, Year 1 to February 1, Year 1), an FDII-eligible related party of DC (DS) leases a substantially similar property (Asset B) from a specified related party (FS2), DC's transfer of Asset A and lease of Asset B are treated as per se occurring pursuant to a principal purpose of decreasing the amount of its deemed tangible income return. Accordingly, for purposes of determining DC's QBAI, DC is treated as owning Asset A from February 1, Year 1, the later of the date of the transfer of Asset A (January 1, Year 1) and the beginning of the term of the lease of Asset B (February 1, Year 1), until January 31, Year 6, the earlier of the end of the term of the lease of Asset B (January 31, Year 6) or the remaining recovery period of Asset A (December 31, Year 10).

(ii) *Example 2: Sale-leaseback with a related party; lapse of initial lease*.—(A) *Facts*. The facts are the same as in paragraph (h)(6)(i)(A) of this section (the facts in *Example 1*). In addition, DS allows the lease of Asset B to expire on February 1, Year 6. On June 1, Year 6, DS and FS2 renew the lease for a five-year term ending on May 31, Year 11.

(B) *Analysis*. Because DC is treated as owning Asset A under paragraph (h)(1) of this section, the lapse of the lease of Asset B is treated as a transfer of Asset A to FS2 on February 1, Year 6, under paragraph (h)(4)(iv) of this section. Further, because DC is deemed to transfer specified tangible property (Asset A) to a specified related party (FS2) upon the lapse of the lease, and within a six month period (February 1, Year 6 to June 1, Year 6), an FDII-eligible related party of DC (DS) leases a substantially similar property (Asset B), DC's deemed transfer of Asset A under paragraph (h)(4)(iv) of this section and lease of Asset B are treated as per se occurring pursuant to a principal purpose of decreasing the amount of its deemed tangible income return. Accordingly, for purposes of determining DC's QBAI, DC is treated as owning Asset A from June 1, Year 6, the later of the date of the deemed transfer of Asset A (February 1, Year 6) and the beginning of the term of the lease of Asset B (June 1, Year 6), until December 31, Year 10, the earlier of the end of the term of the lease of Asset B (May 31, Year 11) or the remaining recovery period of Asset A (December 31, Year 10). [Reg. § 1.250(b)-2.]

☐ [*T.D. 9901, 7-9-2020. (corrected 9-28-2020). Amended by T.D. 9956, 9-21-2021.*]

§ 1.250(b)-3. Foreign-derived deduction eligible income (FDDEI) transactions.—(a) *Scope*.—This section provides rules related to the determination of whether a sale of property or provision of a service is a FDDEI transaction. Paragraph (b) of this section provides definitions related to the determination of whether a sale of property or provision of a service is a FDDEI transaction. Paragraph (c) of this section provides rules regarding a sale of property or provision of a service to a foreign government or an agency or instrumentality thereof. Paragraph (d) of this section provides a rule for characterizing a transaction with both sales and services elements. Paragraph (e) of this section provides a rule for determining whether a sale of property or provision of a service to a partnership is a FDDEI transaction. Paragraph (f) of this section provides rules for substantiating certain FDDEI transactions.

(b) *Definitions*.—This paragraph (b) provides definitions that apply for purposes of this section and §§ 1.250(b)-4 through 1.250(b)-6.

(1) *Digital content*.—The term *digital content* means a computer program or any other content in digital format. For example, digital content includes books in digital format, movies in digital format, and music in digital format. For purposes of this section, a computer program is a set of statements or instructions to be used directly or indirectly in a computer or other electronic device in order to bring about a certain result, and includes any media, user manuals, documentation, data base, or similar item if the media, user manuals, documentation, data base, or other similar item is incidental to the operation of the computer program.

(2) *End user*.—Except as modified by § 1.250(b)-4(d)(2)(ii), the term *end user* means the person that ultimately uses or consumes property or a person that acquires property in a foreign retail sale. A person that acquires property for resale or otherwise as an intermediary is not an end user.

(3) *FDII filing date*.—The term *FDII filing date* means, with respect to a sale of property by a seller or provision of a service by a renderer, the date, including extensions, by which the seller or renderer is required to file an income tax return (or in the case of a seller or renderer that is a partnership, a return of partnership income) for

the taxable year in which the gross income from the sale of property or provision of a service is included in the gross income of the seller or renderer.

(4) *Finished goods.*—The term *finished goods* means general property that is acquired by an end user.

(5) *Foreign person.*—The term *foreign person* means a person (as defined in section 7701(a)(1)) that is not a United States person and includes a foreign government or an international organization.

(6) *Foreign related party.*—The term *foreign related party* means, with respect to a seller or renderer, any foreign person that is a related party of the seller or renderer.

(7) *Foreign retail sale.*—The term *foreign retail sale* means a sale of general property to a recipient that acquires the general property at a physical retail location (such as a store or warehouse) outside the United States.

(8) *Foreign unrelated party.*—The term *foreign unrelated party* means, with respect to a seller, a foreign person that is not a related party of the seller.

(9) *Fungible mass of general property.*—The term *fungible mass of general property* means multiple units of property for sale with similar or identical characteristics for which the seller does not know the specific identity of the recipient or the end user for a particular unit.

(10) *General property.*—The term *general property* means any property other than: intangible property (as defined in paragraph (b)(11) of this section); a security (as defined in section 475(c)(2)); an interest in a partnership, trust, or estate; a commodity described in section 475(e)(2)(A) that is not a physical commodity; or a commodity described in section 475(e)(2)(B) through (D). A physical commodity described in section 475(e)(2)(A) is treated as general property, including if it is sold pursuant to a forward or option contract (including a contract described in section 475(e)(2)(C), but not a section 1256 contract as defined in section 1256(b) or other similar contract that is traded on a U.S. or non-U.S. regulated exchange and cleared by a central clearing organization in a manner similar to a section 1256 contract) that is physically settled by delivery of the commodity (provided that the taxpayer physically settled the contract pursuant to a consistent practice adopted for business purposes of determining whether to cash or physically settle such contracts under similar circumstances).

(11) *Intangible property.*—The term *intangible property* has the meaning set forth in section 367(d)(4). For purposes of section 250, intangible property does not include a copyrighted article as defined in § 1.861-18(c)(3).

(12) *International transportation property.*—The term *international transportation property* means aircraft, railroad rolling stock, vessel, motor vehicle, or similar property that provides a mode of transportation and is capable of traveling internationally.

(13) *IP address.*—The term *IP address* means a device's Internet Protocol address.

(14) *Recipient.*—The term *recipient* means a person that purchases property or services from a seller or renderer.

(15) *Renderer.*—The term *renderer* means a person that provides a service to a recipient.

(16) *Sale.*—The term *sale* means any sale, lease, license, sublicense, exchange, or other disposition of property, and includes any transfer of property in which gain or income is recognized under section 367. In addition, the term *sell* (and any form of the word sell) means any transfer by sale.

(17) *Seller.*—The term *seller* means a person that sells property to a recipient.

(18) *United States.*—The term *United States* has the meaning set forth in section 7701(a)(9), as expanded by section 638(1) with respect to mines, oil and gas wells, and other natural deposits.

(19) *United States person.*—The term *United States person* has the meaning set forth in section 7701(a)(30), except that the term does not include an individual that is a bona fide resident of a United States territory within the meaning of section 937(a).

(20) *United States territory.*—The term *United States territory* means American Samoa, Guam, the Northern Mariana Islands, Puerto Rico, or the U.S. Virgin Islands.

(c) *Foreign military sales and services.*—If a sale of property or a provision of a service is made to the United States or an instrumentality thereof pursuant to 22 U.S.C. 2751 et seq. under which the United States or an instrumentality thereof purchases the property or service for resale or on-service to a foreign government or agency or instrumentality thereof, then the sale of property or provision of a service is treated as a FDDEI sale or FDDEI service without regard to § 1.250(b)-4 or § 1.250(b)-5.

(d) *Transactions with multiple elements.*—A transaction is classified according to its overall predominant character for purposes of determining whether the transaction is a FDDEI sale under § 1.250(b)-4 or a FDDEI service under § 1.250(b)-5. For example, whether a transaction that includes both a sales component and a service component is subject to § 1.250(b)-4 or § 1.250(b)-5 is determined based on whether the overall predominant character, taking into account all relevant facts and circumstances, is a sale or service. In addition, whether a transaction that includes both a sale of general property and a sale of intangible property is subject to § 1.250(b)-4(d)(1) or § 1.250(b)-4(d)(2) is determined based on whether the overall predominant character, taking into account all relevant facts and circumstances, is a sale of general property or a sale of intangible property.

(e) *Treatment of partnerships.*—(1) *In general.*—For purposes of determining whether a sale of property to or by a partnership or a provision of a service to or by a partnership is a FDDEI transaction, a partnership is treated as a person. Accordingly, for example, a partnership may be a seller, renderer, recipient, or related party, including a foreign related party (as defined in paragraph (b)(6) of this section).

(2) *Examples.*—The following examples illustrate the application of this paragraph (e).

(i) *Example 1: Domestic partner sale to foreign partnership with a foreign branch.*—(A) *Facts.* DC, a domestic corporation, is a partner in PRS, a foreign partnership. DC and PRS are not related parties. PRS has a foreign branch within the meaning of § 1.904-4(f)(3)(iii). DC and PRS both use the calendar year as their taxable year. For the taxable year, DC recognizes $20x of gain on the sale of general property to PRS for a foreign use (as determined under § 1.250(b)-4(d)). During the same taxable year, PRS recognizes $20x of gain on the sale of other general property to a foreign person for a foreign use (as determined under § 1.250(b)-4(d)). PRS's income on the sale of the property is attributable to its foreign branch.

(B) *Analysis.* DC's sale of property to PRS, a foreign partnership, is a FDDEI sale because it is a sale to a foreign person for a foreign use. Therefore, DC's gain of $20x on the sale to PRS is included in DC's gross DEI and gross FDDEI. However, PRS's gain of $20x is not included in the gross DEI or gross FDDEI of PRS because the gain is foreign branch income within the meaning of § 1.250(b)-1(c)(11). Accordingly, none of PRS's gain on the sale of property is included in DC's gross DEI or gross FDDEI under § 1.250(b)-1(e)(1).

(ii) *Example 2: Domestic partner sale to domestic partnership without a foreign branch.*—(A) *Facts.* The facts are the same as in paragraph (e)(2)(i)(A) of this section (the facts in *Example 1*), except PRS is a domestic partnership that does not have a foreign branch within the meaning of § 1.904-4(f)(3)(iii).

(B) *Analysis.* DC's sale of property to PRS, a domestic partnership, is not a FDDEI sale because the sale is to a United States person. Therefore, the gross income from DC's sale to PRS is included in DC's gross DEI but is not included in its gross FDDEI. However, PRS's sale of other general property is a FDDEI sale, and therefore the gain of $20x is included in the gross DEI and gross FDDEI of PRS. Accordingly, DC includes its distributive share of PRS's gain from the sale in determining DC's gross DEI and gross FDDEI for the taxable year under § 1.250(b)-1(e)(1).

(f) *Substantiation for certain FDDEI transactions.*—(1) *In general.*—Except as provided in paragraph (f)(2) of this section, for purposes of § 1.250(b)-4(d)(1)(ii)(C) (foreign use for sale of general property for resale), § 1.250(b)-4(d)(1)(iii) (foreign use for sale of general property subject to manufacturing, assembly, or processing outside the United States), § 1.250(b)-4(d)(2) (foreign use for sale of intangible property), and § 1.250(b)-5(e) (general services provided to business recipients located outside the United States), a transaction is a FDDEI transaction only if the taxpayer substantiates its determination of foreign use (in the case of sales of property) or location outside the United States (in the case of general services provided to a business recipient) as described in the applicable paragraph of § 1.250(b)-4(d)(3) or § 1.250(b)-5(e)(4). The substantiating documents must be in existence as of the FDII filing date with respect to the FDDEI transaction, and a taxpayer must provide the required substantiating documents within 30 days of a request by the Commissioner or another period as agreed between the Commissioner and the taxpayer.

(2) *Exception for small businesses.*—Paragraph (f)(1) of this section, and the specific substantiation requirements described in the applicable paragraph of § 1.250(b)-4(d)(3) or § 1.250(b)-5(e)(4), do not apply to a taxpayer if the taxpayer and all related parties of the taxpayer, in the aggregate, receive less than $25,000,000 in gross receipts during the taxable year prior to the FDDEI transaction. If the taxpayer's prior taxable year was less than 12 months (a short period), gross receipts are annualized by multiplying the gross receipts for the short period by 365 and dividing the result by the number of days in the short period.

(3) *Treatment of certain loss transactions.*—(i) *In general.*—If a domestic corporation fails to satisfy the substantiation requirements described in the applicable paragraph of § 1.250(b)-4(d)(3) or § 1.250(b)-5(e)(4) with respect to a transaction (including in connection with a related party transaction described in § 1.250(b)-6), the gross income from the transaction will be treated as gross FDDEI if—

(A) In the case of a sale of property, the seller knows or has reason to know that property is sold to a foreign person for a foreign use (within the meaning of § 1.250(b)-4(d)(1) or (2));

(B) In the case of the provision of a general service to a business recipient, the renderer knows or has reason to know that a service is provided to a business recipient located outside the United States; and

(C) Not treating the transaction as a FDDEI transaction would increase the amount of the corporation's FDDEI for the taxable year relative to its FDDEI that would be determined if the transaction were treated as a FDDEI transaction.

(ii) *Reason to know.*—(A) *Sales to a foreign person for a foreign use.*—For purposes of paragraph (f)(3)(i)(A) of this section, a seller has reason to know that a sale is to a foreign person for a foreign use if the information received as part of the sales process contains information that indicates that the recipient is a foreign person or that the sale is for a foreign use, and the seller fails to obtain evidence establishing that the recipient is not in fact a foreign person or that the sale is not in fact for a foreign use. Information that indicates that a recipient is a foreign person or that the sale is for a foreign use includes, but is not limited to, a foreign phone number, billing address, shipping address, or place of residence; and, with respect to an entity, evidence that the entity is incorporated, formed, or managed outside the United States.

(B) *General services provided to a business recipient located outside the United States.*—For purposes of paragraph (f)(3)(i)(B) of this section, a renderer has reason to know that the provision of a general service is to a business recipient located outside the United States if the information received as part of the sales process contains information that indicates that the recipient is a business recipient located outside the United States and the seller fails to obtain evidence establishing that the recipient is not in fact a business recipient located outside the United States. Information that indicates that a recipient is a business recipient includes, but is not limited to, indicia of a business status (such as "LLC" or "Company," or similar indicia under applicable domestic or foreign law, in the name) or statements by the recipient indicating that it is a business. Information that indicates that a business recipient is located outside the United States includes, but is not limited to, a foreign phone number, billing address, and evidence that the entity or business is incorporated, formed, or managed outside the United States.

(iii) *Multiple transactions.*—If a seller or renderer engages in more than one transaction described in paragraph (f)(3)(i) of this section in a taxable year, paragraph (f)(3)(i) of this section applies by comparing the corporation's FDDEI if each such transaction were not treated as a FDDEI transaction to its FDDEI if each such transaction were treated as a FDDEI transaction.

(iv) *Example.*—The following example illustrates the application of this paragraph (f)(3).

(A) *Facts.* During a taxable year, DC, a domestic corporation, manufactures products A and B in the United States. DC sells product A and product B to Y, a foreign person that is a distributor, for $200x and $800x, respectively. DC knows or has reason to know that all of its sales of product A and product B will ultimately be sold to end users located outside the United States. Y provides DC with a statement that satisfies the substantiation requirement of paragraph (f)(1) of this section and § 1.250(b)-4(d)(3)(ii) that establishes that its sales of product B are for a foreign use but does not obtain substantiation establishing that any sales of product A are for a foreign use. DC's cost of goods sold is $450x. For purposes of determining gross FDDEI, under § 1.250(b)-1(d)(1) DC attributes $250x of cost of goods sold to product A and $200x of cost of goods sold to product B, and then attributes the cost of goods sold for each product ratably between the gross receipts of such product sold to foreign persons and the gross receipts of such product not sold to foreign persons. The manner in which DC attributes the cost of goods sold is a reasonable method. DC has no other items of income, loss, or deduction.

Table 1 to paragraph (f)(3)(iv)(A)

	Product A	Product B	Total
Gross receipts	$200x	$800x	$1,000x
Cost of Goods Sold	$250x	$200x	$450x
Gross Income (Loss)	($50x)	$600x	$550x

(B) *Analysis.* By not treating the sales of product A as FDDEI sales, the amount of DC's FDDEI would increase by $50x relative to its FDDEI if the sales of product A were treated as FDDEI sales. Accordingly, because DC knows or has reason to know that its sales of product A are to foreign persons for a foreign use, the sales of product A constitute FDDEI sales under paragraph (f)(3) of this section, and thus the $50x loss from the sale of product A is included in DC's gross FDDEI. [Reg. § 1.250(b)-3.]

☐ [*T.D. 9901, 7-9-2020.*]

§ 1.250(b)-4. Foreign-derived deduction eligible income (FDDEI) sales.—(a) *Scope.*—This section provides rules for determining whether a sale of property is a FDDEI sale. Paragraph (b) of this section defines a FDDEI sale. Paragraph (c) of this section provides rules for determining whether a recipient is a foreign person. Paragraph (d) of this section provides rules for determining whether property is sold for a foreign use. Paragraph (e) of this section provides a special rule for the sale of interests in a disregarded entity. Paragraph (f) of this section provides a rule regarding certain hedging transactions with respect to FDDEI sales.

(b) *Definition of FDDEI sale.*—Except as provided in § 1.250(b)-6(c), the term *FDDEI sale* means a sale of general property or intangible property to a recipient that is a foreign person (see paragraph (c) of this section for presumption rules relating to determining foreign person status) and that is for a foreign use (as determined under paragraph (d) of this section). A sale of any property other than general property or intangible property is not a FDDEI sale.

(c) *Presumption of foreign person status.*—(1) *In general.*—The sale of property is presumed to be to a recipient that is a foreign person for purposes of paragraph (b) of this section if the sale is described in paragraph (c)(2) of this section. However, this presumption does not apply if the seller knows or has reason to know that the sale is not to a foreign person. A seller has reason to know that a sale is not to a foreign person if the information received as part of the sales process contains information that indicates that the recipient is not a foreign person and the seller fails to obtain evidence establishing that the recipient is in fact a foreign person. Information that indicates that a recipient is not a foreign person include, but are not limited to, a United States phone number, billing address, shipping address, or place of residence; and, with respect to an entity, evidence that the entity is incorporated, formed, or managed in the United States.

(2) *Sales of property.*—A sale of a property is described in this paragraph (c)(2) if:

(i) The sale is a foreign retail sale;

(ii) In the case of a sale of general property that is not a foreign retail sale and the general property is delivered (such as through a commercial carrier) to the recipient or an end user, the shipping address of the recipient or end user is outside the United States;

(iii) In the case of a sale of general property that is not described in either paragraph (c)(2)(i) or (ii) of this section, the billing address of the recipient is outside the United States; or

(iv) In the case of a sale of intangible property, the billing address of the recipient is outside the United States.

(d) *Foreign use.*—(1) *Foreign use for general property.*—(i) *In general.*—The sale of general property is for a foreign use for purposes of paragraph (b) of this section if the seller determines that the sale is for a foreign use under the rules of paragraph (d)(1)(ii) or (iii) of this section and the exception in paragraph (d)(1)(iv) of this section does not apply.

(ii) *Rules for determining foreign use.*—(A) *Sales that are delivered to an end user by a carrier or freight forwarder.*—Except as otherwise provided in this paragraph (d)(1)(ii)(A), a sale of general property (other than a sale of general property described in paragraphs (d)(1)(ii)(D) through (F) of this section) that is delivered through a carrier or freight forwarder to a recipient that is an end user is for a foreign use if the end user receives delivery of the general property outside the United States. However, a sale described in the preceding sentence is not treated as a sale to an end user for a foreign use if the sale is made with a principal purpose of having the property transported from its location outside the United States to a location within the United States for ultimate use or consumption.

(B) *Sales to an end user without the use of a carrier or freight forwarder.*—With respect to sales that are not delivered through the use of a carrier or freight forwarder, a sale of general property (other than a sale of general property described in paragraphs (d)(1)(ii)(D) through (F) of this section) to a recipient that is an end user is for a foreign use if the property is located outside the United States at the time of the sale (including as part of foreign retail sales).

(C) *Sales for resale.*—A sale of general property (other than a sale of general property described in paragraphs (d)(1)(ii)(D) through (F) of this section) to a recipient (such as a distributor or retailer) that will resell the general property is for a foreign use if the general property will ultimately be sold to end users outside the United States (including in foreign retail sales) and such sales to end users outside the United States are substantiated under paragraph (d)(3)(ii) of this section. In the case of sales of a fungible mass of general property, the taxpayer may presume that the proportion of its sales that are ultimately sold to end users outside the United States is the same as the proportion of the recipient's resales of that fungible mass to end users outside the United States.

(D) *Sales of digital content.*—A sale of general property that primarily contains digital content that is transferred electronically rather than in a physical medium is for a foreign use if the end user downloads, installs, receives, or accesses the purchased digital content on the end user's device outside the United States (see § 1.250(b)-5(d)(2) and (e)(2)(iii) for rules that apply in the case of digital content that is not purchased in a sale but is electronically supplied as a service). If information about where the digital content is downloaded, installed, received, or accessed (such as the device's IP address) is unavailable, and the gross receipts from all sales with respect to the end user (which may be a business) are in the aggregate less than $50,000 for the seller's taxable year, a sale of general property described in the preceding sentence is for a foreign use if it is to an end user that has a billing address located outside the United States.

(E) *Sales of international transportation property used for compensation or hire.*—A sale of international transportation property used for compensation or hire is for a foreign use if the end user registers the property with a foreign jurisdiction.

(F) *Sales of international transportation property not used for compensation or hire.*—A sale of international transportation property not used for compensation or hire is for a foreign use if the end user registers the property in a foreign jurisdiction and hangars or stores the property primarily outside the United States.

(iii) *Sales for manufacturing, assembly, or other processing.*—(A) *In general.*—A sale of general property is for a foreign use if the sale is to a foreign unrelated party that subjects the property to manufacture, assembly, or other processing outside the United States and such manufacturing, assembly, or other processing outside the United States is substantiated under paragraph (d)(3)(iii) of this section. Property is subject to manufacture, assembly, or other processing only if the property is physically and materially changed (as described in paragraph (d)(1)(iii)(B) of this section) or the property is incorporated as a component into another product (as described in paragraph (d)(1)(iii)(C) of this section).

(B) *Property subject to a physical and material change.*—The determination of whether general property is subject to a physical and material change is made based on all the relevant facts and circumstances. General property is subject to a physical and material change if it is substantially transformed and is distinguishable from and cannot be readily returned to its original state.

(C) *Property incorporated into a product as a component.*—General property is a component incorporated into another product if the incorporation of the general property into another product involves activities that are substantial in nature and generally considered to constitute the manufacture, assembly, or processing of property based on all the relevant facts and circumstances. However, general property is not considered a component incorporated into another product if it is subject only to packaging, repackaging, labeling, or minor assembly operations. In addition, general property is treated as a component if the seller expects, using reliable estimates, that the fair market value of the property when it is delivered to the recipient will constitute no more than 20 percent of the fair market value of the finished good into which the general property is directly or indirectly incorporated when the finished good is sold to end users (the "20-percent rule"). If the property could be incorporated into a number of different finished goods, a reliable estimate of the fair market value of the finished good may include the average fair market value of a representative range of such goods. For purposes of the 20-percent rule, all general property that is sold by the seller and incorporated into the finished good is treated as a single item of property if the seller sells the property to the recipient and the seller knows or has reason to know that the components will be incorporated into a single item of property (for example, where multiple components are sold as a kit). A seller knows or has reason to know that the components will be incorporated into a single item of property if the information received as part of the sales process indicates that the components will be included in the same second product or the nature of the components compels inclusion into the second product and the seller fails to obtain evidence to the contrary.

(iv) *Sales of property subject to manufacturing, assembly, or other processing in the United States.*—If the seller sells general property to a recipient (other than a related party) for manufacturing, assembly, or other processing within the United States, such property is not sold for a foreign use even if the requirements of paragraph (d)(1)(ii) or (iii) of this section are subsequently satisfied. See § 1.250(b)-6(c) for rules governing sales of general property to a foreign person that is a related party. Property is subject to manufacture, assembly, or other processing only if the property is physically and materially changed (as described in paragraph (d)(1)(iii)(B) of this section) or the property is incorporated as a component into another product (as described in paragraph (d)(1)(iii)(C) of this section).

(v) *Examples.*—The following examples illustrate the application of this paragraph (d)(1).

(A) *Assumed facts.*—The following facts are assumed for purposes of the examples—

(1) DC is a domestic corporation.

(2) FP is a foreign person that is a foreign unrelated party with respect to DC.

(3) To the extent a sale is for a foreign use, any applicable substantiation requirements described in paragraph (d)(3)(ii) or (iii) of this section are satisfied.

(B) *Examples*—

(1) Example 1: Manufacturing outside the United States.—(i) Facts. DC sells batteries for $18x to FP. DC expects that FP will insert the batteries into tablets as part of the process of assembling tablets outside the United States. While the tablets are manufactured in a way that end users would not easily be able to remove the batteries, the batteries could be removed from the tablets and would resemble

their original state following the removal. The finished tablets will be sold to end users within and outside the United States. DC's batteries are used in two types of tablets, Tablet A and Tablet B. Based on an economic analysis, DC determines that the fair market value of Tablet A is $90x and the fair market value of Tablet B is $110x. FP informs DC that the number of sales of Tablet A is approximately equal to the number of sales of Tablet B.

(ii) *Analysis*. Because the batteries could be removed from the tablets and be returned to their original state, the insertion of the batteries into the tablets does not constitute a physical and material change described in paragraph (d)(1)(iii)(B) of this section. However, the average fair market value of a representative range of tablets that incorporate the batteries is $100x (the average of $90x for Tablet A and $110x for Tablet B because their sales are approximately equal), and $18x is less than 20 percent of $100x. Therefore, the batteries are considered components of the tablets and treated as subject to manufacture, assembly, or other processing outside the United States. See paragraphs (d)(1)(iii)(A) and (C) of this section. As a result, notwithstanding that some tablets incorporating the batteries may be sold to an end user in the United States, DC's sale of batteries is considered for a foreign use. Accordingly, DC's sale of batteries to FP is for a foreign use under paragraph (d)(1)(iii)(A) and (C) of this section, and the sale is a FDDEI sale.

(2) *Example 2: Manufacturing outside the United States.*—(i) *Facts*. The facts are the same as in paragraph (d)(1)(v)(B)(*1*) of this section (the facts in *Example 1*), except FP purchases the batteries from DC for $25x. In addition, FP purchased other components of tablets from other parties. FP has a substantial investment in machinery and tools that are used to assemble tablets.

(ii) *Analysis*. Even though the fair market value of the batteries that FP purchases from DC and incorporates into the tablets exceeds 20 percent of the fair market value of the tablets, because the batteries are used by FP in activities that are substantial in nature and generally considered to constitute the manufacture, assembly or other processing of property, the batteries are components of the tablets. As a result, DC's sale of property to FP is still for a foreign use under paragraph (d)(1)(iii)(A) and (C) of this section, and the sale is a FDDEI sale.

(3) *Example 3: Sale of products to distributor outside the United States.*—(i) *Facts*. DC sells smartphones to FP, a distributor of electronics located within Country A. The sales contract between DC and FP provides that FP may sell the smartphones it purchases from DC only to specified retailers located within Country A. The specified retailers only sell electronics, including smartphones, in foreign retail sales.

(ii) *Analysis*. Although FP does not sell the smartphones it purchases from DC to end users, FP sells to retailers that sell the smartphones in foreign retail sales. All of the sales of smartphones from DC to FP are sales of general property for a foreign use under paragraph (d)(1)(ii)(C) of this section because FP is only allowed to sell the smartphones to retailers who sell such property in foreign retail sales. As a result, DC's sales of smartphones to FP are FDDEI sales.

(4) *Example 4: Sale of a fungible mass of products.*—(i) *Facts*. DC and persons other than DC sell multiple units of printer paper that is considered fungible general property to FP during the taxable year. FP is a distributor that sells paper to retail stores within and outside the United States. FP informs DC that approximately 25 percent of FP's sales of the paper are to retail stores located outside of the United States for foreign retail sales.

(ii) *Analysis*. The sale of paper to FP is for a foreign use to the extent that the paper will be sold to end users located outside the United States under paragraph (d)(1)(ii)(C) of this section. Because a portion of DC's sales to FP are not for a foreign use, DC must determine the amount of paper that is sold for a foreign use. Based on the information provided by FP about its own sales, DC determines under paragraph (d)(1)(ii)(C) of this section that 25 percent of the total units of paper that is fungible general property that FP purchased from all persons in the taxable year will ultimately be sold to end users located outside the United States. Accordingly, DC satisfies the test for a foreign use under paragraph (d)(1)(ii)(C) of this section with respect to 25 percent of its sales of the paper to FP.

(5) *Example 5: Limited use license of copyrighted computer software.*—(i) *Facts*. DC provides FP with a limited use license to copyrighted computer software in exchange for an annual fee of $100x. The limited use license restricts FP's use of the computer software to 100 of FP's employees, who download the software onto their computers. The limited use license prohibits FP from using the computer software in any way other than as an end user, which includes prohibiting sublicensing, selling, reverse engineering, or modifying the computer software. All of FP's employees download the software onto computers that are physically located outside the United States.

(ii) *Analysis*. The software licensed to FP is digital content as defined in § 1.250(b)-3(b)(1), and is downloaded by an end user as defined in § 1.250(b)-3(b)(2). Accordingly, because the software is downloaded solely onto computers outside the United States, DC's license to FP is for a foreign use and therefore a FDDEI sale under paragraph (d)(1)(ii)(D) of this section. The entire $100x of the license fee is included in DC's gross FDDEI for the taxable year.

(6) *Example 6: Limited use license of copyrighted computer software used within and outside the United States.*—(i) *Facts*. The facts are the same as in paragraph (d)(1)(v)(B)(*5*) of this section (the facts in *Example 5*), except that FP has offices both within and outside the United States, and DC's internal records indicates that 50 percent of the downloads of the software are onto computers located outside the United States.

(ii) *Analysis*. Because 50 percent of the downloads of the software are onto computers located outside the United States, a portion of DC's license to FP is for a foreign use and therefore such portion is a FDDEI sale. The $50x of license fee derived with respect to such portion is included in DC's gross FDDEI for the taxable year.

(7) *Example 7: Sale of a copyrighted article.*—(i) *Facts*. DC sells copyrighted music available for download on its website. Once downloaded, the recipient listens to the music on electronic devices that do not need to be connected to the internet. DC has data that an individual accesses the website to purchase a song for download on a device located outside the United States. The terms of the sale permit the recipient to use the song for personal use, but convey no other rights to the copyrighted music to the recipient.

(ii) *Analysis*. The music acquired through download is digital content as defined in § 1.250(b)-3(b)(1). Because the recipient acquires no ownership in copyright rights to the music, the sale is considered a sale of a copyrighted article, and thus is a sale of general property. See § 1.250(b)-3(b)(10) and (11). As a result, the sale is considered for a foreign use under paragraph (d)(1)(ii)(D) of this section because the digital content was installed, received, or accessed on the end user's device outside the United States. The income derived with respect to the sale of the music is included in DC's gross FDDEI for the taxable year. See § 1.250(b)-5(d)(3) for an example of digital content provided to consumers as a service rather than as a sale.

(2) *Foreign use for intangible property.*—(i) *In general.*—A sale of rights to exploit intangible property solely outside the United States is for a foreign use. A sale of rights to exploit intangible property solely within the United States is not for a foreign use. A sale of rights to exploit intangible property worldwide is partially for a foreign use and partially not for a foreign use. Whether intangible property is exploited within versus outside the United States is determined based on revenue earned from end users located within versus outside the United States. Therefore, a sale of rights to exploit intangible property both within and outside the United States is for a foreign use in proportion to the revenue earned from end users located outside the United States over the total revenue earned from the exploitation of the intangible property. A sale of intangible property will be treated as a FDDEI sale only if the substantiation requirements of paragraph (d)(3)(iv) of this section are satisfied. For rules specific to determining end users and revenue earned from end users for intangible property used in sales of general property, provision of services, research and development, or consisting of a manufacturing method or process, see paragraph (d)(2)(ii) of this section.

(ii) *Determination of end users and revenue earned from end users.*—(A) *Intangible property embedded in general property or used in connection with the sale of general property.*—If intangible property is embedded in general property that is sold, or used in connection with a sale of general property, then the end user of the intangible property is the end user of the general property. Revenue is earned from the end user of the general property outside the United States to the extent the sale of the general property is for a foreign use under paragraph (d)(1)(ii) or (iii) of this section.

(B) *Intangible property used in providing a service.*—If intangible property is used to provide a service, then the end user of that intangible property is the recipient, consumer, or business recipient of the service or, in the case of a property service or a transportation service that involves the transportation of property, the end user is the owner of the property on which such service is being performed. Such end users are treated as located outside the United States only to the extent the service qualifies as a FDDEI service under § 1.250(b)-5. Therefore, in the case of a recipient of a sale of intangible property that uses such intangible property to provide a property service that qualifies as a FDDEI service to another person, that person is the end user and is treated as located outside the United States.

(C) *Intangible property consisting of a manufacturing method or process.—(1) In general.*—Except as provided in paragraph (d)(2)(ii)(C)(*2*) of this section, if intangible property consists of a manufacturing method or process (as defined in paragraph (d)(2)(ii)(C)(*3*) of this section) and is sold to a foreign unrelated party (including in a sale by a foreign related party), then the foreign unrelated party is treated as an end user located outside the United States, unless the seller knows or has reason to know that the manufacturing method or process will be used in the United States, in which case the foreign unrelated party is treated as an end user located within the United States. A seller has reason to know that the manufacturing method or process will be used in the United States if the information received from the recipient as part of the sales process contains information that indicates that the recipient intends to use the manufacturing method or process in the United States and the seller fails to obtain evidence establishing that the recipient does not intend to use the manufacturing method or process in the United States.

(*2*) *Exception for certain manufacturing arrangements.*—A sale of intangible property consisting of a manufacturing method or process (including a sale by a foreign related party) to a foreign unrelated party for use in manufacturing products for or on behalf of the seller or any person related to the seller does not qualify as a sale to a foreign unrelated party for purposes of determining the end user under paragraph (d)(2)(ii)(C)(*1*) of this section.

(*3*) *Manufacturing method or process.*—For purposes of this section, a manufacturing method or process consists of a sequence of actions or steps that comprise an overall method or process that is used to manufacture a product or produce a particular manufacturing result, which may be in the form of a patent or know-how. Intangible property consisting of the right to make and sell an item of property is not a manufacturing method or process, whereas intangible property consisting of the right to apply a series of actions or steps to be performed to achieve a particular manufacturing result is a manufacturing method or process. For example, a utility or design patent on an article of manufacture, machine, composition of matter, design, or providing the right to sell equipment to perform a process is not a manufacturing method or process, whereas a utility patent covering a method or process of manufacturing is a manufacturing method or process for purposes of this section.

(D) *Intangible property used in research and development.*—If intangible property (primary IP) is used to develop new or modify other intangible property (secondary IP), then the end user of the primary IP is the end user (applying paragraph (d)(2)(ii)(A), (B), or (C) of this section) of the secondary IP.

(iii) *Determination of revenue for periodic payments versus lump sums.*—(A) *Sales in exchange for periodic payments.*—In the case of a sale of intangible property, other than intangible property consisting of a manufacturing method or process that is sold to a foreign unrelated party, to a recipient in exchange for periodic payments, the extent to which the sale is for a foreign use is determined annually based on the actual revenue earned by the recipient from any use of the intangible property for the taxable year in which a periodic payment is received. If actual revenue earned by the recipient cannot be obtained after reasonable efforts, then estimated revenue earned by a recipient that is not a related party of the seller from the use of the intangible property may be used based on the principles of paragraph (d)(2)(iii)(B) of this section.

(B) *Sales in exchange for a lump sum.*—In the case of a sale of intangible property, other than intangible property consisting of a manufacturing method or process that is sold to a foreign unrelated party, for a lump sum, the extent to which the sale is for a foreign use is determined based on the ratio of the total net present value of revenue the seller would have expected to earn from the exploitation of the intangible property outside the United States to the total net present value of revenue the seller would have expected to earn from the exploitation of the intangible property. In the case of a recipient that is a foreign unrelated party, net present values of revenue that the recipient expected to earn from the exploitation of the intangible property within and outside the United States may also be used if the seller obtained such revenue data from the recipient near the time of the sale and such revenue data was used to negotiate the lump sum price paid for the intangible property. Net present values must be determined using reliable inputs including, but not limited to, reliable revenue, expenses, and discount rates. The extent to which the inputs are used by the parties to determine the sales price agreed to between the seller and a foreign unrelated party purchasing the intangible property will be a factor in determining whether such inputs are reliable. If the intangible property is sold to a foreign related party, the reliability of the inputs used to determine net present values and the net present values are determined under section 482.

(C) *Sales to a foreign unrelated party of intangible property consisting of a manufacturing method or process.*—In the case of a sale to an unrelated foreign party of intangible property consisting of a manufacturing method or process, the revenue earned from the end user is equal to the amount received from the recipient in exchange for the manufacturing method or process. In the case of a bundled sale of intangible property consisting of a manufacturing method or process and intangible property not consisting of a manufacturing method or process, the revenue earned from the intangible property consisting of the manufacturing method or process equals the total amount paid for the bundled sale multiplied by the proportion that the value of the manufacturing method or process bears to the total value of the intangible property. The value of the manufacturing method or process to the total value of the intangible property must be determined using the principles of section 482.

(iv) *Examples.*—The following examples illustrate the application of this paragraph (d)(2).

(A) *Assumed facts.*—The following facts are assumed for purposes of the examples—

(*1*) DC is a domestic corporation.

(*2*) Except as otherwise provided, FP and FP2 are foreign persons that are foreign unrelated parties with respect to DC.

(*3*) All of DC's income is DEI.

(*4*) Except as otherwise provided, the substantiation requirements described in paragraph (d)(3)(iv) of this section are satisfied.

(*5*) Except as otherwise provided, inputs used to determine the net present values of the revenue are reliable.

(B) *Examples*—

(*1*) *Example 1: License of worldwide rights with actual revenue data from recipient.*—(*i*) *Facts.* DC licenses to FP worldwide rights to the copyright to composition A in exchange for annual royalties of 60 percent of revenue from FP's sales of composition A. FP sells composition A to customers through digital downloads from servers. In the taxable year, FP earns $100x in revenue from sales of copies of composition A to customers, of which $60x is from customers located in the United States and the remaining $40x is from customers located outside the United States. FP provides DC with reliable records showing the amount of revenue earned in the taxable year from sales of composition A to establish the royalties owed to DC. These records also provide DC with the amount of revenue earned from sales of composition A to customers located within the United States.

(*ii*) *Analysis.* FP is not the end user of the copyright to composition A under paragraph (d)(2)(ii)(A) of this section because the copyright is used in the sale of general property (the sale of copyrighted articles to customers). The customers that purchase a copy of composition A from FP are the end users (as defined in § 1.250(b)-3(b)(2) and paragraph (d)(2)(ii)(A) of this section) because those customers are the recipients of composition A when sold as general property. Based on the actual revenue earned by FP from sales of composition A, 40 percent ($40x/$100x) of the revenue generated by the copyright during the taxable year is earned outside the United States. Accordingly, a portion of DC's license to FP is for a foreign use under paragraph (d)(2) of this section and therefore such portion is a FDDEI sale. The $24x of royalty (0.40 x $60x of total royalties owed to DC during the taxable year) derived with respect to such portion is included in DC's gross FDDEI for the taxable year.

(*2*) *Example 2: Fixed annual payments for worldwide rights without actual revenue data from recipient.*—(*i*) *Facts.* The facts are the same as in paragraph (d)(2)(iv)(B)(*1*)(*i*) of this section (the facts in *Example 1*), except FP pays DC a fixed annual payment of $60x each year for the worldwide rights to the copyright to composition A and does not provide DC with data showing how much revenue FP earned from sales of composition A, even after DC requests that FP provide it with such information. DC also is unable to determine how much revenue FP earned from sales of composition A to customers within the United States from the data it has with respect to FP and publicly available data with respect to FP. However, DC's economic analysis of the revenue DC expected it could earn annually from use of composition A as part of determining the annual payments DC would receive from FP from the license of composition A supports a determination that 40 percent of sales of composition A during the tax year would be to customers located outside the United States. During an examination of DC's return for the taxable year, DC provides the IRS with data explaining the economic analysis, inputs, and results from its valuation of composition A used in determining the amount of annual payments agreed to by DC and FP.

(*ii*) *Analysis*. For the same reasons provided in paragraph (d)(2)(iv)(B)(*1*)(*ii*) of this section (the analysis in *Example 1*), the customers that purchase copies of composition A from FP are the end users. DC is allowed to use reliable economic analysis to estimate revenue earned by FP from the use of the copyright to composition A under paragraph (d)(2)(iii)(A) of this section because DC was unable to obtain actual revenue earned by FP from use of the copyright to composition A during the taxable year after reasonable efforts to obtain the actual revenue data. Based on DC's economic analysis, a portion of DC's license to FP is for a foreign use under paragraph (d)(2) of this section and therefore such portion is a FDDEI sale. $24x of the $60x fixed payment to DC (0.40 x $60x) is included in DC's gross FDDEI for the taxable year.

(*3*) *Example 3: Sale of patent rights protected in the United States and other countries; use of financial projections in sale to foreign unrelated party*.—(*i*) *Facts*. DC owns a patent for an active pharmaceutical ingredient ("API") approved for treatment of disease A ("indication A") in the United States and in Countries A, B, and C. The patent is registered in the United States and in Countries A, B, and C. DC sells to FP all of its patent rights to the API for indication A for a lump sum payment of $1,000x. DC has no basis in the patent rights. To determine the sales price for the patent rights, DC projected that the net present value of the revenue it would earn from selling a pharmaceutical product incorporating the API for indication A was $5,000x, with 15 percent of the net present value of revenue earned from sales within the United States and 85 percent of the net present value of revenue earned from sales outside the United States. DC did not obtain revenue projections from the recipient.

(*ii*) *Analysis*. FP is not the end user of the patent under paragraph (d)(2)(ii)(A) of this section because the patent is used in the sale of general property (the sale of pharmaceutical products to customers) and FP is not the recipient of that general property. The unrelated party customers that purchase the finished pharmaceutical product from FP are the end users (as defined in § 1.250(b)-3(b)(2) and paragraph (d)(2)(ii)(A) of this section) because those customers are the unrelated party recipients of the pharmaceutical product when sold as general property. Based on the financial projections DC used to determine the sales price of the patent that FP purchased, a portion of DC's sale to FP is for a foreign use under paragraph (d)(2) of this section and such portion is a FDDEI sale. The $850x (85 percent x $1,000x) of gain derived with respect to such portion is included in DC's gross FDDEI for the taxable year.

(*4*) *Example 4: Sale of patent rights protected in the United States and other countries; use of financial projections in sale to foreign related party*.—(*i*) *Facts*. The facts are the same as in paragraph (d)(2)(iv)(B)(*3*)(*i*) of this section (the facts in *Example 3*), except that FP is a foreign related party with respect to DC, and DC projected that the net present value of the revenue it would earn from selling a pharmaceutical product incorporating the API for indication A would result in 1 percent of the revenue earned from sales within the United States and 99 percent of the revenue earned from sales outside the United States. During the examination of DC's return for the taxable year, the IRS determines that DC's substantiation allocating the projected revenue from sales within the United States and outside the United States does not reflect reliable inputs to determine the net present values of revenues under section 482, but determines that the total lump sum price FP paid for DC's patent rights is an arm's length price. The IRS determines that the most reliable net present values of revenue DC would have earned from sales within the United States and outside the United States is $750x and $4250x, respectively.

(*ii*) *Analysis*. For the same reasons provided in paragraph (d)(2)(iv)(B)(*3*)(*ii*) of this section (the analysis in *Example 3*), the customers that purchase the finished pharmaceutical product from FP are the end users. Under paragraph (d)(2)(iii)(B) of this section, the reliability of the inputs DC used to determine the net present values and the net present values are determined under section 482. Based on the sales price of the patent that FP purchased and the IRS-determined net present values of revenue DC would have earned from sales within the United States and outside the United States, a portion of DC's sale to FP is for a foreign use under paragraph (d)(2) of this section and such portion is a FDDEI sale. DC is allowed to include $850x (($4250x divided by $5000x) x $1,000x) of gain in DC's gross FDDEI for the taxable year.

(*5*) *Example 5: Sale of patent of manufacturing method or process protected in the United States and other countries; foreign unrelated party*.—(*i*) *Facts*. DC owns the worldwide rights to a patent covering a process for refining crude oil. DC sells to FP the right to DC's patented process for refining crude oil for a lump sum payment of $100x. DC has no basis in the patent rights. DC does not know or have reason to know that FP will use the patented process to refine crude oil within the United States or will sell or license the rights to the patent to a person to refine crude oil within the United States.

(*ii*) *Analysis*. DC's patent covering a process for refining crude oil is a manufacturing method or process as defined in paragraph (d)(2)(ii)(C)(*3*) of this section. Under paragraph (d)(2)(ii)(C)(*1*) of this section, FP is treated as the end user of the patent, and is treated as located outside the United States because FP is a foreign unrelated party and DC does not know or have reason to know that the patented process will be used in the United States. As a result, all of the sale to FP is for a foreign use under paragraph (d)(2) of this section and therefore is a FDDEI sale. The entire $100x lump sum payment is included in DC's gross FDDEI for the taxable year.

(*6*) *Example 6: License of intangible property that includes a patented manufacturing method or process protected in the United States and other countries; foreign unrelated party*.—(*i*) *Facts*. DC owns worldwide rights to patents, know-how, and a trademark and tradename for product Z. The patents consist of: a patent covering the right to make, use, and sell product Z (article of manufacture), a patent covering the rights to make, use, and sell a composition of substances used in certain components of product Z (composition of matter), and a patent covering the right to use a manufacturing process consisting of a series of manufacturing steps to manufacture product Z (manufacturing method or process as defined in paragraph (d)(2)(ii)(C)(*3*) of this section) and to sell the product Z that FP manufactures using the manufacturing method or process. The know-how consists entirely of manufacturing know-how used to implement the manufacturing steps that comprise the manufacturing method or process. DC licenses the worldwide rights to the patents, know-how, and the trademark and tradename for product Z to FP in exchange for annual royalties of 60 percent of revenue from sales of product Z. FP manufactures product Z in country X and sells product Z to DC2, a domestic corporation and unrelated party to DC and FP, for resale to customers located within the United States. FP also sells product Z to FP2, a foreign unrelated party with respect to DC and FP, for resale to customers located outside the United States. During the taxable year, FP sells to DC2 $140x of product Z. Also, during the taxable year, FP sells to FP2 $60x of product Z. DC determines under the principles of section 482 that the licensed know-how and the patented manufacturing method or process comprise 10 percent of the arm's length price of the intangible property DC licenses to FP.

(*ii*) *Analysis*—(A) *End users*. Under paragraph (d)(2)(ii)(C)(*1*) of this section, FP is treated as the end user of the patent covering the right to use the manufacturing process and the manufacturing know-how used to implement the manufacturing method or process, and is treated as located outside the United States because FP is a foreign unrelated party and DC does not know or have reason to know that the patented process and know-how will be used in the United States. DC2, FP, and FP2 are not the end users of the remaining intangible property under paragraph (d)(2)(ii)(A) of this section because that intangible property is used in the sale of general property (the sale of product Z) and DC2, FP, and FP2 are not the end users of that general property. The unrelated party customers that purchase product Z from DC2 and FP2 are the end users (as defined in § 1.250(b)-3(b)(2) and paragraph (d)(2)(ii)(A) of this section) because those customers are the unrelated party recipients of product Z.

(B) *Foreign use*. Under paragraph (d)(2)(ii)(A) of this section, revenue from royalties paid for the intangible property other than the manufacturing method or process is earned from end users outside the United States to the extent the sale of the general property is for a foreign use under paragraph (d)(1) of this section. FP2 is a reseller of product Z to end users outside the United States, so all sales of product Z to FP2 are for a foreign use under paragraph (d)(1)(ii)(C) of this section. Because DC has determined that 10 percent of the value of the intangible property consists of a manufacturing method or process (as defined in paragraph (d)(2)(ii)(C)(3) of this section) used to manufacture product Z, $12x of the $120x royalty FP pays to DC during the taxable year is for foreign use ($120x total royalty x 0.10) based on the location of FP's manufacturing utilizing the know-how or all of the sequence of actions that comprise the manufacturing method or process under paragraph (d)(2)(ii)(C)(3) of this section. Based on the sales of product Z within and outside the United States, $32.4x of the royalties FP pays DC for rights to the licensed intangible property during the taxable year (($60x of revenue from sales to FP2 for resale to customers located outside the United States divided by $200x total worldwide sales revenue FP receives from DC2 and FP2) x ($120x total royalties less $12 of those royalties attributable to the manufacturing method or process)) qualifies as income earned from the sale of intangible property for a foreign use under paragraph (d)(2) of this section and therefore such portion is a FDDEI sale. As a result, $44.40x of royalties ($12x + $32.40x) is included in DC's gross FDDEI for the taxable year.

(7) *Example 7: License of intangible property that includes a patented manufacturing method or process protected in the United States and other countries; foreign related party with third-party manufacturer.*—(*i*) *Facts.* The facts are the same as in paragraph (d)(2)(iv)(B)(6)(*i*) of this section (the facts in *Example 6*), except that FP is a foreign related party with respect to DC and FP engages FP2, a foreign unrelated party, to manufacture product Z. FP sublicenses to FP2 the rights to the intangible property FP licenses from DC solely to manufacture product Z and sell product Z to FP. FP2 manufactures product Z in country Y and sells all of product Z it manufactures to FP. During the taxable year, FP sold $80x of product Z to DC2, which DC2 resold to customers located within the United States. Also, during the taxable year, FP sold $120x of product Z to customers located outside the United States.

(*ii*) *Analysis*—(A) *End users.* Under paragraph (d)(2)(ii)(C)(*1*) of this section, FP is not treated as the end user of the patent covering the right to use the manufacturing process and the manufacturing know-how used to implement the manufacturing method or process because FP is a foreign related party with respect to DC. Under paragraph (d)(2)(ii)(C)(2) of this section, FP2 is also not treated as the end user of the patent covering the right to use the manufacturing process and the manufacturing know-how used to implement the manufacturing method or process because FP2 is using that intangible property to manufacture product Z for FP. DC2 is also not treated as the end user of the patent covering the right to use the manufacturing process and the manufacturing know-how used to implement the manufacturing method or process because DC2 does not use the patent or know-how in manufacturing. DC2, FP, and FP2 are not the end users of the remaining intangible property under paragraph (d)(2)(ii)(A) of this section because that intangible property is used in the sale of general property (the sale of product Z) and DC2, FP, and FP2 are not the end users of that general property. The unrelated party customers that purchase the Product Z from DC2 and FP are the end users (as defined in § 1.250(b)-3(b)(2) and paragraph (d)(2)(ii)(A) of this section) of the intangible property because those customers are the persons that ultimately use or consume product Z.

(B) *Foreign use.* Based on the sales of product Z to customers located within and outside the United States, $72x of the royalties FP pays DC for rights to the licensed intangible property during the taxable year (($120x of revenue from sales to customers located outside the United States divided by $200x total worldwide sales revenue) x $120x total royalties) qualifies as income earned from the sale of intangible property for a foreign use under paragraph (d)(2) of this section and therefore such portion is a FDDEI sale. As a result, $72x of royalties is included in DC's gross FDDEI for the taxable year.

(8) *Example 8: Deemed sale in exchange for contingent payments under section 367(d).*—(*i*) *Facts.* DC owns 100 percent of the stock of FP, a foreign related party with respect to DC. FP manufactures and sells product A. For the taxable year, DC contributes to FP exclusive worldwide rights to patents, trademarks, know-how, customer lists, and goodwill and going concern value (collectively, intangible property) related to product A in an exchange described in section 351. DC is required to report an annual income inclusion on its Federal income tax return based on the productivity, use, or disposition of the contributed intangible property under section 367(d). DC includes a percentage of FP's revenue in its gross income under section 367(d) each year. In the current taxable year, FP earns $1,000x of revenue from sales of product A. Based on reliable sales records kept by FP for the taxable year, $300x of FP's revenue is earned from sales of product A to customers within the United States, and $700x of its revenue is earned from sales of product A to customers outside the United States.

(*ii*) *Analysis.* DC's deemed sale of the intangible property to FP in exchange for payments contingent upon the productivity, use, or disposition of the intangible property related to product A under section 367(d) is a sale for purposes of section 250 and this section. See § 1.250(b)-3(b)(16). Based on FP's sales records for the taxable year, 70 percent of DC's deemed sale to FP is for a foreign use, and 70 percent of DC's income inclusion under section 367(d) derived with respect to such portion is included in DC's gross FDDEI for the taxable year.

(9) *Example 9: License of intangible property followed by a sale of general property in which the intangible property is embedded; unrelated parties.*—(*i*) *Facts.* DC owns the worldwide rights to a patent on a silicon chip used in computers, tablets, and smartphones. The patent does not qualify as a manufacturing method or process (as defined in paragraph (d)(2)(ii)(C)(3) of this section). DC licenses the worldwide rights to the patent to FP in exchange for annual royalties of 30 percent of revenue from sales of the silicon chips. During the taxable year, FP manufactures silicon chips protected by the patent and sells all of those chips to FP2 for $1,000x. FP2 also purchases similar silicon chips from other suppliers. FP2 uses the silicon chips in computers, tablets, smartphones, and motherboards that FP2 manufactures in country X and sells to its customers located within the United States and foreign countries. For purposes of this example, FP2's manufacturing qualifies as subjecting the silicon chips to manufacture, assembly, or other processing outside the United States as provided in paragraph (d)(1)(iii) of this section.

(*ii*) *Analysis.* FP is not the end user or treated as an end user (as defined in § 1.250(b)-3(b)(2) and paragraph (d)(2)(ii)(A) of this section) because FP is not the unrelated party recipient of the general property in which the patent is embedded, and the patent does not qualify as a manufacturing method or process. Under paragraph (d)(2)(ii)(A) of this section, revenue from royalties paid for the patent is earned from end users outside the United States to the extent the sale of the general property is for a foreign use under paragraph (d)(1) of this section. Because FP2 is subjecting the silicon chips to manufacture, assembly, or other processing outside the United States, the revenue from royalties FP pays to DC qualifies for foreign use based on the location of FP2's manufacturing and qualifies as a FDDEI sale. As a result, the entire $300x of annual royalties paid by FP to DC during the taxable year is included in DC's gross FDDEI for the taxable year.

(10) *Example 10: License of intangible property followed by a sale of general property in which the intangible property is embedded; related parties.*—(*i*) *Facts.* The facts are the same as in paragraph (d)(2)(iv)(B)(9)(*i*) of this section (the facts in *Example 9*), except that FP and FP2 are foreign related parties with respect to DC. FP2 sells and ships computers, tablets, and smartphones it manufactures with the silicon chips it purchases from FP to unrelated party wholesalers located within and outside the United States. The wholesalers within the United States only sell to retailers located within the United States and the wholesalers outside the United States only sell to retailers located outside the United States. The retailers within the United States only sell to customers located within the United States and the retailers located outside the United States only sell to customers located outside the United States. FP2 earns $15,000x of revenue from sales to unrelated party wholesalers located outside the United States and $10,000x of revenue from sales to unrelated party wholesalers located within the United States. FP2 also sells and ships motherboards with the silicon chips it purchases from FP to unrelated party manufacturers located outside the United States. FP2 does not sell motherboards with the silicon chips it purchases from FP to unrelated party manufacturers located within the United States. FP2 earns $5,000x of revenue from the sales of these motherboards to manufacturers located outside the United States. For purposes of this example, these manufacturers subject the motherboards to manufacture, assembly, or other processing outside the United States as provided in paragraph (d)(1)(iii) of this section.

(*ii*) *Analysis.* FP is not the end user or treated as an end user (as defined in § 1.250(b)-3(b)(2) and paragraph (d)(2)(ii)(A) of this section) of the intangible property because FP is not the end user of the general property in which the patent is embedded (the silicon chips). FP2 is also not the end user (as defined in § 1.250(b)-3(b)(2) and paragraph (d)(2)(ii)(A) of this section) of the intangible property because FP2 is not the end user of the silicon chips. Under paragraph (d)(2)(ii)(A) of this section, the customers of the retailers that purchase from the unrelated party wholesalers are the end users. Because the wholesalers located outside the United States only sell to retailers located outside the United States that sell to end users located outside the United States, the location of the wholesalers is a reliable basis for determining the location of the end users. Revenue from royalties paid for the patent is earned from end users outside the United States to the extent the sale of the general property is for a foreign use under paragraph (d)(1) of this section. A portion of the sales to the unrelated party wholesalers qualify as foreign use under paragraph (d)(1) of this section and the sales to the unrelated party manufacturers qualify as foreign use under paragraph (d)(1)(iii) of this section. Accordingly, revenue from royalties FP pays to DC is from a FDDEI sale to the extent of such sales to the unrelated party manufacturers and such portion of sales to unrelated party wholesalers that qualify for foreign use. As a result, $200x of annual royalties paid by FP to DC during the taxable year ((($15,000x of sales to wholesalers located outside the United States plus $5,000x of sales to manufacturers located outside the United States) divided by $30,000x total sales) x $300x) is included in DC's gross FDDEI for the taxable year.

(11) *Example 11: License of intangible property followed by a sale of general property that incorporates the intangible property; unrelated parties with manufacturing within the United States.*—(*i*) *Facts.* The facts are the same as in paragraph (d)(2)(iv)(B)(*9*)(*i*) of this section (the facts in *Example 9*), except that FP2 manufactures its computers, tablets, smartphones, and motherboards in the United States.

(*ii*) *Analysis.* FP is not the end user or treated as an end user (as defined in § 1.250(b)-3(b)(2) and paragraph (d)(2)(ii)(A) of this section) because FP is not the unrelated party recipient of the general property in which the patent is embedded (the silicon chips) and the patent does not qualify as a manufacturing method or process. Under paragraph (d)(2)(ii)(A) of this section, revenue from royalties paid for the patent is earned from end users outside the United States to the extent the sale of the general property is for a foreign use under paragraph (d)(1) of this section. Because FP2 is subjecting the silicon chips to manufacture, assembly, or other processing within the United States, the revenue from royalties FP pays to DC does not qualify as foreign use based on the location of FP2's manufacturing and therefore does not qualify as a FDDEI sale. As a result, none of the $300x of annual royalties paid by FP to DC during the taxable year is included in DC's gross FDDEI for the taxable year.

(12) *Example 12: License of intangible property used to provide a service.*—(*i*) *Facts.* DC licenses to FP worldwide rights to the copyrights on movies in exchange for an annual royalty of $100x. FP also licenses copyrights on movies from persons other than DC. FP provides a streaming service that meets the definition of an electronically supplied service in § 1.250(b)-5(c)(5) to its customers within the United States and foreign countries. FP's streaming service provides its customers a catalog of movies to choose to stream. These movies include the copyrighted movies FP licenses from DC. FP does not provide DC with data showing how much revenue FP earned from streaming services during the taxable year, even after DC requests that FP provide it with such information. DC also is unable to determine how much revenue FP earned from streaming services to customers within the United States from the data it has with respect to FP and publicly available data with respect to FP. However, DC's economic analysis of the revenue DC expected it could earn annually from use of the copyrights as part of determining the annual payments DC would receive from FP from the license of the copyrights supports a determination that $10,000x of revenue would be earned during the taxable year from customers worldwide, and that 40 percent of that revenue would be earned from customers located outside the United States. During an examination of DC's return for the taxable year, DC provides the IRS with data explaining the economic analysis, inputs, and results from its valuation of the copyrights used in determining the amount of annual payments agreed to by DC and FP.

(*ii*) *Analysis.* Under paragraph (d)(2)(ii)(B) of this section, FP's customers are the end users of the copyrights FP licenses from DC because FP uses those copyrights to provide the general service to FP's customers. Under paragraph (d)(2)(ii)(B) of this section, revenue from royalties paid for the copyrights is earned from end users outside the United States to the extent the service qualifies as a FDDEI service under § 1.250(b)-5. DC is allowed to use reliable economic analysis to estimate revenue earned by FP from streaming the licensed movies under paragraph (d)(2)(iii)(A) of this section because DC was unable to obtain actual revenue earned by FP from use of the copyrights during the taxable year after reasonable efforts to obtain the actual revenue data. Based on DC's reliable economic analysis, $40x of the annual royalty payment to DC (0.40 x $100x total annual royalty payment) is included in DC's gross FDDEI for the taxable year.

(13) *Example 13: License of intangible property used in research and development of other intangible property.*—(*i*) *Facts.* DC owns a patent ("patent A") for an active pharmaceutical ingredient ("API") approved for treatment of disease A in the United States and in foreign countries. DC licenses to FP worldwide rights to patent A for an annual royalty of $100x. FP uses patent A in research and development of a new API for treatment of disease B. Patent A does not consist of a manufacturing method or process (as defined in paragraph (d)(2)(ii)(C)(*3*) of this section). FP's research and development is successful, resulting in FP obtaining both a patent for the new API for treatment of disease B and approval for use in the United States and foreign countries. FP does not earn any revenue from sales of finished pharmaceutical products containing the API during years 1 through 4 of the license of patent A. In year 5 of the license of patent A, FP earns $800x of revenue from sales of finished pharmaceutical products containing the API to customers located within the United States and $200x of revenue from sales to customers located in foreign countries.

(*ii*) *Analysis.* FP is not the end user (as defined in § 1.250(b)-3(b)(2) and paragraph (d)(2)(ii)(D) of this section) of patent A because FP is not the end user described in paragraph (d)(2)(ii)(A) of this section of the product in which the API that was developed from patent A is embedded. The unrelated party customers that purchase the finished pharmaceutical product from FP are the end users (as defined in § 1.250(b)-3(b)(2) and paragraph (d)(2)(ii)(D) of this section) because those customers are the end users described in paragraph (d)(2)(ii)(A) of this section of the pharmaceutical product in which the newly developed patent is embedded. During the taxable years that include years 1 through 4 of the license of patent A, FP earns no revenue from sales of the API to a foreign person for a foreign use. Under paragraph (d)(2)(ii)(D) of this section, none of the $100x annual royalty payments to DC for each of the tax years that include years 1 through 4 of the license of patent A is included in DC's gross FDDEI. Based on FP's sales of the API during the tax year that includes year 5 of the license of patent A, $20x of the annual royalty payment to DC ($200x of revenue from sales of API to customers located outside the United States divided by $1,000x total worldwide revenue earned from sales of the API) x $100x annual royalty) is included in DC's gross FDDEI for the taxable year.

(3) *Foreign use substantiation for certain sales of property.*—(i) *In general.*—Except as provided in § 1.250(b)-3(f)(3) (relating to certain loss transactions), a sale of property described in paragraphs (d)(1)(ii)(C) of this section (foreign use for sale of general property for resale), (d)(1)(iii) of this section (foreign use for sale of general property subject to manufacturing, assembly, or processing outside the United States), or (d)(2) of this section (foreign use for sale of intangible property) is a FDDEI transaction only if the taxpayer satisfies the substantiation requirements described in paragraphs (d)(3)(ii), (iii), or (iv) of this section, as applicable.

(ii) *Substantiation of foreign use for resale.*—A seller satisfies the substantiation requirements with respect to a sale of property described in paragraph (d)(1)(ii)(C) of this section (sales of general property for resale) only if the seller maintains one or more of the following items—

(A) A binding contract that specifically limits subsequent sales to sales outside the United States;

(B) Proof that property is specifically designed, labeled, or adapted for a foreign market;

(C) Proof that the cost of shipping the property back to the United States relative to the value of the property makes it impractical that the property will be resold in the United States;

(D) Credible evidence obtained or created in the ordinary course of business from the recipient evidencing that property will be sold to an end user outside the United States (or, in the case of sales of fungible mass property, stating what portion of the property will be sold to end users outside the United States); or

(E) A written statement prepared by the seller containing the information described in paragraphs (d)(3)(ii)(E)(*1*) through (*7*) of this section corroborated by evidence that is credible and sufficient to support the information provided.

(*1*) The name and address of the recipient;

(*2*) The date or dates the property was shipped or delivered to the recipient;

(*3*) The amount of gross income from the sale;

(*4*) A full description of the property subject to resale;

(5) A description of the method of sales to the end users, such as direct sales by the recipient or sales by the recipient to retail stores;

(6) If known, a description of the end users; and

(7) A description of how the seller determined that property will be ultimately sold to an end user outside the United States (or, in the case of sales of fungible mass property, of how the taxpayer determined what portion of the property that will ultimately be sold to end users outside the United States).

(iii) *Substantiation of foreign use for manufacturing, assembly, or other processing outside the United States.*—A seller satisfies the substantiation requirements with respect to a sale of property described in paragraph (d)(1)(iii) of this section (sales of general property subject to manufacturing, assembly, or other processing outside the United States) if the seller maintains one or more of the following items—

(A) Credible evidence that the property has been sold to a foreign unrelated party that is a manufacturer and such property generally cannot be sold to end users without being subject to a physical and material change (for example, the sale of raw materials that cannot be used except in a manufacturing process);

(B) Credible evidence obtained or created in the ordinary course of business from the recipient to support that the product purchased will be subject to manufacture, assembly, or other processing outside the United States within the meaning of paragraph (d)(1)(iii) of this section; or

(C) A written statement prepared by the seller containing the information described in paragraphs (d)(3)(iii)(C)*(1)* through *(7)* of this section corroborated by evidence that is credible and sufficient to support the information provided.

(1) The name and address of the manufacturer of the property;

(2) The date or dates the property was shipped or delivered to the recipient;

(3) The amount of gross income from the sale;

(4) A full description of the general property sold and the type or types of finished goods that will incorporate the general property the taxpayer sold;

(5) A description of the manufacturing, assembly, or other processing operations, including the location or locations of manufacture, assembly, or other processing; how the general property will be used in the finished good; and the nature of the finished good's manufacturing, assembly, or other processing operations as compared to the process used to make the general property used to make the finished good;

(6) A description of how the seller determined the general property was substantially transformed or the activities were substantial in nature within the meaning of paragraph (d)(1)(iii)(B) or (C) of this section, whichever the case may be; and,

(7) If the seller is relying on the rule described in paragraph (d)(1)(iii)(C) of this section (that the fair market value of the general property be no more than twenty percent of the fair market value when incorporated into the finished goods sold to end users), an explanation of how the seller satisfies the requirements in that paragraph.

(iv) *Substantiation of foreign use of intangible property.*—A taxpayer satisfies the substantiation requirements with respect to a sale of property described in paragraph (d)(2) of this section (foreign use for intangible property) if the seller maintains one or more of the following items—

(A) A binding contract that specifically provides that the intangible property can be exploited solely outside the United States;

(B) Credible evidence obtained or created in the ordinary course of business from the recipient establishing the portion of its revenue for a taxable year that was derived from exploiting the intangible property outside the United States; or

(C) A written statement prepared by the seller containing the information described in paragraphs (d)(3)(iv)(C)*(1)* through *(9)* of this section corroborated by evidence that is credible and sufficient to support the information provided.

(1) The name and address of the recipient;

(2) The date of the sale;

(3) The amount of gross income from the sale;

(4) A description of the intangible property;

(5) An explanation of how the intangible property will be used by the recipient (embedded in general property, used to provide a service, used as a manufacturing method or process, or used in research and development);

(6) An explanation of how the seller determined what portion of the sale is a FDDEI sale;

(7) If the intangible property consists of a manufacturing method or process, an explanation of how the elements of paragraph (d)(2)(ii)(C) of this section are satisfied;

(8) If the sale is for periodic payments, an explanation of how the seller determined the extent of foreign use based on the actual revenue earned by the recipient from the use of the intangible property for the taxable year in which a periodic payment is received as required by paragraph (d)(2)(iii)(A) of this section, or, if actual revenue cannot be obtained after reasonable efforts, an explanation of why actual revenue is unavailable and how the seller determined the extent of foreign use based on estimated revenue; and

(9) If the sale is for a lump sum, an explanation of how the seller determined the total net present value of revenue it expected to earn from the exploitation of the intangible property outside the United States and the total net present value of revenue it expected to earn from the exploitation of the intangible property as required by paragraph (d)(2)(iii)(B) of this section.

(v) *Examples.*—The following examples illustrate the application of this paragraph (d)(3).

(A) *Assumed facts.*—The following facts are assumed for purposes of the examples—

(1) DC is a domestic corporation.

(2) FP is a foreign person located within Country A that is a foreign unrelated party with respect to DC.

(3) All of DC's income is DEI.

(4) Except as otherwise provided, the substantive rule for foreign use as described in paragraphs (d)(1) and (2) of this section are satisfied.

(B) *Examples*—

(1) Example 1: Substantiation by seller of sale of products to distributor outside the United States with taxpayer statement and corroborating evidence.—*(i) Facts.* DC sells smartphones to FP, a distributor of electronics that sells property to end users. As part of their regular business process and pursuant to DC's terms and conditions of sales, DC issues commercial invoices to FP that contain a condition that any subsequent sales must be to end users outside the United States. At or near the time of the FDII filing date, DC prepares a statement containing the information required in paragraph (d)(3)(ii)(E) of this section. During an examination of DC's return for the taxable year, the IRS requests substantiation information of foreign use. DC submits the commercial invoices issued to FP as supporting information that FP's customers are end users outside the United States and all other corroborating evidence to the IRS.

(ii) Analysis. DC's sale to FP is a sale of general property for resale subject to the substantiation requirements of paragraph (d)(3)(ii) of this section. DC satisfies the substantiation requirement by providing the statement that satisfies the requirements of paragraph (d)(3)(ii)(E) of this section. The commercial invoices issued pursuant to the terms and conditions of sales sufficiently corroborate DC's statement that the smartphones will ultimately be sold to end users outside of the United States.

(2) Example 2: Substantiation of sale of products to distributor outside the United States with recipient provided information.—*(i) Facts.* DC sells cameras to FP, a distributor of electronics that sells property to end users outside the United States. FP issues sales invoices to its end users. The invoices contain detailed information about the nature of the subsequent sales of the cameras and the location of the end users for value added tax (VAT) purposes. DC is able to obtain copies of FP's VAT invoices with respect to the camera sales that were maintained and submitted pursuant to Country A law. Rather than prepare a statement described in paragraph (d)(3)(ii)(E) of this section, DC submits FP's invoices to the IRS as substantiation of foreign use.

(ii) Analysis. DC's sale to FP is a sale of general property for resale subject to the substantiation requirements of paragraph (d)(3)(ii) of this section. DC satisfies the substantiation requirements by providing the invoices that satisfy the requirements of paragraph (d)(3)(ii)(D) of this section. The VAT invoices issued by FP pursuant to Country A law constitute credible evidence from FP that ultimate sales are to end users located outside the United States.

(e) *Sales of interests in a disregarded entity.*—Under Federal income tax principles, the sale of any interest in an entity that is disregarded for Federal income tax purposes is considered the sale of the assets of that entity, and this section applies to the sale of each such asset that is general property or intangible property for purposes of determining whether such sale qualifies as a FDDEI sale.

(f) *FDDEI sales hedging transactions.*—(1) *In general.* —The amount of a corporation's or partnership's gross FDDEI from FDDEI sales of general property in a taxable year is increased by any gain, or decreased by any loss, taken into account in that taxable year with respect to any FDDEI sales hedging transactions (determined by taking into account the applicable Federal income tax accounting rules, including § 1.446-4).

(2) *FDDEI sales hedging transaction.*—The term *FDDEI sales hedging transaction* means a transaction that meets the requirements of § 1.1221-2(a) through (e) and that is identified in accordance with the requirements of § 1.1221-2(f), except that the transaction must manage risk of price changes or currency fluctuations with respect to ordinary property, as provided in § 1.1221-2(b)(1), and the ordinary property whose price risk is being hedged must be general property that is sold in a FDDEI sale. [Reg. § 1.250(b)-4.]

☐ [*T.D.* 9901, 7-9-2020 (*corrected* 9-28-2020 *and* 10-27-2020).]

§ 1.250(b)-5. Foreign-derived deduction eligible income (FDDEI) services.—(a) *Scope.*—This section provides rules for determining whether a provision of a service is a FDDEI service. Paragraph (b) of this section defines a FDDEI service. Paragraph (c) of this section provides definitions relevant for determining whether a provision of a service is a FDDEI service. Paragraph (d) of this section provides rules for determining whether a general service is provided to a consumer located outside the United States. Paragraph (e) of this section provides rules for determining whether a general service is provided to a business recipient located outside the United States. Paragraph (f) of this section provides rules for determining whether a proximate service is provided to a recipient located outside the United States. Paragraph (g) of this section provides rules for determining whether a service is provided with respect to property located outside the United States. Paragraph (h) of this section provides rules for determining whether a transportation service is provided to a recipient, or with respect to property, located outside the United States.

(b) *Definition of FDDEI service.*—Except as provided in § 1.250(b)-6(d), the term *FDDEI service* means a provision of a service described in any one of paragraphs (b)(1) through (5) of this section. If only a portion of a service is treated as provided to a person, or with respect to property, outside the United States, the provision of the service is a FDDEI service only to the extent of the gross income derived with respect to such portion.

(1) The provision of a general service to a consumer located outside the United States (as determined under paragraph (d) of this section).

(2) The provision of a general service to a business recipient located outside the United States (as determined under paragraph (e) of this section).

(3) The provision of a proximate service to a recipient located outside the United States (as determined under paragraph (f) of this section).

(4) The provision of a property service with respect to tangible property located outside the United States (as determined under paragraph (g) of this section).

(5) The provision of a transportation service to a recipient, or with respect to property, located outside the United States (as determined under paragraph (h) of this section).

(c) *Definitions.*—This paragraph (c) provides definitions that apply for purposes of this section and § 1.250(b)-6.

(1) *Advertising service.*—The term *advertising service* means a general service that consists primarily of transmitting or displaying content (including via the internet) with a purpose to generate revenue based on the promotion of a product or service.

(2) *Benefit.*—The term *benefit* has the meaning set forth in § 1.482-9(l)(3).

(3) *Business recipient.*—The term *business recipient* means a recipient other than a consumer and includes all related parties of the recipient. However, if the recipient is a related party of the taxpayer, the term does not include the taxpayer.

(4) *Consumer.*—The term *consumer* means a recipient that is an individual that purchases a general service for personal use.

(5) *Electronically supplied service.*—The term *electronically supplied service* means, with respect to a general service other than an advertising service, a service that is delivered primarily over the internet or an electronic network and for which value of the service to the end user is derived primarily from automation or electronic delivery. Electronically supplied services include the provision of access to digital content (as defined in § 1.250(b)-3), such as streaming content; on-demand network access to computing resources, such as networks, servers, storage, and software; the provision or support of a business or personal presence on a network, such as a website or a web page; online intermediation platform services; services automatically generated from a computer via the internet or other network in response to data input by the recipient; and similar services. Electronically supplied services do not include services that primarily involve the application of human effort by the renderer (not considering the human effort involved in the development or maintenance of the technology enabling the electronically supplied services). Accordingly, electronically supplied services do not include certain services (such as legal, accounting, medical, or teaching services) involving primarily human effort that are provided electronically.

(6) *General service.*—The term *general service* means any service other than a property service, proximate service, or transportation service. The term *general service* includes advertising services and electronically supplied services.

(7) *Property service.*—The term *property service* means a service, other than a transportation service, provided with respect to tangible property, but only if substantially all of the service is performed at the location of the property and results in physical manipulation of the property such as through manufacturing, assembly, maintenance, or repair. Substantially all of a service is performed at the location of property only if the renderer spends more than 80 percent of the time providing the service at or near the location of the property.

(8) *Proximate service.*—The term *proximate service* means a service, other than a property service or a transportation service, provided to a consumer or business recipient, but only if substantially all of the service is performed in the physical presence of the consumer or, in the case of a business recipient, substantially all of the service is performed in the physical presence of persons working for the business recipient such as employees, contractors, or agents. Substantially all of a service is performed in the physical presence of a consumer or persons working for a business recipient only if the renderer spends more than 80 percent of the time providing the service in the physical presence of such persons.

(9) *Transportation service.*—The term *transportation service* means a service to transport a person or property using aircraft, railroad rolling stock, vessel, motor vehicle, or any other mode of transportation. Transportation services include freight forwarding and similar services.

(d) *General services provided to consumers.*—(1) *In general.*—A general service is provided to a consumer located outside the United States if the consumer of a general service resides outside of the United States when the service is provided. Except as provided in paragraph (d)(2) of this section, if the renderer does not have or cannot after reasonable efforts obtain the consumer's location of residence when the service is provided, the consumer of a general service is treated as residing at the location of the consumer's billing address. However, the rule in the preceding sentence allowing for the use of a consumer's billing address does not apply if the renderer knows or has reason to know that the consumer does not reside outside the United States. A renderer has reason to know that the consumer does not reside outside the United States if the information received as part of the provision of the service indicates that the consumer resides in the United States and the renderer fails to obtain evidence establishing that the consumer resides outside the United States.

(2) *Electronically supplied services.*—The consumer of an electronically supplied service is deemed to reside at the location of the device used to receive the service. Such location may be determined based on the location of the IP address when the electronically supplied service is provided. However, if the renderer does not have or cannot after reasonable efforts obtain the consumer's device location, then the location of the device is treated as being outside the United States if the renderer's billing address for the consumer is outside of the United States, subject to the knowledge and reason to know standards described in paragraph (d)(1) of this section.

(3) *Example.*—The following example illustrates the application of paragraph (d) of this section.

(i) *Facts.* DC, a domestic corporation, provides a streaming movie service on its website. The terms of the service allow consumers to watch movies over the internet. The terms of the service permit the consumer to view the movies for personal use, but convey no ownership of movies to the consumers.

(ii) *Analysis.* The streaming service is a FDDEI service under paragraph (d)(1) of this section to the extent that the service is provided to consumers that reside outside the United States. The service that DC provides is a general service, provided to consumers that is an electronically supplied service under paragraph (c)(5) of this section. Therefore, the consumers are deemed to reside at the location of the devices used to receive the service under paragraph (d)(2) of this section. However, if the renderer cannot reasonably obtain the consumers' device location (such as IP addresses), the device location is treated as being outside the United States if their billing addresses are outside the United States. See § 1.250(b)-4(d)(1)(v)(B)(7) for an example of digital content provided to consumers as a sale rather than a service.

(e) *General services provided to business recipients.*—(1) *In general.*—A general service is provided to a business recipient located outside the United States to the extent that the service confers a benefit on the business recipient's operations outside the United States under the rules in paragraph (e)(2) of this section. The location of residence, incorporation, or formation of a business recipient is not relevant to determining the location of the business recipient's operations that benefit from a general service.

(2) *Determination of business operations that benefit from the service.*—(i) *In general.*—Except as otherwise provided in paragraph (e)(2)(ii) and (iii) of this section, the determination of which operations of the business recipient located outside the United States benefit from a general service, and the extent to which such operations benefit, is made under the principles of § 1.482-9 by treating the taxpayer as one controlled taxpayer, the portions of the business recipient's operations within the United States (if any) that may benefit from the general service as one or more controlled taxpayers, and the portions of the business recipient's operations outside the United States (if any) that may benefit from the general service, each as one or more controlled taxpayers. The extent to which a business recipient's operations within or outside of the United States are treated as one or more separate controlled taxpayers is determined under any reasonable method (for example, separate controlled taxpayers may be determined on a per entity or per country basis, or by aggregating all of the business recipient's operations outside the United States as one controlled taxpayer). The determination of the amount of the benefit conferred on the business recipient's operations that are treated as controlled taxpayers is determined under a reasonable method consistent with the principles of § 1.482-9(k), treating the renderer's gross income from the services provided to the business recipient as if it were a "cost" as that term is used in § 1.482-9(k). Reasonable methods may include, for example, allocations based on time spent or costs incurred by the renderer or sales, profits, or assets of the business recipient.

The determination is made when the service is provided based on information obtained from the business recipient or on the renderer's own records (such as time spent working with the business recipient's offices located outside the United States).

(ii) *Advertising services.*—With respect to advertising services, the operations of the business recipient that benefit from the advertising service provided by the renderer are deemed to be located where the advertisements are viewed by individuals. If advertising services are displayed via the internet, the advertising services are viewed at the location of the device on which the advertisements are viewed. For this purpose, the IP address may be used to establish the location of a device on which an advertisement is viewed.

(iii) *Electronically supplied services.*—With respect to an electronically supplied service, the operations of the business recipient that benefit from that service provided by the renderer are deemed to be located where the business recipient (including employees, contractors, or agents) accesses or otherwise uses the service. If it cannot be determined whether the location is within or outside the United States (such as where the location of access cannot be reliably determined using the location of the IP address of the device used to receive the service), and the gross receipts from all services with respect to the business recipient are in the aggregate less than $50,000 for the renderer's taxable year, the operations of the business recipient that benefit from the service provided by the renderer are deemed to be located at the recipient's billing address; otherwise, the operations of the business recipient that benefit are deemed to be located in the United States. If the renderer provides a service that is partially an electronically supplied service and partially a general service that is not an electronically supplied service (such as a service that is performed partially online and partially by mail or in person), the location of the business recipient is determined using the rule for electronically supplied services in this paragraph (e)(2)(iii) if the primary purpose of the service is to provide electronically supplied services; otherwise, the rule for general services described in paragraph (e)(2)(i) of this section applies.

(3) *Identification of business recipient's operations.*—(i) *In general.*—For purposes of this paragraph (e), except with respect to advertising services and electronically supplied services, a business recipient is treated as having operations where it maintains an office or other fixed place of business. In general, an office or other fixed place of business is a fixed facility, that is, a place, site, structure, or other similar facility, through which the business recipient engages in a trade or business. For purposes of making the determination in this paragraph (e)(3)(i), the renderer may make reliable assumptions based on the information available to it.

(ii) *Advertising services and electronically supplied services.*—The location of a business recipient that receives advertising services or electronically supplied services will be determined under the rules of paragraph (e)(2)(ii) and (iii) of this section, respectively, even if the business recipient does not maintain an office or other fixed place of business in the locations where the advertisements are viewed (in the case of advertising services) or where the general service is accessed (in the case of electronically supplied services).

(iii) *No office or fixed place of business.*—In the case of general services other than advertising services and other than electronically supplied services, if the business recipient does not have an identifiable office or fixed place of business (including the office of a principal manager or managing owner), the business recipient is deemed to be located at its primary billing address.

(4) *Substantiation of the location of a business recipient's operations outside the United States.*—Except as provided in § 1.250(b)-3(f)(3) (relating to certain loss transactions), a general service provided to a business recipient is treated as a FDDEI service only if the renderer substantiates its determination of the extent to which the service benefits a business recipient's operations outside the United States. A renderer satisfies the preceding sentence if the renderer maintains one or more of the following items—

(i) Credible evidence obtained or created in the ordinary course of business from the business recipient establishing the extent to which operations of the business recipient outside the United States benefit from the service; or

(ii) A written statement prepared by the renderer containing the information described in paragraphs (e)(4)(ii)(A) through (F) of this section corroborated by evidence that is credible and sufficient to support the information provided.

(A) The name of the business recipient;

(B) The date or dates of the service;

(C) The amount of gross income from the service;

(D) A full description of the service;

(E) A description of how the service will benefit the business recipient; and

(F) An explanation of how the renderer determined what portion of the service will benefit the business recipient's operations located outside the United States.

(5) *Examples.*—The following examples illustrate the application of this paragraph (e).

(i) *Assumed facts.*—The following facts are assumed for purposes of the examples—

(A) DC is a domestic corporation.

(B) A and R are not related parties of DC.

(C) Except as otherwise provided, the substantiation requirements described in paragraph (e)(4) of this section are satisfied.

(ii) *Examples*—

(A) *Example 1: Determination of business operations that benefit from the service.*—(*1*) *Facts.* For the taxable year, DC provides a consulting service to R, a company that operates restaurants within and outside of the United States, in exchange for $150x. Fifty percent of the sales earned by R and its related parties are from customers located outside of the United States. However, the consulting service that DC provides relates specifically to a single chain of fast food restaurants that R operates. Sales information that R provides to DC indicates that 70 percent of the sales of the fast food restaurant chain are from locations within the United States and 30 percent of the sales are from Country X. DC determines that the use of sales is a reasonable method under the principles of § 1.482-9(k) to allocate the benefit of the consulting service among R's fast food operations.

(2) *Analysis.* Under paragraph (e)(1) of this section, DC's service is provided to a person located outside the United States to the extent that DC's service confers a benefit to R's operations outside the United States. Under paragraph (e)(2)(i) of this section, DC, R's fast food operations within the United States, and R's fast food operations in Country X, are treated as if they were controlled taxpayers because only these operations may benefit from DC's service. The principles of § 1.482-9(k) apply to determine the amount of DC's service that benefits R's operations outside the United States. DC's gross income is allocated based on the sales of the fast food chain of restaurants that benefits from DC's service because using sales is a reasonable method. Therefore, 30 percent of the provision of the consulting service is treated as the provision of a service to a person located outside the United States and a FDDEI service under paragraph (b)(2) of this section. Accordingly, $45x ($150x x 0.30) of DC's gross income from the provision of the consulting service is included in DC's gross FDDEI for the taxable year.

(B) *Example 2: Determination of business operations that benefit from the service; alternative facts.*—(1) *Facts.* The facts are the same as in paragraph (e)(5)(ii)(A)(*1*) of this section (the facts in *Example 1*), except that DC provides an information technology service to R that benefits R's entire business. DC determines that the use of sales is a reasonable method under the principles of § 1.482-9(k) to allocate the benefit of the information technology service among R's entire business.

(2) *Analysis.* DC, R's operations within the United States, and R's operations in Country X, are treated as if they were controlled taxpayers because the service that DC provides relates to R's entire business. DC's gross income is allocated based on sales of the entire business because using sales is a reasonable method to determine the amount of DC's service that benefits R's operations outside the United States under the principles of § 1.482-9(k). Therefore, 50 percent of the provision of the information technology service is treated as a service to a person located outside the United States and a FDDEI service under paragraph (b)(2) of this section. Accordingly, $75x ($150x x 0.50) of DC's gross income from the provision of the information technology service is included in DC's gross FDDEI for the taxable year.

(C) *Example 3: Advertising services.*—(1) *Facts.* The facts are the same as in paragraph (e)(5)(ii)(A)(*1*) of this section (the facts in *Example 1*), except that DC provides an advertising service to R. DC displays advertisements for R's restaurant chain on its social media website and smartphone application. Based on the IP addresses of the devices on which the advertisements are viewed, 20 percent of the views of the advertisements were from devices located outside the United States.

(2) *Analysis.* Because the service that DC provides is an advertising service, under paragraph (e)(2)(i) of this section, as modified by paragraph (e)(2)(ii) of this section, R's operations that benefit from DC's advertising service are deemed to be where the advertisements are viewed. Therefore, 20 percent of the provision of the advertising service is treated as a service to a person located outside the United States and a FDDEI service under paragraph (b)(2) of this section. Accordingly, $30x ($150x x 0.20) of DC's gross income from the provision of the advertising service is included in DC's gross FDDEI for the taxable year.

(D) *Example 4: No reliable information about which operations benefit from the service or publicly available information.*—(1) *Facts.* For the taxable year, DC provides a consulting service to R, a business-facing company that does not advertise its business. All of DC's interaction with R is through R's employees that report to an office in the United States. Statements made by R's employees indicate that the service will benefit R's business operations located within and outside the United States, but do not provide information that would allow DC to reliably determine the extent to which its service will confer a benefit on R's business operations located outside the United States.

(2) *Analysis.* DC is unable to determine the extent to which its service will confer a benefit on R's business operations located outside the United States under paragraph (e)(2)(i) of this section. Accordingly, DC cannot substantiate a determination of the extent to which the service benefits a business recipient's operations outside the United States under paragraph (e)(4) of this section. Therefore, no portion of DC's service is a FDDEI service.

(E) *Example 5: Electronically supplied services that are accessed by the business recipient's employees.*—(1) *Facts.* DC provides payroll services for R. As part of this service, DC maintains a website through which R can enter payroll information for its employees and through which R's employees can enter and change their personal information. DC also causes R's employees' paychecks to be directly deposited into their bank accounts and pays R's employment taxes on R's behalf. The primary purpose of the service is to pay R's employees. R has 100 user accounts that access DC's website. Sixty of the user accounts that access DC's website access the website from devices that are located outside the United States and forty of the user accounts access the website from devices that are located inside the United States.

(2) *Analysis.* Under paragraph (e)(1) of this section, DC's service is provided to a person located outside the United States to the extent that DC's service confers a benefit to R's operations outside the United States. The service that DC provides to R is an electronically supplied service under paragraph (c)(5) of this section. Accordingly, under paragraph (e)(2)(i) of this section, as modified by paragraph (e)(2)(iii) of this section, R's operations that benefit from DC's services are deemed to be located where R accesses the service, which is where R's employees access the website. See paragraph (e)(2)(iii) of this section. Accordingly, the portion of the payroll service that is treated as a service to a person located outside the United States and a FDDEI service under paragraph (b)(2) of this section is determined based on the extent to which the locations where R accesses the website are located outside the United States. Because 60 percent (60/100) of user accounts access DC's website from locations outside the United States, 60 percent of the provision of the payroll service is treated as a service to a person located outside the United States and a FDDEI service under paragraph (b)(2) of this section.

(F) *Example 6: Electronically supplied services that are accessed by the business recipient's.*—(1) *Facts.* DC maintains an inventory management website for R, a company that sells consumer goods online. R's offices and all of its employees, who use the website, are located in the United States, but R sells its products to customers both within and outside the United States.

(2) *Analysis.* Under paragraph (e)(1) of this section, DC's service is provided to a person located outside the United States to the extent that DC's service confers a benefit to R's operations outside the United States. The service that DC provides to R is an electronically supplied service under paragraph (c)(5) of this section. Accordingly, under paragraph (e)(2)(i) of this section, as modified by paragraph (e)(2)(iii) of this section, R's operations that benefit from DC's services are deemed to be located where the service is accessed by employees. Therefore, none of the provision of the inventory management website is treated as a service to a person located outside the United States and none is a FDDEI service under paragraph (b)(2) of this section.

(G) *Example 7: Service provided to a domestic person.*—(1) *Facts.* A, a domestic corporation that operates solely in the United States, enters into a services agreement with R, a company that operates solely outside the United States. Under the agreement, A agrees to perform a consulting service for R. A hires DC to provide a service to A that A will use in the provision of a consulting service to R.

(2) *Analysis.* Because DC provides a service to A, a person located within the United States, DC's provision of the service to A is not a FDDEI service under paragraph (b)(2) of this section, even though the service is used by A in providing a service to R, a person located outside the United States. See also section 250(b)(5)(B)(ii). However, A's provision of the consulting service to R may be a FDDEI service, in which case A's gross income from the provision of such service would be included in A's gross FDDEI.

(f) *Proximate services.*—A proximate service is provided to a recipient located outside the United States if the proximate service is performed outside the United States. In the case of a proximate service performed partly within the United States and partly outside of the United States, a proportionate amount of the service is treated as provided to a recipient located outside the United States corresponding to the portion of time the renderer spends providing the service outside of the United States.

(g) *Property services.*—(1) *In general.*—Except as provided in paragraph (g)(2) of this section, a property service is provided with respect to tangible property located outside the United States only if the property is located outside the United States for the duration of the period the service is performed.

(2) *Exception for services provided with respect to property temporarily in the United States.*—A property service is deemed to be provided with respect to tangible property located outside the United States if the following conditions are satisfied—

(i) The property is temporarily in the United States for the purpose of receiving the property service;

(ii) After the completion of the service, the property will be primarily hangared, stored, or used outside the United States;

(iii) The property is not used to generate revenue in the United States at any point during the duration of the service; and

(iv) The property is owned by a foreign person that resides or primarily operates outside the United States.

(h) *Transportation services.*—Except as provided in this paragraph (h), a transportation service is provided to a recipient, or with respect to property, located outside the United States only if both the origin and the destination of the service are outside of the United States. However, in the case of a transportation service provided to a recipient, or with respect to property, where either the origin or the destination of the service is outside of the United States, but not both, then 50 percent of the gross income from the transportation service is considered derived from services provided to a recipient, or with respect to property, located outside the United States. [Reg. § 1.250(b)-5.]

☐ [*T.D.* 9901, 7-9-2020 (*corrected* 9-28-2020 *and* 10-27-2020). *Amended by T.D.* 9959, 12-28-2021.]

§ 1.250(b)-6. Related party transactions.—(a) *Scope.*—This section provides rules for determining whether a sale of property or a provision of a service to a related party is a FDDEI transaction. Paragraph (b) of this section provides definitions relevant for determining whether a sale of property or a provision of a service to a related party is a FDDEI transaction. Paragraph (c) of this section provides rules for determining whether a sale of general property to a foreign related party is a FDDEI sale. Paragraph (d) of this section provides rules for determining whether the provision of a general service to a business recipient that is a related party is a FDDEI service.

(b) *Definitions.*—This paragraph (b) provides definitions that apply for purposes of this section.

(1) *Related party sale.*—The term *related party sale* means a sale of general property to a foreign related party. See § 1.250(b)-1(e)(3)(ii)(D) (*Example 4*) for an illustration of a related party sale in the case of a seller that is a partnership.

(2) *Related party service.*—The term *related party service* means a provision of a general service to a business recipient that is a related party of the renderer and that is described in § 1.250(b)-5(b)(2) without regard to paragraph (d) of this section.

(3) *Unrelated party transaction.*—The term *unrelated party transaction* means, with respect to property purchased by a foreign related party (the "purchased property") in a related party sale from a seller—

(i) A sale of the purchased property by the foreign related party in the ordinary course of its business to a foreign unrelated party with respect to the seller;

(ii) A sale of property by the foreign related party to a foreign unrelated party with respect to the seller, if the purchased property is a constituent part of the property sold to the foreign unrelated party;

(iii) A sale of property by the foreign related party to a foreign unrelated party with respect to the seller, if the purchased property is not a constituent part of the product sold to the foreign unrelated party but rather is used in connection with producing the property sold to the foreign unrelated party; or

(iv) A provision of a service by the foreign related party to a foreign unrelated party with respect to the seller, if the purchased property was used in connection with the provision of the service.

(c) *Related party sales.*—(1) *In general.*—A related party sale of general property is a FDDEI sale only if the requirements described in either paragraph (c)(1)(i) or (ii) of this section are satisfied with respect to the related party sale. This paragraph (c) does not apply in determining whether a sale of intangible property to a foreign related party is a FDDEI sale.

(i) *Sale of property in an unrelated party transaction.*—A related party sale is a FDDEI sale if an unrelated party transaction described in paragraph (b)(3)(i) or (ii) of this section occurs with respect to the property purchased in the related party sale and such unrelated party transaction is described in § 1.250(b)-4(b) (definition of FDDEI sale). The seller in the related party sale may establish that an unrelated party transaction will occur with respect to the property, or what portion of the property will be sold in an unrelated party transaction in the case of sale of a fungible mass of general property, based on contractual terms (including, for example, that the related party is contractually bound to only sell the product to foreign unrelated parties), past practices of the foreign related party (such as practices to only sell products to foreign unrelated parties), a showing that the product sold is designed specifically for a foreign market, or books and records otherwise evidencing that sales will be made to foreign unrelated parties.

(ii) *Use of property in an unrelated party transaction.*—A related party sale is a FDDEI sale if one or more unrelated party transactions described in paragraph (b)(3)(iii) or (iv) of this section occurs with respect to the property purchased in the related party sale and such unrelated party transaction or transactions would be described in § 1.250(b)-4(b) or § 1.250(b)-5(b) (definition of FDDEI service). If the property purchased in the related party sale will be used in unrelated party transactions described in the preceding sentence and other transactions, the amount of gross income from the related party sale that is attributable to a FDDEI sale is equal to the gross income from the related party sale multiplied by a fraction, the numerator of which is the revenue that the related party reasonably expects (as of the FDII filing date) to earn from all unrelated party transactions with respect to the property purchased in the related party sale that would be described in § 1.250(b)-4(b) or § 1.250(b)-5(b) and the denominator of which is the total revenue that the related party reasonably expects (as of the FDII filing date) to earn from all transactions with respect to the property purchased in the related party sale.

(2) *Treatment of foreign related party as seller or renderer.*—For purposes of determining whether a sale of property or provision of a service by a foreign related party is, or would be, described in § 1.250(b)-4(b) or § 1.250(b)-5(b), the foreign related party that sells the property or provides the service is treated as a seller or renderer, as applicable, and the foreign unrelated party is treated as the recipient.

(3) *Transactions between related parties.*—For purposes of determining whether an unrelated party sale has occurred and satisfies the requirements of paragraphs (c)(1) or (2) of this section with respect to a sale to a foreign related party (and not for purposes of determining whether a sale is to a foreign person as required by § 1.250(b)-4(b)), the seller and all related parties of the seller are treated as if they are part of a single foreign related party. For purposes of the preceding sentence, in determining whether a United States person is a member of the seller's modified affiliated group, and therefore a related party of the seller, the definition of the term *modified affiliated group* in § 1.250(b)-1(c)(17) applies without the substitution of "more than 50 percent" for "at least 80 percent" each place it appears. Accordingly, if a foreign related party sells or uses property purchased in a related party sale in a transaction with a second related party of the seller, transactions between the second related party and an unrelated party may be treated as an unrelated party transaction for purposes of applying paragraph (c)(1) of this section to a related party sale.

(4) *Example.*—The following example illustrates the application of this paragraph (c).

(i) *Facts.* DC, a domestic corporation, sells a machine to FC, a foreign related party of DC in a transaction described in § 1.250(b)-4(b) (without regard to this paragraph (c)). FC uses the machine solely to manufacture product A. As of the FDII filing date for the taxable year, 75 percent of future revenue from sales by FC to unrelated parties of product A will be from sales that would be described in § 1.250(b)-4(b).

(ii) *Analysis.* The sale by DC to FC is a related party sale. Because FC uses the machine to make product A, but the machine is not a constituent part of product A because FC does not undertake further manufacturing with respect to the machine itself, FC's sale of product

A is an unrelated party transaction described in paragraph (b)(3)(iii) of this section. Therefore, DC's sale of the machine is only a FDDEI sale if the requirements of paragraph (c)(1)(ii) of this section are satisfied. Because 75 percent of the revenue from future sales of product A will be from unrelated party transactions that would be described in § 1.250(b)-4(b), 75 percent of the revenues from DC's sale of the machine to FC constitute FDDEI sales.

(d) *Related party services.*—(1) *In general.*—Except as provided in this paragraph (d)(1), a related party service is a FDDEI service only if the related party service is not substantially similar to a service that has been provided or will be provided by the related party to a person located within the United States. However, if a related party service is substantially similar to a service provided (in whole or in part) by the related party to a person located in the United States solely by reason of paragraph (d)(2)(ii) of this section, the amount of gross income from the related party service attributable to a FDDEI service is equal to the difference between the gross income from the related party service and the amount of the price paid by persons located within the United States that is attributable to the related party service. Section 250(b)(5)(C)(ii) and this paragraph (d)(1) apply only to a general service provided to a related party that is a business recipient and are not applicable with respect to any other service provided to a related party.

(2) *Substantially similar services.*—A related party service is substantially similar to a service provided by the related party to a person located within the United States only if the related party service is used by the related party in whole or part to provide a service to a person located within the United States and either—

(i) 60 percent or more of the benefits conferred by the related party service are directly used by the related party to confer benefits on consumers or business recipients located within the United States; or

(ii) 60 percent or more of the price paid by consumers or business recipients located within the United States for the service provided by the related party is attributable to the related party service.

(3) *Special rules.*—For purposes of paragraph (d) of this section, the rules in paragraphs (d)(3)(i) and (ii) of this section apply.

(i) *Rules for determining the location of and price paid by recipients of a service provided by a related party.*—The location of a consumer or business recipient with respect to services provided by the related party is determined under § 1.250(b)-5(d) and (e)(2), respectively, but treating the related party as the renderer. Accordingly, if the related party provides a service to a business recipient, the related party is treated as conferring benefits on a person located within the United States to the extent that the service confers a benefit on the business recipient's operations located within the United States. Similarly, for purposes of applying paragraph (d)(2)(ii) of this section with respect to business recipients, the price paid by a business recipient to the related party for services is allocated proportionally based on the locations of the business recipient that benefit from the services provided by the related party.

(ii) *Rules for allocating the benefits provided by and price paid to the renderer of a related party service.*—For purposes of applying paragraph (d)(2)(i) of this section with respect to benefits that are directly used by the related party to confer benefits on its recipients, the benefits provided by the renderer to the related party are allocated to the related party's consumers or business recipients within the United States based on the proportion of benefits conferred by the related party on consumers or business recipients located within the United States. For purposes of determining the amount of the price paid by persons located within the United States that is attributable to the related party service in applying paragraph (d)(2)(ii) of this section, if the related party provides services that confer benefits on persons located within the United States and outside the United States, the price paid for the related party service by the related party to the renderer is allocated proportionally based on the benefits conferred on each location by the related party to its recipients.

(4) *Examples.*—The following examples illustrate the application of this paragraph (d).

(i) *Assumed facts.*—The following facts are assumed for purposes of the examples—

(A) DC is a domestic corporation.

(B) FC is a foreign corporation and a foreign related party of DC that operates solely outside the United States.

(C) The service DC provides to FC is a general service provided to a business recipient located outside the United States as described in § 1.250(b)-5(b)(2) without regard to the application of paragraph (d) of this section.

(D) The benefits conferred by DC's service to FC's customers are not indirect or remote within the meaning of § 1.482-9(l)(3)(ii).

(ii) *Examples*—

(A) *Example 1: Services that are substantially similar services under paragraph (d)(2)(i) of this section.*—(*1*) *Facts.* FC enters into a services agreement with R, a company that operates restaurant chains within and outside the United States. Under the agreement, FC agrees to furnish a design for the renovation of a chain of restaurants that R owns; the design will include architectural plans. FC hires DC to provide an architectural service to FC that FC will use in the provision of its design service to R. The architectural service that DC provides to FC will serve no other purpose than to enable FC to provide its service to R. The service that FC provides will benefit only R's operations within the United States. FC pays an arm's length price of $50x to DC for the architectural service and DC recognizes $50x of gross income from the service. FC incurs additional costs to add additional design elements to the plans and charges R a total of $100x for its service.

(*2*) *Analysis.* All of the service that DC provides to FC is directly used in the provision of a service to R because FC uses DC's architectural service to provide its design service to R, and the architectural service that DC provides to FC will serve no purpose other than to enable FC to provide its service to R. In addition, FC is treated as conferring benefits only to persons located within the United States under paragraph (d)(3)(i) of this section because only R's operations within the United States benefit from the service provided by FC that used the service provided by DC. Therefore, the service provided by DC to FC is substantially similar to the service provided by FC to R under paragraph (d)(2)(i) of this section. Accordingly, DC's provision of the architectural service to FC is not a FDDEI service under paragraph (d)(1) of this section, and DC's gross income from the architectural service ($50x) is not included in its gross FDDEI.

(B) *Example 2: Services that are not substantially similar services under paragraph (d)(2)(i) of this section.*—(*1*) *Facts.* The facts are the same as paragraph (d)(4)(ii)(A)(*1*) of this section (the facts in *Example 1*), except that 90 percent of R's operations that will benefit from FC's service are located outside the United States.

(*2*) *Analysis*—(*i*) *Analysis under paragraph (d)(2)(i) of this section.* All of the service that DC provides to FC is directly used in the provision of a service to R. However, because 90 percent of R's operations that will benefit from FC's service are located outside the United States under paragraph (d)(3)(i) of this section, only 10 percent of the benefits of FC's service are conferred on persons located within the United States. Further, because FC's service confers a benefit on R's operations located within and outside the United States, the benefit provided by DC to FC is allocated proportionately based on the locations of R that benefit from the services provided by FC under paragraph (d)(3)(ii) of this section. Therefore, only 10 percent of DC's architectural service are directly used by FC to confer benefits on persons located within the United States under paragraph (d)(3)(ii) of this section. Therefore, the architectural service provided by DC to FC is not substantially similar to the design service provided by FC to persons located within the United States under paragraph (d)(2)(i) of this section.

(C) *Example 3: Services that are substantially similar services under paragraph (d)(2)(ii) of this section.*—(*1*) *Facts.* The facts are the same as paragraph (d)(4)(ii)(B)(*1*) of this section (the facts in *Example 2*), except that FC pays an arm's length price of $75x to DC for the architectural service and DC recognizes $75x of gross income from the service. As in paragraph (d)(4)(ii)(A)(*1*) and (d)(4)(ii)(B)(*1*) of this section (the facts in *Example 1* and *Example 2*), FC charges R a total of $100x for its service.

(*2*) *Analysis*—(*i*) *Price paid by persons located within the United States.* Under paragraph (d)(3)(i) of this section, FC is treated as conferring benefits on a person located within the United States to the extent that R's operations that will benefit from FC's service are located within the United States. Further, because FC's service confers a benefit on R's operations located within and outside the United States, the price paid by R to FC ($100x) is allocated proportionately based on the locations of R that benefit from the services provided by FC under paragraph (d)(3)(i) of this section. Accordingly, because 10 percent of R's operations that will benefit from FC's services are located within the United States, persons located within the United States are treated as paying $10x ($100x x 0.10) for FC's services for purposes of applying the test in paragraph (d)(2)(ii) of this section

(ii) *Amount attributable to the related party service.* The service that FC provides to R is attributable in part to DC's service because FC uses the architectural plans that DC provides to provide a service to R. Under paragraph (d)(3)(ii) of this section, because the benefits of the service provided by FC are conferred on persons located within the United States and outside the United States, a proportionate amount (10 percent) of the price paid to DC for the related party service ($75x), or $7.5x, is treated as attributable to the services provided to persons located within the United States.

(iii) *Application of test in paragraph (d)(2)(ii) of this section.* For purposes of applying the test described in paragraph (d)(2)(ii) of this section, the price paid by persons located within the United States for the service provided by the related party (FC) is $10x, as determined in paragraph (d)(4)(ii)(C)(2)(*i*) of this section (the analysis of this *Example 3*). The amount of the price that is attributable to DC's service is $7.5x, as determined in paragraph (d)(4)(ii)(C)(2)(*ii*) of this section (the analysis of this *Example 3*). Accordingly, of the price treated as paid to FC by persons located within the United States, 75 percent ($7.5x/$10x) is attributable to the related party service. Because more than 60 percent of the price treated as paid by persons within the United States for FC's service is attributable to DC's service, the service provided by DC to FC is substantially similar to the design service provided by FC to persons located within the United States under paragraph (d)(2)(ii) of this section.

(*iv*) *Conclusion.* Under paragraph (d)(1) of this section, because the related party service provided by DC is substantially similar to the service provided by FC to a person located in the United States solely by reason of paragraph (d)(2)(ii) of this section, the difference between DC's gross income from the related party service and the amount of the price paid by persons located within the United States that is attributable to the related party service is treated as a FDDEI service. Accordingly, $67.5x ($75x - $7.5x) of DC's gross income from the provision of the service to FC is treated as a FDDEI service. [Reg. § 1.250(b)-6.]

☐ [*T.D. 9901, 7-9-2020 (corrected 9-28-2020 and 10-27-2020).*]

Items Not Deductible

§ 1.267(a)-3. Deduction of amounts owed to related foreign persons.—(a) *Purpose and scope.*—This section provides rules under section 267(a)(2) and (3) governing when an amount owed to a related foreign person that is otherwise deductible under Chapter 1 may be deducted. Paragraph (b) of this section provides the general rules, and paragraph (c) of this section provides exceptions and special rules.

(b) *Deduction of amount owed to related foreign person.*—(1) *In general.*—Except as provided in paragraph (c) of this section, section 267(a)(3) requires a taxpayer to use the cash method of accounting with respect to the deduction of amounts owed to a related foreign person. An amount that is owed to a related foreign person and that is otherwise deductible under Chapter 1 thus may not be deducted by the taxpayer until such amount is paid to the related foreign person. For purposes of this section, a related foreign person is any person that is not a United States person within the meaning of section 7701(a)(30), and that is related (within the meaning of section 267(b)) to the taxpayer at the close of the taxable year in which the amount incurred by the taxpayer would otherwise be deductible. Section 267(f) defines "controlled group" for purposes of section 267(b) without regard to the limitations of section 1563(b). An amount is treated as paid for purposes of this section if the amount is considered paid for purposes of section 1441 or section 1442 (including an amount taken into account pursuant to section 884(f)).

(2) *Amounts covered.*—This section applies to otherwise deductible amounts that are of a type described in section 871(a)(1)(A), (B) or (D), or in section 881(a)(1), (2) or (4). The rules of this section also apply to interest that is from sources outside the United States. Amounts other than interest that are from sources outside the United States, and that are not income of a related foreign person effectively connected with the conduct by such related foreign person of a trade or business within the United States, are not subject to the rules of section 267(a)(2) or (3) or this section. See paragraph (c) of this section for rules governing the treatment of amounts that are income of a related foreign person effectively connected with the conduct of a trade or business within the United States by such related foreign person.

(3) *Change in method of accounting.*—A taxpayer that uses a method of accounting other than that required by the rules of this section must change its method of accounting to conform its method to the rules of this section. The taxpayer's change in method must be made pursuant to the rules of section 446(e), the regulations thereunder, and any applicable administrative procedures prescribed by the Commissioner. Because the rules of this section prescribe a method of accounting, these rules apply in the determination of a taxpayer's earnings and profits pursuant to § 1.1312-6(a).

(4) *Examples.*—The provisions of this paragraph (b) may be illustrated by the following examples:

Example 1. (i) FC, a corporation incorporated in Country X, owns 100 percent of the stock of C, a domestic corporation. C uses the accrual method of accounting in computing its income and deductions, and is a calendar year taxpayer. In Year 1, C accrues an amount owed to FC for interest. C makes an actual payment of the amount owed to FC in Year 2.

(ii) Regardless of its source, the interest owed to FC is an amount to which this section applies. Pursuant to the rules of this paragraph (b), the amount owed to FC by C will not be allowable as a deduction in Year 1. Section 267 does not preclude the deduction of this amount in Year 2.

Example 2. (i) RS, a domestic corporation, is the sole shareholder of FSC, a foreign sales corporation. Both RS and FSC use the accrual method of accounting. In Year 1, RS accrues $z owed to FSC for commissions earned by FSC in Year 1. Pursuant to the foreign sales company provisions, sections 921 through 927, a portion of this amount, $x, is treated as effectively connected income of FSC from sources outside the United States. Accordingly, the rules of section 267(a)(3) and paragraph (b) of this section do not apply. See paragraph (c) of this section for the rules governing the treatment of amounts that are effectively connected income of FSC.

(ii) The remaining amount of the commission, $y, is classified as exempt foreign trade income under section 923(a)(3) and is treated as income of FSC from sources outside the United States that is not effectively connected income. This amount is one to which the provisions of this section do not apply, since it is an amount other than interest from sources outside the United States and is not effectively connected income. Therefore, a deduction for $y is allowable to RS as of the day on which it accrues the otherwise deductible amount, without regard to section 267(a)(2) and (a)(3) and the regulations thereunder.

(c) *Exceptions and special rules.*—(1) *Effectively connected income subject to United States tax.*—The provisions of section 267(a)(2) and the regulations thereunder, and not the provisions of paragraph (b) of this section, apply to an amount that is income of the related foreign person that is effectively connected with the conduct of a United States trade or business of such related foreign person. An amount described in this paragraph (c)(1) thus is allowable as a deduction as of the day on which the amount is includible in the gross income of the related foreign person as effectively connected income under sections 872(a)(2) or 882(b) (or, if later, as of the day on which the deduction would be so allowable but for section 267(a)(2)). However, this paragraph (c)(1) does not apply if the related foreign person is exempt from United States income tax on the amount owed, or is subject to a reduced rate of tax, pursuant to a treaty obligation of the United States (such as under an article relating to the taxation of business profits).

(2) *Items exempt from tax by treaty.*—Except with respect to interest, neither paragraph (b) of this section nor section 267(a)(2) applies to any amount that is income of a related foreign person with respect to which the related foreign person is exempt from United States taxation on the amount owed pursuant to a treaty obligation of the United States (such as under an article relating to the taxation of business profits). Interest that is effectively connected income of the related foreign person under sections 872(a)(2) or 882(b) is an amount covered by paragraph (c)(1) of this section. Interest that is not effectively connected income of the related foreign person is an amount covered by paragraph (b) of this section, regardless of whether the related foreign person is exempt from United States taxation on the amount owed pursuant to a treaty obligation of the United States.

(3) *Items subject to reduced rate of tax by treaty.*—Paragraph (b) of this section applies to amounts that are income of a related foreign person with respect to which the related foreign person claims a reduced rate of United States income tax on the amount owed pursuant to a treaty obligation of the United States (such as under an article relating to the taxation of royalties).

(4) *Certain amounts owed to certain controlled foreign corporations.*—An amount that is income of a related foreign person is exempt from the application of section 267(a)(3)(B)(i) if the related foreign person is a controlled foreign corporation that does not have any United States shareholders (as defined in section 951(b)) that own (within the meaning of section 958(a)) stock of the controlled foreign corporation. However, in this case, the amount is subject to the application of section 267(a)(3)(A) in the same manner as if the related foreign person were a foreign corporation that is not a controlled foreign corporation.

(d) *Effective date.*—The rules of this section are effective with respect to interest that is allowable as a deduction under chapter 1 (without regard to the rules of this section) in taxable years beginning after December 31, 1983, but are not effective with respect to interest that is incurred with respect to indebtedness incurred on or before September 29, 1983, or incurred after that date pursuant to a contract that was binding on that date and at all times thereafter (unless the indebtedness or the contract was renegotiated, extended, renewed, or revised after that date). Except as otherwise provided in this paragraph (d), the regulations in this section issued under section 267 apply to all other deductible amounts that are incurred after July 31, 1989, but do not apply to amounts that are incurred pursuant to a contract that was binding on September 29, 1983, and at all times thereafter (unless the contract was renegotiated, extended, renewed, or revised after that date). Paragraph (c)(2) of this section applies to payments accrued on or after October 22, 2004. For payments accrued before October 22, 2004, see § 1.267(a)-3(c)(2), as contained in 26 CFR part 1, revised as of April 1, 2004. Paragraph (c)(4) of this section applies to payments accrued on or after October 1, 2019. For payments accrued before October 1, 2019, a taxpayer may apply paragraph (c)(4) of this section for payments accrued during the last taxable year of a foreign corporation beginning before January 1, 2018, and each subsequent taxable year of the foreign corporation, provided that the taxpayer and United States persons that are related (within the meaning of section 267 or 707) to the taxpayer consistently apply such paragraph with respect to all foreign corporations. For payments accrued before October 22, 2004, see § 1.267(a)-3(c)(4), as contained in 26 CFR part 1, revised as of April 1, 2004. [Reg. § 1.267(a)-3.]

☐ [*T.D. 8465, 12-31-92. Amended by T.D. 9908, 9-21-2020.*]

§ 1.267A-1. Disallowance of certain interest and royalty deductions.—(a) *Scope.*—This section and §§ 1.267A-2 through 1.267A-5 provide rules regarding when a deduction for any interest or royalty paid or accrued is disallowed under section 267A. Section 1.267A-2 describes hybrid and branch arrangements. Section 1.267A-3 provides rules for determining income inclusions and provides that certain amounts are not amounts for which a deduction is disallowed. Section 1.267A-4 provides an imported mismatch rule. Section 1.267A-5 sets forth definitions and special rules that apply for purposes of section 267A. Section 1.267A-6 illustrates the application of section 267A through examples. Section 1.267A-7 provides applicability dates.

(b) *Disallowance of deduction.*—This paragraph (b) sets forth the exclusive circumstances in which a deduction is disallowed under section 267A. Except as provided in paragraph (c) of this section, a specified party's deduction for any interest or royalty paid or accrued (the amount paid or accrued with respect to the specified party, a *specified payment*) is disallowed under section 267A to the extent that the specified payment is described in this paragraph (b). *See also* § 1.267A-5(b)(5) (treating structured payments as interest paid or accrued for purposes of section 267A and the regulations in this part under section 267A). A specified payment is described in this paragraph (b) to the extent that it is—

(1) A disqualified hybrid amount, as described in § 1.267A-2 (hybrid and branch arrangements);

(2) A disqualified imported mismatch amount, as described in § 1.267A-4 (payments offset by a hybrid deduction); or

(3) A specified payment for which the requirements of the anti-avoidance rule of § 1.267A-5(b)(6) are satisfied.

(c) *De minimis exception.*—Paragraph (b) of this section does not apply to a specified party for a taxable year in which the sum of the specified party's specified payments that but for this paragraph (c) would be described in paragraph (b) of this section is less than $50,000. For purposes of this paragraph (c), specified parties that are related (within the meaning of § 1.267A-5(a)(14)) are treated as a single specified party. [Reg. § 1.267(A) 1.]

☐ [*T.D. 9896, 4-7-2020.*]

§ 1.267A-2. Hybrid and branch arrangements.—(a) *Payments pursuant to hybrid transactions.*—(1) *In general.*—If a specified payment is made pursuant to a hybrid transaction, then, subject to § 1.267A-3(b) (amounts included or includible in income), the payment is a disqualified hybrid amount to the extent that—

(i) A specified recipient of the payment does not include the payment in income, as determined under § 1.267A-3(a) (to such extent, a *no-inclusion*); and

(ii) The specified recipient's no-inclusion is a result of the payment being made pursuant to the hybrid transaction. For purposes of this paragraph (a)(1)(ii), the specified recipient's no-inclusion is a result of the specified payment being made pursuant to the hybrid transaction to the extent that the no-inclusion would not occur were the specified recipient's tax law to treat the payment as interest or a royalty, as applicable. See § 1.267A-6(c)(1) and (2) for examples illustrating the application of paragraph (a) of this section.

(2) *Definition of hybrid transaction.*—(i) *In general.*—The term *hybrid transaction* means any transaction, series of transactions, agreement, or instrument one or more payments with respect to which are treated as interest or royalties for U.S. tax purposes but are not so treated for purposes of the tax law of a specified recipient of the payment. Examples of a hybrid transaction include an instrument a payment with respect to which is treated as interest for U.S. tax purposes but, for purposes of a specified recipient's tax law, is treated as a distribution with respect to equity or a recovery of principal with respect to indebtedness.

(ii) *Special rules.*—(A) *Long-term deferral.*—A specified payment is deemed to be made pursuant to a hybrid transaction if the taxable year in which a specified recipient of the payment takes the payment into account in income under its tax law (or, based on all the facts and circumstances, is reasonably expected to take the payment into account in income under its tax law) ends more than 36 months after the end of the taxable year in which the specified party would be allowed a deduction for the payment under U.S. tax law. In addition, if the tax law of a specified recipient of the specified payment does not impose an income tax, then such tax law does not cause the payment to be deemed to be made pursuant to a hybrid transaction under this paragraph (a)(2)(ii)(A). See § 1.267A-6(c)(8) for an example illustrating the application of this paragraph (a)(2)(ii)(A) in the context of the imported mismatch rule.

(B) *Royalties treated as payments in exchange for property under foreign law.*—In the case of a specified payment that is a royalty for U.S. tax purposes and for purposes of the tax law of a specified recipient of the payment is consideration received in exchange for property, the tax law of the specified recipient is not treated as causing the payment to be made pursuant to a hybrid transaction.

(C) *Coordination with disregarded payment rule.*—A specified payment is not considered made pursuant to a hybrid transaction if the payment is a disregarded payment, as described in paragraph (b)(2) of this section.

(3) *Payments pursuant to securities lending transactions, sale-repurchase transactions, or similar transactions.*—This paragraph (a)(3) applies if a specified payment is made pursuant to a repo transaction and is not regarded under a foreign tax law, but another amount connected to the payment (the *connected amount*) is regarded under such foreign tax law. For purposes of this paragraph (a)(3), a *repo transaction* means a transaction one or more payments with respect to which are treated as interest (as defined in § 1.267A-5(a)(12)) or a structured payment (as defined in § 1.267A-5(b)(5)(ii)) for U.S. tax purposes and that is a securities lending transaction or sale-repurchase transaction (including as described in § 1.861-2(a)(7)), or other similar transaction or series of related transactions in which legal title to property is transferred and the property (or similar property, such as securities of the same class and issue) is reacquired or expected to be reacquired. For example, this paragraph (a)(3) applies if a specified payment arising from characterizing a repo transaction of stock in accordance with its substance (that is, characterizing the specified

payment as interest) is not regarded as such under a foreign tax law but an amount consistent with the form of the transaction (such as a dividend) is regarded under such foreign tax law. When this paragraph (a)(3) applies, the determination of the identity of a specified recipient of the specified payment under the foreign tax law is made with respect to the connected amount. In addition, if the specified recipient includes the connected amount in income (as determined under § 1.267A-3(a), by treating the connected amount as the specified payment), then the amount of the specified recipient's no-inclusion with respect to the specified payment is correspondingly reduced. Further, the principles of this paragraph (a)(3) apply to cases similar to repo transactions in which a foreign tax law does not characterize the transaction in accordance with its substance. See § 1.267A-6(c)(2) for an example illustrating the application of this paragraph (a)(3).

(4) *Payments pursuant to interest-free loans and similar arrangements.*—In the case of a specified payment that is interest for U.S. tax purposes, the following special rules apply:

(i) The payment is deemed to be made pursuant to a hybrid transaction to the extent that—

(A) Under U.S. tax law, the payment is imputed (for example, under section 482 or 7872, including because the instrument pursuant to which it is made is indebtedness but the terms of the instrument provide for an interest rate equal to or less than the risk-free rate or the rate on sovereign debt with similar terms in the relevant foreign currency); and

(B) A tax resident or taxable branch to which the payment is made does not take the payment into account in income under its tax law because such tax law does not impute any interest. The rules of paragraph (b)(4) of this section apply for purposes of determining whether the specified payment is made indirectly to a tax resident or taxable branch.

(ii) A tax resident or taxable branch the tax law of which causes the payment to be deemed to be made pursuant to a hybrid transaction under paragraph (a)(4)(i) of this section is deemed to be a specified recipient of the payment for purposes of paragraph (a)(1) of this section.

(b) *Disregarded payments.*—(1) *In general.*—Subject to § 1.267A-3(b) (amounts included or includible in income), the excess (if any) of the sum of a specified party's disregarded payments for a taxable year over its dual inclusion income for the taxable year is a disqualified hybrid amount. See § 1.267A-6(c)(3) and (4) for examples illustrating the application of paragraph (b) of this section.

(2) *Definition of disregarded payment.*—(i) *In general.*—The term *disregarded payment* means a specified payment to the extent that, under the tax law of a tax resident or taxable branch to which the payment is made, the payment is not regarded (for example, because under such tax law it is a payment involving a single taxpayer or members of a group) and, were the payment to be regarded (and treated as interest or a royalty, as applicable) under such tax law, the tax resident or taxable branch would include the payment in income, as determined under § 1.267A-3(a).

(ii) *Special rules.*—(A) *Foreign consolidation and similar regimes.*—A disregarded payment includes a specified payment that, under the tax law of a tax resident or taxable branch to which the payment is made, is a payment that gives rise to a deduction or similar offset allowed to the tax resident or taxable branch (or group of entities that include the tax resident or taxable branch) under a foreign consolidation, fiscal unity, group relief, loss sharing, or any similar regime.

(B) *Certain payments of a U.S. taxable branch.*—In the case of a specified payment of a U.S. taxable branch, the payment is not a disregarded payment to the extent that under the tax law of the tax resident to which the payment is made the payment is otherwise taken into account. See paragraph (c)(2) of this section for an example of when an amount may be otherwise taken into account.

(C) *Coordination with other hybrid and branch arrangements.*—A disregarded payment does not include a deemed branch payment described in paragraph (c)(2) of this section, a specified payment pursuant to a repo transaction or similar transaction described in paragraph (a)(3) of this section, or a specified payment pursuant to an interest-free loan or similar transaction described in paragraph (a)(4) of this section.

(3) *Definition of dual inclusion income.*—(i) *In general.*—With respect to a specified party, the term *dual inclusion income* means the excess, if any, of—

(A) The sum of the specified party's items of income or gain for U.S. tax purposes that are included in the specified party's income, as determined under § 1.267A-3(a) (by treating the items of income or gain as the specified payment; and, in the case of a specified party that is a CFC, by treating U.S. tax law as the CFC's tax law), to the extent the items of income or gain are included in the income of the tax resident or taxable branch to which the disregarded payments are made, as determined under § 1.267A-3(a) (by treating the items of income or gain as the specified payment); over

(B) The sum of the specified party's items of deduction or loss for U.S. tax purposes (other than deductions for disregarded payments), to the extent the items of deduction or loss are allowable (or have been or will be allowable during a taxable year that ends no more than 36 months after the end of the specified party's taxable year) under the tax law of the tax resident or taxable branch to which the disregarded payments are made.

(ii) *Special rule for certain dividends.*—An item of income or gain of a specified party that is included in the specified party's income but not included in the income of the tax resident or taxable branch to which the disregarded payments are made is considered described in paragraph (b)(3)(i)(A) of this section to the extent that, under the tax resident's or taxable branch's tax law, the item is a dividend that would have been included in the income of the tax resident or taxable branch but for an exemption, exclusion, deduction, credit, or other similar relief particular to the item, provided that the party paying the item is not allowed a deduction or other tax benefit for it under its tax law. Similarly, an item of income or gain of a specified party that is included in the income of the tax resident or taxable branch to which the disregarded payments are made but not included in the specified party's income is considered described in paragraph (b)(3)(ii)(A) of this section to the extent that, under U.S. tax law, the item is a dividend that would have been included in the income of the specified party but for a dividends received deduction with respect to the dividend (for example, a deduction under section 245A(a)), provided that the party paying the item is not allowed a deduction or other tax benefit for it under its tax law. See § 1.267A-6(c)(3)(iv) for an example illustrating the application of this paragraph (b)(3)(ii).

(4) *Payments made indirectly to a tax resident or taxable branch.*—A specified payment made to an entity an interest of which is directly or indirectly (determined under the rules of section 958(a) without regard to whether an intermediate entity is foreign or domestic, or under substantially similar rules under a tax resident's or taxable branch's tax law) owned by a tax resident or taxable branch is considered made to the tax resident or taxable branch to the extent that, under the tax law of the tax resident or taxable branch, the entity to which the payment is made is fiscally transparent (and all intermediate entities, if any, are also fiscally transparent).

(c) *Deemed branch payments.*—(1) *In general.*—If a specified payment is a deemed branch payment, then the payment is a disqualified hybrid amount if the tax law of the home office provides an exclusion or exemption for income attributable to the branch. See § 1.267A-6(c)(4) for an example illustrating the application of this paragraph (c).

(2) *Definition of deemed branch payment.*—The term *deemed branch payment* means, with respect to a U.S. taxable branch that is a U.S. permanent establishment of a treaty resident eligible for benefits under an income tax treaty between the United States and the treaty country, any amount of interest or royalties allowable as a deduction in computing the business profits of the U.S. permanent establishment, to the extent the amount is deemed paid to the home office (or other branch of the home office), is not regarded (or otherwise taken into account) under the home office's tax law (or the other branch's tax law), and, were the payment to be regarded (and treated as interest or a royalty, as applicable) under the home office's tax law (or other branch's tax law), the home office (or other branch) would include the payment in income, as determined under § 1.267A-3(a). An amount may be otherwise taken into account for purposes of this paragraph (c)(2) if, for example, under the home office's tax law a corresponding amount of interest or royalties is allocated and attributable to the U.S. permanent establishment and is therefore not deductible.

(d) *Payments to reverse hybrids.*—(1) *In general.*—If a specified payment is made to a reverse hybrid, then, subject to § 1.267A-3(b) (amounts included or includible in income), the payment is a disqualified hybrid amount to the extent that—

(i) An investor, the tax law of which treats the reverse hybrid as not fiscally transparent, does not include the payment in income, as determined under § 1.267A-3(a) (to such extent, a *no-inclusion*); and

(ii) The investor's no-inclusion is a result of the payment being made to the reverse hybrid. For purposes of this paragraph (d)(1)(ii), the investor's no-inclusion is a result of the specified payment being made to the reverse hybrid to the extent that the no-inclusion would not occur were the investor's tax law to treat the reverse hybrid as fiscally transparent (and treat the payment as interest or a royalty, as applicable). See § 1.267A-6(c)(5) for an example illustrating the application of paragraph (d) of this section.

(2) *Definition of reverse hybrid.*—The term *reverse hybrid* means an entity (regardless of whether domestic or foreign) that is fiscally transparent under the tax law of the country in which it is created, organized, or otherwise established but not fiscally transparent under the tax law of an investor of the entity.

(3) *Payments made indirectly to a reverse hybrid.*—A specified payment made to an entity an interest of which is directly or indirectly (determined under the rules of section 958(a) without regard to whether an intermediate entity is foreign or domestic, or under substantially similar rules under a tax resident's or taxable branch's tax law) owned by a reverse hybrid is considered made to the reverse hybrid to the extent that, under the tax law of an investor of the reverse hybrid, the entity to which the payment is made is fiscally transparent (and all intermediate entities, if any, are also fiscally transparent).

(4) *Exception for inclusion by taxable branch in establishment country.*—Paragraph (d)(1) of this section does not apply to a specified payment made to a reverse hybrid to the extent that a taxable branch located in the country in which the reverse hybrid is created, organized, or otherwise established (and the activities of which are carried on by one or more investors of the reverse hybrid) includes the payment in income, as determined under § 1.267A-3(a).

(e) *Branch mismatch payments.*—(1) *In general.*—If a specified payment is a branch mismatch payment, then, subject to § 1.267A-3(b) (amounts included or includible in income), the payment is a disqualified hybrid amount to the extent that—

(i) A home office, the tax law of which treats the payment as income attributable to a branch of the home office, does not include the payment in income, as determined under § 1.267A-3(a) (to such extent, a *no-inclusion*); and

(ii) The home office's no-inclusion is a result of the payment being a branch mismatch payment. For purposes of this paragraph (e)(1)(ii), the home office's no-inclusion is a result of the specified payment being a branch mismatch payment to the extent that the no-inclusion would not occur were the home office's tax law to treat the payment as income that is not attributable a branch of the home office (and treat the payment as interest or a royalty, as applicable). See § 1.267A-6(c)(6) for an example illustrating the application of paragraph (e) of this section.

(2) *Definition of branch mismatch payment.*—The term *branch mismatch payment* means a specified payment for which the following requirements are satisfied:

(i) Under a home office's tax law, the payment is treated as income attributable to a branch of the home office; and

(ii) Either—

(A) The branch is not a taxable branch; or

(B) Under the branch's tax law, the payment is not treated as income attributable to the branch.

(f) *Relatedness or structured arrangement limitation.*—A specified recipient, a tax resident or taxable branch to which a specified payment is made, an investor, or a home office is taken into account for purposes of paragraphs (a), (b), (d), and (e) of this section, respectively, only if the specified recipient, the tax resident or taxable branch, the investor, or the home office, as applicable, is related (as defined in § 1.267A-5(a)(14)) to the specified party or is a party to a structured arrangement (as defined in § 1.267A-5(a)(20)) pursuant to which the specified payment is made. [Reg. § 1.267(A)-2.]

□ [*T.D.* 9896, 4-7-2020.]

§ 1.267A-3. Income inclusions and amounts not treated as disqualified hybrid amounts.—(a) *Income inclusions.*—(1) *General rule.*—For purposes of section 267A, a tax resident or taxable branch includes in income a specified payment to the extent that, under the tax law of the tax resident or taxable branch—

(i) It takes the payment into account (or has taken the payment into account, or, based on all the facts and circumstances, is reasonably expected to take the payment into account during a taxable year that ends no more than 36 months after the end of the specified party's taxable year) in its income or tax base at the full marginal rate imposed on ordinary income (or, if different, the full marginal rate imposed on interest or a royalty, as applicable); and

(ii) The payment is not reduced or offset by an exemption, exclusion, deduction, credit (other than for withholding tax imposed on the payment), or other similar relief particular to such type of payment. Examples of such reductions or offsets include a participation exemption, a dividends received deduction, a deduction or exclusion with respect to a particular category of income (such as income attributable to a branch, or royalties under a patent box regime), a credit for underlying taxes paid by a corporation from which a dividend is received, and a recovery of basis with respect to stock or a recovery of principal with respect to indebtedness. A specified payment is not considered reduced or offset by a deduction or other similar relief particular to the type of payment if it is offset by a generally applicable deduction or other tax attribute, such as a deduction for depreciation or a net operating loss. For purposes of this paragraph (a)(1)(ii), a deduction may be treated as being generally applicable even if it arises from a transaction related to the specified payment (for example, if the deduction and payment are in connection with a back-to-back financing arrangement).

(2) *Coordination with foreign hybrid mismatch rules.*—Whether a tax resident or taxable branch includes in income a specified payment is determined without regard to any defensive or secondary rule contained in hybrid mismatch rules, if any, under the tax law of the tax resident or taxable branch. For purposes of this paragraph (a)(2), a defensive or secondary rule means a provision of hybrid mismatch rules that requires a tax resident or taxable branch to include an amount in income if a deduction for the amount is not disallowed under the payer's tax law. However, a defensive or secondary rule does not include a rule pursuant to which a participation exemption or similar relief particular to a dividend is inapplicable as to a dividend for which the payer is allowed a deduction or other tax benefit under its tax law. Thus, a defensive or secondary rule does not include a rule consistent with recommendation 2.1 in Chapter 2 of OECD/G-20, *Neutralising the Effects of Hybrid Mismatch Arrangements, Action 2: 2015 Final Report* (October 2015).

(3) *Inclusions with respect to reverse hybrids.*—With respect to a tax resident or taxable branch that is an investor of a reverse hybrid, whether the investor includes in income a specified payment made to the reverse hybrid is determined without regard to a distribution from the reverse hybrid (or the right to a distribution from the reverse hybrid triggered by the payment). However, if the reverse hybrid distributes all of its income during a taxable year, then, for that year, the determination of whether an investor includes in income a specified payment made to the reverse hybrid is made with regard to one or more distributions from the reverse hybrid during the year, by treating a portion of the specified payment as relating to each distribution during the year. For purposes of this paragraph (a)(3), the portion of the specified payment that is considered to relate to a distribution is the lesser of—

(i) The specified payment multiplied by a fraction, the numerator of which is the amount of the distribution and the denominator of which is the aggregate amount of distributions from the reverse hybrid during the taxable year; and

(ii) The amount of the distribution multiplied by a fraction, the numerator of which is the specified payment and the denominator of which is the sum of all specified payments made to the reverse hybrid during the taxable year.

(4) *Inclusions with respect to certain payments pursuant to hybrid transactions.*—This paragraph (a)(4) applies to a specified payment that is interest and that is made pursuant to a hybrid transaction, to the extent that, under the tax law of a specified recipient of the payment, the payment is a recovery of basis with respect to stock or a recovery of principal with respect to indebtedness such that, but for this paragraph (a)(4), a no-inclusion would occur with respect to the specified recipient. In such a case, an amount that is a repayment of principal for U.S. tax purposes and that is or has been paid (or, based on all the facts and circumstances, is reasonably expected to be paid) by the specified party pursuant to the hybrid transaction (such amount, the *principal payment*) is, to the extent included in the income

of the specified recipient, treated as correspondingly reducing the specified recipient's no-inclusion with respect to the specified payment. For purposes of this paragraph (a)(4), whether the specified recipient includes the principal payment in income is determined under paragraph (a)(1) of this section, by treating the principal payment as the specified payment and the taxable year period described in paragraph (a)(1) as being composed of taxable years of the specified recipient ending no more than 36 months after the end of the specified party's taxable year during which the specified payment is made (as opposed to, for example, being composed of taxable years of the specified recipient ending no more than 36 months after the end of the specified party's taxable year during which the principal payment is reasonably expected to be made). Moreover, once a principal payment reduces a no-inclusion with respect to a specified payment, it is not again taken into account for purposes of applying this paragraph (a)(4) to another specified payment. See §1.267A-6(c)(1)(vi) for an example illustrating the application of this paragraph (a)(4).

(5) *Deemed full inclusions and de minimis inclusions.*—A preferential rate, exemption, exclusion, deduction, credit, or similar relief particular to a type of payment that reduces or offsets 90 percent or more of the payment is considered to reduce or offset 100 percent of the payment. In addition, a preferential rate, exemption, exclusion, deduction, credit, or similar relief particular to a type of payment that reduces or offsets 10 percent or less of the payment is considered to reduce or offset none of the payment.

(b) *Certain amounts not treated as disqualified hybrid amounts to extent included or includible in income for U.S. tax purposes.*—(1) *In general.*—A specified payment, to the extent that but for this paragraph (b) it would be a disqualified hybrid amount (such amount, a *tentative disqualified hybrid amount*), is reduced under the rules of paragraphs (b)(2) through (4) of this section, as applicable. The tentative disqualified hybrid amount, as reduced under such rules, is the disqualified hybrid amount. See §1.267A-6(c)(3) and (7) for examples illustrating the application of paragraph (b) of this section.

(2) *Included in income of United States tax resident or U.S. taxable branch.*—A tentative disqualified hybrid amount is reduced to the extent that a specified recipient that is a tax resident of the United States or a U.S. taxable branch takes the tentative disqualified hybrid amount into account in determining its gross income.

(3) *Includible in income under section 951(a)(1)(A).*—A tentative disqualified hybrid amount is reduced to the extent that the tentative disqualified hybrid amount is received by a CFC and includible under section 951(a)(1)(A) (determined without regard to properly allocable deductions of the CFC, qualified deficits under section 952(c)(1)(B), and the earnings and profits limitation under §1.952-1(c)) in the gross income of a United States shareholder of the CFC. However, if the United States shareholder is a domestic partnership, then the amount includible under section 951(a)(1)(A) in the gross income of the United States shareholder reduces the tentative disqualified hybrid amount only to the extent that a tax resident of the United States would take into account the amount.

(4) *Includible in income under section 951A(a).*—A tentative disqualified hybrid amount is reduced to the extent that the tentative disqualified hybrid amount increases a United States shareholder's pro rata share of tested income (as determined under §§1.951A-1(d)(2) and 1.951A-2(b)(1)) with respect to a CFC, reduces the shareholder's pro rata share of tested loss (as determined under §§1.951A-1(d)(4) and 1.951A-2(b)(2)) of the CFC, or both. However, to the extent that a deduction for the tentative disqualified hybrid amount would be allowed to a tax resident of the United States or a U.S. taxable branch, or would be allowed to a CFC but would be allocated and apportioned to gross income of the CFC that is gross income taken into account in determining subpart F income (as described in section 952) or gross income that is effectively connected (or treated as effectively connected) with the conduct of a trade or business in the United States (as described in §1.882-4(a)(1)), the reduction provided under this paragraph (b)(4) is equal to the reduction that would be provided under this paragraph (b)(4) but for this sentence multiplied by the difference of 100 percent and the percentage described in section 250(a)(1)(B).

(5) *Includible in income under section 1293.*—A tentative disqualified hybrid amount is reduced to the extent that the tentative disqualified hybrid amount is received by a qualified electing fund (as described in section 1295) and is includible under section 1293 in the gross income of a United States person that owns stock of that fund. However, if the United States person is a domestic partnership, then the amount includible under section 1293 in the gross income of the United States person reduces the tentative disqualified hybrid amount only to the extent that a tax resident of the United States would take into account the amount. [Reg. §1.267(A)-3.]

□ [*T.D. 9896*, 4-7-2020.]

§1.267A-4. Disqualified imported mismatch amounts.—(a) *Disqualified imported mismatch amounts.*—(1) *Rule.*—An imported mismatch payment is a disqualified imported mismatch amount to the extent that, under the set-off rules of paragraph (c) of this section, the income attributable to the payment is directly or indirectly offset by a hybrid deduction incurred by a foreign tax resident or foreign taxable branch that is related to the imported mismatch payer (or that is a party to a structured arrangement pursuant to which the payment is made). See §1.267A-6(c)(8) through (12) for examples illustrating the application of this section.

(2) *Definitions of certain terms.*—The following definitions apply for purposes of this section:

(i) A *foreign tax resident* means a tax resident that is not a tax resident of the United States.

(ii) A *foreign taxable branch* means a taxable branch that is not a U.S. taxable branch.

(iii) An *imported mismatch payee* means, with respect to an imported mismatch payment, a foreign tax resident or foreign taxable branch that includes the payment in income, as determined under §1.267A-3(a).

(iv) An *imported mismatch payer* means, with respect to an imported mismatch payment, the specified party.

(v) An *imported mismatch payment* means a specified payment to the extent that it is neither a disqualified hybrid amount nor included or includible in income in the United States. For purposes of this paragraph (a)(2)(v), a specified payment is included or includible in income in the United States to the extent that, if the payment were a tentative disqualified hybrid amount (as described in §1.267A-3(b)(1)), it would be reduced under the rules of §1.267A-3(b)(2) through (5).

(b) *Hybrid deduction.*—(1) *In general.*—A *hybrid deduction* means any of the following:

(i) A deduction allowed to a foreign tax resident or foreign taxable branch under its tax law for an amount paid or accrued that is interest (including an amount that would be a structured payment under the principles of §1.267A-5(b)(5)(ii)) or royalty under such tax law, to the extent that a deduction for the amount would be disallowed if such tax law contained rules substantially similar to those under §§1.267A-1 through 1.267A-3 and 1.267A-5. Such a deduction is a hybrid deduction regardless of whether or how the amount giving rise to the deduction would be recognized under U.S. tax law.

(ii) A deduction allowed to a foreign tax resident or foreign taxable branch under its tax law with respect to equity (including deemed equity), such as a notional interest deduction (or similar deduction determined with respect to the foreign tax resident's or foreign taxable branch's equity). However, a deduction allowed to a foreign tax resident or foreign taxable branch with respect to equity is a hybrid deduction only to the extent that an investor of the foreign tax resident, or the home office of the foreign taxable branch, would include the amount in income if, for purposes of the investor's or home office's tax law, the amount were interest paid by the foreign tax resident ratably (by value) with respect to the interests of the foreign tax resident, or interest paid by the foreign taxable branch to the home office. For purposes of this paragraph (b)(1)(ii), the rules of §1.267A-3(a) apply to determine the extent that an investor or home office would include an amount in income, by treating the amount as the specified payment.

(2) *Special rules.*—(i) *Foreign tax law contains hybrid mismatch rules.*—In the case of a foreign tax resident or foreign taxable branch the tax law of which contains hybrid mismatch rules, only the following deductions allowed to the foreign tax resident or foreign taxable branch under its tax law are hybrid deductions:

(A) A deduction described in paragraph (b)(1)(i) of this section, to the extent that the deduction would be disallowed if the foreign tax resident's or foreign taxable branch's tax law—

(1) Contained a rule substantially similar to §1.267A-2(a)(4) (payments pursuant to interest-free loans and similar arrangements); or

(2) Did not permit an inclusion in income in a third country to discharge the application of its hybrid mismatch rules as

to the amount giving rise to the deduction when the amount is not included in income in another country as a result of a hybrid or branch arrangement.

(B) A deduction described in paragraph (b)(1)(ii) of this section (deductions with respect to equity).

(ii) *Dual inclusion income used to determine hybrid deductions arising from deemed branch payments in certain cases.*—In the case of a foreign taxable branch the tax law of which permits a loss of the foreign taxable branch to be shared with a tax resident or taxable branch (without regard to whether it is in fact so shared or whether there is a tax resident or taxable branch with which the loss can be shared), a deduction allowed to the foreign taxable branch for an amount that would be a deemed branch payment were such tax law to contain a provision substantially similar to § 1.267A-2(c) is a hybrid deduction to the extent of the excess (if any) of the sum of all such amounts over the foreign taxable branch's dual inclusion income (as determined under the principles of § 1.267A-2(b)(3)). The rule in this paragraph (b)(2)(ii) applies without regard to whether the tax law of the home office provides an exclusion or exemption for income attributable to the branch.

(iii) *Certain deductions are hybrid deductions only if allowed for an accounting period beginning on or after December 20, 2018.*—A deduction described in paragraph (b)(1)(ii) of this section (deductions with respect to equity), or a deduction that would be disallowed if the foreign tax resident's or foreign taxable branch's tax law contained a rule substantially similar to § 1.267A-2(a)(4) (payments pursuant to interest-free loans and similar arrangements), is a hybrid deduction only if allowed for an accounting period beginning on or after December 20, 2018.

(iv) *Certain deductions of a CFC are not hybrid deductions.*—A deduction that but for this paragraph (b)(2)(iv) would be a hybrid deduction is not a hybrid deduction to the extent that the amount paid or accrued giving rise to the deduction is—

(A) A disqualified hybrid amount (but subject to the special rule of paragraph (g) of this section); or

(B) Included or includible in income in the United States. For purposes of this paragraph (b)(2)(iv)(B), an amount is included or includible in income in the United States to the extent that, if the amount were a tentative disqualified hybrid amount (as described in § 1.267A-3(b)(1)), it would be reduced under the rules of § 1.267A-3(b)(2) through (5).

(v) *Loss carryovers.*—A hybrid deduction for a particular accounting period includes a loss carryover from another accounting period, but only to the extent that a hybrid deduction incurred in an accounting period ending on or after December 20, 2018, comprises the loss carryover.

(c) *Set-off rules.*—(1) *In general.*—In the order described in paragraph (c)(2) of this section, a hybrid deduction directly or indirectly offsets the income attributable to an imported mismatch payment to the extent that, under paragraph (c)(3) of this section, the payment directly or indirectly funds the hybrid deduction. The rules of paragraphs (c)(2) and (3) of this section are applied by taking into account the application of paragraph (c)(4) of this section (adjustments to ensure that amounts not taken into account more than once).

(2) *Ordering rules.*—The following ordering rules apply for purposes of determining the extent that a hybrid deduction directly or indirectly offsets income attributable to imported mismatch payments.

(i) First, the hybrid deduction offsets income attributable to a factually-related imported mismatch payment that directly or indirectly funds the hybrid deduction. For purposes of this paragraph (c)(2)(i), a *factually-related imported mismatch payment* means an imported mismatch payment that is made pursuant to a transaction, agreement, or instrument entered into pursuant to the same plan or series of related transactions that includes the transaction, agreement, or instrument pursuant to which the hybrid deduction is incurred, provided that a design of the plan or series of related transactions was for the hybrid deduction to offset income attributable to the payment (as determined under the principles of § 1.267A-5(a)(20)(i), by treating the offset as the "hybrid mismatch" described in § 1.267A-5(a)(20)(i)).

(ii) Second, to the extent remaining, the hybrid deduction offsets income attributable to an imported mismatch payment (other than a factually-related imported mismatch payment) that directly funds the hybrid deduction.

(iii) Third, to the extent remaining, the hybrid deduction offsets income attributable to an imported mismatch payment (other than a factually-related imported mismatch payment) that indirectly funds the hybrid deduction.

(3) *Funding rules.*—The following funding rules apply for purposes of determining the extent that an imported mismatch payment directly or indirectly funds a hybrid deduction.

(i) The imported mismatch payment directly funds a hybrid deduction to the extent that the imported mismatch payee incurs the hybrid deduction.

(ii) The imported mismatch payment indirectly funds a hybrid deduction to the extent that the imported mismatch payee is allocated the hybrid deduction, and provided that the imported mismatch payee is related to the imported mismatch payer (or is a party to a structured arrangement pursuant to which the imported mismatch payment is made).

(iii) The imported mismatch payee is allocated a hybrid deduction to the extent that the imported mismatch payee directly or indirectly makes a funded taxable payment to the foreign tax resident or foreign taxable branch that incurs the hybrid deduction.

(iv) An imported mismatch payee indirectly makes a funded taxable payment to the foreign tax resident or foreign taxable branch that incurs a hybrid deduction to the extent that a chain of funded taxable payments connects the imported mismatch payee, each intermediary foreign tax resident or foreign taxable branch, and the foreign tax resident or foreign taxable branch that incurs the hybrid deduction, and provided that each intermediary foreign tax resident or foreign taxable branch is related to the imported mismatch payer (or is a party to a structured arrangement pursuant to which the imported mismatch payment is made).

(v) The term *funded taxable payment* means an amount paid or accrued by a foreign tax resident or foreign taxable branch under its tax law (other than an amount that gives rise to a hybrid deduction), to the extent that—

(A) The amount is deductible (but, if such tax law contains hybrid mismatch rules, determined without regard to a provision substantially similar to this section);

(B) Another foreign tax resident or foreign taxable branch includes the amount in income, as determined under § 1.267A-3(a) (by treating the amount as the specified payment); and

(C) The amount is neither a disqualified hybrid amount (but subject to the special rule of paragraph (g) of this section) nor included or includible in income in the United States. For purposes of this paragraph (c)(3)(v)(C), an amount is included or includible in income in the United States to the extent that, if the amount were a tentative disqualified hybrid amount (as described in § 1.267A-3(b)(1)), it would be reduced under the rules of § 1.267A-3(b)(2) through (5).

(vi) If a deduction or loss that is not incurred by a foreign tax resident or foreign taxable branch is directly or indirectly made available to offset income of the foreign tax resident or foreign taxable branch under its tax law, then, for purposes of this paragraph (c), the foreign tax resident or foreign taxable branch to which the deduction or loss is made available and the foreign tax resident or foreign taxable branch that incurs the deduction or loss are treated as a single foreign tax resident or foreign taxable branch. For example, if a deduction or loss of one foreign tax resident is made available to offset income of another foreign tax resident under a tax consolidation, fiscal unity, group relief, loss sharing, or any similar regime, then the foreign tax residents are treated as a single foreign tax resident for purposes of this paragraph (c).

(vii) An imported mismatch payee that directly makes a funded taxable payment to the foreign tax resident or foreign taxable branch that incurs a hybrid deduction is allocated the hybrid deduction before the hybrid deduction (to the extent remaining) is allocated to an imported mismatch payee that indirectly makes a funded taxable payment to the foreign tax resident or foreign taxable branch that incurs the hybrid deduction.

(viii) An imported mismatch payee that, through a chain of funded taxable payments consisting of a particular number of funded taxable payments, indirectly makes a funded taxable payment to the foreign tax resident or foreign taxable branch that incurs a hybrid deduction is allocated the hybrid deduction before the hybrid deduction (to the extent remaining) is allocated to an imported mismatch payee that, through a chain of funded taxable payments consisting of a greater number of funded taxable payments, indirectly makes a funded taxable payment to the foreign tax resident or foreign taxable branch that incurs the hybrid deduction.

(4) *Adjustments to ensure amounts not taken into account more than once.*—To the extent that the income attributable to an imported mismatch payment is directly or indirectly offset by a hybrid deduction, the imported mismatch payment, the hybrid deduction, and, if applicable, each funded taxable payment comprising the chain of funded taxable payments connecting the imported mismatch payee, each intermediary foreign tax resident or foreign taxable branch, and the foreign tax resident or foreign taxable branch that incurs the hybrid deduction is correspondingly reduced; as a result, such amounts are not again taken into account under this section.

(d) *Calculations based on aggregate amounts during accounting period.*—For purposes of this section, amounts are determined on an accounting period basis. Thus, for example, the amount of imported mismatch payments made by an imported mismatch payer to a particular imported mismatch payee is equal to the aggregate amount of all such payments made by the imported mismatch payer during the accounting period.

(e) *Pro rata adjustments.*—Amounts are allocated on a pro rata basis if there would otherwise be more than one permissible manner in which to allocate the amounts. Thus, for example, if multiple imported mismatch payers make an imported mismatch payment to a single imported mismatch payee, the sum of such payments exceeds the hybrid deduction incurred by the imported mismatch payee, and the payments are not factually-related imported mismatch payments, then a pro rata portion of each imported mismatch payer's payment is considered to directly fund the hybrid deduction. See § 1.267A-6(c)(9) and (12) for examples illustrating the application of this paragraph (e).

(f) *Special rules regarding manner in which this section is applied.*—(1) *Initial application of this section.*—This section is first applied without regard to paragraph (f)(2) of this section and by taking into account only the following hybrid deductions:

(i) A hybrid deduction described in paragraph (b)(1)(i) of this section, to the extent that—

(A) The deduction would be disallowed if the foreign tax resident's or foreign taxable branch's tax law contained a rule substantially similar to § 1.267A-2(a)(4) (payments pursuant to interest-free loans and similar arrangements); or

(B) The paid or accrued amount giving rise to the deduction is included in income in a third country but is not included in income in another country as a result of a hybrid or branch arrangement.

(ii) A hybrid deduction described in paragraph (b)(1)(ii) of this section (deductions with respect to equity).

(2) *Subsequent application of this section takes into account certain amounts deemed to be imported mismatch payments.*—After this section is applied pursuant to the rules of paragraph (f)(1) of this section, the section is then applied by taking into account only hybrid deductions other than those described in paragraph (f)(1) of this section. In addition, when applying this section in the manner described in the previous sentence, for purposes of determining the extent to which the income attributable to an imported mismatch payment is directly or indirectly offset by a hybrid deduction, an amount paid or accrued by a foreign tax resident or foreign taxable branch that is not a specified party is deemed to be an imported mismatch payment (and such foreign tax resident or foreign taxable branch and a foreign tax resident or foreign taxable branch that includes the amount in income, as determined under § 1.267A-3(a), by treating the amount as the specified payment, are deemed to be an imported mismatch payer and an imported mismatch payee, respectively) to the extent that—

(i) The tax law of such foreign tax resident or foreign taxable branch contains hybrid mismatch rules; and

(ii) The amount is subject to disallowance under a provision of the hybrid mismatch rules substantially similar to this section. See § 1.267A-6(c)(10) and (12) for examples illustrating the application of paragraph (f)(2) of this section.

(g) *Special rule regarding extent to which a disqualified hybrid amount of a CFC prevents a hybrid deduction or a funded taxable payment.*—A disqualified hybrid amount of a CFC is taken into account for purposes of paragraph (b)(2)(iv)(A) or (c)(3)(v)(C) of this section (certain deductions not hybrid deductions or funded taxable payments to the extent the amount giving rise to the deduction is a disqualified hybrid amount) only to the extent of the excess (if any) of the disqualified hybrid amount over the sum of the amounts described in paragraphs (g)(1) through (3) of this section. See § 1.267A-6(c)(11) for an example illustrating the application of this paragraph (g).

(1) The disqualified hybrid amount to the extent that, if allowed as a deduction, it would be allocated and apportioned to residual CFC gross income (as described in § 1.951A-2(c)(5)(iii)(B)) of the CFC.

(2) The disqualified hybrid amount to the extent that, if allowed as a deduction, it would be allocated and apportioned (under the rules of section 954(b)(5)) to gross income that is taken into account in determining the CFC's subpart F income (as described in section 952 and § 1.952-1), multiplied by the difference of 100 percent and the percentage of stock (by value) of the CFC that, for purposes of sections 951 and 951A, is owned (within the meaning of section 958(a), and determined by treating a domestic partnership as foreign) by one or more tax residents of the United States that are United States shareholders of the CFC.

(3) The disqualified hybrid amount to the extent that, if allowed as a deduction, it would be allocated and apportioned (under the rules of § 1.951A-2(c)(3)) to gross tested income of the CFC (as described in section 951A(c)(2)(A) and § 1.951A-2(c)(1)), multiplied by the difference of 100 percent and the percentage of stock (by value) of the CFC that, for purposes of sections 951 and 951A, is owned (within the meaning of section 958(a), and determined by treating a domestic partnership as foreign) by one or more tax residents of the United States that are United States shareholders of the CFC. [Reg. § 1.267(A)-4.]

☐ [*T.D.* 9896, 4-7-2020.]

§ 1.267A-5. Definitions and special rules.—(a) *Definitions.*—For purposes of §§ 1.267A-1 through 1.267A-7 the following definitions apply.

(1) The term *accounting period* means a taxable year, or a period of similar length over which, under a provision of hybrid mismatch rules substantially similar to § 1.267A-4, computations similar to those under § 1.267A-4 are made under a foreign tax law.

(2) The term *branch* means a taxable presence of a tax resident in a country other than its country of residence as determined under either the tax resident's tax law or such other country's tax law.

(3) The term *branch mismatch payment* has the meaning provided in § 1.267A-2(e)(2).

(4) The term *controlled foreign corporation* (or *CFC*) has the meaning provided in section 957.

(5) The term *deemed branch payment* has the meaning provided in § 1.267A-2(c)(2).

(6) The term *disregarded payment* has the meaning provided in § 1.267A-2(b)(2).

(7) The term *entity* means any person as described in section 7701(a)(1), including an entity that under §§ 301.7701-1 through 301.7701-3 of this chapter is disregarded as an entity separate from its owner, other than an individual.

(8) The term *fiscally transparent* means, with respect to an entity, fiscally transparent with respect to an item of income as determined under the principles of § 1.894-1(d)(3)(ii) and (iii), without regard to whether a tax resident (either the entity or interest holder in the entity) that derives the item of income is a resident of a country that has an income tax treaty with the United States. In addition, the following special rules apply with respect to an item of income received by an entity:

(i) The entity is fiscally transparent with respect to the item under the tax law of the country in which the entity is created, organized, or otherwise established if, under that tax law, the entity does not take the item into account in its income (without regard to whether such tax law requires an investor of the entity, wherever resident, to separately take into account on a current basis the investor's respective share of the item), and the effect under that tax law is that an investor of the entity is required to take the item into account in its income as if the item were realized directly from the source from which realized by the entity, whether or not distributed.

(ii) The entity is fiscally transparent with respect to the item under the tax law of an investor of the entity if, under that tax law, an investor of the entity takes the item into account in its income (without regard to whether such tax law requires the investor to separately take into account on a current basis the investor's respective share of the item) as if the item were realized directly from the source from which realized by the entity, whether or not distributed.

(iii) The entity is fiscally transparent with respect to the item under the tax law of the country in which the entity is created, organized, or otherwise established if—

(A) That tax law imposes a corporate income tax; and

(B) Under that tax law, neither the entity is required to take the item into account in its income nor an investor of the entity is required to take the item into account in its income as if the item were realized directly from the source from which realized by the entity, whether or not distributed.

(9) The term *home office* means a tax resident that has a branch.

(10) The term *hybrid mismatch rules* means rules, regulations, or other tax guidance substantially similar to section 267A, and includes rules the purpose of which is to neutralize the deduction/no-inclusion outcome of hybrid and branch mismatch arrangements. Examples of such rules would include rules based on, or substantially similar to, the recommendations contained in OECD/G-20, *Neutralising the Effects of Hybrid Mismatch Arrangements, Action 2: 2015 Final Report* (October 2015), and OECD/G-20, *Neutralising the Effects of Branch Mismatch Arrangements, Action 2: Inclusive Framework on BEPS* (July 2017).

(11) The term *hybrid transaction* has the meaning provided in § 1.267A-2(a)(2).

(12) The term *interest* means any amount described in paragraph (a)(12)(i) or (ii) of this section that is paid or accrued, or treated as paid or accrued, for the taxable year or that is otherwise designated as interest expense in paragraph (a)(12)(i) or (ii) of this section.

(i) *In general.*—Interest is an amount paid, received, or accrued as compensation for the use or forbearance of money under the terms of an instrument or contractual arrangement, including a series of transactions, that is treated as a debt instrument for purposes of section 1275(a) and § 1.1275-1(d), and not treated as stock under § 1.385-3, or an amount that is treated as interest under other provisions of the Internal Revenue Code (Code) or the regulations in this part. Thus, interest includes, but is not limited to, the following—

(A) Original issue discount (OID);

(B) Qualified stated interest, as adjusted by the issuer for any bond issuance premium;

(C) OID on a synthetic debt instrument arising from an integrated transaction under § 1.1275-6;

(D) Repurchase premium to the extent deductible by the issuer under § 1.163-7(c);

(E) Deferred payments treated as interest under section 483;

(F) Amounts treated as interest under a section 467 rental agreement;

(G) Forgone interest under section 7872;

(H) De minimis OID taken into account by the issuer;

(I) Amounts paid in connection with a sale-repurchase agreement treated as indebtedness under Federal tax principles;

(J) Redeemable ground rent treated as interest under section 163(c); and

(K) Amounts treated as interest under section 636.

(ii) *Swaps with significant nonperiodic payments.*—(A) *In general.*—Except as provided in paragraphs (a)(12)(ii)(B) and (C) of this section, a swap with significant nonperiodic payments is treated as two separate transactions consisting of an on-market, level payment swap and a loan. The loan must be accounted for by the parties to the contract independently of the swap. The time value component associated with the loan, determined in accordance with § 1.446-3(f)(2)(iii)(A), is recognized as interest expense to the payor.

(B) *Exception for cleared swaps.*—Paragraph (a)(12)(ii)(A) of this section does not apply to a cleared swap. The term *cleared swap* means a swap that is cleared by a derivatives clearing organization, as such term is defined in section 1a of the Commodity Exchange Act (7 U.S.C. 1a), or by a clearing agency, as such term is defined in section 3 of the Securities Exchange Act of 1934 (15 U.S.C. 78c), that is registered as a derivatives clearing organization under the Commodity Exchange Act or as a clearing agency under the Securities Exchange Act of 1934, respectively, if the derivatives clearing organization or clearing agency requires the parties to the swap to post and collect margin or collateral.

(C) *Exception for non-cleared swaps subject to margin or collateral requirements.*—Paragraph (a)(12)(ii)(A) of this section does not apply to a non-cleared swap that requires the parties to meet the margin or collateral requirements of a Federal regulator or that provides for margin or collateral requirements that are substantially similar to a cleared swap or a non-cleared swap subject to the margin or collateral requirements of a Federal regulator. For purposes of this paragraph (a)(12)(ii)(C), the term *Federal regulator* means the Securities and Exchange Commission (SEC), the Commodity Futures Trading Commission (CFTC), or a prudential regulator, as defined in section 1a(39) of the Commodity Exchange Act (7 U.S.C. 1a), as amended by section 721 of the Dodd-Frank Wall Street Reform and Consumer Protection Act of 2010, Public Law No. 111-203, 124 Stat. 1376, Title VII.

(13) The term *investor* means, with respect to an entity, any tax resident or taxable branch that directly or indirectly (determined under the rules of section 958(a) without regard to whether an intermediate entity is foreign or domestic, or under substantially similar rules under a tax resident's or taxable branch's tax law) owns an interest in the entity.

(14) The term *related* has the meaning provided in this paragraph (a)(14). A tax resident or taxable branch is related to a specified party if the tax resident or taxable branch is a related person within the meaning of section 954(d)(3), determined by treating the specified party as the "controlled foreign corporation" referred to in section 954(d)(3) and the tax resident or taxable branch as the "person" referred to in section 954(d)(3). In addition, for the purposes of this paragraph (a)(14), a tax resident that under §§ 301.7701-1 through 301.7701-3 of this chapter is disregarded as an entity separate from its owner for U.S. tax purposes, as well as a taxable branch, is treated as a corporation. *See also* § 1.954-1(f)(2)(iv)(B)(*1*) (neither section 318(a)(3), nor § 1.958-2(d) or the principles thereof, applies to attribute stock or other interests).

(15) The term *reverse hybrid* has the meaning provided in § 1.267A-2(d)(2).

(16) The term *royalty* includes amounts paid or accrued as consideration for the use of, or the right to use—

(i) Any copyright, including any copyright of any literary, artistic, scientific or other work (including cinematographic films and software);

(ii) Any patent, trademark, design or model, plan, secret formula or process, or other similar property (including goodwill); or

(iii) Any information concerning industrial, commercial or scientific experience, but does not include—

(A) Amounts paid or accrued for after-sales services;

(B) Amounts paid or accrued for services rendered by a seller to the purchaser under a warranty;

(C) Amounts paid or accrued for pure technical assistance; or

(D) Amounts paid or accrued for an opinion given by an engineer, lawyer or accountant.

(17) The term *specified party* means a tax resident of the United States, a CFC (other than a CFC with respect to which there is not a tax resident of the United States that, for purposes of sections 951 and 951A, owns (within the meaning of section 958(a), and determined by treating a domestic partnership as foreign) at least ten percent (by vote or value) of the stock of the CFC), and a U.S. taxable branch. Thus, an entity that is fiscally transparent for U.S. tax purposes is not a specified party, though an owner of the entity may be a specified party. For example, in the case of a payment by a partnership, a domestic corporation that is a partner of the partnership is a specified party and a deduction for its allocable share of the payment is subject to disallowance under section 267A.

(18) The term *specified payment* has the meaning provided in § 1.267A-1(b).

(19) The term *specified recipient* means, with respect to a specified payment, any tax resident that derives the payment under its tax law or any taxable branch to which the payment is attributable under its tax law (or any tax resident that, based on all the facts and circumstances, is reasonably expected to derive the payment under its tax law, or any taxable branch to which, based on all the facts and circumstances, the payment is reasonably expected to be attributable under its tax law). The principles of § 1.894-1(d)(1) apply for purposes of determining whether a tax resident derives (or is reasonably expected to derive) a specified payment under its tax law, without regard to whether the tax resident is a resident of a country that has an income tax treaty with the United States. There may be more than one specified recipient with respect to a specified payment.

(20) The terms *structured arrangement* and *party to a structured arrangement* have the meaning set forth in this paragraph (a)(20).

(i) *Structured arrangement.*—A structured arrangement means an arrangement with respect to which one or more specified payments would be a disqualified hybrid amount (or a disqualified imported mismatch amount) without regard to the relatedness limitation in § 1.267A-2(f) (or without regard to the phrase "that is related to the specified party" in § 1.267A-4(a)) (either such outcome, a *hybrid mismatch*), provided that, based on all the facts and circumstances (including the terms of the arrangement), the arrangement is designed to produce the hybrid mismatch. Facts and circumstances that indicate the arrangement is designed to produce the hybrid mismatch include the following:

(A) The hybrid mismatch is priced into the terms of the arrangement, including—

(1) The pricing of the arrangement is different from what the pricing would have been absent the hybrid mismatch;

(2) Features that alter the terms of the arrangement, including its return if the hybrid mismatch is no longer available; or

(3) A below-market return absent the tax effects or benefits resulting from the hybrid mismatch.

(B) The arrangement is marketed as tax-advantaged where some or all of the tax advantage derives from the hybrid mismatch.

(C) The arrangement is marketed to tax residents of a country the tax law of which enables the hybrid mismatch.

(ii) *Party to a structured arrangement.*—A party to a structured arrangement means a tax resident, a taxable branch, or an entity that participates in the structured arrangement. For purposes of this paragraph (a)(20)(ii), in the case of an entity, the entity's participation in a structured arrangement is imputed to its investors. However, a tax resident, a taxable branch or an entity (the *relevant party*) is considered to participate in the structured arrangement only if—

(A) The relevant party (or a related tax resident or taxable branch, determined under paragraph (a)(14) of this section by treating the relevant party as a specified party) could, based on all the facts and circumstances, reasonably be expected to be aware of the hybrid mismatch; and

(B) The relevant party or one or more of its investors (or a related tax resident or taxable branch, determined under paragraph (a)(14) of this section by treating the relevant party or an investor as a specified party) shares in the value of the tax benefit resulting from the hybrid mismatch.

(21) The term *tax law* of a country includes statutes, regulations, administrative or judicial rulings, and income tax treaties of the country. If a country has an income tax treaty with the United States that applies to taxes imposed by a political subdivision or other local authority of that country, then the tax law of the political subdivision or other local authority is deemed to be a tax law of a country. When used with respect to a tax resident or branch, tax law refers to—

(i) In the case of a tax resident, the tax law of the country or countries where the tax resident is resident; and

(ii) In the case of a branch, the tax law of the country where the branch is located.

(22) The term *taxable branch* means a branch that has a taxable presence under its tax law.

(23) The term *tax resident* means either of the following:

(i) A body corporate or other entity or body of persons liable to tax under the tax law of a country as a resident. For purposes of this paragraph (a)(23)(i), an entity that is created, organized, or otherwise established under the tax law of a country that does not impose a corporate income tax is treated as liable to tax under the tax law of such country as a resident if under the corporate or commercial laws of such country the entity is treated as a body corporate or a company. A body corporate or other entity or body of persons may be a tax resident of more than one country.

(ii) An individual liable to tax under the tax law of a country as a resident. An individual may be a tax resident of more than one country.

(24) The term *United States shareholder* has the meaning provided in section 951(b).

(25) The term *U.S. taxable branch* means a trade or business carried on in the United States by a tax resident of another country, except that if an income tax treaty applies, the term means a permanent establishment of a tax treaty resident eligible for benefits under an income tax treaty between the United States and the treaty country. Thus, for example, a U.S. taxable branch includes a U.S. trade or business of a foreign corporation taxable under section 882(a) or a U.S. permanent establishment of a tax treaty resident.

(b) *Special rules.*—For purposes of §§1.267A-1 through 1.267A-7, the following special rules apply.

(1) *Coordination with other provisions.*—(i) *In general.*—Except as provided in paragraph (b)(1)(ii) of this section, a specified payment is subject to section 267A after the application of any other applicable provisions of the Code and regulations in this part. Thus, the determination of whether a deduction for a specified payment is disallowed under section 267A is made with respect to the taxable year for which a deduction for the payment would otherwise be allowed for U.S. tax purposes. *See, for example,* sections 163(e)(3) and 267(a)(3) for rules that may defer the taxable year for which a deduction is allowed. *See also* §1.882-5(a)(5) (providing that provisions that disallow interest expense apply after the application of §1.882-5). In addition, provisions that characterize amounts paid or accrued as something other than interest or royalties, such as §1.894-1(d)(2), govern the treatment of such amounts and therefore such amounts would not be treated as specified payments. Moreover, to the extent that a specified payment is not described in §1.267A-1(b) when it is subject to section 267A, the payment is not again subject to section 267A at a later time. For example, if for the taxable year in which a specified payment is paid the payment is not described in §1.267A-1(b) but under section 163(j) a deduction for the payment is deferred, the payment is not again subject to section 267A in the taxable year for which section 163(j) no longer defers the deduction.

(ii) *Section 267A applied before certain provisions.*—In addition to the extent provided in any other applicable provision of the Code or regulations in this part, section 267A applies before the application of sections 163(j), 461(l), 465, and 469.

(iii) *Coordination with capitalization and recovery provisions.*—To the extent a specified payment is described in §1.267A-1(b), a deduction for the payment is considered permanently disallowed for all purposes of the Code and regulations in this part and, therefore, the payment is not taken into account for purposes of computing costs that are required to be capitalized and recovered through depreciation, amortization, cost of goods sold, adjustment to basis, or similar forms of recovery under any applicable provision of the Code or in regulations in this part. Thus, for example, to the extent an interest or royalty payment is a specified payment described in §1.267A-1(b), the payment is not capitalized and included in inventory cost or added to basis under section 263A. As an additional example, to the extent that a debt issuance cost is a specified payment described in §1.267A-1(b), it is neither capitalized under section 263 or the regulations in this part under section 263 nor recoverable under §1.446-5.

(iv) *Specified payments arising in taxable years beginning before January 1, 2018.*—Section 267A does not apply to a specified payment that is paid or accrued in a taxable year beginning before January 1, 2018, regardless of whether under a provision of the Code or regulations in this part (for example, section 267(a)(3)) a deduction for the payment is deferred to a taxable year beginning after December 31, 2017, or whether the payment is carried over to another taxable year and under another provision of the Code (for example, section 163(j)) is considered paid or accrued in such taxable year.

(2) *Foreign currency gain or loss.*—Except as set forth in this paragraph (b)(2), section 988 gain or loss is not taken into account under section 267A. Foreign currency gain or loss recognized with respect to a specified payment is taken into account under section 267A to the extent that a deduction for the specified payment is disallowed under section 267A, provided that the foreign currency gain or loss is described in §1.988-2(b)(4) (relating to exchange gain or loss recognized by the issuer of a debt instrument with respect to accrued interest) or §1.988-2(c) (relating to items of expense or gross income or receipts which are to be paid after the date accrued). If a deduction for a specified payment is disallowed under section 267A, then a proportionate amount of foreign currency loss under section 988 with respect to the specified payment is also disallowed, and a proportionate amount of foreign currency gain under section 988 with respect to the specified payment reduces the amount of the disallowance. For purposes of this paragraph (b)(2), the proportionate amount is the amount of the foreign currency gain or loss under section 988 with respect to the specified payment multiplied by a fraction, the numerator of which is the amount of the specified payment for which a deduction is disallowed under section 267A and the denominator of which is the total amount of the specified payment.

(3) *U.S. taxable branch payments.*—(i) *Amounts considered paid or accrued by a U.S. taxable branch.*—For purposes of section 267A, a U.S. taxable branch is considered to pay or accrue an amount of interest or royalty equal to either—

(A) The amount of interest or royalty allocable to effectively connected income of the U.S. taxable branch under section 873(a) or 882(c)(1), as applicable; or

(B) In the case of a U.S. taxable branch that is a U.S. permanent establishment of a treaty resident eligible for benefits under an income tax treaty between the United States and the treaty country, the amount of interest or royalty allowable in computing the business profits attributable to the U.S. permanent establishment.

(ii) *Treatment of U.S. taxable branch payments.*—(A) *Interest.*—Interest considered paid or accrued by a U.S. taxable branch of a foreign corporation under paragraph (b)(3)(i) of this section (the "U.S. taxable branch interest payment") is treated as a payment directly to the person to which the interest is payable, to the extent it is paid or accrued with respect to a liability described in § 1.882-5(a)(1)(ii)(A) or (B) (resulting in directly allocable interest) or with respect to a U.S. booked liability, as described in § 1.882-5(d)(2). If the U.S. taxable branch interest payment exceeds in the aggregate the interest paid or accrued on the U.S. taxable branch's directly allocable interest and interest paid or accrued on U.S. booked liabilities, the excess amount is treated as paid or accrued by the U.S. taxable branch on a pro-rata basis to the same persons and pursuant to the same terms that the home office paid or accrued interest, excluding any directly allocable interest or interest paid or accrued on a U.S. booked liability. The rules of this paragraph (b)(3)(ii) for determining to whom interest is paid or accrued apply without regard to whether the U.S. taxable branch interest payment is determined under the method described in § 1.882-5(b) through (d) or the method described in § 1.882-5(e).

(B) *Royalties.*—Royalties considered paid or accrued by a U.S. taxable branch under paragraph (b)(3)(i) of this section are treated solely for purposes of section 267A as paid or accrued on a pro-rata basis by the U.S. taxable branch to the same persons and pursuant to the same terms that the home office paid or accrued such royalties.

(C) *Permanent establishments and interbranch payments.*—If a U.S. taxable branch is a permanent establishment in the United States, the principles of the rules in paragraphs (b)(3)(ii)(A) and (B) of this section apply with respect to interest and royalties allowed in computing the business profits of a treaty resident eligible for treaty benefits. This paragraph (b)(3)(ii)(C) does not apply to interbranch interest or royalty payments allowed as deduction under certain U.S. income tax treaties (as described in § 1.267A-2(c)(2)).

(4) *Effect on earnings and profits.*—The disallowance of a deduction under section 267A does not affect whether the amount paid or accrued that gave rise to the deduction reduces earnings and profits of a corporation. However, for purposes of section 952(c)(1) and § 1.952-1(c), a CFC's earnings and profits are not reduced by a specified payment a deduction for which is disallowed under section 267A, if a principal purpose of the transaction pursuant to which the payment is made is to reduce or limit the CFC's subpart F income.

(5) *Application to structured payments.*—(i) *In general.*—For purposes of section 267A and the regulations in this part under section 267A, a structured payment (as defined in paragraph (b)(5)(ii) of this section) is treated as interest. Thus, a structured payment is treated as subject to section 267A and the regulations in this part under section 267A to the same extent as if the payment were an amount of interest paid or accrued.

(ii) *Structured payment.*—A structured payment means any amount described in paragraph (b)(5)(ii)(A) or (B) of this section.

(A) *Substitute interest payments.*—A substitute interest payment described in § 1.861-2(a)(7) is treated as a structured payment for purposes of section 267A, unless the payment relates to a sale-repurchase agreement or a securities lending transaction that is entered into by the payor in the ordinary course of the payor's business. This paragraph (b)(5)(ii)(A) does not apply to an amount described in paragraph (a)(12)(i)(I) of this section.

(B) *Amounts economically equivalent to interest.*—(1) *Principal purpose to reduce interest expense.*—Any expense or loss economically equivalent to interest is treated as a structured payment for purposes of section 267A if a principal purpose of structuring the transaction(s) is to reduce an amount incurred by the taxpayer that otherwise would have been described in paragraph (a)(12) or (b)(5)(ii)(A) of this section. For purposes of this paragraph (b)(5)(ii)(B)(*1*), the fact that the taxpayer has a business purpose for obtaining the use of funds does not affect the determination of whether the manner in which the taxpayer structures the transaction(s) is with a principal purpose of reducing the taxpayer's interest expense. In addition, the fact that the taxpayer has obtained funds at a lower pre-tax cost based on the structure of the transaction(s) does not affect the determination of whether the manner in which the taxpayer structures the transaction(s) is with a principal purpose of reducing the taxpayer's interest expense. For purposes of this paragraph (b)(5)(ii)(B), any expense or loss is economically equivalent to interest to the extent that the expense or loss is—

(*i*) Deductible by the taxpayer;

(*ii*) Incurred by the taxpayer in a transaction or series of integrated or related transactions in which the taxpayer secures the use of funds for a period of time;

(*iii*) Substantially incurred in consideration of the time value of money; and

(*iv*) Not described in paragraph (a)(12) or (b)(5)(ii)(A) of this section.

(*2*) *Principal purpose.*—Whether a transaction or a series of integrated or related transactions is entered into with a principal purpose described in paragraph (b)(5)(ii)(B)(*1*) of this section depends on all the facts and circumstances related to the transaction(s). A purpose may be a principal purpose even though it is outweighed by other purposes (taken together or separately). Factors to be taken into account in determining whether one of the taxpayer's principal purposes for entering into the transaction(s) include the taxpayer's normal borrowing rate in the taxpayer's functional currency, whether the taxpayer would enter into the transaction(s) in the ordinary course of the taxpayer's trade or business, whether the parties to the transaction(s) are related persons (within the meaning of section 267(b) or 707(b)), whether there is a significant and bona fide business purpose for the structure of the transaction(s), whether the transactions are transitory, for example, due to a circular flow of cash or other property, and the substance of the transaction(s).

(6) *Anti-avoidance rule.*—A specified party's deduction for a specified payment is disallowed to the extent that both of the following requirements are satisfied:

(i) The payment (or income attributable to the payment) is not included in the income of a tax resident or taxable branch, as determined under § 1.267A-3(a) (but without regard to the deemed full inclusion rule in § 1.267A-3(a)(5)).

(ii) A principal purpose of the terms or structure of the arrangement (including the form and the tax laws of the parties to the arrangement) is to avoid the application of the regulations in this part under section 267A in a manner that is contrary to the purposes of section 267A and the regulations in this part under section 267A. [Reg. § 1.267(A)-5.]

☐ [*T.D.* 9896, 4-7-2020 (*corrected* 8-11-2020).]

§ 1.267A-6. Examples.—(a) *Scope.*—This section provides examples that illustrate the application of § § 1.267A-1 through 1.267A-5.

(b) *Presumed facts.*—For purposes of the examples in this section, unless otherwise indicated, the following facts are presumed:

(1) US1, US2, and US3 are domestic corporations that are tax residents solely of the United States.

(2) FW, FX, and FZ are bodies corporate established in, and tax residents of, Country W, Country X, and Country Z, respectively. They are not fiscally transparent under the tax law of any country. They are not specified parties.

(3) Under the tax law of each country, interest and royalty payments are deductible.

(4) The tax law of each country provides a 100 percent participation exemption for dividends received from non-resident corporations.

(5) The tax law of each country, other than the United States, provides an exemption for income attributable to a branch.

(6) Except as provided in paragraphs (b)(4) and (5) of this section, all amounts derived (determined under the principles of § 1.894-1(d)(1)) by a tax resident, or attributable to a taxable branch, are included in income, as determined under § 1.267A-3(a).

(7) Only the tax law of the United States contains hybrid mismatch rules.

(c) *Examples.*—(1) *Example 1. Payment pursuant to a hybrid financial instrument.*—(i) *Facts.* FX holds all the interests of US1. FX also holds an instrument issued by US1 that is treated as equity for Country X tax purposes and indebtedness for U.S. tax purposes (the FX-US1 instrument). On date 1, US1 pays $50x to FX pursuant to the instrument. The amount is treated as an excludible dividend for Country X tax purposes (by reason of the Country X participation exemption) and as interest for U.S. tax purposes.

(ii) *Analysis.* US1 is a specified party and thus a deduction for its $50x specified payment is subject to disallowance under section 267A. As described in paragraphs (c)(1)(ii)(A) through (C) of this section, the entire $50x payment is a disqualified hybrid amount under the hybrid transaction rule of § 1.267A-2(a) and, as a result, a deduction for the payment is disallowed under § 1.267A-1(b)(1).

(A) US1's payment is made pursuant to a hybrid transaction because a payment with respect to the FX-US1 instrument is treated as interest for U.S. tax purposes but not for purposes of Country X tax law (the tax law of FX, a specified recipient that is related to US1). *See* § 1.267A-2(a)(2) and (f). Therefore, § 1.267A-2(a) applies to the payment.

(B) For US1's payment to be a disqualified hybrid amount under § 1.267A-2(a), a no-inclusion must occur with respect to FX. *See* § 1.267A-2(a)(1)(i). As a consequence of the Country X participation exemption, FX includes $0 of the payment in income and therefore a $50x no-inclusion occurs with respect to FX. *See* § 1.267A-3(a)(1). The result is the same regardless of whether, under the Country X participation exemption, the $50x payment is simply excluded from FX's taxable income or, instead, is reduced or offset by other means, such as a $50x dividends received deduction. *See* § 1.267A-3(a)(1).

(C) Pursuant to § 1.267A-2(a)(1)(ii), FX's $50x no-inclusion gives rise to a disqualified hybrid amount to the extent that it is a result of US1's payment being made pursuant to the hybrid transaction. FX's $50x no-inclusion is a result of the payment being made pursuant to the hybrid transaction because, were the payment to be treated as interest for Country X tax purposes, FX would include $50x in income and, consequently, the no-inclusion would not occur.

(iii) *Alternative facts – multiple specified recipients.* The facts are the same as in paragraph (c)(1)(i) of this section, except that FX holds all the interests of FZ, which is fiscally transparent for Country X tax purposes, and FZ holds all of the interests of US1. Moreover, the FX-US1 instrument is held by FZ (rather than by FX) and US1 makes its $50x payment to FZ (rather than to FX); the payment is derived by FZ under its tax law and by FX under its tax law and, accordingly, both FZ and FX are specified recipients of the payment. Further, the payment is treated as interest for Country Z tax purposes and FZ includes it in income. For the reasons described in paragraph (c)(1)(ii) of this section, FX's no-inclusion causes the payment to be a disqualified hybrid amount. FZ's inclusion in income (regardless of whether Country Z has a low or high tax rate) does not affect the result, because the hybrid transaction rule of § 1.267A-2(a) applies if any no-inclusion occurs with respect to a specified recipient of the payment as a result of the payment being made pursuant to the hybrid transaction.

(iv) *Alternative facts – preferential rate.* The facts are the same as in paragraph (c)(1)(i) of this section, except that for Country X tax purposes US1's payment is treated as a dividend subject to a 4% tax rate, whereas the marginal rate imposed on ordinary income is 20%. FX includes $10x of the payment in income, calculated as $50x multiplied by 0.2 (.04, the rate at which the particular type of payment (a dividend for Country X tax purposes) is subject to tax in Country X, divided by 0.2, the marginal tax rate imposed on ordinary income). *See* § 1.267A-3(a)(1). Thus, a $40x no-inclusion occurs with respect to FX ($50x less $10x). The $40x no-inclusion is a result of the payment being made pursuant to the hybrid transaction because, were the payment to be treated as interest for Country X tax purposes, FX would include the entire $50x in income at the full marginal rate imposed on ordinary income (20%) and, consequently, the no-inclusion would not occur. Accordingly, $40x of US1's payment is a disqualified hybrid amount.

(v) *Alternative facts – no-inclusion not the result of hybridity.* The facts are the same as in paragraph (c)(1)(i) of this section, except that Country X has a pure territorial regime (that is, Country X only taxes income with a domestic source). Although US1's payment is pursuant to a hybrid transaction and a $50x no-inclusion occurs with respect to FX, FX's no-inclusion is not a result of the payment being made pursuant to the hybrid transaction. This is because if Country X tax law were to treat the payment as interest, FX would include $0 in income and, consequently, the $50x no-inclusion would still occur. Accordingly, US1's payment is not a disqualified hybrid amount. *See* § 1.267A-2(a)(1)(ii). The result would be the same if Country X instead did not impose a corporate income tax.

(vi) *Alternative facts – indebtedness under both tax laws but different ordering rules give rise to hybrid transaction; reduction of no-inclusion by reason of inclusion of a principal payment.* The facts are the same as in paragraph (c)(1)(i) of this section, except that the FX-US1 instrument is indebtedness for both U.S. and Country X tax purposes. In addition, the $50x date 1 payment is treated as interest for U.S. tax purposes and a repayment of principal for Country X tax purposes. On date 1, based on all the facts and circumstances (including the terms of the FX-US1 instrument, the tax laws of the United States and Country X, and an absence of a plan pursuant to which FX would dispose of the FX-US1 instrument), it is reasonably expected that on date 2 (a date that is within 36 months after the end of the taxable year of US1 that includes date 1), US1 will pay a total of $200x to FX and that, for U.S. tax purposes, $25x will be treated as interest and $175x as a repayment of principal, and, for Country X tax purposes, $75x will be treated as interest (and included in FX's income) and $125x as a repayment of principal. US1's $50x specified payment is made pursuant to a hybrid transaction and, but for § 1.267A-3(a)(4), a $50x no-inclusion would occur with respect to FX. *See* § § 1.267A-2(a)(2) and 1.267A-3(a)(1). However, pursuant to § 1.267A-3(a)(4), FX's inclusion in income with respect to $50x of the date 2 amount that is a repayment of principal for U.S. tax purposes is treated as correspondingly reducing FX's no-inclusion with respect to the specified payment. As a result, as to US1's $50x specified payment, a no-inclusion does not occur with respect to FX. *See* § 1.267A-3(a)(4). Therefore, US1's $50x specified payment is not a disqualified hybrid amount. *See* § 1.267A-2(a)(1)(i).

(2) *Example 2. Payment pursuant to a repo transaction.*—(i) *Facts.* FX holds all the interests of US1, and US1 holds all the interests of US2. On date 1, US1 and FX enter into a sale and repurchase transaction. Pursuant to the transaction, US1 transfers shares of preferred stock of US2 to FX in exchange for $1,000x, subject to a binding commitment of US1 to reacquire those shares on date 3 for an agreed price, which represents a repayment of the $1,000x plus a financing or time value of money return reduced by the amount of any distributions paid with respect to the preferred stock between dates 1 and 3 that are retained by FX. On date 2, US2 pays a $100x dividend on its preferred stock to FX. For Country X tax purposes, FX is treated as owning the US2 preferred stock and therefore is the beneficial owner of the dividend. For U.S. tax purposes, the transaction is treated as a loan from FX to US1 that is secured by the US2 preferred stock. Thus, for U.S. tax purposes, US1 is treated as owning the US2 preferred stock and is the beneficial owner of the dividend. In addition, for U.S. tax purposes, US1 is treated as paying $100x of interest to FX (an amount corresponding to the $100x dividend paid by US2 to FX). Further, the marginal tax rate imposed on ordinary income under Country X tax law is 25%. Moreover, instead of a participation exemption, Country X tax law provides its tax residents a credit for underlying foreign taxes paid by a non-resident corporation from which a dividend is received; with respect to the $100x dividend received by FX from US2, the credit is $10x.

(ii) *Analysis.* US1 is a specified party and thus a deduction for its $100x specified payment is subject to disallowance under section 267A. As described in paragraphs (c)(2)(ii)(A) through (D) of this section, $40x of the payment is a disqualified hybrid amount under the hybrid transaction rule of § 1.267A-2(a) and, as a result, $40x of the deduction is disallowed under § 1.267A-1(b)(1).

(A) Although US1's $100x interest payment is not regarded under Country X tax law, a connected amount (US2's dividend payment) is regarded and derived by FX under such tax law. Thus, FX is considered a specified recipient with respect to US1's interest payment. *See* § 1.267A-2(a)(3).

(B) US1's payment is made pursuant to a hybrid transaction because a payment with respect to the sale and repurchase transaction is treated as interest for U.S. tax purposes but not for purposes of Country X tax law (the tax law of FX, a specified recipient that is related to US1), which does not regard the payment. *See* § 1.267A-2(a)(2) and (f). Therefore, § 1.267A-2(a) applies to the payment.

(C) For US1's payment to be a disqualified hybrid amount under § 1.267A-2(a), a no-inclusion must occur with respect to FX. *See* § 1.267A-2(a)(1)(i). As a consequence of Country X tax law not regarding US1's payment, FX includes $0 of the payment in income and therefore a $100x no-inclusion occurs with respect to FX. *See* § 1.267A-3(a). However, FX includes $60x of a connected amount (US2's dividend payment) in income, calculated as $100x (the amount of the dividend) less $40x (the portion of the connected amount that is not included in income in Country X due to the foreign tax credit, determined by dividing the amount of the credit, $10x, by 0.25, the tax rate in Country X). *See* § 1.267A-3(a). Pursuant to § 1.267A-2(a)(3), FX's inclusion in income with respect to the connected amount correspondingly reduces the amount of its no-inclusion with respect to US1's payment. Therefore, for purposes of § 1.267A-2(a), FX's no-inclusion with respect to US1's payment is $40x ($100x less $60x). *See* § 1.267A-2(a)(3).

(D) Pursuant to § 1.267A-2(a)(1)(ii), FX's $40x no-inclusion gives rise to a disqualified hybrid amount to the extent that FX's no-inclusion is a result of US1's payment being made pursuant to the hybrid transaction. FX's $40x no-inclusion is a result of US1's payment being made pursuant to the hybrid transaction because, were the sale and repurchase transaction to be treated as a loan from FX to US1 for Country X tax purposes, FX would include US1's $100x interest payment in income (because it would not be entitled to a foreign tax credit) and, consequently, the no-inclusion would not occur.

(iii) *Alternative facts – structured arrangement.* The facts are the same as in paragraph (c)(2)(i) of this section, except that FX is a bank that is unrelated to US1. In addition, the sale and repurchase transaction is a structured arrangement and FX is a party to the structured arrangement. The result is the same as in paragraph (c)(2)(ii) of this section. That is, even though FX is not related to US1, it is taken into account with respect to the determinations under § 1.267A-2(a) because it is a party to a structured arrangement pursuant to which the payment is made. *See* § 1.267A-2(f).

(3) *Example 3. Disregarded payment.*—(i) *Facts.* FX holds all the interests of US1. For Country X tax purposes, US1 is a disregarded entity of FX. During taxable year 1, US1 pays $100x to FX pursuant to a debt instrument. The amount is treated as interest for U.S. tax purposes but is disregarded for Country X tax purposes as a transaction involving a single taxpayer. During taxable year 1, US1's only other items of income, gain, deduction, or loss are $125x of gross income (the entire amount of which is included in US1's income) and a $60x item of deductible expense. The $125x item of gross income is included in FX's income, and the $60x item of deductible expense is allowable for Country X tax purposes.

(ii) *Analysis.* US1 is a specified party and thus a deduction for its $100x specified payment is subject to disallowance under section 267A. As described in paragraphs (c)(3)(ii)(A) and (B) of this section, $35x of the payment is a disqualified hybrid amount under the disregarded payment rule of § 1.267A-2(b) and, as a result, $35x of the deduction is disallowed under § 1.267A-1(b)(1).

(A) US1's $100x payment is not regarded under the tax law of Country X (the tax law of FX, a related tax resident to which the payment is made) because under such tax law the payment involves a single taxpayer. *See* § 1.267A-2(b)(2) and (f). In addition, were the tax law of Country X to regard the payment (and treat it as interest), FX would include it in income. Therefore, the payment is a disregarded payment to which § 1.267A-2(b) applies. *See* § 1.267A-2(b)(2).

(B) Under § 1.267A-2(b)(1), the excess (if any) of US1's disregarded payments for taxable year 1 ($100x) over its dual inclusion income for the taxable year is a disqualified hybrid amount. US1's dual inclusion income for taxable year 1 is $65x, calculated as $125x (the amount of US1's gross income that is included in FX's income) less $60x (the amount of US1's deductible expenses, other than deductions for disregarded payments, that are allowable for Country X tax purposes). *See* § 1.267A-2(b)(3). Therefore, $35x is a disqualified hybrid amount ($100x less $65x). *See* § 1.267A-2(b)(1).

(iii) *Alternative facts – non-dual inclusion income arising from hybrid transaction.* The facts are the same as in paragraph (c)(3)(i) of this section, except that US1 holds all the interests of FZ (a specified party that is a CFC) and US1's only item of income, gain, deduction, or loss during taxable year 1 (other than the $100x payment to FX) is $80x paid to US1 by FZ pursuant to an instrument treated as indebtedness for U.S. and Country Z tax purposes and equity for Country X tax purposes (the US1-FZ instrument). The $80x is treated as interest for Country Z and U.S. tax purposes (the entire amount of which is included in US1's income) and is treated as an excludible dividend for Country X tax purposes (by reason of the Country X participation exemption). Paragraphs (c)(3)(iii)(A) and (B) of this section describe the extent to which the specified payments by FZ and US1, each of which is a specified party, are disqualified hybrid amounts.

(A) The hybrid transaction rule of § 1.267A-2(a) applies to FZ's payment because the payment is made pursuant to a hybrid transaction, as a payment with respect to the US1-FZ instrument is treated as interest for U.S. tax purposes but not for purposes of Country X's tax law (the tax law of FX, a specified recipient that is related to FZ). As a consequence of the Country X participation exemption, an $80x no-inclusion occurs with respect to FX, and such no-inclusion is a result of the payment being made pursuant to the hybrid transaction. Thus, but for § 1.267A-3(b), the entire $80x of FZ's payment would be a disqualified hybrid amount. However, because US1 (a tax resident of the United States that is also a specified recipient of the payment) takes the entire $80x payment into account in its gross income, no portion of the payment is a disqualified hybrid amount. *See* § 1.267A-3(b)(2).

(B) The disregarded payment rule of § 1.267A-2(b) applies to US1's $100x payment to FX, for the reasons described in paragraph (c)(3)(ii)(A) of this section. In addition, US1 has no dual inclusion income for taxable year 1 because, as a result of the Country X participation exemption, no portion of FZ's $80x payment to US1 (which is derived by FX under its tax law) is included in FX's income. *See* §§ 1.267A-2(b)(3) and 1.267A-3(a). Therefore, the entire $100x payment from US1 to FX is a disqualified hybrid amount, calculated as $100x (the amount of the payment) less $0 (the amount of dual inclusion income). *See* § 1.267A-2(b)(1).

(iv) *Alternative facts – dual inclusion income despite participation exemption.* The facts are the same as in paragraph (c)(3)(iii) of this section, except that the US1-FZ instrument is treated as indebtedness for U.S. tax purposes and equity for Country Z and Country X tax purposes. In addition, the $80x paid to US1 by FZ is treated as interest for U.S. tax purposes (the entire amount of which is included in US1's income), a dividend for Country Z tax purposes (for which FZ is not allowed a deduction or other tax benefit), and an excludible dividend for Country X tax purposes (by reason of the Country X participation exemption). For the reasons described in paragraph (c)(3)(iii)(A) of this section, the hybrid transaction rule of § 1.267A-2(a) applies to FZ's payment but no portion of the payment is a disqualified hybrid amount. In addition, the disregarded payment rule of § 1.267A-2(b) applies to US1's $100x payment to FX, for the reasons described in paragraph (c)(3)(ii)(B) of this section. US1's dual inclusion income for taxable year 1 is $80x. This is because the $80x paid to US1 by FZ is included in US1's income and, although not included in FX's income, it is a dividend for Country X tax purposes that would have been included in FX's income but for the Country X participation exemption, and FZ is not allowed a deduction or other tax benefit for it under Country Z tax law. *See* § 1.267A-2(b)(3)(ii). Therefore, $20x of US1's $100x payment is a disqualified hybrid amount ($100x less $80x). *See* § 1.267A-2(b)(1).

(4) *Example 4. Payment allocable to a U.S. taxable branch.*—(i) *Facts.* FX1 and FX2 are foreign corporations that are bodies corporate established in and tax residents of Country X. FX1 holds all the interests of FX2, and FX1 and FX2 file a consolidated return under Country X tax law. FX2 has a U.S. taxable branch ("USB"). During taxable year 1, FX2 pays $50x to FX1 pursuant to an instrument (the "FX1-FX2 instrument"). The amount paid pursuant to the instrument is treated as interest for U.S. tax purposes but, as a consequence of the Country X consolidation regime, is treated as a disregarded transaction between group members for Country X tax purposes. Also during taxable year 1, FX2 pays $100x of interest to an unrelated bank that is not a party to a structured arrangement (the instrument pursuant to which the payment is made, the "bank-FX2 instrument"). FX2's only other item of income, gain, deduction, or loss for taxable year 1 is $200x of gross income. Under Country X tax law, the $200x of gross income is attributable to USB, but is not included in FX2's income because Country X tax law exempts income attributable to a branch. Under U.S. tax law, the $200x of gross income is effectively connected income of USB. Further, under section 882(c)(1), $75x of interest is, for taxable year 1, allocable to USB's effectively connected income. USB has neither liabilities that are directly allocable to it, as described in § 1.882-5(a)(1)(ii)(A), nor U.S. booked liabilities, as defined in § 1.882-5(d)(2).

(ii) *Analysis.* USB is a specified party and thus any interest or royalty allowable as a deduction in determining its effectively connected income is subject to disallowance under section 267A. Pursuant to § 1.267A-5(b)(3)(i)(A), USB is treated as paying $75x of interest, and such interest is thus a specified payment. Of that $75x, $25x is treated as paid to FX1, calculated as $75x (the interest allocable to USB under section 882(c)(1)) multiplied by 1/3 ($50x, FX2's payment to FX1, divided by $150x, the total interest paid by FX2). *See* § 1.267A-5(b)(3)(ii)(A). As described in paragraphs (c)(4)(ii)(A) and (B) of this section, the $25x of the specified payment treated as paid by USB to FX1 is a disqualified hybrid amount under the disregarded payment rule of § 1.267A-2(b) and, as a result, a deduction for that amount is disallowed under § 1.267A-1(b)(1).

(A) USB's $25x payment to FX1 is not regarded under the tax law of Country X (the tax law of FX1, a related tax resident to which the payment is made) because under such tax law it is a disregarded transaction between group members. *See* § 1.267A-2(b)(2) and (f). In addition, were the tax law of Country X to regard the payment (and treat it as interest), FX1 would include it in income. Therefore, the payment is a disregarded payment to which § 1.267A-2(b) applies. *See* § 1.267A-2(b)(2).

(B) Under § 1.267A-2(b)(1), the excess (if any) of USB's disregarded payments for taxable year 1 ($25x) over its dual inclusion income for the taxable year is a disqualified hybrid amount. USB's dual inclusion income for taxable year 1 is $0. This is because, as a result of the Country X exemption for income attributable to a branch, no portion of USB's $200x item of gross income is included in FX2's income. *See* § 1.267A-2(b)(3). Therefore, the entire $25x of the specified payment treated as paid by USB to FX1 is a disqualified hybrid amount, calculated as $25x (the amount of the payment) less $0 (the amount of dual inclusion income). *See* § 1.267A-2(b)(1).

(iii) *Alternative facts – deemed branch payment.* The facts are the same as in paragraph (c)(4)(i) of this section, except that FX2 does not pay any amounts during taxable year 1 (thus, it does not pay the $50x to FX1 or the $100x to the bank). However, under an income tax treaty between the United States and Country X, USB is a U.S. permanent establishment and, for taxable year 1, $25x of royalties is allowable as a deduction in computing the business profits of USB and is deemed paid to FX2. Under Country X tax law, the $25x is not regarded. Accordingly, the $25x is a specified payment that is a deemed branch payment. *See* §§1.267A-2(c)(2) and 1.267A-5(b)(3)(i)(B). In addition, the entire $25x is a disqualified hybrid amount for which a deduction is disallowed because the tax law of Country X provides an exclusion or exemption for income attributable to a branch. *See* §1.267A-2(c)(1).

(5) *Example 5. Payment to a reverse hybrid.*—(i) *Facts.* FX holds all the interests of US1 and FY, and FY holds all the interests of FV. FY is an entity established in Country Y, and FV is an entity established in Country V. FY is fiscally transparent for Country Y tax purposes but is not fiscally transparent for Country X tax purposes. FV is fiscally transparent for Country X tax purposes. On date 1, US1 pays $100x to FY. The payment is treated as interest for U.S. tax purposes and Country X tax purposes.

(ii) *Analysis.* US1 is a specified party and thus a deduction for its $100x specified payment is subject to disallowance under section 267A. As described in paragraphs (c)(5)(ii)(A) through (C) of this section, the entire $100x payment is a disqualified hybrid amount under the reverse hybrid rule of §1.267A-2(d) and, as a result, a deduction for the payment is disallowed under §1.267A-1(b)(1).

(A) US1's payment is made to a reverse hybrid because FY is fiscally transparent under the tax law of Country Y (the tax law of the country in which it is established) but is not fiscally transparent under the tax law of Country X (the tax law of FX, an investor that is related to US1). *See* §1.267A-2(d)(2) and (f). Therefore, §1.267A-2(d) applies to the payment. The result would be the same if the payment were instead made to FV. *See* §1.267A-2(d)(3).

(B) For US1's payment to be a disqualified hybrid amount under §1.267A-2(d), a no-inclusion must occur with respect to FX, an investor the tax law of which treats FY as not fiscally transparent. *See* §1.267A-2(d)(1)(i). Because FX does not derive the $100x payment under Country X tax law (as FY is not fiscally transparent under such tax law), FX includes $0 of the payment in income and therefore a $100x no-inclusion occurs with respect to FX. *See* §1.267A-3(a).

(C) Pursuant to §1.267A-2(d)(1)(ii), FX's $100x no-inclusion gives rise to a disqualified hybrid amount to the extent that it is a result of US1's payment being made to the reverse hybrid. FX's $100x no-inclusion is a result of the payment being made to the reverse hybrid because, were FY to be treated as fiscally transparent for Country X tax purposes, FX would include $100x in income and, consequently, the no-inclusion would not occur. The result would be the same if Country X tax law instead viewed US1's payment as a dividend, rather than interest. *See* §1.267A-2(d)(1)(ii).

(iii) *Alternative facts – inclusion under anti-deferral regime.* The facts are the same as in paragraph (c)(5)(i) of this section, except that, under a Country X anti-deferral regime, FX takes into account $100x attributable to the $100x payment received by FY. If under the rules of §1.267A-3(a) FX includes the entire attributed amount in income (that is, if FX takes the amount into account in its income at the full marginal rate imposed on ordinary income and the amount is not reduced or offset by certain relief particular to the amount), then a no-inclusion does not occur with respect to FX. As a result, in such a case, no portion of US1's payment would be a disqualified hybrid amount under §1.267A-2(d).

(iv) *Alternative facts – multiple investors.* The facts are the same as in paragraph (c)(5)(i) of this section, except that FX holds all the interests of FZ, which is fiscally transparent for Country X tax purposes; FZ holds all the interests of FY, which is fiscally transparent for Country Z tax purposes; and FZ includes the $100x payment in income. Thus, each of FZ and FX is an investor of FY, as each directly or indirectly holds an interest of FY. *See* §1.267A-5(a)(13). A $100x no-inclusion occurs with respect to FX, an investor the tax law of which treats FY as not fiscally transparent. FX's no-inclusion is a result of the payment being made to the reverse hybrid because, were FY to be treated as fiscally transparent for Country X tax purposes, then FX would include $100x in income (as FZ is fiscally transparent for Country X tax purposes). Accordingly, FX's no-inclusion is a result of US1's payment being made to the reverse hybrid and, consequently, the entire $100x payment is a disqualified hybrid amount. However, if instead FZ were not fiscally transparent for Country X tax purposes, then FX's no-inclusion would not be a result of US1's payment being made to the reverse hybrid and, therefore, the payment would not be a disqualified hybrid amount under §1.267A-2(d).

(v) *Alternative facts – portion of no-inclusion not the result of hybridity.* The facts are the same as in paragraph (c)(5)(i) of this section, except that the $100x is viewed as a royalty for U.S. tax purposes and Country X tax purposes, and Country X tax law contains a patent box regime that provides an 80% deduction with respect to certain royalty income. If the royalty payment would qualify for the Country X patent box deduction were FY to be treated as fiscally transparent for Country X tax purposes, then only $20x of FX's $100x no-inclusion would be the result of the payment being paid to a reverse hybrid, calculated as $100x (the no-inclusion with respect to FX that actually occurs) less $80x (the no-inclusion with respect to FX that would occur if FY were to be treated as fiscally transparent for Country X tax purposes). *See* §1.267A-2(d)(1)(ii) and 1.267A-3(a)(1)(ii). Accordingly, in such a case, only $20x of US1's payment would be a disqualified hybrid amount under §1.267A-2(d).

(vi) *Alternative facts – payment to a discretionary trust*—(A) *Facts.* The facts are the same as in paragraph (c)(5)(i) of this section, except that FY is a discretionary trust established in, and a tax resident of, Country Y (and as a result, FY is generally not fiscally transparent for Country Y tax purposes under the principles of §1.894-1(d)(3)(ii)). In general, under Country Y tax law, FX, an investor of FY, is not required to separately take into account in its income US1's $100x payment received by FY; instead, FY is required to take the payment into account in its income. However, under the trust agreement, the trustee of FY may, with respect to certain items of income received by FY, allocate such an item to FY's beneficiary, FX. When this occurs, then, for Country Y tax purposes, FY does not take the item into account in its income, and FX is required to take the item into account in its income as if it received the item directly from the source from which realized by FY. For Country X tax purposes, FX in all cases does not take into account in its income any item of income received by FY. With respect to the $100x paid from US1 to FY, the trustee allocates the $100x to FX.

(B) *Analysis.* FY is fiscally transparent with respect to US1's $100x payment under the tax law of Country Y (the tax law of the country in which FY is established). *See* §1.267A-5(a)(8)(i). In addition, FY is not fiscally transparent with respect to US1's $100x payment under the tax law of Country X (the tax law of FX, the investor of FY). *See* §1.267A-5(a)(8)(ii). Thus, FY is a reverse hybrid with respect to the payment. *See* §1.267A-2(d)(2) and (f). Therefore, for reasons similar to those discussed in paragraphs (c)(5)(ii)(B) and (C) of this section, the entire $100x payment is a disqualified hybrid amount.

(6) *Example 6. Branch mismatch payment.*—(i) *Facts.* FX holds all the interests of US1 and FZ. FZ owns BB, a Country B branch that gives rise to a taxable presence in Country B under Country Z tax law but not under Country B tax law. On date 1, US1 pays $50x to FZ. The amount is treated as a royalty for U.S. tax purposes and Country Z tax purposes. Under Country Z tax law, the amount is treated as income attributable to BB and, as a consequence of County Z tax law exempting income attributable to a branch, is excluded from FZ's income.

(ii) *Analysis.* US1 is a specified party and thus a deduction for its $50x specified payment is subject to disallowance under section 267A. As described in paragraphs (c)(6)(ii)(A) through (C) of this section, the entire $50x payment is a disqualified hybrid amount under the branch mismatch rule of §1.267A-2(e) and, as a result, a deduction for the payment is disallowed under §1.267A-1(b)(1).

(A) US1's payment is a branch mismatch payment because under Country Z tax law (the tax law of FZ, a home office that is related to US1) the payment is treated as income attributable to BB, and BB is not a taxable branch (that is, under Country B tax law, BB does not give rise to a taxable presence). *See* §1.267A-2(e)(2) and (f). Therefore, §1.267A-2(e) applies to the payment. The result would be the same if instead BB were a taxable branch and, under Country B tax law, US1's payment were treated as income attributable to FZ, the home office, and not BB. *See* §1.267A-2(e)(2).

(B) For US1's payment to be a disqualified hybrid amount under §1.267A-2(e), a no-inclusion must occur with respect to FZ. *See* §1.267A-2(e)(1)(i). As a consequence of the Country Z branch exemption, FZ includes $0 of the payment in income and therefore a $50x no-inclusion occurs with respect to FZ. *See* §1.267A-3(a).

(C) Pursuant to §1.267A-2(e)(1)(ii), FZ's $50x no-inclusion gives rise to a disqualified hybrid amount to the extent that it is a result of US1's payment being a branch mismatch payment. FZ's $50x no-inclusion is a result of the payment being a branch mismatch payment because, were the payment to not be treated as income attributable to BB for Country Z tax purposes, FZ would include $50x in income and, consequently, the no-inclusion would not occur.

(7) *Example 7. Reduction of disqualified hybrid amount for certain amounts includible in income.*—(i) *Facts.* US1 and FW hold 60% and 40%, respectively, of the interests of FX, and FX holds all the interests of FZ. Each of FX and FZ is a specified party that is a CFC. FX holds an instrument issued by FZ that it is treated as equity for Country X tax purposes and as indebtedness for U.S. tax purposes (the FX-FZ instrument). On date 1, FZ pays $100x to FX pursuant to the FX-FZ instrument. The amount is treated as a dividend for Country X tax purposes and as interest for U.S. tax purposes. In addition, pursuant to section 954(c)(6), the amount is not foreign personal holding company income of FX and, under section 951A, the amount is gross tested income (as described in § 1.951A-2(c)(1)) of FX. Further, were FZ allowed a deduction for the amount, it would be allocated and apportioned to gross tested income (as described in § 1.951A-2(c)(1)) of FZ. Lastly, Country X tax law provides an 80% participation exemption for dividends received from nonresident corporations and, as a result of such participation exemption, FX includes $20x of FZ's payment in income.

(ii) *Analysis.* FZ, a CFC, is a specified party and thus a deduction for its $100x specified payment is subject to disallowance under section 267A. But for § 1.267A-3(b), $80x of FZ's payment would be a disqualified hybrid amount (such amount, a "tentative disqualified hybrid amount"). *See* § § 1.267A-2(a) and 1.267A-3(b)(1). Pursuant to § 1.267A-3(b), the tentative disqualified hybrid amount is reduced by $48x. *See* § 1.267A-3(b)(4). The $48x is the tentative disqualified hybrid amount to the extent that it increases US1's pro rata share of tested income with respect to FX under section 951A (calculated as $80x multiplied by 60%). *See* § 1.267A-3(b)(4). Accordingly, $32x of FZ's payment ($80x less $48x) is a disqualified hybrid amount under § 1.267A-2(a) and, as a result, $32x of the deduction is disallowed under § 1.267A-1(b)(1).

(iii) *Alternative facts – United States shareholder is a domestic partnership.* The facts are the same as in paragraph (c)(7)(i) of this section, except that US1 is a domestic partnership, 90% of the interests of which are held by US2 and the remaining 10% of which are held by an individual that is a nonresident alien (as defined in section 7701(b)(1)(B)). Thus, although each of US1 and US2 is a United States shareholder of FX, only US2 has a pro rata share of any tested item of FX. *See* § 1.951A-1(e). In addition, $43.2x of the $80x tentative disqualified hybrid amount increases US2's pro rata share of the tested income of FX (calculated as $80x multiplied by 60% multiplied by 90%). Thus, $36.8x of FZ's payment ($80x less $43.2x) is a disqualified hybrid amount under § 1.267A-2(a). *See* § 1.267A-3(b)(4).

(8) *Example 8. Imported mismatch rule – direct offset.*—(i) *Facts.* FX holds all the interests of FW, and FW holds all the interests of US1. FX holds an instrument issued by FW that is treated as equity for Country X tax purposes and indebtedness for Country W tax purposes (the FX-FW instrument). FW holds an instrument issued by US1 that is treated as indebtedness for Country W and U.S. tax purposes (the FW-US1 instrument). In accounting period 1, FW pays $100x to FX pursuant to the FX-FW instrument. The amount is treated as an excludible dividend for Country X tax purposes (by reason of the Country X participation exemption) and as interest for Country W tax purposes. Also in accounting period 1, US1 pays $100x to FW pursuant to the FW-US1 instrument. The amount is treated as interest for Country W and U.S. tax purposes and is included in FW's income. The FX-FW instrument was not entered into pursuant to the same plan or series of related transactions pursuant to which the FW-US1 instrument was entered into.

(ii) *Analysis.* US1 is a specified party and thus a deduction for its $100x specified payment is subject to disallowance under section 267A. US1's $100x payment is neither a disqualified hybrid amount nor included or includible in income in the United States. *See* § 1.267A-4(a)(2)(v). In addition, FW's $100x deduction is a hybrid deduction because it is a deduction allowed to FW that results from an amount paid that is interest under Country W tax law, and were Country W law to have rules substantially similar to those under § § 1.267A-1 through 1.267A-3 and 1.267A-5, a deduction for the payment would be disallowed (because under such rules the payment would be pursuant to a hybrid transaction and FX's no-inclusion would be a result of the hybrid transaction). *See* § § 1.267A-2(a) and 1.267A-4(b). Under § 1.267A-4(a)(2), US1's payment is an imported mismatch payment, US1 is an imported mismatch payer, and FW (the foreign tax resident that includes the imported mismatch payment in income) is an imported mismatch payee. The imported mismatch payment is a disqualified imported mismatch amount to the extent that the income attributable to the payment is directly or indirectly offset by the hybrid deduction incurred by FW (a foreign tax resident that is related to US1). *See* § 1.267A-4(a)(1). Under § 1.267A-4(c)(1), the $100x hybrid deduction directly or indirectly offsets the income attributable to US1's imported mismatch payment to the extent that the payment directly or indirectly funds the hybrid deduction. The entire $100x of US1's payment directly funds the hybrid deduction because FW (the imported mismatch payee) incurs at least that amount of the hybrid deduction. *See* § 1.267A-4(c)(3)(i). Accordingly, the entire $100x payment is a disqualified imported mismatch amount under § 1.267A-4(a)(1) and, as a result, a deduction for the payment is disallowed under § 1.267A-1(b)(2).

(iii) *Alternative facts – long-term deferral.* The facts are the same as in paragraph (c)(8)(i) of this section, except that the FX-FW instrument is treated as indebtedness for Country X and Country W tax purposes, and FW does not pay any amounts pursuant to the instrument during accounting period 1. In addition, under Country W tax law, FW is allowed to deduct interest under the FX-FW instrument as it accrues, whereas under Country X tax law FX does not take into account in its income interest under the FX-FW instrument until the interest is paid. Further, FW accrues $100x of interest during accounting period 1, and FW will not pay such amount to FX for more than 36 months after the end of accounting period 1. The results are the same as in paragraph (c)(8)(ii) of this section. That is, FW's $100x deduction for the accrued interest is a hybrid deduction, *see* § § 1.267A-2(a), 1.267A-3(a), and 1.267A-4(b), and the income attributable to US1's $100x imported mismatch payment is offset by the hybrid deduction for the reasons described in paragraph (c)(8)(ii) of this section. As a result, a deduction for the payment is disallowed under § 1.267A-1(b)(2). The result would be the same even if the FX-FW instrument is expected to be redeemed or capitalized before the $100x of interest is paid such that FX will never take into account in its income (and therefore will not include in income) the $100x of interest.

(iv) *Alternative facts – notional interest deduction.* The facts are the same as in paragraph (c)(8)(i) of this section, except that there is no FX-FW instrument and thus FW does not pay any amounts to FX during accounting period 1. However, during accounting period 1, FW is allowed a $100x notional interest deduction with respect to its equity under Country W tax law. Pursuant to § 1.267A-4(b)(1)(ii), FW's notional interest deduction is a hybrid deduction. The results are the same as in paragraph (c)(8)(ii) of this section. That is, the income attributable to US1's $100x imported mismatch payment is offset by FW's hybrid deduction for the reasons described in paragraph (c)(8)(ii) of this section. As a result, a deduction for the payment is disallowed under § 1.267A-1(b)(2). The result would be the same if the tax law of Country W contains hybrid mismatch rules because FW's deduction is a deduction with respect to equity. *See* § 1.267A-4(b)(2)(i).

(v) *Alternative facts – foreign hybrid mismatch rules prevent hybrid deduction.* The facts are the same as in paragraph (c)(8)(i) of this section, except that the tax law of Country W contains hybrid mismatch rules, and under such rules FW is not allowed a deduction for the $100x that it pays to FX pursuant to the FX-FW instrument. The $100x paid by FW therefore does not give rise to a hybrid deduction. *See* § 1.267A-4(b). Accordingly, because the income attributable to US1's payment to FW is not directly or indirectly offset by a hybrid deduction, the payment is not a disqualified imported mismatch amount. Therefore, a deduction for the payment is not disallowed under § 1.267A-1(b)(2).

(9) *Example 9. Imported mismatch rule – indirect offsets and pro rata allocations.*—(i) *Facts.* FX holds all the interests of FZ, and FZ holds all the interests of US1 and US2. FX has a Country B branch that, for Country X and Country B tax purposes, gives rise to a taxable presence in Country B and is therefore a taxable branch ("BB"). Under the Country B-Country X income tax treaty, BB is a permanent establishment entitled to deduct expenses properly attributable to BB for purposes of computing its business profits under the treaty. In addition, BB is deemed to pay a royalty to FX for the right to use intangibles developed by FX equal to cost plus y%. The deemed royalty is a deductible expense properly attributable to BB under the Country B-Country X income tax treaty. For Country X tax purposes, any transactions between BB and X are disregarded. The deemed royalty is $80x for accounting period 1. Country B tax law does not permit a loss of a taxable branch to be shared with a tax resident or another taxable branch. In addition, an instrument issued by FZ to FX is properly reflected as an asset on the books and records of BB (the FX-FZ instrument). The FX-FZ instrument is treated as indebtedness for Country X, Country Z, and Country B tax purposes. In accounting period 1, FZ pays $80x to FX pursuant to the FX-FZ instrument; the amount is treated as interest for Country X, Country Z, and Country B tax purposes, and is treated as income attributable to BB for Country X and Country B tax purposes (but, for Country X

tax purposes, is excluded from FX's income as a consequence of the Country X exemption for income attributable to a branch). Further, in accounting period 1, US1 and US2 pay $60x and $40x, respectively, to FZ pursuant to instruments that are treated as indebtedness for Country Z and U.S. tax purposes; the amounts are treated as interest for Country Z and U.S. tax purposes and are included in FZ's income. Lastly, neither the instrument pursuant to which US1 pays the $60x nor the instrument pursuant to which US2 pays the $40x was entered into pursuant to a plan or series of related transactions that includes the transaction or agreement giving rise to BB's deduction for the deemed royalty.

(ii) *Analysis.* US1 and US2 are specified parties and thus deductions for their specified payments are subject to disallowance under section 267A. Neither of the payments is a disqualified hybrid amount, nor is either of the payments included or includible in income in the United States. *See* § 1.267A-4(a)(2)(v). In addition, BB's $80x deduction for the deemed royalty is a hybrid deduction because it is a deduction allowed to BB that results from an amount paid that is treated as a royalty under Country B tax law (regardless of whether a royalty deduction would be allowed under U.S. law), and were Country B tax law to have rules substantially similar to those under § § 1.267A-1 through 1.267A-3 and 1.267A-5, a deduction for the payment would be disallowed because under such rules the payment would be a deemed branch payment and Country X has an exclusion for income attributable to a branch. *See* § § 1.267A-2(c) and 1.267A-4(b). Under § 1.267A-4(a)(2), each of US1's and US2's payments is an imported mismatch payment, US1 and US2 are imported mismatch payers, and FZ (the foreign tax resident that includes the imported mismatch payments in income) is an imported mismatch payee. The imported mismatch payments are disqualified imported mismatch amounts to the extent that the income attributable to the payments is directly or indirectly offset by the hybrid deduction incurred by BB (a foreign taxable branch that is related to US1 and US2). *See* § 1.267A-4(a). Under § 1.267A-4(c)(1), the $80x hybrid deduction directly or indirectly offsets the income attributable to the imported mismatch payments to the extent that the payments directly or indirectly fund the hybrid deduction. Paragraphs (c)(9)(ii)(A) and (B) of this section describe the extent to which the imported mismatch payments directly or indirectly fund the hybrid deduction.

(A) Neither US1's nor US2's payment directly funds the hybrid deduction because FZ (the imported mismatch payee) does not incur the hybrid deduction. *See* § 1.267A-4(c)(3)(i). To determine the extent to which the payments indirectly fund the hybrid deduction, the amount of the hybrid deduction that is allocated to FZ must be determined. *See* § 1.267A-4(c)(3)(ii). FZ is allocated the hybrid deduction to the extent that it directly or indirectly makes a funded taxable payment to BB (the foreign taxable branch that incurs the hybrid deduction). *See* § 1.267A-4(c)(3)(iii). The $80x that FZ pays pursuant to the FX-FZ instrument is a funded taxable payment of FZ to BB. *See* § 1.267A-4(c)(3)(v). Therefore, because FZ makes a funded taxable payment to BB that is at least equal to the amount of the hybrid deduction, FZ is allocated the entire amount of the hybrid deduction. *See* § 1.267A-4(c)(3)(iii).

(B) But for US2's imported mismatch payment, the entire $60x of US1's imported mismatch payment would indirectly fund the hybrid deduction because FZ is allocated at least that amount of the hybrid deduction. *See* § 1.267A-4(c)(3)(ii). Similarly, but for US1's imported mismatch payment, the entire $40x of US2's imported mismatch payment would indirectly fund the hybrid deduction because FZ is allocated at least that amount of the hybrid deduction. *See* § 1.267A-4(c)(3)(ii). However, because the sum of US1's and US2's imported mismatch payments to FZ ($100x) exceeds the hybrid deduction allocated to FZ ($80x), pro rata adjustments must be made. *See* § 1.267A-4(e). Thus, $48x of US1's imported mismatch payment is considered to indirectly fund the hybrid deduction, calculated as $80x (the amount of the hybrid deduction) multiplied by 60% ($60x, the amount of US1's imported mismatch payment to FZ, divided by $100x, the sum of the imported mismatch payments that US1 and US2 make to FZ). Similarly, $32x of US2's imported mismatch payment is considered to indirectly fund the hybrid deduction, calculated as $80x (the amount of the hybrid deduction) multiplied by 40% ($40x, the amount of US2's imported mismatch payment to FZ, divided by $100x, the sum of the imported mismatch payments that US1 and US2 make to FZ). Accordingly, $48x of US1's imported mismatch payment, and $32x of US2's imported mismatch payment, are disqualified imported mismatch amounts under § 1.267A-4(a)(1) and, as a result, deductions for such amounts are disallowed under § 1.267A-1(b)(2).

(iii) *Alternative facts – loss made available through foreign group relief regime.* The facts are the same as in paragraph (c)(9)(i) of this section, except that FZ holds all the interests in FZ2, a body corporate that is a tax resident of Country Z, FZ2 (rather than FZ) holds all the interests of US1 and US2, and US1 and US2 make their respective $60x and $40x payments to FZ2 (rather than to FZ). Further, in accounting period 1, a $10x loss of FZ is made available to offset income of FZ2 through a Country Z foreign group relief regime. Pursuant to § 1.267A-4(c)(3)(vi), FZ and FZ2 are treated as a single foreign tax resident for purposes of § 1.267A-4(c) because a loss that is not incurred by FZ2 (FZ's $10x loss) is made available to offset income of FZ2 under the Country Z group relief regime. Accordingly, the results are the same as in paragraph (c)(9)(ii) of this section. That is, by treating FZ and FZ2 as a single foreign tax resident for purposes of § 1.267A-4(c), BB's hybrid deduction offsets the income attributable to US1's and US2's imported mismatch payments to the same extent as described in paragraph (c)(9)(ii) of this section.

(10) *Example 10. Imported mismatch rule – ordering rules and rule deeming certain payments to be imported mismatch payments.*—(i) *Facts.* FX holds all the interests of FW, and FW holds all the interests of US1, US2, and FZ. FZ holds all the interests of US3. FX transfers cash to FW in exchange for an instrument that is treated as equity for Country X tax purposes and indebtedness for Country W tax purposes (the FX-FW instrument). FW transfers cash to US1 in exchange for an instrument that is treated as indebtedness for Country W and U.S. tax purposes (the FW-US1 instrument). The FX-FW instrument and the FW-US1 instrument were entered into pursuant to a plan a design of which was for deductions incurred by FW pursuant to the FX-FW instrument to offset income attributable to payments by US1 pursuant to the FW-US1 instrument. In accounting period 1, FW pays $125x to FX pursuant to the FX-FW instrument; the amount is treated as an excludible dividend for Country X tax purposes (by reason of the Country X participation exemption regime) and as interest for Country W tax purposes. Also in accounting period 1, US1 pays $50x to FW pursuant to the FW-US1 instrument; US2 pays $50x to FW pursuant to an instrument treated as indebtedness for Country W and U.S. tax purposes (the FW-US2 instrument); US3 pays $50x to FZ pursuant to an instrument treated as indebtedness for Country Z and U.S. tax purposes (the FZ-US3 instrument); and FZ pays $50x to FW pursuant to an instrument treated as indebtedness for Country W and Country Z tax purposes (FW-FZ instrument). The amounts paid by US1, US2, US3, and FZ are treated as interest for purposes of the relevant tax laws and are included in the income of FW (in the case of US1's, US2's and FZ's payment) or FZ (in the case of US3's payment). Lastly, neither the FW-US2 instrument, the FW-FZ instrument, nor the FZ-US3 instrument was entered into pursuant to a plan or series of related transactions that includes the transaction pursuant to which the FX-FW instrument was entered into.

(ii) *Analysis.* US1, US2, and US3 are specified parties (but FZ is not a specified party, see § 1.267A-5(a)(17)) and thus deductions for US1's, US2's, and US3's specified payments are subject to disallowance under section 267A. None of the specified payments is a disqualified hybrid amount, nor is any of the payments included or includible in income in the United States. *See* § 1.267A-4(a)(2)(v). Under § 1.267A-4(a)(2), each of the payments is an imported mismatch payment, US1, US2, and US3 are imported mismatch payers, and FW and FZ (the foreign tax residents that include the imported mismatch payments in income) are imported mismatch payees. The imported mismatch payments are disqualified imported mismatch amounts to the extent that the income attributable to the payments is directly or indirectly offset by FW's $125x hybrid deduction. *See* § 1.267A-4(a)(1) and (b). Under § 1.267A-4(c)(1), the $125x hybrid deduction directly or indirectly offsets the income attributable to the imported mismatch payments to the extent that the payments directly or indirectly fund the hybrid deduction. Paragraphs (c)(10)(ii)(A) through (C) of this section describe the extent to which the imported mismatch payments directly or indirectly fund the hybrid deduction and are therefore disqualified hybrid amounts for which a deduction is disallowed under § 1.267A-1(b)(2).

(A) First, the $125x hybrid deduction offsets the income attributable to US1's imported mismatch payment, a factually-related imported mismatch payment that directly funds the hybrid deduction. *See* § 1.267A-4(c)(2)(i). The entire $50x of US1's payment directly funds the hybrid deduction because FW (the imported mismatch payee) incurs at least that amount of the hybrid deduction. *See* § 1.267A-4(c)(3)(i). Accordingly, the entire $50x of the payment is a disqualified imported mismatch amount under § 1.267A-4(a)(1).

(B) Second, the remaining $75x hybrid deduction offsets the income attributable to US2's imported mismatch payment, a factually-unrelated imported mismatch payment that directly funds the remaining hybrid deduction. *See* § 1.267A-4(c)(2)(ii). The entire $50x of US2's payment directly funds the remaining hybrid deduction because FW (the imported mismatch payee) incurs at least that amount of the remaining hybrid deduction. *See* § 1.267A-4(c)(3)(i).

Accordingly, the entire $50x of the payment is a disqualified imported mismatch amount under § 1.267A-4(a)(1).

(C) Third, the remaining $25x hybrid deduction offsets the income attributable to US3's imported mismatch payment, a factually-unrelated imported mismatch payment that indirectly funds the remaining hybrid deduction. *See* § 1.267A-4(c)(2)(iii). The imported mismatch payment indirectly funds the remaining hybrid deduction to the extent that FZ (the imported mismatch payee) is allocated the remaining hybrid deduction. *See* § 1.267A-4(c)(3)(iii). FZ is allocated the remaining hybrid deduction to the extent that it directly or indirectly makes a funded taxable payment to FW (the tax resident that incurs the hybrid deduction). *See* § 1.267A-4(c)(3)(iii). The $50x that FZ pays to FW pursuant to the FW-FZ instrument is a funded taxable payment of FZ to FW. *See* § 1.267A-4(c)(3)(v). Therefore, because FZ makes a funded taxable payment to FW that is at least equal to the amount of the remaining hybrid deduction, FZ is allocated the remaining hybrid deduction. *See* § 1.267A-4(c)(3)(iii). Accordingly, $25x of US3's payment indirectly funds the $25x remaining hybrid deduction and, consequently, $25x of US3's payment is a disqualified imported mismatch amount under § 1.267A-4(a)(2).

(iii) *Alternative facts – amount deemed to be an imported mismatch payment.* The facts are the same as in paragraph (c)(10)(i) of this section, except that US1 is not a domestic corporation but instead is a body corporate that is only a tax resident of Country E (hereinafter, "FE") (thus, for purposes of this paragraph (c)(10)(iii), the FW-US1 instrument is instead issued by FE and is the "FW-FE instrument"). In addition, the tax law of Country E contains hybrid mismatch rules and the $50x FE pays to FW pursuant to the FW-FE instrument is subject to disallowance under a provision of the hybrid mismatch rules substantially similar to § 1.267A-4. Pursuant to § 1.267A-4(f)(2), the $50x that FE pays to FW pursuant to the FW-FE instrument is deemed to be an imported mismatch payment for purposes of determining the extent to which the income attributable to an imported mismatch payment is offset by FW's hybrid deduction (a hybrid deduction other than one described in § 1.267A-4(f)(1)). The results are the same as in paragraphs (c)(10)(ii)(B) and (C) of this section. That is, by treating the $50x that FE pays to FW as an imported mismatch payment, and for reasons similar to those described in paragraphs (c)(10)(ii)(A) through (C) of this section, $50x of FW's $125x hybrid deduction offsets income attributable to FE's imported mismatch payment, $50x of the remaining $75x hybrid deduction offsets income attributable to US2's imported mismatch payment, and the remaining $25x hybrid deduction offsets income attributable to US3's imported mismatch payment. Accordingly, the entire $50x of US2's payment is a disqualified imported mismatch amount, and $25x of US3's payment is a disqualified imported mismatch amount.

(iv) *Alternative facts – amount deemed to be an imported mismatch payment and "waterfall" approach.* The facts are the same as in paragraph (c)(10)(i) of this section, except that FZ holds all of the interests of US3 indirectly through FE, a body corporate that is only a tax resident of Country E (hereinafter, "FE"), and US3 makes its $50x payment to FE (rather than to FZ); such amount is treated as interest for Country E tax purposes and is included in FE's income. In addition, during accounting period 1, FE pays $50x to FZ pursuant to an instrument; such amount is treated as interest for Country E and Country Z tax purposes, and is included in FZ's income. Further, the tax law of Country E contains hybrid mismatch rules and the $50x FE pays to FZ pursuant to the instrument is subject to disallowance under a provision of the hybrid mismatch rules substantially similar to § 1.267A-4. For purposes of determining the extent to which the income attributable to an imported mismatch payment is directly or indirectly offset by a hybrid deduction, the $50x that FE pays to FZ is deemed to be an imported mismatch payment (and FE and FZ are deemed to be an imported mismatch payer and imported mismatch payee, respectively). *See* § 1.267A-4(f)(2). With respect to US1 and US2, the results are the same as described in paragraphs (c)(10)(ii)(A) and (B) of this section. No portion of US3's payment is a disqualified imported mismatch amount because, by treating the $50x that FE pays to FZ as an imported mismatch payment, the remaining $25x of FW's hybrid deduction offsets income attributable to FE's imported mismatch payment. This is because the remaining $25x of FW's hybrid deduction is indirectly funded solely by FE's imported mismatch payment (as opposed to also being funded by US3's imported mismatch payment), as FZ (the imported mismatch payee with respect to FE's payment) directly makes a funded taxable payment to FW, whereas FE (the imported mismatch payee with respect to US3's payment) indirectly makes a funded taxable payment to FW. *See* § 1.267A-4(c)(3)(ii) through (v) and (vii).

(11) *Example 11. Imported mismatch rule – hybrid deduction of a CFC.*—(i) *Facts.* FX holds all the interests of US1, and FX and US1 hold 80% and 20%, respectively, of the interests of FZ, a specified party that is a CFC. US1 also holds all the interests of US2, and FX also holds all the interests of FY. FY is an entity established in Country Y, and is fiscally transparent for Country Y tax purposes but is not fiscally transparent for Country X tax purposes. In accounting period 1, US2 pays $100x to FZ pursuant to an instrument (the FZ-US2 instrument). The amount is treated as interest for U.S. tax purposes and Country Z tax purposes, and is included in FZ's income; in addition, for U.S. tax purposes, the amount is foreign personal holding company income of FZ. Also in accounting period 1, FZ pays $100x to FY pursuant to an instrument (the FY-FZ instrument). The amount is treated as interest for U.S. tax purposes and Country Z tax purposes, and none of the amount is included in FX's income. Under Country Z tax law, FZ is allowed a deduction for its entire $100x payment. Under § 1.267A-2(d), the entire $100x of FZ's payment is a disqualified hybrid amount (by reason of being made to a reverse hybrid) and, as a result, a deduction for the payment is disallowed under § 1.267A-1(b)(1); in addition, if a deduction were allowed for the $100x, it would be allocated and apportioned (under the rules of section 954(b)(5)) to gross subpart F income of FZ. Lastly, the FZ-US2 instrument was not entered into pursuant to a plan or series of related transactions that includes the transaction pursuant to which the FY-FZ instrument was entered into.

(ii) *Analysis.* US2 is a specified party and thus a deduction for its $100x specified payment is subject to disallowance under section 267A. As described in paragraphs (c)(11)(ii)(A) through (C) of this section, $80x of US2's payment is a disqualified imported mismatch amount for which a deduction is disallowed under § 1.267A-1(b)(2).

(A) $80x of US2's specified payment is an imported mismatch payment, calculated as $100x (the amount of the payment) less $0 (the disqualified hybrid amount with respect to the payment) less $20 (the amount of the payment that is included or includible in income in the United States). *See* § 1.267A-4(a)(2)(v). US2 is an imported mismatch payer and FZ (a foreign tax resident that includes the imported mismatch in income) is an imported mismatch payee. *See* § 1.267A-4(a)(2).

(B) But for § 1.267A-4(b)(2)(iv), the entire $100x deduction allowed to FZ under its tax law would be a hybrid deduction. *See* §§ 1.267A-2(d) and 1.267A-4(b)(1). However, pursuant to § 1.267A-4(b)(2)(iv), only $80x of the deduction is a hybrid deduction, calculated as $100x (the deduction to the extent that it would be a hybrid deduction but for § 1.267A-4(b)(2)(iv)) less $20x (the extent that FZ's payment giving rise to the deduction is a disqualified hybrid amount that is taken into account for purposes of § 1.267A-4(b)(2)(iv)(A)), less $0 (the extent that FZ's payment giving rise to the deduction is included or includible in income in the United States). *See* § 1.267A-4(b)(2)(iv). The $20x disqualified hybrid amount that is taken into account for purposes of § 1.267A-4(b)(2)(iv)(A) is calculated as $100x (the extent that FZ's payment is a disqualified hybrid amount) less $80x ($100x, the disqualified hybrid amount to the extent that, if allowed as a deduction, it would be allocated and apportioned to gross subpart F income, multiplied by 80%, the difference of 100% and the percentage of the stock (by value) of FZ that is owned by US1)). *See* § 1.267A-4(g).

(C) The $80x hybrid deduction offsets the income attributable to US2's imported mismatch payment, an imported mismatch payment that directly funds the hybrid deduction. *See* § 1.267A-4(c)(2)(ii). The entire $80x of US2's imported mismatch payment directly funds the hybrid deduction because FZ (the imported mismatch payee) incurs at least that amount of the hybrid deduction. *See* § 1.267A-4(c)(3)(i). Accordingly, the entire $80x of US2's imported mismatch payment is a disqualified imported mismatch amount under § 1.267A-4(a)(1).

(12) *Example 12. Imported mismatch rule – application first with respect to certain hybrid deductions, then with respect to other hybrid deductions.*—(i) *Facts.* FX holds all the interests of FZ, and FZ holds all the interests of each of US1 and FE. The tax law of Country E contains hybrid mismatch rules. FX holds an instrument issued by FZ that is treated as equity for Country X tax purposes and indebtedness for Country Z tax purposes (the FX-FZ instrument). In accounting period 1, FZ pays $10x to FX pursuant to the FX-FZ instrument. The amount is treated as an excludible dividend for Country X tax purposes (by reason of the Country X participation exemption) and as interest for Country Z tax purposes. Also in accounting period 1, FZ is allowed a $90x notional interest deduction with respect to its equity under Country Z tax law. In addition, in accounting period 1, US1 pays $100x to FZ pursuant to an instrument (the FZ-US1 instrument); the amount is treated as interest for U.S. tax purposes and Country Z tax purposes, and is included in FZ's income. Further, in accounting period 1, FE pays $40x to FZ pursuant to an instrument (the FZ-FE instrument); the amount is treated as interest for Country E and Country Z tax purposes, is included in FZ's income, and is

subject to disallowance under a provision of Country E hybrid mismatch rules substantially similar to § 1.267A-4. Lastly, neither the FZ-US1 instrument nor the FZ-FE instrument was entered into pursuant to a plan or series of related transactions that includes the transaction pursuant to which the FX-FZ instrument was entered into.

(ii) *Analysis*. US1 is a specified party and thus a deduction for its $100x specified payment is subject to disallowance under section 267A. As described in paragraphs (c)(12)(ii)(A) through (D) of this section, $92x of US1's payment is a disqualified imported mismatch amount for which a deduction is disallowed under § 1.267A-1(b)(2).

(A) The entire $100x of US1's specified payment is an imported mismatch payment. *See* § 1.267A-4(a)(2)(v). US1 is an imported mismatch payer and FZ (a foreign tax resident that includes the imported mismatch payment in income) is an imported mismatch payee. *See* § 1.267A-4(a)(2).

(B) FZ has $100x of hybrid deductions (the $10x deduction for the payment pursuant to the FX-FZ instrument plus the $90x notional interest deduction). *See* § 1.267A-4(b). Pursuant to § 1.267A-4(f)(1), § 1.267A-4 is first applied by taking into account only the $90x hybrid deduction consisting of the notional interest deduction; in addition, for purposes of applying § 1.267A-4 in this manner, FE's $40x payment is not treated as an imported mismatch payment. Thus, the $90x hybrid deduction offsets the income attributable to US1's imported mismatch payment, an imported mismatch payment that directly funds the hybrid deduction. *See* § 1.267A-4(c)(2)(ii). Moreover, $90x of US1's imported mismatch payment directly funds the hybrid deduction because FZ (the imported mismatch payee) incurs at least that amount of the hybrid deduction. *See* § 1.267A-4(c)(3)(i).

(C) Section § 1.267A-4 is next applied by taking into account only the $10x hybrid deduction consisting of the deduction for the payment pursuant to the FX-FZ instrument. *See* § 1.267A-4(f)(2). When applying § 1.267A-4 in this manner, and for purposes of determining the extent to which the income attributable to an imported mismatch payment is directly or indirectly offset by a hybrid deduction, FE's $40x payment is treated as an imported mismatch payment. *See* § 1.267A-4(f)(2). In addition, US1's imported mismatch payment is reduced from $100x to $10x. *See* § 1.267A-4(c)(4). But for FE's imported mismatch payment, the entire $10x of US1's imported mismatch payment would directly fund the $10x hybrid deduction because FZ incurred at least that amount of the hybrid deduction. *See* § 1.267A-4(c)(3)(i). Similarly, but for US1's imported mismatch payment, the entire $40x of FE's imported mismatch payment would directly fund the $10x hybrid deduction because FZ incurred at least that amount of the hybrid deduction. *See* § 1.267A-4(c)(3)(i). However, because the sum of US1's and FE's imported mismatch payments to FZ ($50x) exceeds the hybrid deduction incurred by FZ ($10x), pro rata adjustments must be made. *See* § 1.267A-4(e). Thus, $2x of US1's imported mismatch payment is considered to directly fund the hybrid deduction, calculated as $10x (the amount of the hybrid deduction) multiplied by 20% ($10x, the amount of US1's imported mismatch payment to FZ, divided by $50x, the sum of the imported mismatch payments that US1 and FE make to FZ). Similarly, $8x of FE's imported mismatch payment is considered to directly fund the hybrid deduction, calculated as $10x (the amount of the hybrid deduction) multiplied by 80% ($40x, the amount of FE's imported mismatch payment to FZ, divided by $50x, the sum of the imported mismatch payments that US1 and FE make to FZ). Accordingly, $2x of FZ's $10x hybrid deduction offsets income attributable to US1's $10x imported mismatch payment, and $8x of the hybrid deduction offsets income attributable to FE's $40x imported mismatch payment.

(D) Therefore, $92x of US1's imported mismatch payment is a disqualified imported mismatch amount, calculated as $90x (the amount that is a disqualified imported mismatch amount determined by applying § 1.267A-4 in the manner set forth in § 1.267A-4(f)(1)) plus $2x (the amount that is a disqualified imported mismatch amount determined by applying § 1.267A-4 in the manner set forth in § 1.267A-4(f)(2)). *See* § 1.267A-4(a)(1) and (f).

(iii) *Alternative facts – amount deemed to be an imported mismatch payment solely funds hybrid instrument deduction*. The facts are the same as in paragraph (c)(12)(i) of this section, except that FZ holds all of the interests of US1 indirectly through FE, and US1 makes its $100x payment to FE (rather than to FZ); such amount is treated as interest for U.S. and Country E tax purposes, and is included in FE's income. Moreover, FE pays $100x to FZ (rather than $40x); such amount is included in FZ's income, and is subject to disallowance under a provision of Country E hybrid mismatch rules substantially similar to § 1.267A-4. As described in paragraphs (c)(12)(iii)(A) through (D) of this section, $90x of US1's payment is a disqualified imported mismatch amount for which a deduction is disallowed under § 1.267A-1(b)(2).

(A) The entire $100x of US1's specified payment is an imported mismatch payment. *See* § 1.267A-4(a)(2)(v). US1 is an imported mismatch payer and FE (a foreign tax resident that includes the imported mismatch payment in income) is an imported mismatch payee. *See* § 1.267A-4(a)(2).

(B) FZ has $100x of hybrid deductions. *See* § 1.267A-4(b). Pursuant to § 1.267A-4(f)(1), § 1.267A-4 is first applied by taking into account only the $90x hybrid deduction consisting of the notional interest deduction; in addition, for purposes of applying § 1.267A-4 in this manner, FE's $100x payment is not treated as an imported mismatch payment. Thus, the $90x hybrid deduction offsets the income attributable to US1's imported mismatch payment, an imported mismatch payment that indirectly funds the hybrid deduction. *See* § 1.267A-4(c)(2)(iii). The imported mismatch payment indirectly funds the hybrid deduction because FE (the imported mismatch payee) is allocated the deduction, as FE makes a funded taxable payment (the $100x payment to FZ) that is at least equal to the amount of the deduction. *See* § 1.267A-4(c)(3)(ii), (iii), and (v).

(C) Section § 1.267A-4 is next applied by taking into account only the $10x hybrid deduction consisting of the deduction for the payment pursuant to the FX-FZ instrument. *See* § 1.267A-4(f)(2). For purposes of applying § 1.267A-4 in this manner, FE's $100x payment is reduced from $100x to $10x, and similarly US1's imported mismatch payment is reduced from $100x to $10x. *See* § 1.267A-4(c)(4). Further, FE's $10x payment is treated as an imported mismatch payment. *See* § 1.267A-4(f)(2). The entire $10x of FE's imported mismatch payment directly funds the hybrid deduction because FZ (the imported mismatch payee with respect to FE's imported mismatch payment) incurs at least that amount of the hybrid deduction. *See* § 1.267A-4(c)(3)(i). Accordingly, the $10x hybrid deduction offsets the income attributable to FE's imported mismatch payment, and none of the income attributable to US1's imported mismatch payment.

(D) Therefore, $90x of US1's imported mismatch payment is a disqualified imported mismatch amount, calculated as $90x (the amount that is a disqualified imported mismatch amount determined by applying § 1.267A-4 in the manner set forth in § 1.267A-4(f)(1)) plus $0 (the amount that is a disqualified imported mismatch amount determined by applying § 1.267A-4 in the manner set forth in § 1.267A-4(f)(2)). *See* § 1.267A-4(a)(1) and (f). [Reg. § 1.267(A)-6.]

☐ [*T.D.* 9896, 4-7-2020.]

§ 1.267A-7. Applicability dates.—(a) *General rule*.—Except as provided in paragraph (b) of this section, §§ 1.267A-1 through 1.267A-6 apply to taxable years ending on or after December 20, 2018, provided that such taxable years begin after December 31, 2017. However, taxpayers may apply the regulations in §§ 1.267A-1 through 1.267A-6 in their entirety (including by taking into account paragraph (b) of this section) for taxable years beginning after December 31, 2017, and ending before December 20, 2018. In lieu of applying the regulations in §§ 1.267A-1 through 1.267A-6 (including paragraph (b) of this section), taxpayers may apply the provisions matching §§ 1.267A-1 through 1.267A-6 (including by taking into account the provision matching paragraph (b) of this section) from the Internal Revenue Bulletin (IRB) 2019-03 (https://www.irs.gov/pub/irs-irbs/irb19-03.pdf) in their entirety for all taxable years ending on or before April 8, 2020.

(b) *Special rules*.—The following special rules apply regarding applicability dates:

(1) Sections 1.267A-2(a)(4) (payments pursuant to interest-free loans and similar arrangements), (b) (disregarded payments), (c) (deemed branch payments), and (e) (branch mismatch transactions), 1.267A-4 (imported mismatch rule), and 1.267A-5(b)(5) (structured payments), except as provided in paragraph (b)(5) of this section, apply to taxable years beginning on or after December 20, 2018.

(2) Section 1.267A-5(a)(20) (defining structured arrangement), as well as the portions of §§ 1.267A-1 through 1.267A-3 that relate to structured arrangements and that are not otherwise described in paragraph (b) of this section, apply to taxable years beginning on or after December 20, 2018. However, in the case of a specified payment made pursuant to an arrangement entered into before December 22, 2017, § 1.267A-5(a)(20), and the portions of §§ 1.267A-1 through 1.267A-3 that relate to structured arrangements and that are not otherwise described in paragraph (b) of this section, apply to taxable years beginning after December 31, 2020.

(3) Except as provided in paragraph (b)(4) of this section, the rules provided in § 1.267A-5(a)(12)(ii) (swaps with significant nonperiodic payments) apply to notional principal contracts entered into on or after April 8, 2021. However, taxpayers may apply the

rules provided in § 1.267A-5(a)(12)(ii) to notional principal contracts entered into before April 8, 2021.

(4) For a notional principal contract entered into before April 8, 2021, the interest equivalent rules provided in § 1.267A-5(b)(5)(ii)(B) (applied without regard to the references to § 1.267A-5(a)(12)(ii)) apply to a notional principal contract entered into on or after April 8, 2020.

(5) Section 1.267A-5(b)(5)(ii)(B) (interest equivalent rules) applies to transactions entered into on or after April 8, 2020. [Reg. § 1.267(A)-7.]

□ [*T.D. 9896, 4-7-2020 (corrected 8-11-2020).*]

Stapled Foreign Corporations

§ 1.269B-1. Stapled foreign corporations.—(a) *Treatment as a domestic corporation.*—(1) *General rule.*—Except as otherwise provided, if a foreign corporation is a stapled foreign corporation within the meaning of paragraph (b)(1) of this section, such foreign corporation will be treated as a domestic corporation for U.S. Federal income tax purposes. Accordingly, for example, the worldwide income of such corporation will be subject to the tax imposed by section 11. For application of the branch profits tax under section 884, and application of sections 871(a), 881, 1441, and 1442 to dividends and interest paid by a stapled foreign corporation, see § § 1.884-1(h) and 1.884-4(d).

(2) *Foreign owned exception.*—Paragraph (a)(1) of this section will not apply if a foreign corporation and a domestic corporation are stapled entities (as provided in paragraph (b) of this section) and such foreign and domestic corporations are foreign owned within the meaning of this paragraph (a)(2). A corporation will be treated as foreign owned if it is established to the satisfaction of the Commissioner that United States persons hold directly (or indirectly applying section 958(a)(2) and (3) and section 318(a)(4)) less than 50 percent of the total combined voting power of all classes of stock entitled to vote and less than 50 percent of the total value of the stock of such corporation. For the consequences of a stapled foreign corporation becoming or ceasing to be foreign owned, therefore converting its status as either a foreign or domestic corporation within the meaning of this paragraph (a)(2), see paragraph (c) of this section.

(b) *Definition of a stapled foreign corporation.*—(1) *General rule.*—A foreign corporation is a stapled foreign corporation if such foreign corporation and a domestic corporation are stapled entities. A foreign corporation and a domestic corporation are stapled entities if more than 50 percent of the aggregate value of each corporation's beneficial ownership consists of interests that are stapled. In the case of corporations with more than one class of stock, it is not necessary for a class of stock representing more than 50 percent of the beneficial ownership of the foreign corporation to be stapled to a class of stock representing more than 50 percent of the beneficial ownership of the domestic corporation, provided that more than 50 percent of the aggregate value of each corporation's beneficial ownership (taking into account all classes of stock) are in fact stapled. Interests are stapled if a transferor of one or more interests in one entity is required, by form of ownership, restrictions on transfer, or other terms or conditions, to transfer interests in the other entity. The determination of whether interests are stapled for this purpose is based on the relevant facts and circumstances, including, but not limited to, the corporations' by-laws, articles of incorporation or association, and stock certificates, shareholder agreements, agreements between the corporations, and voting trusts with respect to the corporations. For the consequences of a foreign corporation becoming or ceasing to be a stapled foreign corporation (e.g., a corporation that is no longer foreign owned) under this paragraph (b)(1), see paragraph (c) of this section.

(2) *Related party ownership rule.*—For purposes of determining whether a foreign corporation is a stapled foreign corporation, the Commissioner may, at his discretion, treat interests that otherwise would be stapled interests as not being stapled if the same person or related persons (within the meaning of section 267(b) or 707(b)) hold stapled interests constituting more than 50 percent of the beneficial ownership of both corporations, and a principal purpose of the stapling of those interests is the avoidance of U.S. income tax. A stapling of interests may have a principal purpose of tax avoidance even though the tax avoidance purpose is outweighed by other purposes when taken together.

(3) *Example.*—The principles of paragraph (b)(1) of this section are illustrated by the following example:

Example. USCo, a domestic corporation, and FCo, a foreign corporation, are publicly traded companies, each having two classes of stock outstanding. USCo's class A shares, which constitute 75% of the value of all beneficial ownership in USCo, are stapled to FCo's class B shares, which constitute 25% of the value of all beneficial ownership in F Co. USCo's class B shares, which constitute 25% of the value of all beneficial ownership in USCo, are stapled to FCo class A shares, which constitute 75% of the value of all beneficial ownership in FCo. Because more than 50% of the aggregate value of the stock of each corporation is stapled to the stock of the other corporation, USCo and FCo are stapled entities within the meaning of section 269B(c)(2).

(c) *Changes in domestic or foreign status.*—The deemed conversion of a foreign corporation to a domestic corporation under section 269B is treated as a reorganization under section 368(a)(1)(F). Similarly, the deemed conversion of a corporation that is treated as a domestic corporation under section 269B to a foreign corporation is treated as a reorganization under section 368(a)(1)(F). For the consequences of a deemed conversion, including the closing of a corporation's taxable year, see § § 1.367(a)-1(e), (f) and 1.367(b)-2(f).

(d) *Includible corporation.*—(1) Except as provided in paragraph (d)(2) of this section, a stapled foreign corporation treated as a domestic corporation under section 269B nonetheless is treated as a foreign corporation in determining whether it is an includible corporation within the meaning of section 1504(b). Thus, for example, a stapled foreign corporation is not eligible to join in the filing of a consolidated return under section 1501, and a dividend paid by such corporation is not a qualifying dividend under section 243(b), unless a valid section 1504(d) election is made with respect to such corporation.

(2) A stapled foreign corporation is treated as a domestic corporation in determining whether it is an includible corporation under section 1504(b) for purposes of applying § § 1.904(i)-1 and 1.861-11T(d)(6).

(e) *U.S. treaties.*—(1) A stapled foreign corporation that is treated as a domestic corporation under section 269B may not claim an exemption from U.S. income tax or a reduction in U.S. tax rates by reason of any treaty entered into by the United States.

(2) The principles of this paragraph (e) are illustrated by the following example:

Example. FCo, a Country X corporation, is a stapled foreign corporation that is treated as a domestic corporation under section 269B. FCo qualifies as a resident of Country X pursuant to the income tax treaty between the United States and Country X. Under such treaty, the United States is permitted to tax business profits of a Country X resident only to the extent that the business profits are attributable to a permanent establishment of the Country X resident in the United States. While FCo earns income from sources within and without the United States, it does not have a permanent establishment in the United States within the meaning of the relevant treaty. Under paragraph (e)(1) of this section, however, FCo is subject to U.S. Federal income tax on its income as a domestic corporation without regard to the provisions of the U.S.- Country X treaty and therefore without regard to the fact that FCo has no permanent establishment in the United States.

(f) *Tax assessment and collection procedures.*—(1) *In general.*—(i) Any income tax imposed on a stapled foreign corporation by reason of its treatment as a domestic corporation under section 269B (whether such income tax is shown on the stapled foreign corporation's U.S. Federal income tax return or determined as a deficiency in income tax) shall be assessed as the income tax liability of such stapled foreign corporation.

(ii) Any income tax assessed as a liability of a stapled foreign corporation under paragraph (f)(1)(i) of this section shall be considered as having been properly assessed as an income tax liability of the stapled domestic corporation (as defined in paragraph (f)(4)(i) of this section) and all 10-percent shareholders of the stapled foreign corporation (as defined in paragraph (f)(4)(ii) of this section). The date of such deemed assessment shall be the date the income tax liability of the stapled foreign corporation was properly assessed. The Commissioner may collect such income tax from the stapled domestic corporation under the circumstances set forth in paragraph (f)(2) of this section and may collect such income tax from any 10-percent shareholders of the stapled foreign corporation under the circumstances set forth in paragraph (f)(3) of this section.

(2) *Collection from domestic stapled corporation.*—If the stapled foreign corporation does not pay its income tax liability that was properly assessed, the unpaid balance of such income tax or any portion thereof may be collected from the stapled domestic corporation, provided that the following conditions are satisfied—

(i) The Commissioner has issued a notice and demand for payment of such income tax to the stapled foreign corporation in accordance with § 301.6303-1 of this Chapter;

(ii) The stapled foreign corporation has failed to pay the income tax by the date specified in such notice and demand;

(iii) The Commissioner has issued a notice and demand for payment of the unpaid portion of such income tax to the stapled domestic corporation in accordance with § 301.6303-1 of this Chapter.

(3) *Collection from 10-percent shareholders of the stapled foreign corporation.*—The unpaid balance of the stapled foreign corporation's income tax liability may be collected from a 10-percent shareholder of the stapled foreign corporation, limited to each such shareholder's income tax liability as determined under paragraph (f)(4)(iv) of this section, provided the following conditions are satisfied—

(i) The Commissioner has issued a notice and demand to the stapled domestic corporation for the unpaid portion of the stapled foreign corporation's income tax liability, as provided in paragraph (f)(2)(iii) of this section;

(ii) The stapled domestic corporation has failed to pay the income tax by the date specified in such notice and demand;

(iii) The Commissioner has issued a notice and demand for payment of the unpaid portion of such income tax to such 10-percent shareholder of the stapled foreign corporation in accordance with § 301.6303-1 of this Chapter.

(4) *Special rules and definitions.*—For purposes of this paragraph (f), the following rules and definitions apply:

(i) *Stapled domestic corporation.*—A domestic corporation is a *stapled domestic corporation* with respect to a stapled foreign corporation if such domestic corporation and the stapled foreign corporation are stapled entities as described in paragraph (b)(1) of this section.

(ii) *10-percent shareholder.*—A *10-percent shareholder* of a stapled foreign corporation is any person that owned directly 10 percent or more of the total value or total combined voting power of all classes of stock in the stapled foreign corporation for any day of the stapled foreign corporation's taxable year with respect to which the income tax liability relates.

(iii) *10-percent shareholder in the case of indirect ownership of stapled foreign corporation stock.*—[Reserved].

(iv) *Determination of a 10-percent shareholder's income tax liability.*—The income tax liability of a 10-percent shareholder of a stapled foreign corporation, for the income tax of the stapled foreign corporation under section 269B and this section, is determined by assigning an equal portion of the total income tax liability of the stapled foreign corporation for the taxable year to each day in such corporation's taxable year, and then dividing that portion ratably among the shares outstanding for that day on the basis of the relative values of such shares. The liability of any 10-percent shareholder for this purpose is the sum of the income tax liability allocated to the shares held by such shareholder for each day in the taxable year.

(v) *Income tax.*—The term *income tax* means any income tax liability imposed on a domestic corporation under title 26 of the United States Code, including additions to tax, additional amounts, penalties, and interest related to such income tax liability.

(g) *Effective dates.*—(1) Except as provided in this paragraph (g), the provisions of this section are applicable for taxable years that begin after July 29, 2005.

(2) Paragraphs (d)(1) and (f) of this section (except as applied to the collection of tax from any 10-percent shareholder of a stapled foreign corporation that is a foreign person) are applicable beginning on—

(i) July 18, 1984, for any foreign corporation that became stapled to a domestic corporation after June 30, 1983; and

(ii) January 1, 1987, for any foreign corporation that was stapled to a domestic corporation as of June 30, 1983.

(3) Paragraph (d)(2) of this section is applicable for taxable years beginning after July 22, 2003, except that in the case of a foreign corporation that becomes stapled to a domestic corporation on or after July 22, 2003, paragraph (d)(2) of this section applies for taxable years ending on or after July 22, 2003.

(4) Paragraph (e) of this section is applicable beginning on July 18, 1984, except as provided in paragraph (g)(5) of this section.

(5) In the case of a foreign corporation that was stapled to a domestic corporation as of June 30, 1983, which was entitled to claim benefits under an income tax treaty as of that date, and which remains eligible for such treaty benefits, paragraph (e) of this section will not apply to such foreign corporation and for all purposes of the Internal Revenue Code such corporation will continue to be treated as a foreign entity. The prior sentence will continue to apply even if such treaty is subsequently modified by protocol, or superseded by a new treaty, so long as the stapled foreign corporation continues to be eligible to claim such treaty benefits. If the treaty benefits to which the stapled foreign corporation was entitled as of June 30, 1983, are terminated, then a deemed conversion of the foreign corporation to a domestic corporation shall occur pursuant to paragraph (c) of this section as of the date of such termination. [[Reg. § 1.269B-1.]

☐ [*T.D. 9216*, 7-28-2005. Amended by *T.D. 9739*, 9-18-2015.]

Distributions by Corporations

§ 1.304-4. Special rules for the use of related corporations to avoid the application of section 304.—(a) *Scope and purpose.*—This section applies to determine the amount of a property distribution constituting a dividend (and the source thereof) under section 304(b)(2), for certain transactions involving controlled corporations. The purpose of this section is to prevent the avoidance of the application of section 304 to a controlled corporation.

(b) *Amount and source of dividend.*—For purposes of determining the amount constituting a dividend (and source thereof) under section 304(b)(2), the following rules shall apply:

(1) *Deemed acquiring corporation.*—A corporation (deemed acquiring corporation) shall be treated as acquiring for property the stock of a corporation (issuing corporation) acquired for property by another corporation (acquiring corporation) that is controlled by the deemed acquiring corporation, if a principal purpose for creating, organizing, or funding the acquiring corporation by any means (including through capital contributions or debt) is to avoid the application of section 304 to the deemed acquiring corporation. See paragraph (c) *Example 1* of this section for an illustration of this paragraph.

(2) *Deemed issuing corporation.*—The acquiring corporation shall be treated as acquiring for property the stock of a corporation (deemed issuing corporation) controlled by the issuing corporation if, in connection with the acquisition for property of stock of the issuing corporation by the acquiring corporation, the issuing corporation acquired stock of the deemed issuing corporation with a principal purpose of avoiding the application of section 304 to the deemed issuing corporation. See paragraph (c) *Example 2* of this section for an illustration of this paragraph.

(c) *Examples.*—The rules of this section are illustrated by the following examples:

Example 1. (i) *Facts.* P, a domestic corporation, wholly owns CFC1, a controlled foreign corporation with substantial accumulated earnings and profits. CFC1 is organized in Country X, which imposes a high rate of tax on the income of CFC1. P also wholly owns CFC2, a controlled foreign corporation with accumulated earnings and profits of $200x. CFC2 is organized in Country Y, which imposes a low rate of tax on the income of CFC2. P wishes to own all of its foreign corporations in a direct chain and to repatriate the cash of CFC2. In order to avoid having to obtain Country X approval for the acquisition of CFC1 (a Country X corporation) by CFC2 (a Country Y corporation) and to avoid the dividend distribution from CFC2 to P that would result if CFC2 were the acquiring corporation, P causes CFC2 to form CFC3 in Country X and to contribute $100x to CFC3. CFC3 then acquires all of the stock of CFC1 from P for $100x.

(ii) *Result.* Because a principal purpose for creating, organizing, or funding CFC3 (acquiring corporation) is to avoid the application of section 304 to CFC2 (deemed acquiring corporation), under paragraph (b)(1) of this section, for purposes of determining the amount of the $100x distribution constituting a dividend (and source thereof) under section 304(b)(2), CFC2 shall be treated as acquiring the stock of CFC1 (issuing corporation) from P for $100x. As a result, P receives a $100x distribution out of the earnings and profits of CFC2 to which section 301(c)(1) applies.

Example 2. (i) *Facts.* P, a domestic corporation, wholly owns CFC1, a controlled foreign corporation with substantial accumulated earnings and profits. The CFC1 stock has a basis of $100x. CFC1 is organized in Country X. P also wholly owns CFC2, a controlled foreign corporation with zero accumulated earnings and profits. CFC2 is organized in Country Y. P wishes to own all of its foreign corporations in a direct chain and to repatriate the cash of CFC2. In order to avoid having to obtain Country X approval for the acquisition of CFC1 (a Country X corporation) by CFC2 (a Country Y corporation) and to avoid a dividend distribution from CFC1 to P, P forms a new corporation (CFC3) in Country X and transfers the stock of CFC1 to CFC3 in exchange for CFC3 stock. P then transfers the stock of CFC3 to CFC2 in exchange for $100x.

(ii) *Result.* Because a principal purpose for the transfer of the stock of CFC1 (deemed issuing corporation) by P to CFC3 (issuing corporation) is to avoid the application of section 304 to CFC1, under paragraph (b)(2) of this section, for purposes of determining the amount of the $100x distribution constituting a dividend (and source thereof) under section 304(b)(2), CFC2 (acquiring corporation) shall be treated as acquiring the stock of CFC1 from P for $100x. As a result, P receives a $100x distribution out of the earnings and profits of CFC1 to which section 301(c)(1) applies.

(d) *Effective/applicability date.*—This section applies to acquisitions of stock occurring on or after December 29, 2009. [Reg. § 1.304-4.]

□ [*T.D. 9477, 12-29-2009. Amended by T.D. 9606, 12-21-2012.*]

§ 1.304-6. Amount constituting a dividend.— [Reserved]

□ [*T.D. 9761, 4-4-2016.*]

§ 1.304-7. Certain acquisitions by foreign acquiring corporations.—(a) *Scope.*—This section provides rules regarding the application of section 304(b)(5)(B) to an acquisition of stock described in section 304 by an acquiring corporation that is foreign (foreign acquiring corporation). Paragraph (b) of this section provides the rule for determining which earnings and profits are taken into account for purposes of applying section 304(b)(5)(B). Paragraph (c) of this section provides rules addressing the use of a partnership, option (or similar interest), or other arrangement. Paragraph (d) of this section provides examples that illustrate the rules of this section. Paragraph (e) of this section provides the applicability date.

(b) *Earnings and profits taken into account.*—For purposes of applying section 304(b)(5)(B), only the earnings and profits of the foreign acquiring corporation are taken into account in determining whether more than 50 percent of the dividends arising from the acquisition (determined without regard to section 304(b)(5)(B)) would neither be subject to tax under chapter 1 of subtitle A of the Internal Revenue Code for the taxable year in which the dividends arise (subject to tax) nor be includible in the earnings and profits of a controlled foreign corporation (includible by a controlled foreign corporation). For purposes of this section, a controlled foreign corporation has the meaning provided in section 957 and without regard to section 953(c), determined without applying subparagraphs (A), (B), and (C) of section 318(a)(3) so as to consider a United States person as owning stock which is owned by a person who is not a United States person.

(c) *Use of a partnership, option (or similar interest), or other arrangement.*—If a partnership, option (or similar interest), or other arrangement, is used with a principal purpose of avoiding the application of this section (for example, to treat a transferor as a controlled foreign corporation), then the partnership, option (or similar interest), or other arrangement will be disregarded for purposes of applying this section.

(d) *Examples.*—The following examples illustrate the rules of this section. For purposes of the examples, assume the following facts in addition to the facts stated in the examples:

(1) FA is a foreign corporation that is not a controlled foreign corporation;

(2) FA wholly owns DT, a domestic corporation;

(3) DT wholly owns FS1, a controlled foreign corporation; and

(4) No portion of a dividend from FS1 would be treated as from sources within the United States under section 861.

Example 1—(i) *Facts.* DT has earnings and profits of $51x, and FS1 has earnings and profits of $49x. FA transfers DT stock with a fair market value of $100x to FS1 in exchange for $100x of cash.

(ii) *Analysis.* Under section 304(a)(2), the $100x of cash is treated as a distribution in redemption of the stock of DT. The redemption of the DT stock is treated as a distribution to which section 301 applies pursuant to section 302(d), which ordinarily would be sourced first from FS1 under section 304(b)(2)(A). Without regard to the application of section 304(b)(5)(B), more than 50 percent of the dividend arising from the acquisition, taking into account only the earnings and profits of FS1 pursuant to paragraph (b) of this section, would neither be subject to tax nor includible by a controlled foreign corporation. In particular, no portion of a dividend from FS1 would be subject to tax or includible by a controlled foreign corporation. Accordingly, section 304(b)(5)(B) and paragraph (b) of this section apply to the transaction, and no portion of the distribution of $100x is treated under section 301(c)(1) as a dividend out of the earnings and profits of FS1. Furthermore, the $100x of cash is treated as a dividend to the extent of the earnings and profits of DT ($51x).

Example 2—(i) *Facts.* FA and DT own 40 percent and 60 percent, respectively, of the capital and profits interests of PRS, a foreign partnership. PRS wholly owns FS2, a controlled foreign corporation. The FS2 stock has a fair market value of $100x. FS1 has earnings and profits of $150x. PRS transfers all of its FS2 stock to FS1 in exchange for $100x of cash. DT enters into a gain recognition agreement that complies with the requirements set forth in section 4.01 of Notice 2012-15, 2012-9 I.R.B 424, with respect to the portion (60 percent) of the FS2 stock that DT is deemed to transfer to FS1 in an exchange described in section 367(a)(1). See § 1.367(a)-1T(c)(3)(i)(A).

(ii) *Analysis.* Under section 304(a)(1), PRS and FS1 are treated as if PRS transferred its FS2 stock to FS1 in an exchange described in section 351(a) solely for FS1 stock, and, in turn, FS1 redeemed such FS1 stock in exchange for $100x of cash. The redemption of the FS1 stock is treated as a distribution to which section 301 applies pursuant to section 302(d). Without regard to the application of section 304(b)(5)(B), more than 50 percent of a dividend arising from the acquisition, taking into account only the earnings and profits of FS1 pursuant to paragraph (b) of this section, would be subject to tax. In particular, 60 percent of a dividend from FS1 would be included in DT's distributive share of PRS's partnership income and therefore would be subject to tax. Accordingly, section 304(b)(5)(B) does not apply, and the entire distribution of $100x is treated under section 301(c)(1) as a dividend out of the earnings and profits of FS1.

(e) *Applicability date.*—This section applies to acquisitions that are completed on or after September 22, 2014. [Reg. § 1.304-7.]

□ [*T.D. 9834, 7-11-2018.*]

§ 1.332-8. Recognition of gain on liquidation of certain holding companies.—(a) *Definition of controlled foreign corporation.*—For purposes of section 332(d)(3), a controlled foreign corporation has the meaning provided in section 957, determined without applying section 318(a)(3)(A), (B), and (C) so as to consider a United States person as owning stock which is owned by a person who is not a United States person.

(b) *Applicability date.*—This section applies to distributions in complete liquidation occurring on or after October 1, 2019, and to distributions in complete liquidation occurring before October 1, 2019, that result from an entity classification election made under § 301.7701-3 of this chapter that is filed on or after October 1, 2019. For distributions in complete liquidation occurring before October 1, 2019, other than distributions in complete liquidation occurring before October 1, 2019, that result from an entity classification election made under § 301.7701-3 of this chapter that is filed on or after October 1, 2019, a taxpayer may apply this section to distributions in complete liquidation occurring during the last taxable year of a distributee foreign corporation beginning before January 1, 2018, and each subsequent taxable year of the foreign corporation, provided that the taxpayer and United States persons that are related (within the meaning of section 267 or 707) to the taxpayer consistently apply this section with respect to all foreign corporations. [Reg. § 1.332-8.]

□ [*T.D. 9908, 9-21-2020.*]

§ 1.334-1. Basis of property received in liquidations.—(a) *In general.*—Section 334 sets forth rules for determining a distributee's basis in property received in a distribution in complete liquidation of a corporation. The general rule is set forth in section 334(a) and provides that, if property is received in a distribution in complete liquidation of a corporation and if gain or loss is recognized on the receipt of the property, then the distributee's basis in the property is the fair market value of the property at the time of the distribution. However, if property is received in a complete liquidation to which section 332 applies, including property received in satisfaction of an indebtedness described in section 337(b)(1), see section 334(b)(1) and paragraph (b) of this section.

(b) *Liquidations under section 332.*—(1) *General rule.*—Except as otherwise provided in paragraph (b)(2) or (3) of this section, if a corporation (P) meeting the ownership requirements of section 332(b)(1) receives property from a subsidiary (S) in a complete liquidation to which section 332 applies (section 332 liquidation), including property received in a transfer in satisfaction of indebtedness that satisfies the requirements of section 337(b)(1), P's basis in the property received is the same as S's basis in the property immediately before the property was distributed. However, see § 1.460-4(k)(3)(iv)(B)(2) for rules relating to adjustments to the basis of certain contracts accounted for using a long-term contract method of accounting that are acquired in a section 332 liquidation.

(2) *Basis in property with respect to which gain or loss was recognized.*—Except as otherwise provided in Subtitle A of the Internal Revenue Code (Code) and this subchapter of the Income Tax Regulations, if S recognizes gain or loss on the distribution of property to P in a section 332 liquidation, P's basis in that property is the fair market value of the property at the time of the distribution. Section 334(b)(1)(A) (certain tax-exempt distributions under section 337(b)(2)); see also, for example, § 1.367(e)-2(b)(3)(i).

(3) *Basis in importation property received in loss importation transaction.*—(i) *Purpose.*—The purpose of section 334(b)(1)(B) and this paragraph (b)(3) is to modify the application of this section to prevent P from importing a net built-in loss in a transaction described in section 332. See paragraph (b)(3)(iii)(A) of this section for definitions of terms used in this paragraph (b)(3).

(ii) *Determination of basis.*—Notwithstanding paragraph (b)(1) of this section, if a section 332 liquidation is a loss importation transaction, P's basis in each importation property received from S in the liquidation is an amount that is equal to the value of the property. The basis of property received in a section 332 liquidation that is not importation property received in a loss importation transaction is determined under generally applicable basis rules without regard to whether the liquidation also involves the receipt of importation property in a loss importation transaction.

(iii) *Operating rules.*—(A) *In general.*—For purposes of section 334(b)(1)(B) and this paragraph (b)(3), the provisions of § 1.362-3 (basis of importation property received in a loss importation transaction) apply, adjusted as appropriate to apply to section 332 liquidations. Thus, when used in this paragraph (b)(3), the terms "importation property," "loss importation transaction," and "value" have the same meaning as in § 1.362-3(c)(2), (3), and (4), respectively, except that "the section 332(b)(1) distributee corporation" is substituted for "Acquiring" and "section 332 liquidation" is substituted for "section 362 transaction." Similarly, when gain or loss on property would be owned or treated as owned by multiple persons, the provisions of § 1.362-3(d)(2) apply to tentatively divide the property in applying this section, substituting "section 332 liquidation" for "section 362 transaction" and making such other adjustments as necessary.

(B) *Time for making determinations.*—For purposes of section 334(b)(1)(B) and this paragraph (b)(3)—

(1) P's basis in distributed property.—P's basis in each property S distributes to P in the section 332 liquidation is determined immediately after S distributes each such property;

(2) Value of distributed property.—The value of each property S distributes to P in the section 332 liquidation is determined immediately after S distributes the property;

(3) Importation property.—The determination of whether each property distributed by S is importation property is made as of the time S distributes each such property;

(4) Loss importation transaction.—The determination of whether a section 332 liquidation is a loss importation transaction is made immediately after S makes the final liquidating distribution to P.

(C) *Effect of basis determination under this paragraph (b)(3).*—*(1) Determination by reference to transferor's basis.*—A determination of basis under section 334(b)(1)(B) and this paragraph (b)(3) is a determination by reference to the transferor's basis, including for purposes of sections 1223(2) and 7701(a)(43). However, solely for purposes of applying section 755, a determination of basis under this paragraph (b)(3) is treated as a determination not by reference to the transferor's basis.

(2) Not tax-exempt income or noncapital, nondeductible expense.—The application of this paragraph (b)(3) does not give rise to an item treated as tax-exempt income under § 1.1502-32(b)(2)(ii) or as a noncapital, nondeductible expense under § 1.1502-32(b)(2)(iii)

(3) No effect on earnings and profits.—Any determination of basis under this paragraph (b)(3) does not reduce or otherwise affect the calculation of the all earnings and profits amount provided in § 1.367(b)-2(d).

(iv) *Examples.*—The examples in this paragraph (b)(3)(iv) illustrate the application of section 334(b)(1)(B) and the provisions of this paragraph (b)(3). Unless the facts indicate otherwise, the examples use the following nomenclature and assumptions: USP is a domestic corporation that has not elected to be an S corporation within the meaning of section 1361(a)(1); FC, CFC1, and CFC2 are controlled foreign corporations within the meaning of section 957(a), which are not engaged in a U.S. trade or business, have no U.S. real property interests, and have no other relationships, activities, or interests that would cause their property to be subject to any tax imposed under subtitle A of the Code (federal income tax); there is no applicable income tax treaty; and all persons and transactions are unrelated. All other relevant facts are set forth in the examples:

Example 1. Basic application of this paragraph (b)(3). (i) *Distribution of importation property in a loss importation transaction.* (A) *Facts.* USP owns the sole outstanding share of FC stock. FC owns three assets, A1 (basis $40, value $50), A2 (basis $120, value $30), and A3 (basis $140, value $20). On Date 1, FC distributes A1, A2, and A3 to USP in a complete liquidation that qualifies under section 332.

(B) *Importation property.* Under § 1.362-3(d)(2), the fact that any gain or loss recognized by a CFC may affect an income inclusion under section 951(a) does not alone cause gain or loss recognized by the CFC to be treated as taken into account in determining a federal income tax liability for purposes of this section. Thus, if FC had sold either A1, A2, or A3 immediately before the transaction, no gain or loss recognized on the sale would have been taken into account in determining a federal income tax liability. Further, if USP had sold A1, A2, or A3 immediately after the transaction, USP would take into account any gain or loss recognized on the sale in determining its federal income tax liability. Therefore, A1, A2, and A3 are all importation properties. See paragraph (b)(3)(iii)(A) of this section and § 1.362-3(c)(2).

(C) *Loss importation transaction.* Immediately after the distribution, USP's aggregate basis in the importation properties, A1, A2, and A3, would, but for section 334(b)(1)(B) and this section, be $300 ($40 + $120 + $140) and the properties' aggregate value would be $100 ($50 + $30 + $20). Therefore, the importation properties' aggregate basis would exceed their aggregate value and the distribution is a loss importation transaction. See paragraph (b)(3)(iii)(A) of this section and § 1.362-3(c)(3).

(D) *Basis of importation property distributed in loss importation transaction.* Because the importation properties, A1, A2, and A3, were transferred in a loss importation transaction, the basis in each of the importation properties received is equal to its value immediately after FC distributes the property. Accordingly, USP's basis in A1 is $50; USP's basis in A2 is $30; and USP's basis in A3 is $20.

(ii) *Distribution of both importation and non-importation property in a loss importation transaction.* (A) *Facts.* The facts are the same as in paragraph (i)(A) of this *Example 1* except that FC is engaged in a U.S. trade or business and A3 is used in that U.S. trade or business.

(B) *Importation property.* A1 and A2 are importation properties for the reasons set forth in paragraph (i)(B) of this *Example 1.* However, if FC had sold A3 immediately before the transaction, FC would take into account any gain or loss recognized on the sale in determining its federal income tax liability. Therefore, A3 is not importation property. See paragraph (b)(3)(iii)(A) of this section and § 1.362-3(c)(2).

(C) *Loss importation transaction.* Immediately after the distribution, USP's aggregate basis in the importation properties, A1 and A2, would, but for section 334(b)(1)(B) and this section, be $160 ($40 + $120). Further, the properties' aggregate value would be $80 ($50 + $30). Therefore, the importation properties' aggregate basis would exceed their aggregate value and the distribution is a loss importation transaction. See paragraph (b)(3)(iii)(A) of this section and § 1.362-3(c)(3).

(D) *Basis of importation property distributed in loss importation transaction.* Because the importation properties, A1 and A2, were transferred in a loss importation transaction, the basis in each of the importation properties received is equal to its value immediately after FC distributes the property. Accordingly, USP's basis in A1 is $50 and USP's basis in A2 is $30.

(E) *Basis of other property.* Because A3 is not importation property distributed in a loss importation transaction, USP's basis in A3 is determined under generally applicable basis rules. Accordingly, USP's basis in A3 is $140, the adjusted basis that FC had in the property immediately before the distribution. See section 334(b)(1).

(iii) *FC not wholly owned.* The facts are the same as in paragraph (i)(A) of this *Example 1* except that USP owns only 80% of the sole outstanding class of FC stock and the remaining 20% is owned by individual X. Further, on Date 1 and pursuant to the plan of liquidation, FC distributes A1 and A2 to USP and A3 to X. A1 and A2 are importation properties, the distribution to USP is a loss importation transaction, and USP's bases in A1 and A2 are equal to their value ($50 and $30, respectively) for the reasons set forth in paragraphs (ii)(C) and (D) of this *Example 1.* Under section 334(a), X's basis in A3 is $20.

(iv) *Importation property, no net built in loss.* (A) *Facts.* The facts are the same as in paragraph (i)(A) of this *Example 1* except that the value of A2 is $230.

(B) *Importation property.* A1, A2, and A3, are importation properties for the reasons set forth in paragraph (i)(B) of this *Example 1.*

(C) *Loss importation transaction.* Immediately after the distribution, USP's aggregate basis in the importation properties, A1, A2, and A3, would, but for section 334(b)(1)(B) and this section, be $300 ($40 + $120 + $140). However, the properties' aggregate value would also be $300 ($50 + $230 + $20). Therefore, the importation properties' aggregate basis would not exceed their aggregate value and the distribution is not a loss importation transaction. See paragraph (b)(3)(iii)(A) of this section and § 1.362-3(c)(3).

(D) *Basis of importation property not distributed in loss importation transaction.* Because the importation properties, A1, A2, and A3, were not distributed in a loss importation transaction, the basis of each of the importation properties is determined under the generally applicable basis rules. Accordingly, immediately after the distribution, USP's basis in A1 is $40, USP's basis in A2 is $120, and USP's basis in A3 is $140, the adjusted bases that FC had in the properties immediately before the distribution. See section 334(b)(1).

(v) *CFC stock as importation property distributed in loss importation transaction.* (A) *Facts.* USP owns the sole outstanding share of FC stock. FC owns the sole outstanding share of CFC1 stock (basis $80, value $100) and the sole outstanding share of CFC2 stock (basis $100, value $5). On Date 1, FC distributes its shares of CFC1 and CFC2 stock to USP in a complete liquidation that qualifies under section 332.

(B) *Importation property.* No special rule applies to the treatment of property that is the stock of a CFC. Thus, if FC had sold either the CFC1 share or the CFC2 share immediately before the transaction, no gain or loss recognized on the sale would have been taken into account in determining a federal income tax liability. Further, if USP had sold either the CFC1 share or the CFC2 share immediately after the transaction, USP would take into account any gain or loss recognized on the sale in determining its federal income tax liability. Thus, the CFC1 share and the CFC2 share are importation property. See paragraph (b)(3)(iii)(A) of this section and § 1.362-3(c)(2).

(C) *Loss importation transaction.* Immediately after the distribution, USP's aggregate basis in importation property (the CFC1 share and the CFC2 share) would, but for section 334(b)(1)(B) and this section, be $180 ($80 + $100) and the shares' aggregate value is $105 ($100 + $5). Therefore, the importation property's aggregate basis would exceed their aggregate value and the distribution is a loss importation transaction. See paragraph (b)(3)(iii)(A) of this section and § 1.362-3(c)(3).

(D) *Basis of importation property distributed in loss importation transaction.* Because the importation property (the CFC1 share and the CFC2 share) was transferred in a loss importation transaction, USP's basis in each of the shares received is equal to its value immediately after FC distributes the shares. Accordingly, USP's basis in the CFC1 share is $100 and USP's basis in the CFC2 share is $5.

Example 2. Multiple step liquidation. (i) *Facts.* USP owns the sole outstanding share of FC stock. On January 1 of year 1, FC adopts a plan of liquidation. FC makes the following distributions to USP in a transaction that qualifies as a complete liquidation under section 332. In year 1, FC distributes A1 and, immediately before the distribution, FC's basis in A1 is $100 and A1's value is $120. In Year 2, FC distributes A2, and, immediately before the distribution, FC's basis in A2 is $100 and A2's value is $120. In year 3, in its final liquidating distribution, FC distributes A3 and, immediately before the distribution, FC's basis in A3 is $100 and A3's value is $120. As of the time of the final distribution, USP had depreciated the bases of A1 and A2 to $90 and $95, respectively; the value of A1 had appreciated to $160; and, the value of A2 has declined to $0.

(ii) *Importation property.* If FC had sold either A1, A2, or A3 immediately before it was distributed, no gain or loss recognized on the sale would have been taken into account in determining a federal income tax liability. Further, if USP had sold either A1, A2, or A3 immediately after it was distributed, USP would take into account any gain or loss recognized on the sale in determining its federal income tax liability. Therefore, A1, A2, and A3 are all importation properties. See paragraph (b)(3)(iii)(A) of this section and § 1.362-3(c)(2).

(iii) *Loss importation transaction.* Immediately after it was distributed, USP's basis in each of the importation properties, A1, A2, and A3, would, but for section 334(b)(1)(B) and this section, have been $100. Further, immediately after each such property was distributed, its value was $120. Thus, the properties' aggregate basis, $300, would not have exceeded the properties' aggregate value, $360. Accordingly, the distribution is not a loss importation transaction irrespective of the fact that, when the liquidation was completed, the properties' aggregate basis was $285 and the properties' aggregate value was $280. See paragraph (b)(3)(iii)(B) of this section and § 1.362-3(c)(3).

(iv) *Basis of importation property not distributed in loss importation transaction.* Because the importation properties, A1, A2, and A3, were not distributed in a loss importation transaction, the basis of each of the importation properties is determined under the generally applicable basis rules. Accordingly, USP takes each of the properties with a basis of $100 and, immediately after the final distribution, has an adjusted basis of $90 in A1 (USP's $100 basis less the $10 depreciation), $95 in A2 (USP's $100 basis less the $5 depreciation), and $100 in A3. See section 334(b).

(c) *Applicability date.*—This section applies with respect to liquidations occurring on or after March 28, 2016, and also with respect to liquidations occurring before such date as a result of an entity classification election under § 301.7701-3 of this chapter filed on or after March 28, 2016, unless such liquidation is pursuant to a binding agreement that was in effect prior to March 28, 2016 and at all times thereafter. In addition, taxpayers may apply this section to any section 332 liquidation occurring after October 22, 2004. [Reg. § 1.334-1.]

☐ [*T.D.* 6152, 12-2-55. *Amended by T.D.* 6298, 6-23-58; *T.D.* 7231, 12-21-72; *T.D.* 8474, 4-26-93, *T.D.* 8995, 5-14-2002 *and T.D.* 9759, 3-25-2016.]

§ 1.336-2. Availability, mechanics, and consequences of section 336(e) election.—

* * *

(g) * * *

(3) *International provisions.*—(i) *Source and foreign tax credit.*—The principles of section 338(h)(16) apply to section 336(e) elections for targets with foreign operations to ensure that the source and foreign tax credit limitation are properly determined.

(ii) *Allocation of foreign income taxes.*—(A) *General rule.*—Except as provided in paragraph (g)(3)(ii)(B) of this section, if a section 336(e) election is made for target and target's taxable year under foreign law (if any) does not close at the end of the disposition date, foreign income tax as defined in § 1.960-1(b) (other than a withholding tax as defined in section 901(k)(1)(B)) paid or accrued by new target with respect to such foreign taxable year is allocated between old target and new target. If there is more than one section 336(e) election with respect to target during target's foreign taxable year, foreign income tax paid or accrued with respect to that foreign taxable year is allocated among all old targets and new targets. The allocation is made based on the respective portions of the taxable income (as determined under foreign law) for the foreign taxable year that are attributable under the principles of § 1.1502-76(b) to the period of existence of each old target and new target during the foreign taxable year.

(B) *Foreign income taxes imposed on partnerships and disregarded entities.*—If a section 336(e) election is made for target and target holds an interest in a disregarded entity (as described in § 301.7701-2(c)(2)(i) of this chapter) or partnership, the rules of § 1.901-2(f)(4) and (5) apply to determine the person who is considered for Federal income tax purposes to pay foreign income tax imposed at the entity level on the income of the disregarded entity or partnership.

(iii) *Disallowance of foreign tax credits under section 901(m).*—For rules that may apply to disallow foreign tax credits by reason of a section 336(e) election, see section 901(m) and § § 1.901(m)-1 through 1.901(m)-8.

* * *

☐ [*T.D. 9619, 5-10-2013 (corrected 8-27-2013). Amended by T.D.* 9959, 12-28-2021.]

§ 1.336-5. Applicability dates.—Except as otherwise provided in this section, the provisions of § § 1.336-1 through 1.336-4 apply to any qualified stock disposition for which the disposition date is on or after May 15, 2013. The provisions of § 1.336-1(b)(5)(i)(A) relating to section 1022 apply on and after January 19, 2017. The provisions of § 1.336-2(g)(3)(ii) and (iii) apply to foreign income taxes paid or accrued in taxable years beginning on or after December 28, 2021. [Reg. § 1.336-5.]

☐ [*T.D. 9619, 5-10-2013. Amended by T.D. 9811, 1-18-2017 and T.D.* 9959, 12-28-2021.]

§ 1.337-1. Nonrecognition for property distributed to parent in complete liquidation of subsidiary.—(a) *General rule.*—If sections 332(a) and 337 are applicable with respect to the receipt of a subsidiary's property in complete liquidation, no gain or loss is recognized to the liquidating subsidiary with respect to such property (including property distributed with respect to indebtedness, see section 337(b)(1) and § 1.332-7), except as provided in section 337(b)(2) (distributions to certain tax-exempt distributees), section 367(e)(2) (distributions to foreign corporations), and section 897(d) (distributions of U.S. real property interests by foreign corporations).

(b) *Aplicability date.*—This section applies to any taxable year beginning on or after March 28, 2016. [Reg. § 1.337-1.]

☐ [*T.D. 9759, 3-25-2016.*]

Section 338 Elections

§ 1.338-1. General principles; status of old target and new target.—(a) *In general.*—(1) *Deemed transaction.*—Elections are available under section 338 when a purchasing corporation acquires the stock of another corporation (the target) in a qualified stock purchase. One type of election, under section 338(g), is available to the purchasing corporation. Another type of election, under section 338(h)(10), is, in more limited circumstances, available jointly to the purchasing corporation and the sellers of the stock. (Rules concerning eligibility for these elections are contained in § § 1.338-2, 1.338-3, and 1.338(h)(10)-1.) However, if, as a result of the deemed purchase of old target's assets pursuant to a section 336(e) election, there would be both a qualified stock purchase and a qualified stock disposition (as defined in § 1.336-1(b)(6)) of the stock of a subsidiary of target, neither a section 338(g) election nor a section 338(h)(10) election may be made with respect to the qualified stock purchase of the subsidiary. Instead, a section 336(e) election may be made with respect to such purchase. See § 1.336-1(b)(6)(ii). Although target is a single corporation under corporate law, if a section 338 election is made, then two separate corporations, old target and new target, generally are considered to exist for purposes of subtitle A of the Internal Revenue Code. Old target is treated as transferring all of its assets to an unrelated person in exchange for consideration that includes the discharge of its liabilities (see § 1.1001-2(a)), and new target is treated as acquiring all of its assets from an unrelated person in exchange for consideration that includes the assumption of those liabilities. (Such transaction is, without regard to its characterization for Federal income tax purposes, referred to as the deemed asset sale and the income tax consequences thereof as the deemed sale tax consequences.) If a section 338(h)(10) election is made, old target is deemed to liquidate following the deemed asset sale.

(2) *Application of other rules of law.*—Other rules of law apply to determine the tax consequences to the parties as if they had actually engaged in the transactions deemed to occur under section 338 and the regulations thereunder except to the extent otherwise provided in those regulations. See also § 1.338-6(c)(2). Other rules of law may characterize the transaction as something other than or in addition to a sale and purchase of assets; however, the transaction between old and new target must be a taxable transaction. For example, if the target is an insurance company for which a section 338 election is made, the deemed asset sale results in an assumption reinsurance transaction for the insurance contracts deemed transferred from old target to new target. See, generally, § 1.817-4(d), and for special rules regarding the acquisition of insurance company targets, § 1.338-11. See also § 1.367(a)-8(k)(13) for a rule applicable to gain recognition agreements (filed under section § § 1.367(a)-3(b)(1)(ii) and 1.367(a)-8) and deemed asset sales as a result of an election under section 338(g).

(3) *Overview.*—Definitions and special nomenclature and rules for making the section 338 election are provided in § 1.338-2. Qualification for the section 338 election is addressed in § 1.338-3. The amount for which old target is treated as selling all of its assets (the aggregate deemed sale price, or ADSP) is addressed in § 1.338-4. The amount for which new target is deemed to have purchased all its assets (the adjusted grossed-up basis, or AGUB) is addressed in § 1.338-5. Section 1.338-6 addresses allocation both of ADSP among the assets old target is deemed to have sold and of AGUB among the assets new target is deemed to have purchased. Section 1.338-7 addresses allocation of ADSP or AGUB when those amounts subsequently change. Asset and stock consistency are addressed in § 1.338-8. International aspects of section 338 are covered in § 1.338-9. Rules for the filing of returns are provided in § 1.338-10. Section 1.338-11 provides special rules for insurance company targets. Eligibility for and treatment of section 338(h)(10) elections is addressed in § 1.338(h)(10)-1.

(b) *Treatment of target under other provisions of the Internal Revenue Code.*—(1) *General rule for subtitle A.*—Except as provided in this section, new target is treated as a new corporation that is unrelated to old target for purposes of subtitle A of the Internal Revenue Code. Thus—

(i) New target is not considered related to old target for purposes of section 168 and may make new elections under section 168 without taking into account the elections made by old target; and

(ii) New target may adopt, without obtaining prior approval from the Commissioner, any taxable year that meets the requirements of section 441 and any method of accounting that meets the requirements of section 446. Notwithstanding § 1.441-1T(b)(2), a new target may adopt a taxable year on or before the last day for making the election under section 338 by filing its first return for the desired taxable year on or before that date.

(2) *Exceptions for subtitle A.*—New target and old target are treated as the same corporation for purposes of—

(i) The rules applicable to employee benefit plans (including those plans described in sections 79, 104, 105, 106, 125, 127, 129, 132, 137, and 220), qualified pension, profit-sharing, stock bonus and annuity plans (sections 401(a) and 403(a)), simplified employee pensions (section 408(k)), tax qualified stock option plans (sections 422 and 423), welfare benefit funds (sections 419, 419A, 512(a)(3), and 4976), voluntary employees' beneficiary associations (section 501(c)(9) and the regulations thereunder), and tax on excess tax-exempt organization executive compensation (section 4960) and the regulations in part 53 under section 4960;

(ii) Sections 1311 through 1314 (relating to the mitigation of the effect of limitations), if a section 338(h)(10) election is not made for target;

(iii) Section 108(e)(5) (relating to the reduction of purchase money debt);

(iv) Section 45A (relating to the Indian Employment Credit), section 51 (relating to the Work Opportunity Credit), section 51A (relating to the Welfare to Work Credit), and section 1396 (relating to the Empowerment Zone Act);

(v) Sections 401(h) and 420 (relating to medical benefits for retirees);

(vi) Section 414 (relating to definitions and special rules); and

(vii) Section 846(e) (relating to an election to use an insurance company's historical loss payment pattern).

(viii) Any other provision designated in the Internal Revenue Bulletin by the Internal Revenue Service. See § 601.601(d)(2)(ii) of this chapter. See, for example, § 1.1001-3(e)(4)(i)(F) providing that an election under section 338 does not result in the substitution of a new obligor on target's debt. See also, for example, § 1.1502-77(c)(8), providing that an election under section 338 does not result in a deemed termination of target's existence for purposes of the rules applicable to the agent for a consolidated group.

(3) *General rule for other provisions of the Internal Revenue Code.*—Except as provided in the regulations under section 338 or in the Internal Revenue Bulletin by the Internal Revenue Service (see § 601.601(d)(2)(ii) of this chapter), new target is treated as a continuation of old target for purposes other than subtitle A of the Internal Revenue Code. For example—

(i) New target is liable for old target's Federal income tax liabilities, including the tax liability for the deemed sale tax consequences and those tax liabilities of the other members of any consolidated group that included old target that are attributable to taxable years in which those corporations and old target joined in the same consolidated return (see § 1.1502-6(a));

(ii) Wages earned by the employees of old target are considered wages earned by such employees from new target for purposes of sections 3101 and 3111 (Federal Insurance Contributions Act) and section 3301 (Federal Unemployment Tax Act); and

(iii) Old target and new target must use the same employer identification number.

(c) *Anti-abuse rule.*—(1) *In general.*—The rules of this paragraph (c) apply for purposes of applying the regulations under sections 336(e), 338, and 1060. The Commissioner is authorized to treat any property (including cash) transferred by old target in connection with the transactions resulting in the application of the residual method (and not held by target at the close of the acquisition date) as, nonetheless, property of target at the close of the acquisition date if the property so transferred is, within 24 months after the deemed asset sale, owned by new target, or is owned, directly or indirectly, by a member of the affiliated group of which new target is a member and continues after the acquisition date to be held or used primarily in connection with one or more of the activities of new target. In addition, the Commissioner is authorized to treat any property (including cash) transferred to old target in connection with the transactions resulting in the application of the residual method (and held by target at the close of the acquisition date) as, nonetheless, not being property of target at the close of the acquisition date if the property so transferred is, within 24 months after the deemed asset sale, not owned by new target but owned, directly or indirectly, by a member of the affiliated group of which new target is a member, or owned by new target but held or used primarily in connection with an activity conducted, directly or indirectly, by another member of the affiliated group of which new target is a member in combination with other property retained by or acquired, directly or indirectly, from the transferor of the property (or a member of the same affiliated group) to old target. For purposes of this paragraph (c)(1), an interest in an entity is considered held or used in connection with an activity if property of the entity is so held or used. The authority of the Commissioner under this paragraph (c)(1) includes the making of any appropriate correlative adjustments (avoiding, to the extent possible, the duplication or omission of any item of income, gain, loss, deduction, or basis).

(2) *Examples.*—The following examples illustrate this paragraph (c):

Example 1. Prior to a qualified stock purchase under section 338, target transfers one of its assets to a related party. The purchasing corporation then purchases the target stock and also purchases the transferred asset from the related party. After its purchase of target, the purchasing corporation and target are members of the same affiliated group. A section 338 election is made. Under an arrangement with the purchaser, the separately transferred asset is used primarily in connection with target's activities. Applying the anti-abuse rule of this paragraph (c), the Commissioner may consider target to own the transferred asset for purposes of applying the residual method under section 338.

Example 2. T owns all the stock of T1. T1 leases intellectual property to T, which T uses in connection with its own activities. P, a purchasing corporation, wishes to buy the T-T1 chain of corporations. P, in connection with its planned purchase of the T stock, contracts to consummate a purchase of all the stock of T1 on March 1 and of all the stock of T on March 2. Section 338 elections are thereafter made for both T and T1. Immediately after the purchases, P, T and T1 are members of the same affiliated group. T continues to lease the intellectual property from T1 and that is the primary use of the intellectual property. Thus, an asset of T, the T1 stock, was removed from T's own assets prior to the qualified stock purchase of the T stock, T1's own assets are used after the deemed asset sale in connection with T's own activities, and the T1 stock is after the deemed asset sale owned by P, a member of the same affiliated group of which T is a member. Applying the anti-abuse rule of this paragraph (c), the Commissioner may, for purposes of application of the residual method under section 338 both to T and to T1, consider P to have bought only the stock of T, with T at the time of the qualified stock purchases of both T and T1 (the qualified stock purchase of T1 being triggered by the deemed sale under section 338 of T's assets) owning T1. The Commissioner accordingly would allocate consideration to T's assets as though the T1 stock were one of those assets, and then allocate consideration within T1 based on the amount allocated to the T1 stock at the T level.

(d) *Next day rule for post-closing transactions.*—If a target corporation for which an election under section 338 is made engages in a transaction outside the ordinary course of business on the acquisition date after the event resulting in the qualified stock purchase of the target or a higher tier corporation, the target and all persons related thereto (either before or after the qualified stock purchase) under section 267(b) or section 707 must treat the transaction for all Federal income tax purposes as occurring at the beginning of the day following the transaction and after the deemed purchase by new target.

(e) *Effective/applicability date.*—Paragraphs (a)(1) and (c)(1) of this section are applicable to any qualified stock disposition for which the disposition date (as defined in § 1.336-1(b)(8)) is on or after May 15, 2013. [Reg. § 1.338-1.]

☐ [*T.D.* 8940, 2-12-2001. *Amended by T.D.* 9002, 6-27-2002; *T.D.* 9257, 4-7-2006; *T.D.* 9377, 1-22-2008; *T.D.* 9446, 2-9-2009; *T.D.* 9619, 5-10-2013; *T.D.* 9715, 3-31-2015; *T.D.* 9932, 12-28-2020 *and T.D.* 9938, 1-15-2021.]

§ 1.338-2. Nomenclature and definitions; mechanics of the section 338 election.—(a) *Scope.*—This section prescribes rules relating to elections under section 338.

(b) *Nomenclature.*—For purposes of the regulations under section 338 (except as otherwise provided):

(1) T is a domestic target corporation that has only one class of stock outstanding. Old T refers to T for periods ending on or before the close of T's acquisition date; new T refers to T for subsequent periods.

(2) P is the purchasing corporation.

(3) The P group is an affiliated group of which P is a member.

(4) P1, P2, etc., are domestic corporations that are members of the P group.

(5) T1, T2, etc., are domestic corporations that are target affiliates of T. These corporations (T1, T2, etc.) have only one class of stock outstanding and may also be targets.

(6) S is a domestic corporation (unrelated to P and B) that owns T prior to the purchase of T by P. (S is referred to in cases in which it is appropriate to consider the effects of having all of the outstanding stock of T owned by a domestic corporation.)

(7) A, a U.S. citizen or resident, is an individual (unrelated to P and B) who owns T prior to the purchase of T by P. (A is referred to in cases in which it is appropriate to consider the effects of having all of the outstanding stock of T owned by an individual who is a U.S. citizen or resident. Ownership of T by A and ownership of T by S are mutually exclusive circumstances.)

(8) B, a U.S. citizen or resident, is an individual (unrelated to T, S, and A) who owns the stock of P.

(9) F, used as a prefix with the other terms in this paragraph (b), connotes foreign, rather than domestic, status. For example, FT is a foreign corporation (as defined in section 7701(a)(5)) and FA is an individual other than a U.S. citizen or resident.

(10) CFC, used as a prefix with the other terms in this paragraph (b) referring to a corporation, connotes a controlled foreign corporation (as defined in section 957, taking into account section 953(c)). A corporation identified with the prefix F may be a controlled foreign corporation. (The prefix CFC is used when the corporation's status as a controlled foreign corporation is significant.)

(c) *Definitions.*—For purposes of the regulations under section 338 (except as otherwise provided):

(1) *Acquisition date.*—The term *acquisition date* has the same meaning as in section 338(h)(2).

(2) *Acquisition date assets.*— *Acquisition date assets* are the assets of the target held at the beginning of the day after the acquisition date (but see § 1.338-1(d) (regarding certain transactions on the acquisition date)).

(3) *Affiliated group.*—The term *affiliated group* has the same meaning as in section 338(h)(5). Corporations are affiliated on any day they are members of the same affiliated group.

(4) *Common parent.*—The term *common parent* has the same meaning as in section 1504.

(5) *Consistency period.*—The *consistency period* is the period described in section 338(h)(4)(A) unless extended pursuant to § 1.338-8(j)(1).

(6) *Deemed asset sale.*—The *deemed asset sale* is the transaction described in § 1.338-1(a)(1) that is deemed to occur for purposes of subtitle A of the Internal Revenue Code if a section 338 election is made.

(7) *Deemed sale tax consequences.*— *Deemed sale tax consequences* refers to, in the aggregate, the Federal income tax consequences (generally, the income, gain, deduction, and loss) of the deemed asset sale. Deemed sale tax consequences also refers to the Federal income tax consequences of the transfer of a particular asset in the deemed asset sale.

(8) *Deemed sale return.*—The *deemed sale return* is the return on which target's deemed sale tax consequences are reported that does not include any other items of target. Target files a deemed sale return when a section 338 election (but not a section 338(h)(10) election) is filed for target and target is a member of a selling group (defined in paragraph (c)(16) of this section) that files a consolidated return for the period that includes the acquisition date. See § 1.338-10. If target is an S corporation for the period that ends on the day before the acquisition date and a section 338 election (but not a section 338(h)(10) election) is filed for target, see § 1.338-10(a)(3).

(9) *Domestic corporation.*—A *domestic corporation* is a corporation—

(i) That is domestic within the meaning of section 7701(a)(4) or that is treated as domestic for purposes of subtitle A of the Internal Revenue Code (e.g., to which an election under section 953(d) or 1504(d) applies); and

(ii) That is not a DISC, a corporation described in section 1248(e), or a corporation to which an election under section 936 applies.

(10) *Old target's final return.*— *Old target's final return* is the income tax return of old target for the taxable year ending at the close of the acquisition date that includes the deemed sale tax consequences. However, if a deemed sale return is filed for old target, the deemed sale return is considered old target's final return.

(11) *Purchasing corporation.*—The term *purchasing corporation* has the same meaning as in section 338(d)(1). The purchasing corporation may also be referred to as purchaser. Unless otherwise provided, any reference to the purchasing corporation is a reference to all members of the affiliated group of which the purchasing corporation is a member. See sections 338(h)(5) and (8). Also, unless otherwise provided, any reference to the purchasing corporation is, with respect to a deemed purchase of stock under section 338(a)(2), a reference to new target with respect to its own deemed purchase of stock in another target.

(12) *Qualified stock purchase.*—The term *qualified stock purchase* has the same meaning as in section 338(d)(3).

(13) *Related persons.*—Two persons are related if stock in a corporation owned by one of the persons would be attributed under section 318(a) (other than section 318(a)(4)) to the other.

(14) *Section 338 election.*—A *section 338 election* is an election to apply section 338(a) to target. A section 338 election is made by filing a statement of section 338 election pursuant to paragraph (d) of this section. The form on which this statement is filed is referred to in the regulations under section 338 as the Form 8023, "Elections Under Section 338 For Corporations Making Qualified Stock Purchases."

(15) *Section 338(h)(10) election.*—A *section 338(h)(10) election* is an election to apply section 338(h)(10) to target. A section 338(h)(10) election is made by making a joint election for target under § 1.338(h)(10)-1 on Form 8023.

(16) *Selling group.*—The *selling group* is the affiliated group (as defined in section 1504) eligible to file a consolidated return that includes target for the taxable period in which the acquisition date occurs. However, a selling group is not an affiliated group of which target is the common parent on the acquisition date.

(17) *Target; old target; new target.*— *Target* is the target corporation as defined in section 338(d)(2). *Old target* refers to target for periods ending on or before the close of target's acquisition date. *New target* refers to target for subsequent periods.

(18) *Target affiliate.*—The term *target affiliate* has the same meaning as in section 338(h)(6) (applied without section 338(h)(6)(B)(i)). Thus, a corporation described in section 338(h)(6)(B)(i) is considered a target affiliate for all purposes of section 338. If a target affiliate is acquired in a qualified stock purchase, it is also a target.

(19) *12-month acquisition period.*—The *12-month acquisition period* is the period described in section 338(h)(1), unless extended pursuant to § 1.338-8(j)(2).

(d) *Time and manner of making election.*—The purchasing corporation makes a section 338 election for target by filing a statement of section 338 election on Form 8023 in accordance with the instructions to the form. The section 338 election must be made not later than the 15th day of the 9th month beginning after the month in which the acquisition date occurs. A section 338 election is irrevocable. See § 1.338(h)(10)-1(c)(2) for section 338(h)(10) elections.

(e) *Special rules for foreign corporations or DISCs.*—(1) *Elections by certain foreign purchasing corporations.*—(i) *General rule.*—A qualifying foreign purchasing corporation is not required to file a statement of section 338 election for a qualifying foreign target before the earlier of 3 years after the acquisition date and the 180th day after the close of the purchasing corporation's taxable year within which a triggering event occurs.

(ii) *Qualifying foreign purchasing corporation.*—A purchasing corporation is a *qualifying foreign purchasing corporation* only if, during the acquisition period of a qualifying foreign target, all the corporations in the purchasing corporation's affiliated group are foreign corporations that are not subject to United States tax.

(iii) *Qualifying foreign target.*—A target is a *qualifying foreign target* only if target and its target affiliates are foreign corporations that, during target's acquisition period, are not subject to United States tax (and will not become subject to United States tax during such period because of a section 338 election). A target affiliate is taken into account for purposes of the preceding sentence only if, during target's 12-month acquisition period, it is or becomes a member of the affiliated group that includes the purchasing corporation.

(iv) *Triggering event.*—A *triggering event* occurs in the taxable year of the qualifying foreign purchasing corporation in which either that corporation or any corporation in its affiliated group becomes subject to United States tax.

(v) *Subject to United States tax.*—For purposes of this paragraph (e)(1), a foreign corporation is considered subject to United States tax—

(A) For the taxable year for which that corporation is required under § 1.6012-2(g) (other than § 1.6012-2(g)(2)(i)(B)(2)) to file a United States income tax return; or

(B) For the period during which that corporation is a controlled foreign corporation, a passive foreign investment company for which an election under section 1295 is in effect, a foreign investment company, or a foreign corporation the stock ownership of which is described in section 552(a)(2).

(2) *Acquisition period.*—For purposes of this paragraph (e), the term *acquisition period* means the period beginning on the first day of the 12-month acquisition period and ending on the acquisition date.

(3) *Statement of section 338 election may be filed by United States shareholders in certain cases.*—The United States shareholders (as defined in section 951(b)) of a foreign purchasing corporation that is a controlled foreign corporation (as defined in section 957 (taking into account section 953(c))) may file a statement of section 338 election on behalf of the purchasing corporation if the purchasing corporation is not required under § 1.6012-2(g) (other than § 1.6012-2(g)(2)(i)(B)(2)) to file a United States income tax return for its taxable year that includes the acquisition date. Form 8023 must be filed as described in the form and its instructions and also must be attached to the Form 5471, "Information Returns Of U.S. Persons With Respect To Certain Foreign Corporations," filed with respect to the purchasing corporation by each United States shareholder for the purchasing corporation's taxable year that includes the acquisition date (or, if paragraph (e)(1)(i) of this section applies to the election, for the purchasing corporation's taxable year within which it becomes a controlled foreign corporation). The provisions of § 1.964-1(c) (including § 1.964-1(c)(7)) do not apply to an election made by the United States shareholders.

(4) *Notice requirement for U.S. persons holding stock in foreign target.*—(i) *General rule.*—If a target subject to a section 338 election was a controlled foreign corporation, a passive foreign investment company, or a foreign personal holding company at any time during the portion of its taxable year that ends on its acquisition date, the purchasing corporation must deliver written notice of the election (and a copy of Form 8023, its attachments and instructions) to—

(A) Each U.S. person (other than a member of the affiliated group of which the purchasing corporation is a member (the purchasing group member)) that, on the acquisition date of the foreign target, holds stock in the foreign target; and

(B) Each U.S. person (other than a purchasing group member) that sells stock in the foreign target to a purchasing group member during the foreign target's 12-month acquisition period.

(ii) *Limitation.*—The notice requirement of this paragraph (e)(4) applies only where the section 338 election for the foreign target affects income, gain, loss, deduction, or credit of the U.S. person described in paragraph (e)(4)(i) of this section under section 551, 951, 1248, or 1293.

(iii) *Form of notice.*—The notice to U.S. persons must be identified prominently as a notice of section 338 election and must—

(A) Contain the name, address, and employer identification number (if any) of, and the country (and, if relevant, the lesser political subdivision) under the laws of which are organized the purchasing corporation and the relevant target (i.e., the target the stock of which the particular U.S. person held or sold under the circumstances described in paragraph (e)(4)(i) of this section);

(B) Identify those corporations as the purchasing corporation and the foreign target, respectively; and

(C) Contain the following declaration (or a substantially similar declaration):

THIS DOCUMENT SERVES AS NOTICE OF AN ELECTION UNDER SECTION 338 FOR THE ABOVE CITED FOREIGN TARGET THE STOCK OF WHICH YOU EITHER HELD OR SOLD UNDER THE CIRCUMSTANCES DESCRIBED IN TREASURY REGULATIONS SECTION 1.338-2(e)(4). FOR POSSIBLE UNITED STATES FEDERAL INCOME TAX CONSEQUENCES UNDER SECTION 551, 951, 1248, OR 1293 OF THE INTERNAL REVENUE CODE OF 1986 THAT MAY APPLY TO YOU, SEE TREASURY REGULATIONS SECTION 1.338-9(b). YOU MAY BE REQUIRED TO ATTACH THE INFORMATION ATTACHED TO THIS NOTICE TO CERTAIN RETURNS.

(iv) *Timing of notice.*—The notice required by this paragraph (e)(4) must be delivered to the U.S. person on or before the later of the 120th day after the acquisition date of the particular target or the day on which Form 8023 is filed. The notice is considered delivered on the date it is mailed to the proper address (or an address similar enough to complete delivery), unless the date it is mailed cannot be reasonably determined. The date of mailing will be determined under the rules of section 7502. For example, the date of mailing is the date of U.S. postmark or the applicable date recorded or marked by a designated delivery service.

(v) *Consequence of failure to comply.*—A statement of section 338 election is not valid if timely notice is not given to one or more U.S. persons described in this paragraph (e)(4). If the form of notice fails to comply with all requirements of this paragraph (e)(4), the section 338 election is valid, but the waiver rule of § 1.338-10(b)(1) does not apply.

(vi) *Good faith effort to comply.*—The purchasing corporation will be considered to have complied with this paragraph (e)(4), even though it failed to provide notice or provide timely notice to each person described in this paragraph (e)(4), if the Commissioner determines that the purchasing corporation made a good faith effort to identify and provide timely notice to those U.S. persons. [Reg. § 1.338-2.]

☐ [*T.D.* 8940, 2-12-2001.]

§ 1.338-4. Aggregate deemed sale price; various aspects of taxation of the deemed asset sale.—(a) *Scope.*—This section provides rules under section 338(a)(1) to determine the aggregate deemed sale price (ADSP) for target. ADSP is the amount for which old target is deemed to have sold all of its assets in the deemed asset sale. ADSP is allocated among target's assets in accordance with § 1.338-6 to determine the amount for which each asset is deemed to have been sold. When a subsequent increase or decrease is required under general principles of tax law with respect to an element of ADSP, the redetermined ADSP is allocated among target's assets in accordance with § 1.338-7. This § 1.338-4 also provides rules regarding the recognition of gain or loss on the deemed sale of target affiliate stock. Notwithstanding section 338(h)(6)(B)(ii), stock held by a target affiliate in a foreign corporation or in a corporation that is a DISC or that is described in section 1248(e) is not excluded from the operation of section 338.

* * *

(h) *Deemed sale of target affiliate stock.*—(1) *Scope.*—This paragraph (h) prescribes rules relating to the treatment of gain or loss realized on the deemed sale of stock of a target affiliate when a section 338 election (but not a section 338(h)(10) election) is made for the target affiliate. For purposes of this paragraph (h), the definition of domestic corporation in § 1.338-2(c)(9) is applied without the exclusion therein for DISCs, corporations described in section 1248(e), and corporations to which an election under section 936 applies.

(2) *In general.*—Except as otherwise provided in this paragraph (h), if a section 338 election is made for target, target recognizes no gain or loss on the deemed sale of stock of a target affiliate having the same acquisition date and for which a section 338 election is made if—

(i) Target directly owns stock in the target affiliate satisfying the requirements of section 1504(a)(2);

(ii) Target and the target affiliate are members of a consolidated group filing a final consolidated return described in § 1.338-10(a)(1); or

(iii) Target and the target affiliate file a combined return under § 1.338-10(a)(4).

(3) *Deemed sale of foreign target affiliate by a domestic target.*—A domestic target recognizes gain or loss on the deemed sale of stock of a foreign target affiliate. For the proper treatment of such gain or loss, see, e.g., sections 1246, 1248, 1291 et seq., and 338(h)(16) and § 1.338-9.

(4) *Deemed sale producing effectively connected income.*—A foreign target recognizes gain or loss on the deemed sale of stock of a foreign target affiliate to the extent that such gain or loss is effectively connected (or treated as effectively connected) with the conduct of a trade or business in the United States.

* * *

(6) *Deemed sale of DISC target affiliate.*—A foreign or domestic target recognizes gain (but not loss) on the deemed sale of stock of a target affiliate that is a DISC or a former DISC (as defined in section 992(a)) in an amount equal to the lesser of the gain realized or the amount of accumulated DISC income determined with respect to such stock under section 995(c). Such gain is included in gross income as a dividend as provided in sections 995(c)(2) and 996(g).

* * *

(8) *Examples.*—The following examples illustrate this paragraph (h):

* * *

Example 4. (i) T's sole asset, all of the FT1 stock, has a basis of $25 and a fair market value of $150. FT1's sole asset, all of the FT2 stock, has a basis of $75 and a fair market value of $150. FT1 and FT2 each have $50 of accumulated earnings and profits for purposes of section 1248(c) and (d). FT2's assets have a basis of $125 and a fair market value of $150, and their sale would not generate subpart F income under section 951. The sale of the FT2 stock or assets would not generate income effectively connected with the conduct of a trade or business within the United States. FT1 does not have an election in effect under section 953(d) and neither FT1 nor FT2 is a passive foreign investment company.

(ii) P makes a qualified stock purchase of T and makes a section 338 election for T. T's deemed purchase of the FT1 stock results in a qualified stock purchase of FT1 and a section 338 election is made for M. Similarly, FT1's deemed purchase of the FT2 stock results in a qualified stock purchase of FT2 and a section 338 election is made for FT2.

(iii) T recognizes $125 of gain on the deemed sale of the FT1 stock under paragraph (h)(3) of this section. FT1 does not recognize $75 of gain on the deemed sale of the FT2 stock under paragraph (h)(2) of this section. FT2 recognizes $25 of gain on the deemed sale of its assets. The $125 gain T recognizes on the deemed sale of the FT1 stock is included in T's income as a dividend under section 1248, because FT1 and FT2 have sufficient earnings and profits for full recharacterization ($50 of accumulated earnings and profits in FT1, $50 of accumulated earnings and profits in FT2, and $25 of deemed sale earnings and profits in FT2). Section 1.338-9(b). For purposes of sections 901 through 908, the source and foreign tax credit limitation basket of $25 of the recharacterized gain on the deemed sale of the FT1 stock is determined under section 338(h)(16).

[Reg. § 1.338-4.]

□ [*T.D. 8940, 2-12-2001.*]

§ 1.338-8. Asset and stock consistency.

* * *

(g) *Extension of consistency if dividends qualifying for 100 percent dividends received deduction are paid.*—(1) *General rule for direct acquisitions from target.*—Unless a section 338 election is made for target, the basis rules of paragraph (d) of this section apply to an asset if—

(i) Target recognizes gain (whether or not deferred) on disposition of the asset during the portion of the target consistency period that ends on the target acquisition date;

(ii) The asset is owned, immediately after the asset disposition and on the target acquisition date, by a corporation that acquires stock of target in the qualified stock purchase (or by an affiliate of an acquiring corporation); and

(iii) During the portion of the target consistency period that ends on the target acquisition date, the aggregate amount of dividends paid by target, to which section 243(a)(3) applies, exceeds the greater of—

(A) $250,000; or

(B) 125 percent of the yearly average amount of dividends paid by target, to which section 243(a)(3) applies, during the three calendar years immediately preceding the year in which the target consistency period begins (or, if shorter, the period target was in existence).

(2) *Other direct acquisitions having same effect.*—The basis rules of paragraph (d) of this section also apply to an asset if the effect of a transaction described in paragraph (g)(1) of this section is achieved through any combination of disposition of assets and payment of dividends to which section 243(a)(3) applies (or any other dividends eligible for a 100 percent dividends received deduction). *See* paragraph (h)(4) of this section for additional rules relating to target affiliates that are controlled foreign corporations.

(3) *Indirect acquisitions.*—The principles of paragraph (f) of this section also apply for purposes of this paragraph (g).

(4) *Examples.*—This paragraph (g) may be illustratedby the following examples:

Example 1. Asset acquired from target paying dividends to which section 243(a)(3) applies. (a) The S group does not file a consolidated return. In Year 1, Year 2, and Year 3, T pays dividends to S to which section 243(a)(3) applies of $200,000, $250,000, and $300,000, respectively. On February 1 of Year 4, T sells an asset to P and recognizes gain. On January 1 of Year 5, P makes a qualified stock purchase of T from S. No section 338 election is made for T. During the portion of T's consistency period that ends on T's acquisition date, T pays S dividends to which section 243(a)(3) applies of $1,000,000.

(b) Under paragraph (g)(1) of this section, paragraph (d) of this section applies to the asset. T recognizes gain on disposition of the asset during the portion of T's consistency period that ends on T's acquisition date, the asset is owned by P immediately after the disposition and on T's acquisition date, and T pays dividends described in paragraph (g)(1)(iii) of this section. Consequently, under paragraph (d)(1) of this section, P's basis in the asset is T's adjusted basis in the asset immediately before the sale to P.

(c) If T is a controlled foreign corporation, the results would be the same if T pays dividends in the amount described in paragraph (g)(1)(iii) of this section that qualify for a 100 percent dividends received deduction. See sections 243(e) and 245.

(d) If S and T3 file a consolidated return in which T, T1, and T2 do not join, the results would be the same because the dividends paid by T are still described in paragraph (g)(1)(iii) of this section.

(e) If T, T1, and T2 file a consolidated return in which S and T3 do not join, the results would be the same because the dividends paid by T are still described in paragraph (g)(1)(iii) of this section.

Example 2. Asset disposition by target affiliate achieving same effect. (a) The S group does not file a consolidated return. On February 1 of Year 1, T2 sells an asset to P and recognizes gain. T pays dividends to S described in paragraph (g)(1)(iii) of this section. On January 1 of Year 2, P makes a qualified stock purchase of T from S. No section 338 election is made for T.

(b) Paragraph (g)(1) of this section does not apply to the asset because T did not recognize gain on the disposition of the asset. However, under paragraph (g)(2) of this section, because the asset disposition by T2 and the dividends paid by T achieve the effect of a transaction described in paragraph (g)(1) of this section, the carryover basis rule of paragraph (d)(1) of this section applies to the asset. The effect was achieved because T2 is a lower-tier affiliate of T and the dividends paid by T to S reduce the value to S of T and its lower-tier affiliates.

(c) If T2 is a controlled foreign corporation, the results would be the same because T2 is a lower-tier affiliate of T and the dividends paid by T to S reduce the value to S of T and its lower-tier affiliates.

(d) If P buys an asset from T3, rather than T2, the asset disposition and the dividends do not achieve the effect of a transaction described in paragraph (g)(1) of this section because T3 is not a lower-tier affiliate of T. Thus, the basis rules of paragraph (d) of this section do not apply to the asset. The results would be the same whether or not P also acquires the T3 stock (whether or not in a qualified stock purchase).

Example 3. Dividends by target affiliate achieving same effect. (a) The S group does not file a consolidated return. On February 1 of Year 1, T1 sells an asset to P and recognizes gain. On January 1 of Year 2, P makes a qualified stock purchase of T from S. No section 338 election is made for T. T does not pay dividends to S described in paragraph (g)(1)(iii) of this section. However, T1 pays dividends to T that would be described in paragraph (g)(1)(iii) of this section if T1 were a target.

(b) Paragraph (g)(1) of this section does not apply to the asset because T did not recognize gain on the disposition of the asset and did not pay dividends described in paragraph (g)(1)(iii) of this section. Further, paragraph (g)(2) of this section does not apply because the dividends paid by T1 to T do not reduce the value to S of T and its lower-tier affiliates.

(c) If both S and T own T1 stock and T1 pays dividends to S that would be described in paragraph (g)(1)(iii) of this section if T1 were a target, paragraph (g)(2) of this section would apply because the dividends paid by T1 to S reduce the value to S of T and its lower-tier affiliates. If T, rather than T1, sold the asset to P, the results would be the same. Further, if T and T1 pay dividends to S that, only when aggregated, would be described in paragraph (g)(1)(iii) of this section (if they were all paid by T), the results would be the same.

Example 4. Gain reflected by reason of dividends. (a) S and T file a consolidated return in which T1 and T2 do not join. On February 1 of Year 1, T1 sells an asset to P and recognizes gain. On January 1 of Year 2, P makes a qualified stock purchase of T from S. No section 338 election is made for T. T1 pays dividends to T that would be described in paragraph (g)(1)(iii) of this section if T1 were a target.

(b) The requirements of paragraph (b) of this section are not satisfied because, under paragraph (c)(3) of this section, gain from T1's sale is not reflected in S's basis in the T stock by reason of the dividends paid by T1 to T.

(c) Although the dividends paid by T1 to T do not reduce the value to S of T and its lower-tier affiliates, paragraph (g)(2) of this section applies because the dividends paid by T1 to T are taken into account under § 1.1502-32 in determining S's basis in the T stock.

Consequently, the carryover basis rule of paragraph (d)(1) of this section applies to the asset.

(h) *Consistency for target affiliates that are controlled foreign corporations.*—(1) *In general.*—This paragraph (h) applies only if target is a domestic corporation. For additional rules that may apply with respect to controlled foreign corporations, see paragraph (g) of this section. The definitions and nomenclature of § 1.338-2(b) and (c) and paragraph (e) of this section apply for purposes of this section.

(2) *Income or gain resulting from asset dispositions.*—(i) *General rule.*—Income or gain of a target affiliate that is a controlled foreign corporation from the disposition of an asset is not reflected in the basis of target stock under paragraph (c) of this section unless the income or gain results in an inclusion under section 951(a)(1)(A), 951(a)(1)(C), 1291 or 1293.

(ii) *Basis of controlled foreign corporation stock.*—If, by reason of paragraph (h)(2)(i) of this section, the carryover basis rules of this section apply to an asset, no increase in basis in the stock of a controlled foreign corporation under section 961(a) or 1293(d)(1), or under regulations issued pursuant to section 1297(b)(5), is allowed to target or a target affiliate to the extent the increase is attributable to income or gain described in paragraph (h)(2)(i) of this section. A similar rule applies to the basis of any property by reason of which the stock of the controlled foreign corporation is considered owned under section 958(a)(2) or 1297(a).

(iii) *Operating rule.*—For purposes of this paragraph (h)(2)—

(A) If there is an income inclusion under section 951 (a)(1)(A) or (C), the shareholder's income inclusion is first attributed to the income or gain of the controlled foreign corporation from the disposition of the asset to the extent of the shareholder's pro rata share of such income or gain; and

(B) Any income or gain under section 1293 is first attributed to the income or gain from the disposition of the asset to the extent of the shareholder's pro rata share of the income or gain.

(iv) *Increase in asset or stock basis.*—(A) If the carryover basis rules under paragraph (h)(2)(i) of this section apply to an asset, and the purchasing corporation disposes of the asset to an unrelated party in a taxable transaction and recognizes and includes in its U.S. gross income or the U.S. gross income of its shareholders the greater of the income or gain from the disposition of the asset by the selling controlled foreign corporation that was reflected in the basis of the target stock under paragraph (c) of this section, or the gain recognized on the asset by the purchasing corporation on the disposition of the asset, then the purchasing corporation or the target or a target affiliate, as appropriate, shall increase the basis of the selling controlled foreign corporation stock subject to paragraph (h)(2)(ii) of this section, as of the date of the disposition of the asset by the purchasing corporation, by the amount of the basis increase that was denied under paragraph (h)(2)(ii) of this section. The preceding sentence shall apply only to the extent that the controlled foreign corporation stock is owned (within the meaning of section 958(a)) by a member of the purchasing corporation's affiliated group.

(B) If the carryover basis rules under paragraph (h)(2)(i) of this section apply to an asset, and the purchasing corporation or the target or a target affiliate, as appropriate, disposes of the stock of the selling controlled foreign corporation to an unrelated party in a taxable transaction and recognizes and includes in its U.S. gross income or the U.S. gross income of its shareholders the greater of the gain equal to the basis increase that was denied under paragraph (h)(2)(ii) of this section, or the gain recognized in the stock by the purchasing corporation or by the target or a target affiliate, as appropriate, on the disposition of the stock, then the purchasing corporation shall increase the basis of the asset, as of the date of the disposition of the stock of the selling controlled foreign corporation by the purchasing corporation or by the target or a target affiliate, as appropriate, by the amount of the basis increase that was denied pursuant to paragraph (h)(2)(i) of this section. The preceding sentence shall apply only to the extent that the asset is owned (within the meaning of section 958(a)) by a member of the purchasing corporation's affiliated group.

(3) *Stock issued by target affiliate that is a controlled foreign corporation.*—The exception to the carryover basis rules of this section provided in paragraph (d)(2)(iii) of this section does not apply to stock issued by a target affiliate that is a controlled foreign corporation. After applying the carryover basis rules of this section to the stock, the basis in the stock is increased by the amount treated as a dividend under section 1248 on the disposition of the stock (or that would have been so treated but for section 1291), except to the extent the basis increase is attributable to the disposition of an asset in which a carryover basis is taken under this section.

(4) *Certain distributions.*—(i) *General rule.*—In the case of a target affiliate that is a controlled foreign corporation, paragraph (g) of this section applies with respect to the target affiliate by treating any reference to a dividend to which section 243(a)(3) applies as a reference to any amount taken into account under § 1.1502-32 in determining the basis of target stock that is—

(A) A dividend;

(B) An amount treated as a dividend under section 1248 (or that would have been so treated but for section 1291); or

(C) An amount included in income under section 951(a)(1)(B).

(ii) *Basis of controlled foreign corporation stock.*—If the carryover basis rules of this section apply to an asset, the basis in the stock of the controlled foreign corporation (or any property by reason of which the stock is considered owned under section 958(a)(2)) is reduced (but not below zero) by the sum of any amounts that are treated, solely by reason of the disposition of the asset, as a dividend, amount treated as a dividend under section 1248 (or that would have been so treated but for section 1291), or amount included in income under section 951(a)(1)(B). For this purpose, any dividend, amount treated as a dividend under section 1248 (or that would have been so treated but for section 1291), or amount included in income under section 951(a)(1)(B) is considered attributable first to earnings and profits resulting from the disposition of the asset.

(iii) *Increase in asset or stock basis.*—(A) If the carryover basis rules under paragraphs (g) and (h)(4)(i) of this section apply to an asset, and the purchasing corporation disposes of the asset to an unrelated party in a taxable transaction and recognizes and includes in its U.S. gross income or the U.S. gross income of its shareholders the greater of the gain equal to the basis increase denied in the asset pursuant to paragraphs (g) and (h)(4)(i) of this section, or the gain recognized on the asset by the purchasing corporation on the disposition of the asset, then the purchasing corporation or the target or a target affiliate, as appropriate, shall increase the basis of the selling controlled foreign corporation stock subject to paragraph (h)(4)(ii) of this section, as of the date of the disposition of the asset by the purchasing corporation, by the amount of the basis reduction under paragraph (h)(4)(ii) of this section. The preceding sentence shall apply only to the extent that the controlled foreign corporation stock is owned (within the meaning of section 958(a)) by a member of the purchasing corporation's affiliated group.

(B) If the carryover basis rules under paragraphs (g) and (h)(4)(i) of this section apply to an asset, and the purchasing corporation or the target or a target affiliate, as appropriate, disposes of the stock of the selling controlled foreign corporation to an unrelated party in a taxable transaction and recognizes and includes in its U.S. gross income or the U.S. gross income of its shareholders the greater of the amount of the basis reduction under paragraph (h)(4)(ii) of this section, or the gain recognized in the stock by the purchasing corporation or by the target or a target affiliate, as appropriate, on the disposition of the stock, then the purchasing corporation shall increase the basis of the asset, as of the date of the disposition of the stock of the selling controlled foreign corporation by the purchasing corporation or by the target or a target affiliate, as appropriate, by the amount of the basis increase that was denied pursuant to paragraphs (g) and (h)(4)(i) of this section. The preceding sentence shall apply only to the extent that the asset is owned (within the meaning of section 958(a)) by a member of the purchasing corporation's affiliated group.

(5) *Examples.*—This paragraph (h) may be illustrated by the following examples:

Example 1. Stock of target affiliate that is a CFC. (a) The S group files a consolidated return; however, T2 is a controlled foreign corporation. On December 1 of Year 1, T1 sells the T2 stock to P and recognizes gain. On January 2 of Year 2, P makes a qualified stock purchase of T from S. No section 338 election is made for T.

(b) Under paragraph (b)(1) of this section, paragraph (d) of this section applies to the T2 stock. Under paragraph (h)(3) of this section, paragraph (d)(2)(iii) of this section does not apply to the T2 stock. Consequently, paragraph (d)(1) of this section applies to the T2 stock. However, after applying paragraph (d)(1) of this section, P's basis in the T2 stock is increased by the amount of T1's gain on the sale of the T2 stock that is treated as a dividend under section 1248. Because P has a carryover basis in the T2 stock, the T2 stock is not considered purchased within the meaning of section 338(h)(3) and no section 338 election may be made for T2.

Example 2. Stock of target affiliate CFC; inclusion under subpart F. (a) The S group files a consolidated return; however, T2 is a controlled foreign corporation. On December 1 of Year 1, T2 sells an asset to P and recognizes subpart F income that results in an inclusion in T1's gross income under section 951(a)(1)(A). On January 2 of Year 2, P makes a qualified stock purchase of T from S. No section 338 election is made for T.

(b) Because gain from the disposition of the asset results in an inclusion under section 951(a)(1)(A), the gain is reflected in the basis of the T stock as of T's acquisition date. See paragraph (h)(2)(i) of this section. Consequently, under paragraph (b)(1) of this section, paragraph (d)(1) of this section applies to the asset. In addition, under paragraph (h)(2)(ii) of this section, T1's basis in the T2 stock is not increased under section 961(a) by the amount of the inclusion that is attributable to the sale of the asset.

(c) If, in addition to making a qualified stock purchase of T, P acquires the T2 stock from T1 on January 1 of Year 2, the results are the same for the asset sold by T2. In addition, under paragraph (h)(2)(ii) of this section, T1's basis in the T2 stock is not increased by the amount of the inclusion that is attributable to the gain on the sale of the asset. Further, under paragraph (h)(3) of this section, paragraph (d)(1) of this section applies to the T2 stock. However, after applying paragraph (d)(1) of this section, P's basis in the T2 stock is increased by the amount of T1's gain on the sale of the T2 stock that is treated as a dividend under section 1248. Finally, because P has a carryover basis in the T2 stock, the T2 stock is not considered purchased within the meaning of section 338(h)(3) and no section 338 election may be made for T2.

(d) If P makes a qualified stock purchase of T2 from T1, rather than of T from S, and T1's gain on the sale of T2 is treated as a dividend under section 1248, under paragraph (h)(1) of this section, paragraphs (h)(2) and (3) of this section do not apply because there is no target that is a domestic corporation. Consequently, the carryover basis rules of paragraph do not apply to the asset sold by T2 or the T2 stock.

Example 3. Gain reflected by reason of section 1248 dividend; gain from non-subpart F asset. (a) The S group files a consolidated return; however, T2 is a controlled foreign corporation. In Years 1 through 4, T2 does not pay any dividends to T1 and no amount is included in T1's income under section 951(a)(1)(B). On December 1 of Year 4, T2 sells an asset with a basis of $400,000 to P for $900,000. T2's gain of $500,000 is not subpart F income. On December 15 of Year 4, T1 sells T2, in which it has a basis of $600,000, to P for $1,600,000. Under section 1248, $800,000 of T1's gain of $1,000,000 is treated as a dividend. However, in the absence of the sale of the asset by T2 to P, only $300,000 would have been treated as a dividend under section 1248. On December 30 of Year 4, P makes a qualified stock purchase of T1 from T. No section 338 election is made for T1.

(b) Under paragraph (h)(4) of this section, paragraph (g)(2) of this section applies by reference to the amount treated as a dividend under section 1248 on the disposition of the T2 stock. Because the amount treated as a dividend is taken into account in determining T's basis in the T1 stock under §1.150232, the sale of the T2 stock and the deemed dividend have the effect of a transaction described in paragraph (g)(1) of this section. Consequently, paragraph (d)(1) of this section applies to the asset sold by T2 to P and P's basis in the asset is $400,000 as of December 1 of Year 4.

(c) Under paragraph (h)(3) of this section, paragraph (d)(1) of this section applies to the T2 stock and P's basis in the T2 stock is $600,000 as of December 15 of Year 4. Under paragraphs (h)(3) and (4)(ii) of this section, however, P's basis in the T2 stock is increased by $300,000 (the amount of T1's gain treated as a dividend under section 1248 ($800,000), other than the amount treated as a dividend solely as a result of the sale of the asset by T2 to P ($500,000)) to $900,000.

***

[Reg. §1.338-8.]

☐ *[T.D. 8515, 1-12-94. Amended by T.D. 8597, 7-12-95 and T.D. 8710, 1-22-97. Redesignated by T.D. 8858, 1-5-2000. Amended by T.D. 8940, 2-12-2001.]*

§1.338-9. International aspects of section 338.—(a) *Scope.*—This section provides guidance regarding international aspects of section 338. As provided in §1.338-2(c)(18), a foreign corporation, a DISC, or a corporation for which a section 936 election has been made is considered a target affiliate for all purposes of section 338. In addition, stock described in section 338(h)(6)(B)(ii) held by a target affiliate is not excluded from the operation of section 338.

(b) *Application of section 338 to foreign targets.*—(1) *In general.*—For purposes of subtitle A, the deemed sale tax consequences, as defined in §1.338-2(c)(7), of a foreign target for which a section 338 election is made (FT), and the corresponding earnings and profits, are taken into account in determining the taxation of FT and FT's direct and indirect shareholders. See, however, section 338(h)(16). For example, the income and earnings and profits of FT are determined, for purposes of sections 551, 951, 1248, and 1293, by taking into account the deemed sale tax consequences.

(2) *Ownership of FT stock on the acquisition date.*—A person who transfers FT stock to the purchasing corporation on FT's acquisition date is considered to own the transferred stock at the close of FT's acquisition date. See, e.g., §1.951-1(f) (relating to determination of holding period for purposes of sections 951 through 964). If on the acquisition date the purchasing corporation owns a block of FT stock that was acquired before FT's acquisition date, the purchasing corporation is considered to own such block of stock at the close of the acquisition date.

(3) *Carryover FT stock.*—(i) *Definition.*—FT stock is carryover FT stock if—

(A) FT was a controlled foreign corporation within the meaning of section 957 (taking into account section 953(c)) at any time during the portion of the 12-month acquisition period that ends on the acquisition date; and

(B) Such stock is owned as of the beginning of the day after FT's acquisition date by a person other than a purchasing corporation, or by a purchasing corporation if the stock is nonrecently purchased and is not subject to a gain recognition election under §1.338-5(d).

(ii) *Carryover of earnings and profits.*—The earnings and profits of old FT (and associated foreign taxes) attributable to the carryover FT stock (adjusted to reflect deemed sale tax consequences) carry over to new FT solely for purposes of—

(A) Characterizing an actual distribution with respect to a share of carryover FT stock as a dividend;

(B) Characterizing gain on a post-acquisition date transfer of a share of carryover FT stock as a dividend under section 1248 (if such section is otherwise applicable);

(C) Characterizing an investment of earnings in United States property as income under sections 951(a)(1)(B) and 956 (if such sections are otherwise applicable); and

(D) Determining foreign taxes deemed paid under sections 902 and 960 with respect to the amount treated as a dividend or income by virtue of this paragraph (b)(3)(ii) (subject to the operation of section 338(h)(16)).

(iii) *Cap on carryover of earnings and profits.*—The amount of earnings and profits of old FT taken into account with respect to a share of carryover FT stock is limited to the amount that would have been included in gross income of the owner of such stock as a dividend under section 1248 if—

(A) The shareholder transferred that share to the purchasing corporation on FT's acquisition date for a consideration equal to the fair market value of that share on that date; or

(B) In the case of nonrecently purchased FT stock treated as carryover FT stock, a gain recognition election under section 338(b)(3)(A) applied to that share. For purposes of the preceding sentence, a shareholder that is a controlled foreign corporation is considered to be a United States person, and the principle of section 1248(c)(2)(D)(ii) (concerning a United States person's indirect ownership of stock in a foreign corporation) applies in determining the correct holding period.

(iv) *Post-acquisition date distribution of old FT earnings and profits.*—A post-acquisition date distribution with respect to a share of carryover FT stock is considered to be derived first from earnings and profits derived after FT's acquisition date and then from earnings and profits derived on or before FT's acquisition date.

(v) *Old FT earnings and profits unaffected by post-acquisition date deficits.*—The carryover amount for a share of carryover FT stock is not reduced by deficits in earnings and profits incurred by new FT. This rule applies for purposes of determining the amount of foreign taxes deemed paid regardless of the fact that there are no accumulated earnings and profits. For example, a distribution by new FT with respect to a share of carryover FT stock is treated as a dividend by the distributee to the extent of the carryover amount for that share notwithstanding that new FT has no earnings and profits.

(vi) *Character of FT stock as carryover FT stock eliminated upon disposition.*—A share of FT stock is not considered carryover FT stock after it is disposed of provided that all gain realized on the transfer is recognized at the time of the transfer, or that, if less than all of the realized gain is recognized, the recognized amount equals or exceeds the remaining carryover amount for that share.

(4) *Passive foreign investment company stock.*—Stock that is owned as of the beginning of the day after FT's acquisition date by a person other than a purchasing corporation, or by a purchasing corporation if the FT stock is nonrecently purchased stock not subject to a gain recognition election under § 1.338-5(d), is treated as passive foreign investment company stock to the extent provided in section 1297(b)(1).

(c) *Dividend treatment under section 1248(e).*—The principles of this paragraph (b) apply to shareholders of a domestic corporation subject to section 1248(e).

(d) *Allocation of foreign income taxes.*—(1) *In general.*—Except as provided in paragraph (d)(3) of this section, if a section 338 election is made for target (whether foreign or domestic), and target's taxable year under foreign law (if any) does not close at the end of the acquisition date, foreign income tax as defined in § 1.901-2(a)) (other than a withholding tax as defined in section 901(k)(1)(B)) paid or accrued by new target with respect to such foreign taxable year is allocated between old target and new target. If there is more than one section 338 election with respect to target during target's foreign taxable year, foreign income tax paid or accrued with respect to that foreign taxable year is allocated among all old targets and new targets. The allocation is made based on the respective portions of the taxable income (as determined under foreign law) for the foreign taxable year that are attributable under the principles of § 1.1502-76(b) to the period of existence of each old target and new target during the foreign taxable year.

(2) *Foreign income taxes imposed on partnerships and disregarded entities.*—If a section 338 election is made for target and target holds an interest in a disregarded entity (as described in § 301.7701-2(c)(2)(i) of this chapter) or partnership, the rules of § 1.901-2(f)(4) and (5) apply to determine the person who is considered for Federal income tax purposes to pay foreign income tax imposed at the entity level on the income of the disregarded entity or partnership.

(3) *Disallowance of foreign tax credits under section 901(m).*—For rules that may apply to disallow foreign tax credits by reason of a section 338 election, see section 901(m) and §§ 1.901(m)-1 through 1.901(m)-8.

(4) *Applicability date.*—This paragraph (d) applies to foreign income taxes paid or accrued in taxable years beginning on or after December 28, 2021.

(e) *Operation of section 338(h)(16).*—[Reserved]

(f) *Examples.*—(1) Except as otherwise provided, all corporations use the calendar year as the taxable year, have no earnings and profits (or deficit) accumulated for any taxable year, and have only one class of outstanding stock.

(2) This section may be illustrated by the following examples:

Example 1. Gain recognition election for carryover FT stock. (a) A has owned 90 of the 100 shares of CFCT stock since CFCT was organized on March 13, 1989. P has owned the remaining 10 shares of CFCT stock since CFCT was organized. Those 10 shares constitute nonrecently purchased stock in P's hands within the meaning of section 338(b)(6)(B). On November 1, 1994, P purchases A's 90 shares of CFCT stock for $90,000 and makes a section 338 election for CFCT. P also makes a gain recognition election under section 338(b)(3)(A) and § 1.338-5(d).

(b) CFCT's earnings and profits for its short taxable year ending on November 1, 1994, are $50,000, determined without taking into account the deemed asset sale. Assume A recognizes gain of $81,000 on the sale of the CFCT stock. Further, assume that CFCT recognizes gain of $40,000 by reason of its deemed sale of assets under section 338(a)(1).

(c) A's sale of CFCT stock to P is a transfer to which section 1248 and paragraphs (b)(1) and (2) of this section apply. For purposes of applying section 1248(a) to A, the earnings and profits of CFCT for its short taxable year ending on November 1, 1994, are $90,000 (the earnings and profits for that taxable year as determined under § 1.1248-2(e) ($50,000) plus earnings from the deemed sale ($40,000)). Thus, A's entire gain is characterized as a dividend under section 1248 (but see section 338(h)(16)).

(d) Assume that P recognizes a gain of $9,000 with respect to the 10 shares of nonrecently purchased CFCT stock by reason of the gain recognition election. Because P is treated as selling the nonrecently purchased stock for all purposes of the Internal Revenue Code, section 1248 applies. Thus, under § 1.1248-2(e), $9,000 of the $90,000 of earnings and profits for 1994 are attributable to the block of 10 shares of CFCT stock deemed sold by P at the close of November 1, 1994 ($90,000 × 10/100). Accordingly, P's entire gain on the deemed sale of 10 shares of CFCT stock is included under section 1248(a) in P's gross income as a dividend (but see section 338(h)(16)).

Example 2. No gain recognition election for carryover FT stock. (a) Assume the same facts as in *Example 1*, except that P does not make a gain recognition election.

(b) The 10 shares of nonrecently purchased CFCT stock held by P is carryover FT stock under paragraph (b)(3) of this section. Accordingly, the earnings and profits (and attributable foreign taxes) of old CFCT carry over to new CFCT solely for purposes of that block of 10 shares. The amount of old CFCT's earnings and profits taken into account with respect to that block in the event, for example, of a distribution by new CFCT with respect to that block is the amount of the section 1248 dividend that P would have recognized with respect to that block had it made a gain recognition election under section 338(b)(3)(A). Under the facts of *Example 1*, P would have recognized a gain of $9,000 with respect to that block, all of which would have been a section 1248 dividend ($90,000 × 10/100). Accordingly, the carryover amount for the block of 10 shares of nonrecently purchased CFCT stock is $9,000.

Example 3. Sale of controlled foreign corporation stock prior to and on the acquisition date. (a) X and Y, both U.S. corporations, have each owned 50% of the CFCT stock since 1986. Among CFCT's assets are assets the sale of which would generate subpart F income. On December 31, 1994, X sells its CFCT stock to P. On June 30, 1995, Y sells its CFCT stock to P. P makes a section 338 election for CFCT. In both 1994 and 1995, CFCT has subpart F income resulting from operations.

(b) For taxable year 1994, X and Y are United States shareholders on the last day of CFCT's taxable year, so pursuant to section 951(a)(1)(A) each must include in income its pro rata share of CFCT's subpart F income for 1994. Because P's holding period in the CFCT stock acquired from X does not begin until January 1, 1995, P is not a United States shareholder on the last day of 1994 for purposes of section 951(a)(1)(A) (see § 1.951-1(f)). X must then determine the extent to which section 1248 recharacterizes its gain on the sale of CFCT stock as a dividend.

(c) For the short taxable year ending June 30, 1995, Y is considered to own the CFCT stock sold to P at the close of CFCT's acquisition date. Because the acquisition date is the last day of CFCT's taxable year, Y and P are United States shareholders on the last day of CFCT's taxable year. Pursuant to section 951(a)(1)(A), each must include its pro rata share of CFCT's subpart F income for the short taxable year ending June 30, 1995. This includes any income generated on the deemed sale of CFCT's assets. Y must then determine the extent to which section 1248 recharacterizes its gain on the sale of the CFCT stock as a dividend, taking into account any increase in CFCT's earnings and profits due to the deemed sale of assets.

Example 4. Acquisition of control for purposes of section 951 prior to the acquisition date. FS owns 100% of the FT stock. On July 1, 1994, P buys 60% of the FT stock. On December 31, 1994, P buys the remaining 40% of the FT stock and makes a section 338 election for FT. For tax year 1994, FT has earnings and profits of $1,000 (including earnings resulting from the deemed sale). The section 338 election results in $500 of subpart F income. As a result of the section 338 election, P must include in gross income the following amount under section 951(a)(1)(A) (see § 1.951-[1](b)(2)):

FT's subpart F income for 1994	$500.00
Less: reduction under section 951(a)(2)(A) for period (1-1-94 through 7-1-94) during which FT is not a controlled foreign corporation ($500 × 182/365)	249.32
Subpart F income as limited by section 951 (a)(2)(A)	$250.68
P's pro rata share of subpart F income as determined under section 951(a)(2)(A) (60% × 250.68)	$150.41

Example 5. Coordination with section 936. (a) T is a corporation for which a section 936 election has been made. P makes a qualified stock purchase of T and makes a section 338 election for T.

(b) T's deemed sale of assets under section 338 constitutes a sale for purposes of subtitle A of the Internal Revenue Code, including section 936(a)(1)(A)(ii). To the extent that the assets deemed sold are used in the conduct of an active trade or business in a possession for purposes of section 936(a)(1)(A)(i), and assuming all the other conditions of section 936 are satisfied, the income from the deemed sale qualifies for the credit granted by section 936(a). The source of income from the deemed sale is determined as if the assets had actually been sold and is not affected for purposes of section 936 by section 338(h)(16).

(c) Because new T is treated a new corporation for purposes of subtitle A of the Internal Revenue Code, the three year testing period in section 936(a)(2)(A) begins again for new T on the day following T's acquisition date. Thus, if the character or source of old T's gross income disqualified it for the credit under section 936, a fresh start is allowed by a section 338 election. [Reg. § 1.338-9.]

☐ [*T.D.* 8515, 1-12-94. *Redesignated by T.D.* 8858, 1-5-2000. *Amended by T.D.* 8940, 2-12-2001 *and T.D.* 9959, 12-28-2021 (*corrected* 7-26-2022).]

Corporate Organizations and Reorganizations

§ 1.362-3. Basis of importation property acquired in loss importation transaction.—(a) *Purpose.*—The purpose of section 362(e)(1) and this section is to modify the application of section 362(a) (section 351 transfers, contributions to capital, or paid-in surplus) and section 362(b) (reorganizations) to prevent a corporation (Acquiring) from importing a net built-in loss in a transaction described in either section. See paragraph (c) of this section for definitions of terms used in this section.

(b) *Basis determinations under this section.*—(1) *Basis of importation property received in loss importation transaction.*—Notwithstanding the general rules of section 362(a) and (b), Acquiring's basis in importation property (as defined in paragraph (c)(2) of this section) acquired in a loss importation transaction (as defined in paragraph (c)(3) of this section) is equal to the value of the property immediately after the transaction.

(2) *Adjustment to basis of subsidiary stock in triangular reorganizations.*—If a corporation (P) computes its basis in stock of a subsidiary (whether S or T) under § 1.358-6 (stock basis in certain triangular reorganizations), P's basis in property treated as acquired by P in § 1.358-6(c) is determined under section 362(e)(1) and this section to the extent such property, if actually acquired by P, would be importation property acquired in a loss importation transaction. See § 1.358-6(c)(1)(i)(A), (c)(2)(ii)(B), and (c)(3)(i). The subsidiary's basis in the property actually acquired in the transaction is determined under applicable law (including this section), without regard to the amount of any adjustment to P's basis in the subsidiary's stock. Thus, the basis of the property in S's or T's hands may differ from the amount of the adjustment to P's basis in its stock of S or T.

(3) *Acquiring's basis in other property transferred.*—In general, Acquiring's basis in property received in a section 362 transaction (as defined in paragraph (c)(1) of this section) that is not determined under section 362(e)(1) and this section is determined under section 362(a) or section 362(b). However, if the transaction is described in section 362(a) (without regard to whether it is also described in any other section), further adjustment may be required under section 362(e)(2). See § 1.362-4.

(4) *Other effects of basis determination under this section.*—(i) *Determination by reference to transferor's basis.*—A determination of basis under this section is a determination by reference to the transferor's basis, including for purposes of sections 1223(2) and 7701(a)(43). However, solely for purposes of applying section 755, a determination of basis under this section is treated as a determination not by reference to the transferor's basis.

(ii) *Not tax-exempt income or noncapital, nondeductible expense.*—The application of this section does not give rise to an item treated as tax-exempt income under § 1.1502-32(b)(2)(ii) or as a noncapital, nondeductible expense under § 1.1502-32(b)(2)(iii).

(iii) *No effect on earnings and profits.*—Any determination of basis under this section does not reduce or otherwise affect the calculation of the all earnings and profits amount provided in § 1.367(b)-2(d).

(c) *Definitions.*—For purposes of this section, the following definitions apply:

(1) *Section 362 transaction.*—The term *section 362 transaction* means any transaction described in section 362(a) or in section 362(b).

(2) *Importation property.*—(i) *General rule.*—The term *importation property* means any property (including separate portions determined under paragraph (d)(4) of this section and separate portions of property tentatively divided under paragraph (e)(2) of this section) with respect to which—

(A) Any gain or loss that would be recognized on its sale by the transferor immediately before the transaction (the transferor's hypothetical sale) would not be subject to tax imposed under any provision of subtitle A of the Internal Revenue Code (federal income tax) (taking into account the provisions of paragraph (d) of this section); and

(B) Any gain or loss that would be recognized on its sale by Acquiring immediately after the transaction (Acquiring's hypothetical sale) would be subject to federal income tax (taking into account the provisions of paragraph (d) of this section).

(ii) *Special rules for applying this paragraph (c)(2).*—See paragraph (d) of this section for rules for determining whether gain or loss on a hypothetical sale would be taken into account in determining a federal income tax liability and paragraph (e) of this section for rules applicable when more than one person would take such gain or loss into account.

(3) *Loss importation transaction.*—The term *loss importation transaction* means any section 362 transaction in which Acquiring's aggregate basis in all importation property received from all transferors in the transaction would exceed the aggregate value of such property immediately after the transaction. For this purpose, Acquiring's basis in property received is determined without regard to this section or section 362(e)(2).

(4) *Value.*—(i) *General rule.*—The term *value* means fair market value.

(ii) *Special rule for transfers of partnership interests.*—Notwithstanding the general rule in paragraph (c)(4)(i) of this section, when referring to a partnership interest, for purposes of this section, the term *value* means the sum of the cash that Acquiring would receive for the interest, assuming an exchange between a willing buyer and a willing seller (neither being under any compulsion to buy or sell and both having reasonable knowledge of relevant facts), increased by any § 1.752-1 liabilities (as defined in § 1.752-1(a)(4)) of the partnership allocated to Acquiring with regard to such transferred interest under section 752 immediately after the transfer to Acquiring. If a partnership has elected under section 754, or if section 743(b) would require a downward basis adjustment to the partnership property, the partnership must apply the rules of § 1.743-1 to determine the amount of the basis adjustment to the partnership property.

(d) *Rules for determining whether gain or loss would be taken into account in determining a federal income tax liability.*—(1) *General rule.*—In general, any gain or loss that would be recognized on a hypothetical sale described in paragraph (c)(2) of this section is considered to be subject to federal income tax if, taking into account all relevant facts and circumstances, such gain or loss would affect or be taken into account in determining the federal income tax liability of the transferor or Acquiring, respectively. This determination is made without regard to whether such person has or would have any actual federal income tax liability for the taxable year of the transaction.

(2) *Look-through rule in the case of certain pass-through entities.*—Notwithstanding the general rule in paragraph (d)(1) of this section, the determination of whether any gain or loss on a hypothetical sale would be treated as subject to federal income tax is made by reference to the person that would be required to include such gain or loss in its taxable income if the hypothetical seller is—

(i) A trust treated as owned by its grantors or others (see section 671);

(ii) A partnership (see section 701); or

(iii) An S corporation (see sections 1363 and 1366).

(3) *Controlled foreign corporation (CFC), passive foreign investment company (PFIC).*—For purposes of this section, gain or loss that would be recognized by a CFC (as defined in section 957(a)) or a PFIC (as defined in section 1297(a)) is not deemed taken into account in determining a federal income tax liability solely because it could affect an inclusion under section 951(a) or section 1293(a).

(4) *Special rule for debt-financed property subject to section 512.*—If property is debt-financed property (as defined in section 514(b)) owned by an organization subject to the unrelated business income tax described in section 511(a)(2) and, as a result, a portion of any gain or loss on a sale of the property would be included in unrelated taxable business income (UBTI) under section 512, such property is treated as divided into separate portions in proportion to the amount of such gain or loss that would be includible in UBTI. The rules of paragraph (e) of this section apply to determine the characterization of such portions (as includible in the determination of a federal income tax liability or not), and the tax treatment and consequences of the transaction in which such portions are transferred.

(5) *Look-through treatment in the case of certain avoidance transactions.*—(i) *Application of this paragraph (d)(5).*—This paragraph (d)(5) applies if—

(A) The transferor is a domestic entity that is a trust (other than a trust described in paragraph (d)(2)(i) of this section), estate, regulated investment company (as defined in section 851(a)), a real estate investment trust (as defined in section 856(a)), or a cooperative (as described in section 1381); and

(B) The transferor transfers, directly or indirectly, property that was transferred to or acquired by it as part of a plan (whether of transferor, Acquiring, or any other person) to avoid the application of section 362(e)(1) and this section to a section 362 transaction.

(ii) *Effect of application of this paragraph (d)(5).*—Notwithstanding paragraph (d)(1) of this section, if a transferor is described in both paragraphs (d)(5)(i)(A) and (B) of this section—

(A) The transferor is treated as though it distributes the proceeds of the hypothetical sale (which, for this purpose, are presumed to be an amount greater than zero);

(B) To the fullest extent possible under the transferor's organizing instrument, the deemed distribution is treated as made to a distributee or distributees that would not take distributions from the transferor into account in determining a federal income tax liability; and

(C) The determination of whether the gain or loss on the hypothetical sale is treated as subject to federal income tax is made by reference to the deemed distributee or distributees.

(iii) *Tiered entities.*—If a deemed distributee is an entity described in paragraph (d)(5)(i)(A) of this section, the determination of whether gain or loss on the hypothetical sale is taken into account in determining a federal income tax liability is made by treating the deemed distributee, and any successive such deemed distributees, as a transferor and applying the rules in paragraphs (d)(5)(i) and (ii) of this section to its deemed distribution (and to all successive deemed distributions), until no deemed distributee or successive deemed distributee is an entity described in paragraph (d)(5)(i)(A) of this section.

(e) *Special rules for gain or loss that would be taken into account by multiple persons.*—(1) *In general.*—If gain or loss from a disposition of property would be includible in income by more than one person, the property is treated as tentatively divided into separate portions in proportion to the amount of gain or loss recognized with respect to the property that would be allocated to each such person. If an entity's organizing instrument specially allocates gain and loss, the tentative division of property under this paragraph (e) must reflect the manner in which gain or loss on the disposition of such property would be allocated under the terms of the organizing instrument and any applicable rules of law, taking into account the net gain or loss actually recognized by the entity in that tax year.

(2) *Application of section.*—The rules of this section apply independently to each tentatively divided portion to determine if the portion is importation property. Each tentatively divided portion that is determined to be importation property is included with all other importation property in the determination of whether the transaction is a loss importation transaction.

(3) *Acquiring's basis in property tentatively divided into separate portions.*—Immediately after the application of section 362(e)(1) and this section and before the application of section 362(e)(2), each property treated as tentatively divided into separate portions for purposes of applying section 362(e)(1) and this section ceases to be treated as tentatively divided and Acquiring has a single, undivided basis in such property that is equal to the sum of—

(i) The value of each tentatively divided portion that is importation property, if the transaction is a loss importation transaction; and

(ii) Acquiring's basis in each tentatively divided portion that is not importation property received in a loss importation transaction, as determined under section 362(a) or section 362(b), as applicable, and without regard to any potential application of section 362(e)(2).

(f) *Examples.*—The examples in this paragraph (f) illustrate the application of section 362(e)(1) and the provisions of this section. Unless otherwise indicated, the examples use the following nomenclature and assumptions: A and B are U.S. citizens. DC, DC1, and P are domestic corporations that have not elected to be S corporations within the meaning of section 1361(a)(1) and that are not members of a consolidated group. F is a foreign individual. FP is a foreign partnership. FC, FC1, and FC2 are foreign corporations. Unless the facts indicate otherwise, the foreign individuals, corporations, and partnerships are not engaged in a U.S. trade or business, have no U.S. real property interests, and have no other relationships, activities, or interests that would cause them, their shareholders, their partners, or their property to be subject to federal income tax. There is no applicable income tax treaty, all persons' tax years are calendar years, and all persons and transactions are unrelated unless the facts indicate otherwise.

Example 1. Basic application of section. (i) *Section 351 transfer of importation property in a loss importation transaction.* (A) *Facts.* FC owns three assets, A1 (basis $40, value $150), A2 (basis $120, value $30), and A3 (basis $140, value $20). On Date 1, FC transfers A1, A2, and A3 to DC in a transaction to which section 351 applies.

(B) *Importation property.* If FC had sold A1, A2, or A3 immediately before the transaction, no gain or loss recognized on the sale would have been taken into account in determining a federal income tax liability. Further, if DC had sold A1, A2, or A3 immediately after the transaction, DC would take into account any gain or loss recognized on the sale in determining its federal income tax liability. Therefore, A1, A2, and A3 are all importation properties. See paragraph (c)(2) of this section.

(C) *Loss importation transaction.* FC's transfer of A1, A2, and A3 is a section 362 transaction. Furthermore, but for section 362(e)(1) and this section and section 362(e)(2), DC's aggregate basis in the importation properties, A1, A2, and A3, would be $300 ($40 + $120 + $140) under section 362(a) and the properties' aggregate value would be $200 ($150 + $30 + $20). Therefore, the importation properties' aggregate basis would exceed their aggregate value and the transaction is a loss importation transaction. See paragraph (c)(3) of this section.

(D) *Application of section 362(e)(1) and this section to importation property received in loss importation transaction.* Because the importation properties, A1, A2, and A3, were transferred in a loss importation transaction, paragraph (b)(1) of this section applies and DC's basis in A1, A2, and A3 will each be equal to the property's value ($150, $30, and $20, respectively) immediately after the transfer.

(E) *Basis of property received in transaction.* Following the application of section 362(e)(1) and this section, the provisions of section 362(e)(2) must be taken into account because the transfer is a section 362(a) transaction. Taking into account the application of section 362(e)(1) and this section, DC's aggregate basis in the transferred properties would not exceed their aggregate value immediately after the transfer. Therefore, FC does not have a net built-in loss, FC's transfer is not a loss duplication transaction, and section 362(e)(2) does not apply to this transaction. DC's bases in A1, A2, and A3, as determined under paragraph (i)(D) of this *Example 1*, are $150, $30, and $20, respectively. Under section 358(a), FC receives the DC stock with a basis of $300 (the sum of FC's bases in A1, A2, and A3 immediately before the exchange).

(ii) *Reorganization.* The facts are the same as in paragraph (i)(A) of this *Example 1* except that, instead of transferring property to DC in a section 351 exchange, FC merges with and into DC in a transaction described in section 368(a)(1)(A). The analysis and results are the same as set forth in paragraphs (i)(B), (C), and (D) of this *Example 1.* However, the analysis in paragraph (i)(E) of this *Example 1* does not apply to these facts because the transaction is not subject to 362(e)(2) and § 1.362-4. Under section 358(a), FC's shareholders will take the DC stock with a basis determined by reference to their FC stock basis.

(iii) *FC's property used in U.S. trade or business.* (A) *Facts.* The facts are the same as in paragraph (i)(A) of this *Example 1*, except that FC is engaged in a U.S. trade or business and uses all the properties in that U.S. trade or business. In this case, none of the properties would be importation property because FC would take any gain or loss on the disposition of the properties into account in determining its federal income tax liability. Accordingly, this section does not apply to the transaction.

(B) *Basis of property received in transaction.* Following the application of section 362(e)(1) and this section, the provisions of section 362(e)(2) must be taken into account because the transfer is a section 362(a) transaction. Taking into account the application of section 362(e)(1) and this section but without taking into account the provisions of section 362(e)(2), DC's aggregate basis in the transferred properties would be $300 ($40 + $120 + $140) under section 362(a) and the properties' aggregate value immediately after the transfer would be $200 ($150 + $30 + $20). Therefore, FC has a net built-in loss and FC's transfer of A1, A2, and A3 is a loss duplication transaction. Accordingly, under the general rule of section 362(e)(2), FC's $100 net built-in loss ($300 aggregate basis over $200 aggregate value) would be allocated proportionately (by the amount of built-in loss in each property) to reduce DC's basis in the loss properties, A2 and A3. See § 1.362-4. As a result, DC's basis in A2 would be $77.14 ($120 basis under section 362(a) reduced by $42.86, A2's proportionate share of FC's net built-in loss, computed as $90/$210 x $100) and DC's basis in A3 would be $82.86 ($140 basis under section 362(a) reduced by $57.14, A3's proportionate share of FC's net built-in loss, computed as $120/$210 x $100). However, if FC and DC were to elect under section 362(e)(2)(C) to apply the $100 basis reduction to FC's basis in the DC stock received in the transaction, DC's bases in A2 and A3 would remain their section 362(a) bases of $120 and $140, respectively. Under section 362(a), DC's basis in A1 is $40 (irrespective of whether the section 362(e)(2)(C) election is made). If FC and DC do not make a section 362(e)(2)(C) election, FC's basis in the DC stock received in the exchange will be $300; if FC and DC do make the election, FC's basis in the DC stock will be $200 ($300 - $100 net built-in loss). See § 1.362-4(b).

Example 2. Multiple transferors. (i) *Facts.* The facts are the same as in paragraph (i)(A) of *Example 1* of this paragraph (f), except that FC only owns A1 (basis $40, value $150) and A2 (basis $120, value $30) and F owns A3 (basis $140, value $20). On Date 1, FC transfers A1 and A2, and F transfers A3, to DC in a single transaction described in section 351.

(ii) *Importation property.* A1 and A2 are importation properties for the reasons set forth in paragraph (i)(B) of *Example 1* of this paragraph (f). A3 is also an importation property because, if F had sold A3 immediately before the transaction, no gain or loss recognized on the sale would have been taken into account in determining a federal income tax liability, and, further, if DC had sold A3 immediately after the transaction, DC would take into account any gain or loss recognized on the sale in determining its federal income tax liability.

(iii) *Loss importation transaction.* The transfers by FC and F are a section 362 transaction. The transaction is a loss importation transaction for the reasons set forth in paragraph (i)(C) of *Example 1* of this paragraph (f) (notwithstanding that one of the transferors, FC, did not transfer a net built-in loss). See paragraph (c)(3) of this section.

(iv) *Application of section 362(e)(1) and this section to importation property received in loss importation transaction.* Because the importation properties, A1, A2, and A3, were transferred in a loss importation transaction, paragraph (b)(1) of this section applies and DC's basis in A1, A2, and A3 will each be equal to the property's value ($150, $30, and $20, respectively) immediately after the transfer.

(v) *Basis of property received in transaction.* Following the application of section 362(e)(1) and this section, the provisions of section 362(e)(2) must be taken into account because the transfer is a section 362(a) transaction. The application of section 362(e)(2) is determined separately for each transferor. See § 1.362-4(b). Taking into account the application of section 362(e)(1) and this section, neither DC's aggregate basis in FC's properties nor DC's basis in F's property would exceed the properties' respective values immediately after the transaction. Therefore neither FC nor F has a net built-in loss, neither transfer is a loss duplication transaction, and section 362(e)(2) does not apply to either transfer. DC's bases in A1, A2, and A3, as determined under paragraph (iv) of this *Example 2*, are $150, $30, and $20, respectively. Under section 358(a), FC's basis in the DC stock received is $160 ($40 + $120) and F's basis in the DC stock received in the exchange is $140.

Example 3. Transfer of importation and non-importation property. (i) *Facts.* As in paragraph (i) of *Example 2*, FC owns A1 (basis $40, value $150) and A2 (basis $120, value $30), and F owns A3 (basis $140, value $20). In addition, A2 is a U.S. real property interest as defined in section 897(c)(1). On Date 1, FC transfers A1 and A2, and F transfers A3, to DC in a single transaction described in section 351.

(ii) *Importation property.* A1 and A3 are importation properties for the reasons set forth in paragraph (i)(B) of *Example 1* and paragraph (ii) of *Example 2* of this paragraph (f), respectively. However, A2 is not importation property because, if FC had sold A2 immediately before the transaction, FC would take into account any gain or loss recognized on the sale in determining its federal income tax liability.

(iii) *Loss importation transaction.* FC's and F's transfer is a section 362 transaction. Furthermore, but for section 362(e)(1) and this section and section 362(e)(2), DC's aggregate basis in the importation properties, A1 and A3, would be $180 ($40 + $140) and the properties' aggregate value would be $170 ($150 + $20) immediately after the transaction. Therefore, the importation properties' aggregate basis would exceed their aggregate value immediately after the transaction, and the transfer is a loss importation transaction.

(iv) *Application of section 362(e)(1) and this section to importation property received in loss importation transaction.* Because the importation properties, A1 and A3, were transferred in a loss importation transaction, paragraph (b)(1) of this section applies and DC's basis in A1 and in A3 will each be equal to the property's value ($150 and $20, respectively) immediately after the transfer.

(v) *Basis of property received in transaction.* Following the application of section 362(e)(1) and this section, the provisions of section 362(e)(2) must be taken into account because the transfer is a section 362(a) transaction. The application of section 362(e)(2) is determined separately for each transferor. See § 1.362-4(b).

(A) *FC's transfer.* Taking into account the application of section 362(e)(1) and this section but without taking into account the provisions of section 362(e)(2), DC would have an aggregate basis of $270 in the transferred properties ($150 in A1, as determined under paragraph (iv) of this *Example 3*, plus $120 in A2, determined under section 362(a)), and the properties would have an aggregate value of $180 ($150 + $30) immediately after the transfer. Therefore, FC has a net built-in loss and FC's transfer of A1 and A2 is a loss duplication transaction. Accordingly, under the general rule of section 362(e)(2), FC's $90 net built-in loss ($270 aggregate basis to DC over $180 aggregate value) would be allocated proportionately to reduce DC's basis in the loss property transferred by FC. As a result, FC's entire net built-in loss would be allocated to A2, the only loss property transferred by FC, and DC's basis in A2 would be $30 ($120 basis under section 362(a) reduced by $90 net built-in loss). However, if FC and DC were to elect under section 362(e)(2)(C) to apply the $90 basis reduction to FC's basis in the DC stock received in the transaction, DC's basis in A2 would remain its section 362(a) basis of $120. DC's basis in A1 is $150 as determined under paragraph (iv) of this *Example 3* (irrespective of whether the section 362(e)(2)(C) election is made). If FC and DC do not make a section 362(e)(2)(C) election, FC's basis in the DC stock received in the exchange will be $160; if FC and DC do make the election, FC's basis in the DC stock will be $70 ($160 - $90 net built-in loss). See § 1.362-4.

(B) *F's transfer of A3.* Taking into account the application of section 362(e)(1) and this section, DC's basis in A3, the property transferred by F, would not exceed its value immediately after the transfer. Therefore, F does not have a built-in loss, F's transfer is not a loss duplication transaction, and section 362(e)(2) does not apply to F's transfer. DC's basis in A3, as determined under paragraph (iv) of this *Example 3*, is $20. Under section 358(a), F receives the DC stock with a basis of $140.

Example 4. Multiple transferors of non-importation properties. (i) *Facts.* DC1 owns A1 (basis $40, value $150). In addition, as in *Example 3* of this paragraph (f), FC owns A2 (basis $120, value $30), a U.S. real property interest as defined in section 897(c)(1), and F owns A3 (basis $140, value $20). On Date 1, DC1 transfers A1, FC transfers A2, and F transfers A3, to DC in a single transaction described in section 351.

(ii) *Importation property.* A2 is not importation property and A3 is importation property for the reasons set forth in paragraph (ii) of *Example 3* and paragraph (i)(B) of *Example 1* of this paragraph (f), respectively. A1 is not importation property because, if DC1 had sold A2 immediately before the transaction, DC1 would take into account any gain or loss recognized on the sale in determining its federal income tax liability.

(iii) *Loss importation transaction.* The transfer of A1, A2, and A3 is a section 362 transaction. Furthermore, but for section 362(e)(1) and this section and section 362(e)(2), DC's basis in importation property, A3, would be $140 and the value of the property would be $20 immediately after the transaction. Therefore, the importation property's basis would exceed value and the transfer is a loss importation transaction.

(iv) *Application of section 362(e)(1) and this section to importation property received in loss importation transaction.* Because the importation property, A3, was transferred in a loss importation transaction, section 362(e)(1) and paragraph (b)(1) of this section apply and DC's basis in A3 will be equal to A3's $20 value immediately after the transfer.

(v) *Basis of property received in transaction.* Following the application of section 362(e)(1) and this section, the provisions of section 362(e)(2) must be taken into account because the transfer is a section 362(a) transaction. The application of section 362(e)(2) is determined separately for each transferor. See § 1.362-4.

(A) *DC1's transfer.* Taking into account the application of section 362(e)(1) and this section, DC's basis in A1 ($40 under section 362(a)) would not exceed its value immediately after the transfer. Therefore, DC1 does not have a net built-in loss, DC1's transfer is not a loss duplication transaction, and section 362(e)(2) does not apply to DC1's transfer. DC's basis in A1, determined under section 362(a), is $40. Under section 358(a), DC1 receives the DC stock with a basis of $40.

(B) *FC's transfer.* Taking into account the application of section 362(e)(1) and this section, but without taking into account the provisions of section 362(e)(2), DC would have a section 362(a) basis of $120 in A2, which would exceed A2's $30 value immediately after the transfer. Therefore, FC has a net built-in loss and FC's transfer of A2 is a loss duplication transaction. Accordingly, under the general rule of section 362(e)(2), FC's $90 net built-in loss (DC's $120 basis in A2 over A2's $30 value) would be applied to reduce DC's basis in A2, the only loss property transferred by FC. As a result, DC's basis in A2 would be $30 ($120 basis under section 362(a), reduced by the $90 net built-in loss). However, if FC and DC were to elect under section 362(e)(2)(C) to apply the $90 basis reduction to FC's basis in the DC stock received in the transaction, DC's basis in A2 would be its $120 basis determined under section 362(a). If FC and DC do not make a section 362(e)(2)(C) election, FC's basis in the DC stock received in the exchange will be $120; if FC and DC do make the election, FC's basis in the DC stock will be $30 ($120 - $90). See § 1.362-4.

(C) *F's transfer.* F's transfer of A3 is a transaction described in section 362(a). However, taking into account the application of section 362(e)(1) and this section, DC's basis in A3 ($20) would not exceed its value immediately after the transfer. Therefore, F does not have a built-in loss, F's transfer is not a loss duplication transaction, and section 362(e)(2) does not apply to F's transfer. DC's basis in A3, as determined under paragraph (iv) of this *Example 4*, is $20. Under section 358(a), F receives the DC stock with a basis of $140.

Example 5. Partnership transactions. (i) *Transfer by foreign partnership, foreign and domestic partners.* (A) *Facts.* A and F are equal partners in FP. FP owns A1 (basis $100, value $70). Under the terms of the FP partnership agreement, FP's items of income, gain, deduction, and loss are allocated equally between A and F. Section 704(c) does not apply with respect to the partnership property. FP transfers A1 to DC in a transfer to which section 351 applies. No election is made under section 362(e)(2)(C).

(B) *Importation property.* If FP had sold A1 immediately before the transaction, any gain or loss recognized on the sale would be allocated to and includible by A and F equally under the partnership agreement. Thus, under paragraph (d)(2) of this section, A1 is treated as tentatively divided into two equal portions, one treated as owned by A and one treated as owned by F. If FP had sold A1 immediately before the transaction, any gain or loss recognized on the portion treated as owned by A would have been taken into account in determining a federal income tax liability (A's); thus A's tentatively divided portion of A1 is not importation property. However, no gain or loss recognized on the tentatively divided portion treated as owned by F would have been taken into account in determining a federal income tax liability. Further, if DC had sold A1 immediately after the transaction, any gain or loss recognized on the sale would have been taken into account in determining a federal income tax liability (DC's); thus, F's tentatively divided portion of A1 is importation property.

(C) *Loss importation transaction.* FP's transfer of A1 is a section 362 transaction. Furthermore, but for section 362(e)(1) and this section and section 362(e)(2), DC's basis in the importation property, F's portion of A1, would be $50 under section 362(a) and the property's value would be $35 immediately after the transaction. Therefore, the importation property's basis would exceed its value and the transfer is a loss importation transaction.

(D) *Application of section 362(e)(1) and this section to importation property received in loss importation transaction.* Because the importation property, F's tentatively divided portion of A1, was transferred in a loss importation transaction, section 362(e)(1) and paragraph (b)(1) of this section apply and DC's basis in F's portion of A1 will be equal to its $35 value.

(E) *Basis of property received in transaction.* Following the application of section 362(e)(1) and this section, the provisions of section 362(e)(2) must be taken into account because the transfer is a section 362(a) transaction. Taking into account the application of section 362(e)(1) and this section but without taking into account the provisions of section 362(e)(2), DC's aggregate basis in A1 would be $85 (the sum of the $35 basis in F's tentatively divided portion of A1, as determined under paragraph (i)(D) of this *Example 5*, and the $50 basis in A's tentatively divided portion of A1, determined under section 362(a), see paragraphs (d)(2) and (e)(3) of this section) and A1's value immediately after the transfer would be $70. Therefore, FP has a net built-in loss and FP's transfer of A1 is a loss duplication transaction. Accordingly, under the general rule of section 362(e)(2), FP's $15 net built-in loss ($85 basis over $70 value) would be allocated to reduce DC's basis in the loss asset, A1, the only loss property transferred by FP. As a result, DC's basis in A1 would be $70 ($85 basis under section 362(a) and this section, reduced by the $15 net built-in loss). Under section 358, FP's basis in the DC stock received in the exchange will be $100. See § 1.362-4.

(ii) *Transfer with election to apply section 362(e)(2)(C).* The facts are the same as in paragraph (i)(A) of this *Example 5*, except that FP and DC elect to apply section 362(e)(2)(C) to reduce FP's basis in the DC stock received in the exchange. The analysis and results are the same as in paragraphs (i)(B), (C), (D), and (E) of this *Example 5*, except that the $15 reduction to DC's basis in A1 is not made and, as a result, DC's basis in A1 remains $85, and FP's basis in the DC stock received in the exchange is reduced from $100 to $85. The $15 reduction to FP's basis in DC stock reduces A's basis in its FP interest under section 705(a)(2)(B). See § 1.362-4(e)(1).

(iii) *Transfer by domestic partnership.* The facts are the same as in paragraph (i)(A) of this *Example 5* except that FP is a domestic partnership. The analysis and results are the same as in paragraphs (i)(B), (C), (D), and (E) of this *Example 5*.

(iv) *Transfer of interest in partnership with liability.* (A) *Facts.* F and two other individuals are equal partners in FP. F's basis in its partnership interest is $247. F's share of FP's § 1.752-1 liabilities (as defined in § 1.752-1(a)(4)) is $150. F transfers his partnership interest to DC in a transaction to which section 351 applies. If DC were to sell the FP interest immediately after the transfer, DC would receive $100 in cash or other property. In addition, taking into account the rules under § 1.752-4, DC's share of FP's § 1.752-1 liabilities (as defined in § 1.752-1(a)(4)) is $145 immediately after the transfer.

(B) *Importation property.* If F had sold his partnership interest immediately before the transaction, no gain or loss recognized on the sale would have been taken into account in determining a federal income tax liability. Further, if DC had sold the partnership interest immediately after the transaction, any gain or loss recognized on the sale would have been taken into account in determining a federal income tax liability. Therefore, F's partnership interest is importation property.

(C) *Loss importation transaction.* F's transfer is a section 362 transaction. However, but for section 362(e)(1) and this section and section 362(e)(2), DC's basis in the importation property, the partnership interest, determined under section 362(a) and taking into account the rules under section 752, would be $242 (F's $247 basis reduced by F's $150 share of FP liabilities and increased by DC's $145 share of FP liabilities) and, under paragraph (c)(4)(ii) of this section, the value of the FP interest would be $245 (the sum of $100, the cash DC would receive if DC immediately sold the partnership interest, and $145, DC's share of the § 1.752-1 liabilities (as defined in § 1.752-1(a)(4)) under section 752 immediately after the transfer to DC). Therefore, the importation property's basis ($242) would not exceed its value ($245), and the transfer is not a loss importation transaction.

(D) *Basis in property received in transaction.* Following the application of section 362(e)(1) and this section, the provisions of section 362(e)(2) must be taken into account because the transfer is a section 362(a) transaction. As described in paragraph (iv)(C) of this *Example 5*, taking into account the application of section 362(e)(1) and this section, DC's basis in the partnership interest would not exceed its value. Therefore, under § 1.362-4, F does not have a net built-in loss, the transfer is not a loss duplication transaction, and section 362(e)(2) does not apply to the transfer. DC's basis in F's partnership interest is $242, determined under sections 362(a) and 752. Under section 358, taking into account the rules under section 752, F's basis in the DC stock received in the exchange is $97 ($247 reduced by F's $150 share of FP liabilities). If FP had elected under section 754, or if section 743(b) required a downward basis adjustment to the partnership property, FP would apply the rules of § 1.743-1 to determine the amount of the basis adjustment to the partnership property.

Example 6. Transactions involving tax-exempt entities. (i) *Exempt transferor.* (A) *Facts.* InsCo is a benevolent life insurance association of a purely local character exempt from federal income tax under section 501(a) because it is described in section 501(c)(12). InsCo owns shares of stock of DC1 (basis $100, value $70) for investment purposes, which are not debt-financed property (as defined in section 514). On December 31, Year 1, InsCo transfers the DC1 stock to DC in exchange for DC stock in a transaction to which section 351 applies. No election is made under section 362(e)(2)(C).

(B) *Importation property*. If InsCo had sold the DC1 stock immediately before the transaction, any gain or loss realized would be excluded from UBTI under section 512(b)(5), and thus no gain or loss recognized on the sale would have been taken into account in determining federal income tax liability. Further, if DC had sold the DC1 stock immediately after the transaction, any gain or loss recognized on the sale would have been taken into account in determining federal income tax liability. Therefore, the DC1 stock is importation property.

(C) *Loss importation transaction*. InsCo's transfer is a section 362 transaction. Furthermore, but for section 362(e)(1) and this section and section 362(e)(2), DC's basis in importation property, the DC1 stock, would be $100, and the stock's value would be $70 immediately after the transaction. Therefore, the importation property's basis would exceed its value and the transfer is a loss importation transaction.

(D) *Application of section 362(e)(1) and this section to importation property received in loss importation transaction*. Because the importation property, the DC1 stock, was transferred in a loss importation transaction, paragraph (b)(1) of this section applies and DC's basis in the stock will be equal to its $70 value.

(E) *Basis of property received in transaction*. Following the application of section 362(e)(1) and this section, the provisions of section 362(e)(2) must be taken into account because the transfer is a section 362(a) transaction. Taking into account the application of section 362(e)(1) and this section, DC's basis in the DC1 stock does not exceed its value immediately after the transaction. Therefore, InsCo does not have a net built-in loss, InsCo's transfer is not a loss duplication transaction, and section 362(e)(2) has no application to the transaction. DC's basis in the DC1 stock, as determined under paragraph (i)(D) of this *Example 6*, is $70. Under section 358, InsCo's basis in the DC stock received in the exchange will be $100.

(ii) *Transferor loses tax-exempt status*. (A) *Facts*. The facts are the same as in paragraph (i)(A) of this *Example 6* except that InsCo fails to be described in section 501(c)(12) in Year 1.

(B) *Importation property*. If InsCo had sold the DC1 stock immediately before the transaction, any gain or loss recognized on the sale would have been taken into account in determining a federal income tax liability. Therefore, the DC1 stock is not importation property and this section does not apply to the transaction.

(C) *Basis of property received in transaction*. Following the application of section 362(e)(1) and this section, the provisions of section 362(e)(2) must be taken into account because the transfer is a section 362(a) transaction. Taking into account the application of section 362(e)(1) and this section but without taking into account the provisions of section 362(e)(2), DC would have a section 362(a) basis of $100 in the stock, which would exceed its value of $70 immediately after the transfer. Therefore, InsCo has a net built-in loss and InsCo's transfer of the DC1 stock is a loss duplication transaction. Accordingly, under the general rule of section 362(e)(2), InsCo's $30 net built-in loss ($100 basis over $70 value) would be allocated to reduce DC's basis in the loss asset, the DC1 stock, the only loss property transferred by InsCo. As a result, DC's basis in the DC1 stock would be $70 ($100 basis under section 362(a), reduced by the $30 net built-in loss). Under section 358, InsCo's basis in the DC stock received in the exchange will be $100.

(iii) *Transfer of property that is subject to unrelated business tax*. (A) *Facts*. The facts are the same as in paragraph (i)(A) of this *Example 6* except that, on December 31, Year 1, instead of the DC1 stock, InsCo transfers A1 (basis $200, value $150) to DC. A1 is real property that InsCo owned from January 1 to December 31 of Year 1. During the entirety of this period, A1's basis was $200, and in the twelve months prior to December 31, Year 1, the highest amount of outstanding principal indebtedness on A1 was $40. For purposes of the UBTI rules under section 512, A1 is debt-financed property within the meaning of section 514(b).

(B) *Importation property*. If InsCo had sold A1 immediately before the transaction, 20 percent of any gain or loss recognized on that sale (that is, $40 of acquisition indebtedness on A1 divided by A1's $200 basis in Year 1) would, under sections 512 and 514, be includible in UBTI at the end of Year 1, and 80 percent would not. Thus, under paragraph (d)(4) of this section, A1 is treated as tentatively divided into two portions, one reflecting the gain or loss that would be taken into account in determining a federal income tax liability in InsCo's hands immediately before the transfer (the 20 percent portion) and one that would not (the 80 percent portion). Further, if DC sold A1 immediately after the transfer, any gain or loss on both portions would be taken into account in determining a federal income tax liability. Accordingly, the 20 percent portion is not importation property, but the 80 percent portion is.

(C) *Loss importation transaction*. InsCo's transfer of A1 is a section 362 transaction. Furthermore, but for section 362(e)(1) and this section and section 362(e)(2), DC's basis in the importation property, the 80 percent portion of A1, would be $160 (80 percent of InsCo's $200 basis) under section 362(a) and the property's value would be $120 (80% of A1's $120 value) immediately after the transaction. Therefore, the importation property's basis would exceed its value and the transfer is a loss importation transaction.

(D) *Application of section 362(e)(1) and this section to importation property received in loss importation transaction*. Because the importation property, the 80 percent portion of A1, was transferred in a loss importation transaction, section 362(e)(1) and paragraph (b)(1) of this section apply and DC's basis in that portion of A1 will be equal to its $120 value.

(E) *Basis of property received in transaction*. Following the application of section 362(e)(1) and this section, the provisions of section 362(e)(2) must be taken into account because the transfer is a section 362(a) transaction. Taking into account the application of section 362(e)(1) and this section but without taking into account the provisions of section 362(e)(2), DC's aggregate basis in A1 would be $160 (the sum of the $120 basis in the 80 percent importation portion of A1, as determined under paragraph (iii)(D) of this *Example 6*, and the $40 basis in the 20 percent portion of A1 that is not importation property, determined under section 362(a). See paragraph (e)(3) of this section). Further, A1's value immediately after the transfer would be $150. Therefore, InsCo has a net built-in loss in A1, and InsCo's transfer of A1 is a loss duplication transaction. Accordingly, under the general rule of section 362(e)(2), InsCo's $10 net built-in loss ($160 basis over $150 value) would be allocated to reduce DC's basis in the loss asset, A1, the only loss property transferred by InsCo. As a result, DC's basis in A1 would be $150 ($160 basis under section 362(a) and this section, reduced by the $10 net built-in loss). Under section 358, InsCo's basis in the DC stock received in the exchange will be $200. See § 1.362-4.

(iv) *Transfer with election to apply section 362(e)(2)(C)*. The facts are the same as in paragraph (iii)(A) of this *Example 6*, except that InsCo and DC elect to apply section 362(e)(2)(C) to reduce InsCo's basis in the DC stock received in the exchange. The analysis and results are the same as in paragraphs (iii)(B), (C), (D), and (E) of this *Example 6*, except that the $10 reduction to DC's basis in A1 is not made and, as a result, DC's basis in A1 remains $160; however, InsCo's basis in the DC stock received in the exchange is reduced from $200 to $190.

Example 7. Transactions involving CFCs. (i) *Transfer by CFC*. (A) *Facts*. FC is a CFC with 100 shares of stock outstanding. A owns 60 of the shares and F owns the remaining 40 shares. FC owns two assets, A1 (basis $70, value $100), which is used in the conduct of a U.S. trade or business, and A2 (basis $100, value $75), which is not used in the conduct of a U.S. trade or business. FC transfers both assets to DC in a transaction to which section 351 applies.

(B) *Importation property*. If FC had sold A1 immediately before the transaction, any gain or loss recognized on the sale would have been taken into account in determining a federal income tax liability (FC's). See section 882(a). Therefore, A1 is not importation property. If FC had sold A2 immediately before the transaction, FC would not take the gain or loss recognized into account in determining its federal income tax liability, but the gain or loss could be taken into account in determining a section 951 inclusion to FC's U.S. shareholders. However, under paragraph (d)(3) of this section, gain or loss is not deemed taken into account in determining a federal income tax liability solely because it could affect an inclusion under section 951(a). Further, if DC had sold A2 immediately after the transaction, any gain or loss recognized on the sale would have been taken into account in determining a federal income tax liability. Therefore, A2 is importation property.

(C) *Loss importation transaction*. FC's transfer is a section 362 transaction. Furthermore, but for section 362(e)(1) and this section and section 362(e)(2), DC's basis in the importation property, A2, would be $100 and the property's value would be $75 immediately after the transaction. Therefore, the importation property's basis would exceed its value and the transfer is a loss importation transaction.

(D) *Application of section 362(e)(1) and this section to importation property received in loss importation transaction*. Because the importation property, A2, was transferred in a loss importation transaction, paragraph (b)(1) of this section applies and DC's basis in A2 will be equal to A2's $75 value immediately after the transfer.

(E) *Basis of property received in transaction*. Following the application of section 362(e)(1) and this section, the provisions of section

362(e)(2) must be taken into account because the transfer is a section 362(a) transaction. Taking into account the application of section 362(e)(1) and this section but without taking into account the provisions of section 362(e)(2), DC would have an aggregate basis of $145 in the transferred properties ($70 in A1, determined under section 362(a), plus $75 in A2, determined under this section) and the properties would have an aggregate value of $175 ($100 + $75) immediately after the transfer. Therefore, FC does not have a net built-in loss, FC's transfer is not a loss duplication transaction, and section 362(e)(2) does not apply to the transaction. DC's basis in A1 will be $70, determined under section 362(a), and DC's basis in A2 will be $75, as determined under paragraph (i)(D) of this *Example 7*. Under the general rule in section 358(a), FC receives the DC stock with a basis of $170 ($70 attributable to A1 plus $100 attributable to A2).

(ii) *Transfer of CFC stock.* (A) *Facts.* The facts are the same as in paragraph (i)(A) of this *Example 7*, except that A transfers its 60 shares of FC stock (basis $80, value $105) and F transfers its 40 shares of FC stock (basis $100, value $70) to DC in an exchange that qualifies under section 351.

(B) *Importation property.* If A had sold its FC shares immediately before the transaction, any gain or loss recognized on the sale would have been taken into account in determining a federal income tax liability (A's). Therefore, A's FC shares are not importation property. However, if F had sold its FC shares immediately before the transaction, no gain or loss recognized on the sale would have been taken into account in determining a federal income tax liability. Further, if DC had sold F's FC shares immediately after the transaction, any gain or loss recognized on the sale would have been taken into account in determining a federal income tax liability. Therefore, F's FC shares are importation property.

(C) *Loss importation transaction.* The transfer of the FC shares is a section 362 transaction. Furthermore, but for section 362(e)(1) and this section and section 362(e)(2), DC's aggregate basis in the importation property, F's shares of FC stock, would be $100 under section 362(a) and the shares' aggregate value would be $70. Therefore, the importation property's aggregate basis would exceed its aggregate value, and the transfer is a loss importation transaction.

(D) *Application of section 362(e)(1) and this section to importation property received in loss importation transaction.* Because the importation property, F's shares of FC stock, was transferred in a loss importation transaction, paragraph (b)(1) of this section applies and DC's aggregate basis in the shares will be equal to their $70 aggregate value immediately after the transfer.

(E) *Basis of property received in transaction.* Following the application of section 362(e)(1) and this section, the provisions of section 362(e)(2) must be taken into account because the transfer is a section 362(a) transaction. The application of section 362(e)(2) is determined separately for each transferor. See § 1.362-4(b).

(1) A's transfer. Taking into account the application of section 362(e)(1) and this section, DC's aggregate basis in the shares ($80 under section 362(a)) would not exceed the shares' value ($105) immediately after the transaction. Therefore A does not have a built-in loss, A's transfer is not a loss duplication transaction, and section 362(e)(2) does not apply to A's transfer. DC's aggregate basis in A's shares, determined under section 362(a), is $80. Under section 358(a), A receives the DC stock with a basis of $80.

(2) F's transfer. Taking into account the application of section 362(e)(1) and this section, DC's aggregate basis in the shares would not exceed their value immediately after the transaction. Therefore, F does not have a built-in loss, F's transfer is not a loss duplication transaction, and section 362(e)(2) does not apply to F's transfer. DC's aggregate basis in F's shares, as determined under paragraph (ii)(D) of this *Example 7*, is $70. Under section 358(a), F receives the DC stock with a basis of $100.

Example 8. Property subject to withholding tax. (i) *Facts.* FC owns a share of DC1 stock (basis $100, value $70) as an investment. FC receives dividends on the share that are subject to federal withholding tax of 30 percent of the amount received under section 881(a); under section 1442(a), DC1 must withhold tax on the dividends paid. FC transfers the DC1 share to DC in a transaction to which section 351 applies.

(ii) *Importation property.* Although any dividends received with respect to the DC1 stock were subject to withholding tax, if FC had sold the share of stock of DC1, no gain or loss recognized on the sale would have been taken into account in determining a federal income tax liability. See section 865(a)(2). Further, if DC had sold the share of DC1 stock immediately after the transaction, any gain or loss recognized on the sale would be taken into account in determining federal income tax liability. Therefore, the share of DC1 stock is importation property.

(iii) *Loss importation transaction.* FC's transfer is a section 362 transaction. Furthermore, but for section 362(e)(1) and this section and section 362(e)(2), DC's basis in the importation property, the share of DC1 stock, would be $100 and the share's value would be $70 immediately after the transaction. Therefore, the share's basis would exceed its value and the transfer is a loss importation transaction.

(iv) *Application of section 362(e)(1) and this section to importation property received in loss importation transaction.* Because the importation property, the DC1 share, was transferred in a loss importation transaction, paragraph (b)(1) of this section applies and DC's basis in the share will be equal to the share's $70 value.

(v) *Basis of property received in transaction.* Following the application of section 362(e)(1) and this section, the provisions of section 362(e)(2) must be taken into account because the transfer is a section 362(a) transaction. Taking into account the application of section 362(e)(1) and this section, DC's basis in the DC1 share would not exceed the share's value immediately after the transaction. Therefore, FC does not have a net built-in loss, FC's transfer is not a loss duplication transaction, and section 362(e)(2) does not apply to the transaction. DC's basis in the DC1 share, as determined under paragraph (iv) of this *Example 8*, is $70. Under section 358, FC's basis in the DC stock received in the exchange will be $100.

Example 9. Property transferred in triangular reorganization. (i) *Foreign subsidiary.* (A) *Facts.* P owns the sole outstanding share of stock of FC (basis $1), FC1 owns the sole outstanding share of FC2 (basis $100), and FC2 owns one asset, A1 (basis $100, value $20). In a forward triangular merger described in § 1.358-6(b)(2)(i), FC2 merges with and into FC, and FC1 receives shares of P stock in exchange for its FC2 stock. The forward triangular merger is a transaction described in section 368(a)(2)(D) and, therefore, in section 362(b).

(B) *Determining P's basis in its FC share.* Pursuant to § 1.358-6, for purposes of determining the adjustment to P's basis in its FC shares, P is treated as though it first received A1 in a transaction in which its basis in A1 would be determined under section 362(b) and then it transferred A1 to FC in a transaction in which P's basis in its FC stock would be determined under section 358.

(1) P's deemed acquisition and transfer of A1. If FC2 had sold A1 for its value immediately before the deemed transaction, no gain or loss recognized on the sale would have been taken into account in determining a federal income tax liability. If P had sold A1 immediately after the deemed transaction, any gain or loss recognized on the sale would have been taken into account in determining a federal income tax liability (P's). Therefore, with respect to P's deemed acquisition, A1 is importation property. Furthermore, immediately after the deemed transaction, P's basis in A1, but for section 362(e)(1) and this section and section 362(e)(2), would be $100 and A1's value is $20. Therefore, the importation property's basis would exceed its value and the transfer is a loss importation transaction. Accordingly, P's deemed basis in A1 will be equal to A1's $20 value.

(2) P's FC stock basis. As a result of P's deemed transfer of A1 to FC (and applying the principles of § 1.367(b)-13), P's basis in its FC stock is increased by its $20 deemed basis in A1. Accordingly, following the transaction, P's basis in its share of FC stock will be $21 (the sum of its original $1 basis and the $20 adjustment for the deemed transfer of A1).

(C) *FC's basis in A1.* FC's basis in A1 is determined under the rules of this section without regard to the determination of P's adjustment to its basis in FC stock. If FC2 had sold A1 for its value immediately before the transaction, no gain or loss recognized on the sale would have been taken into account in determining a federal income tax liability. However, if FC had sold A1 immediately after the transaction, no gain or loss recognized on the sale would have been taken into account in determining a federal income tax liability, so A1 is not importation property. Accordingly, this section will not apply to the transaction. Although there is a net built-in loss in A1, the transaction is not described in section 362(a), and so section 362(e)(2) and § 1.362-4 will not apply to the transaction. Thus, under section 362(b), FC's basis in A1 will be $100.

(D) *FC1's basis in P stock.* Under section 358, FC1's basis in the P stock it receives in the exchange will be $100.

(ii) *Property transferred to U.S. subsidiary in triangular reorganization.* (A) *Facts.* The facts are the same as in paragraph (i)(A) of this *Example 9*, except that P also owns the sole outstanding share of DC (basis $1) and, instead of merging into FC, FC2 merged into DC.

(B) *Determining P's basis in its DC share.* As determined under paragraph (i)(B)(2) of this *Example 9*, P's basis in its DC share is $21, the sum of its original $1 basis plus the $20 adjustment for the deemed transfer of A1.

(C) *DC's basis in A1.* If FC2 had sold A1 for its value immediately before the transaction, no gain or loss recognized on the sale would have been taken into account in determining a federal income tax liability. However, if DC had sold A1 immediately after the transaction, any gain or loss recognized on the sale would have been taken into account in determining a federal income tax liability, so A1 is importation property with respect to DC. Furthermore, immediately after the transaction, DC's basis in A1, but for section 362(e)(1) and this section and section 362(e)(2), would be $100 and A1's value is $20. Therefore, the importation property's basis would exceed its value and the transfer is a loss importation transaction. Accordingly, DC's basis in A1 will be $20, A1's value immediately after the transaction.

(D) *FC1's basis in P stock.* Under section 358, FC1's basis in the P stock it receives in the exchange is $100.

(g) *Applicability date.*—This section applies with respect to any transaction occurring on or after March 28, 2016, and also with respect to any transaction occurring before such date as a result of an entity classification election under § 301.7701-3 of this chapter filed on or after March 28, 2016, unless such transaction is pursuant to a binding agreement that was in effect prior to March 28, 2016 and at all times thereafter. In addition, taxpayers may apply this section to any transaction occurring after October 22, 2004. [Reg. § 1.362-3.]

☐ [*T.D.* 9759, 3-25-2016.]

§ 1.362-4. Basis of loss duplication property.—(a) *Purpose and scope.*—(1) *In general.*—The purpose of section 362(e)(2) and this section is to prevent the duplication of net loss in transfers to which section 351 applies, capital contributions, and paid-in surplus (each, a section 362(a) transaction). See paragraph (g) of this section for definitions of terms used in this section.

(2) *Intercompany transactions.*—For rules relating to the application of section 362(e)(2) to transfers between members of a consolidated group on or after October 22, 2004, see § 1.1502-80(h).

(b) *Basis determinations under section 362(e)(2) and this section.*—Notwithstanding section 362(a), if a corporation (Acquiring) receives loss duplication property (as defined in paragraph (g)(1) of this section) from a person (Transferor) in a loss duplication transaction (as defined in paragraph (g)(2) of this section), Acquiring's basis in such property is equal to the basis of the property determined without regard to section 362(e)(2) and this section (as described in paragraph (g)(1)(ii) of this section), reduced by the property's allocable portion of Transferor's net built-in loss (as defined in paragraph (g)(3) of this section). If more than one Transferor transfers property to a corporation in a section 362(a) transaction, whether and the extent to which section 362(e)(2) and this section apply is determined separately for each Transferor.

(c) *Exceptions and special rules.*—(1) *Transactions in which net built-in loss is eliminated without recognition.*—Section 362(e)(2) does not apply to a transaction to the extent that—

(i) Without recognizing gain or loss, Transferor distributes the Acquiring stock received in the transaction; and

(ii) Upon completion of the transaction, no person holds Acquiring stock or any other asset with a basis determined, in whole or in part, by reference to Transferor's basis in the distributed Acquiring stock.

(2) *Certain transactions outside of the United States.*—Section 362(e)(2) does not apply to a transaction if—

(i) Neither Transferor nor Acquiring is a U.S. person (as defined in section 7701(a)(30)), a person otherwise required to file a U.S. return for the year of the transaction, a controlled foreign corporation (CFC, as defined in paragraph (g)(7) of this section), or a controlled foreign partnership (CFP, as defined in paragraph (g)(9) of this section) on the date of the transaction;

(ii) The transfer occurs more than two years prior to the date of any event described in paragraph (d)(3)(ii)(E), (F), or (G) of this section; and

(iii) The original transaction and the event or events described in paragraph (d)(3)(ii)(E), (F), or (G) of this section were not entered into with a view to reducing or avoiding the Federal income tax liability of any person by avoiding the application of section 362(e)(2) and this section to the original transaction.

(3) *Other effects of basis determination under this section.*—(i) *Determination by reference to transferor's basis.*—A determination of basis under this section is a determination by reference to the transferor's basis, including for purposes of sections 755, 1223(2), and 7701(a)(43).

(ii) *Treatment as tax-exempt income or noncapital, nondeductible expense.*—A determination of basis under paragraph (b) of this section does not give rise to an item treated as a noncapital, nondeductible expense under § 1.1502-32(b)(2)(iii). However, a determination of basis under paragraph (d) of this section does give rise to an item treated as a noncapital, nondeductible expense under § 1.1502-32(b)(2)(iii).

(d) *Election to reduce Transferor's stock basis instead of Acquiring's asset basis.*—(1) *In general.*—In lieu of making the basis reductions otherwise required under paragraph (b) of this section, Transferor and Acquiring may elect to reduce Transferor's basis in Acquiring stock that is received in the transaction without the recognition of gain or loss (the section 362(e)(2)(C) election). The section 362(e)(2)(C) election may be made protectively and will have no effect to the extent that property transferred in the transaction is determined not to be subject to section 362(e)(2) and this section. However, the election is irrevocable once it is made. A section 362(e)(2)(C) election is made and effective if—

(i) Prior to the filing of a Section 362(e)(2)(C) Statement (described in paragraph (d)(3)(i) of this section), Transferor and Acquiring enter into a written, binding agreement to elect to apply section 362(e)(2)(C); and

(ii) The Section 362(e)(2)(C) Statement is filed in accordance with the provisions of paragraph (d)(3) of this section.

(2) *Effect of section 362(e)(2)(C) election.*—If a section 362(e)(2)(C) election is made and in effect—

(i) An amount equal to the portion of Transferor's net built-in loss (as defined in paragraph (g)(3) of this section) that would otherwise be applied to reduce asset basis under paragraph (b) of this section is allocated among the Acquiring shares received or deemed received in the exchange (in proportion to the value of such shares) and applied to reduce Transferor's basis (determined without regard to section 362(e)(2) and this section) in each such share; and

(ii) Acquiring's basis in loss duplication property received from Transferor in the transaction is not determined under section 362(e)(2) and this section.

(3) *Section 362(e)(2)(C) Statement.*—(i) *Form and contents of statement.*—The Section 362(e)(2)(C) Statement is to be titled "Section 362(e)(2)(C) Statement." The Section 362(e)(2)(C) Statement must—

(A) Identify (by name and tax identification number, if any) Transferor and Acquiring;

(B) State that Transferor and Acquiring have entered into a written, binding agreement to elect to apply section 362(e)(2)(C) as required in paragraph (d)(1)(i) of this section; and

(C) State the date of the transaction (or, if the transaction includes transfers on more than one date, then the dates of all transfers) to which the election applies.

(ii) *Filing the Section 362(e)(2)(C) Statement.*—In general, the Section 362(e)(2)(C) Statement is filed by the person or entity described in the applicable paragraph of this paragraph (d)(3)(ii). Thus, if Transferor is a partnership, S corporation, trust (including a subpart E trust), or other pass-through entity, or Acquiring is an S corporation, the entity (and not the partners, shareholders, or other persons having an interest in the entity or its property) is the person that must file the Section 362(e)(2)(C) Statement, without regard to whether such entity is foreign or domestic. However, in the case of a CFC or CFP, the controlling U.S. shareholders of the CFC or the reporting U.S. partners of the CFP, respectively, file the Section 362(e)(2)(C) Statement.

(A) *Transferor is a person required to file a U.S. return.*—If Transferor is a person required to file a U.S. return for the year of the transfer, Transferor must include the Section 362(e)(2)(C) Statement on or with its timely filed (including extensions) original U.S. return for the taxable year in which the transfer occurred.

(B) *Transferor is a CFC or CFP and not required to file a U.S. return.*—If paragraph (d)(3)(ii)(A) of this section does not apply and Transferor is either a CFC or a CFP on the date of the transfer, all of Transferor's controlling U.S. shareholders (in the case of a CFC) or all of Transferor's reporting U.S. partners (in the case of a CFP) must include the Section 362(e)(2)(C) Statement on or with their timely filed (including extensions) original U.S. returns for their taxable years in which the transfer occurred.

(C) *Transferor is not a person required to file a U.S. return, a CFC, or a CFP, but Acquiring is required to file U.S. return.*—If paragraphs (d)(3)(ii)(A) and (B) of this section do not apply and Acquiring is a person required to file a U.S. return for the year of the transfer, Acquiring must include the Section 362(e)(2)(C) Statement on or with its timely filed (including extensions) original U.S. return for the taxable year in which the transfer occurred.

(D) *Transferor is not a person required to file a U.S. return, a CFC, or a CFP, Acquiring is not required to file a U.S. return, but Acquiring is a CFC.*—If paragraphs (d)(3)(ii)(A) through (C) of this section do not apply and Acquiring is a CFC on the date of the transfer, all of Acquiring's controlling U.S. shareholders must include the Section 362(e)(2)(C) Statement on or with their timely filed (including extensions) original U.S. returns for their taxable years in which the transfer occurred.

(E) *Neither Transferor nor Acquiring is a person required to file a U.S. return, a CFC, or a CFP, but Transferor later becomes a person required to file a U.S. return, a CFC, or a CFP.*—If paragraphs (d)(3)(ii)(A) through (D) of this section do not apply and Transferor becomes a person required to file a U.S. return, a CFC, or a CFP, Transferor (if required to file a U.S. return), all of Transferor's controlling U.S. shareholders (if Transferor becomes a CFC not otherwise required to file a U.S. return), or all of Transferor's reporting U.S. partners (if Transferor becomes a CFP not otherwise required to file a U.S. return) must include the Section 362(e)(2)(C) Statement on or with their timely filed (including extensions) original U.S. returns for their taxable years in which an event described in this paragraph (d)(3)(ii)(E) first occurs. For purposes of this paragraph (d)(3)(ii)(E), the term Transferor includes any person holding property with a basis determined directly or indirectly by reference to Transferor's basis in the Acquiring stock received in the transaction.

(F) *Transferor is not and does not become a person required to file a U.S. return, a CFC, or a CFP, Acquiring is not, but later becomes either a person required to file a U.S. return, a CFC, or a CFP.*—If paragraphs (d)(3)(ii)(A) through (E) of this section do not apply and Acquiring becomes a person required to file a U.S. return, a CFC, or a CFP, Acquiring (if required to file a U.S. return), all of Acquiring's controlling U.S. shareholders (if Acquiring becomes a CFC not otherwise required to file a U.S. return), or all of Acquiring's reporting U.S. partners (if Acquiring becomes a CFP not otherwise required to file a U.S. return) must include the Section 362(e)(2)(C) Statement on or with their timely filed (including extensions) original U.S. returns for their taxable years in which an event described in this paragraph (d)(3)(ii)(F) first occurs. For purposes of this paragraph (d)(3)(ii)(F), the term Acquiring includes any person holding property with a basis determined directly or indirectly by reference to Acquiring's basis in loss duplication property received in the transaction.

(G) *Transferor and Acquiring are not and do not become a person required to file a U.S. return, a CFC, or a CFP, but the basis of the loss duplication property or Acquiring stock later becomes relevant for Federal tax purposes.*—If paragraphs (d)(3)(ii)(A) through (F) of this section do not apply and, in a transferred basis transaction, a person required to file a U.S. return, a CFC, or a CFP acquires either loss duplication property or Acquiring stock that was received in the loss duplication transaction, or any property the basis of which is determined in whole or in part by reference to any such property or stock, all such persons (or, in the case of a CFC or CFP not required to file a U.S. return, all the controlling U.S. shareholders or all the reporting U.S. partners, as applicable) must include the Section 362(e)(2)(C) Statement on or with their timely filed (including extensions) original U.S. returns for their first taxable year(s) in which there occurs an event or events described in this paragraph (d)(3)(ii)(G).

(e) *Transfers by partnerships and S corporations.*—(1) *Transfers by partnerships.*—If a partnership transfers property in a loss duplication transaction with respect to which a section 362(e)(2)(C) election is made, the resulting reduction to the partnership's basis in the Acquiring stock received in exchange for the loss duplication property is treated as an expenditure of the partnership described in section 705(a)(2)(B).

(2) *Transfers by S corporations.*—If an S corporation transfers property in a loss duplication transaction with respect to which a section 362(e)(2)(C) election is made, the resulting reduction to the S corporation's basis in the Acquiring stock received in exchange for the loss duplication property is treated as an expense of the S corporation described in section 1367(a)(2)(D).

(f) *Transfers to S corporations.*—If a person transfers property to an S corporation in a loss duplication transaction, any resulting reduction under section 362(e)(2) and this section to the S corporation's basis in the property received is not treated as an expense of the S corporation described in section 1367(a)(2)(D).

(g) *Definitions.*—For purposes of section 362(e)(2) and this section—

(1) *Loss duplication property* is any property—

(i) That is transferred by Transferor to Acquiring in a loss duplication transaction (as defined in paragraph (g)(2) of this section); and

(ii) That Acquiring would take with a basis in excess of value immediately after the transaction; for this purpose, the basis Acquiring would take in the property is determined immediately after the transaction and without regard to section 362(e)(2) and this section, but otherwise taking into account all applicable provisions of law, including, without limitation, section 362(e)(1).

(2) A *loss duplication transaction* is a section 362(a) transaction in which Acquiring's aggregate basis in the property received from Transferor would, but for section 362(e)(2) and this section, exceed the aggregate value of such property immediately after the transaction. For this purpose—

(i) A transaction is a section 362(a) transaction if it is described in section 362(a) without regard to whether it is also described in any other provision of the Internal Revenue Code (Code), including, without limitation, section 362(b); and

(ii) Acquiring's aggregate basis in the property received from Transferor is determined immediately after the transaction and without regard to section 362(e)(2) and this section, but otherwise taking into account all applicable provisions of law, including, without limitation, section 362(e)(1).

(3) *Transferor's net built-in loss* is the excess of—

(i) Acquiring's aggregate basis (determined under paragraph (g)(2)(ii) of this section) in all property received from Transferor in a loss duplication transaction, over

(ii) The aggregate value of such property immediately after the transaction.

(4) A property's *built-in loss* is the excess of Acquiring's basis in the property (determined as described in paragraph (g)(1)(ii) of this section) over the property's value (determined immediately after the transaction).

(5) A property's *allocable portion of Transferor's net built-in loss* is the portion of Transferor's net built-in loss that bears the same ratio to Transferor's net built-in loss that the property's built-in loss bears to the aggregate built-in losses reflected in the bases of loss duplication property transferred by Transferor in the transaction.

(6) A *U.S. return* is a return of income under section 6012 or an information return under Subtitle F, Chapter 61, Subchapter A, Part III of the Code (sections 6031 and following) or the regulations thereunder, that the taxpayer is unconditionally required to file. Thus, the term does not include elective forms or statements that are required to be filed only to obtain a particular tax treatment, including forms filed to make an election or to reduce or avoid withholding by a person not otherwise required to file a U.S. return (as described in this paragraph (g)(6)) (for example, a notice of nonrecognition under § 1.1445-2(d)).

(7) A *controlled foreign corporation* (CFC) is any corporation described in section 957 or section 953(c).

(8) A *controlling U.S. shareholder* is any person that is treated as a controlling U.S. shareholder under § 1.964-1(c)(5) because such person either owns a direct interest in the CFC or is treated as owning an interest in the CFC by reason of section 318(a)(2) (attribution from partnerships, estates, trusts, and corporations).

(9) A *controlled foreign partnership* (CFP) is any partnership treated as a controlled foreign partnership for purposes of section 6038.

(10) A *reporting U.S. partner* is any partner of a CFP that is required to file an information return with respect to the CFP pursuant to section 6038 or the regulations thereunder, without regard to § 1.6038-3(c) or (j). In addition, in applying the constructive ownership rules of § 1.6038-3(b)(4), the term "nonresident alien" is replaced by the term "individual."

(11) The term *stock* means both Acquiring stock and Acquiring securities received by Transferor in the transaction if gain or loss on the receipt of the stock or securities is not recognized in whole or in part.

(12) *Value.*—(i) *General rule.*—The term *value* means fair market value.

(ii) *Special rule for transfers of partnership interests.*—Notwithstanding the general rule in paragraph (g)(12)(i) of this section, when referring to a partnership interest, for purposes of section 362(e)(2) and this section, the term *value* means the sum of the cash that Acquiring would receive for the interest, assuming an exchange between a willing buyer and a willing seller (neither being under any compulsion to buy or sell and both having reasonable knowledge of relevant facts), increased by any § 1.752-1 liabilities (as defined in § 1.752-1(a)(4)) of the partnership allocated to Acquiring with regard to such transferred interest under section 752 immediately after the transfer to Acquiring. See § 1.743-1 regarding the application of section 743(b) following a section 362(e) basis reduction.

(h) *Examples.*—The examples in this paragraph (h) illustrate the application of section 362(e)(2) and the provisions of this section. Unless the facts otherwise indicate, the examples use the following nomenclature and assumptions: X, Y, P, S, S1, and S2 are domestic corporations; A and B are U.S. individuals; FC1 and FC2 are foreign corporations and are not engaged in a U.S. trade or business, have no U.S. real property interests, and have no other relationships, activities, or interests that would cause them, their shareholders, or their property to be subject to tax imposed under any provision of subtitle A of the Internal Revenue Code (federal income tax); there is no applicable income tax treaty; PRS is a domestic partnership; no election is made under section 362(e)(2)(C); and the transferred property is not importation property (as defined in § 1.362-3(c)(2)) and the transfers are not loss importation transactions (as defined in § 1.362-3(c)(3)), so that the basis of no property is determined under section 362(e)(1). All persons and transactions are unrelated unless the facts indicate otherwise, all taxpayers are on a calendar tax year, and all other relevant facts are set forth in the examples. See § 1.362-3(f) for additional examples illustrating the application of section 362(e)(2) and this section, including to transactions that are subject to section 362(e)(2), and section 362(e)(1).

Example 1. Transfer described in section 351. (i) *Basic application of section.* (A) *Facts.* A owns Asset 1 (basis $90, value $60) and Asset 2 (basis $110, value $120). In a transaction to which section 351 applies, A transfers Asset 1 and Asset 2 to X in exchange for a single outstanding share of X stock representing all the outstanding X stock immediately after the transaction.

(B) *Analysis. (1) Loss duplication transaction.* A's transfer of Asset 1 and Asset 2 is a section 362(a) transaction. But for section 362(e)(2) and this section, X's aggregate basis in those assets would be $200 ($90 + $110), which would exceed the aggregate value of the assets $180 ($60 + $120) immediately after the transaction. Accordingly, the transfer is a loss duplication transaction and A has a net built-in loss of $20 ($200 - $180).

(2) Identifying loss duplication property. But for section 362(e)(2) and this section, X's basis in Asset 1 would be $90, which would exceed Asset 1's $60 value immediately after the transaction. Accordingly, Asset 1 is loss duplication property. But for section 362(e)(2) and this section, X's basis in Asset 2 would be $110, which would not exceed Asset 2's $120 value immediately after the transaction. Accordingly, Asset 2 is not loss duplication property.

(C) *Basis in loss duplication property.* X's basis in Asset 1 is $70, computed as its $90 basis under section 362(a) reduced by A's $20 net built-in loss.

(D) *Basis in other property.* Under section 362(a), X has a transferred basis of $110 in Asset 2. Under section 358(a), A has an exchanged basis of $200 in the X stock it receives in the transaction.

(ii) *Section 362(e)(2)(C) election.* The facts are the same as in paragraph (i)(A) of this *Example 1*, except that A and X make an election under section 362(e)(2)(C). Under paragraph (d)(2)(i) of this section, A reduces its basis in the X stock, as determined without regard to section 362(e)(2) and this section, by the amount of A's net built-in loss that would have been applied to reduce X's basis in Asset 1 had the section 362(e)(2)(C) election not been made. In addition, no reduction is made to X's basis in Asset 1, as determined without regard to section 362(e)(2) and this section. As a result, A's basis in the X stock is $180 ($200 - $20), X's basis in Asset 1 is $90, and X's basis in Asset 2 is $110.

Example 2. Transfer described in both section 351 and section 368(a)(1)(B). (i) *Basic application of section.* (A) *Facts.* P owns the sole outstanding share of S1 stock and the ten outstanding shares of S2 stock. In a transaction to which section 351 applies and that is described in section 368(a)(1)(B), P transfers its ten S2 shares to S1 in exchange for an additional ten shares of S1 voting stock. At the time of the transfer, P has a basis of $10 each in five of its S2 shares (Shares 1 - 5) and a basis of $5 each in its other five S2 shares (Shares 6 - 10), and the value of each share is $7.

(B) *Analysis. (1) Loss duplication transaction.* P's transfer of the S2 shares is a section 362(a) transaction notwithstanding that it is also a transaction described in section 368(a)(1)(B) and therefore section 362(b). But for section 362(e)(2) and this section, S1's aggregate basis in the S2 shares would be $75 ($10 × 5, or $50, for Shares 1-5 + $5 × 5, or $25, for Shares 6-10). Thus, S1's $75 aggregate basis in the shares would exceed the aggregate value of the shares, $70 ($7 × 10 shares), immediately after the transaction. Accordingly, the transfer is a loss duplication transaction and P has a net built-in loss of $5 ($75 - $70).

(2) Identifying loss duplication property. But for section 362(e)(2) and this section, S1's basis in each of Shares 1-5 would be $10, which would exceed each share's $7 value immediately after the transaction. Accordingly, Shares 1-5 are each loss duplication property. But for section 362(e)(2) and this section, S1's basis in each of Shares 6-10 would be $5, which would not exceed each share's $7 value immediately after the transaction. Accordingly, Shares 6-10 are not loss duplication property.

(C) *Basis in loss duplication property.* S1's basis in each of Shares 1 - 5 is $9, computed as its $10 basis (determined without regard to section 362(e)(2) and this section) reduced by $1, the share's allocable portion (1/5) of P's net built-in loss ($5).

(D) *Basis in other property.* Under section 362(a), S1 has a transferred basis of $5 in each of Shares 6 - 10. Under section 358(a), P has an exchanged basis in the ten S1 shares it receives in the exchange ($10 in each of the five S1 shares received in exchange for Shares 1-5 and $5 in each of the five S1 shares received in exchange for Shares 5 - 10).

(ii) *Section 362(e)(2)(C) election.* The facts are the same as in paragraph (i)(A) of this *Example 2*, except that an election under section 362(e)(2)(C) is made to reduce P's basis in the shares of S1 stock received in the exchange. Under paragraph (d)(2)(i) of this section, P reduces its basis in the S1 stock by $5, the amount of P's net built-in loss that S1's basis in the S2 shares would have been reduced under section 362(e)(2) and this section had the section 362(e)(2)(C) election not been made, and no reduction is made to S1's basis in the S2 stock (as determined without regard to section 362(e)(2) and this section). Because an election is being made under section 362(e)(2)(C), P's basis in the new S1 shares is not determined under the general rule of § 1.358-2(a)(2)(i) (under which P's basis in each new S1 share would be equal to the basis of the S2 share transferred in exchange for the S1 share). Section 1.358-2(a)(2)(viii)(B). Accordingly, P's basis in each new S1 share will be $7, the share's allocable portion of P's $75 aggregate basis in the S2 shares transferred in the transaction (or, $7.50 per share), reduced under paragraph (d)(2)(i) of this section by the $5 that would have been applied to reduce S1's basis in the S2 shares had the section 362(e)(2)(C) election not been made (or $.50 per share). Under paragraph (d)(2)(ii) of this section and section 362(a), S1 receives five shares of the S2 stock with a basis of $10 each and five shares of the S2 stock with a basis of $5 each.

Example 3. Transfer described in both section 351 and section 368(a)(1)(A), multiple transferors, elimination of duplicated loss. (i) *Facts.* A owns Asset 1 (basis $120, value $130) and all the outstanding shares of X stock. B owns all the outstanding shares of Y stock (basis $150). Y owns Asset 2 (basis $250, value $210). Pursuant to a single plan, A transfers Asset 1 to X in exchange for additional X shares and, in a transaction qualifying as a reorganization described in section 368(a)(1)(A), Y merges with and into X. In the merger, B receives X stock with a basis equal to B's basis in its Y stock immediately before the merger. A's transfer of Asset 1 to X in exchange for X stock and Y's transfer of Asset 2 to X in the merger are both transactions to which section 351 applies. Notwithstanding that the transfers by A and Y are pursuant to a single plan forming one transaction, section 362(e)(2) and this section apply to each transferor separately.

(ii) *Application of section to A's transfer of Asset 1.* A's transfer of Asset 1 is a section 362(a) transaction. But for section 362(e)(2) and this section, X's basis in Asset 1 would be $120, which would not exceed Asset 1's $130 value immediately after the transaction. Accordingly, A's transfer of Asset 1 is not a loss duplication transaction notwithstanding that, taking both A's transfer and Y's transfer into account, X has an aggregate net loss in Asset 1 and Asset 2. Because Asset 1 is not received in a loss duplication transaction, it is not loss duplication property and section 362(e)(2) and this section do not apply to A's transfer of Asset 1.

(iii) *Application of section to Y's transfer of Asset 2.* (A) *Analysis. (1) Loss duplication transaction.* Y's transfer of Asset 2 to X is a section 362(a) transaction, notwithstanding that it is also a transaction described in section 368(a)(1)(A) and therefore section 362(b). But for section 362(e)(2) and this section, X's basis in Asset 2 would be $250, which would exceed Asset 2's $210 value immediately after the transaction. Accordingly, Y's transfer is a loss duplication transaction and Y has a net built-in loss of $40.

(2) *Identifying loss duplication property.* But for section 362(e)(2) and this section, X's basis in Asset 2 would be $250, which would exceed Asset 2's $210 value immediately after the transaction. Accordingly, Asset 2 is loss duplication property.

(B) *Basis in loss duplication property.* Although Asset 2 is loss duplication property, section 362(e)(2) does not apply to Y's transfer of Asset 2 to X because Y distributes all of the X stock received in the exchange without recognizing gain or loss, and, upon completion of the transaction, no person will hold the X stock or any other asset with a basis determined in whole or in part by reference to Y's basis in such stock. Accordingly, under paragraph (c)(1) of this section, X's basis in Asset 2 is not determined under section 362(e)(2) and this section. Thus, under section 362(a), X's basis in Asset 2 is $250.

(iv) *Basis in other property.* Under section 358, A's basis in the X stock received in exchange for Asset 1 is $120 and B's basis in the X stock received in the merger is $150. Under section 362(a), X's basis in Asset 1 is $120.

Example 4. Transfer described in both section 351 and section 368(a)(1)(D), followed by a distribution qualifying under section 355. (i) *Basic transaction.* (A) *Facts.* A and B each own one of the two outstanding shares of X common stock. X's assets include Asset 1 (basis $120, value $70), Asset 2 (basis $160, value $110), and Asset 3 (basis $220, value $240). In a transaction to which section 351 applies and that is described in section 368(a)(1)(D), X transfers Asset 1, Asset 2, and Asset 3 to Y in exchange for all the Y stock; then, in a distribution that qualifies under section 355, X distributes all the Y stock received in the exchange to A in exchange for all of A's X stock. Under section 361(c)(1), X does not recognize gain or loss as a result of the distribution of all the Y stock.

(B) *Analysis. (1) Loss duplication transaction.* X's transfer of Asset 1, Asset 2, and Asset 3 is a section 362(a) transaction. But for section 362(e)(2) and this section, Y's aggregate basis in those assets would be $500 ($120 + $160 + $220). The aggregate value of the assets immediately after the transaction is $420 ($70 + $110 + $240). Thus, Y's aggregate basis in the assets would exceed the aggregate value of the assets immediately after the transaction. Accordingly, the transfer is a loss duplication transaction and X has a net built-in loss of $80 ($500 - $420).

(2) *Identifying loss duplication property.* But for section 362(e)(2) and this section, Y's basis in Asset 1 would be $120, which would exceed Asset 1's $70 value immediately after the transaction. Accordingly, Asset 1 is loss duplication property. But for section 362(e)(2) and this section, Y's basis in Asset 2 would be $160, which would exceed Asset 2's $110 value immediately after the transaction. Accordingly, Asset 2 is also loss duplication property. But for section 362(e)(2) and this section, Y's basis in Asset 3 would be $220 and would therefore not exceed Asset 3's $240 value immediately after the transaction. Accordingly, Asset 3 is not loss duplication property.

(C) *Basis in loss duplication property.* Although Asset 1 and Asset 2 are each loss duplication property, X will distribute the Y stock received in exchange for Asset 1 and Asset 2 without recognition of gain or loss, and, upon completion of the transaction, no person will hold the Y stock received by X or any other asset with a basis determined in whole or in part by reference to X's basis in the Y stock received in the exchange. (A's basis in the Y stock will be determined by reference to his basis in his X stock.) Accordingly, under paragraph (c)(1) of this section, Y's bases in Asset 1 and Asset 2 are determined under section 362(a) and not under section 362(e)(2) and this section. Thus, Y's basis in Asset 1 is $120 and Y's basis in Asset 2 is $160.

(D) *Basis in other property.* Under section 358, A's basis in the Y stock received in exchange for his X stock is determined by reference to his basis in his X stock surrendered. Under section 362(a), Y's basis in Asset 3 is $220.

(ii) *Section 355(e).* (A) *Facts.* The facts are the same as in paragraph (i)(A) of this *Example 4*, except that, after the section 355 distribution, Y is acquired pursuant to a plan (within the meaning of § 1.355-7), resulting in the application of section 355(e) to the transactions.

(B) *Analysis.* Because section 361(c)(2), and not section 361(c)(1), will apply to X's distribution of Y stock, X will not qualify for nonrecognition treatment on the distribution of the Y stock. As a result, paragraph (c)(1) of this section does not apply to the transaction, and Y's bases in Asset 1 and Asset 2, the loss duplication property, are determined under section 362(e)(2) and this section. Asset 1 has a built-in loss of $50 ($120 - $70), and Asset 2 has a built-in loss of $50 ($160 - $110). Thus, Asset 1's allocable portion of X's net built-in loss is $40 ($50/$100 × $80), and Asset 2's allocable portion of X's net built-in loss is $40 ($50/$100 × $80). Accordingly, Y receives Asset 1 with a basis of $80 ($120 - $40) and Asset 2 with a basis of $120 ($160 - $40).

(iii) *Retained stock and securities.* (A) *Facts.* The facts are the same as in paragraph (i)(A) of this *Example 4*, except that X transfers Asset 1, Asset 2, and Asset 3 to Y in exchange for Y stock and Y securities, each constituting half of the consideration. In addition, for a valid business purpose, X retains Y stock and Y securities each worth 1 percent of the total consideration.

(B) *Analysis.* Paragraph (c)(1) of this section applies only to the extent that stock received in a transaction is distributed without recognition of gain or loss. Thus, section 362(e)(2) and this section apply to the extent that property was exchanged for the retained Y stock and Y securities (2 percent of the total). Accordingly, Y reduces its basis in Asset 1 and in Asset 2, the loss duplication property, by $1.60 (two percent of X's $80 net built-in loss). Asset 1 has a built-in loss of $50 ($120 - $70), and Asset 2 has a built-in loss of $50 ($160 - $110). Thus, Asset 1's allocable portion of X's net built-in loss is $.80 ($50/$100 × $1.60), and Asset 2's allocable portion of X's net built-in loss is $.80 ($50/$100 × $1.60). As a result, Y receives Asset 1 with a basis of $119.20 ($120 - $.80) and Asset 2 with a basis of $159.20 ($160 - $.80).

(iv) *Retained stock and securities with a section 362(e)(2)(C) election.* (A) *Facts.* The facts are the same as in paragraph (iii)(A) of this *Example 4*, except that an election under section 362(e)(2)(C) is made to reduce X's bases in its retained Y stock and retained Y securities.

(B) *Analysis.* Under paragraph (d)(2)(i) of this section, X reduces its basis in the retained Y stock and the retained Y securities (determined without regard to section 362(e)(2) and this section) by $1.60, the portion of X's $80 net built-in loss that would have been applied to reduce Y's basis in the transferred assets had the election to apply section 362(e)(2)(C) not been made. (Because the value of the Y stock and the value of the Y securities are equal, X's $500 basis in the transferred property would be allocated equally between the Y stock and the Y securities, $250 to each, under § 1.358-2(b)(2), and the retained Y stock and Y securities have a basis of $2.50 each (one percent of $250).) For the reasons set forth in paragraph (iii)(B) of this *Example 4*, Y would have been required to reduce its basis in the transferred assets by $1.60. Accordingly, X must reduce its aggregate basis in the retained Y stock and Y securities by $1.60. Under paragraph (d)(2)(i) of this section, the $1.60 basis reduction is allocated and applied to reduce X's bases in the retained Y stock and Y securities in proportion to the value of each. Because X retained Y stock and Y securities with equal values, X holds each of the retained Y stock and securities with an adjusted basis of $1.70 ($2.50 - $.80). Under paragraph (d)(2)(ii) of this section, Y receives Asset 1 with a basis of $120, Asset 2 with a basis of $160, and Asset 3 with a basis of $220.

Example 5. Transfer of liabilities. (i) *Liabilities described in section 358(d)(1).* (A) *Basic application of section, no section 362(e)(2)(C) election. (1) Facts.* A owns Asset 1 (basis $800, value $700). A also has a $200 liability that has been taken into account for tax purposes and is thus described in section 358(d)(1), and not in sections 357(c)(3), 358(d)(2), and 358(h)(1). A transfers Asset 1 to X in exchange for a single outstanding share of X stock representing all the outstanding X stock immediately after the transaction and X's assumption of the liability. The transfer is a transaction to which section 351 applies.

(2) *Analysis. (i) Loss duplication transaction.* A's transfer of Asset 1 is a section 362(a) transaction. But for section 362(e)(2) and this section, X's basis in Asset 1 would be $800, which would exceed Asset 1's $700 value immediately after the transaction. Accordingly, the transfer is a loss duplication transaction and A has a net built-in loss of $100 ($800 - $700).

(ii) *Identifying loss duplication property.* But for section 362(e)(2) and this section, X's basis in Asset 1 would be $800, which would exceed the $700 value of Asset 1 immediately after the transaction. Accordingly, Asset 1 is loss duplication property.

(3) *Basis in loss duplication property.* X's basis in Asset 1 is $700, computed as its $800 basis determined under section 362(a) reduced by A's $100 net built-in loss.

(4) *Basis in other property.* Under sections 358(a) and (d)(1), A's basis in the X stock is $600 ($800 basis in property transferred - $200 liability assumed).

(B) *Section 362(e)(2)(C) election.* The facts are the same as in paragraph (i)(A)(*1*) of this *Example 5*, except that A and X make an election under section 362(e)(2)(C). In this case, A's $100 net built-in loss that would have been applied to reduce X's basis in Asset 1 is applied to reduce A's basis in the X stock received. As a result, A's basis in the X stock is $500 ($600, as determined in paragraph (i)(A)(*4*) of this *Example 5*, reduced by $100) and X's basis in Asset 1 is $800.

(ii) *Contingent liabilities described in section 358(h)(1), section 358(h)(2)(A) exception applies.* (A) *Facts.* The facts are the same as in paragraph (i)(A)(*1*) of this Example 5, except that A's liability (valued at $200) has not been taken into account for tax purposes and is described in sections 358(d)(2) and 358(h)(1). However, Asset 1 is a trade or business and the liability is associated with the trade or business; as a result, the liability is described in section 358(h)(2)(A) and is excepted from the general rule of section 358(h)(1).

(B) *Analysis.* For the reasons set forth in paragraph (i)(A)(2) of this *Example 5*, A's transfer of Asset 1 is a loss duplication transaction, A has a net built-in loss of $100, and Asset 1 is loss duplication property.

(C) *Basis in loss duplication property.* For the reasons set forth in paragraph (i)(A)(3) of this *Example 5*, X's basis in Asset 1 is $700.

(D) *Basis in other property.* A's basis in the X stock is $800 under sections 358(a), 358(d)(2), and 358(h)(2)(A).

(E) *Section 362(e)(2)(C) election.* The facts are the same as in paragraph (ii)(A) of this *Example 5*, except that A and X make an election under section 362(e)(2)(C). In this case, A's $100 net built-in loss that would have applied to reduce X's basis in Asset 1 is applied to reduce A's basis in the X stock received. As a result, A's basis in the X stock is $700 ($800, as determined in paragraph (ii)(D) of this *Example 5*, reduced by $100). X's basis in Asset 1 is $800.

Example 6. Section 351 transfer with boot. (i) *Basic transaction.* (A) *Facts.* A owns Asset 1 (basis $80, value $100) and Asset 2 (basis $30, value $25). In a transaction to which section 351 applies, A transfers Asset 1 and Asset 2 to X in exchange for 10 shares of X stock and $25.

(B) *Analysis. (1) Loss duplication transaction.* A's transfer of Asset 1 and Asset 2 is a section 362(a) transaction. But for section 362(e)(2) and this section, X's aggregate basis in those assets would be $130, computed as follows. Under section 362(a), a corporation's basis in property acquired in a transaction to which section 351 applies is the same as the property's basis in the hands of the transferor, increased by any gain recognized to the transferor on such transfer. Under section 351(b), gain (but not loss) is recognized to the extent a transferor in a section 351 exchange receives other property or money in addition to the stock permitted to be received without the recognition of gain. To determine the amount of gain recognized under section 351(b), the consideration is allocated proportionately (by value) among the transferred properties. A's gain on the transfer is therefore computed as follows: Asset 1 reflects 80 percent of the value transferred ($100/$125) and Asset 2 reflects 20 percent of the value transferred ($25/$125). Thus, 80 percent of the stock (eight shares) and the cash ($20) are treated as being received in exchange for Asset 1 and 20 percent of the stock (two shares) and the cash ($5) are treated as being received in exchange for Asset 2. Thus, under section 351(b), A recognizes $20 of gain for the cash received in exchange for Asset 1, but A recognizes no loss for the amount received for Asset 2. As a result, under section 362(a), X would have a basis of $100 in Asset 1 and $30 in Asset 2. Thus, X's aggregate basis in the assets would be $130, which exceeds the $125 aggregate value of the assets ($100 + $25)). The transfer is a loss duplication transaction and A has a net built-in loss of $5 ($130 - $125).

(2) Identifying loss duplication property. But for section 362(e)(2) and this section, X's basis in Asset 1 would be $100 (A's $80 basis increased by A's $20 gain recognized), which would not exceed Asset 1's $100 value immediately after the transaction. Accordingly, Asset 1 is not loss duplication property. But for section 362(e)(2) and this section, X's basis in Asset 2 would be $30, which would exceed Asset 2's $25 value immediately after the transaction. Accordingly, Asset 2 is loss duplication property.

(C) *Basis in loss duplication property.* X's basis in Asset 2 is $25, computed as its $30 basis under section 362(a) reduced by A's $5 net built-in loss.

(D) *Basis in other property.* Under section 362(a), X's basis in Asset 1 is $100 (A's $80 basis increased by the $20 gain recognized). Under section 358, A's basis in the X stock is $105 (the sum of its $80 basis in Asset 1, its $30 basis in Asset 2, and its $20 gain recognized, reduced by the $25 cash received in the exchange).

(ii) *Section 362(e)(2)(C) election.* The facts are the same as in paragraph (i)(A) of this *Example 6*, except that A and X elect to reduce A's stock basis under section 362(e)(2)(C). Under paragraph (d)(2)(i) of this section, A reduces its $105 basis in the X stock by $5, the amount of A's net built-in loss of that would have been applied to reduce X's basis in Asset 2 had the section 362(e)(2)(C) election not been made. As a result, A's basis in the X stock is $100, and X's basis in Asset 2 is $30.

Example 7. Section 304 sale of built-in loss stock. (i) *Basic transaction.* (A) *Facts.* A owns all the stock of X (basis $90, value $60) and all the stock of Y. A sells all his X stock to Y for $60. Under section 304, A is treated as though he transferred the X stock to Y in exchange for Y stock in a transaction to which section 351 applies. Then, Y is treated as redeeming the Y stock it was treated as having issued to A in the deemed section 351 transaction.

(B) *Analysis. (1) Loss duplication transaction.* A's deemed transfer of X stock to Y is a section 362(a) transaction. But for section 362(e)(2) and this section, Y's aggregate basis in the X stock would be $90, which would exceed the X stock's value of $60 immediately after the transaction. Accordingly, the transfer is a loss duplication transaction and A has a net built-in loss of $30.

(2) Identifying loss duplication property. But for section 362(e)(2) and this section, Y's basis in the X stock would be $90, which would exceed the X stock's $60 value immediately after the transaction. Accordingly, the X stock is loss duplication property.

(C) *Basis in loss duplication property.* Y's basis in the X stock is $60, its $90 basis determined without regard to section 362(e)(2) and this section, reduced by A's $30 net built-in loss.

(D) *Basis in other property.* Under section 358(a), A has an exchanged basis of $90 in the Y stock he is deemed to receive in the exchange; the effect of the deemed redemption of that stock is then determined under section 302.

(ii) *Section 362(e)(2)(C) election.* The facts are the same as in paragraph (i)(A) of this *Example 7*, except that the parties elect to reduce A's stock basis under section 362(e)(2)(C). For the reasons set forth in paragraphs (i)(B) and (C) of this *Example 7*, Y's basis in the X stock would be reduced by $30. Accordingly, A's basis in the deemed-issued Y stock is $60, his $90 basis otherwise determined under section 358(a) reduced by the $30 that would have been applied to reduce Y's basis in the X stock under section 362(e)(2) and this section; the effect of the deemed redemption of that stock is then determined under section 302. Y's basis in the X stock is $90.

Example 8. Transactions involving partnerships. (i) *Transfer by a partnership.* (A) *Basic application of section. (1) Facts.* PRS owns Asset 1 (basis $100, value $70). PRS contributes Asset 1 to X in a transaction to which section 351 applies.

(2) Analysis. (i) Loss duplication transaction. PRS's transfer of Asset 1 is a section 362(a) transaction. But for section 362(e)(2) and this section, X's basis in Asset 1 would be $100, which would exceed Asset 1's $70 value immediately after the transaction. Accordingly, the transfer is a loss duplication transaction and PRS has a net built-in loss of $30 ($100 - $70).

(ii) Identifying loss duplication property. But for section 362(e)(2) and this section, X's basis in Asset 1 would be $100, which would exceed Asset 1's $70 value immediately after the transaction. Accordingly, Asset 1 is loss duplication property.

(3) Basis in loss duplication property. X's basis in Asset 1 is $70, computed as its $100 basis under section 362(a) reduced by PRS's $30 net built-in loss.

(4) Basis in other property. Under section 358(a), PRS has an exchanged basis of $100 in the X stock it receives in the exchange.

(B) *Section 362(e)(2)(C) election.* The facts are the same as in paragraph (i)(A)(*1*) of this *Example 8*, except that PRS and X elect to reduce PRS's stock basis under section 362(e)(2)(C). In this case, PRS's $30 net built-in loss (as determined in paragraph (i)(A)*(2)(i)* of this *Example 8*) that would have been applied to reduce X's basis in Asset 1 is applied to reduce PRS's basis in the X stock received. As a result, PRS's basis in the X stock is $70 ($100 - $30) and X's basis in Asset 1 is $100. The $30 reduction to PRS's basis in the X stock is treated as an expenditure of PRS under section 705(a)(2)(B) and paragraph (e)(1) of this section. As a result, the partners of PRS must reduce their bases in their PRS interests.

(ii) *Transfer of interest in partnership with liability.* (A) *Basic application of section. (1) Facts.* A and two other individuals are equal partners in PRS. A's basis in its partnership interest is $247. A's share of PRS's § 1.752-1 liabilities (as defined in § 1.752-1(a)(4)) is $145. A transfers his partnership interest to X in a transaction to which section 351 applies. PRS has no election in effect under section 754. If X were to sell the PRS interest immediately after the transfer, X would receive $100 in cash or other property. In addition, assume that, taking into account the rules under § 1.752-4, X's share of PRS's § 1.752-1 liabilities (as defined in § 1.752-1(a)(4)) is $150 immediately after the transfer.

(2) Analysis. (i) Loss duplication transaction. A's transfer of its PRS interest is a section 362(a) transaction. But for section 362(e)(2) and this section, X's basis in the PRS interest, would be $252 (A's basis of $247, reduced by A's $145 share of PRS liabilities, increased by X's $150 share of PRS liabilities) and, under paragraph (g)(12)(ii) of this section, the value of the PRS interest would be $250 (the sum of $100, the cash X would receive if X immediately sold the interest, and $150, X's share of the § 1.752-1 liabilities (as defined in § 1.752-1(a)(4)) under section 752 immediately after the transfer to X). Therefore, the transfer is a loss duplication transaction and A has a net built-in loss of $2 ($252 - $250).

(ii) Identifying loss duplication property. But for section 362(e)(2) and this section, X's basis in the PRS interest would be $252, which would

exceed the PRS interest's $250 value immediately after the transaction. Accordingly, the PRS interest is loss duplication property.

(3) *Basis in loss duplication property*. X's basis in the PRS interest is $250, computed as its $252 basis under section 362(a), taking into account the rules under section 752, reduced by A's $2 net built-in loss.

(4) *Basis in other property*. Under section 358, taking into account the rules under section 752, A has a basis of $102 ($247 reduced by A's $145 share of PRS liabilities) in the X stock he receives in the transaction.

(B) *Section 362(e)(2)(C) election*. The facts are the same as in paragraph (i)(A) of this *Example 8*, except that A and X make an election under section 362(e)(2)(C). Under paragraph (d)(2)(i) of this section, A reduces his basis in the X stock, as determined without regard to section 362(e)(2) and this section, by the amount of A's net built-in loss that would have been applied to reduce X's basis in the PRS interest had the section 362(e)(2)(C) election not been made. In addition, no reduction is made to X's basis in the PRS interest, as determined without regard to section 362(e)(2) and this section. As a result, A's basis in the X stock is $100 ($102 - $2) and X's basis in the PRS interest is $252.

(C) *Transfer of partnership interest with liability, not loss duplication transaction*. The facts are the same as in paragraph (ii)(A)(1) of this *Example 8*, except that A's share of PRS's §1.752-1 liabilities (as defined in §1.752-1(a)(4)) is $155. But for section 362(e)(2) and this section, X's basis in the PRS interest would be $242 (A's basis of $247, reduced by A's $155 share of PRS liabilities, increased by X's $150 share of PRS liabilities), which would not exceed the PRS interest's $250 value immediately after the transaction. Accordingly, A's transfer of the PRS interest is not a loss duplication transaction and section 362(e)(2) and this section have no application to the transaction. Under section 362(a), X's basis in the PRS interest is $242 and, under section 358, taking into account the rules under section 752, A has a basis of $92 ($247 reduced by A's $155 share of PRS liabilities) in the X stock he receives in the transaction.

Example 9. Transactions involving S Corporations. (i) *Transfer by S Corporation*. (A) *No section 362(e)(2)(C) election*. (1) *Facts*. S, an S corporation as defined in section 1361(a)(1), owns Asset 1 (basis $100, value $70). S transfers Asset 1 to X in exchange for a single outstanding share of X stock representing all the outstanding X stock immediately after the transaction. S does not elect to treat X as a qualified subchapter S subsidiary. The transaction is one to which section 351 applies.

(2) *Analysis*. (*i*) *Loss duplication transaction*. S's transfer of Asset 1 is a section 362(a) transaction. But for section 362(e)(2) and this section, X's basis in Asset 1 would be $100, which would exceed Asset 1's $70 value immediately after the transaction. Accordingly, the transfer is a loss duplication transaction and S has a net built-in loss of $30 ($100 - $70).

(*ii*) *Identifying loss duplication property*. But for section 362(e)(2) and this section, X's basis in Asset 1 would be $100, which would exceed Asset 1's $70 value immediately after the transaction. Accordingly, Asset 1 is loss duplication property.

(*iii*) *Basis in loss duplication property*. X's basis in Asset 1 is $70, computed as its $100 basis under section 362(a) reduced by S's $30 net built-in loss.

(*iv*) *Basis in other property*. Under section 358(a), S has an exchanged basis of $100 in the X stock it receives in the exchange.

(B) *Section 362(e)(2)(C) election*. The facts are the same as in paragraph (i)(A)(1) of this *Example 9*, except that S and X elect to reduce S's stock basis under section 362(e)(2). In this case, S's $30 built-in loss (as determined in paragraph (i)(A)(2)(*i*) of this *Example 9*) that would have been applied to reduce X's basis in Asset 1 is applied to reduce S's basis in the X stock received. As a result, S's basis in the X stock is $70 ($100 - $30) and X's basis in Asset 1 is $100. The $30 reduction to S's basis in the X stock is treated as an expense of S under section 1367(a)(2)(D) and paragraph (e)(2) of this section. As a result, the shareholders of S must reduce their bases in their S stock.

(ii) *Transfer to S Corporation*. (A) *Basic application of section*. (1) *Facts*. A owns Asset 1 (basis $90, value $60) and Asset 2 (basis $110, value $120). In a transaction to which section 351 applies, A transfers Asset 1 and Asset 2 to S, an S corporation as defined in section 1361(a)(1), in exchange for a single share of S stock representing all the outstanding S stock immediately after the transaction.

(2) *Analysis*. (*i*) *Loss duplication transaction*. A's transfer of Asset 1 and Asset 2 is a section 362(a) transaction. But for section 362(e)(2) and this section, S's aggregate basis in those assets would be $200 ($90 + $110), which would exceed the aggregate value of the assets $180 ($60 + $120) immediately after the transaction. Accordingly, the transfer is a loss duplication transaction and A has a net built-in loss of $20 ($200 - $180).

(*ii*) *Identifying loss duplication property*. But for section 362(e)(2) and this section, S's basis in Asset 1 would be $90, which would exceed Asset 1's $60 value immediately after the transaction. As a result, Asset 1 is loss duplication property. But for section 362(e)(2) and this section, S's basis in Asset 2 would be $110, which would not exceed Asset 2's $120 value immediately after the transaction. As a result, Asset 2 is not loss duplication property.

(3) *Basis in loss duplication property*. S's basis in Asset 1 is $70, computed as its $90 basis under section 362(a) reduced by S's $20 net built-in loss. The $20 reduction to S's basis in Asset 1 does not require a reduction to A's basis in its S stock under section 1367(a)(2)(D). See paragraph (f) of this section.

(4) *Basis in other property*. Under section 362(a), S has a transferred basis of $110 in Asset 2. Under section 358(a), A has a basis of $200 in the S stock it receives in the exchange.

(B) *Section 362(e)(2)(C) election*. (1) *Application of section to transaction*. The facts are the same as in paragraph (ii)(A)(1) of this *Example 9*, except that A and S elect to reduce A's stock basis under section 362(e)(2)(C). In this case, A's $20 built-in loss (as determined in paragraph (ii)(A)(2) of this *Example 9*) that would have been applied to reduce S's basis in Asset 1 is applied to reduce A's basis in the S stock received. As a result, A's basis in the S stock is $180 ($200 - $20), S's basis in Asset 1 is $90, and S's basis in Asset 2 is $110.

(2) *Tax consequences of subsequent disposition of transferred assets*. The facts are the same as in paragraph (ii)(B)(1) of this *Example 9* except that, in addition, the year after the transaction, S sells Asset 1 (basis $90, value $60) and Asset 2 (basis $110, value $120) for $180, recognizing the $20 net built-in loss. The loss is allocated to A and reduces A's basis in the S stock from $180 to $160 under section 1367(a)(2)(B). If A then sells its S stock for its $180 value, A will recognize a gain of $20.

Example 10. Triangular reorganizations. (i) *Facts*. P owns all the stock of S1 and X owns all the stock of S2. In a merger described in section 368(a)(2)(D), S2 merges with and into S1, and X receives stock of P in exchange for its S2 stock. S2 has a net built-in loss in its assets acquired by S1 in the transaction.

(ii) *Analysis*. The reorganization is not a section 362(a) transaction, notwithstanding that, under §1.358-6(c), P is treated as acquiring and then transferring S2's assets to S1 for purposes of determining P's adjustment to its basis in its S1 stock. Accordingly, S1's basis in the property acquired in the transaction is not determined under section 362(e)(2) and this section; it is determined under section 362(b).

Example 11. Transfers of importation property with non-importation property. (i) *Single transferor, loss importation transaction*. (A) *Facts*. FC1 transfers Asset 1 (basis $80, value $50), Asset 2 (basis $120, value $110), and Asset 3 (basis $32, value $40) to DC in a transaction to which section 351 applies. Asset 1 is not importation property within the meaning of §1.362-3(c)(2). Asset 2 and Asset 3 are importation property within the meaning of §1.362-3(c)(2).

(B) *Application of section 362(e)(1)*. Immediately after the transfer, and without regard to section 362(e)(1) or section 362(e)(2) and this section, DC's aggregate basis in importation property (Asset 2 and Asset 3) would be $152. The aggregate value of the importation property immediately after the transfer is $150. Accordingly, the transaction is a loss importation transaction within the meaning of §1.362-3(c)(3) and, under section 362(e)(1), DC's bases in Asset 2 and Asset 3 would equal the value of each, $110 and $40, respectively.

(C) *Application of section 362(e)(2) and this section*. (1) *Analysis*. (*i*) *Loss duplication transaction*. FC1's transfer of Asset 1, Asset 2, and Asset 3 is a transaction described in section 362(a). But for section 362(e)(2) and this section, DC's aggregate basis in those assets would be $230 ($80 under section 362(a) + $110 +$40 under section 362(e)(1)), which would exceed the aggregate value of the assets $200 ($50 + $110 +$40) immediately after the transaction. Accordingly, the transfer is a loss duplication transaction and FC1 has a net built-in loss of $30 ($230 - $200).

(*ii*) *Identifying loss duplication property*. But for section 362(e)(2) and this section, DC's basis in Asset 1 would be $80, which would exceed Asset 1's $50 value immediately after the transaction. Accordingly, Asset 1 is loss duplication property. But for section 362(e)(2) and this section, DC's basis in Asset 2 would be $110, which would not exceed Asset 2's $110 value immediately after the transaction. Accordingly, Asset 2 is not loss duplication property. But for section 362(e)(2) and this section, DC's basis in Asset 3 would be $40, which would not exceed Asset 3's $40 value immediately after the transaction. Accordingly, Asset 3 is not loss duplication property.

(D) *Basis in loss duplication property*. DC's basis in Asset 1 is $50, computed as its $80 basis under section 362(a) reduced by FC1's $30 net built-in loss.

(E) *Basis in other property*. Under section 362(e)(1), DC's basis in Asset 2 is $110 and DC's basis in Asset 3 is $40. Under section 358(a),

FC1 has an exchanged basis of $232 in the DC stock it receives in the transaction.

(ii) *Multiple transferors, no importation of loss.* (A) *Facts.* The facts are the same as paragraph (i)(A) of this *Example 11,* except that, in addition, FC2 transfers Asset 4 (basis $100, value $150) to DC as part of the same transaction. Asset 4 is importation property within the meaning of § 1.362-3(c)(2).

(B) *Application of section 362(e)(1).* Immediately after the transfer, and without regard to section 362(e)(1) or section 362(e)(2) and this section, DC's aggregate basis in importation property (Asset 2, Asset 3, and Asset 4) would be $252 ($120 + $32 + $100). The aggregate value of the importation property immediately after the transfer is $300 ($110 + $40 + $150). Accordingly, the transaction is not a loss importation transaction within the meaning of § 1.362-3(c)(3) and DC's bases in the importation property is not determined under section 362(e)(1).

(C) *Application of section 362(e)(2) and this section.* Notwithstanding that the transfers by FC1 and FC2 are pursuant to a single plan forming one transaction, section 362(e)(2) and this section apply to each transferor separately.

(1) Application of section to FC1. (i) Loss duplication transaction. FC1's transfer of Asset 1, Asset 2, and Asset 3 is a transaction described in section 362(a). But for section 362(e)(2) and this section, DC's aggregate basis in those assets would be $232 ($80 + $120 +$32), which would exceed the aggregate value of the assets $200 ($50 + $110 + $40) immediately after the transaction. Accordingly, the transfer is a loss duplication transaction and FC1 has a net built-in loss of $32 ($232 - $200).

(ii) Identifying loss duplication property. But for section 362(e)(2) and this section, DC's basis in Asset 1 would be $80, which would exceed Asset 1's $50 value immediately after the transaction. Accordingly, Asset 1 is loss duplication property. But for section 362(e)(2) and this section, DC's basis in Asset 2 would be $120, which would exceed Asset 2's $110 value immediately after the transaction. Accordingly, Asset 2 is also loss duplication property. But for section 362(e)(2) and this section, DC's basis in Asset 3 would be $32, which would not exceed Asset 3's $40 value immediately after the transaction. Accordingly, Asset 3 is not loss duplication property.

(iii) Basis in loss duplication property. DC's basis in Asset 1 is $56, computed as its $80 basis under section 362(a) reduced by $24, its allocable portion of FC1's $32 net built-in loss ($30/40 x $32). DC's basis in Asset 2 is $112, computed as its $120 basis under section 362(a) reduced by $8, its allocable portion of FC1's $40 net built-in loss ($10/$40 x $32).

(iv) Basis in other property. Under section 358(a), FC1 has an exchanged basis of $232 in the DC stock it receives in the transaction.

(2) Application of section to FC2. FC2's transfer of Asset 3 is not a loss duplication transaction because Asset 3's value exceeds its basis immediately after the transaction. Accordingly, under section 362(a), DC's basis in Asset 3 is $100.

Example 12. Section 362(e)(2)(C) elections with respect to transfers between persons that are not required to file a U.S. return and that are not CFCs or CFPs. (i) *Basic application of section.* On June 30, Year 1, FC1 transfers Asset 1 to FC2 in a transaction to which section 351 applies (the original transfer) and that is therefore a section 362(a) transaction. But for section 362(e)(2) and this section, FC2's basis in Asset 1 (determined immediately after the transfer, taking into account all applicable law, including section 362(e)(1)) exceeds the value of Asset 1 immediately after the transaction. Accordingly, the transaction is a loss duplication transaction and Asset 1 is loss duplication property. FC1 and FC2 executed a written, binding agreement to apply section 362(e)(2)(C) at some point before any Section 362(e)(2)(C) Statement is filed. However, the transfer was not entered into with a view to reducing or avoiding the Federal income tax liability of any person by avoiding the application of section 362(e)(2) and this section; further, no event described in paragraph (d)(3)(ii)(E), (F), or (G) of this section occurs prior to June 30, Year 3. As a result, under paragraph (c)(2) of this section, section 362(e)(2) and this section do not apply to the transfer. Accordingly, FC2's basis in Asset 1 is determined under section 362(a), no section 362(e)(2)(C) election can be made, and any protective filing of a Section 362(e)(2)(C) Statement will have no effect.

(ii) *Loss duplication property later acquired by a person required to file U.S. return.* The facts are the same as in paragraph (i) of this *Example 12,* except that, in addition, on January 1, Year 2, FC2 transfers Asset 1 to DC in an exchange to which section 351 applies. FC2's transfer is an event described in paragraph (d)(3)(ii)(G) of this section. As a result, paragraph (c)(2) does not except the original transfer from the application of section 362(e)(2) and this section. Under paragraph (d)(3)(ii)(G) of this section, DC must include the Section 362(e)(2)(C) Statement for the original transfer on or with its Year 2 U.S. return in order for that election to be effective. The result would be the same if, instead of FC2 transferring Asset 1 to DC, FC1 transferred its FC2 stock to DC in an exchange to which section 351 applies. (Further, if an asset transferred by FC1 or FC2 to DC is a loss asset immediately after its transfer to DC, DC's basis in that asset may be subject to section 362(e)(1).)

(iii) *Party to exchange later becomes a person required to file U.S. return.* The facts are the same as in paragraph (i) of this *Example 12,* except that, in addition, on January 1, Year 2, FC2 becomes engaged in a U.S. business. FC2's becoming engaged in a U.S. business is an event described in paragraph (d)(3)(ii)(F) of this section because it will cause FC2 to become a person required to file a U.S. return. As a result, paragraph (c)(2) of this section does not except the transfer from the application of section 362(e)(2) and this section. Under paragraph (d)(3)(ii)(F) of this section, FC2 must include the Section 362(e)(2)(C) Statement for the original transfer on or with its Year 2 U.S. return in order for the section 362(e)(2)(C) election for the original transfer to be effective.

(iv) *Statement not filed with respect to designated event.* The facts are the same as in paragraph (iii) of this *Example 12,* except that, in addition, FC1 became engaged in a U.S. trade or business on October 31, Year 1 and as a result became a person required to file a U.S. return, an event described in paragraph (d)(3)(ii)(E) of this section. As a result, paragraph (c)(2) of this section does not except the transfer from the application of section 362(e)(2) and this section. Further, in order for the election to be effective, FC1 must file the Section 362(e)(2)(C) Statement on or with its Year 1 U.S. return. See paragraph (d)(3)(ii)(E) of this section. A statement filed by FC2 on or with its Year 2 U.S. return has no effect. Thus, if FC1 does not file the statement, the election does not become effective and basis is determined under the general rule of section 362(e)(2).

(v) *Nonrecognition transfer of loss duplication property outside United States, transferee later becomes engaged in U.S. trade or business.* The facts are the same as in paragraph (i) of this *Example 12,* except that, in addition, on December 31, Year 1, FC2 transfers Asset 1 to FC3 in a transferred basis transaction. In Year 2, FC3 becomes engaged in a U.S. trade or business and as a result becomes a person required to file a U.S. return; Asset 1 is not used in or connected with the U.S. trade or business or otherwise subject to Federal income tax. FC3's becoming engaged in a U.S. trade or business is an event described in paragraph (d)(3)(ii)(F) of this section because FC3, a person who holds loss duplication property with a basis determined by FC2's basis in the property, will be required to file a U.S. return as a result of its becoming engaged in a U.S. business. As a result, paragraph (c)(2) of this section does not except the transfer from the application of section 362(e)(2) and this section. Under paragraph (d)(3)(ii)(F) of this section, FC3 must include the Section 362(e)(2)(C) Statement for the original transfer on or with its Year 2 U.S. return in order for the section 362(e)(2)(C) election for the original transfer to be effective.

(i) [Reserved].

(j) *Effective/applicability date.*—This section applies to transactions occurring after September 3, 2013, unless effected pursuant to a binding agreement that was in effect prior to September 3, 2013, and at all times thereafter. In addition, taxpayers may apply these regulations to transactions occurring after October 22, 2004. The introductory text and *Example 11* of paragraph (h) of this section apply with respect to transactions occurring on or after March 28, 2016, and also with respect to transactions occurring before such date as a result of an entity classification election under § 301.7701-3 of this chapter filed on or after March 28, 2016, unless such transaction is pursuant to a binding agreement that was in effect prior to March 28, 2016 and at all times thereafter. In addition, taxpayers may apply such provisions to any transaction occurring after October 22, 2004. [Reg. § 1.362-4.]

☐ *[T.D. 9424, 9-9-2008. Amended by T.D. 9633, 8-30-2013 and T.D. 9759, 3-25-2016.]*

International Tax-Free Exchanges

§ 1.367(a)-1. Transfers to foreign corporations subject to section 367(a): In general.—(a) *Scope.*—Section 367(a)(1) provides the general rule concerning certain transfers of property by a United States person (referred to at times in this section as the "U.S. person" or "U.S. transferor") to a foreign corporation. Paragraph (b) of this section provides general rules explaining the effect of section 367(a)(1). Paragraph (c) of this section describes transfers of property that are described in section 367(a)(1). Paragraph (d) of this section provides definitions that apply for purposes of sections 367(a) and (d) and the regulations thereunder. Paragraphs (e) and (f) of this section provide rules that apply to certain reorganizations described in section 368(a)(1)(F). Paragraph (g) of this section provides dates of applicability. For rules concerning the reporting requirements under section 6038B for certain transfers of property to a foreign corporation, see § 1.6038B-1.

(b) *General rules.*—(1) *Foreign corporation not considered a corporation for purposes of certain transfers.*—If a U.S. person transfers property to a foreign corporation in connection with an exchange described in section 351, 354, 356, or 361, then, pursuant to section 367(a)(1), the foreign corporation will not be considered to be a corporation for purposes of determining the extent to which gain is recognized on the transfer. Section 367(a)(1) denies nonrecognition treatment only to transfers of items of property on which gain is realized. Thus, the amount of gain recognized because of section 367(a)(1) is unaffected by the transfer of items of property on which loss is realized (but not recognized).

(2) *Cases in which foreign corporate status is not disregarded.*—For circumstances in which section 367(a)(1) does not apply to a U.S. transferor's transfer of property to a foreign corporation, and thus the foreign corporation is considered to be a corporation, see §§ 1.367(a)-2, 1.367(a)-3, and 1.367(a)-7.

(3) *Determination of value.*—In cases in which a U.S. transferor's transfer of property to a foreign corporation constitutes a controlled transaction as defined in § 1.482-1(i)(8), the value of the property transferred is determined in accordance with section 482 and the regulations thereunder.

(4) *Character, source, and adjustments.*—(i) *In general.*—If a U.S. person is required to recognize gain under section 367 upon a transfer of property to a foreign corporation, then —

(A) The character and source of such gain are determined as if the property had been disposed of in a taxable exchange with the transferee foreign corporation (unless otherwise provided by regulation); and

(B) Appropriate adjustments to earnings and profits, basis, and other affected items will be made according to otherwise applicable rules, taking into account the gain recognized under section 367(a)(1). For purposes of applying section 362, the foreign corporation's basis in the property received is increased by the amount of gain recognized by the U.S. transferor under section 367(a) and the regulations issued pursuant to that section. To the extent the regulations provide that the U.S. transferor recognizes gain with respect to a particular item of property, the foreign corporation increases its basis in that item of property by the amount of such gain recognized. For example, §§ 1.367(a)-2, 1.367(a)-3, and 1.367(a)-4 provide that gain is recognized with respect to particular items of property. To the extent the regulations do not provide that gain recognized by the U.S. transferor is with respect to a particular item of property, such gain is treated as recognized with respect to items of property subject to section 367(a) in proportion to the U.S. transferor's gain realized in such property, after taking into account gain recognized with respect to particular items of property transferred under any other provision of section 367(a). For example, § 1.367(a)-6 provides that branch losses must be recaptured by the recognition of gain realized on the transfer but does not associate the gain with particular items of property. See also § 1.367(a)-1(c)(3) for rules concerning transfers by partnerships or of partnership interests.

(C) The transfer will not be recharacterized for U.S. Federal tax purposes solely because the U.S. person recognizes gain in connection with the transfer under section 367(a)(1). For example, if a U.S. person transfers appreciated stock or securities to a foreign corporation in an exchange described in section 351, the transfer is not recharacterized as other than an exchange described in section 351 solely because the U.S. person recognizes gain in the transfer under section 367(a)(1).

(ii) *Example.*—The rules of this paragraph (b)(4) are illustrated by the following example.

Example. Domestic corporation DC transfers inventory with a fair market value of $ 1 million and adjusted basis of $ 800,000 to foreign corporation FC in exchange for stock of FC that is described in section 351(a). Title passes within the United States. Pursuant to section 367(a), DC is required to recognize gain of $200,000 upon the transfer. Under the rule of this paragraph (b)(4), the gain is treated as ordinary income (sections 1201 and 1221) from sources within the United States (section 861) arising from a taxable exchange with FC. Appropriate adjustments to earnings and profits, basis, etc., will be made as if the transfer were subject to section 351. Thus, for example, DC's basis in the FC stock received, and FC's basis in the transferred inventory, will each be increased by the $200,000 gain recognized by DC, pursuant to sections 358(a)(1) and 362(a), respectively.

(5) *Treatment of certain property as subject to section 367(d).*—A U.S. transferor may apply section 367(d) and § 1.367(d)-1, rather than section 367(a) and the regulations thereunder, to a transfer of property to a foreign corporation that otherwise would be subject to section 367(a), provided that the property is not eligible property, as defined in § 1.367(a)-2(b) but determined without regard to § 1.367(a)-2(c). A U.S. transferor and any other U.S. transferor that is related (within the meaning of section 267(b) or 707(b)(1)) to the U.S. transferor must consistently apply this paragraph (b)(5) to all property described in this paragraph (b)(5) that is transferred to one or more foreign corporations pursuant to a plan. A U.S. transferor applies the provisions of this paragraph (b)(5) in the form and manner set forth in § 1.6038B-1(d)(1)(iv) and (v).

(c)(1) through (c)(3)(i) reserved. For further guidance, see § 1.367(a)-1T(c)(1) through (c)(3)(i).

(ii) *Transfer of partnership interest treated as transfer of proportionate share of assets.*—(A) *In general.*—If a U.S. person transfers an interest as a partner in a partnership (whether foreign or domestic) in an exchange described in section 367(a)(1), then that person is treated as having transferred a proportionate share of the property of the partnership in an exchange described in section 367(a)(1). Accordingly, the applicability of the exception to section 367(a)(1) provided in § 1.367(a)-2 is determined with reference to the property of the partnership rather than the partnership interest itself. A U.S. person's proportionate share of partnership property is determined under the rules and principles of sections 701 through 761 and the regulations thereunder.

(c)(3)(i)(A) *Example* through (7) reserved. For further guidance, see § 1.367(a)-1T(c)(3)(i)(A) *Example* through (7).

(d) *Definitions.*—The following definitions apply for purposes of sections 367(a) and (d) and the regulations thereunder.

(1) *United States person.*—The term "United States person" includes those persons described in section 7701(a)(30). The term includes a citizen or resident of the United States, a domestic partnership, a domestic corporation, and any estate or trust other than a foreign estate or trust. (For definitions of these terms, see section 7701 and the regulations thereunder.) For purposes of this section, an individual with respect to whom an election has been made under section 6013(g) or (h) is considered to be a resident of the United States while such election is in effect. A nonresident alien or a foreign corporation will not be considered a United States person because of its actual or deemed conduct of a trade or business within the United States during a taxable year.

(2) *Foreign corporation.*—The term "foreign corporation" has the meaning set forth in section 7701(a)(3) and (5) and § 301.7701-5.

(3) *Transfer.*—For purposes of section 367 and regulations thereunder, the term "transfer" means any transaction that constitutes a transfer for purposes of section 332, 351, 354, 355, 356, or 361, as applicable. A person's entering into a cost sharing arrangement under § 1.482-7 or acquiring rights to intangible property under such an arrangement shall not be considered a transfer of property described in section 367(a)(1). See § 1.6038B-1T(b)(4) for the date on which the transfer is considered to be made.

(4) *Property.*—For purposes of section 367 and the regulations thereunder, the term "property" means any item that constitutes property for purposes of section 351, 354, 355, 356, or 361, as applicable.

(5) *Intangible property.*—The term "intangible property" means either property described in section 936(h)(3)(B) or property to which a U.S. person applies section 367(d) pursuant to paragraph (b)(5) of this section, but does not include property described in section 1221(a)(3) or a working interest in oil and gas property.

(6) *Operating intangibles.*—An operating intangible is any property described in section 936(h)(3)(B) of a type not ordinarily licensed or otherwise transferred in transactions between unrelated parties for

consideration contingent upon the licensee's or transferee's use of the property. Examples of operating intangibles may include longterm purchase or supply contracts, surveys, studies, and customer lists.

(e) *Close of taxable year in certain section 368(a)(1)(F) reorganizations.*—If a domestic corporation is the transferor corporation in a reorganization described in section 368(a)(1)(F) after March 30, 1987, in which the acquiring corporation is a foreign corporation, then the taxable year of the transferor corporation shall end with the close of the date of the transfer and the taxable year of the acquiring corporation shall end with the close of the date on which the transferor's taxable year would have ended but for the occurrence of the transfer. With regard to the consequences of the closing of the taxable year, see section 381 and the regulations thereunder.

(f) *Exchanges under sections 354(a) and 361(a) in certain section 368(a)(1)(F) reorganizations.*—(1) *Rule.*—In every reorganization under section 368(a)(1)(F), where the transferor corporation is a domestic corporation, and the acquiring corporation is a foreign corporation, there is considered to exist—

(i) A transfer of assets by the transferor corporation to the acquiring corporation under section 361(a) in exchange for stock (or stock and securities) of the acquiring corporation and the assumption by the acquiring corporation of the transferor corporation's liabilities;

(ii) A distribution of the stock (or stock and securities) of the acquiring corporation by the transferor corporation to the shareholders (or shareholders and security holders) of the transferor corporation; and

(iii) An exchange by the transferor corporation's shareholders (or shareholders and security holders) of their stock (or stock and securities) of the transferor corporation for stock (or stock and securities) of the acquiring corporation under section 354(a).

(2) *Rule applies regardless of whether a continuance under applicable law.*—For purposes of paragraph (f)(1) of this section, it shall be immaterial that the applicable foreign or domestic law treats the acquiring corporation as a continuance of the transferor corporation.

(g) *Effective/applicability dates.*—(1) through (3) [Reserved]. For further guidance, *see* § 1.367(a)-1T(g)(1) through (3).

(4) The rules in paragraphs (b)(4)(i)(B) and (b)(4)(i)(C) of this section apply to transfers occurring on or after April 18, 2013. For guidance with respect to paragraph (b)(4)(i)(B) of this section before April 18, 2013, see 26 CFR part 1 revised as of April 1, 2012. The rules in paragraph (e) of this section apply to transactions occurring on or after March 31, 1987. The rules in paragraph (f) of this section apply to transactions occurring on or after January 1, 1985.

(5) Paragraphs (a), (b)(1) through (b)(4)(i)(B), (b)(4)(ii) through (b)(5), (c)(3)(ii)(A), (d) introductory text through (d)(2), (d)(4) through (d)(6) of this section apply to transfers occurring on or after September 14, 2015, and to transfers occurring before September 14, 2015, resulting from entity classification elections made under § 301.7701-3 that are filed on or after September 14, 2015. For transfers occurring before this section is applicable, see §§ 1.367(a)-1 and 1.367(a)-1T as contained in 26 CFR part 1 revised as of April 1, 2016. [Reg. § 1.367(a)-1.]

□ [*T.D.* 9441, 12-31-2008. *Amended by T.D.* 9568, 12-16-2011, *T.D.* 9614, 3-18-2013, *T.D.* 9739, 9-18-2015 *and T.D.* 9803, 12-15-2016 (*corrected* 11-14-2017).]

§ 1.367(a)-1T. Transfers to foreign corporations subject to section 367(a): In general (temporary).—(a) [Reserved].

(b) *General rules.*—(1) [Reserved].

(2) [Reserved].

(3) [Reserved].

(4) *Character, source, and adjustments.*—(i) *In general.*—If a U.S. person is required to recognize gain under section 367 upon a transfer of property to a foreign corporation, then—

(A) [Reserved].

(B) [Reserved]. For further guidance see § 1.367(a)-1(b)(4)(i)(B).

(C) [Reserved]. For further guidance see § 1.367(a)-1(b)(4)(i)(C).

(ii) [Reserved].

(5) [Reserved].

(c) *Transfers described in section 367(a)(1).*—(1) *In general.*—A transfer described in section 367 (a)(1) is any transfer of property by a U.S. person to a foreign corporation pursuant to an exchange described in section 332, 351, 354, 355, 356, or 361. Section 367(a)(1) applies to such a transfer whether it is made directly, indirectly, or constructively. Indirect or constructive transfers that are described in section 367(a)(1) include the transfers described in subparagraphs (2) through (7) of this paragraph (c).

(2) *Indirect transfers in certain reorganizations.*—[Reserved.]For further guidance, see § 1.367(a)-3(d).

(3) *Indirect transfers involving partnerships and interests therein.*—(i) *Transfer by partnership treated as transfer by partners.*—(A) *In general.*—If a partnership (whether foreign or domestic) transfers property to a foreign corporation in an exchange described in section 367(a)(1), then a U.S. person that is a partner in the partnership shall be treated as having transferred a proportionate share of the property in an exchange described in section 367(a)(1). A U.S. person's proportionate share of partnership property shall be determined under the rules and principles of section 701 through 761 and the regulations thereunder. The rule of this paragraph (c)(3)(i)(A) is illustrated by the following example.

Example. P is a partnership having five equal general partners, two of whom are United States persons. P transfers property to F, a foreign corporation, in connection with an exchange described in section 351. The exchange includes an indirect transfer of property by the partners to F. The transfers of property attributable to those partners who are United States persons, that is, 40 percent of each asset transferred to F, are transfers described in section 367(a)(1). The gain (if any) recognized on the transfer of 40 percent of each asset to F is attributable to the two partners who are United States persons.

(B) *Special adjustments to basis.*—If a U.S. person is treated under the rule of this paragraph (c)(3)(i) as having transferred a proportionate share of the property of a partnership in an exchange described in section 367(a), and is therefore required to recognize gain upon the transfer, then—

(1) The U.S. person's basis in the partnership shall be increased by the amount of gain recognized by him;

(2) Solely for purposes of determining the basis of the partnership in the stock of the transferee foreign corporation, the U.S. person shall be treated as having newly acquired an interest in the partnership (for an amount equal to the gain recognized), permitting the partnership to make an optional adjustment to basis pursuant to sections 743 and 754; and

(3) The transferee foreign corporation's basis in the property acquired from the partnership shall be increased by the amount of gain recognized by U.S. persons under this paragraph (c)(3)(i).

(ii) *Transfer of partnership interest treated as transfer of proportionate share of assets.*—(A) [Reserved].

(B) *Special adjustments to basis.*—If a U.S. person is treated under the rule of paragraph (c)(3)(ii)(A) of this section as having transferred a proportionate share of the property of a partnership in an exchange described in section 367(a), and is therefore required to recognize gain upon the transfer, then—

(1) The U.S. person's basis in the stock of the transferee foreign corporation shall be increased by the amount of gain so recognized by that person;

(2) The transferee foreign corporation's basis in the transferred partnership interest shall be increased by the amount of gain recognized by the U.S. person; and

(3) Solely for purposes of determining the partnership's basis in the property held by it, the U.S. person shall be treated as having newly acquired an interest in the partnership (for an amount equal to the gain recognized), permitting the partnership to make an optional adjustment to basis pursuant to sections 743 and 754.

(C) *Limited partnership interest.*—The transfer by a U.S. person of an interest in a partnership shall not be subject to the rules of paragraph (c)(3)(ii)(A) and (B) if—

(1) The interest transferred is a limited partnership interest; and

(2) Such interest is regularly traded on an established securities market.

Instead, the transfer of such an interest shall be treated in the same manner as a transfer of stock or securities. Thus, the consequences of such a transfer shall be determined under the rules of § 1.367(a)-3. For purposes of this section, a limited partnership interest is an interest as a limited partner in a partnership that is organized under the laws of any State of the United States or the District of Columbia.

Whether such an interest is regularly traded on an established securities market shall be determined under the provisions of paragraph (c)(3)(ii)(D) of this section.

(D) *Regularly traded on an established securities market.*—*(1) Established securities market.*—For purposes of this paragraph (c)(3)(ii), an established securities market is—

(i) A national securities exchange which is registered under section 6 of the Securities Exchange Act of 1934 (15 USC 78f);

(ii) A foreign national securities exchange which is officially recognized, sanctioned, or supervised by governmental authority; and

(iii) An over-the-counter market. An over-the-counter market is any market reflected by the existence of an inter-dealer quotation system. An inter-dealer quotation system is any system of general circulation to brokers and dealers which regularly disseminates quotations of stock and securities by identified brokers or dealers, other than by quotation sheets which are prepared and distributed by a broker or dealer in the regular course of business and which contain only quotations of such broker or dealer.

(2) Regularly traded.—A class of interest that is traded on an established securities market is considered to be regularly traded if it is regularly quoted by brokers or dealers making a market in such interests. A class of interests shall be presumed to be regularly traded if the entity has a total of 500 or more interest-holders.

(4) *Transfers by trusts and estates.*—(i) *In general.*—For purposes of section 367(a), a transfer of property by an estate or trust shall be treated as a transfer by the entity itself and not as an indirect transfer by its beneficiaries. Thus, a transfer of property by a foreign trust or estate (as defined in section 7701(a)(31)) is not described in section 367(a)(1), regardless of whether the beneficiaries of the trust or estate are U.S. persons. Similarly, a transfer of property by a domestic trust or estate may be described in section 367(a)(1), regardless of whether the beneficiaries of the trust or estate are foreign persons.

(ii) *Grantor trusts.*—A transfer of a portion or all of the assets of a foreign or domestic trust to a foreign corporation in an exchange described in section 367(a)(1) is considered a transfer by any U.S. person who is treated as the owner of any such portion or all of the assets of the trust under sections 671 through 679.

(5) *Termination of election under section 1504(d).*—Section 367(a) applies to the constructive reorganization and transfer of property from a domestic corporation to a foreign corporation that occurs upon the termination of an election under section 1504(d), which permits the treatment of certain contiguous country corporations as domestic corporations. The rule of this paragraph (c)(5) is illustrated by the following example.

Example. Domestic corporation Y previously made a valid election under section 1504(d) to have its wholly owned Canadian subsidiary, C, treated as a domestic corporation. On July 1, 1986, C fails to continue to qualify for the election under section 1504(d). A constructive reorganization described in section 368(a)(1)(D) occurs. The resulting constructive transfer of assets by "domestic" corporation C to Canadian corporation C upon the termination of the election is a transfer of property described in section 367(a)(1).

(6) *Changes in classification of an entity.*—If a foreign entity is classified as an entity other than an association taxable as a corporation for United States tax purposes, and subsequently a change is made in the governing documents, articles, or agreements of the entity so that the entity is thereafter classified as an association taxable as a corporation, the change in classification is considered a transfer of property to a foreign corporation in connection with an exchange described in section 351. For purposes of section 367(a)(1), the transfer of property is considered as made by the persons determined under the rules set forth in paragraph (c)(3) of this section, with respect to partnerships, and paragraph (c)(4)(i) or (ii), with respect to trusts and estates, and the rules of such paragraphs apply in determining whether a transfer described in section 367(a)(1) has been made.

(7) *Contributions to capital.*—For rules with respect to the treatment of a contribution to the capital of a foreign corporation as a transfer described in section 367(a)(1), see section 367(c)(2) and the regulations thereunder.

(d) [Reserved].

(1) [Reserved].

(2) [Reserved].

(3) [Reserved]. For further guidance, see § 1.367(a)-1(d)(3).

(4) [Reserved].

(5) [Reserved].

(6) [Reserved].

(e) [Reserved]. For further guidance, *see* § 1.367(a)-1(e).

(f) [Reserved]. For further guidance, *see* § 1.367(a)-1(f).

(g) *Effective date of certain sections.*—(1) *In general.*—Except as specifically provided to the contrary elsewhere in these sections, §§ 1.367(a)-1T through 1.367(a)-6T apply to transfers occurring after December 31, 1984.

(2) *Private rulings.*—The taxpayer may rely on a private ruling under section 367(a) received by him before June 16, 1986.

(3) *Certain indirect transfers.*—Sections 1.367(a)-1T(c)(2)(i) and (iii) and 1.367(a)-1T(c)(3) apply to transfers made after June 16, 1986. For transfers made before that date, see 26 CFR § 1.367(a)-1(b) (revised as of April 1, 1986).

(4) [Reserved]. For further guidance see § 1.367(a)-1(g)(4). [Temporary Reg. § 1.367(a)-1T.]

□ [*T.D.* 8087, 5-15-86. *Amended by T.D.* 8280, 1-12-90; *T.D.* 8770, 6-18-98; *T.D.* 9441, 12-31-2008; *T.D.* 9568, 12-16-2011; *T.D.* 9614, 3-18-2013, *T.D.* 9739, 9-18-2015 *and T.D.* 9803, 12-15-2016.]

§ 1.367(a)-2. Exception for transfers of property for use in the active conduct of a trade or business.—(a) *Scope and general rule.*—(1) *Scope.*—Paragraph (a)(2) of this section provides the general exception to section 367(a)(1) for certain property transferred for use in the active conduct of a trade or business. Paragraph (b) of this section describes property that is eligible for the exception provided in paragraph (a)(2) of this section. Paragraph (c) of this section describes property that is not eligible for the exception provided in paragraph (a)(2) of this section. Paragraph (d) of this section provides general rules, and paragraphs (e) through (h) of this section provide special rules, for determining whether property is used in the active conduct of a trade or business outside of the United States. Paragraph (i) of this section is reserved. Paragraph (j) of this section provides relief for certain failures to comply with the reporting requirements under paragraph (a)(2)(iii) of this section that are not willful. Paragraph (k) of this section provides dates of applicability. The rules of this section do not apply to a transfer of stock or securities in an exchange subject to § 1.367(a)-3.

(2) *General rule.*—Except as otherwise provided in §§ 1.367(a)-4, 1.367(a)-6, and 1.367(a)-7, section 367(a)(1) does not apply to property transferred by a United States person (U.S. transferor) to a foreign corporation if—

(i) The property constitutes eligible property;

(ii) The property is transferred for use by the foreign corporation in the active conduct of a trade or business outside of the United States, as determined under paragraph (d), (e), (f), (g), or (h) of this section, as applicable; and

(iii) The U.S. transferor complies with the reporting requirements of section 6038B and the regulations thereunder.

(b) *Eligible property.*—Except as provided in paragraph (c) of this section, eligible property means—

(1) Tangible property;

(2) A working interest in oil and gas property; and

(3) A financial asset. For purposes of this section, a financial asset is—

(i) A cash equivalent;

(ii) A security within the meaning of section 475(c)(2), without regard to the last sentence of section 475(c)(2) (referencing section 1256) and without regard to section 475(c)(4), but excluding an interest in a partnership;

(iii) A commodities position described in section 475(e)(2)(B), 475(e)(2)(C), or 475(e)(2)(D); and

(iv) A notional principal contract described in § 1.446-3(c)(1).

(c) *Exception for certain property.*—Notwithstanding paragraph (b) of this section, property described in paragraph (c)(1), (2), (3), or (4) of this section does not constitute eligible property.

(1) *Inventory.*—Stock in trade of the taxpayer or other property of a kind which would properly be included in the inventory of the taxpayer if on hand at the close of the taxable year, or property held by the taxpayer primarily for sale to customers in the ordinary course

of its trade or business (including raw materials and supplies, partially completed goods, and finished products).

(2) *Installment obligations, etc.*—Installment obligations, accounts receivable, or similar property, but only to the extent that the principal amount of any such obligation has not previously been included by the taxpayer in its taxable income.

(3) *Nonfunctional currency, etc.*—(i) *In general.*—Property that gives rise to a section 988 transaction of the taxpayer described in section 988(c)(1)(A) through (C), without regard to section 988(c)(1)(D) and (E), or that would give rise to such a section 988 transaction if it were acquired, accrued, entered into, or disposed of directly by the taxpayer.

(ii) *Limitation of gain required to be recognized.*—If section 367(a)(1) applies to a transfer of property described in paragraph (c)(3)(i) of this section, then the gain required to be recognized is limited to the gain realized as part of the same transaction upon the transfer of property described in paragraph (c)(3)(i) of this section, less any loss realized as part of the same transaction upon the transfer of property described in paragraph (c)(3)(i) of this section. This limitation applies in lieu of the rule in § 1.367(a)-1(b)(1). No loss is recognized with respect to property described in this paragraph (c)(3).

(4) *Certain leased tangible property.*—Tangible property with respect to which the transferor is a lessor at the time of the transfer, unless either the foreign corporation is the lessee at the time of the transfer or the foreign corporation will lease the property to third persons.

(d) *Active conduct of a trade or business outside the United States.*—(1) *In general.*—Except as provided in paragraphs (e), (f), (g), and (h) of this section, to determine whether property is transferred for use by the foreign corporation in the active conduct of a trade or business outside of the United States, four factual determinations must be made:

(i) What is the trade or business of the foreign corporation (see paragraph (d)(2) of this section);

(ii) Do the activities of the foreign corporation constitute the active conduct of that trade or business (see paragraph (d)(3) of this section);

(iii) Is the trade or business conducted outside of the United States (see paragraph (d)(4) of this section); and

(iv) Is the transferred property used or held for use in the trade or business (see paragraph (d)(5) of this section)?

(2) *Trade or business.*—Whether the activities of the foreign corporation constitute a trade or business is determined based on all the facts and circumstances. In general, a trade or business is a specific unified group of activities that constitute (or could constitute) an independent economic enterprise carried on for profit. For example, the activities of a foreign selling subsidiary could constitute a trade or business if they could be independently carried on for profit, even though the subsidiary acts exclusively on behalf of, and has operations fully integrated with, its parent corporation. To constitute a trade or business, a group of activities must ordinarily include every operation which forms a part of, or a step in, a process by which an enterprise may earn income or profit. In this regard, one or more of such activities may be carried on by independent contractors under the direct control of the foreign corporation. (However, see paragraph (d)(3) of this section.) The group of activities must ordinarily include the collection of income and the payment of expenses. If the activities of the foreign corporation do not constitute a trade or business, then the exception provided by this section does not apply, regardless of the level of activities carried on by the corporation. The following activities are not considered to constitute by themselves a trade or business for purposes of this section:

(i) Any activity giving rise to expenses that would be deductible only under section 212 if the activities were carried on by an individual; or

(ii) The holding for one's own account of investments in stock, securities, land, or other property, including casual sales thereof.

(3) *Active conduct.*—Whether a trade or business is actively conducted by the foreign corporation is determined based on all the facts and circumstances. In general, a corporation actively conducts a trade or business only if the officers and employees of the corporation carry out substantial managerial and operational activities. A corporation may be engaged in the active conduct of a trade or business even though incidental activities of the trade or business are carried out on behalf of the corporation by independent contractors. In determining whether the officers and employees of the corporation carry out substantial managerial and operational activities, however, the activities of independent contractors are disregarded. On the other hand, the officers and employees of the corporation are considered to include the officers and employees of related entities who are made available to and supervised on a day-to-day basis by, and whose salaries are paid by (or reimbursed to the lending related entity by), the foreign corporation. See paragraph (d)(6) of this section for the standard that applies to determine whether a trade or business that produces rents or royalties is actively conducted. The rule of this paragraph (d)(3) is illustrated by the following example.

Example. X, a domestic corporation, and Y, a foreign corporation not related to X, transfer property to Z, a newly formed foreign corporation organized for the purpose of combining the research activities of X and Y. Z contracts all of its operational and research activities to Y for an arm's-length fee. Z's activities do not constitute the active conduct of a trade or business.

(4) *Outside of the United States.*—Whether the foreign corporation conducts a trade or business outside of the United States is determined based on all the facts and circumstances. Generally, the primary managerial and operational activities of the trade or business must be conducted outside the United States and immediately after the transfer the transferred assets must be located outside the United States. Thus, the exception provided by this section would not apply to the transfer of the assets of a domestic business to a foreign corporation if the domestic business continued to operate in the United States after the transfer. In such a case, the primary operational activities of the business would continue to be conducted in the United States. Moreover, the transferred assets would be located in the United States. However, it is not necessary that every item of property transferred be used outside of the United States. As long as the primary managerial and operational activities of the trade or business are conducted outside of the United States and substantially all of the transferred assets are located outside the United States, incidental items of transferred property located in the United States may be considered to have been transferred for use in the active conduct of a trade or business outside of the United States.

(5) *Use in the trade or business.*—Whether property is used or held for use by the foreign corporation in a trade or business is determined based on all the facts and circumstances. In general, property is used or held for use in the foreign corporation's trade or business if it is—

(i) Held for the principal purpose of promoting the present conduct of the trade or business;

(ii) Acquired and held in the ordinary course of the trade or business; or

(iii) Otherwise held in a direct relationship to the trade or business. Property is considered held in a direct relationship to a trade or business if it is held to meet the present needs of that trade or business and not its anticipated future needs. Thus, property will not be considered to be held in a direct relationship to a trade or business if it is held for the purpose of providing for future diversification into a new trade or business, future expansion of trade or business activities, future plant replacement, or future business contingencies.

(6) *Active leasing and licensing.*—For purposes of paragraph (d)(3) of this section, whether a trade or business that produces rents or royalties is actively conducted is determined under the principles of section 954(c)(2)(A) and the regulations thereunder, but without regard to whether the rents or royalties are received from an unrelated party. See §§ 1.954-2(c) and (d).

(e) *Special rules for certain property to be leased.*—(1) *Leasing business of the foreign corporation.*—Except as otherwise provided in this paragraph (e), tangible property that will be leased to another person by the foreign corporation will be considered to be transferred for use by the foreign corporation in an active trade or business outside the United States only if—

(i) The foreign corporation's leasing of the property constitutes the active conduct of a leasing business, as determined under paragraph (d)(6) of this section;

(ii) The lessee of the property is not expected to, and does not, use the property in the United States; and

(iii) The foreign corporation has a need for substantial investment in assets of the type transferred.

(2) *De minimis leasing by the foreign corporation.*—Tangible property that will be leased to another person by the foreign corporation but that does not satisfy the conditions of paragraph (e)(1) of this section will, nevertheless, be considered to be transferred for use in the active conduct of a trade or business if either—

(i) The property transferred will be used by the foreign corporation in the active conduct of a trade or business but will be leased during occasional brief periods when the property would otherwise be idle, such as an airplane leased during periods of excess capacity; or

(ii) The property transferred is real property located outside the United States and—

(A) The property will be used primarily in the active conduct of a trade or business of the foreign corporation; and

(B) Not more than ten percent of the square footage of the property will be leased to others.

(3) *Aircraft and vessels leased in foreign commerce.*—For purposes of satisfying paragraph (e)(1) of this section, an aircraft or vessel, including component parts such as an engine leased separately from the aircraft or vessel, that will be leased to another person by the foreign corporation will be considered to be transferred for use in the active conduct of a trade or business if—

(i) The employees of the foreign corporation perform substantial managerial and operational activities of leasing aircraft or vessels outside the United States; and

(ii) The leased property is predominantly used outside the United States, as determined under § 1.954-2(c)(2)(v).

(f) *Special rules for oil and gas working interests.*—(1) *In general.*—A working interest in oil and gas property will be considered to be transferred for use in the active conduct of a trade or business if—

(i) The transfer satisfies the conditions of paragraph (f)(2) or (f)(3) of this section;

(ii) At the time of the transfer, the foreign corporation has no intention to farm out or otherwise transfer any part of the transferred working interest; and

(iii) During the first three years after the transfer there are no farmouts or other transfers of any part of the transferred working interest as a result of which the foreign corporation retains less than a 50-percent share of the transferred working interest.

(2) *Active use of working interest.*—A working interest in oil and gas property that satisfies the conditions in paragraphs (f)(1)(ii) and (iii) of this section will be considered to be transferred for use in the active conduct of a trade or business if—

(i) The U.S. transferor is regularly and substantially engaged in exploration for and extraction of minerals, either directly or through working interests in joint ventures, other than by reason of the property that is transferred;

(ii) The terms of the working interest transferred were actively negotiated among the joint venturers;

(iii) The working interest transferred constitutes at least a five percent working interest;

(iv) Before and at the time of the transfer, through its own employees or officers, the U.S. transferor was regularly and actively engaged in—

(A) Operating the working interest, or

(B) Analyzing technical data relating to the activities of the venture;

(v) Before and at the time of the transfer, through its own employees or officers, the U.S. transferor was regularly and actively involved in decision making with respect to the operations of the venture, including decisions relating to exploration, development, production, and marketing; and

(vi) After the transfer, the foreign corporation will for the foreseeable future satisfy the requirements of subparagraphs (iv) and (v) of this paragraph (f)(2).

(3) *Start-up operations.*—A working interest in oil and gas property that satisfies the conditions in paragraphs (f)(1)(ii) and (iii) of this section but that does not satisfy all the requirements of paragraph (f)(2) of this section will, nevertheless, be considered to be transferred for use in the active conduct of a trade or business if—

(i) The working interest was acquired by the U.S. transferor immediately before the transfer and for the specific purpose of transferring it to the foreign corporation;

(ii) The requirements of paragraphs (f)(2)(ii) and (iii) of this section are satisfied; and

(iii) The foreign corporation will for the foreseeable future satisfy the requirements of paragraph (f)(2)(iv) and (v) of this section.

(4) *Other applicable rules.*—A working interest in oil and gas property that is not described in paragraph (f)(1) of this section may nonetheless qualify for the exception to section 367(a)(1) contained in this section depending upon the facts and circumstances.

(g) *Property retransferred by the foreign corporation.*—(1) *General rule.*—Property will not be considered to be transferred for use in the active conduct of a trade or business outside of the United States if—

(i) At the time of the transfer, it is reasonable to believe that, in the reasonably foreseeable future, the foreign corporation will sell or otherwise dispose of any material portion of the property other than in the ordinary course of business; or

(ii) Except as provided in paragraph (g)(2) of this section, the foreign corporation receives the property in an exchange described in section 367(a)(1), and, as part of the same transaction, transfers the property to another person. For purposes of the preceding sentence, a subsequent transfer within six months of the initial transfer will be considered to be part of the same transaction, and a subsequent transfer more than six months after the initial transfer may be considered to be part of the same transaction under step-transaction principles.

(2) *Exception.*—Notwithstanding paragraph (g)(1) of this section, the active conduct exception provided by this section shall apply to the initial transfer if—

(i) The initial transfer is followed by one or more subsequent transfers described in section 351 or 721; and

(ii) Each subsequent transferee is either a partnership in which the preceding transferor is a general partner or a corporation in which the preceding transferor owns common stock; and

(iii) The ultimate transferee uses the property in the active conduct of a trade or business outside the United States.

(h) *Compulsory transfers of property.*—Property is presumed to be transferred for use in the active conduct of a trade or business outside of the United States, if—

(1) The property was previously in use in the country in which the foreign corporation is organized; and

(2) The transfer is either:

(i) Legally required by the foreign government as a necessary condition of doing business; or

(ii) Compelled by a genuine threat of immediate expropriation by the foreign government.

(i) [Reserved].

(j) *Failure to comply with reporting requirements of section 6038B.*—(1) *Failure to comply.*—For purposes of the exception to the application of section 367(a)(1) provided in paragraph (a)(2) of this section, a failure to comply with the reporting requirements of section 6038B and the regulations thereunder (failure to comply) has the meaning set forth in § 1.6038B-1(f)(2).

(2) *Relief for certain failures to comply that are not willful.*—(i) *In general.*—A failure to comply described in paragraph (j)(1) of this section will be deemed not to have occurred for purposes of satisfying the requirements of this section if the taxpayer demonstrates that the failure was not willful using the procedure set forth in this paragraph (j)(2). For this purpose, willful is to be interpreted consistent with the meaning of that term in the context of other civil penalties, which would include a failure due to gross negligence, reckless disregard, or willful neglect. Whether a failure to comply was a willful failure will be determined by the Director of Field Operations, Cross Border Activities Practice Area, Large Business & International (or any successor to the roles and responsibilities of such position, as appropriate) (Director) based on all the facts and circumstances. The taxpayer must submit a request for relief and an explanation as provided in paragraph (j)(2)(ii)(A) of this section. Although a taxpayer whose failure to comply is determined not to be willful will not be subject to gain recognition under this section, the taxpayer will be subject to a penalty under section 6038B if the taxpayer fails to demonstrate that the failure was due to reasonable cause and not willful neglect. See § 1.6038B-1(b)(1) and (f). The determination of whether the failure to comply was willful under this section has no effect on any request for relief made under § 1.6038B-1(f).

(ii) *Procedures for establishing that a failure to comply was not willful.*—(A) *Time and manner of submission.*—A taxpayer's statement that the failure to comply was not willful will be considered only if, promptly after the taxpayer becomes aware of the failure, an amended return is filed for the taxable year to which the failure relates that includes the information that should have been included with the original return for such taxable year or that otherwise complies with the rules of this section, and that includes a written statement explaining the reasons for the failure to comply. The amended return must be filed with the Internal Revenue Service at the location where the taxpayer filed its original return. The taxpayer may submit a request for relief from the penalty under section 6038B as part of the same submission. See § 1.6038B-1(f).

(B) *Notice requirement.*—In addition to the requirements of paragraph (j)(2)(ii)(A) of this section, the taxpayer must comply with the notice requirements of this paragraph (j)(2)(ii)(B). If any taxable year of the taxpayer is under examination when the amended return is filed, a copy of the amended return and any information required to be included with such return must be delivered to the Internal Revenue Service personnel conducting the examination. If no taxable year of the taxpayer is under examination when the amended return is filed, a copy of the amended return and any information required to be included with such return must be delivered to the Director.

(3) For illustrations of the application of the willfulness standard of this paragraph (j), see the examples in § 1.367(a)-8(p)(3).

(4) Paragraph (j) applies to requests for relief submitted on or after November 19, 2014.

(k) *Effective/applicability dates.*—(1) *In general.*—Except as provided in paragraphs (j)(4) and (k)(2) of this section, the rules of this section apply to transfers occurring on or after September 14, 2015, and to transfers occurring before September 14, 2015, resulting from entity classification elections made under § 301.7701-3 that are filed on or after September 14, 2015. For transfers occurring before this section is applicable, see §§ 1.367(a)-2, -2T, -4, -4T, -5, and -5T as contained in 26 CFR part 1 revised as of April 1, 2016.

(2) *Foreign currency exception.*—Notwithstanding paragraph (c)(3)(i) of this section, § 1.367(a)-5T(d)(2) as contained in 26 CFR part 1 revised as of April 1, 2016, applies to transfers of property denominated in a foreign currency occurring before December 16, 2016, other than transfers occurring before that date resulting from entity classification elections made under § 301.7701-3 that are filed on or after that date. [Reg. § 1.367(a)-2.]

☐ *[T.D. 9525, 5-5-2011. Amended by T.D. 9704, 11-18-2014 and T.D. 9803, 12-15-2016.]*

§ 1.367(a)-3. Treatment of transfers of stock or securities to foreign corporations.—(a) *In general.*—(1) *Overview.*—This section provides rules concerning the transfer of stock or securities by a U.S. person to a foreign corporation in an exchange described in section 367(a)(1). In general, a transfer of stock or securities (including an indirect stock transfer described in paragraph (d) of this section) by a U.S. person to a foreign corporation that is described in section 351, 354 (including a section 354 exchange pursuant to a reorganization described in section 368(a)(1)(B)), 356, or section 361(a) or (b) is subject to section 367(a)(1). Therefore, gain is recognized on such a transfer unless one of the exceptions set forth in paragraph (a)(2) of this section (regarding general exceptions for certain exchanges of stock or securities), paragraph (b) of this section (regarding transfers of foreign stock or securities), paragraph (c) of this section (regarding transfers of domestic stock or securities), or paragraph (e) of this section (regarding transfers of stock or securities in a section 361 exchange) applies to the transfer. For rules applicable when, pursuant to section 304(a)(1), a U.S. person is treated as transferring stock of a domestic or foreign corporation to a foreign corporation in exchange for stock of such foreign corporation in a transaction to which section 351(a) applies, see § 1.367(a)-9T.

(2) *Exceptions for certain exchanges of stock or securities.*—Unless otherwise provided, the following exchanges are not subject to section 367(a)(1) and therefore gain is not recognized under section 367(a)(1).

(i) *Section 368(a)(1)(E) reorganizations.*—In an exchange under section 354 or 356, a U.S. person exchanges stock or securities of a foreign corporation in a reorganization described in section 368(a)(1)(E).

(ii) *Certain section 368(a)(1) asset reorganizations.*—In an exchange under section 354 or 356, a U.S. person exchanges stock or securities of a domestic or foreign corporation pursuant to an asset reorganization that is not treated as an indirect stock transfer under paragraph (d) of this section. See paragraph (d)(3) *Example 16* of this section. For purposes of this section, an *asset reorganization* is defined as a reorganization described in section 368(a)(1) involving a transfer of property under section 361.

(iii) *Certain reorganizations described in sections 368(a)(1)(A) and (a)(2)(E).*—If, in an exchange described in section 361, a domestic merging corporation transfers stock of a controlling corporation to a foreign surviving corporation in a reorganization described in section 368(a)(1)(A) and (a)(2)(E), the stock of the controlling corporation transferred in such section 361 exchange is not subject to section 367(a)(1) if the stock of the controlling corporation is provided to the merging corporation by the controlling corporation pursuant to the plan of reorganization. However, a section 361 exchange of other property, including stock of the controlling corporation not provided by the controlling corporation pursuant to the plan of reorganization, by the domestic merging corporation to the foreign surviving corporation pursuant to such a reorganization is described in section 367(a)(1) and therefore subject to section 367(a)(1) unless an exception to section 367(a)(1) applies.

(iv) *Certain triangular reorganizations described in § 1.367(b)-10.*—If, in an exchange under section 354 or 356, one or more U.S. persons exchange stock or securities of T (as defined in § 1.358-6(b)(1)(iii)) in connection with a transaction described in § 1.367(b)-10 (applying to certain acquisitions of parent stock or securities for property in triangular reorganizations), section 367(a)(1) shall not apply to such U.S. persons with respect to the exchange of the stock or securities of T if the condition specified in this paragraph (iv) is satisfied. The condition specified in this paragraph (iv) is that the amount of gain in the T stock or securities that would otherwise be recognized under section 367(a)(1) (without regard to any exceptions thereto) pursuant to the indirect stock transfer rules of paragraph (d) of this section is less than the sum of the amount of the deemed distribution under § 1.367(b)-10 treated as a dividend under section 301(c)(1) and the amount of such deemed distribution treated as gain from the sale or exchange of property under section 301(c)(3). See § 1.367(b)-10(a)(2)(iii) (providing a similar rule that excludes certain transactions from the application of § 1.367(b)-10).

(3) *Cross-references.*—For rules regarding other indirect or constructive transfers of stock or securities subject to section 367(a)(1) (unless an exception applies) see § 1.367(a)-1(c). For additional rules regarding a transfer of stock or securities in an exchange described in section 361(a) or (b), see § 1.367(a)-7. For special basis and holding period rules involving foreign corporations that are parties to certain triangular reorganizations under section 368(a)(1), see § 1.367(b)-13. For additional rules relating to certain nonrecognition exchanges involving a foreign corporation, see section 367(b) and the regulations under that section. For rules regarding reporting requirements with respect to transfers described under section 367(a), see section 6038B and the regulations thereunder. For rules related to expatriated entities, see section 7874 and the regulations thereunder.

(b) *Transfers of stock or securities of foreign corporations.*—(1) *General rule.*—Except as provided in paragraph (e) of this section, a transfer of stock or securities of a foreign corporation by a U.S. person to a foreign corporation that would otherwise be subject to section 367(a)(1) under paragraph (a) of this section will not be subject to section 367(a)(1) if either—

(i) *Less than 5-percent shareholder.*—The U.S. person owns less than five percent (applying the attribution rules of section 318, as modified by section 958(b)) of both the total voting power and the total value of the stock of the transferee foreign corporation immediately after the transfer; or

(ii) *5-percent shareholder.*—The U.S. person enters into a five-year gain recognition agreement with respect to the transferred stock or securities as provided in § 1.367(a)-8.

(2) *Certain transfers subject to sections 367(a) and (b).*—(i) *In general.*—A transfer of stock or securities described in section 367(a) or the regulations thereunder as well as in section 367(b) or the regulations thereunder shall be subject concurrently to sections 367(a) and (b) and the respective regulations thereunder, except as provided in paragraph (b)(2)(i)(A) through (C) of this section. See paragraph (d)(3) *Examples 11* and *14* of this section.

(A) Section 367(b) and the regulations thereunder shall not apply if a foreign corporation is not treated as a corporation under section 367(a)(1). See the example in paragraph (b)(2)(ii) of this section and paragraph (d)(3) *Example 14* of this section.

(B) If a foreign corporation transfers assets to a domestic corporation in a transaction to which § 1.367(b)-3(a) and (b) and the indirect stock transfer rules of paragraph (d) of this section apply, and all the earnings and profits amount attributable to the stock of an exchanging shareholder under § 1.367(b)-3(b) is greater than the amount of gain in such stock subject to section 367(a) pursuant to the indirect stock transfer rules of paragraph (d) of this section, then the rules of section 367(b), and not the rules of section 367(a), shall apply to the exchange. See paragraph (d)(3) *Example 15* of this section.

(C) [Reserved]. For further guidance, see § 1.367(a)-3T(b)(2)(i)(C).

(ii) *Example.*—The following example illustrates the provisions of this paragraph (b)(2):

Example. (i) *Facts.* DC, a domestic corporation, owns all of the stock of FC1, a controlled foreign corporation within the meaning of section 957(a). DC's basis in the stock of FC1 is $50, and the value of such stock is $100. The section 1248 amount with respect to such stock is $30. FC2, also a foreign corporation, is owned entirely by foreign individuals who are not related to DC or FC1. In a reorganization described in section 368(a)(1)(B), FC2 acquires all of the stock of FC1 from DC in exchange for 20 percent of the voting stock of FC2. FC2 is not a controlled foreign corporation after the reorganization.

(ii) *Result without gain recognition agreement.* Under the provisions of this paragraph (b), if DC fails to enter into a gain recognition agreement, DC is required to recognize in the year of the transfer the $50 of gain that it realized upon the transfer, $30 of which will be treated as a dividend under section 1248.

(iii) *Result with gain recognition agreement.* If DC enters into a gain recognition agreement under § 1.367(a)-8 with respect to the transfer of FC1 stock, the exchange will also be subject to the provisions of section 367(b) and the regulations thereunder to the extent that it is not subject to tax under section 367(a)(1). In such case, DC will be required to recognize the section 1248 amount of $30 on the exchange of FC1 for FC2 stock. See § 1.367(b)-4(b). The deemed dividend of $30 recognized by DC will increase its basis in the FC1 stock exchanged in the transaction and, therefore, the basis of the FC2 stock received in the transaction. The remaining gain of $20 realized by DC (otherwise recognizable under section 367(a)) in the exchange of FC1 stock will not be recognized if DC enters into a gain recognition agreement with respect to the transfer. (The result would be unchanged if, for example, the exchange of FC1 stock for FC2 stock qualified as a section 351 exchange, or as an exchange described in both sections 351 and 368(a)(1)(B).)

(c) *Transfers of stock or securities of domestic corporations.*—(1) *General rule.*—Except as provided in paragraph (e) of this section, a transfer of stock or securities of a domestic corporation by a U.S. person to a foreign corporation that would otherwise be subject to section 367(a)(1) under paragraph (a) of this section will not be subject to section 367(a)(1) if the domestic corporation the stock or securities of which are transferred (referred to as the U.S. target company) complies with the reporting requirements in paragraph (c)(6) of this section and if each of the following four conditions is met:

(i) Fifty percent or less of both the total voting power and the total value of the stock of the transferee foreign corporation is received in the transaction, in the aggregate, by U.S. transferors (*i.e.*, the amount of stock received does not exceed the 50-percent ownership threshold).

(ii) Fifty percent or less of each of the total voting power and the total value of the stock of the transferee foreign corporation is owned, in the aggregate, immediately after the transfer by U.S. persons that are either officers or directors of the U.S. target company or that are five-percent target shareholders (as defined in paragraph (c)(5)(iii) of this section) (*i.e.*, there is no control group). For purposes of this paragraph (c)(1)(ii), any stock of the transferee foreign corporation owned by U.S. persons immediately after the transfer will be taken into account, whether or not it was received in the exchange for stock or securities of the U.S. target company.

(iii) Either—

(A) The U.S. person is not a five-percent transferee shareholder (as defined in paragraph (c)(5)(ii) of this section); or

(B) The U.S. person is a five-percent transferee shareholder and enters into a five-year agreement to recognize gain with respect to the U.S. target company stock or securities it exchanged in the form provided in § 1.367(a)-8; and

(iv) The active trade or business test (as defined in paragraph (c)(3) of this section) is satisfied.

(2) *Ownership presumption.*—For purposes of paragraph (c)(1) of this section, persons who transfer stock or securities of the U.S. target company in exchange for stock of the transferee foreign corporation are presumed to be U.S. persons. This presumption may be rebutted in accordance with paragraph (c)(7) of this section.

(3) *Active trade or business test.*—(i) *In general.*—The tests of this paragraph (c)(3), collectively referred to as the active trade or business test, are satisfied if:

(A) The transferee foreign corporation or any qualified subsidiary (as defined in paragraph (c)(5)(vii) of this section) or any qualified partnership (as defined in paragraph (c)(5)(viii) of this section) is engaged in an active trade or business outside the United States, within the meaning of § 1.367(a)-2(d)(2), (3) and (4), for the entire 36-month period immediately before the transfer;

(B) At the time of the transfer, neither the transferors nor the transferee foreign corporation (and, if applicable, the qualified subsidiary or qualified partnership engaged in the active trade or business) have an intention to substantially dispose of or discontinue such trade or business; and

(C) The substantiality test (as defined in paragraph (c)(3)(iii) of this section) is satisfied.

(ii) *Special rules.*—For purposes of paragraphs (c)(3)(i)(A) and (B) of this section, the following special rules apply:

(A) The transferee foreign corporation, a qualified subsidiary, or a qualified partnership will be considered to be engaged in an active trade or business for the entire 36-month period preceding the exchange if it acquires at the time of, or any time prior to, the exchange a trade or business that has been active throughout the entire 36-month period preceding the exchange. This special rule shall not apply, however, if the acquired active trade or business assets were owned by the U.S. target company or any affiliate (within the meaning of section 1504(a) but excluding the exceptions contained in section 1504(b) and substituting "50 percent" for "80 percent" where it appears therein) at any time during the 36-month period prior to the acquisition. Nor will this special rule apply if the principal purpose of such acquisition is to satisfy the active trade or business test.

(B) An active trade or business does not include the making or managing of investments for the account of the transferee foreign corporation or any affiliate (within the meaning of section 1504(a) but excluding the exceptions contained in section 1504(b) and substituting "50 percent" for "80 percent" where it appears therein). (This paragraph (c)(3)(ii)(B) shall not create any inference as to the scope of § 1.367(a)-2(d)(2) and (3) for other purposes.)

(iii) *Substantiality test.*—(A) *General rule.*—A transferee foreign corporation will be deemed to satisfy the substantiality test if, at the time of the transfer, the fair market value of the transferee foreign corporation is at least equal to the fair market value of the U.S. target company.

(B) *Special rules for transferee foreign corporation value.*—*(1)* For purposes of paragraph (c)(3)(iii)(A) of this section, the value of the transferee foreign corporation shall include assets acquired outside the ordinary course of business by the transferee foreign corporation within the 36-month period preceding the exchange only if either—

(i) Both—

(A) At the time of the exchange, such assets or, as applicable, the proceeds thereof, do not produce, and are not held for the production of, passive income as defined in section 1297(b); and

(B) Such assets are not acquired for the principal purpose of satisfying the substantiality test; or

(ii) Such assets consist of the stock of a qualified subsidiary or an interest in a qualified partnership. See paragraph (c)(3)(iii)(B)(2) of this section.

(2) For purposes of paragraph (c)(3)(iii)(A) of this section, the value of the transferee foreign corporation shall not include the value of the stock of any qualified subsidiary or the value of any interest in a qualified partnership, held directly or indirectly, to the extent that such value is attributable to assets acquired by such qualified subsidiary or partnership outside the ordinary course of business and within the 36-month period preceding the exchange unless those assets satisfy the requirements in paragraph (c)(3)(iii)(B)(*1*) of this section.

(3) For purposes of paragraph (c)(3)(iii)(A) of this section, the value of the transferee foreign corporation shall not include the value of assets received within the 36-month period prior to the acquisition, notwithstanding the special rule in paragraph

(c)(3)(iii)(B)(*1*) of this section, if such assets were owned by the U.S. target company or an affiliate (within the meaning of section 1504(a) but without the exceptions under section 1504(b) and substituting "50 percent" for "80 percent" where it appears therein) at any time during the 36-month period prior to the transaction.

(C) *Special rule for U.S. target company value.*—For purposes of § 1.367(a)-3(c)(3)(iii)(A), the fair market value of the U.S. target company includes the aggregate amount of non-ordinary course distributions (NOCDs) made by the U.S. target company. To calculate the aggregate value of NOCDs, the principles of § 1.7874-10, including the rule regarding predecessors in § 1.7874-10(e) and the rule regarding a deemed distribution of stock in certain cases in § 1.7874-10(g), apply. However, this paragraph (c)(3)(iii)(C) does not apply if the principles of the de minimis exception in § 1.7874-10(d) are satisfied.

(4) *Special rules.*—(i) *Treatment of partnerships.*—For purposes of this paragraph (c), if a partnership (whether domestic or foreign) owns stock or securities in the U.S. target company or the transferee foreign corporation, or transfers stock or securities in an exchange described in section 367(a), each partner in the partnership, and not the partnership itself, is treated as owning and as having transferred, or as owning, a proportionate share of the stock or securities. See § 1.367(a)-1(c)(3).

(ii) *Treatment of options.*—For purposes of this paragraph (c), one or more options (or an interest similar to an option) will be treated as exercised and thus will be counted as stock for purposes of determining whether the 50percent threshold is exceeded or whether a control group exists if a principal purpose of the issuance or the acquisition of the option (or other interest) was the avoidance of the general rule contained in section 367(a)(1).

(iii) *U.S. target has a vestigial ownership interest in transferee foreign corporation.*—In cases where, immediately after the transfer, the U.S. target company owns, directly or indirectly (applying the attribution rules of sections 267(c)(1) and (5)), stock of the transferee foreign corporation, that stock will not in any way be taken into account (and, thus, will not be treated as outstanding) in determining whether the 50-percent threshold under paragraph (c)(1)(i) of this section is exceeded or whether a control group under paragraph (c)(1)(ii) of this section exists.

(iv) *Attribution rule.*—Except as otherwise provided in this section, the rules of section 318, as modified by the rules of section 958(b), shall apply for purposes of determining the ownership or receipt of stock, securities or other property under this paragraph (c).

(5) *Definitions.*—(i) *Ownership statement.*—An ownership statement is a statement, signed under penalties of perjury, stating—

(A) The identity and taxpayer identification number, if any, of the person making the statement;

(B) That the person making the statement is not a U.S. person (as defined in paragraph (c)(5)(iv) of this section);

(C) That the person making the statement either—

(*1*) Owns less than 1 percent of the total voting power and total value of a U.S. target company the stock of which is described in Rule 13d-1(d) of Regulation 13D (17 CFR 240.13d-1(d)) (or any rule or regulation to generally the same effect) promulgated by the Securities and Exchange Commission under the Securities and Exchange Act of 1934 (15 USC 78m), and such person did not acquire the stock with a principal purpose to enable the U.S. transferors to satisfy the requirement contained in paragraph (c)(1)(i) of this section; or

(*2*) Is not related to any U.S. person to whom the stock or securities owned by the person making the statement are attributable under the rules of section 958(b), and did not acquire the stock with a principal purpose to enable the U.S. transferors to satisfy the requirement contained in paragraph (c)(1)(i) of this section;

(D) The citizenship, permanent residence, home address, and U.S. address, if any, of the person making the statement; and

(E) The ownership such person has (by voting power and by value) in the U.S. target company prior to the exchange and the amount of stock of the transferee foreign corporation (by voting power and value) received by such person in the exchange.

(ii) *Five-percent transferee shareholder.*—A five-percent transferee shareholder is a person that owns at least five percent of either the total voting power or the total value of the stock of the transferee foreign corporation immediately after the transfer described in section 367(a)(1). For special rules involving cases in which stock is held by a partnership, see paragraph (c)(4)(i) of this section.

(iii) *Five-percent target shareholder and certain other 5-percent shareholders.*—A five-percent target shareholder is a person that owns at least five percent of either the total voting power or the total value of the stock of the U.S. target company immediately prior to the transfer described in section 367(a)(1). If the stock of the U.S. target company (or any company through which stock of the U.S. target company is owned indirectly or constructively) is described in Rule 13d-1(d) of Regulation 13D (17 CFR 240.13d-1(d)) (or any rule or regulation to generally the same effect), promulgated by the Securities and Exchange Commission under the Securities Exchange Act of 1934 (15 USC 78m), then, in the absence of actual knowledge to the contrary, the existence or absence of filings of Schedule 13-D or 13-G (or any similar schedules) may be relied upon for purposes of identifying five-percent target shareholders (or a five-percent shareholder of a corporation which itself is a five-percent shareholder of the U.S. target company). For special rules involving cases in which U.S. target company stock is held by a partnership, see paragraph (c)(4)(i) of this section.

(iv) *U.S. person.*—For purposes of this section, a U.S. person is defined by reference to § 1.367(a)-1(d)(1). For application of the rules of this section to stock or securities owned or transferred by a partnership that is a U.S. person, however, see paragraph (c)(4)(i) of this section.

(v) *U.S. transferor.*—A U.S. transferor is a U.S. person (as defined in paragraph (c)(5)(iv) of this section) that transfers stock or securities of one or more U.S. target companies in exchange for stock of the transferee foreign corporation in an exchange described in section 367.

(vi) *Transferee foreign corporation.*—Except as provided in paragraph (d)(2)(i)(B) of this section, a transferee foreign corporation is the foreign corporation whose stock is received in the exchange by U.S. persons.

(vii) *Qualified subsidiary.*—A qualified subsidiary is a foreign corporation whose stock is at least 80-percent owned (by total voting power and total value), directly or indirectly, by the transferee foreign corporation. However, a corporation will not be treated as a qualified subsidiary if it was affiliated with the U.S. target company (within the meaning of section 1504(a) but without the exceptions under section 1504(b) and substituting "50 percent" for "80 percent" where it appears therein) at any time during the 36-month period prior to the transfer. Nor will a corporation be treated as a qualified subsidiary if it was acquired by the transferee foreign corporation at any time during the 36-month period prior to the transfer for the principal purpose of satisfying the active trade or business test, including the substantiality test.

(viii) *Qualified partnership.*—(A) Except as provided in paragraph (c)(5)(viii)(B) or (C) of this section, a qualified partnership is a partnership in which the transferee foreign corporation—

(*1*) Has active and substantial management functions as a partner with regard to the partnership business; or

(*2*) Has an interest representing a 25 percent or greater interest in the partnership's capital and profits.

(B) A partnership is not a qualified partnership if the U.S. target company or any affiliate of the U.S. target company (within the meaning of section 1504(a) but without the exceptions under section 1504(b) and substituting "50 percent" for "80 percent" where it appears therein) held a 5 percent or greater interest in the partnership's capital and profits at any time during the 36-month period prior to the transfer.

(C) A partnership is not a qualified partnership if the transferee foreign corporation's interest was acquired by that corporation at any time during the 36-month period prior to the transfer for the principal purpose of satisfying the active trade or business test, including the substantiality test.

(6) *Reporting requirements of U.S. target company.*—(i) In order for a U.S. person that transfers stock or securities of a domestic corporation to qualify for the exception provided by this paragraph (c) to the general rule under section 367(a)(1), in cases where 10 percent or more of the total voting power or the total value of the stock of the U.S. target company is transferred by U.S. persons in the transaction, the U.S. target company must comply with the reporting requirements contained in this paragraph (c)(6). The U.S. target company

must attach to its timely filed U.S. income tax return for the taxable year in which the transfer occurs a statement titled "Section 367(a)—Reporting of Cross-Border Transfer Under Reg. § 1.367(a)-3(c)(6)," signed under penalties of perjury by an officer of the corporation to the best of the officer's knowledge and belief, disclosing the following information—

(A) A description of the transaction in which a U.S. person or persons transferred stock or securities in the U.S. target company to the transferee foreign corporation in a transfer otherwise subject to section 367(a)(1);

(B) The amount (specified as to the percentage of the total voting power and the total value) of stock of the transferee foreign corporation received in the transaction, in the aggregate, by persons who transferred stock or securities of the U.S. target company. For additional information that may be required to rebut the ownership presumption of paragraph (c)(2) of this section in cases where more than 50 percent of either the total voting power or the total value of the stock of the transferee foreign corporation is received in the transaction, in the aggregate, by persons who transferred stock or securities of the U.S. target company, see paragraph (c)(7) of this section;

(C) The amount (if any) of transferee foreign corporation stock owned directly or indirectly (applying the attribution rules of sections 267(c)(1) and (5)) immediately after the exchange by the U.S. target company;

(D) A statement that there is no control group within the meaning of paragraph (c)(1)(ii) of this section;

(E) A list of U.S. persons who are officers, directors or five-percent target shareholders and the percentage of the total voting power and the total value of the stock of the transferee foreign corporation owned by such persons both immediately before and immediately after the transaction; and

(F) A statement that includes the following—

(1) A statement that the active trade or business test described in paragraph (c)(3) of this section is satisfied by the transferee foreign corporation and a description of such business;

(2) A statement that on the day of the transaction, there was no intent on the part of the transferors or the transferee foreign corporation (or any qualified subsidiary or any qualified partnership, if relevant) to substantially dispose of or discontinue its active trade or business; and

(3) A statement that the substantiality test described in paragraph (c)(3)(iii) of this section is satisfied, and documentation that such test is satisfied, including the value of the transferee foreign corporation and the value of the U.S. target company on the day of the transfer, and either one of the following—

(i) A statement demonstrating that the value of the transferee foreign corporation 36 months prior to the acquisition, plus the value of any assets described in paragraph (c)(3)(iii)(B) of this section (including stock) acquired by the transferee foreign corporation within the 36-month period, less the amount of any liabilities acquired during that period, equals or exceeds the value of the U.S. target company on the acquisition date; or

(ii) A statement demonstrating that the value of the transferee foreign corporation on the date of the acquisition, reduced by the value of any assets not described in paragraph (c)(3)(iii)(B) of this section (including stock) acquired by the transferee foreign corporation within the 36-month period, equals or exceeds the value of the U.S. target company on the date of the acquisition.

(ii) Except as provided in paragraph (f) of this section, for purposes of this paragraph (c)(6), a U.S. income tax return will be considered timely filed if it is filed on or before the last date prescribed for filing (taking into account any extensions of time therefor) for the taxable year in which the transfer occurs.

(7) *Ownership statements.*—To rebut the ownership presumption of paragraph (c)(2) of this section, the U.S. target company must obtain ownership statements (described in paragraph (c)(5)(i) of this section) from a sufficient number of persons that transfer U.S. target company stock or securities in the transaction that are not U.S. persons to demonstrate that the 50-percent threshold of paragraph (c)(1)(i) of this section is not exceeded. In addition, the U.S. target company must attach to its timely filed U.S. income tax return (as described in paragraph (c)(6)(ii) of this section) for the taxable year in which the transfer occurs a statement, titled "Section 367(a) - Compilation of Ownership Statements under Reg. § 1.367(a)-3(c)," signed under penalties of perjury by an officer of the corporation, disclosing the following information:

(i) The amount (specified as to the percentage of the total voting power and the total value) of stock of the transferee foreign corporation received, in the aggregate, by U.S. transferors;

(ii) The amount (specified as to the percentage of total voting power and total value) of stock of the transferee foreign corporation received, in the aggregate, by foreign persons that filed ownership statements;

(iii) A summary of the information tabulated from the ownership statements, including—

(A) The names of the persons that filed ownership statements stating that they are not U.S. persons;

(B) The countries of residence and citizenship of such persons; and

(C) Each of such person's ownership (by voting power and by value) in the U.S. target company prior to the exchange and the amount of stock of the transferee foreign corporation (by voting power and value) received by such persons in the exchange.

(8) *Certain transfers in connection with performance of services.*—Section 367(a)(1) shall not apply to a domestic corporation's transfer of its own stock or securities in connection with the performance of services, if the transfer is considered to be to a foreign corporation solely by reason of § 1.83-6(d)(1). The transfer may still, however, be reportable under section 6038B. See § 1.6038B-1(b)(2)(i)(A)*(4)* and (b)(2)(i)(B)*(4)*.

(9) *Private letter ruling option.*—The Internal Revenue Service may, in limited circumstances, issue a private letter ruling to permit the taxpayer to qualify for an exception to the general rule under section 367(a)(1) if—

(i) A taxpayer is unable to satisfy all of the requirements of paragraph (c)(3) of this section relating to the active trade or business test of paragraph (c)(1)(iv) of this section, but such taxpayer meets all of the other requirements contained in paragraphs (c)(1)(i) through (c)(1)(iii) of this section, and such taxpayer is substantially in compliance with the rules set forth in paragraph (c)(3) of this section; or

(ii) A taxpayer is unable to satisfy any requirement of paragraph (c)(1) of this section due to the application of paragraph (c)(4)(iv) of this section. Notwithstanding the preceding sentence, in no event will the Internal Revenue Service rule on the issue of whether the principal purpose of an acquisition was to satisfy the active trade or business test, including the substantiality test.

(10) *Examples.*—This paragraph (c) may be illustrated by the following examples:

Example 1. Ownership presumption. (i) FC, a foreign corporation, issues 51 percent of its stock to the shareholders of S, a domestic corporation, in exchange for their S stock, in a transaction described in section 367(a)(1).

(ii) Under paragraph (c)(2) of this section, all shareholders of S who receive stock of FC in the exchange are presumed to be U.S. persons. Unless this ownership presumption is rebutted, the condition set forth in paragraph (c)(1)(i) of this section will not be satisfied, and the exception in paragraph (c)(1) of this section will not be available. As a result, all U.S. persons that transferred S stock will recognize gain on the exchange. To rebut the ownership presumption, S must comply with the reporting requirements contained in paragraph (c)(7) of this section, obtaining ownership statements (described in paragraph (c)(5)(i) of this section) from a sufficient number of non-U.S. persons who received FC stock in the exchange to demonstrate that the amount of FC stock received by U.S. persons in the exchange does not exceed 50 percent.

Example 2. Filing of gain recognition agreement. (i) The facts are the same as in *Example 1*, except that FC issues only 40 percent of its stock to the shareholders of S in the exchange. FC satisfies the active trade or business test of paragraph (c)(1)(iv) of this section. A, a U.S. person, owns 10 percent of S's stock immediately before the transfer. All other shareholders of S own less than five percent of its stock. None of S's officers or directors owns any stock in FC immediately after the transfer. A will own 15 percent of the stock of FC immediately after the transfer, 4 percent received in the exchange, and the balance being stock in FC that A owned prior to and independent of the transaction. No S shareholder besides A owns five percent or more of FC immediately after the transfer. The reporting requirements under paragraph (c)(6) of this section are satisfied.

(ii) The condition set forth in paragraph (c)(1)(i) of this section is satisfied because, even after application of the presumption in paragraph (c)(2) of this section, U.S. transferors could not receive more than 50 percent of FC's stock in the transaction. There is no control group because five-percent target shareholders and officers and directors of S do not, in the aggregate, own more than 50 percent of the stock of FC immediately after the transfer (A, the sole five-percent target shareholder, owns 15 percent of the stock of FC immediately after the transfer, and no officers or directors of S own any stock of

FC immediately after the transfer). Therefore, the condition set forth in paragraph (c)(1)(ii) of this section is satisfied. The facts assume that the condition set forth in paragraph (c)(1)(iv) of this section is satisfied. Thus, U.S. persons that are not five-percent transferee shareholders will not recognize gain on the exchange of S shares for FC shares. A, a five-percent transferee shareholder, will not be required to include in income any gain realized on the exchange in the year of the transfer if he files a 5-year gain recognition agreement (GRA) and complies with section 6038B.

Example 3. Control group. (i) The facts are the same as in *Example 2*, except that B, another U.S. person, is a 5-percent target shareholder, owning 25 percent of S's stock immediately before the transfer. B owns 40 percent of the stock of FC immediately after the transfer, 10 percent received in the exchange, and the balance being stock in FC that B owned prior to and independent of the transaction.

(ii) A control group exists because A and B, each a five-percent target shareholder within the meaning of paragraph (c)(5)(iii) of this section, together own more than 50 percent of FC immediately after the transfer (counting both stock received in the exchange and stock owned prior to and independent of the exchange). As a result, the condition set forth in paragraph (c)(1)(ii) of this section is not satisfied, and all U.S. persons (not merely A and B) who transferred S stock will recognize gain on the exchange.

Example 4. Partnerships. (i) The facts are the same as in *Example 3*, except that B is a partnership (domestic or foreign) that has five equal partners, only two of whom, X and Y, are U.S. persons. Under paragraph (c)(4)(i) of this section, X and Y are treated as the owners and transferors of 5 percent each of the S stock owned and transferred by B and as owners of 8 percent each of the FC stock owned by B immediately after the transfer. U.S. persons that are five-percent target shareholders thus own a total of 31 percent of the stock of FC immediately after the transfer (A's 15 percent, plus X's 8 percent, plus Y's 8 percent).

(ii) Because no control group exists, the condition in paragraph (c)(1)(ii) of this section is satisfied. The conditions in paragraphs (c)(1)(i) and (iv) of this section also are satisfied. Thus, U.S. persons that are not five-percent transferee shareholders will not recognize gain on the exchange of S shares for FC shares. A, X, and Y, each a five-percent transferee shareholder, will not be required to include in income in the year of the transfer any gain realized on the exchange if they file 5-year GRAs and comply with section 6038B.

(11) *Applicability date of this paragraph (c).*—(i) *In general.*—Except as otherwise provided, this paragraph (c) applies to transfers occurring after January 29, 1997. A U.S. person exchanges stock or securities of a corporation (the acquired corporation) for stock or securities of a foreign corporation that controls the acquiring corporation in a reorganization described in either sections 368(a)(1)(A) and (a)(2)(D), or in sections 368(a)(1)(G) and (a)(2)(D). See paragraph (d)(3) *Example 1* of this section for an example of a reorganization described in sections 368(a)(1)(A) and (a)(2)(D) involving domestic acquired and acquiring corporations, and see paragraph (d)(3) *Example 10* of this section for an example involving a domestic acquired corporation and a foreign acquiring corporation.

(ii) *Applicability date of certain provisions of this paragraph (c).*—The first and second sentence of paragraph (c)(3)(iii)(C) of this section apply to transfers completed on or after September 22, 2014. The third sentence of paragraph (c)(3)(iii)(C) of this section applies to transfers completed on or after November 19, 2015. Taxpayers may, however, elect to apply the third sentence of paragraph (c)(3)(iii)(C) of this section to transfers completed on or after September 22, 2014, and before November 19, 2015.

(d) *Indirect stock transfers in certain nonrecognition transfers.*—(1) *In general.*—For purposes of this section, a U.S. person who exchanges, under section 354 (or section 356) stock or securities in a domestic or foreign corporation for stock or securities in a foreign corporation (or in a domestic corporation in control of a foreign acquiring corporation in a triangular section 368(a)(1)(B) reorganization) in connection with a transaction described in paragraphs (d)(1)(i) through (v) of this section (or who is deemed to make such an exchange under paragraph (d)(1)(vi) of this section) shall, except as provided in paragraph (d)(2)(vii) of this section, be treated as having made an indirect transfer of such stock or securities to a foreign corporation that is subject to the rules of this section, including, for example, the requirement, where applicable, that the U.S. transferor enter into a gain recognition agreement to preserve nonrecognition treatment under section 367(a). If the U.S. person exchanges stock or securities of a foreign corporation, see also section 367(b) and the regulations thereunder. For examples of the concurrent application of the indirect stock transfer rules under section 367(a) and the rules of section 367(b), see paragraph (d)(3) *Examples 14* and *15* of this section. For purposes of this paragraph (d), if a corporation acquiring assets in an asset reorganization transfers all or a portion of such assets to a corporation controlled (within the meaning of section 368(c)) by the acquiring corporation as part of the same transaction, the subsequent transfer of assets to the controlled corporation will be referred to as a controlled asset transfer. See section 368(a)(2)(C).

(i) *Mergers described in sections 368(a)(1)(A) and (a)(2)(D) and reorganizations described in sections 368(a)(1)(G) and (a)(2)(D).*—A U.S. person exchanges stock or securities of a corporation (the acquired corporation) for stock or securities of a foreign corporation that controls the acquiring corporation in a reorganization described in either sections 368(a)(1)(A) and (a)(2)(D), or in sections 368(a)(1)(G) and (a)(2)(D). See paragraph (d)(3) *Example 1* of this section for an example of a reorganization described in sections 368(a)(1)(A) and (a)(2)(D) involving domestic acquired and acquiring corporations, and see paragraph (d)(3) *Example 10* of this section for an example involving a domestic acquired corporation and a foreign acquiring corporation.

(ii) *Mergers described in sections 368(a)(1)(A) and (a)(2)(E).*—A U.S. person exchanges stock or securities of a corporation (the acquiring corporation) for stock or securities in a foreign corporation that controls the acquired corporation in a reorganization described in sections 368(a)(1)(A) and (a)(2)(E). See paragraph (d)(3) *Example 2* of this section for an example of a reorganization described in sections 368(a)(1)(A) and (a)(2)(E) involving domestic acquired and acquiring corporations, and see paragraph (d)(3) *Example 11* of this section for an example involving a domestic acquired corporation and a foreign acquiring corporation.

(iii) *Triangular reorganizations described in section 368(a)(1)(B).*—(A) A U.S. person exchanges stock or securities of the acquired corporation for voting stock or securities of a foreign corporation that is in control (as defined in section 368(c)) of the acquiring corporation in a reorganization described in section 368(a)(1)(B). See paragraph (d)(3) *Example 5* of this section.

(B) A U.S. person exchanges stock or securities of the acquired corporation for voting stock or securities of a domestic corporation that is in control (as defined in section 368(c)) of a foreign acquiring corporation in a reorganization described in section 368(a)(1)(B). See paragraph (d)(3) *Example 5A* of this section.

(iv) *Triangular reorganizations described in section 368(a)(1)(C).*—A U.S. person exchanges stock or securities of a corporation (the acquired corporation) for voting stock or securities of a foreign corporation that controls the acquiring corporation in a reorganization described in section 368(a)(1)(C). See, e.g., paragraph (d)(3) *Example 6* of this section (for an example of a triangular section 368(a)(1)(C) reorganization involving domestic acquired and acquiring corporations), and paragraph (d)(3) *Example 8* of this section (for an example involving a domestic acquired corporation and a foreign acquiring corporation). If the acquired corporation is a foreign corporation, see paragraph (d)(3) *Example 14* of this section, and section 367(b) and the regulations thereunder.

(v) *Transfers of assets to subsidiaries in certain section 368(a)(1) reorganizations.*—A U.S. person exchanges stock or securities of a corporation (the acquired corporation) for stock or securities of a foreign acquiring corporation in an asset reorganization (other than a triangular section 368(a)(1)(C) reorganization described in paragraph (d)(1)(iv) of this section, a reorganization described in sections 368(a)(1)(A) and (a)(2)(D) or sections 368(a)(1)(G) and (a)(2)(D) described in paragraph (d)(1)(i) of this section, a reorganization described in sections 368(a)(1)(A) and (a)(2)(E) described in paragraph (d)(1)(ii) of this section, or a same-country section 368(a)(1)(F) reorganization) that is followed by a controlled asset transfer. For purposes of this section, a same-country section 368(a)(1)(F) reorganization is a reorganization described in section 368(a)(1)(F) in which both the acquired corporation and the acquiring corporation are foreign corporations and are created or organized under the laws of the same foreign country. In the case of a transaction described in this paragraph (d)(1)(v) in which some but not all of the assets of the acquired corporation are transferred in a controlled asset transfer, the transaction shall be considered to be an indirect transfer of stock or securities subject to this paragraph (d) only to the extent of the assets so transferred. The remaining assets shall be treated as having been transferred by the acquired corporation in an asset transfer rather than an indirect stock transfer, and, if the acquired corporation is a domestic corporation, such asset transfer shall be subject to the other provisions of section 367, including sections 367(a)(1), (3), and (5), and (d). See paragraph (d)(3) *Examples 6A* and *6B* of this section.

(vi) *Successive transfers of property to which section 351 applies.*—A U.S. person transfers property (other than stock or securities) to a foreign corporation in an exchange described in section 351, and all or a portion of such assets transferred to the foreign corporation by such person are, in connection with the same transaction, transferred to a second corporation that is controlled by the foreign corporation in one or more exchanges described in section 351. For purposes of this paragraph (d)(1) and § 1.367(a)-8, the initial transfer by the U.S. person shall be deemed to be a transfer of stock described in section 354. (Any assets transferred to the foreign corporation that are not transferred by the foreign corporation to a second corporation shall be treated as a transfer of assets subject to the general rules of section 367, including sections 367(a)(1), (3), (5) and (d), and not as an indirect stock transfer under the rules of this paragraph (d).) See, e.g., paragraph (d)(3) *Example 13* and *Example 13A* of this section.

(2) *Special rules for indirect transfers.*—If a U.S. person is considered to make an indirect transfer of stock or securities described in paragraph (d)(1) of this section, the rules of this section and § 1.367(a)-8 shall apply to the transfer. For purposes of applying the rules of this section and § 1.367(a)-8:

(i) *Transferee foreign corporation.*—(A) *General rule.*—Except as provided in paragraph (d)(2)(i)(B) of this section, the transferee foreign corporation shall be the foreign corporation that issues stock or securities to the U.S. person in the exchange.

(B) *Special rule for triangular reorganizations described in paragraph (d)(1)(iii)(B) of this section.*—In the case of a triangular reorganization described in paragraph (d)(1)(iii)(B) of this section, the transferee foreign corporation shall be the foreign acquiring corporation. See paragraph (d)(3) *Example 5A* of this section.

(ii) *Transferred corporation.*—The transferred corporation shall be the acquiring corporation, except as provided in this paragraph (d)(2)(ii). In the case of a triangular section 368(a)(1)(B) reorganization described in paragraph (d)(1)(iii) of this section, the transferred corporation shall be the acquired corporation. In the case of an indirect stock transfer described in paragraph (d)(1)(i), (ii), or (iv) of this section followed by a controlled asset transfer, or an indirect stock transfer described in paragraph (d)(1)(v) of this section, the transferred corporation shall be the controlled corporation to which the assets are transferred. In the case of successive section 351 transfers described in paragraph (d)(1)(vi) of this section, the transferred corporation shall be the corporation to which the assets are transferred in the final section 351 transfer. The transferred property shall be the stock or securities of the transferred corporation, as appropriate under the circumstances.

(iii) *Amount of gain.*—For purposes of determining the amount of gain that a U.S. person is required to include in income as a result of a triggering event, see § 1.367(a)-8(c)(1)(i).

(iv) *Gain recognition agreements involving multiple parties.*—The U.S. person's agreement to recognize gain, as provided in § 1.367(a)-8, shall include appropriate provisions consistent with the principles of § 1.367(a)-8. See *Examples 5* and *5A* of this section and § 1.367(a)-8(j)(9).

(v) *Determination of whether substantially all of the transferred corporation's assets are disposed of.*—For purposes of applying § 1.367(a)-8(j)(2)(i) to determine whether substantially all of the assets of the transferred corporation have been disposed of, the following assets shall be taken into account (but only if such assets are not fully taxable under section 367 in the taxable year that includes the indirect transfer)—

(A) In the case of a reorganization described in paragraph (d)(1)(i) of this section (a reorganization described in sections 368(a)(1)(A) and (a)(2)(D) or sections 368(a)(1)(G) and (a)(2)(D)) or a reorganization described in section (d)(1)(iv) of this section (a triangular section 368(a)(1)(C) reorganization), the assets of the acquired corporation;

(B) In the case of a sections 368(a)(1)(A) and (a)(2)(E) reorganization described in paragraph (d)(1)(ii) of this section, the assets of the acquiring corporation immediately prior to the transaction;

(C) In the case of an asset reorganization followed by a controlled asset transfer, as described in paragraph (d)(1)(v) of this section, the assets of the acquired corporation that are transferred to the corporation controlled by the acquiring corporation;

(D) In the case of a triangular reorganization described in section 368(a)(1)(C) followed by a controlled asset transfer, a reorganization described in sections 368(a)(1)(A) and (a)(2)(D) followed by a controlled asset transfer, or a reorganization described in sections 368(a)(1)(G) and (a)(2)(D) followed by a controlled asset transfer, the assets of the acquired corporation including those transferred to the corporation controlled by the acquiring corporation;

(E) In the case of a reorganization described in sections 368(a)(1)(A) and (a)(2)(E) followed by a controlled asset transfer, the assets of the acquiring corporation including those transferred to the corporation controlled by the acquiring corporation; and

(F) In the case of successive section 351 exchanges described in paragraph (d)(1)(vi) of this section, the assets that are both transferred initially to the foreign corporation, and transferred by the foreign corporation to a second corporation.

(vi) *Coordination between asset transfer rules and indirect stock transfer rules.*—(A) *General rule.*—Except as otherwise provided in this paragraph (d)(2)(vi), if, pursuant to any of the transactions described in paragraph (d)(1) of this section, a U.S. person transfers (or is deemed to transfer) assets to a foreign corporation in an exchange described in section 351 or section 361, the rules of section 367, including sections 367(a)(1), (a)(3), and (a)(5), as well as section 367(d), and the regulations thereunder shall apply prior to the application of the rules of this section.

(B) *Exceptions.*—*(1)* If a transaction is described in paragraph (d)(2)(vi)(A) of this section, section 367(a) and (d) will not apply to the extent a domestic corporation (domestic acquired corporation) transfers assets to a foreign corporation (foreign acquiring corporation) in an asset reorganization, and those assets (re-transferred assets) are transferred to a domestic corporation (domestic controlled corporation) in a controlled asset transfer, provided that each of the following conditions is satisfied:

(i) The domestic controlled corporation's adjusted basis in the re-transferred assets is not greater than the domestic acquired corporation's adjusted basis in those assets. For this purpose, any increase in basis in the re-transferred assets that results because the domestic acquired corporation recognized gain or income with respect to the re-transferred assets in the transaction is not taken into account.

(ii) The domestic acquired corporation includes a statement described in paragraph (d)(2)(vi)(C) of this section with its timely filed U.S. income tax return for the taxable year of the transfer; and

(iii) The requirements of paragraphs (c)(1)(i), (ii), and (iv) and (c)(6) of this section are satisfied with respect to the indirect transfer of stock in the domestic acquired corporation.

(2) Sections 367(a) and (d) shall not apply to transfers described in paragraph (d)(1)(vi) of this section if a U.S. person transfers assets to a foreign corporation in a section 351 exchange, to the extent that such assets are transferred by such foreign corporation to a domestic corporation in another section 351 exchange, but only if the domestic transferee's adjusted basis in the assets is not greater than the adjusted basis that the U.S. person had in such assets. Any increase in adjusted basis in the assets that results because the U.S. person recognized gain or income with respect to such assets in the initial section 351 exchange is not taken into account for purposes of determining whether the domestic transferee's adjusted basis in the assets is not greater than the U.S. person's adjusted basis in such assets. This paragraph (d)(2)(vi)(B)*(2)* will not, however, apply to an exchange described in section 351 that is also an exchange described in section 361(a) or (b). An exchange described in section 351 that is also an exchange described in section 361(a) or (b) is only eligible for the exception in paragraph (d)(2)(vi)(B)*(1)* of this section.

(C) *Required statement.*—The statement required by paragraph (d)(2)(vi)(B)*(1)(ii)* of this section shall be entitled "Required Statement under § 1.367(a)-3(d) for Assets Transferred to a Domestic Corporation" and shall be signed under penalties of perjury by an authorized officer of the domestic acquired corporation and by an authorized officer of the foreign acquiring corporation. The required statement shall contain a certification that, if the foreign acquiring corporation disposes of any stock of the domestic controlled corporation in a transaction described in paragraph (d)(2)(vi)(D) of this section, the domestic acquired corporation shall recognize gain as described in paragraph (d)(2)(vi)(E) of this section. The domestic acquired corporation (or the foreign acquiring corporation on behalf of the domestic acquired corporation) shall file a U.S. income tax return (or an amended U.S. tax return, as the case may be) for the year of the transfer reporting such gain.

(D) *Gain recognition transaction.—(1)* A transaction described in this paragraph (d)(2)(vi)(D) is one where a principal purpose of the transfer by the domestic acquired corporation is the avoidance of U.S. tax that would have been imposed on the domestic acquired corporation on the disposition of the re-transferred assets. A transfer may have a principal purpose of tax avoidance even though the tax avoidance purpose is outweighed by other purposes when taken together.

(2) For purposes of paragraph (d)(2)(vi)(D)*(1)* of this section, a transaction is deemed to have a principal purpose of tax avoidance if the foreign acquiring corporation disposes of any stock of the domestic controlled corporation (whether in a recognition or non-recognition transaction) within 2 years of the transfer described in paragraph (d)(2)(vi)(A) of this section. The rule in this paragraph (d)(2)(vi)(D)*(2)* shall not apply if the domestic acquired corporation (or the foreign acquiring corporation on behalf of the domestic acquired corporation) demonstrates to the satisfaction of the Commissioner that the avoidance of U.S. tax was not a principal purpose of the transaction. For this purpose, a disposition by the foreign acquiring corporation of stock of the domestic controlled corporation more than 5 years after completion of the transfer described in paragraph (d)(2)(vi)(A) of this section is deemed to not have a principal purpose of tax avoidance.

(E) *Amount of gain recognized and other matters.—(1)* In the case of a transaction described in paragraph (d)(2)(vi)(D) of this section, solely for purposes of this paragraph (d)(2)(vi)(E), the domestic acquired corporation shall be treated as if, immediately prior to the transfer described in paragraph (d)(2)(vi)(A) of this section, it transferred the re-transferred assets, including any intangible assets, directly to a domestic corporation in exchange for stock of such domestic corporation in a transaction that is treated as a section 351 exchange, and immediately sold such stock to an unrelated party for its fair market value in a sale in which it shall recognize gain, if any (but not loss). Any gain recognized by the domestic acquired corporation pursuant to this paragraph (d)(2)(vi)(E) will increase the basis that the foreign acquiring corporation has in the stock of the domestic controlled corporation immediately before the transaction described in paragraph (d)(2)(vi)(D) of this section, but will not increase the basis of the re-transferred assets held by the domestic controlled corporation. Section 1.367(d)-1T(g)(6) shall not apply with respect to any intangible property included in the re-transferred assets described in this paragraph.

(2) If additional tax is required to be paid as a result of a transaction described in paragraph (d)(2)(vi)(D) of this section, then interest must be paid on that amount at rates determined under section 6621 with respect to the period between the date prescribed for filing the domestic acquired corporation's income tax return for the year of the transfer and the date on which the additional tax for that year is paid.

(F) *Examples.*—For illustrations of the rules in paragraph (d)(2)(vi) of this section, see paragraph (d)(3) *Examples 6B, 6C, 9,* and *13A* of this section.

(vii) *Change in status of a domestic acquired corporation to a foreign corporation.*—(A) A U.S. person that exchanges stock or securities of a domestic corporation for stock or securities of a foreign corporation under section 354 (or section 356) will be treated for purposes of this section as having made an indirect stock transfer of the stock or securities of a foreign corporation (and not of a domestic corporation) to a foreign corporation under paragraph (b) of this section (but not paragraph (c) of this section), if the acquired domestic corporation is a subsidiary member (within the meaning of § 1.1502-1(c)) of a consolidated group (within the meaning of § 1.1502-1(h)) immediately before the transaction, and if the transaction is either of the following:

(1) Described in paragraph (d)(1)(i) or (iv) of this section, but only if the acquiring corporation is foreign. See paragraph (d)(3) *Examples 8, 9, 10* and *12* of this section.

(2) Described in paragraph (d)(1)(v) of this section, but only to the extent the controlled asset transfer is to a foreign corporation. See paragraph (d)(3) *Example 6A* of this section.

(B) The rules of paragraph (d)(2)(vii)(A) of this section will not apply to the extent assets transferred to the foreign acquiring corporation in a transaction described in paragraph (d)(2)(vii)(A)*(1)* of this section, or assets transferred to a foreign corporation in a controlled asset transfer in a transaction described in paragraph (d)(2)(vii)(A)*(2)* of this section, are retransferred to a domestic controlled corporation in one or more successive transfers as part of the same transaction. See paragraph (d)(3) *Example 9* of this section.

(3) *Examples.*—The rules of this paragraph (d) and § 1.367(a)-8 are illustrated by the following examples. For purposes of these examples, assume section 7874 does not apply.

Example 1. Section 368(a)(1)(A)/(a)(2)(D) reorganization—(i) *Facts.* F, a foreign corporation, owns all the stock of Newco, a domestic corporation. A, a domestic corporation, owns all of the stock of W, also a domestic corporation. A and W file a consolidated Federal income tax return. A does not own any stock in F (applying the attribution rules of section 318, as modified by section 958(b)). In a reorganization described in sections 368(a)(1)(A) and (a)(2)(D), Newco acquires all of the assets of W, and A receives 40% of the stock of F in an exchange described in section 354.

(ii) *Result.* Pursuant to paragraph (d)(1)(i) of this section, the reorganization is subject to the indirect stock transfer rules. F is treated as the transferee foreign corporation, and Newco is treated as the transferred corporation. Provided that the requirements of paragraph (c)(1) of this section are satisfied, including the requirement that A enter into a five-year gain recognition agreement as described in § 1.367(a)-8, A's exchange of W stock for F stock under section 354 will not be subject to section 367(a)(1). If F disposes (within the meaning of § 1.367(a)-8(j)(1)) of all (or a portion) of Newco's stock within the five-year term of the agreement (and A has not made a valid election under § 1.367(a)-8(c)(2)(vi)), A is required to file an amended return for the year of the transfer and include in income, with interest, the gain realized but not recognized on the initial section 354 exchange. If A has made a valid election under § 1.367(a)-8(c)(2)(vi) to include the amount subject to the gain recognition agreement in the year of the triggering event, A would instead include the gain on its tax return for the taxable year that includes the triggering event, together with interest.

Example 1A. Transferor is a subsidiary in consolidated group—(i) *Facts.* The facts are the same as in *Example 1,* except that A is owned by P, a domestic corporation, and for the taxable year in which the transaction occurred, P, A and W filed a consolidated Federal income tax return.

(ii) *Result.* Even though A is the U.S. transferor, P is required under § 1.367(a)-8(d)(3) and (e)(1)(i) to enter into the gain recognition agreement and comply with the requirements under § 1.367(a)-8. If A leaves the P group, the gain recognition agreement would be triggered pursuant to § 1.367(a)-8(j)(5), unless the exception provided under § 1.367(a)-8(k)(10) applies.

Example 2. Section 368(a)(1)(A)/(a)(2)(E) reorganization—(i) *Facts.* The facts are the same as in *Example 1,* except that Newco merges into W and Newco receives stock of W which it distributes to F in a reorganization described in sections 368(a)(1)(A) and (a)(2)(E). Pursuant to the reorganization, A receives 40 percent of the stock of F in an exchange described in section 354.

(ii) *Result.* The consequences of the transfer are similar to those described in *Example 1.* Pursuant to paragraph (d)(1)(ii) of this section, A is considered to have transferred its W stock to F pursuant to the indirect stock transfer rules. F is treated as the transferee foreign corporation, and W is treated as the transferred corporation. Provided that the requirements of paragraph (c)(1) of this section are satisfied, including the requirement that A enter into a five-year gain recognition agreement as described in § 1.367(a)-8, A's exchange of W stock for F stock under section 354 will not be subject to section 367(a)(1).

Example 3. Taxable transaction pursuant to indirect stock transfer rules—(i) *Facts.* The facts are the same as in *Example 1,* except that A receives 55 percent of either the total voting power or the total value of the stock of F in the transaction.

(ii) *Result.* A is required to include in income in the year of the exchange the amount of gain realized on such exchange. See paragraph (c)(1)(i) of this section. If A fails to include the income on its timely-filed return, A will also be liable for the penalty under section 6038B (together with interest and other applicable penalties) unless A's failure to include the income is due to reasonable cause and not willful neglect. See § 1.6038B-1(f).

Example 4. Disposition by U.S. transferred corporation of substantially all of its assets—(i) *Facts.* The facts are the same as in *Example 1,* except that, during the third year of the gain recognition agreement, Newco disposes of substantially all (as described in § 1.367(a)-8(j)(2)(i)) of the assets described in paragraph (d)(2)(v)(A) of this section for cash and recognizes currently all of the gain realized on the disposition.

(ii) *Result.* Under § 1.367(a)-8(j)(2), the gain recognition agreement is generally triggered when the transferred corporation disposes of substantially all of its assets. However, under the special rule contained in § 1.367(a)-8(o)(4), because A owned an amount of stock in W described in section 1504(a)(2) immediately before the transaction, and Newco, the transferred corporation, is a domestic corporation, the gain recognition agreement is terminated and has no further effect.

Example 5. Triangular section 368(a)(1)(B) reorganization—(i) *Facts.* F, a foreign corporation, owns all the stock of S, a domestic corporation. U, a domestic corporation, owns all of the stock of Y, also a domestic corporation. U does not own any of the stock of F (applying the attribution rules of section 318, as modified by section 958(b)). In a triangular reorganization described in section 368(a)(1)(B) and paragraph (d)(1)(iii)(A) of this section, S acquires all the stock of Y, and U receives 10% of the voting stock of F.

(ii) *Result.* U's exchange of Y stock for F stock will not be subject to section 367(a)(1), provided that all of the requirements of paragraph (c)(1) are satisfied, including the requirement that U enter into a five-year gain recognition agreement. For purposes of this section, F is treated as the transferee foreign corporation and Y is treated as the transferred corporation. See paragraphs (d)(2)(i) and (ii) of this section. Under § 1.367(a)-8(j)(9), the gain recognition agreement would be triggered if F sold all or a portion of the stock of S.

Example 5A. Triangular section 368(a)(1)(B) reorganization—(i) *Facts.* The facts are the same as in *Example 5*, except that F is a domestic corporation and S is a foreign corporation.

(ii) *Result.* U's exchange of Y stock for stock of F, a domestic corporation in control of S, the foreign acquiring corporation, is treated as an indirect transfer of Y stock to a foreign corporation under paragraph (d)(1)(iii)(B) of this section. U's exchange of Y stock for F stock will not be subject to section 367(a)(1) provided that all of the requirements of paragraph (c)(1) of this section are satisfied, including the requirement that U enter into a five-year gain recognition agreement. In satisfying the 50 percent or less ownership requirements of paragraphs (c)(1)(i) and (ii) of this section, U's indirect ownership of S stock (through its direct ownership of F) will determine whether the requirement of paragraph (c)(1)(i) of this section is satisfied and will be taken into account in determining whether the requirement of paragraph (c)(1)(ii) of this section is satisfied. See paragraph (c)(4)(iv) of this section. For purposes of this section, S is treated as the transferee foreign corporation (see paragraph (d)(2)(i)(B) of this section). If Y sold substantially all of its assets (within the meaning of section 368(a)(1)(C)), the gain recognition agreement would be terminated because U owned an amount of stock in Y described in section 1504(a)(2) immediately before the transaction and Y is a domestic corporation. See § 1.367(a)-8(o)(4).

Example 6. Triangular section 368(a)(1)(C) reorganization—(i) *Facts.* F, a foreign corporation, owns all of the stock of R, a domestic corporation that operates an historical business. V, a domestic corporation, owns all of the stock of Z, also a domestic corporation. V does not own any of the stock of F (applying the attribution rules of section 318 as modified by section 958(b)). In a triangular reorganization described in section 368(a)(1)(C) (and paragraph (d)(1)(iv) of this section), R acquires all of the assets of Z, and V receives 30% of the voting stock of F.

(ii) *Result.* The consequences of the transfer are similar to those described in *Example 1*; V is required to enter into a 5-year gain recognition agreement under § 1.367(a)-8 to secure nonrecognition treatment under section 367(a). Under paragraphs (d)(2)(i) and (ii) of this section, F is treated as the transferee foreign corporation and R is treated as the transferred corporation. In determining whether, in a later transaction, R has disposed of substantially all of its assets under § 1.367(a)-8(j)(2)(i), see paragraph (d)(2)(v)(A) of this section.

Example 6A. Section 368(a)(1)(C) reorganization followed by a controlled asset transfer—(i) *Facts.* The facts are the same as in *Example 6*, except that the transaction is structured as a section 368(a)(1)(C) reorganization with Z transferring its assets to F, followed by a controlled asset transfer, and R is a foreign corporation. The following additional facts are present. Z has 3 businesses: Business A with a basis of $10 and a value of $50, Business B with a basis of $10 and a value of $40, and Business C with a basis of $10 and a value of $30. V and Z file a consolidated Federal income tax return and V has a basis of $30 in the Z stock, which has a value of $120. Assume that Businesses A and B consist solely of assets that will satisfy the section 367(a)(3) active trade or business exception; none of Business C's assets will satisfy the exception. Z transfers all 3 businesses to F in exchange for 30 percent of the F stock, which Z distributes to V pursuant to a section 368(a)(1)(C) reorganization. F then contributes Businesses B and C to R in a controlled asset transfer.

(ii) *Result.* The transfer of the Business A assets by Z to F does not constitute an indirect stock transfer under paragraph (d) of this section, and, subject to the conditions and requirements of section 367(a)(5) and § 1.367(a)-7(c), the Business A assets qualify for the section 367(a)(3) active trade or business exception and are not subject to section 367(a)(1). The transfer of the Business B and C assets by Z to F must first be tested under sections 367(a)(1), (a)(3), and (a)(5). Z recognizes $20 of gain on the outbound transfer of the Business C assets, as those assets do not qualify for an exception to section 367(a)(1). Subject to the conditions and requirements of section 367(a)(5) and § 1.367(a)-7(c), the Business B assets qualify for the active trade or business exception under section 367(a)(3). Pursuant to paragraphs (d)(1) and (d)(2)(vii)(A)(2) of this section, V is deemed to transfer the stock of a foreign corporation to F in a section 354 exchange subject to the rules of paragraphs (b) and (d) of this section. V must enter into the gain recognition agreement in the amount of $30 to preserve Z's nonrecognition treatment with respect to its transfer of Business B assets. Under paragraphs (d)(2)(i) and (d)(2)(ii) of this section, F is the transferee foreign corporation and R is the transferred corporation.

Example 6B. Section 368(a)(1)(C) reorganization followed by a controlled asset transfer to a domestic controlled corporation—(i) *Facts.* The facts are the same as in paragraph (d)(3), *Example 6A*, of this section, except that R is a domestic corporation.

(ii) *Result.* As in paragraph (d)(3), *Example 6A*, of this section, the outbound transfer of the Business A assets to F is not affected by the rules of § 1.367-3(d) and is subject to the general rules under section 367. Subject to the conditions and requirements of section 367(a)(5) and § 1.367(a)-7(c), the Business A assets qualify for the section 367(a)(3) active trade or business exception and are not subject to section 367(a)(1). The Business B and C assets are part of an indirect stock transfer under § 1.367-3(d), but must first be tested under section 367(a) and (d). The Business B assets qualify for the active trade or business exception under section 367(a)(3); the Business C assets do not. However, pursuant to paragraph (d)(2)(vi)(B)(*1*) of this section, the Business B and C assets are not subject to section 367(a) or (d), provided that the basis of the Business B and C assets in the hands of R is not greater than the basis of the assets in the hands of Z, the requirements of paragraphs (c)(1)(i), (ii), and (iv) and (c)(6) of this section are satisfied, and Z attaches a statement described in paragraphs (d)(2)(vi)(C) of this section to its U.S. income tax return for the taxable year of the transfer. V also is deemed to make an indirect transfer of Z stock under the rules of paragraph (d) of this section to the extent the assets are transferred to R. To preserve nonrecognition treatment, and assuming the other requirements of paragraph (c) of this section are satisfied, V must enter into a gain recognition agreement in the amount of $50, which equals the aggregate gain in the Business B and C assets, because the transfer of those assets by Z was not taxable under section 367(a)(1) and constitute an indirect stock transfer.

Example 6C. Section 368(a)(1)(C) reorganization followed by a controlled asset transfer to a domestic controlled corporation—(i) *Facts.* The facts are the same as in paragraph (d)(3), *Example 6B*, of this section, except that Z is owned by U.S. individuals, none of whom qualify as five-percent target shareholders with respect to Z within the meaning of paragraph (c)(5)(iii) of this section. The following additional facts are present. No U.S. persons that are either officers or directors of Z own any stock of F immediately after the transfer. F is engaged in an active trade or business outside the United States that satisfies the test set forth in paragraph (c)(3) of this section.

(ii) *Result.* The Business A assets transferred to F are not retransferred to R and therefore Z's transfer of these assets is not subject to the rules of paragraph (d) of this section. However, gain must be recognized on the transfer of those assets under section 367(a)(1) because the section 367(a)(3) active trade or business exception is inapplicable pursuant to section 367(a)(5) and § 1.367(a)-7(b). The Business B and C assets are part of an indirect stock transfer under paragraph (d) of this section, but must first be tested with respect to Z under section 367(a) and (d), as provided in paragraph (d)(2)(vi) of this section. The transfer of the Business B assets (which otherwise would satisfy the section 367(a)(3) active trade or business exception) generally is subject to section 367(a)(1) pursuant to section 367(a)(5) and § 1.367(a)-7(b). The transfer of the Business C assets generally is subject to section 367(a)(1) because these assets do not qualify for the active trade or business exception under section 367(a)(3). However, pursuant to paragraph (d)(2)(vi)(B) of this section, the transfer of the Business B and C assets is not subject to sections 367(a)(1) and (d), provided the basis of the Business B and C assets in the hands of R is no greater than the basis in the hands of Z and certain other requirements are satisfied. Z may avoid immediate gain recognition under section 367(a) and (d) on the transfers of the Business B and Business C assets to F if, pursuant to paragraph (d)(2)(vi)(B) of this section, the indirect transfer of Z stock satisfies the requirements of paragraphs (c)(1)(i), (ii), and (iv) and (c)(6) of this section, and Z attaches a statement described in paragraph (d)(2)(vi)(C) of this section to its U.S. income tax return for the taxable year of the transfer. In general, the statement must contain a certification that, if F disposes of the stock of R (in a recognition or nonrecognition transaction) and a principal purpose of the transfer is the avoidance of U.S. tax that would have been imposed on Z on the disposition of the Business B and C assets transferred to R, then Z (or F on behalf of Z) will file a return (or amended return as the case may be) recognizing gain ($50), as if, immediately prior to the reorganization, Z transferred the Business B and C assets to a domestic corporation in exchange for stock in a transaction treated as a section 351 exchange and immediately sold such stock to an unrelated party for its fair market value. A transaction is deemed to have a principal purpose of U.S. tax avoidance if F disposes of R stock within two years of the transfer, unless Z (or F on behalf of Z) can rebut the presumption to the satisfaction of the Commissioner. See paragraph (d)(2)(vi)(D)(2) of this section. With respect to the indirect transfer of Z stock, assume the requirements of paragraphs (c)(1)(i), (ii), and (iv) of this section are satisfied. Thus, assuming Z attaches the statement described in paragraph (d)(2)(vi)(C) of this section to its U.S. income tax return and satisfies the reporting requirements of paragraph (c)(6) of this section, the transfer of Business B and C assets is not subject to immediate gain recognition under section 367(a) or (d).

Example 7. Triangular section 368(a)(1)(C) reorganization followed by 351 exchange—(i) *Facts*. The facts are the same as in *Example 6*, except that, during the fourth year of the gain recognition agreement, R transfers substantially all of the assets received from Z to K, a wholly-owned domestic subsidiary of R, in an exchange described in section 351.

(ii) *Result*. The disposition by R, the transferred corporation, of substantially all of its assets would terminate the gain recognition agreement if the assets were disposed of in a taxable transaction because V owned an amount of stock in Z described in section 1504(a)(2) immediately before the transaction, and R is a domestic corporation. See § 1.367(a)-8(o)(4). Because the assets were transferred in an exchange to which section 351 applies, such transfer does not trigger the gain recognition agreement if V complies with the requirements contained in § 1.367(a)-8(k)(4). See also paragraph (d)(2)(iv) of this section. To determine whether substantially all of the assets are disposed of, any assets of Z that were transferred by Z to R and then contributed by R to K are taken into account.

Example 7A. Triangular section 368(a)(1)(C) reorganization followed by section 351 exchange with foreign transferee—(i) *Facts*. The facts are the same as in *Example 7* except that K is a foreign corporation.

(ii) *Result*. This transfer of assets by R to K must be analyzed to determine its effect upon the gain recognition agreement, and such transfer is also an outbound transfer of assets that is taxable under section 367(a)(1) unless the active trade or business exception under section 367(a)(3) applies. If the transfer is fully taxable under section 367(a)(1), the transfer is treated as if the transferred company, R, sold substantially all of its assets. Thus, the gain recognition agreement would terminate because V owned an amount of stock in Z described in section 1504(a)(2) immediately before the transaction, and R is a domestic corporation. See § 1.367(a)-8(o)(4). If each asset transferred qualifies for nonrecognition treatment under section 367(a)(3) and the regulations thereunder (which require, under § 1.367(a)-2(a)(2)(iii), the transferor to comply with the reporting requirements under section 6038B), the result is the same as in *Example 7*. If a portion of the assets transferred qualify for nonrecognition treatment under section 367(a)(3) and a portion are taxable under section 367(a)(1) (but such portion does not result in the disposition of substantially all of the assets), the gain recognition agreement will not be triggered if such information is reported as required under § 1.367(a)-8(g) and V satisfies the requirements contained in § 1.367(a)-8(k)(4).

Example 8. Concurrent application of asset transfer and indirect stock transfer rules in consolidated return setting—(i) *Facts*. Assume the same facts as in *Example 6*, except that R is a foreign corporation and V and Z file a consolidated return for Federal income tax purposes. The properties of Z consist of Business A assets, with an adjusted basis of $50 and fair market value of $90, and Business B assets, with an adjusted basis of $50 and a fair market value of $110. Assume that the Business A assets do not qualify for the active trade or business exception under section 367(a)(3), but that the Business B assets do qualify for the exception. V's basis in the Z stock is $100, and the value of such stock is $200.

(ii) *Result*. Under paragraph (d)(2)(vi), the assets of Businesses A and B that are transferred to R must be tested under sections 367(a)(3) and (a)(5) prior to consideration of the indirect stock transfer rules of this paragraph (d). Thus, Z must recognize $40 of income under section 367(a)(1) on the outbound transfer of Business A assets. Subject to the conditions and requirements of section 367(a)(5) and § 1.367(a)-7(c), the Business B assets qualify for the active trade or business exception under section 367(a)(3). Under § 1.1502-32, because V and Z file a consolidated return, V's basis in its Z stock increases from $100 to $140 as a result of Z's $40 gain. Pursuant to paragraphs (d)(1) and (d)(2)(vii)(A)(*1*) of this section, V is deemed to transfer the stock of a foreign corporation to F in a section 354 exchange subject to the rules of paragraphs (b) and (d) of this section, and therefore must enter into a gain recognition agreement in the amount of $60 (the gain realized but not recognized by V in the stock of Z after the $40 basis adjustment). If F sells a portion of its stock in R during the term of the agreement, V will be required to recognize a portion of the $60 gain subject to the agreement. To determine whether R disposes of substantially all of its assets (under § 1.367(a)-8(j)(2)(i)), only the Business B assets will be considered (because the transfer of the Business A assets was taxable to Z under section 367). See paragraph (d)(2)(v)(A) of this section.

Example 8A. Concurrent application without consolidated returns—(i) *Facts*. The facts are the same as in *Example 8*, except that V and Z do not file consolidated income tax returns.

(ii) *Result*. Z would still recognize $40 of gain on the transfer of its Business A assets, and the Business B assets would still qualify for the active trade or business exception under section 367(a)(3). However, V's basis in its stock of Z would not be increased by the amount of Z's gain. V's indirect transfer of stock will be taxable unless V enters into a gain recognition agreement (as described in § 1.367(a)-8) for the $100 of gain realized but not recognized with respect to the stock of Z.

Example 8B. Concurrent application with individual U.S. shareholder—(i) *Facts*. The facts are the same as in *Example 8*, except that V is an individual U.S. citizen.

(ii) *Result*. Under section 367(a)(5) and § 1.367(a)-7(b), the active trade or business exception under section 367(a)(3) does not apply to Z's transfer of assets to R. Thus, Z's transfer of assets to R would be fully taxable under section 367(a)(1). Z would recognize $100 of income. V's basis in its stock of Z is not increased by this amount. V is taxable with respect to its indirect transfer of its Z stock unless V enters into a gain recognition agreement in the amount of the $100, the gain realized but not recognized with respect to its Z stock.

Example 8C. Concurrent application with nonresident alien shareholder—(i) *Facts*. The facts are the same as in *Example 8*, except that V is a nonresident alien.

(ii) *Result*. Under section 367(a)(5) and § 1.367(a)-7(b), the active trade or business exception under section 367(a)(3) does not apply to Z's transfer of assets to R. Thus, Z has $100 of gain with respect to the Business A and B assets. Because V is a nonresident alien, however, V is not subject to section 367(a) with respect to its indirect transfer of Z stock.

Example 9. Indirect stock transfer by reason of a controlled asset transfer—(i) *Facts*. The facts are the same as in paragraph (d)(3), *Example 8*, of this section, except that R transfers the Business A assets to M, a wholly owned domestic subsidiary of R, in a controlled asset transfer. In addition, V's basis in its Z stock is $90.

(ii) *Result*. Pursuant to paragraph (d)(2)(vi)(B) of this section, sections 367(a) and (d) do not apply to Z's transfer of the Business A assets to R if M's basis in the Business A assets is not greater than the basis of the assets in the hands of Z, the requirements of paragraphs (c)(1)(i), (ii), and (iv) and (c)(6) of this section are satisfied, and Z includes a statement described in paragraph (d)(2)(vi)(C) of this section with its U.S. income tax return for the taxable year of the transfer. Subject to the conditions and requirements of section 367(a)(5) and § 1.367(a)-7(c), Z's transfer of the Business B assets to R (which are not re-transferred to M) qualifies for the active trade or business exception under section 367(a)(3). Pursuant to paragraphs (d)(1) and (d)(2)(vii)(A)(*1*) of this section, V is generally deemed to transfer the stock of a foreign corporation to F in a section 354 exchange subject to the rules of paragraphs (b) and (d) of this section, including the requirement that V enter into a gain recognition agreement and comply with the requirements of § 1.367(a)-8. However, pursuant to paragraph (d)(2)(vii)(B) of this section, paragraph (d)(2)(vii)(A) of this section does not apply to the extent of the transfer of business A assets by R to M, a domestic corporation. As a result, to the extent of the business A assets transferred by R to M, V is deemed to transfer the stock of Z (a domestic corporation) to F in a section 354 exchange subject to the rules of paragraphs (c) and (d) of this section. Thus, with respect to V's indirect transfer of stock of a domestic corporation to F, such transfer is not subject to gain recognition under section 367(a)(1) if the requirements of paragraph (c) of this section are satisfied, including the requirement that V enter into a gain recognition agreement (separate from the gain recognition agreement described above with respect to the deemed transfer of stock of a foreign corporation to F) and comply with the requirements of § 1.367(a)-8. Under paragraphs (d)(2)(i) and (ii) of this section, the transferee foreign corporation is F and the transferred corporation is R (with respect to the transfer of stock of a foreign corporation) and M (with respect to the transfer of stock of a domestic corporation). Pursuant to paragraph (d)(2)(iv) of this section, a disposition by F of the stock of R would trigger both gain recognition agreements. In addition, a disposition by R of the stock of M would trigger the gain recognition agreement filed with respect to the transfer of the stock of a domestic corporation. To determine whether there is a triggering event under § 1.367(a)-8(j)(2)(i) for the gain recognition agreement filed with respect to the transfer of stock of the domestic corporation, the Business A assets in M must be considered. To determine whether there is such a triggering event for the gain recognition agreement filed with respect to the transfer of stock of the foreign corporation, the Business B assets in R must be considered.

Example 10. Concurrent application of asset transfer and indirect stock transfer rules in section 368(a)(1)(A)/(a)(2)(D) reorganization—(i) *Facts*. The facts are the same as in *Example 8*, except that R acquires all of the assets of Z in a reorganization described in sections 368(a)(1)(A) and (a)(2)(D). Pursuant to the reorganization, V receives 30 percent of the stock of F in a section 354 exchange.

(ii) *Result*. The consequences of the transaction are similar to those in *Example 8*. The assets of Businesses A and B that are transferred to R must be tested under section 367(a) and (d) prior to the consideration of the indirect stock transfer rules of this paragraph (d). Subject to the conditions and requirements of section 367(a)(5) and § 1.367(a)-7(c), the Business B assets qualify for the active trade or business exception under section 367(a)(3). Because the Business A assets do not qualify for the exception, Z must recognize $40 of gain under section 367(a) on the transfer of Business A assets to R. Further, because V and Z file a consolidated return, V's basis in the stock of Z is increased from $100 to $140 as a result of Z's $40 gain. Pursuant to paragraphs (d)(1) and (d)(2)(vii)(A)(*1*) of this section, V is deemed to transfer the stock of a foreign corporation to F in a section 354 exchange subject to the rules of paragraph (b) and (d) of this section. V's indirect transfer of foreign stock will be taxable under section 367(a) unless V enters into a gain recognition agreement in the amount of $60 ($200 value of Z stock less $140 adjusted basis).

Example 11. Concurrent application of section 367(a) and (b) in section 368(a)(1)(A)/(a)(2)(E) reorganization—(i) *Facts*. F, a foreign corporation, owns all the stock of D, a domestic corporation. V, a domestic corporation, owns all the stock of Z, a foreign corporation. V has a basis of $100 in the stock of Z which has a fair market value of $200. D is an operating corporation with assets valued at $100 with a basis of $60. In a reorganization described in sections 368(a)(1)(A) and (a)(2)(E), D merges into Z, and V exchanges its Z stock for 55 percent of the outstanding F stock.

(ii) *Result*. Under paragraph (d)(1)(ii) of this section, V is treated as indirectly transferring Z stock to F. V must recognize gain on its indirect transfer of Z stock to F under section 367(a) (and section 1248 will be applicable) if V does not enter into a gain recognition agreement with respect to the indirect stock transfer in accordance with § 1.367(a)-8. Under paragraph (b)(2) of this section, if V enters into a gain recognition agreement with respect to the indirect stock transfer, the exchange will be subject to the provisions of section 367(b) and the regulations pursuant to such section as well as section 367(a). Under § 1.367(b)-4(b), however, no income inclusion is required because, immediately after the exchange, F and Z are controlled foreign corporations with respect to which V is a section 1248 shareholder. Under paragraphs (d)(2)(i) and (d)(2)(ii) of this section, the transferee foreign corporation is F, and the transferred corporation is Z (the acquiring corporation). If F disposes (within the meaning of § 1.367(a)-8(j)(1)) of all (or a portion) of Z stock within the term of the gain recognition agreement, V must either file an amended return for the year of the indirect stock transfer and include in income, with interest, the gain realized but not recognized on the initial exchange or if a valid election under § 1.367(a)-8(c)(2)(vi) was made, currently recognize the gain and pay the related interest. Under paragraph (d)(2)(v)(B) of this section, to determine whether, for purposes of the gain recognition agreement, Z (the transferred corporation) disposes of substantially all of its assets, only the assets held by Z immediately before the transaction are taken into account. Because D is wholly owned by F, a foreign corporation, the control requirement of section 367(a)(5) and § 1.367(a)-7(c)(1) cannot be satisfied. Therefore, section 367(a)(5) and § 1.367(a)-7(b) preclude the application of the active trade or business exception under section 367(a)(3) to any property transferred by D to Z. Thus, under section 367(a)(1), D must recognize the gross amount of gain in each asset transferred to Z, or $40.

Example 12. Concurrent application of direct and indirect stock transfer rules—(i) *Facts*. F, a foreign corporation, owns all of the stock of O, also a foreign corporation. D, a domestic corporation, owns all of the stock of E, also a domestic corporation, which owns all of the stock of N, also a domestic corporation. Prior to the transactions described in this *Example 12*, D, E and N filed a consolidated income tax return. D has a basis of $100 in the stock of E, which has a fair market value of $160. The N stock has a fair market value of $100, and E has a basis of $60 in such stock. In addition to the stock of N, E owns the assets of Business X. The assets of Business X have a fair market value of $60, and E has a basis of $50 in such assets. Assume that the Business X assets qualify for nonrecognition treatment under section 367(a)(3). D does not own any stock in F (applying the attribution rules of section 318 as modified by section 958(b)). In a triangular reorganization described in section 368(a)(1)(C) and paragraph (d)(1)(iv) of this section, O acquires all of the assets of E, and D exchanges its stock in E for 40% of the voting stock of F.

(ii) *Result*. E's transfer of its assets, including the N stock, must be tested under the general rules of section 367(a) before consideration of D's indirect transfer of the stock of E. Subject to the conditions and requirements of section 367(a)(5) and § 1.367(a)-7(c), the active trade or business exception under section 367(a)(3) applies to E's transfer of Business X assets. E's transfer of its N stock could qualify for nonrecognition treatment if D satisfies the requirements in § 1.367(a)-3(e)(3). O is the transferee foreign corporation; N is the transferred corporation. Pursuant to paragraphs (d)(1) and (d)(2)(vii)(A)(*1*) of this section, D is deemed to transfer the stock of a foreign corporation to F in a section 354 exchange subject to the rules of paragraphs (b) and (d) of this section, and therefore may enter into a gain recognition agreement for such indirect stock transfer as provided in paragraph (b) of this section and § 1.367(a)-8. As to this transfer, F is the transferee foreign corporation; O is the transferred corporation. The amount of the gain recognition agreement is $60.

Example 13. Successive section 351 exchanges—(i) *Facts*. D, a domestic corporation, owns all the stock of X, a controlled foreign corporation that operates an historical business, which owns all the stock of Y, a controlled foreign corporation that also operates an historical business. The properties of D consist of Business A assets, with an adjusted basis of $50 and a fair market value of $90, and Business B assets, with an adjusted basis of $50 and a fair market value of $110. Assume that the Business B assets qualify for the exception under section 367(a)(3) and § 1.367(a)-2(g)(2), but that the Business A assets do not qualify for the exception. In an exchange described in section 351, D transfers the assets of Businesses A and B to X, and, in connection with the same transaction, X transfers the assets of Business B to Y in another exchange described in section 351.

(ii) *Result*. Under paragraph (d)(1)(vi) of this section, this transaction is treated as an indirect stock transfer for purposes of section 367(a), but the transaction is not recharacterized for purposes of section 367(b). Moreover, under paragraph (d)(2)(vi) of this section, the assets of Businesses A and B that are transferred to X must be tested under section 367(a)(3). The Business A assets, which were not transferred to Y, are subject to the general rules of section 367(a), and not the indirect stock transfer rules described in this paragraph (d). D must recognize $40 of income on the outbound transfer of Business A assets. The transfer of the Business B assets is subject to both the asset transfer rules (under section 367(a)(3)) and the indirect stock transfer rules of this paragraph (d) and § 1.367(a)-8. Thus, D's transfer of the Business B assets will not be subject to section 367(a)(1) if D enters into a five-year gain recognition agreement with respect to the stock of Y. Under paragraphs (d)(2)(i) and (ii) of this section, X will be treated as the transferee foreign corporation and Y will be treated as the transferred corporation for purposes of applying the terms of the agreement. If X sells all or a portion of the stock of Y during the term of the agreement, D will be required to recognize a proportionate amount of the $60 gain that was realized by D on the initial transfer of the Business B assets.

Example 13A. Successive section 351 exchanges with ultimate domestic transferee—(i) *Facts*. The facts are the same as in *Example 13*, except that Y is a domestic corporation.

(ii) *Result*. As in *Example 13*, D must recognize $40 of income on the outbound transfer of the Business A assets. Although the Business B assets qualify for the exception under section 367(a)(3) (and end up in U.S. corporate solution, in Y), the $60 of gain realized on the Business B assets is nevertheless taxable under paragraphs (c)(1) and (d)(1)(vi) of this section because the transaction is considered to be a transfer by D of stock of a domestic corporation, Y, in which D receives more than 50 percent of the stock of the transferee foreign corporation, X. A gain recognition agreement is not permitted.

Example 14. Concurrent application of indirect stock transfer rules and section 367(b)—(i) *Facts*. F, a foreign corporation, owns all of the stock of Newco, which is also a foreign corporation. P, a domestic corporation, owns all of the stock of S, a foreign corporation that is a controlled foreign corporation within the meaning of section 957(a). P's basis in the stock of S is $50 and the value of S is $100. The section 1248 amount with respect to S stock is $30. In a reorganization described in section 368(a)(1)(C) (and paragraph (d)(1)(iv) of this section), Newco acquires all of the properties of S, and P exchanges its stock in S for 49 percent of the stock of F.

(ii) *Result*. P's exchange of S stock for F stock under section 354 will be taxable under section 367(a) (and section 1248 will be applicable) if P fails to enter into a 5-year gain recognition agreement in accordance with § 1.367(a)-8. Under paragraph (b)(2) of this section, if P enters into a gain recognition agreement, the exchange will be subject to the provisions of section 367(b) and the regulations thereunder as well as section 367(a). Under § 1.367(b)-4(b) of this chapter, P must recognize the section 1248 amount of $30 because P exchanged stock of a controlled foreign corporation, S, for stock of a foreign corporation that is not a controlled foreign corporation, F. The indirect stock transfer rules do not apply with respect to section 367(b). The deemed dividend of $30 recognized by P will increase P's basis in the F stock received in the transaction, and F's basis in the Newco stock. Thus, the amount of the gain recognition agreement is $20 ($50 gain realized on the transfer less the $30 inclusion under section 367(b)). Under paragraphs (d)(2)(i) and (ii) of this section, F is treated as the transferee foreign corporation and Newco is the transferred corporation.

Example 14A. Triangular section 368(a)(1)(C) reorganization involving foreign acquired corporation—(i) *Facts*. Assume the same facts as in *Example 14*, except that P receives 51 percent of the stock of F.

(ii) *Result*. P may still enter into a gain recognition agreement to avoid taxation under section 367(a). Assuming § 1.367(b)-4(b) does not apply, there is no income inclusion under section 367(b), and the amount of the gain recognition agreement is $50.

Example 15. Concurrent application of indirect stock transfer rules and section 367(b)—(i) *Facts*. F, a foreign corporation, owns all of the stock of Newco, a domestic corporation. P, a domestic corporation, owns all of the stock of FC, a foreign corporation. P's basis in the stock of FC is $50 and the value of FC stock is $100. The all earnings and profits amount with respect to the FC stock held by P is $60. See § 1.367(b)-2(d). In a reorganization described in sections 368(a)(1)(A) and (a)(2)(D) (and paragraph (d)(1)(i) of this section), Newco acquires all of the properties of FC, and P exchanges its stock in FC for 20 percent of the stock in F.

(ii) *Result*. P's section 354 exchange is considered an indirect stock transfer under paragraph (d)(1)(i) of this section. Further, because the assets of FC were acquired by Newco, a domestic corporation, in an asset reorganization, the transaction is within § 1.367(b)-3(a) and (b). Because the transactions is subject to § 1.367(b)-3 and the indirect stock rules of paragraph (d) of this section, and because the all earnings and profits amount with respect to the FC stock exchanged by P ($60) is greater than the gain in such stock subject to section 367(a) ($50), the section 367(b) rules (and not the section 367(a) rules) apply to the exchange. See § 1.367(a)-3(b)(2)(i)(B). Under the rules of section 367(b), P must include in income the all earnings and profits amount of $60 with respect to its FC stock. See § 1.367(b)-3. Alternatively, if P's all earnings and profits amount with respect to its FC stock were $30 (which is less than the gain in such stock subject to section 367(a) ($50)), section 367(b) and the regulations thereunder would not apply if there is gain recognition under section 367(a). Thus, if P failed to enter into a 5-year gain recognition agreement in accordance with § 1.367(a)-8, then P would recognize $50 of gain under section 367(a) and there would be no income inclusion under section 367(b). If, instead, P enters into a 5-year gain recognition agreement under § 1.367(a)-8, thereby avoiding immediate gain recognition on the entire $50 of section 367(a) gain, P is required to include in income the all earnings and profits amount of $30. In such a case, P will adjust its basis in the FC stock pursuant to § 1.367(b)-2(e)(3)(ii) and enter into a gain recognition agreement in the amount of $20.

Example 16. Direct asset reorganization not subject to stock transfer rules—(i) *Facts*. D is a domestic corporation that owns all the stock of F1 and F2, both foreign corporations. In a reorganization described in section 368(a)(1)(D), F2 acquires all of the assets of F1, and D receives 30 percent of the stock of F2 in an exchange described in section 354.

(ii) *Result*. The section 368(a)(1)(D) reorganization is not an indirect stock transfer described in paragraph (d) of this section. Moreover, the section 354 exchange by D of F1 stock for F2 stock is not an exchange described under section 367(a). See paragraph (a)(2)(ii) of this section.

(e) *Transfers of stock or securities by a domestic corporation to a foreign corporation in a section 361 exchange*.—(1) *Overview*.—(i) *Scope and definitions*.—This paragraph (e) applies to a domestic corporation (U.S. transferor) that transfers stock or securities of a domestic or foreign corporation (transferred stock or securities) to a foreign corporation (foreign acquiring corporation) in a section 361 exchange. Except as otherwise provided in this paragraph (e), paragraphs (b) and (c) of this section do not apply to the U.S. transferor's transfer of the transferred stock or securities in the section 361 exchange. For purposes of this paragraph (e), the definitions of control group, control group member, and non-control group member in § 1.367(a)-7(f)(1), ownership interest percentage in § 1.367(a)-7(f)(7), section 361 exchange in § 1.367(a)-7(f)(8), and U.S. transferor shareholder in § 1.367(a)-7(f)(13), apply.

(ii) *Ordering rules*.—Except as otherwise provided, this paragraph (e) applies to the transfer of the transferred stock or securities in the section 361 exchange prior to the application of any other provision of section 367 to such transfer. Furthermore, any gain recognized (including gain treated as a deemed dividend pursuant to section 1248(a)) by the U.S. transferor under this paragraph (e) shall be taken into account for purposes of applying any other provision of section 367 (including §§ 1.367(a)-6, 1.367(a)-7, and 1.367(b)-4) to the transfer of the transferred stock or securities.

(2) *General rule*.—Except as provided in paragraph (e)(3) of this section, the transfer by the U.S. transferor of the transferred stock or securities to the foreign acquiring corporation in the section 361 exchange shall be subject to section 367(a)(1), and therefore the U.S. transferor shall recognize any gain (but not loss) realized with respect to the transferred stock or securities. Realized gain is recognized pursuant to the prior sentence notwithstanding that the transfer is described in any other nonrecognition provision enumerated in section 367(a)(1) (such as section 351 or 354).

(3) *Exception*.—The general rule of paragraph (e)(2) of this section shall not apply if the conditions of paragraphs (e)(3)(i), (ii), and (iii) of this section are satisfied.

(i) The conditions set forth in § 1.367(a)-7(c) are satisfied with respect to the section 361 exchange.

(ii) If the transferred stock or securities are of a domestic corporation, the U.S. target company (as defined in paragraph (c)(1) of this section) complies with the reporting requirements of paragraph (c)(6) of this section, and the conditions of paragraphs (c)(1)(i), (ii), and (iv) of this section are satisfied with respect to the transferred stock or securities.

(iii) If the U.S. transferor owns (applying the attribution rules of section 318, as modified by section 958(b)) five percent or more of the total voting power or the total value of the stock of the transferee foreign corporation immediately after the transfer of the transferred stock or securities in the section 361 exchange, then the conditions set forth in paragraphs (e)(3)(iii)(A), (B), and (C) of this section are satisfied.

(A) Except as otherwise provided in this paragraph (e)(3)(iii)(A), each U.S. transferor shareholder that is a qualified U.S. person (as defined in paragraph (e)(6)(vii) of this section) owning (applying the attribution rules of section 318, as modified by section 958(b)) five percent or more of the total voting power or the total value of the stock of the transferee foreign corporation immediately after the reorganization enters into a gain recognition agreement that satisfies the conditions of paragraph (e)(6) of this section and § 1.367(a)-8. A U.S. transferor shareholder is not required to enter into a gain recognition agreement pursuant to this paragraph if the amount of gain that would be subject to the gain recognition agreement (as determined under paragraph (e)(6)(i) of this section) is zero.

(B) With respect to non-control group members that are not described in paragraph (e)(3)(iii)(A) of this section, the U.S. transferor recognizes gain equal to the product of the aggregate ownership interest percentage of such non-control group members multiplied by the gain realized by the U.S. transferor on the transfer of the transferred stock or securities.

(C) With respect to each control group member that is not described in paragraph (e)(3)(iii)(A) of this section, the U.S. transferor recognizes gain equal to the product of the ownership interest percentage of such control group member multiplied by the gain realized by the U.S. transferor on the transfer of the transferred stock or securities.

(4) *Application of certain rules at U.S. transferor-level*.—For purposes of paragraphs (c)(5)(iii) and (e)(3)(ii) and (iii) of this section, ownership of the stock of the transferee foreign corporation is determined by reference to stock owned by the U.S. transferor immediately after the transfer of the transferred stock or securities to the foreign acquiring corporation in the section 361 exchange, but prior to and without taking into account the U.S. transferor's distribution under section 361(c)(1) of the stock received.

(5) *Transferee foreign corporation.*—(i) *General rule.*—Except as provided in paragraph (e)(5)(ii) of this section, the transferee foreign corporation for purposes of applying paragraph (e) of this section and § 1.367(a)-8 shall be the foreign corporation that issues stock or securities to the U.S. transferor in the section 361 exchange.

(ii) *Special rule for triangular asset reorganizations involving the receipt of stock or securities of a domestic corporation.*—In the case of a triangular asset reorganization described in § 1.358-(6)(b)(2)(i), (ii), or (iii) or (b)(2)(v) (triangular asset reorganization) in which the U.S. transferor receives stock or securities of a domestic corporation that is in control (within the meaning of section 368(c)) of the foreign acquiring corporation, the transferee foreign corporation shall be the foreign acquiring corporation.

(6) *Special requirements for gain recognition agreements.*—A gain recognition agreement filed by a U.S. transferor shareholder pursuant to paragraph (e)(3)(iii)(A) of this section is, in addition to the terms and conditions of § 1.367(a)-8, subject to the conditions of this paragraph (e)(6).

(i) The amount of gain subject to the gain recognition agreement shall equal the product of the ownership interest percentage of the U.S. transferor shareholder multiplied by the gain realized by the U.S. transferor on the transfer of the transferred stock or securities, reduced (but not below zero) by the sum of the amounts described in paragraphs (e)(6)(i)(A),(B), (C), and (D) of this section.

(A) Gain recognized by the U.S. transferor with respect to the transferred stock or securities under section 367(a)(1) (including any portion treated as a deemed dividend under section 1248(a)) that is attributable to such U.S. transferor shareholder pursuant to § 1.367(a)-7(c)(2) or (e)(5).

(B) A deemed dividend included in the income of the U.S. transferor with respect to the transferred stock under § 1.367(b)-4(b)(1)(i) that is attributable to such U.S. transferor shareholder pursuant to § 1.367(a)-7(e)(4).

(C) If the U.S. transferor shareholder is subject to an election under § 1.1248(f)-2(c)(1), a deemed dividend included in the income of the U.S. transferor pursuant to § 1.1248(f)-2(c)(3) that is attributable to the U.S. transferor shareholder.

(D) If the U.S. transferor shareholder is not subject to an election under § 1.1248(f)-2(c)(1), the hypothetical section 1248 amount (as defined in § 1.1248(f)-1(c)(4)) with respect to the stock of each foreign corporation transferred in the section 361 exchange attributable to the U.S. transferor shareholder.

(ii) The gain recognition agreement shall include the election described in § 1.367(a)-8(c)(2)(vi).

(iii) The gain recognition agreement shall designate the U.S. transferor shareholder as the U.S. transferor for purposes of § 1.367(a)-8.

(iv) If the transfer of the transferred stock or securities in the section 361 exchange is pursuant to a triangular asset reorganization, the gain recognition agreement shall include appropriate provisions that are consistent with the principles of § 1.367(a)-8 for gain recognition agreements involving multiple parties. See § 1.367(a)-8(j)(9).

(v) The gain recognition agreement shall not be eligible for termination upon a taxable disposition pursuant to § 1.367(a)-8(o)(1) unless the value of the stock or securities received by the U.S. transferor shareholder in exchange for the stock or securities of the U.S. transferor under section 354 or 356 is at least equal to the amount of gain subject to the gain recognition agreement filed by such U.S. transferor shareholder.

(vi) Except as otherwise provided in this paragraph (e)(6)(vi), if gain is subsequently recognized by the U.S. transferor shareholder under the terms of the gain recognition agreement pursuant to § 1.367(a)-8(c)(1)(i), the increase in stock basis provided under § 1.367(a)-8(c)(4)(i) with respect to the stock received by the U.S. transferor shareholder shall not exceed the amount of the stock basis adjustment made pursuant to § 1.367(a)-7(c)(3) with respect to the stock received by the U.S. transferor shareholder. This paragraph (e)(6)(vi) shall not apply if the U.S. transferor shareholder and the U.S. transferor are members of the same consolidated group at the time of the reorganization.

(vii) For purposes of this section, a qualified U.S. person means a U.S. person, as defined in § 1.367(a)-1T(d)(1), but for this purpose does not include domestic partnerships, regulated investment companies (as defined in section 851(a)), real estate investment trusts (as defined in section 856(a)), and S corporations (as defined in section 1361(a)).

(7) *Gain subject to section 1248(a).*—If the U.S. transferor recognizes gain under paragraphs (e)(3)(iii)(B) or (C) of this section with respect to transferred stock that is stock in a foreign corporation to which section 1248(a) applies, then the portion of such gain treated as a deemed dividend under section 1248(a) is the product of the amount of the gain multiplied by the section 1248(a) ratio. The section 1248(a) ratio is the ratio of the amount that would be treated as a deemed dividend under section 1248(a) if all the gain in the transferred stock were recognized to the amount of gain realized in all the transferred stock.

(8) *Examples.*—The following examples illustrate the provisions of paragraph (e) of this section. Except as otherwise indicated: US1, US2, and UST are domestic corporations that are not members of a consolidated group; X is a United States citizen; US1, US2, and X are unrelated parties; CFC1, CFC2, and FA are foreign corporations; each corporation described herein has a single class of stock issued and outstanding and a tax year ending on December 31; the section 1248 amount (within the meaning of § 1.367(b)-2(c)) with respect to the stock of CFC1 and CFC2 is zero; Asset A is section 367(a) property that, but for the application of section 367(a)(5), would qualify for the active foreign trade or business exception under § 1.367(a)-2T; the requirements of § 1.367(a)-7(c)(2) through (5) are satisfied with respect to a section 361 exchange; the provisions of § 1.367(a)-6T (regarding branch loss recapture) are not applicable; and none of the foreign corporations in the examples is a surrogate foreign corporation (within the meaning of section 7874) as a result of the transactions described in the examples because one or more of the conditions of section 7874(a)(2)(B) is not satisfied.

Example 1. U.S. transferor owns less than 5% of stock of transferee foreign corporation—(i) *Facts.* US1, US2, and X own 80%, 5%, and 15%, respectively, of the stock of UST with a fair market value of $160x, $10x, and $30x, respectively. UST has two assets, Asset A and 100% of the stock of CFC1. UST has no liabilities. Asset A has a $150x basis and $100x fair market value (as defined in § 1.367(a)-7(f)(3)), and the CFC1 stock has a $0x basis and $100x fair market value. UST transfers Asset A and the CFC1 stock to FA solely in exchange for $200x of FA voting stock in a reorganization described in section 368(a)(1)(C). UST's transfer of Asset A and the CFC1 stock to FA qualifies as a section 361 exchange. UST distributes the FA stock received in the section 361 exchange to US1, US2, and X pursuant to the plan of reorganization, and liquidates. US1 receives $160x of FA stock, US2 receives $10x of FA stock, and X receives $30x of FA stock in exchange for the UST stock. Immediately after the transfer of Asset A and the CFC1 stock to FA in the section 361 exchange, but prior to and without taking into account UST's distribution of the FA stock pursuant to section 361(c)(1), UST does not own (applying the attribution rules of section 318, as modified by section 958(b)) five percent or more of the total voting power or the total value of the stock of FA.

(ii) *Result*—(A) UST's transfer of the CFC1 stock to FA in the section 361 exchange is subject to the provisions of this paragraph (e), and this paragraph (e) applies to the transfer of the CFC1 stock prior to the application of any other provision of section 367 to such transfer. See paragraphs (e)(1)(i) and (ii) of this section. Pursuant to the general rule of paragraph (e)(2) of this section, UST must recognize the gain realized of $100x on the transfer of the CFC1 stock (computed as the excess of the $100x fair market value over the $0x basis) unless the requirements for the exception provided in paragraph (e)(3) of this section are satisfied. In this case, the requirements of paragraph (e)(3) of this section are satisfied. First, the requirement of paragraph (e)(3)(i) of this section is satisfied because the control requirement of § 1.367(a)-7(c)(1) is satisfied, and a stated assumption is that the requirements of § 1.367(a)-7(c)(2) through (5) will be satisfied. The control requirement is satisfied because US1 and US2, each a control group member, own in the aggregate 85% of the stock of UST immediately before the reorganization. Second, the requirement of paragraph (e)(3)(ii) of this section is not applicable because that paragraph applies to the transfer of stock of a domestic corporation and CFC1 is a foreign corporation. Third, paragraph (e)(3)(iii) of this section is not applicable because immediately after the section 361 exchange, but prior to and without taking into account UST's distribution of the FA stock pursuant to section 361(c)(1), UST does not own (applying the attribution rules of section 318, as modified by section 958(b)) 5% or more of the total voting power or the total value of the stock of FA. See paragraph (e)(4) of this section. Accordingly, UST does not recognize the $100x of gain realized in the CFC1 stock pursuant to this section.

(B) In order to meet the requirements of § 1.367(a)-7(c)(2)(i), UST must recognize gain equal to the portion of the inside gain (as defined in § 1.367(a)-7(f)(5)) attributable to non-control group members (X), or $7.50x. The $7.50x of gain is computed as the product of the inside gain ($50x) multiplied by X's ownership interest percentage in UST (15%). Pursuant to § 1.367(a)-7(f)(5), the $50x of inside gain is the amount by which the aggregate fair market value ($200x) of the section 367(a) property (as defined in § 1.367(a)-7(f)(10), or Asset A and the CFC1 stock) exceeds the sum of the inside basis ($150x) of such property and the product of the section 367(a) percentage (as defined in § 1.367(a)-7(f)(9), or 100%) multiplied by UST's deductible liabilities (as defined in § 1.367(a)-7(f)(2), or $0x). Pursuant to § 1.367(a)-7(f)(4), the inside basis equals the aggregate basis of the section 367(a) property transferred in the section 361 exchange ($150x), increased by any gain or deemed dividends recognized by UST with respect to the section 367(a) property under section 367 ($0x), but not including the $7.50x of gain recognized by UST under § 1.367(a)-7(c)(2)(i). Pursuant to § 1.367(a)-7(e)(1), the $7.50x of gain recognized by UST is treated as recognized with respect to the CFC1 stock and Asset A in proportion to the amount of gain realized in each. However, because there is no gain realized by UST with respect to Asset A, all $7.50x of the gain is allocated to the CFC1 stock. Furthermore, FA's basis in the CFC1 stock, as determined under section 362 is increased by the $7.50x of gain recognized by UST. See § 1.367(a)-1(b)(4)(i)(B).

(C) The requirement to recognize gain under § 1.367(a)-7(c)(2)(ii) is not applicable because the portion of the inside gain attributable to US1 and US2 (control group members) can be preserved in the stock received by each such shareholder. As described in paragraph (ii)(B) of this *Example 1*, the inside gain is $50x. US1's attributable inside gain of $40x (equal to the product of $50x inside gain multiplied by US1's 80% ownership interest percentage, reduced by $0x, the sum of the amounts described in § 1.367(a)-7(c)(2)(ii)(A)(*1*) through (*3*)) does not exceed $160x (equal to the product of the section 367(a) percentage of 100% multiplied by $160x fair market value of FA stock received by US1). Similarly, US2's attributable inside gain of $2.50x (equal to the product of $50x inside gain multiplied by US2's 5% ownership interest percentage, reduced by $0x, the sum of the amounts described in § 1.367(a)-7(c)(2)(ii)(A)(*1*) through (*3*)) does not exceed $10x (equal to the product of the section 367(a) percentage of 100% multiplied by $10x fair market value of FA stock received by US2).

(D) Each control group member (US1 and US2) must separately compute any required adjustment to stock basis under § 1.367(a)-7(c)(3).

Example 2. U.S. transferor owns 5% or more of the stock of the transferee foreign corporation—(i) *Facts.* The facts are the same as in paragraph (e), *Example 1*, of this section except that immediately after the section 361 exchange, but prior to and without taking into account UST's distribution of the FA stock pursuant to section 361(c)(1), UST owns (applying the attribution rules of section 318, as modified by section 958(b)) 5% or more of the total voting power or value of the stock of FA. Furthermore, immediately after the reorganization, US1 and X (but not US2) each own (applying the attribution rules of section 318, as modified by section 958(b)) five percent or more of the total voting power or value of the stock of FA.

(ii) *Result*—(A) As is the case with paragraph (e), *Example 1*, of this section, UST's transfer of the CFC1 stock to FA in the section 361 exchange is subject to the provisions of this paragraph (e), and this paragraph (e) applies to the transfer of the CFC1 stock prior to the application of any other provision of section 367 to such transfer. See paragraphs (e)(1)(i) and (ii) of this section. In addition, UST must recognize the gain realized of $100x on the transfer of the CFC1 stock (computed as the excess of the $100x fair market value over the $0x basis) unless the requirements for the exception provided in paragraph (e)(3) of this section are satisfied. For the same reasons provided in *Example 1*, the requirement in paragraph (e)(3)(i) of this section is satisfied and the requirement of paragraph (e)(3)(ii) of this section is not applicable.

(B) Unlike paragraph (e), *Example 1*, of this section, however, UST owns 5% or more of the voting power or value of the stock of FA immediately after the transfer of the CFC1 stock in the section 361 exchange, but prior to and without taking into account UST's distribution of the FA stock under section 361(c)(1). As a result, paragraph (e)(3)(iii) of this section is applicable to the section 361 exchange of the CFC1 stock. Accordingly, in order to meet the requirements of paragraph (e)(3)(iii)(A) of this section US1 and X must enter into gain recognition agreements that satisfy the requirements of paragraph (e)(6) of this section and § 1.367(a)-8. See paragraph (ii)(G) of this *Example 2* for the computation of the amount of gain subject to each gain recognition agreement.

(C) In order to meet the requirements of paragraph (e)(3)(iii)(C) of this section, UST must recognize $5x of gain attributable to US2 (computed as the product of the $100x of gain realized with respect to the transfer of the CFC1 stock multiplied by the 5% ownership interest percentage of US2). The $5x of gain recognized is not included in the computation of inside basis (see § 1.367(a)-7(f)(4)(i)), but reduces (but not below zero) the amount of gain recognized by UST pursuant to § 1.367(a)-7(c)(2)(ii) that is attributable to US2. Furthermore, FA's basis in the CFC1 stock as determined under section 362 is increased for the $5x of gain recognized. See § 1.367(a)-1(b)(4)(i)(B). Assuming US1 and X enter into the gain recognition agreements described in paragraph (ii)(B) of this *Example 2*, and UST recognizes the $5x of gain described in this example, the requirements of paragraph (e)(3) of this section are satisfied and, accordingly, UST does not recognize the remaining $95x of gain realized in the CFC1 stock pursuant to this section.

(D) As described in paragraph (ii)(B) of *Example 1* of this paragraph (e), UST must recognize $7.50x of gain pursuant to § 1.367(a)-7(c)(2)(i), the amount of the $50x of inside gain attributable to X. Pursuant to § 1.367(a)-7(e)(1), the $7.50x of gain recognized by UST is treated as recognized with respect to the CFC1 stock and Asset A in proportion to the amount of gain realized in each. However, because there is no gain realized by UST with respect to Asset A, all $7.50x of the gain is allocated to the CFC1 stock. Furthermore, FA's basis in the CFC1 stock as determined under section 362 is increased for the $7.50x of gain recognized. See § 1.367(a)-1(b)(4)(i)(B).

(E) As described in paragraph (ii)(C) of *Example 1* of this paragraph (e), the requirement to recognize gain pursuant to § 1.367(a)-7(c)(2)(ii) is not applicable because the attributable inside gain of US1 and US2 can be preserved in the stock received by each shareholder. However, if UST were required to recognize gain pursuant to § 1.367(a)-7(c)(2)(ii) for inside gain attributable to US2 (for example, if US2 received solely cash rather than FA stock in the reorganization), the amount of such gain would be reduced (but not below zero) by the amount of gain recognized by UST pursuant to paragraph (e)(3)(iii)(C) of this section that is attributable to US2 (computed as $5x in paragraph (ii)(C) of this *Example 2*). See § 1.367(a)-7(c)(2)(ii)(A)(*1*).

(F) Each control group member (US1 and US2) must separately compute any required adjustment to stock basis under § 1.367(a)-7(c)(3).

(G) The amount of gain subject to the gain recognition agreement filed by each of US1 and X is determined pursuant to paragraph (e)(6)(i) of this section. With respect to US1, the amount of gain subject to the gain recognition agreement is $80x. The $80x is computed as the product of US1's ownership interest percentage (80%) multiplied by the gain realized by UST in the CFC1 stock as determined prior to taking into account the application of any other provision of section 367 ($100x), reduced by the sum of the amounts described in paragraphs (e)(6)(i)(A) through (D) of this section attributable to US1 ($0x). With respect to X, the amount of gain subject to the gain recognition agreement is $7.50x. The $7.50x is computed as the product of X's ownership interest percentage (15%) multiplied by the gain realized by UST in the CFC1 stock as determined prior to taking into account the application of any other provision of section 367 ($100x), reduced by the sum of the amounts described in paragraphs (e)(6)(i)(A) through (D) of this section attributable to X ($7.50x, as computed in paragraph (ii)(D) of this *Example 2*).

(H) In order the meet the requirements of paragraph (e)(6)(ii) of this section, each gain recognition agreement must include the election described in § 1.367(a)-8(c)(2)(vi). Furthermore, pursuant to paragraph (e)(6)(iii) of this section, US1 and X must be designated as the U.S. transferor on their respective gain recognition agreements for purposes of § 1.367(a)-8.

Example 3. U.S. transferor owns 5% or more of the stock of the transferee foreign corporation; interaction with section 1248(f)—(i) *Facts.* US1, US2, and X own 50%, 30%, and 20%, respectively, of the stock of UST. The UST stock owned by US1 has a $180x basis and $200x fair market value; the UST stock owned by US2 has a $100x basis and $120x fair market value; and the UST stock owned by X has a $80x fair market value. UST owns Asset A, and all the stock of CFC1 and CFC2. UST has no liabilities. Asset A has a $10x basis and $200x fair market value. The CFC1 stock is a single block of stock (as defined in § 1.1248(f)-1(c)(2)) with a $20x basis, $40x fair market value, and $30x of earnings and profits attributable to it for purposes of section 1248 (with the result that the section 1248 amount (as defined in § 1.1248(f)-1(c)(9)) is $20x). The CFC2 stock is also a single block of stock with a $30x basis, $160x fair market value, and $150x of earnings and profits attributable to it for purposes of section 1248 (with the result that the section 1248 amount is $130x). On December 31, Year 3, in a reorganization described in section 368(a)(1)(D), UST transfers the CFC1 stock, CFC2 stock, and Asset A to FA in exchange for 60 shares of FA stock with a $400x fair market value. UST's transfer of the CFC1 stock, CFC2 stock, and Asset A to FA in exchange for the 60 shares of FA stock qualifies as a section 361 exchange. UST distributes the FA stock received in the section 361 exchange to US1, US2, and X pursuant to section 361(c)(1). US1, US2, and X exchange their UST stock for 30, 18, and 12 shares, respectively, of FA stock pursuant to section 354. Immediately after the reorganization, FA has 100 shares of stock outstanding, and US1 and US2 are each a section 1248 shareholder with respect to FA.

(ii) *Result*—(A) UST's transfer of the CFC1 stock and CFC2 stock to FA in the section 361 exchange is subject to the provisions of this paragraph (e), and this paragraph (e) applies to the transfer of the CFC1 stock and CFC2 stock prior to the application of any other provision of section 367 to such transfer. See paragraphs (e)(1)(i) and (ii) of this section. Pursuant to the general rule of paragraph (e)(2) of this section, UST must recognize the gain realized of $20x on the transfer of the CFC1 stock (the excess of $40x fair market value over $20x basis) and the gain realized of $130x on the transfer of the CFC2 stock (the excess of $160x fair market value over $30x basis), subject to the application of section 1248(a), unless the requirements for the exception provided in paragraph (e)(3) of this section are satisfied. In this case, the requirement of paragraph (e)(3)(i) of this section is satisfied because the control requirement of § 1.367(a)-7(c)(1) is satisfied, and a stated assumption is that the requirements of § 1.367(a)-7(c)(2) through (5) will be satisfied. The control requirement is satisfied because US1 and US2, each a control group member, own in the aggregate 80% of the UST stock immediately before the reorganization. The requirement of paragraph (e)(3)(ii) of this section is not applicable because paragraph (e)(3)(ii) applies to the transfer of stock of a domestic corporation, and CFC1 and CFC2 are foreign corporations. UST owns 5% or more of the total voting power or value of the stock of FA (60%, or 60 of the 100 shares of FA stock outstanding) immediately after the transfer of the CFC1 stock and CFC2 stock in the section 361 exchange, but prior to and without taking into account UST's distribution of the FA stock under section 361(c)(1). As a result, paragraph (e)(3)(iii) of this section is applicable to the section 361 exchange of the CFC1 stock and CFC2 stock. US1, US2, and X each own (applying the attribution rules of section 318, as modified by section 958(b)) 5% or more of the total voting power or value of the FA stock immediately after the reorganization, or 30%, 18%, and 12%, respectively. Accordingly, in order to meet the requirements of paragraph (e)(3)(iii)(A) of this section, US1 and US2 must enter into gain recognition agreements with respect to the CFC1 stock and CFC2 stock that satisfy the requirements of paragraph (e)(6) of this section and § 1.367(a)-8. X is not required to enter into a gain recognition agreement because the amount of gain that would be subject to the gain recognition agreement is zero. See paragraph (ii)(J) of this *Example 3* for the computation of the amount of gain subject to each gain recognition agreement. Assuming US1 and US2 enter into the gain recognitions agreements described above, the requirements of paragraph (e)(3) of this section are satisfied and accordingly, UST does not recognize the gain realized of $20x in the stock of CFC1 or the gain realized of $130x in the stock of CFC2 pursuant to this section.

(B) UST's transfer of the CFC1 stock and CFC2 stock to FA pursuant to the section 361 exchange is subject to § 1.367(b)-4(b)(1)(i), which applies prior to the application of § 1.367(a)-7(c). See paragraph (e)(1) of this section. UST (the exchanging shareholder) is a U.S. person and a section 1248 shareholder with respect to CFC1 and CFC2 (each a foreign acquired corporation). However, UST is not required to include in income as a deemed dividend the section 1248 amount with respect to the CFC1 stock ($20x) or CFC2 stock ($130x) under § 1.367(b)-4(b)(1)(i) because, immediately after UST's section 361 exchange of the CFC1 stock and CFC2 stock for FA stock (and before the distribution of the FA stock to US1, US2, and X under section 361(c)(1), FA, CFC1, and CFC2 are controlled foreign corporations as to which UST is a section 1248 shareholder. See § 1.367(b)-4(b)(1)(ii)(A). However, if UST were required to include in income as a deemed dividend the section 1248 amount with respect to the CFC1 stock or CFC2 stock (for example, if FA were not a controlled foreign corporation), such deemed dividend would be taken into account prior to the application of § 1.367(a)-7(c). Furthermore, because US1, US2, and X are all persons described in paragraph (e)(3)(iii)(A) of this section, any such deemed dividend would increase inside basis. See § 1.367(a)-7(f)(4).

(C) In order to meet the requirements of § 1.367(a)-7(c)(2)(i), UST must recognize gain equal to the portion of the inside gain attributable to non-control group members (X), or $68x. The $68x of gain is computed as the product of the inside gain ($340x) multiplied by X's ownership interest percentage in UST (20%), reduced (but not below zero) by $0x, the sum of the amounts described in § 1.367(a)-7(c)(2)(i)(A) through (C). Pursuant to § 1.367(a)-7(f)(5), the $340x of inside gain is the amount by which the aggregate fair market value ($400x) of the section 367(a) property (Asset A, CFC1 stock, and CFC2 stock) exceeds the sum of the inside basis ($60x) and $0x (the product of the section 367(a) percentage (100%) multiplied by UST's deductible liabilities ($0x)). Pursuant to § 1.367(a)-7(f)(4), the inside basis equals the aggregate basis of the section 367(a) property transferred in the section 361 exchange ($60x), increased by any gain or deemed dividends recognized by UST with respect to the section 367(a) property under section 367 ($0x), but not including the $68x of gain recognized by UST under § 1.367(a)-7(c)(2)(i). Under § 1.367(a)-7(e)(1), the $68x gain recognized is treated as being with respect to the CFC1 stock, CFC2 stock, and Asset A in proportion to the amount of gain realized by UST on the transfer of the property. The amount treated as recognized with respect to the CFC1 stock is $4x ($68x gain multiplied by $20x/$340x). The amount treated as recognized with respect to the CFC2 stock is $26x ($68x gain multiplied by $130x/$340x). The amount treated as recognized with respect to Asset A is $38x ($68x gain multiplied by $190x/$340x). Under section 1248(a), UST must include in gross income as a dividend the $4x gain recognized with respect to the CFC1 stock and the $26x gain recognized with respect to CFC2 stock. Furthermore, FA's basis in the CFC1 stock, CFC2 stock, and Asset A, as determined under section 362, is increased by the amount of gain recognized by UST with respect to such property. See § 1.367(a)-1(b)(4)(i)(B). Thus, FA's basis in the CFC1 stock is $24x ($20x increased by $4x of gain), the CFC2 stock is $56x ($30x increased by $26x of gain), and Asset A is $48x ($10x increased by $38x of gain).

(D) The requirement to recognize gain under § 1.367(a)-7(c)(2)(ii) is not applicable because the portion of the inside gain attributable to US1 and US2 (control group members) can be preserved in the stock received by each such shareholder. As described in paragraph (ii)(C) of this Example 3, the inside gain is $340x. US1's attributable inside gain of $170x (equal to the product of $340x inside gain multiplied by US1's 50% ownership interest percentage, reduced by $0x, the sum of the amounts described in § 1.367(a)-7(c)(2)(ii)(A)(*1*) through (*3*)) does not exceed $200x (equal to the product of the section 367(a) percentage of 100% multiplied by $200x fair market value of FA stock received by US1). Similarly, US2's attributable inside gain of $102x (equal to the product of $340x inside gain multiplied by US2's 30% ownership interest percentage, reduced by $0x, the sum of the amounts described in § 1.367(a)-7(c)(2)(ii)(A)(*1*) through (*3*)) does not exceed $120x (equal to the product of the section 367(a) percentage of 100% multiplied by $120x fair market value of FA stock received by US2).

(E) Each control group member (US1 and US2) separately computes any required adjustment to stock basis under § 1.367(a)-7(c)(3). US1's section 358 basis in the FA stock received of $180x (equal to US1's basis in the UST stock exchanged) is reduced to preserve the attributable inside gain with respect to US1, less any gain recognized with respect to US1 under § 1.367(a)-7(c)(2)(ii). Because UST does not recognize gain on the section 361 exchange with respect to US1 under § 1.367(a)-7(c)(2)(ii) (as determined in paragraph (ii)(D) of this *Example 3*), the attributable inside gain of $170x with respect to US1 is not reduced under § 1.367(a)-7(c)(3)(i)(A). US1's outside gain (as defined in § 1.367(a)-7(f)(6)) in the FA stock is $20x, the product of the section 367(a) percentage (100%) multiplied by the $20x gain (equal to the difference between $200x fair market value and $180x section 358 basis in the FA stock). Thus, US1's $180x section 358 basis in the FA stock must be reduced by $150x (the excess of $170x attributable inside gain, reduced by $0x, over $20x outside gain) to $30x. Similarly, US2's section 358 basis in the FA stock received of $100x (equal to US2's basis in the UST stock exchanged) is reduced to preserve the attributable inside gain with respect to US2, less any gain recognized with respect to US2 under § 1.367(a)-7(c)(2)(ii). Because UST does not recognize gain on the section 361 exchange with respect to US2 under § 1.367(a)-7(c)(2)(ii) (as determined in paragraph (ii)(D) of this *Example 3*), the attributable inside gain of $102x with respect to US2 is not reduced under § 1.367(a)-7(c)(3)(i)(A). US2's outside gain in the FA stock is $20x, the product of the section 367(a) percentage (100%) multiplied by the $20x gain (equal to the difference between $120x fair market value and $100x section 358 basis in FA stock). Thus, US2's $100x section 358 basis in the FA stock must be reduced by $82x (the excess of $102x attributable inside gain, reduced by $0x, over $20x outside gain) to $18x.

(F) UST's distribution of the FA stock to US1, US2, and X under section 361(c)(1) (new stock distribution) is subject to § 1.1248(f)-1(b)(3). Except as provided in § 1.1248(f)-2(c), under § 1.1248(f)-1(b)(3) UST must include in gross income as a dividend the total section 1248(f) amount (as defined in § 1.1248(f)-1(c)(14)). The total section 1248(f) amount is $120x, the sum of the section 1248(f) amount (as defined in § 1.1248(f)-1(c)(10)) with respect to the CFC1 stock ($16x) and CFC2 stock ($104x). The $16x section 1248(f) amount with respect to the CFC1 stock is the amount that UST would have included in income as a dividend under § 1.367(b)-4(b)(1)(i) with respect to the CFC1 stock if the requirements of § 1.367(b)-4(b)(1)(ii)(A) had not been satisfied ($20x), reduced by the amount of gain recognized by UST under § 1.367(a)-7(c)(2) allocable to the CFC1 stock and treated as a dividend under section 1248(a) ($4x, as described in paragraph (ii)(C) of this *Example 3*). Similarly, the section 1248(f) amount with respect to the CFC2 stock is $104x ($130x reduced by $26x).

(G) If, however, UST along with US1 and US2 (each a section 1248 shareholder of FA immediately after the distribution) elect to apply the provisions of § 1.1248(f)-2(c) (as provided in § 1.1248(f)-2(c)(1)), the amount that UST is required to include in income as a dividend under § 1.1248(f)-1(b)(3) ($120x total section 1248(f) amount as computed in paragraph (ii)(F) of this *Example 3*) is reduced by the sum of the portions of the section 1248(f) amount with respect to the CFC1 stock and CFC2 stock that is attributable (under the rules of § 1.1248(f)-2(d)) to the FA stock distributed to US1 and US2. Assume that the election is made to apply § 1.1248(f)-2(c).

(*1*) Under § 1.1248(f)-2(d)(1), the portion of the section 1248(f) amount with respect to the CFC1 stock that is attributed to the 30 shares of FA stock distributed to US1 is equal to the hypothetical section 1248 amount (as defined in § 1.1248(f)-1(c)(4)) with respect to the CFC1 stock that is attributable to US1's ownership interest percentage in UST. US1's hypothetical section 1248 amount with respect to the CFC1 stock is the amount that UST would have included in income as a deemed dividend under § 1.367(b)-4(b)(1)(i) with respect to the CFC1 stock if the requirements of § 1.367(b)-4(b)(1)(ii)(A) had not been satisfied ($20x) and that would be attributable to US1's ownership interest percentage in UST (50%), reduced by the amount of gain recognized by UST under § 1.367(a)-7(c)(2) attributable to US1 and allocable to the CFC1 stock, but only to the extent such gain is treated as a dividend under section 1248(a) ($0x, as described in paragraphs (ii)(C) and (D) of this *Example 3*). Thus, US1's hypothetical section 1248 amount with respect to the CFC1 stock is $10x ($20x multiplied by 50%, reduced by $0x). The $10x hypothetical section 1248 amount is attributed pro rata (based on relative values) among the 30 shares of FA stock distributed to US1, and the attributable share amount (as defined in § 1.1248(f)-2(d)(1)) is $.33x ($10x/30 shares). Similarly, US1's hypothetical section 1248 amount with respect to the CFC2 stock is $65x ($130x multiplied by 50%, reduced by $0x), and the attributable share amount is $2.17x ($65x/30 shares). Similarly, US2's hypothetical section 1248 amount with respect to the CFC1 stock is $6x ($20x multiplied by 30%, reduced by $0x), and the attributable share amount is also $.33x ($6x/18 shares). Finally, US2's hypothetical section 1248 amount with respect to the CFC2 stock is $39x ($130x multiplied by 30%, reduced by $0x), and the attributable share amount is also $2.17x ($39x/18 shares). Thus, the sum of the portion of the section 1248(f) amount with respect to the CFC1 stock and CFC2 stock attributable to shares of stock of FA distributed to US1 and US2 is $120x ($10x plus $65x plus $6x plus $39x).

(*2*) If the shares of FA stock are divided into portions, § 1.1248(f)-2(d)(2) applies to attribute the attributable share amount to portions of shares of FA stock distributed to US1 and US2. Under § 1.1248(f)-2(c)(2) each share of FA stock received by US1 (30 shares) and US2 (18 shares) is divided into three portions, one attributable to the single block of stock of CFC1, one attributable to the single block of stock of CFC2, and one attributable to Asset A. Thus, the attributable share amount of $.33x with respect to the CFC1 stock is attributed to the portion of each of the 30 shares and 18 shares of FA stock received by US1 and US2, respectively, that relates to the CFC1 stock. Similarly, the attributable share amount of $2.17x with respect to the CFC2 stock is attributed to the portion of each of the 30 shares and 18 shares of FA stock received by US1 and US2, respectively, that relates to the CFC2 stock.

(*3*) The total section 1248(f) amount ($120x) that UST is otherwise required to include in gross income as a dividend under § 1.1248(f)-1(b)(3) is reduced by $120x, the sum of the portions of the section 1248(f) amount with respect to the CFC1 stock and CFC2 stock that are attributable to the shares of FA stock distributed to US1 and US2. Thus, the amount DC is required to include in gross income as a dividend under § 1.1248(f)-1(b)(3) is $0x ($120x reduced by $120x).

(H) As stated in paragraph (ii)(G)(*2*) of this *Example 3*, under § 1.1248(f)-2(c)(2) each share of FA stock received by US1 (30 shares) and US2 (18 shares) is divided into three portions, one attributable to the CFC1 stock, one attributable to the CFC2 stock, and one attributable to Asset A. Under § 1.1248(f)-2(c)(4)(i), the basis of each portion is the product of US1's and US2's section 358 basis in the share of FA stock multiplied by the ratio of the section 362 basis of the property (CFC1 stock, CFC2 stock, or Asset A, as applicable) received by FA in the section 361 exchange to which the portion relates, to the aggregate section 362 basis of all property received by FA in the section 361 exchange. Under § 1.1248(f)-2(c)(4)(ii), the fair market value of each portion is the product of the fair market value of the share of FA stock multiplied by the ratio of the fair market value of the property (CFC1 stock, CFC2 stock, or Asset A, as applicable) to which the portion relates, to the aggregate fair market value of all property received by FA in the section 361 exchange. The section 362 basis of the CFC1 stock, CFC2 stock, and Asset A is $24x, $56x, and $48x, respectively, for an aggregate section 362 basis of $128x. See paragraph (ii)(C) of this *Example 3*. The fair market value of the CFC1 stock, CFC2 stock, and Asset A is $40x, $160x, and $200x, for an aggregate fair market value of $400x. Furthermore, US1's 30 shares of FA stock have an aggregate fair market value of $200x and section 358 basis of $30x (resulting in aggregate gain of $170x), and US2's 18 shares of FA stock have an aggregate fair market value of $120x and section 358 basis of $18x (resulting in aggregate gain of $102x). See paragraph (ii)(E) of this *Example 3*.

(*1*) With respect to US1's 30 shares of FA stock, the portions attributable to the CFC1 stock have an aggregate basis of $5.63x ($30x multiplied by $24x/$128x) and fair market value of $20x ($200x multiplied by $40x/$400x), resulting in aggregate gain in such portions of $14.38x (or $.48x gain in each such portion of the 30 shares). The portions attributable to the CFC2 stock have an aggregate basis of $13.13x ($30x multiplied by $56x/$128x) and fair market value of $80x ($200x multiplied by $160x/$400x), resulting in aggregate gain in such portions of $66.88x (or $2.23x in each such portion of the 30 shares). The portions attributable to Asset A have an aggregate basis of $11.25x ($30x multiplied by $48x/$128x) and fair market value of $100x ($200x multiplied by $200x/$400x), resulting in aggregate gain in such portions of $88.75x (or $2.96x in each such portion of the 30 shares). Thus, the aggregate gain in all the portions of the 30 shares is $170x ($14.38x plus $66.88x plus $88.75x).

(*2*) With respect to US2's 18 shares of FA stock, the portions attributable to the CFC1 stock have an aggregate basis of $3.38x ($18x multiplied by $24x/$128x) and fair market value of $12x ($120x multiplied by $40x/$400x), resulting in aggregate gain in such portions of $8.63x (or $.48x in each such portion of the 18 shares). The portions attributable to the CFC2 stock have an aggregate basis of $7.88x ($18x multiplied by $56x/$128x) and fair market value of $48x ($120x multiplied by $160x/$400x), resulting in aggregate gain of $40.13x (or $2.23x in each such portion of the 18 shares). The portions attributable to Asset A have an aggregate basis of $6.75x ($18x multiplied by $48x/$128x) and fair market value of $60x ($120x multiplied by $200x/$400x), resulting in aggregate gain of $53.25x (or $2.96x in each such portion of the 18 shares). Thus, the aggregate gain in all the portions of the 18 shares is $102x ($8.63x plus $40.13x plus $53.25x).

(*3*) Under § 1.1248-8(b)(2)(iv), the earnings and profits of CFC1 attributable to the portions of US1's 30 shares of FA stock that relate to the CFC1 stock is $15x (the product of US1's 50% ownership interest percentage in UST multiplied by $30x of earnings and profits attributable to the CFC1 stock before the section 361 exchange, reduced by $0x of dividend included in UST's income with respect to the CFC1 stock under section 1248(a) attributable to US1). The earnings and profits of CFC2 attributable to the portions of US1's 30 shares of FA stock that relate to the CFC2 stock is $75x (the product of US1's 50% ownership interest percentage in UST multiplied by $150x of earnings and profits attributable to the CFC2 stock before the section 361 exchange, reduced by $0x of dividend included in UST's income with respect to the CFC2 stock under section 1248(a) attributable to US1). Similarly, the earnings and profits of CFC1 attributable to the portions of US2's 18 shares of FA stock that relate to the CFC1 stock is $9x (the product of US2's 30% ownership interest percentage in UST multiplied by $30x of earnings and profits attributable to the CFC1 stock before the section 361 exchange, reduced by $0x of dividend included in UST's income with respect to the CFC1 stock under section 1248(a) attributable to US2). Finally, the earnings and profits of CFC2 attributable to the portions of US2's 18 shares of FA stock that relate to the CFC2 stock is $45x (the product of US2's 30% ownership interest percentage in UST multiplied by $150x of earnings and profits attributable to the CFC2 stock before the section 361 exchange, reduced by $0x of dividend included in UST's income with respect to the CFC2 stock under section 1248(a) attributable to US2).

(I) Under § 1.1248(f)-2(c)(3), neither US1 nor US2 is required to reduce the aggregate section 358 basis in the portions of their respective shares of FA stock, and UST is not required to include in gross income any additional deemed dividend.

(*1*) US1 is not required to reduce the aggregate section 358 basis of the portions of its 30 shares of FA stock that relate to the CFC1 stock because the $10x section 1248(f) amount with respect to the CFC1 stock attributable to the portions of the shares of FA stock received by US1 (as computed in paragraph (ii)(G) of this *Example 3*) does not exceed US1's postdistribution amount (as defined in § 1.1248(f)-1(c)(6), or $14.38x) in those portions. The $14.38x postdistribution amount equals the amount that US1 would be required to include in income as a dividend under section 1248(a) with respect to such portion if it sold the 30 shares of FA stock immediately after the distribution in a transaction in which all realized gain is recognized, without taking into account basis adjustments or income inclusions under § 1.1248(f)-2(c)(3) ($20x fair market value, $5.63x basis, and $15x earnings and profits attributable to the portions for purposes of section 1248). Similarly, US1 is not required to reduce the aggregate section 358 basis of the portions of its 30 shares of FA stock that relate to the CFC2 stock because the $65x section 1248(f) amount with respect to the CFC2 stock attributable to the portions of the shares of FA stock received by US1 (as computed in paragraph (ii)(G) of this *Example 3*) does not exceed US1's postdistribution amount ($66.88x) in those portions. The $66.88x postdistribution amount equals the amount that US1 would be required to include in income as a dividend under section 1248(a) with respect to such portion if it sold the 30 shares of FA stock immediately after the distribution in a transaction in which all realized gain is recognized, without taking into account basis adjustments or income inclusions under § 1.1248(f)-2(c)(3) ($80x fair market value, $13.13x basis, and $75x earnings and profits attributable to the portions for purposes of section 1248).

(2) US2 is not required to reduce the aggregate section 358 basis of the portions of its 18 shares of FA stock that relate to the CFC1 stock because the $6x section 1248(f) amount with respect to the CFC1 stock attributable to the portions of the shares of FA stock received by US2 (as computed in paragraph (ii)(G) of this *Example 3*) does not exceed US2's postdistribution amount ($8.63x) in those portions. The $8.63x postdistribution amount equals the amount that US2 would be required to include in income as a dividend under section 1248(a) with respect to such portion if it sold the 18 shares of FA stock immediately after the distribution in a transaction in which all realized gain is recognized, without taking into account basis adjustments or income inclusions under § 1.1248(f)-2(c)(3) ($12x fair market value, $3.38x basis, and $9x earnings and profits attributable to the portions for purposes of section 1248). Similarly, US2 is not required to reduce the aggregate section 358 basis of the portions of its 18 shares of FA stock that relate to the CFC2 stock because the $39x section 1248(f) amount with respect to the CFC2 stock attributable to the portions of the shares of FA stock received by US2 (as computed in paragraph (ii)(G) of this *Example 3*) does not exceed US1's postdistribution amount ($40.13x) in those portions. The $40.13x postdistribution amount equals the amount that US2 would be required to include in income as a dividend under section 1248(a) with respect to such portion if it sold the 18 shares of FA stock immediately after the distribution in a transaction in which all realized gain is recognized, without taking into account basis adjustments or income inclusions under § 1.1248(f)-2(c)(3) ($48x fair market value, $7.88x basis, and $45x earnings and profits attributable to the portions for purposes of section 1248).

(J) The amount of gain subject to the gain recognition agreement filed by each of US1 and US2 is determined pursuant to paragraph (e)(6)(i) of this section. The amount of gain subject to the gain recognition agreement filed by US1 with respect to the stock of CFC1 and CFC2 is $10x and $65x, respectively. The $10x and $65x are computed as the product of US1's ownership interest percentage (50%) multiplied by the gain realized by UST in the CFC1 stock ($20x) and CFC2 stock ($130x), respectively, as determined prior to taking into account the application of any other provision of section 367, reduced by the sum of the amounts described in paragraphs (e)(6)(i)(A) through (D) of this section with respect to the CFC1 stock and CFC2 stock attributable to US1 ($0x with respect to the CFC1 stock, and $0x with respect to the CFC2 stock). The amount of gain subject to the gain recognition agreement filed by US2 with respect to the stock of CFC1 and CFC2 is $6x and $39x, respectively. The $6x and $39x are computed as the product of US2's ownership interest percentage (30%) multiplied by the gain realized by UST in the CFC1 stock ($20x) and CFC2 stock ($130x), respectively, as determined prior to taking into account the application of any other provision of section 367, reduced by the sum of the amounts described in paragraphs (e)(6)(i)(A) through (D) of this section with respect to the CFC1 stock and CFC2 stock attributable to US2 ($0x with respect to the CFC1 stock, and $0x with respect to the CFC2 stock). X is not required to enter into a gain recognition agreement because the amount of gain that would be subject to the gain recognition agreement is $0x with respect to the CFC1 stock, and $0x with respect to the CFC2 stock, computed as X's ownership percentage (20%) multiplied by the gain realized in the stock of CFC1 ($20x multiplied by 20%, or $4x) and CFC2 ($130x multiplied by 20%, or $26x), reduced by the amount of gain recognized by UST with respect to the stock of CFC1 and CFC2 that is attributable to X pursuant to § 1.367(a)-7(c)(2) ($4x and $26x, respectively, as determined in paragraph (ii)(C) of this *Example 3*). Pursuant to paragraph (e)(6)(ii) of this section, each gain recognition agreement must include the election described in § 1.367(a)-8(c)(2)(vi). Furthermore, pursuant to paragraph (e)(6)(iii) of this section, US1 and US2 must be designated as the U.S. transferor on their respective gain recognition agreements for purposes of § 1.367(a)-8.

(9) *Illustration of rules.*—For rules relating to certain distributions of stock of a foreign corporation by a domestic corporation, see section 1248(f) and §§ 1.1248(f)-1 through 1.1248(f)-3.

(f) *Failure to file statements.*—(1) *Failure to file.*—For purposes of the exceptions to the application of section 367(a)(1) provided in paragraphs (c) and (d)(2)(vi)(B) of this section, there is a failure to file a statement described in paragraph (c)(6), (c)(7), or (d)(2)(vi)(C) of this section (failure to file) if the statement is not filed with a timely filed U.S. income tax return or is not completed in all material respects.

(2) *Relief for certain failures to file that are not willful.*—(i) *In general.*—A failure to file described in paragraph (f)(1) of this section will be deemed not to have occurred for purposes of satisfying the requirements of the applicable regulation if the taxpayer demonstrates that the failure was not willful using the procedure set forth in this paragraph (f)(2). For this purpose, willful is to be interpreted consistent with the meaning of that term in the context of other civil penalties, which would include a failure due to gross negligence, reckless disregard, or willful neglect. Whether a failure to file was a willful failure will be determined by the Director of Field Operations International, Large Business & International (or any successor to the roles and responsibilities of such position, as appropriate) (Director) based on all the facts and circumstances. The taxpayer must submit a request for relief and an explanation as provided in paragraph (f)(2)(ii)(A) of this section. Although a taxpayer whose failure to file is determined not to be willful will not be subject to gain recognition under this section, the taxpayer will be subject to a penalty under section 6038B if the taxpayer fails to satisfy the reporting requirements, if any, under that section and does not demonstrate that the failure was due to reasonable cause and not willful neglect. See § 1.6038B-1(b) and (f). The determination of whether the failure to file was willful under this section has no effect on any request for relief made under § 1.6038B-1(f).

(ii) *Procedures for establishing that a failure to file was not willful.*—(A) *Time and manner of submission.*—A taxpayer's statement that the failure to file was not willful will be considered only if, promptly after the taxpayer becomes aware of the failure, an amended return is filed for the taxable year to which the failure relates that includes the information that should have been included with the original return for such taxable year or that otherwise complies with the rules of this section, and that includes a written statement explaining the reasons for the failure to file. The amended return must be filed with the Internal Revenue Service at the location where the taxpayer filed its original return. The taxpayer may submit a request for relief from the penalty under section 6038B as part of the same submission. See § 1.6038B-1(f).

(B) *Notice requirement.*—In addition to the requirements of paragraph (f)(2)(ii)(A) of this section, the taxpayer must comply with the notice requirements of this paragraph (f)(2)(ii)(B). If any taxable year of the taxpayer is under examination when the amended return is filed, a copy of the amended return and any information required to be included with such return must be delivered to the Internal Revenue Service personnel conducting the examination. If no taxable year of the taxpayer is under examination when the amended return is filed, a copy of the amended return and any information required to be included with such return must be delivered to the Director.

(3) For illustrations of the application of the willfulness standard of this paragraph (f), see the examples in § 1.367(a)-8(p)(3).

(g) *Effective/applicability dates.*—(1) *Rules of applicability.*—(i) Except as otherwise provided in this paragraph (g), the rules in paragraphs (a), (b), and (d) of this section apply to transfers occurring on or after July 20, 1998.

(ii) The following rules apply to transactions occurring on or after January 23, 2006—

(A) The rules in paragraphs (a) and (d) of this section, as they apply to section 368(a)(1)(A) reorganizations (including reorganizations described in section 368(a)(2)(D) or (E)) involving a foreign acquiring or foreign acquired corporation;

(B) The rules in paragraph (b)(2)(i)(B) of this section;

(C) The rules in paragraph (d) of this section, as they apply to section 368(a)(1)(G) reorganizations (including reorganizations described in section 368(a)(2)(D));

(D) The rules of paragraph (d)(1) and (d)(2)(iv), as they relate to exchanges by a U.S. person of securities of an acquired corporation for voting stock or securities of a foreign corporation in control of the acquiring corporation in a triangular section 368(a)(1)(B) reorganization;

(E) The rules in paragraph (d)(1) and (d)(2)(iv) of this section, as they relate to exchanges by a U.S. person of stock or securities of an acquired corporation for voting stock or securities of a domestic corporation in control of the foreign acquiring corporation in a triangular section 368(a)(1)(B) reorganization; and

(F) The rules in paragraph (d)(2)(vii) of this section.

(iii) The rules of paragraph (a) of this section that apply to transfers of securities in a section 354 or 356 exchange (pursuant to a section 368(a)(1)(E) reorganization or an asset reorganization that is not treated as an indirect stock transfer) that is not subject to section 367(a) apply only to transfers occurring after January 5, 2005 (although taxpayers may apply such provision to transfers of securities occurring on or after July 20, 1998, and on or before January 5, 2005, if done consistently to all transactions).

(iv) The rules in paragraph (d)(1)(v) of this section apply to:

(A) A reorganization described in section 368(a)(1)(C) followed by a controlled asset transfer if such reorganization occurs on or after July 20, 1998;

(B) A reorganization described in section 368(a)(1)(D) followed by a controlled asset transfer if such reorganization occurs after December 9, 2002 (for additional guidance concerning such reorganizations that occur on or after July 20, 1998 and on or before December 9, 2002, see Rev. Rul. 2002-85 (2002-2 C.B. 986) and § 601.601(d)(2) of this chapter); and

(C) A reorganization described in section 368(a)(1)(A), (F), or (G) followed by a controlled asset transfer if such reorganization occurs on or after January 23, 2006.

(v) The rules of paragraph (d)(2)(vi) of this section apply only to transactions occurring on or after January 23, 2006. See § 1.367(a)-3(d)(2)(vi), as contained in 26 CFR Part 1 revised as of April 1, 2005, for transactions occurring on or after July 20, 1998 and before January 23, 2006.

(A) Except as provided in paragraphs (g)(1)(v)(B) of this section and § 1.367(a)-3T(g)(1)(ix), the rules of paragraph (d)(2)(vi) of this section apply only to transactions occurring on or after January 23, 2006. See § 1.367(a)-3(d)(2)(vi), as contained in 26 CFR part 1 revised as of April 1, 2005, for transactions occurring on or after July 20, 1998, and before January 23, 2006.

(B)(*1*) For purposes of paragraph (d)(2)(vi)(B)(*1*) of this section as contained in 26 CFR part 1 revised as of April 1, 2007, except as provided in paragraph (g)(1)(v)(B)(*3*) of this section, the following conditions must be satisfied for transactions occurring on or after December 28, 2007, and before March 18, 2013: the conditions and requirements of section 367(a)(5) and paragraph (g)(1)(v)(B)(*2*) of this section must be satisfied with respect to the domestic acquired corporation's transfer of assets to the foreign acquiring corporation and those conditions and requirements apply before the application of the exception under paragraph (d)(2)(vi)(B)(*1*) of this section as contained in 26 CFR part 1 revised as of April 1, 2007.

(*2*) The domestic acquired corporation is controlled (within the meaning of section 368(c)) by five or fewer (but at least one) domestic corporations (controlling domestic corporations) immediately before the reorganization, appropriate basis adjustments under section 367(a)(5) are made to the stock received by the controlling domestic corporations in the reorganization, and any other conditions as provided in regulations under section 367(a)(5) are satisfied. For purposes of determining whether the domestic acquired corporation is controlled by five or fewer domestic corporations, all members of the same affiliated group within the meaning of section 1504 are treated as one corporation. Any adjustments to stock basis required under section 367(a)(5) must be made to the stock received by the controlling domestic corporation in the reorganization so the appropriate amount of built-in gain in the property transferred by the domestic acquired corporation to the foreign acquiring corporation in the section 361 exchange is reflected in the stock received. The basis adjustment requirement cannot be satisfied by adjusting the basis in stock of the foreign acquiring corporation held by the controlling domestic corporation before the reorganization. To the extent the appropriate amount of built-in gain in the property transferred by the domestic acquired corporation to the foreign acquiring corporation in the section 361 exchange cannot be preserved in the stock received by the controlling domestic corporation in the reorganization, the domestic acquired corporation's transfer of property to the foreign acquiring corporation is subject to section 367(a) and (d).

(*3*) For transactions occurring on or after August 19, 2008, and before March 18, 2013, the following condition also applies: to the extent any of the re-transferred assets constitute property to which section 367(d) applies, the exception under paragraph (d)(2)(iv)(B)(*1*) of this section, as contained in 26 CFR part 1 revised as of April 1, 2007, applies only if the property to which section 367(d) applies is treated as property subject to section 367(a) for purposes of satisfying the conditions and requirements of section 367(a)(5).

(vi) With respect to certain transfers of domestic stock or securities, the rules in paragraph (c) of this section are generally applicable for transfers occurring after January 29, 1997. See § 1.367(a)-3(c)(11). For transition rules regarding certain transfers of domestic stock or securities after December 16, 1987, and before January 30, 1997, and transfers of foreign stock or securities after December 16, 1987, and before July 20, 1998, see paragraph (j) of this section.

(vii)(A) Except as provided in this paragraph (g)(1)(vii), the rules of paragraph (e) of this section apply to transfers of stock or securities occurring on or after April 17, 2013. For matters covered in this section for periods before April 17, 2013, but on or after March 13, 2009, see § 1.367(a)-3(e) as contained in 26 CFR part 1 revised as of April 1, 2012. For matters covered in this section for periods before March 13, 2009, but on or after March 7, 2007, see § 1.367(a)-3T(e) as contained in 26 CFR part 1 revised as of April 1, 2007. For matters covered in this section for periods before March 7, 2007, but on or after July 20, 1998, see § 1.367(a)-8(f)(2)(i) as contained in 26 CFR part 1 revised as of April 1, 2006.

(B) Taxpayers may apply the rules of § 1.367(a)-3(e) to transfers occurring before March 13, 2009 and during a taxable year for which the period of limitations on assessments under section 6501(a) has not closed, if done consistently to all such transfers occurring during each taxable year. A taxpayer applies the rules of § 1.367(a)-3(e) to transfers occurring before March 13, 2009 and during a taxable year for which the period of limitations on assessments under section 6501(a) has not closed, by including the gain recognition agreement, annual certification, or other information filing, that is required as a result of the rules of § 1.367(a)-3(e) applying to such a transfer, with an amended tax return for the taxable year in which the transfer occurs that is filed on or before *August 10, 2009*. A taxpayer that wishes to apply the rules of § 1.367(a)-3(e) to transfers occurring before March 13, 2009 and during a taxable year for which the period of limitations on assessments under section 6501(a) has not closed but that fails to meet the filing requirement described in the preceding sentence must request relief for reasonable cause for such failure as provided in § 1.367(a)-8.

(viii) Paragraph (a)(2)(iv) of this section applies to exchanges occurring on or after May 17, 2011. For exchanges that occur prior to May 17, 2011, see § 1.367(a)-3T(b)(2)(i)(C) as contained in 26 CFR part 1 revised as of April 1, 2011.

(ix) Paragraphs (d)(2)(vi)(B)(*1*)(*i*) and (*iii*), (d)(2)(vi)(B)(*2*), and (d)(3), *Examples 6B, 6C,* and *9* of this section apply to transfers that occur on or after March 18, 2013. See paragraphs (d)(2)(vi)(B)(*1*)(*i*) and (*iii*), (d)(2)(vi)(B)(*2*), and (d)(3), *Examples 6B, 6C,* and *9* of this section, as contained in 26 CFR part 1 revised as of April 1, 2012, for transfers that occur on or after January 23, 2006, and before March 18, 2013. Paragraph (d)(2)(vi)(B)(*1*)(*ii*) of this section applies to statements that are required to be filed on or after November 19, 2014. See paragraph (d)(2)(vi)(B)(*1*)(*ii*) of this section, as contained in 26 CFR part 1 revised as of April 1, 2014, for statements required to be filed on or after March 18, 2013, and before November 19, 2014.

(x) Paragraphs (c)(6)(ii) and (f) of this section apply to statements that are required to be filed on or after November 19, 2014, as well as to requests for relief submitted on or after November 19, 2014.

(2) *Election.*—Notwithstanding paragraphs (g)(1) and (j) of this section, taxpayers may, by timely filing an original or amended return, elect to apply paragraphs (b) and (d) of this section to all transfers of foreign stock or securities occurring after December 16, 1987, and before July 20, 1998, except to the extent that a gain recognition agreement has been triggered prior to July 20, 1998. If an election is made under this paragraph (g)(2), the provisions of § 1.367(a)-3T(g) (see 26 CFR part 1, revised April 1, 1998) shall apply, and, for this purpose, the term *substantial portion* under § 1.367(a)-3T(g)(3)(iii) (see 26 CFR part 1, revised April 1, 1998) shall be interpreted to mean *substantially all* as defined in section 368(a)(1)(C). In addition, if such an election is made, the taxpayer must apply the rules under section 367(b) and the regulations thereunder to any transfers occurring within that period as if the election

to apply § 1.367(a)-3(b) and (d) to transfers occurring within that period had not been made, except that in the case of an exchange described in section 351 the taxpayer must apply section 367(b) and the regulations thereunder as if the exchange was described in § 7.367(b)-7 of this chapter (as in effect before February 23, 2000; see 26 CFR part 1, revised as of April 1, 1999). For example, if a U.S. person, pursuant to a section 351 exchange, transfers stock of a controlled foreign corporation in which it is a United States shareholder but does not receive back stock of a controlled foreign corporation in which it is a United States shareholder, the U.S. person must include in income under § 7.367(b)-7 of this chapter (as in effect before February 23, 2000; see 26 CFR part 1, revised as of April 1, 1999) the section 1248 amount attributable to the stock exchanged (to the extent that the fair market value of the stock exchanged exceeds its adjusted basis). Such inclusion is required even though § 7.367(b)-7 of this chapter (as in effect before February 23, 2000; see 26 CFR part 1, revised as of April 1, 1999), by its terms, did not apply to section 351 exchanges.

(h) *Former 10-year gain recognition agreements.*—If a taxpayer elects to apply the rules of this section to all prior transfers occurring after December 16, 1987, any 10-year gain recognition agreement that remains in effect (has not been triggered in full) on July 20, 1998 will be considered by the Internal Revenue Service to be a 5-year gain recognition agreement with a duration of five full taxable years following the close of the taxable year of the initial transfer.

(i) [Reserved].

(j) *Transition rules regarding certain transfers of domestic or foreign stock or securities after December 16, 1987, and prior to July 20, 1998.*—(1) *Scope.*—Transfers of domestic stock or securities described under section 367(a) that occurred after December 16, 1987, and prior to April 17, 1994, and transfers of foreign stock or securities described under section 367(a) that occur after December 16, 1987, and prior to July 20, 1998 are subject to the rules contained in section 367(a) and the regulations thereunder, as modified by the rules contained in paragraph (j)(2) of this section. For transfers of domestic stock or securities described under section 367(a) that occurred after April 17, 1994 and before January 30, 1997, see Temporary Income Regulations under section 367(a) in effect at the time of the transfer (§ 1.367(a)-3T(a) and (c), 26 CFR part 1, revised April 1, 1996) and paragraph (c)(11) of this section. For transfers of domestic stock or securities described under section 367(a) that occur after January 29, 1997, see § 1.367(a)-3(c).

(2) *Transfers of domestic or foreign stock or securities: additional substantive rules.*—(i) *Rule for less than 5-percent shareholders.*—Unless paragraph (j)(2)(iii) of this section applies (in the case of domestic stock or securities) or paragraph (j)(2)(iv) of this section applies (in the case of foreign stock or securities), a U.S. transferor that transfers stock or securities of a domestic or foreign corporation in an exchange described in section 367(a) and owns less than 5 percent of both the total voting power and the total value of the stock of the transferee foreign corporation immediately after the transfer (taking into account the attribution rules of section 958) is not subject to section 367(a)(1) and is not required to enter into a gain recognition agreement.

(ii) *Rule for 5-percent shareholders.*—Unless paragraph (j)(2)(iii) or (iv) of this section applies, a U.S. transferor that transfers domestic or foreign stock or securities in an exchange described in section 367(a) and owns at least 5 percent of either the total voting power or the total value of the stock of the transferee foreign corporation immediately after the transfer (taking into account the attribution rules under section 958) may qualify for nonrecognition treatment by filing a gain recognition agreement in accordance with § 1.367(a)-3T(g) in effect prior to July 20, 1998 (see 26 CFR part 1, revised April 1, 1998) for a duration of 5 or 10 years. The duration is 5 years if the U.S. transferor (5-percent shareholder) determines that all U.S. transferors, in the aggregate, own less than 50 percent of both the total voting power and the total value of the transferee foreign corporation immediately after the transfer. The duration is 10 years in all other cases. See, however, § 1.367(a)-3(h). If a 5-percent shareholder fails to properly enter into a gain recognition agreement, the exchange is taxable to such shareholder under section 367(a)(1).

(iii) *Gain recognition agreement option not available to controlling U.S. transferor if U.S. stock or securities are transferred.*—Notwithstanding the provisions of paragraph (j)(2)(ii) of this section, in no event will any exception to section 367(a)(1) apply to the transfer of stock or securities of a domestic corporation where the U.S. transferor owns (applying the attribution rules of section 958) more than 50 percent of either the total voting power or the total value of the stock of the transferee foreign corporation immediately after the transfer (i.e., the use of a gain recognition agreement to qualify for nonrecognition treatment is unavailable in this case).

(iv) *Loss of United States shareholder status in the case of a transfer of foreign stock.*—Notwithstanding the provisions of paragraphs (j)(2)(i) and (ii) of this section, in no event will any exception to section 367(a)(1) apply to the transfer of stock of a foreign corporation in which the U.S. transferor is a United States shareholder (as defined in § 7.367(b)-2(b) of this chapter (as in effect before February 23, 2000; see 26 CFR part 1, revised as of April 1, 1999) or section 953(c)) unless the U.S. transferor receives back stock in a controlled foreign corporation (as defined in section 953(c), section 957(a) or section 957(b)) as to which the U.S. transferor is a United States shareholder immediately after the transfer.

(k) [Reserved]. For further guidance, see § 1.367-3T(k). [Reg. § 1.367(a)-3.]

☐ [*T.D.* 8702, 12-27-96. *Amended by T.D.* 8770, 6-18-98 (*corrected* 3-31-99); *T.D.* 8850, 12-27-99; *T.D.* 8862, 1-21-2000; *T.D.* 9243, 1-23-2006; *T.D.* 9250, 2-17-2006; *T.D.* 9311, 2-1-2007 *T.D.* 9400, 5-23-2008; *T.D.* 9446, 2-9-2009 (*corrected* 3-26-2009); *T.D.* 9444, 2-10-2009; *T.D.* 9526, 5-17-2011; *T.D.* 9614, 3-18-2013; *T.D.* 9615, 3-18-2013; *T.D.* 9704, 11-18-2014; *T.D.* 9760, 3-18-2016; *T.D.* 9761, 4-4-2016; *T.D.* 9803, 12-15-2016 *and T.D.* 9834, 7-11-2018.]

Proposed Amendments to Regulation

§ 1.367(a)-3. Treatment of transfers of stock or securities to foreign corporations.—

* * *

(c) * * *

(4) * * *

(iv) *Attribution rule.*—Except as otherwise provided in this section, the rules of section 318, as modified by the rules of section 958(b) but without applying section 318(a)(3)(A), (B), and (C) so as to consider a U.S. person as owning stock which is owned by a person who is not a U.S. person, apply for purposes of determining the ownership or receipt of stock, securities, or other property under this paragraph. For purposes of determining whether a U.S. person is a five-percent transferee shareholder under paragraph (c)(1)(iii) of this section, however, the rules of section 318, as modified by the rules of section 958(b) (taking into account section 318(a)(3)(A), (B), and (C) so as to consider a U.S. person as owning stock which is owned by a person who is not a U.S. person), apply.

* * *

(11) * * *

(ii) * * * Paragraph (c)(4)(iv) of this section applies to transfers occurring on or after September 21, 2020. For transfers occurring before September 21, 2020, a taxpayer may apply paragraph (c)(4)(iv) of this section to transfers occurring during the last taxable year of a foreign corporation beginning before January 1, 2018, and each subsequent taxable year of the foreign corporation, provided that the taxpayer and persons that are related (within the meaning of section 267 or 707) to the taxpayer consistently apply this paragraph with respect to all transfers to all foreign corporations.

* * *

[Prop. Reg. § 1.367(a)-3.]

[Proposed 9-22-2020.]

§ 1.367(a)-4. Special rules applicable to specified transfers of property.—(a) *Depreciated property used in the United States.*—(1) *In general.*—A U.S. person that transfers U.S. depreciated property (as defined in paragraph (a)(2) of this section) to a foreign corporation in an exchange described in section 367(a)(1), must include in its gross income for the taxable year in which the transfer occurs ordinary income equal to the gain realized that would have been includible in the transferor's gross income as ordinary income under section 617(d)(1), 1245(a), 1250(a), 1252(a), 1254(a), or 1255(a), whichever is applicable, if at the time of the transfer the U.S. person had sold the property at its fair market value. Recapture of depreciation under this paragraph (a) is required regardless of whether the exception to section 367(a)(1) provided by § 1.367(a)-2(a)(2) applies to the transfer of the U.S. depreciated property. However, the transfer of the U.S. depreciated property may qualify for the exception with respect to realized gain that is not included in ordinary income pursuant to this paragraph (a).

(2) *U.S. depreciated property.*—U.S. depreciated property subject to the rules of this paragraph (a) is any property that—

(i) Is either mining property (as defined in section 617(f)(2)), section 1245 property (as defined in section 1245(a)(3)), section 1250 property (as defined in section 1250(c)), farm land (as defined in section 1252(a)(2)), section 1254 property (as defined in section 1254(a)(3)), or section 126 property (as defined in section 1255(a)(2)); and

(ii) Has been used in the United States or has been described in section 168(g)(4) before its transfer.

(3) *Property used within and without the United States.*—(i) If U.S. depreciated property has been used partly within and partly without the United States, then the amount required to be included in ordinary income pursuant to this paragraph (a) is reduced to an amount determined in accordance with the following formula:

$$\text{Full recapture amount} \times \frac{\text{U.S use}}{\text{Total use}}$$

(ii) For purposes of the fraction in paragraph (a)(3)(i) of this section, the "full recapture amount" is the amount that would otherwise be included in the transferor's income under paragraph (a)(1) of this section. "U.S. use" is the number of months that the property either was used within the United States or has been described in section 168(g)(4), and was subject to depreciation by the transferor or a related person. "Total use" is the total number of months that the property was used (or available for use), and subject to depreciation, by the transferor or a related person. For purposes of this paragraph (a)(3), property is not considered to have been in use outside of the United States during any period in which such property was, for purposes of section 168, treated as property not used predominantly outside the United States pursuant to section 168(g)(4). For purposes of this paragraph (a)(3), the term "related person" has the meaning set forth in § 1.367(d)-1(h).

(b) *Effective/applicability dates.*—The rules of this section apply to transfers occurring on or after September 14, 2015, and to transfers occurring before September 14, 2015, resulting from entity classification elections made under § 301.7701-3 that are filed on or after September 14, 2015. For transfers occurring before this section is applicable, see §§ 1.367(a)-4 and 1.367(a)-4T as contained in 26 CFR part 1 revised as of April 1, 2016. [Reg. § 1.367(a)-4.]

☐ [*T.D.* 9525, 5-5-2011. *Amended by T.D.* 9803, 12-15-2016.]

§ 1.367(a)-5. [Reserved].

☐ [*T.D.* 9525, 5-5-2011. *Removed and reserved by T.D.* 9803, 12-15-2016.]

§ 1.367(a)-6. Transfer of foreign branch with previously deducted losses.—(a) through (b)(1) [Reserved]. For further guidance, see § 1.367(a)-6T(a) through (b)(1).

(b)(2) *No active conduct exception.*—The rules of this paragraph (b) apply regardless of whether any of the assets of the foreign branch satisfy the active trade or business exception of § 1.367(a)-2(a)(2).

(c)(1) [Reserved]. For further guidance, see § 1.367(a)-6T(c)(1).

(2) *Gain limitation.*—The gain required to be recognized under paragraph (b)(1) of this section will not exceed the aggregate amount of gain realized on the transfer of all branch assets (without regard to the transfer of any assets on which loss is realized but not recognized).

(3) [Reserved].

(4) *Transfers of certain intangible property.*—Gain realized on the transfer of intangible property (computed with reference to the fair market value of the intangible property as of the date of the transfer) that is an asset of a foreign branch is taken into account in computing the limitation on loss recapture under paragraph (c)(2) of this section. For rules relating to the crediting of gain recognized under this section against income deemed to arise by operation of section 367(d), see § 1.367(d)-1(g)(3).

(d) through (i) [Reserved]. For further guidance, see § 1.367(a)-6T(d) through (i).

(j) *Effective/applicability dates.*—The rules of this section apply to transfers occurring on or after September 14, 2015, and to transfers occurring before September 14, 2015, resulting from entity classification elections made under § 301.7701-3 that are filed on or after September 14, 2015. For transfers occurring before this section is applicable, see § 1.367(a)-6T as contained in 26 CFR part 1 revised as of April 1, 2016. [Reg. § 1.367(a)-6.]

☐ [*T.D.* 9760, 3-18-2016. *Amended by T.D.* 9803, 12-15-2016.]

§ 1.367(a)-6T. Transfer of foreign branch with previously deducted losses (temporary).—Transfer of foreign branch with previously deducted losses (temporary).—(a) *In general.*—This section provides special rules relating to the transfer of the assets of a foreign branch with previously deducted losses. Paragraph (b) of this section provides generally that such losses must be recaptured by the recognition of the gain realized on the transfer. Paragraph (c) of this section sets forth rules concerning the character of, and limitations on, the gain required to be recognized. Paragraph (d) of this section defines the term "previously deducted losses." Paragraph (e) of this section describes certain reductions that are made to the previously deducted losses before they are taken into income under this section. Finally, paragraph (g) of this section defines the term "foreign branch."

(b) *Recognition of gain required.*—(1) *In general.*—If a U.S. person transfers any assets of a foreign branch to a foreign corporation in an exchange described in section 367(a)(1), then the transferor shall recognize gain equal to—

(i) The sum of the previously deducted branch ordinary losses as defined and reduced in paragraphs (d) and (e) of this section; and

(ii) The sum of the previously deducted branch capital losses as defined and reduced in paragraphs (d) and (e) of this section.

(2) [Reserved].

(c) *Special rules concerning gain recognized.*—(1) *Character and source of gain.*—The gain described in paragraph (b)(1)(i) of this section shall be treated as ordinary income of the transferor, and the gain described in paragraph (b)(1)(ii) of this section shall be treated as long-term capital gain of the transferor. Gain that is recognized pursuant to the rules of this section shall be treated as income from sources outside the United States. Such recognized gain shall be treated as foreign oil and gas extraction income (as defined in section 907) in the same proportion that previously deducted foreign oil and gas extraction losses bore to the total amount of previously deducted losses.

(2) [Reserved].

(3) *Foreign goodwill and going concern value.*—For purposes of this section, the assets of a foreign branch shall include foreign goodwill and going concern value related to the business of the foreign branch, as defined in § 1.367(a)-1T(d)(5)(iii). Thus, gain realized upon the transfer of the foreign goodwill or going concern value of a foreign branch to a foreign corporation will be taken into account in computing the limitation on loss recapture under paragraph (c)(2) of this section.

(4) [Reserved].

(d) *Previously deducted losses.*—(1) *In general.*—This paragraph (d) provides rules for determining, for purposes of paragraph (b)(1) of this section, the previously deducted losses of a foreign branch any of whose assets are transferred to a foreign corporation in an exchange described in section 367(a)(1). Initially, the two previously deducted losses of a foreign branch for a taxable year are the total ordinary loss ("previously deducted branch ordinary loss") and the total capital loss ("previously deducted branch capital loss") that were realized by the foreign branch in that taxable year (a "branch loss year") prior to the transfer and that were or will be reflected on a U.S. income tax return of the transferor. The previously deducted branch ordinary loss for each branch loss year is reduced by expired net ordinary losses under paragraph (d)(2) of this section, while the previously deducted capital loss for each loss year is reduced by expired net capital losses under paragraph (d)(3) of this section. For each branch loss year, the remaining previously deducted branch ordinary loss and the remaining previously deducted branch capital loss are then reduced, proceeding from the first branch loss year to the last branch loss year, to reflect expired foreign tax credits under paragraph (d)(4) of this section. The reductions are made in the order of the taxable years in which the foreign tax credits arose. Finally, similar reductions are made to reflect expired investment credits under paragraph (d)(5) of this section.

(2) *Reduction by expired net ordinary loss.*—(i) *In general.*—The previously deducted branch ordinary loss for each branch loss year shall be reduced under this paragraph (d)(2) by the amount of any expired net ordinary loss with respect to that branch loss year.

Expired net ordinary losses arising in years other than the branch loss year shall reduce the previously deducted branch ordinary loss for the branch loss year only to the extent that the previously deducted branch ordinary loss exceeds the net operating loss, if any, incurred by the transferor in the branch loss year. The previously deducted branch ordinary losses shall be reduced proceeding from the first branch loss year to the last branch loss year. For each branch loss year, expired net operating losses shall be applied to reduce the previously deducted branch ordinary loss for that year in the order in which the expired net ordinary losses arose.

(ii) *Existence of expired net ordinary loss.*—An expired net ordinary loss exists with respect to a branch loss year to the extent that—

(A) The transferor incurred a net operating loss (within the meaning of section 172(c));

(B) That net operating loss arose in the branch loss year or was available for carryover or carryback to the branch loss year under section 172(b)(1);

(C) That net operating loss has neither given rise to a net operating loss deduction (within the meaning of section 172(a)) for any taxable year prior to the year of the transfer, nor given rise to a reduction of any previously deducted branch ordinary loss (pursuant to paragraph (d)(2) of this section) of any foreign branch of the transferor upon a previous transfer to a foreign corporation; and

(D) The period during which the transferor may claim a net operating loss deduction with respect to that net operating loss has expired.

(3) *Reduction by expired net capital loss.*—(i) *In general.*—The previously deducted branch capital loss for each branch loss year shall be reduced under this paragraph (d)(3) by the amount of any expired net capital loss with respect to that branch loss year. Expired net capital losses arising in years other than the branch loss year shall reduce the previously deducted branch capital loss for the branch loss year only to the extent that the previously deducted branch capital loss exceeds the net capital loss, if any, incurred by the transferor in the branch loss year. The previously deducted branch capital losses shall be reduced proceeding from the first branch loss year to the last branch loss year. For each branch loss year, expired net capital losses shall be applied to reduce the previously deducted branch capital loss for that year in the order in which the expired net capital losses arose.

(ii) *Existence of expired net capital loss.*—An expired net capital loss exists with respect to a branch loss year to the extent that—

(A) The transferor incurred a net capital loss (within the meaning of section 1222(10));

(B) That net capital loss arose in the branch loss year or was available for carryover or carryback to the branch loss year under section 1212;

(C) That net capital loss has neither been allowed for any taxable year prior to the year of the transfer, nor given rise to a reduction of any previously deducted branch capital loss (pursuant to paragraph (d)(3) of this section) of any foreign branch of the transferor upon any previous transfer to a foreign corporation; and

(D) The period during which the transferor may claim a capital loss deduction with respect to that net capital loss has expired.

(4) *Reduction for expired foreign tax credits.*—(i) *In general.*—The previously deducted branch ordinary loss and the previously deducted branch capital loss for each branch loss year remaining after the reductions described in paragraph (d)(2) and (3) of this section shall be further reduced under this paragraph (d)(4) proportionately by the amount of any expired foreign tax credit loss equivalent with respect to that branch loss year. The previously deducted branch losses shall be reduced proceeding from the first branch loss year to the last branch loss year. For each branch loss year, expired foreign tax credit loss equivalents shall be applied to reduce the previously deducted branch loss for the year in the order in which the expired foreign tax credits arose.

(ii) *Existence of foreign tax credit loss equivalent.*—A foreign tax credit loss equivalent exists with respect to a branch loss year if—

(A) The transferor paid, accrued, or is deemed under section 902 or 960 to have paid creditable foreign taxes in a taxable year;

(B) The creditable foreign taxes were paid, accrued, or deemed paid in the branch loss year or were available for carryover or carryback to the branch loss year under section 904(c);

(C) No foreign tax credit with respect to the foreign taxes paid, accrued, or deemed paid has been taken because of the operation of section 904(a) or similar limitations provided by the Code or an applicable treaty, and such taxes have not given rise to a reduction (pursuant to this paragraph (d)(5)) of any previously deducted branch loss of the foreign branch for a prior taxable year or of any previously deducted branch losses of any foreign branch of the transferor upon a prior transfer to a foreign corporation; and

(D) The period during which the transferor may claim a foreign tax credit for the foreign taxes paid, accrued, or deemed paid has expired.

(iii) *Amount of foreign tax credit loss equivalent.*—The amount of the foreign tax credit loss equivalent for the branch loss year with respect to the creditable foreign taxes described in paragraph (d)(4)(ii) of this section is the amount of those creditable foreign taxes divided by the highest rate of tax to which the transferor was subject in the loss year.

(5) *Reduction for expired investment credits.*—(i) *In general.*—The previously deducted branch ordinary loss and the previously deducted branch capital loss for each branch loss year shall be further reduced under this paragraph (d)(5) proportionately by the amount of any expired investment credit loss equivalent with respect to that branch year. The previously deducted branch losses shall be reduced proceeding from the first branch loss year to the last branch loss year. For each branch loss year, expired investment credit loss equivalents shall be applied to reduce the previously deducted branch loss for that year in the order in which the expired investment credits were earned.

(ii) *Existence of investment credit loss equivalent.*—An investment credit loss equivalent exists with respect to a branch loss year if—

(A) The transferor earned an investment credit (within the meaning of section 46(a)) in a taxable year;

(B) The investment credit was earned in the branch loss year or was available for carryover or carryback to the branch loss year under section 39;

(C) The investment credit earned by the transferor in the credit year has been denied by section 38(a) or by similar provisions of the Code and has not given rise to a reduction (pursuant to this paragraph (d)(5)) of any previously deducted branch loss of the foreign branch for a preceding taxable year or of the previously deducted losses of any foreign branch of the transferor upon any previous transfer to a foreign corporation; and

(D) The period during which the transferor may claim the investment credit has expired.

(iii) *Amount of investment tax credit loss equivalent.*—The amount of the investment credit loss equivalent for the branch loss year with respect to the investment credit described in paragraph (d)(5)(ii) of this section is 85 percent of the amount of that investment credit divided by the highest rate of tax to which the transferor was subject in the loss year.

(e) *Amounts that reduce previously deducted losses subject to recapture.*—(1) *In general.*—This paragraph (e) describes five amounts that reduce the sum of the previously deducted branch ordinary losses and the sum of the previously deducted branch capital losses before they are taken into income under paragraph (b) of this section. Amounts representing ordinary income shall be applied to reduce first the sum of the previously deducted branch ordinary losses to the extent thereof, and then the sum of the previously deducted branch capital losses to the extent thereof. Similarly, amounts representing capital gains shall be applied to reduce first the sum of the previously deducted branch capital losses and then the sum of the previously deducted branch ordinary losses.

(2) *Taxable income.*—The previously deducted losses shall be reduced by any taxable income of the foreign branch recognized through the close of the taxable year of the transfer, whether before or after any taxable year in which losses were incurred.

(3) *Amounts currently recaptured under section 904(f)(3).*—The previously deducted losses shall be reduced by the amount recognized under section 904(f)(3) on account of the transfer.

(4) [Reserved.]

(5) *Amounts previously recaptured under section 904(f)(3).*—(i) *In general.*—The previously deducted branch losses shall be reduced by the portion of any amount recognized under section 904(f)(3) upon a previous transfer of property that was attributable to the losses of the

foreign branch, provided that the amount did not reduce any gain otherwise required to be recognized under section 367(a)(3)(C) and this section (or Revenue Ruling 78-201, 1978-1 C.B. 91).

(ii) *Portion attributable to the losses of the foreign branch.*—(A) *Branch property.*—The full amount recognized under section 904(f)(3) upon a previous transfer of property of the branch shall be treated as attributable to the losses of the foreign branch.

(B) *Non-branch property.*—The portion of the amount previously recognized under section 904(f)(3) upon a transfer of non-branch property that was attributable to the losses of the foreign branch shall be the sum, over the taxable years in which the transferor sustained an overall foreign loss some portion of which was recaptured on the disposition, of the recaptured portions of those overall foreign losses after multiplication by the following fraction:

$$\frac{\text{Losses of the foreign branch for the year}}{\text{All foreign losses for the year}}$$

For purposes of this fraction, the term "losses of the foreign branch for the year" means the losses of the foreign branch that were taken into account under section 904(f)(2) in determining the amount of the transferor's overall foreign loss for the year, and the term "all foreign losses for the year" means all of the lossses of the transferor that were taken into account under section 904(f)(2).

(6) *Amounts previously recognized under the rules of this section.*—The previously deducted losses shall be reduced by the amounts previously recognized under the rules of this section upon a previous transfer of assets of the foreign branch.

(f) *Example.*—The rules of paragraphs (b) through (e) of this section are illustrated by the following example.

Example. (i) *Facts.* X, a U.S. corporation, is a calendar year taxpayer. On January 1, 1981, X established a branch in foreign country A to manufacture and sell X's products in country A. On July 1, 1986, X organized corporation Y, a country A subsidiary, and transferred to Y all of the assets of its country A branch, including goodwill and going concern value. During the period from January 1, 1981, through July 1, 1986, X's country A branch earned income and incurred losses in the following amounts:

Country A branch

Year	*Ordinary income (loss)*	*Capital gain (loss)*
1981	(200)	0
1982	(300)	(100)
1983	(400)	0
1984	200	0
1985	(100)	0
1986	50	0

At the time of the transfer of X's country A branch assets to Y, those assets had a fair market value of $2,500 and an adjusted basis of $1,000. For each of the assets, fair market value exceeded adjusted basis. X had no net capital loss or unused investment credit during any taxable year relevant to the transfer. In 1984, X incurred a net operating loss of $400, $200 of which was carried back to prior years. An additional $50 of the 1984 net operating loss was carried over to 1985. The remaining $150 of the 1984 net operating loss was not used in any year prior to the transfer. In 1979, X paid creditable foreign taxes of $330 that could not be claimed as a credit in that year or any earlier year because of section 904. Of those foreign taxes, $100 were carried over and claimed as a credit in 1983, but the remaining $230 were not used in any year prior to the transfer. X was not required to recognize any gain under section 904(f)(3) on account of the 1986 transfer or any prior transfer. X was not required to recognize gain upon the transfer under section 367(a) (other than by reason of the provisions of this section).

(ii) *Previously deducted losses.* The previously deducted losses of X's country A branch are $575 of ordinary losses and $25 of capital losses, computed as follows: Initially, the branch has previously deducted ordinary losses of $1,000 ($200 + $300 + $400 + $100), and previously deducted capital losses of $100. (See paragraph (d)(1) of this section.)

(iii) *Expired losses and credits.* Under the facts of this example, there are no reductions for expired net ordinary losses or expired net capital losses under paragraph (d)(2) or (3) of this section. However, the previously deducted losses are reduced proceeding from the first branch loss year to the last branch loss year to reflect the expired foreign tax credit from 1979. The amount of the foreign tax credit loss equivalent with respect to 1981 is $500 ($230 / .46). It reduces the previously deducted losses for 1981 proportionately. Thus, the previously deducted ordinary loss for 1981 is reduced from $200 to $0. (See paragraph (d)(4) of this section.) The amount of the foreign tax credit loss equivalent with respect to 1982 is $300 ($500 – $200, *i.e.*, $138 / .46). (See paragraph (d)(4)(ii)(C) of this section.) It reduces the previously deducted losses for 1982 proportionately. Thus, the previously deducted ordinary loss for 1982 is reduced from $300 to $75, and the previously deducted capital loss for 1982 is reduced from $100 to $25.

(iv) *Further reductions.* The previously deducted ordinary losses of $575 and the previously deducted capital losses of $25 are reduced by the taxable income earned by the branch prior to the date of the transfer ($250). (See paragraph (e)(2) of this section.) Since that income was ordinary income, it is applied first to reduce the previously deducted ordinary losses of $575 to $325. (See paragraph (e)(1) of this section.)

(v) *Recapture.* Since the gain realized by X upon its transfer of the branch assets to Y exceeds the sum of the previously deducted branch losses as defined and reduced above ($325 + $25), the limitation in paragraph (c)(2) of this section does not apply. Thus, X is required to recognize $325 of ordinary income and $25 of long-term capital gain upon the transfer. (See paragraph (b) and (c)(1) of this section.)

(g) *Definition of foreign branch.*—(1) *In general.*—For purposes of this section, the term "foreign branch" means an integral business operation carried on by a U.S. person outside the United States. Whether the activities of a U.S. person outside the United States constitute a foreign branch operation must be determined under all the facts and circumstances. Evidence of the existence of a foreign branch includes, but is not limited to, the existence of a separate set of books and records, and the existence of an office or other fixed place of business used by employees or officers of the U.S. person in carrying out business activities outside the United States. Activities outside the United States shall be deemed to constitute a foreign branch for purposes of this section if the activities constitute a permanent establishment under the terms of a treaty between the United States and the country in which the activities are carried out. Any U.S. person may be treated as having a foreign branch for purposes of this section, whether that person is a corporation, partnership, trust, estate, or individual.

(2) *More than one branch.*—If a U.S. person carries on more than one branch operation outside the United States, then the rules of this section must be separately applied with respect to each foreign branch that is transferred to a foreign corporation. Thus, the previously deducted losses of one branch may not be offset, for purposes of determining the gain required to be recognized under the rules of this section, by the income of another branch that is also transferred to a foreign corporation. Similarly, the losses of one branch shall not be recaptured upon a transfer of the assets of a separate branch. Whether the foreign activities of a U.S. person are carried out through more than one branch must be determined under all of the facts and circumstances. In general, a separate branch exists if a particular group of activities is sufficiently integrated to constitute a single business that could be operated as an independent enterprise. For purposes of determining the combination of activities that constitute a branch operation as defined in this paragraph (g), the nominal relationship among those activities shall not be controlling. Factors suggesting that nominally separate business operations constitute a single foreign branch include a substantial identity of products, customers, operational facilities, operational processes, accounting and record-keeping functions, management, employees, distribution channels, or sales and purchasing forces. For examples of the application of the principles of this paragraph (g)(2), see Revenue Ruling 81-82, 1981-1 C.B. 127.

(3) *Consolidated group.*—For purposes of this section, the activities of each of two domestic corporations outside the United States will be considered to constitute a single foreign branch if—

(i) The two corporations are members of the same consolidated group of corporations; and

(ii) The activities of the two corporations in the aggregate would constitute a single foreign branch if conducted by a single corporation.

Notwithstanding the preceding rule of this paragraph (g)(3), gains of a foreign branch of a domestic corporation arising in a year in which that corporation did not file a consolidated return with a second domestic corporation shall not be applied to reduce the previously deducted losses of a foreign branch of the second corporation (but may be applied to reduce such losses of the foreign branch of the first corporation) upon the transfer of the two branches to a foreign corporation, even though the two domestic corporations file a consolidated return for the year in which the transfer occurs and the two branches are considered at that time to constitute a single foreign branch. For an example of the application of the principles of this paragraph (g)(3), see Revenue Ruling 81-89, 1981-1 C.B. 129.

(4) *Property not transferred.*—A U.S. transferor's failure to transfer any property of a foreign branch shall be irrelevant to the determination of the previously deducted losses of the branch subject to recapture under the rules of this section. Thus, if the activities with respect to untransferred property constituted a part of the branch operation under the rules of this paragraph (g), then the losses generated by those activities shall be subject to recapture, notwithstanding the failure to transfer the property. For an example of the application of the principles of this paragraph (g)(4), see Revenue Ruling 80-247, 1980-2 C.B. 127, relating to property abandoned by the U.S. transferor.

(h) *Anti-abuse rule.*—If—

(1) A U.S. person transfers property of a foreign branch to a domestic corporation for a principal purpose of avoiding the effect of this section; and

(2) The domestic corporation thereafter transfers the property of the foreign branch to a foreign corporation,

then, solely for purposes of this section, that U.S. person shall be treated as having transferred the property of the branch directly to the foreign corporation. A U.S. person shall be presumed to have transferred property of a foreign branch for a principal purpose of avoiding the effect of this section if the property is transferred to the domestic corporation less than two years prior to the domestic corporation's transfer of the property to a foreign corporation. This presumption may be rebutted by clear evidence that the subsequent transfer of the property was not contemplated at the time of the initial transfer to the domestic corporation and that avoidance of the effect of this section was not a principal purpose for the transaction. A transfer may have more than one principal purpose.

(i) *Basis adjustments.*—Basis adjustments reflecting gain recognized pursuant to this section shall be made as described in § 1.367(a)-1T(b)(4)(ii).

(j) [Reserved]. [Temporary Reg. § 1.367(a)-6T]

☐ [*T.D. 8087, 5-15-86. Amended by T.D. 9615, 3-18-2013, T.D. 9760, 3-18-2016 and T.D. 9803, 12-15-2016.*]

§ 1.367(a)-7. Outbound transfers of property described in section 361(a) or (b).—(a) *Scope and purpose.*—This section provides rules under section 367(a)(5) that apply to the transfer of certain property (including stock or securities) by a domestic corporation (U.S. transferor) to a foreign corporation (foreign acquiring corporation) in a section 361 exchange. This section applies only to the transfer of section 367(a) property. See section 367(d) for rules applicable to transfers of section 367(d) property. Paragraph (b) of this section provides the general rule requiring the recognition of gain on the transfer of section 367(a) property, while paragraph (c) of this section provides an elective exception to the general rule that is available if certain requirements are satisfied. Paragraph (d) of this section provides rules for applying the elective exception to a section 361 exchange followed by successive distributions to which section 355 applies. Paragraph (e) of this section provides rules for recognizing gain on section 367(a) property, not willful relief provisions, an anti-abuse rule, and special rules that take into account income inclusions under § 1.367(b)-4 and gain recognition under § 1.367(a)-6. Paragraph (f) of this section provides definitions, and paragraph (g) of this section provides examples. Paragraph (h) of this section provides applicable cross-references, paragraph (i) of this section is reserved, and paragraph (j) of this section provides effective/applicability dates.

(b) *General rule.*—(1) *Nonrecognition exchanges enumerated in section 367(a)(1).*—Except to the extent provided in paragraphs (b)(2) and (c) of this section, the exceptions to section 367(a)(1) provided in section 367(a) and the regulations under that section do not apply to a transfer of section 367(a) property by a U.S. transferor to a foreign acquiring corporation in a section 361 exchange, and the U.S. transferor shall recognize any gain (but not loss) realized with respect to the section 367(a) property under section 367(a)(1). Realized gain is recognized pursuant to the prior sentence notwithstanding the application of any other nonrecognition provision enumerated in section 367(a)(1) to the transfer (such as section 351 or 354).

(2) *Nonrecognition exchanges not enumerated in section 367(a)(1).*—To the extent a transfer of items of property described in paragraph (b)(1) of this section also qualifies for nonrecognition under a provision that is not enumerated in section 367(a)(1) (such as section 1036), the U.S. transferor recognizes gain or loss realized on the transfer of such items of property, but the amount of loss recognized on the property shall not exceed the amount of gain recognized on the property. See section 337(d).

(c) *Elective exception.*—Except to the extent provided in paragraph (d) of this section, paragraph (b) of this section does not apply to the transfer of section 367(a) property by a U.S. transferor to a foreign acquiring corporation in a section 361 exchange if the conditions of paragraphs (c)(1), (c)(2), (c)(3), and (c)(4) of this section are satisfied, and an election to apply the exception provided by this paragraph (c) is made in the manner provided by paragraph (c)(5) of this section. If this paragraph (c) applies to the section 361 exchange, see, for example, §§ 1.367(a)-2, 1.367(a)-3, 1.367(a)-4, or 1.367(a)-6, as applicable, for additional requirements that must be satisfied in order for the U.S. transferor to not recognize gain under section 367(a)(1) on the transfer of section 367(a) property in the section 361 exchange. Nothing in this section provides for the nonrecognition of gain not otherwise permitted under another provision of the Internal Revenue Code (Code) or the regulations.

(1) *Control.*—Immediately before the reorganization, the U.S. transferor is controlled (within the meaning of section 368(c)) by five or fewer, but at least one, control group members. For illustrations of this rule, see paragraph (g) of this section, *Example 4* and *Example 5*.

(2) *Gain recognition.*—(i) *Non-control group members.*—The U.S. transferor recognizes gain equal to the product of the inside gain multiplied by the aggregate ownership interest percentage of all non-control group members, reduced (but not below zero) by the sum of the amounts described in paragraphs (c)(2)(i)(A), (c)(2)(i)(B), and (c)(2)(i)(C) of this section.

(A) Gain recognized with respect to stock or securities under § 1.367(a)-3(e)(3)(iii)(B) (including any portion treated as a deemed dividend under section 1248(a));

(B) Gain recognized with respect to stock or securities under § 1.367(a)-6 (including any portion treated as a deemed dividend under section 1248(a)) attributable to non-control group members (as determined pursuant to § 1.367(a)-7(e)(5)); and

(C) A deemed dividend included in income under § 1.367(b)-4 attributable to non-control group members (as determined pursuant to § 1.367(a)-7(e)(4)).

(ii) *Control group members.*—With respect to each control group member, the U.S. transferor recognizes gain equal to the amount, if any, by which the amount described in paragraph (c)(2)(ii)(A) of this section exceeds the amount described in paragraph (c)(2)(ii)(B) of this section.

(A) The product of the inside gain multiplied by such control group member's ownership interest percentage, reduced (but not below zero) by the sum of the amounts described in paragraphs (c)(2)(ii)(A)(*1*), (c)(2)(ii)(A)(*2*), and (c)(2)(ii)(A)(*3*) of this section (attributable inside gain).

(*1*) Gain recognized with respect to stock or securities under § 1.367(a)-3(e)(3)(iii)(C) (including any portion treated as a deemed dividend under section 1248(a)) attributable to the control group member;

(*2*) Gain recognized with respect to stock or securities under § 1.367(a)-6 (including any portion treated as a deemed dividend under section 1248(a)) attributable to the control group member (as determined pursuant to § 1.367(a)-7(e)(5)); and

(*3*) A deemed dividend included in income under § 1.367(b)-4 attributable to the control group member (as determined pursuant to § 1.367(a)-7(e)(4)).

(B) The product of the section 367(a) percentage multiplied by the fair market value of the stock received by the U.S. transferor in the section 361 exchange and distributed to the control group member under section 354, 355, or 356.

(iii) *Illustration of rules.*—For an illustration of gain recognition under paragraph (c)(2)(i) of this section, see paragraph (g) of this section, *Example 1*. For an illustration of gain recognition under paragraph (c)(2)(ii) of this section, see paragraph (g) of this section, *Example 2*.

(3) *Basis adjustments required for control group members.*—(i) *General rule.*—Except as provided in paragraph (c)(3)(iv) of this section, if there is any attributable inside gain (determined under paragraph (c)(2)(ii)(A) of this section) with respect to a control group member, then such control group member's aggregate basis in the stock received in exchange for (or with respect to, as applicable) stock or securities of the U.S. transferor under section 354, 355, or 356, as determined under section 358 and the regulations under that section (section 358 basis), is reduced by the amount in paragraph (c)(3)(i)(A), (c)(3)(i)(B), or (c)(3)(i)(C) of this section, as applicable.

(A) If the control group member has outside gain, the amount, if any, by which the attributable inside gain, reduced by any gain recognized by the U.S. transferor with respect to the control group member under paragraph (c)(2)(ii) of this section, exceeds the control group member's outside gain.

(B) If the control group member has outside loss, the amount, if any, by which the attributable inside gain, reduced by any gain recognized by the U.S. transferor with respect to the control group member under paragraph (c)(2)(ii) of this section, exceeds the control group member's outside loss (for this purpose, treating the outside loss as a negative amount).

(C) If the control group member has no outside gain or outside loss, the amount of the attributable inside gain, reduced by any gain recognized by the U.S. transferor with respect to the control group member under paragraph (c)(2)(ii) of this section.

(ii) *Stock received in the section 361 exchange.*—This paragraph (c)(3) applies only to stock received by the U.S. transferor in the section 361 exchange and distributed to the control group member in exchange for (or with respect to, as applicable) stock or securities of the U.S. transferor.

(iii) *Pro rata adjustments.*—The section 358 basis of each share of stock received by the control group member must be reduced pro rata based on the relative section 358 basis of all shares of stock received by the control group member.

(iv) *Successive distributions to which section 355 applies.*—Paragraph (c)(3) of this section does not apply to a control group member that distributes the stock of a foreign acquiring corporation received from the U.S. transferor in a distribution satisfying the requirements of section 355 (section 355 distribution) that is in connection with a transaction described in paragraph (d) of this section (relating to successive section 355 distributions). If paragraph (c)(3) of this section does not apply to a control group member pursuant to this paragraph (c)(3)(iv), then paragraph (c)(3) of this section shall apply to the final distributee (as defined in paragraph (d) of this section) that receives the stock of the foreign acquiring corporation in the final section 355 distribution described in paragraph (d) of this section.

(v) *Illustration of rules.*—For illustrations of the adjustment to stock basis under paragraph (c)(3)(i) of this section, see paragraph (g) of this section, *Example 1* and *Example 2*, § 1.367(a)-3(e)(8), *Example 3*, and § 1.1248(f)-2(e), *Example 3*. For an illustration of the adjustment to stock basis under paragraph (c)(3)(iii) of this section, see paragraph (g) of this section, *Example 3*.

(4) *Agreement to amend or file a U.S. income tax return.*—(i) *General rule.*—Except as provided in paragraph (c)(4)(ii) of this section, the U.S. transferor complies with the requirements of § 1.6038B-1(c)(6)(iii), relating to the requirement to report gain that was not recognized by the U.S. transferor upon certain subsequent dispositions by the foreign acquiring corporation of section 367(a) property received from the U.S. transferor in the section 361 exchange.

(ii) *Exception.*—To the extent section 367(a) property transferred in the section 361 exchange is subject to § 1.367(a)-3(e) (relating to transfers of stock or securities by a domestic corporation to a foreign corporation in a section 361 exchange), § 1.6038B-1(c)(6)(iii) does not apply with respect to the transfer of that property.

(5) *Election and reporting requirements.*—(i) *General rule.*—The U.S. transferor and each control group member elect to apply the provisions of paragraph (c) of this section in the manner provided under paragraph (c)(5)(ii) or (c)(5)(iii) of this section, as applicable, and by entering into a written agreement described in paragraph (c)(5)(iv) of this section. If a control group member distributes the stock of the foreign acquiring corporation received from the U.S. transferor in a section 355 distribution that is in connection with a transaction described in paragraph (d) of this section, the final distributee that receives that stock in the final section 355 distribution elects to apply the provisions of this paragraph (c) and enters into the written agreement instead of the control group member. For this purpose, the term *control group member* will be replaced by the term *final distributee*, as appropriate.

(ii) *Control group member.*—(A) *Time and manner of making election.*—Each control group member elects to apply the provisions of paragraph (c) of this section by including a statement (in the form and with the content specified in paragraph (c)(5)(ii)(B) of this section) on or with a timely filed return for the taxable year in which the reorganization occurs. If the control group member is a member of a consolidated group but is not the common parent of the consolidated group, the common parent makes the election on behalf of the control group member.

(B) *Form and content of election statement.*—The statement must be entitled, "ELECTION TO APPLY EXCEPTION UNDER § 1.367(a)-7(c)," and set forth:

(1) The name and taxpayer identification number (if any) of the control group member, the U.S. transferor, the foreign acquiring corporation and, in the case of a triangular reorganization (within the meaning of § 1.358-6(b)(2)), the corporation that controls the foreign acquiring corporation; the control group member's ownership interest percentage in the U.S. transferor; and the percentage of voting stock and non-voting stock of the U.S. transferor owned by the control group member for purposes of satisfying the control requirement of paragraph (c)(1) of this section;

(2) If the control group member is a member of a consolidated group but is not the common parent, the name and taxpayer identification number of the common parent;

(3) The amount of the adjustment (if any) to stock basis required under paragraph (c)(3) of this section, the resulting adjusted basis in the stock, and the fair market value of the stock, or if no stock was received, indicate no stock was received; and

(4) The date on which the written agreement described in paragraph (c)(5)(iv) of this section was entered into.

(iii) *Statement by U.S. transferor.*—The U.S. transferor elects to apply the provisions of paragraph (c) of this section in the form and manner set forth in § 1.6038B-1(c)(6)(ii).

(iv) *Written agreement.*—The U.S. transferor and each control group member must enter into a written agreement satisfying the conditions of this paragraph on or before the due date (including extensions) for the U.S. transferor's tax return for the taxable year in which the reorganization occurs. Each party to the agreement must retain the original or a copy of the agreement in the manner specified by § 1.6001-1(e). Each party to the agreement must provide a copy of the agreement to the Internal Revenue Service within 30 days of the receipt of a request for the copy of the agreement. The written agreement must—

(A) State the document constitutes an agreement entered into pursuant to paragraph (c)(5) of this section;

(B) Identify the U.S. transferor, the foreign acquiring corporation, the corporation that controls the foreign acquiring corporation (in the case of a triangular reorganization within the meaning of § 1.358-6(b)(2)), and each control group member, and provide the taxpayer identification number (if any) for each corporation;

(C) State the amount of gain (if any) recognized by the U.S. transferor under paragraph (c)(2) of this section; and

(D) With respect to each control group member, state the amount of the adjustment (if any) to stock basis required under paragraph (c)(3) of this section, the resulting adjusted basis in the stock, and the fair market value of the stock. Alternatively, if a control group member did not receive any stock, indicate that no stock was received.

(d) *Section 361 exchange followed by successive distributions to which section 355 applies.*—If the U.S. transferor distributes stock of the foreign acquiring corporation received in the section 361 exchange to a control group member in a section 355 distribution and, as part of a plan or series of related transactions, that stock is further distributed in one or more successive section 355 distributions, paragraph (c) of this section can apply to the section 361 exchange only to the extent each subsequent section 355 distribution is to a member of the affiliated group (within the meaning of section 1504) that includes the U.S. transferor immediately before the reorganization. In that case, each affiliated group member that receives stock of the foreign acquiring corporation in the final section 355 distribution (final distributee) is subject to the requirements of paragraphs (c)(3) and (c)(5) of this section. If this paragraph (d) applies, then for purposes of applying paragraphs (c)(3), (c)(5) or (e)(2) of this section the term *control group member* is replaced by the term *final distributee*, as appropriate.

(e) *Other rules.*—(1) *Section 367(a) property with respect to which gain is recognized.*—Except as otherwise provided in this paragraph (e)(1), gain recognized by the U.S. transferor pursuant to paragraph (c)(2) of this section will be treated as recognized with respect to the section 367(a) property transferred in the section 361 exchange in proportion to the amount of gain realized by the U.S. transferor on the transfer of each item of section 367(a) property. This paragraph (e)(1) will be applied after taking into account any gain or deemed dividends (including any deemed dividends under section 1248(a)) recognized by the U.S. transferor on the transfer of the section 367(a) property in the section 361 exchange pursuant to all other provisions of sections 367(a) and (b) and the regulations under that section. See, for example, §§1.367(a)-2, 1.367(a)-3(e), 1.367(a)-4, 1.367(a)-6, and 1.367(b)-4. If the U.S. transferor recognizes gain (including gain treated as a deemed dividend under section 1248(a)) pursuant to §1.367(a)-3(e)(3)(iii)(B) or (e)(3)(iii)(C) with respect to stock or securities transferred in the section 361 exchange, the realized gain in such stock or securities shall not be taken into account for purposes of applying this paragraph (e)(1) to gain recognized under paragraph (c)(2) of this section attributable to U.S. transferor shareholders described in §1.367(a)-3(e)(3)(iii)(B) or (e)(3)(iii)(C). Accordingly, gain recognized under paragraph (c)(2) attributable to such U.S. transferor shareholders shall not be treated as recognized with respect to such stock or securities under this paragraph. Furthermore, to the extent gain recognized by the U.S. transferor under paragraph (c)(2) is treated as recognized with respect to stock in a foreign corporation transferred in the section 361 exchange to which section 1248(a) applies, the portion of such gain treated as a deemed dividend under section 1248(a) is the product of the amount of the gain multiplied by the ratio of the amount that would be treated as a deemed dividend under section 1248(a) if all gain in the transferred stock were recognized under §1.367(a)-7(b) and the amount of gain realized in the transferred stock. See §1.367(a)-1(b)(4) for additional rules on the character, source, and adjustments relating to gain recognized under section 367(a)(1), and §1.367(b)-2(e) for rules on the timing, treatment, and effect of amounts included in income as deemed dividends pursuant to regulations under section 367(b).

(2) *Relief for certain failures to comply that are not willful.*—(i) *In general.*—A control group member or U.S. transferor's failure to comply with any requirement of this section will be deemed not to have occurred for purposes of satisfying the requirements of this section if the control group member or U.S. transferor (or the foreign acquiring corporation on behalf of the U.S. transferor), as applicable, demonstrates that the failure was not willful using the procedure set forth in paragraph (e)(2)(ii) of this section. For this purpose, willful is to be interpreted consistent with the meaning of that term in the context of other civil penalties, which would include a failure due to gross negligence, reckless disregard, or willful neglect. Whether the failure to comply was a willful failure will be determined by the Director of Field Operations, Cross Border Activities Practice Area of Large Business & International (or any successor to the roles and responsibilities of such person) (Director) based on all the facts and circumstances. The control group member or U.S. transferor (or the foreign acquiring corporation on behalf of the U.S. transferor), as applicable, must submit a request for relief and an explanation as provided in paragraph (e)(2)(ii) of this section. Although a U.S transferor whose failure to comply is determined not to be willful will not be subject to gain recognition under this section, the U.S. transferor will be subject to a penalty under section 6038B if the U.S. transferor fails to demonstrate that the failure was due to reasonable cause and not willful neglect. See §1.6038B-1(b) and (f). The determination of whether the failure to comply was willful under this section has no effect on any request for relief made under §1.6038B-1(f).

(ii) *Procedures for establishing that a failure to comply was not willful.*—(A) *Time and manner of submission.*—A control group member or U.S. transferor's statement that the failure to comply was not willful will be considered only if, promptly after the control group member or U.S. transferor, as applicable, becomes aware of the failure, an amended return is filed for the taxable year to which the failure relates that includes the information that should have been included with the original return for such taxable year or that otherwise complies with the rules of this section, and that includes a written statement explaining the reasons for the failure to comply. The amended return must be filed with the Internal Revenue Service at the location where the taxpayer filed its original return. The U.S. transferor may submit a request for relief from the penalty under section 6038B as part of the same submission. See §1.6038B-1(f).

(B) *Notice requirement.*—In addition to the requirements of paragraph (e)(2)(ii)(A) of this section, a control group member or U.S. transferor, as applicable, must comply with the notice requirements of this paragraph (e)(2)(ii)(B). If any taxable year of the control group member or U.S. transferor, as applicable, is under examination when the amended return is filed, a copy of the amended return and any information required to be included with such return must be delivered to the Internal Revenue Service personnel conducting the examination. If no taxable year of the control group member or U.S transferor, as applicable, is under examination when the amended return is filed, a copy of the amended return and any information required to be included with such return must be delivered to the Director.

(iii) For illustrations of the application of the willfulness standard of this paragraph (e)(2), see the examples in §1.367(a)-8(p)(3).

(3) *Anti-abuse rule.*—Any property of the U.S. transferor acquired with a principal purpose of affecting any determination under this section (including, for example, the section 367(a) percentage, inside gain, or inside basis) shall not be taken in account for purposes of any determination under this section. Nothing in this paragraph (e)(3) constitutes a limitation on or modification to judicial doctrines, including step-transaction or substance-over-form.

(4) *Certain income inclusions under §1.367(b)-4.*—(i) *Income inclusion attributable to U.S. transferor shareholder described in §1.367(a)-3(e)(3)(iii)(A).*—If pursuant to §1.367(a)-3(e)(3)(iii)(B) or (e)(3)(iii)(C) the U.S. transferor is required to recognize gain on the transfer of foreign stock (all or a portion of which is treated as a deemed dividend under section 1248(a)), and if pursuant to §1.367(b)-4(b)(1)(i) the U.S. transferor is also required to include in income as a deemed dividend the section 1248 amount (within the meaning of §1.367(b)-2(c)) in the foreign stock, then the section 1248 amount included in income under §1.367(b)-4(b)(1)(i) is attributable to each U.S. transferor shareholder described in §1.367(a)-3(e)(3)(iii)(A) pursuant to this paragraph (e)(4)(i). The portion of the section 1248 amount attributable to each U.S. transferor shareholder described in §1.367(a)-3(e)(3)(iii)(A) is the portion of the section 1248 amount that bears the same ratio as such U.S. transferor shareholder's ownership interest percentage bears to the aggregate ownership interest percentage of all U.S. transferor shareholders described in §1.367(a)-3(e)(3)(iii)(A).

(ii) *Ordering rules for determining section 1248 amount.*—The section 1248 amount (within the meaning of §1.367(b)-2(c)) included in income as a deemed dividend under §1.367(b)-4(b)(1)(i) is determined after taking into account any gain recognized under §§1.367(a)-3(e)(3)(iii)(B) or (e)(3)(iii)(C) or 1.367(a)-6 that is treated as a deemed dividend under section 1248(a). See §1.367(a)-3(e)(7) and paragraph (e)(5)(ii) of this section for rules to determine the amount of gain recognized under §§1.367(a)-3(e)(3)(iii)(B) or (e)(3)(iii)(C) or 1.367(a)-6, respectively, that is treated as a deemed dividend under section 1248(a).

(5) *Certain gain under §1.367(a)-6.*—(i) *Gain attributable to U.S. transferor shareholder described in §1.367(a)-3(e)(3)(iii)(A).*—If pursuant to §1.367(a)-3(e)(3)(iii)(B) or (e)(3)(iii)(C), the U.S. transferor is required to recognize gain on the transfer of stock or securities, and if pursuant to §1.367(a)-6 the U.S. transferor is also required to recognize gain, then gain recognized under §1.367(a)-6 (including any portion treated as a deemed dividend under section 1248(a)) to the extent treated as recognized with respect to the stock or securities, is attributable to each U.S. transferor shareholder described in §1.367(a)-3(e)(3)(iii)(A) pursuant to this paragraph (e)(5)(i). The portion of the gain (including any portion treated as a deemed dividend under section 1248(a)) that is attributable to each U.S. transferor shareholder described in §1.367(a)-3(e)(3)(iii)(A) is the portion of the gain that bears the same ratio as such U.S. transferor shareholder's ownership interest percentage bears to the aggregate ownership interest percentage of all U.S. transferor shareholders described in §1.367(a)-3(e)(3)(iii)(A).

(ii) *Gain subject to section 1248(a).*—If the U.S. transferor recognizes gain under § 1.367(a)-6 with respect to transferred stock that is stock in a foreign corporation to which section 1248(a) applies, the portion of such gain treated as a deemed dividend under section 1248(a) is determined after taking into account any gain recognized under § 1.367(a)-3(e)(3)(iii)(B) or (e)(3)(iii)(C) and the amount of such gain treated as a deemed dividend under section 1248(a) pursuant to § 1.367(a)-3(e)(7).

(f) *Definitions.*—The following definitions apply for purposes of this section:

(1) *Control group, control group member, and non-control group member.*—(i) *General rule.*—Except as provided in paragraph (f)(1)(ii) of this section, the *control group* is the group of five or fewer, but at least one, domestic corporations that controls (within the meaning of section 368(c)) the U.S. transferor immediately before the reorganization. If the U.S. transferor is owned directly by more than five domestic corporations immediately before the reorganization, but some combination of five or fewer domestic corporations controls the U.S. transferor, the U.S. transferor must designate the five or fewer domestic corporations that comprise the control group on Form 926, "Return by a U.S. Transferor of Property to a Foreign Corporation." For purposes of identifying the control group, members of an affiliated group (within the meaning of section 1504) are treated as a single corporation. Except as provided in paragraph (f)(1)(ii) of this section, a *control group member* is a domestic corporation that is part of the control group. A *non-control group member* is a shareholder of the U.S. transferor immediately before the reorganization that is not a control group member.

(ii) *Exception for certain entities.*—Regulated investment companies (as defined in section 851(a)), real estate investment trusts (as defined in section 856(a)), and S corporations (as defined in section 1361(a)) cannot be control group members.

(2) *Deductible liability* is any liability of the U.S. transferor that is assumed in the section 361 exchange if payment of the liability would give rise to a deduction.

(3) *Fair market value* is the fair market value determined without regard to mortgages, liens, pledges, or other liabilities. For this purpose, the fair market value of any property subject to a nonrecourse indebtedness shall be treated as being not less than the amount of any nonrecourse indebtedness to which such property is subject.

(4) *Inside basis* is the aggregate basis of the section 367(a) property transferred by the U.S. transferor in the section 361 exchange and, except as otherwise provided in this paragraph (f)(4), increased by any gain recognized or any deemed dividend included in income by the U.S. transferor under section 367 on the transfer of the section 367(a) property in the section 361 exchange, but not including any gain recognized under paragraph (c)(2) of this section. If the U.S. transferor transfers stock or securities and recognizes gain under § 1.367(a)-3(e)(3)(iii)(B) or (e)(3)(iii)(C) with respect to such stock or securities, then inside basis is not increased for gain recognized or deemed dividends included in income that are described in paragraph (f)(4)(i), (f)(4)(ii), or (f)(4)(iii) of this section.

(i) Gain recognized under § 1.367(a)-3(e)(3)(iii)(B) or (e)(3)(iii)(C) (including any portion treated as a deemed dividend under section 1248(a));

(ii) Gain recognized under § 1.367(a)-6 (including any portion treated as a deemed dividend under section 1248(a)) attributable to U.S. transferor shareholders described in § 1.367(a)-3(e)(3)(iii)(A) (as determined pursuant to § 1.367(a)-7(e)(5));

(iii) A deemed dividend included in income under § 1.367(b)-4(b) attributable to U.S. transferor shareholders described in § 1.367(a)-3(e)(3)(iii)(A) (as determined pursuant to § 1.367(a)-7(e)(4)).

(5) *Inside gain* is the amount (but not below zero) by which the aggregate fair market value of the section 367(a) property transferred in the section 361 exchange exceeds the sum of:

(i) The inside basis; and

(ii) The product of the section 367(a) percentage multiplied by the aggregate deductible liabilities of the U.S. transferor.

(6) *Outside gain or loss* is the product of the section 367(a) percentage multiplied by the difference between—

(i) The aggregate fair market value of the stock received by a control group member in exchange for (or with respect to, as applicable) stock or securities of the U.S. transferor under section 354, 355, or 356, and

(ii) The control group member's aggregate section 358 basis (as defined in paragraph (c)(3) of this section) in such stock received, determined without regard to any adjustment to that basis under paragraph (c)(3) of this section.

(7) *Ownership interest percentage* is the ratio of the fair market value of the stock in the U.S. transferor owned by a shareholder to the fair market value of all of the outstanding stock of the U.S. transferor. Except as provided in this paragraph (f)(7), the ownership interest percentage of a shareholder is determined immediately before the reorganization. For purposes of determining the ownership interest percentage with respect to each shareholder, however, the numerator and denominator of the fraction are first reduced as described in this paragraph (f)(7). The numerator is reduced (but not below zero) by any distributions by the U.S. transferor of money or other property (within the meaning of section 356) to such shareholder pursuant to the plan of reorganization, but only to the extent such money or other property is not provided by the foreign acquiring corporation in exchange for property of the U.S. transferor acquired in the section 361 exchange. Furthermore, the denominator of the fraction is reduced (but not below zero) by all such distributions by the U.S. transferor to all shareholders. For illustrations of this definition, see paragraph (g) of this section, *Example 4* and *Example 5*.

(8) *Section 361 exchange* is an exchange described in section 361(a) or (b).

(9) *Section 367(a) percentage* is the ratio of the aggregate fair market value of the section 367(a) property transferred by the U.S. transferor in the section 361 exchange to the aggregate fair market value of all property transferred by the U.S. transferor in the section 361 exchange.

(10) *Section 367(a) property.*—Except as provided in paragraph (e)(3) of this section, *section 367(a) property* is any property, as defined in § 1.367(a)-1T(d)(4), other than section 367(d) property.

(11) Section 367(d) property is intangible property as defined in § 1.367(a)-1(d)(5).

(12) *Timely filed return* is a U.S. income tax return filed on or before the due date set forth in section 6072(b), including any extensions of time to file the return granted under section 6081.

(13) *U.S. transferor shareholder* is a person that is either a control group member or a non-control group member.

(g) *Examples.*—The rules of this section are illustrated by the examples set forth in this paragraph (g). See also § 1.367(a)-3(e)(8), *Example 2* and *Example 3*. The analysis of the following examples is limited to a discussion of issues under this section. Unless otherwise indicated, for purposes of the following examples: DP1, DP2, and DC are domestic corporations that do not join in the filing of a consolidated return and none of which is a regulated investment company, a real estate investment trust, or an S corporation; FP and FA are foreign corporations created or organized under the laws of Country B and are unrelated to DP1, DP2, and DC; each corporation has a single class of stock outstanding; each share of stock of DC owned by a shareholder of DC has an identical stock basis; Business A consists solely of section 367(a) property whose fair market value exceeds its basis and that, but for the application of this section, would qualify for the active foreign trade or business exception under § 1.367(a)-2; the fair market value of any FA stock received in a reorganization is equal to the fair market value of property exchanged therefor; FA is not a surrogate foreign corporation for purposes of section 7874 because one or more of the conditions of section 7874(a)(2)(B) is not satisfied; DC has no liabilities; DP1 and DP2 satisfy the requirements of paragraph (c)(5) of this section, and DC satisfies the requirements of § 1.6038B-1(c)(6)(ii).

Example 1. Tainted assets and non-control group ownership. (i) *Facts.* DP1, DP2, and FP own 50%, 30%, and 20%, respectively, of the outstanding stock of DC. DP1 and DP2 are members of the same affiliated group within the meaning of section 1504. DP1's DC stock has a $120x basis and $100x fair market value. DP2's DC stock has a $50x basis and $60x fair market value. DC owns inventory with a $40x basis and a $100x fair market value. DC also owns Business A (excluding the inventory) with a $10x basis and $100x fair market value. In a reorganization described in section 368(a)(1)(F), DC transfers the inventory and Business A to FA, a newly formed corporation, in exchange for all of the outstanding stock of FA. DC's transfer of the inventory and Business A to FA qualifies as a section 361 exchange. DP1, DP2, and FP exchange the DC stock for a proportionate amount of FA stock pursuant to section 354.

(ii) *Result.* (A) Under section 367(a)(3)(B)(i), DC must recognize $60x gain ($100x fair market value less $40x basis) on the transfer of the inventory to FA. The basis of the inventory in the hands of FA is increased by the gain recognized of $60x (that is, increased from $40x to $100x). See § 1.367(a)-1(b)(4)(i)(B). Under section 367(a)(5) and paragraph (b) of this section, DC's transfer of Business A to FA is subject to the general rule of section 367(a)(1). As a result, DC must also generally recognize $90x gain ($100x fair market value less $10x basis) on the transfer of Business A to FA notwithstanding the application of section 361 (or any other nonrecognition provision enumerated in section 367(a)(1)). However, if the conditions and requirements of paragraph (c) of this section are met, DC's transfer of Business A to FA would qualify for the active foreign trade or business exception provided by section 367(a)(3) and § 1.367(a)-2.

(B) The requirement of paragraph (c)(1) of this section is satisfied because DC is controlled (within the meaning of section 368(c)) by five or fewer domestic corporations immediately before the reorganization (in this case, by a single domestic corporation because DP1 and DP2 together own 80% of the stock of DC). DP1 and DP2 are treated as a single domestic corporation for this purpose under paragraph (f)(1)(i) of this section because DP1 and DP2 are members of the same affiliated group.

(C) Paragraph (c)(2)(i) of this section would be satisfied only if DC recognizes $18x gain on the transfer of Business A, which is the amount of inside gain attributable to FP, a non-control group member. The $18x gain equals the product of the inside gain ($90x) multiplied by FP's ownership interest percentage (20%) in DC, reduced by $0x (the sum of the amounts described in paragraphs (c)(2)(i)(A) through (c)(2)(i)(C) of this section). Under paragraph (f)(5) of this section, the $90x inside gain is the amount by which the aggregate fair market value ($200x) of the section 367(a) property (inventory and Business A) exceeds $110x, the sum of the inside basis of $110x and the product of the section 367(a) percentage (100%) multiplied by the deductible liabilities of DC ($0x). Under paragraph (f)(4) of this section, the inside basis equals the $50x aggregate basis of the section 367(a) property transferred in the section 361 exchange, increased by the $60x gain recognized by DC on the transfer of the inventory to FA, but not by the $18x gain recognized by DC under paragraph (c)(2)(i) of this section attributable to FP. The section 367(a) percentage is 100% because the only assets transferred are the inventory and Business A, which are section 367(a) property. Under paragraph (e)(1) of this section, the $18x gain recognized under paragraph (c)(2)(i) of this section is treated as recognized with respect to Business A. FA's basis in Business A as determined under section 362 is increased for the $18x gain recognized. See § 1.367(a)-1(b)(4)(i)(B).

(D) Paragraph (c)(2)(ii) of this section is not applicable with respect to either DP1 or DP2 because the attributable inside gain with respect to each such shareholder can be preserved in the FA stock received. As stated in paragraph (ii)(C) of this *Example 1*, the amount of the inside gain is $90x. The attributable inside gain with respect to DP1 of $45x (equal to the product of $90x inside gain multiplied by DP1's 50% ownership interest percentage, reduced by $0x (the sum of the amounts described in paragraphs (c)(2)(ii)(A)(*1*) through (c)(2)(ii)(A)(*3*) of this section)) does not exceed $100x (equal to the product of the section 367(a) percentage of 100% multiplied by $100x fair market value of FA stock received by DP1). Similarly, the attributable inside gain with respect to DP2 of $27x (equal to the product of $90x inside gain multiplied by DP2's 30% ownership interest percentage, reduced by $0x (the sum of the amounts described in paragraphs (c)(2)(ii)(A)(*1*) through (c)(2)(ii)(A)(*3*) of this section)) does not exceed $60x (equal to the product of the section 367(a) percentage of 100% multiplied by $60x fair market value of FA stock received by DP2).

(E) Each control group member (DP1 and DP2) separately computes any required adjustment to stock basis under paragraph (c)(3) of this section. DP1's section 358 basis in the FA stock received of $120x (the amount of DP1's basis in the DC stock exchanged) is reduced to preserve the attributable inside gain with respect to DP1, less any gain recognized with respect to DP1 under paragraph (c)(2)(ii) of this section. Because DC does not recognize gain on the section 361 exchange with respect to DP1 under paragraph (c)(2)(ii) of this section (as determined in paragraph (ii)(D) of this *Example 1*), the attributable inside gain of $45x with respect to DP1 is not reduced under paragraph (c)(3)(i)(B) of this section. DP1's outside loss in the FA stock is $20x, the product of the section 367(a) percentage of 100% multiplied by $20x loss (equal to the difference between $100x fair market value and $120x section 358 basis in FA stock). Thus, DP1's $120x section 358 basis in the FA stock must be reduced by $65x (excess of $45x, reduced by $0x, over $20x outside loss) to $55x.

(F) DP2's aggregate section 358 basis in the FA stock received of $50x (the amount of DP2's basis in the DC stock exchanged) is reduced to preserve the attributable inside gain with respect to DP2, less any gain recognized with respect to DP2 under paragraph (c)(2)(ii) of this section. Because DC does not recognize gain on the section 361 exchange with respect to DP2 (as determined in paragraph (ii)(D) of this *Example 1*), the attributable inside gain of $27x with respect to DP2 is not reduced under paragraph (c)(3)(i)(A) of this section. DP2's outside gain in the FA stock is $10x, the product of the section 367(a) percentage of 100% multiplied by $10x gain (equal to the difference between $60x fair market value and $50x section 358 basis in FA stock). Thus, DP2's $50x section 358 basis in the FA stock must be reduced by $17x (excess of $27x, reduced by $0x, over the $10x outside gain) to $33x.

(G) Paragraph (c)(4) of this section would be satisfied only if DC complies with the requirements of § 1.6038B-1(c)(6)(iii), including filing with its timely filed return for the year of the reorganization a statement agreeing to file an amended return reporting the gain realized but not recognized on the section 361 exchange in certain cases if a significant amount of the section 367(a) property received in the section 361 exchange is disposed of, directly or indirectly, in one or more related transactions within the prescribed 60-month period.

Example 2. Triangular reorganization involving an exchange of section 367(a) property for foreign stock and cash. (i) *Facts.* (A) DP1 wholly owns DC. DP1 and DC file a consolidated return. DP1's DC stock has a $170x basis and $200x fair market value. DC owns Business A, which has a $10x basis and $200x fair market value. FP wholly owns FA.

(B) In a triangular reorganization described in section 368(a)(1)(A) by reason of section 368(a)(2)(D), DC transfers Business A to FA in exchange for $180x of FP stock and $20x cash. DC's transfer of Business A to FA qualifies as a section 361 exchange. DP1 exchanges its DC stock for $180x of FP stock and $20x cash pursuant to section 356. The triangular reorganization constitutes an indirect stock transfer under § 1.367(a)-3(d)(1)(i), and DP1 properly files a gain recognition agreement under § 1.367(a)-8 with respect to the transfer. See also § 1.367(a)-3(d)(2)(vii).

(ii) *Result.* (A) Under section 367(a)(5) and paragraph (b) of this section, DC's transfer of Business A to FA is subject to the general rule of section 367(a)(1). As a result, DC must generally recognize $190x gain ($200x fair market value less $10x basis) on the transfer of Business A to FA notwithstanding the application of section 361 (or any other nonrecognition exchange enumerated in section 367(a)(1)). However, if the requirements of paragraph (c) of this section are satisfied, DC's transfer of Business A to FA would qualify for the active foreign trade or business exception provided in section 367(a)(3) and § 1.367(a)-2.

(B) The requirement of paragraph (c)(1) of this section is satisfied because DC is controlled (within the meaning of section 368(c)) by five or fewer domestic corporations immediately before the reorganization (in this case, by a single domestic corporation, DP1).

(C) DC is not required to recognize gain under paragraph (c)(2)(i) of this section because, immediately before the reorganization, DC is wholly owned by DP1, a control group member. In addition, DP1's ownership interest percentage is 100%. Paragraph (c)(2)(ii) of this section would be satisfied only if DC recognizes $10x gain, computed as the amount by which the attributable inside gain with respect to DP1 of $190x (the product of $190x inside gain multiplied by DP1's ownership interest percentage of 100%, reduced by $0x (the sum of the amounts in paragraphs (c)(2)(ii)(A)(*1*) through (c)(2)(ii)(A)(*3*) of this section)) exceeds $180x (the product of the section 367(a) percentage of 100% multiplied by $180x fair market value of FP stock received by DP1). Under paragraph (f)(5) of this section, the $190x inside gain is the amount by which the $200x aggregate fair market value of Business A exceeds $10x (the sum of the inside basis of $10x and the product of the section 367(a) percentage (100%) multiplied by the deductible liabilities of DC ($0x)). Under paragraph (f)(4) of this section, the inside basis equals the $10x aggregate basis of the section 367(a) property transferred in the section 361 exchange (not increased by the $10x gain recognized by DC under paragraph (c)(2)(ii) of this section). The section 367(a) percentage is 100% because the only asset transferred is Business A, which is section 367(a) property. Under § 1.1502-32(b)(2), DP1 increases the basis of its DC stock by the $10x gain recognized, that is, from $170x to $180x. Under paragraph (e)(1) of this section, the $10x gain recognized under paragraph (c)(2)(ii) of this section is treated as recognized with respect to Business A. FA's basis in Business A as determined under section 362 is increased for the $10x gain recognized. See § 1.367(a)-1(b)(4)(i)(B).

(D) Paragraph (c)(3) of this section would be satisfied only if DP1's section 358 basis in the FP stock is reduced by the amount by which the attributable inside gain with respect to DP1, reduced by any gain recognized by DC with respect to DP1 under paragraph (c)(2)(ii) of this section, exceeds DP1's outside gain in the FP stock. DP1's section 358 basis in the FP stock is $180x, computed as $180x basis in DC stock, as determined in paragraph (ii)(C) of this *Example 2*, decreased by $20x cash received and increased by $20x gain recognized under section 356 (such amount equal to the lesser of the $20x cash received and the $20x gain in the DC stock, computed as $200x fair market value less $180x basis). Because DC recognizes $10x gain on the section 361 exchange with respect to DP1 under paragraph (c)(2)(ii) of this section as determined in paragraph (ii)(C) of this *Example 2*, the $190x attributable inside gain with respect to DP1 is reduced by $10x to $180x under paragraph (c)(3)(i)(C) of this section. DP1's outside gain in the FP stock is $0x, the product of the section 367(a) percentage of 100% multiplied by $0x gain (the difference between $180x fair market value and $180x section 358 basis in FP stock). Thus, DP1's section 358 basis in the FP stock ($180x) must be reduced by $180x ($190x attributable inside gain reduced by $10x) to $0x.

(E) Paragraph (c)(4)(i) of this section would be satisfied only if DC complies with the requirements of § 1.6038B-1(c)(6)(iii), including filing with its tax return for the year of the reorganization a statement agreeing to file an amended return reporting the gain on the section 361 exchange in certain cases if a significant amount of the section 367(a) property received in the section 361 exchange is disposed of, directly or indirectly, in one or more related transactions within the prescribed 60-month period.

Example 3. Adjustment to basis of multiple blocks of stock; transfer of section 367(d) property. (i) *Facts.* (A) DP1 wholly owns DC. One half of DP1's shares of stock in DC, each with an identical basis, has an aggregate basis of $60x and fair market value of $100x (Block 1). The other one half of DP's shares of stock in DC, each with an identical basis, has an aggregate basis of $120x and fair market value of $100x (Block 2). DC owns Business A ($15x basis and $150x fair market value) (excluding the patent) and a patent ($0x basis and $50x fair market value). The patent is section 367(d) property.

(B) In a reorganization described in section 368(a)(1)(F), DC transfers Business A and the patent to FA, a newly formed corporation, in exchange for 2 shares of FA stock. DC's transfer of Business A and the patent to FA qualifies as a section 361 exchange. DP1 exchanges Block 1 and Block 2 for the two shares of FA stock pursuant to section 354. Pursuant to § 1.358-2(a)(2)(i), one share of the FA stock corresponds to Block 1 (Share 1) and the other share of FA stock corresponds to Block 2 (Share 2). The basis of Share 1 and Share 2 correspond to the basis of Block 1 and Block 2, respectively.

(ii) *Result.* (A) Under section 367(a)(5) and paragraph (b) of this section, DC's transfer of Business A to FA is subject to the general rule of section 367(a)(1). As a result, DC must generally recognize $135x of gain on the transfer of Business A to FA notwithstanding the application of section 361 (or any other nonrecognition exchange described in section 367(a)(1)). However, if the requirements of paragraph (c) of this section are met, DC's transfer of Business A to FA would qualify for the active foreign trade or business exception provided in section 367(a)(3). For rules applicable to DC's transfer of the patent to FA, see section 367(d).

(B) The requirement of paragraph (c)(1) of this section is satisfied because DC is controlled (within the meaning of section 368(c)) by five or fewer domestic corporations immediately before the reorganization (in this case, by a single domestic corporation, DP1).

(C) Paragraph (c)(2)(i) of this section is not applicable because, immediately before the reorganization, DC is wholly owned by DP1, a control group member. In addition, DP1's ownership interest percentage is 100%. Paragraph (c)(2)(ii) of this section is not applicable because the attributable inside gain with respect to DP1 can be preserved in the FA stock received. The attributable inside gain with respect to DP1 of $135x (equal to the product of $135x inside gain multiplied by DP1's 100% ownership interest percentage, reduced by $0x (the sum of the amounts in paragraphs (c)(2)(ii)(A)(*1*) through (c)(2)(ii)(A)(3) of this section)) does not exceed $150x (equal to the product of the section 367(a) percentage of 75% multiplied by $200x fair market value of FA stock received by DP1). Under paragraph (f)(5) of this section, the $135x inside gain is the amount by which the aggregate fair market value of Business A ($150x) exceeds $15x, the sum of the inside basis of Business A ($15x) and the product of the section 367(a) percentage (75%) multiplied by the deductible liabilities of DC ($0x). Under paragraph (f)(4) of this section, the inside basis equals the $15x aggregate basis of the section 367(a) property transferred in the exchange. The section 367(a) percentage of 75% is equal to the ratio of the fair market value of the section 367(a) property ($150x for Business A) to the fair market value of all the property transferred ($200x, the sum of $150x for Business A and $50x for the patent).

(D) Under paragraph (c)(3) of this section, DP1's aggregate section 358 basis of $180x in the stock of FA (computed as the sum of $60x basis in Share 1 and $120x basis in Share 2) is reduced by the amount by which the attributable inside gain with respect to DP1, reduced by any gain recognized by DC with respect to DP1 under paragraph (c)(2)(ii) of this section, exceeds DP1's outside gain in the FP stock received. Because DC recognizes no gain on the section 361 exchange with respect to DP1 under paragraph (c)(2)(ii) of this section as determined in paragraph (ii)(C) of this *Example 3*, the $135x attributable inside gain with respect to DP1 is not reduced under paragraph (c)(3)(i)(A) of this section. DP1's outside gain in Share 1 and Share 2 in the aggregate is $15x, the product of the section 367(a) percentage of 75% multiplied by $20x (the difference between $200x aggregate fair market value and $180x aggregate section 358 basis in the FA stock received by DP1). Thus, DP1's section 358 basis in the FA stock ($180x) must be reduced by $120x (the excess of $135x attributable inside gain, reduced by $0x, over $15x outside gain) to $60x.

(E) Under paragraph (c)(3)(iii) of this section, the $120x reduction to basis is allocated between Share 1 and Share 2 based on the relative section 358 basis of each share. Therefore, the basis in Share 1 is reduced by $40x ($120x multiplied by $60x/$180x). As adjusted, DP1's basis in Share 1 is $20x ($60x less $40x). The basis in Share 2 is reduced by $80x ($120x multiplied by $120x/$180x). As adjusted, DP1's basis in Share 2 is $40x ($120x less $80x).

(F) Paragraph (c)(4)(i) of this section would be satisfied only if DC complies with the requirements of § 1.6038B-1(c)(6)(iii), including filing with its tax return for the year of the reorganization, a statement agreeing to file an amended return reporting the gain realized but not recognized on the section 361 exchange in certain cases if a significant amount of the section 367(a) property received in the section 361 exchange is disposed of, directly or indirectly, in one or more related transactions within the prescribed 60-month period.

Example 4. Control requirement and ownership interest percentage; nonqualified property provided by foreign acquiring corporation. (i) *Facts.* DP1 and FP own 80% and 20%, respectively, of the outstanding stock of DC. DC owns Business A with a basis of $0x and $100x fair market value. DP1's DC stock has a fair market value of $80x, and FP's DC stock has a fair market value of $20x. In a reorganization described in section 368(a)(1)(D), DC transfers Business A to FA in exchange for $80x of FA stock and $20x cash. DC's transfer of Business A to FA qualifies as a section 361 exchange. DP1 exchanges its $80x of DC stock for $60x of FA stock and $20x cash, and FP exchanges its $20x of DC stock for $20x of FA stock.

(ii) *Result.* (A) The requirement of paragraph (c)(1) of this section is satisfied because DC is controlled (within the meaning of section 368(c)) by five or fewer domestic corporations immediately before the reorganization (in this case, by a single domestic corporation, DP1). The fact that the $20x cash is distributed solely to DP1 does not change the analysis of the control requirement. The control requirement is determined immediately before the reorganization and is not affected by distributions of property.

(B) Pursuant to paragraph (f)(7) of this section, the ownership interest percentages of DP1 and FP immediately before the reorganization are 80% ($80x/($80x + $20x)) and 20% ($20x/($80x + $20x)), respectively. The fact that the $20x of cash is distributed solely to DP1 does not change this result. The distribution of the $20x of cash is not taken into account for purposes of the ownership interest percentage computation because the $20x of cash distributed by DC is provided by FA to DC in the section 361 exchange.

Example 5. Control requirement and ownership interest percentage; nonqualified property provided by U.S. transferor. (i) *Facts.* The facts are the same as in *Example 4*, except as follows. Business A has a fair market value of $80x (and not $100x) and DC also owns inventory with a basis of $0x and fair market value of $20x. DC transfers Business A, but not the inventory, to FA in exchange for $80x of FA stock. DP1 exchanges its $80x of DC stock for $60x of FA stock and the $20x of inventory, and FP exchanges its $20x of DC stock for $20x of FA stock.

(ii) *Result.* (A) The requirement of paragraph (c)(1) of this section is satisfied because DC is controlled (within the meaning of section 368(c)) by five or fewer domestic corporations immediately before the reorganization (in this case, by a single domestic corporation, DP1). The fact that the $20x of inventory is not transferred to FA, but is instead distributed solely to DP1, does not change the analysis of the control requirement. The control requirement is determined immediately before the reorganization, and is not affected by distributions of property.

(B) Pursuant to the general rule of paragraph (f)(7) of this section, the ownership interest percentages of DP1 and FP immediately before the reorganization would be 80% ($80x/($80x + $20x)) and 20% ($20x/($80x + $20x)), respectively. In this case, however, the distribution of the $20x inventory to DP1 is taken into account for purposes of computing the ownership interest percentage of DP1 and FP because the inventory is not provided by FA to DC in the section 361 exchange. With respect to DP1, the numerator of the ownership interest percentage computation is $60x, computed as the fair market value of DC stock owned by DP1 immediately before the reorganization but reduced by the fair market value of the inventory distributed to DP1 ($80x less $20x). With respect to FP, the numerator of the ownership interest percentage computation is $20x, the fair market value of the DC stock owned by FP immediately before the reorganization. With respect to both DP1 and FP, the denominator of the ownership interest percentage computation is $80x, computed as the fair market value of all DC stock immediately before the reorganization, but reduced by the fair market value of the inventory distributed to DP1 ($100x, less $20x). Accordingly, the ownership interest percentage of DP1 is 75% ($60x/$80x), and the ownership interest percentage of FP is 25% ($20x/$80x).

(h) *Applicable cross-references.*—For rules relating to the character, source, and adjustments resulting from gain recognized by a U.S. transferor under section 367(a), see § 1.367(a)-1(b)(4). For rules relating to transfers of stock or securities in a section 361 exchange, see § 1.367(a)-3(e). For rules relating to the acquisition of the stock or assets of a foreign corporation by another foreign corporation, see § 1.367(b)-4. For rules relating to transfers of section 367(d) property by a U.S. transferor to a foreign corporation, see section 367(d). For rules relating to distributions of stock of a foreign corporation by a domestic corporation under section 355 or 361, see §§ 1.367(b)-5, 1.367(e)-1, and 1.1248(f)-1 through 1.1248(f)-3. For additional rules relating to certain reporting requirements of a U.S. transferor, see § 1.6038B-1. For rules regarding expatriated entities, see section 7874 and the regulations under that section.

(i) [Reserved].

(j) *Effective/applicability dates.*—(1) *In general.*—Except for paragraph (e)(2) of this section, and as provided in paragraph (j)(2) of this section, this section applies to transfers occurring on or after April 18, 2013. Paragraph (e)(2) applies to requests for relief submitted on or after November 19, 2014. Paragraph (e)(2) of this section also applies to requests for relief submitted before November 19, 2014 if the statute of limitations on the assessment of tax has not expired for any year to which the request relates and the control group member or U.S. transferor, as applicable, resubmits the request under paragraph (e)(2) of this section and notes, on the request, that the request is being submitted pursuant to the third sentence of this paragraph (j). See paragraph (e)(2) of this section, as contained in 26 CFR part 1 revised as of April 1, 2014, for requests for relief submitted after April 17, 2013, and before November 19, 2014, that are not resubmitted under paragraph (e)(2) of this section.

(2) *Section 367(d) property.*—The definition provided in paragraph (f)(11) of this section applies to transfers occurring on or after September 14, 2015, and to transfers occurring before September 14, 2015, resulting from entity classification elections made under § 301.7701-3 that are filed on or after September 14, 2015. For transfers occurring before this section is applicable, see § 1.367(a)-7 as contained in 26 CFR part 1 revised as of April 1, 2016. [Reg. § 1.367(a)-7.]

☐ [*T.D.* 9614, 3-18-2013 *Amended by T.D.* 9704, 11-18-2014, *T.D.* 9760, 3-18-2016 *and T.D.* 9803, 12-15-2016.]

§ 1.367(a)-8. Gain recognition agreement requirements.—(a) *Scope.*—This section provides the terms and conditions for a gain recognition agreement entered into by a United States person pursuant to § 1.367(a)-3(b) through (e) in connection with a transfer of stock or securities to a foreign corporation pursuant to an exchange that would otherwise be subject to section 367(a)(1). Paragraph (b) of this section provides definitions and special rules. Paragraphs (c) through (h) of this section identify the form, content, and other conditions of a gain recognition agreement. Paragraph (i) of this section is reserved. Paragraph (j) of this section identifies certain events that may require gain to be recognized under a gain recognition agreement. Paragraph (k) of this section provides exceptions for certain events that would otherwise require gain to be recognized under a gain recognition agreement. Paragraph (l) of this section is reserved. Paragraph (m) of this section provides rules that require gain to be recognized under a gain recognition agreement in connection with certain events to which an exception under paragraph (k) of this section otherwise applies. Paragraph (n) of this section provides special rules in the case of a distribution of property with respect to stock to which section 301 applies. Paragraph (o) of this section provides rules for certain transactions that terminate or reduce the amount of gain subject to a gain recognition agreement. Paragraph (p) of this section provides relief for certain failures to file an initial gain recognition agreement (as defined in paragraph (b)(1)(vi) of this section) or to comply with the requirements of this section with respect to a gain recognition agreement (as described in paragraph (c) of this section). Paragraph (q) of this section provides examples that illustrate the rules of the section. Paragraph (r) of this section provides effective dates for the provisions of this section.

(b) *Definitions and special rules.*—The following definitions and special rules apply for purposes of this section.

(1) *Definitions.*—(i) *Asset reorganization.*—(A) *General rule.*—Except as provided in paragraph (b)(1)(i)(B) of this section, an *asset reorganization* is a reorganization described in section 368(a)(1) that involves an exchange of property described in section 361(a) or (b) (a section 361 exchange).

(B) *Exceptions.*—An asset reorganization does not include the following:

(1) A reorganization described in section 368(a)(1)(D) or (G) if the requirements of section 354(b)(1)(A) and (B) are not met.

(2) For purposes of paragraphs (j)(2)(ii)(B), (k)(6)(ii), and (k)(6)(iii) of this section, a triangular asset reorganization. For rules applicable to a triangular asset reorganization, see paragraph (k)(7) of this section.

(ii) A *consolidated group* has the meaning set forth in § 1.1502-1(h).

(iii) *Disposition.*—Except as provided in this paragraph (b)(1)(iii), a *disposition* includes any transfer that would constitute a disposition for any purpose of the Internal Revenue Code. A disposition includes an indirect disposition of the stock of the transferred corporation as described in § 1.367(a)-3(d). Except as provided in paragraph (n)(1) of this section, a disposition does not include the receipt of a distribution of property with respect to stock to which section 301 applies (including by reason of section 302(d)). See paragraphs (n)(2) and (o)(3) of this section for rules that apply if gain is recognized under section 301(c)(3). A complete or partial disposition by installment sale (under section 453) shall be treated as a disposition in the year of the installment sale.

(iv) A *gain recognition agreement document* means any agreement, statement, schedule, or form required to be filed under this section, including an initial gain recognition agreement (as defined in paragraph (b)(1)(vi) of this section), a new gain recognition agreement described in paragraph (c)(5) of this section, a Form 8838 extending the period of limitations on assessment of tax described in paragraph (f) of this section, and an annual certification described in paragraph (g) of this section.

(v) A *gain recognition event* is an event described in paragraphs (j) through (o) of this section that requires gain to be recognized under a gain recognition agreement.

(vi) An *initial gain recognition agreement* means the gain recognition agreement entered into under paragraph (c) of this section with respect to the initial transfer.

(vii) The *initial transfer* means a transfer of stock or securities (transferred stock or securities) to a foreign corporation pursuant to an exchange that would otherwise be subject to section 367(a)(1) but with respect to which a gain recognition agreement is entered into by a United States person pursuant to § 1.367(a)-3(b) through (e).

(viii) An *intercompany item* has the meaning set forth in § 1.1502-13(b)(2).

(ix) An *intercompany transaction* has the meaning set forth in § 1.1502-13(b)(1).

(x) A *nonrecognition transaction* has the meaning set forth in section 7701(a)(45). In addition, a nonrecognition transaction includes an exchange described in section 351(b) or 356 even if all gain realized in the exchange is recognized.

(xi) The terms *P, S,* and *T* have the meanings set forth in § 1.358-6(b)(1)(i), (ii), and (iii), respectively.

(xii) The determination of whether *substantially all* of the assets of the transferred corporation have been disposed of is based on all the facts and circumstances.

(xiii) A *timely filed return* means a Federal income tax return filed on or before the last date prescribed for filing (taking into account any extensions of time therefor) such return.

(xiv) *Transferee foreign corporation.*—Except as provided in this paragraph (b)(1)(xiv), the *transferee foreign corporation* is the foreign corporation to which the transferred stock or securities are transferred in an initial transfer. In the case of an indirect stock transfer, the transferee foreign corporation has the meaning set forth in § 1.367(a)-3(d)(2)(i). The transferee foreign corporation also includes a corporation designated as the transferee foreign corporation in the case of a new gain recognition agreement entered into under this section.

(xv) *Transferred corporation.*—Except as provided in this paragraph (b)(1)(xv), the *transferred corporation* is the corporation the stock or securities of which are transferred in the initial transfer. In the case of an indirect stock transfer, the transferred corporation has the meaning set forth in § 1.367(a)-3(d)(2)(ii). The transferred corporation also includes a corporation designated as the transferred corporation in the case of a new gain recognition agreement entered into under this section.

(xvi) A *triangular asset reorganization* is a reorganization described in § 1.358-6(b)(2)(i), (ii), (iii), or (v).

(xvii) The *U.S. transferor* is the United States person (as defined in § 1.367(a)-1(d)(1)) that transfers the transferred stock or securities to the transferee foreign corporation in the initial transfer. For purposes of determining the U.S. transferor in the case of a transfer by a partnership, see § 1.367(a)-1(c)(3)(i). The *U.S. transferor* also includes the United States person designated as the U.S. transferor in the case of a new gain recognition agreement entered into under this section including, for example, under paragraph (k)(14) of this section.

(2) *Special rules.*—(i) *Stock deemed received or transferred.*—References to stock received include stock deemed received (for example, pursuant to section 367(c)(2)). References to a transfer of stock or securities include a deemed transfer of stock or securities.

(ii) *Stock of the transferee foreign corporation.*—References to stock of the transferee foreign corporation includes any stock of the transferee foreign corporation the basis of which is determined, in whole or in part, by reference to the basis of the stock of the transferee foreign corporation received by the U.S. transferor in the initial transfer.

(iii) *Transferred stock or securities.*—References to transferred stock or securities includes any stock or securities of the transferred corporation the basis of which is determined, in whole or in part, by reference to the basis of the stock or securities transferred in the initial transfer.

(c) *Gain recognition agreement.*—(1) *Terms of agreement.*—(i) *General rule.*—Except as provided in this paragraph (c)(1)(i), if a gain recognition event occurs during the period beginning on the date of the initial transfer and ending as of the close of the fifth full taxable year (not less than 60 months) following the close of the taxable year in which the initial transfer occurs (GRA term), the U.S. transferor must include in income the gain realized but not recognized on the initial transfer by reason of entering into the gain recognition agreement. In the case of a gain recognition event that occurs as a result of a partial disposition of stock, securities, or a partnership interest, as applicable, the U.S. transferor is required to recognize a proportionate amount of the gain subject to the gain recognition agreement, determined based on the fair market value of the stock, securities, or partnership interest, as applicable, disposed of (measured at the time of the partial disposition) as compared to the fair market value of all the stock, securities, or partnership interest, as applicable (measured at the time of the partial disposition). If the U.S. transferor must recognize gain under this paragraph as a result of an event described in paragraph (m) or (n) of this section, see those paragraphs to determine the amount of the gain that must be recognized. The amount of gain subject to the gain recognition agreement shall be reduced by the amount of gain recognized under this paragraph. If the amount of gain subject to the gain recognition agreement is reduced to zero, the gain recognition agreement shall terminate without further effect.

(ii) *Ordering rule for gain recognized under multiple gain recognition agreements.*—If a gain recognition event occurs that requires gain to be recognized under multiple gain recognition agreements, gain shall first be recognized under the gain recognition agreement that relates to the earliest initial transfer, then under the gain recognition agreement that relates to the immediately following initial transfer and so forth until the appropriate amount of gain has been recognized under each gain recognition agreement. The amount of gain recognized under a gain recognition agreement shall be determined after taking into account, as appropriate, any increase to basis (including the basis of the transferred stock or securities) under paragraph (c)(4) of this section resulting from gain recognized under another gain recognition agreement. For an illustration of this ordering rule, see paragraph (q)(2)(vi) of this section.

(iii) *Taxable year in which gain is reported.*—(A) *Year of initial transfer.*—Except as provided in paragraph (c)(1)(iii)(B) of this section, the U.S. transferor must report any gain recognized under paragraph (c)(1)(i) of this section on an amended Federal income tax return for the taxable year of the initial transfer. The amended return must be filed on or before the 90th day following the date on which the gain recognition event occurs.

(B) *Year of gain recognition event.*—If an election under paragraph (c)(2)(vi) of this section is made with the gain recognition agreement or if paragraph (c)(5)(ii) of this section applies to the gain recognition agreement, the U.S. transferor must report any gain recognized under paragraph (c)(1)(i) of this section on its Federal income tax return for the taxable year during which the gain recognition event occurs. If an election under paragraph (c)(2)(vi) of this section is made with the gain recognition agreement or if paragraph (c)(5)(ii) of this section applies to the gain recognition agreement but the U.S. transferor does not report the gain recognized on its Federal income tax return for the taxable year during which the gain recognition event occurs, the Commissioner may require the U.S. transferor to report the gain on an amended Federal income tax return for the taxable year during which the initial transfer occurred.

(iv) *Offsets.*—No special limitations apply with respect to offsetting gain recognized under paragraph (c)(1)(i) of this section with net operating losses, capital losses, credits against tax, or similar items.

(v) *Payment and reporting of interest.*—Interest must be paid on any additional tax due with respect to gain recognized by the U.S. transferor under paragraph (c)(1)(i) of this section. Any interest due shall be determined based on the rates under section 6621 for the period between the date that was prescribed for filing the Federal income tax return of the U.S. transferor for the year of the initial transfer and the date on which the additional tax due is paid. If paragraph (c)(1)(iii)(B) of this section applies, any interest due must be included with the payment of tax due with the Federal income tax return of the U.S. transferor for the taxable year during which the gain recognition event occurs (or should reduce the amount of any refund due to the U.S. transferor for such taxable year). A schedule entitled "Calculation of Section 367 Tax and Interest" that separately identifies and calculates any additional tax and interest due must be included with the Federal income tax return on which any interest due is reported.

(2) *Content of gain recognition agreement.*—The gain recognition agreement must be entitled "GAIN RECOGNITION AGREEMENT UNDER § 1.367(a)-8" and include the information described in paragraphs (c)(2)(i) through (viii) of this paragraph with the corresponding paragraph numbers. The information required under this paragraph (c)(2) and paragraph (c)(3) of this section must be included in the gain recognition agreement as filed.

(i) A statement that the document constitutes an agreement by the U.S. transferor to recognize gain in accordance with the requirements of this section.

(ii) A description of the transferred stock or securities and other information as required in paragraph (c)(3) of this section.

(iii) A statement that the U.S. transferor agrees to comply with all the conditions and requirements of this section, including to recognize gain under the gain recognition agreement in accordance with paragraph (c)(1)(i) of this section, to extend the period of limitations on assessment of tax as provided in paragraph (f) of this section, to file the certification described in paragraph (g) of this section, and, as provided in paragraph (j)(8) of this section, to treat a failure to comply (as described in paragraph (j)(8) of this section) as extending the period of limitations on assessment of tax for the taxable year in which gain is required to be reported.

(iv) A statement that arrangements have been made to ensure that the U.S. transferor is informed of any events that affect the gain recognition agreement, including triggering events or other gain recognition events.

(v) In the case of a new gain recognition agreement filed under this section—

(A) A description of the event (such as a triggering event) and the applicable exception, if any, that gave rise to the new gain recognition agreement (such as a triggering event exception), including the date of the event and the name, address, and taxpayer identification number (if any) of each person that is a party to the event;

(B) As applicable, a description of the class, amount, and characteristics of the stock, securities or partnership interest received in the transaction; and

(C) As applicable, a calculation of the amount of gain that remains subject to the new gain recognition agreement as a result of the application of paragraph (m), (n), or (o) of this section.

(vi) A statement whether the U.S. transferor elects to include in income any gain recognized under paragraph (c)(1)(i) of this section in the taxable year during which a gain recognition event occurs. See paragraph (c)(5)(ii) of this section for a rule that requires, in certain cases, for the gain recognized pursuant to a new gain recognition agreement to be included in income during the taxable year in which the gain recognition event occurs.

(vii) A statement whether a gain recognition event has occurred during the taxable year of the initial transfer.

(viii) A statement describing any disposition of assets of the transferred corporation during such taxable year other than in the ordinary course of business.

(3) *Description of transferred stock or securities and other information.*—The gain recognition agreement shall include the following:

(i) A description of the transferred stock or securities including—

(A) The type or class, amount, and characteristics of the transferred stock or securities;

(B) A calculation of the amount of the built-in gain in the transferred stock or securities that are subject to the gain recognition agreement, reflecting the basis and fair market value on the date of the initial transfer;

(C) The amount of any gain recognized by the U.S. transferor on the initial transfer; and

(D) The percentage (by voting power and value) that the transferred stock (if any) represents of the total stock outstanding of the transferred corporation on the date of the initial transfer.

(ii) The name, address, place of incorporation, and taxpayer identification number (if any) of the transferred corporation.

(iii) The date on which the U.S. transferor acquired the transferred stock or securities.

(iv) The name, address and place of incorporation of the transferee foreign corporation, and a description of the stock or securities received by the U.S. transferor in the initial transfer, including the percentage of stock (by vote and value) of the transferee foreign corporation received in such exchange.

(v) If the initial transfer is described in § 1.367(a)-3(e), a statement that the conditions of section 367(a)(5) and any regulations under that section have been satisfied, and a description of any adjustments to the basis of the stock received in the transaction or other adjustments made pursuant to section 367(a)(5) and any regulations under that section.

(vi) If the transferred corporation is domestic, a statement describing the application of section 7874 to the transaction, and indicating that the requirements of § 1.367(a)-3(c)(1) are satisfied.

(vii) If the transferred corporation is foreign, a statement indicating whether the U.S. transferor was a section 1248 shareholder (as defined in § 1.367(b)-2(b)) of the transferred corporation immediately before the initial transfer, and whether the U.S. transferor is a section 1248 shareholder with respect to the transferee foreign corporation immediately after the initial transfer, and whether any reporting requirements or other rules contained in regulations under section 367(b) are applicable, and, if so, whether they have been satisfied.

(viii) If the initial transfer involves a transfer by a partnership (see § 1.367(a)-1(c)(3)(i)) or a transfer of a partnership interest (see section 367(a)(4) and § 1.367(a)-1(c)(3)(ii)) a complete description of the transfer, including a description of the partners in the partnership.

(ix) If the transaction involved the transfer of property other than the transferred stock or securities and the transaction was subject to the indirect stock transfer rules of § 1.367(a)-3(d), a statement indicating whether—

(A) The reporting requirements under section 6038B have been satisfied with respect to the transfer of such other property;

(B) Whether gain was recognized under section 367(a)(1);

(C) Whether section 367(d) applied to the transfer of such property; and

(D) Whether the other property transferred qualified for the active foreign trade or business exception under section 367(a)(3).

(4) *Basis adjustments for gain recognized.*—The following basis adjustments shall be made if gain is recognized under paragraph (c)(1)(i) of this section.

(i) *Stock or securities of transferee foreign corporation.*—The basis of the stock or securities, as applicable, of the transferee foreign corporation received by the U.S. transferor in the initial transfer shall be increased as of the date of the initial transfer by the amount of gain recognized.

(ii) *Transferred stock or securities.*—The basis of the transferred stock or securities shall be increased as of the date of the initial transfer by the amount of the gain recognized.

(iii) *Other appropriate adjustments.*—The basis of other stock, securities, or a partnership interest shall be increased, as appropriate, in accordance with the principles of this paragraph (c)(4). Under no circumstances shall the basis of stock, securities, or of a partnership interest held by a U.S. person that does not recognize gain under paragraph (c)(1)(i) of this section be increased under this paragraph (c)(4). In addition, under no circumstances shall the basis of any property be increased by the amount of any additional tax due or interest paid with respect to such tax, nor shall the basis of the assets of the transferred corporation be increased as a result of gain recognized by the U.S. transferor under paragraph (c)(1)(i) of this section.

(iv) *Cross-reference.*—See paragraphs (q)(2)(i), (ii), (iii), and (v) of this section for illustrations of the rules of this paragraph (c)(4). See also § 1.367(a)-1(b)(4) for rules that determine the increase to basis of property resulting from the application of section 367(a).

(5) *Terms and conditions of a new gain recognition agreement.*—(i) *General rule.*—A new gain recognition agreement entered into pursuant to this section shall replace the existing gain recognition agreement, which shall terminate without further effect. The term of the new gain recognition agreement shall be the remaining term of the existing gain recognition agreement. The amount of gain subject to the new gain recognition agreement shall equal the amount of gain subject to the existing gain recognition agreement, reduced by any gain recognized under paragraph (c)(1)(i) of this section with respect to the existing gain recognition agreement by reason of the gain recognition event that gives rise to the new gain recognition agreement. The new gain recognition agreement shall, as applicable, be subject to the conditions and requirements of this section to the same extent as the existing gain recognition agreement. For example, a triggering event with respect to the new gain recognition agreement will generally include a disposition of the transferred stock or securities or of substantially all the assets of the transferred corporation. If, however, the transferred stock is canceled or redeemed pursuant to the disposition or other event that gives rise to the new gain recognition agreement (for example, pursuant to a liquidation where the transferee foreign corporation is the corporate distributee (within the meaning of section 334(b)(2)), or an asset reorganization where the transferee foreign corporation is the acquiring corporation) the transferred stock is not subject to the new gain recognition agreement.

(ii) *Special rule for inclusion of gain.*—If the U.S. transferor with respect to the new gain recognition agreement is not the U.S. transferor with respect to the existing gain recognition agreement, or a member of the consolidated group of which the U.S. transferor with respect to the existing gain recognition agreement was a member on the date of the initial transfer, then any gain recognized under paragraph (c)(1)(i) of this section with respect to the new gain recognition agreement must be included in income in the taxable year during which the gain recognition event occurs.

(6) *Cross-reference.*—For gain recognition agreements entered into pursuant to certain outbound asset reorganizations, see § 1.367(a)-3(e)(6).

(d) *Filing requirements.*—(1) *General rule.*—An initial gain recognition agreement must be timely filed in order for the U.S. transferor to avoid recognizing gain under section 367(a)(1) with respect to the transferred stock or securities by reason of the applicable exceptions provided under § 1.367(a)-3. Except as provided in paragraph (p) of this section, an initial gain recognition agreement is timely filed only if—

(i) The initial gain recognition agreement and any other gain recognition agreement document required to be filed with the initial gain recognition agreement are included with a timely filed return of the U.S. transferor for the taxable year during which the initial transfer occurs; and

(ii) Each gain recognition agreement document identified in paragraph (d)(1)(i) of this section is completed in all material respects.

(2) *Special requirements.*—(i) *New gain recognition agreement.*—A new gain recognition agreement entered into under this section must be included with the timelyfiled return of the U.S. transferor (as identified in the new gain recognition agreement) for the taxable year during which the disposition or event that requires the new gain

recognition agreement occurs. If the new gain recognition agreement is entered into by the U.S. transferor that entered into the existing gain recognition agreement, the new gain recognition agreement is in lieu of the annual certification otherwise required for such taxable year under paragraph (g) of this section with respect to the existing gain recognition agreement.

(ii) *Multiple events within a taxable year.*—Except as otherwise provided in this paragraph (d)(2)(ii), if the initial transfer and one or more dispositions or other events (even if a triggering event exception applies) that affect the gain recognition agreement entered into by the U.S. transferor with respect to the initial transfer occur within the same taxable year of such U.S. transferor, or if multiple dispositions or other events occur in a taxable year of the U.S. transferor that does not include the initial transfer, only one gain recognition agreement is required to be entered into and included with the timely-filed return of the U.S. transferor for such taxable year. The gain recognition agreement must describe the initial transfer and/or each disposition or other event that affects the gain recognition agreement (even if a triggering event exception applies). This paragraph does not apply, however, if any such disposition or other event requires a new gain recognition agreement to be entered into by a United States person other than the U.S. transferor with respect to the initial transfer or that entered into the existing gain recognition agreement, as applicable.

(3) *Common parent as agent for U.S. transferor.*—If the U.S. transferor is a member but not the common parent of a consolidated group, the common parent of the consolidated group is the agent for the U.S. transferor under § 1.1502-77(a)(1). Thus, the common parent must file the gain recognition agreement on behalf of the U.S. transferor. References in this section to the timely-filed return of the U.S. transferor include the timely-filed return of the consolidated group of which the U.S. transferor is a member, as applicable.

(e) *Signatory.*—(1) *General rule.*—The gain recognition agreement must be signed under penalties of perjury by an agent of the U.S. transferor that is authorized to sign under a general or specific power of attorney, or by the appropriate party based on the category of the U.S. transferor described in this paragraph (e)(1).

(i) If the U.S. transferor is a corporation but not a member of a consolidated group, a responsible officer of the U.S. transferor. If the U.S. transferor is a member of a consolidated group, a responsible officer of the common parent of the consolidated group.

(ii) If the U.S. transferor is an individual, the individual.

(iii) If the U.S. transferor is a trust or estate, a trustee, executor, or equivalent fiduciary of the U.S. transferor.

(iv) In a bankruptcy case under Title 11, United States Code, a debtor in possession or trustee.

(2) *Signature requirement.*—The inclusion of an unsigned copy of the gain recognition agreement with the timely-filed return of the U.S. transferor shall satisfy the signature requirement of paragraph (e)(1) of this section if the U.S. transferor retains the original signed gain recognition agreement in the manner specified by § 1.6001-1(e).

(f) *Extension of period of limitations on assessments of tax.*—(1) *General rule.*—In connection with the filing of a gain recognition agreement, the U.S. transferor must extend the period of limitations on assessments of tax with respect to the gain realized but not recognized on the initial transfer through the close of the eighth full taxable year following the taxable year during which the initial transfer occurs. The U.S. transferor extends the period of limitations by filing Form 8838 "Consent to Extend the Time to Assess Tax Under Section 367—Gain Recognition Agreement." The Form 8838 must be signed by a person authorized to sign the gain recognition agreement under paragraph (e)(1) of this section.

(2) *New gain recognition agreement.*—If a new gain recognition agreement is entered into under this section, the U.S. transferor must extend the period of limitations on assessments of tax on the initial transfer through the close of the eighth full taxable year following the taxable year during which the initial transfer occurs, consistent with paragraph (f)(1) of this section, unless the U.S. transferor with respect to the new gain recognition agreement is the U.S. transferor with respect to the existing gain recognition agreement, or a member of the consolidated group of which the U.S. transferor with respect to the existing gain recognition agreement was a member on the date of the initial transfer.

(g) *Annual certification.*—Except as provided in paragraph (d)(2)(i) of this section, the U.S. transferor must include with its timely-filed return for each of the five full taxable years following the taxable year of the initial transfer a certification (annual certification) that includes the information described in paragraphs (g)(1) through (3) of this section, as appropriate. The annual certification must be signed by a person authorized under paragraph (e)(1) of this section to sign the gain recognition agreement for the initial transfer. The inclusion of an unsigned copy of the annual certification with the relevant timely-filed return of the U.S. transferor shall satisfy the signature requirement of paragraph (e)(1) of this section provided the U.S. transferor retains the original signed certification in the manner specified by § 1.6001-1(e).

(1) A statement of whether a gain recognition event has or has not occurred during such taxable year. If a gain recognition event has occurred during such taxable year, the annual certification must state:

(i) The amount of gain subject to the gain recognition agreement at the time of the gain recognition event;

(ii) The amount of gain recognized under the gain recognition agreement by reason of the gain recognition event; and

(iii) A calculation of the reduction to the amount of gain subject to the gain recognition agreement by reason of the gain recognition event (for example, in the case of a gain recognition event described in paragraph (n)(2) of this section).

(2) A complete description of any event occurring during such taxable year that has terminated or reduced the amount of gain subject to the gain recognition agreement (for example, an event described in paragraph (o) of this section), including a calculation of any reduction to the amount of gain subject to the gain recognition agreement.

(3) A statement describing any disposition of assets of the transferred corporation during the taxable year not in the ordinary course of business.

(h) *Use of security.*—The U.S. transferor may be required to furnish a bond or other security that satisfies the requirements of § 301.7101-1 if the Area Director, Field Examination, Small Business/Self Employed or the Director of Field Operations, Large and Mid-Size Business (Director) determines that such security is necessary to ensure the payment of any tax on the gain realized, but not recognized, upon the initial transfer. Such bond or security generally will be required only if the transferred stock or securities are a principal asset of the U.S. transferor and the Director has reason to believe that a disposition of the stock or securities may be contemplated.

(i) [Reserved.]

(j) *Triggering events.*—Except as provided in this section, if an event described in paragraphs (j)(1) through (10) of this section (triggering event) occurs during the GRA term, the U.S. transferor must recognize gain under the gain recognition agreement in accordance with paragraph (c)(1)(i) of this section. This paragraph (j) generally requires the U.S. transferor to recognize gain (and pay applicable interest with respect to any additional tax due as provided in paragraph (c)(1)(v) of this section) under the gain recognition agreement to the extent the transferred stock or securities are disposed of, directly or indirectly. This paragraph (j) also requires the U.S. transferor to recognize gain under the gain recognition agreement in certain cases where it is not appropriate for the gain recognition agreement to continue. See paragraph (k) of this section for exceptions available for certain events that would otherwise constitute triggering events under this paragraph (j). See paragraph (o) of this section for certain events that terminate or reduce the amount of gain subject to a gain recognition agreement.

(1) *Disposition of transferred stock or securities.*—A complete or partial disposition of the transferred stock or securities. See paragraph (q)(2)(ii) of this section for an illustration of the rule of this paragraph (j)(1).

(2) *Disposition of substantially all of the assets of the transferred corporation.*—(i) *General rule.*—Except as provided in paragraph (j)(2)(ii) of this section, a disposition in one or more related transactions of substantially all of the assets of the transferred corporation (including stock or securities in a subsidiary corporation or a partnership interest). If the transferred corporation is domestic, see paragraph (o)(4) of this section.

(ii) *Exceptions.*—For purposes of paragraph (j)(2)(i) of this section, the following dispositions shall be disregarded—

(A) Dispositions of property described in section 1221(a)(1) occurring in the ordinary course of business;

(B) An exchange of stock or securities described in section 354 that is pursuant to an asset reorganization; and

(C) An exchange of stock by a corporate distributee (as defined in section 334(b)(2)) pursuant to a complete liquidation to which section 332 applies.

(3) *Disposition of certain partnership interests.*—If the initial transfer occurs by reason of the transfer of a partnership interest, a complete or partial disposition of such partnership interest. See section 367(a)(4) and § 1.367(a)-1(c)(3)(ii).

(4) *Disposition of stock of the transferee foreign corporation.*—A complete or partial disposition of the stock of the transferee foreign corporation received by the U.S. transferor in the initial transfer. For purposes of this section, an individual U.S. transferor that loses U.S. citizenship or ceases to be a lawful permanent resident of the United States (within the meaning of section 7701(b)(6)) shall be treated as disposing of all the stock of the transferee foreign corporation received in the initial transfer as of the date before the loss of such status.

(5) *Deconsolidation.*—A U.S. transferor that is a member of a consolidated group ceases to be a member of the consolidated group, other than by reason of an acquisition of the assets of the U.S. transferor in a transaction to which section 381(a) applies, or by reason of the U.S. transferor joining another consolidated group as part of the same transaction.

(6) *Consolidation.*—A U.S. transferor becomes a member of a consolidated group, including a U.S. transferor that is a member of a consolidated group and that becomes a member of another consolidated group.

(7) *Death of an individual; trust or estate ceases to exist.*—A U.S. transferor that is an individual dies, or a U.S. transferor that is a trust or estate ceases to exist.

(8) *Failure to comply.*—A U.S. transferor fails to comply in any material respect with any requirement of this section, or the terms of the gain recognition agreement as described in paragraph (c)(1) of this section. A failure to comply under this paragraph (j)(8) will extend the period of limitations on assessment of tax for the taxable year in which gain is required to be reported until the close of the third full taxable year ending after the date on which the U.S. transferor furnishes to the Director of Field Operations, Cross Border Activities Practice Area of Large Business & International (or any successor to the roles and responsibilities of such person) (Director) the information that should have been provided under this section. Except as provided in paragraph (p) of this section, for purposes of this paragraph (j)(8), a failure to comply includes—

(i) If there is a gain recognition event in a taxable year, a failure to report gain or pay any additional tax or interest due under the terms of the gain recognition agreement; and

(ii) A failure to file a gain recognition agreement document, other than an initial gain recognition agreement or a document required to be filed with the initial gain recognition agreement. For this purpose, there is a failure to file a gain recognition agreement document if—

(A) The gain recognition agreement document is not timely filed as required under this section, or

(B) The gain recognition agreement document is not completed in all material respects.

(9) *Gain recognition agreement filed in connection with indirect stock transfers and certain triangular asset reorganizations.*—With respect to a gain recognition agreement entered into in connection with an indirect stock transfer (as defined in § 1.367(a)-3(d)), or a triangular asset reorganization described in § 1.367(a)-3(e)(6)(iv), an indirect disposition of the transferred stock or securities. For example, in the case of an indirect stock transfer described in § 1.367(a)-3(d)(1)(iii)(A), a complete or partial disposition of the stock of the acquiring corporation.

(10) *Gain recognition agreement filed pursuant to paragraph (k)(14) of this section.*—In the case of a gain recognition agreement entered into pursuant to paragraph (k)(14) of this section, in addition to any disposition or other event described in paragraphs (j)(1) through (9) of this section,—

(i) Any disposition or other event identified as a triggering event in a new gain recognition agreement as required under paragraph (k)(14)(iii) of this section; and

(ii) Any disposition or other event that is inconsistent with the principles of paragraph (k) of this section including, for example, an indirect disposition of the transferred stock or securities.

(k) *Triggering event exceptions.*—Notwithstanding paragraph (j) of this section, a disposition or other event described in paragraphs (k)(1) through (14) of this section shall not constitute a triggering event. This paragraph (k) generally provides exceptions for certain dispositions that constitute nonrecognition transactions but only if, immediately after the disposition, a U.S. transferor retains, as applicable, a direct or indirect interest in the transferred stock or securities, or in the assets of the transferred corporation, and a new gain recognition agreement is entered into with respect to the initial transfer in accordance with this paragraph (k). Notwithstanding the application of this paragraph (k), if a gain recognition event described under paragraphs (m) and (n) of this section occurs during the GRA term the U.S. transferor may be required to recognize gain under the gain recognition agreement in accordance with paragraph (c)(1)(i) of this section. See paragraph (o) of this section which provides that, notwithstanding paragraph (j) of this section, certain dispositions or other events shall instead terminate or reduce the amount of gain subject to a gain recognition agreement.

(1) *Transfers of stock of the transferee foreign corporation to a corporation or partnership.*—A disposition of stock of the transferee foreign corporation received in the initial transfer pursuant to an exchange to which section 351, 354 (but only in a reorganization described in section 368(a)(1)(B) that is not a triangular reorganization), 361 (but only in a divisive reorganization to which section 355 applies), or 721 applies, shall not constitute a triggering event if a new gain recognition agreement is entered into in accordance with paragraphs (k)(1)(i) through (iv) of this section, as applicable. In the case of an exchange to which section 354 applies that is pursuant to a triangular reorganization described in section 368(a)(1)(B), see paragraph (k)(14) of this section and paragraph (q)(2)(iv) of this section.

(i) In the case of an exchange to which section 351 or 354 applies in which stock of a foreign acquiring corporation is received, the U.S. transferor includes with the new gain recognition agreement a statement that a complete or partial disposition of the stock of the foreign acquiring corporation received in the exchange shall constitute a triggering event. The principles of paragraph (o)(1)(i) or (ii), as appropriate, shall be applied to determine whether a subsequent complete or partial disposition of the stock of the foreign acquiring corporation received in the exchange shall instead terminate or reduce the amount of the new gain recognition agreement.

(ii) In the case of an exchange to which section 351 or 354 applies in which stock of a domestic acquiring corporation is received, the domestic acquiring corporation enters into the new gain recognition agreement, which must designate the domestic acquiring corporation as the U.S. transferor for purposes of this section. For an illustration of the rule provided by this paragraph (k)(1)(ii), see paragraph (q)(2)(iii) of this section.

(iii) In the case of a section 361 exchange that is pursuant to a divisive reorganization to which section 355 applies and in which stock of a domestic corporation (domestic controlled corporation) is received, the domestic controlled corporation enters into the new gain recognition agreement, which must designate the domestic controlled corporation as the U.S. transferor for purposes of this section. For an illustration of the rule provided by this paragraph (k)(1)(iii), see paragraph (q)(2)(xi) of this section.

(iv) In the case of an exchange to which section 721 applies, the U.S. transferor includes with the new gain recognition agreement a statement that a complete or partial disposition of the partnership interest received in the exchange shall constitute a triggering event for purposes of the new gain recognition agreement.

(2) *Complete liquidation of U.S. transferor under sections 332 and 337.*—A distribution by the U.S. transferor of the stock of the transferee foreign corporation received in the initial transfer to which section 337 applies, that is pursuant to a complete liquidation under section 332, shall not constitute a triggering event if the corporate distributee (as defined in section 334(b)(2)) is a domestic corporation (domestic corporate distributee) and the domestic corporate distributee enters into a new gain recognition agreement. The new gain recognition agreement must designate the domestic corporate distributee as the U.S. transferor for purposes of this section.

(3) *Transfers of transferred stock or securities to a corporation or partnership.*—A disposition of the transferred stock or securities pursuant to an exchange to which section 351, 354 (but only in a reorganization described in section 368(a)(1)(B)), or 721 applies, shall not constitute a triggering event if the U.S. transferor enters in to a new gain recognition agreement that provides that the dispositions described in paragraphs (k)(3)(i) and (ii) of this section shall constitute triggering events for purposes of the new gain recognition agreement.

(i) A complete or partial disposition of the stock, securities, or partnership interest (as applicable) received in exchange for the transferred stock or securities.

(ii) Any other event that is inconsistent with the principles of this paragraph (k), including the indirect disposition of the transferred stock or securities.

(4) *Transfers of substantially all of the assets of the transferred corporation.*—A disposition of substantially all of the assets of the transferred corporation pursuant to an exchange to which section 351, 354 (but only in a reorganization described in section 368(a)(1)(B)), or 721 applies, shall not constitute a triggering event if the U.S. transferor enters into a new gain recognition agreement that provides that a complete or partial disposition of the stock, securities, or partnership interest (as applicable) received in exchange for the assets shall constitute a triggering event for purposes of the new gain recognition agreement.

(5) *Recapitalizations and section 1036 exchanges.*—A complete or partial disposition of the transferred stock or securities, or of the stock of the transferee foreign corporation received in the initial transfer, pursuant to a reorganization described under section 368(a)(1)(E), or pursuant to a transaction to which section 1036 applies, shall not constitute a triggering event if the U.S. transferor enters into a new gain recognition agreement.

(6) *Certain asset reorganizations.*—(i) *Stock of transferee foreign corporation.*—If stock of the transferee foreign corporation received in the initial transfer is transferred to a domestic acquiring corporation in a section 361 exchange that is pursuant to an asset reorganization, the exchanges made pursuant to the asset reorganization shall not constitute triggering events if the domestic acquiring corporation enters into a new gain recognition agreement that designates the domestic acquiring corporation as the U.S. transferor for purposes of this section. For an illustration of the rule provided by this paragraph (k)(6), see paragraph (q)(2)(v) of this section. If the acquiring corporation is foreign, see paragraph (k)(14) of this section and paragraph (q)(2)(vi) of this section.

(ii) *Transferred stock or securities.*—If the transferred stock or securities are transferred to a foreign acquiring corporation in a section 361 exchange that is pursuant to an asset reorganization, the exchanges made pursuant to the asset reorganization shall not constitute triggering events if the U.S. transferor enters into a new gain recognition agreement that designates the foreign acquiring corporation as the transferee foreign corporation for purposes of this section. For an illustration of the rule provided by this paragraph, see paragraph (q)(2)(vii) of this section. If the transfer is to a domestic acquiring corporation, or is pursuant to a triangular asset reorganization, see paragraph (k)(14) or (o)(5) of this section.

(iii) *Assets of transferred corporation.*—If substantially all of the assets of the transferred corporation are transferred to a foreign or domestic acquiring corporation in a section 361 exchange that is pursuant to an asset reorganization, the exchanges made pursuant to the asset reorganization shall not constitute triggering events if the U.S. transferor enters into a new gain recognition agreement that, unless the acquiring corporation is the transferee foreign corporation, designates the acquiring corporation as the transferred corporation for purposes of this section. Only the assets of the transferred corporation received by the acquiring corporation shall be treated as assets of the transferred corporation for purposes of this section (for example, only such assets will be taken into account for purposes of paragraph (j)(2) of this section). For an illustration of the rule provided by this paragraph, see paragraph (q)(2)(viii) of this section. If the transferred corporation is domestic, see section 367(a)(1) and (a)(5), and paragraph (o)(4) of this section. If the transfer is pursuant to a triangular asset reorganization, see paragraph (k)(14) of this section.

(7) *Certain triangular reorganizations.*—(i) *Transferee foreign corporation.*—If substantially all of the assets of the transferee foreign corporation are transferred to a foreign acquiring corporation in a section 361 exchange that is pursuant to a triangular asset reorganization, the exchanges made pursuant to the reorganization shall not constitute triggering events if a new gain recognition agreement is entered into in accordance with paragraphs (k)(7)(i)(A) through (C) of this section. If the acquiring corporation is domestic, see paragraph (k)(14) of this section. For rules that apply to gain recognition agreements entered into as a result of an indirect stock transfer, see § 1.367(a)-3(d)(2)(iv) and paragraph (j)(9) of this section.

(A) If P is foreign, the new gain recognition agreement designates P as the transferee foreign corporation and includes a statement that the U.S. transferor agrees to treat a complete or partial disposition of the S stock held by P as a triggering event.

(B) Except as provided in paragraph (k)(7)(i)(C) of this section, if P is domestic, P enters into the new gain recognition agreement that designates P as the U.S. transferor and S as the transferee foreign corporation.

(C) If the triangular asset reorganization is described in section 368(a)(1)(A) by reason of section 368(a)(2)(E) and the transferee foreign corporation is the merged corporation, the U.S. transferor enters into the new gain recognition agreement and designates the surviving corporation as the transferee foreign corporation.

(ii) *Transferred corporation.*—If substantially all of the assets of the transferred corporation are transferred in a section 361 exchange pursuant to a triangular asset reorganization, the exchanges made pursuant to the reorganization shall not constitute triggering events if the U.S. transferor enters into a new gain recognition agreement in accordance with paragraph (k)(7)(ii)(A) of this section and, as applicable, paragraph (k)(7)(ii)(B) or (C) of this section.

(A) The new gain recognition agreement includes a statement that the U.S. transferor agrees to treat a complete or partial disposition of the P stock received in the reorganization as a triggering event.

(B) If the triangular asset reorganization is described in section 368(a)(1)(C), or section 368(a)(1)(A) or (G) by reason of section 368(a)(2)(D), the new gain recognition agreement includes a statement that the U.S. transferor agrees to treat a complete or partial disposition of the S stock held by P as a triggering event.

(C) If the triangular asset reorganization is described in section 368(a)(1)(A) by reason of section 368(a)(2)(E) and the transferred corporation is the merged corporation, the new gain recognition agreement includes a statement that the U.S. transferor agrees to treat a complete or partial disposition of the stock of the surviving corporation as a triggering event.

(8) *Complete liquidation of transferred corporation.*—A distribution of substantially all of the assets of the transferred corporation to which section 337 applies, and the related exchange of the transferred stock to which section 332 applies, shall not constitute triggering events, if the U.S. transferor enters into a new gain recognition agreement. If the transferred corporation is domestic, see § 1.367(e)-2 and paragraph (o)(4) of this section. See paragraph (q)(2)(ix) of this section for an illustration of the rules provided in this paragraph (k)(8).

(9) *Death of U.S. transferor.*—The death of a U.S. transferor shall not constitute a triggering event if the person winding up the affairs of the U.S. transferor—

(i) Retains sufficient assets of the U.S. transferor to satisfy any possible Federal tax liability of the U.S. transferor under the gain recognition agreement for the duration of the extended period of limitations on assessments of tax on the gain realized but not recognized in the initial transfer;

(ii) Provides security as required under paragraph (h) of this section for any possible Federal tax liability of the U.S. transferor under the gain recognition agreement; or

(iii) Obtains a ruling from the Internal Revenue Service providing for one or more successors to the U.S. transferor under the gain recognition agreement.

(10) *Deconsolidation.*—A deconsolidation of the U.S. transferor shall not constitute a triggering event if the U.S. transferor enters into a new gain recognition agreement.

(11) *Consolidation.*—A consolidation of the U.S. transferor shall not constitute a triggering event if the U.S. transferor enters into a new gain recognition agreement. See paragraph (d)(3) of this section.

(12) *Intercompany transactions.*—(i) *General rule.*—If, pursuant to an intercompany transaction, the U.S. transferor disposes of stock of the transferee foreign corporation received in the initial transfer, this

paragraph (k)(12) applies to such disposition to the extent the intercompany transaction creates an intercompany item that is not taken into account in the taxable year during which the intercompany transaction occurs. To the extent this paragraph (k)(12) applies, the disposition shall not constitute a triggering event, and the U.S. transferor shall remain subject to the gain recognition agreement if the conditions of paragraphs (k)(12)(i)(A) and (B) of this section are satisfied. To the extent the intercompany transaction does not create an intercompany item see, for example, paragraph (k)(1) and paragraph (q)(2)(xx) of this section. See paragraph (o)(6) of this section for the effect on a gain recognition agreement when an intercompany item from an intercompany transaction to which this paragraph (k)(12)(i) applies is taken into account.

(A) At the time of the disposition, the basis of the stock of the transferee foreign corporation received in the initial transfer that is disposed of in the intercompany transaction is not greater than the sum of the amounts described in paragraphs (k)(12)(i)(A)(*1*) through (*3*) of this section. If only a portion of the stock of the transferee foreign corporation received in the initial transfer is disposed of, then the basis of such stock shall be compared with a proportionate amount (measured by value as determined at the time of the disposition) of the amounts described in paragraph (k)(12)(i)(A)(*1*) through (*3*) of this section. To satisfy the basis condition of this paragraph (k)(12)(i)(A), the U.S. transferor may reduce the basis of the stock of the transferee foreign corporation received in the initial transfer that is disposed of in the intercompany transaction in accordance with the principles of paragraph (o)(1)(iii) of this section.

(*1*) The aggregate basis of the transferred stock or securities at the time of the initial transfer;

(*2*) The amount of any increase to the basis of the transferred stock or securities by reason of gain recognized by the U.S. transferor on the initial transfer; and

(*3*) The amount of any increase to the basis of the stock disposed of by reason of an income inclusion by the U.S. transferor with respect to such stock (for example, pursuant to section 961(a)).

(B) The annual certification filed with respect to the existing gain recognition agreement for the taxable year during which the intercompany transaction occurs includes a complete description of the intercompany transaction and a schedule illustrating how the basis condition of paragraph (k)(12)(i)(A) of this section is satisfied.

(ii) *Certain dispositions following intercompany transaction.*—A subsequent disposition of stock of the transferee foreign corporation that is transferred in an intercompany transaction to which the exception provided by paragraph (k)(12)(i) of this section applies shall not constitute a triggering event if—

(A) The stock is transferred to a member of the consolidated group that includes the U.S. transferor immediately after the disposition, and

(B) The annual certification filed with respect to the existing gain recognition agreement for the taxable year during which the subsequent disposition occurs includes a complete description of the disposition.

(13) *Deemed asset sales pursuant to section 338(g) elections.*—A deemed sale of the assets of the transferred corporation or the transferee foreign corporation as a result of an election under section 338(g) shall not constitute a triggering event. This paragraph does not apply to the sale of the stock of the target corporation (within the meaning of section 338(d)(2)) with respect to which such election is made.

(14) *Other dispositions or events.*—A disposition or other event that would constitute a triggering event, without regard to this paragraph (k)(14), shall not constitute a triggering event if the conditions of paragraph (k)(14)(i) through (iii) of this section, as applicable, are satisfied. See paragraphs (q)(2)(iv), (vi), (x), (xii), (xvii), (xxi), and (xxiii) of this section for illustrations of the rules provided by this paragraph (k)(14).

(i) The disposition qualifies as a nonrecognition transaction.

(ii) Immediately after the disposition or other event, a U.S. transferor retains a direct or indirect interest in the transferred stock or securities or, as applicable, in substantially all of the assets of the transferred corporation (for example, in a case where the transferred corporation has been liquidated pursuant to section 332). If, as a result of the disposition or other event, a foreign corporation acquires the transferred stock or securities or, as applicable, substantially all the assets of the transferred corporation, the condition of this paragraph (k)(14)(ii) is satisfied only if the U.S. transferor owns at least five percent (applying the attribution rules of section 318, as modified by section 958(b) but without applying section 318(a)(3)(A), (B), and (C) so as to consider the U.S. transferor as owning stock which is owned by a person who is not a United States person) of the total voting power and the total value of the outstanding stock of such foreign corporation.

(iii) A new gain recognition agreement is entered into by the U.S. transferor described in paragraph (k)(14)(ii) of this section that includes—

(A) An explanation of why this paragraph (k)(14) applies to the disposition or other event; and

(B) A description of each subsequent disposition or other event that would constitute a triggering event, other than those described in paragraph (j) of this section, with respect to the new gain recognition agreement based on the principles of paragraphs (j) and (k) of this section including, for example, an indirect disposition of the transferred stock or securities.

(l) [Reserved.]

(m) *Receipt of boot in nonrecognition transactions.*—(1) *Dispositions of transferred stock or securities.*—Notwithstanding paragraph (k) of this section, if gain is required to be recognized (not including any gain that would be treated as a dividend under section 356(a)(2)) in connection with a disposition of the transferred stock or securities to which an exception under paragraph (k) of this section otherwise applies (triggering event exception), the U.S. transferor shall recognize gain under paragraph (c)(1)(i) of this section equal to the amount of gain required to be recognized in connection with the disposition, but not in excess of the amount of gain subject to the gain recognition agreement. For purposes of this paragraph (m)(1), the amount of gain required to be recognized in connection with the disposition shall be determined before taking into account any increase to the basis of the transferred stock or securities under paragraph (c)(4)(ii) of this section. See paragraph (q)(2)(xiii) of this section, for an illustration of the rule provided by this paragraph (m)(1).

(2) *Dispositions of assets of transferred corporation.*—If gain is required to be recognized (not including any gain that would be treated as a dividend under section 356(a)(2)) in connection with a disposition of substantially all of the assets of the transferred corporation to which a triggering event exception otherwise applies, the U.S. transferor shall recognize gain under paragraph (c)(1)(i) of this section equal to the amount of gain required to be recognized in connection with the disposition, but not in excess of the amount of gain subject to the gain recognition agreement.

(n) *Special rules for distributions with respect to stock.*—(1) *Certain dividend equivalent redemptions treated as dispositions.*—A redemption of the transferred stock or of stock of the transferee foreign corporation received in the initial transfer that is treated by reason of section 302(d) as a distribution of property to which section 301 applies shall constitute a disposition for purposes of this section unless the U.S. transferor enters into a new gain recognition agreement that includes appropriate provisions to account for the redemption. For an illustration of the rule of this paragraph (n)(1), see paragraph (q)(2)(xiv) of this section.

(2) *Gain recognized under section 301(c)(3).*—If gain is required to be recognized under section 301(c)(3) with respect to the transferred stock, the U.S. transferor shall recognize gain under the gain recognition agreement in accordance with paragraph (c)(1)(i) of this section in an amount equal to the gain required to be recognized under section 301(c)(3), but not in excess of the amount of gain subject to the gain recognition agreement. For this purpose, the amount of gain required to be recognized under section 301(c)(3) shall be determined before taking into account any increase in the basis of the transferred stock under paragraph (c)(4)(ii) of this section.

(o) *Dispositions or other events that terminate or reduce the amount of gain subject to the gain recognition agreement.*—Notwithstanding paragraph (j) of this section, the following dispositions or other events shall not constitute triggering events but instead shall terminate or reduce the amount of gain subject to the gain recognition agreement.

(1) *Taxable disposition of stock of the transferee foreign corporation.*—(i) *Complete disposition.*—Except as otherwise provided in this paragraph (o)(1)(i), if the U.S. transferor disposes of all the stock of the transferee foreign corporation received in the initial transfer in a transaction in which all gain realized is recognized and included in taxable income during the taxable year of the disposition, the gain recognition agreement shall terminate without further effect if, at the time of the disposition, the aggregate basis of such stock is not

greater than the sum of the amounts described in paragraphs (o)(1)(i)(A) through (C) of this section. This paragraph shall not apply to a disposition of stock of the transferee foreign corporation pursuant to an intercompany transaction to which paragraph (k)(12) of this section applies. This paragraph shall also not apply to an individual U.S. transferor that loses U.S. citizenship or ceases to be a lawful permanent resident of the United States (within the meaning of section 7701(b)(6)).

(A) The aggregate basis of the transferred stock or securities at the time of the initial transfer;

(B) The amount of any increase to the basis of the transferred stock or securities by reason of gain recognized by the U.S. transferor on the initial transfer; and

(C) The amount of any increase to the basis of the stock disposed of by reason of an income inclusion by the U.S. transferor with respect to such stock (for example, pursuant to section 961(a)).

(ii) *Partial dispositions.*—A partial disposition by the U.S. transferor of the stock of the transferee foreign corporation received in the initial transfer in a transaction otherwise described in paragraph (o)(1)(i) of this section shall reduce the amount of gain subject to the gain recognition agreement based on the relative fair market value of the stock disposed of (measured at the time of the disposition) compared to the fair market value of all of the stock of the transferee foreign corporation received in the initial transfer (measured at the time of the disposition). For determining whether the basis condition of paragraph (o)(1)(i) of this section is satisfied in the case of a partial disposition, the aggregate basis of the stock disposed of is compared to a proportionate amount (based on fair market value, as measured at the time of the partial disposition) of the amounts described in paragraphs (o)(1)(i)(A) through (C) of this section. For an illustration of the rules of this paragraph (o)(1)(ii), see paragraph (q)(2)(xv) of this section, of this section.

(iii) *Reduction of stock basis.*—For purposes of satisfying the basis condition of paragraph (o)(1)(i) or (ii) of this section, the U.S. transferor may reduce the aggregate basis of the stock of the transferee foreign corporation received in the initial transfer, effective immediately before the disposition. For an illustration of the rules of this paragraph (o)(1)(iii), see paragraph (q)(2)(xvi) of this section, of this section. The U.S. transferor reduces the basis of the stock of the transferee foreign corporation by including a statement with the timely-filed return of the U.S. transferor for the taxable year in which the disposition occurs, entitled "Election to Reduce Stock Basis Under § 1.367(a)-8(o)(1)(iii)" and that includes—

(A) A description, including the date, of the disposition;

(B) A description of the stock of the transferee foreign corporation disposed of and the basis adjustments made under this paragraph (o)(1)(iii); and

(C) The fair market value of all the stock of the transferee foreign corporation held by the U.S. transferor at the time of the disposition.

(2) *Gain recognized in connection with certain nonrecognition transactions.*—If the U.S. transferor recognizes gain in connection with a complete or partial disposition of stock of the transferee foreign corporation received in the initial transfer that is described in paragraph (k) of this section, and the basis condition of paragraph (o)(1)(i) or (ii) of this section, as applicable, is satisfied with the respect to such disposition, the amount of gain subject to the new gain recognition agreement filed under paragraph (k) of this section as a result of such disposition shall equal the amount of gain subject to the existing gain recognition agreement reduced by the amount of gain recognized by the U.S. transferor on the disposition. If the U.S. transferor recognizes gain in connection with a complete or partial disposition of the stock of the transferee foreign corporation received in the initial transfer that is described in paragraph (k) of this section, and the condition of paragraph (o)(1)(i) or (ii) of this section, as applicable, is satisfied with the respect to the disposition, but a new gain recognition agreement is not filed with respect to such disposition so that a triggering event exception does not apply to the disposition, the amount of gain required to be recognized by the U.S. transferor under the existing gain recognition agreement shall be reduced by the amount of the gain recognized on the disposition.

(3) *Gain recognized under section 301(c)(3).*—If the U.S. transferor recognizes gain under section 301(c)(3) with respect to the stock of the transferee foreign corporation received in the initial transfer, the amount of gain subject to the gain recognition agreement shall be reduced by the amount of such recognized gain.

(4) *Dispositions of substantially all of the assets of a domestic transferred corporation.*—Except as otherwise provided in this paragraph (o)(4), the gain recognition agreement shall terminate without further effect if substantially all of the assets of the transferred corporation are disposed of in a transaction in which all gain realized is recognized and included in taxable income during the taxable year of the disposition, but only if, at the time of the initial transfer, the U.S. transferor owned stock in the transferred corporation satisfying the requirements of section 1504(a)(2) and the U.S. transferor and the transferred corporation were members of the same consolidated group. If the initial transfer was part of an indirect stock transfer, the gain recognition agreement shall terminate without further effect if substantially all of the assets of the transferred corporation (taking into account § 1.367(a)-3(d)(2)(v)) are disposed of in a transaction in which all gain realized is recognized and included in taxable income during the taxable year of the disposition, but only if at the time of the initial transfer the U.S. transferor owned stock in the transferred corporation satisfying the requirements of section 1504(a)(2) (for example, in the case of a reorganization described in section 368(a)(1)(A) by reason of section 368(a)(2)(E)) and the U.S. transferor and the transferred corporation were members of the same consolidated group.

(5) *Certain distributions or transfers of transferred stock or securities to U.S. persons.*—To the extent a distribution or transfer of the transferred stock or securities satisfies the conditions of paragraphs (o)(5)(i) through (iii) of this section, the gain recognition agreement shall terminate without further effect, or the amount of gain subject to the gain recognition agreement shall be reduced, as appropriate.

(i) *Distributions or transfers described in section 337, 355, or 361.*—The transferred stock or securities are distributed or transferred pursuant to a transaction described in paragraph (o)(5)(i)(A) through (D) of this section, as appropriate.

(A) A distribution described in section 337 that is pursuant to a complete liquidation described in section 332. See paragraph (q)(2)(xviii) of this section, for an illustration of the rule provided by this paragraph (o)(5)(i)(A).

(B) A distribution to which section 355 applies. See paragraph (q)(2)(xix) of this section, for an illustration of the rule provided by this paragraph (o)(5)(i)(B).

(C) A section 361 exchange that is pursuant to an asset reorganization. See paragraph (q)(2)(xxii) of this section, for an illustration of the rule provided by this paragraph (o)(5)(i)(C).

(D) A distribution to which section 361(c) applies that is pursuant to an asset reorganization. See paragraph (q)(2)(xxii) of this section, for an illustration of the rule provided by this paragraph (o)(5)(i)(D).

(ii) *Qualified recipient.*—The recipient of the transferred stock or securities in the relevant transaction described in paragraph (o)(5)(i) of this section (qualified recipient) is—

(A) The U.S. transferor;

(B) A member of the consolidated group that includes the U.S. transferor immediately after the transaction; or

(C) An individual that is a United States person.

(iii) *Basis requirement.*—(A) *General rule.*—Immediately after the relevant transaction described in paragraph (o)(5)(i) of this section, the aggregate basis of the transferred stock or securities received by the qualified recipient is not greater than the aggregate basis of such stock or securities at the time of the initial transfer (as adjusted for gain recognized by the U.S. transferor on the initial transfer attributable to such stock or securities). For this purpose, the basis of the transferred stock in the hands of the qualified recipient shall be determined without regard to any basis attributable to income inclusions with respect to the stock (for example, under section 961(a)). In the case of a distribution to which section 355 applies, any adjustments to basis under § 1.367(b)-5(c) shall be made before determining whether the basis condition of this paragraph is satisfied.

(B) *Election to reduce basis in transferred stock or securities.*—If the basis condition of paragraph (o)(5)(iii)(A) of this section is not satisfied, each qualified recipient may reduce the basis of the transferred stock or securities received in the transaction to the extent necessary to satisfy the basis condition. A qualified recipient reduces the basis of the transferred stock or securities by including a statement with its timely-filed return for the taxable year during which the distribution or transfer occurs entitled "Election to Reduce Stock Basis Under § 1.367(a)-8(o)(5)(iii)(B)" and that includes—

(1) A complete description and the date of the distribution or transfer;

(2) The fair market value of the transferred stock or securities received by the qualified recipient in the transaction; and

(3) The basis of the transferred stock or securities received by the qualified recipient immediately before and after the basis reduction.

(6) *Dispositions or other event following certain intercompany transactions.*—If, subsequent to an intercompany transaction to which paragraph (k)(12) of this section applies, a disposition or other event occurs that requires the U.S. transferor to take into account the intercompany item related to the intercompany transaction (under the provisions of § 1.1502-13), the gain recognition agreement shall terminate without further effect or the amount of gain subject to the gain recognition agreement shall be reduced based on the principles of paragraph (o)(1)(i) or (ii) of this section, as appropriate. For an illustration of the rules of this paragraph (o)(6), see paragraph (q)(2)(xx) of this section.

(7) *Expropriations under foreign law.*—The amount of gain subject to the gain recognition agreement shall be reduced to the extent the stock or securities of the transferee foreign corporation received in the initial transfer, the transferred stock or securities, or substantially all the assets of the transferred corporation, are expropriated, seized, or subjected to a similar taking of such property by the government of a foreign country, any political subdivision thereof, or any agency or instrumentality of the foregoing. Principles similar to those of paragraph (o)(1)(i) or (o)(1)(ii) of this paragraph, as relevant, shall be applied to determine the amount of the reduction.

(p) *Relief for certain failures to file or failures to comply that are not willful.*—(1) *In general.*—This paragraph (p) provides relief if there is a failure to file an initial gain recognition agreement as required under paragraph (d)(1) of this section (failure to file), or a failure to comply that is a triggering event under paragraph (j)(8) of this section (failure to comply). A failure to file or failure to comply will be deemed not to have occurred for purposes of paragraph (d)(1) of this section or paragraph (j)(8) of this section if the U.S. transferor demonstrates that the failure was not willful using the procedure set forth in this paragraph (p). For this purpose, willful is to be interpreted consistent with the meaning of that term in the context of other civil penalties, which would include a failure due to gross negligence, reckless disregard, or willful neglect. Whether a failure to file or failure to comply was willful will be determined by the Director (as described in paragraph (j)(8) of this section) based on all the facts and circumstances. The U.S. transferor must submit a request for relief and an explanation as provided in paragraph (p)(2)(i) of this section. Although a U.S. transferor whose failure to file or failure to comply is determined not to be willful will not be subject to gain recognition under paragraph (b), (c), or (e) of § 1.367(a)-3 or paragraph (c)(1) of this section, as applicable, the U.S. transferor will be subject to a penalty under section 6038B if the U.S. transferor fails to satisfy the reporting requirements under that section and does not demonstrate that the failure was due to reasonable cause and not willful neglect. See § 1.6038B-1(b)(2) and (f). The determination of whether the failure to file or failure to comply was willful under this section has no effect on any request for relief made under § 1.6038B-1(f).

(2) *Procedures for establishing that a failure to file or failure to comply was not willful.*—(i) *Time and manner of submission.*—A U.S. transferor's statement that a failure to file or failure to comply was not willful will be considered only if, promptly after the U.S. transferor becomes aware of the failure, an amended return is filed for the taxable year to which the failure relates that includes the information that should have been included with the original return for such taxable year or that otherwise complies with the rules of this section, and that includes a written statement explaining the reasons for the failure to file or failure to comply. The U.S. transferor must file, with the amended return, a Form 8838 extending the period of limitations on assessment of tax with respect to the gain realized but not recognized on the initial transfer to the later of: the close of the eighth full taxable year following the taxable year during which the initial transfer occurred (date one); or the close of the third full taxable year ending after the date on which the required information is provided to the Director (date two). However, the U.S. transferor is not required to file a Form 8838 with the amended return if both date one is later than date two and a Form 8838 was previously filed extending the period of limitations on assessment of tax with respect to the gain realized but not recognized on the initial transfer to date one. If a Form 8838 is not required to be filed with the amended return pursuant to the previous sentence, a copy of the previously filed Form 8838 must be filed with the amended return. The amended return and either a Form 8838 or a copy of the previously filed Form 8838, as the case may be, must be filed with the Internal Revenue Service at the location where the U.S. transferor filed its original return. The U.S. transferor may submit a request for relief from the penalty under section 6038B as part of the same submission. See § 1.6038B-1(f).

(ii) *Notice requirement.*—In addition to the requirements of paragraph (p)(2)(i) of this section, the U.S. transferor must comply with the notice requirements of this paragraph (p)(2)(ii). If any taxable year of the U.S. transferor is under examination when the amended return is filed, a copy of the amended return and any information required to be included with such return must be delivered to the Internal Revenue Service personnel conducting the examination. If no taxable year of the U.S. transferor is under examination when the amended return is filed, a copy of the amended return and any information required to be included with such return must be delivered to the Director.

(3) *Examples.*—The following examples illustrate the application of this paragraph (p). All of the examples are based solely on the following facts and any additional facts stated in the particular example. DC, a domestic corporation, wholly owns FS and FA, each a foreign corporation. In Year 1, pursuant to a transaction qualifying both as an exchange under section 351 and a reorganization under section 368(a)(1)(B), DC transferred all the FS stock to FA solely in exchange for voting stock of FA (FS Transfer). The fair market value of the FS stock exceeded DC's tax basis in the stock at the time of the FS transfer. Absent the application of section 367 to the transaction, DC's exchange of the FS stock for the stock of FA qualified as a tax-free exchange under sections 351(a) and section 354. Immediately after the transaction, both FA and FS were controlled foreign corporations (as defined in section 957). Furthermore, DC was a section 1248 shareholder (as defined in § 1.367(b)-2(b)) with respect to FA and FS, and a 5-percent shareholder with respect to FA for purposes of § 1.367(a)-3(b)(ii). Thus, DC was required to recognize gain under section 367(a)(1) by reason of the FS Transfer unless DC timely filed an initial gain recognition agreement (GRA) as required by paragraph (d)(1) of this section and complies in all material respects with the requirements of this section throughout the term of the GRA. The application of section 6038B is not addressed in these examples. DC may be subject to a penalty under section 6038B even if DC demonstrates under this section that a failure to file or failure to comply was not willful. See § 1.6038B-1(b) and (f) for the application of section 6038B.

(i) *Example 1.—Taxpayer failed to file a GRA due to accidental oversight.* (A) *Facts.* DC filed its tax return for the year of the FS Transfer, reporting no gain with respect to the exchange of the FS stock. DC, through its tax department, was aware of the requirement to file a GRA in order for DC to avoid recognizing gain with respect to the FS Transfer under section 367(a)(1), and had the experience and competency to properly prepare the GRA. DC had filed many GRAs over the years and had never failed to timely file a GRA. However, although DC prepared the GRA with respect to the FS Transfer, it was not filed with DC's tax return for the year of the FS Transfer due to an accidental oversight. During the preparation of the following year's tax return, DC discovered that the GRA was not filed. DC filed an amended return to file the GRA and complied with the procedures set forth under paragraph (p)(2) of this section promptly after it became aware of the failure.

(B) *Result.* Because DC failed to file a GRA with its timely filed tax return for the year of the FS Transfer, there is a failure to timely file the GRA as required by paragraph (d)(1) of this section. However, based on the facts of in paragraph (p)(3)(i)(A) of this section (the facts of this *Example 1*), including that the failure to timely file the GRA was an isolated and accidental oversight, the failure to timely file is not a willful failure to file. Accordingly, the timely filed requirement of paragraph (d)(1) of this section is considered to be satisfied, and DC is not required to recognize the gain realized on the FS Transfer under section 367(a)(1).

(ii) *Example 2.—Taxpayer's course of conduct is taken into account in determination.* (A) *Facts.* DC filed its tax return for the year of the FS Transfer, reporting no gain with respect to the exchange of the FS stock, but failed to file a GRA. DC, through its tax department, was aware of the requirement to file a GRA in order for DC to avoid recognizing gain with respect to the FS Transfer under section 367(a)(1). DC had not consistently and in a timely manner filed GRAs in the past, and also had an established history of failing to timely file other tax and information returns for which it was subject to penalties. In a year subsequent to Year 1, DC transferred stock of another foreign subsidiary with respect to which DC had a built-in gain (FS2) to FA in a transaction that qualified as both a reorganization under section 368(a)(1)(B) and an exchange described under section 351 (FS2 Transfer). DC was required to recognize gain on the FS2 Transfer under section 367(a)(1) unless DC timely filed a GRA as required by paragraph (d)(1) of this section and complied with the requirements of this section during the term of the GRA. DC reported no gain on the FS2 Transfer on its tax return, but failed to file a GRA. At the time of the FS2 Transfer, DC was already aware of its failure to file the GRA required for the prior FS Transfer, but had not implemented any safeguards to ensure that it would timely file GRAs for future transactions. DC filed an amended return to file the GRA for the FS2 Transfer and complied with the procedures set forth under paragraph (p)(2) of this section promptly after it became aware of the failure. DC asserts that its failure to timely file a GRA with respect to the FS2 Transfer was due to an isolated oversight similar to the one that occurred with respect to the FS Transfer. At issue is DC's failure to timely file a GRA for the FS2 Transfer.

(B) *Result*. Because DC failed to file a GRA with its timely filed tax return for the year of the FS2 Transfer, there is a failure to timely file the GRA as required by paragraph (d)(1) of this section. DC's course of conduct is taken into account in determining whether its failure to timely file a GRA for the FS2 Transfer was willful. Based on the facts of in paragraph (p)(3)(ii)(A) of this section (the facts of this *Example 2*), including DC's history of failing to file required tax and information returns in general and GRAs in particular, and its failure to implement safeguards to ensure that it would timely file GRAs, the failure to timely file a GRA with respect to the FS2 Transfer rises to the level of a willful failure to timely file. Accordingly, DC is ineligible for relief under paragraph (p) of this section, the GRA is not considered timely filed for purposes of paragraph (d)(1) of this section, and DC must recognize the full amount of the gain realized on the FS2 Transfer.

(iii) *Example 3.—GRA not completed in all material respects.* (A) *Facts.* DC timely filed its tax return for the year of the FS Transfer, reporting no gain with respect to the exchange of the FS stock. DC was aware of the requirement to file a GRA to avoid recognizing gain under section 367(a)(1), including the requirement to provide the basis and fair market value of the transferred stock. However, DC filed a purported GRA that did not contain the fair market value of the FS stock. Instead, the GRA was filed with the statement that the fair market value information was "available upon request." Other than the omission of the fair market value of the FS stock, the GRA contained all other information required by this section.

(B) *Result.* Because DC omitted the fair market value of the FS stock from the GRA, the GRA was not completed in all material respects. Accordingly, there is a failure to timely file the GRA. Furthermore, because DC knowingly omitted such information, DC's omission is a willful failure to timely file a GRA. Accordingly, DC is ineligible for relief under paragraph (p) of this section, the GRA is not considered timely filed for purposes of paragraph (d)(1) of this section, and DC must recognize the full amount of the gain realized on the FS Transfer. The same result would arise if DC had included the fair market value of the FS stock, but knowingly omitted its tax basis from the GRA.

(iv) *Example 4.—Taxpayer knew of GRA filing requirement, but intentionally chose not to file.* (A) *Facts.* When DC filed its tax return for the tax year of the FS Transfer, it was aware of the requirement to file a GRA to avoid recognizing gain under section 367(a)(1). However, because DC anticipated selling Business A in the following tax year, which was expected to produce a capital loss that could be carried back to fully offset the gain recognized on the FS Transfer, DC intentionally chose not to file a GRA. DC recognized the gain from the FS Transfer under section 367(a)(1) and reported the gain on its timely filed tax return. At the end of the following year, a large class action lawsuit was filed against Business A and, consequently, DC was unable to sell the business. As a result, DC did not realize the expected capital loss, and it was not able to offset the gain from the FS Transfer. DC now seeks to file a GRA for the FS Transfer.

(B) *Result.* Because DC failed to file a GRA with its timely filed tax return for the year of the FS Transfer, there is a failure to timely file the GRA as required by paragraph (d)(1) of this section. Furthermore, because DC intentionally chose not to file a GRA for the FS Transfer, its actions constitute a willful failure to timely file a GRA. Accordingly, DC is ineligible for relief under paragraph (p) of this section, the GRA is not considered timely filed for purposes of paragraph (d)(1) of this section, and DC must recognize the full amount of the gain realized on the FS Transfer in Year 1.

(q) *Examples.*—(1) *Presumed facts and references.*—For purposes of the examples in paragraph (q)(2) of this section, and except where otherwise indicated, the following is presumed.

(i) UST, USP, and DC are domestic corporations that each use a calendar taxable year.

(ii) USP wholly owns UST and is the common parent of the consolidated group of which UST is a member.

(iii) TFC, TFD, F1, and FA are foreign corporations.

(iv) UST wholly owns TFD.

(v) In a section 351 exchange, UST transfers all of the stock of TFD (TFD stock) to TFC in exchange solely for stock of TFC (the initial transfer).

(vi) Pursuant to § 1.367(a)-3(b)(1)(ii) and this section, UST enters into a gain recognition agreement in connection with the initial transfer and makes the election described under paragraph (c)(2)(vi) of this section with respect to the gain recognition agreement.

(vii) As applicable, the section 1248 amount (within the meaning of § 1.367(b)-2(c)) or all earnings and profits amount (within the meaning of § 1.367(b)-2(d)) attributable to the stock of a foreign corporation is zero.

(viii) All transactions are respected under general principles of tax law, including the step transaction doctrine.

(ix) References to a U.S. transferor entering into a gain recognition agreement mean, where applicable, that the common parent of the consolidated group of which the U.S. transferor is a member has filed the gain recognition agreement on behalf of the U.S. transferor in accordance with paragraph (d)(3) of this section.

(x) Taxable years during the GRA term are referred to, for example, as year 1 and year 2.

(2) *Examples.*—The following examples illustrate the application of the rules of this section.

(i) *Example 1.—Basis adjustments from gain recognized under the gain recognition agreement.* (A) *Facts.* TFC wholly owns F1. In year 3, pursuant to a section 351 exchange, TFC transfers all of the TFD stock to F1 in exchange solely for voting stock of F1. UST enters into a new gain recognition agreement with respect to the initial transfer under paragraph (k)(3) of this section, and therefore the transfer by TFC of the TFD stock to F1 is not a triggering event. Under paragraph (c)(5)(i) of this section, the existing gain recognition agreement terminates without further effect. In year 4, in an exchange to which section 721 applies, UST contributes the TFC stock received in the initial transfer to PRS, a domestic partnership, in exchange for a partnership interest. UST enters into a new gain recognition agreement with respect to the initial transfer under paragraph (k)(1) of this section, and therefore the transfer by UST of the TFC stock to PRS is not a triggering event. Under paragraph (c)(5)(i) of this section, the new gain recognition agreement filed by UST in year 3 terminates without further effect. In year 5, TFD disposes of substantially all of its assets in a transaction that constitutes a triggering event under paragraph (j)(2)(i) of this section. Under paragraph (c)(1)(i) of this section, UST recognizes the gain realized but not recognized on the initial transfer by reason of entering into the gain recognition agreement.

(B) *Result.* Under paragraph (c)(4) of this section, the basis of the PRS interest held by UST, the TFC stock held by PRS that was received from UST in year 4, the F1 stock held by TFC that was received in exchange for the TFD stock in year 3, and the TFD stock held by F1 that was received from TFC in year 3 is increased by the amount of gain recognized by UST (but not by the additional tax or interest paid as result of such gain) with respect to the initial transfer under the gain recognition agreement. However, the basis of the assets of TFD (including the assets disposed of in year 5) is not increased as a result of the gain recognized by UST.

(ii) *Example 2.—Impact of gain recognition event on computation of income.* (A) *Facts.* At the time of the initial transfer, the TFD stock has a $50x basis, a $100x fair market value, and a $30x section 1248 amount. The amount of gain subject to the gain recognition agreement is $50x. UST did not make an election under paragraph (c)(2)(vi) of this section with respect to the gain recognition agreement. In year 3, TFC disposes of the TFD stock received in the initial transfer in exchange for $120x cash.

(B) *Result*—(1) *Gain recognition without an election.* The disposition by TFC of the TFD stock in year 3 is a triggering event under paragraph (j)(1) of this section. As a result, under paragraph (c)(1)(i) of this section, UST must recognize and include in income $50x gain under the gain recognition agreement. Under paragraph (c)(1)(iii)(A) of this section, UST must report the $50x gain on an amended return filed for the taxable year of the initial transfer. Under paragraph (c)(1)(v) of this section, UST must pay applicable interest on any additional tax due with respect to the $50x gain recognized. Under section 1248(a), $30x of the gain recognized by UST under the gain recognition agreement is recharacterized as a dividend. Under paragraph (c)(4) of this section, as of the date of the initial transfer, the basis of the TFC stock received by UST in the initial transfer and the TFD stock received by TFC in the initial transfer, respectively, is increased by $50x. After taking into account the increase to the basis of the TFD stock, TFC recognizes $20x gain on the disposition of the TFD stock in year 3.

(2) *Gain recognition with an election.* If UST made an election under paragraph (c)(2)(vi) of this section with the gain recognition agreement filed for the initial transfer, the result would be the same as in paragraph (q)(2)(ii)(B)(*1*) of this section (paragraph (*1*) in the results in this *Example 2*), except that UST must include in income the $50x gain recognized under the gain recognition agreement on its tax return filed for year 3. Any additional tax due with respect to the $50x gain and applicable interest on the additional tax due must be included with such return. The amount, if any, of the $50x gain recognized by UST under the gain recognition agreement that is characterized as a dividend under section 1248(a) is determined in year 3.

(iii) *Example 3.—Transfer of stock of the transferee foreign corporation to a domestic corporation in a section 351 exchange.* (A) *Facts.* UST wholly owns DC. In year 3, pursuant to a section 351 exchange, UST transfers all of the TFC stock received in the initial transfer to DC in an exchange solely for voting stock of DC.

(B) *Result.* The year 3 transfer of the TFC stock by UST to DC constitutes a triggering event under paragraph (j)(4) of this section. However, the transfer shall not constitute a triggering event pursuant to paragraph (k)(1)(ii) of this section if DC enters into a new gain recognition agreement with respect to the initial transfer that designates DC as the U.S. transferor for purposes of this section. Pursuant to paragraphs (c)(4)(i) and (ii) of this section, if DC is required to recognize gain under the new gain recognition agreement, the basis of the stock of TFC and TFD would be increased by the amount of gain recognized. However, pursuant to paragraph (c)(4)(iii) of this section, no adjustment would be made to the basis of the DC voting stock received by UST in year 3 as a result of such gain recognition. Alternatively, if the conditions for the application of paragraph (k)(14) of this section are satisfied UST could instead enter into the new gain recognition agreement with respect to the initial transfer.

(iv) *Example 4.—Transfer of stock of the transferee foreign corporation in a triangular section 368(a)(1)(B) reorganization.* (A) *Facts.* DC wholly owns FA. In year 3, pursuant to a triangular reorganization described in section 368(a)(1)(B), UST transfers all of the TFC stock received in the initial transfer to FA in exchange solely for 20% of the outstanding voting stock of DC. At the time of the reorganization, the TFC stock has a basis in excess of fair market value.

(B) *Result.* (1) The transfer by UST of the TFC stock to FA is an indirect stock transfer under § 1.367(a)-3(d)(1)(iii)(B). Accordingly, to preserve nonrecognition treatment, UST must enter into a separate gain recognition agreement under this section with respect to such transfer.

(2) With respect to the gain recognition agreement filed for the initial transfer of the TFD stock, the transfer by UST of the TFC stock to FA is a triggering event under paragraph (j)(4) of this section. However, the transfer shall not constitute a triggering event if the conditions of the exception provided by paragraph (k)(14) of this section are satisfied.

(*i*) The condition of paragraph (k)(14)(i) of this section is satisfied because the transfer qualifies as a nonrecognition transaction (assuming UST enters into a gain recognition agreement as described in paragraph (q)(2)(iv)(B)(*1*) of this section (paragraph (*1*) in the results in this *Example 4*).

(*ii*) The condition of paragraph (k)(14)(ii) of this section is satisfied because immediately after the transfer DC, a domestic corporation that is eligible to be a U.S. transferor, owns at least 5% (determined as provided in paragraph (k)(14)(ii) of this section) of the total voting power and total fair market value of the outstanding stock of FA. As a result, DC is treated as retaining an indirect interest in the TFD stock immediately following the transfer.

(*iii*) The condition of paragraph (k)(14)(iii) of this section is satisfied if DC enters into a new gain recognition agreement with respect to the initial transfer of the TFD stock that, based on the principles of paragraph (j) of this section, describes the subsequent dispositions or other events that would constitute triggering events for purposes of the new gain recognition agreement (other than the dispositions and other events described in paragraph (j) of this section). For example, a complete or partial disposition of the stock of FA would constitute a triggering event for purposes of the new gain recognition agreement.

(v) *Example 5.—Transfer of stock of the transferee foreign corporation to a domestic corporation pursuant to an asset reorganization.* (A) *Facts.* At the time of the initial transfer the TFD stock has a $50x basis and a $100x fair market value. Therefore, the amount of gain subject to the gain recognition agreement is $50x. In year 3, pursuant to an asset reorganization described in section 368(a)(1)(A), UST transfers its assets to DC in exchange solely for 20% of the outstanding stock of DC. UST distributes the stock of DC to USP pursuant to the plan of reorganization.

(B) *Result.* The transfer by UST of the TFC stock to DC constitutes a triggering event under paragraph (j)(4) of this section. However, pursuant to paragraph (k)(6)(i) of this section, if DC enters into a new gain recognition agreement with respect to the initial transfer that designates DC as the U.S. transferor, the transfer shall not constitute a triggering event.

(vi) *Example 6.—Transfer of stock of the transferee foreign corporation to a foreign corporation pursuant to an asset reorganization.* (A) *Facts.* The facts are the same as in *Example 5*, except the acquiring corporation in the asset reorganization is FA, and, at the time of the asset reorganization, the TFC stock transferred by UST to FA has a $50x basis and a $150x fair market value. All of the conditions under section 367(a)(5) and the regulations under that section are satisfied, and no adjustment is required to the basis of the FA stock received by USP in the transaction.

(B) *Result.* (1) The transfer by UST of the TFC stock to FA is described in section 361(a) and is therefore subject to section 367(a)(5). In general, UST cannot file a gain recognition agreement with respect to such transfer, and the transfer therefore is subject to the general rule of section 367(a)(1). However, if the conditions of § 1.367(a)-3(e)(1)(i) through (iv) are satisfied, USP can enter into a gain recognition agreement with respect to the transfer to avoid the recognition of gain by UST on the transfer under section 367(a)(1). If the exception provided by paragraph (k)(14) of this section applies so that the transfer by UST of the TFC stock to FA is not a triggering event with respect to the gain recognition agreement filed for the initial transfer (discussed in paragraph (q)(2)(vi)(B)(*2*) of this section (paragraph (*2*) in the results in this *Example 6*), the amount of gain subject to the gain recognition agreement (if entered into) with respect to the transfer by UST of the TFC stock to FA in the asset reorganization is $100x.

(2) Under paragraph (j)(4) of this section, the transfer of the TFC stock by UST to FA is a triggering event with respect to the gain recognition agreement for the initial transfer. The exception provided by paragraph (k)(6)(i) of this section does not apply to such transfer because FA, the acquiring corporation in the asset reorganization, is foreign. However, the transfer shall not constitute a triggering event if the conditions of the exception provided by paragraph (k)(14) of this section are satisfied.

(*i*) The condition of paragraph (k)(14)(i) of this section is satisfied because the transfer of the TFC stock to FA qualifies as a nonrecognition transaction (assuming USP enters into a gain recognition agreement with respect to such transfer).

(*ii*) The condition of paragraph (k)(14)(ii) of this section is satisfied because immediately after the transfer USP, a domestic corporation that is eligible to be a U.S. transferor, owns at least 5% (determined as provided in paragraph (k)(14)(ii) of this section) of the total voting power and total fair market value of the outstanding stock of FA. As a result, USP is treated as retaining an indirect interest in the TFD stock immediately following the transfer.

(*iii*) The condition of paragraph (k)(14)(iii) of this section is satisfied if USP enters into a new gain recognition agreement with respect to the initial transfer of the TFD stock that, based on the principles of paragraph (j) of this section, describes the subsequent dispositions or other events that would constitute triggering events for purposes of the new gain recognition agreement, other than those already provided in paragraph (j) of this section. For example, a disposition of the stock of FA would constitute such a triggering event for purposes of the new gain recognition agreement.

(C) *Alternate facts.* Assume the same facts as in paragraph (q)(2)(vi)(A) of this section (the facts in this *Example 6*), including that paragraph (k)(14) of this section applies to the year 3 reorganization so that USP enters into a new gain recognition agreement with respect to the initial transfer of the TFD stock that occurred in year 1 (GRA 1), and that under § 1.367(a)-3(e) USP enters into a separate gain recognition agreement with respect to the initial transfer of the

TFC stock by UST to FA pursuant to the year 3 asset reorganization (GRA 2). Assume further that in year 4 TFC disposes of 10% of the TFD stock pursuant to a transaction that constitutes a triggering event with respect to GRA 1. The disposition of the TFD stock is not a triggering event with respect to GRA 2 because the TFD stock disposed of does not constitute substantially all the assets of TFC. Under paragraphs (j)(1) and (c)(1)(i) of this section, USP must recognize $5x gain (10% of $50x) under GRA 1. Under paragraph (c)(4)(i) and (ii) of this section, as of the date of the initial transfer (with respect to which GRA 1 was filed), the basis of the TFC stock and TFD stock, respectively, is increased by $5x. Under paragraph (c)(1)(i) of this section, the amount of gain subject to GRA 1 is reduced from $50x to $45x. Similarly, because the transferred stock for purposes of GRA 2 is the TFC stock, the amount of gain subject to GRA 2 is reduced from $100x to $95x to reflect the increase to the basis of the TFC stock.

(vii) *Example 7.—Transfer of transferred stock to a foreign corporation pursuant to an asset reorganization.* (A) *Facts.* UST wholly owns FA. In year 4, pursuant to a reorganization described in section 368(a)(1)(D), TFC transfers all of the TFD stock to FA in exchange solely for stock of FA. TFC distributes the FA stock to UST pursuant to the plan of reorganization.

(B) *Analysis.* In general, the year 4 transfer by TFC of the TFD stock to FA and the exchange by UST of the TFC stock for FA stock constitute triggering events under paragraphs (j)(1) and (4) of this section, respectively. However, under paragraph (k)(6)(ii) of this section, the transfers shall not constitute triggering events if UST enters into a new gain recognition agreement with respect to the initial transfer that designates FA as the transferee foreign corporation.

(viii) *Example 8.—Transfer of substantially all the assets of the transferred corporation pursuant to an asset reorganization.* (A) *Facts.* In year 4, pursuant to an asset reorganization described in section 368(a)(1)(C), TFD transfers all of its assets to FA in exchange solely for voting stock of FA. TFD distributes the FA voting stock to TFC pursuant to the plan of reorganization.

(B) *Analysis.* The year 4 transfer by TFD of all its assets to FA and the exchange by TFC of its TFD stock for FA voting stock pursuant to the reorganization constitute triggering events under paragraphs (j)(2) and (j)(1) of this section, respectively. However, under paragraph (k)(6)(iii) of this section, the transfers shall not constitute triggering events if UST enters into a new gain recognition agreement with respect to the initial transfer that designates FA as the transferred corporation. In addition, under paragraph (k)(6)(iii) of this section only the assets of TFD acquired by FA in the asset reorganization shall be treated as assets of the transferred corporation for purposes of the new gain recognition agreement.

(ix) *Example 9.—Complete liquidation of transferred corporation into transferee foreign corporation.* (A) *Facts.* UST does not make an election under paragraph (c)(2)(vi) of this section in connection with the gain recognition agreement entered into with respect to the initial transfer. In year 3, TFD distributes all of its assets to TFC pursuant to a complete liquidation to which sections 332 and 337 apply. Under paragraph (k)(8) of this section, UST enters into a new gain recognition agreement with respect to the initial transfer such that the liquidation is not a triggering event. Under paragraph (c)(5)(i) of this section, the new gain recognition agreement is subject to the conditions and requirements of this section to the same extent as the existing gain recognition agreement, except that the transferred stock is no longer subject to the gain recognition agreement because the transferred stock is cancelled by reason of the liquidation. In year 5 TFC disposes of substantially all of the assets received from TFD in the year 3 liquidation.

(B) *Result.* The year 5 disposition by TFC of substantially all of the assets received from TFD in the year 3 liquidation is a triggering event under paragraph (j)(2) of this section, and therefore UST must recognize the gain subject to the gain recognition agreement. UST must report the gain recognized on an amended return for the taxable year during which the initial transfer occurred. UST must also pay applicable interest on any additional tax due with respect to the gain recognized. Under paragraph (c)(4)(i) of this section, the basis of the TFC stock received by UST in the initial transfer is increased as of the date of the initial transfer by the amount of gain recognized under the gain recognition agreement. The basis of the assets of TFD, however, is not increased.

(x) *Example 10.—Transfer of transferred stock to foreign corporation in section 351 exchange, followed by a section 332 liquidation of the foreign corporation.* (A) *Facts.* In year 3, pursuant to a section 351 exchange, TFC transfers the TFD stock to F1, a newly formed corporation, in exchange solely for voting stock of F1. The transfer by TFC of the TFD stock to F1 is not a triggering event because UST complies with the conditions of paragraph (k)(3) of this section. In year 5, F1 distributes all of its assets to TFC in a complete liquidation to which sections 332 and 337 apply.

(B) *Result.* The distribution of the TFD stock by F1, and the exchange of F1 stock by TFC pursuant to the year 5 liquidation of F1 constitute triggering events under paragraphs (j)(1) and (k)(3)(i) of this section, respectively. However, if paragraph (k)(14) of this section applies, neither the distribution of the TFD stock by F1, nor the exchange by TFC of the F1 stock, shall constitute a triggering event.

(*1*) The condition of paragraph (k)(14)(i) of this section is satisfied because the distribution of the TFD stock, and the exchange of F1 stock, both qualify as nonrecognition transactions.

(*2*) The condition of paragraph (k)(14)(ii) of this section is satisfied because immediately after the distribution UST, a domestic corporation that is eligible to be a U.S. transferor, owns at least 5% (determined as provided in paragraph (k)(14)(ii) of this section) of the stock of TFC. As a result, UST is treated as retaining an indirect interest in the TFD stock following the complete liquidation of F1.

(*3*) The condition of paragraph (k)(14)(iii) of this section is satisfied if UST enters into a new gain recognition agreement. Because after the complete liquidation of F1, UST wholly owns TFC, which wholly owns TFD, as was the case immediately after the initial transfer, UST is not required to describe, with the new gain recognition agreement, other dispositions or events that would constitute triggering events based on the principles of paragraph (j) of this section, other than the dispositions or events described in paragraph (j) of this section.

(xi) *Example 11.—Disposition of stock of transferee foreign corporation pursuant to a divisive reorganization.* (A) *Facts.* In year 3, pursuant to a divisive reorganization described in section 368(a)(1)(D), UST transfers all of the TFC stock to DC, a newly-formed corporation, in exchange solely for stock of DC. UST then distributes all of the DC stock to USP in a transaction to which section 355 applies.

(B) *Result.* The transfer of the TFC stock by UST to DC constitutes a triggering event under paragraph (j)(4) of this section. However, under paragraph (k)(1)(iii) of this section, the transfer of the TFC stock shall not constitute a triggering event if DC enters into a new gain recognition agreement that designates DC as the U.S. transferor for purposes of this section.

(C) *Alternate facts.* The facts are the same as in paragraph (q)(2)(xi)(A) of this section (the facts in this *Example 11*), except that UST transfers only 90% of the TFC stock to DC. Paragraph (k)(1)(iii) of this section applies only with respect to the TFC stock transferred to DC. Thus, the conditions of paragraph (k)(1)(iii) of this section are satisfied if DC enters into a new gain recognition agreement with respect to the TFC stock received from UST. The amount of gain subject to the new gain recognition agreement entered into by DC equals 90% of the amount of gain subject to the gain recognition agreement entered into by UST with respect to the initial transfer. The amount of gain subject to the gain recognition agreement entered into by UST with respect to the initial transfer is reduced by the amount of gain subject to the new gain recognition agreement entered into by DC. The gain recognition agreement entered into by UST with respect to the initial transfer continues to apply to the remaining TFC stock held by UST.

(xii) *Example 12.—Disposition of transferred stock pursuant to a divisive reorganization.* (A) *Facts.* In year 3, pursuant to a divisive reorganization described in section 368(a)(1)(D), TFC transfers all of the TFD stock to F1, a newly formed corporation, in exchange solely for all of the outstanding stock of F1. TFC then distributes all of the F1 stock to UST in a transaction to which section 355 applies.

(B) *Result.* The transfer by TFC of the TFD stock to F1 constitutes a triggering event under paragraph (j)(1) of this section. However, if paragraph (k)(14) of this section applies, neither the transfer of the TFD stock by TFC to F1, nor the distribution of the F1 stock by TFC to UST, shall constitute triggering events.

(*1*) The condition of paragraph (k)(14)(i) of this section is satisfied because the dispositions of the TFD stock and F1 stock qualify as nonrecognition transactions.

(*2*) The condition of paragraph (k)(14)(ii) of this section is satisfied because immediately after the transfer UST, an eligible U.S. transferor, owns at least 5% (determined as provided in paragraph (k)(14)(ii) of this section) of the total voting power and the total fair market value of the outstanding stock of F1. As a result, UST is treated as retaining an indirect interest in the TFD stock following the dispositions.

(3) The condition of paragraph (k)(14)(iii) of this section is satisfied if UST enters into a new gain recognition agreement with respect to the initial transfer that describes the subsequent dispositions or other events that would constitute triggering events based on the principles of paragraph (j) of this section, other than those described in paragraph (j) of this section. For example, a complete or partial disposition of the F1 stock would constitute a triggering event for purposes of the new gain recognition agreement (subject to the exceptions provided by paragraph (k) of this section).

(xiii) *Example 13.—Receipt of boot by the transferee foreign corporation in a subsequent section 351 exchange.* (A) *Facts.* At the time of the initial transfer, the TFD stock has a $50x basis and $100x fair market value. The amount of gain subject to the gain recognition agreement is $50x. In year 3, TFC and X, an unrelated foreign corporation, form F1. TFC transfers the TFD stock to F1 in exchange for $35x cash and $65x stock of F1. At the time of the transfer, the TFD stock has a $50x basis and $100x fair market value. The F1 stock received by TFC represents 25% of the outstanding stock of F1. Without regard to the gain recognized under the gain recognition agreement and any adjustments to basis under paragraph (c)(4)(ii) of this section, under section 351(b) TFC would recognize $35x gain in connection with the transfer of the TFD stock to F1. UST complies with the conditions of paragraph (k)(3) of this section, and therefore the disposition by TFC of the TFD stock does not constitute a triggering event.

(B) *Result.* Under paragraph (m)(1) of this section, UST must recognize $35x gain under the gain recognition agreement as a result of the year 3 disposition by TFC of the TFD stock. Thus, the amount of gain subject to the new gain recognition agreement entered into by UST pursuant to paragraph (k)(3) of this section is $15x. Under paragraph (c)(4)(ii) of this section, as of the date of the initial transfer, the basis of the TFD stock held by TFC is increased by $35x, the amount of the gain recognized by UST under the gain recognition agreement. Under paragraph (c)(4)(i) of this section, the basis of the TFC stock received by UST in the initial transfer is also increased by $35x. After taking into account the increase to the basis of the TFD stock under paragraph (c)(4)(ii) of this section, TFC recognizes $15x gain under section 351(b) in connection with the year 3 transfer of the TFD stock to F1. Under section 362(a), the basis of the TFD stock in the hands of F1 is $100x.

(xiv) *Example 14.—Complete disposition of transferred stock pursuant to a section 304(a)(1) transaction.* (A) *Facts.* UST wholly owns FA. In year 3, in a transaction to which section 304(a)(1) applies, TFC transfers all of the TFD stock to FA in exchange for cash. Under section 304(a)(1), TFC and FA are treated as if TFC transferred the TFD stock to FA in a section 351 exchange in exchange solely for FA stock, and then FA redeemed the FA stock deemed issued in exchange for the cash. Under section 302(d), the redemption of the FA stock deemed issued by FA to TFC under section 304(a)(1) is treated as a distribution to which section 301 applies.

(B) *Result.* (1) In general, the deemed contribution by TFC of the TFD stock to FA in the section 351 exchange is a triggering event under paragraph (j)(1) of this section. However, under paragraph (k)(3) of this section the deemed contribution shall not be a triggering event if UST enters into a new gain recognition agreement with respect to the initial transfer in which it agrees to treat as a triggering event a complete or partial disposition of the FA stock deemed received by TFC.

(2) Under paragraph (n)(1) of this section, the redemption of the FA stock deemed received by TFC in exchange for the TFD stock shall not constitute a disposition if UST enters into a new gain recognition agreement with respect to the initial transfer that includes appropriate provisions to take into account such redemption. Therefore, under the new gain recognition agreement UST must agree to treat as a triggering event a complete or partial disposition of the stock of FA. Pursuant to paragraph (d)(2)(ii) of this section, UST is permitted to enter into a single new gain recognition agreement in year 3, but the gain recognition agreement must provide a complete description of the section 304(a)(1) transaction including the deemed section 351 exchange and redemption of the FA stock.

(xv) *Example 15.—Reduction in amount of gain subject to gain recognition agreement, followed by triggering event.* (A) *Facts.* In year 3, UST disposes of 60% of the TFC stock received in the initial transfer in a transaction in which the conditions of paragraph (o)(1)(ii) of this section are satisfied. Thus, the amount of gain subject to the gain recognition agreement is reduced by 60%. In year 5, TFC disposes of 50% of the TFD stock in a transaction that constitutes a triggering event.

(B) *Result.* As a result of the year 5 disposition by TFC of 50% of the TFD stock, under paragraphs (j)(1) and (c)(1)(i) of this section, UST must recognize and include in income 50% of the gain subject to the gain recognition agreement (because of the year 3 disposition of TFC stock, the amount of gain subject to the gain recognition agreement equals 40% of the gain realized, but not recognized, on the initial transfer). UST must pay applicable interest on any additional tax due with respect to the gain recognized. The amount of gain subject to the gain recognition agreement is reduced by the amount of gain recognized by UST (the remaining gain equals 20% of the gain realized, but not recognized, by UST on the initial transfer).

(xvi) *Example 16.—Taxable sale of stock of transferee foreign corporation and election to reduce stock basis.* (A) *Facts.* UST wholly owns F1 and TFD. The F1 stock has a $100x basis and $90x fair market value, and the TFD stock has a $0x basis and $100x fair market value. UST also owns real property with a $10x basis and $10x fair market value. In year 1, pursuant to a section 351 exchange, UST transfers the real property, the TFD stock, and the F1 stock to TFC in exchange solely for 20 shares of TFC stock. UST enters into a gain recognition agreement with respect to the transfer of the TFD stock. The amount of the gain recognition agreement is $100x. UST takes the position that the basis of each share of TFC stock received in the exchange is $5.5x (a proportionate amount of the $110x aggregate basis of the transferred property). In year 3, UST disposes of all its TFC stock in a transaction in which all gain realized is recognized and included in taxable income.

(B) *Result.* The year 3 disposition of the TFC stock is a triggering event under paragraph (j)(4) of this section. The disposition does not terminate the gain recognition agreement pursuant to paragraph (o)(1)(i) of this section because the basis of each share of TFC stock received in exchange for the TFD stock in the initial transfer is $5.5×, which exceeds the $0× basis of the TFD stock at time of the initial transfer. However, under paragraph (o)(1)(iii) of this section, to satisfy the basis condition of paragraph (o)(1)(i) of this section, UST can reduce the basis of the 10 shares of the TFC stock received in exchange for the TFD stock to $0x. If UST reduces the basis of the 10 shares of TFC stock to $0x, under paragraph (o)(1)(i) of this section the disposition of the TFC stock shall not constitute a triggering event but instead shall terminate the gain recognition agreement without further effect.

(xvii) *Example 17.—Successive section 351 exchanges, section 301 distributions, and transactions involving partnerships.* (A) *Facts.* UST owns a 40 percent capital and profits interest in a foreign partnership (PRS). PRS wholly owns TFD and other assets with basis equal to fair market value. The TFD stock has a $50x basis and $200x fair market value. TFC wholly owns F1. On day 1 of year 1, in a section 351 exchange, UST transfers its PRS interest to TFC in exchange solely for stock of TFC (initial transfer). On that same day, in a section 351 exchange, TFC transfers the PRS interest received from UST to F1 in exchange solely for stock of F1. In year 3, PRS receives a $150x distribution from TFD to which section 301 applies. Under section 301(c), $25x of the distribution constitutes a dividend, $50x is applied against and reduces the basis of the TFD stock held by PRS, and the remaining $75x is treated as gain from the sale or exchange of property. With respect to the TFD stock deemed transferred by UST in the initial transfer, under section 301(c), $10x (40% of $25x) of the distribution constitutes a dividend, $20x (40% of $50x) is applied against and reduces the basis of TFD stock, and $30x (40% of $75x) is treated as gain from the sale or exchange of property. In year 5, pursuant to a distribution to which section 731 applies, PRS distributes all of the TFD stock to F1.

(B) *Result.* (1) *Successive section 351 transfers.* Under section 367(a)(4) and § 1.367(a)-1T(c)(3)(ii), the transfer of the PRS interest by UST to TFC is treated, for purposes of section 367(a), as a transfer by UST to TFC of its proportionate share of the TFD stock held by PRS (the initial transfer). The initial transfer by UST of the TFD stock to TFC is subject to the general rule of section 367(a)(1), unless UST enters into a gain recognition agreement with respect to such transfer pursuant to § 1.367(a)-3(b)(1)(ii) and this section. Under paragraph (c)(3)(viii) of this section, the gain recognition agreement must include a complete description of the transfer, including a description of the partners of PRS. Even if UST enters into a gain recognition agreement with respect to the initial transfer, under paragraph (j)(3) of this section, the subsequent transfer by TFC of the PRS interest to F1 is a triggering event unless UST enters into a new gain recognition agreement with respect to the initial transfer under paragraph (k)(14) that provides that, in addition to the triggering events provided in paragraph (j) of this section, a complete or partial disposition of the F1 stock received by TFC in exchange for the PRS interest shall constitute a triggering event for purposes of the gain recognition agreement. The new gain recognition agreement must also provide that any other disposition that is inconsistent with the principles of paragraph (k), including an indirect disposition of the TFD stock or of substantially all of the assets of TFD, shall constitute a triggering event for purposes of the new gain recognition agreement. Under paragraph (d)(2)(ii) of this section, UST is permitted to enter into a single gain recognition agreement with respect to the initial transfer and the subsequent transfer by TFC of the PRS interest, but the agreement must include a complete description of the initial transfer and the subsequent transfer of the PRS interest.

(2) *Section 301 distribution from TFD to PRS.* Under paragraph (b)(1)(iii) of this section, the section 301 distribution received by PRS from TFD is not a disposition (and therefore does not affect the gain recognition agreement) to the extent it is described in section 301(c)(1) or (2). However, under paragraph (n)(2) of this section, to the extent the distribution is described in section 301(c)(3), UST must recognize gain ($30x) under the gain recognition agreement. For this purpose, the amount of the distribution that is described in section 301(c)(3) is determined before taking into account the increase to the basis of the TFD stock under paragraph (c)(4)(ii) of this section.

(3) *Distribution of TFD stock by PRS to F1.* The year 5 distribution of the TFD stock by PRS to F1 is a triggering event under paragraph (j)(1) of this section, unless paragraph (k)(14) of this section applies.

(*i*) The condition of paragraph (k)(14)(i) of this section is satisfied because the distribution qualifies as a nonrecognition transaction.

(*ii*) The condition of paragraph (k)(14)(ii) of this section is satisfied because immediately after the distribution UST, a domestic corporation that is eligible to be a U.S. transferor, owns at least 5% (determined as provided in paragraph (k)(14)(ii) of this section) of the total voting power and total value of the outstanding stock of F1. As a result, UST is treated as retaining an indirect interest in the TFD stock following the distribution.

(*ii*) The condition of paragraph (k)(14)(iii) of this section is satisfied if UST enters into a new gain recognition agreement with respect to the initial transfer. The new gain recognition agreement need not describe additional dispositions or other events that would constitute triggering events because, pursuant to paragraph (c)(5) of this section, the dispositions or other events described in paragraph (j) of this section or in the existing gain recognition agreement apply to the new gain recognition agreement.

(xviii) *Example 18.—Complete liquidation of transferee foreign corporation.* (A) *Facts.* TFD has 10 shares of stock outstanding immediately before the initial transfer. On the date of the initial transfer, the TFD stock has a $0x basis and $90x fair market value. In year 2, in exchange for 1 share of TFD stock TFC transfers real estate to TFD with a $10x basis and $10x fair market value. In year 4, TFC distributes the 11 shares of TFD stock to UST in a complete liquidation to which sections 332 and 337 apply.

(B) *Result.* In determining whether the gain recognition agreement entered into by UST with respect to the initial transfer is terminated under paragraph (o)(5) of this section, or triggered under paragraphs (j)(1) and (j)(4) of this section, only the 10 shares of TFD stock transferred by UST in the initial transfer are considered. Thus, the 1 share of TFD stock received by TFC in exchange for the real estate in year 2 is not taken into account.

(xix) *Example 19.—Spin-off of transferred corporation.* (A) *Facts.* Before the initial transfer, the TFD stock has an $80x basis and a $100x fair market value, and the TFC stock has a $100x basis and a $100x fair market value. In year 4, TFC distributes all of the TFD stock to UST in a transaction to which section 355 applies. At the time of the distribution, the TFD stock has a $200x fair market value, and the TFC stock (without regard to the value of the TFD stock held by TFC) has a $100x fair market value. At such time, the TFC stock has a $180x basis. As determined under section 358, immediately after the distribution, the TFC stock has a $60x basis, and the TFD stock has a $120x basis.

(B) *Result.* The distribution of the TFD stock by TFC in year 4 is a triggering event under paragraph (j)(1) of this section. The distribution does not terminate the gain recognition agreement under paragraph (o)(5) of this section because after the distribution, the basis of the TFD stock in the hands of UST ($120x) is greater than the basis of the TFD stock at the time of the initial transfer ($80x). However, if UST reduces the basis of the TFD stock to $80x (as provided under paragraph (o)(5)(iii) of this section) the gain recognition agreement will terminate without further effect. If UST does not elect to reduce the basis of the TFD stock, see paragraph (k)(14) of this section.

(xx) *Example 20.—Intercompany transaction followed by disposition to nonmember.* (A) *Facts.* At the time of the initial transfer, the TFD stock has a $50x basis and $100x fair market value. The amount of the gain recognition agreement is $50x. In year 3, UST distributes all of the TFC stock to USP in a transaction to which section 301 applies. At the time of the distribution, the TFC stock has a $50x basis and $90x fair market value. Under section 311(b), UST must recognize $40x gain (the intercompany item) on the distribution, but because the distribution is an intercompany transaction, under the provisions of § 1.1502-13, the $40x gain is not taken into account in year 3. In year 4, USP sells all of the TFC stock to X, an unrelated corporation. Under the provisions of § 1.1502-13, in year 4 UST takes into account the $40x intercompany item as a result of the sale of the TFC stock to X.

(B) *Result.* (1) The year 3 distribution of the TFC stock by UST to USP does not terminate the gain recognition agreement under paragraph (o)(1) of this section because UST does not include the $40x gain in taxable income during year 3. Under paragraph (j)(4) of this section, the year 3 distribution of the TFC stock by UST to USP is generally a triggering event; however, because the distribution is an intercompany transaction that creates an intercompany item, the distribution shall not constitute a triggering event if the conditions of paragraph (k)(12)(i) of this section are satisfied.

(i) The condition of paragraph (k)(12)(i)(A) of this section is satisfied because the aggregate basis of the TFC stock distributed ($50x) is not greater than the sum of the aggregate basis of the TFD stock at the time of the initial transfer ($50x).

(ii) The condition of paragraph (k)(12)(i)(B) of this section is satisfied if the next annual certification for the existing gain recognition agreement includes a complete description of the intercompany transaction and an explanation of how the basis condition of paragraph (k)(12)(i)(A) of this section is satisfied.

(2) Under paragraph (o)(6) of this section and the principles of paragraph (o)(1)(i) of this section, because the year 4 sale of the TFC stock to X requires UST to take into account the $40x gain (the intercompany item) from the year 3 distribution, the year 4 sale terminates the gain recognition agreement. If, alternatively, in year 4 USP had sold only 30% of the TFC stock, then under paragraph (o)(6) of this section and the principles of paragraph (o)(1)(ii) of this section the amount of gain subject to the gain recognition agreement would be reduced by 30%.

(C) *Alternate facts. Intercompany transaction followed by sale of transferee foreign corporation to member.* Assume the same facts as in paragraph (q)(2)(xx)(A) of this section (the facts in this *Example 20*), except that, instead of USP selling the TFC stock to X, in year 4 USP sells the TFC stock to USS in exchange for $90× cash. UST and USS are members of the USP consolidated group immediately after the sale. The results of the year 3 distribution of the TFC stock by UST to USP are the same as in paragraph (q)(2)(xx)(B) of this section (the results in this *Example 20*). In addition, under paragraph (k)(12)(ii) of this section, the year 4 sale by USP of the TFC stock to USS is not a triggering event, provided UST includes a complete description of the sale with the annual certification filed for the gain recognition agreement in year 4.

(D) *Alternate facts. Intercompany transaction followed by complete liquidation of transferee foreign corporation.* Assume the same facts as in paragraph (q)(2)(xx)(A) of this section (the facts in this *Example 20*), except that, instead of USP selling the TFC stock to X, in year 4 TFC distributes all of its assets to USP in a complete liquidation to which sections 332 and 337 apply. The result is the same as in paragraph (q)(2)(xx)(B) of this section (the facts in this *Example 20*) because, under the provisions of § 1.1502-13, in year 4 UST takes into account the $40x gain (the intercompany item) from the year 3 distribution.

(E) *Alternate facts. Intercompany transaction followed by triggering event.* Assume the same facts as in paragraph (q)(2)(xx)(A) of this section (the facts in this *Example 20*), except that instead of USP selling the TFC stock to X, in year 4 TFC disposes of all of the TFD stock in a transaction that constitutes a triggering event under paragraph (j)(1) of this section. Under paragraph (c)(1)(i) of this section UST must recognize $50x gain under the gain recognition agreement. Under paragraphs (c)(4)(i) and (ii) of this section, as of the date of the initial transfer the basis of the TFC stock and TFD stock, respectively, is increased by $50x.

(F) *Alternate facts. Intercompany transaction followed by section 351 transfer to member.* The facts are the same as in paragraph (q)(2)(xx)(A) of this section (the facts in this *Example 20*), except that, in year 3, in a section 351 exchange UST transfers all of the TFC stock to USS in exchange for $10x cash and $80x of stock of USS. USS is a member of the USP consolidated group immediately after the exchange. The transfer of the TFC stock by UST to USS is an intercompany transaction. Under section 351(b), UST must generally recognize $10x gain (intercompany item) in connection with the transfer; however, under the provisions of § 1.1502-13, UST does not take the $10x gain into account in year 3. Under paragraph (k)(12) of this section, as result of the intercompany transaction creating an intercompany item ($10x gain), the existing gain recognition agreement ($50x gain) must be divided between UST and USS. UST shall remain subject to a gain recognition agreement of $10x (equal to the amount of the intercompany item). The amount of the gain recognition agreement entered into by USS under paragraph (k)(1) of this section is $40x (equal to the amount of the existing gain recognition agreement, reduced by the amount of the of the gain recognition agreement to which UST remains subject).

(xxi) *Example 21.—Transfer of transferred stock to United States person other than U.S. transferor.* (A) *Facts.* An individual (A) that is a United States citizen wholly owns TFD, TFC, and DC. A transfers the TFD stock to TFC in a section 351 exchange and enters into a gain recognition agreement with respect to such transfer. In year 5, pursuant to an asset reorganization, TFC transfers all of its assets to DC in exchange solely for DC stock. TFC distributes the DC stock to A pursuant to the plan of reorganization.

(B) *Result.* The transfer by TFC of the TFD stock to DC and the exchange by A of the TFC stock for DC stock pursuant to the asset reorganization are triggering events under paragraphs (j)(1) and (j)(4) of this section, respectively. The gain recognition agreement does not terminate under paragraph (o)(5) of this section because DC is neither the U.S. transferor, nor an individual that is a United States person, nor a member of the same consolidated group of which the U.S. transferor is a member. However, if paragraph (k)(14) of this section applies the exchanges shall not constitute triggering events.

(1) The condition of paragraph (k)(14)(i) of this section is satisfied because the transfer of the TFD stock to DC qualifies as a nonrecognition transaction.

(2) The condition of paragraph (k)(14)(ii) of this section is satisfied because immediately after the transfer DC, a domestic corporation that is eligible to be a U.S. transferor, retains a direct interest in the TFD stock following the transfer.

(3) The condition of paragraph (k)(14)(iii) of this section is satisfied if DC enters into a new gain recognition agreement with respect to the initial transfer. Under paragraph (k)(14)(iii)(B) of this section, DC is not required to describe any subsequent dispositions or other events that (based on the principles of paragraph (j) of this section) would constitute triggering events for purposes of the new gain recognition agreement, other than the dispositions or other events described in paragraph (j) of this section, because DC holds a direct interest in TFD after the asset reorganization.

(xxii) *Example 22.—Transfer of transferred stock to consolidated group member.* (A) *Facts.* UST wholly owns DC, a member of the USP consolidated group that includes UST. In year 5, pursuant to an asset reorganization described in section 368(a)(1)(A) TFC merges with and into DC. Immediately after the asset reorganization, DC wholly owns TFD, and the basis of the TFD stock is not greater than the aggregate basis of such stock at the time of the initial transfer.

(B) *Result.* The gain recognition agreement filed by UST with respect to the initial transfer terminates without further effect if the conditions of paragraph (o)(5) of this section are satisfied.

(1) The condition of paragraph (o)(5)(i) of this section is satisfied because the transfer of the TFD stock is a section 361 exchange.

(2) The condition of paragraph (o)(5)(ii) of this section is satisfied because DC is a member of the consolidated group that includes UST immediately after the section 361 exchange.

(3) The condition of paragraph (o)(5)(iii) of this section is satisfied because the aggregate basis of the TFD stock immediately after the section 361 exchange is not greater than the aggregate basis of the TFD stock at the time of the initial transfer (as adjusted for any gain recognized by UST on such transfer). If the basis condition of paragraph (o)(5)(iii) were not satisfied, under paragraph (o)(5)(iii) of this section, DC could reduce the basis of the TFD stock received in the reorganization. Alternatively, a new gain recognition agreement could be entered into if paragraph (k)(14) of this section applied to the disposition of the TFD stock pursuant to the section 361 exchange.

(C) *Alternate facts.* The facts are the same as in paragraph (q)(2)(xxii)(A) of this section (the facts in this *Example 22*), except that instead of TFC merging into DC, TFC merges into TFD in a reorganization described in section 368(a)(1)(A). The gain recognition agreement terminates without further effect if the conditions of paragraph (o)(5) of this section are satisfied.

(1) The condition of paragraph (o)(5)(i) of this section is satisfied because the TFD stock issued by TFD to TFC in the reorganization, which is treated as transferred stock under paragraph (b)(2)(iii) of this section, is distributed by TFC to UST pursuant to section 361(c).

(2) The condition of paragraph (o)(5)(ii) of this section is satisfied because UST is the U.S. transferor.

(3) The condition of paragraph (o)(5)(iii) of this section is satisfied if the aggregate basis of the TFD stock received by UST from TFC is not greater than the aggregate basis of the TFD stock at the time of the initial transfer (as adjusted for any gain recognized by UST on such transfer). If the basis condition of paragraph (o)(5)(iii) were not satisfied, under paragraph (o)(5)(iii) of this section, UST could reduce the basis of the TFD stock received in the reorganization.

(xxiii) *Example 23.—Split-off of transferred stock.* (A) *Facts.* X, a domestic corporation that is unrelated to USP and UST, wholly owns TFC. Pursuant to a reorganization described in section 368(a)(1)(B), UST transfers all of the TFD stock to TFC in exchange for 50% of the outstanding voting stock of TFC. UST enters into a gain recognition agreement with respect to such transfer. In year 4, in a split-off transaction to which section 355 applies, TFC distributes all of the TFD stock to X in exchange for all the TFC stock held by X.

(B) *Result.* Under paragraph (j)(1) of this section, the year 4 distribution of the TFD stock to X constitutes a triggering event. However, the distribution shall not constitute a triggering event if paragraph (k)(14) of this section applies. The gain recognition agreement does not terminate under paragraph (o)(5) of this section because X is not a recipient described in paragraph (o)(5)(ii) of this section.

(1) The condition of paragraph (k)(14)(i) of this section is satisfied because the distribution of the TFD stock qualifies as a nonrecognition transaction.

(2) The condition of paragraph (k)(14)(ii) of this section is satisfied because immediately after the distribution X, a domestic corporation that is eligible to be a U.S. transferor, retains a direct interest in the TFD stock.

(3) The condition of paragraph (k)(14)(iii) of this section is satisfied if X enters into a new gain recognition agreement with respect to the initial transfer. Under paragraph (k)(14)(iii)(B) of this section, X is not required to describe, with the new gain recognition agreement, any subsequent dispositions or other events that (based on the principles of paragraph (j) of this section) would constitute triggering events, other than the dispositions described in paragraph (j) of this section, because X directly owns TFD after the distribution.

(4) If X were a United States citizen, the gain recognition agreement would terminate if the condition of paragraph (o)(5)(iii) of this section were satisfied. Alternatively, the gain recognition agreement would continue for its remaining term if the conditions for the application of paragraph (k)(14) of this section were satisfied.

(C) *Alternate facts. Distribution to unrelated foreign corporation.* The facts are the same as in paragraph (q)(2)(xxiii)(A) of this section (the facts in this *Example 23*), except that X is a foreign corporation wholly owned by DC. DC is unrelated to UST. The results are the same as in paragraph (q)(2)(xxiii)(B) of this section (the results in this *Example 23*), except as follows.

(1) The condition of paragraph (k)(14)(ii) of this section is satisfied because immediately after the distribution DC, a domestic corporation that is eligible to be a U.S. transferor, owns at least 5% (determined as provided in paragraph (k)(14)(ii) of this section) of the total voting power and total value of the outstanding stock of X. As a result, DC is treated as retaining an indirect interest in the TFD stock immediately following the distribution.

(2) The condition of paragraph (k)(14)(iii) of this section is satisfied if DC enters into a new gain recognition agreement with respect to the initial transfer. Under paragraph (k)(14)(iii)(B) of this section, DC must, in addition to the dispositions described in paragraph (j) of this section, include as a triggering event a complete or partial disposition of the stock of X.

(D) *Alternate facts. Distribution to nonresident alien individual.* The facts are the same as in paragraph (q)(2)(xxiii)(A) of this section (the facts in this *Example 23*), except that X is a nonresident alien individual. Paragraph (k)(14) of this section does not apply to the distribution because the conditions of paragraph (k)(14)(ii) and (iii) of this section cannot be satisfied. Therefore, the distribution is a triggering event, and UST will recognize gain under the gain recognition agreement as required under paragraphs (c)(1)(i) and (v) of this section. The result would be the same if X were a foreign corporation and, immediately after the distribution, no United States person owned at least 5% (determined as provided in paragraph (k)(14)(ii) of this section) of the total voting power and value of the outstanding stock of X.

(xxiv) *Example 24.—Applicability of this section to gain recognition agreements filed before March 13, 2009.* (A) *Facts.* The facts are the same as in paragraph (q)(2)(vi)(A) of this section (the facts in *Example 6*), except that the initial transfer occurred on March 7, 2007, and the asset reorganization occurred on July 1, 2008.

(B) *Result.* Under paragraph (r)(1)(ii) of this section, the rules of § 1.367(a)-8T (see 26 CFR part 1, revised April 1, 2007) apply to the transfers pursuant to the asset reorganization because the initial transfer occurred on March 7, 2007. As a result of the disposition of the TFC stock pursuant to the asset reorganization, under § 1.367(a)-8T(d), USP is required to recognize the gain subject to the gain recognition agreement and pay applicable interest on any additional tax due with respect to such gain. Because the acquiring corporation in the asset reorganization is foreign, an exception under § 1.367(a)-8T(e) is not available for the exchange of TFC stock by USP. However, pursuant to paragraph (r)(2)(i) of this section, because the exception provided by paragraph (k)(14) of this section is not included in § 1.367(a)-8T, USP may apply paragraph (k)(14) of this section to such exchange (provided the conditions of paragraph (k)(14) of this section are satisfied), if the statute of limitations on assessments of tax for the 2007 tax year has not closed. If USP applies paragraph (k)(14) of this section to its exchange of the TFC stock pursuant to the asset reorganization, under paragraph (r)(2)(ii) of this section USP must include the new gain recognition agreement required under paragraph (k)(14)(iii) of this section with an amended Federal income tax return for its 2008 tax year that is filed August 10, 2009.

(xxv) *Example 25.—Applicability of this section to gain recognition agreements filed before March 13, 2009.* (A) *Facts.* The initial transfer occurs in 2004. In 2005, pursuant to a section 351 exchange, TFC transfers the TFD stock to F1 in exchange solely for F1 voting stock. UST does not file a new gain recognition agreement under § 1.367(a)-8(g)(2) with respect to the exchange.

(B) *Result.* Under paragraph (r)(1)(ii) of this section, the rules of § 1.367(a)-8 (see 26 CFR part 1, revised April 1, 2006) apply to the year 2005 disposition of the TFD stock because UST filed the gain recognition agreement after July 20, 1998, but before March 7, 2007. Under § 1.367(a)-8(e) (see 26 CFR part 1, revised April 1, 2006), as a result of the disposition of the TFD stock by TFC, UST must recognize the amount of gain subject to the gain recognition agreement. Paragraph (r)(2)(i) of this section does not apply because the rule provided by paragraph (k)(3) of this section was included in § 1.367(a)-8(g)(2) (see 26 CFR part 1, revised April 1, 2006). However, UST may request relief for reasonable cause under § 1.367(a)-8(c)(2) (see 26 CFR part 1, revised April 1, 2006) to file a new gain recognition agreement with respect to the disposition of the TFD stock by TFC in 2005.

(r) *Applicability dates.—*(1) *General rule.—*(i) *Transfers occurring on or after March 13, 2009; relief for certain failures that are not willful.—*The rules of this section apply to gain recognition agreements filed with respect to transfers of stock or securities occurring on or after March 13, 2009. However, the rules of this section do not apply to gain recognition agreements filed with respect to any such transfer occurring on or after March 13, 2009, if such transfer was entered into pursuant to a written agreement that was (subject to customary conditions) binding before February 11, 2009, and at all times thereafter. Solely for purposes of this paragraph (r), a transfer described in the preceding sentence shall be deemed to be a transfer occurring before March 13, 2009 to which the rules of § 1.367(a)-8 (see 26 CFR part 1, revised April 1, 2006) apply. See paragraph (r)(2)(iii) of this section for the ability to apply the rules of this section with respect to gain recognition agreements filed for taxable years ending before March 13, 2009. The eleventh sentence of paragraph (a) and paragraphs (b)(1)(iv), (b)(1)(vi), (b)(1)(xiii), (d)(1), (j)(8), and (p) of this section will apply to gain recognition agreement documents that are required to be filed on or after November 19, 2014, as well as to requests for relief submitted on or after November 19, 2014. Paragraph (k)(14)(ii) of this section applies to transfers occurring on or after October 1, 2019, and to transfers occurring before October 1, 2019, that result from an entity classification election made under § 301.7701-3 of this chapter that is filed on or after October 1, 2019. For transfers occurring before October 1, 2019, other than transfers occurring before October 1, 2019, that result from an entity classification election made under § 301.7701-3 of this chapter that is filed on or after October 1, 2019, a taxpayer may apply paragraph (k)(14)(ii) of this section to transfers occurring during the last taxable year of a transferee foreign corporation beginning before January 1, 2018, and each subsequent taxable year of the foreign corporation, provided that the taxpayer and United States persons that are related (within the meaning of section 267 or 707) to the taxpayer consistently apply such paragraph with respect to all foreign corporations. For transfers occurring before October 1, 2019, other than transfers occurring before October 1, 2019, that result from an entity classification election made under § 301.7701-3 of this chapter that is filed on or after October 1, 2019, where the taxpayer does not apply paragraph (k)(14)(ii) of this section as described in the preceding sentence, see paragraph (k)(14)(ii) of this section as in effect and contained in 26 CFR part 1, as revised April 1, 2020.

(ii) *Transfers occurring before March 13, 2009.—*For matters covered in this section for periods before March 13, 2009 but on or after March 7, 2007, the corresponding rules of § 1.367(a)-8T (see 26 CFR part 1, revised April 1, 2007) apply. For matters covered in this section for periods before March 7, 2007 but on or after July 20, 1998, the corresponding rules of § 1.367(a)-8 (see 26 CFR part 1, revised April 1, 2006) apply. For matters covered in this section for periods before July 20, 1998, the corresponding rules of § 1.367(a)-3T(g) (see 26 CFR part 1, revised April 1, 1998) and Notice 87-85 (1987-2 CB 395) apply. In addition, if a U.S. transferor entered into a gain recognition agreement for transfers before July 20, 1998, then the rules of § 1.367(a)-3T(g) (see 26 CFR part 1, revised April 1, 1998) continue to apply in lieu of this section in the event of any direct or indirect nonrecognition transfer of the same property. See also, § 1.367(a)-3(h).

(2) *Applicability to transfers occurring before March 13, 2009.—*(i) *General rule.—*Taxpayers may apply the rules of this regulation § 1.367(a)-8 that were not included in § 1.367(a)-8T (see 26 CFR part 1, revised April 1, 2007), to gain recognition agreements filed with respect to transfers of stock or securities for all open taxable years, if done consistently to all transfers. A U.S. transferor subject to section 877 and § 1.367(a)-8T(d)(6) shall not apply the rules of this regulation to reach a contrary result. A taxpayer that failed to file a gain recognition agreement for a transfer, or to comply materially with any requirement of this section with respect to an existing gain recognition agreement, must obtain relief for reasonable cause for such failure under § 1.367(a)-8T(e)(10) before applying the rules of this regulation § 1.367(a)-8 that were not included in § 1.367(a)-8T as permitted by this paragraph (r)(2). See paragraphs (q)(2)(xxiv) and (xxv) of this section for illustrations of the rule provided by this paragraph (r)(2)(i).

(ii) *Taxable years ending before March 13, 2009.—*Notwithstanding the requirements of § 1.367(a)-8(d), any gain recognition agreement or other filing required by reason of electing to apply the rules of this regulation § 1.367(a)-8 that were not included in § 1.367(a)-8T, as permitted by this paragraph (r)(2), for a taxable year ending before Applicability to gain recognition agreements filed before March 13, 2009 shall be considered filed in accordance with the requirements of § 1.367(a)-8(d), provided the gain recognition agreement or other filing is attached to an original or amended return for such taxable year. An amended return required to be filed by reason of electing to apply the rules of this regulation § 1.367(a)-8 that were not included in § 1.367(a)-8T, as permitted by this paragraph (r)(2), must be filed on or before August 10, 2009. A taxpayer that wishes to apply the rules of this regulation § 1.367(a)-8 that were not included in § 1.367(a)-8T, as permitted by this paragraph (r)(2), but that fails to meet the filing requirement described in the preceding sentence must request relief for reasonable cause under paragraph (p) of this section.

(iii) *Taxable years ending after effective date.—*A taxpayer that entered into a gain recognition agreement to which § 1.367(a)-8T (see 26 CFR part 1, revised April 1, 2007) applies may apply the rules of this section in a tax year ending on or after Applicability to gain recognition agreements filed before March 13, 2009 by attaching the agreement, certification, or other information related to such gain recognition agreement that the rules of this section require in accordance with the rules of this section and with the time and manner rules provided in § 1.367(a)-8(d).

(3) *Applicability to requests for relief submitted before November 19, 2014.—*The eleventh sentence of paragraph (a) and paragraphs (b)(1)(iv), (b)(1)(vi), (b)(1)(xiii), (d)(1), (j)(8), and (p) of this section will apply to requests for relief submitted before November 19, 2014 if—

(i) The statute of limitations on the assessment of tax has not expired for any year to which the request relates; and

(ii) The U.S. transferor resubmits the request under paragraph (p) of this section, notes on the request that the request is being submitted pursuant to this paragraph (r)(3), and acknowledges on the request that the last sentence of § 1.6038B-1(g)(6) provides a special rule regarding the application of § 1.6038B-1 to any transfer that is the subject of the request. [Reg. § 1.367(a)-8.]

□ [*T.D.* 8770, 6-18-98. *Amended by T.D.* 9243, 1-23-2006; *T.D.* 9311, 2-1-2007; *T.D.* 9446, 2-9-2009 (*corrected* 3-9-2009 and 3-26-2009); *T.D.* 9614, 3-18-2013, *T.D.* 9704, 11-18-2014 (*corrected* 1-2-2015), *T.D.* 9760, 3-18-2016, *T.D.* 9803, 12-15-2016 *and T.D.* 9908, 9-21-2020.]

§ 1.367(a)-9T. Treatment of deemed section 351 exchanges pursuant to section 304(a)(1) (temporary).—(a) *Scope and general rule.*—This section applies to the extent that, pursuant to section 304(a)(1), a United States person is treated as transferring stock of a domestic or foreign corporation to a foreign corporation (foreign acquiring corporation) in exchange for stock of the foreign acquiring corporation in a transaction to which section 351(a) applies (deemed section 351 exchange). Except to the extent provided in paragraph (b) of this section, a transfer of stock by a United States person to a foreign acquiring corporation in a deemed section 351 exchange is not subject to section 367(a)(1).

(b) *Special rule.*—Notwithstanding paragraph (a) of this section, if the distribution received by the United States person in redemption of the stock of the foreign acquiring corporation deemed issued in the deemed section 351 exchange is applied against and reduces (in whole or in part), pursuant to section 301(c)(2), the basis of stock of the foreign acquiring corporation held by the United States person other than the stock deemed issued in the deemed section 351 exchange, the United States person shall recognize gain pursuant to this paragraph (b). The exceptions described in § 1.367(a)-3(b)(1) and (c)(1) shall not apply to a transfer of stock described in paragraph (a) of this section. The amount of gain recognized by a United States person pursuant to this paragraph (b) shall equal the amount, if any, by which—

(1) The gain realized by the United States person with respect to the transferred stock in connection with the deemed section 351 exchange exceeds;

(2) The amount of the distribution received by the United States person in redemption of the stock of the foreign acquiring corporation deemed issued in the deemed section 351 exchange that is treated as a dividend under section 301(c)(1) and included in gross income by the United States person.

(c) *Ordering rule.*—For purposes of paragraph (b)(1) of this section, the amount of gain realized by the United States person in connection with the deemed section 351 exchange shall be determined without regard to the amount of gain recognized by the United States person under paragraph (b) of this section.

(d) *Allocation of recognized gain.*—Gain recognized by a United States person pursuant to paragraph (b) of this section shall be treated as recognized with respect to the stock transferred in the deemed section 351 exchange in proportion to the amount of gain realized by the United States person with respect to such stock. See § 1.367(a)-1T(b)(4) for additional rules on the character, source, and adjustments relating to gain recognized under section 367(a).

(e) *Example.*—The following example illustrates the rules of this section:

Example. (i) *Facts.* (A) USP, a domestic corporation, wholly owns FC1 and FC2, each a foreign corporation. USP, FC1 and FC2 use a calendar taxable year. The FC1 stock has a $40x basis and $100x fair market value. The FC2 stock has a $100x basis and $100x fair market value. As of December 31, year 1, FC1 has zero earnings and profits, and FC2 has $20x earnings and profits. On December 31, year 1, in a transaction described in section 304(a)(1), USP sells the FC1 stock to FC2 for $100x cash.

(B) Because USP wholly owns FC1 before the transactions and is treated, under section 318, as indirectly owning 100% of the FC1 stock after the transfer, under section 304(a)(1), USP and FC2 are treated in the same manner as if USP contributed the FC1 stock to FC2 in a deemed section 351 exchange in exchange solely for $100x of FC2 stock, and then FC2 redeemed for $100x cash its stock deemed issued to USP. Because USP wholly owns FC1 before the sale and is treated as owning 100% of FC1 after the sale, section 302(a) does not apply to the redemption. Instead, under section 302(d), the redemption is treated as a distribution to which section 301 applies. Pursuant to section 304(b)(2), $20x of the distribution is treated as a dividend from FC2. With respect to the remaining $80x, USP takes the position that $40x is applied against and reduces the basis of the FC2 stock issued in the deemed section 351 exchange, and $40x is applied against and reduces the basis of the FC2 stock held by USP prior to (and after) the transaction.

(ii) *Analysis.* Under paragraph (b) of this section, USP must recognize gain of $40x on its transfer of the FC1 stock to FC2 in the deemed section 351 exchange (the amount by which the $60x gain realized by USP on the deemed section 351 exchange with respect to the F1 stock exceeds the $20x dividend inclusion). Pursuant to paragraph (b) of this section, the exception under § 1.367(a)-3(b) is not available to the transfer of the FC1 stock by USP to FC2 in the deemed section 351 exchange. Thus, USP cannot avoid gain recognition under paragraph (b) of this section by entering into a gain recognition agreement with respect to its transfer of the FC1 stock to FC2 in the deemed section 351 exchange. Under paragraph (d) of this section, the $40x gain recognized is allocated among the shares of FC1 stock transferred to FC2 in the deemed section 351 exchange in proportion to the gain realized by USP on the transfer of such shares. Under paragraph (c) of this section, the application of paragraph (b) of this section is determined prior to taking into account the $40x increase to the basis of the FC1 stock transferred by USP. Under section 362, the basis of the FC1 stock in the hands of FC2 is increased by $40x, the amount of gain recognized by the USP on the transfer of the FC1 stock under paragraph (b) of this section. Under section 358, the basis of the FC2 stock received by USP in the deemed section 351 exchange is similarly increased by $40x. See § 1.367(a)-1T(b)(4). The $40x increase to the basis of the FC2 stock is taken into account before determining the consequences of the redemption of such stock under section 304(a)(1).

(f) *Effective/applicability date.*—This section applies to transfers occurring on or after February 10, 2009. See § 1.367(a)-3(a), as contained in 26 CFR part 1 revised as of April 1, 2008, for transfers occurring on or after February 21, 2006, and before February 10, 2009.

(g) *Expiration date.*—This section expires on or before February 10, 2012. [Temporary Reg. § 1.367(a)-9T.]

□ [*T.D.* 9444, 2-10-2009 (*corrected* 3-9-2009).]

§ 1.367(b)-1. Other transfers.—(a) *Scope.*—The regulations promulgated under section 367(b) (the section 367(b) regulations) set forth rules regarding the proper inclusions and adjustments that must be made as a result of an exchange described in section 367(b) (a section 367(b) exchange). A section 367(b) exchange is any exchange described in section 332, 351, 354, 355, 356 or 361, with respect to which the status of a foreign corporation as a corporation is relevant for determining the extent to which income shall be recognized or for determining the effect of the transaction on earnings and profits, basis of stock or securities, basis of assets, or other relevant tax attributes. For rules coordinating the concurrent application of sections 367(a) and (b), see § 1.367(a)-3(b)(2).

(b) *General rules.*—(1) *Rules.*—The following general rules apply under the section 367(b) regulations—

(i) A foreign corporation in a section 367(b) exchange is considered to be a corporation and, as a result, all of the related provisions (e.g., section 381) shall apply, except to the extent provided in the section 367(b) regulations; and

(ii) Nothing in the section 367(b) regulations shall permit—

(A) The nonrecognition of income that would otherwise be required to be recognized under another provision of the Internal Revenue Code or the regulations thereunder; or

(B) The recognition of a loss or deduction that would otherwise not be recognized under another provision of the Internal Revenue Code or the regulations thereunder.

(2) *Example.*—The following example illustrates the rules of this paragraph (b):

Example—(i) *Facts.* DC, a domestic corporation, owns 90 percent of P, a partnership. The remaining 10 percent of P is owned by a person unrelated to DC. P owns all of the outstanding stock of FC, a controlled foreign corporation. FC liquidates into P.

(ii) *Result.* FC's liquidation is not a transaction described in section 332. Nothing in the section 367(b) regulations, including § 1.367(b)-2(k), permits FC's liquidation to qualify as a liquidation described in section 332.

(c) *Notice required.*—(1) *In general.*—A notice under this paragraph (c) (section 367(b) notice) must be filed with regard to any person described in paragraph (c)(2) of this section. A section 367(b) notice must be filed in the time and manner described in paragraph (c)(3) of this section and must include the information described in paragraph (c)(4) of this section.

(2) *Persons subject to section 367(b) notice*.—The following persons are described in this paragraph (c)(2)—

(i) A shareholder described in § 1.367(b)-3(b)(1) that realizes income in a transaction described in § 1.367(b)-3(a);

(ii) A shareholder that makes the election described in § 1.367(b)-3(c)(3);

(iii) A shareholder described in § 1.367(b)-4(b)(1)(i)(A)(*1*) or (*2*) that realizes income in a transaction described in § 1.367(b)-4(a);

(iv) A shareholder that realizes income in a transaction described in § 1.367(b)-5(c) or 1.367(b)-5(d) and that is either—

(A) A section 1248 shareholder of the distributing or controlled corporation; or

(B) A foreign corporation with one or more shareholders that are described in paragraph (c)(2)(iv)(A) of this section; and

(v) A foreign surviving corporation described in § 1.367(b)-7(a).

(3) *Time and manner for filing notice*.—(i) *United States persons described in § 1.367(b)-1(c)(2)*.—A United States person described in paragraph (c)(2) of this section must file a section 367(b) notice attached to a timely filed Federal tax return (including extensions) for the person's taxable year in which income is realized in the section 367(b) exchange. In the case of a shareholder that makes the election described in § 1.367(b)-3(c)(3), notification of such election must be sent to the foreign acquired corporation (or its successor in interest) on or before the date the section 367(b) notice is filed, so that appropriate corresponding adjustments can be made in accordance with the rules of § 1.367(b)-2(e).

(ii) *Foreign corporations described in § 1.367(b)-1(c)(2)*.—Each United States person listed in this paragraph (c)(3)(ii) must file a section 367(b) notice with regard to a foreign corporation described in paragraph (c)(2) of this section. Such notice must be attached to a timely filed Federal tax return (including extensions) for the United States person's taxable year in which income is realized in the section 367(b) exchange and, if the United States person is required to file a Form 5471 (Information Return of U.S. Persons With Respect To Certain Foreign Corporations), the section 367(b) notice must be attached to the Form 5471. The following persons are listed in this paragraph (c)(3)(ii)—

(A) United States shareholders (as defined in § 1.367(b)-3(b)(2)) of foreign corporations described in paragraph (c)(2)(i) or (v) of this section; and

(B) Section 1248 shareholders of foreign corporations described in paragraph (c)(2)(iii) or (iv) of this section.

(4) *Information required*.—Except as provided in paragraph (c)(5) of this section, a section 367(b) notice shall include the following information—

(i) A statement that the exchange is a section 367(b) exchange;

(ii) A complete description of the exchange;

(iii) A description of any stock, securities or other consideration transferred or received in the exchange;

(iv) A statement that describes any amount required, under the section 367(b) regulations, to be taken into account as income or loss or as an adjustment to basis, earnings and profits, or other tax attributes as a result of the exchange;

(v) Any information that is or would be required to be furnished with a Federal income tax return pursuant to regulations under section 332, 351, 354, 355, 356, 361 or 368 (whether or not a Federal income tax return is required to be filed), if such information has not otherwise been provided by the person filing the section 367(b) notice;

(iv) A statement that describes any amount (or amounts) required, under the section 367(b) regulations, to be taken into account as income or loss or as an adjustment (including an adjustment under § 1.367(b)-7 or 1.367(b)-9) to basis, earnings and profits, or other tax attributes as a result of the exchange;

(v) Any information that is or would be required to be furnished with a Federal income tax return pursuant to regulations under section 332, 351, 354, 355, 356, 361, 368, or 381 (whether or not a Federal income tax return is required to be filed), if such information has not otherwise been provided by the person filing the section 367(b) notice;

(vi) Any information required to be furnished with respect to the exchange under sections 6038, 6038A, 6038B, 6038C or 6046, or the regulations under those sections, if such information has not otherwise been provided by the person filing the section 367(b) notice; and

(vii) If applicable, a statement that the shareholder is making the election described in § 1.367(b)-3(c)(3). This statement must include—

(A) A copy of the information the shareholder received from the foreign acquired corporation (or its successor in interest) establishing and substantiating the shareholder's all earnings and profits amount with respect to the shareholder's stock in the foreign acquired corporation; and

(B) A representation that the shareholder has notified the foreign acquired corporation (or its successor in interest) that the shareholder is making the election described in § 1.367(b)-3(c)(3).

(5) *Abbreviated notice provision for shareholders that make the election described in § 1.367(b)-3(c)(3)*.—In the case of a foreign acquired corporation that has never had earnings and profits that would result in any shareholder having an all earnings and profits amount, a shareholder making the election described in § 1.367(b)-3(c)(3) may satisfy the information requirements of paragraph (c)(4) of this section by filing a section 367(b) notice that includes—

(i) A statement from the foreign acquired corporation (or its successor in interest) that the foreign acquired corporation has never had any earnings and profits that would result in any shareholder having an all earnings and profits amount; and

(ii) The information described in paragraphs (c)(4)(i) through (iii) of this section.

(6) *Supplemental published guidance*.—The section 367(b) notice requirements may be updated or amended by revenue procedure or other published guidance. [Reg. § 1.367(b)-1.]

☐ [*T.D. 8770, 6-18-98. Amended by T.D. 8862, 1-21-2000 (corrected 11-3-2000); T.D. 9243, 1-23-2006 and T.D. 9273, 8-7-2006.*]

§ 1.367(b)-2. Definitions and special rules.—(a) *Controlled foreign corporation*.—The term *controlled foreign corporation* means a controlled foreign corporation as defined in section 957 (taking into account section 953(c)).

(b) *Section 1248 shareholder*.—The term *section 1248 shareholder* means any United States person that satisfies the ownership requirements of section 1248(a)(2) or (c)(2) with respect to a foreign corporation.

(c) *Section 1248 amount*.—(1) *Rule*.—The term *section 1248 amount* with respect to stock in a foreign corporation means the net positive earnings and profits (if any) that would have been attributable to such stock and includible in income as a dividend under section 1248 and the regulations thereunder if the stock were sold by the shareholder. In the case of a transaction in which the shareholder is a foreign corporation (foreign shareholder), the following additional rules shall apply—

(i) The foreign shareholder shall be deemed to be a United States person for purposes of this paragraph (c), except that the foreign shareholder shall not be considered a United States person for purposes of determining whether the stock owned by the foreign shareholder is stock of a controlled foreign corporation; and

(ii) The foreign shareholder's holding period in the stock of the foreign corporation shall be determined by reference to the period that the foreign shareholder's section 1248 shareholders held (directly or indirectly) an interest in the foreign corporation. This paragraph (c)(1)(ii) applies in addition to the section 1248 regulations' incorporation of section 1223 holding periods. See § 1.1248–8.

(2) *Examples*.—The following examples illustrate the rules of this paragraph (c):

Example 1—(i) *Facts*. DC, a domestic corporation, owns all of the outstanding stock of FC1, a controlled foreign corporation (CFC). FC1 owns all of the outstanding stock of FC2, a CFC. DC has always owned all of the stock of FC1, and FC1 has always owned all of the stock of FC2.

(ii) *Result*. Under this paragraph (c), DC's section 1248 amount with respect to its FC1 stock is computed by reference to all of FC1's and FC2's earnings and profits. See section 1248(c)(2). Because FC1's section 1248 shareholder (DC) always indirectly held all of the stock of FC2, FC1's section 1248 amount with respect to its FC2 stock is computed by reference to all of FC2's earnings and profits.

Example 2—(i) *Facts*. DC, a domestic corporation, owns 40 percent of the outstanding stock of FC1, a foreign corporation. The other 60 percent of FC1 stock is owned (directly and indirectly) by foreign persons that are unrelated to DC. FC1 owns all of the outstanding stock of FC2, a foreign corporation. On January 1, 2001, DC purchases the remaining 60 percent of FC1 stock.

(ii) *Result.* Under this paragraph (c), DC's section 1248 amount with respect to its FC1 stock is computed by reference to FC1's and FC2's earnings and profits that accumulated on or after January 1, 2001, the date FC1 and FC2 became controlled foreign corporations (CFCs). See section 1248(a). Because FC1 is not considered a United States person for purposes of determining whether FC2 is a CFC, FC1's section 1248 amount with respect to its FC2 stock is computed by reference to FC2's earnings and profits that accumulated on or after January 1, 2001, the date FC2 became an actual CFC.

Example 3—(i) *Facts.* FC1, a foreign corporation, owns all of the outstanding stock of FC2, a foreign corporation. DC is a domestic corporation that is unrelated to FC1, FC2, and their direct and indirect owners. On January 1, 2001, DC purchases all of the outstanding stock of FC1.

(ii) *Result.* Under this paragraph (c), DC's section 1248 amount with respect to its FC1 stock is computed by reference to FC1's and FC2's earnings and profits that accumulated on or after January 1, 2001, the first day DC held the stock of FC1. See section 1248(a). FC1's section 1248 amount with respect to its FC2 stock is computed by reference to FC2's earnings and profits that accumulated on or after January 1, 2001, the first day FC1's section 1248 shareholder (DC) indirectly held the stock of FC2.

(d) *All earnings and profits amount.*—(1) *General rule.*—The term *all earnings and profits amount* with respect to stock in a foreign corporation means the net positive earnings and profits (if any) determined as provided under paragraph (d)(2) of this section and attributable to such stock as provided under paragraph (d)(3) of this section. The all earnings and profits amount shall be determined without regard to the amount of gain that would be realized on a sale or exchange of the stock of the foreign corporation.

(2) *Rules for determining earnings and profits.*—(i) *Domestic rules generally applicable.*—For purposes of this paragraph (d), except as provided in sections 312(k)(4) and (n)(8), 964 and 986, the earnings and profits of a foreign corporation for any taxable year shall be determined according to principles substantially similar to those applicable to domestic corporations.

(ii) *Certain adjustments to earnings and profits.*—Notwithstanding paragraph (d)(2)(i) of this section, for purposes of this paragraph (d), the earnings and profits of a foreign corporation for any taxable year shall not include the amounts specified in section 1248(d). In the case of amounts specified in section 1248(d)(4), the preceding sentence requires that the earnings and profits for any taxable year be decreased by the net positive amount (if any) of earnings and profits attributable to activities described in section 1248(d)(4), and increased by the net reduction (if any) in earnings and profits attributable to activities described in section 1248(d)(4).

(iii) *Effect of section 332 liquidating distribution.*—The all earnings and profits amount with respect to stock of a corporation that distributes all of its property in a liquidation described in section 332 shall be determined without regard to the adjustments prescribed by section 312(a) and (b) resulting from the distribution of such property in liquidation, except that gain or loss realized by the corporation on the distribution shall be taken into account to the extent provided in section 312(f)(1). See § 1.367(b)-3(b)(3)(ii) *Example 3.*

(3) *Amount attributable to a block of stock.*—(i) *Application of section 1248 principles.*—(A) *In general.*—*(1) Rule.*—The all earnings and profits amount with respect to stock of a foreign corporation is determined according to the attribution principles of section 1248 and the regulations thereunder. The attribution principles of section 1248 shall apply without regard to the requirements of section 1248 that are not relevant to the determination of a shareholder's pro rata portion of earnings and profits. Thus, for example, the all earnings and profits amount is determined without regard to whether the foreign corporation was a controlled foreign corporation at any time during the five years preceding the section 367(b) exchange in question, without regard to whether the shareholder owned a 10 percent or greater interest in the stock, and without regard to whether the earnings and profits of the foreign corporation were accumulated in post-1962 taxable years or while the corporation was a controlled foreign corporation.

(2) Example.—The following example illustrates the rules of this paragraph (d)(3)(i)(A):

Example—(i) *Facts.* On January 1, 2001, DC, a domestic corporation, purchases 9 percent of the outstanding stock of FC, a foreign corporation. On January 1, 2002, DC purchases an additional 1 percent of FC stock. On January 1, 2003, DC exchanges its stock in FC in a section 367(b) exchange in which DC is required to include the all earnings and profits amount in income. FC was not a controlled foreign corporation during the entire period DC held its FC stock.

(ii) *Result.* The all earnings and profits amount with respect to DC's stock in FC is computed by reference to 9 percent of FC's earnings and profits from January 1, 2001, through December 31, 2001, and by reference to 10 percent of FC's earnings and profits from January 1, 2002, through January 1, 2003.

(B) *Foreign shareholders.*—In the case of a transaction in which the exchanging shareholder is a foreign corporation (foreign shareholder), the following additional rules shall apply—

(1) The attribution principles of section 1248 shall apply without regard to whether the person directly owning the stock is a United States person; and

(2) The foreign shareholder's holding period in the stock of the foreign acquired corporation shall be determined by reference to the period that the foreign shareholder's United States shareholders (as defined in § 1.367(b)-3(b)(2)) held (directly or indirectly) an interest in the foreign acquired corporation. This paragraph (d)(3)(i)(B)(2) applies in addition to the section 1248 regulations' incorporation of section 1223 holding periods. See § 1.1248–8.

(ii) *Exclusion of lower-tier earnings.*—In applying the attribution principles of section 1248 and the regulations thereunder to determine the all earnings and profits amount with respect to stock of a foreign corporation, the earnings and profits of subsidiaries of the foreign corporation shall not be taken into account notwithstanding section 1248(c)(2).

(e) *Treatment of deemed dividends.*—(1) *In general.*—In certain circumstances these regulations provide that an exchanging shareholder shall include an amount in income as a deemed dividend. This paragraph provides rules for the treatment of the deemed dividend.

(2) *Consequences of dividend characterization.*—A deemed dividend described in paragraph (e)(1) of this section shall be treated as a dividend for purposes of the Internal Revenue Code. The deemed dividend shall be considered as paid out of the earnings and profits with respect to which the amount of the deemed dividend was determined. Thus, for example, a deemed dividend that is determined by reference to the all earnings and profits amount or the section 1248 amount will never be considered as paid out of (and therefore will never reduce) earnings and profits specified in section 1248(d), because such earnings and profits are excluded in computing the all earnings and profits amount (under paragraph (d)(2)(ii) of this section) and the section 1248 amount (under section 1248(d) and paragraph (c)(1) of this section). If the deemed dividend is determined by reference to the earnings and profits of a foreign corporation that is owned indirectly (i.e., through one or more tiers of intermediate owners) by the person that is required to include the deemed dividend in income, the deemed dividend shall be considered as having been paid by such corporation to such person through the intermediate owners, rather than directly to such person.

(3) *Ordering rules.*—In the case of an exchange of stock in which the exchanging shareholder is treated as receiving a deemed dividend from a foreign corporation, the following ordering rules concerning the timing, treatment, and effect of such a deemed dividend shall apply. See also paragraph (j)(2) of this section.

(i) For purposes of the section 367(b) regulations, the gain realized by an exchanging shareholder shall be determined before increasing (as provided in paragraph (e)(3)(ii) of this section) the basis in the stock of the foreign corporation by the amount of the deemed dividend.

(ii) Except as provided in paragraph (e)(3)(i) of this section, the deemed dividend shall be considered to be received immediately before the exchanging shareholder's receipt of consideration for its stock in the foreign corporation, and the shareholder's basis in the stock exchanged shall be increased by the amount of the deemed dividend. Such basis increase shall be taken into account before determining the gain otherwise recognized on the exchange (for example, under section 356), the basis that the exchanging shareholder takes in the property that it receives in the exchange (under section 358(a)(1)), and the basis that the transferee otherwise takes in the transferred stock (under section 362).

(iii) Except as provided in paragraph (e)(3)(i) of this section, the earnings and profits of the appropriate foreign corporation shall be reduced by the deemed dividend amount before determining the consequences of the recognition of gain in excess of the deemed dividend amount (for example, under section 356(a)(2) or sections 356(a)(1) and 1248).

(4) *Examples.*—The following examples illustrate the rules of this paragraph (e):

Example 1. DC, a domestic corporation, exchanges stock in FC, a foreign corporation, in a section 367(b) exchange in which DC includes the all earnings and profits amount in income as a deemed dividend. Under paragraph (e)(2) of this section, a deemed dividend is treated as a dividend for purposes of the Internal Revenue Code.

Example 2. DC, a domestic corporation, exchanges stock in FC1, a foreign corporation that is a controlled foreign corporation, in a transaction in which DC is required to include the section 1248 amount in income as a deemed dividend. A portion of the section 1248 amount is determined by reference to the earnings and profits of FC1 (the upper-tier portion of the section 1248 amount), and the remainder of the section 1248 amount is determined by reference to the earnings and profits of FC2, which is a wholly owned foreign subsidiary of FC1 (the lower-tier portion of the section 1248 amount). Under paragraph (e)(2) of this section, DC computes its deemed paid foreign tax credit as if the lower-tier portion of the section 1248 amount were distributed as a dividend by FC2 to FC1, and as if such portion and the upper-tier portion of the section 1248 amount were then distributed as a dividend by FC1 to DC.

Example 3. DC, a domestic corporation, exchanges stock in FC, a foreign corporation that is a controlled foreign corporation, in a transaction in which DC realizes gain of $100 (prior to the application of the section 367(b) regulations). In connection with the transaction, DC is required to include $40 in income as a deemed dividend under the section 367(b) regulations. In addition to receiving property permitted to be received under section 354 without the recognition of gain, DC also receives cash in the amount of $70. Under paragraph (e)(3) of this section, the $40 deemed dividend increases DC's basis in its FC stock before determining the gain to be recognized under section 356. Thus, in applying section 356, DC is considered to realize $60 of gain on the exchange, all of which is recognized under section 356(a)(1).

(f) *Deemed asset transfer and closing of taxable year in certain section 368(a)(1)(F) reorganizations.*—(1) *Scope.*—This paragraph applies to a reorganization described in section 368(a)(1)(F) in which the transferor corporation is a foreign corporation.

(2) *Deemed asset transfer.*—In a reorganization described in paragraph (f)(1) of this section, there is considered to exist—

(i) A transfer of assets by the foreign transferor corporation to the acquiring corporation in exchange for stock (or stock and securities) of the acquiring corporation and the assumption by the acquiring corporation of the foreign transferor corporation's liabilities;

(ii) A distribution of such stock (or stock and securities) by the foreign transferor corporation to its shareholders (or shareholders and security holders); and

(iii) An exchange by the foreign transferor corporation's shareholders (or shareholders and security holders) of their stock (or stock and securities) for stock (or stock and securities) of the acquiring corporation.

(3) *Other applicable rules.*—For purposes of this paragraph (f), it is immaterial that the applicable foreign or domestic law treats the acquiring corporation as a continuation of the foreign transferor corporation.

(4) *Closing of taxable year.*—In a reorganization described in paragraph (f)(1) of this section, the taxable year of the foreign transferor corporation shall end with the close of the date of the transfer and, except as otherwise required under the Internal Revenue Code (e.g. section 1502 and the regulations thereunder), the taxable year of the acquiring corporation shall end with the close of the date on which the transferor's taxable year would have ended but for the occurrence of the reorganization if—

(i) The acquiring corporation is a domestic corporation; or

(ii) The foreign transferor corporation has effectively connected earnings and profits (as defined in section 884(d)) or accumulated effectively connected earnings and profits (as defined in section 884(b)(2)(B)(ii)).

(g) *Stapled stock under section 269B.*—For rules addressing the deemed conversion of a foreign corporation to a domestic corporation under section 269B, see § 1.269B-1(c).

(h) *Section 953(d) domestication elections.*—(1) *Effect of election.*—A foreign corporation that elects under section 953(d) to be treated as a domestic corporation shall be treated for purposes of section 367(b) as transferring, as of the first day of the first taxable year for which the election is effective, all of its assets to a domestic corporation in a reorganization described in section 368(a)(1)(F). Notwithstanding paragraph (d) of this section, for purposes of determining the consequences of the reorganization under § 1.367(b)-3, the all earnings and profits amount shall not be considered to include earnings and profits accumulated in taxable years beginning before January 1, 1988.

(2) *Post-election exchanges.*—For purposes of applying section 367(b) to post-election exchanges with respect to a corporation that has made a valid election under section 953(d) to be treated as a domestic corporation, such corporation shall be treated as a domestic corporation as to earnings and profits that were taken into account at the time of the section 953(d) election or which accrue after such election, and shall be treated as a foreign corporation as to earnings and profits accumulated in taxable years beginning before January 1, 1988. Thus, for example, if the section 953(d) corporation subsequently transfers its assets to a domestic corporation (other than another section 953(d) corporation) in a transaction described in section 381(a), the rules of § 1.367(b)-3 shall apply to such transaction to the extent of the section 953(d) corporation's earnings and profits accumulated in taxable years beginning before January 1, 1988.

(i) *Section 1504(d) elections.*—An election under section 1504(d), which permits certain foreign corporations to be treated as domestic corporations, is treated as a transfer of property to a domestic corporation and will generally constitute a reorganization described in section 368(a)(1)(F). However, if an election under section 1504(d) is made with respect to a foreign corporation from the first day of the foreign corporation's existence, then the foreign corporation shall be treated as a domestic corporation, and the section 367(b) regulations will not apply.

(j) *Sections 985 through 989.*—(1) *Change in functional currency of a qualified business unit.*—(i) *Rule.*—If, as a result of a section 367(b) exchange described in section 381(a), a qualified business unit (as defined in section 989(a)) (QBU) has a different functional currency determined under the rules of section 985(b) than it used prior to the transaction, then the QBU shall be deemed to have automatically changed its functional currency immediately prior to the transaction. A QBU that is deemed to change its functional currency pursuant to this paragraph (j) must make the adjustments described in § 1.985-5.

(ii) *Example.*—The following example illustrates the rule of this paragraph (j)(1):

Example—(i) *Facts.* DC, a domestic corporation, owns 100 percent of FC1, a foreign corporation. FC1 owns and operates a qualified business unit (QBU) (B1) in France, whose functional currency is the euro. FC2, an unrelated foreign corporation, owns and operates a QBU (B2) in France, whose functional currency is the dollar. FC2 acquires FC1's assets (including B1) in a reorganization described in section 368(a)(1)(C). As a part of the reorganization, B1 and B2 combine their operations into one QBU. Applying the rules of section 985(b), the functional currency of the combined operations of B1 and B2 is the euro.

(ii) *Result.* FC2's acquisition of FC1's assets is a section 367(b) exchange that is described in section 381(a). Because the functional currency of the combined operations of B1 and B2 after the exchange is the euro, B2 is deemed to have automatically changed its functional currency to the euro immediately prior to the section 367(b) exchange. B2 must make the adjustments described in § 1.985-5.

(2) *Previously taxed earnings and profits.*—(i) *Exchanging shareholder that is a United States person.*—If an exchanging shareholder that is a United States person is required to include in income either the all earnings and profits amount or the section 1248 amount under the provisions of § 1.367(b)-3 or 1.367(b)-4, then immediately prior to the exchange, and solely for the purpose of computing exchange gain or loss under section 986(c), the exchanging shareholder shall be treated as receiving a distribution of previously taxed earnings and profits from the appropriate foreign corporation that is attributable (under the principles of section 1248) to the exchanged stock. If an exchanging shareholder that is a United States person is a distributee in an exchange described in § 1.367(b)-5(c) or (d), then immediately

prior to the exchange, and solely for the purpose of computing exchange gain or loss under section 986(c), the exchanging shareholder shall be treated as receiving a distribution of previously taxed earnings and profits from the appropriate foreign corporation to the extent such shareholder has a diminished interest in such previously taxed earnings and profits after the exchange. The exchange gain or loss recognized under this paragraph (j)(2)(i) will increase or decrease the exchanging shareholder's adjusted basis in the stock of the foreign corporation, including for purposes of computing gain or loss realized with respect to the stock on the transaction. The exchanging shareholder's dollar basis with respect to each account of previously taxed income shall be increased or decreased by the exchange gain or loss recognized.

(ii) *Exchanging shareholder that is a foreign corporation.*—If an exchanging shareholder that is a foreign corporation is required to include in income either the all earnings and profits amount or the section 1248 amount under the provisions of §1.367(b)-3 or 1.367(b)-4, then, immediately prior to the exchange, the exchanging shareholder shall be treated as receiving a distribution of previously taxed earnings and profits from the appropriate foreign corporation that is attributable (under the principles of section 1248) to the exchanged stock. If an exchanging shareholder that is a foreign corporation is a distributee in an exchange described in §1.367(b)-5(c) or (d), then the exchanging shareholder shall be treated as receiving (immediately prior to the exchange) a distribution of previously taxed earnings and profits from the appropriate foreign corporation. Such distribution shall be measured by the extent to which the exchanging shareholder's direct or indirect United States shareholders (as defined in section 951(b)) have a diminished interest in such previously taxed earnings and profits after the exchange.

(3) *Other rules.*—See sections 985 through 989 for other currency rules that may apply in connection with a section 367(b) exchange.

(k) *Partnerships, trusts and estates.*—In applying the section 367(b) regulations, stock of a corporation that is owned by a foreign partnership, trust or estate shall be considered as owned proportionately by its partners, owners, or beneficiaries under the principles of §1.367(e)-1(b)(2). Stock owned by an entity that is disregarded as an entity separate from its owner under §301.7701-3 is owned directly by the owner of such entity. In applying §1.367(b)-5(b), the principles of §1.367(e)-1(b)(2) shall also apply to a domestic partnership, trust or estate.

(l) *Additional definitions.*—(1) *Foreign income taxes.*—The term *foreign income taxes* has the meaning set forth in §1.902-1(a)(7).

(2) *Post-1986 undistributed earnings.*—The term *post-1986 undistributed earnings* has the meaning set forth in §1.902-1(a)(9).

(3) *Post-1986 foreign income taxes.*—The term *post-1986 foreign income taxes* has the meaning set forth in §1.902-1(a)(8).

(4) *Pre-1987 accumulated profits.*—The term *pre-1987 accumulated profits* means the earnings and profits described in §1.902-1(a)(10)(i), computed in accordance with the rules of §1.902-1(a)(10)(ii).

(5) *Pre-1987 foreign income taxes.*—The term *pre-1987 foreign income taxes* has the meaning set forth in §1.902-1(a)(10)(iii).

(6) *Pre-1987 section 960 earnings and profits.*—The term *pre-1987 section 960 earnings and profits* means the earnings and profits of a foreign corporation accumulated in taxable years beginning before January 1, 1987, computed under §1.964-1(a) through (e), and translated into the functional currency (as determined under section 985) of the foreign corporation at the spot rate on the first day of the foreign corporation's first taxable year beginning after December 31, 1986. For further guidance, see Notice 88-70 (1988-2 C.B. 369, 370) (see also §601.601(d)(2) of this chapter). The term pre-1987 section 960 earnings and profits does not include earnings and profits that represent previously taxed earnings and profits described in section 959.

(7) *Pre-1987 section 960 foreign income taxes.*—The term *pre-1987 section 960 foreign income taxes* means the foreign income taxes related to pre-1987 section 960 earnings and profits, determined in accordance with the principles of §1.902-1(a)(10)(iii), except that the U.S. dollar amounts of pre-1987 section 960 foreign income taxes are determined by reference to the exchange rates in effect when the taxes were paid or accrued.

(8) *Earnings and profits.*—For purposes of §§1.367(b)-7 and 1.367(b)-9, the term *earnings and profits* means post-1986 undistributed earnings, pre-1987 accumulated profits, and pre-1987 section 960 earnings and profits.

(9) *Pooling corporation.*—The term *pooling corporation* means a foreign corporation with respect to which the requirements of section 902(c)(3)(B) have been met in the current taxable year or any prior taxable year.

(10) *Nonpooling corporation.*—The term *nonpooling corporation* means a foreign corporation that is not a pooling corporation.

(11) *Separate category.*—The term *separate category* has the meaning set forth in section 904(d)(1), and shall also include any other category of income to which section 904(a), (b), and (c) are applied separately under any other provision of the Internal Revenue Code (e.g., sections 56(g)(4)(C)(iii)(IV), 245(a)(10), 865(h), 901(j), and 904(h)(10) (or section 904(g)(10) for taxable years beginning on or before December 31, 2006).

(12) *Passive category.*—The term *passive category* means the separate category that includes income described in section 904(d)(1)(A).

(13) *General category.*—The term *general category* means the separate category that includes income described in section 904(d)(1)(B) (or section 904(d)(1)(I) for taxable years beginning on or before December 31, 2006). [Reg. §1.367(b)-2.]

☐ [*T.D.* 8397, 2-25-92. *Amended by T.D.* 8862, 1-21-2000 (*corrected* 11-3-2000); *T.D.* 9216, 7-28-2005; *T.D.* 9273, 8-7-2006; *T.D.* 9345, 7-27-2007, *T.D.* 9400, 5-23-2008 *and T.D.* 9959, 12-28-2021.]

§1.367(b)-3. Repatriation of foreign corporate assets in certain nonrecognition transactions.—(a) *Scope.*—This section applies to an acquisition by a domestic corporation (the domestic acquiring corporation) of the assets of a foreign corporation (the foreign acquired corporation) in a liquidation described in section 332 or an asset acquisition described in section 368(a)(1).

(b) *Exchange of stock owned directly by a United States shareholder or by certain foreign corporate shareholders.*—(1) *Scope.*—This paragraph (b) applies in the case of an exchanging shareholder that is either—

(i) A United States shareholder of the foreign acquired corporation; or

(ii) A foreign corporation with respect to which there are one or more United States shareholders.

(2) *United States shareholder.*—For purposes of this section (and for purposes of the other section 367(b) regulation provisions that specifically refer to this paragraph (b)(2)), the term *United States shareholder* means any shareholder described in section 951(b) (without regard to whether the foreign corporation is a controlled foreign corporation), and also any shareholder described in section 953(c)(1)(A) (but only if the foreign corporation is a controlled foreign corporation as defined in section 953(c)(1)(B) subject to the rules of section 953(c)).

(3) *Income inclusion.*—(i) *Inclusion of all earnings and profits amount.*—An exchanging shareholder shall include in income as a deemed dividend the all earnings and profits amount with respect to its stock in the foreign acquired corporation. For the consequences of the deemed dividend, see §1.367(b)-2(e). Notwithstanding §1.367(b)-2(e), however, a deemed dividend from the foreign acquired corporation to an exchanging foreign corporate shareholder shall not qualify for the exception from foreign personal holding company income provided by section 954(c)(3)(A)(i), although it may qualify for the look-through treatment provided by section 904(d)(3) if the requirements of that section are met with respect to the deemed dividend.

(ii) *Examples.*—The following examples illustrate the rules of paragraph (b)(3)(i) of this section:

Example 1—(i) *Facts.* DC, a domestic corporation, owns all of the outstanding stock of FC, a foreign corporation. The stock of FC has a value of $100, and DC has a basis of $30 in such stock. The all earnings and profits amount attributable to the FC stock owned by DC is $20, of which $15 is described in section 1248(a) and the remaining $5 is not (for example, because it accumulated prior to 1963). FC has a basis of $50 in its assets. In a liquidation described in section 332, FC distributes all of its property to DC, and the FC stock held by DC is canceled.

(ii) *Result.* Under paragraph (b)(3)(i) of this section, DC must include $20 in income as a deemed dividend from FC. Under section 337(a) FC does not recognize gain or loss in the assets that it distributes to DC, and under section 334(b), DC takes a basis of $50 in such assets.

Example 2—(i) *Facts.* DC, a domestic corporation, owns all of the outstanding stock of FC, a foreign corporation. The stock of FC has a value of $100, and DC has a basis of $30 in such stock. The all earnings and profits amount attributable to the FC stock owned by DC is $75. FC has a basis of $50 in its assets. In a liquidation described in section 332, FC distributes all of its property to DC, and the FC stock held by DC is canceled.

(ii) *Result.* Under paragraph (b)(3)(i) of this section, DC must include $75 in income as a deemed dividend from FC. Under section 337(a) FC does not recognize gain or loss in the assets that it distributes to DC, and under section 334(b), DC takes a basis of $50 in such assets.

Example 3—(i) *Facts.* DC, a domestic corporation, owns 80 percent of the outstanding stock of FC, a foreign corporation. DC has owned its 80 percent interest in FC since FC was incorporated. The remaining 20 percent of the outstanding stock of FC is owned by a person unrelated to DC (the minority shareholder). The stock of FC owned by DC has a value of $80, and DC has a basis of $24 in such stock. The stock of FC owned by the minority shareholder has a value of $20, and the minority shareholder has a basis of $18 in such stock. FC's only asset is land having a value of $100, and FC has a basis of $50 in the land. Gain on the land would not generate earnings and profits qualifying under section 1248(d) for an exclusion from earnings and profits for purposes of section 1248. FC has earnings and profits of $20 (determined under the rules of § 1.367(b)-2(d)(2)(i) and (ii)), $16 of which is attributable to the stock owned by DC under the rules of § 1.367(b)-2(d)(3). FC subdivides the land and distributes to the minority shareholder land with a value of $20 and a basis of $10. As part of the same transaction, in a liquidation described in section 332, FC distributes the remainder of its land to DC, and the FC stock held by DC and the minority shareholder is canceled.

(ii) *Result.* Under section 336, FC must recognize the $10 of gain it realizes in the land it distributes to the minority shareholder, and under section 331 the minority shareholder recognizes its gain of $2 in the stock of FC. Such gain is included in income by the minority shareholder as a dividend to the extent provided in section 1248 if the minority shareholder is a United States person that is described in section 1248(a)(2). Under § 1.367(b)-2(d)(2)(iii), the $10 of gain recognized by FC increases its earnings and profits for purposes of computing the all earnings and profits amount and, as a result, $8 of such increase (80 percent of $10) is considered to be attributable to the FC stock owned by DC under § 1.367(b)-2(d)(3)(i)(A)(*1*). DC's all earnings and profits amount with respect to its stock in FC is $24 (the $16 of initial all earnings and profits amount with respect to the FC stock held by DC, plus the $8 addition to such amount that results from FC's recognition of gain on the distribution to the minority shareholder). Under paragraph (b)(3)(i) of this section, DC must include the $24 all earnings and profits amount in income as a deemed dividend from FC.

Example 4—(i) *Facts.* DC1, a domestic corporation, owns all of the outstanding stock of DC2, a domestic corporation. DC1 also owns all of the outstanding stock of FC, a foreign corporation. The stock of FC has a value of $100, and DC1 has a basis of $30 in such stock. The assets of FC have a value of $100. The all earnings and profits amount with respect to the FC stock owned by DC1 is $20. In a reorganization described in section 368(a)(1)(D), DC2 acquires all of the assets of FC solely in exchange for DC2 stock. FC distributes the DC2 stock to DC1, and the FC stock held by DC1 is canceled.

(ii) *Result.* DC1 must include $20 in income as a deemed dividend from FC under paragraph (b)(3)(i) of this section. Under section 361, FC does not recognize gain or loss in the assets that it transfers to DC2 or in the DC2 stock that it distributes to DC1, and under section 362(b) DC2 takes a basis in the assets that it acquires from FC equal to the basis that FC had therein. Under § 1.367(b)-2(e)(3)(ii) and section 358(a)(1), DC1 takes a basis of $50 (its $30 basis in the stock of FC, plus the $20 that was treated as a deemed dividend to DC1) in the stock of DC2 that it receives in exchange for the stock of FC. Under § 1.367(b)-2(e)(3)(iii) and section 312(a), the earnings and profits of FC are reduced by the $20 deemed dividend.

Example 5—(i) *Facts.* DC1, a domestic corporation, owns all of the outstanding stock of FC1, a foreign corporation. FC1 owns all of the outstanding stock of FC2, a foreign corporation. The all earnings and profits amount with respect to the FC2 stock owned by FC1 is $20. In a reorganization described in section 368(a)(1)(A), DC2, a domestic corporation unrelated to FC1 or FC2, acquires all of the assets and liabilities of FC2 pursuant to a State W merger. FC2 receives DC2 stock and distributes such stock to FC1. The FC2 stock held by FC1 is canceled, and FC2 ceases its separate legal existence.

(ii) *Result.* FC1 must include $20 in income as a deemed dividend from FC2 under paragraph (b)(3)(i) of this section. The deemed dividend is treated as a dividend for purposes of the Internal Revenue Code as provided in § 1.367(b)-2(e)(2); however, under paragraph (b)(3)(i) of this section the deemed dividend cannot qualify for the exception from foreign personal holding company income provided by section 954(c)(3)(A)(i), even if the provisions of that section would otherwise have been met in the case of an actual dividend.

Example 6—(i) *Facts.* DC1, a domestic corporation, owns 99 percent of USP, a domestic partnership. The remaining 1 percent of USP is owned by a person unrelated to DC1. DC1 and USP each directly own 9 percent of the outstanding stock of FC, a foreign corporation that is not a controlled foreign corporation subject to the rule of section 953(c). In a reorganization described in section 368(a)(1)(C), DC2, a domestic corporation, acquires all of the assets and liabilities of FC in exchange for DC2 stock. FC distributes to its shareholders DC2 stock, and the FC stock held by its shareholders is canceled.

(ii) *Result.* (A) DC1 and USP are United States persons that are exchanging shareholders in a transaction described in paragraph (a) of this section. As a result, DC1 and USP are subject to the rules of paragraph (b) of this section if they qualify as United States shareholders as defined in paragraph (b)(2) of this section. Alternatively, if they do not qualify as United States shareholders as defined in paragraph (b)(2) of this section, DC1 and USP are subject to the rules of paragraph (c) of this section. Paragraph (b)(2) of this section defines the term United States shareholder to include any shareholder described in section 951(b) (without regard to whether the foreign corporation is a controlled foreign corporation). A shareholder described in section 951(b) is a United States person that is considered to own, applying the rules of section 958(a) and 958(b), 10 percent or more of the total combined voting power of all classes of stock entitled to vote of a foreign corporation. Under section 958(b), the rules of section 318(a), as modified by section 958(b) and the regulations thereunder, apply so that, in general, stock owned directly or indirectly by a partnership is considered as owned proportionately by its partners, and stock owned directly or indirectly by a partner is considered as owned by the partnership. Thus, under section 958(b), DC1 is treated as owning its proportionate share of FC stock held by USP, and USP is treated as owning all of the FC stock held by DC1.

(B) Accordingly, for purposes of determining whether DC1 is a United States shareholder under paragraph (b)(2) of this section, DC1 is considered as owning 99 percent of the 9 percent of FC stock held by USP. Because DC1 also owns 9 percent of FC stock directly, DC1 is considered as owning more than 10 percent of FC stock. DC1 is thus a United States shareholder of FC under paragraph (b)(2) of this section and, as a result, is subject to the rules of paragraph (b) of this section. However, for purposes of determining DC1's all earnings and profits amount, DC1 is not treated as owning the FC stock held by USP. Under § 1.367(b)-2(d)(3), DC1's all earnings and profits amount is determined by reference to the 9 percent of FC stock that it directly owns.

(C) For purposes of determining whether USP is a United States shareholder under paragraph (b)(2) of this section, USP is considered as owning the 9 percent of FC stock held by DC1. Because USP also owns 9 percent of FC stock directly, USP is considered as owning more than 10 percent of FC stock. USP is thus a United States shareholder of FC under paragraph (b)(2) of this section and, as a result, is subject to the rules of paragraph (b) of this section. However, for purposes of determining USP's all earnings and profits amount, USP is not treated as owning the FC shares held by DC1. Under § 1.367(b)-2(d)(3), USP's all earnings and profits amount is determined by reference to the 9 percent of FC stock that it directly owns.

(iii) *Recognition of exchange gain or loss with respect to capital.*—[Reserved]

(4) *Reserved.*—For further guidance concerning section 367(b) exchanges occurring before February 24, 2001, see § 1.367(b)-3T(b)(4).

(c) *Exchange of stock owned by a United States person that is not a United States shareholder.*—(1) *Scope.*—This paragraph (c) applies in the case of an exchanging shareholder that is a United States person not described in paragraph (b)(1)(i) of this section (i.e., a United States person that is not a United States shareholder of the foreign acquired corporation).

(2) *Requirement to recognize gain.*—An exchanging shareholder described in paragraph (c)(1) of this section shall recognize realized gain (but not loss) with respect to the stock of the foreign acquired corporation.

(3) *Election to include all earnings and profits amount.*—In lieu of the treatment prescribed by paragraph (c)(2) of this section, an exchanging shareholder described in paragraph (c)(1) of this section may instead elect to include in income as a deemed dividend the all earnings and profits amount with respect to its stock in the foreign acquired corporation. For the consequences of a deemed dividend, see § 1.367(b)-2(e). Such election may be made only if—

(i) The foreign acquired corporation (or its successor in interest) has provided the exchanging shareholder information to substantiate the exchanging shareholder's all earnings and profits amount with respect to its stock in the foreign acquired corporation; and

(ii) The exchanging shareholder complies with the section 367(b) notice requirement described in § 1.367(b)-1(c), including the specific rules contained therein concerning the time and manner for electing to apply the rules of this paragraph (c)(3).

(4) *De minimis exception.*—This paragraph (c) shall not apply in the case of an exchanging shareholder whose stock in the foreign acquired corporation has a fair market value of less than $50,000 on the date of the section 367(b) exchange.

(5) *Examples.*—The following examples illustrate the rules of this paragraph (c):

Example 1—(i) *Facts.* DC1, a domestic corporation, owns 5 percent of the outstanding stock of FC, a foreign corporation that is not a controlled foreign corporation subject to the rule of section 953(c). Persons unrelated to DC1 own the remaining 95 percent of the outstanding stock of FC. DC1 has owned its 5 percent interest in FC since FC was incorporated. DC1's stock in FC has a basis of $40,000 and a value of $100,000. The all earnings and profits amount with respect to DC1's stock in FC is $50,000. In a reorganization described in section 368(a)(1)(C), DC2, a domestic corporation, acquires all of the assets and liabilities of FC in exchange for DC2 stock. FC distributes DC2 stock to its shareholders, and the FC stock held by its shareholders is canceled.

(ii) *Alternate result 1.* If DC1 does not make the election described in paragraph (c)(3) of this section, then the general rule of paragraph (c)(2) of this section applies and DC1 must recognize its $60,000 gain in the FC stock. Under section 358(a)(1), DC1 has a $100,000 basis (its $40,000 basis in the FC stock, plus the $60,000 recognized gain) in the DC2 stock that it receives in exchange for its FC stock. Because DC1 is not a shareholder described in section 1248(a)(2), section 1248 does not apply to recharacterize any of DC1's gain as a dividend.

(iii) *Alternate result 2.* If DC1 makes a valid election under paragraph (c)(3) of this section, then DC1 must include in income as a deemed dividend the $50,000 all earnings and profits amount with respect to its FC stock. Under § 1.367(b)-2(e)(3) and section 358(a)(1), DC1 has a $90,000 basis (its $40,000 basis in the FC stock, plus the $50,000 that was treated as a deemed dividend to DC1) in the DC2 stock that it receives in exchange for its FC stock.

Example 2—(i) *Facts.* The facts are the same as in *Example 1*, except that DC1's stock in FC has a fair market value of $48,000 on the date DC1 receives the DC2 stock.

(ii) *Result.* Because DC1's stock in FC has a fair market value of less than $50,000 on the date of the section 367(b) exchange, the de minimis exception of paragraph (c)(4) of this section applies. As a result, DC1 is not subject to the gain or income inclusion requirements of this paragraph (c).

(d) *Carryover of certain foreign taxes.*—(1) *Rule.*—Excess foreign taxes under section 904(c) allowable to the foreign acquired corporation under section 906 shall carry over to the domestic acquiring corporation and become allowable under section 901, subject to the limitations prescribed by the Internal Revenue Code (for example, sections 383, 904 and 907). The domestic acquiring corporation shall not succeed to any other foreign taxes paid or incurred by the foreign acquired corporation.

(2) *Example.*—The following example illustrates the rules of this paragraph (d):

Example—(i) *Facts.* DC, a domestic corporation owns 100 percent of the outstanding stock of FC, a foreign corporation. FC has net positive earnings and profits, none of which are attributable to DC's FC stock under § 1.367(b)-2(d)(3). FC has paid foreign taxes that are not eligible for credit under section 906. In a liquidation described in section 332, FC distributes all of its property to DC, and the FC stock held by DC is canceled.

(ii) *Result.* The liquidation of FC into DC is a section 367(b) exchange. Thus, DC is subject to the section 367(b) regulations, and must file a section 367(b) notice pursuant to § 1.367(b)-1(c). Pursuant to the provisions of paragraph (d)(1) of this section, the foreign taxes paid by FC do not carryover to DC because FC's foreign taxes are not eligible for credit under section 906.

(e) *Net operating loss and capital loss carryovers.*—A net operating loss or capital loss carryover of the foreign acquired corporation is described in section 381(c)(1) and (c)(3) and thus is eligible to carry over from the foreign acquired corporation to the domestic acquiring corporation only to the extent the underlying deductions or losses were allowable under chapter 1 of subtitle A of the Internal Revenue Code. Thus, only a net operating loss or capital loss carryover that is effectively connected with the conduct of a trade or business within the United States (or that is attributable to a permanent establishment, in the context of an applicable United States income tax treaty) is eligible to be carried over under section 381. For further guidance, see Rev. Rul. 72-421 (1972-2 C.B. 166) (see also § 601.601(d)(2) of this chapter).

(f) *Carryover of earnings and profits.*—(1) *General rule.*—Except to the extent otherwise specifically provided (see, e.g., Notice 89-79 (1989-2 C.B. 392) (see also § 601.601(d)(2) of this chapter)), earnings and profits of the foreign acquired corporation that are not included in income as a deemed dividend under the section 367(b) regulations (or deficit in earnings and profits) are eligible to carry over from the foreign acquired corporation to the domestic acquiring corporation under section 381(c)(2) only to the extent such earnings and profits (or deficit in earnings and profits) are effectively connected with the conduct of a trade or business within the United States (or are attributable to a permanent establishment in the United States, in the context of an applicable United States income tax treaty). All other earnings and profits (or deficit in earnings and profits) of the foreign acquired corporation shall not carry over to the domestic acquiring corporation and, as a result, shall be eliminated.

(2) *Previously taxed earnings and profits.*—[Reserved]
[Reg. § 1.367(b)-3.]

☐ [*T.D.* 8862, 1-21-2000 (*corrected* 11-3-2000). *Amended by T.D.* 9243, 1-23-2006, *T.D.* 9273, 8-7-2006 *and T.D.* 9959, 12-28-2021.]

§ 1.367(b)-3T. Repatriation of foreign corporate assets in certain nonrecognition transactions (temporary).—(a) through (b)(3). [Reserved]. For further guidance, see § 1.367(b)-3(a) through (b)(3).

(b)(4) *Election of taxable exchange treatment.*—(i) *Rules.*—(A) *In general.*—In lieu of the treatment prescribed by § 1.367(b)-3(b)(3)(i), an exchanging shareholder described in § 1.367(b)-3(b)(1) may instead elect to recognize the gain (but not loss) that it realizes in the exchange (taxable exchange election). To make a taxable exchange election, the following requirements must be satisfied—

(1) The exchanging shareholder (and its direct or indirect owners that would be affected by the election, in the case of an exchanging shareholder that is a foreign corporation) reports the exchange in a manner consistent therewith (see, e.g., sections 954(c)(1)(B)(i), 1001 and 1248);

(2) The notification requirements of paragraph (b)(4)(i)(C) of this section are satisfied; and

(3) The adjustments described in paragraph (b)(4)(i)(B) of this section are made when the following circumstances are present—

(i) The transaction is described in section 332 or is an asset acquisition described in section 368(a)(1), with regard to which one U.S. person owns (directly or indirectly) 100 percent of the foreign acquired corporation; and

(ii) The all earnings and profits amount described in § 1.367(b)-3(b)(3)(i) with respect to the exchange exceeds the gain recognized by the exchanging shareholder.

(B) *Attribute reduction.*—*(1) Reduction of NOL carryovers.*—The amount by which the all earnings and profits amount exceeds the gain recognized by the exchanging shareholder (the excess earnings and profits amount) shall be applied to reduce the net operating loss carryovers (if any) of the foreign acquired corporation to which the domestic acquiring corporation would otherwise succeed under section 381(a) and (c)(1). See also Rev. Rul. 72-421 (1972-2 C.B. 166) (see § 601.601(d)(2) of this chapter).

(2) *Reduction of capital loss carryovers.*—After the application of paragraph (b)(4)(i)(B)(*1*) of this section, any remaining excess earnings and profits amount shall be applied to reduce the capital loss carryovers (if any) of the foreign acquired corporation to which the domestic acquiring corporation would otherwise succeed under section 381(a) and (c)(3).

(3) *Reduction of basis.*—After the application of paragraph (b)(4)(i)(B)(2) of this section, any remaining excess earnings and profits amount shall be applied to reduce (but not below zero) the basis of the assets (other than dollar-denominated money) of the foreign acquired corporation that are acquired by the domestic acquiring corporation. Such remaining excess earnings and profits amount shall be applied to reduce the basis of such assets in the following order: first, tangible depreciable or depletable assets, according to their class lives (beginning with those assets with the shortest class life); second, other non-inventory tangible assets; third, intangible assets that are amortizable; and finally, the remaining assets of the foreign acquired corporation that are acquired by the domestic acquiring corporation. Within each of these categories, if the total basis of all assets in the category is greater than the excess earnings and profits amount to be applied against such basis, the taxpayer may choose to which specific assets in the category the basis reduction first applies.

(C) *Notification.*—The exchanging shareholder shall elect to apply the rules of this paragraph (b)(4)(i) by attaching a statement of its election to its section 367(b) notice. See § 1.367(b)-1(c) for the rules concerning filing a section 367(b) notice.

(D) *Example.*—The following example illustrates the rules of this paragraph (b)(4)(i):

Example—(i) *Facts.* DC, a domestic corporation, owns all of the outstanding stock of FC, a foreign corporation. The stock of FC has a value of $100, and DC has a basis of $80 in such stock. The assets of FC are one parcel of land with a value of $60 and a basis of $30, and tangible depreciable assets with a value of $40 and a basis of $80. FC has no net operating loss carryovers or capital loss carryovers. The all earnings and profits amount with respect to the FC stock owned by DC is $30, of which $19 is described in section 1248(a) and the remaining $11 is not (for example, because it was earned prior to 1963). In a liquidation described in section 332, FC distributes all of its property to DC, and the FC stock held by DC is canceled. Rather than including in income as a deemed dividend the all earnings and profits amount of $30 as provided in § 1.367(b)-3(b)(3)(i), DC instead elects taxable exchange treatment under paragraph (b)(4)(i)(A) of this section.

(ii) *Result.* DC recognizes the $20 of gain it realizes on its stock in FC. Of this $20 amount, $19 is included in income by DC as a dividend pursuant to section 1248(a). (For the source of the remaining $1 of gain recognized by DC, see section 865. For the treatment of the $1 for purposes of the foreign tax credit limitation, see generally section 904(d)(2)(A)(i).) Because the transaction is described in section 332 and because the all earnings and profits amount with respect to the FC stock held by DC ($30) exceeds by $10 the income recognized by DC ($20), the attribute reduction rules of paragraph (b)(4)(i)(B) of this section apply. Accordingly, the $10 excess earnings and profits amount is applied to reduce the basis of the tangible depreciable assets of FC, beginning with those assets with the shortest class lives. Under section 337(a) FC does not recognize gain or loss in the assets that it distributes to DC, and under section 334(b) (which is applied taking into account the basis reduction prescribed by paragraph (b)(4)(i)(A)(3) of this section) DC takes a basis of $30 in the land and $70 in the tangible depreciable assets that it receives from FC.

(ii) *Effective date.*—This paragraph (b)(4) applies for section 367(b) exchanges that occur between February 23, 2000 and February 23, 2001.

(c) and (d) [Reserved]. For further guidance, see § 1.367(b)-3(c) through (d). [Temporary Reg. § 1.367(b)-3T.]

□ [*T.D.* 8863, 1-21-2000.]

§ 1.367(b)-4. Acquisition of foreign corporate stock or assets by a foreign corporation in certain nonrecognition transactions.—(a) *Scope.*—This section applies to certain acquisitions by a foreign corporation of the stock or assets of a foreign corporation in an exchange described in section 351 or in a reorganization described in section 368(a)(1). Paragraph (b) of this section provides a rule regarding when an exchanging shareholder is required to include in income as a deemed dividend the section 1248 amount attributable to the stock that it exchanges. Paragraph (c) of this section provides a rule excluding deemed dividends from foreign personal holding company income. Paragraph (d) of this section provides rules for subsequent sales or exchanges. Paragraphs (e) and (f) of this section provide rules regarding certain exchanges following inversion transactions. Paragraph (g) of this section provides definitions and special rules, including special rules regarding triangular reorganizations and recapitalizations. Paragraph (h) of this section provides the applicability dates for certain paragraphs of this section. See also § 1.367(a)-3(b)(2) for transactions subject to the concurrent application of sections 367(a) and (b) and § 1.367(b)-2 for additional definitions that apply.

(b) *Income inclusion.*—If a foreign corporation (the transferee foreign corporation) acquires the stock of a foreign corporation in an exchange described in section 351 or the stock or assets of a foreign corporation in a reorganization described in section 368(a)(1) (in either case, the foreign acquired corporation), then an exchanging shareholder must, if its exchange is described in paragraph (b)(1)(i), (b)(2)(i), or (b)(3) of this section, include in income as a deemed dividend the section 1248 amount attributable to the stock that it exchanges.

(1) *Exchange that results in loss of status as section 1248 shareholder.*—(i) *General rule.*—Except as provided in paragraph (b)(1)(ii) of this section, an exchange is described in this paragraph (b)(1)(i) if—

(A) Immediately before the exchange, the exchanging shareholder is—

(*1*) A United States person that is a section 1248 shareholder with respect to the foreign acquired corporation; or

(*2*) A foreign corporation, and a United States person is a section 1248 shareholder with respect to such foreign corporation and with respect to the foreign acquired corporation;

(B) Either of the following conditions is satisfied—

(*1*) Immediately after the exchange, the stock received in the exchange is not stock in a corporation that is a controlled foreign corporation as to which the United States person described in paragraph (b)(1)(i)(A) of this section is a section 1248 shareholder; or

(*2*) Immediately after the exchange, the transferee foreign corporation or the foreign acquired corporation (in the case of the acquisition of the stock of a foreign acquired corporation) is not a controlled foreign corporation as to which the United States person described in paragraph (b)(1)(i)(A) of this section is a section 1248 shareholder; and

(C) The exchange is not a specified exchange to which paragraph (e)(1) of this section applies.

(ii) *Special rules.*—(A) *Receipt of foreign stock in an exchange to which § 1.367(a)-7(c) applies.*—If an exchanging shareholder is a domestic corporation that transfers stock of a foreign acquired corporation in an exchange under section 361(a) or (b) (section 361 exchange) to which the exception to section 367(a)(5) in § 1.367(a)-7(c) applies, and the exchanging shareholder receives stock in either the transferee foreign corporation or foreign controlling corporation (in the case of a triangular reorganization), such exchange will not be described in paragraph (b)(1)(i) of this section only if immediately after the exchanging shareholder's receipt of the foreign stock in the section 361 exchange, but prior to, and without taking into account, the exchanging shareholder's distribution of the foreign stock under section 361(c)(1), the foreign acquired corporation, transferee foreign corporation, and foreign controlling corporation (in the case of a triangular reorganization) are controlled foreign corporations as to which the exchanging shareholder is a section 1248 shareholder. See paragraph (b)(1)(iii) of this section, *Example 4*, for an illustration of this rule. If an exchange is not described in paragraph (b)(1)(i) of this section as a result of the application of this paragraph, see §§ 1.1248(f)-1(b)(3) and 1.1248(f)-2(c), as applicable. For adjustments to the basis of stock of the foreign surviving corporation in certain triangular reorganizations, see paragraph (b)(1)(ii)(B)(2)(*i*) of this section.

(B) *Special rules for certain triangular reorganizations.*—(*1*) *Receipt of domestic stock.*—In the case of a triangular reorganization in which the stock received in the exchange is stock of a domestic controlling corporation, such exchange is not described in paragraph (b)(1)(i) of this section if immediately after the exchange the following foreign corporations are controlled foreign corporations as to which the domestic controlling corporation is a section 1248 shareholder—

(*i*) The foreign acquired corporation and foreign surviving corporation, in the case of a section 354 exchange of the stock of the foreign acquired corporation pursuant to a triangular B reorganization.

(*ii*) The foreign surviving corporation, in the case of a section 354 or section 356 exchange of the stock of the foreign acquired corporation pursuant to a forward triangular merger, triangular C reorganization, reverse triangular merger, or triangular G reorganization. See paragraph (b)(1)(iii) of this section, *Example 3B* for an illustration of this rule.

(*iii*) The foreign acquired corporation and foreign surviving corporation, in the case of a section 361 exchange of the stock of the foreign acquired corporation by an exchanging shareholder that is a foreign corporation described in paragraph (b)(1)(i)(A)(*2*) of this section and that is a foreign acquired corporation the assets of which are acquired in a triangular reorganization described in paragraph (b)(1)(ii)(B)(*1*)(*ii*) of this section.

(*iv*) The foreign acquired corporation and foreign surviving corporation, in the case of a section 361 exchange of the stock of the foreign acquired corporation by an exchanging shareholder that is a domestic corporation described in paragraph (b)(1)(i)(A)(*1*) of this section and that is acquired in a triangular reorganization to which the exception to section 367(a)(5) in §1.367(a)-7(c) applies. See paragraph (b)(1)(iii) of this section, *Example 5* for an illustration of this rule.

(*2*) *Adjustments to basis of stock of foreign surviving corporation.*—(*i*) *Section 361 exchanges to which §1.367(a)-7(c) applies.*—If stock of the foreign acquired corporation is acquired by the foreign surviving corporation in a section 361 exchange by reason of a triangular reorganization (other than a triangular B reorganization) to which the exception to section 367(a)(5) provided in §1.367(a)-7(c) applies, and if paragraph (b)(1)(i) of this section does not apply to the section 361 exchange by reason of (b)(1)(ii)(A) of this section (if the stock received is stock of a foreign controlling corporation) or by reason of (b)(1)(ii)(B)(*1*)(*iv*) of this section (if the stock received is stock of a domestic controlling corporation), then the controlling corporation (foreign or domestic) must apply the principles of §1.367(b)-13 to adjust the basis of the stock of the foreign surviving corporation so that the section 1248 amount in the stock of the foreign acquired corporation (determined when the foreign surviving corporation acquires such stock) is reflected in the stock of the foreign surviving corporation immediately after the exchange. See paragraph (b)(1)(iii) of this section, *Example 5*, for an illustration of this rule.

(*ii*) *Other exchanges.*—See §1.367(b)-13 for rules regarding the adjustment to the basis of the stock of the foreign surviving corporation in exchanges pursuant to triangular reorganizations that are not subject to paragraph (b)(1)(ii)(B)(*2*)(*i*) of this section.

(iii) *Examples.*—The following examples illustrate the rules of this paragraph (b)(1):

Example 1—(i) *Facts.* FC1 is a foreign corporation that is owned, directly and indirectly (applying the ownership rules of section 958), solely by foreign persons. DC is a domestic corporation that is unrelated to FC1. DC owns all of the outstanding stock of FC2, a foreign corporation. Thus, under §1.367(b)-2(a) and (b), DC is a section 1248 shareholder with respect to FC2, and FC2 is a controlled foreign corporation. Under §1.367(b)-2(c)(1), the section 1248 amount attributable to the stock of FC2 held by DC is $20. In a reorganization described in section 368(a)(1)(C), FC1 acquires all of the assets and assumes all of the liabilities of FC2 in exchange for FC1 voting stock. The FC1 voting stock received does not represent more than 50 percent of the voting power or value of FC1's stock. FC2 distributes the FC1 stock to DC, and the FC2 stock held by DC is canceled.

(ii) *Result.* FC1 is not a controlled foreign corporation immediately after the exchange. As a result, the exchange is described in paragraph (b)(1)(i) of this section. Under paragraph (b) of this section, DC must include in income, as a deemed dividend from FC2, the section 1248 amount ($20) attributable to the FC2 stock that DC exchanged.

Example 2—(i) *Facts.* The facts are the same as in *Example 1*, except that the voting stock of FC1, which is received by FC2 in exchange for its assets and distributed by FC2 to DC, represents more than 50 percent of the voting power of FC1's stock under the rules of section 957(a).

(ii) *Result.* Paragraph (b)(1)(i) of this section does not apply to require inclusion in income of the section 1248 amount, because FC1 is a controlled foreign corporation as to which DC is a section 1248 shareholder immediately after the exchange.

Example 3—(i) *Facts.* The facts are the same as in *Example 1*, except that FC2 receives and distributes voting stock of FP, a foreign corporation that is in control (within the meaning of section 368(c)) of FC1, instead of receiving and distributing voting stock of FC1.

(ii) *Result.* For purposes of section 367(a), the transfer is an indirect stock transfer subject to section 367(a). See §1.367(a)-3(d)(1)(iv). Accordingly, DC's exchange of FC2 stock for FP stock under section 354 will be taxable under section 367(a) (and section 1248 will be applicable) if DC fails to enter into a gain recognition agreement in accordance with §1.367(a)-8. Under §1.367(a)-3(b)(2), if DC enters into a gain recognition agreement, the exchange will be subject to the provisions of section 367(b) and the regulations thereunder, as well as section 367(a). If FP and FC1 are controlled foreign corporations as to which DC is a (direct or indirect) section 1248 shareholder immediately after the reorganization, then the section 367(b) result is the same as in *Example 2*—that is, paragraph (b)(1)(i) of this section does not apply to require inclusion in income of the section 1248 amount. Under these circumstances, the amount of the gain recognition agreement would equal the amount of the gain realized on the indirect stock transfer. If FP or FC1 is not a controlled foreign corporation as to which DC is a (direct or indirect) section 1248 shareholder immediately after the exchange, then the section 367(b) result is the same as in *Example 1*—that is, DC must include in income, as a deemed dividend from FC2, the section 1248 amount ($20) attributable to the FC2 stock that DC exchanged. Under these circumstances, the amount of the gain recognition agreement would equal the amount of the gain realized on the indirect stock transfer, less the $20 section 1248 amount inclusion.

Example 3A. (i) *Facts.* The facts are the same as in *Example 3*, except that FC1 merges into FC2 in a reorganization described in sections 368(a)(1)(A) and (a)(2)(E). Pursuant to the reorganization, DC exchanges its FC2 stock for stock of FP.

(ii) *Result.* The result is similar to the result in *Example 3*. The transfer is an indirect stock transfer subject to section 367(a). See §1.367(a)-3(d)(1)(ii). Accordingly, DC's exchange of FC2 stock for FP stock will be taxable under section 367(a) (and section 1248 will be applicable) if DC fails to enter into a gain recognition agreement. If DC enters into a gain recognition agreement, the exchange will be subject to the provisions of section 367(b) and the regulations thereunder, as well as section 367(a). If FP and FC2 are controlled foreign corporations as to which DC is a section 1248 shareholder immediately after the reorganization, then paragraph (b)(1)(i) of this section does not apply to require DC to include in income the section 1248 amount attributable to the FC2 stock that was exchanged and the amount of the gain recognition agreement is the amount of gain realized on the indirect stock transfer. If FP or FC2 is not a controlled foreign corporation as to which DC is a section 1248 shareholder immediately after the exchange, then DC must include in income as a deemed dividend from FC2 the section 1248 amount ($20) attributable to the FC2 stock that DC exchanged. Under these circumstances, the gain recognition agreement would be the amount of gain realized on the indirect transfer, less the $20 section 1248 amount inclusion.

Example 3B. (i) *Facts.* The facts are the same as *Example 3*, except that USP, a domestic corporation, owns the controlling interest (within the meaning of section 368(c)) in FC1 stock. In addition, FC2 merges into FC1 in a reorganization described in sections 368(a)(1)(A) and (a)(2)(D). Pursuant to the reorganization, DC exchanges its FC2 stock for USP stock.

(ii) *Result.* Because DC receives stock of a domestic corporation, USP, in the section 354 exchange, the transfer is not an indirect stock transfer subject to section 367(a). Accordingly, the exchange will be subject only to the provisions of section 367(b) and the regulations thereunder. Under paragraph (b)(1)(ii) of this section, because the stock received is stock of a domestic corporation (USP) and, immediately after the exchange, USP is a section 1248 shareholder of FC1 (the surviving corporation) and FC1 is a controlled foreign corporation, the exchange is not described in paragraph (b)(1)(i) of this section and DC is not required to include in income the section 1248 amount attributable to the FC2 stock that was exchanged. See §1.367(b)-13(c) for the basis and holding period rules applicable to this transaction, which cause USP's adjusted basis and holding period in the stock of FC1 after the transaction to reflect the basis and holding period that DC had in its FC2 stock.

Example 4. (i) *Facts.* DC1, a domestic corporation, owns all of the outstanding stock of DC2, a domestic corporation. DC2 owns various assets, including all of the outstanding stock of FC2, a foreign corporation. The stock of FC2 has a value of $100, and DC2 has a basis of $30 in the stock. The section 1248 earnings and profits attributable to the FC2 stock held by DC2 is $20. DC2 does not own any stock other than the FC2 stock. FC1 is a foreign corporation that is unrelated to DC1, DC2, and FC2. In a reorganization described in section 368(a)(1)(C), FC1 acquires all of the assets of DC2 in exchange for the assumption of DC2's liabilities and voting stock of FC1 that represents 20% of the outstanding voting stock of FC1. DC2 distributes the FC1 stock to DC1 under section 361(c)(1), and the DC2 stock held by DC1 is canceled. The exception to section 367(a)(5) provided in § 1.367(a)-7(c) applies to the section 361 exchange. DC1 properly files a gain recognition agreement that satisfies the conditions of § § 1.367(a)-T(e)(6) and 1.367(a)-8 to qualify for nonrecognition treatment under section 367(a) with respect to DC2's transfer of the FC2 stock to FC1. See § 1.367(a)-3(e). FC1 is not a surrogate foreign corporation (within the meaning of section 7874) because DC1 does not hold at least 60% of the stock of FC1 by reason of holding stock of DC2.

(ii) *Result.* DC2, the exchanging shareholder, is a U.S. person and a section 1248 shareholder with respect to FC2, the foreign acquired corporation. Whether DC2 is required to include in income the section 1248 amount attributable to the FC2 stock under paragraph (b)(1)(i) of this section depends on whether, immediately after DC2's section 361 exchange of the FC2 stock for FC1 stock (and before the distribution of the FC1 stock to DC1 under section 361(c)(1)), FC1 and FC2 are controlled foreign corporations as to which DC2 is a section 1248 shareholder. See paragraph (b)(1)(ii)(A) of this section. If, immediately after the section 361 exchange (and before the distribution of the FC1 stock to DC1 under section 361(c)(1)), FC1 and FC2 are both controlled foreign corporations as to which DC2 is a section 1248 shareholder, then DC2 is not required to include in income the section 1248 amount attributable to the FC2 stock under paragraph (b)(1)(i) of this section because neither condition in paragraph (b)(1)(i)(B) of this section is satisfied. Alternatively, if immediately after the section 361 exchange (and before the distribution of the FC1 stock to DC1 under section 361(c)(1)) either FC1 or FC2 is not a controlled foreign corporation as to which DC2 is a section 1248 shareholder, then, pursuant to paragraph (b)(1)(i) of this section, DC2 must include in income the section 1248 amount attributable to the FC2 stock. For the treatment of DC2's transfer of assets other than the FC2 stock to FC1, see section 367(a)(1) and (a)(3) and the regulations under that section. Furthermore, because DC2's transfer of any other assets to FC1 is pursuant to a section 361 exchange, see section 367(a)(5) and § 1.367(a)-7. If any of the assets transferred are intangible assets for purposes of section 367(d), see section 367(d). With respect to DC2's distribution of the FC1 stock to DC1 under section 361(c)(1), see section 1248(f)(1), and § § 1.1248(f)-1 and 1.1248(f)-2.

Example 5. (i) *Facts.* DC1, a domestic corporation, wholly owns DC2, a domestic corporation. The DC2 stock has a $100x fair market value, and DC1 has a basis of $30x in the stock. DC2's only asset is all of the outstanding stock of FC2, a foreign corporation. The FC2 stock has a $100x fair market value, and DC2 has a basis of $30x in the stock. There are $20x of earnings and profits attributable to the FC2 stock for purposes of section 1248. USP, a domestic corporation unrelated to DC1, DC2, and FC2, wholly owns FC1, a foreign corporation. In a triangular reorganization described in section 368(a)(1)(C), DC2 transfers all the FC2 stock to FC1 in exchange solely for voting stock of USP, and distributes the USP stock to DC1 under section 361(c)(1). DC1 exchanges its DC2 stock for the USP stock under section 354. DC2's transfer of the FC2 stock to FC1 is described in section 361(a) and therefore, under section 367(a)(5) and § 1.367(a)-7, is generally subject to section 367(a)(1). However, the exception to section 367(a)(5) provided in § 1.367(a)-7(c) applies to the section 361 exchange. In addition, DC1 is not required to adjust the basis of its USP stock (determined under section 358) under section 367(a)(5) and § 1.367(a)-7(c)(3). DC1 properly files a gain recognition agreement that satisfies the conditions of § § 1.367(a)-3(e)(6) and 1.367(a)-8 to qualify for nonrecognition treatment under section 367(a) with respect to DC2's transfer of the FC2 stock to FC1. See § 1.367(a)-3(e).

(ii) *Result.* Immediately after the exchange, FC1 and FC2 are controlled foreign corporations as to which USP is a section 1248 shareholder because USP directly and indirectly owns all the FC1 stock and FC2 stock, respectively. Because DC2 receives stock of a domestic corporation (USP) in exchange for the FC2 stock and, immediately after the exchange, FC1 and FC2 are controlled foreign corporations as to which USP is a section 1248 shareholder, DC2's exchange of the FC2 stock for the USP stock is not described in paragraph (b)(1)(i) of this section. See paragraph (b)(1)(ii)(B)(*1*)(*iv*) of this section. Therefore, DC2 is not required to include in income the section 1248 amount in the FC2 stock. Under paragraph (b)(1)(ii)(B)(*2*)(*i*) of this section, USP must apply the principles of § 1.367(b)-13 to adjust the basis of its FC1 stock to preserve the section 1248 amount ($20x) in the FC2 stock. Under the principles of § 1.367(b)-13, each share of FC1 stock held by USP after the exchange must be divided into portions, one portion attributable to the FC1 stock owned before the exchange and one portion attributable to the FC2 stock received in the exchange. The $30x basis in the FC2 stock and the $20x earnings and profits attributable to the FC2 stock before the exchange are attributable to the divided portions of the FC1 stock to which the FC2 stock relates.

(2) *Receipt by exchanging shareholder of preferred or other stock in certain instances.*—(i) *Rule.*—An exchange is described in this paragraph (b)(2)(i) if—

(A) Immediately before the exchange, the foreign acquired corporation and the transferee foreign corporation are not members of the same affiliated group (within the meaning of section 1504(a), but without regard to the exceptions set forth in section 1504(b), and substituting the words "more than 50" in place of the words "at least 80" in sections 1504(a)(2)(A) and (B));

(B) Immediately after the exchange, a domestic corporation directly or indirectly owns 10 percent or more of the voting power or value of the transferee foreign corporation; and

(C) The exchanging shareholder receives preferred stock (other than preferred stock that is fully participating with respect to dividends, redemptions and corporate growth) in consideration for common stock or preferred stock that is fully participating with respect to dividends, redemptions and corporate growth, or, in the discretion of the Commissioner or the Commissioner's delegate (and without regard to whether the stock exchanged is common stock or preferred stock), receives stock that entitles it to participate (through dividends, redemption payments or otherwise) disproportionately in the earnings generated by particular assets of the foreign acquired corporation or transferee foreign corporation.

(ii) *Examples.*—The following examples illustrate the rules of this paragraph (b)(2):

Example 1—(i) *Facts.* FC1 is a foreign corporation. DC is a domestic corporation that is unrelated to FC1. DC owns all of the outstanding stock of FC2, a foreign corporation, and FC2 has no outstanding preferred stock. The value of FC2 is $100 and DC has a basis of $50 in the stock of FC2. Under § 1.367(b)-2(c)(1), the section 1248 amount attributable to the stock of FC2 held by DC is $20. In a reorganization described in section 368(a)(1)(B), FC1 acquires all of the stock of FC2 and, in exchange, DC receives FC1 voting preferred stock that constitutes 10 percent of the voting stock of FC1 for purposes of section 902(a). Immediately after the exchange, FC1 and FC2 are controlled foreign corporations and DC is a section 1248 shareholder of FC1 and FC2, so paragraph (b)(1)(i) of this section does not require inclusion in income of the section 1248 amount.

(ii) *Result.* Pursuant to § 1.367(a)-3(b)(2), the transfer is subject to both section 367(a) and section 367(b). Under § 1.367(a)-3(b)(1), DC will not be subject to tax under section 367(a)(1) if it enters into a gain recognition agreement in accordance with § 1.367(a)-8. Even though paragraph (b)(1)(i) of this section does not apply to require inclusion in income by DC of the section 1248 amount, DC must nevertheless include the $20 section 1248 amount in income as a deemed dividend from FC2 under paragraph (b)(2)(i) of this section. Thus, if DC enters into a gain recognition agreement, the amount is $30 (the $50 gain realized less the $20 recognized under section 367(b)). If DC fails to enter into a gain recognition agreement, it must include in income under section 367(a)(1) the $50 of gain realized ($20 of which is treated as a dividend under section 1248). Section 367(b) does not apply in such case.

Example 2—(i) *Facts.* The facts are the same as in *Example 1,* except that DC owns all of the outstanding stock of FC1 immediately before the transaction.

(ii) *Result.* Both section 367(a) and section 367(b) apply to the transfer. Paragraph (b)(2)(i) of this section does not apply to require inclusion of the section 1248 amount. Under paragraph (b)(2)(i)(A) of this section, the transaction is outside the scope of paragraph (b)(2)(i) of this section because FC1 and FC2 are, immediately before the transaction, members of the same affiliated group (within the meaning of such paragraph). Thus, if DC enters into a gain recognition agreement in accordance with § 1.367(a)-8, the amount of such agreement is $50. As in *Example 1,* if DC fails to enter into a gain recognition agreement, it must include in income $50, $20 of which will be treated as a dividend under section 1248.

Example 3—(i) *Facts.* FC1 is a foreign corporation. DC is a domestic corporation that is unrelated to FC1. DC owns all of the outstanding stock of FC2, a foreign corporation. The section 1248 amount attributable to the stock of FC2 held by DC is $20. In a reorganization described in section 368(a)(1)(B), FC1 acquires all of the stock of FC2 in exchange for FC1 voting stock that constitutes 10 percent of the voting stock of FC1 for purposes of section 902(a). The FC1 voting stock received by DC in the exchange carries voting rights in FC1, but by agreement of the parties the shares entitle the holder to dividends, amounts to be paid on redemption, and amounts to be paid on liquidation, that are to be determined by reference to the earnings or value of FC2 as of the date of such event, and that are affected by the earnings or value of FC1 only if FC1 becomes insolvent or has insufficient capital surplus to pay dividends.

(ii) *Result.* Under § 1.367(a)-3(b)(1), DC will not be subject to tax under section 367(a)(1) if it enters into a gain recognition agreement with respect to the transfer of FC2 stock to FC1. Under § 1.367(a)-3(b)(2), the exchange will be subject to the provisions of section 367(b) and the regulations thereunder to the extent that it is not subject to tax under section 367(a)(1). Furthermore, even if DC would not otherwise be required to recognize income under this section, the Commissioner or the Commissioner's delegate may nevertheless require that DC include the $20 section 1248 amount in income as a deemed dividend from FC2 under paragraph (b)(2)(i) of this section.

(3) *Certain recapitalizations.*—An exchange pursuant to a recapitalization under section 368(a)(1)(E) shall be deemed to be an exchange described in this paragraph (b)(3) if the following conditions are satisfied—

(i) During the 24-month period immediately preceding or following the date of the recapitalization, the corporation that undergoes the recapitalization (or a predecessor of, or successor to, such corporation) also engages in a transaction that would be described in paragraph (b)(2)(i) of this section but for paragraph (b)(2)(i)(C) of this section, either as the foreign acquired corporation or the transferee foreign corporation; and

(ii) The exchange in the recapitalization is described in paragraph (b)(2)(i)(C) of this section.

(c) *Exclusion of deemed dividend from foreign personal holding company income.*—(1) *Rule.*—In the event the section 1248 amount is included in income as a deemed dividend by a foreign corporation under paragraph (b) of this section, such deemed dividend shall not be included as foreign personal holding company income under section 954(c).

(2) *Example.*—The following example illustrates the rule of this paragraph (c):

Example—(i) *Facts.* FC1 is a foreign corporation that is owned, directly and indirectly (applying the ownership rules of section 958), solely by foreign persons. DC is a domestic corporation that is unrelated to FC1. DC owns all of the outstanding stock of FC2, a foreign corporation. FC2 owns all of the outstanding stock of FC3, a foreign corporation. Under § 1.367(b)-2(c)(1), the section 1248 amount attributable to the stock of FC3 held by FC2 is $20. In a reorganization described in section 368(a)(1)(B), FC1 acquires from FC2 all of the stock of FC3 in exchange for FC1 voting stock. The FC1 voting stock received by FC2 does not represent more than 50 percent of the voting power or value of FC1's stock.

(ii) *Result.* FC1 is not a controlled foreign corporation immediately after the exchange. Under paragraph (b)(1) of this section, FC2 must include in income, as a deemed dividend from FC3, the section 1248 amount ($20) attributable to the FC3 stock that FC2 exchanged. The deemed dividend is treated as a dividend for purposes of the Internal Revenue Code as provided in § 1.367(b)-2(e)(2); however, under this paragraph (c) the deemed dividend is not foreign personal holding company income to FC2.

(d) *Rules for subsequent sales or exchanges.*—(1) *Rule.*—If an exchanging shareholder (as defined in § 1.1248-8(b)(1)(iv)) is not required to include in income as a deemed dividend the section 1248 amount under paragraph (b) or paragraph (e)(1) of this section (noninclusion exchange), then, for purposes of applying section 367(b) or 1248 to subsequent sales or exchanges, and subject to the limitation of § 1.367(b)-2(d)(3)(ii) (in the case of a transaction described in § 1.367(b)-3), the determination of the earnings and profits attributable to the stock an exchanging shareholder receives in the noninclusion exchange is determined pursuant to the rules of section 1248 and the regulations under that section.

(2) *Example.*—The following example illustrates the rules of this section. For purposes of the example, assume that

(i) There is no immediate gain recognition pursuant to section 367(a)(1) and the regulations under that section (either through operation of the rules or because the appropriate parties have entered into a gain recognition agreement under §§ 1.367(a)-3(b) and 1.367(a)-8);

(ii) References to earnings and profits are to earnings and profits that would be includible in income as a dividend under section 1248 and the regulations under that section if stock to which the earnings and profits are attributable were sold or exchanged by its shareholder;

(iii) Each corporation has only a single class of stock outstanding and uses the calendar year as its taxable year; and

(iv) Each transaction is unrelated to all other transactions.

Example. Acquisition of the stock of a foreign corporation that controls a transferee foreign corporation in a reorganization described in section 368(a)(1)(C). (i) *Facts.* DC1, a domestic corporation, has owned all the stock of CFC1, a controlled foreign corporation, since its formation on January 1, year 1. CFC1 has owned all the stock of CFC2, a controlled foreign corporation, since its formation on January 1, year 1. FC, a foreign corporation that is not a controlled foreign corporation, has owned all of the stock of FC2, a foreign corporation, since its formation on January 1, year 2. On December 31, year 3, pursuant to a restructuring transaction that was a triangular reorganization described in section 368(a)(1)(C), CFC1 transfers all of its assets, including the CFC2 stock, to FC2 in exchange for 80% of the voting stock of FC. CFC1 transfers the voting stock of FC to DC1 and the CFC1 stock is cancelled. Pursuant to section 1223(1), DC1 is considered to have held the stock of FC since January 1, year 1. Under section 1223(2), FC2 is considered to have held the stock of CFC2 since January 1, year 1. On December 31, year 3, CFC1 has $100 of earnings and profits. From January 1, year 4, until December 31, year 5, FC (a controlled foreign corporation after the restructuring transaction) accumulates an additional $50 of earnings and profits. FC2, a controlled foreign corporation after the restructuring transaction, accumulates $100 of earnings and profits from January 1, year 4, until December 31, year 5. On December 31, year 5, FC is liquidated into DC1 in a transaction described in section 332.

(ii) *Result.* Generally, this paragraph (d) requires that DC1 include in income the earnings and profits attributable to its stock in FC as determined under § 1.1248-8. However, since the liquidation of FC into DC1 is a transaction described in § 1.367(b)-3, the earnings and profits attributable to the stock of FC are limited by § 1.367(b)-2(d) (3)(ii) to that portion of the earnings and profits accumulated by FC itself before or after the restructuring transaction, and do not include the earnings and profits of FC's subsidiaries accumulated before or after the restructuring transaction. Thus, DC1 will include $40 of earnings and profits in income (80% of the $50 of earnings and profits accumulated by FC after the restructuring transaction).

(e) *Income inclusion and gain recognition in certain exchanges following an inversion transaction.*—(1) *General rule.*—If a foreign corporation (the transferee foreign corporation) acquires stock of a foreign corporation in an exchange described in section 351 or stock or assets of a foreign corporation in a reorganization described in section 368(a)(1) (in either case, the foreign acquired corporation), then an exchanging shareholder must, if its exchange is a specified exchange and the exception in paragraph (e)(3) of this section does not apply—

(i) Include in income as a deemed dividend the section 1248 amount attributable to the stock that it exchanges; and

(ii) After taking into account the increase in basis provided in § 1.367(b)-2(e)(3)(ii) resulting from the deemed dividend (if any), recognize all realized gain with respect to the stock that would not otherwise be recognized.

(2) *Specified exchanges.*—An exchange is a specified exchange if—

(i) Immediately before the exchange, the foreign acquired corporation is an expatriated foreign subsidiary and the exchanging shareholder is either an expatriated entity described in paragraph (b)(1)(i)(A)(*1*) of this section or an expatriated foreign subsidiary described in paragraph (b)(1)(i)(A)(*2*) of this section;

(ii) The stock received in the exchange is stock of a foreign corporation; and

(iii) The exchange occurs during the applicable period.

(3) *De minimis exception.*—The exception in this paragraph (e)(3) applies if—

(i) Immediately after the exchange, the foreign acquired corporation (in the case of an acquisition of stock of the foreign acquired corporation) or the transferee foreign corporation (in the case of an acquisition of assets of the foreign acquired corporation) is a controlled foreign corporation;

(ii) The post-exchange ownership percentage with respect to the foreign acquired corporation (in the case of an acquisition of stock of the foreign acquired corporation) or the transferee foreign corporation (in the case of an acquisition of assets of the foreign acquired corporation) is at least 90 percent of the pre-exchange ownership percentage with respect to the foreign acquired corporation; and

(iii) The post-exchange ownership percentage with respect to each lower-tier expatriated foreign subsidiary of the foreign acquired corporation is at least 90 percent of the pre-exchange ownership percentage with respect to the lower-tier expatriated foreign subsidiary.

(4) *Certain exceptions from foreign personal holding company not available.*—An income inclusion of a foreign corporation under paragraph (e)(1) of this section does not qualify for the exceptions from foreign personal holding company income provided by sections 954(c)(3)(A)(i) and 954(c)(6) (to the extent in effect).

(5) *Examples.*—The following examples illustrate the application of this paragraph (e). For purposes of all of the examples, unless otherwise indicated: FP, a foreign corporation, owns all of the stock of USP, a domestic corporation, and all 40 shares of stock of FS, a controlled foreign corporation for its taxable year beginning January 1, 2017, but not for prior taxable years, except as a result of a transaction described in the facts of an example. USP owns all 50 shares of stock of FT1, a controlled foreign corporation, which, in turn, owns all 50 shares of FT2, a controlled foreign corporation. FP acquired all of the stock of USP in an inversion transaction that was completed on July 1, 2016. Therefore, with respect to that inversion transaction, USP is an expatriated entity; FT1 and FT2 are expatriated foreign subsidiaries; and FP and FS are each a non-EFS foreign related person. All entities have a calendar year tax year for U.S. tax purposes. All shares of stock have a fair market value of $1x, and each corporation has a single class of stock outstanding.

Example 1. Specified exchange to which general rule applies—(i) *Facts.* During the applicable period, and pursuant to a reorganization described in section 368(a)(1)(B), FT1 transfers all 50 shares of FT2 stock to FS in exchange solely for 50 newly issued voting shares of FS. Immediately before the exchange, USP is a section 1248 shareholder with respect to FT1 and FT2. At the time of the exchange, the FT2 stock owned by FT1 has a fair market value of $50x and an adjusted basis of $5x, such that the FT2 stock has a built-in gain of $45x. In addition, the earnings and profits of FT2 attributable to FT1's stock in FT2 for purposes of section 1248 is $30x, taking into account the rules of § 1.367(b)-2(c)(1)(i) and (ii), and therefore the section 1248 amount with respect to the FT2 stock is $30x (the lesser of the $45x of built-in gain and the $30x of earnings and profits attributable to the stock).

(ii) *Analysis.* FT1's exchange is a specified exchange because the requirements set forth in paragraphs (e)(2)(i) through (iii) of this section are satisfied. The requirement set forth in paragraph (e)(2)(i) of this section is satisfied because, immediately before the exchange, FT2 (the foreign acquired corporation) is an expatriated foreign subsidiary and FT1 (the exchanging shareholder) is an expatriated foreign subsidiary that is described in paragraph (b)(1)(i)(A)(2) of this section. The requirement set forth in paragraph (e)(2)(ii) of this section is also satisfied because the stock received in the exchange (FS stock) is stock of a foreign corporation. The requirement set forth in paragraph (e)(2)(iii) of this section is satisfied because the exchange occurs during the applicable period. Accordingly, under paragraph (e)(1)(i) of this section, FT1 must include in income as a deemed dividend $30x, the section 1248 amount with respect to its FT2 stock. In addition, under paragraph (e)(1)(ii) of this section, FT1 must, after taking into account the increase in basis provided in § 1.367(b)-2(e)(3)(ii) resulting from the deemed dividend (which increases FT1's basis in its FT2 stock from $5x to $35x), recognize $15x ($50x amount realized less $35x basis), the realized gain with respect to the FT2 stock that would not otherwise be recognized.

Example 2. De minimis shift to non-EFS foreign related persons—(i) *Facts.* The facts are the same as in the introductory sentences of this paragraph (e)(5), except as follows. FT1 does not own any shares of FT2, and all 40 shares of FS are owned by DX, a domestic corporation wholly owned by individual A, and thus FS is not a non-EFS foreign related person. During the applicable period and pursuant to a reorganization described in section 368(a)(1)(D), FT1 transfers all of its assets to FS in exchange for 50 newly issued FS shares, FT1 distributes the 50 FS shares to USP in liquidation under section 361(c)(1), and USP exchanges its 50 shares of FT1 stock for the 50 FS shares under section 354. Further, immediately after the exchange, FS is a controlled foreign corporation.

(ii) *Analysis.* Although USP's exchange is a specified exchange, paragraph (e)(1) of this section does not apply to the exchange because, as described in paragraphs (ii)(A) through (C) of this *Example 2*, the requirements of paragraph (e)(3) of this section are satisfied.

(A) Because the assets, rather than the stock, of FT1 (the foreign acquired corporation) are acquired, the requirement set forth in paragraph (e)(3)(i) of this section is satisfied if FS (the transferee foreign corporation) is a controlled foreign corporation immediately after the exchange. As stated in the facts, FS is a controlled foreign corporation immediately after the exchange.

(B) The requirement set forth in paragraph (e)(3)(ii) of this section is satisfied if the post-exchange ownership percentage with respect to FS is at least 90% of the pre-exchange ownership percentage with respect to FT1. Because USP, a domestic corporation that is an expatriated entity, directly owns 50 shares of FT1 stock immediately before the exchange, none of those shares are treated as indirectly owned by FP (a non-EFS foreign related person) for purposes of calculating the pre-exchange ownership percentage with respect to FT1. See paragraph (g)(1) of this section. Thus, for purposes of calculating the pre-exchange ownership percentage with respect to FT1, FP is treated as directly or indirectly owning 0%, or 0 of 50 shares, of the stock of FT1. Accordingly, the pre-exchange ownership percentage with respect to FT1 is 100 (calculated as 100% less 0%, the percentage of FT1 stock that non-EFS foreign related persons are treated as directly or indirectly owning immediately before the exchange). Consequently, for the requirement set forth in paragraph (e)(3)(ii) of this section to be satisfied, the post-exchange ownership percentage with respect to FS must be at least 90. Because USP, a domestic corporation that is an expatriated entity, directly owns 50 shares of FS stock immediately after the exchange, none of those shares are treated as indirectly owned by FP (a non-EFS foreign related person) for purposes of calculating the post-exchange ownership percentage with respect to FS. See paragraph (g)(1) of this section. Thus, for purposes of calculating the post-exchange ownership percentage with respect to FS, FP is treated as directly or indirectly owning 0%, or 0 of 90 shares, of the stock of FS. As a result, the post-exchange ownership percentage with respect to FS is 100 (calculated as 100% less 0%, the percentage of FS stock that non-EFS foreign related persons are treated as directly or indirectly owning immediately after the exchange). Therefore, because the post-exchange ownership percentage with respect to FS (100) is at least 90, the requirement set forth in paragraph (e)(3)(ii) of this section is satisfied.

(C) Because there is not a lower-tier expatriated foreign subsidiary of FT1, the requirement set forth in paragraph (e)(3)(iii) of this section does not apply.

(f) *Gain recognition upon certain transfers of property described in section 351 following an inversion transaction.*—(1) *General rule.*—If, during the applicable period, an expatriated foreign subsidiary transfers specified property to a foreign corporation (the transferee foreign corporation) in an exchange described in section 351, then the expatriated foreign subsidiary must recognize all realized gain with respect to the specified property transferred that would not otherwise be recognized, unless the exception in paragraph (f)(2) of this section applies.

(2) *De minimis exception.*—The exception in this paragraph (f)(2) applies if—

(i) Immediately after the transfer, the transferee foreign corporation is a controlled foreign corporation; and

(ii) The post-exchange ownership percentage with respect to the transferee foreign corporation is at least 90 percent of the pre-exchange ownership percentage with respect to the expatriated foreign subsidiary.

(3) *Examples.*—The following examples illustrate the application of this paragraph (f). For purposes of all of the examples, unless otherwise indicated: FP, a foreign corporation, owns all of the stock of USP, a domestic corporation, and all 10 shares of stock of FS, a controlled foreign corporation for its taxable year beginning January 1, 2017, but not for prior taxable years, except as a result of a transaction described in the facts of an example. USP owns all 50 shares of stock of FT, a controlled foreign corporation. FT owns Asset A, which is specified property with a fair market value of $50x and an adjusted basis of $10x. FP acquired all of the stock of USP in an inversion transaction that was completed on or after September 22, 2014. Accordingly, with respect to that inversion transaction, USP is an expatriated entity, FT is an expatriated foreign subsidiary, and FP and FS are each a non-EFS foreign related person. All entities have a calendar year tax year for U.S. tax purposes. All shares of stock have a fair market value of $1x, and each corporation has a single class of stock outstanding.

Example 1. Transfer to which general rule applies—(i) *Facts.* In addition to the stock of USP and FS, FP owns Asset B, which has a fair market value of $40x. During the applicable period, and pursuant to an exchange described in section 351, FT transfers Asset A to FS in exchange for 50 newly issued shares of FS stock, and FP transfers Asset B to FS in exchange for 40 newly issued shares of FS stock.

(ii) *Analysis.* Paragraph (f)(1) of this section applies to the transfer by FT (an expatriated foreign subsidiary) of Asset A, which is specified property, to FS (the transferee foreign corporation). Thus, FT must recognize gain of $40x under paragraph (f)(1) of this section, which is the realized gain with respect to Asset A that would not otherwise be recognized ($50x amount realized less $10x basis). For rules regarding whether the FS stock held by FT is treated as United States property for purposes of section 956, see § 1.956-2(a)(4)(i).

Example 2. De minimis shift to non-EFS foreign related persons—(i) *Facts.* Individual, a United States person, owns Asset B, which has a fair market value of $40x. During the applicable period, and pursuant to an exchange described in section 351, FT transfers Asset A to FS in exchange for 50 newly issued shares of FS stock, and Individual transfers Asset B to FS in exchange for 40 newly issued shares of FS stock.

(ii) *Analysis.* Paragraph (f)(1) of this section does not apply to the transfer by FT (an expatriated foreign subsidiary) of Asset A, which is specified property, to FS (the transferee foreign corporation)) because the requirements set forth in paragraph (f)(2) of this section are satisfied. The requirement set forth in paragraph (f)(2)(i) of this section is satisfied because FS is a controlled foreign corporation immediately after the transfer. The requirement set forth in paragraph (f)(2)(ii) of this section is satisfied if the post-exchange ownership percentage with respect to FS is at least 90 percent of the pre-exchange ownership percentage with respect to FT. Because USP, a domestic corporation that is an expatriated entity, directly owns 50 shares of FT stock immediately before the transfer, none of those shares are treated as indirectly owned by FP (a non-EFS foreign related person) for purposes of calculating the pre-exchange ownership percentage with respect to FT. See paragraph (g)(1) of this section. Thus, for purposes of calculating the pre-exchange ownership percentage with respect to FT, FP is treated as directly or indirectly owning 0 percent, or 0 of 50 shares, of the stock of FT. Accordingly, the pre-exchange ownership percentage with respect to FT is 100 (calculated as 100 percent less 0 percent, the percentage of FT stock that non-EFS foreign related persons are treated as directly or indirectly owning immediately before the transfer). Consequently, for the requirement set forth in paragraph (f)(2)(ii) of this section to be satisfied, the post-exchange ownership percentage with respect to FS must be at least 90. Although FP directly owns 10 FS shares, none of the 50 FS shares that FP owns through USP (a domestic corporation that is an expatriated entity) are treated as indirectly owned by FP for purposes of calculating the post-exchange ownership percentage with respect to FS because USP directly owns them. See paragraph (g)(1) of this section. Thus, for purposes of calculating the post-exchange ownership percentage with respect to FS, FP is treated as directly or indirectly owning 10 percent, or 10 of 100 shares, of the stock of FS. As a result, the post-exchange ownership percentage with respect to FS is 90 (calculated as 100 percent less 10 percent, the percentage of FS stock that non-EFS foreign related persons are treated as directly or indirectly owning immediately after the transfer). Therefore, because the post-exchange ownership percentage with respect to FS (90) is at least 90, the requirement set forth in paragraph (f)(2)(ii) of this section is satisfied.

(g) *Definitions and special rules.*—In addition to the definitions and special rules in §§ 1.367(b)-2 and 1.7874-12, the following definitions and special rules apply for purposes of this section.

(1) *Indirect ownership.*—To determine indirect ownership of the stock of a corporation for purposes of calculating a pre-exchange ownership percentage or post-exchange ownership percentage with respect to that corporation, the principles of section 958(a) apply without regard to whether an intermediate entity is foreign or domestic. For this purpose, stock of the corporation that is directly or indirectly (applying the principles of section 958(a) without regard to whether an intermediate entity is foreign or domestic) owned by a domestic corporation that is an expatriated entity is not treated as indirectly owned by a non-EFS foreign related person.

(2) A *lower-tier expatriated foreign subsidiary* means an expatriated foreign subsidiary whose stock is directly or indirectly owned (under the principles of section 958(a)) by an expatriated foreign subsidiary.

(3) *Pre-exchange ownership percentage* means, with respect to a corporation, 100 percent less the percentage of stock (by value) in the corporation that, immediately before an exchange, is owned, in the aggregate, directly or indirectly by non-EFS foreign related persons.

(4) *Post-exchange ownership percentage* means, with respect to a corporation, 100 percent less the percentage of stock (by value) in the corporation that, immediately after the exchange, is owned, in the aggregate, directly or indirectly by non-EFS foreign related persons.

(5) *Specified property* means any property other than stock of a lower-tier expatriated foreign subsidiary.

(6) *Recapitalizations.*—A foreign corporation that undergoes a reorganization described in section 368(a)(1)(E) is treated as both the foreign acquired corporation and the transferee foreign corporation.

(7) *Triangular reorganizations.*—(i) *Definition.*—A triangular reorganization means a reorganization described in § 1.358-6(b)(2)(i) (forward triangular merger), (ii) (triangular C reorganization), (iii) (reverse triangular merger), (iv) (triangular B reorganization), and (v) (triangular G reorganization).

(ii) *Special rules.*—(A) *Triangular reorganizations other than a reverse triangular merger.*—In the case of a triangular reorganization other than a reverse triangular merger, the surviving corporation is the transferee foreign corporation that acquires the assets or stock of the foreign acquired corporation, and the reference to controlling corporation (foreign or domestic) is to the corporation that controls the surviving corporation.

(B) *Reverse triangular merger.*—In the case of a reverse triangular merger, the surviving corporation is the entity that survives the merger, and the controlling corporation (foreign or domestic) is the corporation that before the merger controls the merged corporation. In the case of a reverse triangular merger, this section applies only if stock of the foreign surviving corporation is exchanged for stock of a foreign corporation in control of the merging corporation; in such a case, the foreign surviving corporation is treated as a foreign acquired corporation.

(h) *Applicability date of certain paragraphs in this section.*—Except as otherwise provided in this paragraph (h), paragraphs (a), (b) introductory text, (b)(1)(i)(C), (d)(1), (e), (f), and (g) of this section apply to exchanges completed on or after September 22, 2014, but only if the inversion transaction was completed on or after September 22, 2014. Paragraph (e)(1)(ii) of this section applies to exchanges completed on or after November 19, 2015, but only if the inversion transaction was completed on or after September 22, 2014. The portion of paragraph (e)(2)(i) of this section that requires the exchanging shareholder to be an expatriated entity or an expatriated foreign subsidiary apply to exchanges completed on or after April 4, 2016, but only if the inversion transaction was completed on or after September 22, 2014. For inversion transactions completed on or after September 22, 2014, however, taxpayers may elect to apply the portion of paragraph (e)(2)(i) of this section that requires the exchanging shareholder to be an expatriated entity or an expatriated foreign subsidiary to exchanges completed on or after September 22, 2014, and before April 4, 2016. Paragraphs (f) and (g)(5) of this section apply to transfers completed on or after April 4, 2016, but only if the inversion transaction was completed or after September 22, 2014. See § 1.367(b)-4, as contained in 26 CFR part 1 revised as of April 1, 2016, for exchanges completed before September 22, 2014. Paragraph (b)(2)(i)(B) of this section applies to exchanges completed in taxable years of exchanging shareholders ending on or after November 2, 2020, and to taxable years of exchanging shareholders ending before November 2, 2020, resulting from an entity classification election made under § 301.7701-3 of this chapter that was effective on or before November 2, 2020, but was filed on or after November 2, 2020. [Reg. § 1.367(b)-4.]

☐ [*T.D.* 8770, 6-18-98 (*corrected* 3-31-99). *Amended by T.D.* 8862, 1-21-2000 (*corrected* 11-3-2000); *T.D.* 9243, 1-23-2006; *T.D.* 9250, 2-17-2006; *T.D.* 9311, 2-1-2007 *T.D.* 9345, 7-27-2007; *T.D.* 9446, 2-9-2009; *T.D.* 9444, 2-10-2009; *T.D.* 9614, 3-18-2013 *T.D.* 9760, 3-18-2016; *T.D.* 9761, 4-4-2016 (corrected 6-22-2016). *T.D.* 9834, 7-11-2018 *and T.D.* 9959, 12-28-2021 (*corrected* 7-26-2022).]

§ 1.367(b)-5. Distributions of stock described in section 355.—(a) *In general.*—(1) *Scope.*—This section provides rules relating to a distribution described in section 355 (or so much of section 356 as relates to section 355) and to which section 367(b) applies. For purposes of this section, the terms *distributing corporation*, *controlled corporation*, and *distributee* have the same meaning as used in section 355 and the regulations thereunder.

(2) *Treatment of distributees as exchanging shareholders.*—For purposes of the section 367(b) regulations, all distributees in a transaction described in paragraph (b), (c), or (d) of this section shall be

treated as exchanging shareholders that realize income in a section 367(b) exchange.

(b) *Distribution by a domestic corporation.*—(1) *General rule.*—In a distribution described in section 355, if the distributing corporation is a domestic corporation and the controlled corporation is a foreign corporation, the following general rules shall apply—

(i) If the distributee is a corporation, then the controlled corporation shall be considered to be a corporation; and

(ii) If the distributee is an individual, then, solely for purposes of determining the gain recognized by the distributing corporation, the controlled corporation shall not be considered to be a corporation, and the distributing corporation shall recognize any gain (but not loss) realized on the distribution.

(2) *Section 367(e) transactions.*—The rules of paragraph (b)(1) of this section shall not apply to a foreign distributee to the extent gain is recognized under section 367(e)(1) and the regulations thereunder.

(3) *Determining whether distributees are individuals.*—All distributees in a distribution described in paragraph (b)(1) of this section are presumed to be individuals. However, the shareholder identification principles of §1.367(e)-1(d) (including the reporting procedures in §1.367(e)-1(d)(2) and (3)) shall apply for purposes of rebutting this presumption.

(4) *Applicable cross-references.*—For rules with respect to a distributee that is a partnership, trust or estate, see §1.367(b)-2(k). For additional rules relating to a distribution of stock of a foreign corporation by a domestic corporation, see section 1248(f) and the regulations thereunder. For additional rules relating to a distribution described in section 355 by a domestic corporation to a foreign distributee, see section 367(e)(1) and the regulations thereunder.

(c) *Pro rata distribution by a controlled foreign corporation.*—(1) *Scope.*—This paragraph (c) applies to a distribution described in section 355 in which the distributing corporation is a controlled foreign corporation and in which the stock of the controlled corporation is distributed pro rata to each of the distributing corporation's shareholders.

(2) *Adjustment to basis in stock and income inclusion.*—If the distributee's postdistribution amount (as defined in paragraph (e)(2) of this section) with respect to the distributing or controlled corporation is less than the distributee's predistribution amount (as defined in paragraph (e)(1) of this section) with respect to such corporation, then the distributee's basis in such stock immediately after the distribution (determined under the normal principles of section 358) shall be reduced by the amount of the difference. However, the distributee's basis in such stock shall not be reduced below zero, and to the extent the foregoing reduction would have reduced basis below zero, the distributee shall instead include such amount in income as a deemed dividend from such corporation.

(3) *Interaction with §1.367(b)-2(e)(3)(ii).*—The basis increase provided in §1.367(b)-2(e)(3)(ii) shall not apply to a deemed dividend that is included in income pursuant to paragraph (c)(2) of this section.

(4) *Basis redistribution.*—If a distributee reduces the basis in the stock of the distributing or controlled corporation (or has an inclusion with respect to such stock) under paragraph (c)(2) of this section, the distributee shall increase its basis in the stock of the other corporation by the amount of the basis decrease (or deemed dividend inclusion) required by paragraph (c)(2) of this section. However, the distributee's basis in such stock shall not be increased above the fair market value of such stock and shall not be increased to the extent the increase diminishes the distributee's postdistribution amount with respect to such corporation.

(d) *Non-pro rata distribution by a controlled foreign corporation.*—(1) *Scope.*—This paragraph (d) applies to a distribution described in section 355 in which the distributing corporation is a controlled foreign corporation and in which the stock of the controlled corporation is not distributed pro rata to each of the distributing corporation's shareholders.

(2) *Treatment of certain shareholders as distributees.*—For purposes of the section 367(b) regulations, all persons owning stock of the distributing corporation immediately after a transaction described in paragraph (d)(1) of this section shall be treated as distributees of such stock. For other applicable rules, see paragraph (a)(2) of this section.

(3) *Inclusion of excess section 1248 amount by exchanging shareholder.*—If the distributee's postdistribution amount (as defined in paragraph (e)(2) of this section) with respect to the distributing or controlled corporation is less than the distributee's predistribution amount (as defined in paragraph (e)(1) of this section) with respect to such corporation, then the distributee shall include in income as a deemed dividend the amount of the difference. For purposes of this paragraph (d)(3), if a distributee owns no stock in the distributing or controlled corporation immediately after the distribution, the distributee's postdistribution amount with respect to such corporation shall be zero.

(4) *Interaction with §1.367(b)-2(e)(3)(ii).*—(i) *Limited application.*—The basis increase provided in §1.367(b)-2(e)(3)(ii) shall apply to a deemed dividend that is included in income pursuant to paragraph (d)(3) of this section only to the extent that such basis increase does not increase the distributee's basis above the fair market value of such stock and does not diminish the distributee's postdistribution amount with respect to such corporation.

(ii) *Interaction with predistribution amount.*—For purposes of this paragraph (d), the distributee's predistribution amount (as defined in paragraph (e)(1) of this section) shall be determined without regard to any basis increase permitted under paragraph (d)(4)(i) of this section.

(e) *Definitions.*—(1) *Predistribution amount.*—For purposes of this section, the predistribution amount with respect to a distributing or controlled corporation is the distributee's section 1248 amount (as defined in §1.367(b)-2(c)(1)) computed immediately before the distribution (and after any section 368(a)(1)(D) transfer connected with the section 355 distribution), but only to the extent that such amount is attributable to the distributing corporation and any corporations controlled by it immediately before the distribution (the distributing group) or the controlled corporation and any corporations controlled by it immediately before the distribution (the controlled group), as the case may be, under the principles of §§1.1248-1(d)(3), 1.1248-2 and 1.1248-3. However, the predistribution amount with regard to the distributing group shall be computed without taking into account the distributee's predistribution amount with respect to the controlled group.

(2) *Postdistribution amount.*—For purposes of this section, the postdistribution amount with respect to a distributing or controlled corporation is the distributee's section 1248 amount (as defined in §1.367(b)-2(c)(1)) with respect to such stock, computed immediately after the distribution (but without regard to paragraph (c) or (d) of this section (whichever is applicable)). The postdistribution amount under this paragraph (e)(2) shall be computed before taking into account the effect (if any) of any inclusion under section 356(a) or (b).

(f) *Exclusion of deemed dividend from foreign personal holding company income.*—In the event an amount is included in income as a deemed dividend by a foreign corporation under paragraph (c) or (d) of this section (including amounts received as an intermediate owner under the rule of §1.367(b)-2(e)(2)), such deemed dividend shall not be included as foreign personal holding company income under section 954(c).

(g) *Examples.*—The following examples illustrate the rules of this section:

Example 1—(i) *Facts.* USS, a domestic corporation, owns 40 percent of the outstanding stock of FD, a controlled foreign corporation (CFC). USS has owned the stock since FD was incorporated, and FD has always been a CFC. USS has a basis of $80 in its FD stock, which has a fair market value of $200. FD owns 100 percent of the outstanding stock of FC, a foreign corporation. FD has owned the stock since FC was incorporated. Neither FD nor FC own stock in any other corporation. FD has earnings and profits of $0 and a fair market value of $250 (not considering its ownership of FC). FC has earnings and profits of $300, none of which is described in section 1248(d), and a fair market value of $250. In a pro rata distribution described in section 355, FD distributes to USS stock in FC worth $100; thereafter, USS's FD stock is worth $100 as well.

(ii) *Result*—(A) FD's distribution is a transaction described in paragraph (c)(1) of this section. Under paragraph (c)(2) of this section, USS must compare its predistribution amounts with respect to FD and FC to its respective postdistribution amounts. Under paragraph (e)(1) of this section, USS's predistribution amount with respect to FD or FC is its section 1248 amount computed immediately before the distribution, but only to the extent such amount is attributable to FD or FC. Under § 1.367(b)-2(c)(1), USS's section 1248 amount computed immediately before the distribution is $120, all of which is attributable to FC. Thus, USS's predistribution amount with respect to FD is $0, and its predistribution amount with respect to FC is $120. These amounts are computed as follows: If USS had sold its FD stock immediately before the transaction, it would have recognized $120 of gain ($200 fair market value – $80 basis). All of the gain would have been treated as a dividend under section 1248, and all of the section 1248 amount would have been attributable to FC (based on USS's pro rata share of FC's earnings and profits (40 percent × $300)).

(B) Under paragraph (e)(2) of this section, USS's postdistribution amount with respect to FD or FC is its section 1248 amount with respect to such corporation, computed immediately after the distribution (but without regard to paragraph (c) of this section). Under § 1.367(b)-2(c)(1), USS's section 1248 amounts computed immediately after the distribution with respect to FD and FC are $0 and $60, respectively. These amounts, which are USS's postdistribution amounts, are computed as follows: Under the normal principles of section 358, USS allocates its $80 predistribution basis in FD between FD and FC according to the stock blocks' relative values, yielding a $40 basis in each block. If USS sold its FD stock immediately after the distribution, none of the resulting gain would be treated as a dividend under section 1248. If USS sold its FC stock immediately after the distribution, it would have a $60 gain ($100 fair market value – $40 basis), all of which would be treated as a dividend under section 1248.

(C) The basis adjustment and income inclusion rules of paragraph (c)(2) of this section apply to the extent of any difference between USS's postdistribution and predistribution amounts. In the case of FD, there is no difference between the two amounts and, as a result, no adjustment or income inclusion is required. In the case of FC, USS's postdistribution amount is $60 less than its predistribution amount. Accordingly, under paragraph (c)(2) of this section, USS is required to reduce its basis in its FC stock from $40 to $0 and include $20 in income as a deemed dividend. Under § 1.367(b)-2(e)(2), the $20 deemed dividend is considered as having been paid by FC to FD, and by FD to USS, immediately prior to the distribution. Under paragraph (f) of this section, the deemed dividend is not included by FD as foreign personal holding company income under section 954(c). Under paragraph (c)(3) of this section, the basis increase provided in § 1.367(b)-2(e)(3)(ii) does not apply with regard to the $20 deemed dividend. Under the rules of paragraph (c)(4) of this section, USS increases its basis in FD by the amount by which it decreased its basis in FC, as well as by the amount of its deemed dividend inclusion ($40 + $40 + $20 = $100).

Example 2—(i) *Facts*. USS1 and USS2, domestic corporations, each own 50 percent of the outstanding stock of FD, a controlled foreign corporation (CFC). USS1 and USS2 have owned their FD stock since it was incorporated, and FD has always been a CFC. USS1 and USS2 each have a basis of $500 in their FD stock, and the fair market value of each block of FD stock is $750. FD owns 100 percent of the outstanding stock of FC, a foreign corporation. FD owned the stock since FC was incorporated. Neither FD nor FC own stock in any other corporation. FD has earnings and profits of $0 and a fair market value of $750 (not considering its ownership of FC). FC has earnings and profits of $500, none of which is described in section 1248(d), and a fair market value of $750. In a non-pro rata distribution described in section 355, FD distributes all of the stock of FC to USS2 in exchange for USS2's FD stock.

(ii) *Result*—(A) FD's distribution is a transaction described in paragraph (d)(1) of this section. Under paragraph (d)(2) of this section, USS1 is considered a distributee of FD stock. Under paragraph (d)(3) of this section, USS1 and USS2 must compare their predistribution amounts with respect to FD and FC stock to their respective postdistribution amounts. Under paragraph (e)(1) of this section, USS1's predistribution amount with respect to FD or FC is USS1's section 1248 amount computed immediately before the distribution, but only to the extent such amount is attributable to FD or FC. USS2's predistribution amount is determined in the same manner. Under § 1.367(b)-2(c)(1), USS1 and USS2 each have a section 1248 amount computed immediately before the distribution of $250, all of which is attributable to FC. Thus, USS1 and USS2 each have a predistribution amount with respect to FD of $0, and each have a predistribution amount with respect to FC of $250. These amounts are computed as follows: If either USS1 or USS2 had sold its FD stock immediately before the transaction, it would have recognized $250 of gain ($750 fair market value – $500 basis). All of the gain would have been treated as a dividend under section 1248, and all of the section 1248 amount would have been attributable to FC (based on USS1's and USS2's pro rata shares of FC's earnings and profits (50 percent × $500)).

(B) Under paragraph (d)(3) of this section, a distributee that owns no stock in the distributing or controlled corporation immediately after the distribution has a postdistribution amount with regard to that stock of zero. Accordingly, USS2 has a postdistribution amount of $0 with respect to FD and USS1 has a postdistribution amount of $0 with respect to FC. Under paragraph (e)(2) of this section, USS1's postdistribution amount with respect to FD is its section 1248 amount with respect to such corporation, computed immediately after the distribution (but without regard to paragraph (d) of this section). USS2's postdistribution amount with respect to FC is determined in the same manner. Under § 1.367(b)-2(c)(1), USS1's section 1248 amount computed immediately after the distribution with respect to FD is $0 and USS2's section 1248 amount computed immediately after the distribution with respect to FC is $250. These amounts, which are USS1's and USS2's postdistribution amounts, are computed as follows: After the non-pro rata distribution, USS1 owns all the stock of FD and USS2 owns all the stock of FC. If USS1 sold its FD stock immediately after the distribution, none of the resulting $250 gain ($750 fair market value – $500 basis) would be treated as a dividend under section 1248. If USS2 sold its FC stock immediately after the distribution, it would have a $250 gain ($750 fair market value – $500 basis), all of which would be treated as a dividend under section 1248.

(C) The income inclusion rule of paragraph (d)(3) of this section applies to the extent of any difference between USS1's and USS2's postdistribution and predistribution amounts. In the case of USS2, there is no difference between the two amounts with respect to either FD or FC and, as a result, no income inclusion is required. In the case of USS1, there is no difference between the two amounts with respect to its FD stock. However, USS1's postdistribution amount with respect to FC is $250 less than its predistribution amount. Accordingly, under paragraph (d)(3) of this section, USS1 is required to include $250 in income as a deemed dividend. Under § 1.367(b)-2(e)(2), the $250 deemed dividend is considered as having been paid by FC to FD, and by FD to USS1, immediately prior to the distribution. This deemed dividend increases USS1's basis in FD ($500 + $250 = $750). Under paragraph (f) of this section, the deemed dividend is not included by FD as foreign personal holding company income under section 954(c).

[Reg. § 1.367(b)-5.]

☐ [*T.D.* 8862, 1-21-2000 (*corrected* 11-3-2000).]

Proposed Amendments to Regulation

§ 1.367(b)-5. Distributions of stock described in section 355.—

* * *

(b) * * *

(1) * * *

(ii) If the distributee is an individual or a tax-exempt entity as described in § 1.337(d)-4(c)(2) then, solely for purposes of determining the gain recognized by the distributing corporation, the controlled corporation shall not be considered to be a corporation, and the distributing corporation shall recognize any gain (but not loss) realized on the distribution.

* * *

(c) * * *

(2) *Adjustment to basis in stock and income inclusion.*—(i) *In general.*—If the distributee's postdistribution amount (as defined in paragraph (e)(2) of this section) with respect to the distributing or controlled corporation is less than the distributee's predistribution amount (as defined in paragraph (e)(1) of this section) with respect to such corporation, then the distributee's basis in such stock immediately after the distribution (determined under the normal principles of section 358) shall be reduced by the amount of the difference. However, the distributee's basis in such stock shall not be reduced below zero, and to the extent the foregoing reduction would have reduced basis below zero, the distributee shall instead include such amount in income as a deemed dividend from such corporation. See, e.g., paragraph (g) *Example 1* of this section.

(ii) *Exception.*—The basis reduction rule of paragraph (c)(2)(i) of this section shall apply only to the extent such reduction increases the distributee's section 1248 amount (as defined in § 1.367(b)-2(c)(1)) with respect to the distributing or controlled corporation; otherwise such basis reduction shall be replaced by the income inclusion rule of paragraph (c)(2)(i) of this section. See, e.g., § 1.367(b)-8(d)(6) *Example 2*.

* * *

(e) * * *

(3) *Divisive D reorganization with a preexisting controlled corporation.*—In the case of a transaction described in § 1.367(b)-8(b)(4), the predistribution amount with respect to a distributing or controlled corporation shall be computed after the allocation of the distributing corporation's earnings and profits described in § 1.367(b)-8(b)(4)(i)(A) and (b)(4)(ii)(A) (without regard to the parenthetical phrase in § 1.367(b)-8(b)(4)(ii)(A)), but before the reduction in the distributing corporation's earnings and profits described in § 1.367(b)-8(b)(4)(i)(B). See, e.g., § 1.367(b)-8(d)(6) *Example 3* and § 1.367(b)-8(e)(7) *Example 3.*

* * *

[Prop. Reg. § 1.367(b)-5.]

[Proposed 11-15-2000.]

§ 1.367(b)-6. Effective/applicability dates and coordination rules.—(a) *Effective/applicability dates.*—(1) *In general.*—(i) Except as otherwise provided in this paragraph (a)(1) and paragraph (a)(2) of this section, §§ 1.367(b)-1 through 1.367(b)-5, and this section, apply to section 367(b) exchanges that occur on or after February 23, 2000.

(ii) The rules of §§ 1.367(b)-3 and 1.367(b)-4, as they apply to reorganizations described in section 368(a)(1)(A) (including reorganizations described in section 368(a)(2)(D) or (a)(2)(E)) involving a foreign acquiring or foreign acquired corporation, apply only to transfers occurring on or after January 23, 2006.

(iii) Section 1.367(b)-1(c)(2)(v), (c)(3)(ii)(A), (c)(4)(iv), (c)(4)(v), § 1.367(b)-2(j)(1)(i) and (l), and § 1.367(b)-3(e) and (f), apply to section 367(b) exchanges that occur on or after November 6, 2006. For guidance with respect to § 1.367(b)-1(c)(3)(ii)(A), (c)(4)(iv), and (c)(4)(v) and § 1.367(b)-2(j)(1)(i) for exchanges that occur before November 6, 2006, see 26 CFR part 1 revised as of April 1, 2006.

(iv) Section 1.367(b)-4(b)(1)(i)(B)(2), § 1.367(b)-4(b)(1)(ii), § 1.367(b)-4(b)(1)(iii), *Example 4* and *Example 5* apply to section 367(b) exchanges that occur on or after April 18, 2013. For guidance with respect to § 1.367(b)-4(b)(1)(i)(B)(2), § 1.367(b)-4(b)(1)(ii) and § 1.367(b)-4(b)(1)(iii), *Example 4*, for exchanges that occur before April 18, 2013, see 26 CFR part 1 revised as of April 1, 2012.

(2) *Exception.*—A taxpayer may, however, elect to have §§ 1.367(b)-1 through 1.367(b)-5, and this section, apply to section 367(b) exchanges that occur (or occurred) before February 23, 2000, if the due date for the taxpayer's timely filed Federal tax return (including extensions) for the taxable year in which the section 367(b) exchange occurs (or occurred) is after February 23, 2000. The election under this paragraph (a)(2) will be valid only if—

(i) The electing taxpayer makes the election on a timely filed section 367(b) notice;

(ii) In the case of an exchanging shareholder that is a foreign corporation, the election is made on the section 367(b) notice that is filed by each of its shareholders listed in § 1.367(b)-1(c)(3)(ii); and

(iii) The electing taxpayer provides notice of the election to all corporations (or their successors in interest) whose earnings and profits are affected by the election on or before the date the section 367(b) notice is filed.

(b) *Certain recapitalizations described in § 1.367(b)-4(b)(3).*—In the case of a recapitalization described in § 1.367(b)-4(b)(3) that occurred prior to July 20, 1998, the exchanging shareholder shall include the section 1248 amount on its tax return for the taxable year that includes the exchange described in § 1.367(b)-4(b)(3)(i) (and not in the taxable year of the recapitalization), except that no inclusion is required if both the recapitalization and the exchange described in § 1.367(b)-4(b)(3)(i) occurred prior to July 20, 1998.

(c) *Use of reasonable method to comply with prior published guidance.*—(1) *Prior exchanges.*—The taxpayer may use a reasonable method to comply with the following prior published guidance to the extent such guidance relates to section 367(b): Notice 88-71 (1988-2 C.B. 374); Notice 89-30 (1989-1 C.B. 670); and Notice 89-79 (1989-2 C.B. 392) (see § 601.601(d)(2) of this chapter). This rule applies to section 367(b) exchanges that occur (or occurred) before February 23, 2000, or, if a taxpayer makes the election described in paragraph (a)(2) of this section, for section 367(b) exchanges that occur (or occurred) before the date described in paragraph (a)(2) of this section. This rule also applies to section 367(b) exchanges and distributions described in paragraph (d) of this section.

(2) *Future exchanges.*—Section 367(b) exchanges that occur on or after February 23, 2000, (or, if a taxpayer makes the election described in paragraph (a)(2) of this section, for section 367(b) exchanges that occur on or after the date described in paragraph (a)(2) of this section) are governed by the section 367(b) regulations and, as a result, paragraph (c)(1) of this section shall not apply.

(d) *Effect of removal of attribution rules.*—To the extent that the rules under §§ 7.367(b)-9 and 7.367(b)-10(h) of this chapter, as in effect prior to February 23, 2000 (see 26 CFR part 1 revised as of April 1, 1999), attributed earnings and profits to the stock of a foreign corporation in connection with an exchange described in section 351, 354, 355, or 356 before February 23, 2000, the foreign corporation shall continue to be subject to the rules of § 7.367(b)-12 of this chapter in the event of any subsequent exchanges and distributions with respect to such stock, notwithstanding the fact that such subsequent exchange or distribution occurs on or after the effective date described in paragraph (a) of this section. [Reg. § 1.367(b)-6.]

☐ [*T.D.* 8862, 1-21-2000. *Amended by T.D.* 9243, 1-23-2006 (*corrected* 5-15-2006); *T.D.* 9250, 2-17-2006; *T.D.* 9273, 8-7-2006 (*corrected* 3-17-2008); *T.D.* 9614, 3-18-2013 *and T.D.* 9834, 7-11-2018.]

§ 1.367(b)-7. Carryover of earnings and profits and foreign income taxes in certain foreign-to-foreign nonrecognition transactions.—(a) *Scope.*—This section applies to an acquisition by a foreign corporation (foreign acquiring corporation) of the assets of another foreign corporation (foreign target corporation) in a transaction described in section 381 (foreign section 381 transaction). This section describes the manner and extent to which earnings and profits and foreign income taxes of the foreign acquiring corporation and the foreign target corporation carry over to the surviving foreign corporation (foreign surviving corporation) and the ordering of distributions by the foreign surviving corporation. See § 1.367(b)-9 for special rules governing reorganizations described in section 368(a)(1)(F) and foreign section 381 transactions involving foreign corporations that hold no property and have no tax attributes immediately before the transaction, other than a nominal amount of assets (and related tax attributes).

(b) *General rules.*—(1) *Non-previously taxed earnings and profits and related taxes.*—Earnings and profits and related foreign income taxes of the foreign acquiring corporation and the foreign target corporation (pre-transaction earnings and pre-transaction taxes, respectively) shall carry over to the foreign surviving corporation in the manner described in paragraphs (d), (e), and (f) of this section. Dividend distributions by the foreign surviving corporation (post-transaction distributions) shall be out of earnings and profits and shall reduce related foreign income taxes in the manner described in paragraph (c) of this section. See paragraph (g) of this section for rules applicable to taxable years of foreign corporations beginning on or after January 1, 2018, and taxable years of United States shareholders in which or with which such taxable years of foreign corporations end ("post-2017 taxable years").

(2) *Previously taxed earnings and profits.*—[Reserved]

(c) *Ordering rule for post-transaction distributions.*—Dividend distributions out of a foreign surviving corporation's earnings and profits shall be ordered in accordance with the rules of paragraph (c)(1) or (2) of this section, depending on whether the foreign surviving corporation is a pooling corporation or a nonpooling corporation.

(1) *If foreign surviving corporation is a pooling corporation.*—In the case of a foreign surviving corporation that is a pooling corporation, post-transaction distributions shall be first out of the post-1986 pool (as described in paragraph (d) of this section) and second out of the pre-pooling annual layers (as described in paragraph (e)(1) of this section) under an annual last-in, first-out (LIFO) method.

(2) *If foreign surviving corporation is a nonpooling corporation.*—In the case of a foreign surviving corporation that is a nonpooling corporation, post-transaction distributions shall be out of the pre-pooling annual layers (as described in paragraph (e)(2) of this section) under the LIFO method.

(d) *Post-1986 pool.*—If the foreign surviving corporation is a pooling corporation, then the post-1986 pool shall be determined under the rules of this paragraph (d).

(1) *In general.*—(i) *Qualifying earnings and taxes.*—The post-1986 pool shall consist of the post-1986 undistributed earnings and related

post-1986 foreign income taxes of the foreign acquiring corporation and the foreign target corporation.

(ii) *Carryover rule.*—Subject to paragraph (d)(2) of this section, the amounts described in paragraph (d)(1)(i) of this section attributable to the foreign acquiring corporation and the foreign target corporation shall carry over to the foreign surviving corporation and shall be combined on a separate category-by-separate category basis.

(2) *Hovering deficit.* (i) *In general.* If immediately prior to the foreign section 381 transaction either the foreign acquiring corporation or the foreign target corporation has a deficit in one or more separate categories of post-1986 undistributed earnings or an aggregate deficit in pre-1987 accumulated profits, such deficit will be a hovering deficit of the foreign surviving corporation. The rules of this paragraph (d)(2) apply to hovering deficits in separate categories of post-1986 undistributed earnings. See paragraphs (e)(1)(iii) and (e)(2)(iii) of this section for rules that apply to hovering deficits in pre-1987 accumulated profits. If the foreign acquiring corporation and the foreign target corporation each have a post-1986 hovering deficit in the same separate category of post-1986 undistributed earnings, such deficits and their related post-1986 foreign income taxes shall be combined for purposes of applying this paragraph (d)(2). See also paragraphs (f)(1) and (4) of this section (describing other rules applicable to a deficit described in this paragraph (d)(2)).

(ii) *Offset rule.*—A hovering deficit in a separate category of post-1986 undistributed earnings shall offset only earnings and profits accumulated by the foreign surviving corporation after the foreign section 381 transaction (post-transaction earnings) in the same separate category of post-1986 undistributed earnings. For purposes of this rule, however, post-transaction earnings do not include post-1986 undistributed earnings in the same category that are earned after the foreign section 381 transaction, but are distributed or deemed distributed in the same year they are earned (that is, that do not become accumulated). The offset shall occur as of the first day of the foreign surviving corporation's first taxable year following the year in which the post-transaction earnings accumulated.

(iii) *Related taxes.*—Post-1986 foreign income taxes that are related to a hovering deficit in a separate category of post-1986 undistributed earnings shall only be added to the foreign surviving corporation's post-1986 foreign income taxes in that separate category on a pro rata basis as the hovering deficit is absorbed. Pro rata means in the same proportion as the portion of the hovering deficit that offsets post-transaction earnings in the separate category under paragraph (d)(2)(ii) of this section bears to the total amount of the hovering deficit.

(3) *Examples.*—The following examples illustrate the rules of this paragraph (d). The examples assume the following facts: foreign corporations A and B are controlled foreign corporations (CFCs) that were incorporated after December 31, 1986, have always been pooling corporations, and have always had calendar taxable years. None of the shareholders of foreign corporations A and B are required to include any amount in income under § 1.367(b)-4 as a result of the foreign section 381 transaction. Foreign corporations A and B (and all of their respective qualified business units as defined in section 989) maintain a "u" functional currency. Finally, unless otherwise stated, any post-1986 undistributed earnings in the passive category resulted from a look-through dividend that was paid by a lower-tier CFC out of earnings accumulated when the CFC was a noncontrolled section 902 corporation and that qualified for the subpart F same-country exception under section 954(c)(3)(A). The examples are as follows:

Example 1. (i) *Facts.* (A) On December 31, 2006, foreign corporations A and B have the following post-1986 undistributed earnings and post-1986 foreign income taxes:

Foreign Corporation A

Separate Category	*E&P*	*Foreign Taxes*
General	300u	$60
Passive	100u	$40
	400u	$100

Foreign Corporation B

Separate Category	*E&P*	*Foreign Taxes*
General	300u	$70

(B) On January 1, 2007, foreign corporation B acquires the assets of foreign corporation A in a reorganization described in section 368(a)(1)(C). Immediately following the foreign section 381 transaction, foreign surviving corporation is a CFC.

(ii) *Result.* Under the rules described in paragraph (d)(1) of this section, foreign surviving corporation has the following post-1986 undistributed earnings and post-1986 foreign income taxes:

Separate Category	*E&P*	*Foreign Taxes*
General	600u	$130
Passive	100u	$40
	700u	$170

(iii) *Post-transaction distribution.* (A) During 2007, foreign surviving corporation does not accumulate any earnings and profits or pay or accrue any foreign income taxes. On December 31, 2007, foreign surviving corporation distributes 350u to its shareholders. Under the rules described in § 1.902-1(d)(1) and paragraph (c)(1) of this section, the distribution is out of, and reduces, post-1986 undistributed earnings and post-1986 foreign income taxes in the separate categories on a pro rata basis, as follows:

Separate Category	*E&P*	*Foreign Taxes*
General	300u	$65
Passive	50u	$20
	350u	$85

(B) The foreign income taxes deemed paid by qualifying shareholders of foreign surviving corporation upon the distribution are subject to generally applicable rules and limitations, such as those of sections 78, 902, and 904(d).

(C) Immediately after the distribution, foreign surviving corporation has the following post-1986 undistributed earnings and post-1986 foreign income taxes:

Separate Category	*E&P*	*Foreign Taxes*
General	300u	$65
Passive	50u	$20
	350u	$85

Example 2. (i) *Facts.* (A) On December 31, 2006, foreign corporations A and B have the following post-1986 undistributed earnings and post-1986 foreign income taxes:

Foreign Corporation A

Separate Category	*E&P*	*Foreign Taxes*
General	200u	$30
Passive	(100u)	$10
	100u	$40

Foreign Corporation B

Separate Category	*E&P*	*Foreign Taxes*
General	300u	$60
Passive	100u	$30
	400u	$90

(B) On January 1, 2007, foreign corporation B acquires the assets of foreign corporation A in a reorganization described in section 368(a)(1)(C). Immediately following the foreign section 381 transaction, foreign surviving corporation is a CFC.

(ii) *Result*. Under the rules described in paragraphs (d)(1) and (2) of this section, foreign surviving corporation has the following post-1986 undistributed earnings and post-1986 foreign income taxes:

	Earnings & Profits:		*Foreign Taxes:*	
Separate Category	*Positive E&P*	*Hovering Deficit*	*Foreign Taxes Available*	*Foreign Taxes Associated with Hovering Deficit*
General	500u		$ 90	
Passive	100u	(100u)	$ 30	$10
	600u	(100u)	$120	$10

(iii) *Post-transaction distribution*. (A) During 2007, foreign surviving corporation does not accumulate any earnings and profits or pay or accrue any foreign income taxes. On December 31, 2007, foreign surviving corporation distributes 300u to its shareholders. Under the rules described in § 1.902-1(d)(1) and paragraph (c)(1) of this section, the distribution is out of, and reduces, post-1986 undistributed earnings and post-1986 foreign income taxes on a pro rata basis as follows:

Separate Category	*E&P*	*Foreign Taxes*
General	250u	$45
Passive	50u	$15
	300u	$60

(B) The foreign income taxes deemed paid by qualifying shareholders of foreign surviving corporation upon the distribution are subject to generally applicable rules and limitations, such as those of sections 78, 902, and 904(d).

(C) Immediately after the distribution, foreign surviving corporation has the following post-1986 undistributed earnings and post-1986 foreign income taxes:

	Earnings & Profits:		*Foreign Taxes:*	
Separate Category	*Positive E&P*	*Hovering Deficit*	*Foreign Taxes Available*	*Foreign Taxes Associated with Hovering Deficit*
General	250u		$45	
Passive	50u	(100u)	$15	$10
	300u	(100u)	$60	$10

(iv) *Post-transaction earnings*—(A) In its taxable year ending on December 31, 2008, foreign surviving corporation accumulates earnings and profits and pays related foreign income taxes as follows:

Separate Category	*E&P*	*Foreign Taxes*
General	100u	$20
Passive	50u	$10
	150u	$40

(B) None of foreign surviving corporation's earnings and profits for its 2008 taxable year qualifies as subpart F income as defined in section 952(a). Under the rules described in paragraphs (d)(2)(ii) and (iii) of this section, the hovering deficit in the passive category will offset the post-transaction earnings in that category and a proportionate amount of the foreign taxes related to the hovering deficit will be added to the post-1986 foreign income taxes pool. Because the post-transaction earnings in the passive category are half of the amount of the hovering deficit, half of the related taxes are added to the post-1986 foreign income taxes pool. Accordingly, foreign surviving corporation has the following post-1986 undistributed earnings and post-1986 foreign income taxes on January 1, 2009:

	Earnings & Profits:		*Foreign Taxes:*	
Separate Category	*Positive E&P*	*Hovering Deficit*	*Foreign Taxes Available*	*Foreign Taxes Associated with Hovering Deficit*
General	350u		$65	
Passive	50u	(50u)	$30	$5
	400u	(50u)	$95	$5

Example 3. (i) *Facts*. The facts are the same as *Example* 2, except that the 50u of earnings in the passive category accrued by foreign surviving corporation during 2008 is subpart F income, all of which is included in income under section 951(a) by United States shareholders (as defined in section 951(b)). This example assumes that none of the United States shareholders are able to reduce their subpart F income inclusion with a qualified deficit under section 952(c)(1)(B).

(ii) *Result*. (A) Under the rule described in paragraph (f)(1) of this section, the (100u) hovering deficit in the passive category does not reduce foreign surviving corporation's current passive earnings and profits for purposes of determining subpart F income or associated deemed paid credits. Thus, foreign surviving corporation's United States shareholders include their pro rata shares of 50u in taxable income for the year and are eligible for a deemed paid foreign tax credit under section 960, computed by reference to their pro rata shares of $12.50 (50u subpart F inclusion / (50u + 50u post-1986 undistributed earnings in the passive category = 100u) = 50%, × $25 post-1986 foreign income taxes in the passive category = $12.50). The United States shareholders will also include their pro rata shares of the deemed-paid taxes of $12.50 in taxable income for the year as a deemed dividend pursuant to section 78.

(B) Immediately after the subpart F inclusion and section 960 deemed paid taxes (and taking into account the taxable year 2008 earnings and profits and related taxes in the general category), foreign surviving corporation has the following post-1986 undistributed earnings and post-1986 foreign income taxes:

	Earnings & Profits:		*Foreign Taxes:*	
Separate Category	*Positive E&P*	*Hovering Deficit*	*Foreign Taxes Available*	*Foreign Taxes Associated with Hovering Deficit*
General	350u		$65.00	
Passive	50u	(100u)	$12.50	$10
	400u	(100u)	$77.50	$10

(C) The 50u included as subpart F income constitutes previously taxed earnings and profits under section 959.

Example 4. (i) *Facts.* (A) On December 31, 2006, foreign corporations A and B have the following post-1986 undistributed earnings and post-1986 foreign income taxes:

Foreign Corporation A		
Separate Category	*E&P*	*Foreign Taxes*
General	50u	$10
Foreign Corporation B		
Separate Category	*E&P*	*Foreign Taxes*
General	(100u)	$20

(B) On January 1, 2007, foreign corporation B acquires the assets of foreign corporation A in a reorganization described in section 368(a)(1)(C). Immediately following the foreign section 381 transaction, foreign surviving corporation is a CFC.

(ii) *Result.* Under the rules described in paragraphs (d)(1) and (2) of this section, foreign surviving corporation has the following post-1986 undistributed earnings and post-1986 foreign income taxes:

	Earnings & Profits:		*Foreign Taxes:*	
Separate Category	*Positive E&P*	*Hovering Deficit*	*Foreign Taxes Available*	*Foreign Taxes Associated with Hovering Deficit*
General	50u	(100u)	$10	$20

(iii) *Post-transaction earnings and distribution.* (A) In its taxable year ending on December 31, 2007, foreign surviving corporation earns 100u in the general category and pays related foreign income taxes of $24. On December 31, 2007, foreign surviving corporation distributes 75u to its shareholders.

(B) *Result.* For purposes of determining the dividend amount under section 316 and the foreign income taxes deemed paid with respect to that dividend under section 902, under paragraph (d)(2)(ii) of this section the hovering deficit does not offset the post-transaction current year earnings. Accordingly, the full 75u will be a dividend under section 316. The deemed paid taxes on that dividend are $17 (75u distribution / (100u current earnings + 50u accumulated earnings) = 50%, × ($10 accumulated foreign taxes + $24 current year foreign taxes) = $17). The 25u of undistributed earnings and profits in 2007 will be offset by (25u) of the hovering deficit for purposes of determining the opening balance of the post-1986 undistributed earnings pool in 2008. Because the amount of earnings offset by the hovering deficit is 25% of the amount of the hovering deficit, under paragraph (d)(2)(iii) of this section $5 (25% of $20) of the related taxes are added to the post-1986 foreign income taxes pool at the beginning of the next taxable year. Accordingly, foreign surviving corporation has the following post-1986 undistributed earnings and post-1986 foreign income taxes on January 1, 2008:

	Earnings & Profits:		*Foreign Taxes:*	
Separate Category	*Positive E&P*	*Hovering Deficit*	*Foreign Taxes Available*	*Foreign Taxes Associated with Hovering Deficit*
General	50u	(75u)	$22	$15

(e) *Pre-pooling annual layers.*—(1) *If foreign surviving corporation is a pooling corporation.*—If the foreign surviving corporation is a pooling corporation, the pre-pooling annual layers shall be determined under the rules of this paragraph (e)(1).

(i) *Qualifying earnings and taxes.*—The pre-pooling annual layers shall consist of the pre-1987 accumulated profits and the pre-1987 foreign income taxes of the foreign acquiring corporation and the foreign target corporation.

(ii) *Carryover rule.*—Subject to paragraph (e)(1)(iii) of this section, the amounts described in paragraph (e)(1)(i) of this section shall carry over to the foreign surviving corporation but shall not be combined. If the foreign acquiring corporation and the foreign target corporation have pre-1987 accumulated profits in the same year and a distribution is made therefrom, the rules of § 1.902-1(b)(2)(ii) and (b)(3) shall apply separately to reduce pre-1987 accumulated profits and pre-1987 foreign income taxes of the foreign acquiring corporation and the foreign target corporation on a pro rata basis. For further guidance, see Rev. Rul. 68-351 (1968-2 C.B. 307); Rev. Rul. 70-373 (1970-2 C.B. 152) (see also § 601.601(d)(2) of this chapter); see also paragraph (f)(2) of this section (governing the reconciliation of taxable years).

(iii) *Deficit.*—(A) *In general.*—The rules of this paragraph (e)(1)(iii) apply when, immediately prior to the foreign section 381 transaction, the foreign acquiring corporation or the foreign target corporation (or both) has a deficit in earnings and profits for one or more of the years that comprise its pre-1987 accumulated profits (see also paragraphs (f)(1) and (4) of this section, describing other rules applicable to a deficit described in this paragraph (e)(1)(iii)).

(B) *Aggregate positive pre-1987 accumulated profits.*—If the foreign acquiring corporation or the foreign target corporation (or both) has an aggregate positive (or zero) amount of pre-1987 accumulated profits, but a deficit in earnings and profits for one or more years, then the rules otherwise applicable to such deficits shall apply separately to the pre-1987 accumulated profits and related pre-1987 foreign income taxes of such corporation. A deficit in pre-1987 accumulated profits for one or more years is applied to reduce pre-1987 accumulated profits on a LIFO basis. Any remaining deficit shall be applied to reduce pre-1987 accumulated profits in succeeding years. See Rev. Rul. 74-550 (1974-2 C.B. 209) (see also § 601.601(d)(2) of this chapter); *Champion Int'l Corp. v. Commissioner*, 81 T.C. 424 (1983), acq. in result, 1987-2 C.B. 1; Rev. Rul. 87-72 (1987-2 C.B. 170) (see also § 601.601(d)(2) of this chapter). As a result, no amount in excess of the aggregate positive amount of pre-1987 accumulated profits shall be distributed from the pre-transaction earnings of the foreign acquiring corporation or the foreign target corporation.

(C) *Aggregate deficit in pre-1987 accumulated profits.*—If the foreign acquiring corporation or the foreign target corporation (or both) has an aggregate deficit in pre-1987 accumulated profits, a hovering deficit as defined under paragraph (d)(2)(i) of this section, then the rules under § 1.902-2(b) shall apply to such hovering deficit (and related pre-1987 foreign income taxes) immediately prior to the transaction, except that the aggregate hovering deficit that is carried forward into the foreign surviving corporation's post-1986 pool shall offset only post-transaction earnings accumulated by the foreign surviving corporation in the same separate category of post-1986 undistributed earnings to which the relevant portion of the hovering deficit is attributable. Post-transaction earnings do not include earnings and profits that are earned after the foreign section 381 transaction but distributed or deemed distributed in the same year they are earned.

(D) *Deficit and positive separate categories within annual layers.*—For purposes of applying the rules of paragraphs (e)(1)(iii)(B) and (C) of this section, if within a single pre-pooling annual layer, the foreign acquiring corporation or the foreign target corporation (or both) has a deficit in pre-1987 accumulated profits in a separate category and positive pre-1987 accumulated profits in another separate category, the deficit shall first be used to offset the positive pre-1987 accumulated profits in the other separate category in the same pre-pooling annual layer. Any remaining deficit shall be carried forward or back to other years according to the rules of paragraph (e)(1)(iii)(B) or (C) of this section as applicable.

(iv) *Pre-1987 section 960 earnings and profits and foreign income taxes.*—The pre-1987 section 960 earnings and profits and pre-1987 section 960 foreign income taxes of the foreign acquiring corporation and the foreign target corporation shall carry over to the foreign surviving corporation but shall not be combined. The rules otherwise applicable to such amounts shall apply separately to the pre-1987 section 960 earnings and profits and pre-1987 section 960 foreign income taxes of the foreign acquiring corporation and the foreign target corporation on a pro rata basis. For further guidance, see Notice 88-70 (1988-2 C.B. 369) (see also § 601.601(d)(2) of this chapter).

(v) *Examples.*—The following examples illustrate the rules of this paragraph (e)(1). The examples assume the following facts: foreign corporation A was incorporated in 2003 and was a nonpooling corporation through December 31, 2004. Foreign corporation A became a CFC on January 1, 2005 and, as a result, began to maintain a pool of post-1986 undistributed earnings on that date. Foreign corporation B was incorporated in 2003 and has always been owned by foreign shareholders (and thus never has met the requirements of section 902(c)(3)(B)). Both foreign corporation A and foreign corporation B have always had calendar taxable years. Foreign corporations A and B (and all of their respective qualified business units as defined in section 989) maintain a "u" functional currency. Finally, unless otherwise stated, all earnings and profits of foreign corporations A and B are in the general category. The examples are as follows:

Example 1. (i) *Facts.* (A) On December 31, 2006, foreign corporations A and B have the following earnings and profits and foreign income taxes:

Foreign Corporation A	*E&P*	*Foreign Taxes*
Post-1986 pool	1,000u	$350
2004	400u	160u
2003	100u	5u
	1,500u	

Foreign Corporation B	*E&P*	*Foreign Taxes*
2006	100u	20u
2005	150u	30u
2004	0u	50u
2003	50u	5u
	300u	105u

(B) On January 1, 2007, foreign corporation B acquires the assets of foreign corporation A in a reorganization described in section 368(a)(1)(C). Immediately following the foreign section 381 transaction, foreign surviving corporation is a CFC.

(ii) *Result.* Under the rules described in paragraphs (e)(1)(i) and (ii) of this section, foreign surviving corporation has the following earnings and profits and foreign income taxes:

	E&P	*Foreign Taxes*
Post-1986 pool	1,000u	$350
2006	100u	20u
2005	150u	30u
Two Side-by-Side Layers of 2004 E&P:		
2004 layer #1 (from Corp A)	400u	160u
2004 layer #2 (from Corp B)	0u	50u
Two Side-by-Side Layers of 2003 E&P:		
2003 layer #1 (from Corp A)	100u	5u
2003 layer #2 (from Corp B)	50u	5u
	1,800u	

(iii) *Post-transaction distribution.* (A) During 2007, foreign surviving corporation does not accumulate any earnings and profits or pay or accrue any foreign income taxes. On December 31, 2007, foreign surviving corporation distributes 1,725u to its shareholders. Under the rules of paragraph (c)(1) of this section, the distribution is first out of the post-1986 pool, and then out of the pre-pooling annual layers under the LIFO method, as follows:

	E&P	*Foreign Taxes*
Post-1986 pool	1,000u	$350
2006	100u	20u
2005	150u	30u
Two Side-by-Side Layers of 2004 E&P:		
2004 layer #1	400u	160u
2004 layer #2	0u	0u
Two Side-by-Side Layers of 2003 E&P:		
2003 layer #1	50u	2.5u
(100u in layer / 150u aggregate 2003 earnings = 66.67% × 75u distribution)		
2003 layer #2	25u	2.5u
(50u in layer / 150u aggregate 2003 earnings = 33.33% × 75u distribution)		
	1,725u	

(B) The foreign income taxes deemed paid by qualifying shareholders of foreign surviving corporation upon the distribution are subject to generally applicable rules and limitations, such as those of sections 78, 902, and 904(d).

(C) Immediately after the distribution, foreign surviving corporation has the following earnings and profits and foreign income taxes:

	E&P	Foreign Taxes
2004 layer #2	0u	50u
Two Side-by-Side Layers of 2003 E&P:		
2003 layer #1	50u	2.5u
2003 layer #2	25u	2.5u
	75u	55u

(iv) *Post-transaction earnings.* For the taxable year ending on December 31, 2008, foreign surviving corporation has 500u of current earnings and profits in the general category, none of which qualify as subpart F income under section 952(a), and pays $70 in foreign income taxes. As of the close of the 2008 taxable year, foreign surviving corporation has the following earnings and profits and foreign income taxes:

	E&P	Foreign Taxes
Post-1986 pool	500u	$70
2004	0u	50u
Two Side-by-Side Layers of 2003 E&P:		
2003 layer #1	50u	2.5u
2003 layer #2	25u	2.5u
	575u	

Example 2. (i) *Facts.* (A) On December 31, 2006, foreign corporations A and B have the following earnings and profits and foreign income taxes:

Foreign Corporation A	E&P	Foreign Taxes
Post-1986 pool	1,000u	$350
2004	100u	20u
2003	(50u)	5u
	1,050u	

Foreign Corporation B	E&P	Foreign Taxes
2006	100u	20u
2005	(50u)	5u
2004	0u	50u
2003	100u	10u
	150u	85u

(B) On January 1, 2007, foreign corporation B acquires the assets of foreign corporation A in a reorganization described in section 368(a)(1)(C). Immediately following the foreign section 381 transaction, foreign surviving corporation is a CFC.

(ii) *Result.* Because foreign corporations A and B have aggregate positive amounts of pre-1987 accumulated profits with a deficit in one or more years, the rules of paragraph (e)(1)(iii)(B) of this section apply. Accordingly, after the foreign section 381 transaction, foreign surviving corporation has the following earnings and profits and foreign income taxes:

	Earnings & Profits:		*Foreign Taxes:*	
	Positive E&P	Deficit E&P	Foreign Taxes Available	Foreign Taxes Associated with Deficit E&P
Post-1986 pool	1,000u		$350	
2006	100u		20u	
2005		(50u)		5u
Two Side-by-Side Layers of 2004 E&P:				
2004 layer #1 (from Corp A)	100u		20u	
2004 layer #2 (from Corp B)	0u		50u	
Two Side-by-Side Layers of 2003 E&P:				
2003 layer #1 (from Corp A)		(50u)		5u
2003 layer #2 (from Corp B)	100u		10u	
	1,300u	(100u)		10u

(iii) *Post-transaction distribution.* (A) During 2007, foreign surviving corporation does not accumulate any earnings and profits or pay or accrue any foreign income taxes. On December 31, 2007, foreign surviving corporation distributes 1,175u to its shareholders. Under the rules described in paragraphs (c)(1) and (e)(1)(iii)(B) of this section, the distribution is first out of the post-1986 pool, and then out of the pre-pooling annual layers, as follows:

Distribution	E&P	Foreign Taxes
Post-1986 pool	1,000u	$350
2006	100u	20u
2005	0u	0u
Two Side-by-Side Layers of 2004 E&P:		
2004 layer #1	50u	20u
2004 layer #2	0u	0u
Two Side-by-Side Layers of 2003 E&P:		
2003 layer #1	0u	0u
2003 layer #2	25u	5u
	1,175u	

(B) Under paragraph (e)(1)(iii)(B) of this section, the rules otherwise applicable when a foreign corporation has an aggregate positive (or zero) amount of pre-1987 accumulated profits, but a deficit in one or more years, apply separately to the pre-1987 accumulated profits and related foreign income taxes of foreign corporation A and foreign corporation B. As a result, distributions out of the pre-pooling annual layers of foreign corporation A and foreign corporation B cannot exceed the aggregate positive amount of pre-1987 accumulated profits of each corporation. Accordingly, only 50u can be distributed from foreign corporation A's pre-pooling annual layers and is out of its 2004 layer #1 (after rolling forward the (50u) deficit in 2003 layer #1 to reduce earnings in 2004 layer #1 to 50u

(100u - 50u)). Under the principles of § 1.902-1(b)(3), the full 20u of taxes related to 2004 layer #1 is reduced or deemed paid ($20 × (50/50)). 100u is distributed from foreign corporation B's 2006 annual layer. Foreign corporation B's (50u) deficit in 2005 is then rolled back to offset its 2003 annual layer to reduce earnings in that layer to 50u, 25u of which is distributed. Thus, after the distribution, 25u remains in 2003 layer # 2 along with 5u of foreign income taxes (10u × (25u / 50u)).

(C) The foreign income taxes deemed paid by qualifying shareholders of foreign surviving corporation upon the distribution are subject to generally applicable rules and limitations, such as those of sections 78, 902, and 904(d).

(D) Immediately after the distribution, foreign surviving corporation has the following earnings and profits and foreign income taxes:

	E&P	*Foreign Taxes*
2005	0u	5u
2004 layer #2	0u	50u
Two Side-by-Side Layers of 2003 E&P:		
2003 layer #1	0u	5u
2003 layer #2	25u	5u
	25u	65u

(E) Under paragraph (e)(1)(iii)(B) of this section, the 5u, 50u, and 5u of pre-1987 foreign income taxes related to foreign surviving corporation's 2005 layer, 2004 layer #2, and 2003 layer #1, respectively, remain in those layers. These foreign income taxes generally will not be reduced or deemed paid unless a foreign tax refund restores a positive balance to the associated earnings pursuant to section 905(c), and thus will be trapped. See § 1.902-2(b)(2).

Example 3. (i) *Facts.* (A) On December 31, 2006, foreign corporations A and B have the following earnings and profits and foreign income taxes:

Foreign Corporation A	*E&P*	*Foreign Taxes*
Post-1986 pool	1,000u	$350
2004	150u	20u
2003	100u	5u
	1,250u	

Foreign Corporation B	*E&P*	*Foreign Taxes*
2006	100u	20u
2005	(250u)	5u
2004	0u	50u
2003	100u	10u
	(50u)	85u

(B) On January 1, 2007, foreign corporation B acquires the assets of foreign corporation A in a reorganization described in section 368(a)(1)(C). Immediately following the foreign section 381 transaction, foreign surviving corporation is a CFC.

(ii) *Result.* (A) Because foreign corporation B has an aggregate hovering deficit in pre-1987 accumulated profits, the rules of paragraph (e)(1)(iii)(C) of this section apply. Accordingly, § 1.902-2(b) applies immediately prior to the foreign section 381 transaction, except that the hovering deficit is carried forward into the foreign surviving corporation's post-1986 undistributed earnings pool and will offset only post-transaction earnings accumulated by foreign surviving corporation in the general category. Accordingly, after the foreign section 381 transaction, foreign surviving corporation has the following earnings and profits and foreign income taxes:

	Earnings & Profits:		*Foreign Taxes:*	
	Positive E&P	*Hovering Deficit*	*Foreign Taxes Available*	*Foreign Taxes Associated with Hovering Deficit*
Post-1986 pool	1,000u	(50u)	$350	$0
2006	0u		20u	
2005	0u		5u	
Two Side-by-Side Layers of 2004 E&P:				
2004 layer #1 (from Corp A)	150u		20u	
2004 layer #2 (from Corp B)	0u		50u	
Two Side-by-Side Layers of 2003 E&P:				
2003 layer #1 (from Corp A)	100u		5u	
2003 layer #2 (from Corp B)	0u		10u	
	1,250u	(50u)		$0

(B) Under paragraph (e)(1)(iii)(C) of this section, the 20u, 5u, 50u, and 10u of pre-1987 foreign income taxes associated with foreign corporation B's pre-1987 accumulated profits for 2006, 2005, 2004 layer #2, and 2003 layer #2, respectively, remain in those layers. These foreign income taxes generally will not be reduced or deemed paid unless a foreign tax refund restores a positive balance to the associated earnings pursuant to section 905(c), and thus will be trapped. See § 1.902-2(b)(2).

(2) *If foreign surviving corporation is a nonpooling corporation.*—If the foreign surviving corporation is a nonpooling corporation, then the pre-pooling annual layers shall be determined under the rules of this paragraph (e)(2).

(i) *Qualifying earnings and taxes.*—The pre-pooling annual layers shall consist of the pre-1987 accumulated profits and the pre-1987 foreign income taxes of the foreign acquiring corporation and the foreign target corporation. If the foreign acquiring corporation or the foreign target corporation (or both) has post-1986 undistributed earnings or a deficit in post-1986 undistributed earnings, then those earnings or deficits and any related post-1986 foreign income taxes shall be recharacterized as pre-1987 accumulated profits or deficits and pre-1987 foreign income taxes of the foreign acquiring corporation or the foreign target corporation accumulated immediately prior to the foreign section 381 transaction.

(ii) *Carryover rule.*—Subject to paragraph (e)(2)(iii) of this section, the amounts described in paragraph (e)(2)(i) of this section shall carry over to the foreign surviving corporation but shall not be combined. If the foreign acquiring corporation and the foreign target corporation have pre-1987 accumulated profits in the same year and a distribution is made therefrom, the principles of § 1.902-1(b)(2)(ii) and (3) shall apply separately to reduce pre-1987 accumulated profits and pre-1987 foreign income taxes of the foreign acquiring corporation and the foreign target corporation on a pro rata basis. For further guidance, see Rev. Rul. 68-351 (1968-2 C.B. 307); Rev. Rul. 70-373 (1970-2 C.B. 152) (see also § 601.601(d)(2) of this chapter); see also paragraph (f)(2) of this section (governing the reconciliation of taxable years).

(iii) *Deficits.*—(A) *In general.*—The rules of this paragraph (e)(2)(iii) apply when, immediately prior to the foreign section 381 transaction (and after application of the last sentence of paragraph (e)(2)(i) of this section), the foreign acquiring corporation or the foreign target corporation (or both) has a deficit in one or more years that comprise its pre-1987 accumulated profits. See also paragraphs (f)(1) and (4) of this section (describing other rules applicable to a deficit described in this paragraph (e)(2)(iii)).

(B) *Aggregate positive pre-1987 accumulated profits.*—If the foreign acquiring corporation or the foreign target corporation (or both) has an aggregate positive (or zero) amount of pre-1987 accumulated profits, but a deficit in pre-1987 accumulated profits in one or more years, then the rules otherwise applicable to such deficits shall apply separately to the pre-1987 accumulated profits and related foreign income taxes of such corporation. A deficit in pre-1987 accumulated profits for one or more years is applied to reduce pre-1987 accumulated profits on a LIFO basis. Any remaining deficit shall be applied to reduce pre-1987 accumulated profits in succeeding years. See Rev. Rul. 74-550 (1974-2 C.B. 209) (see also § 601.601(d)(2) of this chapter); *Champion Int'l Corp. v. Commissioner*, 81 T.C. 424 (1983), acq. in result, 1987-2 C.B. 1; Rev. Rul. 87-72 (1987-2 C.B. 170) (see also § 601.601(d)(2) of this chapter). As a result, no amount in excess of the aggregate positive amount of pre-1987 accumulated profits shall be distributed from the pre-transaction earnings of the foreign acquiring corporation or the foreign target corporation.

(C) *Aggregate deficit in pre-1987 accumulated profits.*—If the foreign acquiring corporation or the foreign target corporation (or both) has an aggregate deficit in pre-1987 accumulated profits, a hovering deficit as defined under paragraph (d)(2)(i) of this section, then the rules otherwise applicable to such hovering deficits shall apply separately to the pre-transaction earnings and profits and related taxes of the relevant corporation. See, e.g., sections 316(a) and 381(c)(2)(B). Thus, any hovering deficit shall offset only post-transaction earnings accumulated by the foreign surviving corporation in the same separate category of earnings and profits to which the relevant portion of the hovering deficit is attributable. Post-transaction earnings do not include earnings and profits that are earned after the foreign section 381 transaction but distributed or deemed distributed in the same year they are earned. Following the principles of § 1.902-2(b), if there is an aggregate deficit in pre-1987 accumulated profits, any related pre-1987 foreign income taxes generally will not be reduced or deemed paid unless a foreign tax refund restores a positive balance to the associated earnings pursuant to section 905(c), and creates a pre-transaction aggregate positive balance for pre-1987 accumulated profits.

(D) *Deficit and positive separate categories within annual layers.*—For purposes of applying the rules of paragraphs (e)(2)(iii)(B) and (C) of this section, if within a single pre-pooling annual layer, the foreign acquiring corporation or the foreign target corporation (or both) has a deficit in pre-1987 accumulated profits in a separate category and positive pre-1987 accumulated profits in another separate category, the deficit shall first be used to offset the positive pre-1987 accumulated profits in the other separate category in the same pre-pooling annual layer. Any remaining deficit shall be carried forward or back to other years according to the rules of paragraph (e)(2)(iii)(B) or (C) as applicable.

(iv) *Pre-1987 section 960 earnings and profits and foreign income taxes.*—The pre-1987 section 960 earnings and profits and pre-1987 section 960 foreign income taxes of the foreign acquiring corporation and the foreign target corporation shall carry over to the foreign surviving corporation but shall not be combined. The rules otherwise applicable to such amounts shall apply separately to the pre-1987 section 960 earnings and profits and pre-1987 section 960 foreign income taxes of the foreign acquiring corporation and the foreign target corporation on a pro rata basis. For further guidance, see Notice 88-70 (1988-2 C.B. 369) (see also § 601.601(d)(2) of this chapter).

(v) *Examples.*—The following examples illustrate the rules of this paragraph (e)(2). The examples assume the following facts: both foreign corporation A and foreign corporation B have always had calendar taxable years. Foreign corporations A and B (and all of their respective qualified business units as defined in section 989) maintain a "u" functional currency, and 1u = US$1 at all times. Finally, unless otherwise stated, all earnings and profits of foreign corporations A and B are in the general category. The examples are as follows:

Example 1. (i) *Facts.* (A) Foreign corporations A and B both were incorporated in 2003. Nine percent of the voting stock of foreign corporation A is owned by domestic corporate shareholder C. Nine percent of the voting stock of foreign corporation B is owned by domestic corporate shareholder D. Shareholders C and D are unrelated. The remaining 91% of the voting stock of each foreign corporation is owned by unrelated foreign shareholders. Thus, neither corporation meets the requirements of section 902(c)(3)(B). On December 31, 2006, foreign corporations A and B have the following earnings and profits and foreign income taxes:

Foreign Corporation A	*E&P*	*Foreign Taxes*
2006	500u	350u
2005	400u	300u
2004	400u	160u
2003	100u	5u
	1,400u	815u

Foreign Corporation B	*E&P*	*Foreign Taxes*
2006	100u	20u
2005	300u	60u
2004	0u	50u
2003	50u	5u
	450u	135u

(B) On January 1, 2007, foreign corporation B acquires the assets of foreign corporation A in a reorganization described in section 368(a)(1)(C). Immediately following the foreign section 381 transaction, foreign surviving corporation is a nonpooling corporation that does not meet the requirements of section 902(c)(3)(B).

(ii) *Result.* Under the rules described in paragraphs (e)(2)(i) and (ii) of this section, foreign surviving corporation has the following earnings and profits and foreign income taxes:

	E&P	*Foreign Taxes*
Two Side-by-Side Layers of 2006 E&P:		
2006 layer #1 (from Corp A)	500u	350u
2006 layer #2 (from Corp B)	100u	20u
Two Side-by-Side Layers of 2005 E&P:		
2005 layer #1 (from Corp A)	400u	300u
2005 layer #2 (from Corp B)	300u	60u
Two Side-by-Side Layers of 2004 E&P:		
2004 layer #1 (from Corp A)	400u	160u
2004 layer #2 (from Corp B)	0u	50u
Two Side-by-Side Layers of 2003 E&P:		
2003 layer #1 (from Corp A)	100u	5u
2003 layer #2 (from Corp B)	50u	5u
	1,850u	950u

(iii) *Post-transaction distribution.* (A) During 2007, foreign surviving corporation does not accumulate any earnings and profits or pay or accrue any foreign income taxes. On December 31, 2007, foreign surviving corporation distributes 600u to its shareholders. Under the rules of paragraph (c)(3) of this section, the distribution is out of pre-pooling annual layers under the LIFO method as follows:

	E&P	Foreign Taxes
Two Side-by-Side Layers of 2006 E&P:		
2006 layer #1 (from Corp A)	500u	350u
2006 layer #2 (from Corp B)	100u	20u
	600u	370u

(B) Foreign surviving corporation's foreign income tax accounts are reduced to reflect the distribution of earnings and profits notwithstanding that no shareholders are eligible to claim deemed paid foreign income taxes under section 902. See § 1.902-1(a)(10)(iii).

(C) Immediately after the distribution, foreign surviving corporation has the following earnings and profits and foreign income taxes:

	E&P	Foreign Taxes
Two Side-by-Side Layers of 2005 E&P:		
2005 layer #1 (from Corp A)	400u	300u
2005 layer #2 (from Corp B)	300u	60u
Two Side-by-Side Layers of 2004 E&P:		
2004 layer #1 (from Corp A)	400u	160u
2004 layer #2 (from Corp B)	0u	50u
Two Side-by-Side Layers of 2003 E&P:		
2003 layer #1 (from Corp A)	100u	5u
2003 layer #2 (from Corp B)	50u	5u
	1,250u	580u

Example 2. (i) *Facts.* (A) The facts are the same as in *Example 1* (i)(A), except that foreign corporation A met the requirements of section 902(c)(3)(B) on January 1, 2005, when U.S. corporate shareholder C acquired an additional 1% of voting stock for a total ownership interest of 10%; foreign corporation A thereby became a pooling corporation. On December 31, 2006, foreign corporations A and B have the following earnings and profits and foreign income taxes:

Foreign Corporation A	E&P	Foreign Taxes
Post-1986 pool	900u	$650
2004	400u	160u
2003	100u	5u
	1,400u	

Foreign Corporation B	E&P	Foreign Taxes
2006	100u	20u
2005	300u	60u
2004	0u	50u
2003	50u	5u
	450u	135u

(B) On January 1, 2007, foreign corporation B acquires the assets of foreign corporation A in a reorganization described in section 368(a)(1)(C). Immediately following the foreign section 381 transaction, foreign surviving corporation is a nonpooling corporation that does not meet the requirements of section 902(c)(3)(B).

(ii) *Result.* Under the rules described in paragraphs (e)(2)(i) and (ii) of this section, foreign surviving corporation has the following earnings and profits and foreign income taxes:

	E&P	Foreign Taxes
Two Side-by-Side Layers of 2006 E&P:		
2006 layer #1 (from Corp A's pool)	900u	$650
2006 layer #2 (from Corp B's layer)	100u	20u
2005 (from Corp B)	300u	60u
Two Side-by-Side Layers of 2004 E&P:		
2004 layer #1 (from Corp A)	400u	160u
2004 layer #2 (from Corp B)	0u	50u
Two Side-by-Side Layers of 2003 E&P:		
2003 layer #1 (from Corp A)	100u	5u
2003 layer #2 (from Corp B)	50u	5u
	1,850u	

(iii) *Subsequent ownership change.* On July 1, 2010, USS (a domestic corporation) acquires 100% of the stock of foreign surviving corporation. Under the rules of paragraph (f)(3) of this section, foreign surviving corporation begins to pool its earnings and profits under section 902(c)(3) as of January 1, 2010. Foreign surviving corporation's earnings and profits and foreign income taxes accrued before January 1, 2010 retain their character as pre-1987 accumulated profits and pre-1987 foreign income taxes.

Example 3. (i) *Facts.* (A) The facts are the same as in *Example 2* (i)(A), except that on December 31, 2006, foreign corporations A and B have the following earnings and profits and foreign income taxes:

Foreign Corporation A	E&P	Foreign Taxes
Post-1986 pool	1,000u	$500
2004	(200u)	10u
2003	400u	5u
	1,200u	

Foreign Corporation B	E&P	Foreign Taxes
2006	300u	20u
2005	(100u)	60u
2004	0u	50u
2003	50u	5u
	250u	135u

(B) On January 1, 2007, foreign corporation B acquires the assets of foreign corporation A in a reorganization described in section 368(a)(1)(C). Immediately following the foreign section 381 transaction, foreign surviving corporation is a nonpooling corporation that does not meet the requirements of section 902(c)(3)(B).

(ii) *Result.* Because foreign corporations A and B have aggregate positive amounts of pre-1987 accumulated profits with a deficit in one or more years, the rules of paragraph (e)(2)(iii)(B) of this section apply. Accordingly, after the foreign section 381 transaction, foreign surviving corporation has the following earnings and profits and foreign income taxes:

	Earnings & Profits:		*Foreign Taxes:*	
	Positive E&P	*Deficit E&P*	*Foreign Taxes Available*	*Foreign Taxes Associated with Deficit E&P*
Two Side-by-Side Layers of 2006 E&P:				
2006 layer #1 (from Corp A's pool)	1,000u		$500	
2006 layer #2 (from Corp B's layer)	300u		20u	
2005 (from Corp B)		(100u)		60u
Two Side-by-Side Layers of 2004 E&P:				
2004 layer #1 (from Corp A)		(200u)		10u
2004 layer #2 (from Corp B)	0u		50u	
Two Side-by-Side Layers of 2003 E&P:				
2003 layer #1 (from Corp A)	400u		5u	
2003 layer #2 (from Corp B)	50u		5u	
	1,750u	(300u)		70u

(iii) *Post-transaction distribution.* (A) During 2007, foreign surviving corporation does not accumulate any earnings and profits or pay or accrue any foreign income taxes. On December 31, 2007, foreign surviving corporation distributes 1,300u to its shareholders. Under the rules described in paragraphs (c)(3) and (e)(2)(iii)(B) of this section, the distribution is out of the pre-pooling annual layers, as follows:

	E&P	*Foreign Taxes*
Two Side-by-Side Layers of 2006 E&P:		
2006 layer #1	1,000u	$500
2006 layer #2	250u	20u
2003 E&P:		
2003 layer #1	50u	1.25u (25% of 5u taxes)
	1,300u	

(B) Under paragraph (e)(2)(iii)(B) of this section, the rules otherwise applicable when a foreign corporation has an aggregate positive (or zero) amount of pre-1987 accumulated profits, but a deficit in one or more years, apply separately to the pre-1987 accumulated profits and related pre-1987 foreign income taxes of foreign corporation A and foreign corporation B. As a result, distributions out of the pre-pooling annual layers of foreign corporation A and foreign corporation B cannot exceed the aggregate positive amount of pre-1987 accumulated profits of each corporation. Accordingly, only 1,200u and 250u can be distributed out of foreign corporation A's and foreign corporation B's pre-pooling annual layers, respectively. Thus, 1,000u of the distribution is out of foreign corporation A's 2006 layer #1 and 250u is out of foreign corporation B's 2006 layer #2. (after rolling forward (50u) of the deficit in 2005 layer to reduce earnings in 2006 layer #1 to 250u (300u - 50u)) Under the principles of § 1.902-1(b)(3), all of the taxes in each of those respective layers are reduced. The remaining 50u is distributed from foreign corporation A's 2003 layer #1 (after rolling back the (200u) deficit in 2004 layer #1 to reduce earnings in 2003 layer #1 to 200u (400u - 200u)). Thus, after the distribution, 150u remains in the 2003 layer #1 along with 3.75u of foreign income taxes (5u × (150u ÷ 200u)).

(C) Foreign surviving corporation's foreign income tax accounts are reduced to reflect the distribution of earnings and profits notwithstanding that no shareholders are eligible to claim a credit for deemed paid foreign income taxes under section 902. See § 1.902-1(a)(10)(iii).

(D) Immediately after the distribution, foreign surviving corporation has the following earnings and profits and foreign income taxes:

	E&P	*Foreign Taxes*
2005	0u	60u
Two Side-by-Side Layers of 2004 E&P:		
2004 layer #1	0u	10u
2004 layer #2	0u	50u
Two Side-by-Side Layers of 2003 E&P:		
2003 layer #1	150u	3.75u
2003 layer #2	0u	5u
	150u	128.75u

(E) Under paragraph (e)(2)(iii)(B) of this section, the 60u, 10u, 50u, and 5u of foreign income taxes related to foreign surviving corporation's 2005 layer, 2004 layer #1, 2004 layer #2, and 2003 layer #2, respectively, remain in those layers. These foreign income taxes generally will not be reduced or deemed paid unless a foreign tax refund restores a positive balance to the associated earnings pursuant to section 905(c), and thus will be trapped. See § 1.902-2(b)(2).

Example 4. (i) *Facts.* (A) The facts are the same as in *Example 2* (i)(A), except that on December 31, 2006, foreign corporations A and B have the following earnings and profits and foreign income taxes:

Foreign Corporation A	*E&P*	*Foreign Taxes*
Post-1986 pool	(1,000u)	$20
2004	(200u)	10u
2003	400u	5u
	(800u)	

Foreign Corporation B	*E&P*	*Foreign Taxes*
2006	100u	20u
2005	300u	60u
2004	0u	50u
2003	50u	5u
	450u	135u

(B) On January 1, 2007, foreign corporation A acquires the assets of foreign corporation B in a reorganization described in section 368(a)(1)(C). Immediately following the foreign section 381 transaction, foreign surviving corporation is a nonpooling corporation.

(ii) *Result.* (A) Under paragraph (e)(2)(i) of this section, foreign corporation A's post-1986 pool is recharacterized as a 2006 layer of pre-1987 accumulated profits. Because after the foreign section 381 transaction foreign corporation A has an aggregate deficit in pre-1987 accumulated profits, the rules of paragraph (e)(2)(iii)(C) of this section apply and the rules otherwise applicable apply separately to the pre-1987 accumulated profits that carry over to foreign surviving corporation from foreign corporation A. The (800u) aggregate deficit in foreign corporation A's pre-1987 accumulated profits is a hovering deficit that will offset only post-transaction earnings accumulated by foreign surviving corporation in the general category. Accordingly, after the foreign section 381 transaction, foreign surviving corporation has the following earnings and profits and foreign income taxes:

	Earnings & Profits:		*Foreign Taxes:*	
	Positive E&P	*Deficit E&P*	*Foreign Taxes Available*	*Foreign Taxes Associated with Deficit E&P*
Hovering deficit from Corp A's annual layers		(800u)		0
Two Side-by-Side Layers of 2006 E&P:				
2006 layer #1 (from Corp A's pool)		0u		$20
2006 layer #2 (from Corp B's layer)	100u		20u	
2005 (from Corp B)	300u		60u	
Two Side-by-Side Layers of 2004 E&P:				
2004 layer #1 (from Corp A)		0u		10u
2004 layer #2 (from Corp B)	0u		50u	
Two Side-by-Side Layers of 2003 E&P:				
2003 layer #1 (from Corp A)	0u		5u	
2003 layer #2 (from Corp B)	50u		5u	
	450u	(800u)	140u	

(B) Under paragraph (e)(2)(iii)(C) of this section, the $20, 10u, and 5u of pre-1987 foreign income taxes associated with foreign corporation A's pre-1987 accumulated profits for 2006 layer #1, 2004 layer #1, and 2003 layer #1, respectively, remain in those layers. These foreign income taxes generally will not be reduced or deemed paid unless a foreign tax refund restores a positive balance to the associated earnings pursuant to section 905(c), and thus will be trapped. See § 1.902-2(b)(2).

(iii) *Post-transaction distribution.* (A) During 2007, foreign surviving corporation does not accumulate any earnings and profits or pay or accrue any foreign income taxes. On December 31, 2007, foreign surviving corporation distributes 200u to its shareholders. Under the rules described in paragraph (e)(2)(iii)(C) of this section, no distribution can be made out of the pre-1987 accumulated profits of foreign corporation A (and the (800u) aggregate hovering deficit will offset only post-transaction earnings accumulated by foreign surviving corporation). Thus, the distribution is out of prepooling annual layers as follows:

	E&P	*Foreign Taxes Paid*
2006 layer #2	100u	20u
2005	100u	20u
	200u	40u

(B) Foreign surviving corporation's foreign income tax accounts are reduced to reflect the distribution of earnings and profits notwithstanding that no shareholders are eligible to claim deemed paid foreign income taxes under section 902. See § 1.902-1(a)(10)(iii).

(C) Immediately after the distribution, foreign surviving corporation has the following earnings and profits and foreign income taxes:

	Earnings & Profits:		*Foreign Taxes:*	
	Positive E&P	*Deficit E&P*	*Foreign Taxes Available*	*Foreign Taxes Associated with Deficit E&P*
Hovering deficit From Corp A's annual layers		(800u)		0
Two Side-by-Side Layers of 2006 E&P:				
2006 layer #1 (from Corp A's pool)		0u		$20
2006 layer #2 (from Corp B's layer)	0u		0u	
2005 (from Corp B)	200u		40u	
Two Side-by-Side Layers of 2004 E&P:				
2004 layer #1 (from Corp A)		0u		10u
2004 layer #2 (from Corp B)	0u		50u	
Two Side-by-Side Layers of 2003 E&P:				
2003 layer #1 (from Corp A)	0u		5u	
2003 layer #2 (from Corp B)	50u		5u	
	250u	(800u)	140u	

(f) *Special rules.*—(1) *Treatment of deficit.*—(i) *General rule.*—Any deficit described in paragraph (d)(2), (e)(1)(iii), or (e)(2)(iii) of this section shall not be taken into account in determining current or accumulated earnings and profits of a foreign surviving corporation other than to offset post-transaction accumulated earnings, as defined in paragraph (d)(2)(ii) of this section, including for purposes of calculating—

(A) The earnings and profits limitation of section 952(c)(1)(A); and

(B) the amount of the foreign surviving corporation's subpart F income as defined in section 952(a).

(ii) *Exceptions.*—The rule in paragraph (i) shall not apply for purposes of calculating an earnings and profits limitation under section 952(c)(1)(B) or (C).

(iii) *Examples.*—The following examples illustrate the principles of this paragraph (f)(1). The examples assume the following facts: foreign corporation A, incorporated in 2002, is and always has been a wholly owned subsidiary of USP, a domestic corporation. Foreign corporation B, incorporated in 2004, is and always has been a wholly owned subsidiary of foreign corporation A. Both foreign corporation A and foreign corporation B are organized under the laws of foreign country X and have always had a calendar taxable year. Foreign corporations A and B (and all of their respective qualified business units as defined in section 989) maintain a "u" functional currency. Unless otherwise stated, any earnings and profits or deficit in earnings and profits of foreign corporation A and B in the general category are attributable to subpart F income derived from foreign base company sales income. Foreign corporation C is a wholly owned subsidiary of USP2 and was organized in 2004 under the laws of foreign country Y. Foreign corporation C (and all of its qualified business units as defined in section 989) maintains a "u" functional currency. Earnings and profits of foreign corporation C in the general category are not attributable to subpart F income. The examples are as follows:

Example 1. (i) *Facts.* (A) On December 31, 2007, foreign corporations A and B have the following post-1986 undistributed earnings and post-1986 foreign income taxes:

Foreign Corporation A Separate Category	*E&P*	*Foreign Taxes*
General	(100u)	$25

Foreign Corporation B Separate Category	*E&P*	*Foreign Taxes*
General	0u	$10

(B) On January 1, 2008, foreign corporation B elects under § 301.7701-3(c) of this chapter to be disregarded as an entity separate from foreign corporation A. Accordingly, foreign corporation B is deemed to have distributed all its property to foreign corporation A in a liquidation described in section 332.

(ii) *Result*. Under the rules described in paragraphs (d)(1) and (2) of this section, foreign surviving corporation A has the following post-1986 undistributed earnings and post-1986 foreign income taxes.

	Earnings & Profits:		*Foreign Taxes:*	
Separate Category	*Positive E&P*	*Hovering Deficit*	*Foreign Taxes Available*	*Foreign Taxes Associated with Hovering Deficit*
General	0u	(100u)	$10	$25

(iii) *Post-transaction earnings and subpart F limitations.* (A) In its taxable year ending on December 31, 2008, foreign surviving corporation A earns 300u of subpart F general category income with respect to which it pays $50 in foreign income taxes. The hovering deficit of (100u) meets the requirements under section 952(c)(1)(B) and therefore is taken into account as a qualified deficit that may be used by USP to offset a portion of its income inclusion related to foreign surviving corporation A's subpart F income of 300u in the 2008 taxable year. Accordingly, USP includes 200u in taxable income for the year and is eligible for a deemed paid foreign tax credit under section 960 of $40 (200u subpart F inclusion / 300 post-1986 undistributed earnings in the general category = 66.67%, × $60 foreign income taxes in the general category = $40). USP will also include the deemed paid foreign taxes of $40 in taxable income for the year as a deemed dividend pursuant to section 78. The 100u offset under section 952(c)(1)(B) does not result in a reduction of the hovering deficit for purposes of section 316 or section 902.

(B) Foreign surviving corporation A's 100u of subpart F income not included in income by USP will accumulate and be added to its post-1986 undistributed earnings as of the beginning of 2009. This 100u of post-transaction earnings will be offset by the (100u) hovering deficit. Because the amount of earnings offset by the hovering deficit is 100% of the total amount of the hovering deficit, all $25 of the related taxes are added to the post-1986 foreign income taxes pool as well. Accordingly, foreign surviving corporation A has the following post-1986 undistributed earnings and post-1986 foreign income taxes on January 1, 2009:

	Earnings & Profits:	
Separate Category	*Positive E&P*	*Hovering Deficit*
General	0u	(0u)

(C) The 200u included as subpart F income constitutes previously taxed earnings under section 959.

Example 2. (i) *Facts.* (A) On July 1, 2007, foreign corporation B elects under § 301.7701-3(c) of this chapter to be disregarded as an entity separate from foreign corporation A. Accordingly, foreign corporation B is deemed to have distributed all of its property to foreign corporation A in a liquidation described in section 332.

(B) Neither foreign corporation A nor B has any post-1986 undistributed earnings or post-1986 foreign income taxes as of the beginning of the 2007 taxable year. For its short taxable year ending on June 30, 2007, foreign corporation B has the following post-1986 undistributed earnings and post-1986 foreign income taxes:

Foreign Corporation B Separate Category	*E&P*	*Foreign Taxes*
General	(200u)	$30

(C) For the 2007 taxable year, foreign surviving corporation A earns a total of 200u of subpart F foreign based company sales income in the general category with respect to which it pays $40 in foreign income taxes.

(ii) *Result.* (A) Under paragraph (d)(2) of this section, foreign corporation B's (200u) deficit carries over to foreign surviving corporation A as a hovering deficit. Nevertheless, because it is a deficit of a qualified chain member for a taxable year ending within the 2007 taxable year of foreign surviving corporation A, the (200u) deficit meets the requirements under section 952(c)(1)(C) and therefore may still be taken into account for purposes of limiting foreign surviving corporation A's subpart F income. Accordingly, foreign surviving corporation A's 200u of subpart F income for the 2007 taxable year is fully offset by the (200u) deficit of foreign corporation B, and USP will have no subpart F income inclusion for the 2007 taxable year. The offset under section 952(c)(1)(C) does not result in a reduction of the hovering deficit for purposes of section 316 or section 902. The hovering deficit may not also be taken into account under section 952(c)(1)(B).

(B) Because USP has no subpart F income inclusion, foreign surviving corporation A's subpart F earnings of 200u will accumulate and be added to its post-1986 undistributed earnings as of the beginning of 2008. Under the rules of paragraph (f)(5) of this section, a pro rata amount, in this case 50% or 100u, will be deemed to have been accumulated prior to the foreign section 381 transaction and the other 50%, or 100u, will be deemed to have been accumulated after the foreign section 381 transaction. The 100u of post-transaction earnings will be offset by (100u) of the hovering deficit for purposes of determining the opening balance of the post-1986 undistributed earnings pool in 2008. Because the amount of earnings offset by the hovering deficit is 50% of the total amount of the hovering deficit, $15 (50% of $30) of the related taxes are added to the post-1986 foreign income taxes pool as well. The 100u of pre-transaction earnings remain in the post-1986 undistributed earnings pool. Accordingly, foreign surviving corporation A has the following post-1986 undistributed earnings and post-1986 foreign income taxes on January 1, 2008:

	Earnings & Profits:		*Foreign Taxes:*	
Separate Category	*Positive E&P*	*Hovering Deficit*	*Foreign Taxes Available*	*Foreign Taxes Associated with Hovering Deficit*
General	100u	(100u)	$55	$15

Example 3. (i) *Facts.* (A) On January 1, 2007, foreign corporation B and foreign corporation C have the following post-1986 undistributed earnings and post-1986 foreign income taxes:

Foreign Corporation B		
Separate Category	*E&P*	*Foreign Taxes*
General	(100u)	$0

Foreign Corporation C		
Separate Category	*E&P*	*Foreign Taxes*
General	0u	$10

(B) On July 1, 2007, foreign corporation B acquires the assets of foreign corporation C in a reorganization described in section 368(a)(1)(C). Immediately following the foreign section 381 transaction, foreign surviving corporation B is a CFC.

(C) During the 2007 taxable year foreign surviving corporation B has a current deficit of (400u) and $60 of related foreign income taxes. During its short taxable year ending on June 30, 2007, foreign corporation C has no additional earnings and pays or accrues no foreign income taxes.

(ii) *Result.* (A) Under the rules of paragraph (f)(5) of this section, a pro rata amount, in this case 50% or (200u), of foreign surviving corporation B's (400u) current year deficit for the 2007 taxable year will be deemed to have been accumulated prior to the foreign section 381 transaction and be treated as a hovering deficit. The other 50%, or (200u) of the deficit will be deemed to have been accumulated after the foreign section 381 transaction. The related foreign income taxes of $60 will also be allocated on a similar 50/50 basis.

(B) Under the rules described in paragraphs (d)(1) and (2) of this section, foreign surviving corporation B has the following post-1986 undistributed earnings and post-1986 foreign income taxes as of January 1, 2008:

	Earnings & Profits:		*Foreign Taxes:*	
Separate Category	*Positive E&P*	*Hovering Deficit*	*Foreign Taxes Available*	*Foreign Taxes Associated with Hovering Deficit*
General	(200u)	(300u)	$40	$30

(iii) *Subpart F income limitations.* Even though (200u) of the current year deficit is treated as a hovering deficit, the full (400u) current year deficit in 2007 of foreign surviving corporation B meets the requirements under section 952(c)(1)(C) and therefore is available as a limitation on subpart F income, to the extent foreign corporation A, which wholly owns foreign surviving corporation B, earns any subpart F income in the 2007 taxable year. Any such offset under section 952(c)(1)(C) will have no effect on the earnings and profits and foreign income tax accounts above of foreign surviving corporation B for purposes of sections 316 and 902. Moreover, to the extent the hovering deficit reduces subpart F income under section 952(c)(1)(C), it may not also be taken into account under section 952(c)(1)(B).

(2) *Reconciling taxable years.*—If a foreign acquiring corporation and a foreign target corporation had taxable years ending on different dates, then the pro rata distribution rules of paragraphs (e)(1)(ii) and (e)(2)(ii) of this section shall apply with respect to the taxable years that end within the same calendar year.

(3) *Post-transaction change of status.*—If a foreign surviving corporation that is subject to the rules of paragraph (c)(2) of this section subsequently becomes a pooling corporation (by reason, for example, of a reorganization, liquidation, or change of ownership), then post-1986 undistributed earnings and post-1986 foreign income taxes that were recharacterized as pre-1987 accumulated profits and pre-1987 foreign income taxes, respectively, under paragraph (e)(2)(i) of this section retain their characterization as a pre-pooling annual layer.

(4) *Ordering rule for multiple hovering deficits.*—(i) *Rule.*—A foreign surviving corporation shall apply the deficit rules of paragraphs (d)(2), (e)(1)(iii), and (e)(2)(iii) of this section in that order if more than one of such rules applies to the foreign surviving corporation.

(ii) *Example.*—The following example illustrates the principles of this paragraph (f)(4). The example assumes the following facts: foreign corporation A has been a pooling corporation since its incorporation on January 1, 1998. Foreign corporation B has been a nonpooling corporation since its incorporation on January 1, 2000. Foreign corporations A and B have always had calendar taxable years. Foreign corporations A and B (and all of their respective qualified business units as defined in section 989) maintain a "u" functional currency. All earnings and profits of foreign corporation B are in the general category. Finally, unless otherwise stated, any earnings and profits in the passive category resulted from a look-through dividend that was paid by a lower-tier CFC out of earnings accumulated when the CFC was a noncontrolled section 902 corporation and that qualified for the subpart F same-country exception under section 954(c)(3)(A). The example is as follows:

Example—(i) *Facts.* (A) On December 31, 2006, foreign corporations A and B have the following earnings and profits and foreign income taxes:

Foreign Corporation A		
Post-1986 Pool Separate Category:	*E&P*	*Foreign Taxes*
Passive	400u	$160
General	(300u)	$ 25
	100u	$185

Foreign Corporation B	*E&P*	*Foreign Taxes*
2006	(300u)	50u
2005	100u	25u
	(200u)	75u

(B) On January 1, 2007, foreign corporation B acquires the assets of foreign corporation A in a reorganization described in section 368(a)(1)(C). Immediately following the foreign section 381 transaction, foreign surviving corporation is a CFC.

(ii) *Result.* Under the rules described in paragraphs (d)(1), (d)(2), (e)(1)(i), (e)(1)(ii), and (e)(1)(iii) of this section, foreign surviving corporation has the following earnings and profits and foreign income taxes:

	Earnings & Profits:		*Foreign Taxes:*	
	Positive E&P	*Hovering Deficit*	*Foreign Taxes Available*	*Foreign Taxes Associated with Hovering Deficit*
Post-1986 Pool Separate Category				
Passive	400u		$160	
General		(300u)		$25
Carryforward pre-pooling deficit from Corp B		(200u)		0
2006 (from Corp B)	0u		50u	
2005 (from Corp B)	0u		25u	
	400u	(500u)		$25

(iii) *Post-transaction earnings.* (A) In the taxable year ending on December 31, 2007, foreign surviving corporation accumulates earnings and profits and pays related foreign income taxes as follows:

	E&P	*Foreign Taxes*
Post-1986 Pool Separate Category		
Passive	150u	$ 40
General	400u	$ 60
	550u	$100

(B) None of the earnings and profits qualify as subpart F income as defined in section 952(a). Under paragraph (f)(4)(i) of this section, the rules of paragraph (d)(2) of this section apply before the rules of paragraph (e)(1)(iii) of this section. Accordingly, post-transaction earnings in a separate category are first offset by a hovering deficit in the same separate category in the post-1986 pool. Thus, foreign surviving corporation's (300u) deficit in the general category offsets 300u of post-transaction earnings in the general category. After application of paragraph (d)(2) of this section, the (200u) deficit in the general category carried forward from foreign corporation B's pre-pooling aggregate deficit offsets the remaining 100u of post-transaction earnings in the general category. Accordingly, foreign surviving corporation has the following earnings and profits and foreign income taxes at the end of 2007:

	Earnings & Profits:		*Foreign Taxes:*	
	Positive E&P	*Hovering Deficit*	*Foreign Taxes Available*	*Foreign Taxes Associated with Hovering Deficit*
Post-1986 Pool Separate Category				
Passive	550u		$200	
General			$85	
Carryforward pre-pooling deficit from Corp B		(100u)		$0
2006 (from Corp B)	0u		50u	
2005 (from Corp B)	0u		25u	
	550u	(100u)		$0

(C) Under paragraph (d)(2)(iii) of this section, all of the $25 of post-1986 foreign income taxes related to the (300u) hovering deficit in the general category is added to the foreign surviving corporation's post-1986 foreign income taxes of $60 in that category (because post-transaction earnings in the general category have exceeded the deficit in that category). Under paragraph (e)(1)(iii)(C) of this section, the 50u and 25u of foreign income taxes associated with foreign corporation B's pre-1987 accumulated profits for 2006 and 2005 remain in those layers. These foreign income taxes generally will not be reduced or deemed paid unless a foreign tax refund restores a positive balance to the associated earnings pursuant to section 905(c), and thus will be trapped. See § 1.902-2(b)(2).

(5) *Pro rata rule for earnings and deficits during transaction year.*—(i) For purposes of offsetting post-transaction earnings of a foreign surviving corporation under the rules described in paragraphs (d)(2), (e)(1)(iii), and (e)(2)(iii) of this section, the earnings and profits, and any related foreign income taxes, in each separate category for the taxable year of the foreign surviving corporation in which the transaction occurs shall be deemed to have been accumulated after such transaction in an amount which bears the same ratio to the undistributed earnings and profits of the foreign surviving corporation for such taxable year (computed without regard to any earnings and profits carried over) as the number of days in the taxable year after the date of transaction bears to the total number of days in the taxable year. See, e.g., § 1.381(c)(2)-1(a)(7) *Example 2* (illustrating application of this rule with respect to domestic corporations).

(ii) For purposes of determining the amount of pre-transaction deficits described in paragraphs (d)(2), (e)(1)(iii), and (e)(2)(iii) of this section, of a foreign surviving corporation that has a deficit in earnings and profits in any separate category for its taxable year in which the transaction occurs, unless the actual accumulated earnings and profits, or deficit, as of such date can be shown, such pre-transaction deficit, and any related foreign income taxes, shall be deemed to have accumulated in a manner similar to that described in paragraph (f)(5)(i) of this section. See, e.g., § 1.381(c)(2)-1(a)(7) *Example 4* (illustrating application of this rule with respect to domestic corporations).

(g) *Post-2017 taxable years.*—As a result of the repeal of section 902 effective for taxable years of foreign corporations beginning on or after January 1, 2018, all foreign target corporations, foreign acquiring corporations, and foreign surviving corporations are treated as nonpooling corporations in post-2017 taxable years. Any amounts remaining in post-1986 undistributed earnings and post-1986 foreign income taxes of any such corporation in any separate category as of the end of the foreign corporation's last taxable year beginning before January 1, 2018, are treated as earnings and taxes in a single pre-pooling annual layer in the foreign corporation's post-2017 taxable years for purposes of this section. Foreign income taxes that are related to non-previously taxed earnings of a foreign acquiring corporation and a foreign target corporation that were accumulated in taxable years before the current taxable year of the foreign corporation, or in a foreign target's taxable year that ends on the date of the section 381 transaction, are not treated as current year taxes (as defined in § 1.960-1(b)(4)) of a foreign surviving corporation in any post-2017 taxable year. In addition, foreign income taxes that are related to a hovering deficit are not treated as current year taxes of the foreign surviving corporation in any post-2017 taxable year, regardless of whether the hovering deficit is absorbed.

(h) *Applicability dates.*—Except as otherwise provided in this paragraph (h), this section applies to foreign section 381 transactions that occur on or after November 6, 2006. Paragraph (g) of this section applies to taxable years of foreign corporations ending on or after November 2, 2020, and to taxable years of United States shareholders in which or with which such taxable years of foreign corporations end. [Reg. § 1.367(b)-7.]

☐ [*T.D.* 9273, 8-7-2006 (*corrected* 12-6-2006). *Amended by T.D.* 9959, 12-28-2021.]

§ 1.367(b)-8. Allocation of earnings and profits and foreign income taxes in certain foreign corporate separation.—[Reserved]

☐ [*T.D.* 9273, 8-7-2006.]

Proposed Regulation

§ 1.367(b)-8. Allocation of earnings and profits and foreign income taxes in certain foreign corporate separations.—(a) *Scope.*—This section applies to distributions to which section 355 (or so much of section 356 as relates to section 355) applies, whether or not in connection with a section 368(a)(1)(D) reorganization (D reorganization), in which the distributing corporation or the controlled corporation (or both) is a foreign corporation (foreign divisive transaction). For purposes of this section, the terms distributing corporation and controlled corporation have the same meaning as used in section 355 and the regulations thereunder. Paragraph (b) of this section provides general rules governing the allocation and reduction of a distributing corporation's earnings and profits and foreign income taxes (pre-transaction earnings and pre-transaction taxes, respectively) in foreign divisive transactions. Paragraphs (c), (d), and (e) of this section describe special rules for the application of paragraph (b) of this section to specific situations, depending upon whether the distributing corporation or the controlled corporation (or both the distributing and the controlled corporation) is a foreign corporation.

(b) *General rules.*—(1) *Application of § 1.312-10.*—(i) *In general.*—Pre-transaction earnings of a distributing corporation shall be allocated between the distributing corporation and the controlled corporation in accordance with the rules of § 1.312-10(a) and shall be reduced in accordance with the rules of § 1.312-10(b), except to the extent otherwise provided in this section.

(ii) *Special rules for application of § 1.312-10(b).*—(A) *Distributing corporation.*—The pre-transaction earnings of a distributing corporation shall be reduced without taking into account § 1.312-10(b)(2).

(B) *Controlled corporation.*—Section 1.312-10(b) shall not apply to increase or replace the earnings and profits of a controlled corporation by the amount of any decrease in the pre-transaction earnings of a distributing corporation.

(iii) *Net deficit in pre-transaction earnings.*—Nothing in this section shall permit any portion of the pre-transaction earnings of a distributing corporation that has a net deficit in pre-transaction earnings to be allocated or reduced under paragraph (b)(1)(i) of this section. See § 1.312-10(c). Compare paragraph (b)(2) of this section (requiring an allocation or reduction of a pro rata portion of deficits in statutory groupings of earnings and profits when a distributing corporation has a net positive amount of pre-transaction earnings).

(iv) *Use of net bases.*—All allocations and reductions described in paragraph (b)(1)(i) of this section shall be determined in accordance with the net bases in assets. Net basis shall have the same meaning as under § 1.312-10(a).

(v) *Gain recognized by distributing corporation.*—The pre-transaction earnings that are subject to allocation or reduction under paragraph (b)(1)(i) of this section shall include any increase in earnings and profits from gain recognized or income included by the distributing corporation as a result of the foreign divisive transaction. See, for example, section 367(a) and (e), section 1248(f), and § 1.367(b)-5(b).

(vi) *Coordination with branch profits tax.*—An allocation or reduction in a distributing corporation's pre-transaction earnings under paragraph (b)(1)(i) of this section shall not be out of or reduce effectively connected earnings and profits or non-previously taxed accumulated effectively connected earnings and profits, as defined in section 884. See also § 1.884-2T(d)(5)(iii) (providing that such earnings and profits are not subject to reduction under § 1.312-10(b)).

(2) *Cross-section of earnings and profits.*—Except to the extent provided in paragraphs (b)(1)(iii), (b)(1)(vi), (d)(2)(ii), (d)(4), and (e)(4) of this section and other than any portion attributable to an inclusion under § 1.367(b)-5 or paragraph (d)(2)(i) of this section, an allocation or reduction of pre-transaction earnings described in paragraph (b)(1)(i) of this section shall decrease, on a pro rata basis, the statutory groupings of earnings and profits (or deficits in statutory groupings of earnings and profits) of the distributing corporation. Thus, for example, a pro rata portion of a foreign distributing corporation's separate categories, post-1986 undistributed earnings, and annual layers of pre-1987 accumulated profits and pre-1987 section 960 earnings and profits shall be allocated or reduced.

(3) *Foreign income taxes.*—Pre-transaction taxes of a distributing corporation shall be ratably allocated or reduced only to the extent described in paragraphs (d)(3) and (e)(3) of this section. Thus, a distributing corporation's excess foreign taxes described in section 904(c) shall not be allocated or reduced under this section.

(4) *Divisive D reorganization with a preexisting controlled corporation.*—In the case of a foreign divisive transaction that includes a D reorganization with a controlled corporation that is not newly created (a preexisting controlled corporation), paragraph (b)(1)(i) of this section shall apply in the following manner:

(i) *Calculation of earnings and profits of distributing corporation.*—The pre-transaction earnings of a distributing corporation shall be reduced by the sum of—

(A) The amount of the reduction in the pre-transaction earnings of the distributing corporation as described in § 1.312-10(a) (as determined under this section); and

(B) The amount of the reduction in the pre-transaction earnings of the distributing corporation as described in § 1.312-10(b) (as determined under this section).

(ii) *Calculation of earnings and profits of controlled corporation.*—The amount of earnings and profits of the controlled corporation immediately after the foreign divisive transaction shall equal the sum of—

(A) The amount described in paragraph (b)(4)(i)(A) of this section (except to the extent such amounts are included in income as a deemed dividend pursuant to the foreign divisive transaction or are subject to the rule of § 1.367(b)-3(f)); and

(B) The amount of earnings and profits of the controlled corporation immediately before the foreign divisive transaction.

(c) *Foreign divisive transactions involving a domestic distributing corporation and a foreign controlled corporation.*—(1) *Scope.*—The rules of this paragraph (c) apply to a foreign divisive transaction involving a domestic distributing corporation and a foreign controlled corporation.

(2) *Earnings and profits allocated to a foreign controlled corporation.*—Pre-transaction earnings of a domestic distributing corporation that are allocated to a foreign controlled corporation under the rules described in paragraph (b)(1)(i) of this section shall not be included in the foreign controlled corporation's post-1986 undistributed earnings, pre-1987 accumulated profits, or pre-1987 section 960 earnings and profits. In addition, if a distribution by the domestic distributing corporation out of pre-transaction earnings immediately before the foreign divisive transaction would have been treated as a U.S. source dividend under section 861(a)(2)(A) that would not be exempt from tax under section 871(i)(2)(B) or 881(d), a distribution out of such earnings and profits by the foreign controlled corporation shall be treated as a U.S. source dividend under section 904(g) and for purposes of Chapter 3 of subtitle A of the Internal Revenue Code. See *Georday Enterprises v. Commissioner*, 126 F.2d 384 (4th Cir. 1942). See also sections 243(e) and 861(a)(2)(C) and § 1.367(b)-2(j) for other rules that may apply.

(3) *Examples.*—The following examples illustrate the application of the rules of this section to transactions described in paragraph (c)(1) of this section. The examples presume the following facts: USD is a domestic corporation engaged in manufacturing and shipping activities through Business A and Business B, respectively. FC is a foreign corporation that is wholly owned by USD. USD and FC use calendar taxable years. FC (and all of its qualified business units as defined in section 989) maintains a "u" functional currency and, except as otherwise specified, 1u = US$1 at all times. The examples are as follows:

Example 1—(i) *Facts.* The stock of USD is owned in equal parts by three shareholders, USP (a domestic corporation), USI (a United States citizen), and FP (a foreign corporation). USD owns assets with total net bases of $260 (including $100 attributable to the Business B shipping assets, which have a $160 fair market value). USD has $500 of earnings and profits (that it accumulated). The entire $500 would have been treated as a U.S. source dividend under section 861(a)(2)(A) that would not be exempt from tax under sections 871(i)(2)(B) or 881(d) if distributed by USD immediately before the foreign divisive transaction. On January 1, 2002, USD incorporates FC and transfers to FC the Business B shipping assets. USD then distributes the FC stock pro rata to USP, USI, and FP. The transaction meets the requirements of sections 368(a)(1)(D) and 355.

(ii) Result—(A) *Gain Recognition.* Under section 367(a)(5), USD recognizes gain equal to the difference between the fair market value and USD's adjusted basis in the Business B shipping assets ($160 – $100 = $60).

(B) *Calculation of USD's earnings and profits.* Under paragraph (b)(1)(v) of this section, USD's pre-transaction earnings include any gain recognized or income included as a result of the foreign divisive transaction. As described in this *Example 1* (ii)(A), USD recognizes $60 of gain as a result of the foreign divisive transaction. Accordingly, USD has $560 of pre-transaction earnings ($500 + $60). Under paragraph (b)(1)(i) of this section, USD's pre-transaction earnings are reduced by an amount equal to its pre-transaction earnings times the net bases of the assets transferred to FC divided by the net bases of the assets held by USD immediately before the foreign divisive transaction ($560 × ($160 ÷ $320) = $280). Following this reduction, USD has $280 of earnings and profits ($560 – $280).

(C) *Calculation of FC's earnings and profits.* Under paragraph (b)(1)(i) of this section, the $280 reduction in USD's pre-transaction earnings is allocated to FC. Under § 1.367(b)-2(j)(1), the $280 is translated into "u" at the spot rate on January 1, 2002, to 280u. Under paragraph (c)(2) of this section, the 280u is not included as part of FC's post-1986 undistributed earnings, pre-1987 accumulated profits, or section 960 earnings and profits.

(iii) *Post-transaction distribution.* During 2002, FC does not accumulate any earnings and profits or pay or accrue any foreign income taxes. On December 31, 2002, at a time when US$1 = 0.5u, FC distributes 180u (or $360) to its shareholders. Thus, FP, USP, and USI each receive a $120 dividend. See section 989(b)(1). Under paragraph (c)(2) of this section and § 1.367(b)-2(j)(4), $93.33 of the distribution to FP is subject to withholding under Chapter 3 of subtitle A of the Internal Revenue Code ($280 ÷ 3 = $93.33). Under section 243(e) and § 1.367(b)-2(j)(3), $93.33 of the distribution to USP is eligible for the dividends received deduction. See also section 861(a)(2)(C). Under paragraph (c)(2) of this section, the remaining $26.67 distribution to USP is treated as U.S. source under section 904(g) (and is not eligible for the dividends received deduction under section 243(e)). Under paragraph (c)(2) of this section, the $120 dividend distribution to USI is treated as U.S. source under section 904(g).

Example 2—(i) *Facts.* The stock of USD is owned by the following unrelated persons: 20 percent by USP (a domestic corporation), 20 percent by USI (a United States citizen), and 60 percent by FP (a foreign corporation). FC is a preexisting controlled corporation that was incorporated in 1995 and USD always has owned all of the FC stock. USD owns assets with total net bases of $320 (including $160 attributable to the FC stock), and USD has $500 of earnings and profits. FC has 150u of earnings and profits in the section 904(d)(1)(D) shipping separate category and has $60 of related foreign income taxes. FC's earnings and profits qualified for the high tax exception from subpart F income under section 954(b)(4), and USD elected to exclude the earnings and profits from subpart F income under section 954(b)(4) and § 1.954-1(d)(5). On January 1, 2002, USD distributes the stock of FC to its shareholders in a transaction that meets the requirements of section 355. FC is not a controlled foreign corporation after the foreign divisive transaction. On the date of the foreign divisive transaction, the FC stock has a $460 fair market value.

(ii) *Result*—(A) *Gain Recognition.* Under § 1.367(b)-5(b)(1)(ii), USD recognizes gain equal to the difference between the fair market value and USD's adjusted basis in the FC stock distributed to USI. Under § 1.367(e)-1(b)(1), USD recognizes gain equal to the difference between the fair market value and USD's adjusted basis in the FC stock distributed to FP. As a result of the transfers to USI and FP, USD recognizes gain of $240 (4/5 × ($460 – $160)), $120 of which is included in USD's income as a dividend under section 1248(a) and (f)(1) (4/5 × 150u, translated at the spot rate under section 989(b)(2)). Under section 1248(a) and (f)(1), USD includes as a dividend the difference between the fair market value and its adjusted basis in the FC stock distributed to USP to the extent of FC's earnings and profits attributable to the distributed stock. For further guidance, see also Notice 87-64 (1987-2 C.B. 375) (see also § 601.601(d)(2) of this chapter). As a result of this transfer, USD includes a $30 dividend under section 1248(a) and (f)(1) (1/5 × 150u). USD qualifies for a section 902 deemed paid foreign tax credit with respect to its $150 of section 1248 dividends.

(B) *Calculation of USD's earnings and profits.* Under paragraph (b)(1)(v) of this section, USD's pre-transaction earnings include any gain recognized or income included as a result of the foreign divisive transaction. As described in this *Example 2* (ii)(A), USD recognizes and includes a total of $270 of gain and dividend income as a result of the foreign divisive transaction. Accordingly, USD has $770 of pre-transaction earnings ($500 + $270). Under paragraphs (b)(1)(i) and (b)(1)(ii)(A) of this section, USD's pre-transaction earnings are reduced by the amount of the reduction that would have been required if USD had transferred the stock of FC to a new corporation in a D reorganization. Thus, USD's pre-transaction earnings are reduced by an amount equal to its pre-transaction earnings times its net basis in the FC stock divided by the net bases of the assets held by USD immediately before the foreign divisive transaction ($770 × ($430 ÷ $590) = $561.19). Following this reduction, USD has $208.81 of earnings and profits ($770 – $561.19).

(C) *Calculation of FC's earnings and profits.* Under paragraph (b)(1)(ii)(B) of this section, FC's earnings and profits are not increased (or replaced) as a result of the foreign divisive transaction.

Example 3—(i) *Facts.* USP, a domestic corporation, owns all of the stock of USD. FC is a preexisting controlled corporation and USD has owned all of the FC stock since FC was incorporated in 1995. USD owns assets with total net bases of $320 (including $100 attributable to the FC stock and $160 attributable to the Business B shipping assets). USD has $500 of pre-transaction earnings. FC has 150u of earnings and profits in the section 904(d)(1)(D) shipping separate category and has $60 of related foreign income taxes. FC's earnings and profits qualified for the high tax exception from subpart F income under section 954(b)(4), and USD elected to exclude the earnings and profits from subpart F income under section 954(b)(4) and § 1.954-1(d)(5). On January 1, 2002, USD transfers to FC the Business B shipping assets. USD then distributes the FC stock to USP. The transaction meets the requirements of sections 368(a)(1)(D) and 355. USD's transfer of the Business B shipping assets to FC falls within the active trade or business exception to section 367(a)(1) described in § 1.367(a)-2T. Immediately after the foreign divisive transaction, the FC stock has a $460 fair market value. USP and USD meet and comply with the requirements of section 367(a)(5) and 1248(f)(2) (and any regulations thereunder). (Sections 1.367(b)-5(b)(1)(ii) and 1.367(e)-1(b)(1) do not apply with respect to the foreign divisive transaction because the distributee, USP, is a domestic corporation.)

(ii) *Result*—(A) *Calculation of USD's earnings and profits.* Under paragraph (b)(4)(i) of this section, USD's pre-transaction earnings are reduced by the sum of the amounts described in paragraphs (b)(4)(i)(A) and (b)(4)(i)(B) of this section. Under paragraph (b)(4)(i)(A) of this section, USD's pre-transaction earnings are reduced by an amount equal to USD's pre-transaction earnings times the net bases of the assets transferred to FC divided by the total net bases of the assets held by USD immediately before the foreign divisive transaction ($500 × ($160 ÷ $320) = $250). Under paragraph (b)(4)(i)(B) of this section, USD's pre-transaction earnings are reduced by an amount equal to USD's pre-transaction earnings times USD's net basis in the stock of FC (immediately before USD's transfer of the shipping assets) divided by the total net bases of the assets held by USD immediately before the foreign divisive transaction ($500 × ($100 ÷ $320) = $156.25). The sum of the amounts described in paragraphs (b)(4)(i)(A) and (B) of this section is $406.25 ($250 + $156.25). Following the reduction described in paragraph (b)(4)(i) of this section, USD has $93.75 of earnings and profits ($500 – $406.25).

(B) *Calculation of FC's earnings and profits.* Under paragraphs (b)(4)(ii) of this section, the earnings and profits of FC immediately after the foreign divisive transaction are increased by the amount of the reduction in USD's pre-transaction earnings described in paragraph (b)(4)(i)(A) of this section ($250). Under § 1.367(b)-2(j)(1), this $250 is translated into "u" at the spot rate on January 1, 2002, to 250u. Under paragraph (c)(2) of this section, the 250u is not included as part of FC's post-1986 undistributed earnings. FC has 400u in earnings and profits (250u + 150u) immediately after the foreign divisive transaction.

(iii) *Post-transaction distribution.* FC does not accumulate any earnings and profits or pay or accrue any foreign income taxes during 2002. On December 31, 2002, FC distributes 100u as a dividend to USP, which has remained its sole shareholder. Under section 989(b)(1), the 100u distribution is translated into US$ at the spot rate on December 31, 2002, to $100. Proportionate parts of the $100 dividend are attributable to the pre-transaction earnings of FC ($37.50 = $100 × (150 ÷ 400)) and USD ($62.50 = $100 × (250 ÷ 400)). See sections 243(e) and 245. Thus, under sections 243(e) and § 1.367(b)-2(j)(3), $62.50 of the distribution is eligible for the dividends received deduction. See also section 861(a)(2)(C). The remaining $37.50 of the distribution (and $15 of related foreign income taxes) is subject to the generally applicable rules concerning dividends paid by foreign corporations.

(d) *Foreign divisive transactions involving a foreign distributing corporation and a domestic controlled corporation.*—(1) *Scope.*—The rules of this paragraph (d) apply to a foreign divisive transaction involving a foreign distributing corporation and a domestic controlled corporation.

(2) *Coordination with § 1.367(b)-3.*—(i) *In general.*—In the case of a foreign divisive transaction that includes a D reorganization, the rules of § 1.367(b)-3 are applicable with respect to the pre-transaction earnings of a foreign distributing corporation that are allocable to a domestic controlled corporation under paragraph (b)(1)(i) of this section.

(ii) *Determination of all earnings and profits amount.*—An all earnings and profits amount inclusion under paragraph (d)(2)(i) of this section shall be computed with respect to the pre-transaction earnings that are allocable to the domestic controlled corporation, without regard to the parenthetical phrase in paragraph (b)(4)(ii)(A) of this section.

(iii) *Interaction with section 358 and § 1.367(b)-2(e)(3)(ii).*—The basis increase provided in § 1.367(b)-2(e)(3)(ii) shall apply to an all earnings and profits amount inclusion under paragraph (d)(2)(i) of this section, subject to the following rules—

(A) Section 358 shall apply to determine the distributee's basis in the foreign distributing and domestic controlled corporation without regard to the all earnings and profits amount inclusion;

(B) After application of the rule in paragraph (d)(2)(iii)(A) of this section, the basis increase provided in § 1.367(b)-2(e)(3)(ii) shall be applied in a manner that attributes such basis increase solely to the exchanging shareholder's stock in the domestic controlled corporation; and

(C) the rule of paragraph (d)(2)(iii)(B) of this section shall apply prior to § 1.367(b)-5(c)(4) and (d)(4).

(iv) *Coordination with § 1.367(b)-3(c).*—In applying the rule of § 1.367(b)-3(c)(2), an exchanging shareholder described in § 1.367(b)-3(c)(1) shall recognize gain with respect to the stock of the domestic controlled corporation after the foreign divisive transaction.

(v) *Special rule for U.S. persons that own foreign distributing corporation stock after a non pro rata distribution.*—[Reserved]

(3) *Foreign income taxes.*—Pre-transaction taxes related to a foreign distributing corporation's pre-transaction earnings that are allocable or are reduced under the rules described in paragraph (b)(1)(i) of this section shall be ratably reduced. Pre-transaction taxes related to a foreign distributing corporation's pre-transaction earnings that are allocable to a domestic controlled corporation under the rules described in paragraph (b)(1)(i) of this section shall not carry over to the domestic controlled corporation. Nothing in this paragraph (d)(3) shall affect the deemed paid taxes that otherwise would accompany an inclusion under § 1.367(b)-5 or paragraph (d)(2)(i) of this section.

(4) *Previously taxed earnings and profits.*—[Reserved]

(5) *Coordination with § 1.367(b)-5.*—See also § 1.367(b)-5(c) and (d) for other rules that may apply to a foreign divisive transaction described in paragraph (d)(1) of this section.

(6) *Examples.*—The following examples illustrate the application of the rules of this section to transactions described in paragraph (d)(1) of this section. The examples presume the following facts: FD is a foreign corporation engaged in manufacturing and shipping activities through Business A and Business B, respectively. Any earnings and profits of FD described in section 904(d)(1)(D) (shipping income) qualified for the high tax exception from subpart F income under section 954(b)(4), and FD'S United States shareholders elected to exclude the earnings and profits from subpart F income under section 954(b)(4) and § 1.954-1(d)(5). USC is a domestic corporation that is wholly owned by FD. FD and USC use calendar taxable years. FD (and all of its qualified business units as defined in section 989) maintains a "u" functional currency, and 1u = US$1 at all times. The examples are as follows:

Example 1—(i) *Facts.* (A) USP, a domestic corporation, has owned all of the stock of FD since FD's incorporation in 1995. USP's adjusted basis in the FD stock is $100, and the FD stock has a fair market value of $800. FD owns assets with total net bases of 320u (including 160u attributable to the Business B shipping assets), and has the following pre-transaction earnings and pre-transaction taxes accounts:

Separate Category	*E&P*	*Foreign Taxes*
General	300u	$60
Shipping	200u	$80
	500u	$140

(B) On January 1, 2002, FD incorporates USC and transfers to USC the Business B shipping assets. FD then distributes the USC stock to USP. The transaction meets the requirements of sections 368(a)(1)(D) and 355. Immediately after the foreign divisive transaction, the FD stock and the USC stock each have a fair market value of $400.

(ii) *Results*—(A) *Calculation of FD's earnings and profits.* Under paragraph (b)(1)(i) of this section, FD's pre-transaction earnings are reduced by an amount equal to its pre-transaction earnings times the net bases of the assets transferred to USC divided by the net bases of the assets held by FD immediately before the foreign divisive transaction (500u × (160u ÷ 320u) = 250u). Following this reduction, FD has 250u of earnings and profits (500u – 250u).

(B) *All earnings and profits amount inclusion.* Under § 1.367(b)-3 and paragraph (d)(2)(i) of this section, USP includes in income as an all earnings and profits amount the pre-transaction earnings of FD that are allocable to USC under paragraph (b)(1)(i) of this section. Thus, USP's all earnings and profits amount inclusion is $250. See also section 989(b)(1) and paragraph (d)(2)(ii) of this section. Under § 1.367(b)-3(b)(3)(i) and § 1.367(b)-2(e), USP includes the all earnings and profits amount as a deemed dividend received from FD immediately before the foreign divisive transaction. Because the requirements of section 902 are met, USP qualifies for a deemed paid foreign tax credit with respect to the deemed dividend that it receives from FD. Under § 1.902-1(d)(1), the $250 deemed dividend is out of FD's separate categories and reduces foreign income taxes as follows:

Separate Category	*E&P*	*Foreign Taxes*
General	150u	$30
Shipping	100u	$40
	250u	$70

(C) *Calculation of USP's basis in USC and USC's earnings and profits.* Under paragraph (d)(2)(iii) of this section, the § 1.367(b)-2(e)(3)(ii) basis increase applies with respect to USP's all earnings and profits amount inclusion from FD and is attributed solely to USP's basis in USC (after application of section 358). Accordingly, USP has a $300 basis in the USC stock ($50 section 358 basis, determined by reference to the relative values of USP's FD and USC stock: $100 pre-transaction basis × ($400 ÷ $800) + $250 § 1.367(b)-2(e)(3)(ii) basis increase = $300). Because USP included in income as a deemed dividend under § 1.367(b)-3 and paragraph (d)(2) of this section the pre-transaction earnings of FD that are allocable to USC under paragraph (b)(1)(i) of this section, such earnings and profits are not available to increase USC's earnings and profits. As a result, USC has zero earnings and profits immediately after the foreign divisive transaction.

(D) *Application of § 1.367(b)-5(c).* The basis adjustment and income inclusion rules of § 1.367(b)-5(c)(2) apply if USP's postdistribution amount with respect to FD stock is less than its predistribution amount with respect to FD stock. Under § 1.367(b)-5(e)(1), USP's predistribution amount with respect to FD stock is USP's section 1248 amount attributable to such stock computed immediately before the distribution but after taking into account the allocation of earnings and profits as a result of the D reorganization. Thus, USP's predistribution amount with respect to FD stock is $250 (500u – 250u). See also section 989(b)(2). Under section 358, USP allocates its $100 basis in FD stock between FD stock and USC stock according to the stock blocks' relative values, yielding a $50 ($100 × ($400 ÷ $800)) basis in FD stock. See also paragraph (d)(2)(iii) of this section. Under § 1.367(b)-5(e)(2), USP's postdistribution amount with respect to FD stock is USP's section 1248 amount with respect to such stock, computed immediately after the distribution. Accordingly, USP's postdistribution amount with respect to FD stock is $250. Because USP's, postdistribution amount with respect to FD stock is not less than its predistribution amount, USP is not required to make any basis adjustment or include any income under § 1.367(b)-5(c).

(E) *FD's earnings and profits after the foreign divisive transaction.* Following the reduction described in this *Example 1* (ii)(A) and (B), FD has the following earnings and profits and foreign income taxes accounts:

Separate Category	E&P	Foreign Taxes
General	150u	$30
Shipping	100u	$40
	250u	$70

Example 2—(i) *Facts.* (A) USP, a domestic corporation, has owned all of the stock of FD since FD's incorporation in 1995. USP's adjusted basis in the FD stock is $400 and the FD stock has a fair market value of $800. USC is a preexisting controlled corporation. FD owns assets with net total bases of 320u (including 160u attributable to the USC stock), and has the following pre-transaction earnings and pre-transaction taxes accounts:

Separate Category	E&P	Foreign Taxes
General	300u	$60
Shipping	200u	$80
	500u	$140

(B) On January 1, 2002, FD distributes the USC stock to USP in a transaction that meets the requirements of section 355. Immediately after the foreign divisive transaction, the FD stock and the USC stock each have a $400 fair market value.

(ii) *Results*—(A) *Calculation of FD's earnings and profits.* Under paragraphs (b)(1)(i) and (b)(1)(ii)(A) of this section, FD's pre-transaction earnings are reduced by the amount of the reduction that would have been required if FD had transferred the stock of USC to a new corporation in a D reorganization. Thus, FD's pre-transaction earnings are reduced by an amount equal to its pre-transaction earnings times its net basis in the USC stock divided by the net bases of the assets held by FD immediately before the foreign divisive transaction (500u × (160u ÷ 320u) = 250u). Following this reduction, FD has 250u of earnings and profits (500u – 250u).

(B) *Calculation of USC's earnings and profits.* Under paragraph (b)(1)(ii)(B) of this section, USC's earnings and profits are not increased (or replaced) as a result of the foreign divisive transaction. As a result, USP is not required to include an amount in income under paragraph (d)(2)(i) of this section.

(C) *Application of §1.367(b)-5(c).* The basis adjustment and income inclusion rules of §1.367(b)-5(c)(2) apply if USP's postdistribution amount with respect to FD stock is less than its predistribution amount with respect to FD stock. Under §1.367(b)-5(e)(1), USP's predistribution amount with respect to FD stock is USP's section 1248 amount attributable to such stock computed immediately before the distribution. Thus, USP's predistribution amount with respect to FD stock is $400 (the predistribution amount is limited to USP's built-in gain in FD stock immediately before the distribution ($800 – $400)). See also section 989(b)(2). Under section 358, USP allocates its $400 basis in FD stock between FD stock and USC stock according to the stock blocks' relative values, yielding a $200 ($400 × ($400 ÷ $800)) basis in each block. Under §1.367(b)-5(e)(2), USP's postdistribution amount with respect to FD stock is USP's section 1248 amount with respect to such stock, computed immediately after the distribution. Accordingly, USP's postdistribution amount with respect to FD stock is $200 (the postdistribution amount is limited to USP's built-in gain in FD stock immediately after the distribution ($400 – $200)). Because USP's postdistribution amount with respect to FD stock is $200 less than its predistribution amount with respect to such stock ($400 – $200), §1.367(b)-5(c)(2)(i) and (ii) require USP to reduce its basis in FD stock by the $200 difference, but only to the extent such reduction increases USP's section 1248 amount with respect to the FD stock. As a result, USP reduces its basis in the FD stock from $200 to $150 and includes $150 in income as a deemed dividend from FD. Because the requirements of section 902 are met, USP qualifies for a deemed paid foreign tax credit with respect to the deemed dividend that it receives from FD. Under §1.902-1(d)(1), the $150 deemed dividend is out of FD's separate categories and reduces foreign income taxes as follows:

Separate Category	E&P	Foreign Taxes
General	90u	$18
Shipping	60u	$24
	150u	$42

(D) *Basis adjustment.* Under §1.367(b)-5(c)(3), USP does not increase its basis in FD stock as a result of USP's $150 deemed dividend from FD. Under §1.367(b)-5(c)(4), USP increases its basis in the USC stock by the amount by which it decreased its basis in the FD stock, as well as by the amount of its deemed dividend inclusion. The §1.367(b)-5(c)(4) basis increase applies in full because USP's basis in the USC stock is not increased above the fair market value of such stock. Thus, USP increases its basis in USC stock to $400 ($200 + $50 + $150).

(E) *Reduction in FD's statutory groupings of earnings and profits.* Under paragraph (b)(2) of this section, the reduction in FD's pre-transaction earnings that is not attributable to USP's inclusion under §1.367(b)-5 decreases FD's statutory groupings of earnings and profits on a pro rata basis. Under paragraph (d)(3) of this section, FD's pre-transaction taxes also are ratably reduced. As described in this *Example 2* (ii)(A), the reduction in FD's pre-transaction earnings is 250u. As described in this *Example 2* (ii)(C), 150u of the 250u reduction is attributable to an inclusion under §1.367(b)-5. As a result, under paragraphs (b)(2) and (d)(3) of this section the remaining 100u reduction in FD's pre-transaction earnings is out of the following separate categories of earnings and profits and foreign income taxes:

Separate Category	E&P	Foreign Taxes
General	60u	$12
Shipping	40u	$16
	100u	$28

(F) *FD's earnings and profits after the foreign divisive transaction.* After the reductions described in this *Example 2* (ii)(C) and (E), FD has the following earnings and profits and foreign income taxes accounts:

Separate Category	E&P	Foreign Taxes
General	150u	$30
Shipping	100u	$40
	250u	$70

Example 3—(i) *Facts.* (A) USP, a domestic corporation, has owned all of the stock of FD since FD's incorporation in 1995. USP's adjusted basis in the FD stock is $400 and the FD stock has a fair market value of $800. USC is a preexisting controlled corporation. FD owns assets with total net bases of 320u (including 160u attributable to the USC stock and 80u attributable to the Business B shipping assets), and has the following pre-transaction earnings and pre-transaction taxes accounts:

Separate Category	E&P	Foreign Taxes
General	300u	$ 60
Shipping	200u	$80
	500u	$140

(B) On January 1, 2002, FD transfers to USC the Business B shipping assets. FD then distributes the USC stock to USP. The transaction meets the requirements of sections 368(a)(1)(D) and 355. Immediately after the foreign divisive transaction, the FD stock has a $200 fair market value and the USC stock has a $600 fair market value.

(ii) *Results*—(A) *Calculation of FD's earnings and profits.* Under paragraph (b)(4)(i) of this section, FD's pre-transaction earnings are reduced by the sum of the amounts described in paragraphs (b)(4)(i)(A) and (B) of this section. Under paragraph (b)(4)(i)(A) of this section, FD's pre-transaction earnings are reduced by an amount equal to FD's pre-transaction earnings times the net bases of the Business B shipping assets transferred to USC divided by the total net bases of the assets held by FD immediately before the foreign divisive transaction (500u × (80u ÷ 320u) = 125u). Under paragraph (b)(4)(i)(B) of this section, FD's pre-transaction earnings are reduced by an amount equal to FD's pre-transaction earnings times FD's net basis in the stock of USC divided by the total net bases of the assets held by FD immediately before the foreign divisive transaction (500u ×(160u ÷ 320u) = 250u). The sum of the amounts described in paragraphs (b)(4)(i)(A) and (B) of this section is 375u (125u + 250u).

(B) *All earnings and profits amount inclusion.* Under § 1.367(b)-3 and paragraph (d)(2)(i) of this section, USP is required to include in income as an all earnings and profits amount the pre-transaction earnings of FD that are allocable to USC under paragraph (b)(1)(i) of this section. Under paragraph (b)(4)(ii)(A) of this section, the 125u of pre-transaction earnings described in paragraph (b)(4)(i)(A) are allocable to USC. Thus, the all earnings and profits amount is $125. See also section 989(b)(1) and paragraph (d)(2)(ii) of this section. Under § § 1.367(b)-3(b)(3)(i) and 1.367(b)-2(e), USP includes the all earnings and profits amount as a deemed dividend received from FD immediately before the foreign divisive transaction. Because the requirements of section 902 are met, USP qualifies for a deemed paid foreign tax credit with respect to the deemed dividend that it receives from FD. Under § 1.902-1(d)(1), the $125 deemed dividend is out of FD's separate categories and reduces foreign income taxes as follows:

Separate Category	*E&P*	*Foreign Taxes*
General	75u	$15
Shipping	50u	$20
	125u	$35

(C) *Calculation of USP's basis in USC and USC's earnings and profits.* Under paragraph (d)(2)(iii) of this section, the § 1.367(b)-2(e)(3)(ii) basis increase applies with respect to USP's all earnings and profits amount inclusion and is attributed solely to USP's basis in USC (after application of section 358). Accordingly, USP has a $425 basis in the USC stock ($300 section 358 basis, determined by reference to the relative values of USP's FD and USC stock: $400 pre-transaction basis × ($600 ÷ $800) + $125 § 1.367(b)-2(e)(3)(ii) basis increase = $425). Because USP included in income as a deemed dividend under § 1.367(b)-3 and paragraph (d)(2) of this section the pre-transaction earnings of FD that are allocable to USC under paragraph (b)(1)(i) of this section, such earnings and profits are not available to increase USC's earnings and profits. As a result, USC's earnings and profits are not increased as a result of the foreign divisive transaction.

(D) *Application of § 1.367(b)-5(c).* The basis adjustment and income inclusion rules of § 1.367(b)-5(c)(2) apply if USP's postdistribution amount with respect to FD stock is less than its predistribution amount with respect to FD stock. Under § 1.367(b)-5(e)(1) and (3), USP's predistribution amount with respect to FD stock is USP's section 1248 amount attributable to such stock computed immediately before the distribution, after the allocation of FD's pre-transaction earnings described in paragraphs (b)(4)(i)(A) and (ii)(A) of this section, but without regard to the reduction in FD's pre-transaction earnings described in paragraph (b)(4)(i)(B) of this section. Thus, USP's predistribution amount with respect to FD stock is $375 ($500 – $125). See also section 989(b)(2). Under section 358, USP allocates its $400 basis in FD stock between FD stock and USC stock according to the stock blocks' relative values, yielding a $100 ($400 × ($200 ÷ $800)) basis in FD stock. See also paragraph (d)(2)(iii) of this section. Under § 1.367(b)-5(e)(2), USP's postdistribution amount with respect to FD stock is USP's section 1248 amount with respect to such stock, computed immediately after the distribution. Accordingly, USP's postdistribution amount with respect to FD stock is $100. (While FD has earnings and profits of 125u immediately after the foreign divisive transaction, USP's postdistribution amount is limited to its built-in gain in FD stock immediately after the distribution ($200 – $100).) Because USP's postdistribution amount with respect to FD stock is $275 less than its predistribution amount with respect to such stock ($375 – $100), § 1.367(b)-5(c)(2)(i) and (ii) require USP to reduce its basis in FD stock, but only to the extent such reduction increases USP's section 1248 amount with respect to the FD stock. As a result, USP reduces its basis in the FD stock from $100 to $75 and includes $250 in income as a deemed dividend from FD. Because the requirements of section 902 are met, USP qualifies for a deemed paid foreign tax credit with respect to the deemed dividend that it receives from FD. Under § 1.902-1(d)(1), the $250 deemed dividend is out of FD's separate categories and reduces foreign income taxes as follows:

Separate Category	*E&P*	*Foreign Taxes*
General	150u	$30
Shipping	100u	$40
	250u	$70

(E) *Basis adjustment.* Under § 1.367(b)-5(c)(3), USP does not increase its basis in FD stock as a result of USP's $250 deemed dividend from FD. Under § 1.367(b)-5(c)(4), USP increases its basis in the USC stock by the amount by which it decreased its basis in the FD stock, as well as by the amount of its deemed dividend inclusion, but only up to the fair market value of USP's USC stock. As described in this *Example 3* (ii)(C), USP has already increased its basis in the USC stock to $425. Because the fair market value of FD's USC stock is $600, USP's basis increase under § 1.367(b)-5(c)(4) is limited to $175. See also paragraph (d)(2)(iii)(C) of this section. Thus, USP has a $600 basis in the USC stock immediately after the foreign divisive transaction.

(F) *Reduction in FD's statutory groupings of earnings and profits.* Under paragraph (b)(2) of this section, the reduction in FD's pre-transaction earnings that is not attributable to USP's inclusion under paragraph (d)(2)(i) of this section or § 1.367(b)-5 decrease FD's statutory groupings of earnings and profits on a pro rata basis. Under paragraph (d)(3) of this section, FD's pre-transaction taxes are also ratably reduced. As described in this *Example 3* (ii)(A), the reduction in FD's pre-transaction earnings is 375u. As described in this *Example 3* (ii)(B) and (D), the entire 375u reduction was subject to inclusion as a deemed dividend by USP under paragraph (d)(2)(i) of this section or § 1.367(b)-5. Thus, none of FD's pre-transaction earnings remain to be reduced under paragraph (b)(2) of this section.

(G) *FD's earnings and profits after the foreign divisive transaction.* After the reductions described in this *Example 3* (ii)(B) and (D), FD has the following earnings and profits and foreign income taxes accounts:

Separate Category	*E&P*	*Foreign Taxes*
General	75u	$15
Shipping	50u	$20
	125u	$35

(e) *Foreign divisive transactions involving a foreign distributing corporation and a foreign controlled corporation.*—(1) *Scope.*—The rules of this paragraph (e) apply to a foreign divisive transaction involving a foreign distributing corporation and a foreign controlled corporation.

(2) *Earnings and profits of foreign controlled corporation.*—(i) *In general.*—Except to the extent specified in paragraph (e)(2)(ii) of this section, pre-transaction earnings of a foreign distributing corporation that are allocated to a foreign controlled corporation under the rules

described in paragraphs (b)(1)(i) and (4) of this section shall carry over to the foreign controlled corporation in accordance with the rules described in § 1.367(b)-7.

(ii) *Special rule for pre-transaction earnings allocated to a newly created controlled corporation.*—Section 1.367(b)-9 shall apply to pre-transaction earnings that are allocated from a foreign distributing corporation to a newly created foreign controlled corporation under the rules described in paragraph (b)(1)(i) of this section.

(3) *Foreign income taxes.*—Pre-transaction taxes related to a foreign distributing corporation's pre-transaction earnings that are allocated or reduced under the rules described in paragraph (b)(1)(i) of this section shall be ratably reduced. Pre-transaction taxes related to a foreign distributing corporation's pre-transaction earnings that are allocated to a foreign controlled corporation under the rules described in paragraph (b)(1)(i) of this section shall carry over to the foreign controlled corporation in accordance with the rules of § 1.367(b)-7. Section 1.367(b)-9 shall apply to pre-transaction taxes that are allocated from a foreign distributing corporation to a newly created foreign controlled corporation under the rules described in paragraph (b)(1)(i) of this section.

(4) *Previously taxed earnings and profits.*—[Reserved]

(5) *Coordination with § 1.367(b)-5.*—See also § 1.367(b)-5(c) and (d) for other rules that may apply to a foreign divisive transaction described in paragraph (e)(1) of this section.

(6) *Examples.*—The following examples illustrate the application of the rules of this section to transactions described in paragraph (e)(1) of this section. The examples presume the following facts: FD is a foreign corporation engaged in manufacturing and shipping activities through Business A and Business B, respectively. FC is a foreign corporation that is wholly owned by FD. Any earnings and profits of FD or FC described in section 904(d)(1)(D) (shipping income) qualified for the high tax exception from subpart F income under section 954(b)(4), and FD's and FC's United States shareholders elected to exclude the earnings and profits from subpart F income under section 954(b)(4) and § 1.954-1(d)(1). FD and FC have calendar taxable years. FD and FC (and all of their respective qualified business units as defined in section 989) maintain a "u" functional currency, and 1u = US$1 at all times. The examples are as follows:

Example 1—(i) *Facts.* (A) USP, a domestic corporation, has owned all of the stock of FD since FD's incorporation in 1995. USP's adjusted basis in the FD stock is $400 and the FD stock has a fair market value of $800. FD owns assets with total net bases of 320u (including 160u attributable to the Business B shipping assets), and has the following pre-transaction earnings and pre-transaction taxes accounts:

Separate Category	*E&P*	*Foreign Taxes*
General	300u	$60
Shipping	200u	$80
	500u	$140

(B) On January 1, 2002, FD incorporates FC and transfers to FC the Business B shipping assets. FD then distributes the FC stock to USP. The transaction meets the requirements of sections 368(a)(1)(D) and 355. Immediately after the foreign divisive transaction, the FD stock and the FC stock each have a $400 fair market value.

(ii) *Result*—(A) *Calculation of FD's earnings and profits.* Under paragraph (b)(1)(i) of this section, FD's pre-transaction earnings are reduced by an amount equal to its pre-transaction earnings times the net bases of the assets transferred to FC divided by the net bases of the assets held by FD immediately before the foreign divisive transaction (500u × (160u ÷ 320u) = 250u). Following this reduction, FD has 250u of earnings and profits (500u – 250u).

(B) *Application of § 1.367(b)-5(c).* The basis adjustment and income inclusion rules of § 1.367(b)-5(c)(2) apply if USP's postdistribution amount with respect to FD or FC stock is less than its predistribution amount with respect to such stock. Under § 1.367(b)-5(e)(1), USP's predistribution amount with respect to FD or FC stock is USP's section 1248 amount attributable to such stock computed immediately before the distribution but after taking into account the allocation of earnings and profits as a result of the D reorganization. Thus, USP's predistribution amounts with respect to FD and FC stock are both $200. See also section 989(b)(2) and § 1.1248-1(d)(3). Under section 358, USP allocates its $400 basis in FD stock between FD stock and FC stock according to the stock blocks' relative values, yielding a $200 ($400 × ($400 ÷ $800)) basis in each block. Under § 1.367(b)-5(e)(2), USP's postdistribution amount with respect to FD or FC stock is USP's section 1248 amount with respect to such stock, computed immediately after the distribution. Accordingly, USP's postdistribution amounts with respect to FD and FC stock are both $200. Because USP's postdistribution amounts with respect to FD and FC stock are not less than USP's respective predistribution amounts, USP is not required to make any basis adjustment or include any income under § 1.367(b)-5(c).

(C) *Reduction in FD's statutory groupings of earnings and profits.* Under paragraph (b)(2) of this section, the 250u reduction in FD's pre-transaction earnings decreases FD's statutory groupings of earnings and profits on a pro rata basis. Under paragraph (e)(3) of this section, FD's pre-transaction taxes also are ratably reduced. Accordingly, FD's pre-transaction earnings and pre-transaction taxes are reduced by the following amounts:

Separate Category	*E&P*	*Foreign Taxes*
General	150u	$30
Shipping	100u	$40
	250u	$70

(D) *Calculation of FC's earnings and profits.* Under paragraph (e)(2) of this section, the pre-transaction earnings of FD that are allocated to FC under paragraph (b)(1)(i) of this section carry over to FC in accordance with the rules of § 1.367(b)-7, subject to the rule of § 1.367(b)-9. Under paragraph (e)(3) of this section, FD's pre-transaction taxes related to the pre-transaction earnings that are allocated to FC similarly carry over to FC in accordance with the rules of § 1.367(b)-7, subject to the rule of § 1.367(b)-9. As a result, under § 1.367(b)-7(d), FC has the following earnings and profits and foreign income taxes accounts immediately after the foreign divisive transaction:

Separate Category	*E&P*	*Foreign Taxes*
General	150u	$30
Shipping	100u	$40
	250u	$70

Example 2—(i) *Facts.* (A) USP, a domestic corporation, has owned all of the stock of FD since FD's incorporation in 1995. USP's adjusted basis in the FD stock is $300 and the FD stock has a fair market value of $1,500. FC is a preexisting controlled corporation and FD has always owned all of the FC stock. FD owns assets with total net bases of 320u (including 160u attributable to the FC stock). FD and FC have the following earnings and profits and foreign income taxes accounts:

FD:

Separate Category	*E&P*	*Foreign Taxes*
General	400u	$50
Passive	(100u)	$6
Shipping	200u	$80
	500u	$136

FC:

Separate Category	E&P	Foreign Taxes
General	600u	$100
Passive	(50u)	$6
Shipping	100u	$40
	650u	$146

(B) On January 1, 2002, FD distributes the FC stock to USP in a transaction that meets the requirements of section 355. Immediately after the foreign divisive transaction, the FD stock and the FC stock each have a $750 fair market value.

(ii) *Result*—(A) *Calculation of FD's earnings and profits.* Under paragraph (b)(1)(i) and (ii)(A) of this section, FD's pre-transaction earnings are reduced by the amount of the reduction that would have been required if FD had transferred the stock of FC to a new corporation in a D reorganization. Thus, FD's pre-transaction earnings are reduced by an amount equal to its pre-transaction earnings times its net basis in the FC stock divided by the net bases of the assets held by FD immediately before the foreign divisive transaction (500u × (160u ÷ 320u) = 250u). Following this reduction, FD has 250u of earnings and profits (500u – 250u).

(B) *Application of § 1.367(b)-5(c).* The basis adjustment and income inclusion rules of § 1.367(b)-5(c) apply if USP's postdistribution amount with respect to FD or FC stock is less than its predistribution amount with respect to such stock. Under § 1.367(b)-5(e)(1), USP's predistribution amount with respect to FD or FC stock is USP's section 1248 amount attributable to such stock computed immediately before the distribution. Thus, USP's predistribution amounts with respect to FD and FC stock are $500 and $650, respectively. See also section 989(b)(2). Under section 358, USP allocates its $300 basis in FD stock between FD stock and FC stock according to the stock blocks' relative values, yielding a $150 ($300 × ($750 ÷ $1,500)) basis in each block. Under § 1.367(b)-5(e)(2), USP's postdistribution amount with respect to FD or FC stock is USP's section 1248 amount with respect to such stock, computed immediately after the distribution. Accordingly, USP's postdistribution amount with respect to FD stock is $250 (500u – 250u), and its postdistribution amount with respect to FC stock is $600 (while FC has 650u of earnings and profits immediately after the foreign divisive transaction, USP's postdistribution amount is limited to its built-in gain in FC stock immediately after the distribution ($750 – $150)). USP's postdistribution amount with respect to both the FD and FC stock is less than its predistribution amount with respect to such stock. This difference is $50 with respect to FC ($650 – $600), and $250 with respect to FD ($500 – $250). Under § 1.367(b)-5(c)(2)(i) and (ii), USP is required to reduce its basis in the FD and FC stock, but only to the extent such reductions increase USP's section 1248 amount with respect to the stock. Accordingly, USP reduces its basis in the FC stock by $50, and thereafter USP has a $100 basis in such stock ($150 – $100). Because a reduction in USP's basis in FD stock would not increase any of USP's section 1248 amount with respect to such stock, USP includes the entire $250 difference between its predistribution and postdistribution amounts with respect to the FD stock as a deemed dividend from FD. Because the requirements of section 902 are met, USP qualifies for a deemed paid foreign tax credit with respect to the deemed dividend that it receives from FD. Under § 1.960-1(i)(4), the 100u deficit in the section 904(d)(1)(A) passive separate category is allocated proportionately against the other separate categories for purposes of computing the deemed paid credit on the distribution. Thus, there are 333.33u (400u – (100u × (400u ÷ 600u))) of available earnings in the section 904(d)(1)(I) general separate category (along with $50 of foreign income taxes) and 166.67u (200u – (100u × (200u ÷ 600u))) of available earnings in the section 904(d)(1)(D) shipping separate category (along with $80 of foreign income taxes). Under § 1.902-1(d)(1), the $250 deemed dividend is out of FD's separate categories and reduces foreign income taxes as follows:

Separate Category	E&P	Foreign Taxes
General	166.67u	$25
Passive	0u	$0
Shipping	83.33u	$40
	250u	$65

(C) *Basis adjustments.* Under § 1.367(b)-5(c)(3), USP does not increase its basis in FD stock as a result of USP's $250 deemed dividend from FD. Under § 1.367(b)-5(c)(4), USP increases its basis in the FD and FC stock by the amount of its basis decrease or deemed dividend inclusion with respect to the other corporation, but only to the extent such basis increase does not diminish USP's postdistribution amount with respect to that other corporation and only to the extent of the other corporation's fair market value. Under these rules, USP increases its basis in the FD stock by the full amount by which it decreased its basis in FC ($150 + $50 = $200). USP does not increase its basis in the FC stock as a result of its deemed dividend from FD because any increase in the FC stock basis would diminish USP's postdistribution amount with respect to such stock.

(D) *FD's earnings and profits after the foreign divisive transaction.* Because the entire $250 reduction in FD's pre-transaction earnings was subject to inclusion under § 1.367(b)-5 (as described in this *Example 2* (ii)(B)), paragraph (b)(2) of this section does not apply. FD has the following earnings and profits and foreign income taxes accounts immediately after the foreign divisive transaction (see § 1.960-1(i)(4)):

Separate Category	E&P	Foreign Taxes
General	233.33u	$25
Passive	(100u)	$6
Shipping	116.67u	$40
	250u	$71

(E) *Calculation of FC's earnings and profits.* Under paragraph (b)(1)(ii)(B) of this section, FC's earnings and profits are not increased (or replaced) as a result of the foreign divisive transaction. FC's earnings and profits also are not reduced because USP was not required to include a deemed dividend out of FC under § 1.367(b)-5.

Example 3—(i) *Facts.* (A) USP, a domestic corporation, has owned all of the stock of FD since FD's incorporation in 1995. USP's adjusted basis in the FD stock is $100 and the FD stock has a fair market value of $2,000. FC is a preexisting controlled corporation and FD has always owned all of the FC stock. FD owns assets with total net bases of 320u (including 100u attributable to the FC stock and 160u attributable to the Business B shipping assets). FD and FC have the following earnings and profits and foreign income taxes accounts:

FD:

Separate Category	E&P	Foreign Taxes
General	300u	$50
10/50 dividends from FC1, a noncontrolled section 902 corporation	100u	$6
Shipping	200u	$80
	600u	$136

FC:

Separate Category	E&P	Foreign Taxes
General	100u	$10
Passive	(50u)	$6
Shipping	100u	$40
	150u	$56

(B) On January 1, 2002, FD transfers to FC the Business B shipping assets. FD then distributes the FC stock to USP. The transaction meets the requirements of sections 368(a)(1)(D) and 355. Immediately after the foreign divisive transaction, the FD stock and the FC stock each have a $1,000 fair market value.

(ii) *Result*—(A) *Calculation of FD's earnings and profits.* Under paragraph (b)(4)(i) of this section, FD's pre-transaction earnings are reduced by the sum of the amounts described in paragraphs (b)(4)(i)(A) and (B) of this section. Under paragraph (b)(4)(i)(A) of this section, FD's pre-transaction earnings are reduced by an amount equal to FD's pre-transaction earnings times the net bases of the Business B shipping assets transferred to FC divided by the total net bases in the assets held by FD immediately before the foreign divisive transaction (600u × (160u ÷ 320u) = 300u). Under paragraph (b)(4)(i)(B) of this section, FD's pre-transaction earnings are reduced by an amount equal to FD's pre-transaction earnings times FD's net bases in the stock of FC divided by the total net bases of the assets held by FD immediately before the foreign divisive transaction (600u × (100u ÷ 320u) = 187.50u). The sum of the amounts described in paragraphs (b)(4)(i)(A) and (B) of this section is 487.50u.

(B) *Application of § 1.367(b)-5(c).* The basis adjustment and income inclusion rules of § 1.367(b)-5(c)(2) apply if USP's postdistribution amount with respect to FD or FC stock is less than its predistribution amount with respect to such stock. Under § 1.367(b)-5(e)(1) and (3), USP's predistribution amount with respect to FD or FC stock is USP's section 1248 amount attributable to such stock computed immediately before the distribution, after the allocation of FD's pre-transaction earnings described in paragraphs (b)(4)(i)(A) and (ii)(A) of this section, but before the reduction in FD's pre-transaction earnings described in paragraph (b)(4)(i)(B) of this section. Thus, USP's predistribution amounts with respect to FD and FC stock are $300 (600u – 300u) and $450 (150u + 300u), respectively. See also section 989(b)(2). Under section 358, USP allocates its $100 basis in FD stock between FD stock and FC stock according to the stock blocks' relative values, yielding a $50 ($100 × ($1,000 ÷ $2,000)) basis in each block. Under § 1.367(b)-5(e)(2), USP's postdistribution amount with respect to FD or FC stock is USP's section 1248 amount with respect to such stock, computed immediately after the distribution. Accordingly, USP's postdistribution amount with respect to FD stock is $112.50 (600u – 300u – 187.50u), and its postdistribution amount with respect to FC stock is $450 (150u + 300u). Because USP's postdistribution amount with respect to FC stock is not less than its predistribution amount with respect to such stock, the § 1.367(b)-5(c)(2) basis adjustment and income inclusion rules do not apply with respect to the FC stock. Because USP's postdistribution amount with respect to FD stock is $187.50 less than its predistribution amount with respect to such stock ($300 – $112.50), § 1.367(b)-5(c)(2)(i) and (ii) require USP to reduce its basis in FD stock, but only to the extent such reduction increases USP's section 1248 amount with respect to the FD stock. Because a reduction in USP's basis in the FD stock would not increase any of USP's section 1248 amount with respect to such stock, USP includes the entire $187.50 difference between its predistribution and postdistribution amounts with respect to the FD stock as a deemed dividend from FD. Because the requirements of section 902 are met, USP qualifies for a deemed paid foreign tax credit with respect to the deemed dividend that it receives from FD. Under § 1.902-1(d)(1), the $187.50 deemed dividend is out of FD's separate categories and reduces foreign income taxes as follows:

Separate Category	*E&P*	*Foreign Taxes*
General	93.75u	$15.63
10/50 dividends from FC1	31.25u	$1.88
Shipping	62.50u	$25
	187.50u	$42.51

(C) *Basis adjustment.* Under § 1.367(b)-5(c)(3), the basis increase provided in § 1.367(b)-2(e)(3)(ii) does not apply with respect to USP's $187.50 deemed dividend from FD. Under § 1.367(b)-5(c)(4), USP increases its basis in the FC stock by the amount of its deemed dividend inclusion from FD, but only to the extent such basis increase does not diminish USP's postdistribution amount with respect to FC stock and only up to the fair market value of the FC stock. Under these rules, USP increases its basis in the FC stock by the full amount of its deemed dividend from FD ($50 + $187.50 = $237.50).

(D) *Reduction in FD's statutory groupings of earnings and profits.* Under paragraph (b)(2) of this section, the reduction in FD's pre-transaction earnings that is not attributable to USP's inclusion under § 1.367(b)-5 decreases FD's statutory groupings of earnings and profits on a pro rata basis. Under paragraph (e)(3) of this section, FD's pre-transaction taxes are also ratably reduced. As described in this *Example 3* (ii)(A), the reduction in FD's pre-transaction earnings is 487.50u. As described in this *Example 3* (ii)(B), 187.50u of the 487.50u reduction is attributable to a deemed dividend inclusion by USP under § 1.367(b)-5. Thus, under paragraphs (b)(2) and (e)(3) of this section, the remaining 300u reduction in FD's pre-transaction earnings and related pre-transaction taxes is out of FD's separate categories and reduces foreign income taxes as follows:

Separate Category	*E&P*	*Foreign Taxes*
General	150u	$25
10/50 dividends from FC1	50u	$3
Shipping	100u	$40
	300u	$68

(E) *Calculation of FC's earnings and profits.* Under paragraph (b)(4)(ii) of this section, FC's earnings and profits immediately after the foreign divisive transaction equal the sum of FC's earnings and profits immediately before the foreign divisive transaction, plus the amount of the reduction in FD's earnings and profits described in paragraph (b)(4)(i)(A) of this section, except to the extent such amount was included in income as a deemed dividend pursuant to the foreign divisive transaction. The reduction in FD's earnings and profits described in paragraph (b)(4)(i)(A) of this section is 300u, none of which was included in income by USP as a deemed dividend pursuant to the foreign divisive transaction. Under paragraphs (e)(2) and (3) of this section, the 300u of pre-transaction earnings and related pre-transaction taxes carry over to FC and combine with FC's earnings and profits and foreign income taxes accounts in accordance with the rules described in § 1.367(b)-7. Under § 1.367(b)-7(d), FC has the following earnings and profits and foreign income taxes accounts immediately after the foreign divisive transaction:

Separate Category	*E&P*	*Hovering Deficit*	*Taxes*	*Taxes Associated w/ Hovering Deficit*
General	250u		$35	
10/50 dividends from FC1	50u		$3	
Passive		(50u)		$6
Shipping	200u		$80	
	500u	(50u)	$118	$6

(F) *FD's earnings and profits after the foreign divisive transaction.* Following the reductions described in this *Example 3* (ii)(B) and (D), FD has the following earnings and profits and foreign income taxes accounts:

Separate Category	*E&P*	*Foreign Taxes*
General	56.25u	$9.37
10/50 dividends from FC1	18.75u	$1.12
Shipping	37.50u	$15
	112.50u	$25.49

(f) *Effective date.*—This section shall apply to section 367(b) exchanges that occur on or after the date 30 days after these regulations are published as final regulations in the Federal Register. [Prop. Reg. § 1.367(b)-8.]

[Proposed 11-15-2000 (corrected 3-12-2001).]

§1.367(b)-9. Special rule for F reorganizations and similar transactions.—(a) *Scope.*—This section applies to a foreign section 381 transaction (as defined in §1.367(b)-7(a)) either—

(1) That is described in section 368(a)(1)(F); or

(2) That involves—

(i) At least one foreign corporation that holds no property and has no tax attributes immediately before the transaction, other than a nominal amount of assets (and related tax attributes) to facilitate its organization or preserve its existence as a corporation; and

(ii) No more than one foreign corporation that holds more than a nominal amount of property or has more than a nominal amount of tax attributes immediately before the transaction.

(b) *Hovering deficit rules inapplicable.*—If a transaction is described in paragraph (a) of this section, a foreign surviving corporation shall succeed to earnings and profits, deficits in earnings and profits, and foreign income taxes without regard to the hovering deficit rules of §1.367(b)-7(d)(2), (e)(1)(iii), and (e)(2)(iii).

(c) *Foreign divisive transactions.*—[Reserved]

(d) *Examples.*—The following examples illustrate the principles of this section:

Example 1. (i) *Facts.* (A) Foreign corporation A is and always has been a wholly owned subsidiary of USP, a domestic corporation. Foreign corporation A was incorporated in 1995, and has always had a calendar taxable year. Foreign corporation A (and all of its respective qualified business units as defined in section 989) maintains a "u" functional currency. On December 31, 2006, foreign corporation A has the following post-1986 undistributed earnings and post-1986 foreign income taxes:

Separate Category	*E&P*	*Foreign Taxes*
Passive	(1,000u)	$ 5
General	200u	$200
	(800u)	$205

(B) On January 1, 2007, foreign corporation A moves its place of incorporation from Country 1 to Country 2 in a reorganization described in section 368(a)(1)(F).

(ii) *Result.* Under §1.367(b)-7(d), as modified by paragraph (b) of this section, the pre-transaction deficit of foreign corporation A will not hover. Accordingly, foreign surviving corporation has the following post-1986 undistributed earnings and post-1986 foreign income taxes immediately after the foreign section 381 transaction:

Separate Category	*E&P*	*Foreign Taxes*
Passive	(1,000u)	$ 5
General	200u	$200
	(800u)	$205

Example 2. (i) *Facts.* (A) Foreign corporations B, C and D are and always have been wholly owned subsidiaries of USP, a domestic corporation. Foreign corporation B was incorporated in 2000 and foreign corporations C and D were incorporated in 2001. Foreign corporation B does not own any significant property and has no earnings and profits or foreign income taxes accounts. Both foreign corporations C and D have always had a calendar taxable year. Foreign corporations C and D (and all of their respective qualified business units as defined in section 989) maintain a "u" functional currency. On December 31, 2006, foreign corporations C and D have the following post-1986 undistributed earnings and post-1986 foreign income taxes:

Foreign corporation C

Separate Category	*E&P*	*Foreign Taxes*
Passive	(900u)	$ 50
General	(200u)	$100
	(1100u)	$150

Foreign corporation D

Separate Category	*E&P*	*Foreign Taxes*
Passive	1200u	$400
General	400u	$100
	1600u	$500

(B) On January 1, 2007, USP foreign corporations C and D merge into foreign corporation B in a reorganization described in section 368(a)(1)(A).

(ii) *Result.* Although the merger is a foreign section 381 transaction involving a foreign corporation with no property or tax attributes, paragraph (b) of this section does not apply because more than one foreign corporation with significant tax attributes is involved in the foreign section 381 transaction. Accordingly, under §1.367(b)-7(d), foreign surviving corporation B has the following post-1986 undistributed earnings and post-1986 foreign income taxes immediately after the foreign section 381 transaction:

	Earnings & Profits:		*Foreign Taxes:*	
Separate Category	*Positive E&P*	*Hovering Deficit*	*Foreign Taxes Available*	*Foreign Taxes Associated with Hovering Deficit*
General	1200u	(900u)	$400	$ 50
Passive	400u	(200u)	$100	$100
	1600u	(1100u)	$500	$150

(e) *Effective date.*—This section shall apply to section 367(b) transactions that occur on or after November 6, 2006. [Reg. §1.367(b)-9.]

□ [*T.D.* 9273, 8-7-2006.]

§1.367(b)-10. Acquisition of parent stock or securities for property in triangular reorganizations.—(a) *In general.*—(1) *Scope.*—Except as provided in paragraphs (a)(2)(i) through (iii) of this section, this section applies to a triangular reorganization if P or S (or both) is a foreign corporation and, in connection with the reorganization, S acquires in exchange for property all or a portion of the P stock or P securities (P acquisition) that are used to acquire the stock, securities or property of T in the triangular reorganization. This section applies to a triangular reorganization regardless of whether P controls (within the meaning of section 368(c)) S at the time of the P acquisition.

(2) *Exceptions.*—This section shall not apply if—

(i) P and S are foreign corporations and neither P nor S is a controlled foreign corporation (within the meaning of §1.367(b)-2(a)) immediately before or immediately after the triangular reorganization;

(ii) S is a domestic corporation, P's stock in S is not a United States real property interest (within the meaning of section 897(c)), and P would not be subject to U.S. tax on a dividend (as determined under section 301(c)(1)) from S under either section 881 (for example, by reason of an applicable treaty) or section 882; or

(iii) In an exchange under section 354 or 356, one or more U.S. persons exchange stock or securities of T and the amount of gain in the T stock or securities recognized by such U.S. persons under section 367(a)(1) is equal to or greater than the sum of the amount of the deemed distribution that would be treated by P as a dividend under section 301(c)(1) and the amount of such deemed distribution that would be treated by P as gain from the sale or exchange of property under section 301(c)(3) if this section would otherwise apply to the triangular reorganization. See § 1.367(a)-3(a)(2)(iv) (providing a similar rule that excludes certain transactions from the application of section 367(a)(1)).

(3) *Definitions.*—For purposes of this section, the following definitions apply:

(i) The terms *P, S,* and *T* have the meanings set forth in § 1.358-6(b)(1)(i), (ii), and (iii), respectively.

(ii) The term *property* has the meaning set forth in section 317(a), except that the term property also includes —

(A) A liability assumed by S to acquire the P stock or securities; and

(B) S stock (or any rights to acquire S stock) to the extent such S stock (or rights to acquire S stock) is used by S to acquire P stock or securities from a person other than P.

(iii) The term *security* means an instrument that constitutes a security for purposes of section 354 or 356.

(iv) The term *triangular reorganization* has the meaning set forth in § 1.358-6(b)(2).

(b) *General rules.*—(1) *Deemed distribution.*—If this section applies, adjustments shall be made that have the effect of a distribution of property (with no built-in gain or loss) from S to P under section 301 (deemed distribution). The amount of the deemed distribution shall equal the sum of the amount of money transferred by S, the amount of any liabilities that are assumed by S and constitute property, and the fair market value of other property transferred by S in the P acquisition in exchange for the P stock or P securities described in paragraph (i) or (ii), respectively, of this paragraph (b)(1)—

(i) P stock received by T shareholders or securityholders in an exchange to which section 354 or 356 applies.

(ii) P securities received by T shareholders or securityholders to the extent such securities are "other property" (within the meaning of section 356(d)).

(2) *Deemed contribution.*—If this section applies, adjustments shall be made that have the effect of a contribution of property (with no built-in gain or loss) by P to S in an amount equal to the amount of the deemed distribution from S to P under paragraph (b)(1) of this section (deemed contribution).

(3) *Timing of deemed distribution and deemed contribution.*—If P controls (within the meaning of section 368(c)) S at the time of the P acquisition, the adjustments described in paragraphs (b)(1) and (2) of this section shall be made as if the deemed distribution and deemed contribution, respectively, are separate transactions occurring immediately before the P acquisition. If P does not control (within the meaning of section 368(c)) S at the time of the P acquisition, the adjustments described in paragraphs (b)(1) and (2) of this section shall be made as if the deemed distribution and deemed contribution, respectively, are separate transactions occurring immediately after P acquires control of S, but prior to the triangular reorganization.

(4) *Application of other provisions.*—Nothing in this section shall prevent the application of other provisions of the Internal Revenue Code from applying to the P acquisition. For example, section 304 may apply to the P acquisition. Furthermore, section 1001 or 267 may apply to S's transfer of property to acquire P stock or securities from P or a person other than P. In addition, generally applicable provisions that apply to triangular reorganizations, such as § 1.358-6 and § 1.1032-2, shall apply to the triangular reorganization in a manner consistent with S acquiring the P stock or securities in exchange for property from P or a person other than P, as the case may be.

(5) *Example.*—The rules of this paragraph (b) are illustrated by the following example:

(i) *Facts.* P, a publicly traded domestic corporation, owns all of the outstanding stock of FS, a foreign corporation, and all of the outstanding stock of US1, a domestic corporation that is a member of the P consolidated group. US1 owns all of the outstanding stock of FT, a foreign corporation, the fair market value of which is $100x. US1's basis in the FT stock is $100x, such that there is a no built-in gain or loss in the FT stock. FS has earnings and profits in excess of $100x. FS purchases $100x of P stock from the public on the open market in exchange for $100x of cash. Pursuant to foreign law, FT merges with and into FS in a triangular reorganization that qualifies under section 368(a)(1)(A) by reason of section 368(a)(2)(D). In an exchange to which section 354 applies, US1 exchanges all the outstanding stock of FT for the $100x of P stock purchased by FS on the open market.

(ii) *Analysis.* The triangular reorganization is described in paragraph (a)(1) of this section. P is a domestic corporation and FS is a foreign corporation. In connection with FS purchasing the $100x of P stock in exchange for property (cash), FS uses the P stock to acquire the FT property in a triangular reorganization, and US1 receives the P stock in an exchange to which section 354 applies. Furthermore, none of the exceptions of paragraphs (a)(2)(i) through (iii) of this section apply. Therefore, pursuant to paragraph (b)(1) of this section, adjustments are made that have the effect of a deemed distribution of property (with no built-in gain or loss) in the amount of $100x from FS to P under section 301. Pursuant to paragraph (b)(2) of this section, adjustments are made that have the effect of a deemed contribution of property (with no built-in gain or loss) in the amount of $100x by P to FS. Pursuant to paragraph (b)(3) of this section, the adjustments described in paragraphs (b)(1) and (2) of this section are made as if the deemed distribution and deemed contribution, respectively, are separate transactions occurring immediately before FS's purchase of the P stock on the open market. Generally applicable provisions apply to FS's purchase of the P stock on the open market (see, for example, section 304) and in determining certain tax consequences to P and FS as a result of the triangular reorganization (see, for example, § 1.358-6(d) and § 1.1032-2(c)).

(c) *Collateral adjustments.*—This paragraph (c) provides additional rules that apply by reason of the deemed distribution and deemed contribution described in paragraphs (b)(1) and (b)(2), respectively, of this section.

(1) *Deemed distribution.*—A deemed distribution described in paragraph (b)(1) of this section shall be treated as occurring for all purposes of the Internal Revenue Code. Thus, for example, the ordering rules of section 301(c) apply to characterize the deemed distribution to P as a dividend from the earnings and profits of S, return of stock basis, or gain from the sale or exchange of property, as the case may be. Furthermore, section 959 may apply to the deemed distribution if S is a foreign corporation, and sections 881, 882, 897, 1442, or 1445 may apply to the deemed distribution if S is a domestic corporation. Appropriate corresponding adjustments shall be made to S's earnings and profits consistent with the principles of section 312.

(2) *Deemed contribution.*—A deemed contribution described in paragraph (b)(2) of this section shall be treated as occurring for all purposes of the Internal Revenue Code. Thus, for example, appropriate adjustments shall be made to P's basis in the S stock.

(d) *Anti-abuse rule.*—Appropriate adjustments shall be made pursuant to this section if, in connection with a triangular reorganization, a transaction is engaged in with a view to avoid the purpose of this section. For example, if S is created, organized, or funded to avoid the application of this section with respect to the earnings and profits of a corporation related (within the meaning of section 267(b)) to P or S, the earnings and profits of S will be deemed to include the earnings and profits of such related corporation for purposes of determining the consequences of the adjustments provided in this section, and appropriate corresponding adjustments will be made to account for the application of this section to the earnings and profits of such related corporation.

(e) *Applicability dates.*—This section applies to triangular reorganizations occurring on or after May 17, 2011. For triangular reorganizations that occur prior to May 17, 2011, see § 1.367(b)-14T as contained in 26 CFR part 1 revised as of April 1, 2011. Paragraph (c)(1) of this section applies to deemed distributions that occur in taxable years ending on or after November 2, 2020. [Reg. § 1.367(b)-10.]

☐ [*T.D. 9526, 5-17-2011. Amended by T.D. 9959, 12-28-2021.*]

§ 1.367(b)-12. Subsequent treatment of amounts attributed or included in income.—(a) *In general.*—This section applies to distributions with respect to, or a disposition of, stock—

(1) To which, in connection with an exchange occurring before February 23, 2000, an amount has been attributed pursuant to § 7.367(b)-9 or 7.367(b)-10 of this chapter (as in effect prior to February 23, 2000, see 26 CFR part 1 revised as of April 1, 1999); or

(2) In respect of which, before February 23, 2000, an amount has been included in income or added to earnings and profits pursuant to § 7.367(b)-7 or 7.367(b)-10 of this chapter (as in effect prior to February 23, 2000, see 26 CFR part 1 revised as of April 1, 1999).

(b) *Applicable rules.*—See §7.367(b)-12(b) through (e) of this chapter (as in effect prior to January 11, 2001, see 26 CFR part 1 revised as of April 1, 2000) for purposes of applying paragraph (a) of this section.

(c) *Effective date.*—This section applies to distributions or dispositions that occur on or after January 11, 2001. [Reg. §1.367(b)-12.]

□ [*T.D. 8937, 1-10-2001.*]

§1.367(b)-13. Special rules for determining basis and holding period.—(a) *Scope and definitions.*—(1) *Scope.*—This section provides special basis and holding period rules to determine the basis and holding period of stock of certain foreign surviving corporations held by a controlling corporation whose stock is issued in an exchange under section 354 or 356 in a triangular reorganization. This section applies to transactions that are subject to section 367(b) as well as section 367(a), including transactions concurrently subject to sections 367(a) and (b).

(2) *Definitions.*—For purposes of this section, the following definitions apply:

(i) A block of stock has the meaning provided in §1.1248-2(b).

(ii) The terms *P, S,* and *T* have the meanings set forth in §1.358-6(b)(1)(i), (ii), and (iii), respectively.

(iii) A triangular reorganization is a reorganization described in §1.358-6(b)(2)(i), (ii), (iii), or (v) (a forward triangular merger, triangular C reorganization, reverse triangular merger, or triangular G reorganization, respectively).

(b) *Determination of basis for exchanges of foreign stock or securities under section 354 or 356.*—For rules determining the basis of stock or securities in a foreign corporation received in a section 354 or 356 exchange, see §1.358-2.

(c) *Determination of basis and holding period for triangular reorganizations.*—(1) *Application.*—In the case of a triangular reorganization described in paragraph (a)(2)(ii) of this section, this paragraph (c) applies, if—

(i)(A) Immediately before the transaction, either P is a section 1248 shareholder with respect to S, or P is a foreign corporation and a United States person is a section 1248 shareholder with respect to both P and S; and

(B) In the case of a reverse triangular merger, P's exchange of S stock is not described in §1.367(b)-3(a) and (b) or in §1.367(b)-4(b)(1)(i), (2)(i), or (3); or

(ii)(A) Immediately before the transaction, a shareholder of T is a section 1248 shareholder with respect to T, or a shareholder of T is a foreign corporation and a United States person is a section 1248 shareholder with respect to both such foreign corporation and T; and

(B) With respect to at least one of the exchanging shareholders described in paragraph (c)(1)(ii)(A) of this section, the exchange of T stock is not described in §1.367(b)-3(a) and (b) or in §1.367(b)-4(b)(1)(i), (2)(i), or (3).

(2) *Basis and holding period rules.*—In the case of a triangular reorganization described in paragraph (c)(1) of this section, each share of stock of the surviving corporation (S or T) held by P must be divided into portions attributable to the S stock and the T stock immediately before the exchange. See paragraph (e) of this section *Examples 1* through *4* for illustrations of this rule.

(i) *Portions attributable to S stock.*—(A) In the case of a forward triangular merger, a triangular C reorganization, or a triangular G reorganization, the basis and holding period of the portion of each share of surviving corporation stock attributable to the S stock is the basis and holding period of such share of stock immediately before the exchange.

(B) In the case of a reverse triangular merger, the basis and holding period of the portion of each share of surviving corporation stock attributable to the S stock is the basis and the holding period immediately before the exchange of a proportionate amount of the S stock to which the portion relates. If P is a shareholder described in paragraph (c)(1)(i)(A) of this section with respect to S, and P exchanges two or more blocks of S stock pursuant to the transaction, then each share of the surviving corporation (T) attributable to the S stock must be further divided into separate portions to account for the separate blocks of stock in S.

(C) If the value of S stock immediately before the triangular reorganization is less than one percent of the value of the surviving corporation stock immediately after the triangular reorganization, then P may determine its basis in the surviving corporation stock by applying the rules of paragraph (c)(2)(ii) of this section to determine the basis and holding period of the surviving corporation stock attributable to the T stock, and then increasing the basis of each share of surviving corporation stock by the proportionate amount of P's aggregate basis in the S stock immediately before the exchange (without dividing the stock of the surviving corporation into separate portions attributable to the S stock).

(ii) *Portions attributable to T stock.*—(A) If any exchanging shareholder of T stock is described in paragraph (c)(1)(ii) of this section, the basis and holding period of the portion of each share of stock in the surviving corporation attributable to the T stock is the basis and holding period immediately before the exchange of a proportionate amount of the T stock to which such portion relates. If any exchanging shareholder of T stock is described in paragraph (c)(1)(ii) of this section, and such shareholder exchanges two or more blocks of T stock pursuant to the transaction, then each share of surviving corporation stock attributable to the T stock must be further divided into separate portions to account for the separate blocks of T stock.

(B) If no exchanging shareholder of T stock is described in paragraph (c)(1)(ii) of this section, the rules of §1.358-6 apply to determine the basis of the portion of each share of the surviving corporation attributable to T immediately before the exchange.

(d) *Special rules applicable to divided shares of stock.*—(1) *In general.*—(i) Shares of stock in different blocks are aggregated into one divided portion for basis purposes, if such shares immediately before the exchange are owned by one or more shareholders that are—

(A) Not section 1248 shareholders with respect to the corporation; or

(B) Foreign corporate shareholders, provided that no United States persons are section 1248 shareholders with respect to both such foreign corporate shareholders and the corporation.

(ii) For purposes of determining the amount of gain realized on the sale or exchange of stock that has a divided portion pursuant to paragraph (c) of this section, any amount realized on such sale or exchange will be allocated to each divided portion of the stock based on the relative fair market value of the stock to which the portion is attributable at the time the portions were created. See paragraph (e) *Example 5* of this section.

(iii) Shares of stock will no longer be required to be divided if section 1248 or section 964(e) would not apply to a disposition or exchange of such stock.

(2) *Pre-exchange earnings and profits.*—All earnings and profits (or deficits) accumulated by a foreign corporation before the reorganization and attributable to a share (or block) of stock for purposes of section 1248 are attributable to the divided portion of stock with the basis and holding period of that share (or block). See §1.367(b)-4(d).

(3) *Post-exchange earnings and profits.*—Any earnings and profits (or deficits) accumulated by the surviving corporation subsequent to the reorganization are attributed to each divided share of stock pursuant to section 1248 and the regulations thereunder. The amount of earnings and profits (or deficits) attributable to a divided share of stock is further attributed to the divided portions of such share of stock based on the relative fair market value of each divided portion of stock. See paragraph (e) *Example 5* of this section.

(e) *Examples.*—The rules of this section are illustrated by the following examples:

Example 1. Blocks of stock exchanged in a triangular reorganization—(i) *Facts.* (A) US1, a domestic corporation, owns all the stock of F1, a foreign corporation. F1 owns all the stock of FT, a foreign corporation, with 100 shares of stock outstanding. Each share of FT stock is valued at $10x. Because F1 acquired the stock of FT at two different dates, F1 owns two blocks of FT stock for purposes of section 1248. The first block consists of 60 shares. The shares in the first block have a basis of $300x ($5x per share), a holding period of 10 years, and $240x ($4x per share) of earnings and profits attributable to the shares for purposes of section 1248. The second block consists of 40 shares. The shares in the second block have a basis of $600x ($15x per share), a holding period of 2 years, and $80x ($2x per share) of earnings and profits attributable to the shares for purposes of section 1248.

(B) US2, a domestic corporation, owns all of the stock of FP, a foreign corporation, which owns all of the stock of FS, a foreign corporation. FP owns two blocks of FS stock. Each block consists of 10 shares with a value of $200x ($20x per share). The shares in the first block have a basis of $50x ($5x per share), a holding period of 10 years, and $50x ($5x per share) of earnings and profits attributable to such shares for purposes of section 1248. The shares in the second block had a basis of $100x ($10x per share), a holding period of 5 years, and $20x ($2x per share) of earnings and profits attributable to such shares for purposes of section 1248.

(C) FT merges into FS, with FS surviving, and F1 receives 50 shares of FP stock with a value of $1,000x in exchange for its FT stock. The merger of FT into FS qualifies as forward triangular merger, and immediately after the exchange US1 is a section 1248 shareholder with respect to F1, the exchanging shareholder, FP and FS, all of which are controlled foreign corporations.

(ii) *Basis and holding period determination.* (*1*) US1 is a section 1248 shareholder of F1, the exchanging shareholder, and FT (both of which are controlled foreign corporations) immediately before the transaction. Moreover, F1 is not required to include amounts in income under § 1.367(b)-3(b) or 1.367(b)-4(b) as described in paragraph (c)(1)(ii)(B) of this section. Accordingly, the basis and holding period of the FS stock held by FP immediately after the triangular reorganization is determined pursuant to paragraph (c) of this section.

(2) Pursuant to paragraph (c) of this section, each share of FS stock is divided into portions attributable to the basis and holding period of the FS stock held by FP immediately before the exchange (the FS portion) and the FT stock held by F1 immediately before the exchange (the FT portion). The basis and holding period of the FS portion is the basis and holding period of the FS stock held by FP immediately before the exchange. Thus, each share of FS stock in the first block has a portion with a basis of $5x, a value of $20x, a holding period of 10 years, and $5x of earnings and profits attributable to such portion for purposes of section 1248. Each share of FS stock in the second block has a portion with a basis of $10x, a value of $20x, a holding period of 5 years, and $2x of earnings and profits attributable to such portion for purposes of section 1248.

(3) Because the exchanging shareholder of FT stock (F1) has a section 1248 shareholder (US1), the holding period and basis of the FT portion is the holding period and the proportionate amount of the basis of the FT stock immediately before the exchange to which such portion relates. Further, because F1 exchanged two blocks of FT stock, the FT portion must be divided into two separate portions attributable to the two blocks of FT stock. Thus, each share of FS stock will have a second portion with a basis of $15x ($300x basis / 20 shares), a value of $30x ($600x value / 20 shares), a holding period of 10 years, and $12x of earnings and profits ($240x / 20 shares) attributable to such portion for purposes of section 1248. Each share of FS stock will have a third portion with a basis of $30x ($600x basis / 20 shares), a value of $20x ($400x value / 20 shares), a holding period of 2 years, and $4x of earnings and profits ($80x / 20 shares) attributable to such portion for purposes of section 1248.

(iii) *Subsequent disposition—first block.* Assume, immediately after the transaction, FP disposes of a share of FS stock from the first block. When FP disposes of any share of its FS stock, it is treated as disposing of each divided portion of such share. With respect to the first portion (attributable to the FS stock), FP recognizes a gain of $15x ($20x value - $5x basis), $5x of which is treated as a dividend under section 1248. With respect to the second portion (attributable to the first block of FT stock), FP recognizes a gain of $15x ($30x value - $15x basis), $12x of which is treated as a dividend under section 1248. With respect to the third portion (attributable to the second block of FT stock), FP recognizes a capital loss of $10x ($20x value - $30x basis).

(iv) *Subsequent disposition—second block.* Assume further, immediately after the transaction, FP also disposes of a share of stock from the second block of FS stock. With respect to the first portion (attributable to the FS stock), FP recognizes a gain of $10x ($20x value - $10x basis), $2x of which is treated as a dividend under section 1248. With respect to the second portion (attributable to the first block of FT stock), FP recognizes a gain of $15x ($30x value - $15x basis), $12x of which is treated as a dividend under section 1248. With respect to the third portion (attributable to the second block of FT stock), FP recognizes a capital loss of $10x ($20x value - $30x basis).

Example 2. (i) *Facts.* The facts are the same as in *Example 1,* except that FS merges into FT with FT surviving in a reverse triangular merger. Pursuant to the merger, F1 receives FP stock with a value of $1,000x in exchange for its FT stock, and FP receives 10 shares of FT stock with a value of $1,000x in exchange for its FS stock. Immediately after the exchange, US1 is a section 1248 shareholder with respect to F1, the exchanging shareholder, FP, and FT, all of which are controlled foreign corporations.

(ii) *Basis and holding period determination*—(A) The basis and holding period of the stock of the surviving corporation held by FP are the same as in *Example 1,* except that each share of the surviving corporation (FT, instead of FS) will be divided into four portions instead of three portions. Because FP exchanges two blocks of FS stock, the FS portion must be divided into two separate portions attributable to the two blocks of FS stock. Because F1 exchanges two blocks of FT stock, the FT portion must be divided into two separate portions attributable to the two blocks of FT stock.

(B) Thus, each share of the surviving corporation (FT) will have a first portion (attributable to the first block of FS stock) with a basis of $5x ($50x / 10 shares), a value of $20x ($200x / 10 shares), a holding period of 10 years, and $5x of earnings and profits ($50x / 10 shares) attributable to such portion for purposes of section 1248. Each share of F1 stock will have a second portion (attributable to the second block of FS stock) with a basis of $10x ($100x / 10 shares), a value of $20x ($200x / 10 shares), a holding period of 5 years, and $2x of earnings and profits ($20x / 10 shares) attributable to such portion for purposes of section 1248. Moreover, each share of FT stock will have a third portion (attributable to the first block of FT stock) with a basis of $30x ($300x basis / 10 shares), a value of $60x ($600x value / 10 shares), a holding period of 10 years, and $24x of earnings and profits ($240x / 10 shares) attributable to such portion for purposes of section 1248. Lastly, each share of FT stock will have a fourth portion (attributable to the second block of FT stock) with a basis of $60x ($600x basis / 10 shares), a value of $40x ($400x value / 10 shares), a holding period of 2 years, and $8x of earnings and profits ($80x / 10 shares) attributable to such portion for purposes of section 1248.

Example 3. (i) *Facts.* USP, a domestic corporation, owns all the stock of FS, a foreign corporation with 10 shares of stock outstanding. Each share of FS stock has a value of $10x, a basis of $5x, a holding period of 10 years, and $7x of earnings and profits attributable to such share for purposes of section 1248. FP, a foreign corporation, owns the stock of FT, another foreign corporation. FP and FT do not have any section 1248 shareholders. FT has assets with a value of $100x, a basis of $50x, and no liabilities. The FT stock held by FP has a value of $100x and a basis of $75x. FT merges into FS with FS surviving in a forward triangular merger. Pursuant to the reorganization, FP receives USP stock with a value of $100x in exchange for its FT stock.

(ii) *Basis and holding period determination*—(A) Because USP is a section 1248 shareholder of FS immediately before the transaction, the basis and holding period of the FS stock held by USP immediately after the triangular reorganization is determined pursuant to paragraph (c) of this section.

(B) Pursuant to paragraph (c) of this section, each share of FS stock is divided into portions attributable to the basis and holding period of the FS stock held by USP immediately before the exchange (the FS portion) and the FT portion immediately before the exchange. Because FT does not have a section 1248 shareholder immediately before the transaction, the rules of § 1.358-6 apply to determine the basis of the FT portion of each share of FS stock. Those rules determine the basis of FS stock held by USP by reference to the basis of FT's net assets. The basis and holding period of the FS portion is the basis and holding period of the FS stock held by USP immediately before the exchange. Thus, each share of FS stock has a portion with a basis of $5x, a value of $10x, a holding period of 10 years, and $7x of earnings and profits attributable to such portion for section 1248 purposes. The basis of the FT portion is the basis of the FT assets to which such portion relates. Thus, each share of FS stock has a second portion with a basis of $5x ($50x basis in FT's assets / 10 shares) and a value of $10x ($100x value of FT's assets / 10 shares). All of FS's earnings and profits prior to the transaction ($70x) is attributed solely to the FS portion in each share of FS stock. As a result of each share of stock being divided into portions, the basis of the FS stock is not averaged with the basis of the FT assets to increase the section 1248 amount with respect to the stock of the surviving corporation (FS).

Example 4. (i) *Facts.* US, a domestic corporation, owns all of the stock of FT, a foreign corporation. The FT stock held by US constitutes a single block of stock with a value of $1,000x, a basis of $600x, and holding period of 5 years. USP, a domestic corporation, forms FS, a foreign corporation, pursuant to the plan of reorganization and capitalizes it with $10x of cash. FS merges into FT with FT surviving in a reverse triangular merger and a reorganization described in section 368(a)(1)(B). Pursuant to the reorganization, US receives USP stock with a value of $1,000x in exchange for its FT stock, and USP receives 10 shares of FT stock with a value of $1,010x in exchange for its FS stock.

(ii) *Basis and holding period determination.* (A) US and USP are section 1248 shareholders of FT and FS, respectively, immediately before the transaction. Neither US nor USP is required to include amounts in income under § 1.367(b)-3(b) or 1.367(b)-4(b) as described in paragraph (c)(1)(i)(B) or (c)(1)(ii)(B) of this section. The basis and holding period of the FT stock held by USP is determined pursuant to paragraph (c) of this section.

(B) Pursuant to paragraph (c) of this section, because the exchanging shareholder of FT stock (US) is a section 1248 shareholder of FT, each share of the surviving corporation (FT) has a proportionate amount of the basis and holding period of the FT stock immediately before the exchange to which such share relates. Thus, the portion of each share of FT stock attributable to the FT stock has a basis of $60x ($600x basis / 10 shares), a value of $100x ($1,000x value / 10 shares), and a holding period of 5 years. Because the value of FS stock immediately before the triangular reorganization ($10x) is less than one percent of the value of the surviving corporation (FT) immediately after the triangular reorganization ($1,010x), USP may determine its basis in the stock of the surviving corporation (FT) attributable to its FS stock basis held prior to the reorganization by increasing the basis of each share of FT stock by the proportionate amount of USP's aggregate basis in the FS stock immediately before the exchange (without dividing each share of FT stock into separate portions to account for FS and FT). If USP so elects, USP's basis in each share of FT stock is increased by $1x ($10x basis in FS stock / 10 shares). As a result, each share of FT stock has a basis of $61x, a value of $101x, and a holding period of 5 years.

Example 5. (i) *Facts.* US, a domestic corporation, owns all of the stock of F1, a foreign corporation, which owns all the stock of FT, a foreign corporation. The FT stock held by F1 constitutes one block of stock with a basis of $170x, a value of $200x, a holding period of 5 years, and $10x of earnings and profits attributable to such stock for purposes of section 1248. FP, a foreign corporation, owns all the stock of FS, a foreign corporation. FS has 10 shares of stock outstanding. No United States person is a section 1248 shareholder with respect to FP or FS. The FS stock held by FP has a value of $100x and a basis of $50x ($5x per share). FT merges into FS with FS surviving in a forward triangular merger. Pursuant to the merger, F1 receives FP stock with a value of $200x for its FT stock in an exchange that qualifies for non-recognition under section 354. US is a section 1248 shareholder with respect to F1, the exchanging shareholder, FP, and FS (all of which are controlled foreign corporations) immediately after the exchange.

(ii) *Basis and holding period determination.* (A) Because US is a section 1248 shareholder of F1, the exchanging shareholder, and FT immediately before the transaction, and US is a section 1248 shareholder of F1, FP, and FS immediately after the transactions, F1 is not required to include amounts in income under §§ 1.367(b)-3(b) and 1.367(b)-4(b) as described in paragraph (c)(1)(ii)(B) of this section. Thus, the basis and holding period of the FS stock held by FP immediately after the triangular reorganization is determined pursuant to paragraph (c) of this section.

(B) Pursuant to paragraph (c) of this section, each share of FS stock is divided into portions attributable to the basis and holding period of the FS stock held by FP immediately before the exchange (the FS portion) and the FT stock held by F1 immediately before the exchange (the FT portion). The basis and holding period of the FS portion is the basis and holding period of the FS stock held by FP immediately before the exchange. Thus, each share of FS stock has a portion with a basis of $5x and a value of $10x. Because the exchanging shareholder of FT stock (F1) has a section 1248 shareholder of both F1 and FT, the basis and holding period of the FT portion is the proportionate amount of the basis and the holding period of the FT stock immediately before the exchange to which such portion relates. Thus, each share of FS stock will have a second portion with a basis of $17x ($170x basis / 10 shares), a value of $20x ($200x value / 10 shares), a holding period of 5 years, and $1x of earnings and profits ($10x earnings and profits / 10 shares) attributable to such portion for purposes of section 1248.

(iii) *Subsequent disposition.* (A) Several years after the merger, FP disposes of all of its FS stock in a transaction governed by section 964(e). At the time of the disposition, FS stock has decreased in value to $210x (a post-merger reduction in value of $90x), and FS has incurred a post-merger deficit in earnings and profits of $30x.

(B) Pursuant to paragraph (d)(1)(ii) of this section, for purposes of determining the amount of gain realized on the sale or exchange of stock that has a divided portion, any amount realized on such sale or exchange is allocated to each divided portion of the stock based on the relative fair market value of the stock to which the portion is attributable at the time the portions were created. Immediately before the merger, the value of the FS stock in relation to the value of both the FS stock and the FT stock was one-third ($100x / ($100x plus $200x)). Likewise, immediately before the merger, the value of the FT stock in relation to the value of both the FT stock and the FS stock was two-thirds ($200x / $100x plus $200x). Accordingly, one-third of the $210x amount realized is allocated to the FS portion of each share and two-thirds to the FT portion of each share. Thus, the amount realized allocated to the FS portion of each share is $7x (one-third of $210x divided by 10 shares). The amount realized allocated to the FT portion of each share is $14x (two-thirds of $210x divided by 10 shares).

(C) Pursuant to paragraph (d)(3) of this section, any earnings and profits (or deficits) accumulated by the surviving corporation subsequent to the reorganization are attributed to the divided portions of shares of stock based on the relative fair market value of each divided portion of stock. Accordingly, one-third of the post-merger earnings and profits deficit of $30x is allocated to the FS portion of each share and two-thirds to the FT portion of each share. Thus, the deficit in earnings and profits allocated to the FS portion of each share is $1x (one-third of $30x divided by 10 shares). The deficit in earnings and profits allocated to the FT portion of each share is $2x (two-thirds of $30x divided by 10 shares).

(D) When FP disposes of its FS stock, FP is treated as disposing of each divided portion of a share of stock. With respect to the FS portion of each share of stock, FP recognizes a gain of $2x ($7x value - $5x basis), which is not recharacterized as a dividend because a deficit in earnings and profits of $1x is attributable to such portion for purposes of section 1248. With respect to the FT portion of each share of stock, FP recognizes a loss of $3x ($14x value - $17x basis).

(f) *Effective date.*—This section applies to exchanges occurring on or after January 23, 2006. [Reg. § 1.367(b)-13.]

☐ [*T.D. 9243, 1-23-2006. Amended by T.D. 9400, 5-23-2008 and T.D. 9446, 2-9-2009.*]

§ 1.367(d)-1. Transfers of intangible property to foreign corporations.—(a) [Reserved]. For further guidance, see § 1.367(d)-1T(a).

(b) *Property subject to section 367(d).*—Section 367(d) and the rules of this section apply to the transfer of intangible property, as defined in § 1.367(a)-1(d)(5), by a U.S. person to a foreign corporation in an exchange described in section 351 or 361. See section 367(a) and the regulations thereunder for the rules that apply to the transfer of any property other than intangible property.

(c)(1) through (2) [Reserved]. For further guidance, see § 1.367(d)-1T(c)(1) and (2).

(3) *Useful life.*—(i) *In general.*—For purposes of determining the period of inclusions for deemed payments under § 1.367(d)-1T(c)(1), the useful life of intangible property is the entire period during which exploitation of the intangible property is reasonably anticipated to affect the determination of taxable income, as of the time of transfer. Exploitation of intangible property includes any direct or indirect use or transfer of the intangible property, including use without further development, use in the further development of the intangible property itself (and any exploitation of the further developed intangible property), and use in the development of other intangible property (and any exploitation of the other developed intangible property).

(ii) *Procedure to limit inclusions to 20 years.*—In cases where the useful life of the transferred property is indefinite or is reasonably anticipated to exceed twenty years, taxpayers may, in lieu of including amounts during the entire useful life of the intangible property, choose in the year of transfer to increase annual inclusions during the 20-year period beginning with the first year in which the U.S transferor takes into account income pursuant to section 367(d), to reflect amounts that, but for this paragraph (c)(3)(ii), would have been required to be included following the end of the 20-year period. See § 1.6038B-1(d)(1)(iv) for guidance on reporting this choice of method. If the taxpayer applies this method during the 20-year period, no adjustments will be made for taxable years beginning after the conclusion of the 20-year period. However, for purposes of determining whether amounts included during the 20-year period are commensurate with the income attributable to the transferred intangible property, the Commissioner may take into account information with respect to taxable years after that period, such as the income attributable to the transferred property during those later years. The application of this paragraph (c)(3)(ii) must be reflected in a statement (titled "Application of 20-Year Inclusion Period to Section 367(d) Transfers") attached to a timely filed original federal income tax return (including extensions) for the year of the transfer. An increase to the deemed payment rate made pursuant to this paragraph (c)(3)(ii) will be irrevocable, and a failure to timely file the statement under this paragraph (c)(3)(ii) may not be remedied.

(iii) *Example.* Property subject to section 367(d) is transferred from USP, a domestic corporation, to FA, a foreign corporation wholly owned by USP. The useful life of the transferred property, inclusive of derivative works, at the time of transfer is indefinite but is reasonably anticipated to exceed 20 years. In the first five years following the transfer, sales related to the property are expected to be $100x, $130x, $160x, $180x and $187.2x, respectively. Thereafter, for the remainder of the property's useful life, sales are expected to grow by four percent annually. In the first five years following the transfer, operating profits attributable to the property are expected to be $5x, $8x, $11x, $12.5x, and $13x, respectively. Thereafter, for the remainder of the property's useful life, operating profits are expected to grow by four percent annually. It is determined that the appropriate discount rate for sales and operating profits is 10 percent. The present value of operating profits through the property's indefinite useful life is $185x. The present value of sales through the property's indefinite useful life is $2698x. Accordingly, the sales based royalty rate during the property's useful life is 6.8 percent ($185x/$2698x). The taxpayer may choose to take income inclusions into account over a 20-year period. The present value of sales through the 20-year period is $1787x. Accordingly, the sales based royalty rate under the 20-year option is increased to 10.3 percent ($185x/$1787x).

(c)(4) through (g)(2) (introductory text) [Reserved]. For further guidance, see § 1.367(d)-1T(c)(4) through (g)(2) (introductory text).

(g)(2)(i) The intangible property transferred constitutes an operating intangible, as defined in § 1.367(a)-1(d)(6).

(g)(2)(ii) through (iii)(D) [Reserved]. For further guidance, see § 1.367(d)-1T(g)(2)(ii) through (iii)(D).

(E) The transferred intangible property will be used in the active conduct of a trade or business outside of the United States within the meaning of § 1.367(a)-2 and will not be used in connection with the manufacture or sale of products in or for use or consumption in the United States.

(g)(2)(iii) undesignated concluding paragraph [Reserved]. For further guidance, see § 1.367(d)-1T(g)(2)(iii) undesignated concluding paragraph.

(3) *Intangible property transferred from branch with previously deducted losses.*—(i) If income is required to be recognized under section 904(f)(3) and the regulations thereunder or under § 1.367(a)-6 upon the transfer of intangible property of a foreign branch that had previously deducted losses, then the income recognized under those sections with respect to that property is credited against amounts that would otherwise be required to be recognized with respect to that same property under paragraphs (c) through (f) of this section in either the current or future taxable years. The amount recognized under section 904(f)(3) or § 1.367(a)-6 with respect to the transferred intangible property is determined in accordance with the following formula:

$$\text{Loss recapture income} \times \frac{\text{gain from intangible property}}{\text{gain from all branch assets}}$$

(ii) For purposes of the formula in paragraph (g)(3)(i) of this section, the "loss recapture income" is the total amount required to be recognized by the U.S. transferor pursuant to section 904(f)(3) or § 1.367(a)-6. The "gain from intangible property" is the total amount of gain realized by the U.S. transferor pursuant to section 904(f)(3) and § 1.367(a)-6 upon the transfer of items of property that are subject to section 367(d). "Gain from intangible property" does not include gain realized with respect to intangible property by reason of an election under paragraph (g)(2) of this section. The "gain from all branch assets" is the total amount of gain realized by the transferor upon the transfer of items of property of the branch for which gain is realized.

(g)(4) through (i) [Reserved]. For further guidance, see § 1.367(d)-1T(g)(4) through (i).

(j) *Effective/applicability dates.*—This section applies to transfers occurring on or after September 14, 2015, and to transfers occurring before September 14, 2015, resulting from entity classification elections made under § 301.7701-3 that are filed on or after September 14, 2015. For transfers occurring before this section is applicable, see § 1.367(d)-1T as contained in 26 CFR part 1 revised as of April 1, 2016. [Reg. § 1.367(d)-1.]

☐ [*T.D.* 9803, 12-15-2016.]

§ 1.367(d)-1T. Transfers of intangible property to foreign corporations (temporary).—(a) *Purpose and scope.*—This section provides rules under section 367(d) concerning transfers of intangible property by U.S. persons to foreign corporations pursuant to section 351 or 361. Paragraph (b) of this section specifies the transfers that are subject to section 367(d) and the rules of this section, while paragraph (c) provides rules concerning the consequences of such a transfer. In general, the U.S. transferor will be treated as receiving annual payments contingent on productivity or use of the transferred property, over the useful life of the property (regardless of whether such payments are in fact made by the transferee). Paragraphs (d), (e), and (f) of this section provide rules for cases in which there is a later direct or indirect disposition of the intangible property transferred. In general, deemed annual license payments will continue if a transfer is made to a related person, while gain must be recognized immediately if the transfer is to an unrelated person. Paragraph (g) of this section provides several special rules, including a rule allowing appropriate adjustments where deemed payments under section 367(d) are not in fact received by the U.S. transferor of the intangible property, and a rule providing for a limited election to treat certain transfers of intangible property as sales at fair market value (in lieu of applying the general useful life-contingent payment rule). In addition, paragraph (g) of this section provides rules coordinating the application of section 367(d) with other relevant Code sections. Paragraph (h) of this section defines the term "related person" for purposes of this section. Finally, paragraph (i) of this section provides the effective date of this section. For rules concerning transfers of intangible property pursuant to section 332, see § 1.367(a)-5T(e). For purposes of determining whether a U.S. person has made a transfer of intangible property that is subject to the rules of section 367(d), the rules of § 1.367(a)-1T(c) shall apply.

(b) [Reserved].

(c) *Deemed payments upon transfer of intangible property to foreign corporation.*—(1) *In general.*—If a U.S. person transfers intangible property that is subject to section 367(d) and the rules of this section to a foreign corporation in an exchange described in section 351 or 361, then such person shall be treated as having transferred that property in exchange for annual payments contingent on the productivity or use of the property. Such person shall, over the useful life of the property, annually include in gross income an amount that represents an appropriate arms-length charge for the use of the property. The appropriate charge shall be determined in accordance with the provisions of section 482 and regulations thereunder. See § 1.482-2(d). The amount of the deemed payment thus calculated shall be reduced by any royalty or other periodic payment made or accrued by the transferee to an unrelated person during that taxable year for the right to use the intangible property. Amounts so included in the transferor's income shall be treated as ordinary income from sources within the United States. For purposes of computing estimated tax payments, deemed payments under this paragraph (c) shall be treated as received by the transferor on the last day of its taxable year.

(2) *Required adjustments.*—The following adjustments shall be made with respect to a U.S. person's recognition of a deemed payment for the use of intangible property under this paragraph (c):

(i) For purposes of chapter 1 of the Code, the earnings and profits of the transferee foreign corporation shall be reduced by the amount of such deemed payment; and

(ii) For purposes of subpart F of part III of subchapter N of the Code, the transferee foreign corporation may treat such deemed payment as an expense (whether or not that amount is actually paid), properly allocated and apportioned to gross income subject to subpart F, in accordance with the provisions of § § 1.954-1(c) and 1.861-8. No other special adjustments to earnings and profits, basis, or gross income shall be permitted by reason of the recognition of a deemed payment under this paragraph (c). However, see paragraph (g)(1) of this section for rules permitting the establishment of an account receivable with respect to deemed payments not actually received by the U.S. person.

(3) [Reserved].

(4) *Blocked income.*—No deemed payment included in a taxpayer's income under paragraph (c)(1) of this section shall be treated as deferrable income for purposes of applying rules relating to blocked foreign income. See Revenue Ruling 74-351, 1974-2 C.B. 144.

(d) *Subsequent transfer of stock of transferee foreign corporation to unrelated person.*—(1) *Treatment as sale of intangible property.*—If a U.S. person transfers intangible property that is subject to section 367(d) and the rules of this section to a foreign corporation in an exchange described in section 351 or 361, and within the useful life of the intangible property that U.S. transferor subsequently disposes of the stock of the transferee foreign corporation to a person that is not a related person (within the meaning of paragraph (h) of this section), then the U.S. transferor shall be treated as having simultaneously sold the intangible property to the person acquiring the stock of the transferee foreign corporation. The U.S. transferor shall be required to recognize gain (but not loss) from sources within the United States in an amount equal to the difference between the fair market value of the transferred intangible property on the date of the subsequent disposition and the U.S. transferor's former adjusted basis in that property (determined as of the original transfer). If the U.S. transferor's disposition of the stock of the transferee foreign corporation is subject to U.S. tax other than by reason of this paragraph (d), then the amount of gain otherwise required to be recognized with respect to the stock of the transferee foreign corporation shall be reduced by the amount of gain recognized with respect to the intangible property pursuant to this paragraph (d).

(2) *Required adjustments.*—If a U.S. person disposes of the stock of a transferee foreign corporation, and under paragraph (d)(1) of this section is treated as having simultaneously sold intangible property, then, for purposes of computing basis and earnings and profits, the person acquiring the stock of the transferee foreign corporation shall be deemed to have purchased that property at fair market value and to have immediately thereafter contributed it to the transferee foreign corporation in a transaction not covered by section 367(d). Therefore, for purposes of chapter 1 of the Code—

(i) The transferee foreign corporation's basis in the intangible property will be equal to its fair market value (as calculated for purposes of determining the gain required to be recognized by the U.S. transferor);

(ii) The acquiring person's basis in the stock of the transferee foreign corporation shall be determined as if no portion of the consideration given by the acquiring person for the stock is attributable to the intangible property; and

(iii) The earnings and profits of the transferee foreign corporation will not be affected by the transfer of its stock or the deemed transfer to it of the intangible property.

(e) *Subsequent transfer of stock of transferee foreign corporation to related person.*—(1) *Transfer to related U.S. person treated as disposition of intangible property.*—If a U.S. person transfers intangible property that is subject to section 367(d) and the rules of this section to a foreign corporation in an exchange described in section 351 or 361 and, within the useful life of the transferred intangible property, that U.S. transferor subsequently transfers the stock of the transferee foreign corporation to U.S. persons that are related to the transferor within the meaning of paragraph (h) of this section, then the following rules shall apply:

(i) Each such related U.S. person shall be treated as having received (with the stock of the transferee foreign corporation) a right to receive a proportionate share of the contingent annual payments that would otherwise be deemed to be received by the U.S. transferor under paragraph (c) of this section.

(ii) Each such related U.S. person shall, over the useful life of the property, annually include in gross income a proportionate share of the amount that would have been included in the income of the U.S. transferor pursuant to paragraph (c) of this section. Such amounts shall be treated as ordinary income from sources within the United States.

(iii) The amount of income required to be recognized by the U.S. transferor pursuant to the rule of paragraph (d)(1) of this section shall be reduced to the amount determined in accordance with the following formula:

$$\text{(d)(1) amount} \times (100\% - \text{(e) percentage}).$$

For purposes of the above formula, the "(d)(1) amount" is the income that would otherwise be required to be recognized by the transferor corporation pursuant to paragraph (d)(1) of this section, and the "(e) percentage" is the percentage of the transferor corporation's total deemed rights to receive contingent annual payments under paragraph (c) of this section that is deemed to be transferred to related U.S. persons under the rules of this paragraph (e).

(iv) The rules of paragraphs (d) and (e) of this section shall be reapplied in the case of any later transfer of the stock of the transferee foreign corporation by a related U.S. person that received such stock in a transfer that was subject to the rules of this paragraph (e). For purposes of reapplying the rules of paragraphs (d) and (e), each such related U.S. person shall be treated as a U.S. transferor of intangible property to the transferee foreign corporation (to the extent of the interest attributed to such person pursuant to subdivision (i) of this paragraph (e)(1)).

(2) *Required adjustments.*—If a U.S. person transfers stock of a transferee foreign corporation to a U.S. related person in a transaction that is subject to the rules of paragraph (e)(1) of this section, the following adjustments shall be made:

(i) For purposes of chapter 1 of the Code, the earnings and profits of the transferee foreign corporation shall be reduced by the amount of any payment deemed to be received by a related U.S. person under paragraph (e)(1)(ii) of this section;

(ii) For purposes of subpart F of part III of subchapter N of the Code, the transferee foreign corporation may allocate and apportion such deemed payments (whether or not such payments are actually made) to gross income subject to subpart F to the extent appropriate under the provisions of § § 1.954-1(c) and 1.861-8;

(iii) For purposes of reapplying the rules of paragraphs (d) and (e) of this section, if the related U.S. person is deemed to have received a right to contingent annual payments for the use of intangible property, then the U.S. related person shall be deemed to have held a proportionate share of the property with a basis equal to a proportionate share of the U.S. transferor's adjusted basis plus the gain, if any, recognized by the U.S. transferor on the earlier transfer of the stock to the U.S. related person, and then to have transferred that proportionate share of the property to the foreign corporation in a transfer subject to section 367(d); and

(iv) If the U.S. transferor is itself required to recognize gain upon the transfer by reason of the operation of paragraphs (d)(1) and (e)(1)(iii) of this section (because stock of the transferee foreign corporation is also transferred to unrelated persons), then those unrelated persons shall be deemed to have purchased a proportionate share of the transferred intangible property at fair market value and immediately contributed that property to the transferee foreign corporation, consistent with the general rule of paragraph (d)(2) of this section concerning transfers of stock to unrelated persons. Therefore, for purposes of chapter 1 of the Code—

(A) Each unrelated person's basis in the stock of the transferee foreign corporation shall be increased to the extent of the gain recognized by the U.S. transferor upon the deemed purchase of intangible property by that person; and

(B) The transferee foreign corporation will receive an increase in its basis in the transferred intangible property equal to the fair market value of that portion of the intangible property deemed to be contributed to the transferee foreign corporation by unrelated persons (as calculated for purposes of determining the gain required to be recognized by the U.S. transferor).

(3) *Transfer to related foreign person not treated as disposition of intangible property.*—If a U.S. person transfers intangible property that is subject to section 367(d) and the rules of this section to a foreign corporation in an exchange described in section 351 or 361, and within the useful life of the transferred intangible property that U.S. transferor subsequently transfers any of the stock of the transferee foreign corporation to one or more foreign persons that are related to the transferor within the meaning of paragraph (h) of this section, then the U.S. transferor shall continue to include in its income the deemed payments described in paragraph (c) of this section in the same manner as if the subsequent transfer of stock had not occurred. The rule of this paragraph (e)(3) shall not apply with respect to the subsequent transfer by the U.S. person of any of the remaining stock to any related U.S. person or unrelated person.

(4) *Proportionate share.*—For purposes of this paragraph (e), any "proportionate share" shall be determined by reference to the fair market value (at the time of the original transfer) of the stock of the transferee foreign corporation that was transferred by the U.S. transferor and the fair market value of all of the stock of the transferee foreign corporation originally received by the U.S. transferor.

(f) *Subsequent disposition of transferred intangible property by transferee foreign corporation.*—(1) *In general.*—If a U.S. person transfers intangible property that is subject to section 367(d) and the rules of this section to a foreign corporation in an exchange described in section 351 or 361, and within the useful life of the intangible property that transferee foreign corporation subsequently disposes of the intangible property to an unrelated person, then—

(i) The U.S. transferor of the intangible property (or any person treated as such pursuant to paragraph (e)(1) of this section) shall be required to recognize gain from U.S. sources (but not loss) in an amount equal to the difference between the fair market value of the transferred intangible property on the date of the subsequent disposition and the U.S. transferor's former adjusted basis in that property (determined as of the original transfer); and

(ii) the U.S. transferor shall be required to recognize a deemed payment under paragraph (c) of this section for that part of its taxable year that the intangible property was held by the transferee foreign corporation and thereafter shall not be required to recognize any further deemed payments under paragraph (c) or (e)(1) of this section with respect to the transferred intangible property disposed of by the transferee foreign corporation.

(2) *Required adjustments.*—If a U.S. transferor is required to recognize gain under paragraph (f)(1) of this section, then—

(i) For purposes of chapter 1 of the Code, the earnings and profits of the transferee foreign corporation shall be reduced by the amount of gain required to be recognized; and

(ii) The U.S. transferor's recognition of gain will permit the establishment of an account receivable from the transferee foreign corporation, in accordance with paragraph (g)(1) of this section.

(3) *Subsequent transfer of intangible property to related person.*—The requirement that a U.S. person recognize gain under paragraph (c) or (e) of this section shall not be affected by the transferee foreign corporation's subsequent disposition of the transferred intangible property to a related person. For purposes of any required adjustments, and of any accounts receivable created under paragraph (g)(1) of this section, the related person that receives the intangible property shall be treated as the transferee foreign corporation.

(g) *Special rules.*—(1) *Establishment of accounts receivable.*—(i) *In general.*—If a U.S. person is required to recognize income under the provisions of paragraph (c), (e), or (f) of this section, and the amount deemed to be received is not actually paid by the transferee foreign corporation, then the U.S. person may establish an account receivable from the transferee foreign corporation equal to the amount deemed paid that was not actually paid. A separate account receivable must be established for each taxable year in which payments deemed to be received are not actually made. Payments received from the transferee foreign corporation must be designated as payments upon a particular account and must be deducted from that account. Accounts receivable under this paragraph (g)(1) may be established and paid without further U.S. income tax consequences to the U.S. transferor or the transferee foreign corporation. No interest shall be paid or accrued on an account receivable created under this paragraph (g)(1), nor shall any bad debt deduction be allowed under section 166 with respect to any failure to receive payment on an account.

(ii) *Unpaid receivable treated as contribution to capital.*—If any portion of an account receivable established under this paragraph (g)(1) remains unpaid as of the last day of the third taxable year following the taxable year to which the account relates, then—

(A) Such portion shall be deemed to have been paid on that date; and

(B) The U.S. person shall be deemed to have contributed an equivalent amount to the capital of the foreign corporation, and the U.S. person's basis in the stock of the foreign corporation shall, therefore, be increased by that amount.

(2) *Election to treat transfer as sale.*—A U.S. person that transfers intangible property to a foreign corporation in a transaction subject to section 367(d) may elect to recognize income in accordance with the rules of this paragraph (g)(2), if—

(i) [Reserved].

(ii) The transfer of the intangible property is either legally required by the government of the country in which the transferee corporation is organized as a condition of doing business in that country, or compelled by a genuine threat of immediate expropriation by the foreign government; or

(iii)(A) The U.S. person transferred the intangible property to the foreign corporation within three months of the organization of that corporation and as part of the original plan of capitalization of that corporation;

(B) Immediately after the transfer, the U.S. person owns at least 40 percent but not more than 60 percent of the total voting power and total value of the stock of the transferee foreign corporation;

(C) Immediately after the transfer, at least 40 percent of the total voting power and total value of the stock of the transferee foreign corporation is owned by foreign persons unrelated to the U.S. person;

(D) Intangible property constitutes at least 50 percent of the fair market value of the property transferred to the foreign corporation by the U.S. transferor; and

(E) [Reserved].

A person that makes the election under this paragraph (g)(2) shall not be subject to the provisions of paragraphs (c) through (f) of this section. Such person shall instead recognize in the year of the transfer ordinary income from sources within the United States in an amount equal to the difference between the fair market value of the intangible property transferred and its adjusted basis. A U.S. person shall make an election under this paragraph (g)(2) by notifying the Internal Revenue Service of the election in accordance with the requirements of section 6038B and regulations thereunder, and subsequently including the appropriate amounts in gross income in a timely filed tax return for the year of the transfer.

(3) [Reserved].

(4) *Coordination with section 482.*—(i) *In general.*—Section 367(d) and the rules of this section shall not apply in the case of an actual sale or license of intangible property by a U.S. person to a foreign corporation. If an adjustment under section 482 is required with respect to an actual sale or license of intangible property, then section 367(d) and the rules of this section shall not apply with respect to the required adjustment. If a U.S. person transfers intangible property to a related foreign corporation without consideration, or in exchange for stock or securities of the transferee in a transaction described in section 351 or 361, no sale or license subject to adjustment under section 482 will be deemed to have occurred. Instead, the U.S. person shall be treated as having made a transfer of the intangible property that is subject to section 367(d).

(ii) *Sham licenses and sales.*—For purposes of paragraph (g)(4)(i) of this section, a purported sale or license of intangible property may be disregarded, and treated as a transfer subject to section 367(d) and the rules of this section, if—

(A) The purported sale or license is made to a foreign corporation in which the transferor holds (or is acquiring) an interest; and

(B) The terms of the purported sale or license differ so greatly from the economic substance of the transaction or the terms that would obtain between unrelated persons that the purported sale or license is a sham.

The terms of a purported sale or license, for purposes of applying the rule of this paragraph (g)(4)(ii), shall be determined by reference not only to the nominal terms of the agreement but also to the actual practice of the parties under that agreement. A sale or license of intangible property shall not be disregarded under this paragraph (g)(4)(ii) solely because other property of an integrated business is simultaneously transferred to the foreign corporation by the U.S. transferor in a transaction described in section 367(a)(1) or any statutory or regulatory exception to section 367(a)(1).

(5) *Determination of fair market value.*—For purposes of determining the gain required to be recognized immediately under paragraph (d), (f) or (g)(2) or this section, the fair market value of transferred property shall be the single payment arm's-length price that would be paid for the property by an unrelated purchaser determined in accordance with the principles of section 482 and regulations thereunder. The allocation of a portion of the purchase price to intangible property agreed to by the parties to the transaction shall not necessarily be controlling for this purpose.

(6) *Anti-abuse rule.*—If a U.S. person—

(i) Transfers intangible property to a domestic corporation with a principal purpose of avoiding the effect of section 367(d) and the rules of this section; and

(ii) Thereafter transfers the stock of that domestic corporation to a related foreign corporation,

then solely for purposes of section 367(d) that U.S. person shall be treated as having transferred the intangible property directly to the foreign corporation. A U.S. person shall be presumed to have transferred intangible property for a principal purpose of avoiding the effect of section 367(d) if the property is transferred to the domestic corporation less than two years prior to the transfer of the stock of that domestic corporation to a foreign corporation. The presumption created by the previous sentence may be rebutted by clear evidence that the subsequent transfer of the stock of the domestic transferee corporation was not contemplated at the time the intangible property was transferred to that corporation and that avoidance of section 367(d) and the rules of this section was not a principal purpose of the transaction. A transfer may have more than one principal purpose.

(h) *Related person.*—For purposes of this section, persons are considered to be related if—

(1) They are partners or partnerships described in section 707(b)(1) of the Code; or

(2) They are related within the meaning of section 267(b), (c), and (f) of the Code, except that—

(i) "10 percent or more" shall be substituted for "more than 50 percent" each place it appears; and

(ii) Section 1563 shall apply (for purposes of section 267(f)), without regard to section 1563(b)(2).

(i) *Effective date.*—Except as specifically provided to the contrary elsewhere in this section, this section applies to transfers occurring after December 31, 1984. [Temporary Reg. § 1.367(d)-1T.]

☐ [*T.D. 8087, 5-15-86. Amended by T.D. 8770, 6-18-98 and T.D. 9803, 12-15-2016.*]

Proposed Amendments to Regulation

§ 1.367(d)-1. Transfers of intangible property to foreign corporations.—

* * *

(c) *Deemed payments upon transfer of intangible property to foreign corporation.*—(1) *In general.*—For further guidance, see § 1.367(d)-1T(c)(1).

(2) *Required adjustments.*—For further guidance, see § 1.367(d)-1T(c)(2) introductory text and (c)(2)(i).

(i) [Reserved]

(ii) The deemed payment is treated as an allowable deduction (whether or not that amount is paid) of the transferee foreign corporation properly allocated and apportioned to the appropriate classes of gross income in accordance with §§ 1.882-4(b)(1), 1.951A-2(c)(3), 1.954-1(c), 1.960-1(c), and 1.960-1(d), as applicable.

* * *

(4) *Blocked income.*—For further guidance, see § 1.367(d)-1T(c)(4).

(d) *Subsequent transfer of stock of transferee corporation to unrelated person.*—For further guidance, see § 1.367(d)-1T(d).

(e) *Subsequent transfer of stock of transferee foreign corporation to related person.*—(1) *Transfer to related U.S. person treated as disposition of intangible property.*—For further guidance, see § 1.367(d)-1T(e)(1)

(2) *Required adjustments.*—For further guidance, see § 1.367(d)-1T(e)(2) introductory text and (e)(2)(i).

(i) [Reserved]

(ii) The deemed payment is treated as an allowable deduction (whether or not that amount is paid) of the transferee foreign corporation properly allocated and apportioned to the appropriate classes of gross income in accordance with §§ 1.882-4(b)(1), 1.951A-2(c)(3), 1.954-1(c), 1.960-1(c), and 1.960-1(d), as applicable.

(iii) For further guidance, see § 1.367(d)-1T(e)(2)(iii) through (e)(4).

(iv) [Reserved]

(3) through (4) [Reserved]

(f) *Subsequent disposition of transferred intangible property by transferee foreign Corporation.*—(1) *In general.*—For further guidance, see § 1.367(d)-1T(f)(1).

(2) *Required adjustments.*—If a U.S. transferor is required to recognize gain under paragraph (f)(4)(i)(A) of this section or § 1.367(d)-1T(f)(1), then, in addition to the adjustments described in paragraph (c)(2)(ii) of this section and § 1.367(d)-1T(c)(2) with respect to the deemed payment described in § 1.367(d)-1T(f)(1)(ii)—

(i) For purposes of chapter 1 of the Code, the transferee foreign corporation reduces (but not below zero) the portion of its earnings and profits and gross income arising by reason of the subsequent disposition of the intangible property by the amount of gain recognized by the U.S. transferor under paragraph (f)(4)(i)(A) of this section or § 1.367(d)-1T(f)(1); and

(ii) The U.S. transferor may establish an account receivable from the transferee foreign corporation equal to the amount of gain recognized under paragraph (f)(4)(i)(A) of this section or § 1.367(d)-1T(f)(1) in accordance with § 1.367(d)-1T(g)(1).

(3) *Subsequent transfer of intangible property to related person.*—Except as provided in paragraph (f)(4)(i)(B) of this section, a U.S. person's requirement to recognize income under § 1.367(d)-1T(c) or (e) is not affected by the transferee foreign corporation's subsequent disposition of the transferred intangible property to a related person. For purposes of any required adjustments, and of any accounts receivable created under § 1.367(d)-1T(g)(1), the related person that receives the intangible property is treated as the transferee foreign corporation.

(4) *Subsequent transfer of intangible property to qualified domestic person.*—(i) *In general.*—Except as provided in paragraph (f)(4)(v) of this section, if a U.S. person transfers intangible property subject to section 367(d) and the rules of this section and § 1.367(d)-1T to a foreign corporation in an exchange described in section 351 or 361 and, within the useful life of the intangible property, that transferee foreign corporation subsequently disposes of the intangible property to a qualified domestic person, then—

(A) The U.S. transferor of the intangible property (or any person treated as such pursuant to § 1.367(d)-1T(e)(1)) is required to recognize gain, as applicable, equal to the amount described in paragraph (f)(4)(ii) of this section; and

(B) If the U.S. transferor provides the information described in § 1.6038B-1(d)(2)(iv), then—

(*1*) The U.S. transferor is required to recognize a deemed payment as provided in § 1.367(d)-1T(f)(1)(ii); and

(*2*) The intangible property is no longer subject to section 367(d), this section, and § 1.367(d)-1T after applying paragraphs (f)(4)(i)(A) and (f)(4)(i)(B)(1) of this section.

(ii) *Gain recognition for U.S. transferor.*—The amount of gain a U.S. transferor must recognize under paragraph (f)(4)(i)(A) of this section is determined as follows—

(A) If the intangible property is transferred basis property (as defined in section 7701(a)(43)) by reason of the subsequent disposition (determined without regard to section 367(d), this section, and § 1.367(d)-1T), the amount of gain, if any, the transferee foreign corporation would recognize if its adjusted basis in the intangible property were equal to the U.S. transferor's former adjusted basis in the property; or

(B) If the intangible property is not transferred basis property by reason of the subsequent disposition (determined without regard to section 367(d), this section, and § 1.367(d)-1T), the excess, if any, of the fair market value of the intangible property on the date of the subsequent disposition and the U.S. transferor's former adjusted basis in that property.

(iii) *Qualified domestic person.*—For purposes of paragraph (f)(4) of this section, a qualified domestic person means—

(A) The U.S. transferor that initially transferred intangible property subject to section 367(d);

(B) A U.S. person treated as a U.S. transferor under § 1.367(d)-1T(e)(1), provided such person is an individual or a corporation other than a corporation exempt from tax under section 501(a), a regulated investment company (as defined in section 851(a)), a real estate investment trust (as defined in section 856(a)), a domestic international sales corporation (DISC) (as defined in section 992(a)(1)), or an S corporation (as defined in section 1361(a));

(C) A U.S. person that is an individual related, within the meaning of paragraph (h)(2)(ii) of this section and § 1.367(d)-1T(h), to the person described in paragraph (f)(4)(iii)(A) or (B) of this section; or

(D) A U.S. person that is a corporation related, within the meaning of paragraph (h)(2)(ii) of this section and § 1.367(d)-1T(h), to the person described in paragraph (f)(4)(iii)(A) or (B) of this section, other than a corporation exempt from tax under section 501(a), a regulated investment company (as defined in section 851(a)), a real estate investment trust (as defined in section 856(a)), a DISC (as defined in section 992(a)(1)), or an S corporation (as defined in section 1361(a)).

(iv) *Qualified domestic person's basis in the intangible property.*—The qualified domestic person's adjusted basis in the intangible property is—

(A) In the case of a subsequent disposition of intangible property described in paragraph (f)(4)(ii)(A) of this section, and subject to any applicable limitations that may apply under the Code, the lesser of the U.S. transferor's former adjusted basis in the intangible property or the transferee foreign corporation's adjusted basis in the intangible property (as determined immediately before the subsequent disposition), in each case increased by the greater of the amount of gain (if any) described in paragraph (f)(4)(ii)(A) of this section and recognized by the U.S. transferor or the amount of gain (if any) recognized by the transferee foreign corporation as to the intangible property by reason of the subsequent disposition; or

(B) In the case of a subsequent disposition of intangible property described in paragraph (f)(4)(ii)(B) of this section, the fair market value of the intangible property (as determined on the date of the subsequent disposition).

(v) *Special rule for related transactions.*—If the transferee foreign corporation subsequently disposes of the transferred intangible property to a person that would, absent this paragraph (f)(4)(v), be a qualified domestic person (initial transferee) and, as part of a series of related transactions, the intangible property is subsequently disposed of to any other person, including by reason of multiple dispositions, then the initial transferee is treated as a qualified domestic person only if the ultimate recipient of the intangible property is a qualified domestic person. *See* paragraphs (f)(6)(ii)(D) and (E) of this section *(Examples* 4 and 5), for illustrations of the application of this paragraph (f)(4)(v).

(5) *Relief for certain failures to comply.*—This paragraph (f)(5) provides relief if paragraph (f)(4)(i)(B)(2) of this section would apply but for the U.S. transferor's failure to provide the information required by paragraph (f)(4)(i)(B) of this section (a "failure to comply"). When a failure to comply occurs, the subsequent disposition of the transferred intangible property is generally subject to paragraphs (f)(3) and (f)(4)(i)(A) of this section, and not paragraph (f)(4)(i)(B)(2) of this section. Nevertheless, a failure to comply is deemed not to have occurred (regardless of whether the U.S. transferor continued to include amounts in gross income under § 1.367(d)-1T(c) or (e) after the subsequent disposition), and the requirements of paragraph (f)(4)(i)(B) of this section are treated as satisfied as of the date of the subsequent disposition if, promptly after the U.S. transferor becomes aware of the failure, the U.S. transferor provides such information and provides a reasonable explanation for its failure to comply to the Director of Field Operations, Cross Border Activities Practice Area of Large Business & International (or any successor to the roles and responsibilities of such position, as appropriate). Additionally, the U.S. transferor must timely file an amended return for the taxable year in which the subsequent disposition occurred (and, if applicable, for each taxable year starting with the taxable year immediately after the taxable year in which the subsequent disposition occurred and ending with the taxable year in which the U.S. transferor seeks relief under this paragraph (f)(5)) that includes the information required by paragraph (f)(4)(i)(B) of this section. If any taxable year of the U.S. transferor is under examination when an amended return is filed, a copy of the amended return (or, if applicable, amended returns) must be provided to the Internal Revenue Service personnel conducting the examination.

(6) *Examples.*—(i) *Assumed facts.*—For purposes of the examples in paragraph (f)(6)(ii) of this section, and except where otherwise indicated, the following facts are assumed.

(A) USP and USS are domestic corporations that each use a calendar taxable year.

(B) TFC is a foreign corporation whose functional currency is the U.S. dollar.

(C) In year 1, USP transfers intangible property, as defined in section 367(d)(4), with a $0 adjusted basis, to TFC in a section 351 exchange (the "transferred IP"), and such transfer is subject to section 367(d).

(D) Each annual inclusion (including any amount described in § 1.367(d)-1T(f)(1)(ii)) is taken into account under section 367(d)(2)(A)(ii)(I) and § 1.367(d)-1T(c)(1).

(E) Any subsequent transfer or disposition of stock of TFC or the transferred IP occurs within the useful life of the transferred IP.

(F) All transactions are respected under general principles of tax law.

(ii) *Examples.*—The following examples illustrate the application of paragraph (f)(4) of this section and other paragraphs of this section that relate to paragraph (f)(4).

(A) *Example 1: Complete liquidation of transferee foreign corporation into a qualified domestic person.—(1) Facts.*—In year 2, USP transfers all the stock of TFC to USS, a related person within the meaning of § 1.367(d)-1T(h) and paragraph (h)(2)(ii) of this section, in a section 351 exchange to which § 1.367(d)-1T(e)(1) applies (the "year 2 transfer"). In year 3, TFC distributes all its property (including the transferred IP) to USS pursuant to a complete liquidation to which sections 332 and 337 apply (the "year 3 liquidation"). The all earnings and profits amount determined under § 1.367(b)-2(d) with respect to the stock of TFC held by USS is $0. The information described in § 1.6038B-1(d)(2) is provided by USS for the taxable year in which the year 3 liquidation occurs.

(2) Analysis.—(i) The year 2 transfer.—Because the year 2 transfer involves a transfer of all the stock of TFC by USP (the initial U.S. transferor) to a related U.S. person (USS), under § 1.367(d)-1T(e)(1)(i) USS (a successor U.S. transferor) is treated as receiving the right to receive a proportionate share of the contingent annual payments that USP would have otherwise taken into account under § 1.367(d)-1T(c). As determined under § 1.367(d)-1T(e)(4), USS's proportionate share of such payments is 100 percent. Accordingly, USS will annually include in its gross income the full amount of each of the annual payments that USP would otherwise have taken into account under § 1.367(d)-1T(c) over the useful life of the transferred IP, and USP will not recognize any gain upon the year 2 transfer. *See* § 1.367(d)-1T(e)(1)(ii) and (iii).

(ii) The year 3 liquidation.—The year 3 liquidation results in a subsequent disposition of the transferred IP to USS. USS, a U.S. person treated as the U.S. transferor pursuant to § 1.367(d)-1T(e)(1), is a qualified domestic person within the meaning of paragraph (f)(4)(iii) of this section. Pursuant to paragraph (f)(4)(i)(A) of this section, USS must recognize the amount of gain described in paragraph (f)(4)(ii) of this section. Because the year 3 liquidation is a complete liquidation to which sections 332 and 337 apply, the intangible property is transferred basis property (as defined in section 7701(a)(43) and determined without regard to section 367(d), this section, and § 1.367(d)-1T), and therefore paragraph (f)(4)(ii)(A) applies to determine the amount of any gain USS must recognize. Because TFC does not recognize gain with respect to the transferred IP (regardless of the adjusted basis in the intangible property) by reason of the year 3 liquidation, the amount of gain described in paragraph (f)(4)(ii)(A) of this section is $0. Accordingly, USS does not recognize gain pursuant to paragraph (f)(4)(i)(A) of this section by reason of the year 3 liquidation. Additionally, because USS provides the information described in § 1.6038B-1(d)(2), paragraph (f)(4)(i)(B) of this section applies to the year 3 liquidation. USS therefore recognizes a deemed payment representing the part of USS's taxable year during which TFC held the transferred IP pursuant to paragraph (f)(4)(i)(B)(1) of this section, and the required adjustments described in paragraph (c)(2)(ii) of this section and § 1.367(d)-1T(c)(2)(i) apply as to the deemed payment. Also, because USS does not recognize gain pursuant to paragraph (f)(4)(i)(A) of this section, the required adjustments described in paragraph (f)(2) of this section do not apply. Pursuant to paragraph (f)(4)(i)(B)(2) of this section, after taking the deemed payment into account, the transferred IP is no longer subject to section 367(d), this section, and § 1.367(d)-1T. Finally, pursuant to paragraph (f)(4)(iv)(A) of this section, USS's adjusted basis in the transferred IP is $0, which is equal to USP's former adjusted basis in the transferred IP ($0), increased by the greater of the amount of gain recognized by USS under paragraph (f)(4)(i)(A) of this section ($0) or the amount of gain recognized by TFC upon the year 3 distribution ($0).

(B) *Example 2: Taxable distribution of the transferred intangible property to a qualified domestic person.—(1) Facts.*—The facts are the same as in paragraph (f)(6)(ii)(A) of this section *(Example 1),* except that, instead of in year 3 TFC distributing all its property to USS pursuant to a complete liquidation, in year 3 TFC distributes the transferred IP to USS in a distribution described in section 311(b) when the fair market value of the transferred IP is $100x (the "year 3 distribution"). TFC's adjusted basis in the transferred IP immediately before the distribution is $0.

(2) Analysis.—The consequence of the year 2 transfer is the same as described in paragraph (f)(6)(ii)(A)(2)(i) of this section *(Example 1).* Like the consequences described in paragraph (f)(6)(ii)(A)(2) of this section *(Example 1),* the year 3 distribution is a subsequent disposition of the transferred IP to USS, a qualified domestic person. Pursuant to paragraph (f)(4)(i)(A) of this section, USS must recognize the amount of gain described in paragraph (f)(4)(ii) of this section. Because the year 3 distribution is described in section 311(b) the intangible property is not transferred basis property (as defined in section 7701(a)(43) and determined without regard to section 367(d), this section, and § 1.367(d)-1T), and therefore USS must recognize $100x gain under paragraph (f)(4)(ii)(B) of this section. The $100x gain amount equals the excess of the fair market value of the transferred IP on the date of the year 3 distribution

($100x) over USP's former adjusted basis in the property ($0). TFC, because of USS's gain recognition under paragraph (f)(4)(i)(A) of this section, reduces (but not below zero) the portion of its earnings and profits and gross income arising by reason of the year 3 distribution by the amount of such gain under paragraph (f)(2)(i) of this section. Specifically, because the year 3 distribution requires USS to recognize $100x of gain, TFC reduces the portion of its earnings and profits and gross income that arise by reason of the year 3 distribution, which is $100x (the excess of the fair market value of the transferred IP ($100x) over TFC's adjusted basis in the transferred IP ($0)), by $100x (the amount of gain USS recognizes pursuant to paragraph (f)(4)(i)(A) of this section). As a result, after taking into account the reduction, TFC has no earnings and profits or gross income that arise by reason of the year 3 distribution. Furthermore, USS may establish an account receivable from TFC equal to $100x under paragraph (f)(2)(ii) of this section. Additionally, and as described in paragraph (f)(6)(ii)(A)(2) of this section *(Example 1)*, pursuant to paragraph (f)(4)(i)(B)(1) of this section, USS recognizes a deemed payment for the portion of USS's taxable year during which TFC held the transferred IP, and the required adjustments described in paragraph (c)(2)(ii) of this section and § 1.367(d)-1T(c)(2) apply to this deemed payment. After taking these consequences into account, pursuant to paragraph (f)(4)(i)(B)(2) of this section, the transferred IP is no longer subject to section 367(d), this section, and § 1.367(d)-1T. Finally, pursuant to paragraph (f)(4)(iv)(B) of this section, USS's adjusted basis in the transferred IP is $100x, which is the fair market value of the transferred IP on the date of the year 3 distribution.

(C) *Example 3: Qualified domestic person's basis in intangible property when intangible property is repatriated in an exchange described in section 351(b).—(1) Facts.*—The facts are the same as in paragraph (f)(6)(ii)(A) of this section *(Example 1)*, except that the transfer of stock of TFC to USS in year 2 does not occur and instead of the year 3 liquidation, in year 3 TFC transfers the intangible property to USS (a qualified domestic person as defined in paragraph (f)(4)(iii) of this section) in an exchange described in section 351(b) pursuant to which TFC recognizes $50x of gain and USP recognizes $50x of gain under paragraph (f)(4)(i)(A) of this section (the "year 3 exchange").

(2) *Analysis.*—Pursuant to paragraph (f)(4)(iv)(A) of this section, USS's adjusted basis in the intangible property is $50x, which is the amount equal to the lesser of USP's former adjusted basis in the property ($0) or TFC's adjusted basis in the property ($0), increased by the greater of the amount of gain recognized by USP under paragraph (f)(4)(i)(A) of this section ($50x) or the amount of gain recognized by TFC upon the year 3 exchange ($50x).

(D) *Example 4: Repatriation as part of a series of related transactions culminating in transfer to a foreign corporation.—(1) Facts.*—The facts are the same as in paragraph (f)(6)(ii)(A)(1) of this section *(Example 1)*, except that the year 3 liquidation occurs as part of a series of related transactions pursuant to which USS transfers the transferred IP that it receives from TFC to a related foreign corporation (FC1) in exchange for stock in FC1.

(2) *Analysis.*—Because the year 3 liquidation occurs as part of a series of related transactions pursuant to which the transferred IP is ultimately contributed to a FC1, a foreign corporation, and because a foreign corporation is not a qualified domestic person pursuant to paragraph (f)(4)(iii) of this section, then, under paragraph (f)(4)(v) of this section, the year 3 liquidation is not treated as a subsequent disposition described in paragraph (f)(4)(i) of this section, but is instead treated as a subsequent disposition described in paragraph (f)(3) of this section.

(E) *Example 5: Repatriation as part of a series of related transactions culminating in transfer to a qualified domestic person.—(1) Facts.*—The facts are the same as in paragraph (f)(6)(ii)(B)(1) of this section *(Example 2)*, except that the year 3 distribution occurs as part of a series of related transactions pursuant to which USS disposes of the transferred IP that it receives from TFC to USP.

(2) *Analysis.*—Because the year 3 distribution occurs as part of a series of related transactions pursuant to which the transferred IP is distributed to USP, and because USP is a qualified domestic person pursuant to paragraph (f)(4)(iii) of this section, paragraph (f)(4)(v) of this section does not prevent paragraph (f)(4)(i) of this section from applying to the year 3 distribution. Accordingly, the consequences under section 367(d) of the year 3 distribution are the same as those described in paragraph (f)(6)(ii)(B)(2) of this section *(Example 2)*, and the consequences of the subsequent disposition of the transferred IP by USS to USP are determined after applying paragraph (f)(4) of this section to the transfer of the transferred IP by TFC to USS.

(g) *Special rules.*—(1) *Establishment of accounts receivable.*—For further guidance, see § 1.367(d)-1T(g)(1).

(2) *Election to treat transfer as sale.*—For further guidance, see § 1.367(d)-1T(g)(2) introductory text.

* * *

(ii) For further guidance, see § 1.367-1T(g)(2)(ii) through (g)(2)(iii)(D).

(iii) [Reserved]

(A) through (D) [Reserved]

* * *

(4) *Coordination with section 482.*—For further guidance, see § 1.367(d)-1T(g)(4).

(5) *Determination of fair market value.*—For further guidance, see § 1.367(d)-1T(g)(5).

(6) *Anti-abuse rule.*—For further guidance, see § 1.367(d)-1T(g)(6).

(h) *Related person.*—For further guidance, see § 1.367(d)-1T(h) introductory text and (h)(1).

(1) [Reserved]

(2) For further guidance, see § 1.367(d)-1T(h)(2) introductory text and (h)(2)(i).

(i) [Reserved]

(ii) Section 1563 applies (for purposes of section 267(f)) without regard to section 1563(b)(2).

(i) *Effective date.*—For further guidance, see § 1.367(d)-1T(i).

(j) *Applicability dates.*—(1) *In general.*—This section applies to transfers occurring on or after September 14, 2015, and to transfers occurring before September 14, 2015, resulting from entity classification elections made under § 301.7701-3 of this chapter that are filed on or after September 14, 2015. For transfers occurring before this section is applicable, see § 1.367(d)-1T as contained in 26 CFR part 1 revised as of April 1, 2016.

(2) *Certain subsequent dispositions of intangible property.*—Paragraphs (c)(2)(ii), (e)(2)(ii), (f)(2) through (5), and (h)(2)(ii) of this section apply to subsequent dispositions of intangible property occurring on or after [date of publication of final regulations in the **Federal Register**]. For subsequent dispositions of intangible property occurring before [date of publication of final regulations in the **Federal Register**], see § 1.367(d)-1T (as contained in 26 CFR part 1, revised as of April 1, 2022). [Prop. Reg. § 1.367(d)-1.]

[Proposed 5-3-2023.]

§ 1.367(e)-1. Distributions described in section 367(e)(1).—(a) *Purpose and scope.*—This section provides rules for recognition (and nonrecognition) of gain by a domestic corporation (distributing corporation) on a distribution of stock or securities of a corporation (controlled corporation) to foreign persons that is described in section 355. Paragraph (b) of this section contains the general rule that gain is recognized on the distribution to the extent stock or securities of controlled are distributed to foreign persons. Paragraph (c) of this section provides an exception to the gain recognition rule for distributions of stock or securities of a domestic corporation. Paragraph (d) of this section contains rules for determining whether distributees of stock or securities in a section 355 distribution are qualified U.S. persons. Paragraph (e) of this section provides cross-references. Finally, paragraph (f) of this section specifies the effective date of this section.

(b) *Gain recognition.*—(1) *General rule.*—If a domestic corporation makes a distribution of stock or securities of a corporation that qualifies for nonrecognition under section 355 to a person who is not a qualified U.S. person, then, except as provided in paragraph (c) of this section, the distributing corporation shall recognize gain (but not loss) on the distribution under section 367(e)(1). A distributing corporation shall not recognize gain under this section with respect to a section 355 distribution to a qualified U.S. person. For purposes of this section, a qualified U.S. person is—

(A) A citizen or resident of the United States; or

(B) A domestic corporation.

(2) *Stock owned through partnerships, disregarded entities, trusts, and estates.*—For purposes of this section, distributing corporation stock or securities owned by or for a partnership (whether foreign or domestic) are owned proportionately by its partners. A partner's proportionate share of the stock or securities of the distributing corporation shall be equal to the partner's distributive share of the gain that would have been recognized had the partnership sold the stock or securities (at a taxable gain) immediately before the distribution. The partner's distributive share of gain shall be determined under the rules and principles of sections 701 through 761 and the regulations thereunder. For purposes of this section, stock or securities owned by or for an entity that is disregarded as an entity separate from its owner (disregarded entity) under § 301.7701-3 of this chapter are owned directly by the owner of such disregarded entity. For purposes of this section, stock or securities owned by or for a trust or estate (whether foreign or domestic) are owned proportionately by the persons who would be treated as owning such stock or securities under section 318(a)(2)(A) and (B). In applying section 318(a)(2)(B)(i), if a trust includes interests that are not actuarially ascertainable, all such interests shall be considered to be owned by foreign persons. In a case where an interest holder in a partnership, a disregarded entity, trust, or estate that (directly or indirectly) owns stock of the distributing corporation is itself a partnership, disregarded entity, trust, or estate, the rules of this paragraph (b)(2) apply to such interest holder.

(3) *Gain computation.*—Gain recognized under paragraph (b)(1) of this section shall be equal to the excess of the fair market value of the stock or securities distributed to persons who are not qualified U.S. persons (determined as of the time of the distribution) over the distributing corporation's adjusted basis in the stock or securities distributed to such distributees. For purposes of the preceding sentence, the distributing corporation's adjusted basis in each unit of each class of stock or securities distributed to a distributee shall be equal to the distributing corporation's total adjusted basis in all of the units of the respective class of stock or securities owned immediately before the distribution, divided by the total number of units of the class of stock or securities owned immediately before the distribution.

(4) *Treatment of distributee.*—If the distribution otherwise qualifies for nonrecognition under section 355, each distributee shall be considered to have received stock or securities in a distribution qualifying for nonrecognition under section 355, even though the distributing corporation may recognize gain on the distribution under this section. Thus, the distributee shall not be considered to have received a distribution described in section 301 or a distribution in an exchange described in section 302(b) upon the receipt of the stock or securities of the controlled corporation, and the domestic distributing corporation shall have no withholding responsibilities under section 1441. Except where section 897(e)(1) and the regulations thereunder cause gain to be recognized by the distributee, the basis of the distributed domestic or foreign corporation stock in the hands of the foreign distributee shall be the basis of the distributed stock determined under section 358 without any increase for any gain recognized by the domestic corporation on the distribution.

(c) *Nonrecognition of gain.*—A domestic distributing corporation shall not recognize gain under paragraph (b)(1) of this section on the distribution of stock or securities of a domestic corporation.

(d) *Determining whether distributees are qualified U.S. persons.*—(1) *General rule—presumption of foreign status.*—Except as provided in paragraphs (d)(2) and (3) of this section, all distributions of stock or securities in a distribution described in section 355 in which the distributing corporation is domestic and the controlled corporation is foreign are presumed to be to persons who are not qualified U.S. persons, as defined in paragraph (b)(1) of this section.

(2) *Non-publicly traded distributing corporations.*—If the class of stock or securities of the distributing corporation (in respect to which stock or securities of the controlled corporation are distributed) is not regularly traded on a qualified exchange or other market (as defined in paragraph (d)(4) of this section), then the distributing corporation may only rebut the presumption contained in paragraph (d)(1) of this section by identifying the qualified U.S. persons to which controlled corporation stock or securities were distributed and by certifying the amount of stock or securities that were distributed to the qualified U.S. persons.

(3) *Publicly traded distributing corporations.*—If the class of stock or securities of the distributing corporation (in respect to which stock or securities of the controlled corporation are distributed) is regularly traded on a qualified exchange or other market (as defined in paragraph (d)(4) of this section), then the distributing corporation may only rebut the presumption contained in paragraph (d)(1) of this section as described in this paragraph (d)(3).

(i) *Five percent shareholders.*—A publicly traded distributing corporation may only rebut the presumption contained in paragraph (d)(1) of this section with respect to distributees that are five percent shareholders of the class of stock or securities of the distributing corporation (in respect to which stock or securities of the controlled corporation are distributed) by identifying the qualified U.S. persons to which controlled corporation stock or securities were distributed and by certifying the amount of stock or securities that were distributed to the qualified U.S. persons. A five percent shareholder is a distributee who is required under U.S. securities laws to file with the Securities and Exchange Commission (SEC) a Schedule 13D or 13G under 17 CFR 240.13d-1 or 17 CFR 240.13d-2, and provide a copy of same to the distributing corporation under 17 CFR 240.13d-7.

(ii) *Other distributees.*—A distributing corporation that has made a distribution described in paragraph (d)(3) of this section may rebut the presumption contained in paragraph (d)(1) of this section with respect to distributees that are not five percent shareholders (as defined in this paragraph (d)(3)) by relying on and providing a reasonable analysis of shareholder records and other relevant information that demonstrates a number of distributees that are qualified U.S. persons. Taxpayers may rely on such analysis, unless it is subsequently determined that there are actually fewer distributees who are qualified U.S. persons than were demonstrated in the analysis.

(4) *Qualified exchange or other market.*—For purposes of paragraph (d) of this section, the term qualified exchange or other market means, for any taxable year—

(i) A national securities exchange which is registered with the SEC or the national market system established pursuant to section 11A of the Securities Exchange Act of 1934 (15 U.S.C. 78f); or

(ii) A foreign securities exchange that is regulated or supervised by a governmental authority of the country in which the market is located and which has the following characteristics—

(A) The exchange has trading volume, listing, financial disclosure, and other requirements designed to prevent fraudulent and manipulative acts and practices, to remove impediments to and perfect the mechanism of a free and open market, and to protect investors; and the laws of the country in which the exchange is located and the rules of the exchange ensure that such requirements are actually enforced; and

(B) The rules of the exchange ensure active trading of listed stocks.

(e) *Cross-references.*—For additional rules relating to the distribution of the stock of a foreign corporation by a domestic corporation, see §§ 1.367(a)-3(e), 1.367(a)-7, 1.367(b)-5, and 1.1248(f)-1 through 1.1248(f)-3. See the regulations under section 6038B for reporting requirements for distributions under this section.

(f) *Effective/applicability date.*—This section shall be applicable to distributions occurring in taxable years ending after August 8, 1999. [Reg. § 1.367(e)-1.]

☐ [*T.D.* 8834, 8-6-99 (*corrected* 3-2-2000). *Amended by T.D.* 9614, 3-18-2013 *and T.D.* 9760, 3-18-2016.]

Proposed Amendments to Regulation

§ 1.367(e)-1. Distributions described in section 367(e)(1).—(a) * * * See § 1.367(b)-8(c)(3) for an example illustrating the interaction of § 1.367(e)-1 with other sections of the Internal Revenue Code (such as sections 367(b) and 1248).

* * *

[Proposed 11-15-2000.]

§ 1.367(e)-2. Distributions described in section 367(e)(2).—(a) *Purpose and scope.*—(1) *In general.*—This section provides rules requiring gain and loss recognition by a corporation on its distribution of property to a foreign corporation in a complete liquidation described in section 332. Paragraph (b)(1) of this section contains the general rule that gain and loss are recognized when a domestic corporation makes a distribution of property in complete liquidation under section 332 to a foreign corporation that meets the stock ownership requirements of section 332(b) with respect to stock in the domestic corporation. Paragraph (b)(2) of this section provides the only exceptions to the gain and loss recognition rule of paragraph (b)(1) of this section. Paragraph (b)(3) of this section refers to other consequences of distributions described in paragraphs (b)(1) and (2) of this section. Paragraph (c)(1) of this section contains the general rule that gain and loss are not recognized when a foreign corporation makes a distribution of property in complete liquidation under section 332 to a foreign corporation that meets the stock ownership requirements of section 332(b) with respect to stock in the foreign liquidating corporation. Paragraph (c)(2) of this section provides the only exceptions to the nonrecognition rule of paragraph (c)(1) of this section. Paragraph (c)(3) of this section refers to other consequences of distributions described in paragraphs (c)(1) and (2) of this section. Paragraph (d) of this section contains an anti-abuse rule. Paragraph (e) of this section provides rules regarding failures to file statements or other documents required under this section or failures to comply with the requirements of this section. Paragraph (f) of this section provides relief for certain failures to file or comply. Finally, paragraph (g) of this section specifies the effective/applicability dates for the rules of this section. The rules of this section are issued pursuant to the authority conferred by section 367(e)(2).

(2) *Nonapplicability of section 367(a)*.—Section 367(a) shall not apply to a complete liquidation described in section 332 by a domestic liquidating corporation into a foreign corporation that meets the stock ownership requirements of section 332(b).

(b) *Distribution by a domestic corporation*.—(1) *General rule*.—(i) *Recognition of gain and loss*.—If a domestic corporation (domestic liquidating corporation) makes a distribution of property in complete liquidation under section 332 to a foreign corporation (foreign distributee corporation) that meets the stock ownership requirements of section 332(b) with respect to stock in the domestic liquidating corporation, then—

(A) Section 337(a) and (b)(1) will not apply; and

(B) The domestic liquidating corporation will recognize gain or loss on the distribution of property to the foreign distributee corporation, except as provided in paragraph (b)(2) of this section.

(ii) *Operating rules*.—(A) *General rule*.—Except as provided in paragraphs (b)(1)(ii)(B) and (C) of this section, the rules contained in section 336 will apply to the gain and loss recognized pursuant to this section.

(B) *Overall loss limitation*.—*(1) Overall loss limitation rule*.—Loss in excess of gain from the distribution shall not be recognized. If realized losses exceed recognized losses, the losses shall be recognized on a pro rata basis with respect to the realized loss attributable to each distributed loss asset in the category of assets (i.e., capital or ordinary) to which the realized but unrecognized loss relates. For additional limitations on the recognition of losses, see, e.g., section 1211.

(2) Example.—The following example illustrates the overall loss limitation rule, the pro rata loss allocation method, and the general capital loss limitation rule in section 1211(a):

Example. F, a foreign corporation, owns all stock of US1, a domestic corporation. US1 owns the following capital assets: Asset A, which has a fair market value of $100 and an adjusted basis of $40; Asset B, which has a fair market value of $60 and an adjusted basis of $80; and, Asset C, which has a fair market value of $40 and an adjusted basis of $100. US1 also owns the following business assets that will generate ordinary income (or loss) upon disposition: Asset D, which has a fair market value of $100 and an adjusted basis of $40; Asset E, which has a fair market value of $60 and an adjusted basis of $100; and, Asset F, which has a fair market value of $40 and an adjusted basis of $80. US1 liquidates into F and distributes all assets to F in liquidation. None of the assets qualify for nonrecognition under paragraph (b)(2) of this section. US1's total realized capital loss is $80, but it may only recognize $60 of that loss. See section 1211(a). US1's total realized ordinary loss is $80, but it may only recognize $60 of that loss. See paragraph (b)(1)(ii)(B)*(1)* of this section. US1 will allocate $15 (60 × .25) of the recognized capital loss to Asset B and will allocate the remaining $45 (60 × .75) of recognized capital loss to Asset C. See paragraph (b)(1)(ii)(B)*(1)* of this section. US1 will allocate $30 (60 × .50) of the recognized ordinary loss to Asset E and will allocate the remaining $30 (60 × .50) to Asset F. See paragraph (b)(1)(ii)(B)*(1)* of this section.

(C) *Special rules for built-in gains and losses attributable to property received in liquidations and reorganizations*.—Built-in losses attributable to property received in a transaction described in sections 332 or 361 (during the two-year period ending on the date of the distribution in liquidation covered by this section) shall not offset gain from property not received in the same transaction. Built-in gains attributable to property received in a transaction described in sections 332 or 361 (during the two-year period ending on the date of the distribution in liquidation covered by this section) shall not be offset by a loss from property not received in the same transaction. Built-in gain or loss is that amount of gain or loss on property that existed at the time the domestic liquidating corporation acquired such property. See sections 336(d) and 382 for additional limitations on the recognition of losses.

(iii) *Distribution of partnership interest*.—(A) *General rule*.—If a domestic corporation distributes a partnership interest (whether foreign or domestic) in a distribution described in paragraph (b)(1)(i) of this section, then for purposes of applying this section the domestic liquidating corporation shall be treated as having distributed a proportionate share of partnership property. Accordingly, the applicability of the recognition rules of paragraphs (b)(1)(i) and (ii) of this section, and of any exception to recognition provided in this section shall be determined with reference to the partnership property, rather than to the partnership interest itself. Where the partnership property includes an interest in a lower-tier partnership, the applicability of any exception with respect to the interest in the lower-tier partnership shall be determined with reference to the lower-tier partnership property. In the case of multiple tiers of partnerships, the applicability of an exception shall be determined with reference to the property of each partnership, applying the rule contained in the preceding sentence. A domestic liquidating corporation's proportionate share of partnership property shall be determined under the rules and principles of sections 701 through 761 and the regulations thereunder.

(B) *Gain or loss calculation*.—[Reserved]

(C) *Basis adjustments*.—The foreign distributee corporation's basis in the distributed partnership interest shall be equal to the domestic liquidating corporation's basis in such partnership interest immediately prior to the distribution, increased by the amount of gain and reduced by the amount of loss recognized by the domestic liquidating corporation on the distribution of the partnership interest. Solely for purposes of sections 743 and 754, the foreign distributee corporation shall be treated as having purchased the partnership interest for an amount equal to the foreign corporation's adjusted basis therein.

(D) *Publicly traded partnerships*.—The distribution by a domestic liquidating corporation of an interest in a publicly traded partnership that is treated as a corporation for U.S. income tax purposes under section 7704(a) shall not be subject to the rules of paragraphs (b)(1)(iii)(A) and (B) of this section. Instead, the distribution of such an interest shall be treated in the same manner as a distribution of stock. Thus, a transfer of an interest in a publicly traded partnership that is treated as a U.S. corporation for U.S. income tax purposes shall be treated in the same manner as stock in a domestic corporation, and a transfer of an interest in a publicly traded partnership that is treated as a foreign corporation for U.S. income tax purposes shall be treated in the same manner as stock in a foreign corporation.

(2) *Exceptions*.—(i) *Distribution of property used in a U.S. trade or business*.—(A) *Conditions for nonrecognition*.—A domestic liquidating corporation shall not recognize gain or loss under paragraph (b)(1) of this section on its distribution of property (including inventory) used by the domestic liquidating corporation in the conduct of a trade or business within United States, if—

(1) The foreign distributee corporation, immediately thereafter and for the ten-year period beginning on the date of the distribution of such property, uses the property in the conduct of a trade or business within the United States;

(2) The domestic liquidating corporation attaches the statement described in paragraph (b)(2)(i)(C) of this section to its timely filed U.S. income tax returns for the taxable years that include the distributions in liquidation; and

(3) The foreign distributee corporation attaches a copy of the property description contained in paragraph (b)(2)(i)(C)(2) of this section to its timely filed U.S. income tax return for the tax year that includes the date of distribution.

(B) *Qualifying property.*—Property is used by the foreign distributee corporation in the conduct of a trade or business in the United States within the meaning of this paragraph (b)(2)(i) only if all income from the use of the property and all income or gain from the sale or exchange of the property would be subject to taxation under section 882(a) as effectively connected income. Also, stock held by a dealer as inventory or for sale in the ordinary course of its trade or business shall be treated as inventory and not as stock in the hands of both the domestic liquidating corporation and the distributee foreign corporation. Notwithstanding the foregoing, the exception provided in this paragraph (b)(2)(i) shall not apply to intangibles described in section 936(h)(3)(B).

(C) *Required statement.*—The statement required by paragraph (b)(2)(i)(A) of this section shall be entitled "Required Statement under § 1.367(e)-2(b)(2)(i)" and shall be prepared by the domestic liquidating corporation and signed under penalties of perjury by an authorized officer of the domestic liquidating corporation and by an authorized officer of the foreign distributee corporation. The statement shall contain the following items:

(1) Declaration and certification.—A declaration that the distribution to the foreign distributee corporation is one to which the rules of this paragraph (b)(2)(i) apply and a certification that the domestic liquidating corporation and the foreign distributee corporation agree to comply with all the conditions and requirements of this section, including, as provided in paragraph (e)(4)(ii)(B) of this section, to treat a failure to comply (as described in paragraph (e)(4)(i) of this section) as extending the period of limitations on assessment of tax for the taxable year in which gain is required to be reported.

(2) Property description.—A description of all property distributed by the domestic liquidating corporation (irrespective of whether the property qualifies for nonrecognition). Such description shall be entitled "Master Property Description" and shall identify the property that continues to be used by the foreign distributee corporation in the conduct of a trade or business within the United States, including the location, adjusted basis, estimated fair market value, a summary of the method (including appraisals if any) used for determining such value, and the date of distribution of such items of property. The description shall also identify the property excepted from gain recognition under paragraphs (b)(2)(ii) and (iii) of this section.

(3) Distributee identification.—An identification of the foreign distributee corporation, including its name and address, taxpayer identification number, residence, and place of incorporation.

(4) Treaty benefits waiver.—With respect to property entitled to nonrecognition pursuant to this paragraph (b)(2)(i), a declaration by the foreign distributee corporation that it irrevocably waives any right under any treaty (whether or not currently in force at the time of the liquidation) to sell or exchange any item of such property without U.S. income taxation or at a reduced rate of taxation, or to derive income from the use of any item of such property without U.S. income taxation or at a reduced rate of taxation.

(5) Statute of limitations extension.—An agreement by the domestic liquidating corporation and the foreign distributee corporation to extend the statute of limitations on assessments and collections (under section 6501) with respect to the domestic liquidating corporation on the distribution of each item of property until three years after the date on which all such items of property have ceased to be used in a trade or business within the United States, but in no event shall the extension be for a period longer than 13 years from the filing of the original U.S. income tax return for the taxable year of the last distribution of any such item of property. The agreement to extend the statute of limitation shall be executed on a Form 8838, "Consent to Extend the Time to Assess Tax Under Section 367—Gain Recognition Agreement."

(D) *Failure to file statement.*—If a domestic liquidating corporation that would otherwise qualify for nonrecognition on the distribution of property under this paragraph (b)(2)(i) fails to file the statement described in paragraph (b)(2)(i)(C) of this section or files a statement that does not comply with the requirements of paragraph (b)(2)(i)(C) of this section, the Commissioner may treat the domestic liquidating corporation as if it had claimed nonrecognition under this paragraph (b)(2)(i) and met all the requirements of paragraph (b)(2)(i)(C) of this section, if such treatment is necessary to prevent the domestic liquidating corporation or the foreign distributee corporation from otherwise deriving a tax benefit by such failure.

(E) *Operating rules.*—By the domestic liquidating corporation's claiming nonrecognition under this paragraph (b)(2)(i) and filing a statement described in paragraph (b)(2)(i)(C) of this section, the domestic liquidating corporation and the foreign distributee corporation agree to be subject to the rules of this paragraph (b)(2)(i)(E).

(1) Gain or loss recognition by the foreign distributee corporation.—*(i) Taxable dispositions.*—If, within the ten-year period from the date of a distribution of qualifying property, the foreign distributee corporation disposes of any qualifying property in a transaction subject to tax under section 882(a), then the foreign distributee corporation shall recognize such gain (or loss) and properly report it on a timely filed U.S. income tax return. If the foreign distributee corporation recognizes gain (or loss) under this paragraph (b)(2)(i)(E)*(1)*(*i*) and properly reports such gain (or loss) on its U.S. income tax return, then the domestic liquidating corporation shall not recognize gain attributable to such property under paragraph (b)(2)(i)(E)*(2)* of this section.

(ii) Other triggering events.—If, within the ten-year period from the date of distribution, any qualifying property ceases to be used by the foreign distributee corporation in the conduct of a trade or business in the United States (other than by reason of a taxable disposition described in paragraph (b)(2)(i)(E)*(1)*(*i*) of this section, a nontriggering event described in paragraph (b)(2)(i)(E)*(4)* of this section, or a nontriggering transfer described in paragraph (b)(2)(i)(E)*(5)* of this section), then the foreign distributee corporation shall recognize gain (but not loss) attributable to such property and properly report it on a timely filed U.S. income tax return. If the foreign distributee corporation properly reports gain under this paragraph (or if such qualified property is not gain property on the date that it ceases to be used in the foreign distributee corporation's U.S. trade or business), then the domestic liquidating corporation shall not recognize gain attributable to such property under paragraph (b)(2)(i)(E)*(2)* of this section. The gain recognized under this paragraph (b)(2)(i)(E)*(1)*(*ii*) shall be an amount equal to the fair market value of the property on the date it ceases to be used in the foreign distributee corporation's U.S. trade or business less the foreign distributee corporation's adjusted basis in such property.

(2) Gain recognition by the domestic liquidating corporation.—*(i) General rule.*—If, within the ten-year period from the date of distribution, any qualifying property described in paragraph (b)(2)(i)(B) of this section ceases to be used by the foreign distributee corporation (or a qualifying transferee described in paragraph (b)(2)(i)(E)*(5)* of this section) in the conduct of a trade or business in the United States for any reason (including but not limited to the sale or exchange of such property or the removal of the property from conduct of the trade or business), then, except to the extent gain (or loss) is recognized under paragraph (b)(1)(i)(E)*(1)* of this section, the domestic liquidating corporation shall recognize the gain (but not loss) realized but not recognized upon the initial distribution of such item of property. The domestic liquidating corporation shall recognize gain pursuant to this paragraph (b)(2)(i)(E)*(2)*(*i*) on the amended U.S. income tax return described in paragraph (b)(2)(i)(E)*(2)*(*ii*) of this section.

(ii) Amended return.—If gain recognition is required pursuant to paragraph (b)(2)(i)(E)*(2)*(*i*) of this section, the foreign distributee corporation shall file an amended U.S. income tax return on behalf of the domestic liquidating corporation for the year of the distribution of such item of property. On the amended return, the domestic liquidating corporation may use any losses (or credits) existing in the year of the distribution to offset the gain recognized pursuant to paragraph (b)(2)(i)(E)*(2)*(*i*) of this section (or the tax thereon), provided that the losses (or credits) were otherwise available in the year distribution and were not used in another year. The amended return shall be filed no later than the due date (including extensions) for the return of the foreign distributee corporation for the taxable year in which the property ceases to be used by the foreign distributee corporation in the conduct of a trade or business in the United States.

(iii) Interest.—If the domestic liquidating corporation owes additional tax pursuant to paragraph (b)(2)(i)(E)*(2)*(*i*) of this section for the year of liquidation, then interest must be paid on that amount at the rates determined under section 6621. The interest due will be calculated from the due date of the domestic liquidating corporation's U.S. income tax return for the year of the distribution to the date on which the additional tax for that year is paid.

(iv) Joint and several liability.—The foreign distributee corporation shall be jointly and severally liable for any tax owed by the domestic liquidating corporation as a result of the application of this section, and shall succeed to the domestic liquidating corporation's agreement to extend the statute of limitations on assessments and collections under section 6501.

(3) Schedule for property no longer used in a U.S. trade or business.—If qualifying property (other than inventory) ceases to be used by the foreign distributee corporation in the conduct of a U.S. trade or business in the ten-year period beginning on the date of distribution of such property from the domestic liquidating corporation to the foreign distributee corporation, then the foreign distributee corporation shall list on a separate schedule (attached to its timely filed U.S. income tax return for the year of cessation) all such qualifying property. For purposes of this paragraph (b)(2)(i)(E)(*3*), property ceases to be used in a U.S. trade or business whenever such property is sold, exchanged, or otherwise removed from the U.S. trade or business, irrespective of whether the domestic liquidating corporation filed an amended return under paragraph (b)(2)(i)(E)(*2*) of this section, and irrespective of whether the property ceases to be used in the foreign distributee corporation's U.S. trade or business by virtue of a nontriggering event described in paragraph (b)(2)(i)(E)(*4*) of this section or a nontriggering transfer described in paragraph (b)(2)(i)(E)(*5*) of this section.

(4) Nontriggering events.—*(i) Conversions, certain exchanges, and abandonment.*—Gain (or loss) under this paragraph (b)(2)(i)(E) shall not be triggered if qualifying property described in paragraph (b)(2)(i)(B) of this section is involuntarily converted into, or exchanged for, similar qualifying property used in the conduct of a trade or business in the United States, to the extent such conversion or exchange qualifies for nonrecognition under sections 1033 or 1031. Also, the abandonment or disposal of worthless or obsolete property shall not trigger gain (or loss) under this paragraph (b)(2)(i)(E).

(ii) Amendment to Master Property Description.—If the foreign distributee corporation acquires replacement property by virtue of a conversion or exchange of the qualifying property under this paragraph (b)(2)(i)(E)(*4*), then the foreign distributee corporation shall attach to its timely filed U.S. income tax return for the year of the acquisition such replacement property a schedule entitled "Amendment to Master Property Description Required by § 1.367(e)-2(b)(2)(i)" that lists the replacement property and the property being replaced.

(5) Nontriggering transfers to qualified transferees.—Gain (or loss) under this paragraph (b)(2)(i)(E) will not be triggered if qualifying property described in paragraph (b)(2)(i)(B) of this section is transferred to another person (qualified transferee) in a transaction qualifying for nonrecognition under the Internal Revenue Code (other than transactions described in paragraphs (b)(2)(i)(E)(*4*)(*i*) and (c)(1) of this section), if—

(i) The qualified transferee (and all other subsequent qualified transferees), immediately thereafter and for the ten-year period beginning on the date of the initial distribution of such qualifying property from the domestic liquidating corporation to the foreign distributee corporation, uses the property in the conduct of a trade or business in the United States;

(ii) The foreign distributee corporation (or its successor in interest) prepares and attaches to its timely filed U.S. income tax return for the year of transfer a statement entitled "Required Statement under § 1.367(e)-2(b)(2)(i)(E)(*5*) for Property Transferred to a Qualified Transferee" that is signed under penalties of perjury by an authorized officer of the foreign distributee corporation and by a person similarly authorized by the qualified transferee;

(iii) The statement described in paragraph (b)(2)(i)(E)(*5*)(*ii*) of this section shall contain a description of all qualifying property transferred by the foreign distributee corporation (or qualified transferee) to the qualified transferee (or subsequent qualified transferee);

(iv) The statement described in paragraph (b)(2)(i)(E)(*5*)(*ii*) of this section shall also contain an identification of the qualified transferee (or subsequent qualified transferee), including its name and address, taxpayer identification number, residence, and place of incorporation (if applicable);

(v) The statement described in paragraph (b)(2)(i)(E)(*5*)(*ii*) of this section shall also contain a declaration by the qualifying transferee (or subsequent qualifying transferee) that it irrevocably waives any right under any treaty (whether or not currently in force at the time of the liquidation) to sell or exchange any item of such property without U.S. income taxation or at a reduced rate of taxation, or to derive income from the use of any item of such qualifying property without U.S. income taxation or at a reduced rate of taxation; and

(vi) A declaration that the transfer to the qualifying transferee (or subsequent qualifying transferee) is one to which the rules of this paragraph (b)(2)(i)(E)(*5*) apply and a certification that the foreign distributee corporation (or its successor in interest) and the qualifying transferee (or subsequent qualifying transferee) agree to all of the terms and conditions set forth in paragraph (b)(2)(i)(E)(*1*) of this section, replacing "foreign distributee corporation" with "qualifying transferee" and replacing references to "section 882(a)" with "section 871(b)" (as the case may be).

(ii) *Distribution of certain U.S. real property interests.*—A domestic liquidating corporation shall not recognize gain (or loss) under paragraph (b)(1) of this section on the distribution of a U.S. real property interest (other than stock in a former U.S. real property holding corporation that is treated as a U.S. real property interest for five years under section 897(c)(1)(A)(ii)). If property distributed by the domestic liquidating corporation is a U.S. real property interest that qualifies for nonrecognition under this paragraph (b)(2)(ii) in addition to nonrecognition provided by paragraph (b)(2)(i) of this section, then the domestic liquidating corporation shall secure nonrecognition pursuant to this paragraph (b)(2)(ii) and not pursuant to the provisions of paragraph (b)(2)(i) of this section.

(iii) *Distribution of stock of domestic subsidiary corporations.*—(A) *Conditions for nonrecognition.*—A domestic liquidating corporation shall not recognize gain or loss under paragraph (b)(1) of this section on a distribution of stock of an 80 percent domestic subsidiary corporation, if the domestic liquidating corporation attaches a statement described in paragraph (b)(2)(iii)(D) of this section to its timely filed U.S. income tax return for the year of the distribution of such stock. For purposes of this paragraph (b)(2)(iii), a corporation is an 80 percent domestic subsidiary corporation, if—

(1) The subsidiary corporation is a domestic corporation (but not a foreign corporation that has made an election under section 897(i) to be treated as a U.S. corporation for purposes of section 897);

(2) The domestic liquidating corporation owns (directly and without regard to paragraph (b)(1)(iii) of this section) at least 80 percent of the total voting power of the stock of such corporation; and

(3) The domestic liquidating corporation owns (directly and without regard to paragraph (b)(1)(iii) of this section) at least 80 percent of the total value of all stock of such corporation.

(B) *Exceptions when the liquidating corporation is a U.S. real property holding corporation.*—If the domestic liquidating corporation is a U.S. real property holding corporation (as defined in section 897(c)(2)) at the time of liquidation (or is a former U.S. real property holding corporation the stock of which is treated as a U.S. real property interest for five years under section 897(c)(1)(A)(ii)), then the exception in paragraph (b)(2)(iii)(A) of this section shall apply only to the distribution of stock of an 80 percent domestic subsidiary corporation that is a U.S. real property holding corporation (as defined in section 897(c)(2)) at the time of the liquidation and immediately thereafter.

(C) *Anti-abuse rule.*—*(1)* The exception in paragraph (b)(2)(iii)(A) of this section shall not apply, if a principal purpose of the distribution of the 80 percent domestic subsidiary corporation's stock is the avoidance of U.S. tax that would have been imposed on the domestic liquidating corporation's disposition of such stock (directly or indirectly) to an unrelated party. A distribution may have a principal purpose of tax avoidance even though the tax avoidance purpose is outweighed by other purposes when taken together.

(2) For purposes of paragraph (b)(2)(iii)(C)(*1*) of this section, a distribution of stock of the 80 percent domestic subsidiary corporation will be deemed to have been made pursuant to a plan, one of the principal purposes of which was the avoidance of U.S. tax, if the foreign distributee corporation disposes of (whether in a recognition or nonrecognition transaction) any such stock within two years of such distribution. The rule in this paragraph (b)(2)(iii)(C)(*2*) will not apply if the foreign distributee corporation can demonstrate to the satisfaction of the Commissioner that the avoidance of U.S. tax was not a principal purpose of the liquidation.

(D) *Required statement.*—The statement required by paragraph (b)(2)(iii)(A) of this section shall be entitled "Required Statement under §1.367(e)-2(b)(2)(iii) for Stock of 80 Percent Domestic Subsidiary Corporations" and shall be prepared by the domestic liquidating corporation and shall be signed under penalties of perjury by an authorized officer of the domestic liquidating corporation and by an authorized officer of the foreign distributee corporation. The required statement shall contain a certification that states that if the foreign distributee corporation disposes of any stock subject to paragraph (b)(2)(iii)(A) of this section in a transaction described in paragraph (b)(2)(iii)(C) of this section, then the domestic liquidating corporation shall recognize all realized gain attributable to the distributed stock at the time of distribution, and the domestic liquidating corporation (or the foreign distributee corporation on behalf of the domestic liquidating corporation) shall file a U.S. income tax return (or amended U.S. income tax return, as the case may be) for the year of distribution reporting the gain attributable to such stock. The required statement shall also state that the domestic liquidating corporation agrees, as provided in paragraph (e)(4)(ii)(B) of this section, to treat a failure to comply (as described in paragraph (e)(4)(i) of this section) as extending the period of limitations on assessment of tax for the taxable year in which gain is required to be reported.

(3) *Other consequences.*—(i) *Distributee basis in property.*—The foreign distributee corporation's basis in property subject to this paragraph (b) shall be the same as the domestic liquidating corporation's basis in such property immediately before the liquidation, increased by any gain, or reduced by any loss recognized by the domestic liquidating corporation on such property pursuant to paragraph (b)(1) of this section.

(ii) *Reporting under section 6038B.*—Section 6038B and the regulations thereunder apply to a domestic liquidating corporation's transfer of property to a foreign distributee corporation under section 367(e)(2).

(iii) *Other rules.*—For other rules that may apply, see sections 381, 897, 1248, and §1.482-1(f)(2)(i)(C).

(c) *Distribution by a foreign corporation.*—(1) *General rule—gain and loss not recognized.*—If a foreign corporation (foreign liquidating) makes a distribution of property in complete liquidation under section 332 to a foreign corporation (foreign distributee) that meets the stock ownership requirements of section 332(b) with respect to stock in the foreign liquidating corporation, then, except as provided in paragraph (c)(2) of this section, section 337(a) and (b)(1) shall apply and the foreign liquidating corporation shall not recognize gain (or loss) on the distribution under section 367(e)(2). If a foreign liquidating corporation distributes a partnership interest (whether foreign or domestic), then such corporation shall be treated as having distributed a proportionate share of partnership property in accordance with the principles of paragraph (b)(1)(iii) of this section.

(2) *Exceptions.*—(i) *Property used in a U.S. trade or business.*—(A) *General rule.*—A foreign liquidating corporation (including a corporation that has made an effective election under section 897(i)) that makes a distribution described in paragraph (c)(1) of this section shall recognize gain (or loss in accordance with principles contained in paragraph (b)(1)(ii) of this section) on the distribution of qualified property, as described in paragraph (b)(2)(i)(B) of this section (other than U.S. real property interests), that is used by the foreign liquidating corporation in the conduct of a trade or business within the United States at the time of distribution.

(B) *Ten-year active U.S. business exception.*—A foreign liquidating corporation shall not recognize gain under paragraph (c)(2)(i)(A) of this section, if—

(1) The foreign distributee corporation, immediately thereafter and for the ten-year period beginning on the date of the distribution of such property, uses the property in the conduct of a trade or business in the United States;

(2) The foreign distributee corporation is not entitled to benefits under a comprehensive income tax treaty (this requirement shall apply only if the foreign liquidating corporation (or predecessor corporation) was not entitled to benefits under a comprehensive income tax treaty); and

(3) The foreign liquidating corporation and foreign distributee corporation attach the statement described in paragraph (c)(2)(i)(C) of this section to their timely filed U.S. income tax returns for their taxable years that include the distribution.

(C) *Required statement.*—The statement required by paragraph (c)(2)(i)(B)(3) of this section shall be entitled "Required Statement under §1.367(e)-2(c)(2)(i)," shall be prepared by foreign liquidating corporation, shall be signed under penalties of perjury by an authorized officer of the foreign liquidating corporation and by an authorized officer of the foreign distributee corporation, and shall be identical to the statement described in paragraph (b)(2)(i)(C) of this section, except that "§1.367(e)-2(c)(2)(i)(B)" shall be substituted for references to "§1.367(e)-2(b)(2)(i)" and "foreign liquidating corporation" shall be substituted for "domestic liquidating corporation" each time it appears. References in the rules of paragraph (b)(2)(i)(C) of this section to various rules in paragraph (b) of this section shall be applied as if such references were to this paragraph (c). However, the statement described in this paragraph (c)(2)(i)(C) shall be modified as follows:

(1) The foreign distributee corporation shall not be required to waive its income tax treaty benefits as required by §1.367(e)-2(b)(2)(i)(C)(*4*), unless—

(i) The foreign liquidating corporation was required to waive its treaty benefits under paragraph (b)(2)(i)(C)(4) of this section in connection with the distribution of such property in a prior liquidation distribution subject to the provisions of this section; or

(ii) The foreign distributee corporation is entitled benefits under a treaty to which the foreign liquidating corporation was not entitled.

(2) If the foreign distributee is required to waive treaty benefits because of paragraph (c)(2)(i)(C)(*1*)(*ii*) of this section, then the foreign distributee shall only be required to waive benefits that were not available to the foreign liquidating corporation (or a predecessor corporation) prior to liquidation.

(3) The property description described in paragraph (b)(2)(i)(C)(2) of this section shall include only the qualified U.S. trade or business property described in paragraph (c)(2)(i) of this section.

(D) *Operating rules.*—By the foreign liquidating corporation's claiming nonrecognition under paragraph (c)(2)(i)(B) of this section and filing a statement described in paragraph (c)(2)(i)(C) of this section, the foreign liquidating corporation and the foreign distributee corporation agree to be subject to the rules of paragraph (c)(2)(i) of this section, as well as the rules of paragraphs (b)(2)(i)(D) and (E) of this section. In applying the rules of paragraphs (b)(2)(i)(D) and (E) of this section, "foreign liquidating corporation" shall be used instead of "domestic liquidating corporation" each time it appears. References in the rules of paragraphs (b)(2)(i)(D) and (E) of this section to various rules in paragraph (b) of this section shall be applied as if such references were to this paragraph (c).

(ii) *Property formerly used in a United States trade or business.*—A foreign liquidating corporation that makes a distribution described in paragraph (c)(1) of this section shall recognize gain (but not loss) on the distribution of property (other than U.S. real property interests) that had ceased to be used by the foreign liquidating corporation in the conduct of a U.S. trade or business within the ten-year period ending on the date of distribution and that would have been subject to section 864(c)(7) had it been disposed. Section 864(c)(7) shall govern the treatment of any gain recognized on the distribution of assets described in this paragraph as income effectively connected with the conduct of a trade or business within the United States.

(3) *Other consequences.*—(i) *Distributee basis in property.*—The foreign distributee corporation's basis in property subject to this paragraph (c) shall be the same as the foreign liquidating corporation's basis in such property immediately before the liquidation, increased by any gain, or reduced by any loss recognized by the foreign liquidating corporation on such property, pursuant to paragraph (c)(2) of this section.

(ii) *Other rules.*—For other rules that may apply, see sections 367(b) and 381.

(d) *Anti-abuse rule.*—The Commissioner may require a domestic liquidating corporation to recognize gain on a distribution in liquidation described in paragraph (b) of this section (or treat the liquidating corporation as if it had recognized loss on a distribution in liquidation), if a principal purpose of the liquidation is the avoidance of U.S. tax (including, but not limited to, the distribution of a liquidating corporation's earnings and profits with a principal purpose of avoiding U.S. tax). A liquidation may have a principal purpose of tax avoidance even though the tax avoidance purpose is outweighed by other purposes when taken together.

(e) *Failures to file or failures to comply.*—(1) *Scope.*—This paragraph (e) provides rules regarding a failure to file an initial liquidation document with respect to one or more liquidating distributions by a domestic liquidating corporation that, absent such failure, would qualify for nonrecognition treatment under paragraph (b)(2)(i) or (iii) of this section, or with respect to one or more liquidating distributions by a foreign liquidating corporation that, absent such failure, would qualify for nonrecognition treatment under paragraph (c)(2)(i)(B) of this section (failure to file). This paragraph (e) also provides rules regarding failures to comply in all material respects with the terms of this section with respect to one or more liquidating distributions for which nonrecognition treatment was initially claimed under paragraph (b)(2)(i), (b)(2)(iii), or (c)(2)(i)(B) of this section, as applicable (failure to comply).

(2) *Definitions.*—The following definitions apply for purposes of this section.

(i) An *initial liquidation document* means any statement, schedule, or form required to be filed under this section in order for the domestic liquidating corporation or foreign liquidating corporation, as applicable, to initially qualify to claim nonrecognition treatment with respect to one or more liquidating distributions described in this section, including—

(A) The statement and attachments described in paragraph (b)(2)(i)(C) of this section;

(B) The statement described in paragraph (b)(2)(iii)(D) of this section; and

(C) The statement and attachments described in paragraph (c)(2)(i)(C) of this section.

(ii) A *subsequent liquidation document* means any statement, schedule, or form (other than an initial liquidation document) required to be filed under this section in order for the domestic liquidating corporation or foreign liquidating corporation, as applicable, to continue to qualify for nonrecognition treatment with respect to one or more liquidating distributions described in this section, including—

(A) The schedule described in paragraph (b)(2)(i)(E)(*3*) of this section;

(B) The schedule described in paragraph (b)(2)(i)(E)(*4*)(*ii*) of this section; and

(C) The statement and attachments described in paragraph (b)(2)(i)(E)(*5*) of this section.

(iii) A *timely filed U.S. income tax return* means a Federal income tax return filed on or before the last date prescribed for filing (taking into account any extensions of time therefor) such return.

(3) *Failure to file.*—(i) *General rule.*—For purposes of this section and except as provided in paragraph (b)(2)(i)(D) or (f) of this section, there is a failure to file an initial liquidation document if—

(A) An initial liquidation document is not filed with the timely filed U.S. income tax return specified under this section, or

(B) An initial liquidation document is not completed in all material respects.

(ii) *Consequences of a failure to file.*—If there is a failure to file an initial liquidation document, then nonrecognition treatment under paragraph (b)(2)(i), (b)(2)(iii), or (c)(2)(i)(B) of this section (as appropriate) will not apply.

(4) *Failure to comply.*—(i) *General rule.*—For purposes of this section and except as provided in paragraph (b)(2)(i)(D) or (f) of this section, a failure to comply includes –

(A) A failure to report gain, or pay any additional tax or interest due, in accordance with the requirements under this section; and

(B) A failure to file a subsequent liquidation document, as determined by applying paragraph (e)(3)(i) of this section, but replacing the term "initial liquidation document" with the term "subsequent liquidation document."

(ii) *Consequences of a failure to comply.*—If there is a failure to comply in any material respect with the terms of paragraph (b)(2)(i), (b)(2)(iii), or (c)(2)(i) of this section, as applicable, then—

(A) Any gain (but not loss) that was not previously recognized by the domestic liquidating corporation or foreign liquidating corporation, as applicable, under paragraph (b)(2)(i), (b)(2)(iii), or (c)(2)(i)(B) of this section must be recognized; and

(B) The period of limitations on assessment of tax for the taxable year in which gain is required to be reported will be extended until the close of the third full taxable year ending after the date on which the domestic liquidating corporation, foreign distributee corporation, or foreign liquidating corporation, as applicable, furnishes to the Director of Field Operations, Cross Border Activities Practice Area of Large Business & International (or any successor to the roles and responsibilities of such position, as appropriate) (Director) the information that should have been provided under this section.

(f) *Relief for certain failures to file or failures to comply that are not willful.*—(1) *In general.*—This paragraph (f) provides relief if there is a failure to file an initial liquidation document as described in paragraph (e)(3)(i) of this section (failure to file), or a failure to comply in any material respect with the terms of this section as described in paragraph (e)(4)(i) of this section (failure to comply). A failure to file or a failure to comply will be deemed not to have occurred for purposes of paragraph (e)(3)(ii) or (e)(4)(ii) of this section if the taxpayer demonstrates that the failure was not willful using the procedure set forth in this paragraph (f). For this purpose, willful is to be interpreted consistent with the meaning of that term in the context of other civil penalties, which would include a failure due to gross negligence, reckless disregard, or willful neglect. Whether a failure to file or failure to comply was willful will be determined by the Director (as described in paragraph (e)(4)(ii)(B) of this section) based on all the facts and circumstances. The taxpayer must submit a request for relief and an explanation as provided in paragraph (f)(2)(i) of this section. Although a taxpayer whose failure to file or failure to comply is determined not to be willful will not be subject to gain or loss recognition under this section, the taxpayer will be subject to a penalty under section 6038B if the taxpayer fails to satisfy the reporting requirements, if any, under that section and does not demonstrate that the failure was due to reasonable cause and not willful neglect. See § 1.6038B-1(e)(4) and (f). The determination of whether the failure to file or failure to comply was willful under this section has no effect on any request for relief made under § 1.6038B-1(f).

(2) *Procedures for establishing that a failure to file or failure to comply was not willful.*—(i) *Time and manner of submission.*—A taxpayer's statement that a failure to file or failure to comply was not willful will be considered only if, promptly after the taxpayer becomes aware of the failure, an amended return is filed for the taxable year to which the failure relates that includes the information that should have been included with the original return for such taxable year or that otherwise complies with the rules of this section, and that includes a written statement explaining the reasons for the failure. In the case of a liquidating distribution described in paragraph (b)(2)(iii) of this section, the taxpayer must file, with the amended return, a Form 8838 extending the period of limitations on assessment of tax with respect to the gain realized but not recognized with respect to the liquidating distribution to the close of the third full taxable year ending after the date on which the required information is provided to the Director. In the case of a liquidating distribution described in paragraph (b)(2)(i) or (c)(2)(i)(B) of this section, the taxpayer must file, with the amended return, a Form 8838 extending the period of limitations on the assessment of tax with respect to the gain realized but not recognized with respect to the liquidating distribution to the later of: the date provided in paragraph (b)(2)(i)(C)(5), taking into account paragraph (c)(2)(i)(C) and (D), as applicable (date one); or, the close of the third full taxable year ending after the date on which the required information is provided to the Director (date two). However, the taxpayer is not required to file a Form 8838 with the amended return if both date one is later than date two and a Form 8838 was previously filed extending the period of limitations on assessment of tax with respect to the gain realized but not recognized with respect to the liquidating distribution to date one. If a Form 8838 is not required to be filed pursuant to the previous sentence, a copy of the previously filed Form 8838 must be filed with the amended return. The amended return and either a Form 8838 or a copy of the previously filed Form 8838, as the case may be, must be filed with the Internal Revenue Service at the location where the taxpayer filed its original return. The taxpayer may submit a request for relief from the penalty under section 6038B as part of the same submission. See § 1.6038B-1(f).

(ii) *Notice requirement.*—In addition to the requirements of paragraph (f)(2)(i) of this section, the taxpayer must comply with the notice requirements of this paragraph (f)(2)(ii). If any taxable year of the taxpayer is under examination when the amended return is filed, a copy of the amended return and any information required to be included with such return must be delivered to the Internal Revenue Service personnel conducting the examination. If no taxable year of the taxpayer is under examination when the amended return is filed, a copy of the amended return and any information required to be included with such return must be delivered to the Director.

(3) For illustrations of the application of the willfulness standard of this paragraph (f), see the examples in § 1.367(a)-8(p)(3).

(g) *Effective/applicability dates*.—Except as otherwise provided, this section applies to distributions occurring on or after September 7, 1999 or, if the taxpayer so elects, to distributions in taxable years ending after August 8, 1999. The ninth, tenth, and eleventh sentences of paragraph (a) of this section, and paragraphs (b)(1)(i), (b)(2)(i)(A)(*2*), (b)(2)(i)(A)(*3*), (b)(2)(i)(E)(*3*), (b)(2)(i)(E)(*4*)(*ii*), (b)(2)(i)(E)(*5*)(*ii*), (b)(2)(iii)(A), (c)(2)(i)(B)(*3*), (e), and (f) of this section will apply to liquidation documents that are required to be filed on or after November 19, 2014, as well as to requests for relief submitted on or after November 19, 2014. [Reg. § 1.367(e)-2.]

☐ [*T.D.* 8834, 8-6-99 (*corrected* 3-2-2000), *Amended by T.D.* 9066, 7-1-2003, *T.D.* 9704 11-18-2014 (*corrected* 1-2-2015) *and T.D.* 9803, 12-15-2016.]

§ 1.368-2. Definition of terms.—

* * *

(m) *Qualification as a reorganization under section 368(a)(1)(F)*.—(1) *Mere change*.—To qualify as a reorganization under section 368(a)(1)(F), a transaction must result in a mere change in identity, form, or place of organization of one corporation, however effected (a mere change). A mere change can consist of a transaction that involves an actual or deemed transfer of property from one corporation (a transferor corporation) to one other corporation (a resulting corporation). Such a transaction is a mere change and qualifies as a reorganization under section 368(a)(1)(F) only if all the requirements set forth in paragraphs (m)(1)(i) through (vi) of this section are satisfied. For purposes of this paragraph (m), a transaction or a series of related transactions that can be tested against the requirements set forth in paragraphs (m)(1)(i) through (vi) of this section (a potential F reorganization) begins when the transferor corporation begins transferring (or is deemed to begin transferring) its assets, directly or indirectly, to the resulting corporation, and it ends when the transferor corporation has distributed (or is deemed to have distributed) to its shareholders the consideration it receives (or is deemed to receive) from the resulting corporation and has completely liquidated for federal income tax purposes. For purposes of this paragraph (m), deemed transfers include, for example, those provided in § 301.7701-3(g)(1)(iv) of this chapter (when an entity disregarded as separate from its owner elects under paragraph § 301.7701-3(c)(1)(i) of this chapter to be classified as an association, the owner of the entity is deemed to transfer all of the assets and liabilities of the entity to the association in exchange for stock of the association). Deemed transfers also include those resulting from the application of step transaction principles. For example, step transaction principles may disregard a transitory holding of property by an individual after a liquidation of the transferor corporation and before a subsequent transfer of the transferor corporation's property to the resulting corporation. Step transaction principles may also treat a contribution of all the stock of the transferor corporation to the resulting corporation, followed by a liquidation (or deemed liquidation) of the transferor corporation, as a deemed transfer of the transferor corporation's property to the resulting corporation, followed by a distribution of stock of the resulting corporation in complete liquidation of the transferor corporation.

(i) *Resulting corporation stock distributed in exchange for transferor corporation stock*.—Immediately after the potential F reorganization, all the stock of the resulting corporation, including any stock of the resulting corporation issued before the potential F reorganization, must have been distributed (or deemed distributed) in exchange for stock of the transferor corporation in the potential F reorganization. However, for purposes of this paragraph (m)(1)(i) and paragraph (m)(1)(ii) of this section, a de minimis amount of stock issued by the resulting corporation other than in respect of stock of the transferor corporation to facilitate the organization of the resulting corporation or maintain its legal existence is disregarded.

(ii) *Identity of stock ownership*.—The same person or persons must own all of the stock of the transferor corporation, determined immediately before the potential F reorganization, and of the resulting corporation, determined immediately after the potential F reorganization, in identical proportions. However, this requirement is not violated if one or more holders of stock in the transferor corporation exchange stock in the transferor corporation for stock of equivalent value in the resulting corporation, but having different terms from those of the stock in the transferor corporation, or receive a distribution of money or other property from either the transferor corporation or the resulting corporation, whether or not in exchange for stock in the transferor corporation or the resulting corporation.

(iii) *Prior assets or attributes of resulting corporation*.—The resulting corporation may not hold any property or have any tax attributes (including those specified in section 381(c)) immediately before the potential F reorganization. However, this requirement is not violated if the resulting corporation holds or has held a de minimis amount of assets to facilitate its organization or maintain its legal existence, and has tax attributes related to holding those assets, or holds the proceeds of borrowings undertaken in connection with the potential F reorganization.

(iv) *Liquidation of transferor corporation*.—The transferor corporation must completely liquidate, for federal income tax purposes, in the potential F reorganization. However, the transferor corporation is not required to dissolve under applicable law and may retain a de minimis amount of assets for the sole purpose of preserving its legal existence.

(v) *Resulting corporation is the only acquiring corporation*.—Immediately after the potential F reorganization, no corporation other than the resulting corporation may hold property that was held by the transferor corporation immediately before the potential F reorganization, if such other corporation would, as a result, succeed to and take into account the items of the transferor corporation described in section 381(c).

(vi) *Transferor corporation is the only acquired corporation*.—Immediately after the potential F reorganization, the resulting corporation may not hold property acquired from a corporation other than the transferor corporation if the resulting corporation would, as a result, succeed to and take into account the items of such other corporation described in section 381(c).

(2) *Non-application of continuity of interest and continuity of business enterprise requirements*.—A continuity of the business enterprise and a continuity of interest are not required for a potential F reorganization to qualify as a reorganization under section 368(a)(1)(F). *See* § 1.368-1(b).

(3) *Related transactions*.—(i) *Series of transactions*.—A potential F reorganization consisting of a series of related transactions that together result in a mere change of one corporation may qualify as a reorganization under section 368(a)(1)(F), whether or not certain steps in the series, viewed in isolation, could be subject to other Code provisions, such as sections 304(a), 331, 332, or 351. However, *see* paragraph (k) of this section for transactions that qualify as reorganizations under section 368(a) and will not be recharacterized as a mere change as a result of one or more subsequent transfers of assets or stock.

(ii) *Mere change within a larger transaction*.—A potential F reorganization that qualifies as a reorganization under section 368(a)(1)(F) may occur before, within, or after other transactions that effect more than a mere change, even if the resulting corporation has only transitory existence. Related events that precede or follow the potential F reorganization generally will not cause that potential F reorganization to fail to qualify as a reorganization under section 368(a)(1)(F). Qualification of a potential F reorganization as a reorganization under section 368(a)(1)(F) will not alter the character of other transactions for federal income tax purposes, and step transaction principles may be applied to other transactions without regard to whether certain steps qualify as a reorganization or part of a reorganization under section 368(a)(1)(F).

(iii) *Distributions treated as separate transactions*.—As provided in paragraph (m)(1)(ii) of this section, a potential F reorganization may qualify as a mere change even though a holder of stock in the transferor corporation receives a distribution of money or other property from either the transferor corporation or the resulting corporation. If a shareholder receives money or other property (including in exchange for its shares) from the transferor corporation or the resulting corporation in a potential F reorganization that qualifies as a reorganization under section 368(a)(1)(F), then the receipt of money or other property (including any exchanged for shares) is treated as an unrelated, separate transaction from the reorganization, whether or not connected in a formal sense. See § 1.301-1(j).

(iv) *Transactions also qualifying under other provisions of section 368(a)(1).*—In certain cases, a potential F reorganization would (but for this paragraph (m)(3)(iv)) qualify both as a reorganization under section 368(a)(1)(F) and as a reorganization or part of a reorganization under another provision of section 368(a)(1). The following rules determine which of these overlapping qualifications applies.

(A) If the potential F reorganization or a step thereof qualifies as a reorganization or part of a reorganization under another provision of section 368(a)(1), and if a corporation in control (within the meaning of section 368(c)) of the resulting corporation is a party to such other reorganization (within the meaning of section 368(b)), the potential F reorganization will not qualify as a reorganization under section 368(a)(1)(F).

(B) Except as provided in paragraph (m)(3)(iv)(A) of this section, if, but for this paragraph (m)(3)(iv)(B), the potential F reorganization would qualify as a reorganization under both section 368(a)(1)(F) and one or more of sections 368(a)(1)(A), 368(a)(1)(C), or 368(a)(1)(D), then for all federal income tax purposes the potential F reorganization will qualify as a reorganization only under section 368(a)(1)(F).

(4) *Examples.*—The following examples illustrate the application of this paragraph (m). Unless the facts otherwise indicate, A, B, and C are domestic individuals; P, S, T, X, Y, and Z (and similar designations) are domestic corporations; each transaction is entered into for a valid business purpose; all persons and transactions are unrelated; and all other relevant facts are set forth in the examples.

Example 1. Cash contribution and redemption – no mere change. C owns all of the stock of X, a State A corporation. The net value of X's assets and liabilities is $1,000,000. Y, a State B corporation, seeks to acquire the assets of X for cash. To effect the acquisition, Y and X enter into an agreement under which Y will contribute $1,000,000 to Z, a newly formed corporation of which Y is the sole shareholder, in exchange for Z stock and X will merge into Z. In the merger, C surrenders all of the X stock and receives the $1,000,000 Y contributed to Z. C receives no Z stock in the transaction. After the merger, Y holds all of the Z stock, and Z holds all of the assets and liabilities previously held by X. Z stock is not distributed to the shareholders of X in exchange for their stock in X as required by paragraph (m)(1)(i) of this section, and the transaction results in a change in the ownership of X that does not result from an exchange or distribution described in paragraph (m)(1)(ii) of this section. Therefore, the merger of X into Z is not a mere change of X and does not qualify as a reorganization under section 368(a)(1)(F).

Example 2. Cash redemption – mere change. A owns 75%, and B owns 25%, of the stock of X, a State A corporation. The management of X determines that it would be in the best interest of X to reorganize under the laws of State B. Accordingly, X forms Y, a State B corporation, and X and Y enter into an agreement under which X will merge into Y. A does not wish to own stock in Y. In the merger, A surrenders A's X stock and receives cash, and B surrenders all of B's X stock and receives all the stock of Y. The change in ownership caused by A's surrender of X stock results from a distribution and exchange described in paragraph (m)(1)(ii) of this section. Therefore, the merger of X into Y is a mere change of X and qualifies as a reorganization under section 368(a)(1)(F). Under paragraph (m)(3)(iii) of this section, A's surrender of X stock for cash is treated as a transaction, separate from the reorganization, to which section 302(a) applies.

Example 3. Pre-transaction de minimis stock issuance – mere change – other provisions of section 368(a)(1). P owns all of the stock of S, a Country A corporation. The management of P determines that it would be in the best interest of S to change its place of incorporation to Country B. Under Country B law, a corporation must have at least two shareholders to enjoy limited liability. P is advised by its Country B advisors that the new corporation should issue 1% of its stock to a shareholder that is not P's nominee to assure satisfaction of the two-shareholder requirement. As part of an integrated plan, C, an officer of S, organizes Y, a Country B corporation with 1,000 shares of common stock authorized, and contributes cash to Y in exchange for ten of the common shares. S then merges into Y under the laws of Country A and Country B. Pursuant to the plan of merger, P surrenders its shares of S stock and receives 990 shares of Y common stock. The ten shares of Y stock issued to C not in respect of the S stock are de minimis and are used to facilitate the organization of Y within the meaning of paragraph (m)(1)(i) of this section. Therefore, the issuance of this stock to a new shareholder does not prevent the merger of S into Y from qualifying as a mere change of S. Accordingly, the merger is a reorganization under section 368(a)(1)(F). Without regard to the merger's qualification under section 368(a)(1)(F), the merger would also qualify as a reorganization under both section 368(a)(1)(A) and section 368(a)(1)(D). Under paragraph (m)(3)(iv)(B) of this section, if a potential F reorganization qualifies as a reorganization under section 368(a)(1)(F), and would also qualify under one or more of sections 368(a)(1)(A) or 368(a)(1)(D), the potential F reorganization qualifies only as a reorganization under 368(a)(1)(F), and neither section 368(a)(1)(A) nor section 368(a)(1)(D) will apply.

Example 4. Pre-transaction assets, attributes – no mere change. A owns all of the stock of P, and P owns all of the stock of S, which is engaged in a manufacturing business. P has owned the stock of S for many years. P owns no assets other than the stock of S. A decides to eliminate the holding company structure by merging P into S. Because it operates a manufacturing business, the potential resulting corporation, S, holds property and has tax attributes immediately before the potential F reorganization. Therefore, under paragraph (m)(1)(iii) of this section, the merger of P into S is not a mere change of P and does not qualify as a reorganization under section 368(a)(1)(F). The same result would occur under paragraph (m)(1)(iii) of this section if, instead of P merging into S, S merged into P, because P, the potential resulting corporation, holds property (the stock of S) and has tax attributes immediately before the potential F reorganization.

Example 5. Series of related transactions – mere change. P owns all of the stock of S1, a State A corporation. The management of P determines that it would be in the best interest of S1 to change its place of incorporation to State B. Accordingly, under an integrated plan, P forms S2, a new State B corporation; P contributes the S1 stock to S2; and S1 merges into S2 under the laws of State A and State B. Under paragraph (m)(3)(i) of this section, a series of transactions that together result in a mere change of one corporation may qualify as a reorganization under section 368(a)(1)(F). The contribution of S1 stock to S2 and the merger of S1 into S2 together constitute a mere change of S1. Therefore, the potential F reorganization qualifies as a reorganization under section 368(a)(1)(F). Without regard to its qualification under section 368(a)(1)(F), the potential F reorganization would also qualify as a reorganization under both section 368(a)(1)(A) and section 368(a)(1)(D). Under paragraph (m)(3)(iv)(B) of this section, if a potential F reorganization qualifies as a reorganization under section 368(a)(1)(F) and would also qualify under one or more of sections 368(a)(1)(A) or 368(a)(1)(D), it qualifies only as a reorganization under 368(a)(1)(F), and neither section 368(a)(1)(A) nor section 368(a)(1)(D) will apply. The result would be the same with respect to qualification under section 368(a)(1)(F) if, instead of merging into S2, S1 completely liquidates or is deemed to liquidate by reason of a conversion in an entity disregarded as separate from its owner under § 301.7701-3 of this chapter.

Example 6. Post-transaction stock sale – mere change. P owns all of the stock of S1, a State A corporation. The management of P determines that it would be in the best interest of S1 to change its place of incorporation to State B. Accordingly, P forms S2, a new State B corporation. S1 then merges into S2 under the laws of State A and State B. Immediately thereafter, and as part of the same plan, P sells all of its stock in S2 to an unrelated party. Without regard to P's sale of S2 stock, the merger of S1 into S2 is a potential F reorganization that qualifies as a mere change of S1 within the meaning of paragraph (m)(1) of this section. Under paragraph (m)(3)(ii) of this section, related events that occur before or after a potential F reorganization that qualifies as a mere change generally do not cause that potential F reorganization to fail to qualify as a reorganization under section 368(a)(1)(F). Therefore, P's sale of the S2 stock is disregarded in determining whether the merger of S1 into S2 is a mere change of S1. Accordingly, the merger of S1 into S2 qualifies as a reorganization under section 368(a)(1)(F). The result would be the same if, instead of the S2 stock being sold by P, S2 merges into a previously unrelated corporation and terminates its separate existence.

Example 7. Post-transaction redemption – mere change. A owns all of the stock of T. P owns all of the stock of S. Each of T, P, and S is a State A corporation engaged in a manufacturing business. The following transactions occur pursuant to a single plan. First, T merges into S with A receiving solely stock in P. Second, P changes its state of incorporation to State B by merging into newly incorporated New P under the laws of State A and State B. Third, New P redeems all the New P stock issued to A in respect of A's P stock (initially issued to A in respect of A's T stock) for cash. Without regard to the other steps, the merger of P into New P is a potential F reorganization that qualifies as a reorganization under section 368(a)(1)(F). Under paragraph (m)(3)(ii) of this section, related events that occur before or after a potential F reorganization that qualifies as a mere change generally do not prevent that potential F reorganization from qualifying as a reorganization under section 368(a)(1)(F). Therefore, the merger of P into New P qualifies as a reorganization under section 368(a)(1)(F). Under paragraph (m)(3)(ii) of this section, the qualification of the merger of P into New P as a reorganization under section 368(a)(1)(F) does not alter the tax treatment of the merger of T into S. Because the P shares received by A in respect of the T shares (exchanged for New P shares in the mere change of P into New P) are redeemed for cash pursuant to the plan, the merger of T into S does not satisfy the continuity of interest requirement of § 1.368-1(e) and therefore does not qualify as a reorganization under section 368(a).

Example 8. Series of related transactions –mere change. P owns all of the stock of S, a State A corporation. The management of P determines that it would be in the best interest of S to change its form from a State A corporation to a State A limited partnership but to continue to be treated as a corporation for federal tax purposes. Accordingly, P contributes 1% of the S stock to newly formed LLC, a limited liability company, in exchange for all of the membership interests in LLC. P is the sole member of LLC. Under § 301.7701-3 of this chapter, LLC is disregarded as an entity separate from its owner, P. Then, under a State A statute, S converts to a State A limited partnership. In the conversion, P's interest as a 99% shareholder of S is converted into a 99% limited partner interest, and LLC's interest as a 1% shareholder of S is converted into a 1% general partner interest. S also elects, under § 301.7701-3(c) of this chapter, to be classified as a corporation for federal income tax purposes, effective on the same day as the conversion. Under paragraph (m)(3)(i) of this section, the conversion of S from a State A corporation to a State A limited partnership, together with the election to treat S as a corporation for federal tax purposes, results in a mere change of S and qualifies as a reorganization under section 368(a)(1)(F).

Example 9. Other acquiring corporation – no mere change. P owns 80%, and A owns 20%, of the stock of S. A and the management of P determine that it would be in the best interest of S to completely liquidate while A continues to operate part of the business of S in corporate form. Accordingly, S distributes 80% of its assets to P and 20% of its assets to A; S dissolves; and A contributes the assets it receives from S to newly incorporated New S in exchange for all of the stock of New S. S's distribution of 80% of its property to P as part of the complete liquidation of S meets the requirements of section 332. Thus, section 381(a)(1) applies to P's acquisition of 80% of the property held by S immediately before the transaction. Under paragraph (m)(1)(v) of this section, the potential F reorganization in which 20% of the property held by S immediately before the transaction is transferred to New S cannot be a mere change of S, because section 381(a) applies to P's acquisition of property held by S immediately before the potential F reorganization. Accordingly, sections 331 and 336 apply to A's acquisition of property from S and S's distribution of property to A, and section 351 applies to A's contribution of that property to New S.

Example 10. Other acquiring corporation –no mere change. P owns all of the stock of S1. The management of P determines that it would be in the best interest of S1 to merge S1 into P. Accordingly, pursuant to a state merger statute, S1 merges into P. Immediately afterward and as part of the same plan, P contributes 50% of the former assets of S1 to newly incorporated S2 in exchange for all of the stock of S2. The transaction does not qualify as a complete liquidation of S1 under section 332 (because of the reincorporation of some of S1's assets) but does qualify as a reorganization under section 368(a)(1)(A) by reason of section 368(a)(2)(C) and paragraph (k) of this section. Under paragraph (m)(1)(v) of this section, the potential F reorganization in which some of the former assets of S1 are transferred (in form) first to P, and then to S2, is not a mere change of S1, because section 381(a) applies to P's acquisition of property held by S1 immediately before the potential F reorganization. Furthermore, under paragraph (m)(3)(iv)(A) of this section, P, the corporation in control of S2 within the meaning of section 368(c), is a party to the reorganization within the meaning of section 368(b). Thus, the indirect transfer of property from S1 to S2 does not qualify under section 368(a)(1)(F).

Example 11. Other acquiring corporation –mere change. P owns all of the stock of S1. S1's only asset is all of the equity interest in LLC2, a domestic limited liability company. Under § 301.7701-3 of this chapter, LLC2 is disregarded as an entity separate from its owner, S1. Pursuant to an integrated plan to undergo a reorganization under 368(a)(1)(F), S1 and LLC2 undergo the following two state law conversions. First, under state law LLC2 converts into S2, a corporation. Second, under state law S1 converts into LLC1, a domestic limited liability company. Under § 301.7701-3 of this chapter, LLC1 is disregarded as an entity separate from its owner, P. As a result of the two conversions, S1 is deemed to transfer its assets to S2 in exchange for all of the stock in S2 and then distribute the S2 stock to P in complete liquidation of S1. The two conversions, viewed as a potential F reorganization, constitute a mere change of S1, and that potential F reorganization qualifies as a reorganization under section 368(a)(1)(F). The result would be the same if, instead of converting into S2 pursuant to state law, LLC2 elected under § 301.7701-3(c) to change its classification for federal tax purposes and be treated as an association taxable as a corporation, provided the effective date of the election (and its resulting deemed transactions) occurs before the conversion of S1.

Example 12. Other acquiring corporation – no mere change. The facts are the same facts as in *Example 11*, except that S1 converts into LLC1 prior to the conversion of LLC2 into S2. As a result of these conversions, S1 is deemed to distribute all of its assets to P in exchange for all of P's S1 stock, and P is deemed to transfer all of those assets to S2 in exchange for all of the stock in S2. The transaction does not qualify as a complete liquidation of S1 under section 332 (because of the reincorporation of S1's assets), but does qualify as a reorganization under section 368(a)(1)(C) by reason of section 368(a)(2)(C) and paragraph (k) of this section. Under paragraph (m)(1)(v) of this section, the potential F reorganization in which the former assets of S1 are deemed transferred, first by S1 to P, and then by P to S2, is not a mere change of S1 because section 381(a) applies to P's acquisition of property held by S1 immediately before the potential F reorganization. Furthermore, the corporation in control of S2, within the meaning of section 368(c), is a party to the reorganization within the meaning of section 368(b). Thus, the indirect transfer of property from S1 to S2 does not qualify under section 368(a)(1)(F).

Example 13. *Series of related transactions – no mere change.* X owns all of the stock of T. P acquires all of the stock of T in exchange for consideration consisting of $50 cash and P voting stock with $50 value. No election is made under section 338. Immediately thereafter and as part of the same plan, P forms S as a wholly-owned subsidiary, and T is merged into S. Viewed in isolation as a potential F reorganization, the merger of T into S appears to constitute a mere change of T. However, the acquisition of the T stock by P and the merger of T into S, viewed together, qualify as a reorganization under section 368(a)(1)(A) by reason of section 368(a)(2)(D). The step transaction doctrine is applied treat the transaction as a statutory merger of T into S in exchange for $50 cash and $50 of P's voting stock (and S's assumption of T's liabilities), P's momentary ownership of T stock is disregarded. Under paragraph (m)(3)(iv)(A) of this section, P, the corporation in control of S, is a party to the reorganization within the meaning of section 368(b). Thus, the transfer of property from T to S does not qualify under section 368(a)(1)(F).

Example 14. *Multiple transferor corporations – no mere change.* P owns all the stock of S1 and S2. The management of P determines it would be in the best interest of S1 and S2 to operate as a single corporation. P forms S3 and, under applicable corporate law,S1 and S2 simultaneously merge into S3. Immediately after the merger, P owns all the stock of S3. Each of the mergers can be tested as a potential F reorganization. However, immediately after the simultaneous mergers. the resulting corporation, S3, holds property acquired from a corporation other than the transferor corporation, and section 381(a) would apply to the acquisition of such property. Therefore, under paragraph (m)(1)(vi) of this section, neither potential F reorganization is a mere change, and neither merger into S3 qualifies as a reorganization under section 386(a)(1)(F). The result would be different if the mergers were not simultaneous. If S1 completed its merger into S3 before S2 began its merger into S3, the merger of S1 into S3 would qualify as a reorganization under section 368(a)(1)(F), but the merger of S2 into S3 would not so qualify (although it would qualify as a reorganization under sections 368(a)(1)(A) and 368(a)(1)(D)).

(5) *Effective/Applicability Date.*—This paragraph (m) applies to transactions occurring on or after September 21, 2015. [Reg. § 1.368-2.]

☐ [*T.D.* 6152, 12-2-55. *Amended by T.D.* 7281, 7-11-73; *T.D.* 7422, 6-25-76; *T.D.* 8059, 10-21-85; *T.D.* 8760, 1-23-98; *T.D.* 8885, 5-18-2000; *T.D.* 9038, 1-23-2003; *T.D.* 9242, 1-23-2006; *T.D.* 9259, 4-24-2006; *T.D.* 9303, 12-18-2006; *T.D.* 9361, 10-24-2007; *T.D.* 9396, 5-8-2008, *T.D.* 9475, 12-17-2009 (*corrected* 1-19-2010), *T.D.* 9739, 9-18-2015 (*corrected* 12-7-2015) *and T.D.* 9954, 9-21-2021.]

Corporate Interests as Stock or Debt

§ 1.385-1. General provisions.—(a) *Overview of section 385 regulations.*—This section and §§ 1.385-3 through 1.385-4 (collectively, the section 385 regulations) provide rules under section 385 to determine the treatment of an interest in a corporation as stock or indebtedness (or as in part stock and in part indebtedness) in particular factual situations. Paragraph (b) of this section provides the general rule for determining the treatment of an interest based on provisions of the Internal Revenue Code and on common law, including the factors prescribed under common law. Paragraphs (c), (d), and (e) of this section provide definitions and rules of general application for purposes of the section 385 regulations. Section 1.385-3 sets forth additional factors that, when present, control the determination of whether an interest in a corporation that is held by a member of the corporation's expanded group is treated (in whole or in part) as stock or indebtedness.

(b) *General rule.*—Except as otherwise provided in the Internal Revenue Code and the regulations thereunder, including the section 385 regulations, whether an interest in a corporation is treated for purposes of the Internal Revenue Code as stock or indebtedness (or as in part stock and in part indebtedness) is determined based on common law, including the factors prescribed under such common law.

(c) *Definitions.*—The definitions in this paragraph (c) apply for purposes of the section 385 regulations. For additional definitions that apply for purposes of their respective sections, see §§1.385-3(g) and 1.385-4(e).

(1) *Controlled partnership.*—The term controlled partnership means, with respect to an expanded group, a partnership with respect to which at least 80 percent of the interests in partnership capital or profits are owned, directly or indirectly, by one or more members of the expanded group. For purposes of identifying a controlled partnership, indirect ownership of a partnership interest is determined by applying the principles of paragraph (c)(4)(iii) of this section. Such determination is separate from the determination of the status of a corporation as a member of an expanded group. An unincorporated organization described in §1.761-2 that elects to be excluded from all of subchapter K of chapter 1 of the Internal Revenue Code is not a controlled partnership.

(2) *Covered member.*—The term covered member means a member of an expanded group that is—

(i) A domestic corporation; and

(ii) [Reserved]

(3) *Disregarded entity.*—The term disregarded entity means a business entity (as defined in §301.7701-2(a) of this chapter) that is disregarded as an entity separate from its owner for federal income tax purposes under §§301.7701-1 through 301.7701-3 of this chapter.

(4) *Expanded group.*—(i) *In general.*—The term expanded group means one or more chains of corporations (other than S corporations) connected through stock ownership with a common parent corporation that is not an S corporation or a regulated investment company or a real estate investment trust subject to tax under subchapter M of chapter 1 of the Internal Revenue Code (a RIC or a REIT, respectively) (such common parent corporation, an expanded group parent), but only if—

(A) The expanded group parent owns directly or indirectly stock meeting the requirements of section 1504(a)(2) (modified by substituting "or" for "and" in section 1504(a)(2)(A)) in at least one of the other corporations; and

(B) Stock meeting the requirements of section 1504(a)(2) (modified by substituting "or" for "and" in section 1504(a)(2)(A)) in each of the other corporations (except the expanded group parent) is owned directly or indirectly by one or more of the other corporations.

(ii) *Definition of stock.*—For purposes of paragraph (c)(4)(i) of this section, the term stock has the same meaning as "stock" in section 1504 (without regard to §1.1504-4) and all shares of stock within a single class are considered to have the same value. Thus, control premiums and minority and blockage discounts within a single class are not taken into account.

(iii) *Indirect stock ownership.*—For purposes of paragraph (c)(4)(i) of this section, indirect stock ownership is determined by applying the constructive ownership rules of section 318(a) with the following modifications:

(A) Section 318(a)(1) and (a)(3) do not apply except as set forth in paragraph (c)(4)(v) of this section;

(B) Section 318(a)(2)(C) applies by substituting "5 percent" for "50 percent;" and

(C) Section 318(a)(4) only applies to options (as defined in §1.1504-4(d)) that are reasonably certain to be exercised as described in §1.1504-4(g).

(iv) *Member of an expanded group or expanded group member.*—The expanded group parent and each of the other corporations described in paragraphs (c)(4)(i)(A) and (c)(4)(i)(B) of this section is a member of an expanded group (also referred to as an expanded group member). For purposes of the section 385 regulations, a corporation is a member of an expanded group if it is described in this paragraph (c)(4)(iv) immediately before the relevant time for determining membership (for example, immediately before the issuance of a debt instrument (as defined in §1.385-3(g)(4)) or immediately before a distribution or acquisition that may be subject to §1.385-3(b)(2) or (3)).

(v) *Brother-sister groups with non-corporate owners.*—[Reserved]

(vi) *Special rule for indirect ownership through options for certain members of consolidated groups.*—In the case of an option of which a member of a consolidated group, other than the common parent, is the issuing corporation (as defined in §1.1504-4(c)(1)), section 318(a)(4) only applies (for purposes of applying paragraph (c)(4)(iii)(C) of this section) to the option if the option is treated as stock or as exercised under §1.1504-4(b) for purposes of determining whether a corporation is a member of an affiliated group.

(vii) *Examples.*—The following examples illustrate the rules of this paragraph (c)(4). Except as otherwise stated, for purposes of the examples in this paragraph (c)(4)(vii), all persons described are corporations that have a single class of stock outstanding and file separate federal tax returns and are not an S corporation, a RIC, or a REIT. In addition, the stock of each publicly traded corporation is widely held such that no person directly or indirectly owns stock in the publicly traded corporation meeting the requirements of section 1504(a)(2) (as modified by this paragraph (c)(4)).

(A) *Example 1. Two different expanded group parents. (1) Facts.* P has two classes of common stock outstanding: Class A and Class B. X, a publicly traded corporation, directly owns all shares of P's Class A common stock, which is high-vote common stock representing 85% of the vote and 15% of the value of the stock of P. Y, a publicly traded corporation, directly owns all shares of P's Class B common stock, which is low-vote common stock representing 15% of the vote and 85% of the value of the stock of P. P directly owns 100% of the stock of S1.

(2) Analysis. X owns directly 85% of the vote of the stock of P, which is stock meeting the requirements of section 1504(a)(2) (as modified by paragraph (c)(4)(i)(A) of this section). Therefore, X is an expanded group parent described in paragraph (c)(4)(i) of this section with respect to P. Y owns 85% of the value of the stock of P, which is stock meeting the requirements of section 1504(a)(2) (as modified by paragraph (c)(4)(i)(A) of this section). Therefore, Y is also an expanded group parent described in paragraph (c)(4)(i) of this section with respect to P. P owns directly 100% of the voting power and value of the stock of S1, which is stock meeting the requirements of section 1504(a)(2) (as modified by paragraph (c)(4)(i)(B) of this section). Therefore, X, P, and S1 constitute an expanded group as defined in paragraph (c)(4)(i) of this section. Additionally, Y, P, and S1 constitute an expanded group as defined in paragraph (c)(4) of this section. X and Y are not members of the same expanded group under paragraph (c)(4) of this section because X does not directly or indirectly own any of the stock of Y and Y does not directly or indirectly own any of the stock of X, such that X and Y do not comprise a chain of corporations described in paragraph (c)(4)(i) of this section.

(B) *Example 2. Inclusion of a REIT within an expanded group. (1) Facts.* All of the stock of P is publicly traded. In addition to other assets representing 85% of the value of its total assets, P directly owns all of the stock of S1. S1 owns 99% of the stock of S2. The remaining 1% of the stock of S2 is owned by 100 unrelated individuals. In addition to other assets representing 85% of the value of its total assets, S2 owns all of the stock of S3, which has elected to be treated as a taxable REIT subsidiary of S2 under section 856(l)(1). Both P and S2 are REITs.

(2) Analysis. P directly owns 100% of the stock of S1. However, under paragraph (c)(4)(i) of this section, P cannot be the expanded group parent because P is a REIT. Because no other corporation owns stock in P meeting the requirements described in paragraph (c)(4)(i) of this section, P is not an expanded group member. S1 directly owns 99% of the stock of S2, which is stock meeting the requirements of section 1504(a)(2) (as modified by paragraph (c)(4)(i)(A) of this section). Although S2 is a corporation that is a REIT, a REIT may be a member of an expanded group described under paragraph (c)(4)(i) of this section provided the corporation is not the expanded group parent. In this case, S1 is the expanded

group parent. S2 directly owns 100% of the stock of S3, which is stock meeting the requirements of section 1504(a)(2) (as modified by paragraph (c)(4)(i)(B) of this section). Therefore, S1, S2, and S3 constitute an expanded group as defined in paragraph (c)(4) of this section.

(C) *Example 3. Attribution of hook stock. (1) Facts.* P, a publicly traded corporation, directly owns 50% of the stock of S1. S1 directly owns 100% of the stock of S2. S2 directly owns the remaining 50% of the stock of S1.

(2) Analysis. (i) P directly owns 50% of the stock of S1. Under paragraph (c)(4)(iii) of this section (which applies section 318(a)(2) with modifications), P constructively owns 50% of the stock of S2 because P directly owns 50% of the stock of S1, which directly owns 100% of S2. Under section 318(a)(5)(A), stock constructively owned by P by reason of the application of section 318(a)(2) is, for purposes of section 318(a)(2), considered as actually owned by P.

(ii) S2 directly owns 50% of the stock of S1. Thus, under paragraph (c)(4)(iii) of this section, P is treated as constructively owning an additional 25% of the stock of S1. For purposes of determining the expanded group, P's ownership must be recalculated treating the additional 25% of S1 stock as actually owned. Under the second application of section 318(a)(2)(C) as modified by paragraph (c)(4)(iii) of this section, P constructively owns an additional 12.5% of the stock of S1 as follows: 25% (P's new attributed ownership of S1) x 100% (S1's ownership of S2) x 50% (S2's ownership of S1) = 12.5%. After two iterations, P's ownership in S1 is 87.5% (50% direct ownership + 25% first order constructive ownership + 12.5% second order constructive ownership) and thus S1 is a member of the expanded group that includes P and S2. Subsequent iterative calculations of P's ownership, treating constructive ownership as actual ownership, would demonstrate that P owns, directly and indirectly, 100% of the stock of S1. P, S1, and S2 therefore constitute an expanded group as defined in paragraph (c)(4) of this section and P is the expanded group parent.

(D) *Example 4. Attribution of hook stock when an intermediary has multiple owners. (1) Facts.* The facts are the same as in paragraph (c)(4)(vii)(C) *(1)* of this section (*Example 3*), except that P directly owns only 25% of the stock of S1. X, a corporation unrelated to P, also directly owns 25% of the stock of S1.

(2) Analysis. (i) P and X each directly owns 25% of the stock of S1. Under paragraph (c)(4)(iii) of this section, P and X each constructively owns 25% of the stock of S2 because P and X each directly owns 25% of the stock of S1, which directly owns 100% of the stock of S2. Under section 318(a)(5)(A), stock constructively owned by P or X by reason of the application of section 318(a)(2) is, for purposes of section 318(a)(2), considered as actually owned by P or X, respectively.

(ii) S2 directly owns 50% of the stock of S1. Thus, under paragraph (c)(4)(iii) of this section, P and X each is treated as constructively owning an additional 12.5% of the stock of S1. Under a second application of section 318(a)(2)(C) as modified by paragraph (c)(4)(iii) of this section, P and X each constructively owns an additional 6.25% of the stock of S1 as follows: 12.5% (each of P's and X's new attributed ownership of S1) x 100% (S1's ownership of S2) x 50% (S2's ownership of S1) = 6.25%. After two iterations, each of P's and X's ownership in S1 is 43.75% (25% direct ownership + 12.5% first order constructive ownership + 6.25% second order constructive ownership). Subsequent iterative calculations of each of P's and X's ownership, treating constructive ownership as actual ownership, would demonstrate that P and X each owns, directly and indirectly, 50% of the stock of S1.

(iii) S1 and S2 constitute an expanded group as defined under paragraph (c)(4)(i) of this section because S1 directly owns 100% of the stock of S2. S1 is the expanded group parent of the expanded group and neither P nor X are a member of the expanded group that includes S1 and S2.

(5) *Regarded owner.*—The term *regarded owner* means a person (which cannot be a disregarded entity) that is the single owner (within the meaning of §301.7701-2(c)(2)(i) of this chapter) of a disregarded entity.

(d) *Treatment of deemed exchanges.*—(1) *Debt instrument deemed to be exchanged for stock.*—(i) *In general.*—If a debt instrument (as defined in §1.385-3(g)(4)) is deemed to be exchanged under the section 385 regulations, in whole or in part, for stock, the holder is treated for all Federal tax purposes as having realized an amount equal to the holder's adjusted basis in that portion of the debt instrument as of the date of the deemed exchange (and as having basis in the stock deemed to be received equal to that amount), and, except as provided in paragraph (d)(1)(iv)(B) of this section, the issuer is treated for all Federal tax purposes as having retired that portion of the debt instrument for an amount equal to its adjusted issue price as of the date of the deemed exchange. In addition, neither party accounts for any accrued but unpaid qualified stated interest on the debt instrument or any foreign exchange gain or loss with respect to that accrued but unpaid qualified stated interest (if any) as of the deemed exchange. This paragraph (d)(1)(i) does not affect any rules in Title 26 of the United States Code that otherwise apply to the debt instrument prior to the date of the deemed exchange (for example, this paragraph (d)(1)(i) does not affect the issuer's deduction of accrued but unpaid qualified stated interest otherwise deductible prior to the date of the deemed exchange). Moreover, the stock issued in the deemed exchange is not treated as a payment of accrued but unpaid original issue discount or qualified stated interest on the debt instrument for Federal tax purposes.

(ii) *Section 988.*—Notwithstanding the first sentence of paragraph (d)(1)(i) of this section, the rules of §1.988-2(b)(13) apply to require the holder and the issuer of a debt instrument that is deemed to be exchanged under the section 385 regulations, in whole or in part, for stock to recognize any exchange gain or loss, other than any exchange gain or loss with respect to accrued but unpaid qualified stated interest that is not taken into account under paragraph (d)(1)(i) of this section at the time of the deemed exchange. For purposes of this paragraph (d)(1)(ii), in applying §1.988-2(b)(13) the exchange gain or loss under section 988 is treated as the total gain or loss on the exchange.

(iii) *Section 108(e)(8).*—For purposes of section 108(e)(8), if the issuer of a debt instrument is treated as having retired all or a portion of the debt instrument in exchange for stock under paragraph (d)(1)(i) of this section, the stock is treated as having a fair market value equal to the adjusted issue price of that portion of the debt instrument as of the date of the deemed exchange.

(iv) *Issuer of stock deemed exchanged for debt.*—For purposes of applying paragraph (d)(1)(i) of this section—

(A) A debt instrument that is issued by a disregarded entity is deemed to be exchanged for stock of the regarded owner under §1.385-3(d)(4);

(B) A debt instrument that is issued by a partnership that becomes a deemed transferred receivable, in whole or in part, is deemed to be exchanged by the holder for deemed partner stock under §1.385-3(f)(4) and the partnership is therefore not treated for any federal tax purpose as having retired any portion of the debt instrument; and

(C) A debt instrument that is issued in any situation not described in paragraph (d)(1)(iv)(A) or (B) of this section is deemed to be exchanged for stock of the issuer of the debt instrument.

(2) *Stock deemed to be exchanged for newly-issued debt instrument.*—(i) [Reserved].

(ii) *Debt instruments recharacterized under §1.385-3.*—If a debt instrument treated as stock under §1.385-3(b) is deemed to be exchanged under §1.385-3(d)(2), in whole or in part, for a newly-issued debt instrument, the issue price of the newly-issued debt instrument is determined under either section 1273(b)(4) or 1274, as applicable.

(e) *Indebtedness in part.*—[Reserved]

(f) *Applicability date.*—This section applies to taxable years ending on or after January 19, 2017. [Reg. §1.385-1.]

☐ [*T.D.* 9790, 10-13-2016 (*corrected* 1-23-2017). *Amended by T.D.* 9880, 10-31-2019 *and T.D.* 9897, 5-13-2020.]

§1.385-3. Certain distributions of debt instruments and similar transactions.—(a) *Scope.*—This section sets forth factors that control the determination of whether an interest is treated as stock or indebtedness. Specifically, this section addresses the issuance of a covered debt instrument to a related person as part of a transaction or series of transactions that does not result in new investment in the operations of the issuer. Paragraph (b) of this section sets forth rules for determining when these factors are present, such that a covered debt instrument is treated as stock under this section. Paragraph (c) of this section provides exceptions to the application of paragraph (b) of this section. Paragraph (d) of this section provides operating rules. Paragraph (e) of this section reserves on the affirmative use of this section. Paragraph (f) of this section provides rules for the aggregate treatment of controlled partnerships. Paragraph (g) of this section provides definitions. Paragraph (h) of this section provides examples illustrating the application of the rules of this section. Paragraph (j) of this section provides dates of applicability. For rules regarding the application of this section to members of a consolidated group, see generally § 1.385-4.

(b) *Covered debt instrument treated as stock.*—(1) *Effect of characterization as stock.*—Except as otherwise provided in paragraph (d)(7) of this section, to the extent a covered debt instrument is treated as stock under paragraphs (b)(2), (3), or (4) of this section, it is treated as stock for all federal tax purposes.

(2) *General rule.*—Except as otherwise provided in paragraphs (c) and (e) of this section, a covered debt instrument is treated as stock to the extent the covered debt instrument is issued by a covered member to a member of the covered member's expanded group in one or more of the following transactions:

(i) In a distribution;

(ii) In exchange for expanded group stock, other than in an exempt exchange; or

(iii) In exchange for property in an asset reorganization, but only to the extent that, pursuant to the plan of reorganization, a shareholder in the transferor corporation that is a member of the issuer's expanded group immediately before the reorganization receives the covered debt instrument with respect to its stock in the transferor corporation.

(3) *Funding rule.*—(i) *In general.*—Except as otherwise provided in paragraphs (c) and (e) of this section, a covered debt instrument that is not a qualified short-term debt instrument (as defined in paragraph (b)(3)(vii) of this section) is treated as stock to the extent that it is both issued by a covered member to a member of the covered member's expanded group in exchange for property and, pursuant to paragraph (b)(3)(iii) or (b)(3)(iv) of this section, treated as funding a distribution or acquisition described in one or more of paragraphs (b)(3)(i)(A) through (C) of this section. A covered member that makes a distribution or acquisition described in paragraphs (b)(3)(i)(A) through (C) is referred to as a "funded member," regardless of when it issues a covered debt instrument in exchange for property.

(A) A distribution of property by the funded member to a member of the funded member's expanded group, other than in an exempt distribution;

(B) An acquisition of expanded group stock, other than an exempt exchange, by the funded member from a member of the funded member's expanded group in exchange for property other than expanded group stock; or

(C) An acquisition of property by the funded member in an asset reorganization but only to the extent that, pursuant to the plan of reorganization, a shareholder in the transferor corporation that is a member of the funded member's expanded group immediately before the reorganization receives other property or money within the meaning of section 356 with respect to its stock in the transferor corporation.

(ii) *Transactions described in more than one paragraph.*—For purposes of this section, to the extent that a distribution or acquisition by a funded member is described in more than one of paragraphs (b)(3)(i)(A) through (C) of this section, the funded member is treated as making only a single distribution or acquisition described in paragraph (b)(3)(i) of this section. In the case of an asset reorganization, to the extent an acquisition by the transferee corporation is described in paragraph (b)(3)(i)(C) of this section, a distribution or acquisition by the transferor corporation is not also described in paragraph (b)(3)(i)(A) through (C) of this section. For purposes of this paragraph (b)(3)(ii), whether a distribution or acquisition is described in paragraphs (b)(3)(i)(A) through (C) of this section is determined without regard to paragraph (c) of this section.

(iii) *Per se funding rule.*—(A) *In general.*—A covered debt instrument is treated as funding a distribution or acquisition described in paragraphs (b)(3)(i)(A) through (C) of this section if the covered debt instrument is issued by a funded member during the period beginning 36 months before the date of the distribution or acquisition, and ending 36 months after the date of the distribution or acquisition (*per se period*).

(B) *Multiple interests.*—If, pursuant to paragraph (b)(3)(iii)(A) of this section, two or more covered debt instruments may be treated as stock by reason of this paragraph (b)(3), the covered debt instruments are tested under paragraph (b)(3)(iii)(A) of this section based on the order in which they are issued, with the earliest issued covered debt instrument tested first. See paragraph (h)(3) of this section, *Example 6*, for an illustration of this rule.

(C) *Multiple distributions or acquisitions.*—If, pursuant to paragraph (b)(3)(iii)(A) of this section, a covered debt instrument may be treated as funding more than one distribution or acquisition described in paragraphs (b)(3)(i)(A) through (C) of this section, the covered debt instrument is treated as funding one or more distributions or acquisitions based on the order in which the distributions or acquisitions occur, with the earliest distribution or acquisition treated as the first distribution or acquisition that is funded. See paragraph (h)(3) of this section, *Example 9*, for an illustration of this rule.

(D) *Transactions that straddle different expanded groups.*—*(1) In general.*—For purposes of paragraph (b)(3)(iii)(A) of this section, a covered debt instrument is not treated as issued by a funded member during the per se period with respect to a distribution or acquisition described in paragraphs (b)(3)(i)(A) through (C) of this section if all of the conditions described in paragraphs (b)(3)(iii)(D)(*1*)(*i*) through (*iii*) of this section are satisfied.

(*i*) The distribution or acquisition occurs prior to the issuance of the covered debt instrument by the funded member or, if the funded member is treated as making the distribution or acquisition of a predecessor or a successor, the predecessor or successor is not a member of the expanded group of which the funded member is a member on the date on which the distribution or the acquisition occurs.

(*ii*) The distribution or acquisition is made by the funded member when the funded member is a member of an expanded group that does not have an expanded group parent that is the funded member's expanded group parent when the covered debt instrument is issued. For purposes of the preceding sentence, a reference to an expanded group parent includes a reference to a predecessor or successor of the expanded group parent.

(*iii*) On the date of the issuance of the covered debt instrument, the recipient member (as defined in paragraph (b)(3)(iii)(D)(*2*) of this section) is neither a member nor a controlled partnership of an expanded group of which the funded member is a member.

(2) Recipient member.—For purposes of this paragraph (b)(3)(iii)(D), the term *recipient member* means, with respect to a distribution or acquisition by a funded member described in paragraphs (b)(3)(i)(A) through (C) of this section, the expanded group member that receives a distribution of property, property in exchange for expanded group stock, or other property or money within the meaning of section 356 with respect to its stock in the transferor corporation. For purposes of this paragraph (b)(3)(iii)(D), a reference to the recipient member includes a predecessor or successor of the recipient member or one or more other entities that, in the aggregate, acquire substantially all of the property of the recipient member.

(E) *Modifications of a covered debt instrument.*—*(1) In general.*—For purposes of paragraph (b)(3)(iii)(A) of this section, if a covered debt instrument is treated as exchanged for a modified covered debt instrument pursuant to § 1.1001-3(b), the modified covered debt instrument is treated as issued on the original issue date of the covered debt instrument.

(2) Effect of certain modifications.—Notwithstanding paragraph (b)(3)(iii)(E)(1) of this section, if a covered debt instrument is treated as exchanged for a modified covered debt instrument pursuant to § 1.1001–3(b) and the modification, or one of the modifications, that results in the deemed exchange includes the substitution of an obligor on the covered debt instrument, the addition or deletion of a co-obligor on the covered debt instrument, or the material deferral of scheduled payments due under the covered debt instrument, then the modified covered debt instrument is treated as issued on the date of the deemed exchange for purposes of paragraph (b)(3)(iii)(A) of this section.

(3) Additional principal amount.—For purposes of paragraph (b)(3)(iii)(A) of this section, if the principal amount of a covered debt instrument is increased, the portion of the covered debt instrument attributable to such increase is treated as issued on the date of such increase.

(iv) *Principal purpose rule.*—For purposes of this paragraph (b)(3), a covered debt instrument that is not issued by a funded member during the per se period with respect to a distribution or acquisition described in paragraphs (b)(3)(i)(A) through (C) of this section is treated as funding the distribution or acquisition to the extent that it is issued by a funded member with a principal purpose of funding a distribution or acquisition described in paragraphs (b)(3)(i)(A) through (C) of this section. Whether a covered debt instrument is issued with a principal purpose of funding a distribution or acquisition described in paragraphs (b)(3)(i)(A) through (C) of this section is determined based on all the facts and circumstances. A covered debt instrument may be treated as issued with a principal purpose of funding a distribution or acquisition described in paragraphs (b)(3)(i)(A) through (C) of this section regardless of whether it is issued before or after the distribution or acquisition.

(v) *Predecessors and successors.*—(A) *In general.*—Subject to the limitations in paragraph (b)(3)(v)(B) of this section, for purposes of this paragraph (b)(3), references to a funded member include references to any predecessor or successor of such member. See paragraph (h)(3) of this section, *Examples 9* and *10*, for illustrations of this rule.

(B) *Limitations to the application of the per se funding rule.*—For purposes of paragraph (b)(3)(iii)(A) of this section, a covered debt instrument issued by a funded member that satisfies the condition described in paragraph (b)(3)(iii)(A) with respect to a distribution or acquisition described in paragraphs (b)(3)(i)(A) through (C) of this section made by a predecessor or successor of the funded member is not treated as issued during the per se period with respect to the distribution or acquisition unless the conditions described in paragraphs (b)(3)(v)(B)(*1*) and (2) of this section are satisfied:

(*1*) The covered debt instrument is issued by the funded member during the period beginning 36 months before the date of the transaction in which the predecessor or successor becomes a predecessor or successor and ending 36 months after the date of the transaction.

(*2*) The distribution or acquisition is made by the predecessor or successor during the period beginning 36 months before the date of the transaction in which the predecessor or successor becomes a predecessor or successor of the funded member and ending 36 months after the date of the transaction.

(vi) *Treatment of funded transactions.*—When a covered debt instrument is treated as stock pursuant to paragraph (b)(3) of this section, the distribution or acquisition described in paragraphs (b)(3)(i)(A) through (C) of this section that is treated as funded by such covered debt instrument is not recharacterized as a result of the treatment of the covered debt instrument as stock.

(vii) *Qualified short-term debt instrument.*—The term qualified short-term debt instrument means a covered debt instrument that is described in paragraphs (b)(3)(vii)(A) though (D) of this section.

(A) *Short-term funding arrangement.*—A covered debt instrument is described in this paragraph (b)(3)(vii)(A) if the requirements of the specified current assets test described in paragraph (b)(3)(vii)(A)(*1*) of this section or the 270-day test described in paragraph (b)(3)(vii)(A)(2) of this section (the alternative tests) are satisfied, provided that an issuer may only claim the benefit of one of the alternative tests with respect to covered debt instruments issued by the issuer in the same taxable year.

(*1*) *Specified current assets test.*—(*i*) *In general.*—The requirements of this paragraph (b)(3)(vii)(A)(*1*) are satisfied with respect to a covered debt instrument if the requirement of paragraph (b)(3)(vii)(A)(*1*)(*ii*) of this section is satisfied, but only to the extent the requirement of paragraph (b)(3)(vii)(A)(*1*)(*iii*) of this section is satisfied.

(*ii*) *Maximum interest rate.*—The rate of interest charged with respect to the covered debt instrument does not exceed an arm's length interest rate, as determined under section 482 and §§1.482-1 through 1.482-9, that would be charged with respect to a comparable debt instrument of the issuer with a term that does not exceed the longer of 90 days and the issuer's normal operating cycle.

(*iii*) *Maximum outstanding balance.*—The amount owed by the issuer under covered debt instruments issued to members of the issuer's expanded group that satisfy the requirements of paragraph (b)(3)(vii)(A)(*1*)(*ii*), (b)(3)(vii)(A)(2) (if the covered debt instrument was issued in a prior taxable year), or (b)(3)(vii)(B) or (C) of this section immediately after the covered debt instrument is issued does not exceed the maximum of the amounts of specified current assets reasonably expected to be reflected, under applicable accounting principles, on the issuer's balance sheet as a result of transactions in the ordinary course of business during the subsequent 90-day period or the issuer's normal operating cycle, whichever is longer. For purposes of the preceding sentence, in the case of an issuer that is a qualified cash pool header, the amount owed by the issuer shall not take into account deposits described in paragraph (b)(3)(vii)(D) of this section. Additionally, the amount owed by any issuer shall be reduced by the amount of the issuer's deposits with a qualified cash pool header, but only to the extent of amounts borrowed from the same qualified cash pool header that satisfy the requirements of paragraph (b)(3)(vii)(A)(2) (if the covered debt instrument was issued in a prior taxable year) or (b)(3)(vii)(A)(*1*)(*ii*) of this section.

(*iv*) *Specified current assets.*—For purposes of paragraph (b)(3)(vii)(A)(*1*)(*iii*) of this section, the term *specified current assets* means assets that are reasonably expected to be realized in cash or sold (including by being incorporated into inventory that is sold) during the normal operating cycle of the issuer, other than cash, cash equivalents, and assets that are reflected on the books and records of a qualified cash pool header.

(*v*) *Normal operating cycle.*—For purposes of paragraph (b)(3)(vii)(A)(*1*) of this section, the term *normal operating cycle* means the issuer's normal operating cycle as determined under applicable accounting principles, except that if the issuer has no single clearly defined normal operating cycle, then the normal operating cycle is determined based on a reasonable analysis of the length of the operating cycles of the multiple businesses and their sizes relative to the overall size of the issuer.

(*vi*) *Applicable accounting principles.*—For purposes of paragraph (b)(3)(vii)(A)(*1*) of this section, the term *applicable accounting principles* means the financial accounting principles generally accepted in the United States, or an international financial accounting standard, that is applicable to the issuer in preparing its financial statements, computed on a consistent basis.

(2) *270-day test.*—(*i*) *In general.*—A covered debt instrument is described in this paragraph (b)(3)(vii)(A)(2) if the requirements of paragraphs (b)(3)(vii)(A)(2)(*ii*) through (*iv*) of this section are satisfied.

(*ii*) *Maximum term and interest rate.*—The covered debt instrument must have a term of 270 days or less or be an advance under a revolving credit agreement or similar arrangement and must bear a rate of interest that does not exceed an arm's length interest rate, as determined under section 482 and §§1.482-1 through 1.482-9, that would be charged with respect to a comparable debt instrument of the issuer with a term that does not exceed 270 days.

(*iii*) *Lender-specific indebtedness limit.*—The issuer is a net borrower from the lender for no more than 270 days during the taxable year of the issuer, and in the case of a covered debt instrument outstanding during consecutive tax years, the issuer is a net borrower from the lender for no more than 270 consecutive days, in both cases taking into account only covered debt instruments that satisfy the requirement of paragraph (b)(3)(vii)(A)(2)(*ii*) of this section other than covered debt instruments described in paragraph (b)(3)(vii)(B) or (C) of this section.

(*iv*) *Overall indebtedness limit.*—The issuer is a net borrower under all covered debt instruments issued to members of the issuer's expanded group that satisfy the requirements of paragraphs (b)(3)(vii)(A)(2)(*ii*) and (*iii*) of this section, other than covered debt instruments described in paragraph (b)(3)(vii)(B) or (C) of this section, for no more than 270 days during the taxable year of the issuer, determined without regard to the identity of the lender under such covered debt instruments.

(*v*) *Inadvertent error.*—An issuer's failure to satisfy the 270-day test will be disregarded if the failure is reasonable in light of all the facts and circumstances and the failure is promptly cured upon discovery. A failure to satisfy the 270-day test will be considered reasonable if the taxpayer maintains due diligence procedures to prevent such failures, as evidenced by having written policies and operational procedures in place to monitor compliance with the 270-day test and management-level employees of the expanded group having undertaken reasonable efforts to establish, follow, and enforce such policies and procedures.

(B) *Ordinary course loans.*—A covered debt instrument is described in this paragraph (b)(3)(vii)(B) if the covered debt instrument is issued as consideration for the acquisition of property other than money in the ordinary course of the issuer's trade or business, provided that the obligation is reasonably expected to be repaid within 120 days of issuance.

(C) *Interest-free loans.*—A covered debt instrument is described in this paragraph (b)(3)(vii)(C) if the instrument does not provide for stated interest or no interest is charged on the instrument, the instrument does not have original issue discount (as defined in section 1273 and § § 1.1273-1 and 1.1273-2), interest is not imputed under section 483 or section 7872 and § § 1.483-1 through 1.483-4 or § § 1.7872-1 through 1.7872-16, respectively, and interest is not required to be charged under section 482 and § § 1.482-1 through 1.482-9.

(D) *Deposits with a qualified cash pool header.*—*(1) In general.*—A covered debt instrument is described in this paragraph (b)(3)(vii)(D) if it is a demand deposit received by a qualified cash pool header described in paragraph (b)(3)(vii)(D)(2) of this section pursuant to a cash-management arrangement described in paragraph (b)(3)(vii)(D)(3) of this section. This paragraph (b)(3)(vii)(D) does not apply if a purpose for making the demand deposit is to facilitate the avoidance of the purposes of this section with respect to a qualified business unit (as defined in section 989(a) and § 1.989(a)-1) (QBU) that is not a qualified cash pool header.

(2) Qualified cash pool header.—The term *qualified cash pool header* means an expanded group member, controlled partnership, or QBU described in § 1.989(a)-1(b)(2)(ii), that has as its principal purpose managing a cash-management arrangement for participating expanded group members, provided that the excess (if any) of funds on deposit with such expanded group member, controlled partnership, or QBU (header) over the outstanding balance of loans made by the header is maintained on the books and records of the header in the form of cash or cash equivalents, or invested through deposits with, or the acquisition of obligations or portfolio securities of, persons that do not have a relationship to the header (or, in the case of a header that is a QBU described in § 1.989(a)-1(b)(2)(ii), its owner) described in section 267(b) or section 707(b).

(3) Cash-management arrangement.—The term cash-management arrangement means an arrangement the principal purpose of which is to manage cash for participating expanded group members. For purposes of the preceding sentence, managing cash means borrowing excess funds from participating expanded group members and lending funds to participating expanded group members, and may also include foreign exchange management, clearing payments, investing excess cash with an unrelated person, depositing excess cash with another qualified cash pool header, and settling intercompany accounts, for example through netting centers and pay-on-behalf-of programs.

(viii) *Distributions or acquisitions occurring before April 5, 2016.*—A distribution or acquisition that occurs before April 5, 2016, is not taken into account for purposes of applying this paragraph (b)(3).

(4) *Anti-abuse rule.*—If a member of an expanded group enters into a transaction with a principal purpose of avoiding the purposes of this section or § 1.385-3, an interest issued or held by that member or another member of the member's expanded group may, depending on the relevant facts and circumstances, be treated as stock. Paragraphs (b)(4)(i) and (ii) of this section include a non-exhaustive list of transactions that could result in an interest being treated as stock under this paragraph (b)(4).

(i) *Interests.*—An interest is treated as stock if it is issued with a principal purpose of avoiding the purposes of this section or § 1.385-3. Interests subject to this paragraph (b)(4)(i) may include:

(A) An interest that is not a covered debt instrument for purposes of this section (for example, a contract to which section 483 applies that is not otherwise a covered debt instrument or a nonperiodic swap payment that is not otherwise a covered debt instrument).

(B) A covered debt instrument issued to a person that is not a member of the issuer's expanded group, if the covered debt instrument is later acquired by a member of the issuer's expanded group or such person later becomes a member of the issuer's expanded group.

(C) A covered debt instrument issued to an entity that is not taxable as a corporation for federal tax purposes.

(D) A covered debt instrument issued in connection with a reorganization or similar transaction.

(E) A covered debt instrument issued as part of a plan or a series of transactions to expand the applicability of the transition rules described in § 1.385-3(j)(2) or § 1.385-3(k)(2).

(ii) *Other transactions.*—A covered debt instrument is treated as stock if the funded member or any member of the expanded group engages in a transaction (including a distribution or acquisition) with a principal purpose of avoiding the purposes of this section or § 1.385-3. Transactions subject to this paragraph (b)(4)(ii) may include:

(A) A member of the issuer's expanded group is substituted as a new obligor or added as a co-obligor on an existing covered debt instrument.

(B) A covered debt instrument is transferred in connection with a reorganization or similar transaction.

(C) A covered debt instrument funds a distribution or acquisition where the distribution or acquisition is made by a member other than the funded member and the funded member acquires the assets of the other member in a transaction that does not make the other member a predecessor to the funded member.

(D) Members of a consolidated group engage in transactions as part of a plan or a series of transactions through the use of the consolidated group rules set forth in § 1.385-4, including through the use of the departing member rules.

(5) *Coordination between general rule and funding rule.*—For purposes of this section, a distribution or acquisition described in paragraph (b)(2) of this section is not also described in paragraph (b)(3)(i) of this section. In the case of an asset reorganization, an acquisition described in paragraph (b)(2)(iii) of this section by the transferee corporation is not also a distribution or acquisition described in paragraph (b)(3)(i) of this section by the transferor corporation. For purposes of this paragraph (b)(5), whether a distribution or acquisition is described in paragraphs (b)(2)(i) through (iii) of this section is determined without regard to paragraph (c) of this section.

(6) *Non-duplication.*—Except as otherwise provided in paragraph (d)(2) of this section, to the extent a distribution or acquisition described in paragraphs (b)(3)(i)(A) through (C) of this section is treated as funded by a covered debt instrument under paragraph (b)(3) of this section, the distribution or acquisition is not treated as funded by another covered debt instrument and the covered debt instrument is not treated as funding another distribution or acquisition for purposes of paragraph (b)(3).

(c) *Exceptions.*—(1) *In general.*—This paragraph (c) provides exceptions for purposes of applying paragraphs (b)(2) and (b)(3) of this section to a covered member. These exceptions are applied in the following order: first, paragraph (c)(2) of this section; second, paragraph (c)(3) of this section; and, third, paragraph (c)(4) of this section. The exceptions under § 1.385-3(c)(2) and (c)(3) apply to distributions and acquisitions that are otherwise described in paragraph (b)(2) or (b)(3)(i) of this section after applying paragraphs (b)(3)(ii) and (b)(5) of this section. Except as otherwise provided, the exceptions are applied by taking into account the aggregate treatment of controlled partnerships described in § 1.385-3(f).

(2) *Exclusions for transactions otherwise described in paragraph (b)(2) or (b)(3)(i) of this section.*—(i) *Exclusion for certain acquisitions of subsidiary stock.*—(A) *In general.*—An acquisition of expanded group stock (including by issuance) is not treated as described in paragraph (b)(2)(ii) or (b)(3)(i)(B) of this section if, immediately after the acquisition, the covered member that acquires the expanded group stock (acquirer) controls the member of the expanded group from which the expanded group stock is acquired (seller), and the acquirer does not relinquish control of the seller pursuant to a plan that existed on the date of the acquisition, other than in a transaction in which the seller ceases to be a member of the expanded group of which the acquirer is a member. For purposes of the preceding sentence, an acquirer and seller do not cease to be members of the same expanded group by reason of a complete liquidation described in section 331.

(B) *Control.*—For purposes of this paragraph (c)(2)(i) and paragraph (c)(3)(ii)(E) of this section, control of a corporation means the direct or indirect ownership of more than 50 percent of the total combined voting power of all classes of stock of the corporation entitled to vote and more than 50 percent of the total value of the stock of the corporation. For purposes of the preceding sentence, indirect ownership is determined by applying the principles of section 958(a) without regard to whether an intermediate entity is foreign or domestic.

(C) *Rebuttable presumption.*—For purposes of paragraph (c)(2)(i)(A) of this section, the acquirer is presumed to have a plan to relinquish control of the seller on the date of the acquisition if the acquirer relinquishes control of the seller within the 36-month period following the date of the acquisition. The presumption created by the previous sentence may be rebutted by facts and circumstances clearly establishing that the loss of control was not contemplated on the date of the acquisition and that the avoidance of the purposes of this section or § 1.385-3 was not a principal purpose for the subsequent loss of control.

(ii) *Exclusion for compensatory stock acquisitions.*—An acquisition of expanded group stock is not treated as described in paragraph (b)(2)(ii) or (b)(3)(i)(B) of this section if the expanded group stock is delivered to individuals that are employees, directors, or independent contractors in consideration for services rendered by such individuals to a member of the expanded group or a controlled partnership in which a member of the expanded group is an expanded group partner.

(iii) *Exclusion for distributions or acquisitions resulting from transfer pricing adjustments.*—A distribution or acquisition deemed to occur under § 1.482-1(g) (including adjustments made pursuant to Revenue Procedure 99-32, 1999-2 C.B. 296) is not treated as described in paragraph (b)(3)(i)(A) or (B) of this section.

(iv) *Exclusion for acquisitions of expanded group stock by a dealer in securities.*—An acquisition of expanded group stock by a dealer in securities (within the meaning of section 475(c)(1)), or by an expanded group partner treated as acquiring expanded group stock pursuant to § 1.385-3(f)(2) if the relevant controlled partnership is a dealer in securities, is not treated as described in paragraph (b)(2)(ii) or (b)(3)(i)(B) of this section to the extent the expanded group stock is acquired in the ordinary course of the dealer's business of dealing in securities. The preceding sentence applies solely to the extent that—

(A) The dealer accounts for the stock as securities held primarily for sale to customers in the ordinary course of business;

(B) The dealer disposes of the stock within a period of time that is consistent with the holding of the stock for sale to customers in the ordinary course of business, taking into account the terms of the stock and the conditions and practices prevailing in the markets for similar stock during the period in which it is held; and

(C) The dealer does not sell or otherwise transfer the stock to a person in the same expanded group, other than in a sale to a dealer that in turn satisfies the requirements of paragraph (c)(2)(iv) of this section.

(v) *Exclusion for certain acquisitions of expanded group stock resulting from application of this section.*—The following deemed acquisitions are not treated as acquisitions of expanded group stock described in paragraph (b)(3)(i)(B) of this section, provided that they are not part of a plan or arrangement to prevent the application of paragraph (b)(3)(i) to a covered debt instrument:

(A) An acquisition of a covered debt instrument that is treated as stock by means of paragraph (b)(3) of this section.

(B) An acquisition of stock of a regarded owner that is deemed to be issued under § 1.385-3(d)(4).

(C) An acquisition of deemed partner stock pursuant to a deemed transfer or a specified event described in § 1.385-3(f)(4) or (5).

(3) *Reductions for transactions described in paragraph (b)(2) or (b)(3)(i) of this section.*—(i) *Reduction for expanded group earnings.*—(A) *In general.*—The aggregate amount of any distributions or acquisitions by a covered member described in paragraph (b)(2) or (b)(3)(i) of this section in a taxable year during the covered member's expanded group period is reduced by the covered member's expanded group earnings account (as defined in paragraph (c)(3)(i)(B) of this section) for the expanded group period as of the close of the taxable year. The reduction described in this paragraph (c)(3)(i)(A) applies to one or more distributions or acquisitions based on the order in which the distributions or acquisitions occur, regardless of whether any distribution or acquisition would be treated as funded by a covered debt instrument without regard to this paragraph (c)(3).

(B) *Expanded group earnings account.*—The term *expanded group earnings account* means, with respect to a covered member and an expanded group period (as defined in paragraph (c)(3)(i)(E) of this section) of the covered member, the excess, if any, of the covered member's expanded group earnings (as defined in paragraph (c)(3)(i)(C) of this section) for the expanded group period over the covered member's expanded group reductions (as defined in paragraph (c)(3)(i)(D) of this section) for the expanded group period.

(C) *Expanded group earnings.*—*(1) In general.*—The term expanded group earnings means, with respect to a covered member and an expanded group period of the covered member, the earnings and profits accumulated by the covered member during the expanded group period, computed as of the close of the taxable year of the covered member, without diminution by reason of any distributions or acquisitions by the covered member described in paragraphs (b)(2) and (b)(3)(i) of this section. Notwithstanding the preceding sentence, the expanded group earnings of a covered member do not include earnings and profits accumulated by the covered member in any taxable year ending before April 5, 2016.

(2) Special rule for change in expanded group within a taxable year.—For purposes of calculating a covered member's expanded group earnings for a taxable year that is not wholly included in an expanded group period, the covered member's expanded group earnings are ratably allocated among the portion of the taxable year included in the expanded group period and the portion of the taxable year not included in the expanded group period. For purposes of the preceding sentence, the expanded group period is determined by excluding the day on which the covered member becomes a member of an expanded group with the same expanded group parent and including the day on which the covered member ceases to be a member of an expanded group with the same expanded group parent.

(3) Look-through rule for dividends.—*(i) In general.*—For purposes of paragraph (c)(3)(i)(C)*(1)* of this section, a dividend from a member of the same expanded group (*distributing member*) is not taken into account for purposes of calculating a covered member's expanded group earnings, except to the extent the dividend is attributable to earnings and profits accumulated by the distributing member in a taxable year ending after April 4, 2016, during its expanded group period (*qualified earnings and profits*). For purposes of the preceding sentence, a dividend received from a member (*intermediate distributing member*) is not taken into account for purposes of calculating the qualified earnings and profits of a distributing member (or another intermediate distributing member), except to the extent the dividend is attributable to qualified earnings and profits of the intermediate distributing member. A dividend from distributing member or an intermediate distributing member is considered to be attributable to qualified earnings and profits to the extent thereof. If a controlled partnership receives a dividend from a distributing member and a portion of the dividend is allocated (including through one or more partnerships) to a covered member, then, for purposes of this paragraph (c)(3)(i)(C)*(3)*, the covered member is treated as receiving the dividend from the distributing member.

(ii) Dividend.—For purposes of paragraph (c)(3)(i)(C)*(3)*(*i*) of this section, the term dividend has the meaning specified in section 316, including the portion of gain recognized under section 1248 that is treated as a dividend and deemed dividends under section 367(b) and the regulations thereunder. In addition, the term dividend includes inclusions with respect to stock (for example, inclusions under sections 951(a) and 1293).

(4) Effect of interest deductions.—For purposes of calculating the expanded group earnings of a covered member for a taxable year, expanded group earnings are calculated without regard to the application of this section during the taxable year to a covered debt instrument issued by the covered member that was not treated as stock under paragraph (b) of this section as of the close of the preceding taxable year, or, if the covered member is an expanded group partner in a controlled partnership that is the issuer of a debt instrument, without regard to the application of § 1.385-3(f)(4)(i) during the taxable year with respect to the covered member's share of the debt instrument. To the extent that the application of this paragraph (c)(3)(i)(C)*(4)* reduces the expanded group earnings of the covered member for the taxable year, the expanded group earnings of the covered member are increased as of the beginning of the succeeding taxable year during the expanded group period.

(D) *Expanded group reductions.*—The term expanded group reductions means, with respect to a covered member and an expanded group period of the covered member, the amounts by which acquisitions or distributions described in paragraph (b)(2) or (b)(3)(i) of this section were reduced by reason of paragraph (c)(3)(i)(A) of this section during the portion of the expanded group period preceding the taxable year.

(E) *Expanded group period.—(1) In general.*—For purposes of this paragraph (c)(3)(i) and paragraph (c)(3)(ii) of this section, the term expanded group period means, with respect to a covered member, the period during which a covered member is a member of an expanded group with the same expanded group parent.

(2) Mere change.—For purposes of paragraph (c)(3)(i)(E)(*1*) of this section, an expanded group parent that is a resulting corporation (within the meaning of § 1.368-2(m)(1)) in a reorganization described in section 368(a)(1)(F) is treated as the same expanded group parent as an expanded group parent that is a transferor corporation (within the meaning of § 1.368-2(m)(1)) in the same reorganization, provided that either—

(i) The transferor corporation is not a covered member; or

(ii) Both the transferor corporation and the resulting corporation are covered members.

(F) *Special rules for certain corporate transactions.—(1) Reduction for expanded group earnings in an asset reorganization.*—For purposes of applying paragraph (c)(3)(i) of this section, a distribution or acquisition described in paragraph (b)(2) or (b)(3)(i) of this section that occurs pursuant to a reorganization described in section 381(a)(2) is reduced solely by the expanded group earnings account of the acquiring member after taking into account the adjustment to its expanded group earnings account provided in paragraph (c)(3)(i)(F)(*2*)(*ii*) of this section.

(2) Effect of certain corporate transactions on the calculation of expanded group earnings account.—(i) In general.—Section 381 and § 1.312-10 are not taken into account for purposes of calculating a covered member's expanded group earnings account for an expanded group period. The expanded group earnings account that a covered member succeeds to under paragraphs (c)(3)(i)(F)(*2*)(*ii*) through (*iv*) of this section is attributed to the covered member's expanded group period as of the close of the date of the distribution or transfer.

(ii) Section 381 transactions.—If a covered member (*acquiring member*) acquires the assets of another covered member (*acquired member*) in a transaction described in section 381(a), and, immediately before the transaction, both corporations are members of the same expanded group, then the acquiring member succeeds to the expanded group earnings account of the acquired member, if any, determined after application of paragraph (c)(3)(i) of this section with respect to the final taxable year of the acquired member.

(iii) Section 1.312-10(a) transactions.—If a covered member (*transferor member*) transfers property to another covered member (*transferee member*) in a transaction described in § 1.312-10(a), the expanded group earnings account of the transferor member is allocated between the transferor member and the transferee member in the same proportion as the earnings and profits of the transferor member are allocated between the transferor member and the transferee member under § 1.312-10(a).

(iv) Section 1.312-10(b) transactions.—If a covered member (*distributing member*) distributes the stock of another covered member (*controlled member*) in a transaction described in § 1.312-10(b), the expanded group earnings account of the distributing member is decreased by the amount that the expanded group earnings account of the distributing member would have been decreased under paragraph (c)(3)(i)(F)(*2*)(*iii*) of this section if the distributing member had transferred the stock of the controlled member to a newly formed corporation in a transaction described in § 1.312-10(a). If the amount of the decrease described in the preceding sentence exceeds the expanded group earnings account of the controlled member immediately before the transaction described in § 1.312-10(b), then the expanded group earnings account of the controlled member after the transaction is equal to the amount of the decrease.

(G) *Overlapping expanded groups.*—A covered member that is a member of two expanded groups at the same time has a single expanded group earnings account with respect to a single expanded group period. In this case, the expanded group period is determined by reference to the shorter of the two periods during which the covered member is a member of an expanded group with the same expanded group parent.

(ii) *Reduction for qualified contributions.*—(A) *In general.*—The amount of a distribution or acquisition by a covered member described in paragraph (b)(2) or (b)(3)(i) of this section is reduced by the aggregate fair market value of the stock issued by the covered member in one or more qualified contributions (as defined in paragraph (c)(3)(ii)(B) of this section) during the qualified period (as defined in paragraph (c)(3)(ii)(C) of this section), but only to the extent the qualified contribution or qualified contributions have not reduced another distribution or acquisition. The reduction described in this paragraph (c)(3)(ii)(A) applies to one or more distributions or acquisitions based on the order in which the distributions or acquisitions occur, regardless of whether any distribution or acquisition would be treated as funded by a covered debt instrument without regard to this paragraph (c)(3).

(B) *Qualified contribution.*—The term *qualified contribution* means, with respect to a covered member, except as provided in paragraph (c)(3)(ii)(E) of this section, a contribution of property, other than excluded property (defined in paragraph (c)(3)(ii)(D) of this section), to the covered member by a member of the covered member's expanded group (or by a controlled partnership of the expanded group) in exchange for stock.

(C) *Qualified period.*—The term *qualified period* means, with respect to a covered member, a qualified contribution, and a distribution or acquisition described in paragraph (b)(2) or (b)(3)(i) of this section, the period beginning on the later of the beginning of the periods described in paragraphs (c)(3)(ii)(C)(*1*) and (2) of this section, and ending on the earlier of the ending of the periods described in paragraphs (c)(3)(ii)(C)(*1*) and (2) of this section or the date described in paragraph (c)(3)(ii)(C)(*3*) of this section.

(1) The period beginning 36 months before the date of the distribution or acquisition, and ending 36 months after the date of the distribution or acquisition.

(2) The covered member's expanded group period (as defined in paragraph (c)(3)(i)(E) of this section) that includes the distribution or acquisition.

(3) The last day of the first taxable year that a covered debt instrument issued by the covered member would, absent the application of this paragraph (c)(3)(ii) with respect to the distribution or acquisition, be treated, in whole or in part, as stock under paragraph (b) of this section or, in the case of a covered debt instrument issued by a controlled partnership in which the covered member is an expanded group partner, the covered debt instrument would be treated, in whole or in part, as a specified portion.

(D) *Excluded property.*—The term *excluded property* means—

(1) Expanded group stock;

(2) Property acquired by the covered member in an asset reorganization from a member of the expanded group of which the covered member is a member;

(3) A covered debt instrument of any member of the same expanded group, including a covered debt instrument issued by the covered member;

(4) Property acquired by the covered member in exchange for a covered debt instrument issued by the covered member that is recharacterized under paragraph (b)(3) of this section;

(5) A debt instrument issued by a controlled partnership of the expanded group of which the covered member is a member, including the portion of such a debt instrument that is a deemed transferred receivable or a retained receivable; and

(6) Any other property acquired by the covered member with a principal purpose to avoid the purposes of this section or § 1.385-3, including a transaction involving an indirect transfer of property described in paragraphs (c)(3)(ii)(D)(*1*) through (5) of this section.

(E) *Excluded contributions.—(1) Upstream contributions from certain subsidiaries.*—For purposes of paragraph (c)(3)(ii)(B) of this section, a contribution of property from a corporation (*controlled member*) that the covered member controls, within the meaning of paragraph (c)(2)(i)(B) of this section, is not a qualified contribution.

(2) Contributions to a predecessor or successor.—For purposes of paragraph (c)(3)(ii)(B) of this section, a contribution of property to a covered member from a corporation of which the covered member is a predecessor or successor, or from a corporation

controlled by that corporation within the meaning of paragraph (c)(2)(i)(B) of this section, is not a qualified contribution.

(3) Contributions that do not increase fair market value.—A contribution of property to a covered member that is not described in paragraph (c)(3)(ii)(E)(*1*) or (2) of this section is not a qualified contribution to the extent that the contribution does not increase the aggregate fair market value of the outstanding stock of the covered member immediately after the transaction and taking into account all related transactions, other than distributions and acquisitions described in paragraphs (b)(2) and (b)(3)(i) of this section.

(4) Contributions that become excluded contributions after the date of the contribution.—If a contribution of property described in paragraph (c)(3)(ii)(E)(*1*) or (2) of this section occurs before the covered member acquires control of the controlled member described in paragraph (c)(3)(ii)(E)(*1*) or before the transaction in which the corporation described in paragraph (c)(3)(ii)(E)(2) becomes a predecessor or successor to the covered member, the contribution of property ceases to be a qualified contribution on the date that the covered member acquires control of the controlled member or on the date of the transaction in which the corporation becomes a predecessor or successor to the covered member (*transaction date*). If the contribution of property occurs within 36 months before the transaction date, the covered member is treated as making a distribution described in paragraph (b)(3)(i)(A) of this section on the transaction date equal to the amount by which any distribution or acquisition described in paragraph (b)(2) or (b)(3)(i) of this section was reduced under paragraph (c)(3)(ii)(A) of this section because the contribution of property was treated as a qualified contribution.

(F) *Special rules for certain corporate transactions.—(1) Reduction for qualified contributions in an asset reorganization.*—For purposes of applying paragraph (c)(3)(ii)(A) of this section, a distribution or acquisition described in paragraph (b)(2) or (b)(3)(i) of this section that occurs pursuant to a reorganization described in section 381(a)(2) is reduced solely by the qualified contributions of the acquiring member after taking into account the adjustment to its qualified contributions provided in paragraph (c)(3)(ii)(F)(2) of this section.

(2) Effect of certain corporate transactions on the calculation of qualified contributions.—(i) In general.—This paragraph (c)(3)(ii)(F)(2) provides rules for allocating or reducing the qualified contributions of a covered member as a result of certain corporation transactions. For purposes of paragraph (c)(3)(ii)(C)(*1*) of this section, a qualified contribution that a covered member succeeds to under paragraphs (c)(3)(ii)(F)(2)(*ii*) and (*iii*) of this section is treated as made to the covered member on the date on which the qualified contribution was made to the covered member that received the qualified contribution. For purposes of paragraph (c)(3)(ii)(C)(2) of this section, a qualified contribution that a covered member succeeds to under paragraphs (c)(3)(ii)(F)(2)(*ii*) and (*iii*) of this section is attributed to the covered member's expanded group period as of the close of the date of the distribution or transfer. For purposes of paragraph (c)(3)(ii)(C)(*3*) of this section, a qualified contribution a covered member succeeds to under paragraphs (c)(3)(ii)(F)(2)(*ii*) and (*iii*) of this section is treated as made to the covered member as of the close of the date of the distribution or transfer.

(ii) Section 381 transactions.—If a covered member (acquiring member) acquires the assets of another covered member (acquired member) in a transaction described in section 381(a), and, immediately before the transaction, both corporations are members of the same expanded group, the acquiring member succeeds to the qualified contributions of the acquired member, if any, adjusted for the application of paragraph (c)(3)(ii)(E)(4) of this section.

(iii) Section 1.312-10(a) transactions.—If a covered member (transferor member) transfers property to another covered member (transferee member) in a transaction described in § 1.312-10(a), each qualified contribution of the transferor member is allocated between the transferor member and the transferee member in the same proportion as the earnings and profits of the transferor member are allocated between the transferor member and the transferee member under § 1.312-10(a).

(iv) Section 1.312-10(b) transactions.—If a covered member (distributing member) distributes the stock of another covered member (controlled member) in a transaction described in § 1.312-10(b), each qualified contribution of the distributing member is decreased by the amount that each qualified contribution of the distributing member would have been decreased under paragraph (c)(3)(ii)(F)(2)(*iii*) of this section if the distributing member had transferred the stock of the controlled member to a newly formed corporation in a transaction described in § 1.312-10(a). No amount of the qualified contributions of the distributing member is allocated to the controlled member.

(iii) *Predecessors and successors.*—For purposes of this paragraph (c)(3), references to a covered member do not include references to any corporation of which the covered member is a predecessor or successor. Accordingly, a distribution or acquisition by a covered member described in paragraphs (b)(3)(i)(A) through (C) is reduced solely by the expanded group earnings account of the covered member (taking into account the application of paragraph (c)(3)(i)(F)(2) of this section) and the qualified contributions of the covered member (taking into account the application of paragraph (c)(3)(ii)(F)(2) of this section), notwithstanding that the distribution or acquisition is treated as made by a funded member of which the covered member is a predecessor or successor.

(iv) *Ordering rule.*—The exceptions described in this paragraph (c)(3) are applied in the following order: first, paragraph (c)(3)(i) of this section; and, second, paragraph (c)(3)(ii) of this section.

(4) *Threshold exception.*—A covered debt instrument is not treated as stock under this section if, immediately after the covered debt instrument would be treated as stock under this section but for the application of this paragraph (c)(4), the aggregate adjusted issue price of covered debt instruments held by members of the issuer's expanded group that would be treated as stock under this section but for the application of this paragraph (c)(4) does not exceed $50 million. To the extent a debt instrument issued by a controlled partnership would be treated as a specified portion (as defined in paragraph (g)(23) of this section) but for the application of this paragraph (c)(4), the debt instrument is treated as a covered debt instrument described in the preceding sentence for purposes of this paragraph (c)(4). To the extent that, immediately after a covered debt instrument would be treated as stock under this section but for the application of this paragraph (c)(4), the aggregate adjusted issue price of covered debt instruments held by members of the issuer's expanded group that would be treated as stock under this section but for the application of this paragraph (c)(4) exceeds $50 million, only the amount of the covered debt instrument in excess of $50 million is treated as stock under this section. For purposes of this rule, any covered debt instrument that is not denominated in U.S. dollars is translated into U.S. dollars at the spot rate (as defined in § 1.988-1(d)) on the date that the covered debt instrument is issued.

(d) *Operating rules.*—(1) *Timing.*—This paragraph (d)(1) provides rules for determining when a covered debt instrument is treated as stock under paragraph (b) of this section. For special rules regarding the treatment of a deemed exchange of a covered debt instrument that occurs pursuant to paragraphs (d)(1)(ii), (d)(1)(iii), or (d)(1)(iv) of this section, see § 1.385-1(d).

(i) *General timing rule.*—Except as otherwise provided in this paragraph (d)(1), when paragraph (b) of this section applies to treat a covered debt instrument as stock, the covered debt instrument is treated as stock when the covered debt instrument is issued. When paragraph (b)(3) of this section applies to treat a covered debt instrument as stock when the covered debt instrument is issued, see also paragraph (b)(3)(vi) of this section.

(ii) *Exception when a covered debt instrument is treated as funding a distribution or acquisition that occurs after the issuance of the covered debt instrument.*—When paragraph (b)(3)(iii) of this section applies to treat a covered debt instrument as funding a distribution or acquisition described in paragraph (b)(3)(i)(A) through (C) of this section that occurs after the covered debt instrument is issued, the covered debt instrument is deemed to be exchanged for stock on the date that the distribution or acquisition occurs. See paragraph (h)(3) of this section, *Examples 4* and *9*, for an illustration of this rule.

(iii) *Exception for certain predecessor and successor transactions.*—To the extent that a covered debt instrument would not be treated as stock but for the fact that a funded member is treated as the predecessor or successor of another expanded group member under paragraph (b)(3)(v) of this section, the covered debt instrument is deemed to be exchanged for stock on the later of the date that the funded member completes the transaction causing it to become a predecessor or successor of the other expanded group member or the date that the covered debt instrument would be treated as stock under paragraph (d)(1)(i) or (ii) of this section.

(iv) *Exception when a covered debt instrument is re-tested under paragraph (d)(2) of this section.*—When paragraph (b)(3)(iii) of this section applies to treat a covered debt instrument as funding a distribution or acquisition described in paragraphs (b)(3)(i)(A) through (C) of this section as a result of a re-testing described in paragraph (d)(2)(ii) of this section that occurs in a taxable year subsequent to the taxable year in which the covered debt instrument is issued, the covered debt instrument is deemed to be exchanged for stock on the later of the date of the re-testing or the date that the covered debt instrument would be treated as stock under paragraph (d)(1)(i) or (ii) of this section. See paragraph (h)(3) of this section, *Example 7*, for an illustration of this rule.

(2) *Covered debt instrument treated as stock that leaves the expanded group.*—(i) *Events that cause a covered debt instrument to cease to be treated as stock.*—Subject to paragraph (b)(4) of this section, this paragraph (d)(2)(i) applies with respect to a covered debt instrument that is treated as stock under this section when the holder and issuer of a covered debt instrument cease to be members of the same expanded group, either because the covered debt instrument is transferred to a person that is not a member of the expanded group that includes the issuer or because the holder or the issuer ceases to be a member of the same expanded group, or in the case of a holder that is a controlled partnership, when the holder ceases to be a controlled partnership with respect to the expanded group of which the issuer is a member, either because the partnership ceases to be a controlled partnership or because the issuer ceases to be a member of the same expanded group with respect to which the holder is a controlled partnership. In such a case, the covered debt instrument ceases to be treated as stock under this section. For this purpose, immediately before the transaction that causes the holder and issuer of the covered debt instrument to cease to be members of the same expanded group, or, if the holder is a controlled partnership, that causes the holder to cease to be a controlled partnership with respect to the expanded group of which the issuer is a member, the issuer is deemed to issue a new covered debt instrument to the holder in exchange for the covered debt instrument that was treated as stock in a transaction that is disregarded for purposes of paragraphs (b)(2) and (b)(3) of this section.

(ii) *Re-testing of covered debt instruments and certain distributions and acquisitions.*—(A) *General rule.*—For purposes of paragraph (b)(3)(iii) of this section, when paragraph (d)(2)(i) of this section or § 1.385-4(c)(2) causes a covered debt instrument that previously was treated as stock pursuant to paragraph (b)(3) of this section to cease to be treated as stock, all other covered debt instruments of the issuer that are not treated as stock on the date that the transaction occurs that causes paragraph (d)(2)(i) of this section to apply are re-tested to determine whether those other covered debt instruments are treated as funding the distribution or acquisition that previously was treated as funded by the covered debt instrument that ceases to be treated as stock pursuant to paragraph (d)(2)(i) of this section. In addition, a covered debt instrument that is issued after an application of paragraph (d)(2)(i) of this section and within the per se period may also be treated as funding that distribution or acquisition. See paragraph (h)(3) of this section, *Example 7*, for an illustration of this rule.

(B) *Re-testing upon a specified event with respect to a debt instrument issued by a controlled partnership.*—If, with respect to a covered member that is an expanded group partner and a debt instrument issued by the controlled partnership, there is reduction in the covered member's specified portion under § 1.385-3(f)(5)(i) by reason of a specified event, the covered member must re-test its debt instruments as described in paragraph (d)(2)(ii)(A) of this section.

(3) *Inapplicability of section 385(c)(1).*—Section 385(c)(1) does not apply with respect to a covered debt instrument to the extent that it is treated as stock under this section.

(4) *Treatment of disregarded entities.*—This paragraph (d)(4) applies to the extent that a covered debt instrument issued by a disregarded entity, the regarded owner of which is a covered member, would, absent the application of this paragraph (d)(4), be treated as stock under this section. In this case, rather than the covered debt instrument being treated as stock to such extent (applicable portion), the covered member that is the regarded owner of the disregarded entity is deemed to issue its stock in the manner described in this paragraph (d)(4). If the applicable portion otherwise would have been treated as stock under paragraph (b)(2) of this section, then the covered member is deemed to issue its stock to the expanded group member to which the covered debt instrument was, in form, issued (or transferred) in the transaction described in paragraph (b)(2) of this section. If the applicable portion otherwise would have been treated as stock under paragraph (b)(3)(i) of this section, then the covered member is deemed to issue its stock to the holder of the covered debt instrument in exchange for a portion of the covered debt instrument equal to the applicable portion. In each case, the covered member that is the regarded owner of the disregarded entity is treated as the holder of the applicable portion of the debt instrument issued by the disregarded entity, and the actual holder is treated as the holder of the remaining portion of the covered debt instrument and the stock deemed to be issued by the regarded owner. Under Federal tax principles, the applicable portion of the debt instrument issued by the disregarded entity generally is disregarded. This paragraph (d)(4) must be applied in a manner that is consistent with the principles of paragraph (f)(4) of this section. Thus, for example, stock deemed issued is deemed to have the same terms as the covered debt instrument issued by the disregarded entity, other than the identity of the issuer, and payments on the stock are determined by reference to payments made on the covered debt instrument issued by the disregarded entity. See § 1.385-4(b)(3) for additional rules that apply if the regarded owner of the disregarded entity is a member of a consolidated group. If the regarded owner of a disregarded entity is a controlled partnership, then paragraph (f) of this section applies as though the controlled partnership were the issuer in form of the debt instrument.

(5) *Payments with respect to partially recharacterized covered debt instruments.*—(i) *General rule.*—Except as otherwise provided in paragraph (d)(5)(ii) of this section, a payment with respect to an instrument that is partially recharacterized as stock is treated as made pro rata to the portion treated as stock and to the portion treated as indebtedness.

(ii) *Special rule for payments not required pursuant to the terms of the instrument..*—A payment with respect to an instrument that is partially recharacterized as stock and that is a payment that is not required to be made pursuant to the terms of the instrument (for example, a prepayment of principal) may be designated by the issuer and the holder as with respect to the portion treated as stock or to the portion treated as indebtedness, in whole or in part. In the absence of such designation, see paragraph (d)(5)(i) of this section.

(6) *Treatment of a general rule transaction to which an exception applies.*—To the extent a covered member would, absent the application of paragraph (c)(2) or (c)(3) of this section, be treated as making a distribution or acquisition described in paragraph (b)(2) of this section, then, solely for purposes of applying paragraph (b)(3) of this section, the covered member is treated as issuing the covered debt instrument issued in the distribution or acquisition to a member of the covered member's expanded group in exchange for property.

(7) *Treatment for purposes of section 1504(a).*—(i) *Debt instruments treated as stock.*—A covered debt instrument that is treated as stock under paragraph (b)(2), (3), or (4) of this section and that is not described in section 1504(a)(4) is not treated as stock for purposes of determining whether the issuer is a member of an affiliated group (within the meaning of section 1504(a)).

(ii) *Deemed partner stock and stock deemed issued by a regarded owner.*—If deemed partner stock or stock that is deemed issued by a regarded owner under § 1.385-3(d)(4) is not described in section 1504(a)(4), then that stock is not treated as stock for purposes of determining whether the issuer of the stock is a member of an affiliated group (within the meaning of section 1504(a)).

(e) *No affirmative use.*—[Reserved]

(f) *Treatment of controlled partnerships.*—(1) *In general.*—For purposes of this section and § 1.385-4, a controlled partnership is treated as an aggregate of its partners in the manner described in this paragraph (f). Paragraph (f)(2) of this section sets forth rules concerning the aggregate treatment when a controlled partnership acquires property from a member of the expanded group. Paragraph (f)(3) of this section sets forth rules concerning the aggregate treatment when a controlled partnership issues a debt instrument. Paragraph (f)(4) of this section deems a debt instrument issued by a controlled partnership to be held by an expanded group partner rather than the holder-in-form in certain cases. Paragraph (f)(5) of this section sets forth the rules concerning events that cause the deemed results described in paragraph (f)(4) of this section to cease. Paragraph (f)(6) of this section exempts certain issuances of a controlled partnership's debt to a partner and a partner's debt to a controlled partnership from the application of this section. For definitions applicable for this section, see paragraph (g) of this section. For examples illustrating the application of this section, see paragraph (h) of this section.

(2) *Acquisitions of property by a controlled partnership.*—(i) *Acquisitions of property when a member of the expanded group is a partner on the date of the acquisition.*—(A) *Aggregate treatment.*—Except as otherwise provided in paragraphs (f)(2)(i)(C) and (f)(6) of this section, if a controlled partnership, with respect to an expanded group, acquires property from a member of the expanded group (transferor member), then, for purposes of this section, a member of the expanded group that is an expanded group partner on the date of the acquisition is treated as acquiring its share (as determined under paragraph (f)(2)(i)(B) of this section) of the property. The expanded group partner is treated as acquiring its share of the property from the transferor member in the manner (for example, in a distribution, in an exchange for property, or in an issuance), and on the date on which, the property is actually acquired by the controlled partnership from the transferor member. Accordingly, this section applies to a member's acquisition of property described in this paragraph (f)(2)(i)(A) in the same manner as if the member actually acquired the property from the transferor member, unless explicitly provided otherwise.

(B) *Expanded group partner's share of property.*—For purposes of paragraph (f)(2)(i)(A) of this section, a partner's share of property acquired by a controlled partnership is determined in accordance with the partner's liquidation value percentage (as defined in paragraph (g)(17) of this section) with respect to the controlled partnership. The liquidation value percentage is determined on the date on which the controlled partnership acquires the property.

(C) *Exception if transferor member is an expanded group partner.*—If a transferor member is an expanded group partner in the controlled partnership, paragraph (f)(2)(i)(A) of this section does not apply to such partner.

(ii) *Acquisitions of expanded group stock when a member of the expanded group becomes a partner after the acquisition.*—(A) *Aggregate treatment.*—Except as otherwise provided in paragraph (f)(2)(ii)(C) of this section, if a controlled partnership, with respect to an expanded group, owns expanded group stock, and a member of the expanded group becomes an expanded group partner in the controlled partnership, then, for purposes of this section, the member is treated as acquiring its share (as determined under paragraph (f)(2)(ii)(B) of this section) of the expanded group stock owned by the controlled partnership. The member is treated as acquiring its share of the expanded group stock on the date on which the member becomes an expanded group partner. Furthermore, the member is treated as if it acquires its share of the expanded group stock from a member of the expanded group in exchange for property other than expanded group stock, regardless of the manner in which the partnership acquired the stock and in which the member acquires its partnership interest. Accordingly, this section applies to a member's acquisition of expanded group stock described in this paragraph (f)(2)(ii)(A) in the same manner as if the member actually acquired the stock from a member of the expanded group in exchange for property other than expanded group stock, unless explicitly provided otherwise.

(B) *Expanded group partner's share of expanded group stock.*—For purposes of paragraph (f)(2)(ii)(A) of this section, a partner's share of expanded group stock owned by a controlled partnership is determined in accordance with the partner's liquidation value percentage with respect to the controlled partnership. The liquidation value percentage is determined on the date on which a member of the expanded group becomes an expanded group partner in the controlled partnership.

(C) *Exception if an expanded group partner acquires its interest in a controlled partnership in exchange for expanded group stock.*—Paragraph (f)(2)(ii)(A) of this section does not apply to a member of an expanded group that acquires its interest in a controlled partnership either from another partner in exchange solely for expanded group stock or upon a partnership contribution to the controlled partnership comprised solely of expanded group stock.

(3) *Issuances of debt instruments by a controlled partnership to a member of an expanded group.*—(i) *Aggregate treatment.*—If a controlled partnership, with respect to an expanded group, issues a debt instrument to a member of the expanded group, then, for purposes of this section, a covered member that is an expanded group partner is treated as the issuer with respect to its share (as determined under paragraph (f)(3)(ii) of this section) of the debt instrument issued by the controlled partnership. This section applies to the portion of the debt instrument treated as issued by the covered member as described in this paragraph (f)(3)(i) in the same manner as if the covered member actually issued the debt instrument to the holder-in-form, unless otherwise provided. See paragraph (f)(4) of this section, which deems a debt instrument issued by a controlled partnership to be held by an expanded group partner rather than the holder-in-form in certain cases.

(ii) *Expanded group partner's share of a debt instrument issued by a controlled partnership.*—(A) *General rule.*—An expanded group partner's share of a debt instrument issued by a controlled partnership is determined on each date on which the partner makes a distribution or acquisition described in paragraph (b)(2) or (b)(3)(i) of this section (testing date). An expanded group partner's share of a debt instrument issued by a controlled partnership to a member of the expanded group is determined in accordance with the partner's issuance percentage (as defined in paragraph (g)(16) of this section) on the testing date. A partner's share determined under this paragraph (f)(3)(ii)(A) is adjusted as described in paragraph (f)(3)(ii)(B) of this section.

(B) *Additional rules if there is a specified portion with respect to a debt instrument.*—*(1)* An expanded group partner's share (as determined under paragraph (f)(3)(ii)(A) of this section) of a debt instrument issued by a controlled partnership is reduced, but not below zero, by the sum of all of the specified portions (as defined in paragraph (g)(23) of this section), if any, with respect to the debt instrument that correspond to one or more deemed transferred receivables (as defined in paragraph (g)(8) of this section) that are deemed to be held by the partner.

(2) If the aggregate of all of the expanded group partners' shares (as determined under paragraph (f)(3)(ii)(A) of this section and reduced under paragraph (f)(3)(ii)(B)*(1)* of this section) of the debt instrument exceeds the adjusted issue price of the debt, reduced by the sum of all of the specified portions with respect to the debt instrument that correspond to one or more deemed transferred receivables that are deemed to be held by one or more expanded group partners (excess amount), then each expanded group partner's share (as determined under paragraph (f)(3)(ii)(A) of this section and reduced under paragraph (f)(3)(ii)(B)*(1)* of this section) of the debt instrument is reduced. The amount of an expanded group partner's reduction is the excess amount multiplied by a fraction, the numerator of which is the partner's share, and the denominator of which is the aggregate of all of the expanded group partners' shares.

(iii) *Qualified short-term debt instrument.*—The determination of whether a debt instrument is a qualified short-term debt instrument for purposes of paragraph (b)(3)(vii) of this section is made at the partnership-level without regard to paragraph (f)(3)(i) of this section.

(4) *Recharacterization when there is a specified portion with respect to a debt instrument issued by a controlled partnership.*—(i) *General rule.*—A specified portion, with respect to a debt instrument issued by a controlled partnership and an expanded group partner, is not treated as stock under paragraph (b)(2) or (b)(3)(i) of this section. Except as otherwise provided in paragraphs (f)(4)(ii) and (iii) of this section, the holder-in-form (as defined in paragraph (g)(15) of this section) of the debt instrument is deemed to transfer a portion of the debt instrument (a deemed transferred receivable, as defined in paragraph (g)(8) of this section) with a principal amount equal to the adjusted issue price of the specified portion to the expanded group partner in exchange for stock in the expanded group partner (deemed partner stock, as defined in paragraph (g)(6) of this section) with a fair market value equal to the principal amount of the deemed transferred receivable. Except as otherwise provided in paragraph (f)(4)(vi) of this section (concerning the treatment of a deemed transferred receivable for purposes of section 752) and paragraph (f)(5) of this section (concerning specified events subsequent to the deemed transfer), the deemed transfer described in this paragraph (f)(4)(i) is deemed to occur for all Federal tax purposes.

(ii) *Expanded group partner is the holder-in-form of a debt instrument.*—If the specified portion described in paragraph (f)(4)(i) of this section is with respect to an expanded group partner that is the holder-in-form of the debt instrument, then paragraph (f)(4)(i) of this section will not apply with respect to that specified portion except that only the first sentence of paragraph (f)(4)(i) of this section is applicable.

(iii) *Expanded group partner is a consolidated group member.*—This paragraph (f)(4)(iii) applies when one or more expanded group partners is a member of a consolidated group that files (or is required to file) a consolidated U.S. Federal income tax return. In this case, notwithstanding § 1.385-4(b)(1) (which generally treats members of a consolidated group as one corporation for purposes of this section), the holder-inform of the debt instrument issued by the controlled partnership is deemed to transfer the deemed transferred receivable or receivables to the expanded group partner or partners that are members of a consolidated group that make, or are treated as making under paragraph (f)(2) of this section, the regarded distributions or acquisitions (within the meaning of § 1.385-4(e)(5)) described in paragraph (b)(2) or (b)(3)(i) of this section in exchange for deemed partner stock in such partner or partners. To the extent those regarded distributions or acquisitions are made by a member of the consolidated group that is not an expanded group partner (excess amount), the holder-in-form is deemed to transfer a portion of the deemed transferred receivable or receivables to each member of the consolidated group that is an expanded group partner in exchange for deemed partner stock in the expanded group partner. The portion is the excess amount multiplied by a fraction, the numerator of which is the portion of the consolidated group's share (as determined under paragraph (f)(3)(ii) of this section) of the debt instrument issued by the controlled partnership that would have been the expanded group partner's share if the partner was not a member of a consolidated group, and the denominator of which is the consolidated group's share of the debt instrument issued by the controlled partnership.

(iv) *Rules regarding deemed transferred receivables and deemed partner stock.*—(A) *Terms of deemed partner stock.*—Deemed partner stock has the same terms as the deemed transferred receivable with respect to the deemed transfer, other than the identity of the issuer.

(B) *Treatment of payments with respect to a debt instrument for which there is one or more deemed transferred receivables.*—When a payment is made with respect to a debt instrument issued by a controlled partnership for which there is one or more deemed transferred receivables, then, if the amount of the retained receivable (as defined in paragraph (g)(22) of this section) held by the holder-in-form is zero and a single deemed holder is deemed to hold all of the deemed transferred receivables, the entire payment is allocated to the deemed transferred receivables held by the single deemed holder. If the amount of the retained receivable held by the holder-in-form is greater than zero or there are multiple deemed holders of deemed transferred receivables, or both, the payment is apportioned among the retained receivable, if any, and each deemed transferred receivable in proportion to the principal amount of all the receivables. The portion of a payment allocated or apportioned to a retained receivable or a deemed transferred receivable reduces the principal amount of, or accrued interest with respect to, as applicable depending on the payment, the retained receivable or deemed transferred receivable. When a payment allocated or apportioned to a deemed transferred receivable reduces the principal amount of the receivable, the expanded group partner that is the deemed holder with respect to the deemed transferred receivable is deemed to redeem the same amount of deemed partner stock, and the specified portion with respect to the debt instrument is reduced by the same amount. When a payment allocated or apportioned to a deemed transferred receivable reduces accrued interest with respect to the receivable, the expanded group partner that is the deemed holder with respect to the deemed transferred receivable is deemed to make a matching distribution in the same amount with respect to the deemed partner stock. The controlled partnership is treated as the paying agent with respect to the deemed partner stock.

(v) *Holder-in-form transfers debt instrument in a transaction that is not a specified event.*—If the holder-in-form transfers the debt instrument (which is disregarded for Federal tax purposes) to a member of the expanded group or a controlled partnership (and therefore the transfer is not a specified event described in paragraph (f)(5)(iii)(F) of this section), then, for Federal tax purposes, the holder-in-form is deemed to transfer the retained receivable and the deemed partner stock to the transferee.

(vi) *Allocation of deemed transferred receivable under section 752.*—A partnership liability that is a debt instrument with respect to which there is one or more deemed transferred receivables is allocated for purposes of section 752 without regard to any deemed transfer.

(5) *Specified events affecting ownership following a deemed transfer.*—(i) *General rule.*—If a specified event (within the meaning of paragraph (f)(5)(iii) of this section) occurs with respect to a deemed transfer, then, immediately before the specified event, the expanded group partner that is both the issuer of the deemed partner stock and the deemed holder of the deemed transferred receivable is deemed to distribute the deemed transferred receivable (or portion thereof, as determined under paragraph (f)(5)(iv) of this section) to the holder-in-form in redemption of the deemed partner stock (or portion thereof, as determined under paragraph (f)(5)(iv) of this section) deemed to be held by the holder-in-form. The deemed distribution is deemed to occur for all Federal tax purposes, except that the distribution is disregarded for purposes of paragraph (b) of this section. Except when the deemed transferred receivable (or portion thereof, as determined under paragraph (f)(5)(iv) of this section) is deemed to be retransferred under paragraph (f)(5)(ii) of this section, the principal amount of the retained receivable held by the holder-in-form is increased by the principal amount of the deemed transferred receivable, the deemed transferred receivable ceases to exist for Federal tax purposes, and the specified portion (or portion thereof) that corresponds to the deemed transferred receivable (or portion thereof) ceases to be treated as a specified portion for purposes of this section.

(ii) *New deemed transfer when a specified event involves a transferee that is a covered member that is an expanded group partner.*—If the specified event is described in paragraph (f)(5)(iii)(E) of this section, the holder-in-form of the debt instrument is deemed to retransfer the deemed transferred receivable (or portion thereof, as determined under paragraph (f)(5)(iv) of this section) that the holder-in-form is deemed to have received pursuant to paragraph (f)(5)(i) of this section, to the transferee expanded group partner in exchange for deemed partner stock issued by the transferee expanded group partner with a fair market value equal to the principal amount of the deemed transferred receivable (or portion thereof) that is retransferred. For purposes of this section, this deemed transfer is treated in the same manner as a deemed transfer described in paragraph (f)(4)(i) of this section.

(iii) *Specified events.*—A specified event, with respect to a deemed transfer, occurs when, immediately after the transaction and taking into account all related transactions:

(A) The controlled partnership that is the issuer of the debt instrument either ceases to be a controlled partnership or ceases to have an expanded group partner that is a covered member.

(B) The holder-in-form is a member of the expanded group immediately before the transaction, and the holder-in-form and the deemed holder cease to be members of the same expanded group for the reasons described in paragraph (d)(2) of this section.

(C) The holder-in-form is a controlled partnership immediately before the transaction, and the holder-in-form ceases to be a controlled partnership.

(D) The expanded group partner that is both the issuer of deemed partner stock and the deemed holder transfers (directly or indirectly through one or more partnerships) all or a portion of its interest in the controlled partnership to a person that neither is a covered member nor a controlled partnership with an expanded group partner that is a covered member. If there is a transfer of only a portion of the interest, see paragraph (f)(5)(iv) of this section.

(E) The expanded group partner that is both the issuer of deemed partner stock and the deemed holder transfers (directly or indirectly through one or more partnerships) all or a portion of its interest in the controlled partnership to a covered member or a controlled partnership with an expanded group partner that is a covered member. If there is a transfer of only a portion of the interest, see paragraph (f)(5)(iv) of this section.

(F) The holder-in-form transfers the debt instrument (which is disregarded for Federal tax purposes) to a person that is neither a member of the expanded group nor a controlled partnership. See paragraph (f)(4)(v) of this section if the holder-in-form transfers the debt instrument to a member of the expanded group or a controlled partnership.

(iv) *Specified event involving a transfer of only a portion of an interest in a controlled partnership.*—If, with respect to a specified event described in paragraph (f)(5)(iii)(D) or (E) of this section, an expanded group partner transfers only a portion of its interest in a controlled partnership, then, only a portion of the deemed transferred receivable that is deemed to be held by the expanded group partner is deemed to be distributed in redemption of an equal portion of the deemed partner stock. The portion of the deemed transferred receivable referred to in the preceding sentence is equal to the product of the entire principal amount of the deemed transferred receivable deemed to be held by the expanded group partner multiplied by a fraction, the numerator of which is the portion of the expanded group partner's capital account attributable to the interest that is transferred, and the denominator of which is the expanded group partner's capital account with respect to its entire interest, determined immediately before the specified event.

(6) *Issuance of a partnership's debt instrument to a partner and a partner's debt instrument to a partnership.*—If a controlled partnership, with respect to an expanded group, issues a debt instrument to an expanded group partner, or if a covered member that is an expanded group partner issues a covered debt instrument to a controlled partnership, and in each case, no partner deducts or receives an allocation of expense with respect to the debt instrument, then this section does not apply to the debt instrument.

(g) *Definitions.*—The definitions in this paragraph (g) apply for purposes of this section and §§1.385-3 and 1.385-4.

(1) *Asset reorganization.*—The term asset reorganization means a reorganization described in section 368(a)(1)(A), (C), (D), (F), or (G).

(2) *Consolidated group.*—The term consolidated group has the meaning specified in §1.1502-1(h).

(3) *Covered debt instrument.*—(i) *In general.*—The term covered debt instrument means a debt instrument issued after April 4, 2016, that is not a qualified dealer debt instrument (as defined in paragraph (g)(3)(ii) of this section) or an excluded statutory or regulatory debt instrument (as defined in paragraph (g)(3)(iii) of this section), and that is issued by a covered member that is not an excepted regulated financial company (as defined in paragraph (g)(3)(iv) of this section) or a regulated insurance company (as defined in paragraph (g)(3)(v) of this section).

(ii) *Qualified dealer debt instrument.*—For purposes of this paragraph (g)(3), the term qualified dealer debt instrument means a debt instrument that is issued to or acquired by an expanded group member that is a dealer in securities (within the meaning of section 475(c)(1)) in the ordinary course of the dealer's business of dealing in securities. The preceding sentence applies solely to the extent that—

(A) The dealer accounts for the debt instruments as securities held primarily for sale to customers in the ordinary course of business;

(B) The dealer disposes of the debt instruments (or the debt instruments mature) within a period of time that is consistent with the holding of the debt instruments for sale to customers in the ordinary course of business, taking into account the terms of the debt instruments and the conditions and practices prevailing in the markets for similar debt instruments during the period in which it is held; and

(C) The dealer does not sell or otherwise transfer the debt instrument to a member of the dealer's expanded group unless that sale or transfer is to a dealer that satisfies the requirements of this paragraph (g)(3)(ii).

(iii) *Excluded statutory or regulatory debt instrument.*—For purposes of this paragraph (g)(3), the term excluded statutory or regulatory debt instrument means a debt instrument that is described in any of the following paragraphs:

(A) Production payments treated as a loan under section 636(a) or (b).

(B) A "regular interest" in a real estate mortgage investment conduit described in section 860G(a)(1).

(C) A debt instrument that is deemed to arise under §1.482-1(g)(3) (including adjustments made pursuant to Revenue Procedure 99-32, 1999-2 C.B. 296).

(D) A stripped bond or coupon described in section 1286, unless such instrument was issued with a principal purpose of avoiding the purposes of this section or §1.385-3.

(E) A lease treated as a loan under section 467.

(iv) *Excepted regulated financial company.*—For purposes of this paragraph (g)(3), the term excepted regulated financial company means a covered member that is a regulated financial company (as defined in paragraph (g)(3)(iv)(A) of this section) or a member of a regulated financial group (as defined in paragraph (g)(3)(iv)(B) of this section).

(A) *Regulated financial company.*—For purposes of paragraph (g)(3)(iv), the term regulated financial company means—

(*1*) A bank holding company, as defined in 12 U.S.C. 1841;

(*2*) A covered savings and loan holding company, as defined in 12 CFR 217.2;

(*3*) A national bank;

(*4*) A bank that is a member of the Federal Reserve System and is incorporated by special law of any State, or organized under the general laws of any State, or of the United States, including a Morris Plan bank, or other incorporated banking institution engaged in a similar business;

(*5*) An insured depository institution, as defined in 12 U.S.C. 1813(c)(2);

(*6*) A nonbank financial company subject to a determination under 12 U.S.C. 5323(a)(1) or (b)(1);

(*7*) A U.S. intermediate holding company formed by a foreign banking organization in compliance with 12 C.F.R. 252.153;

(*8*) An Edge Act corporation organized under section 25A of the Federal Reserve Act (12 U.S.C. 611-631);

(*9*) Corporations having an agreement or undertaking with the Board of Governors of the Federal Reserve System under section 25 of the Federal Reserve Act (12 U.S.C. 601-604a);

(*10*) A supervised securities holding company, as defined in 12 U.S.C. 1850a(a)(5);

(*11*) A broker or dealer that is registered with the Securities and Exchange Commission under 15 U.S.C. 78o(b);

(*12*) A futures commission merchant, as defined in 7 U.S.C. 1a(28);

(*13*) A swap dealer, as defined in 7 U.S.C. 1a(49);

(*14*) A security-based swap dealer, as defined in 15 U.S.C. 78c(a)(71);

(*15*) A Federal Home Loan Bank, as defined in 12 U.S.C. 1422(1)(A);

(*16*) A Farm Credit System Institution chartered and subject to the provisions of the Farm Credit Act of 1971 (12 U.S.C. 2001 et seq.); or

(*17*) A small business investment company, as defined in 15 U.S.C. 662(3).

(B) *Regulated financial group.*—(*1*) *General rule.*—For purposes of paragraph (g)(3)(iv) of this section, except as otherwise provided in paragraph (g)(3)(iv)(B)(*2*) of this section, the term regulated financial group means any expanded group of which a covered member that is a regulated financial company within the meaning of paragraphs (g)(3)(iv)(A)(*1*) through (*10*) of this section would be the expanded group parent if no person owned, directly or indirectly (as defined in §1.385-1(c)(4)(iii)), the regulated financial company. A domestic eligible entity (within the meaning of §301.7701-5(a) of this chapter) treated as a partnership or disregarded as an entity separate from its owner is, for purposes of this paragraph (g)(3)(iv)(B), also treated as a covered member.

(*2*) *Exception for certain non-financial entities.*—A corporation is not a member of a regulated financial group if it is held by a regulated financial company pursuant to 12 U.S.C. 1843(k)(1)(B), 12 U.S.C. 1843(k)(4)(H), or 12 U.S.C. 1843(o).

(v) *Regulated insurance company.*—For purposes of this paragraph (g)(3), the term regulated insurance company means a covered member that is—

(A) Subject to tax under subchapter L of chapter 1 of the Internal Revenue Code;

(B) Domiciled or organized under the laws of one of the 50 states or the District of Columbia (for purposes of paragraph (g)(3)(v) of this section, each being a "state");

(C) Licensed, authorized, or regulated by one or more states to sell insurance, reinsurance, or annuity contracts to persons other than related persons (within the meaning of section 954(d)(3)) in such states, but in no case will a corporation satisfy the requirements of this paragraph (g)(3)(v)(C) if a principal purpose for obtaining such license, authorization, or regulation was to qualify the issuer as a regulated insurance company; and

(D) Engaged in regular issuances of (or subject to ongoing liability with respect to) insurance, reinsurance, or annuity contracts with persons that are not related persons (within the meaning of section 954(d)(3)).

(4) *Debt instrument.*—The term debt instrument means an interest that would, but for the application of this section, be treated as a debt instrument as defined in section 1275(a) and §1.1275-1(d).

(5) *Deemed holder*.—The term *deemed holder* means, with respect to a deemed transfer, the expanded group partner that is deemed to hold a deemed transferred receivable by reason of the deemed transfer.

(6) *Deemed partner stock*.—The term *deemed partner stock* means, with respect to a deemed transfer, the stock deemed issued by an expanded group partner as described in paragraphs (f)(4)(i) and (iii) and (f)(5)(ii) of this section. The amount of deemed partner stock is reduced as described in paragraphs (f)(4)(iv)(B) and (f)(5)(i) of this section.

(7) *Deemed transfer*.—The term *deemed transfer* means, with respect to a specified portion, the transfer described in paragraph (f)(4)(i) or (iii) or (f)(5)(ii) of this section.

(8) *Deemed transferred receivable*.—The term *deemed transferred receivable* means, with respect to a deemed transfer, the portion of the debt instrument described in paragraph (f)(4)(i) or (iii) or (f)(5)(ii) of this section. The deemed transferred receivable is reduced as described in paragraphs (f)(4)(iv)(B) and (f)(5)(i) of this section.

(9) *Distribution*.—The term distribution means any distribution made by a corporation with respect to its stock.

(10) *Exempt distribution*.—The term exempt distribution means either—

(i) A distribution of stock that is permitted to be received without the recognition of gain or income under section 354(a)(1) or 355(a)(1), or, if section 356 applies, that is not treated as other property or money described in section 356; or

(ii) A distribution of property in a complete liquidation under section 336(a) or 337(a).

(11) *Exempt exchange*.—The term exempt exchange means an acquisition of expanded group stock in which either—

(i) In a case in which the transferor and transferee of the expanded group stock are parties to an asset reorganization, either—

(A) Section 361(a) or (b) applies to the transferor of the expanded group stock and the stock is not transferred by issuance; or

(B) Section 1032 or § 1.1032-2 applies to the transferor of the expanded group stock and the stock is distributed by the transferee pursuant to the plan of reorganization;

(ii) The transferor of the expanded group stock is a shareholder that receives property in a complete liquidation to which section 331 or 332 applies; or

(iii) The transferor of the expanded group stock is an acquiring entity that is deemed to issue the stock in exchange for cash from an issuing corporation in a transaction described in § 1.1032-3(b).

(12) *Expanded group partner*.—The term expanded group partner means, with respect to a controlled partnership of an expanded group, a member of the expanded group that is a partner (directly or indirectly through one or more partnerships).

(13) *Expanded group stock*.—The term expanded group stock means, with respect to a member of an expanded group, stock of a member of the same expanded group.

(14) *Funded member*.—The term funded member has the meaning provided in paragraph (b)(3)(i) of this section.

(15) *Holder-in-form*.—The term *holder-in-form* means, with respect to a debt instrument issued by a controlled partnership, the person that, absent the application of paragraph (f)(4) of this section, would be the holder of the debt instrument for Federal tax purposes. Therefore, the term holder-in-form does not include a deemed holder (as defined in paragraph (g)(5) of this section).

(16) *Issuance percentage*.—The term *issuance percentage* means, with respect to a controlled partnership and an expanded group partner, the ratio (expressed as a percentage) of the partner's reasonably anticipated distributive share of all the partnership's interest expense over a reasonable period, divided by all of the partnership's reasonably anticipated interest expense over that same period, taking into account any and all relevant facts and circumstances. The relevant facts and circumstances include, without limitation, the term of the debt instrument; whether the partnership anticipates issuing other debt instruments; and the partnership's anticipated section 704(b) income and expense, and the partners' respective anticipated allocation percentages, taking into account anticipated changes to those allocation percentages over time resulting, for example, from anticipated contributions, distributions, recapitalizations, or provisions in the controlled partnership agreement.

(17) *Liquidation value percentage*.—The term *liquidation value percentage* means, with respect to a controlled partnership and an expanded group partner, the ratio (expressed as a percentage) of the liquidation value of the expanded group partner's interest in the partnership divided by the aggregate liquidation value of all the partners' interests in the partnership. The liquidation value of an expanded group partner's interest in a controlled partnership is the amount of cash the partner would receive with respect to the interest if the partnership (and any partnership through which the partner indirectly owns an interest in the controlled partnership) sold all of its property for an amount of cash equal to the fair market value of the property (taking into account section 7701(g)), satisfied all of its liabilities (other than those described in § 1.752-7), paid an unrelated third party to assume all of its § 1.752-7 liabilities in a fully taxable transaction, and then the partnership (and any partnership through which the partner indirectly owns an interest in the controlled partnership) liquidated.

(18) *Member of a consolidated group*.—The term member of a consolidated group means a corporation described in § 1.1502-1(b).

(19) *Per se period*.—The term per se period has the meaning provided in paragraph (b)(3)(iii)(A) of this section.

(20) *Predecessor*.—(i) *In general*.—Except as otherwise provided in paragraph (g)(20)(ii) of this section, the term predecessor means, with respect to a corporation—

(A) The distributor or transferor corporation in a transaction described in section 381(a) in which the corporation is the acquiring corporation; or

(B) The distributing corporation in a distribution or exchange to which section 355 (or so much of section 356 that relates to section 355) applies in which the corporation is a controlled corporation.

(ii) *Predecessor ceasing to be a member of the same expanded group as corporation*.—The term predecessor does not include the distributing corporation described in paragraph (g)(20)(i)(B) of this section from the date that the distributing corporation ceases to be a member of the expanded group of which the controlled corporation is a member.

(iii) *Multiple predecessors*.—A corporation may have more than one predecessor, including by reason of a predecessor of the corporation having a predecessor or successor. Accordingly, references to a corporation also include references to a predecessor or successor of a predecessor of the corporation.

(21) *Property*.—The term property has the meaning specified in section 317(a).

(22) *Retained receivable*.—The term *retained receivable* means, with respect to a debt instrument issued by a controlled partnership, the portion of the debt instrument that is not transferred by the holder-in-form pursuant to one or more deemed transfers. The retained receivable is adjusted for decreases described in paragraph (f)(4)(iv)(B) of this section and increases described in paragraph (f)(5)(i) of this section.

(23) *Specified portion*.—The term *specified portion* means, with respect to a debt instrument issued by a controlled partnership and a covered member that is an expanded group partner, the portion of the debt instrument that is treated under paragraph (f)(3)(i) of this section as issued on a testing date (within the meaning of paragraph (f)(3)(ii) of this section) by the covered member and that, absent the application of paragraph (f)(4)(i) of this section, would be treated as stock under paragraph (b)(2) or (b)(3)(i) of this section on the testing date. A specified portion is reduced as described in paragraphs (f)(4)(iv)(B) and (f)(5)(i) of this section.

(24) *Successor*.—(i) *In general*.—Except as otherwise provided in paragraph (g)(24)(iii) of this section, the term successor means, with respect to a corporation—

(A) The acquiring corporation in a transaction described in section 381(a) in which the corporation is the distributor or transferor corporation;

(B) A controlled corporation in a distribution or exchange to which section 355 (or so much of section 356 that relates to section 355) applies in which the corporation is the distributing corporation; or

(C) Subject to the rules in paragraph (g)(24)(ii) of this section, a seller in an acquisition described in paragraph (c)(2)(i)(A) of this section in which the corporation is the acquirer.

(ii) *Special rules for certain acquisitions of subsidiary stock.*—The following rules apply with respect to a successor described in paragraph (g)(24)(i)(C) of this section:

(A) The seller is a successor to the acquirer only to the extent of the value (adjusted as described in paragraph (g)(24)(ii)(C) of this section) of the expanded group stock acquired from the seller in exchange for property (other than expanded group stock) in the acquisition described in paragraph (c)(2)(i)(A) of this section.

(B) A distribution or acquisition by either the seller or a successor seller to or from either the acquirer, the seller, or a successor seller is not treated as described in paragraph (b)(3) of this section for purposes of applying paragraph (b)(3) of this section to a covered debt instrument of the acquirer. For purposes of the preceding sentence, the term successor seller means a member of the expanded group that receives property (other than expanded group stock) in a distribution or acquisition from the seller or another successor seller and is controlled by the acquirer as determined under the principles of paragraph (c)(2)(i) of this section. A successor seller is treated as a successor to the acquirer to the extent of the value of the property received in a distribution or acquisition described in the preceding sentence and, for purposes of applying this paragraph (g)(24)(ii)(B).

(C) To the extent that a covered debt instrument of the acquirer is treated as funding a distribution or acquisition by the seller or successor seller described in paragraphs (b)(3)(i)(A) through (C) of this section, or would be treated but for the exceptions described in paragraphs (c)(3)(i) and (ii) of this section, the value of the expanded group stock described in paragraph (g)(24)(ii)(A) of this section is reduced by an amount equal to the distribution or acquisition for purposes of any further application of paragraph (g)(24)(ii)(A) of this section with respect to the acquirer and seller.

(iii) *Successor ceasing to be a member of the same expanded group as corporation.*.—The term successor does not include a controlled corporation described in paragraph (g)(24)(i)(B) of this section with respect to a distributing corporation or a seller described in paragraph (g)(24)(i)(C) of this section with respect to an acquirer from the date that the controlled corporation or the seller ceases to be a member of the expanded group of which the controlled corporation or acquirer, respectively, is a member.

(iv) *Multiple successors.*—A corporation may have more than one successor, including by reason of a successor of the corporation having a predecessor or successor. Accordingly, references to a corporation also include references to a predecessor or successor of a successor of the corporation.

(25) *Taxable year.*—The term taxable year refers to the taxable year of the issuer of the covered debt instrument.

(h) *Examples.*—(1) *Assumed facts.*—Except as otherwise stated, the following facts are assumed for purposes of the examples in paragraph (h)(3) of this section:

(i) FP is a foreign corporation that owns 100% of the stock of USS1, a covered member, 100% of the stock of USS2, a covered member, and 100% of the stock of FS, a foreign corporation;

(ii) USS1 owns 100% of the stock of DS, a covered member, and CFC, which is a controlled foreign corporation within the meaning of section 957;

(iii) At the beginning of Year 1, FP is the common parent of an expanded group comprised solely of FP, USS1, USS2, FS, DS, and CFC (the FP expanded group);

(iv) The FP expanded group has more than $50 million of covered debt instruments described in paragraph (c)(4) of this section at all times;

(v) No issuer of a covered debt instrument has a positive expanded group earnings account within the meaning of paragraph (c)(3)(i)(B) of this section or has received qualified contributions within the meaning of paragraph (c)(3)(ii) of this section;

(vi) All notes are covered debt instruments (as defined in paragraph (g)(3) of this section) and are not qualified short-term debt instruments (as defined in paragraph (b)(3)(vii) of this section);

(vii) Each entity has as its taxable year the calendar year;

(viii) PRS is a partnership for federal income tax purposes;

(ix) No corporation is a member of a consolidated group;

(x) No domestic corporation is a United States real property holding corporation within the meaning of section 897(c)(2);

(xi) Each note is issued with adequate stated interest (as defined in section 1274(c)(2)); and

(xii) Each transaction occurs after January 19, 2017.

(2) *No inference.*—Except as otherwise provided in this section, it is assumed for purposes of the examples in paragraph (h)(3) of this section that the form of each transaction is respected for federal tax purposes. No inference is intended, however, as to whether any particular note would be respected as indebtedness or as to whether the form of any particular transaction described in an example in paragraph (h)(3) of this section would be respected for federal tax purposes.

(3) *Examples.*—The following examples illustrate the rules of this section.

(i) *Example 1: Distribution of a covered debt instrument.*—(A) *Facts.* On Date A in Year 1, FS lends $100x to USS1 in exchange for USS1 Note A. On Date B in Year 2, USS1 issues USS1 Note B, which is has a value of $100x, to FP in a distribution.

(B) *Analysis.* USS1 Note B is a covered debt instrument that is issued by USS1 to FP, a member of the expanded group of which USS1 is a member, in a distribution. Accordingly, USS1 Note B is treated as stock under paragraph (b)(2)(i) of this section. Under paragraph (d)(1)(i) of this section, USS1 Note B is treated as stock when it is issued by USS1 to FP on Date B in Year 2. Accordingly, USS1 is treated as distributing USS1 stock to its shareholder FP in a distribution that is subject to section 305. Under paragraph (b)(5) of this section, because the distribution of USS1 Note B is described in paragraph (b)(2)(i) of this section, the distribution of USS1 Note B is not treated as a distribution of property described in paragraph (b)(3)(i)(A) of this section. Accordingly, USS1 Note A is not treated as funding the distribution of USS1 Note B for purposes of paragraph (b)(3)(i)(A) of this section.

(ii) *Example 2: Covered debt instrument issued for expanded group stock that is exchanged for stock in a corporation that is not a member of the same expanded group.*—(A) *Facts.* UST is a publicly traded domestic corporation. On Date A in Year 1, USS1 issues USS1 Note to FP in exchange for FP stock. Subsequently, on Date B of Year 1, USS1 transfers the FP stock to UST's shareholders, which are not members of the FP expanded group, in exchange for all of the stock of UST.

(B) *Analysis.* (*1*) Because USS1 and FP are both members of the FP expanded group, USS1 Note is treated as stock when it is issued by USS1 to FP in exchange for FP stock on Date A in Year 1 under paragraphs (b)(2)(ii) and (d)(1)(i) of this section. This result applies even though, pursuant to the same plan, USS1 transfers the FP stock to persons that are not members of the FP expanded group. The exchange of USS1 Note for FP stock is not an exempt exchange within the meaning of paragraph (g)(11) of this section.

(*2*) Because USS1 Note is treated as stock for federal tax purposes when it is issued by USS1, pursuant to section § 1.367(b)-10(a)(3)(ii) (defining property for purposes of § 1.367(b)-10) there is no potential application of § 1.367(b)-10(a) to USS1's acquisition of the FP stock.

(iii) *Example 3: Issuance of a note in exchange for expanded group stock.*—(A) *Facts.* On Date A in Year 1, USS1 issues USS1 Note to FP in exchange for 40% of the FS stock owned by FP.

(B) *Analysis.* (*1*) Because USS1 and FP are both members of the FP expanded group, USS1 Note is treated as stock when it is issued by USS1 to FP in exchange for FS stock on Date A in Year 1 under paragraphs (b)(2)(ii) and (d)(1)(i) of this section. The exchange of USS1 Note for FS stock is not an exempt exchange within the meaning of paragraph (g)(11) of this section.

(*2*) Because USS1 Note is treated as stock for federal tax purposes when it is issued by USS1, USS1 Note is not treated as property for purposes of section 304(a) because it is not property within the meaning specified in section 317(a). Therefore, USS1's acquisition of FS stock from FP in exchange for USS1 Note is not an acquisition described in section 304(a)(1).

(iv) *Example 4: Funding occurs in same taxable year as distribution.*—(A) *Facts.* On Date A in Year 1, FP lends $200x to DS in exchange for DS Note A. On Date B in Year 1, DS distributes $400x of cash to USS1 in a distribution.

(B) *Analysis.* Under paragraph (b)(3)(iii)(A) of this section, DS Note A is treated as funding the distribution by DS to USS1 because DS Note A is issued to a member of the FP expanded group during the per se period with respect to DS's distribution to USS1. Accordingly, under paragraphs (b)(3)(i)(A) and (d)(1)(ii) of this section, DS Note A is treated as stock on Date B in Year 1.

(v) *Example 5: Additional funding.*—(A) *Facts.* The facts are the same as in paragraph (h)(3)(iv)(A) of this section (*Example 4*), except that, in addition, on Date C in Year 2, FP lends an additional $300x to DS in exchange for DS Note B.

(B) *Analysis.* The analysis is the same as in paragraph (h)(3)(iv)(B) of this section (*Example 4*) with respect to DS Note A. DS Note B is also issued to a member of the FP expanded group during the per se period with respect to DS's distribution to USS1. Under paragraphs (b)(3)(iii)(A) and (b)(6) of this section, DS Note B is treated as funding only the remaining portion of DS's distribution to USS1, which is $200x. Accordingly, $200x of DS Note B is treated as stock under paragraph (b)(3)(i)(A) of this section. Under paragraph (d)(1)(i) of this section, $200x of DS Note B is treated as stock when it is issued by DS to FP on Date C in Year 2. The remaining $100x of DS Note B continues to be treated as indebtedness.

(vi) *Example 6. Funding involving multiple interests.*—(A) *Facts.* On Date A in Year 1, FP lends $300x to USS1 in exchange for USS1 Note A. On Date B in Year 2, USS1 distributes $300x of cash to FP. On Date C in Year 3, FP lends another $300x to USS1 in exchange for USS1 Note B.

(B) *Analysis.* (*1*) Under paragraph (b)(3)(iii)(B) of this section, USS1 Note A is tested under paragraph (b)(3) of this section before USS1 Note B is tested. USS1 Note A is issued during the per se period with respect to USS1's $300x distribution to FP and, therefore, is treated as funding the distribution under paragraph (b)(3)(iii)(A) of this section. Beginning on Date B in Year 2, USS1 Note A is treated as stock under paragraphs (b)(3)(i)(A) and (d)(1)(ii) of this section.

(*2*) Under paragraph (b)(3)(iii)(B) of this section, USS1 Note B is tested under paragraph (b)(3) of this section after USS1 Note A is tested. Because USS1 Note A is treated as funding the entire $300x distribution by USS1 to FP, USS1 Note B will continue to be treated as indebtedness. See paragraph (b)(6) of this section.

(vii) *Example 7. Re-testing.*—(A) *Facts.* The facts are the same as in paragraph (h)(3)(vi)(A) of this section (*Example 6*), except that on Date D in Year 4, FP sells USS1 Note A to Bank.

(B) *Analysis.* (*1*) Under paragraph (d)(2)(i) of this section, USS1 Note A ceases to be treated as stock when FP sells USS1 Note A to Bank on Date D in Year 4. Immediately before FP sells USS1 Note A to Bank, USS1 is deemed to issue a debt instrument to FP in exchange for USS1 Note A in a transaction that is disregarded for purposes of paragraphs (b)(2) and (b)(3) of this section.

(*2*) Under paragraph (d)(2)(ii) of this section, after USS1 Note A is deemed exchanged for a new debt instrument, USS1's other covered debt instruments that are not treated as stock as of Date D in Year 4 (USS1 Note B) are re-tested for purposes of paragraph (b)(3)(iii) of this section to determine whether the instruments are treated as funding the $300x distribution by USS1 to FP on Date B in Year 2. USS1 Note B was issued by USS1 to FP during the per se period. Accordingly, USS1 Note B is re-tested under paragraph (b)(3)(iii) of this section. Under paragraph (b)(3)(iii) of this section, USS1 Note B is treated as funding the distribution on Date C in Year 3 and, accordingly, is treated as stock under paragraph (b)(3)(i)(A) of this section. USS1 Note B is deemed to be exchanged for stock on Date D in Year 4, the re-testing date, under paragraph (d)(1)(iv) of this section. See § 1.385-1(d) for rules regarding the treatment of this deemed exchange.

(viii) *Example 8. Distribution of expanded group stock and covered debt instrument in a reorganization that qualifies under section 355.*—(A) *Facts.* On Date A in Year 1, FP lends $200x to USS2 in exchange for USS2 Note. In a transaction that is treated as independent from the transaction on Date A in Year 1, on Date B in Year 2, USS2 transfers a portion of its assets to DS2, a newly formed domestic corporation, in exchange for all of the stock of DS2 and DS2 Note. Immediately afterwards, USS2 distributes all of the DS2 stock and the DS2 Note to FP with respect to FP's USS2 stock in a transaction that qualifies under section 355. USS2's transfer of a portion of its assets to DS2 qualifies as a reorganization described in section 368(a)(1)(D). The DS2 stock has a value of $150x and DS2 Note has a value of $50x. The DS2 stock is not non-qualified preferred stock as defined in section 351(g)(2). Absent the application of this section, DS2 Note would be treated by FP as other property within the meaning of section 356.

(B) *Analysis.* (*1*) The contribution and distribution transaction is a reorganization described in section 368(a)(1)(D) involving a transfer of property by USS2 to DS2 in exchange for DS2 stock and DS2 Note. The transfer of property by USS2 to DS2 is a contribution of excluded property described in paragraph (c)(3)(ii)(D)(*2*) of this section and an excluded contribution described in paragraph (c)(3)(ii)(E)(*2*) of this section. Accordingly, USS2's contribution of property to DS2 is not a qualified contribution described in paragraph (c)(3)(ii)(B) of this section.

(*2*) DS2 Note is a covered debt instrument that is issued by DS2 to USS2, both members of the FP expanded group, in exchange for property of USS2 in an asset reorganization (as defined in paragraph (g)(1) of this section), and received by FP, another FP expanded group member immediately before the reorganization, as other property with respect to FP's USS2 stock. Accordingly, the transaction is described in paragraph (b)(2)(iii) of this section, and DS2 Note is treated as stock when it is issued by DS2 to USS2 on Date B in Year 2 pursuant to paragraphs (b)(2)(iii) and (d)(1)(i) of this section.

(*3*) Because the issuance of DS2 Note by DS2 in exchange for the property of USS2 in an asset reorganization is described in paragraph (b)(2)(iii) of this section, the distribution and acquisition of DS2 Note by USS2 is not treated as a distribution or acquisition described in paragraph (b)(3)(i) of this section. Accordingly, USS2 Note is not treated as funding the distribution of DS2 Note for purposes of paragraph (b)(3)(i) of this section.

(*4*) USS2's acquisition of DS2 stock is not an acquisition described in paragraph (b)(3)(i)(B) of this section because it is an exempt exchange (as defined in paragraph (g)(11) of this section). USS2's acquisition of DS2 stock is an exempt exchange because USS2 and DS2 are both parties to a reorganization that is an asset reorganization, section 1032 applies to DS2, the transferor of the expanded group stock, and the DS2 stock is distributed by USS2, the transferee of the expanded group stock, pursuant to the plan of reorganization.

(*5*) USS2's distribution of $150x of the DS2 stock is a distribution of stock that is permitted to be received by FP without recognition of gain under section 355(a)(1). Accordingly, USS2's distribution of the DS2 stock (other than the DS2 Note) to FP is an exempt distribution, and is not described in paragraph (b)(3)(i)(A) of this section.

(*6*) Because USS2 has not made a distribution or acquisition that is described in paragraph (b)(3)(i)(A), (B), or (C) of this section, USS2 Note is not treated as stock.

(ix) *Example 9. Funding a distribution by a successor to funded member.*—(A) *Facts.* The facts are the same as in *Example 8* of this paragraph (h)(3), except that on Date C in Year 3, DS2 distributes $200x of cash to FP and, subsequently, on Date D in Year 3, USS2 distributes $100x of cash to FP.

(B) *Analysis.* (*1*) USS2 is a predecessor of DS2 under paragraph (g)(20)(i)(B) of this section and DS2 is a successor to USS2 under paragraph (g)(24)(i)(B) of this section because USS2 is the distributing corporation and DS2 is the controlled corporation in a distribution to which section 355 applies. Accordingly, under paragraph (b)(3)(v) of this section, a distribution by DS2 is treated as a distribution by USS2. Under paragraphs (b)(3)(iii)(A) and (b)(3)(v)(B) of this section, USS2 Note is treated as funding the distribution by DS2 to FP because USS2 Note was issued during the per se period with respect to DS2's $200x cash distribution, and because both the issuance of USS2 Note and the distribution by DS2 occur during the per se period with respect to the section 355 distribution. Accordingly, under paragraphs (b)(3)(i)(A) and (d)(1)(ii) of this section, USS2 Note is treated as stock beginning on Date C in Year 3. See § 1.385-1(d) for rules regarding the treatment of this deemed exchange.

(*2*) Because the entire amount of USS2 Note is treated as funding DS2's $200x distribution to FP, under paragraph (b)(3)(iii)(C) of this section, USS2 Note is not treated as funding the subsequent distribution by USS2 on Date D in Year 3.

(x) *Example 10. Asset reorganization; section 354 qualified property.*—(A) *Facts.* On Date A in Year 1, FS lends $100x to USS2 in exchange for USS2 Note. On Date B in Year 2, in a transaction that qualifies as a reorganization described in section 368(a)(1)(D), USS2 transfers all of its assets to USS1 in exchange for stock of USS1 and the assumption by USS1 of all of the liabilities of USS2, and USS2 distributes to FP, with respect to FP's USS2 stock, all of the USS1 stock that USS2 receives. FP does not recognize gain under section 354(a)(1).

(B) *Analysis.* (*1*) USS1 is a successor to USS2 under paragraph (g)(24)(i)(A) of this section. For purposes of paragraph (b)(3) of this section, USS2 and, under paragraph (b)(3)(v)(A) of this section, its successor, USS1, are funded members with respect to USS2 Note. Although USS2, a funded member, distributes property (USS1 stock) to its shareholder, FP, pursuant to the reorganization, the distribution of USS1 stock is not described in paragraph (b)(3)(i)(A) of this section because the stock is distributed in an exempt distribution (as defined in paragraph (g)(10) of this section). In addition, neither USS1's acquisition of the assets of USS2 nor USS2's acquisition of USS1 stock is described in paragraph (b)(3)(i)(C) of this section because FP does not receive other property within the meaning of section 356 with respect to its stock in USS2.

(2) USS2's acquisition of USS1 stock is not an acquisition described in paragraph (b)(3)(i)(B) of this section because it is an exempt exchange (as defined in paragraph (g)(11) of this section). USS2's acquisition of USS1 stock is an exempt exchange because USS1 and USS2 are both parties to an asset reorganization, section 1032 applies to USS1, the transferor of the USS1 stock, and the USS1 stock is distributed by USS2, the transferee, pursuant to the plan of reorganization. Furthermore, USS2's acquisition of its own stock from FS is not an acquisition described in paragraph (b)(3)(i)(B) of this section because USS2 acquires its stock in exchange for USS1 stock.

(3) Because neither USS1 nor USS2 has made a distribution or acquisition described in paragraph (b)(3)(i)(A), (B), or (C) of this section, USS2 Note is not treated as stock under paragraph (b)(3)(iii)(A) of this section.

(xi) *Example 11. Distribution of a covered debt instrument and issuance of a covered debt instrument with a principal purpose of avoiding the purposes of this section.*—(A) Facts. On Date A in Year 1, USS1 issues USS1 Note A, which has a value of $100x, to FP in a distribution. On Date B in Year 1, with a principal purpose of avoiding the purposes of this section, FP sells USS1 Note A to Bank for $100x of cash and lends $100x to USS1 in exchange for USS1 Note B.

(B) *Analysis.* USS1 Note A is a covered debt instrument that is issued by USS1 to FP, a member of USS1's expanded group, in a distribution. Accordingly, under paragraphs (b)(2)(i) and (d)(1)(i) of this section, USS1 Note A is treated as stock when it is issued by USS1 to FP on Date A in Year 1. Accordingly, USS1 is treated as distributing USS1 stock to FP. Because the distribution of USS1 Note A is described in paragraph (b)(2)(i) of this section, the distribution of USS1 Note A is not described in paragraph (b)(3)(i)(A) of this section under paragraph (b)(5) of this section. Under paragraph (d)(2)(i) of this section, USS1 Note A ceases to be treated as stock when FP sells USS1 Note A to Bank on Date B in Year 1. Immediately before FP sells USS1 Note A to Bank, USS1 is deemed to issue a debt instrument to FP in exchange for USS1 Note A in a transaction that is disregarded for purposes of paragraphs (b)(2) and (b)(3)(i) of this section. USS1 Note B is not treated as stock under paragraph (b)(3)(i)(A) of this section because the funded member, USS1, has not made a distribution of property. However, because the transactions occurring on Date B of Year 1 were undertaken with a principal purpose of avoiding the purposes of this section, USS1 Note B is treated as stock on Date B of Year 1 under paragraph (b)(4) of this section.

(xii) *Example 12: Distribution of a covered debt instrument to a controlled partnership.*—(A) *Facts.* CFC and FS are equal partners in PRS. PRS owns 100% of the stock in X Corp, a domestic corporation. On Date A in Year 1, X Corp issues X Note to PRS in a distribution.

(B) *Analysis.* (*1*) Under § 1.385-1(c)(4), in determining whether X Corp is a member of the FP expanded group that includes CFC and FS, CFC and FS are each treated as owning 50% of the X Corp stock held by PRS. Accordingly, 100% of X Corp's stock is treated as owned by CFC and FS, and X Corp is a member of the FP expanded group.

(*2*) Together CFC and FS own 100% of the interests in PRS capital and profits, such that PRS is a controlled partnership under § 1.385-1(c)(1). CFC and FS are both expanded group partners on the date on which PRS acquired X Note. Therefore, pursuant to paragraph (f)(2)(i)(A) of this section, each of CFC and FS is treated as acquiring its share of X Note in the same manner (in this case, by a distribution of X Note), and on the date on which, PRS acquired X Note. Likewise, X Corp is treated as issuing to each of CFC and FS its share of X Note. Under paragraph (f)(2)(i)(B) of this section, each of CFC's and FS's share of X Note, respectively, is determined in accordance with its liquidation value percentage determined on Date A in Year 1, the date X Corp distributed X Note to PRS. On Date A in Year 1, pursuant to paragraph (g)(17) of this section, each of CFC's and FS's liquidation value percentages is 50%. Accordingly, on Date A in Year 1, under paragraph (f)(2)(i)(A) of this section, for purposes of this section, CFC and FS are each treated as acquiring 50% of X Note in a distribution.

(*3*) Under paragraphs (b)(2)(i) and (d)(1)(i) of this section, X Note is treated as stock on the date of issuance, which is Date A in Year 1. Under paragraph (f)(2)(i)(A) of this section, each of CFC and FS are treated as acquiring 50% of X Note in a distribution for purposes of this section. Therefore, X Corp is treated as distributing its stock to PRS in a distribution described in section 305.

(xiii) *Example 13: Loan to a controlled partnership; proportionate distributions by expanded group partners.*—(A) *Facts.* DS, USS2, and USP are partners in PRS. USP is a domestic corporation that is not a member of the FP expanded group. Each of DS and USS2 own 45% of the interests in PRS profits and capital, and USP owns 10% of the interests in PRS profits and capital. The PRS partnership agreement provides that all items of PRS income, gain, loss, deduction, and credit are allocated in accordance with the percentages in the preceding sentence. On Date A in Year 1, FP lends $200x to PRS in exchange for PRS Note with stated principal amount of $200x, which is payable at maturity. PRS Note also provides for annual payments of interest that are qualified stated interest. PRS uses all $200x in its business and does not distribute any money or other property to a partner. Subsequently, on Date B in Year 1, DS distributes $90x to USS1, USS2 distributes $90x to FP, and USP distributes $20x to its shareholder. Each of DS's and USS2's issuance percentage is 45% on Date B in Year 1, the date of the distributions and therefore a testing date under paragraph (f)(3)(ii)(A) of this section.

(B) *Analysis.* (*1*) DS and USS2 together own 90% of the interests in PRS profits and capital and therefore PRS is a controlled partnership under § 1.385-1(c)(1). Under § 1.385-1(c)(2), each of DS and USS2 is a covered member.

(*2*) Under paragraph (f)(3)(i) of this section, each of DS and USS2 is treated as issuing its share of PRS Note, and under paragraph (f)(3)(ii)(A) of this section, DS's and USS2's share is each $90x (45% of $200x). USP is not an expanded group partner and therefore has no issuance percentage and is not treated as issuing any portion of PRS Note.

(*3*) The $90x distributions made by DS to USS1 and by USS2 to FP are described in paragraph (b)(3)(i)(A) of this section. Under paragraph (b)(3)(iii)(A) of this section, the portions of PRS Note treated as issued by each of DS and USS2 are treated as funding the distribution made by DS and USS2 because the distributions occurred within the per se period with respect to PRS Note. Under paragraph (b)(3)(i) of this section, the portions of PRS Note treated as issued by each of DS and USS2 would, absent the application of paragraph (f)(4)(i) of this section, be treated as stock of DS and USS2 on Date B in Year 1, the date of the distributions. See paragraph (d)(1)(ii) of this section. Under paragraph (g)(23) of this section, each of the $90x portions is a specified portion.

(*4*) Under paragraph (f)(4)(i) of this section, the specified portions are not treated as stock under paragraph (b)(3)(i) of this section. Instead, FP is deemed to transfer a portion of PRS Note with a principal amount equal to $90x (the adjusted issue price of the specified portion with respect to DS) to DS in exchange for deemed partner stock in DS with a fair market value of $90x. Similarly, FP is deemed to transfer a portion of PRS Note with a principal amount equal to $90x (the adjusted issue price of the specified portion with respect to USS2) to USS2 in exchange for deemed partner stock in USS2 with a fair market value of $90x. The principal amount of the retained receivable held by FP is $20x ($200x – $90x – $90x).

(xiv) *Example 14: Loan to a controlled partnership; disproportionate distributions by expanded group partners.*—(A) *Facts.* The facts are the same as in paragraph (h)(3)(xiii)(A) of this section (*Example 13*), except that on Date B in Year 1, DS distributes $45x to USS1 and USS2 distributes $135x to FP.

(B) *Analysis.* (*1*) The analysis is the same as in paragraph (h)(3)(xiii)(B)(*1*) of this section (*Example 13*).

(*2*) The analysis is the same as in paragraph (h)(3)(xiii)(B)(2) of this section (*Example 13*).

(*3*) The $45x and $135x distributions made by DS to USS1 and by USS2 to FP, respectively, are described in paragraph (b)(3)(i)(A) of this section. Under paragraph (b)(3)(iii)(A) of this section, the portion of PRS Note treated as issued by DS is treated as funding the distribution made by DS because the distribution occurred within the per se period with respect to PRS Note, but under paragraph (b)(3)(i) of this section, only to the extent of DS's $45x distribution. USS2 is treated as issuing $90x of PRS Note, all of which is treated as funding $90x of USS2's $135x distribution under paragraph (b)(3)(iii)(A) of this section. Under paragraph (b)(3)(i) of this section, absent the application of paragraph (f)(4)(i) of this section, $45x of PRS Note would be treated as stock of DS and $90x of PRS Note would be treated as stock of USS2 on Date B in Year 1, the date of the distributions. See paragraph (d)(1)(ii) of this section. Under paragraph (g)(23) of this section, $45x of PRS Note is a specified portion with respect to DS and $90x of PRS Note is a specified portion with respect to USS2.

(*4*) Under paragraph (f)(4)(i) of this section, the specified portions are not treated as stock under paragraph (b)(3)(i) of this section. Instead, FP is deemed to transfer a portion of PRS Note with a principal amount equal to $45x (the adjusted issue price of the specified portion with respect to DS) to DS in exchange for stock of DS with a fair market value of $90x. Similarly, FP is deemed to transfer a portion of PRS Note with a principal amount equal to $90x (the adjusted issue price of the specified portion with respect to USS2) to USS2 in exchange for stock of USS2 with a fair market value of $90x. The principal amount of the retained receivable held by FP is $65x ($200x-$45x-$90x).

(xv) *Example 15: Loan to partnership; distribution in later year.*—(A) *Facts.* The facts are the same as in paragraph (h)(3)(xiii)(A) of this section (*Example 13*), except that USS2 does not distribute $90x to FP until Date C in Year 2, which is less than 36 months after Date A in Year 1. On Date C in Year 2, DS's, USS2's, and USP's issuance percentages under paragraph (g)(16) of this section are unchanged at 45%, 45%, and 10%, respectively.

(B) *Analysis.* (*1*) The analysis is the same as in paragraph (h)(3)(xiii)(B)(*1*) of this section (*Example 13*).

(*2*) The analysis is the same as in paragraph (h)(3)(xiii)(B)(*2*) of this section (*Example 13*).

(*3*) With respect to the distribution made by DS, the analysis is the same as in paragraph (h)(3)(xiii)(B)(*3*) of this section (*Example 13*).

(*4*) With respect to the deemed transfer to DS, the analysis is the same as in paragraph (h)(3)(xiii)(B)(*4*) of this section (*Example 13*). Accordingly, the amount of the retained receivable held by FP as of Date B in Year 1 is $110x ($200x-$90x).

(*5*) Under paragraph (f)(3)(ii)(A) of this section, USS2's share of PRS Note is determined on Date C in Year 2. On Date C in Year 2, DS's, USS2's, and USP's respective shares of PRS Note under paragraph (f)(3)(ii)(A) of this section are $90x, $90x, and $20x. However, because DS is treated as the issuer with respect to a $90x specified portion of PRS Note, DS's share of PRS Note is reduced by $90x to $0 under paragraph (f)(3)(ii)(B)(*1*) of this section. No reduction to either of USS2's or USP's share of PRS Note is required under paragraph (f)(3)(ii)(B)(*2*) of this section because the aggregate of DS's, USS2's, and USP's shares of PRS Note as reduced is $110x (DS has a $0 share, USS2 has a $90x share, and USP has a $20x share), which does not exceed $110x (the $200x adjusted issue price of PRS Note reduced by the $90x specified portion with respect to DS). Under paragraph (f)(3)(i) of this section, USS2 is treated as issuing its share of PRS Note.

(*6*) The $90x distribution made by USS2 to FP is described in paragraph (b)(3)(i)(A) of this section. Under paragraph (b)(3)(iii)(A) of this section, the portion of PRS Note treated as issued by USS2 is treated as funding the distribution made by USS2, because the distribution occurred within the per se period with respect to PRS Note. Accordingly, the portion of PRS Note treated as issued by USS2 would, absent the application of paragraph (f)(4)(i) of this section, be treated as stock of USS2 under paragraph (b)(3)(i) of this section on Date C in Year 2. See paragraph (d)(1)(ii) of this section. Under paragraph (g)(23) of this section, the $90x portion is a specified portion.

(*7*) Under paragraph (f)(4)(i) of this section, the specified portion of PRS Note treated as issued by USS2 is not treated as stock under paragraph (b)(3)(i) of this section. Instead, on Date C in Year 2, FP is deemed to transfer a portion of PRS Note with a principal amount equal to $90x (the adjusted issue price of the specified portion with respect to USS2) to USS2 in exchange for stock in USS2 with a fair market value of $90x. The principal amount of the retained receivable held by FP is reduced from $110x to $20x.

(xvi) *Example 16: Loan to a controlled partnership; partnership ceases to be a controlled partnership.*—(A) *Facts.* The facts are the same as in paragraph (h)(3)(xiii)(A) of this section (*Example 13*), except that on Date C in Year 4, USS2 sells its entire interest in PRS to an unrelated person.

(B) *Analysis.* (*1*) On date C in Year 4, PRS ceases to be a controlled partnership with respect to the FP expanded group under §1.385-1(c)(1). This is the case because DS, the only remaining partner that is a member of the FP expanded group, only owns 45% of the total interest in PRS profits and capital. Because PRS ceases to be a controlled partnership, a specified event (within the meaning of paragraph (f)(5)(iii)(A) of this section) occurs with respect to the deemed transfers with respect to each of DS and USS2.

(*2*) Under paragraph (f)(5)(i) of this section, on Date C in Year 4, immediately before PRS ceases to be a controlled partnership, each of DS and USS2 is deemed to distribute its deemed transferred receivable to FP in redemption of FP's deemed partner stock in DS and USS2. The specified portion that corresponds to each of the deemed transferred receivables ceases to be treated as a specified portion. Furthermore, the deemed transferred receivables cease to exist, and the retained receivable held by FP increases from $20x to $200x.

(xvii) *Example 17: Transfer of an interest in a partnership to a covered member.*—(A) *Facts.* The facts are the same as in paragraph (h)(3)(xiii)(A) of this section (*Example 13*), except that on Date C in Year 4, USS2 sells its entire interest in PRS to USS1.

(B) *Analysis.* (*1*) After USS2 sells its interest in PRS to USS1, DS and USS1 together own 90% of the interests in PRS profits and capital and therefore PRS continues to be a controlled partnership under §1.385-1(c)(1). A specified event (within the meaning of paragraph (f)(5)(iii)(E) of this section) occurs as result of the sale only with respect to the deemed transfer with respect to USS2.

(*2*) Under paragraph (f)(5)(i) of this section, on Date C in Year 4, immediately before USS2 sells its entire interest in PRS to USS1, USS2 is deemed to distribute its deemed transferred receivable to FP in redemption of FP's deemed partner stock in USS2. Because the specified event is described in paragraph (f)(5)(iii)(E) of this section, under paragraph (f)(5)(ii) of this section, FP is deemed to retransfer the deemed transferred receivable deemed received from USS2 to USS1 in exchange for deemed partner stock in USS1 with a fair market value equal to the principal amount of the deemed transferred receivable that is retransferred to USS1.

(xviii) *Example 18: Loan to partnership and all partners are members of a consolidated group.*—(A) *Facts.* USS1 and DS are equal partners in PRS. USS1 and DS are members of a consolidated group, as defined in §1.1502-1(h). The PRS partnership agreement provides that all items of PRS income, gain, loss, deduction, and credit are allocated equally between USS1 and DS. On Date A in Year 1, FP lends $200x to PRS in exchange for PRS Note. PRS uses all $200x in its business and does not distribute any money or other property to any partner. On Date B in Year 1, DS distributes $200x to USS1, and USS1 distributes $200x to FP. If neither of USS1 or DS were a member of the consolidated group, each would have an issuance percentage under paragraph (g)(16) of this section, determined as of Date A in Year 1, of 50%.

(B) *Analysis.* (*1*) Pursuant to §1.385-4(b)(6), PRS is treated as a partnership for purposes of this section. Under §1.385-4(b)(1), DS and USS1 are treated as one corporation for purposes of this section, and thus a single covered member under §1.385-1(c)(2). For purposes of this section, the single covered member owns 100% of the PRS profits and capital and therefore PRS is a controlled partnership under §1.385-1(c)(1). Under paragraph (f)(3)(i) of this section, the single covered member is treated as issuing all $200x of PRS Note to FP, a member of the same expanded group as the single covered member. DS's distribution to USS1 is a disregarded distribution because it is a distribution between members of a consolidated group that is disregarded under the one-corporation rule described in §1.385-4(b)(1). However, under paragraph (b)(3)(iii)(A) of this section, PRS Note, treated as issued by the single covered member, is treated as funding the distribution by USS1 to FP, which is described in paragraph (b)(3)(i)(A) of this section and which is a regarded distribution. Accordingly, PRS Note, absent the application of paragraph (f)(4)(i) of this section, would be treated as stock under paragraph (b) of this section on Date B in Year 1. Thus, pursuant to paragraph (g)(23) of this section, the entire PRS Note is a specified portion.

(*2*) Under paragraphs (f)(4)(i) and (iii) of this section, the specified portion is not treated as stock and, instead, FP is deemed to transfer PRS Note with a principal amount equal to $200x to USS1 in exchange for stock of USS1 with a fair market value of $200x. Under paragraph (f)(4)(iii) of this section, FP is deemed to transfer PRS Note to USS1 because only USS1 made a regarded distribution described in paragraph (b)(3)(i) of this section.

(xix) *Example 19: Loan to a disregarded entity.*—(A) *Facts.* DS owns DRE, a disregarded entity within the meaning of §1.385-1(c)(3). On Date A in Year 1, FP lends $200x to DRE in exchange for DRE Note. Subsequently, on Date B in Year 1, DS distributes $100x of cash to USS1.

(B) *Analysis.* Under paragraph (b)(3)(iii)(A) of this section, $100x of DRE Note would be treated as funding the distribution by DS to USS1 because DRE Note is issued to a member of the FP expanded group during the per se period with respect to DS's distribution to USS1. Accordingly, under paragraphs (b)(3)(i)(A) and (d)(1)(ii) of this section, $100x of DRE Note would be treated as stock on Date B in Year 1. However, under paragraph (d)(4) of this section, DS, as the regarded owner, within the meaning of § 1.385-1(c)(5), of DRE is deemed to issue its stock to FP in exchange for a portion of DRE Note equal to the $100x applicable portion (as defined in paragraph (d)(4) of this section). Thus, DS is treated as the holder of $100x of DRE Note, which is disregarded, and FP is treated as the holder of the remaining $100x of DRE Note. The $100x of stock deemed issued by DS to FP has the same terms as DRE Note, other than the issuer, and payments on the stock are determined by reference to payments on DRE Note.

(i) [*Reserved*]

(j) *Applicability date and transition rules.*—(1) *In general.*—Except as provided in paragraph (j)(2) or (3) or (k) of this section, this section applies to taxable years ending on or after January 19, 2017.

(2) *Transition rules.*—(i) *Transition rule for covered debt instruments that would be treated as stock in taxable years ending before January 19, 2017.* If paragraphs (b) and (d)(1) of this section, taking into account § § 1.385-1, 1.385-3, and 1.385-4, would have treated a covered debt instrument as stock in a taxable year ending before January 19, 2017 but for the application of paragraph (j)(1) of this section, to the extent that the covered debt instrument is held by a member of the expanded group of which the issuer is a member immediately after January 19, 2017, then the covered debt instrument is deemed to be exchanged for stock immediately after January 19, 2017.

(ii) *Transition rule for certain covered debt instruments treated as stock in taxable years ending on or after January 19, 2017.* If paragraphs (b) and (d)(1) of this section, taking into account § § 1.385-1, 1.385-3, and 1.385-4, would treat a covered debt instrument as stock on or before January 19, 2017 but in a taxable year ending on or after January 19, 2017, that covered debt instrument is not treated as stock during the 90-day period after January 19, 2017. Instead, to the extent that the covered debt instrument is held by a member of the expanded group of which the issuer is a member immediately after January 19, 2017, the covered debt instrument is deemed to be exchanged for stock immediately after January 19, 2017.

(iii) *Transition funding rule.*—When a covered debt instrument would be recharacterized as stock after April 4, 2016, and on or before January 19, 2017 (the *transition period*), but that covered debt instrument is not recharacterized as stock on such date due to the application of paragraph (j)(1), (j)(2)(i), or (j)(2)(ii) of this section, any payments made with respect to such covered debt instrument (other than stated interest), including pursuant to a refinancing, after the date that the covered debt instrument would have been recharacterized as stock and through the remaining portion of the transition period are treated as distributions for purposes of applying paragraph (b)(3) of this section for taxable years ending on or after January 19, 2017. In addition, to the extent that the holder and the issuer of the covered debt instrument cease to be members of the same expanded group during the transition period, the distribution or acquisition that would have caused the covered debt instrument to be treated as stock is available to be treated as funded by other covered debt instruments of the issuer for purposes of paragraph (b)(3) of this section (to the extent provided in paragraph (b)(3)(iii) of this section). The prior sentence is applied in a manner that is consistent with the rules set forth in paragraph (d)(2) of this section.

(iv) *Coordination between the general rule and funding rule.*—When a covered debt instrument would be recharacterized as stock pursuant to paragraph (b)(2) of this section after April 4, 2016, and on or before January 19, 2017, but that covered debt instrument is not recharacterized as stock on such date due to the application of paragraph (j)(1), (j)(2)(i), or (j)(2)(ii) of this section, the issuance of such covered debt instrument is not treated as a distribution or acquisition described in § 1.385-3(b)(3)(i), but only to the extent that the covered debt instrument is held by a member of the expanded group of which the issuer is a member immediately after January 19, 2017.

(v) *Option to apply proposed regulations.*—In lieu of applying § § 1.385-1, 1.385-3, and 1.385-4, taxpayers may apply the provisions matching § § 1.385-1, 1.385-3, and 1.385-4 from the Internal Revenue Bulletin (IRB) 2016-17 (*https://www.irs.gov/pub/irs-irbs/irb16-17.pdf*) to all debt instruments issued by a particular issuer (and members of its expanded group that are covered members) after April 4, 2016, and before October 13, 2016, solely for purposes of determining whether a debt instrument is treated as stock, provided that those sections are consistently applied. [Reg. § 1.385-3.]

(3) *Paragraph (f)(4)(iii) of this section.*—Paragraph (f)(4)(iii) of this section applies to taxable years for which the U.S. Federal income tax return is due, without extensions, after May 14, 2020. For taxable years ending on or after January 19, 2017, and for which the U.S. Federal income tax return is due, without extensions, on or before May 14, 2020, see § 1.385-3T(f)(4)(iii), as contained in 26 CFR in part 1 in effect on April 1, 2019. In the case of a taxable year that ends after October 13, 2019, and on or before May 14, 2020, a taxpayer may choose to apply paragraph (f)(4)(iii) of this section to the portion of the taxable year that occurs after the expiration of § 1.385-3T on October 13, 2019, provided that all members of the taxpayer's expanded group apply such paragraph.

(k) *Additional transition rules.*—See transition rules in § 1.385-3T(k)(2) as contained in 26 CFR in part 1 in effect on April 1, 2019. [Reg. § 1.385-3.]

☐ [*T.D.* 9790, 10-13-2016 (*corrected* 1-23-2017). *Amended by T.D.* 9880, 10-31-2019 *and T.D.* 9897, 5-13-2020.]

§ 1.385-4. Treatment of consolidated groups.—(a) *Scope.*—This section provides rules for applying § 1.385-3 to members of consolidated groups. Paragraph (b) of this section sets forth rules concerning the extent to which, solely for purposes of applying § 1.385-3, members of a consolidated group that file (or that are required to file) a consolidated U.S. Federal income tax return are treated as one corporation. Paragraph (c) of this section sets forth rules concerning the treatment of a debt instrument that ceases to be, or becomes, a consolidated group debt instrument. Paragraph (d) of this section provides rules for applying the funding rule of § 1.385-3(b)(3) to members that depart a consolidated group. For definitions applicable to this section, see paragraph (e) of this section and § § 1.385-1(c) and 1.385-3(g). For examples illustrating the application of this section, see paragraph (f) of this section.

(b) *Treatment of consolidated groups.*—(1) *Members treated as one corporation.*—For purposes of this section and § 1.385-3, and except as otherwise provided in this section and § 1.385-3, all members of a consolidated group (as defined in § 1.1502-1(h)) that file (or that are required to file) a consolidated U.S. Federal income tax return are treated as one corporation. Thus, for example, when a member of a consolidated group issues a covered debt instrument that is not a consolidated group debt instrument, the consolidated group generally is treated as the issuer of the covered debt instrument for purposes of this section and § 1.385-3. Also, for example, when one member of a consolidated group issues a covered debt instrument that is not a consolidated group debt instrument and therefore is treated as issued by the consolidated group, and another member of the consolidated group makes a distribution or acquisition described in § 1.385-3(b)(3)(i)(A) through (C) with an expanded group member that is not a member of the consolidated group, § 1.385-3(b)(3)(i) may treat the covered debt instrument as funding the distribution or acquisition made by the consolidated group. In addition, except as otherwise provided in this section, acquisitions and distributions described in § 1.385-3(b)(2) and (b)(3)(i) in which all parties to the transaction are members of the same consolidated group both before and after the transaction are disregarded for purposes of this section and § 1.385-3.

(2) *One-corporation rule inapplicable to expanded group member determination.*—The one-corporation rule described in paragraph (b)(1) of this section does not apply in determining the members of an expanded group. Notwithstanding the previous sentence, an expanded group does not exist for purposes of this section and § 1.385-3 if it consists only of members of a single consolidated group.

(3) *Application of § 1.385-3 to debt instruments issued by members of a consolidated group.*—(i) *Debt instrument treated as stock of the issuing member of a consolidated group.*—If a covered debt instrument treated as issued by a consolidated group under the one-corporation rule described in paragraph (b)(1) of this section is treated as stock under § 1.385-3, the covered debt instrument is treated as stock in the member of the consolidated group that would be the issuer of such debt instrument without regard to this section. But see § 1.385-3(d)(7) (providing that a covered debt instrument that is treated as stock under § 1.385-3(b)(2), (3), or (4) and that is not described in section

1504(a)(4) is not treated as stock for purposes of determining whether the issuer is a member of an affiliated group (within the meaning of section 1504(a)).

(ii) *Application of the covered debt instrument exclusions.*—For purposes of determining whether a debt instrument issued by a member of a consolidated group is a covered debt instrument, each test described in § 1.385-3(g)(3) is applied on a separate member basis without regard to the one-corporation rule described in paragraph (b)(1) of this section.

(iii) *Qualified short-term debt instrument.*—The determination of whether a member of a consolidated group has issued a qualified short-term debt instrument for purposes of § 1.385-3(b)(3)(vii) is made on a separate member basis without regard to the one-corporation rule described in paragraph (b)(1) of this section.

(4) *Application of the reductions of § 1.385-3(c)(3) to members of a consolidated group.*—(i) *Application of the reduction for expanded group earnings.*—(A) *In general.*—A consolidated group maintains one expanded group earnings account with respect to an expanded group period, and only the earnings and profits, determined in accordance with § 1.1502-33 (without regard to the application of § 1.1502-33(b)(2), (e), and (f)), of the common parent (within the meaning of section 1504) of the consolidated group are considered in calculating the expanded group earnings for the expanded group period of the consolidated group. Accordingly, a regarded distribution or acquisition made by a member of a consolidated group is reduced to the extent of the expanded group earnings account of the consolidated group.

(B) *Effect of certain corporate transactions on the calculation of expanded group earnings.*—*(1) Consolidation.*—A consolidated group succeeds to the expanded group earnings account of a joining member under the principles of § 1.385-3(c)(3)(i)(F)*(2)*(*ii*).

(2) Deconsolidation.—*(i) In general.*—Except as otherwise provided in paragraph (b)(4)(i)(B)*(2)*(*ii*) of this section, no amount of the expanded group earnings account of a consolidated group for an expanded group period, if any, is allocated to a departing member. Accordingly, immediately after leaving the consolidated group, the departing member has no expanded group earnings account with respect to its expanded group period.

(ii) Allocation of expanded group earnings to a departing member in a distribution described in section 355.—If a departing member leaves the consolidated group by reason of an exchange or distribution to which section 355 (or so much of section 356 that relates to section 355) applies, the expanded group earnings account of the consolidated group is allocated between the consolidated group and the departing member in proportion to the earnings and profits of the consolidated group and the earnings and profits of the departing member immediately after the transaction.

(ii) *Application of the reduction for qualified contributions.*—(A) *In general.*—For purposes of applying § 1.385-3(c)(3)(ii)(A) to a consolidated group—

(1) A qualified contribution to any member of a consolidated group that remains a member of the consolidated group immediately after the qualified contribution from a person other than a member of the same consolidated group is treated as made to the one corporation described in paragraph (b)(1) of this section;

(2) A qualified contribution that causes a member of a consolidated group to become a departing member of that consolidated group is treated as made to the departing member and not to the consolidated group of which the departing member was a member immediately prior to the qualified contribution; and

(3) No contribution of property by a member of a consolidated group to any other member of the consolidated group is a qualified contribution.

(B) *Effect of certain corporate transactions on the calculation of qualified contributions.*—*(1) Consolidation.*—A consolidated group succeeds to the qualified contributions of a joining member under the principles of § 1.385-3(c)(3)(ii)(F)*(2)*(*ii*).

(2) Deconsolidation.—*(i) In general.*—Except as otherwise provided in paragraph (b)(4)(ii)(B)*(2)*(*ii*) of this section, no amount of the qualified contributions of a consolidated group for an expanded group period, if any, is allocated to a departing member. Accordingly, immediately after leaving the consolidated group, the departing member has no qualified contributions with respect to its expanded group period.

(ii) Allocation of qualified contributions to a departing member in a distribution described in section 355.—If a departing member leaves the consolidated group by reason of an exchange or distribution to which section 355 (or so much of section 356 that relates to section 355) applies, each qualified contribution of the consolidated group is allocated between the consolidated group and the departing member in proportion to the earnings and profits of the consolidated group and the earnings and profits of the departing member immediately after the transaction.

(5) *Order of operations.*—For purposes of this section and § 1.385-3, the consequences of a transaction involving one or more members of a consolidated group are determined as provided in paragraphs (b)(5)(i) and (ii) of this section.

(i) First, determine the characterization of the transaction under Federal tax law without regard to the one-corporation rule described in paragraph (b)(1) of this section.

(ii) Second, apply this section and § 1.385-3 to the transaction as characterized to determine whether to treat a debt instrument as stock, treating the consolidated group as one corporation under paragraph (b)(1) of this section, unless otherwise provided.

(6) *Partnership owned by a consolidated group.*—For purposes of this section and § 1.385-3, and notwithstanding the one-corporation rule described in paragraph (b)(1) of this section, a partnership that is wholly owned by members of a consolidated group is treated as a partnership. Thus, for example, if members of a consolidated group own all of the interests in a controlled partnership that issues a debt instrument to a member of the consolidated group, such debt instrument would be treated as a consolidated group debt instrument because, under § 1.385-3(f)(3)(i), for purposes of this section and § 1.385-3, a consolidated group member that is an expanded group partner is treated as the issuer with respect to its share of the debt instrument issued by the partnership.

(7) *Predecessor and successor.*—(i) *In general.*—Pursuant to paragraph (b)(5) of this section, the determination as to whether a member of an expanded group is a predecessor or successor of another member of the consolidated group is made without regard to paragraph (b)(1) of this section. For purposes of § 1.385-3(b)(3), if a consolidated group member is a predecessor or successor of a member of the same expanded group that is not a member of the same consolidated group, the consolidated group is treated as a predecessor or successor of the expanded group member (or the consolidated group of which that expanded group member is a member). Thus, for example, a departing member that departs a consolidated group in a distribution or exchange to which section 355 applies is a successor to the consolidated group and the consolidated group is a predecessor of the departing member.

(ii) *Joining members.*—For purposes of § 1.385-3(b)(3), the term *predecessor* also means, with respect to a consolidated group, a joining member and the term successor also means, with respect to a joining member, a consolidated group.

(c) *Consolidated group debt instruments.*—(1) *Debt instrument ceases to be a consolidated group debt instrument but continues to be issued and held by expanded group members.*—(i) *Consolidated group member leaves the consolidated group.*—For purposes of this section and § 1.385-3, when a debt instrument ceases to be a consolidated group debt instrument as a result of a transaction in which the member of the consolidated group that issued the instrument (the issuer) or the member of the consolidated group holding the instrument (the holder) ceases to be a member of the same consolidated group but both the issuer and the holder continue to be members of the same expanded group, the issuer is treated as issuing a new debt instrument to the holder in exchange for property immediately after the debt instrument ceases to be a consolidated group debt instrument. To the extent the newly-issued debt instrument is a covered debt instrument that is treated as stock under § 1.385-3(b)(3), the covered debt instrument is then immediately deemed to be exchanged for stock of the issuer. For rules regarding the treatment of the deemed exchange, see § 1.385-1(d). For examples illustrating the rule in this paragraph (c)(1)(i), see paragraphs (f)(3)(iv) and (v) of this section (*Examples 4 and 5*).

(ii) *Consolidated group debt instrument that is transferred outside of the consolidated group.*—For purposes of this section and § 1.385-3, when a member of a consolidated group that holds a consolidated group debt instrument transfers the debt instrument to an expanded group member that is not a member of the same consolidated group (transferee expanded group member), the debt instrument is treated as issued by the consolidated group to the transferee expanded group member immediately after the debt instrument ceases to be a consolidated group debt instrument. Thus, for example, for purposes of this section and § 1.385-3, the sale of a consolidated group debt instrument to a transferee expanded group member is treated as an issuance of the debt instrument by the consolidated group to the transferee expanded group member in exchange for property. To the extent the newly-issued debt instrument is a covered debt instrument that is treated as stock upon being transferred, the covered debt instrument is deemed to be exchanged for stock of the member of the consolidated group treated as the issuer of the debt instrument (determined under paragraph (b)(3)(i) of this section) immediately after the covered debt instrument is transferred outside of the consolidated group. For rules regarding the treatment of the deemed exchange, see § 1.385-1(d). For examples illustrating the rule in this paragraph (c)(1)(ii), see paragraphs (f)(3)(ii) and (iii) of this section (*Examples* 2 and 3).

(iii) *Overlap transactions.*—If a debt instrument ceases to be a consolidated group debt instrument in a transaction to which both paragraphs (c)(1)(i) and (ii) of this section apply, then only the rules of paragraph (c)(1)(ii) of this section apply with respect to such debt instrument.

(iv) *Subgroup exception.*—A debt instrument is not treated as ceasing to be a consolidated group debt instrument for purposes of paragraphs (c)(1)(i) and (ii) of this section if both the issuer and the holder of the debt instrument are members of the same consolidated group immediately after the transaction described in paragraph (c)(1)(i) or (ii) of this section.

(2) *Covered debt instrument treated as stock becomes a consolidated group debt instrument.*—When a covered debt instrument that is treated as stock under § 1.385-3 becomes a consolidated group debt instrument, then immediately after the covered debt instrument becomes a consolidated group debt instrument, the issuer is deemed to issue a new covered debt instrument to the holder in exchange for the covered debt instrument that was treated as stock. In addition, in a manner consistent with § 1.385-3(d)(2)(ii)(A), when the covered debt instrument that previously was treated as stock becomes a consolidated group debt instrument, other covered debt instruments issued by the issuer of that instrument (including a consolidated group that includes the issuer) that are not treated as stock when the instrument becomes a consolidated group debt instrument are retested to determine whether those other covered debt instruments are treated as funding the regarded distribution or acquisition that previously was treated as funded by the instrument (unless such distribution or acquisition is disregarded under paragraph (b)(1) of this section). Further, also in a manner consistent with § 1.385-3(d)(2)(ii)(A), a covered debt instrument that is issued by the issuer (including a consolidated group that includes the issuer) after the application of this paragraph (c)(2) and within the per se period may also be treated as funding that regarded distribution or acquisition.

(3) *No interaction with the intercompany obligation rules of § 1.1502-13(g).*—The rules of this section do not affect the application of the rules of § 1.1502-13(g). Thus, any deemed satisfaction and reissuance of a debt instrument under § 1.1502-13(g) and any deemed issuance and deemed exchange of a debt instrument under this paragraph (c) that arise as part of the same transaction or series of transactions are not integrated. Rather, each deemed satisfaction and reissuance under the rules of § 1.1502-13(g), and each deemed issuance and exchange under the rules of this section, are respected as separate steps and treated as separate transactions.

(d) *Application of the funding rule of § 1.385-3(b)(3) to members departing a consolidated group.*—This paragraph (d) provides rules for applying the funding rule of § 1.385-3(b)(3) when a departing member ceases to be a member of a consolidated group, but only if the departing member and the consolidated group are members of the same expanded group immediately after the deconsolidation.

(1) *Continued application of the one-corporation rule.*—A disregarded distribution or acquisition by any member of the consolidated group continues to be disregarded when the departing member ceases to be a member of the consolidated group.

(2) *Continued recharacterization of a departing member's covered debt instrument as stock.*—A covered debt instrument of a departing member that is treated as stock of the departing member under § 1.385-3(b) continues to be treated as stock when the departing member ceases to be a member of the consolidated group.

(3) *Effect of issuances of covered debt instruments that are not consolidated group debt instruments on the departing member and the consolidated group.*—If a departing member has issued a covered debt instrument (determined without regard to the one-corporation rule described in paragraph (b)(1) of this section) that is not a consolidated group debt instrument and that is not treated as stock immediately before the departing member ceases to be a consolidated group member, then the departing member (and not the consolidated group) is treated as issuing the covered debt instrument on the date and in the manner the covered debt instrument was issued. If the departing member is not treated as the issuer of a covered debt instrument pursuant to the preceding sentence, then the consolidated group continues to be treated as issuing the covered debt instrument on the date and in the manner the covered debt instrument was issued.

(4) *Treatment of prior regarded distributions or acquisitions.*—This paragraph (d)(4) applies when a departing member ceases to be a consolidated group member in a transaction other than a distribution to which section 355 (or so much of section 356 as relates to section 355) applies, and the consolidated group has made a regarded distribution or acquisition. In this case, to the extent the distribution or acquisition has not caused a covered debt instrument of the consolidated group to be treated as stock under § 1.385-3(b) on or before the date the departing member leaves the consolidated group, then—

(i) If the departing member made the regarded distribution or acquisition (determined without regard to the one-corporation rule described in paragraph (b)(1) of this section), the departing member (and not the consolidated group) is treated as having made the regarded distribution or acquisition.

(ii) If the departing member did not make the regarded distribution or acquisition (determined without regard to the one-corporation rule described in paragraph (b)(1) of this section), then the consolidated group (and not the departing member) continues to be treated as having made the regarded distribution or acquisition.

(e) *Definitions.*—The definitions in this paragraph (e) apply for purposes of this section.

(1) *Consolidated group debt instrument.*—The term *consolidated group debt instrument* means a covered debt instrument issued by a member of a consolidated group and held by a member of the same consolidated group.

(2) *Departing member.*—The term *departing member* means a member of an expanded group that ceases to be a member of a consolidated group but continues to be a member of the same expanded group. In the case of multiple members leaving a consolidated group as a result of a single transaction that continue to be members of the same expanded group, if such members are treated as one corporation under paragraph (b)(1) of this section immediately after the transaction, that one corporation is a departing member with respect to the consolidated group.

(3) *Disregarded distribution or acquisition.*—The term *disregarded distribution or acquisition* means a distribution or acquisition described in § 1.385-3(b)(2) or (b)(3)(i) between members of a consolidated group that is disregarded under the one-corporation rule described in paragraph (b)(1) of this section.

(4) *Joining member.*—The term *joining member* means a member of an expanded group that becomes a member of a consolidated group and continues to be a member of the same expanded group. In the case of multiple members joining a consolidated group as a result of a single transaction that continue to be members of the same expanded group, if such members were treated as one corporation under paragraph (b)(1) of this section immediately before the transaction, that one corporation is a joining member with respect to the consolidated group.

(5) *Regarded distribution or acquisition.*—The term *regarded distribution or acquisition* means a distribution or acquisition described in § 1.385-3(b)(2) or (b)(3)(i) that is not disregarded under the one-corporation rule described in paragraph (b)(1) of this section.

(f) *Examples.*—(1) *Assumed facts.*—Except as otherwise stated, the following facts are assumed for purposes of the examples in paragraph (f)(3) of this section:

(i) FP is a foreign corporation that owns 100% of the stock of USS1, a covered member, and 100% of the stock of FS, a foreign corporation;

(ii) USS1 owns 100% of the stock of DS1 and DS3, both covered members;

(iii) DS1 owns 100% of the stock of DS2, a covered member;

(iv) FS owns 100% of the stock of UST, a covered member;

(v) At the beginning of Year 1, FP is the common parent of an expanded group comprised solely of FP, USS1, FS, DS1, DS2, DS3, and UST (the FP expanded group);

(vi) USS1, DS1, DS2, and DS3 are members of a consolidated group of which USS1 is the common parent (the USS1 consolidated group);

(vii) The FP expanded group has outstanding more than $50 million of debt instruments described in § 1.385-3(c)(4) at all times;

(viii) No issuer of a covered debt instrument has a positive expanded group earnings account, within the meaning of § 1.385-3(c)(3)(i)(B), or has received a qualified contribution, within the meaning of § 1.385-3(c)(3)(ii)(B);

(ix) All notes are covered debt instruments, within the meaning of § 1.385-3(g)(3), and are not qualified short-term debt instruments, within the meaning of § 1.385-3(b)(3)(vii);

(x) All notes between members of a consolidated group are intercompany obligations within the meaning of § 1.1502-13(g)(2)(ii);

(xi) Each entity has as its taxable year the calendar year;

(xii) No domestic corporation is a United States real property holding corporation within the meaning of section 897(c)(2);

(xiii) Each note is issued with adequate stated interest (as defined in section 1274(c)(2)); and

(xiv) Each transaction occurs after January 19, 2017.

(2) *No inference.*—Except as otherwise provided in this section, it is assumed for purposes of the examples in paragraph (f)(3) of this section that the form of each transaction is respected for Federal tax purposes. No inference is intended, however, as to whether any particular note would be respected as indebtedness or as to whether the form of any particular transaction described in an example in paragraph (f)(3) of this section would be respected for Federal tax purposes.

(3) *Examples.*—The following examples illustrate the rules of this section.

(i) *Example 1: Order of operations.*—(A) *Facts.* On Date A in Year 1, UST issues UST Note to USS1 in exchange for DS3 stock representing less than 20% of the value and voting power of DS3.

(B) *Analysis.* UST is acquiring the stock of DS3, the non-common parent member of a consolidated group. Pursuant to paragraph (b)(5)(i) of this section, the transaction is first analyzed without regard to the one-corporation rule described in paragraph (b)(1) of this section, and therefore UST is treated as issuing a covered debt instrument in exchange for expanded group stock. The exchange of UST Note for DS3 stock is not an exempt exchange within the meaning of § 1.385-3(g)(11) because UST and USS1 are not parties to an asset reorganization. Pursuant to paragraph (b)(5)(ii) of this section, § 1.385-3 (including § 1.385-3(b)(2)(ii)) is then applied to the transaction, thereby treating UST Note as stock for Federal tax purposes when it is issued by UST to USS1. The UST Note is not treated as property for purposes of section 304(a) because it is not property within the meaning specified in section 317(a). Therefore, UST's acquisition of DS3 stock from USS1 in exchange for UST Note is not an acquisition described in section 304(a)(1).

(ii) *Example 2: Distribution of consolidated group debt instrument.*—(A) *Facts.* On Date A in Year 1, DS1 issues DS1 Note to USS1 in a distribution. On Date B in Year 2, USS1 distributes DS1 Note to FP.

(B) *Analysis.* Under paragraph (b)(1) of this section, the USS1 consolidated group is treated as one corporation for purposes of § 1.385-3. Accordingly, when DS1 issues DS1 Note to USS1 in a distribution on Date A in Year 1, DS1 is not treated as issuing a debt instrument to another member of DS1's expanded group in a distribution for purposes of § 1.385-3(b)(2), and DS1 Note is not treated as stock under § 1.385-3. When USS1 distributes DS1 Note to FP, DS1 Note is deemed satisfied and reissued under § 1.1502-13(g)(3)(ii), immediately before DS1 Note ceases to be an intercompany obligation. Under paragraph (c)(1)(ii) of this section, when USS1 distributes DS1 Note to FP, the USS1 consolidated group is treated as issuing DS1 Note to FP in a distribution on Date B in Year 2. Accordingly, DS1 Note is treated as stock under § 1.385-3(b)(2)(i). Under paragraph (c)(1)(ii) of this section, DS1 Note is deemed to be exchanged for stock of the issuing member, DS1, immediately after DS1 Note is transferred outside of the USS1 consolidated group. Under paragraph (c)(3) of this section, the deemed satisfaction and reissuance under § 1.1502-13(g)(3)(ii) and the deemed issuance and exchange under paragraph (c)(1)(ii) of this section, are respected as separate steps and treated as separate transactions.

(iii) *Example 3: Sale of consolidated group debt instrument.*—(A) *Facts.* On Date A in Year 1, DS1 lends $200x of cash to USS1 in exchange for USS1 Note. On Date B in Year 2, USS1 distributes $200x of cash to FP. Subsequently, on Date C in Year 2, DS1 sells USS1 Note to FS for $200x.

(B) *Analysis.* Under paragraph (b)(1) of this section, the USS1 consolidated group is treated as one corporation for purposes of § 1.385-3. Accordingly, when USS1 issues USS1 Note to DS1 for property on Date A in Year 1, the USS1 consolidated group is not treated as a funded member, and when USS1 distributes $200x to FP on Date B in Year 2, that distribution is a transaction described in § 1.385-3(b)(3)(i)(A), but does not cause USS1 Note to be recharacterized under § 1.385-3(b)(3). When DS1 sells USS1 Note to FS, USS1 Note is deemed satisfied and reissued under § 1.1502-13(g)(3)(ii), immediately before USS1 Note ceases to be an intercompany obligation. Under paragraph (c)(1)(ii) of this section, when the USS1 Note is transferred to FS for $200x on Date C in Year 2, the USS1 consolidated group is treated as issuing USS1 Note to FS in exchange for $200x on that date. Because USS1 Note is issued by the USS1 consolidated group to FS within the per se period as defined in § 1.385-3(g)(19) with respect to the distribution by the USS1 consolidated group to FP, USS1 Note is treated as funding the distribution under § 1.385-3(b)(3)(iii)(A) and, accordingly, is treated as stock under § 1.385-3(b)(3). Under § 1.385-3(d)(1)(i) and paragraph (c)(1)(ii) of this section, USS1 Note is deemed to be exchanged for stock of the issuing member, USS1, immediately after USS1 Note is transferred outside of the USS1 consolidated group. Under paragraph (c)(3) of this section, the deemed satisfaction and reissuance under § 1.1502-13(g)(3)(ii) and the deemed issuance and exchange under paragraph (c)(1)(ii) of this section are respected as separate steps and treated as separate transactions.

(iv) *Example 4: Treatment of consolidated group debt instrument and departing member's regarded distribution or acquisition when the issuer of the instrument leaves the consolidated group.*—(A) *Facts.* The facts are the same as provided in paragraph (f)(1) of this section, except that USS1 and FS own 90% and 10% of the stock of DS1, respectively. On Date A in Year 1, DS1 distributes $80x of cash and newly-issued DS1 Note, which has a value of $10x, to USS1. Also on Date A in Year 1, DS1 distributes $10x of cash to FS. On Date B in Year 2, FS purchases all of USS1's stock in DS1 (90% of the stock of DS1), resulting in DS1 ceasing to be a member of the USS1 consolidated group.

(B) *Analysis.* Under paragraph (b)(1) of this section, the USS1 consolidated group is treated as one corporation for purposes of § 1.385-3. Accordingly, DS1's distribution of $80x of cash to USS1 on Date A in Year 1 is a disregarded distribution or acquisition, and under paragraph (d)(1) of this section, continues to be a disregarded distribution or acquisition when DS1 ceases to be a member of the USS1 consolidated group. In addition, when DS1 issues DS1 Note to USS1 in a distribution on Date A in Year 1, DS1 is not treated as issuing a debt instrument to a member of DS1's expanded group in a distribution for purposes of § 1.385-3(b)(2)(i), and DS1 Note is not treated as stock under § 1.385-3(b)(2)(i). DS1's issuance of DS1 Note to USS1 is also a disregarded distribution or acquisition, and under paragraph (d)(1) of this section, continues to be a disregarded distribution or acquisition when DS1 ceases to be a member of the USS1 consolidated group. The distribution of $10x cash by DS1 to FS on Date A in Year 1 is a regarded distribution or acquisition. When FS purchases 90% of the stock of DS1's from USS1 on Date B in Year 2 and DS1 ceases to be a member of the USS1 consolidated group, DS1 Note is deemed satisfied and reissued under § 1.1502-13(g)(3)(ii), immediately before DS1 Note ceases to be an intercompany obligation. Under paragraph (c)(1)(i) of this section, for purposes of § 1.385-3, DS1 is treated as issuing a new debt instrument to USS1 in exchange for property immediately after DS1 Note ceases to be a consolidated group debt instrument. Under paragraph (d)(4)(i) of this section, the departing member, DS1 (and not the USS1 consolidated group) is treated as having distributed $10x to FS on Date A in Year 1 (a regarded distribution or acquisition) for purposes of applying § 1.385-3(b)(3) after DS1 ceases to be a member of the USS1 consolidated group. Because DS1 Note is reissued by DS1 to USS1 within the per se period (as defined in § 1.385-3(g)(19)) with respect to DS1's regarded distribution to FS, DS1 Note is treated as funding the distribution under § 1.385-3(b)(3)(iii)(A) and, accordingly, is treated as stock under § 1.385-3(b)(3). Under § 1.385-3(d)(1)(i) and paragraph (c)(1)(i) of this section, DS1 Note is immediately deemed to be exchanged for stock of DS1 on Date B in Year 2. Under paragraph (c)(3) of this section, the deemed satisfaction and reissuance under § 1.1502-13(g)(3)(ii) and the deemed issuance and exchange under paragraph (c)(1)(i) of this section are respected as separate steps and treated as separate transactions. Under § 1.385-3(d)(7)(i), after DS1 Note is treated as stock held by USS1, DS1 Note is not treated as stock for purposes of determining whether DS1 is a member of the USS1 consolidated group.

(v) *Example 5: Treatment of consolidated group debt instrument and consolidated group's regarded distribution or acquisition.*—(A) *Facts.* On Date A in Year 1, DS1 issues DS1 Note to USS1. On Date B in Year 2, USS1 distributes $100x of cash to FP. On Date C in Year 3, USS1 sells all of its interest in DS1 to FS, resulting in DS1 ceasing to be a member of the USS1 consolidated group.

(B) *Analysis.* Under paragraph (b)(1) of this section, the USS1 consolidated group is treated as one corporation for purposes of § 1.385-3. Accordingly, when DS1 issues DS1 Note to USS1 in a distribution on Date A in Year 1, DS1 is not treated as issuing a debt instrument to a member of DS1's expanded group in a distribution for purposes of § 1.385-3(b)(2)(i), and DS1 Note is not treated as stock under § 1.385-3(b)(2)(i). DS1's issuance of DS1 Note to USS1 is also a disregarded distribution or acquisition, and under paragraph (d)(1) of this section, continues to be a disregarded distribution or acquisition when DS1 ceases to be a member of the USS1 consolidated group. The distribution of $100x cash by DS1 to USS1 on Date B in Year 2 is a regarded distribution or acquisition. When FS purchases all of the stock of DS1 from USS1 on Date C in Year 3 and DS1 ceases to be a member of the USS1 consolidated group, DS1 Note is deemed satisfied and reissued under § 1.1502-13(g)(3)(ii), immediately before DS1 Note ceases to be an intercompany obligation. Under paragraph (c)(1)(i) of this section, for purposes of § 1.385-3, DS1 is treated as issuing a new debt instrument to USS1 in exchange for property immediately after DS1 Note ceases to be a consolidated group debt instrument. Under paragraph (d)(4)(ii) of this section, the USS1 consolidated group (and not DS1) is treated as having distributed $100x to FP on Date B in Year 2 (a regarded distribution or acquisition) for purposes of applying § 1.385-3(b)(3) after DS1 ceases to be a member of the USS1 consolidated group. Because DS1 has not engaged in a regarded distribution or acquisition that would have been treated as funded by the reissued DS1 Note, the reissued DS1 Note is not treated as stock.

(vi) *Example 6: Treatment of departing member's issuance of a covered debt instrument.*—(A) *Facts.* On Date A in Year 1, FS lends $100x of cash to DS1 in exchange for DS1 Note. On Date B in Year 2, USS1 distributes $30x of cash to FP. On Date C in Year 2, USS1 sells all of its DS1 stock to FP, resulting in DS1 ceasing to be a member of the USS1 consolidated group.

(B) *Analysis.* Under paragraph (b)(1) of this section, the USS1 consolidated group is treated as one corporation for purposes of § 1.385-3. Accordingly, on Date A in Year 1, the USS1 consolidated group is treated as issuing DS1 Note to FS, and on Date B in Year 2, the USS1 consolidated group is treated as distributing $30x of cash to FP. Because DS1 Note is issued by the USS1 consolidated group to FS within the per se period as defined in § 1.385-3(g)(19) with respect to the distribution by the USS1consoldiated group of $30x cash to FP, $30x of DS1 Note is treated as funding the distribution under § 1.385-3(b)(3)(iii)(A), and, accordingly, is treated as stock on Date B in Year 2 under § 1.385-3(b)(3) and § 1.385-3(d)(1)(ii). Under paragraph (d)(3) of this section, DS1 (and not the USS1 consolidated group) is treated as the issuer of the remaining portion of DS1 Note for purposes of applying § 1.385-3(b)(3) after DS1 ceases to be a member of the USS1 consolidated group.

(g) *Applicability date.*—This section applies to taxable years for which the U.S. Federal income tax return is due, without extensions, after May 14, 2020. For taxable years ending on or after January 19, 2017, and for which the U.S. Federal income tax return is due, without extensions, on or before May 14, 2020, see § 1.385-4T, as contained in 26 CFR in part 1 in effect on April 1, 2019. In the case of a taxable year that ends after October 13, 2019, and on or before May 14, 2020, a taxpayer may choose to apply this section to the portion of the taxable year that occurs after the expiration of § 1.385-4T on October 13, 2019, provided that all members of the taxpayer's expanded group apply this section in its entirety. [Reg. § 1.385-4.]

☐ [*T.D.* 9897, 5-13-2020.]

Notional Principal Contracts

Proposed Amendments to Regulation

§ 1.446-3. Notional principal contracts.

* * *

(c) *Definitions and scope.*—(1) *Notional principal contract.*—(i) *In general.*—A notional principal contract is a financial instrument that requires one party to make two or more payments to the counterparty at specified intervals calculated by reference to a specified index upon a notional principal amount in exchange for specified consideration or a promise to pay similar amounts. An agreement between a taxpayer and a qualified business unit (as defined in section 989(a)) of the taxpayer, or among qualified business units of the same taxpayer, is not a notional principal contract because a taxpayer cannot enter into a contract with itself.

(ii) *Payment defined.*—For purposes of paragraph (c)(1)(i) of this section, a payment includes an amount that is fixed on one date and paid or otherwise taken into account on a later date. Thus, for example, a contract that provides for a settlement payment referenced to the appreciation or depreciation on a specified number of shares of common stock, adjusted for actual dividends paid during the term of the contract, is treated as a contract with more than one payment with respect to that leg of the contract. See *Example 2* of this paragraph (c).

(iii) *Included contracts.*—Notional principal contracts governed by this section include contracts commonly referred to as interest rate swaps, currency swaps, basis swaps, interest rate caps, interest rate floors, commodity swaps, equity swaps, equity index swaps, credit default swaps, weather-related swaps, and similar agreements that satisfy the requirements of paragraph (c)(1)(i). A collar is not itself a notional principal contract, but a cap and a floor that comprise a collar may be treated as a single notional principal contract under paragraph (f)(2)(v)(C) of this section. A contract may be a notional principal contract governed by this section even though the term of the contract is subject to termination or extension. Each confirmation under a master agreement to enter into an agreement covered by this section is treated as a separate notional principal contract (or as more than one notional principal contract if the confirmation creates more than one notional principal contract). Notwithstanding the rule under paragraph (c)(3) of this section—

(A) *Special rule for credit default swaps.*—A credit default swap contract that permits or requires the delivery of specified debt instruments in satisfaction of one leg of the contract is a notional principal contract if it otherwise satisfies the requirements of paragraph (c)(1)(i) of this section.

(B) *Special rule for nonfunctional currency notional principal contracts.*—A notional principal contract that permits or requires the delivery of specified currency in satisfaction of one or both legs of the contract but that otherwise qualifies as a nonfunctional currency notional principal contract under § 1.988-1(a)(2)(iii)(B) is a notional principal contract.

(iv) *Excluded contracts.*—A forward contract, an option, and a guarantee are not notional principal contracts. An instrument or contract that constitutes indebtedness under general Federal income tax law is not a notional principal contract. An option or forward contract that entitles or obligates a person to enter into a notional principal contract is not a notional principal contract, but payments made under such an option or forward contract may be governed by paragraph (g)(3) of this section.

(v) *Transactions within section 475.*—To the extent that the rules provided in paragraphs (e) and (f) of this section are inconsistent with the rules that apply to any notional principal contract that is governed by section 475 and the regulations thereunder, the rules of section 475 and the regulations thereunder govern.

(vi) *Transactions within section 988*.—To the extent that the rules provided in this section are inconsistent with the rules that apply to any notional principal contract that is also a section 988 transaction or that is integrated with other property or debt pursuant to section 988(d), the rules of section 988 and the regulations thereunder govern. The rules of § 1.446-3(g)(4) are not considered to be inconsistent with the rules of section 988. See § 1.988-2(e)(3)(iv).

(2) *Specified index*.—A specified index may be either a specified financial index or a specified non-financial index.

(i) *Specified financial index*.—A specified financial index is—

(A) A fixed rate, price, or amount;

(B) A fixed rate, price, or amount applicable in one or more specified periods followed by one or more different fixed rates, prices, or amounts applicable in other periods;

(C) An index that is based on objective financial information (as defined in paragraph (c)(4)(ii) of this section); and

(D) An interest rate index that is regularly used in normal lending transactions between a party to the contract and unrelated persons.

(ii) *Specified non-financial index*.—A specified non-financial index is any objectively determinable information that—

(A) Is not within the control of any of the parties to the contract and is not unique to one of the parties' circumstances;

(B) Is not financial information; and

(C) Cannot be reasonably expected to front-load or back-load payments accruing under the contract.

(3) *Notional principal amount*.—For purposes of this section, a notional principal amount is any specified amount of money or property that, when multiplied by either a specified financial index or a specified non-financial index, measures a party's rights and obligations under the contract, but is not borrowed, loaned, or sold between the parties as part of the contract. The notional principal amount may vary over the term of the contract, provided that it is set in advance or varies based on objective financial information (as defined in paragraph (c)(4)(ii) of this section). If a notional principal contract references a notional principal amount that varies, or that references a different notional principal amount for each party, and a principal purpose for entering into the contract is to avoid the application of the rules in this section, the Commissioner may recharacterize the contract according to its substance, including by separating the contract into a series of notional principal contracts for purposes of applying the rules of this section or by treating the contract, in whole or in part, as a loan.

* * *

(5) [Reserved]

(6) *Examples*.—The following examples illustrate the application of paragraph (c) of this section.

Example 1. Forward rate agreement. (i) On January 1, 2012, A enters into a contract with unrelated counterparty B under which on December 31, 2013, A will pay or receive from B, as the case may be, an amount determined by subtracting 6% multiplied by a notional amount of $10 million from 3 month LIBOR on December 31, 2013 multiplied by the same notional amount ((3 month LIBOR × $10,000,000) - (6% × $10,000,000)). The contract provides for no other payments.

(ii) Because this contract provides for a single net payment between A and B determined by interest rates in effect on the settlement date of the contract, the contract is not a notional principal contract defined in § 1.446-3(c)(1)(i).

Example 2. Equity total return contract with dividend adjustments. (i) On January 1, 2012, A enters into a contract with unrelated counterparty B under which on December 31, 2013, A will receive from B an amount equal to the appreciation (if any) on a notional amount of 1 million shares of XYZ common stock, plus any dividends or other distributions that are paid on 1 million shares of XYZ common stock during the term of the contract. In return, on December 31, 2013 A will pay B an amount equal to any depreciation on 1 million shares of XYZ common stock, and an amount equal to 3 month LIBOR multiplied by the notional value of 1 million shares of XYZ stock on January 1, 2012 compounded over the term of the contract. All payments are netted such that A and B are only liable for the net payment due under the contract on December 31, 2013.

(ii) Because both legs of this contract provide for payments that become fixed during the term of the contract (the dividend payments and the LIBOR-based payments), each leg of the contract is treated as providing for more than one payment. In addition, since the indices referenced in the contract are specified indices described in paragraph (c)(2)(i) of this section, and the 1 million shares of XYZ common stock are a notional principal amount described in paragraph (c)(3) of this section, the contract is a notional principal contract defined in § 1.446-3(c)(1)(i).

* * *

[Prop. Reg. § 1.446-3.]

[Proposed 9-16-2011.]

Hedging Transactions

Proposed Amendments to Regulation

§ 1.446-4. Hedging transactions.—(a) *In general*.—Except as provided in this paragraph (a), a hedging transaction as defined in § 1.1221-2(b) (whether or not the character of gain or loss from the transaction is determined under § 1.1221-2) and a bona fide hedging transaction as defined in § 1.954-2(a)(4)(ii) must be accounted for under the rules of this section. * * *

* * *

(g) *Applicability date*.—* * * This section applies to a bona fide hedging transaction (as defined in § 1.954-2(a)(4)(ii)) entered into on or after the date that these regulations are published as final regulations in the *Federal Register*. [Prop. Reg. § 1.446-4.]

[Proposed 12-19-2017.]

Section 482 Adjustments

§ 1.482-1. Allocation of income and deductions among taxpayers.—(a) *In general*.—(1) *Purpose and scope*.—The purpose of section 482 is to ensure that taxpayers clearly reflect income attributable to controlled transactions and to prevent the avoidance of taxes with respect to such transactions. Section 482 places a controlled taxpayer on a tax parity with an uncontrolled taxpayer by determining the true taxable income of the controlled taxpayer. This section sets forth general principles and guidelines to be followed under section 482. Section 1.482-2 provides rules for the determination of the true taxable income of controlled taxpayers in specific situations, including controlled transactions involving loans or advances or the use of tangible property. Sections 1.482-3 through 1.482-6 provide rules for the determination of the true taxable income of controlled taxpayers in cases involving the transfer of property. Section 1.482-7T sets forth the cost sharing provisions applicable to taxable years beginning on or after January 5, 2009. Section 1.482-8 provides examples illustrating the application of the best method rule. Finally, § 1.482-9 provides rules for the determination of the true taxable income of controlled taxpayers in cases involving the performance of services.

(2) *Authority to make allocations*.—The district director may make allocations between or among the members of a controlled group if a controlled taxpayer has not reported its true taxable income. In such case, the district director may allocate income, deductions, credits, allowances, basis, or any other item or element affecting taxable income (referred to as allocations). The appropriate allocation may take the form of an increase or decrease in any relevant amount.

(3) *Taxpayer's use of section 482*.—If necessary to reflect an arm's length result, a controlled taxpayer may report on a timely filed U.S. income tax return (including extensions) the results of its controlled transactions based upon prices different from those actually charged. Except as provided in this paragraph, section 482 grants no other right to a controlled taxpayer to apply the provisions of section 482 at will or to compel the district director to apply such provisions. Therefore, no untimely or amended returns will be permitted to decrease taxable income based on allocations or other adjustments with respect to controlled transactions. See § 1.6662-6T(a)(2) or successor regulations.

(b) *Arm's length standard.*—(1) *In general.*—In determining the true taxable income of a controlled taxpayer, the standard to be applied in every case is that of a taxpayer dealing at arm's length with an uncontrolled taxpayer. A controlled transaction meets the arm's length standard if the results of the transaction are consistent with the results that would have been realized if uncontrolled taxpayers had engaged in the same transaction under the same circumstances (arm's length result). However, because identical transactions can rarely be located, whether a transaction produces an arm's length result generally will be determined by reference to the results of comparable transactions under comparable circumstances. See § 1.482-1(d)(2) (Standard of comparability). Evaluation of whether a controlled transaction produces an arm's length result is made pursuant to a method selected under the best method rule described in § 1.482-1(c).

(2) *Arm's length methods.*—(i) *Methods.*—Sections 1.482-2 through 1.482-7 and 1.482-9 provide specific methods to be used to evaluate whether transactions between or among members of the controlled group satisfy the arm's length standard, and if they do not, to determine the arm's length result. This section provides general principles applicable in determining arm's length results of such controlled transactions, but do not provide methods, for which reference must be made to those other sections in accordance with paragraphs (b)(2)(ii) and (iii) of this section. Section 1.482-7 provides the specific methods to be used to evaluate whether a cost sharing arrangement as defined in § 1.482-7 produces results consistent with an arm's length result.

(ii) *Selection of category of method applicable to transaction.*—The methods listed in § 1.482-2 apply to different types of transactions, such as transfers of property, services, loans or advances, and rentals. Accordingly, the method or methods most appropriate to the calculation of arm's length results for controlled transactions must be selected, and different methods may be applied to interrelated transactions if such transactions are most reliably evaluated on a separate basis. For example, if services are provided in connection with the transfer of property, it may be appropriate to separately apply the methods applicable to services and property in order to determine an arm's length result. But see § 1.482-1(f)(2)(i) (Aggregation of transactions). In addition, other applicable provisions of the Code may affect the characterization of a transaction, and therefore affect the methods applicable under section 482. See for example section 467.

(iii) *Coordination of methods applicable to certain intangible development arrangements.*—Section 1.482-7 provides the specific methods to be used to determine arm's length results of controlled transactions in connection with a cost sharing arrangement as defined in § 1.482-7. Sections 1.482-4 and 1.482-9, as appropriate, provide the specific methods to be used to determine arm's length results of arrangements, including partnerships, for sharing the costs and risks of developing intangibles, other than a cost sharing arrangement covered by § 1.482-7. See also §§ 1.482-4(g) (Coordination with rules governing cost sharing arrangements) and 1.482-9(m)(3) (Coordination with rules governing cost sharing arrangements).

(c) *Best method rule.*—(1) *In general.*—The arm's length result of a controlled transaction must be determined under the method that, under the facts and circumstances, provides the most reliable measure of an arm's length result. Thus, there is no strict priority of methods, and no method will invariably be considered to be more reliable than others. An arm's length result may be determined under any method without establishing the inapplicability of another method, but if another method subsequently is shown to produce a more reliable measure of an arm's length result, such other method must be used. Similarly, if two or more applications of a single method provide inconsistent results, the arm's length result must be determined under the application that, under the facts and circumstances, provides the most reliable measure of an arm's length result. See § 1.482-8 for examples of the application of the best method rule. See § 1.482-7 for the applicable methods in the case of a cost sharing arrangement.

(2) *Determining the best method.*—Data based on the results of transactions between unrelated parties provides the most objective basis for determining whether the results of a controlled transaction are arm's length. Thus, in determining which of two or more available methods (or applications of a single method) provides the most reliable measure of an arm's length result, the two primary factors to take into account are the degree of comparability between the controlled transaction (or taxpayer) and any uncontrolled comparables, and the quality of the data and assumptions used in the analysis. In addition, in certain circumstances, it also may be relevant to consider whether the results of an analysis are consistent with the results of an analysis under another method. These factors are explained in paragraphs (c)(2)(i), (ii), and (iii) of this section.

(i) *Comparability.*—The relative reliability of a method based on the results of transactions between unrelated parties depends on the degree of comparability between the controlled transaction or taxpayers and the uncontrolled comparables, taking into account the factors described in § 1.482-1(d)(3) (Factors for determining comparability), and after making adjustments for differences, as described in § 1.482-1(d)(2) (Standard of comparability). As the degree of comparability increases, the number and extent of potential differences that could render the analysis inaccurate is reduced. In addition, if adjustments are made to increase the degree of comparability, the number, magnitude, and reliability of those adjustments will affect the reliability of the results of the analysis. Thus, an analysis under the comparable uncontrolled price method will generally be more reliable than analyses obtained under other methods if the analysis is based on closely comparable uncontrolled transactions, because such an analysis can be expected to achieve a higher degree of comparability and be susceptible to fewer differences than analyses under other methods. See § 1.482-3(b)(2)(ii)(A). An analysis will be relatively less reliable, however, as the uncontrolled transactions become less comparable to the controlled transaction.

(ii) *Data and assumptions.*—Whether a method provides the most reliable measure of an arm's length result also depends upon the completeness and accuracy of the underlying data, the reliability of the assumptions, and the sensitivity of the results to possible deficiencies in the data and assumptions. Such factors are particularly relevant in evaluating the degree of comparability between the controlled and uncontrolled transactions. These factors are discussed in paragraphs (c)(2)(ii)(A), (B), and (C) of this section.

(A) *Completeness and accuracy of data.*—The completeness and accuracy of the data affects the ability to identify and quantify those factors that would affect the result under any particular method. For example, the completeness and accuracy of data will determine the extent to which it is possible to identify differences between the controlled and uncontrolled transactions, and the reliability of adjustments that are made to account for such differences. An analysis will be relatively more reliable as the completeness and accuracy of the data increases.

(B) *Reliability of assumptions.*—All methods rely on certain assumptions. The reliability of the results derived from a method depends on the soundness of such assumptions. Some assumptions are relatively reliable. For example, adjustments for differences in payment terms between controlled and uncontrolled transactions may be based on the assumption that at arm's length such differences would lead to price differences that reflect the time value of money. Although selection of the appropriate interest rate to use in making such adjustments involves some judgement, the economic analysis on which the assumption is based is relatively sound. Other assumptions may be less reliable. For example, the residual profit split method may be based on the assumption that capitalized intangible development expenses reflect the relative value of the intangible property contributed by each party. Because the costs of developing an intangible may not be related to its market value, the soundness of this assumption will affect the reliability of the results derived from this method.

(C) *Sensitivity of results to deficiencies in data and assumptions.*—Deficiencies in the data used or assumptions made may have a greater effect on some methods than others. In particular, the reliability of some methods is heavily dependent on the similarity of property or services involved in the controlled and uncontrolled transaction. For certain other methods, such as the resale price method, the analysis of the extent to which controlled and uncontrolled taxpayers undertake the same or similar functions, employ similar resources, and bear similar risks is particularly important. Finally, under other methods, such as the profit split method, defining the relevant business activity and appropriate allocation of costs, income, and assets may be of particular importance. Therefore, a difference between the controlled and uncontrolled transactions for which an accurate adjustment cannot be made may have a greater effect on the reliability of the results derived under one method than the results derived under another method. For example, differences in management efficiency may have a greater effect on a comparable profits method analysis than on a comparable uncontrolled price method analysis, while differences in product characteristics will ordinarily have a greater effect on a comparable uncontrolled price method analysis than on a comparable profits method analysis.

(iii) *Confirmation of results by another method.*—If two or more methods produce inconsistent results, the best method rule will be applied to select the method that provides the most reliable measure of an arm's length result. If the best method rule does not clearly indicate which method should be selected, an additional factor that may be taken into account in selecting a method is whether any of the competing methods produce results that are consistent with the results obtained from the appropriate application of another method. Further, in evaluating different applications of the same method, the fact that a second method (or another application of the first method) produces results that are consistent with one of the competing applications may be taken into account.

(d) *Comparability.*—(1) *In general.*—Whether a controlled transaction produces an arm's length result is generally evaluated by comparing the results of that transaction to results realized by uncontrolled taxpayers engaged in comparable transactions under comparable circumstances. For this purpose, the comparability of transactions and circumstances must be evaluated considering all factors that could affect prices or profits in arm's length dealings (comparability factors). While a specific comparability factor may be of particular importance in applying a method, each method requires analysis of all of the factors that affect comparability under that method. Such factors include the following—

(i) Functions;
(ii) Contractual terms;
(iii) Risks;
(iv) Economic conditions; and
(v) Property or services.

(2) *Standard of comparability.*—In order to be considered comparable to a controlled transaction, an uncontrolled transaction need not be identical to the controlled transaction, but must be sufficiently similar that it provides a reliable measure of an arm's length result. If there are material differences between the controlled and uncontrolled transactions, adjustments must be made if the effect of such differences on prices or profits can be ascertained with sufficient accuracy to improve the reliability of the results. For purposes of this section, a material difference is one that would materially affect the measure of an arm's length result under the method being applied. If adjustments for material differences cannot be made, the uncontrolled transaction may be used as a measure of an arm's length result, but the reliability of the analysis will be reduced. Generally, such adjustments must be made to the results of the uncontrolled comparable and must be based on commercial practices, economic principles, or statistical analyses. The extent and reliability of any adjustments will affect the relative reliability of the analysis. See § 1.482-1(c)(1) (Best method rule). In any event, unadjusted industry average returns themselves cannot establish arm's length results.

(3) *Factors for determining comparability.*—The comparability factors listed in § 1.482-1(d)(1) are discussed in this section. Each of these factors must be considered in determining the degree of comparability between transactions or taxpayers and the extent to which comparability adjustments may be necessary. In addition, in certain cases involving special circumstances, the rules under paragraph (d)(4) of this section must be considered.

(i) *Functional analysis.*—Determining the degree of comparability between controlled and uncontrolled transactions requires a comparison of the functions performed, and associated resources employed, by the taxpayers in each transaction. This comparison is based on a functional analysis that identifies and compares the economically significant activities undertaken, or to be undertaken, by the taxpayers in both controlled and uncontrolled transactions. A functional analysis should also include consideration of the resources that are employed, or to be employed, in conjunction with the activities undertaken, including consideration of the type of assets used, such as plant and equipment, or the use of valuable intangibles. A functional analysis is not a pricing method and does not itself determine the arm's length result for the controlled transaction under review. Functions that may need to be accounted for in determining the comparability of two transactions include—

(A) Research and development;
(B) Product design and engineering;
(C) Manufacturing, production and process engineering;
(D) Product fabrication, extraction, and assembly;
(E) Purchasing and materials management;
(F) Marketing and distribution functions, including inventory management, warranty administration, and advertising activities;
(G) Transportation and warehousing; and
(H) Managerial, legal, accounting and finance, credit and collection, training, and personnel management services.

(ii) *Contractual terms.*—(A) *In general.*—Determining the degree of comparability between the controlled and uncontrolled transactions requires a comparison of the significant contractual terms that could affect the results of the two transactions. These terms include—

(1) The form of consideration charged or paid;
(2) Sales or purchase volume;
(3) The scope and terms of warranties provided;
(4) Rights to updates, revisions or modifications;
(5) The duration of relevant license, contract or other agreements, and termination or renegotiation rights;
(6) Collateral transactions or ongoing business relationships between the buyer and the seller, including arrangements for the provision of ancillary or subsidiary services; and
(7) Extension of credit and payment terms. Thus, for example, if the time for payment of the amount charged in a controlled transaction differs from the time for payment of the amount charged in an uncontrolled transaction, an adjustment to reflect the difference in payment terms should be made if such difference would have a material effect on price. Such comparability adjustment is required even if no interest would be allocated or imputed under § 1.482-2(a) or other applicable provisions of the Internal Revenue Code or regulations.

(B) *Identifying contractual terms.*—*(1) Written agreement.*—The contractual terms, including the consequent allocation of risks, that are agreed to in writing before the transactions are entered into will be respected if such terms are consistent with the economic substance of the underlying transactions. In evaluating economic substance, greatest weight will be given to the actual conduct of the parties, and the respective legal rights of the parties (see, for example, § 1.482-4(f)(3) (Ownership of intangible property)). If the contractual terms are inconsistent with the economic substance of the underlying transaction, the district director may disregard such terms and impute terms that are consistent with the economic substance of the transaction.

(2) No written agreement.—In the absence of a written agreement, the district director may impute a contractual agreement between the controlled taxpayers consistent with the economic substance of the transaction. In determining the economic substance of the transaction, greatest weight will be given to the actual conduct of the parties and their respective legal rights (see, for example, § 1.482-4(f)(3) (Ownership of intangible property)). For example, if, without a written agreement, a controlled taxpayer operates at full capacity and regularly sells all of its output to another member of its controlled group, the district director may impute a purchasing contract from the course of conduct of the controlled taxpayers, and determine that the producer bears little risk that the buyer will fail to purchase its full output. Further, if an established industry convention or usage of trade assigns a risk or resolves an issue, that convention or usage will be followed if the conduct of the taxpayers is consistent with it. See UCC § 1-205. For example, unless otherwise agreed, payment generally is due at the time and place at which the buyer is to receive goods. See UCC § 2-310.

(C) *Examples.*—The following examples illustrate this paragraph (d)(3)(ii).

Example 1—Differences in volume. USP, a United States agricultural exporter, regularly buys transportation services from FSub, its foreign subsidiary, to ship its products from the United States to overseas markets. Although FSub occasionally provides transportation services to URA, an unrelated domestic corporation, URA accounts for only 10% of the gross revenues of FSub, and the remaining 90% of FSub's gross revenues are attributable to FSub's transactions with USP. In determining the degree of comparability between FSub's uncontrolled transaction with URA and its controlled transaction with USP, the difference in volumes involved in the two transactions and the regularity with which these services are provided must be taken into account if such difference would have a material effect on the price charged. Inability to make reliable adjustments for these differences would affect the reliability of the results derived from the uncontrolled transaction as a measure of the arm's length result.

Example 2—Reliability of adjustment for differences in volume. (i) FS manufactures product XX and sells that product to its parent corporation, P. FS also sells product XX to uncontrolled taxpayers at a price of $100 per unit. Except for the volume of each transaction, the sales to P and to uncontrolled taxpayers take place under substantially the same economic conditions and contractual terms. In uncontrolled transactions, FS offers a 2% discount for quantities of 20 per order, and a 5% discount for quantities of 100 per order. If P purchases product XX in quantities of 60 per order, in the absence of other reliable information, it may reasonably be concluded that the arm's length price to P would be $100, less a discount of 3.5%.

(ii) If P purchases product XX in quantities of 1,000 per order, a reliable estimate of the appropriate volume discount must be based on proper economic or statistical analysis, not necessarily a linear extrapolation from the 2% and 5% catalog discounts applicable to sales of 20 and 100 units, respectively.

Example 3—Contractual terms imputed from economic substance. (i) FP, a foreign producer of wristwatches, is the registered holder of the YY trademark in the United States and in other countries worldwide. In year 1, FP enters the United States market by selling YY wristwatches to its newly organized United States subsidiary, USSub, for distribution in the United States market. USSub pays FP a fixed price per wristwatch. USSub and FP undertake, without separate compensation, marketing activities to establish the YY trademark in the United States market. Unrelated foreign producers of trademarked wristwatches and their authorized United States distributors respectively undertake similar marketing activities in independent arrangements involving distribution of trademarked wristwatches in the United States market. In years 1 through 6, USSub markets and sells YY wristwatches in the United States. Further, in years 1 through 6, USSub undertakes incremental marketing activities in addition to the activities similar to those observed in the independent distribution transactions in the United States market. FP does not directly or indirectly compensate USSub for performing these incremental activities during years 1 through 6. Assume that, aside from these incremental activities, and after any adjustments are made to improve the reliability of the comparison, the price paid per wristwatch by the independent, authorized distributors of wristwatches would provide the most reliable measure of the arm's length price paid per YY wristwatch by USSub.

(ii) By year 7, the wristwatches with the YY trademark generate a premium return in the United States market, as compared to wristwatches marketed by the independent distributors. In year 7, substantially all the premium return from the YY trademark in the United States market is attributed to FP, for example through an increase in the price paid per watch by USSub, or by some other means.

(iii) In determining whether an allocation of income is appropriate in year 7, the Commissioner may consider the economic substance of the arrangements between USSub and FP, and the parties' course of conduct throughout their relationship. Based on this analysis, the Commissioner determines that it is unlikely that, ex ante, an uncontrolled taxpayer operating at arm's length would engage in the incremental marketing activities to develop or enhance intangible property owned by another party unless it received contemporaneous compensation or otherwise had a reasonable anticipation of receiving a future benefit from those activities. In this case, USSub's undertaking the incremental marketing activities in years 1 through 6 is a course of conduct that is inconsistent with the parties' attribution to FP in year 7 of substantially all the premium return from the enhanced YY trademark in the United States market. Therefore, the Commissioner may impute one or more agreements between USSub and FP, consistent with the economic substance of their course of conduct, which would afford USSub an appropriate portion of the premium return from the YY trademark wristwatches. For example, the Commissioner may impute a separate services agreement that affords USSub contingent-payment compensation for its incremental marketing activities in years 1 through 6, which benefited FP by contributing to the value of the trademark owned by FP. In the alternative, the Commissioner may impute a long-term, exclusive agreement to exploit the YY trademark in the United States that allows USSub to benefit from the incremental marketing activities it performed. As another alternative, the Commissioner may require FP to compensate USSub for terminating USSub's imputed long-term, exclusive agreement to exploit the YY trademark in the United States, an agreement that USSub made more valuable at its own expense and risk. The taxpayer may present additional facts that could indicate which of these or other alternative agreements best reflects the economic substance of the underlying transactions, consistent with the parties' course of conduct in the particular case.

Example 4—Contractual terms imputed from economic substance. (i) FP, a foreign producer of athletic gear, is the registered holder of the AA trademark in the United States and in other countries worldwide. In year 1, FP enters into a licensing agreement that affords its newly organized United States subsidiary, USSub, exclusive rights to certain manufacturing and marketing intangible property (including the AA trademark) for purposes of manufacturing and marketing athletic gear in the United States under the AA trademark. The contractual terms of this agreement obligate USSub to pay FP a royalty based on sales, and also obligate both FP and USSub to undertake without separate compensation specified types and levels of marketing activities. Unrelated foreign businesses license independent United States businesses to manufacture and market athletic gear in the United States, using trademarks owned by the unrelated foreign businesses. The contractual terms of these uncontrolled transactions require the licensees to pay royalties based on sales of the merchandise, and obligate the licensors and licensees to undertake without separate compensation specified types and levels of marketing activities. In years 1 through 6, USSub manufactures and sells athletic gear under the AA trademark in the United States. Assume that, after adjustments are made to improve the reliability of the comparison for any material differences relating to marketing activities, manufacturing or marketing intangible property, and other comparability factors, the royalties paid by independent licensees would provide the most reliable measure of the arm's length royalty owed by USSub to FP, apart from the additional facts in paragraph (ii) of this *Example 4*.

(ii) In years 1 through 6, USSub performs incremental marketing activities with respect to the AA trademark athletic gear, in addition to the activities required under the terms of the license agreement with FP, that are also incremental as compared to those observed in the comparables. FP does not directly or indirectly compensate USSub for performing these incremental activities during years 1 through 6. By year 7, AA trademark athletic gear generates a premium return in the United States, as compared to similar athletic gear marketed by independent licensees. In year 7, USSub and FP enter into a separate services agreement under which FP agrees to compensate USSub on a cost basis for the incremental marketing activities that USSub performed during years 1 through 6, and to compensate USSub on a cost basis for any incremental marketing activities it may perform in year 7 and subsequent years. In addition, the parties revise the license agreement executed in year 1, and increase the royalty to a level that attributes to FP substantially all the premium return from sales of the AA trademark athletic gear in the United States.

(iii) In determining whether an allocation of income is appropriate in year 7, the Commissioner may consider the economic substance of the arrangements between USSub and FP and the parties' course of conduct throughout their relationship. Based on this analysis, the Commissioner determines that it is unlikely that, ex ante, an uncontrolled taxpayer operating at arm's length would engage in the incremental marketing activities to develop or enhance intangible property owned by another party unless it received contemporaneous compensation or otherwise had a reasonable anticipation of a future benefit. In this case, USSub's undertaking the incremental marketing activities in years 1 through 6 is a course of conduct that is inconsistent with the parties' adoption in year 7 of contractual terms by which FP compensates USSub on a cost basis for the incremental marketing activities that it performed. Therefore, the Commissioner may impute one or more agreements between USSub and FP, consistent with the economic substance of their course of conduct, which would afford USSub an appropriate portion of the premium return from the AA trademark athletic gear. For example, the Commissioner may impute a separate services agreement that affords USSub contingent-payment compensation for the incremental activities it performed during years 1 through 6, which benefited FP by contributing to the value of the trademark owned by FP. In the alternative, the Commissioner may impute a longterm, exclusive United States license agreement that allows USSub to benefit from the incremental activities. As another alternative, the Commissioner may require FP to compensate USSub for terminating USSub's imputed long-term United States license agreement, a license that USSub made more valuable at its own expense and risk. The taxpayer may present additional facts that could indicate which of these or other alternative agreements best reflects the economic substance of the underlying transactions, consistent with the parties' course of conduct in this particular case.

Example 5—Non-arm's length compensation. (i) The facts are the same as in paragraph (i) of *Example 4*. As in *Example 4*, assume that, after adjustments are made to improve the reliability of the comparison for any material differences relating to marketing activities, manufacturing or marketing intangible property, and other comparability factors, the royalties paid by independent licensees would provide the most reliable measure of the arm's length royalty owed by USSub to FP, apart from the additional facts described in paragraph (ii) of this *Example 5.*

(ii) In years 1 through 4, USSub performs certain incremental marketing activities with respect to the AA trademark athletic gear, in addition to the activities required under the terms of the basic license agreement, that are also incremental as compared with those activities observed in the comparables. At the start of year 1, FP enters into a separate services agreement with USSub, which states that FP will compensate USSub quarterly, in an amount equal to specified costs plus X%, for these incremental marketing functions. Further, these written agreements reflect the intent of the parties that USSub receive such compensation from FP throughout the term of the agreement, without regard to the success or failure of the promotional activities. During years 1 through 4, USSub performs marketing activities pursuant to the separate services agreement and in each year USSub receives the specified compensation from FP on a cost of services plus basis.

(iii) In evaluating year 4, the Commissioner performs an analysis of independent parties that perform promotional activities comparable to those performed by USSub and that receive separately-stated compensation on a current basis without contingency. The Commissioner determines that the magnitude of the specified cost plus X% is outside the arm's length range in each of years 1 through 4. Based on an evaluation of all the facts and circumstances, the Commissioner makes an allocation to require payment of compensation to USSub for the promotional activities performed in year 4, based on the median of the interquartile range of the arm's length markups charged by the uncontrolled comparables described in paragraph (e)(3) of this section.

(iv) Given that based on facts and circumstances, the terms agreed by the controlled parties were that FP would bear all risks associated with the promotional activities performed by USSub to promote the AA trademark product in the United States market, and given that the parties' conduct during the years examined was consistent with this allocation of risk, the fact that the cost of services plus markup on USSub's services was outside the arm's length range does not, without more, support imputation of additional contractual terms based on alternative views of the economic substance of the transaction, such as terms indicating that USSub, rather than FP, bore the risk associated with these activities.

Example 6—Contractual terms imputed from economic substance. (i) Company X is a member of a controlled group that has been in operation in the pharmaceutical sector for many years. In years 1 through 4, Company X undertakes research and development activities. As a result of those activities, Company X developed a compound that may be more effective than existing medications in the treatment of certain conditions.

(ii) Company Y is acquired in year 4 by the controlled group that includes Company X. Once Company Y is acquired, Company X makes available to Company Y a large amount of technical data concerning the new compound, which Company Y uses to register patent rights with respect to the compound in several jurisdictions, making Company Y the legal owner of such patents. Company Y then enters into licensing agreements with group members that afford Company Y 100% of the premium return attributable to use of the intangible property by its subsidiaries.

(iii) In determining whether an allocation is appropriate in year 4, the Commissioner may consider the economic substance of the arrangements between Company X and Company Y, and the parties' course of conduct throughout their relationship. Based on this analysis, the Commissioner determines that it is unlikely that an uncontrolled taxpayer operating at arm's length would make available the results of its research and development or perform services that resulted in transfer of valuable know how to another party unless it received contemporaneous compensation or otherwise had a reasonable anticipation of receiving a future benefit from those activities. In this case, Company X's undertaking the research and development activities and then providing technical data and know-how to Company Y in year 4 is inconsistent with the registration and subsequent exploitation of the patent by Company Y. Therefore, the Commissioner may impute one or more agreements between Company X and Company Y consistent with the economic substance of their course of conduct, which would afford Company X an appropriate portion of the premium return from the patent rights. For example, the Commissioner may impute a separate services agreement that affords Company X contingent-payment compensation for its services in year 4 for the benefit of Company Y, consisting of making available to Company Y technical data, know-how, and other fruits of research and development conducted in previous years. These services benefited Company Y by giving rise to and contributing to the value of the patent rights that were ultimately registered by Company Y. In the alternative, the Commissioner may impute a transfer of patentable intangible property rights from Company X to Company Y immediately preceding the registration of patent rights by Company Y. The taxpayer may present additional facts that could indicate which of these or other alternative agreements best reflects the economic substance of the underlying transactions, consistent with the parties' course of conduct in the particular case.

(iii) *Risk.*—(A) *Comparability.*—Determining the degree of comparability between controlled and uncontrolled transactions requires a comparison of the significant risks that could affect the prices that would be charged or paid, or the profit that would be earned, in the two transactions. Relevant risks to consider include—

(1) Market risks, including fluctuations in cost, demand, pricing, and inventory levels;

(2) Risks associated with the success or failure of research and development activities;

(3) Financial risks, including fluctuations in foreign currency rates of exchange and interest rates;

(4) Credit and collection risks;

(5) Product liability risks; and

(6) General business risks related to the ownership of property, plant, and equipment.

(B) *Identification of taxpayer that bears risk.*—In general, the determination of which controlled taxpayer bears a particular risk will be made in accordance with the provisions of § 1.482-1(d)(3)(ii)(B) (Identifying contractual terms). Thus, the allocation of risks specified or implied by the taxpayer's contractual terms will generally be respected if it is consistent with the economic substance of the transaction. An allocation of risk between controlled taxpayers after the outcome of such risk is known or reasonably knowable lacks economic substance. In considering the economic substance of the transaction, the following facts are relevant—

(1) Whether the pattern of the controlled taxpayer's conduct over time is consistent with the purported allocation of risk between the controlled taxpayers; or where the pattern is changed, whether the relevant contractual arrangements have been modified accordingly;

(2) Whether a controlled taxpayer has the financial capacity to fund losses that might be expected to occur as the result of the assumption of a risk, or whether, at arm's length, another party to the controlled transaction would ultimately suffer the consequences of such losses; and

(3) The extent to which each controlled taxpayer exercises managerial or operational control over the business activities that directly influence the amount of income or loss realized. In arm's length dealings, parties ordinarily bear a greater share of those risks over which they have relatively more control.

(C) *Examples.*—The following examples illustrate this paragraph (d)(3)(iii).

Example 1. FD, the wholly-owned foreign distributor of USM, a U.S. manufacturer, buys widgets from USM under a written contract. Widgets are a generic electronic appliance. Under the terms of the contract, FD must buy and take title to 20,000 widgets for each of the five years of the contract at a price of $10 per widget. The widgets will be sold under FD's label, and FD must finance any marketing strategies to promote sales in the foreign market. There are no rebate or buy back provisions. FD has adequate financial capacity to fund its obligations under the contract under any circumstances that could reasonably be expected to arise. In Years 1, 2 and 3, FD sold only 10,000 widgets at a price of $11 per unit. In Year 4, FD sold its entire inventory of widgets at a price of $25 per unit. Since the contractual terms allocating market risk were agreed to before the outcome of such risk was known or reasonably knowable, FD had the financial capacity to bear the market risk that it would be unable to sell all of the widgets it purchased currently, and its conduct was consistent over time, FD will be deemed to bear the risk.

Example 2. The facts are the same as in *Example 1,* except that in Year 1 FD had only $100,000 in total capital, including loans. In subsequent years USM makes no additional contributions to the capital of FD, and FD is unable to obtain any capital through loans from an unrelated party. Nonetheless, USM continues to sell 20,000 widgets annually to FD under the terms of the contract, and USM extends credit to FD to enable it to finance the purchase. FD does not have the financial capacity in Years 1, 2 and 3 to finance the purchase of the widgets given that it could not sell most of the widgets it purchased during those years. Thus, notwithstanding the terms of the contract, USM and not FD assumed the market risk that a substantial portion of the widgets could not be sold, since in that event FD would not be able to pay USM for all of the widgets it purchased.

Example 3. S, a Country X corporation, manufactures small motors that it sells to P, its U.S. parent. P incorporates the motors into various products and sells those products to uncontrolled customers in the United States. The contract price for the motors is expressed in U.S. dollars, effectively allocating the currency risk for these transactions to S for any currency fluctuations between the time the contract is signed and payment is made. As long as S has adequate financial capacity to bear this currency risk (including by hedging all or part of the risk) and the conduct of S and P is consistent with the terms of the contract (i.e., the contract price is not adjusted to reflect exchange rate movements), the agreement of the parties to allocate the exchange risk to S will be respected.

Example 4. USSub is the wholly-owned U.S. subsidiary of FP, a foreign manufacturer. USSub acts as a distributor of goods manufactured by FP. FP and USSub execute an agreement providing that FP will bear any ordinary product liability costs arising from defects in the goods manufactured by FP. In practice, however, when ordinary product liability claims are sustained against USSub and FP, USSub pays the resulting damages. Therefore, the district director disregards the contractual arrangement regarding product liability costs between FP and USSub, and treats the risk as having been assumed by USSub.

(iv) *Economic conditions.*—Determining the degree of comparability between controlled and uncontrolled transactions requires a comparison of the significant economic conditions that could affect the prices that would be charged or paid, or the profit that would be earned in each of the transactions. These factors include—

(A) The similarity of geographic markets;

(B) The relative size of each market, and the extent of the overall economic development in each market;

(C) The level of the market (e.g., wholesale, retail, etc.);

(D) The relevant market shares for the products, properties, or services transferred or provided;

(E) The location-specific costs of the factors of production and distribution;

(F) The extent of competition in each market with regard to the property or services under review;

(G) The economic condition of the particular industry, including whether the market is in contraction or expansion; and

(H) The alternatives realistically available to the buyer and seller.

(v) *Property or services.*—Evaluating the degree of comparability between controlled and uncontrolled transactions requires a comparison of the property or services transferred in the transactions. This comparison may include any intangible property that is embedded in tangible property or services being transferred (embedded intangibles). The comparability of the embedded intangibles will be analyzed using the factors listed in § 1.482-4(c)(2)(iii)(B)(1) (comparable intangible property). The relevance of product comparability in evaluating the relative reliability of the results will depend on the method applied. For guidance concerning the specific comparability considerations applicable to transfers of tangible and intangible property and performance of services, *see* § § 1.482-3 through 1.482-6 and § 1.482-9; *see also* § § 1.482-3(f), 1.482-4(f)(4), and 1.482-9(m), dealing with the coordination of intangible and tangible property and performance of services rules.

(4) *Special circumstances.*—(i) *Market share strategy.*—In certain circumstances, taxpayers may adopt strategies to enter new markets or to increase a product's share of an existing market (market share strategy). Such a strategy would be reflected by temporarily increased market development expenses or resale prices that are temporarily lower than the prices charged for comparable products in the same market. Whether or not the strategy is reflected in the transfer price depends on which party to the controlled transaction bears the costs of the pricing strategy. In any case, the effect of a market share strategy on a controlled transaction will be taken into account only if it can be shown that an uncontrolled taxpayer engaged in a comparable strategy under comparable circumstances for a comparable period of time, and the taxpayer provides documentation that substantiates the following—

(A) The costs incurred to implement the market share strategy are borne by the controlled taxpayer that would obtain the future profits that result from the strategy, and there is a reasonable likelihood that the strategy will result in future profits that reflect an appropriate return in relation to the costs incurred to implement it;

(B) The market share strategy is pursued only for a period of time that is reasonable, taking into consideration the industry and product in question; and

(C) The market share strategy, the related costs and expected returns, and any agreement between the controlled taxpayers to share the related costs, were established before the strategy was implemented.

(ii) *Different geographic markets.*—(A) *In general.*—Uncontrolled comparables ordinarily should be derived from the geographic market in which the controlled taxpayer operates, because there may be significant differences in economic conditions in different markets. If information from the same market is not available, an uncontrolled comparable derived from a different geographic market may be considered if adjustments are made to account for differences between the two markets. If information permitting adjustments for such differences is not available, then information derived from uncontrolled comparables in the most similar market for which reliable data is available may be used, but the extent of such differences may affect the reliability of the method for purposes of the best method rule. For this purpose, a geographic market is any geographic area in which the economic conditions for the relevant product or service are substantially the same, and may include multiple countries, depending on the economic conditions.

(B) *Example.*—The following example illustrates this paragraph (d)(4)(ii).

Example. Manuco, a wholly-owned foreign subsidiary of P, a U.S. corporation, manufactures products in Country Z for sale to P. No uncontrolled transactions are located that would provide a reliable measure of the arm's length result under the comparable uncontrolled price method. The district director considers applying the cost plus method or the comparable profits method. Information on uncontrolled taxpayers performing comparable functions under comparable circumstances in the same geographic market is not available. Therefore, adjusted data from uncontrolled manufacturers in other markets may be considered in order to apply the cost plus method. In this case, comparable uncontrolled manufacturers are found in the United States. Accordingly, data from the comparable U.S. uncontrolled manufacturers, as adjusted to account for differences between the United States and Country Z's geographic market, is used to test the arm's length price paid by P to Manuco. However, the use of such data may affect the reliability of the results for purposes of the best method rule. See § 1.482-1(c).

(C) *Location savings.*—If an uncontrolled taxpayer operates in a different geographic market than the controlled taxpayer, adjustments may be necessary to account for significant differences in costs attributable to the geographic markets. These adjustments must be based on the effect such differences would have on the consideration charged or paid in the controlled transaction given the relative competitive positions of buyers and sellers in each market. Thus, for example, the fact that the total costs of operating in a controlled manufacturer's geographic market are less than the total costs of operating in other markets ordinarily justifies higher profits to the manufacturer only if the cost differences would increase the profits of comparable uncontrolled manufacturers operating at arm's length, given the competitive positions of buyers and sellers in that market.

(D) *Example.*—The following example illustrates the principles of this paragraph (d)(4)(ii)(C).

Example. Couture, a U.S. apparel design corporation, contracts with Sewco, its wholly owned Country Y subsidiary, to manufacture its clothes. Costs of operating in Country Y are significantly lower than the operating costs in the United States. Although clothes with the Couture label sell for a premium price, the actual production of the clothes does not require significant specialized knowledge that could not be acquired by actual or potential competitors to Sewco at reasonable cost. Thus, Sewco's functions could be performed by several actual or potential competitors to Sewco in geographic markets that are similar to Country Y. Thus, the fact that production is less costly in Country Y will not, in and of itself, justify additional profits derived from lower operating costs in Country Y inuring to Sewco, because the competitive positions of the other actual or potential producers in similar geographic markets capable of performing the same functions at the same low costs indicate that at arm's length such profits would not be retained by Sewco.

(iii) *Transactions ordinarily not accepted as comparables.*—(A) *In general.*—Transactions ordinarily will not constitute reliable measures of an arm's length result for purposes of this section if—

(1) They are not made in the ordinary course of business; or

(2) One of the principal purposes of the uncontrolled transaction was to establish an arm's length result with respect to the controlled transaction.

(B) *Examples.*—The following examples illustrate the principle of this paragraph (d)(4)(iii).

Example 1—Not in the ordinary course of business. USP, a United States manufacturer of computer software, sells its products to FSub, its foreign distributor in country X. Compco, a United States competitor of USP, also sells its products in X through unrelated distributors. However, in the year under review, Compco is forced into bankruptcy, and Compco liquidates its inventory by selling all of its products to unrelated distributors in X for a liquidation price. Because the sale of its entire inventory was not a sale in the ordinary course of business, Compco's sale cannot be used as an uncontrolled comparable to determine USP's arm's length result from its controlled transaction.

Example 2—Principal purpose of establishing an arm's length result. USP, a United States manufacturer of farm machinery, sells its products to FSub, its wholly-owned distributor in Country Y. USP, operating at nearly full capacity, sells 95% of its inventory to FSub. To make use of its excess capacity, and also to establish a comparable uncontrolled price for its transfer price to FSub, USP increases its production to full capacity. USP sells its excess inventory to Compco, an unrelated foreign distributor in Country X. Country X has approximately the same economic conditions as that of Country Y. Because one of the principal purposes of selling to Compco was to establish an arm's length price for its controlled transactions with FSub, USP's sale to Compco cannot be used as an uncontrolled comparable to determine USP's arm's length result from its controlled transaction.

(e) *Arm's length range.*—(1) *In general.*—In some cases, application of a pricing method will produce a single result that is the most reliable measure of an arm's length result. In other cases, application of a method may produce a number of results from which a range of reliable results may be derived. A taxpayer will not be subject to adjustment if its results fall within such range (arm's length range).

(2) *Determination of arm's length range.*—(i) *Single method.*—The arm's length range is ordinarily determined by applying a single pricing method selected under the best method rule to two or more uncontrolled transactions of similar comparability and reliability. Use of more than one method may be appropriate for the purposes described in paragraph (c)(2)(iii) of this section (Best method rule).

(ii) *Selection of comparables.*—Uncontrolled comparables must be selected based upon the comparability criteria relevant to the method applied and must be sufficiently similar to the controlled transaction that they provide a reliable measure of an arm's length result. If material differences exist between the controlled and uncontrolled transactions, adjustments must be made to the results of the uncontrolled transaction if the effect of such differences on price or profits can be ascertained with sufficient accuracy to improve the reliability of the results. See § 1.482-1(d)(2) (Standard of comparability). The arm's length range will be derived only from those uncontrolled comparables that have, or through adjustments can be brought to, a similar level of comparability and reliability, and uncontrolled comparables that have a significantly lower level of comparability and reliability will not be used in establishing the arm's length range.

(iii) *Comparables included in arm's length range.*—(A) *In general.*—The arm's length range will consist of the results of all of the uncontrolled comparables that meet the following conditions: the information on the controlled transaction and the uncontrolled comparables is sufficiently complete that it is likely that all material differences have been identified, each such difference has a definite and reasonably ascertainable effect on price or profit, and an adjustment is made to eliminate the effect of each such difference.

(B) *Adjustment of range to increase reliability.*—If there are no uncontrolled comparables described in paragraph (e)(2)(iii)(A) of this section, the arm's length range is derived from the results of all the uncontrolled comparables, selected pursuant to paragraph (e)(2)(ii) of this section, that achieve a similar level of comparability and reliability. In such cases the reliability of the analysis must be increased, where it is possible to do so, by adjusting the range through application of a valid statistical method to the results of all of the uncontrolled comparables so selected. The reliability of the analysis is increased when statistical methods are used to establish a range of results in which the limits of the range will be determined such that there is a 75 percent probability of a result falling above the lower end of the range and a 75 percent probability of a result falling below the upper end of the range. The interquartile range ordinarily provides an acceptable measure of this range; however a different statistical method may be applied if it provides a more reliable measure.

(C) *Interquartile range.*—For purposes of this section, the interquartile range is the range from the 25th to the 75th percentile of the results derived from the uncontrolled comparables. For this purpose, the 25th percentile is the lowest result derived from an uncontrolled comparable such that at least 25 percent of the results are at or below the value of that result. However, if exactly 25 percent of the results are at or below a result, then the 25th percentile is equal to the average of that result and the next higher result derived from the uncontrolled comparables. The 75th percentile is determined analogously.

(3) *Adjustment if taxpayer's results are outside arm's length range.*—If the results of a controlled transaction fall outside the arm's length range, the district director may make allocations that adjust the controlled taxpayer's result to any point within the arm's length range. If the interquartile range is used to determine the arm's length range, such adjustment will ordinarily be to the median of all the results. The median is the 50th percentile of the results, which is determined in a manner analogous to that described in paragraph (e)(2)(iii)(C) of this section (Interquartile range). In other cases, an adjustment normally will be made to the arithmetic mean of all the results. See § 1.482-1(f)(2)(iii)(D) for determination of an adjustment when a controlled taxpayer's result for a multiple year period falls outside an arm's length range consisting of the average results of uncontrolled comparables over the same period.

(4) *Arm's length range not prerequisite to allocation.*—The rules of this paragraph (e) do not require that the district director establish an arm's length range prior to making an allocation under section 482. Thus, for example, the district director may properly propose an allocation on the basis of a single comparable uncontrolled price if the comparable uncontrolled price method, as described in § 1.482-3(b), has been properly applied. However, if the taxpayer subsequently demonstrates that the results claimed on its income tax return are within the range established by additional equally reliable comparable uncontrolled prices in a manner consistent with the requirements set forth in § 1.482-1(e)(2)(iii), then no allocation will be made.

(5) *Examples.*—The following examples illustrate the principles of this paragraph (e).

Example 1—Selection of comparables. (i) To evaluate the arm's length result of a controlled transaction between USSub, the United States taxpayer under review, and FP, its foreign parent, the district director considers applying the resale price method. The district director identifies ten potential uncontrolled transactions. The distributors in all ten uncontrolled transactions purchase and resell similar products and perform similar functions to those of USSub.

(ii) Data with respect to three of the uncontrolled transactions is very limited, and although some material differences can be identified and adjusted for, the level of comparability of these three uncontrolled comparables is significantly lower than that of the other seven. Further, of those seven, adjustments for the identified material differences can be reliably made for only four of the uncontrolled transactions. Therefore, pursuant to § 1.482-1(e)(2)(ii) only these four uncontrolled comparables may be used to establish an arm's length range.

Example 2—Arm's length range consists of all the results. (i) The facts are the same as in *Example 1*. Applying the resale price method to the four uncontrolled comparables, and making adjustments to the uncontrolled comparables pursuant to § 1.482-1(d)(2), the district director derives the following results:

Comparable	*Result ($ price)*
1	44.00
2	45.00
3	45.00
4	45.50

(ii) The district director determines that data regarding the four uncontrolled transactions is sufficiently complete and accurate so that it is likely that all material differences between the controlled and uncontrolled transactions have been identified, such differences have a definite and reasonably ascertainable effect, and appropriate adjustments were made for such differences. Accordingly, if the resale price method is determined to be the best method pursuant to § 1.482-1(c), the arm's length range for the controlled transaction will consist of the results of all of the uncontrolled comparables, pursuant to paragraph (e)(2)(iii)(A) of this section. Thus, the arm's length range in this case would be the range from $44 to $45.50.

Example 3—Arm's length range limited to interquartile range. (i) The facts are the same as in *Example 2*, except in this case there are some product and functional differences between the four uncontrolled comparables and USSub. However, the data is insufficiently complete to determine the effect of the differences. Applying the resale price method to the four uncontrolled comparables, and making adjustments to the uncontrolled comparables pursuant to § 1.482-1(d)(2), the district director derives the following results:

Uncontrolled Comparable	*Result ($ price)*
1	42.00
2	44.00
3	45.00
4	47.50

(ii) It cannot be established in this case that all material differences are likely to have been identified and reliable adjustments made for those differences. Accordingly, if the resale price method is determined to be the best method pursuant to § 1.482-1(c), the arm's length range for the controlled transaction must be established pursuant to paragraph (e)(2)(iii)(B) of this section. In this case, the district director uses the interquartile range to determine the arm's length range, which is the range from $43 to $46.25. If USSub's price falls outside this range, the district director may make an allocation. In this case that allocation would be to the median of the results, or $44.50.

Example 4—Arm's length range limited to interquartile range. (i) To evaluate the arm's length result of controlled transactions between USP, a United States manufacturing company, and FSub, its foreign subsidiary, the district director considers applying the comparable profits method. The district director identifies 50 uncontrolled taxpayers within the same industry that potentially could be used to apply the method.

(ii) Further review indicates that only 20 of the uncontrolled manufacturers engage in activities requiring similar capital investments and technical know-how. Data with respect to five of the uncontrolled manufacturers is very limited, and although some material differences can be identified and adjusted for, the level of comparability of these five uncontrolled comparables is significantly lower than that of the other 15. In addition, for those five uncontrolled comparables it is not possible to accurately allocate costs between the business activity associated with the relevant transactions and other business activities. Therefore, pursuant to § 1.482-1(e)(2)(ii) only the other fifteen uncontrolled comparables may be used to establish an arm's length range.

(iii) Although the data for the fifteen remaining uncontrolled comparables is relatively complete and accurate, there is a significant possibility that some material differences may remain. The district director has determined, for example, that it is likely that there are material differences in the level of technical expertise or in management efficiency. Accordingly, if the comparable profits method is determined to be the best method pursuant to § 1.482-1(c), the arm's length range for the controlled transaction may be established only pursuant to paragraph (e)(2)(iii)(B) of this section.

(f) *Scope of review.*—(1) *In general.*—The authority to determine true taxable income extends to any case in which either by inadvertence or design the taxable income, in whole or in part, of a controlled taxpayer is other than it would have been had the taxpayer, in the conduct of its affairs, been dealing at arm's length with an uncontrolled taxpayer.

(i) *Intent to evade or avoid tax not a prerequisite.*—In making allocations under section 482, the district director is not restricted to the case of improper accounting, to the case of a fraudulent, colorable, or sham transaction, or to the case of a device designed to reduce or avoid tax by shifting or distorting income, deductions, credits, or allowances.

(ii) *Realization of income not a prerequisite.*—(A) *In general.*—The district director may make an allocation under section 482 even if the income ultimately anticipated from a series of transactions has not been or is never realized. For example, if a controlled taxpayer sells a product at less than an arm's length price to a related taxpayer in one taxable year and the second controlled taxpayer resells the product to an unrelated party in the next taxable year, the district director may make an appropriate allocation to reflect an arm's length price for the sale of the product in the first taxable year, even though the second controlled taxpayer had not realized any gross income from the resale of the product in the first year. Similarly, if a controlled taxpayer lends money to a related taxpayer in a taxable year, the district director may make an appropriate allocation to reflect an arm's length charge for interest during such taxable year even if the second controlled taxpayer does not realize income during such year. Finally, even if two controlled taxpayers realize an overall loss that is attributable to a particular controlled transaction, an allocation under section 482 is not precluded.

(B) *Example.*—The following example illustrates this paragraph (f)(1)(ii).

Example. USSub is a U.S. subsidiary of FP, a foreign corporation. Parent manufactures product X and sells it to USSub. USSub functions as a distributor of product X to unrelated customers in the United States. The fact that FP may incur a loss on the manufacture and sale of product X does not by itself establish that USSub, dealing with FP at arm's length, also would incur a loss. An independent distributor acting at arm's length with its supplier would in many circumstances be expected to earn a profit without regard to the level of profit earned by the supplier.

(iii) *Nonrecognition provisions may not bar allocation.*—(A) *In general.*—If necessary to prevent the avoidance of taxes or to clearly reflect income, the district director may make an allocation under section 482 with respect to transactions that otherwise qualify for nonrecognition of gain or loss under applicable provisions of the Internal Revenue Code (such as section 351 or 1031).

(B) *Example.*—The following example illustrates this paragraph (f)(1)(iii).

Example. (i) In Year 1 USP, a United States corporation, bought 100 shares of UR, an unrelated corporation, for $100,000. In Year 2, when the value of the UR stock had decreased to $40,000, USP contributed all 100 shares of UR stock to its wholly-owned subsidiary in exchange for subsidiary's capital stock. In Year 3, the subsidiary sold all of the UR stock for $40,000 to an unrelated buyer, and on its U.S. income tax return, claimed a loss of $60,000 attributable to the sale of the UR stock. USP and its subsidiary do not file a consolidated return.

(ii) In determining the true taxable income of the subsidiary, the district director may disallow the loss of $60,000 on the ground that the loss was incurred by USP. *National Securities Corp. v. Commissioner*, 137 F.2d 600 (3rd Cir. 1943), cert. denied, 320 U.S. 794 (1943).

(iv) *Consolidated returns.*—Section 482 and the regulations thereunder apply to all controlled taxpayers, whether the controlled taxpayer files a separate or consolidated U.S. income tax return. If a controlled taxpayer files a separate return, its true separate taxable income will be determined. If a controlled taxpayer is a party to a consolidated return, the true consolidated taxable income of the affiliated group and the true separate taxable income of the controlled taxpayer must be determined consistently with the principles of a consolidated return.

(2) *Rules relating to determination of true taxable income.*—The following rules must be taken into account in determining the true taxable income of a controlled taxpayer.

(i)(A) through (E) [Reserved]. For further guidance see § 1.482-1T(f)(2)(i)(A) through (E).

(ii) *Allocation based on taxpayer's actual transactions.*—(A) *In general.*—The Commissioner will evaluate the results of a transaction as actually structured by the taxpayer unless its structure lacks economic substance. However, the Commissioner may consider the alternatives available to the taxpayer in determining whether the terms of the controlled transaction would be acceptable to an uncontrolled taxpayer faced with the same alternatives and operating under comparable circumstances. In such cases the Commissioner may adjust the consideration charged in the controlled transaction based on the cost or profit of an alternative as adjusted to account for material differences between the alternative and the controlled transaction, but will not restructure the transaction as if the alternative had been adopted by the taxpayer. See paragraph (d)(3) of this section (factors for determining comparability; contractual terms and risk); §§ 1.482-3(e), 1.482-4(d), and 1.482-9(h) (unspecified methods).

(B) [Reserved]. For further guidance see § 1.482-1T(f)(2)(ii)(B).

(iii) *Multiple year data.*—(A) *In general.*—The results of a controlled transaction ordinarily will be compared with the results of uncontrolled comparables occurring in the taxable year under review. It may be appropriate, however, to consider data relating to the uncontrolled comparables or the controlled taxpayer for one or more years before or after the year under review. If data relating to uncontrolled comparables from multiple years is used, data relating to the controlled taxpayer for the same years ordinarily must be considered. However, if such data is not available, reliable data from other years, as adjusted under paragraph (d)(2) (Standard of comparability) of this section may be used.

(B) *Circumstances warranting consideration of multiple year data.*—The extent to which it is appropriate to consider multiple year data depends on the method being applied and the issue being addressed. Circumstances that may warrant consideration of data from multiple years include the extent to which complete and accurate data are available for the taxable year under review, the effect of business cycles in the controlled taxpayer's industry, or the effects of life cycles of the product or intangible property being examined. Data from one or more years before or after the taxable year under review must ordinarily be considered for purposes of applying the provisions of paragraph (d)(3)(iii) of this section (risk), paragraph (d)(4)(i) of this section (market share strategy), § 1.482-4(f)(2) (periodic adjustments), § 1.482-5 (comparable profits method), § 1.482-9(f) (comparable profits method for services), and § 1.482-9(i) (contingent-payment contractual terms for services). On the other hand, multiple year data ordinarily will not be considered for purposes of applying the comparable uncontrolled price method of § 1.482-3(b) or the comparable uncontrolled services price method of § 1.482-9(c) (except to the extent that risk or market share strategy issues are present).

(C) *Comparable effect over comparable period.*—Data from multiple years may be considered to determine whether the same economic conditions that caused the controlled taxpayer's results had a comparable effect over a comparable period of time on the uncontrolled comparables that establish the arm's length range. For example, given that uncontrolled taxpayers enter into transactions with the ultimate expectation of earning a profit, persistent losses among controlled taxpayers may be an indication of non-arm's length dealings. Thus, if a controlled taxpayer that realizes a loss with respect to a controlled transaction seeks to demonstrate that the loss is within the arm's length range, the district director may take into account data from taxable years other than the taxable year of the transaction to determine whether the loss was attributable to arm's length dealings. The rule of this paragraph (f)(2)(iii)(C) is illustrated by *Example 3* of paragraph (f)(2)(iii)(E) of this section.

(D) *Applications of methods using multiple year averages.*—If a comparison of a controlled taxpayer's average result over a multiple year period with the average results of uncontrolled comparables over the same period would reduce the effect of short-term variations that may be unrelated to transfer pricing, it may be appropriate to establish a range derived from the average results of uncontrolled comparables over a multiple year period to determine if an adjustment should be made. In such a case the district director may make an adjustment if the controlled taxpayer's average result for the multiple year period is not within such range. Such a range must be determined in accordance with § 1.482-1(e) (Arm's length range). An adjustment in such a case ordinarily will be equal to the difference, if any, between the controlled taxpayer's result for the taxable year and the mid-point of the uncontrolled comparables' results for that year. If the interquartile range is used to determine the range of average results for the multiple year period, such adjustment will ordinarily be made to the median of all the results of the uncontrolled comparables for the taxable year. See *Example 2* of § 1.482-5(e). In other cases, the adjustment normally will be made to the arithmetic mean of all the results of the uncontrolled comparables for the taxable year. However, an adjustment will be made only to the extent that it would move the controlled taxpayer's multiple year average closer to the arm's length range for the multiple year period or to any point within such range. In determining a controlled taxpayer's average result for a multiple year period, adjustments made under this section for prior years will be taken into account only if such adjustments have been finally determined, as described in § 1.482-1(g)(2)(iii). See *Example 3* of § 1.482-5(e).

(E) *Examples.*—The following examples, in which S and P are controlled taxpayers, illustrate this paragraph (f)(2)(iii). *Examples 1* and *4* also illustrate the principle of the arm's length range of paragraph (e) of this section.

Example 1. P sold product Z to S for $60 per unit in 1995. Applying the resale price method to data from uncontrolled comparables for the same year establishes an arm's length range of prices for the controlled transaction from $52 to $59 per unit. Since the price charged in the controlled transaction falls outside the range, the district director would ordinarily make an allocation under section 482. However, in this case there are cyclical factors that affect the results of the uncontrolled comparables (and that of the controlled transaction) that cannot be adequately accounted for by specific adjustments to the data for 1995. Therefore, the district director considers results over multiple years to account for these factors. Under these circumstances, it is appropriate to average the results of the uncontrolled comparables over the years 1993, 1994, and 1995 to determine an arm's length range. The averaged results establish an arm's length range of $56 to $58 per unit. For consistency, the results of the controlled taxpayers must also be averaged over the same years. The average price in the controlled transaction over the three years is $57. Because the controlled transfer price of product Z falls within the arm's length range, the district director makes no allocation.

Example 2. (i) FP, a Country X corporation, designs and manufactures machinery in Country X. FP's costs are incurred in Country X currency. USSub is the exclusive distributor of FP's machinery in the United States. The price of the machinery sold by FP to USSub is expressed in Country X currency. Thus, USSub bears all of the currency risk associated with fluctuations in the exchange rate between the time the contract is signed and the payment is made. The prices charged by FP to USSub for 1995 are under examination. In that year, the value of the dollar depreciated against the currency of Country X, and as a result, USSub's gross margin was only 8%.

(ii) UD is an uncontrolled distributor of similar machinery that performs distribution functions substantially the same as those performed by USSub, except that UD purchases and resells machinery in transactions where both the purchase and resale prices are denominated in U.S. dollars. Thus, UD had no currency exchange risk. UD's gross margin in 1995 was 10%. UD's average gross margin for the period 1990 to 1998 has been 12%.

(iii) In determining whether the price charged by FP to USSub in 1995 was arm's length, the district director may consider USSub's average gross margin for an appropriate period before and after 1995 to determine whether USSub's average gross margin during the period was sufficiently greater than UD's average gross margin during the same period such that USSub was sufficiently compensated for the currency risk it bore throughout the period. See § 1.482-1(d)(3)(iii) (Risk).

Example 3. FP manufactures product X in Country M and sells it to USSub, which distributes X in the United States. USSub realizes losses with respect to the controlled transactions in each of five consecutive taxable years. In each of the five consecutive years a different uncontrolled comparable realized a loss with respect to comparable transactions equal to or greater than USSub's loss. Pursuant to paragraph (f)(3)(iii)(C) of this section, the district director examines whether the uncontrolled comparables realized similar losses over a comparable period of time, and finds that each of the five comparables realized losses in only one of the five years, and their average result over the five-year period was a profit. Based on this data, the district director may conclude that the controlled taxpayer's results are not within the arm's length range over the five year period, since the economic conditions that resulted in the controlled taxpayer's loss did not have a comparable effect over a comparable period of time on the uncontrolled comparables.

Example 4. (i) USP, a U.S. corporation, manufactures product Y in the United States and sells it to FSub, which acts as USP's exclusive distributor of product Y in Country N. The resale price method described in § 1.482-3(c) is used to evaluate whether the transfer price charged by USP to FSub for the 1994 taxable year for product Y was arm's length. For the period 1992 through 1994, FSub had a gross profit margin for each year of 13%. A, B, C and D are uncontrolled distributors of products that compete directly with product Y in country N. After making appropriate adjustments in accordance with §§ 1.482-1(d)(2) and 1.482-3(c), the gross profit margins for A, B, C, and D are as follows:

	1992	*1993*	*1994*	*Average*
A	13	3	8	8.00
B	11	13	2	8.67
C	4	7	13	8.00
D	7	9	6	7.33

(ii) Applying the provisions of § 1.482-1(e), the district director determines that the arm's length range of the average gross profit margins is between 7.33 and 8.67. The district director concludes that FSub's average gross margin of 13% is not within the arm's length range, despite the fact that C's gross profit margin for 1994 was also 13%, since the economic conditions that caused S's result did not have a comparable effect over a comparable period of time on the results of C or the other uncontrolled comparables. In this case, the district director makes an allocation equivalent to adjusting FSub's gross profit margin for 1994 from 13% to the mean of the uncontrolled comparables' results for 1994 (7.25%).

(iv) *Product lines and statistical techniques.*—The methods described in §§1.482-2 through 1.482-6 are generally stated in terms of individual transactions. However, because a taxpayer may have controlled transactions involving many different products, or many separate transactions involving the same product, it may be impractical to analyze every individual transaction to determine its arm's length price. In such cases, it is permissible to evaluate the arm's length results by applying the appropriate methods to the overall results for product lines or other groupings. In addition, the arm's length results of all related party transactions entered into by a controlled taxpayer may be evaluated by employing sampling and other valid statistical techniques.

(v) *Allocations apply to results, not methods.*—(A) *In general.*—In evaluating whether the result of a controlled transaction is arm's length, it is not necessary for the district director to determine whether the method or procedure that a controlled taxpayer employs to set the terms for its controlled transactions corresponds to the method or procedure that might have been used by a taxpayer dealing at arm's length with an uncontrolled taxpayer. Rather, the district director will evaluate the result achieved rather than the method the taxpayer used to determine its prices.

(B) *Example.*—The following example illustrates this paragraph (f)(2)(v).

Example. (i) FS is a foreign subsidiary of P, a U.S. corporation. P manufactures and sells household appliances. FS operates as P's exclusive distributor in Europe. P annually establishes the price for each of its appliances sold to FS as part of its annual budgeting, production allocation and scheduling, and performance evaluation processes. FS's aggregate gross margin earned in its distribution business is 18%.

(ii) ED is an uncontrolled European distributor of competing household appliances. After adjusting for minor differences in the level of inventory, volume of sales, and warranty programs conducted by FS and ED, ED's aggregate gross margin is also 18%. Thus, the district director may conclude that the aggregate prices charged by P for its appliances sold to FS are arm's length, without determining whether the budgeting, production, and performance evaluation processes of P are similar to such processes used by ED.

(g) *Collateral adjustments with respect to allocations under section 482.*—(1) *In general.*—The district director will take into account appropriate collateral adjustments with respect to allocations under section 482. Appropriate collateral adjustments may include correlative allocations, conforming adjustments, and setoffs, as described in this paragraph (g).

(2) *Correlative allocations.*—(i) *In general.*—When the district director makes an allocation under section 482 (referred to in this paragraph (g)(2) as the primary allocation), appropriate correlative allocations will also be made with respect to any other member of the group affected by the allocation. Thus, if the district director makes an allocation of income, the district director will not only increase the income of one member of the group, but correspondingly decrease the income of the other member. In addition, where appropriate, the district director may make such further correlative allocations as may be required by the initial correlative allocation.

(ii) *Manner of carrying out correlative allocation.*—The district director will furnish to the taxpayer with respect to which the primary allocation is made a written statement of the amount and nature of the correlative allocation. The correlative allocation must be reflected in the documentation of the other member of the group that is maintained for U.S. tax purposes, without regard to whether it affects the U.S. income tax liability of the other member for any open year. In some circumstances the allocation will have an immediate U.S. tax effect, by changing the taxable income computation of the other member (or the taxable income computation of a shareholder of the other member, for example, under the provisions of subpart F of the Internal Revenue Code). Alternatively, the correlative allocation may not be reflected on any U.S. tax return until a later year, for example when a dividend is paid.

(iii) *Events triggering correlative allocation.*—For purposes of this paragraph (g)(2), a primary allocation will not be considered to have been made (and therefore, correlative allocations are not required to be made) until the date of a final determination with respect to the allocation under section 482. For this purpose, a final determination includes—

(A) Assessment of tax following execution by the taxpayer of a Form 870 (Waiver of Restrictions on Assessment and Collection of Deficiency in Tax and Acceptance of Overassessment) with respect to such allocation;

(B) Acceptance of a Form 870-AD (Offer of Waiver of Restriction on Assessment and Collection of Deficiency in Tax and Acceptance of Overassessment);

(C) Payment of the deficiency;

(D) Stipulation in the Tax Court of the United States; or

(E) Final determination of tax liability by offer-in-compromise, closing agreement, or final resolution (determined under the principles of section 7481) of a judicial proceeding.

(iv) *Examples.*—The following examples illustrate this paragraph (g)(2). In each example, X and Y are members of the same group of controlled taxpayers and each regularly computes its income on a calendar year basis.

Example 1. (i) In 1996, Y, a U.S. corporation, rents a building owned by X, also a U.S. corporation. In 1998 the district director determines that Y did not pay an arm's length rental charge. The district director proposes to increase X's income to reflect an arm's length rental charge. X consents to the assessment reflecting such adjustment by executing Form 870, a Waiver of Restrictions on Assessment and Collection of Deficiency in Tax and Acceptance of Overassessment. The assessment of the tax with respect to the adjustment is made in 1998. Thus, the primary allocation, as defined in paragraph (g)(2)(i) of this section, is considered to have been made in 1998.

(ii) The adjustment made to X's income under section 482 requires a correlative allocation with respect to Y's income. The district director notifies X in writing of the amount and nature of the adjustment made with respect to Y. Y had net operating losses in 1993, 1994, 1995, 1996, and 1997. Although a correlative adjustment will not have an effect on Y's U.S. income tax liability for 1996, an adjustment increasing Y's net operating loss for 1996 will be made for purposes of determining Y's U.S. income tax liability for 1998 or a later taxable year to which the increased net operating loss may be carried.

Example 2. (i) In 1995, X, a U.S. construction company, provided engineering services to Y, a U.S. corporation, in the construction of Y's factory. In 1997, the district director determines that the fees paid by Y to X for its services were not arm's length and proposes to make an adjustment to the income of X. X consents to an assessment reflecting such adjustment by executing Form 870. An assessment of the tax with respect to such adjustment is made in 1997. The district director notifies X in writing of the amount and nature of the adjustment to be made with respect to Y.

(ii) The fees paid by Y for X's engineering services properly constitute a capital expenditure. Y does not place the factory into service until 1998. Therefore, a correlative adjustment increasing Y's basis in the factory does not affect Y's U.S. income tax liability for 1997. However, the correlative adjustment must be made in the books and records maintained by Y for its U.S. income tax purposes and such adjustment will be taken into account in computing Y's allowable depreciation or gain or loss on a subsequent disposition of the factory.

Example 3. In 1995, X, a U.S. corporation, makes a loan to Y, its foreign subsidiary not engaged in a U.S. trade or business. In 1997, the district director, upon determining that the interest charged on the loan was not arm's length, proposes to adjust X's income to reflect an arm's length interest rate. X consents to an assessment reflecting such allocation by executing Form 870, and an assessment of the tax with respect to the section 482 allocation is made in 1997. The district director notifies X in writing of the amount and nature of the correlative allocation to be made with respect to Y. Although the correlative adjustment does not have an effect on Y's U.S. income tax liability, the adjustment must be reflected in the documentation of Y that is maintained for U.S. tax purposes. Thus, the adjustment must be reflected in the determination of the amount of Y's earnings and profits for 1995 and subsequent years, and the adjustment must be made to the extent it has an effect on any person's U.S. income tax liability for any taxable year.

(3) *Adjustments to conform accounts to reflect section 482 allocations.*—(i) *In general.*—Appropriate adjustments must be made to conform a taxpayer's accounts to reflect allocations made under section 482. Such adjustments may include the treatment of an allo-

cated amount as a dividend or a capital contribution (as appropriate), or, in appropriate cases, pursuant to such applicable revenue procedures as may be provided by the Commissioner (see § 601.601(d)(2) of this chapter), repayment of the allocated amount without further income tax consequences.

(ii) *Example.*—The following example illustrates the principles of this paragraph (g)(3).

Example—Conforming cash accounts. (i) USD, a United States corporation, buys Product from its foreign parent, FP. In reviewing USD's income tax return, the district director determines that the arm's length price would have increased USD's taxable income by $5 million. The district director accordingly adjusts USD's income to reflect its true taxable income.

(ii) To conform its cash accounts to reflect the section 482 allocation made by the district director, USD applies for relief under Rev. Proc. 65-17, 1965-1 C.B. 833 (see § 601.601(d)(2)(ii)(*b*) of this chapter), to treat the $5 million adjustment as an account receivable from FP, due as of the last day of the year of the transaction, with interest accruing therefrom.

(4) *Setoffs.*—(i) *In general.*—If an allocation is made under section 482 with respect to a transaction between controlled taxpayers, the Commissioner will take into account the effect of any other non-arm's length transaction between the same controlled taxpayers in the same taxable year which will result in a setoff against the original section 482 allocation. Such setoff, however, will be taken into account only if the requirements of paragraph (g)(4)(ii) of this section are satisfied. If the effect of the setoff is to change the characterization or source of the income or deductions, or otherwise distort taxable income, in such a manner as to affect the U.S. tax liability of any member, adjustments will be made to reflect the correct amount of each category of income or deductions. For purposes of this setoff provision, the term arm's length refers to the amount defined in paragraph (b) of this section (arm's length standard), without regard to the rules in § 1.482-2(a) that treat certain interest rates as arm's length rates of interest.

(ii) *Requirements.*—The district director will take a setoff into account only if the taxpayer—

(A) Establishes that the transaction that is the basis of the setoff was not at arm's length and the amount of the appropriate arm's length charge;

(B) Documents, pursuant to paragraph (g)(2) of this section, all correlative adjustments resulting from the proposed setoff; and

(C) Notifies the district director of the basis of any claimed setoff within 30 days after the earlier of the date of a letter by which the district director transmits an examination report notifying the taxpayer of proposed adjustments or the date of the issuance of the notice of deficiency.

(iii) *Examples.*—The following examples illustrate this paragraph (g)(4).

Example 1. P, a U.S. corporation, renders construction services to S, its foreign subsidiary in Country Y, in connection with the construction of S's factory. An arm's length charge for such services determined under § 1.482-9 would be $100,000. During the same taxable year P makes available to S the use of a machine to be used in the construction of the factory, and the arm's length rental value of the machine is $25,000. P bills S $125,000 for the services, but does not charge S for the use of the machine. No allocation will be made with respect to the undercharge for the machine if P notifies the district director of the basis of the claimed setoff within 30 days after the date of the letter from the district director transmitting the examination report notifying P of the proposed adjustment, establishes that the excess amount charged for services was equal to an arm's length charge for the use of the machine and that the taxable income and income tax liabilities of P are not distorted, and documents the correlative allocations resulting from the proposed setoff.

Example 2. The facts are the same as in *Example 1*, except that, if P had reported $25,000 as rental income and $25,000 less as service income, it would have been subject to the tax on personal holding companies. Allocations will be made to reflect the correct amounts of rental income and service income.

(h) *Special rules.*—(1) *Small taxpayer safe harbor.*—[Reserved]

(2) *Effect of foreign legal restrictions.*—(i) *In general.*—The district director will take into account the effect of a foreign legal restriction to the extent that such restriction affects the results of transactions at arm's length. Thus, a foreign legal restriction will be taken into account only to the extent that it is shown that the restriction affected an uncontrolled taxpayer under comparable circumstances for a comparable period of time. In the absence of evidence indicating the effect of the foreign legal restriction on uncontrolled taxpayers, the restriction will be taken into account only to the extent provided in paragraphs (h)(2)(iii) and (iv) of this section (Deferred income method of accounting).

(ii) *Applicable legal restrictions.*—Foreign legal restrictions (whether temporary or permanent) will be taken into account for purposes of this paragraph (h)(2) only if, and so long as, the conditions set forth in paragraphs (h)(2)(ii)(A) through (D) of this section are met.

(A) The restrictions are publicly promulgated, generally applicable to all similarly situated persons (both controlled and uncontrolled), and not imposed as part of a commercial transaction between the taxpayer and the foreign sovereign;

(B) The taxpayer (or other member of the controlled group with respect to which the restrictions apply) has exhausted all remedies prescribed by foreign law or practice for obtaining a waiver of such restrictions (other than remedies that would have a negligible prospect of success if pursued);

(C) The restrictions expressly prevented the payment or receipt, in any form, of part or all of the arm's length amount that would otherwise be required under section 482 (for example, a restriction that applies only to the deductibility of an expense for tax purposes is not a restriction on payment or receipt for this purpose); and

(D) The related parties subject to the restriction did not engage in any arrangement with controlled or uncontrolled parties that had the effect of circumventing the restriction, and have not otherwise violated the restriction in any material respect.

(iii) *Requirement for electing the deferred income method of accounting.*—If a foreign legal restriction prevents the payment or receipt of part or all of the arm's length amount that is due with respect to a controlled transaction, the restricted amount may be treated as deferrable if the following requirements are met—

(A) The controlled taxpayer establishes to the satisfaction of the district director that the payment or receipt of the arm's length amount was prevented because of a foreign legal restriction and circumstances described in paragraph (h)(2)(ii) of this section; and

(B) The controlled taxpayer whose U.S. tax liability may be affected by the foreign legal restriction elects the deferred income method of accounting, as described in paragraph (h)(2)(iv) of this section, on a written statement attached to a timely U.S. income tax return (or an amended return) filed before the IRS first contacts any member of the controlled group concerning an examination of the return for the taxable year to which the foreign legal restriction applies. A written statement furnished by a taxpayer subject to the Coordinated Examination Program will be considered an amended return for purposes of this paragraph (h)(2)(iii)(B) if it satisfies the requirements of a qualified amended return for purposes of § 1.6664-2(c)(3) as set forth in those regulations or as the Commissioner may prescribe by applicable revenue procedures. The election statement must identify the affected transactions, the parties to the transactions, and the applicable foreign legal restrictions.

(iv) *Deferred income method of accounting.*—If the requirements of paragraph (h)(2)(ii) of this section are satisfied, any portion of the arm's length amount, the payment or receipt of which is prevented because of applicable foreign legal restrictions, will be treated as deferrable until payment or receipt of the relevant item ceases to be prevented by the foreign legal restriction. For purposes of the deferred income method of accounting under this paragraph (h)(2)(iv), deductions (including the cost or other basis of inventory and other assets sold or exchanged) and credits properly chargeable against any amount so deferred, are subject to deferral under the provisions of § 1.461-1(a)(4). In addition, income is deferrable under this deferred income method of accounting only to the extent that it exceeds the related deductions already claimed in open taxable years to which the foreign legal restriction applied.

(v) *Examples.*—The following examples, in which Sub is a Country FC subsidiary of U.S. corporation, Parent, illustrate this paragraph (h)(2).

Example 1. Parent licenses an intangible to Sub. FC law generally prohibits payments by any person within FC to recipients outside the country. The FC law meets the requirements of paragraph (h)(2)(ii) of this section. There is no evidence of unrelated parties entering into transactions under comparable circumstances for a comparable period of time, and the foreign legal restrictions will not be taken into account in determining the arm's length amount. The arm's length royalty rate for the use of the intangible property in the absence of the foreign restriction is 10% of Sub's sales in country FC. However, because the requirements of paragraph (h)(2)(ii) of this section are satisfied, Parent can elect the deferred income method of accounting by attaching to its timely filed U.S. income tax return a written statement that satisfies the requirements of paragraph (h)(2)(iii)(B) of this section.

Example 2. (i) The facts are the same as in *Example 1,* except that Sub, although it makes no royalty payment to Parent, arranges with an unrelated intermediary to make payments equal to an arm's length amount on its behalf to Parent.

(ii) The district director makes an allocation of royalty income to Parent, based on the arm's length royalty rate of 10%. Further, the district director determines that because the arrangement with the third party had the effect of circumventing the FC law, the requirements of paragraph (h)(2)(ii)(D) of this section are not satisfied. Thus, Parent could not validly elect the deferred income method of accounting, and the allocation of royalty income cannot be treated as deferrable. In appropriate circumstances, the district director may permit the amount of the distribution to be treated as payment by Sub of the royalty allocated to Parent, under the provisions of § 1.482-1(g) (Collateral adjustments).

Example 3. The facts are the same as in *Example 1,* except that the laws of FC do not prevent distributions from corporations to their shareholders. Sub distributes an amount equal to 8% of its sales in country FC. Because the laws of FC did not expressly prevent all forms of payment from Sub to Parent, Parent cannot validly elect the deferred income method of accounting with respect to any of the arm's length royalty amount. In appropriate circumstances, the district director may permit the 8% that was distributed to be treated as payment by Sub of the royalty allocated to Parent, under the provisions of § 1.482-1(g) (Collateral adjustments).

Example 4. The facts are the same as in *Example 1,* except that Country FC law permits the payment of a royalty, but limits the amount to 5% of sales, and Sub pays the 5% royalty to Parent. Parent demonstrates the existence of a comparable uncontrolled transaction for purposes of the comparable uncontrolled transaction method in which an uncontrolled party accepted a royalty rate of 5%. Given the evidence of the comparable uncontrolled transaction, the 5% royalty rate is determined to be the arm's length royalty rate.

(3) *Coordination with section 936.*—(i) *Cost sharing under section 936.*—If a possessions corporation makes an election under section 936(h)(5)(C)(i)(I), the corporation must make a section 936 cost sharing payment that is at least equal to the payment that would be required under section 482 if the electing corporation were a foreign corporation. In determining the payment that would be required under section 482 for this purpose, the provisions of § § 1.482-1 and 1.482-4 will be applied, and to the extent relevant to the valuation of intangibles, § § 1.482-5 and 1.482-6 will be applied. The provisions of section 936(h)(5)(C)(i)(II) (Effect of Election—electing corporation treated as owner of intangible property) do not apply until the payment that would be required under section 482 has been determined.

(ii) *Use of terms.*—A cost sharing payment, for the purposes of section 936(h)(5)(C)(i)(I), is calculated using the provisions of section 936 and the regulations thereunder and the provisions of this paragraph (h)(3). The provisions relating to cost sharing under section 482 do not apply to payments made pursuant to an election under section 936(h)(5)(C)(i)(I). Similarly, a profit split payment, for the purposes of section 936(h)(5)(C)(ii)(I), is calculated using the provisions of section 936 and the regulations thereunder, not section 482 and the regulations thereunder.

(i) *Definitions.*—The definitions set forth in paragraphs (i)(1) through (i)(10) of this section apply to this section and § § 1.482-2 through 1.482-9.

(1) *Organization* includes an organization of any kind, whether a sole proprietorship, a partnership, a trust, an estate, an association, or a corporation (as each is defined or understood in the Internal Revenue Code or the regulations thereunder), irrespective of the place of organization, operation, or conduct of the trade or business, and regardless of whether it is a domestic or foreign organization, whether it is an exempt organization, or whether it is a member of an affiliated group that files a consolidated U.S. income tax return, or a member of an affiliated group that does not file a consolidated U.S. income tax return.

(2) *Trade* or *business* includes a trade or business activity of any kind, regardless of whether or where organized, whether owned individually or otherwise, and regardless of the place of operation. Employment for compensation will constitute a separate trade or business from the employing trade or business.

(3) *Taxpayer* means any person, organization, trade or business, whether or not subject to any internal revenue tax.

(4) *Controlled* includes any kind of control, direct or indirect, whether legally enforceable or not, and however exercisable or exercised, including control resulting from the actions of two or more taxpayers acting in concert or with a common goal or purpose. It is the reality of the control that is decisive, not its form or the mode of its exercise. A presumption of control arises if income or deductions have been arbitrarily shifted.

(5) *Controlled taxpayer* means any one of two or more taxpayers owned or controlled directly or indirectly by the same interests, and includes the taxpayer that owns or controls the other taxpayers. *Uncontrolled taxpayer* means any one of two or more taxpayers not owned or controlled directly or indirectly by the same interests.

(6) *Group, controlled group,* and *group of controlled taxpayers* mean the taxpayers owned or controlled directly or indirectly by the same interests.

(7) *Transaction* means any sale, assignment, lease, license, loan, advance, contribution, or any other transfer of any interest in or a right to use any property (whether tangible or intangible, real or personal) or money, however such transaction is effected, and whether or not the terms of such transaction are formally documented. A transaction also includes the performance of any services for the benefit of, or on behalf of, another taxpayer.

(8) *Controlled transaction* or *controlled transfer* means any transaction or transfer between two or more members of the same group of controlled taxpayers. The term *uncontrolled transaction* means any transaction between two or more taxpayers that are not members of the same group of controlled taxpayers.

(9) *True taxable income* means, in the case of a controlled taxpayer, the taxable income that would have resulted had it dealt with the other member or members of the group at arm's length. It does not mean the taxable income resulting to the controlled taxpayer by reason of the particular contract, transaction, or arrangement the controlled taxpayer chose to make (even though such contract, transaction, or arrangement is legally binding upon the parties thereto).

(10) *Uncontrolled comparable* means the uncontrolled transaction or uncontrolled taxpayer that is compared with a controlled transaction or taxpayer under any applicable pricing methodology. Thus, for example, under the comparable profits method, an uncontrolled comparable is any uncontrolled taxpayer from which data is used to establish a comparable operating profit.

(j) *Effective dates.*—(1) These regulations are generally effective for taxable years beginning after October 6, 1994.

(2) Taxpayers may elect to apply retroactively all of the provisions of these regulations for any open taxable year. Such election will be effective for the year of the election and all subsequent taxable years.

(3) Although these regulations are generally effective for taxable years as stated, the final sentence of section 482 (requiring that the income with respect to transfers or licenses of intangible property be commensurate with the income attributable to the intangible) is generally effective for taxable years beginning after December 31, 1986. For the period prior to the effective date of these regulations, the final sentence of section 482 must be applied using any reasonable method not inconsistent with the statute. The IRS considers a method that applies these regulations or their general principles to be a reasonable method.

(4) These regulations will not apply with respect to transfers made or licenses granted to foreign persons before November 17, 1985, or before August 17, 1986, for transfers or licenses to others. Nevertheless, they will apply with respect to transfers or licenses before such dates if, with respect to property transferred pursuant to an earlier and continuing transfer agreement, such property was not in existence or owned by the taxpayer on such date.

(5) The last sentences of paragraphs (b)(2)(i) and (c)(1) of this section and of paragraph (c)(2)(iv) of § 1.482-5 apply for taxable years beginning on or after August 26, 2003.

(6)(i) The provisions of paragraphs (a)(1), (d)(3)(ii)(C) *Example 3, Example 4, Example 5,* and *Example 6,* (d)(3)(v), (f)(2)(ii)(A), (f)(2)(iii)(B), (g)(4)(i), (g)(4)(iii), and (i) of this section are generally applicable for taxable years beginning after July 31, 2009. The provision of paragraph (b)(2)(iii) of this section is generally applicable on January 5, 2009.

(ii) A person may elect to apply the provisions of paragraphs (a)(1), (b)(2)(i), (d)(3)(ii)(C) *Example 3, Example 4, Example 5,* and *Example 6,* (d)(3)(v), (f)(2)(ii)(A), (f)(2)(iii)(B), (g)(4)(i), (g)(4)(iii), and (i) of this section to earlier taxable years in accordance with the rules set forth in § 1.482-9(n)(2).

(7) [Reserved]. For further guidance see § 1.482-1T(j)(7). [Reg. § 1.482-1.]

☐ [*T.D.* 8552, 7-1-94. *Amended by T.D.* 9088, 8-25-2003; *T.D.* 9278, 7-31-2006 (*corrected* 12-21-2006); *T.D.* 9441, 12-31-2008; *T.D.* 9456, 7-31-2009 (*corrected* 9-8-2009), *T.D.* 9568, 12-16-2011 (*corrected* 1-24-2012) *and T.D.* 9738, 9-14-2015.]

§ 1.482-1T. Allocation of income and deductions among taxpayers (temporary).—(a) through (f)(2) [Reserved]. For further guidance see § 1.482-1(a) through (f)(2).

(i) *Compensation independent of the form or character of controlled transaction.*—(A) *In general.*—All value provided between controlled taxpayers in a controlled transaction requires an arm's length amount of compensation determined under the best method rule of § 1.482-1(c). Such amount must be consistent with, and must account for all of, the value provided between the parties in the transaction, without regard to the form or character of the transaction. For this purpose, it is necessary to consider the entire arrangement between the parties, as determined by the contractual terms, whether written or imputed in accordance with the economic substance of the arrangement, in light of the actual conduct of the parties. See, e.g., § 1.482-1(d)(3)(ii)(B) (identifying contractual terms) and (f)(2)(ii)(A) (regarding reference to realistic alternatives).

(B) *Aggregation.*—The combined effect of two or more separate transactions (whether before, during, or after the year under review), including for purposes of an analysis under multiple provisions of the Code or regulations, may be considered if the transactions, taken as a whole, are so interrelated that an aggregate analysis of the transactions provides the most reliable measure of an arm's length result determined under the best method rule of § 1.482-1(c). Whether two or more transactions are evaluated separately or in the aggregate depends on the extent to which the transactions are economically interrelated and on the relative reliability of the measure of an arm's length result provided by an aggregate analysis of the transactions as compared to a separate analysis of each transaction. For example, consideration of the combined effect of two or more transactions may be appropriate to determine whether the overall compensation in the transactions is consistent with the value provided, including any synergies among items and services provided.

(C) *Coordinated best method analysis and evaluation.*—Consistent with the principles of paragraphs (f)(2)(i)(A) and (B) of this section, a coordinated best method analysis and evaluation of two or more controlled transactions to which one or more provisions of the Code or regulations apply may be necessary to ensure that the overall value provided, including any synergies, is properly taken into account. A coordinated best method analysis would include a consistent consideration of the facts and circumstances of the functions performed, resources employed, and risks assumed in the relevant transactions, and a consistent measure of the arm's length results, for purposes of all relevant statutory and regulatory provisions.

(D) *Allocations of value.*—In some cases, it may be necessary to allocate one or more portions of the arm's length result that was properly determined under a coordinated best method analysis described in paragraph (f)(2)(i)(C) of this section. Any such allocation of the arm's length result determined under the coordinated best method analysis must be made using the method that, under the facts and circumstances, provides the most reliable measure of an arm's length result for each allocated amount. For example, if the full value of compensation due in controlled transactions whose tax treatment is governed by multiple provisions of the Code or regulations has been most reliably determined on an aggregate basis, then that full value must be allocated in a manner that provides the most reliable measure of each allocated amount.

(E) *Examples.*—The following examples illustrate the provisions of this paragraph (f)(2)(i). For purposes of the examples in this paragraph (E), P is a domestic corporation, and S1, S2, and S3 are foreign corporations that are wholly owned by P.

Example 1. Aggregation of interrelated licensing, manufacturing, and selling activities. P enters into a license agreement with S1 that permits S1 to use a proprietary manufacturing process and to sell the output from this process throughout a specified region. S1 uses the manufacturing process and sells its output to S2, which in turn resells the output to uncontrolled parties in the specified region. In evaluating whether the royalty paid by S1 to P is an arm's length amount, it may be appropriate to evaluate the royalty in combination with the transfer prices charged by S1 to S2 and the aggregate profits earned by S1 and S2 from the use of the manufacturing process and the sale to uncontrolled parties of the products produced by S1.

Example 2. Aggregation of interrelated manufacturing, marketing, and services activities. S1 is the exclusive Country Z distributor of computers manufactured by P. S2 provides marketing services in connection with sales of P computers in Country Z and in this regard uses significant marketing intangibles provided by P. S3 administers the warranty program with respect to P computers in Country Z, including maintenance and repair services. In evaluating whether the transfer prices paid by S1 to P, the fees paid by S2 to P for the use of P marketing intangibles, and the service fees earned by S2 and S3 are arm's length amounts, it would be appropriate to perform an aggregate analysis that considers the combined effects of these interrelated transactions if they are most reliably analyzed on an aggregated basis.

Example 3. Aggregation and reliability of comparable uncontrolled transactions. The facts are the same as in *Example 2.* In addition, U1, U2, and U3 are uncontrolled taxpayers that carry out functions comparable to those of S1, S2, and S3, respectively, with respect to computers produced by unrelated manufacturers. R1, R2, and R3 constitute a controlled group of taxpayers (unrelated to the P controlled group) that carry out functions comparable to those of S1, S2, and S3 with respect to computers produced by their common parent. Prices charged to uncontrolled customers of the R group differ from the prices charged to customers of U1, U2, and U3. In determining whether the transactions of U1, U2, and U3, or the transactions of R1, R2, and R3, would provide a more reliable measure of the arm's length result, it is determined that the interrelated R group transactions are more reliable than the wholly independent transactions of U1, U2, and U3, given the interrelationship of the P group transactions.

Example 4. Non-aggregation of transactions that are not interrelated. P enters into a license agreement with S1 that permits S1 to use a proprietary process for manufacturing product X and to sell product X to uncontrolled parties throughout a specified region. P also sells to S1 product Y, which is manufactured by P in the United States and unrelated to product X. Product Y is resold by S1 to uncontrolled parties in the specified region. There is no connection between product X and product Y other than the fact that they are both sold in the same specified region. In evaluating whether the royalty paid by S1 to P for the use of the manufacturing process for product X and the transfer prices charged for unrelated product Y are arm's length amounts, it would not be appropriate to consider the combined effects of these separate and unrelated transactions.

Example 5. Aggregation of interrelated patents. P owns 10 individual patents that, in combination, can be used to manufacture and sell a successful product. P anticipates that it could earn profits of $25x from the patents based on a discounted cash flow analysis that provides a more reliable measure of the value of the patents exploited as a bundle rather than separately. P licenses all 10 patents to S1 to be exploited as a bundle. Evidence of uncontrolled licenses of similar individual patents indicates that, exploited separately, each license of each patent would warrant a price of $1x, implying a total price for the patents of $10x. Under paragraph (f)(2)(i)(B) of this section, in determining the arm's length royalty for the license of the bundle of patents, it would not be appropriate to use the uncontrolled licenses as comparables for the license of the bundle of patents, because, unlike the discounted cash flow analysis, the uncontrolled licenses considered separately do not reliably reflect the enhancement to value resulting from the interrelatedness of the 10 patents exploited as a bundle.

Example 6. Consideration of entire arrangement, including imputed contractual terms—(i) P conducts a business ("Business") from the United States, with a worldwide clientele, but until Date X has no foreign operations. The success of Business significantly depends on intangibles (including marketing, manufacturing, technological, and goodwill or going concern value intangibles, collectively the "IP"), as well as ongoing support activities performed by P (including related research and development, central marketing, manufacturing process enhancement, and oversight activities, collectively "Support"), to maintain and improve the IP and otherwise maximize the profitability of Business.

(ii) On Date X, Year 1, P contributes the foreign rights to conduct Business, including the foreign rights to the IP, to newly incorporated S1. S1, utilizing the IP of which it is now the owner, commences foreign operations consisting of local marketing, manufacturing, and back office activities in order to conduct and expand Business in the foreign market.

(iii) Later, on Date Y, Year 1, P and S1 enter into a cost sharing arrangement ("CSA") to develop and exploit the rights to conduct the Business. Under the CSA, P is entitled to the U.S. rights to conduct the Business, and S1 is entitled to the rest-of-the-world ("ROW") rights to conduct the Business. P continues after Date Y to perform the Support, employing resources, capabilities, and rights that as a factual matter were not contributed to S1 in the Date X transaction, for the benefit of the Business worldwide. Pursuant to the CSA, P and S1 share the costs of P's Support in proportion to their reasonably anticipated benefit shares from their respective rights to the Business.

(iv) P treats the Date X transaction as a transfer described in section 351 that is subject to 367 and treats the Date Y transaction as the commencement of a CSA subject to section 482 and § 1.482-7. P takes the position that the only platform contribution transactions ("PCTs") in connection with the Date Y CSA consist of P's contribution of the U.S. Business IP rights and S1's contribution of the ROW Business IP rights of which S1 had become the owner on account of the prior Date X transaction.

(v) Pursuant to paragraph (f)(2)(i)(A) of this section, in determining whether an allocation of income is appropriate in Year 1 or subsequent years, the Commissioner may consider the economic substance of the entire arrangement between P and S1, including the parties' actual conduct throughout their relationship, regardless of the form or character of the contractual arrangement the parties have expressly adopted. The Commissioner determines that the parties' formal arrangement fails to reflect the full scope of the value provided between the parties in accordance with the economic substance of their arrangement. Therefore, the Commissioner may impute one or more agreements between P and S1, consistent with the economic substance of their arrangement, that fully reflect their respective reasonably anticipated commitments in terms of functions performed, resources employed, and risks assumed over time. For example, because P continues after Date Y to perform the Support, employing resources, capabilities, and rights not contributed to S1, for the benefit of the Business worldwide, the Commissioner may impute another PCT on Date Y pursuant to which P commits to so continuing the Support. See § 1.482-7(b)(1)(ii). The taxpayer may present additional facts that could indicate whether this or another alternative agreement best reflects the economic substance of the underlying transactions and course of conduct, provided that the taxpayer's position fully reflects the value of the entire arrangement consistent with the realistic alternatives principle.

Example 7. Distinguishing provision of value from characterization—(i) P developed a collection of resources, capabilities, and rights ("Collection") that it uses on an interrelated basis in ongoing research and development of computer code that is used to create a successful line of software products. P can continue to use the Collection on such interrelated basis in the future to further develop computer code and, thus, further build on its successful line of software products. Under § 1.482-7(g)(2)(ix), P determines that the interquartile range of the net present value of its own use of the Collection in future research and development and software product marketing is between $1000x and $1100x, and this range provides the most reliable measure of the value to P of continuing to use the Collection on an interrelated basis in future research, development, and exploitation. Instead, P enters into an exchange described in section 351 in which it transfers certain intangible property related to the Collection to S1 for use in future research, development, and exploitation but continues to perform the same development functions that it did prior to the exchange, now on behalf of S1, under express or implied commitments in connection with S1's use of the intangible property. P takes the position that a portion of the Collection, consisting of computer code and related instruction manuals and similar intangible property (Portion 1), was transferrable intangible property and was the subject of the section 351 exchange and compensable under section 367(d). P claims that another portion of the Collection consists of items that either do not constitute property for purposes of section 367 or are not transferrable (Portion 2). P then takes the position that the value of Portion 2 does not give rise to income under section 367(d) or gain under section 367(a).

(ii) Under paragraphs (f)(2)(i)(A) and (C) of this section, any part of the value in Portion 2 that is not taken into account in an exchange under section 367 must nonetheless be evaluated under section 482 and the regulations thereunder to determine arm's length compensation for any value provided to S1. Accordingly, even if P's assertion that certain items were either not property or not capable of being transferred were correct, arm's length compensation is nonetheless required for all of the value associated with P's contributions under the section 482 regulations. Alternatively, the Commissioner may determine under all the facts and circumstances that P's assertion is incorrect and that the transaction in fact constitutes an exchange of property subject to, and therefore to be taken into account under, section 367. Thus, whether any item that P identifies as being within Portion 2 is properly characterized as property under section 367 (transferable or otherwise) is irrelevant because any value in Portion 2 that is provided to S1 must be compensated by S1 in a manner consistent with the $1000x to $1100x interquartile range of the overall value.

Example 8. Arm's length compensation for equivalent provisions of intangibles under sections 351 and 482. P owns the worldwide rights to manufacturing and marketing intangibles that it uses to manufacture and market a product in the United States ("US intangibles") and the rest of the world ("ROW intangibles"). P transfers all the ROW intangibles to S1 in an exchange described in section 351 and retains the US intangibles. Immediately after the exchange, P and S1 entered into a CSA described in § 1.482-7(b) that covers all research and development of intangibles conducted by the parties. A realistic alternative that was available to P and that would have involved the controlled parties performing similar functions, employing similar resources, and assuming similar risks as in the controlled transaction, was to transfer all ROW intangibles to S1 upon entering into the CSA in a platform contribution transaction described in § 1.482-7(c), rather than in an exchange described in section 351 immediately before entering into the CSA. Under paragraph (f)(2)(i)(A) of this section, the arm's length compensation for the ROW intangibles must correspond to the value provided between the parties, regardless of the form of the transaction. Accordingly, the arm's length compensation for the ROW intangibles is the same in both scenarios, and the analysis of the amount to be taken into account under section 367(d) pursuant to § § 1.367(d)-1T(c) and 1.482-4 should include consideration of the amount that P would have charged for the realistic alternative determined under § 1.482-7(g) (and § 1.482-4, to the extent of any make-or-sell rights transferred). See § § 1.482-1(b)(2)(iii) and 1.482-4(g).

Example 9. Aggregation of interrelated manufacturing and marketing intangibles governed by different statutes and regulations. The facts are the same as in *Example 8* except that P transfers only the ROW intangibles related to manufacturing to S1 in an exchange described in section 351 and, upon entering into the CSA, then transfers the ROW intangibles related to marketing to S1 in a platform contribution transaction described in § 1.482-7(c) (rather than transferring all ROW intangibles only upon entering into the CSA or only in a prior exchange described in section 351). The value of the ROW intangibles that P transferred in the two transactions is greater in the aggregate, due to synergies among the different types of ROW intangibles, than if valued as two separate transactions. Under paragraph (f)(2)(i)(B) of this section, the arm's length standard requires these synergies to be taken into account in determining the arm's length results for the transactions.

Example 10. Services provided using intangibles.—(i) P's worldwide group produces and markets Product X and subsequent generations of products, which result from research and development performed by P's R&D Team. Through this collaboration with respect to P's proprietary products, the members of the R&D Team have individually and as a group acquired specialized knowledge and expertise subject to non-disclosure agreements (collectively, "knowhow").

(ii) P arranges for the R&D Team to provide research and development services to create a new line of products, building on the Product X platform, to be owned and exploited by S1 in the overseas market. P asserts that the arm's length charge for the services is only reimbursement to P of its associated R&D Team compensation costs.

(iii) Even though P did not transfer the platform or the R&D Team to S1, P is providing value associated with the use of the platform, along with the value associated with the use of the knowhow, to S1 by way of the services performed by the R&D Team for S1 using the platform and the knowhow. The R&D Team's use of intangible property, and any other valuable resources, in P's provision of services (regardless of whether the service effects a transfer of intangible property or valuable resources and regardless of whether the property is relatively high or low value) must be evaluated under the section 482 regulations, including the regulations specifically applicable to controlled services transactions in § 1.482-9, to ensure that P receives arm's length compensation for any value (attributable to such property or services) provided to S1 in a controlled transaction. See § § 1.482-4 and 1.482-9(m). Under paragraph (f)(2)(i)(A) of this section, the arm's length compensation for the services performed by the R&D Team for S1 must be consistent with the value provided to S1, including the value of the knowhow and any synergies with the platform. Under paragraphs (f)(2)(i)(B) and (C) of this section, the best method analysis may determine that the compensation is most reliably determined on an aggregate basis reflecting the interrelated value of the services and embedded value of the platform and knowhow.

(iv) In the alternative, the facts are the same as above, except that P assigns to S1 all or a pertinent portion of the R&D Team and the relevant rights in the platform. P takes the position that, although the transferred platform rights must be compensated, the knowhow does not have substantial value independent of the services of any individual on the R&D Team and therefore is not an intangible within the meaning of § 1.482-4(b). In P's view, S1 owes no compensation to P on account of the R&D Team, as S1 will directly bear the cost of the relevant R&D Team compensation. However, in assembling and arranging to assign the relevant R&D Team, and thereby making available the value of the knowhow to S1, rather than other employees without the knowhow, P is performing services for S1 under imputed contractual terms based on the parties' course of conduct. Therefore, even if P's position were correct that the knowhow is not an intangible under § 1.482-4(b), a position that the Commissioner may challenge, arm's length compensation is required for all of the value that P provides to S1 through the interrelated provision of platform rights, knowhow, and services under paragraphs (f)(2)(i)(A), (B), and (C) of this section.

Example 11. Allocating arm's length compensation determined under an aggregate analysis —(i) P provides services to S1, which is incorporated in Country A. In connection with those services, P licenses intellectual property to S2, which is incorporated in Country B. S2 sublicenses the intellectual property to S1.

(ii) Under paragraph (f)(2)(i)(B) of this section, if an aggregate analysis of the service and license transactions provides the most reliable measure of an arm's length result, then an aggregate analysis must be performed. Under paragraph (f)(2)(i)(D) of this section, if an allocation of the value that results from such an aggregate analysis is necessary, for example, for purposes of sourcing the services income that P receives from S1 or determining deductible expenses incurred by S1, then the value determined under the aggregate analysis must be allocated using the method that provides the most reliable measure of the services income and deductible expenses.

(ii)(A) [Reserved]. For further guidance see § 1.482-1(f)(2)(ii)(A).

(B) *Example*.—The following example illustrates this paragraph (f)(2)(ii):

Example. P and S are controlled taxpayers. P licenses a proprietary process to S for S's use in manufacturing product X. Using its sales and marketing employees, S sells product X to related and unrelated customers outside the United States. If the license between P and S has economic substance, the Commissioner ordinarily will not restructure the taxpayer's transaction to treat P as if it had elected to exploit directly the manufacturing process. However, because P could have directly exploited the manufacturing process and manufactured product X itself, this realistic alternative may be taken into account under § 1.482-4(d) in determining the arm's length consideration for the controlled transaction. For examples of such an analysis, see *Examples* 7 and 8 in paragraph (f)(2)(i)(E) of this section and the *Example* in § 1.482-4(d)(2).

(iii) through (j)(6) [Reserved]. For further guidance see § 1.482-1(f)(2)(iii) through (j)(6).

(7) *Certain effective/applicability dates*.—(i) Paragraphs (f)(2)(i)(A) through (E) and (f)(2)(ii)(B) of this section apply to taxable years ending on or after September 14, 2015.

(ii) *Expiration date*.—The applicability of paragraphs (f)(2)(i)(A) through (E) and (f)(2)(ii)(B) of this section expires on or before September 14, 2018. [Temporary Reg.§ 1.482.1T.]

☐ *T.D.* 9738, 9-14-2015.]

§ 1.482-2. Determination of taxable income in specific situations.—(a) *Loans or advances*.—(1) *Interest on bona fide indebtedness*.—(i) *In general*.—Where one member of a group of controlled entities makes a loan or advance directly or indirectly to, or otherwise becomes a creditor of, another member of such group and either charges no interest, or charges interest at a rate which is not equal to an arm's length rate of interest (as defined in paragraph (a)(2) of this section) with respect to such loan or advance, the district director may make appropriate allocations to reflect an arm's length rate of interest for the use of such loan or advance.

(ii) *Application of paragraph (a) of this section*.—(A) *Interest on bona fide indebtedness*.—Paragraph (a) of this section applies only to determine the appropriateness of the rate of interest charged on the principal amount of a bona fide indebtedness between members of a group of controlled entities, including—

(1) Loans or advances of money or other consideration (whether or not evidenced by a written instrument); and

(2) Indebtedness arising in the ordinary course of business from sales, leases, or the rendition of services by or between members of the group, or any other similar extension of credit.

(B) *Alleged indebtedness*.—This paragraph (a) does not apply to so much of an alleged indebtedness which is not in fact a bona fide indebtedness, even if the stated rate of interest thereon would be within the safe haven rates prescribed in paragraph (a)(2)(iii) of this section. For example, paragraph (a) of this section does not apply to payments with respect to all or a portion of such alleged indebtedness where in fact all or a portion of an alleged indebtedness is a contribution to the capital of a corporation or a distribution by a corporation with respect to its shares. Similarly, this paragraph (a) does not apply to payments with respect to an alleged purchase-money debt instrument given in consideration for an alleged sale of property between two controlled entities where in fact the transaction constitutes a lease of the property. Payments made with respect to alleged indebtedness (including alleged stated interest thereon) shall be treated according to their substance. See § 1.482-2(a)(3)(i).

(iii) *Period for which interest shall be charged*.—(A) *General rule*.—This paragraph (a)(1)(iii) is effective for indebtedness arising after June 30, 1988. See § 1.482-2(a)(3) (26 CFR Part 1 edition revised as of April 1, 1988) for indebtedness arising before July 1, 1988. Except as otherwise provided in paragraphs (a)(1)(iii)(B) through (E) of this section, the period for which interest shall be charged with respect to a bona fide indebtedness between controlled entities begins on the day after the day the indebtedness arises and ends on the day the indebtedness is satisfied (whether by payment, offset, cancellation, or otherwise). Paragraphs (a)(1)(iii)(B) through (E) of this section provide certain alternative periods during which interest is not required to be charged on certain indebtedness. These exceptions apply only to indebtedness described in paragraph (a)(1)(ii)(A)(2) of this section (relating to indebtedness incurred in the ordinary course of business from sales, services, etc., between members of the group) and not evidenced by a written instrument requiring the payment of interest. Such amounts are hereinafter referred to as intercompany trade receivables. The period for which interest is not required to be charged on intercompany trade receivables under this paragraph (a)(1)(iii) is called the interest-free period. In general, an intercompany trade receivable arises at the time economic performance occurs (within the meaning of section 461(h) and the regulations thereunder) with respect to the underlying transaction between controlled entities. For purposes of this paragraph (a)(1)(iii), the term United States includes any possession of the United States, and the term foreign country excludes any possession of the United States.

(B) *Exception for certain intercompany transactions in the ordinary course of business*.—Interest is not required to be charged on an intercompany trade receivable until the first day of the third calendar month following the month in which the intercompany trade receivable arises.

(C) *Exception for trade or business of debtor member located outside the United States*.—In the case of an intercompany trade receivable arising from a transaction in the ordinary course of a trade or business which is actively conducted outside the United States by the debtor member, interest is not required to be charged until the first day of the fourth calendar month following the month in which such intercompany trade receivable arises.

(D) *Exception for regular trade practice of creditor member or others in creditor's industry*.—If the creditor member or unrelated persons in the creditor member's industry, as a regular trade practice, allow unrelated parties a longer period without charging interest than that described in paragraph (a)(1)(iii)(B) or (C) of this section (whichever is applicable) with respect to transactions which are similar to transactions that give rise to intercompany trade receivables, such longer interest-free period shall be allowed with respect to a comparable amount of intercompany trade receivables.

(E) *Exception for property purchased for resale in a foreign country*.—*(1) General rule*.—If in the ordinary course of business one member of the group (related purchaser) purchases property from another member of the group (related seller) for resale to unrelated persons located in a particular foreign country, the related purchaser and the related seller may use as the interest-free period for the intercompany trade receivables arising during the related seller's taxable year from the purchase of such property within the same product group an interest-free period equal the sum of—

(*i*) The number of days in the related purchaser's average collection period (as determined under paragraph (a)(1)(iii)(E)(2) of this section) for sales of property within the same product group sold in the ordinary course of business to unrelated persons located in the same foreign country; plus

(*ii*) Ten (10) calendar days.

(2) *Interest-free period.*—The interest-free period under this paragraph (a)(1)(iii)(E), however, shall in no event exceed 183 days. The related purchaser does not have to conduct business outside the United States in order to be eligible to use the interest-free period of this paragraph (a)(1)(iii)(E). The interest-free period under this paragraph (a)(1)(iii)(E) shall not apply to intercompany trade receivables attributable to property which is manufactured, produced, or constructed (within the meaning of § 1.954-3(a)(4)) by the related purchaser. For purposes of this paragraph (a)(1)(iii)(E) a product group includes all products within the same three-digit Standard Industrial Classification (SIC) Code (as prepared by the Statistical Policy Division of the Office of Management and Budget, Executive Office of the President.)

(3) *Average collection period.*—An average collection period for purposes of this paragraph (a)(1)(iii)(E) is determined as follows—

(*i*) *Step 1.*—Determine total sales (less returns and allowances) by the related purchaser in the product group to unrelated persons located in the same foreign country during the related purchaser's last taxable year ending on or before the first day of the related seller's taxable year in which the intercompany trade receivable arises.

(*ii*) *Step 2.*—Determine the related purchaser's average month-end accounts receivable balance with respect to sales described in paragraph (a)(1)(iii)(E)(2)(*i*) of this section for the related purchaser's last taxable year ending on or before the first day of the related seller's taxable year in which the intercompany trade receivable arises.

(*iii*) *Step 3.*—Compute a receivables turnover rate by dividing the total sales amount described in paragraph (a)(1)(iii)(E)(2)(*i*) of this section by the average receivables balance described in paragraph (a)(1)(iii)(E)(2)(*ii*) of this section.

(*iv*) *Step 4.*—Divide the receivables turnover rate determined under paragraph (a)(1)(iii)(E)(2)(*iii*) of this section into 365, and round the result to the nearest whole number to determine the number of days in the average collection period.

(*v*) *Other considerations.*—If the related purchaser makes sales in more than one foreign country, or sells property in more than one product group in any foreign country, separate computations of an average collection period, by product group within each country, are required. If the related purchaser resells fungible property in more than one foreign country and the intercompany trade receivables arising from the related party purchase of such fungible property cannot reasonably be identified with resales in particular foreign countries, then solely for the purpose of assigning an interest-free period to such intercompany trade receivables under this paragraph (a)(1)(iii)(E), an amount of each such intercompany trade receivable shall be treated as allocable to a particular foreign country in the same proportion that the related purchaser's sales of such fungible property in such foreign country during the period described in paragraph (a)(1)(iii)(E)(2)(*i*) of this section bears to the related purchaser's sales of all such fungible property in all such foreign countries during such period. An interest-free period under this paragraph (a)(1)(iii)(E) shall not apply to any intercompany trade receivables arising in a taxable year of the related seller if the related purchaser made no sales described in paragraph (a)(1)(iii)(E)(2)(*i*) of this section from which the appropriate interest-free period may be determined.

(4) *Illustration.*—The interest-free period provided under paragraph (a)(1)(iii)(E) of this section may be illustrated by the following example:

Example—(i) *Facts.* X and Y use the calendar year as the taxable year and are members of the same group of controlled entities within the meaning of section 482. For Y's 1988 calendar taxable year X and Y intend to use the interest-free period determined under this paragraph (a)(1)(iii)(E) for intercompany trade receivables attributable to X's purchases of certain products from Y for resale by X in the ordinary course of business to unrelated persons in country Z. For its 1987 calendar taxable year all of X's sales in country Z were of products within a single product group based upon a three-digit SIC code, were not manufactured, produced, or constructed (within the meaning of § 1.954-3(a)(4)) by X, and were sold in the ordinary course of X's trade or business to unrelated persons located only in country Z. These sales and the month-end accounts receivable balances (for such sales and for such sales uncollected from prior months) are as follows:

Month	*Sales*	*Accounts Receivable*
January 1987	$500,000	$2,835,850
February	600,000	2,840,300
March	450,000	2,850,670
April	550,000	2,825,700
May	650,000	2,809,360
June	525,000	2,803,200
July	400,000	2,825,850
August	425,000	2,796,240
September	475,000	2,839,390
October	525,000	2,650,550
November	450,000	2,775,450
December 1987	650,000	2,812,600
TOTALS	$6,200,000	$33,665,160

(ii) *Average collection period.* X's total sales within the same product group to unrelated persons within country Z for the period are $6,200,000. The average receivables balance for the period is $2,805,430 ($ 33,665,160/12). The average collection period in whole days is determined as follows:

$$\text{Receivables Turnover Rate} = \frac{\$6{,}200{,}000}{\$2{,}805{,}430} = 2.21$$

$$\text{Average Collection Period days.} = \frac{365}{2.21} = 165.16 \text{ days, rounded to the nearest whole day} = 165$$

(iii) *Interest-free period.* Accordingly, for intercompany trade receivables incurred by X during Y's 1988 calendar taxable year attributable to the purchase of property from Y for resale to unrelated persons located in country Z and included in the product group, X may use an interest-free period of 175 days (165 days in the average collection period plus 10 days, but not in excess of a maximum of 183 days). All other intercompany trade receivables incurred by X are subject to the interest-free periods described in paragraphs (a)(1)(iii)(B), (C), or (D), whichever are applicable. If X makes sales in other foreign countries in addition to country Z or makes sales of property in more than one product group in any foreign country, separate computations of X's average collection period, by product group within each country, are required in order for X and Y to determine an interest-free period for such product groups in such foreign countries under this paragraph (a)(1)(iii)(E).

(iv) *Payment; book entries.*—(A) Except as otherwise provided in this paragraph (a)(1)(iv), in determining the period of time for which an amount owed by one member of the group to another member is outstanding, payments or other credits to an account are considered to be applied against the earliest amount outstanding, that is, payments or credits are applied against amounts in a first-in, first-out (FIFO) order. Thus, tracing payments to individual intercompany trade receivables is generally not required in order to determine whether a particular intercompany trade receivable has been paid within the applicable interest-free period determined under paragraph (a)(1)(iii) of this section. The application of this paragraph (a)(1)(iv)(A) may be illustrated by the following example:

Example—(i) *Facts.* X and Y are members of a group of controlled entities within the meaning of section 482. Assume that the balance of intercompany trade receivables owed by X to Y on June 1 is $100, and that all of the $100 balance represents amounts incurred by X to Y during the month of May. During the month of June X incurs an additional $200 of intercompany trade receivables to Y. Assume that on July 15, $60 is properly credited against X's intercompany account to Y, and that $240 is properly credited against the intercompany account on August 31. Assume that under paragraph (a)(1)(iii)(B) of this section interest must be charged on X's intercompany trade receivables to Y beginning with the first day of the third calendar month following the month the intercompany trade receivables arise, and that no alternative interest-free period applies. Thus, the interest-free period for intercompany trade receivables incurred during the month of May ends on July 31, and the interest-free period for intercompany trade receivables incurred during the month of June ends on August 31.

(ii) *Application of payments.* Using a FIFO payment order, the aggregate payments of $300 are applied first to the opening June balance, and then to the additional amounts incurred during the month of June. With respect to X's June opening balance of $100, no interest is required to be accrued on $60 of such balance paid by X on July 15, because such portion was paid within its interest-free period. Interest for 31 days, from August 1 to August 31 inclusive, is required to be accrued on the $40 portion of the opening balance not paid until August 31. No interest is required to be accrued on the $200 of intercompany trade receivables X incurred to Y during June because the $240 credited on August 31, after eliminating the $40 of indebtedness remaining from periods before June, also eliminated the $200 incurred by X during June prior to the end of the interest-free period for that amount. The amount of interest incurred by X to Y on the $40 amount during August creates bona fide indebtedness between controlled entities and is subject to the provisions of paragraph (a)(1)(iii)(A) of this section without regard to any of the exceptions contained in paragraphs (a)(1)(iii)(B) through (E).

(B) Notwithstanding the first-in, first-out payment application rule described in paragraph (a)(1)(iv)(A) of this section, the taxpayer may apply payments or credits against amounts owed in some other order on its books in accordance with an agreement or understanding of the related parties if the taxpayer can demonstrate that either it or others in its industry, as a regular trade practice, enter into such agreements or understandings in the case of similar balances with unrelated parties.

(2) *Arm's length interest rate.*—(i) *In general.*—For purposes of section 482 and paragraph (a) of this section, an arm's length rate of interest shall be a rate of interest which was charged, or would have been charged, at the time the indebtedness arose, in independent transactions with or between unrelated parties under similar circumstances. All relevant factors shall be considered, including the principal amount and duration of the loan, the security involved, the credit standing of the borrower, and the interest rate prevailing at the situs of the lender or creditor for comparable loans between unrelated parties.

(ii) *Funds obtained at situs of borrower.*—Notwithstanding the other provisions of paragraph (a)(2) of this section, if the loan or advance represents the proceeds of a loan obtained by the lender at the situs of the borrower, the arm's length rate for any taxable year shall be equal to the rate actually paid by the lender increased by an amount which reflects the costs or deductions incurred by the lender in borrowing such amounts and making such loans, unless the taxpayer establishes a more appropriate rate under the standards set forth in paragraph (a)(2)(i) of this section.

(iii) *Safe haven interest rates for certain loans and advances made after May 8, 1986.*—(A) *Applicability.*—(*1*) *General rule.*—Except as otherwise provided in paragraph (a)(2) of this section, paragraph (a)(2)(iii)(B) applies with respect to the rate of interest charged and to the amount of interest paid or accrued in any taxable year—

(*i*) Under a term loan or advance between members of a group of controlled entities where (except as provided in paragraph (a)(2)(iii)(A)(*2*)(*ii*) of this section) the loan or advance is entered into after May 8, 1986; and

(*ii*) After May 8, 1986 under a demand loan or advance between such controlled entities.

(*2*) *Grandfather rule for existing loans.*—The safe haven rates prescribed in paragraph (a)(2)(iii)(B) of this section shall not apply, and the safe haven rates prescribed in § 1.482-2(a)(2)(iii) (26 CFR part 1 edition revised as of April 1, 1985), shall apply to—

(*i*) Term loans or advances made before May 9, 1986; and

(*ii*) Term loans or advances made before August 7, 1986, pursuant to a binding written contract entered into before May 9, 1986.

(B) *Safe haven interest rate based on applicable Federal rate.*—Except as otherwise provided in this paragraph (a)(2), in the case of a loan or advance between members of a group of controlled entities, an arm's length rate of interest referred to in paragraph (a)(2)(i) of this section shall be for purposes of chapter 1 of the Internal Revenue Code—

(*1*) The rate of interest actually charged if that rate is—

(*i*) Not less than 100 percent of the applicable Federal rate (lower limit); and

(*ii*) Not greater than 130 percent of the applicable Federal rate (upper limit); or

(*2*) If either no interest is charged or if the rate of interest charged is less than the lower limit, then an arm's length rate of interest shall be equal to the lower limit, compounded semiannually; or

(*3*) If the rate of interest charged is greater than the upper limit, then an arm's length rate of interest shall be equal to the upper limit, compounded semiannually, unless the taxpayer establishes a more appropriate compound rate of interest under paragraph (a)(2)(i) of this section. However, if the compound rate of interest actually charged is greater than the upper limit and less than the rate determined under paragraph (a)(2)(i) of this section, or if the compound rate actually charged is less than the lower limit and greater than the rate determined under paragraph (a)(2)(i) of this section, then the compound rate actually charged shall be deemed to be an arm's length rate under paragraph (a)(2)(i). In the case of any sale-leaseback described in section 1274(e), the lower limit shall be 110 percent of the applicable Federal rate, compounded semiannually.

(C) *Applicable Federal rate.*—For purposes of paragraph (a)(2)(iii)(B) of this section, the term applicable Federal rate means, in the case of a loan or advance to which this section applies and having a term of—

(*1*) Not over 3 years, the Federal short-term rate;

(*2*) Over 3 years but not over 9 years, the Federal mid-term rate; or

(*3*) Over 9 years, the Federal long-term rate,

as determined under section 1274(d) in effect on the date such loan or advance is made. In the case of any sale or exchange between controlled entities, the lower limit shall be the lowest of the applicable Federal rates in effect for any month in the 3-calendar-month period ending with the first calendar month in which there is a binding written contract in effect for such sale or exchange (lowest 3-month rate, as defined in section 1274(d)(2)). In the case of a demand loan or advance to which this section applies, the applicable Federal rate means the Federal short-term rate determined under section 1274(d) (determined without regard to the lowest 3-month short term rate determined under section 1274(d)(2)) in effect for each day on which any amount of such loan or advance (including unpaid accrued interest determined under paragraph (a)(2) of this section) is outstanding.

(D) *Lender in business of making loans.*—If the lender in a loan or advance transaction to which paragraph (a)(2) of this section applies is regularly engaged in the trade or business of making loans or advances to unrelated parties, the safe haven rates prescribed in paragraph (a)(2)(iii)(B) of this section shall not apply, and the arm's length interest rate to be used shall be determined under the standards described in paragraph (a)(2)(i) of this section, including reference to the interest rates charged in such trade or business by the lender on loans or advances of a similar type made to unrelated parties at and about the time the loan or advance to which paragraph (a)(2) of this section applies was made.

(E) *Foreign currency loans.*—The safe haven interest rates prescribed in paragraph (a)(2)(iii)(B) of this section do not apply to any loan or advance the principal or interest of which is expressed in a currency other than U.S. dollars.

(3) *Coordination with interest adjustments required under certain other Code sections.*—If the stated rate of interest on the stated principal amount of a loan or advance between controlled entities is subject to adjustment under section 482 and is also subject to adjustment under any other section of the Internal Revenue Code (for example, section 467, 483, 1274 or 7872), section 482 and paragraph (a) of this section may be applied to such loan or advance in addition to such other Internal Revenue Code section. After the enactment of the Tax Reform Act of 1964, Pub. L. 98-369, and the enactment of Pub. L. 99-121, such other Internal Revenue Code sections include sections 467, 483, 1274 and 7872. The order in which the different provisions shall be applied is as follows—

(i) First, the substance of the transaction shall be determined; for this purpose, all the relevant facts and circumstances shall be considered and any law or rule of law (assignment of income, step transaction, etc.) may apply. Only the rate of interest with respect to the stated principal amount of the bona fide indebtedness (within the meaning of paragraph (a)(1) of this section), if any, shall be subject to adjustment under section 482, paragraph (a) of this section, and any other Internal Revenue Code section.

(ii) Second, the other Internal Revenue Code section shall be applied to the loan or advance to determine whether any amount other than stated interest is to be treated as interest, and if so, to determine such amount according to the provisions of such other Internal Revenue Code section.

(iii) Third, whether or not the other Internal Revenue Code section applies to adjust the amounts treated as interest under such loan or advance, section 482 and paragraph (a) of this section may then be applied by the district director to determine whether the rate of interest charged on the loan or advance, as adjusted by any other Code section, is greater or less than an arm's length rate of interest, and if so, to make appropriate allocations to reflect an arm's length rate of interest.

(iv) Fourth, section 482 and paragraphs (b) through (d) of this section and §§1.482-3 through 1.482-7, if applicable, may be applied by the district director to make any appropriate allocations, other than an interest rate adjustment, to reflect an arm's length transaction based upon the principal amount of the loan or advance and the interest rate as adjusted under paragraph (a)(3)(i), (ii) or (iii) of this section. For example, assume that two commonly controlled taxpayers enter into a deferred payment sale of tangible property and no interest is provided, and assume also that section 483 is applied to treat a portion of the stated sales price as interest, thereby reducing the stated sales price. If after this recharacterization of a portion of the stated sales price as interest, the recomputed sales price does not reflect an arm's length sales price under the principles of §1.482-3, the district director may make other appropriate allocations (other than an interest rate adjustment) to reflect an arm's length sales price.

(4) *Examples.*—The principles of paragraph (a)(3) of this section may be illustrated by the following examples:

Example 1. An individual, A, transfers $20,000 to a corporation controlled by A in exchange for the corporation's note which bears adequate stated interest. The district director recharacterizes the transaction as a contribution to the capital of the corporation in exchange for preferred stock. Under paragraph (a)(3)(i) of this section, section 1.482-2(a) does not apply to the transaction because there is no bona fide indebtedness.

Example 2. B, an individual, is an employee of Z corporation, and is also the controlling shareholder of Z. Z makes a term loan of $15,000 to B at a rate of interest that is less than the applicable Federal rate. In this instance the other operative Code section is section 7872. Under section 7872(b), the difference between the amount loaned and the present value of all payments due under the loan using a discount rate equal to 100 percent of the applicable Federal rate is treated as an amount of cash transferred from the corporation to B and the loan is treated as having original issue discount equal to such amount. Under paragraph (a)(3)(iii) of this section, section 482 and paragraph (a) of this section may also be applied by the district director to determine if the rate of interest charged on this $15,000 loan (100 percent of the AFR, compounded semiannually, as adjusted by section 7872) is an arm's length rate of interest. Because the rate of interest on the loan, as adjusted by section 7872, is within the safe haven range of 100-130 percent of the AFR, compounded semiannually, no further interest rate adjustments under section 482 and paragraph (a) of this section will be made to this loan.

Example 3. The facts are the same as in *Example 2* except that the amount lent by Z to B is $9,000, and that amount is the aggregate outstanding amount of loans between Z and B. Under the $10,000 de minimis exception of section 7872(c)(3), no adjustment for interest will be made to this $9,000 loan under section 7872. Under paragraph (a)(3)(iii) of this section, the district director may apply section 482 and paragraph (a) of this section to this $9,000 loan to determine whether the rate of interest charged is less than an arm's length rate of interest, and if so, to make appropriate allocations to reflect an arm's length rate of interest.

Example 4. X and Y are commonly controlled taxpayers. At a time when the applicable Federal rate is 12 percent, compounded semiannually, X sells property to Y in exchange for a note with a stated rate of interest of 18 percent, compounded semiannually. Assume that the other applicable Code section to the transaction is section 483. Section 483 does not apply to this transaction because, under section 483(d), there is no total unstated interest under the contract using the test rate of interest equal to 100 percent of the applicable Federal rate. Under paragraph (a)(3)(iii) of this section, section 482 and paragraph (a) of this section may be applied by the district director to determine whether the rate of interest under the note is excessive, that is, to determine whether the 18 percent stated interest rate under the note exceeds an arm's length rate of interest.

Example 5. Assume that A and B are commonly controlled taxpayers and that the applicable Federal rate is 10 percent, compounded semiannually. On June 30, 1986, A sells property to B and receives in exchange B's purchase-money note in the amount of $2,000,000. The stated interest rate on the note is 9%, compounded semiannually, and the stated redemption price at maturity on the note is $2,000,000. Assume that the other applicable Code section to this transaction is section 1274. As provided in section 1274A(a) and (b), the discount rate for purposes of section 1274 will be nine percent, compounded semiannually, because the stated principal amount of B's note does not exceed $2,800,000. Section 1274 does not apply to this transaction because there is adequate stated interest on the debt instrument using a discount rate equal to 9%, compounded semiannually, and the stated redemption price at maturity does not exceed the stated principal amount. Under paragraph (a)(3)(iii) of this section, the district director may apply section 482 and paragraph (a) of this section to this $2,000,000 note to determine whether the 9% rate of interest charged is less than an arm's length rate of interest, and if so, to make appropriate allocations to reflect an arm's length rate of interest.

(b) *Rendering of services.*—For rules governing allocations under section 482 to reflect an arm's length charge for controlled transactions involving the rendering of services, see §1.482-9.

(c) *Use of tangible property.*—(1) *General rule.*—Where possession, use, or occupancy of tangible property owned or leased by one member of a group of controlled entities (referred to in this paragraph as the owner) is transferred by lease or other arrangement to another member of such group (referred to in this paragraph as the user) without charge or at a charge which is not equal to an arm's length rental charge (as defined in paragraph (c)(2)(i) of this section) the district director may make appropriate allocations to properly reflect such arm's length charge. Where possession, use, or occupancy of only a portion of such property is transferred, the determination of the arm's length charge and the allocation shall be made with reference to the portion transferred.

(2) *Arm's length charge.*—(i) *In general.*—For purposes of paragraph (c) of this section, an arm's length rental charge shall be the amount of rent which was charged, or would have been charged for the use of the same or similar property, during the time it was in use, in independent transactions with or between unrelated parties under similar circumstances considering the period and location of the use, the owner's investment in the property or rent paid for the property, expenses of maintaining the property, the type of property involved, its condition, and all other relevant facts.

(ii) *Safe haven rental charge.*—See §1.482-2(c)(2)(ii) (26 CFR Part 1 revised as of April 1, 1985), for the determination of safe haven rental charges in the case of certain leases entered into before May 9, 1986, and for leases entered into before August 7, 1986, pursuant to a binding written contract entered into before May 9, 1986.

(iii) *Subleases.*—(A) Except as provided in paragraph (c)(2)(iii)(B) of this section, where possession, use, or occupancy of tangible property, which is leased by the owner (lessee) from an unrelated party is transferred by sublease or other arrangement to the user, an arm's length rental charge shall be considered to be equal to all the deductions claimed by the owner (lessee) which are attributable to the property for the period such property is used by the user. Where only a portion of such property was transferred, any allocations shall be made with reference to the portion transferred. The deductions to be considered include the rent paid or accrued by the owner (lessee) during the period of use and all other deductions directly and indirectly connected with the property paid or accrued by the owner (lessee) during such period. Such deductions include deductions for maintenance and repair, utilities, management and other similar deductions.

(B) The provisions of paragraph (c)(2)(iii)(A) of this section shall not apply if either—

(1) The taxpayer establishes a more appropriate rental charge under the general rule set forth in paragraph (c)(2)(i) of this section; or

(2) During the taxable year, the owner (lessee) or the user was regularly engaged in the trade or business of renting property of the same general type as the property in question to unrelated persons.

(d) *Transfer of property.*—For rules governing allocations under section 482 to reflect an arm's length consideration for controlled transactions involving the transfer of property, see §§1.482-3 through 1.482-6.

(e) *Cost sharing arrangement.*—For rules governing allocations under section 482 to reflect an arm's length consideration for controlled transactions involving a cost sharing arrangement, see §1.482-7.

(f) *Effective/applicability date.*—(1) *In general.*—The provision of paragraph (b) of this section is generally applicable for taxable years beginning after December 31, 2006. The provision of paragraph (e) of this section is generally applicable on January 5, 2009.

(2) *Election to apply paragraph (b) to earlier taxable years.*—A person may elect to apply the provisions of paragraph (b) of this section to earlier taxable years in accordance with the rules set forth in §1.482-9(n)(2). [Reg. §1.482-2.]

☐ [*T.D. 8552, 7-1-94. Amended by T.D. 9278, 7-31-2006; T.D. 9456, 7-31-2009 and T.D. 9568, 12-16-2011.*]

§1.482-3. Methods to determine taxable income in connection with a transfer of tangible property.—(a) *In general.*—The arm's length amount charged in a controlled transfer of tangible property must be determined under one of the six methods listed in this paragraph (a). Each of the methods must be applied in accordance with all of the provisions of §1.482-1, including the best method rule of §1.482-1(c), the comparability analysis of §1.482-1(d), and the arm's length range of §1.482-1(e). The methods are—

(1) The comparable uncontrolled price method, described in paragraph (b) of this section;

(2) The resale price method, described in paragraph (c) of this section;

(3) The cost plus method, described in paragraph (d) of this section;

(4) The comparable profits method, described in §1.482-5;

(5) The profit split method, described in §1.482-6; and

(6) Unspecified methods, described in paragraph (e) of this section.

(b) *Comparable uncontrolled price method.*—(1) *In general.*—The comparable uncontrolled price method evaluates whether the amount charged in a controlled transaction is arm's length by reference to the amount charged in a comparable uncontrolled transaction.

(2) *Comparability and reliability considerations.*—(i) *In general.*—Whether results derived from applications of this method are the most reliable measure of the arm's length result must be determined using the factors described under the best method rule in §1.482-1(c). The application of these factors under the comparable uncontrolled price method is discussed in paragraph (b)(2)(ii) and (iii) of this section.

(ii) *Comparability.*—(A) *In general.*—The degree of comparability between controlled and uncontrolled transactions is determined by applying the provisions of §1.482-1(d). Although all of the factors described in §1.482-1(d)(3) must be considered, similarity of products generally will have the greatest effect on comparability under this method. In addition, because even minor differences in contractual terms or economic conditions could materially affect the amount charged in an uncontrolled transaction, comparability under this method depends on close similarity with respect to these factors, or adjustments to account for any differences. The results derived from applying the comparable uncontrolled price method generally will be the most direct and reliable measure of an arm's length price for the controlled transaction if an uncontrolled transaction has no differences with the controlled transaction that would affect the price, or if there are only minor differences that have a definite and reasonably ascertainable effect on price and for which appropriate adjustments are made. If such adjustments cannot be made, or if there are more than minor differences between the controlled and uncontrolled transactions, the comparable uncontrolled price method may be used, but the reliability of the results as a measure of the arm's length price will be reduced. Further, if there are material product differences for which reliable adjustments cannot be made, this method ordinarily will not provide a reliable measure of an arm's length result.

(B) *Adjustments for differences between controlled and uncontrolled transactions.*—If there are differences between the controlled and uncontrolled transactions that would affect price, adjustments should be made to the price of the uncontrolled transaction according to the comparability provisions of §1.482-1(d)(2). Specific examples of the factors that may be particularly relevant to this method include—

(1) Quality of the product;

(2) Contractual terms, (e.g., scope and terms of warranties provided, sales or purchase volume, credit terms, transport terms);

(3) Level of the market (i.e., wholesale, retail, etc.);

(4) Geographic market in which the transaction takes place;

(5) Date of the transaction;

(6) Intangible property associated with the sale;

(7) Foreign currency risks; and

(8) Alternatives realistically available to the buyer and seller.

(iii) *Data and assumptions.*—The reliability of the results derived from the comparable uncontrolled price method is affected by the completeness and accuracy of the data used and the reliability of the assumptions made to apply the method. See §1.482-1(c) (Best method rule).

(3) *Arm's length range.*—See §1.482-1(e)(2) for the determination of an arm's length range.

(4) *Examples.*—The principles of this paragraph (b) are illustrated by the following examples.

Example 1—Comparable Sales of Same Product. USM, a U.S. manufacturer, sells the same product to both controlled and uncontrolled distributors. The circumstances surrounding the controlled and uncontrolled transactions are substantially the same, except that the controlled sales price is a delivered price and the uncontrolled sales are made f.o.b. USM's factory. Differences in the contractual terms of transportation and insurance generally have a definite and reasonably ascertainable effect on price, and adjustments are made to the results of the uncontrolled transaction to account for such differences. No other material difference has been identified between the controlled and uncontrolled transactions. Because USM sells in both the controlled and uncontrolled transactions, it is likely that all material differences between the two transactions have been identified. In addition, because the comparable uncontrolled price method is applied to an uncontrolled comparable with no product differences, and there are only minor contractual differences that have a definite and reasonably ascertainable effect on price, the results of this application of the comparable uncontrolled price method will provide the most direct and reliable measure of an arm's length result. See §1.482-3(b)(2)(ii)(A).

Example 2—Effect of Trademark. The facts are the same as in *Example 1,* except that USM affixes its valuable trademark to the property sold in the controlled transactions, but does not affix its trademark to the property sold in the uncontrolled transactions. Under the facts of this case, the effect on price of the trademark is material and cannot be reliably estimated. Because there are material product differences for which reliable adjustments cannot be made, the comparable uncontrolled price method is unlikely to provide a reliable measure of the arm's length result. See §1.482-3(b)(2)(ii)(A).

Example 3—Minor Product Differences. The facts are the same as in *Example 1,* except that USM, which manufactures business machines, makes minor modifications to the physical properties of the machines to satisfy specific requirements of a customer in controlled sales, but does not make these modifications in uncontrolled sales. If the minor physical differences in the product have a material affect on prices, adjustments to account for these differences must be made to the results of the uncontrolled transactions according to the provisions of § 1.482-1(d)(2), and such adjusted results may be used as a measure of the arm's length result.

Example 4—Effect of Geographic Differences. FM, a foreign specialty radio manufacturer, sells its radios to a controlled U.S. distributor, AM, that serves the West Coast of the United States. FM sells its radios to uncontrolled distributors to serve other regions in the United States. The product in the controlled and uncontrolled transactions is the same, and all other circumstances surrounding the controlled and uncontrolled transactions are substantially the same, other than the geographic differences. If the geographic differences are unlikely to have a material effect on price, or they have definite and reasonably ascertainable effects for which adjustments are made, then the adjusted results of the uncontrolled sales may be used under the comparable uncontrolled price method to establish an arm's length range pursuant to § 1.482-1(e)(2)(iii)(A). If the effects of the geographic differences would be material but cannot be reliably ascertained, then the reliability of the results will be diminished. However, the comparable uncontrolled price method may still provide the most reliable measure of an arm's length result, pursuant to the best method rule of § 1.482-1(c), and, if so, an arm's length range may be established pursuant to § 1.482-1(e)(2)(iii)(B).

(5) *Indirect evidence of comparable uncontrolled transactions.*—(i) *In general.*—A comparable uncontrolled price may be derived from data from public exchanges or quotation media, but only if the following requirements are met—

(A) The data is widely and routinely used in the ordinary course of business in the industry to negotiate prices for uncontrolled sales;

(B) The data derived from public exchanges or quotation media is used to set prices in the controlled transaction in the same way it is used by uncontrolled taxpayers in the industry; and

(C) The amount charged in the controlled transaction is adjusted to reflect differences in product quality and quantity, contractual terms, transportation costs, market conditions, risks borne, and other factors that affect the price that would be agreed to by uncontrolled taxpayers.

(ii) *Limitation.*—Use of data from public exchanges or quotation media may not be appropriate under extraordinary market conditions.

(iii) *Examples.*—The following examples illustrate this paragraph (b)(5).

Example 1—Use of Quotation Medium. (i) On June 1, USOil, a United States corporation, enters into a contract to purchase crude oil from its foreign subsidiary, FS, in Country Z. USOil and FS agree to base their sales price on the average of the prices published for that crude in a quotation medium in the five days before August 1, the date set for delivery. USOil and FS agree to adjust the price for the particular circumstances of their transactions, including the quantity of the crude sold, contractual terms, transportation costs, risks borne, and other factors that affect the price.

(ii) The quotation medium used by USOil and FS is widely and routinely used in the ordinary course of business in the industry to establish prices for uncontrolled sales. Because USOil and FS use the data to set their sales price in the same way that unrelated parties use the data from the quotation medium to set their sales prices, and appropriate adjustments were made to account for differences, the price derived from the quotation medium used by USOil and FS to set their transfer prices will be considered evidence of a comparable uncontrolled price.

Example 2—Extraordinary Market Conditions. The facts are the same as in *Example 1*, except that before USOil and FS enter into their contract, war breaks out in Countries X and Y, major oil producing countries, causing significant instability in world petroleum markets. As a result, given the significant instability in the price of oil, the prices listed on the quotation medium may not reflect a reliable measure of an arm's length result. See § 1.482-3(b)(5)(ii).

(c) *Resale price method.*—(1) *In general.*—The resale price method evaluates whether the amount charged in a controlled transaction is arm's length by reference to the gross profit margin realized in comparable uncontrolled transactions. The resale price method measures the value of functions performed, and is ordinarily used in cases involving the purchase and resale of tangible property in which the reseller has not added substantial value to the tangible goods by physically altering the goods before resale. For this purpose, packaging, repackaging, labelling, or minor assembly do not ordinarily constitute physical alteration. Further the resale price method is not ordinarily used in cases where the controlled taxpayer uses its intangible property to add substantial value to the tangible goods.

(2) *Determination of arm's length price.*—(i) *In general.*—The resale price method measures an arm's length price by subtracting the appropriate gross profit from the applicable resale price for the property involved in the controlled transaction under review.

(ii) *Applicable resale price.*—The applicable resale price is equal to either the resale price of the particular item of property involved or the price at which contemporaneous resales of the same property are made. If the property purchased in the controlled sale is resold to one or more related parties in a series of controlled sales before being resold in an uncontrolled sale, the applicable resale price is the price at which the property is resold to an uncontrolled party, or the price at which contemporaneous resales of the same property are made. In such case, the determination of the appropriate gross profit will take into account the functions of all members of the group participating in the series of controlled sales and final uncontrolled resales, as well as any other relevant factors described in § 1.482-1(d)(3).

(iii) *Appropriate gross profit.*—The appropriate gross profit is computed by multiplying the applicable resale price by the gross profit margin (expressed as a percentage of total revenue derived from sales) earned in comparable uncontrolled transactions.

(iv) *Arm's length range.*—See § 1.482-1(e)(2) for determination of the arm's length range.

(3) *Comparability and reliability considerations.*—(i) *In general.*—Whether results derived from applications of this method are the most reliable measure of the arm's length result must be determined using the factors described under the best method rule in § 1.482-1(c). The application of these factors under the resale price method is discussed in paragraphs (c)(3)(ii) and (iii) of this section.

(ii) *Comparability.*—(A) *Functional comparability.*—The degree of comparability between an uncontrolled transaction and a controlled transaction is determined by applying the comparability provisions of § 1.482-1(d). A reseller's gross profit provides compensation for the performance of resale functions related to the product or products under review, including an operating profit in return for the reseller's investment of capital and the assumption of risks. Therefore, although all of the factors described in § 1.482-1(d)(3) must be considered, comparability under this method is particularly dependent on similarity of functions performed, risks borne, and contractual terms, or adjustments to account for the effects of any such differences. If possible, appropriate gross profit margins should be derived from comparable uncontrolled purchases and resales of the reseller involved in the controlled sale, because similar characteristics are more likely to be found among different resales of property made by the same reseller than among sales made by other resellers. In the absence of comparable uncontrolled transactions involving the same reseller, an appropriate gross profit margin may be derived from comparable uncontrolled transactions of other resellers.

(B) *Other comparability factors.*—Comparability under this method is less dependent on close physical similarity between the products transferred than under the comparable uncontrolled price method. For example, distributors of a wide variety of consumer durables might perform comparable distribution functions without regard to the specific durable goods distributed. Substantial differences in the products may, however, indicate significant functional differences between the controlled and uncontrolled taxpayers. Thus, it ordinarily would be expected that the controlled and uncontrolled transactions would involve the distribution of products of the same general type (e.g., consumer electronics). Furthermore, significant differences in the value of the distributed goods due, for example, to the value of a trademark, may also affect the reliability of the comparison. Finally, the reliability of profit measures based on gross profit may be adversely affected by factors that have less effect on prices. For example, gross profit may be affected by a variety of other factors, including cost structures (as reflected, for example, in the age of plant and equipment), business experience (such as whether the business is in a start-up phase or is mature), or management efficiency (as indicated, for example, by expanding or contracting sales or executive compensation over time). Accordingly, if material differences in these factors are identified based on objective evidence, the reliability of the analysis may be affected.

(C) *Adjustments for differences between controlled and uncontrolled transactions.*—If there are material differences between the controlled and uncontrolled transactions that would affect the gross profit margin, adjustments should be made to the gross profit margin earned with respect to the uncontrolled transaction according to the comparability provisions of § 1.482-1(d)(2). For this purpose, consideration of operating expenses associated with functions performed and risks assumed may be necessary, because differences in functions performed are often reflected in operating expenses. If there are differences in functions performed, however, the effect on gross profit of such differences is not necessarily equal to the differences in the amount of related operating expenses. Specific examples of the factors that may be particularly relevant to this method include—

(1) Inventory levels and turnover rates, and corresponding risks, including any price protection programs offered by the manufacturer;

(2) Contractual terms (e.g., scope and terms of warranties provided, sales or purchase volume, credit terms, transport terms);

(3) Sales, marketing, advertising programs and services, (including promotional programs, rebates, and co-op advertising);

(4) The level of the market (e.g., wholesale, retail, etc.); and

(5) Foreign currency risks.

(D) *Sales agent.*—If the controlled taxpayer is comparable to a sales agent that does not take title to goods or otherwise assume risks with respect to ownership of such goods, the commission earned by such sales agent, expressed as a percentage of the uncontrolled sales price of the goods involved, may be used as the comparable gross profit margin.

(iii) *Data and assumptions.*—(A) *In general.*—The reliability of the results derived from the resale price method is affected by the completeness and accuracy of the data used and the reliability of the assumptions made to apply this method. See § 1.482-1(c) (Best method rule).

(B) *Consistency in accounting.*—The degree of consistency in accounting practices between the controlled transaction and the uncontrolled comparables that materially affect the gross profit margin affects the reliability of the result. Thus, for example, if differences in inventory and other cost accounting practices would materially affect the gross profit margin, the ability to make reliable adjustments for such differences would affect the reliability of the results. Further, the controlled transaction and the uncontrolled comparable should be consistent in the reporting of items (such as discounts, returns and allowances, rebates, transportation costs, insurance, and packaging) between cost of goods sold and operating expenses.

(4) *Examples.*—The following examples illustrate the principles of this paragraph (c).

Example 1. A controlled taxpayer sells property to another member of its controlled group that resells the property in uncontrolled sales. There are no changes in the beginning and ending inventory for the year under review. Information regarding an uncontrolled comparable is sufficiently complete to conclude that it is likely that all material differences between the controlled and uncontrolled transactions have been identified and adjusted for. If the applicable resale price of the property involved in the controlled sale is $100 and the appropriate gross profit margin is 20%, then an arm's length result of the controlled sale is a price of $80 ($100 minus (20% × $100)).

Example 2. (i) S, a U.S. corporation, is the exclusive distributor for FP, its foreign parent. There are no changes in the beginning and ending inventory for the year under review. S's total reported cost of goods sold is $800, consisting of $600 for property purchased from FP and $200 of other costs of goods sold incurred to unrelated parties. S's applicable resale price and reported gross profit are as follows:

Applicable resale price		$1000
Cost of goods sold		
Cost of purchases from FP	600	
Costs incurred to unrelated parties	200	
Reported gross profit		$200

(ii) The district director determines that the appropriate gross profit margin is 25%. Therefore, S's appropriate gross profit is $250 (i.e., 25% of the applicable resale price of $1000). Because S is incurring costs of sales to unrelated parties, an arm's length price for property purchased from FP must be determined under a two-step process. First, the appropriate gross profit ($250) is subtracted from the applicable resale price ($1000). The resulting amount ($750) is then reduced by the costs of sales incurred to unrelated parties ($200). Therefore, an arm's length price for S's cost of sales of FP's product in this case equals $550 (i.e., $750 minus $200).

Example 3. FP, a foreign manufacturer, sells Product to USSub, its U.S. subsidiary, which in turn sells Product to its domestic affiliate Sister. Sister sells Product to unrelated buyers. In this case, the applicable resale price is the price at which Sister sells Product in uncontrolled transactions. The determination of the appropriate gross profit margin for the sale from FP to USSub will take into account the functions performed by USSub and Sister, as well as other relevant factors described in § 1.482-1(d)(3).

Example 4. USSub, a U.S. corporation, is the exclusive distributor of widgets for its foreign parent. To determine whether the gross profit margin of 25% earned by USSub is an arm's length result, the district director considers applying the resale price method. There are several uncontrolled distributors that perform similar functions under similar circumstances in uncontrolled transactions. However, the uncontrolled distributors treat certain costs such as discounts and insurance as cost of goods sold, while USSub treats such costs as operating expenses. In such cases, accounting reclassifications, pursuant to § 1.482-3(c)(3)(iii)(B), must be made to ensure consistent treatment of such material items. Inability to make such accounting reclassifications will decrease the reliability of the results of the uncontrolled transactions.

Example 5. (i) USP, a U.S. corporation, manufactures Product X, an unbranded widget, and sells it to FSub, its wholly owned foreign subsidiary. FSub acts as a distributor of Product X in country M, and sells it to uncontrolled parties in that country. Uncontrolled distributors A, B, C, D, and E distribute competing products of approximately similar value in country M. All such products are unbranded.

(ii) Relatively complete data is available regarding the functions performed and risks borne by the uncontrolled distributors and the contractual terms under which they operate in the uncontrolled transactions. In addition, data is available to ensure accounting consistency between all of the uncontrolled distributors and FSub. Because the available data is sufficiently complete and accurate to conclude that it is likely that all material differences between the controlled and uncontrolled transactions have been identified, such differences have a definite and reasonably ascertainable effect, and reliable adjustments are made to account for such differences, the results of each of the uncontrolled distributors may be used to establish an arm's length range pursuant to § 1.482-1(e)(2)(iii)(A).

Example 6. The facts are the same as *Example 5,* except that sufficient data is not available to determine whether any of the uncontrolled distributors provide warranties or to determine the payment terms of the contracts. Because differences in these contractual terms could materially affect price or profits, the inability to determine whether these differences exist between the controlled and uncontrolled transactions diminishes the reliability of the results of the uncontrolled comparables. However, the reliability of the results may be enhanced by the application of a statistical method when establishing an arm's length range pursuant to § 1.4821(e)(2)(iii)(B).

Example 7. The facts are the same as in *Example 5,* except that Product X is branded with a valuable trademark that is owned by P. A, B, and C distribute unbranded competing products, while D and E distribute products branded with other trademarks. D and E do not own any rights in the trademarks under which their products are sold. The value of the products that A, B, and C sold are not similar to the value of the products sold by S. The value of products sold by D and E, however, is similar to that of Product X. Although close product similarity is not as important for a reliable application of the resale price method as for the comparable uncontrolled price method, significant differences in the value of the products involved in the controlled and uncontrolled transactions may affect the reliability of the results. In addition, because in this case it is difficult to determine the effect the trademark will have on price or profits, reliable adjustments for the differences cannot be made. Because D and E have a higher level of comparability than A, B, and C with respect to S, pursuant to § 1.482-1(e)(2)(ii), only D and E may be included in an arm's length range.

(d) *Cost plus method.*—(1) *In general.*—The cost plus method evaluates whether the amount charged in a controlled transaction is arm's length by reference to the gross profit markup realized in comparable uncontrolled transactions. The cost plus method is ordinarily used in cases involving the manufacture, assembly, or other production of goods that are sold to related parties.

(2) *Determination of arm's length price.*—(i) *In general.*—The cost plus method measures an arm's length price by adding the appropriate gross profit to the controlled taxpayer's costs of producing the property involved in the controlled transaction.

(ii) *Appropriate gross profit.*—The appropriate gross profit is computed by multiplying the controlled taxpayer's cost of producing the transferred property by the gross profit markup, expressed as a percentage of cost, earned in comparable uncontrolled transactions.

(iii) *Arm's length range.*—See § 1.482-1(e)(2) for determination of an arm's length range.

(3) *Comparability and reliability considerations.*—(i) *In general.*—Whether results derived from the application of this method are the most reliable measure of the arm's length result must be determined using the factors described under the best method rule in § 1.482-1(c).

(ii) *Comparability.*—(A) *Functional comparability.*—The degree of comparability between controlled and uncontrolled transactions is determined by applying the comparability provisions of § 1.482-1(d). A producer's gross profit provides compensation for the performance of the production functions related to the product or products under review, including an operating profit for the producer's investment of capital and assumption of risks. Therefore, although all of the factors described in § 1.482-1(d)(3) must be considered, comparability under this method is particularly dependent on similarity of functions performed, risks borne, and contractual terms, or adjustments to account for the effects of any such differences. If possible, the appropriate gross profit markup should be derived from comparable uncontrolled transactions of the taxpayer involved in the controlled sale, because similar characteristics are more likely to be found among sales of property by the same producer than among sales by other producers. In the absence of such sales, an appropriate gross profit markup may be derived from comparable uncontrolled sales of other producers whether or not such producers are members of the same controlled group.

(B) *Other comparability factors.*—Comparability under this method is less dependent on close physical similarity between the products transferred than under the comparable uncontrolled price method. Substantial differences in the products may, however, indicate significant functional differences between the controlled and uncontrolled taxpayers. Thus, it ordinarily would be expected that the controlled and uncontrolled transactions involve the production of goods within the same product categories. Furthermore, significant differences in the value of the products due, for example, to the value of a trademark, may also affect the reliability of the comparison. Finally, the reliability of profit measures based on gross profit may be adversely affected by factors that have less effect on prices. For example, gross profit may be affected by a variety of other factors, including cost structures (as reflected, for example, in the age of plant and equipment), business experience (such as whether the business is in a start-up phase or is mature), or management efficiency (as indicated, for example, by expanding or contracting sales or executive compensation over time). Accordingly, if material differences in these factors are identified based on objective evidence, the reliability of the analysis may be affected.

(C) *Adjustments for differences between controlled and uncontrolled transactions.*—If there are material differences between the controlled and uncontrolled transactions that would affect the gross profit markup, adjustments should be made to the gross profit markup earned in the comparable uncontrolled transaction according to the provisions of § 1.482-1(d)(2). For this purpose, consideration of the operating expenses associated with the functions performed and risks assumed may be necessary, because differences in functions performed are often reflected in operating expenses. If there are differences in functions performed, however, the effect on gross profit of such differences is not necessarily equal to the differences in the amount of related operating expenses. Specific examples of the factors that may be particularly relevant to this method include—

(1) The complexity of manufacturing or assembly;

(2) Manufacturing, production, and process engineering;

(3) Procurement, purchasing, and inventory control activities;

(4) Testing functions;

(5) Selling, general, and administrative expenses;

(6) Foreign currency risks; and

(7) Contractual terms (e.g., scope and terms of warranties provided, sales or purchase volume, credit terms, transport terms).

(D) *Purchasing agent.*—If a controlled taxpayer is comparable to a purchasing agent that does not take title to property or otherwise assume risks with respect to ownership of such goods, the commission earned by such purchasing agent, expressed as a percentage of the purchase price of the goods, may be used as the appropriate gross profit markup.

(iii) *Data and assumptions.*—(A) *In general.*—The reliability of the results derived from the cost plus method is affected by the completeness and accuracy of the data used and the reliability of the assumptions made to apply this method. See § 1.482-1(c) (Best method rule).

(B) *Consistency in accounting.*—The degree of consistency in accounting practices between the controlled transaction and the uncontrolled comparables that materially affect the gross profit markup affects the reliability of the result. Thus, for example, if differences in inventory and other cost accounting practices would materially affect the gross profit markup, the ability to make reliable adjustments for such differences would affect the reliability of the results. Further, the controlled transaction and the comparable uncontrolled transaction should be consistent in the reporting of costs between cost of goods sold and operating expenses. The term *cost of producing* includes the cost of acquiring property that is held for resale.

(4) *Examples.*—The following examples illustrate the principles of this paragraph (d).

Example 1. (i) USP, a domestic manufacturer of computer components, sells its products to FS, its foreign distributor. UT1, UT2, and UT3 are domestic computer component manufacturers that sell to uncontrolled foreign purchasers.

(ii) Relatively complete data is available regarding the functions performed and risks borne by UT1, UT2, and UT3, and the contractual terms in the uncontrolled transactions. In addition, data is available to ensure accounting consistency between all of the uncontrolled manufacturers and USP. Because the available data is sufficiently complete to conclude that it is likely that all material differences between the controlled and uncontrolled transactions have been identified, the effect of the differences are definite and reasonably ascertainable, and reliable adjustments are made to account for the differences, an arm's length range can be established pursuant to § 1.482-1(e)(2)(iii)(A).

Example 2. The facts are the same as in *Example 1*, except that USP accounts for supervisory, general, and administrative costs as operating expenses, which are not allocated to its sales to FS. The gross profit markups of UT1, UT2, and UT3, however, reflect supervisory, general, and administrative expenses because they are accounted for as costs of goods sold. Accordingly, the gross profit markups of UT1, UT2, and UT3 must be adjusted as provided in paragraph (d)(3)(iii)(B) of this section to provide accounting consistency. If data is not sufficient to determine whether such accounting differences exist between the controlled and uncontrolled transactions, the reliability of the results will be decreased.

Example 3. The facts are the same as in *Example 1*, except that under its contract with FS, USP uses materials consigned by FS. UT1, UT2, and UT3, on the other hand, purchase their own materials, and their gross profit markups are determined by including the costs of materials. The fact that USP does not carry an inventory risk by purchasing its own materials while the uncontrolled producers carry inventory is a significant difference that may require an adjustment if the difference has a material effect on the gross profit markups of the uncontrolled producers. Inability to reasonably ascertain the effect of the difference on the gross profit markups will affect the reliability of the results of UT1, UT2, and UT3.

Example 4. (i) FS, a foreign corporation, produces apparel for USP, its U.S. parent corporation. FS purchases its materials from unrelated suppliers and produces the apparel according to designs provided by USP. The district director identifies 10 uncontrolled foreign apparel producers that operate in the same geographic market and are similar in many respect to FS.

(ii) Relatively complete data is available regarding the functions performed and risks borne by the uncontrolled producers. In addition, data is sufficiently detailed to permit adjustments for differences in accounting practices. However, sufficient data is not available to determine whether it is likely that all material differences in contractual terms have been identified. For example, it is not possible to determine which parties in the uncontrolled transactions bear currency risks. Because differences in these contractual terms could materially affect price or profits, the inability to determine whether differences exist between the controlled and uncontrolled transactions will diminish the reliability of these results. Therefore, the reliability of the results of the uncontrolled transactions must be enhanced by the application of a statistical method in establishing an arm's length range pursuant to § 1.482-1(e)(2)(iii)(B).

(e) *Unspecified methods.*—(1) *In general.*—Methods not specified in paragraphs (a)(1), (2), (3), (4), and (5) of this section may be used to evaluate whether the amount charged in a controlled transaction is arm's length. Any method used under this paragraph (e) must be applied in accordance with the provisions of § 1.482-1. Consistent with the specified methods, an unspecified method should take into account the general principle that uncontrolled taxpayers evaluate the terms of a transaction by considering the realistic alternatives to that transaction, and only enter into a particular transaction if none of the alternatives is preferable to it. For example, the comparable uncontrolled price method compares a controlled transaction to similar uncontrolled transactions to provide a direct estimate of the price to which the parties would have agreed had they resorted directly to a market alternative to the controlled transaction. Therefore, in establishing whether a controlled transaction achieved an arm's length result, an unspecified method should provide information on the prices or profits that the controlled taxpayer could have realized by choosing a realistic alternative to the controlled transaction. As with any method, an unspecified method will not be applied unless it provides the most reliable measure of an arm's length result under the principles of the best method rule. See § 1.482-1(c). Therefore, in accordance with § 1.482-1(d) (Comparability), to the extent that a method relies on internal data rather than uncontrolled comparables, its reliability will be reduced. Similarly, the reliability of a method will be affected by the reliability of the data and assumptions used to apply the method, including any projections used.

(2) *Example.*—The following example illustrates an application of the principle of this paragraph (e).

Example. Amcan, a U.S. company, produces unique vessels for storing and transporting toxic waste, toxicans, at its U.S. production facility. Amcan agrees by contract to supply its Canadian subsidiary, Cancan, with 4000 toxicans per year to serve the Canadian market for toxicans. Prior to entering into the contract with Cancan, Amcan had received a bona fide offer from an independent Canadian waste disposal company, Cando, to serve as the Canadian distributor for toxicans and to purchase a similar number of toxicans at a price of $5,000 each. If the circumstances and terms of the Cancan supply contract are sufficiently similar to those of the Cando offer, or sufficiently reliable adjustments can be made for differences between them, then the Cando offer price of $5,000 may provide reliable information indicating that an arm's length consideration under the Cancan contract will not be less than $5,000 per toxican.

(f) *Coordination with intangible property rules.*—The value of an item of tangible property may be affected by the value of intangible property, such as a trademark affixed to the tangible property (embedded intangible). Ordinarily, the transfer of tangible property with an embedded intangible will not be considered a transfer of such intangible if the controlled purchaser does not acquire any rights to exploit the intangible property other than rights relating to the resale of the tangible property under normal commercial practices. Pursuant to § 1.482-1(d)(3)(v), however, the embedded intangible must be accounted for in evaluating the comparability of the controlled transaction and uncontrolled comparables. For example, because product comparability has the greatest effect on an application of the comparable uncontrolled price method, trademarked tangible property may be insufficiently comparable to unbranded tangible property to permit a reliable application of the comparable uncontrolled price method. The effect of embedded intangibles on comparability will be determined under the principles of § 1.482-4. If the transfer of tangible property conveys to the recipient a right to exploit an embedded intangible (other than in connection with the resale of that item of tangible property), it may be necessary to determine the arm's length consideration for such intangible separately from the tangible property, applying methods appropriate to determining the arm's length result for a transfer of intangible property under § 1.482-4. For example, if the transfer of a machine conveys the right to exploit a manufacturing process incorporated in the machine, then the arm's length consideration for the transfer of that right must be determined separately under § 1.482-4. [Reg. § 1.482-3.]

☐ [*T.D.* 8552, 7-1-94.]

§ 1.482-4. Methods to determine taxable income in connection with a transfer of intangible property.—(a) *In general.*—The arm's length amount charged in a controlled transfer of intangible property must be determined under one of the four methods listed in this paragraph (a). Each of the methods must be applied in accordance with all of the provisions of § 1.482-1, including the best method rule of § 1.482-1(c), the comparability analysis of § 1.482-1(d), and the arm's length range of § 1.482-1(e). The arm's length consideration for the transfer of an intangible determined under this section must be commensurate with the income attributable to the intangible. See § 1.482-4(f)(2) (Periodic adjustments). The available methods are—

(1) The comparable uncontrolled transaction method, described in paragraph (c) of this section;

(2) The comparable profits method, described in § 1.482-5;

(3) The profit split method, described in § 1.482-6; and

(4) Unspecified methods described in paragraph (d) of this section.

(b) *Definition of intangible.*—For purposes of section 482, an intangible is an asset that comprises any of the following items and has substantial value independent of the services of any individual—

(1) Patents, inventions, formulae, processes, designs, patterns, or know-how;

(2) Copyrights and literary, musical, or artistic compositions;

(3) Trademarks, trade names, or brand names;

(4) Franchises, licenses, or contracts;

(5) Methods, programs, systems, procedures, campaigns, surveys, studies, forecasts, estimates, customer lists, or technical data; and

(6) Other similar items. For purposes of section 482, an item is considered similar to those listed in paragraph (b)(1) through (5) of this section if it derives its value not from its physical attributes but from its intellectual content or other intangible properties.

(c) *Comparable uncontrolled transaction method.*—(1) *In general.*—The comparable uncontrolled transaction method evaluates whether the amount charged for a controlled transfer of intangible property was arm's length by reference to the amount charged in a comparable uncontrolled transaction. The amount determined under this method may be adjusted as required by paragraph (f)(2) of this section (Periodic adjustments).

(2) *Comparability and reliability considerations.*—(i) *In general.*—Whether results derived from applications of this method are the most reliable measure of an arm's length result is determined using the factors described under the best method rule in § 1.482-1(c). The application of these factors under the comparable uncontrolled transaction method is discussed in paragraphs (c)(2)(ii), (iii), and (iv) of this section.

(ii) *Reliability.*—If an uncontrolled transaction involves the transfer of the same intangible under the same, or substantially the same, circumstances as the controlled transaction, the results derived from applying the comparable uncontrolled transaction method will generally be the most direct and reliable measure of the arm's length result for the controlled transfer of an intangible. Circumstances between the controlled and uncontrolled transactions will be considered substantially the same if there are at most only minor differences that have a definite and reasonably ascertainable effect on the amount charged and for which appropriate adjustments are made. If such uncontrolled transactions cannot be identified, uncontrolled transactions that involve the transfer of comparable intangibles under comparable circumstances may be used to apply this method, but the reliability of the analysis will be reduced.

(iii) *Comparability.*—(A) *In general.*—The degree of comparability between controlled and uncontrolled transactions is determined by applying the comparability provisions of § 1.482-1(d). Although all of the factors described in § 1.482-1(d)(3) must be considered, specific factors may be particularly relevant to this method. In particular, the application of this method requires that the controlled and uncontrolled transactions involve either the same intangible property or comparable intangible property, as defined in paragraph (c)(2)(iii)(B)(*1*) of this section. In addition, because differences in contractual terms, or the economic conditions in which transactions take place, could materially affect the amount charged, comparability under this method also depends on similarity with respect to these factors, or adjustments to account for material differences in such circumstances.

(B) *Factors to be considered in determining comparability.— (1) Comparable intangible property.*—In order for the intangible property involved in an uncontrolled transaction to be considered comparable to the intangible property involved in the controlled transaction, both intangibles must—

(i) Be used in connection with similar products or processes within the same general industry or market; and

(ii) Have similar profit potential. The profit potential of an intangible is most reliably measured by directly calculating the net present value of the benefits to be realized (based on prospective profits to be realized or costs to be saved) through the use or subsequent transfer of the intangible, considering the capital investment and start-up expenses required, the risks to be assumed, and other relevant considerations. The need to reliably measure profit potential increases in relation to both the total amount of potential profits and the potential rate of return on investment necessary to exploit the intangible. If the information necessary to directly calculate net present value of the benefits to be realized is unavailable, and the need to reliably measure profit potential is reduced because the potential profits are relatively small in terms of total amount and rate of return, comparison of profit potential may be based upon the factors referred to in paragraph (c)(2)(iii)(B)(*2*) of this section. See *Example 3* of § 1.482-4(c)(4). Finally, the reliability of a measure of profit potential is affected by the extent to which the profit attributable to the intangible can be isolated from the profit attributable to other factors, such as functions performed and other resources employed.

(2) Comparable circumstances.—In evaluating the comparability of the circumstances of the controlled and uncontrolled transactions, although all of the factors described in § 1.482-1(d)(3) must be considered, specific factors that may be particularly relevant to this method include the following—

(i) The terms of the transfer, including the exploitation rights granted in the intangible, the exclusive or nonexclusive character of any rights granted, any restrictions on use, or any limitations on the geographic area in which the rights may be exploited;

(ii) The stage of development of the intangible (including, where appropriate, necessary governmental approvals, authorizations, or licenses) in the market in which the intangible is to be used;

(iii) Rights to receive updates, revisions, or modifications of the intangible;

(iv) The uniqueness of the property and the period for which it remains unique, including the degree and duration of protection afforded to the property under the laws of the relevant countries;

(v) The duration of the license, contract, or other agreement, and any termination or renegotiation rights;

(vi) Any economic and product liability risks to be assumed by the transferee;

(vii) The existence and extent of any collateral transactions or ongoing business relationships between the transferee and transferor; and

(viii) The functions to be performed by the transferor and transferee, including any ancillary or subsidiary services.

(iv) *Data and assumptions.*—The reliability of the results derived from the comparable uncontrolled transaction method is affected by the completeness and accuracy of the data used and the reliability of the assumptions made to apply this method. See § 1.482-1(c) (Best method rule).

(3) *Arm's length range.*—See § 1.482-1(e)(2) for the determination of an arm's length range.

(4) *Examples.*—The following examples illustrate the principles of this paragraph (c).

Example 1. (i) USpharm, a U.S. pharmaceutical company, develops a new drug Z that is a safe and effective treatment for the disease zeezee. USpharm has obtained patents covering drug Z in the United States and in various foreign countries. USpharm has also obtained the regulatory authorizations necessary to market drug Z in the United States and in foreign countries.

(ii) USpharm licenses its subsidiary in country X, Xpharm, to produce and sell drug Z in country X. At the same time, it licenses an unrelated company, Ydrug, to produce and sell drug Z in country Y, a neighboring country. Prior to licensing the drug, USpharm had obtained patent protection and regulatory approvals in both countries and both countries provide similar protection for intellectual property rights. Country X and country Y are similar countries in terms of population, per capita income and the incidence of disease zeezee. Consequently, drug Z is expected to sell in similar quantities and at similar prices in both countries. In addition, costs of producing and marketing drug Z in each country are expected to be approximately the same.

(iii) USpharm and Xpharm establish terms for the license of drug Z that are identical in every material respect, including royalty rate, to the terms established between USpharm and Ydrug. In this case the district director determines that the royalty rate established in the Ydrug license agreement is a reliable measure of the arm's length royalty rate for the Xpharm license agreement.

Example 2. The facts are the same as in *Example 1*, except that the incidence of the disease zeezee in Country Y is much higher than in Country X. In this case, the profit potential from exploitation of the right to make and sell drug Z is likely to be much higher in country Y than it is in Country X. Consequently, the Ydrug license agreement is unlikely to provide a reliable measure of the arm's length royalty rate for the Xpharm license.

Example 3. (i) FP is a foreign company that designs, manufactures and sells industrial equipment. FP has developed proprietary components that are incorporated in its products. These components are important in the operation of FP's equipment and some of them have distinctive features, but other companies produce similar components and none of these components by itself accounts for a substantial part of the value of FP's products.

(ii) FP licenses its U.S. subsidiary, USSub, exclusive North American rights to use the patented technology for producing component X, a heat exchanger used for cooling operating mechanisms in industrial equipment. Component X incorporates proven technology that makes it somewhat more efficient than the heat exchangers commonly used in industrial equipment. FP also agrees to provide technical support to help adapt component X to USSub's products and to assist with initial production. Under the terms of the license agreement USSub pays FP a royalty equal to 3 percent of sales of USSub equipment incorporating component X.

(iii) FP does not license unrelated parties to use component X, but many similar components are transferred between uncontrolled taxpayers. Consequently, the district director decides to apply the comparable uncontrolled transaction method to evaluate whether the 3 percent royalty for component X is an arm's length royalty.

(iv) The district director uses a database of company documents filed with the Securities and Exchange Commission (SEC) to identify potentially comparable license agreements between uncontrolled taxpayers that are on file with the SEC. The district director identifies 40 license agreements that were entered into in the same year as the controlled transfer or in the prior or following year, and that relate to transfers of technology associated with industrial equipment that has similar applications to USSub's products. Further review of these uncontrolled agreements indicates that 25 of them involved components that have a similar level of technical sophistication as component X and could be expected to play a similar role in contributing to the total value of the final product.

(v) The district director makes a detailed review of the terms of each of the 25 uncontrolled agreements and finds that 15 of them are similar to the controlled agreement in that they all involve—

(A) The transfer of exclusive rights for the North American market;

(B) Products for which the market could be expected to be of a similar size to the market for the products into which USSub incorporates component X;

(C) The transfer of patented technology;

(D) Continuing technical support;

(E) Access to technical improvements;

(F) Technology of a similar age; and

(G) A similar duration of the agreement.

(vi) Based on these factors and the fact that none of the components to which these license agreements relate accounts for a substantial part of the value of the final products, the district director concludes that these fifteen intangibles have similar profit potential to the component X technology.

(vii) The 15 uncontrolled comparables produce the following royalty rates:

License	Royalty rate (percent)
1	1.0
2	1.0
3	1.25
4	1.25
5	1.5
6	1.5
7	1.75
8	2.0
9	2.0
10	2.0
11	2.25
12	2.5
13	2.5
14	2.75
15	3.0

(viii) Although the uncontrolled comparables are clearly similar to the controlled transaction, it is likely that unidentified material differences exist between the uncontrolled comparables and the controlled transaction. Therefore, an appropriate statistical technique must be used to establish the arm's length range. In this case the district director uses the interquartile range to determine the arm's length range. Therefore, the arm's length range covers royalty rates from 1.25 to 2.5 percent, and an adjustment is warranted to the 3 percent royalty charged in the controlled transfer. The district director determines that the appropriate adjustment corresponds to a reduction in the royalty rate to 2.0 percent, which is the median of the uncontrolled comparables.

Example 4. (i) USdrug, a U.S. pharmaceutical company, has developed a new drug, Nosplit, that is useful in treating migraine headaches and produces no significant side effects. Nosplit replaces another drug, Lessplit, that USdrug had previously produced and marketed as a treatment for migraine headaches. A number of other drugs for treating migraine headaches are already on the market, but Nosplit can be expected rapidly to dominate the worldwide market for such treatments and to command a premium price since all other treatments produce side effects. Thus, USdrug projects that extraordinary profits will be derived from Nosplit in the U.S. market and other markets.

(ii) USdrug licenses its newly established European subsidiary, Eurodrug, the rights to produce and market Nosplit in the European market. In setting the royalty rate for this license, USdrug considers the royalty that it established previously when it licensed the right to produce and market Lessplit in the European market to an unrelated European pharmaceutical company. In many respects the two license agreements are closely comparable. The drugs were licensed at the same stage in their development and the agreements conveyed identical rights to the licensees. Moreover, there appear to have been no significant changes in the European market for migraine headache treatments since Lessplit was licensed. However, at the time that Lessplit was licensed there were several other similar drugs already on the market to which Lessplit was not in all cases superior. Consequently, the projected and actual Lessplit profits were substantially less than the projected Nosplit profits. Thus, USdrug concludes that the profit potential of Lessplit is not similar to the profit potential of Nosplit, and the Lessplit license agreement consequently is not a comparable uncontrolled transaction for purposes of this paragraph (c) in spite of the other indicia of comparability between the two intangibles.

(d) *Unspecified methods.*—(1) *In general.*—Methods not specified in paragraphs (a)(1), (2), and (3) of this section may be used to evaluate whether the amount charged in a controlled transaction is arm's length. Any method used under this paragraph (d) must be applied in accordance with the provisions of § 1.482-1. Consistent with the specified methods, an unspecified method should take into account the general principle that uncontrolled taxpayers evaluate the terms of a transaction by considering the realistic alternatives to that transaction, and only enter into a particular transaction if none of the alternatives is preferable to it. For example, the comparable uncontrolled transaction method compares a controlled transaction to similar uncontrolled transactions to provide a direct estimate of the price the parties would have agreed to had they resorted directly to a market alternative to the controlled transaction. Therefore, in establishing whether a controlled transaction achieved an arm's length result, an unspecified method should provide information on the prices or profits that the controlled taxpayer could have realized by choosing a realistic alternative to the controlled transaction. As with any method, an unspecified method will not be applied unless it provides the most reliable measure of an arm's length result under the principles of the best method rule. See § 1.482-1(c). Therefore, in accordance with § 1.482-1(d) (Comparability), to the extent that a method relies on internal data rather than uncontrolled comparables, its reliability will be reduced. Similarly, the reliability of a method will be affected by the reliability of the data and assumptions used to apply the method, including any projections used.

(2) *Example.* The following example illustrates an application of the principle of this paragraph (d).

Example. (i) USbond is a U.S. company that licenses to its foreign subsidiary, Eurobond, a proprietary process that permits the manufacture of Longbond, a long-lasting industrial adhesive, at a substantially lower cost than otherwise would be possible. Using the proprietary process, Eurobond manufactures Longbond and sells it to related and unrelated parties for the market price of $550 per ton. Under the terms of the license agreement, Eurobond pays USbond a royalty of $100 per ton of Longbond sold. USbond also manufactures and markets Longbond in the United States.

(ii) In evaluating whether the consideration paid for the transfer of the proprietary process to Eurobond was arm's length, the district director may consider, subject to the best method rule of § 1.482-1(c), USbond's alternative of producing and selling Longbond itself. Reasonably reliable estimates indicate that if USbond directly supplied Longbond to the European market, a selling price of $300 per ton would cover its costs and provide a reasonable profit for its functions, risks and investment of capital associated with the production of Longbond for the European market. Given that the market price of Longbond was $550 per ton, by licensing the proprietary process to Eurobond, USbond forgoes $250 per ton of profit over the profit that would be necessary to compensate it for the functions, risks and investment involved in supplying Longbond to the European market itself. Based on these facts, the district director concludes that a royalty of $100 for the proprietary process is not arm's length.

(e) *Coordination with tangible property rules.*—See § 1.482-3(f) for the provisions regarding the coordination between the tangible property and intangible property rules.

(f) *Special rules for transfers of intangible property.*—(1) *Form of consideration.*—If a transferee of an intangible pays nominal or no consideration and the transferor has retained a substantial interest in the property, the arm's length consideration shall be in the form of a royalty, unless a different form is demonstrably more appropriate.

(2) *Periodic adjustments.*—(i) *General rule.*—If an intangible is transferred under an arrangement that covers more than one year, the consideration charged in each taxable year may be adjusted to ensure that it is commensurate with the income attributable to the intangible. Adjustments made pursuant to this paragraph (f)(2) shall be consistent with the arm's length standard and the provisions of § 1.482-1. In determining whether to make such adjustments in the taxable year under examination, the district director may consider all relevant facts and circumstances throughout the period the intangible is used. The determination in an earlier year that the amount charged for an intangible was an arm's length amount will not preclude the district director in a subsequent taxable year from making an adjustment to the amount charged for the intangible in the subsequent year. A periodic adjustment under the commensurate with income requirement of section 482 may be made in a subsequent taxable year without regard to whether the taxable year of the original transfer remains open for statute of limitation purposes. For exceptions to this rule see paragraph (f)(2)(ii) of this section.

(ii) *Exceptions.*—(A) *Transactions involving the same intangible.*—If the same intangible was transferred to an uncontrolled taxpayer under substantially the same circumstances as those of the controlled transaction; this transaction serves as the basis for the application of the comparable uncontrolled transaction method in the first taxable year in which substantial periodic consideration was required to be paid; and the amount paid in that year was an arm's length amount, then no allocation in a subsequent year will be made under paragraph (f)(2)(i) of this paragraph for a controlled transfer of intangible property.

(B) *Transactions involving comparable intangible.*—If the arm's length result is derived from the application of the comparable uncontrolled transaction method based on the transfer of a comparable intangible under comparable circumstances to those of the controlled transaction, no allocation will be made under paragraph (f)(2)(i) of this section if each of the following facts is established—

(1) The controlled taxpayers entered into a written agreement (controlled agreement) that provided for an amount of consideration with respect to each taxable year subject to such agreement, such consideration was an arm's length amount for the first taxable year in which substantial periodic consideration was required to be paid under the agreement, and such agreement remained in effect for the taxable year under review;

(2) There is a written agreement setting forth the terms of the comparable uncontrolled transaction relied upon to establish the arm's length consideration (uncontrolled agreement), which contains no provisions that would permit any change to the amount of consideration, a renegotiation, or a termination of the agreement, in circumstances comparable to those of the controlled transaction in the taxable year under review (or that contains provisions permitting only specified, non-contingent, periodic changes to the amount of consideration);

(3) The controlled agreement is substantially similar to the uncontrolled agreement, with respect to the time period for which it is effective and the provisions described in paragraph (f)(2)(ii)(B)(2) of this section;

(4) The controlled agreement limits use of the intangible to a specified field or purpose in a manner that is consistent with industry practice and any such limitation in the uncontrolled agreement;

(5) There were no substantial changes in the functions performed by the controlled transferee after the controlled agreement was executed, except changes required by events that were not foreseeable; and

(6) The aggregate profits actually earned or the aggregate cost savings actually realized by the controlled taxpayer from the exploitation of the intangible in the year under examination, and all past years, are not less than 80% nor more than 120% of the prospective profits or cost savings that were foreseeable when the comparability of the uncontrolled agreement was established under paragraph (c)(2) of this section.

(C) *Methods other than comparable uncontrolled transaction.*—If the arm's length amount was determined under any method other than the comparable uncontrolled transaction method, no allocation will be made under paragraph (f)(2)(i) of this section if each of the following facts is established—

(1) The controlled taxpayers entered into a written agreement (controlled agreement) that provided for an amount of consideration with respect to each taxable year subject to such agreement, and such agreement remained in effect for the taxable year under review;

(2) The consideration called for in the controlled agreement was an arm's length amount for the first taxable year in which substantial periodic consideration was required to be paid, and relevant supporting documentation was prepared contemporaneously with the execution of the controlled agreement;

(3) There have been no substantial changes in the functions performed by the transferee since the controlled agreement was executed, except changes required by events that were not foreseeable; and

(4) The total profits actually earned or the total cost savings realized by the controlled transferee from the exploitation of the intangible in the year under examination, and all past years, are not less than 80% nor more than 120% of the prospective profits or cost savings that were foreseeable when the controlled agreement was entered into.

(D) *Extraordinary events.*—No allocation will be made under paragraph (f)(2)(i) of this section if the following requirements are met—

(1) Due to extraordinary events that were beyond the control of the controlled taxpayers and that could not reasonably have been anticipated at the time the controlled agreement was entered into, the aggregate actual profits or aggregate cost savings realized by the taxpayer are less than 80% or more than 120% of the prospective profits or cost savings; and

(2) All of the requirements of paragraph (f)(2)(ii)(B) or (C) of this section are otherwise satisfied.

(E) *Five-year period.*—If the requirements of § 1.482-4(f)(2)(ii)(B) or (f)(2)(ii)(C) are met for each year of the five-year period beginning with the first year in which substantial periodic consideration was required to be paid, then no periodic adjustment will be made under paragraph (f)(2)(i) of this section in any subsequent year.

(iii) *Examples.*—The following examples illustrate this paragraph (f)(2).

Example 1. (i) USdrug, a U.S. pharmaceutical company, has developed a new drug, Nosplit, that is useful in treating migraine headaches and produces no significant side effects. A number of other drugs for treating migraine headaches are already on the market, but Nosplit can be expected rapidly to dominate the worldwide market for such treatments and to command a premium price since all other treatments produce side effects. Thus, USdrug projects that extraordinary profits will be derived from Nosplit in the U.S. and European markets.

(ii) USdrug licenses its newly established European subsidiary, Eurodrug, the rights to produce and market Nosplit for the European market for 5 years. In setting the royalty rate for this license, USdrug makes projections of the annual sales revenue and the annual profits to be derived from the exploitation of Nosplit by Eurodrug. Based on the projections, a royalty rate of 3.9% is established for the term of the license.

(iii) In Year 1, USdrug evaluates the royalty rate it received from Eurodrug. Given the high profit potential of Nosplit, USdrug is unable to locate any uncontrolled transactions dealing with licenses of comparable intangible property. USdrug therefore determines that the comparable uncontrolled transaction method will not provide a reliable measure of an arm's length royalty. However, applying the comparable profits method to Eurodrug, USdrug determines that a royalty rate of 3.9% will result in Eurodrug earning an arm's length return for its manufacturing and marketing functions.

(iv) In Year 5, the U.S. income tax return for USdrug is examined, and the district director must determine whether the royalty rate between USdrug and Eurodrug is commensurate with the income attributable to Nosplit. In making this determination, the district director considers whether any of the exceptions in § 1.482-4(f)(2)(ii) are applicable. In particular, the district director compares the profit projections attributable to Nosplit made by USdrug against the actual profits realized by Eurodrug. The projected and actual profits are as follows:

	Profit projections	*Actual profits*
Year 1	200	250
Year 2	250	300
Year 3	500	600
Year 4	350	200
Year 5	100	100
Total	1400	1450

(v) The total profits earned through Year 5 were not less than 80% nor more than 120% of the profits that were projected when the license was entered into. If the district director determines that the other requirements of § 1.482-4(f)(2)(ii)(C) were met, no adjustment will be made to the royalty rate between USdrug and Eurodrug for the license of Nosplit.

Example 2. (i) The facts are the same as in *Example 1*, except that Eurodrug's actual profits earned were much higher than the projected profits, as follows:

	Profit projections	Actual profits
Year 1	200	250
Year 2	250	500
Year 3	500	800
Year 4	350	700
Year 5	100	600
Total	1400	2850

(ii) In examining USdrug's tax return for Year 5, the district director considers the actual profits realized by Eurodrug in Year 5, and all past years. Accordingly, although Years 1 through 4 may be closed under the statute of limitations, for purposes of determining whether an adjustment should be made with respect to the royalty rate in Year 5 with respect to Nosplit, the district director aggregates the actual profits from those years with the profits of Year 5. However, the district director will make an adjustment, if any, only with respect to Year 5.

Example 3. (i) FP, a foreign corporation, licenses to USS, its U.S. subsidiary, a new air-filtering process that permits manufacturing plants to meet new environmental standards. The license runs for a 10-year period, and the profit derived from the new process is projected to be $15 million per year, for an aggregate profit of $150 million.

(ii) The royalty rate for the license is based on a comparable uncontrolled transaction involving a comparable intangible under comparable circumstances. The requirements of paragraphs (f)(2)(ii)(B)(*1*) through (*5*) of this section have been met. Specifically, FP and USS have entered into a written agreement that provides for a royalty in each year of the license, the royalty rate is considered arm's length for the first taxable year in which a substantial royalty was required to be paid, the license limited the use of the process to a specified field, consistent with industry practice, and there are no substantial changes in the functions performed by USS after the license was entered into.

(iii) In examining Year 4 of the license, the district director determines that the aggregate actual profits earned by USS through Year 4 are $30 million, less than 80% of the projected profits of $60 million. However, USS establishes to the satisfaction of the district director that the aggregate actual profits from the process are less than 80% of the projected profits in Year 3 because an earthquake severely damaged USS's manufacturing plant. Because the difference between the projected profits and actual profits was due to an extraordinary event that was beyond the control of USS, and could not reasonably have been anticipated at the time the license was entered into, the requirement under § 1.482-4(f)(2)(ii)(D) has been met, and no adjustment under this section is made.

(3) *Ownership of intangible property.*—(i) *Identification of owner.*—(A) *In general.*—The legal owner of intangible property pursuant to the intellectual property law of the relevant jurisdiction, or the holder of rights constituting an intangible property pursuant to contractual terms (such as the terms of a license) or other legal provision, will be considered the sole owner of the respective intangible property for purposes of this section unless such ownership is inconsistent with the economic substance of the underlying transactions. See § 1.482-1(d)(3)(ii)(B) (identifying contractual terms). If no owner of the respective intangible property is identified under the intellectual property law of the relevant jurisdiction, or pursuant to contractual terms (including terms imputed pursuant to § 1.482-1(d)(3)(ii)(B)) or other legal provision, then the controlled taxpayer who has control of the intangible property, based on all the facts and circumstances, will be considered the sole owner of the intangible property for purposes of this section.

(B) *Cost sharing arrangements.*—The rules in this paragraph (f)(3) regarding ownership with respect to cost shared intangibles and cost sharing arrangements will apply only as provided in § 1.482-7.

(ii) *Examples.*—The principles of this paragraph (f)(3) are illustrated by the following examples:

Example 1. FP, a foreign corporation, is the registered holder of the AA trademark in the United States. FP licenses to its U.S. subsidiary, USSub, the exclusive rights to manufacture and market products in the United States under the AA trademark. FP is the owner of the trademark pursuant to intellectual property law. USSub is the owner of the license pursuant to the terms of the license, but is not the owner of the trademark. See paragraphs (b)(3) and (4) of this section (defining an intangible as, among other things, a trademark or a license).

Example 2. The facts are the same as in *Example 1.* As a result of its sales and marketing activities, USSub develops a list of several hundred creditworthy customers that regularly purchase AA trademarked products. Neither the terms of the contract between FP and USSub nor the relevant intellectual property law specify which party owns the customer list. Because USSub has knowledge of the contents of the list, and has practical control over its use and dissemination, USSub is considered the sole owner of the customer list for purposes of this paragraph (f)(3).

(4) *Contribution to the value of intangible property owned by another.*—(i) *In general.*—The arm's length consideration for a contribution by one controlled taxpayer that develops or enhances the value, or may be reasonably anticipated to develop or enhance the value, of intangible property owned by another controlled taxpayer will be determined in accordance with the applicable rules under section 482. If the consideration for such a contribution is embedded within the contractual terms for a controlled transaction that involves such intangible property, then ordinarily no separate allocation will be made with respect to such contribution. In such cases, pursuant to § 1.482-1(d)(3), the contribution must be accounted for in evaluating the comparability of the controlled transaction to uncontrolled comparables, and accordingly in determining the arm's length consideration in the controlled transaction.

(ii) *Examples.*—The principles of this paragraph (f)(4) are illustrated by the following examples:

Example 1. A, a member of a controlled group, allows B, another member of the controlled group, to use tangible property, such as laboratory equipment, in connection with B's development of an intangible that B owns. By furnishing tangible property, A makes a contribution to the development of intangible property owned by another controlled taxpayer, B. Pursuant to paragraph (f)(4)(i) of this section, the arm's length charge for A's furnishing of tangible property will be determined under the rules for use of tangible property in § 1.482-2(c).

Example 2. (i) *Facts.* FP, a foreign producer of wristwatches, is the registered holder of the YY trademark in the United States and in other countries worldwide. FP enters into an exclusive, five-year, renewable agreement with its newly organized U.S. subsidiary, USSub. The contractual terms of the agreement grant USSub the exclusive right to re-sell YY trademark wristwatches in the United States, obligate USSub to pay a fixed price per wristwatch throughout the entire term of the contract, and obligate both FP and USSub to undertake without separate compensation specified types and levels of marketing activities.

(ii) The consideration for FP's and USSub's marketing activities, as well as the consideration for the exclusive right to re-sell YY trademarked merchandise in the United States, are embedded in the transfer price paid for the wristwatches. Accordingly, pursuant to paragraph (f)(4)(i) of this section, ordinarily no separate allocation would be appropriate with respect to these embedded contributions.

(iii) Whether an allocation is warranted with respect to the transfer price for the wristwatches is determined under §§ 1.482-1, 1.482-3, and this section through § 1.482-6. The comparability analysis would include consideration of all relevant factors, including the nature of the intangible property embedded in the wristwatches and the nature of the marketing activities required under the agreement. This analysis would also take into account that the compensation for the activities performed by USSub and FP, as well as the consideration for USSub's use of the YY trademark, is embedded in the transfer price for the wristwatches, rather than provided for in separate agreements. See §§ 1.482-3(f) and 1.482-9(m)(4).

Example 3. (i) *Facts.* FP, a foreign producer of athletic gear, is the registered holder of the AA trademark in the United States and in other countries. In year 1, FP licenses to a newly organized U.S. subsidiary, USSub, the exclusive rights to use certain manufacturing and marketing intangible property to manufacture and market athletic gear in the United States under the AA trademark. The license agreement obligates USSub to pay a royalty based on sales of trademarked merchandise. The license agreement also obligates FP and USSub to perform without separate compensation specified types and levels of marketing activities. In year 1, USSub manufactures and sells athletic gear under the AA trademark in the United States.

(ii) The consideration for FP's and USSub's respective marketing activities is embedded in the contractual terms of the license for the AA trademark. Accordingly, pursuant to paragraph (f)(4)(i) of this section, ordinarily no separate allocation would be appropriate with respect to the embedded contributions in year 1. See § 1.482-9(m)(4).

(iii) Whether an allocation is warranted with respect to the royalty under the license agreement would be analyzed under § 1.482-1, and this section through § 1.482-6. The comparability analysis would include consideration of all relevant factors, such as the term and geographical exclusivity of the license, the nature of the intangible property subject to the license, and the nature of the marketing activities required to be undertaken pursuant to the license. Pursuant to paragraph (f)(4)(i) of this section, the analysis would also take into account the fact that the compensation for the marketing services is embedded in the royalty paid for use of the AA trademark, rather than provided for in a separate services agreement. For illustrations of application of the best method rule, see § 1.482-8 *Examples 10, 11,* and *12.*

Example 4. (i) *Facts.* The year 1 facts are the same as in *Example 3,* with the following exceptions. In year 2, USSub undertakes certain incremental marketing activities in addition to those required by the contractual terms of the license for the AA trademark executed in year 1. The parties do not execute a separate agreement with respect to these incremental marketing activities performed by USSub. The license agreement executed in year 1 is of sufficient duration that it is reasonable to anticipate that USSub will obtain the benefit of its incremental activities, in the form of increased sales or revenues of trademarked products in the U.S. market.

(ii) To the extent that it was reasonable to anticipate that USSub's incremental marketing activities would increase the value only of USSub's intangible property (that is, USSub's license to use the AA trademark for a specified term), and not the value of the AA trademark owned by FP, USSub's incremental activities do not constitute a contribution for which an allocation is warranted under paragraph (f)(4)(i) of this section.

Example 5. (i) *Facts.* The year 1 facts are the same as in *Example 3.* In year 2, FP and USSub enter into a separate services agreement that obligates USSub to perform certain incremental marketing activities to promote AA trademark athletic gear in the United States, above and beyond the activities specified in the license agreement executed in year 1. In year 2, USSub begins to perform these incremental activities, pursuant to the separate services agreement with FP.

(ii) Whether an allocation is warranted with respect to USSub's incremental marketing activities covered by the separate services agreement would be evaluated under § § 1.482-1 and 1.482-9, including a comparison of the compensation provided for the services with the results obtained under a method pursuant to § 1.482-9, selected and applied in accordance with the best method rule of § 1.482-1(c).

(iii) Whether an allocation is warranted with respect to the royalty under the license agreement is determined under § 1.482-1, and this section through § 1.482-6. The comparability analysis would include consideration of all relevant factors, such as the term and geographical exclusivity of the license, the nature of the intangible property subject to the license, and the nature of the marketing activities required to be undertaken pursuant to the license. The comparability analysis would take into account that the compensation for the incremental activities by USSub is provided for in the separate services agreement, rather than embedded in the royalty paid for use of the AA trademark. For illustrations of application of the best method rule, see § 1.482-8 *Examples 10, 11,* and *12.*

Example 6. (i) *Facts.* The year 1 facts are the same as in *Example 3.* In year 2, FP and USSub enter into a separate services agreement that obligates FP to perform incremental marketing activities, not specified in the year 1 license, by advertising AA trademarked athletic gear in selected international sporting events, such as the Olympics and the soccer World Cup. FP's corporate advertising department develops and coordinates these special promotions. The separate services agreement obligates USSub to pay an amount to FP for the benefit to USSub that may reasonably be anticipated as the result of FP's incremental activities. The separate services agreement is not a qualified cost sharing arrangement under § 1.482-7T. FP begins to perform the incremental activities in year 2 pursuant to the separate services agreement.

(ii) Whether an allocation is warranted with respect to the incremental marketing activities performed by FP under the separate services agreement would be evaluated under § 1.482-9. Under the circumstances, it is reasonable to anticipate that FP's activities would increase the value of USSub's license as well as the value of FP's trademark. Accordingly, the incremental activities by FP may constitute in part a controlled services transaction for which USSub must compensate FP. The analysis of whether an allocation is warranted would include a comparison of the compensation provided for the services with the results obtained under a method pursuant to § 1.482-9, selected and applied in accordance with the best method rule of § 1.482-1(c).

(iii) Whether an allocation is appropriate with respect to the royalty under the license agreement would be evaluated under § § 1.482-1 through 1.482-3, this section, and § § 1.482-5 and 1.482-6. The comparability analysis would include consideration of all relevant factors, such as the term and geographical exclusivity of USSub's license, the nature of the intangible property subject to the license, and the marketing activities required to be undertaken by both FP and USSub pursuant to the license. This comparability analysis would take into account that the compensation for the incremental activities performed by FP was provided for in the separate services agreement, rather than embedded in the royalty paid for use of the AA trademark. For illustrations of application of the best method rule, see § 1.482-8, *Example 10, Example 11,* and *Example 12.*

(5) *Consideration not artificially limited.*—The arm's length consideration for the controlled transfer of an intangible is not limited by the consideration paid in any uncontrolled transactions that do not meet the requirements of the comparable uncontrolled transaction method described in paragraph (c) of this section. Similarly, the arm's length consideration for an intangible is not limited by the prevailing rates of consideration paid for the use or transfer of intangibles within the same or similar industry.

(6) *Lump sum payments.*—(i) *In general.*—If an intangible is transferred in a controlled transaction for a lump sum, that amount must be commensurate with the income attributable to the intangible. A lump sum is commensurate with income in a taxable year if the equivalent royalty amount for that taxable year is equal to an arm's length royalty. The equivalent royalty amount for a taxable year is the amount determined by treating the lump sum as an advance payment of a stream of royalties over the useful life of the intangible (or the period covered by an agreement, if shorter), taking into account the projected sales of the licensee as of the date of the transfer. Thus, determining the equivalent royalty amount requires a present value calculation based on the lump sum, an appropriate discount rate, and the projected sales over the relevant period. The equivalent royalty amount is subject to periodic adjustments under § 1.482-4(f)(2)(i) to the same extent as an actual royalty payment pursuant to a license agreement.

(ii) *Exceptions.*—No periodic adjustment will be made under paragraph (f)(2)(i) of this section if any of the exceptions to periodic adjustments provided in paragraph (f)(2)(ii) of this section apply.

(iii) *Example.*—The following example illustrates the principle of this paragraph (f)(5).

Example. Calculation of the equivalent royalty amount. (i) FSub is the foreign subsidiary of USP, a U.S. company. USP licenses FSub the right to produce and sell the whopperchopper, a patented new kitchen appliance, for the foreign market. The license is for a period of five years, and payment takes the form of a single lump-sum charge of $500,000 that is paid at the beginning of the period.

(ii) The equivalent royalty amount for this license is determined by deriving an equivalent royalty rate equal to the lump-sum payment divided by the present discounted value of FSub's projected sales of whopperchoppers over the life of the license. Based on the riskiness of the whopperchopper business, an appropriate discount rate is determined to be 10 percent. Projected sales of whopperchoppers for each year of the license are as follows:

Year	*Projected Sales ($)*
1	2,500,000
2	2,600,000
3	2,700,000
4	2,700,000
5	2,750,000

(iii) Based on this information, the present discounted value of the projected whopperchopper sales is approximately $10 million, yielding an equivalent royalty rate of approximately 5%. Thus, the equivalent royalty amounts for each year are as follows:

Year	Projected Sales ($)	Equivalent royalty amount ($)
1	2,500,000	125,000
2	2,600,000	130,000
3	2,700,000	135,000
4	2,700,000	135,000
5	2,750,000	137,500

(iv) If in any of the five taxable years the equivalent royalty amount is determined not to be an arm's length amount, a periodic adjustment may be made pursuant to § 1.482-4(f)(2)(i). The adjustment in such case would be equal to the difference between the equivalent royalty amount and the arm's length royalty in that taxable year.

(g) *Coordination with rules governing cost sharing arrangements.*—Section 1.482-7 provides the specific methods to be used to determine arm's length results of controlled transactions in connection with a cost sharing arrangement. This section provides the specific methods to be used to determine arm's length results of a transfer of intangible property, including in an arrangement for sharing the costs and risks of developing intangibles other than a cost sharing arrangement covered by § 1.482-7. In the case of such an arrangement, consideration of the principles, methods, comparability, and reliability considerations set forth in § 1.482-7 is relevant in determining the best method, including an unspecified method, under this section, as appropriately adjusted in light of the differences in the facts and circumstances between such arrangement and a cost sharing arrangement.

(h) *Effective/applicability date.*—(1) *In general.*—Except as provided in the succeeding sentence, the provisions of paragraphs (f)(3) and (4) of this section are generally applicable for taxable years beginning after December 31, 2006. The provisions of paragraphs (f)(3)(i)(B) and (g) of this section are generally applicable on January 5, 2009.

(2) *Election to apply regulation to earlier taxable years.*—A person may elect to apply the provisions of paragraphs (f)(3) and (4) of this section to earlier taxable years in accordance with the rules set forth in § 1.482-9(n)(2). [Reg. § 1.482-4.]

☐ [*T.D.* 8552, 7-1-94. *Amended by T.D.* 9278, 7-31-2006; *T.D.* 9456, 7-31-2009 *and T.D.* 9568, 12-16-2011.]

§ 1.482-5. Comparable profits method.—(a) *In general.*—The comparable profits method evaluates whether the amount charged in a controlled transaction is arm's length based on objective measures of profitability (profit level indicators) derived from uncontrolled taxpayers that engage in similar business activities under similar circumstances.

(b) *Determination of arm's length result.*—(1) *In general.*—Under the comparable profits method, the determination of an arm's length result is based on the amount of operating profit that the tested party would have earned on related party transactions if its profit level indicator were equal to that of an uncontrolled comparable (comparable operating profit). Comparable operating profit is calculated by determining a profit level indicator for an uncontrolled comparable, and applying the profit level indicator to the financial data related to the tested party's most narrowly identifiable business activity for which data incorporating the controlled transaction is available (relevant business activity). To the extent possible, profit level indicators should be applied solely to the tested party's financial data that is related to controlled transactions. The tested party's reported operating profit is compared to the comparable operating profits derived from the profit level indicators of uncontrolled comparables to determine whether the reported operating profit represents an arm's length result.

(2) *Tested party.*—(i) *In general.*—For purposes of this section, the tested party will be the participant in the controlled transaction whose operating profit attributable to the controlled transactions can be verified using the most reliable data and requiring the fewest and most reliable adjustments, and for which reliable data regarding uncontrolled comparables can be located. Consequently, in most cases the tested party will be the least complex of the controlled taxpayers and will not own valuable intangible property or unique assets that distinguish it from potential uncontrolled comparables.

(ii) *Adjustments for tested party.*—The tested party's operating profit must first be adjusted to reflect all other allocations under section 482, other than adjustments pursuant to this section.

(3) *Arm's length range.*—See § 1.482-1(e)(2) for the determination of the arm's length range. For purposes of the comparable profits method, the arm's length range will be established using comparable operating profits derived from a single profit level indicator.

(4) *Profit level indicators.*—Profit level indicators are ratios that measure relationships between profits and costs incurred or resources employed. A variety of profit level indicators can be calculated in any given case. Whether use of a particular profit level indicator is appropriate depends upon a number of factors, including the nature of the activities of the tested party, the reliability of the available data with respect to uncontrolled comparables, and the extent to which the profit level indicator is likely to produce a reliable measure of the income that the tested party would have earned had it dealt with controlled taxpayers at arm's length, taking into account all of the facts and circumstances. The profit level indicators should be derived from a sufficient number of years of data to reasonably measure returns that accrue to uncontrolled comparables. Generally, such a period should encompass at least the taxable year under review and the preceding two taxable years. This analysis must be applied in accordance with § 1.482-1(f)(2)(iii)(D). Profit level indicators that may provide a reliable basis for comparing operating profits of the tested party and uncontrolled comparables include the following—

(i) *Rate of return on capital employed.*—The rate of return on capital employed is the ratio of operating profit to operating assets. The reliability of this profit level indicator increases as operating assets play a greater role in generating operating profits for both the tested party and the uncontrolled comparable. In addition, reliability under this profit level indicator depends on the extent to which the composition of the tested party's assets is similar to that of the uncontrolled comparable. Finally, difficulties in properly valuing operating assets will diminish the reliability of this profit level indicator.

(ii) *Financial ratios.*—Financial ratios measure relationships between profit and costs or sales revenue. Since functional differences generally have a greater effect on the relationship between profit and costs or sales revenue than the relationship between profit and operating assets, financial ratios are more sensitive to functional differences than the rate of return on capital employed. Therefore, closer functional comparability normally is required under a financial ratio than under the rate of return on capital employed to achieve a similarly reliable measure of an arm's length result. Financial ratios that may be appropriate include the following—

(A) Ratio of operating profit to sales; and

(B) Ratio of gross profit to operating expenses.

Reliability under this profit level indicator also depends on the extent to which the composition of the tested party's operating expenses is similar to that of the uncontrolled comparables.

(iii) *Other profit level indicators.*—Other profit level indicators not described in this paragraph (b)(4) may be used if they provide reliable measures of the income that the tested party would have earned had it dealt with controlled taxpayers at arm's length. However, profit level indicators based solely on internal data may not be used under this paragraph (b)(4) because they are not objective measures of profitability derived from operations of uncontrolled taxpayers engaged in similar business activities under similar circumstances.

(c) *Comparability and reliability considerations.*—(1) *In general.*—Whether results derived from application of this method are the most reliable measure of the arm's length result must be determined using the factors described under the best method rule in § 1.482-1(c).

(2) *Comparability.*—(i) *In general.*—The degree of comparability between an uncontrolled taxpayer and the tested party is determined by applying the provisions of § 1.482-1(d)(2). The comparable profits method compares the profitability of the tested party, measured by a profit level indicator (generally based on operating profit), to the profitability of uncontrolled taxpayers in similar circumstances. As with all methods that rely on external market benchmarks, the greater the degree of comparability between the tested party and the uncontrolled taxpayer, the more reliable will be the results derived from the application of this method. The determination of the degree of comparability between the tested party and the uncontrolled taxpayer depends upon all the relevant facts and circumstances, including the relevant lines of business, the product or service markets involved, the asset composition employed (including the nature

and quantity of tangible assets, intangible assets and working capital), the size and scope of operations, and the stage in a business or product cycle.

(ii) *Functional, risk and resource comparability.*—An operating profit represents a return for the investment of resources and assumption of risks. Therefore, although all of the factors described in §1.482-1(d)(3) must be considered, comparability under this method is particularly dependent on resources employed and risks assumed. Moreover, because resources and risks usually are directly related to functions performed, it is also important to consider functions performed in determining the degree of comparability between the tested party and an uncontrolled taxpayer. The degree of functional comparability required to obtain a reliable result under the comparable profits method, however, is generally less than that required under the resale price or cost plus methods. For example, because differences in functions performed often are reflected in operating expenses, taxpayers performing different functions may have very different gross profit margins but earn similar levels of operating profit.

(iii) *Other comparability factors.*—Other factors listed in §1.482-1(d)(3) also may be particularly relevant under the comparable profits method. Because operating profit usually is less sensitive than gross profit to product differences, reliability under the comparable profits method is not as dependent on product similarity as the resale price or cost plus method. However, the reliability of profitability measures based on operating profit may be adversely affected by factors that have less effect on results under the comparable uncontrolled price, resale price, and cost plus methods. For example, operating profit may be affected by varying cost structures (as reflected, for example, in the age of plant and equipment), differences in business experience (such as whether the business is in a start-up phase or is mature), or differences in management efficiency (as indicated, for example, by objective evidence such as expanding or contracting sales or executive compensation over time). Accordingly, if material differences in these factors are identified based on objective evidence, the reliability of the analysis may be affected.

(iv) *Adjustments for the differences between the tested party and the uncontrolled taxpayers.*—If there are differences between the tested party and an uncontrolled comparable that would materially affect the profits determined under the relevant profit level indicator, adjustments should be made according to the comparability provisions of §1.482-1(d)(2). In some cases, the assets of an uncontrolled comparable may need to be adjusted to achieve greater comparability between the tested party and the uncontrolled comparable. In such cases, the uncontrolled comparable's operating income attributable to those assets must also be adjusted before computing a profit level indicator in order to reflect the income and expense attributable to the adjusted assets. In certain cases it may also be appropriate to adjust the operating profit of the tested party and comparable parties. For example, where there are material differences in accounts payable among the comparable parties and the tested party, it will generally be appropriate to adjust the operating profit of each party by increasing it to reflect an imputed interest charge on each party's accounts payable. As another example, it may be appropriate to adjust the operating profit of a party to account for material differences in the utilization of or accounting for stock-based compensation (as defined by §1.482-7(d)(3)(i)) among the tested party and comparable parties.

(3) *Data and assumptions.*—(i) *In general.*—The reliability of the results derived from the comparable profits method is affected by the quality of the data and assumptions used to apply this method.

(ii) *Consistency in accounting.*—The degree of consistency in accounting practices between the controlled transaction and the uncontrolled comparables that materially affect operating profit affects the reliability of the result. Thus, for example, if differences in inventory and other cost accounting practices would materially affect operating profit, the ability to make reliable adjustments for such differences would affect the reliability of the results.

(iii) *Allocations between the relevant business activity and other activities.*—The reliability of the allocation of costs, income, and assets between the relevant business activity and other activities of the tested party or an uncontrolled comparable will affect the reliability of the determination of operating profit and profit level indicators. If it is not possible to allocate costs, income, and assets directly based on factual relationships, a reasonable allocation formula may be used. To the extent direct allocations are not made, the reliability of the results derived from the application of this method is reduced relative to the results of a method that requires fewer allocations of costs, income, and assets. Similarly, the reliability of the results derived from the application of this method is affected by the extent to which it is possible to apply the profit level indicator to the tested party's financial data that is related solely to the controlled transactions. For example, if the relevant business activity is the assembly of components purchased from both controlled and uncontrolled suppliers, it may not be possible to apply the profit level indicator solely to financial data related to the controlled transactions. In such a case, the reliability of the results derived from the application of this method will be reduced.

(d) *Definitions.*—The definitions set forth in paragraphs (d)(1) through (6) of this section apply for purposes of this section.

(1) *Sales revenue.*—means the amount of the total receipts from sale of goods and provision of services, less returns and allowances. Accounting principles and conventions that are generally accepted in the trade or industry of the controlled taxpayer under review must be used.

(2) *Gross profit.*—means sales revenue less cost of goods sold.

(3) *Operating expenses.*—includes all expenses not included in cost of goods sold except for interest expense, foreign income taxes (as defined in §1.901-2(a)), domestic income taxes, and any other expenses not related to the operation of the relevant business activity. Operating expenses ordinarily include expenses associated with advertising, promotion, sales, marketing, warehousing and distribution, administration, and a reasonable allowance for depreciation and amortization.

(4) *Operating profit.*—means gross profit less operating expenses. Operating profit includes all income derived from the business activity being evaluated by the comparable profits method, but does not include interest and dividends, income derived from activities not being tested by this method, or extraordinary gains and losses that do not relate to the continuing operations of the tested party.

(5) *Reported operating profit.*—means the operating profit of the tested party reflected on a timely filed U.S. income tax return. If the tested party files a U.S. income tax return, its operating profit is considered reflected on a U.S. income tax return if the calculation of taxable income on its return for the taxable year takes into account the income attributable to the controlled transaction under review. If the tested party does not file a U.S. income tax return, its operating profit is considered reflected on a U.S. income tax return in any taxable year for which income attributable to the controlled transaction under review affects the calculation of the U.S. taxable income of any other member of the same controlled group. If the comparable operating profit of the tested party is determined from profit level indicators derived from financial statements or other accounting records and reports of comparable parties, adjustments may be made to the reported operating profit of the tested party in order to account for material differences between the tested party's operating profit reported for U.S. income tax purposes and the tested party's operating profit for financial statement purposes. In addition, in accordance with §1.482-1(f)(2)(iii)(D), adjustments under section 482 that are finally determined may be taken into account in determining reported operating profit.

(6) *Operating assets.*—The term operating assets means the value of all assets used in the relevant business activity of the tested party, including fixed assets and current assets (such as cash, cash equivalents, accounts receivable, and inventories). The term does not include investments in subsidiaries, excess cash, and portfolio investments. Operating assets may be measured by their net book value or by their fair market value, provided that the same method is consistently applied to the tested party and the comparable parties, and consistently applied from year to year. In addition, it may be necessary to take into account recent acquisitions, leased assets, intangibles, currency fluctuations, and other items that may not be explicitly recorded in the financial statements of the tested party or uncontrolled comparable. Finally, operating assets must be measured by the average of the values for the beginning of the year and the end of the year, unless substantial fluctuations in the value of operating assets during the year make this an inaccurate measure of the average value over the year. In such a case, a more accurate measure of the average value of operating assets must be applied.

(e) *Examples.*—The following examples illustrate the application of this section.

Example 1—Transfer of tangible property resulting in no adjustment. (i) FP is a publicly traded foreign corporation with a U.S. subsidiary, USSub, that is under audit for its 1996 taxable year. FP manufactures a consumer product for worldwide distribution. USSub imports the assembled product and distributes it within the United States at the wholesale level under the FP name.

(ii) FP does not allow uncontrolled taxpayers to distribute the product. Similar products are produced by other companies but none of them is sold to uncontrolled taxpayers or to uncontrolled distributors.

(iii) Based on all the facts and circumstances, the district director determines that the comparable profits method will provide the most reliable measure of an arm's length result. USSub is selected as the tested party because it engages in activities that are less complex than those undertaken by FP. There is data from a number of independent operators of wholesale distribution businesses. These potential comparables are further narrowed to select companies in the same industry segment that perform similar functions and bear similar risks to USSub. An analysis of the information available on these taxpayers shows that the ratio of operating profit to sales is the most appropriate profit level indicator, and this ratio is relatively stable where at least three years are included in the average. For the taxable years 1994 through 1996, USSub shows the following results:

	1994	*1995*	*1996*	*Average*
Sales	500,000	560,000	500,000	520,000
Cost of Goods Sold	393,000	412,400	400,000	401,800
Operating Expenses	80,000	110,000	104,600	98,200
Operating Profit	27,000	37,600	(4,600)	20,000

(iv) After adjustments have been made to account for identified material differences between USSub and the uncontrolled distributors, the average ratio of operating profit to sales is calculated for each of the uncontrolled distributors. Applying each ratio to USSub would lead to the following comparable operating profit (COP) for USSub:

Uncontrolled Distributor	*OP/S*	*USSub COP*
A	1.7%	$8,840
B	3.1%	16,120
C	3.8%	19,760
D	4.5%	23,400
E	4.7%	24,440
F	4.8%	24,960
G	4.9%	25,480
H	6.7%	34,840
I	9.9%	51,480
J	10.5%	54,600

(v) The data is not sufficiently complete to conclude that it is likely that all material differences between USSub and the uncontrolled distributors have been identified. Therefore, an arm's length range can be established only pursuant to § 1.482-1(e)(2)(iii)(B). The district director measures the arm's length range by the interquartile range of results, which consists of the results ranging from $19,760 to $34,840. Although USSub's operating income for 1996 shows a loss of $4,600, the district director determines that no allocation should be made, because USSub's average reported operating profit of $20,000 is within this range.

Example 2—Transfer of tangible property resulting in adjustment. (i) The facts are the same as in *Example 1* except that USSub reported the following income and expenses:

	1994	*1995*	*1996*	*Average*
Sales	500,000	560,000	500,000	520,000
Cost of Goods Sold	370,000	460,000	400,000	410,000
Operating Expenses	110,000	110,000	110,000	110,000
Operating Profit	20,000	(10,000)	(10,000)	0

(ii) The interquartile range of comparable operating profits remains the same as derived in *Example 1:* $19,760 to $34,840. USSub's average operating profit for the years 1994 through 1996 ($0) falls outside this range. Therefore, the district director determines that an allocation may be appropriate.

(iii) To determine the amount, if any, of the allocation, the district director compares USSub's reported operating profit for 1996 to comparable operating profits derived from the uncontrolled distributors' results for 1996. The ratio of operating profit to sales in 1996 is calculated for each of the uncontrolled comparables and applied to USSub's 1996 sales to derive the following results:

Uncontrolled Distributor	*OP/S*	*USSub COP*
C	0.5%	$2,500
D	1.5%	7,500
E	2.0%	10,000
A	1.6%	13,000
F	2.8%	14,000
B	2.9%	14,500
J	3.0%	15,000
I	4.4%	22,000
H	6.9%	34,500
G	7.4%	37,000

(iv) Based on these results, the median of the comparable operating profits for 1996 is $14,250. Therefore, USSub's income for 1996 is increased by $24,250, the difference between USSub's reported operating profit for 1996 and the median of the comparable operating profits for 1996.

Example 3—Multiple year analysis. (i) The facts are the same as in *Example 2*. In addition, the district director examines the taxpayer's results for the 1997 taxable year. As in *Example 2*, the district director increases USSub's income for the 1996 taxable year by $24,250. The results for the 1997 taxable year, together with the 1995 and 1996 taxable years, are as follows:

	1995	*1996*	*1997*	*Average*
Sales	560,000	500,000	530,000	530,000
Cost of Goods Sold	460,000	400,000	430,000	430,000
Operating Expenses	110,000	110,000	110,000	110,000
Operating Profit	(10,000)	(10,000)	(10,000)	(10,000)

(ii) The interquartile range of comparable operating profits, based on average results from the uncontrolled comparables and average sales for USSub for the years 1995 through 1997, ranges from $15,500 to $30,000. In determining whether an allocation for the 1997 taxable year may be made, the district director compares USSub's average reported operating profit for the years 1995 through 1997 to the interquartile range of average comparable operating profits over this period. USSub's average reported operating profit is determined without regard to the adjustment made with respect to the 1996 taxable year. See § 1.482-1(f)(2)(iii)(D). Therefore, USSub's average reported operating profit for the years 1995 through 1997 is ($10,000). Because this amount of income falls outside the interquartile range, the district director determines that an allocation may be appropriate.

(iii) To determine the amount, if any, of the allocation for the 1997 taxable year, the district director compares USSub's reported operating profit for 1997 to the median of the comparable operating profits derived from the uncontrolled distributors' results for 1997. The median of the comparable operating profits derived from the uncontrolled comparables results for the 1997 taxable year is $12,000. Based on this comparison, the district director increases USSub's 1997 taxable income by $22,000, the difference between the median of the comparable operating profits for the 1997 taxable year and USSub's reported operating profit of ($10,000) for the 1997 taxable year.

Example 4—Transfer of intangible to offshore manufacturer. (i) DevCo is a U.S. developer, producer and marketer of widgets. DevCo develops a new "high tech widget" (htw) that is manufactured by its foreign subsidiary ManuCo located in Country H. ManuCo sells the htw to MarkCo (a U.S. subsidiary of DevCo) for distribution and marketing in the United States. The taxable year 1996 is under audit, and the district director examines whether the royalty rate of 5 percent paid by ManuCo to DevCo is an arm's length consideration for the htw technology.

(ii) Based on all the facts and circumstances, the district director determines that the comparable profits method will provide the most reliable measure of an arm's length result. ManuCo is selected as the tested party because it engages in relatively routine manufacturing activities, while DevCo engages in a variety of complex activities using unique and valuable intangibles. Finally, because ManuCo engages in manufacturing activities, it is determined that the ratio of operating profit to operating assets is an appropriate profit level indicator.

(iii) Uncontrolled taxpayers performing similar functions cannot be found in country H. It is determined that data available in countries M and N provides the best match of companies in a similar market performing similar functions and bearing similar risks. Such data is sufficiently complete to identify many of the material differences between ManuCo and the uncontrolled comparables, and to make adjustments to account for such differences. However, data is not sufficiently complete so that it is likely that no material differences remain. In particular, the differences in geographic markets might have materially affected the results of the various companies.

(iv) In a separate analysis, it is determined that the price that ManuCo charged to MarkCo for the htw's is an arm's length price under § 1.482-3(b). Therefore, ManuCo's financial data derived from its sales to MarkCo are reliable. ManuCo's financial data from 1994-1996 is as follows:

	1994	*1995*	*1996*	*Average*
Assets	$24,000	$25,000	$26,000	$25,000
Sales to MarkCo	25,000	30,000	35,000	30,000
Cost of Goods Sold	6,250	7,500	8,750	7,500
Royalty to DevCo (5%)	1,250	1,500	1,750	1,500
Other	5,000	6,000	7,000	6,000
Operating Expenses	1,000	1,000	1,000	1,000
Operating Profit	17,750	21,500	25,250	21,500

(v) Applying the ratios of average operating profit to operating assets for the 1994 through 1996 taxable years derived from a group of similar uncontrolled comparables located in country M and N to Manuco's average operating assets for the same period provides a set of comparable operating profits. The interquartile range for these average comparable operating profits is $3,000 to $4,500. ManuCo's average reported operating profit for the years 1994 through 1996 ($21,500) falls outside this range. Therefore, the district director determines that an allocation may be appropriate for the 1996 taxable year.

(vi) To determine the amount, if any, of the allocation for the 1996 taxable year, the district director compares ManuCo's reported operating profit for 1996 to the median of the comparable operating profits derived from the uncontrolled distributors' results for 1996. The median result for the uncontrolled comparables for 1996 is $3,750. Based on this comparison, the district director increases royalties that ManuCo paid by $21,500 (the difference between $25,250 and the median of the comparable operating profits, $3,750).

Example 5—Adjusting operating assets and operating profit for differences in accounts receivable. (i) USM is a U.S. company that manufactures parts for industrial equipment and sells them to its foreign parent corporation. For purposes of applying the comparable profits method, 15 uncontrolled manufacturers that are similar to USM have been identified.

(ii) USM has a significantly lower level of accounts receivable than the uncontrolled manufacturers. Since the rate of return on capital employed is to be used as the profit level indicator, both operating assets and operating profits must be adjusted to account for this difference. Each uncontrolled comparable's operating assets is reduced by the amount (relative to sales) by which they exceed USM's accounts receivable. Each uncontrolled comparable's operating profit is adjusted by deducting imputed interest income on the excess accounts receivable. This imputed interest income is calculated by multiplying the uncontrolled comparable's excess accounts receivable by an interest rate appropriate for short-term debt.

Example 6—Adjusting operating profit for differences in accounts payable. (i) USD is the U.S. subsidiary of a foreign corporation. USD purchases goods from its foreign parent and sells them in the U.S. market. For purposes of applying the comparable profits method, 10 uncontrolled distributors that are similar to USD have been identified.

(ii) There are significant differences in the level of accounts payable among the uncontrolled distributors and USD. To adjust for these differences, the district director increases the operating profit of the uncontrolled distributors and USD to reflect interest expense imputed to the accounts payable. The imputed interest expense for each company is calculated by multiplying the company's accounts payable by an interest rate appropriate for its short-term debt. [Reg. § 1.482-5.]

☐ *[T.D. 8552, 7-1-94. Amended by T.D. 9088, 8-25-2003 T.D. 9441, 12-31-2008 and T.D. 9568, 12-16-2011.]*

§ 1.482-6. Profit split method.—(a) *In general.*—The profit split method evaluates whether the allocation of the combined operating profit or loss attributable to one or more controlled transactions is arm's length by reference to the relative value of each controlled taxpayer's contribution to that combined operating profit or loss. The combined operating profit or loss must be derived from the most narrowly identifiable business activity of the controlled taxpayers for which data is available that includes the controlled transactions (relevant business activity).

(b) *Appropriate share of profits and losses.*—The relative value of each controlled taxpayer's contribution to the success of the relevant business activity must be determined in a manner that reflects the functions performed, risks assumed, and resources employed by each participant in the relevant business activity, consistent with the comparability provisions of § 1.482-1(d)(3). Such an allocation is intended to correspond to the division of profit or loss that would result from an arrangement between uncontrolled taxpayers, each performing functions similar to those of the various controlled taxpayers engaged in the relevant business activity. The profit allocated to any particular member of a controlled group is not necessarily limited to the total operating profit of the group from the relevant business activity. For example, in a given year, one member of the group may earn a profit while another member incurs a loss. In addition, it may not be assumed that the combined operating profit or loss from the relevant business activity should be shared equally, or in any other arbitrary proportion. The specific method of allocation must be determined under paragraph (c) of this section.

(c) *Application.*—(1) *In general.*—The allocation of profit or loss under the profit split method must be made in accordance with one of the following allocation methods—

(i) The comparable profit split, described in paragraph (c)(2) of this section; or

(ii) The residual profit split, described in paragraph (c)(3) of this section.

(2) *Comparable profit split.*—(i) *In general.*—A comparable profit split is derived from the combined operating profit of uncontrolled taxpayers whose transactions and activities are similar to those of the controlled taxpayers in the relevant business activity. Under this method, each uncontrolled taxpayer's percentage of the combined

operating profit or loss is used to allocate the combined operating profit or loss of the relevant business activity.

(ii) *Comparability and reliability considerations.*—(A) *In general.*—Whether results derived from application of this method are the most reliable measure of the arm's length result is determined using the factors described under the best method rule in § 1.482-1(c).

(B) *Comparability.*—*(1) In general.*—The degree of comparability between the controlled and uncontrolled taxpayers is determined by applying the comparability provisions of § 1.482-1(d). The comparable profit split compares the division of operating profits among the controlled taxpayers to the division of operating profits among uncontrolled taxpayers engaged in similar activities under similar circumstances. Although all of the factors described in § 1.482-1(d)(3) must be considered, comparability under this method is particularly dependent on the considerations described under the comparable profits method in § 1.482-5(c)(2) or § 1.482-9(f)(2)(iii) because this method is based on a comparison of the operating profit of the controlled and uncontrolled taxpayers. In addition, because the contractual terms of the relationship among the participants in the relevant business activity will be a principal determinant of the allocation of functions and risks among them, comparability under this method also depends particularly on the degree of similarity of the contractual terms of the controlled and uncontrolled taxpayers. Finally, the comparable profit split may not be used if the combined operating profit (as a percentage of the combined assets) of the uncontrolled comparables varies significantly from that earned by the controlled taxpayers.

(2) Adjustments for differences between the controlled and uncontrolled taxpayers.—If there are differences between the controlled and uncontrolled taxpayers that would materially affect the division of operating profit, adjustments must be made according to the provisions of § 1.482-1(d)(2).

(C) *Data and assumptions.*—The reliability of the results derived from the comparable profit split is affected by the quality of the data and assumptions used to apply this method. In particular, the following factors must be considered—

(1) The reliability of the allocation of costs, income, and assets between the relevant business activity and the participants' other activities will affect the accuracy of the determination of combined operating profit and its allocation among the participants. If it is not possible to allocate costs, income, and assets directly based on factual relationships, a reasonable allocation formula may be used. To the extent direct allocations are not made, the reliability of the results derived from the application of this method is reduced relative to the results of a method that requires fewer allocations of costs, income, and assets. Similarly, the reliability of the results derived from the application of this method is affected by the extent to which it is possible to apply the method to the parties' financial data that is related solely to the controlled transactions. For example, if the relevant business activity is the assembly of components purchased from both controlled and uncontrolled suppliers, it may not be possible to apply the method solely to financial data related to the controlled transactions. In such a case, the reliability of the results derived from the application of this method will be reduced.

(2) The degree of consistency between the controlled and uncontrolled taxpayers in accounting practices that materially affect the items that determine the amount and allocation of operating profit affects the reliability of the result. Thus, for example, if differences in inventory and other cost accounting practices would materially affect operating profit, the ability to make reliable adjustments for such differences would affect the reliability of the results. Further, accounting consistency among the participants in the controlled transaction is required to ensure that the items determining the amount and allocation of operating profit are measured on a consistent basis.

(D) *Other factors affecting reliability.*—Like the methods described in §§ 1.482-3, 1.482-4, 1.482-5, and 1.482-9, the comparable profit split relies exclusively on external market benchmarks. As indicated in § 1.482-1(c)(2)(i), as the degree of comparability between the controlled and uncontrolled transactions increases, the relative weight accorded the analysis under this method will increase. In addition, the reliability of the analysis under this method may be enhanced by the fact that all parties to the controlled transaction are evaluated under the comparable profit split. However, the reliability of the results of an analysis based on information from all parties to a transaction is affected by the reliability of the data and the assumptions pertaining to each party to the controlled transaction. Thus, if the data and assumptions are significantly more reliable with respect to one of the parties than with respect to the others, a different method, focusing solely on the results of that party, may yield more reliable results.

(3) *Residual profit split.*—(i) *In general.*—Under this method, the combined operating profit or loss from the relevant business activity is allocated between the controlled taxpayers following the two-step process set forth in paragraphs (c)(3)(i)(A) and (B) of this section.

(A) *Allocate income to routine contributions.*—The first step allocates operating income to each party to the controlled transactions to provide a market return for its routine contributions to the relevant business activity. Routine contributions are contributions of the same or a similar kind to those made by uncontrolled taxpayers involved in similar business activities for which it is possible to identify market returns. Routine contributions ordinarily include contributions of tangible property, services and intangible property that are generally owned by uncontrolled taxpayers engaged in similar activities. A functional analysis is required to identify these contributions according to the functions performed, risks assumed, and resources employed by each of the controlled taxpayers. Market returns for the routine contributions should be determined by reference to the returns achieved by uncontrolled taxpayers engaged in similar activities, consistent with the methods described in §§ 1.482-3, 1.482-4, 1.482-5 and 1.482-9.

(B) *Allocate residual profit.*—*(1) Nonroutine contributions generally.*—The allocation of income to the controlled taxpayer's routine contributions will not reflect profits attributable to each controlled taxpayer's contributions to the relevant business activity that are not routine (nonroutine contributions). A nonroutine contribution is a contribution that is not accounted for as a routine contribution. Thus, in cases where such nonroutine contributions are present, there normally will be an unallocated residual profit after the allocation of income described in paragraph (c)(3)(i)(A) of this section. Under this second step, the residual profit generally should be divided among the controlled taxpayers based upon the relative value of their nonroutine contributions to the relevant business activity. The relative value of the nonroutine contributions of each taxpayer should be measured in a manner that most reliably reflects each nonroutine contribution made to the controlled transaction and each controlled taxpayer's role in the nonroutine contributions. If the nonroutine contribution by one of the controlled taxpayers is also used in other business activities (such as transactions with other controlled taxpayers), an appropriate allocation of the value of the nonroutine contribution must be made among all the business activities in which it is used.

(2) Nonroutine contributions of intangible property.—In many cases, nonroutine contributions of a taxpayer to the relevant business activity may be contributions of intangible property. For purposes of paragraph (c)(3)(i)(B)*(1)* of this section, the relative value of nonroutine intangible property contributed by taxpayers may be measured by external market benchmarks that reflect the fair market value of such intangible property. Alternatively, the relative value of nonroutine intangible property contributions may be estimated by the capitalized cost of developing the intangible property and all related improvements and updates, less an appropriate amount of amortization based on the useful life of each intangible property. Finally, if the intangible property development expenditures of the parties are relatively constant over time and the useful life of the intangible property contributed by all parties is approximately the same, the amount of actual expenditures in recent years may be used to estimate the relative value of nonroutine intangible property contributions.

(ii) *Comparability and reliability considerations.*—(A) *In general.*—Whether results derived from this method are the most reliable measure of the arm's length result is determined using the factors described under the best method rule in § 1.482-1(c). Thus, comparability and the quality of data and assumptions must be considered in determining whether this method provides the most reliable measure of an arm's length result. The application of these factors to the residual profit split is discussed in paragraph (c)(3)(ii)(B), (C), and (D) of this section.

(B) *Comparability.*—The first step of the residual profit split relies on market benchmarks of profitability. Thus, the comparability considerations that are relevant for the first step of the residual profit split are those that are relevant for the methods that are used to determine market returns for the routine contributions. The second step of the residual profit split, however, may not rely so directly on market benchmarks. Thus, the reliability of the results under this method is reduced to the extent that the allocation of profits in the second step does not rely on market benchmarks.

(C) *Data and assumptions*.—The reliability of the results derived from the residual profit split is affected by the quality of the data and assumptions used to apply this method. In particular, the following factors must be considered—

(1) The reliability of the allocation of costs, income, and assets as described in paragraph (c)(2)(ii)(C)*(1)* of this section;

(2) Accounting consistency as described in paragraph (c)(2)(ii)(C)*(2)* of this section;

(3) The reliability of the data used and the assumptions made in valuing the intangible property contributed by the participants. In particular, if capitalized costs of development are used to estimate the value of intangible property, the reliability of the results is reduced relative to the reliability of other methods that do not require such an estimate, for the following reasons. First, in any given case, the costs of developing the intangible may not be related to its market value. Second, the calculation of the capitalized costs of development may require the allocation of indirect costs between the relevant business activity and the controlled taxpayer's other activities, which may affect the reliability of the analysis. Finally, the calculation of costs may require assumptions regarding the useful life of the intangible property.

(D) *Other factors affecting reliability*.—Like the methods described in §§1.482-3, 1.482-4, 1.482-5, and 1.482-9, the first step of the residual profit split relies exclusively on external market benchmarks. As indicated in §1.482-1(c)(2)(i), as the degree of comparability between the controlled and uncontrolled transactions increases, the relative weight accorded the analysis under this method will increase. In addition, to the extent the allocation of profits in the second step is not based on external market benchmarks, the reliability of the analysis will be decreased in relation to an analysis under a method that relies on market benchmarks. Finally, the reliability of the analysis under this method may be enhanced by the fact that all parties to the controlled transaction are evaluated under the residual profit split. However, the reliability of the results of an analysis based on information from all parties to a transaction is affected by the reliability of the data and the assumptions pertaining to each party to the controlled transaction. Thus, if the data and assumptions are significantly more reliable with respect to one of the parties than with respect to the others, a different method, focusing solely on the results of that party, may yield more reliable results.

(iii) *Example*.—The provisions of this paragraph (c)(3) are illustrated by the following example.

Example—Application of Residual Profit Split. (i) XYZ is a U.S. corporation that develops, manufactures and markets a line of products for police use in the United States. XYZ's research unit developed a bulletproof material for use in protective clothing and headgear (Nulon). XYZ obtains patent protection for the chemical formula for Nulon. Since its introduction in the U.S., Nulon has captured a substantial share of the U.S. market for bulletproof material.

(ii) XYZ licensed its European subsidiary, XYZ-Europe, to manufacture and market Nulon in Europe. XYZ-Europe is a well-established company that manufactures and markets XYZ products in Europe. XYZ-Europe has a research unit that adapts XYZ products for the defense market, as well as a well-developed marketing network that employs brand names that it developed.

(iii) XYZ-Europe's research unit alters Nulon to adapt it to military specifications and develops a high-intensity marketing campaign directed at the defense industry in several European countries. Beginning with the 1995 taxable year, XYZ-Europe manufactures and sells Nulon in Europe through its marketing network under one of its brand names.

(iv) For the 1995 taxable year, XYZ has no direct expenses associated with the license of Nulon to XYZ-Europe and incurs no expenses related to the marketing of Nulon in Europe. For the 1995 taxable year, XYZ-Europe's Nulon sales and pre-royalty expenses are $500 million and $300 million, respectively, resulting in net pre-royalty profit of $200 million related to the Nulon business. The operating assets employed in XYZ-Europe's Nulon business are $200 million. Given the facts and circumstances, the district director determines under the best method rule that a residual profit split will provide the most reliable measure of an arm's length result. Based on an examination of a sample of European companies performing functions similar to those of XYZ-Europe, the district director determines that an average market return on XYZ-Europe's operating assets in the Nulon business is 10 percent, resulting in a market return of $20 million (10% × $200 million) for XYZ-Europe's Nulon business, and a residual profit of $180 million.

(v) Since the first stage of the residual profit split allocated profits to XYZ-Europe's contributions other than those attributable to highly valuable intangible property, it is assumed that the residual profit of $180 million is attributable to the valuable intangibles related to Nulon, i.e., the European brand name for Nulon and the Nulon formula (including XYZ-Europe's modifications). To estimate the relative values of these intangibles, the district director compares the ratios of the capitalized value of expenditures as of 1995 on Nulon-related research and development and marketing over the 1995 sales related to such expenditures.

(vi) Because XYZ's protective product research and development expenses support the worldwide protective product sales of the XYZ group, it is necessary to allocate such expenses among the worldwide business activities to which they relate. The district director determines that it is reasonable to allocate the value of these expenses based on worldwide protective product sales. Using information on the average useful life of its investments in protective product research and development, the district director capitalizes and amortizes XYZ's protective product research and development expenses. This analysis indicates that the capitalized research and development expenditures have a value of $0.20 per dollar of global protective product sales in 1995.

(vii) XYZ-Europe's expenditures on Nulon research and development and marketing support only its sales in Europe. Using information on the average useful life of XYZ-Europe's investments in marketing and research and development, the district director capitalizes and amortizes XYZ-Europe's expenditures and determines that they have a value in 1995 of $0.40 per dollar of XYZ-Europe's Nulon sales.

(viii) Thus, XYZ and XYZ-Europe together contributed $0.60 in capitalized intangible development expenses for each dollar of XYZ-Europe's protective product sales for 1995, of which XYZ contributed one-third (or $0.20 per dollar of sales). Accordingly, the district director determines that an arm's length royalty for the Nulon license for the 1995 taxable year is $60 million, i.e., one-third of XYZ-Europe's $180 million in residual Nulon profit.

(d) *Effective/applicability date*.—(1) *In general*.—The provisions of paragraphs (c)(2)(ii)(B)*(1)* and (D), (c)(3)(i)(A) and (B), and (c)(3)(ii)(D) of this section are generally applicable for taxable years beginning after July 31, 2009.

(2) *Election to apply regulation to earlier taxable years*.—A person may elect to apply the provisions of paragraphs (c)(2)(ii)(B)*(1)* and (D), (c)(3)(i)(A) and (B), and (c)(3)(ii)(D) of this section to earlier taxable years in accordance with the rules set forth in §1.482-9(n)(2). [Reg. §1.482-6.]

☐ [*T.D. 8552, 7-1-94. Amended by T.D. 9278, 7-31-2006 and T.D. 9456, 7-31-2009 (corrected 9-8-2009).*]

§1.482-7. Methods to determine taxable income in connection with a cost sharing arrangement.—(a) *In general*.—The arm's length amount charged in a controlled transaction reasonably anticipated to contribute to developing intangibles pursuant to a cost sharing arrangement (CSA), as described in paragraph (b) of this section, must be determined under a method described in this section. Each method must be applied in accordance with the provisions of §1.482-1, except as those provisions are modified in this section.

(1) *RAB share method for cost sharing transactions (CSTs)*.—See paragraph (b)(1)(i) of this section regarding the requirement that controlled participants, as defined in section (j)(1)(i) of this section, share intangible development costs (IDCs) in proportion to their shares of reasonably anticipated benefits (RAB shares) by entering into cost sharing transactions (CSTs).

(2) *Methods for platform contribution transactions (PCTs)*.—The arm's length amount charged in a platform contribution transaction (PCT) described in paragraph (b)(1)(ii) of this section must be determined under the method or methods applicable under the other section or sections of the section 482 regulations, as supplemented by paragraph (g) of this section. See §1.482-1(b)(2)(ii) (Selection of category of method applicable to transaction), §1.482-1(b)(2)(iii) (Coordination of methods applicable to certain intangible development arrangements), and paragraph (g) of this section (Supplemental guidance on methods applicable to PCTs).

(3) *Methods for other controlled transactions.*—(i) *Contribution to a CSA by a controlled taxpayer that is not a controlled participant.*—If a controlled taxpayer that is not a controlled participant contributes to developing a cost shared intangible, as defined in section (j)(1)(i) of this section, it must receive consideration from the controlled participants under the rules of § 1.482-4(f)(4) (Contribution to the value of an intangible owned by another). Such consideration will be treated as an intangible development cost for purposes of paragraph (d) of this section.

(ii) *Transfer of interest in a cost shared intangible.*—If at any time (during the term, or upon or after the termination, of a CSA) a controlled participant transfers an interest in a cost shared intangible to another controlled taxpayer, the controlled participant must receive an arm's length amount of consideration from the transferee under the rules of § § 1.482-4 through 1.482-6 as supplemented by paragraph (f)(4) of this section regarding arm's length consideration for a change in participation. For this purpose, a capability variation described in paragraph (f)(3) of this section is considered to be a controlled transfer of interests in cost shared intangibles.

(iii) *Other controlled transactions in connection with a CSA.*—Controlled transactions between controlled participants that are not PCTs or CSTs and are not described in paragraph (a)(3)(ii) of this section (for example, provision of a cross operating contribution, as defined in paragraph (j)(1)(i) of this section, or make-or-sell rights, as defined in paragraph (c)(4) of this section) require arm's length consideration under the rules of § § 1.482-1 through 1.482-6, and 1.482-9 as supplemented by paragraph (g)(2)(iv) of this section.

(iv) *Controlled transactions in the absence of a CSA.*—If a controlled transaction is reasonably anticipated to contribute to developing intangibles pursuant to an arrangement that is not a CSA described in paragraph (b)(1) or (5) of this section, whether the results of any such controlled transaction are consistent with an arm's length result must be determined under the applicable rules of the other sections of the regulations under section 482. For example, an arrangement for developing intangibles in which one controlled taxpayer's costs of developing the intangibles significantly exceeds its share of reasonably anticipated benefits from exploiting the developed intangibles would not in substance be a CSA, as described in paragraphs (b)(1)(i) through (iii) of this section or paragraph (b)(5)(i) of this section. In such a case, unless the rules of this section are applicable by reason of paragraph (b)(5) of this section, the arrangement must be analyzed under other applicable sections of regulations under section 482 to determine whether it achieves arm's length results, and if not, to determine any allocations by the Commissioner that are consistent with such other regulations under section 482. See § 1.482-1(b)(2)(ii) (Selection of category of method applicable to transaction) and (iii) (Coordination of methods applicable to certain intangible development arrangements).

(4) *Coordination with the arm's length standard.*—A CSA produces results that are consistent with an arm's length result within the meaning of § 1.482-1(b)(1) if, and only if, each controlled participant's IDC share (as determined under paragraph (d)(4) of this section) equals its RAB share, each controlled participant compensates its RAB share of the value of all platform contributions by other controlled participants, and all other requirements of this section are satisfied.

(b) *Cost sharing arrangement.*—A cost sharing arrangement is an arrangement by which controlled participants share the costs and risks of developing cost shared intangibles in proportion to their RAB shares. An arrangement is a CSA if and only if the requirements of paragraphs (b)(1) through (4) of this section are met.

(1) *Substantive requirements.*—(i) *CSTs.*—All controlled participants must commit to, and in fact, engage in cost sharing transactions. In CSTs, the controlled participants make payments to each other (CST Payments) as appropriate, so that in each taxable year each controlled participant's IDC share is in proportion to its respective RAB share.

(ii) *PCTs.*—All controlled participants must commit to, and in fact, engage in platform contributions transactions to the extent that there are platform contributions pursuant to paragraph (c) of this section. In a PCT, each other controlled participant (PCT Payor) is obligated to, and must in fact, make arm's length payments (PCT Payments) to each controlled participant (PCT Payee) that provides a platform contribution. For guidance on determining such arm's length obligation, see paragraph (g) of this section.

(iii) *Divisional interests.*—Each controlled participant must receive a non-overlapping interest in the cost shared intangibles without further obligation to compensate another controlled participant for such interest.

(iv) *Examples.*—The following examples illustrate the principles of this paragraph (b)(1):

Example 1. Company A and Company B, who are members of the same controlled group, execute an agreement to jointly develop vaccine X and own the exclusive rights to commercially exploit vaccine X in their respective territories, which together comprise the whole world. The agreement provides that they will share some, but not all, of the costs for developing Vaccine X in proportion to RAB share. Such agreement is not a CSA because Company A and Company B have not agreed to share all of the IDCs in proportion to their respective RAB shares.

Example 2. Company A and Company B agree to share all the costs of developing Vaccine X. The agreement also provides for employing certain resources and capabilities of Company A in this program including a skilled research team and certain research facilities, and provides for Company B to make payments to Company A in this respect. However, the agreement expressly provides that the program will not employ, and so Company B is expressly relieved of the payments in regard to, certain software developed by Company A as a medical research tool to model certain cellular processes expected to be implicated in the operation of Vaccine X even though such software would reasonably be anticipated to be relevant to developing Vaccine X and, thus, would be a platform contribution. See paragraph (c) of this section. Such agreement is not a CSA because Company A and Company B have not engaged in a necessary PCT for purposes of developing Vaccine X.

Example 3. Companies C and D, who are members of the same controlled group, enter into a CSA. In the first year of the CSA, C and D conduct the intangible development activity, as described in paragraph (d)(1) of this section. The total IDCs in regard to such activity are $3,000,000 of which C and D pay $2,000,000 and $1,000,000, respectively, directly to third parties. As between C and D, however, their CSA specifies that they will share all IDCs in accordance with their RAB shares (as described in paragraph (e)(1) of this section), which are 60% for C and 40% for D. It follows that C should bear $1,800,000 of the total IDCs (60% of total IDCs of $3,000,000) and D should bear $1,200,000 of the total IDCs (40% of total IDCs of $3,000,000). D makes a CST payment to C of $200,000, that is, the amount by which D's share of IDCs in accordance with its RAB share exceeds the amount of IDCs initially borne by D ($1,200,000 - $1,000,000), and which also equals the amount by which the total IDCs initially borne by C exceeds its share of IDCS in accordance with its RAB share ($2,000,000 - $1,800,000). As a result of D's CST payment to C, the IDC shares of C and D are in proportion to their respective RAB shares.

(2) *Administrative requirements.*—The CSA must meet the requirements of paragraph (k) of this section.

(3) *Date of a PCT.*—The controlled participants must enter into a PCT as of the earliest date on or after the CSA is entered into on which a platform contribution is reasonably anticipated to contribute to developing cost shared intangibles.

(4) *Divisional interests.*—(i) *In general.*—Pursuant to paragraph (b)(1)(iii) of this section, each controlled participant must receive a non-overlapping interest in the cost shared intangibles without further obligation to compensate another controlled participant for such interest. Each controlled participant must be entitled to the perpetual and exclusive right to the profits from transactions of any member of the controlled group that includes the controlled participant with uncontrolled taxpayers to the extent that such profits are attributable to such interest in the cost shared intangibles.

(ii) *Territorial based divisional interests.*—The CSA may divide all interests in cost shared intangibles on a territorial basis as follows. The entire world must be divided into two or more non-overlapping geographic territories. Each controlled participant must receive at least one such territory, and in the aggregate all the participants must receive all such territories. Each controlled participant will be assigned the perpetual and exclusive right to exploit the cost shared intangibles through the use, consumption, or disposition of property or services in its territories. Thus, compensation will be required if other members of the controlled group exploit the cost shared intangibles in such territory.

(iii) *Field of use based divisional interests.*—The CSA may divide all interests in cost shared intangibles on the basis of all uses (whether or not known at the time of the division) to which cost shared intangibles are to be put as follows. All anticipated uses of cost shared intangibles must be identified. Each controlled participant must be assigned at least one such anticipated use, and in the aggregate all the participants must be assigned all such anticipated uses. Each controlled participant will be assigned the perpetual and exclusive right to exploit the cost shared intangibles through the use or uses assigned to it and one controlled participant must be assigned the exclusive and perpetual right to exploit cost shared intangibles through any unanticipated uses.

(iv) *Other divisional bases.*—(A) In the event that the CSA does not divide interests in the cost shared intangibles on the basis of exclusive territories or fields of use as described in paragraphs (b)(4)(ii) and (iii) of this section, the CSA may adopt some other basis on which to divide all interests in the cost shared intangibles among the controlled participants, provided that each of the following criteria is met:

(1) The basis clearly and unambiguously divides all interests in cost shared intangibles among the controlled participants.

(2) The consistent use of such basis for the division of all interests in the cost shared intangibles can be dependably verified from the records maintained by the controlled participants.

(3) The rights of the controlled participants to exploit cost shared intangibles are non-overlapping, exclusive, and perpetual.

(4) The resulting benefits associated with each controlled participant's interest in cost shared intangibles are predictable with reasonable reliability.

(B) See paragraph (f)(3) of this section for rules regarding the requirement of arm's length consideration for changes in participation in CSAs involving divisions of interest described in this paragraph (b)(4)(iv).

(v) *Examples.*—The following examples illustrate the principles of this paragraph (b)(4):

Example 1. Companies P and S, both members of the same controlled group, enter into a CSA to develop product Z. Under the CSA, P receives the interest in product Z in the United States and S receives the interest in product Z in the rest of the world, as described in paragraph (b)(4)(ii) of this section. Both P and S have plants for manufacturing product Z located in their respective geographic territories. However, for commercial reasons, product Z is nevertheless manufactured by P in the United States for sale to customers in certain locations just outside the United States in close proximity to P's U.S. manufacturing plant. Because S owns the territorial rights outside the United States, P must compensate S to ensure that S realizes all the cost shared intangible profits from P's sales of product Z in S's territory. The pricing of such compensation must also ensure that P realizes an appropriate return for its manufacturing efforts. Benefits projected with respect to such sales will be included for purposes of estimating S's, but not P's, RAB share.

Example 2. The facts are the same as in *Example 1* except that P and S agree to divide their interest in product Z based on site of manufacturing. P will have exclusive and perpetual rights in product Z manufactured in facilities owned by P. S will have exclusive and perpetual rights to product Z manufactured in facilities owned by S. P and S agree that neither will license manufacturing rights in product Z to any related or unrelated party. Both P and S maintain books and records that allow production at all sites to be verified. Both own facilities that will manufacture product Z and the relative capacities of these sites are known. All facilities are currently operating at near capacity and are expected to continue to operate at near capacity when product Z enters production so that it will not be feasible to shift production between P's and S's facilities. P and S have no plans to build new facilities and the lead time required to plan and build a manufacturing facility precludes the possibility that P or S will build a new facility during the period for which sales of Product Z are expected. Based on these facts, this basis for the division of interests in Product Z is a division described in paragraph (b)(4)(iv) of this section. The basis for the division of interest is unambiguous and clearly defined and its use can be dependably verified. P and S both have non-overlapping, exclusive and perpetual rights in Product Z. The division of interest results in the participant's relative benefits being predictable with reasonable reliability.

Example 3. The facts are the same as in *Example 2* except that P's and S's manufacturing facilities are not expected to operate at full capacity when product Z enters production. Production of Product Z can be shifted at any time between sites owned by P and sites owned by S, although neither P nor S intends to shift production as a result of the agreement. The division of interests in Product Z between P and S based on manufacturing site is not a division described in paragraph (b)(4)(iv) of this section because their relative shares of benefits are not predictable with reasonable reliability. The fact that neither P nor S intends to shift production is irrelevant.

(5) *Treatment of certain arrangements as CSAs.*—(i) *Situation in which Commissioner must treat arrangement as a CSA.*—The Commissioner must apply the rules of this section to an arrangement among controlled taxpayers if the administrative requirements of paragraph (b)(2) of this section are met with respect to such arrangement and the controlled taxpayers reasonably concluded that such arrangement was a CSA meeting the requirements of paragraphs (b)(1), (3), and (4) of this section.

(ii) *Situation in which Commissioner may treat arrangement as a CSA.*—For arrangements among controlled taxpayers not described in paragraph (b)(5)(i) of this section, the Commissioner may apply the provisions of this section if the Commissioner concludes that the administrative requirements of paragraph (b)(2) of this section are met, and, notwithstanding technical failure to meet the substantive requirements of paragraph (b)(1), (3), or (4) of this section, the rules of this section will provide the most reliable measure of an arm's length result. See § 1.482-1(c)(1) (the best method rule). For purposes of applying this paragraph (b)(5)(ii), any such arrangement shall be interpreted by reference to paragraph (k)(1)(iv) of this section.

(iii) *Examples.*—The following examples illustrate the principles of this paragraph (b)(5). In the examples, assume that Companies P and S are both members of the same controlled group.

Example 1. (i) P owns the patent on a formula for a capsulated pain reliever, P-Cap. P reasonably anticipates, pending further research and experimentation, that the P-Cap formula could form the platform for a formula for P-Ves, an effervescent version of P-Cap. P also owns proprietary software that it reasonably anticipates to be critical to the research efforts. P and S execute a contract that purports to be a CSA by which they agree to proportionally share the costs and risks of developing a formula for P-Ves. The agreement reflects the various contractual requirements described in paragraph (k)(1) of this section and P and S comply with the documentation, accounting, and reporting requirements of paragraphs (k)(2) through (4) of this section. Both the patent rights for P-Cap and the software are reasonably anticipated to contribute to the development of P-Ves and therefore are platform contributions for which compensation is due from S as part of PCTs. Though P and S enter into and implement a PCT for the P-Cap patent rights that satisfies the arm's length standard, they fail to enter into a PCT for the software.

(ii) In this case, P and S have substantially complied with the contractual requirements of paragraph (k)(1) of this section and the documentation, accounting, and reporting requirements of paragraphs (k)(2) through (4) of this section and therefore have met the administrative requirements of paragraph (b)(2) of this section. However, because they did not enter into a PCT, as required under paragraphs (b)(1)(ii) and (b)(3) of this section, for the software that was reasonably anticipated to contribute to the development of P-Ves (see paragraph (c) of this section), they cannot reasonably conclude that their arrangement was a CSA. Accordingly, the Commissioner is not required under paragraph (b)(5)(i) of this section to apply the rules of this section to their arrangement.

(iii) Nevertheless, the arrangement between P and S closely resembles a CSA. If the Commissioner concludes that the rules of this section provide the most reliable measure of an arm's length result for such arrangement, then pursuant to paragraph (b)(5)(ii) of this section, the Commissioner may apply the rules of this section and treat P and S as entering into a PCT for the software in accordance with the requirements of paragraph (b)(1)(ii) of this section, and make any appropriate allocations under paragraph (i) of this section. Alternatively, the Commissioner may conclude that the rules of this section do not provide the most reliable measure of an arm's length result. In such case, the arrangement would be analyzed under the methods under other sections of the 482 regulations to determine whether the arrangement reaches an arm's length result.

Example 2. The facts are the same as in *Example 1* except that P and S do enter into and implement a PCT for the software as required under this paragraph (b). The Commissioner determines that the PCT Payments for the software were not arm's length; nevertheless, under the facts and circumstances at the time they entered into the CSA and PCTs, P and S reasonably concluded their arrangement to be a CSA. Because P and S have met the requirements of paragraph (b)(2) of this section and reasonably concluded their arrangement is a CSA, pursuant to paragraph (b)(5)(i) of this section, the Commissioner must apply the rules of this section to their arrangement. Accordingly, the Commissioner treats the arrangement as a CSA and makes adjustments to the PCT Payments as appropriate under this section to achieve an arm's length result for the PCT for the software.

Example 3. (i) The facts are the same as in *Example 1* except that P and S do enter into a PCT for the software as required under this paragraph (b). The agreement entered into by P and S provides for a fixed consideration of $50 million per year for four years, payable at the end of each year. This agreement satisfies the arm's length standard. However, S actually pays P consideration at the end of each year in the form of four annual royalties equal to two percent of sales. While such royalties at the time of the PCT were expected to be $50 million per year, actual sales during the first year were less than anticipated and the first royalty payment was only $25 million.

(ii) In this case, P and S failed to implement the terms of their agreement. Under these circumstances, P and S could not reasonably conclude that their arrangement was a CSA, as described in paragraph (b)(1) of this section. Accordingly, the Commissioner is not required under paragraph (b)(5)(i) of this section to apply the rules of this section to their arrangement.

(iii) Nevertheless, the arrangement between P and S closely resembles a CSA. If the Commissioner concludes that that the rules of this section provide the most reliable measure of an arm's length result for such arrangement, then pursuant to paragraph (b)(5)(ii) of this section, the Commissioner may apply the rules of this section and make any appropriate allocations under paragraph (i) of this section. Alternatively, the Commissioner may conclude that the rules of this section do not provide the most reliable measure of an arm's length result. In such case, the arrangement would be analyzed under the methods under other sections of the 482 regulations to determine whether the arrangement reaches an arm's length result.

Example 4. (i) The facts are the same as in Example 1 except that P does not own proprietary software and P and S use a method for determining the arm's length amount of the PCT Payment for the P-Cap patent rights different from the method used in *Example 1*.

(ii) P and S determine that the arm's length amount of the PCT Payments for the P-Cap patent is $10 million. However, the Commissioner determines the best method for determining the arm's length amount of the PCT Payments for the P-Cap patent rights and under such method the arm's length amount is $100 million. To determine this $10 million present value, P and S assumed a useful life of eight years for the platform contribution, because the P-Cap patent rights will expire after eight years. However, the P-Cap patent rights are expected to lead to benefits attributable to exploitation of the cost shared intangibles extending many years beyond the expiration of the P-Cap patent, because use of the P-Cap patent rights will let P and S bring P-Ves to market before the competition, and because P and S expect to apply for additional patents covering P-Ves, which would bar competitors from selling that product for many future years. The assumption by P and S of a useful life for the platform contribution that is less than the anticipated period of exploitation of the cost shared intangibles is contrary to paragraph (g)(2)(ii) of this section, and reduces the reliability of the method used by P and S.

(iii) The method used by P and S employs a declining royalty. The royalty starts at 8% of sales, based on an application of the CUT method in which the purported CUTs all involve licenses to manufacture and sell the current generation of P-Cap, and declines to 0% over eight years, declining by 1% each year. Such make-or-sell rights are fundamentally different from use of the P-Cap patent rights to generate a new product. This difference raises the issue of whether the make-or-sell rights are sufficiently comparable to the rights that are the subject of the PCT Payment. See § 1.482-4(c). While a royalty rate for make-or-sell rights can form the basis for a reliable determination of an arm's length PCT Payment in the CUT-based implementation of the income method described in paragraph (g)(4) of this section, under that method such royalty rate does not decline to zero. Therefore, the use of a declining royalty rate based on an initial rate for make-or-sell rights further reduces the reliability of the method used by P and S.

(iv) Sales of the next-generation product are not anticipated until after seven years, at which point the royalty rate will have declined to 1%. The temporal mismatch between the period of the royalty rate decline and the period of exploitation raises further concerns about the method's reliability.

(v) For the reasons given in paragraphs (ii) through (iv) of this *Example 4*, the method used by P and S is so unreliable and so contrary to provisions of this section that P and S could not reasonably conclude that they had contracted to make arm's length PCT Payments as required by paragraphs (b)(1)(ii) and (b)(3) of this section, and thus could not reasonably conclude that their arrangement was a CSA. Accordingly, the Commissioner is not required under paragraph (b)(5)(i) of this section to apply the rules of this section to their arrangement.

(vi) Nevertheless, the arrangement between P and S closely resembles a CSA. If the Commissioner concludes that that the rules of this section provide the most reliable measure of an arm's length result for such arrangement, then pursuant to paragraph (b)(5)(ii) of this section, the Commissioner may apply the rules of this section and make any appropriate allocations under paragraph (i) of this section. Alternatively, the Commissioner may conclude that the rules of this section do not provide the most reliable measure of an arm's length result. In such case, the arrangement would be analyzed under the methods under other section 482 regulations to determine whether the arrangement reaches an arm's length result.

(6) *Entity classification of CSAs.*—See § 301.7701-1(c) of this chapter for the classification of CSAs for purposes of the Internal Revenue Code.

(c) *Platform contributions.*—(1) *In general.*—A platform contribution is any resource, capability, or right that a controlled participant has developed, maintained, or acquired externally to the intangible development activity (whether prior to or during the course of the CSA) that is reasonably anticipated to contribute to developing cost shared intangibles. The determination whether a resource, capability, or right is reasonably anticipated to contribute to developing cost shared intangibles is ongoing and based on the best available information. Therefore, a resource, capability, or right reasonably determined not to be a platform contribution as of an earlier point in time, may be reasonably determined to be a platform contribution at a later point in time. The PCT obligation regarding a resource or capability or right once determined to be a platform contribution does not terminate merely because it may later be determined that such resource or capability or right has not contributed, and no longer is reasonably anticipated to contribute, to developing cost shared intangibles. Notwithstanding the other provisions of this paragraph (c), platform contributions do not include rights in land or depreciable tangible property, and do not include rights in other resources acquired by IDCs. See paragraph (d)(1) of this section.

(2) *Terms of platform contributions.*—(i) *Presumed to be exclusive.*—For purposes of a PCT, the PCT Payee's provision of a platform contribution is presumed to be exclusive. Thus, it is presumed that the platform resource, capability, or right is not reasonably anticipated to be committed to any business activities other than the CSA Activity, as defined in paragraph (j)(1)(i) of this section, whether carried out by the controlled participants, other controlled taxpayers, or uncontrolled taxpayers.

(ii) *Rebuttal of exclusivity.*—The controlled participants may rebut the presumption set forth in paragraph (c)(2)(i) of this section to the satisfaction of the Commissioner. For example, if the platform resource is a research tool, then the controlled participants could rebut the presumption by establishing to the satisfaction of the Commissioner that, as of the date of the PCT, the tool is reasonably anticipated not only to contribute to the CSA Activity but also to be licensed to an uncontrolled taxpayer. In such case, the PCT Payments may need to be prorated as described in paragraph (c)(2)(iii) of this section.

(iii) *Proration of PCT Payments to the extent allocable to other business activities.*—(A) *In general.*—Some transfer pricing methods employed to determine the arm's length amount of the PCT Payments do so by considering the overall value of the platform contributions as opposed to, for example, the value of the anticipated use of the platform contributions in the CSA Activity. Such a transfer pricing method is consistent with the presumption that the platform contribution is exclusive (that is, that the resources, capabilities or rights that are the subject of a platform contribution are reasonably anticipated to contribute only to the CSA Activity). See paragraph (c)(2)(i) (Terms of platform contributions - Presumed to be exclusive) of this section. The PCT Payments determined under such transfer pricing method may have to be prorated if the controlled participants can rebut the presumption that the platform contribution is exclusive to the satisfaction of the Commissioner as provided in paragraph (c)(2)(ii) of this section. In the case of a platform contribution that also contributes to lines of business of a PCT Payor that are not reasonably anticipated to involve exploitation of the cost shared intangibles, the need for explicit proration may in some cases be avoided through aggregation of transactions. See paragraph (g)(2)(iv) of this section (Aggregation of transactions).

(B) *Determining the proration of PCT Payments.*—Proration will be done on a reasonable basis in proportion to the relative economic value, as of the date of the PCT, reasonably anticipated to be derived from the platform contribution by the CSA Activity as compared to the value reasonably anticipated to be derived from the platform contribution by other business activities. In the case of an aggregate valuation done under the principles of paragraph (g)(2)(iv) of this section that addresses payment for resources, capabilities, or rights used for business activities other than the CSA Activity (for example, the right to exploit an existing intangible without further development), the proration of the aggregate payments may have to reflect the economic value attributable to such resources, capabilities, or rights as well. For purposes of the best method rule under § 1.482-1(c), the reliability of the analysis under a method that requires proration pursuant to this paragraph is reduced relative to the reliability of an analysis under a method that does not require proration.

(3) *Categorization of the PCT.*—For purposes of § 1.482-1(b)(2)(ii) and paragraph (a)(2) of this section, a PCT must be identified by the controlled participants as a particular type of transaction (for example, a license for royalty payments). See paragraph (k)(2)(ii)(H) of this section. Such designation must be consistent with the actual conduct of the controlled participants. If the conduct is consistent with different , economically equivalent types of transactions then the controlled participants may designate the PCT as being any of such types of transactions. If the controlled participants fail to make such designation in their documentation, the Commissioner may make a designation consistent with the principles of paragraph (k)(1)(iv) of this section.

(4) *Certain make-or-sell rights excluded.*—(i) *In general.*—Any right to exploit an existing resource, capability, or right without further development of such item, such as the right to make, replicate, license, or sell existing products, does not constitute a platform contribution to a CSA (and the arm's length compensation for such rights (make-or-sell rights) does not satisfy the compensation obligation under a PCT) unless exploitation without further development of such item is reasonably anticipated to contribute to developing or further developing a cost shared intangible.

(ii) *Examples.*—The following examples illustrate the principles of this paragraph (c)(4):

Example 1. P and S, which are members of the same controlled group, execute a CSA. Under the CSA, P and S will bear their RAB shares of IDCs for developing the second generation of ABC, a computer software program. Prior to that arrangement, P had incurred substantial costs and risks to develop ABC. Concurrent with entering into the arrangement, P (as the licensor) executes a license with S (as the licensee) by which S may make and sell copies of the existing ABC. Such make-or-sell rights do not constitute a platform contribution to the CSA. The rules of § § 1.482-1 and 1.482-4 through 1.482-6 must be applied to determine the arm's length consideration in connection with the make-or-sell licensing arrangement. In certain circumstances, this determination of the arm's length consideration may be done on an aggregate basis with the evaluation of compensation obligations pursuant to the PCTs entered into by P and S in connection with the CSA. See paragraph (g)(2)(iv) of this section.

Example 2. (i) P, a software company, has developed and currently exploits software program ABC. P and S enter into a CSA to develop future generations of ABC. The ABC source code is the platform on which future generations of ABC will be built and is therefore a platform contribution of P for which compensation is due from S pursuant to a PCT. Concurrent with entering into the CSA, P licenses to S the make-or-sell rights for the current version of ABC. P has entered into similar licenses with uncontrolled parties calling for sales-based royalty payments at a rate of 20%. The current version of ABC has an expected product life of three years. P and S enter into a contingent payment agreement to cover both the PCT Payments due from S for P's platform contribution and payments due from S for the make-or-sell license. Based on the uncontrolled make-or-sell licenses, P and S agree on a sales-based royalty rate of 20% in Year 1 that declines on a straight line basis to 0% over the 3 year product life of ABC.

(ii) The make-or-sell rights for the current version of ABC are not platform contributions, though paragraph (g)(2)(iv) of this section provides for the possibility that the most reliable determination of an arm's length charge for the platform contribution and the make-or-sell license may be one that values the two transactions in the aggregate. A contingent payment schedule based on the uncontrolled make-or-sell licenses may provide an arm's length charge for the separate make-or-sell license between P and S, provided the royalty rates in the uncontrolled licenses similarly decline, but as a measure of the aggregate PCT and licensing payments it does not account for the arm's length value of P's platform contributions which include the rights in the source code and future development rights in ABC.

Example 3. S is a controlled participant that owns Patent Q, which protects S's use of a research tool that is helpful in developing and testing new pharmaceutical compounds. The research tool, which is not itself such a compound, is used in the CSA Activity to develop such compounds. However, the CSA Activity is not anticipated to result in the further development of the research tool or in patents based on Patent Q. Although the right to use Patent Q is not anticipated to result in the further development of Patent Q or the technology that it protects, that right constitutes a platform contribution (as opposed to make-or-sell rights) because it is anticipated to contribute to the research activity to develop cost shared intangibles relating to pharmaceutical compounds covered by the CSA.

(5) *Examples.*—The following examples illustrate the principles of this paragraph (c). In each example, Companies P and S are members of the same controlled group, and execute a CSA providing that each will have the exclusive right to exploit cost shared intangibles in its own territory. See paragraph (b)(4)(ii) of this section (Territorial based divisional interests).

Example 1. Company P has developed and currently markets version 1.0 of a new software application XYZ. Company P and Company S execute a CSA under which they will share the IDCs for developing future versions of XYZ. Version 1.0 is reasonably anticipated to contribute to the development of future versions of XYZ and therefore Company P's rights in version 1.0 constitute a platform contribution from Company P that must be compensated by Company S pursuant to a PCT. Pursuant to paragraph (c)(3) of this section, the controlled participants designate the platform contribution as a transfer of intangibles that would otherwise be governed by § 1.482-4, if entered into by controlled parties. Accordingly, pursuant to paragraph (a)(2) of this section, the applicable method for determining the arm's length value of the compensation obligation under the PCT between Company P and Company S will be governed by § 1.482-4 as supplemented by paragraph (g) of this section. Absent a showing to the contrary by P and S, the platform contribution in this case is presumed to be the exclusive provision of the benefit of all rights in version 1.0, other than the rights described in paragraph (c)(4) of this section (Certain make-or-sell rights excluded). This includes the right to use version 1.0 for purposes of research and the exclusive right in S's territory to exploit any future products that incorporated the technology of version 1.0, and would cover a term extending as long as the controlled participants were to exploit future versions of XYZ or any other product based on the version 1.0 platform. The compensation obligation of Company S pursuant to the PCT will reflect the full value of the platform contribution, as limited by Company S's RAB share.

Example 2. Company P and Company S execute a CSA under which they will share the IDCs for developing Vaccine Z. Company P will commit to the project its research team that has successfully developed a number of other vaccines. The expertise and existing integration of the research team is a unique resource or capability of Company P which is reasonably anticipated to contribute to the development of Vaccine Z. Therefore, P's provision of the capabilities of the research team constitute a platform contribution for which compensation is due from Company S as part of a PCT. Pursuant to paragraph (c)(3) of this section, the controlled parties designate the platform contribution as a provision of services that would otherwise be governed by § 1.482-9(a) if entered into by controlled parties. Accordingly, pursuant to paragraph (a)(2) of this section, the applicable method for determining the arm's length value of the compensation obligation under the PCT between Company P and Company S will be governed by § 1.482-9(a) as supplemented by paragraph (g) of this section. Absent a showing to the contrary by P and S, the platform contribution in this case is presumed to be the exclusive provision of the benefits by Company P of its research team to the development of Vaccine Z. Because the IDCs include the ongoing compensation of the researchers, the compensation obligation under the PCT is only for the value of the commitment of the research team by Company P to the CSA's development efforts net of such researcher compensation. The value of the compensation obligation of Company S for the PCT will reflect the full value of the provision of services, as limited by Company S's RAB share.

(d) *Intangible development costs.*—(1) *Determining whether costs are IDCs.*—Costs included in IDCs are determined by reference to the scope of the intangible development activity (IDA).

(i) *Definition and scope of the IDA.*—For purposes of this section, the IDA means the activity under the CSA of developing or attempting to develop reasonably anticipated cost shared intangibles. The scope of the IDA includes all of the controlled participants' activities that could reasonably be anticipated to contribute to developing the reasonably anticipated cost shared intangibles. The IDA cannot be described merely by a list of particular resources, capabilities, or rights that will be used in the CSA, because such a list would not identify reasonably anticipated cost shared intangibles. Also, the scope of the IDA may change as the nature or identity of the reasonably anticipated cost shared intangibles changes or the nature of the activities necessary for their development become clearer. For example, the relevance of certain ongoing work to developing reasonably anticipated cost shared intangibles or the need for additional work may only become clear over time.

(ii) *Reasonably anticipated cost shared intangible.*—For purposes of this section, *reasonably anticipated cost shared intangible* means any intangible, within the meaning of § 1.482-4(b), that, at the applicable point in time, the controlled participants intend to develop under the CSA. Reasonably anticipated cost shared intangibles may change over the course of the CSA. The controlled participants may at any time change the reasonably anticipated cost shared intangibles but must document any such change pursuant to paragraph (k)(2)(ii)(A)(*1*) of this section. Removal of reasonably anticipated cost shared intangibles does not affect the controlled participants' interests in cost shared intangibles already developed under the CSA. In addition, the reasonably anticipated cost shared intangibles automatically expand to include the intended result of any further development of a cost shared intangible already developed under the CSA, or applications of such an intangible. However, the controlled participants may override this automatic expansion in a particular case if they separately remove specified further development of such intangible (or specified applications of such intangible) from the IDA, and document such separate removal pursuant to paragraph (k)(2)(ii)(A)(3) of this section.

(iii) *Costs included in IDCs.*—For purposes of this section, IDCs mean all costs, in cash or in kind (including stock-based compensation, as described in paragraph (d)(3) of this section), but excluding acquisition costs for land or depreciable property, in the ordinary course of business after the formation of a CSA that, based on analysis of the facts and circumstances, are directly identified with, or are reasonably allocable to, the IDA. Thus, IDCs include costs incurred in attempting to develop reasonably anticipated cost shared intangibles regardless of whether such costs ultimately lead to development of those intangibles, other intangibles developed unexpectedly, or no intangibles. IDCs shall also include the arm's length rental charge for the use of any land or depreciable tangible property (as determined under § 1.482-2(c) (Use of tangible property)) directly identified with, or reasonably allocable to, the IDA. Reference to generally accepted accounting principles or Federal income tax accounting rules may provide a useful starting point but will not be conclusive regarding inclusion of costs in IDCs. IDCs do not include interest expense, foreign income taxes (as defined in § 1.901-2(a)), or domestic income taxes.

(iv) *Examples.*—The following examples illustrate the principles of this paragraph (d)(1):

Example 1. A contract that purports to be a CSA provides that the IDA to which the agreement applies consists of all research and development activity conducted at laboratories A, B, and C but not at other facilities maintained by the controlled participants. The contract does not describe the reasonably anticipated cost shared intangibles with respect to which research and development is to be undertaken. The contract fails to meet the requirements set forth in paragraph (k)(1)(ii)(B) of this section because it fails to adequately describe the scope of the IDA to be undertaken.

Example 2. A contract that purports to be a CSA provides that the IDA to which the agreement applies consists of all research and development activity conducted by any of the controlled participants with the goal of developing a cure for a particular disease. Such a cure is thus a reasonably anticipated cost shared intangible. The contract also contains a provision that the IDA will exclude any activity that builds on the results of the controlled participants' prior research concerning Enzyme X even though such activity could reasonably be anticipated to contribute to developing such cure. The contract fails to meet the requirement set forth in paragraph (d)(1)(i) of this section that the scope of the IDA include all of the controlled participants' activities that could reasonably be anticipated to contribute to developing reasonably anticipated cost shared intangibles.

(2) *Allocation of costs.*—If a particular cost is directly identified with, or reasonably allocable to, a function the results of which will benefit both the IDA and other business activities, the cost must be allocated on a reasonable basis between the IDA and such other business activities in proportion to the relative economic value that the IDA and such other business activities are anticipated to derive from such results.

(3) *Stock-based compensation.*—(i) *In general.*—As used in this section, the term *stock-based compensation* means any compensation provided by a controlled participant to an employee or independent contractor in the form of equity instruments, options to acquire stock (stock options), or rights with respect to (or determined by reference to) equity instruments or stock options, including but not limited to property to which section 83 applies and stock options to which section 421 applies, regardless of whether ultimately settled in the form of cash, stock, or other property.

(ii) *Identification of stock-based compensation with the IDA.*—The determination of whether stock-based compensation is directly identified with, or reasonably allocable to, the IDA is made as of the date that the stock-based compensation is granted. Accordingly, all stock-based compensation that is granted during the term of the CSA and, at date of grant, is directly identified with, or reasonably allocable to, the IDA is included as an IDC under paragraph (d)(1) of this section. In the case of a repricing or other modification of a stock option, the determination of whether the repricing or other modification constitutes the grant of a new stock option for purposes of this paragraph (d)(3)(ii) will be made in accordance with the rules of section 424(h) and related regulations.

(iii) *Measurement and timing of stock-based compensation IDC.*—(A) *In general.*—Except as otherwise provided in this paragraph (d)(3)(iii), the cost attributable to stock-based compensation is equal to the amount allowable to the controlled participant as a deduction for federal income tax purposes with respect to that stock-based compensation (for example, under section 83(h)) and is taken into account as an IDC under this section for the taxable year for which the deduction is allowable.

(1) Transfers to which section 421 applies.—Solely for purposes of this paragraph (d)(3)(iii)(A), section 421 does not apply to the transfer of stock pursuant to the exercise of an option that meets the requirements of section 422(a) or 423(a).

(2) Deductions of foreign controlled participants.—Solely for purposes of this paragraph (d)(3)(iii)(A), an amount is treated as an allowable deduction of a foreign controlled participant to the extent that a deduction would be allowable to a United States taxpayer.

(3) Modification of stock option.—Solely for purposes of this paragraph (d)(3)(iii)(A), if the repricing or other modification of a stock option is determined, under paragraph (d)(3)(ii) of this section, to constitute the grant of a new stock option not identified with, or reasonably allocable to, the IDA, the stock option that is repriced or otherwise modified will be treated as being exercised immediately before the modification, provided that the stock option is then exercisable and the fair market value of the underlying stock then exceeds the price at which the stock option is exercisable. Accordingly, the amount of the deduction that would be allowable (or treated as allowable under this paragraph (d)(3)(iii)(A)) to the controlled participant upon exercise of the stock option immediately before the modification must be taken into account as an IDC as of the date of the modification.

(4) Expiration or termination of CSA.—Solely for purposes of this paragraph (d)(3)(iii)(A), if an item of stock-based compensation identified with, or reasonably allocable to, the IDA is not exercised during the term of a CSA, that item of stock-based compensation will be treated as being exercised immediately before the expiration or termination of the CSA, provided that the stock-based compensation is then exercisable and the fair market value of the underlying stock then exceeds the price at which the stock-based compensation is exercisable. Accordingly, the amount of the deduction that would be allowable (or treated as allowable under this paragraph (d)(3)(iii)(A)) to the controlled participant upon exercise of the stock-based compensation must be taken into account as an IDC as of the date of the expiration or termination of the CSA.

(B) *Election with respect to options on publicly traded stock.*—*(1) In general.*—With respect to stock-based compensation in the form of options on publicly traded stock, the controlled participants in a

CSA may elect to take into account all IDCs attributable to those stock options in the same amount, and as of the same time, as the fair value of the stock options reflected as a charge against income in audited financial statements or disclosed in footnotes to such financial statements, provided that such statements are prepared in accordance with United States generally accepted accounting principles by or on behalf of the company issuing the publicly traded stock.

(2) Publicly traded stock.—As used in this paragraph (d)(3)(iii)(B), the term *publicly traded stock* means stock that is regularly traded on an established United States securities market and is issued by a company whose financial statements are prepared in accordance with United States generally accepted accounting principles for the taxable year.

(3) Generally accepted accounting principles.—For purposes of this paragraph (d)(3)(iii)(B), a financial statement prepared in accordance with a comprehensive body of generally accepted accounting principles other than United States generally accepted accounting principles is considered to be prepared in accordance with United States generally accepted accounting principles provided that either—

(i) The fair value of the stock options under consideration is reflected in the reconciliation between such other accounting principles and United States generally accepted accounting principles required to be incorporated into the financial statement by the securities laws governing companies whose stock is regularly traded on United States securities markets; or

(ii) In the absence of a reconciliation between such other accounting principles and United States generally accepted accounting principles that reflects the fair value of the stock options under consideration, such other accounting principles require that the fair value of the stock options under consideration be reflected as a charge against income in audited financial statements or disclosed in footnotes to such statements.

(4) Time and manner of making the election.—The election described in this paragraph (d)(3)(iii)(B) is made by an explicit reference to the election in the written contract required by paragraph (k)(1) of this section or in a written amendment to the CSA entered into with the consent of the Commissioner pursuant to paragraph (d)(3)(iii)(C) of this section. In the case of a CSA in existence on August 26, 2003, the election by written amendment to the CSA may be made without the consent of the Commissioner if such amendment is entered into not later than the latest due date (with regard to extensions) of a federal income tax return of any controlled participant for the first taxable year beginning after August 26, 2003.

(C) *Consistency.*—Generally, all controlled participants in a CSA taking options on publicly traded stock into account under paragraph (d)(3)(ii), (d)(3)(iii)(A), or (d)(3)(iii)(B) of this section must use that same method of identification, measurement and timing for all options on publicly traded stock with respect to that CSA. Controlled participants may change their method only with the consent of the Commissioner and only with respect to stock options granted during taxable years subsequent to the taxable year in which the Commissioner's consent is obtained. All controlled participants in the CSA must join in requests for the Commissioner's consent under this paragraph (d)(3)(iii)(C). Thus, for example, if the controlled participants make the election described in paragraph (d)(3)(iii)(B) of this section upon the formation of the CSA, the election may be revoked only with the consent of the Commissioner, and the consent will apply only to stock options granted in taxable years subsequent to the taxable year in which consent is obtained. Similarly, if controlled participants already have granted stock options that have been or will be taken into account under the general rule of paragraph (d)(3)(iii)(A) of this section, then except in cases specified in the last sentence of paragraph (d)(3)(iii)(B)(4) of this section, the controlled participants may make the election described in paragraph (d)(3)(iii)(B) of this section only with the consent of the Commissioner, and the consent will apply only to stock options granted in taxable years subsequent to the taxable year in which consent is obtained.

(4) *IDC share.*—A controlled participant's IDC share for a taxable year is equal to the controlled participant's cost contribution for the taxable year, divided by the sum of all IDCs for the taxable year. A controlled participant's cost contribution for a taxable year means all of the IDCs initially borne by the controlled participant, plus all of the CST Payments that the participant makes to other controlled participants, minus all of the CST Payments that the participant receives from other controlled participants.

(5) *Examples.*—The following examples illustrate this paragraph (d):

Example 1. Foreign parent (FP) and its U.S. subsidiary (USS) enter into a CSA to develop a better mousetrap. USS and FP share the costs of FP's R&D facility that will be exclusively dedicated to this research, the salaries of the researchers at the facility, and overhead costs attributable to the project. They also share the cost of a conference facility that is at the disposal of the senior executive management of each company. Based on the facts and circumstances, the cost of the conference facility cannot be directly identified with, and is not reasonably allocable to, the IDA. In this case, the cost of the conference facility must be excluded from the amount of IDCs.

Example 2. U.S. parent (USP) and its foreign subsidiary (FS) enter into a CSA to develop intangibles for producing a new device. USP and FS share the costs of an R&D facility, the salaries of the facility's researchers, and overhead costs attributable to the project. Although USP also incurs costs related to field testing of the device, USP does not include those costs in the IDCs that USP and FS will share under the CSA. The Commissioner may determine, based on the facts and circumstances, that the costs of field testing are IDCs that the controlled participants must share.

Example 3. U.S. parent (USP) and its foreign subsidiary (FS) enter into a CSA to develop a new process patent. USP assigns certain employees to perform solely R&D to develop a new mathematical algorithm to perform certain calculations. That algorithm will be used both to develop the new process patent and to develop a new design patent the development of which is outside the scope of the CSA. During years covered by the CSA, USP compensates such employees with cash salaries, stock-based compensation, or a combination of both. USP and FS anticipate that the economic value attributable to the R&D will be derived from the process patent and the design patent in a relative proportion of 75% and 25%, respectively. Applying the principles of paragraph (d)(2) of this section, 75% of the compensation of such employees must be allocated to the development of the new process patent and, thus, treated as IDCs. With respect to the cash salary compensation, the IDC is 75% of the face value of the cash. With respect to the stock-based compensation, the IDC is 75% of the value of the stock-based compensation as determined under paragraph (d)(3)(iii) of this section.

Example 4. Foreign parent (FP) and its U.S. subsidiary (USS) enter into a CSA to develop a new computer source code. FP has an executive officer who oversees a research facility and employees dedicated solely to the IDA. The executive officer also oversees other research facilities and employees unrelated to the IDA, and performs certain corporate overhead functions. The full amount of the costs of the research facility and employees dedicated solely to the IDA can be directly identified with the IDA and, therefore, are IDCs. In addition, based on the executive officer's records of time worked on various matters, the controlled participants reasonably allocate 20% of the executive officer's compensation to supervision of the facility and employees dedicated to the IDA, 50% of the executive officer's compensation to supervision of the facilities and employees unrelated to the IDA, and 30% of the executive officer's compensation to corporate overhead functions. The controlled participants also reasonably determine that the results of the executive officer's corporate overhead functions yield equal economic benefit to the IDA and the other business activities of FP. Applying the principles of paragraph (d)(1) of this section, the executive officer's compensation allocated to supervising the facility and employees dedicated to the IDA (amounting to 20% of the executive officer's total compensation) must be treated as IDCs. Applying the principles of paragraph (d)(2) of this section, half of the executive officer's compensation allocated to corporate overhead functions (that is, half of 30% of the executive officer's total compensation), must be treated as IDCs. Therefore, a total of 35% (20% plus 15%) of the executive officer's total compensation must be treated as IDCs.

(e) *Reasonably anticipated benefits share.*—(1) *Definition.*—(i) *In general.*—A controlled participant's share of reasonably anticipated benefits is equal to its reasonably anticipated benefits divided by the sum of the reasonably anticipated benefits, as defined in paragraph (j)(1)(i) of this section, of all the controlled participants. RAB shares must be updated to account for changes in economic conditions, the business operations and practices of the participants, and the ongoing development of intangibles under the CSA. For purposes of determining RAB shares at any given time, reasonably anticipated benefits must be estimated over the entire period, past and future, of exploitation of the cost shared intangibles, and must reflect appropriate updates to take into account the most reliable data regarding past and projected future results available at such time. RAB shares determined for a particular purpose shall not be further updated for that purpose based on information not available at the time that determination needed to be made. For example, RAB shares determined in order to determine IDC shares for a particular taxable year (as set forth in paragraphs (b)(1)(i) and (d)(4) of this section) shall not be recomputed based on information not available at that time. Similarly, RAB shares determined for the purpose of using a particular method such as the acquisition price method (as set forth in paragraph (g)(5)(ii) of this section) to evaluate the arm's length amount charged in a PCT shall not be recomputed based on information not available at the date of that PCT. However, nothing in this paragraph (e)(1)(i) shall limit the Commissioner's use of subsequently available information for purposes of its allocation determinations in accordance with the provisions of paragraph (i) (Allocations by the Commissioner in connection with a CSA) of this section.

(ii) *Reliability*.—A controlled participant's RAB share must be determined by using the most reliable estimate. In determining which of two or more available estimates is most reliable, the quality of the data and assumptions used in the analysis must be taken into account, consistent with § 1.482-1(c)(2)(ii) (Data and assumptions). Thus, the reliability of an estimate will depend largely on the completeness and accuracy of the data, the soundness of the assumptions, and the relative effects of particular deficiencies in data or assumptions on different estimates. If two estimates are equally reliable, no adjustment should be made based on differences between the estimates. The following factors will be particularly relevant in determining the reliability of an estimate of RAB shares:

(A) The basis used for measuring benefits, as described in paragraph (e)(2)(ii) of this section.

(B) The projections used to estimate benefits, as described in paragraph (e)(2)(iii) of this section.

(iii) *Examples*.—The following examples illustrate the principles of this paragraph (e)(1):

Example 1. (i) USP and FS plan to conduct research to develop Product Lines A and B. USP and FS reasonably anticipate respective benefits from Product Line A of 100X and 200X and respective benefits from Product Line B, respectively, of 300X and 400X. USP and FS thus reasonably anticipate combined benefits from Product Lines A and B of 400X and 600X, respectively.

(ii) USP and FS could enter into a separate CSA to develop Product Line A with respective RAB shares of 33 1/3 percent and 66 2/3 percent (reflecting a ratio of 100X to 200X), and into a separate CSA to develop Product Line B with respective RAB shares of 42 6/7 percent and 57 1/7 percent (reflecting a ratio of 300X to 400X). Alternatively, USP and FS could enter into a single CSA to develop both Product Lines A and B with respective RAB shares of 40 percent and 60 percent (in the ratio of 400X to 600X). If the separate CSAs are chosen, then any costs for activities that contribute to developing both Product Line A and Product Line B will constitute IDCs of the respective CSAs as required by paragraphs (d)(1) and (2) of this section.

Example 2. (i) USP, a US company, wholly owns foreign subsidiary, FS. USP and FS enter into a CSA at the start of Year 1. The CSA's total IDCs are $100,000 in each year for Years 1 through 4. In Year 1, USP correctly estimates its RAB share as 50%, based on information available at the time, and therefore correctly computes $50,000 as its cost contribution for Year 1.

(ii) In Year 4, USP correctly estimates its RAB share to be 70%, based on information available at the time and, therefore, correctly computes $70,000 as its cost contribution for Year 4.

(iii) In Year 4, USP also files an amended return for Year 1 in which USP deducts a cost contribution of $70,000, asserting that, for this purpose, it should revise its Year 1 estimated RAB share to 70% based on the information that is now available to it in Year 4. The Commissioner determines that USP is incorrect for two reasons. First, a RAB share determined for a particular purpose (here, to determine USP's IDC shares and thus USP's cost contributions in Year 1) should not be revised based on information not available to USP until Year 4. See paragraph (e)(1)(i) of this section. Second, more generally, USP is not permitted to file an amended return for this purpose under § 1.482-1(a)(3). Therefore, for both of these reasons, Commissioner adjusts USP's amended return for Year 1 by disallowing $20,000 of the $70,000 deduction.

(2) *Measure of benefits*.—(i) *In general*.—In order to estimate a controlled participant's RAB share, the amount of each controlled participant's reasonably anticipated benefits must be measured on a basis that is consistent for all such participants. See paragraph (e)(2)(ii)(E) *Example 9* of this section. If a controlled participant transfers a cost shared intangible to another controlled taxpayer, other than by way of a transfer described in paragraph (f) of this section, that controlled participant's benefits from the transferred intangible must be measured by reference to the transferee's benefits, disregarding any consideration paid by the transferee to the controlled participant (such as a royalty pursuant to a license agreement). Reasonably anticipated benefits are measured either on a direct basis, by reference to estimated benefits to be generated by the use of cost shared intangibles (generally based on additional revenues plus cost savings less any additional costs incurred), or on an indirect basis, by reference to certain measurements that reasonably can be assumed to relate to benefits to be generated. Such indirect bases of measurement of anticipated benefits are described in paragraph (e)(2)(ii) of this section. A controlled participant's reasonably anticipated benefits must be measured on the basis, whether direct or indirect, that most reliably determines RAB shares. In determining which of two bases of measurement is most reliable, the factors set forth in § 1.482-1(c)(2)(ii) (Data and assumptions) must be taken into account. It normally will be expected that the basis that provided the most reliable estimate for a particular year will continue to provide the most reliable estimate in subsequent years, absent a material change in the factors that affect the reliability of the estimate. Regardless of whether a direct or indirect basis of measurement is used, adjustments may be required to account for material differences in the activities that controlled participants undertake to exploit their interests in cost shared intangibles. See *Examples* 4 and 7 of paragraph (e)(2)(ii)(E) of this section.

(ii) *Indirect bases for measuring anticipated benefits*.—Indirect bases for measuring anticipated benefits from participation in a CSA include the following:

(A) *Units used, produced, or sold*.—Units of items used, produced, or sold by each controlled participant in the business activities in which cost shared intangibles are exploited may be used as an indirect basis for measuring its anticipated benefits. This basis of measurement will more reliably determine RAB shares to the extent that each controlled participant is expected to have a similar increase in net profit or decrease in net loss attributable to the cost shared intangibles per unit of the item or items used, produced, or sold. This circumstance is most likely to arise when the cost shared intangibles are exploited by the controlled participants in the use, production, or sale of substantially uniform items under similar economic conditions.

(B) *Sales*.—Sales by each controlled participant in the business activities in which cost shared intangibles are exploited may be used as an indirect basis for measuring its anticipated benefits. This basis of measurement will more reliably determine RAB shares to the extent that each controlled participant is expected to have a similar increase in net profit or decrease in net loss attributable to cost shared intangibles per dollar of sales. This circumstance is most likely to arise if the costs of exploiting cost shared intangibles are not substantial relative to the revenues generated, or if the principal effect of using cost shared intangibles is to increase the controlled participants' revenues (for example, through a price premium on the products they sell) without affecting their costs substantially. Sales by each controlled participant are unlikely to provide a reliable basis for measuring RAB shares unless each controlled participant operates at the same market level (for example, manufacturing, distribution, etc.).

(C) *Operating profit*.—Operating profit of each controlled participant from the activities in which cost shared intangibles are exploited, as determined before any expense (including amortization) on account of IDCs, may be used as an indirect basis for measuring anticipated benefits. This basis of measurement will more reliably determine RAB shares to the extent that such profit is largely attributable to the use of cost shared intangibles, or if the share of profits attributable to the use of cost shared intangibles is expected to be similar for each controlled participant. This circumstance is most likely to arise when cost shared intangibles are closely associated with the activity that generates the profit and the activity could not be carried on or would generate little profit without use of those intangibles.

(D) *Other bases for measuring anticipated benefits*.—Other bases for measuring anticipated benefits may in some circumstances be appropriate, but only to the extent that there is expected to be a reasonably identifiable relationship between the basis of measurement used and additional revenue generated or net costs saved by the use of cost shared intangibles. For example, a division of costs based on employee compensation would be considered unreliable unless there were a relationship between the amount of compensation and the expected additional revenue generated or net costs saved by the controlled participants from using the cost shared intangibles.

(E) *Examples.*—The following examples illustrates this paragraph (e)(2)(ii):

Example 1. Controlled parties A and B enter into a CSA to develop product and process intangibles for already existing Product P. Without such intangibles, A and B would each reasonably anticipate revenue, in present value terms, of $100M from sales of Product P until it becomes obsolete. With the intangibles, A and B each reasonably anticipate selling the same number of units each year, but reasonably anticipate that the price will be higher. Because the particular product intangible is more highly regarded in A's market, A reasonably anticipates an increase of $20M in present value revenue from the product intangible, while B reasonably anticipates an increase of only $10M in present value from the product intangible. Further, A and B each reasonably anticipate spending an additional amount equal to $5M in present value in production costs to include the feature embodying the product intangible. Finally, A and B each reasonably anticipate saving an amount equal to $2M in present value in production costs by using the process intangible. A and B reasonably anticipate no other economic effects from exploiting the cost shared intangibles. A's reasonably anticipated benefits from exploiting the cost shared intangibles equal its reasonably anticipated increase in revenue ($20M) plus its reasonably anticipated cost savings ($2M) less its reasonably anticipated increased costs ($5M), which equals $17M. Similarly, B's reasonably anticipated benefits from exploiting the cost shared intangibles equal its reasonably anticipated increase in revenue ($10M) plus its reasonably anticipated cost savings ($2M) less its reasonably anticipated increased costs ($5M), which equals $7M. Thus A's reasonably anticipated benefits are $17M and B's reasonably anticipated benefits are $7M.

Example 2. Foreign Parent (FP) and U.S. Subsidiary (USS) both produce a feedstock for the manufacture of various high-performance plastic products. Producing the feedstock requires large amounts of electricity, which accounts for a significant portion of its production cost. FP and USS enter into a CSA to develop a new process that will reduce the amount of electricity required to produce a unit of the feedstock. FP and USS currently both incur an electricity cost of $2 per unit of feedstock produced and rates for each are expected to remain similar in the future. The new process, if it is successful, will reduce the amount of electricity required by each company to produce a unit of the feedstock by 50%. Switching to the new process would not require FP or USS to incur significant investment or other costs. Therefore, the cost savings each company is expected to achieve after implementing the new process are $1 per unit of feedstock produced. Under the CSA, FP and USS divide the costs of developing the new process based on the units of the feedstock each is anticipated to produce in the future. In this case, units produced is the most reliable basis for measuring RAB shares and dividing the IDCs because each controlled participant is expected to have a similar $1 (50% of current charge of $2) decrease in costs per unit of the feedstock produced.

Example 3. The facts are the same as in *Example 2*, except that currently USS pays $3 per unit of feedstock produced for electricity while FP pays $6 per unit of feedstock produced. In this case, units produced is not the most reliable basis for measuring RAB shares and dividing the IDCs because the participants do not expect to have a similar decrease in costs per unit of the feedstock produced. The Commissioner determines that the most reliable measure of RAB shares may be based on units of the feedstock produced if FP's units are weighted relative to USS's units by a factor of 2. This reflects the fact that FP pays twice as much as USS for electricity and, therefore, FP's savings of $3 per unit of the feedstock (50% reduction of current charge of $6) would be twice USS's savings of $1.50 per unit of feedstock (50% reduction of current charge of $3) from any new process eventually developed.

Example 4. The facts are the same as in *Example 3*, except that to supply the particular needs of the U.S. market USS manufactures the feedstock with somewhat different properties than FP's feedstock. This requires USS to employ a somewhat different production process than does FP. Because of this difference, USS would incur significant construction costs in order to adopt any new process that may be developed under the cost sharing agreement. In this case, units produced is not the most reliable basis for measuring RAB shares. In order to reliably determine RAB shares, the Commissioner measures the reasonably anticipated benefits of USS and FP on a direct basis. USS's reasonably anticipated benefits are its reasonably anticipated total savings in electricity costs, less its reasonably anticipated costs of adopting the new process. FS's reasonably anticipated benefits are its reasonably anticipated total savings in electricity costs.

Example 5. U.S. Parent (USP) and Foreign Subsidiary (FS) enter into a CSA to develop new anesthetic drugs. USP obtains the right to market any resulting drugs in the United States and FS obtains the right to market any resulting drugs in the rest of the world. USP and FS determine RAB shares on the basis of their respective total anticipated operating profit from all drugs under development. USP anticipates that it will receive a much higher profit than FS per unit sold because the price of the drugs is not regulated in the United States, whereas the price of the drugs is regulated in many non-U.S. jurisdictions. In both controlled participants' territories, the anticipated operating profits are almost entirely attributable to the use of the cost shared intangibles. In this case, the controlled participants' basis for measuring RAB shares is the most reliable.

Example 6. (i) Foreign Parent (FP) and U.S. Subsidiary (USS) manufacture and sell fertilizers. They enter into a CSA to develop a new pellet form of a common agricultural fertilizer that is currently available only in powder form. Under the CSA, USS obtains the rights to produce and sell the new form of fertilizer for the U.S. market while FP obtains the rights to produce and sell the new form of fertilizer in the rest of the world. The costs of developing the new form of fertilizer are divided on the basis of the anticipated sales of fertilizer in the controlled participants' respective markets.

(ii) If the research and development is successful, the pellet form will deliver the fertilizer more efficiently to crops and less fertilizer will be required to achieve the same effect on crop growth. The pellet form of fertilizer can be expected to sell at a price premium over the powder form of fertilizer based on the savings in the amount of fertilizer that needs to be used. This price premium will be a similar premium per dollar of sales in each territory. If the research and development is successful, the costs of producing pellet fertilizer are expected to be approximately the same as the costs of producing powder fertilizer and the same for both FP and USS. Both FP and USS operate at approximately the same market levels, selling their fertilizers largely to independent distributors.

(iii) In this case, the controlled participants' basis for measuring RAB shares is the most reliable.

Example 7. The facts are the same as in *Example 6*, except that FP distributes its fertilizers directly while USS sells to independent distributors. In this case, sales of USS and FP are not the most reliable basis for measuring RAB shares unless adjustments are made to account for the difference in market levels at which the sales occur.

Example 8. Foreign Parent (FP) and U.S. Subsidiary (USS) enter into a CSA to develop materials that will be used to train all new entry-level employees. FP and USS determine that the new materials will save approximately ten hours of training time per employee. Because their entry-level employees are paid on differing wage scales, FP and USS decide that they should not measure benefits based on the number of entry-level employees hired by each. Rather, they measure benefits based on compensation paid to the entry-level employees hired by each. In this case, the basis used for measuring RAB shares is the most reliable because there is a direct relationship between compensation paid to new entry-level employees and costs saved by FP and USS from the use of the new training materials.

Example 9. U.S. Parent (USP), Foreign Subsidiary 1 (FS1), and Foreign Subsidiary 2 (FS2) enter into a CSA to develop computer software that each will market and install on customers' computer systems. The controlled participants measure benefits on the basis of projected sales by USP, FS1, and FS2 of the software in their respective geographic areas. However, FS1 plans not only to sell but also to license the software to unrelated customers, and FS1's licensing income (which is a percentage of the licensees' sales) is not counted in the projected benefits. In this case, the basis used for measuring the benefits of each controlled participant is not the most reliable because all of the benefits received by controlled participants are not taken into account. In order to reliably determine RAB shares, FS1's projected benefits from licensing must be included in the measurement on a basis that is the same as that used to measure its own and the other controlled participants' projected benefits from sales (for example, all controlled participants might measure their benefits on the basis of operating profit).

(iii) *Projections used to estimate benefits.*—(A) *In general.*—The reliability of an estimate of RAB shares also depends upon the reliability of projections used in making the estimate. Projections required for this purpose generally include a determination of the time period between the inception of the research and development activities under the CSA and the receipt of benefits, a projection of the time over which benefits will be received, and a projection of the benefits anticipated for each year in which it is anticipated that the cost shared intangible will generate benefits. A projection of the relevant basis for measuring anticipated benefits may require a projection of the factors that underlie it. For example, a projection of operating profits may require a projection of sales, cost of sales, operating expenses, and other factors that affect operating profits. If it is anticipated that there will be significant variation among controlled participants in the timing of their receipt of benefits, and consequently benefit shares are expected to vary significantly over the years in which benefits will be received, it normally will be necessary to use the present value of the projected benefits to reliably determine RAB shares. See paragraph (g)(2)(v) of this section for best method considerations regarding discount rates used for this purpose. If it is not anticipated that benefit shares will significantly change over time, current annual benefit shares may provide a reliable projection of RAB shares. This circumstance is most likely to occur when the CSA is a long-term arrangement, the arrangement covers a wide variety of intangibles, the composition of the cost shared intangibles is unlikely to change, the cost shared intangibles are unlikely to generate unusual profits, and each controlled participant's share of the market is stable.

(B) *Examples.*—The following examples illustrate the principles of this paragraph (e)(2)(iii):

Example 1. (i) Foreign Parent (FP) and U.S. Subsidiary (USS) enter into a CSA to develop a new car model. The controlled participants plan to spend four years developing the new model and four years producing and selling the new model. USS and FP project total sales of $4 billion and $2 billion, respectively, over the planned four years of exploitation of the new model. The controlled participants determine RAB shares for each year of 66 2/3% for USS and 33 1/3% for FP, based on projected total sales.

(ii) USS typically begins producing and selling new car models a year after FP begins producing and selling new car models. In order to reflect USS's one-year lag in introducing new car models, a more reliable projection of each participant's RAB share would be based on a projection of all four years of sales for each participant, discounted to present value.

Example 2. U.S. Parent (USP) and Foreign Subsidiary (FS) enter into a CSA to develop new and improved household cleaning products. Both controlled participants have sold household cleaning products for many years and have stable worldwide market shares. The products under development are unlikely to produce unusual profits for either controlled participant. The controlled participants determine RAB shares on the basis of each controlled participant's current sales of household cleaning products. In this case, the controlled participants' RAB shares are reliably projected by current sales of cleaning products.

Example 3. The facts are the same as in *Example 2,* except that FS's market share is rapidly expanding because of the business failure of a competitor in its geographic area. The controlled participants' RAB shares are not reliably projected by current sales of cleaning products. FS's benefit projections should take into account its growth in market share.

Example 4. Foreign Parent (FP) and U.S. Subsidiary (USS) enter into a CSA to develop synthetic fertilizers and insecticides. FP and USS share costs on the basis of each controlled participant's current sales of fertilizers and insecticides. The market shares of the controlled participants have been stable for fertilizers, but FP's market share for insecticides has been expanding. The controlled participants' projections of RAB shares are reliable with regard to fertilizers, but not reliable with regard to insecticides; a more reliable projection of RAB shares would take into account the expanding market share for insecticides.

(f) *Changes in participation under a CSA.*—(1) *In general.*—A change in participation under a CSA occurs when there is either a controlled transfer of interests or a capability variation. A change in participation requires arm's length consideration under paragraph (a)(3)(ii) of this section, and as more fully described in this paragraph (f).

(2) *Controlled transfer of interests.*—A controlled transfer of interests occurs when a participant in a CSA transfers all or part of its interests in cost shared intangibles under the CSA in a controlled transaction, and the transferee assumes the associated obligations under the CSA. For example, a change in the territorial based divisional interests or field of use based divisional interests, as described in paragraph (b)(4), is a controlled transfer of interests. After the controlled transfer of interests occurs, the CSA will still exist if at least two controlled participants still have interests in the cost shared intangibles. In such a case, the transferee will be treated as succeeding to the transferor's prior history under the CSA as pertains to the transferred interests, including the transferor's cost contributions, benefits derived, and PCT Payments attributable to such rights or obligations. A transfer that would otherwise constitute a controlled transfer of interests for purposes of this paragraph (f)(2) shall not constitute a controlled transfer of interests if it also constitutes a capability variation for purposes of paragraph (f)(3) of this section.

(3) *Capability variation.*—A capability variation occurs when, in a CSA in which interests in cost shared intangibles are divided as described in paragraph (b)(4)(iv) of this section, the controlled participants' division of interests or their relative capabilities or capacities to benefit from the cost shared intangibles are materially altered. For purposes of paragraph (a)(3)(ii) of this section, a capability variation is considered to be a controlled transfer of interests in cost shared intangibles, in which any controlled participant whose RAB share decreases as a result of the capability variation is a transferor, and any controlled participant whose RAB share thus increases is the transferee of the interests in cost shared intangibles.

(4) *Arm's length consideration for a change in participation.*—In the event of a change in participation, the arm's length amount of consideration from the transferee, under the rules of §§1.482-1 and 1.482-4 through 1.482-6 and paragraph (a)(3)(ii) of this section, will be determined consistent with the reasonably anticipated incremental change in the returns to the transferee and transferor resulting from such change in participation. Such changes in returns will themselves depend on the reasonably anticipated incremental changes in the benefits from exploiting the cost shared intangibles, IDCs borne, and PCT Payments (if any). However, any arm's length consideration required under this paragraph (f)(4) with respect to a capability variation shall be reduced as necessary to prevent duplication of an adjustment already performed under paragraph (i)(2)(ii)(A) of this section that resulted from the same capability variation. If an adjustment has been performed already under this paragraph (f)(4) with respect to a capability variation, then for purposes of any adjustment to be performed under paragraph (i)(2)(ii)(A) of this section, the controlled participants' projected benefit shares referred to in paragraph (i)(2)(ii)(A) of this section shall be considered to be the controlled participants' respective RAB shares after the capability variation occurred.

(5) *Examples.*—The following examples illustrate the principles of this paragraph (f):

Example 1. X, Y, and Z are the only controlled participants in a CSA. The CSA divides interests in cost shared intangibles on a territorial basis as described in paragraph (b)(4)(ii) of this section. X is assigned the territories of the Americas, Y is assigned the territory of the UK and Australia, and Z is assigned the rest of the world. When the CSA is formed, X has a platform contribution T. Under the PCTs for T, Y and Z are each obligated to pay X royalties equal to five percent of their respective sales. Aside from T, there are no platform contributions. Two years after the formation of the CSA, Y transfers to Z its interest in cost shared intangibles relating to the UK territory, and the associated obligations, in a controlled transfer of interests described in paragraph (f)(2) of this section. At that time the reasonably anticipated benefits from exploiting cost shared intangibles in the UK have a present value of $11M, the reasonably anticipated IDCs to be borne relating to the UK territory have a present value of $3M, and the reasonably anticipated PCT Payments to be made to X relating to sales in the UK territory have a present value of $2M. As arm's length consideration for the change in participation due to the controlled transfer of interests, Z must pay Y compensation with an anticipated present value of $11M, less $3M, less $2M, which equals $6M.

Example 2. As in *Example 2* of paragraph (b)(4)(v) of this section, companies P and S, both members of the same controlled group, enter into a CSA to develop product Z. P and S agree to divide their interest in product Z based on site of manufacturing. P will have exclusive and perpetual rights in product Z manufactured in facilities owned by P. S will have exclusive and perpetual rights to product Z manufactured in facilities owned by S. P and S agree that neither will license manufacturing rights in product Z to any related or unrelated party. Both P and S maintain books and records that allow production at all sites to be verified. Both own facilities that will manufacture product Z and the relative capacities of these sites are known. All facilities are currently operating at near capacity and are expected to continue to operate at near capacity when product Z enters production so that it will not be feasible to shift production between P's and S's facilities. P and S have no plans to build new facilities and the lead time required to plan and build a manufacturing facility precludes the possibility that P or S will build a new facility during the period for which sales of Product Z are expected. When the CSA is formed, P has a platform contribution T. Under the PCT for T, S is obligated to pay P sales-based royalties according to a certain formula. Aside from T, there are no other platform contributions. Two years after the formation of the CSA, owing to a change in plans not reasonably foreseeable at the time the CSA was entered into, S acquires additional facilities F for the manufacture of Product Z. Such acquisition constitutes a capability variation described in paragraph (f)(3) of this section. Under this capability variation, S's RAB share increases from 50% to 60%. Accordingly, there is a compensable change in participation under paragraph (f)(3) of this section.

(g) *Supplemental guidance on methods applicable to PCTs.*—(1) *In general.*—This paragraph (g) provides supplemental guidance on applying the methods listed in this paragraph (g)(1) for purposes of evaluating the arm's length amount charged in a PCT. Each method will yield a value for the compensation obligation of each PCT Payor consistent with the product of the combined pre-tax value to all controlled participants of the platform contribution that is the subject of the PCT and the PCT Payor's RAB share. Each method must yield results consistent with measuring the value of a platform contribution by reference to the future income anticipated to be generated by the resulting cost shared intangibles. The methods are—

(i) The comparable uncontrolled transaction method described in § 1.482-4(c), or the comparable uncontrolled services price method described in § 1.482-9(c), as further described in paragraph (g)(3) of this section;

(ii) The income method, described in paragraph (g)(4) of this section;

(iii) The acquisition price method, described in paragraph (g)(5) of this section;

(iv) The market capitalization method, described in paragraph (g)(6) of this section;

(v) The residual profit split method, described in paragraph (g)(7) of this section; and

(vi) Unspecified methods, described in paragraph (g)(8) of this section.

(2) *Best method analysis applicable for evaluation of a PCT pursuant to a CSA.*—(i) *In general.*—Each method must be applied in accordance with the provisions of § 1.482-1, including the best method rule of § 1.482-1(c), the comparability analysis of § 1.482-1(d), and the arm's length range of § 1.482-1(e), except as those provisions are modified in this paragraph (g).

(ii) *Consistency with upfront contractual terms and risk allocation - the investor model.*—(A) *In general.*—Although all of the factors entering into a best method analysis described in § 1.482-1(c) and (d) must be considered, specific factors may be particularly relevant in the context of a CSA. In particular, the relative reliability of an application of any method depends on the degree of consistency of the analysis with the applicable contractual terms and allocation of risk under the CSA and this section among the controlled participants as of the date of the PCT, unless a change in such terms or allocation has been made in return for arm's length consideration. In this regard, a CSA involves an upfront division of the risks as to both reasonably anticipated obligations and reasonably anticipated benefits over the reasonably anticipated term of the CSA Activity. Accordingly, the relative reliability of an application of a method also depends on the degree of consistency of the analysis with the assumption that, as of the date of the PCT, each controlled participant's aggregate net investment in the CSA Activity (including platform contributions, operating contributions, as such term is defined in paragraph (j)(1)(i) of this section, operating cost contributions, as such term is defined in paragraph (j)(1)(i) of this section, and cost contributions) is reasonably anticipated to earn a rate of return (which might be reflected in a discount rate used in applying a method) appropriate to the riskiness of the controlled participant's CSA Activity over the entire period of such CSA Activity. If the cost shared intangibles themselves are reasonably anticipated to contribute to developing other intangibles, then the period described in the preceding sentence includes the period, reasonably anticipated as of the date of the PCT, of developing and exploiting such indirectly benefited intangibles.

(B) *Example.*—The following example illustrates the principles of this paragraph (g)(2)(ii):

Example. (i) P, a U.S. corporation, has developed a software program, DEF, which applies certain algorithms to reconstruct complete DNA sequences from partially-observed DNA sequences. S is a wholly-owned foreign subsidiary of P. On the first day of Year 1, P and S enter into a CSA to develop a new generation of genetic tests, GHI, based in part on the use of DEF. DEF is therefore a platform contribution of P for which compensation is due from S pursuant to a PCT. S makes no platform contributions to the CSA. Sales of GHI are projected to commence two years after the inception of the CSA and then to continue for eight more years. Based on industry experience, P and S are confident that GHI will be replaced by a new type of genetic testing based on technology unrelated to DEF or GHI and that, at that point, GHI will have no further value. P and S project that that replacement will occur at the end of Year 10.

(ii) For purposes of valuing the PCT for P's platform contribution of DEF to the CSA, P and S apply a type of residual profit split method that is not described in paragraph (g)(7) of this section and which, accordingly, constitutes an unspecified method. See paragraph (g)(7)(i) (last sentence) of this section. The principles of this paragraph (g)(2) apply to any method for valuing a PCT, including the unspecified method used by P and S.

(iii) Under the method employed by P and S, in each year, a portion of the income from sales of GHI in S's territory is allocated to certain routine contributions made by S. The residual of the profit or loss from GHI sales in S's territory after the routine allocation step is divided between P and S pro rata to their capital stocks allocable to S's territory. Each controlled participant's capital stock is computed by capitalizing, applying a capital growth factor to, and amortizing its historical expenditures regarding DEF allocable to S's territory (in the case of P), or its ongoing cost contributions towards developing GHI (in the case of S). The amortization of the capital stocks is effected on a straight-line basis over an assumed four-year life for the relevant expenditures. The capital stocks are grown using an assumed growth factor that P and S consider to be appropriate.

(iv) The assumption that all expenditures amortize on a straight-line basis over four years does not appropriately reflect the principle that as of the date of the PCT regarding DEF, every contribution to the development of GHI, including DEF, is reasonably anticipated to have value throughout the entire period of exploitation of GHI which is projected to continue through Year 10. Under this method as applied by P and S, the share of the residual profit in S's territory that is allocated to P as a PCT Payment from S will decrease every year. After Year 4, P's capital stock in DEF will necessarily be $0, so that P will receive none of the residual profit or loss from GHI sales in S's territory after Year 4 as a PCT Payment.

(v) As a result of this limitation of the PCT Payments to be made by S, the anticipated return to S's aggregate investment in the CSA, over the whole period of S's CSA Activity, is at a rate that is significantly higher than the appropriate rate of return for S's CSA Activity (as determined by a reliable method). This discrepancy is not consistent with the investor model principle that S should anticipate a rate of return to its aggregate investment in the CSA, over the whole period of its CSA Activity, appropriate for the riskiness of its CSA Activity. The inconsistency of the method with the investor model materially lessens its reliability for purposes of a best method analysis. See § 1.482-1(c)(2)(ii)(B).

(iii) *Consistency of evaluation with realistic alternatives.*—(A) *In general.*—The relative reliability of an application of a method also depends on the degree of consistency of the analysis with the assumption that uncontrolled taxpayers dealing at arm's length would have evaluated the terms of the transaction, and only entered into such transaction, if no alternative is preferable. This condition is not met, therefore, where for any controlled participant the total anticipated present value of its income attributable to its entering into the CSA, as of the date of the PCT, is less than the total anticipated present value of its income that could be achieved through an alternative arrangement realistically available to that controlled participant. In principle, this comparison is made on a post-tax basis but, in many cases, a comparison made on a pre-tax basis will yield equivalent results. See also paragraph (g)(2)(v)(B)(1) of this section (Discount rate variation between realistic alternatives).

(B) *Examples.*—The following examples illustrate the principles of this paragraph (g)(2)(iii):

Example 1. (i) P, a corporation, and S, a wholly-owned subsidiary of P, enter into a CSA to develop a personal transportation device (the product). Under the arrangement, P will undertake all of the R&D, and manufacture and market the product in Country X. S will make CST Payments to P for its appropriate share of P's R&D costs, and manufacture and market the product in the rest of the world. P owns existing patents and trade secrets that are reasonably anticipated to contribute to the development of the product. Therefore the rights in the patents and trade secrets are platform contributions for which compensation is due from S as part of a PCT.

(ii) S's manufacturing and distribution activities under the CSA will be routine in nature, and identical to the activities it would undertake if it alternatively licensed the product from P.

(iii) Reasonably reliable estimates indicate that P could develop the product without assistance from S and license the product outside of Country X for a royalty of 20% of sales. Based on reliable financial projections that include all future development costs and licensing revenue that are allocable to the non-Country X market, and using a discount rate appropriate for the riskiness of P's role as a licensor (see paragraph (g)(2)(v) of this section), the post-tax present value of this licensing alternative to P for the non-Country X market (measured as of the date of the PCT) would be $500 million. Thus, based on this realistic alternative, the anticipated post-tax present value under the CSA to P in the non-Country X market (measured as of the date of the PCT), taking into account anticipated development costs allocable to the non-Country X market, and anticipated CST Payments and PCT Payments from S, and using a discount rate appropriate for the riskiness of P's role as a participant in the CSA, should not be less than $500 million.

Example 2. (i) The facts are the same as in *Example 1*, except that there are no reliable estimates of the value to P from the licensing alternative to the CSA. Further, reasonably reliable estimates indicate that an arm's length return for S's routine manufacturing and distribution activities is a 10% mark-up on total costs of goods sold plus operating expenses related to those activities. Finally, the Commissioner determines that the respective activities undertaken by P and S (other than licensing payments, cost contributions, and PCT Payments) would be identical regardless of whether the arrangement was undertaken as a CSA (cost sharing alternative) or as a long-term licensing arrangement (licensing alternative). In particular, in both alternatives, P would perform all research activities and S would undertake routine manufacturing and distribution activities associated with its territory.

(ii) P undertakes an economic analysis that derives S's cost contributions under the CSA, based on reliable financial projections. Based on this and further economic analysis, P determines S's PCT Payment as a certain lump sum amount to be paid as of the date of the PCT (Date D).

(iii) Based on reliable financial projections that include S's cost contributions and that incorporate S's PCT Payment, as computed by P, and using a discount rate appropriate for the riskiness of S's role as a CSA participant (see paragraphs (g)(2)(v) and (4)(vi)(F) of this section), the anticipated post-tax net present value to S in the cost sharing alternative (measured as of Date D) is $800 million. Further, based on these same reliable projections (but incorporating S's licensing payments instead of S's cost contributions and PCT Payment), and using a discount rate appropriate for the riskiness of S's role as a long-term licensee, the anticipated post-tax net present value to S in the licensing alternative (measured as of Date D) is $100 million. Thus, S's anticipated post-tax net present value is $700 million greater in the cost sharing alternative than in the licensing alternative. This result suggests that P's anticipated post-tax present value must be significantly less under the cost sharing alternative than under the licensing alternative. This means that the reliability of P's analysis as described in paragraph (ii) of this *Example 2* is reduced, because P would not be expected to enter into a CSA if its alternative of being a long-term licensor is preferable.

Example 3. (i) The facts are the same as in paragraphs (i) and (ii) of *Example 2*. In addition, based on reliable financial projections that include S's cost contributions and S's PCT Payment, and using a discount rate appropriate for the riskiness of S's role as a CSA participant, the anticipated post-tax net present value to S under the CSA (measured as of the date of the PCT) is $50 million. Also, instead of entering the CSA, S has the realistic alternative of manufacturing and distributing product Z unrelated to the personal transportation device, with the same anticipated 10% mark-up on total costs that it would anticipate for its routine activities in *Example 2*. Under its realistic alternative, at a discount rate appropriate for the riskiness of S's role with respect to product Z, S anticipates a present value of $100 million.

(ii) Because the lump sum PCT Payment made by S results in S having a considerably lower anticipated net present value than S could achieve through an alternative arrangement realistically available to it, the reliability of P's calculation of the lump sum PCT Payment is reduced.

(iv) *Aggregation of transactions.*—The combined effect of multiple contemporaneous transactions, consisting either of multiple PCTs, or of one or more PCT and one or more other transactions in connection with a CSA that are not governed by this section (such as transactions involving cross operating contributions or make-or-sell rights), may require evaluation in accordance with the principles of aggregation described in § 1.482-1(f)(2)(i). In such cases, it may be that the multiple transactions are reasonably anticipated, as of the date of the PCT(s), to be so interrelated that the method that provides the most reliable measure of an arm's length charge is a method under this section applied on an aggregate basis for the PCT(s) and other transactions. A section 482 adjustment may be made by comparing the aggregate arm's length charge so determined to the aggregate payments actually made for the multiple transactions. In such a case, it generally will not be necessary to allocate separately the aggregate arm's length charge as between various PCTs or as between PCTs and such other transactions. However, such an allocation may be necessary for other purposes, such as applying paragraph (i)(6) (Periodic adjustments) of this section. An aggregate determination of the arm's length charge for multiple transactions will often yield a payment for a controlled participant that is equal to the aggregate value of the platform contributions and other resources, capabilities, and rights covered by the multiple transactions multiplied by that controlled participant's RAB share. Because RAB shares only include benefits from cost shared intangibles, the reliability of an aggregate determination of payments for multiple transactions may be reduced to the extent that it includes transactions covering resources, capabilities, and rights for which the controlled participants' expected benefit shares differ substantially from their RAB shares.

(v) *Discount rate.*—(A) *In general.*—The best method analysis in connection with certain methods or forms of payment may depend on a rate or rates of return used to convert projected results of transactions to present value, or to otherwise convert monetary amounts at one or more points in time to equivalent amounts at a different point or points in time. For this purpose, a discount rate or rates should be used that most reliably reflect the market-correlated risks of activities or transactions and should be applied to the best estimates of the relevant projected results, based on all the information potentially available at the time for which the present value calculation is to be performed. Depending on the particular facts and circumstances, the market-correlated risk involved and thus, the discount rate, may differ among a company's various activities or transactions. Normally, discount rates are most reliably determined by reference to market information.

(B) *Considerations in best method analysis of discount rate.*—*(1) Discount rate variation between realistic alternatives.*—Realistic alternatives may involve varying risk exposure and, thus, may be more reliably evaluated using different discount rates. See paragraphs (g)(4)(i)(F) and (vi)(F) of this section. In some circumstances, a party may have less risk as a licensee of intangibles needed in its operations, and so require a lower discount rate, than it would have by entering into a CSA to develop such intangibles, which may involve the party's assumption of additional risk in funding its cost contributions to the IDA. Similarly, self-development of intangibles and licensing out may be riskier for the licensor, and so require a higher discount rate, than entering into a CSA to develop such intangibles, which would relieve the licensor of the obligation to fund a portion of the IDCs of the IDA.

(2) Implied discount rates.—In some circumstances, the particular discount rate or rates used for certain activities or transactions logically imply that certain other activities will have a particular discount rate or set of rates (implied discount rates). To the extent that an implied discount rate is inappropriate in light of the facts and circumstances, which may include reliable direct evidence of the appropriate discount rate applicable for such other activities, the reliability of any method is reduced where such method is based on the discount rates from which such an inappropriate implied discount rate is derived. See paragraphs (g)(4)(vi)(F)(2) and (g)(4)(viii), *Example 8* of this section.

(3) Discount rate variation between forms of payment.—Certain forms of payment may involve different risks than others. For example, ordinarily a royalty computed on a profits base would be more volatile, and so require a higher discount rate to discount projected payments to present value, than a royalty computed on a sales base.

(4) Post-tax rate.—In general, discount rate estimates that may be inferred from the operations of the capital markets are post-tax discount rates. Therefore, an analysis would in principle apply post-tax discount rates to income net of expense items including

taxes (post-tax income). However, in certain circumstances the result of applying a post-tax discount rate to post-tax income is equivalent to the product of the result of applying a post-tax discount rate to income net of expense items other than taxes (pre-tax income), and the difference of one minus the tax rate (as defined in paragraph (j)(1)(i) of this section). Therefore, in such circumstances, calculation of pre-tax income, rather than post-tax income, may be sufficient. See, for example, paragraph (g)(4)(i)(G) of this section.

(C) *Example.*—The following example illustrates the principles of this paragraph (g)(2)(v).

Example. (i) P and S form a CSA to develop intangible X, which will be used in product Y. P will develop X, and S will make CST Payments as its cost contributions. At the start of the CSA, P has a platform contribution, for which S commits to make a PCT Payment of 5% of its sales of product Y. As part of the evaluation of whether that PCT Payment is arm's length, the Commissioner considers whether P had a more favorable realistic alternative (see paragraph (g)(2)(iii) of this section). Specifically, the Commissioner compares P's anticipated post-tax discounted present value of the financial projections under the CSA (taking into account S's PCT payment of 5% of its sale of product Y) with P's anticipated post-tax discounted present value of the financial projections under a reasonably available licensing alternative that consists of developing intangible X on its own and then licensing X to S or to an uncontrolled party similar to S. In undertaking the analysis, the Commissioner determines that, because it would be funding the entire development of the intangible, P undertakes greater risks in the licensing alternative than in the cost sharing alternative (in the cost sharing alternative P would be funding only part of the development of the intangible).

(ii) The Commissioner determines that, as between the two scenarios, all of the components of P's anticipated financial flows are identical, except for the CST and PCT Payments under the CSA, compared to the licensing payments under the licensing alternative. Accordingly, the Commissioner concludes that the differences in market-correlated risks between the two scenarios, and therefore the differences in discount rates between the two scenarios, relate to the differences in these components of the financial projections.

(vi) *Financial projections.*—The reliability of an estimate of the value of a platform or operating contribution in connection with a PCT will often depend upon the reliability of projections used in making the estimate. Such projections should reflect the best estimates of the items projected (normally reflecting a probability weighted average of possible outcomes and thus also reflecting non-market-correlated risk). Projections necessary for this purpose may include a projection of sales, IDCs, costs of developing operating contributions, routine operating expenses, and costs of sales. Some method applications directly estimate projections of items attributable to separate development and exploitation by the controlled participants within their respective divisions. Other method applications indirectly estimate projections of items from the perspective of the controlled group as a whole, rather than from the perspective of a particular participant, and then apportion the items so estimated on some assumed basis. For example, in some applications, sales might be directly projected by division, but worldwide projections of other items such as operating expenses might be apportioned among divisions in the same ratio as the divisions' respective sales. Which approach is more reliable depends on which provides the most reliable measure of an arm's length result, considering the competing perspectives under the facts and circumstances in light of the completeness and accuracy of the underlying data, the reliability of the assumptions, and the sensitivity of the results to possible deficiencies in the data and assumptions. For these purposes, projections that have been prepared for non-tax purposes are generally more reliable than projections that have been prepared solely for purposes of meeting the requirements in this paragraph (g).

(vii) *Accounting principles.*—(A) *In general.*—Allocations or other valuations done for accounting purposes may provide a useful starting point but will not be conclusive for purposes of the best method analysis in evaluating the arm's length charge in a PCT, particularly where the accounting treatment of an asset is inconsistent with its economic value.

(B) *Examples.*—The following examples illustrate the principles of this paragraph (g)(2)(vii):

Example 1. (i) USP, a U.S. corporation and FSub, a wholly-owned foreign subsidiary of USP, enter into a CSA in Year 1 to develop software programs with application in the medical field. Company X is an uncontrolled software company located in the United States that is engaged in developing software programs that could significantly enhance the programs being developed by USP and FSub. Company X is still in a startup phase, so it has no currently exploitable products or marketing intangibles and its workforce consists of a team of software developers. Company X has negligible liabilities and tangible property. In Year 2, USP purchases Company X as part of an uncontrolled transaction in order to acquire its in-process technology and workforce for purposes of the development activities of the CSA. USP files a consolidated return that includes Company X. For accounting purposes, $50 million of the $100 million acquisition price is allocated to the in-process technology and workforce, and the residual $50 million is allocated to goodwill.

(ii) The in-process technology and workforce of Company X acquired by USP are reasonably anticipated to contribute to developing cost shared intangibles and therefore the rights in the in-process technology and workforce of Company X are platform contributions for which FSub must compensate USP as part of a PCT. In determining whether to apply the acquisition price or another method for purposes of evaluating the arm's length charge in the PCT, relevant best method analysis considerations must be weighed in light of the general principles of paragraph (g)(2) of this section. The allocation for accounting purposes raises an issue as to the reliability of using the acquisition price method in this case because it suggests that a significant portion of the value of Company X's nonroutine contributions to USP's business activities is allocable to goodwill, which is often difficult to value reliably and which, depending on the facts and circumstances, might not be attributable to platform contributions that are to be compensated by PCTs. See paragraph (g)(5)(iv)(A) of this section.

(iii) Paragraph (g)(2)(vii)(A) of this section provides that accounting treatment may be a starting point, but is not determinative for purposes of assessing or applying methods to evaluate the arm's length charge in a PCT. The facts here reveal that Company X has nothing of economic value aside from its in-process technology and assembled workforce. The $50 million of the acquisition price allocated to goodwill for accounting purposes, therefore, is economically attributable to either of, or both, the in-process technology and the workforce. That moots the potential issue under the acquisition price method of the reliability of valuation of assets not to be compensated by PCTs, since there are no such assets. Assuming the acquisition price method is otherwise the most reliable method, the aggregate value of Company X's in-process technology and workforce is the full acquisition price of $100 million. Accordingly, the aggregate value of the arm's length PCT Payments due from FSub to USP for the platform contributions consisting of the rights in Company X's in-process technology and workforce will equal $100 million multiplied by FSub's RAB share.

Example 2. (i) The facts are the same as in *Example 1*, except that Company X is a mature software business in the United States with a successful current generation of software that it markets under a recognized trademark, in addition to having the research team and new generation software in process that could significantly enhance the programs being developed under USP's and FSub's CSA. USP continues Company X's existing business and integrates the research team and the in-process technology into the efforts under its CSA with FSub. For accounting purposes, the $100 million price for acquiring Company X is allocated $50 million to existing software and trademark, $25 million to inprocess technology and research workforce, and the residual $25 million to goodwill and going concern value.

(ii) In this case an analysis of the facts indicates a likelihood that, consistent with the allocation under the accounting treatment (although not necessarily in the same amount), a significant amount of the nonroutine contributions to the USP's business activities consist of goodwill and going concern value economically attributable to the existing U.S. software business rather than to the platform contributions consisting of the rights in the in-process technology and research workforce. In addition, an analysis of the facts indicates that a significant amount of the nonroutine contributions to USP's business activities consist of the make-or-sell rights under the existing software and trademark, which are not platform contributions and might be difficult to value. Accordingly, further consideration must be given to the extent to which these circumstances reduce the relative reliability of the acquisition price method in comparison to other potentially applicable methods for evaluating the PCT Payment.

Example 3. (i) USP, a U.S. corporation, and FSub, a wholly-owned foreign subsidiary of USP, enter into a CSA in Year 1 to develop Product A. Company Y is an uncontrolled corporation that owns Technology X, which is critical to the development of Product A. Company Y currently markets Product B, which is dependent on Technology X. USP is solely interested in acquiring Technology X, but is only able to do so through the acquisition of Company Y in its entirety for $200 million in an uncontrolled transaction in Year 2. For accounting purposes, the acquisition price is allocated as follows: $120 million to Product B and the underlying Technology X, $30 million to trademark and other marketing intangibles, and the residual $50 million to goodwill and going concern value. After the acquisition of Company Y, Technology X is used to develop Product A. No other part of Company Y is used in any manner. Immediately after the acquisition, product B is discontinued, and, therefore, the accompanying marketing intangibles become worthless. None of the previous employees of Company Y is retained.

(ii) The Technology X of Company Y acquired by USP is reasonably anticipated to contribute to developing cost shared intangibles and is therefore a platform contribution for which FSub must compensate USP as part of a PCT. Although for accounting purposes a significant portion of the acquisition price of Company Y was allocated to items other than Technology X, the facts demonstrate that USP had no intention of using and therefore placed no economic value on any part of Company Y other than Technology X. If USP was willing to pay $200 million for Company Y solely for purposes of acquiring Technology X, then assuming the acquisition price method is otherwise the most reliable method, the value of Technology X is the full $200 million acquisition price. Accordingly, the value of the arm's length PCT Payment due from FSub to USP for the platform contribution consisting of the rights in Technology X will equal the product of $200 million and FSub's RAB share.

(viii) *Valuations of subsequent PCTs.*—(A) *Date of subsequent PCT.*—The date of a PCT may occur subsequent to the inception of the CSA. For example, an intangible initially developed outside the IDA may only subsequently become a platform contribution because that later time is the earliest date on which it is reasonably anticipated to contribute to developing cost shared intangibles within the IDA. In such case, the date of the PCT, and the analysis of the arm's length amount charged in the subsequent PCT, is as of such later time.

(B) *Best method analysis for subsequent PCT.*—In cases where PCTs occur on different dates, the determination of the arm's length amount charged, respectively, in the prior and subsequent PCTs must be coordinated in a manner that provides the most reliable measure of an arm's length result. In some circumstances, a subsequent PCT may be reliably evaluated independently of other PCTs, as may be possible for example, under the acquisition price method. In other circumstances, the results of prior and subsequent PCTs may be interrelated and so a subsequent PCT may be most reliably evaluated under the residual profit split method of paragraph (g)(7) of this section. In those cases, for purposes of allocating the present value of nonroutine residual divisional profit or loss, and so determining the present value of the subsequent PCT Payments, in accordance with paragraph (g)(7)(iii)(C) of this section, the PCT Payor's interest in cost shared intangibles, both already developed and in process, are treated as additional PCT Payor operating contributions as of the date of the subsequent PCT.

(ix) *Arm's length range.*—(A) *In general.*—The guidance in § 1.482-1(e) regarding determination of an arm's length range, as modified by this section, applies in evaluating the arm's length amount charged in a PCT under a transfer pricing method provided in this section (applicable method). Section 1.482-1(e)(2)(i) provides that the arm's length range is ordinarily determined by applying a single pricing method selected under the best method rule to two or more uncontrolled transactions of similar comparability and reliability although use of more than one method may be appropriate for the purposes described in § 1.482-1(c)(2)(iii). The rules provided in § 1.482-1(e) and this section for determining an arm's length range shall not override the rules provided in paragraph (i)(6) of this section for periodic adjustments by the Commissioner. The provisions in paragraphs (g)(2)(ix)(C) and (D) of this section apply only to applicable methods that are based on two or more input parameters as described in paragraph (g)(2)(ix)(B) of this section. For an example of how the rules of this section for determining an arm's length range of PCT Payments are applied, see paragraph (g)(4)(viii) of this section.

(B) *Methods based on two or more input parameters.*—An applicable method may determine PCT Payments based on calculations involving two or more parameters whose values depend on the facts and circumstances of the case (input parameters). For some input parameters (market-based input parameters), the value is most reliably determined by reference to data that derives from uncontrolled transactions (market data). For example, the value of the return to a controlled participant's routine contributions, as such term is defined in paragraph (j)(1)(i) of this section, to the CSA Activity (which value is used as an input parameter in the income method described in paragraph (g)(4) of this section) may in some cases be most reliably determined by reference to the profit level of a company with rights, resources, and capabilities comparable to those routine contributions. See § 1.482-5. As another example, the value for the discount rate that reflects the riskiness of a controlled participant's role in the CSA (which value is used as an input parameter in the income method described in paragraph (g)(4) of this section) may in some cases be most reliably determined by reference to the stock beta of a company whose overall risk is comparable to the riskiness of the controlled participant's role in the CSA.

(C) *Variable input parameters.*—For some market-based input parameters (variable input parameters), the parameter's value is most reliably determined by considering two or more observations of market data that have, or with adjustment can be brought to, a similar reliability and comparability, as described in § 1.482-1(e)(2)(ii) (for example, profit levels or stock betas of two or more companies). See paragraph (g)(2)(ix)(B) of this section.

(D) *Determination of arm's length PCT Payment.*—For purposes of applying this paragraph (g)(2)(ix), each input parameter is assigned a single most reliable value, unless it is a variable input parameter as described in paragraph (g)(2)(ix)(C) of this section. The determination of the arm's length payment depends on the number of variable input parameters.

(1) No variable input parameters.—If there are no variable input parameters, the arm's length PCT Payment is a single value determined by using the single most reliable value determined for each input parameter.

(2) One variable input parameter.—If there is exactly one variable input parameter, then under the applicable method, the arm's length range of PCT Payments is the interquartile range, as described in § 1.482-1(e)(2)(iii)(C), of the set of PCT Payment values calculated by selecting—

(i) Iteratively, the value of the variable input parameter that is based on each observation as described in paragraph (g)(2)(ix)(C) of this section; and

(ii) The single most reliable values for each other input parameter.

(3) More than one variable input parameter.—If there are two or more variable input parameters, then under the applicable method, the arm's length range of PCT Payments is the interquartile range, as described in § 1.482-1(e)(2)(iii)(C), of the set of PCT Payment values calculated iteratively using every possible combination of permitted choices of values for the input parameters. For input parameters other than a variable input parameter, the only such permitted choice is the single most reliable value. For variable input parameters, such permitted choices include any value that is—

(i) Based on one of the observations described in paragraph (g)(2)(ix)(C) of this section; and

(ii) Within the interquartile range (as described in § 1.482-1(e)(2)(iii)(C)) of the set of all values so based.

(E) *Adjustments.*—Section 1.482-1(e)(3), applied as modified by this paragraph (g)(2)(ix), determines when the Commissioner may make an adjustment to a PCT Payment due to the taxpayer's results being outside the arm's length range. Adjustment will be to the median, as defined in § 1.482-1(e)(3). Thus, the Commissioner is not required to establish an arm's length range prior to making an allocation under section 482.

(x) *Valuation undertaken on a pre-tax basis.*—PCT Payments in general may increase the PCT Payee's tax liability and decrease the PCT Payor's tax liability. The arm's length amount of a PCT Payment determined under the methods in this paragraph (g) is the value of the PCT Payment itself, without regard to such tax effects. Therefore, the methods under this section must be applied, with suitable adjustments if needed, to determine the PCT Payments on a pre-tax basis. See paragraphs (g)(2)(v)(B) and (4)(i)(G) of this section.

(3) *Comparable uncontrolled transaction method.*—The comparable uncontrolled transaction (CUT) method described in § 1.482-4(c), and the comparable uncontrolled services price (CUSP) method described in § 1.482-9(c), may be applied to evaluate whether the amount charged in a PCT is arm's length by reference to the amount charged in a comparable uncontrolled transaction. Although all of the factors

entering into a best method analysis described in § 1.482-1(c) and (d) must be considered, comparability and reliability under this method are particularly dependent on similarity of contractual terms, degree to which allocation of risks is proportional to reasonably anticipated benefits from exploiting the results of intangible development, similar period of commitment as to the sharing of intangible development risks, and similar scope, uncertainty, and profit potential of the subject intangible development, including a similar allocation of the risks of any existing resources, capabilities, or rights, as well as of the risks of developing other resources, capabilities, or rights that would be reasonably anticipated to contribute to exploitation within the parties' divisions, that is consistent with the actual allocation of risks between the controlled participants as provided in the CSA in accordance with this section. When applied in the manner described in § 1.482-4(c) or 1.482-9(c), the CUT or CUSP method will typically yield an arm's length total value for the platform contribution that is the subject of the PCT. That value must then be multiplied by each PCT Payor's respective RAB share in order to determine the arm's length PCT Payment due from each PCT Payor. The reliability of a CUT or CUSP that yields a value for the platform contribution only in the PCT Payor's division will be reduced to the extent that value is not consistent with the total worldwide value of the platform contribution multiplied by the PCT Payor's RAB share.

(4) *Income method.*—(i) *In general.*—(A) *Equating cost sharing and licensing alternatives.*—The income method evaluates whether the amount charged in a PCT is arm's length by reference to a controlled participant's best realistic alternative to entering into a CSA. Under this method, the arm's length charge for a PCT Payment will be an amount such that a controlled participant's present value, as of the date of the PCT, of its cost sharing alternative of entering into a CSA equals the present value of its best realistic alternative. In general, the best realistic alternative of the PCT Payor to entering into the CSA would be to license intangibles to be developed by an uncontrolled licensor that undertakes the commitment to bear the entire risk of intangible development that would otherwise have been shared under the CSA. Similarly, the best realistic alternative of the PCT Payee to entering into the CSA would be to undertake the commitment to bear the entire risk of intangible development that would otherwise have been shared under the CSA and license the resulting intangibles to an uncontrolled licensee. Paragraphs (g)(4)(i)(B) through (vi) of this section describe specific applications of the income method, but do not exclude other possible applications of this method.

(B) *Cost sharing alternative.*—The PCT Payor's cost sharing alternative corresponds to the actual CSA in accordance with this section, with the PCT Payor's obligation to make the PCT Payments to be determined and its commitment for the duration of the IDA to bear cost contributions.

(C) *Licensing alternative.*—The licensing alternative is derived on the basis of a functional and risk analysis of the cost sharing alternative, but with a shift of the risk of cost contributions to the licensor. Accordingly, the PCT Payor's licensing alternative consists of entering into a license with an uncontrolled party, for a term extending for what would be the duration of the CSA Activity, to license the make-or-sell rights in to-be-developed resources, capabilities, or rights of the licensor. Under such license, the licensor would undertake the commitment to bear the entire risk of intangible development that would otherwise have been shared under the CSA. Apart from any difference in the allocation of the risks of the IDA, the licensing alternative should assume contractual provisions with regard to non-overlapping divisional intangible interests, and with regard to allocations of other risks, that are consistent with the actual CSA in accordance with this section. For example, the analysis under the licensing alternative should assume a similar allocation of the risks of any existing resources, capabilities, or rights, as well as of the risks of developing other resources, capabilities, or rights that would be reasonably anticipated to contribute to exploitation within the parties' divisions, that is consistent with the actual allocation of risks between the controlled participants as provided in the CSA in accordance with this section. Accordingly, the financial projections associated with the licensing and cost sharing alternatives are necessarily the same except for the licensing payments to be made under the licensing alternative and the cost contributions and PCT Payments to be made under the CSA.

(D) *Only one controlled participant with nonroutine platform contributions.*—This method involves only one of the controlled participants providing nonroutine platform contributions as the PCT Payee. For a method under which more than one controlled participant may be a PCT Payee, see the application of the residual profit method pursuant to paragraph (g)(7) of this section.

(E) *Income method payment forms.*—The income method may be applied to determine PCT Payments in any form of payment (for example, lump sum, royalty on sales, or royalty on divisional profit). For converting to another form of payment, see generally paragraph (h) (Form of payment rules) of this section.

(F) *Discount rates appropriate to cost sharing and licensing alternatives.*—The present value of the cost sharing and licensing alternatives, respectively, should be determined using the appropriate discount rates in accordance with paragraphs (g)(2)(v) and (g)(4)(vi)(F) of this section. See, for example, § 1.482-7(g)(2)(v)(B)(1) (Discount rate variation between realistic alternatives). In circumstances where the market-correlated risks as between the cost sharing and licensing alternatives are not materially different, a reliable analysis may be possible by using the same discount rate with respect to both alternatives.

(G) *The effect of taxation on determining the arm's length amount.*—*(1)* In principle, the present values of the cost sharing and licensing alternatives should be determined by applying post-tax discount rates to post-tax income (including the post-tax value to the controlled participant of the PCT Payments). If such approach is adopted, then the post-tax value of the PCT Payments must be appropriately adjusted in order to determine the arm's length amount of the PCT Payments on a pre-tax basis. See paragraph (g)(2)(x) of this section.

(2) In certain circumstances, post-tax income may be derived as the product of the result of applying a post-tax discount rate to pre-tax income, and a factor equal to one minus the tax rate (as defined in (j)(1)(i)). See paragraph (g)(2)(v)(B) of this section.

(3) To the extent that a controlled participant's tax rate is not materially affected by whether it enters into the cost sharing or licensing alternative (or reliable adjustments may be made for varying tax rates), the factor (that is, one minus the tax rate) may be cancelled from both sides of the equation of the cost sharing and licensing alternative present values. Accordingly, in such circumstance it is sufficient to apply post-tax discount rates to projections of pre-tax income for the purpose of equating the cost sharing and licensing alternatives. The specific applications of the income method described in paragraphs (g)(4)(ii) through (iv) of this section and the examples set forth in paragraph (g)(4)(viii) of this section assume that a controlled participant's tax rate is not materially affected by whether it enters into the cost sharing or licensing alternative.

(ii) *Evaluation of PCT Payor's cost sharing alternative.*—The present value of the PCT Payor's cost sharing alternative is the present value of the stream of the reasonably anticipated residuals over the duration of the CSA Activity of divisional profits or losses, minus operating cost contributions, minus cost contributions, minus PCT Payments.

(iii) *Evaluation of PCT Payor's licensing alternative.*—(A) *Evaluation based on CUT.*—The present value of the PCT Payor's licensing alternative may be determined using the comparable uncontrolled transaction method, as described in § 1.482-4(c)(1) and (2). In this case, the present value of the PCT Payor's licensing alternative is the present value of the stream, over what would be the duration of the CSA Activity under the cost sharing alternative, of the reasonably anticipated residuals of the divisional profits or losses that would be achieved under the cost sharing alternative, minus operating cost contributions that would be made under the cost sharing alternative, minus the licensing payments as determined under the comparable uncontrolled transaction method.

(B) *Evaluation based on CPM.*—The present value of the PCT Payor's licensing alternative may be determined using the comparable profits method, as described in § 1.482-5. In this case, the present value of the licensing alternative is determined as in paragraph (g)(4)(iii)(A) of this section, except that the PCT Payor's licensing payments, as defined in paragraph (j)(1)(i) of this section, are determined in each period to equal the reasonably anticipated residuals of the divisional profits or losses that would be achieved under the cost sharing alternative, minus operating cost contributions that would be made under the cost sharing alternative, minus market returns for routine contributions, as defined in paragraph (j)(1)(i) of this section. However, treatment of net operating contributions as operating cost contributions shall be coordinated with the treatment of other routine contributions pursuant to this paragraph so as to avoid duplicative market returns to such contributions.

(iv) *Lump sum payment form*.—Where the form of PCT Payment is a lump sum as of the date of the PCT, then, based on paragraphs (g)(4)(i) through (iii) of this section, the PCT Payment equals the difference between—

(A) The present value, using the discount rate appropriate for the cost sharing alternative, of the stream of the reasonably anticipated residuals over the duration of the CSA Activity of divisional profits or losses, minus cost contributions and operating cost contributions; and

(B) The present value of the licensing alternative.

(v) *Application of income method using differential income stream*.—In some cases, the present value of an arm's length PCT Payment may be determined as the present value, discounted at the appropriate rate, of the PCT Payor's reasonably anticipated stream of additional positive or negative income over the duration of the CSA Activity that would result (before PCT Payments) from undertaking the cost sharing alternative rather than the licensing alternative (differential income stream). See *Example 9* of paragraph (g)(4)(viii) of this section.

(vi) *Best method analysis considerations*.—(A) *Coordination with §1.482-1(c)*.—Whether results derived from this method are the most reliable measure of an arm's length result is determined using the factors described under the best method rule in §1.482-1(c). Thus, comparability and the quality of data, the reliability of the assumptions, and the sensitivity of the results to possible deficiencies in the data and assumptions, must be considered in determining whether this method provides the most reliable measure of an arm's length result.

(B) *Assumptions Concerning Tax Rates*.—This method will be more reliable to the extent that the controlled participants' respective tax rates are not materially affected by whether they enter into the cost sharing or licensing alternative. Even if this assumption of invariant tax rates across alternatives does not hold, this method may still be reliable to the extent that reliable adjustments can be made to reflect the variation in tax rates.

(C) *Coordination with §1.482-4(c)(2)*.—If the licensing alternative is evaluated using the comparable uncontrolled transactions method, as described in paragraph (g)(4)(iii)(A) of this section, any additional comparability and reliability considerations stated in §1.482-4(c)(2) may apply.

(D) *Coordination with §1.482-5(c)*.—If the licensing alternative is evaluated using the comparable profits method, as described in paragraph (g)(4)(iii)(B) of this section, any additional comparability and reliability considerations stated in §1.482-5(c) may apply.

(E) *Certain Circumstances Concerning PCT Payor*.—This method may be used even if the PCT Payor furnishes significant operating contributions, or commits to assume the risk of significant operating cost contributions, to the PCT Payor's division. However, in such a case, any comparable uncontrolled transactions described in paragraph (g)(4)(iii)(A) of this section, and any comparable transactions used under §1.482-5(c) as described in paragraphs (g)(4)(iii)(B) of this section, should be consistent with such contributions (or reliable adjustments must be made for material differences).

(F) *Discount rates*.—*(1) Reflection of similar risk profiles of cost sharing alternative and licensing alternative*.—Because the financial projections associated with the licensing and cost sharing alternatives are the same, except for the licensing payments to be made under the licensing alternative and the cost contributions and PCT Payments to be made under the cost sharing alternative, the analysis of the risk profile and financial projections for a realistic alternative to the cost sharing alternative must be closely associated with the risk profile and financial projections associated with the cost sharing alternative, differing only in the treatment of licensing payments, cost contributions, and PCT Payments. When using discount rates in applying the income method, this means that even if different discount rates are warranted for the two alternatives, the risk profiles for the two discount rates are closely related to each other because the discount rate for the licensing alternative and the discount rate for the cost sharing alternative are both derived from the single probability-weighted financial projections associated with the CSA Activity. The difference, if any, in market-correlated risks between the licensing and cost sharing alternatives is due solely to the different effects on risks of the PCT Payor making licensing payments under the licensing alternative, on the one hand, and the PCT Payor making cost contributions and PCT Payments under the cost sharing alternative, on the other hand. That is, the difference in the risk profile between the two scenarios solely reflects the incremental risk, if any, associated with the cost contributions taken on by the PCT Payor in developing the cost shared intangible under the cost sharing alternative, and the difference, if any, in risk associated with the particular payment forms of the licensing payments and the PCT Payments, in light of the fact that the licensing payments in the licensing alternative are partially replaced by cost contributions and partially replaced by PCT Payments in the cost sharing alternative, each with its own payment form. An analysis under the income method that uses a different discount rate for the cost sharing alternative than for the licensing alternative will be more reliable the greater the extent to which the difference, if any, between the two discount rates reflects solely these differences in the risk profiles of these two alternatives. See, for example, paragraph (g)(2)(iii), *Example 2* of this section.

(2) Use of differential income stream as a consideration in assessing the best method.—An analysis under the income method that uses a different discount rate for the cost sharing alternative than for the licensing alternative will be more reliable the greater the extent to which the implied discount rate for the projected present value of the differential income stream is consistent with reliable direct evidence of the appropriate discount rate applicable for activities reasonably anticipated to generate an income stream with a similar risk profile to the differential income stream. Such differential income stream is defined as the stream of the reasonably anticipated residuals of the PCT Payor's licensing payments to be made under the licensing alternative, minus the PCT Payor's cost contributions to be made under the cost sharing alternative. See *Example 8* of paragraph (g)(4)(viii) of this section.

(vii) *Routine platform and operating contributions*.—For purposes of this paragraph (g)(4), any routine contributions that are platform or operating contributions, the valuation and PCT Payments for which are determined and made independently of the income method, are treated similarly to cost contributions and operating cost contributions, respectively. Accordingly, wherever used in this paragraph (g)(4), the term "routine contributions" shall not include routine platform or operating contributions, and wherever the terms "cost contributions" and "operating cost contributions" appear in this paragraph, they shall include net routine platform contributions and net routine operating contributions, respectively. Net routine platform contributions are the value of a controlled participant's total reasonably anticipated routine platform contributions, plus its reasonably anticipated PCT Payments to other controlled participants in respect of their routine platform contributions, minus the reasonably anticipated PCT Payments it is to receive from other controlled participants in respect of its routine platform contributions. Net routine operating contributions are the value of a controlled participant's total reasonably anticipated routine operating contributions, plus its reasonably anticipated arm's length compensation to other controlled participants in respect of their routine operating contributions, minus the reasonably anticipated arm's length compensation it is to receive from other controlled participants in respect of its routine operating contributions.

(viii) *Examples*.—The following examples illustrate the principles of this paragraph (g)(4):

Example 1. (i) For simplicity of calculation in this *Example 1*, all financial flows are assumed to occur at the beginning of each period. USP, a software company, has developed version 1.0 of a new software application that it is currently marketing. In Year 1 USP enters into a CSA with its wholly-owned foreign subsidiary, FS, to develop future versions of the software application. Under the CSA, USP will have the rights to exploit the future versions in the United States, and FS will have the rights to exploit them in the rest of the world. The future rights in version 1.0, and USP's development team, are reasonably anticipated to contribute to the development of future versions and therefore the rights in version 1.0 and the research and development team are platform contributions for which compensation is due from FS as part of a PCT. USP does not transfer the current exploitation rights in version 1.0 to FS. FS will not perform any research or development activities and does not furnish any platform contributions nor does it control any operating intangibles at the inception of the CSA that would be relevant to the exploitation of version 1.0 or future versions of the software.

(ii) FS undertakes financial projections in its territory of the CSA:

(1) Year	(2) Sales	(3) Operating costs	(4) Cost contributions	(5) Operating income under cost sharing alternative (excluding PCT)
1	0	0	50	–50
2	0	0	50	–50
3	200	100	50	50
4	400	200	50	150
5	600	300	60	240
6	650	325	65	260
7	700	350	70	280
8	750	375	75	300
9	750	375	75	300
10	675	338	68	269
11	608	304	61	243
12	547	273	55	219
13	410	205	41	164
14	308	154	31	123
15	231	115	23	93

FS anticipates that activity on this application will cease after Year 15. The application was derived from software developed by Company Q, an uncontrolled party. FS has a license under Company Q's copyright, but that license expires after Year 15 and will not be renewed.

(iii) In evaluating the cost sharing alternative, FS concludes that the cost sharing alternative represents a riskier alternative for FS than the licensing alternative because, in cost sharing, FS will take on the additional risks associated with cost contributions. Taking this difference into account, FS concludes that the appropriate discount rate to apply in assessing the licensing alternative, based on discount rates of comparable uncontrolled companies undertaking comparable licensing transactions, would be 13% per year, whereas the appropriate discount rate to apply in assessing the cost sharing alternative would be 15% per year. FS determines that the arm's length rate USP would have charged an uncontrolled licensee for a license of future versions of the software (if USP had further developed version 1.0 on its own) is 35% of the sales price, as determined under the CUT method in § 1.482-4(c). FS also determines that the tax rate applicable to it will be the same in the licensing alternative as in the CSA. Accordingly, the financial projections associated with the licensing alternative are:

(6) Year	(7) Sales	(8) Operating costs	(9) Licensing payments	(10) Operating income under licensing alternative	(11) Operating income under cost sharing alternative minus operating income under licensing alternative
1	0	0	0	0	–50
2	0	0	0	0	–50
3	200	100	70	30	20
4	400	200	140	60	90
5	600	300	210	90	150
6	650	325	228	97	163
7	700	350	245	105	175
8	750	375	263	112	188
9	750	375	263	112	188
10	675	338	236	101	168
11	608	304	213	91	152
12	547	273	191	83	136
13	410	205	144	61	103
14	308	154	108	46	77
15	231	115	81	35	58

(iv) Based on these projections and applying the appropriate discount rate, FS determines that under the cost sharing alternative, the present value of the stream of residuals of its anticipated divisional profits, reduced by the anticipated operating cost contributions and cost contributions, but not reduced by any PCT Payments (that is, the stream of anticipated operating income as shown in column 5) would be $889 million. Under the licensing alternative, the present value of the stream of residuals of its anticipated divisional profits and losses minus the operating cost contributions (that is, the stream of anticipated operating income before licensing payments, which is the present value of column 7 reduced by column 8) would be $1.419 billion, and the present value of the licensing payments would be $994 million. Therefore, the total value of the licensing alternative would be $425 million. In order for the present value of the cost sharing alternative to equal the present value of the licensing alternative, the present value of the PCT Payments must equal $464 million. Therefore, the taxpayer makes and reports PCT Payments with a present value of $464 million.

Example 2. Arm's length range. (i) The facts are the same as in *Example 1*. The Commissioner accepts the financial projections undertaken by FS. Further, the Commissioner determines that the licensing discount rate and the CUT licensing rate are most reliably determined by reference to comparable uncontrolled discount rates and license rates, respectively. The observations that are in the interquartile range of the respective input parameters (see paragraph (g)(2)(ix) of this section) are as follows:

Observations that are within interquartile range	Comparable uncontrolled discount rate
1	11%
2	12%
3 (Median)	13%
4	15%
5	17%

Observations that are within interquartile range	Comparable uncontrolled licensing rate
1	30%
2	32%
3 (Median)	35%
4	37%
5	40%

(ii) Following the principles of paragraph (g)(2)(ix) of this section, the Commissioner undertakes 25 different applications of the income method, using each combination of the discount rate and licensing rate parameters. In undertaking this analysis, the Commissioner assumes that the ratio of the median discount rate for the cost sharing alternative to the median discount rate for the licensing alternative (that is, 15% to 13%) is maintained. The results of the 25 applications of the income method, sorted in ascending order of calculated present value of the PCT Payment, are as follows:

INCOME METHOD APPLICATION NUMBER:	Comparable uncontrolled licensing discount rate	Comparable uncontrolled CSA discount rate	Comparable uncontrolled licensing rate	Calculated lump sum PCT Payment	Interquartile range of PCT Payments
1	17%	19.6%	30%	217	
2	17%	19.6%	32%	263	
3	15%	17.3%	30%	264	
4	15%	17.3%	32%	315	
5	13%	15%	30%	321	
6	17%	19.6%	35%	331	
7	12%	13.8%	30%	354	LQ = 354
8	17%	19.6%	37%	376	
9	13%	15%	32%	378	
10	11%	12.7%	30%	391	
11	15%	17.3%	35%	391	
12	12%	13.8%	32%	415	
13	15%	17.3%	37%	442	Median = 442
14	17%	19.6%	40%	444	
15	11%	12.7%	32%	455	
16	13%	15%	35%	464	
17	12%	13.8%	35%	505	
18	15%	17.3%	40%	517	
19	13%	15%	37%	520	UQ = 520
20	11%	12.7%	35%	551	
21	12%	13.8%	37%	566	
22	13%	15%	40%	605	
23	11%	12.7%	37%	615	
24	12%	13.8%	40%	655	
25	11%	12.7%	40%	710	

(iii) Accordingly, the Commissioner determines that a taxpayer will not be subject to adjustment if its initial (ex ante) determination of the present value of PCT Payments is between $354 million and $520 million (the lower and upper quartile results as shown in the last column). Because FS's determination of the 112 present value of the PCT Payments, $464 million, is within the interquartile range, no adjustments are warranted.

Example 3. (i) For simplicity of calculation in this *Example 3*, all financial flows are assumed to occur at the beginning of each period. USP, a U.S. software company, has developed version 1.0 of a new software application, employed to store and retrieve complex data sets in certain types of storage media. Version 1.0 is currently being marketed. In Year 1, USP enters into a CSA with its wholly-owned foreign subsidiary, FS, to develop future versions of the software application. Under the CSA, USP will have the exclusive rights to exploit the future versions in the U.S., and FS will have the exclusive rights to exploit them in the rest of the world. USP's rights in version 1.0, and its development team, are reasonably anticipated to contribute to the development of future versions of the software application and, therefore, the rights in version 1.0 are platform contributions for which compensation is due from FS as part of a PCT. USP also transfers the current exploitation rights in version 1.0 to FS and the arm's length amount of the compensation for such transfer is determined in the aggregate with the arm's length PCT Payments in this *Example 3*. FS does not furnish any platform contributions to the CSA nor does it control any operating intangibles at the inception of the CSA that would be relevant to the exploitation of version 1.0 or future versions of the software. It is reasonably anticipated that FS will have gross sales of $1000X in its territory for 5 years attributable to its exploitation of version 1.0 and the cost shared intangibles, after which time the software application will be rendered obsolete and unmarketable by the obsolescence of the storage medium technology to which it relates. FS's costs reasonably attributable to the CSA, other than cost contributions and operating cost contributions, are anticipated to be $250X per year. Certain operating cost contributions that will be borne by FS are reasonably anticipated to equal $200X per annum for 5 years. In addition, FS is reasonably anticipated to pay cost contributions of $200X per year as a controlled participant in the CSA.

(ii) FS concludes that its realistic alternative would be to license software from an uncontrolled licensor that would undertake the commitment to bear the entire risk of software development. Applying CPM using the profit levels experienced by uncontrolled licensees with contractual provisions and allocations of risk that are comparable to those of FS's licensing alternative, FS determines that it could, as a licensee, reasonably expect a (pre-tax) routine return equal to 14% of gross sales or $140X per year for 5 years. The remaining net revenue would be paid to the uncontrolled licensor as a license fee of $410X per year. FS determines that the discount rate that would be applied to determine the present value of income and costs attributable to its participation in the licensing alternative would be 12.5% as compared to the 15% discount rate that would be applicable in determining the present value of the net income attributable to its participation in the CSA (reflecting the increased risk borne by FS in bearing a share of the R & D costs in the cost sharing alternative). FS also determines that the tax rate applicable to it will be the same in the licensing alternative as in the CSA.

(iii) On these facts, the present value to FS of entering into the cost sharing alternative equals the present value of the annual divisional profits ($1,000X minus $250X) minus operating cost contributions ($200X) minus cost contributions ($200X) minus PCT Payments, determined over 5 years by discounting at a discount rate of 15%.

Thus, the present value of the residuals, prior to subtracting the present value of the PCT Payments, is $1349X.

(iv) On these facts, the present value to FS of entering into the licensing alternative would be $561X determined by discounting, over 5 years, annual divisional profits ($1,000X minus $250X) minus operating cost contributions ($200X) and licensing payments ($410X) at a discount rate of 12.5% per annum. The present value of the cost sharing alternative must also equal $561X but equals $1349X prior to subtracting the present value of the PCT Payments. Consequently, the PCT Payments must have a present value of $788X.

Example 4. Pre-tax PCT Payment derived from post-tax information. (i) For simplicity of calculation in this *Example 4*, it is assumed that all payments are made at the end of each year. Domestic controlled participant USP has developed a technology, Z, that it would like to exploit for three years in a CSA. USP enters into a CSA with its wholly-owned foreign subsidiary, FS, that provides for PCT Payments from FS to USP with respect to USP's platform contribution to the CSA of Z in the form of three annual installment payments due from FS to USP on the last day of each of the first three years of the CSA. FS makes no platform contributions to the CSA. Prior to entering into the CSA, FS considers that it has the realistic alternative available to it of licensing Z from USP rather than entering into a CSA with USP to further develop Z for three years.

(ii) FS undertakes financial projections for both the licensing and cost sharing alternatives for exploitation of Z in its territory of the CSA. These projections are set forth in the following tables. The example assumes that there is a reasonably anticipated effective tax rate of 25% in each of years 1 through 3 under both the licensing and cost sharing alternatives. FS determines that the appropriate post-tax discount rate under the licensing alternative is 12.5%, and that the appropriate post-tax discount rate under the cost sharing alternative is 15%.

	Licensing Alternative	Present Value (12.5% DR)	Year 1	Year 2	Year 3
(1)	Sales		$1000	$1100	$1210
(2)	License Fee		400	440	484
(3)	Operating costs		500	550	605
(4)	Operating Income	$261	100	110	121
(5)	Tax (25%)		25	28	30
(6)	Post-tax income	$196	$75	$82	$91

	Cost Sharing Alternative	Present Value (15% DR)	Year 1	Year 2	Year 3
(7)	Sales		$1000	$1100	$1210
(8)	Cost Contributions		200	220	242
(9)	PCT Payments	D	A	B	C
(10)	Operating costs		500	550	605
(11)	Operating income Excluding PCT	$749	300	330	363
(12)	Operating income	H	E	F	G
(13)	Tax				
(14)	Post-tax income excluding PCT	$562	$225	$248	$272
(15)	Post-tax income	L	I	J	K

(iii) Under paragraph (g)(4) of this section, the arm's length charge for a PCT Payment will be an amount such that a controlled participant's present value, as of the date of the PCT of its cost sharing alternative of entering into a CSA equals the present value of its best realistic alternative. This requires that L, the present value of the post-tax income under the CSA, equals the present value of the post-tax income under the licensing alternative, or $196.

(iv) FS determines that PCT Payments for Z should be $196 in Year 1 (A), $215 in Year 2 (B), and $236 in Year 3 (C). By using these amounts for A, B, and C in the table above, FS is able to derive the values of E, F, G, I, J, and K in the table above. Based on these PCT Payments for Z, the post-tax income will be $78 in Year 1 (I), $86 in Year 2 (J), and $95 in Year 3 (K). When this post-tax income stream is discounted at the appropriate rate for the cost sharing alternative (15%), the net present value is $196 (L). The present value of the PCT Payments, when discounted at the appropriate post-tax rate, is $488 (D).

(v) The Commissioner undertakes an audit of the PCT Payments made by FS to USP for Z in Years 1 through 3. The Commissioner concludes that the PCT Payments for Z are arm's length in accordance with this paragraph (g)(4).

Example 5. Pre-tax PCT Payment derived from post-tax information. (i) The facts are the same as in paragraphs (i) and (ii) of Example 4. In addition, under this paragraph (g)(4), the arm's length charge for a PCT Payment will be an amount such that a controlled participant's present value, as of the date of the PCT of its cost sharing alternative equals the present value of its best realistic alternative. This requires that L, the present value of the post-tax income under the CSA, equals the present value of the post-tax income under the licensing alternative, or $196.

(ii) FS determines that the post-tax present value of the cost sharing alternative (excluding PCT Payments) is $562. The post-tax present value of the licensing alternative is $196. Accordingly, payments with a post-tax present value of $366 are required.

(iii) The Commissioner undertakes an audit of the PCT Payments made by FS to USP for Z in Years 1 through 3. In correspondence to the Commissioner, USP maintains that the arm's length PCT Payment for Z should have a present value of $366 (D).

(iv) The Commissioner considers that if FS makes PCT Payments for Z with a present value of $366, then the post-tax present value under the CSA (considering the deductibility of the PCT Payments) will be $287, substantially higher than the post-tax present value of the licensing arrangement, $196. The Commissioner determines that, under the specific facts and assumptions of this example, the present value of the post-tax payments may be grossed up by a factor of (one minus the tax rate), resulting in a present value of pre-tax payments of $488. Accordingly, FS must make yearly PCT Payments (A, B, and C) such that the present value of the Payments is $488 (D). (When FS's post-tax income after these PCT Payments for Z is discounted at the appropriate rate for the cost sharing alternative (15%), the net present value is $196 (L), which is equal to the present value of post-tax income under the licensing alternative.) The Commissioner concludes that the calculations that it has made for the PCT Payments for Z are arm's length in accordance with this paragraph (g)(4) and, accordingly, makes the appropriate adjustments to USP's income tax return to account for the gross-up required by paragraph (g)(2)(x) of this section.

Example 6. Pre-tax PCT Payment derived from pre-tax information. (i) The facts are the same as in paragraphs (i) and (ii) of *Example 4*. In addition, under paragraph (g)(4) of this section, the arm's length charge for a PCT Payment will be an amount such that a controlled participant's present value, as of the date of the PCT of its cost sharing alternative of entering into a CSA equals the present value of its best realistic alternative. This requires that "L," the present value of the post-tax income under the CSA, equals the present value of the post-tax income under the licensing alternative, or $196.

(ii) Under the specific facts and assumptions of this *Example 6* (see paragraph (g)(4)(i)(G) of this section), and using the same (post-tax) discount rates as in *Example 4*, the present value of pre-tax income under the licensing alternative (that is, the operating income) is $261, and the present value of pre-tax income under the cost sharing alternative (excluding PCT Payments) is $749. Accordingly, FS determines that its PCT Payments for Z should have a present value equal to the difference between the two, or $488 (D). Such PCT Payments for Z result in a present value of post-tax income under the cost sharing alternative of $196 (L), which is equal to the present value of post-tax income under the licensing alternative.

(iii) The Commissioner undertakes an audit of the PCT Payments for Z made by FS to USP in Years 1 through 3. The Commissioner concludes that the PCT Payments for Z are arm's length in accordance with this paragraph (g)(4).

Example 7. Application of income method with a terminal value calculation. (i) For simplicity of calculation in this *Example 7*, all financial flows are assumed to occur at the beginning of each period. USP's research and development team, Q, has developed a technology, Z, for which it has several applications on the market now and several planned for release at future dates. In Year 1, USP, enters into a CSA with its wholly-owned subsidiary, FS, to develop future applications of Z. Under the CSA, USP will have the rights to further develop and exploit the future applications of Z in the United States, and FS will have the rights to further develop and exploit the future applications of Z in the rest of the world. Both Q and the rights to further develop and exploit future applications of Z are reasonably anticipated to contribute to the development of future applications of Z. Therefore, both Q and the rights to further develop and exploit the future applications of Z are platform contributions for which compensation is due from FS to USP as part of a PCT. USP does not transfer the current exploitation rights for current applications of Z to FS. FS will not perform any research or development activities on Z and does not furnish any platform contributions to the CSA, nor does it control any operating intangibles at the inception of the CSA that would be relevant to the exploitation of either current or future applications of Z.

(ii) At the outset of the CSA, FS undertakes an analysis of the PCTs involving Q and the rights with respect to Z in order to determine the arm's length PCT Payments owing from FS to USP under the CSA. In that evaluation, FS concludes that the cost sharing alternative represents a riskier alternative for FS than the licensing alternative. FS further concludes that the appropriate discount rate to apply in assessing the licensing alternative, based on discount rates of comparable uncontrolled companies undertaking comparable licensing transactions, would be 13% per annum, whereas the appropriate discount rate to apply in assessing the cost sharing alternative would be 14% per annum. FS undertakes financial projections and anticipates making $100 million in sales during the first two years of the CSA in its territory with sales in Years 3 through 8 increasing to $200 million, $400 million, $600 million, $650 million, $700 million, and $750 million, respectively. After Year 8, FS expects its sales of all products based upon exploitation of Z in the rest of the world to grow at 3% per annum for the future. FS and USP do not anticipate cessation of the CSA Activity with respect to Z at any determinable date. FS anticipates that its manufacturing and distribution costs for exploiting Z (including its operating cost contributions), will equal 60% of gross sales of Z from Year 1 onwards, and anticipates its cost contributions will equal $25 million per annum for Years 1 and 2, $50 million per annum for Years 3 and 4, and 10% of gross sales per annum thereafter.

(iii) Based on this analysis, FS determines that the arm's length royalty rate that USP would have charged an uncontrolled licensee for a license of future applications of Z if USP had further developed future applications of Z on its own is 30% of the sales price of the Z-based product, as determined under the comparable uncontrolled transaction method in § 1.482-4(c). In light of the expected sales growth and anticipation that the CSA Activity will not cease as of any determinable date, FS's determination includes a terminal value calculation. FS further determines that under the cost sharing alternative, the present value of FS's divisional profits, reduced by the present values of the anticipated operating cost contributions and cost contributions, would be $1,361 million. Under the licensing alternative, the present value of the operating divisional profits and losses, reduced by the operating cost contributions, would be $2,113 million, and the present value of the licensing payments would be $1,585 million. Therefore, the total value of the licensing alternative would be $528 million. In order for the present value of the cost sharing alternative to equal the present value of the licensing alternative, the present value of the PCT Payments must equal $833 million. Accordingly, FS pays USP a lump sum PCT Payment of $833 million in Year 1 for USP's platform contributions of Z and Q.

(iv) The Commissioner undertakes an audit of the PCTs and concludes, based on his own analysis, that this lump sum PCT Payment is within the interquartile range of arm's length results for these platform contributions. The calculations made by FS in determining the PCT Payment in this *Example 7* are set forth in the following tables:

COST SHARING ALTERNATIVE

	Time Period (Y = Year, TV = Terminal Value)	Y1	Y2	Y3	Y4	Y5	Y6	Y7	Y8	TV
	Discount Period	0	1	2	3	4	5	6	7	7
	Items of Income/Expense at Beginning of Year									
1	Sales	100	100	200	400	600	650	700	750	(3% annual growth in each year from previous year)
2	Routine Cost and Operating Cost Contributions (60% of sales amount in row 1 of relevant year)	60	60	120	240	360	390	420	450	(60% of annual sales in row 1 for each year)
3	Cost Contributions (10% of sales amount in row 1 for relevant year after Year 5)	25	25	50	50	60	65	70	75	(10% of annual sales in row 1 for each year)
4	Profit = amount in row 1 reduced by amounts in rows 2 and 3	15	15	30	110	180	195	210	225	(row 1 minus rows 2 and 3 for each year)
5	PV (using 14% discount rate)	15	13.2	23.1	74.2	107	101	95.7	89.9	842
6	TOTAL PV of Cost Sharing Alternative = Sum of all PV amounts in Row 5 for all Time Periods = $1,361 million.									

LICENSING ALTERNATIVE

Time Period (Y = Year, TV = Terminal Value)	Y1	Y2	Y3	Y4	Y5	Y6	Y7	Y8	TV
Discount Period	0	1	2	3	4	5	6	7	7
Items of Income/Expense at Beginning of Year									
7 Sales	100	100	200	400	600	650	700	750	(3% annual growth in each year from previou s year)
8 Routine Cost and Operating Cost Contributions (60% of sales amount in row 7 of relevant year)	60	60	120	240	360	390	420	450	(60% of annual sales in row 7 for each year)
9 Operating Profit = amount in Row 7 reduced by amount in Row 8	40	40	80	160	240	260	280	300	(Row 7 minus row 8 for each year)
10 PV of row 9 (using 13% discount rate)	40	35.4	62.7	111	147	141	135	128	1313
11 TOTAL PV FOR ALL AMOUNTS IN ROW 10 = $2,112.7 million									
12 Licensing Payments (30% of sales amount in row 7)	30	30	60	120	180	195	210	225	(30% of amount in row 7 for each year)
13 PV of amount in row 12 (using 13% discount rate)	30	26.5	47	83.2	110	106	101	95.6	985
14 TOTAL PV FOR ALL AMOUNTS IN ROW 13 = $1,584.5 million.									
15 TOTAL PV of Licensing Alternative = Row 11 minus Row 14 = $528 million.									

CALCULATION OF PCT PAYMENT

16	TOTAL PV OF COST SHARING ALTERNATIVE (FROM ROW 6 ABOVE) =	$1,361 million
17	TOTAL PV OF LICENSING ALTERNATIVE (FROM ROW 15 ABOVE) =	$528 million
18	LUMP SUM PCT PAYMENT = ROW 16 - ROW 17 =	$833 million

Example 8. (i) The facts are the same as in *Example 1*, except that the taxpayer determines that the appropriate discount rate for the cost sharing alternative is 20%. In addition, the taxpayer determines that the appropriate discount rate for the licensing alternative is 10%. Accordingly, the taxpayer determines that the appropriate present value of the PCT Payment is $146 million.

(ii) Based on the best method analysis described in *Example 2*, the Commissioner determines that the taxpayer's calculation of the present value of the PCT Payments is outside of the interquartile range (as shown in the sixth column of *Example 2*), and thus warrants an adjustment. Furthermore, in evaluating the taxpayer's analysis, the Commissioner undertakes an analysis based on the difference in the financial projections between the cost sharing and licensing alternatives (as shown in column 11 of *Example 1*). This column shows the anticipated differential income stream of additional positive or negative income for FS over the duration of the CSA Activity that would result from undertaking the cost sharing alternative (before any PCT Payments) rather than the licensing alternative. This anticipated differential income stream thus reflects the anticipated incremental undiscounted profits to FS from the incremental activity of undertaking the risk of developing the cost shared intangibles and enjoying the value of its divisional interests. Taxpayer's analysis logically implies that the present value of this stream must be $146 million, since only then would FS have the same anticipated value in both the cost sharing and licensing alternatives. A present value of $146 million implies that the discount rate applicable to this stream is 34.4%. Based on a reliable calculation of discount rates applicable to the anticipated income streams of uncontrolled companies whose resources, capabilities, and rights consist primarily of software applications intangibles and research and development teams similar to USP's platform contributions to the CSA, and which income streams, accordingly, may be reasonably anticipated to reflect a similar risk profile to the differential income stream, the Commissioner concludes that an appropriate discount rate for the anticipated income stream associated with USP's platform contributions (that is, the additional positive or negative income over the duration of the CSA Activity that would result, before PCT Payments, from switching from the licensing alternative to the cost sharing alternative) is 16%, which is significantly less than 34.4%. This conclusion further suggests that Taxpayer's analysis is unreliable. See paragraphs (g)(2)(v)(B)(*2*) and (g)(4)(vi)(F)(*1*) and (*2*) of this section.

(iii) The Commissioner makes an adjustment of $296 million, so that the present value of the PCT Payments is $442 million (the median results as shown in column 6 of *Example 2*).

Example 9. The facts are the same as in *Example 1*, except that additional data on discount rates are available that were not available in *Example 1*. The Commissioner determines the arm's length charge for the PCT Payment by discounting at an appropriate rate the differential income stream associated with the rights contributed by USP in the PCT (that is, the stream of income in column (11) of *Example 1*). Based on an analysis of a set of public companies whose resources, capabilities, and rights consist primarily of resources, capabilities, and rights similar to those contributed by USP in the PCT, the Commissioner determines that 15% to 17% is an appropriate range of discount rates to use to assess the value of the differential income stream associated with the rights contributed by USP in the PCT. The Commissioner determines that applying a discount rate of 17% to the differential income stream associated with the rights contributed by USP in the PCT yields a present value of $446 million, while applying a discount rate of 15% to the differential income stream associated with the rights contributed by USP in the PCT yields a present value of $510 million. Because the taxpayer's result, $464 million, is within the interquartile range determined by the Commissioner, no adjustments are warranted. See paragraphs (g)(2)(v)(B)(*2*), (g)(4)(v), and (g)(4)(vi)(F)(*1*) of this section.

(5) *Acquisition price method.*—(i) *In general.*—The acquisition price method applies the comparable uncontrolled transaction method of § 1.482-4(c), or the comparable uncontrolled services price method described in § 1.482-9(c), to evaluate whether the amount charged in a PCT, or group of PCTs, is arm's length by reference to the amount charged (the acquisition price) for the stock or asset purchase of an entire organization or portion thereof (the target) in an uncontrolled transaction. The acquisition price method is ordinarily used where substantially all the target's nonroutine contributions, as such term is defined in paragraph (j)(1)(i) of this section, made to the PCT Payee's business activities are covered by a PCT or group of PCTs.

(ii) *Determination of arm's length charge.*—Under this method, the arm's length charge for a PCT or group of PCTs covering resources, capabilities, and rights of the target is equal to the adjusted acquisition price, as divided among the controlled participants according to their respective RAB shares.

(iii) *Adjusted acquisition price.*—The adjusted acquisition price is the acquisition price of the target increased by the value of the target's liabilities on the date of the acquisition, other than liabilities not assumed in the case of an asset purchase, and decreased by the value of the target's tangible property on that date and by the value on that date of any other resources, capabilities, and rights not covered by a PCT or group of PCTs.

(iv) *Best method analysis considerations.*—The comparability and reliability considerations stated in § 1.482-4(c)(2) apply. Consistent with those considerations, the reliability of applying the acquisition price method as a measure of the arm's length charge for the PCT Payment normally is reduced if—

(A) A substantial portion of the target's nonroutine contributions to the PCT Payee's business activities is not required to be covered by a PCT or group of PCTs, and that portion of the nonroutine contributions cannot reliably be valued;

(B) A substantial portion of the target's assets consists of tangible property that cannot reliably be valued; or

(C) The date on which the target is acquired and the date of the PCT are not contemporaneous.

(v) *Example.*—The following example illustrates the principles of this paragraph (g)(5):

Example. USP, a U.S. corporation, and its newly incorporated, whollyowned foreign subsidiary (FS) enter into a CSA at the start of Year 1 to develop Group Z products. Under the CSA, USP and FS will have the exclusive rights to exploit the Group Z products in the U.S. and the rest of the world, respectively. At the start of Year 2, USP acquires Company X for cash consideration worth $110 million. At this time USP's RAB share is 60%, and FS's RAB share is 40% and is not reasonably anticipated to change as a result of this acquisition. Company X joins in the filing of a U.S. consolidated income tax return with USP. Under paragraph (j)(2)(i) of this section, Company X and USP are treated as one taxpayer for purposes of this section. Accordingly, the rights in any of Company X's resources and capabilities that are reasonably anticipated to contribute to the development activities of the CSA will be considered platform contributions furnished by USP. Company X's resources and capabilities consist of its workforce, certain technology intangibles, $15 million of tangible property and other assets and $5 million in liabilities. The technology intangibles, as well as Company X's workforce, are reasonably anticipated to contribute to the development of the Group Z products under the CSA and, therefore, the rights in the technology intangibles and the workforce are platform contributions for which FS must make a PCT Payment to USP. None of Company X's existing intangible assets or any of its workforce are anticipated to contribute to activities outside the CSA. For purposes of this example, it is assumed that no additional adjustment on account of tax liabilities is needed. Applying the acquisition price method, the value of USP's platform contributions is the adjusted acquisition price of $100 million ($110 million acquisition price plus $5 million liabilities less $15 million tangible property and other assets). FS must make a PCT Payment to USP for these platform contributions with a reasonably anticipated present value of $40 million, which is the product of $100 million (the value of the platform contributions) and 40% (FS's RAB share).

(6) *Market capitalization method.*—(i) *In general.*—The market capitalization method applies the comparable uncontrolled transaction method of § 1.482-4(c), or the comparable uncontrolled services price method described in § 1.482-9(c), to evaluate whether the amount charged in a PCT, or group of PCTs, is arm's length by reference to the average market capitalization of a controlled participant (PCT Payee) whose stock is regularly traded on an established securities market. The market capitalization method is ordinarily used where substantially all of the PCT Payee's nonroutine contributions to the PCT Payee's business are covered by a PCT or group of PCTs.

(ii) *Determination of arm's length charge.*—Under the market capitalization method, the arm's length charge for a PCT or group of PCTs covering resources, capabilities, and rights of the PCT Payee is equal to the adjusted average market capitalization, as divided among the controlled participants according to their respective RAB shares.

(iii) *Average market capitalization.*—The average market capitalization is the average of the daily market capitalizations of the PCT Payee over a period of time beginning 60 days before the date of the PCT and ending on the date of the PCT. The daily market capitalization of the PCT Payee is calculated on each day its stock is actively traded as the total number of shares outstanding multiplied by the adjusted closing price of the stock on that day. The adjusted closing price is the daily closing price of the stock, after adjustments for stock-based transactions (dividends and stock splits) and other pending corporate (combination and spin-off) restructuring transactions for which reliable arm's length adjustments can be made.

(iv) *Adjusted average market capitalization.*—The adjusted average market capitalization is the average market capitalization of the PCT Payee increased by the value of the PCT Payee's liabilities on the date of the PCT and decreased by the value on such date of the PCT Payee's tangible property and of any other resources, capabilities, or rights of the PCT Payee not covered by a PCT or group of PCTs.

(v) *Best method analysis considerations.*—The comparability and reliability considerations stated in § 1.482-4(c)(2) apply. Consistent with those considerations, the reliability of applying the comparable uncontrolled transaction method using the adjusted market capitalization of a company as a measure of the arm's length charge for the PCT Payment normally is reduced if—

(A) A substantial portion of the PCT Payee's nonroutine contributions to its business activities is not required to be covered by a PCT or group of PCTs, and that portion of the nonroutine contributions cannot reliably be valued;

(B) A substantial portion of the PCT Payee's assets consists of tangible property that cannot reliably be valued; or

(C) Facts and circumstances demonstrate the likelihood of a material divergence between the average market capitalization of the PCT Payee and the value of its resources, capabilities, and rights for which reliable adjustments cannot be made.

(vi) *Examples.*—The following examples illustrate the principles of this paragraph (g)(6):

Example 1. (i) USP, a publicly traded U.S. company, and its newly incorporated wholly-owned foreign subsidiary (FS) enter into a CSA on Date 1 to develop software. At that time USP has in-process software but has no software ready for the market. Under the CSA, USP and FS will have the exclusive rights to exploit the software developed under the CSA in the United States and the rest of the world, respectively. On Date 1, USP's RAB share is 70% and FS's RAB share is 30%. USP's assembled team of researchers and its in-process software are reasonably anticipated to contribute to the development of the software under the CSA. Therefore, the rights in the research team and in-process software are platform contributions for which compensation is due from FS. Further, these rights are not reasonably anticipated to contribute to any business activity other than the CSA Activity.

(ii) On Date 1, USP had an average market capitalization of $205 million, tangible property and other assets that can be reliably valued worth $5 million, and no liabilities. Aside from those assets, USP had no assets other than its research team and in-process software. Applying the market capitalization method, the value of USP's platform contributions is $200 million ($205 million average market capitalization of USP less $5 million of tangible property and other assets). The arm's length value of the PCT Payments FS must make to USP for the platform contributions, before any adjustment on account of tax liability as described in paragraph (g)(2)(ii) of this section, is $60 million, which is the product of $200 million (the value of the platform contributions) and 30% (FS's RAB share on Date 1).

Example 2. Aggregation with make-or-sell rights. (i) The facts are the same as in *Example 1*, except that on Date 1 USP also has existing software ready for the market. USP separately enters into a license agreement with FS for make-or-sell rights for all existing software outside the United States. No marketing has occurred, and USP has no marketing intangibles. This license of current make-or-sell rights is a transaction governed by § 1.482-4. However, after analysis, it is determined that the arm's length PCT Payments and the arm's length payments for the make-or-sell license may be most reliably determined in the aggregate using the market capitalization method, under principles described in paragraph (g)(2)(iv) of this section, and it is further determined that those principles are most reliably implemented by computing the aggregate arm's length charge as the product of the aggregate value of the existing and inprocess software and FS's RAB share on Date 1.

(ii) Applying the market capitalization method, the aggregate value of USP's platform contributions and the make-or-sell rights in its existing software is $250 million ($255 million average market capitalization of USP less $5 million of tangible property and other assets). The total arm's length value of the PCT Payments and licensing payments FS must make to USP for the platform contributions and current make-or-sell rights, before any adjustment on account of tax liability, if any, is $75 million, which is the product of $250 million (the value of the platform contributions and the make-or-sell rights) and 30% (FS's RAB share on Date 1).

Example 3. Reduced reliability. The facts are the same as in *Example 1* except that USP also has significant nonroutine assets that will be used solely in a nascent business division that is unrelated to the subject of the CSA and that cannot themselves be reliably valued. Those nonroutine contributions are not platform contributions and accordingly are not required to be covered by a PCT. The reliability of using the market capitalization method to determine the value of USP's platform contributions to the CSA is significantly reduced in this case because that method would require adjusting USP's average market capitalization to account for the significant nonroutine contributions that are not required to be covered by a PCT.

(7) *Residual profit split method*.—(i) *In general*.—The residual profit split method evaluates whether the allocation of combined operating profit or loss attributable to one or more platform contributions subject to a PCT is arm's length by reference to the relative value of each controlled participant's contribution to that combined operating profit or loss. The combined operating profit or loss must be derived from the most narrowly identifiable business activity (relevant business activity) of the controlled participants for which data are available that include the CSA Activity. The residual profit split method may not be used where only one controlled participant makes significant nonroutine contributions (including platform or operating contributions) to the CSA Activity. The provisions of § 1.482-6 shall apply to CSAs only to the extent provided and as modified in this paragraph (g)(7). Any other application to a CSA of a residual profit method not described in paragraphs (g)(7)(ii) and (iii) of this section will constitute an unspecified method for purposes of sections 482 and 6662(e) and the regulations under those sections.

(ii) *Appropriate share of profits and losses*.—The relative value of each controlled participant's contribution to the success of the relevant business activity must be determined in a manner that reflects the functions performed, risks assumed, and resources employed by each participant in the relevant business activity, consistent with the best method analysis described in § 1.482-1(c) and (d). Such an allocation is intended to correspond to the division of profit or loss that would result from an arrangement between uncontrolled taxpayers, each performing functions similar to those of the various controlled participants engaged in the relevant business activity. The profit allocated to any particular controlled participant is not necessarily limited to the total operating profit of the group from the relevant business activity. For example, in a given year, one controlled participant may earn a profit while another controlled participant incurs a loss. In addition, it may not be assumed that the combined operating profit or loss from the relevant business activity should be shared equally, or in any other arbitrary proportion.

(iii) *Profit split*.—(A) *In general*.—Under the residual profit split method, the present value of each controlled participant's residual divisional profit or loss attributable to nonroutine contributions (nonroutine residual divisional profit or loss) is allocated between the controlled participants that each furnish significant nonroutine contributions (including platform or operating contributions) to the relevant business activity in that division.

(B) *Determine nonroutine residual divisional profit or loss*.—The present value of each controlled participant's nonroutine residual divisional profit or loss must be determined to reflect the most reliable measure of an arm's length result. The present value of nonroutine residual divisional profit or loss equals the present value of the stream of the reasonably anticipated residuals over the duration of the CSA Activity of divisional profit or loss, minus market returns for routine contributions, minus operating cost contributions, minus cost contributions, using a discount rate appropriate to such residuals in accordance with paragraph (g)(2)(v) of this section. As used in this paragraph (g)(7), the phrase "market returns for routine contributions" includes market returns for operating cost contributions and excludes market returns for cost contributions.

(C) *Allocate nonroutine residual divisional profit or loss*.—*(1) In general*.—The present value of nonroutine residual divisional profit or loss in each controlled participant's division must be allocated among all of the controlled participants based upon the relative values, determined as of the date of the PCTs, of the PCT Payor's as compared to the PCT Payee's nonroutine contributions to the PCT Payor's division. For this purpose, the PCT Payor's nonroutine contribution consists of the sum of the PCT Payor's nonroutine operating contributions and the PCT Payor's RAB share of the PCT Payor's nonroutine platform contributions. For this purpose, the PCT Payee's nonroutine contribution consists of the PCT Payor's RAB share of the PCT Payee's nonroutine platform contributions.

(2) Relative value determination.—The relative values of the controlled participants' nonroutine contributions must be determined so as to reflect the most reliable measure of an arm's length result. Relative values may be measured by external market benchmarks that reflect the fair market value of such nonroutine contributions. Alternatively, the relative value of nonroutine contributions may be estimated by the capitalized cost of developing the nonroutine contributions and updates, as appropriately grown or discounted so that all contributions may be valued on a comparable dollar basis as of the same date. If the nonroutine contributions by a controlled participant are also used in other business activities (such as the exploitation of make-or-sell rights described in paragraph (c)(1) of this section), an allocation of the value of the nonroutine contributions must be made on a reasonable basis among all the business activities in which they are used in proportion to the relative economic value that the relevant business activity and such other business activities are anticipated to derive over time as the result of such nonroutine contributions.

(3) Determination of PCT Payments.—Any amount of the present value of a controlled participant's nonroutine residual divisional profit or loss that is allocated to another controlled participant represents the present value of the PCT Payments due to that other controlled participant for its platform contributions to the relevant business activity in the relevant division. For purposes of paragraph (j)(3)(ii) of this section, the present value of a PCT Payor's PCT Payments under this paragraph shall be deemed reduced to the extent of the present value of any PCT Payments owed to it from other controlled participants under this paragraph (g)(7). The resulting remainder may be converted to a fixed or contingent form of payment in accordance with paragraph (h) (Form of payment rules) of this section.

(4) Routine platform and operating contributions.—For purposes of this paragraph (g)(7), any routine platform or operating contributions, the valuation and PCT Payments for which are determined and made independently of the residual profit split method, are treated similarly to cost contributions and operating cost contributions, respectively. Accordingly, wherever used in this paragraph (g)(7), the term "routine contributions" shall not include routine platform or operating contributions, and wherever the terms "cost contributions" and "operating cost contributions" appear in this paragraph (g)(7), they shall include net routine platform contributions and net routine operating contributions, respectively, as defined in paragraph (g)(4)(vii) of this section. However, treatment of net operating contributions as operating cost contributions shall be coordinated with the treatment of other routine contributions pursuant to paragraphs (g)(4)(iii)(B) and (7)(iii)(B) of this section so as to avoid duplicative market returns to such contributions.

(iv) *Best method analysis considerations*.—(A) *In general*.—Whether results derived from this method are the most reliable measure of the arm's length result is determined using the factors described under the best method rule in § 1.482-1(c). Thus, comparability and quality of data, reliability of assumptions, and sensitivity of results to possible deficiencies in the data and assumptions, must be considered in determining whether this method provides the most reliable measure of an arm's length result. The application of these factors to the residual profit split in the context of the relevant business activity of developing and exploiting cost shared intangibles is discussed in paragraphs (g)(7)(iv)(B) through (D) of this section.

(B) *Comparability*.—The derivation of the present value of nonroutine residual divisional profit or loss includes a carveout on account of market returns for routine contributions. Thus, the comparability considerations that are relevant for that purpose include those that are relevant for the methods that are used to determine market returns for the routine contributions.

(C) *Data and assumptions*.—The reliability of the results derived from the residual profit split is affected by the quality of the data and assumptions used to apply this method. In particular, the following factors must be considered:

(1) The reliability of the allocation of costs, income, and assets between the relevant business activity and the controlled participants' other activities that will affect the reliability of the determination of the divisional profit or loss and its allocation among the controlled participants. See § 1.482-6(c)(2)(ii)(C)(1).

(2) The degree of consistency between the controlled participants and uncontrolled taxpayers in accounting practices that materially affect the items that determine the amount and allocation of operating profit or loss affects the reliability of the result. See § 1.482-6(c)(2)(ii)(C)(2).

(3) The reliability of the data used and the assumptions made in estimating the relative value of the nonroutine contributions by the controlled participants. In particular, if capitalized costs of development are used to estimate the relative value of nonroutine contributions, the reliability of the results is reduced relative to the reliability of other methods that do not require such an estimate. This is because, in any given case, the costs of developing a nonroutine contribution may not be related to its market value and because the calculation of the capitalized costs of development may require the allocation of indirect costs between the relevant business activity and the controlled participant's other activities, which may affect the reliability of the analysis.

(D) *Other factors affecting reliability.*—Like the methods described in §§1.482-3 through 1.482-5 and §1.482-9(c), the carveout on account of market returns for routine contributions relies exclusively on external market benchmarks. As indicated in §1.482-1(c)(2)(i), as the degree of comparability between the controlled participants and uncontrolled transactions increases, the relative weight accorded the analysis under this method will increase. In addition, to the extent the allocation of nonroutine residual divisional profit or loss is not based on external market benchmarks, the reliability of the analysis will be decreased in relation to an analysis under a method that relies on market benchmarks. Finally, the reliability of the analysis under this method may be enhanced by the fact that all the controlled participants are evaluated under the residual profit split. However, the reliability of the results of an analysis based on information from all the controlled participants is affected by the reliability of the data and the assumptions pertaining to each controlled participant. Thus, if the data and assumptions are significantly more reliable with respect to one of the controlled participants than with respect to the others, a different method, focusing solely on the results of that party, may yield more reliable results.

(v) *Examples.*—The following examples illustrate the principles of this paragraph (g)(7):

Example 1. (i) For simplicity of calculation in this Example 1, all financial flows are assumed to occur at the beginning of each period. USP, a U.S. electronic data storage company, has partially developed technology for a type of extremely small compact storage devices (nanodisks) which are expected to provide a significant increase in data storage capacity in various types of portable devices such as cell phones, MP3 players, laptop computers and digital cameras. At the same time, USP's wholly-owned subsidiary, FS, has developed significant marketing intangibles outside the United States in the form of customer lists, ongoing relations with various OEMs, and trademarks that are well recognized by consumers due to a long history of marketing successful data storage devices and other hardware used in various types of consumer electronics. At the beginning of Year 1, USP enters into a CSA with FS to develop nanodisk technologies for eventual commercial exploitation. Under the CSA, USP will have the right to exploit nanodisks in the United States, while FS will have the right to exploit nanodisks in the rest of the world. The partially developed nanodisk technologies owned by USP are reasonably anticipated to contribute to the development of commercially exploitable nanodisks and therefore the rights in the nanodisk technologies constitute platform contributions of USP for which compensation is due under PCTs. FS does not have any platform contributions for the CSA. Due to the fact that nanodisk technologies have yet to be incorporated into any commercially available product, neither USP nor FS transfers rights to make or sell current products in conjunction with the CSA.

(ii) Because only in FS's territory do both controlled participants make significant nonroutine contributions, USP and FS determine that they need to determine the relative value of their respective contributions to residual divisional profit or loss attributable to the CSA Activity only in FS's territory. FS anticipates making no nanodisk sales during the first year of the CSA in its territory with revenues in Year 2 reaching $200 million. Revenues through Year 5 are reasonably anticipated to increase by 50% per year. The annual growth rate for revenues is then expected to decline to 30% per annum in Years 6 and 7, 20% per annum in Years 8 and 9 and 10% per annum in Year 10. Revenues are then expected to decline 10% in Year 11 and 5% per annum, thereafter. The routine costs (defined here as costs other than cost contributions, routine platform and operating contributions, and nonroutine contributions) that are allocable to this revenue in calculating FS's divisional profit or loss, are anticipated to equal $40 million for the first year of the CSA and $130 for the second year and $200 and $250 million in Years 3 and 4. Total operating expenses attributable to product exploitation (including operating cost contributions) equal 52% of sales per year. FS undertakes routine distribution activities in its markets that constitute routine contributions to the relevant business activity of exploiting nanodisk technologies. USP and FS estimate that the total market return on these routine contributions will amount to 6% of the routine costs. FS expects its cost contributions to be $60 million in Year 1, rise to $100 million in Years 2 and 3, and then decline again to $60 million in Year 4. Thereafter, FS's cost contributions are expected to equal 10% of revenues.

(iii) USP and FS determine the present value of the stream of the reasonably anticipated residuals in FS's territory over the duration of the CSA Activity of the divisional profit or loss (revenues minus routine costs), minus the market returns for routine contributions, the operating cost contributions, and the cost contributions. USP and FS determine, based on the considerations discussed in paragraph (g)(2)(v) of this section, that the appropriate discount rate is 17.5% per annum. Therefore, the present value of the nonroutine residual divisional profit is $1,395 million.

(iv) After analysis, USP and FS determine that the relative value of the nanodisk technologies contributed by USP to CSA (giving effect only to its value in FS's territory) is roughly 150% of the value of FS's marketing intangibles (which only have value in FS's territory). Consequently, 60% of the nonroutine residual divisional profit is attributable to USP's platform contribution. Therefore, FS's PCT Payments should have an expected present value equal to $837 million (.6 × $1,395 million).

(v) The calculations for this *Example 1* are displayed in the following table:

Time Period (Y = Year)	Y1	Y2	Y3	Y4	Y5	Y6	Y7	Y8	Y9	Y10	Y11	TV
(TV = Terminal Value)												
Discount Period	0	1	2	3	4	5	6	7	8	9	10	10
[1] Sales	0	200	300	450	675	878	1141	1369	1643	1807	1626	...
[2] Growth Rate	—	—	50%	50%	50%	30%	30%	20%	20%	10%	–10%	...
[3] Exploitation Costs and Operating Cost Contributions (52% of Sales [1])	40	130	200	250	351	456	593	712	854	940	846	...
[4] Return on [3] (6% of [3])	2.4	8	12	15	21	27	36	43	51	56	51	...
[5] Cost Contributions (10% of Sales [1] after Year 5)	60	100	100	60	68	88	114	137	164	181	163	...
[6] Residual Profit = [1] minus {[3] + [4] + [5]}	–102	–38	–12	125	235	306	398	477	573	630	567	2395
[7] Residual Profit [6] Discounted at 17.5% discount rate	–102	–32	–9	77	124	137	151	154	158	148	113	477
[8] Sum of all amounts in [7] for all time periods = $1,395 million												
[9] Relative value in FS's division of USP's nanotechnology to FS's marketing intangibles = 150%												
[10] Profit Split (USP)	60% = 1.5 × [11]											
[11] Profit Split (FS)	40%											
[12] FS's PCT Payments	[8] × [10] = $1,395 million × 60% = $837 million											

Example 2. (i) For simplicity of calculation in this *Example 2*, all financial flows are assumed to occur at the beginning of each period. USP is a U.S. automobile manufacturing company that has completed significant research on the development of diesel-electric hy-

brid engines that, if they could be successfully manufactured, would result in providing a significant increased fuel economy for a wide variety of motor vehicles. Successful commercialization of the diesel-electric hybrid engine will require the development of a new class of advanced battery that will be light, relatively cheap to manufacture and yet capable of holding a substantial electric charge. FS, a foreign subsidiary of USP, has completed significant research on developing lithium-ion batteries that appear likely to have the requisite characteristics. At the beginning of Year 1, USP enters into a CSA with FS to further develop diesel-electric hybrid engines and lithium-ion battery technologies for eventual commercial exploitation. Under the CSA, USP will have the right to exploit the diesel-electric hybrid engine and lithium-ion battery technologies in the United States, while FS will have the right to exploit such technologies in the rest of the world. The partially developed diesel-electric hybrid engine and lithium-ion battery technologies owned by USP and FS, respectively, are reasonably anticipated to contribute to the development of commercially exploitable automobile engines and therefore the rights in both these technologies constitute platform contributions of USP and of FS for which compensation is due under PCTs. At the time of inception of the CSA, USP owns operating intangibles in the form of self-developed marketing intangibles which have significant value in the United States, but not in the rest of the world, and that are relevant to exploiting the cost shared intangibles. Similarly, FS owns self-developed marketing intangibles which have significant value in the rest of the world, but not in the United States, and that are relevant to exploiting the cost shared intangibles. Although the new class of diesel-electric hybrid engine using lithium-ion batteries is not yet ready for commercial exploitation, components based on this technology are beginning to be incorporated in current-generation gasoline-electric hybrid engines and the rights to make and sell such products are transferred from USP to FS and vice-versa in conjunction with the inception of the CSA, following the same territorial division as in the CSA.

(ii) USP's estimated RAB share is 66.7%. During Year 1, it is anticipated that sales in USP's territory will be $1000X in Year 1. Sales in FS's territory are anticipated to be $500X. Thereafter, as revenue from the use of components in gasoline-electric hybrids is supplemented by revenues from the production of complete diesel-electric hybrid engines using lithium-ion battery technology, anticipated sales in both territories will increase rapidly at a rate of 50% per annum through Year 4. Anticipated sales are then anticipated to increase at a rate of 40% per annum for another 4 years. Sales are then anticipated to increase at a rate of 30% per annum through Year 10. Thereafter, sales are anticipated to decrease at a rate of 5% per annum for the foreseeable future as new automotive drivetrain technologies displace diesel-electric hybrid engines and lithium-ion batteries. Total operating expenses attributable to product exploitation (including operating cost contributions) equal 40% of sales per year for both USP and FS. USP and FS estimate that the total market return on these routine contributions to the CSA will amount to 6% of these operating expenses. USP is expected to bear 2/3 of the total cost contributions for the foreseeable future. Cost contributions are expected to total $375X in Year 1 (of which $250X are borne by USP) and increase at a rate of 25% per annum through Year 6. In Years 7 through 10, cost contributions are expected to increase 10% a year. Thereafter, cost contributions are expected to decrease by 5% a year for the foreseeable future.

(iii) USP and FS determine the present value of the stream of FS's reasonably anticipated residual divisional profit, which is the stream of FS's reasonably anticipated divisional profit or loss, minus the market returns for routine contributions, minus operating cost contributions, minus cost contributions. USP and FS determine, based on the considerations discussed in paragraph (g)(2)(v) of this section, that the appropriate discount rate is 12% per year. Therefore, the present value of the nonroutine residual divisional profit in USP's territory is $41,727X and in CFC's territory is $20,864X.

(iv) After analysis, USP and FS determine that, in the United States the relative value of the technologies contributed by USP and FS to the CSA and of the operating intangibles used by USP in the exploitation of the cost shared intangibles (reported as equaling 100 in total), equals: USP's platform contribution (59.5); FS's platform contribution (25.5); and USP's operating intangibles (15). Consequently, the present value of the arm's length amount of the PCT Payments that USP should pay to FS for FS's platform contribution is $10,640X (.255 × $41,727X). Similarly, USP and FS determine that, in the rest of the world, the relative value of the technologies contributed by USP and FS to the CSA and of the operating intangibles used by FS in the exploitation of the cost shared intangibles can be divided as follows: USP's platform contribution (63); FS's platform contribution (27); and FS's operating intangibles (10). Consequently, the present value of the arm's length amount of the PCT Payments that FS should pay to USP for USP's platform contribution is $13,144X (.63 × $20,864X). Therefore, FS is required to make a net payment to USP with a present value of $2,504X ($13,144X - 10,640X).

(v) The calculations for this *Example 2* are displayed in the following tables:

CALCULATION OF USP's PCT PAYMENT TO FS

Time Period (Y = Year) (TV = Terminal Value)	Y1	Y2	Y3	Y4	Y5	Y6	Y7	Y8	Y9	Y10	TV
Discount Period	0	1	2	3	4	5	6	7	8	9	9
[1] Sales	1000	1500	2250	3375	4725	6615	9261	12965	16855	21912	. . .
[2] Growth Rate	—	50%	50%	50%	40%	40%	40%	40%	30%	30%	. . .
[3] Exploitation Costs and Operating Cost Contributions (40% of Sales [1])	400	600	900	1350	1890	2646	3704	5186	6742	8765	. . .
[4] Return on [3] = 6% of [3]	24	36	54	81	113	159	222	311	405	526	. . .
[5] Cost Contributions	250	313	391	488	610	763	839	923	1015	1117	. . .
[6] Residual Profit = [1] minus {[3] + [4] + [5]}	326	552	905	1456	2111	3047	4495	6545	8693	11504	64287
[7] Residual Profit [6] Discounted at 12% discount rate	326	492	722	1036	1342	1729	2277	2961	3511	4148	23183

[8] Sum of all amounts in [7] for all time periods = $41,727X

Profit Split for Calculation of USP's PCT Payment to FS: [Total of US contributions = 74.5%]

[9] USP's Platform Contribution = 59.5%

[10] FS's Platform Contribution = 25.5%

[11] USP's Operating Intangibles = 15%

[12] USP's PCT Payment to FS = [8] × [10] = $41,727X multiplied by 25.5% = $10,640X

CALCULATION OF FS's NET PCT PAYMENTS TO USP

Time Period (Y = Year) (TV = Terminal Value)	Y1	Y2	Y3	Y4	Y5	Y6	Y7	Y8	Y9	Y10	TV
Discount Period	0	1	2	3	4	5	6	7	8	9	9
[13] Sales	500	750	1125	1688	2363	3308	4631	6483	8428	10956	. . .
[14] Growth Rate	—	50%	50%	50%	40%	40%	40%	40%	30%	30%	. . .

Time Period (Y = Year) (TV = Terminal Value)	Y1	Y2	Y3	Y4	Y5	Y6	Y7	Y8	Y9	Y10	TV
Discount Period	0	1	2	3	4	5	6	7	8	9	9
[15] Exploitation Costs and Operating Cost Contributions (40% of Sales [13])	200	300	450	675	945	1323	1852	2593	3371	4382	. . .
[16] Return on [15] = 6% of [15]	12	18	27	41	57	79	111	156	202	263	. . .
[17] Cost Contributions	125	156	195	244	305	381	420	462	508	559	. . .
[18] Residual Profit = [13] minus {[15] + [16] + [17]}	163	276	453	728	1056	1524	2248	3272	4347	5752	32144
[19] Residual Profit [18] Discounted at 12% discount rate	163	246	361	518	671	865	1139	1480	1755	2074	11591
[20] Sum of all amounts in [19] for all time periods = $20,864X											

Profit Split for Calculation of FS's PCT Payment to USP: [Total of FS's contributions = 37%]
[21] USP's Platform Contribution = 63%
[22] FS's Platform Contribution = 27%
[23] FS's Operating Intangibles =10%

[24] FS's PCT Payment to USP = [20] × [21] = $20,864X multiplied by 63% = $13,144X

[25] FS's Net PCT Payment to USP z [24] minus [12] = $13,144X minus $10,640X = $2,504X

(8) *Unspecified methods.*—Methods not specified in paragraphs (g)(3) through (7) of this section may be used to evaluate whether the amount charged for a PCT is arm's length. Any method used under this paragraph (g)(8) must be applied in accordance with the provisions of § 1.482-1 and of paragraph (g)(2) of this section. Consistent with the specified methods, an unspecified method should take into account the general principle that uncontrolled taxpayers evaluate the terms of a transaction by considering the realistic alternatives to that transaction, and only enter into a particular transaction if none of the alternatives is preferable to it. Therefore, in establishing whether a PCT achieved an arm's length result, an unspecified method should provide information on the prices or profits that the controlled participant could have realized by choosing a realistic alternative to the CSA. See paragraph (k)(2)(ii)(J) of this section. As with any method, an unspecified method will not be applied unless it provides the most reliable measure of an arm's length result under the principles of the best method rule. See § 1.482-1(c) (Best method rule). In accordance with § 1.482-1(d) (Comparability), to the extent that an unspecified method relies on internal data rather than uncontrolled comparables, its reliability will be reduced. Similarly, the reliability of a method will be affected by the reliability of the data and assumptions used to apply the method, including any projections used.

(h) *Form of payment rules.*—(1) *CST Payments.*—CST Payments may not be paid in shares of stock in the payor (or stock in any member of the controlled group that includes the controlled participants).

(2) *PCT Payments.*—(i) *In general.*—The consideration under a PCT for a platform contribution may take one or a combination of both of the following forms:

(A) Payments of a fixed amount (fixed payments), either paid in a lump sum payment or in installment payments spread over a specified period, with interest calculated in accordance with § 1.482-2(a) (Loans or advances).

(B) Payments contingent on the exploitation of cost shared intangibles by the PCT Payor (contingent payments). Accordingly, controlled participants have flexibility to adopt a form and period of payment, provided that such form and period of payment are consistent with an arm's length charge as of the date of the PCT. See also paragraphs (h)(2)(iv) and (3) of this section.

(ii) *No PCT Payor Stock.*—PCT Payments may not be paid in shares of stock in the PCT Payor (or stock in any member of the controlled group that includes the controlled participants).

(iii) *Specified form of payment.*—(A) *In general.*—The form of payment selected (subject to the rules of this paragraph (h)) for any PCT, including, in the case of contingent payments, the contingent base and structure of the payments as set forth in paragraph (h)(2)(iii)(B) of this section, must be specified no later than the due date of the applicable tax return (including extensions) for the later of the taxable year of the PCT Payor or PCT Payee that includes the date of that PCT.

(B) *Contingent payments.*—In accordance with paragraph (k)(1)(iv)(A) of this section, a provision of a written contract described in paragraph (k)(1) of this section, or of the additional documentation described in paragraph (k)(2) of this section, that provides for payments for a PCT (or group of PCTs) to be contingent on the exploitation of cost shared intangibles will be respected as consistent with economic substance only if the allocation between the controlled participants of the risks attendant on such form of payment is determinable before the outcomes of such allocation that would have materially affected the PCT pricing are known or reasonably knowable. A contingent payment provision must clearly and unambiguously specify the basis on which the contingent payment obligations are to be determined. In particular, the contingent payment provision must clearly and unambiguously specify the events that give rise to an obligation to make PCT Payments, the royalty base (such as sales or revenues), and the computation used to determine the PCT Payments. The royalty base specified must be one that permits verification of its proper use by reference to books and records maintained by the controlled participants in the normal course of business (for example, books and records maintained for financial accounting or business management purposes).

(C) *Examples.*—The following examples illustrate the principles of this paragraph (h)(2).

Example 1. A CSA provides that PCT Payments with respect to a particular platform contribution shall be contingent payments equal to 15% of the revenues from sales of products that incorporate cost shared intangibles. The terms further permit (but do not require) the controlled participants to adjust such contingent payments in accordance with a formula set forth in the arrangement so that the 15% rate is subject to adjustment by the controlled participants at their discretion on an after-the-fact, uncompensated basis. The Commissioner may impute payment terms that are consistent with economic substance with respect to the platform contribution because the contingent payment provision does not specify the computation used to determine the PCT Payments.

Example 2. Taxpayer, an automobile manufacturer, is a controlled participant in a CSA that involves research and development to perfect certain manufacturing techniques necessary to the actual manufacture of a state-of-the-art, hybrid fuel injection system known as DRL337. The arrangement involves the platform contribution of a design patent covering DRL337. Pursuant to paragraph (h)(2)(iii)(B) of this section, the CSA provides for PCT Payments with respect to the platform contribution of the patent in the form of royalties contingent on sales of automobiles that contain the DRL337 system. However, Taxpayer's system of book- and record-keeping does not enable Taxpayer to track which automobile sales involve automobiles that contain the DRL337 system. Because Taxpayer has not complied with paragraph (h)(2)(iii)(B) of this section, the Commissioner may impute payment terms that are consistent with economic substance and susceptible to verification by the Commissioner.

Example 3. (i) Controlled participants A and B enter into a CSA that provides for PCT Payments from A to B with respect to B's platform contribution, Z, in the form of three annual installment payments due from A to B on the last day of each of the first three years of the CSA.

(ii) On audit, based on all the facts and circumstances, the Commissioner determines that the installment PCT Payments are consistent with an arm's length charge as of the date of the PCT. Accordingly, the Commissioner does not make an adjustment with respect to the PCT Payments in any year.

Example 4. (i) The facts are the same as in *Example 3* except that the CSA contains an additional term with respect to the PCT Payments. Under this provision, A and B further agreed that, if the present value (as of the CSA Start Date) of A's actual divisional operating profit or loss during the three-year period is less than the present value (as of the CSA Start Date) of the divisional operating profit or loss that the parties projected for A upon formation of the CSA for that period, then the third installment payment shall be subject to a compensating adjustment in the amount necessary to reduce the present value (as of the CSA Start Date) of the aggregate PCT Payments for those three years to the amount that would have been calculated if the actual results had been used for the calculation instead of the projected results.

(ii) This provision further specifies that A will pay B an additional amount, $Q, in the first year of the CSA to compensate B for taking on additional downside risk through the contingent payment term described in paragraph (i) of this *Example 4*.

(iii) During the first two years, A pays B installment payments as agreed, as well as the additional amount, $Q. In the third year, A and B determine that the present value (as of the CSA Start Date) of A's actual divisional operating profit or loss during the three-year period is less than the present value (as of the CSA Start Date) of the divisional operating profit or loss that the parties projected for A upon formation of the CSA for that period. A reduces the PCT Payment to B in the third year in the amount necessary to reduce the present value (as of the CSA Start Date) of the aggregate PCT Payments for those three years to the amount that would have been calculated if the actual results had been used for the calculation instead of the projected results.

(iv) On audit, based on all the facts and circumstances, the Commissioner determines that the installment PCT Payments agreed to be paid by A to B were consistent with an arm's length charge as of the date of the PCT. The Commissioner further determines that the contingency was sufficiently specified such that its occurrence or nonoccurrence was unambiguous and determinable; that the projections were reliable; and that the contingency did, in fact, occur. Finally, the Commissioner determines, based on all the facts and circumstances, that $Q was within the arm's length range for the additional allocation of risk to B. Accordingly, no adjustment is made with respect to the installment PCT Payments, or the additional PCT Payment for the contingent payment term, in any year.

Example 5. (i) The facts are the same as in *Example 4* except that the CSA states the amount that A will pay B for the contingent payment term is $X, an amount that is less than $Q, and A pays B $X in the first year of the CSA.

(ii) On audit, based on all the facts and circumstances, the Commissioner determines that the installment PCT Payments agreed to be paid by A to B were consistent with an arm's length charge as of the date of the PCT. The Commissioner further determines that the contingency was sufficiently specified such that its occurrence or nonoccurrence was unambiguous and determinable; that the projections were reliable; and that the contingency did, in fact, occur. However, the Commissioner also determines, based on all the facts and circumstances, that the additional PCT Payment of $X from A to B for the contingent payment term was not an arm's length charge for the additional allocation of risk as of the CSA Start Date in connection with the contingent payment term. Accordingly, the Commissioner makes an adjustment to B's results equal to the difference between $X and the median of the arm's length range of charges for the contingent payment term.

Example 6. (i) The facts are the same as in Example 3 except that A and B further agreed that, if the present value (as of the CSA Start Date) of A's actual divisional operating profit or loss during the three-year period is either less or greater than the present value (as of the CSA Start Date) of the divisional operating profit or loss that the parties projected for A upon formation of the CSA for that period, then A may make a compensating adjustment to the third installment payment in the amount necessary to reduce (if actual divisional operating profit or loss is less than the projections) or increase (if actual divisional operating profit or loss exceeds the projections) the present value (as of the CSA Start Date) of the aggregate PCT Payments for those three years to the amount that would have been calculated if the actual results had been used for the calculation instead of the projected results.

(ii) On audit, the Commissioner determines that the contingent payment term lacks economic substance under §§1.482-1(d)(3)(iii)(B) and 1.482-7(h)(2)(iii)(B). It lacks economic substance because the allocation of the risks between A and B was indeterminate as of the CSA Start Date due to the elective nature of the potential compensating adjustments. Specifically, the parties agreed upfront only that A might make compensating adjustments to the installment payments. By the terms of the agreement, A could decide whether to make such adjustments after the outcome of the risks was known or reasonably knowable. Even though the contingency and potential compensating adjustments were clearly defined in the CSA, no compensating adjustments were required by the CSA regardless of the occurrence or nonoccurrence of the contingency. As a result, the contingent payment terms did not clearly and unambiguously specify the events that give rise to an obligation to make PCT Payments, and, accordingly, the obligation to make compensating adjustments pursuant to the contingency was indeterminate. The contingent payment term allows the taxpayer to make adjustments that are favorable to its overall tax position in those years where the agreement allows it to make such adjustments, but decline to exercise its right to make any adjustment in those years in which such an adjustment would be unfavorable to its overall tax position. Such terms do not reflect a substantive upfront allocation of risk. In addition, the vagueness of the agreement makes it impossible to determine whether such contingent payment term warrants an additional arm's length charge and, if so, how much.

(iii) Accordingly, the Commissioner may disregard the contingent payment term under §§1.482-1(d)(3)(ii)(B)(1) and 1.482-7(k)(1)(iv) and may impute other contractual terms in its place consistent with the economic substance of the CSA.

Example 7. (i) The facts are the same as in *Example 6* except that the contingent payment term provides that, if the present value (as of the CSA Start Date) of A's actual divisional operating profit or loss during the three-year period is either less or greater than the present value (as of the CSA Start Date) of the divisional operating profit or loss that the parties projected for A upon formation of the CSA for that period, then A will make a compensating adjustment to the third installment payment. The CSA does not specify the amount of (or a formula for) any such compensating adjustments.

(ii) On audit, the Commissioner determines that the contingent payment term lacks economic substance under §§1.482-1(d)(3)(iii)(B) and 1.482-7(h)(2)(iii)(B). It lacks economic substance because the allocation of the risks between A and B was indeterminate as of the CSA Start Date due to the failure to specify the amount of (or a formula for) the compensating adjustments that must be made if a contingency occurs. The basis on which the compensating adjustments were to be determined was neither clear nor unambiguous. Even though the contingency was clearly defined in the CSA and the requirement of a compensating adjustment in the event of a contingency was clearly specified in the CSA, the parties had no agreement regarding the amount of such compensating adjustments. As a result, the computation used to determine the PCT Payments was indeterminate. The parties could choose to make a small positive compensating adjustment if the actual results turned out to be much greater than the projections, and could choose to make a significant negative compensating adjustment if the actual results turned out to be less than the projections. Such terms do not reflect a substantive upfront allocation of risk. In addition, the vagueness of the agreement makes it impossible to determine whether such contingent payment term warrants an additional arm's length charge and, if so, how much.

(iii) Accordingly, the Commissioner may disregard the contingent price term under §§1.482-1(d)(3)(ii)(B)(1) and 1.482-7(k)(1)(iv) and may impute other contractual terms in its place consistent with economic substance of the CSA.

(iv) *Conversion from fixed to contingent form of payment.*—With regard to a conversion of a fixed present value to a contingent form of payment, see paragraphs (g)(2)(v) (Discount rate) and (vi) (Financial projections) of this section.

(3) *Coordination of best method rule and form of payment.*—A method described in paragraph (g)(1) of this section evaluates the arm's length amount charged in a PCT in terms of a form of payment (method payment form). For example, the method payment form for the acquisition price method described in paragraph (g)(5) of this section, and for the market capitalization method described in paragraph (g)(6) of this section, is fixed payment. Applications of the income method provide different method payment forms. See paragraphs (g)(4)(i)(E) and (iv) of this section. The method payment form may not necessarily correspond to the form of payment specified pursuant to paragraphs (h)(2)(iii) and (k)(2)(ii)(l) of this section (specified payment form). The determination under §1.482-1(c) of the method that provides the most reliable measure of an arm's length

result is to be made without regard to whether the respective method payment forms under the competing methods correspond to the specified payment form. If the method payment form of the method determined under § 1.482-1(c) to provide the most reliable measure of an arm's length result differs from the specified payment form, then the conversion from such method payment form to such specified payment form will be made to the satisfaction of the Commissioner.

(i) *Allocations by the Commissioner in connection with a CSA.*—(1) In general. The Commissioner may make allocations to adjust the results of a controlled transaction in connection with a CSA so that the results are consistent with an arm's length result, in accordance with the provisions of this paragraph (i).

(2) *CST allocations.*—(i) *In general.*—The Commissioner may make allocations to adjust the results of a CST so that the results are consistent with an arm's length result, including any allocations to make each controlled participant's IDC share, as determined under paragraph (d)(4) of this section, equal to that participant's RAB share, as determined under paragraph (e)(1) of this section. Such allocations may result from, for purposes of CST determinations, adjustments to—

(A) Redetermine IDCs by adding any costs (or cost categories) that are directly identified with, or are reasonably allocable to, the IDA, or by removing any costs (or cost categories) that are not IDCs;

(B) Reallocate costs between the IDA and other business activities;

(C) Improve the reliability of the selection or application of the basis used for measuring benefits for purposes of estimating a controlled participant's RAB share;

(D) Improve the reliability of the projections used to estimate RAB shares, including adjustments described in paragraph (i)(2)(ii) of this section; and

(E) Allocate among the controlled participants any unallocated interests in cost shared intangibles.

(ii) *Adjustments to improve the reliability of projections used to estimate RAB shares.*—(A) *Unreliable projections.*—A significant divergence between projected benefit shares and benefit shares adjusted to take into account any available actual benefits to date (adjusted benefit shares) may indicate that the projections were not reliable for purposes of estimating RAB shares. In such a case, the Commissioner may use adjusted benefit shares as the most reliable measure of RAB shares and adjust IDC shares accordingly. The projected benefit shares will not be considered unreliable, as applied in a given taxable year, based on a divergence from adjusted benefit shares for every controlled participant that is less than or equal to 20% of the participant's projected benefits share. Further, the Commissioner will not make an allocation based on such divergence if the difference is due to an extraordinary event, beyond the control of the controlled participants, which could not reasonably have been anticipated at the time that costs were shared. The Commissioner generally may adjust projections of benefits used to calculate benefit shares in accordance with the provisions of § 1.482-1. In particular, if benefits are projected over a period of years, and the projections for initial years of the period prove to be unreliable, this may indicate that the projections for the remaining years of the period are also unreliable and thus should be adjusted. For purposes of this paragraph (i)(2)(ii)(A), all controlled participants that are not U.S. persons are treated as a single controlled participant. Therefore, an adjustment based on an unreliable projection of RAB shares will be made to the IDC shares of foreign controlled participants only if there is a matching adjustment to the IDC shares of controlled participants that are U.S. persons. Nothing in this paragraph (i)(2)(ii)(A) prevents the Commissioner from making an allocation if a taxpayer did not use the most reliable basis for measuring anticipated benefits. For example, if the taxpayer measures its anticipated benefits based on units sold, and the Commissioner determines that another basis is more reliable for measuring anticipated benefits, then the fact that actual units sold were within 20% of the projected unit sales will not preclude an allocation under this section.

(B) *Foreign-to-foreign adjustments.*—Adjustments to IDC shares based on an unreliable projection also may be made among foreign controlled participants if the variation between actual and projected benefits has the effect of substantially reducing U.S. tax.

(C) *Correlative adjustments to PCTs.*—Correlative adjustments will be made to any PCT Payments of a fixed amount that were determined based on RAB shares that are subsequently adjusted on a finding that they were based on unreliable projections. No correlative adjustments will be made to contingent PCT Payments regardless of whether RAB shares were used as a parameter in the valuation of those payments.

(D) *Examples.*—The following examples illustrate the principles of this paragraph (i)(2)(ii):

Example 1. U.S. Parent (USP) and Foreign Subsidiary (FS) enter into a CSA to develop new food products, dividing costs on the basis of projected sales two years in the future. In Year 1, USP and FS project that their sales in Year 3 will be equal, and they divide costs accordingly. In Year 3, the Commissioner examines the controlled participants' method for dividing costs. USP and FS actually accounted for 42% and 58% of total sales, respectively. The Commissioner agrees that sales two years in the future provide a reliable basis for estimating benefit shares. Because the differences between USP's and FS's adjusted and projected benefit shares are less than 20% of their projected benefit shares, the projection of future benefits for Year 3 is reliable.

Example 2. The facts are the same as in *Example 1*, except that in Year 3 USP and FS actually accounted for 35% and 65% of total sales, respectively. The divergence between USP's projected and adjusted benefit shares is greater than 20% of USP's projected benefit share and is not due to an extraordinary event beyond the control of the controlled participants. The Commissioner concludes that the projected benefit shares were unreliable, and uses adjusted benefit shares as the basis for an adjustment to the cost shares borne by USP and FS.

Example 3. U.S. Parent (USP), a U.S. corporation, and its foreign subsidiary (FS) enter into a CSA in Year 1. They project that they will begin to receive benefits from cost shared intangibles in Years 4 through 6, and that USP will receive 60% of total benefits and FS 40% of total benefits. In Years 4 through 6, USP and FS actually receive 50% each of the total benefits. In evaluating the reliability of the controlled participants' projections, the Commissioner compares the adjusted benefit shares to the projected benefit shares. Although USP's adjusted benefit share (50%) is within 20% of its projected benefit share (60%), FS's adjusted benefit share (50%) is not within 20% of its projected benefit share (40%). Based on this discrepancy, the Commissioner may conclude that the controlled participants' projections were unreliable and may use adjusted benefit shares as the basis for an adjustment to the cost shares borne by USP and FS.

Example 4. Three controlled taxpayers, USP, FS1, and FS2 enter into a CSA. FS1 and FS2 are foreign. USP is a domestic corporation that controls all the stock of FS1 and FS2. The controlled participants project that they will share the total benefits of the cost shared intangibles in the following percentages: USP 50%; FS1 30%; and FS2 20%. Adjusted benefit shares are as follows: USP 45%; FS1 25%; and FS2 30%. In evaluating the reliability of the controlled participants' projections, the Commissioner compares these adjusted benefit shares to the projected benefit shares. For this purpose, FS1 and FS2 are treated as a single controlled participant. The adjusted benefit share received by USP (45%) is within 20% of its projected benefit share (50%). In addition, the non-US controlled participant' adjusted benefit share (55%) is also within 20% of their projected benefit share (50%). Therefore, the Commissioner concludes that the controlled participant's projections of future benefits were reliable, despite the fact that FS2's adjusted benefit share (30%) is not within 20% of its projected benefit share (20%).

Example 5. The facts are the same as in *Example 4*. In addition, the Commissioner determines that FS2 has significant operating losses and has no earnings and profits, and that FS1 is profitable and has earnings and profits. Based on all the evidence, the Commissioner concludes that the controlled participants arranged that FS1 would bear a larger cost share than appropriate in order to reduce FS1's earnings and profits and thereby reduce inclusions USP otherwise would be deemed to have on account of FS1 under subpart F. Pursuant to paragraph (i)(2)(ii)(B) of this section, the Commissioner may make an adjustment solely to the cost shares borne by FS1 and FS2 because FS2's projection of future benefits was unreliable and the variation between adjusted and projected benefits had the effect of substantially reducing USP's U.S. income tax liability (on account of FS1 subpart F income).

Example 6. (i)(A) Foreign Parent (FP) and U.S. Subsidiary (USS) enter into a CSA in 1996 to develop a new treatment for baldness. USS's interest in any treatment developed is the right to produce and sell the treatment in the U.S. market while FP retains rights to produce and sell the treatment in the rest of the world. USS and FP measure their anticipated benefits from the CSA based on their respective projected future sales of the baldness treatment. The following sales projections are used:

Sales [In millions of dollars]

Year	USS	FP
1	5	10
2	20	20
3	30	30
4	40	40
5	40	40
6	40	40
7	40	40
8	20	20
9	10	10
10	5	5

(B) In Year 1, the first year of sales, USS is projected to have lower sales than FP due to lags in U.S. regulatory approval for the baldness treatment. In each subsequent year, USS and FP are projected to have equal sales. Sales are projected to build over the first three years of the period, level off for several years, and then decline over the final years of the period as new and improved baldness treatments reach the market.

(ii) To account for USS's lag in sales in the Year 1, the present discounted value of sales over the period is used as the basis for measuring benefits. Based on the risk associated with this venture, a discount rate of 10 percent is selected. The present discounted value of projected sales is determined to be approximately $154.4 million for USS and $158.9 million for FP. On this basis USS and FP are projected to obtain approximately 49.3% and 50.7% of the benefit, respectively, and the costs of developing the baldness treatment are shared accordingly.

(iii) (A) In Year 6, the Commissioner examines the CSA. USS and FP have obtained the following sales results through Year 5:

Sales [In millions of dollars]

Year	USS	FP
1	0	17
2	17	35
3	25	41
4	38	41
5	39	41

(B) USS's sales initially grew more slowly than projected while FP's sales grew more quickly. In each of the first three years of the period, the share of total sales of at least one of the parties diverged by over 20% from its projected share of sales. However, by Year 5 both parties' sales had leveled off at approximately their projected values. Taking into account this leveling off of sales and all the facts and circumstances, the Commissioner determines that it is appropriate to use the original projections for the remaining years of sales. Combining the actual results through Year 5 with the projections for subsequent years, and using a discount rate of 10%, the present discounted value of sales is approximately $141.6 million for USS and $187.3 million for FP. This result implies that USS and FP obtain approximately 43.1% and 56.9%, respectively, of the anticipated benefits from the baldness treatment. Because these adjusted benefit shares are within 20% of the benefit shares calculated based on the original sales projections, the Commissioner determines that, based on the difference between adjusted and projected benefit shares, the original projections were not unreliable. No adjustment is made based on the difference between adjusted and projected benefit shares.

Example 7. (i) The facts are the same as in *Example 6*, except that the actual sales results through Year 5 are as follows:

Sales [In millions of dollars]

Year	USS	FP
1	0	17
2	17	35
3	25	44
4	34	54
5	36	55

(ii) Based on the discrepancy between the projections and the actual results and on consideration of all the facts, the Commissioner determines that for the remaining years the following sales projections are more reliable than the original projections:

Sales [In millions of dollars]

Year	USS	FP
6	36	55
7	36	55
8	18	28
9	9	14
10	4.5	7

(iii) Combining the actual results through Year 5 with the projections for subsequent years, and using a discount rate of 10%, the present discounted value of sales is approximately $131.2 million for USS and $229.4 million for FP. This result implies that USS and FP obtain approximately 35.4% and 63.6%, respectively, of the anticipated benefits from the baldness treatment. These adjusted benefit shares diverge by greater than 20% from the benefit shares calculated based on the original sales projections, and the Commissioner determines that, based on the difference between adjusted and projected benefit shares, the original projections were unreliable. The Commissioner adjusts cost shares for each of the taxable years under examination to conform them to the recalculated shares of anticipated benefits.

(iii) *Timing of CST allocations.*—If the Commissioner makes an allocation to adjust the results of a CST, the allocation must be reflected for tax purposes in the year in which the IDCs were incurred. When a CST payment is owed by one controlled participant to another controlled participant, the Commissioner may make appropriate allocations to reflect an arm's length rate of interest for the time value of money, consistent with the provisions of § 1.482-2(a) (Loans or advances).

(3) *PCT allocations.*—The Commissioner may make allocations to adjust the results of a PCT so that the results are consistent with an arm's length result in accordance with the provisions of the applicable sections of the regulations under section 482, as determined pursuant to paragraph (a)(2) of this section.

(4) *Allocations regarding changes in participation under a CSA.*—The Commissioner may make allocations to adjust the results of any controlled transaction described in paragraph (f) of this section if the controlled participants do not reflect arm's length results in relation to any such transaction.

(5) *Allocations when CSTs are consistently and materially disproportionate to RAB shares.*—If a controlled participant bears IDC shares that are consistently and materially greater or lesser than its RAB

share, then the Commissioner may conclude that the economic substance of the arrangement between the controlled participants is inconsistent with the terms of the CSA. In such a case, the Commissioner may disregard such terms and impute an agreement that is consistent with the controlled participants' course of conduct, under which a controlled participant that bore a disproportionately greater IDC share received additional interests in the cost shared intangibles. See §§1.482-1(d)(3)(ii)(B) (Identifying contractual terms) and 1.482-4(f)(3)(ii) (Identification of owner). Such additional interests will consist of partial undivided interests in the other controlled participant's interest in the cost shared intangible. Accordingly, that controlled participant must receive arm's length consideration from any controlled participant whose IDC share is less than its RAB share over time, under the provisions of §§1.482-1 and 1.482-4 through 1.482-6 to provide compensation for the latter controlled participants' use of such partial undivided interest.

(6) *Periodic adjustments.*—(i) *In general.*—Subject to the exceptions in paragraph (i)(6)(vi) of this section, the Commissioner may make periodic adjustments for an open taxable year (the Adjustment Year) and for all subsequent taxable years for the duration of the CSA Activity with respect to all PCT Payments, if the Commissioner determines that, for a particular PCT (the Trigger PCT), a particular controlled participant that owes or owed a PCT Payment relating to that PCT (such controlled participant being referred to as the PCT Payor for purposes of this paragraph (i)(6)) has realized an Actually Experienced Return Ratio (AERR) that is outside the Periodic Return Ratio Range (PRRR). The satisfaction of the condition stated in the preceding sentence is referred to as a Periodic Trigger. See paragraphs (i)(6)(ii) through (vi) of this section regarding the PRRR, the AERR, and periodic adjustments. In determining whether to make such adjustments, the Commissioner may consider whether the outcome as adjusted more reliably reflects an arm's length result under all the relevant facts and circumstances, including any information known as of the Determination Date. The Determination Date is the date of the relevant determination by the Commissioner. The failure of the Commissioner to determine for an earlier taxable year that a PCT Payment was not arm's length will not preclude the Commissioner from making a periodic adjustment for a subsequent year. A periodic adjustment under this paragraph (i)(6) may be made without regard to whether the taxable year of the Trigger PCT or any other PCT remains open for statute of limitations purposes or whether a periodic adjustment has previously been made with respect to any PCT Payment.

(ii) *PRRR.*—Except as provided in the next sentence, the *PRRR* will consist of return ratios that are not less than .667 nor more than 1.5. Alternatively, if the controlled participants have not substantially complied with the documentation requirements referenced in paragraph (k) of this section, as modified, if applicable, by paragraphs (m)(2) and (3) of this section, the PRRR will consist of return ratios that are not less than .8 nor more than 1.25.

(iii) *AERR.*—(A) *In general.*—The *AERR* is the present value of total profits (PVTP) divided by the present value of investment (PVI). In computing PVTP and PVI, present values are computed using the applicable discount rate (ADR), and all information available as of the Determination Date is taken into account.

(B) *PVTP.*—The *PVTP* is the present value, as of the CSA Start Date, as defined in section (j)(1)(i) of this section, of the PCT Payor's actually experienced divisional profits or losses from the CSA Start Date through the end of the Adjustment Year.

(C) *PVI.*—The *PVI* is the present value, as of the CSA Start Date, of the PCT Payor's investment associated with the CSA Activity, defined as the sum of its cost contributions and its PCT Payments, from the CSA Start Date through the end of the Adjustment Year. For purposes of computing the PVI, PCT Payments means all PCT Payments due from a PCT Payor before netting against PCT Payments due from other controlled participants pursuant to paragraph (j)(3)(ii) of this section.

(iv) *ADR.*—(A) *In general.*—Except as provided in paragraph (i)(6)(iv)(B) of this section, the ADR is the discount rate pursuant to paragraph (g)(2)(v) of this section, subject to such adjustments as the Commissioner determines appropriate.

(B) *Publicly traded companies.*—If the PCT Payor meets the conditions of paragraph (i)(6)(iv)(C) of this section, the ADR is the PCT Payor WACC as of the date of the Trigger PCT. However, if the Commissioner determines, or the controlled participants establish to the satisfaction of the Commissioner, that a discount rate other than the PCT Payor WACC better reflects the degree of risk of the CSA Activity as of such date, the ADR is such other discount rate.

(C) *Publicly traded.*—A PCT Payor meets the conditions of this paragraph (i)(6)(iv)(C) if—

(1) Stock of the PCT Payor is publicly traded; or

(2) Stock of the PCT Payor is not publicly traded, provided the PCT Payor is included in a group of companies for which consolidated financial statements are prepared; and a publicly traded company in such group owns, directly or indirectly, stock in PCT Payor. Stock of a company is publicly traded within the meaning of this paragraph (i)(6)(iv)(C) if such stock is regularly traded on an established United States securities market and the company issues financial statements prepared in accordance with United States generally accepted accounting principles for the taxable year.

(D) *PCT Payor WACC.*—The *PCT Payor WACC* is the WACC, as defined in paragraph (j)(1)(i) of this section, of the PCT Payor or the publicly traded company described in paragraph (i)(6)(iv)(C)(2)(ii) of this section, as the case may be.

(E) *Generally accepted accounting principles.*—For purposes of paragraph (i)(6)(iv)(C) of this section, a financial statement prepared in accordance with a comprehensive body of generally accepted accounting principles other than United States generally accepted accounting principles is considered to be prepared in accordance with United States generally accepted accounting principles provided that the amounts of debt, equity, and interest expense are reflected in any reconciliation between such other accounting principles and United States generally accepted accounting principles required to be incorporated into the financial statement by the securities laws governing companies whose stock is regularly traded on United States securities markets.

(v) *Determination of periodic adjustments.*—In the event of a Periodic Trigger, subject to paragraph (i)(6)(vi) of this section, the Commissioner may make periodic adjustments with respect to all PCT Payments between all PCT Payors and PCT Payees for the Adjustment Year and all subsequent years for the duration of the CSA Activity pursuant to the residual profit split method as provided in paragraph (g)(7) of this section, subject to the further modifications in this paragraph (i)(6)(v). A periodic adjustment may be made for a particular taxable year without regard to whether the taxable years of the Trigger PCT or other PCTs remain open for statute of limitation purposes.

(A) *In general.*—Periodic adjustments are determined by the following steps:

(1) First, determine the present value, as of the date of the Trigger PCT, of the PCT Payments under paragraph (g)(7)(iii)(C)(3) of this section pursuant to the Adjusted RPSM as defined in paragraph (i)(6)(v)(B) of this section (first step result).

(2) Second, convert the first step result into a stream of contingent payments on a base of reasonably anticipated divisional profits or losses over the entire duration of the CSA Activity, using a level royalty rate (second step rate). See paragraph (h)(2)(iv) of this section (Conversion from fixed to contingent form of payment). This conversion is made based on all information known as of the Determination Date.

(3) Third, apply the second step rate to the actual divisional profit or loss for taxable years preceding and including the Adjustment Year to yield a stream of contingent payments for such years, and convert such stream to a present value as of the CSA Start Date under the principles of paragraph (g)(2)(v) of this section (third step result). For this purpose, the second step rate applied to a loss for a particular year will yield a negative contingent payment for that year.

(4) Fourth, convert any actual PCT Payments up through the Adjustment Year to a present value as of the CSA Start Date under the principles of paragraph (g)(2)(v) of this section. Then subtract such amount from the third step result. Determine the nominal amount in the Adjustment Year that would have a present value as of the CSA Start Date equal to the present value determined in the previous sentence to determine the periodic adjustment in the Adjustment Year.

(5) Fifth, apply the second step rate to the actual divisional profit or loss for each taxable year after the Adjustment Year up to and including the taxable year that includes the Determination Date to yield a stream of contingent payments for such years. For this purpose, the second step rate applied to a loss will yield a negative contingent payment for that year. Then subtract from each such

payment any actual PCT Payment made for the same year to determine the periodic adjustment for such taxable year.

(6) For each taxable year subsequent to the year that includes the Determination Date, the periodic adjustment for such taxable year (which is in lieu of any PCT Payment that would otherwise be payable for that year under the taxpayer's position) equals the second step rate applied to the actual divisional profit or loss for that year. For this purpose, the second step rate applied to a loss for a particular year will yield a negative contingent payment for that year.

(7) If the periodic adjustment for any taxable year is a positive amount, then it is an additional PCT Payment owed from the PCT Payor to the PCT Payee for such year. If the periodic adjustment for any taxable year is a negative amount, then it is an additional PCT Payment owed by the PCT Payee to the PCT Payor for such year.

(B) *Adjusted RPSM as of Determination Date.*—The Adjusted RPSM is the residual profit split method pursuant to paragraph (g)(7) of this section applied to determine the present value, as of the date of the Trigger PCT, of the PCT Payments under paragraph (g)(7)(iii)(C)(3) of this section, with the following modifications.

(1) Actual results up through the Determination Date shall be substituted for what otherwise were the projected results over such period, as reasonably anticipated as of the date of the Trigger PCT.

(2) Projected results for the balance of the CSA Activity after the Determination Date, as reasonably anticipated as of the Determination Date, shall be substituted for what otherwise were the projected results over such period, as reasonably anticipated as of the date of the Trigger PCT.

(3) The requirement in paragraph (g)(7)(i) of this section, that at least two controlled participants make significant nonroutine contributions, does not apply.

(vi) *Exceptions to periodic adjustments.*—(A) *Controlled participants establish periodic adjustment not warranted.*—No periodic adjustment will be made under paragraphs (i)(6)(i) and (v) of this section if the controlled participants establish to the satisfaction of the Commissioner that all the conditions described in one of paragraphs (i)(6)(vi)(A)(1) through (4) of this section apply with respect to the Trigger PCT.

(1) Transactions involving the same platform contribution as in the Trigger PCT.

(i) The same platform contribution is furnished to an uncontrolled taxpayer under substantially the same circumstances as those of the relevant Trigger PCT and with a similar form of payment as the Trigger PCT;

(ii) This transaction serves as the basis for the application of the comparable uncontrolled transaction method described in paragraph (g)(3) of this section, in the first year and all subsequent years in which substantial PCT Payments relating to the Trigger PCT were required to be paid; and

(iii) The amount of those PCT Payments in that first year was arm's length.

(2) Results not reasonably anticipated.—The differential between the AERR and the nearest bound of the PRRR is due to extraordinary events beyond the control of the controlled participants that could not reasonably have been anticipated as of the date of the Trigger PCT.

(3) Reduced AERR does not cause Periodic Trigger.—The Periodic Trigger would not have occurred had the PCT Payor's divisional profits or losses used to calculate its PVTP both taken into account expenses on account of operating cost contributions and routine platform contributions, and excluded those profits or losses attributable to the PCT Payor's routine contributions to its exploitation of cost shared intangibles, nonroutine contributions to the CSA Activity, operating cost contributions, and routine platform contributions.

(4) Increased AFRR does not cause Periodic Trigger.—*(i)* The Periodic Trigger would not have occurred had the divisional profits or losses of the PCT Payor used to calculate its PVTP included its reasonably anticipated divisional profits or losses after the Adjustment Year from the CSA Activity, including from its routine contributions, its operating cost contributions, and its nonroutine contributions to that activity, and had the cost contributions and PCT Payments of the PCT Payor used to calculate its PVI included its reasonably anticipated cost contributions and PCT Payments after the Adjustment Year. The reasonably anticipated amounts in the previous sentence are determined based on all information available as of the Determination Date.

(ii) For purposes of this paragraph (i)(6)(vi)(A)(4), the controlled participants may, if they wish, assume that the average yearly divisional profits or losses for all taxable years prior to and including the Adjustment Year, in which there has been substantial exploitation of cost shared intangibles resulting from the CSA (exploitation years), will continue to be earned in each year over a period of years equal to 15 minus the number of exploitation years prior to and including the Determination Date.

(B) *Circumstances in which Periodic Trigger deemed not to occur.*—No Periodic Trigger will be deemed to have occurred at the times and in the circumstances described in paragraph (i)(6)(vi)(B)(1) or (2) of this section.

(1) 10-year period.—In any year subsequent to the 10-year period beginning with the first taxable year in which there is substantial exploitation of cost shared intangibles resulting from the CSA, if the AERR determined is within the PRRR for each year of such 10-year period.

(2) 5-year period.—In any year of the 5-year period beginning with the first taxable year in which there is substantial exploitation of cost shared intangibles resulting from the CSA, if the AERR falls below the lower bound of the PRRR.

(vii) *Examples.*—The following examples illustrate the rules of this paragraph (i)(6):

Example 1. (i) For simplicity of calculation in this *Example 1*, all financial flows are assumed to occur at the beginning of the year. At the beginning of Year 1, USP, a publicly traded U.S. company, and FS, its wholly-owned foreign subsidiary, enter into a CSA to develop new technology for cell phones. USP has a platform contribution, the rights for an in-process technology that when developed will improve the clarity of calls, for which compensation is due from FS. FS has no platform contributions to the CSA, no operating contributions, and no operating cost contributions. USP and FS agree to fixed PCT payments of $40 million in Year 1 and $10 million per year for Years 2 through 10. At the beginning of Year 1, the weighted average cost of capital of the controlled group that includes USP and FS is 15%. In Year 9, the Commissioner audits Years 5 through 7 of the CSA and considers whether any periodic adjustments should be made. USP and FS have substantially complied with the documentation requirements of paragraph (k) of this section.

(ii) FS experiences the results reported in the following table from its participation in the CSA through Year 7. In the table, all present values (PV) are reported as of the CSA Start Date, which is the same as the date of the PCT (and reflect a 15% discount rate as discussed in paragraph (iii) of this *Example 1*). Thus, in any year the present value of the cumulative investment is PVI and of the cumulative divisional profit or loss is PVTP. All amounts in this table and the tables that follow are reported in millions of dollars and cost contributions are referred to as "CCs" (for simplicity of calculation in this *Example 1*, all financial flows are assumed to occur at the beginning of the year).

a	b	c	d	e	f	g	h
Year	Sales	Non-CC Costs	CCs	PCT Payments	Investment (d+e)	Divisional Profit or Loss (b-c)	AERR (PVTP/PVI) (g/f)
1	0	0	15	40	55	0	
2	0	0	17	10	27	0	
3	0	0	18	10	28	0	
4	705	662	20	10	30	46	
5	886	718	22	10	32	168	
6	1,113	680	24	10	34	433	

a	b	c	d	e	f	g	h
Year	Sales	Non-CC Costs	CCs	PCT Payments	Investment (d+e)	Divisional Profit or Loss (b-c)	AERR (PVTP/PVI) (g/f)
7	1,179	747	27	10	37	432	
PV through Year 5	970	846	69	69	138	124	0.90
PV through Year 6	1,523	1,184	81	74	155	340	2.20
PV through Year 7	2,033	1,507	93	78	171	526	3.09

(iii) Because USP is publicly traded in the United States and is a member 163 of the controlled group to which FS (the PCT Payor) belongs, for purposes of calculating the AERR for FS, the present values of its PVTP and PVI are determined using an ADR of 15%, the weighted average cost of capital of the controlled group. (It is assumed that no other rate was determined or established, under paragraph (i)(6)(iv)(B) of this section, to better reflect the relevant degree of risk.) At a 15% discount rate, the PVTP, calculated as of Year 1, and based on actual profits realized by FS through Year 7 from exploiting the new cell phone technology developed by the CSA, is $526 million. The PVI, based on FS's cost contributions and its PCT Payments, is $171 million. The AERR for FS is equal to its PVTP divided by its PVI, $526 million/$171 million, or 3.09. There is a Periodic Trigger because FS's AERR of 3.09 falls outside the PRRR of .67 to 1.5, the applicable PRRR for controlled participants complying with the documentation requirements of this section.

(iv) At the time of the Determination Date, it is determined that the first Adjustment Year in which a Periodic Trigger occurred was Year 6, when the AERR of FS was determined to be 2.20. It is also determined that for Year 6 none of the exceptions to periodic adjustments described in paragraph (i)(6)(vi) of this section applies. The Commissioner exercises its discretion under paragraph (i)(6)(i) of this section to make periodic adjustments using Year 6 as the Adjustment Year. Therefore, the arm's length PCT Payments from FS to USP shall be determined for each taxable year using the adjusted residual profit split method described in paragraphs (g)(7) and (i)(6)(v)(B) of this section. Periodic adjustments will be made for each year to the extent the PCT Payments actually made by FS differ from the PCT Payment calculation under the adjusted residual profit split method.

(v) It is determined, as of the Determination Date, that the cost shared intangibles will be exploited through Year 10. FS's return for routine contributions (determined by the Commissioner, based on the return for comparable functions undertaken by comparable uncontrolled companies, to be 8% of non-CC costs), and its actual and projected results, are described in the following table.

a	b	c	d	e	f	g
Year	Sales	Non-CC Costs	Divisional profit or loss (b-c)	CCs	Routine Return	Residual Profit (d-e-f)
1	0	0	0	15	0	-15
2	0	0	0	17	0	-17
3	0	0	0	18	0	-18
4	705	662	43	20	53	-30
5	886	718	168	22	57	89
6	1,113	680	433	24	54	355
7	1,179	747	432	27	60	345
8	1,238	822	416	29	66	321
9	1,300	894	406	32	72	302
10	1,365	974	391	35	78	278
Cumulative PV through Year 10 as of CSA Start Date	3,312	2,385	927	124	191	612

(vi) The periodic adjustments are calculated in a series of steps set out in paragraph (i)(6)(v)(A) of this section. First, a lump sum for the PCT Payment is determined using the adjusted residual profit split method. Under the method, based on the considerations discussed in paragraph (g)(2)(v) of this section, the appropriate discount rate is 15% per year. The nonroutine residual divisional profit or loss described in paragraph (g)(7)(iii)(B) of this section is $612 million. Further, under paragraph (g)(7)(iii)(C) of this section, the entire nonroutine residual divisional profit constitutes the PCT Payment because only USP has nonroutine contributions.

(vii) In step two, the first step result ($612 million) is converted into a level royalty rate based on the reasonably anticipated divisional profit or losses of the CSA Activity, the PV of which is reported in the table above (net PV of divisional profit or loss for Years 1 through 10 is $927 million). Consequently, the step two result is a level royalty rate of 66.0% ($612/$927) of the divisional profit in Years 1 through 10.

(viii) In step three, the Commissioner calculates the PCT Payments due through Year 6 by applying the step two royalty rate to the actual divisional profits for each year and then determines the aggregate PV of these PCT Payments as of the CSA Start Date ($224 million as reported in the following table). In step four, the PCT Payments actually made through Year 6 are similarly converted to PV as of the CSA Start Date ($74 million) and subtracted from the amount determined in step three ($224 million - $74 million = $150 million). That difference of $150 million, representing a net PV as of the CSA Start Date, is then converted to a nominal amount, as of the Adjustment Year, of equivalent present value (again using a discount rate of 15%). That nominal amount is $302 million (not shown in the table), and is the periodic adjustment in Year 6.

a	b	c	d	e
Year	Divisional Profit	Royalty Rate	Nominal Royalty Due under adjusted RPSM (b*c)	Nominal Payments made
Year 1	0	66.0%	$0	$40
Year 2	0	66.0%	$0	$10
Year 3	0	66.0%	$0	$10
Year 4	43	66.0%	$28	$10
Year 5	168	66.0%	$111	$10
Year 6	433	66.0%	$286	$10
Cumulative PV as of Year 1			$224	$74

(ix) Under step five, the royalties due from FS to USP for Year 7 (the year after the Adjustment Year) through Year 9 (the year including the Determination Date) are determined. (These determinations are made for Years 8 and 9 after the divisional profit for those years becomes available.) For each year, the periodic adjustment is a PCT Payment due in addition to the $10 million PCT Payment that must otherwise be paid under the CSA as described in paragraph (i) of this *Example 1.* That periodic adjustment is calculated as the product of the step two royalty rate and the divisional profit, minus the $10 million that was otherwise paid for that year. The calculations are shown in the following table:

a	b	c	d	E	f
Year	Divisional profit	Royalty rate	Royalty due (b*c)	PCT Payments otherwise paid	Periodic adjustment (d-e)
7	432	66.0%	$285	$10	$275
8	416	66.0%	$275	$10	$265
9	406	66.0%	$268	$10	$258

(x) Under step six, the periodic adjustment for Year 10 (the only exploitation year after the year containing the Determination Date) will be determined by applying the step two royalty rate to the divisional profit. This periodic adjustment is a PCT Payment payable from FS to USP, and is in lieu of the $10 payment otherwise due. The calculations are shown in the following table, based on a divisional profit of $391 million. USP and FS experienced the following results in Year 10.

Year	Divisional profit	Royalty rate	Royalty due	PCT Payment called for under original agreement but not made	Periodic adjustment
10	391	66.0%	$258	$10 (not paid)	$258

Example 2. The facts are the same as in paragraphs (i) through (iii) of *Example 1.* At the time of the Determination Date, it is determined that the first Adjustment Year in which a Periodic Trigger occurred was Year 6, when the AERR of FS was determined to be 2.73. Upon further investigation as to what may have caused the high return in FS's market, the Commissioner learns that, in Years 4 through 6, USP's leading competitors experienced severe, unforeseen disruptions in their supply chains resulting in a significant increase in USP's and FS's market share for cell phones. Further analysis determines that without this unforeseen occurrence the Periodic Trigger would not have occurred. Based on paragraph (i)(6)(vi)(A)(2) of this section, the Commissioner determines to his satisfaction that no adjustments are warranted.

Example 3. (i) USP, a U.S. corporation, and its wholly-owned foreign subsidiaries FS1, FS2, and FS3 enter into a CSA at the start of Year 1 to develop version 2.0 of a computer program. USP makes a platform contribution, version 1.0 of the program (upon which version 2.0 will be based), for which compensation is due from FS1, FS2, and FS3. None of the foreign subsidiaries makes any platform contributions.

(ii) In Year 6, the Commissioner audits Years 3 through 5 of the CSA and considers whether any periodic adjustments should be made. At the time of the Determination Date, the Commissioner determines that the first Adjustment Year in which a Periodic Trigger occurred was Year 3, and further determines that none of the exceptions to periodic adjustments described in paragraph (i)(6)(vi) of this section applies. The Commissioner exercises his discretion under paragraph (i)(6)(i) of this section to make periodic adjustments using Year 3 as the Adjustment Year. Therefore, the arm's length PCT Payments from FS1, FS2, and FS3 to USP shall be determined using the adjusted residual profit split method described in paragraphs (g)(7)(v)(B) and (i)(6)(v)(B) of this section. Periodic adjustments will be made for each year to the extent the PCT Payments actually made by FS1, FS2, and FS3 differ from the PCT Payment calculation under the adjusted residual profit split method.

(iii) The periodic adjustments are calculated in a series of steps set out in paragraph (i)(6)(v)(A) of this section. First, a lump sum for the PCT Payments is determined using the adjusted residual profit split method. The following results are calculated (based on actual results for years for which actual results are available and projected results for all years thereafter) in order to apply the adjusted residual profit split method (it is determined that the cost shared intangibles will be exploited through Year 7, so the results reported in the following table are cumulative values through Year 7):

Participant	Divisional Profits (cumulative PV through Year 7 as of the CSA Start Date)	Residual Profits (cumulative PV through Year 7 as of the CSA Start Date)
FS1	$667	$314
FS2	$271	$159
FS3	$592	$295

Because only USP had nonroutine contributions, under paragraph (g)(7)(iii)(C) of this section, the entire nonroutine residual divisional profit constitutes the PCT Payment owed to USP. Therefore, the present values (as of the CSA Start Date) of the PCT Payments owed are as follows:

PCT Payment owed from FS1 to USP: $314 million

PCT Payment owed from FS2 to USP: $159 million

PCT Payment owed from FS3 to USP: $295 million

Pursuant to paragraph (i)(6)(v)(A) of this section, the steps in paragraphs (i)(6)(v)(A)(2) through (7) of this section are performed separately for the PCT Payments that are owed to USP by each of FS1, FS2, and FS3.

(iv) First, the steps are performed with respect to FS1. In step two, the first step result ($314 million) is converted into a level royalty rate based on FS1's reasonably anticipated divisional profits or losses through Year 7 (the PV of which is $667 million). Consequently, the step two result is a level royalty rate of 47.1% ($314/$667) of the divisional profits in Years 1 through 7. In step three, the Commissioner calculates the PCT Payments due through Year 3 (the Adjustment Year) by applying the step two royalty rate (47.1%) to FS1's actual divisional profits for each year up to and including Year 3 and then determining the aggregate PV of these PCT Payments as of Year 3. In step four, the PCT Payments actually made by FS1 to USP through Year 3 are similarly converted to a PV as of Year 3 and subtracted from the amount determined in step three. That difference is the periodic adjustment in Year 3 with respect to the PCT Payments made for Years 1 through 3 from FS1 to USP. Under step five, the royalties due from FS1 to USP for Year 4 (the year after the Adjustment Year) through Year 6 (the year including the Determination Date) are determined. The periodic adjustment for each of these years is calculated as the product of the step two royalty rate and the divisional profit for that year, minus any actual PCT Payment made by FS1 to USP in that year. The periodic adjustment for each such year is a PCT Payment due in addition to the PCT Payment from FS1 to USP that was already made under the CSA. Under step six, the periodic adjustment for Year 7 (the only exploitation year after the year containing the Determination Date) will be determined by applying the step two royalty rate to FS1's divisional profit for that year. This periodic adjustment for Year 7 is a PCT Payment payable from FS1 to USP and is in lieu of any PCT Payment from FS1 to USP otherwise due.

(v) Next, the steps in paragraphs (i)(6)(v)(A)(2) through (7) of this section are performed with respect to FS2. In step two, the first step result ($159 million) is converted into a level royalty rate based on FS2's reasonably anticipated divisional profits or losses through Year 7 (the PV of which is $271 million). Consequently, the step two result is a level royalty rate of 58.7% ($159/$271) of the divisional profits in Years 1 through 7. In step three, the Commissioner calculates the PCT Payments due through Year 3 (the Adjustment Year) by applying the step two royalty rate (58.7%) to FS2's actual divisional profits for each year up to and including Year 3 and then determining the aggregate PV of these PCT Payments as of Year 3. In step four, the PCT Payments actually made by FS2 to USP through Year 3 are similarly converted to a PV as of Year 3 and subtracted from the amount determined in step three. That difference is the periodic adjustment in Year 3 with respect to the PCT Payments made for Years 1 through 3 from FS2 to USP. Under step five, the royalties due from FS2 to USP for Year 4 (the year after the Adjustment Year) through Year 6 (the year including the Determination Date) are determined. The periodic adjustment for each of these years is calculated as the product of the step two royalty rate and the divisional profit for that year, minus any actual PCT Payment made by FS2 to USP in that year. The periodic adjustment for each such year is a PCT Payment due in addition to the PCT Payment from FS2 to USP that was already made under the CSA. Under step six, the periodic adjustment for Year 7 (the only exploitation year after the year containing the Determination Date) will be determined by applying the step two royalty rate to FS2's divisional profit for that year. This periodic adjustment for Year 7 is a PCT Payment payable from FS2 to USP and is in lieu of any PCT Payment from FS2 to USP otherwise due.

(vi) Finally, the steps in paragraphs (i)(6)(v)(A)(2) through (7) of this section are performed with respect to FS3. In step two, the first step result ($295 million) is converted into a level royalty rate based on FS3's reasonably anticipated divisional profits or losses through Year 7 (the PV of which is $592 million). Consequently, the step two result is a level royalty rate of 49.8% ($295/$592) of the divisional profits in Years 1 through 7. In step three, the Commissioner calculates the PCT Payments due through Year 3 (the Adjustment Year) by applying the step two royalty rate (49.8%) to FS3's actual divisional profits for each year up to and including Year 3 and then determining the aggregate PV of these PCT Payments as of Year 3. In step four, the PCT Payments actually made by FS3 to USP through Year 3 are similarly converted to a PV as of Year 3 and subtracted from the amount determined in step three. That difference is the periodic adjustment in Year 3 with respect to the PCT Payments made for Years 1 through 3 from FS3 to USP. Under step five, the royalties due from FS3 to USP for Year 4 (the year after the Adjustment Year) through Year 6 (the year including the Determination Date) are determined. The periodic adjustment for each of these years is calculated as the product of the step two royalty rate and the divisional profit for that year, minus any actual PCT Payment made by FS3 to USP in that year. The periodic adjustment for each such year is a PCT Payment due in addition to the PCT Payment from FS3 to USP that was already made under the CSA. Under step six, the periodic adjustment for Year 7 (the only exploitation year after the year containing the Determination Date) will be determined by applying the step two royalty rate to FS3's divisional profit for that year. This periodic adjustment for Year 7 is a PCT Payment payable from FS3 to USP and is in lieu of any PCT Payment from FS3 to USP otherwise due.

(j) *Definitions and special rules.*—(1) *Definitions.*—(i) *In general.*—For purposes of this section—

Term	Definition	Main Cross References
Acquisition price		§ 1.482-7(g)(5)(i)
Adjusted acquisition price		§ 1.482-7(g)(5)(iii)
Adjusted average market capitalization		§ 1.482-7(g)(6)(iv)
Adjusted benefit shares		§ 1.482-7(i)(2)(ii)(A)
Adjusted RPSM		§ 1.482-7(i)(6)(v)(B)
Adjustment Year		§ 1.482-7(i)(6)(i)
ADR		§ 1.482-7(i)(6)(iv)
AERR		§ 1.482-7(i)(6)(iii)
Applicable Method		§ 1.482-7(g)(2)(ix)(A)
Average market capitalization		§ 1.482-7(g)(6)(iii)
Benefits	*Benefits* mean the sum of additional revenue generated, plus cost savings, minus any cost increases from exploiting cost shared intangibles.	§ 1.482-7(e)(1)(i)
Capability variation		§ 1.482-7(f)(3)
Change in participation under a CSA		§ 1.482-7(f)
Consolidated group		§ 1.482-7(j)(2)(i)
Contingent payments		§ 1.482-7(h)(2)(i)(B)
Controlled participant	*Controlled participant* means a controlled taxpayer, as defined under § 1.482-1(i)(5), that is a party to the contractual agreement that underlies the CSA, and that reasonably anticipates that it will derive benefits, as defined in paragraph (e)(1)(i) of this section, from exploiting one or more cost shared intangibles.	§ 1.482-7(a)(1)
Controlled transfer of interests		§ 1.482-7(f)(2)
Cost contribution		§ 1.482-7(d)(4)
Cost shared intangible	*Cost shared intangible* means any intangible, within the meaning of § 1.482-4(b), that is developed by the IDA, including any portion of such intangible that reflects a platform contribution. Therefore, an intangible developed by the IDA is a cost shared intangible even though the intangible was not always or was never a reasonably anticipated cost shared intangible.	§ 1.482-7(b)
Cost sharing alternative		§ 1.482-7(g)(4)(i)(B)
Cost sharing arrangement or CSA		§ 1.482-7(a), (b)
Cost sharing transactions or CSTs		§ 1.482-7(a)(1), (b)(1)(i)

Term	Definition	Main Cross References
Cross operating contributions	A *cross operating contribution* is any resource or capability or right, other than a platform contribution, that a controlled participant has developed, maintained, or acquired prior to the CSA Start Date, or subsequent to the CSA start date by means other than operating cost contributions or cost contributions, that is reasonably anticipated to contribute to the CSA Activity within another controlled participant's division.	§ 1.482-7(a)(3)(iii), (g)(2)(iv)
CSA Activity	*CSA Activity* is the activity of developing and exploiting cost shared intangibles.	§ 1.482-7(c)(2)(i)
CSA Start Date	The *CSA Start Date* is the earlier of the date of the CSA contract or the first occurrence of any IDC to which the CSA applies, in accordance with § 1.482-7(k)(1)(iii).	§ 1.482-7(i)(6)(iii)(B) and (k)(1)(ii) and (iii).
CST Payments		§ 1.482-7(b)(1)
Date of PCT		§ 1.482-7(b)(3)
Determination Date		§ 1.482-7(i)(6)(i)
Differential income stream		§ 1.482-7(g)(4)(vi)(F)(2)
Division	*Division* means the territory or other division that serves as the basis of the division of interests under the CSA in the cost shared intangibles pursuant to § 1.482-7(b)(4).	See definitions of divisional profit or loss, operating contribution, and operating cost contribution
Divisional interest		§ 1.482-7(b)(1)(iii), (b)(4)
Divisional profit or loss	*Divisional profit or loss* means the operating profit or loss as separately earned by each controlled participant in its division from the CSA Activity, determined before any expense (including amortization) on account of cost contributions, operating cost contributions, routine platform and operating contributions, nonroutine contributions (including platform and operating contributions), and tax.	§ 1.482-7(g)(4)(iii)
Fixed payments		§ 1.482-7(h)(2)(i)(A)
Implied discount rate		§ 1.482-7(g)(2)(v)(B)(2)
IDC share		§ 1.482-7(d)(4)
Input parameters		§ 1.482-7(g)(2)(ix)(B)
Intangible development activity or IDA		§ 1.482-7(d)(1)
Intangible development costs or IDCs		§ 1.482-7(a)(1), (d)(1)
Licensing alternative		§ 1.482-7(g)(4)(i)(C)
Licensing payments	*Licensing payments* means payments pursuant to the licensing obligations under the licensing alternative.	§ 1.482-7(g)(4)(iii)
Make-or-sell rights		§ 1.482-7(c)(4), (g)(2)(iv)
Market-based input parameter		§ 1.482-7(g)(2)(ix)(B)
Market returns for routine contributions	*Market returns for routine contributions* means returns determined by reference to the returns achieved by uncontrolled taxpayers engaged in activities similar to the relevant business activity in the controlled participant's division, consistent with the methods described in §§ 1.482-3, 1.482-4, 1.482-5, or § 1.482-9(c).	§ 1.482-7(g)(4), (g)(7)
Method payment form		§ 1.482-7(h)(3)
Nonroutine contributions	*Nonroutine contributions* means a controlled participant's contributions to the relevant business activities that are not routine contributions. Nonroutine contributions ordinarily include both nonroutine platform contributions and nonroutine operating contributions used by controlled participants in the commercial exploitation of their interests in the cost shared intangibles (for example, marketing intangibles used by a controlled participant in its division to sell products that are based on the cost shared intangible).	§ 1.482-7(g)
Nonroutine residual divisional profit or loss		§ 1.482-7(g)(7)(iii)

Term	Definition	Main Cross References
Operating contributions	An *operating contribution* is any resource or capability or right, other than a platform contribution, that a controlled participant has developed, maintained, or acquired prior to the CSA Start Date, or subsequent to the CSA Start Date by means other than operating cost contributions or cost contributions, that is reasonably anticipated to contribute to the CSA Activity within the controlled participant's division.	§ 1.482-7(g)(2)(ii), (g)(4)(vi)(E), (g)(7)(iii)(A) and (C)
Operating cost contributions	*Operating cost contributions* means all costs in the ordinary course of business on or after the CSA Start Date that, based on analysis of the facts and circumstances, are directly identified with, or are reasonably allocable to, developing resources, capabilities, or rights (other than reasonably anticipated cost shared intangibles) that are reasonably anticipated to contribute to the CSA Activity within the controlled participant's division.	§ 1.482-7(g)(2)(ii), (g)(4)(iii), (g)(7)(iii)(B)
PCT Payee		§ 1.482-7(b)(1)(ii)
PCT Payment		§ 1.482-7(b)(1)(ii)
PCT Payor		§ 1.482-7(b)(1)(ii), (i)(6)(i)
PCT Payor WACC		§ 1.482-7(i)(6)(iv)(D)
Periodic adjustments		§ 1.482-7(i)(6)(i)
Periodic Trigger		§ 1.482-7(i)(6)(i)
Platform contribution transaction or PCT		§ 1.482-7(a)(2), (b)(1)(ii)
Platform contributions		§ 1.482-7(c)(1)
Post-tax income		§ 1.482-7(g)(2)(v)(B)(4), (g)(4)(i)(G)
Pre-tax income		§ 1.482-7(g)(2)(v)(B)(4), (g)(4)(i)(G)
Projected benefit shares		§ 1.482-7(i)(2)(ii)(A)
PRRR		§ 1.482-7(i)(6)(ii)
PVI		§ 1.482-7(i)(6)(iii)(C)
PVTP		§ 1.482-7(i)(6)(iii)(B)
Reasonably anticipated benefits	A controlled participant's *reasonably anticipated benefits* mean the benefits that reasonably may be anticipated to be derived from exploiting cost shared intangibles. For purposes of this definition, benefits mean the sum of additional revenue generated, plus cost savings, minus any cost increases from exploiting cost shared intangibles	§ 1.482-7(e)(1)
Reasonably anticipated benefits or RAB shares		§ 1.482-7(a)(1), (e)(1)
Reasonably anticipated cost shared intangible		§ 1.482-7(d)(1)(ii)
Relevant business activity		§ 1.482-7(g)(7)(i)
Routine contributions	*Routine contributions* means a controlled participant's contributions to the relevant business activities that are of the same or similar kind to those made by uncontrolled taxpayers involved in similar business activities for which it is possible to identify market returns. Routine contributions ordinarily include contributions of tangible property, services and intangibles that are generally owned by uncontrolled taxpayers engaged in similar activities. A functional analysis is required to identify these contributions according to the functions performed, risks assumed, and resources employed by each of the controlled participants.	§ 1.482-7(g)(4), (g)(7)
Routine platform and operating contributions, and net routine platform and operating contributions		§ 1.482-7(g)(4)(vii), 1.482-7(g)(7)(iii)(C)(4)
Specified payment form		§ 1.482-7(h)(3)
Stock-based compensation		§ 1.482-7(d)(3)
Stock options		§ 1.482-7(d)(3)(i)
Subsequent PCT		§ 1.482-7(g)(2)(viii)
Target		§ 1.482-7(g)(5)(i)

Term	Definition	Main Cross References
Tax rate	Reasonably anticipated effective tax rate with respect to the pre-tax income to which the tax rate is being applied. For example, under the income method, this rate would be the reasonably anticipated effective tax rate of the PCT Payor or PCT Payee under the cost sharing alternative or the licensing alternative, as appropriate.	§ 1.482-7(g)(2)(v)(B)(4)(ii), (g)(4)(i)(G)
Trigger PCT		§ 1.482-7(i)(6)(i)
Variable input parameter		§ 1.482-7(g)(2)(ix)(C)
WACC	*WACC* means weighted average cost of capital.	§ 1.482-7(i)(6)(iv)(D)

(ii) *Examples.*—The following examples illustrate certain definitions in paragraph (j)(1)(i) of this section:

Example 1. Controlled participant. Foreign Parent (FP) is a foreign corporation engaged in the extraction of a natural resource. FP has a U.S. subsidiary (USS) to which FP sells supplies of this resource for sale in the United States. FP enters into a CSA with USS to develop a new machine to extract the natural resource. The machine uses a new extraction process that will be patented in the United States and in other countries. The CSA provides that USS will receive the rights to exploit the machine in the extraction of the natural resource in the United States, and FP will receive the rights in the rest of the world. This resource does not, however, exist in the United States. Despite the fact that USS has received the right to exploit this process in the United States, USS is not a controlled participant because it will not derive a benefit from exploiting the intangible developed under the CSA.

Example 2. Controlled participants. (i) U.S. Parent (USP), one foreign subsidiary (FS), and a second foreign subsidiary constituting the group's research arm (R+D) enter into a CSA to develop manufacturing intangibles for a new product line A. USP and FS are assigned the exclusive rights to exploit the intangibles respectively in the United States and the rest of the world, where each presently manufactures and sells various existing product lines. R+D is not assigned any rights to exploit the intangibles. R+D's activity consists solely in carrying out research for the group. It is reliably projected that the RAB shares of USP and FS will be 66 2/3% and 33 1/3%, respectively, and the parties' agreement provides that USP and FS will reimburse 66 2/3% and 33 1/3%, respectively, of the IDCs incurred by R+D with respect to the new intangible.

(ii) R+D does not qualify as a controlled participant within the meaning of paragraph (j)(1)(i) of this section, because it will not derive any benefits from exploiting cost shared intangibles. Therefore, R+D is treated as a service provider for purposes of this section and must receive arm's length consideration for the assistance it is deemed to provide to USP and FS, under the rules of paragraph (a)(3) of this section and §§ 1.482-4(f)(3)(iii) and (4), and 1.482-9, as appropriate. Such consideration must be treated as IDCs incurred by USP and FS in proportion to their RAB shares (that is, 66 2/3% and 33 1/3%, respectively). R+D will not be considered to bear any share of the IDCs under the arrangement.

Example 3. Cost shared intangible, reasonably anticipated cost shared intangible. U.S. Parent (USP) has developed and currently exploits an antihistamine, XY, which is manufactured in tablet form. USP enters into a CSA with its wholly-owned foreign subsidiary (FS) to develop XYZ, a new improved version of XY that will be manufactured as a nasal spray. Work under the CSA is fully devoted to developing XYZ, and XYZ is developed. During the development period, XYZ is a reasonably anticipated cost shared intangible under the CSA. Once developed, XYZ is a cost shared intangible under the CSA.

Example 4. Cost shared intangible. The facts are the same as in *Example 3*, except that in the course of developing XYZ, the controlled participants by accident discover ABC, a cure for disease D. ABC is a cost shared intangible under the CSA.

Example 5. Reasonably anticipated benefits. Controlled parties A and B enter into a cost sharing arrangement to develop product and process intangibles for an already existing Product P. Without such intangibles, A and B would each reasonably anticipate revenue, in present value terms, of $100M from sales of Product P until it became obsolete. With the intangibles, A and B each reasonably anticipate selling the same number of units each year, but reasonably anticipate that the price will be higher. Because the particular product intangible is more highly regarded in A's market, A reasonably anticipates an increase of $20M in present value revenue from the product intangible, while B reasonably anticipates only an increase of $10M. Further, A and B each reasonably anticipate spending an extra $5M present value in production costs to include the feature embodying the product intangible. Finally, A and B each reasonably anticipate saving $2M present value in production costs by using the process intangible. A and B reasonably anticipate no other economic effects from exploiting the cost shared intangibles. A's reasonably anticipated benefits from exploiting the cost shared intangibles equal its reasonably anticipated increase in revenue ($20M) plus its reasonably anticipated cost savings ($2M) minus its reasonably anticipated increased costs ($5M), which equals $17M. Similarly, B's reasonably anticipated benefits from exploiting the cost shared intangibles equal its reasonably anticipated increase in revenue ($10M) plus its reasonably anticipated cost savings ($2M) minus its reasonably anticipated increased costs ($5M), which equals $7M. Thus A's reasonably anticipated benefits are $17M and B's reasonably anticipated benefits are $7M.

(2) *Special rules.*—(i) *Consolidated group.*—For purposes of this section, all members of the same consolidated group shall be treated as one taxpayer. For these purposes, the term *consolidated group* means all members of a group of controlled entities created or organized within a single country and subjected to an income tax by such country on the basis of their combined income.

(ii) *Trade or business.*—A participant that is a foreign corporation or nonresident alien individual will not be treated as engaged in a trade or business within the United States solely by reason of its participation in a CSA. See generally § 1.864-2(a).

(iii) *Partnership.*—A CSA, or an arrangement to which the Commissioner applies the rules of this section, will not be treated as a partnership to which the rules of subchapter K of the Internal Revenue Code apply. See § 301.7701-1(c) of this chapter.

(3) *Character.*—(i) *CST Payments.*—CST Payments generally will be considered the payor's costs of developing intangibles at the location where such development is conducted. For these purposes, IDCs borne directly by a controlled participant that are deductible are deemed to be reduced to the extent of any CST Payments owed to it by other controlled participants pursuant to the CSA. Each cost sharing payment received by a payee will be treated as coming pro rata from payments made by all payors and will be applied pro rata against the deductions for the taxable year that the payee is allowed in connection with the IDCs. Payments received in excess of such deductions will be treated as in consideration for use of the land and tangible property furnished for purposes of the CSA by the payee. For purposes of the research credit determined under section 41, CST Payments among controlled participants will be treated as provided for intra-group transactions in § 1.41-6(i). Any payment made or received by a taxpayer pursuant to an arrangement that the Commissioner determines not to be a CSA will be subject to the provisions of §§ 1.482-1 through 1.482-6 and 1.482-9. Any payment that in substance constitutes a cost sharing payment will be treated as such for purposes of this section, regardless of its characterization under foreign law.

(ii) *PCT Payments.*—A PCT Payor's payment required under paragraph (b)(1)(ii) of this section is deemed to be reduced to the extent of any payments owed to it under such paragraph from other controlled participants. Each PCT Payment received by a PCT Payee will be treated as coming pro rata out of payments made by all PCT Payors. PCT Payments will be characterized consistently with the designation of the type of transaction pursuant to paragraphs (c)(3) and (k)(2)(ii)(H) of this section. Depending on such designation, such payments will be treated as either consideration for a transfer of an interest in intangible property or for services.

(iii) *Examples.*—The following examples illustrate this paragraph (j)(3):

Example 1. U.S. Parent (USP) and its wholly owned Foreign Subsidiary (FS) form a CSA to develop a miniature widget, the Small R. Based on RAB shares, USP agrees to bear 40% and FS to bear 60% of the costs incurred during the term of the agreement. The principal IDCs are operating costs incurred by FS in Country Z of 100X annually, and costs incurred by USP in the United States also of 100X annually. Of the total costs of 200X, USP's share is 80X and FS's share is 120X so that FS must make a payment to USP of 20X. The payment will be treated as a reimbursement of 20X of USP's costs in the United States. Accordingly, USP's Form 1120 will reflect an 80X deduction on account of activities performed in the United States for purposes of allocation and apportionment of the deduction to source. The Form 5471 "Information Return of U.S. Persons With Respect to Certain Foreign Corporations" for FS will reflect a 100X deduction on account of activities performed in Country Z and a 20X deduction on account of activities performed in the United States.

Example 2. The facts are the same as in *Example 1*, except that the 100X of costs borne by USP consist of 5X of costs incurred by USP in the United States and 95X of arm's length rental charge, as described in paragraph (d)(1)(iii) of this section, for the use of a facility in the United States. The depreciation deduction attributable to the U.S. facility is 7X. The 20X net payment by FS to USP will first be applied in reduction pro rata of the 5X deduction for costs and the 7X depreciation deduction attributable to the U.S. facility. The 8X remainder will be treated as rent for the U.S. facility.

Example 3. (i) Four members (A, B, C, and D) of a controlled group form a CSA to develop the next generation technology for their business. Based on RAB shares, the participants agree to bear shares of the costs incurred during the term of the agreement in the following percentages: A 40%; B 15%; C 25%; and D 20%. The arm's length values of the platform contributions they respectively own are in the following amounts for the taxable year: A 80X; B 40X; C 30X; and D 30X. The provisional (before offsets) and final PCT Payments among A, B, C, and D are shown in the table as follows:

(All amounts stated in X's)

	A	B	C	D
Payments	<40>	<21>	<37.5>	<30>
Receipts	48	34	22.5	24
Final	8	13	<15>	<6>

(ii) The first row/first column shows A's provisional PCT Payment equal to the product of 100X (sum of 40X, 30X, and 30X) and A's RAB share of 40%. The second row/first column shows A's provisional PCT receipts equal to the sum of the products of 80X and B's, C's, and D's RAB shares (15%, 25%, and 20%, respectively). The other entries in the first two rows of the table are similarly computed. The last row shows the final PCT receipts/payments after offsets. Thus, for the taxable year, A and B are treated as receiving the 8X and 13X, respectively, pro rata out of payments by C and D of 15X and 6X, respectively.

(k) *CSA administrative requirements.*—A controlled participant meets the requirements of this paragraph if it substantially complies, respectively, with the CSA contractual, documentation, accounting, and reporting requirements of paragraphs (k)(1) through (4) of this section.

(1) *CSA contractual requirements.*—(i) *In general.*—A CSA must be recorded in writing in a contract that is contemporaneous with the formation (and any revision) of the CSA and that includes the contractual provisions described in this paragraph (k)(1).

(ii) *Contractual provisions.*—The written contract described in this paragraph (k)(1) must include provisions that—

(A) List the controlled participants and any other members of the controlled group that are reasonably anticipated to benefit from the use of the cost shared intangibles, including the address of each domestic entity and the country of organization of each foreign entity;

(B) Describe the scope of the IDA to be undertaken and each reasonably anticipated cost shared intangible or class of reasonably anticipated cost shared intangibles;

(C) Specify the functions and risks that each controlled participant will undertake in connection with the CSA;

(D) Divide among the controlled participants all divisional interests in cost shared intangibles and specify each controlled participant's divisional interest in the cost shared intangibles, as described in paragraphs (b)(1)(iii) and (4) of this section, that it will own and exploit without any further obligation to compensate any other controlled participant for such interest;

(E) Provide a method to calculate the controlled participants' RAB shares, based on factors that can reasonably be expected to reflect the participants' shares of anticipated benefits, and require that such RAB shares must be updated, as described in paragraph (e)(1) of this section (see also paragraph (k)(2)(ii)(F) of this section);

(F) Enumerate all categories of IDCs to be shared under the CSA;

(G) Specify that the controlled participant must use a consistent method of accounting to determine IDCs and RAB shares, as described in paragraphs (d) and (e) of this section, respectively, and must translate foreign currencies on a consistent basis;

(H) Require the controlled participant to enter into CSTs covering all IDCs, as described in paragraph (b)(1)(i) of this section, in connection with the CSA;

(I) Require the controlled participants to enter into PCTs covering all platform contributions, as described in paragraph (b)(1)(ii) of this section, in connection with the CSA;

(J) Specify the form of payment due under each PCT (or group of PCTs) in existence at the formation (and any revision) of the CSA, including information and explanation that reasonably supports an analysis of applicable provisions of paragraph (h) of this section; and

(K) Specify the date on which the CSA is entered into (CSA Start Date) and the duration of the CSA, the conditions under which the CSA may be modified or terminated, and the consequences of a modification or termination (including consequences described under the rules of paragraph (f) of this section).

(iii) *Meaning of contemporaneous.*—(A) *In general.*—For purposes of this paragraph (k)(1), a written contractual agreement is contemporaneous with the formation (or revision) of a CSA if, and only if, the controlled participants record the CSA, in its entirety, in a document that they sign and date no later than 60 days after the first occurrence of any IDC described in paragraph (d) of this section to which such agreement (or revision) is to apply.

(B) *Example.*—The following example illustrates the principles of this paragraph (k)(1)(iii):

Example. Companies A and B, both of which are members of the same controlled group, commence an IDA on March 1, Year 1. Company A pays the first IDCs in relation to the IDA, as cash salaries to A's research staff, for the staff's work during the first week of March, Year 1. A and B, however, do not sign and date any written contractual agreement until August 1, Year 1, whereupon they execute a "Cost Sharing Agreement" that purports to be "effective as of" March 1 of Year 1. The arrangement fails the requirement that the participants record their arrangement in a written contractual agreement that is contemporaneous with the formation of a CSA. The arrangement has failed to meet the requirements set forth in paragraph (b)(2) of this section and, pursuant to paragraph (b) of this section, cannot be a CSA.

(iv) *Interpretation of contractual provisions.*—(A) *In general The provisions of a written contract described in this paragraph (k)(1) and of the additional documentation described in paragraph (k)(2) of this section must be clear and unambiguous.*—The provisions will be interpreted by reference to the economic substance of the transaction and the actual conduct of the controlled participants. See § 1.482-1(d)(3)(ii)(B) (Identifying contractual terms). Accordingly, the Commissioner may impute contractual terms in a CSA consistent with the economic substance of the CSA and may disregard contractual terms that lack economic substance. An allocation of risk between controlled participants after the outcome of such risk is known or reasonably knowable lacks economic substance. See § 1.482-1(d)(3)(iii)(B) (Identification of taxpayer that bears risk). A contractual term that is disregarded due to a lack of economic substance does not satisfy a contractual requirement set forth in this paragraph (k)(1) or documentation requirement set forth in paragraph (k)(2) of this section. See paragraph (b)(5) of this section for the treatment of an arrangement among controlled taxpayers that fails to comply with the requirements of this section.

(B) *Examples.*—The following examples illustrate the principles of this paragraph (k)(1)(iv). In each example, it is assumed that the Commissioner will exercise the discretion granted pursuant to paragraph (b)(5)(ii) of this section to apply the provisions of this section to the arrangement that purports to be a CSA.

Example 1. The contractual provisions recorded upon formation of an arrangement that purports to be a CSA provide that PCT Payments with respect to a particular platform contribution will consist of payments contingent on sales. Contrary to the contractual provisions, the PCT Payments actually made are contingent on profits. Because the controlled participants' actual conduct is different from the contractual terms, the Commissioner may determine, based on the facts and circumstances, that—

(i) The actual payments have economic substance and, therefore, impute payment terms in the CSA consistent with the actual payments; or

(ii) The contract terms reflect the economic substance of the arrangement and, therefore, the actual payments must be adjusted to conform to the terms.

Example 2. An arrangement that purports to be a CSA provides that PCT Payments with respect to a particular platform contribution shall be contingent payments equal to 10% of sales of products that incorporate cost shared intangibles. The contract terms further provide that the controlled participants must adjust such contingent payments in accordance with a formula set forth in the terms. During the first three years of the arrangement, the controlled participants fail to make the adjustments required by the terms with respect to the PCT Payments. The Commissioner may determine, based on the facts and circumstances, that—

(i) The contingent payment terms with respect to the platform contribution do not have economic substance because the controlled participants did not act in accordance with their upfront risk allocation; or

(ii) The contract terms reflect the economic substance of the arrangement and, therefore, the actual payments must be adjusted to conform to the terms.

(2) *CSA documentation requirements.*—(i) *In general.*—The controlled participants must timely update and maintain sufficient documentation to establish that the participants have met the CSA contractual requirements of paragraph (k)(1) of this section and the additional CSA documentation requirements of this paragraph (k)(2).

(ii) *Additional CSA documentation requirements.*—The controlled participants to a CSA must timely update and maintain documentation sufficient to—

(A) Describe the current scope of the IDA and identify—

(1) Any additions or subtractions from the list of reasonably anticipated cost shared intangibles reported pursuant to paragraph (k)(1)(ii)(B) of this section;

(2) Any cost shared intangible, together with each controlled participant's interest therein; and

(3) Any further development of intangibles already developed under the CSA or of specified applications of such intangible which has been removed from the IDA (see paragraphs (d)(1)(ii) and (j)(1)(i) of this section for the definitions of reasonably anticipated cost shared intangible and cost shared intangible) and the steps (including any accounting classifications and allocations) taken to implement such removal;

(B) Establish that each controlled participant reasonably anticipates that it will derive benefits from exploiting cost shared intangibles;

(C) Describe the functions and risks that each controlled participant has undertaken during the term of the CSA;

(D) Provide an overview of each controlled participant's business segments, including an analysis of the economic and legal factors that affect CST and PCT pricing;

(E) Establish the amount of each controlled participant's IDCs for each taxable year under the CSA, including all IDCs attributable to stock-based compensation, as described in paragraph (d)(3) of this section (including the method of measurement and timing used in determining such IDCs, and the data, as of the date of grant, used to identify stock-based compensation with the IDA);

(F) Describe the method used to estimate each controlled participant's RAB share for each year during the course of the CSA, including—

(1) All projections used to estimate benefits;

(2) All updates of the RAB shares in accordance with paragraph (e)(1) of this section; and

(3) An explanation of why that method was selected and why the method provides the most reliable measure for estimating RAB shares;

(G) Describe all platform contributions;

(H) Designate the type of transaction involved for each PCT or group of PCTs;

(I) Specify, within the time period provided in paragraph (h)(2)(iii) of this section, the form of payment due under each PCT or group of PCTs, including information and explanation that reasonably supports an analysis of applicable provisions of paragraph (h) of this section;

(J) Describe and explain the method selected to determine the arm's length payment due under each PCT, including—

(1) An explanation of why the method selected constitutes the best method, as described in § 1.482-1(c)(2), for measuring an arm's length result;

(2) The economic analyses, data, and projections relied upon in developing and selecting the best method, including the source of the data and projections used;

(3) Each alternative method that was considered, and the reason or reasons that the alternative method was not selected;

(4) Any data that the controlled participant obtains, after the CSA takes effect, that would help determine if the controlled participant's method selected has been applied in a reasonable manner;

(5) The discount rate or rates, where applicable, used for purposes of evaluating PCT Payments, including information and explanation that reasonably supports an analysis of applicable provisions of paragraph (g)(2)(v) of this section;

(6) The estimated arm's length values of any platform contributions as of the dates of the relevant PCTs, in accordance with paragraph (g)(2)(ii) of this section;

(7) A discussion, where applicable, of why transactions were or were not aggregated under the principles of paragraph (g)(2)(iv) of this section;

(8) The method payment form and any conversion made from the method payment form to the specified payment form, as described in paragraph (h)(3) of this section; and

(9) If applicable under paragraph (i)(6)(iv) of this section, the WACC of the parent of the controlled group that includes the controlled participants.

(iii) *Coordination rules and production of documents.*—(A) *Coordination with penalty regulations.*—See § 1.6662-6(d)(2)(iii)(D) regarding coordination of the rules of this paragraph (k) with the documentation requirements for purposes of the accuracy-related penalty under section 6662(e) and (h).

(B) *Production of documentation.*—Each controlled participant must provide to the Commissioner, within 30 days of a request, the items described in this paragraph (k)(2) and paragraph (k)(3) of this section. The time for compliance described in this paragraph (k)(2)(iii)(B) may be extended at the discretion of the Commissioner.

(3) *CSA accounting requirements.*—(i) *In general.*—The controlled participants must maintain books and records (and related or underlying data and information) that are sufficient to—

(A) Establish that the controlled participants have used (and are using) a consistent method of accounting to measure costs and benefits;

(B) Permit verification that the amount of any contingent PCT Payments due have been (and are being) properly determined;

(C) Translate foreign currencies on a consistent basis; and

(D) To the extent that the method of accounting used materially differs from U.S. generally accepted accounting principles, explain any such material differences.

(ii) *Reliance on financial accounting.*—For purposes of this section, the controlled participants may not rely solely upon financial accounting to establish satisfaction of the accounting requirements of this paragraph (k)(3). Rather, the method of accounting must clearly reflect income. *Thor Power Tools Co. v. Commissioner*, 439 U.S. 522 (1979).

(4) *CSA reporting requirements.*—(i) *CSA Statement.*—Each controlled participant must file with the Internal Revenue Service, in the manner described in this paragraph (k)(4), a "Statement of Controlled Participant to § 1.482-7 Cost Sharing Arrangement" (CSA

Statement) that complies with the requirements of this paragraph (k)(4).

(ii) *Content of CSA Statement*.—The CSA Statement of each controlled participant must—

(A) State that the participant is a controlled participant in a CSA;

(B) Provide the controlled participant's taxpayer identification number;

(C) List the other controlled participants in the CSA, the country of organization of each such participant, and the taxpayer identification number of each such participant;

(D) Specify the earliest date that any IDC described in paragraph (d)(1) of this section occurred; and

(E) Indicate the date on which the controlled participants formed (or revised) the CSA and, if different from such date, the date on which the controlled participants recorded the CSA (or any revision) contemporaneously in accordance with paragraphs (k)(1)(i) and (iii) of this section.

(iii) *Time for filing CSA Statement*.—(A) *90-day rule*.—Each controlled participant must file its original CSA Statement with the Internal Revenue Service Ogden Campus (addressed as follows: "Attn: CSA Statements, Mail Stop 4912, Internal Revenue Service, 1973 North Rulon White Blvd., Ogden, Utah 84404-0040"), no later than 90 days after the first occurrence of an IDC to which the newly-formed CSA applies, as described in paragraph (k)(1)(iii)(A) of this section, or, in the case of a taxpayer that became a controlled participant after the formation of the CSA, no later than 90 days after such taxpayer became a controlled participant. A CSA Statement filed in accordance with this paragraph (k)(4)(iii)(A) must be dated and signed, under penalties of perjury, by an officer of the controlled participant who is duly authorized (under local law) to sign the statement on behalf of the controlled participant.

(B) *Annual return requirement*.—*(1) In general*.—Each controlled participant must attach to its U.S. income tax return, for each taxable year for the duration of the CSA, a copy of the original CSA Statement that the controlled participant filed in accordance with the 90-day rule of paragraph (k)(4)(iii)(A) of this section. In addition, the controlled participant must update the information reflected on the original CSA Statement annually by attaching a schedule that documents changes in such information over time.

(2) Special filing rule for annual return requirement.—If a controlled participant is not required to file a U.S. income tax return, the participant must ensure that the copy or copies of the CSA Statement and any updates are attached to Schedule M of any Form 5471, any Form 5472 "Information Return of a Foreign Owned Corporation," or any Form 8865 "Return of U.S. Persons With Respect to Certain Foreign Partnerships," filed with respect to that participant.

(iv) *Examples*.—The following examples illustrate this paragraph (k)(4). In each example, Companies A and B are members of the same controlled group.

Example 1. A and B, both of which file U.S. tax returns, agree to share the costs of developing a new chemical formula in accordance with the provisions of this section. On March 30, Year 1, A and B record their agreement in a written contract styled, "Cost Sharing Agreement." The contract applies by its terms to IDCs occurring after March 1, Year 1. The first IDCs to which the CSA applies occurred on March 15, Year 1. To comply with paragraph (k)(4)(iii)(A) of this section, A and B individually must file separate CSA Statements no later than 90 days after March 15, Year 1 (June 13, Year 1). Further, to comply with paragraph (k)(4)(iii)(B) of this section, A and B must attach copies of their respective CSA Statements to their respective Year 1 U.S. income tax returns.

Example 2. The facts are the same as in *Example 1*, except that a year has passed and C, which files a U.S. tax return, joined the CSA on May 9, Year 2. To comply with the annual filing requirement described in paragraph (k)(4)(iii)(B) of this section, A and B must each attach copies of their respective CSA Statements (as filed for Year 1) to their respective Year 2 income tax returns, along with a schedule updated appropriately to reflect the changes in information described in paragraph (k)(4)(ii) of this section resulting from the addition of C to the CSA. To comply with both the 90-day rule described in paragraph (k)(4)(iii)(A) of this section and the annual filing requirement described in paragraph (k)(4)(iii)(B) of this section, C must file a CSA Statement no later than 90 days after May 9, Year 2 (August 7, Year 2), and must attach a copy of such CSA Statement to its Year 2 income tax return.

(l) *Effective/applicability dates*.—Except as otherwise provided in this paragraph (l), this section applies on December 16, 2011. Paragraphs (g)(2)(v)(B)(2), (g)(4)(vi)(F)(2), and (g)(4)(viii), *Example 8* of this section apply to taxable years beginning on or after December 19, 2011. Paragraphs (g)(4)(v) and (g)(4)(viii), *Example 9* apply to taxable years beginning on or after August 27, 2013.

(m) *Transition rule*.—(1) *In general*.—An arrangement in existence on January 5, 2009, will be considered a CSA, as described under paragraph (b) of this section, if, prior to such date, it was a qualified cost sharing arrangement under the provisions of § 1.482-7 (as contained in the 26 CFR part 1 edition revised as of January 1, 1996, hereafter referred to as "former § 1.482-7"), but only if the written contract, as described in paragraph (k)(1) of this section, is amended, if necessary, to conform with, and only if the activities of the controlled participants substantially comply with, the provisions of this section, as modified by paragraphs (m)(2) and (m)(3) of this section, by July 6, 2009.

(2) *Transitional modification of applicable provisions*.—For purposes of this paragraph (m), conformity and substantial compliance with the provisions of this section shall be determined with the following modifications:

(i) CSTs and PCTs occurring prior to January 5, 2009, shall be subject to the provisions of former § 1.482-7 rather than this section.

(ii) Except to the extent provided in paragraph (m)(3) of this section, PCTs that occur under a CSA that was a qualified cost sharing arrangement under the provisions of former § 1.482-7 and remained in effect on January 5, 2009, shall be subject to the periodic adjustment rules of § 1.482-4(f)(2) rather than the rules of paragraph (i)(6) of this section.

(iii) Paragraphs (b)(1)(iii) and (b)(4) of this section shall not apply.

(iv) Paragraph (k)(1)(ii)(D) of this section shall not apply.

(v) Paragraphs (k)(1)(ii)(H) and (I) of this section shall be construed as applying only to transactions entered into on or after January 5, 2009.

(vi) The deadline for recordation of the revised written contractual agreement pursuant to paragraph (k)(1)(iii) of this section shall be no later than July 6, 2009.

(vii) Paragraphs (k)(2)(ii)(G) through (J) of this section shall be construed as applying only with reference to PCTs entered into on or after January 5, 2009.

(viii) Paragraph (k)(4)(iii)(A) of this section shall be construed as requiring a CSA Statement with respect to the revised written contractual agreement described in paragraph (m)(2)(vi) of this section no later than September 2, 2009.

(ix) Paragraph (k)(4)(iii)(B) of this section shall be construed as only applying for taxable years ending after the filing of the CSA Statement described in paragraph (m)(2)(viii) of this section.

(3) *Special rule for certain periodic adjustments*.—The periodic adjustment rules in paragraph (i)(6) of this section (rather than the rules of § 1.482-4(f)(2)) shall apply to PCTs that occur on or after the date of a material change in the scope of the CSA from its scope as of January 5, 2009. A material change in scope would include a material expansion of the activities undertaken beyond the scope of the intangible development area, as described in former § 1.482-7(b)(4)(iv). For this purpose, a contraction of the scope of a CSA, absent a material expansion into one or more lines of research and development beyond the scope of the intangible development area, does not constitute a material change in scope of the CSA. Whether a material change in scope has occurred is determined on a cumulative basis. Therefore, a series of expansions, any one of which is not a material expansion by itself, may collectively constitute a material expansion. [Reg. § 1.482-7.]

☐ [*T.D.* 9568, 12-16-2011 (*corrected* 1-24-2012 *and* 2-13-2012). *Amended by T.D.* 9569, 12-19-2011 *and T.D.* 9630, 8-26-2013 (*corrected* 10-21-2013).]

§ 1.482-8. Examples of the best method rule.—(a) *Introduction*.—In accordance with the best method rule of § 1.482-1(c), a method may be applied in a particular case only if the comparability, quality of data, and reliability of assumptions under that method make it more reliable than any other available measure of the arm's length result. The following examples illustrate the comparative analysis required to apply this rule. As with all of the examples in these regulations, these examples are based on simplified facts, are provided solely for purposes of illustrating the type of analysis required under the relevant rule, and do not provide rules of general application. Thus, conclusions reached in these examples as to the relative reliability of methods are based on the assumed facts of the examples, and are not general conclusions concerning the relative reliability of any method.

(b) *Examples.—Example 1—Preference for comparable uncontrolled price method.* Company A is the U.S. distribution subsidiary of Company B, a foreign manufacturer of consumer electrical appliances. Company A purchases toaster ovens from Company B for resale in the U.S. market. To exploit other outlets for its toaster ovens, Company B also sells its toaster ovens to Company C, an unrelated U.S. distributor of toaster ovens. The products sold to Company A and Company C are identical in every respect and there are no material differences between the transactions. In this case application of the CUP method, using the sales of toaster ovens to Company C, generally will provide a more reliable measure of an arm's length result for the controlled sale of toaster ovens to Company A than the application of any other method. See §§1.482-1(c)(2)(i) and -3(b)(2)(ii)(A).

Example 2—Resale price method preferred to comparable uncontrolled price method. The facts are the same as in *Example 1*, except that the toaster ovens sold to Company A are of substantially higher quality than those sold to Company C and the effect on price of such quality differences cannot be accurately determined. In addition, in order to round out its line of consumer appliances Company A purchases blenders from unrelated parties for resale in the United States. The blenders are resold to substantially the same customers as the toaster ovens, have a similar resale value to the toaster ovens, and are purchased under similar terms and in similar volumes. The distribution functions performed by Company A appear to be similar for toaster ovens and blenders. Given the product differences between the toaster ovens, application of the resale price method using the purchases and resales of blenders as the uncontrolled comparables is likely to provide a more reliable measure of an arm's length result than application of the comparable uncontrolled price method using Company B's sales of toaster ovens to Company C.

Example 3—Resale price method preferred to comparable profits method. (i) The facts are the same as in *Example 2* except that Company A purchases all its products from Company B and Company B makes no uncontrolled sales into the United States. However, six uncontrolled U.S. distributors are identified that purchase a similar line of products from unrelated parties. The uncontrolled distributors purchase toaster ovens from unrelated parties, but there are significant differences in the characteristics of the toaster ovens, including the brandnames under which they are sold.

(ii) Under the facts of this case, reliable adjustments for the effect of the different brandnames cannot be made. Except for some differences in payment terms and inventory levels, the purchases and resales of toaster ovens by the three uncontrolled distributors are closely similar to the controlled purchases in terms of the markets in which they occur, the volume of the transactions, the marketing activities undertaken by the distributor, inventory levels, warranties, allocation of currency risk, and other relevant functions and risks. Reliable adjustments can be made for the differences in payment terms and inventory levels. In addition, sufficiently detailed accounting information is available to permit adjustments to be made for differences in accounting methods or in reporting of costs between cost of goods sold and operating expenses. There are no other material differences between the controlled and uncontrolled transactions.

(iii) Because reliable adjustments for the differences between the toaster ovens, including the trademarks under which they are sold, cannot be made, these uncontrolled transactions will not serve as reliable measures of an arm's length result under the comparable uncontrolled price method. There is, however, close functional similarity between the controlled and uncontrolled transactions and reliable adjustments have been made for material differences that would be likely to affect gross profit. Under these circumstances, the gross profit margins derived under the resale price method are less likely to be susceptible to any unidentified differences than the operating profit measures used under the comparable profits method. Therefore, given the close functional comparability between the controlled and uncontrolled transactions, and the high quality of the data, the resale price method achieves a higher degree of comparability and will provide a more reliable measure of an arm's length result. See §1.482-1(c) (Best method rule).

Example 4—Comparable profits method preferred to resale price method. The facts are the same as in *Example 3*, except that the accounting information available for the uncontrolled comparables is not sufficiently detailed to ensure consistent reporting between cost of goods sold and operating expenses of material items such as discounts, insurance, warranty costs, and supervisory, general and administrative expenses. These expenses are significant in amount. Therefore, whether these expenses are treated as costs of goods sold or operating expenses would have a significant effect on gross margins. Because in this case reliable adjustments can not be made for such accounting differences, the reliability of the resale price method is significantly reduced. There is, however, close functional similarity between the controlled and uncontrolled transactions and reliable adjustments have been made for all material differences other than the potential accounting differences. Because the comparable profits method is not adversely affected by the potential accounting differences, under these circumstances the comparable profits method is likely to produce a more reliable measure of an arm's length result than the resale price method. See §1.482-1(c) (Best method rule).

Example 5—Cost plus method preferred to comparable profits method. (i) USS is a U.S. company that manufactures machine tool parts and sells them to its foreign parent corporation, FP. Four U.S. companies are identified that also manufacture various types of machine tool parts but sell them to uncontrolled purchasers.

(ii) Except for some differences in payment terms, the manufacture and sales of machine tool parts by the four uncontrolled companies are closely similar to the controlled transactions in terms of the functions performed and risks assumed. Reliable adjustments can be made for the differences in payment terms. In addition, sufficiently detailed accounting information is available to permit adjustments to be made for differences between the controlled transaction and the uncontrolled comparables in accounting methods and in the reporting of costs between cost of goods sold and operating expenses.

(iii) There is close functional similarity between the controlled and uncontrolled transactions and reliable adjustments can be made for material differences that would be likely to affect gross profit. Under these circumstances, the gross profit markups derived under the cost plus method are less likely to be susceptible to any unidentified differences than the operating profit measures used under the comparable profits method. Therefore, given the close functional comparability between the controlled and uncontrolled transactions, and the high quality of the data, the cost plus method achieves a higher degree of comparability and will provide a more reliable measure of an arm's length result. See §1.482-1(c) (Best method rule).

Example 6—Comparable profits method preferred to cost plus method. The facts are the same as in *Example 5*, except that there are significant differences between the controlled and uncontrolled transactions in terms of the types of parts and components manufactured and the complexity of the manufacturing process. The resulting functional differences are likely to materially affect gross profit margins, but it is not possible to identify the specific differences and reliably adjust for their effect on gross profit. Because these functional differences would be reflected in differences in operating expenses, the operating profit measures used under the comparable profits method implicitly reflect to some extent these functional differences. Therefore, because in this case the comparable profits method is less sensitive than the cost plus method to the potentially significant functional differences between the controlled and uncontrolled transactions, the comparable profits method is likely to produce a more reliable measure of an arm's length result than the cost plus method. See §1.482-1(c) (Best method rule).

Example 7—Preference for comparable uncontrolled transaction method. (i) USpharm, a U.S. pharmaceutical company, develops a new drug Z that is a safe and effective treatment for the disease zeezee. USpharm has obtained patents covering drug Z in the United States and in various foreign countries. USpharm has also obtained the regulatory authorizations necessary to market drug Z in the United States and in foreign countries.

(ii) USpharm licenses its subsidiary in country X, Xpharm, to produce and sell drug Z in country X. At the same time, it licenses an unrelated company, Ydrug, to produce and sell drug Z in country Y, a neighboring country. Prior to licensing the drug, USpharm had obtained patent protection and regulatory approvals in both countries and both countries provide similar protection for intellectual property rights. Country X and country Y are similar countries in terms of population, per capita income and the incidence of disease zeezee. Consequently, drug Z is expected to sell in similar quantities and at similar prices in both countries. In addition, costs of producing drug Z in each country are expected to be approximately the same.

(iii) USpharm and Xpharm establish terms for the license of drug Z that are identical in every material respect, including royalty rate, to the terms established between USpharm and Ydrug. In this case the district director determines that the royalty rate established in the Ydrug license agreement is a reliable measure of the arm's length royalty rate for the Xpharm license agreement. Given that the same property is transferred in the controlled and uncontrolled transactions, and that the circumstances under which the transactions occurred are substantially the same, in this case the comparable uncontrolled transaction method is likely to provide a more reliable measure of an arm's length result than any other method. See § 1.482-4(c)(2)(ii).

Example 8—Residual profit split method preferred to other methods. (i) USC is a U.S. company that develops, manufactures and sells communications equipment. EC is the European subsidiary of USC. EC is an established company that carries out extensive research and development activities and develops, manufactures and sells communications equipment in Europe. There are extensive transactions between USC and EC. USC licenses valuable technology it has developed to EC for use in the European market but EC also licenses valuable technology it has developed to USC. Each company uses components manufactured by the other in some of its products and purchases products from the other for resale in its own market.

(ii) Detailed accounting information is available for both USC and EC and adjustments can be made to achieve a high degree of consistency in accounting practices between them. Relatively reliable allocations of costs, income and assets can be made between the business activities that are related to the controlled transactions and those that are not. Relevant marketing and research and development expenditures can be identified and reasonable estimates of the useful life of the related intangibles are available so that the capitalized value of the intangible development expenses of USC and EC can be calculated. In this case there is no reason to believe that the relative value of these capitalized expenses is substantially different from the relative value of the intangible property of USC and EC. Furthermore, comparables are identified that could be used to estimate a market return for the routine contributions of USC and EC. Based on these facts, the residual profit split could provide a reliable measure of an arm's length result.

(iii) There are no uncontrolled transactions involving property that is sufficiently comparable to much of the tangible and intangible property transferred between USC and EC to permit use of the comparable uncontrolled price method or the comparable uncontrolled transaction method. Uncontrolled companies are identified in Europe and the United States that perform somewhat similar activities to USC and EC; however, the activities of none of these companies are as complex as those of USC and EC and they do not use similar levels of highly valuable intangible property that they have developed themselves. Under these circumstances, the uncontrolled companies may be useful in determining a market return for the routine contributions of USC and EC, but that return would not reflect the value of the intangible property employed by USC and EC. Thus, none of the uncontrolled companies is sufficiently similar so that reliable results would be obtained using the resale price, cost plus, or comparable profits methods. Moreover, no uncontrolled companies can be identified that engaged in sufficiently similar activities and transactions with each other to employ the comparable profit split method.

(iv) Given the difficulties in applying the other methods, the reliability of the internal data on USC and EC, and the fact that acceptable comparables are available for deriving a market return for the routine contributions of USC and EC, the residual profit split method is likely to provide the most reliable measure of an arm's length result in this case.

Example 9—Comparable profits method preferred to profit split. (i) Company X is a large, complex U.S. company that carries out extensive research and development activities and manufactures and markets a variety of products. Company X has developed a new process by which compact disks can be fabricated at a fraction of the cost previously required. The process is expected to prove highly profitable, since there is a large market for compact disks. Company X establishes a new foreign subsidiary, Company Y, and licenses it the rights to use the process to fabricate compact disks for the foreign market as well as continuing technical support and improvements to the process. Company Y uses the process to fabricate compact disks which it supplies to related and unrelated parties.

(ii) The process licensed to Company Y is unique and highly valuable and no uncontrolled transfers of intangible property can be found that are sufficiently comparable to permit reliable application of the comparable uncontrolled transaction method. Company X is a large, complex company engaged in a variety of activities that owns unique and highly valuable intangible property. Consequently, no uncontrolled companies can be found that are similar to Company X. Furthermore, application of the profit split method in this case would involve the difficult and problematic tasks of allocating Company X's costs and assets between the relevant business activity and other activities and assigning a value to Company X's intangible contributions. On the other hand, Company Y performs relatively routine manufacturing and marketing activities and there are a number of similar uncontrolled companies. Thus, application of the comparable profits method using Company Y as the tested party is likely to produce a more reliable measure of an arm's length result than a profit split in this case.

Example 10—Cost of services plus method preferred to other methods. (i) FP designs and manufactures consumer electronic devices that incorporate advanced technology. In year 1, FP introduces Product X, an entertainment device targeted primarily at the youth market. FP's wholly-owned, exclusive U.S. distributor, USSub, sells Product X in the U.S. market. USSub hires an independent marketing firm, Agency A, to promote Product X in the U.S. market. Agency A has successfully promoted other electronic products on behalf of other uncontrolled parties. USSub executes a one-year, renewable contract with Agency A that requires it to develop the market for Product X, within an annual budget set by USSub. In years 1 through 3, Agency A develops advertising, buys media, and sponsors events featuring Product X. Agency A receives a markup of 25% on all expenses of promoting Product X, with the exception of media buys, which are reimbursed at cost. During year 3, sales of Product X decrease sharply, as Product X is displaced by competitors' products. At the end of year 3, sales of Product X are discontinued.

(ii) Prior to the start of year 4, FP develops a new entertainment device, Product Y. Like Product X, Product Y is intended for sale to the youth market, but it is marketed under a new trademark distinct from that used for Product X. USSub decides to perform all U.S. market promotion for Product Y. USSub hires key Agency A staff members who handled the successful Product X campaign. To promote Product Y, USSub intends to use methods similar to those used successfully by Agency A to promote Product X (print advertising, media, event sponsorship, etc.). FP and USSub enter into a one-year, renewable agreement concerning promotion of Product Y in the U.S. market. Under the agreement, FP compensates USSub for promoting Product Y, based on a cost of services plus markup of A%. Third-party media buys by USSub in connection with Product Y are reimbursed at cost.

(iii) Assume that under the contractual arrangements between FP and USSub, the arm's length consideration for Product Y and the trademark or other intangible property may be determined reliably under one or more transfer pricing methods. At issue in this example is the separate evaluation of the arm's length compensation for the year 4 promotional activities performed by USSub pursuant to its contract with FP.

(iv) USSub's accounting records contain reliable data that separately state the costs incurred to promote Product Y. A functional analysis indicates that USSub's activities to promote Product Y in year 4 are similar to activities performed by Agency A during years 1 through 3 under the contract with USSub. In other respects, no material differences exist in the market conditions or the promotional activities performed in year 4, as compared to those years 1 through 3.

(v) It is possible to identify uncontrolled distributors or licensees of electronic products that perform, as one component of their business activities, promotional activities similar to those performed by USSub. However, it is unlikely that publicly available accounting data from these companies would allow computation of the comparable transactional costs or total services costs associated with the marketing or promotional activities that these entities perform, as one component of business activities. If that were possible, the comparable profits method for services might provide a reliable measure of an arm's length result. The functional analysis of the marketing activities performed by USSub in year 4 indicates that they are similar to the activities performed by Agency A in years 1 through 3 for Product X. Because reliable information is available concerning the markup on costs charged in a comparable uncontrolled transaction, the most reliable measure of an arm's length price is the cost of services plus method in § 1.482-9(e).

Example 11—CPM for services preferred to other methods. (i) FP manufactures furniture and accessories for residential use. FP sells its products to retailers in Europe under the trademark, "Moda." FP holds all worldwide rights to the trademark, including in the United States. USSub is FP's wholly-owned subsidiary in the U.S. market and the exclusive U.S. distributor of FP's merchandise. Historically, USSub dealt only with specialized designers in the U.S. market and advertised in trade publications targeted to this market. Although items sold in the U.S. and Europe are physically identical, USSub's U.S. customers generally resell the merchandise as non-branded merchandise.

(ii) FP retains an independent firm to evaluate the feasibility of selling FP's trademarked merchandise in the general wholesale and retail market in the United States. The study concludes that this segment of the U.S. market, which is not exploited by USSub, may generate substantial profits. Based on this study, FP enters into a separate agreement with USSub, which provides that USSub will develop this market in the United States for the benefit of FP. USSub separately accounts for personnel expenses, overhead, and out-of-pocket costs attributable to the initial stage of the marketing campaign (Phase I). USSub receives as compensation its costs, plus a markup of X%, for activities in Phase I. At the end of Phase I, FP will evaluate the program. If success appears likely, USSub will begin full-scale distribution of trademarked merchandise in the new market segment, pursuant to agreements negotiated with FP at that time.

(iii) Assume that under the contractual arrangements in effect between FP and USSub, the arm's length consideration for the merchandise and the trademark or other intangible property may be determined reliably under one or more transfer pricing methods. At issue in this example is the separate evaluation of the arm's length compensation for the marketing activities conducted by USSub in years 1 and following.

(iv) A functional analysis reveals that USSub's activities consist primarily of modifying the promotional materials created by FP, negotiating media buys, and arranging promotional events. FP separately compensates USSub for all Phase I activities, and detailed accounting information is available regarding the costs of these activities. The Phase I activities of USSub are similar to those of uncontrolled companies that perform, as their primary business activity, a range of advertising and media relations activities on a contract basis for uncontrolled parties.

(v) No information is available concerning the comparable uncontrolled prices for services in transactions similar to those engaged in by FP and USSub. Nor is any information available concerning uncontrolled transactions that would allow application of the cost of services plus method. It is possible to identify uncontrolled distributors or licensees of home furnishings that perform, as one component of their business activities, promotional activities similar to those performed by USSub. However, it is unlikely that publicly available accounting data from these companies would allow computation of the comparable transactional costs or total services costs associated with the marketing or promotional activities that these entities performed, as one component of their business activities. On the other hand, it is possible to identify uncontrolled advertising and media relations companies, the principal business activities of which are similar to the Phase I activities of USSub. Under these circumstances, the most reliable measure of an arm's length price is the comparable profits method of § 1.482-9(f). The uncontrolled advertising comparables' treatment of material items, such as classification of items as cost of goods sold or selling, general, and administrative expenses, may differ from that of USSub. Such inconsistencies in accounting treatment between the uncontrolled comparables and the tested party, or among the comparables, are less important when using the ratio of operating profit to total services costs under the comparable profits method for services in § 1.482-9(f). Under this method, the operating profit of USSub from the Phase I activities is compared to the operating profit of uncontrolled parties that perform general advertising and media relations as their primary business activity.

Example 12—Residual profit split preferred to other methods. (i) USP is a manufacturer of athletic apparel sold under the AA trademark, to which FP owns the worldwide rights. USP sells AA trademark apparel in countries throughout the world, but prior to year 1, USP did not sell its merchandise in Country X. In year 1, USP acquires an uncontrolled Country X company which becomes its wholly-owned subsidiary, XSub. USP enters into an exclusive distribution arrangement with XSub in Country X. Before being acquired by USP in year 1, XSub distributed athletic apparel purchased from uncontrolled suppliers and resold that merchandise to retailers. After being acquired by USP in year 1, XSub continues to distribute merchandise from uncontrolled suppliers and also begins to distribute AA trademark apparel. Under a separate agreement with USP, XSub uses its best efforts to promote the AA trademark in Country X, with the goal of maximizing sales volume and revenues from AA merchandise.

(ii) Prior to year 1, USP executed long-term endorsement contracts with several prominent professional athletes. These contracts give USP the right to use the names and likenesses of the athletes in any country in which AA merchandise is sold during the term of the contract. These contracts remain in effect for five years, starting in year 1. Before being acquired by USP, XSub renewed a long-term agreement with SportMart, an uncontrolled company that owns a nationwide chain of sporting goods retailers in Country X. XSub has been SportMart's primary supplier from the time that SportMart began operations. Under the agreement, SportMart will provide AA merchandise preferred shelf-space and will feature AA merchandise at no charge in its print ads and seasonal promotions. In consideration for these commitments, USP and XSub grant SportMart advance access to new products and the right to use the professional athletes under contract with USP in SportMart advertisements featuring AA merchandise (subject to approval of content by USP).

(iii) Assume that it is possible to segregate all transactions by XSub that involve distribution of merchandise acquired from uncontrolled distributors (non-controlled transactions). In addition, assume that, apart from the activities undertaken by USP and XSub to promote AA apparel in Country X, the arm's length compensation for other functions performed by USP and XSub in the Country X market in years 1 and following can be reliably determined. At issue in this Example 12 is the application of the residual profit split analysis to determine the appropriate division between USP and XSub of the balance of the operating profits from the Country X market, that is the portion attributable to nonroutine contributions to the marketing and promotional activities.

(iv) A functional analysis of the marketing and promotional activities conducted in the Country X market, as described in this example, indicates that both USP and XSub made nonroutine contributions to the business activity. USP contributed the long-term endorsement contracts with professional athletes. XSub contributed its long-term contractual rights with SportMart, which were made more valuable by its successful, long-term relationship with SportMart.

(v) Based on the facts and circumstances, including the fact that both USP and XSub made valuable nonroutine contributions to the marketing and promotional activities and an analysis of the availability (or lack thereof) of comparable and reliable market benchmarks, the Commissioner determines that the most reliable measure of an arm's length result is the residual profit split method in § 1.482-9(g). The residual profit split analysis would take into account both routine and nonroutine contributions by USP and XSub, in order to determine an appropriate allocation of the combined operating profits in the Country X market from the sale of AA merchandise and from related promotional and marketing activities.

Example 13. Preference for acquisition price method. (i) USP develops, manufactures, and distributes pharmaceutical products. USP and FS, USP's wholly-owned subsidiary, enter into a CSA to develop a new oncological drug, Oncol. Immediately prior to entering into the CSA, USP acquires Company X, an unrelated U.S. pharmaceutical company. Company X is solely engaged in oncological pharmaceutical research, and its only significant resources and capabilities are its workforce and its sole patent, which is associated with Compound X, a promising molecular compound derived from a rare plant, which USP reasonably anticipates will contribute to developing Oncol. All of Company X researchers will be engaged solely in research that is reasonably anticipated to contribute to developing Oncol as well. The rights in the Compound X and the commitment of Company X's researchers to the development of Oncol are platform contributions for which compensation is due from FS as part of a PCT.

(ii) In this case, the acquisition price method, based on the lump sum price paid by USP for Company X, is likely to provide a more reliable measure of an arm's length PCT Payment due to USP than the application of any other method. See §§ 1.482-4(c)(2) and 1.482-7(g)(5)(iv)(A).

Example 14. Preference for market capitalization method. (i) Company X is a publicly traded U.S. company solely engaged in oncological pharmaceutical research and its only significant resources and capabilities are its workforce and its sole patent, which is associated with Compound Y, a promising molecular compound derived from a rare plant. Company X has no marketable products. Company X enters into a CSA with FS, a newly-formed foreign subsidiary, to develop a new oncological drug, Oncol, derived from Compound Y. Compound Y is reasonably anticipated to contribute to developing Oncol. All of Company X researchers will be engaged solely in research that is reasonably anticipated to contribute to developing Oncol under the CSA. The rights in Compound Y and the commitment of Company X's researchers are platform contributions for which compensation is due from FS as part of a PCT.

(ii) In this case, given that Company X's platform contributions covered by PCTs relate to its entire economic value, the application of the market capitalization method, based on the market capitalization of Company X, provides a reliable measure of an arm's length result for Company X's PCTs to the CSA. See §§ 1.482-4(c)(2) and 1.482-7(g)(6)(v)(A).

Example 15. Preference for market capitalization method. (i) MicroDent, Inc. (MDI) is a publicly traded company that developed a new dental surgical microscope ScopeX-1, which drastically shortens many surgical procedures. On January 1 of Year 1, MDI entered into a CSA with a wholly-owned foreign subsidiary (FS) to develop ScopeX-2, the next generation of ScopeX-1. In the CSA, divisional interests are divided on a territorial basis. The rights associated with ScopeX-1, as well as MDI's research capabilities are reasonably anticipated to contribute to the development of ScopeX-2 and are therefore platform contributions for which compensation is due from FS as part of a PCT. At the time of the PCT, MDI's only product was the ScopeX-I microscope, although MDI was in the process of developing ScopeX-2. Concurrent with the CSA, MDI separately transfers exclusive and perpetual exploitation rights associated with ScopeX-1 to FS in the same territory as assigned to FS in the CSA.

(ii) Although the transactions between MDI and FS under the CSA are distinct from the transactions between MDI and FS relating to the exploitation rights for ScopeX-1, it is likely to be more reliable to evaluate the combined effect of the transactions than to evaluate them in isolation. This is because the combined transactions between MDI and FS relate to all of the economic value of MDI (that is, the exploitation rights and research rights associated with ScopeX-1, as well as the research capabilities of MDI). In this case, application of the market capitalization method, based on the enterprise value of MDI on January 1 of Year 1, is likely to provides a reliable measure of an arm's length payment for the aggregated transactions. See §§1.482-4(c)(2) and 1.482-7(g)(6)(v)(A).

(iii) Notwithstanding that the market capitalization method provides the most reliable measure of the aggregated transactions between MDI and FS, see §1.482-7(g)(2)(iv) for further considerations of when further analysis may be required to distinguish between the remuneration to MDI associated with PCTs under the CSA (for research rights and capabilities associated with ScopeX-1) and the remuneration to MDI for the exploitation rights associated with ScopeX-1.

Example 16. Income method (applied using CPM) preferred to acquisition price method. The facts are the same as in *Example 13,* except that the acquisition occurred significantly in advance of formation of the CSA, and reliable adjustments cannot be made for this time difference. In addition, Company X has other valuable molecular patents and associated research capabilities, apart from Compound X, that are not reasonably anticipated to contribute to the development of Oncol and that cannot be reliably valued. The CSA divides divisional interests on a territorial basis. Under the terms of the CSA, USP will undertake all R&D (consisting of laboratory research and clinical testing) and manufacturing associated with Oncol, as well as the distribution activities for its territory (the United States). FS will distribute Oncol in its territory (the rest of the world). FS's distribution activities are routine in nature, and the profitability from its activities may be reliably determined from third-party comparables. FS does not furnish any platform contributions. At the time of the PCT, reliable (ex ante) financial projections associated with the development of Oncol and its separate exploitation in each of USP's and FSub's assigned geographical territories are undertaken. In this case, application of the income method using CPM is likely to provide a more reliable measure of an arm's length result than application of the acquisition price method based on the price paid by USP for Company X. See §1.482-7(g)(4)(vi) and (5)(iv)(C).

Example 17. Evaluation of alternative methods. (i) The facts are the same as in *Example 13,* except that the acquisition occurred sometime prior to the CSA, and Company X has some areas of promising research that are not reasonably anticipated to contribute to developing Oncol. For purposes of this example, the CSA is assumed to divide divisional interests on a territorial basis. In general, the Commissioner determines that the acquisition price data is useful in informing the arm's length price, but not necessarily determinative. Under the terms of the CSA, USP will undertake all R&D (consisting of laboratory research and clinical testing) and manufacturing associated with Oncol, as well as the distribution activities for its territory (the United States). FS will distribute Oncol in its territory (the rest of the world). FS's distribution activities are routine in nature, and the profitability from its activities may be reliably determined from third-party comparables. At the time of the PCT, financial projections associated with the development of Oncol and its separate exploitation in each of USP's and FSub's assigned geographical territories are undertaken.

(ii) Under the facts, it is possible that the acquisition price method or the income method using CPM might reasonably be applied. Whether the acquisition price method or the income method provides the most reliable evidence of the arm's length price of USP's contributions depends on a number of factors, including the reliability of the financial projections, the reliability of the discount rate chosen, and the extent to which the acquisition price of Company X can be reliably adjusted to account for changes in value over the time period between the acquisition and the formation of the CSA and to account for the value of the in-process research done by Company X that does not constitute platform contributions to the CSA. See §1.482-7(g)(4)(vi) and (5)(iv)(A) and (C).

Example 18. Evaluation of alternative methods. (i) The facts are the same as in *Example 17,* except that FS has a patent on Compound Y, which the parties reasonably anticipate will be useful in mitigating potential side effects associated with Compound X and thereby contribute to the development of Oncol. The rights in Compound Y constitute a platform contribution for which compensation is due from USP as part of a PCT. The value of FS's platform contribution cannot be reliably measured by market benchmarks.

(ii) Under the facts, it is possible that either the acquisition price method and the income method together or the residual profit split method might reasonably be applied to determine the arm's length PCT Payments due between USP and FS. Under the first option the PCT Payment for the platform contributions related to Company X's workforce and Compound X would be determined using the acquisition price method referring to the lump sum price paid by USP for Company X. Because the value of these platform contributions can be determined by reference to a market benchmark, they are considered routine platform contributions. Accordingly, under this option, the platform contribution related to Compound Y would be the only nonroutine platform contribution and the relevant PCT Payment is determined using the income method. Under the second option, rather than looking to the acquisition price for Company X, all the platform contributions are considered nonroutine and the RPSM is applied to determine the PCT Payments for each platform contribution. Under either option, the PCT Payments will be netted against each other.

(iii) Whether the acquisition price method together with the income method or the residual profit split method provides the most reliable evidence of the arm's length price of the platform contributions of USP and FS depends on a number of factors, including the reliability of the determination of the relative values of the platform contributions for purposes of the RPSM, and the extent to which the acquisition price of Company X can be reliably adjusted to account for changes in value over the time period between the acquisition and the formation of the CSA and to account for the value of the rights in the in-process research done by Company X that does not constitute platform contributions to the CSA. In these circumstances, it is also relevant to consider whether the results of each method are consistent with each other, or whether one or both methods are consistent with other potential methods that could be applied. See §1.482-7(g)(4)(vi), (5)(iv), and (7)(iv).

(c) *Effective/applicability date.*—(1) *In general.*—Paragraphs (a) and (b) *Examples 10* through *12* of this section are generally applicable for taxable years beginning after December 31, 2006. Paragraph (b) *Examples 13* through *18* of this section are generally applicable on January 5, 2009.

(2) *Election to apply regulation to earlier taxable years.*—A person may elect to apply the provisions of paragraph (b) *Examples 10, 11,* and *12* of this section to earlier taxable years in accordance with the rules set forth in §1.482-9(n)(2). [Reg. §1.482-8.]

□ [*T.D. 8552, 7-1-94. Amended by T.D. 9278, 7-31-2006; T.D. 9441, 12-31-2008 and T.D. 9456, 7-31-2009* (corrected 9-8-2009) *and T.D. 9568, 12-16-2011.*]

Proposed Regulation

Section 1.482-8 is redesignated as §1.482-9 and a new §1.482-8 is added to read as follows:

§1.482-8. Allocation of income earned in a global securities dealing operation.—(a) *General requirements and definitions.*—(1) *In general.*—Where two or more controlled taxpayers are participants in a global dealing operation, the allocation of income, gains, losses, deductions, credits and allowances (referred to herein as income and deductions) from the global dealing operation is determined under this section. The arm's length allocation of income and deductions related to a global dealing operation must be determined under one of the methods listed in paragraphs (b) through (f) of this section. Each of the methods must be applied in accordance with all of the provisions of §1.482-1, including the best method rule of §1.482-1(c), the comparability analysis of §1.482-1(d), and the arm's length range of §1.482-1(e), as those sections are supplemented or modified in paragraphs (a)(3) and (a)(4) of this section. The available methods are—

(i) The comparable uncontrolled financial transaction method, described in paragraph (b) of this section;

(ii) The gross margin method, described in paragraph (c) of this section;

(iii) The gross markup method, described in paragraph (d) of this section;

(iv) The profit split method, described in paragraph (e) of this section; and

(v) Unspecified methods, described in paragraph (f) of this section.

(2) *Definitions.*—(i) *Global dealing operation.*—A global dealing operation consists of the execution of customer transactions, including marketing, sales, pricing and risk management activities, in a particular financial product or line of financial products, in multiple tax jurisdictions and/or through multiple participants, as defined in paragraph (a)(2)(ii) of this section. The taking of proprietary positions is not included within the definition of a global dealing operation unless the proprietary positions are entered into by a regular dealer in securities in its capacity as such a dealer under paragraph (a)(2)(iii) of this section. Lending activities are not included within the definition of a global dealing operation. Therefore, income earned from such lending activities or from securities held for investment is not income from a global dealing operation and is not governed by this section. A global dealing operation may consist of several different business activities engaged in by participants. Whether a separate business activity is a global dealing operation shall be determined with respect to each type of financial product entered on the taxpayer's books and records.

(ii) *Participant.*—(A) A participant is a controlled taxpayer, as defined in § 1.482-1(i)(5), that is—

(1) A regular dealer in securities as defined in paragraph (a)(2)(iii) of this section; or

(2) A member of a group of controlled taxpayers which includes a regular dealer in securities, but only if that member conducts one or more activities related to the activities of such dealer.

(B) For purposes of paragraph (a)(2)(ii)(A)(2) of this section, such related activities are marketing, sales, pricing, risk management or brokering activities. Such related activities do not include credit analysis, accounting services, back office services, general supervision and control over the policies of the controlled taxpayer, or the provision of a guarantee of one or more transactions entered into by a regular dealer in securities or other participant.

(iii) *Regular dealer in securities.*—For purposes of this section, a regular dealer in securities is a taxpayer that—

(A) Regularly and actively offers to, and in fact does, purchase securities from and sell securities to customers who are not controlled taxpayers in the ordinary course of a trade or business; or

(B) Regularly and actively offers to, and in fact does, enter into, assume, offset, assign or otherwise terminate positions in securities with customers who are not controlled entities in the ordinary course of a trade or business.

(iv) *Security.*—For purposes of this section, a security is a security as defined in section 475(c)(2) or foreign currency.

(3) *Factors for determining comparability for a global dealing operation.*—The comparability factors set out in this paragraph (a)(3) must be applied in place of the comparability factors described in § 1.482-1(d)(3) for purposes of evaluating a global dealing operation.

(i) *Functional analysis.*—In lieu of the list set forth in § 1.482-1(d)(3)(i)(A) through (H), functions that may need to be accounted for in determining the comparability of two transactions are—

(A) Product research and development;

(B) Marketing;

(C) Pricing;

(D) Brokering; and

(E) Risk management.

(ii) *Contractual terms.*—In addition to the terms set forth in § 1.482-1(d)(3)(ii)(A), and subject to § 1.482-1(d)(3)(ii)(B), significant contractual terms for financial products transactions include—

(A) Sales or purchase volume;

(B) Rights to modify or transfer the contract;

(C) Contingencies to which the contract is subject or that are embedded in the contract;

(D) Length of the contract;

(E) Settlement date;

(F) Place of settlement (or delivery);

(G) Notional principal amount;

(H) Specified indices;

(I) The currency or currencies in which the contract is denominated;

(J) Choice of law and jurisdiction governing the contract to the extent chosen by the parties; and

(K) Dispute resolution, including binding arbitration.

(iii) *Risk.*—In lieu of the list set forth in § 1.482-1(d)(3), significant risks that could affect the prices or profitability include—

(A) Market risks, including the volatility of the price of the underlying property;

(B) Liquidity risks, including the fact that the property (or the hedges of the property) trades in a thinly traded market;

(C) Hedging risks;

(D) Creditworthiness of the counterparty; and

(E) Country and transfer risk.

(iv) *Economic conditions.*—. In lieu of the list set forth in § 1.482-1(d)(3)(iv)(A) through (H), significant economic conditions that could affect the prices or profitability include—

(A) The similarity of geographic markets;

(B) The relative size and sophistication of the markets;

(C) The alternatives reasonably available to the buyer and seller;

(D) The volatility of the market; and

(E) The time the particular transaction is entered into.

(4) *Arm's length range.*—(i) *General rule.*—Except as modified in this paragraph (a)(4), § 1.482-1(e) will apply to determine the arm's length range of transactions entered into by a global dealing operation as defined in paragraph (a)(2)(i) of this section. In determining the arm's length range, whether the participant is a buyer or seller is a relevant factor.

(ii) *Reliability.*—In determining the reliability of an arm's length range, it is necessary to consider the fact that the market for financial products is highly volatile and participants in a global dealing operation frequently earn only thin profit margins. The reliability of using a statistical range in establishing a comparable price of a financial product in a global dealing operation is based on facts and circumstances. In a global dealing operation, close proximity in time between a controlled transaction and an uncontrolled transaction may be a relevant factor in determining the reliability of the uncontrolled transaction as a measure of the arm's length price. The relevant time period will depend on the price volatility of the particular product.

(iii) *Authority to make adjustments.*—The district director may, notwithstanding § 1.482-1(e)(1), adjust a taxpayer's results under a method applied on a transaction by transaction basis if a valid statistical analysis demonstrates that the taxpayer's controlled prices, when analyzed on an aggregate basis, provide results that are not arm's length. See § 1.482-1(f)(2)(iv). This may occur, for example, when there is a pattern of prices in controlled transactions that are higher or lower than the prices of comparable uncontrolled transactions.

(5) *Examples.*—The following examples illustrate the principles of this paragraph (a).

Example 1. Identification of participants. (i) B is a foreign bank that acts as a market maker in foreign currency in country X, the country of which it is a resident. C, a country Y resident corporation, D, a country Z resident corporation, and USFX, a U.S. resident corporation are all members of a controlled group of taxpayers with B, and each acts as a market maker in foreign currency. In addition to market-making activities conducted in their respective countries, C, D, and USFX each employ marketers and traders, who also perform risk management with respect to their foreign currency operations. In a typical business day, B, C, D, and USFX each enter into several hundred spot and forward contracts to purchase and sell Deutsche marks (DM) with unrelated third parties on the interbank market. In the ordinary course of business, B, C, D, and USFX also enter into contracts to purchase and sell DM with each other.

(ii) Under § 1.482-8(a)(2)(iii), B, C, D, and USFX are each regular dealers in securities because they each regularly and actively offer to, and in fact do, purchase and sell currencies to customers who are not controlled taxpayers, in the ordinary course of their trade or business. Consequently, each controlled taxpayer is also a participant. Together, B, C, D, and USFX conduct a global dealing operation within the meaning of § 1.482-8(a)(2)(i) because they execute customer transactions in multiple tax jurisdictions. Accordingly, the controlled transactions between B, C, D, and USFX are evaluated under the rules of § 1.482-8.

(2) *Determination of an arm's length price.*—(i) *In general.*—The gross margin method measures an arm's length price by subtracting the appropriate gross profit from the applicable resale price for the financial product involved in the controlled transaction under review.

(ii) *Applicable resale price.*—The applicable resale price is equal to either the price at which the financial product involved is sold in an uncontrolled sale or the price at which contemporaneous resales of the same product are made. If the product purchased in the controlled sale is resold to one or more related parties in a series of controlled sales before being resold in an uncontrolled sale, the applicable resale price is the price at which the product is resold to an uncontrolled party, or the price at which contemporaneous resales of the same product are made. In such case, the determination of the appropriate gross profit will take into account the functions of all members of the controlled group participating in the series of controlled sales and final uncontrolled resales, as well as any other relevant factors described in paragraph (a)(3) of this section.

(iii) *Appropriate gross profit.*—The appropriate gross profit is computed by multiplying the applicable resale price by the gross profit margin, expressed as a percentage of total revenue derived from sales, earned in comparable uncontrolled transactions.

(3) *Comparability and reliability.*—(i) *In general.*—The provisions of § 1.482-1(d), as modified by paragraph (a)(3) of this section, apply in determining whether a controlled transaction is comparable to a particular uncontrolled transaction. All of the factors described in paragraph (a)(3) of this section must be considered in determining the comparability of two financial products transactions, including the functions performed. The gross margin method considers whether a participant has earned a sufficient gross profit margin on the resale of a financial product (or line of products) given the functions performed by the participant. A reseller's gross profit margin provides compensation for performing resale functions related to the product or products under review, including an operating profit in return for the reseller's investment of capital and the assumption of risks. Accordingly, where a participant does not take title, or does not become a party to a financial product, the reseller's return to capital and assumption of risk are additional factors that must be considered in determining an appropriate gross profit margin. An appropriate gross profit margin primarily should be derived from comparable uncontrolled purchases and resales of the reseller involved in the controlled sale. This is because similar characteristics are more likely to be found among different resales of a financial product or products made by the same reseller than among sales made by other resellers. In the absence of comparable uncontrolled transactions involving the same reseller, an appropriate gross profit margin may be derived from comparable uncontrolled transactions of other resellers.

(ii) *Adjustments for differences between controlled and uncontrolled transactions.*—If there are material differences between controlled and uncontrolled transactions that would affect the gross profit margin, adjustments should be made to the gross profit margin earned in the uncontrolled transaction according to the comparability provisions of § 1.482-1(d)(2) and paragraph (a)(3) of this section. For this purpose, consideration of operating expenses associated with functions performed and risks assumed may be necessary because differences in functions performed are often reflected in operating expenses. The effect of a difference in functions performed on gross profit, however, is not necessarily equal to the difference in the amount of related operating expenses.

(iii) *Reliability.*—In order for the gross margin method to be considered a reliable measure of an arm's length price, the gross profit should ordinarily represent an amount that would allow the participant who resells the product to recover its expenses (whether directly related to selling the product or more generally related to maintaining its operations) and to earn a profit commensurate with the functions it performed. The gross margin method may be a reliable means of establishing an arm's length price where there is a purchase and resale of a financial product and the participant who resells the property does not substantially participate in developing a product or in tailoring the product to the unique requirements of a customer prior to the resale.

(iv) *Data and assumptions.*—(A) *In general.*—The reliability of the results derived from the gross margin method is affected by the completeness and accuracy of the data used and the reliability of the assumptions made to apply the method. See § 1.482-1(c)(2)(ii). A participant may establish the gross margin by comparing the bid and offer prices on a public exchange or quotation media. In such case, the prices must be contemporaneous to the controlled transaction, and the participant must retain records of such data.

(B) *Consistency in accounting.*—The degree of consistency in accounting practices between the controlled transaction and the uncontrolled transactions may affect the reliability of the gross margin method. For example, differences as between controlled and uncontrolled transactions in the method used to value similar financial products (including methods of accounting, methods of estimation, and the timing for changes of such methods) could affect the gross profit. The ability to make reliable adjustments for such differences could affect the reliability of the results.

(4) *Arm's length range.*—See § 1.482-1(e)(2) and paragraph (a)(4) of this section for the determination of an arm's length range.

(5) *Example.*—The following example illustrates the principles of this paragraph (c).

Example 1. Gross margin method. (i) T is a U.S. resident financial institution that acts as a market maker in debt and equity instruments issued by U.S. corporations. Most of T's sales are to U.S.-based customers. TS, T's U.K. subsidiary, acts as a market maker in debt and equity instruments issued by European corporations and conducts most of its business with European-based customers. On occasion, however, a customer of TS wishes to purchase a security that is either held by or more readily accessible to T. To facilitate this transaction, T sells the security it owns or acquires to TS, who then promptly sells it to the customer. T and TS generally derive the majority of their profit on the difference between the price at which they purchase and the price at which they sell securities (the bid/offer spread). On average, TS's gross profit margin on its purchases and sales of securities from unrelated persons is 2%. Applying the comparability factors specified in § 1.482-8(a)(3), T's purchases and sales with unrelated persons are comparable to the purchases and sales between T and TS.

(ii) Under § 1.482-8(a)(2), T and TS are participants in a global dealing operation that deals in debt and equity securities. Since T's related purchases and sales are comparable to its unrelated purchases and sales, if TS's gross profit margin on purchases and sales of comparable securities from unrelated persons is 2%, TS should also typically earn a 2% gross profit on the securities it purchases from T. Thus, when TS resells for $100 a security that it purchased from T, the arm's length price at which TS would have purchased the security from T would normally be $98 ($100 sales price minus (2% gross profit margin x $100)).

(d) *Gross markup method.*—(1) *General rule.*—The gross markup method evaluates whether the amount allocated to a participant in a global dealing operation is arm's length by reference to the gross profit markup realized in comparable uncontrolled transactions. The gross markup method may be used to establish an arm's length price for a transaction where a participant purchases a financial product from an unrelated party that the participant sells to a related party. This method may apply to transactions involving the purchase and resale of debt and equity instruments. The method may also be used to evaluate whether a participant has received an arm's length commission for its role in a global dealing operation when the participant has not taken title to a security or has not become a party to a derivative financial product. To meet the arm's length standard, the gross profit markup on controlled transactions should be similar to that of comparable uncontrolled transactions.

(2) *Determination of an arm's length price.*—(i) *In general.*—The gross markup method measures an arm's length price by adding the appropriate gross profit to the participant's cost or anticipated cost, of purchasing, holding, or structuring the financial product involved in the controlled transaction under review (or in the case of a derivative financial product, the initial net present value, measured by the anticipated cost of purchasing, holding, or structuring the product).

(ii) *Appropriate gross profit.*—The appropriate gross profit is computed by multiplying the participant's cost or anticipated cost of purchasing, holding, or structuring a transaction by the gross profit markup, expressed as a percentage of cost, earned in comparable uncontrolled transactions.

(3) *Comparability and reliability.*—(i) *In general.*—The provisions of § 1.482-1(d), as modified by paragraph (a)(3) of this section, apply in determining whether a controlled transaction is comparable to a

particular uncontrolled transaction. All of the factors described in paragraph (a)(3) of this section must be considered in determining the comparability of two financial products transactions, including the functions performed. The gross markup method considers whether a participant has earned a sufficient gross markup on the sale of a financial product, or line of products, given the functions it has performed. A participant's gross profit markup provides compensation for purchasing, hedging, and transactional structuring functions related to the transaction under review, including an operating profit in return for the investment of capital and the assumption of risks. Accordingly, where a participant does not take title, or does not become a party to a financial product, the reseller's return to capital and assumption of risk are additional factors that must be considered in determining the gross profit markup. An appropriate gross profit markup primarily should be derived from comparable uncontrolled purchases and sales of the participant involved in the controlled sale. This is because similar characteristics are more likely to be found among different sales of property made by the same participant than among sales made by other resellers. In the absence of comparable uncontrolled transactions involving the same participant, an appropriate gross profit markup may be derived from comparable uncontrolled transactions of other parties whether or not such parties are members of the same controlled group.

(ii) *Adjustments for differences between controlled and uncontrolled transactions.*—If there are material differences between controlled and uncontrolled transactions that would affect the gross profit markup, adjustments should be made to the gross profit markup earned in the uncontrolled transaction according to the comparability provisions of § 1.482-1(d)(2) and paragraph (a)(3) of this section. For this purpose, consideration of operating expenses associated with the functions performed and risks assumed may be necessary, because differences in functions performed are often reflected in operating expenses. The effect of a difference in functions on gross profit, however, is not necessarily equal to the difference in the amount of related operating expenses.

(iii) *Reliability.*—In order for the gross markup method to be considered a reliable measure of an arm's length price, the gross profit should ordinarily represent an amount that would allow the participant who purchases the product to recover its expenses (whether directly related to selling the product or more generally related to maintaining its operations) and to earn a profit commensurate with the functions it performed. As with the gross margin method, the gross markup method may be a reliable means of establishing an arm's length price where there is a purchase and resale of a financial product and the participant who resells the property does not substantially participate in developing a product or in tailoring the product to the unique requirements of a customer prior to the resale.

(iv) *Data and assumptions.*—(A) *In general.*—The reliability of the results derived from the gross markup method is affected by the completeness and accuracy of the data used and the reliability of the assumptions made to apply the method. See § 1.482-1(c)(2)(ii). A participant may establish the gross markup by comparing the bid and offer prices on a public exchange or quotation media. In such case, the prices must be contemporaneous with the controlled transaction, and the participant must retain records of such data.

(B) *Consistency in accounting.*—The degree of consistency in accounting practices between the controlled transaction and the uncontrolled transactions may affect the reliability of the gross markup method. For example, differences as between controlled and uncontrolled transactions in the method used to value similar financial products (including methods in accounting, methods of estimation, and the timing for changes of such methods) could affect the gross profit. The ability to make reliable adjustments for such differences could affect the reliability of the results.

(4) *Arm's length range.*—See § 1.482-1(e)(2) and paragraph (a)(4) of this section for the determination of an arm's length range.

(e) *Profit split method.*—(1) *General rule.*—The profit split method evaluates whether the allocation of the combined operating profit or loss of a global dealing operation to one or more participants is at arm's length by reference to the relative value of each participant's contribution to that combined operating profit or loss. The combined operating profit or loss must be derived from the most narrowly identifiable business activity of the participants for which data is available that includes the controlled transactions (relevant business activity).

(2) *Appropriate share of profit and loss.*—(i) *In general.*—The relative value of each participant's contribution to the global dealing activity must be determined in a manner that reflects the functions performed, risks assumed, and resources employed by each participant in the activity, consistent with the comparability provisions of § 1.482-1(d), as modified by paragraph (a)(3) of this section. Such an allocation is intended to correspond to the division of profit or loss that would result from an arrangement between uncontrolled taxpayers, each performing functions similar to those of the various controlled taxpayers engaged in the relevant business activity. The relative value of the contributions of each participant in the global dealing operation should be measured in a manner that most reliably reflects each contribution made to the global dealing operation and each participant's role in that contribution. In appropriate cases, the participants may find that a multi-factor formula most reliably measures the relative value of the contributions to the profitability of the global dealing operation. The profit allocated to any particular participant using a profit split method is not necessarily limited to the total operating profit from the global dealing operation. For example, in a given year, one participant may earn a profit while another participant incurs a loss, so long as the arrangement is comparable to an arrangement to which two uncontrolled parties would agree. In addition, it may not be assumed that the combined operating profit or loss from the relevant business activity should be shared equally or in any other arbitrary proportion. The specific method must be determined under paragraph (e)(4) of this section.

(ii) *Adjustment of factors to measure contribution clearly.*—In order to reliably measure the value of a participant's contribution, the factors, for example, those used in a multi-factor formula, must be expressed in units of measure that reliably quantify the relative contribution of the participant. If the data or information is influenced by factors other than the value of the contribution, adjustments must be made for such differences so that the factors used in the formula only measure the relative value of each participant's contribution. For example, if trader compensation is used as a factor to measure the value added by the participants' trading expertise, adjustments must be made for variances in compensation paid to traders due solely to differences in the cost of living.

(3) *Definitions.*—The definitions in this paragraph (e)(3) apply for purposes of applying the profit split methods in this paragraph (e).

Gross profit is gross income earned by the global dealing operation.

Operating expenses includes all expenses not included in the computation of gross profit, except for interest, foreign income taxes as defined in § 1.901-2(a), domestic income taxes, and any expenses not related to the global dealing activity that is evaluated under the profit split method. With respect to interest expense, see section 864(e) and the regulations thereunder and § 1.882-5.

Operating profit or loss is gross profit less operating expenses, and includes all income, expense, gain, loss, credits or allowances attributable to each global dealing activity that is evaluated under the profit split method. It does not include income, expense, gain, loss, credits or allowances from activities that are not evaluated under the profit split method, nor does it include extraordinary gains or losses that do not relate to the continuing global dealing activities of the participant.

(4) *Application.*—Profit or loss shall be allocated under the profit split method using either the total profit split, described in paragraph (e)(5) of this section, or the residual profit split, described in paragraph (e)(6) of this section.

(5) *Total profit split.*—(i) *In general.*—The total profit split derives the percentage of the combined operating profit of the participants in a global dealing operation allocable to a participant in the global dealing operation by evaluating whether uncontrolled taxpayers who perform similar functions, assume similar risks, and employ similar resources would allocate their combined operating profits in the same manner.

(ii) *Comparability.*—The total profit split evaluates the manner by which comparable uncontrolled taxpayers divide the combined operating profit of a particular global dealing activity. The degree of comparability between the controlled and uncontrolled taxpayers is determined by applying the comparability standards of § 1.482-1(d), as modified by paragraph (a)(3) of this section. In particular, the functional analysis required by § 1.482-1(d)(3)(i) and paragraph (a)(3)(i) of this section is essential to determine whether two situations are comparable. Nevertheless, in certain cases, no comparable ventures between uncontrolled taxpayers may exist. In this situation, it is necessary to analyze the remaining factors set forth in paragraph (a)(3) of this section that could affect the division of operating profits between parties. If there are differences between the controlled and uncontrolled taxpayers that would materially affect the division of operating profit, adjustments must be made according to the provisions of § 1.482-1(d)(2) and paragraph (a)(3) of this section.

(iii) *Reliability.*—As indicated in § 1.482-1(c)(2)(i), as the degree of comparability between the controlled and uncontrolled transactions increases, the reliability of a total profit split also increases. In a global dealing operation, however, the absence of external market benchmarks (for example, joint ventures between uncontrolled taxpayers) on which to base the allocation of operating profits does not preclude use of this method if the allocation of the operating profit takes into account the relative contribution of each participant. The reliability of this method is increased to the extent that the allocation has economic significance for purposes other than tax (for example, satisfying regulatory standards and reporting, or determining bonuses paid to management or traders). The reliability of the analysis under this method may also be enhanced by the fact that all parties to the controlled transaction are evaluated under this method. The reliability of the results, however, of an analysis based on information from all parties to a transaction is affected by the reliability of the data and assumptions pertaining to each party to the controlled transaction. Thus, if the data and assumptions are significantly more reliable with respect to one of the parties than with respect to the others, a different method, focusing solely on the results of that party, may yield more reliable results.

(iv) *Data and assumptions.*—(A) *In general.*—The reliability of the results derived from the total profit split method is affected by the quality of the data used and the assumptions used to apply the method. See§ 1.482-1(c)(2)(ii). The reliability of the allocation of income, expense, or other attributes between the participants' relevant business activities and the participants' other activities will affect the reliability of the determination of the combined operating profit and its allocation among the participants. If it is not possible to allocate income, expense, or other attributes directly based on factual relationships, a reasonable allocation formula may be used. To the extent direct allocations are not made, the reliability of the results derived from application of this method is reduced relative to the results of a method that requires fewer allocations of income, expense, and other attributes. Similarly, the reliability of the results derived from application of this method is affected by the extent to which it is possible to apply the method to the participants' financial data that is related solely to the controlled transactions. For example, if the relevant business activity is entering into interest rate swaps with both controlled and uncontrolled taxpayers, it may not be possible to apply the method solely to financial data related to the controlled transactions. In such case, the reliability of the results derived from application of this method will be reduced.

(B) *Consistency in accounting.*—The degree of consistency between the controlled and uncontrolled taxpayers in accounting practices that materially affect the items that determine the amount and allocation of operating profit affects the reliability of the result. Thus, for example, if differences in financial product valuation or in cost allocation practices would materially affect operating profit, the ability to make reliable adjustments for such differences would affect the reliability of the results.

(6) *Residual profit split.*—(i) *In general.*—The residual profit split allocates the combined operating profit or loss between participants following the two-step process set forth in paragraphs (e)(6)(ii) and (iii) of this section.

(ii) *Allocate income to routine contributions.*—The first step allocates operating income to each participant to provide an arm's length return for its routine contributions to the global dealing operation. Routine contributions are contributions of the same or similar kind as those made by uncontrolled taxpayers involved in similar business activities for which it is possible to identify market returns. Routine contributions ordinarily include contributions of tangible property, services, and intangibles that are generally owned or performed by uncontrolled taxpayers engaged in similar activities. For example, transactions processing and credit analysis are typically routine contributions. In addition, a participant that guarantees obligations of or otherwise provides credit support to another controlled taxpayer in a global dealing operation is regarded as making a routine contribution. A functional analysis is required to identify the routine contributions according to the functions performed, risks assumed, and resources employed by each of the participants. Market returns for the routine contributions should be determined by reference to the returns achieved by uncontrolled taxpayers engaged in similar activities, consistent with the methods described in §§ 1.482-2 through 1.482-4 and this § 1.482-8.

(iii) *Allocate residual profit.*—The allocation of income to the participant's routine contributions will not reflect profits attributable to each participant's valuable nonroutine contributions to the global dealing operation. Thus, in cases where valuable nonroutine contributions are present, there normally will be an unallocated residual profit after the allocation of income described in paragraph (e)(6)(ii) of this section. Under this second step, the residual profit generally should be divided among the participants based upon the relative value of each of their nonroutine contributions. Nonroutine contributions are contributions so integral to the global dealing operation that it is impossible to segregate them from the operation and find a separate market return for the contribution. Pricing and risk managing financial products almost invariably involve nonroutine contributions. Similarly, product development and information technology are generally nonroutine contributions. Marketing may be a nonroutine contribution if the marketer substantially participates in developing a product or in tailoring the product to the unique requirements of a customer. The relative value of the nonroutine contributions of each participant in the global dealing operation should be measured in a manner that most reliably reflects each nonroutine contribution made to the global dealing operation and each participant's role in the nonroutine contributions.

(iv) *Comparability.*—The first step of the residual profit split relies on external market benchmarks of profitability. Thus, the comparability considerations that are relevant for the first step of the residual profit split are those that are relevant for the methods that are used to determine market returns for routine contributions. In the second step of the residual profit split, however, it may not be possible to rely as heavily on external market benchmarks. Nevertheless, in order to divide the residual profits of a global dealing operation in accordance with each participant's nonroutine contributions, it is necessary to apply the comparability standards of § 1.482-1(d), as modified by paragraph (a)(3) of this section. In particular, the functional analysis required by § 1.482-1(d)(3)(i) and paragraph (a)(3)(i) of this section is essential to determine whether two situations are comparable. Nevertheless, in certain cases, no comparable ventures between uncontrolled taxpayers may exist. In this situation, it is necessary to analyze the remaining factors set forth in paragraph (a)(3) of this section that could affect the division of operating profits between parties. If there are differences between the controlled and uncontrolled taxpayers that would materially affect the division of operating profit, adjustments must be made according to the provisions of § 1.482-1(d)(2) and paragraph (a)(3) of this section.

(v) *Reliability.*—As indicated in § 1.482-1(c)(2)(i), as the degree of comparability between the controlled and uncontrolled transactions increases, the reliability of a residual profit split also increases. In a global dealing operation, however, the absence of external market benchmarks (for example, joint ventures between uncontrolled taxpayers) on which to base the allocation of operating profits does not preclude use of this method if the allocation of the residual profit takes into account the relative contribution of each participant. The reliability of this method is increased to the extent that the allocation has economic significance for purposes other than tax (for example, satisfying regulatory standards and reporting, or determining bonuses paid to management or traders). The reliability of the analysis under this method may also be enhanced by the fact that all parties to the controlled transaction are evaluated under this method. The reliability of the results, however, of an analysis based on information from all parties to a transaction is affected by the reliability of the data and assumptions pertaining to each party to the controlled transaction. Thus, if the data and assumptions are significantly more reliable with respect to one of the parties than with respect to the others, a different method, focusing solely on the results of that party, may yield more reliable results.

(vi) *Data and assumptions.*—(A) *General rule.*—The reliability of the results derived from the residual profit split is measured under the standards set forth in paragraph (e)(5)(iv)(A) of this section.

(B) *Consistency in accounting.*—The degree of accounting consistency between controlled and uncontrolled taxpayers is measured under the standards set forth in paragraph (e)(5)(iv)(B) of this section.

(7) *Arm's length range.*—See § 1.482-1(e)(2) and paragraph (a)(4) of this section for the determination of an arm's length range.

(8) *Examples.*—The following examples illustrate the principles of this paragraph (e).

Example 1. Total profit split. (i) P, a U.S. corporation, establishes a separate U.S. subsidiary (USsub) to conduct a global dealing operation in over-the-counter derivatives. USsub in turn establishes subsidiaries incorporated and doing business in the U.K. (UKsub) and Japan (Jsub). Ussub, Uksub, and Jsub each employ marketers and traders who work closely together to design and sell derivative products to meet the particular needs of customers. Each also employs personnel who process and confirm trades, reconcile trade tickets and provide ongoing administrative support (back office services) for the global dealing operation. The global dealing operation maintains a single common book for each type of risk, and the book is maintained where the head trader for that type of risk is located. Thus, notional principal contracts denominated in North and South American currencies are booked in USsub, notional principal contracts denominated in European currencies are booked in UKsub, and notional principal contracts denominated in Japanese yen are booked in Jsub. However, each of the affiliates has authorized a trader located in each of the other affiliates to risk manage its books during periods when the booking location is closed. This grant of authority is necessary because marketers, regardless of their location, are expected to sell all of the group's products, and need to receive pricing information with respect to products during their clients' business hours, even if the booking location is closed. Moreover, P is known for making a substantial amount of its profits from trading activities, and frequently does not hedge the positions arising from its customer transactions in an attempt to profit from market changes. As a result, the traders in "off-hours" locations must have a substantial amount of trading authority in order to react to market changes.

(ii) Under § 1.482-8(a)(2), USsub, UKsub and Jsub are participants in a global dealing operation in over-the-counter derivatives. P determines that the total profit split method is the best method to allocate an arm's length amount of income to each participant. P allocates the operating profit from the global dealing operation between USsub, UKsub and Jsub on the basis of the relative compensation paid to marketers and traders in each location. In making the allocation, P adjusts the compensation amounts to account for factors unrelated to job performance, such as the higher cost of living in certain jurisdictions. Because the traders receive significantly greater compensation than marketers in order to account for their greater contribution to the profits of the global dealing operation, P need not make additional adjustments or weight the compensation of the traders more heavily in allocating the operating profit between the affiliates. For rules concerning the source of income allocated to Ussub, Uksub and Jsub (and any U.S. trade or business of the participants), see § 1.863-3(h).

Example 2. Total profit split. The facts are the same as in Example 1, except that the labor market in Japan is such that traders paid by Jsub are paid the same as marketers paid by Jsub at the same seniority level, even though the traders contribute substantially more to the profitability of the global dealing operation. As a result, the allocation method used by P is unlikely to compensate the functions provided by each affiliate so as to be a reliable measure of an arm's length result under §§ 1.482-8(e)(2) and 1.482-1(c)(1), unless P weights the compensation of traders more heavily than the compensation of marketers or develops another method of measuring the contribution of traders to the profitability of the global dealing operation.

Example 3. Total profit split. The facts are the same as in Example 2, except that, in P's annual report to shareholders, P divides its operating profit from customer business into "dealing profit" and "trading profit." Because both marketers and traders are involved in the dealing function, P divides the "dealing profit" between the affiliates on the basis of the relative compensation of marketers and traders. However, because only the traders contribute to the trading profit, P divides the trading profit between the affiliates on the basis of the relative compensation only of the traders. In making that allocation, P must adjust the compensation of traders in Jsub in order to account for factors not related to job performance.

Example 4. Total profit split. The facts are the same as in Example 1, except that P is required by its regulators to hedge its customer positions as much as possible and therefore does not earn any "trading profit." As a result, the marketing intangibles, such as customer relationships, are relatively more important than the intangibles used by traders. Accordingly, P must weight the compensation of marketers more heavily than the compensation of traders in order to take into account accurately the contribution each function makes to the profitability of the business.

Example 5. Residual profit split. (i) P is a U.S. corporation that engages in a global dealing operation in foreign currency options directly and through controlled taxpayers that are incorporated and operate in the United Kingdom (UKsub) and Japan (Jsub). Each controlled taxpayer is a participant in a global dealing operation. Each participant employs marketers and traders who work closely together to design and sell foreign currency options that meet the particular needs of customers. Each participant also employs salespeople who sell foreign currency options with standardized terms and conditions, as well as other financial products offered by the controlled group. The traders in each location risk manage a common book of transactions during the relevant business hours of each location. P has a AAA credit rating and is the legal counterparty to all third party transactions. The traders in each location have discretion to execute contracts in the name of P. UKsub employs personnel who process and confirm trades, reconcile trade tickets, and provide ongoing administrative support (back office services) for all the participants in the global dealing operation. The global dealing operation has generated $192 of operating profit for the period.

(ii) After analyzing the foreign currency options business, P has determined that the residual profit split method is the best method to allocate the operating profit of the global dealing operation and to determine an arm's length amount of compensation allocable to each participant in the global dealing operation.

(iii) The first step of the residual profit split method (§ 1.482-8(e)(6)(ii)) requires P to identify the routine contributions performed by each participant. P determines that the functions performed by the salespeople are routine. P determines that the arm's length compensation for salespeople is $3, $4, and $5 in the United States, the United Kingdom, and Japan, respectively. Thus, P allocates $3, $4, and $5 to P, UKsub, and Jsub, respectively.

(iv) Although the back office function would not give rise to participant status, in the context of a residual profit split allocation, the back office function is relevant for purposes of receiving remuneration for routine contributions to a global dealing operation. P determines that an arm's length compersation for the back office is $20. Since the back office services constitute routine contributions, $20 of income is allocated to UKsub under step 1 of the residual profit split method. In addition, P determines that the comparable arm's length compensation for the risk to which P is subject as counterparty is $40. Accordingly, $40 is allocated to P as compensation for acting as counterparty to the transactions entered into in P's name by Jsub and UKsub.

(v) The second step of the residual profit split method (§ 1.482-8(e)(6)(iii)) requires that the residual profit be allocated to participants according to the relative value of their nonroutine contributions. Under P's transfer pricing method, P allocates the residual profit of $120 ($192 gross income minus $12 salesperson commissions minus $20 payment for back office services minus $40 compensation for the routine contribution of acting as counterparty) using a multifactor formula that reflects the relative value of the nonroutine contributions. Applying the comparability factors set out in § 1.482-8(a)(3), P allocates 40% of the residual profit to UKsub, 35% of the residual profit to P, and the remaining 25% of residual profit to Jsub. Accordingly, under step 2, $48 is allocated to UKsub, $42 is allocated to P, and $30 is allocated to Jsub. See § 1.863-3(h) for the source of income allocated to P with respect to its counterparty function.

(f) *Unspecified methods.*—Methods not specified in paragraphs (b), (c), (d), or (e) of this section may be used to evaluate whether the amount charged in a controlled transaction is at arm's length. Any method used under this paragraph (f) must be applied in accordance with the provisions of§ 1.482-1 as modified by paragraph (a)(3) of this section.

(g) *Source rule for qualified business units.*—See § 1.863-3(h) for application of the rules of this section for purposes of determining the source of income, gain or loss from a global dealing operation among qualified business units (as defined in section 989(c) and §§ 1.863-3(h)(3)(iv) and 1.989(a)-1). [Prop. Reg. § 1.482-8.]

[Proposed 3-6-98.]

§ 1.482-9. Methods to determine taxable income in connection with a controlled services transaction.—(a) *In general.*—The arm's length amount charged in a controlled services transaction must be determined under one of the methods provided for in this section.

Each method must be applied in accordance with the provisions of § 1.482-1, including the best method rule of § 1.482-1(c), the comparability analysis of § 1.482-1(d), and the arm's length range of § 1.482-1(e), except as those provisions are modified in this section. The methods are-

(1) The services cost method, described in paragraph (b) of this section;

(2) The comparable uncontrolled services price method, described in paragraph (c) of this section;

(3) The gross services margin method, described in paragraph (d) of this section;

(4) The cost of services plus method, described in paragraph (e) of this section;

(5) The comparable profits method, described in § 1.482-5 and in paragraph (f) of this section;

(6) The profit split method, described in § 1.482-6 and in paragraph (g) of this section; and

(7) Unspecified methods, described in paragraph (h) of this section.

(b) *Services cost method.*—(1) *In general.*—The services cost method evaluates whether the amount charged for certain services is arm's length by reference to the total services costs (as defined in paragraph (j) of this section) with no markup. If a taxpayer applies the services cost method in accordance with the rules of this paragraph (b), then it will be considered the best method for purposes of § 1.482-1(c), and the Commissioner's allocations will be limited to adjusting the amount charged for such services to the properly determined amount of such total services costs.

(2) *Eligibility for the services cost method.*—To apply the services cost method to a service in accordance with the rules of this paragraph (b), all of the following requirements must be satisfied with respect to the service—

(i) The service is a covered service as defined in paragraph (b)(3) of this section;

(ii) The service is not an excluded activity as defined in paragraph (b)(4) of this section;

(iii) The service is not precluded from constituting a covered service by the business judgment rule described in paragraph (b)(5) of this section; and

(iv) Adequate books and records are maintained as described in paragraph (b)(6) of this section.

(3) *Covered services.*—For purposes of this paragraph (b), covered services consist of a controlled service transaction or a group of controlled service transactions (see § 1.482-1(f)(2)(i) (aggregation of transactions)) that meet the definition of specified covered services or low margin covered services.

(i) *Specified covered services.*—Specified covered services are controlled services transactions that the Commissioner specifies by revenue procedure. Services will be included in such revenue procedure based upon the Commissioner's determination that the specified covered services are support services common among taxpayers across industry sectors and generally do not involve a significant median comparable markup on total services costs. For the definition of the median comparable markup on total services costs, see paragraph (b)(3)(ii) of this section. The Commissioner may add to, subtract from, or otherwise revise the specified covered services described in the revenue procedure by subsequent revenue procedure, which amendments will ordinarily be prospective only in effect.

(ii) *Low margin covered services.*—Low margin covered services are controlled services transactions for which the median comparable markup on total services costs is less than or equal to seven percent. For purposes of this paragraph (b), the median comparable markup on total services costs means the excess of the arm's length price of the controlled services transaction determined under the general section 482 regulations without regard to this paragraph (b), using the interquartile range described in § 1.482-1(e)(2)(iii)(C) and as necessary adjusting to the median of such interquartile range, over total services costs, expressed as a percentage of total services costs.

(4) *Excluded activity.*—The following types of activities are excluded activities:

(i) Manufacturing.

(ii) Production.

(iii) Extraction, exploration, or processing of natural resources.

(iv) Construction.

(v) Reselling, distribution, acting as a sales or purchasing agent, or acting under a commission or other similar arrangement.

(vi) Research, development, or experimentation.

(vii) Engineering or scientific.

(viii) Financial transactions, including guarantees.

(ix) Insurance or reinsurance.

(5) *Not services that contribute significantly to fundamental risks of business success or failure.*—A service cannot constitute a covered service unless the taxpayer reasonably concludes in its business judgment that the service does not contribute significantly to key competitive advantages, core capabilities, or fundamental risks of success or failure in one or more trades or businesses of the controlled group, as defined in § 1.482-1(i)(6). In evaluating the reasonableness of the conclusion required by this paragraph (b)(5), consideration will be given to all the facts and circumstances.

(6) *Adequate books and records.*—Permanent books of account and records are maintained for as long as the costs with respect to the covered services are incurred by the renderer. Such books and records must include a statement evidencing the taxpayer's intention to apply the services cost method to evaluate the arm's length charge for such services. Such books and records must be adequate to permit verification by the Commissioner of the total services costs incurred by the renderer, including a description of the services in question, identification of the renderer and the recipient of such services, and sufficient documentation to allow verification of the methods used to allocate and apportion such costs to the services in question in accordance with paragraph (k) of this section.

(7) *Shared services arrangement.*—(i) *In general.*—If the services cost method is used to evaluate the amount charged for covered services, and such services are the subject of a shared services arrangement, then the arm's length charge to each participant for such services will be the portion of the total costs of the services otherwise determined under the services cost method of this paragraph (b) that is properly allocated to such participant pursuant to the arrangement.

(ii) *Requirements for shared services arrangement.*—A shared services arrangement must meet the requirements described in this paragraph (b)(7).

(A) *Eligibility.*—To be eligible for treatment under this paragraph (b)(7), a shared services arrangement must—

(1) Include two or more participants;

(2) Include as participants all controlled taxpayers that reasonably anticipate a benefit (as defined under paragraph (l)(3)(i) of this section) from one or more covered services specified in the shared services arrangement; and

(3) Be structured such that each covered service (or each reasonable aggregation of services within the meaning of paragraph (b)(7)(iii)(B) of this section) confers a benefit on at least one participant in the shared services arrangement.

(B) *Allocation.*—The costs for covered services must be allocated among the participants based on their respective shares of the reasonably anticipated benefits from those services, without regard to whether the anticipated benefits are in fact realized. Reasonably anticipated benefits are benefits as defined in paragraph (l)(3)(i) of this section. The allocation of costs must provide the most reliable measure of the participants' respective shares of the reasonably anticipated benefits under the principles of the best method rule. See § 1.482-1(c). The allocation must be applied on a consistent basis for all participants and services. The allocation to each participant in each taxable year must reasonably reflect that participant's respective share of reasonably anticipated benefits for such taxable year. If the taxpayer reasonably concluded that the shared services arrangement (including any aggregation pursuant to paragraph (b)(7)(iii)(B) of this section) allocated costs for covered services on a basis that most reliably reflects the participants' respective shares of the reasonably anticipated benefits attributable to such services, as provided for in this paragraph (b)(7), then the Commissioner may not adjust such allocation basis.

(C) *Documentation.*—The taxpayer must maintain sufficient documentation to establish that the requirements of this paragraph (b)(7) are satisfied, and include—

(1) A statement evidencing the taxpayer's intention to apply the services cost method to evaluate the arm's length charge for covered services pursuant to a shared services arrangement;

(2) A list of the participants and the renderer or renderers of covered services under the shared services arrangement;

(3) A description of the basis of allocation to all participants, consistent with the participants' respective shares of reasonably anticipated benefits; and

(4) A description of any aggregation of covered services for purposes of the shared services arrangement, and an indication whether this aggregation (if any) differs from the aggregation used to evaluate the median comparable markup for any low margin covered services described in paragraph (b)(3)(ii) of this section.

(iii) *Definitions and special rules.*—(A) *Participant.*—A participant is a controlled taxpayer that reasonably anticipates benefits from covered services subject to a shared services arrangement that substantially complies with the requirements described in this paragraph (b)(7).

(B) *Aggregation.*—Two or more covered services may be aggregated in a reasonable manner taking into account all the facts and circumstances, including whether the relative magnitude of reasonably anticipated benefits of the participants sharing the costs of such aggregated services may be reasonably reflected by the allocation basis employed pursuant to paragraph (b)(7)(ii)(B) of this section. The aggregation of services under a shared services arrangement may differ from the aggregation used to evaluate the median comparable markup for any low margin covered services described in paragraph (b)(3)(ii) of this section, provided that such alternative aggregation can be implemented on a reasonable basis, including appropriately identifying and isolating relevant costs, as necessary.

(C) *Coordination with cost sharing arrangements.*—To the extent that an allocation is made to a participant in a shared services arrangement that is also a participant in a cost sharing arrangement subject to § 1.482-7T, such amount with respect to covered services is first allocated pursuant to the shared services arrangement under this paragraph (b)(7). Costs allocated pursuant to a shared services arrangement may (if applicable) be further allocated between the intangible property development activity under § 1.482-7T and other activities of the participant.

(8) *Examples.*—The application of this section is illustrated by the following examples. No inference is intended whether the presence or absence of one or more facts is determinative of the conclusion in any example. For purposes of *Examples 1* through *14*, assume that Company P and its subsidiaries, Company Q and Company R, are corporations and members of the same group of controlled entities (PQR Controlled Group). For purposes of *Example 15*, assume that Company P and its subsidiary, Company S, are corporations and members of the same group of controlled entities (PS Controlled Group). For purposes of *Examples 16* through *24*, assume that Company P and its subsidiaries, Company X, Company Y, and Company Z, are corporations and members of the same group of controlled entities (PXYZ Group) and that Company P and its subsidiaries satisfy all of the requirements for a shared services arrangement specified in paragraphs (b)(7)(ii) and (iii) of this section.

Example 1. Data entry services. (i) Company P, Company Q, and Company R own and operate hospitals. Each owns an electronic database of medical information gathered by doctors and nurses during interviews and treatment of its patients. All three databases are maintained and updated by Company P's administrative support employees who perform data entry activities by entering medical information from the paper records of Company P, Company Q, and Company R into their respective databases.

(ii) Assume that these services relating to data entry are specified covered services within the meaning of paragraph (b)(3)(i) of this section. Under the facts and circumstances of the business of the PQR Controlled Group, the taxpayer could reasonably conclude that these services do not contribute significantly to the controlled group's key competitive advantages, core capabilities, or fundamental risks of success or failure in the group's business. If these services meet the other requirements of this paragraph (b), Company P will be eligible to charge these services to Company Q and Company R in accordance with the services cost method.

Example 2. Data entry services. (i) Company P, Company Q, and Company R specialize in data entry, data processing, and data conversion. Company Q and Company R's data entry activities involve converting medical information data contained in paper records to a digital format. Company P specializes in data entry activities. This specialization reflects, in part, proprietary quality control systems and specially trained data entry experts used to ensure the highest degree of accuracy of data entry services. Company P is engaged by Company Q and Company R to perform these data entry activities for them. Company Q and Company R then charge their customers for the data entry activities performed by Company P.

(ii) Assume that these services performed by Company P relating to data entry are specified covered services within the meaning of paragraph (b)(3)(i) of this section. Under the facts and circumstances, the taxpayer is unable to reasonably conclude that these services do not contribute significantly to the controlled group's key competitive advantages, core capabilities, or fundamental risks of success or failure in the group's business. Company P is not eligible to charge these services to Company Q and Company R in accordance with the services cost method.

Example 3. Recruiting services. (i) Company P, Company Q, and Company R are manufacturing companies that sell their products to unrelated retail establishments. Company P's human resources department recruits mid-level managers and engineers for itself as well as for Company Q and Company R by attending job fairs and other recruitment events. For recruiting higher-level managers and engineers, each of these companies uses recruiters from unrelated executive search firms.

(ii) Assume that these services relating to recruiting are specified covered services within the meaning of paragraph (b)(3)(i) of this section. Under the facts and circumstances of the business of the PQR Controlled Group, the taxpayer could reasonably conclude that these services do not contribute significantly to the controlled group's key competitive advantages, core capabilities, or fundamental risks of success or failure in the group's business. If these services meet the other requirements of this paragraph (b), Company P will be eligible to charge these services to Company Q and Company R in accordance with the services cost method.

Example 4. Recruiting services. (i) Company Q and Company R are executive recruiting service companies that are hired by other companies to recruit professionals. Company P is a recruiting agency that is engaged by Company Q and Company R to perform recruiting activities on their behalf in certain geographic areas.

(ii) Assume that the services performed by Company P are specified covered services within the meaning of paragraph (b)(3)(i) of this section. Under the facts and circumstances, the taxpayer is unable to reasonably conclude that these services do not contribute significantly to the controlled group's key competitive advantages, core capabilities, or fundamental risks of success or failure in the group's business. Company P is not eligible to charge these services to Company Q and Company R in accordance with the services cost method.

Example 5. Credit analysis services. (i) Company P is a manufacturer and distributor of clothing for retail stores. Company Q and Company R are distributors of clothing for retail stores. As part of its operations, personnel in Company P perform credit analysis on its customers. Most of the customers have a history of purchases from Company P, and the credit analysis involves a review of the recent payment history of the customer's account. For new customers, the personnel in Company P perform a basic credit check of the customer using reports from a credit reporting agency. On behalf of Company Q and Company R, Company P performs credit analysis on customers who order clothing from Company Q and Company R using the same method as Company P uses for itself.

(ii) Assume that these services relating to credit analysis are specified covered services within the meaning of paragraph (b)(3)(i) of this section. Under the facts and circumstances of the business of the PQR Controlled Group, the taxpayer could reasonably conclude that these services do not contribute significantly to the controlled group's key competitive advantages, core capabilities, or fundamental risks of success or failure in the group's business. If these services meet the other requirements of this paragraph (b), Company P will be eligible to charge these services to Company Q and Company R in accordance with the services cost method.

Example 6. Credit analysis services. (i) Company P, Company Q, and Company R lease furniture to retail customers who present a significant credit risk and are generally unable to lease furniture from other providers. As part of its leasing operations, personnel in Company P perform credit analysis on each of the potential lessees. The personnel have developed special expertise in determining whether a particular customer who presents a significant credit risk (as indicated by credit reporting agencies) will be likely to make the requisite lease payments on a timely basis. Also, as part of its operations, Company P performs similar credit analysis services for Company Q and Company R, which charge correspondingly high monthly lease payments.

(ii) Assume that these services relating to credit analysis are specified covered services within the meaning of paragraph (b)(3)(i) of this section. Under the facts and circumstances, the taxpayer is unable to reasonably conclude that these services do not contribute significantly to the controlled group's key competitive advantages, core capabilities, or fundamental risks of success or failure in the group's business. Company P is not eligible to charge these services to Company Q and Company R in accordance with the services cost method.

Example 7. Credit analysis services. (i) Company P is a large full-service bank, which provides products and services to corporate and consumer markets, including unsecured loans, secured loans, lines of credit, letters of credit, conversion of foreign currency, consumer loans, trust services, and sales of certificates of deposit. Company Q makes routine consumer loans to individuals, such as auto loans and home equity loans. Company R makes only business loans to small businesses.

(ii) Company P performs credit analysis and prepares credit reports for itself, as well as for Company Q and Company R. Company P, Company Q and Company R regularly employ these credit reports in the ordinary course of business in making decisions regarding extensions of credit to potential customers (including whether to lend, rate of interest, and loan terms).

(iii) Assume that these services relating to credit analysis are specified covered services within the meaning of paragraph (b)(3)(i) of this section. Under the facts and circumstances, the credit analysis services constitute part of a "financial transaction" described in paragraph (b)(4)(viii) of this section. Company P is not eligible to charge these services to Company Q and Company R in accordance with the services cost method.

Example 8. Data verification services. (i) Company P, Company Q and Company R are manufacturers of industrial supplies. Company P's accounting department performs periodic reviews of the accounts payable information of Company P, Company Q and Company R, and identifies any inaccuracies in the records, such as double-payments and double-charges.

(ii) Assume that these services relating to verification of data are specified covered services within the meaning of paragraph (b)(3)(i) of this section. Under the facts and circumstances of the business of the PQR Controlled Group, the taxpayer could reasonably conclude that these services do not contribute significantly to the controlled group's key competitive advantages, core capabilities, or fundamental risks of success or failure in the group's business. If these services meet the other requirements of this paragraph (b), Company P will be eligible to charge these services to Company Q and Company R in accordance with the services cost method.

Example 9. Data verification services. (i) Company P gathers and inputs information regarding accounts payable and accounts receivable from unrelated parties and utilizes its own computer system to analyze that information for purposes of identifying errors in payment and receipts (data mining). Company P is compensated for these services based on a fee that reflects a percentage of amounts collected by customers as a result of the data mining services. These activities constitute a significant portion of Company P's business. Company P performs similar activities for Company Q and Company R by analyzing their accounts payable and accounts receivable records.

(ii) Assume that these services relating to data mining are specified covered services within the meaning of paragraph (b)(3)(i) of this section. Under the facts and circumstances, the taxpayer is unable to reasonably conclude that these services do not contribute significantly to the controlled group's key competitive advantages, core capabilities, or fundamental risks of success or failure in the group's business. Company P is not eligible to charge these services to Company Q and Company R in accordance with the services cost method.

Example 10. Legal services. (i) Company P is a domestic corporation with two wholly-owned foreign subsidiaries, Company Q and Company R. Company P and its subsidiaries manufacture and distribute equipment used by industrial customers. Company P maintains an in-house legal department consisting of attorneys experienced in a wide range of business and commercial matters. Company Q and Company R maintain small legal departments, consisting of attorneys experienced in matters that most frequently arise in the normal course of business of Company Q and Company R in their respective jurisdictions.

(ii) Company P seeks to maintain in-house legal staff with the ability to address the majority of legal matters that arise in the United States with respect to the operations of Company P, as well as any U.S. reporting or compliance obligations of Company Q or Company R. These include the preparation and review of corporate contracts relating to, for example, product sales, equipment purchases and leases, business liability insurance, real estate, employee salaries and benefits. Company P relies on outside attorneys for major business transactions and highly technical matters such as patent licenses. The in-house legal staffs of Company Q and Company R are much more limited. It is necessary for Company P to retain several local law firms to handle litigation and business disputes arising from the activities of Company Q and Company R. Although Company Q and Company R pay the fees of these law firms, the hiring authority and general oversight of the firms' representation is in the legal department of Company P.

(iii) In determining what portion of the legal expenses of Company P may be allocated to Company Q and Company R, Company P first excludes any expenses relating to legal services that constitute shareholder activities and other items that are not properly analyzed as controlled services. Assume that the remaining services relating to general legal functions performed by in-house legal counsel are specified covered services within the meaning of paragraph (b)(3)(i) of this section. Under the facts and circumstances of the business of the PQR Controlled Group, the taxpayer could reasonably conclude that these latter services do not contribute significantly to the controlled group's key competitive advantages, core capabilities, or fundamental risks of success or failure in the group's business. If these services meet the other requirements of this paragraph (b), Company P will be eligible to charge these services to Company Q and Company R in accordance with the services cost method.

Example 11. Legal services. (i) Company P is a domestic holding company whose operating companies, Company Q and Company R, generate electric power for consumers by operating nuclear plants. Assume that, although Company P owns 100% of the stock of Companies Q and R, the companies do not elect to file a consolidated Federal income tax return with Company P.

(ii) Company P maintains an in-house legal department that includes attorneys who are experts in the areas of Federal utilities regulation, Federal labor and environmental law, and securities law. Companies Q and R maintain their own, smaller in-house legal staffs comprising experienced attorneys in the areas of state and local utilities regulation, state labor and employment law, and general commercial law. The legal department of Company P performs general oversight of the legal affairs of the company and determines whether a particular matter would be more efficiently handled by the Company P legal department, by the legal staffs in the operating companies, or in rare cases, by retained outside counsel. In general, Company P has succeeded in minimizing duplication and overlap of functions between the legal staffs of the various companies or by retained outside counsel.

(iii) The domestic nuclear power plant operations of Companies Q and R are subject to extensive regulation by the U.S. Nuclear Regulatory Commission (NRC). Operators are required to obtain pre-construction approval, operating licenses, and, at the end of the operational life of the nuclear reactor, nuclear decommissioning certificates. Company P files consolidated financial statements on behalf of itself, as well as Companies Q and R, with the United States Securities and Exchange Commission (SEC). In these SEC filings, Company P discloses that failure to obtain any of these licenses (and the related periodic renewals) or agreeing to licenses on terms less favorable than those granted to competitors would have a material adverse impact on the operations of Company Q or Company R. Company Q and Company R do not have in-house legal staff with experience in the NRC area. Company P maintains a group of in-house attorneys with specialized expertise in the NRC area that exclusively represents Company Q and Company R before the NRC. Although Company P occasionally hires an outside law firm or industry expert to assist on particular NRC matters, the majority of the work is performed by the specialized legal staff of Company P.

(iv) Certain of the legal services performed by Company P constitute duplicative or shareholder activities that do not confer a benefit on the other companies and therefore do not need to be allocated to the other companies, while certain other legal services are eligible to be charged to Company Q and Company R in accordance with the services cost method.

(v) Assume that the specialized legal services relating to nuclear licenses performed by in-house legal counsel of Company P are specified covered services within the meaning of paragraph (b)(3)(i) of this section. Under the facts and circumstances, the taxpayer is unable to reasonably conclude that these services do not contribute significantly to the controlled group's key competitive advantages, core capabilities, or fundamental risks of success or failure in the group's business. Company P is not eligible to charge these services to Company Q and Company R in accordance with the services cost method.

Example 12. Group of services. (i) Company P, Company Q, and Company R are manufacturing companies that sell their products to unrelated retail establishments. Company P has an enterprise resource planning (ERP) system that maintains data relating to accounts payable and accounts receivable information for all three companies. Company P's personnel perform the daily operations on this ERP system such as inputting data relating to accounts payable and accounts receivable into the system and extracting data relating to accounts receivable and accounts payable in the form of reports or electronic media and providing those data to all three companies. Periodically, Company P's computer specialists also modify the ERP system to adapt to changing business functions in all three companies. Company P's computer specialists make these changes by either modifying the underlying software program or by purchasing additional software or hardware from unrelated third party vendors.

(ii) Assume that the services relating to accounts payable and accounts receivable are specified covered services within the meaning of paragraph (b)(3)(i) of this section. Under the facts and circumstances of the business of the PQR Controlled Group, the taxpayer could reasonably conclude that these services do not contribute significantly to the controlled group's key competitive advantages, core capabilities, or fundamental risks of success or failure in the group's business. If these services meet the other requirements of this paragraph (b), Company P will be eligible to charge these services to Company Q and Company R in accordance with the services cost method.

(iii) Assume that the services performed by Company P's computer specialists that relate to modifying the ERP system are specifically excluded from the services described in a revenue procedure referenced in paragraph (b)(3) of this section as developing hardware or software solutions (such as systems integration, Website design, writing computer programs, modifying general applications software, or recommending the purchase of commercially available hardware or software). If these services do not constitute low margin covered services within the meaning of paragraph (b)(3)(ii) of this section, then Company P is not eligible to charge these services to Company Q and Company R in accordance with the services cost method.

Example 13. Group of services. (i) Company P manufactures and sells widgets under an exclusive contract to Customer 1. Company Q and Company R sell widgets under exclusive contracts to Customer 2 and Customer 3, respectively. At least one year in advance, each of these customers can accurately forecast its need for widgets. Using these forecasts, each customer over the course of the year places orders for widgets with the appropriate company, Company P, Company Q, or Company R. A customer's actual need for widgets seldom deviates from that customer's forecasted need.

(ii) It is most efficient for the PQR Controlled Group companies to manufacture and store an inventory of widgets in advance of delivery. Although all three companies sell widgets, only Company P maintains a centralized warehouse for widgets. Pursuant to a contract, Company P provides storage of these widgets to Company Q and Company R at an arm's length price.

(iii) Company P's personnel also obtain orders from all three companies' customers to draw up purchase orders for widgets as well as make payment to suppliers for widget replacement parts. In addition, Company P's personnel use data entry to input information regarding orders and sales of widgets and replacement parts for all three companies into a centralized computer system. Company P's personnel also maintain the centralized computer system and extract data for all three companies when necessary.

(iv) Assume that these services relating to tracking purchases and sales of inventory are specified covered services within the meaning of paragraph (b)(3)(i) of this section. Under the facts and circumstances of the business of the PQR Controlled Group, the taxpayer could reasonably conclude that these services do not contribute significantly to the controlled group's key competitive advantages, core capabilities, or fundamental risks of success or failure in the group's business. If these services meet the other requirements of this paragraph (b), Company P will be eligible to charge these services to Company Q and Company R in accordance with the services cost method.

Example 14. Group of services. (i) Company P, Company Q, and Company R assemble and sell gadgets to unrelated customers. Each of these companies purchases the components necessary for assembly of the gadgets from unrelated suppliers. As a service to its subsidiaries, Company P's personnel obtain orders for components from all three companies, prepare purchase orders, and make payment to unrelated suppliers for the components. In addition, Company P's personnel use data entry to input information regarding orders and sales of gadgets for all three companies into a centralized computer. Company P's personnel also maintain the centralized computer system and extract data for all three companies on an as-needed basis. The services provided by Company P personnel, in conjunction with the centralized computer system, constitute a state-of-the-art inventory management system that allows Company P to order components necessary for assembly of the gadgets on a "just-in-time" basis.

(ii) Unrelated suppliers deliver the components directly to Company P, Company Q and Company R. Each company stores the components in its own facilities for use in filling specific customer orders. The companies do not maintain any inventory that is not identified in specific customer orders. Because of the efficiencies associated with services provided by personnel of Company P, all three companies are able to significantly reduce their inventory-related costs. Company P's Chief Executive Officer makes a statement in one of its press conferences with industry analysts that its inventory management system is critical to the company's success.

(iii) Assume that these services relating to tracking purchases and sales of inventory are specified covered services within the meaning of paragraph (b)(3)(i) of this section. Under the facts and circumstances, the taxpayer is unable to reasonably conclude that these services do not contribute significantly to the controlled group's key competitive advantages, core capabilities, or fundamental risks of success or failure in the group's business. Company P is not eligible to charge these services to Company Q and Company R in accordance with the services cost method.

Example 15. Low margin covered services. Company P renders certain accounting services to Company S. Company P uses the services cost method for the accounting services, and determines the amount charged as its total cost of rendering the services, with no markup. Based on an application of the section 482 regulations without regard to this paragraph (b), the interquartile range of arm's length markups on total services costs for these accounting services is between 3% and 9%, and the median is 6%. Because the median comparable markup on total services costs is 6%, which is less than 7%, the accounting services constitute low margin covered services within the meaning of paragraph (b)(3)(ii) of this section.

Example 16. Shared services arrangement and reliable measure of reasonably anticipated benefit (allocation key). (i) Company P operates a centralized data processing facility that performs automated invoice processing and order generation for all of its subsidiaries, Companies X, Y, Z, pursuant to a shared services arrangement.

(ii) In evaluating the shares of reasonably anticipated benefits from the centralized data processing services, the total value of the merchandise on the invoices and orders may not provide the most reliable measure of reasonably anticipated benefits shares, because value of merchandise sold does not bear a relationship to the anticipated benefits from the underlying covered services.

(iii) The total volume of orders and invoices processed may provide a more reliable basis for evaluating the shares of reasonably anticipated benefits from the data processing services. Alternatively, depending on the facts and circumstances, total central processing unit time attributable to the transactions of each subsidiary may provide a more reliable basis on which to evaluate the shares of reasonably anticipated benefits.

Example 17. Shared services arrangement and reliable measure of reasonably anticipated benefit (allocation key). (i) Company P operates a centralized center that performs human resources functions, such as administration of pension, retirement, and health insurance plans that are made available to employees of its subsidiaries, Companies X, Y, Z, pursuant to a shared services arrangement.

(ii) In evaluating the shares of reasonably anticipated benefits from these centralized services, the total revenues of each subsidiary may not provide the most reliable measure of reasonably anticipated benefit shares, because total revenues do not bear a relationship to the shares of reasonably anticipated benefits from the underlying services.

(iii) Employee headcount or total compensation paid to employees may provide a more reliable basis for evaluating the shares of reasonably anticipated benefits from the covered services.

Example 18. Shared services arrangement and reliable measure of reasonably anticipated benefit (allocation key). (i) Company P performs human resource services (service A) on behalf of the PXYZ Group that qualify for the services cost method. Under that method, Company P determines the amount charged for these services pursuant to a shared services arrangement based on an application of paragraph (b)(7) of this section. Service A constitutes a specified covered service described in a revenue procedure pursuant to paragraph (b)(3)(i) of this section. The total services costs for service A otherwise determined under the services cost method is 300.

(ii) Companies X, Y and Z reasonably anticipate benefits from service A. Company P does not reasonably anticipate benefits from service A. Assume that if relative reasonably anticipated benefits were precisely known, the appropriate allocation of charges pursuant to paragraph (k) of this section to Company X, Y and Z for service A is as follows:

Company	Service A [Total cost 300]
X	150
Y	75
Z	75

(iii) The total number of employees (employee headcount) in each company is as follows:

Company X - 600 employees
Company Y - 250 employees
Company Z - 250 employees

(iv) Company P allocates the 300 total services costs of service A based on employee headcount as follows:

Service A [Total cost 300]		
Allocation Key	Company	
	Headcount	Amount
X	600	164
Y	250	68
Z	250	68

(v) Based on these facts, Company P may reasonably conclude that the employee headcount allocation basis most reliably reflects the participants' respective shares of the reasonably anticipated benefits attributable to service A.

Example 19. Shared services arrangement and reliable measure of reasonably anticipated benefit (allocation key). (i) Company P performs accounts payable services (service B) on behalf of the PXYZ Group and determines the amount charged for the services under such method pursuant to a shared services arrangement based on an application of paragraph (b)(7) of this section. Service B is a specified covered service described in a revenue procedure pursuant to paragraph (b)(3)(i) of this section. The total services costs for service B otherwise determined under the services cost method is 500.

(ii) Companies X, Y and Z reasonably anticipate benefits from service B. Company P does not reasonably anticipate benefits from service B. Assume that if relative reasonably anticipated benefits were precisely known, the appropriate allocation of charges pursuant to paragraph (k) of this section to Companies X, Y and Z for service B is as follows:

Company	Service B [Total cost 500]
X	125
Y	205
Z	170

(iii) The total number of employees (employee headcount) in each company is as follows:

Company X - 600
Company Y - 200
Company Z - 200

(iv) The total number of transactions (transaction volume) with uncontrolled customers by each company is as follows:

Company X - 2,000
Company Y - 4,000
Company Z - 3,500

(v) If Company P allocated the 500 total services costs of service B based on employee headcount, the resulting allocation would be as follows:

Service B [Total cost 500]		
Allocation key	Company	
	Headcount	Amount
X	600	300
Y	200	100
Z	200	100

(vi) In contrast, if Company P used volume of transactions with uncontrolled customers as the allocation basis under the shared services arrangement, the allocation would be as follows:

Service B [Total cost 500]		
Allocation key	Company	
	Transaction Volume	Amount
X	2,000	105
Y	4,000	211
Z	3,500	184

(vii) Based on these facts, Company P may reasonably conclude that the transaction volume, but not the employee headcount, allocation basis most reliably reflects the participants' respective shares of the reasonably anticipated benefits attributable to service B.

Example 20. Shared services arrangement and aggregation. (i) Company P performs human resource services (service A) and accounts payable services (service B) on behalf of the PXYZ Group that qualify for the services cost method. Company P determines the amount charged for these services under such method pursuant to a shared services arrangement based on an application of paragraph (b)(7) of this section. Service A and service B are specified covered services described in a revenue procedure pursuant to paragraph (b)(3)(i) of this section. The total services costs otherwise determined under the services cost method for service A is 300 and for service B is 500; total services costs for services A and B are 800. Company P determines that aggregation of services A and B for purposes of the arrangement is appropriate.

(ii) Companies X, Y and Z reasonably anticipate benefits from services A and B. Company P does not reasonably anticipate benefits from services A and B. Assume that if relative reasonably anticipated benefits were precisely known, the appropriate allocation of total charges pursuant to paragraph (k) of this section to Companies X, Y and Z for services A and B is as follows:

Company	Services A and B [Total cost 800]
X	350
Y	100
Z	350

(iii) The total volume of transactions with uncontrolled customers in each company is as follows:

Company X - 2,000
Company Y - 4,000
Company Z - 4,000

(iv) The total number of employees in each company is as follows:

Company X - 600
Company Y - 200
Company Z - 200

(v) If Company P allocated the 800 total services costs of services A and B based on transaction volume or employee headcount, the resulting allocation would be as follows:

Aggregated Services AB [Total cost 800]				
Company	Allocation key		Allocation key	
	Transaction Volume	Amount	Headcount	Amount
X	2,000	160	600	480
Y	4,000	320	200	160
Z	4,000	320	200	160

(vi) In contrast, if aggregated services AB were allocated by reference to the total U.S. dollar value of sales to uncontrolled parties (trade sales) by each company, the following results would obtain:

Aggregated Services AB
[Total cost 800]

Company	Allocation Key	
	Trade sales (millions)	Amount
X	$400	314
Y	$120	94
Z	$500	392

(vii) Based on these facts, Company P may reasonably conclude that the trade sales, but not the transaction volume or the employee headcount, allocation basis most reliably reflects the participants' respective shares of the reasonably anticipated benefits attributable to services AB.

Example 21. Shared services arrangement and aggregation. (i) Company P performs services A through P on behalf of the PXYZ Group that qualify for the services cost method. Company P determines the amount charged for these services under such method pursuant to a shared services arrangement based on an application of paragraph (b)(7) of this section. All of these services A through P constitute either specified covered services or low margin covered services described in paragraph (b)(3) of this section. The total services costs for services A through P otherwise determined under the services cost method is 500. Company P determines that aggregation of services A through P for purposes of the arrangement is appropriate.

(ii) Companies X and Y reasonably anticipate benefits from services A through P and Company Z reasonably anticipates benefits from services A through M but not from services N through P (Company Z performs services similar to services N through P on its own behalf). Company P does not reasonably anticipate benefits from services A through P. Assume that if relative reasonably anticipated benefits were precisely known, the appropriate allocation of total charges pursuant to paragraph (k) of this section to Company X, Y, and Z for services A through P is as follows:

Company	Services A - M (cost 490)	Services N - P (cost 10)	Services A - P (total cost 500)
X	90	5	95
Y	240	5	245
Z	160	...	160

(iii) The total volume of transactions with uncontrolled customers in each company is as follows:

Company X - 2,000

Company Y - 4,500

Company Z - 3,500

(iv) Company P allocates the 500 total services costs of services A through P based on transaction volume as follows:

Aggregated Services A - Z
[Total costs 500]

Company	Allocation Key	
	Transaction Volume	Amount
X	2,000	100
Y	4,500	225
Z	3,500	175

(v) Based on these facts, Company P may reasonably conclude that the transaction volume allocation basis most reliably reflects the participants' respective shares of the reasonably anticipated benefits attributable to services A through P.

Example 22. Renderer reasonably anticipates benefits. (i) Company P renders services on behalf of the PXYZ Group that qualify for the services cost method. Company P determines the amount charged for these services under such method. Company P's share of reasonably anticipated benefits from services A, B, C, and D is 20% of the total reasonably anticipated benefits of all participants. Company P's total services cost for services A, B, C, and D charged within the group is 100.

(ii) Based on an application of paragraph (b)(7) of this section, Company P charges 80 which is allocated among Companies X, Y, and Z. No charge is made to Company P under the shared services arrangement for activities that it performs on its own behalf.

Example 23. Coordination with cost sharing arrangement. (i) Company P performs human resource services (service A) on behalf of the PXYZ Group that qualify for the services cost method. Company P determines the amount charged for these services under such method pursuant to a shared services arrangement based on an application of paragraph (b)(7) of this section. Service A constitutes a specified covered service described in a revenue procedure pursuant to paragraph (b)(3)(i) of this section. The total services costs for service A otherwise determined under the services cost method is 300.

(ii) Company X, Y, Z, and P reasonably anticipate benefits from service A. Using a basis of allocation that is consistent with the controlled participants' respective shares of the reasonably anticipated benefits from the shared services, the total charge of 300 is allocated as follows:

X - 100

Y - 50

Z - 25

P - 125

(iii) In addition to performing services, P undertakes 500 of R&D and incurs manufacturing and other costs of 1,000.

(iv) Companies P and X enter into a cost sharing arrangement in accordance with § 1.482-7T. Under the arrangement, Company P will undertake all intangible property development activities. All of Company P's research and development (R&D) activity is devoted to the intangible property development activity under the cost sharing arrangement. Company P will manufacture, market, and otherwise exploit the product in its defined territory. Companies P and X will share intangible property development costs in accordance with their reasonably anticipated benefits from the intangible property, and Company X will make payments to Company P as required under § 1.482-7T. Company X will manufacture, market, and otherwise exploit the product in the rest of the world.

(v) A portion of the charge under the shared services arrangement is in turn allocable to the intangible property development activity undertaken by Company P. The most reliable estimate of the proportion allocable to the intangible property development activity is determined to be 500 (Company P's R&D expenses) divided by 1,500 (Company P's total non-covered services costs), or one-third. Accordingly, onethird of Company P's charge of 125, or 42, is allocated to the intangible property development activity. Companies P and X must share the intangible property development costs of the cost shared intangible property (including the charge of 42 that is allocated under the shared services arrangement) in proportion to their respective shares of reasonably anticipated benefits under the cost sharing arrangement. That is, the reasonably anticipated benefit shares under the cost sharing arrangement are determined separately from reasonably anticipated benefit shares under the shared services arrangement.

Example 24. Coordination with cost sharing arrangement. (i) The facts and analysis are the same as in *Example 25*, except that Company X also performs intangible property development activities related to the cost sharing arrangement. Using a basis of allocation that is consistent with the controlled participants' respective shares of the reasonably anticipated benefits from the shared services, the 300 of service costs is allocated as follows:

X - 100
Y - 50
Z - 25
P - 125

(ii) In addition to performing services, Company P undertakes 500 of R&D and incurs manufacturing and other costs of 1,000. Company X undertakes 400 of R&D and incurs manufacturing and other costs of 600.

(iii) Companies P and X enter into a cost sharing arrangement in accordance with § 1.482-7T. Under the arrangement, both Companies P and X will undertake intangible property development activities. All of the research and development activity conducted by Companies P and X is devoted to the intangible property development activity under the cost sharing arrangement. Both Companies P and X will manufacture, market, and otherwise exploit the product in their respective territories and will share intangible property development costs in accordance with their reasonably anticipated benefits from the intangible property, and both will make payments as required under § 1.482-7T.

(iv) A portion of the charge under the shared services arrangement is in turn allocable to the intangible property development activities undertaken by Companies P and X. The most reliable estimate of the portion allocable to Company P's intangible property development activity is determined to be 500 (Company P's R&D expenses) divided by 1,500 (P's total non-covered services costs), or one-third. Accordingly, onethird of Company P's allocated services cost method charge of 125, or 42, is allocated to its intangible property development activity.

(v) In addition, it is necessary to determine the portion of the charge under the shared services arrangement to Company X that should be further allocated to Company X's intangible property development activities under the cost sharing arrangement. The most reliable estimate of the portion allocable to Company X's intangible property development activity is 400 (Company X's R&D expenses) divided by 1,000 (Company X's costs), or 40%. Accordingly, 40% of the 100 that was allocated to Company X, or 40, is allocated in turn to Company X's intangible property development activities. Company X makes a payment to Company P of 100 under the shared services arrangement and includes 40 of services cost method charges in the pool of intangible property development costs.

(vi) The parties' respective contributions to intangible property development costs under the cost sharing arrangement are as follows:

P:	500 + (0.333 * 125)	=	542
X:	400 + (0.40 * 100)	=	440

(c) *Comparable uncontrolled services price method.*—(1) *In general.*—The comparable uncontrolled services price method evaluates whether the amount charged in a controlled services transaction is arm's length by reference to the amount charged in a comparable uncontrolled services transaction.

(2) *Comparability and reliability considerations.*—(i) *In general.*—Whether results derived from application of this method are the most reliable measure of the arm's length result must be determined using the factors described under the best method rule in § 1.482-1(c). The application of these factors under the comparable uncontrolled services price method is discussed in paragraphs (c)(2)(ii) and (iii) of this section.

(ii) *Comparability.*—(A) *In general.*—The degree of comparability between controlled and uncontrolled transactions is determined by applying the provisions of § 1.482-1(d). Although all of the factors described in § 1.482-1(d)(3) must be considered, similarity of the services rendered, and of the intangible property (if any) used in performing the services, generally will have the greatest effects on comparability under this method. In addition, because even minor differences in contractual terms or economic conditions could materially affect the amount charged in an uncontrolled transaction, comparability under this method depends on close similarity with respect to these factors, or adjustments to account for any differences. The results derived from applying the comparable uncontrolled services price method generally will be the most direct and reliable measure of an arm's length price for the controlled transaction if an uncontrolled transaction has no differences from the controlled transaction that would affect the price, or if there are only minor differences that have a definite and reasonably ascertainable effect on price and for which appropriate adjustments are made. If such adjustments cannot be made, or if there are more than minor differences between the controlled and uncontrolled transactions, the comparable uncontrolled services price method may be used, but the reliability of the results as a measure of the arm's length price will be reduced. Further, if there are material differences for which reliable adjustments cannot be made, this method ordinarily will not provide a reliable measure of an arm's length result.

(B) *Adjustments for differences between controlled and uncontrolled transactions.*—If there are differences between the controlled and uncontrolled transactions that would affect price, adjustments should be made to the price of the uncontrolled transaction according to the comparability provisions of § 1.482-1(d)(2). Specific examples of factors that may be particularly relevant to application of this method include-

(1) Quality of the services rendered;

(2) Contractual terms (for example, scope and terms of warranties or guarantees regarding the services, volume, credit and payment terms, allocation of risks, including any contingent-payment terms and whether costs were incurred without a provision for current reimbursement);

(3) Intangible property (if any) used in rendering the services;

(4) Geographic market in which the services are rendered or received;

(5) Risks borne (for example, costs incurred to render the services, without provision for current reimbursement);

(6) Duration or quantitative measure of services rendered;

(7) Collateral transactions or ongoing business relationships between the renderer and the recipient, including arrangement for the provision of tangible property in connection with the services; and

(8) Alternatives realistically available to the renderer and the recipient.

(iii) *Data and assumptions.*—The reliability of the results derived from the comparable uncontrolled services price method is affected by the completeness and accuracy of the data used and the reliability of the assumptions made to apply the method. See § 1.482-1(c) (best method rule).

(3) *Arm's length range.*—See § 1.482-1(e)(2) for the determination of an arm's length range.

(4) *Examples.*—The principles of this paragraph (c) are illustrated by the following examples:

Example 1. Internal comparable uncontrolled services price. Company A, a United States corporation, performs shipping, stevedoring, and related services for controlled and uncontrolled parties on a short-term or as-needed basis. Company A charges uncontrolled parties in Country X a uniform fee of $60 per container to place loaded cargo containers in Country X on oceangoing vessels for marine transportation. Company A also performs identical services in Country X for its wholly-owned subsidiary, Company B, and there are no substantial differences between the controlled and uncontrolled transactions. In evaluating the appropriate measure of the arm's length price for the container-loading services performed for Company B, because Company A renders substantially identical services in Country X to both controlled and uncontrolled parties, it is determined that the comparable uncontrolled services price constitutes the best method for determining the arm's length price for the controlled services transaction. Based on the reliable data provided by Company A concerning the price charged for services in comparable uncontrolled transactions, a loading charge of $60 per cargo container will be considered the most reliable measure of the arm's length price for the services rendered to Company B. See paragraph (c)(2)(ii)(A) of this section.

Example 2. External comparable uncontrolled services price. (i) The facts are the same as in *Example 1*, except that Company A performs services for Company B, but not for uncontrolled parties. Based on information obtained from unrelated parties (which is determined to be reliable under the comparability standards set forth in paragraph (c)(2) of this section), it is determined that uncontrolled parties in Country X perform services comparable to those rendered by Company A to Company B, and that such parties charge $60 per cargo container.

(ii) In evaluating the appropriate measure of an arm's length price for the loading services that Company A renders to Company B, the $60 per cargo container charge is considered evidence of a comparable uncontrolled services price. See paragraph (c)(2)(ii)(A) of this section.

Example 3. External comparable uncontrolled services price. The facts are the same as in *Example 2,* except that uncontrolled parties in Country X render similar loading and stevedoring services, but only under contracts that have a minimum term of one year. If the difference in the duration of the services has a material effect on prices, adjustments to account for these differences must be made to the results of the uncontrolled transactions according to the provisions of § 1.482-1(d)(2), and such adjusted results may be used as a measure of the arm's length result.

Example 4. Use of valuable intangible property. (i) Company A, a United States corporation in the biotechnology sector, renders research and development services exclusively to its affiliates. Company B is Company A's wholly-owned subsidiary in Country X. Company A renders research and development services to Company B.

(ii) In performing its research and development services function, Company A uses proprietary software that it developed internally. Company A uses the software to evaluate certain genetically engineered compounds developed by Company B. Company A owns the copyright on this software and does not license it to uncontrolled parties.

(iii) No uncontrolled parties can be identified that perform services identical or with a high degree of similarity to those performed by Company A. Because there are material differences for which reliable adjustments cannot be made, the comparable uncontrolled services price method is unlikely to provide a reliable measure of the arm's length price. See paragraph (c)(2)(ii)(A) of this section.

Example 5. Internal comparable. (i) Company A, a United States corporation, and its subsidiaries render computer consulting services relating to systems integration and networking to business clients in various countries. Company A and its subsidiaries render only consulting services, and do not manufacture computer hardware or software nor distribute such products. The controlled group is organized according to industry specialization, with key industry specialists working for Company A. These personnel typically form the core consulting group that teams with consultants from the localcountry subsidiaries to serve clients in the subsidiaries' respective countries.

(ii) Company A and its subsidiaries sometimes undertake engagements directly for clients, and sometimes work as subcontractors to unrelated parties on more extensive supply-chain consulting engagements for clients. In undertaking the latter engagements with third party consultants, Company A typically prices its services based on consulting hours worked multiplied by a rate determined for each category of employee. The company also charges, at no markup, for out-of-pocket expenses such as travel, lodging, and data acquisition charges. The Company has established the following schedule of hourly rates:

Category	Rate
Project managers	$400 per hour
Technical staff	$300 per hour

(iii) Thus, for example, a project involving 100 hours of the time of project managers and 400 hours of technical staff time would result in the following project fees (without regard to any out-of-pocket expenses): ([100 hrs. × $400/hr.] + [400 hrs. × $300/hr.]) = $40,000 + $120,000 = $160,000.

(iv) Company B, a Country X subsidiary of Company A, contracts to perform consulting services for a Country X client in the banking industry. In undertaking this engagement, Company B uses its own consultants and also uses Company A project managers and technical staff that specialize in the banking industry for 75 hours and 380 hours, respectively. In determining an arm's length charge, the price that Company A charges for consulting services as a subcontractor in comparable uncontrolled transactions will be considered evidence of a comparable uncontrolled services price. Thus, in this case, a payment of $144,000, (or [75 hrs. × $400/hr.] + [380 hrs. × $300/hr.] = $30,000 + $114,000) may be used as a measure of the arm's length price for the work performed by Company A project mangers and technical staff. In addition, if the comparable uncontrolled services price method is used, then, consistent with the practices employed by the comparables with respect to similar types of expenses, Company B must reimburse Company A for appropriate out-of-pocket expenses. See paragraph (c)(2)(ii)(A) of this section.

Example 6. Adjustments for differences. (i) The facts are the same as in *Example 5,* except that the engagement is undertaken with the client on a fixed fee basis. That is, prior to undertaking the engagement Company B and Company A estimate the resources required to undertake the engagement, and, based on hourly fee rates, charge the client a single fee for completion of the project. Company A's portion of the engagement results in fees of $144,000.

(ii) The engagement, once undertaken, requires 20% more hours by each of Companies A and B than originally estimated. Nevertheless, the unrelated client pays the fixed fee that was agreed upon at the start of the engagement. Company B pays Company A $144,000, in accordance with the fixed fee arrangement.

(iii) Company A often enters into similar fixed fee engagements with clients. In addition, Company A's records for similar engagements show that when it experiences cost overruns, it does not collect additional fees from the client for the difference between projected and actual hours. Accordingly, in evaluating whether the fees paid by Company B to Company A are arm's length, it is determined that no adjustments to the intercompany service charge are warranted. See § 1.482-1(d)(3)(ii) and paragraph (c)(2)(ii)(A) of this section.

(5) *Indirect evidence of the price of a comparable uncontrolled services transaction.*—(i) *In general.*—The price of a comparable uncontrolled services transaction may be derived based on indirect measures of the price charged in comparable uncontrolled services transactions, but only if—

(A) The data are widely and routinely used in the ordinary course of business in the particular industry or market segment for purposes of determining prices actually charged in comparable uncontrolled services transactions;

(B) The data are used to set prices in the controlled services transaction in the same way they are used to set prices in uncontrolled services transactions of the controlled taxpayer, or in the same way they are used by uncontrolled taxpayers to set prices in uncontrolled services transactions; and

(C) The amount charged in the controlled services transaction may be reliably adjusted to reflect differences in quality of the services, contractual terms, market conditions, risks borne (including contingent-payment terms), duration or quantitative measure of services rendered, and other factors that may affect the price to which uncontrolled taxpayers would agree.

(ii) *Example.*—The following example illustrates this paragraph (c)(5):

Example. Indirect evidence of comparable uncontrolled services price. (i) Company A is a United States insurance company. Company A's wholly-owned Country X subsidiary, Company B, performs specialized risk analysis for Company A as well as for uncontrolled parties. In determining the price actually charged to uncontrolled entities for performing such risk analysis, Company B uses a proprietary, multi-factor computer program, which relies on the gross value of the policies in the customer's portfolio, the relative composition of those policies, their location, and the estimated number of personnel hours necessary to complete the project. Uncontrolled companies that perform comparable risk analysis in the same industry or marketsegment use similar proprietary computer programs to price transactions with uncontrolled customers (the competitors' programs may incorporate different inputs, or may assign different weights or values to individual inputs, in arriving at the price).

(ii) During the taxable year subject to audit, Company B performed risk analysis for uncontrolled parties as well as for Company A. Because prices charged to uncontrolled customers reflected the composition of each customer's portfolio together with other factors, the prices charged in Company B's uncontrolled transactions do not provide a reliable basis for determining the comparable uncontrolled services price for the similar services rendered to Company A. However, in evaluating an arm's length price for the studies performed by Company B for Company A, Company B's proprietary computer program may be considered as indirect evidence of the comparable uncontrolled services price that would be charged to perform the services for Company A. The reliability of the results obtained by application of this internal computer program as a measure of an arm's length price for the services will be increased to the extent that Company A used the internal computer program to generate actual transaction prices for risk-analysis studies performed for uncontrolled parties during the same taxable year under audit; Company A used data that are widely and routinely used in the ordinary course of business in the insurance industry to determine the price charged; and Company A reliably adjusted the price charged in the controlled services transaction to reflect differences that may affect the price to which uncontrolled taxpayers would agree.

(d) *Gross services margin method.*—(1) *In general.*—The gross services margin method evaluates whether the amount charged in a controlled services transaction is arm's length by reference to the gross profit margin realized in comparable uncontrolled transactions. This method ordinarily is used in cases where a controlled taxpayer performs services or functions in connection with an uncontrolled transaction between a member of the controlled group and an uncontrolled taxpayer. This method may be used where a controlled taxpayer renders services (agent services) to another member of the controlled group in connection with a transaction between that other member and an uncontrolled taxpayer. This method also may be used in cases where a controlled taxpayer contracts to provide services to an uncontrolled taxpayer (intermediary function) and another member of the controlled group actually performs a portion of the services provided.

(2) *Determination of arm's length price.*—(i) *In general.*—The gross services margin method evaluates whether the price charged or amount retained by a controlled taxpayer in the controlled services transaction in connection with the relevant uncontrolled transaction is arm's length by determining the appropriate gross profit of the controlled taxpayer.

(ii) *Relevant uncontrolled transaction.*—The relevant uncontrolled transaction is a transaction between a member of the controlled group and an uncontrolled taxpayer as to which the controlled taxpayer performs agent services or an intermediary function.

(iii) *Applicable uncontrolled price.*—The applicable uncontrolled price is the price paid or received by the uncontrolled taxpayer in the relevant uncontrolled transaction.

(iv) *Appropriate gross services profit.*—The appropriate gross services profit is computed by multiplying the applicable uncontrolled price by the gross services profit margin in comparable uncontrolled transactions. The determination of the appropriate gross services profit will take into account any functions performed by other members of the controlled group, as well as any other relevant factors described in § 1.482-1(d)(3). The comparable gross services profit margin may be determined by reference to the commission in an uncontrolled transaction, where that commission is stated as a percentage of the price charged in the uncontrolled transaction.

(v) *Arm's length range.*—See § 1.482-1(e)(2) for determination of the arm's length range.

(3) *Comparability and reliability considerations.*—(i) *In general.*—Whether results derived from application of this method are the most reliable measure of the arm's length result must be determined using the factors described under the best method rule in § 1.482-1(c). The application of these factors under the gross services margin method is discussed in paragraphs (d)(3)(ii) and (iii) of this section.

(ii) *Comparability.*—(A) *Functional comparability.*—The degree of comparability between an uncontrolled transaction and a controlled transaction is determined by applying the comparability provisions of § 1.482-1(d). A gross services profit provides compensation for services or functions that bear a relationship to the relevant uncontrolled transaction, including an operating profit in return for the investment of capital and the assumption of risks by the controlled taxpayer performing the services or functions under review. Therefore, although all of the factors described in § 1.482-1(d)(3) must be considered, comparability under this method is particularly dependent on similarity of services or functions performed, risks borne, intangible property (if any) used in providing the services or functions, and contractual terms, or adjustments to account for the effects of any such differences. If possible, the appropriate gross services profit margin should be derived from comparable uncontrolled transactions by the controlled taxpayer under review, because similar characteristics are more likely found among different transactions by the same controlled taxpayer than among transactions by other parties. In the absence of comparable uncontrolled transactions involving the same controlled taxpayer, an appropriate gross services profit margin may be derived from transactions of uncontrolled taxpayers involving comparable services or functions with respect to similarly related transactions.

(B) *Other comparability factors.*—Comparability under this method is not dependent on close similarity of the relevant uncontrolled transaction to the related transactions involved in the uncontrolled comparables. However, substantial differences in the nature of the relevant uncontrolled transaction and the relevant transactions involved in the uncontrolled comparables, such as differences in the type of property transferred or service provided in the relevant uncontrolled transaction, may indicate significant differences in the services or functions performed by the controlled and uncontrolled taxpayers with respect to their respective relevant transactions. Thus, it ordinarily would be expected that the services or functions performed in the controlled and uncontrolled transactions would be with respect to relevant transactions involving the transfer of property within the same product categories or the provision of services of the same general type (for example, information-technology systems design). Furthermore, significant differences in the intangible property (if any) used by the controlled taxpayer in the controlled services transaction as distinct from the uncontrolled comparables may also affect the reliability of the comparison. Finally, the reliability of profit measures based on gross services profit may be adversely affected by factors that have less effect on prices. For example, gross services profit may be affected by a variety of other factors, including cost structures or efficiency (for example, differences in the level of experience of the employees performing the service in the controlled and uncontrolled transactions). Accordingly, if material differences in these factors are identified based on objective evidence, the reliability of the analysis may be affected.

(C) *Adjustments for differences between controlled and uncontrolled transactions.*—If there are material differences between the controlled and uncontrolled transactions that would affect the gross services profit margin, adjustments should be made to the gross services profit margin, according to the comparability provisions of § 1.482-1(d)(2). For this purpose, consideration of the total services costs associated with functions performed and risks assumed may be necessary because differences in functions performed are often reflected in these costs. If there are differences in functions performed, however, the effect on gross services profit of such differences is not necessarily equal to the differences in the amount of related costs. Specific examples of factors that may be particularly relevant to this method include—

(1) Contractual terms (for example, scope and terms of warranties or guarantees regarding the services or function, volume, credit and payment terms, and allocation of risks, including any contingent-payment terms);

(2) Intangible property (if any) used in performing the services or function;

(3) Geographic market in which the services or function are performed or in which the relevant uncontrolled transaction takes place; and

(4) Risks borne, including, if applicable, inventory-type risk.

(D) *Buy-sell distributor.*—If a controlled taxpayer that performs an agent service or intermediary function is comparable to a distributor that takes title to goods and resells them, the gross profit margin earned by such distributor on uncontrolled sales, stated as a percentage of the price for the goods, may be used as the comparable gross services profit margin.

(iii) *Data and assumptions.*—(A) *In general.*—The reliability of the results derived from the gross services margin method is affected by the completeness and accuracy of the data used and the reliability of the assumptions made to apply this method. See § 1.482-1(c) (best method rule).

(B) *Consistency in accounting.*—The degree of consistency in accounting practices between the controlled transaction and the uncontrolled comparables that materially affect the gross services profit margin affects the reliability of the results under this method.

(4) *Examples.*—The principles of this paragraph (d) are illustrated by the following examples:

Example 1. Agent services. Company A and Company B are members of a controlled group. Company A is a foreign manufacturer of industrial equipment. Company B is a U.S. company that acts as a commission agent for Company A by arranging for Company A to make direct sales of the equipment it manufactures to unrelated purchasers in the U.S. market. Company B does not take title to the equipment but instead receives from Company A commissions that are determined as a specified percentage of the sales price for the equipment that is charged by Company A to the unrelated purchaser. Company B also arranges for direct sales of similar equipment by unrelated foreign manufacturers to unrelated purchasers in the U.S. market. Company B charges these unrelated foreign manufacturers a commission fee of 5% of the sales price charged by the unrelated foreign manufacturers to the unrelated U.S. purchasers for the equipment. Information regarding the comparable agent services provided by Company B to unrelated foreign manufacturers is sufficiently complete to conclude that it is likely that all material differences between the controlled and uncontrolled transactions have been identified and adjustments for such differences have been made. If the comparable gross services profit margin is 5% of the price charged in the relevant transactions involved in the uncontrolled comparables, then the appropriate gross services profit that Company B may earn and the arm's length price that it may charge Company A for its agent services is equal to 5% of the applicable uncontrolled price charged by Company A in sales of equipment in the relevant uncontrolled transactions.

Example 2. Agent services. The facts are the same as in *Example 1*, except that Company B does not act as a commission agent for unrelated parties and it is not possible to obtain reliable information concerning commission rates charged by uncontrolled commission agents that engage in comparable transactions with respect to relevant sales of property. It is possible, however, to obtain reliable information regarding the gross profit margins earned by unrelated parties that briefly take title to and then resell similar property in uncontrolled transactions, in which they purchase the property from foreign manufacturers and resell the property to purchasers in the U.S. market. Analysis of the facts and circumstances indicates that, aside from certain minor differences for which adjustments can be made, the uncontrolled parties that resell property perform similar functions and assume similar risks as Company B performs and assumes when it acts as a commission agent for Company A's sales of property. Under these circumstances, the gross profit margin earned by the unrelated distributors on the purchase and resale of property may be used, subject to any adjustments for any material differences between the controlled and uncontrolled transactions, as a comparable gross services profit margin. The appropriate gross services profit that Company B may earn and the arm's length price that it may charge Company A for its agent services is therefore equal to this comparable gross services margin, multiplied by the applicable uncontrolled price charged by Company A in its sales of equipment in the relevant uncontrolled transactions.

Example 3. Agent services. (i) Company A and Company B are members of a controlled group. Company A is a U.S. corporation that renders computer consulting services, including systems integration and networking, to business clients.

(ii) In undertaking engagements with clients, Company A in some cases pays a commission of 3% of its total fees to unrelated parties that assist Company A in obtaining consulting engagements. Typically, such fees are paid to non-computer consulting firms that provide strategic management services for their clients. When Company A obtains a consulting engagement with a client of a non-computer consulting firm, Company A does not subcontract with the other consulting firm, nor does the other consulting firm play any role in Company A's consulting engagement.

(iii) Company B, a Country X subsidiary of Company A, assists Company A in obtaining an engagement to perform computer consulting services for a Company B banking industry client in Country X. Although Company B has an established relationship with its Country X client and was instrumental in arranging for Company A's engagement with the client, Company A's particular expertise was the primary consideration in motivating the client to engage Company A. Based on the relative contributions of Companies A and B in obtaining and undertaking the engagement, Company B's role was primarily to facilitate the consulting engagement between Company A and the Country X client. Information regarding the commissions paid by Company A to unrelated parties for providing similar services to facilitate Company A's consulting engagements is sufficiently complete to conclude that it is likely that all material differences between these uncontrolled transactions and the controlled transaction between Company B and Company A have been identified and that appropriate adjustments have been made for any such differences. If the comparable gross services margin earned by unrelated parties in providing such agent services is 3% of total fees charged in the relevant transactions involved in the uncontrolled comparables, then the appropriate gross services profit that Company B may earn and the arm's length price that it may charge Company A for its agent services is equal to this comparable gross services margin (3%), multiplied by the applicable uncontrolled price charged by Company A in its relevant uncontrolled consulting engagement with Company B's client.

Example 4. Intermediary function. (i) The facts are the same as in *Example 3*, except that Company B contracts directly with its Country X client to provide computer consulting services and Company A performs the consulting services on behalf of Company B. Company A does not enter into a consulting engagement with Company B's Country X client. Instead, Company B charges its Country X client an uncontrolled price for the consulting services, and Company B pays a portion of the uncontrolled price to Company A for performing the consulting services on behalf of Company B.

(ii) Analysis of the relative contributions of Companies A and B in obtaining and undertaking the consulting contract indicates that Company B functioned primarily as an intermediary contracting party, and the gross services margin method is the most reliable method for determining the amount that Company B may retain as compensation for its intermediary function with respect to Company A's consulting services. In this case, therefore, because Company B entered into the relevant uncontrolled transaction to provide services, Company B receives the applicable uncontrolled price that is paid by the Country X client for the consulting services. Company A technically performs services for Company B when it performs, on behalf of Company B, the consulting services Company B contracted to provide to the Country X client. The arm's length amount that Company A may charge Company B for performing the consulting services on Company B's behalf is equal to the applicable uncontrolled price received by Company B in the relevant uncontrolled transaction, less Company B's appropriate gross services profit, which is the amount that Company B may retain as compensation for performing the intermediary function.

(iii) Reliable data concerning the commissions that Company A paid to uncontrolled parties for assisting it in obtaining engagements to provide consulting services similar to those it has provided on behalf of Company B provide useful information in applying the gross services margin method. However, consideration should be given to whether the third party commission data may need to be adjusted to account for any additional risk that Company B may have assumed as a result of its function as an intermediary contracting party, compared with the risk it would have assumed if it had provided agent services to assist Company A in entering into an engagement to provide its consulting service directly. In this case, the information regarding the commissions paid by Company A to unrelated parties for providing agent services to facilitate its performance of consulting services for unrelated parties is sufficiently complete to conclude that all material differences between these uncontrolled transactions and the controlled performance of an intermediary function, including possible differences in the amount of risk assumed in connection with performing that function, have been identified and that appropriate adjustments have been made. If the comparable gross services margin earned by unrelated parties in providing such agent services is 3% of total fees charged in Company B's relevant uncontrolled transactions, then the appropriate gross services profit that Company B may retain as compensation for performing an intermediary function (and the amount, therefore, that is deducted from the applicable uncontrolled price to arrive at the arm's length price that Company A may charge Company B for performing consulting services on Company B's behalf) is equal to this comparable gross services margin (3%), multiplied by the applicable uncontrolled price charged by Company B in its contract to provide services to the uncontrolled party.

Example 5. External comparable. (i) The facts are the same as in *Example 4*, except that neither Company A nor Company B engages in transactions with third parties that facilitate similar consulting engagements.

(ii) Analysis of the relative contributions of Companies A and B in obtaining and undertaking the contract indicates that Company B's role was primarily to facilitate the consulting arrangement between Company A and the Country X client. Although no reliable internal data are available regarding comparable transactions with uncontrolled entities, reliable data exist regarding commission rates for similar facilitating services between uncontrolled parties. These data indicate that a 3% commission (3% of total engagement fee) is charged in such transactions. Information regarding the uncontrolled comparables is sufficiently complete to conclude that it is likely that all material differences between the controlled and uncontrolled transactions have been identified and adjusted for. If the appropriate gross services profit margin is 3% of total fees, then an arm's length result of the controlled services transaction is for Company B to retain an amount equal to 3% of total fees paid to it.

(e) *Cost of services plus method.*—(1) *In general.*—The cost of services plus method evaluates whether the amount charged in a controlled services transaction is arm's length by reference to the gross services profit markup realized in comparable uncontrolled transactions. The cost of services plus method is ordinarily used in cases where the controlled service renderer provides the same or similar services to both controlled and uncontrolled parties. This method is ordinarily not used in cases where the controlled services transaction involves a contingent-payment arrangement, as described in paragraph (i)(2) of this section.

(2) *Determination of arm's length price.*—(i) *In general.*—The cost of services plus method measures an arm's length price by adding the appropriate gross services profit to the controlled taxpayer's comparable transactional costs.

(ii) *Appropriate gross services profit.*—The appropriate gross services profit is computed by multiplying the controlled taxpayer's comparable transactional costs by the gross services profit markup, expressed as a percentage of the comparable transactional costs earned in comparable uncontrolled transactions.

(iii) *Comparable transactional costs.*—Comparable transactional costs consist of the costs of providing the services under review that are taken into account as the basis for determining the gross services profit markup in comparable uncontrolled transactions. Depending on the facts and circumstances, such costs typically include all compensation attributable to employees directly involved in the performance of such services, materials and supplies consumed or made available in rendering such services, and may include as well other costs of rendering the services. Comparable transactional costs must be determined on a basis that will facilitate comparison with the comparable uncontrolled transactions. For that reason, comparable transactional costs may not necessarily equal total services costs, as defined in paragraph (j) of this section, and in appropriate cases may be a subset of total services costs. Generally accepted accounting principles or Federal income tax accounting rules (where Federal income tax data for comparable transactions or business activities are available) may provide useful guidance but will not conclusively establish the appropriate comparable transactional costs for purposes of this method.

(iv) *Arm's length range.*—See § 1.482-1(e)(2) for determination of an arm's length range.

(3) *Comparability and reliability considerations.*—(i) *In general.*—Whether results derived from the application of this method are the most reliable measure of the arm's length result must be determined using the factors described under the best method rule in § 1.482-1(c).

(ii) *Comparability.*—(A) *Functional comparability.*—The degree of comparability between controlled and uncontrolled transactions is determined by applying the comparability provisions of § 1.482-1(d). A service renderer's gross services profit provides compensation for performing services related to the controlled services transaction under review, including an operating profit for the service renderer's investment of capital and assumptions of risks. Therefore, although all of the factors described in § 1.482-1(d)(3) must be considered, comparability under this method is particularly dependent on similarity of services or functions performed, risks borne, intangible property (if any) used in providing the services or functions, and contractual terms, or adjustments to account for the effects of any such differences. If possible, the appropriate gross services profit markup should be derived from comparable uncontrolled transactions of the same taxpayer participating in the controlled services transaction because similar characteristics are more likely to be found among services provided by the same service provider than among services provided by other service providers. In the absence of such services transactions, an appropriate gross services profit markup may be derived from comparable uncontrolled services transactions of other service providers. If the appropriate gross services profit markup is derived from comparable uncontrolled services transactions of other service providers, in evaluating comparability the controlled taxpayer must consider the results under this method expressed as a markup on total services costs of the controlled taxpayer, because differences in functions performed may be reflected in differences in service costs other than those included in comparable transactional costs.

(B) *Other comparability factors.*—Comparability under this method is less dependent on close similarity between the services provided than under the comparable uncontrolled services price method. Substantial differences in the services may, however, indicate significant functional differences between the controlled and uncontrolled taxpayers. Thus, it ordinarily would be expected that the controlled and uncontrolled transactions would involve services of the same general type (for example, information-technology systems design). Furthermore, if a significant amount of the controlled taxpayer's comparable transactional costs consists of service costs incurred in a tax accounting period other than the tax accounting period under review, the reliability of the analysis would be reduced. In addition, significant differences in the value of the services rendered, due for example to the use of valuable intangible property, may also affect the reliability of the comparison. Finally, the reliability of profit measures based on gross services profit may be adversely affected by factors that have less effect on prices. For example, gross services profit may be affected by a variety of other factors, including cost structures or efficiency-related factors (for example, differences in the level of experience of the employees performing the service in the controlled and uncontrolled transactions). Accordingly, if material differences in these factors are identified based on objective evidence, the reliability of the analysis may be affected.

(C) *Adjustments for differences between the controlled and uncontrolled transactions.*—If there are material differences between the controlled and uncontrolled transactions that would affect the gross services profit markup, adjustments should be made to the gross services profit markup earned in the comparable uncontrolled transaction according to the provisions of § 1.482-1(d)(2). For this purpose, consideration of the comparable transactional costs associated with the functions performed and risks assumed may be necessary, because differences in the functions performed are often reflected in these costs. If there are differences in functions performed, however, the effect on gross services profit of such differences is not necessarily equal to the differences in the amount of related comparable transactional costs. Specific examples of the factors that may be particularly relevant to this method include—

(1) The complexity of the services;

(2) The duration or quantitative measure of services;

(3) Contractual terms (for example, scope and terms of warranties or guarantees provided, volume, credit and payment terms, allocation of risks, including any contingent-payment terms);

(4) Economic circumstances; and

(5) Risks borne.

(iii) *Data and assumptions.*—(A) *In general.*—The reliability of the results derived from the cost of services plus method is affected by the completeness and accuracy of the data used and the reliability of the assumptions made to apply this method. See § 1.482-1(c) (Best method rule).

(B) *Consistency in accounting.*—The degree of consistency in accounting practices between the controlled transaction and the uncontrolled comparables that materially affect the gross services profit markup affects the reliability of the results under this method. Thus, for example, if differences in cost accounting practices would materially affect the gross services profit markup, the ability to make reliable adjustments for such differences would affect the reliability of the results obtained under this method. Further, reliability under this method depends on the extent to which the controlled and uncontrolled transactions reflect consistent reporting of comparable transactional costs. For purposes of this paragraph (e)(3)(iii)(B), the term *comparable transactional costs* includes the cost of acquiring tangible property that is transferred (or used) with the services, to the extent that the arm's length price of the tangible property is not separately evaluated as a controlled transaction under another provision.

(4) *Examples.*—The principles of this paragraph (e) are illustrated by the following examples:

Example 1. Internal comparable. (i) Company A designs and assembles information-technology networks and systems. When Company A renders services for uncontrolled parties, it receives compensation based on time and materials as well as certain other related costs necessary to complete the project. This fee includes the cost of hardware and software purchased from uncontrolled vendors and incorporated in the final network or system, plus a reasonable allocation of certain specified overhead costs incurred by Company A in providing these services. Reliable accounting records maintained by Company A indicate that Company A earned a gross services profit markup of 10% on its time, materials and specified overhead in providing design services during the year under examination on information technology projects for uncontrolled entities.

(ii) Company A designed an information-technology network for its Country X subsidiary, Company B. The services rendered to Company B are similar in scope and complexity to services that Company A rendered to uncontrolled parties during the year under examination. Using Company A's accounting records (which are determined to be reliable under paragraph (e)(3) of this section), it is possible to identify the comparable transactional costs involved in the controlled services transaction with reference to the costs incurred by Company A in rendering similar design services to uncontrolled parties. Company A's records indicate that it does not incur any additional types of costs in rendering similar services to uncontrolled customers. The data available are sufficiently complete to conclude that it is likely that all material differences between the controlled and uncontrolled transactions have been identified and adjusted for. Based on the gross services profit markup data derived from Company A's uncontrolled transactions involving similar design services, an arm's length result for the controlled services transaction is equal to the price that will allow Company A to earn a 10% gross services profit markup on its comparable transactional costs.

Example 2. Inability to adjust for differences in comparable transactional costs. The facts are the same as in *Example 1*, except that Company A's staff that rendered the services to Company B consisted primarily of engineers in training status or on temporary rotation from other Company A subsidiaries. In addition, the Company B network incorporated innovative features, including specially designed software suited to Company B's requirements. The use of less-experienced personnel and staff on temporary rotation, together with the special features of the Company B network, significantly increased the time and costs associated with the project as compared to time and costs associated with similar projects completed for uncontrolled customers. These factors constitute material differences between the controlled and the uncontrolled transactions that affect the determination of Company A's comparable transactional costs associated with the controlled services transaction, as well as the gross services profit markup. Moreover, it is not possible to perform reliable adjustments for these differences on the basis of the available accounting data. Under these circumstances, the reliability of the cost of services plus method as a measure of an arm's length price is substantially reduced.

Example 3. Operating loss by reference to total services costs. The facts and analysis are the same as in *Example 1*, except that an unrelated Company C, instead of Company A, renders similar services to uncontrolled parties and publicly available information indicates that Company C earned a gross services profit markup of 10% on its time, materials and certain specified overhead in providing those services. As in *Example 1*, Company A still provides services for its Country X subsidiary, Company B. In accordance with the requirements in paragraph (e)(3)(ii) of this section, the taxpayer performs additional analysis and restates the results of Company A's controlled services transaction with its Country X subsidiary, Company B, in the form of a markup on Company A's total services costs. This analysis by reference to total services costs shows that Company A generated an operating loss on the controlled services transaction, which indicates that functional differences likely exist between the controlled services transaction performed by Company A and uncontrolled services transactions performed by Company C, and that these differences may not be reflected in the comparable transactional costs. Upon further scrutiny, the presence of such functional differences between the controlled and uncontrolled transactions may indicate that the cost of services plus method does not provide the most reliable measure of an arm's length result under the facts and circumstances.

Example 4. Internal comparable. (i) Company A, a U.S. corporation, and its subsidiaries perform computer consulting services relating to systems integration and networking for business clients in various countries. Company A and its subsidiaries render only consulting services and do not manufacture or distribute computer hardware or software to clients. The controlled group is organized according to industry specialization, with key industry specialists working for Company A. These personnel typically form the core consulting group that teams with consultants from the localcountry subsidiaries to serve clients in the subsidiaries' respective countries.

(ii) On some occasions, Company A and its subsidiaries undertake engagements directly for clients. On other occasions, they work as subcontractors for uncontrolled parties on more extensive consulting engagements for clients. In undertaking the latter engagements with third-party consultants, Company A typically prices its services at four times the compensation costs of its consultants, defined as the consultants' base salary plus estimated fringe benefits, as defined in this table:

Category	Rate
Project managers	$100 per hour
Technical staff	$75 per hour

(iii) In uncontrolled transactions, Company A also charges the customer, at no markup, for out-of-pocket expenses such as travel, lodging, and data acquisition charges. Thus, for example, a project involving 100 hours of time from project managers, and 400 hours of technical staff time would result in total compensation costs to Company A of (100 hrs. × $100/hr.) + (400 hrs. × $75/hr.) = $10,000 + $30,000 = $40,000. Applying the markup of 300%, the total fee charged would thus be (4 × $40,000), or $160,000, plus out of pocket expenses.

(iv) Company B, a Country X subsidiary of Company A, contracts to render consulting services to a Country X client in the banking industry. In undertaking this engagement, Company B uses its own consultants and also uses the services of Company A project managers and technical staff that specialize in the banking industry for 75 hours and 380 hours, respectively. The data available are sufficiently complete to conclude that it is likely that all material differences between the controlled and uncontrolled transactions have been identified and adjusted for. Based on reliable data concerning the compensation costs to Company A, an arm's length result for the controlled services transaction is equal to $144,000. This is calculated as follows: [4 × (75 hrs. × $100/hr.)] + [4 × (380 hrs. × $75/hr.)]= $30,000 + $114,000 = $144,000, reflecting a 300% markup on the total compensation costs for Company A project managers and technical staff. In addition, consistent with Company A's pricing of uncontrolled transactions, Company B must reimburse Company A for appropriate out-of-pocket expenses incurred in performing the services.

(f) *Comparable profits method.*—(1) *In general.*—The comparable profits method evaluates whether the amount charged in a controlled transaction is arm's length, based on objective measures of profitability (profit level indicators) derived from uncontrolled taxpayers that engage in similar business activities under similar circumstances. The rules in § 1.482-5 relating to the comparable profits method apply to controlled services transactions, except as modified in this paragraph (f).

(2) *Determination of arm's length result.*—(i) *Tested party.*—This paragraph (f) applies where the relevant business activity of the tested party as determined under § 1.482-5(b)(2) is the rendering of services in a controlled services transaction. Where the tested party determined under § 1.482-5(b)(2) is instead the recipient of the controlled services, the rules under this paragraph (f) are not applicable to determine the arm's length result.

(ii) *Profit level indicators.*—In addition to the profit level indicators provided in § 1.482-5(b)(4), a profit level indicator that may provide a reliable basis for comparing operating profits of the tested party involved in a controlled services transaction and uncontrolled comparables is the ratio of operating profit to total services costs (as defined in paragraph (j) of this section).

(iii) *Comparability and reliability considerations—Data and assumptions—Consistency in accounting.*—Consistency in accounting practices between the relevant business activity of the tested party and the uncontrolled service providers is particularly important in determining the reliability of the results under this method, but less than in applying the cost of services plus method. Adjustments may be appropriate if materially different treatment is applied to particular cost items related to the relevant business activity of the tested party and the uncontrolled service providers. For example, adjustments may be appropriate where the tested party and the uncontrolled comparables use inconsistent approaches to classify similar expenses as "cost of goods sold" and "selling, general, and administrative expenses." Although distinguishing between these two categories may be difficult, the distinction is less important to the extent that the ratio of operating profit to total services costs is used as the appropriate profit level indicator. Determining whether adjustments are necessary under these or similar circumstances requires thorough analysis of the functions performed and consideration of the cost accounting practices of the tested party and the uncontrolled comparables. Other adjustments as provided in § 1.482-5(c)(2)(iv) may also be necessary to increase the reliability of the results under this method.

(3) *Examples.*—The principles of this paragraph (f) are illustrated by the following examples:

Example 1. Ratio of operating profit to total services costs as the appropriate profit level indicator. (i) A Country T parent firm, Company A, and its Country Y subsidiary, Company B, both engage in manufacturing as their principal business activity. Company A also performs certain advertising services for itself and its affiliates. In year 1, Company A renders advertising services to Company B.

(ii) Based on the facts and circumstances, it is determined that the comparable profits method will provide the most reliable measure of an arm's length result. Company A is selected as the tested party. No data are available for comparable independent manufacturing firms that render advertising services to third parties. Financial data are available, however, for ten independent firms that render similar advertising services as their principal business activity in Country X. The ten firms are determined to be comparable under § 1.482-5(c). Neither Company A nor the comparable companies use valuable intangible property in rendering the services.

(iii) Based on the available financial data of the comparable companies, it cannot be determined whether these comparable companies report costs for financial accounting purposes in the same manner as the tested party. The publicly available financial data of the comparable companies segregate total services costs into cost of goods sold and sales, general and administrative costs, with no further segmentation of costs provided. Due to the limited information available regarding the cost accounting practices used by the comparable companies, the ratio of operating profits to total services costs is determined to be the most appropriate profit level indicator. This ratio includes total services costs to minimize the effect of any inconsistency in accounting practices between Company A and the comparable companies.

Example 2. Application of the operating profit to total services costs profit level indicator. (i) Company A is a foreign subsidiary of Company B, a U.S. corporation. Company B is under examination for its year 1 taxable year. Company B renders management consulting services to Company A. Company B's consulting function includes analyzing Company A's operations, benchmarking Company A's financial performance against companies in the same industry, and to the extent necessary, developing a strategy to improve Company A's operational performance. The accounting records of Company B allow reliable identification of the total services costs of the consulting staff associated with the management consulting services rendered to Company A. Company A reimburses Company B for its costs associated with rendering the consulting services, with no markup.

(ii) Based on all the facts and circumstances, it is determined that the comparable profits method will provide the most reliable measure of an arm's length result. Company B is selected as the tested party, and its rendering of management consulting services is identified as the relevant business activity. Data are available from ten domestic companies that operate in the industry segment involving management consulting and that perform activities comparable to the relevant business activity of Company B. These comparables include entities that primarily perform management consulting services for uncontrolled parties. The comparables incur similar risks as Company B incurs in performing the consulting services and do not make use of valuable intangible property or special processes.

(iii) Based on the available financial data of the comparables, it cannot be determined whether the comparables report their costs for financial accounting purposes in the same manner as Company B reports its costs in the relevant business activity. The available financial data for the comparables report only an aggregate figure for costs of goods sold and operating expenses, and do not segment the underlying services costs. Due to this limitation, the ratio of operating profits to total services costs is determined to be the most appropriate profit level indicator.

(iv) For the taxable years 1 through 3, Company B shows the following results for the services performed for Company A:

	Year 1	Year 2	Year 3	Average
Revenues	1,200,000	1,100,000	1,300,000	1,200,000
Cost of Goods Sold	100,000	100,000	N/A	66,667
Operating Expenses	1,100,000	1,000,000	1,300,000	1,133,333
Operating Profit	0	0	0	0

(v) After adjustments have been made to account for identified material differences between the relevant business activity of Company B and the comparables, the average ratio for the taxable years 1 through 3 of operating profit to total services costs is calculated for each of the uncontrolled service providers. Applying each ratio to Company B's average total services costs from the relevant business activity for the taxable years 1 through 3 would lead to the following comparable operating profit (COP) for the services rendered by Company B:

Uncontrolled Service Provider	*OP/Total Service Costs*	*Company B COP*
Company 1	15.75%	$189,000
Company 2	15.00%	$180,000
Company 3	14.00%	$168,000
Company 4	13.30%	$159,600
Company 5	12.00%	$144,000
Company 6	11.30%	$135,600
Company 7	11.25%	$135,000
Company 8	11.18%	$134,160
Company 9	11.11%	$133,320
Company 10	10.75%	$129,000

(vi) The available data are not sufficiently complete to conclude that it is likely that all material differences between the relevant business activity of Company B and the comparables have been identified. Therefore, an arm's length range can be established only pursuant to § 1.482-1(e)(2)(iii)(B). The arm's length range is established by reference to the interquartile range of the results as calculated under § 1.482-1(e)(2)(iii)(C), which consists of the results ranging from $168,000 to $134,160. Company B's reported average operating profit of zero ($0) falls outside this range. Therefore, an allocation may be appropriate.

(vii) Because Company B reported income of zero, to determine the amount, if any, of the allocation, Company B's reported operating profit for year 3 is compared to the comparable operating profits derived from the comparables' results for year 3. The ratio of operating profit to total services costs in year 3 is calculated for each of the comparables and applied to Company B's year 3 total services costs to derive the following results:

Uncontrolled Service Provider	*OP/Total Service Costs (for year 3)*	*Company B COP*
Company 1	15.00%	$195,000
Company 2	14.75%	$191,750
Company 3	14.00%	$182,000
Company 4	13.50%	$175,500
Company 5	12.30%	$159,900
Company 6	11.05%	$143,650
Company 7	11.03%	$143,390
Company 8	11.00%	$143,000
Company 9	10.50%	$136,500
Company 10	10.25%	$133,250

(viii) Based on these results, the median of the comparable operating profits for year 3 is $151,775. Therefore, Company B's income for year 3 is increased by $151,775, the difference between Company B's reported operating profit for year 3 of zero and the median of the comparable operating profits for year 3.

Example 3. Material difference in accounting for stock-based compensation. (i) Taxpayer, a U.S. corporation the stock of which is publicly traded, performs controlled services for its wholly-owned subsidiaries. The arm's length price of these controlled services is evaluated under the comparable profits method for services in paragraph (f) of this section by reference to the net cost plus profit level indicator (PLI). Taxpayer is the tested party under paragraph (f)(2)(i) of this section. The Commissioner identifies the most narrowly identifiable business activity of the tested party for which data are available that incorporate the controlled transaction (the relevant business activity). The Commissioner also identifies four uncontrolled domestic service providers, Companies A, B, C, and D, each of which performs exclusively activities similar to the relevant business activity of Taxpayer that is subject to analysis under paragraph (f) of this section. The stock of Companies A, B, C, and D is publicly traded on a U.S. stock exchange. Assume that Taxpayer makes an election to apply these regulations to earlier taxable years.

(ii) Stock options are granted to the employees of Taxpayer that engage in the relevant business activity. Assume that, as determined under a method in accordance with U.S. generally accepted accounting principles, the fair value of such stock options attributable to the employees' performance of the relevant business activity is 500 for the taxable year in question. In evaluating the controlled services, Taxpayer includes salaries, fringe benefits, and related compensation of these employees in "total services costs," as defined in paragraph (j) of this section. Taxpayer does not include any amount attributable to stock options in total services costs, nor does it deduct that amount in determining "reported operating profit" within the meaning of §1.482-5(d)(5), for the year under examination.

(iii) Stock options are granted to the employees of Companies A, B, C, and D. Under a fair value method in accordance with U.S. generally accepted accounting principles, the comparables include in total compensation the value of the stock options attributable to the employees' performance of the relevant business activity for the annual financial reporting period, and treat this amount as an expense in determining operating profit for financial accounting purposes. The treatment of employee stock options is summarized in the following table:

	Salaries and other non-option compensation	Stock options fair value	Stock options expensed
Taxpayer	1,000	500	0
Company A	7,000	2,000	2,000
Company B	4,300	250	250
Company C	12,000	4,500	4,500
Company D	15,000	2,000	2,000

(iv) A material difference in accounting for stock-based compensation (within the meaning of §1.482-7T(d)(3)(i)) exists. Analysis indicates that this difference would materially affect the measure of an arm's length result under this paragraph (f). In making an adjustment to improve comparability under §§1.482-1(d)(2) and 1.482-5(c)(2)(iv), the Commissioner includes in total services costs of the tested party the total compensation costs of 1,500 (including stock option fair value). In addition, the Commissioner calculates the net cost plus PLI by reference to the financial-accounting data of Companies A, B, C, and D, which take into account compensatory stock options.

Example 4. Material difference in utilization of stock-based compensation. (i) The facts are the same as in paragraph (i) of Example 3.

(ii) No stock options are granted to the employees of Taxpayer that engage in the relevant business activity. Thus, no deduction for stock options is made in determining "reported operating profit" (within the meaning of §1.482-5(d)(5)) for the taxable year under examination.

(iii) Stock options are granted to the employees of Companies A, B, C, and D, but none of these companies expense stock options for financial accounting purposes. Under a method in accordance with U.S. generally accepted accounting principles, however, Companies A, B, C, and D disclose the fair value of the stock options for financial accounting purposes. The utilization and treatment of employee stock options is summarized in the following table:

	Salaries and other non-option compensation	Stock options fair value	Stock options expensed
Taxpayer	1,000	0	N/A
Company A	7,000	2,000	0
Company B	4,300	250	0
Company C	12,000	4,500	0
Company D	15,000	2,000	0

(iv) A material difference in the utilization of stock-based compensation (within the meaning of §1.482-7T(d)(3)(i)) exists. Analysis indicates that these differences would materially affect the measure of an arm's length result under this paragraph (f). In evaluating the comparable operating profits of the tested party, the Commissioner uses Taxpayer's total services costs, which include total compensation costs of 1,000. In considering whether an adjustment is necessary to improve comparability under §§1.482-1(d)(2) and 1.482-5(c)(2)(iv), the Commissioner recognizes that the total compensation provided to employees of Taxpayer is comparable to the total compensation provided to employees of Companies A, B, C, and D. Because Companies A, B, C, and D do not expense stock-based compensation for financial accounting purposes, their reported operating profits must be adjusted in order to improve comparability with the tested party. The Commissioner increases each comparable's total services costs, and also reduces its reported operating profit, by the fair value of the stock-based compensation incurred by the comparable company.

(v) The adjustments to the data of Companies A, B, C, and D described in paragraph (iv) of this *Example 4* are summarized in the following table:

	Salaries and other nonoption compensation	Stock options fair value	Total services costs (A)	Operating profit (B)	Net cost plus PLI (B/A)
Per financial statements:					
Company A	7,000	2,000	25,000	6,000	24.00%
Company B	4,300	250	12,500	2,500	20.00%
Company C	12,000	4,500	36,000	11,000	30.56%
Company D	15,000	2,000	27,000	7,000	25.93%
As adjusted:					
Company A	7,000	2,000	27,000	4,000	14.81%
Company B	4,300	250	12,750	2,250	17.65%
Company C	12,000	4,500	40,500	6,500	16.05%
Company D	15,000	2,000	29,000	5,000	17.24%

Example 5. Non-material difference in utilization of stock-based compensation. (i) The facts are the same as in paragraph (i) of *Example 3*.

(ii) Stock options are granted to the employees of Taxpayer that engage in the relevant business activity. Assume that, as determined under a method in accordance with U.S. generally accepted accounting principles, the fair value of such stock options attributable to the employees' performance of the relevant business activity is 50 for the taxable year. Taxpayer includes salaries, fringe benefits, and all other compensation of these employees (including the stock option fair value) in "total services costs," as defined in paragraph (j) of this section, and deducts these amounts in determining "reported operating profit" within the meaning of §1.482-5(d)(5), for the taxable year under examination.

(iii) Stock options are granted to the employees of Companies A, B, C, and D, but none of these companies expense stock options for financial accounting purposes. Under a method in accordance with U.S. generally accepted accounting principles, however, Companies A, B, C, and D disclose the fair value of the stock options for financial accounting purposes. The utilization and treatment of employee stock options is summarized in the following table:

	Salaries and other non-option compensation	Stock options fair value	Stock options expensed
Taxpayer	1,000	50	50
Company A	7,000	100	0
Company B	4,300	40	0
Company C	12,000	130	0
Company D	15,000	75	0

(iv) Analysis of the data reported by Companies A, B, C, and D indicates that an adjustment for differences in utilization of stock-based compensation would not have a material effect on the determination of an arm's length result.

	Salaries and other non-option compensation	Stock options fair value	Total services costs (A)	Operating profit (B)	Net cost plus PLI (B/A)
Per financial statements:					
Company A	7,000	100	25,000	6,000	24.00%
Company B	4,300	40	12,500	2,500	20.00%
Company C	12,000	130	36,000	11,000	30.56%
Company D	15,000	75	27,000	7,000	25.93%
As adjusted:					
Company A	7,000	100	25,100	5,900	23.51%
Company B	4,300	40	12,540	2,460	19.62%
Company C	12,000	130	36,130	10,870	30.09%
Company D	15,000	75	27,075	6,925	25.58%

(v) Under the circumstances, the difference in utilization of stock-based compensation would not materially affect the determination of the arm's length result under this paragraph (f). Accordingly, in calculating the net cost plus PLI, no comparability adjustment is made to the data of Companies A, B, C, or D pursuant to §§1.482-1(d)(2) and 1.482-5(c)(2)(iv).

Example 6. Material difference in comparables' accounting for stock-based compensation. (i) The facts are the same as in paragraph (i) of *Example 3*.

(ii) Stock options are granted to the employees of Taxpayer that engage in the relevant business activity. Assume that, as determined under a method in accordance with U.S. generally accepted accounting principles, the fair value of such stock options attributable to employees' performance of the relevant business activity is 500 for the taxable year. Taxpayer includes salaries, fringe benefits, and all other compensation of these employees (including the stock option fair value) in "total services costs," as defined in paragraph (j) of this section, and deducts these amounts in determining "reported operating profit" (within the meaning of §1.482-5(d)(5)) for the taxable year under examination.

(iii) Stock options are granted to the employees of Companies A, B, C, and D. Companies A and B expense the stock options for financial accounting purposes in accordance with U.S. generally accepted accounting principles. Companies C and D do not expense the stock options for financial accounting purposes. Under a method in accordance with U.S. generally accepted accounting principles, however, Companies C and D disclose the fair value of these options in their financial statements. The utilization and accounting treatment of options are depicted in the following table:

	Salary and other non-option compensation	Stock options fair value	Stock options expensed
Taxpayer	1,000	500	500
Company A	7,000	2,000	2,000
Company B	4,300	250	250
Company C	12,000	4,500	0
Company D	15,000	2,000	0

(iv) A material difference in accounting for stock-based compensation (within the meaning of §1.482-7T(d)(3)(i)) exists. Analysis indicates that this difference would materially affect the measure of the arm's length result under paragraph (f) of this section. In evaluating the comparable operating profits of the tested party, the Commissioner includes in total services costs Taxpayer's total compensation costs of 1,500 (including stock option fair value of 500). In considering whether an adjustment is necessary to improve comparability under §§1.482-1(d)(2) and 1.482-5(c)(2)(iv), the Commissioner recognizes that the total employee compensation (including stock options provided by Taxpayer and Companies A, B, C, and D) provides a reliable basis for comparison. Because Companies A and B expense stock-based compensation for financial accounting purposes, whereas Companies C and D do not, an adjustment to the comparables' operating profit is necessary. In computing the net cost plus PLI, the Commissioner uses the financial-accounting data of Companies A and B, as reported. The Commissioner increases the total services costs of Companies C and D by amounts equal to the fair value of their respective stock options, and reduces the operating profits of Companies C and D accordingly.

(v) The adjustments described in paragraph (iv) of this *Example 6* are depicted in the following table. For purposes of illustration, the unadjusted data of Companies A and B are also included.

	Salaries and other non-option compensation	Stock options fair value	Total services costs (A)	Operating profit (B)	Net cost plus PLI (B/A)
Per financial Statements:					
Company A	7,000	2,000	27,000	4,000	14.80%
Company B	4,300	250	12,750	2,250	17.65%
As adjusted:					
Company C	12,000	4,500	40,500	6,500	16.05%
Company D	15,000	2,000	29,000	5,000	17.24%

(g) *Profit split method.*—(1) *In general.*—The profit split method evaluates whether the allocation of the combined operating profit or loss attributable to one or more controlled transactions is arm's length by reference to the relative value of each controlled taxpayer's contribution to that combined operating profit or loss. The relative value of each controlled taxpayer's contribution is determined in a manner that reflects the functions performed, risks assumed and resources employed by such controlled taxpayer in the relevant business activity. For application of the profit split method (both the comparable profit split and the residual profit split), see §1.482-6. The residual profit split method may not be used where only one controlled taxpayer makes significant nonroutine contributions.

(2) *Examples.*—The principles of this paragraph (g) are illustrated by the following examples:

Example 1. Residual profit split. (i) Company A, a corporation resident in Country X, auctions spare parts by means of an interactive database. Company A maintains a database that lists all spare parts available for auction. Company A developed the software used to run the database. Company A's database is managed by Company A employees in a data center located in Country X, where storage and manipulation of data also take place. Company A has a wholly-owned subsidiary, Company B, located in Country Y. Company B performs marketing and advertising activities to promote Company A's interactive database. Company B solicits unrelated companies to auction spare parts on Company A's database, and solicits customers interested in purchasing spare parts online. Company B owns and maintains a computer server in Country Y, where it receives information on spare parts available for auction. Company B has also designed a specialized communications network that connects its data center to Company A's data center in Country X. The communications network allows Company B to enter data from uncontrolled companies on Company A's database located in Country X. Company B's communications network also allows uncontrolled companies to access Company A's interactive database and purchase spare parts. Company B bore the risks and cost of developing this specialized communications network. Company B enters into contracts with uncontrolled companies and provides the companies access to Company A's database through the Company B network.

(ii) Analysis of the facts and circumstances indicates that both Company A and Company B possess valuable intangible property that they use to conduct the spare parts auction business. Company A bore the economic risks of developing and maintaining software and the interactive database. Company B bore the economic risks of developing the necessary technology to transmit information from its server to Company A's data center, and to allow uncontrolled companies to access Company A's database. Company B helped to enhance the value of Company A's trademark and to establish a network of customers in Country Y. In addition, there are no market comparables for the transactions between Company A and Company B to reliably evaluate them separately. Given the facts and circumstances, the Commissioner determines that a residual profit split method will provide the most reliable measure of an arm's length result.

(iii) Under the residual profit split method, profits are first allocated based on the routine contributions of each taxpayer. Routine contributions include general sales, marketing or administrative functions performed by Company B for Company A for which it is possible to identify market returns. Any residual profits will be allocated based on the nonroutine contributions of each taxpayer. Since both Company A and Company B provided nonroutine contributions, the residual profits are allocated based on these contributions.

Example 2. Residual profit split. (i) Company A, a Country 1 corporation, provides specialized services pertaining to the processing and storage of Level 1 hazardous waste (for purposes of this example, the most dangerous type of waste). Under long-term contracts with private companies and governmental entities in Country 1, Company A performs multiple services, including transportation of Level 1 waste, development of handling and storage protocols, recordkeeping, and supervision of waste-storage facilities owned and maintained by the contracting parties. Company A's research and development unit has also developed new and unique processes for transport and storage of Level 1 waste that minimize environmental and occupational effects. In addition to this novel technology, Company A has substantial know-how and a long-term record of safe operations in Country 1.

(ii) Company A's subsidiary, Company B, has been in operation continuously for a number of years in Country 2. Company B has successfully completed several projects in Country 2 involving Level 2 and Level 3 waste, including projects with government-owned entities. Company B has a license in Country 2 to handle Level 2 waste (Level 3 does not require a license). Company B has established a reputation for completing these projects in a responsible manner. Company B has cultivated contacts with procurement officers, regulatory and licensing officials, and other government personnel in Country 2.

(iii) Country 2 government publishes invitations to bid on a project to handle the country's burgeoning volume of Level 1 waste, all of which is generated in governmentowned facilities. Bidding is limited to companies that are domiciled in Country 2 and that possess a license from the government to handle Level 1 or Level 2 waste. In an effort to submit a winning bid to secure the contract, Company B points to its Level 2 license and its record of successful completion of projects, and also demonstrates to Country 2 government that it has access to substantial technical expertise pertaining to processing of Level 1 waste.

(iv) Company A enters into a long-term technical services agreement with Company B. Under this agreement, Company A agrees to supply to Company B project managers and other technical staff who have detailed knowledge of Company A's proprietary Level 1 remediation techniques. Company A commits to perform under any long-term contracts entered into by Company B. Company B agrees to compensate Company A based on a markup on Company A's marginal costs (pro rata compensation and current expenses of Company A personnel). In the bid on the Country 2 contract for Level 1 waste remediation, Company B proposes to use a multi-disciplinary team of specialists from Company A and Company B. Project managers from Company A will direct the team, which will also include employees of Company B and will make use of physical assets and facilities owned by Company B. Only Company A and Company B personnel will perform services under the contract. Country 2 grants Company B a license to handle Level 1 waste.

(v) Country 2 grants Company B a five-year, exclusive contract to provide processing services for all Level 1 hazardous waste generated in County 2. Under the contract, Company B is to be paid a fixed price per ton of Level 1 waste that it processes each year. Company B undertakes that all services provided will meet international standards applicable to processing of Level 1 waste. Company B begins performance under the contract.

(vi) Analysis of the facts and circumstances indicates that both Company A and Company B make nonroutine contributions to the Level 1 waste processing activity in Country 2. In addition, it is determined that reliable comparables are not available for the services that Company A provides under the long-term contract, in part because those services incorporate specialized knowledge and process intangible property developed by Company A. It is also determined that reliable comparables are not available for the Level 2 license in Country 2, the successful track record, the government contacts with Country 2 officials, and other intangible property that Company B provided. In view of these facts, the Commissioner determines that the residual profit split method for services in paragraph (g) of this section provides the most reliable means of evaluating the arm's length results for the transaction. In evaluating the appropriate returns to Company A and Company B for their respective contributions, the Commissioner takes into account that the controlled parties incur different risks, because the contract between the controlled parties provides that Company A will be compensated on the basis of marginal costs incurred, plus a markup, whereas the contract between Company B and the government of Country 2 provides that Company B will be compensated on a fixed-price basis per ton of Level 1 waste processed.

(vii) In the first stage of the residual profit split, an arm's length return is determined for routine activities performed by Company B in Country 2, such as transportation, recordkeeping, and administration. In addition, an arm's length return is determined for routine activities performed by Company A (administrative, human resources, etc.) in connection with providing personnel to Company B. After the arm's length return for these functions is determined, residual profits may be present. In the second stage of the residual profit split, any residual profit is allocated by reference to the relative value of the nonroutine contributions made by each taxpayer. Company A's nonroutine contributions include its commitment to perform under the contract and the specialized technical knowledge made available through the project managers under the services agreement with Company B. Company B's nonroutine contributions include its licenses to handle Level 1 and Level 2 waste in Country 2, its knowledge of and contacts with procurement, regulatory and licensing officials in the government of Country 2, and its record in Country 2 of successfully handling non-Level 1 waste.

(h) *Unspecified methods.*—Methods not specified in paragraphs (b) through (g) of this section may be used to evaluate whether the amount charged in a controlled services transaction is arm's length. Any method used under this paragraph (h) must be applied in accordance with the provisions of §1.482-1. Consistent with the specified methods, an unspecified method should take into account the general principle that uncontrolled taxpayers evaluate the terms of a transaction by considering the realistic alternatives to that transaction, including economically similar transactions structured as other than services transactions, and only enter into a particular transaction if none of the alternatives is preferable to it. For example, the comparable uncontrolled services price method compares a controlled services transaction to similar uncontrolled transactions to provide a direct estimate of the price to which the parties would have agreed had they resorted directly to a market alternative to the controlled services transaction. Therefore, in establishing whether a controlled services transaction achieved an arm's length result, an unspecified method should provide information on the prices or profits that the controlled taxpayer could have realized by choosing a realistic alternative to the controlled services transaction (for example, outsourcing a particular service function, rather than performing the function itself). As with any method, an unspecified method will not be applied unless it provides the most reliable measure of an arm's length result under the principles of the best method rule. See §1.482-1(c). Therefore, in accordance with §1.482-1(d) (comparability), to the extent that an unspecified method relies on internal data rather than uncontrolled comparables, its reliability will be reduced.

Similarly, the reliability of a method will be affected by the reliability of the data and assumptions used to apply the method, including any projections used.

Example. (i) Company T, a U.S. corporation, develops computer software programs including a real estate investment program that performs financial analysis of commercial real properties. Companies U, V, and W are owned by Company T. The primary business activity of Companies U, V, and W is commercial real estate development. For business reasons, Company T does not sell the computer program to its customers (on a compact disk or via download from Company T's server through the Internet). Instead, Company T maintains the software program on its own server and allows customers to access the program through the Internet by using a password. The transactions between Company T and Companies U, V, and W are structured as controlled services transactions whereby Companies U, V, and W obtain access via the Internet to Company T's software program for financial analysis. Each year, Company T provides a revised version of the computer program including the most recent data on the commercial real estate market, rendering the old version obsolete.

(ii) In evaluating whether the consideration paid by Companies U, V, and W to Company T was arm's length, the Commissioner may consider, subject to the best method rule of § 1.482-1(c), Company T's alternative of selling the computer program to Companies U, V, and W on a compact disk or via download through the Internet. The Commissioner determines that the controlled services transactions between Company T and Companies U, V, and W are comparable to the transfer of a similar software program on a compact disk or via download through the Internet between uncontrolled parties. Subject to adjustments being made for material differences between the controlled services transactions and the comparable uncontrolled transactions, the uncontrolled transfers of tangible property may be used to evaluate the arm's length results for the controlled services transactions between Company T and Companies U, V, and W.

(i) *Contingent-payment contractual terms for services.*—(1) *Contingent-payment contractual terms recognized in general.*—In the case of a contingent-payment arrangement, the arm's length result for the controlled services transaction generally would not require payment by the recipient to the renderer in the tax accounting period in which the service is rendered if the specified contingency does not occur in that period. If the specified contingency occurs in a tax accounting period subsequent to the period in which the service is rendered, the arm's length result for the controlled services transaction generally would require payment by the recipient to the renderer on a basis that reflects the recipient's benefit from the services rendered and the risks borne by the renderer in performing the activities in the absence of a provision that unconditionally obligates the recipient to pay for the activities performed in the tax accounting period in which the service is rendered.

(2) *Contingent-payment arrangement.*—For purposes of this paragraph (i), an arrangement will be treated as a contingent-payment arrangement if it meets all of the requirements in paragraph (i)(2)(i) of this section and is consistent with the economic substance and conduct requirement in paragraph (i)(2)(ii) of this section.

(i) *General requirements.*—(A) *Written contract.*—The arrangement is set forth in a written contract entered into prior to, or contemporaneous with the start of the activity or group of activities constituting the controlled services transaction.

(B) *Specified contingency.*—The contract states that payment for a controlled services transaction is contingent (in whole or in part) upon the happening of a future benefit (within the meaning of § 1.482-9(l)(3)) for the recipient directly related to the activity or group of activities. For purposes of the preceding sentence, whether the future benefit is directly related to the activity or group of activities is evaluated based on all the facts and circumstances.

(C) *Basis for payment.*—The contract provides for payment on a basis that reflects the recipient's benefit from the services rendered and the risks borne by the renderer.

(ii) *Economic substance and conduct.*—The arrangement, including the contingency and the basis for payment, is consistent with the economic substance of the controlled transaction and the conduct of the controlled parties. See § 1.482-1(d)(3)(ii)(B).

(3) *Commissioner's authority to impute contingent-payment terms.*—Consistent with the authority in § 1.482-1(d)(3)(ii)(B), the Commissioner may impute contingentpayment contractual terms in a controlled services transaction if the economic substance of the transaction is consistent with the existence of such terms.

(4) *Evaluation of arm's length charge.*—Whether the amount charged in a contingent-payment arrangement is arm's length will be evaluated in accordance with this section and other applicable regulations under section 482. In evaluating whether the amount charged in a contingent-payment arrangement for the manufacture, construction, or development of tangible or intangible property owned by the recipient is arm's length, the charge determined under the rules of §§ 1.482-3 and 1.482-4 for the transfer of similar property may be considered. See § 1.482-1(f)(2)(ii).

(5) *Examples.*—The principles of this paragraph (i) are illustrated by the following examples:

Example 1. (i) Company X is a member of a controlled group that has operated in the pharmaceutical sector for many years. In year 1, Company X enters into a written services agreement with Company Y, another member of the controlled group, whereby Company X will perform certain research and development activities for Company Y. The parties enter into the agreement before Company X undertakes any of the research and development activities covered by the agreement. At the time the agreement is entered into, the possibility that any new products will be developed is highly uncertain and the possible market or markets for any products that may be developed are not known and cannot be estimated with any reliability. Under the agreement, Company Y will own any patent or other rights that result from the activities of Company X under the agreement and Company Y will make payments to Company X only if such activities result in commercial sales of one or more derivative products. In that event, Company Y will pay Company X, for a specified period, x% of Company Y's gross sales of each of such products. Payments are required with respect to each jurisdiction in which Company Y has sales of such a derivative product, beginning with the first year in which the sale of a product occurs in the jurisdiction and continuing for six additional years with respect to sales of that product in that jurisdiction.

(ii) As a result of research and development activities performed by Company X for Company Y in years 1 through 4, a compound is developed that may be more effective than existing medications in the treatment of certain conditions. Company Y registers the patent rights with respect to the compound in several jurisdictions in year 4. In year 6, Company Y begins commercial sales of the product in Jurisdiction A and, in that year, Company Y makes the payment to Company X that is required under the agreement. Sales of the product continue in Jurisdiction A in years 7 through 9 and Company Y makes the payments to Company X in years 7 through 9 that are required under the agreement.

(iii) The years under examination are years 6 through 9. In evaluating whether the contingent-payment terms will be recognized, the Commissioner considers whether the conditions of paragraph (i)(2) of this section are met and whether the arrangement, including the specified contingency and basis of payment, is consistent with the economic substance of the controlled services transaction and with the conduct of the controlled parties. The Commissioner determines that the contingent-payment arrangement is reflected in the written agreement between Company X and Company Y; that commercial sales of products developed under the arrangement represent future benefits for Company Y directly related to the controlled services transaction; and that the basis for the payment provided for in the event such sales occur reflects the recipient's benefit and the renderer's risk. Consistent with § 1.482-1(d)(3)(ii)(B) and (iii)(B), the Commissioner determines that the parties' conduct over the term of the agreement has been consistent with their contractual allocation of risk; that Company X has the financial capacity to bear the risk that its research and development services may be unsuccessful and that it may not receive compensation for such services; and that Company X exercises managerial and operational control over the research and development, such that it is reasonable for Company X to assume the risk of those activities. Based on all these facts, the Commissioner determines that the contingentpayment arrangement is consistent with economic substance.

(iv) In determining whether the amount charged under the contingent-payment arrangement in each of years 6 through 9 is arm's length, the Commissioner evaluates under this section and other applicable rules under section 482 the compensation paid in each year for the research and development services. This analysis takes into account that under the contingent-payment terms Company X bears the risk that it might not receive payment for its services in the event that those services do not result in marketable products and the risk that the magnitude of its payment depends on the magnitude of product sales, if any. The Commissioner also considers the alternatives reasonably available to the parties in connection with the controlled services transaction. One such alternative, in view of Company X's willingness and ability to bear the risk and expenses of research and development activities, would be for Company X to undertake such activities on its own behalf and to license the rights to products successfully developed as a result of such activities. Accordingly, in evaluating whether the compensation of x% of gross sales that is paid to Company X during the first four years of commercial sales of derivative products is arm's length, the Commissioner may consider the royalties (or other consideration) charged for intangible property that are comparable to those incorporated in the derivative products and that resulted from Company X's research and development activities under the contingentpayment arrangement.

Example 2. (i) The facts are the same as in *Example 1*, except that no commercial sales ever materialize with regard to the patented compound so that, consistent with the agreement, Company Y makes no payments to Company X in years 6 through 9.

(ii) Based on all the facts and circumstances, the Commissioner determines that the contingent-payment arrangement is consistent with economic substance, and the result (no payments in years 6 through 9) is consistent with an arm's length result.

Example 3. (i) The facts are the same as in *Example 1*, except that, in the event that Company X's activities result in commercial sales of one or more derivative products by Company Y, Company Y will pay Company X a fee equal to the research and development costs borne by Company X plus an amount equal to x% of such costs, with the payment to be made in the first year in which any such sales occur. The x% markup on costs is within the range, ascertainable in year 1, of markups on costs of independent contract researchers that are compensated under terms that unconditionally obligate the recipient to pay for the activities performed in the tax accounting period in which the service is rendered. In year 6, Company Y makes the single payment to Company X that is required under the arrangement.

(ii) The years under examination are years 6 through 9. In evaluating whether the contingent-payment terms will be recognized, the Commissioner considers whether the requirements of paragraph (i)(2) of this section were met at the time the written agreement was entered into and whether the arrangement, including the specified contingency and basis for payment, is consistent with the economic substance of the controlled services transaction and with the conduct of the controlled parties. The Commissioner determines that the contingent-payment terms are reflected in the written agreement between Company X and Company Y and that commercial sales of products developed under the arrangement represent future benefits for Company Y directly related to the controlled services transaction. However, in this case, the Commissioner determines that the basis for payment provided for in the event such sales occur (costs of the services plus x%, representing the markup for contract research in the absence of any nonpayment risk) does not reflect the recipient's benefit and the renderer's risks in the controlled services transaction. Based on all the facts and circumstances, the Commissioner determines that the contingent-payment arrangement is not consistent with economic substance.

(iii) Accordingly, the Commissioner determines to exercise its authority to impute contingent-payment contractual terms that accord with economic substance, pursuant to paragraph (i)(3) of this section and § 1.482-1(d)(3)(ii)(B). In this regard, the Commissioner takes into account that at the time the arrangement was entered into, the possibility that any new products would be developed was highly uncertain and the possible market or markets for any products that may be developed were not known and could not be estimated with any reliability. In such circumstances, it is reasonable to conclude that one possible basis of payment, in order to reflect the recipient's benefit and the renderer's risks, would be a charge equal to a percentage of commercial sales of one or more derivative products that result from the research and development activities. The Commissioner in this case may impute terms that require Company Y to pay Company X a percentage of sales of the products developed under the agreement in each of years 6 through 9.

(iv) In determining an appropriate arm's length charge under such imputed contractual terms, the Commissioner conducts an analysis under this section and other applicable rules under section 482, and considers the alternatives reasonably available to the parties in connection with the controlled services transaction. One such alternative, in view of Company X's willingness and ability to bear the risks and expenses of research and development activities, would be for Company X to undertake such activities on its own behalf and to license the rights to products successfully developed as a result of such activities. Accordingly, for purposes of its determination, the Commissioner may consider the royalties (or other consideration) charged for intangible property that are comparable to those incorporated in the derivative products that resulted from Company X's research and development activities under the contingent-payment arrangement.

(j) *Total services costs.*—For purposes of this section, total services costs means all costs of rendering those services for which total services costs are being determined. Total services costs include all costs in cash or in kind (including stock-based compensation) that, based on analysis of the facts and circumstances, are directly identified with, or reasonably allocated in accordance with the principles of paragraph (k)(2) of this section to, the services. In general, costs for this purpose should comprise provision for all resources expended, used, or made available to achieve the specific objective for which the service is rendered. Reference to generally accepted accounting principles or Federal income tax accounting rules may provide a useful starting point but will not necessarily be conclusive regarding inclusion of costs in total services costs. Total services costs do not include interest expense, foreign income taxes (as defined in § 1.901-2(a)), or domestic income taxes.

(k) *Allocation of costs.*—(1) *In general.*—In any case where the renderer's activity that results in a benefit (within the meaning of paragraph (l)(3) of this section) for one recipient in a controlled services transaction also generates a benefit for one or more other members of a controlled group (including the benefit, if any, to the renderer), and the amount charged under this section in the controlled services transaction is determined under a method that makes reference to costs, costs must be allocated among the portions of the activity performed for the benefit of the first mentioned recipient and such other members of the controlled group under this paragraph (k). The principles of this paragraph (k) must also be used whenever it is appropriate to allocate and apportion any class of costs (for example, overhead costs) in order to determine the total services costs of rendering the services. In no event will an allocation of costs based on a generalized or non-specific benefit be appropriate.

(2) *Appropriate method of allocation and apportionment.*—(i) *Reasonable method standard.*—Any reasonable method may be used to allocate and apportion costs under this section. In establishing the appropriate method of allocation and apportionment, consideration should be given to all bases and factors, including, for example, total services costs, total costs for a relevant activity, assets, sales, compensation, space utilized, and time spent. The costs incurred by supporting departments may be apportioned to other departments on the basis of reasonable overall estimates, or such costs may be reflected in the other departments' costs by applying reasonable departmental overhead rates. Allocations and apportionments of costs must be made on the basis of the full cost, as opposed to the incremental cost.

(ii) *Use of general practices.*—The practices used by the taxpayer to apportion costs in connection with preparation of statements and analyses for the use of management, creditors, minority shareholders, joint venturers, clients, customers, potential investors, or other parties or agencies in interest will be considered as potential indicators of reliable allocation methods, but need not be accorded conclusive weight by the Commissioner. In determining the extent to which allocations are to be made to or from foreign members of a controlled group, practices employed by the domestic members in apportioning costs among themselves will also be considered if the relationships with the foreign members are comparable to the relationships among the domestic members of the controlled group. For example, if for purposes of reporting to public stockholders or to a governmental agency, a corporation apportions the costs attributable to its executive officers among the domestic members of a controlled group on a reasonable and consistent basis, and such officers exercise comparable control over foreign members of the controlled group, such domestic apportionment practice will be considered in determining the allocations to be made to the foreign members.

(3) *Examples.*—The principles of this paragraph (k) are illustrated by the following examples:

Example 1. Company A pays an annual license fee of 500x to an uncontrolled taxpayer for unlimited use of a database within the corporate group. Under the terms of the license with the uncontrolled taxpayer, Company A is permitted to use the database for its own use and in rendering research services to its subsidiary, Company B. Company B obtains benefits from the database that are similar to those that it would obtain if it had independently licensed the database from the uncontrolled taxpayer. Evaluation of the arm's length charge (under a method in which costs are relevant) to Company B for the controlled services that incorporate use of the database must take into account the full amount of the license fee of 500x paid by Company A, as reasonably allocated and apportioned to the relevant benefits, although the incremental use of the database for the benefit of Company B did not result in an increase in the license fee paid by Company A.

Example 2. (i) Company A is a consumer products company located in the United States. Companies B and C are wholly-owned subsidiaries of Company A and are located in Countries B and C, respectively. Company A and its subsidiaries manufacture products for sale in their respective markets. Company A hires a consultant who has expertise regarding a manufacturing process used by Company A and its subsidiary, Company B. Company C, the Country C subsidiary, uses a different manufacturing process, and accordingly will not receive any benefit from the outside consultant hired by Company A. In allocating and apportioning the cost of hiring the outside consultant (100), Company A determines that sales constitute the most appropriate allocation key.

(ii) Company A and its subsidiaries have the following sales:

Company	A	B	C	Total
Sales	400	100	200	700

(iii) Because Company C does not obtain any benefit from the consultant, none of the costs are allocated to it. Rather, the costs of 100 are allocated and apportioned ratably to Company A and Company B as the entities that obtain a benefit from the campaign, based on the total sales of those entities (500). An appropriate allocation of the costs of the consultant is as follows:

Company	A	B	Total
Allocation	400/500	100/500	....
Amount	80	20	100

(l) *Controlled services transaction.*—(1) *In general.*—A controlled services transaction includes any activity (as defined in paragraph (l)(2) of this section) by one member of a group of controlled taxpayers (the renderer) that results in a benefit (as defined in paragraph (l)(3) of this section) to one or more other members of the controlled group (the recipient(s)).

(2) *Activity.*—An activity includes the performance of functions, assumptions of risks, or use by a renderer of tangible or intangible property or other resources, capabilities, or knowledge, such as knowledge of and ability to take advantage of particularly advantageous situations or circumstances. An activity also includes making available to the recipient any property or other resources of the renderer.

(3) *Benefit.*—(i) *In general.*—An activity is considered to provide a benefit to the recipient if the activity directly results in a reasonably identifiable increment of economic or commercial value that enhances the recipient's commercial position, or that may reasonably be anticipated to do so. An activity is generally considered to confer a benefit if, taking into account the facts and circumstances, an uncontrolled taxpayer in circumstances comparable to those of the recipient would be willing to pay an uncontrolled party to perform the same or similar activity on either a fixed or contingentpayment basis, or if the recipient otherwise would have performed for itself the same activity or a similar activity. A benefit may result to the owner of intangible property if the renderer engages in an activity that is reasonably anticipated to result in an increase in the value of that intangible property. Paragraphs (l)(3)(ii) through (v) of this section provide guidelines that indicate the presence or absence of a benefit for the activities in the controlled services transaction.

(ii) *Indirect or remote benefit.*—An activity is not considered to provide a benefit to the recipient if, at the time the activity is performed, the present or reasonably anticipated benefit from that activity is so indirect or remote that the recipient would not be willing to pay, on either a fixed or contingent-payment basis, an uncontrolled party to perform a similar activity, and would not be willing to perform such activity for itself for this purpose. The determination whether the benefit from an activity is indirect or remote is based on the nature of the activity and the situation of the recipient, taking into consideration all facts and circumstances.

(iii) *Duplicative activities.*—If an activity performed by a controlled taxpayer duplicates an activity that is performed, or that reasonably may be anticipated to be performed, by another controlled taxpayer on or for its own account, the activity is generally not considered to provide a benefit to the recipient, unless the duplicative activity itself provides an additional benefit to the recipient.

(iv) *Shareholder activities.*—An activity is not considered to provide a benefit if the sole effect of that activity is either to protect the renderer's capital investment in the recipient or in other members of the controlled group, or to facilitate compliance by the renderer with reporting, legal, or regulatory requirements applicable specifically to the renderer, or both. Activities in the nature of day-to-day management generally do not relate to protection of the renderer's capital investment. Based on analysis of the facts and circumstances, activities in connection with a corporate reorganization may be considered to provide a benefit to one or more controlled taxpayers.

(v) *Passive association.*—A controlled taxpayer generally will not be considered to obtain a benefit where that benefit results from the controlled taxpayer's status as a member of a controlled group. A controlled taxpayer's status as a member of a controlled group may, however, be taken into account for purposes of evaluating comparability between controlled and uncontrolled transactions.

(4) *Disaggregation of transactions.*—A controlled services transaction may be analyzed as two separate transactions for purposes of determining the arm's length consideration, if that analysis is the most reliable means of determining the arm's length consideration for the controlled services transaction. See the best method rule under § 1.482-1(c).

(5) *Examples.*—The principles of this paragraph (l) are illustrated by the following examples. In each example, assume that Company X is a U.S. corporation and Company Y is a wholly-owned subsidiary of Company X in Country B.

Example 1. In general. In developing a worldwide advertising and promotional campaign for a consumer product, Company X pays for and obtains designation as an official sponsor of the Olympics. This designation allows Company X and all its subsidiaries, including Company Y, to identify themselves as sponsors and to use the Olympic logo in advertising and promotional campaigns. The Olympic sponsorship campaign generates benefits to Company X, Company Y, and other subsidiaries of Company X.

Example 2. Indirect or remote benefit. Based on recommendations contained in a study performed by its internal staff, Company X implements certain changes in its management structure and the compensation of managers of divisions located in the United States. No changes were recommended or considered for Company Y in Country B. The internal study and the resultant changes in its management may increase the competitiveness and overall efficiency of Company X. Any benefits to Company Y as a result of the study are, however, indirect or remote. Consequently, Company Y is not considered to obtain a benefit from the study.

Example 3. Indirect or remote benefit. Based on recommendations contained in a study performed by its internal staff, Company X decides to make changes to the management structure and management compensation of its subsidiaries, in order to increase their profitability. As a result of the recommendations in the study, Company X implements substantial changes in the management structure and management compensation scheme of Company Y. The study and the changes implemented as a result of the recommendations are anticipated to increase the profitability of Company X and its subsidiaries. The increased management efficiency of Company Y that results from these changes is considered to be a specific and identifiable benefit, rather than remote or speculative.

Example 4. Duplicative activities. At its corporate headquarters in the United States, Company X performs certain treasury functions for Company X and for its subsidiaries, including Company Y. These treasury functions include raising capital, arranging medium and long-term financing for general corporate needs, including cash management. Under these circumstances, the treasury functions performed by Company X do not duplicate the functions performed by

Company Y's staff. Accordingly, Company Y is considered to obtain a benefit from the functions performed by Company X.

Example 5. Duplicative activities. The facts are the same as in *Example 4*, except that Company Y's functions include ensuring that the financing requirements of its own operations are met. Analysis of the facts and circumstances indicates that Company Y independently administers all financing and cash-management functions necessary to support its operations, and does not utilize financing obtained by Company X. Under the circumstances, the treasury functions performed by Company X are duplicative of similar functions performed by Company Y's staff, and the duplicative functions do not enhance Company Y's position. Accordingly, Company Y is not considered to obtain a benefit from the duplicative activities performed by Company X.

Example 6. Duplicative activities. Company X's in-house legal staff has specialized expertise in several areas, including intellectual property. The intellectual property legal staff specializes in technology licensing, patents, copyrights, and negotiating and drafting intellectual property agreements. Company Y is involved in negotiations with an unrelated party to enter into a complex joint venture that includes multiple licenses and cross-licenses of patents and copyrights. Company Y retains outside counsel that specializes in intellectual property law to review the transaction documents. Company Y does not have in-house counsel of its own to review intellectual property transaction documents. Outside counsel advises that the terms for the proposed transaction are advantageous to Company Y and that the contracts are valid and fully enforceable. Company X's intellectual property legal staff possess valuable knowledge of Company Y's patents and technological achievements. They are capable of identifying particular scientific attributes protected under patent that strengthen Company Y's negotiating position, and of discovering flaws in the patents offered by the unrelated party. To reduce risk associated with the transaction, Company X's intellectual property legal staff reviews the transaction documents before Company Y executes the contracts. Company X's intellectual property legal staff also separately evaluates the patents and copyrights with respect to the licensing arrangements and concurs in the opinion provided by outside counsel. The activities performed by Company X substantially duplicate the legal services obtained by Company Y, but they also reduce risk associated with the transaction in a way that confers an additional benefit on Company Y.

Example 7. Shareholder activities. Company X is a publicly held corporation. U.S. laws and regulations applicable to publicly held corporations such as Company X require the preparation and filing of periodic reports that show, among other things, profit and loss statements, balance sheets, and other material financial information concerning the company's operations. Company X, Company Y and each of the other subsidiaries maintain their own separate accounting departments that record individual transactions and prepare financial statements in accordance with their local accounting practices. Company Y, and the other subsidiaries, forward the results of their financial performance to Company X, which analyzes and compiles these data into periodic reports in accordance with U.S. laws and regulations. Because Company X's preparation and filing of the reports relate solely to its role as an investor of capital or shareholder in Company Y or to its compliance with reporting, legal, or regulatory requirements, or both, these activities constitute shareholder activities and therefore Company Y is not considered to obtain a benefit from the preparation and filing of the reports.

Example 8. Shareholder activities. The facts are the same as in *Example 7*, except that Company Y's accounting department maintains a general ledger recording individual transactions, but does not prepare any financial statements (such as profit and loss statements and balance sheets). Instead, Company Y forwards the general ledger data to Company X, and Company X analyzes and compiles financial statements for Company Y, as well as for Company X's overall operations, for purposes of complying with U.S. reporting requirements. Company Y is subject to reporting requirements in Country B similar to those applicable to Company X in the United States. Much of the data that Company X analyzes and compiles regarding Company Y's operations for purposes of complying with the U.S. reporting requirements are made available to Company Y for its use in preparing reports that must be filed in Country B. Company Y incorporates these data, after minor adjustments for differences in local accounting practices, into the reports that it files in Country B. Under these circumstances, because Company X's analysis and compilation of Company Y's financial data does not relate solely to its role as an investor of capital or shareholder in Company Y, or to its compliance with reporting, legal, or regulatory requirements, or both, these activities do not constitute shareholder activities.

Example 9. Shareholder activities. Members of Company X's internal audit staff visit Company Y on a semiannual basis in order to review the subsidiary's adherence to internal operating procedures issued by Company X and its compliance with U.S. anti-bribery laws, which apply to Company Y on account of its ownership by a U.S. corporation. Because the sole effect of the reviews by Company X's audit staff is to protect Company X's investment in Company Y, or to facilitate Company X's compliance with U.S. anti-bribery laws, or both, the visits are shareholder activities and therefore Company Y is not considered to obtain a benefit from the visits.

Example 10. Shareholder activities. Country B recently enacted legislation that changed the foreign currency exchange controls applicable to foreign shareholders of Country B corporations. Company X concludes that it may benefit from changing the capital structure of Company Y, thus taking advantage of the new foreign currency exchange control laws in Country B. Company X engages an investment banking firm and a law firm to review the Country B legislation and to propose possible changes to the capital structure of Company Y. Because Company X's retention of the firms facilitates Company Y's ability to pay dividends and other amounts and has the sole effect of protecting Company X's investment in Company Y, these activities constitute shareholder activities and Company Y is not considered to obtain a benefit from the activities.

Example 11. Shareholder activities. The facts are the same as in *Example 10*, except that Company Y bears the full cost of retaining the firms to evaluate the new foreign currency control laws in Country B and to make appropriate changes to its stock ownership by Company X. Company X is considered to obtain a benefit from the rendering by Company Y of these activities, which would be shareholder activities if conducted by Company X (see *Example 10*).

Example 12. Shareholder activities. The facts are the same as in *Example 10*, except that the new laws relate solely to corporate governance in Country B, and Company X retains the law firm and investment banking firm in order to evaluate whether restructuring would increase Company Y's profitability, reduce the number of legal entities in Country B, and increase Company Y's ability to introduce new products more quickly in Country B. Because Company X retained the law firm and the investment banking firm primarily to enhance Company Y's profitability and the efficiency of its operations, and not solely to protect Company X's investment in Company Y or to facilitate Company X's compliance with Country B's corporate laws, or to both, these activities do not constitute shareholder activities.

Example 13. Shareholder activities. Company X establishes detailed personnel policies for its subsidiaries, including Company Y. Company X also reviews and approves the performance appraisals of Company Y's executives, monitors levels of compensation paid to all Company Y personnel, and is involved in hiring and firing decisions regarding the senior executives of Company Y. Because this personnelrelated activity by Company X involves day-to-day management of Company Y, this activity does not relate solely to Company X's role as an investor of capital or a shareholder of Company Y, and therefore does not constitute a shareholder activity.

Example 14. Shareholder activities. Each year, Company X conducts a twoday retreat for its senior executives. The purpose of the retreat is to refine the longterm business strategy of Company X and its subsidiaries, including Company Y, and to produce a confidential strategy statement. The strategy statement identifies several potential growth initiatives for Company X and its subsidiaries and lists general means of increasing the profitability of the company as a whole. The strategy statement is made available without charge to Company Y and the other subsidiaries of Company X. Company Y independently evaluates whether to implement some, all, or none of the initiatives contained in the strategy statement. Because the preparation of the strategy statement does not relate solely to Company X's role as an investor of capital or a shareholder of Company Y, the expense of preparing the document is not a shareholder expense.

Example 15. Passive association/benefit. Company X is the parent corporation of a large controlled group that has been in operation in the information-technology sector for ten years. Company Y is a small corporation that was recently acquired by the Company X controlled group from local Country B owners. Several months after the acquisition of Company Y, Company Y obtained a contract to redesign and assemble the information-technology networks and systems of a large financial institution in Country B. The project was significantly larger and more complex than any other project undertaken to date by Company Y. Company Y did not use Company X's marketing intangible property to solicit the contract, and Company X had no involvement in the solicitation, negotiation, or anticipated execution of the contract. For purposes of this section, Company Y is not considered to obtain a benefit from Company X or any other member of the controlled group because the ability of Company Y to obtain the contract, or to obtain the contract on more favorable terms than would have been possible prior to its acquisition by the Company X controlled group, was due to Company Y's status as a member of the Company X controlled group and not to any specific activity by Company X or any other member of the controlled group.

Example 16. Passive association/benefit. The facts are the same as in *Example 15*, except that Company X executes a performance guarantee with respect to the contract, agreeing to assist in the project if Company Y fails to meet certain mileposts. This performance guarantee allowed Company Y to obtain the contract on materially more favorable terms than otherwise would have been possible. Company Y is considered to obtain a benefit from Company X's execution of the performance guarantee.

Example 17. Passive association/benefit. The facts are the same as in *Example 15*, except that Company X began the process of negotiating the contract with the financial institution in Country B before acquiring Company Y. Once Company Y was acquired by Company X, the contract with the financial institution was entered into by Company Y. Company Y is considered to obtain a benefit from Company X's negotiation of the contract.

Example 18. Passive association/benefit. The facts are the same as in *Example 15*, except that Company X sent a letter to the financial institution in Country B, which represented that Company X had a certain percentage ownership in Company Y and that Company X would maintain that same percentage ownership interest in Company Y until the contract was completed. This letter allowed Company Y to obtain the contract on more favorable terms than otherwise would have been possible. Since this letter from Company X to the financial institution simply affirmed Company Y's status as a member of the controlled group and represented that this status would be maintained until the contract was completed, Company Y is not considered to obtain a benefit from Company X's furnishing of the letter.

Example 19. Passive association/benefit. (i) S is a company that supplies plastic containers to companies in various industries. S establishes the prices for its containers through a price list that offers customers discounts based solely on the volume of containers purchased.

(ii) Company X is the parent corporation of a large controlled group in the information technology sector. Company Y is a wholly-owned subsidiary of Company X located in Country B. Company X and Company Y both purchase plastic containers from unrelated supplier S. In year 1, Company X purchases 1 million units and Company Y purchases 100,000 units. S, basing its prices on purchases by the entire group, completes the order for 1.1 million units at a price of $0.95 per unit, and separately bills and ships the orders to each company. Companies X and Y undertake no bargaining with supplier S with respect to the price charged, and purchase no other products from supplier S.

(iii) R1 and its wholly-owned subsidiary R2 are a controlled group of taxpayers (unrelated to Company X or Company Y) each of which carries out functions comparable to those of Companies X and Y and undertakes purchases of plastic containers from supplier S, identical to those purchased from S by Company X and Company Y, respectively. S, basing its prices on purchases by the entire group, charges R1 and R2 $0.95 per unit for the 1.1 million units ordered. R1 and R2 undertake no bargaining with supplier S with respect to the price charged, and purchase no other products from supplier S.

(iv) U is an uncontrolled taxpayer that carries out comparable functions and undertakes purchases of plastic containers from supplier S identical to Company Y. U is not a member of a controlled group, undertakes no bargaining with supplier S with respect to the price charged, and purchases no other products from supplier S. U purchases 100,000 plastic containers from S at the price of $1.00 per unit.

(v) Company X charges Company Y a fee of $5,000, or $0.05 per unit of plastic containers purchased by Company Y, reflecting the fact that Company Y receives the volume discount from supplier S.

(vi) In evaluating the fee charged by Company X to Company Y, the Commissioner considers whether the transactions between R1, R2, and S or the transactions between U and S provide a more reliable measure of the transactions between Company X, Company Y and S. The Commissioner determines that Company Y's status as a member of a controlled group should be taken into account for purposes of evaluating comparability of the transactions, and concludes that the transactions between R1, R2, and S are more reliably comparable to the transactions between Company X, Company Y, and S. The comparable charge for the purchase was $0.95 per unit. Therefore, obtaining the plastic containers at a favorable rate (and the resulting $5,000 savings) is entirely due to Company Y's status as a member of the Company X controlled group and not to any specific activity by Company X or any other member of the controlled group. Consequently, Company Y is not considered to obtain a benefit from Company X or any other member of the controlled group.

Example 20. Disaggregation of transactions. (i) X, a domestic corporation, is a pharmaceutical company that develops and manufactures ethical pharmaceutical products. Y, a Country B corporation, is a distribution and marketing company that also performs clinical trials for X in Country B. Because Y does not possess the capability to conduct the trials, it contracts with a third party to undertake the trials at a cost of $100. Y also incurs $25 in expenses related to the third-party contract (for example, in hiring and working with the third party).

(ii) Based on a detailed functional analysis, the Commissioner determines that Y performed functions beyond merely facilitating the clinical trials for X, such as audit controls of the third party performing those trials. In determining the arm's length price, the Commissioner may consider a number of alternatives. For example, for purposes of determining the arm's length price, the Commissioner may determine that the intercompany service is most reliably analyzed on a disaggregated basis as two separate transactions: in this case, the contract between Y and the third party could constitute an internal CUSP with a price of $100. Y would be further entitled to an arm's length remuneration for its facilitating services. If the most reliable method is one that provides a markup on Y's costs, then "total services cost" in this context would be $25. Alternatively, the Commissioner may determine that the intercompany service is most reliably analyzed as a single transaction, based on comparable uncontrolled transactions involving the facilitation of similar clinical trial services performed by third parties. If the most reliable method is one that provides a markup on all of Y's costs, and the base of the markup determined by the comparable companies includes the third-party clinical trial costs, then such a markup would be applied to Y's total services cost of $125.

Example 21. Disaggregation of transactions. (i) X performs a number of administrative functions for its subsidiaries, including Y, a distributor of widgets in Country B. These services include those relating to working capital (inventory and accounts receivable/payable) management. To facilitate provision of these services, X purchases an ERP system specifically dedicated to optimizing working capital management. The system, which entails significant third-party costs and which includes substantial intellectual property relating to its software, costs $1000.

(ii) Based on a detailed functional analysis, the Commissioner determines that in providing administrative services for Y, X performed functions beyond merely operating the ERP system itself, since X was effectively using the ERP as an input to the administrative services it was providing to Y. In determining arm's length price for the services, the Commissioner may consider a number of alternatives. For example, if the most reliable uncontrolled data is derived from companies that use similar ERP systems purchased from third parties to perform similar administrative functions for uncontrolled parties, the Commissioner may determine that a CPM is the best method for measuring the functions performed by X, and, in addition, that a markup on total services costs, based on the markup from the comparable companies, is the most reliable PLI. In this case, total services cost, and the basis for the markup, would include appropriate reflection of the ERP costs of $1000. Alternatively, X's functions may be most reliably measured based on comparable uncontrolled companies that perform similar administrative functions using their customers' own ERP systems. Under these circumstances, the total services cost would equal X's costs of providing the administrative services excluding the ERP cost of $1000.

(m) *Coordination with transfer pricing rules for other transactions.*—(1) *Services transactions that include other types of transactions.*—A transaction structured as a controlled services transaction may include other elements for which a separate category or categories of methods are provided, such as a loan or advance, a rental, or a transfer of tangible or intangible property. See §§1.482-1(b)(2) and 1.482-2(a), (c), and (d). Whether such an integrated transaction is evaluated as a controlled services transaction under this section or whether one or more elements should be evaluated separately under other sections of the section 482 regulations depends on which approach will provide the most reliable measure of an arm's length result. Ordinarily, an integrated transaction of this type may be evaluated under this section and its separate elements need not be evaluated separately, provided that each component of the transaction may be adequately accounted for in evaluating the comparability of the controlled transaction to the uncontrolled comparables and, accordingly, in determining the arm's length result in the controlled transaction. See §1.482-1(d)(3).

(2) *Services transactions that effect a transfer of intangible property.*—A transaction structured as a controlled services transaction may in certain cases include an element that constitutes the transfer of intangible property or may result in a transfer, in whole or in part, of intangible property. Notwithstanding paragraph (m)(1) of this section, if such element relating to intangible property is material to the evaluation, the arm's length result for the element of the transaction that involves intangible property must be corroborated or determined by an analysis under § 1.482-4.

(3) *Coordination with rules governing cost sharing arrangements.*—Section 1.482-7 provides the specific methods to be used to determine arm's length results of controlled transactions in connection with a cost sharing arrangement. This section provides the specific methods to be used to determine arm's length results of a controlled service transaction, including in an arrangement for sharing the costs and risks of developing intangibles other than a cost sharing arrangement covered by § 1.482-7. In the case of such an arrangement, consideration of the principles, methods, comparability, and reliability considerations set forth in § 1.482-7 is relevant in determining the best method, including an unspecified method, under this section, as appropriately adjusted in light of the differences in the facts and circumstances between such arrangement and a cost sharing arrangement.

(4) *Other types of transactions that include controlled services transactions.*—A transaction structured other than as a controlled services transaction may include one or more elements for which separate pricing methods are provided in this section. Whether such an integrated transaction is evaluated under another section of the section 482 regulations or whether one or more elements should be evaluated separately under this section depends on which approach will provide the most reliable measure of an arm's length result. Ordinarily, a single method may be applied to such an integrated transaction, and the separate services component of the transaction need not be separately analyzed under this section, provided that the controlled services may be adequately accounted for in evaluating the comparability of the controlled transaction to the uncontrolled comparables and, accordingly, in determining the arm's length results in the controlled transaction. See § 1.482-1(d)(3).

(5) *Examples.*—The principles of this paragraph (m) are illustrated by the following examples:

Example 1. (i) U.S. parent corporation Company X enters into an agreement to maintain equipment of Company Y, a foreign subsidiary. The maintenance of the equipment requires the use of spare parts. The cost of the spare parts necessary to maintain the equipment amounts to approximately 25 percent of the total costs of maintaining the equipment. Company Y pays a fee that includes a charge for labor and parts.

(ii) Whether this integrated transaction is evaluated as a controlled services transaction or is evaluated as a controlled services transaction and the transfer of tangible property depends on which approach will provide the most reliable measure of an arm's length result. If it is not possible to find comparable uncontrolled services transactions that involve similar services and tangible property transfers as the controlled transaction between Company X and Company Y, it will be necessary to determine the arm's length charge for the controlled services, and then to evaluate separately the arm's length charge for the tangible property transfers under § 1.482-1 and §§ 1.482-3 through 1.482-6. Alternatively, it may be possible to apply the comparable profits method of § 1.482-5 to evaluate the arm's length profit of Company X or Company Y from the integrated controlled transaction. The comparable profits method may provide the most reliable measure of an arm's length result if uncontrolled parties are identified that perform similar, combined functions of maintaining and providing spare parts for similar equipment.

Example 2. (i) U.S. parent corporation Company X sells industrial equipment to its foreign subsidiary, Company Y. In connection with this sale, Company X renders to Company Y services that consist of demonstrating the use of the equipment and assisting in the effective start-up of the equipment. Company X structures the integrated transaction as a sale of tangible property and determines the transfer price under the comparable uncontrolled price method of § 1.482-3(b).

(ii) Whether this integrated transaction is evaluated as a transfer of tangible property or is evaluated as a controlled services transaction and a transfer of tangible property depends on which approach will provide the most reliable measure of an arm's length result. In this case, the controlled services may be similar to services rendered in the transactions used to determine the comparable uncontrolled price, or they may appropriately be considered a difference between the controlled transaction and comparable transactions with a definite and reasonably ascertainable effect on price for which appropriate adjustments can be made. See § 1.482-1(d)(3)(ii)(A)(*6*). In either case, application of the comparable uncontrolled price method to evaluate the integrated transaction may provide a reliable measure of an arm's length result, and application of a separate transfer pricing method for the controlled services element of the transaction is not necessary.

Example 3. (i) The facts are the same as in *Example 2* except that, after assisting Company Y in start-up, Company X also renders ongoing services, including instruction and supervision regarding Company Y's ongoing use of the equipment. Company X structures the entire transaction, including the incremental ongoing services, as a sale of tangible property, and determines the transfer price under the comparable uncontrolled price method of § 1.482-3(b).

(ii) Whether this integrated transaction is evaluated as a transfer of tangible property or is evaluated as a controlled services transaction and a transfer of tangible property depends on which approach will provide the most reliable measure of an arm's length result. It may not be possible to identify comparable uncontrolled transactions in which a seller of merchandise renders services similar to the ongoing services rendered by Company X to Company Y. In such a case, the incremental services in connection with ongoing use of the equipment could not be taken into account as a comparability factor because they are not similar to the services rendered in connection with sales of similar tangible property. Accordingly, it may be necessary to evaluate separately the transfer price for such services under this section in order to produce the most reliable measure of an arm's length result. Alternatively, it may be possible to apply the comparable profits method of § 1.482-5 to evaluate the arm's length profit of Company X or Company Y from the integrated controlled transaction. The comparable profits method may provide the most reliable measure of an arm's length result if uncontrolled parties are identified that perform the combined functions of selling equipment and rendering ongoing after-sale services associated with such equipment. In that case, it would not be necessary to separately evaluate the transfer price for the controlled services under this section.

Example 4. (i) Company X, a U.S. corporation, and Company Y, a foreign corporation, are members of a controlled group. Both companies perform research and development activities relating to integrated circuits. In addition, Company Y manufactures integrated circuits. In years 1 through 3, Company X engages in substantial research and development activities, gains significant know-how regarding the development of a particular high-temperature resistant integrated circuit, and memorializes that research in a written report. In years 1 through 3, Company X generates overall net operating losses as a result of the expenditures associated with this research and development effort. At the beginning of year 4, Company X enters into a technical assistance agreement with Company Y. As part of this agreement, the researchers from Company X responsible for this project meet with the researchers from Company Y and provide them with a copy of the written report. Three months later, the researchers from Company Y apply for a patent for a high-temperature resistant integrated circuit based in large part upon the know-how obtained from the researchers from Company X.

(ii) The controlled services transaction between Company X and Company Y includes an element that constitutes the transfer of intangible property (such as, knowhow). Because the element relating to the intangible property is material to the arm's length evaluation, the arm's length result for that element must be corroborated or determined by an analysis under § 1.482-4.

(6) *Global dealing operations.*—[Reserved].

(n) *Effective/applicability date.*—(1) *In general.*—This section is generally applicable for taxable years beginning after July 31, 2009. In addition, a person may elect to apply the provisions of this section to earlier taxable years. See paragraph (n)(2) of this section.

(2) *Election to apply regulations to earlier taxable years.*—(i) *Scope of election.*—A taxpayer may elect to apply § 1.482-1(a)(1), (b)(2)(i), (d)(3)(ii)(C) *Examples 3* through *6*, (d)(3)(v), (f)(2)(ii)(A), (f)(2)(iii)(B), (g)(4)(i), (g)(4)(iii) *Example 1*, (i), (j)(6)(i) and (j)(6)(ii), § 1.482-2(b), (f)(1) and (2), § 1.482-4(f)(3)(i)(A), (f)(3)(ii) *Examples 1* and *2*, (f)(4), (h)(1) and (2), § 1.482-6(c)(2)(ii)(B)(1), (c)(2)(ii)(D), (c)(3)(i)(A), (c)(3)(i)(B), (c)(3)(ii)(D), and (d), § 1.482-8(b) *Examples 10* through *12*, (c)(1) and (c)(2), § 1.482-9(a) through (m)(2), and (m)(4) through (n)(2), § 1.861-8(a)(5)(ii), (b)(3), (e)(4), (f)(4)(i), (g) *Examples 17, 18*, and *30*, § 1.6038A-3(a)(3) *Example 4* and (i), § 1.6662-6(d)(2)(ii)(B), (d)(2)(iii)(B)(*4*), (d)(2)(iii)(B)(*6*), and (g), and § 31.3121(s)-1(c)(2)(iii)

and (d) of this chapter to any taxable year beginning after September 10, 2003. Such election requires that all of the provisions of such sections be applied to such taxable year and all subsequent taxable years (earlier taxable years) of the taxpayer making the election.

(ii) *Effect of election.*—An election to apply the regulations to earlier taxable years has no effect on the limitations on assessment and collection or on the limitations on credit or refund (see Chapter 66 of the Internal Revenue Code).

(iii) *Time and manner of making election.*—An election to apply the regulations to earlier taxable years must be made by attaching a statement to the taxpayer's timely filed U.S. tax return (including extensions) for its first taxable year beginning after July 31, 2009.

(iv) *Revocation of election.*—An election to apply the regulations to earlier taxable years may not be revoked without the consent of the Commissioner. [Reg. § 1.482-9.]

☐ [*T.D. 9456, 7-31-2009 (corrected 9-8-2009). Amended by T.D. 9568, 12-16-2011.*]

Corporations Improperly Accumulating Surplus

§ 1.532-1. Corporations subject to accumulated earnings tax.—

* * *

(c) *Foreign corporations.*—Section 531 is applicable to any foreign corporation, whether resident or nonresident, with respect to any income derived from sources within the United States, if any of its shareholders are subject to income tax on the distributions of the corporation by reason of being (1) citizens or residents of the United States, or (2) nonresident alien individuals to whom section 871 is applicable, or (3) foreign corporations if a beneficial interest therein is owned directly or indirectly by any shareholder specified in subparagraph (1) or (2) of this paragraph. [Reg. § 1.532-1.]

☐ [*T.D. 6377, 5-12-59.*]

§ 1.535-1. Definition.—

* * *

(b) In the case of a foreign corporation, whether resident or nonresident, which files or causes to be filed a return, the accumulated taxable income shall be the taxable income from sources within the United States with the adjustments prescribed by section 535(b) and § 1.535-2 minus the sum of the dividends paid deduction and the accumulated earnings credit. In the case of a foreign corporation which files no return, the accumulated taxable income shall be the gross income from sources within the United States without allowance of any deductions (including the accumulated earnings credit). [Reg. § 1.535-1.]

☐ [*T.D. 6377, 5-12-59. Amended by T.D. 7244, 12-29-72.*]

§ 1.535-2. Adjustments to taxable income.—(a) *Taxes.*—

* * *

(2) *Taxes of foreign countries and United States possessions.*—In determining accumulated taxable income for any taxable year, if the taxpayer chooses the benefits of section 901 for such taxable year, a deduction shall be allowed for—

(i) The income, war profits, and excess profits taxes imposed by foreign countries or possessions of the United States and accrued during such taxable year, and

(ii) In the case of a domestic corporation, the foreign income taxes deemed to be paid for such taxable year under section 902(a) in accordance with §§ 1.902-1 and 1.902-2 or section 960(a)(1) in accordance with § 1.960-7. In no event shall the amount under subdivision (ii) of this subparagraph exceed the amount includible in gross income with respect to such taxes under section 78 and § 1.78-1. The credit for such taxes provided by section 901 shall not be allowed against the accumulated earnings tax imposed by section 531. See section 901(a).

* * *

[Reg. § 1.535-2.]

☐ [*T.D. 6377, 5-12-59. Amended by T.D. 6805, 3-8-65; T.D. 6841, 7-26-65; T.D. 7301, 1-3-74 and T.D. 7649, 10-17-79.*]

Estates, Trusts, and Beneficiaries

§ 1.679-1. U.S. transferor treated as owner of foreign trust.—(a) *In general.*—A U.S. transferor who transfers property to a foreign trust is treated as the owner of the portion of the trust attributable to the property transferred if there is a U.S. beneficiary of any portion of the trust, unless an exception in § 1.679-4 applies to the transfer.

(b) *Interaction with sections 673 through 678.*—The rules of this section apply without regard to whether the U.S. transferor retains any power or interest described in sections 673 through 677. If a U.S. transferor would be treated as the owner of a portion of a foreign trust pursuant to the rules of this section and another person would be treated as the owner of the same portion of the trust pursuant to section 678, then the U.S. transferor is treated as the owner and the other person is not treated as the owner.

(c) *Definitions.*—The following definitions apply for purposes of this section and §§ 1.679-2 through 1.679-7:

(1) *U.S. transferor.*—The term *U.S. transferor* means any U.S. person who makes a transfer (as defined in § 1.679-3) of property to a foreign trust.

(2) *U.S. person.*—The term *U.S. person* means a United States person as defined in section 7701(a)(30), a nonresident alien individual who elects under section 6013(g) to be treated as resident of the United States, and an individual who is a dual resident taxpayer within the meaning of § 301.7701(b)-7(a) of this chapter.

(3) *Foreign trust.*—Section 7701(a)(31)(B) defines the term *foreign trust*. See also § 301.7701-7 of this chapter.

(4) *Property.*—The term *property* means any property including cash.

(5) *Related person.*—A person is a *related person* if, without regard to the transfer at issue, the person is—

(i) A grantor of any portion of the trust (within the meaning of § 1.671-2(e)(1));

(ii) An owner of any portion of the trust under sections 671 through 679;

(iii) A beneficiary of the trust; or

(iv) A person who is related (within the meaning of section 643(i)(2)(B)) to any grantor, owner or beneficiary of the trust.

(6) *Obligation.*—The term *obligation* means any bond, note, debenture, certificate, bill receivable, account receivable, note receivable, open account, or other evidence of indebtedness, and, to the extent not previously described, any annuity contract.

(d) *Examples.*—The following examples illustrate the rules of paragraph (a) of this section. In these examples, *A* is a resident alien, *B* is *A*'s son, who is a resident alien, *C* is *A*'s father, who is a resident alien, *D* is *A*'s uncle, who is a nonresident alien, and *FT* is a foreign trust. The examples are as follows:

Example 1. Interaction with section 678. A creates and funds *FT*. *FT* may provide for the education of *B* by paying for books, tuition, room and board. In addition, *C* has the power to vest the trust corpus or income in himself within the meaning of section 678(a)(1). Under paragraph (b) of this section, *A* is treated as the owner of the portion of *FT* attributable to the property transferred to *FT* by *A* and *C* is not treated as the owner thereof.

Example 2. U.S. person treated as owner of a portion of FT. D creates and funds *FT* for the benefit of *B*. *D* retains a power described in section 676 and § 1.672(f)-3(a)(1). *A* transfers property to *FT*. Under sections 676 and 672(f), *D* is treated as the owner of the portion of *FT* attributable to the property transferred by *D*. Under paragraph (a) of this section, *A* is treated as the owner of the portion of *FT* attributable to the property transferred by *A*.
[Reg. § 1.679-1.]

☐ [*T.D. 8955, 7-19-2001.*]

§1.679-2. Trusts treated as having a U.S. beneficiary.—(a) *Existence of U.S. beneficiary.*—(1) *In general.*—The determination of whether a foreign trust has a U.S. beneficiary is made on an annual basis. A foreign trust is treated as having a U.S. beneficiary unless during the taxable year of the U.S. transferor—

(i) No part of the income or corpus of the trust may be paid or accumulated to or for the benefit of, directly or indirectly, a U.S. person; and

(ii) If the trust is terminated at any time during the taxable year, no part of the income or corpus of the trust could be paid to or for the benefit of, directly or indirectly, a U.S. person.

(2) *Benefit to a U.S. person.*—(i) *In general.*—For purposes of paragraph (a)(1) of this section, income or corpus may be paid or accumulated to or for the benefit of a U.S. person during a taxable year of the U.S. transferor if during that year, directly or indirectly, income may be distributed to, or accumulated for the benefit of, a U.S. person, or corpus may be distributed to, or held for the future benefit of, a U.S. person. This determination is made without regard to whether income or corpus is actually distributed to a U.S. person during that year, and without regard to whether a U.S. person's interest in the trust income or corpus is contingent on a future event.

(ii) *Certain unexpected beneficiaries.*—Notwithstanding paragraph (a)(2)(i) of this section, for purposes of paragraph (a)(1) of this section, a person who is not named as a beneficiary and is not a member of a class of beneficiaries as defined under the trust instrument is not taken into consideration if the U.S. transferor demonstrates to the satisfaction of the Commissioner that the person's contingent interest in the trust is so remote as to be negligible. The preceding sentence does not apply with respect to persons to whom distributions could be made pursuant to a grant of discretion to the trustee or any other person. A class of beneficiaries generally does not include heirs who will benefit from the trust under the laws of intestate succession in the event that the named beneficiaries (or members of the named class) have all deceased (whether or not stated as a named class in the trust instrument).

(iii) *Examples.*—The following examples illustrate the rules of paragraphs (a)(1) and (2) of this section. In these examples, *A* is a resident alien, *B* is *A*'s son, who is a resident alien, *C* is *A*'s daughter, who is a nonresident alien, and *FT* is a foreign trust. The examples are as follows:

Example 1. Distribution of income to U.S. person. A transfers property to *FT*. The trust instrument provides that all trust income is to be distributed currently to *B*. Under paragraph (a)(1) of this section, *FT* is treated as having a U.S. beneficiary.

Example 2. Income accumulation for the benefit of a U.S. person. In 2001, *A* transfers property to *FT*. The trust instrument provides that from 2001 through 2010, the trustee of *FT* may distribute trust income to *C* or may accumulate the trust income. The trust instrument further provides that in 2011, the trust will terminate and the trustee may distribute the trust assets to either or both of *B* and *C*, in the trustee's discretion. If the trust terminates unexpectedly prior to 2011, all trust assets must be distributed to *C*. Because it is possible that income may be accumulated in each year, and that the accumulated income ultimately may be distributed to *B*, a U.S. person, under paragraph (a)(1) of this section *FT* is treated as having a U.S. beneficiary during each of *A*'s tax years from 2001 through 2011. This result applies even though no U.S. person may receive distributions from the trust during the tax years 2001 through 2010.

Example 3. Corpus held for the benefit of a U.S. person. The facts are the same as in *Example 2*, except that from 2001 through 2011, all trust income must be distributed to *C*. In 2011, the trust will terminate and the trustee may distribute the trust corpus to either or both of *B* and *C*, in the trustee's discretion. If the trust terminates unexpectedly prior to 2011, all trust corpus must be distributed to *C*. Because during each of *A*'s tax years from 2001 through 2011 trust corpus is held for possible future distribution to *B*, a U.S. person, under paragraph (a)(1) of this section *FT* is treated as having a U.S. beneficiary during each of those years. This result applies even though no U.S. person may receive distributions from the trust during the tax years 2001 through 2010.

Example 4. Distribution upon U.S. transferor's death. A transfers property to *FT*. The trust instrument provides that all trust income must be distributed currently to *C* and, upon *A*'s death, the trust will terminate and the trustee may distribute the trust corpus to either or both of *B* and *C*. Because *B* may receive a distribution of corpus upon the termination of *FT*, and *FT* could terminate in any year, *FT* is treated as having a U.S. beneficiary in the year of the transfer and in subsequent years.

Example 5. Distribution after U.S. transferor's death. The facts are the same as in *Example 4*, except the trust instrument provides that the trust will not terminate until the year following *A*'s death. Upon termination, the trustee may distribute the trust assets to either or both of *B* and *C*, in the trustee's discretion. All trust assets are invested in the stock of *X*, a foreign corporation, and *X* makes no distributions to *FT*. Although no U.S. person may receive a distribution until the year after *A*'s death, and *FT* has no realized income during any year of its existence, during each year in which *A* is living corpus may be held for future distribution to *B*, a U.S. person. Thus, under paragraph (a)(1) of this section *FT* is treated as having a U.S. beneficiary during each of *A*'s tax years from 2001 through the year of *A*'s death.

Example 6. Constructive benefit to U.S. person. A transfers property to *FT*. The trust instrument provides that no income or corpus may be paid directly to a U.S. person. However, the trust instrument provides that trust corpus may be used to satisfy *B*'s legal obligations to a third party by making a payment directly to the third party. Under paragraphs (a)(1) and (2) of this section, *FT* is treated as having a U.S. beneficiary.

Example 7. U.S. person with negligible contingent interest. A transfers property to *FT*. The trust instrument provides that all income is to be distributed currently to *C*, and upon *C*'s death, all corpus is to be distributed to whomever of *C*'s three children is then living. All of *C*'s children are nonresident aliens. Under the laws of intestate succession that would apply to *FT*, if all of *C*'s children are deceased at the time of *C*'s death, the corpus would be distributed to *A*'s heirs. *A*'s living relatives at the time of the transfer consist solely of two brothers and two nieces, all of whom are nonresident aliens, and two first cousins, one of whom, *E*, is a U.S. citizen. Although it is possible under certain circumstances that *E* could receive a corpus distribution under the applicable laws of intestate succession, for each year the trust is in existence *A* is able to demonstrate to the satisfaction of the Commissioner under paragraph (a)(2)(ii) of this section that *E*'s contingent interest in *FT* is so remote as to be negligible. Provided that paragraph (a)(4) of this section does not require a different result, *FT* is not treated as having a U.S. beneficiary.

Example 8. U.S. person with non-negligible contingent interest. A transfers property to *FT*. The trust instrument provides that all income is to be distributed currently to *D*, *A*'s uncle, who is a nonresident alien, and upon *A*'s death, the corpus is to be distributed to D if he is then living. Under the laws of intestate succession that would apply to *FT*, *B* and *C* would share equally in the trust corpus if *D* is not living at the time of *A*'s death. *A* is unable to demonstrate to the satisfaction of the Commissioner that *B*'s contingent interest in the trust is so remote as to be negligible. Under paragraph (a)(2)(ii) of this section, *FT* is treated as having a U.S. beneficiary as of the year of the transfer.

Example 9. U.S. person as member of class of beneficiaries. A transfers property to *FT*. The trust instrument provides that all income is to be distributed currently to *D*, *A*'s uncle, who is a nonresident alien, and upon *A*'s death, the corpus is to be distributed to *D* if he is then living. If *D* is not then living, the corpus is to be distributed to *D*'s descendants. *D*'s grandson, *E*, is a resident alien. Under paragraph (a)(2)(ii) of this section, *FT* is treated as having a U.S. beneficiary as of the year of the transfer.

Example 10. Trustee's discretion in choosing beneficiaries. A transfers property to *FT*. The trust instrument provides that the trustee may distribute income and corpus to, or accumulate income for the benefit of, any person who is pursuing the academic study of ancient Greek, in the trustee's discretion. Because it is possible that a U.S. person will receive distributions of income or corpus, or will have income accumulated for his benefit, *FT* is treated as having a U.S. beneficiary. This result applies even if, during a tax year, no distributions or accumulations are actually made to or for the benefit of a U.S. person. *A* may not invoke paragraph (a)(2)(ii) of this section because a U.S. person could benefit pursuant to a grant of discretion in the trust instrument.

Example 11. Appointment of remainder beneficiary. A transfers property to *FT*. The trust instrument provides that the trustee may distribute current income to *C*, or may accumulate income, and, upon termination of the trust, trust assets are to be distributed to *C*. However, the trust instrument further provides that *D*, *A*'s uncle, may appoint a different remainder beneficiary. Because it is possible that a U.S. person could be named as the remainder beneficiary, and because corpus could be held in each year for the future benefit of that U.S. person, *FT* is treated as having a U.S. beneficiary for each year.

Example 12. Trust not treated as having a U.S. beneficiary. A transfers property to *FT*. The trust instrument provides that the trustee may distribute income and corpus to, or accumulate income for the benefit of C. Upon termination of the trust, all income and corpus must be distributed to C. Assume that paragraph (a)(4) of this section is not applicable under the facts and circumstances and that A establishes to the satisfaction of the Commissioner under paragraph (a)(2)(ii) of this section that no U.S. persons are reasonably expected to benefit from the trust. Because no part of the income or corpus of the trust may be paid or accumulated to or for the benefit of, either directly or indirectly, a U.S. person, and if the trust is terminated no part of the income or corpus of the trust could be paid to or for the benefit of, either directly or indirectly, a U.S. person, *FT* is not treated as having a U.S. beneficiary.

Example 13. U.S. beneficiary becomes non-U.S. person. In 2001, *A* transfers property to *FT*. The trust instrument provides that, as long as *B* remains a U.S. resident, no distributions of income or corpus may be made from the trust to *B*. The trust instrument further provides that if *B* becomes a nonresident alien, distributions of income (including previously accumulated income) and corpus may be made to him. If *B* remains a U.S. resident at the time of *FT's* termination, all accumulated income and corpus is to be distributed to *C*. In 2007, *B* becomes a nonresident alien and remains so thereafter. Because income may be accumulated during the years 2001 through 2007 for the benefit of a person who is a U.S. person during those years, *FT* is treated as having a U.S. beneficiary under paragraph (a)(1) of this section during each of those years. This result applies even though *B* cannot receive distributions from *FT* during the years he is a resident alien and even though *B* might remain a resident alien who is not entitled to any distribution from *FT*. Provided that paragraph (a)(4) of this section does not require a different result and that *A* establishes to the satisfaction of the Commissioner under paragraph (a)(2)(ii) of this section that no other U.S. persons are reasonably expected to benefit from the trust, *FT* is not treated as having a U.S. beneficiary under paragraph (a)(1) of this section during tax years after 2007.

(3) *Changes in beneficiary's status.*—(i) *In general.*—For purposes of paragraph (a)(1) of this section, the possibility that a person that is not a U.S. person could become a U.S. person will not cause that person to be treated as a U.S. person for purposes of paragraph (a)(1) of this section until the tax year of the U.S. transferor in which that individual actually. becomes a U.S. person. However, if a person who is not a U.S. person becomes a U.S. person for the first time more than 5 years after the date of a transfer to the foreign trust by a U.S. transferor, that person is not treated as a U.S. person for purposes of applying paragraph (a)(1) of this section with respect to that transfer.

(ii) *Examples.*—The following examples illustrate the rules of paragraph (a)(3) of this section. In these examples, *A* is a resident alien, *B* is *A's* son, who is a resident alien, *C* is *A's* daughter, who is a nonresident alien, and *FT* is a foreign trust. The examples are as follows:

Example 1. Non-U.S. beneficiary becomes U.S. person. In 2001, *A* transfers property to *FT*. The trust instrument provides that all income is to be distributed currently to *C* and that, upon the termination of *FT*, all corpus is to be distributed to *C*. Assume that paragraph (a)(4) of this section is not applicable under the facts and circumstances and that *A* establishes to the satisfaction of the Commissioner under paragraph (a)(2)(ii) of this section that no U.S. persons are reasonably expected to benefit from the trust. Under paragraph (a)(3)(i) of this section, *FT* is not treated as having a U.S. beneficiary during the tax years of *A* in which *C* remains a nonresident alien. If *C* first becomes a resident alien in 2004, *FT* is treated as having a U.S. beneficiary commencing in that year under paragraph (a)(3) of this section. See paragraph (c) of this section regarding the treatment of *A* upon *FT's* acquisition of a U.S. beneficiary.

Example 2. Non-U.S. beneficiary becomes U.S. person more than 5 years after transfer. The facts are the same as in *Example 1*, except *C* first becomes a resident alien in 2007. *FT* is treated as not having a U.S. beneficiary under paragraph (a)(3)(i) of this section with respect to the property transfer by *A*. However, if *C* had previously been a U.S. person during any prior period, the 5-year exception in paragraph (a)(3)(i) of this section would not apply in 2007 because it would not have been the first time *C* became a U.S. person.

(4) *General rules.*—(i) *Records and documents.*—Even if, based on the terms of the trust instrument, a foreign trust is not treated as having a U.S. beneficiary within the meaning of paragraph (a)(1) of this section, the trust may nevertheless be treated as having a U.S. beneficiary pursuant to paragraph (a)(1) of this section based on the following—

(A) All written and oral agreements and understandings relating to the trust;

(B) Memoranda or letters of wishes;

(C) All records that relate to the actual distribution of income and corpus; and

(D) All other documents that relate to the trust, whether or not of any purported legal effect.

(ii) *Additional factors.*—For purposes of determining whether a foreign trust is treated as having a U.S. beneficiary within the meaning of paragraph (a)(1) of this section, the following additional factors are taken into account—

(A) If the terms of the trust instrument allow the trust to be amended to benefit a U.S. person, all potential benefits that could be provided to a U.S. person pursuant to an amendment must be taken into account;

(B) If the terms of the trust instrument do not allow the trust to be amended to benefit a U.S. person, but the law applicable to a foreign trust may require payments or accumulations of income or corpus to or for the benefit of a U.S. person (by judicial reformation or otherwise), all potential benefits that could be provided to a U.S. person pursuant to the law must be taken into account, unless the U.S. transferor demonstrates to the satisfaction of the Commissioner that the law is not reasonably expected to be applied or invoked under the facts and circumstances; and

(C) If the parties to the trust ignore the terms of the trust instrument, or if it is reasonably expected that they will do so, all benefits that have been, or are reasonably expected to be, provided to a U.S. person must be taken into account.

(iii) *Examples.*—The following examples illustrate the rules of paragraph (a)(4) of this section. In these examples, *A* is a resident alien, *B* is *A's* son, who is a resident alien, *C* is *A's* daughter, who is a nonresident alien, and *FT* is a foreign trust. The examples are as follows:

Example 1. Amendment pursuant to local law. *A* creates and funds *FT* for the benefit of *C*. The terms of *FT* (which, according to the trust instrument, cannot be amended) provide that no part of the income or corpus of *FT* may be paid or accumulated during the taxable year to or for the benefit of any U.S. person, either during the existence of *FT* or at the time of its termination. However, pursuant to the applicable foreign law, *FT* can be amended to provide for additional beneficiaries, and there is an oral understanding between *A* and the trustee that *B* can be added as a beneficiary. Under paragraphs (a)(1) and (a)(4)(ii)(B) of this section, *FT* is treated as having a U.S. beneficiary.

Example 2. Actions in violation of the terms of the trust. *A* transfers property to *FT*. The trust instrument provides that no U.S. person can receive income or corpus from *FT* during the term of the trust or at the termination of *FT*. Notwithstanding the terms of the trust instrument, a letter of wishes directs the trustee of *FT* to provide for the educational needs of *B*, who is about to begin college. The letter of wishes contains a disclaimer to the effect that its contents are only suggestions and recommendations and that the trustee is at all times bound by the terms of the trust as set forth in the trust instrument. Under paragraphs (a)(1) and (a)(4)(ii)(C) of this section, *FT* is treated as having a U.S. beneficiary.

(b) *Indirect U.S. beneficiaries.*—(1) *Certain foreign entities.*—For purposes of paragraph (a)(1) of this section, an amount is treated as paid or accumulated to or for the benefit of a U.S. person if the amount is paid to or accumulated for the benefit of—

(i) A controlled foreign corporation, as defined in section 957(a);

(ii) A foreign partnership, if a U.S. person is a partner of such partnership; or

(iii) A foreign trust or estate, if such trust or estate has a U.S. beneficiary (within the meaning of paragraph (a)(1) of this section).

(2) *Other indirect beneficiaries.*—For purposes of paragraph (a)(1) of this section, an amount is treated as paid or accumulated to or for the benefit of a U.S. person if the amount is paid to or accumulated for the benefit of a U.S. person through an intermediary, such as an agent or nominee, or by any other means where a U.S. person may obtain an actual or constructive benefit.

(3) *Examples.*—The following examples illustrate the rules of this paragraph (b). Unless otherwise noted, *A* is a resident alien. *B* is *A's* son and is a resident alien. *FT* is a foreign trust. The examples are as follows:

Example 1. Trust benefitting foreign corporation. A transfers property to *FT*. The beneficiary of *FT* is *FC*, a foreign corporation. *FC* has outstanding solely 100 shares of common stock. *B* owns 49 shares of the *FC* stock and *FC2*, also a foreign corporation, owns the remaining 51 shares. *FC2* has outstanding solely 100 shares of common stock. *B* owns 49 shares of *FC2* and nonresident alien individuals own the remaining 51 *FC2* shares. *FC* is a controlled foreign corporation (as defined in section 957(a), after the application of section 958(a)(2)). Under paragraphs (a)(1) and (b)(1)(i) of this section, *FT* is treated as having a U.S. beneficiary.

Example 2. Trust benefitting another trust. A transfers property to *FT*. The terms of *FT* permit current distributions of income to *B*. *A* transfers property to another foreign trust, *FT2*. The terms of *FT2* provide that no U.S. person can benefit either as to income or corpus, but permit current distributions of income to *FT*. Under paragraph (a)(1) of this section, *FT* is treated as having a U.S. beneficiary and, under paragraphs (a)(1) and (b)(1)(iii) of this section, *FT2* is treated as having a U.S. beneficiary.

Example 3. Trust benefitting another trust after transferor's death. A transfers property to *FT*. The terms of *FT* require that all income from *FT* be accumulate during *A*'s lifetime. In the year following *A*'s death, a share of *FT* is to be distributed to *FT2*, another foreign trust, for the benefit of *B*. Under paragraphs (a)(1) and (b)(1)(iii) of this section, *FT* is treated as having a U.S. beneficiary beginning with the year of *A*'s transfer of property to *FT*.

Example 4. Indirect benefit through use of debit card. A transfers property to *FT*. The trust instrument provides that no U.S. person can benefit either as to income or corpus. However, *FT* maintains an account with *FB*, a foreign bank, and *FB* issues a debit card to *B* against the account maintained by *FT* and *B* is allowed to make withdrawals. Under paragraphs (a)(1) and (b)(2) of this section, *FT* is treated as having a U.S. beneficiary.

Example 5. Other indirect benefit. A transfers property to *FT*. *FT* is administered by *FTC*, a foreign trust company. *FTC* forms *IBC*, an international business corporation formed under the laws of a foreign jurisdiction. *IBC* is the beneficiary of *FT*. *IBC* maintains an account with *FB*, a foreign bank. *FB* issues a debit card to *B* against the account maintained by *IBC* and *B* is allowed to make withdrawals. Under paragraphs (a)(1) and (b)(2) of this section, *FT* is treated as having a U.S. beneficiary.

(c) *Treatment of U.S. transferor upon foreign trust's acquisition or loss of U.S. beneficiary.*—(1) *Trusts acquiring a U.S. beneficiary.*—If a foreign trust to which a U.S. transferor has transferred property is not treated as having a U.S. beneficiary (within the meaning of paragraph (a) of this section) for any taxable year of the U.S. transferor, but the trust is treated as having a U.S. beneficiary (within the meaning of paragraph (a) of this section) in any subsequent taxable year, the U.S. transferor is treated as having additional income in the first such taxable year of the U.S. transferor in which the trust is treated as having a U.S. beneficiary. The amount of the additional income is equal to the trust's undistributed net income, as defined in section 665(a), at the end of the U.S. transferor's immediately preceding taxable year and is subject to the rules of section 668, providing for an interest charge on accumulation distributions from foreign trusts.

(2) *Trusts ceasing to have a U.S. beneficiary.*—If, for any taxable year of a U.S. transferor, a foreign trust that has received a transfer of property from the U.S. transferor ceases to be treated as having a U.S. beneficiary, the U.S. transferor ceases to be treated as the owner of the portion of the trust attributable to the transfer beginning in the first taxable year following the last taxable year of the U.S. transferor during which the trust was treated as having a U.S. beneficiary (unless the U.S. transferor is treated as an owner thereof pursuant to sections 673 through 677). The U.S. transferor is treated as making a transfer of property to the foreign trust on the first day of the first taxable year following the last taxable year of the U.S. transferor during which the trust was treated as having a U.S. beneficiary. The amount of the property deemed to be transferred to the trust is the portion of the trust attributable to the prior transfer to which paragraph (a)(1) of this section applied. For rules regarding the recognition of gain on transfers to foreign trusts, see section 684.

(3) *Examples.*—The rules of this paragraph (c) are illustrated by the following examples. *A* is a resident alien, *B* is *A*'s son, and *FT* is a foreign trust. The examples are as follows:

Example 1. Trust acquiring U.S. beneficiary. (i) In 2001, *A* transfers stock with a fair market value of $100,000 to *FT*. The stock has an adjusted basis of $50,000 at the time of the transfer. The trust instrument provides that income may be paid currently to, or accumulated for the benefit of, *B* and that, upon the termination of the trust, all income and corpus is to be distributed to *B*. At the time of the transfer, *B* is a nonresident alien. *A* is not treated as the owner of any portion of *FT* under sections 673 through 677. *FT* accumulates a total of $30,000 of income during the taxable years 2001 through 2003. In 2004, *B* moves to the United States and becomes a resident alien. Assume paragraph (a)(4) of this section is not applicable under the facts and circumstances.

(ii) Under paragraph (c) (1) of this section, *A* is treated as receiving an accumulation distribution in the amount of $30,000 in 2004 and immediately transferring that amount back to the trust. The accumulation distribution is subject to the rules of section 668, providing for an interest charge on accumulation distributions.

(iii) Under paragraphs (a)(1) and (3) of this section, beginning in 2005, *A* is treated as the owner of the portion of *FT* attributable to the stock transferred by *A* to *FT* in 2001 (which includes the portion attributable to the accumulated income deemed to be retransferred in 2004).

Example 2. Trust ceasing to have U.S. beneficiary. (i) The facts are the same as in *Example 1*. In 2008, *B* becomes a nonresident alien. On the date *B* becomes a nonresident alien, the stock transferred by *A* to *FT* in 2001 has a fair market value of $125,000 and an adjusted basis of $50,000.

(ii) Under paragraph (c)(2) of this section, beginning in 2009, *FT* is not treated as having a U.S. beneficiary, and *A* is not treated as the owner of the portion of the trust attributable to the prior transfer of stock. For rules regarding the recognition of gain on the termination of ownership status, see section 684.

[Reg. § 1.679-2.]

☐ [*T.D. 8955, 7-19-2001.*]

§ 1.679-3. Transfers.—(a) *In general.*—A transfer means a direct, indirect, or constructive transfer.

(b) *Transfers by certain trusts.*—(1) *In general.*—If any portion of a trust is treated as owned by a U.S. person, a transfer of property from that portion of the trust to a foreign trust is treated as a transfer from the owner of that portion to the foreign trust.

(2) *Example.*—The following example illustrates this paragraph (b):

Example. In 2001, *A*, a U.S. citizen, creates and funds *DT*, a domestic trust. *A* has the power to revest absolutely in himself the title to the property in *DT* and is treated as the owner of *DT* pursuant to section 676. In 2004, *DT* transfers property to *FT*, a foreign trust. *A* is treated as having transferred the property to *FT* in 2004 for purposes of this section.

(c) *Indirect transfers.*—(1) *Principal purpose of tax avoidance.*—A transfer to a foreign trust by any person (intermediary) to whom a U.S. person transfers property is treated as an indirect transfer by a U.S. person to the foreign trust if such transfer is made pursuant to a plan one of the principal purposes of which is the avoidance of United States tax.

(2) *Principal purpose of tax avoidance deemed to exist.*—For purposes of paragraph (c)(1) of this section, a transfer is deemed to have been made pursuant to a plan one of the principal purposes of which was the avoidance of United States tax if—

(i) The U.S. person is related (within the meaning of paragraph (c)(4) of this section) to a beneficiary of the foreign trust, or has another relationship with a beneficiary of the foreign trust that establishes a reasonable basis for concluding that the U.S. transferor would make a transfer to the foreign trust; and

(ii) The U.S. person cannot demonstrate to the satisfaction of the Commissioner that—

(A) The intermediary has a relationship with a beneficiary of the foreign trust that establishes a reasonable basis for concluding that the intermediary would make a transfer to the foreign trust;

(B) The intermediary acted independently of the U.S. person;

(C) The intermediary is not an agent of the U.S. person under generally applicable United States agency principles; and

(D) The intermediary timely complied with the reporting requirements of section 6048, if applicable.

(3) *Effect of disregarding intermediary .*—(i) *In general.*—Except as provided in paragraph (c)(3)(ii) of this section, if a transfer is treated as an indirect transfer pursuant to paragraph (c)(1) of this section, then the intermediary is treated as an agent of the U.S. person, and the property is treated as transferred to the foreign trust by the U.S.

person in the year the property is transferred, or made available, by the intermediary to the foreign trust. The fair market value of the property transferred is determined as of the date of the transfer by the intermediary to the foreign trust.

(ii) *Special rule.*—If the Commissioner determines, or if the taxpayer can demonstrate to the satisfaction of the Commissioner, that the intermediary is an agent of the foreign trust under generally applicable United states agency principles, the property will be treated as transferred to the foreign trust in the year the U.S. person transfers the property to the intermediary. The fair market value of the property transferred will be determined as of the date of the transfer by the U.S. person to the intermediary.

(iii) *Effect on intermediary.*—If a transfer of property is treated as an indirect transfer under paragraph (c)(1) of this section, the intermediary is not treated as having transferred the property to the foreign trust.

(4) *Related parties.*—For purposes of this paragraph (c), a U.S. transferor is treated as related to a U.S. beneficiary of a foreign trust if the U.S. transferor and the beneficiary are related for purposes of section 643(i)(2)(B), with the following modifications—

(i) For purposes of applying section 267 (other than section 267(f)) and section 707(b)(1), "at least 10 percent" is used instead of "more than 50 percent" each place it appears; and

(ii) The principles of section 267(b)(10), using "at least 10 percent" instead of "more than 50 percent," apply to determine whether two corporations are related.

(5) *Examples.*—The rules of this paragraph (c) are illustrated by the following examples:

Example 1. Principal purpose of tax avoidance. A, a U.S. citizen, creates and funds *FT*, a foreign trust, for the benefit of *A*'s children, who are U.S. citizens. In 2004, *A* decides to transfer an additional 1000X to the foreign trust. Pursuant to a plan with a principal purpose of avoiding the application of section 679, A transfers 1000X to *I*, a foreign person. *I* subsequently transfers 1000X to *FT*. Under paragraph (c)(1) of this section, *A* is treated as having made a transfer of 1000X to *FT*.

Example 2. U.S. person unable to demonstrate that intermediary acted independently. A, a U.S. citizen, creates and funds *FT*, a foreign trust, for the benefit of *A*'s children, who are U.S. citizens. On July 1, 2004, *A* transfers XYZ stock to *D*, *A*'s uncle, who is a nonresident alien. *D* immediately sells the XYZ stock and uses the proceeds to purchase ABC stock. On January 1, 2007, *D* transfers the ABC stock to *FT*. *A* is unable to demonstrate to the satisfaction of the Commissioner, pursuant to paragraph (c)(2) of this section, that D acted independently of *A* in making the transfer to *FT*. Under paragraph (c)(1) of this section, *A* is treated as having transferred the ABC stock to *FT*. Under paragraph (c)(3) of this section, *D* is treated as an agent of *A*, and the transfer is deemed to have been made on January 1, 2007.

Example 3. Indirect loan to foreign trust. A, a U.S. citizen, previously created and funded *FT*, a foreign trust, for the benefit of *A*'s children, who are U.S. citizens. On July 1, 2004, *A* deposits 500X with *FB*, a foreign bank. On January 1, 2005, *FB* loans 450X to *FT*. *A* is unable to demonstrate to the satisfaction of the Commissioner, pursuant to paragraph (c)(2) of this section, that *FB* has a relationship with *FT* that establishes a reasonable basis for concluding that *FB* would make a loan to *FT* or that *FB* acted independently of *A* in making the loan. Under paragraph (c)(1) of this section, *A* is deemed to have transferred 450X directly to *FT* on January 1, 2005. Under paragraph (c)(3) of this section, *FB* is treated as an agent of *A*. For possible exceptions with respect to qualified obligations of the trust, and the treatment of principal repayments with respect to obligations of the trust that are not qualified obligations, see § 1.679-4.

Example 4. Loan to foreign trust prior to deposit of funds in foreign bank. The facts are the same as in *Example 3*, except that *A* makes the 500X deposit with *FB* on January 2, 2005, the day after *FB* makes the loan to *FT*. The result is the same as in *Example 3*.

(d) *Constructive transfers.*—(1) *In general.*—For purposes of paragraph (a) of this section, a constructive transfer includes any assumption or satisfaction of a foreign trust's obligation to a third party.

(2) *Examples.*—The rules of this paragraph (d) are illustrated by the following examples. In each example, *A* is a U.S. citizen and *FT* is a foreign trust. The examples are as follows:

Example 1. Payment of debt of foreign trust. FT owes 1000X to *Y*, an unrelated foreign corporation, for the performance of services by *Y* for *FT*. In satisfaction of FT's liability to *Y*, *A* transfers to *Y* property with a fair market value of 1000X. Under paragraph (d) (1) of this section, *A* is treated as having made a constructive transfer of the property to *FT*.

Example 2. Assumption of liability of foreign trust. FT owes 1000X to *Y*, an unrelated foreign corporation, for the performance of services by *Y* for *FT*. *A* assumes *FT*'s liability to pay *Y*. Under paragraph (d) (1) of this section, *A* is treated as having made a constructive transfer of property with a fair market value of 1000X to *FT*.

(e) *Guarantee of trust obligations.*—(1) *In general.*—If a foreign trust borrows money or other property from any person who is not a related person (within the meaning of § 1.679-1(c)(5)) with respect to the trust (lender) and a U.S. person (U.S. guarantor) that is a related person with respect to the trust guarantees (within the meaning of paragraph (e)(4) of this section) the foreign trust's obligation, the U.S. guarantor is treated for purposes of this section as a U.S. transferor that has made a transfer to the trust on the date of the guarantee in an amount determined under paragraph (e)(2) of this section. To the extent this paragraph causes the U.S. guarantor to be treated as having made a transfer to the trust, a lender that is a U.S. person shall not be treated as having transferred that amount to the foreign trust.

(2) *Amount transferred.*—The amount deemed transferred by a U.S. guarantor described in paragraph (e)(1) of this section is the guaranteed portion of the adjusted issue price of the obligation (within the meaning of § 1.1275-1(b)) plus any accrued but unpaid qualified stated interest (within the meaning of § 1.1273-1(c)).

(3) *Principal repayments.*—If a U.S. person is treated under this paragraph (e) having made a transfer by reason of the guarantee of an obligation, payments of principal to the lender by the foreign trust with respect to the obligation are taken into account on and after the date of the payment in determining the portion of the trust attributable to the property deemed transferred by the U.S. guarantor.

(4) *Guarantee.*—For purposes of this section, the term guarantee—

(i) Includes any arrangement under which a person, directly or indirectly, assures, on a conditional or unconditional basis, the payment of another's obligation;

(ii) Encompasses any form of credit support, and includes a commitment to make a capital contribution to the debtor or otherwise maintain its financial viability; and

(iii) Includes an arrangement reflected in a comfort letter, regardless of whether the arrangement gives rise to a legally enforceable obligation. If an arrangement is contingent upon the occurrence of an event, in determining whether the arrangement is a guarantee, it is assumed that the event has occurred.

(5) *Examples.*—The rules of this paragraph (e) are illustrated by the following examples. In all of the examples, *A* is a U.S. resident and *FT* is a foreign trust. The examples are as follows:

Example 1. Foreign lender. X, a foreign corporation, loans 1000X of cash to *FT* in exchange for *FT*'s obligation to repay the loan. *A* guarantees the repayment of 600X of *FT*'s obligation. Under paragraph (e)(2) of this section, *A* is treated as having transferred 600X to *FT*.

Example 2. Unrelated U.S. lender. The facts are the same as in *Example 1*, except *X* is a U.S. person that is not a related person within the meaning of § 1.679-1(c)(5). The result is the same as in *Example 1*.

(f) *Transfers to entities owned by a foreign trust.*—(1) *General rule.*—If a U.S. person is a related person (as defined in § 1.679-1(c)(5)) with respect to a foreign trust, any transfer of property by the U.S. person to an entity in which the foreign trust holds an ownership interest is treated as a transfer of such property by the U.S. person to the foreign trust followed by a transfer of the property from the foreign trust to the entity owned by the foreign trust, unless the U.S. person demonstrates to the satisfaction of the Commissioner that the transfer to the entity is properly attributable to the U.S. person's ownership interest in the entity.

(2) *Examples.*—The rules of this paragraph (f) are illustrated by the following examples. In all of the examples, *A* is a U.S. citizen, *FT* is a foreign trust, and *FC* is a foreign corporation. The examples are as follows:

Example 1. Transfer treated as transfer to trust. A creates and funds *FT*, which is treated as having a U.S. beneficiary under § 1.679-2. *FT* owns all of the outstanding stock of *FC*. *A* transfers property directly to FC. Because FT is the sole shareholder of FC, A is unable to demonstrate to the satisfaction of the Commissioner that the transfer is properly attributable to A's ownership interest in FC. Accordingly, under this paragraph (f), A is treated as having transferred the property to FT, followed by a transfer of such property by FT to FC. Under § 1.679-1(a), A is treated as the owner of the portion of FT attributable to the property treated as transferred directly to FT. Under § 1.367(a)-1T(c)(4)(ii), the transfer of property by FT to FC is treated as a transfer of the property by A to FC.

Example 2. Transfer treated as transfer to trust. The facts are the same as in *Example 1*, except that FT is not treated as having a U.S. beneficiary under § 1.679-2. Under this paragraph (f), A is treated as having transferred the property to FT, followed by a transfer of such property by FT to FC. A is not treated as the owner of FT for purposes of § 1.679-1(a). For rules regarding the recognition of gain on the transfer, see section 684.

Example 3. Transfer not treated as transfer to trust. A creates and funds FT. FC has outstanding solely 100 shares of common stock. FT owns 50 shares of FC stock, and A owns the remaining 50 shares. On July 1, 2001, FT and A each transfer 1000X to FC. A is able to demonstrate to the satisfaction of the Commissioner that A's transfer to FC is properly attributable to A's ownership interest in FC. Accordingly, under this paragraph (f), A's transfer to FC is not treated as a transfer to FT.

[Reg. § 1.679-3.]

□ *[T.D. 8955, 7-19-2001.]*

§ 1.679-4. Exceptions to general rule.—(a) *In general.*—Section 1.679-1 does not apply to—

(1) Any transfer of property to a foreign trust by reason of the death of the transferor;

(2) Any transfer of property to a foreign trust described in sections 402(b), 404(a)(4), or 404A;

(3) Any transfer of property to a foreign trust described in section 501(c)(3) (without regard to the requirements of section 508(a)); and

(4) Any transfer of property to a foreign trust to the extent the transfer is for fair market value.

(b) *Transfers for fair market value.*—(1) *In general.*—For purposes of this section, a transfer is for fair market value only to the extent of the value of property received from the trust, services rendered by the trust, or the right to use property of the trust. For example, rents, royalties, interest, and compensation paid to a trust are transfers for fair market value only to the extent that the payments reflect an arm's length price for the use of the property of, or for the services rendered by, the trust. For purposes of this determination, an interest in the trust is not property received from the trust. For purposes of this section, a distribution to a trust with respect to an interest held by such trust in an entity other than a trust or an interest in certain investment trusts described in § 301.7701-4(c) of this chapter, liquidating trusts described in § 301.7701-4(d) of this chapter, or environmental remediation trusts described in § 301.7701-4(e) of this chapter is considered to be a transfer for fair market value.

(2) *Special rule.*—(i) *Transfers for partial consideration.*—For purposes of this section, if a person transfers property to a foreign trust in exchange for property having a fair market value that is less than the fair market value of the property transferred, the exception in paragraph (a)(4) of this section applies only to the extent of the fair market value of the property received.

(ii) *Example.*—This paragraph (b) is illustrated by the following example:

Example. A, a U.S. citizen, transfers property that has a fair market value of 1000X to FT, a foreign trust, in exchange for 600X of cash. Under this paragraph (b), § 1.679-1 applies with respect to the transfer of 400X (1000X less 600X) to FT.

(c) *Certain obligations not taken into account.*—Solely for purposes of this section, in determining whether a transfer by a U.S. transferor that is a related person (as defined in § 1.679-1(c)(5)) with respect to the foreign trust is for fair market value, any obligation (as defined in § 1.679-1(c)(6)) of the trust or a related person (as defined in § 1.679-1(c)(5)) that is not a qualified obligation within the meaning of paragraph (d)(1) of this section shall not be taken into account.

(d) *Qualified obligations.*—(1) *In general.*—For purposes of this section, an obligation is treated as a qualified obligation only if—

(i) The obligation is reduced to writing by an express written agreement;

(ii) The term of the obligation does not exceed five years (for purposes of determining the term of an obligation, the obligation's maturity date is the last possible date that the obligation can be outstanding under the terms of the obligation);

(iii) All payments on the obligation are denominated in U.S. dollars;

(iv) The yield to maturity is not less than 100 percent of the applicable Federal rate and not greater that 130 percent of the applicable Federal rate (the applicable Federal rate for an obligation is the applicable Federal rate in effect under section 1274(d) for the day on which the obligation is issued, as published in the Internal Revenue Bulletin (see § 601.601(d)(2) of this chapter));

(v) The U.S. transferor extends the period for assessment of any income or transfer tax attributable to the transfer and any consequential income tax changes for each year that the obligation is outstanding, to a date not earlier than three years after the maturity date of the obligation (this extension is not necessary if the maturity date of the obligation does not extend beyond the end of the U.S. transferor's taxable year for the year of the transfer and is paid within such period); when properly executed and filed, such an agreement is deemed to be consented to for purposes of § 301.6501(c)-1(d) of this chapter; and

(vi) The U.S. transferor reports the status of the loan, including principal and interest payments, on Form 3520 for every year that the loan is outstanding.

(2) *Additional loans.*—If, while the original obligation is outstanding, the U.S. transferor or a person related to the trust (within the meaning of § 1.679-1(c)(5)) directly or indirectly obtains another obligation issued by the trust, or if the U.S. transferor directly or indirectly obtains another obligation issued by a person related to the trust, the original obligation is deemed to have the maturity date of any such subsequent obligation in determining whether the term of the original obligation exceeds the specified 5-year term. In addition, a series of obligations issued and repaid by the trust (or a person related to the trust) is treated as a single obligation if the transactions giving rise to the obligations are structured with a principal purpose to avoid the application of this provision.

(3) *Obligations that cease to be qualified.*—If an obligation treated as a qualified obligation subsequently fails to be a qualified obligation (e.g., renegotiation of the terms of the obligation causes the term of the obligation to exceed five years), the U.S. transferor is treated as making a transfer to the trust in an amount equal to the original obligation's adjusted issue price (within the meaning of § 1.1275-1(b)) plus any accrued but unpaid qualified stated interest (within the meaning of § 1.1273-1(c)) as of the date of the subsequent event that causes the obligation to no longer be a qualified obligation. If the maturity date is extended beyond five years by reason of the issuance of a subsequent obligation by the trust (or person related to the trust), the amount of the transfer will not exceed the issue price of the subsequent obligation. The subsequent obligation is separately tested to determine if it is a qualified obligation.

(4) *Transfers resulting from failed qualified obligations.*—In general, a transfer resulting from a failed qualified obligation is deemed to occur on the date of the subsequent event that causes the obligation to no longer be a qualified obligation. However, based on all of the facts and circumstances, the Commissioner may deem a transfer to have occurred on any date on or after the issue date of the original obligation. For example, if at the time the original obligation was issued, the transferor knew or had reason to know that the obligation would not be repaid, the Commissioner could deem the transfer to have occurred on the issue date of the original obligation.

(5) *Renegotiated loans.*—Any loan that is renegotiated, extended, or revised is treated as a new loan, and any transfer of funds to a foreign trust after such renegotiation, extension, or revision under a pre-existing loan agreement is treated as a transfer subject to this section.

(6) *Principal repayments.*—The payment of principal with respect to any obligation that is not treated as a qualified obligation under this paragraph is taken into account on and after the date of the payment in determining the portion of the trust attributable to the property transferred.

(7) *Examples.*—The rules of this paragraph (d) are illustrated by the following examples. In the examples, *A* and *B* are U.S. residents and *FT* is a foreign trust. The examples are as follows:

Example 1. Demand loan. A transfers 500X to *FT* in exchange for a demand note that permits *A* to require repayment by *FT* at any time. *A* is a related person (as defined in § 1.679-1(c)(5)) with respect to *FT*. Because *FT*'s obligation to *A* could remain outstanding for more than five years, the obligation is not a qualified obligation within the meaning of paragraph (d) of this section and, pursuant to paragraph (c) of this section, it is not taken into account for purposes of determining whether *A*'s transfer is eligible for the fair market value exception of paragraph (a)(4) of this section. Accordingly, § 1.679-1 applies with respect to the full 500X transfer to *FT*.

Example 2. Private annuity. A transfers 4000X to *FT* in exchange for an annuity from the foreign trust that will pay *A* 100X per year for the rest of *A*'s life. *A* is a related person (as defined in § 1.679-1(c)(5)) with respect to *FT*. Because *FT*'s obligation to *A* could remain outstanding for more than five years, the obligation is not a qualified obligation within the meaning of paragraph (d)(1) of this section and, pursuant to paragraph (c) of this section, it is not taken into account for purposes of determining whether *A*'s transfer is eligible for the fair market value exception of paragraph (a)(4) of this section. Accordingly, § 1.679-1 applies with respect to the full 4000X transfer to *FT*.

Example 3. Loan to unrelated foreign trust. B transfers 1000X to *FT* in exchange for an obligation of the trust. The term of the obligation is fifteen years. *B* is not a related person (as defined in § 1.679-1(c)(5)) with respect to *FT*. Because *B* is not a related person, the fair market value of the obligation received by *B* is taken into account for purposes of determining whether *B*'s transfer is eligible for the fair market value exception of paragraph (a)(4) of this section, even though the obligation is not a qualified obligation within the meaning of paragraph (d)(1) of this section.

Example 4. Transfer for an obligation with term in excess of 5 years. A transfers property that has a fair market value of 5000X to *FT* in exchange for an obligation of the trust. The term of the obligation is ten years. *A* is a related person (as defined in § 1.679-1(c)(5)) with respect to *FT*. Because the term of the obligation is greater than five years, the obligation is not a qualified obligation within the meaning of paragraph (d)(1) of this section and, pursuant to paragraph (c) of this section, it is not taken into account for purposes of determining whether *A*'s transfer is eligible for the fair market value exception of paragraph (a)(4) of this section. Accordingly, § 1.679-1 applies with respect to the full 5000X transfer to *FT*.

Example 5. Transfer for a qualified obligation. The facts are the same as in *Example 4*, except that the term of the obligation is 3 years. Assuming the other requirements of paragraph (d)(1) of this section are satisfied, the obligation is a qualified obligation and its adjusted issue price is taken into account for purposes of determining whether *A*'s transfer is eligible for the fair market value exception of paragraph (a)(4) of this section.

Example 6. Effect of subsequent obligation on original obligation. A transfers property that has a fair market value of 1000X to *FT* in exchange for an obligation that satisfies the requirements of paragraph (d)(1) of this section. *A* is a related person (as defined in § 1.679-1(c)(5)) with respect to *FT*. Two years later, *A* transfers an additional 2000X to *FT* and receives another obligation from *FT* that has a maturity date four years from the date that the second obligation was issued. Under paragraph (d)(2) of this section, the original obligation is deemed to have the maturity date of the second obligation. Under paragraph (a) of this section, *A* is treated as having made a transfer in an amount equal to the original obligation's adjusted issue price (within the meaning of § 1.1275-1(b)) plus any accrued but unpaid qualified stated interest (within the meaning of § 1.1273-1(c)) as of the date of issuance of the second obligation. The second obligation is tested separately to determine whether it is a qualified obligation for purposes of applying paragraph (a) of this section to the second transfer.

[Reg. § 1.679-4.]

☐ [*T.D. 8955, 7-19-2001.*]

§ 1.679-5. Pre-immigration trusts.—(a) *In general.*—If a nonresident alien individual becomes a U.S. person and the individual has a residency starting date (as determined under section 7701(b)(2)(A)) within 5 years after directly or indirectly transferring property to a foreign trust (the original transfer), the individual is treated as having transferred to the trust on the residency starting date an amount equal to the portion of the trust attributable to the property transferred by the individual in the original transfer.

(b) *Special rules.*—(1) *Change in grantor trust status.*—For purposes of paragraph (a) of this section, if a nonresident alien individual who is treated as owning any portion of a trust under the provisions of subpart E of part I of subchapter J, chapter 1 of the Internal Revenue Code, subsequently ceases to be so treated, the individual is treated as having made the original transfer to the foreign trust immediately before the trust ceases to be treated as owned by the individual.

(2) *Treatment of undistributed income.*—For purposes of paragraph (a) of this section, the property deemed transferred to the foreign trust on the residency starting date includes undistributed net income, as defined in section 665(a), attributable to the property deemed transferred. Undistributed net income for periods before the individual's residency starting date is taken into account only for purposes of determining the amount of the property deemed transferred.

(c) *Examples.*—The rules of this section are illustrated by the following examples:

Example 1. Nonresident alien becomes resident alien. On January 1, 2002, *A*, a nonresident alien individual, transfers property to a foreign trust, *FT*. On January 1, 2006, *A* becomes a resident of the United States within the meaning of section 7701(b)(1)(A) and has a residency starting date of January 1, 2006, within the meaning of section 7701(b)(2)(A). Under paragraph (a) of this section, *A* is treated as a U.S. transferor and is deemed to transfer the property to *FT* on January 1, 2006. Under paragraph (b)(2) of this section, the property deemed transferred to *FT* on January 1, 2006, includes the undistributed net income of the trust, as defined in section 665(a), attributable to the property originally transferred.

Example 2. Nonresident alien loses power to revest property. On January 1, 2002, *A*, a nonresident alien individual, transfers property to a foreign trust, *FT*. *A* has the power to revest absolutely in himself the title to such property transferred and is treated as the owner of the trust pursuant to sections 676 and 672(f). On January 1, 2008, the terms of *FT* are amended to remove *A*'s power to revest in himself title to the property transferred, and *A* ceases to be treated as the owner of *FT*. On January 1, 2010, *A* becomes a resident of the United States. Under paragraph (b)(1) of this section, for purposes of paragraph (a) of this section *A* is treated as having originally transferred the property to *FT* on January 1, 2008. Because this date is within five years of *A*'s residency starting date, *A* is deemed to have made a transfer to the foreign trust on January 1, 2010, his residency starting date. Under paragraph (b)(2) of this section, the property deemed transferred to the foreign trust on January 1, 2010, includes the undistributed net income of the trust, as defined in section 665(a), attributable to the property deemed transferred.

[Reg. § 1.679-5.]

☐ [*T.D. 8955, 7-19-2001.*]

§ 1.679-6. Outbound migrations of domestic trusts.—(a) *In general.*—Subject to the provisions of paragraph (b) of this section, if an individual who is a U.S. person transfers property to a trust that is not a foreign trust, and such trust becomes a foreign trust while the U.S. person is alive, the U.S. individual is treated as a U.S. transferor and is deemed to transfer the property to a foreign trust on the date the domestic trust becomes a foreign trust.

(b) *Amount deemed transferred.*—For purposes of paragraph (a) of this section, the property deemed transferred to the trust when it becomes a foreign trust includes undistributed net income, as defined in section 665(a), attributable to the property previously transferred. Undistributed net income for periods prior to the migration is taken into account only for purposes of determining the portion of the trust that is attributable to the property transferred by the U.S. person.

(c) *Example.*—The following example illustrates the rules of this section. For purposes of the example, *A* is a resident alien, *B* is *A*'s son, who is a resident alien, and *DT* is a domestic trust. The example is as follows:

Example. Outbound migration of domestic trust. On January 1, 2002, *A* transfers property to *DT*, for the benefit of *B*. On January 1, 2003, *DT* acquires a foreign trustee who has the power to determine whether and when distributions will be made to *B*. Under section 7701(a)(30)(E) and § 301.7701-7(d)(ii)(A) of this chapter, *DT* becomes a foreign trust on January 1, 2003. Under paragraph (a) of this section, *A* is treated as transferring property to a foreign trust on January 1, 2003. Under paragraph (b) of this section, the property deemed transferred to the trust when it becomes a foreign trust includes undistributed net income, as defined in section 665(a), attributable to the property deemed transferred.

[Reg. § 1.679-6.]

☐ [*T.D. 8955, 7-19-2001.*]

§ 1.684-1. Recognition of gain on transfers to certain foreign trusts and estates.—(a) *Immediate recognition of gain.*—(1) *In general.*—Any U.S. person who transfers property to a foreign trust or foreign estate shall be required to recognize gain at the time of the transfer equal to the excess of the fair market value of the property transferred over the adjusted basis (for purposes of determining gain) of such property in the hands of the U.S. transferor unless an exception applies under the provisions of § 1.684-3. The amount of gain recognized is determined on an asset-by-asset basis.

(2) *No recognition of loss.*—Under this section a U.S. person may not recognize loss on the transfer of an asset to a foreign trust or foreign estate. A U.S. person may not offset gain realized on the transfer of an appreciated asset to a foreign trust or foreign estate by a loss realized on the transfer of a depreciated asset to the foreign trust or foreign estate.

(b) *Definitions.*—The following definitions apply for purposes of this section:

(1) *U.S. person.*—The term *U.S. person* means a United States person as defined in section 7701(a)(30), and includes a nonresident alien individual who elects under section 6013(g) to be treated as a resident of the United States.

(2) *U.S. transferor.*—The term *U.S. transferor* means any U.S. person who makes a transfer (as defined in § 1.684-2) of property to a foreign trust or foreign estate.

(3) *Foreign trust.*—Section 7701(a)(31)(B) defines foreign trust. See also § 301.7701-7 of this chapter.

(4) *Foreign estate.*—Section 7701(a)(31)(A) defines foreign estate.

(c) *Reporting requirements.*—A U.S. person who transfers property to a foreign trust or foreign estate must comply with the reporting requirements under section 6048.

(d) *Examples.*—The following examples illustrate the rules of this section. In all examples, *A* is a U.S. person and *FT* is a foreign trust. The examples are as follows:

Example 1. Transfer to foreign trust. A transfers property that has a fair market value of 1000X to *FT*. *A*'s adjusted basis in the property is 400X. *FT* has no U.S. beneficiary within the meaning of § 1.679-2, and no person is treated as owning any portion of *FT*. Under paragraph (a)(1) of this section, *A* recognizes gain at the time of the transfer equal to 600X.

Example 2. Transfer of multiple properties. A transfers property Q, with a fair market value of 1000X, and property R, with a fair market value of 2000X, to *FT*. At the time of the transfer, *A*'s adjusted basis in property Q is 700X, and *A*'s adjusted basis in property R is 2200X. *FT* has no U.S. beneficiary within the meaning of § 1.679-2, and no person is treated as owning any portion of *FT*. Under paragraph (a)(1) of this section, *A* recognizes the 300X of gain attributable to property Q. Under paragraph (a)(2) of this section, *A* does not recognize the 200X of loss attributable to property R, and may not offset that loss against the gain attributable to property Q.

Example 3. Transfer for less than fair market value. A transfers property that has a fair market value of 1000X to *FT* in exchange for 400X of cash. *A*'s adjusted basis in the property is 200X. *FT* has no U.S. beneficiary within the meaning of § 1.679-2, and no person is treated as owning any portion of *FT*. Under paragraph (a)(1) of this section, *A* recognizes gain at the time of the transfer equal to 800X.

Example 4. Exchange of property for private annuity. A transfers property that has a fair market value of 1000X to *FT* in exchange for *FT*'s obligation to pay *A* 50X per year for the rest of *A*'s life. *A*'s adjusted basis in the property is 100X. *FT* has no U.S. beneficiary within the meaning of § 1.679-2, and no person is treated as owning any portion of *FT*. *A* is required to recognize gain equal to 900X immediately upon transfer of the property to the trust. This result applies even though *A* might otherwise have been allowed to defer recognition of gain under another provision of the Internal Revenue Code.

Example 5. Transfer of property to related foreign trust in exchange for qualified obligation. A transfers property that has a fair market value of 1000X to *FT* in exchange for *FT*'s obligation to make payments to *A* during the next four years. *FT* is related to *A* as defined in § 1.679-1(c)(5). The obligation is treated as a qualified obligation within the meaning of § 1.679-4(d), and no person is treated as owning any portion of *FT*. *A*'s adjusted basis in the property is 100X. *A* is required to recognize gain equal to 900X immediately upon transfer of the property to the trust. This result applies even though *A* might otherwise have been allowed to defer recognition of gain under another provision of the Internal Revenue Code. Section 1.684-3(d) provides rules relating to transfers for fair market value to unrelated foreign trusts.

[Reg. § 1.684-1.]

☐ [*T.D. 8956, 7-19-2001.*]

§ 1.684-2. Transfers.—(a) *In general.*—A transfer means a direct, indirect, or constructive transfer.

(b) *Indirect transfers.*—(1) *In general.*—Section 1.679-3(c) shall apply to determine if a transfer to a foreign trust or foreign estate, by any person, is treated as an indirect transfer by a U.S. person to the foreign trust or foreign estate.

(2) *Examples.*—The following examples illustrate the rules of this paragraph (b). In all examples, *A* is a U.S. citizen, *FT* is a foreign trust, and *I* is *A*'s uncle, who is a nonresident alien. The examples are as follows:

Example 1. Principal purpose of tax avoidance. A creates and funds *FT* for the benefit of *A*'s cousin, who is a nonresident alien. *FT* has no U.S. beneficiary within the meaning of § 1.679-2, and no person is treated as owning any portion of *FT*. In 2004, *A* decides to transfer additional property with a fair market value of 1000X and an adjusted basis of 600X to *FT*. Pursuant to a plan with a principal purpose of avoiding the application of section 684, *A* transfers the property to *I*. *I* subsequently transfers the property to *FT*. Under paragraph (b) of this section and § 1.679-3(c), *A* is treated as having transferred the property to *FT*.

Example 2. U.S. person unable to demonstrate that intermediary acted independently. A creates and funds *FT* for the benefit of *A*'s cousin, who is a nonresident alien. *FT* has no U.S. beneficiary within the meaning of § 1.679-2, and no person is treated as owning any portion of *FT*. On July 1, 2004, *A* transfers property with a fair market value of 1000X and an adjusted basis of 300X to *I*, a foreign person. On January 1, 2007, at a time when the fair market value of the property is 1100X, *I* transfers the property to *FT*. *A* is unable to demonstrate to the satisfaction of the Commissioner, under § 1.679-3(c)(2)(ii), that *I* acted independently of *A* in making the transfer to *FT*. Under paragraph (b) of this section and § 1.679-3(c), *A* is treated as having transferred the property to *FT*. Under paragraph (b) of this section and § 1.679-3(c)(3), *I* is treated as an agent of *A*, and the transfer is deemed to have been made on January 1, 2007. Under § 1.684-1(a), *A* recognizes gain equal to 800X on that date.

(c) *Constructive transfers.*—Section 1.679-3(d) shall apply to determine if a transfer to a foreign trust or foreign estate is treated as a constructive transfer by a U.S. person to the foreign trust or foreign estate.

(d) *Transfers by certain trusts.*—(1) *In general.*—If any portion of a trust is treated as owned by a U.S. person, a transfer of property from that portion of the trust to a foreign trust is treated as a transfer from the owner of that portion to the foreign trust.

(2) *Examples.*—The following examples illustrate the rules of this paragraph (d). In all examples, *A* is a U.S. person, *DT* is a domestic trust, and *FT* is a foreign trust. The examples are as follows:

Example 1. Transfer by a domestic trust. On January 1, 2001, *A* transfers property which has a fair market value of 1000X and an adjusted basis of 200X to *DT*. *A* retains the power to revoke *DT*. On January 1, 2003, *DT* transfers property which has a fair market value of 500X and an adjusted basis of 100X to *FT*. At the time of the transfer, *FT* has no U.S. beneficiary as defined in § 1.679-2 and no person is treated as owning any portion of *FT*. *A* is treated as having transferred the property to *FT* and is required to recognize gain of 400X, under § 1.684-1, at the time of the transfer by *DT* to *FT*.

Example 2. Transfer by a foreign trust. On January 1, 2001, *A* transfers property which has a fair market value of 1000X and an adjusted basis of 200X to *FT1*. At the time of the transfer, *FT1* has a U.S. beneficiary as defined in § 1.679-2 and *A* is treated as the owner of *FT1* under section 679. On January 1, 2003, *FT1* transfers property which has a fair market value of 500X and an adjusted basis of 100X to *FT2*. At the time of the transfer, *FT2* has no U.S. beneficiary as defined in § 1.679-2 and no person is treated as owning any portion of *FT2*. *A* is treated as having transferred the property to *FT2* and is required to recognize gain of 400X, under § 1.684-1, at the time of the transfer by *FT1* to *FT2*.

(e) *Deemed transfers when foreign trust no longer treated as owned by a U.S. person.*—(1) *In general.*—If any portion of a foreign trust is treated as owned by a U.S. person under subpart E of part I of subchapter J, chapter 1 of the Internal Revenue Code, and such portion ceases to be treated as owned by that person under such subpart (other than by reason of an actual transfer of property from the trust to which § 1.684-2(d) applies), the U.S. person shall be treated as having transferred, immediately before (but on the same date that) the trust is no longer treated as owned by that U.S. person, the assets of such portion to a foreign trust.

(2) *Examples.*—The following examples illustrate the rules of this paragraph (e). In all examples, *A* is a U.S. citizen and *FT* is a foreign trust. The examples are as follows:

Example 1. Loss of U.S. beneficiary. (i) On January 1, 2001, *A* transfers property, which has a fair market value of 1000X and an adjusted basis of 400X, to *FT*. At the time of the transfer, *FT* has a U.S. beneficiary within the meaning of § 1.679-2, and *A* is treated as owning *FT* under section 679. Under § 1.684-3(a), § 1.684-1 does not cause *A* to recognize gain at the time of the transfer.

(ii) On July 1, 2003, *FT* ceases to have a U.S. beneficiary as defined in § 1.679-2(c) and as of that date neither *A* nor any other person is treated as owning any portion of *FT*. Pursuant to § 1.679-2(c)(2), if *FT* ceases to be treated as having a U.S. beneficiary, *A* will cease to be treated as owner of *FT* beginning on the first day of the first taxable year following the last taxable year in which there was a U.S. beneficiary. Thus, on January 1, 2004, *A* ceases to be treated as owner of *FT*. On that date, the fair market value of the property is 1200X and the adjusted basis is 350X. Under paragraph (e)(1) of this section, *A* is treated as having transferred the property to *FT* on January 1, 2004, and must recognize 850X of gain at that time under § 1.684-1.

Example 2. Death of grantor. (i) The initial facts are the same as in paragraph (i) of *Example 1*.

(ii) On July 1, 2003, *A* dies, and as of that date no other person is treated as the owner of *FT*. On that date, the fair market value of the property is 1200X, and its adjusted basis equals 350X. Under paragraph (e)(1) of this section, *A* is treated as having transferred the property to *FT* immediately before his death, and generally is required to recognize 850X of gain at that time under § 1.684-1. However, an exception may apply under § 1.684-3(c).

Example 3. Release of a power. (i) On January 1, 2001, *A* transfers property that has a fair market value of 500X and an adjusted basis of 200X to *FT*. At the time of the transfer, FT does not have a U.S. beneficiary within the meaning of § 1.679-2. However, *A* retains the power to revoke the trust. *A* is treated as the owner of the trust under section 676 and, therefore, under § 1.684-3(a), *A* is not required to recognize gain under § 1.684-1 at the time of the transfer.

(ii) On January 1, 2007, *A* releases the power to revoke the trust and, as of that date, neither *A* nor any other person is treated as owning any portion of FT. On that date, the fair market value of the property is 900X, and its adjusted basis is 200X. Under paragraph (e)(1) of this section, *A* is treated as having transferred the property to *FT* on January 1, 2007, and must recognize 700X of gain at that time.

(f) *Transfers to entities owned by a foreign trust.*—Section 1.679-3(f) provides rules that apply with respect to transfers of property by a U.S. person to an entity in which a foreign trust holds an ownership interest. [Reg. § 1.684-2.]

☐ [*T.D. 8956, 7-19-2001.*]

§ 1.684-3. Exceptions to general rule of gain recognition.—(a) *Transfers to grantor trusts.*—The general rule of gain recognition under § 1.684-1 shall not apply to any transfer of property by a U.S. person to a foreign trust to the extent that any person is treated as the owner of the trust under section 671. Section 1.684-2(e) provides rules regarding a subsequent change in the status of the trust.

(b) *Transfers to charitable trusts.*—The general rule of gain recognition under § 1.684-1 shall not apply to any transfer of property to a foreign trust that is described in section 501(c)(3) (without regard to the requirements of section 508(a)).

(c) *Certain transfers at death.*—(1) *Section 1014 basis.*—The general rule of gain recognition under § 1.684-1 shall not apply to any transfer of property to a foreign trust or foreign estate or, in the case of a transfer of property by a U.S. transferor decedent dying in 2010, to a foreign trust, foreign estate, or a nonresident alien, by reason of death of the U.S. transferor, if the basis of the property in the hands of the transferee is determined under section 1014(a).

(2) *Section 1022 basis election.*—For U.S. transferor decedents dying in 2010, the general rule of gain recognition under § 1.684-1 shall apply to any transfer of property by reason of death of the U.S. transferor if the basis of the property in the hands of the foreign trust, foreign estate, or the nonresident alien individual is determined under section 1022. The gain on the transfer shall be calculated as set out under § 1.684-1(a), except that adjusted basis will reflect any increases allocated to such property under section 1022.

(d) *Transfers for fair market value to unrelated trusts.*—The general rule of gain recognition under § 1.684-1 shall not apply to any transfer of property for fair market value to a foreign trust that is not a related foreign trust as defined in § 1.679-1(c)(5). Section 1.671-2(e)(2)(ii) defines fair market value.

(e) *Transfers to which section 1032 applies.*—The general rule of gain recognition under § 1.684-1 shall not apply to any transfer of stock (including treasury stock) by a domestic corporation to a foreign trust if the domestic corporation is not required to recognize gain on the transfer under section 1032.

(f) *Certain distributions to trusts.*—For purposes of this section, a transfer does not include a distribution to a trust with respect to an interest held by such trust in an entity other than a trust or an interest in certain investment trusts described in § 301.7701-4(c) of this chapter, liquidating trusts described in § 301.7701-4(d) of this chapter, or environmental remediation trusts described in § 301.7701-4(e) of this chapter.

(g) *Examples.*—The following examples illustrate the rules of this section. In all examples, *A* is a U.S. citizen and *FT* is a foreign trust. The examples are as follows:

Example 1. Transfer to owner trust. In 2001, *A* transfers property which has a fair market value of 1000X and an adjusted basis equal to 400X to *FT*. At the time of the transfer, *FT* has a U.S. beneficiary within the meaning of § 1.679-2, and *A* is treated as owning *FT* under section 679. Under paragraph (a) of this section, § 1.684-1 does not cause *A* to recognize gain at the time of the transfer. See § 1.684-2(e) for rules that may require *A* to recognize gain if the trust is no longer owned by *A*.

Example 2. Transfer of property at death: Basis determined under section 1014(a). (i) The initial facts are the same as *Example 1*.

(ii) *A* dies on July 1, 2004. The fair market value at *A*'s death of all property transferred to *FT* by *A* is 1500X. The basis in the property is 400X. *A* retained the power to revoke *FT*, thus, the value of all property owned by *FT* at *A*'s death is includible in *A*'s gross estate for U.S. estate tax purposes. Pursuant to paragraph (c) of this section, *A* is not required to recognize gain under § 1.684-1 because the basis of the property in the hands of the foreign trust is determined under section 1014(a).

Example 3. Transfer of property at death: Basis not determined under section 1014(a). (i) The initial facts are the same as *Example 1*.

(ii) *A* dies on July 1, 2004. The fair market value at *A*'s death of all property transferred to *FT* by *A* is 1500X. The basis in the property is 400X. *A* retains no power over *FT*, and *FT*'s basis in the property transferred is not determined under section 1014(a). Under § 1.684-2(e)(1), *A* is treated as having transferred the property to *FT* immediately before his death, and must recognize 1100X of gain at that time under § 1.684-1.

Example 4. Transfer of property for fair market value to an unrelated foreign trust. A sells a house with a fair market value of 1000X to *FT* in exchange for a 30-year note issued by *FT*. *A* is not related to *FT* as defined in § 1.679-1(c)(5). *FT* is not treated as owned by any person. Pursuant to paragraph (d) of this section, *A* is not required to recognize gain under § 1.684-1.

[Reg. § 1.684-3.]

☐ [*T.D. 8956, 7-19-2001. Amended by T.D. 9811, 1-18-2017.*]

§ 1.684-4. Outbound migrations of domestic trusts.—(a) *In general.*—If a U.S. person transfers property to a domestic trust, and such trust becomes a foreign trust, and neither trust is treated as owned by any person under subpart E of part I of subchapter J, chapter 1 of the Internal Revenue Code, the trust shall be treated for purposes of this section as having transferred all of its assets to a foreign trust and the trust is required to recognize gain on the transfer under § 1.684-1(a). The trust must also comply with the rules of section 6048.

(b) *Date of transfer.*—The transfer described in this section shall be deemed to occur immediately before, but on the same date that, the trust meets the definition of a foreign trust set forth in section 7701(a)(31)(B).

(c) *Inadvertent migrations.*—In the event of an inadvertent migration, as defined in § 301.7701-7(d)(2) of this chapter, a trust may avoid the application of this section by complying with the procedures set forth in § 301.7701-7(d)(2) of this chapter.

(d) *Examples.*—The following examples illustrate the rules of this section. In all examples, *A* is a U.S. citizen, *B* is a U.S. citizen, *C* is a nonresident alien, and *T* is a trust. The examples are as follows:

Example 1. Migration of domestic trust with U.S. beneficiaries. A transfers property which has a fair market value of 1000X and an adjusted basis equal to 400X to *T*, a domestic trust, for the benefit of *A*'s children who are also U.S. citizens. *B* is the trustee of *T*. On January 1, 2001, while *A* is still alive, *B* resigns as trustee and *C* becomes successor trustee under the terms of the trust. Pursuant to § 301.7701-7(d) of this chapter, *T* becomes a foreign trust. *T* has U.S. beneficiaries within the meaning of § 1.679-2 and *A* is, therefore, treated as owning *FT* under section 679. Pursuant to § 1.684-3(a), neither *A* nor *T* is required to recognize gain at the time of the migration. Section 1.684-2(e) provides rules that may require *A* to recognize gain upon a subsequent change in the status of the trust.

Example 2. Migration of domestic trust with no U.S. beneficiaries. A transfers property which has a fair market value of 1000X and an adjusted basis equal to 400X to *T*, a domestic trust for the benefit of *A*'s mother who is not a citizen or resident of the United States. *T* is not treated as owned by another person. *B* is the trustee of *T*. On January 1, 2001, while *A* is still alive, *B* resigns as trustee and *C* becomes successor trustee under the terms of the trust. Pursuant to § 301.7701-7(d) of this chapter, *T* becomes a foreign trust, *FT*. *FT* has no U.S. beneficiaries within the meaning of § 1.679-2 and no person is treated as owning any portion of *FT*. *T* is required to recognize gain of 600X on January 1, 2001. Paragraph (c) of this section provides rules with respect to an inadvertent migration of a domestic trust.

[Reg. § 1.684-4.]

☐ [*T.D.* 8956, 7-19-2001.]

Partnerships

§ 1.701-2. Anti-abuse rule.—(a) *Intent of subchapter K.*—Subchapter K is intended to permit taxpayers to conduct joint business (including investment) activities through a flexible economic arrangement without incurring an entity-level tax. Implicit in the intent of subchapter K are the following requirements—

(1) The partnership must be bona fide and each partnership transaction or series of related transactions (individually or collectively, the transaction) must be entered into for a substantial business purpose.

(2) The form of each partnership transaction must be respected under substance over form principles.

(3) Except as otherwise provided in this paragraph (a)(3), the tax consequences under subchapter K to each partner of partnership operations and of transactions between the partner and the partnership must accurately reflect the partners' economic agreement and clearly reflect the partner's income (collectively, *proper reflection of income*). However, certain provisions of subchapter K and the regulations thereunder were adopted to promote administrative convenience and other policy objectives, with the recognition that the application of those provisions to a transaction could, in some circumstances, produce tax results that do not properly reflect income. Thus, the proper reflection of income requirement of this paragraph (a)(3) is treated as satisfied with respect to a transaction that satisfies paragraphs (a)(1) and (2) of this section to the extent that the application of such a provision to the transaction and the ultimate tax results, taking into account all the relevant facts and circumstances, are clearly contemplated by that provision. See, for example, paragraph (d) *Example 6* of this section (relating to the value-equals-basis rule in § 1.704-1(b)(2)(iii)(*c*)), paragraph (d) *Example 9* of this section (relating to the election under section 754 to adjust basis in partnership property), and paragraph (d) *Examples 10 and 11* of this section (relating to the basis in property distributed by a partnership under section 732). See also, for example, §§ 1.704-3(e)(1) and 1.752-2(e)(4) (providing certain de minimis exceptions).

(b) *Application of subchapter K rules.*—The provisions of subchapter K and the regulations thereunder must be applied in a manner that is consistent with the intent of subchapter K as set forth in paragraph (a) of this section (*intent of subchapter K*). Accordingly, if a partnership is formed or availed of in connection with a transaction a principal purpose of which is to reduce substantially the present value of the partners' aggregate federal tax liability in a manner that is inconsistent with the intent of subchapter K, the Commissioner can recast the transaction for federal tax purposes, as appropriate to achieve tax results that are consistent with the intent of subchapter K, in light of the applicable statutory and regulatory provisions and the pertinent facts and circumstances. Thus, even though the transaction may fall within the literal words of a particular statutory or regulatory provision, the Commissioner can determine, based on the particular facts and circumstances, that to achieve tax results that are consistent with the intent of subchapter K—

(1) The purported partnership should be disregarded in whole or in part, and the partnership's assets and activities should be considered, in whole or in part, to be owned and conducted, respectively, by one or more of its purported partners;

(2) One or more of the purported partners of the partnership should not be treated as a partner;

(3) The methods of accounting used by the partnership or a partner should be adjusted to reflect clearly the partnership's or the partner's income;

(4) The partnership's items of income, gain, loss, deduction, or credit should be reallocated; or

(5) The claimed tax treatment should otherwise be adjusted or modified.

(c) *Facts and circumstances analysis; factors.*—Whether a partnership was formed or availed of with a principal purpose to reduce substantially the present value of the partners' aggregate federal tax liability in a manner inconsistent with the intent of subchapter K is determined based on all of the facts and circumstances, including a comparison of the purported business purpose for a transaction and the claimed tax benefits resulting from the transaction. The factors set forth below may be indicative, but do not necessarily establish, that a partnership was used in such a manner. These factors are illustrative only, and therefore may not be the only factors taken into account in making the determination under this section. Moreover, the weight given to any factor (whether specified in this paragraph or otherwise) depends on all the facts and circumstances. The presence or absence of any factor described in this paragraph does not create a presumption that a partnership was (or was not) used in such a manner. Factors include:

(1) The present value of the partners' aggregate federal tax liability is substantially less than had the partners owned the partnership's assets and conducted the partnership's activities directly;

(2) The present value of the partners' aggregate federal tax liability is substantially less than would be the case if purportedly separate transactions that are designed to achieve a particular end result are integrated and treated as steps in a single transaction. For example, this analysis may indicate that it was contemplated that a partner who was necessary to achieve the intended tax results and whose interest in the partnership was liquidated or disposed of (in whole or in part) would be a partner only temporarily in order to provide the claimed tax benefits to the remaining partners;

(3) One or more partners who are necessary to achieve the claimed tax results either have a nominal interest in the partnership, are substantially protected from any risk of loss from the partnership's activities (through distribution preferences, indemnity or loss guaranty agreements, or other arrangements), or have little or no participation in the profits from the partnership's activities other than a preferred return that is in the nature of a payment for the use of capital;

(4) Substantially all of the partners (measured by number or interests in the partnership) are related (directly or indirectly) to one another;

(5) Partnership items are allocated in compliance with the literal language of §§ 1.704-1 and 1.704-2 but with results that are inconsistent with the purpose of section 704(b) and those regulations. In this regard, particular scrutiny will be paid to partnerships in which income or gain is specially allocated to one or more partners that may be legally or effectively exempt from federal taxation (for example, a foreign person, an exempt organization, an insolvent taxpayer, or a taxpayer with unused federal tax attributes such as net operating losses, capital losses, or foreign tax credits);

(6) The benefits and burdens of ownership of property nominally contributed to the partnership are in substantial part retained (directly or indirectly) by the contributing partner (or a related party); or

(7) The benefits and burdens of ownership of partnership property are in substantial part shifted (directly or indirectly) to the distributee partner before or after the property is actually distributed to the distributee partner (or a related party).

(d) *Examples.*—The following examples illustrate the principles of paragraphs (a), (b), and (c) of this section. The examples set forth below do not delineate the boundaries of either permissible or impermissible types of transactions. Further, the addition of any facts or circumstances that are not specifically set forth in an example (or the deletion of any facts or circumstances) may alter the outcome of the transaction described in the example. Unless otherwise indicated, parties to the transactions are not related to one another.

* * *

Example 3. Choice of entity; avoidance of more restrictive foreign tax credit limitation; use of partnership consistent with the intent of subchapter K. (i) X, a domestic corporation, and Y, a foreign corporation, form partnership PRS under the laws of foreign Country A to conduct a bona fide joint business. X and Y each owns a 50% interest in PRS. PRS is properly classified as a partnership under §§301.7701-2 and 301.7701-3. PRS pays income taxes to Country A. X and Y chose partnership form to enable X to qualify for a direct foreign tax credit under section 901, with look-through treatment under §1.904-5(h)(1). Conversely, if PRS were a foreign corporation for U.S. tax purposes, X would be entitled only to indirect foreign tax credits under section 902 with respect to dividend distributions from PRS. The look-through rules, however, would not apply, and pursuant to section 904(d)(1)(E) and §1.904-4(g), the dividends and associated taxes would be subject to a separate foreign tax credit limitation for dividends from PRS, a noncontrolled section 902 corporation.

(ii) Subchapter K is intended to permit taxpayers to conduct joint business activity through a flexible economic arrangement without incurring an entity-level tax. See paragraph (a) of this section. The decision to organize and conduct business through PRS in order to take advantage of the look-through rules for foreign tax credit purposes, thereby maximizing X's use of its proper share of foreign taxes paid by PRS, is consistent with this intent. In addition, on these facts, the requirements of paragraphs (a)(1), (2), and (3) of this section have been satisfied. The Commissioner therefore cannot invoke paragraph (b) of this section to recast the transaction.

* * *

(e) *Abuse of entity treatment.*—(1) *General rule.*—The Commissioner can treat a partnership as an aggregate of its partners in whole or in part as appropriate to carry out the purpose of any provision of the Internal Revenue Code or the regulations promulgated thereunder.

(2) *Clearly contemplated entity treatment.*—Paragraph (e)(1) of this section does not apply to the extent that—

(i) A provision of the Internal Revenue Code or the regulations promulgated thereunder prescribes the treatment of a partnership as an entity, in whole or in part, and

(ii) That treatment and the ultimate tax results, taking into account all the relevant facts and circumstances, are clearly contemplated by that provision.

(f) *Examples.*—The following examples illustrate the principles of paragraph (e) of this section. The examples set forth below do not delineate the boundaries of either permissible or impermissible types of transactions. Further, the addition of any facts or circumstances that are not specifically set forth in an example (or the deletion of any facts or circumstances) may alter the outcome of the transaction described in the example. Unless otherwise indicated, parties to the transactions are not related to one another.

* * *

Example 3. Prescribed entity treatment of partnership; determination of CFC status clearly contemplated. (i) X, a domestic corporation, and Y, a foreign corporation, intend to conduct a joint venture in foreign Country A. They form PRS, a bona fide domestic general partnership in which X owns a 40% interest and Y owns a 60% interest. PRS is properly classified as a partnership under §§301.7701-2 and 301.7701-3. PRS holds 100% of the voting stock of Z, a Country A entity that is classified as an association taxable as a corporation for federal tax purposes under §301.7701-2. Z conducts its business operations in Country A. By investing in Z through a domestic partnership, X seeks to obtain the benefit of the look-through rules of section 904(d)(3) and, as a result, maximize its ability to claim credits for its proper share of Country A taxes expected to be incurred by Z.

(ii) Pursuant to sections 957(c) and 7701(a)(30), PRS is a United States person. Therefore, because it owns 10% or more of the voting stock of Z, PRS satisfies the definition of a U.S. shareholder under section 951(b). Under section 957(a), Z is a controlled foreign corporation (CFC) because more than 50% of the voting power or value of its stock is owned by PRS. Consequently, under section 904(d)(3), X qualifies for look-through treatment in computing its credit for foreign taxes paid or accrued by Z. In contrast, if X and Y owned their interests in Z directly, Z would not be a CFC because only 40% of its stock would be owned by U.S. shareholders. X's credit for foreign taxes paid or accrued by Z in that case would be subject to a separate foreign tax credit limitation for dividends from Z, a noncontrolled section 902 corporation. See section 904(d)(1)(E) and §1.904-4(g).

(iii) Sections 957(c) and 7701(a)(30) prescribe the treatment of a domestic partnership as an entity for purposes of defining a U.S. shareholder, and thus, for purposes of determining whether a foreign corporation is a CFC. The CFC rules prevent the deferral by U.S. shareholders of U.S. taxation of certain earnings of the CFC and reduce disparities that otherwise might occur between the amount of income subject to a particular foreign tax credit limitation when a taxpayer earns income abroad directly rather than indirectly through a CFC. The application of the look-through rules for foreign tax credit purposes is appropriately tied to CFC status. See sections 904(d)(2)(E) and 904(d)(3). This analysis confirms that Congress clearly contemplated that taxpayers could use a bona fide domestic partnership to subject themselves to the CFC regime, and the resulting application of the look-through rules of section 904(d)(3). Accordingly, under paragraph (e) of this section, the Commissioner cannot treat PRS as an aggregate of its partners for purposes of determining X's foreign tax credit limitation.

* * *

(i) *Application of nonstatutory principles and other statutory authorities.*—The Commissioner can continue to assert and to rely upon applicable nonstatutory principles and other statutory and regulatory authorities to challenge transactions. This section does not limit the applicability of those principles and authorities. [Reg. §1.701-2.]

☐ [*T.D. 8588, 12-29-94. Amended by T.D. 8592, 4-12-95.*]

§1.702-1. Income and credits of partner.—(a) *General rule.*—Each partner is required to take into account separately in his return his distributive share, whether or not distributed, of each class or item of partnership income, gain, loss, deduction, or credit described in subparagraphs (1) through (9) of this paragraph. (For the taxable year in which a partner includes his distributive share of partnership taxable income, see section 706(a) and §1.706-1(a). Such distributive share shall be determined as provided in section 704 and §1.704-1.) Accordingly, in determining his income tax:

(1) Each partner shall take into account, as part of his gains and losses from sales or exchanges of capital assets held for not more than 1 year (6 months for taxable years beginning before 1977; 9 months for taxable years beginning in 1977), his distributive share of the combined net amount of such gains and losses of the partnership.

(2) Each partner shall take into account, as part of his gains and losses from sales or exchanges of capital assets held for more than 1 year (6 months for taxable years beginning before 1977; 9 months for taxable years beginning in 1977), his distributive share of the combined net amount of such gains and losses of the partnership. Each partner subject to section 1061 must take into account gains and losses from sales of capital assets held for more than one year as provided in section 1061 and §§1.1061-1 through 1.1061-6.

(3) Each partner shall take into account, as part of his gains and losses from sales or exchanges of property described in section 1231 (relating to property used in the trade or business and involuntary conversions), his distributive share of the combined net amount of such gains and losses of the partnership. The partnership shall not combine such items with items set forth in subparagraph (1) or (2) of this paragraph.

(4) Each partner shall take into account, as part of the charitable contributions paid by him, his distributive share of each class of charitable contributions paid by the partnership within the partnership's taxable year. Section 170 determines the extent to which such amount may be allowed as a deduction to the partner. For the definition of the term "charitable contribution", see section 170(c).

(5) Each partner shall take into account, as part of the dividends received by him from domestic corporations, his distributive share of dividends received by the partnership, with respect to which the partner is entitled to a credit under section 34 (for dividends received

on or before December 31, 1964), an exclusion under section 116, or a deduction under part VIII, subchapter B, chapter 1 of the Code.

(6) Each partner shall take into account, as part of his taxes described in section 901 which have been paid or accrued to foreign countries or to possessions of the United States, his distributive share of such taxes which have been paid or accrued by the partnership, according to its method of treating such taxes. A partner may elect to treat his total amount of such taxes, including his distributive share of such taxes of the partnership, as a deduction under section 164 or as a credit under section 901, the subject to the provisions of sections 901 through 905.

(7) Each partner shall take into account, as part of the partially tax-exempt interest received by him on obligations of the United States or on obligations of instrumentalities of the United States, as described in section 35 or section 242, his distributive share of such partially tax-exempt interest received by the partnership. However, if the partnership elects to amortize premiums on bonds as provided in section 171, the amount received on such obligations by the partnership shall be reduced by the amortizable bond premium applicable to such obligations as provided in section 171(a)(3).

(8)(i) Each partner shall take into account separately, as part of any class of income, gain, loss, deduction, or credit, his distributive share of the following items: recoveries of bad debts, prior taxes, and delinquency amounts (section 111); gains and losses from wagering transactions (section 165(d)); soil and water conservation expenditures (section 175); nonbusiness expenses as described in section 212; medical, dental, etc., expenses (section 213); expenses for care of certain dependents (section 214); alimony, etc., payments (section 215); amounts representing taxes and interest paid to cooperative housing corporations (section 216); intangible drilling and developments costs (section 263(c)); pre-1970 exploration expenditures (section 615); certain mining exploration expenditures (section 617); income, gain, or loss to the partnership under section 751(b); and any items of income, gain, loss, deduction, or credit subject to a special allocation under the partnership agreement which differs from the allocation of partnership taxable income or loss generally.

(ii) Each partner must also take into account separately the partner's distributive share of any partnership item which, if separately taken into account by any partner, would result in an income tax liability for that partner, or for any other person, different from that which would result if that partner did not take the item into account separately. Thus, if any partner is a controlled foreign corporation, as defined in section 957, items of income that would be gross subpart F income if separately taken into account by the controlled foreign corporation must be separately stated for all partners. Under section 911(a), if any partner is a bona fide resident of a foreign country who may exclude from gross income the part of the partner's distributive share which qualifies as earned income, as defined in section 911(b), the earned income of the partnership for all partners must be separately stated. Similarly, all relevant items of income or deduction of the partnership must be separately stated for all partners in determining the applicability of section 183 (relating to activities not engaged in for profit) and the recomputation of tax thereunder for any partner. This paragraph (a)(8)(ii) applies to taxable years beginning on or after July 23, 2002.

(iii) Each partner shall aggregate the amount of his separate deductions or exclusions and his distributive share of partnership deductions or exclusions separately stated in determining the amount allowable to him of any deduction or exclusion under subtitle A of the Code as to which a limitation is imposed. For example, partner A has individual domestic exploration expenditures of $300,000. He is also a member of the AB partnership which in 1971, in its first year of operation has foreign exploration expenditures of $400,000. A's distributable share of this item is $200,000. However, the total amount of his distributable share that A can deduct as exploration expenditures under section 617(a) is limited to $100,000 in view of the limitation provided in section 617(h). Therefore, the excess of $100,000 ($200,000 minus $100,000) is not deductible by A.

(9) Each partner shall also take into account separately his distributive share of the taxable income or loss of the partnership, exclusive of items requiring separate computations under subparagraphs (1) through (8) of this paragraph. For limitation on allowance of a partner's distributive share of partnership losses, see section 704(d) and paragraph (d) of § 1.704-1.

(b) *Character of items constituting distributive share.*—The character in the hands of a partner of any item of income, gain, loss, deduction, or credit described in section 702(a)(1) through (8) shall be determined as if such item were realized directly from the source from which realized by the partnership or incurred in the same manner as incurred by the partnership. For example, a partner's distributive share of gain from the sale of depreciable property used in the trade or business of the partnership shall be considered as gain from the sale of such depreciable property in the hands of the partner. Similarly, a partner's distributive share of partnership "hobby losses" (section 270) or his distributive share of partnership charitable contributions to organizations qualifying under section 170(b)(1)(A) retains such character in the hands of the partner.

(c) *Gross income of a partner.*—(1) Where it is necessary to determine the amount or character of the gross income of a partner, his gross income shall include the partner's distributive share of the gross income of the partnership, that is, the amount of gross income of the partnership from which was derived the partner's distributive share of partnership taxable income or loss (including items described in section 702(a)(1) through (8)). For example, a partner is required to include his distributive share of partnership gross income:

(i) In computing his gross income for the purpose of determining the necessity of filing a return (section 6012(a));

(ii) In determining the application of the provisions permitting the spreading of income for services rendered over a 36-month period (section 1301, as in effect for taxable years beginning before January 1, 1964);

(iii) In computing the amount of gross income received from sources within possessions of the United States (section 937);

(iv) In determining a partner's "gross income from farming" (sections 175 and 6073); and

(v) In determining whether the de minimis or full inclusion rules of section 954(b)(3) apply.

(2) In determining the applicability of the 6-year period of limitation on assessment and collection provided in section 6501(e) (relating to omission of more than 25 percent of gross income), a partner's gross income includes his distributive share of partnership gross income (as described in section 6501(e)(1)(A)(i)). In this respect, the amount of partnership gross income from which was derived the partner's distributive share of any item of partnership income, gain, loss, deduction, or credit (as included or disclosed in the partner's return) is considered as an amount of gross income stated in the partner's return for the purposes of section 6501(e). For example, A, who is entitled to one-fourth of the profits of the ABCD partnership, which has $10,000 gross income and $2,000 taxable income, reports only $300 as his distributive share of partnership profits. A should have shown $500 as his distributive share of profits, which amount was derived from $2,500 of partnership gross income. However, since A included only $300 on his return without explaining in the return the difference of $200, he is regarded as having stated in his return only $1,500 ($300/$500 of $2,500) as gross income from the partnership.

* * *

(g) *Applicability date.*—The last sentence of paragraph (a)(2) of this section applies for the taxable years beginning on or after January 19, 2021. [Reg. § 1.702-1.]

☐ [*T.D.* 6175, 5-23-56. *Amended by T.D.* 6605, 8-14-62; *T.D.* 6777, 12-15-64; *T.D.* 6885, 6-1-66; *T.D.* 7192, 6-29-72; *T.D.* 7564, 9-11-78; *T.D.* 7728, 10-31-80; *T.D.* 8247, 4-5-89; *T.D.* 8348, 5-10-91; *T.D.* 9008, 7-22-2002; *T.D.* 9194, 4-6-2005 *and T.D.* 9945, 1-13-2021.]

§ 1.704-1. Partner's distributive share.—(a) *Effect of partnership agreement.*—A partner's distributive share of any item or class of items of income, gain, loss, deduction, or credit of the partnership shall be determined by the partnership agreement, unless otherwise provided by section 704 and paragraphs (b) through (e) of this section. For definition of partnership agreement see section 761(c).

(b) *Determination of partner's distributive share.*—

* * *

(1) *In general.*—(i) *Basic principles.*—Under section 704(b) if a partnership agreement does not provide for the allocation of income, gain, loss, deduction, or credit (or item thereof) to a partner, or if the partnership agreement provides for the allocation of income, gain, loss, deduction, or credit (or item thereof) to a partner but such allocation does not have substantial economic effect, then the partner's distributive share of such income, gain, loss, deduction, or credit (or item thereof) shall be determined in accordance with such partner's interest in the partnership (taking into account all facts and circumstances). If the partnership agreement provides for the allocation of income, gain, loss, deduction, or credit (or item thereof) to a partner, there are three ways in which such allocation will be

respected under section 704(b) and this paragraph. First, the allocation can have substantial economic effect in accordance with paragraph (b)(2) of this section. Second, taking into account all facts and circumstances, the allocation can be in accordance with the partner's interest in the partnership. See paragraph (b)(3) of this section. Third, the allocation can be deemed to be in accordance with the partner's interest in the partnership pursuant to one of the special rules contained in paragraph (b)(4) of this section and § 1.704-2. To the extent an allocation under the partnership agreement of income, gain, loss, deduction, or credit (or item thereof) to a partner does not have substantial economic effect, is not in accordance with the partner's interest in the partnership, and is not deemed to be in accordance with the partner's interest in the partnership, such income, gain, loss, deduction, or credit (or item thereof) will be reallocated in accordance with the partner's interest in the partnership (determined under paragraph (b)(3) of this section).

(ii) *Effective/applicability date.*—*(a) Generally.*—Except as otherwise provided in this section, the provisions of this paragraph are effective for partnership taxable years beginning after December 31, 1975. However, for partnership taxable years beginning after December 31, 1975, but before May 1, 1986 (January 1, 1987, in the case of allocations of nonrecourse deductions as defined in paragraph (b)(4)(iv)(*a*) of this section), an allocation of income, gain, loss deduction, or credit (or item thereof) to a partner that is not respected under this paragraph nevertheless will be respected under section 704(b) if such allocation has substantial economic effect or is in accordance with the partners' interests in the partnership as those terms have been interpreted under the relevant case law, the legislative history of section 210(d) of the Tax Reform Act of 1976, and the provisions of this paragraph in effect for partnership taxable years beginning before May 1, 1986. Paragraphs (b)(2)(iii)(*a*) (last sentence), (b)(2)(iii)(*d*), (b)(2)(iii)(*e*), and (b)(5) *Example 28, Example 29*, and *Example 30* of this section apply to partnership taxable years beginning on or after May 19, 2008. In addition, paragraph (b)(2)(iv)(*d*)(4), paragraph (b)(2)(iv)(*f*)(*1*), paragraph (b)(2)(iv)(*f*)(*5*)(*iv*), paragraph (b)(2)(iv)(*h*)(2), paragraph (b)(2)(iv)(*s*), paragraph (b)(4)(ix), paragraph (b)(4)(x), and *Examples 31* through *35* in paragraph (b)(5) of this section apply to noncompensatory options (as defined in § 1.721-2(f)) that are issued on or after February 5, 2013. The last sentence of paragraph (b)(2)(iv)(g)(3) of this section is applicable for partnership taxable years ending on or after September 24, 2019. However, a partnership may choose to apply the last sentence in paragraph (b)(2)(iv)(g)(3) of this section for the partnership's taxable years ending on or after September 28, 2017. A partnership may rely on the last sentence in paragraph (b)(2)(iv)(g)(3) of this section in regulation project REG-104397-18 (2018-41 I.R.B. 558) (see § 601.601(d)(2)(ii)(*b*) of this chapter) for the partnership's taxable years ending on or after September 28, 2017, and ending before the partnership's taxable year that includes September 24, 2019. Furthermore, the last sentence of paragraph (b)(2)(ii)(*b*)(*3*) of this section and paragraphs (b)(2)(ii)(*b*)(*4*) through (*7*) and (b)(2)(ii)(*c*) of this section apply to partnership taxable years ending on or after October 9, 2019. However, taxpayers may apply the last sentence of paragraph (b)(2)(ii)(*b*)(*3*) of this section and paragraphs (b)(2)(ii)(*b*)(*4*) through (*7*) and (b)(2)(ii)(*c*) of this section for partnership taxable years ending on or after October 5, 2016. For partnership taxable years ending before October 9, 2019, see § 1.704-1 as contained in 26 CFR part 1 revised as of April 1, 2019.

(b) Rules relating to foreign tax expenditures.—*(1) In general.*—Except as otherwise provided in this paragraph (b)(1)(ii)(*b*)(*1*), the provisions of paragraphs (b)(3)(iv) and (b)(4)(viii) of this section (regarding the allocation of creditable foreign taxes) apply for partnership taxable years beginning on or after October 19, 2006. The rules that apply to allocations of creditable foreign taxes made in partnership taxable years beginning before October 19, 2006 are contained in § 1.704-1T(b)(1)(ii)(*b*)(*1*) and (b)(4)(xi) as in effect before October 19, 2006 (see 26 CFR part 1 revised as of April 1, 2005). However, taxpayers may rely on the provisions of paragraphs (b)(3)(iv) and (b)(4)(viii) of this section for partnership taxable years beginning on or after April 21, 2004. Except as provided in the next sentence, the provisions of paragraphs (b)(4)(viii)(*a*)(*1*), (b)(4)(viii)(*c*)(*1*), (b)(4)(viii)(*c*)(*2*)(*ii*) and (*iii*), (b)(4)(viii)(*c*)(*3*) and (*4*), and (b)(4)(viii)(*d*)(*1*) (as in effect on July 24, 2019) and in paragraphs (b)(6)(i), (ii), and (iii) of this section (*Examples 1, 2*, and *3*) apply for partnership taxable years that both begin on or after January 1, 2016, and end after February 4, 2016. For partnership taxable years beginning after December 31, 2019, paragraph (b)(4)(viii)(*d*)(*1*) of this section applies. For the rules that apply to partnership taxable years beginning on or after October 19, 2006, and before January 1, 2016, and to taxable years that both begin on or after January 1, 2016, and end on or before February 4, 2016, see § 1.704-1(b)(1)(ii)(*b*), (b)(4)(viii)(*a*)(*1*), (b)(4)(viii)(*c*)(*1*), (b)(4)(viii)(*c*)(*2*)(*ii*) and (*iii*), (b)(4)(viii)(*c*)(*3*) and (*4*), (b)(4)(viii)(*d*)(*1*), and (b)(5), *Example 25* (as contained in 26 CFR part 1 revised as of April 1, 2015).

(2) Transition rule.—Transition relief is provided herein to partnerships whose agreements were entered into prior to April 21, 2004. In such case, if there has been no material modification to the partnership agreement on or after April 21, 2004, then the partnership may apply the provisions of paragraph (b) of this section as if the amendments made by paragraphs (b)(3)(iv) and (b)(4)(viii) of this section had not occurred. If the partnership agreement was materially modified on or after April 21, 2004, then the rules provided in paragraphs (b)(3)(iv) and (b)(4)(viii) of this section shall apply to the later of the taxable year beginning on or after October 19, 2006, or the taxable year within which the material modification occurred, and to all subsequent taxable years. If the partnership agreement was materially modified on or after April 21, 2004, and before a tax year beginning on or after October 19, 2006, see §§ 1.704-1T(b)(1)(ii)(*b*)(*1*) and 1.704-1T(b)(4)(xi) as in effect prior to October 19, 2006 (26 CFR part 1 revised as of April 1, 2005). For purposes of this paragraph (b)(1)(ii)(*b*)(*2*), any change in ownership constitutes a material modification to the partnership agreement. This transition rule does not apply to any taxable year (and all subsequent taxable years) in which persons that are related to each other (within the meaning of section 267(b) and 707(b)) collectively have the power to amend the partnership agreement without the consent of any unrelated party.

(3) Special rules for certain inter-branch payments.—(i) *In general.*—The provisions of § 1.704-1(b)(4)(viii)(*d*)(*3*) apply for partnership taxable years ending after February 9, 2015. See 26 CFR 1.704-1T(b)(4)(viii)(*d*)(*3*) (revised as of April 1, 2014) for rules applicable to taxable years beginning on or after January 1, 2012, and ending on or before February 9, 2015.

(*ii*) *Transition rule.*—Transition relief is provided by this paragraph (b)(1)(ii)(*b*)(*3*)(*ii*) to partnerships whose agreements were entered into before February 14, 2012. In such cases, if there has been no material modification to the partnership agreement on or after February 14, 2012, then, for taxable years beginning on or after January 1, 2012, and before January 1, 2016, and for taxable years that both begin on or after January 1, 2012, and end on or before February 4, 2016, these partnerships may apply the provisions of § 1.704-1(b)(4)(viii)(*c*)(*3*)(*ii*) and (b)(4)(viii)(*d*)(*3*) (see 26 CFR part 1 revised as of April 1, 2011). For taxable years that both begin on or after January 1, 2016, and end after February 4, 2016, these partnerships may apply the provisions of § 1.704-1(b)(4)(viii)(*d*)(*3*) (see 26 CFR part 1 revised as of April 1, 2011). For purposes of this paragraph (b)(1)(ii)(*b*)(*3*), any change in ownership constitutes a material modification to the partnership agreement. The transition rule in this paragraph (b)(1)(ii)(*b*)(*3*)(*ii*) does not apply to any taxable year in which persons bearing a relationship to each other that is specified in section 267(b) or section 707(b) collectively have the power to amend the partnership agreement without the consent of any unrelated party (and all subsequent taxable years).

(4) Special rules for covered asset acquisitions.—Paragraphs (b)(4)(viii)(*c*)(*4*)(*v*) through (*vii*) of this section apply to covered asset acquisitions (CAAs) (as defined in § 1.901(m)-1(a)(13)) occurring on or after March 23, 2020. Taxpayers may, however, choose to apply paragraphs (b)(4)(viii)(*c*)(*4*)(*v*) through (*vii*) of this section before the date paragraphs (b)(4)(viii)(*c*)(*4*)(*v*) through (*vii*) of this section are applicable provided that they (along with any persons that are related (within the meaning of section 267(b) or 707(b)) to the taxpayer)—

(*i*) Consistently apply paragraphs (b)(4)(viii)(*c*)(*4*)(*v*) through (*vii*) of this section, § 1.901(m)-1, and §§ 1.901(m)-3 through 1.901(m)-8 (excluding § 1.901(m)-4(e)) to all CAAs occurring on or after January 1, 2011, and consistently apply § 1.901(m)-2 (excluding § 1.901(m)-2(d)) to all CAAs occurring on or after December 7, 2016, on any original or amended tax return for each taxable year for which the application of the provisions listed in this paragraph (b)(1)(ii)(*b*)(*4*)(*i*) affects the tax liability and for which the statute of limitations does not preclude assessment or the filing of a claim for refund, as applicable;

(*ii*) File all tax returns described in paragraph (b)(1)(ii)(*b*)(*4*)(*i*) of this section for any taxable year ending on or before March 23, 2020, no later than March 23, 2021; and

(*iii*) Make appropriate adjustments to take into account deficiencies that would have resulted from the consistent application under paragraph (b)(1)(ii)(*b*)(*4*)(*i*) of this section for taxable years that are not open for assessment.

(iii) *Effect of other sections.*—The determination of a partner's distributive share of income, gain, loss, deduction, or credit (or item thereof) under section 704(b) and this paragraph is not conclusive as to the tax treatment of a partner with respect to such distributive share. For example, an allocation of loss or deduction to a partner that is respected under section 704(b) and this paragraph may not be deductible by such partner if the partner lacks the requisite motive for economic gain (see, *e.g.*, *Goldstein v. Commissioner*, 364 F.2d 734 (2d Cir. 1966)), or may be disallowed for that taxable year (and held in suspense) if the limitations of section 465 or section 704(d) are applicable. Similarly, an allocation that is respected under section 704(b) and this paragraph nevertheless may be reallocated under other provisions, such as section 482, section 704(e)(2), section 706(d) (and related assignment of income principles), and paragraph (b)(2)(ii) of § 1.751-1. If a partnership has a section 754 election in effect, a partner's distributive share of partnership income, gain, loss, or deduction may be affected as provided in § 1.743-1 (see paragraph (b)(2)(iv)(*m*)(2) of this section). A deduction that appears to be a nonrecourse deduction deemed to be in accordance with the partners' interests in the partnership may not be such because purported nonrecourse liabilities of the partnership in fact constitute equity rather than debt. The examples in paragraph (b)(5) of this section concern the validity of allocations under section 704(b) and this paragraph and, except as noted, do not address the effect of other sections or limitations on such allocations.

(iv) *Other possible tax consequences.*—Allocations that are respected under section 704(b) and this paragraph may give rise to other tax consequences, such as those resulting from the application of section 61, section 83, section 751, section 2501, paragraph (f) of § 1.46-3, § 1.47-6, paragraph (b)(1) of § 1.721-1 (and related principles), and paragraph (e) of § 1.752-1. The examples in paragraph (b)(5) of this section concern the validity of allocations under section 704(b) and this paragraph and, except as noted, do not address other tax consequences that may result from such allocations.

(v) *Purported allocations.*—Section 704(b) and this paragraph do not apply to a purported allocation if it is made to a person who is not a partner of the partnership (see section 7701(a)(2) and paragraph (d) of § 301.7701-3) or to a person who is not receiving the purported allocation in his capacity as a partner (see section 707(a) and paragraph (a) of § 1.707-1).

(vi) *Section 704(c) determinations.*—Section 704(c) and § 1.704-3 generally require that if property is contributed by a partner to a partnership, the partners' distributive shares of income, gain, loss, and deduction, as computed for tax purposes, with respect to the property are determined so as to take account of the variation between the adjusted tax basis and fair market value of the property. Although section 704(b) does not directly determine the partners' distributive shares of tax items governed by section 704(c), the partners' distributive shares of tax items may be determined under section 704(c) and § 1.704-3 (depending on the allocation method chosen by the partnership under § 1.704-3) with reference to the partners' distributive shares of the corresponding book items, as determined under section 704(b) and this paragraph. (See paragraphs (b)(2)(iv)(*d*) and (b)(4)(i) of this section.) See § 1.704-3 for methods of making allocations under section 704(c), and § 1.704-3(d)(2) for a special rule in determining the amount of book items if the remedial allocation method is chosen by the partnership. See also paragraph (b)(5) *Example (13)* (i) of this section.

(vii) *Bottom line allocations.*—Section 704(b) and this paragraph are applicable to allocations of income, gain, loss, deduction, and credit, allocations of specific items of income, gain, loss, deduction, and credit, and allocations of partnerhip net or"bottom line" taxable income and loss. An allocation to a partner of a share of partnership net or "bottom line" taxable income or loss shall be treated as an allocation to such partner of the same share of each item of income, gain, loss, and deduction that is taken into account in computing such net or "bottom line" taxable income or loss. See example (15)(i) of paragraph (b)(5) of this section.

(2) *Substantial economic effect.*—(i) *Two-part analysis.*—The determination of whether an allocation of income, gain, loss, or deduction (or item thereof) to a partner has substantial economic effect involves a two-part analysis that is made as of the end of the partnership taxable year to which the allocation relates. First, the allocation must have economic effect (within the meaning of paragraph (b)(2)(ii) of this section). Second, the economic effect of the allocation must be substantial (within the meaning of paragraph (b)(2)(iii) of this section).

(ii) *Economic effect.*—*(a) Fundamental principles.*—In order for an allocation to have economic effect, it must be consistent with the underlying economic arrangement of the partners. This means that in the event there is an economic benefit or economic burden that corresponds to an allocation, the partner to whom the allocation is made must receive such economic benefit or bear such economic burden.

(b) Three requirements.—Based on the principles contained in paragraph (b)(2)(ii)(*a*) of this section, and except as otherwise provided in this paragraph, an allocation of income, gain, loss, or deduction (or item thereof) to a partner will have economic effect if, and only if, throughout the full term of the partnership, the partnership agreement provides—

(1) For the determination and maintenance of the partners' capital accounts in accordance with the rules of paragraph (b)(2)(iv) of this section,

(2) Upon liquidation of the partnership (or any partner's interest in the partnership), liquidating distributions are required in all cases to be made in accordance with the positive capital account balances of the partners, as determined after taking into account all capital account adjustments for the partnership taxable year during which such liquidation occurs (other than those made pursuant to this requirement (2) and requirement (3) of this paragraph (b)(2)(ii)(*b*)), by the end of such taxable year (or, if later, within 90 days after the date of such liquidation), and

(3) If such partner has a deficit balance in his capital account following the liquidation of his interest in the partnership, as determined after taking into account all capital account adjustments for the partnership taxable year during which such liquidation occurs (other than those made pursuant to this requirement *(3)*), he is unconditionally obligated to restore the amount of such deficit balance to the partnership by the end of such taxable year (or, if later, within 90 days after the date of such liquidation), which amount shall, upon liquidation of the partnership, be paid to creditors of the partnership or distributed to other partners in accordance with their positive capital account balances (in accordance with requirement (2) of this paragraph (b)(2)(ii)(*b*)). Notwithstanding the partnership agreement, an obligation to restore a deficit balance in a partner's capital account, including an obligation described in paragraph (b)(2)(ii)(*c*)(*1*) of this section, will not be respected for purposes of this section to the extent the obligation is disregarded under paragraph (b)(2)(ii)(*c*)(*4*) of this section.

(4) For purposes of paragraphs (b)(2)(ii)(*b*)(*1*) through (3) of this section, a partnership taxable year shall be determined without regard to section 706(c)(2)(A).

(5) The requirements in paragraphs (b)(2)(ii)(*b*)(2) and (3) of this section are not violated if all or part of the partnership interest of one or more partners is purchased (other than in connection with the liquidation of the partnership) by the partnership or by one or more partners (or one or more persons related, within the meaning of section 267(b) (without modification by section 267(e)(1)) or section 707(b)(1), to a partner) pursuant to an agreement negotiated at arm's length by persons who at the time such agreement is entered into have materially adverse interests and if a principal purpose of such purchase and sale is not to avoid the principles of the second sentence of paragraph (b)(2)(ii)(*a*) of this section.

(6) The requirement in paragraph (b)(2)(ii)(*b*)(2) of this section is not violated if, upon the liquidation of the partnership, the capital accounts of the partners are increased or decreased pursuant to paragraph (b)(2)(iv)(*f*) of this section as of the date of such liquidation and the partnership makes liquidating distributions within the time set out in the requirement in paragraph (b)(2)(ii)(*b*)(2) of this section in the ratios of the partners' positive capital accounts, except that it does not distribute reserves reasonably required to provide for liabilities (contingent or otherwise) of the partnership and installment obligations owed to the partnership, so long as such withheld amounts are distributed as soon as practicable and in the ratios of the partners' positive capital account balances.

(7) See *Examples 1.(i)* and *(ii)*, *4.(i)*, *8.(i)*, and *16.(i)* of paragraph (b)(5) of this section for issues concerning paragraph (b)(2)(ii)(*b*) of this section.

(c) Obligation to restore deficit.—*(1) Other arrangements treated as obligations to restore deficits.*—If a partner is not expressly obligated to restore the deficit balance in such partner's capital account, such partner nevertheless will be treated as obligated to restore the deficit balance in his capital account (in accordance with the requirement in paragraph (b)(2)(ii)(*b*)(3) of this section and subject to paragraph (b)(2)(ii)(*c*)(2) of this section) to the extent of—

(A) The outstanding principal balance of any promissory note (of which such partner is the maker) contributed to the partnership by such partner (other than a promissory note that is readily tradable on an established securities market), and

(B) The amount of any unconditional obligation of such partner (whether imposed by the partnership agreement or by state or local law) to make subsequent contributions to the partnership (other than pursuant to a promissory note of which such partner is the maker).

(2) Satisfaction requirement.—For purposes of paragraph (b)(2)(ii)(*c*)(*1*) of this section, a promissory note or unconditional obligation is taken into account only if it is required to be satisfied at a time no later than the end of the partnership taxable year in which such partner's interest is liquidated (or, if later, within 90 days after the date of such liquidation). If a promissory note referred to in paragraph (b)(2)(ii)(*c*)(*1*) of this section is negotiable, a partner will be considered required to satisfy such note within the time period specified in this paragraph (b)(2)(ii)(*c*)(*2*) if the partnership agreement provides that, in lieu of actual satisfaction, the partnership will retain such note and such partner will contribute to the partnership the excess, if any, of the outstanding principal balance of such note over its fair market value at the time of liquidation. See paragraph (b)(2)(iv)(*d*)(*2*) of this section. See *Examples 1.(ix)* and *(x)* of paragraph (b)(5) of this section.

(3) Related party notes.—For purposes of paragraph (b)(2) of this section, if a partner contributes a promissory note to the partnership during a partnership taxable year beginning after December 29, 1988, and the maker of such note is a person related to such partner (within the meaning of § 1.752-4(b)(1)), then such promissory note shall be treated as a promissory note of which such partner is the maker.

(4) Obligations disregarded.—*(A) General rule.*—A partner in no event will be considered obligated to restore the deficit balance in his capital account to the partnership (in accordance with the requirement in paragraph (b)(2)(ii)(*b*)(*3*) of this section) to the extent such partner's obligation is a bottom dollar payment obligation that is not recognized under § 1.752-2(b)(3) or is not legally enforceable, or the facts and circumstances otherwise indicate a plan to circumvent or avoid such obligation. See paragraphs (b)(2)(ii)(*f*), (b)(2)(ii)(*h*), and (b)(4)(vi) of this section for other rules regarding such obligation. To the extent a partner is not considered obligated to restore the deficit balance in the partner's capital account to the partnership (in accordance with the requirement in paragraph (b)(2)(ii)(*b*)(*3*) of this section), the obligation is disregarded and paragraph (b)(2) of this section and § 1.752-2 are applied as if the obligation did not exist.

(B) Factors indicating plan to circumvent or avoid obligation.—In the case of an obligation to restore a deficit balance in a partner's capital account upon liquidation of a partnership, paragraphs (b)(2)(ii)(*c*)(*4*)(B)(i) through (iv) of this section provide a non-exclusive list of factors that may indicate a plan to circumvent or avoid the obligation. For purposes of making determinations under this paragraph (b)(2)(ii)(*c*)(*4*), the weight to be given to any particular factor depends on the particular case and the presence or absence of any particular factor is not, in itself, necessarily indicative of whether or not the obligation is respected. The following factors are taken into consideration for purposes of this paragraph (b)(2):

(i) The partner is not subject to commercially reasonable provisions for enforcement and collection of the obligation.

(ii) The partner is not required to provide (either at the time the obligation is made or periodically) commercially reasonable documentation regarding the partner's financial condition to the partnership.

(iii) The obligation ends or could, by its terms, be terminated before the liquidation of the partner's interest in the partnership or when the partner's capital account as provided in § 1.704-1(b)(2)(iv) is negative other than when a transferee partner assumes the obligation.

(iv) The terms of the obligation are not provided to all the partners in the partnership in a timely manner.

(d) Alternate test for economic effect.—If—

(1) Requirements *(1)* and *(2)* of paragraph (b)(2)(ii)(*b*) of this section are satisfied, and

(2) The partner to whom an allocation is made is not obligated to restore the deficit balance in his capital account to the partnership (in accordance with requirement *(3)* of paragraph (b)(2)(ii)(*b*) of this section), or is obligated to restore only a limited dollar amount of such deficit balance, and

(3) The partnership agreement contains a "qualified income offset,"

such allocation will be considered to have economic effect under this paragraph (b)(2)(ii)(*d*) to the extent such allocation does not cause or increase a deficit balance in such partner's capital account (in excess of any limited dollar amount of such deficit balance that such partner is obligated to restore) as of the end of the partnership taxable year to which such allocation relates. In determining the extent to which the previous sentence is satisfied, such partner's capital account also shall be reduced for—

(4) Adjustments that, as of the end of such year, reasonably are expected to be made to such partner's capital account under paragraph (b)(2)(iv)(*k*) of this section for depletion allowances with respect to oil and gas properties of the partnership, and

(5) Allocations of loss and deduction that, as of the end of such year, reasonably are expected to be made to such partner pursuant to section 704(e)(2), section 706(d), and paragraph (b)(2)(ii) of § 1.751-1, and

(6) Distributions that, as of the end of such year, reasonably are expected to be made to such partner to the extent they exceed offsetting increases to such partner's capital account that reasonably are expected to occur during (or prior to) the partnership taxable years in which such distributions reasonably are expected to be made (other than increases pursuant to a minimum gain chargeback under paragraph (b)(4)(iv)(*e*) of this section or under § 1.704-2(f); however, increases to a partner's capital account pursuant to a minimum gain chargeback requirement are taken into account as an offset to distributions of nonrecourse liability proceeds that are reasonably expected to be made and that are allocable to an increase in partnership minimum gain).

For purposes of determining the amount of expected distributions and expected capital account increases described in *(6)* above, the rule set out in paragraph (b)(2)(iii)(*c*) of this section concerning the presumed value of partnership property shall apply. The partnership agreement contains a "qualified income offset" if, and only if, it provides that a partner who unexpectedly receives an adjustment, allocation, or distribution described in *(4)*, *(5)*, or *(6)* above, will be allocated items of income and gain (consisting of a pro rata portion of each item of partnership income, including gross income, and gain for such year) in an amount and manner sufficient to eliminate such deficit balance as quickly as possible. Allocations of items of income and gain made pursuant to the immediately preceding sentence shall be deemed to be made in accordance with the partners' interests in the partnership if requirements *(1)* and *(2)* of paragraph (b)(2)(ii)(*b*) of this section are satisfied. See examples (1)(iii), (iv), (v), (vi), (viii), (ix), and (x), (15), and (16)(ii) of paragraph (b)(5) of this section.

(e) Partial economic effect.—If only a portion of an allocation made to a partner with respect to a partnership taxable year has economic effect, both the portion that has economic effect and the portion that is reallocated shall consist of a proportionate share of all items that made up the allocation to such partner for such year. See examples (15)(ii) and (iii) of paragraph (b)(5) of this section.

(f) Reduction of obligation to restore.—If requirements *(1)* and *(2)* of paragraph (b)(2)(ii)(*b*) of this section are satisfied, a partner's obligation to restore the deficit balance in his capital account (or any limited dollar amount thereof) to the partnership may be eliminated or reduced as of the end of a partnership taxable year without affecting the validity of prior allocations (see paragraph (b)(4)(vi) of this section) to the extent the deficit balance (if any) in such partner's capital account, after reduction for the items described in *(4)*, *(5)*, and *(6)* of paragraph (b)(2)(ii)(*d*) of this section, will not exceed the partner's remaining obligation (if any) to restore the deficit balance in his capital account. See example (l)(viii) of paragraph (b)(5) of this section.

(g) Liquidation defined.—For purposes of this paragraph, a liquidation of a partner's interest in the partnership occurs upon the earlier of (1) the date upon which there is a liquidation of the partnership, or (2) the date upon which there is a liquidation of the partner's interest in the partnership under paragraph (d) of § 1.761-1. For purposes of this paragraph, the liquidation of a partnership occurs upon the earlier of (3) the date upon which the partnership is terminated under section 708(b)(1), or (4) the date upon which the partnership ceases to be a going concern (even though it may continue in existence for the purpose of winding up its affairs, paying its debts, and distributing any remaining balance to its partners). Requirements (2) and (3) of paragraph (b)(2)(ii)(*b*) of this section will be

considered unsatisfied if the liquidation of a partner's interest in the partnership is delayed after its primary business activities have been terminated (for example, by continuing to engage in a relatively minor amount of business activity, if such actions themselves do not cause the partnership to terminate pursuant to section 708(b)(1)) for a principal purpose of deferring any distribution pursuant to requirement (2) of paragraph (b)(2)(ii)(*b*) of this section or deferring any partner's obligation under requirement (3) of paragraph (b)(2)(ii)(*b*) of this section.

(*h*) *Partnership agreement defined.*—For purposes of this paragraph, the partnership agreement includes all agreements among the partners, or between one or more partners and the partnership, concerning affairs of the partnership and responsibilities of partners, whether oral or written, and whether or not embodied in a document referred to by the partners as the partnership agreement. Thus, in determining whether distributions are required in all cases to be made in accordance with the partners' positive capital account balances (requirement (2) of paragraph (b)(2)(ii)(*b*) of this section), and in determining the extent to which a partner is obligated to restore a deficit balance in his capital account (requirement (3) of paragraph (b)(2)(ii)(*b*) of this section), all arrangements among partners, or between one or more partners and the partnership relating to the partnership, direct and indirect, including puts, options, and other buy-sell agreements, and any other "stop-loss" arrangement, are considered to be part of the partnership agreement. (Thus, for example, if one partner who assumes a liability of the partnership is indemnified by another partner for a portion of such liability, the indemnifying partner (depending upon the particular facts) may be viewed as in effect having a partial deficit makeup obligation as a result of such indemnity agreement.) In addition, the partnership agreement includes provisions of Federal, State, or local law that govern the affairs of the partnership or are considered under such law to be a part of the partnership agreement (see the last sentence of paragraph (c) of §1.761-1). For purposes of this paragraph (b)(2)(ii)(*h*), an agreement with a partner or a partnership shall include an agreement with a person related, within the meaning of section 267(b) (without modification by section 267(e)(1)) or section 707(b)(1), to such partner or partnership. For purposes of the preceding sentence, sections 267(b) and 707(b)(1) shall be applied for partnership taxable years beginning after December 29, 1988, by (*1*) substituting "80 percent or more" for "more than 50 percent" each place it appears in such sections, (*2*) excluding brothers and sisters from the members of a person's family, and (*3*) disregarding section 267(f)(1)(A).

(*i*) *Economic effect equivalence.*—Allocations made to a partner that do not otherwise have economic effect under this paragraph (b)(2)(ii) shall nevertheless be deemed to have economic effect, provided that as of the end of each partnership taxable year a liquidation of the partnership at the end of such year or at the end of any future year would produce the same economic results to the partners as would occur if requirements (*1*), (*2*), and (*3*) of paragraph (b)(2)(ii)(*b*) of this section had been satisfied, regardless of the economic performance of the partnership. See examples (4)(ii) and (iii) of paragraph (b)(5) of this section.

(iii) *Substantiality.*—*(a) General rules.*—Except as otherwise provided in this paragraph (b)(2)(iii), the economic effect of an allocation (or allocations) is substantial if there is a reasonable possibility that the allocation (or allocations) will affect substantially the dollar amounts to be received by the partners from the partnership, independent of tax consequences. Notwithstanding the preceding sentence, the economic effect of an allocation (or allocations) is not substantial if, at the time the allocation becomes part of the partnership agreement, (*1*) the after-tax economic consequences of at least one partner may, in present value terms, be enhanced compared to such consequences if the allocation (or allocations) were not contained in the partnership agreement, and (2) there is a strong likelihood that the after-tax economic consequences of no partner will, in present value terms, be substantially diminished compared to such consequences if the allocation (or allocations) were not contained in the partnership agreement. In determining the after-tax economic benefit or detriment to a partner, tax consequences that result from the interaction of the allocation with such partner's tax attributes that are unrelated to the partnership will be taken into account. See examples (5) and (9) of paragraph (b)(5) of this section. The economic effect of an allocation is not substantial in the two situations described in paragraphs (b)(2)(iii)(*b*) and (*c*) of this section. However, even if an allocation is not described therein, its economic effect may be insubstantial under the general rules stated in this paragraph (b)(2)(iii)(*a*). References in this paragraph (b)(2)(iii) to allocations includes capital account adjustments made pursuant to paragraph (b)(2)(iv)(*k*) of this section. References in this paragraph (b)(2)(iii) to a comparison to consequences arising if an allocation (or allocations) were not contained in the partnership agreement mean that the allocation (or allocations) is determined in accordance with the partners' interests in the partnership (within the meaning of paragraph (b)(3) of this section), disregarding the allocation (or allocations) being tested under this paragraph (b)(2)(iii).

(*b*) *Shifting tax consequences.*—The economic effect of an allocation (or allocations) in a partnership taxable year is not substantial if, at the time the allocation (or allocations) becomes part of the partnership agreement, there is a strong likelihood that—

(*1*) The net increases and decreases that will be recorded in the partners' respective capital accounts for such taxable year will not differ substantially from the net increases and decreases that would be recorded in such partners' respective capital accounts for such year if the allocations were not contained in the partnership agreement, and

(*2*) The total tax liability of the partners (for their respective taxable years in which the allocations will be taken into account) will be less than if the allocations were not contained in the partnership agreement (taking into account tax consequences that result from the interaction of the allocation (or allocations) with partner tax attributes that are unrelated to the partnership).

If, at the end of a partnership taxable year to which an allocation (or allocations) relates, the net increases and decreases that are recorded in the partners' respective capital accounts do not differ substantially from the net increases and decreases that would have been recorded in such partners' respective capital accounts had the allocation (or allocations) not been contained in the partnership agreement, and the total tax liability of the partners is (as described in (2) above) less than it would have been had the allocation (or allocations) not been contained in the partnership agreement, it will be presumed that, at the time the allocation (or allocations) became part of such partnership agreement, there was a strong likelihood that these results would occur. This presumption may be overcome by a showing of facts and circumstances that prove otherwise. See examples (6), (7)(ii) and (iii), and (10)(ii) of paragraph (b)(5) of this section.

(*c*) *Transitory allocations.*—If a partnership agreement provides for the possibility that one or more allocations (the "original allocation(s)") will be largely offset by one or more other allocations (the "offsetting allocations(s)"), and, at the time the allocations become part of the partnership agreement, there is a strong likelihood that—

(*1*) The net increases and decreases that will be recorded in the partners' respective capital accounts for the taxable years to which the allocations relate will not differ substantially from the net increases and decreases that would be recorded in such partners' respective capital accounts for such years if the original allocation(s) and offsetting allocation(s) were not contained in the partnership agreement, and

(*2*) The total tax liability of the partners (for their respective taxable years in which the allocations will be taken into account) will be less than if the allocations were not contained in the partnership agreement (taking into account tax consequences that result from the interaction of the allocation (or allocations) with partner tax attributes that are unrelated to the partnership)

the economic effect of the original allocation(s) and offsetting allocation(s) will not be substantial. If, at the end of a partnership taxable year to which an offsetting allocation(s) relates, the net increases and decreases recorded in the partners' respective capital accounts do not differ substantially from the net increases and decreases that would have been recorded in such partners' respective capital accounts had the original allocation(s) and the offsetting allocation(s) not been contained in the partnership agreement, and the total tax liability of the partners is (as described in (2) above) less than it would have been had such allocations not been contained in the partnership agreement, it will be presumed that, at the time the allocations became part of the partnership agreement, there was a strong likelihood that these results would occur. This presumption may be overcome by a showing of facts and circumstances that prove otherwise. See examples (1)(xi), (2), (3), (7), (8)(ii), and (17) of paragraph (b)(5) of this section. Notwithstanding the foregoing, the original allocation(s) and the offsetting allocation(s) will not be insubstantial (under this paragraph (b)(2)(iii)(*c*)) and, for purposes of paragraph (b)(2)(iii)(*a*), it will be presumed that there is a reasonable possibility that the allocations will affect substantially the dollar amounts to be received by the partners from the partnership if, at the time the allocations become part of the partnership agreement, there is a strong likelihood that the offsetting allocation(s) will not, in large part, be made within five years after the original allocation(s) is made (determined on a first-in, first-out basis). See example (2) of paragraph (b)(5) of this section. For purposes of applying the provisions of this paragraph (b)(2)(iii) (and paragraphs (b)(2)(ii)(*d*)(6) and (b)(3)(iii) of this section), the adjusted tax basis of partnership property (or, if partnership property is properly reflected on the books of the partnership at a book value that differs from its adjusted tax basis, the book value of such property) will be presumed to be the fair market value of such property, and adjustments to the adjusted tax basis (or book value) of such property will be presumed to be matched by corresponding changes in such property's fair market value. Thus, there cannot be a strong likelihood that the economic effect of an allocation (or allocations) will be largely offset by an allocation (or allocations) of gain or loss from the disposition of partnership property. See examples (1)(vi) and (xi) of paragraph (b)(5) of this section.

(d) Partners that are look-through entities or members of a consolidated group.—(1) In general.—For purposes of applying paragraphs (b)(2)(iii)(*a*), (*b*), and (*c*) of this section to a partner that is a look-through entity, the tax consequences that result from the interaction of the allocation with the tax attributes of any person that is an owner, or in the case of a trust or estate, the beneficiary, of an interest in such a partner, whether directly or indirectly through one or more look-through entities, must be taken into account. For purposes of applying paragraphs (b)(2)(iii)(*a*), (*b*), and (*c*) of this section to a partner that is a member of a consolidated group (within the meaning of §1.1502- 1(h)), the tax consequences that result from the interaction of the allocation with the tax attributes of the consolidated group and with the tax attributes of another member with respect to a separate return year must be taken into account. See paragraph (b)(5) *Example 29* of this section.

(2) Look-through entity.—For purposes of this paragraph (b)(2)(iii)(*d*), a *look-through entity* means—

(i) A partnership;

(ii) A subchapter S corporation;

(iii) A trust or an estate;

(iv) An entity that is disregarded for Federal tax purposes, such as a qualified subchapter S subsidiary under section 1361(b)(3), an entity that is disregarded as an entity separate from its owner under §§301.7701-1 through 301.7701-3 of this chapter, or a qualified REIT subsidiary within the meaning of section 856(i)(2); or

(v) A controlled foreign corporation if United States shareholders of the controlled foreign corporation in the aggregate own, directly or indirectly, at least 10 percent of the capital or profits of the partnership on any day during the partnership's taxable year. In such case, the controlled foreign corporation shall be treated as a look-through entity, but only with respect to allocations of income, gain, loss, or deduction (or items thereof) that enter into the computation of a United States shareholder's inclusion under section 951(a) with respect to the controlled foreign corporation, enter into any person's income attributable to a United States shareholder's inclusion under section 951(a) with respect to the controlled foreign corporation, or would enter into the computations described in this paragraph if such items were allocated to the controlled foreign corporation. See paragraph (b)(2)(iii)(*d*)(6) for the definition of indirect ownership.

(3) Controlled foreign corporations.—For purposes of this section, the term *controlled foreign corporation* means a controlled foreign corporation as defined in section 957(a) or section 953(c). In the case of a controlled foreign corporation that is a look-through entity, the tax attributes to be taken into account are those of any person that is a United States shareholder (as defined in paragraph (b)(2)(iii)(*d*)(5) of this section) of the controlled foreign corporation, or, if the United States shareholder is a look-through entity, a United States person that owns an interest in such shareholder directly or indirectly through one or more look-through entities.

(4) United States person.—For purposes of this section, a *United States person* is a person described in section 7701(a)(30).

(5) United States shareholder.—For purposes of this section, a *United States shareholder* is a person described in section 951(b) or section 953(c).

(6) Indirect ownership.—For purposes of this section, indirect ownership of stock or another equity interest (such as an interest in a partnership) shall be determined in accordance with the principles of section 318, substituting the phrase "10 percent" for the phrase "50 percent" each time it appears.

(e) De minimis rule.—(1) Partnership taxable years beginning after May 19, 2008 and beginning before December 28, 2012.—Except as provided in paragraph (b)(2)(iii)(*e*)(*2*) of this section, for purposes of applying this paragraph (b)(2)(iii), for partnership taxable years beginning after May 19, 2008 and beginning before December 28, 2012, the tax attributes of de minimis partners need not be taken into account. For purposes of this paragraph (b)(2)(iii)(*e*)(*1*), a de minimis partner is any partner, including a look-through entity that owns, directly or indirectly, less than 10 percent of the capital and profits of a partnership, and who is allocated less than 10 percent of each partnership item of income, gain, loss, deduction, and credit. See paragraph (b)(2)(iii)(*d*)(*6*) of this section for the definition of indirect ownership.

(2) Nonapplicability of de minimis rule.—(i) Allocations that become part of the partnership agreement on or after December 28, 2012. Paragraph (b)(2)(iii)(*e*)(*1*) of this section does not apply to allocations that become part of the partnership agreement on or after December 28, 2012.

(ii) Retest for allocations that become part of the partnership agreement prior to December 28, 2012. If the de minimis partner rule of paragraph (b)(2)(iii)(*e*)(*1*) of this section was relied upon in testing the substantiality of allocations that became part of the partnership agreement before December 28, 2012, such allocations must be retested on the first day of the first partnership taxable year beginning on or after December 28, 2012, without regard to paragraph (b)(2)(iii)(*e*)(*1*) of this section.

(iv) *Maintenance of capital accounts.—(a) In general.*—The economic effect test described in paragraph (b)(2)(ii) of this section requires an examination of the capital accounts of the partners of a partnership, as maintained under the partnership agreement. Except as otherwise provided in paragraph (b)(2)(ii)(*i*) of this section, an allocation of income, gain, loss, or deduction will not have economic effect under paragraph (b)(2)(ii) of this section, and will not be deemed to be in accordance with a partner's interest in the partnership under paragraph (b)(4) of this section, unless the capital accounts of the partners are determined and maintained throughout the full term of the partnership in accordance with the capital accounting rules of this paragraph (b)(2)(iv).

(b) Basic rules.—Except as otherwise provided in this paragraph (b)(2)(iv), the partners' capital accounts will be considered to be determined and maintained in accordance with the rules of this paragraph (b)(2)(iv) if, and only if, each partner's capital account is increased by (*1*) the amount of money contributed by him to the partnership, (*2*) the fair market value of property contributed by him to the partnership (net of liabilities that the partnership is considered to assume or take subject to), and (*3*) allocations to him of partnership income and gain (or items thereof), including income and gain exempt from tax and income and gain described in paragraph (b)(2)(iv)(*g*) of this section, but excluding income and gain described in paragraph (b)(4)(i) of this section; and is decreased by (*4*) the amount of money distributed to him by the partnership, (*5*) the fair market value of property distributed to him by the partnership (net of liabilities that such partner is considered to assume or take subject to), (*6*) allocations to him of expenditures of the partnership described in section 705(a)(2)(B), and (*7*) allocations of partnership loss and deduction (or item thereof), including loss and deduction described in paragraph (b)(2)(iv)(*g*) of this section, but excluding items described in (*6*) above and loss or deduction described in paragraphs (b)(4)(i) or (b)(4)(iii) of this section; and is otherwise adjusted in accordance with the additional rules set forth in this paragraph (b)(2)(iv). For purposes of this paragraph, a partner who has more than one interest in a partnership shall have a single capital account that reflects all such interests, regardless of the class of interests owned by such partner (*e.g.*, general or limited) and regardless of the time or manner in which such interests were acquired. For liabilities assumed before June 24, 2003, references to liabilities in this paragraph (b)(2)(iv)(*b*) shall include only liabilities secured by the contributed or distributed property that are taken into account under section 752(a) and (b).

(c) Treatment of liabilities.—For purposes of this paragraph (b)(2)(iv), (*1*) money contributed by a partner to a partnership includes the amount of any partnership liabilities that are assumed by such partner (other than liabilities described in paragraph (b)(2)(iv)(*b*)(*5*) of this section that are assumed by a distributee partner) but does not include increases in such partner's share of partner-

ship liabilities (see section 752(a)), and (2) money distributed to a partner by a partnership includes the amount of such partner's individual liabilities that are assumed by the partnership (other than liabilities described in paragraph (b)(2)(iv)(*b*)(2) of this section that are assumed by the partnership) but does not include decreases in such partner's share of partnership liabilities (see section 752(b)). For purposes of this paragraph (b)(2)(iv)(*c*), liabilities are considered assumed only to the extent the assuming party is thereby subjected to personal liability with respect to such obligation, the obligee is aware of the assumption and can directly enforce the assuming party's obligation, and, as between the assuming party and the party from whom the liability is assumed, the assuming party is ultimately liable.

(d) Contributed property.—(1) In general.—The basic capital accounting rules contained in paragraph (b)(2)(iv)(*b*) of this section require that a partner's capital account be increased by the fair market value of property contributed to the partnership by such partner on the date of contribution. See *Example 13*(i) of paragraph (b)(5) of this section. Consistent with section 752(c), section 7701(g) does not apply in determining such fair market value.

(2) Contribution of promissory notes.—Notwithstanding the general rule of paragraph (b)(2)(iv)(*b*)(2) of this section, except as provided in this paragraph (b)(2)(iv)(*d*)(2), if a promissory note is contributed to a partnership by a partner who is the maker of such note, such partner's capital account will be increased with respect to such note only when there is a taxable disposition of such note by the partnership or when the partner makes principal payments on such note. See example (1)(ix) of paragraph (b)(5) of this section. The first sentence of this paragraph (b)(2)(iv)(*d*)(2) shall not apply if the note referred to therein is readily tradable on an established securities market. See also paragraph (b)(2)(ii)(*c*) of this section. Furthermore, a partner whose interest is liquidated will be considered as satisfying his obligation to restore the deficit balance in his capital account to the extent of (*i*) the fair market value, at the time of contribution, of any negotiable promissory note (of which such partner is the maker) that such partner contributes to the partnership on or after the date his interest is liquidated and within the time specified in paragraph (b)(2)(ii)(*b*)(3) of this section, and (*ii*) the fair market value, at the time of liquidation, of the unsatisfied portion of any negotiable promissory note (of which such partner is the maker) that such partner previously contributed to the partnership. For purposes of the preceding sentence, the fair market value of a note will be no less than the outstanding principal balance of such note, provided that such note bears interest at a rate no less than the applicable federal rate at the time of valuation.

(3) Section 704(c) considerations.—Section 704(c) and § 1.704-3 govern the determination of the partners' distributive shares of income, gain, loss, and deduction, as computed for tax purposes, with respect to property contributed to a partnership (see paragraph (b)(1)(vi) of this section). In cases where section 704(c) and § 1.704-3 apply to partnership property, the capital accounts of the partners will not be considered to be determined and maintained in accordance with the rules of this paragraph (b)(2)(iv) unless the partnership agreement requires that the partners' capital accounts be adjusted in accordance with paragraph (b)(2)(iv)(*g*) of this section for allocations to them of income, gain, loss, and deduction (including depreciation, depletion, amortization, or other cost recovery) as computed for book purposes, with respect to the property. See, however, § 1.704-3(d)(2) for a special rule in determining the amount of book items if the partnership chooses the remedial allocation method. See also *Example (13)* (i) of paragraph (b)(5) of this section. Capital accounts are not adjusted to reflect allocations under section 704(c) and § 1.704-3 (e.g., tax allocations of precontribution gain or loss).

(4) Exercise of noncompensatory options.—Solely for purposes of paragraph (b)(2)(iv)(*b*)(2) of this section, the fair market value of the property contributed on the exercise of a noncompensatory option (as defined in § 1.721-2(f)) does not include the fair market value of the option privilege, but does include the consideration paid to the partnership to acquire the option and the fair market value of any property (other than the option) contributed to the partnership on the exercise of the option. With respect to convertible debt, the fair market value of the property contributed on the exercise of the option is the adjusted issue price of the debt and the accrued but unpaid qualified stated interest (as defined in § 1.1273-1(c)) on the debt immediately before the conversion, plus the fair market value of any property (other than the convertible debt) contributed to the partnership on the exercise of the option. See *Examples 31* through *35* of paragraph (b)(5) of this section.

(e) Distributed property.—(1) In general.—The basic capital accounting rules contained in paragraph (b)(2)(iv)(*b*) of this section require that a partner's capital account be decreased by the fair market value of property distributed by the partnership (without regard to section 7701(g)) to such partner (whether in connection with a liquidation or otherwise). To satisfy this requirement, the capital accounts of the partners first must be adjusted to reflect the manner in which the unrealized income, gain, loss, and deduction inherent in such property (that has not been reflected in the capital accounts previously) would be allocated among the partners if there were a taxable disposition of such property for the fair market value of such property (taking section 7701(g) into account) on the date of distribution. See example (14)(v) of paragraph (b)(5) of this section.

(2) Distribution of promissory notes.—Notwithstanding the general rule of paragraph (b)(2)(iv)(*b*)(5), except as provided in this paragraph (b)(2)(iv)(*e*)(2), if a promissory note is distributed to a partner by a partnership that is the maker of such note, such partner's capital account will be decreased with respect to such note only when there is a taxable disposition of such note by the partner or when the partnership makes principal payments on the note. The previous sentence shall not apply if a note distributed to a partner by a partnership who is the maker of such note is readily tradable on an established securities market. Furthermore, the capital account of a partner whose interest in a partnership is liquidated will be reduced to the extent of (*i*) the fair market value, at the time of distribution, of any negotiable promissory note (of which such partnership is the maker) that such partnership distributes to the partner on or after the date such partner's interest is liquidated and within the time specified in paragraph (b)(2)(ii)(*b*)(2) of this section, and (*ii*) the fair market value, at the time of liquidation, of the unsatisfied portion of any negotiable promissory note (of which such partnership is the maker) that such partnership previously distributed to the partner. For purposes of the preceding sentence, the fair market value of a note will be no less than the outstanding principal balance of such note, provided that such note bears interest at a rate no less than the applicable federal rate at the time of valuation.

(f) Revaluations of property.—A partnership agreement may, upon the occurrence of certain events, increase or decrease the capital accounts of the partners to reflect a revaluation of partnership property (including intangible assets such as goodwill) on the partnership's books. Capital accounts so adjusted will not be considered to be determined and maintained in accordance with the rules of this paragraph (b)(2)(iv) unless—

(1) The adjustments are based on the fair market value of partnership property (taking section 7701(g) into account) on the date of adjustment, as determined under paragraph (b)(2)(iv)(*h*) of this section. See *Example 33* of paragraph (b)(5) of this section.

(2) The adjustments reflect the manner in which the unrealized income, gain, loss, or deduction inherent in such property (that has not been reflected in the capital accounts previously) would be allocated among the partners if there were a taxable disposition of such property for such fair market value on that date, and

(3) The partnership agreement requires that the partners' capital accounts be adjusted in accordance with paragraph (b)(2)(iv)(*g*) of this section for allocations to them of depreciation, depletion, amortization, and gain or loss, as computed for book purposes, with respect to such property, and

(4) The partnership agreement requires that the partners' distributive shares of depreciation, depletion, amortization, and gain or loss, as computed for tax purposes, with respect to such property be determined so as to take account of the variation between the adjusted tax basis and book value of such property in the same manner as under section 704(c) (see paragraph (b)(4)(i) of this section), and

(5) The adjustments are made principally for a substantial non-tax business purpose—

(i) In connection with a contribution of money or other property (other than a *de minimis* amount) to the partnership by a new or existing partner as consideration for an interest in the partnership, or

(ii) In connection with the liquidation of the partnership or a distribution of money or other property (other than a *de minimis* amount) by the partnership to a retiring or continuing partner as consideration for an interest in the partnership, or

(iii) In connection with the grant of an interest in the partnership (other than a *de minimis* interest) on or after May 6, 2004, as consideration for the provision of services to or for the benefit of the partnership by an existing partner acting in a partner capacity, or

by a new partner acting in a partner capacity or in anticipation of being a partner, or

(iv) In connection with the issuance by the partnership of a noncompensatory option (other than an option for a de minimis partnership interest), or

(v) Under generally accepted industry accounting practices, provided substantially all of the partnership's property (excluding money) consists of stock, securities, commodities, options, warrants, futures, or similar instruments that are readily tradable on an established securities market.

See examples (14) and (18) of paragraph (b)(5) of this section. If the capital accounts of the partners are not adjusted to reflect the fair market value of partnership property when an interest in the partnership is acquired from or relinquished to the partnership, paragraphs (b)(1)(iii) and (b)(1)(iv) of this section should be consulted regarding the potential tax consequences that may arise if the principles of section 704(c) are not applied to determine the partners' distributive shares of depreciation, depletion, amortization, and gain or loss, as computed for tax purposes, with respect to such property.

(6) Notwithstanding paragraph (b)(2)(iv)(*f*)(*5*) of this section, the revaluation is required under § 1.721(c)-3(d)(1) as a condition of the application of the gain deferral method (as described in § 1.721(c)-3(b)) and is pursuant to an event described in this paragraph (b)(2)(iv)(*f*)(*6*). If an interest in a partnership is contributed to a section 721(c) partnership (as defined in § 1.721(c)-1(b)(14)), the partnership whose interest is contributed may revalue its property in accordance with this section. In this case, the revaluation by the partnership whose interest was contributed must occur immediately before the contribution. If a partnership that revalues its property pursuant to this paragraph owns an interest in another partnership, the partnership in which it owns an interest may also revalue its property in accordance with this section. When multiple partnerships revalue under this paragraph (b)(2)(iv)(*f*)(*6*), the revaluations occur in order from the lowest-tier partnership to the highest-tier partnership.

(g) Adjustments to reflect book value.—(1) In general.—Under paragraphs (b)(2)(iv)(*d*) and (b)(2)(iv)(*f*) of this section, property may be properly reflected on the books of the partnership at a book value that differs from the adjusted tax basis of such property. In these circumstances, paragraphs (b)(2)(iv)(*d*)(*3*) and (b)(2)(iv)(*f*)(*3*) of this section provide that the capital accounts of the partners will not be considered to be determined and maintained in accordance with the rules of this paragraph (b)(2)(iv) unless the partnership agreement requires the partners' capital accounts to be adjusted in accordance with this paragraph (b)(2)(iv)(*g*) for allocations to them of depreciation, depletion, amortization, and gain or loss, as computed for book purposes, with respect to such property. In determining whether the economic effect of an allocation of book items is substantial, consideration will be given to the effect of such allocation on the determination of the partners' distributive shares of corresponding tax items under section 704(c) and paragraph (b)(4)(i) of this section. See example (17) of paragraph (b)(5) of this section. If an allocation of book items under the partnership agreement does not have substantial economic effect (as determined under paragraphs (b)(2)(ii) and (b)(2)(iii) of this section), or is not otherwise respected under this paragraph, such items will be reallocated in accordance with the partners' interests in the partnership, and such reallocation will be the basis upon which the partners' distributive shares of the corresponding tax items are determined under section 704(c) and paragraph (b)(4)(i) of this section. See examples (13), (14), and (18) of paragraph (b)(5) of this section.

(2) Payables and receivables.—References in this paragraph (b)(2)(iv) and paragraph (b)(4)(i) of this section to book and tax depreciation, depletion, amortization, and gain or loss with respect to property that has an adjusted tax basis that differs from book value include, under analogous rules and principles, the unrealized income or deduction with respect to accounts receivable, accounts payable, and other accrued but unpaid items.

(3) Determining amount of book items.—The partners' capital accounts will not be considered adjusted in accordance with this paragraph (b)(2)(iv)(*g*) unless the amount of book depreciation, depletion, or amortization for a period with respect to an item of partnership property is the amount that bears the same relationship to the book value of such property as the depreciation (or cost recovery deduction), depletion, or amortization computed for tax purposes with respect to such property for such period bears to the adjusted tax basis of such property. If such property has a zero adjusted tax basis, the book depreciation, depletion, or amortization may be determined under any reasonable method selected by the partnership. For purposes of the preceding sentence, additional first year depreciation deduction under section 168(k) is not a reasonable method.

(h) Determinations of fair market value.—(1) In general.—For purposes of this paragraph (b)(2)(iv), the fair market value assigned to property contributed to a partnership, property distributed by a partnership, or property otherwise revalued by a partnership, will be regarded as correct, provided that (*1*) such value is reasonably agreed to among the partners in arm's-length negotiations, and (*2*) the partners have sufficiently adverse interests. If, however, these conditions are not satisfied and the value assigned to such property is overstated or understated (by more than an insignificant amount), the capital accounts of the partners will not be considered to be determined and maintained in accordance with the rules of this paragraph (b)(2)(iv). Valuation of property contributed to the partnership, distributed by the partnership, or otherwise revalued by the partnership shall be on a property-by-property basis, except to the extent the regulations under section 704(c) permit otherwise.

(2) Adjustments for noncompensatory options.—The value of partnership property as reflected on the books of the partnership must be adjusted to account for any outstanding noncompensatory options (as defined in § 1.721-2(f)) at the time of a revaluation of partnership property under paragraph (b)(2)(iv)(*f*) or (*s*) of this section. If the fair market value of outstanding noncompensatory options (as defined in § 1.721-2(f)) as of the date of the adjustment exceeds the consideration paid to the partnership to acquire the options, then the value of partnership property as reflected on the books of the partnership must be reduced by that excess to the extent of the unrealized income or gain in partnership property (that has not been reflected in the capital accounts previously). This reduction is allocated only to properties with unrealized appreciation in proportion to their respective amounts of unrealized appreciation. If the consideration paid to the partnership to acquire the outstanding noncompensatory options (as defined in § 1.721-2(f)) exceeds the fair market value of such options as of the date of the adjustment, then the value of partnership property as reflected on the books of the partnership must be increased by that excess to the extent of the unrealized loss in partnership property (that has not been reflected in the capital accounts previously). This increase is allocated only to properties with unrealized loss in proportion to their respective amounts of unrealized loss. However, any reduction or increase shall take into account the economic arrangement of the partners with respect to the property.

(i) Section 705(a)(2)(B) expenditures.—(1) In general.—The basic capital accounting rules contained in paragraph (b)(2)(iv)(*b*) of this section require that a partner's capital account be decreased by allocations made to such partner of expenditures described in section 705(a)(2)(B). See example (11) of paragraph (b)(5) of this section. If an allocation of these expenditures under the partnership agreement does not have substantial economic effect (as determined under paragraphs (b)(2)(ii) and (b)(2)(iii) of this section), or is not otherwise respected under this paragraph, such expenditures will be reallocated in accordance with the partners' interest in the partnership.

(2) Expenses described in section 709.—Except for amounts with respect to which an election is properly made under section 709(b), amounts paid or incurred to organize a partnership or to promote the sale of (or to sell) an interest in such a partnership shall, solely for purposes of this paragraph, be treated as section 705(a)(2)(B) expenditures, and upon liquidation of the partnership no further capital account adjustments will be made in respect thereof.

(3) Disallowed losses.—If a deduction for a loss incurred in connection with the sale or exchange of partnership property is disallowed to the partnership under section 267(a)(1) or section 707(b), that deduction shall, solely for purposes of this paragraph, be treated as a section 705(a)(2)(B) expenditure.

(j) Basis adjustments to section 38 property.—The capital accounts of the partners will not be considered to be determined and maintained in accordance with the rules of this paragraph (b)(2)(iv) unless such capital accounts are adjusted by the partners' shares of any upward or downward basis adjustments allocated to them under this paragraph (b)(2)(iv)(*j*). When there is a reduction in the adjusted tax basis of partnership section 38 property under section 48(q)(1) or section 48(q)(3), section 48(q)(6) provides for an equivalent downward adjustment to the aggregate basis of partnership interests (and no additional adjustment is made under section 705(a)(2)(B)). These downward basis adjustments shall be shared among the partners in

the same proportion as the adjusted tax basis or cost of (or the qualified investment in) such section 38 property is allocated among the partners under paragraph (f) of § 1.46-3 (or paragraph (a)(4)(iv) of § 1.48-8). Conversely, when there is an increase in the adjusted tax basis of partnership section 38 property under section 48(q)(2), section 48(q)(6) provides for an equivalent upward adjustment to the aggregate basis or partnership interests. These upward adjustments shall be allocated among the partners in the same proportion as the investment tax credit from such property is recaptured by the partners under § 1.47-6.

(k) Depletion of oil and gas properties.—(1) In general.—The capital accounts of the partners will not be considered to be determined and maintained in accordance with the rules of this paragraph (b)(2)(iv) unless such capital accounts are adjusted for depletion and gain or loss with respect to the oil or gas properties of the partnership in accordance with this paragraph (b)(2)(iv)(*k*).

(2) Simulated depletion.—Except as provided in paragraph (b)(2)(iv)(*k*)(*3*) of this section, a partnership shall, solely for purposes of maintaining capital accounts under this paragraph, compute simulated depletion allowances with respect to its oil and gas properties at the partnership level. These allowances shall be computed on each depletable oil or gas property of the partnership by using either the cost depletion method or the percentage depletion method (computed in accordance with section 613 at the rates specified in section 613A(c)(5) without regard to the limitations of section 613A, which theoretically could apply to any partner) for each partnership taxable year that the property is owned by the partnership and subject to depletion. The choice between the simulated cost depletion method and the simulated percentage depletion method shall be made on a property-by-property basis in the first partnership taxable year beginning after April 30, 1986, for which it is relevant for the property, and shall be binding for all partnership taxable years during which the oil or gas property is held by the partnership. The partnership shall make downward adjustments to the capital accounts of the partners for the simulated depletion allowance with respect to each oil or gas property of the partnership, in the same proportion as such partners (or their predecessors in interest) were properly allocated the adjusted tax basis of each such property. The aggregate capital account adjustments for simulated percentage depletion allowances with respect to an oil or gas property of the partnership shall not exceed the aggregate adjusted tax basis allocated to the partners with respect to such property. Upon the taxable disposition of an oil or gas property by a partnership, such partnership's simulated gain or loss shall be determined by subtracting its simulated adjusted basis in such property from the amount realized upon such disposition. (The partnership's simulated adjusted basis in an oil or gas property is determined in the same manner as adjusted tax basis except that simulated depletion allowances are taken into account instead of actual depletion allowances.) The capital accounts of the partners shall be adjusted upward by the amount of any simulated gain in proportion to such partners' allocable shares of the portion of the total amount realized from the disposition of such property that exceeds the partnership's simulated adjusted basis in such property. The capital accounts of such partners shall be adjusted downward by the amount of any simulated loss in proportion to such partners' allocable shares of the total amount realized from the disposition of such property that represents recovery of the partnership's simulated adjusted basis in such property. See section 613A(c)(7)(D) and the regulations thereunder and paragraph (b)(4)(v) of this section. See example (19)(iv) of paragraph (b)(5) of this section.

(3) Actual depletion.—Pursuant to section 613A(c)(7)(D) and the regulations thereunder, the depletion allowance under section 611 with respect to the oil and gas properties of a partnership is computed separately by the partners. Accordingly, in lieu of adjusting the partners' capital accounts as provided in paragraph (b)(2)(iv)(*k*)(2) of this section, the partnership may make downward adjustments to the capital account of each partner equal to such partner's depletion allowance with respect to each oil or gas property of the partnership (for the partner's taxable year that ends with or within the partnership's taxable year). The aggregate adjustments to the capital account of a partner for depletion allowances with respect to an oil or gas property of the partnership shall not exceed the adjusted tax basis allocated to such partner with respect to such property. Upon the taxable disposition of an oil or gas property by a partnership, the capital account of each partner shall be adjusted upward by the amount of any excess of such partner's allocable share of the total amount realized from the disposition of such property over such partner's remaining adjusted tax basis in such property. If there is no such excess, the capital account of such partner shall be adjusted downward by the amount of any excess of such partner's remaining adjusted tax basis in such property over such partner's allocable share of the total amount realized from the disposition thereof. See section 613A(c)(7)(4)(D) and the regulations thereunder and paragraph (b)(4)(v) of this section.

(4) Effect of book values.—If an oil or gas property of the partnership is, under paragraphs (b)(2)(iv)(*d*) or (b)(2)(iv)(*f*) of this section, properly reflected on the books of the partnership at a book value that differs from the adjusted tax basis of such property, the rules contained in this paragraph (b)(2)(iv)(*k*) and paragraph (b)(4)(v) of this section shall be applied with reference to such book value. A revaluation of a partnership oil or gas property under paragraph (b)(2)(iv)(*f*) of this section may give rise to a reallocation of the adjusted tax basis of such property, or a change in the partners' relative shares of simulated depletion from such property, only to the extent permitted by section 613A(c)(7)(D) and the regulations thereunder.

(l) Transfers of partnership interests.—The capital accounts of the partners will not be considered to be determined and maintained in accordance with the rules of this paragraph (b)(2)(iv) unless, upon the transfer of all or a part of an interest in the partnership, the capital account of the transferor that is attributable to the transferred interest carries over to the transferee partner. (See paragraph (b)(2)(iv)(*m*) of this section for rules concerning the effect of a section 754 election on the capital accounts of the partners.) If the transfer of an interest in a partnership causes a termination of the partnership under section 708(b)(1)(B), the capital account of the transferee partner and the capital accounts of the other partners of the terminated partnership carry over to the new partnership that is formed as a result of the termination of the partnership under § 1.708-1(b)(1)(iv). Moreover, the deemed contribution of assets and liabilities by the terminated partnership to a new partnership and the deemed liquidation of the terminated partnership that occur under § 1.708-1(b)(1)(iv) are disregarded for purposes of paragraph (b)(2)(iv) of this section. See Example 13 of paragraph (b)(5) of this section and the example in § 1.708-1(b)(1)(iv). The previous three sentences apply to terminations of partnerships under section 708(b)(1)(B) occurring on or after May 9, 1997; however, the sentences may be applied to terminations occurring on or after May 9, 1996, provided that the partnership and its partners apply the sentences to the termination in a consistent manner.

(m) Section 754 elections.—(1) In general.—The capital accounts of the partners will not be considered to be determined and maintained in accordance with the rules of this paragraph (b)(2)(iv) unless, upon adjustment to the adjusted tax basis of partnership property under section 732, 734, or 743, the capital accounts of the partners are adjusted as provided in this paragraph (b)(2)(iv)(*m*).

(2) Section 743 adjustments.—In the case of a transfer of all or a part of an interest in a partnership that has a section 754 election in effect for the partnership taxable year in which such transfer occurs, adjustments to the adjusted tax basis of partnership property under section 743 shall not be reflected in the capital account of the transferee partner or on the books of the partnership, and subsequent capital account adjustments for distributions (see paragraph (b)(2)(iv)(*e*)(1) of this section) and for depreciation, depletion, amortization, and gain or loss with respect to such property will disregard the effect of such basis adjustment. The preceding sentence shall not apply to the extent such basis adjustment is allocated to the common basis of partnership property under paragraph (b)(1) of § 1.734-2; in these cases, such basis adjustment shall, except as provided in paragraph (b)(2)(iv)(*m*)(*5*) of this section, give rise to adjustments to the capital accounts of the partners in accordance with their interests in the partnership under paragraph (b)(3) of this section. See examples (13)(iii) and (iv) of paragraph (b)(5) of this section.

(3) Section 732 adjustments.—In the case of a transfer of all or a part of an interest in a partnership that does not have a section 754 election in effect for the partnership taxable year in which such transfer occurs, adjustments to the adjusted tax basis of partnership property under section 732(d) will be treated in the capital accounts of the partners in the same manner as section 743 basis adjustments are treated under paragraph (b)(2)(iv)(*m*)(2) of this section.

(4) Section 734 adjustments.—Except as provided in paragraph (b)(2)(iv)(*m*)(*5*) of this section, in the case of a distribution of property in liquidation of a partner's interest in the partnership by a partnership that has a section 754 election in effect for the partnership taxable year in which the distribution occurs, the partner who

receives the distribution that gives rise to the adjustment to the adjusted tax basis of partnership property under section 734 shall have a corresponding adjustment made to his capital account. If such distribution is made other than in liquidation of a partner's interest in the partnership, however, except as provided in paragraph (b)(2)(iv)(*m*)(*5*) of this section, the capital accounts of the partners shall be adjusted by the amount of the adjustment to the adjusted tax basis of partnership property under section 734, and such capital account adjustment shall be shared among the partners in the manner in which the unrealized income and gain that is displaced by such adjustment would have been shared if the property whose basis is adjusted were sold immediately prior to such adjustment for its recomputed adjusted tax basis.

(*5*) *Limitations on adjustments.*—Adjustments may be made to the capital account of a partner (or his successor in interest) in respect of basis adjustments to partnership property under sections 732, 734, and 743 only to the extent that such basis adjustments (i) are permitted to be made to one or more items of partnership property under section 755, and (ii) result in an increase or a decrease in the amount at which such property is carried on the partnership's balance sheet, as computed for book purposes. For example, if the book value of partnership property exceeds the adjusted tax basis of such property, a basis adjustment to such property may be reflected in a partner's capital account only to the extent such adjustment exceeds the difference between the book value of such property and the adjusted tax basis of such property prior to such adjustment.

(*n*) *Partnership level characterization.*—Except as otherwise provided in paragraph (b)(2)(iv)(*k*) of this section, the capital accounts of the partners will not be considered to be determined and maintained in accordance with the rules of this paragraph (b)(2)(iv) unless adjustments to such capital accounts in respect of partnership income, gain, loss, deduction, and section 705(a)(2)(B) expenditures (or item thereof) are made with reference to the Federal tax treatment of such items (and in the case of book items, with reference to the Federal tax treatment of the corresponding tax items) at the partnership level, without regard to any requisite or elective tax treatment of such items at the partner level (for example, under section 58(i)). However, a partnership that incurs mining exploration expenditures will determine the Federal tax treatment of income, gain, loss, and deduction with respect to the property to which such expenditures relate at the partnership level only after first taking into account the elections made by its partners under section 617 and section 703(b)(4).

(*o*) *Guaranteed payments.*—Guaranteed payments to a partner under section 707(c) cause the capital account of the recipient partner to be adjusted only to the extent of such partner's distributive share of any partnership deduction, loss, or other downward capital account adjustment resulting from such payment.

(*p*) *Minor discrepancies.*—Discrepancies between the balances in the respective capital accounts of the partners and the balances that would be in such respective capital accounts if they had been determined and maintained in accordance with this paragraph (b)(2)(iv) will not adversely affect the validity of an allocation, provided that such discrepancies are minor and are attributable to good faith error by the partnership.

(*q*) *Adjustments where guidance is lacking.*—If the rules of this paragraph (b)(2)(iv) fail to provide guidance on how adjustments to the capital accounts of the partners should be made to reflect particular adjustments to partnership capital on the books of the partnership, such capital accounts will not be considered to be determined and maintained in accordance with those rules unless such capital account adjustments are made in a manner that (*1*) maintains equality between the aggregate governing capital accounts of the partners and the amount of partnership capital reflected on the partnership's balance sheet, as computed for book purposes, (*2*) is consistent with the underlying economic arrangement of the partners, and (*3*) is based, wherever practicable, on Federal tax accounting principles.

(*r*) *Restatement of capital accounts.*—With respect to partnerships that began operating in a taxable year beginning before May 1, 1986, the capital accounts of the partners of which have not been determined and maintained in accordance with the rules of this paragraph (b)(2)(iv) since inception, such capital accounts shall not be considered to be determined and maintained in accordance with the rules of this paragraph (b)(2)(iv) for taxable years beginning after April 30, 1986, unless either—

(*1*) such capital accounts are adjusted, effective for the first partnership taxable year beginning after April 30, 1986, to reflect the fair market value of partnership property as of the first day of such taxable year, and in connection with such adjustment, the rules contained in paragraph (b)(2)(iv)(*f*)(*2*), (*3*), and (*4*) of this section are satisfied, or

(*2*) the differences between the balance in each partner's capital account and the balance that would be in such partner's capital account if capital accounts had been determined and maintained in accordance with this paragraph (b)(2)(iv) throughout the full term of the partnership are not significant (for example, such differences are solely attributable to a failure to provide for treatment of section 709 expenses in accordance with the rules of paragraph (b)(2)(iv)(*i*)(*2*) of this section or to a failure to follow the rules in paragraph (b)(2)(iv)(*m*) of this section), and capital accounts are adjusted to bring them into conformity with the rules of this paragraph (b)(2)(iv) no later than the end of the first partnership taxable year beginning after April 30, 1986.

(*3*) With respect to a partnership that began operating in a taxable year beginning before May 1, 1986, modifications to the partnership agreement adopted on or before November 1, 1988, to make the capital account adjustments required to comply with this paragraph, and otherwise to satisfy the requirements of this paragraph, will be treated as if such modifications were included in the partnership agreement before the end of the first partnership taxable year beginning after April 30, 1986. However, compliance with the previous sentences will have no bearing on the validity of allocations that relate to partnership taxable years beginning before May 1, 1986.

(*s*) *Adjustments on the exercise of a noncompensatory option.*—A partnership agreement may grant a partner, on the exercise of a noncompensatory option (as defined in § 1.721-2(f)), a right to share in partnership capital that exceeds (or is less than) the sum of the consideration paid to the partnership to acquire and exercise such option. Where such an agreement exists, capital accounts will not be considered to be determined and maintained in accordance with the rules of this paragraph (b)(2)(iv) unless the following requirements are met:

(*1*) In lieu of revaluing partnership property under paragraph (b)(2)(iv)(*f*) of this section immediately before the exercise of the option, the partnership revalues partnership property in accordance with the provisions of paragraphs (b)(2)(iv)(*f*)(*1*) through (*f*)(*4*) of this section immediately after the exercise of the option.

(*2*) In determining the capital accounts of the partners (including the exercising partner) under paragraph (b)(2)(iv)(*s*)(*1*) of this section, the partnership first allocates any unrealized income, gain, or loss in partnership property (that has not been reflected in the capital accounts previously) to the exercising partner to the extent necessary to reflect that partner's right to share in partnership capital under the partnership agreement, and then allocates any remaining unrealized income, gain, or loss (that has not been reflected in the capital accounts previously) to the existing partners, to reflect the manner in which the unrealized income, gain, or loss in partnership property would be allocated among those partners if there were a taxable disposition of such property for its fair market value on that date. For purposes of the preceding sentence, if the exercising partner's initial capital account as determined under § 1.704-1(b)(2)(iv)(*b*) and (*d*)(*4*) of this section would be less than the amount that reflects the exercising partner's right to share in partnership capital under the partnership agreement, then only income or gain may be allocated to the exercising partner from partnership properties with unrealized appreciation, in proportion to their respective amounts of unrealized appreciation. If the exercising partner's initial capital account, as determined under § 1.704-1(b)(2)(iv)(*b*) and (*d*)(*4*) of this section, would be greater than the amount that reflects the exercising partner's right to share in partnership capital under the partnership agreement, then only loss may be allocated to the exercising partner from partnership properties with unrealized loss, in proportion to their respective amounts of unrealized loss. However, any allocation must take into account the economic arrangement of the partners with respect to the property.

(*3*) If, after making the allocations described in paragraph (b)(2)(iv)(*s*)(*2*) of this section, the exercising partner's capital account does not reflect that partner's right to share in partnership capital under the partnership agreement, then the partnership reallocates partnership capital between the existing partners and the exercising partner so that the exercising partner's capital account reflects the exercising partner's right to share in partnership capital under the partnership agreement (a capital account reallocation). Any increase or decrease in the capital accounts of existing partners that occurs as a result of a capital account reallocation under this paragraph (b)(2)(iv)(*s*)(*3*) must be allocated among the existing partners in accordance with the principles of this section. See *Example 32* of paragraph (b)(5) of this section.

(*4*) The partnership agreement requires corrective allocations so as to take into account all capital account reallocations made under paragraph (b)(2)(iv)(*s*)(*3*) of this section (see paragraph (b)(4)(x) of this section). See *Example 32* of paragraph (b)(5) of this section.

(3) *Partner's interest in the partnership.*—(i) *In general.*—References in section 704(b) and this paragraph to a partner's interest in the partnership, or to the partners' interests in the partnership, signify the manner in which the partners have agreed to share the economic benefit or burden (if any) corresponding to the income, gain, loss, deduction, or credit (or item thereof) that is allocated. Except with respect to partnership items that cannot have economic effect (such as nonrecourse deductions of the partnership), this sharing arrangement may or may not correspond to the overall economic arrangement of the partners. (For example, in the case of an unexpected downward adjustment to the capital account of a partner who does not have a deficit makeup obligation that causes such partner to have a negative capital account, it may be necessary to allocate a disproportionate amount of gross income of the partnership to such partner for such year so as to bring that partner's capital account back up to zero.) Thus, a partner who has a 50 percent overall interest in the partnership may have a 90 percent interest in a particular item of income or deduction. The determination of a partner's interest in a partnership shall be made by taking into account all facts and circumstances relating to the economic arrangement of the partners.

(ii) *Factors considered.*—In determining a partner's interest in the partnership, the following factors are among those that will be considered:

(*a*) The partners' relative contributions to the partnership,

(*b*) The interests of the partners in economic profits and losses (if different than that in taxable income or loss),

(*c*) The interests of the partners in cash flow and other nonliquidating distributions, and

(*d*) The rights of the partners to distributions of capital upon liquidation.

The provisions of this subparagraph (b)(3) are illustrated by examples (1)(i) and (ii), (4)(i), (5)(i) and (ii), (6), (7)(i), (ii), and (iv), (8), (10)(ii), (16)(i), and (19)(iii) of paragraph (b)(5) of this section. See paragraph (b)(4)(i) of this section concerning rules for determining the partners' interests in the partnership with respect to certain tax items.

(iii) *Certain determinations.*—If—

(*a*) Requirements (*1*) and (*2*) of paragraph (b)(2)(ii)(*b*) of this section are satisfied, and

(*b*) All or a portion of an allocation of income, gain, loss, or deduction made to a partner for a partnership taxable year does not have economic effect under paragraph (b)(2)(ii) of this section,

the partners' interests in the partnership with respect to the portion of the allocation that lacks economic effect will be determined by comparing the manner in which distributions (and contributions) would be made if all partnership property were sold at book value and the partnership were liquidated immediately following the end of the taxable year to which the allocation relates with the manner in which distributions (and contributions) would be made if all partnership property were sold at book value and the partnership were liquidated immediately following the end of the prior taxable year, and adjusting the result for the items described in (*4*), (*5*), and (*6*) of paragraph (b)(2)(ii)(*d*) of this section. A determination made under this paragraph (b)(3)(iii) will have no force if the economic effect of valid allocations made in the same manner is insubstantial under paragraph (b)(2)(iii) of this section. See examples (1)(iv), (v), and (vi), and (15)(ii) and (iii) of paragraph (b)(5) of this section.

(iv) *Special rule for creditable foreign tax expenditures.*—In determining whether an allocation of a partnership item is in accordance with the partners' interests in the partnership, the allocation of the creditable foreign tax expenditure (CFTE) (as defined in paragraph (b)(4)(viii)(*b*) of this section) must be disregarded. This paragraph (b)(3)(iv) shall not apply to the extent the partners to whom such taxes are allocated reasonably expect to claim a deduction for such taxes in determining their U.S. tax liabilities.

(4) *Special rules.*—(i) *Allocations to reflect revaluations.*—If partnership property is, under paragraphs (b)(2)(iv)(*d*) or (b)(2)(iv)(*f*) of this section, properly reflected in the capital accounts of the partners and on the books of the partnership at a book value that differs from the adjusted tax basis of such property, then depreciation, depletion, amortization, and gain or loss, as computed for book purposes, with respect to such property will be greater or less than the depreciation, depletion, amortization, and gain or loss, as computed for tax purposes, with respect to such property. In these cases the capital accounts of the partners are required to be adjusted solely for allocations of the book items to such partners (see paragraph (b)(2)(iv)(*g*) of this section), and the partners' shares of the corresponding tax items are not independently reflected by further adjustments to the partners' capital accounts. Thus, separate allocations of these tax items cannot have economic effect under paragraph (b)(2)(ii)(*b*)(*1*) of this section, and the partners' distributive shares of such tax items must (unless governed by section 704(c)) be determined in accordance with the partners' interests in the partnership. These tax items must be shared among the partners in a manner that takes account of the variation between the adjusted tax basis of such property and its book value in the same manner as variations between the adjusted tax basis and fair market value of property contributed to the partnership are taken into account in determining the partners' shares of tax items under section 704(c). See examples (14) and (18) of paragraph (b)(5) of this section.

(ii) *Credits.*—Allocations of tax credits and tax credit recapture are not reflected by adjustments to the partners' capital accounts (except to the extent that adjustments to the adjusted tax basis of partnership section 38 property in respect of tax credits and tax credit recapture give rise to capital account adjustments under paragraph (b)(2)(iv)(*j*) of this section). Thus, such allocations cannot have economic effect under paragraph (b)(2)(ii)(*b*)(*1*) of this section, and the tax credits and tax credit recapture must be allocated in accordance with the partners' interests in the partnership as of the time the tax credit or credit recapture arises. With respect to the investment tax credit provided by section 38, allocations of cost or qualified investment made in accordance with paragraph (f) of § 1.46-3 and paragraph (a)(4)(iv) of § 1.48-8 shall be deemed to be made in accordance with the partners' interests in the partnership. With respect to other tax credits, if a partnership expenditure (whether or not deductible) that gives rise to a tax credit in a partnership taxable year also gives rise to valid allocations of partnership loss or deduction (or other downward capital account adjustments) for such year, then the partners' interests in the partnership with respect to such credit (or the cost giving rise thereto) shall be in the same proportion as such partners' respective distributive shares of such loss or deduction (and adjustments). See example (11) of paragraph (b)(5) of this section. Identical principles shall apply in determining the partners' interests in the partnership with respect to tax credits that arise from receipts of the partnership (whether or not taxable).

(iii) *Excess percentage depletion.*—To the extent the percentage depletion in respect of an item of depletable property of the partnership exceeds the adjusted tax basis of such property, allocations of such excess percentage depletion are not reflected by adjustments to the partners' capital accounts. Thus, such allocations cannot have economic effect under paragraph (b)(2)(ii)(*b*)(*1*) of this section, and such excess percentage depletion must be allocated in accordance with the partners' interests in the partnership. The partners' interests in the partnership for a partnership taxable year with respect to such excess percentage depletion shall be in the same proportion as such partners' respective distributive shares of gross income from the depletable property (as determined under section 613(c)) for such year. See example (12) of paragraph (b)(5) of this section. See paragraphs (b)(2)(iv)(*k*) and (b)(4)(v) of this section for special rules concerning oil and gas properties of the partnership.

(iv) *Allocations attributable to nonrecourse liabilities.*—The rules for allocations attributable to nonrecourse liabilities are contained in § 1.704-2.

(v) *Allocations under section 613A(c)(7)(D).*—Allocations of the adjusted tax basis of a partnership oil or gas property are controlled by section 613A(c)(7)(D) and the regulations thereunder. However, if the partnership agreement provides for an allocation of the adjusted tax basis of an oil or gas property among the partners, and such allocation is not otherwise governed under section 704(c) (or related principles under paragraph (b)(4)(i) of this section), that allocation will be recognized as being in accordance with the partners' interests in partnership capital under section 613A(c)(7)(D), provided (*a*) such allocation does not give rise to capital account adjustments under paragraph (b)(2)(iv)(*k*) of this section the economic effect of which is insubstantial (as determined under paragraph (b)(2)(iii) of this section), and (*b*) all other material allocations and capital account adjustments under the partnership agreement are recognized under this paragraph (b). Otherwise, such adjusted tax basis must be allocated among the partners pursuant to section 613A(c)(7)(D) in accordance with the partners' actual interests in partnership capital or income. For purposes of section 613A(c)(7)(D) the partners' allocable shares of the amount realized upon the partnership's taxable disposition of an oil or gas property will, except to the extent governed by section 704(c) (or related principles under paragraph (b)(4)(i) of this section), be determined under this paragraph (b)(4)(v). If, pursuant to paragraph (b)(2)(iv)(*k*)(2) of this section, the partners' capital accounts are adjusted to reflect the simulated depletion of an oil or gas property of the partnership, the portion of the total amount realized by the partnership upon the taxable disposition of such property that represents recovery of its simulated adjusted tax basis therein will be allocated to the partners in the same proportion as the aggregate adjusted tax basis of such property was allocated to such partners (or their predecessors in interest). If, pursuant to paragraph (b)(2)(iv)(*k*)(*3*) of this section, the partners' capital accounts are adjusted to reflect the actual depletion of an oil or gas property of the partnership, the portion of the total amount realized by the partnership upon the taxable disposition of such property that equals the partners' aggregate remaining adjusted basis therein will be allocated to the partners in proportion to their respective remaining adjusted tax bases in such property. An allocation provided by the partnership agreement of the portion of the total amount realized by the partnership on its taxable disposition of an oil or gas property that exceeds the portion of the total amount realized allocated under either of the previous two sentences (whichever is applicable) shall be deemed to be made in accordance with the partners' allocable shares of such amount realized, provided (*c*) such allocation does not give rise to capital account adjustments under paragraph (b)(2)(iv)(*k*) of this section the economic effect of which is insubstantial (as determined under paragraph (b)(2)(ii) of this section), and (*d*) all other allocations and capital account adjustments under the partnership agreement are recognized under this paragraph. Otherwise, the partners' allocable shares of the total amount realized by the partnership on its taxable disposition of an oil or gas property shall be determined in accordance with the partners' interests in the partnership under paragraph (b)(3) of this section. See example (19) of paragraph (b)(5) of this section. (See paragraph (b)(2)(iv)(*k*) of this section for the determination of appropriate adjustments to the partners' capital accounts relating to section 613A(c)(7)(D).)

(vi) *Amendments to partnership agreement.*—If an allocation has substantial economic effect under paragraph (b)(2) of this section or is deemed to be made in accordance with the partners' interests in the partnership under paragraph (b)(4) of this section under the partnership agreement that is effective for the taxable year to which such allocation relates, and such partnership agreement thereafter is modified, both the tax consequences of the modification and the facts and circumstances surrounding the modification will be closely scrutinized to determine whether the purported modification was part of the original agreement. If it is determined that the purported modification was part of the original agreement, prior allocations may be reallocated in a manner consistent with the modified terms of the agreement, and subsequent allocations may be reallocated to take account of such modified terms. For example, if a partner is obligated by the partnership agreement to restore the deficit balance in his capital account or any limited dollar amount thereof) in accordance with requirement (*3*) of paragraph (b)(2)(ii)(*b*) of this section and, thereafter, such obligation is eliminated or reduced (other than as provided in paragraph (b)(2)(ii)(*f*) of this section), or is not complied with in a timely manner, such elimination, reduction, or noncompliance may be treated as if it always were part of the partnership agreement for purposes of making any reallocations and determining the appropriate limitations period.

(vii) *Recapture.*—For special rules applicable to the allocation of recapture income or credit, see paragraph (e) of § 1.1245-1, paragraph (f) of § 1.1250-1, paragraph (c) of § 1.1254-1, and paragraph (a) of § 1.47-6.

(viii) *Allocation of creditable foreign taxes.*—(*a*) *In general.*—Allocations of creditable foreign taxes do not have substantial economic effect within the meaning of paragraph (b)(2) of this section and, accordingly, such expenditures must be allocated in accordance with the partners' interests in the partnership. See paragraph (b)(3)(iv) of this section. An allocation of a creditable foreign tax expenditure (CFTE) will be deemed to be in accordance with the partners' interests in the partnership if—

(*1*) The CFTE is allocated (whether or not pursuant to an express provision in the partnership agreement) to each partner and reported on the partnership return in proportion to the partners' CFTE category shares of income to which the CFTE relates; and

(*2*) Allocations of all other partnership items that, in the aggregate, have a material effect on the amount of CFTEs allocated to a partner pursuant to paragraph (b)(4)(viii)(*a*)(*1*) of this section are valid.

(*b*) *Creditable foreign tax expenditures (CFTEs).*—For purposes of this section, a CFTE is a foreign tax paid or accrued by a partnership that is eligible for a credit under section 901(a) or an applicable U.S. income tax treaty. A foreign tax is a CFTE for these purposes without regard to whether a partner receiving an allocation of such foreign tax elects to claim a credit for such tax. Foreign taxes paid or accrued by a partner with respect to a distributive share of partnership income, and foreign taxes deemed paid under section 902 or 960 by a corporate partner with respect to stock owned, directly or indirectly, by or for a partnership, are not taxes paid or accrued by a partnership and, therefore, are not CFTEs subject to the rules of this section. See paragraphs (e) and (f) of § 1.901-2 for rules for determining when and by whom a foreign tax is paid or accrued.

(*c*) *Income to which CFTEs relate.*—(*1*) *In general.*—For purposes of paragraph (b)(4)(viii)(*a*) of this section, CFTEs are related to net income in the partnership's CFTE category or categories to which the CFTE is allocated and apportioned in accordance with the rules of paragraph (b)(4)(viii)(*d*) of this section. Paragraph (b)(4)(viii)(*c*)(*2*) of this section provides rules for determining a partnership's CFTE categories. Paragraph (b)(4)(viii)(*c*)(*3*) of this section provides rules for determining the net income in each CFTE category. Paragraph (b)(4)(viii)(*c*)(*4*) of this section provides rules for determining a partner's CFTE category share of income, including rules that require adjustments to net income in a CFTE category for purposes of determining the partners' CFTE category share of income with respect to certain CFTEs. Paragraph (b)(4)(viii)(*c*)(*5*) of this section provides a special rule for allocating CFTEs when a partnership has no net income in a CFTE category.

(*2*) *CFTE category.*—(*i*) *Income from activities.*—A CFTE category is a category of net income (or loss) attributable to one or more activities of the partnership. Net income (or loss) from all the partnership's activities shall be included in a single CFTE category unless the allocation of net income (or loss) from one or more activities differs from the allocation of net income (or loss) from other activities, in which case income from each activity or group of activities that is subject to a different allocation shall be treated as net income (or loss) in a separate CFTE category.

(*ii*) *Different allocations.*—Different allocations of net income (or loss) generally will result from provisions of the partnership agreement providing for different sharing ratios for net income (or loss) from separate activities. Different allocations of net income (or loss) from separate activities generally will also result if any partnership item is shared in a different ratio than any other partnership item. A guaranteed payment described in paragraph (b)(4)(viii)(*c*)(*4*)(*ii*) of this section, gross income allocation, or other preferential allocation will result in different allocations of net income (or loss) from separate activities only if the amount of the payment or the allocation is determined by reference to income from less than all of the partnership's activities.

(*iii*) *Activity.*—Whether a partnership has one or more activities, and the scope of each activity, is determined in a reasonable manner taking into account all the facts and circumstances. In evaluating whether aggregating or disaggregating income from particular business or investment operations constitutes a reasonable method of determining the scope of an activity, the principal consideration is whether the proposed determination has the effect of separating CFTEs from the related foreign income. Relevant considerations include whether the partnership conducts business in more than one geographic location or through more than one entity or branch, and whether certain types of income are exempt from foreign tax or subject to preferential foreign tax treatment. In addition, income from a divisible part of a single activity is treated as income from a separate activity if necessary to prevent separating CFTEs from the related foreign income, such as when income from divisible parts of a single activity is subject to different allocations. See, for example, paragraph (b)(4)(viii)(*c*)(*3*)(*iv*) of this section (special allocations related to disregarded payments can give rise to subdivision of an activity into divisible parts). A guaranteed payment, gross income allocation, or other preferential allocation of income that is determined by reference to all the income from a single activity generally will not result in the division of an activity into divisible parts. See

Example 22 in paragraph (b)(5)(xxii) of this section and *Example 1* in paragraph (b)(6)(i) of this section. The partnership's activities must be determined consistently from year to year absent a material change in facts and circumstances.

(*3*) *Net income in a CFTE category*.—(*i*) *In general*.—A partnership computes net income in a CFTE category as follows: First, the partnership determines for U.S. Federal income tax purposes all of its partnership items, including items of gross income, gain, loss, deduction, and expense, and items allocated pursuant to section 704(c). For the purpose of this paragraph (b)(4)(viii)(*c*)(*3*)(*i*), the items of the partnership are determined without regard to any adjustments under section 743(b) that its partners may have to the basis of property of the partnership. However, if the partnership is a transferee partner that has a basis adjustment under section 743(b) in its capacity as a direct or indirect partner in a lower-tier partnership, the partnership does take such basis adjustment into account. Second, the partnership must assign those partnership items to its activities pursuant to paragraph (b)(4)(viii)(*c*)(*3*)(*ii*) of this section. Third, partnership items attributable to each activity are aggregated within the relevant CFTE category as determined under paragraph (b)(4)(viii)(*c*)(2) of this section in order to compute the net income in a CFTE category.

(*ii*) *Assignment of partnership items to activities*.—The items of gross income attributable to an activity must be determined in a consistent manner under any reasonable method taking into account all the facts and circumstances. Except as otherwise provided in paragraph (b)(4)(viii)(*c*)(*3*)(*iii*) of this section, expenses, losses, or other deductions must be allocated and apportioned to gross income attributable to an activity in accordance with the rules of §§1.861-8 and 1.861-8T. Under the rules §§1.861-8 and 1.861-8T, if an expense, loss, or other deduction is allocated to gross income from more than one activity, such expense, loss, or deduction must be apportioned among each such activity using a reasonable method that reflects to a reasonably close extent the factual relationship between the deduction and the gross income from such activities. See §1.861-8T(c). For the effect of disregarded payments in determining the amount of net income attributable to an activity, see paragraph (b)(4)(viii)(*c*)(*3*)(*iv*) of this section.

(*iii*) *Interest expense and research and experimental expenditures*.—The partnership's interest expense and research and experimental expenditures described in section 174 may be allocated and apportioned under any reasonable method, including but not limited to the methods prescribed in §§1.861-9 through 1.861-13T (interest expense) and §1.861-17 (research and experimental expenditures).

(*iv*) *Disregarded payments*.—An item of gross income is assigned to the activity that generates the item of income that is recognized for U.S. Federal income tax purposes. Consequently, disregarded payments are not taken into account in determining the amount of net income attributable to an activity, although a special allocation of income used to make a disregarded payment may result in the subdivision of an activity into divisible parts. See paragraph (b)(4)(viii)(*c*)(2)(*iii*) of this section, *Example 24* in paragraph (b)(5)(xxiv) of this section, and *Examples* 2 and 3 in paragraphs (b)(6)(ii) and (iii), respectively, of this section (relating to inter-branch payments).

(*4*) *CFTE category share of income*.—(*i*) *In general*.—CFTE category share of income means the portion of the net income in a CFTE category, determined in accordance with paragraph (b)(4)(viii)(*c*)(*3*) of this section as modified by paragraphs (b)(4)(viii)(*c*)(*4*)(*ii*) through (*iv*) of this section, that is allocated to a partner. To the extent provided in paragraph (b)(4)(viii)(*c*)(*4*)(*ii*) of this section, a guaranteed payment is treated as an allocation to the recipient of the guaranteed payment for this purpose. If more than one partner receives positive income allocations (income in excess of expenses) from a CFTE category, which in the aggregate exceed the total net income in the CFTE category, then such partner's CFTE category share of income equals the partner's positive income allocation from the CFTE category, divided by the aggregate positive income allocations from the CFTE category, multiplied by the net income in the CFTE category. Paragraphs (b)(4)(viii)(*c*)(*4*)(*ii*) through (*iv*) of this section require adjustments to the net income in a CFTE category for purposes of determining the partners' CFTE category share of income if one or more foreign jurisdictions impose a tax that provides for certain exclusions or deductions from the foreign taxable base. Such adjustments apply only with respect to CFTEs attributable to the taxes that allow such exclusions or deductions. Thus, net income in a CFTE category may vary for purposes of applying paragraph (b)(4)(viii)(*a*)(*1*) of this section to different CFTEs within that CFTE category.

(*ii*) *Guaranteed payments*.—Except as otherwise provided in this paragraph (b)(4)(viii)(*c*)(*4*)(*ii*), solely for purposes of applying the safe harbor provisions of paragraph (b)(4)(viii)(*a*)(*1*) of this section, net income in the CFTE category from which a guaranteed payment (within the meaning of section 707(c)) is made is increased by the amount of the guaranteed payment that is deductible for U.S. Federal income tax purposes, and such amount is treated as an allocation to the recipient of such guaranteed payment for purposes of determining the partners' CFTE category shares of income. If a foreign tax allows (whether in the current or in a different taxable year) a deduction from its taxable base for a guaranteed payment, then solely for purposes of applying the safe harbor provisions of paragraph (b)(4)(viii)(*a*)(*1*) of this section to allocations of CFTEs that are attributable to that foreign tax, net income in the CFTE category is increased only to the extent that the amount of the guaranteed payment that is deductible for U.S. Federal income tax purposes exceeds the amount allowed as a deduction for purposes of the foreign tax, and such excess is treated as an allocation to the recipient of the guaranteed payment for purposes of determining the partners' CFTE category shares of income. See *Example 1* in paragraph (b)(6)(i) of this section.

(*iii*) *Preferential allocations*.—To the extent that a foreign tax allows (whether in the current or in a different taxable year) a deduction from its taxable base for an allocation (or distribution of an allocated amount) to a partner, then solely for purposes of applying the safe harbor provisions of paragraph (b)(4)(viii)(*a*)(*1*) of this section to allocations of CFTEs that are attributable to that foreign tax, the net income in the CFTE category from which the allocation is made is reduced by the amount of the allocation, and that amount is not treated as an allocation for purposes of determining the partners' CFTE category shares of income. See *Example 1* in paragraph (b)(6)(i) of this section.

(*iv*) *Foreign law exclusions due to status of partner*.—If a foreign tax excludes an amount from its taxable base as a result of the status of a partner, then solely for purposes of applying the safe harbor provisions of paragraph (b)(4)(viii)(*a*)(*1*) of this section to allocations of CFTEs that are attributable to that foreign tax, the net income in the relevant CFTE category is reduced by the excluded amounts that are allocable to such partners. See *Example 27* in paragraph (b)(5)(xxvii) of this section.

(*v*) *Adjustments related to section 901(m)*.—If one or more assets owned by a partnership are relevant foreign assets (or RFAs) with respect to a foreign income tax, then, solely for purposes of applying the safe harbor provisions of paragraph (b)(4)(viii)(*a*)(*1*) of this section to allocations of CFTEs with respect to that foreign income tax, the net income in a CFTE category that includes partnership items of income, deduction, gain, or loss attributable to the RFA shall be increased by the amount described in paragraph (b)(4)(viii)(*c*)(*4*)(*vi*) of this section and reduced by the amount described in paragraph (b)(4)(viii)(*c*)(*4*)(*vii*) of this section. Similarly, a partner's CFTE category share of income shall be increased by the portion of the amount described in paragraph (b)(4)(viii)(*c*)(*4*)(*vi*) of this section that is allocated to the partner under §1.901(m)-5(d) and reduced by the portion of the amount described in paragraph (b)(4)(viii)(*c*)(*4*)(*vii*) of this section that is allocated to the partner under §1.901(m)-5(d). The principles of this paragraph (b)(4)(viii)(*c*)(*4*)(*v*) apply similarly when a partnership owns an RFA indirectly through one or more other partnerships. For purposes of this paragraph (b)(4)(viii)(*c*)(*4*)(*v*) and paragraphs (b)(4)(viii)(*c*)(*4*)(*vi*) and (b)(4)(viii)(*c*)(*4*)(*vii*) of this section, basis difference is defined in §1.901(m)-4, cost recovery amount is defined in §1.901(m)-5(b)(2), disposition amount is defined in §1.901(m)-5(c)(2), foreign income tax is defined in §1.901(m)-1(a)(26), RFA is defined in §1.901(m)-2(c), U.S. disposition gain is defined in §1.901(m)-1(a)(52), and U.S. disposition loss is defined in §1.901(m)-1(a)(53).

(*vi*) *Adjustment amounts for RFAs with a positive basis difference*.—With respect to RFAs with a positive basis difference, the amount referenced in paragraph (b)(4)(viii)(*c*)(*4*)(*v*) of this section is the sum of any cost recovery amounts and disposition amounts attributable to U.S. disposition loss that correspond to partnership items that are included in the net income in the CFTE category and that are taken into account for the U.S. taxable year of the partnership under §1.901(m)-5(d).

(vii) *Adjustment amounts for RFAs with a negative basis difference.*—With respect to RFAs with a negative basis difference, the amount referenced in paragraph (b)(4)(viii)(*c*)(*4*)(*v*) of this section is the sum of any cost recovery amounts and disposition amounts attributable to U.S. disposition gain that correspond to partnership items that are included in the net income in the CFTE category and that are taken into account for the U.S. taxable year of the partnership under § 1.901(m)-5(d).

(*5*) *No net income in a CFTE category.*—If a CFTE is allocated or apportioned to a CFTE category that does not have net income for the year in which the foreign tax is paid or accrued, the CFTE shall be deemed to relate to the aggregate of the net income (disregarding net losses) recognized by the partnership in that CFTE category in each of the three preceding taxable years. Accordingly, except as provided below, such CFTE must be allocated in the current taxable year in the same proportion as the allocation of the aggregate net income for the prior three-year period in order to satisfy the requirements of paragraph (b)(4)(viii)(*a*)(*1*) of this section. If the partnership does not have net income in the applicable CFTE category in either the current year or any of the previous three taxable years, the CFTE must be allocated in the same proportion that the partnership reasonably expects to allocate the aggregate net income (disregarding net losses) in the CFTE category for the succeeding three taxable years. If the partnership does not reasonably expect to have net income in the CFTE category for the succeeding three years and the partnership has net income in one or more other CFTE categories for the year in which the foreign tax is paid or accrued, the CFTE shall be deemed to relate to such other net income and must be allocated in proportion to the allocations of such other net income. If any CFTE is not allocated pursuant to the above provisions of this paragraph then the CFTE must be allocated in proportion to the partners' outstanding capital contributions.

(*d*) *Allocation and apportionment of CFTEs to CFTE categories.*—(*1*) *In general.*—CFTEs are allocated and apportioned to CFTE categories in accordance with § 1.861-20 by treating each CFTE category as a statutory grouping (with no residual grouping). See paragraphs (b)(6)(ii) and (iii) of this section (*Examples* 2 and 3), which illustrate the application of this paragraph (b)(4)(viii)(d)(1) in the case of serial disregarded payments subject to withholding tax. In addition, if as described in § 1.861-20(e), foreign law does not provide for the direct allocation or apportionment of expenses, losses or other deductions allowed under foreign law to a CFTE category of income, then such expenses, losses or other deductions must be allocated and apportioned to gross income as determined under foreign law in a manner that is consistent with the allocation and apportionment of such items for purposes of determining the net income in the CFTE categories for Federal income tax purposes pursuant to paragraph (b)(4)(viii)(*c*)(*3*) of this section.

(*2*) *Timing and base differences.*—A foreign tax imposed on an item that would be income under U.S. tax principles in another year (a timing difference) is allocated to the CFTE category that would include the income if the income were recognized for U.S. tax purposes in the year in which the foreign tax is imposed. A foreign tax imposed on an item that would not constitute income under U.S. tax principles in any year (a base difference) is allocated to the CFTE category that includes the partnership items attributable to the activity with respect to which the foreign tax is imposed. See paragraph (b)(5) *Example* 23 of this section.

(*3*) *Special rules for inter-branch payments.*—For rules relating to foreign tax paid or accrued in partnership taxable years beginning before January 1, 2012, in respect of certain inter-branch payments, see 26 CFR 1.704-1(b)(4)(viii)(*d*)(3) (revised as of April 1, 2011).

(ix) *Allocations with respect to noncompensatory options.*—(*a*) *In general.*—A partnership agreement may grant to a partner that exercises a noncompensatory option (as defined in § 1.721-2(f)) a right to share in partnership capital that exceeds (or is less than) the sum of the amounts paid to the partnership to acquire and exercise the option. In such a case, allocations of income, gain, loss, and deduction to the partners while the noncompensatory option is outstanding cannot have economic effect because, if the noncompensatory option is exercised, the exercising partner, rather than the existing partners, may receive the economic benefit or bear the economic detriment associated with that income, gain, loss, or deduction. However, allocations of partnership income, gain, loss, and deduction to the partners while the noncompensatory option is outstanding will be deemed to be in accordance with the partners' interests in the partnership only if—

(*1*) The holder of the noncompensatory option is not treated as a partner under § 1.761-3;

(*2*) The partnership agreement requires that, while a noncompensatory option is outstanding, the partnership comply with the rules of paragraph (b)(2)(iv)(*f*) of this section and that, on the exercise of the noncompensatory option, the partnership comply with the rules of paragraph (b)(2)(iv)(*s*) of this section; and

(*3*) All material allocations and capital account adjustments under the partnership agreement would be respected under section 704(b) if there were no outstanding noncompensatory options issued by the partnership. See *Examples 31* through *35* of paragraph (b)(5) of this section.

(*b*) *Substantial economic effect under sections 168(h) and 514(c)(9)(E)(i)(II).*—An allocation of partnership income, gain, loss, or deduction to the partners will be deemed to have substantial economic effect for purposes of sections 168(h) and 514(c)(9)(E)(i)(II) if—

(*1*) The allocation would meet the substantial economic effect requirements of paragraph (b)(2) of this section if there were no outstanding noncompensatory options issued by the partnership; and

(*2*) The partnership satisfies the requirements of paragraph (b)(4)(ix)(*a*)(*1*), (2), and (3) of this section.

(x) *Corrective allocations.*—(*a*) *In general.*—If partnership capital is reallocated between existing partners and a partner exercising a noncompensatory option under paragraph (b)(2)(iv)(*s*)(*3*) of this section (a capital account reallocation), then the partnership must, beginning with the taxable year of the exercise and in all succeeding taxable years until the required allocations are fully taken into account, make corrective allocations so as to take into account the capital account reallocation. A corrective allocation is an allocation (consisting of a pro rata portion of each item) for tax purposes of gross income and gain, or gross loss and deduction, that differs from the partnership's allocation of the corresponding book item. See *Example 32* of paragraph (b)(5) of this section.

(*b*) *Timing.*—Section 706 and the regulations and principles thereunder apply in determining the items of income, gain, loss, and deduction that may be subject to corrective allocation.

(*c*) *Allocation of gross income and gain and gross loss and deduction.*—If the capital account reallocation is from the historic partners to the exercising option holder, then the corrective allocations must first be made with gross income and gain. If an allocation of gross income and gain alone does not completely take into account the capital account reallocation in a given year, then the partnership must also make corrective allocations using a pro rata portion of items of gross loss and deduction as to further take into account the capital account reallocation. Conversely, if the capital account reallocation is from the exercising option holder to the historic partners, then the corrective allocations must first be made with gross loss and deduction. If an allocation of gross loss and deduction alone does not completely take into account the capital account reallocation in a given year, then the partnership must also make corrective allocations using a pro rata portion of items of gross income and gain as to further take into account the capital account reallocation.

(xi) *Section 163(j) excess items.*—Allocations of section 163(j) excess items as defined in § 1.163(j)-6(b)(6) do not have substantial economic effect under paragraph (b)(2) of this section and, accordingly, such expenditures must be allocated in accordance with the partners' interests in the partnership. See paragraph (b)(3)(iv) of this section. Allocations of section 163(j) excess items will be deemed to be in accordance with the partners' interests in the partnership if such allocations are made in accordance with § 1.163(j)-6(f).

(5) *Examples.*—The operation of the rules in this paragraph is illustrated by the following examples:

Example (1). (i) A and B form a general partnership with cash contributions of $40,000 each, which cash is used to purchase depreciable personal property at a cost of $80,000. The partnership elects under section 48(q)(4) to reduce the amount of investment tax credit in lieu of adjusting the tax basis of such property. The partnership agreement provides that A and B will have equal shares of taxable income and loss (computed without regard to cost recovery deductions) and cash flow and that all cost recovery deductions on the property will be allocated to A. The agreement further provides that the partners' capital accounts will be determined and maintained in accordance with paragraph (b)(2)(iv) of this section, but that upon liquidation of the partnership, distributions will be made equally between the partners (regardless of capital account balances) and no partner will be required to restore the deficit balance in his capital account for distribution to partners with positive capital accounts balances. In the partnership's first taxable year, it recognizes operating income equal to its operating expenses and has an additional $20,000 cost recovery deduction, which is allocated entirely to A. That A and B will be entitled to equal distributions on liquidation, even though A is allocated the entire $20,000 cost recovery deduction, indicates A will not bear the full risk of the economic loss corresponding to such deduction if such loss occurs. Under paragraph (b)(2)(ii) of this section, the allocation lacks economic effect and will be disregarded. The partners made equal contributions to the partnership, share equally in other taxable income and loss and in cash flow, and will share equally in liquidation proceeds, indicating that their actual economic arrangement is to bear the risk imposed by the potential decrease in the value of the property equally. Thus, under paragraph (b)(3) of this section the partners' interests in the partnership are equal, and the cost recovery deduction will be reallocated equally between A and B.

(ii) Assume the same facts as in (i) except that the partnership agreement provides that liquidation proceeds will be distributed in accordance with capital account balances if the partnership is liquidated during the first five years of its existence but that liquidation proceeds will be distributed equally if the partnership is liquidated thereafter. Since the partnership agreement does not provide for the requirement contained in paragraph (b)(2)(ii)(*b*)(*2*) of this section to be satisfied throughout the term of the partnership, the partnership allocations do not have economic effect. Even if the partnership agreement provided for the requirement contained in paragraph (b)(2)(ii)(*b*)(*2*) to be satisfied throughout the term of the partnership, such allocations would not have economic effect unless the requirement contained in paragraph (b)(2)(ii)(*b*)(*3*) of this section or the alternate economic effect test contained in paragraph (b)(2)(ii)(*d*) of this section were satisfied.

(iii) Assume the same facts as in (i) except that distributions in liquidation of the partnership (or any partner's interest) are to be made in accordance with the partners' positive capital account balances throughout the term of the partnership (as set forth in paragraph (b)(2)(ii)(*b*)(*2*) of this section). Assume further that the partnership agreement contains a qualified income offset (as defined in paragraph (b)(2)(ii)(*d*) of this section) and that, as of the end of each partnership taxable year, the items described in paragraphs (b)(2)(ii)(*d*)(*4*), (*5*), and (*6*) of this section are not reasonably expected to cause or increase a deficit balance in A's capital account.

	A	*B*
Capital account upon formation	$40,000	$40,000
Less: year 1 cost recovery deduction	(20,000)	0
Capital account at end of year 1	$20,000	$40,000

Under the alternate economic effect test contained in paragraph (b)(2)(ii)(*d*) of this section, the allocation of the $20,000 cost recovery deduction to A has economic effect.

(iv) Assume the same facts as in (iii) and that in the partnership's second taxable year it recognizes operating income equal to its operating expenses and has a $25,000 cost recovery deduction which, under the partnership agreement, is allocated entirely to A.

	A	*B*
Capital account at beginning of year 2	$20,000	$40,000
Less: year 2 cost recovery deduction	(25,000)	0
Capital account at end of year 2	($5,000)	$40,000

The allocation of the $25,000 cost recovery deduction to A satisfies the alternate economic effect test contained in paragraph (b)(2)(ii)(*d*) of this section only to the extent of $20,000. Therefore, only $20,000 of such allocation has economic effect, and the remaining $5,000 must be reallocated in accordance with the partners' interests in the partnership. Under the partnership agreement, if the property were sold immediately following the end of the partnership's second taxable year for $35,000 (its adjusted tax basis), the $35,000 would be distributed to B. Thus, B, and not A, bears the economic burden corresponding to $5,000 of the $25,000 cost recovery deduction allocated to A. Under paragraph (b)(3)(iii) of this section, $5,000 of such cost recovery deduction will be reallocated to B.

(v) Assume the same facts as in (iv) except that the cost recovery deduction for the partnership's second taxable year is $20,000 instead of $25,000. The allocation of such cost recovery deduction to A has economic effect under the alternate economic effect test contained in paragraph (b)(2)(ii)(*d*) of this section. Assume further that the property is sold for $35,000 immediately following the end of the partnership's second taxable year, resulting in a $5,000 taxable loss ($40,000 adjusted tax basis less $35,000 sales price), and the partnership is liquidated.

	A	*B*
Capital account at beginning of year 2	$20,000	$40,000
Less: year 2 cost recovery deduction	(20,000)	0
Capital account at end of year 2	0	$40,000
Less: loss on sale	(2,500)	(2,500)
Capital account before liquidation	($2,500)	$37,500

Under the partnership agreement the $35,000 sales proceeds are distributed to B. Since B bears the entire economic burden corresponding to the $5,000 taxable loss from the sale of the property, the allocation of $2,500 of such loss to A does not have economic effect and must be reallocated in accordance with the partners' interests in the partnership. Under paragraph (b)(3)(iii) of this section, such $2,500 loss will be reallocated to B.

(vi) Assume the same facts as in (iv) except that the cost recovery deduction for the partnership's second taxable year is $20,000 instead of $25,000, and that as of the end of the partnership's second taxable year it is reasonably expected that during its third taxable year the partnership will (1) have operating income equal to its operating expenses (but will have no cost recovery deductions), (2) borrow $10,000 (recourse) and distribute such amount $5,000 to A and $5,000 to B, and (3) thereafter sell the partnership property, repay the $10,000 liability, and liquidate. In determining the extent to which the alternate economic effect test contained in paragraph (b)(2)(ii)(*d*) of this section is satisfied as of the end of the partnership's second taxable year, the fair market value of partnership property is presumed to be equal to its adjusted tax basis (in accordance with paragraph (b)(2)(iii)(*c*) of this section). Thus, it is presumed that the selling price of such property during the partnership's third taxable year will be its $40,000 adjusted tax basis. Accordingly, there can be no reasonable expectation that there will be increases to A's capital account in the partnership's third taxable year that will offset the expected $5,000 distribution to A. Therefore, the distribution of the loan proceeds must be taken into account in determining to what extent the alternate economic effect test contained in paragraph (b)(2)(ii)(*d*) is satisfied.

	A	*B*
Capital account at beginning of year 2	$20,000	$40,000
Less: expected future distribution	(5,000)	(5,000)
Less: year 2 cost recovery deduction	(20,000)	(0)
Hypothetical capital account at end of year 2	($5,000)	$35,000

Upon sale of the partnership property, the $40,000 presumed sales proceeds would be used to repay the $10,000 liability, and the remaining $30,000 would be distributed to B. Under these circumstances the allocation of the $20,000 cost recovery deduction to A in the partnership's second taxable year satisfies the alternate economic effect test contained in paragraph (b)(2)(ii)(*d*) of this section only to the extent of $15,000. Under paragraph (b)(3)(iii) of this section, the remaining $5,000 of such deduction will be reallocated to B. The results in this example would be the same even if the partnership agreement also provided that any gain (whether ordinary income or capital gain) upon the sale of the property would be allocated to A to the extent of the prior allocations of cost recovery deductions to him, and, at end of the partnership's second taxable year, the partners were confident that the gain on the sale of the property in the partnership's third taxable year would be sufficient to offset the expected $5,000 distribution to A.

(vii) Assume the same facts as in (iv) except that the partnership agreement also provides that any partner with a deficit balance in his capital account following the liquidation of his interest must restore that deficit to the partnership (as set forth in paragraph (b)(2)(ii)(*b*)(3) of this section). Thus, if the property were sold for $35,000 immediately after the end of the partnership's second taxable year, the $35,000 would be distributed to B, A would contribute $5,000 (the deficit balance in his capital account) to the partnership, and that $5,000 would be distributed to B. The allocation of the entire $25,000 cost recovery deduction to A in the partnership's second taxable year has economic effect.

(viii) Assume the same facts as in (vii) except that A's obligation to restore the deficit balance in his capital account is limited to a maximum of $5,000. The allocation of the $25,000 cost recovery deduction to A in the partnership's second taxable year has economic effect under the alternate economic effect test contained in paragraph (b)(2)(ii)(*d*) of this section. At the end of such year, A makes an additional $5,000 contribution to the partnership (thereby eliminating the $5,000 deficit balance in his capital account). Under paragraph (b)(2)(ii)(*f*) of this section, A's obligation to restore up to $5,000 of the deficit balance in his capital account may be eliminated after he contributes the additional $5,000 without affecting the validity of prior allocations.

(ix) Assume the same facts as in (iv) except that upon formation of the partnership A also contributes to the partnership his negotiable promissory note with a $5,000 principal balance. The note unconditionally obligates A to pay an additional $5,000 to the partnership at the earlier of (a) the beginning of the partnership's fourth taxable year, or (b) the end of the partnership taxable year in which A's interest is liquidated. Under paragraph (b)(2)(ii)(*c*) of this section, A is considered obligated to restore up to $5,000 of the deficit balance in his capital account to the partnership. Accordingly, under the alternate economic effect test contained in paragraph (b)(2)(ii)(*d*) of this section, the allocation of the $25,000 cost recovery deduction to A in the partnership's second taxable year has economic effect. The results in this example would be the same if (1) the note A contributed to the partnership were payable only at the end of the partnership's fourth taxable year (so that A would not be required to satisfy the note upon liquidation of his interest in the partnership), and (2) the partnership agreement provided that upon liquidation of A's interest, the partnership would retain A's note, and A would contribute to the partnership the excess of the outstanding principal balance of the note over its then fair market value.

(x) Assume the same facts as in (ix) except that A's obligation to contribute an additional $5,000 to the partnership is not evidenced by a promissory note. Instead, the partnership agreement imposes upon A the obligation to make an additional $5,000 contribution to the partnership at the earlier of (a) the beginning of the partnership's fourth taxable year, or (b) the end of the partnership taxable year in which A's interest is liquidated. Under paragraph (b)(2)(ii)(*c*) of this section, as a result of A's deferred contribution requirement, A is considered obligated to restore up to $5,000 of the deficit balance in his capital account to the partnership. Accordingly, under the alternate economic effect test contained in paragraph (b)(2)(*ii*)(*d*) of this section, the allocation of the $25,000 cost recovery deduction to A in the partnership's second taxable year has economic effect.

(xi) Assume the same facts as in (vii) except that the partnership agreement also provides that any gain (whether ordinary income or capital gain) upon the sale of the property will be allocated to A to the extent of the prior allocations to A of cost recovery deductions from such property, and additional gain will be allocated equally between A and B. At the time the allocations of cost recovery deductions were made to A, the partners believed there would be gain on the sale of the property in an amount sufficient to offset the allocations of cost recovery deductions to A. Nevertheless, the existence of the gain chargeback provision will not cause the economic effect of the allocations to be insubstantial under paragraph (b)(2)(iii)(*c*) of this section, since in testing whether the economic effect of such allocations is substantial, the recovery property is presumed to decrease in value by the amount of such deductions.

Example (2). C and D form a general partnership solely to acquire and lease machinery that is 5-year recovery property under section 168. Each contributes $100,000, and the partnership obtains an $800,000 recourse loan to purchase the machinery. The partnership elects under section 48(q)(4) to reduce the amount of investment tax credit in lieu of adjusting the tax basis of such machinery. The partnership, C, and D have calendar taxable years. The partnership agreement provides that the partners' capital accounts will be determined and maintained in accordance with paragraph (b)(2)(iv) of this section, distributions in liquidation of the partnership (or any partner's interest) will be made in accordance with the partners' positive capital account balances, and any partner with a deficit balance in his capital account following the liquidation of his interest must restore that deficit to the partnership (as set forth in paragraphs (b)(2)(ii)(*b*)(2) and (3) of this section). The partnership agreement further provides that (a) partnership net taxable loss will be allocated 90 percent to C and 10 percent to D until such time as there is partnership net taxable income, and thereafter C will be allocated 90 percent of such taxable income until he has been allocated partnership net taxable income equal to the partnership net taxable loss previously allocated to him, (b) all further partnership net taxable income or loss will be allocated equally between C and D, and (c) distributions of operating cash flow will be made equally between C and D. The partnership enters into a 12-year lease with a financially secure corporation under which the partnership expects to have a net taxable loss in each of its first 5 partnership taxable years due to cost recovery deductions with respect to the machinery and net taxable income in each of its following 7 partnership taxable years, in part due to the absence of such cost recovery deductions. There is a strong likelihood that the partnership's net taxable loss in partnership taxable years 1 through 5 will be $100,000, $90,000, $80,000, $70,000, and $60,000, respectively, and the partnership's net taxable income in partnership taxable years 6 through 12 will be $40,000, $50,000, $60,000, $70,000, $80,000, $90,000, and $100,000, respectively. Even though there is a strong likelihood that the allocations of net taxable loss in years 1 through 5 will be largely offset by other allocations in partnership taxable years 6 through 12, and even if it is assumed that the total tax liability of the partners in years 1 through 12 will be less than if the allocations had not been provided in the partnership agreement, the economic effect of the allocations will not be insubstantial under paragraph (b)(2)(iii)(*c*) of this section. This is because at the time such allocations became part of the partnership agreement, there was a strong likelihood that the allocations of net taxable loss in years 1 through 5 would not be largely offset by allocations of income within 5 years (determined on a first-in, first-out basis). The year 1 allocation will not be offset until years 6, 7, and 8, the year 2 allocation will not be offset until years 8 and 9, the year 3 allocation will not be offset until years 9 and 10, the year 4 allocation will not be offset until years 10 and 11, and the year 5 allocation will not be offset until years 11 and 12.

Example (3). E and F enter into a partnership agreement to develop and market experimental electronic devices. E contributes $2,500 cash and agrees to devote his full-time services to the partnership. F contributes $100,000 cash and agrees to obtain a loan for the partnership for any additional capital needs. The partnership agreement provides that all deductions for research and experimental expenditures and interest on partnership loans are to be allocated to F. In addition, F will be allocated 90 percent, and E 10 percent, of partnership taxable income or loss, computed net of the deductions for such research and experimental expenditures and interest, until F has received allocations of such taxable income equal to the sum of such research and experimental expenditures, such interest expense, and his share of such taxable loss. Thereafter, E and F will share all taxable income and loss equally. Operating cash flow will be distributed equally between E and F. The partnership agreement also provides that E's and F's capital accounts will be determined and maintained in accordance with paragraph (b)(2)(iv) of this section, distributions in liquidation of the partnership (or any partner's interest) will be made in accordance with the partners' positive capital account balances, and any partner with a deficit balance in his capital account following the liquidation of his interest must restore that deficit to the partnership (as set forth in paragraphs (b)(2)(ii)(*b*)(2) and (3) of this section). These allocations have economic effect. In addition, in view of the nature of the partnership's activities, there is not a strong likelihood at the time the allocations become part of the partnership agreement that the economic effect of the allocations to F of deductions for research and experimental expenditures and interest on partnership loans will be largely offset by allocations to F of partnership net taxable income. The economic effect of the allocations is substantial.

Example (4). (i) G and H contribute $75,000 and $25,000, respectively, in forming a general partnership. The partnership agreement provides that all income, gain, loss, and deduction will be allocated equally between the partners, that the partners' capital accounts will be determined and maintained in accordance with paragraph (b)(2)(iv) of this section, but that all partnership distributions will, regardless of capital account balances, be made 75 percent to G and 25 percent to H. Following the liquidation of the partnership, neither partner is required to restore the deficit balance in his capital account to the partnership for distribution to partners with positive capital account balances. The allocations in the partnership agreement do not have economic effect. Since contributions were made in a 75/25 ratio and the partnership agreement indicates that all economic profits and losses of the partnership are to be shared in a 75/25 ratio, under paragraph (b)(3) of this section, partnership income, gain, loss, and deduction will be reallocated 75 percent to G and 25 percent to H.

(ii) Assume the same facts as in (i) except that the partnership maintains no capital accounts and the partnership agreement provides that all income, gain, loss, deduction, and credit will be allocated 75 percent to G and 25 percent to H. G and H are ultimately liable (under a State law right of contribution) for 75 percent and 25 percent, respectively, of any debts of the partnership. Although the allocations do not satisfy the requirements of paragraph (b)(2)(ii)(*b*) of this section, the allocations have economic effect under the economic effect equivalence test of paragraph (b)(2)(ii)(*i*) of this section.

(iii) Assume the same facts as in (i) except that the partnership agreement provides that any partner with a deficit balance in his capital account must restore that deficit to the partnership (as set forth in paragraph (b)(2)(ii)(*b*)(*2*) of this section). Although the allocations do not satisfy the requirements of paragraph (b)(2)(ii)(*b*) of this section, the allocations have economic effect under the economic effect equivalence test of paragraph (b)(2)(ii)(*i*) of this section.

Example (5). (i) Individuals I and J are the only partners of an investment partnership. The partnership owns corporate stocks, corporate debt instruments, and tax-exempt debt instruments. Over the next several years, I expects to be in the 50 percent marginal tax bracket, and J expects to be in the 15 percent marginal tax bracket. There is a strong likelihood that in each of the next several years the partnership will realize between $450 and $550 of tax-exempt interest and between $450 and $550 of a combination of taxable interest and dividends from its investments. I and J made equal capital contributions to the partnership, and they have agreed to share equally in gains and losses from the sale of the partnership's investment securities. I and J agree, however, that rather than share interest and dividends of the partnership equally, they will allocate the partnership's tax-exempt interest 80 percent to I and 20 percent to J and will distribute cash derived from interest received on the tax-exempt bonds in the same percentages. In addition, they agree to allocate 100 percent of the partnership's taxable interest and dividends to J and to distribute cash derived from interest and dividends received on the corporate stocks and debt instruments 100 percent to J. The partnership agreement further provides that the partners' capital accounts will be determined and maintained in accordance with paragraph (b)(2)(iv) of this section, distributions in liquidation of the partnership (or any partner's interest) will be made in accordance with the partner's positive capital account balances, and any partner with a deficit balance in his capital account following the liquidation of his interest must restore that deficit to the partnership (as set forth in paragraphs (b)(2)(ii)(*b*)(*2*) and (*3*) of this section). The allocation of taxable interest and dividends and tax-exempt interest has economic effect, but that economic effect is not substantial under the general rules set forth in paragraph (b)(2)(iii) of this section. Without the allocation I would be allocated between $225 and $275 of tax-exempt interest and between $225 and $275 of a combination of taxable interest and dividends, which (net of Federal income taxes he would owe on such income) would give I between $337.50 and $412.50 after tax. With the allocation, however, I will be allocated between $360 and $440 of tax-exempt interest and no taxable interest and dividends, which (net of Federal income taxes) will give I between $360 and $440 after tax. Thus, at the time the allocations became part of the partnership agreement, I is expected to enhance his after-tax economic consequences as a result of the allocations. On the other hand, there is a strong likelihood that neither I nor J will substantially diminish his after-tax economic consequences as a result of the allocations. Under the combination of likely investment outcomes least favorable for J, the partnership would realize $550 of tax-exempt interest and $450 of taxable interest and dividends, giving J $492.50 after tax (which is more than the $466.25 after tax J would have received if each of such amounts had been allocated equally between the partners). Under the combination of likely investment outcomes least favorable for I, the partnership would realize $450 of tax-exempt interest and $550 of taxable interest and dividends, giving I $360 after tax (which is not substantially less than the $362.50 he would have received if each of such amounts had been allocated equally between the partners). Accordingly, the allocations in the partnership agreement must be reallocated in accordance with the partners' interests in the partnership under paragraph (b)(3) of this section.

(ii) Assume the same facts as in (i). In addition, assume that in the first partnership taxable year in which the allocation arrangement described in (i) applies, the partnership realizes $450 of tax-exempt interest and $550 of taxable interest and dividends, so that, pursuant to the partnership agreement, I's capital account is credited with $360 (80 percent of the tax-exempt interest), and J's capital account is credited with $640 (20 percent of the tax-exempt interest and 100 percent of the taxable interest and dividends). The allocations of tax-exempt interest and taxable interest and dividends (which do not have substantial economic effect for the reasons stated in (i)) will be disregarded and will be reallocated. Since under the partnership agreement I will receive 36 percent (360/1,000) and J will receive 64 percent (640/1,000) of the partnership's total investment income in such year, under paragraph (b)(3) of this section the partnership's tax-exempt interest and taxable interest and dividends each will be reallocated 36 percent to I and 64 percent to J.

Example (6). K and L are equal partners in a general partnership formed to acquire and operate property described in section 1231(b). The partnership, K, and L have calendar taxable years. The partnership agreement provides that the partners' capital accounts will be determined and maintained in accordance with paragraph (b)(2)(iv) of this section, that distributions in liquidation of the partnership (or any partner's interest) will be made in accordance with the partners' positive capital account balances, and that any partner with a deficit balance in his capital account following the liquidation of his interest must restore that deficit to the partnership (as set forth in paragraphs (b)(2)(ii)(*b*) and (*3*) of this section). For a taxable year in which the partnership expects to incur a loss on the sale of a portion of such property, the partnership agreement is amended (at the beginning of the taxable year) to allocate such loss to K, who expects to have no gains from the sale of depreciable property described in section 1231(b) in that taxable year, and to allocate an equivalent amount of partnership loss and deduction for that year of a different character to L, who expects to have such gains. Any partnership loss and deduction in excess of these allocations will be allocated equally between K and L. The amendment is effective only for that taxable year. At the time the partnership agreement is amended, there is a strong likelihood that the partnership will incur deduction or loss in the taxable year other than loss from the sale of property described in section 1231(b) in an amount that will substantially equal or exceed the expected amount of the section 1231(b) loss. The allocations in such taxable year have economic effect. However, the economic effect of the allocations is insubstantial under the test described in paragraph (b)(2)(iii)(*b*) of this section because there is a stong likelihood, at the time the allocations become part of the partnership agreement, that the net increases and decreases to K's and L's capital accounts will be the same at the end of the taxable year to which they apply with such allocations in effect as they would have been in the absence of such allocations, and that the total taxes of K and L for such year will be reduced as a result of such allocations. If in fact the partnership incurs deduction or loss, other than loss from the sale of property described in section 1231(b), in an amount at least equal to the section 1231(b) loss, the loss and deduction in such taxable year will be reallocated equally between K and L under paragraph (b)(3) of this section. If not, the loss from the sale of property described in section 1231(b) and the items of deduction and other loss realized in such year will be reallocated between K and L in proportion to the net decreases in their capital accounts due to the allocation of such items under the partnership agreement.

Example (7). (i) M and N are partners in the MN general partnership, which is engaged in an active business. Income, gain, loss, and deduction from MN's business is allocated equally between M and N. The partnership, M, and N have calendar taxable years. Under the partnership agreement the partners' capital accounts will be determined and maintained in accordance with paragraph (b)(2)(iv) of this section, distributions in liquidation of the partnership (or any partner's interest) will be made in accordance with the partners' positive capital account balances, and any partner with a deficit balance in his capital account following the liquidation of his interest must restore that deficit to the partnership (as set forth in paragraphs (b)(2)(ii)(*b*)(*2*) and (*3*) of this section). In order to enhance the credit standing of the partnership, the partners contribute surplus funds to the partnership, which the partners agree to invest in equal dollar amounts of tax-exempt bonds and corporate stock for the partnership's first 3 taxable years. M is expected to be in a higher marginal tax bracket than N during those 3 years. At the time the decision to make these investments is made, it is agreed that, during the 3-year period of the investment, M will be allocated 90 percent and N 10 percent of the interest income from the tax-exempt bonds as well as any gain or loss from the sale thereof, and that M will be allocated 10 percent and N 90 percent of the dividend income from the corporate stock as well as any gain or loss from the sale thereof. At the time the allocations concerning the investments become part of the partnership agreement, there is not a strong likelihood that the gain or loss from the sale of the stock will be substantially equal to the gain or loss from the sale of the tax-exempt bonds, but there is a strong likelihood that the tax-exempt interest and the taxable dividends realized from these investments during the 3-year period will not differ substantially. These allocations have economic effect, and the economic effect of the allocations of the gain or loss on the sale of the tax-exempt bonds and corporate stock is substantial. The economic effect of the allocations of the tax-exempt interest and the taxable dividends, however, is not substantial under the test described in paragraph (b)(2)(iii)(*c*) of this section because there is a strong likelihood, at the time the allocations become part of the partnership agreement, that at the end of the 3-year period to which such allocations relate, the net increases and decreases to M's and N's capital accounts will be the same with such allocations as they would have been in the absence of such allocations, and that the total taxes of M and N for the taxable years to which such allocations relate will be reduced as a result of such allocations. If in fact the amounts of tax-exempt interest and taxable dividends earned by the partnership during the 3-year period are equal, the tax-exempt interest and taxable dividends will be reallocated to the partners in equal shares under paragraph (b)(3) of this section. If not, the tax-exempt interest and taxable dividends will be reallocated between M and N in proportion to the net increases in their capital accounts during such 3-year period due to the allocation of such items under the partnership agreement.

(ii) Assume the same facts as in (i) except that gain or loss from the sale of the tax-exempt bonds and corporate stock will be allocated equally between M and N and the partnership agreement provides that the 90/10 allocation arrangement with respect to the investment income applies only to the first $10,000 of interest income from the tax-exempt bonds and the first $10,000 of dividend income from the corporate stock, and only to the first taxable year of the partnership. There is a strong likelihood at the time the 90/10 allocation of the investment income became part of the partnership agreement that in the first taxable year of the partnership, the partnership will earn more than $10,000 of tax-exempt interest and more than $10,000 of taxable dividends. The allocations of tax-exempt interest and taxable dividends provided in the partnership agreement have economic effect, but under the test contained in paragraph (b)(2)(iii)(*b*) of this section, such economic effect is not substantial for the same reasons stated in (i) (but applied to the 1 taxable year, rather than to a 3-year period). If in fact the partnership realizes at least $10,000 of tax-exempt interest and at least $10,000 of taxable dividends in such year, the allocations of such interest income and dividend income will be reallocated equally between M and N under paragraph (b)(3) of this section. If not, the tax-exempt interest and taxable dividends will be reallocated between M and N in proportion to the net increases in their capital accounts due to the allocations of such items under the partnership agreement.

(iii) Assume the same facts as in (ii) except that at the time the 90/10 allocation of investment income becomes part of the partnership agreement, there is not a strong likelihood that (1) the partnership will earn $10,000 or more of tax-exempt interest and $10,000 or more of taxable dividends in the partnership's first taxable year, and (2) the amount of tax-exempt interest and taxable dividends earned during such year will be substantially the same. Under these facts the economic effect of the allocations generally will be substantial. (Additional facts may exist in certain cases, however, so that the allocation is insubstantial under the second sentence of paragraph (b)(2)(iii). See example (5) above.)

Example (8). (i) O and P are equal partners in the OP general partnership. The partnership, O, and P have calendar taxable years. Partner O has a net operating loss carryover from another venture that is due to expire at the end of the partnership's second taxable year. Otherwise, both partners expect to be in the 50 percent marginal tax bracket in the next several taxable years. The partnership agreement provides that the partners' capital accounts will be determined and maintained in accordance with paragraph (b)(2)(iv) of this section, distributions in liquidation of the partnership (or any partner's interest) will be made in accordance with the partners' positive capital account balances, and any partner with a deficit balance in his capital account following the liquidation of his interest must restore that deficit to the partnership (as set forth in paragraphs (b)(2)(ii)(*b*)(2) and (3) of this section). The partnership agreement is amended (at the beginning of the partnership's second taxable year) to allocate all the partnership net taxable income for that year to O. Future partnership net taxable loss is to be allocated to O, and future partnership net taxable income to P, until the allocation of income to O in the partnership's second taxable year is offset. It is further agreed orally that in the event the partnership is liquidated prior to completion of such offset, O's capital account will be adjusted downward to the extent of one-half of the allocations of income to O in the partnership's second taxable year that have not been offset by other allocations, P's capital account will be adjusted upward by a like amount, and liquidation proceeds will be distributed in accordance with the partners' adjusted capital account balances. As a result of this oral amendment, all allocations of partnership net taxable income and net taxable loss made pursuant to the amendment executed at the beginning of the partnership's second taxable year lack economic effect and will be disregarded. Under the partnership agreement other allocations are made equally to O and P, and O and P will share equally in liquidation proceeds, indicating that the partners' interests in the partnership are equal. Thus, the disregarded allocations will be reallocated equally between the partners under paragraph (b)(3) of this section.

(ii) Assume the same facts as in (i) except that there is no agreement that O's and P's capital accounts will be adjusted downward and upward, respectively, to the extent of one-half of the partnership net taxable income allocated to O in the partnership's second taxable year that is not offset subsequently by other allocations. The income of the partnership is generated primarily by fixed interest payments received with respect to highly rated corporate bonds, which are expected to produce sufficient net taxable income prior to the end of the partnership's seventh taxable year to offset in large part the net taxable income to be allocated to O in the partnership's second taxable year. Thus, at the time the allocations are made part of the partnership agreement, there is a strong likelihood that the allocation of net taxable income to be made to O in the second taxable year will be offset in large part within 5 taxable years thereafter. These allocations have economic effect. However, the economic effect of the allocation of partnership net taxable income to O in the partnership's second taxable year, as well as the offsetting allocations to P, is not substantial under the test contained in paragraph (b)(2)(iii)(*c*) of this section because there is a strong likelihood that the net increases or decreases in O's and P's capital accounts will be the same at the end of the partnership's seventh taxable year with such allocations as they would have been in the absence of such allocations, and the total taxes of O and P for the taxable years to which such allocations relate will be reduced as a result of such allocations. If in fact the partnership, in its taxable years 3 through 7, realizes sufficient net taxable income to offset the amount allocated to O in the second taxable year, the allocations provided in the partnership agreement will be reallocated equally between the partners under paragraph (b)(3) of this section.

Example (9). Q and R form a limited partnership with contributions of $20,000 and $180,000, respectively. Q, the limited partner, is a corporation that has $2,000,000 of net operating loss carryforwards that will not expire for 8 years. Q does not expect to have sufficient income (apart from the income of the partnership) to absorb any of such net operating loss carryforwards. R, the general partner, is a corporation that expects to be in the 46 percent marginal tax bracket for several years. The partnership agreement provides that the partners' capital accounts will be determined and maintained in accordance with paragraph (b)(2)(iv) of this section, distributions in liquidation of the partnership (or any partner's interest) will be made in accordance with the partners' positive capital account balances, and any partner with a deficit balance in his capital account following the liquidation of his interest must restore that deficit to the partnership (as set forth in paragraph (b)(2)(ii)(*b*)(2) and (3) of this section). The partnership's cash, together with the proceeds of an $800,000 loan, are invested in assets that are expected to produce taxable income and cash flow (before debt service) of approximately $150,000 a year for the first 8 years of the partnership's operations. In addition, it is expected that the partnership's total taxable income in its first 8 taxable years will not exceed $2,000,000. The partnership's $150,000 of cash flow in each of its first 8 years will be used to retire the $800,000 loan. The partnership agreement provides that partnership net taxable income will be allocated 90 percent to Q and 10 percent to R in the first through eighth partnership taxable years, and 90 percent to R and 10 percent to Q in all subsequent partnership taxable years. Net taxable loss will be allocated 90 percent to R and 10 percent to Q in all partnership taxable years. All distributions of cash from the partnership to partners (other than the priority distributions to Q described below) will be made 90 percent to R and 10 percent to Q. At the end of the partnership's eighth taxable year, the amount of Q's capital account in excess of one-ninth of R's capital account on such date will be designated as Q's "excess capital account." Beginning in the ninth taxable year of the partnership, the undistributed portion of Q's excess capital account will begin to bear interest (which will be paid and deducted under section 707(c)) at a rate of interest below the rate that the partnership can borrow from commercial lenders, and over the next several years (following the eighth year) the partnership will make priority cash distributions to Q in prearranged percentages of Q's excess capital account designed to amortize Q's excess capital account and the interest thereon over a prearranged period. In addition, the partnership's agreement prevents Q from causing his interest in the partnership from being liquidated (and thereby receiving the balance in his capital account) without R's consent until Q's excess capital account has been eliminated. The below-market rate of interest and the period over which the amortization will take place are prescribed such that, as of the end of the partnership's eighth taxable year, the present value of Q's right to receive such priority distributions is approximately 46 percent of the amount of Q's excess capital account as of such date. However, because the partnership's income for its first 8 taxable years will be realized approximately ratably over that period, the present value of Q's right to receive the priority distributions with respect to its excess capital account is, as of the date the partnership agreement is entered into, less than the present value of the additional Federal income taxes for which R would be liable if, during the partnership's first 8 taxable years, all partnership income were to be allocated 90 percent to R and 10 to Q. The allocations of partnership taxable income to Q and R in the first through eighth partnership taxable years have economic effect. However, such economic effect is not substantial under the general rules set forth in paragraph (b)(2)(iii) of this section. This is true because R may enhance his after-tax economic consequences, on a present value basis, as a result of the allocations to Q of 90 percent of partnership's income during taxable years 1 through 8, and there is a strong likelihood that neither R nor Q will substantially diminish its after-tax economic consequences, on a present value basis, as a result of such allocation. Accordingly, partnership taxable income for partnership taxable years 1 through 8 will be reallocated in accordance with the partners' interests in the partnership under paragraph (b)(3) of this section.

Example (10). (i) S and T form a general partnership to operate a travel agency. The partnership agreement provides that the partners' capital accounts will be determined and maintained in accordance with paragraph (b)(2)(iv) of this section, distributions in liquidation of the partnership (or any partner's interest) will be made in accordance with the partners' positive capital account balances, and any partner with a deficit balance in his capital account following the liquidation of his interest must restore that deficit to the partnership (as set forth in paragraphs (b)(2)(ii)(*b*)(2) and (3) of this section). The partnership agreement provides that T, a resident of a foreign country, will be allocated 90 percent, and S 10 percent, of the income, gain, loss, and deduction derived from operations conducted by T within his country, and all remaining income, gain, loss, and deduction will be allocated equally. The amount of such income, gain, loss, or deduction cannot be predicted with any reasonable certainty. The allocations provided by the partnership agreement have substantial economic effect.

(ii) Assume the same facts as in (i) except that the partnership agreement provides that all income, gain, loss, and deduction of the partnership will be shared equally, but that T will be allocated all income, gain, loss, and deduction derived from operations conducted by him within his country as a part of his equal share of partnership income, gain, loss, and deduction, up to the amount of such share. Assume the total tax liability of S and T for each year to which these allocations relate will be reduced as a result of such allocation. These allocations have economic effect. However, such economic effect is not substantial under the test stated in paragraph (b)(2)(iii)(*b*) of this section because, at the time the allocations became part of the partnership agreement, there is a strong likelihood that the net increases and decreases to S's and T's capital accounts will be the same at the end of each partnership taxable year with such allocations as they would have been in the absense of such allocations, and that the total tax liability of S and T for each year to which such allocations relate will be reduced as a result of such allocations. Thus, all items of partnership income, gain, loss, and income, gain, loss, and deduction will be reallocated equally between S and T under paragraph (b)(3) of this section.

Example (11). (i) U and V share equally all income, gain, loss, and deduction of the UV general partnership, as well as all non-liquidating distributions made by the partnership. The partnership agreement provides that the partners' capital accounts will be determined and maintained in accordance with paragraph (b)(2)(iv) of this section, distributions in liquidation of the partnership (or any partner's interest) will be made in accordance with the partners' positive capital account balances, and any partner with a deficit balance in his capital account following the liquidation of his interest must restore such deficit to the partnership (as set forth in paragraphs (b)(2)(ii)(*b*)(2) and (3) of this section). The agreement further provides that the partners will be allocated equal shares of any section 705(a)(2)(B) expenditures of the partnership. In the partnership's first taxable year, it pays qualified first-year wages of $6,000 and is entitled to a $3,000 targeted jobs tax credit under sections 44B and 51 of the Code. Under section 280C the partnership must reduce its deduction for wages paid by the $3,000 credit claimed (which amount constitutes a section 705(a)(2)(B) expenditure). The partnership agreement allocates the credit to U. Although the allocations of wage deductions and section 705 (a)(2)(B) expenditures have substantial economic effect, the allocation of tax credit cannot have economic effect since it cannot properly be reflected in the partners' capital accounts. Furthermore, the allocation is not in accordance with the special partners' interests in the partnership rule contained in paragraph (b)(4)(ii) of this section. Under that rule, since the expenses that gave rise to the credit are shared equally by the partners, the credit will be shared equally between U and V.

(ii) Assume the same facts as in (i) and that at the beginning of the partnership's second taxable year, the partnership agreement is amended to allocate to U all wage expenses incurred in that year (including wage expenses that constitute section 705(a)(2)(B) expenditures) whether or not such wages qualify for the credit. The partnership agreement contains no offsetting allocations. That taxable year the partnership pays $8,000 in total wages to its employees. Assume that the partnership has operating income equal to its operating expenses (exclusive of expenses for wages). Assume further that $6,000 of the $8,000 wage expense constitutes qualified first-year wages. U is allocated the $3,000 deduction and the $3,000 section 705(a)(2)(B) expenditure attributable to the $6,000 of qualified first-year wages, as well as the deduction for the other $2,000 in wage expenses. The allocations of wage deductions and section 705(a)(2)(B) expenditures have substantial economic effect. Furthermore, since the wage credit is allocated in the same proportion as the expenses that gave rise to the credit, and the allocation of those expenses has substantial economic effect, the allocation of such credit to U is in accordance with the special partners' interests in the partnership rule contained in paragraph (b)(4)(ii) of this section and is recognized thereunder.

Example (12). (i) W and X form a general partnership for the purpose of mining iron ore. W makes an initial contribution of $75,000, and X makes an initial contribution of $25,000. The partnership agreement provides that non-liquidating distributions will be made 75 percent to W and 25 percent to X, and that all items of income, gain, loss, and deduction will be allocated 75 percent to W and 25 percent to X, except that all percentage depletion deductions will be allocated to W. The agreement further provides that the partners' capital accounts will be determined and maintained in accordance with paragraph (b)(2)(iv) of this section, distributions in liquidation of the partnership (or any partner's interest) will be made in accordance with the partners' positive capital account balances, and any partner with a deficit balance in his capital account following the liquidation of his interest must restore such deficit to the partnership (as set forth in paragraphs (b)(2)(ii)(*b*)(2) and (3) of this section). Assume that the adjusted tax basis of the partnership's only depletable iron ore property is $1,000 and that the percentage depletion deduction for the taxable year with respect to such property is $1,500. The allocation of partnership income, gain, loss, and deduction (excluding the percentage depletion deduction) as well as the allocation of $1,000 of the percentage depletion deduction have substantial economic effect. The allocation to W of the remaining $500 of the percentage depletion deduction, representing the excess of percentage depletion over adjusted tax basis of the iron ore property, cannot have economic effect since such amount cannot properly be reflected in the partners' capital accounts. Furthermore, the allocation to W of that $500 excess percentage depletion deduction is not in accordance with the special partners' interests in the partnership rule contained in paragraph (b)(4)(iii) of this section, under which such $500 excess depletion deduction (and all further percentage depletion deductions from the mine) will be reallocated 75 percent to W and 25 percent to X.

(ii) Assume the same facts as in (i) except that the partnership agreement provides that all percentage depletion deductions of the partnership will be allocated 75 percent to W and 25 percent to X. Once again, the allocation of partnership income, gain, loss, and deduction (excluding the percentage depletion deduction) as well as the allocation of $1,000 of the percentage depletion deduction have substantial economic effect. Furthermore, since the $500 portion of the percentage depletion deduction that exceeds the adjusted basis of such iron ore property is allocated in the same manner as valid allocations of the gross income from such property during the taxable year (*i.e.,* 75 percent to W and 25 percent to X), the allocation of the $500 excess percentage depletion contained in the partnership agreement is in accordance with the special partners' interests in the partnership rule contained in paragraph (b)(4)(iii) of this section.

Example (13). (i) Y and Z form a brokerage general partnership for the purpose of investing and trading in marketable securities. Y contributes cash of $10,000, and Z contributes securities of P corporation, which have an adjusted basis of $3,000 and a fair market value of $10,000. The partnership would not be an investment company under section 351(e) if it were incorporated. The partnership agreement provides that the partners' capital accounts will be determined and maintained in accordance with paragraph (b)(2)(iv) of this section, distributions in liquidation of the partnership (or any partner's interest) will be made in accordance with the partners' positive capital account balances, and any partner with a deficit balance in his capital account following the liquidation of his interest must restore that deficit to the partnership (as set forth in paragraphs (b)(2)(ii)(*b*)(2) and (3) of this section). The partnership uses the interim closing of the books method for purposes of section 706. The initial capital accounts of Y and Z are fixed at $10,000 each. The agreement further provides that all partnership distributions, income, gain, loss, deduction, and credit will be shared equally between Y and Z, except that the taxable gain attributable to the precontribution appreciation in the value of the securities of P corporation will be allocated to Z in accordance with section 704(c). During the partnership's first taxable year, it sells the securities of P corporation for $12,000, resulting in a $2,000 book gain ($12,000 less $10,000 book value) and a $9,000 taxable gain ($12,000 less $3,000 adjusted tax basis). The partnership has no other income, gain, loss, or deductions for the taxable year. The gain from the sale of the securities is allocated as follows:

	Y Tax	Y Book	Z Tax	Z Book
Capital account upon formation	$10,000	$10,000	$3,000	$10,000
Plus: gain	1,000	1,000	8,000	1,000
Capital account at end of year 1	$11,000	$11,000	$11,000	$11,000

The allocation of the $2,000 book gain, $1,000 each to Y and Z, has substantial economic effect. Furthermore, under section 704(c) the partners' distributive shares of the $9,000 taxable gain are $1,000 to Y and $8,000 to Z.

(ii) Assume the same facts as in (i) and that at the beginning of the partnership's second taxable year, it invests its $22,000 of cash in securities of G Corp. The G Corp. securities increase in value to $40,000, at which time Y sells 50 percent of his partnership interest (*i.e.*, a 25 percent interest in the partnership) to LK for $10,000. The partnership does not have a section 754 election in effect for the partnership taxable year during which such sale occurs. In accordance with paragraph (b)(2)(iv)(*l*) of this section, the partnership agreement provides that LK inherits 50 percent of Y's $11,000 capital account balance. Thus, following the sale, LK and Y each have a capital account of $5,500, and Z's capital account remains at $11,000. Prior to the end of the partnership's second taxable year, the securities are sold for their $40,000 fair market value, resulting in an $18,000 taxable gain ($40,000 less $22,000 adjusted tax basis). The partnership has no other income, gain, loss, or deduction in such taxable year. Under the partnership agreement the $18,000 taxable gain is allocated as follows:

	Y	Z	LK
Capital account before sale of securities	$5,500	$11,000	$5,500
Plus: gain	4,500	9,000	4,500
Capital account at end of year 2	$10,000	$20,000	$10,000

The allocation of the $18,000 taxable gain has substantial economic effect.

(iii) Assume the same facts as in (ii) except that the partnership has a section 754 election in effect for the partnership taxable year during which Y sells 50 percent of his interest to LK. Accordingly, under § 1.743-1 there is a $4,500 basis increase to the G Corp. securities with respect to LK. Notwithstanding this basis adjustment, as a result of the sale of the G Corp. securities, LK's capital account is, as in (ii), increased by $4,500. The fact that LK recognizes no taxable gain from such sale (due to his $4,500 section 743 basis adjustment) is irrelevant for capital accounting purposes since, in accordance with paragraph (b)(2)(iv)(*m*)(2) of this section, that basis adjustment is disregarded in the maintenance and computation of the partners' capital accounts.

(iv) Assume the same facts as in (iii) except that immediately following Y's sale of 50 percent of this interest to LK, the G Corp. securities decrease in value to $32,000 and are sold. The $10,000 taxable gain ($32,000 less $22,000 adjusted tax basis) is allocated as follows:

	Y	Z	LK
Capital account before sale of securities	$5,500	$11,000	$5,500
Plus: gain	2,500	5,000	2,500
Capital account at end of the year 2	$8,000	$16,000	$8,000

The fact that LK recognizes a $2,000 taxable loss from the sale of the G Corp. securities (due to his $4,500 section 743 basis adjustment) is irrelevant for capital accounting purposes since, in accordance with paragraph (b)(2)(iv)(*m*)(2) of this section, that basis adjustment is disregarded in the maintenance and computation of the partners' capital accounts.

(v) Assume the same facts as in (ii) except that Y sells 100 percent of his partnership interest (*i.e.*, a 50 percent interest in the partnership) to LK for $20,000. Under section 708(b)(1)(B) the partnership terminates. Under paragraph (b)(1)(iv) of § 1.708-1, there is a constructive liquidation of the partnership. Immediately preceding the constructive liquidation, the capital accounts of Z and LK equal $11,000 each (LK having inherited Y s $11,000 capital account) and the book value of the G Corp. securities is $22,000 (original purchase price of securities). Under paragraph (b)(2)(iv)(*l*) of this section, the deemed contribution of assets and liabilities by the terminated partnership to the new partnership and the deemed liquidation of the terminated partnership that occur under § 1.708-1(b)(1)(iv) in connection with the constructive liquidation of the terminated partnership are disregarded in the maintenance and computation of the partners' capital accounts. As a result, the capital accounts of Z and LK in the new partnership equal $11,000 each (their capital accounts in the terminated partnership immediately prior to the termination), and the book value of the G Corp. securities remains $22,000 (its book value immediately prior to the termination). This *Example 13*(v) applies to terminations of partnerships under section 708(b)(1)(B) occurring on or after May 9, 1997; however, this *Example 13*(v) may be applied to terminations occurring on or after May 9, 1996, provided that the partnership and its partners apply this *Example 13*(v) to the termination in a consistent manner.

Example (14). (i) MC and RW form a general partnership to which each contributes $10,000. The $20,000 is invested in securities of Ventureco (which are not readily tradable on an established securities market). In each of the partnership's taxable years, it recognizes operating income equal to its operating deductions (excluding gain or loss from the sale of securities). The partnership agreement provides that the partners' capital accounts will be determined and maintained in accordance with paragraph (b)(2)(iv) of this section, distributions in liquidation of the partnership (or any partner's interest) will be made in accordance with the partners' positive capital account balances, and any partner with a deficit balance in his capital account following the liquidation of his interest must restore that deficit to the partnership (as set forth in paragraphs (b)(2)(ii)(*b*)(2) and (3) of this section). The partnership uses the interim closing of the books method for purposes of section 706. Assume that the Ventureco securities subsequently appreciate in value to $50,000. At that time SK makes a $25,000 cash contribution to the partnership (thereby acquiring a one-third interest in the partnership), and the $25,000 is placed in a bank account. Upon SK's admission to the partnership, the capital accounts of MC and RW (which were $10,000 each prior to SK's admission) are, in accordance with paragraph (b)(2)(iv)(*f*) of this section, adjusted upward (to $25,000 each) to reflect their shares of the unrealized appreciation in the Ventureco securities that occurred before SK was admitted to the partnership. Immediately after SK's admission to the partnership, the securities are sold for their $50,000 fair market value, resulting in taxable gain of $30,000 ($50,000 less $20,000 adjusted tax basis) and no book gain or loss. An allocation of the $30,000 taxable gain cannot have economic effect since it cannot properly be reflected in the partners' book capital accounts. Under paragraph (b)(2)(iv)(*f*) of this section and the special partners' interests in the partnership rule contained in paragraph (b)(4)(i) of this section, unless the partnership agreement provides that the $30,000 taxable gain will, in accordance with section 704(c) principles, be shared $15,000 to MC and $15,000 to RW, the partners' capital accounts will not be considered maintained in accordance with paragraph (b)(2)(iv) of this section.

	MC		RW		SK	
	Tax	*Book*	*Tax*	*Book*	*Tax*	*Book*
Capital account following SK's admission	$10,000	$25,000	$10,000	$25,000	$25,000	$25,000
Plus: gain	15,000	0	15,000	0	0	0
Capital account following sale	$25,000	$25,000	$25,000	$25,000	$25,000	$25,000

(ii) Assume the same facts as (i), except that after SK's admission to the partnership, the Ventureco securities appreciate in value to $74,000 and are sold, resulting in taxable gain of $54,000 ($74,000 less $20,000 adjusted tax basis) and book gain of $24,000 ($74,000 less $50,000 book value). Under the partnership agreement the $24,000 book gain (the appreciation in value occurring after SK became a partner) is allocated equally among MC, RW, and SK, and such allocations have substantial economic effect. An allocation of the $54,000 taxable gain cannot have economic effect since it cannot properly be reflected in the partners' book capital accounts. Under paragraph (b)(2)(iv)(*f*) of this section and the special partners' interests in the partnership rule contained in paragraph (b)(4)(i) of this section, unless the partnership agreement provides that the taxable gain will, in accordance with section 704(c) principles, be shared $23,000 to MC, $23,000 to RW, and $8,000 to SK, the partners' capital accounts will not be considered maintained in accordance with paragraph (b)(2)(iv) of this section.

	MC		RW		SK	
	Tax	*Book*	*Tax*	*Book*	*Tax*	*Book*
Capital account following SK's admission	$10,000	$25,000	$10,000	$25,000	$25,000	$25,000
Plus: gain	23,000	8,000	23,000	8,000	8,000	8,000
Capital account following sale	$33,000	$33,000	$33,000	$33,000	$33,000	$33,000

(iii) Assume the same facts as (i) except that after SK's admission to the partnership, the Ventureco securities depreciate in value to $44,000 and are sold, resulting in taxable gain of $24,000 ($44,000 less $20,000 adjusted tax basis) and a book loss of $6,000 ($50,000 book value less $44,000). Under the partnership agreement the $6,000 book loss is allocated equally among MC, RW, and SK, and such allocations have substantial economic effect. An allocation of the $24,000 taxable gain cannot have economic effect since it cannot properly be reflected in the partners' book capital accounts. Under paragraph (b)(2)(iv)(*f*) of this section and the special partners' interests in the partnership rule contained in paragraph (b)(4)(i) of this section, unless the partnership agreement provides that the $24,000 taxable gain will, in accordance with section 704(c) principles, be shared equally between MC and RW, the partners' capital accounts will not be considered maintained in accordance with paragraph (b)(2)(iv) of this section.

	MC		RW		SK	
	Tax	*Book*	*Tax*	*Book*	*Tax*	*Book*
Capital account following SK's admission	$10,000	$25,000	$10,000	$25,000	$25,000	$25,000
Plus: gain	12,000	0	12,000	0	0	0
Less: loss	0	(2,000)	0	(2,000)	0	(2,000)
Capital account following sale	$22,000	$23,000	$22,000	$23,000	$25,000	$23,000

That SK bears an economic loss of $2,000 without a corresponding taxable loss is attributable entirely to the "ceiling rule." See paragraph (c)(2) of § 1.704-1.

(iv) Assume the same facts as in (ii) except that upon the admission of SK the capital accounts of MC and RW are not each adjusted upward from $10,000 to $25,000 to reflect the appreciation in the partnership's securities that occurred before SK was admitted to the partnership. Rather, upon SK's admission to the partnership, the partnership agreement is amended to provide that the first $30,000 of taxable gain upon the sale of such securities will be allocated equally between MC and RW, and that all other income, gain, loss, and deduction will be allocated equally between MC, RW, and SK. When the securities are sold for $74,000, the $54,000 of taxable gain is so allocated. These allocations of taxable gain have substantial economic effect. (If the agreement instead provides for all taxable gain (including the $30,000 taxable gain attributable to the appreciation in the securities prior to SK's admission to the partnership) to be allocated equally between MC, RW, and SK, the partners should consider whether, and to what extent, the provisions of paragraphs (b)(1)(iii) and (iv) of this section are applicable.)

(v) Assume the same facts as in (iv) except that instead of selling the securities, the partnership makes a distribution of the securities (which have a fair market value of $74,000). Assume the distribution does not give rise to a transaction described in section 707(a)(2)(B). In accordance with paragraph (b)(2)(iv)(*e*) of this section, the partners' capital accounts are adjusted immediately prior to the distribution to reflect how taxable gain ($54,000) would have been allocated had the securities been sold for their $74,000 fair market value, and capital account adjustments in respect of the distribution of the securities are made with reference to the $74,000 "booked-up" fair market value.

	MC	RW	SK
Capital account before adjustment	$10,000	$10,000	$25,000
Deemed sale adjustment	23,000	23,000	8,000
Less: distribution	(24,667)	(24,667)	(24,667)
Capital account after distribution	$8,333	$8,333	$8,333

(vi) Assume the same facts as in (i) except that the partnership does not sell the Ventureco securities. During the next 3 years the fair market value of the Ventureco securities remains at $50,000, and the partnership engages in no other investment activities. Thus, at the end of that period the balance sheet of the partnership and the partners' capital accounts are the same as they were at the beginning of such period. At the end of the 3 years, MC's interest in the partnership is liquidated for the $25,000 cash held by the partnership. Assume the distribution does not give rise to a transaction described in section 707(a)(2)(B). Assume further that the partnership has a section 754 election in effect for the taxable year during which such liquidation occurs. Under sections 734(b) and 755 the partnership increases the basis of the Ventureco securities by the $15,000 basis adjustment (the excess of $25,000 over the $10,000 adjusted tax basis of MC's partnership interest).

	MC		RW		SK	
	Tax	*Book*	*Tax*	*Book*	*Tax*	*Book*
Capital account before distribution	$10,000	$25,000	$10,000	$25,000	$25,000	$25,000
Plus: basis adjustment	15,000	0	0	0	0	0
Less: distribution	(25,000)	(25,000)	0	0	0	0
Capital account, account after liquidation	0	0	$10,000	$25,000	$25,000	$25,000

(vii) Assume the same facts as in (vi) except that the partnership has no section 754 election in effect for the taxable year during which such liquidation occurs.

	MC		RW		SK	
	Tax	*Book*	*Tax*	*Book*	*Tax*	*Book*
Capital account before distribution	$10,000	$25,000	$10,000	$25,000	$25,000	$25,000
Less: distribution	25,000	(25,0000	0	0	0	0
Capital account after liquidation	($15,000)	0	$10,000	$25,000	$25,000	$25,000

Following the liquidation of MC's interest in the partnership, the Ventureco securities are sold for their $50,000 fair market value, resulting in no book gain or loss but a $30,000 taxable gain. An allocation of this $30,000 taxable gain cannot have economic effect since it cannot properly be reflected in the partners' book capital accounts. Under paragraph (b)(2)(iv)(*f*) of this section and the special partners' interests in the partnership rule contained in paragraph (b)(4)(i) of this section, unless the partnership agreement provides that $15,000 of such taxable gain will, in accordance with section 704(c) principles, be included in RW's distributive share, the partners' capital accounts will not be considered maintained in accordance with paragraph (b)(2)(iv) of this section. The remaining $15,000 of such gain will, under paragraph (b)(3) of this section, be shared equally between RW and SK.

Example (15). (i) JB and DK form a limited partnership for the purpose of purchasing residential real estate to lease. JB, the limited partner, contributes $13,500, and DK, the general partner, contributes $1,500. The partnership, which uses the cash receipts and disbursements method of accounting, purchases a building for $100,000 (on leased land), incurring a recourse mortgage of $85,000 that requires the payment of interest only for a period of 3 years. The partnership agreement provides that partnership net taxable income and loss will be allocated 90 percent to JB and 10 percent to DK, the partners' capital accounts will be determined and maintained in accordance with paragraph (b)(2)(iv) of this section, distributions in liquidation of the partnership (or any partner's interest) will be made in accordance with the partners' positive capital account balances (as set forth in paragraph (b)(2)(ii)(*b*)(*2*) of this section), and JB is not required to restore any deficit balance in his capital account, but DK is so required. The partnership agreement contains a qualified income offset (as defined in paragraph (b)(2)(ii)(*d*) of this section). As of the end of each of the partnership's first 3 taxable years, the items described in paragraphs (b)(2)(ii)(*d*)(*4*), (*5*), and (*6*) of this section are not reasonably expected to cause or increase a deficit balance in JB's capital account. In the partnership's first taxable year, it has rental income of $10,000, operating expenses of $2,000, interest expense of $8,000, and cost recovery deductions of $12,000. Under the partnership agreement JB and DK are allocated $10,800 and $1,200, respectively, of the $12,000 net taxable loss incurred in the partnership's first taxable year.

	JB	*DK*
Capital account upon formation	$13,500	$1,500
Less: year 1 net loss	(10,800)	(1,200)
Capital account at end of year 1	$2,700	$300

The alternate economic effect test contained in paragraph (b)(2)(ii)(*d*) of this section is satisfied as of the end of the partnership's first taxable year. Thus, the allocation made in the partnership's first taxable year has economic effect.

(ii) Assume the same facts as in (i) and that in the partnership's second taxable year it again has rental income of $10,000, operating expenses of $2,000, interest expense of $8,000, and cost recovery deductions of $12,000. Under the partnership agreement JB and DK are allocated $10,800 and $1,200, respectively, of the $12,000 net taxable loss incurred in the partnership's second taxable year.

	JB	*DK*
Capital account at beginning of year 1	$2,700	$300
Less: year 2 net loss	(10,800)	(1,200)
Capital account at end of year 2	$(8,100)	$(900)

Only $2,700 of the $10,800 net taxable loss allocated to JB satisfies the alternate economic effect test contained in paragraph (b)(2)(ii)(*d*) of this section as of the end of the partnership's second taxable year. The allocation of such $2,700 net taxable loss to JB (consisting of $2,250 of rental income, $450 of operating expenses, $1,800 of interest expense, and $2,700 of cost recovery deductions) has economic effect. The remaining $8,100 of net taxable loss allocated by the partnership agreement to JB must be reallocated in accordance with the partners' interests in the partnership. Under paragraph (b)(3)(iii) of this section, the determination of the partners' interests in the remaining $8,100 net taxable loss is made by comparing how distributions (and contributions) would be made if the partnership sold its property at its adjusted tax basis and liquidated immediately following the end of the partnership's first taxable year with the results of such a sale and liquidation immediately following the end of the partnership's second taxable year. If the partnership's real property were sold for its $88,000 adjusted tax basis and the partnership were liquidated immediately following the end of the partnership's first taxable year, the $88,000 sales proceeds would be used to repay the $85,000 note, and there would be $3,000 remaining in the partnership, which would be used to make liquidating distributions to DK and JB of $300 and $2,700, respectively. If such property were sold for its $76,000 adjusted tax basis and the partnership were liquidated immediately following the end of the partnership's second taxable year, DK would be required to contribute $9,000 to the partnership in order for the partnership to repay the $85,000 note, and there would be no assets remaining in the partnership to distribute. A comparison of these outcomes indicates that JB bore $2,700 and DK $9,300 of the economic burden that corresponds to the $12,000 net taxable loss. Thus, in addition to the $1,200 net taxable loss allocated to DK under the partnership agreement, $8,100 of net taxable loss will be reallocated to DK under paragraph (b)(3)(iii) of this section. Similarly, for subsequent taxable years, absent an increase in JB's capital account, all net taxable loss allocated to JB under the partnership agreement will be reallocated to DK.

(iii) Assume the same facts as in (ii) and that in the partnership's third taxable year there is rental income of $35,000, operating expenses of $2,000, interest expense of $8,000, the cost recovery deductions of $10,000. The capital accounts of the partners maintained on the books of the partnership do not take into account the reallocation to DK of the $8,100 net taxable loss in the partnership's second taxable year. Thus, an allocation of the $15,000 net taxable income $13,500 to JB and $1,500 to DK (as dictated by the partnership agreement and as reflected in the capital accounts of the partners) does not have economic effect. The partners' interests in the partnership with respect to such $15,000 taxable gain again is made in the manner described in paragraph (b)(3)(iii) of this section. If the partnership's real property were sold for its $76,000 adjusted tax basis and the partnership were liquidated immediately following the end of the partnership's second taxable year, DK would be required to contribute $9,000 to the partnership in order for the partnership to repay the $85,000 note, and there would be no assets remaining to distribute. If such property were sold for its $66,000 adjusted tax basis and the partnership were liquidated immediately following the end of the partnership's third taxable year, the $91,000 ($66,000 sales proceeds plus $25,000 cash on hand) would be used to repay the $85,000 note and there would be $6,000 remaining in the partnership, which would be used to make liquidating distributions to DK and JB of $600 and $5,400, respectively. Accordingly, under paragraph (b)(3)(iii) of this section the $15,000 net taxable income in the partnership's third taxable year will be reallocated $9,600 to DK (minus $9,000 at end of the second taxable year to positive $600 at end of the third taxable year) and $5,400 to JB (zero at end of the second taxable year to positive $5,400 at end of the third taxable year).

Example (16). (i) KG and WN form a limited partnership for the purpose of investing in improved real estate. KG, the general partner, contributes $10,000 to the partnership, and WN, the limited partner, contributes $990,000 to the partnership. The $1,000,000 is used to purchase an apartment building on leased land. The partnership agreement provides that (1) the partners' capital accounts will be determined and maintained in accordance with paragraph (b)(2)(iv) of this section; (2) cash will be distributed first to WN until such time as he has received the amount of his original capital contribution ($990,000), next to KG until such time as he has received the amount of his original capital contribution ($10,000), and thereafter equally between WN and KG; (3) partnership net taxable income will be allocated 99 percent to WN and 1 percent to KG until the cumulative net taxable income allocated for all taxable years is equal to the cumulative net taxable loss previously allocated to the partners, and thereafter equally between WN and KG; (4) partnership net taxable loss will be allocated 99 percent to WN and 1 percent to KG, unless net taxable income has previously been allocated equally between WN and KG, in which case such net taxable loss first will be allocated equally until the cumulative net taxable loss allocated for all taxable years is equal to the cumulative net taxable income previously allocated to the partners; and (5) upon liquidation, WN is not required to restore any deficit balance in his capital account, but KG is so required. Since distributions in liquidation are not required to be made in accordance with the partners' positive capital account balances, and since WN is not required, upon the liquidation of his interest, to restore the deficit balance in his capital account to the partnership, the allocations provided by the partnership agreement do not have economic effect and will be reallocated in accordance with the partners' interests in the partnership under paragraph (b)(3) of this section.

(ii) Assume the same facts as in (i) except that the partnership agreement further provides that distributions in liquidation of the partnership (or any partner's interest) are to be made in accordance with the partners' positive capital account balances (as set forth in paragraph (b)(2)(ii)(*b*)(2) of this section). Assume further that the partnership agreement contains a qualified income offset (as defined in paragraph (b)(2)(ii)(*d*) of this section) and that, as of the end of each partnership taxable year, the items described in paragraphs (b)(2)(iii)(*d*)(*4*), (*5*), and (*6*) of this section are not reasonably expected to cause or increase a deficit balance in WN's capital account. The allocations provided by the partnership agreement have economic effect.

Example (17). FG and RP form a partnership with FG contributing cash of $100 and RP contributing property, with 2 years of cost recovery deductions remaining, that has an adjusted tax basis of $80 and a fair market value of $100. The partnership, FG, and RP have calendar taxable years. The partnership agreement provides that the partners' capital accounts will be determined and maintained in accordance with paragraph (b)(2)(iv) of this section, liquidation proceeds will be made in accordance with capital account balances, and each partner is liable to restore the deficit balance in his capital account to the partnership upon liquidation of his interest (as set forth in paragraphs (b)(2)(ii)(*b*)(2) and (3) of this section). FG expects to be in a substantially higher tax bracket than RP in the partnership's first taxable year. In the partnership's second taxable year, and in subsequent taxable years, it is expected that both will be in approximately equivalent tax brackets. The partnership agreement allocates all items equally except that all $50 of book depreciation is allocated to FG in the partnership's first taxable year and all $50 of book depreciation is allocated to RP in the partnership's second taxable year. If the allocation to FG of all book depreciation in the partnership's first taxable year is respected, FG would be entitled under section 704(c) to the entire cost recovery deduction ($40) for such year. Likewise, if the allocation to RP of all the book depreciation in the partnership's second taxable year is respected, RP would be entitled under section 704(c) to the entire cost recovery deduction ($40) for such year. The allocation of book depreciation to FG and RP in the partnership's first 2 taxable years has economic effect within the meaning of paragraph (b)(2)(ii) of this section. However, the economic effect of these allocations is not substantial under the test described in paragraph (b)(2)(iii)(*c*) of this section since there is a strong likelihood at the time such allocations became part of the partnership agreement that at the end of the 2-year period to which such allocations relate, the net increases and decreases to FG's and RP's capital accounts will be the same with such allocations as they would have been in the absence of such allocation, and the total tax liability of FG and RP for the taxable years to which the section 704(c) determinations relate would be reduced as a result of the allocations of book depreciation. As a result the allocations of book depreciation in the partnership agreement will be disregarded. FG and RP will be allocated such book depreciation in accordance with the partners' interests in the partnership under paragraph (b)(3) of this section. Under these facts the book depreciation deductions will be reallocated equally between the partners, and section 704(c) will be applied with reference to such reallocation of book depreciation.

Example (18). (i) WM and JL form a general partnership by each contributing $300,000 thereto. The partnership uses the $600,000 to purchase an item of tangible personal property, which it leases out. The partnership elects under section 48(q)(4) to reduce the amount of investment tax credit in lieu of adjusting the tax basis of such property. The partnership agreement provides that (1) the partners' capital account will be determined and maintained in accordance with paragraph (b)(2)(iv) of this section, (2) distributions in liquidation of the partnership (or any partner's interest) will be made in accordance with the partners' positive capital account balances (as set forth in paragraph (b)(2)(ii)(*b*)(2) of this section), (3) any partner with a deficit balance in his capital account following the liquidation of his interest must restore that deficit to the partnership (as set forth in paragraph (b)(2)(ii)(*b*)(3 of this section), (4) all income, gain, loss, and deduction of the partnership will be allocated equally between the partners, and (5) all non-liquidating distributions of the partnership will be made equally between the partners. Assume that in each of the partnership's taxable years, it recognizes operating income equal to its operating deductions (excluding cost recovery and depreciation deductions and gain or loss on the sale of its property). During its first 2 taxable years, the partnership has an additional $200,000 cost recovery deduction in each year. Pursuant to the partnership agreement these items are allocated equally between WM and JL.

	WM	JL
Capital account upon formation	$300,000	$300,000
Less: net loss for years 1 and 2	(200,000)	(200,000)
Capital account at end of year 2	$100,000	$100,000

The allocations made in the partnership's first 2 taxable years have substantial economic effect.

(ii) Assume the same facts as in (i) and that MK is admitted to the partnership at the beginning of the partnership's third taxable year. At the time of his admission, the fair market value of the partnership property is $600,000. MK contributes $300,000 to the partnership in exchange for an equal one-third interest in the partnership, and, as permitted under paragraph (b)(2)(iv)(*g*), the capital accounts of WM and JL are adjusted upward to $300,000 each to reflect the fair market value of partnership property. In addition, the partnership agreement is modified to provide that depreciation and gain or loss, as computed for tax purposes, with respect to the partnership property that appreciated prior to MK's admission will be shared among the partners in a manner that takes account of the variation between such property's $200,000 adjusted tax basis and its $600,000 book value in accordance with paragraph (b)(2)(iv)(*f*) and the special rule contained in paragraph (b)(4)(i) of this section. Depreciation and gain or loss, as computed for book purposes, with respect to such property will be allocated equally among the partners and, in accordance with paragraph (b)(2)(iv)(*g*) of this section, will be reflected in the partners' capital accounts, as will all other partnership income, gain, loss, and deduction. Since the requirements of (b)(2)(iv)(*g*) of this section are satisfied, the capital accounts of the partners (as adjusted) continue to be maintained in accordance with paragraph (b)(2)(iv) of this section.

(iii) Assume the same facts as in (ii) and that immediately after MK's admission to the partnership, the partnership property is sold for $600,000, resulting in a taxable gain of $400,000 ($600,000 less $200,000 adjusted tax basis) and no book gain or loss, and the partnership is liquidated. An allocation of the $400,000 taxable gain cannot have economic effect because such gain cannot properly be reflected in the partners' book capital accounts. Consistent with the special partners' interests in the partnership rule contained in paragraph (b)(4)(i) of this section, the partnership agreement provides that the $400,000 taxable gain will, in accordance with section 704(c) principles, be shared equally between WM and JL.

	WM Tax	WM Book	JL Tax	JL Book	MK Tax	MK Book
Capital account at beginning of year 3	$100,000	$300,000	$100,000	$300,000	$300,000	$300,000
Plus: gain	200,000	0	200,000	0	0	0
Capital account before liquidation	$300,000	$300,000	$300,000	$300,000	$300,000	$300,000

The $900,000 of partnership cash ($600,000 sales proceeds plus $300,000 contributed by MK) is distributed equally among WM, JL, and MK in accordance with their adjusted positive capital account balances, each of which is $300,000.

(iv) Assume the same facts as in (iii) except that prior to liquidation the property appreciates and is sold for $900,000, resulting in a taxable gain of $700,000 ($900,000 less $200,000 adjusted tax basis) and a book gain of $300,000 ($900,000 less $600,000 book value). Under the partnership agreement the $300,000 of book gain is allocated equally among the partners, and such allocation has substantial economic effect.

	WM Tax	WM Book	JL Tax	JL Book	MK Tax	MK Book
Capital account at beginning of year 3	$100,000	$300,000	$100,000	$300,000	$300,000	$300,000
Plus: gain	300,000	100,000	300,000	100,000	100,000	100,000
Capital account before liquidation	$400,000	$400,000	$400,000	$400,000	$400,000	$400,000

Consistent with the special partners' interests in the partnership rule contained in paragraph (b)(4)(i) of this section, the partnership agreement provides that the $700,000 taxable gain is, in accordance with section 704(c) principles, shared $300,000 to JL, $300,000 to WM, and $100,000 to MK. This ensures that (1) WM and JL share equally the $400,000 taxable gain that is attributable to appreciation in the property that occurred prior to MK's admission to the partnership in the same manner as it was reflected in their capital accounts upon MK's admission, and (2) WM, JL, and MK share equally the additional

$300,000 taxable gain in the same manner as they shared the $300,000 book gain.

(v) Assume the same facts as in (ii) except that shortly after MK's admission the property depreciates and is sold for $450,000, resulting in a taxable gain of $250,000 ($450,000 less $200,000 adjusted tax basis) and a book loss of $150,000 (450,000 less $600,000 book value). Under the partnership agreement these items are allocated as follows:

	WM Tax	WM Book	JL Tax	JL Book	MK Tax	MK Book
Capital account at beginning of year 3	$100,000	$300,000	$100,000	$300,000	$300,000	$300,000
Plus: gain	125,000	0	125,000	0	0	0
Less: loss	0	(50,000)	0	(50,000)	0	(50,000)
Capital account before liquidation	$225,000	$250,000	$225,000	$250,000	$300,000	$250,000

The $150,000 book loss is allocated equally among the partners, and such allocation has substantial economic effect. Consistent with the special partners' interests in the partnership rule contained in paragraph (b)(4)(i) of this section, the partnership agreement provides that the $250,000 taxable gain is, in accordance with section 704(c) principles, shared equally between WM and JL. The fact that MK bears an economic loss of $50,000 without a corresponding taxable loss is attributable entirely to the "ceiling rule." See paragraph (c)(2) of § 1.704-1.

(vi) Assume the same facts as in (ii) except that the property depreciates and is sold for $170,000, resulting in a $30,000 taxable loss ($200,000 adjusted tax basis less $170,000) and a book loss of $430,000 ($600,000 book value less $170,000). The book loss of $430,000 is allocated equally among the partners ($143,333 each) and has substantial economic effect. Consistent with the special partners' interests in the partnership rule contained in paragraph (b)(4)(i) of this section, the partnership agreement provides that the entire $30,000 taxable loss is, in accordance with section 704(c) principles, included in MK's distributive share.

	WM Tax	WM Book	JL Tax	JL Book	MK Tax	MK Book
Capital account at beginning of year 3	$100,000	$300,000	$100,000	$300,000	$300,000	$300,000
Less: loss	0	(143,333)	0	(143,333)	(30,000)	(143,333)
Capital account before liquidation	$100,000	$156,667	$100,000	$156,667	$270,000	$156,667

(vii) Assume the same facts as in (ii) and that during the partnership's third taxable year, the partnership has an additional $100,000 cost recovery deduction and $300,000 book depreciation deduction attributable to the property purchased by the partnership in its first taxable year. The $300,000 book depreciation deduction is allocated equally among the partners, and that allocation has substantial economic effect. Consistent with the special partners' interests in the partnership rule contained in paragraph (b)(4)(i) of this section, the partnership agreement provides that the $100,000 cost recovery deduction for the partnership's third taxable year is, in accordance with section 704(c) principles, included in MK's distributive share. This is because under these facts those principles require MK to include the cost recovery deduction for such property in his distributive share up to the amount of the book depreciation deduction for such property properly allocated to him.

	WM Tax	WM Book	JL Tax	JL Book	MK Tax	MK Book
Capital account at beginning of year 3	$100,000	$300,000	$100,000	$300,000	$300,000	$300,000
Less: recovery/depreciation deduction for year 3 .	0	(100,000)	0	(100,000)	(100,000)	(100,000)
Capital account at the end of year 3	$100,000	$200,000	$100,000	$200,000	$200,000	$200,000

(viii) Assume the same facts as in (vii) except that upon MK's admission the partnership property has an adjusted tax basis of $220,000 (instead of $200,000), and thus the cost recovery deduction for the partnership's third taxable year is $110,000. Assume further that upon MK's admission WM and JL have adjusted capital account balances of $110,000 and $100,000, respectively. Consistent with the special partners' interests in the partnership rule contained in paragraph (b)(4)(i) of this section, the partnership agreement provides that the excess $10,000 cost recovery deduction ($110,000 less $100,000 included in MK's distributive share) is, in accordance with section 704(c) principles, shared equally between WM and JL and is so included in their respective distributive shares for the partnership's third taxable year.

(ix) Assume the same facts as in (vii) except that upon MK's admission the partnership agreement is amended to allocate the first $400,000 of book depreciation and loss on partnership property equally between WM and JL and the last $200,000 of such book depreciation and loss to MK. Assume such allocations have substantial economic effect. Pursuant to this amendment the $300,000 book depreciation deduction in the partnership's third taxable year is allocated equally between WM and JL. Consistent with the special partners' interests in the partnership rule contained in paragraph (b)(4)(i) of this section, the partnership agreement provides that the $100,000 cost recovery deduction is, in accordance with section 704(c) principles, shared equally between WM and JL. In the partnership's fourth taxable year, it has a $60,000 cost recovery deduction and a $180,000 book depreciation deduction. Under the amendment described above, the $180,000 book depreciation deduction is allocated $50,000 to WM, $50,000 to JL, and $80,000 to MK. Consistent with the special partners' interests in the partnership rule contained in paragraph (b)(4)(i) of this section, the partnership agreement provides that the $60,000 cost recovery deduction is, in accordance with section 704(c) principles, included entirely in MK's distributive share.

	WM Tax	WM Book	JL Tax	JL Book	MK Tax	MK Book
Capital account at beginning of year 3	$100,000	$300,000	$100,000	$300,000	$300,000	$300,000
Less: (a) recovery/depreciation deduction for year 3	(50,000)	(150,000)	(50,000)	(150,000)	0	0
(b) recovery/depreciation deduction for year 4 . . .	0	(50,000)	0	(50,000)	(60,000)	(80,000)
Capital account at end of year 4	$50,000	$100,000	$50,000	$100,000	$240,000	$220,000

(x) Assume the same facts as in (vii) and that at the beginning of the partnership's third taxable year, the partnership purchases a second item of tangible personal property for $300,000 and elects under section 48(q)(4) to reduce the amount of investment tax credit in lieu of adjusting the tax basis of such property. The partnership agreement is amended to allocate the first $150,000 of cost recovery deductions and loss from such property to WM and the next $150,000 of cost recovery deductions and loss from such property equally between JL and MK. Thus, in the partnership's third taxable year it has, in addition to the items specified in (vii), a cost recovery and book depreciation deduction of $100,000 attributable to the newly acquired property, which is allocated entirely to WM. As in (vii), the allocation of the $300,000 book depreciation attributable to the property purchased in the partnership's first taxable year equally among the partners has substantial economic effect, and consistent with the special partners' interests in the partnership rule contained in paragraph (b)(4)(i) of this section, the partnership agreement properly provides for the entire $100,000 cost recovery deduction attributable to such property to be included in MK's distributive share. Furthermore, the allocation to WM of the $100,000 cost recovery deduction attributable to the property purchased in the partnership's third taxable year has substantial economic effect.

	WM Tax	WM Book	JL Tax	JL Book	MK Tax	MK Book
Capital account at beginning of year 3	$100,000	$300,000	$100,000	$300,000	$300,000	$300,000
Less: (a) recovery/depreciation deduction for property bought in year 1	0	(100,000)	0	(100,000)	(100,000)	(100,000)
(b) recovery/depreciation deduction for property bought in year 3	(100,000)	(100,000)	0	0	0	0
Capital account at end of year 3	0	$100,000	$100,000	$200,000	$200,000	$200,000

(xi) Assume the same facts as in (x) and that at the beginning of the partnership's fourth taxable year, the properties purchased in the partnership's first and third taxable years are disposed of for $90,000 and $180,000, respectively, and the partnership is liquidated. With respect to the property purchased in the first taxable year, there is a book loss of $210,000 ($300,000 book value less $90,000) and a taxable loss of $10,000 ($100,000 adjusted tax basis less $90,000). The book loss is allocated equally among the partners, and such allocation has substantial economic effect. Consistent with the special partners' interests in the partnership rule contained in paragraph (b)(4)(i) of this section, the partnership agreement provides that the taxable loss of $10,000 will, in accordance with section 704(c) principles, be included entirely in MK's distributive share. With respect to the property purchased in the partnership's third taxable year, there is a book and taxable loss of $20,000. Pursuant to the partnership agreement this loss is allocated entirely to WM, and such allocation has substantial economic effect.

	WM		JL		MK	
	Tax	*Book*	*Tax*	*Book*	*Tax*	*Book*
Capital account at beginning of year 4	0	$100,000	$100,000	$200,000	$200,000	$200,000
Less: (a) loss on property bought in year 1	0	(70,000)	0	(70,000)	(10,000)	(70,000)
(b) loss on property bought in year 3	(20,000)	(20,000)	0	0	0	0
Capital account before liquidation	($20,000)	$10,000	$100,000	$130,000	$190,000	$130,000

Partnership liquidation proceeds ($270,000) are properly distributed in accordance with the partners' adjusted positive book capital account balances ($10,000 to WM, $130,000 to JL and $130,000 to MK).

(xii) Assume the same facts as in (x) and that in the partnership's fourth taxable year it has a cost recovery deduction of $60,000 and book depreciation deduction of $180,000 attributable to the property purchased in the partnership's first taxable year, and a cost recovery and book depreciation deduction of $100,000 attributable to the property purchased in the partnership's third taxable year. The $180,000 book depreciation deduction attributable to the property purchased in the partnership's first taxable year is allocated equally among the partners, and such allocation has substantial economic effect. Consistent with the special partners' interests in the partnership rule contained in paragraph (b)(4)(i) of this section, the partnership agreement provides that the $60,000 cost recovery deduction attributable to the property purchased in the first taxable year is, in accordance with section 704(c) principles, included entirely in MK's distributive share. Furthermore, the $100,000 cost recovery deduction attributable to the property purchased in the third taxable year is allocated $50,000 to WM, $25,000 to JL, and $25,000 to MK, and such allocation has substantial economic effect.

	WM		JL		MK	
	Tax	*Book*	*Tax*	*Book*	*Tax*	*Book*
Capital account at beginning of year 4	—0—	$100,000	$100,000	$200,000	$200,000	$200,000
Less: (a) recovery/depreciation deduction for property bought in year 1	—0—	(60,000)	—0—	(60,000)	(60,000)	(60,000)
(b) recovery/depreciation deduction for property bought in year 3	(50,000)	(50,000)	(25,000)	(25,000)	(25,000)	(25,000)
Capital account at end of year 4	($50,000)	($10,000)	$75,000	$115,000	$115,000	$115,000

At the end of the partnership's fourth taxable year the adjusted tax bases of the partnership properties acquired in its first and third taxable years are $40,000 and $100,000, respectively. If the properties are disposed of at the beginning of the partnership's fifth taxable year for their adjusted tax bases, there would be no taxable gain or loss, a book loss of $80,000 on the property purchased in the partnership's first taxable year ($120,000 book value less $40,000), and cash available for distribution of $140,000.

	WM		JL		MK	
	Tax	*Book*	*Tax*	*Book*	*Tax*	*Book*
Capital account at beginning of year 5	($50,000)	($10,000)	$75,000	$115,000	$115,000	$115,000
Less: loss	—0—	(26,667)	—0—	(26,667)	—0—	(26,667)
Capital account before liquidation	($50,000)	($36,667)	$75,000	$88,333	$115,000	$88,333

If the partnership is then liquidated, the $140,000 of cash on hand plus the $36,667 balance that WM would be required to contribute to the partnership (the deficit balance in his book capital account) would be distributed equally between JL and MK in accordance with their adjusted positive book capital account balances.

(xiii) Assume the same facts as in (i). Any tax preferences under section 57(a)(12) attributable to the partnership's cost recovery deductions in the first 2 taxable years will be taken into account equally by WM and JL. If the partnership agreement instead provides that the partnership's cost recovery deductions in its first 2 taxable years are allocated 25 percent to WM and 75 percent to JL (and such allocations have substantial economic effect), the tax preferences attributable to such cost recovery deductions would be taken into account 25 percent by WM and 75 percent by JL. The conclusion in the previous sentence is unchanged even if the partnership's operating expenses (exclusive of cost recovery and depreciation deductions) exceed its operating income in each of the partnership's first 2 taxable years, the resulting net loss is allocated entirely to WM, and the cost recovery deductions are allocated 25 percent to WM and 75 percent to JL (provided such allocations have substantial economic effect). If the partnership agreement instead provides that all income, gain, loss, and deduction (including cost recovery and depreciation deductions) are allocated equally between JL and WM, the tax preferences attributable to the cost recovery deductions would be taken into account equally by JL and WM. In this case, if the partnership has a $100,000 cost recovery deduction in its first taxable year and an additional net loss of $100,000 in its first taxable year (*i.e.*, its operating expenses exceed its operating income by $100,000) and purports to categorize JL's $100,000 distributive share of partnership loss as being attributable to the cost recovery deduction and WM's $100,000 distributive share of partnership loss as being attributable to the net loss, the economic effect of such allocations is not substantial, and each partner will be allocated one-half of all partnership income, gain, loss, and deduction and will take into account one-half of the tax preferences attributable to the cost recovery deductions.

Example (19). (i) DG and JC form a general partnership for the purpose of drilling oil wells. DG contributes an oil lease, which has a fair market value and adjusted tax basis of $100,000. JC contributes $100,000 in cash, which is used to finance the drilling operations. The partnership agreement provides that DG is credited with a capital account of $100,000, and JC is credited with a capital account of $100,000. The agreement further provides that the partners' capital accounts will be determined and maintained in accordance with paragraph (b)(2)(iv) of this section, distributions in liquidation of the partnership (or any partner's interest) will be made in accordance with the partners' positive capital account balances, and any partner with a deficit balance in his capital account following the liquidation of his interest must restore such deficit to the partnership (as set forth in paragraphs (b)(2)(ii)(b)(2) and (3) of this section). The partnership chooses to adjust capital accounts on a simulated cost depletion basis and elects under section 48(q)(4) to reduce the amount of investment tax credit in lieu of adjusting the basis of its section 38 property. The agreement further provides that (1) all additional cash requirements of the partnership will be borne equally by DG and JC, (2) the deductions attributable to the property (including money) contributed by each partner will be allocated to such partner, (3) all other income, gain, loss, and deductions (and item thereof) will be allocated equally between DG and JC, and (4) all cash from operations will be distributed equally between DG and JC. In the partnership's first taxable year $80,000 of partnership intangible drilling cost deductions and $20,000 of cost recovery deductions on partnership equipment are allocated to JC, and the $100,000 basis of the lease is, for purposes of the depletion allowance under sections 611 and 613A(c)(7)(D), allocated to DG. The allocations of income, gain, loss, and deduction provided in the partnership agreement have substantial economic effect. Furthermore, since the allocation of the entire basis of the lease to DG will not result in capital account adjustments (under paragraph (b)(2)(*iv*)(*k*) of this section) the economic effect of which is insubstantial, and since all other partnership allocations are recognized under this paragraph, the allocation of the $100,000 adjusted basis of the lease to DG is, under paragraph (b)(4)(v) of this section, recognized as being in accordance with the partners' interests in partnership capital for purposes of section 613A(c)(7)(D).

(ii) Assume the same facts as in (i) except that the partnership agreement provides that (1) all additional cash requirements of the partnership for additional expenses will be funded by additional contributions from JC, (2) all cash from operations will first be distributed to JC until the excess of such cash distributions over the amount of such additional expenses equals his initial $100,000 contribution, (3) all deductions attributable to such additional operating expenses will be allocated to JC, and (4) all income will be allocated to JC until the aggregate amount of income allocated to him equals the amount of partnership operating expenses funded by his initial $100,000 contribution plus the amount of additional operating expenses paid from contributions made solely by him. The allocations of income, gain, loss, and deduction provided in the partnership agreement have economic effect. In addition, the economic effect of the allocations provided in the agreement is substantial. Because the partnership's drilling activities are sufficiently speculative, there is not a strong likelihood at the time the disproportionate allocations of loss and deduction to JC are provided for by the partnership agreement that the economic effect of such allocations will be largely offset by allocations of income. In addition, since the allocation of the entire basis of the lease to DG will not result in capital account adjustments (under paragraph (b)(2)(*iv*)(*k*) of this section), the economic effect of which is insubstantial, and since all other partnership allocations are recognized under this paragraph, the allocation of the adjusted basis of the lease to DG is, under paragraph (b)(4)(v) of this section, recognized as being in accordance with the partners' interests in partnership capital under section 613A(c)(7)(D).

(iii) Assume the same facts as in (i) except that all distributions, including those made upon liquidation of the partnership, will be made equally between DG and JC, and no partner is obligated to restore the deficit balance in his capital account to the partnership following the liquidation of his interest for distribution to partners with positive capital account balances. Since liquidation proceeds will be distributed equally between DG and JC irrespective of their capital account balances, and since no partner is required to restore the deficit balance in his capital account to the partnership upon liquidation (in accordance with paragraph (b)(2)(ii)(*b*)(*3*) of this section), the allocations of income, gain, loss, and deduction provided in the partnership agreement do not have economic effect and must be reallocated in accordance with the partners' interests in the partnership under paragraph (b)(3) of this section. Under these facts all partnership income, gain, loss, and deduction (and item thereof) will be reallocated equally between JC and DG. Furthermore, the allocation of the $100,000 adjusted tax basis of the lease to DG is not, under paragraph (b)(4)(v) of this section, deemed to be in accordance with the partners' interests in partnership capital under section 613A(c)(7)(D), and such basis must be reallocated in accordance with the partners' interests in partnership capital or income as determined under section 613A(c)(7)(D). The results in this example would be the same if JC's initial cash contribution were $1,000,000 (instead of $100,000), but in such case the partners should consider whether, and to what extent, the provisions of paragraph (b)(1) of § 1.721-1, and principles related thereto, may be applicable.

(iv) Assume the same facts as in (i) and that for the partnership's first taxable year the simulated depletion deduction with respect to the lease is $10,000. Since DG properly was allocated the entire depletable basis of the lease (such allocation having been recognized as being in accordance with DG's interest in partnership capital with respect to such lease), under paragraph (b)(2)(iv)(*k*)(*1*) of this section the partnership's $10,000 simulated depletion deduction is allocated to DG and will reduce his capital account accordingly. If (prior to any additional simulated depletion deductions) the lease is sold for $100,000, paragraph (b)(4)(v) of this section requires that the first $90,000 (*i.e.,* the partnership's simulated adjusted basis in the lease) out of the $100,000 amount realized on such sale be allocated to DG (but does not directly affect his capital account). The partnersip agreement allocates the remaining $10,000 amount realized equally between JC and DG (but such allocation does not directly affect their capital accounts). This allocation of the $10,000 portion of amount realized that exceeds the partnership's simulated adjusted basis in the lease will be treated as being in accordance with the partners' allocable shares of such amount realized under section 613A(c)(7)(D) because such allocation will not result in capital account adjustments (under paragraph (b)(2)(iv)(*k*) of this section) the economic effect of which is insubstantial, and all other partnership allocations are recognized under this paragraph. Under paragraph (b)(2)(iv)(*k*) of this section, the partners' capital accounts are adjusted upward by the partnership's simulated gain of $10,000 ($100,000 sales price less $90,000 simulated adjusted basis) in proportion to such partners' allocable shares of the $10,000 portion of the total amount realized that exceeds the partnership's $90,000 simulated adjusted basis ($5,000 to JC and $5,000 to DG). If the lease is sold for $50,000, under paragraph (b)(4)(v) of this section the entire $50,000 amount realized on the sale of the lease will be allocated to DG (but will not directly affect his capital account). Under paragraph (b)(2)(iv)(*k*) of this section the partners' capital accounts will be adjusted downward by the partnership's $40,000 simulated loss ($50,000 sales price less $90,000 simulated adjusted basis) in proportion to the partners' allocable shares of the total amount realized from the property that represents recovery of the partnership's simulated adjusted basis therein. Accordingly, DG's capital account will be reduced by such $40,000.

Example 20. (i) A and B form AB, an eligible entity (as defined in § 301.7701-3(a) of this chapter), treated as a partnership for U.S. tax purposes. AB operates business M in country X and earns income from passive investments in country X. Country X imposes a 40 percent tax on business M income, which tax is a CFTE, but exempts from tax income from passive investments. In 2007, AB earns $100,000 of income from business M and $30,000 from passive investments and pays or accrues $40,000 of country X taxes. For purposes of section 904(d), the income from business M is general limitation income and the income from the passive investments is passive income. Pursuant to the partnership agreement, all partnership items, including CFTEs, from business M are allocated 60 percent to A and 40 percent to B, and all partnership items, including CFTEs, from passive investments are allocated 80 percent to A and 20 percent to B. Accordingly, A is allocated 60 percent of the business M income ($60,000) and 60 percent of the country X taxes ($24,000), and B is allocated 40 percent of the business M income ($40,000) and 40 percent of the country X taxes ($16,000). The income from the passive investments is allocated $24,000 to A and $6,000 to B. Assume that allocations of all items other than CFTEs are valid.

(ii) Because the partnership agreement provides for different allocations of the net income attributable to business M and the passive investments, the net income attributable to each is income in a separate CFTE category. See paragraph (b)(4)(viii)(*c*)(*2*) of this section. AB must determine the net income in each CFTE category and the CFTEs allocable to each CFTE category. Under paragraph (b)(4)(viii)(*c*)(*3*) of this section, the net income in the business M CFTE category is the $100,000 attributable to business M and the net income in the passive investments CFTE category is the $30,000 attributable to the passive investments. Under paragraph (b)(4)(viii)(*d*) of this section, the $40,000 of country X taxes is allocated to the business M CFTE category and no portion of the country X taxes is allocated to the passive investments CFTE category. Therefore, the $40,000 of country X taxes are related to the $100,000 of net income in the business M CFTE category. See paragraph (b)(4)(viii)(*c*)(*1*) of this section. Because AB's partnership agreement allocates the net income from the business M CFTE category 60 percent to A and 40 percent to B, and the country X taxes 60 percent to A and 40 percent to B, the allocations of the CFTEs are in proportion to the distributive shares of income to which the CFTEs relate. Because AB satisfies the requirement of paragraph (b)(4)(viii) of this section, the allocations of the country X taxes are deemed to be in accordance with the partners' interests in the partnership. Because the business M income is general limitation income, all $40,000 of taxes are attributable to the general limitation category. See § 1.904-6.

Example 21. (i) A and B form AB, an eligible entity (as defined in § 301.7701-3(a) of this chapter), treated as a partnership for U.S. tax purposes. AB operates business M in country X and business N in country Y. Country X imposes a 40 percent tax on business M income, country Y imposes a 20 percent tax on business N income, and the country X and country Y taxes are CFTEs. In 2007, AB has $100,000 of income from business M and $50,000 of income from business N. Country X imposes $40,000 of tax on the income from business M and country Y imposes $10,000 of tax on the income of business N. Pursuant to the partnership agreement, all partnership items, including CFTEs, from business M are allocated 75 percent to A and 25 percent to B, and all partnership items, including CFTEs, from business N are split evenly between A and B (50 percent each). Accordingly, A is allocated 75 percent of the income from business M ($75,000), 75 percent of the country X taxes ($30,000), 50 percent of the income from business N ($25,000), and 50 percent of the country Y taxes ($5,000). B is allocated 25 percent of the income from business M ($25,000), 25 percent of the country X taxes ($10,000), 50 percent of the income from business N ($25,000), and 50 percent of the country Y taxes ($5,000). Assume that allocations of all items other than CFTEs are valid. The income from business M and business N is general limitation income for purposes of section 904(d).

(ii) Because the partnership agreement provides for different allocations of the net income attributable to businesses M and N, the net income attributable to each business is income in a separate CFTE category even though all of the income is in the general limitation category for section 904(d) purposes. See paragraph (b)(4)(viii)(*c*)(*2*) of this section. Under paragraph (b)(4)(viii)(*c*)(*3*) of this section, the net income in the business M CFTE category is the $100,000 attributable to business M and the net income in the business N CFTE category is $50,000 attributable to business N. Under paragraph (b)(4)(viii)(*d*) of this section, the $40,000 of country X taxes is allocated to the business M CFTE category and the $10,000 of country Y taxes is allocated to the business N CFTE category. Therefore, the $40,000 of country X taxes are related to the $100,000 of net income in the business M CFTE category and the $10,000 of country Y taxes are related to the $50,000 of net income in the business N CFTE category. See paragraph (b)(4)(viii)(*c*)(*1*) of this section. Because AB's partnership agreement allocates the $40,000 of country X taxes in the same proportion as the net income in the business M CFTE category, and the $10,000 of country Y taxes in the same proportion as the net income in the business N CFTE category, the allocations of the country X taxes and the country Y taxes are in proportion to the distributive shares of income to which the foreign taxes relate. Because AB satisfies the requirements of paragraph (b)(4)(viii) of this section, the allocations of the country X and country Y taxes are deemed to be in accordance with the partners' interests in the partnership.

Example 22. (i) The facts are the same as in *Example 21,* except that the partnership agreement provides for the following allocations. Depreciation attributable to machine X, which is used in business M, is allocated 100 percent to A. B is allocated the first $20,000 of gross income attributable to business N, which allocation does not result in a deduction under foreign law. All remaining items, except CFTEs, are allocated 50 percent to A and 50 percent to B. For 2007, assume that business M generates $120,000 of income, before taking into account depreciation attributable to machine X. The total amount of depreciation attributable to machine X is $20,000, which results in $100,000 of net income attributable to business M for U.S. and country X tax purposes. Business N generates $70,000 of gross income and has $20,000 of expenses, resulting in $50,000 of net income for U.S. and country Y tax purposes. Pursuant to the partnership agreement, A is allocated $40,000 of the net income attributable to business M ($60,000 of business M income less $20,000 of depreciation attributable to machine X), and $15,000 of the net income attributable to business N. B is allocated $60,000 of the net income attributable to business M and $35,000 of the net income attributable to business N ($20,000 of gross income, plus $15,000 of net income).

(ii) As a result of the special allocations, the net income attributable to business M ($100,000) is allocated 40 percent to A and 60 percent to B. The net income attributable to business N ($50,000) is allocated 30 percent to A and 70 percent to B. Because the partnership agreement provides for different allocations of the net income attributable to businesses M and N, the net income from each of businesses M and N is income in a separate CFTE category. See paragraph (b)(4)(viii)(*c*)(*2*) of this section. Under paragraph (b)(4)(viii)(*c*)(*3*) of this section, the net income in the business M CFTE category is the $100,000 of net income attributable to business M and the net income in the business N CFTE category is the $50,000 of net income attributable to business N. Under paragraph (b)(4)(viii)(*d*)(*1*) of this section, the $40,000 of country X taxes is allocated to the business M CFTE category and the $10,000 of country Y taxes is allocated to the business N CFTE category. Therefore, the $40,000 of country X taxes relates to the $100,000 of net income in the business M CFTE and the $10,000 of country Y taxes relates to the $50,000 of net income in the business N CFTE category. See paragraph (b)(4)(viii)(*c*)(*1*) of this section. The allocations of the country X taxes will be in proportion to the distributive shares of income to which they relate and will be deemed to be in accordance with the partners' interests in the partnership if such taxes are allocated 40 percent to A and 60 percent to B. The allocations of the country Y taxes will be in proportion to the distributive shares of income to which they relate and will be deemed to be in accordance with the partners' interests in the partnership if such taxes are allocated 30 percent to A and 70 percent to B.

(iii) Assume that for 2008, all the facts are the same as in paragraph (i) of this *Example 22,* except that business M generates $60,000 of income before taking into account depreciation attributable to machine X and country X imposes $16,000 of tax on the $40,000 of net income attributable to business M. Pursuant to the partnership agreement, A is allocated 25 percent of the income from business M ($10,000), and B is allocated 75 percent of the income from business M ($30,000). Allocations of the country X taxes will be in proportion to the distributive shares of income to which they relate and will be deemed to be in accordance with the partners' interests in the partnership if such taxes are allocated 25 percent to A and 75 percent to B.

Example 23. (i) The facts are the same as in *Example 21,* except that AB does not actually receive the $50,000 of income accrued in 2007 with respect to business N until 2008 and AB accrues and receives an additional $100,000 with respect to business N in 2008. Also assume that A, B, and AB each report taxable income on an accrual basis for U.S. tax purposes and AB reports taxable income using the cash receipts and disbursements method of accounting for country X and country Y purposes. In 2007, AB pays or accrues country X taxes of $40,000. In 2008, AB pays or accrues country Y taxes of $30,000. Pursuant to the partnership agreement, in 2007, A is allocated 75 percent of business M income ($75,000) and country X taxes ($30,000) and 50 percent of business N income ($25,000). B is allocated 25 percent of business M income ($25,000) and country X taxes ($10,000) and 50 percent of business N income ($25,000). In 2008, A and B are each allocated 50 percent of the business N income ($50,000) and country Y taxes ($15,000).

(ii) For 2007, the $40,000 of country X taxes paid or accrued by AB relates to the $100,000 of net income in the business M CFTE category. No portion of the country X taxes paid or accrued in 2007 relates to the $50,000 of net income in the business N CFTE category. For 2008, the net income in the business N CFTE category is the $100,000 attributable to business N. See paragraph (b)(4)(viii)(*c*)(*3*) of this section. Under paragraph (b)(4)(viii)(*d*)(*1*) of this section, $20,000 of the country Y tax paid or accrued in 2008 is allocated to the business N CFTE category. The remaining $10,000 of country Y tax is allocated to the business N CFTE category under paragraph (b)(4)(viii)(*d*)(*2*) of this section (relating to timing differences). Therefore, the $30,000 of country Y taxes paid or accrued by AB in 2008 is related to the $100,000 of net income in the business N CFTE category for 2008. See paragraph (b)(4)(viii)(*c*)(*1*) of this section. Because AB's partnership agreement allocates the $40,000 of country X taxes and the $30,000 of country Y taxes in proportion to the distributive shares of income to which the taxes relate, the allocations of the country X and country Y taxes satisfy the requirements of paragraphs (b)(4)(viii)(*a*)(*1*) and (*2*) of this section and the allocations of the country X and Y taxes are deemed to be in accordance with the partners' interests in the partnership under paragraph (b)(4)(viii) of this section.

Example 24. (i) The facts are the same as in *Example 21,* except that businesses M and N are conducted by entities (DE1 and DE2, respectively) that are corporations for country X and Y tax purposes and disregarded entities for U.S. Federal income tax purposes. Also, assume that DE1 makes payments of $75,000 during 2012 to DE2 that are deductible by DE1 for country X tax purposes and includible in income of DE2 for country Y tax purposes. As a result of such payments, DE1 has taxable income of $25,000 for country X purposes on which $10,000 of taxes are imposed and DE2 has taxable income of $125,000 for country Y purposes on which $25,000 of taxes are imposed. For U.S. Federal income tax purposes, $100,000 of AB's income is attributable to the activities of DE1 and $50,000 of AB's income is attributable to the activities of DE2. Pursuant to the partnership agreement, all partnership items from business M, excluding CFTEs paid or accrued by business M, are allocated 75% to A and 25% to B, and all partnership items from business N, excluding CFTEs paid or accrued by business N, are split evenly between A and B (50% each). Accordingly, A is allocated 75% of the income from business M ($75,000), and 50% of the income from business N ($25,000). B is allocated 25% of the income from business M ($25,000), and 50% of the income from business N ($25,000).

(ii) Because the partnership agreement provides for different allocations of the net income attributable to businesses M and N, the net income attributable to each of business M and business N is income in separate CFTE categories. See paragraph (b)(4)(viii)(*c*)(*2*) of this section. Under paragraph (b)(4)(viii)(*c*)(*3*) of this section, the $100,000 of net income attributable to business M is in the business M CFTE category and the $50,000 of net income attributable to business N is in the business N CFTE category. Under paragraph (b)(4)(viii)(*d*)(*1*) of this section, the $10,000 of country X taxes is allocated to the business M CFTE category and $10,000 of the country Y taxes is allocated to the business N CFTE category. The additional $15,000 of country Y tax imposed with respect to the inter-branch payment is assigned to the business M CFTE category because for U.S. Federal income tax purposes, the related $75,000 of income that country Y is taxing is in the business M CFTE category. Therefore, $25,000 of taxes ($10,000 of country X taxes and $15,000 of the country Y taxes) is related to the $100,000 of net income in the business M CFTE category and the other $10,000 of country Y taxes is related to the $50,000 of net income in the business N CFTE category. See paragraph (b)(4)(viii)(*c*)(*1*) of this section. The allocations of country X taxes will be in proportion to the distributive shares of income to which they relate and will be deemed to be in accordance with the partners' interests in the partnership if such taxes are allocated 75% to A and 25% to B. The allocations of country Y taxes will be in proportion to the distributive shares of income to which they relate and will be deemed to be in accordance with the partners' interests in the partnership if $15,000 of such taxes is allocated 75% to A and 25% to B and the other $10,000 of such taxes is allocated 50% to A and 50% to B. No inference is intended with respect to the application of other provisions to arrangements that involve disregarded payments.

(iii) Assume that the facts are the same as in paragraph (i) of this *Example 24*, except that in order to reflect the $75,000 payment from DE1 to DE2, the partnership agreement allocates $75,000 of the income attributable to business M equally between A and B (50% each). In order to prevent separating the CFTEs from the related foreign income, the $75,000 payment is treated as a divisible part of the business M activity and, therefore, a separate activity. See paragraph (b)(4)(viii)(*c*)(*2*)(*iii*) of this section. Because items from the disregarded payment and business N are both shared equally between A and B, the disregarded payment activity and the business N activity are treated as a single CFTE category. See paragraph (b)(4)(viii)(*c*)(*2*)(*i*) of this section. Accordingly, $25,000 of net income attributable to business M is in the business M CFTE category and $75,000 of income of business M attributable to the disregarded payment and the $50,000 of net income attributable to business N are in the business N CFTE category. Under paragraph (b)(4)(viii)(*d*)(*1*) of this section, the $10,000 of country X taxes is allocated to the business M CFTE category and all $25,000 of the country Y taxes is allocated to the business N CFTE category. The allocations of country X taxes will be in proportion to the distributive shares of income to which they relate and will be deemed to be in accordance with the partners' interests in the partnership if such taxes are allocated 75% to A and 25% to B. The allocations of country Y taxes will be in proportion to the distributive shares of income to which they relate and will be deemed to be in accordance with the partners' interests in the partnership if such taxes are allocated 50% to A and 50% to B.

Example 25. [Reserved]. For further guidance, see § 1.704-1T(b)(5) *Example 25*.

Example 26. (i) A and B form AB, an eligible entity (as defined in § 301.7701-3(a) of this chapter), treated as a partnership for U.S. tax purposes. AB operates business M in country X and business N in country Y. A, a U.S. corporation, contributes a building with a fair market value of $200,000 and an adjusted basis of $50,000 for both U.S. and country X purposes. The building contributed by A is used in business M. B, a country X corporation, contributes $800,000 cash. The AB partnership agreement provides that AB will make allocations under section 704(c) using the traditional method under § 1.704-3(b) and that all other items, excluding creditable foreign taxes, will be allocated 20 percent to A and 80 percent to B. The partnership agreement provides that creditable foreign taxes will be allocated in proportion to the partners' distributive shares of net income in each CFTE category, which shall be determined by taking into accounts items allocated pursuant to section 704(c). Country X and Country Y impose tax at a rate of 20 percent and 40 percent, respectively, and such taxes are CFTEs. In 2007, AB sells the building contributed by A for $200,000, thereby recognizing taxable income of $150,000 for U.S. and country X purposes, and recognizes $250,000 of other income from the operation of business M. AB pays or accrues $80,000 of country X tax on such income. Also in 2007, business N recognizes $100,000 of taxable income for U.S. and country Y purposes and pays or accrues $40,000 of country Y tax. Pursuant to the partnership agreement, A is allocated $200,000 of business M income ($150,000 of taxable income in accordance with section 704(c) and $50,000 of other business M income) and $40,000 of country X tax, and 20 percent of both business N income ($20,000) and country Y tax ($8,000). B is allocated $200,000 of business M income and $40,000 of country X tax and 80 percent of both the business N income ($80,000) and country Y tax ($32,000). Assume that allocations of all items other than CFTEs are valid.

(ii) The net income attributable to business M ($400,000) is allocated 50 percent to A and 50 percent to B while the net income attributable to business N ($100,000) is allocated 20 percent to A and 80 percent to B. Because the partnership agreement provides for different allocations of the net income attributable to businesses M and N, the net income attributable to each activity is income in a separate CFTE category. See paragraph (b)(4)(viii)(*c*)(2) of this section. Under paragraph (b)(4)(viii)(*c*)(*3*) of this section, the net income in the business M CFTE category is the $400,000 of net income attributable to business M and the net income in the business N CFTE category is the $100,000 of net income attributable to business N. Under paragraph (b)(4)(viii)(*d*)(*1*) of this section, the $80,000 of country X tax is allocated to the business M CFTE category and the $40,000 of country Y tax is allocated to the business N CFTE category. Therefore, the $80,000 of country X tax relates to the $400,000 of net income in the business M CFTE category and the $40,000 of country Y tax relates to the $100,000 of net income in the business N CFTE category. See paragraph (b)(4)(viii)(*c*)(*1*) of this section. Because AB's partnership agreement allocates the $80,000 of country X taxes and $40,000 of country Y taxes in proportion to the distributive shares of income to which such taxes relate, the allocations are deemed to be in accordance with the partners' interests in the partnership under paragraph (b)(4)(viii) of this section.

Example 27. (i) A, a U.S. citizen, and B, a country X citizen, form AB, a country X eligible entity (as defined in § 301.7701-3(a) of this chapter), treated as a partnership for U.S. tax purposes. AB's only activity is business M, which it operates in country X. Country X imposes a 40 percent tax on the portion of AB's business M income that is the allocable share of AB's owners that are not citizens of country X, which tax is a CFTE. The partnership agreement provides that all partnership items, excluding CFTEs, from business M are allocated 40 percent to A and 60 percent to B. CFTEs are allocated 100 percent to A. In 2007, AB earns $100,000 of net income from business M and pays or accrues $16,000 of country X taxes on A's allocable share of AB's income ($40,000). Pursuant to the partnership agreement, A is allocated 40 percent of the business M income ($40,000) and 100 percent of the country X taxes ($16,000), and B is allocated 60 percent of the business M income ($60,000) and no country X taxes. Assume that allocations of all items other than CFTEs are valid.

(ii) AB has a single CFTE category because all of AB's net income is allocated in the same ratio. See paragraph (b)(4)(viii)(*c*)(2). Under paragraph (b)(4)(viii)(*c*)(*3*) of this section, the $40,000 of business M income that is allocated to A is included in the single CFTE category. Under paragraph (b)(4)(viii)(*c*)(*3*)(*ii*) of this section, no portion of the $60,000 allocated to B is included in the single CFTE category. Under paragraph (b)(4)(viii)(*d*) of this section, the $16,000 of taxes is allocated to the single CFTE category.

Therefore, the $16,000 of country X taxes is related to the $40,000 of net income in the single CFTE category that is allocated to A. See paragraph (b)(4)(viii)(*c*)(*1*) of this section. Because AB's partnership agreement allocates the country X taxes in proportion to the distributive share of income to which the taxes relate, AB satisfies the requirement of paragraph (b)(4)(viii) of this section, and the allocation of the country X taxes is deemed to be in accordance with the partners' interests in the partnership.

Example 28. (i) B, a domestic corporation, and C, a controlled foreign corporation, form BC, a partnership organized under the laws of country X. B and C each contribute 50 percent of the capital of BC. B and C are wholly-owned subsidiaries of A, a domestic corporation. Substantially all of BC's income would not be subpart F income if earned directly by C. The BC partnership agreement provides that, for the first fifteen years, BC's gross income will be allocated 10 percent to B and 90 percent to C, and BC's deductions and losses will be allocated 90 percent to B and 10 percent to C. The partnership agreement also provides that, after the initial fifteen year period, BC's gross income will be allocated 90 percent to B and 10 percent to C, and BC's deductions and losses will be allocated 10 percent to B and 90 percent to C.

(ii) Apart from the application of section 704(b), the Commissioner may reallocate or otherwise not respect the allocations under other sections. See paragraph (b)(1)(iii) of this section. For example, BC's allocations of gross income, deductions, and losses may be evaluated and reallocated (or not respected), as appropriate, if it is determined that the allocations result in the evasion of tax or do not clearly reflect income under section 482.

Example 29. PRS is a partnership with three equal partners, A, B, and C. A is a corporation that is a member of a consolidated group within the meaning of § 1.1502-1(h). B is a subchapter S corporation that is wholly owned by D, an individual. C is a partnership with two partners, E, an individual, and F, a corporation that is a member of a consolidated group within the meaning of § 1.1502-1(h). For purposes of paragraph (b)(2)(iii) of this section, in determining the after-tax economic benefit or detriment of an allocation to A, the tax consequences that result from the interaction of the allocation to A with the tax attributes of the consolidated group of which A is a member must be taken into account. In determining the after-tax economic benefit or detriment of an allocation to B, the tax consequences that result from the interaction of the allocation with the tax attributes of D must be taken into account. In determining the after-tax economic benefit or detriment of an allocation to C, the tax consequences that result from the interaction of the allocation with the tax attributes of E and the consolidated group of which F is a member must be taken into account.

Example 30. (i) A, a controlled foreign corporation, and B, a foreign corporation that is not a controlled foreign corporation, form AB, a partnership organized under the laws of country X. The partnership agreement contains the provisions necessary to comply with the economic effect safe harbor of paragraph (b)(2)(ii)(*b*) of this section. A is wholly-owned by C, a domestic corporation that is not a member of a consolidated group within the meaning of § 1.1502-1(h). B is wholly owned by an individual who is a citizen and resident of country X and is not related to A. Neither A, B, nor AB, is engaged in a trade or business in the United States. A and B each contribute 50 percent of the capital of AB. There is a strong likelihood that in each of the next several years AB will realize equal amounts of gross income that would constitute subpart F income if allocated to A, and gross income that would not constitute subpart F income if allocated to A ("non-subpart F income"). A and B agree to share bottom-line net income from AB equally; however, rather than share all items of gross income equally, A and B agree that B will be allocated all of AB's subpart F income to the extent of its 50 percent share of bottom-line net income. In year 1, AB earns $60x of income, $30x of which is subpart F income and is allocated to B, and $30x of which is non-subpart F income and is allocated to A.

(ii) Although neither A nor B is subject to U.S. tax with respect to its distributive share of the income of AB, under paragraph (b)(2)(iii)(*d*) of this section, the tax attributes of C must be taken into account with respect to A for purposes of applying the tests described in paragraphs (b)(2)(iii)(*a*), (*b*), and (*c*) of this section. The allocations in year 1 have economic effect. However, the economic effect of the allocations is not substantial under the test described in paragraph (b)(2)(iii)(*b*) of this section because there was a strong likelihood, at the time the allocations became part of the AB partnership agreement, that the net increases and decreases to A's and B's capital accounts in year 1 would not differ substantially when compared to the net increases and decreases to A's and B's capital accounts for year 1 if the allocations were not contained in the partnership agreement, and the total tax liability from the income earned by AB in year 1 (taking into account the tax attributes of the allocations to C) would be reduced as a result of such allocations. Under paragraph (b)(3) of this section, the subpart F income and non-subpart F income earned by AB in year 1 must each be reallocated 50 percent to A and 50 percent to B.

Example 31. (i) In Year 1, A and B each contribute cash of $9,000 to LLC, a newly formed limited liability company classified as a partnership for Federal tax purposes, in exchange for 100 units in LLC. Under the LLC agreement, each unit is entitled to participate equally in the profits and losses of LLC. LLC uses the cash contributions to purchase a nondepreciable property, Property A, for $18,000. Later in Year 1, at a time when Property A is valued at $20,000, LLC issues an option to C. The option allows C to buy 100 units in LLC for an exercise price of $15,000 in Year 2. C pays $1,000 to LLC to purchase the option. Assume that the LLC agreement satisfies the requirements of paragraph (b)(2) of this section and requires that, on the exercise of a noncompensatory option, LLC comply with the rules of paragraph (b)(2)(iv)(*s*) of this section. Also assume that C's option is a noncompensatory option under §1.721-2(f), and that C is not treated as a partner with respect to the option. Under paragraph (b)(2)(iv)(*f*)(*5*)(*iv*) of this section, LLC revalues its property in connection with the issuance of the option. The $2,000 unrealized gain in Property A is allocated equally to A and B under the LLC agreement. In Year 2, C exercises the option, contributing the $15,000 exercise price to the partnership. At the time the option is exercised, the value of Property A is $35,000.

Year 1 After Issuance of the Option

Assets	Basis	Value	Liabilities and Capital	Basis	Value
Cash Premium	$1,000	$1,000	Cash Premium	$1,000	$1,000
Property A	$18,000	$20,000	A	$9,000	$10,000
			B	$9,000	$10,000
Total	$19,000	$21,000		$19,000	$21,000

Year 2 After Exercise of the Option

Assets	Basis	Value	Liabilities and Capital	Basis	Value
Property A	$18,000	$35,000	A	$9,000	$17,000
Cash Premium	$1,000	$1,000	B	$9,000	$17,000
Exercise Price	$15,000	$15,000	C	$16,000	$17,000
Total	$34,000	$51,000		$34,000	$51,000

(ii) In lieu of revaluing LLC's property under paragraph (b)(2)(iv)(*f*) of this section immediately before the option is exercised, under paragraph (b)(2)(iv)(*s*)(*1*) of this section LLC must revalue its property under the principles of paragraph (b)(2)(iv)(*f*) of this section immediately after the exercise of the option. Under paragraphs (b)(2)(iv)(*b*) and (b)(2)(iv)(*d*)(*4*) of this section, C's capital account is credited with the amount paid for the option ($1,000) and the exercise price of the option ($15,000). Under the LLC agreement, however, C is entitled to LLC capital corresponding to 100 units of LLC (1/3 of LLC's capital). Immediately after the exercise of the option, LLC's properties are cash of $16,000 ($1,000 premium and $15,000 exercise price contributed by C) and Property A, which has a value of $35,000. Thus, the total value of LLC's property is $51,000. C is entitled to LLC capital equal to 1/3 of this value, or $17,000. As C is entitled to $1,000 more LLC capital than C's capital contributions to LLC, the provisions of paragraph (b)(2)(iv)(*s*) of this section apply.

(iii) Under paragraph (b)(2)(iv)(*s*)(*2*) of this section, LLC must increase C's capital account from $16,000 to $17,000 by, first, revaluing LLC property in accordance with the principles of paragraph (b)(2)(iv)(*f*) of this section. The unrealized gain in LLC's property (Property A) which has not been reflected in the capital accounts previously is $15,000 ($35,000 value less $20,000 book value). Under paragraph (b)(2)(iv)(*s*)(*2*) of this section, the first $1,000 of this gain must be allocated to C, and the remaining $14,000 of this gain is allocated equally to A and B in accordance with the LLC agreement. Because the revaluation of LLC property under paragraph (b)(2)(iv)(*s*)(*2*) of this section increases C's capital account to the amount agreed on by the members, LLC is not required to make a capital account reallocation under paragraph (b)(2)(iv)(*s*)(*3*) of this section. The $17,000 of unrealized booked gain in Property A ($35,000 value less $18,000 basis) is shared $8,000 to each A and B, and $1,000 to C. Under paragraph (b)(2)(iv)(*f*)(*4*) of this section, the tax items from the revalued property must be allocated in accordance with section 704(c) principles.

	A		B		C	
	Tax	Book	Tax	Book	Tax	Book
Capital account after exercise	$9,000	$10,000	$9,000	$10,000	$16,000	$16,000
Revaluation amount	0	$7,000	0	$7,000	0	$1,000
Capital account after revaluation	$9,000	$17,000	$9,000	$17,000	$16,000	$17,000

Example 32. (i) Assume the same facts as in *Example 31*, except that, in Year 2, before the exercise of the option, LLC sells Property A for $40,000, recognizing gain of $22,000. LLC does not distribute the sale proceeds to its partners and it has no other earnings in Year 2. With the proceeds ($40,000), LLC purchases Property B, a nondepreciable property. Also assume that C exercises the noncompensatory option at the beginning of Year 3 and that, at the time C exercises the option, the value of Property B is $41,000. In Year 3, LLC has gross income of $3,000 and deductions of $1,500.

Year 2 After Purchase of Property B

Assets	Basis	Value	Liabilities and Capital	Basis	Value
Cash Premium	$1,000	$1,000	Cash Premium	$1,000	$1,000
Property B	$40,000	$40,000	A	$20,000	$20,000
			B	$20,000	$20,000
Total	$41,000	$41,000		$41,000	$41,000

Year 3 After Exercise of the Option

Assets	Basis	Value	Liabilities and Capital	Basis	Value
Property B	$40,000	$41,000	A	$20,000	$19,000
Cash	$16,000	$16,000	B	$20,000	$19,000
			C	$16,000	$19,000
Total	$56,000	$57,000		$56,000	$57,000

(ii) Under paragraphs (b)(2)(iv)(*b*) and (b)(2)(iv)(*d*)(*4*) of this section, C's capital account is credited with the amount paid for the option ($1,000) and the exercise price of the option ($15,000). Under the LLC agreement, however, C is entitled to LLC capital corresponding to 100 units of LLC (1/3 of LLC's capital). Immediately after the exercise of the option, LLC's properties are $16,000 cash ($1,000 option premium and $15,000 exercise price contributed by C) and Property B, which has a value of $41,000. Thus, the total value of LLC's property is $57,000. C is entitled to LLC capital equal to 1/3 of this amount, or $19,000. As C is entitled to $3,000 more LLC capital than C's capital contributions to LLC, the provisions of paragraph (b)(2)(iv)(*s*) of this section apply.

(iii) In lieu of revaluing LLC's property under paragraph (b)(2)(iv)(*f*) of this section immediately before the option is exercised, under paragraph (b)(2)(iv)(*s*)(*1*) of this section LLC must revalue its property under the principles of paragraph (b)(2)(iv)(*f*) of this section immediately after the exercise of the option. Under paragraph (b)(2)(iv)(*s*) of this section, LLC must increase C's capital account from $16,000 to $19,000 by, first, revaluing LLC property in accordance with the principles of paragraph (b)(2)(iv)(*f*) of this section, and allocating all $1,000 of unrealized gain from the revaluation to C under paragraph (b)(2)(iv)(*s*)(*2*). This brings C's capital account to $17,000.

(iv) Next, under paragraph (b)(2)(iv)(*s*)(*3*) of this section, LLC must reallocate $2,000 of capital from the existing partners (A and B) to C to bring C's capital account to $19,000 (the capital account reallocation). As A and B shared equally in all items from Property A, whose sale gave rise to the need for the capital account reallocation, each member's capital account is reduced by 1/2 of the $2,000 reduction ($1,000).

(v) Under paragraph (b)(2)(iv)(*s*)(*4*) of this section, beginning in the year in which the option is exercised, LLC must make corrective allocations so as to take into account the capital account reallocation. In Year 3, LLC has gross income of $3,000 and deductions of $1,500. Under paragraph (b)(4)(x)(*c*) of this section, LLC must allocate the book gross income of $3,000 equally among A, B, and C, but for tax purposes, however, LLC must allocate all of its gross income ($3,000) to C. LLC's book and tax deductions ($1,500) will then be allocated equally among A, B, and C. The $1,000 unrealized booked gain in Property B has been allocated entirely to C. Under paragraph (b)(2)(iv)(*f*)(*4*) of this section, the tax items from Property B must be allocated in accordance with section 704(c) principles.

	A		B		C	
	Tax	Book	Tax	Book	Tax	Book
Capital account after exercise	$20,000	$20,000	$20,000	$20,000	$16,000	$16,000
Revaluation	0	0	0	0	0	$1,000
Capital account after revaluation	$20,000	$20,000	$20,000	$20,000	$16,000	$17,000
Capital account reallocation	0	($1,000)	0	($1,000)	0	$2,000
Capital account after capital account reallocation	$20,000	$19,000	$20,000	$19,000	$16,000	$19,000
Income allocation (Yr. 3)	0	$1,000	0	$1,000	$3,000	$1,000
Deduction allocation (Yr. 3)	($500)	($500)	($500)	($500)	($500)	($500)
Capital account at end of year 3	$19,500	$19,500	$19,500	$19,500	$18,500	$19,500

Example 33. (i) In Year 1, D and E each contribute cash of $10,000 to LLC, a newly formed limited liability company classified as a partnership for Federal tax purposes, in exchange for 100 units in LLC. Under the LLC agreement, each unit is entitled to participate equally in the profits and losses of LLC. LLC uses the cash contributions to purchase two nondepreciable properties, Property A and Property B, for $10,000 each. Also in Year 1, at a time when Property A and Property B are still valued at $10,000 each, LLC issues an option to F. The option allows F to buy 100 units in LLC for an exercise price of $15,000 in Year 2. F pays $2,000 to LLC to purchase the option. Assume that the LLC agreement satisfies the requirements of paragraph (b)(2) of this section and requires that, on the exercise of a noncompensatory option, LLC comply with the rules of paragraph (b)(2)(iv)(*s*) of this section. Also assume that F's option is a noncompensatory option under § 1.721-2(f), and that F is not treated as a partner with respect to the option.

End of Year 1

Assets	Basis	Value	Liabilities and Capital	Basis	Value
Cash Premium	$2,000	$2,000	Cash Premium	$2,000	$2,000
Property A	$10,000	$10,000	D	$10,000	$10,000
Property B	$10,000	$10,000	E	$10,000	$10,000
Total	$22,000	$22,000		$22,000	$22,000

(ii) In year 2, prior to the exercise of F's option, G contributes $18,000 to LLC for 100 units in LLC. At the time of G's contribution, Property A has a value of $32,000 and a basis of $10,000, Property B has a value of $5,000 and a basis of $10,000, and the fair market value of F's option is $3,000. In year 2, LLC has no item of income, gain, loss, deduction, or credit.

(iii) Upon G's admission to the partnership, the capital accounts of D and E (which were $10,000 each prior to G's admission) are, in accordance with paragraph (b)(2)(iv)(*f*) of this section, adjusted upward to reflect their shares of the unrealized appreciation in the partnership's property. Property A has $22,000 of unrealized gain and Property B has $5,000 of unrealized loss. Under paragraph (b)(2)(iv)(*f*)(*1*) of this section, the adjustments must be based on the fair market value of LLC property (taking section 7701(g) into account) on the date of the adjustment, as determined under paragraph (b)(2)(iv)(*h*) of this section. The fair market value of partnership property must be reduced by the excess of the fair market value of the option as of the date of the adjustment over the consideration paid by F to acquire the option ($3,000 - $2,000 = $1,000) (under paragraph (b)(2)(iv)(*h*)(*2*) of this section), but only to the extent of the unrealized appreciation in LLC property that has not been reflected in the capital accounts previously ($22,000). This $1,000 reduction is allocated entirely to Property A, the only asset having unrealized appreciation not reflected in the capital accounts previously. Therefore, the book value of Property A is $31,000. Accordingly, the revaluation adjustments must reflect only $16,000 of the net appreciation in LLC's property ($21,000 of unrealized gain in Property A and $5,000 of unrealized loss in Property B). Thus, D's and E's capital accounts (which were $10,000 each prior to G's admission) must be adjusted upward (by $8,000) to $18,000 each. The $21,000 of built-in gain in Property A and the $5,000 of built-in loss in Property B must be allocated equally between D and E in accordance with section 704(c) principles.

Assets

	Basis	Value	Option Adjustment	704(b) Book
Property A	$10,000	$32,000	($1,000)	$31,000
Property B	$10,000	$ 5,000	0	$ 5,000
Cash	$ 2,000	$ 2,000	0	$ 2,000
Subtotal	$22,000	$39,000	($1,000)	$38,000
Cash Contributed by G	$18,000	$18,000	0	$18,000
Total	$40,000	$57,000	($1,000)	$56,000

Liabilities and Capital

	Tax	Value	704(b) Book
Cash Premium (option value)	$2,000	$3,000	$2,000
D	$10,000	$18,000	$18,000
E	$10,000	$18,000	$18,000
G	$18,000	$18,000	$18,000
Total	$40,000	$57,000	$56,000

(iv) In year 2, after the admission of G, when Property A still has a value of $32,000 and a basis of $10,000 and Property B still has a value of $5,000 and a basis of $10,000, F exercises the option. On the exercise of the option, F's capital account is credited with the amount paid for the option ($2,000) and the exercise price of the option ($15,000). Under the LLC agreement, however, F is entitled to LLC capital corresponding to 100 units of LLC (1/4 of LLC's capital). Immediately after the exercise of the option, LLC's properties are worth $72,000 ($15,000 contributed by F, plus the value of LLC property prior to the exercise of the option, $57,000). F is entitled to LLC capital equal to 1/4 of this value, or $18,000. As F is entitled to $1,000 more LLC capital than F's capital contributions to LLC, the provisions of paragraph (b)(2)(iv)(*s*) of this section apply.

(v) Under paragraph (b)(2)(iv)(*s*) of this section, LLC must increase F's capital account from $17,000 to $18,000 by, first, revaluing LLC property in accordance with the principles of paragraph (b)(2)(iv)(*f*) of this section and allocating the first $1,000 of unrealized gain to F. The total unrealized gain which has not been reflected in the capital accounts previously is $1,000 (the difference between the actual value of Property A, $32,000, and the book value of Property A, $31,000). The entire $1,000 of book gain is allocated to F under paragraph (b)(2)(iv)(*s*)(*2*) of this section. Because the revaluation of LLC property under paragraph (b)(2)(iv)(*s*)(*2*) of this section increases F's capital account to the amount agreed on by the members, LLC is not required to make a capital account reallocation under paragraph (b)(2)(iv)(*s*)(*3*) of this section. The ($5,000) of unrealized booked loss in Property B has been allocated ($2,500) to each D and E, and the $22,000 of unrealized booked gain in Property A has been allocated $10,500 to each D and E, and $1,000 to F. Under paragraph (b)(2)(iv)(*f*)(*4*) of this section, the tax items from Properties A and B must be allocated in accordance with section 704(c) principles.

	D		E		G		F	
	Tax	Book	Tax	Book	Tax	Book	Tax	Book
Capital account after admission of G	$10,000	$18,000	$10,000	$18,000	$18,000	$18,000	0	0
Capital account after exercise of F's option	$10,000	$18,000	$10,000	$18,000	$18,000	$18,000	$17,000	$17,000
Revaluation	0	0	0	0	0	0	0	$1,000
Capital account after revaluation	$10,000	$18,000	$10,000	$18,000	$18,000	$18,000	$17,000	$18,000

Example 34. (i) On the first day of Year 1, H, I, and J form LLC, a limited liability company classified as a partnership for Federal tax purposes. H and I each contribute $10,000 cash to LLC for 100 units of common interest in LLC. J contributes $10,000 cash for a convertible preferred interest in LLC. J's convertible preferred interest entitles J to receive an annual allocation and distribution of cumulative LLC net profits in an amount equal to 10 percent of J's unreturned capital. J's convertible preferred interest also entitles J to convert, in Year 3, J's preferred interest into 100 units of common interest. If J converts, J has the right to the same share of LLC capital as J would have had if J had held the 100 units of common interest since the formation of LLC. Under the LLC agreement, each unit of common interest has an equal right to share in any LLC net profits that remain after payment of the preferred return. Assume that the LLC agreement satisfies the requirements of paragraph (b)(2) of this section and requires that, on the exercise of a noncompensatory option, LLC comply with the rules of paragraph (b)(2)(iv)(*s*) of this section. Also assume that J's right to convert the preferred interest into a common interest qualifies as a noncompensatory option under § 1.721-2(f), and that, prior to the exercise of the conversion right, the conversion right is not treated as a partnership interest.

(ii) LLC uses the $30,000 to purchase Property Z, a property that is depreciable on a straight-line basis over 15 years. In each of Years 1 and 2, LLC has net income of $2,500, comprised of $4,500 of gross income and $2,000 of depreciation. It allocates $1,000 of net income to J and distributes $1,000 to J in each year. LLC allocates the remaining $1,500 of net income equally to H and I in each year but makes no distributions to H and I.

	H		I		J	
	Tax	Book	Tax	Book	Tax	Book
Capital account upon formation	$10,000	$10,000	$10,000	$10,000	$10,000	$10,000
Allocation of income Years 1 and 2	$1,500	$1,500	$1,500	$1,500	$2,000	$2,000
Distributions Years 1 and 2	0	0	0	0	($2,000)	($2,000)
Capital account at end of Year 2	$11,500	$11,500	$11,500	$11,500	$10,000	$10,000

(iii) At the beginning of Year 3, when Property Z has a value of $38,000 and a basis of $26,000 ($30,000 original basis less $4,000 of depreciation) and LLC has accumulated undistributed cash of $7,000 ($9,000 gross receipts less $2,000 distributions), J converts J's preferred interest into a common interest. Under paragraphs (b)(2)(iv)(*b*) and (b)(2)(iv)(*d*)(*4*) of this section, J's capital account after the conversion equals J's capital account before the conversion, $10,000. On the conversion of the preferred interest, however, J is entitled to LLC capital corresponding to 100 units of common interest in LLC (1/3 of LLC's capital). At the time of the conversion, the total value of LLC property is $45,000. J is entitled to LLC capital equal to 1/3 of this value, or $15,000. As J is entitled to $5,000 more LLC capital than J's capital account immediately after the conversion, the provisions of paragraph (b)(2)(iv)(*s*) of this section apply.

Assets	Basis	Value	Liabilities and Capital	Basis	Value
Property Z	$26,000	$38,000	H	$11,500	$15,000
Undistributed Income	$7,000	$7,000	I	$11,500	$15,000
			J	$10,000	$15,000
Total	$33,000	$45,000	Total	$33,000	$45,000

(iv) Under paragraph (b)(2)(iv)(*s*) of this section, LLC must increase J's capital account from $10,000 to $15,000 by, first, revaluing LLC property in accordance with the principles of paragraph (b)(2)(iv)(*f*) of this section, and allocating the first $5,000 of unrealized gain from that revaluation to J. The unrealized gain in Property Z is $12,000 ($38,000 value less $26,000 basis). The first $5,000 of this unrealized gain must be allocated to J under paragraph (b)(2)(iv)(*s*)(*2*) of this section. The remaining $7,000 of the unrealized gain must be allocated equally to H and I in accordance with the LLC agreement. Because the revaluation of LLC property under paragraph (b)(2)(iv)(*s*)(*2*) of this section increases J's capital account to the amount agreed on by the members, LLC is not required to make a capital account reallocation under paragraph (b)(2)(iv)(*s*)(*3*) of this section. The $12,000 of unrealized booked gain in Property Z has been allocated $3,500 to each H and I, and $5,000 to J. Under paragraph (b)(2)(iv)(*f*)(*4*) of this section, the tax items from the revalued property must be allocated in accordance with section 704(c) principles.

	H Tax	H Book	I Tax	I Book	J Tax	J Book
Capital account prior to conversion	$11,500	$11,500	$11,500	$11,500	$10,000	$10,000
Revaluation on conversion	0	$3,500	0	$3,500	0	$5,000
Capital account after conversion	$11,500	$15,000	$11,500	$15,000	$10,000	$15,000

Example 35. (i) On the first day of Year 1, K and L each contribute cash of $10,000 to LLC, a newly formed limited liability company classified as a partnership for Federal tax purposes, in exchange for 100 units in LLC. Immediately after its formation, LLC borrows $10,000 from M. Under the terms of the debt instrument, interest of $1,000 is unconditionally payable at the end of each year and the $10,000 stated principal is repayable in five years. Throughout the term of the indebtedness, M has the right to convert the debt instrument into 100 units in LLC. If M converts, M has the right to the same share of LLC capital as M would have had if M had held 100 units in LLC since the formation of LLC. Under the LLC agreement, each unit participates equally in the profits and losses of LLC and has an equal right to share in LLC capital. Assume that the LLC agreement satisfies the requirements of paragraph (b)(2) of this section and requires that, on the exercise of a noncompensatory option, LLC comply with the rules of paragraph (b)(2)(iv)(*s*) of this section. Also assume that M's right to convert the debt into an interest in LLC qualifies as a noncompensatory option under § 1.721-2(f), and that, prior to the exercise of the conversion right, M is not treated as a partner with respect to the convertible debt.

(ii) LLC uses the $30,000 to purchase Property D, property that is depreciable on a straight-line basis over 15 years. In each of Years 1, 2, and 3, LLC has net income of $2,000, comprised of $5,000 of gross income, $2,000 of depreciation, and interest expense (representing payments of interest on the loan from M) of $1,000. LLC allocates this income equally to K and L but makes no distributions to either K or L.

	K Tax	K Book	L Tax	L Book	M Tax	M Book
Initial capital account	$10,000	$10,000	$10,000	$10,000	0	0
Year 1 net income	$1,000	$1,000	$1,000	$1,000	0	0
Year 2 net income	$1,000	$1,000	$1,000	$1,000	0	0
Year 3 net income	$1,000	$1,000	$1,000	$1,000	0	0
Year 4 initial capital account	$13,000	$13,000	$13,000	$13,000	0	0

(iii) At the beginning of Year 4, at a time when property D, LLC's only asset, has a value of $33,000 and basis of $24,000 ($30,000 original basis less $6,000 depreciation in Years 1 through 3), and LLC has accumulated undistributed cash of $12,000 ($15,000 gross income less $3,000 of interest payments) in LLC, M converts the debt into a 1/3 interest in LLC. Under paragraphs (b)(2)(iv)(*b*) and (b)(2)(iv)(*d*)(*4*) of this section, M's capital account after the conversion is the adjusted issue price of the debt immediately before M's conversion of the debt, $10,000, plus any accrued but unpaid qualified stated interest on the debt, $0. On the conversion of the debt, however, M is entitled to receive LLC capital corresponding to 100 units of LLC (1/3 of LLC's capital). At the time of the conversion, the total value of LLC's property is $45,000. M is entitled to LLC capital equal to 1/3 of this value, or $15,000. As M is entitled to $5,000 more LLC capital than M's capital contribution to LLC ($10,000), the provisions of paragraph (b)(2)(iv)(*s*) of this section apply.

Assets	Basis	Value	Liabilities and Capital	Basis	Value
Property D	$24,000	$33,000	K	$13,000	$15,000
Cash	$12,000	$12,000	L	$13,000	$15,000
			M	$10,000	$15,000
Total	$36,000	$45,000		$36,000	$45,000

(iv) Under paragraph (b)(2)(iv)(*s*) of this section, LLC must increase M's capital account from $10,000 to $15,000 by, first, revaluing LLC property in accordance with the principles of paragraph (b)(2)(iv)(*f*) of this section, and allocating the first $5,000 of unrealized gain from that revaluation to M. The unrealized gain in Property D is $9,000 ($33,000 value less $24,000 basis). The first $5,000 of this unrealized gain must be allocated to M under paragraph (b)(2)(iv)(*s*)(*2*) of this section, and the remaining $4,000 of the unrealized gain must be allocated equally to K and L in accordance with the LLC agreement. Because the revaluation of LLC property under paragraph (b)(2)(iv)(*s*)(*2*) of this section increases M's capital account to the amount agreed upon by the members, LLC is not required to make a capital account reallocation under paragraph (b)(2)(iv)(*s*)(*3*) of this section. The $9,000 unrealized booked gain in property D has been allocated $2,000 to each K and L, and $5,000 to M. Under paragraph (b)(2)(iv)(*f*)(*4*) of this section, the tax items from the revalued property must be allocated in accordance with section 704(c) principles.

	K Tax	K Book	L Tax	L Book	M Tax	M Book
Year 4 capital account prior to exercise	$13,000	$13,000	$13,000	$13,000	0	0
Capital account after exercise	$13,000	$13,000	$13,000	$13,000	$10,000	$10,000
Revaluation	0	$2,000	0	$2,000	0	$5,000
Capital account after revaluation	$13,000	$15,000	$13,000	$15,000	$10,000	$15,000

Example 36. [Reserved]. For further guidance, see § 1.704-1T(b)(5) *Example 36.*

Example 37. [Reserved]. For further guidance, see § 1.704-1T(b)(5) *Example 37.*

(6) *Examples.*—(i) *Example 1.* (*a*) A contributes $750,000 and B contributes $250,000 to form AB, a country X eligible entity (as defined in § 301.7701-3(a) of this chapter) treated as a partnership for U.S. Federal income tax purposes. AB operates business M in country X. Country X imposes a 20 percent tax on the net income from business M, which tax is a CFTE. In 2016, AB earns $300,000 of gross income, has deductible expenses of $100,000, and pays or accrues $40,000 of country X tax. Pursuant to the partnership agreement, the first $100,000 of gross income each year is specially allocated to A as a preferred return on excess capital contributed by A. All remaining partnership items, including CFTEs, are split evenly between A and B (50 percent each). The gross income allocation is not deductible in determining AB's taxable income under country X law. Assume that allocations of all items other than CFTEs are valid.

(*b*) AB has a single CFTE category because all of AB's net income is allocated in the same ratio. See paragraph (b)(4)(viii)(*c*)(*2*) of this section. Under paragraph (b)(4)(viii)(*c*)(*3*) of this section, the net income in the single CFTE category is $200,000. The $40,000 of taxes is allocated to the single CFTE category and, thus, is related to the $200,000 of net income in the single CFTE category. In 2016, AB's partnership agreement results in an allocation of $150,000 or 75 percent of the net income to A ($100,000 attributable to the gross income allocation plus $50,000 of the remaining $100,000 of net income) and $50,000 or 25 percent of the net income to B. AB's partnership agreement allocates the country X taxes in accordance with the partners' shares of partnership items remaining after the $100,000 gross income allocation. Therefore, AB allocates the country X taxes 50 percent to A ($20,000) and 50 percent to B ($20,000). AB's allocations of country X taxes are not deemed to be in accordance with the partners' interests in the partnership under paragraph (b)(4)(viii) of this section because they are not in proportion to the allocations of the CFTE category shares of income to which the country X taxes relate. Accordingly, the country X taxes will be reallocated according to the partners' interests in the partnership. Assuming that the partners do not reasonably expect to claim a deduction for the CFTEs in determining their U.S. Federal income tax liabilities, a reallocation of the CFTEs under paragraph (b)(3) of this section would be 75 percent to A ($30,000) and 25 percent to B ($10,000). If the reallocation of the CFTEs causes the partners' capital accounts not to reflect their contemplated economic arrangement, the partners may need to reallocate other partnership items to ensure that the tax consequences of the partnership's allocations are consistent with their contemplated economic arrangement over the term of the partnership.

(*c*) The facts are the same as in paragraph (b)(6)(i)(*a*) of this section, except that country X allows a deduction for the $100,000 allocation of gross income and, as a result, AB pays or accrues only $20,000 of foreign tax. Under paragraph (b)(4)(viii)(*c*)(*4*)(*iii*) of this section, the net income in the single CFTE category is $100,000, determined by reducing the net income in the CFTE category by the $100,000 of gross income that is allocated to A and for which country X allows a deduction in determining AB's taxable income. Pursuant to the partnership agreement, AB allocates the country X tax 50 percent to A ($10,000) and 50 percent to B ($10,000). This allocation is in proportion to the partners' CFTE category shares of the $100,000 net income. Accordingly, AB's allocations of country X taxes are deemed to be in accordance with the partners' interests in the partnership under paragraph (b)(4)(viii)(*a*) of this section.

(*d*) The facts are the same as in paragraph (b)(6)(i)(*c*) of this section, except that, in addition to $20,000 of country X tax, AB is subject to $30,000 of country Y withholding tax with respect to the $300,000 of gross income that it earns in 2016. Country Y does not allow any deductions for purposes of determining the withholding tax. As described in paragraph (b)(6)(i)(*b*) of this section, there is a single CFTE category with respect to AB's net income. Both the $20,000 of country X tax and the $30,000 of country Y withholding tax relate to that income and are therefore allocated to the single CFTE category. Under paragraph (b)(4)(viii)(*c*)(*4*)(*iii*) of this section, however, net income in a CFTE category is reduced by the amount of an allocation for which a deduction is allowed in determining a foreign taxable base, but only for purposes of applying paragraph (b)(4)(viii)(*a*) of this section to allocations of CFTEs that are attributable to that foreign tax. Accordingly, because the $100,000 allocation of gross income is deductible for country X tax purposes but not for country Y tax purposes, the allocations of the CFTEs attributable to country X tax and country Y tax are analyzed separately. For purposes of applying paragraph (b)(4)(viii)(*a*)(*1*) of this section to allocations of the CFTEs attributable to the $20,000 tax imposed by country X, the analysis described in paragraph (b)(6)(i)(*c*) of this section applies. For purposes of applying paragraph (b)(4)(viii)(*a*)(*1*) of this section to allocations of the CFTEs attributable to the $30,000 tax imposed by country Y, which did not allow a deduction for the $100,000 gross income allocation, the net income in the single CFTE category is $200,000. Pursuant to the partnership agreement, AB allocates the country Y tax 50 percent to A ($15,000) and 50 percent to B ($15,000). These allocations are not deemed to be in accordance with the partners' interests in the partnership under paragraph (b)(4)(viii) of this section because they are not in proportion to the partners' CFTE category shares of the $200,000 of net income in the category, which is allocated 75 percent to A and 25 percent to B under the partnership agreement. Accordingly, the country Y taxes will be reallocated according to the partners' interests in the partnership as described in paragraph (b)(6)(i)(*b*) of this section.

(*e*) If, rather than being a preferential gross income allocation, the $100,000 was a guaranteed payment to A within the meaning of section 707(c), the amount of net income in the single CFTE category of AB for purposes of applying paragraph (b)(4)(viii)(*a*)(*1*) of this section to allocations of CFTEs would be the same as in the fact patterns described in paragraphs (b)(6)(i)(*b*), (c), and (d) of this section. See paragraph (b)(4)(viii)(*c*)(*4*)(*ii*) of this section.

(ii) *Example 2.* (*a*) A, B, and C form ABC, an eligible entity (as defined in § 301.7701-3(a) of this chapter) treated as a partnership for U.S. Federal income tax purposes. ABC owns three entities, DEX, DEY, and DEZ, which are organized in, and treated as corporations under the laws of, countries X, Y, and Z, respectively, and as disregarded entities for U.S. Federal income tax purposes. DEX operates business X in country X, DEY operates business Y in country Y, and DEZ operates business Z in country Z. Businesses X, Y, and Z relate to the licensing and sublicensing of intellectual property owned by DEZ. During 2016, DEX earns $100,000 of royalty income from unrelated payors on which it pays no withholding taxes. Country X imposes a 30 percent tax on DEX's net income. DEX makes royalty payments of $90,000 during 2016 to DEY that are deductible by DEX for country X purposes and subject to a 10 percent withholding tax imposed by country X. DEY earns no other income in 2016. Country Y does not impose income or withholding taxes. DEY makes royalty payments of $80,000 during 2016 to DEZ. DEZ earns no other income in 2016. Country Z does not impose income or withholding taxes. The royalty payments from DEX to DEY and from DEY to DEZ are disregarded for U.S. Federal income tax purposes.

(*b*) As a result of these payments, DEX has taxable income of $10,000 for country X purposes on which $3,000 of taxes are imposed, and DEY has $90,000 of income for country X withholding tax purposes on which $9,000 of withholding taxes are imposed. Pursuant to the partnership agreement, all partnership items from business X, excluding CFTEs paid or accrued by business X, are allocated 80 percent to A and 10 percent each to B and C. All partnership items from business Y, excluding CFTEs paid or accrued by business Y, are allocated 80 percent to B and 10 percent each to A and C. All partnership items from business Z, excluding CFTEs paid or accrued by business Z, are allocated 80 percent to C and 10 percent each to A and B. Because only business X has items that are regarded for U.S. Federal income tax purposes (the $100,000 of royalty income), only business X has partnership items. Accordingly A is allocated 80 percent of the income from business X ($80,000) and B and C are each allocated 10 percent of the income from business X ($10,000 each). There are no partnership items of income from business Y or Z to allocate.

(*c*) Because the partnership agreement provides for different allocations of partnership net income attributable to businesses X, Y, and Z, the net income attributable to each of businesses X, Y, and Z is income in separate CFTE categories. See paragraph (b)(4)(viii)(*c*)(*2*) of this section. Under paragraph (b)(4)(viii)(*c*)(*3*)(*iv*) of this section, an item of gross income that is recognized for U.S. Federal income tax purposes is assigned to the activity that generated the item, and disregarded inter-branch payments are not taken into account in determining net income attributable to an activity. Consequently, all $100,000 of ABC's income is attributable to the business X activity for U.S. Federal income tax purposes, and no net income is in the business Y or Z CFTE category. Under paragraph (b)(4)(viii)(*d*)(*1*) of this section, the $3,000 of country X taxes imposed on DEX is allocated to the business X CFTE category. The additional $9,000 of country X withholding tax imposed with respect to the inter-branch payment to DEY is also allocated to the business X CFTE category because for U.S. Federal income tax purposes the related $90,000 of income on which the country X withholding tax is imposed is in the business X CFTE category. Therefore, $12,000 of taxes ($3,000 of country X income taxes and $9,000 of the country X withholding taxes) is related to the $100,000 of net income in the business X CFTE. See paragraph (b)(4)(viii)(*c*)(*1*) of this section. The allocations of country X taxes will be in proportion to the CFTE category shares of income to which they relate and will be deemed to be in accordance with the partners' interests in the partnership if such taxes are allocated 80 percent to A and 10 percent each to B and C.

(iii) *Example 3.* (*a*) Assume that the facts are the same as in paragraph (b)(5)(ii)(*a*) of this section, except that in order to reflect the $90,000 payment from DEX to DEY and the $80,000 payment from DEY to DEZ, the partnership agreement treats only $10,000 of the gross income as attributable to the business X activity, which the partnership agreement allocates 80 percent to A and 10 percent each to B and C. Of the remaining $90,000 of gross income, the partnership agreement treats $10,000 of the gross income as attributable to the business Y activity, which the partnership agreement allocates 80 percent to B and 10 percent each to A and C; and the partnership agreement treats $80,000 of the gross income as attributable to the business Z activity, which the partnership agreement allocates 80 percent to C and 10 percent each to A and B. In addition, the partnership agreement allocates the country X taxes among A, B, and C in accordance with which disregarded entity is considered to have paid the taxes for country X purposes. The partnership agreement allocates the $3,000 of country X income taxes 80 percent to A and 10 percent to each of B and C, and allocates the $9,000 of country X withholding taxes 80 percent to B and 10 percent to each of A and C. Thus, ABC allocates the country X taxes $3,300 to A (80 percent of $3,000 plus 10 percent of $9,000), $7,500 to B (10 percent of $3,000 plus 80 percent of $9,000), and $1,200 to C (10 percent of $3,000 plus 10 percent of $9,000).

(*b*) In order to prevent separating the CFTEs from the related foreign income, the special allocations of the $10,000 and $80,000 treated under the partnership agreement as attributable to the business Y and the business Z activities, respectively, which do not follow the allocation ratios that otherwise apply under the partnership agreement to items of income in the business X activity, are treated as divisible parts of the business X activity and, therefore, as separate activities. See paragraph (b)(4)(viii)(*c*)(*2*)(*iii*) of this section. Because the divisible part of the business X activity attributable to the portion of the disregarded payment received by DEY and not paid on to DEZ ($10,000) and the net income from the business Y activity ($0) are both shared 80 percent to B and 10 percent each to A and C, that divisible part of the business X activity and the business Y activity are treated as a single CFTE category. Because the divisible part of the business X activity attributable to the disregarded payment paid to DEZ ($80,000) and the net income from the business Z activity ($0) are both shared 80 percent to C and 10 percent each to A and B, that divisible part of the business X activity and the business Z activity are also treated as a single CFTE category. See paragraph (b)(4)(viii)(*c*)(*2*)(*i*) of this section. Accordingly, $10,000 of net income attributable to business X is in the business X CFTE category, $10,000 of net income of business X attributable to the net disregarded payments of DEY is in the business Y CFTE category, and $80,000 of net income of business X attributable to the disregarded payment to DEZ is in the business Z CFTE category.

(*c*) Under paragraph (b)(4)(viii)(*d*)(*1*) of this section, the $3,000 of country X tax imposed on DEX's income is allocated to the business X CFTE category. Because the $90,000 on which the country X withholding tax is imposed is split between the business Y CFTE category and the business Z CFTE category, those withholding taxes are allocated on a pro rata basis, $1,000 [$9,000 x ($10,000 / $90,000)] to the business Y CFTE category and $8,000 [$9,000 x ($80,000 / $90,000)] to the business Z CFTE category. See paragraph (b)(4)(viii)(*d*)(*1*) of this section. To satisfy the safe harbor of paragraph (b)(4)(viii) of this section, the $3,000 of country X taxes allocated to the business X CFTE category must be allocated in proportion to the CFTE category shares of income to which they relate, and therefore would be deemed to be in accordance with the partners' interests in the partnership if such taxes were allocated 80 percent to A and 10 percent each to B and C. The allocation of the $1,000 of country X withholding taxes allocated to the business Y CFTE category would be in proportion to the CFTE category shares of income to which they relate, and therefore would be deemed to be in accordance with the partners' interests in the partnership if such taxes were allocated 80 percent to B and 10 percent each to A and C. The allocation of the $8,000 of country X withholding taxes allocated to the business Z CFTE category would be in proportion to the CFTE category shares of income to which they relate, and therefore would be deemed to be in accordance with the partners' interests in the partnership if such taxes were allocated 80 percent to C and 10 percent each to A and B. Thus, to satisfy the safe harbor, ABC must allocate the country X taxes $3,300 to A (80 percent of $3,000 plus 10 percent of $1,000 plus 10 percent of $8,000), $1,900 to B (10 percent of $3,000 plus 80 percent of $1,000 plus 10 percent of $8,000), and $6,800 to C (10 percent of $3,000 plus 10 percent of $1,000 plus 80 percent of $8,000).

(*d*) ABC's allocations of country X taxes are not deemed to be in accordance with the partners' interests in the partnership under paragraph (b)(4)(viii) of this section because they are not in proportion to the partners' CFTE category shares of income to which the country X taxes relate. Accordingly, the country X taxes will be reallocated according to the partners' interests in the partnership.

* * *

[Reg. § 1.704-1.]

☐ [*T.D.* 6175, 5-23-56. *Amended by T.D.* 6771, 11-19-64; *T.D.* 8065, 12-24-85; *T.D.* 8099, 9-8-86; *T.D.* 8237, 12-29-88; *T.D.* 8385, 12-26-91; *T.D.* 8500, 12-21-93; *T.D.* 8585, 12-27-94; *T.D.* 8717, 5-8-97; *T.D.* 9121, 4-20-2004; *T.D.* 9126, 5-5-2004; *T.D.* 9207, 5-23-2005; *T.D.* 9292, 10-18-2006 (*corrected* 12-6-2006); *T.D.* 9398, 5-16-2008 (*corrected* 6-11-2008); *T.D.* 9577, 2-9-2012; *T.D.* 9607, 12-21-2012; *T.D.* 9612, 2-4-2013 (*corrected* 3-22-2013 *and* 6-12-2013), *T.D.* 9710, 2-9-2015, *T.D.* 9748, 2-3-2016, *T.D.* 9814, 1-18-2017, *T.D.* 9871, 7-23-2019, *T.D.* 9874, 9-17-2019, *T.D.* 9877, 10-4-2019, *T.D.* 9891, 1-17-2020; *T.D.* 9895, 3-20-2020; *T.D.* 9905, 9-3-2020 *and T.D.* 9922, 11-2-2020.]

§ 1.704-1T. Partner's distributive share (temporary).—(a) For further guidance, see § 1.704-1(a).

(b)(1) For further guidance, see § 1.704-1(b)(1).

(2) For further guidance, see § 1.704-1(b)(2)(i) through (b)(2)(iv)(*f*) (*5*).

(i) through (iii) [Reserved]

(iv)(*a*) through (*e*) [Reserved]

(*f*)(*1*) through (5) [Reserved]

(*g*) For further guidance, see § 1.704-1(b)(2)(iv)(*g*) through (s).

(*h*) through (*s*) [Reserved]

(3) For further guidance, see § 1.704-1(b)(3) through (6).

(4) through (6) [Reserved]

(c) For further guidance, see § 1.704-1(c) through (e).

(d) through (e) [Reserved]

[Temporary Reg. § 1.704-1T.]

☐ *T.D.* 9748, 2-3-2016. *Amended by T.D.* 9814, 1-18-2017, *T.D.* 9871, 7-23-2019 and *T.D.* 9891, 1-17-2020.]

§ 1.704-3. Contributed property.—(a) *In general.*—(1) *General principles.*—The purpose of section 704(c) is to prevent the shifting of tax consequences among partners with respect to precontribution gain or loss. Under section 704(c), a partnership must allocate income, gain, loss, and deduction with respect to property contributed by a partner to the partnership so as to take into account any variation between the adjusted tax basis of the property and its fair market value at the time of contribution. Notwithstanding any other provision of this section, the allocations must be made using a reasonable method that is consistent with the purpose of section 704(c). For this purpose, an allocation method includes the application of all of the rules of this section (e.g., aggregation rules). An allocation method is not necessarily unreasonable merely because another allocation method would result in a higher aggregate tax liability. Paragraphs (b), (c), and (d) of this section describe allocation methods that are generally reasonable. Other methods may be reasonable in appropriate circumstances. Nevertheless, in the absence of specific published guidance, it is not reasonable to use an allocation method in which the basis of property contributed to the partnership is increased (or decreased) to reflect built-in gain (or loss), or a method under which the partnership creates tax allocations of income, gain, loss, or deduction independent of allocations affecting book capital accounts. See § 1.704-3(d). Paragraph (e) of this section contains special rules and exceptions. The principles of this paragraph (a)(1), together with the methods described in paragraphs (b), (c) and (d) of this section, apply only to contributions of property that are otherwise respected. See for example § 1.701-2. Accordingly, even though a partnership's allocation method may be described in the literal language of paragraphs (b), (c) or (d) of this section, based on the particular facts and circumstances, the Commissioner can recast the contribution as appropriate to avoid tax results inconsistent with the intent of subchapter K. One factor that may be considered by the Commissioner is the use of the remedial allocation method by related partners in which allocations of remedial items of income, gain, loss or deduction are made to one partner and the allocations of offsetting remedial items are made to a related partner.

(2) *Operating rules.*—Except as provided in paragraphs (e)(2) and (e)(3) of this section, section 704(c) and this section apply on a property-by-property basis. Therefore, in determining whether there is a disparity between adjusted tax basis and fair market value, the built-in gains and built-in losses on items of contributed property cannot be aggregated. A partnership may use different methods with respect to different items of contributed property, provided that the partnership and the partners consistently apply a single reasonable

method for each item of contributed property and that the overall method or combination of methods are reasonable based on the facts and circumstances and consistent with the purpose of section 704(c). It may be unreasonable to use one method for appreciated property and another method for depreciated property. Similarly, it may be unreasonable to use the traditional method for built-in gain property contributed by a partner with a high marginal tax rate while using curative allocations for built-in gain property contributed by a partner with a low marginal tax rate. A new partnership formed as the result of the termination of a partnership under section 708(b)(1)(B) is not required to use the same method as the terminated partnership with respect to section 704(c) property deemed contributed to the new partnership by the terminated partnership under § 1.7081(b)(1)(iv). The previous sentence applies to terminations of partnerships under section 708(b)(1)(B) occurring on or after May 9, 1997; however, the sentence may be applied to terminations occurring on or after May 9, 1996, provided that the partnership and its partners apply the sentence to the termination in a consistent manner.

(3) *Definitions.*—(i) *Section 704(c) property.*—Property contributed to a partnership is section 704(c) property if at the time of contribution its book value differs from the contributing partner's adjusted tax basis. For purposes of this section, book value is determined as contemplated by § 1.704-1(b). Therefore, book value is equal to fair market value at the time of contribution and is subsequently adjusted for cost recovery and other events that affect the basis of the property. For a partnership that maintains capital accounts in accordance with § 1.704-1(b)(2)(iv), the book value of property is initially the value used in determining the contributing partner's capital account under § 1.704-1(b)(2)(iv)(*d*), and is appropriately adjusted thereafter (e.g., for book cost recovery under § § 1.704-1(b)(2)(iv)(*g*)(3) and 1.704-3(d)(2) and other events that affect the basis of the property). A partnership that does not maintain capital accounts under § 1.704-1(b)(2)(iv) must comply with this section using a book capital account based on the same principles (i.e., a book capital account that reflects the fair market value of property at the time of contribution and that is subsequently adjusted for cost recovery and other events that affect the basis of the property). Property deemed contributed to a new partnership as the result of the termination of a partnership under section 708(b)(1)(B) is treated as section 704(c) property in the hands of the new partnership only to the extent that the property was section 704(c) property in the hands of the terminated partnership immediately prior to the termination. See § 1.708-1(b)(1)(iv) for an example of the application of this rule. The previous two sentences apply to terminations of partnerships under section 708(b)(1)(B) occurring on or after May 9, 1997; however, the sentences may be applied to terminations occurring on or after May 9, 1996, provided that the partnership and its partners apply the sentences to the termination in a consistent manner.

(ii) *Built-in gain and built-in loss.*—The built-in gain on section 704(c) property is the excess of the property's book value over the contributing partner's adjusted tax basis upon contribution. The built-in gain is thereafter reduced by decreases in the difference between the property's book value and adjusted tax basis. The built-in loss on section 704(c) property is the excess of the contributing partner's adjusted tax basis over the property's book value upon contribution. The built-in loss is thereafter reduced by decreases in the difference between the property's adjusted tax basis and book value. See § 1.460-4(k)(3)(v)(A) for a rule relating to the amount of built-in income or built-in loss attributable to a contract accounted for under a long-term contract method of accounting.

(4) *Accounts payable and other accrued but unpaid items.*—Accounts payable and other accrued but unpaid items contributed by a partner using the cash receipts and disbursements method of accounting are treated as section 704(c) property for purposes of applying the rules of this section.

(5) *Other provisions of the Internal Revenue Code.*—Section 704(c) and this section apply to a contribution of property to the partnership only if the contribution is governed by section 721, taking into account other provisions of the Internal Revenue Code. For example, to the extent that a transfer of property to a partnership is a sale under section 707, the transfer is not a contribution of property to which section 704(c) applies.

(6) *Other applications of section 704(c) principles.*—(i) *Revaluations under section 704(b).*—The principles of this section apply to allocations with respect to property for which differences between book value and adjusted tax basis are created when a partnership revalues partnership property pursuant to § 1.704-1(b)(2)(iv)(*f*) or 1.704-1(b)(2)(iv)(*s*) (reverse section 704(c) allocations). Partnerships are not required to use the same allocation method for reverse section 704(c) allocations as for contributed property, even if at the time of revaluation the property is already subject to section 704(c) and paragraph (a) of this section. In addition, partnerships are not required to use the same allocation method for reverse section 704(c) allocations each time the partnership revalues its property. A partnership that makes allocations with respect to revalued property must use a reasonable method that is consistent with the purposes of section 704(b) and (c).

(ii) *Basis adjustments.*—A partnership making adjustments under § 1.743-1(b) or 1.751-1(a)(2) must account for built-in gain or loss under section 704(c) in accordance with the principles of this section.

(7) *Transfer of a partnership interest.*—If a contributing partner transfers a partnership interest, built-in gain or loss must be allocated to the transferee partner as it would have been allocated to the transferor partner. If the contributing partner transfers a portion of the partnership interest, the share of built-in gain or loss proportionate to the interest transferred must be allocated to the transferee partner. This rule does not apply to any person who acquired a partnership interest from a § 1.752-7 liability partner in a transaction to which paragraph (e)(1) of § 1.752-7 applies. See § 1.752-7(c)(1).

(8) *Special rules.*—(i) *Disposition in a nonrecognition transaction.*—If a partnership disposes of section 704(c) property in a nonrecognition transaction, the substituted basis property (within the meaning of section 7701(a)(42)) is treated as section 704(c) property with the same amount of built-in gain or loss as the section 704(c) property disposed of by the partnership. If gain or loss is recognized in such a transaction, appropriate adjustments must be made. The allocation method for the substituted basis property must be consistent with the allocation method chosen for the original property. If a partnership transfers an item of section 704(c) property together with other property to a corporation under section 351, in order to preserve that item's built-in gain or loss, the basis in the stock received in exchange for the section 704(c) property is determined as if each item of section 704(c) property had been the only property transferred to the corporation by the partnership.

(ii) *Disposition in an installment sale.*—If a partnership disposes of section 704(c) property in an installment sale as defined in section 453(b), the installment obligation received by the partnership is treated as the section 704(c) property with the same amount of built-in gain as the section 704(c) property disposed of by the partnership (with appropriate adjustments for any gain recognized on the installment sale). The allocation method for the installment obligation must be consistent with the allocation method chosen for the original property.

(iii) *Contributed contracts.*—If a partner contributes to a partnership a contract that is section 704(c) property, and the partnership subsequently acquires property pursuant to that contract in a transaction in which less than all of the gain or loss is recognized, then the acquired property is treated as the section 704(c) property with the same amount of built-in gain or loss as the contract (with appropriate adjustments for any gain or loss recognized on the acquisition). For this purpose, the term contract includes, but is not limited to, options, forward contracts, and futures contracts. The allocation method for the acquired property must be consistent with the allocation method chosen for the contributed contract.

(iv) *Capitalized amounts.*—To the extent that a partnership properly capitalizes all or a portion of an item as described in paragraph (a)(12) of this section, then the item or items to which such cost is properly capitalized is treated as section 704(c) property with the same amount of built-in loss as corresponds to the amount capitalized.

(9) *Tiered partnerships.*—If a partnership contributes section 704(c) property to a second partnership (the lower-tier partnership), or if a partner that has contributed section 704(c) property to a partnership contributes that partnership interest to a second partnership (the upper-tier partnership), the upper-tier partnership must allocate its distributive share of lower-tier partnership items with respect to that section 704(c) property in a manner that takes into account the contributing partner's remaining built-in gain or loss. Allocations made under this paragraph will be considered to be made in a manner that meets the requirements of

§ 1.704-1(b)(2)(iv)(*q*) (relating to capital account adjustments where guidance is lacking).

(10) *Anti-abuse rule.*—(i) *In general.*—An allocation method (or combination of methods) is not reasonable if the contribution of property (or event that results in reverse section 704(c) allocations) and the corresponding allocation of tax items with respect to the property are made with a view to shifting the tax consequences of built-in gain or loss among the partners in a manner that substantially reduces the present value of the partners' aggregate tax liability. For purposes of this paragraph (a)(10), all references to the partners shall include both direct and indirect partners.

(ii) *Definition of indirect partner.*—An *indirect partner* is any direct or indirect owner of a partnership, S corporation, or controlled foreign corporation (as defined in section 957(a) or 953(c)), or direct or indirect beneficiary of a trust or estate, that is a partner in the partnership, and any consolidated group of which the partner in the partnership is a member (within the meaning of § 1.1502-1(h)). An owner (whether directly or through tiers of entities) of a controlled foreign corporation is treated as an indirect partner only with respect to allocations of items of income, gain, loss, or deduction that enter into the computation of a United States shareholder's inclusion under section 951(a) with respect to the controlled foreign corporation, enter into any person's income attributable to a United States shareholder's inclusion under section 951(a) with respect to the controlled foreign corporation, or would enter into the computations described in this sentence if such items were allocated to the controlled foreign corporation.

(11) *Contributing and noncontributing partners' recapture shares.*—For special rules applicable to the allocation of depreciation recapture with respect to property contributed by a partner to a partnership, see § § 1.1245-1(e)(2) and 1.1250-1(f).

(12) *§ 1.752-7 liabilities.*—Except as otherwise provided in § 1.752-7, § 1.752-7 liabilities (within the meaning of § 1.752-7(b)(2)) are section 704(c) property (built-in loss property that at the time of contribution has a book value that differs from the contributing partner's adjusted tax basis) for purposes of applying the rules of this section. See § 1.752-7(c). To the extent that the built-in loss associated with the § 1.752-7 liability exceeds the cost of satisfying the § 1.752-7 liability (as defined in § 1.752-7(b)(3)), the excess creates a "ceiling rule" limitation, within the meaning of § 1.704-3(b)(1), subject to the methods of allocation set forth in § 1.704-3(b), (c) and (d).

(13) *Rules for tiered section 721(c) partnerships.*—(i) *Revaluations.*—If a partnership revalues its property pursuant to § 1.704-1(b)(2)(iv)(*f*)(*6*) immediately before an interest in the partnership is contributed to another partnership, or if an upper-tier partnership owns an interest in a lower-tier partnership, and both the upper-tier partnership and the lower-tier partnership revalue partnership property pursuant to § 1.704-1(b)(2)(iv)(*f*)(*6*), the principles of paragraph (a)(9) of this section will apply to any reverse section 704(c) allocations made as a result of the revaluation.

(ii) *Basis-derivative items.*—If a lower-tier partnership that is a section 721(c) partnership applies the gain deferral method, then, for purposes of applying this section, the upper-tier partnership must treat its distributive share of lower-tier partnership items of gain, loss, amortization, depreciation, or other cost recovery with respect to the lower-tier partnership's section 721(c) property as though they were items of gain, loss, amortization, depreciation, or other cost recovery with respect to the upper-tier partnership's interest in the lower-tier partnership. For purposes of this paragraph (a)(13)(ii), gain deferral method is defined in § 1.721(c)-1(b)(8), section 721(c) partnership is defined in § 1.721(c)-1(b)(14), and section 721(c) property is defined in § 1.721(c)-1(b)(15).

(b) *Traditional method.*—(1) *In general.*—This paragraph (b) describes the traditional method of making section 704(c) allocations. In general, the traditional method requires that when the partnership has income, gain, loss, or deduction attributable to section 704(c) property, it must make appropriate allocations to the partners to avoid shifting the tax consequences of the built-in gain or loss. Under this rule, if the partnership sells section 704(c) property and recognizes gain or loss, built-in gain or loss on the property is allocated to the contributing partner. If the partnership sells a portion of, or an interest in, section 704(c) property, a proportionate part of the built-in gain or loss is allocated to the contributing partner. For section 704(c) property subject to amortization, depletion, depreciation, or other cost recovery, the allocation of deductions attributable to these items takes into account built-in gain or loss on the property. For example, tax allocations to the noncontributing partners of cost recovery deductions with respect to section 704(c) property generally must, to the extent possible, equal book allocations to those partners. However, the total income, gain, loss, or deduction allocated to the partners for a taxable year with respect to a property cannot exceed the total partnership income, gain, loss, or deduction with respect to that property for the taxable year (the ceiling rule). If a partnership has no property the allocations from which are limited by the ceiling rule, the traditional method is reasonable when used for all contributed property.

(2) *Examples.*—The following examples illustrate the principles of the traditional method.

Example 1. Operation of the traditional method—(i) *Calculation of built-in gain on contribution.* A and B form partnership AB and agree that each will be allocated a 50 percent share of all partnership items and that AB will make allocations under section 704(c) using the traditional method under paragraph (b) of this section. A contributes depreciable property with an adjusted tax basis of $4,000 and a book value of $10,000, and B contributes $10,000 cash. Under paragraph (a)(3) of this section, A has built-in gain of $6,000, the excess of the partnership's book value for the property ($10,000) over A's adjusted tax basis in the property at the time of contribution ($4,000).

(ii) *Allocation of tax depreciation.* The property is depreciated using the straight-line method over a 10-year recovery period. Because the property depreciates at an annual rate of 10 percent, B would have been entitled to a depreciation deduction of $500 per year for both book and tax purposes if the adjusted tax basis of the property equalled its fair market value at the time of contribution. Although each partner is allocated $500 of book depreciation per year, the partnership is allowed a tax depreciation deduction of only $400 per year (10 percent of $4,000). The partnership can allocate only $400 of tax depreciation under the ceiling rule of paragraph (b)(1) of this section, and it must be allocated entirely to B. In AB's first year, the proceeds generated by the equipment exactly equal AB's operating expense. At the end of that year, the book value of the property is $9,000 ($10,000 less the $1,000 book depreciation deduction), and the adjusted tax basis is $3,600 ($4,000 less the $400 tax depreciation deduction). A's built-in gain with respect to the property decreases to $5,400 ($9,000 book value less $3,600 adjusted tax basis). Also, at the end of AB's first year, A has a $9,500 book capital account and a $4,000 tax basis in A's partnership interest. B has a $9,500 book capital account and a $9600 adjusted tax basis in B's partnership interest.

(iii) *Sale of the property.* If AB sells the property at the beginning of AB's second year for $9,000, AB realizes tax gain of $5,400 ($9,000, the amount realized, less the adjusted tax basis of $3,600). Under paragraph (b)(1) of this section, the entire $5,400 gain must be allocated to A because the property A contributed has that much built-in gain remaining. If AB sells the property at the beginning of AB's second year for $10,000, AB realizes tax gain of $6,400 ($10,000, the amount realized, less the adjusted tax basis of $3,600). Under paragraph (b)(1) of this section, only $5,400 of gain must be allocated to A to account for A's built-in gain. The remaining $1,000 of gain is allocated equally between A and B in accordance with the partnership agreement. If AB sells the property for less than the $9,000 book value, AB realizes tax gain of less than $5,400, and the entire gain must be allocated to A.

(iv) *Termination and liquidation of partnership.* If AB sells the property at the beginning of AB's second year for $9,000, and AB engages in no other transactions that year, A will recognize a gain of $5,400, and B will recognize no income or loss. A's adjusted tax basis for A's interest in AB will then be $9,400 ($4,000, A's original tax basis, increased by the gain of $5,400). B's adjusted tax basis for B's interest in AB will be $9,600 ($10,000, B's original tax basis, less the $400 depreciation deduction in he first partnership year). If the partnership then terminates and distributes its assets ($19,000 in cash) to A and B in proportion to their capital account balances, A will recognize a capital gain of $100 ($9,500, the amount distributed to A, less $9,400, the adjusted tax basis of A's interest). B will recognize a capital loss of $100 (the excess of B's adjusted tax basis, $9,600, over the amount received, $9,500).

Example 2. Unreasonable use of the traditional method—(i) *Facts.* C and D form partnership CD and agree that each will be allocated a 50 percent share of all partnership items and that CD will make allocations under section 704(c) using the traditional method under paragraph (b) of this section. C contributes equipment with an adjusted tax basis of $1,000 and a book value of $10,000, with a view to taking advantage of the fact that the equipment has only one year remaining on its cost recovery schedule although its remaining economic life is significantly longer. At the time of contribution, C has a built-in gain of $9,000 and the equipment is section 704(c) property. D contributes $10,000 of cash, which CD uses to buy securities. D has substantial net operating loss carryforwards that D anticipates will otherwise expire unused. Under §1.704-1(b)(2)(iv)(*g*)(3), the partnership must allocate the $10,000 of book depreciation to the partners in the first year of the partnership. Thus, there is $10,000 of book depreciation and $1,000 of tax depreciation in the partnership's first year. CD sells the equipment during the second year for $10,000 and recognizes a $10,000 gain ($10,000, the amount realized, less the adjusted tax basis of $0).

(ii) *Unreasonable use of method*—(A) At the beginning of the second year, both the book value and adjusted tax basis of the equipment are $0. Therefore, there is no remaining built-in gain. The $10,000 gain on the sale of the equipment in the second year is allocated $5,000 each to C and D. The interaction of the partnership's one-year write-off of the entire book value of the equipment and the use of the traditional method results in a shift of $4,000 of the precontribution gain in the equipment from C to D (D's $5,000 share of CD's $10,000 gain, less the $1,000 tax depreciation deduction previously allocated to D).

(B) The traditional method is not reasonable under paragraph (a)(10) of this section because the contribution of property is made, and the traditional method is used, with a view to shifting a significant amount of taxable income to a partner with a low marginal tax rate and away from a partner with a high marginal tax rate.

(C) Under these facts, if the partnership agreement in effect for the year of contribution had provided that tax gain from the sale of the property (if any) would always be allocated first to C to offset the effect of the ceiling rule limitation, the allocation method would not violate the anti-abuse rule of paragraph (a)(10) of this section. See paragraph (c)(3) of this section. Under other facts, (for example, if the partnership holds multiple section 704(c) properties and either uses multiple allocation methods or uses a single allocation method where one or more of the properties are subject to the ceiling rule) the allocation to C may not be reasonable.

(c) *Traditional method with curative allocations.*—(1) *In general.*—To correct distortions created by the ceiling rule, a partnership using the traditional method under paragraph (b) of this section may make reasonable curative allocations to reduce or eliminate disparities between book and tax items of noncontributing partners. A curative allocation is an allocation of income, gain, loss, or deduction for tax purposes that differs from the partnership's allocation of the corresponding book item. For example, if a noncontributing partner is allocated less tax depreciation than book depreciation with respect to an item of section 704(c) property, the partnership may make a curative allocation to that partner of tax depreciation from another item of partnership property to make up the difference, notwithstanding that the corresponding book depreciation is allocated to the contributing partner. A partnership may limit its curative allocations to allocations of one or more particular tax items (e.g., only depreciation from a specific property or properties) even if the allocation of those available items does not offset fully the effect of the ceiling rule.

(2) *Consistency.*—A partnership must be consistent in its application of curative allocations with respect to each item of section 704(c) property from year to year.

(3) *Reasonable curative allocations.*—(i) *Amount.*—A curative allocation is not reasonable to the extent it exceeds the amount necessary to offset the effect of the ceiling rule for the current taxable year or, in the case of a curative allocation upon disposition of the property, for prior taxable years.

(ii) *Timing.*—The period of time over which the curative allocations are made is a factor in determining whether the allocations are reasonable. Notwithstanding paragraph (c)(3)(i) of this section, a partnership may make curative allocations in a taxable year to offset the effect of the ceiling rule for a prior taxable year if those allocations are made over a reasonable period of time, such as over the property's economic life, and are provided for under the partnership agreement in effect for the year of contribution. See paragraph (c)(4) *Example 3* (ii)(C) of this section.

(iii) *Type.*—(A) *In general.*—To be reasonable, a curative allocation of income, gain, loss, or deduction must be expected to have substantially the same effect on each partner's tax liability as the tax item limited by the ceiling rule. The expectation must exist at the time the section 704(c) property is obligated to be (or is) contributed to the partnership and the allocation with respect to that property becomes part of the partnership agreement. However, the expectation is tested at the time the allocation with respect to that property is actually made if the partnership agreement is not sufficiently specific as to the precise manner in which allocations are to be made with respect to that property. Under this paragraph (c), if the item limited by the ceiling rule is loss from the sale of property, a curative allocation of gain must be expected to have substantially the same effect as would an allocation to that partner of gain with respect to the sale of the property. If the item limited by the ceiling rule is depreciation or other cost recovery, a curative allocation of income to the contributing partner must be expected to have substantially the same effect as would an allocation to that partner of partnership income with respect to the contributed property. For example, if depreciation deductions with respect to leased equipment contributed by a tax-exempt partner are limited by the ceiling rule, a curative allocation of dividend or interest income to that partner generally is not reasonable, although a curative allocation of depreciation deductions from other leased equipment to the noncontributing partner is reasonable. Similarly, under this rule, if depreciation deductions apportioned to foreign source income in a particular statutory grouping under section 904(d) are limited by the ceiling rule, a curative allocation of income from another statutory grouping to the contributing partner generally is not reasonable, although a curative allocation of income from the same statutory grouping and of the same character is reasonable.

(B) *Exception for allocation from disposition of contributed property.*—If cost recovery has been limited by the ceiling rule, the general limitation on character does not apply to income from the disposition of contributed property subject to the ceiling rule, but only if properly provided for in the partnership agreement in effect for the year of contribution or revaluation. For example, if allocations of depreciation deductions to a noncontributing partner have been limited by the ceiling rule, a curative allocation to the contributing partner of gain from the sale of that property, if properly provided for in the partnership agreement, is reasonable for purposes of paragraph (c)(3)(iii)(A) of this section even if not of the same character.

(4) *Examples.*—The following examples illustrate the principles of this paragraph (c).

Example 1. Reasonable and unreasonable curative allocations—(i) *Facts.* E and F form partnership EF and agree that each will be allocated a 50 percent share of all partnership items and that EF will make allocations under section 704(c) using the traditional method with curative allocations under paragraph (c) of this section. E contributes equipment with an adjusted tax basis of $4,000 and a book value of $10,000. The equipment has 10 years remaining on its cost recovery schedule and is depreciable using the straight-line method. At the time of contribution, E has a built-in gain of $6,000, and therefore, the equipment is section 704(c) property. F contributes $10,000 of cash, which EF uses to buy inventory for resale. In EF's first year, the revenue generated by the equipment equals EF's operating expenses. The equipment generates $1,000 of book depreciation and $400 of tax depreciation for each of 10 years. At the end of the first year EF sells all the inventory for $10,700, recognizing $700 of income. The partners anticipate that the inventory income will have substantially the same effect on their tax liabilities as income from E's contributed equipment. Under the traditional method of paragraph (b) of this section, E and F would each be allocated $350 of income from the sale of inventory for book and tax purposes and $500 of depreciation for book purposes. The $400 of tax depreciation would all be allocated to F. Thus, at the end of the first year, E and F's book and tax capital accounts would be as follows:

E		F		
Book	*Tax*	*Book*	*Tax*	
$10,000	$4,000	$10,000	$10,000	Initial contribution
<500 >	<0 >	<500 >	<400 >	Depreciation
350	350	350	350	Sales income
$9,850	$4,350	$9,850	$9,950	

(ii) *Reasonable curative allocation.* Because the ceiling rule would cause a disparity of $100 between F's book and tax capital accounts, EF may properly allocate to E under paragraph (c) of this section an additional $100 of income from the sale of inventory for tax purposes. This allocation results in capital accounts at the end of EF's first year as follows:

E Book	E Tax	F Book	F Tax	
$10,000	$4,000	$10,000	$10,000	Initial contribution
<500 >	<0 >	<500 >	<400 >	Depreciation
350	450	350	250	Sales income
$9,850	$4,450	$9,850	$9,850	

(iii) *Unreasonable curative allocation.* (A) The facts are the same as in paragraphs (i) and (ii) of this *Example 1*, except that E and F choose to allocate all the income from the sale of the inventory to E for tax purposes, although they share it equally for book purposes. This allocation results in capital accounts at the end of EF's first year as follows:

E Book	E Tax	F Book	F Tax	
$10,000	$4,000	$10,000	$10,000	Initial contribution
<500 >	<0 >	<500 >	<400 >	Depreciation
350	700	350	0	Sales income
$9,850	$4,700	$9,850	$9,600	

(B) This curative allocation is not reasonable under paragraph (c)(3)(i) of this section because the allocation exceeds the amount necessary to offset the disparity caused by the ceiling rule.

Example 2. Curative allocations limited to depreciation—(i) Facts. G and H form partnership GH and agree that each will be allocated a 50 percent share of all partnership items and that GH will make allocations under section 704(c) using the traditional method with curative allocations under paragraph (c) of this section, but only to the extent that the partnership has sufficient tax depreciation deductions. G contributes property G1, with an adjusted tax basis of $3,000 and a fair market value of $10,000, and H contributes property H1, with an adjusted tax basis of $6,000 and a fair market value of $10,000. Both properties have 5 years remaining on their cost recovery schedules and are depreciable using the straight-line method. At the time of contribution, G1 has a built-in gain of $7,000 and H1 has a built-in gain of $4,000, and therefore, both properties are section 704(c) property. G1 generates $600 of tax depreciation and $2,000 of book depreciation for each of five years. H1 generates $1,200 of tax depreciation and $2,000 of book depreciation for each of 5 years. In addition, the properties each generate $500 of operating income annually. G and H are each allocated $1,000 of book depreciation for each property. Under the traditional method of paragraph (b) of this section, G would be allocated $0 of tax depreciation for G1 and $1,000 for H1, and H would be allocated $600 of tax depreciation for G1 and $200 for H1. Thus, at the end of the first year, G and H's book and tax capital accounts would be as follows:

G Book	G Tax	H Book	H Tax	
$10,000	$3,000	$10,000	$6,000	Initial contribution
<1,000 >	<0 >	<1,000 >	<600 >	G1 depreciation
<1,000 >	<1,000 >	<1,000 >	<200 >	H1 depreciation
500	500	500	500	Operating income
$8,500	$2,500	$8,500	$5,700	

(ii) *Curative allocations.* Under the traditional method, G is allocated more depreciation deductions than H, even though H contributed property with a smaller disparity reflected on GH's book and tax capital accounts. GH makes curative allocations to H of an additional $400 of tax depreciation each year, which reduces the disparities between G and H's book and tax capital accounts ratably each year. These allocations are reasonable provided the allocations meet the other requirements of this section. As a result of their agreement, at the end of the first year, G and H's capital accounts are as follows:

G Book	G Tax	H Book	H Tax	
$10,000	$3,000	$10,000	$6,000	Initial contribution
<1,000 >	<0 >	<1,000 >	<600 >	G1 depreciation
<1,000 >	<600 >	<1,000 >	<600 >	H1 depreciation
500	500	500	500	Operating income
$8,500	$2,900	$8,500	$5,300	

Example 3. Unreasonable use of curative allocations—(i) Facts. J and K form partnership JK and agree that each will receive a 50 percent share of all partnership items and that JK will make allocations under section 704(c) using the traditional method with curative allocations under paragraph (c) of this section. J contributes equipment with an adjusted tax basis of $1,000 and a book value of $10,000, with a view to taking advantage of the fact that the equipment has only one year remaining on its cost recovery schedule although it has an estimated remaining economic life of 10 years. J has substantial net operating loss carryforwards that J anticipates will otherwise expire unused. At the time of contribution, J has a built-in gain of $9,000, and therefore, the equipment is section 704(c) property. K contributes $10,000 of cash, which JK uses to buy inventory for resale. In JK's first year, the revenues generated by the equipment exactly equal JK's operating expenses. Under § 1.704-1(b)(2)(iv)(*g*)(*3*), the partnership must allocate the $10,000 of book depreciation to the partners in the first year of the partnership. Thus, there is $10,000 of book depreciation and $1,000 of tax depreciation in the partnership's first year. In addition, at the end of the first year JK sells all of the inventory for $18,000, recognizing $8,000 of income. The partners anticipate that the inventory income will have substantially the same effect on their tax liabilities as income from J's contributed equipment. Under the traditional method of paragraph (b) of this section, J and K's book and tax capital accounts at the end of the first year would be as follows:

J Book	J Tax	K Book	K Tax	
$10,000	$1,000	$10,000	$10,000	Initial contribution
<5,000 >	<0 >	<5,000 >	<1,000 >	Depreciation
4,000	4,000	4,000	4,000	Sales income
$9,000	$5,000	$9,000	$13,000	

(ii) *Unreasonable use of method.* (A) The use of curative allocations under these facts to offset immediately the full effect of the ceiling rule would result in the following book and tax capital accounts at the end of JK's first year:

J Book	J Tax	K Book	K Tax	
$10,000	$1,000	$10,000	$10,000	Initial contribution
<5,000 >	<0 >	<5,000 >	<1,000 >	Depreciation
4,000	8,000	4,000	0	Sales income
$9,000	$9,000	$9,000	$9,000	

(B) This curative allocation is not reasonable under paragraph (a)(10) of this section because the contribution of property is made and the curative allocation method is used with a view to shifting a significant amount of partnership taxable income to a partner with a low marginal tax rate and away from a partner with a high marginal tax rate, within a period of time significantly shorter than the economic life of the property.

(C) The property has only one year remaining on its cost recovery schedule even though its economic life is considerably longer. Under these facts, if the partnership agreement had provided for curative allocations over a reasonable period of time, such as over the property's economic life, rather than over its remaining cost recovery period, the allocations would have been reasonable. See paragraph (c)(3)(ii) of this section. Thus, in this example, JK would make a curative allocation of $400 of sales income to J in the partnership's first year (10 percent of $4,000). J and K's book and tax capital accounts at the end of the first year would be as follows:

J		K		
Book	*Tax*	*Book*	*Tax*	
$10,000	$1,000	$10,000	$10,000	Initial contribution
<5,000 >	<0 >	<5,000 >	<1,000 >	Depreciation
4,000	4,400	4,000	3,600	Sales income
$9,000	$5,400	$9,000	$12,600	

(d) *Remedial allocation method.*—(1) *In general.*—A partnership may adopt the remedial allocation method described in this paragraph to eliminate distortions caused by the ceiling rule. A partnership adopting the remedial allocation method eliminates those distortions by creating remedial items and allocating those items to its partners. Under the remedial allocation method, the partnership first determines the amount of book items under paragraph (d)(2) of this section and the partners' distributive shares of these items under section 704(b). The partnership then allocates the corresponding tax items recognized by the partnership, if any, using the traditional method described in paragraph (b)(1) of this section. If the ceiling rule (as defined in paragraph (b)(1) of this section) causes the book allocation of an item to a noncontributing partner to differ from the tax allocation of the same item to the noncontributing partner, the partnership creates a remedial item of income, gain, loss, or deduction equal to the full amount of the difference and allocates it to the noncontributing partner. The partnership simultaneously creates an offsetting remedial item in an identical amount and allocates it to the contributing partner.

(2) *Determining the amount of book items.*—Under the remedial allocation method, a partnership determines the amount of book items attributable to contributed property in the following manner rather than under the rules of § 1.704-1(b)(2)(iv)(*g*)(*3*). The portion of the partnership's book basis in the property equal to the adjusted tax basis in the property at the time of contribution is recovered in the same manner as the adjusted tax basis in the property is recovered (generally, over the property's remaining recovery period under section 168(i)(7) or other applicable Internal Revenue Code section). The remainder of the partnership's book basis in the property (the amount by which book basis exceeds adjusted tax basis) is recovered using any recovery period and depreciation (or other cost recovery) method (including first-year conventions) available to the partnership for newly purchased property (of the same type as the contributed property) that is placed in service at the time of contribution. However, the additional first year depreciation deduction under section 168(k) is not a permissible method for purposes of the preceding sentence and, if a partnership has acquired property in a taxable year for which the additional first year depreciation deduction under section 168(k) has been used of the same type as the contributed property, the portion of the contributed property's book basis that exceeds its adjusted tax basis must be recovered under a reasonable method. See § 1.168(k)-2(b)(3)(iv)(B).

(3) *Type.*—Remedial allocations of income, gain, loss, or deduction to the noncontributing partner have the same tax attributes as the tax item limited by the ceiling rule. The tax attributes of offsetting remedial allocations of income, gain, loss, or deduction to the contributing partner are determined by reference to the item limited by the ceiling rule. Thus, for example, if the ceiling rule limited item is loss from the sale of contributed property, the offsetting remedial allocation to the contributing partner must be gain from the sale of that property. Conversely, if the ceiling rule limited item is gain from the sale of contributed property, the offsetting remedial allocation to the contributing partner must be loss from the sale of that property. If the ceiling rule limited item is depreciation or other cost recovery from the contributed property, the offsetting remedial allocation to the contributing partner must be income of the type produced (directly or indirectly) by that property. Any partner level tax attributes are determined at the partner level. For example, if the ceiling rule limited item is depreciation from property used in a rental activity, the remedial allocation to the noncontributing partner is depreciation from property used in a rental activity and the offsetting remedial allocation to the contributing partner is ordinary income from that rental activity. Each partner then applies section 469 to the allocations as appropriate.

(4) *Effect of remedial items.*—(i) *Effect on partnership.*—Remedial items do not affect the partnership's computation of its taxable income under section 703 and do not affect the partnership's adjusted tax basis in partnership property.

(ii) *Effect on partners.*—Remedial items are notional tax items created by the partnership solely for tax purposes and do not affect the partners' book capital accounts. Remedial items have the same effect as actual tax items on a partner's tax liability and on the partner's adjusted tax basis in the partnership interest.

(5) *Limitations on use of methods involving remedial allocations.*—(i) *Limitation on taxpayers.*—In the absence of published guidance, the remedial allocation method described in this paragraph (d) is the only reasonable section 704(c) method permitting the creation of notional tax items.

(ii) *Limitation on Internal Revenue Service.*—In exercising its authority under paragraph (a)(10) of this section to make adjustments if a partnership's allocation method is not reasonable, the Internal Revenue Service will not require a partnership to use the remedial allocation method described in this paragraph (d) or any other method involving the creation of notional tax items.

(iii) *Special rules for a section 721(c) partnership and anti-churning property.*—(A) *In general.*—Solely in the case of a gain deferral contribution of section 721(c) property that is a section 197(f)(9) intangible that was not an amortizable section 197 intangible in the hands of the contributor, the remedial allocation method is modified with respect to allocations to a related person to the U.S. transferor pursuant to paragraphs (d)(5)(iii)(B) through (F) of this section. For purposes of this paragraph (d)(5)(iii), gain deferral contribution is defined in § 1.721(c)-1(b)(7), related person is defined in § 1.721(c)-1(b)(12), section 721(c) partnership is defined in § 1.721(c)-1(b)(14), section 721(c) property is defined in § 1.721(c)-1(b)(15), and U.S. transferor is defined in § 1.721(c)-1(b)(18). For an example applying the rules of this paragraph (d)(5)(iii), see § 1.721(c)-7(b)(6) (*Example 6*).

(B) *Book basis recovery.*—The section 721(c) partnership must amortize the portion of the partnership's book value in the section 197(f)(9) intangible that exceeds the adjusted basis in the property upon contribution using any recovery period and amortization method available to the partnership as if the property had been newly purchased by the partnership from an unrelated party.

(C) *Effect of ceiling rule limitations.*—If the ceiling rule causes the book allocation of the item of amortization of a section 197(f)(9) intangible under paragraph (d)(5)(iii)(B) of this section by a section 721(c) partnership to a related person with respect to the U.S. transferor to differ from the tax allocation of the same item to the related person (a ceiling rule limited related person), the partnership must not create a remedial item of deduction to allocate to the related person but instead must increase the adjusted basis of the section 197(f)(9) intangible by an amount equal to the difference solely with respect to that related person. The partnership simultaneously must create an offsetting remedial item in an amount identical to the increase in adjusted tax basis of the section 197(f)(9) intangible and allocate it to the contributing partner.

(D) *Effect of basis adjustment.*—(*1*) *In general.*—The basis adjustment described in paragraph (d)(5)(iii)(C) of this section constitutes an adjustment to the adjusted basis of a section 197(f)(9) intangible with respect to the ceiling rule limited related person only. No adjustment is made to the common basis of partnership property. Thus, for purposes of calculating gain and loss, the ceiling rule limited related person will have a special basis for that section 197(f)(9) intangible. The adjustment to the basis of partnership property under this section has no effect on the partnership's computation of any item under section 703.

(*2*) *Computation of a partner's distributive share of partnership items.*—The partnership first computes its items of gain or loss at the partnership level under section 703. The partnership then allocates the partnership items among the partners, including the ceiling rule limited related person, in accordance with section 704, and adjusts the partners' capital accounts accordingly. The partnership then adjusts the ceiling rule limited related person's distributive share of the items of partnership gain or loss, in accordance with paragraph (d)(5)(iii)(D)(3) of this section, to reflect the effects of that person's basis adjustment under this section. These adjustments to that person's distributive shares must be reflected on Schedules K and K-1 of the partnership's return (Form 1065) (when otherwise required to be completed) and do not affect that person's capital account.

(3) *Effect of basis adjustment in determining items of income, gain, or loss.*—The amount of a ceiling rule limited related person's gain or loss from the sale or exchange of a section 197(f)(9) intangible in which that person has a tax basis adjustment is equal to that person's share of the partnership's gain or loss from the sale of the asset (including any remedial allocations under this paragraph (d)), minus the amount of that person's tax basis adjustment for the section 197(f)(9) intangible.

(E) *Subsequent transfers.*—(1) *In general.*—Except as provided in paragraph (d)(5)(iii)(E)(2) of this section, if a ceiling rule limited related person transfers all or part of its partnership interest, the portion of the basis adjustment for a section 197(f)(9) intangible attributable to the interest transferred is eliminated. The transferor of the partnership interest remains the ceiling rule limited related person with respect to any remaining basis adjustment for the section 197(f)(9) intangible.

(2) *Special rules for substituted basis transactions.*—Paragraph (d)(5)(iii)(E)(1) of this section does not apply to the extent a ceiling rule limited related person transfers its partnership interest in a transaction in which the transferee's basis in the partnership interest is determined in whole or in part by reference to the ceiling rule limited related person's basis in that interest. Instead, in such a case, the transferee succeeds to that portion of the transferor's basis adjustment for a section 197(f)(9) intangible attributable to the interest transferred. In such a case, the basis adjustment in a section 197(f)(9) intangible to which the transferee succeeds is taken into account for purposes of determining the transferee's share of the adjusted basis to the partnership of the partnership's property for purposes of §§1.743-1(b) and 1.755-1(b)(5). To the extent a transferee would be required to decrease the adjusted basis of a section 197(f)(9) intangible pursuant to §§1.743-1(b)(2) and 1.755-1(b)(5), the decrease first reduces the special basis adjustment described in paragraph (d)(5)(iii)(C) of this section, if any, to which the transferee succeeds.

(F) *Non-amortization of basis adjustment.*—Neither the increase to the adjusted basis of a section 197(f)(9) intangible with respect to a ceiling rule limited related person nor the portion of the basis of any property that was determined by reference to such increase is subject to amortization, depreciation, or other cost recovery.

(6) *Adjustments to application of method.*—The Commissioner may, by published guidance, prescribe adjustments to the remedial allocation method under this paragraph (d) as necessary or appropriate. This guidance may, for example, prescribe adjustments to the remedial allocation method to prevent the duplication or omission of items of income or deduction or to reflect more clearly the partners' income or the income of a transferee of a partner.

(7) *Examples.*—The following examples illustrate the principles of this paragraph (d).

Example 1. Remedial allocation method—(i) *Facts.* On January 1, L and M form partnership LM and agree that each will be allocated a 50 percent share of all partnership items. The partnership agreement provides that LM will make allocations under section 704(c) using the remedial allocation method under this paragraph (d) and that the straight-line method will be used to recover excess book basis. L contributes depreciable property with an adjusted tax basis of $4,000 and a fair market value of $10,000. The property is depreciated using the straight-line method with a 10-year recovery period and has 4 years remaining on its recovery period. M contributes $10,000, which the partnership uses to purchase land. Except for the depreciation deductions, LM's expenses equal its income in each year of the 10 years commencing with the year the partnership is formed.

(ii) *Years 1 through 4.* Under the remedial allocation method of this paragraph (d), LM has book depreciation for each of its first 4 years of $1,600 [$1,000 ($4,000 adjusted tax basis divided by the 4-year remaining recovery period) plus $600 ($6,000 excess of book value over tax basis, divided by the *new* 10-year recovery period)]. (For the purpose of simplifying the example, the partnership's book depreciation is determined without regard to any first-year depreciation conventions.) Under the partnership agreement, L and M are each allocated 50 percent ($800) of the book depreciation. M is allocated $800 of tax depreciation and L is allocated the remaining $200 of tax depreciation ($1,000 – $800). See paragraph (d)(1) of this section. No remedial allocations are made because the ceiling rule does not result in a book allocation of depreciation to M different from the tax allocation. The allocations result in capital accounts at the end of LM's first 4 years as follows:

L Book	L Tax	M Book	M Tax	
$10,000	$4,000	$10,000	$10,000	Initial contribution
<3,200 >	<800 >	<3,200 >	<3,200 >	Depreciation
$6,800	$3,200	$6,800	$6,800	

(iii) *Subsequent years.* (A) For each of years 5 through 10, LM has $600 of book depreciation ($6,000 excess of initial book value over adjusted tax basis divided by the 10-year recovery period that commenced in year 1), but no tax depreciation. Under the partnership agreement, the $600 of book depreciation is allocated equally to L and M. Because of the application of the ceiling rule in year 5, M would be allocated $300 of book depreciation, but no tax depreciation. Thus, at the end of LM's fifth year L's and M's book and tax capital accounts would be as follows:

L Book	L Tax	M Book	M Tax	
$6,800	$3,200	$6,800	$6,800	End of year 4
<300 >		<300 >		Depreciation
$6,500	$3,200	$6,500	$6,800	

(B) Because the ceiling rule would cause an annual disparity of $300 between M's allocations of book and tax depreciation, LM must make remedial allocations of $300 of tax depreciation deductions to M under the remedial allocation method for each of years 5 through 10. LM must also make an offsetting remedial allocation to L of $300 of taxable income, which must be of the same type as income produced by the property. At the end of year 5, LM's capital accounts are as follows:

L Book	L Tax	M Book	M Tax	
$6,800	$3,200	$6,800	$6,800	End of year 4
<300 >		<300 >		Depreciation
	300		<300 >	Remedial allocations
$6,500	$3,500	$6,500	$6,500	

(C) At the end of year 10, LM's capital accounts are as follows:

L Book	L Tax	M Book	M Tax	
$6,500	$3,500	$6,500	$6,500	End of year 5
<1,500 >		<1,500 >		Depreciation
	1,500		<1,500 >	Remedial allocations
$5,000	$5,000	$5,000	$5,000	

Example 2. Remedial allocations on sale—(i) *Facts.* N and P form partnership NP and agree that each will be allocated a 50 percent share of all partnership items. The partnership agreement provides that NP will make allocations under section 704(c) using the remedial allocation method under this paragraph (d). N contributes Blackacre (land) with an adjusted tax basis of $4,000 and a fair market value of $10,000. Because N has a built-in gain of $6,000, Blackacre is section 704(c) property. P contributes Whiteacre (land) with an adjusted tax basis and fair market value of $10,000. At the end of NP's first year, NP sells Blackacre to Q for $9,000 and recognizes a capital gain of $5,000 ($9,000 amount realized less $4,000 adjusted tax basis) and a book loss of $1,000 ($9,000 amount realized less $10,000 book basis). NP has no other items of income, gain, loss, or deduction. If the ceiling rule were applied, N would be allocated the entire $5,000 of tax gain and N and P would each be allocated $500 of book loss. Thus, at the end of NP's first year N's and P's book and tax capital accounts would be as follows:

N Book	N Tax	P Book	P Tax	
$10,000	$4,000	$10,000	$10,000	Initial contribution
<500 >	5,000	<500 >		Sale of Blackacre
$9,500	$9,000	$9,500	$10,000	

(ii) *Remedial allocation.* Because the ceiling rule would cause a disparity of $500 between P's allocation of book and tax loss, NP must make a remedial allocation of $500 of capital loss to P and an offsetting remedial allocation to N of an additional $500 of capital gain. These allocations result in capital accounts at the end of NP's first year as follows:

N Book	N Tax	P Book	P Tax	
$10,000	$4,000	$10,000	$10,000	Initial contribution
<500 >	5,000	<500 >		Sale of Blackacre
	500		<500 >	Remedial allocations
$9,500	$9,500	$9,500	$9,500	

Example 3. Remedial allocation where built-in gain property sold for book and tax loss—(i) *Facts.* The facts are the same as in Example 2, except that at the end of NP's first year, NP sells Blackacre to Q for $3,000 and recognizes a capital loss of $1,000 ($3,000 amount realized less $4,000 adjusted tax basis) and a book loss of $7,000 ($3,000 amount realized less $10,000 book basis). If the ceiling rule were applied, P would be allocated the entire $1,000 of tax loss and N and P would each be allocated $3,500 of book loss. Thus, at the end of NP's first year, N's and P's book and tax capital accounts would be as follows:

N Book	N Tax	P Book	P Tax	
$10,000	$4,000	$10,000	$10,000	Initial contribution
<3,500 >	0	<3,500 >	<1,000 >	Sale of Blackacre
$6,500	$4,000	$6,500	$9,000	

(ii) *Remedial allocation.* Because the ceiling rule would cause a disparity of $2,500 between P's allocation of book and tax loss on the sale of Blackacre, NP must make a remedial allocation of $2,500 of capital loss to P and an offsetting remedial allocation to N of $2,500 of capital gain. These allocations result in capital accounts at the end of NP's first year as follows:

N Book	N Tax	P Book	P Tax	
$10,000	$4,000	$10,000	$10,000	Initial contribution
<3,500 >	0	<3,500 >	<1,000 >	Sale of Blackacre
	<2,500 >		<2,500 >	Remedial allocations
$6,500	$6,500	$6,500	$6,500	

(e) *Exceptions and special rules.*—(1) *Small disparities.*—(i) *General rule.*—If a partner contributes one or more items of property to a partnership within a single taxable year of the partnership, and the disparity between the book value of the property and the contributing partner's adjusted tax basis in the property is a small disparity, the partnership may—

(A) Use a reasonable section 704(c) method;

(B) Disregard the application of section 704(c) to the property; or

(C) Defer the application of section 704(c) to the property until the disposition of the property.

(ii) *Definition of small disparity.*—A disparity between book value and adjusted tax basis is a small disparity if the book value of all properties contributed by one partner during the partnership taxable year does not differ from the adjusted tax basis by more than 15 percent of the adjusted tax basis, and the total gross disparity does not exceed $20,000.

(2) *Aggregation.*—Each of the following types of property may be aggregated for purposes of making allocations under section 704(c) and this section if contributed by one partner during the partnership taxable year.

(i) *Depreciable property.*—All property, other than real property, that is included in the same general asset account of the contributing partner and the partnership under section 168.

(ii) *Zero-basis property.*—All property with a basis equal to zero, other than real property.

(iii) *Inventory.*—For partnerships that do not use a specific identification method of accounting, each item of inventory, other than qualified financial assets (as defined in paragraph (e)(3)(ii) of this section).

(3) *Special aggregation rule for securities partnerships.*—(i) *General rule.*—For purposes of making reverse section 704(c) allocations, a securities partnership may aggregate gains and losses from qualified financial assets using any reasonable approach that is consistent with the purpose of section 704(c). Notwithstanding paragraphs (a)(2) and (a)(6)(i) of this section, once a partnership adopts an aggregate approach, that partnership must apply the same aggregate approach to all of its qualified financial assets for all taxable years in which the partnership qualifies as a securities partnership. Paragraphs (e)(3)(iv) and (e)(3)(v) of this section describe approaches for aggregating reverse section 704(c) gains and losses that are generally reasonable. Other approaches may be reasonable in appropriate circumstances. See, however, paragraph (a)(10) of this section, which describes the circumstances under which section 704(c) methods, including the aggregate approaches described in this paragraph (e)(3), are not reasonable. A partnership using an aggregate approach must separately account for any built-in gain or loss from contributed property.

(ii) *Qualified financial assets.*—(A) *In general.*—A qualified financial asset is any personal property (including stock) that is actively traded. Actively traded means actively traded as defined in § 1.1092(d)-1 (defining actively traded property for purposes of the straddle rules).

(B) *Management companies.*—For a management company, qualified financial assets also include the following, even if not actively traded: shares of stock in a corporation; notes, bonds, debentures, or other evidences of indebtedness; interest rate, currency, or equity notional principal contracts; evidences of an interest in, or derivative financial instruments in, any security, currency, or commodity, including any option, forward or futures contract, or short position; or any similar financial instrument.

(C) *Partnership interests.*—An interest in a partnership is not a qualified financial asset for purposes of this paragraph (e)(3)(ii). However, for purposes of this paragraph (e)(3), a partnership (upper-tier partnership) that holds an interest in a securities partnership (lower-tier partnership) must take into account the lower-tier partnership's assets and qualified financial assets as follows:

(1) In determining whether the upper-tier partnership qualifies as an investment partnership, the upper-tier partnership must treat its proportionate share of the lower-tier securities partnership's assets as assets of the upper-tier partnership; and

(2) If the upper-tier partnership adopts an aggregate approach under this paragraph (e)(3), the upper-tier partnership must aggregate the gains and losses from its directly held qualified financial assets with its distributive share of the gains and losses from the qualified financial assets of the lower-tier securities partnership.

(iii) *Securities partnership.*—(A) *In general.*—A partnership is a securities partnership if the partnership is either a management company or an investment partnership, and the partnership makes all of its book allocations in proportion to the partners' relative book capital accounts (except for reasonable special allocations to a partner that provides management services or investment advisory services to the partnership).

(B) *Definitions.*—*(1) Management company.*—A partnership is a management company if it is registered with the Securities and

Exchange Commission as a management company under the Investment Company Act of 1940, as amended (15 U.S.C. 80a).

(2) *Investment partnership.*—A partnership is an investment partnership if:

(*i*) On the date of each capital account restatement, the partnership holds qualified financial assets that constitute at least 90 percent of the fair market value of the partnership's non-cash assets; and

(*ii*) The partnership reasonably expects, as of the end of the first taxable year in which the partnership adopts an aggregate approach under this paragraph (e)(3) to make revaluations at least annually.

(iv) *Partial netting approach.*—This paragraph (e)(3)(iv) describes the partial netting approach of making reverse section 704(c) allocations. See Example 1 of paragraph (e)(3)(ix) of this section for an illustration of the partial netting approach. To use the partial netting approach, the partnership must establish appropriate accounts for each partner for the purpose of taking into account each partner's share of the book gains and losses and determining each partner's share of the tax gains and losses. Under the partial netting approach, on the date of each capital account restatement, the partnership:

(A) Nets its book gains and book losses from qualified financial assets since the last capital account restatement and allocates the net amount to its partners;

(B) Separately aggregates all tax gains and all tax losses from qualified financial assets since the last capital account restatement; and

(C) Separately allocates the aggregate tax gain and aggregate tax loss to the partners in a manner that reduces the disparity between the book capital account balances and the tax capital account balances (book-tax disparities) of the individual partners.

(v) *Full netting approach.*—This paragraph (e)(3)(v) describes the full netting approach of making reverse section 704(c) allocations on an aggregate basis. See Example 2 of paragraph (e)(3)(ix) of this section for an illustration of the full netting approach. To use the full netting approach, the partnership must establish appropriate accounts for each partner for the purpose of taking into account each partner's share of the book gains and losses and determining each partner's share of the tax gains and losses. Under the full netting approach, on the date of each capital account restatement, the partnership:

(A) Nets its book gains and book losses from qualified financial assets since the last capital account restatement and allocates the net amount to its partners;

(B) Nets tax gains and tax losses from qualified financial assets since the last capital account restatement; and

(C) Allocates the net tax gain (or net tax loss) to the partners in a manner that reduces the book-tax disparities of the individual partners.

(vi) *Type of tax gain or loss.*—The character and other tax attributes of gain or loss allocated to the partners under this paragraph (e)(3) must:

(A) Preserve the tax attributes of each item of gain or loss realized by the partnership;

(B) Be determined under an approach that is consistently applied;

(C) With respect to any person who directly or indirectly holds an Applicable Partnership Interest, as defined in § 1.1061-1(a)(1), take into account the application of section 1061 with respect to such interest in an appropriate manner; and

(D) Not be determined with a view to reducing substantially the present value of the partners' aggregate tax liability.

(vii) *Disqualified securities partnerships.*—A securities partnership that adopts an aggregate approach under this paragraph (e)(3) and subsequently fails to qualify as a securities partnership must make reverse section 704(c) allocations on an asset-by-asset basis after the date of disqualification. The partnership, however, is not required to disaggregate the book gain or book loss from qualified asset revaluations before the date of disqualification when making reverse section 704(c) allocations on or after the date of disqualification.

(viii) *Transitional rule for qualified financial assets revalued after effective date.*—A securities partnership revaluing its qualified financial assets pursuant to § 1.704-1(b)(2)(iv)(*f*) on or after the effective date of this section may use any reasonable approach to coordinate with revaluations that occurred prior to the effective date of this section.

(ix) *Examples.*—The following examples illustrate the principles of this paragraph (e)(3).

Example 1. Operation of the partial netting approach—(i) *Facts.* Two regulated investment companies, X and Y, each contribute $150,000 in cash to form PRS, a partnership that registers as a management company. The partnership agreement provides that book items will be allocated in accordance with the partners' relative book capital accounts, that book capital accounts will be adjusted to reflect daily revaluations of property pursuant to § 1.704-1(b)(2)(iv)(*f*)(*5*)(*iii*), and that reverse section 704(c) allocations will be made using the partial netting approach described in paragraph (e)(3)(iv) of this section. X and Y each have an initial book capital account of $150,000. In addition, the partnership establishes for each of X and Y a revaluation account with a beginning balance of $0. On Day 1, PRS buys Stock 1, Stock 2, and Stock 3 for $100,000 each. On Day 2, Stock 1 increases in value from $100,000 to $102,000, Stock 2 increases in value from $100,000 to $105,000, and Stock 3 declines in value from $100,000 to $98,000. At the end of Day 2, Z, a regulated investment company, joins PRS by contributing $152,500 in cash for a one-third interest in the partnership [$152,500 divided by $300,000 (initial values of stock) + $5,000 (net gain at end of Day 2) + $152,500]. PRS uses this cash to purchase Stock 4. PRS establishes a revaluation account for Z with a $0 beginning balance. As of the close of Day 3, Stock 1 increases in value from $102,000 to $105,000, and Stocks 2, 3, and 4 decrease in value from $105,000 to $102,000, from $98,000 to $96,000, and from $152,500 to $151,500, respectively. At the end of Day 3, PRS sells Stocks 2 and 3.

(ii) *Book allocations—Day 2.* At the end of Day 2, PRS revalues the partnership's qualified financial assets and increases X's and Y's book capital accounts by each partner's 50 percent share of the $5,000 ($2,000 + $5,000 − $2,000) net increase in the value of the partnership's assets during Day 2. PRS increases X's and Y's respective revaluation account balances by $2,500 each to reflect the amount by which each partner's book capital account increased on Day 2. Z's capital account is not affected because Z did not join PRS until the end of Day 2. At the beginning of Day 3, the partnership's accounts are as follows:

Stock 1	*Stock 2*	*Stock 3*	*Stock 4*	
$100,000	$100,000	$100,000	—	Opening Balance
2,000	5,000	(2,000)	—	Day 2 Adjustment
$102,000	$105,000	$98,000	$152,500	Total

Book	X *Tax*	*Revaluation Account*	
$150,000	$150,000	$0	Opening Balance
2,500	0	2,500	Day 2 Adjustment
$152,500	$150,000	$2,500	Closing Balance

Book	Y *Tax*	*Revaluation Account*	
$150,000	$150,000	$0	Opening Balance
2,500	0	2,500	Day 2 Adjustment
$152,500	$150,000	$2,500	Closing Balance

Book	Z *Tax*	*Revaluation Account*	
—	—	—	Opening Balance
—	—	—	Day 2 Adjustment
$152,500	$152,500	$0	Closing Balance

(iii) *Book and tax allocations—Day 3.* At the end of Day 3, PRS decreases the book capital accounts of X, Y, and Z by $1,000 to reflect each partner's share of the $3,000 ($3,000 – $3,000 – $2,000 – $1,000) net decrease in the value of the partnership's qualified financial assets. PRS also reduces each partner's revaluation account balance by $1,000. Accordingly, X's and Y's revaluation account balances are reduced to $1,500 each and Z's revaluation account balance is ($1,000). PRS then separately allocates the tax gain from the sale of Stock 2 and the tax loss from the sale of Stock 3. The $2,000 of tax gain recognized on the sale of Stock 2 ($102,000 – $100,000) is allocated among the partners with positive revaluation account balances in accordance with the relative balances of those revaluation accounts. X's and Y's revaluation accounts have equal positive balances; thus, PRS allocates $1,000 of the gain from the sale of Stock 2 to X and $1,000 of that gain to Y. PRS allocates none of the gain from the sale to Z because Z's revaluation account balance is negative. The $4,000 of tax loss recognized from the sale of Stock 3 ($96,000 – $100,000) is allocated first to the partners with negative revaluation account balances to the extent of those balances. Because Z is the only partner with a negative revaluation account balance, the tax loss is allocated first to Z to the extent of Z's ($1,000) balance. The remaining $3,000 of tax loss is allocated among the partners in accordance with their distributive shares of the loss. Accordingly, PRS allocates $1,000 of tax loss from the sale of Stock 3 to each of X and Y. PRS also allocates an additional $1,000 of the tax loss to Z, so that Z's total share of the tax loss from the sale of Stock 3 is $2,000. PRS then reduces each partner's revaluation account balance by the amount of any tax gain allocated to that partner and increases each partner's revaluation account balance by the amount of any tax loss allocated to that partner. At the beginning of Day 4, the partnership's accounts are as follows:

Stock 1	Stock 2	Stock 3	Stock 4	
$100,000	$100,000	$100,000	$152,500	Opening Balance
2,000	5,000	(2,000)	—	Day 2 Adjustment
3,000	(3,000)	(2,000)	(1,000)	Day 3 Adjustment
$105,000	$102,000	$ 96,000	$151,500	Total

X and Y

Book	Tax	Revaluation Account	
$150,000	$150,000	$0	Opening Balance
2,500	0	2,500	Day 2 Adjustment
(1,000)	0	(1,000)	Day 3 Adjustment
$151,500	$150,000	$1,500	Total
0	1,000	(1,000)	Gain from Stock 2
0	(1,000)	1,000	Loss from Stock 3
$151,500	$150,000	$1,500	Closing Balance

Z

Book	Tax	Revaluation Account	
$152,500	$152,500	$0	Opening Balance
(1,000)	0	(1,000)	Day 3 Adjustment
$151,500	$152,500	($1,000)	Total
0	0	0	Gain from Stock 2
0	(2,000)	2,000	Loss from Stock 3
$151,500	$150,500	$1,000	Closing Balance

Example 2. Operation of the full netting approach—(i) Facts. The facts are the same as in Example 1, except that the partnership agreement provides that PRS will make reverse section 704(c) allocations using the full netting approach described in paragraph (e)(3)(v) of this section.

(ii) *Book allocations—Days 2 and 3.* PRS allocates its book gains and losses in the manner described in paragraphs (ii) and (iii) of Example 1 (the partial netting approach). Thus, at the end of Day 2, PRS increases the book capital accounts of X and Y by $2,500 to reflect the appreciation in the partnership's assets from the close of Day 1 to the close of Day 2 and records that increase in the revaluation account created for each partner. At the end of Day 3, PRS decreases the book capital accounts of X, Y, and Z by $1,000 to reflect each partner's share of the decline in value of the partnership's assets from Day 2 to Day 3 and reduces each partner's revaluation account by a corresponding amount.

(iii) *Tax allocations—Day 3.* After making the book adjustments described in the previous paragraph, PRS allocates its net tax gain (or net tax loss) from its sales of qualified financial assets during Day 3. To do so, PRS first determines its net tax gain (or net tax loss) recognized from its sales of qualified financial assets for the day. There is a $2,000 net tax loss ($2,000 gain from the sale of Stock 2 less $4,000 loss from the sale of Stock 3) on the sale of PRS's qualified financial assets. Because Z is the only partner with a negative revaluation account balance, the partnership's net tax loss is allocated first to Z to the extent of Z's ($1,000) revaluation account balance. The remaining net tax loss is allocated among the partners in accordance with their distributive shares of loss. Thus, PRS allocates $333.33 of the $2,000 net tax loss to each of X and Y. PRS also allocates an additional $333.33 of the net tax loss to Z, so that the total net tax loss allocation to Z is $1,333.33. PRS then increases each partner's revaluation account balance by the amount of net tax loss allocated to that partner. At the beginning of Day 4, the partnership's accounts are as follows:

Stock 1	Stock 2	Stock 3	Stock 4	
$100,000	$100,000	$100,000	$152,500	Opening Balance
2,000	5,000	(2,000)	—	Day 2 Adjustment
3,000	(3,000)	(2,000)	(1,000)	Day 3 Adjustment
$105,000	$102,000	$ 96,000	$151,500	Total

X and Y

Book	Tax	Revaluation Account	
$150,000	$150,000	$0	Opening Balance
2,500	0	2,500	Day 2 Adjustment
(1,000)	0	(1,000)	Day 3 Adjustment
$151,500	$150,000	$1,500	Total
0	(333)	(333)	Net Tax Loss-Stocks 2 & 3
$151,500	$149,667	$1,833	Closing Balance

Z

Book	Tax	Revaluation Account	
$152,500	$152,500	$0	Opening Balance
(1,000)	0	(1,000)	Day 3 Adjustment
$151,500	$152,500	($1,000)	Total
0	(1,333)	1,333	Net Tax Loss-Stocks 2 & 3
$151,500	$151,167	$333	Closing Balance

(4) *Aggregation as permitted by the Commissioner.*—The Commissioner may, by published guidance or by letter ruling, permit:

(i) Aggregation of properties other than those described in paragraphs (e)(2) and (e)(3) of this section;

(ii) Partnerships and partners not described in paragraph (e)(3) of this section to aggregate gain and loss from qualified financial assets; and

(iii) Aggregation of qualified financial assets for purposes of making section 704(c) allocations in the same manner as that described in paragraph (e)(3) of this section.

(f) *Applicability dates.*—With the exception of paragraphs (a)(1), (a)(8)(ii) and (iii), (a)(10) and (11), and (e)(3)(vi)(C) of this section, and of the last sentence of paragraph (d)(2) of this section, this section applies to properties contributed to a partnership and to revaluations pursuant to § 1.704-1(b)(2)(iv)(*f*) or (*s*) on or after December 21, 1993. Paragraph (a)(11) of this section applies to properties contributed by a partner to a partnership on or after August 20, 1997. However, partnerships may rely on paragraph (a)(11) of this section for properties contributed before August 20, 1997, and disposed of on or after August 20, 1997. Paragraph (a)(8)(ii) applies to installment obligations received by a partnership in exchange for section 704(c) property on or after November 24, 2003. Paragraph (a)(8)(iii) applies to property acquired on or after November 24, 2003, by a partnership pursuant to a contract that is section 704(c) property. Except as otherwise provided in § 1.752-7(k), paragraphs (a)(8)(iv) and (a)(12) apply to § 1.752-7 liability transfers, as defined in § 1.752-7(b)(4), occurring on or after June 24, 2003. See § 1.752-7(k). Paragraphs (a)(1) and (a)(10) of this section are applicable for taxable years beginning after June 9, 2010. The last sentence of paragraph (d)(2) of this section applies to property contributed to a partnership on or after September 24, 2019. However, a taxpayer may choose to apply the last sentence in paragraph (d)(2) of this section for property contributed to a partnership on or after September 28, 2017. A taxpayer may rely on the last sentence in paragraph (d)(2) of this section in regulation project REG-104397-18 (2018-41 I.R.B. 558) (see § 601.601(d)(2)(ii)(*b*) of this chapter) for property contributed to a partnership on or after September 28, 2017, and ending before September 24, 2019. Paragraph (e)(3)(vi)(C) of this section applies to taxable years beginning on or after January 19, 2021.

(g) *Applicability dates for rules for section 721(c) partnerships.*—(1) *In general.*—Notwithstanding paragraph (f) of this section, except as provided in paragraph (g)(2) of this section, paragraphs (a)(13) and (d)(5)(iii) of this section apply with respect to contributions occurring on or after January 18, 2017, and with respect to contributions that occurred before January 18, 2017 resulting from an entity classification election made under § 301.7701-3 of this chapter that was effective on or before January 18, 2017 but was filed on or after January 18, 2017.

(2) *Election to apply the provisions described in paragraph (g)(1) of this section retroactively.*—Paragraphs (a)(13) and (d)(5)(iii) of this section may, by election, be applied with respect to a contribution that occurred on or after August 6, 2015 but before January 18, 2017, and with respect to a contribution that occurred before August 6, 2015 resulting from an entity classification election made under § 301.7701-3 of this chapter that was effective on or before August 6, 2015 but was filed on or after August 6, 2015. The election must have been made by applying paragraph (a)(13) or (d)(5)(iii) of this section, as applicable, on a timely filed original return (including extensions) or an amended return filed no later than July 18, 2017. [Reg. § 1.704-3.]

□ [*T.D.* 8500, 12-21-93. *Amended by T.D.* 8585, 12-27-94; *T.D.* 8717, 5-8-97; *T.D.* 8730, 8-19-97; *T.D.* 9137, 7-15-2004; *T.D.* 9193, 3-21-2005 (*corrected* 8-5-2005); *T.D.* 9207, 5-23-2005; *T.D.* 9485, 6-8-2010, *T.D.* 9612, 2-4-2013, *T.D.* 9814, 1-18-2017, *T.D.* 9874, 9-17-2019 *T.D.* 9891, 1-17-2020 *and T.D.* 9945, 1-13-2021.]

§ 1.706-1. Taxable years of partner and partnership.

* * *

(b) * * *

(6) *Certain foreign partners disregarded.*—(i) *Interests of disregarded foreign partners not taken into account.*—In determining the taxable year (the current taxable year) of a partnership under section 706(b) and the regulations thereunder, any interest held by a disregarded foreign partner is not taken into account. A foreign partner is a disregarded foreign partner unless such partner is allocated any gross income of the partnership that was effectively connected (or treated as effectively connected) with the conduct of a trade or business within the United States during the partnership's taxable year immediately preceding the current taxable year (or, if such partner was not a partner during the partnership's immediately preceding taxable year, the partnership reasonably believes that the partner will be allocated any such income during the current taxable year) and taxation of that income is not otherwise precluded under any U.S. income tax treaty.

(ii) *Definition of foreign partner.*—For purposes of this paragraph (b)(6), a foreign partner is any partner that is not a United States person (as defined in section 7701(a)(30)), except that a partner that is a controlled foreign corporation (within the meaning of section 957(a)) in which a United States shareholder (as defined in section 951(b)) owns (within the meaning of section 958(a)) stock is not treated as a foreign partner.

(iii) *Minority interest rule.*—If each partner that is not a disregarded foreign partner under paragraph (b)(6)(i) of this section (regarded partner) holds less than a 10-percent interest, and the regarded partners, in the aggregate, hold less than a 20-percent interest in the capital and profits of the partnership, then paragraph (b)(6)(i) of this section does not apply. In determining ownership in a partnership for purposes of this paragraph (b)(6)(iii), each regarded partner is treated as owning any interest in the partnership owned by a related partner. For this purpose, partners are treated as related if they are related within the meaning of sections 267(b) or 707(b) (using the language "10 percent" instead of "50 percent" each place it appears). However, for purposes of determining if partners hold less than a 20-percent interest in the aggregate, the same interests will not be considered as being owned by more than one regarded partner.

(iv) *Example.*—The provisions of paragraph (b)(6) of this section may be illustrated by the following example:

Example. Partnership B is owned by two partners, F, a foreign corporation that owns a 95-percent interest in the capital and profits of partnership B, and D, a domestic corporation that owns the remaining 5-percent interest in the capital and profits of partnership B. Partnership B is not engaged in the conduct of a trade or business within the United States, and, accordingly, partnership B does not earn any income that is effectively connected with a U.S. trade or business. F uses a March 31 fiscal year, and causes partnership B to maintain its books and records on a March 31 fiscal year as well. D is a calendar year taxpayer. Under paragraph (b)(6)(i) of this section, F would be disregarded and partnership B's taxable year would be determined by reference to D. However, because D owns less than a 10-percent interest in the capital and profits of partnership B, the minority interest rule of paragraph (b)(6)(iii) of this section applies, and partnership B must adopt the March 31 fiscal year for Federal tax purposes.

(v) *Applicability dates.*—(A) *Generally.*—The provisions of this paragraph (b)(6) (other than paragraph (b)(6)(iii) of this section and paragraph (b)(6)(ii) of this section to the extent described in the next sentence) apply to partnership taxable years, other than those of an existing partnership, that begin on or after July 23, 2002. The provisions in paragraph (b)(6)(ii) of this section relating to controlled foreign corporations apply to taxable years of foreign corporations ending on or after October 1, 2019, and taxable years of United States shareholders in which or with which such taxable years of foreign corporations end. For taxable years of foreign corporations ending before October 1, 2019, and taxable years of United States shareholders in which or with which such taxable years of foreign corporations end, a taxpayer may apply such provisions to the last taxable year of a foreign corporation beginning before January 1, 2018, and each subsequent taxable year of the foreign corporation, and to taxable years of United States shareholders in which or with which such taxable years of the foreign corporation end, provided that the taxpayer and United States persons that are related (within the meaning of section 267 or 707) to the taxpayer consistently apply such provisions with respect to all foreign corporations. For taxable years of foreign corporations ending before October 1, 2019, and taxable years of United States shareholders in which or with which such taxable years of foreign corporations end, where the taxpayer does not apply the provisions of paragraph (b)(6)(ii) of this section relating to controlled foreign corporations, see paragraph (b)(6)(ii) of this section as in effect and contained in 26 CFR part 1, as revised April 1, 2020. The provisions of paragraph (b)(6)(iii) of this section apply to partnership taxable years, other than those of an existing partnership or an interim period partnership, that begin on or after August 3, 2015. For partnership taxable years beginning on or after July 23, 2002, and before August 3, 2015, see the provisions of § 1.706-1(b)(6)(iii) as contained in the 26 CFR part 1 on July 31, 2015. For purposes of paragraph (b)(6) of this section, an existing partnership is a partnership that was formed prior to September 23, 2002, and an interim period partnership is a partnership that was formed on or after September 23, 2002, and prior to August 3, 2015.

(B) *Voluntary change in taxable year*.—An existing partnership may change its taxable year to a year determined in accordance with this section. An existing partnership that makes such a change prior to August 3, 2015 will generally cease to be exempted from the requirements of this paragraph (b)(6) of this section, and thus will be subject to the requirements of paragraph (b)(6) of this section, except for paragraph (b)(6)(iii) of this section—instead, such partnership will be subject to the provisions of § 1.706-1(b)(6)(iii) as contained in the 26 CFR part 1 on July 31, 2015. An existing partnership that makes such a change on or after August 3, 2015 will cease to be exempted from the requirements of this paragraph (b)(6). An interim period partnership may change its taxable year to a year determined in accordance with paragraph (b)(6)(iii) of this section. An interim period partnership that makes such a change will cease to be exempted from the requirements of paragraph (b)(6)(iii) of this section.

(C) *Subsequent sale or exchange of interests*.—If an existing partnership or an interim period partnership terminates under section 708(b)(1)(B), the resulting partnership is not an existing partnership or an interim period partnership for purposes of paragraph (b)(6)(v) of this section.

(D) *Transition rule*.—If, in the first taxable year beginning on or after July 23, 2002, an existing partnership voluntarily changes its taxable year to a year determined in accordance with this paragraph (b)(6), then the partners of that partnership may apply the provisions of § 1.702-3T to take into account all items of income, gain, loss, deduction, and credit attributable to the partnership year of change ratably over a four-year period. If, in a partnership taxable year beginning on or after August 3, 2015, an interim period partnership voluntarily changes its taxable year to a year determined in accordance with paragraph (b)(6)(iii) of this section, then the partners of that partnership may apply the provisions of § 1.702-3T to take into account all items of income, gain, loss, deduction, and credit attributable to the partnership year of change ratably over a four-year period.

* * *

(c) * * *

(6) *Foreign taxes*.—For rules relating to the treatment of foreign taxes paid or accrued by a partnership, see § 1.901-2(f)(4)(i) and (f)(4)(ii).

* * *

[Reg. § 1.706-1.]

☐ [*T.D. 6175, 5-23-56. Amended by T.D. 7286, 9-26-73; T.D. 8123, 2-4-87; T.D. 8996, 5-16-2002; T.D. 9009, 7-22-2002; T.D. 9576, 2-9-2012; T.D. 9728, 7-31-2015 (corrected 11-3-2015) and T.D. 9908, 9-21-2020.*]

§ 1.721(c)-1. Overview, definitions, and rules of general application.—(a) *Overview*.—(1) *In general*.—This section and §§ 1.721(c)-2 through 1.721(c)-7 (collectively, the *section 721(c) regulations*) provide rules under section 721(c). This section provides definitions and rules of general application for purposes of the section 721(c) regulations. Section 1.721(c)-2 provides the general operative rules that override section 721(a) nonrecognition of gain upon a contribution of section 721(c) property to a section 721(c) partnership. Section 1.721(c)-3 describes the gain deferral method, which may be applied in order to avoid the immediate recognition of gain upon a contribution of section 721(c) property to a section 721(c) partnership. Section 1.721(c)-4 provides rules regarding acceleration events for purposes of applying the gain deferral method. Section 1.721(c)-5 identifies exceptions to the rules regarding acceleration events provided in § 1.721(c)-4(b). Section 1.721(c)-6 provides procedural and reporting requirements. Section 1.721(c)-7 provides examples illustrating the application of the section 721(c) regulations.

(2) *Scope*.—Paragraph (b) of this section provides definitions. Paragraph (c) of this section describes the treatment of a change in form of a partnership. Paragraph (d) of this section provides an anti-abuse rule. Paragraph (e) of this section provides the dates of applicability.

(b) *Definitions*.—The following definitions apply for purposes of the section 721(c) regulations. Unless otherwise indicated, the definitions apply on a property-by-property basis, as applicable.

(1) *Acceleration event*.—An acceleration event has the meaning provided in § 1.721(c)-4(b).

(2) *Built-in gain*.—Built-in gain is, with respect to property contributed to a partnership, the excess of the book value of the property over the partnership's adjusted tax basis in the property upon the contribution, determined without regard to the application of § 1.721(c)-2(b).

(3) *Consistent allocation method*.—The consistent allocation method is the method described in § 1.721(c)-3(c).

(4) *Controlled partnership*.—A partnership is a controlled partnership with respect to a U.S. transferor if the U.S. transferor and related persons control the partnership. For purposes of this paragraph (b)(4), control is determined based on all the facts and circumstances, except that a partnership will be deemed to be controlled by a U.S. transferor and related persons if those persons, in the aggregate, own (directly or indirectly through one or more partnerships) more than 50 percent of the interests in the partnership capital or profits.

(5) *Direct or indirect partner*.—A direct or indirect partner is a person (other than a partnership) that owns an interest in a partnership directly or indirectly through one or more partnerships.

(6) *Excluded property*.—Excluded property is—

(i) A cash equivalent;

(ii) A security within the meaning of section 475(c)(2), without regard to section 475(c)(4);

(iii) Tangible property with a book value exceeding adjusted tax basis by no more than $20,000 or with an adjusted tax basis in excess of book value; and

(iv) An interest in a partnership in which 90 percent or more of the property (as measured by value) held by the partnership (directly or indirectly through interests in one or more partnerships that are not excluded property) consists of property described in paragraphs (b)(6)(i) through (iii) of this section.

(7) *Gain deferral contribution*.—A gain deferral contribution is a contribution of section 721(c) property to a section 721(c) partnership with respect to which the recognition of gain is deferred under the gain deferral method.

(8) *Gain deferral method*.—The gain deferral method is the method described in § 1.721(c)-3(b).

(9) *Partial acceleration event*.—A partial acceleration event is an event described in § 1.721(c)-5(d)(2) or (3).

(10) *Regulatory allocation*.—A regulatory allocation is—

(i) An allocation pursuant to a minimum gain chargeback, as defined in § 1.704-2(b)(2);

(ii) A partner nonrecourse deduction, as determined in § 1.704-2(i)(2);

(iii) An allocation pursuant to a partner minimum gain chargeback, as described in § 1.704-2(i)(4);

(iv) An allocation pursuant to a qualified income offset, as defined in § 1.704-1(b)(2)(ii)(*d*);

(v) An allocation with respect to the exercise of a noncompensatory option described in § 1.704-1(b)(2)(iv)(*s*); and

(vi) An allocation of partnership level ordinary income or loss described in § 1.751-1(b)(3).

(11) *Related foreign person*.—A related foreign person is, with respect to a U.S. transferor, a related person (other than a partnership) that is not a U.S. person.

(12) *Related person*.—(i) *In general*.—A related person is, with respect to a U.S. transferor, a person that is related (within the meaning of section 267(b) or 707(b)(1)) to the U.S. transferor.

(ii) *Modification to the application of section 267(b)*.—For purposes of determining if a person is a related person with respect to a U.S. transferor, section 267(b) is applied without regard to section 267(c)(3).

(13) *Remaining built-in gain*.—(i) *In general*.—Remaining built-in gain is, with respect to section 721(c) property subject to the gain deferral method, the built-in gain reduced by decreases in the difference between the property's book value and adjusted tax basis, but, for purposes of this paragraph (b)(13)(i), without taking into account increases or decreases to the property's book value pursuant to § 1.704-1(b)(2)(iv)(*f*) or (*s*).

(ii) *Special rule for tiered partnerships.*—If section 721(c) property is described in § 1.721(c)-3(d)(1)(ii), the remaining built-in gain includes the new positive reverse section 704(c) layer described in § 1.721(c)-3(d)(1)(ii), reduced by decreases in the difference between the property's book value and adjusted tax basis, but, for purposes of this paragraph (b)(13)(ii), without taking into account increases or decreases to the property's book value pursuant to § 1.704-1(b)(2)(iv)(*f*) or (*s*) that are unrelated to the revaluation described in § 1.721(c)-3(d)(1)(i).

(14) *Section 721(c) partnership.*—(i) *In general.*—A partnership (domestic or foreign) is a section 721(c) partnership if there is a contribution of section 721(c) property to the partnership and, after the contribution and all transactions related to the contribution—

(A) A related foreign person with respect to the U.S. transferor is a direct or indirect partner in the partnership; and

(B) The U.S. transferor and related persons own 80 percent or more of the interests in partnership capital, profits, deductions, or losses.

(ii) *Special rule for tiered partnerships.*—A partnership described in § 1.721(c)-3(d)(1) or (2) is deemed to be a section 721(c) partnership for purposes of the gain deferral method.

(15) *Section 721(c) property.*—(i) *In general.*—Section 721(c) property is property, other than excluded property, with built-in gain that is contributed to a partnership by a U.S. transferor, including pursuant to a contribution described in § 1.721(c)-2(d) (partnership look-through rule). If the U.S. transferor is treated as contributing its share of property to a partnership pursuant to § 1.721(c)-2(d), the entire property will be section 721(c) property.

(ii) *Special rule for tiered partnerships.*—Property described in § 1.721(c)-3(d)(1)(ii) and an interest in a partnership described in § 1.721(c)-3(d)(2)(ii) is deemed to be section 721(c) property.

(16) *Successor event.*—A successor event is an event described in § 1.721(c)-5(c)(2), (3), (4), or (5).

(17) *Termination event.*—A termination event is an event described in § 1.721(c)-5(b)(2), (3), (4), (5), (6), or (7).

(18) *U.S. transferor.*—(i) *In general.*—A U.S. transferor is a United States person within the meaning of section 7701(a)(30) (a *U.S. person*), other than a domestic partnership.

(ii) *Special rule for tiered partnerships.*—Solely for purposes of applying the consistent allocation method, a U.S. transferor includes a partnership that is treated as a U.S. transferor under § 1.721(c)-3(d)(1)(iii) or (d)(2)(i).

(c) *Change in form of a partnership.*—A mere change in identity, form, or place of organization of a partnership or a recapitalization of a partnership will not cause the partnership to become a section 721(c) partnership.

(d) *Anti-abuse rule.*—If a U.S. transferor engages in a transaction (or series of transactions) or an arrangement with a principal purpose of avoiding the application of the section 721(c) regulations, the transaction (or series of transactions) or the arrangement may be recharacterized (including by aggregating or disregarding steps or disregarding an intermediate entity) in accordance with its substance.

(e) *Applicability dates.*—(1) *In general.*—Except as provided in paragraphs (e)(2) and (3) of this section, this section applies to contributions occurring on or after August 6, 2015, and to contributions that occurred before August 6, 2015 resulting from an entity classification election made under § 301.7701-3 of this chapter that was effective on or before August 6, 2015 but was filed on or after August 6, 2015.

(2) *Certain provisions.*—Except as provided in paragraph (e)(3) of this section, paragraphs (b)(6)(iv) and (c) of this section apply to contributions occurring on or after January 18, 2017, and to contributions that occurred before January 18, 2017 resulting from an entity classification election made under § 301.7701-3 of this chapter that was effective on or before January 18, 2017 but was filed on or after January 18, 2017. Except as provided in paragraph (e)(3) of this section, paragraph (b)(14)(i)(B) of this section applies by replacing "80 percent or more" with "greater than 50 percent" with respect to contributions that occurred on or after August 6, 2015 but before January 18, 2017, and with respect to contributions that occurred before August 6, 2015 resulting from an entity classification election made under § 301.7701-3 of this chapter that was effective on or before August 6, 2015, but was filed on or after August 6, 2015 but before January 18, 2017. Except as provided in paragraph (e)(3) of this section, paragraph (b)(12)(ii) of this section applies to contributions occurring on or after January 17, 2020.

(3) *Election to apply the provisions described in paragraph (e)(2) of this section retroactively.*—Paragraphs (b)(6)(iv) and (c) of this section and paragraph (b)(14)(i)(B) of this section, without the modification described in paragraph (e)(2) of this section, may, by election, be applied to a contribution that occurred on or after August 6, 2015 but before January 18, 2017, and to a contribution that occurred before August 6, 2015 resulting from an entity classification election made under § 301.7701-3 of this chapter that was effective on or before August 6, 2015 but was filed on or after August 6, 2015. The election described in the preceding sentence must have been made by applying paragraph (b)(6)(iv) or (c) as described in paragraph (e)(2) of this section or paragraph (b)(14)(i)(B) of this section, without the modification described in paragraph (e)(2) of this section, as applicable, to the contribution on a timely filed original return (including extensions) or an amended return filed no later than July 18, 2017. Paragraph (b)(12)(ii) of this section, may, by election, be applied to a contribution that occurred on or after August 6, 2015 but before January 17, 2020, and to a contribution that occurred before August 6, 2015 resulting from an entity classification election made under § 301.7701-3 of this chapter that was effective on or before August 6, 2015 but was filed on or after August 6, 2015. The election described in the preceding sentence must be made by applying paragraph (b)(12)(ii) of this section to the contribution on a timely filed original return (including extensions) or an amended return filed no later July 17, 2020. [Reg. § 1.721(c)-1.]

☐ [*T.D.* 9891, 1-17-2020.]

§ 1.721(c)-2. Recognition of gain on certain contributions of property to partnerships with related foreign partners.—(a) *Scope.*—This section provides the general operative rules that override section 721(a) nonrecognition of gain upon a contribution of section 721(c) property to a section 721(c) partnership. Paragraph (b) of this section provides the general rule that nonrecognition of gain under section 721(a) does not apply to a contribution of section 721(c) property to a section 721(c) partnership. Paragraph (c) of this section provides a de minimis exception to the application of the general rule in paragraph (b) of this section. Paragraph (d) of this section provides rules for identifying a section 721(c) partnership when a partnership in which a U.S. transferor is a direct or indirect partner contributes property to another partnership. Paragraph (e) of this section provides the dates of applicability. For definitions that apply for purposes of this section, see § 1.721(c)-1(b).

(b) *General rule for contributions of section 721(c) property.*—Except as provided in this paragraph (b), paragraph (c) of this section, and § 1.721(c)-3 (describing the gain deferral method), nonrecognition under section 721(a) will not apply to gain realized by the contributing partner upon a contribution of section 721(c) property to a section 721(c) partnership. This paragraph (b) does not apply to a direct contribution by a U.S. transferor if the U.S. transferor and related persons with respect to the U.S. transferor do not own 80 percent or more of the interests in partnership capital, profits, deductions, or losses.

(c) *De minimis exception.*—Paragraph (b) of this section will not apply with respect to contributions to a section 721(c) partnership during a taxable year of the section 721(c) partnership for which the sum of the built-in gain with respect to all section 721(c) property contributed in that taxable year does not exceed $1 million. If, pursuant to the last sentence of paragraph (b) of this section, a direct contribution of property to the section 721(c) partnership by a U.S. transferor is not subject to paragraph (b) of this section, then such contribution is not taken into account for purposes of this paragraph (c).

(d) *Rules for identifying a section 721(c) partnership when a partnership contributes property to another partnership.*—(1) *Partnership look-through rule.*—If a U.S. transferor is a direct or indirect partner in a partnership (upper-tier partnership) and the upper-tier partnership contributes all or a portion of its property to another partnership (lower-tier partnership), then, for purposes of determining if the lower-tier partnership is a section 721(c) partnership, the U.S. transferor is treated as contributing to the lower-tier partnership its share of the property actually contributed by the upper-tier partnership to the lower-tier partnership.

(2) *Exception for a technical termination of a partnership.*—Paragraph (d)(1) of this section will not apply to a deemed contribution that occurs as a result of a termination of a partnership described in section 708(b)(1)(B) (technical termination). If a partnership is a section 721(c) partnership immediately before a technical termination, see § 1.721(c)-5(c)(4) (which treats technical terminations as successor events in certain circumstances).

(e) *Applicability dates.*—(1) *In general.*—Except as provided in paragraphs (e)(2) and (3) of this section, this section applies to contributions occurring on or after August 6, 2015, and to contributions that occurred before August 6, 2015 resulting from an entity classification election made under § 301.7701-3 of this chapter that was effective on or before August 6, 2015 but was filed on or after August 6, 2015.

(2) *Certain provisions.*—Except as provided in paragraph (e)(3) of this section, the final sentence of paragraph (b) of this section, the final sentence of paragraph (c) of this section, and paragraph (d)(2) of this section apply to contributions occurring on or after January 18, 2017, and to contributions that occurred before January 18, 2017 resulting from an entity classification election made under § 301.7701-3 of this chapter that was effective on or before January 18, 2017 but was filed on or after January 18, 2017.

(3) *Election to apply the provisions described in paragraph (e)(2) of this section retroactively.*—The final sentence of paragraph (b) of this section, the final sentence of paragraph (c) of this section, and paragraph (d)(2) of this section may, by election, be applied to a contribution that occurred on or after August 6, 2015 but before January 18, 2017, and to a contribution that occurred before August 6, 2015 resulting from an entity classification election made under § 301.7701-3 of this chapter that was effective on or before August 6, 2015 but was filed on or after August 6, 2015. The election must have been made by applying the final sentence of paragraph (b) of this section, the final sentence of paragraph (c) of this section, or paragraph (d)(2) of this section, as applicable, to the contribution on a timely filed original return (including extensions) or an amended return filed no later than July 18, 2017. [Reg. § 1.721(c)-2.]

□ [*T.D.* 9891, 1-17-2020.]

§ 1.721(c)-3. Gain deferral method.—(a) *Scope.*—This section describes the gain deferral method to avoid the immediate recognition of gain upon a contribution of section 721(c) property to a section 721(c) partnership. Paragraph (b) of this section provides the requirements of the gain deferral method, including the requirement to apply the consistent allocation method. Paragraph (c) of this section describes the consistent allocation method. Paragraph (d) of this section provides rules for tiered partnerships. Paragraph (e) of this section provides the dates of applicability. For definitions that apply for purposes of this section, see § 1.721(c)-1(b).

(b) *Requirements of the gain deferral method.*—A contribution of section 721(c) property to a section 721(c) partnership that would be subject to § 1.721(c)-2(b) will not be subject to § 1.721(c)-2(b) if the conditions in paragraphs (b)(1) through (5) of this section are satisfied with respect to that property.

(1) Either—

(i) Both—

(A) The section 721(c) partnership adopts the remedial allocation method described in § 1.704-3(d) with respect to the section 721(c) property; and

(B) The section 721(c) partnership applies the consistent allocation method provided in paragraph (c) of this section; or

(ii) For the period beginning on the date of the contribution of the section 721(c) property and ending on the date on which there is no remaining built-in gain with respect to that property, all distributive shares of income and gain with respect to the section 721(c) property for all direct and indirect partners that are related foreign persons with respect to the U.S. transferor will be subject to taxation as income effectively connected with a trade or business within the United States (under either section 871 or 882), and neither the section 721(c) partnership nor a related foreign person that is a direct or indirect partner in the section 721(c) partnership claims benefits under an income tax convention that would exempt the income or gain from tax or reduce the rate of taxation to which the income or gain is subject.

(2) Upon an acceleration event, the U.S. transferor recognizes an amount of gain equal to the remaining built-in gain with respect to the section 721(c) property or an amount of gain required to be recognized under § 1.721(c)-5(d) or (e), as applicable.

(3) The procedural and reporting requirements provided in § 1.721(c)-6(b) are satisfied.

(4) The U.S. transferor consents to extend the period of limitations on assessment of tax as required by § 1.721(c)-6(b)(5).

(5) If the section 721(c) property is a partnership interest or property described in the partnership look-through rule provided in § 1.721(c)-2(d), the applicable tiered-partnership rules provided in paragraph (d) of this section are applied.

(c) *Consistent allocation method.*—(1) *In general.*—For each taxable year of a section 721(c) partnership in which there is remaining built-in gain in the section 721(c) property, the section 721(c) partnership must allocate each book item of income, gain, deduction, and loss with respect to the section 721(c) property to the U.S. transferor in the same percentage. For purposes of this paragraph (c)(1), upon a variation (as defined in § 1.706-4(a)(1)) of a U.S. transferor's interest in a section 721(c) partnership, a book item of income, gain, deduction, and loss with respect to a section 721(c) property is treated as allocated in the same percentage if the item is allocated under the interim closing method (as described in § 1.706-4), unless the variation results from a transaction undertaken with a principal purpose of avoiding the tax consequences of the gain deferral method. For exceptions to the first sentence in this paragraph (c)(1), see paragraph (c)(4) of this section.

(2) *Determining income or gain with respect to section 721(c) property.*—For purposes of applying paragraph (c)(1) of this section, a section 721(c) partnership must attribute book income and gain to each item of section 721(c) property in a consistent manner using any reasonable method taking into account all the facts and circumstances. All items of book income and gain attributable to an item of section 721(c) property will comprise a single class of gross income for purposes of applying paragraph (c)(3) of this section.

(3) *Determining deduction or loss with respect to section 721(c) property.*—For purposes of applying paragraph (c)(1) of this section, a section 721(c) partnership must use the principles of §§ 1.861-8 and 1.861-8T to allocate and apportion its items of deduction, except for interest expense and research and experimental expenditures, and loss to the class of gross income with respect to each item of section 721(c) property as determined in paragraph (c)(2) of this section. Accordingly, a deduction or loss will be considered to be definitely related and therefore allocable to a class of gross income with respect to particular section 721(c) property whether or not there is any item of gross income in that class that is received or accrued during the taxable year and whether or not the amount of deduction or loss exceeds the amount of gross income in that class during the taxable year. If a deduction or loss is definitely related and therefore allocable to gross income attributable to more than one class of gross income of the section 721(c) partnership or if a deduction or loss is not definitely related to any class of gross income of the section 721(c) partnership, the section 721(c) partnership must apportion that deduction or loss among its classes of gross income using a reasonable method that reflects to a reasonably close extent the factual relationship between the deduction or loss and the classes of gross income. The section 721(c) partnership may allocate and apportion its interest expense and research and experimental expenditures under any reasonable method, including, but not limited to, the methods prescribed in §§ 1.861-9 and 1.861-9T (interest expense) and § 1.861-17 (research and experimental expenditures). For purposes of this paragraph (c)(3), the section 721(c) partnership must allocate and apportion its deductions and losses without regard to the partners' percentage interests in the partnership.

(4) *Exceptions to the consistent allocation method.*—(i) *Regulatory allocations.*—A regulatory allocation (as defined in § 1.721(c)-1(b)(10)) of book income, gain, deduction, or loss with respect to section 721(c) property that otherwise would fail to satisfy paragraph (c)(1) of this section is nevertheless deemed to satisfy paragraph (c)(1) of this section if the allocation is—

(A) An allocation of income or gain to the U.S. transferor (or a member of its consolidated group as defined in § 1.1502-1(h));

(B) An allocation of deduction or loss to a partner other than the U.S. transferor (or a member of its consolidated group); or

(C) Treated as a partial acceleration event pursuant to § 1.721(c)-5(d)(2).

(ii) *Allocation of creditable foreign tax expenditures.*—An allocation of a creditable foreign tax expenditure (as defined in § 1.704-1(b)(4)(viii)(*b*)) is not subject to the consistent allocation method.

(d) *Tiered partnership rules.*—This paragraph (d) provides the tiered partnership rules referred to in paragraph (b)(5) of this section.

(1) *Section 721(c) property is a partnership interest.*—If the section 721(c) property that is contributed to a section 721(c) partnership is an interest in a partnership (lower-tier partnership), then the lower-tier partnership, if it is a controlled partnership with respect to the U.S. transferor, and each partnership in which an interest is owned (directly or indirectly through one or more partnerships) by the lower-tier partnership and that is a controlled partnership with respect to the U.S. transferor, must satisfy the requirements of paragraphs (d)(1)(i), (ii), and (iii) of this section.

(i) The partnership must revalue all its property under § 1.704-1(b)(2)(iv)(*f*)(6) if the revaluation would result in a separate positive difference between book value and adjusted tax basis in at least one property that is not excluded property.

(ii) The partnership must apply the gain deferral method for each property (other than excluded property) for which there is a separate positive difference between book value and adjusted tax basis resulting from the revaluation described in paragraph (d)(1) of this section (*new positive reverse section 704(c) layer*). If the partnership has previously adopted a section 704(c) method other than the remedial allocation method for the property, the partnership satisfies the requirement of paragraph (b)(1)(i)(A) of this section by adopting the remedial allocation method for the new positive reverse section 704(c) layer.

(iii) The partnership must treat a partner that is a partnership in which the U.S. transferor is a direct or indirect partner as if it were the U.S. transferor with respect to the section 721(c) property solely for purposes of applying the consistent allocation method.

(2) *Section 721(c) property is indirectly contributed by a U.S. transferor under the partnership look-through rule.*—If the U.S. transferor is a direct or indirect partner in the upper-tier partnership described in § 1.721(c)-2(d)(1), and under § 1.721(c)-2(d)(1), the U.S. transferor is treated as contributing the section 721(c) property (including an interest in a partnership described in paragraph (d)(1) of this section) to a section 721(c) partnership, then the requirements of paragraphs (d)(2)(i), (ii), and (iii) of this section must be satisfied.

(i) The section 721(c) partnership must treat the upper-tier partnership as the U.S. transferor of the section 721(c) property solely for purposes of applying the consistent allocation method;

(ii) The upper-tier partnership, if it is a controlled partnership with respect to the U.S. transferor, must apply the gain deferral method to its interest in the section 721(c) partnership; and

(iii) If the U.S. transferor is an indirect partner in the upper-tier partnership through one or more partnerships, the principles of paragraphs (d)(2)(i) and (ii) of this section must be applied with respect to those partnerships that are controlled partnerships with respect to the U.S. transferor.

(e) *Applicability dates.*—(1) *In general.*—Except as provided in paragraphs (e)(2) and (3) of this section, this section applies to contributions occurring on or after August 6, 2015, and to contributions that occurred before August 6, 2015 resulting from an entity classification election made under § 301.7701-3 of this chapter that was effective on or before August 6, 2015 but was filed on or after August 6, 2015.

(2) *Certain provisions.*—Except as provided in paragraph (e)(3) of this section, paragraphs (b)(1)(ii), (c)(2) and (3), (c)(4)(i) and (ii), and (d)(1) and (2) of this section apply to contributions occurring on or after January 18, 2017, and to contributions that occurred before January 18, 2017 resulting from an entity classification election made under § 301.7701-3 of this chapter that was effective on or before January 18, 2017 but was filed on or after January 18, 2017. Except as provided in paragraph (e)(3) of this section, the second sentence of paragraph (c)(1) of this section applies to contributions occurring on or after January 17, 2020.

(3) *Election to apply the provisions described in paragraph (e)(2) of this section retroactively.*—Paragraphs (b)(1)(ii), (c)(2) and (3), (c)(4)(i) and (ii), and (d)(1) and (2) of this section may, by election, be applied to a contribution that occurred on or after August 6, 2015 but before January 18, 2017, and to a contribution that occurred before August 6, 2015 resulting from an entity classification election made under § 301.7701-3 of this chapter that was effective on or before August 6, 2015 but was filed on or after August 6, 2015. The election described in the preceding sentence must have been made by applying paragraph (b)(1)(ii), (c)(2) or (3), (c)(4)(i) or (ii), or (d)(1) or (2) of this section, as applicable, to the contribution on a timely filed original return (including extensions) or an amended return filed no later than July 18, 2017. In order to elect to apply paragraph (c)(2) or (3) of this section to a contribution described in this paragraph (e)(3), an election must also have been made to apply paragraph (c)(3) or (2) of this section, respectively, to the contribution. The second sentence of paragraph (c)(1) of this section, may, by election, be applied to a contribution that occurred on or after August 6, 2015 but before January 17, 2020, and to a contribution that occurred before August 6, 2015 resulting from an entity classification election made under § 301.7701-3 of this chapter that was effective on or before August 6, 2015 but was filed on or after August 6, 2015. The election described in the preceding sentence must be made by applying the second sentence of paragraph (c)(1) of this section to the contribution on a timely filed original return (including extensions) or an amended return filed no later than July 17, 2020.

(4) *Transitional rules.*—If a contribution is described in paragraph (e)(2) of this section and no election described in paragraph (e)(3) of this section is made to apply one or more of paragraphs (c)(2) and (3) and (c)(4)(i) and (ii) of this section, as applicable, to the contribution, then, for purposes of paragraph (c)(1) of this section, the section 721(c) partnership must attribute book income, gain, loss, and deduction to the section 721(c) property in a consistent manner under any reasonable method taking into account all the facts and circumstances. If a contribution is described in paragraph (e)(2) of this section and no election described in paragraph (e)(3) of this section is made to apply paragraph (d)(1) or (2) of this section, as applicable, to the contribution, then, this section must be applied in a manner consistent with the purpose of the section 721(c) regulations. Thus, for example, if a U.S. transferor is a direct or indirect partner in a partnership and that partnership contributes section 721(c) property to a lower-tier partnership, or, if a U.S. transferor contributes an interest in a partnership that owns section 721(c) property to a lower-tier partnership, then paragraph (b) of this section applies as though the U.S. transferor contributed its share of the section 721(c) property directly. [Reg. § 1.721(c)-3.]

□ [*T.D.* 9891, 1-17-2020.]

§ 1.721(c)-4. Acceleration events.—(a) *Scope.*—This section provides rules regarding acceleration events for purposes of applying the gain deferral method. Paragraph (b) of this section defines an acceleration event. Paragraph (c) of this section provides the consequences of an acceleration event. Paragraph (d) of this section provides the dates of applicability. For definitions that apply for purposes of this section, see § 1.721(c)-1(b).

(b) *Definition of an acceleration event.*—(1) *General rules.*—Except as provided in this paragraph (b) and § 1.721(c)-5 (acceleration event exceptions), an acceleration event with respect to section 721(c) property is any event that either would reduce the amount of remaining built-in gain that a U.S. transferor would recognize under the gain deferral method if the event had not occurred or could defer the recognition of the remaining built-in gain. An acceleration event includes a contribution of section 721(c) property to another partnership by a section 721(c) partnership and a contribution of an interest in a section 721(c) partnership to another partnership. This paragraph (b) applies on a property-by-property basis.

(2) *Failure to comply with a requirement of the gain deferral method.*—(i) *General rule.*—An acceleration event with respect to section 721(c) property occurs when any party fails to comply with a condition of the gain deferral method with respect to the section 721(c) property.

(ii) *Certain failures to comply with procedural and reporting requirements.*—Notwithstanding paragraph (b)(2)(i) of this section, an acceleration event will not occur solely as a result of a failure to comply with a requirement of § 1.721(c)-3(b)(3) that is not willful. See §§ 1.721(c)-6(f) and 1.6038B-2(h)(3).

(3) *Lower-tier partnership allocations.*—Notwithstanding paragraph (b)(1) of this section, an acceleration event will not occur because of a reduction in remaining built-in gain in an interest in a partnership that is section 721(c) property that occurs as a result of allocations of book items of deduction and loss, or tax items of income and gain.

(4) *Deemed acceleration event.*—A U.S. transferor may treat an acceleration event as having occurred with respect to section 721(c) property by both recognizing gain in an amount equal to the remaining built-in gain that would have been allocated to the U.S. transferor if the section 721(c) partnership had sold the section 721(c) property immediately before the deemed acceleration event for fair market value and satisfying the reporting required by § 1.721(c)-6(b)(3)(i)(D). In this case, see paragraph (c) of this section regarding basis adjustments.

(c) *Consequences of an acceleration event.*—Paragraphs (c)(1) and (2) of this section provide the consequences of an acceleration event with respect to section 721(c) property, a partial acceleration event with respect to section 721(c) property to the extent provided in § 1.721(c)-5(d)(1), and a transfer described in section 367 of section 721(c) property to the extent provided in § 1.721(c)-5(e).

(1) *U.S. transferor.*—The U.S. transferor must recognize gain in an amount equal to the remaining built-in gain that would have been allocated to the U.S. transferor if the section 721(c) partnership had sold the section 721(c) property immediately before the acceleration event for fair market value. The U.S. transferor will increase its basis in its partnership interest by the amount of gain recognized. If the U.S. transferor is an indirect partner in the section 721(c) partnership through one or more tiered partnerships, appropriate basis adjustments will be made to the interests in the tiered partnerships.

(2) *Section 721(c) partnership.*—The section 721(c) partnership will increase its basis in the section 721(c) property by the amount of built-in gain recognized by the U.S. transferor under paragraph (c)(1) of this section. Any tax consequences of the acceleration event will be determined taking into account the increase in the partnership's adjusted tax basis in the section 721(c) property. If the section 721(c) property remains in the partnership after the acceleration event, the increase in basis of the section 721(c) property may be recovered using any applicable recovery period and depreciation (or other cost recovery) method (including first-year conventions) available to the partnership for newly purchased property of the same type placed in service on the date of the acceleration event. The section 721(c) property will no longer be subject to the gain deferral method.

(d) *Applicability dates.*—This section applies to contributions occurring on or after August 6, 2015, and to contributions that occurred before August 6, 2015 resulting from an entity classification election made under § 301.7701-3 of this chapter that was effective on or before August 6, 2015 but was filed on or after August 6, 2015. [Reg. § 1.721(c)-4.]

☐ [*T.D.* 9891, 1-17-2020.]

§ 1.721(c)-5. Acceleration event exceptions.—(a) *Scope.*—This section identifies exceptions to the acceleration events, which, like the rules regarding acceleration events provided in § 1.721(c)-4(b), apply on a property-by-property basis. Paragraph (b) of this section identifies the events that terminate the requirement to apply the gain deferral method. Paragraph (c) of this section identifies the successor events that allow for the continued application of the gain deferral method. Paragraph (d) of this section identifies the partial acceleration events. Paragraph (e) of this section provides special rules for transfers of section 721(c) property to a foreign corporation described in section 367. Paragraph (f) of this section allows for the continued application of the gain deferral method if there is a fully taxable disposition of a portion of an interest in a partnership. Paragraph (g) of this section provides the dates of applicability. For definitions that apply for purposes of this section, see § 1.721(c)-1(b).

(b) *Termination events.*—(1) *In general.*—Notwithstanding § 1.721(c)-4(b)(1), a termination event with respect to section 721(c) property will not constitute an acceleration event. In these cases, the section 721(c) property will no longer be subject to the gain deferral method.

(2) *Transfers of section 721(c) property (other than a partnership interest) to a domestic corporation described in section 351.*—A termination event occurs if a section 721(c) partnership transfers section 721(c) property (other than an interest in a partnership) to a domestic corporation in a transaction to which section 351 applies.

(3) *Certain incorporations of a section 721(c) partnership.*—A termination event occurs upon an incorporation of a section 721(c) partnership into a domestic corporation by any method of incorporation (other than a method involving an actual distribution of partnership property to the partners, followed by a contribution of that property to a corporation), provided that the section 721(c) partnership is liquidated as part of the incorporation transaction.

(4) *Certain distributions of section 721(c) property.*—A termination event occurs if a section 721(c) partnership distributes section 721(c) property either to the U.S. transferor or, if the U.S. transferor is a member of a consolidated group (as defined in § 1.1502-1(h)) at the time of the distribution and the distribution occurs outside the seven-year period described in section 704(c)(1)(B), to a member of the consolidated group.

(5) *Partnership ceases to have a partner that is a related foreign person.*—A termination event occurs when a section 721(c) partnership ceases to have any direct or indirect partners that are related foreign persons with respect to the U.S. transferor, provided there is no plan for a related foreign person to subsequently become a direct or indirect partner in the partnership (or a successor). This paragraph (b)(5) does not apply to a distribution of section 721(c) property in redemption of a related foreign person's interest in a section 721(c) partnership.

(6) *Fully taxable dispositions of section 721(c) property.*—A termination event occurs if a section 721(c) partnership disposes of section 721(c) property in a transaction in which all gain or loss, if any, is recognized.

(7) *Fully taxable dispositions of an entire interest in a section 721(c) partnership.*—A termination event occurs if a U.S. transferor or a partnership in which a U.S. transferor is a direct or indirect partner disposes of its entire interest in a section 721(c) partnership that owns the section 721(c) property in a transaction in which all gain or loss, if any, is recognized. This paragraph (b)(7) does not apply if a U.S. transferor is a member of a consolidated group (as defined in § 1.1502-1(h)) and the interest in the section 721(c) partnership is transferred in an intercompany transaction (as defined in § 1.1502-13(b)(1)); see paragraph (c)(3) of this section for a successor event rule applicable to these intercompany transactions.

(c) *Successor events.*—(1) *In general.*—Notwithstanding § 1.721(c)-4(b)(1), a successor event with respect to section 721(c) property will not constitute an acceleration event. If a portion of an interest in a partnership is transferred in a successor event described in this paragraph (c), the principles of § 1.704-3(a)(7) apply to determine the remaining built-in gain in section 721(c) property that is attributable to the portion of the interest that is transferred and the portion of the interest that is retained.

(2) *Transfers of an interest in a section 721(c) partnership by a U.S. transferor or upper-tier partnership to a domestic corporation in certain nonrecognition transactions.*—A successor event occurs if a U.S. transferor or a partnership in which a U.S. transferor is a direct or indirect partner transfers (directly or indirectly through one or more partnerships) an interest in a section 721(c) partnership to a domestic corporation in a transaction to which section 351 or 381 applies, and the gain deferral method is continued by treating the transferee domestic corporation as the U.S. transferor for purposes of the section 721(c) regulations. If the transfer described in this paragraph (c)(2) also results in a termination under section 708(b)(1)(B) of the section 721(c) partnership, see paragraph (c)(4) of this section.

(3) *Transfers of an interest in a section 721(c) partnership in an intercompany transaction.*—A successor event occurs if a U.S. transferor that is a member of a consolidated group (as defined in § 1.1502-1(h)) transfers (directly or indirectly through one or more partnerships) an interest in a section 721(c) partnership in an intercompany transaction (as defined in § 1.1502-13(b)(1)), and the gain deferral method is continued by treating the transferee member as the U.S. transferor for purposes of the section 721(c) regulations. If the transfer described in this paragraph (c)(3) also results in a termination under section 708(b)(1)(B) of the section 721(c) partnership, see paragraph (c)(4) of this section.

(4) *Termination under section 708(b)(1)(B) of a section 721(c) partnership.*—A successor event occurs if there is a termination under section 708(b)(1)(B) of a section 721(c) partnership, and the gain deferral method is continued by treating the new partnership as the section 721(c) partnership for purposes of the section 721(c) regulations.

(5) *Transactions involving tiered partnerships.*—(i) *Contributions of section 721(c) property to a lower-tier partnership.*—A successor event occurs if a section 721(c) partnership contributes the section 721(c)

property to a partnership that is a controlled partnership with respect to the U.S. transferor (lower-tier section 721(c) partnership) and the requirements of paragraphs (c)(5)(i)(A) through (C) of this section are satisfied.

(A) The lower-tier section 721(c) partnership is a section 721(c) partnership or is treated as a section 721(c) partnership.

(B) The gain deferral method is applied with respect to the section 721(c) property in the hands of the lower-tier section 721(c) partnership.

(C) The gain deferral method is applied with respect to the section 721(c) partnership's interest in the lower-tier section 721(c) partnership. See § 1.721(c)-3(b)(5) and (d)(2).

(ii) *Contributions of an interest in a section 721(c) partnership to an upper-tier partnership.*—A successor event occurs if a U.S. transferor or a partnership in which a U.S. transferor is a direct or indirect partner contributes (directly or indirectly through one or more partnerships) an interest in a section 721(c) partnership to a partnership that is a controlled partnership with respect to the U.S. transferor (upper-tier section 721(c) partnership) and the requirements of paragraphs (c)(5)(ii)(A) through (D) of this section are satisfied.

(A) The gain deferral method is continued with respect to the section 721(c) property in the hands of the section 721(c) partnership.

(B) The upper-tier section 721(c) partnership is, or is treated as, a section 721(c) partnership.

(C) If the upper-tier section 721(c) partnership directly owns its interest in the section 721(c) partnership, the gain deferral method is applied with respect to the upper-tier section 721(c) partnership's interest in the section 721(c) partnership. See § 1.721(c)-3(b)(5) and (d)(1).

(D) If the upper-tier section 721(c) partnership indirectly owns its interest in the section 721(c) partnership through one or more partnerships, the principles of paragraphs (c)(5)(ii)(B) and (C) of this section are applied with respect to each partnership through which the upper-tier section 721(c) partnership indirectly owns an interest in the section 721(c) partnership.

(d) *Partial acceleration events.*—(1) *In general.*—Notwithstanding § 1.721(c)-4, a partial acceleration event with respect to section 721(c) property does not constitute an acceleration event. In these cases, except as provided in paragraph (d)(3) of this section, the rules in § 1.721(c)-4(c) (concerning the consequences of an acceleration event) for making basis adjustments apply to the extent that the U.S. transferor is required to recognize gain under paragraph (d)(2) or (3) of this section. Furthermore, if there is remaining built-in gain with respect to the section 721(c) property after the application of this paragraph (d), the application of the gain deferral method with respect to the section 721(c) property must be continued in the same manner.

(2) *Regulatory allocations.*—If a regulatory allocation is described in § 1.721(c)-3(c)(4)(i) but not in § 1.721(c)-3(c)(4)(i)(A) or (B), a partial acceleration event occurs with respect to section 721(c) property if the U.S. transferor recognizes an amount of gain (but not in excess of remaining built-in gain) equal to the amount of the allocation that, under the consistent allocation method, had the regulatory allocation not occurred, would have been allocated to the U.S. transferor in the case of income or gain, or would not have been allocated to the U.S. transferor in the case of deduction or loss.

(3) *Certain distributions of other partnership property to a partner that result in an adjustment under section 734.*—A partial acceleration event occurs with respect to section 721(c) property if there is a distribution of other property by the section 721(c) partnership that results in a positive basis adjustment to the section 721(c) property under section 734. In these cases, the U.S. transferor must recognize an amount of gain (but not in excess of the remaining built-in gain) equal to the positive basis adjustment to the section 721(c) property under section 734, reduced (but not below zero) by the amount of gain recognized by the U.S. transferor (or a member of its consolidated group (as defined in § 1.1502-1(h))) under section 731(a). In these cases, the partnership will not increase its basis under § 1.721(c)-4(c)(2) by the amount of gain recognized by the U.S. transferor.

(e) *Transfers described in section 367 of section 721(c) property to a foreign corporation.*—If a section 721(c) partnership transfers section 721(c) property, or a U.S. transferor or a partnership in which a U.S. transferor is a direct or indirect partner transfers (directly or indirectly through one or more partnerships) all or a portion of an interest in a section 721(c) partnership that owns section 721(c) property, to a foreign corporation in a transaction described in section 367, then the property will no longer be subject to the gain deferral method. To the extent any U.S. transferor is treated as transferring the section 721(c) property to the foreign corporation for purposes of section 367, the tax consequences will be determined under section 367. In this regard, see §§ 1.367(a)-1T(c)(3)(i) and (ii), 1.367(d)-1T(d)(1), and 1.367(e)-2(b)(1)(iii) (providing for the aggregate treatment of partnerships). However, for the remaining portion of the property (if any), the U.S. transferor must recognize an amount of gain equal to the remaining built-in gain that would have been allocated to the U.S. transferor if the section 721(c) partnership had sold that portion of the section 721(c) property immediately before the transfer for fair market value. The stock in the transferee foreign corporation received will not be subject to the gain deferral method. The rules in § 1.721(c)-4(c) (concerning the consequences of an acceleration event) for making basis adjustments will apply to the extent that the U.S. transferor recognizes gain under this paragraph (e).

(f) *Fully taxable dispositions of a portion of an interest in a partnership.*—If a U.S. transferor or a partnership in which a U.S. transferor is a direct or indirect partner disposes of (directly or indirectly through one or more partnerships) a portion of an interest in a section 721(c) partnership in a transaction in which all gain or loss, if any, is recognized, an acceleration event will not occur with respect to the portion of the interest transferred. The gain deferral method will continue to apply with respect to the section 721(c) property of the section 721(c) partnership. The principles of § 1.704-3(a)(7) will apply to determine the remaining built-in gain in section 721(c) property that is attributable to the portion of the interest in a section 721(c) partnership that is retained. This paragraph (f) will not apply to an intercompany transaction (as defined in § 1.1502-13(b)(1)).

(g) *Applicability dates.*—(1) *In general.*—Except as provided in paragraph (g)(2) of this section, this section applies to contributions occurring on or after January 18, 2017, and to contributions that occurred before January 18, 2017 resulting from an entity classification election made under § 301.7701-3 of this chapter that was effective on or before January 18, 2017 but was filed on or after January 18, 2017.

(2) *Election to apply this section retroactively.*—This section may, by election, be applied to a contribution that occurred on or after August 6, 2015 but before January 18, 2017, and to a contribution that occurred before August 6, 2015 resulting from an entity classification election made under § 301.7701-3 of this chapter that was effective on or before August 6, 2015 but was filed on or after August 6, 2015. The election must have been made by applying this section to the contribution on a timely filed original return (including extensions) or an amended return filed no later than July 18, 2017. [Reg. § 1.721(c)-5.]

☐ [*T.D. 9891*, 1-17-2020.]

§ 1.721(c)-6. Procedural and reporting requirements.—(a) *Scope.*—This section provides procedural and reporting requirements that must be satisfied under § 1.721(c)-3(b)(3) of the gain deferral method. Paragraph (b) of this section describes the procedural and reporting requirements of a U.S. transferor. Paragraph (c) of this section describes information required to be reported with respect to related foreign persons and partnerships. Paragraph (d) of this section describes the procedural and reporting requirements of a section 721(c) partnership with a section 6031 filing obligation. Paragraph (e) of this section provides the proper signatory for the information provided under this section. Paragraph (f) of this section provides relief for certain failures to comply that are not willful. Paragraph (g) of this section provides the dates of applicability. For definitions that apply for purposes of this section, see § 1.721(c)-1(b).

(b) *Procedural and reporting requirements of a U.S. transferor.*—(1) *In general.*—This paragraph (b) describes the procedural and reporting requirements that a U.S. transferor (as defined § 1.721(c)-1(b)(18)(i)) must satisfy in applying the gain deferral method. The information required under this paragraph (b) must be included with the U.S. transferor's timely filed return on (or attached to) the appropriate forms or schedules (or their successors) and must be submitted in the form and manner and to the extent prescribed by the forms and schedules (and their accompanying instructions).

(2) *Reporting of a gain deferral contribution.*—A U.S. transferor must report the following information with respect to a gain deferral contribution:

(i) On Schedule A-1, Certain Foreign Partners, Schedule A-2, Foreign Partners of Section 721(c) Partnership, Schedule G, Statement of Application of the Gain Deferral Method Under Section 721(c), and Schedule H, Acceleration Events and Exceptions Reporting Relating to Gain Deferral Method Under Section 721(c) (for each such Schedule, with respect to Form 8865, Return of U.S. Persons With Respect to Certain Foreign Partnerships), as applicable, the following information with respect to the section 721(c) property—

(A) A description of the property and recovery period (or periods) for the property;

(B) Whether the property is an intangible described in section 197(f)(9);

(C) A calculation of the built-in gain, the basis, and fair market value on the date of the contribution, including the amount of gain recognized by the U.S. transferor, if any, on the gain deferral contribution;

(D) The name, U.S. taxpayer identification number (if any), address, and country of organization (if any) of each direct or indirect partner in the section 721(c) partnership that is a related person with respect to the U.S. transferor, and a description of each partner's interest in capital and profits immediately after the gain deferral contribution; and

(E) When the section 721(c) property is a partnership interest, the information described in paragraphs (b)(2)(i)(A) through (D) of this section with respect to each property of a lower-tier partnership to which the gain deferral method is applied under § 1.721(c)-3(d)(1);

(ii) On Form 8838-P, Consent To Extend the Time To Assess Tax Pursuant to the Gain Deferral Method (Section 721(c)), an extension of the period of limitations on the assessment of tax as described in paragraph (b)(5) of this section;

(iii) A copy of the waiver of treaty benefits described in paragraph (c)(1) of this section (if any);

(iv) On Schedule A-1, Schedule A-2, and Schedule G (for each such Schedule, with respect to Form 8865), as applicable, information relating to the section 721(c) partnership described in paragraph (c)(2) of this section (if any);

(v) On, Schedule O, Transfer of Property to a Foreign Partnership (Form 8865) with respect to any foreign partnership, (or partnership treated as foreign under paragraph (b)(4) of this section), the information required under § 1.6038B-2(c)(1) through (7); and

(vi) The information required under paragraph (b)(3) of this section.

(3) *Annual reporting relating to gain deferral method.*—A U.S. transferor must annually report information for each gain deferral contribution. The information reported must be with respect to the partnership taxable year that ends with, or within, the taxable year of the U.S. transferor, beginning with the partnership's taxable year that includes the date of the gain deferral contribution and ending with the last taxable year in which the gain deferral method is applied to the section 721(c) property. The information reported must include:

(i) For each deferral contribution, the U.S. transferor must report the following information on Schedule G and Schedule H (for each Schedule, with respect to Form 8865), as applicable:

(A) The amount of book income, gain, deduction, and loss and tax items allocated to the U.S. transferor with respect to the section 721(c) property, including a description of any regulatory allocations;

(B) The proportion (expressed as a percentage) in which the book income, gain, deduction, and loss with respect to the section 721(c) property was allocated among the U.S. transferor and related persons that are partners in the section 721(c) partnership under the consistent allocation method;

(C) The amount of remaining built-in gain at the beginning of the taxable year, the remedial income allocated to the U.S. transferor under the remedial allocation method, the amount of built-in gain taken into account by reason of an acceleration event or partial acceleration event (if any), the partnership's adjustment to its tax basis in the section 721(c) property, and the remaining built-in gain at the end of the taxable year;

(D) A declaration stating whether an acceleration event or partial acceleration event occurred during the taxable year, the date of the event, and a description of the event (including a citation to the relevant paragraph of § 1.721(c)-5(d) in the case of a partial acceleration event, and whether the acceleration event is described in § 1.721(c)-4(b)(4));

(E) A description of a termination event or any successor event that occurred during the taxable year with a citation to the relevant paragraph of § 1.721(c)-5(b) or (c), the date of the event, and, in the case of a successor event, the name, address, and U.S. taxpayer identification number (if any) of any successor partnership, lower-tier partnership, upper-tier partnership, or U.S. corporation (as applicable);

(F) A description of all transfers of section 721(c) property to a foreign corporation described in § 1.721(c)-5(e) that occurred during the taxable year, and for each transfer, the date of the transfer, the section 721(c) property transferred, and the name, address, and U.S. taxpayer identification number (if any) of the foreign transferee corporation; and

(G) With respect to section 721(c) property for which a waiver of treaty benefits was filed under paragraph (b)(2)(iii) of this section, a declaration that, after exercising reasonable diligence, to the best of the U.S. transferor's knowledge and belief, all income from the section 721(c) property allocated to the partners during the taxable year remained subject to taxation as income effectively connected with the conduct of a trade or business within the United States (under either section 871 or 882) for all direct or indirect partners that are related foreign persons with respect to the U.S. transferor (regardless of whether any such partner was a partner at the time of the gain deferral contribution), and, that neither the partnership nor any such partner has made any claim under any income tax convention to an exemption from U.S. income tax or a reduced rate of U.S. income taxation on income derived from the use of the section 721(c) property;

(ii) On Form 8838-P, an extension of the period of limitations on the assessment of tax, in the case of a gain deferral contribution, as described in paragraph (b)(5)(ii) of this section, and, in the case of certain contributions on which gain is recognized, as described in paragraph (b)(5)(iii) of this section;

(iii) If the section 721(c) partnership is a partnership that does not have a filing obligation under section 6031, the information described in § 1.6038-3(g) (contents of information returns required of certain United States persons with respect to controlled foreign partnerships), if not already reported elsewhere, without regard to whether the section 721(c) partnership is a controlled foreign partnership within the meaning of section 6038. If the U.S. transferor is not a controlling fifty-percent partner (as defined in § 1.6038-3(a)), the U.S. transferor complies with the requirement of this paragraph (b)(3)(iii) by providing the information described in § 1.6038-3(g)(1);

(iv) On Schedule O (Form 8865), a description of all section 721(c) property contributed by the U.S. transferor to the section 721(c) partnership (including pursuant to a contribution described in § 1.721(c)-2(d)(1)) during the taxable year to which the gain deferral method is not applied; and

(v) The information required in paragraphs (c)(2) and (3) of this section for related foreign persons that are direct or indirect partners in the section 721(c) partnership and the section 721(c) partnership itself (if any).

(4) *Domestic partnerships treated as foreign.*—Solely for purposes of this section, a U.S. transferor must treat a domestic section 721(c) partnership as a foreign partnership if the partnership was formed on or after January 18, 2017. If the section 721(c) partnership has an information return filing obligation under section 6031, that requirement is not affected by the requirement of this paragraph (b)(4) that the U.S. transferor treat the partnership as a foreign partnership.

(5) *Extension of period of limitations on assessment of tax.*—In order to comply with the gain deferral method, a U.S. transferor must extend the period of limitations on the assessment of tax using Form 8838-P:

(i) With respect to the gain realized but not recognized on a gain deferral contribution, through the date that is 96 months after the close of the U.S. transferor's taxable year that includes the date of the gain deferral contribution;

(ii) With respect to all book and tax items with respect to the section 721(c) property allocated to the U.S. transferor in the partnership's taxable year that includes the date of the gain deferral contribution and the subsequent two years, through the date that is 72 months after the close of such taxable year with which, or within which, the partnership's taxable year ends; and

(iii) With respect to the gain recognized on a contribution of section 721(c) property to a section 721(c) partnership for which the gain deferral method is not applied, if the contribution occurs within five partnership taxable years following a partnership taxable year that includes the date of a gain deferral contribution, through the date that is 60 months after the close of the U.S. transferor's taxable year that includes the date of the contribution on which gain is recognized.

(c) *Information with respect to section 721(c) partnerships and related foreign persons.*—(1) *Effectively connected income.*—If the gain deferral method is applied with respect to a contribution of section 721(c) property that satisfies the condition in § 1.721(c)-3(b)(1)(ii), the U.S. transferor must obtain a statement from the section 721(c) partnership and from each related foreign person that is a direct or indirect partner in the section 721(c) partnership, titled "Statement of Waiver of Treaty Benefits under § 1.721(c)-6," pursuant to which the partner and the partnership waive any claim under any income tax convention (whether or not currently in force at the time of the contribution) to an exemption from U.S. income tax or a reduced rate of U.S. income taxation on income derived from the use of the section 721(c) property for the period during which the section 721(c) property is subject to the gain deferral method.

(2) *Partnerships in tiered-partnership structures applying the gain deferral method.*—If the gain deferral method is applied as a result of a transaction described in § 1.721(c)-3(d), the U.S. transferor must supply all the information that a section 721(c) partnership would be required to report under paragraph (b) of this section if the section 721(c) partnership were a U.S. transferor.

(3) *Schedules K-1 for related foreign partners.*—If a section 721(c) partnership does not have a filing obligation under section 6031, the U.S. transferor must obtain a Schedule K-1 (Form 8865), Partner's Share of Income, Deduction, Credits, etc., for all related foreign persons that are direct or indirect partners in the section 721(c) partnership.

(d) *Reporting and procedural requirements of a section 721(c) partnership with a section 6031 filing obligation.*—(1) *Waiver of treaty benefits.*—A section 721(c) partnership with a return filing obligation under section 6031 must include its waiver of treaty benefits described in paragraph (c)(1) of this section with its tax return for the taxable year that includes the date of the gain deferral contribution.

(2) *Information on Schedule K-1.*—A section 721(c) partnership with a return filing obligation under section 6031 must provide the relevant information necessary for the U.S. transferor to comply with the requirements in paragraphs (b)(2) and (3) of this section (using the Forms and Schedules specified in paragraphs (b)(2) and (3) of this section) with the U.S. transferor's Schedule K-1 (Form 1065), Partner's Share of Income, Deductions, Credits, etc. The partnership must also attach a Schedule K-1 (Form 1065) to its Form 1065 for each direct or indirect partner that is a related foreign person with respect to the U.S. transferor.

(e) *Signatory.*—Any statements required in this section must be signed under penalties of perjury by an agent of the U.S. transferor, the related foreign person that is a direct or indirect partner in the section 721(c) partnership, or the section 721(c) partnership, as applicable, that is authorized to sign under a general or specific power of attorney, or by an appropriate party. For the U.S. transferor, an appropriate party is a person described in § 1.367(a)-8(e)(1). For a partnership with a section 6031 filing obligation, an appropriate party is any party authorized to sign Form 1065.

(f) *Relief for certain failures to file or failures to comply that are not willful.*—(1) *In general.*—This paragraph (f)(1) provides relief from the failure to comply with the procedural and reporting requirements of the gain deferral method prescribed by § 1.721(c)-3(b)(3) and provided in paragraph (b) of this section if there is a failure to file or to include information required by this section (failure to comply). A failure to comply will be deemed not to have occurred for purposes of § 1.721(c)-3(b)(3) if the U.S. transferor demonstrates that the failure was not willful using the procedure provided in this paragraph (f). For purposes of this paragraph (f), willful is to be interpreted consistent with the meaning of that term in the context of other civil penalties, which would include a failure due to gross negligence, reckless disregard, or willful neglect. Whether a failure to comply was willful will be determined by the Director of Field Operations, Cross Border Activities Practice Area of Large Business & International (or any successor to the roles and responsibilities of such position, as appropriate) (Director) based on all the facts and circumstances. The U.S. transferor must submit a request for relief and an explanation as provided in paragraph (f)(2) of this section. A U.S. transferor whose failure to comply is determined not to be willful under this paragraph (f) will be subject to a penalty under section 6038B if it fails to satisfy the applicable reporting requirements under that section and does not demonstrate that the failure was due to reasonable cause and not willful neglect. See § 1.6038B-2(h). The determination of whether the failure to comply was willful under this section has no effect on any request for relief made under § 1.6038B-2(h).

(2) *Procedures for establishing that a failure to comply was not willful.*—(i) *Time and manner of submission.*—A U.S. transferor's statement that a failure to comply was not willful will be considered only if, promptly after the U.S. transferor becomes aware of the failure, an amended return is filed for the taxable year to which the failure relates that includes the information that should have been included with the original return for such taxable year or that otherwise complies with the rules of this section as well as a written statement explaining the reasons for the failure to comply. The U.S. transferor also must file, with the amended return, a Schedule O (Form 8865) and Form 8838-P (as described in paragraph (b)(5) of this section), completed and executed as prescribed in forms and instructions, consenting to extend the period of limitations on assessment of tax with respect to the gain realized but not recognized on the gain deferral contribution to the later of the date that is 96 months after the close of the U.S. transferor's taxable year that includes the date of the gain deferral contribution (*date one*), or the date that is 36 months after the date on which the required information is provided to the Director (*date two*). However, the U.S. transferor is not required to file a Schedule O (Form 8865), with the amended return if both date one is later than date two and a consent to extend the period of limitations on assessment of tax with respect to the gain realized but not recognized on the gain deferral contribution for the U.S. transferor's taxable year that includes the date of the contribution was previously submitted with a Schedule O (Form 8865). The amended return and either a Schedule O (Form 8865) or a copy of the previously filed Schedule O (Form 8865), as the case may be, must be filed with the Internal Revenue Service at the location where the U.S. transferor filed its original return. The U.S. transferor may submit a request for relief from the penalty under section 6038B as part of the same submission. See § 1.6038B-2(h)(3).

(ii) *Notice requirement.*—In addition to the requirements of paragraph (f)(2)(i) of this section, the U.S. transferor must comply with the notice requirements of this paragraph (f)(2)(ii). If any taxable year of the U.S. transferor is under examination when the amended return is filed, a copy of the amended return must be delivered to the Internal Revenue Service personnel conducting the examination. If no taxable year of the U.S. transferor is under examination when the amended return is filed, a copy of the amended return must be delivered to the Director.

(g) *Applicability dates.*—(1) *In general.*—Except as provided in paragraphs (g)(2) and (3) of this section, this section applies with respect to contributions occurring on or after January 18, 2017, and with respect to contributions that occurred before January 18, 2017 resulting from an entity classification election made under § 301.7701-3 of this chapter that was effective on or before January 18, 2017 but was filed on or after January 18, 2017.

(2) *Reporting relating to effectively connected income.*—Paragraphs (b)(2)(iii), (b)(3)(i)(G), and (d)(1) of this section apply to a contribution occurring on or after August 6, 2015, and to a contribution that occurred before August 6, 2015 resulting from an entity classification election made under § 301.7701-3 of this chapter that was effective on or before August 6, 2015 but was filed on or after August 6, 2015, and, in either case, provided § 1.721(c)-3(b)(1)(ii) applies to the contribution. To the extent that a previously filed return did not comply with paragraph (b)(2)(iii), (b)(3)(i)(G), or (d)(1) of this section, an amended return complying with such paragraphs must have been filed no later than July 18, 2017.

(3) *Transition rules.*—(i) *Reporting under sections 6038, 6038B, and 6046A.*—For transfers occurring on or after August 6, 2015, and for transfers that occurred before August 6, 2015 resulting from an entity classification election made under § 301.7701-3 of this chapter that was effective on or before August 6, 2015 but was filed on or after August 6, 2015, a U.S. transferor (or a domestic partnership in which a U.S. transferor is a direct or indirect partner) must fulfill any reporting requirements imposed under sections 6038, 6038B, and 6046A with respect to the contribution of the section 721(c) property to the section 721(c) partnership.

(ii) *Reporting using statements instead of prescribed forms and schedules.*—For tax returns filed before July 17, 2020, reporting that met the requirements of § 1.721(c)-6T (see 26 CFR part 1, revised as of April 1, 2019) as in effect before January 1, 2020, will be deemed to satisfy the corresponding requirements of this section. [Reg. § 1.721(c)-6.]

□ [*T.D.* 9891, 1-17-2020 (*corrected* 2-14-2020).]

§1.721(c)-7. Examples.—(a) *Presumed facts.*—For purposes of the examples in paragraph (b) of this section, assume that there are no other transactions that are related to the transactions described in the examples and that all partnership allocations have substantial economic effect under section 704(b). For definitions that apply for purposes of this section, see §1.721(c)-1(b). Except where otherwise indicated, the following facts are presumed—

(1) USP and USX are domestic corporations that each use a calendar taxable year. USX is not a related person with respect to USP.

(2) CFC1, CFC2, FX, and FY are foreign corporations.

(3) USP wholly owns CFC1 and CFC2. Neither FX nor FY is a related person with respect to USP or with respect to each other.

(4) PRS1, PRS2, and PRS3 are foreign entities classified as partnerships for U.S. tax purposes. A partnership interest in PRS1, PRS2, and PRS3 is not described in section 475(c)(2).

(5) A taxable year is referred to, for example, as year 1.

(6) A partner in a partnership has the same percentage interest in income, gain, loss, deduction, and capital of the partnership.

(7) No property is described in section 197(f)(9) in the hands of a contributing partner.

(8) No partnership is a controlled partnership solely under the facts and circumstances test in §1.721(c)-1(b)(4).

(b) *Examples.*—The application of the rules stated in §§1.721(c)-1 through 1.721(c)-6 may be illustrated by the following examples:

(1) *Example 1: Determining if a partnership is a section 721(c) partnership*—(i) *Facts.* In year 1, USP and CFC1 form PRS1 as equal partners. CFC1 contributes cash of $1.5 million to PRS1, and USP contributes three properties to PRS1: a patent with a book value of $1.2 million and an adjusted tax basis of zero, a security (within the meaning of section 475(c)(2)) with a book value of $100,000 and an adjusted tax basis of $20,000, and a machine with a book value of $200,000 and an adjusted tax basis of $600,000.

(ii) *Results.* (A) Under §1.721(c)-1(b)(18)(i), USP is a U.S. transferor because USP is a U.S. person and not a domestic partnership. Under §1.721(c)-1(b)(2), the patent has built-in gain of $1.2 million. The patent is not excluded property under §1.721(c)-1(b)(6). Therefore, under §1.721(c)-1(b)(15)(i), the patent is section 721(c) property because it is property, other than excluded property, with built-in gain that is contributed by a U.S. transferor, USP.

(B) Under §1.721(c)-1(b)(2), the security has built-in gain of $80,000. Under §1.721(c)-1(b)(6)(ii), the security is excluded property because it is described in section 475(c)(2). Therefore, the security is not section 721(c) property.

(C) The tax basis of the machine exceeds its book value. Under §1.721(c)-1(b)(6)(iii), the machine is excluded property and therefore is not section 721(c) property.

(D) Under §1.721(c)-1(b)(12), CFC1 is a related person with respect to USP, and under §1.721(c)-1(b)(11), CFC1 is a related foreign person. Because USP and CFC1 collectively own at least 80 percent of the interests in the capital, profits, deductions, or losses of PRS1, under §1.721(c)-1(b)(14)(i), PRS1 is a section 721(c) partnership upon the contribution by USP of the patent.

(E) The de minimis exception described in §1.721(c)-2(c) does not apply to the contribution because during PRS1's year 1 the sum of the built-in gain with respect to all section 721(c) property contributed in year 1 to PRS1 is $1.2 million, which exceeds the de minimis threshold of $1 million. As a result, under §1.721(c)-2(b), section 721(a) does not apply to USP's contribution of the patent to PRS1, unless the requirements of the gain deferral method are satisfied.

(2) *Example 2: Determining if partnership interest is section 721(c) property*—(i) *Facts.* In year 1, USP and FX form PRS2. USP contributes a security (within the meaning of section 475(c)(2)) with a book value of $100,000 and an adjusted tax basis of $20,000 and a building located in country X with a book value of $30,000 and an adjusted tax basis of $8,000 in exchange for a 40-percent interest. FX contributes a machine with a book value of $195,000 and an adjusted tax basis of $250,000 in exchange for a 60-percent interest.

(ii) *Results.* PRS2 is not a section 721(c) partnership because FX is not a related person with respect to USP. USP's contributions to PRS2 are not subject to §1.721(c)-2(b).

(iii) *Alternative facts and results.* (A) The facts are the same as in paragraph (b)(2)(i) of this section (the facts in *Example* 2). In addition, USP and CFC1 form PRS1 as equal partners. CFC1 contributes cash of $130,000 to PRS1, and USP contributes its 40-percent interest in PRS2.

(B) PRS2's property consists of a security and a machine that are excluded property, and a building with built-in gain in excess of $20,000. Under §1.721(c)-1(b)(6)(iv), because more than 90 percent of the value of the property of PRS2 consists of excluded property described in §1.721(c)-1(b)(6)(i) through (iii) (the security and the machine), any interest in PRS2 is excluded property. Therefore, the 40-percent interest in PRS2 contributed by USP to PRS1 is not section 721(c) property. Accordingly, USP's contribution of its interest in PRS2 to PRS1 is not subject to §1.721(c)-2(b).

(3) *Example 3: Assets-over tiered partnerships*—(i) *Facts.* In year 1, USP and CFC1 form PRS1 as equal partners. USP contributes a patent with a book value of $300 million and an adjusted tax basis of $30 million (USP contribution). CFC1 contributes cash of $300 million. Immediately thereafter, PRS1 contributes the patent to PRS2 in exchange for a two-thirds interest (PRS1 contribution), and CFC2 contributes cash of $150 million in exchange for a one-third interest. The patent has a remaining recovery period of 5 years out of a total of 15 years. With respect to all contributions described in §1.721(c)-2(b), the de minimis exception does not apply, and the gain deferral method is applied. Thus, the partnership agreements of PRS1 and PRS2 provide that the partnership will make allocations under section 704(c) using the remedial allocation method under §1.704-3(d).

(ii) *Results: USP contribution.* PRS1 is a section 721(c) partnership as a result of the USP contribution.

(iii) *Results: PRS1 contribution.* (A) For purposes of determining whether PRS2 is a section 721(c) partnership as a result of the PRS1 contribution, under §1.721(c)-2(d)(1), USP is treated as contributing to PRS2 its share of the patent that PRS1 actually contributes to PRS2. USP and CFC1 are each one-third indirect partners in PRS2. Taking into account the one-third interest in PRS2 directly owned by CFC2, USP, CFC1, and CFC2 collectively own at least 80 percent of the interests in PRS2. Thus, PRS2 is a section 721(c) partnership as a result of the PRS1 contribution.

(B) Under §1.721(c)-2(b), section 721(a) does not apply to PRS1's contribution of the patent to PRS2, unless the requirements of the gain deferral method are satisfied. Under §1.721(c)-3(b), the gain deferral method must be applied with respect to the patent. In addition, under §1.721(c)-3(d)(2), because PRS1 is a controlled partnership with respect to USP, the gain deferral method must be applied with respect to PRS1's interest in PRS2, and, solely for purposes of applying the consistent allocation method, PRS2 must treat PRS1 as the U.S. transferor. As stated in paragraph (b)(3)(i) of this section (the facts in *Example 3*), the gain deferral method is applied. PRS2 is a controlled partnership with respect to USP. Under §1.721(c)-5(c)(5)(i), the PRS1 contribution is a successor event with respect to the USP contribution.

(iv) *Results: application of remedial allocation method.* (A) Under §1.704-3(d)(2), in year 1, PRS2 has $24 million of book amortization with respect to the patent ($6 million ($30 million of book value equal to adjusted tax basis divided by the 5-year remaining recovery period) plus $18 million ($270 million excess of book value over tax basis divided by the new 15-year recovery period)). PRS2 has $6 million of tax amortization. Under the PRS2 partnership agreement, PRS2 allocates $8 million of book amortization to CFC2 and $16 million of book amortization to PRS1. Because of the application of the ceiling rule, PRS2 allocates $6 million of tax amortization to CFC2 and $0 of tax amortization to PRS1. Because the ceiling rule would cause a disparity of $2 million between CFC2's book and tax amortization, PRS2 must make a remedial allocation of $2 million of tax amortization to CFC2 and an offsetting remedial allocation of $2 million of taxable income to PRS1.

(B) PRS1's distributive share of each of PRS2's items with respect to the patent is $16 million of book amortization, $0 of tax amortization, and $2 million of taxable income from the remedial allocation from PRS1. Under §1.704-3(a)(9), PRS1 must allocate its distributive share of each of PRS2's items with respect to the patent in a manner that takes into account USP's remaining built-in gain in the patent. Therefore, PRS1 allocates $2 million of taxable income to USP. Under §1.704-3(a)(13)(ii), PRS1 treats its distributive share of each of PRS2's items of amortization with respect to PRS2's patent as items of amortization with respect to PRS1's interest in PRS2. Under the PRS1 partnership agreement, PRS1 allocates $8 million of book amortization and $0 of tax amortization to CFC1, and $8 million of book amortization and $0 of tax amortization to USP. Because the ceiling rule would cause a disparity of $8 million between CFC1's book and tax amortization, PRS1 must make a remedial allocation of $8 million of tax amortization to CFC1. PRS1 must also make an offsetting remedial allocation of $8 million of taxable income to USP. USP reports $10 million of taxable income ($2 million of remedial income from PRS2 and $8 million of remedial income from PRS1).

(4) *Example 4: Section 721(c) partnership ceases to have a related foreign person as a partner*—(i) *Facts.* In year 1, USP and CFC1 form PRS1. USP contributes a trademark with a built-in gain of $5 million in exchange for a 60-percent interest, and CFC1 contributes other property in exchange for the remaining 40-percent interest. With respect to all contributions described in § 1.721(c)-2(b), the de minimis exception does not apply, and the gain deferral method is applied. On day 1 of year 4, CFC1 sells its entire interest in PRS1 to FX. There is no plan for a related foreign person with respect to USP to subsequently become a partner in PRS1 (or a successor).

(ii) *Results.* (A) PRS1 is a section 721(c) partnership.

(B) With respect to year 4, under § 1.721(c)-5(b)(5), the sale is a termination event because, as a result of CFC1's sale of its interest, PRS1 will no longer have a partner that is a related foreign person, and there is no plan for a related foreign person to subsequently become a partner in PRS1 (or a successor). Thus, under § 1.721(c)-5(b)(1), the trademark is no longer subject to the gain deferral method.

(5) *Example 5: Transfer described in section 367 of section 721(c) property to a foreign corporation*—(i) *Facts.* In year 1, USP, CFC1, and USX form PRS1. USP contributes a patent with a built-in gain of $5 million in exchange for a 60-percent interest, CFC1 contributes other property in exchange for a 30-percent interest, and USX contributes cash in exchange for a 10-percent interest. With respect to all contributions described in § 1.721(c)-2(b), the de minimis exception does not apply, and the gain deferral method is applied. In year 3, when the patent has remaining built-in gain, PRS1 transfers the patent to FX in a transaction described in section 351.

(ii) *Results.* (A) PRS1 is a section 721(c) partnership.

(B) With respect to year 3, the transfer of the patent to FX is a transaction described in section 367(d). Therefore, under § 1.721(c)-5(e), the patent is no longer subject to the gain deferral method. Under §§ 1.367(d)-1T(d)(1) and 1.367(a)-1T(c)(3)(i), for purposes of section 367(d), USP and USX are treated as transferring their proportionate share of the patent actually transferred by PRS1 to FX. Under § 1.721(c)-5(e), to the extent USP and USX are treated as transferring the patent to FX, the tax consequences are determined under section 367(d) and the regulations under section 367(d). With respect to the remaining portion of the patent, if any, which is attributable to CFC1, USP must recognize an amount of gain equal to the remaining built-in gain that would have been allocated to USP if PRS1 had sold that portion of the patent immediately before the transfer for fair market value. Under § 1.721(c)-4(c)(1), USP must increase the basis in its partnership interest in PRS1 by the amount of gain recognized by USP and under § 1.721(c)-4(c)(2), immediately before the transfer, PRS1 must increase its basis in the patent by the same amount. The stock in FX received by PRS1 is not subject to the gain deferral method.

(6) *Example 6: Limited remedial allocation method for anti-churning property with respect to related partners*—(i) *Facts.* USP, CFC1, and FX form PRS1. On January 1 of year 1, USP contributes intellectual property (IP) with a book value of $600 million and an adjusted tax basis of $0 in exchange for a 60-percent interest. The IP is a section 197(f)(9) intangible (within the meaning of § 1.197-2(h)(1)(i)) that was not an amortizable section 197 intangible in USP's hands. CFC1 contributes cash of $300 million in exchange for a 30-percent interest, and FX contributes cash of $100 million in exchange for a 10-percent interest. The IP is section 721(c) property, and PRS1 is a section 721(c) partnership. The gain deferral method is applied. The partnership agreement provides that PRS1 will make allocations under section 704(c) with respect to the IP using the remedial allocation method under § 1.704-3(d)(5)(iii). All of PRS1's allocations with respect to the IP satisfy the requirements of the gain deferral method. On January 1 of year 16, PRS1 sells the IP for cash of $900 million to a person that is not a related person. During years 1 through 16, PRS1 earns no income other than gain from the sale of the IP in year 16, has no expenses or deductions other than from amortization of the IP, and makes no distributions.

(ii) *Results: year 1.* Under § 1.704-3(d)(5)(iii)(B), PRS1 must recover the excess of the book value of the IP over its adjusted tax basis at the time of the contribution ($600 million) using any recovery period and amortization method that would have been available to PRS1 if the property had been newly purchased property from an unrelated party. Thus, under section 197(a), PRS1 must amortize $600 million of the IP's book value ratably over 15 years for book purposes, and PRS1 will have $40 million of book amortization per year without any tax amortization. Under the partnership agreement, in year 1, PRS1 allocates book amortization of $24 million to USP, $12 million to CFC1, and $4 million to FX. Because in year 1 the ceiling rule would cause a disparity between FX's allocations of book and tax amortization, PRS1 makes a remedial allocation of tax amortization of $4 million to FX and an offsetting remedial allocation of $4 million of taxable income to USP. In year 1, the ceiling rule would also cause a disparity between CFC1's allocations of book and tax amortization. However, § 1.197-2(h)(12)(vii)(B) precludes PRS1 from making a remedial allocation of tax amortization to CFC1. Instead, pursuant to § 1.704-3(d)(5)(iii)(C), PRS1 increases the adjusted tax basis in the IP by $12 million, and pursuant to § 1.704-3(d)(5)(iii)(D), that basis adjustment is solely with respect to CFC1. Pursuant to § 1.704-3(d)(5)(iii)(C), PRS1 also makes an offsetting remedial allocation of $12 million of taxable income to USP.

(iii) *Results: years 2-15.* At the end of year 15, PRS1 has book basis and adjusted tax basis of $0 in the IP. PRS1 has amortized $600 million for book purposes by allocating total book amortization deductions of $360 million to USP, $180 million to CFC1, and $60 million to FX. For U.S. tax purposes, by the end of year 15, PRS1 has made remedial allocations of $60 million of tax amortization to FX and increased the adjusted tax basis in the IP by $180 million solely with respect to CFC1. PRS1 has also made total remedial allocations of $240 million of taxable income to USP (attributable to $60 million of remedial tax amortization to FX and $180 million of tax basis adjustments with respect to CFC1). With respect to their partnership interests in PRS1, USP has a capital account and an adjusted tax basis of $240 million, CFC1 has a capital account of $120 million and an adjusted tax basis of $300 million, and FX has a capital account and an adjusted tax basis of $40 million.

(iv) *Results: sale of property in year 16.* PRS1's sale of the IP for cash of $900 million on January 1 of year 16 results in $900 million of book and tax gain ($900 million - $0). PRS1 allocates the book and tax gain 60 percent to USP ($540 million), 10 percent to FX ($90 million), and 30 percent to CFC1 ($270 million). However, under § 1.704-3(d)(5)(iii)(D)(3), CFC1's tax gain is $90 million, equal to its share of PRS1's gain ($270 million), minus the amount of the tax basis adjustment ($180 million). After the sale, PRS1's only property is cash of $1.3 billion. With respect to their partnership interests in PRS1, USP has a capital account and an adjusted tax basis of $780 million, CFC1 has a capital account and an adjusted tax basis of $390 million, and FX has a capital account and an adjusted tax basis of $130 million. [Reg. § 1.721(c)-7.]

□ [*T.D. 9891, 1-17-2020.*]

Determination of Sources of Income

§ 1.861-1. Income from sources within the United States.—(a) *Categories of income.*—Part 1 (section 861 and following), subchapter N, chapter 1 of the Code, and the regulations thereunder determine the sources of income for purposes of the income tax. These sections explicitly allocate certain important sources of income to the United States or to areas outside the United States, as the case may be; and, with respect to the remaining income (particularly that derived partly from sources within and partly from sources without the United States), authorize the Secretary or his delegate to determine the income derived from sources within the United States, either by rules of separate allocation or by processes or formulas of general apportionment. The statute provides for the following three categories of income:

(1) *Within the United States.*—The gross income from sources within the United States, consisting of the items of gross income specified in section 861(a) plus the items of gross income allocated or apportioned to such sources in accordance with section 863(a). See §§ 1.861-2 to 1.861-7, inclusive, and § 1.863-1. The taxable income from sources within the United States, in the case of such income, shall be determined by deducting therefrom, in accordance with sections 861(b) and 863(a), the expenses, losses, and other deductions properly apportioned or allocated thereto and a ratable part of any other expenses, losses, or deductions which cannot definitely be allocated to some item or class of gross income. See §§ 1.861-8 and 1.863-1.

(2) *Without the United States.*—The gross income from sources without the United States, consisting of the items of gross income specified in section 862(a) plus the items of gross income allocated or apportioned to such sources in accordance with section 863(a). See §§ 1.862-1 and 1.863-1. The taxable income from sources without the United States, in the case of such income, shall be determined by deducting therefrom, in accordance with sections 862(b) and 863(a),

the expenses, losses, and other deductions properly apportioned or allocated thereto and a ratable part of any other expenses, losses, or deductions which cannot definitely be allocated to some item or class of gross income. See §§1.862-1 and 1.863-1.

(3) *Partly within and partly without the United States.*—The gross income derived from sources partly within and partly without the United States, consisting of the items specified in section 863(b)(1), (2), and (3). The taxable income allocated or apportioned to sources within the United States, in the case of such income, shall be determined in accordance with section 863(a) or (b). See §§1.863-2 to 1.863-5, inclusive.

(4) *Exceptions.*—An owner of certain aircraft or vessels first leased on or before December 28, 1980, may elect to treat income in respect of these aircraft or vessels as income from sources within the United States for purposes of sections 861(a) and 862(a). See §1.861-9. An owner of certain aircraft, vessels, or spacecraft first leased after December 28, 1980, must treat income in respect of these craft as income from sources within the United States for purposes of sections 861(a) and 862(a). See §1.861-9A.

(b) *Taxable income from sources within the United States.*—The taxable income from sources within the United States shall consist of the taxable income described in paragraph (a)(1) of this section plus the taxable income allocated or apportioned to such sources, as indicated in paragraph (a)(3) of this section.

(c) *Computation of income.*—If a taxpayer has gross income from sources within or without the United States, together with gross income derived partly from sources within and partly from sources without the United States, the amounts thereof, together with the expenses and investment applicable thereto, shall be segregated; and the taxable income from sources within the United States shall be separately computed therefrom. [Reg. §1.861-1.]

☐ [*T.D. 6258, 10-23-57. Amended by T.D. 7635, 8-7-79 and T.D. 7928, 12-15-83.*]

§1.861-2. Interest.—(a) *In general.*—(1) Gross income consisting of interest from the United States or any agency or instrumentality thereof (other than a possession of the United States or an agency or instrumentality of a possession), a State or any political subdivision thereof, or the District of Columbia, and interest from a resident of the United States on a bond, note, or other interest-bearing obligation issued or assumed or incurred by such person shall be treated as income from sources within the United States. Thus, for example, income from sources within the United States includes interest received on any refund of income tax imposed by the United States, a State or any political subdivision thereof, or the District of Columbia. Interest other than that described in this paragraph is not to be treated as income from sources within the United States. See paragraph (a)(7) of this section for special rules concerning substitute interest paid or accrued pursuant to a securities lending transaction.

(2) The term "resident of the United States", as used in this paragraph, includes (i) an individual who at the time of payment of the interest is a resident of the United States, (ii) a domestic corporation, (iii) a domestic partnership which at any time during its taxable year is engaged in trade or business in the United States, or (iv) a foreign corporation or a foreign partnership, which at any time during its taxable year is engaged in trade or business in the United States.

(3) The method by which, or the place where, payment of the interest is made is immaterial in determining whether interest is derived from sources within the United States.

(4) For purposes of this section, the term "interest" includes all amounts treated as interest under section 483, and the regulations thereunder. It also includes original issue discount, as defined in section 1232(b)(1), whether or not the underlying bond, debenture, note, certificate, or other evidence of indebtedness is a capital asset in the hands of the taxpayer within the meaning of section 1221.

(5) If interest is paid on an obligation of a resident of the United States by a nonresident of the United States acting in the nonresident's capacity as a guarantor of the obligation of the resident, the interest will be treated as income from sources within the United States.

(6) In the case of interest received by a nonresident alien individual or foreign corporation this paragraph (a) applies whether or not the interest is effectively connected for the taxable year with the conduct of a trade or business in the United States by such individual or corporation.

(7) A substitute interest payment is a payment, made to the transferor of a security in a securities lending transaction or a sale-repurchase transaction, of an amount equivalent to an interest payment which the owner of the transferred security is entitled to receive during the term of the transaction. A securities lending transaction is a transfer of one or more securities that is described in section 1058(a) or a substantially similar transaction. A sale-repurchase transaction is an agreement under which a person transfers a security in exchange for cash and simultaneously agrees to receive substantially identical securities from the transferee in the future in exchange for cash. A substitute interest payment shall be sourced in the same manner as the interest accruing on the transferred security for purposes of this section and §1.862-1. See also §§1.864-5(b)(2)(iii), 1.871-7(b)(2), 1.881-2(b)(2) and for the character of such payments and §1.894-1(c) for the application tax treaties to these transactions.

(b) *Interest not derived from U.S. sources.*—Notwithstanding paragraph (a) of this section, interest shall be treated as income from sources without the United States to the extent provided by subparagraphs (A) through (H), of section 861(a)(1) and by the following subparagraphs of this paragraph.

(1) *Interest on bank deposits and on similar amounts.*—(i) Interest paid or credited before January 1, 1977, to a nonresident alien individual or foreign corporation on—

(*a*) Deposits with persons, including citizens of the United States or alien individuals and foreign or domestic partnerships or corporations, carrying on the banking business in the United States,

(*b*) Deposits or withdrawable accounts with savings institutions chartered and supervised as savings and loan or similar associations under Federal or State law, or

(*c*) Amounts held by an insurance company under an agreement to pay interest thereon,

shall be treated as income from sources without the United States if such interest is not effectively connected for the taxable year with the conduct of a trade or business in the United States by such nonresident alien individual or foreign corporation. If such interest is effectively connected for the taxable year with the conduct of a trade or business in the United States by such nonresident alien individual or foreign corporation, it shall be treated as income from sources within the United States under paragraph (a) of this section unless it is treated as income from sources without the United States under another subparagraph of this paragraph. For a special rule for determining whether such interest is effectively connected for the taxable year with the conduct of a trade or business in the United States, see paragraph (c)(1)(ii) or §1.864-4.

(ii) Subdivision (i)(*b*) of this subparagraph applies to interest on deposits or withdrawable accounts described therein only to the extent that the interest paid or credited by the savings institution described therein is deductible under section 591 in determining the taxable income of such institution; and, for this purpose, whether an amount is deductible under section 591 shall be determined without regard to section 265, relating to deductions allocable to tax-exempt income. Thus, for example, such subdivision does not apply to amounts paid by a savings and loan or similar association on or with respect to its nonwithdrawable capital stock or on or with respect to funds held in restricted accounts which represent a proprietary interest in such association. Subdivision (i)(*b*) of this subparagraph also applies to so-called dividends paid or credited on deposits or withdrawable accounts if such dividends are deductible under section 591 without reference to section 265.

(iii) For purposes of subdivision (i)(*c*) of this subparagraph, amounts held by an insurance company under an agreement to pay interest thereon include policyholder dividends left with the company to accumulate, prepaid insurance premiums, proceeds of policies left on deposit with the company, and overcharges of premiums. Such subdivision does not apply to (*a*) the so-called "interest element" in the case of annuity or installment payments under life insurance or endowment contracts or (*b*) interest paid by an insurance company to its creditors on notes, bonds, or similar evidences of indebtedness, if the debtor-creditor relationship does not arise by virtue of a contract of insurance with the insurance company.

(iv) For purposes of subdivision (i) of this subparagraph, interest received by a partnership shall be treated as received by each partner of such partnership to the extent of his distributive share of such item.

(2) *Interest from a resident alien individual or domestic corporation deriving substantial income from sources without the United States.*—Interest received from a resident alien individual or a domestic corporation shall be treated as income from sources without the

United States when it is shown to the satisfaction of the district director (or, if applicable, the Director of International Operations) that less than 20 percent of the gross income from all sources of such individual or corporation has been derived from sources within the United States, as determined under the provisions of sections 861 to 863, inclusive, and the regulations thereunder, for the 3-year period ending with the close of the taxable year of such individual or corporation preceding its taxable year in which such interest is paid or credited, or for such part of such period as may be applicable. If 20 percent or more of the gross income from all sources of such individual or corporation has been derived from sources within the United States, as so determined, for such 3-year period (or part thereof), the entire amount of the interest from such individual or corporation shall be treated as income from sources within the United States.

(3) *Interest from a foreign corporation not deriving major portion of its income from a U.S. business.*—(i) Interest from a foreign corporation which, at any time during the taxable year, is engaged in trade or business in the United States shall be treated as income from sources without the United States when it is shown to the satisfaction of the district director (or, if applicable, the Director of International Operations) that (*a*) less than 50 percent of the gross income from all sources of such foreign corporation for the 3-year period ending with the close of its taxable year preceding its taxable year in which such interest is paid or credited (or for such part of such period as the corporation has been in existence) was effectively connected with the conduct by such corporation of a trade or business in the United States, as determined under section 864(c) and § 1.864-3, or (*b*) such foreign corporation had gross income for such 3-year period (or part thereof) but none was effectively connected with the conduct of a trade or business in the United States.

(ii) If 50 percent or more of the gross income from all sources of such foreign corporation for such 3-year period (or part thereof) was effectively connected with the conduct by such corporation of a trade or business in the United States, see section 861(a)(1)(D) and paragraph (c)(1) of this section for determining the portion of interest from such corporation which is treated as income from sources within the United States.

(iii) For purposes of this subparagraph the gross income which is effectively connected with the conduct of a trade or business in the United States includes the gross income which, pursuant to section 882(d) or (e) and the regulations thereunder, is treated as income which is effectively connected with the conduct of a trade or business in the United States.

(iv) This subparagraph does not apply to interest paid or credited after December 31, 1969, by a branch in the United States of a foreign corporation if, at the time of payment or crediting, such branch is engaged in the commercial banking business in the United States; furthermore, such interest is treated under paragraph (a) of this section as income from sources within the United States unless it is treated as income from sources without the United States under subparagraph (1) or (4) of this paragraph.

(4) *Bankers' acceptances.*—Interest derived by a foreign central bank of issue from bankers' acceptances shall be treated as income from sources without the United States. For this purpose, a foreign central bank of issue is a bank which is by law or government sanction the principal authority, other than the government itself, issuing instruments intended to circulate as currency. Such a bank is generally the custodian of the banking reserves of the country under whose law it is organized.

(5) *Foreign banking branch of a domestic corporation or partnership.*—Interest paid or credited on deposits with a branch outside the United States (as defined in section 7701(a)(9)) of a domestic corporation or of a domestic partnership shall be treated as income from sources without the United States if, at the time of payment or crediting, such branch is engaged in the commercial banking business. For purposes of applying this subparagraph, it is immaterial (i) whether the domestic corporation or domestic partnership is carrying on a banking business in the United States, (ii) whether the recipient of the interest is a citizen or resident of the United States, a foreign corporation, or a foreign partnership, (iii) whether the interest is effectively connected with the conduct of a trade or business in the United States by the recipient, or (iv) whether the deposits with the branch located outside the United States are payable in the currency of a foreign country. Notwithstanding the provisions of § 1.863-6, interest to which this subparagraph applies shall be treated as income from sources within the foreign country, possession of the United States, or other territory in which the branch is located.

(6) *Section 4912(c) debt obligations.*—(i) *In general.*—Under section 861(a)(1)(G), interest on a debt obligation shall not be treated as income from sources within the United States if—

(*a*) The debt obligation was part of an issue of debt obligations with respect to which an election has been made under section 4912(c) (relating to the treatment of such debt obligations as debt obligations of a foreign obligor for purposes of the interest equalization tax),

(*b*) The debt obligation had a maturity not exceeding 15 years (within the meaning of subdivision (ii) of this subparagraph) on the date it is originally issued or on the date it is treated under section 4912(c)(2) as issued by reason of being assumed by a certain domestic corporation,

(*c*) The debt obligation, when originally issued, was purchased by one or more underwriters (within the meaning of subdivision (iii) of this subparagraph) with a view to distribution through resale (within the meaning of subdivision (iv) of this subparagraph), and

(*d*) The interest on the debt obligation is attributable to periods after the effective date of an election under section 4912(c) to treat such debt obligations as debt obligations of a foreign obligor for purposes of the interest equalization tax.

(ii) *Maturity not exceeding 15 years.*—The date the debt obligation is issued or treated as issued is not included in the 15 year computation, but the date of maturity of the debt obligation is included in such computation.

(iii) *Purchased by one or more underwriters.*—For purposes of this subparagraph, the debt obligation when originally issued will not be treated as purchased by one or more underwriters unless the underwriter purchases the debt obligation for his own account and bears the risk of gain or loss on resale. Thus, for example, a debt obligation, when originally issued, will not be treated as purchased by one or more underwriters if the underwriter acts only in the capacity of an agent of the issuer. Neither will a debt obligation, when originally issued, be treated as purchased by one or more underwriters if the agreement between the underwriter and issuer is merely for a "best efforts" underwriting, for the purchase by the underwriter of all or a portion of the debt obligations remaining unsold at the expiration of a fixed period of time, or for any other arrangement under the terms of which the debt obligations are not purchased by the underwriter with a view to distribution through resale. The fact that an underwriter is related to the issuer will not prevent the underwriter from meeting the requirements of this subparagraph. In determining whether a related underwriter meets the requirement of this subparagraph consideration shall be given to whether the purchase by the underwriter of the debt obligation from the issuer for resale was effected by a transaction subject to conditions similar to those which would have been imposed between independent persons.

(iv) *With a view to distribution through resale.*—(*a*) An underwriter who purchased a debt obligation shall be deemed to have purchased it with a view to distribution through resale if the requirements of (*b*) or (*c*) of this subdivision (iv) are met.

(*b*) The requirement of this subdivision (*b*) is that—

(*1*) The debt obligation is registered, approved, or listed for trading on one or more foreign securities exchanges or foreign established securities markets within 4 months after the date on which the underwriter purchases the debt obligation, or by the date of the first interest payment on the debt obligation, whichever is later, or

(*2*) The debt obligation, or any substantial portion of the issue of which the debt obligation is a part, is actually traded on one or more foreign securities markets on or within 15 calendar days after the date on which the underwriter purchases the debt obligation.

For purposes of this subdivison (iv), a foreign established securities market includes any foreign over-the-counter market as reflected by the existence of an inter-dealer quotation system for regularly disseminating to brokers and dealers quotations of obligations by identified brokers or dealers, other than quotations prepared and distributed by a broker or dealer in the regular course of his business and containing only quotations of such broker or dealer.

(*c*) The requirements of this subdivision (*c*) are that, except as provided in (*d*) of this subdivision, the underwriter is under no written or implied restriction imposed by the issuer with respect to whom he may resell the debt obligation and either—

(*1*) Within 30 calendar days after he purchased the debt obligation the underwriter or underwriters either (*i*) sold it or (*ii*) sold at least 95 percent of the face amount of the issue of which the debt obligation is a part, or

(2)(i) The debt obligation is evidenced by an instrument which, under the laws of the jurisdiction in which it is issued, is either negotiable or transferable by assignment (whether or not it is registered for trading), and *(ii)* it appears from all the relevant facts and circumstances, including any written statements or assurances made by the purchasing underwriter or underwriters, that such debt obligation was purchased with a view to distribution through resale.

(d) The requirements of *(c)* of this subdivision may be met whether or not the underwriter is restricted from reselling the debt obligations—

(1) To a United States person (as defined in section 7701(a)(30)) or

(2) To any particular person or persons pursuant to a restriction imposed by, or required to be met in order to comply with, United States or foreign securities or other law.

(v) *Statement with return.*—Any taxpayer who is required to file a tax return and who excludes from gross income interest of the type specified in this subparagraph must comply with the requirements of paragraph (d) of this section.

(vi) *Effect of termination of IET.*—If the interest equalization tax expires, the provisions of section 861(a)(1)(G) and this subparagraph shall apply to interest paid on debt obligations only with respect to which a section 4912(c) election was made.

(vii) *Definition of term underwriter.*—For purposes of section 861(a)(1)(G) and this subparagraph, the term "underwriter" shall mean any underwriter as defined in section 4919(c)(1).

(c) *Special rules.*—(1) *Proration of interest from a foreign corporation deriving major portion of its income from U.S. business.*—If, after applying the first sentence of paragraph (b)(3) of this section to interest to which that paragraph applies, it is determined that the interest may not be treated as income from sources without the United States, the amount of the interest from the foreign corporation which at some time during the taxable year is engaged in trade or business in the United States which is to be treated as income from sources within the United States shall be the amount that bears the same ratio to such interest as the gross income of such foreign corporation for the 3-year period ending with the close of its taxable year preceding its taxable year in which such interest is paid or credited (or for such part of such period as the corporation has been in existence) which was effectively connected with the conduct by such corporation of a trade or business in the United States bears to its gross income from all sources for such period.

(2) *Payors having no gross income for period preceding taxable year of payment.*—If the resident alien individual, domestic corporation, or foreign corporation, as the case may be, paying interest has no gross income from any source for the 3-year period (or part thereof) specified in subparagraph (2) or (3) of paragraph (b) of this section, or subparagraph (1) of this paragraph, the 20-percent test or the 50-percent test, or the apportionment formula, as the case may be, described in such subparagraph shall be applied solely with respect to the taxable year of the payor in which the interest is paid or credited. This subparagraph applies whether the lack of gross income for the 3-year period (or part thereof) stems from the business inactivity of the payor, from the fact that the payor is a corporation which is newly created or organized, or from any other cause.

(3) *Transitional rule.*—For purposes of applying paragraph (b)(3) of this section, and subparagraph (1) of this paragraph, the gross income of the foreign corporation for any period before the first taxable year beginning after December 31, 1966, which is from sources within the United States (determined as provided by sections 861 through 863, and the regulations thereunder, as in effect immediately before amendment by section 102 of the Foreign Investors Tax Act of 1966 (Pub. L. 89-809, 80 Stat. 1541)) shall be treated as gross income for such period which is effectively connected with the conduct of a trade or business in the United States by such foreign corporation.

(4) *Gross income determinations.*—In making determinations under subparagraph (2) or (3) of paragraph (b) of this section, or subparagraph (1) or (3) of this paragraph—

(i) The gross income of a domestic corporation or a resident alien individual is to be determined by excluding any items specifically excluded from gross income under chapter 1 of the Code, and

(ii) The gross income of a foreign corporation which is effectively connected with the conduct of a trade or business in the United States is to be determined under section 882(b)(2) and by excluding any items specifically excluded from gross income under chapter 1 of the Code, and

(iii) The gross income from all sources of a foreign corporation is to be determined without regard to section 882(b) and without excluding any items otherwise specifically excluded from gross income under chapter 1 of the Code.

(d) *Statement with return.*—Any taxpayer who is required to file a return and applies any provision of this section to exclude an amount of interest from his gross income must file with his return a statement setting forth the amount so excluded, the date of its receipt, the name and address of the obligor of the interest, and, if known, the location of the records which substantiate the amount of the exclusion. A statement from the obligor setting forth such information and indicating the amount of interest to be treated as income from sources without the United States may be used for this purpose. See §§1.6012-1(b)(1)(i) and 1.6012-2(g)(1)(i).

(e) *Effective dates.*—Except as otherwise provided, this section applies with respect to taxable years beginning after December 31, 1966. For corresponding rules applicable to taxable years beginning before January 1, 1967, (see 26 CFR part 1 revised April 1, 1971). Paragraph (a)(7) of this section is applicable to payments made after November 13, 1997. [Reg. §1.861-2.]

☐ [*T.D. 6258, 10-23-57. Amended by T.D. 6873, 1-24-66; T.D. 7314, 5-22-74; T.D. 7378, 9-29-75; T.D. 8257, 8-1-89 and T.D. 8735, 10-6-97.*]

§1.861-3. Dividends and income inclusions under sections 951, 951A, and 1293 and associated section 78 dividends.—(a) [*In*] *General.*—(1) *Dividends included in gross income.*—Gross income from sources within the United States includes a dividend described in subparagraph (2), (3), (4), or (5) of this paragraph. For purposes of subparagraphs (2), (3), and (4) of this paragraph, the term "dividend" shall have the same meaning as set forth in section 316 and the regulations thereunder. See subparagraph (5) of this paragraph for special rules with respect to certain dividends from a DISC or former DISC. See also paragraph (a)(6) of this section for special rules concerning substitute dividend payments received pursuant to a securities lending transaction.

(2) *Dividend from a domestic corporation.*—A dividend described in this paragraph (a)(2) is a dividend from a domestic corporation other than a corporation that has an election in effect under section 936. See paragraph (a)(5) of this section for the treatment of certain dividends from a DISC or former DISC.

(3) *Dividend from a foreign corporation.*—(i) *In general.*—*(a)* A dividend described in this subparagraph is a dividend from a foreign corporation (other than a dividend to which subparagraph (4) of this paragraph applies) unless less than 50 percent of the gross income from all sources of such foreign corporation for the 3-year period ending with the close of its taxable year preceding the taxable year in which occurs the declaration of such dividend (or for such part of such period as the corporation has been in existence) was effectively connected with the conduct by such corporation of a trade or business in the United States, as determined under section 864(c) and §1.864-3. Thus, no portion of a dividend from a foreign corporation shall be treated as income from sources within the United States under section 861(a)(2)(B) if less than 50 percent of the gross income of such foreign corporation from all sources for such 3-year period (or part thereof) was effectively connected with the conduct of a trade or business in the United States or if such foreign corporation had gross income for such 3-year period (or part thereof) but none was effectively connected with the conduct by such corporation of a trade or business in the United States.

(b) If 50 percent or more of the gross income from all sources of such foreign corporation for such 3-year period (or part thereof) was effectively connected with the conduct by such corporation of a trade or business in the United States, the amount of the dividend which is to be treated as income from sources within the United States under section 861(a)(2)(B) shall be the amount that bears the same ratio to such dividend as the gross income of such foreign corporation for such 3-year period (or part thereof) which was effectively connected with the conduct by such corporation of a trade or business in the United States bears to its gross income from all sources for such period.

(c) For purposes of this subdivision (i), the gross income which is effectively connected with the conduct of a trade or business

in the United States includes the gross income which, pursuant to section 882(d) or (e), is treated as income which is effectively connected with the conduct of a trade or business in the United States.

(ii) *Rule applicable in applying limitation on amount of foreign tax credit.*—For purposes of determining under section 904 the limitation upon the amount of the foreign tax credit—

(a) So much of a dividend from a foreign corporation as exceeds (and only to the extent it so exceeds) the amount which is 100/85ths of the amount of the deduction allowable under section 245(a) in respect of such dividend, plus

(b) An amount which bears the same proportion to any section 78 dividend to which the dividend from the foreign corporation gives rise as the amount of the excess determined under *(a)* of this subdivision bears to the total amount of the dividend from the foreign corporation,

shall, notwithstanding subdivision (i) of this subparagraph, be treated as income from sources without the United States. This subdivision applies to a dividend for which no dividends-received deduction is allowed under section 245 or for which the 85 percent dividends-received deduction is allowed under section 245(a) but does not apply to a dividend for which a deduction is allowable under section 245(b). All of a dividend for which the 100 percent dividends-received deduction is allowed under section 245(b) shall be treated as income from sources within the United States for purposes of determining under section 904 the limitation upon the amount of the foreign tax credit. If the amount of a distribution of property other than money (constituting a dividend under section 316) is determined by applying section 301(b)(1)(C), such amount must be used as the dividend for purposes of applying *(a)* of this subdivision even though the amount used for purposes of section 245(a) is determined by applying section 301(b)(1)(D). In making determinations under this subdivision, a dividend (other than a section 78 dividend referred to in *(b)* of this subdivision) shall be determined without regard to section 78.

(iii) *Illustrations.*—The application of this subparagraph may be illustrated by the following examples:

Example (1). D, a domestic corporation, owns 80 percent of the outstanding stock of M, a foreign manufacturing corporation. M, which makes its returns on the basis of the calendar year, has earnings and profits of $200,000 for 1971 and 60 percent of its gross income for that year is effectively connected for 1971 with the conduct of a trade or business in the United States. For an uninterrupted period of 36 months ending on December 31, 1970, M has been engaged in trade or business in the United States and has received gross income effectively connected with the conduct of a trade or business in the United States amounting to 60 percent of its gross income from all sources for such period. The only distribution by M to D for 1971 is a cash dividend of $100,000; of this amount, $60,000 ($100,000 × 60%) is treated under subdivision (i) of this subparagraph as income from sources within the United States, and $40,000 ($100,000 – $60,000) is treated under § 1.862-1(a)(2) as income from sources without the United States. Accordingly, under section 245(a), D is entitled to a dividends-received deduction of $51,000 ($60,000 × 85%), and under subdivision (ii) of this subparagraph $40,000 ($100,000 – [$51,000 × 100/85]) is treated as income from sources without the United States for purposes of determining under section 904(a)(1) or (2) the limitation upon the amount of the foreign tax credit.

Example (2). (a) The facts are the same as in example (1) except that the distribution for 1971 consists of property which has a fair market value of $100,000 and an adjusted basis of $30,000 in M's hands immediately before the distribution. The amount of the dividend under section 316 is $58,000, determined by applying section 301(b)(1)(C) as follows:

Portion of adjusted basis of property attributable to gross income of M effectively connected for 1971 with conduct of trade or business in United States ($30,000 × 60%)	$18,000
Portion of fair market value of property attributable to gross income of M not effectively connected for 1971 with conduct of trade or business in United States ($100,000 × 40%)	40,000
Total dividend	$58,000

(b) Of the total dividend, $34,800 ($58,000 × 60% (percentage applicable to 3-year period)) is treated under subdivision (i) of this subparagraph as income from sources within the United States, and $23,200 ($58,000 × 40%) is treated under § 1.862-1(a)(2) as income from sources without the United States. However, by reason of section 245(c) the adjusted basis of the property ($30,000) is used under section 245(a) in determining the dividends-received deduction. Thus, under section 245(a), D is entitled to a dividends-received deduction of $15,300 ($30,000 × 60% × 85%).

(c) Under subdivision (ii) of this subparagraph, the amount of the dividend for purposes of applying *(a)* of that subdivision is the amount ($58,000) determined by applying section 301(b)(1)(C) rather than the amount ($30,000) determined by applying section 301(b)(1)(B). Accordingly, under subdivision (ii) of this subparagraph $40,000 ($58,000 – [$15,300 × 100/85]) is treated as income from sources without the United States for purposes of determining under section 904(a) (1) or (2) the limitation upon the amount of the foreign tax credit.

Example (3). (a) D, a domestic corporation which makes its returns on the basis of the calendar year, owns 100 percent of the outstanding stock of N, a foreign corporation which is not a less developed country corporation under section 902(d). N, which makes its returns on the basis of the calendar year, has total gross income for 1971 of $100,000, of which $80,000 (including $60,000 from sources within foreign country X) is effectively connected for that year with the conduct of a trade or business in the United States. For 1971 N is assumed to have paid $27,000 of income taxes to Country X and to have accumulated profits of $81,000 for purposes of section 902(c)(1)(A). N's accumulated profits in excess of foreign income taxes amount to $54,000. For 1971 D receives a cash dividend of $42,000 from N, which is D's only income for that year.

(b) For 1971 D chooses the benefits of the foreign tax credit under section 901, and as a result is required under section 78 to include in gross income an amount equal to the foreign income taxes of $21,000 ($27,000 × $42,000/$54,000) it is deemed to have paid under section 902(a)(1). Thus, assuming no other deductions for the taxable year, D has gross income of $63,000 ($42,000 + $21,000) for 1971 less a dividends-received deduction under section 245(a) of $28,560 ([$42,000 × $80,000/$100,000] × 85%), or taxable income for 1971 of $34,440.

(c) Under subdivision (ii) of this subparagraph, for purposes of determining under section 904(a) (1) or (2) the limitation upon the amount of the foreign tax credit, $12,600 is treated as income from sources without the United States, determined as follows:

Excess of dividend from N over amount which is 100/85ths of amount of sec. 245(a) deduction ($42,000 – [$28,560 × 100/85])	$8,400
Proportionate part of sec. 78 dividend ($21,000 × $8,400/$42,000)	4,200
Taxable income from sources without the United States	$12,600

Example (4). A, an individual citizen of the United States who makes his return on the basis of the calendar year, receives in 1971 a cash dividend of $10,000 from M, a foreign corporation, which makes its return on the basis of the calendar year. For the 3-year period ending with 1970 M has been engaged in trade or business in the United States and has received gross income effectively connected with the conduct of a trade or business in the United States amounting to 80 percent of its gross income from all sources for such period. Of the total dividend, $8,000 ($10,000 × 80%) is treated under subdivision (i) of this subparagraph as income from sources within the United States and $2,000 ($10,000 – $8,000) is treated under § 1.862-1(a)(2) as income from sources without the United States. Since under section 245 no dividends-received deduction is allowable to an individual, A is entitled under subdivision (ii) of this subparagraph to treat the entire dividend of $10,000 ($10,000 – [$0 × 100/85]) as income from sources without the United States for purposes of determining under section 904(a) (1) or (2) the limitation upon the amount of the foreign tax credit.

(4) *Dividend from a foreign corporation succeeding to earnings of a domestic corporation.*—A dividend described in this subparagraph is a dividend from a foreign corporation, if such dividend is received by a corporation after December 31, 1959, but only to the extent that such dividend is treated by such recipient corporation under the provisions of § 1.243-3 as a dividend from a domestic corporation subject to taxation under chapter 1 of the Code. To the extent that this subparagraph applies to a dividend received from a foreign corporation, subparagraph (3) of this paragraph shall not apply to such dividend.

(5) *Certain dividends from a DISC or former DISC.*—(i) *General rule.*—A dividend described in this subparagraph is a dividend from a corporation that is a DISC or former DISC (as defined in section 992(a)) other than a dividend that—

(a) Is deemed paid by a DISC, for taxable years beginning before January 1, 1976, under section 995(b)(1)(D) as in effect for taxable years beginning before January 1, 1976, and for taxable years beginning after December 31, 1975, under section 995(b)(1)(D), (E), and (F) to the extent provided in subdivision (iii) of this subparagraph or

(*b*) Reduces under § 1.996-3(b)(3) accumulated DISC income (as defined in subdivision (ii)(*b*) of this subparagraph) to the extent provided in subdivision (iv) of this subparagraph.

Thus, a dividend deemed paid under section 995(b)(1)(A), (B), or (C) (relating to certain deemed distributions in qualified years) will be treated in full as gross income from sources within the United States. To the extent that a dividend from a DISC or former DISC is paid out of other earnings and profits (as defined in § 1.996-3(d)), subparagraph (2) of this paragraph shall apply. To the extent that a dividend from a DISC or former DISC is paid out of previously taxed income (as defined in § 1.996-3(c)), see section 996(a)(3) (relating to the exclusion from gross income of amounts distributed out of previously taxed income). In determining the source of income of certain dividends from a DISC or former DISC, the source of income from any transaction which gives rise to gross receipts (as defined in § 1.993-6), in the hands of the DISC or former DISC, is immaterial.

(ii) *Definitions.*—For purposes of this subparagraph, the term—

(*a*) "Dividend from" means any amount actually distributed which is a dividend within the meaning of section 316 (including distributions to meet qualification requirements under section 992(c)) and any amount treated as a distribution taxable as a dividend pursuant to section 995(b) (relating to deemed distributions in qualified years or upon disqualification) or included in gross income as a dividend pursuant to section 995(c) (relating to gain on certain dispositions of stock in a DISC or former DISC), and

(*b*) "Accumulated DISC income" means the amount of accumulated DISC income as of the close of the taxable year immediately preceding the taxable year in which the dividend was made increased by the amount of DISC income for the taxable year in which the dividend was made (as determined under § 1.996-3(b)(2)).

(*c*) "Nonqualified export taxable income" means the taxable income of a DISC from any transaction which gives rise to gross receipts (as defined in § 1.993-6) which are not qualified export receipts (as defined in § 1.993-1) other than a transaction giving rise to gain described in section 995(b)(1)(B) or (C).

For purposes of subdivisions (i) (*b*) and (iv) of this subparagraph, if by reason of section 995(c), gain is included in the shareholder's gross income as a dividend, accumulated DISC income shall be treated as if it were reduced under § 1.996-3(b)(3).

(iii) *Determination of source of income for deemed distributions, for taxable years beginning before January 1, 1976, under section 995(b)(1)(D) as in effect for taxable years beginning before January 1, 1976, and for taxable years beginning after December 31, 1975, under section 995(b)(1)(D), (E), and (F).*

(*a*) If for its taxable year a DISC does not have any nonqualified export taxable income, then for such year the entire amount treated, for taxable years beginning before January 1, 1976, under section 995(b)(1)(D) as in effect for taxable years beginning before January 1, 1976, and for taxable years beginning after December 31, 1975, under section 995(b)(1)(D), (E), and (F) as a deemed distribution taxable as a dividend will be treated as gross income from sources without the United States.

(*b*) If for its taxable year a DISC has any nonqualified export taxable income, then for such year the portion of the amount treated, for taxable years beginning before January 1, 1976, under section 995(b)(1)(D) as in effect for taxable years beginning before January 1, 1976, and for taxable years beginning after December 31, 1975, under section 995(b)(1)(D), (E), and (F) as a deemed distribution taxable as a dividend that will be treated as income from sources within the United States shall be equal to the amount of such nonqualified export taxable income multiplied by the following fraction. The numerator of the fraction is the sum of the amounts treated, for taxable years beginning before January 1, 1976, under section 995(b)(1)(D) as in effect for taxable years beginning before January 1, 1976, and for taxable years beginning after December 31, 1975, under section 995(b)(1)(D), (E), and (F) as deemed distributions taxable as dividends. The denominator of the fraction is the taxable income of the DISC for the taxable year, reduced by the amounts treated under section 995(b)(1)(A), (B), and (C) as deemed distributions taxable as dividends. However, in no event shall the numerator exceed the denominator. The remainder of such dividend will be treated as gross income from sources without the United States.

(iv) *Determination of source of income for dividends that reduce accumulated DISC income.—(a)* If no portion of the accumulated DISC income of a DISC or former DISC is attributable to nonqualified export taxable income from any transaction during a year for which it is (or is treated as) a DISC, then the entire amount of any dividend that reduces under § 1.996-3(b)(3) accumulated DISC income will be treated as income from sources without the United States.

(*b*) If any portion of the accumulated DISC income of a DISC or former DISC is attributable to nonqualified export taxable income from any transaction during a year for which it is (or is treated as) a DISC, then the portion of any dividend during its taxable year that reduces under § 1.996-3(b)(3) accumulated DISC income that will be treated as income from sources within the United States shall be equal to the amount of such dividend multiplied by a fraction (determined as of the close of such year) the numerator of which is the amount of accumulated DISC income attributable to nonqualified export taxable income, and the denominator of which is the total amount of accumulated DISC income. The remainder of such dividend will be treated as gross income from sources without the United States.

(v) *Special rules.*—For purposes of subdivisions (iii) and (iv) of this subparagraph—

(*a*) Taxable income shall be determined under § 1.992-3(b)(2)(i) (relating to the computation of deficiency distribution), and

(*b*) The portion of any deemed distribution taxable as a dividend, for taxable years beginning before January 1, 1976, under section 995(b)(1)(D) as in effect for taxable years beginning before January 1, 1976, and for taxable years beginning after December 31, 1975, under section 995(b)(1)(D), (E), and (F) or amount under § 1.996-3(b)(3)(i) through (iv) that is treated as gross income from sources within the United States during the taxable year shall be considered to reduce the amount of nonqualified export taxable income as of the close of such year.

(vi) *Illustrations.*—This subparagraph may be illustrated by the following examples:

Example (1). (a) Y is a corporation which uses the calendar year as its taxable year and which elects to be treated as a DISC beginning with 1972. X is its sole shareholder. In 1973, Y has $18,000 of taxable income from qualified export receipts (none of which are interest and gains described in section 995(b)(1)(A), (B), and (C)) and $1,000 of nonqualified export taxable income. Under these facts, X is deemed to have received a distribution under section 995(b)(1)(D) as in effect for taxable years beginning before January 1, 1976, of $9,500, *i.e.*, $19,000 × 1/2. X is treated under subdivision (iii) (*b*) of this subparagraph as having $500, *i.e.*, $1,000 × $9,500/$19,000, from sources within the United States and $9,000 from sources without the United States.

(b) For 1972, assume that Y did not have any nonqualified export taxable income. Pursuant to subdivision (v)(*b*) of this subparagraph, at the beginning of 1974, $500 of Y's accumulated DISC income is attributable to nonqualified export taxable income, i.e., $1,000 – $500.

Example (2). The facts are the same as in example (1) except that in 1973, in addition to the taxable income described in such example, Y has $450 of taxable income from gross interest from producer's loans described in section 995(b)(1)(A). Under these facts, the deemed distribution of $450 under section 995(b)(1)(A) is treated in full under subdivision (i) of this subparagraph as gross income from sources within the United States. The deemed distribution under section 995(b)(1)(D) as in effect for taxable years beginning before January 1, 1976, of $9,500 will be treated in the same manner as in example (1), *i.e.*, $1,000 × $9,500/($19,450 – $450).

Example (3). (a) The facts are the same as in example (1) except that in 1973, in addition to the distribution described in such example, Y makes a deemed distribution taxable as a dividend of $100 under section 995(b)(1)(G) (relating to foreign investment attributable to producer's loans) and actual distributions of all of its previously taxed income and of $2,000 taxable as a dividend which reduces accumulated DISC income (as defined in subdivision (ii)(*b*) of this subparagraph). Undre § 1.996-3(b)(3), accumulated DISC income is first reduced by the deemed distribution of $100 and then by the actual distribution taxable as a dividend of $2,000. As indicated in example (1), for 1972 Y did not have any nonqualified export taxable income. Assume that Y had accumulated DISC income of $12,000 at the end of 1973, $500 of which under example (1) is attributable to nonqualified export taxable income.

(b) The distribution from previously taxed income is excluded from gross income pursuant to section 996(a)(3).

(c) Of the deemed distribution of $100, X is treated under subdivision (iv)(*b*) as having $4.17, i.e., $100 × 500/12,000, from sources within the United States and $95.83, i.e., $100 – $4.17, from sources without the United States.

(d) Of the actual distribution taxable as a dividend of $2,000, X is treated under subdivision (iv)(*b*) as having $83.33, i.e., $2000 × 500/12,000, from sources within the United States and $1,916.67, i.e., $2,000 – $83.33, from sources without the United States.

(e) The sum of the amounts deemed and actually distributed as dividends for 1973 that are treated as gross income from sources within the United States is as follows:

	Total dividend	Amount of dividend from sources within the United States
Deemed distribution under sec. 995(b)(1)(D) as in effect for taxable years beginning before Jan. 1, 1976	$9,500	$500.00
Deemed distribution under sec. 995(b)(1)(G)	100	4.17
Actual distribution that reduces accumulated DISC income	2,000	83.33
Totals	$11,600	$587.50

Thus, pursuant to subdivision (v)(*b*) of this subparagraph, at the beginning of 1974 Y has $412.50, *i.e.*, $1,000 – $587.50, of nonqualified export taxable income.

(f) The result would be the same if Y made an actual distribution taxable as a dividend of $1,500 on March 30, 1973, and another distribution of $500 on December 31, 1973.

Example (4). (a) Z is a corporation which uses the calendar year as its taxable year and which elects to be treated as a DISC beginning with 1972. W is its sole shareholder. At the end of 1976 Z has previously taxed income of $12,000 and accumulated DISC income of $4,000, $900 of which is attributable to nonqualified export taxable income. In 1977, Z has $20,050 of taxable income from qualified export receipts, of which $550 is from gross income from producer's loans described in section 995(b)(1)(A); Z has $950 of taxable income giving rise to gross receipts which are not qualified export receipts, of which $450 is gain described in section 995(b)(1)(B). Of its total taxable income of $21,000 (which is equal to its earnings and profits for 1977), $1,000 is attributable to sales of military property. Z has an international boycott factor (determined under section 999) of .10, and made an illegal bribe (within the meaning of section 162(c)) of $1,265. The proportion which the amount of Z's adjusted base period export receipts bears to Z's export gross receipts for 1977 is .40 (see section 995(e)(1)). Z makes a deemed distribution taxable as a dividend of $1,000 under section 995(b)(1)(G) (relating to foreign investment attributable to producer's loans) and actual distributions of $32,000.

(b) The deemed distributions of $550 under section 995(b)(1)(A) and $450 under section 995(b)(1)(B) are treated in full under subdivision (i) of this subparagraph as gross income from sources within the United States.

(c) Under these facts, Z has also made the following deemed distributions taxable as dividends to W under the following subdivisions of section 995(b)(1):

(D)	$ 500, *i.e.*, $1/2 \times$ $1,000.
(E)	7,800, *i.e.*, 40 × [$21,000 – $(550 + 450 + 500)].
(F) (i)	5,850, *i.e.*, $1/2 \times$ [$21,000 – $(550 + 450 + 500 + 7,800)].
(F) (ii)	585, *i.e.*, $5,850 × .10.
(F) (iii)	1,265
Total	$16,000

(d) The portion of the total amount of these deemed distributions ($16,000) that is treated under subdivision (iii) (*b*) as gross income from sources within the United States is computed as follows:

(1) The amount of nonqualified export taxable income is $500, *i.e.*, taxable income giving rise to gross receipts which are not qualified export receipts ($950) minus gain described in section 995(b)(1)(B) or (C) ($450).

(2) $500 × {$16,000/$[21,000 – (550 + 450)]} = $400. The remainder of these distributions, $15,600 ($16,000 minus $400), is treated under subdivision (iii)(*b*) of this subparagraph as gross income from sources without the United States.

(e) The earnings and profits accounts of Z at the end of 1977 are computed as follows:

	Total earnings and profits	Previously taxed income	Accumulated DISC income attributable to taxable income from transactions which give rise to gross receipts which are qualified export receipts	Accumulated DISC income attributable to taxable income from transactions which give rise to gross receipts which are not qualified export receipts
(1) Balance—January 1, 1977	$16,000	$12,000	$3,100	$900
(2) Earnings and profits for 1977, before actual and section 995(b)(1)(G) distributions	21,000	17,000	3,900	100 [1]
(3) Balance—December 31, 1977	$37,000	$29,000	$7,000	$1,000
(4) Distribution under section 995(b)(1)(G)		1,000	(875)	(125) [2]
(5) Balance	$37,000	$30,000	$6,125	$875
(6) Actual distribution	(32,000)	(30,000)	(1,750)	(250) [3]
(7) Balance—January 1, 1978	$5,000	. . .	$4,375	$625

[1] The total of nonqualified export taxable income ($500) minus the portion of such income, under subdivision (iii)(*b*) of this subparagraph, deemed distributed pursuant to section 995(b)(1)(D), (E), and (F) ($400), as computed under (d)(2) of this example.

[2] Under subdivision (iv)(*b*) of this subparagraph,

$$\frac{\$1,000}{\$8,000} \times \$1,000.$$

[3] Under subdivision (iv)(*b*) of this subparagraph,

$$\frac{\$1,000}{\$8,000} \times \$2,000 \text{ (amount of actual distribution that reduces accumulated DISC income).}$$

(6) *Substitute dividend payments.*—A substitute dividend payment is a payment, made to the transferor of a security in a securities lending transaction or a sale-repurchase transaction, of an amount equivalent to a dividend distribution which the owner of the transferred security is entitled to receive during the term of the transaction. A securities lending transaction is a transfer of one or more securities that is described in section 1058(a) or a substantially similar transaction. A sale-repurchase transaction is an agreement under which a person transfers a security in exchange for cash and simultaneously agrees to receive substantially identical securities from the transferee in the future in exchange for cash. A substitute dividend payment shall be sourced in the same manner as the distributions with respect to the transferred security for purposes of this section and § 1.862-1. See also §§ 1.864-5(b)(2)(iii), 1.871-7(b)(2) and 1.881-2(b)(2) for the character of such payments and § 1.894-1(c) for the application of tax treaties to these transactions.

(b) *Special rules.*—(1) *Foreign corporation having no gross income for period preceding declaration of dividend.*—If the foreign corporation has no gross income from any source for the 3-year period (or part thereof) specified in paragraph (a)(3)(i) of this section, the 50-percent test, or the apportionment formula, as the case may be, described in such paragraph shall be applied solely with respect to the taxable year of such corporation in which the declaration of the dividend occurs. This subparagraph applies whether the lack of gross income for the 3-year period (or part thereof) stems from the business inactivity of the foreign corporation, from the fact that such corporation is newly created or organized, or from any other cause.

(2) *Transitional rule.*—For purposes of applying paragraph (a)(3)(i) of this section, the gross income of the foreign corporation for any period before the first taxable year beginning after December 31, 1966, which is from sources within the United States (determined as provided by sections 861 through 863, and the regulations thereunder, as in effect immediately before amendment by section 102 of the Foreign Investors Tax Act of 1966 (Pub. L. 89-809, 80 Stat. 1541)) shall be treated as gross income for such period which is effectively connected with the conduct of a trade or business within the United States by such foreign corporation.

(3) *Gross income determinations.*—In making determinations under subparagraph (2) or (3) of paragraph (a) of this section, or subparagraph (2) of this paragraph—

(i) The gross income of a domestic corporation is to be determined by excluding any items specifically excluded from gross income under chapter 1 of the Code,

(ii) The gross income of a foreign corporation which is effectively connected with the conduct of a trade or business in the United States is to be determined under section 882(b)(2) and by excluding any items specifically excluded from gross income under chapter 1 of the Code, and

(iii) The gross income from all sources of a foreign corporation is to be determined without regard to section 882(b) and without excluding any items otherwise specifically excluded from gross income under chapter 1 of the Code.

(c) *Statement with return.*—Any taxpayer who is required to file a return and applies any provision of this section to exclude any dividend from his gross income must file with his return a statement setting forth the amount so excluded, the date of its receipt, the name and address of the corporation paying the dividend, and, if known, the location of the records which substantiate the amount of the exclusion. A statement from the paying corporation setting forth such information and indicating the amount of the dividend to be treated as income from sources within the United States may be used for this purpose. See §§ 1.6012-1(b)(1)(i) and 1.6012-2(g)(1)(i).

(d) *Source of income inclusions under sections 951, 951A, and 1293 and associated section 78 dividends.*—For purposes of sections 861 and sections 862 and §§ 1.861-1 and 1.862-1, and for purposes of applying this section, the amount included in gross income of a United States person under sections 951, sections 951A, and sections 1293 and the associated section 78 dividend for the taxable year with respect to a foreign corporation are treated as dividends received directly by the United States person from the foreign corporation that generated the inclusion. See section 904(h) and § 1.904-5(m) for rules concerning the resourcing of inclusions under sections 951, sections 951A, and sections 1293.

(e) *Applicability dates.*—Except as otherwise provided in this paragraph (e) this section applies with respect to dividends received or accrued after December 31, 1966. Paragraph (a)(5) of this section applies to certain dividends from a DISC or former DISC in taxable years ending after December 31, 1971. Paragraph (a)(6) of this section is applicable to payments made after November 13, 1997. For purposes of paragraph (a)(5) of this section, any reference to a distribution taxable as a dividend under section 995(b)(1)(F)(ii) and (iii) for taxable years beginning after December 31, 1975, shall also constitute a reference to any distribution taxable as a dividend under section 995(b)(1)(F)(ii) and (iii) for taxable years beginning after November 30, 1975, but before January 1, 1976. For corresponding rules applicable with respect to dividends received or accrued before January 1, 1967, see 26 CFR 1.861-3 (Rev. as of Jan. 1, 1972). Paragraph (a)(2) of this section applies to taxable years ending after April 9, 2008. Paragraph (d) of this section applies to taxable years ending on or after November 2, 2020.[Reg. § 1.861-3.]

□ [*T.D.* 6258, 10-23-57. *Amended by T.D.* 6830, 6-22-65, *T.D.* 7378, 9-29-75, *T.D.* 7472, 2-28-77, *T.D.* 7591, 1-19-79; *T.D.* 7854, 11-15-82; *T.D.* 8735, 10-6-97; *T.D.* 9194, 4-6-2005, *T.D.* 9391, 4-4-2008 *and T.D.* 9959, 12-28-2021.]

§ 1.861-4. Compensation for labor or personal services.—(a) *Compensation for labor or personal services performed wholly within the United States.*—(1) Generally, compensation for labor or personal services, including fees, commissions, fringe benefits, and similar items, performed wholly within the United States is gross income from sources within the United States. Gross income from sources within the United States includes compensation for labor or personal services performed in the United States irrespective of the residence of the payer, the place in which the contract for service was made, or the place or time of payment; except that such compensation shall be deemed not to be income from sources within the United States, if—

(i) The labor or services are performed by a nonresident alien individual temporarily present in the United States for a period or periods not exceeding a total of 90 days during his taxable year,

(ii) The compensation for such labor or services does not exceed in the aggregate a gross amount of $3,000, and

(iii) The compensation is for labor or services performed as an employee of, or under any form of contract with—

(*a*) A nonresident alien individual, foreign partnership, or foreign corporation, not engaged in trade or business within the United States, or

(*b*) An individual who is a citizen or resident of the United States, a domestic partnership, or a domestic corporation, if such labor or services are performed for an office or place of business maintained in a foreign country or in a possession of the United States by such individual, partnership, or corporation.

(2) As a general rule, the term "day," as used in subparagraph (1)(i) of this paragraph, means a calendar day during any portion of which the nonresident alien individual is physically present in the United States.

(3) Solely for purposes of applying this paragraph, the nonresident alien individual, foreign partnership, or foreign corporation for which the nonresident alien individual is performing personal services in the United States shall not be considered to be engaged in trade or business in the United States by reason of the performance of such services by such individual.

(4) In determining for purposes of subparagraph (1)(ii) of this paragraph whether compensation received by the nonresident alien individual exceeds in the aggregate a gross amount of $3,000, any amounts received by the individual from an employer as advances or reimbursements for travel expenses incurred on behalf of the employer shall be omitted from the compensation received by the individual, to the extent of expenses incurred, where he was required to account and did account to his employer for such expenses and has met the tests for such accounting provided in § 1.162-17 and paragraph (e)(4) of § 1.274-5. If advances or reimbursements exceed such expenses, the amount of the excess shall be included as compensation for personal services for purposes of such subparagraph. Pensions and retirement pay attributable to labor or personal services performed in the United States are not to be taken into account for purposes of subparagraph (1)(ii) of this paragraph.

(5) For definition of the term "United States," when used in a geographical sense, see sections 638 and 7701(a)(9).

(b) *Compensation for labor or personal services performed partly within and partly without the United States.*—(1) *Compensation for labor or personal services performed by persons other than individuals.*—(i) *In general.*—In the case of compensation for labor or personal services performed partly within and partly without the United States by a person other than an individual, the part of that compensation that is attributable to the labor or personal services performed within the United States, and that is therefore included in gross income as income from sources within the United States, is determined on the basis that most correctly reflects the proper source of the income under the facts and circumstances of the particular case. In many cases, the facts and circumstances will be such that an apportionment on the time basis, as defined in paragraph (b)(2)(ii)(E) of this section, will be acceptable.

(ii) *Example.*—The application of paragraph (b)(1)(i) is illustrated by the following example.

Example. Corp X, a domestic corporation, receives compensation of $150,000 under a contract for services to be performed concurrently in the United States and in several foreign countries by numerous Corp X employees. Each Corp X employee performing services under this contract performs his or her services exclusively in one jurisdiction. Although the number of employees (and hours spent by employees) performing services under the contract within the United States equals the number of employees (and hours spent by employees) performing services under the contract without the United States, the compensation paid to employees performing services under the contract within the United States is higher because of the more sophisticated nature of the services performed by the employees within the United States. Accordingly, the payroll cost for employees performing services under the contract within the United States is $20,000 out of a total contract payroll cost of $30,000. Under these facts and circumstances, a determination based upon relative payroll costs would be the basis that most correctly reflects the proper source of the income received under the contract. Thus, of the $150,000 of compensation included in Corp X's gross income, $100,000 ($150,000 × $20,000/$30,000) is attributable to the labor or personal services performed within the United States and $50,000 ($150,000 × $10,000/$30,000) is attributable to the labor or personal services performed without the United States.

(2) *Compensation for labor or personal services performed by an individual.*—(i) *In general.*—Except as provided in paragraph (b)(2)(ii) of this section, in the case of compensation for labor or personal services performed partly within and partly without the United States by an individual, the part of such compensation that is attributable to the labor or personal services performed within the United States, and that is therefore included in gross income as income from sources within the United States, is determined on the basis that most correctly reflects the proper source of that income under the facts and circumstances of the particular case. In many cases, the facts and circumstances will be such that an apportionment on a time basis, as defined in paragraph (b)(2)(ii)(E) of this section, will be acceptable.

(ii) *Employee compensation.*—(A) *In general.*—Except as provided in paragraph (b)(2)(ii)(B) or (C) of this section, in the case of compensation for labor or personal services performed partly within and partly without the United States by an individual as an employee, the part of such compensation that is attributable to the labor or personal services performed within the United States, and that is therefore included in gross income as income from sources within the United States, is determined on a time basis, as defined in paragraph (b)(2)(ii)(E) of this section.

(B) *Certain fringe benefits sourced on a geographical basis.*—Except as provided in paragraph (b)(2)(ii)(C) of this section, items of compensation of an individual as an employee for labor or personal services performed partly within and partly without the United States that are described in paragraphs (b)(2)(ii)(D)(*1*) through (*6*) of this section are sourced on a geographical basis in accordance with those paragraphs.

(C) *Exceptions and special rules.*—(*1*) *Alternative basis.*—(*i*) *Individual as an employee generally.*—An individual may determine the source of his or her compensation as an employee for labor or personal services performed partly within and partly without the United States under an alternative basis if the individual establishes to the satisfaction of the Commissioner that, under the facts and circumstances of the particular case, the alternative basis more properly determines the source of the compensation than a basis described in paragraph (b)(2)(ii)(A) or (B), whichever is applicable, of this section. An individual that uses an alternative basis must retain in his or her records documentation setting forth why the alternative basis more properly determines the source of the compensation. In addition, the individual must provide the information related to the alternative basis required by applicable Federal tax forms and accompanying instructions.

(*ii*) *Determination by Commissioner.*—The Commissioner may, under the facts and circumstances of the particular case, determine the source of compensation that is received by an individual as an employee for labor or personal services performed partly within and partly without the United States under an alternative basis other than a basis described in paragraph (b)(2)(ii)(A) or (B) of this section if such compensation either is not for a specific time period or constitutes in substance a fringe benefit described in paragraph (b)(2)(ii)(D) of this section notwithstanding a failure to meet any requirement of paragraph (b)(2)(ii)(D) of this section. The Commissioner may make this determination only if such alternative basis determines the source of compensation in a more reasonable manner than the basis used by the individual pursuant to paragraph (b)(2)(ii)(A) or (B) of this section.

(*2*) *Ruling or other administrative pronouncement with respect to groups of taxpayers.*—The Commissioner may, by ruling or other administrative pronouncement applying to similarly situated taxpayers generally, permit individuals to determine the source of their compensation as an employee for labor or personal services performed partly within and partly without the United States under an alternative basis. Any such individual shall be treated as having met the requirement to establish such alternative basis to the satisfaction of the Commissioner under the facts and circumstances of the particular case, provided that the individual meets the other requirements of paragraph (b)(2)(ii)(C)(*1*)(*i*) of this section. The Commissioner also may, by ruling or other administrative pronouncement, indicate the circumstances in which he will require individuals to determine the source of certain compensation as an employee for labor or personal services performed partly within and partly without the United States under an alternative basis pursuant to the authority under paragraph (b)(2)(ii)(C)(*1*)(*ii*) of this section.

(*3*) *Artists and athletes.*—[Reserved.]

(D) *Fringe benefits sourced on a geographical basis.*—Except as provided in paragraph (b)(2)(ii)(C) of this section, compensation of an individual as an employee for labor or personal services performed partly within and partly without the United States in the form of the following fringe benefits is sourced on a geographical basis as indicated in this paragraph (b)(2)(ii)(D). The amount of the compensation in the form of the fringe benefit must be reasonable, and the individual must substantiate such amounts by adequate records or by sufficient evidence under rules similar to those set forth in § 1.274-5T(c) or (h) or § 1.132-5. For purposes of this paragraph (b)(2)(ii)(D), the term *principal place of work* has the same meaning that it has for purposes of section 217 and § 1.217-2(c)(3).

(*1*) *Housing fringe benefit.*—The source of compensation in the form of a housing fringe benefit is determined based on the location of the individual's principal place of work. For purposes of this paragraph (b)(2)(ii)(D)(*1*), a housing fringe benefit includes payments to or on behalf of an individual (and the individual's family if the family resides with the individual) only for rent, utilities (other than telephone charges), real and personal property insurance, occupancy taxes not deductible under section 164 or 216(a), nonrefundable fees paid for securing a leasehold, rental of furniture and accessories, household repairs, residential parking, and the fair rental value of housing provided in kind by the individual's employer. A housing fringe benefit does not include payments for expenses or items set forth in § 1.911-4(b)(2).

(*2*) *Education fringe benefit.*—The source of compensation in the form of an education fringe benefit for the education expenses of the individual's dependents is determined based on the location of the individual's principal place of work. For purposes of this paragraph (b)(2)(ii)(D)(*2*), an education fringe benefit includes payments only for qualified tuition and expenses of the type described in section 530(b)(4)(A)(i) (regardless of whether incurred in connection with enrollment or attendance at a school) and expenditures for room and board and uniforms as described in section 530(b)(4)(A)(ii) with respect to education at an elementary or secondary educational institution.

(3) Local transportation fringe benefit.—The source of compensation in the form of a local transportation fringe benefit is determined based on the location of the individual's principal place of work. For purposes of this paragraph (b)(2)(ii)(D)(*3*), an individual's local transportation fringe benefit is the amount that the individual receives as compensation for local transportation of the individual or the individual's spouse or dependents at the location of the individual's principal place of work. The amount treated as a local transportation fringe benefit is limited to the actual expenses incurred for local transportation and the fair rental value of any vehicle provided by the employer and used predominantly by the individual or the individual's spouse or dependents for local transportation. For this purpose, actual expenses incurred for local transportation do not include the cost (including interest) of the purchase by the individual, or on behalf of the individual, of an automobile or other vehicle.

(4) Tax reimbursement fringe benefit.—The source of compensation in the form of a foreign tax reimbursement fringe benefit is determined based on the location of the jurisdiction that imposed the tax for which the individual is reimbursed.

(5) Hazardous or hardship duty pay fringe benefit.—The source of compensation in the form of a hazardous or hardship duty pay fringe benefit is determined based on the location of the hazardous or hardship duty zone for which the hazardous or hardship duty pay fringe benefit is paid. For purposes of this paragraph (b)(2)(ii)(D)(*5*), a hazardous or hardship duty zone is any place in a foreign country which is either designated by the Secretary of State as a place where living conditions are extraordinarily difficult, notably unhealthy, or where excessive physical hardships exist, and for which a post differential of 15 percent or more would be provided under section 5925(b) of Title 5 of the U.S. Code to any officer or employee of the U.S. Government present at that place, or where a civil insurrection, civil war, terrorism, or wartime conditions threatens physical harm or imminent danger to the health and well-being of the individual. Compensation provided an employee during the period that the employee performs labor or personal services in a hazardous or hardship duty zone may be treated as a hazardous or hardship duty pay fringe benefit only if the employer provides the hazardous or hardship duty pay fringe benefit only to employees performing labor or personal services in a hazardous or hardship duty zone. The amount of compensation treated as a hazardous or hardship duty pay fringe benefit may not exceed the maximum amount that the U. S. government would allow its officers or employees present at that location.

(6) Moving expense reimbursement fringe benefit.—Except as otherwise provided in this paragraph (b)(2)(ii)(D)(*6*), the source of compensation in the form of a moving expense reimbursement is determined based on the location of the employee's new principal place of work. The source of such compensation is determined based on the location of the employee's former principal place of work, however, if the individual provides sufficient evidence that such determination of source is more appropriate under the facts and circumstances of the particular case. For purposes of this paragraph (b)(2)(ii)(D)(*6*), sufficient evidence generally requires an agreement, between the employer and the employee, or a written statement of company policy, which is reduced to writing before the move and which is entered into or established to induce the employee or employees to move to another country. Such written statement or agreement must state that the employer will reimburse the employee for moving expenses that the employee incurs to return to the employee's former principal place of work regardless of whether he or she continues to work for the employer after returning to that location. The writing may contain certain conditions upon which the right to reimbursement is determined as long as those conditions set forth standards that are definitely ascertainable and can only be fulfilled prior to, or through completion of, the employee's return move to the employee's former principal place of work.

(E) *Time basis.*—The amount of compensation for labor or personal services performed within the United States determined on a time basis is the amount that bears the same relation to the individual's total compensation as the number of days of performance of the labor or personal services by the individual within the United States bears to his or her total number of days of performance of labor or personal services. A unit of time less than a day may be appropriate for purposes of this calculation. The time period for which the compensation for labor or personal services is made is presumed to be the calendar year in which the labor or personal services are performed, unless the taxpayer establishes to the satisfaction of the Commissioner, or the Commissioner determines, that another distinct, separate, and continuous period of time is more appropriate. For example, a transfer during a year from a position in the United States to a foreign posting that lasted through the end of that year would generally establish two separate time periods within that taxable year. The first of these time periods would be the portion of the year preceding the start of the foreign posting, and the second of these time periods would be the portion of the year following the start of the foreign posting. However, in the case of a foreign posting that requires short-term returns to the United States to perform services for the employer, such short-term returns would not be sufficient to establish distinct, separate, and continuous time periods within the foreign posting time period but would be relevant to the allocation of compensation relating to the overall time period. In each case, the source of the compensation on a time basis is based upon the number of days (or unit of time less than a day, if appropriate) in that separate time period.

(F) *Multi-year compensation arrangements.*—The source of multi-year compensation is determined generally on a time basis, as defined in paragraph (b)(2)(ii)(E) of this section, over the period to which such compensation is attributable. For purposes of this paragraph (b)(2)(ii)(F), *multi-year compensation* means compensation that is included in the income of an individual in one taxable year but that is attributable to a period that includes two or more taxable years. The determination of the period to which such compensation is attributable, for purposes of determining its source, is based upon the facts and circumstances of the particular case. For example, an amount of compensation that specifically relates to a period of time that includes several calendar years is attributable to the entirety of that multi-year period. The amount of such compensation that is treated as from sources within the United States is the amount that bears the same relationship to the total multi-year compensation as the number of days (or unit of time less than a day, if appropriate) that labor or personal services were performed within the United States in connection with the project bears to the total number of days (or unit of time less than a day, if appropriate) that labor or personal services were performed in connection with the project. In the case of stock options, the facts and circumstances generally will be such that the applicable period to which the compensation is attributable is the period between the grant of an option and the date on which all employment-related conditions for its exercise have been satisfied (the vesting of the option).

(G) *Examples.*—The following examples illustrate the application of this paragraph (b)(2)(ii):

Example 1. B, a nonresident alien individual, was employed by Corp M, a domestic corporation, from March 1 to December 25 of the taxable year, a total of 300 days, for which B received compensation in the amount of $80,000. Under B's employment contract with Corp M, B was subject to call at all times by Corp M and was in a payment status on a 7-day week basis. Pursuant to that contract, B performed services (or was available to perform services) within the United States for 180 days and performed services (or was available to perform services) without the United States for 120 days. None of B's $80,000 compensation was for fringe benefits as identified in paragraph (b)(2)(ii)(D) of this section. B determined the amount of compensation that is attributable to his labor or personal services performed within the United States on a time basis under paragraph (b)(2)(ii)(A) and (E) of this section. B did not assert, pursuant to paragraph (b)(2)(ii)(C)(*1*)(*i*) of this section, that, under the particular facts and circumstances, an alternative basis more properly determines the source of that compensation than the time basis. Therefore, B must include in income from sources within the United States $48,000 ($80,000 × 180/300) of his compensation from Corporation M.

Example 2. (i) Same facts as in *Example 1* except that Corp M had a company-wide arrangement with its employees, including B, that they would receive an education fringe benefit, as described in paragraph (b)(2)(ii)(D)(2) of this section, while working in the United States. During the taxable year, B incurred education expenses for his dependent daughter that qualified for the education fringe benefit in the amount of $10,000, for which B received a reimbursement from Corp M. B did not maintain adequate records or sufficient evidence of this fringe benefit as required by paragraph (b)(2)(ii)(D) of this section. When B filed his Federal income tax return for the taxable year, B did not apply paragraphs (b)(2)(ii)(B) and (D)(2) of this section to treat the compensation in the form of the education fringe benefit as income from sources within the United States, the location of his principal place of work during the 300-day period. Rather, B combined the $10,000 reimbursement with his base compensation of

$80,000 and applied the time basis of paragraph (b)(2)(ii)(A) of this section to determine the source of his gross income.

(ii) On audit, B argues that because he failed to substantiate the education fringe benefit in accordance with paragraph (b)(2)(ii)(D) of this section, his entire employment compensation from Corp M is sourced on a time basis pursuant to paragraph (b)(2)(ii)(A) of this section. The Commissioner, after reviewing Corp M's fringe benefit arrangement, determines, pursuant to paragraph (b)(2)(ii)(C)(*1*)(*ii*) of this section, that the $10,000 educational expense reimbursement constitutes in substance a fringe benefit described in paragraph (b)(2)(ii)(D)(*2*) of this section, notwithstanding a failure to meet all of the requirements of paragraph (b)(2)(ii)(D) of this section, and that an alternative geographic source basis, under the facts and circumstances of this particular case, is a more reasonable manner to determine the source of the compensation than the time basis used by B.

Example 3. (i) A, a United States citizen, is employed by Corp N, a domestic corporation. A's principal place of work is in the United States. A earns an annual salary of $100,000. During the first quarter of the calendar year (which is also A's taxable year), A performed services entirely within the United States. At the beginning of the second quarter of the calendar year, A was transferred to Country X for the remainder of the year and received, in addition to her annual salary, $30,000 in fringe benefits that are attributable to her new principal place of work in Country X. Corp N paid these fringe benefits separately from A's annual salary. Corp N supplied A with a statement detailing that $25,000 of the fringe benefit was paid for housing, as defined in paragraph (b)(2)(ii)(D)(*1*) of this section, and $5,000 of the fringe benefit was paid for local transportation, as defined in paragraph (b)(2)(ii)(D)(*3*) of this section. None of the local transportation fringe benefit is excluded from the employee's gross income as a qualified transportation fringe benefit under section 132(a)(5). Under A's employment contract, A was required to work on a 5-day week basis, Monday through Friday. During the last three quarters of the year, A performed services 30 days in the United States and 150 days in Country X and other foreign countries.

(ii) A determined the source of all of her compensation from Corp N pursuant to paragraphs (b)(2)(ii)(A), (B), and (D)(*1*) and (*3*) of this section. A did not assert, pursuant to paragraph (b)(2)(ii)(C)(*1*)(*i*) of this section, that, under the particular facts and circumstances, an alternative basis more properly determines the source of that compensation than the bases set forth in paragraphs (b)(2)(ii)(A), (B), and (D)(*1*) and (*3*) of this section. However, in applying the time basis set forth in paragraph (b)(2)(ii)(E) of this section, A establishes to the satisfaction of the Commissioner that the first quarter of the calendar year and the last three quarters of the calendar year are two separate, distinct, and continuous periods of time. Accordingly, $25,000 of A's annual salary is attributable to the first quarter of the year (25 percent of $100,000). This amount is entirely compensation that was attributable to the labor or personal services performed within the United States and is, therefore, included in gross income as income from sources within the United States. The balance of A's compensation as an employee of Corp N, $105,000 (which includes the $30,000 in fringe benefits that are attributable to the location of A's principal place of work in Country X), is compensation attributable to the final three quarters of her taxable year. During those three quarters, A's periodic performance of services in the United States does not result in distinct, separate, and continuous periods of time. Of the $75,000 paid for annual salary, $12,500 (30/180 × $75,000) is compensation that was attributable to the labor or personal services performed within the United States and $62,500 (150/180 × $75,000) is compensation that was attributable to the labor or personal services performed outside the United States. Pursuant to paragraphs (b)(2)(ii)(B) and (D)(*1*) and (*3*) of this section, A sourced the $25,000 received for the housing fringe benefit and the $5,000 received for the local transportation fringe benefit based on the location of her principal place of work, Country X. Accordingly, A included the $30,000 in fringe benefits in her gross income as income from sources without the United States.

Example 4. Same facts as in *Example 3.* Of the 150 days during which A performed services in Country X and in other foreign countries (during the final three quarters of A's taxable year), she performed 30 days of those services in Country Y. Country Y is a country designated by the Secretary of State as a place where living conditions are extremely difficult, notably unhealthy, or where excessive physical hardships exist and for which a post differential of 15 percent or more would be provided under section 5925(b) of Title 5 of the U.S. Code to any officer or employee of the U.S. government present at that place. Corp N has a policy of paying its employees a $65 premium per day for each day worked in countries so designated. The $65 premium per day does not exceed the maximum amount that the U. S. government would pay its officers or employees stationed in Country Y. Because A performed services in Country Y for 30 days, she earned additional compensation of $1,950. The $1,950 is considered a hazardous duty or hardship pay fringe benefit and is sourced under paragraphs (b)(2)(ii)(B) and (D)(*5*) of this section based on the location of the hazardous or hardship duty zone, Country Y. Accordingly, A included the amount of the hazardous duty or hardship pay fringe benefit ($1,950) in her gross income as income from sources without the United States.

Example 5. (i) During 2006 and 2007, Corp P, a domestic corporation, employed four United States citizens, E, F, G, and H to work in its manufacturing plant in Country V. As part of his or her compensation package, each employee arranged for local transportation unrelated to Corp P's business needs. None of the local transportation fringe benefit is excluded from the employee's gross income as a qualified transportation fringe benefit under section 132(a)(5) and (f).

(ii) Under the terms of the compensation package that E negotiated with Corp P, Corp P permitted E to use an automobile owned by Corp P. In addition, Corp P agreed to reimburse E for all expenses incurred by E in maintaining and operating the automobile, including gas and parking. Provided that the local transportation fringe benefit meets the requirements of paragraph (b)(2)(ii)(D)(*3*) of this section, E's compensation with respect to the fair rental value of the automobile and reimbursement for the expenses E incurred is sourced under paragraphs (b)(2)(ii)(B) and (D)(*3*) of this section based on E's principal place of work in Country V. Thus, the local transportation fringe benefit will be included in E's gross income as income from sources without the United States.

(iii) Under the terms of the compensation package that F negotiated with Corp P, Corp P let F use an automobile owned by Corp P. However, Corp P did not agree to reimburse F for any expenses incurred by F in maintaining and operating the automobile. Provided that the local transportation fringe benefit meets the requirements of paragraph (b)(2)(ii)(D)(*3*) of this section, F's compensation with respect to the fair rental value of the automobile is sourced under paragraphs (b)(2)(ii)(B) and (D)(*3*) of this section based on F's principal place of work in Country V. Thus, the local transportation fringe benefit will be included in F's gross income as income from sources without the United States.

(iv) Under the terms of the compensation package that G negotiated with Corp P, Corp P agreed to reimburse G for the purchase price of an automobile that G purchased in Country V. Corp P did not agree to reimburse G for any expenses incurred by G in maintaining and operating the automobile. Because the cost to purchase an automobile is not a local transportation fringe benefit as defined in paragraph (b)(2)(ii)(D)(*3*) of this section, the source of the compensation to G will be determined pursuant to paragraph (b)(2)(ii)(A) or (C) of this section.

(v) Under the terms of the compensation package that H negotiated with Corp P, Corp P agreed to reimburse H for the expenses that H incurred in maintaining and operating an automobile, including gas and parking, which H purchased in Country V. Provided that the local transportation fringe benefit meets the requirements of paragraph (b)(2)(ii)(D)(*3*) of this section, H's compensation with respect to the reimbursement for the expenses H incurred is sourced under paragraphs (b)(2)(ii)(B) and (D)(*3*) of this section based on H's principal place of work in Country V. Thus, the local transportation fringe benefit will be included in H's gross income as income from sources without the United States.

Example 6. (i) On January 1, 2006, Company Q compensates employee J with a grant of options to which section 421 does not apply that do not have a readily ascertainable fair market value when granted. The stock options permit J to purchase 100 shares of Company Q stock for $5 per share. The stock options do not become exercisable unless and until J performs services for Company Q (or a related company) for 5 years. J works for Company Q for the 5 years required by the stock option grant. In years 2006-08, J performs all of his services for Company Q within the United States. In 2009, J performs 1/2 of his services for Company Q within the United States and 1/2 of his services for Company Q without the United States. In year 2010, J performs his services entirely without the United States. On December 31, 2012, J exercises the options when the stock is worth $10 per share. J recognizes $500 in taxable compensation (($10-$5) X 100) in 2012.

(ii) Under the facts and circumstances, the applicable period is the 5-year period between the date of grant (January 1, 2006) and the date the stock options become exercisable (December 31, 2010). On the date the stock options become exercisable, J performs all services necessary to obtain the compensation from Company Q. Accordingly, the services performed after the date the stock options become exercisable are not taken into account in sourcing the compensation from the stock options. Therefore, pursuant to paragraph (b)(2)(ii)(A), since J performs 3 1/2 years of services for Company Q within the United States and 1 1/2 years of services for Company Q without the United States during the 5-year period, 7/10 of the $500 of compensation (or $350) recognized in 2012 is income from sources within the United States and the remaining 3/10 of the compensation (or $150) is income from sources without the United States.

(c) *Coastwise travel.*—Except as to income excluded by paragraph (a) of this section, wages received for services rendered inside the territorial limits of the United States and wages of an alien seaman earned on a coastwise vessel are to be regarded as from sources within the United States.

(d) *Effective date.*—This section applies with respect to taxable years beginning after December 31, 1966. For corresponding rules applicable to taxable years beginning before January 1, 1967, see 26 CFR 1.861-4 (Rev. as of Jan. 1, 1972). Paragraph (b) and the first sentence of paragraph (a)(1) of this section apply to taxable years beginning on or after July 14, 2005. [Reg. § 1.861-4.]

□ [*T.D.* 6258, 10-23-57. *Amended by T.D.* 7378, 9-29-75 *and T.D.* 9212, 7-13-2005.]

Proposed Amendments to Regulation

§ 1.861-4. Compensation for labor or personal services.

* * *

(b) * * *

(2) * * *

(ii) * * *

(G) *Event basis.*—The amount of compensation for labor or personal services determined on an event basis is the amount of the person's compensation which, based on the facts and circumstances, is attributable to the labor or personal services performed at the location of a specific event. The source of compensation for labor or personal services determined on an event basis is the location of the specific event. A basis that purports to determine the source of compensation from the performance of labor or personal services at a specific event, whether on a time basis or otherwise, by taking into account the location of labor or personal services performed in preparation for the performance of labor or personal services at the specific event will generally not be the basis that most correctly determines the source of the compensation.

(c) *Examples.*—* * *

Example 7. P, a citizen and resident of Country A, is paid by Company Z to make a presentation in the United States in 2009. In 2010, Company Z pays P to make 10 presentations, four of which are in the United States and six of which are outside the United States. P is compensated separately by Company Z for each presentation. For some presentations P receives a flat fee from Company Z. For the remaining presentations P receives compensation that is based on a formula. Under the facts and circumstances of the particular case, the source of the compensation for each presentation is most correctly reflected on an event basis, as defined in paragraph (b)(2)(ii)(G) of this section. Because P is compensated separately for each presentation, the source of P's compensation from Company Z for the 2009 presentation within the United States and the four 2010 presentations in the United States will be from sources in the United States. The amounts will be determined based on the flat fee or the formula as contractually determined.

Example 8. (i) *Facts.* Group B, a Country N corporation, is a musical group. All of the members of Group B are citizens and residents of Country N. Group B has an employment arrangement with Corp Y, a Country N corporation, to perform as directed by Corp Y. Corp Y and a tour promoter enter into a contract to provide the services of Group B to perform in musical concerts in the United States and Country M during a 45-day period. Under the contract, Group B performs concerts in 15 cities, 10 of which are in the United States. Prior to entering the United States, Group B spends 60 days rehearsing and preparing in Country N. Under the contract with Corp Y, Group B receives a flat fee of $10,000,000 for performing in all 15 cities. The fee is based on expected revenues from the musical concerts. Each concert is expected to require a similar amount and type of labor or personal services by Group B. At the end of the tour, an analysis of the revenues from all of the concerts shows that 80% of the total revenues from the tour were from the performances within the United States.

(ii) *Analysis.* Under the facts and circumstances basis of paragraph (b)(1) of this section, the source of the compensation received under the contract is most correctly reflected on an event basis, as defined in paragraph (b)(2)(ii)(G) of this section, with amounts determined based on the relative gross receipts attributable to the performances within and without the United States. Thus, of the $10,000,000 of compensation included in Group B's gross income, $8,000,000 ($10,000,000 × .80) is attributable to labor or personal services performed by Group B within the United States and $2,000,000 ($10,000,000 × .20) is attributable to the labor or personal services performed by Group B without the United States.

Example 9. (i) *Facts.* A, a citizen and resident of Country M, is an employee of Corp X, a Country M corporation. During 2008, Corp X is contractually obligated to provide A's services to perform in a specific athletic event in the United States. Under A's employment contract with Corp X, A is required to perform at a professional level that requires training and other preparation prior to the event. A undertakes all of this preparation in Country M. Solely as a result of A's performance at the athletic event in the United States, A receives $2,000,000 from Corp. X.

(ii) *Analysis.* The entire $2,000,000 received by A for performing labor or personal services at the athletic event in the United States is income from sources within the United States on an event basis as defined in paragraph (b)(2)(ii)(G) of this section. A's compensation is attributable entirely to labor or personal services performed within the United States at the athletic event. It is inappropriate to conclude that the source of A's compensation for labor or personal services is performed partly within and partly without the United States simply because A's preparation for the athletic event involved activities in Country M.

Example 10. (i) *Facts.* X, a citizen and resident of Country M, is employed under a standard player's contract by a professional sports team (Team) that plays its games both within and without the United States during its season. The term of the contract is for twelve months beginning on October 1. Under the contract, X's salary could be paid in semi-monthly installments beginning with the first game of the regular season and ending with the final game played by the Team. Alternatively, because the regular playing season was shorter than the one-year period covered by the contract, X had the option to receive his salary over a twelve-month period. X elected this option. In addition, during the period of this employment contract, X, as an employee of Team, was required to practice at the direction of the Team as well as to participate in games. During 2008, X participated in all practices and games of Team and received a salary. Team qualified for postseason games in 2008. X also received in 2008 additional amounts for playing in preseason and postseason games for the Team.

(ii) *Analysis.* The salary paid to X by the Team is considered to be personal services compensation of X that X received as an employee of the Team. The source of this compensation within the United States is determined under the time basis method described in paragraph (b)(2)(ii)(A) of this section and accordingly is determined based upon the number of days X performed services for the Team within the United States during 2008 over the total number of days that X performed services for the Team during 2008. The source of the additional amounts X received for playing in preseason and postseason games is determined under the event basis method described in paragraph (b)(2)(ii)(G) of this section and accordingly is determined based on the location where each such preseason or postseason game was played.

* * *

[Prop. Reg. § 1.861-4.]

[Proposed 10-17-2007.]

§ 1.861-5. Rentals and royalties.—Gross income from sources within the United States includes rentals or royalties from property located in the United States or from any interest in such property, including rentals or royalties for the use of, or for the privilege of using, in the United States, patents, copyrights, secret processes and formulas, good will, trademarks, trade brands, franchises, and other like property. The income arising from the rental of property, whether tangible or intangible, located within the United States, or from the use of property, whether tangible or intangible, within the United States, is from sources within the United States. For taxable years beginning after December 31, 1966, gains described in section 871(a)(1)(D) and section 881(a)(4) from the sale or exchange after October 4, 1966, of patents, copyrights, and other like property shall be treated, as provided in section 871(e)(2), as rentals or royalties for the use of, or privilege of using, property or an interest in property. See paragraph (e) of § 1.871-11. [Reg. § 1.861-5.]

□ [*T.D.* 6258, 10-23-57. *Amended by T.D.* 7378, 9-29-75.]

§ 1.861-6. Sale of real property.—Gross income from sources within the United States includes gain, computed under the provisions of section 1001 and the regulations thereunder, derived from the sale or other disposition of real property located in the United States. For the treatment of capital gains and losses, see subchapter P (section 1201 and following) chapter 1 of the Code, and the regulations thereunder. [Reg. § 1.861-6.]

☐ [*T.D. 6258, 10-23-57.*]

§ 1.861-7. Sale of personal property.—(a) *General.*—Gains, profits, and income derived from the purchase and sale of personal property shall be treated as derived entirely from the country in which the property is sold. Thus, gross income from sources within the United States includes gains, profits, and income derived from the purchase of personal property without the United States and its sale within the United States.

(b) *Purchase within a possession.*—Notwithstanding paragraph (a) of this section, income derived from the purchase of personal property within a possession of the United States and its sale within the United States shall be treated as derived partly from sources within and partly from sources without the United States. See section 863(b)(3) and § 1.863-2.

(c) *Country in which sold.*—For the purposes of part I (section 861 and following), subchapter N, chapter 1 of the Code, and the regulations thereunder, a sale of personal property is consummated at the time when, and the place where, the rights, title, and interest of the seller in the property are transferred to the buyer. Where bare legal title is retained by the seller, the sale shall be deemed to have occurred at the time and place of passage to the buyer of beneficial ownership and the risk of loss. However, in any case in which the sales transaction is arranged in a particular manner for the primary purpose of tax avoidance, the foregoing rules will not be applied. In such cases, all factors of the transaction, such as negotiations, the execution of the agreement, the location of the property, and the place of payment, will be considered, and the sale will be treated as having been consummated at the place where the substance of the sale occurred.

(d) *Production and sale.*—For provisions respecting the source of income derived from the sale of personal property produced by the taxpayer, see section 863(b)(2) and paragraphs (b) of § § 1.863-1 and 1.863-2.

(e) *Section 306 stock.*—For determining the source of gain on the disposition of section 306 stock, see section 306(f) and the regulations thereunder. [Reg. § 1.861-7.]

☐ [*T.D. 6258, 10-23-57.*]

Proposed Amendments to Regulation

§ 1.861-7. Sale of personal property.

* * *

(c) *Country in which sold.*—For purposes of part I (section 861 and following), subchapter N, chapter 1 of the Code, and the regulations thereunder, a sale of personal property is consummated at the time when, and the place where, the rights, title, and interest of the seller in the property are transferred to the buyer. Where bare legal title is retained by the seller, the sale shall be deemed to have occurred at the time and place of passage to the buyer of beneficial ownership and the risk of loss. For determining the place of sale of copyrighted articles transferred in electronic medium, see § 1.861-18(f)(2)(ii). However, in any case in which the sales transaction is arranged in a particular manner for the primary purpose of tax avoidance, the foregoing rules will not be applied. In such cases, all factors of the transaction, such as negotiations, the execution of the agreement, the location of the property, and the place of payment, will be considered, and the sale will be treated as having been consummated at the place where the substance of the sale occurred.

* * *

[Prop. Reg. § 1.861-7.]

[Proposed 8-14-2019.]

§ 1.861-8. Computation of taxable income from sources within the United States example 17 of paragraph from other sources and activities.—(a) *In general.*—(1) *Scope.*—Sections 861(b) and 863(a) state in general terms how to determine taxable income of a taxpayer from sources within the United States after gross income from sources within the United States has been determined. Sections 862(b) and 863(a) state in general terms how to determine taxable income of a taxpayer from sources without the United States after gross income from sources without the United States has been determined. This section provides specific guidance for applying the cited Code sections by prescribing rules for the allocation and apportionment of expenses, losses, and other deductions (referred to collectively in this section as "deductions") of the taxpayer. The rules contained in this section apply in determining taxable income of the taxpayer from specific sources and activities under other sections of the Code, referred to in this section as operative sections. See paragraph (f)(1) of this section for a list and description of operative sections. The term *section 861 regulations* means this section and § § 1.861-8T, 1.861-9, 1.861-9T, 1.861-10, 1.861-10T 1.861-11, 1.861-11T, 1.861-12, 1.861-12T, 1.861-13, 1.861-14, 1.861-14T, 1.861-17, and 1.861-20.

(2) *Allocation and apportionment of deductions in general.*—A taxpayer to which this section applies is required to allocate deductions to a class of gross income and, then, if necessary to make the determination required by the operative section of the Code, to apportion deductions within the class of gross income between the statutory grouping of gross income (or among the statutory groupings) and the residual grouping of gross income. Except for deductions, if any, which are not definitely related to gross income (see paragraphs (c)(3) and (e)(9) of this section) and which, therefore, are ratably apportioned to all gross income, all deductions of the taxpayer (except the deductions for personal exemptions enumerated in paragraph (e)(11) of this section) must be so allocated and apportioned. As further detailed below, allocations and apportionments are made on the basis of the factual relationship of deductions to gross income.

(3) *Class of gross income.*—For purposes of this section, the gross income to which a specific deduction is definitely related is referred to as a "class of gross income" and may consist of one or more items (or subdivisions of these items) of gross income enumerated in section 61, namely:

(i) Compensation for services, including fees, commissions, and similar items;

(ii) Gross income derived from business;

(iii) Gains derived from dealings in property;

(iv) Interest;

(v) Rents;

(vi) Royalties;

(vii) Dividends;

(viii) Alimony and separate maintenance payments;

(ix) Annuities;

(x) Income from life insurance and endowment contracts;

(xi) Pensions;

(xii) Income from discharge of indebtedness;

(xiii) Distributive share of partnership gross income;

(xiv) Income in respect of a decedent;

(xv) Income from an interest in an estate or trust.

(4) *Statutory grouping of gross income and residual grouping of gross income.*—For purposes of this section, the term "statutory grouping of gross income" or "statutory grouping" means the gross income from a specific source or activity which must first be determined in order to arrive at taxable income" from such specific source or activity under an operative section. (See paragraph (f)(1) of this section.) Gross income from other sources or activities is referred to as the "residual grouping of gross income" or "residual grouping". In some instances, where the operative section so requires, the statutory grouping or the residual grouping may include, or consist entirely of, excluded income. See paragraph (d)(2) of this section with respect to the allocation and apportionment of deductions to excluded income.

(b) *Allocation.*—(1) *In general.*—For purposes of this section, the gross income to which a specific deduction is definitely related is referred to as a "class of gross income" and may consist of one or more items of gross income. The rules emphasize the factual relationship between the deduction and a class of gross income. See paragraph (d)(1) of this section which provides that in a taxable year there may be no item of gross income in a class or less gross income than deductions allocated to the class, and paragraph (d)(2) of this section which provides that a class of gross income may include excluded income. Allocation is accomplished by determining, with respect to each deduction, the class of gross income to which the deduction is definitely related and then allocating the deduction to such class of gross income (without regard to the taxable year in which such gross income is received or accrued or is expected to be received or accrued). The classes of gross income are not predetermined but must be determined on the basis of the deductions to be allocated. Although most deductions will be definitely related to some class of a taxpayer's total gross income, some deductions are related to all gross income. In addition, some deductions are treated as not definitely related to any gross income and are ratably apportioned to all gross income. (See paragraph (e)(9) of this section.) In allocating deductions it is not necessary to differentiate between deductions related to one item of gross income and deductions related to another item of gross income where both items of gross income are exclusively within the same statutory grouping or exclusively within the residual grouping.

(2) *Relationship to activity or property.*—A deduction shall be considered definitely related to a class of gross income and therefore allocable to such class if it is incurred as a result of, or incident to, an activity or in connection with property from which such class of gross income is derived. Where a deduction is incurred as a result of, or incident to, an activity or in connection with property, which activity or property generates, has generated, or could reasonably have been expected to generate gross income, such deduction shall be considered definitely related to such gross income as a class whether or not there is any item of gross income in such class which is received or accrued during the taxable year and whether or not the amount of deductions exceeds the amount of the gross income in such class. See paragraph (d)(1) of this section with respect to cases in which there is an excess of deductions. In some cases, it will be found that this subparagraph can most readily be applied by determining, with respect to a deduction, the categories of gross income to which it is not related and concluding that it is definitely related to a class consisting of all other gross income.

(3) *Supportive functions.*—Deductions which are supportive in nature (such as overhead, general and administrative, and supervisory expenses) may relate to other deductions which can more readily be allocated to gross income. In such instance, such supportive deductions may be allocated and apportioned along with the deductions to which they relate. On the other hand, it would be equally acceptable to attribute supportive deductions on some reasonable basis directly to activities or property which generate, have generated or could reasonably be expected to generate gross income. This would ordinarily be accomplished by allocating the supportive expenses to all gross income or to another broad class of gross income and apportioning the expenses in accordance with paragraph (c)(1) of this section. For this purpose, reasonable departmental overhead rates may be utilized. For examples of the application of the principles of this paragraph (b)(3) to expenses other than expenses attributable to stewardship activities, see *Examples 19* through *21* of paragraph (g) of this section. See paragraph (e)(4)(ii) of this section for the allocation and apportionment of deductions attributable to stewardship expenses. However, supportive deductions that are described in § 1.861-14T(e)(3) shall be allocated and apportioned in accordance with the rules of § 1.861-14T and shall not be allocated and apportioned by reference only to the gross income of a single member of an affiliated group of corporations as defined in § 1.861-14T(d).

(4) *Deductions related to a class of gross income.*—See paragraph (e) of this section for rules relating to the allocation and apportionment of certain specific deductions definitely related to a class of gross income. See paragraph (c)(1) of this section for rules relating to the apportionment of deductions.

(5) *Deductions related to all gross income.*—If a deduction does not bear a definite relationship to a class of gross income constituting less than all of gross income, it shall ordinarily be treated as definitely related and allocable to all of the taxpayer's gross income except where provided to the contrary under paragraph (e) of this section. Paragraph (e)(9) of this section lists various deductions which generally are not definitely related to any gross income and are ratably apportioned to all gross income.

(c) *Apportionment of deductions.*—(1) *Deductions definitely related to a class of gross income.*—[Reserved] For guidance, see § 1.861-8T(c)(1).

(2) *Apportionment based on assets.*—Certain taxpayers are required by paragraph (e)(2) of this section and § 1.861-9T to apportion interest expense on the basis of assets. A taxpayer may apportion other deductions based on the comparative value of assets that generate income within each grouping, provided that this method reflects the factual relationship between the deduction and the groupings of income and is applied in accordance with the rules of § 1.861-9T(g). In general, such apportionments must be made either on the basis of the tax book value of those assets or, except in the case of interest expense, on the basis of their fair market value. *See* § 1.861-9(h). Taxpayers using the fair market value method for their last taxable year beginning before January 1, 2018, must change to the tax book value method (or the alternative tax book value method) for purposes of apportioning interest expense for their first taxable year beginning after December 31, 2017. The Commissioner's approval is not required for this change. In the case of any corporate taxpayer that both uses tax book value or alternative tax book value, and owns directly or indirectly (within the meaning of § 1.861-12T(c)(2)(ii)(B)) 10 percent or more of the total combined voting power of all classes of stock entitled to vote in any other corporation (domestic or foreign) that is not a member of the affiliated group (as defined in section 864(e)(5)), the taxpayer must adjust its basis in that stock in the manner described in § 1.861-12(c)(2). For the definition of related persons formerly contained in § 1.861-8T(c)(2), see paragraph (c)(4) of this section.

(3) *Deductions not definitely related to any gross income.*—If a deduction is not definitely related to any gross income (see paragraph (e)(9) of this section), the deduction must be apportioned ratably between the statutory grouping (or among the statutory groupings) of gross income and the residual grouping. Thus, the amount apportioned to each statutory grouping shall be equal to the same proportion of the deduction which the amount of gross income in the statutory grouping bears to the total amount of gross income. The amount apportioned to the residual grouping shall be equal to the same proportion of the deduction which the amount of the gross income in the residual grouping bears to the total amount of gross income.

(4) *Cross-referenced definition of related persons.*—The term related persons means two or more persons in a relationship described in section 267(b). In determining whether two or more corporations are members of the same controlled group under section 267(b)(3), a person is considered to own stock owned directly by such person, stock owned by application of section 1563(e)(1), and stock owned by application of section 267(c). In determining whether a corporation is related to a partnership under section 267(b)(10), a person is considered to own the partnership interest owned directly by such person and the partnership interest owned by application of section 267(e)(3).

(d) *Excess of deductions and excluded and eliminated income.*—(1) *Excess of deductions.*—Each deduction which bears a definite relationship to a class of gross income shall be allocated to that class in accordance with paragraph (b)(1) of this section even though, for the taxable year, no gross income in such class is received or accrued or the amount of the deduction exceeds the amount of such class of gross income. In apportioning deductions, it may be that, for the taxable year, there is no gross income in the statutory grouping (or residual grouping), or that deductions exceed the amount of gross income in the statutory grouping (or residual grouping). If there is no gross income in a statutory grouping or the amount of deductions allocated and apportioned to a statutory grouping exceeds the amount of gross income in the statutory grouping, the effects are determined under the operative section. If the taxpayer is a member of a group filing a consolidated return, such excess of deductions allocated or apportioned to a statutory grouping of income of such member is taken into account in determining the consolidated taxable income from such statutory grouping, and such excess of deductions allocated or apportioned to the residual grouping of income is taken into account in determining the consolidated taxable income from the residual grouping. See § 1.1502-12.

(2) *Allocation and apportionment to exempt, excluded, or eliminated income.*—(i) *In general.*—For further guidance, see § 1.861-8T(d)(2)(i).

(ii) *Exempt income and exempt asset defined.*—(A) *In general.*—For purposes of this section, the term *exempt income* means any gross income to the extent that it is exempt, excluded, or eliminated for Federal income tax purposes. The term *exempt asset* means any asset to the extent income from the asset is (or is treated as under paragraph (d)(2)(ii)(B) or (C) of this section) exempt, excluded, or eliminated for Federal income tax purposes.

(B) *Certain stock and dividends.*—The term *exempt income* includes the portion of the dividends that are deductible under section 243(a)(1) or section 243(a)(2) (relating to the dividends received deduction) or section 245(a) (relating to the dividends received deduction for dividends from certain foreign corporations). Thus, for purposes of apportioning deductions using a gross income method, gross income does not include a dividend to the extent that it gives rise to a dividends-received deduction under either section 243(a)(1), section 243(a)(2), or section 245(a). In addition, for purposes of apportioning deductions using an asset method, assets do not include that portion of the value of the stock (determined in accordance with § 1.861-9(g), and, as relevant, §§ 1.861-12 and 1.861-13) equal to the portion of dividends that would be offset by a deduction under either section 243(a)(1), section 243(a)(2), or section 245(a), to the extent the stock generates, has generated, or can reasonably be expected to generate such dividends. For example, in the case of stock for which all dividends would be allowed a deduction of 50 percent under section 243(a)(1), 50 percent of the value of the stock is treated as an exempt asset. In the case of stock which generates, has generated, or can reasonably be expected to generate qualifying dividends deductible under section 243(a)(3), such stock does not constitute an exempt asset. However, such stock and the qualifying dividends thereon are eliminated from consideration in the apportionment of interest expense under the affiliated group rule set forth in § 1.861-11T(c), and in the apportionment of other expenses under the affiliated group rules set forth in § 1.861-14T.

(C) *Foreign-derived intangible income and inclusions under section 951A(a).—(1) Exempt income.*—The term "exempt income" includes an amount of a domestic corporation's gross income included in gross foreign-derived deduction eligible income (or gross FDDEI), and also includes an amount of a domestic corporation's gross income from an inclusion under section 951A(a) and the gross up under section 78 attributable to such an inclusion, in each case equal to the amount of the deduction allowed under section 250(a) for such gross income (taking into account the reduction under section 250(a)(2)(B), if any). Therefore, for purposes of apportioning deductions using a gross income method, gross income does not include gross income included in gross FDDEI, an inclusion under section 951A(a), or the gross up under section 78 attributable to an inclusion under section 951A(a), in an amount equal to the amount of the deduction allowed under section 250(a)(1)(A), (B)(i), or (B)(ii), respectively (taking into account the reduction under section 250(a)(2)(B), if any). The term *gross foreign-derived deduction eligible income*, or *gross FDDEI*, has the meaning provided in § 1.250(b)-1(c)(16).

(2) Exempt assets.—(i) Assets that produce foreign-derived intangible income.—The term "exempt asset" includes the portion of a domestic corporation's assets that produce gross FDDEI equal to the amount of such assets multiplied by the fraction that equals the amount of the domestic corporation's deduction allowed under section 250(a)(1)(A) (taking into account the reduction under section 250(a)(2)(B)(i), if any) divided by its gross FDDEI. No portion of the value of stock in a foreign corporation is treated as an exempt asset by reason of this paragraph (d)(2)(ii)(C)*(2)*(*i*), including by reason of a transfer of intangible property to a foreign corporation subject to section 367(d) that gives rise to gross FDDEI.

(ii) Controlled foreign corporation stock that gives rise to inclusions under section 951A(a).—The term "exempt asset" includes a portion of the value of a United States shareholder's stock in a controlled foreign corporation if the United States shareholder is a domestic corporation that is eligible for a deduction under section 250(a) with respect to income described in section 250(a)(1)(B)(i) and all or a portion of the domestic corporation's stock in the controlled foreign corporation is characterized as GILTI inclusion stock. The portion of foreign corporation stock that is treated as an exempt asset for a taxable year equals the portion of the value of such foreign corporation stock (determined in accordance with §§ 1.861-9(g), 1.861-12, and 1.861-13) that is characterized as GILTI inclusion stock multiplied by a fraction that equals the amount of the domestic corporation's deduction allowed under section 250(a)(1)(B)(i) (taking into account the reduction under section 250(a)(2)(B)(ii), if any) divided by its GILTI inclusion amount (as defined in § 1.951A-1(c)(1) or, in the case of a member of a consolidated group, § 1.1502-51(b)) for such taxable year. The portion of controlled foreign corporation stock treated as an exempt asset under this paragraph (d)(2)(ii)(C)*(2)*(*ii*) is treated as attributable to the relevant categories of GILTI inclusion stock described in each of paragraphs (d)(2)(ii)(C)*(3)*(*i*) through (*v*) of this section based on the relative value of the portion of the stock in each such category.

(3) GILTI inclusion stock.—For purposes of paragraph (d)(2)(ii)(C)*(2)*(*ii*) of this section, the term *GILTI inclusion stock* means the aggregate of the portions of the value of controlled foreign corporation stock that are—

(*i*) Assigned to the section 951A category under § 1.861-13(a)(2);

(*ii*) Assigned to a particular treaty category under § 1.861-13(a)(3)(i) (relating to resourced gross tested income stock);

(*iii*) Assigned under § 1.861-13(a)(1) to the gross tested income statutory grouping within the foreign source passive category less the amount described in § 1.861-13(a)(5)(iii)(A);

(*iv*) Assigned under § 1.861-13(a)(1) to the gross tested income statutory grouping within the U.S. source general category less the amount described in § 1.861-13(a)(5)(iv)(A); and

(*v*) Assigned under § 1.861-13(a)(1) to the gross tested income statutory grouping within the U.S. source passive category less the amount described in § 1.861-13(a)(5)(iv)(B).

(4) Non-applicability to section 250(b).—Paragraphs (d)(2)(ii)(C)*(1)* through *(3)* of this section do not apply when apportioning deductions for purposes of determining deduction eligible income or foreign-derived deduction eligible income under the operative section of section 250(b).

(5) Example.—The following example illustrates the application of the rules in this paragraph (d)(2)(ii)(C).

(*i*) *Facts.* USP, a domestic corporation, directly owns all of the stock of CFC1 and CFC2, both of which are controlled foreign corporations. The tax book value of CFC1 and CFC2's stock is $10,000x and $9,000x, respectively. Pursuant to § 1.861-13(a), $6,100x of the stock of CFC1 is assigned to the section 951A category under § 1.861-13(a)(2) ("section 951A category stock") and the remaining $3,900x of the stock of CFC1 is assigned to the general category ("general category stock"). Additionally, $4,880x of the stock of CFC2 is section 951A category stock and the remaining $4,120x of the stock of CFC2 is general category stock. Under section 951A and the section 951A regulations (as defined in § 1.951A-1(a)(1)), USP's GILTI inclusion amount is $610x. The portion of USP's deduction under section 250 described in section 250(a)(1)(B)(i) is $305x. No portion of USP's deduction is reduced by reason of section 250(a)(2)(B)(ii).

(*ii*) *Analysis.* For purposes of apportioning deductions where section 904 is the operative section, under paragraph (d)(2)(ii)(C)*(1)* of this section, $305x of USP's gross income attributable to its GILTI inclusion amount is exempt income. Under paragraph (d)(2)(ii)(C)*(3)* of this section, the GILTI inclusion stock of CFC1 is the $6,100x of stock that is section 951A category stock and the GILTI inclusion stock of CFC2 is the $4,880x of stock that is section 951A category stock. Under paragraph (d)(2)(ii)(C)*(2)* of this section, the portion of the value of the stock of CFC1 and CFC2 that is treated as an exempt asset equals the portion of the value of the stock of CFC1 and CFC2 that is GILTI inclusion stock multiplied by 50% ($305x/$610x). Accordingly, the exempt portion of the stock of CFC1 is $3,050x (50% x $6,100x) and the exempt portion of CFC2's stock is $2,440x (50% x $4,880x). Therefore, the stock of CFC1 taken into account for purposes of apportioning deductions is $3,050x of non-exempt section 951A category stock and $3,900x of general category stock. The stock of CFC2 taken into account for purposes of apportioning deductions is $2,440x of non-exempt section 951A category stock and $4,120x of general category stock.

(iii) *Income that is not considered tax exempt.*—For further guidance, see § 1.861-8T(d)(2)(iii).

(A) For further guidance, see § 1.861-8T(d)(2)(iii)(A) and (B).

(B) [Reserved]

(C) Dividends for which a deduction is allowed under section 245A;

(D) Foreign earned income as defined in section 911 (however, the rules of § 1.911-6 do not require the allocation and apportionment of certain deductions, including home mortgage interest, to foreign earned income for purposes of determining the deductions disallowed under section 911(d)(6)); and

(E) Inclusions for which a deduction is allowed under section 965(c). *See* § 1.965-6(c).

(iv) *Value of stock attributable to previously taxed earnings and profits.*—No portion of the value of stock in a controlled foreign corporation is treated as an exempt asset by reason of the controlled foreign corporation having previously taxed earnings and profits. For example, no portion of the value of stock in a controlled foreign corporation is treated as an exempt asset by reason of the adjustment under § 1.861-12(c)(2) in respect of previously taxed earnings and profits described in section 959(c)(1) or (c)(2) (including earnings and profits described in section 959(c)(2) by reason of section 951A(f)(1) and § 1.951A-6(b)(1)). *See also* § 1.965-6(c).

(v) *Dividends-received deduction and tax-exempt interest of insurance companies.*—(A) *In general.*—For purposes of characterizing gross income or assets as exempt or not exempt under this section, the following rules apply on a company wide basis pursuant to the rules in paragraphs (d)(2)(v)(A)(*1*) and (*2*) of this section.

(*1*) In the case of an insurance company taxable under section 801, the term *exempt income* includes the portion of dividends received that satisfy the requirements of deductibility under sections 243(a)(1) and (2) and 245(a) but without regard to any disallowance under section 805(a)(4)(A)(ii) of the policyholder's share of the dividends or any similar disallowance under section 805(a)(4)(D), and also includes tax-exempt interest but without reduction for the policyholder's share of tax-exempt interest that reduces the closing balance of items described in section 807(c), as provided under section 807(a)(2)(B) and 807(b)(1)(B). The term *exempt assets* includes the corresponding portion of assets that generates, has generated, or can reasonably be expected to generate exempt income described in the preceding sentence. See § 1.861-8(e)(16) for a special rule concerning the allocation of reserve expenses to dividends received by a life insurance company.

(*2*) In the case of an insurance company taxable under section 831, the term *exempt income* includes the portion of interest and dividends deductible under sections 832(c)(7) and (12) or sections 834(c)(1) and (7). Exempt income also includes the amounts reducing the losses incurred under section 832(b)(5) to the extent such amounts are not already taken into account in the preceding sentence. The term *exempt assets* includes the corresponding portion of assets that give rise to exempt income described in the preceding two sentences.

(B) *Examples.*—The following examples illustrate the application of paragraph (d)(2)(v)(A) of this section.

(*1*) *Example 1.*—(*i*) *Facts.* USC is a domestic life insurance company that has $300x of gross income, consisting of $100x of foreign source general category income and $200x of U.S. source passive category interest income, $100x of the latter of which is tax-exempt interest income from municipal bonds under section 103. USC's opening balance of its section 807(c) reserves is $50,000x and USP's closing balance of its section 807(c) reserves is $50,130x. Under section 807(b)(1)(B), USP's closing balance of its section 807(c) reserves, $50,130x, is reduced by the amount of the policyholder's share of tax-exempt interest. The policyholder's share of tax-exempt interest under section 812(b) is equal to 30 percent of the $100x of tax-exempt interest ($30x). Therefore, under sections 803(a)(2) and 807(b), USP's reserve deduction is $100x ($50,130x of reserve deduction minus $30x (30 percent of $100x of tax-exempt interest), minus $50,000x). USC has no other income or deductions.

(*ii*) *Analysis—allocation.* Under section 818(f)(1), USC's reserve deduction is treated as an item that cannot be definitely allocated to an item or class of gross income. Accordingly, under paragraph (b)(5) of this section, USC's reserve deduction is allocable to all of USC's gross income as a class.

(*iii*) *Analysis—apportionment.* Under paragraph (c)(3) of this section, the reserve deduction is ratably apportioned between the statutory grouping (foreign source general category income) and the residual grouping (U.S. source income) on the basis of the relative amounts of gross income in each grouping. For purposes of apportioning deductions under § 1.861-8T(d)(2)(i)(B), exempt income is not taken into account. Under paragraph (d)(2)(v)(A)(*1*) of this section, in the case of an insurance company taxable under section 801, exempt income includes tax-exempt interest without regard to any reduction for the policyholder's share. USC has U.S. source income of $200x of which $100x is tax-exempt without regard to the reduction for the policyholder's share of tax-exempt interest that reduces the closing balance of items described in section 807(c). Thus, the gross income taken into account in apportioning USC's reserve deduction is $100x of foreign source general category gross income and $100x of U.S. source gross income. Of USC's $100x reserve deduction, $50x ($100x x $100x/$200x) is apportioned to foreign source general category gross income and $50x ($100x x $100x/$200x) is apportioned to U.S. source gross income.

(*2*) *Example 2.*—(*i*) *Facts.* USC is a domestic life insurance company that has $300x of gross income consisting of $100x of foreign source general category income and $200x of U.S. source general category dividend income eligible for the 50% dividends received deduction (DRD) under section 243(a)(1). Under section 805(a)(4)(A)(ii), USC is allowed a 50% DRD on the company's share of the dividend received. Under section 812(a), the company's share of the dividend is equal to 70% of the dividend income eligible for the DRD under section 243(a)(1), which results in a DRD of $70x (50% x 70% x $200x), and under section 812(b), the policyholder's share of the dividend is equal to 30% of the dividend income eligible for the DRD under section 243(a)(1), which would result in a DRD of $30x (50% x 30% x $200x). USC is entitled to a $130x deduction for an increase in its life insurance reserves under sections 803(a)(2) and 807(b). Unlike for tax-exempt interest income, there is no adjustment under section 807(b)(1)(B) to the reserve deduction for the policyholder's share of dividends that would be offset by the DRD under section 243(a)(1). USC has no other income or deductions.

(*ii*) *Analysis—allocation.* Under section 818(f)(1), USC's reserve deduction is treated as an item that cannot be definitely allocated to an item or class of gross income except that, under § 1.861-8(e)(16), an amount of reserve expenses of a life insurance company equal to the DRD that is disallowed because it is attributable to the policyholder's share of dividends is treated as definitely related to such dividends. Thus, USC has a life insurance reserve deduction of $130x, of which $30x (equal to the policyholder's share of the DRD that would have been allowed under section 243(a)(1)) is directly allocated and apportioned to U.S. source dividend income. Under paragraph (b)(5) of this section, the remaining portion of USC's reserve deduction ($100x) is allocable to all of USC's gross income as a class.

(*iii*) *Analysis—apportionment.* Under paragraph (c)(3) of this section, the deduction is ratably apportioned between the statutory grouping (foreign source general category income) and the residual grouping (U.S. source income) on the basis of the relative amounts of gross income in each grouping. For purposes of apportioning deductions under § 1.861-8T(d)(2)(i)(B), exempt income is not taken into account. Under paragraph (d)(2)(v)(A)(*1*) of this section, in the case of an insurance company taxable under section 801, exempt income includes dividends deductible under section 805(a)(4) without regard to any reduction to the DRD for the policyholder's share in section 804(a)(4)(A)(ii). Thus, the gross income taken into account in apportioning $100x of USC's remaining reserve deduction is $100x of foreign source general category gross income and $100x of U.S. source gross income. Of USC's $100x remaining reserve deduction, $50x ($100x x $100x/$200x) is apportioned to foreign source general category gross income and $50x ($100x x $100x/$200x) is apportioned to U.S. source gross income.

(e) *Allocation and apportionment of certain deductions.*—(1) *In general.*—Paragraphs (e)(2) and (e)(3) of this section contain rules with respect to the allocation and apportionment of interest expense and research and development expenditures, respectively. Paragraphs (e)(4) through (e)(8) of this section contain rules with respect to the allocation of certain other deductions. Paragraph (e)(9) of this section lists those deductions which are ordinarily considered as not being definitely related to any class of gross income. Paragraph (e)(10) of this section lists special deductions of corporations which must be allocated and apportioned. Paragraph (e)(11) of this section lists personal exemptions which are neither allocated nor apportioned. Paragraph (e)(12) of this section contains rules with respect to the allocation and apportionment of deductions for charitable contributions. Paragraphs (e)(13) and (14) of this section contain rules with respect to the allocation and apportionment of the deduction allowed under section 250(a). Paragraph (e)(15) of this section contains rules with respect to the allocation and apportionment of a taxpayer's distributive share of a partnership's deductions. Examples of allocation and apportionment are contained in paragraph (g) of this section.

(2) *Interest.*—[Reserved]For guidance, see § 1.861-8T(e)(2).

(3) *Research and experimental expenditures.*—For rules regarding the allocation and apportionment of research and experimental expenditures, see § 1.861-17.

(4) *Stewardship and controlled services.*—(i) *Expenses attributable to controlled services.*—If a taxpayer performs a controlled services transaction (as defined in § 1.482-9(l)(1)), which includes any activity by one member of a group of controlled taxpayers (the renderer) that results in a benefit to a controlled taxpayer (the recipient), and the renderer charges the recipient for such services, section 482 and § 1.482-1 provide for an allocation where the charge is not consistent with an arm's length result. The deductions for expenses incurred by the renderer in performing such services are considered definitely

related to the amounts so charged and are to be allocated to such amounts.

(ii) *Stewardship expenses.*—(A) *In general.*—Stewardship expenses are those expenses resulting from "duplicative activities" (as defined in § 1.482-9(l)(3)(iii)) or "shareholder activities" (as defined in § 1.482-9(l)(3)(iv)) that are undertaken for a person's own benefit as an investor in a related entity, which for purposes of this paragraph (e)(4)(ii) includes a business entity as described in § 301.7701-2(a) of this chapter that is classified for Federal income tax purposes as either a corporation or a partnership, or is disregarded as an entity separate from its owner ("disregarded entity"). Thus, for example, stewardship expenses include expenses of an activity the sole effect of which is to protect the investor's capital investment in the entity or to facilitate compliance by the investor with reporting, legal, or regulatory requirements applicable specifically to the investor. If an investor has a foreign or international department which exercises oversight functions with respect to related entities and, in addition, the department performs other functions that generate other foreign-source income (such as fees for services rendered outside of the United States for the benefit of foreign related corporations or foreign-source royalties), some part of the deductions with respect to that department are considered definitely related to the other foreign-source income. In some instances, the operations of a foreign or international department will also generate U.S. source income (such as fees for services performed in the United States). Stewardship expenses are allocated and apportioned on a separate entity basis without regard to the affiliated group rules in § 1.861-14. See § 1.861-14(e)(1)(i).

(B) *Allocation.*—In the case of stewardship expenses incurred to oversee a corporation, the expenses are considered definitely related and allocable to dividends received or amounts included, or to be received or included, under sections 78, 301, 951, 951A, 1291, 1293, and 1296, from the corporation. In the case of stewardship expenses incurred to oversee a partnership, the expenses are considered definitely related and allocable to a partner's distributive share of partnership income. In the case of stewardship expenses incurred to oversee a disregarded entity, the expenses are considered definitely related and allocable to all gross income attributable to the disregarded entity. Stewardship expenses are allocated to income from a particular entity (or entities) related to the taxpayer if the expense is definitely related to the oversight of that entity or entities as provided in § 1.861-8(b)(1) under all the facts and circumstances.

(C) *Apportionment.*—Stewardship expenses must be apportioned between the statutory and residual groupings based on the relative values of the entity or entities in each grouping that are owned by the investor taxpayer, and without regard to the relative amounts of gross income in the statutory and residual groupings to which the stewardship expense is allocated. In the case of stewardship expenses incurred to oversee a lower-tier entity owned indirectly by the taxpayer, the stewardship expenses must be apportioned based on the relative values of the owner or owners of the lower-tier entity that are owned directly by the taxpayer. In the case of stewardship expenses incurred to oversee a corporation, the corporation's value is the value of its stock as determined and characterized under the asset method in § 1.861-9 (and, as relevant, §§ 1.861-12 and 1.861-13) for purposes of allocating and apportioning the taxpayer's interest expense. For purposes of the preceding sentence, if the corporation is a member of the same affiliated group as the investor, the value of the corporation's stock is determined under the asset method in § 1.861-9 and is characterized by the investor in proportion to how the corporation's assets are characterized for purposes of apportioning the group's interest expense. In the case of stewardship expenses incurred to oversee a partnership, the partnership's value is determined and characterized under the asset method in § 1.861-9 (taking into account any adjustments under sections 734(b) and sections 743(b)). In the case of stewardship expenses incurred to oversee a disregarded entity, the disregarded entity's character and value is determined using the principles of the asset method in § 1.861-9 as if the disregarded entity were treated as a corporation for Federal income tax purposes. For purposes of determining the tax book value of assets under this paragraph (e)(4)(ii)(C), section 864(e)(3) and § 1.861-8(d)(2) do not apply.

(5) *Legal and accounting fees and expenses; damages awards, prejudgment interest, and settlement payments.*—(i) *Legal and accounting fees and expenses.*—Fees and other expenses for legal and accounting services are ordinarily definitely related and allocable to specific classes of gross income or to all the taxpayer's gross income, depending on the nature of the services rendered (and are apportioned as provided in paragraph (c)(1) of this section). For example, accounting fees for the preparation of a study of the costs involved in manufacturing a specific product will ordinarily be definitely related to the class of gross income derived from (or which could reasonably have been expected to be derived from) that specific product. The taxpayer is not relieved from his responsibility to make a proper allocation and apportionment of fees on the grounds that the statement of services rendered does not identify the services performed beyond a generalized designation such as "professional," or does not provide any type of allocation, or does not properly allocate the fees involved.

(ii) *Product liability and other claims for damages.*—Except as otherwise provided in this paragraph (e)(5), awards for litigation or arbitral damages, prejudgment interest, and payments in settlement of or in anticipation of claims for damages, including punitive damages, arising from claims relating to sales, licenses, or leases of products or the provision of services, are definitely related and allocable to the class of gross income of the type produced by the specific sales or leases of the products or provision of services that gave rise to the claims for damage or injury. Such damages and payments may include, but are not limited to, product liability or patent infringement claims. The deductions are apportioned among the statutory and residual groupings on the basis of the relative amounts of gross income in the relevant class in each grouping in the year in which the deductions are allowed. If the claims arise from an event incident to the production or sale of products or provision of services (such as an industrial accident), the payments are definitely related and allocable to the class of gross income ordinarily produced by the assets that are involved in the event. The deductions are apportioned among the statutory and residual groupings on the basis of the relative values (as determined under the asset method in § 1.861-9 for purposes of allocating and apportioning the taxpayer's interest expense) of the assets that were involved in the event or (if the taxpayer no longer owns the assets involved in the event) the assets that are used to produce or sell products or services in the relevant class in each grouping; such values are determined in the year the deductions are allowed.

(iii) *Investor lawsuits.*—If the claims are made by investors in a corporation and arise from negligence, fraud, or other malfeasance of the corporation (or its representatives), then the damages, prejudgment interest, and settlement payments paid by the corporation are definitely related and allocable to all income of the corporation and are apportioned among the statutory and residual groupings based on the relative value of the corporation's assets in each grouping (as determined under the asset method in § 1.861-9 for purposes of allocating and apportioning the taxpayer's interest expense) in the year the deductions are allowed.

(6) *Income taxes.*—(i) *In general.*—The deduction for foreign income, war profits, and excess profits taxes allowed by section 164 is allocated and apportioned among the applicable statutory and residual groupings under § 1.861-20. The deduction for state and local taxes (*state income taxes*) allowed by section 164 is considered definitely related and allocable to the gross income with respect to which such state income taxes are imposed. For example, if a domestic corporation is subject to state income taxation and the state income tax is imposed in part on an amount of foreign source income, then that part of the taxpayer's deduction for state income tax that is attributable to foreign source income is definitely related and allocable to foreign source income. In allocating and apportioning the deduction for state income tax for purposes including (but not limited to) the computation of the foreign tax credit limitation under section 904 of the Code and the consolidated foreign tax credit under § 1.1502-4 of the regulations, the income upon which the state income tax is imposed is determined by reference to the law of the jurisdiction imposing the tax. Thus, if a state attributes taxable income to a corporate taxpayer by applying an apportionment formula that takes into consideration the income and factors of one or more corporations related by ownership to the corporate taxpayer and engaging in activities related to the business of the corporate taxpayer, then the income so attributed is the income upon which the state income tax is imposed. If the income so attributed to the corporate taxpayer includes foreign source income, then, in computing the taxpayer's foreign tax credit limitation under section 904, for example, the taxpayer's deduction for state income tax will be considered definitely related and allocable to a class of gross income that includes the statutory grouping of foreign source income. When the law of the state includes dividends that are treated under section 862(a)(2) as income from sources without the United States in taxable income apportionable to the state, but does not include factors of the corporation paying such dividends in the apportionment formula

used to determine state taxable income, an appropriate portion of the deduction for state income tax will be considered definitely related and allocable to a class of gross income consisting solely of foreign source dividend income. A deduction for state income tax will not be considered definitely related to a hypothetical amount of income calculated under federal tax principles when the jurisdiction imposing the tax computes taxable income under different principles. A corporate taxpayer's deduction for a state franchise tax that is computed on the basis of income attributable to business activities conducted within the state must be allocated and apportioned in the same manner as the deduction for state income taxes. In determining, for example, both the foreign tax credit under section 904 of the Code and the consolidated foreign tax credit limitation under § 1.1502-4 of the regulations, the deduction for state income tax may be allocable and apportionable to foreign source income in a statutory grouping described in section 904(d) in a taxable year in which the taxpayer has no foreign source income in such statutory grouping. Alternatively, such an allocation or apportionment may be appropriate if a taxpayer corporation has no foreign source income in a statutory grouping, but its deduction is attributable to foreign source income in such grouping that is attributed to the taxpayer corporation under the law of a state which attributes taxable income to a corporation by applying an apportionment formula that takes into consideration the income and factors of one or more corporations related by ownership to the taxpayer corporation and engaging in activities related to the business of the taxpayer corporation. *Example 30* of paragraph (g) of this section illustrates the application of this last rule.

(ii) *Methods of allocation and apportionment.*—(A) *In general.*—A taxpayer's deduction for a state income tax is to be allocated (and then apportioned, if necessary, subject to the rules of § 1.861-8(d)) by reference to the taxable income that the law of the taxing jurisdiction attributes to the taxpayer ("state taxable income").

(B) *Effect of subsequent recomputations of state income tax.*—[Reserved]

(C) *Illustrations.*—*(1) In general.*—*Examples* 25 through 32 of paragraph (g) of § 1.861-8 illustrate, in the given factual situations, the application of this paragraph (e)(6) and the general rule of paragraph (b)(1) of this section that a deduction must be allocated to the class of gross income to which the deduction is factually related. In general, these examples employ a presumption that state income taxes are allocable to a class of gross income that includes the statutory grouping of income from sources without the United States when the total amount of taxable income determined under state law exceeds the amount of taxable income determined under the Code (without taking into account the deduction for state income taxes) in the residual grouping of income from sources within the United States. A taxpayer that allocates and apportions the deduction for state income tax in accordance with the methodology of *Example 25* of paragraph (g) of this section must also apply the modifications illustrated in *Examples* 26 and 27 of paragraph (g) of this section, when applicable. The modification illustrated in *Example 26* is applicable when the deduction for state income tax is attributable in part to taxes imposed by a state which factually excludes foreign source income (as determined for federal income tax purposes) from state taxable income. The modification illustrated in *Example 27* is applicable when the taxpayer has income-producing activities in a state which does not impose a corporate income tax. The specific allocation of state income tax illustrated in *Example 28* follows the rule in paragraph (e)(6)(i) of this section, and must be applied whenever a taxpayer's state taxable income includes dividends apportioned to the state under a formula that does not take into account the factors of the corporations paying those dividends, regardless of whether the taxpayer uses the methodology of *Example 25* with respect to the remainder of the deduction for state income taxes.

(2) Modifications.—Before applying a method of allocation and apportionment illustrated in the examples, the computation of state taxable income under state law may be modified, subject to the approval of the District Director, to reflect more accurately the income with respect to which the state income tax is imposed. Any modification to the state law computation of state taxable income must yield an allocation and apportionment of the deduction for state income taxes that is consistent with the rules contained in this paragraph (e)(6), and that accurately reflects the factual relationship between the state income tax and the income on which that tax is imposed. For example, a modification to the computation of taxable income under state law might be appropriate to compensate for differences between the state law definition of taxable income and the federal definition of taxable income, due to a difference in the rate of allowable depreciation or the amount of another deduction that is allowable under both systems. This rule is illustrated in *Example 31* of paragraph (g) of this section. However, a modification to the computation of taxable income under state law will not be appropriate, and will not more accurately reflect the factual relationship between the state tax and the income on which the tax is imposed, to the extent such modification reflects the fact that the state does not follow federal tax principles in attributing income to the taxpayer's activities in the state. This rule is illustrated in *Example 32* of paragraph (g) of this section. A taxpayer may not modify the methods illustrated in the examples, or use an alternative method of allocation and apportionment of the deduction for state income taxes, if the modification or alternative method would be inconsistent with the rules of paragraph (e)(6)(i) of this section. A taxpayer that uses a method of allocation and apportionment other than one illustrated in *Example 25* (as modified by *Examples* 26 and 27), or 29 with respect to a factual situation similar to those of the examples, must describe the alternative method on an attachment to its federal income tax return and establish to the satisfaction of the District Director, upon examination, that the result of the alternative method more accurately reflects the factual relationship between the state income tax and the income on which the tax is imposed.

(D) *Elective safe harbor methods.*—*(1) In general.*—In lieu of applying the rules set forth in paragraphs (e)(6)(ii)(A) through (C) of this section, a taxpayer may elect to allocate and apportion the deduction for state income tax in accordance with one of the two safe harbor methods described in paragraph (e)(6)(ii)(D)(2) and (3) of this section. A taxpayer shall make this election for a taxable year by filing a timely tax return for that year that reflects an allocation and apportionment of the deduction for state income tax under one of the safe harbor methods and attaching to such return a statement that the taxpayer has elected to use the safe harbor method provided in either paragraph (e)(6)(ii)(D)(2) or (3) of this section, as appropriate. Once made, this election is effective for the taxable year for which made and all subsequent taxable years, and may be revoked only with the consent of the Commissioner. *Example 33* of paragraph (g) of this section illustrates the application of these safe harbor methods.

(2) Method One.—*(i) Step One*—*Specific allocation to foreign source portfolio dividends and other income.*—If any portion of the deduction for state income tax is attributable to tax imposed by a state which includes in a corporate taxpayer's taxable income apportionable to the state, portfolio dividends (as defined in paragraph (i) of *Example 28* of paragraph (g) of this section) that are treated under section 862(a)(2) as income from sources without the United States, but does not include factors of the corporations paying the portfolio dividends in the apportionment formula used to determine state taxable income, the taxpayer shall allocate an appropriate portion of the deduction to a class of gross income consisting solely of foreign source portfolio dividends. The portion of the deduction so allocated, and the amount of foreign source portfolio dividends included in such class, shall be determined in accordance with the methodology illustrated in paragraph (ii) of *Example 28* of paragraph (g). If a state income tax is determined based upon formulary apportionment of the total taxable income attributable to the taxpayer's unitary business, the taxpayer must also apply the methodology illustrated in paragraph (ii)(C) through (G) of *Example 29* of paragraph (g) of this section to make specific allocations of appropriate portions of the deduction for state income tax on the basis of income that, under separate accounting, would have been attributed to other members of the unitary group. The taxpayer shall reduce its aggregate state taxable income by the amount of foreign source portfolio dividends and other income to which a specific allocation is made (the reduced amount being referred to hereinafter as "adjusted state taxable income").

(ii) Step Two—*Adjustment of U.S. source federal taxable income.*—If the taxpayer has significant income producing activities in a state which does not impose a corporate income tax or other state tax measured by income derived from business activities in the state, the taxpayer shall reduce its U.S. source federal taxable income (solely for purposes of this safe harbor method) by the amount of federal taxable income attributable to its activities in such state. This amount shall be determined in accordance with the methodology illustrated in paragraph (ii) of *Example 27* of paragraph (g) of this section, provided that the taxpayer shall be required to use the rules of the Uniform Division of Income for Tax Purposes Act to attribute income to the relevant state. The taxpayer's U.S. source federal taxable income, as so reduced, is referred to hereinafter as "adjusted U.S. source federal taxable income."

(iii) *Step Three—Allocation.*—The taxpayer shall allocate the remainder of the deduction for state income tax (after reduction by the portion allocated to foreign source portfolio dividends and other income under Step One) in accordance with the methodology illustrated in paragraph (ii) of *Example 25* of paragraph (g) of this section. However, the taxpayer shall substitute for the comparison of aggregate state taxable income to U.S. source federal taxable income, illustrated in paragraph (ii) of *Example 25* of paragraph (g), a comparison of its adjusted state taxable income to an amount equal to 110% of its adjusted U.S. source federal taxable income.

(iv) *Step Four—Apportionment.*—In the event that apportionment of the remainder of the deduction for state income tax is required, the taxpayer shall apportion that remaining deduction to U.S. source income in accordance with the methodology illustrated in paragraph (iii) of *Example 25* of paragraph (g) of this section, substituting for domestic source income in that paragraph an amount equal to 110% of the taxpayer's adjusted U.S. source federal taxable income. The remaining portion of the deduction shall be apportioned to the statutory groupings of foreign source income described in section 904(d) of the Code in accordance with the proportion of the income in each statutory grouping of foreign source income described in section 904(d) to the taxpayer's total foreign source federal taxable income (after reduction by the amount of foreign source portfolio dividends to which tax has been specifically allocated under Step One, above).

(3) *Method Two.*—(*i*) *Step One—Specific allocation to foreign source portfolio dividends and other income.*—Step One of this method is the same as Step One of Method One (as described in paragraph (e)(6)(ii)(D)(*2*)(*i*) of this section).

(*ii*) *Step Two—Adjustment of U.S. source federal taxable income.*—Step Two of this method is the same as Step Two of Method One (as described in paragraph (e)(6)(ii)(D)(*2*)(*ii*) of this section).

(*iii*) *Step Three—Allocation.*—The taxpayer shall allocate the remainder of the deduction for state income tax (after reduction by the portion allocated to foreign source portfolio dividends and other income under Step One) in accordance with the methodology illustrated in paragraph (ii) of *Example 25* of paragraph (g) of this section. However, the taxpayer shall substitute for the comparison of aggregate state taxable income to U.S. source federal taxable income, illustrated in paragraph (ii) of *Example 25* of paragraph (g) of this section, a comparison of its adjusted state taxable income to its adjusted U.S. source federal taxable income.

(*iv*) *Step Four—Apportionment.*—In the event that apportionment of the deduction is required, the taxpayer shall apportion to U.S. source income that portion of the deduction that is attributable to state income taxes imposed upon an amount of state taxable income equal to adjusted U.S. source federal taxable income. The taxpayer shall apportion the remaining amount of the deduction to U.S. and foreign source income in the same proportions that the taxpayer's adjusted U.S. source federal taxable income and foreign source federal taxable income (after reduction by the amount of foreign source portfolio dividends to which tax has been specifically allocated under Step One, above) bear to its total federal taxable income (taking into account the adjustment of U.S. source federal taxable income under Step Two and after reduction by the amount of foreign source portfolio dividends to which tax has been specifically allocated under Step One). The portion of the deduction apportioned to foreign source income shall be apportioned among the statutory groupings described in section 904(d) of the Code in accordance with the proportions of the taxpayer's total foreign source federal taxable income (after reduction by the amount of foreign source portfolio dividends to which tax has been specifically allocated under Step One, above) in each grouping.

(7) *Losses on the sale, exchange, or other disposition of property.*—See §§1.865-1 and 1.865-2 for rules regarding the allocation and apportionment of certain losses.

(8) *Net operating loss deduction.*—(i) *Components of net operating loss.*—A net operating loss is separated into components that are assigned to statutory or residual groupings by reference to the losses in each such statutory or residual grouping that are not allocated to reduce income in other groupings in the taxable year of the loss. For example, for purposes of applying this paragraph (e)(8)(i) with respect to section 904 as the operative section, the source and separate category components of a net operating loss are determined by reference to the amounts of separate limitation loss and U.S. source loss (determined without regard to adjustments required under section 904(b)) that are not allocated to reduce U.S. source income or income in other separate categories under the rules of sections 904(f) and 904(g) for the taxable year in which the net operating loss arose. See §1.904(g)-3(d)(2). See §1.1502-4 for rules applicable in computing the foreign tax credit limitation and determining the source and separate category of a net operating loss of a consolidated group. Similarly, for purposes of applying this paragraph (e)(8)(i) with respect to another operative section (as described in §1.861-8(f)(1)), a net operating loss is divided into component parts based on the amounts of the deductions that are assigned to the relevant statutory and residual groupings and that are not absorbed in the taxable year in which the loss is incurred under the rules of that operative section. Deductions that are considered absorbed for purposes of an operative section may differ from the deductions that are considered absorbed for purposes of another provision of the Code that requires determining the components of a net operating loss.

(ii) *Allocation and apportionment of section 172 deduction.*—A net operating loss taken as a deduction in computing taxable income for a particular taxable year as allowed under section 172 is allocated and apportioned to statutory and residual groupings by reference to the statutory and residual groupings of the components of the net operating loss (as determined under paragraph (e)(8)(i) of this section) that is deducted in the taxable year. Except as provided under the rules for an operative section, if the full net operating loss carryover is not taken as a deduction in a taxable year, the partial net operating loss deduction is treated as ratably comprising the components of a net operating loss. See, for example, §1.904(g)-3, which is an exception to the general rule described in the previous sentence and provides rules for determining the source and separate category of a partial net operating loss deduction for purposes of section 904 as the operative section.

(9) *Deductions which are not definitely related.*—Deductions which shall generally be considered as not definitely related to any gross income, and therefore are ratably apportioned as provided in paragraph (c)(3) of this section, are—

(i) The deduction allowed by section 163 for interest described in subparagraph (2)(iii) of this paragraph (e);

(ii) The deduction allowed by section 164 for real estate taxes on a personal residence or for sales tax on the purchase of items for personal use;

(iii) The deduction for medical expenses allowed by section 213; and

(iv) The deduction for alimony payments allowed by section 215.

(10) [Reserved]

(11) *Personal exemptions.*—The deductions for the personal exemptions allowed by section 151, 642(b), or 873(b)(3) shall not be taken into account for purposes of allocation and apportionment under this section.

(12) *Deductions for certain charitable contributions.*—(i) *In general.*—The deduction for charitable contributions that is allowed under sections 170, 873(b)(2), and 882(c)(1)(B) is definitely related and allocable to all of the taxpayer's gross income. The deduction allocated under this paragraph (e)(12)(i) shall be apportioned between the statutory grouping (or among the statutory groupings) of gross income and the residual grouping on the basis of the relative amounts of gross income from sources in the United States in each grouping.

(ii) *Treaty provisions.*—If a deduction for charitable contributions not otherwise permitted by sections 170, 873(b)(2), and 882(c)(1)(B) is allowed under a U.S. income tax treaty, and such treaty limits the amount of the deduction based on a percentage of income arising from sources within the treaty partner, the deduction is definitely related and allocable to all of the taxpayer's gross income. The deduction allocated under this paragraph (e)(12)(ii) shall be apportioned between the statutory grouping (or among the statutory groupings) of gross income and the residual grouping on the basis of the relative amounts of gross income from sources within the treaty partner within each grouping.

(iii) *Coordination with §§1.861-14 and 1.861-14T.*—A deduction for a charitable contribution by a member of an affiliated group shall be allocated and apportioned under the rules of this section, §1.861-14(e)(6), and §1.861-14T(c)(1).

(13) *Foreign-derived intangible income.*—The portion of the deduction that is allowed for foreign-derived intangible income under section 250(a)(1)(A) (taking into account the reduction under section 250(a)(2)(B)(i), if any) is considered definitely related and allocable to the class of gross income included in the taxpayer's foreign-derived deduction eligible income (as defined in section 250(b)(4)). If necessary, the portion of the deduction is apportioned within the class ratably between the statutory grouping (or among the statutory groupings) of gross income and the residual grouping of gross income based on the relative amounts of foreign derived deduction eligible income in each grouping.

(14) *Global intangible low-taxed income and related section 78 gross up.*—The portion of the deduction (taking into account the reduction under section 250(a)(2)(B)(ii), if any) that is allowed for the global intangible low-taxed income amount described in section 250(a)(1)(B)(i), and that is allowed for the section 78 gross up under section 250(a)(1)(B)(ii), is considered definitely related and allocable to the class of gross income included under section 951A(a) and section 78, respectively. If necessary (for example, because a portion of the inclusion under section 951A(a) is passive category income or U.S. source income), the portion of the deduction is apportioned within the class ratably between the statutory grouping (or among the statutory groupings) of gross income and the residual grouping of gross income based on the relative amounts of gross income in each grouping.

(15) *Distributive share of partnership deductions.*—In general, if deductions are incurred by a partnership in which the taxpayer is a partner, the taxpayer's deductions that are allocated and apportioned include the taxpayer's distributive share of the partnership's deductions. See §§1.861-9(e), 1.861-17(f), and 1.904-4(n)(1)(ii) for special rules for apportioning a partner's distributive share of deductions of a partnership.

(16) *Special rule for the allocation and apportionment of reserve expenses of a life insurance company.*—An amount of reserve expenses of a life insurance company equal to the dividends received deduction that is disallowed because it is attributable to the policyholders' share of dividends received is treated as definitely related to such dividends. See paragraph (d)(2)(v)(B)(2) of this section (*Example 2*).

(f) *Miscellaneous matters.*—(1) *Operative sections.*—The operative sections of the Code which require the determination of taxable income of the taxpayer from specific sources or activities and which give rise to statutory groupings to which this section is applicable include the sections described below.

(i) [Reserved]

(ii) *Separate foreign tax credit limitations.*—Section 904(d)(1) and other sections described in §1.904-4(m) require that a separate foreign tax credit limitation be determined with respect to each separate category of income specified in those sections. Accordingly, the foreign source income within each separate category described in §1.904-5(a)(4)(v) constitutes a separate statutory grouping of income. U.S. source income is treated as income in the residual grouping for purposes of determining the limitation on the foreign tax credit.

(iii) *DISC and FSC taxable income.*—Sections 925 and 994 provide rules for determining the taxable income of a FSC and DISC, respectively, with respect to qualified sales and leases of export property and qualified services. The combined taxable income method available for determining a DISC's taxable income provides, without consideration of export promotion expenses, that the taxable income of the DISC shall be 50 percent of the combined taxable income of the DISC and the related supplier derived from sales and leases of export property and from services. In the FSC context, the taxable income of the FSC equals 23 percent of the combined taxable income of the FSC and the related supplier. Pursuant to regulations under sections 925 and 994, this section provides rules for determining the deductions to be taken into account in determining combined taxable income, except to the extent modified by the marginal costing rules set forth in the regulations under sections 925(b)(2) and 994(b)(2) if used by the taxpayer. See *Examples* (22) and (23) of paragraph (g) of this section. In addition, the computation of combined taxable income is necessary to determine the applicability of the section 925(d) limitation and the "no loss" rules of the regulations under sections 925 and 994.

(iv) *Effectively connected taxable income.*—Nonresident alien individuals and foreign corporations engaged in trade or business within the United States are taxed, as provided under sections 871(b)(1) and 882(a)(1), on taxable income which is effectively connected with the conduct of a trade or business within the United States. Such taxable income is determined in most instances by initially determining, under section 864(c), the amount of gross income which is effectively connected with the conduct of a trade or business within the United States. Pursuant to sections 873 and 882(c), this section is applicable for purposes of determining the deductions from such gross income (other than the deduction for interest expense allowed to foreign corporations (see §1.882-5)) which are to be taken into account in determining taxable income. See example (21) of paragraph (g) of this section.

(v) *Foreign base company income.*—Section 954 defines the term "foreign base company income" with respect to controlled foreign corporations. Section 954(b)(5) provides that in determining foreign base company income the gross income shall be reduced by the deductions of the controlled foreign corporation "properly allocable to such income". This section provides rules for identifying which deductions are properly allocable to foreign base company income.

(vi) *Other operative sections.*—The rules provided in this section also apply in determining—

(A) The amount of foreign source items of tax preference under section 58(g) determined for purposes of the minimum tax;

(B) The amount of foreign mineral income under section 901(e);

(C) [Reserved];

(D) The amount of foreign oil and gas extraction income and the amount of foreign oil related income under section 907;

(E) The tax base for individuals entitled to the benefits of section 931 and the section 936 tax credit of a domestic corporation that has an election in effect under section 936;

(F) The exclusion for income from Puerto Rico for bona fide residents of Puerto Rico under section 933;

(G) The limitation under section 934 on the maximum reduction in income tax liability incurred to the Virgin Islands;

(H) The income derived from the U.S. Virgin Islands or from a section 935 possession (as defined in §1.935-1(a)(3)(i)).

(I) The special deduction granted to China Trade Act corporations under section 941;

(J) The amount of certain U.S. source income excluded from the subpart F income of a controlled foreign corporation under section 952(b);

(K) The amount of income from the insurance of U.S. risks under section 953(b)(5);

(L) The international boycott factor and the specifically attributable taxes and income under section 999; and

(M) The taxable income attributable to the operation of an agreement vessel under section 607 of the Merchant Marine Act of 1936, as amended, and the Capital Construction Fund Regulations thereunder (26 CFR, pt. 3). See 26 CFR 3.2(b)(3).

(N) Deduction eligible income and foreign-derived deduction eligible income under section 250(b).

(2) *Application to more than one operative section.*—(i) Where more than one operative section applies, it may be necessary for the taxpayer to apply this section separately for each applicable operative section. In such a case, the taxpayer is required to use the same method of allocation and the same principles of apportionment for all operative sections.

(ii) When expenses, losses, and other deductions that have been properly allocated and apportioned between combined gross income of a related supplier and a DISC or former DISC and residual gross income, regardless of which of the administrative pricing methods of section 994 has been applied, such deductions are not also allocated and apportioned to gross income consisting of distributions from the DISC or former DISC attributable to income of the DISC or former DISC as determined under the administrative pricing methods with respect to DISC or former DISC taxable years beginning after December 31, 1986. Accordingly, *Example* (22) of paragraph (g) of this section does not apply to distributions from a DISC or former DISC with respect to DISC or former DISC taxable years beginning after December 31, 1986. This rule does not apply to the extent that the taxable income of the DISC or former DISC is determined under the section 994(a)(3) transfer pricing method. In addition, for taxable years beginning after December 31, 1986, in the case of expenses, losses, and other deductions that have been properly allocated and apportioned between combined gross income of a related supplier and a FSC and residual gross income, regardless of which of the administrative pricing methods of section 925 has been applied, such deductions are not also allocated and apportioned to gross income consisting of distributions from the FSC or former FSC which are attributable to the foreign trade income of the FSC or former FSC as determined under the administrative pricing methods. This rule does not apply to the extent that the foreign trade income of the FSC or former FSC is determined under the section 925(a)(3) transfer pricing method. See *Example* (23) of paragraph (g) of this section.

(3) *Special rules of section 863(b).*—(i) *In general.*—Special rules under section 863(b) provide for the application of rules of general apportionment provided in §§1.863-3 to 1.863-5, to worldwide taxable income in order to attribute part of such worldwide taxable income to U.S. sources and the remainder of such worldwide taxable income to foreign sources. The activities specified in section 863(b) are—

(A) Transportation or other services rendered partly within and partly without the United States,

(B) Sales of personal property produced by the taxpayer within and sold without the United States, or produced by the taxpayer without and sold within the United States, and

(C) Sales within the United States of personal property purchased within a possession of the United States.

In the instances provided in §§1.863-3 and 1.863-4 with respect to the activities described in (A), (B), and (C) of this subsection, this section is applicable only in determining worldwide taxable income attributable to these activities.

(ii) *Relationship of sections 861, 862, 863(a), and 863(b).*—Sections 861, 862, 863(a), and 863(b) are the four provisions applicable in determining taxable income from specific sources. Each of these four provisions applies independently. Where a deduction has been allocated and apportioned to income under one of these four provisions, the deduction shall not again be allocated and apportioned to gross income under any of the other three provisions. However, two or more of these provisions may have to be applied at the same time to determine the proper allocation and apportionment of a deduction. The special rules under section 863(b) take precedence over the general rules of Code sections 861, 862 and 863(a). For example, where a deduction is allocable in whole or in part to gross income to which section 863(b) applies, such deduction or part thereof shall not otherwise be allocated under section 861, 862, or 863(a). However, where the gross income to which the deduction is allocable includes both gross income to which section 863(b) applies and gross income to which section 861, 862, or 863(a) applies, more than one section must be applied at the same time in order to determine the proper allocation and apportionment of the deduction.

(4) *Adjustments made under other provisions of the Code.*—(i) *In general.*—If an adjustment which affects the taxpayer is made under section 482 or any other provision of the Code, it may be necessary to recompute the allocations and apportionments required by this section in order to reflect changes resulting from the adjustment. The recomputation made by the Commissioner shall be made using the same method of allocation and apportionment as was originally used by the taxpayer, provided such method as originally used conformed with paragraph (a)(2) of this section and, in light of the adjustment, such method does not result in a material distortion. In addition to adjustments which would be made aside from this section, adjustments to the taxpayer's income and deductions which would not otherwise be made may be required before applying this section in order to prevent a distortion in determining taxable income from a particular source of activity. For example, if an item included as a part of the cost of goods sold has been improperly attributed to specific sales, and, as a result, gross income under one of the operative sections referred to in paragraph (f)(1) of this section is improperly determined, it may be necessary for the Commissioner to make an adjustment to the cost of goods sold, consistent with the principles of this section, before applying this section. Similarly, if a domestic corporation transfers the stock in its foreign subsidiaries to a domestic subsidiary and the parent corporation continues to incur expenses in connection with protecting its capital investment in the foreign subsidiaries (see paragraph (e)(4) of this section), it may be necessary for the Commissioner to make an allocation under section 482 with respect to such expenses before making allocations and apportionments required by this section, even though the section 482 allocation might not otherwise be made.

(ii) *Example.*—(A) *Facts.* USP, a domestic corporation, purchases and sells consumer items in the United States and foreign markets. Its sales in foreign markets are made to related foreign subsidiaries. USP reported $1,500,000x as sales during the taxable year of which $1,000,000x was domestic sales and $500,000x was foreign sales. USP took a deduction for expenses incurred by its marketing department during the taxable year in the amount of $150,000x. These expenses were determined to be allocable to both domestic and foreign sales and are apportionable between such sales. On audit of USP's return for the taxable year, the IRS adjusted, under section 482, USP's sales to related foreign subsidiaries by increasing the sales price by a total of $100,000x, thereby increasing USP's foreign sales and total sales by the same amount. Before the audit, USP allocated and apportioned the marketing department deduction as follows:

Table 1 to paragraph (f)(4)(ii)(A)

To gross income from domestic sales: $150,000x x ($1,000,000x/$1,500,000x)	$100,000x
To gross income from foreign sales: $150,000x x ($500,000x/$1,500,000x)	$50,000x
Total	$150,000x

(B) *Analysis.* As a result of the section 482 adjustment, the apportionment of the deduction for the marketing department expenses is redetermined as follows:

Table 2 to paragraph (f)(4)(ii)(B)

To gross income from domestic sales: $150,000x x ($1,000,000x/$1,600,000x)	$93,750x
To gross income from foreign sales: $150,000x x ($600,000x/$1,600,000x)	$56,250x
Total	$150,000x

(5) *Verification of allocations and apportionments.*—Since, under this section, allocations and apportionments are made on the basis of the factual relationship between deductions and gross income, the taxpayer is required to furnish, at the request of the District Director, information from which such factual relationships can be determined. In reviewing the overall limitation to the foreign tax credit of a domestic corporation, for example, the District Director should consider information which would enable him to determine the extent to which deductions attributable to functions performed in the United States are related to earning foreign source income, United States source income, or income from both sources. In addition to functions with a specific international purpose, consideration should be given to the functions of management, the direction and results of an acquisition program, the functions of operating units and personnel located at the head office, the functions of support units (including but not limited to engineering, legal, budget, accounting, and industrial relations), the functions of selling and advertising units and personnel, the direction and uses of research and development, and the direction and uses of services furnished by independent contractors. Thus, for example when requested by the District Director, the taxpayer shall make available any of its organization charts, manuals, and other writings which relate to the manner in which its gross income arises and to the functions of organizational units, employees, and assets of the taxpayer and arrange for the interview of such of its employees as the District Director deems desirable in order to determine the gross income to which deductions relate. See section 7602 and the regulations thereunder which generally provide for the examination of books and witnesses. See also section 905(b) and the regulations thereunder which require proof of foreign tax credits to the satisfaction of the Secretary or his delegate.

(g) *Examples.*—The following examples illustrate the principles of the rules in this section. In each example, unless otherwise specified, section 904 is the operative section. In addition, in each example, where a method of allocation or apportionment is illustrated as an acceptable method, it is assumed that such method is used by the taxpayers on a consistent basis from year to year. Further, it is assumed that each party named in each example operates on a calendar year accounting basis and, where the party is a U.S. taxpayer, files returns on a calendar year basis.

(1) through (18) [Reserved]

(15) *Example 15: Payment in settlement of claim for damages allocated to specific class of gross income.*—(i) *Facts.* USP, a domestic corporation, sells Product A in the United States. USP also owns and operates a disregarded entity (FDE) in Country X. FDE, which constitutes a foreign branch of USP within the meaning of § 1.904-4(f)(3)(vii), sells Product A inventory in Country X. FDE's functional currency is the U.S. dollar. In each of its taxable years from 2018 through 2020, USP earns $2,000x of U.S. source gross income from sales of Product A to customers in the United States. USP also sells Product A to FDE for an arm's length price and FDE sells Product A to customers in Country X. After the application of section 862(a)(6), § 1.861-7(c), and the disregarded payment rules of § 1.904-4(f)(2)(vi), the sales of Product A in Country X result in $1,500x of general category foreign source gross income and $500x of foreign branch category foreign source gross income in each of 2018 and 2019 and $2,500x of general category foreign source gross income and $500x of foreign branch category foreign source gross income in 2020. FDE is sued for damages in 2019 after Product A harms a customer in Country X in 2018. In 2020, FDE makes a deductible payment of $60x to the Country X customer in settlement of the legal claims for damages.

(ii) *Analysis.* Under paragraph (e)(5)(ii) of this section, the deductible settlement payment is definitely related and allocable to the class of gross income of the type produced by the specific sales of property that gave rise to the damages claims, that is USP's gross income from sales of Product A in Country X. Claims that might arise from damages caused by Product A to customers in the United States are irrelevant in allocating the deduction for the settlement payments made to the customer in Country X. For purposes of determining USP's foreign tax credit limitation under section 904(d), because in 2020 that class of gross income consists of both foreign source foreign branch category income and foreign source general category income, the settlement payment of $60x is apportioned between gross income in the two categories in proportion to the relative amounts of gross income in each category in 2020, the year the deduction is allowed. Therefore, $10x ($60x x $500x / $3,000x) is apportioned to foreign source foreign branch category income, and the remaining $50x ($60x x $2,500x / $3,000x) is apportioned to foreign source general category income.

(16) *Example 16: Legal damages payment arising from event incident to production and sale.*—(i) *Facts*—The facts are the same as in paragraph (g)(15) of this section (the facts in *Example 15*) except that instead of a product liability lawsuit relating to a 2018 event, in 2019 there is a disaster at a warehouse owned by USP in the United States arising from the negligence of an employee. The warehouse is used to store Product A inventory intended for sale both by USP in the United States and by FDE in Country X. In 2020, the warehouse asset is characterized under § 1.861-9T(g)(3)(ii) as a multiple category asset that is assigned 10% to the foreign source foreign branch category, 50% to the foreign source general category, and 40% to the residual grouping of U.S. source income. The inventory of Product A in the warehouse is destroyed and USP employees as well as residents in the vicinity of the warehouse are injured. USP's reputation in the United States suffers such that USP expects to subsequently lose market share in the United States. In 2020, USP makes deductible damages payments totaling $50x to injured employees and the nearby residents, all of whom are in the United States.

(ii) *Analysis.* USP's warehouse in the United States is used in connection with sales of Product A to customers in both the United States and Country X. Thus, under paragraph (e)(5)(ii) of this section, the $50x damages payment arises from an event incident to the sales of Product A and is therefore definitely related and allocable to the class of gross income ordinarily produced by the asset (the warehouse) that is involved in the event — that is, the gross income from sales of Product A by USP in the United States and by FDE in Country X. Under paragraph (e)(5)(ii) of this section, the $50x deduction for the damages payment is apportioned for purposes of applying section 904(d) on the basis of the relative value in each grouping (as determined under § 1.861-9(g) for purposes of allocating and apportioning USP's interest expense) of USP's warehouse, the asset involved in the event, in 2020, the year the deduction is allowed. USP's warehouse is a multiple category asset as described in § 1.861-9T(g)(3)(ii) and 10% of the value of USP's warehouse is properly characterized as an asset generating foreign source foreign branch category in 2020. Accordingly, $5x (10% x $50x) of the deduction is apportioned to foreign source foreign branch category income. Additionally, 50% of the value of USP's warehouse is properly characterized as an asset generating foreign source general category income in 2020 and, accordingly, $25x (50% x $50x) is apportioned to such grouping. The remaining $20x (40% x $50x) is apportioned to U.S. source income.

(17) *Example 17: Payment following a change in law.*—(i) *Facts.* The facts are the same as in paragraph (g)(16) of this section (the facts in *Example 16*), except that the disaster at USP's warehouse occurred not in 2019 but in 2016 and thus before the enactment of the section 904(d) separate category for foreign branch category income. The deductible damages payments are made in 2020.

(ii) *Analysis.* USP's U.S. warehouse was used in connection with making sales of Product A in both the United States and Country X. Under paragraph (e)(5)(ii) of this section, the 2020 damages payment arises from an event incident to the sales of Product A and is therefore definitely related and allocable to the class of gross income ordinarily produced by the asset (the warehouse) that is involved in the event, that is the gross income from sales of Product A by USP in the United States and by FDE in Country X. Under the law in effect in 2016, the income earned from the Product A sales in Country X was solely general category income. Under paragraph (e)(5)(ii) of this section, the damages payment is definitely related and allocable to the class of gross income consisting of sales of Product A by USP in the United States and by FDE in Country X, and apportioned to the statutory and residual groupings based on the relative value in each grouping (as determined under § 1.861-9(g) for purposes of allocating and apportioning USP's interest expense) of USP's warehouse, the asset involved in the event, in 2020, the year in which the deduction is allowed. Accordingly, for purposes of determining USP's foreign tax credit limitation under section 904(d), the 2020 deductible damages payment of $50x is allocated and apportioned in the same manner as in paragraph (g)(16)(ii) of this section (the analysis in *Example 16*).

(18) *Example 18: Stewardship and supportive expenses.*—(i) *Facts*—(A) *Overview.* USP, a domestic corporation, manufactures and sells Product A in the United States. USP directly owns 100% of the stock of USSub, a domestic corporation, and each of CFC1, CFC2, and CFC3, which are all controlled foreign corporations. USP and USSub file separate returns for U.S. Federal income tax purposes but are members of the same affiliated group as defined in section 243(b)(2). USSub, CFC1, CFC2, and CFC3 perform similar functions in the United States and in the foreign countries T, U, and V, respectively. USP's tax book value in the stock of USSub is $15,000x. USP's tax book value in the stock of each of CFC1, CFC2, and CFC3 is, respectively, $5,000x, $10,000x, and $15,000x.

(B) *USP Department expenses.* USP's supervision department (the Department) incurs expenses of $1,500x. The Department is responsible for the supervision of its four subsidiaries and for rendering certain services to the subsidiaries, and the Department provides all the supportive functions necessary for USP's foreign activities. The Department performs three types of activities. First, the Department performs services that cost $900x outside the United States for the direct benefit of CFC2 for which a marked-up fee is paid by CFC2 to USP. Second, the Department provides services at a cost of $60x related to license agreements that USP maintains with subsidiaries CFC1 and CFC2 and which give rise to foreign source general category income to USP. Third, the Department performs activities described in § 1.482-9(l)(3)(iii) that are in the nature of shareholder oversight, that duplicate functions performed by all four of the subsidiaries' own employees, and that do not provide an additional benefit to the subsidiaries. For example, a team of auditors from USP's accounting department periodically audits the subsidiaries' books and prepares internal reports for use by USP's management. Similarly, USP's treasurer periodically reviews the subsidiaries' financial policies for the board of directors of USP. These activities do not provide an additional benefit to the related corporations. The Department's oversight activities are related to all the subsidiaries. The cost of the duplicative activities is $540x.

(C) *USP's income.* USP earns the following items of income: first, under section 951(a), USP has $2,000x of subpart F income that is passive category income. Second, USP has a GILTI inclusion amount of $2,000x. Third, USP earns $1,000x of royalties, paid by CFC1 and CFC2, that are foreign source general category income. Finally, USP receives a fee of $1,000x from CFC2 that is foreign source general category income.

(i) *Analysis*—(A) *Character of USP Department services.* The first and second activities (the services rendered for the benefit of CFC2, and the provision of services related to license agreements with CFC1 and CFC2) are not properly characterized as stewardship expenses because they are not incurred solely to protect the corporation's capital investment in the related corporation or to facilitate compliance by the corporation with reporting, legal, or regulatory requirements applicable specifically to the corporation. The third activity described is in the nature of shareholder oversight and is characterized as stewardship as described in paragraph (e)(4)(ii)(A) of this section because the expense is related to duplicative activities.

(B) *Allocation*. First, the deduction of $900x for expenses related to services rendered for the benefit of CFC2 is definitely related (and therefore allocable) to the fees for services that USP receives from CFC2. Second, the $60x of deductions attributable to USP's license agreements with CFC1 and CFC2 are definitely related (and therefore allocable) solely to royalties received from CFC1 and CFC2. Third, based on the relevant facts and circumstances and the Department's oversight activities, the stewardship deduction of $540x is related to the oversight of all of USP's subsidiaries and therefore is definitely related (and therefore allocable) to dividends and inclusions received or included from all the subsidiaries.

(C) *Apportionment*. *(1)* No apportionment of USP's deduction of $900x for expenses related to the services performed for CFC2 is necessary because the class of gross income to which the deduction is allocated consists entirely of a single statutory grouping, foreign source general category income.

(2) No apportionment of USP's deduction of $60x attributable to the services related to license agreements is necessary because the class of gross income to which the deduction is allocated consists entirely of a single statutory grouping, foreign source general category income.

(3) For purposes of apportioning USP's $540x stewardship expenses in determining the foreign tax credit limitation, the statutory groupings are foreign source general category income, foreign source passive category income, and foreign source section 951A category income. The residual grouping is U.S. source income.

(4) USP's deduction of $540x for the Department's stewardship expenses which are allocable to dividends and amounts included from the subsidiaries are apportioned using the same value of USP's stock in USSub, CFC1, CFC2, and CFC3 that is used for purposes of allocating and apportioning USP's interest expense. Pursuant to paragraph (e)(4)(ii)(A) of this section and § 1.861-14(e)(1)(i), the value of USP's stock in USSub is included for purposes of apportioning USP's stewardship expense. The value of USSub's stock is $15,000x, and USSub only owns assets that generate income in the residual grouping of gross income from U.S. sources. Therefore, for purposes of apportioning USP's stewardship expense, all of the $15,000x value of the USSub stock is characterized as an asset generating U.S. source income. Although USSub stock would be eliminated from consideration as an asset under paragraph (d)(2)(ii)(B) of this section, for purposes of apportioning USP's stewardship expense section 864(e)(3) and paragraph (d)(2) of this section do not apply. USP uses the asset method described in § 1.861-12T(c)(3)(ii) to characterize the stock in its CFCs. After application of § 1.861-13(a), USP determines that with respect to its three CFCs in the aggregate it has $15,000x of section 951A category stock in the non-section 245A subgroup, $6,000x of general category stock in the section 245A subgroup, and $9,000x of passive category stock in the non-section 245A subgroup. Although under paragraph (d)(2)(ii)(C)*(2)* of this section $7,500x of the stock that is section 951A category stock is an exempt asset, for purposes of apportioning USP's stewardship expense section 864(e)(3) and paragraph (d)(2) of this section do not apply. Finally, even though USP may be allowed a section 245A deduction with respect to dividends from the CFCs, no portion of the value of the stock of the CFCs is eliminated, because the section 245A deduction does not create exempt income or result in the stock being treated as an exempt asset. See section 864(e)(3) and paragraph (d)(2)(iii)(C) of this section.

(5) Taking into account the characterization of USP's stock in USSub, CFC1, CFC2, and CFC3 with a total value of $45,000x ($15,000x + $6,000x + $9,000x + $15,000x), the $540x of Department expenses is apportioned as follows: $180x ($540x x $15,000x / $45,000x) to section 951A category income, $72x ($540x x $6,000x / $45,000x) to general category income, $108x ($540x x $9,000x / $45,000x) to passive category income, and $180x ($540x x $15,000x / $45,000x) to the residual grouping of U.S. source income. Section 904(b)(4)(B)(i) and § 1.904(b)-3 apply to $72x of the stewardship expense apportioned to the CFCs' stock that is characterized as being in the section 245A subgroup in the general category.

(19) *Example 19: Supportive expense*.—(i) *Facts*—(A) USP, a domestic corporation, purchases and sells products both in the United States and in foreign countries. USP has no foreign subsidiary and no international department. During the taxable year, USP incurs the following expenses with respect to its worldwide activities:

Table 3 to paragraph (g)(19)(i)(A)

Personnel department expenses	$50,000x
Training department expenses	$35,000x
General and administrative expenses	$55,000x
President's salary	$40,000x
Sales manager's salary	$20,000x
Total	$200,000x

(B) USP has domestic gross receipts from sales of $750,000x and foreign gross receipts from sales of $500,000x and has gross income from such sales in the same ratio, namely $300,000x from domestic sources and $200,000x from foreign sources that is general category income.

(ii) *Analysis*—(A) *Allocation*. The above expenses are definitely related and allocable to all of USP's gross income derived from both domestic and foreign markets.

(B) *Apportionment*. For purposes of applying the foreign tax credit limitation, the statutory grouping is gross income from sources outside the United States in general category income and the residual grouping is gross income from sources within the United States. USP's deductions for its worldwide sales activities must be apportioned between these groupings. USP does not have a separate international division which performs essentially all of the functions required to manage and oversee its foreign activities. The president and sales manager do not maintain time records. The division of their time between domestic and foreign activities varies from day to day and cannot be estimated on an annual basis with any reasonable degree of accuracy. Similarly, there are no facts which would justify a method of apportionment of their salaries or of one of the other listed deductions based on more specific factors than gross receipts or gross income. An acceptable method of apportionment would be on the basis of gross receipts. The apportionment of the $200,000x deduction is as follows:

Table 4 to paragraph (g)(19)(ii)(B)

Apportionment of the $200,000x expense to the statutory grouping of gross income: $200,000x x [$500,000x/($500,000x + $750,000x)]	$80,000x
Apportionment of the $200,000x expense to the residual grouping of gross income: $200,000x x [$750,000x/($500,000x + $750,000x)]	$120,000x
Total apportioned supportive expense	$200,000x

(20) Example 20: Supportive expense.—(i) *Facts*. Assume the same facts as in paragraph (g)(19)(i) of this section (the facts in *Example 19*), except that USP's president devotes only 5% of his time to the foreign operations and 95% of his time to the domestic operations and that USP's sales manager devotes approximately 10% of her time to foreign sales and 90% of her time to domestic sales.

(ii) *Analysis*—(A) *Allocation*. The expenses incurred by USP with respect to its worldwide activities are definitely related, and therefore allocable to USP's gross income from both its foreign and domestic markets.

(B) *Apportionment*. On the basis of the additional facts it is not acceptable to apportion the salaries of the president and the sales manager on the basis of gross receipts. It is acceptable to apportion such salaries between the statutory grouping (gross income from sources without the United States) and residual grouping (gross income from sources within the United States) on the basis of time devoted to each sales activity. Remaining expenses may still be apportioned on the basis of gross receipts. The apportionment is as follows:

Table 5 to paragraph (g)(20)(ii)(B)

Apportionment of the $200,000x expense to the statutory grouping of gross income:	
President's salary: $40,000x x 5%	$2,000x
Sales manager's salary: $20,000x x 10%	$2,000x
Remaining expenses: $140,000x x [$500,000x/($500,000x + $750,000x)]	$56,000x
Subtotal: Apportionment of expense to statutory grouping	$60,000x
Apportionment of the $200,000x expense to the residual grouping of gross income:	
President's salary: $40,000x x 95%	$38,000x
Sales manager's salary: $20,000x x 90%	$18,000x
Remaining expenses: $140,000x x [$750,000x/($500,000x + $750,000x)]	$84,000x
Subtotal: Apportionment of expense to residual grouping	$140,000x
Total: Apportioned supportive expense	$200,000x

(21) *Example 21: Supportive expense.*—(i) *Facts.* FC, a foreign corporation doing business in the United States, is a manufacturer of metal stamping machines. FC has no U.S. subsidiaries and no separate division to manage and oversee its business in the United States. FC manufactures and sells these machines in the United States and in foreign countries A and B and has a separate manufacturing facility in each country. Sales of these machines are FC's only source of income. In Year 1, FC incurs general and administrative expenses related to both its U.S. and foreign operations of $100,000x. It has machine sales of $500,000x, $1,000,000x, and $1,000,000x on which it earns gross income of $200,000x, $400,000x, and $400,000x in the United States, Country A, and Country B, respectively. The income from the manufacture and sale of the machines in countries A and B is not effectively connected with FC's business in the United States.

(ii) *Analysis*—(A) *Allocation.* The $100,000x of general and administrative expense is definitely related to the income to which it gives rise, namely a part of the gross income from sales of machines in the United States, in Country A, and in Country B. The expenses are allocable to this class of income, even though FC's gross income from sources outside the United States is excluded income since it is not effectively connected with a U.S. trade or business.

(B) *Apportionment.* Since FC is a foreign corporation, the statutory grouping is gross income effectively connected with FC's trade of business in the United States, namely gross income from sources within the United States, and the residual grouping is gross income not effectively connected with a trade or business in the United States, namely gross income from countries A and B. Since there are no facts that would require a method of apportionment other than on the basis of sales or gross income, the amount may be apportioned between the two groupings on the basis of amounts of gross income as follows:

Table 6 to paragraph (g)(21)(ii)(B)

Apportionment of general and administrative expense to the statutory grouping, gross income from sources within the United States: $100,000x x [$200,000x/($200,000x + $400,000x + $400,000x)]	$20,000x
Apportionment of general and administrative expense to the residual grouping, gross income from sources without the United States: $100,000x x [($400,000x + $400,000x)/($200,000x + $400,000x + $400,000x)]	$80,000x
Total apportioned general and administrative expense	$100,000x

(22) through (24) [Reserved]

(25) *Example 25: Income taxes.*—(i) *Facts.* USP, a domestic corporation, is a manufacturer and distributor of electronic equipment with operations in states A, B, and C. USP also has a foreign branch, as defined in section 904(d)(1)(B) and § 1.904-4(f), in Country Y which manufactures and distributes the same type of electronic equipment. In Year 1, USP has taxable income from these activities, as described under the Code (without taking into account the deduction for state income taxes), of $1,000,000x, of which $200,000x is foreign source foreign branch category income and $800,000x is domestic source income. States A, B, and C each determine USP's income subject to tax within their state by making adjustments to USP's taxable income as determined under the Code, and then apportioning the adjusted taxable income on the basis of the relative amounts of USP's payroll, property, and sales within each state as compared to USP's worldwide payroll, property, and sales. The adjustments made by states A, B, and C all involve adding and subtracting enumerated items from taxable income as determined under the Code. However, in making these adjustments to taxable income, none of the states specifically exempts foreign source income as determined under the Code. On this basis, it is determined that USP has taxable income of $550,000x, $200,000x, and $200,000x in states A, B, and C, respectively. The corporate tax rates in states A, B, and C are 10%, 5%, and 2%, respectively, and USP has total state income tax liabilities of $69,000x ($55,000x + $10,000x + $4,000x), which it deducts as an expense for Federal income tax purposes.

(ii) *Analysis*—(A) *Allocation.* USP's deduction of $69,000x for state income taxes is definitely related and thus allocable to the gross income with respect to which the taxes are imposed. Since the statutes of states A, B, and C do not specifically exempt foreign source income (as determined under the Code) from taxation and since, in the aggregate, states A, B, and C tax $950,000x of USP's income while only $800,000x is domestic source income under the Code, it is presumed that state income taxes are imposed on $150,000x of foreign source income. The deduction for state income taxes is therefore related and allocable to both USP's foreign source and domestic source income.

(B) *Apportionment.* For purposes of computing the foreign tax credit limitation, USP's income is comprised of one statutory grouping, foreign source foreign branch category gross income, and one residual grouping, gross income from sources within the United States. The state income tax deduction of $69,000x must be apportioned between these two groupings. Corporation USP calculates the apportionment on the basis of the relative amounts of foreign source foreign branch category taxable income and U.S. source taxable income subject to state taxation. In this case, state income taxes are presumed to be imposed on $800,000x of domestic source income and $150,000x of foreign source general category income.

Table 7 to paragraph (g)(25)(ii)(B)

State income tax deduction apportioned to foreign source foreign branch category income (statutory grouping): $69,000x x ($150,000x/$950,000x)	$10,895x
State income tax deduction apportioned to income from sources within the United States (residual grouping): $69,000x x ($800,000x/$950,000x)	$58,105x
Total apportioned state income tax deduction	$69,000x

(26) *Example 26: Income taxes.*—(i) *Facts.* Assume the same facts as in paragraph (g)(25)(i) of this section (the facts in *Example 25*), except that the language of state A's statute and the statute's operation exempt from taxation all foreign source income, as determined under the Code, so that foreign source income is not included in adjusted taxable income subject to apportionment in state A (and factors relating to USP's Country Y branch are not taken into account in computing the state A apportionment fraction).

(ii) *Analysis*—(A) *Allocation.* USP's deduction of $69,000x for state income taxes is definitely related and thus allocable to the gross income with respect to which the taxes are imposed. Since state A exempts all foreign source income by statute, state A is presumed to impose tax on $550,000x of USP's $800,000x of domestic source income. USP's state A tax of $55,000x is allocable, therefore, solely to domestic source income. Since the statutes of states B and C do not specifically exclude all foreign source income as determined under the Code, and since states B and C impose tax on $400,000x

($200,000x + $200,000x) of USP's income of which only $250,000x ($800,000x − $550,000x) is presumed to be domestic source, the deduction for the $14,000x of income taxes imposed by states B and C is related and allocable to both foreign source and domestic source income.

(B) *Apportionment*—*(1)* For purposes of computing the foreign tax credit limitation, USP's income is comprised of one statutory grouping, foreign source foreign branch category gross income, and one residual grouping, gross income from sources within the United States. The deduction of $14,000x for income taxes of states B and C must be apportioned between these two groupings.

(2) Corporation USP calculates the apportionment on the basis of the relative amounts of foreign source foreign branch category income and U.S. source income subject to state taxation.

Table 8 to paragraph (g)(26)(ii)(B)(2)

States B and C income tax deduction apportioned to foreign source foreign branch category income (statutory grouping):	
$14,000x x ($150,000x/$400,000x)	$5,250x
States B and C income tax deduction apportioned to income from sources within the United States (residual grouping):	
$14,000x x ($250,000x/$400,000x)	$8,750x
Total apportioned state income tax deduction	$14,000x

(3) Of USP's total income taxes of $69,000x, the amount allocated and apportioned to foreign source foreign branch category income equals $5,250x. The total amount of state income taxes allocated and apportioned to U.S. source income equals $63,750x ($55,000x + $8,750x).

(27) *Example 27: Income tax*—(i) *Facts.* Assume the same facts as in paragraph (g)(25)(i) of this section (the facts in *Example 25*), except that state A, in which USP has significant income-producing activities, does not impose a corporate income tax or other state tax computed on the basis of income derived from business activities conducted in state A. USP therefore has a total state income tax liability in Year 1 of $14,000x ($10,000x paid to state B plus $4,000x paid to state C), all of which is subject to allocation and apportionment under paragraph (b) of this section.

(ii) *Analysis*—(A) *Allocation*—*(1)* USP's deduction of $14,000x for state income taxes is definitely related and allocable to the gross income with respect to which the taxes are imposed. However, in these facts, an adjustment is necessary before the aggregate state taxable incomes can be compared with U.S. source income on the Federal income tax return in the manner described in paragraphs (g)(25)(ii) and (g)(26)(ii) of this section (the analysis in *Examples 25* and *26*). Unlike the facts in paragraphs (g)(25)(i) and (g)(26)(i) of this section (the facts in *Examples 25* and *26*), state A imposes no income tax and does not define taxable income attributable to activities in state A. The total amount of USP's income subject to state taxation is, therefore, $400,000x ($200,000x in state B and $200,000x in state C). This total presumptively does not include any income attributable to activities performed in state A and therefore cannot properly be compared to total U.S. source taxable income reported by USP for Federal income tax purposes, which does include income attributable to state A activities.

(2)(i) Accordingly, before applying the method used in paragraphs (g)(25)(ii) and (g)(26)(ii) of this section (the analysis in *Examples 25* and *26*) to the facts of the example in this paragraph (g)(27), it is necessary first to estimate the amount of taxable income that state A could reasonably attribute to USP's activities in state A, and then to reduce federal taxable income by that amount.

(ii) Any reasonable method may be used to attribute taxable income to USP's activities in state A. For example, the rules of the Uniform Division of Income for Tax Purposes Act ("UDITPA") attribute income to a state on the basis of the average of three ratios that are based upon the taxpayer's facts—property within the state over total property, payroll within the state over total payroll, and sales within the state over total sales—and, with adjustments, provide a reasonable method for this purpose. When applying the rules of UDITPA to estimate U.S. source income derived from state A activities, the taxpayer's UDITPA factors must be adjusted to eliminate both taxable income and factors attributable to a foreign branch. Therefore, in the example in this paragraph (g)(27) all taxable income as well as UDITPA apportionment factors (property, payroll, and sales) attributable to USP's Country Y branch must be eliminated.

(3)(i) Since it is presumed that, if state A had had an income tax, state A would not attempt to tax the income derived by USP's Country Y branch, any reasonable estimate of the income that would be taxed by state A must exclude any foreign source income.

(ii) When using the rules of UDITPA to estimate the income that would have been taxable by state A in these facts, foreign source income is excluded by starting with federally defined taxable income (before deduction for state income taxes) and subtracting any income derived by USP's Country Y branch. The hypothetical state A taxable income is then determined by multiplying the resulting difference by the average of USP's state A property, payroll, and sales ratios, determined using the principles of UDITPA (after adjustment by eliminating the Country Y branch factors). The resulting product is presumed to be exclusively U.S. source income, and the allocation and apportionment method described in paragraph (g)(26) of this section (Example 26) must then be applied.

(iii) If, for example, state A taxable income were determined to equal $550,000x, then $550,000x of U.S. source income for Federal income tax purposes would be presumed to constitute state A taxable income. Under paragraph (g)(26) of this section (*Example 26*), the remaining $250,000x ($800,000x − $550,000x) of U.S. source income for Federal income tax purposes would be presumed to be subject to tax in states B and C. Since states B and C impose tax on $400,000x, the application of Example 25 would result in a presumption that $150,000x is foreign source income and $250,000x is domestic source income. The deduction for the $14,000x of income taxes of states B and C would therefore be related and allocable to both foreign source and domestic source income and would be subject to apportionment.

(B) *Apportionment.* The deduction of $14,000x for income taxes of states B and C is apportioned in the same manner as in paragraph (g)(26) of this section (*Example 26*). As a result, $5,250x of the $14,000x of state B and state C income taxes is apportioned to foreign source foreign branch category income ($14,000x x $150,000x/$400,000x), and $8,750x ($14,000x x $250,000x/$400,000x) of the $14,000x of state B and state C income taxes is apportioned to U.S. source income.

(h) *Applicability date.*—(1) Except as provided in this paragraph (h), this section applies to taxable years that both begin after December 31, 2017, and end on or after December 4, 2018.

(2) Paragraphs (d)(2)(ii)(B), (d)(2)(v), (e)(4) and (5), (e)(6)(i), (e)(8) and (16), and (g)(15) through (18) of this section apply to taxable years that begin after December 31, 2019. For taxable years that both begin after December 31, 2017, and end on or after December 4, 2018, and also begin on or before December 31, 2019, see § 1.861-8(d)(2)(ii)(B), (e)(4) and (5), (e)(6)(i), and (e)(8) as in effect on December 17, 2019.

(3) The last sentence of paragraph (d)(2)(ii)(C)(1) of this section and paragraph (f)(1)(vi)(N) of this section apply to taxable years beginning on or after January 1, 2021.

(4) Paragraph (e)(4)(i) of this section applies to taxable years ending on or after November 2, 2020. [Reg. § 1.861-8.]

☐ *[T.D. 6258, 10-23-57. Amended by T.D. 6892, 8-22-66; T.D. 7378, 9-29-75; T.D. 7456, 1-3-77; T.D. 7749, 12-30-80; T.D. 7939, 2-2-84; T.D. 8228, 9-9-88; T.D. 8236, 12-7-88; T.D. 8286, 1-29-90; T.D. 8337, 3-11-91; T.D. 8646, 12-21-95; T.D. 8805, 1-8-99; T.D. 8973, 12-27-2001; T.D. 9143, 7-27-2004; T.D. 9194, 4-6-2005; T.D. 9211, 7-13-2005; T.D. 9278, 7-31-2006; T.D. 9391, 4-4-2008, T.D. 9456, 7-31-2009 (corrected 9-8-2009); T.D. 9882, 12-16-2019 (corrected 5-14-2020), T.D. 9901, 7-9-2020 (corrected 10-27-2020) T.D. 9922, 11-2-2020 (corrected 9-30-2021) and T.D. 9959, 12-28-2021 (corrected 7-26-2022).]*

§ 1.861-8T. Computation of taxable income from sources within the United States and from other sources and activities (Temporary).—(a) *In general.*

(1) [Reserved]

(2) *Allocation and apportionment of deductions in general.*—If an affiliated group of corporations joins in filing a consolidated return under section 1501, the provisions of this section are to be applied separately to each member in that affiliated group for purposes of determining such member's taxable income, except to the extent that expenses, losses, and other deductions are allocated and apportioned as if all domestic members of an affiliated group were a single corporation under section 864(e) and the regulations thereunder. See § 1.861-9T through § 1.861-11T for rules regarding the affiliated group allocation and apportionment of interest expense, and § 1.861-14T for rules regarding the affiliated group allocation and apportionment of expenses other than interest.

(a)(3) through (b) [Reserved]For further guidance, see § 1.861-8(a)(3) through (b).

(c) *Apportionment of deductions.*—(1) *Deductions definitely related to a class of gross income.*—Where a deduction has been allocated in accordance with paragraph (b) of this section to a class of gross income which is included in one statutory grouping and the residual grouping, the deduction must be apportioned between the statutory grouping and the residual grouping. Where a deduction has been allocated to a class of gross income which is included in more than one statutory grouping, such deduction must be apportioned among the statutory groupings and, where necessary, the residual grouping. Thus, in determining the separate limitations on the foreign tax credit imposed by section 904(d)(1) or by section 907, the income within a separate limitation category constitutes a statutory grouping of income and all other income not within that separate limitation category (whether domestic or within a different separate limitation category) constitutes the residual grouping. In this regard, the same method of apportionment must be used in apportioning a deduction to each separate limitation category. Also, see paragraph (f)(1)(iii) of this section with respect to the apportionment of deductions among the statutory groupings designated in section 904(d)(1). If the class of gross income to which a deduction has been allocated consists entirely of a single statutory grouping or the residual grouping, there is no need to apportion that deduction. If a deduction is not definitely related to any gross income, it must be apportioned ratably as provided in paragraph (c)(3) of this section. A deduction is apportioned by attributing the deduction to gross income (within the class to which the deduction has been allocated) which is in one or more statutory groupings and to gross income (within the class) which is in the residual grouping. Such attribution must be accomplished in a manner which reflects to a reasonably close extent the factual relationship between the deduction and the grouping of gross income. In apportioning deductions, it may be that for the taxable year there is no gross income in the statutory grouping or that deductions will exceed the amount of gross income in the statutory grouping. See paragraph (d)(1) of this section with respect to cases in which deductions exceed gross income. In determining the method of apportionment for a specific deduction, examples of bases and factors which should be considered include, but are not limited to—

(i) Comparison of units sold,

(ii) Comparison of the amount of gross sales or receipts,

(iii) Comparison of costs of goods sold,

(iv) Comparison of profit contribution,

(v) Comparison of expenses incurred, assets used, salaries paid, space utilized, and time spent which are attributable to the activities or properties giving rise to the class of gross income, and

(vi) Comparison of the amount of gross income.

Paragraph (e)(2) through (8) of this section provides the applicable rules for allocation and apportionment of deductions for interest, research and development expenses, and certain other deductions. The effects on tax liability of the apportionment of deductions and the burden of maintaining records not otherwise maintained and making computations not otherwise made shall be taken into consideration in determining whether a method of apportionment and its application are sufficiently precise. A method of apportionment described in this paragraph (c)(1) may not be used when it does not reflect, to a reasonably close extent, the factual relationship between the deduction and the groupings of income. Furthermore, certain methods of apportionment described in this paragraph (c)(1) may not be used in connection with any deduction for which another method is prescribed. The principles set forth above are applicable in apportioning both deductions definitely related to a class which constitutes less than all of the taxpayer's gross income and to deductions related to all of the taxpayer's gross income. If a deduction is not related to any class of gross income, it must be apportioned ratably as provided in paragraph (c)(3) of this section.

(2) *Apportionment based on assets.*—For further guidance, see § 1.861-8(c)(2).

(3) [Reserved]

(d) *Excess of deductions and excluded and eliminated items of income.*

(1) [Reserved]

(2) *Allocation and apportionment to exempt, excluded or eliminated income.*—(i) *In general.*—In the case of taxable years beginning after December 31, 1986, except to the extent otherwise permitted by § 1.861-13T, the following rules shall apply to take account of income that is exempt or excluded, or assets generating such income, with respect to allocation and apportionment of deductions.

(A) *Allocation of deductions.*—In allocating deductions that are definitely related to one or more classes of gross income, exempt income (as defined in paragraph (d)(2)(ii) of this section) shall be taken into account.

(B) *Apportionment of deductions.*—In apportioning deductions that are definitely related either to a class of gross income consisting of multiple groupings of income (whether statutory or residual) or to all gross income, exempt income and exempt assets (as defined in paragraph (d)(2)(ii) of this section) shall not be taken into account.

For purposes of apportioning deductions which are not taken into account under § 1.1502-13 in determining gain or loss from intercompany transactions, as defined in § 1.1502-13, income from such transactions shall be taken into account in the year such income is ultimately included in gross income.

(ii) *Exempt income and exempt assets defined.*—(A) *In general.*—For further guidance, see § 1.861-8(d)(2)(ii)(A).

(B) *Certain stock and dividends.*—For further guidance, see § 1.861-8(d)(2)(ii)(B).

(C) *Foreign-derived intangible income and inclusions under section 951A(a).*—For further guidance, see § 1.861-8(d)(2)(ii)(C).

(iii) *Income that is not considered tax exempt.*—The following items are not considered to be exempt, eliminated, or excluded income and, thus, may have expenses, losses, or other deductions allocated and apportioned to them:

(A) In the case of a foreign taxpayer (including a foreign sales corporation (FSC)) computing its effectively connected income, gross income (whether domestic or foreign source) which is not effectively connected to the conduct of a United States trade or business;

(B) In computing the combined taxable income of a DISC or FSC and its related supplier, the gross income of a DISC or a FSC; and

(C) For further guidance, see § 1.861-8(d)(2)(iii)(C) through (d)(2)(iii)(E).

(D) and (E) [Reserved]

(iv) *Value of stock attributable to previously taxed earnings and profits.*—For further guidance, see § 1.861-8(d)(2)(iv).

(e) *Allocation and apportionment of certain deductions.*

(1) [Reserved]. For further guidance, see § 1.861-8(e)(1).

(2) *Interest.*—The rules concerning the allocation and apportionment of interest expense and certain interest equivalents are set forth in § § 1.861-9T through 1.861-13T.

(3) *Research and experimental expenditures.*—For further guidance, see § 1.861-8(e)(3) through (15).

(4) through (15) [Reserved]

(f) *Miscellaneous matters.*—For further guidance, see § 1.861-8(f) through (g).

(g) [Reserved]

(h) *Effective dates.*—(1) Paragraphs (f)(1)(vi)(E), (f)(1)(vi)(F), and (f)(1)(vi)(G) of this section apply to taxable years ending after April 9, 2008.

(2) Paragraph (e)(4), the last sentence of paragraph (f)(4)(i), and paragraph (g), *Examples 17, 18,* and *30* of this section apply to taxable years beginning after July 31, 2009.

(3) Also, see paragraph (e)(12)(iv) of this section and 1.861-14(e)(6) for rules concerning the allocation and apportionment of deductions for charitable contributions. [Temporary Reg. § 1.861-8T.]

☐ [*T.D.* 8228, 9-9-88. *Amended by T.D.* 8236, 12-7-88; *T.D.* 8286, 1-29-90; *T.D.* 8337, 3-11-91; T.D. 8597, 7-12-95; *T.D.* 8805, 1-8-99; *T.D.* 8973, 12-27-2001; *T.D.* 9143, 7-27-2004; *T.D.* 9211, 7-13-2005; *T.D.* 9278, 7-31-2006 (*corrected* 12-21-2006), *T.D.* 9456, 7-31-2009, *T.D.* 9882, 12-16-2019 *and T.D.* 9922, 11-2-2020.]

§ 1.861-9. Allocation and apportionment of interest expense and rules for asset-based apportionment.—(a) *In general.*—For further guidance, see § 1.861-9T(a).

(b) *Interest equivalent.*—(1) *Certain expenses and losses.*—(i) *General rule.*—Any expense or loss (to the extent deductible) incurred in a transaction or series of integrated or related transactions in which the taxpayer secures the use of funds for a period of time is subject to allocation and apportionment under the rules of this section and § 1.861-9T(b) if such expense or loss is substantially incurred in consideration of the time value of money. However, the allocation and apportionment of a loss under this paragraph (b) and § 1.861-9T(b) does not affect the characterization of such loss as capital or ordinary for any purpose other than for purposes of the section 861 regulations (as defined in § 1.861-8(a)(1)).

(ii) *Examples.*—For further guidance, see § 1.861-9T(b)(1)(ii).

(2) *Certain foreign currency borrowings.*—For further guidance, see § 1.861-9T(b)(2) through (7).

(3) through (7) [Reserved]

(8) *Guaranteed payments.*—Any deductions for guaranteed payments for the use of capital under section 707(c) are allocated and apportioned in the same manner as interest expense.

(c) *Allowable deductions.*—For further guidance, see § 1.861-9T(c) introductory text.

(1) *Disallowed deductions.*—For further guidance, see § 1.861-9T(c)(1) through (4).

(2) through (4) [Reserved]

(5) *Section 163(j).*—If a taxpayer is subject to section 163(j), the taxpayer's deduction for business interest expense is limited to the sum of the taxpayer's business interest income, 30 percent of the taxpayer's adjusted taxable income for the taxable year, and the taxpayer's floor plan financing interest expense. In the taxable year that any deduction is permitted for business interest expense with respect to a disallowed business interest carryforward, that business interest expense is apportioned for purposes of this section under rules set forth in paragraph (d), (e), or (f) of this section (as applicable) as though it were incurred in the taxable year in which the expense is deducted.

(d) *Apportionment rules for individuals, estates, and certain trusts.*—For further guidance, see § 1.861-9T(d).

(e) *Partnerships.*—(1) *In general—aggregate rule.*—For further guidance, see § 1.861-9T(e)(1).

(2) *Corporate partners whose interest in the partnership is 10 percent or more.*—A corporate partner shall apportion its interest expense, including the partner's distributive share of partnership interest expense, by reference to the partner's assets, including the partner's pro rata share of partnership assets, under the rules of paragraph (f) of this section if the corporate partner's direct and indirect interest in the partnership (as determined under the attribution rules of section 318) is 10 percent or more. A corporation using the tax book value method or alternative tax book value method of apportionment shall use the partnership's inside basis in its assets, including adjustments under sections 734(b) and 743(b), if any, and adjusted to the extent required under § 1.861-10T(d)(2).

(3) *Individual partners who are general partners or who are limited partners with an interest in the partnership of 10 percent or more.*—An individual partner is subject to the rules of this paragraph (e)(3) if either the individual is a general partner or the individual's direct and indirect interest (as determined under the attribution rules of section 318) in the partnership is 10 percent or more. The individual shall first classify his or her distributive share of partnership interest expense as interest incurred in the active conduct of a trade or business, as passive activity interest, or as investment interest under regulations issued under sections 163 and 469. The individual must then apportion his or her interest expense, including the partner's distributive share of partnership interest expense, under the rules of paragraph (d) of this section. Each such individual partner shall take into account his or her distributive share of the partnership gross income or pro rata share of the partnership assets in applying such rules. An individual using the tax book value or alternative tax book value method of apportionment shall use the partnership's inside basis in its assets, including adjustments under sections 734(b) and 743(b), if any, and adjusted to the extent required under § 1.861-10T(d)(2).

(4) *Entity rule for less than 10 percent limited partners.*—(i) *Partnership interest expense.*—A limited partner (whether individual or corporate), whose ownership, together with ownership by persons that bear a relationship to the partner described in section 267(b) or section 707, of the capital and profits interests of the partnership is less than 10 percent directly allocates its distributive share of partnership interest expense to its distributive share of partnership gross income. Under § 1.904-4(n)(1)(ii), such a partner's distributive share of foreign source income of the partnership is treated as passive income (subject to the high-taxed income exception of section 904(d)(2)(B)(iii)(II)), except in the case of income from a partnership interest held in the ordinary course of the partner's active trade or business, as defined in § 1.904-4(n)(1)(ii)(B). A partner's distributive share of partnership interest expense (other than partnership interest expense that is directly allocated to identified property under § 1.861-10T) is apportioned in accordance with the partner's relative distributive share of gross foreign source income in each separate category and of gross domestic source income from the partnership. To the extent that partnership interest expense is directly allocated under § 1.861-10T, a comparable portion of the income to which such interest expense is allocated is disregarded in determining the partner's relative distributive share of gross foreign source income in each separate category and domestic source income. The partner's distributive share of the interest expense of the partnership that is directly allocable under § 1.861-10T is allocated according to the treatment, after application of § 1.904-4(n)(1), of the partner's distributive share of the income to which the expense is allocated.

(ii) *Other interest expense of the partner.*—For further guidance, see § 1.861-9T(e)(4)(ii).

(5) *Tiered partnerships.*—For further guidance, see § 1.861-9T(e)(5) through (7).

(6) and (7) [Reserved]

(8) *Special rule for downstream partnership loans.*—(i) *In general.*—For purposes of apportioning interest expense that is not directly allocable under paragraph (e)(4) of this section or § 1.861-10T, the disregarded portion of a downstream partnership loan is not considered an asset of a downstream partnership loan lender (DPL lender). The disregarded portion of a downstream partnership loan is the portion of the value of the loan (as determined under paragraph (h)(4)(i) of this section) that bears the same proportion to the total value of the loan as the matching income amount that is included by the DPL lender for a taxable year with respect to the loan bears to the total amount of downstream partnership loan interest income (DPL interest income) that is included directly or indirectly in gross income by the DPL lender with respect to the loan during that taxable year.

(ii) *Treatment of interest expense and interest income attributable to a downstream partnership loan.*—If a DPL lender (or any other person in the same affiliated group as the DPL lender) takes into account a distributive share of downstream partnership loan interest expense (DPL interest expense), the DPL lender must assign an amount of DPL interest income corresponding to the matching income amount for the taxable year that is attributable to the same loan to the same statutory and residual groupings as the statutory and residual groupings of gross income from which the DPL interest expense is deducted (or would be deducted, without regard to any limitations on the deductibility of interest, such as section 163(j)) by the DPL lender (or any other person in the same affiliated group as the DPL lender).

(iii) *Anti-avoidance rule for third party back-to-back loans.*—If, with a principal purpose of avoiding the rules in this paragraph (e)(8), a person makes a loan to a person that is not related (within the meaning of section 267(b) or 707) to the lender, the unrelated person makes a loan to a partnership, and the first loan would constitute a downstream partnership loan if made directly to the partnership, then the rules of this paragraph (e)(8) apply as if the first loan was made directly to the partnership and the interest expense paid by the partnership is treated as made with respect to the first loan. Such a series of loans will be subject to this recharacterization rule without regard to whether there was a principal purpose of avoiding the rules in this paragraph (e)(8) if the loan to the unrelated person would not have been made or maintained on substantially the same terms but for the loan of funds by the unrelated person to the partnership. The principles of this paragraph (e)(8)(iii) also apply to similar transactions that involve more than two loans and regardless of the order in which the loans are made.

(iv) *Anti-avoidance rule for loans held by CFCs.*—A loan receivable held by a controlled foreign corporation with respect to a loan to a partnership in which a United States shareholder (as defined in §1.904-5(a)(4)(vi)) of the controlled foreign corporation owns an interest, directly or indirectly through one or more other partnerships or other pass-through entities (as defined in §1.904-5(a)(4)(iv)), is recharacterized as a loan receivable held directly by the United States shareholder with respect to the loan to such partnership for purposes of this paragraph (e)(8) if the loan was made or transferred with a principal purpose of avoiding the rules in this paragraph (e)(8). An appropriate amount of income derived by the United States shareholder (or any other person in the same affiliated group as the United States shareholder) from the controlled foreign corporation is treated as DPL interest income. Appropriate adjustments must be made to the value and characterization of the stock of the controlled foreign corporation under §§1.861-9 and 1.861-12 in order to reflect the portion of the downstream partnership loan held by the controlled foreign corporation that is disregarded under paragraph (e)(8)(i) of this section.

(v) *Interest equivalents.*—The principles of this paragraph (e)(8) apply in the case of a partner, or any person in the same affiliated group as the partner, that takes into account a distributive share of an expense or loss (to the extent deductible) that is allocated and apportioned in the same manner as interest expense under §§1.861-9(b) and 1.861-9T(b) and has a matching income amount (treating such interest equivalent as interest income or expense for purposes of paragraph (e)(8)(vi)(B) of this section) with respect to the transaction that gives rise to that expense or loss.

(vi) *Definitions.*—For purposes of this paragraph (e)(8), the following definitions apply.

(A) *Affiliated group.*—The term *affiliated group* has the meaning provided in §1.861-11(d)(1).

(B) *Matching income amount.*—The term *matching income amount* means the lesser of the total amount of the DPL interest income included directly or indirectly in gross income by the DPL lender for the taxable year with respect to a downstream partnership loan or the total amount of the distributive shares of the DPL interest expense of the DPL lender (or any other person in the same affiliated group as the DPL lender) with respect to the loan.

(C) *Downstream partnership loan.*—The term *downstream partnership loan* means a loan to a partnership for which the loan receivable is held, directly or indirectly through one or more other partnerships or other pass-through entities (as defined in §1.904-5(a)(4)), by a person (or any person in the same affiliated group as such person) that owns an interest, directly or indirectly through one or more other partnerships or other pass-through entities, in the partnership.

(D) *Downstream partnership loan interest expense (DPL interest expense).*—The term *downstream partnership loan interest expense*, or *DPL interest expense*, means an item of interest expense paid or accrued with respect to a downstream partnership loan, without regard to whether the expense was currently deductible (for example, by reason of section 163(j) or the election to waive deductions pursuant to §1.59A-3(c)(6)).

(E) *Downstream partnership loan interest income (DPL interest income).*—The term *downstream partnership loan interest income*, or *DPL interest income*, means an item of gross interest income received or accrued with respect to a downstream partnership loan.

(F) *Downstream partnership loan lender (DPL lender).*—The term *downstream partnership loan lender*, or *DPL lender*, means the person that holds the receivable with respect to a downstream partnership loan. If a partnership holds the receivable, then any partner in the partnership (other than a partner described in paragraph (e)(4)(i) of this section) is also considered a DPL lender.

(vii) *Examples.*—The following examples illustrate the application of the rules in this paragraph (e)(8).

(A) *Example 1*—(*1*) *Facts.* US1, a domestic corporation, directly owns 60% of PRS, a foreign partnership that is not engaged in a U.S. trade or business. The remaining 40% of PRS is directly owned by US2, a domestic corporation that is unrelated to US1. US1, US2, and PRS all use the calendar year as their taxable year. In Year 1, US1 loans $1,000x to PRS. For Year 1, US1 has $100x of interest income with respect to the loan and PRS has $100x of interest expense with respect to the loan. US1's distributive share of the interest expense is $60x. Under paragraph (e)(2) of this section, $45x of US1's distributive share of the interest expense is apportioned to U.S. source income and $15x is apportioned to foreign source foreign branch category income. Under paragraph (h)(4)(i) of this section, the total value of the loan between US1 and PRS is $1,000x.

(*2*) *Analysis.* The loan by US1 to PRS is a downstream partnership loan and US1 is a DPL lender. Under paragraph (e)(8)(vi)(B) of this section, the matching income amount is $60x, the lesser of the DPL interest income included by US1 with respect to the loan for the taxable year ($100x) and US1's distributive share of the DPL interest expense ($60x). Under paragraph (e)(8)(ii) of this section, US1 assigns $45x of the DPL interest income to U.S. source income and $15x of the DPL interest income to foreign source foreign branch category income. The source and separate category of the remaining $40x of US1's DPL interest income is determined under the generally applicable rules. Under paragraph (e)(8)(i) of this section, the disregarded portion of the downstream partnership loan is $600x ($1,000x x $60x/$100x).

(B) *Example 2*—(*1*) *Facts.* The facts are the same as in paragraph (e)(8)(vii)(A)(*1*) of this section (the facts in *Example 1*), except that US1 and US2 are part of the same affiliated group, US2's distributive share of the interest expense is $40x, and under paragraph (e)(2) of this section, $30x of US2's distributive share of the interest expense is apportioned to U.S. source income and $10x is apportioned to foreign source foreign branch category income.

(*2*) *Analysis.* The loan by US1 to PRS is a downstream partnership loan and US1 is a DPL lender. Under paragraph (e)(8)(vi)(B) of this section, the matching income amount is $100x, the lesser of the DPL interest income included by US1 with respect to the loan for the taxable year ($100x) and the total amount of US1 and US2's distributive shares of the DPL interest expense ($100x). Under paragraph (e)(8)(ii) of this section, US1 assigns $75x of the DPL interest income to U.S. source income and $25x of the DPL interest income to foreign source foreign branch category income. Under paragraph (e)(8)(i) of this section, the disregarded portion of the downstream partnership loan is $1,000x ($1,000x x $100x/$100x).

(C) *Example 3*—(*1*) *Facts.* US1, a domestic corporation, owns 80% of PRS, a foreign partnership that is not engaged in a U.S. trade or business. The remaining 20% of PRS is owned by US2, a domestic corporation that is unrelated to US1. US1, US2, and PRS all use the calendar year as their taxable year. In Year 1, US1 loans $3,000x to Bank and Bank loans $3,000x to PRS. US1 makes the loan to Bank with a principal purpose of avoiding the rules in this paragraph (e)(8). For Year 1, US1 has $150x of interest income with respect to the loan to Bank and PRS has $175x of interest expense with respect to the loan from Bank. US1's distributive share of the interest expense is $140x. Under paragraph (e)(2) of this section, $126x of US1's distributive share of the interest expense is apportioned to U.S. source income and $14x is apportioned to foreign source foreign branch category income. Under paragraph (h)(4)(i) of this section, the total value of the loan between US1 and PRS is $3,000x.

(*2*) *Analysis.* Under paragraph (e)(8)(iii) of this section, because the loan from US1 to Bank is made with a principal purpose of avoiding the rules of this paragraph (e)(8), the rules of this paragraph (e)(8) apply as if the loan by US1 to Bank was made directly to PRS. Accordingly, the loan by US1 to Bank is a downstream partnership loan and US1 is a DPL lender. Under paragraph (e)(8)(vi)(B) of this section, the matching income amount is $140x, the lesser of the DPL interest income included by US1 with respect to the loan for the taxable year ($150x) and US1's distributive share of the DPL interest expense ($140x). Under paragraph (e)(8)(ii) of this section, US1 assigns $126x of the DPL interest income to U.S. source income and $14x of the DPL interest income to foreign source foreign branch category income. The source and separate category of the remaining $10x of US1's DPL interest income is determined under the generally applicable rules. Under paragraph (e)(8)(i) of this section, the disregarded portion of the downstream partnership loan is $2,800x ($3,000x x $140x/$150x).

(D) *Example 4*—(*1*) *Facts.* US1, a domestic corporation, directly owns all of the outstanding stock of CFC, a controlled foreign corporation, and 90% of PRS, a foreign partnership that is not engaged in a U.S. trade or business. The remaining 10% of PRS is owned by US2, a domestic corporation that is unrelated to US1 and CFC. US1, US2, and PRS all use the calendar year as their taxable year. In Year 1, US1 loans $900x to CFC and CFC loans $900x to PRS. CFC makes the loan with a principal purpose of avoiding the rules in this paragraph (e)(8). For Year 1, CFC has $90x of interest income and $90x of interest expense with respect to the loan to PRS, and US1 has $90x of interest income with respect to the loan to CFC. PRS has $90x of interest expense with respect to the loan, and US1's distributive share of the interest expense is $81x. Under paragraph (e)(2) of this section,

$54x of US1's distributive share of the interest expense is apportioned to U.S. source income and $27x is apportioned to foreign source foreign branch category income. Under paragraph (h)(4)(i) of this section, the total value of the loan between CFC and PRS is $900x.

(2) *Analysis*. Under paragraph (e)(8)(iv) of this section, because the loan from CFC to PRS is made with a principal purpose of avoiding the rules of this paragraph (e)(8), the loan from CFC to PRS is recharacterized as a loan receivable held directly by US1, and an appropriate amount of income derived by US1, in this case, the $90x of interest income from the loan to CFC, is treated as DPL interest income. Accordingly, the loan from CFC to PRS is a downstream partnership loan and US1 is a DPL lender. Under paragraph (e)(8)(vi)(B) of this section, the matching income amount is $81x, the lesser of the DPL interest income included by US1 ($90x) and US1's distributive share of the DPL interest expense ($81x). Under paragraph (e)(8)(ii) of this section, US1 assigns $54x of the DPL interest income to U.S. source income and $27x of the DPL interest income to foreign source foreign branch category income. The source and separate category of the remaining $9x of US1's interest income is determined under the generally applicable rules. Under paragraph (e)(8)(i) of this section, the disregarded portion of the downstream partnership loan is $810x ($900x x $81x/$90x). Appropriate adjustments are made to the value and characterization of the stock of CFC under §§1.861-9 and 1.861-12 in order to reflect the $810x disregarded portion of the downstream partnership loan.

(9) *Special rule for upstream partnership loans.*—(i) *In general.*—For purposes of apportioning interest expense that is not directly allocable under paragraph (e)(4) of this section or §1.861-10T, an upstream partnership loan debtor's (UPL debtor) pro rata share of the value of the upstream partnership loan (as determined under paragraph (h)(4)(i) of this section) is not considered an asset of the UPL debtor taken into account as described in paragraphs (e)(2) and (3) of this section.

(ii) *Treatment of interest expense and interest income attributable to an upstream partnership loan.*—If a UPL debtor (or any other person in the same affiliated group as the UPL debtor) takes into account a distributive share of upstream partnership loan interest income (UPL interest income), the UPL debtor (or any other person in the same affiliated group as the UPL debtor) assigns an amount of its distributive share of the UPL interest income equal to the matching expense amount for the taxable year that is attributable to the same loan to the same statutory and residual groupings using the same ratios as the statutory and residual groupings of gross income from which the upstream partnership loan interest expense (UPL interest expense) is deducted by the UPL debtor (or any other person in the same affiliated group as the UPL debtor). Therefore, the amount of the distributive share of UPL interest income that is assigned to each statutory and residual grouping is the amount that bears the same proportion to the matching expense amount as the UPL interest expense in that statutory or residual grouping bears to the total UPL interest expense of the UPL debtor (or any other person in the same affiliated group as the UPL debtor).

(iii) *Anti-avoidance rule for third party back-to-back loans.*—If, with a principal purpose of avoiding the rules in this paragraph (e)(9), a partnership makes a loan to a person that is not related (within the meaning of section 267(b) or 707) to the lender, the unrelated person makes a loan to a direct or indirect partner in the partnership (or any person in the same affiliated group as a direct or indirect partner), and the first loan would constitute an upstream partnership loan if made directly to the direct or indirect partner (or person in the same affiliated group as a direct or indirect partner), then the rules of this paragraph (e)(9) apply as if the first loan was made directly by the partnership to the partner (or affiliate of the partner), and the interest expense paid by the partner is treated as made with respect to the first loan. Such a series of loans will be subject to the recharacterization rule in this paragraph (e)(9)(iii) without regard to whether there was a principal purpose of avoiding the rules in this paragraph (e)(9) if the loan to the unrelated person would not have been made or maintained on substantially the same terms but for the loan of funds by the unrelated person to the direct or indirect partner (or affiliate of the partner). The principles of this paragraph (e)(9)(iii) also apply to similar transactions that involve more than two loans and regardless of the order in which the loans are made.

(iv) *Interest equivalents.*—The principles of this paragraph (e)(9) apply in the case of a partner, or any person in the same affiliated group as the partner, that takes into account a distributive share of income and has a matching expense amount (treating any interest equivalent described in paragraph (b) of this section and §1.861-9T(b) as interest income or expense for purposes of paragraph (e)(9)(v)(B) of this section) that is allocated and apportioned in the same manner as interest expense under paragraph (b) of this section and §1.861-9T(b).

(v) *Definitions.*—For purposes of this paragraph (e)(9), the following definitions apply.

(A) *Affiliated group.*—The term *affiliated group* has the meaning provided in §1.861-11(d)(1).

(B) *Matching expense amount.*—The term *matching expense amount* means the lesser of the total amount of the UPL interest expense taken into account directly or indirectly by the UPL debtor for the taxable year with respect to an upstream partnership loan or the total amount of the distributive shares of the UPL interest income of the UPL debtor (or any other person in the same affiliated group as the UPL debtor) with respect to the loan.

(C) *Upstream partnership loan.*—The term *upstream partnership loan* means a loan by a partnership to a person (or any person in the same affiliated group as such person) that owns an interest, directly or indirectly through one or more other partnerships or other pass-through entities (as defined in §1.904-5(a)(4)(iv)), in the partnership.

(D) *Upstream partnership loan debtor (UPL debtor)*. The term *upstream partnership loan debtor*, or *UPL debtor*, means the person that has the payable with respect to an upstream partnership loan. If a partnership has the payable, then any partner in the partnership (other than a partner described in paragraph (e)(4)(i) of this section) is also considered a UPL debtor.

(E) *Upstream partnership loan interest expense (UPL interest expense)*. The term *upstream partnership loan interest expense*, or *UPL interest expense*, means an item of interest expense paid or accrued with respect to an upstream partnership loan, without regard to whether the expense was currently deductible (for example, by reason of section 163(j) or the election to waive deductions pursuant to §1.59A-3(c)(6)).

(F) *Upstream partnership loan interest income (UPL interest income)*. The term *upstream partnership loan interest income*, or *UPL interest income*, means an item of gross interest income received or accrued with respect to an upstream partnership loan.

(vi) *Examples.*—The following examples illustrate the application of this paragraph (e)(9).

(A) *Example 1.*—(*1*) *Facts.* US1, a domestic corporation, directly owns 60% of PRS, a foreign partnership that is not engaged in a U.S. trade or business. The remaining 40% of PRS is directly owned by US2, a domestic corporation that is unrelated to US1. US1, US2, and PRS all use the calendar year as their taxable year. In Year 1, PRS loans $1,000x to US1. For Year 1, US1 has $100x of interest expense with respect to the loan and PRS has $100x of interest income with respect to the loan. US1's distributive share of the interest income is $60x. Under paragraph (e)(2) of this section, $75x of US1's interest expense with respect to the loan is allocated and apportioned to U.S. source income and $25x is allocated and apportioned to foreign source foreign branch category income. Under paragraph (h)(4)(i) of this section, US1's share of the total value of the loan between US1 and PRS is $600x.

(*2*) *Analysis*. The loan by PRS to US1 is an upstream partnership loan and US1 is an UPL debtor. Under paragraph (e)(9)(iv)(B) of this section, the matching expense amount is $60x, the lesser of the UPL interest expense taken into account by US1 with respect to the loan for the taxable year ($100x) and US1's distributive share of the UPL interest income ($60x). Under paragraph (e)(9)(ii) of this section, US1 assigns $45x of the UPL interest income to U.S. source income ($60x x $75x / $100x) and $15x of the UPL interest income to foreign source foreign branch category income ($60x x $25x / $100x). Under paragraph (e)(9)(i) of this section, the disregarded portion of the upstream partnership loan is $600x, and is not taken into account as described in paragraphs (e)(2) and (3) of this section.

(B) *Example 2.*—(*1*) *Facts.* The facts are the same as in paragraph (e)(9)(vi)(A)(*1*) of this section (the facts in *Example 1*), except that US1 and US2 are part of the same affiliated group with the same ratio of U.S. and foreign assets that US1 had in paragraph (e)(9)(vi)(A)(*1*), US2's distributive share of the interest income is $40x, and under paragraph (h)(4)(i) of this section US2's share of the total value of the loan between US1 and PRS is $400x.

(2) *Analysis.* The loan by PRS to US1 is an upstream partnership loan and US1 is an UPL debtor. Under paragraph (e)(9)(iv)(B) of this section, the matching expense amount is $100x, the lesser of the UPL interest expense taken into account by US1 with respect to the loan for the taxable year ($100x) and the total amount of US1 and US2's distributive shares of the UPL interest income ($100x). Under paragraph (e)(9)(ii) of this section, US1 and US2 assign $75x of their total UPL interest income to U.S. source income ($100x x $75x / $100x) and $25x of their total UPL interest income to foreign source foreign branch category income ($100x x $25x / $100x). Under paragraph (e)(9)(i) of this section, the disregarded portion of the upstream partnership loan is $1,000x, the total amount of US1 and US2's share of the loan between US1 and PRS, and is not taken into account as described in paragraphs (e)(2) and (3) of this section.

(10) *Characterizing certain partnership assets as foreign branch category assets.*—For purposes of applying this paragraph (e) to section 904 as the operative section, a partner that is a United States person that has a distributive share of partnership income that is treated as foreign branch category income under § 1.904-4(f)(1)(i)(B) characterizes its pro rata share of the partnership assets that give rise to such income as assets in the foreign branch category.

(f) *Corporations.*—(1) *Domestic corporations.*—For further guidance, see § 1.861-9T(f)(1).

(2) *Section 987 QBUs of domestic corporations.*—(i) *In general.*—In the application of the asset method described in paragraph (g) of this section, a domestic corporation—

(A) Takes into account the assets of any section 987 QBU (as defined in § 1.987-1(b)(2)), translated according to the rules set forth in paragraph (g) of this section; and

(B) Combines with its own interest expense any deductible interest expense incurred by a section 987 QBU, translated according to the rules under section 987.

(ii) *Coordination with section 987(3).*—For purposes of computing foreign currency gain or loss under section 987(3) (including section 987 gain or loss recognized under § 1.987-5), the rules of this paragraph (f)(2) do not apply. *See* § 1.987-4.

(iii) *Example.*—The following example illustrates the application of the rules in this paragraph (f)(2).

(A) *Facts.* X is a domestic corporation that operates B, a branch doing business in a foreign country. B is a section 987 QBU (as defined in § 1.987-1(b)(2)) as well as a foreign branch (as defined in § 1.904-4(f)(3)(iii)). In 2020, without regard to B, X has gross domestic source income of $1,000x and gross foreign source general category income of $500x and incurs $200 of interest expense. Using the tax book value method of apportionment, X, without regard to B, determines the value of its assets that generate domestic source income to be $6,000x and the value of its assets that generate foreign source general category income to be $1,000x. Applying the translation rules of section 987, X (through B) earned $500 of gross foreign source foreign branch category income and incurred $100x of interest expense. B incurred no other expenses. For 2020, the average functional currency book value of B's assets that generate foreign source foreign branch category income translated at the year-end rate for 2020 is $3,000x.

(B) *Analysis.* The combined assets of X and B for 2020 (averaged under § 1.861-9T(g)(3)) consist 60% ($6,000x/$10,000x) of assets generating domestic source income, 30% ($3,000x/$10,000x) of assets generating foreign source foreign branch category income, and 10% ($1,000x/$10,000x) of assets generating foreign source general category income. The combined interest expense of X and B is $300x. Thus, $180x ($300x x 60%) of the combined interest expense is apportioned to domestic source income, $90x ($300x x 30%) is apportioned to foreign source foreign branch category income, and $30x ($300x x 10%) is apportioned to foreign source general category income, yielding net U.S. source income of $820 ($1,000x – $180x), net foreign source foreign branch category income of $410 ($500x – $90x), and net foreign source general category income of $470x ($500x – $30x).

(3) *Controlled foreign corporations.*—(i) *In general.*—For purposes of computing subpart F income and tested income and computing earnings and profits for all Federal income tax purposes, the interest expense of a controlled foreign corporation may be apportioned using either the asset method described in paragraph (g) of this section or the modified gross income method described in paragraph (j) of this section, subject to the rules of paragraphs (f)(3)(ii) and (iii) of this section.

(f)(3)(ii) *Manner of election.*—The election shall be made by filing the statement and providing the written notice described in § 1.964-1(c)(3)(ii) and (iii), respectively, at the time and in the manner described therein. For further guidance, see § 1.861-9T(f)(3)(ii).

(f)(3)(iii) and (iv) *[Reserved].*—For further guidance, see § 1.861-9T(f)(3)(iii) and (iv).

(f)(4) *Noncontrolled 10-percent owned foreign corporations.*—(i) *In general.*—For purposes of computing earnings and profits of a noncontrolled 10-percent owned foreign corporation (as defined in section 904(d)(2)(E)) for federal tax purposes, the interest expense of a noncontrolled 10-percent owned foreign corporation may be apportioned using either the asset method described in § 1.861-9T(g) or the modified gross income method described in § 1.861-9T(j). A noncontrolled 10-percent owned foreign corporation that is not a controlled foreign corporation may elect to use a different method of apportionment than that elected by one or more of its shareholders. A noncontrolled 10-percent owned foreign corporation must use the same method of apportionment with respect to all its domestic corporate shareholders.

(ii) *Manner of election.*—The election to use the asset method described in § 1.861-9T(g) or the modified gross income method described in § 1.861-9T(j) may be made either by the noncontrolled 10-percent owned foreign corporation or by the majority domestic corporate shareholders (as defined in § 1.964-1(c)(5)(ii)) on behalf of the noncontrolled 10-percent owned foreign corporation. The election shall be made by filing the statement and providing the written notice described in § 1.964-1(c)(3)(ii) and (iii), respectively, at the time and in the manner described therein.

(iii) *Stock characterization.*—The stock of a noncontrolled 10-percent owned foreign corporation is characterized under the rules in § 1.861-12(c)(4).

(5) *Other relevant provisions.*—For further guidance, see § 1.861-9T(f)(5).

(g) *Asset method.*—(1) *In general.*—(i) For further guidance, see § 1.861-9T(g)(1)(i).

(ii) A taxpayer may elect to determine the value of its assets on the basis of either the tax book value or the fair market value of its assets. However, for taxable years beginning after December 31, 2017, the fair market value method is not allowed with respect to allocations and apportionments of interest expense. *See* section 864(e)(2). For rules concerning the application of an alternative method of valuing assets for purposes of the tax book value method, see paragraph (i) of this section. For rules concerning the application of the fair market value method, see paragraph (h) of this section.

(iii) [Reserved]

(iv) For rules relating to earnings and profits adjustments by taxpayers using the tax book value method for the stock in certain 10 percent owned corporations, see § 1.861-12(c)(2).

(v) [Reserved]

(2) *Asset values.*—(i) *General rule.*—(A) *Average of values.*—For purposes of determining the value of assets under this section, an average of values (book or market) within each statutory grouping and the residual grouping is computed for the year on the basis of values of assets at the beginning and end of the year. For the first taxable year beginning after December 31, 2017 (*post-2017 year*), a taxpayer that determined the value of its assets on the basis of the fair market value method for purposes of apportioning interest expense in its prior taxable year may choose to determine asset values under the tax book value method (or the alternative tax book value method) by treating the value of its assets as of the beginning of the post-2017 year as equal to the value of its assets at the end of the first quarter of the post-2017 year, provided that each member of the affiliated group (as defined in § 1.861-11T(d)) determines its asset values on the same basis. Where a substantial distortion of asset values would result from averaging beginning-of-year and end-of-year values, as might be the case in the event of a major corporate acquisition or disposition, the taxpayer must use a different method of asset valuation that more clearly reflects the average value of assets weighted to reflect the time such assets are held by the taxpayer during the taxable year.

(B) *Tax book value method.*—Under the tax book value method, the value of an asset is determined based on the adjusted basis of the asset. For purposes of determining the value of stock in a

10 percent owned corporation at the beginning and end of the year under the tax book value method, the tax book value is determined without regard to any adjustments under section 961(a) or 1293(d), see § 1.861-12(c)(2)(i)(B)(*1*), and before the adjustment required by § 1.861-12(c)(2)(i)(A) to the basis of stock in the 10 percent owned corporation. The average of the tax book value of the stock at the beginning and end of the year is then adjusted with respect to earnings and profits as described in § 1.861-12(c)(2)(i).

(ii) *Special rule for qualified business units of domestic corporations with functional currency other than the U.S. dollar.*—(A) *Tax book value method.*—For further guidance, see § 1.861-9T(g)(2)(ii)(A).

(*1*) *Section 987 QBU.*—For further guidance, see § 1.861-9T(g)(2)(ii)(A)(*1*).

(*2*) *U.S. dollar approximate separate transactions method.*—In the case of a branch to which the U.S. dollar approximate separate transactions method of accounting described in § 1.985-3 applies, the beginning-of-year dollar amount of the assets is determined by reference to the end-of-year balance sheet of the branch for the immediately preceding taxable year, adjusted for U.S. generally accepted accounting principles and Federal income tax accounting principles, and translated into U.S. dollars as provided in § 1.985-3(c). The end-of-year dollar amount of the assets of the branch is determined in the same manner by reference to the end-of-year balance sheet for the current taxable year. The beginning-of-year and end-of-year dollar tax book value of assets, as so determined, within each grouping is then averaged as provided in paragraph (g)(2)(i) of this section.

(B) *Fair market value method.*—For further guidance, see § 1.861-9T(g)(2)(ii)(B).

(iii) *Adjustment for directly allocated interest.*—For further guidance, see § 1.861-9T(g)(2)(iii).

(iv) *Assets in intercompany transactions.*—For further guidance, see § 1.861-9T(g)(2)(iv).

(3) *Characterization of assets.*—For further guidance, see § 1.861-9T(g)(3). In applying § 1.861-9T(g)(3), for purposes of applying section 904 as the operative section, the statutory or residual grouping of income that assets generate, have generated, or may reasonably be expected to generate is determined after taking into account any reallocation of income required under § 1.904-4(f)(2)(vi).

(4) *Characterization of lower tier entities at the level of a CFC.*—In the case of a controlled foreign corporation that is applying the asset method, see for example § 1.861-12T(c)(3)(ii) (requiring the application of § 1.861-9T(g) at the level of the controlled foreign corporation) or paragraph (f)(3)(i) of this section, the controlled foreign corporation (and any lower-tier controlled foreign corporations) must characterize stock of a lower-tier 10 percent owned corporation by applying § 1.861-12 and treating the controlled foreign corporation as the relevant taxpayer for such purposes. In the case of a controlled foreign corporation that owns stock in one or more lower-tier corporations, in applying the asset method, the first-tier controlled foreign corporation must take into account the stock in the lower-tier corporations. Therefore, the controlled foreign corporation (and any lower-tier controlled foreign corporations) must make basis adjustments in lower-tier 10 percent owned corporations under § 1.861-12(c)(2) for purposes of valuing and characterizing the assets of such controlled foreign corporation. For purposes of this paragraph (g)(4), the stock of each such lower-tier corporation is characterized by reference to the assets owned during the lower-tier corporation's taxable year that ends during the first-tier controlled foreign corporation's taxable year. The analysis of assets under this paragraph (g)(4) and § 1.861-12 of a controlled foreign corporation that is in a chain of 10 percent owned corporations must begin at the lowest-tier 10 percent owned corporation and proceed up the chain to the first-tier controlled foreign corporation. *See also* § 1.861-12T(c)(3)(ii).

(h) *Fair market value method.*—An affiliated group (as defined in § 1.861-11T(d)) or other taxpayer (the *taxpayer*) that elects to use the fair market value method of apportionment values its assets according to the methodology described in this paragraph (h). Effective for taxable years beginning after December 31, 2017, the fair market value method is not allowed for purposes of apportioning interest expense. *See* section 864(e)(2). However, a taxpayer may continue to apportion deductions other than interest expense that are properly apportioned based on fair market value according to the methodology described in this paragraph (h). *See* § 1.861-8(c)(2).

(1) *Determination of values.*—For further guidance, see § 1.861-9T(h)(1) through (3).

(2) and (3) [Reserved]

(h)(4) *Valuing related party debt and stock in related persons.*—(i) *Related party debt.*—For purposes of this section, the value of a debt obligation of a related person held by the taxpayer or another person related to the taxpayer equals the amount of the liability of the obligor related person.

(ii) *Stock in related persons.*—The value of stock in a related person held by the taxpayer or by another person related to the taxpayer equals the sum of the following amounts reduced by the taxpayer's pro rata share of liabilities of such related person:

(A) The portion of the value of intangible assets of the taxpayer and related persons that is apportioned to such related person under § 1.861-9T(h)(2);

(B) The taxpayer's pro rata share of tangible assets held by the related person (as determined under § 1.861-9T(h)(1)(ii));

(C) The taxpayer's pro rata share of debt obligations of any related person held by the related person (as valued under paragraph (h)(4)(i) of this section); and

(D) The total value of stock in all related persons held by the related person as determined under this paragraph (h)(4).

(iii) *Example.*—(A) *Facts.*—USP, a domestic corporation, wholly owns CFC1 and owns 80% of CFC2, both foreign corporations. The aggregate trading value of USP's stock traded on established securities markets at the end of Year 1 is $700 and the amount of USP's liabilities to unrelated persons at the end of Year 1 is $400. Neither CFC1 nor CFC2 has liabilities to unrelated persons at the end of Year 1. USP owns plant and equipment valued at $500, CFC1 owns plant and equipment valued at $400, and CFC2 owns plant and equipment valued at $250. The value of these assets has been determined using generally accepted valuation techniques, as required by § 1.861-9T(h)(1)(ii). There is an outstanding loan from CFC2 to CFC1 in an amount of $100. There is also an outstanding loan from USP to CFC1 in an amount of $200.

(B) *Valuation of group assets.*—Pursuant to § 1.861-9T(h)(1)(i), the aggregate value of USP's assets is $1100 (the $700 trading value of USP's stock increased by $400 of USP's liabilities to unrelated persons).

(C) *Valuation of tangible assets.*—Pursuant to § 1.861-9T(h)(1)(ii), the value of USP's tangible assets and pro rata share of assets held by CFC1 and CFC2 is $1100 (the plant and equipment held directly by USP, valued at $500, plus USP's 100% pro rata share of the plant and equipment held by CFC1 valued at $400 and USP's 80% pro rata share of the plant and equipment held by CFC 2 valued at $200 (80% of $250)).

(D) *Computation of intangible asset value.*—Pursuant to § 1.861-9T(h)(1)(iii), the value of the intangible assets of USP, CFC1, and CFC2 is $0 (total aggregate group asset value ($1100) determined in paragraph (B) less total tangible asset value ($1100) determined in paragraph (C)). Because the intangible asset value is zero, the provisions of § 1.861-9T(h)(2) and (3) relating to the apportionment and characterization of intangible assets do not apply.

(E) *Valuing related party debt obligations.*—Pursuant to § 1.861-9(h)(4)(i), the value of the debt obligation of CFC1 held by CFC2 is equal to the amount of the liability, $100. The value of the debt obligation of CFC1 held by USP is equal to the amount of the liability, $200.

(F) *Valuing the stock of CFC1 and CFC2.*—Pursuant to § 1.861-9(h)(4)(ii), the value of the stock of CFC2 held by USP is $280 (USP's 80% pro rata share of tangible assets of CFC2 included in paragraph (C) ($200) plus USP's 80% pro rata share of the debt obligation of CFC1 held by CFC2 valued in paragraph (E) ($80). The value of the stock of CFC1 held by USP is $100 (USP's 100% pro rata share of tangible assets of CFC1 included in paragraph (C) ($400) less USP's 100% pro rata share of the liabilities of CFC1 to USP and CFC2 ($300)).

(5) *Characterizing stock in related persons.*—Stock in a related person held by the taxpayer or by another related person shall be characterized on the basis of the fair market value of the taxpayer's pro rata share of assets held by the related person attributed to each statutory grouping and the residual grouping under the stock charac-

terization rules of § 1.861-12T(c)(3)(ii), except that the portion of the value of intangible assets of the taxpayer and related persons that is apportioned to the related person under § 1.861-9T(h)(2) shall be characterized on the basis of the net income before interest expense of the related person within each statutory grouping or residual grouping (excluding income that is passive under § 1.904-4(b)).

(h)(6) [Reserved].—For further guidance, see § 1.861-9T(h)(6).

(i) *Alternative tax book value method.*—(1) *Alternative value for certain tangible property.*—A taxpayer may elect to determine the tax book value of its tangible property that is depreciated under section 168 (section 168 property) using the rules provided in this paragraph (i)(1) (the alternative tax book value method). The alternative tax book value method applies solely for purposes of apportioning expenses (including the calculation of the alternative minimum tax foreign tax credit pursuant to section 59(a)) under the asset method described in paragraph (g) of this section.

(i) The tax book value of section 168 property placed in service during or after the first taxable year to which the election to use the alternative tax book value method applies shall be determined as though such property were subject to the alternative depreciation system set forth in section 168(g) (or a successor provision) for the entire period that such property has been in service.

(ii) In the case of section 168 property placed in service prior to the first taxable year to which the election to use the alternative tax book value method applies, the tax book value of such property shall be determined under the depreciation method, convention, and recovery period provided for under section 168(g) for the first taxable year to which the election applies.

(iii) If a taxpayer revokes an election to use the alternative tax book value method (the prior election) and later makes another election to use the alternative tax book value method (the subsequent election) that is effective for a taxable year that begins within 3 years of the end of the last taxable year to which the prior election applied, the taxpayer shall determine the tax book value of its section 168 property as though the prior election has remained in effect.

(iv) The tax book value of section 168 property shall be determined without regard to the election to expense certain depreciable assets under section 179.

(v) *Examples.*—The provisions of this paragraph (i)(1) are illustrated in the following examples:

Example 1. In 2000, a taxpayer purchases and places in service section 168 property used solely in the United States. In 2005, the taxpayer elects to use the alternative tax book value method, effective for the current taxable year. For purposes of determining the tax book value of its section 168 property, the taxpayer's depreciation deduction is determined by applying the method, convention, and recovery period rules of the alternative depreciation system under section 168(g)(2) as in effect in 2005 to the taxpayer's original cost basis in such property. In 2006, the taxpayer acquires and places in service in the United States new section 168 property. The tax book value of this section 168 property is determined under the rules of section 168(g)(2) applicable to property placed in service in 2006.

Example 2. Assume the same facts as in *Example 1*, except that the taxpayer revokes the alternative tax book value method election effective for taxable year 2010. Additionally, in 2011, the taxpayer acquires new section 168 property and places it in service in the United States. If the taxpayer elects to use the alternative tax book value method effective for taxable year 2012, the taxpayer must determine the tax book value of its section 168 property as though the prior election still applied. Thus, the tax book value of property placed in service prior to 2005 would be determined by applying the method, convention, and recovery period rules of the alternative depreciation system under section 168(g)(2) applicable to property placed in service in 2005. The tax book value of section 168 property placed in service during any taxable year after 2004 would be determined by applying the method, convention, and recovery period rules of the alternative depreciation system under section 168(g)(2) applicable to property placed in service in such taxable year.

(2) *Timing and scope of election.*—(i) Except as provided in this paragraph (i)(2)(i), a taxpayer may elect to use the alternative tax book value method. For the taxpayer's first taxable year beginning after December 31, 2017, the Commissioner's approval is not required to switch from the fair market value method to the alternative tax book value method for purposes of apportioning interest expense. Any election made pursuant to this paragraph (i)(2)(i) shall apply to all members of an affiliated group of corporations as defined in §§ 1.861-11(d) and 1.861-11T(d). Any election made pursuant to this paragraph (i)(2)(i) shall apply to all subsequent taxable years of the taxpayer unless revoked by the taxpayer. Revocation of such an election, other than in conjunction with an election to use the fair market value method, for a taxable year prior to the sixth taxable year for which the election applies requires the consent of the Commissioner.

(ii) *Example.*—The provisions of this paragraph (i)(2) are illustrated in the following example:

Example. Corporation X, a calendar year taxpayer, elects on its original, timely filed tax return for the taxable year ending December 31, 2007, to use the alternative tax book value method for its 2007 year. The alternative tax book value method applies to Corporation X's 2007 year and all subsequent taxable years. Corporation X may not, without the consent of the Commissioner, revoke its election and determine tax book value using a method other than the alternative tax book value method with respect to any taxable year beginning before January 1, 2012. However, Corporation X may automatically elect to change from the alternative tax book value method to the fair market value method for any open year.

(3) *Certain other adjustments.*—[Reserved.]

(j) *Modified gross income method.*—For further guidance, see § 1.861-9T(j) introductory text.

(1) For further guidance, see § 1.861-9T(j)(1).

(2) For further guidance, see § 1.861-9T(j)(2) introductory text..

(i) *Step 1.*—For further guidance, see § 1.861-9T(j)(2)(i).

(ii) *Step 2.*—Moving to the next higher-tier controlled foreign corporation, combine the gross income of such corporation within each grouping with its pro rata share (as determined under principles similar to section 951(a)(2)) of the gross income net of interest expense of all lower-tier controlled foreign corporations held by such higher-tier corporation within the same grouping adjusted as follows:

(A) Exclude from the gross income of the higher-tier corporation any dividends or other payments received from the lower-tier corporation other than interest income received from the lower-tier corporation;

(B) Exclude from the gross income net of interest expense of any lower-tier corporation any gross subpart F income, net of interest expense apportioned to such income;

(C) Then apportion the interest expense of the higher-tier controlled foreign corporation based on the adjusted combined gross income amounts; and

(D) Repeat paragraphs (j)(2)(ii)(A) through (C) of this section for each next higher-tier controlled foreign corporation in the chain.

(k) *Applicability dates.*—(1) Except as provided in paragraphs (k)(2) and (3) of this section, this section applies to taxable years that both begin after December 31, 2017, and end on or after December 4, 2018.

(2) Paragraphs (b)(1)(i), (b)(8), and (e)(9) of this section apply to taxable years that end on or after December 16, 2019. For taxable years that both begin after December 31, 2017, and end on or after December 4, 2018, and also end before December 16, 2019, see § 1.861-9T(b)(1)(i) as contained in 26 CFR part 1 revised as of April 1, 2019.

(3) The last sentence of paragraph (g)(3) of this section applies to taxable years beginning on or after December 28, 2021. [Reg. § 1.861-9.]

☐ [*T.D.* 8916, 12-29-2000. *Amended by T.D.* 9120, 3-25-2004; *T.D.* 9247, 1-27-2006; *T.D.* 9452, 6-10-2009, *T.D.* 9676, 7-15-2014 (*corrected* 8-21-2014), *T.D.* 9882, 12-16-2019, *T.D.* 9922, 11-2-2020 *and T.D.* 9959, 12-28-2021.]

Caution: The Treasury Department has identified Temporary Reg. §1.861-9T, as amended by T.D. 9794, as a significant tax regulation that imposes an undue financial burden on U.S. taxpayers and/or adds undue complexity to the federal tax laws, pursuant to Executive Order 13789 (issued April 21, 2017) (Notice 2017-38, I.R.B. 2017-30, 147). In a subsequent report, published October 16, 2017, Treasury recommended planned actions that would reduce the burden of these regulations, including an extension of the application date of T.D. 9794 to tax years beginning after December 7, 2023, unless the taxpayer elects to apply them earlier (see Notice 2022-34, I.R.B. 2022-34, 150).

§ 1.861-9T. Allocation and apportionment of interest expense (temporary).—(a) *In general.*—Any expense that is deductible under section 163 (including original issue discount) constitutes interest expense for purposes of this section, as well as for purposes of

§§1.861-10T, 1.861-11T, 1.861-12T, and 1.861-13T. The term interest refers to the gross amount of interest expense incurred by a taxpayer in a given tax year. The method of allocation and apportionment for interest set forth in this section is based on the approach that, in general, money is fungible and that interest expense is attributable to all activities and property regardless of any specific purpose for incurring an obligation on which interest is paid. Exceptions to the fungibility rule are set forth in §1.861-10T. The fungibility approach recognizes that all activities and property require funds and that management has a great deal of flexibility as to the source and use of funds. When borrowing will generally free other funds for other purposes, and it is reasonable under this approach to attribute part of the cost of borrowing to such other purposes. Consistent with the principles of fungibility, except as otherwise provided, the aggregate of deductions for interest in all cases shall be considered related to all income producing activities and assets of the taxpayer and, thus, allocable to all the gross income which the assets of the taxpayer generate, have generated, or could reasonably have been expected to generate. In the case of the interest expense of members of an affiliated group, interest expense shall be considered to be allocable to all the gross income of the members of the group under §1.861-11T. That section requires the members of an affiliated group to allocate and apportion the interest expense of each member of the group as if all members of such group were a single corporation. For the method of determining the interest deduction allowed to foreign corporations under section 882(c), see §1.882-5.

(b) *Interest equivalents.*—(1) *Certain expenses and losses..*—(i) *General rule.*—For further guidance, see §1.861-9(b)(1)(i).

(ii) *Examples.*—The rule of this paragraph (b)(1) may be illustrated by the following example.

Example (1). W, a domestic corporation, borrows from X two ounces of gold at a time when the spot price for gold is $500 per ounce. W agrees to return the two ounces of gold in six months. W sells the two ounces of gold to Y for $1000. W then enters into a contract with Z to purchase two ounces of gold six months in the future for $1,050. In exchange for the use of $1,000 in cash, W has sustained a loss of $50 on related transactions. This loss is subject to allocation and apportionment under the rules of this section in the same manner as interest expense.

Example (2). X, a domestic corporation with a dollar functional currency, borrows 100 pounds on January 1, 1987 for a three-year term at an interest rate greater than the applicable federal rate for dollar loans. At this time, the interest rate on the pound was approximately equal to the interest rate on dollar borrowings and the forward price on the pound, vis-a-vis the dollar, was approximately equal to the spot price. On January 1, 1987, X converted 100 pounds into dollars and entered into a currency swap that substantially hedged X's foreign currency exposure on the pound borrowing, both with respect to interest and principal. The borrowing, coupled with the swap, represents a series of related transactions in which the taxpayer secures the use of funds in its functional currency. Any net foreign currency loss on this series of transactions constitutes a loss incurred substantially in consideration of the time value of money and shall be apportioned in the same manner as interest expense. Thus, if the pound depreciates against the dollar, such that when the first payment on the pound borrowing is due the taxpayer has a currency loss on the swap payment hedging its first interest payment, such loss shall, even if the transaction is not integrated under section 988(d), be allocated and apportioned in the same manner as interest expense under the authority of this paragraph (b)(1).

Example (3). On January 1, 1987, X, a domestic corporation with a dollar functional currency, enters into a dollar interest rate swap contract with Y, a domestic counterparty. Under the terms of this agreement, X agrees to pay Y floating rate interest with respect to a notional principal amount of $100 for five years. In return, Y agrees to pay X fixed rate interest at 10 percent with respect to a notional principal amount of $100 for five years. On the same day, Y prepays the fixed leg of the swap by making a lump sum payment of $37 to X. This lump sum payment represents the present value of five $10 swap payments. Because X secures the use of $37 in this transaction, any net swap expense arising from the transaction represents an expense incurred substantially in consideration of the time value of money. Assuming this lump sum payment is not otherwise characterized as a loan from Y to X, and that X must amortize the $37 lump sum payment under the principles of Notice 89-21, any net swap expense incurred by X with respect to this transaction (*i.e.*, the excess, if any, of X's annual swap payment to Y over the annual amortization of the $37 lump sum payment that is taken into income by X) represents an expense equivalent to interest expense. The result would be the same if X sold the fixed leg to a third party for $37. While this example presents the case of a lump sum payment, the rules of paragraph (b)(1) would also apply to any transaction in which the swap payments are not substantially contemporaneous if the pricing of the transaction is materially affected by the time value of money. Thus, expenses and losses will be subject to apportionment under the rules of this section to the extent that such expenses or losses were incurred in consideration of the time value of money.

(2) *Certain foreign currency borrowings.*—(i) *Rule.*—If a taxpayer borrows in a nonfunctional currency at a rate of interest that is less than the applicable federal rate (or its equivalent in functional currency if the functional currency is not the dollar), any swap, forward, future, option, or similar financial arrangement (or any combination thereof) entered into by the taxpayer or by a related person (as defined in §1.861-8T(c)(2)) that exists during the term of the borrowing and that substantially diminishes currency risk with respect to the borrowing or interest expense thereon will be presumed to constitute a hedge of such borrowing, unless the taxpayer can demonstrate on the basis of facts and circumstances that the two transactions are in fact unrelated. Under this presumption, the currency loss incurred on the borrowing during taxable years beginning after December 31, 1988, in connection with hedged nonfunctional currency borrowings, reduced or increased by the gain or loss on the hedge, will be apportioned in the same manner as interest expense. This presumption can be rebutted by a showing that the financial arrangement was entered into in connection with hedging currency exposure arising in the ordinary course of a trade or business (other than with respect to the borrowing).

(ii) *Examples.*—The principles of this paragraph (b)(2) may be illustrated by the following examples.

Example (1). Taxpayer has a dollar functional currency and does not have any qualified business units with a functional currency other than the dollar. On January 1, 1989, when the unit of foreign currency is worth $1, taxpayer borrows 100 units of foreign currency for a three-year period bearing interest at the annual rate of 3 percent and immediately converts the proceeds of the borrowing into dollars for use in its business. In the ordinary course of its business, taxpayer has no foreign currency exposure in this currency. In March 1989, taxpayer enters into a three-year swap agreement that covers most, but not all, of the payment of interest and principal. Because the swap substantially diminishes currency risk with respect to the borrowing, it is presumed to hedge the loan. Since taxpayer cannot demonstrate that it was hedging currency exposure arising in the ordinary course of its business (other than currency exposure with respect to the borrowing), the net currency loss on the borrowing adjusted for any gain or loss on the swap must be apportioned in the same manner as interest expense.

Example (2). Assume the same facts as in Example 1, except that the taxpayer borrows in two separate foreign currencies on terms described in Example 1 and enters into a swap agreement in a single currency that substantially diminishes the taxpayer's aggregate foreign currency risk. The net currency loss on the borrowings adjusted for any gain or loss on the swap must be apportioned in the same manner as interest expense.

(3) *Losses on sale of certain receivables.*—(i) *General rule.*—Any loss on the sale of a trade receivable (as defined in §1.954-2(h)) shall be allocated and apportioned, solely for purposes of this section and §§1.861-10T, 1.861-11T, 1.861-12T, and 1.861-13T, in the same manner as interest expense, unless at the time of sale of the receivable, it bears interest at a rate which is at least 120 percent of the short term applicable federal rate (as determined under section 1274(d) of the Code), or its equivalent in foreign currency in the case of receivables denominated in foreign currency, determined at the time the receivable arises. This treatment shall not affect the characterization of such expense as interest for other purposes of the Internal Revenue Code.

(ii)(A) *Exceptions.*—To the extent that a loss on the sale of a trade receivable exceeds the discount on the receivable that would be computed applying to the amount received on the sale of the receivable 120 percent of the applicable federal rate (or its equivalent in foreign currency in the case of receivables denominated in foreign currency) for the period commencing with the date on which the receivable is sold and ending with the earlier of the date on which the receivable begins to bear interest at such rate or the anticipated payment date of the receivable, such excess shall not be allocated and apportioned in the same manner as interest expense but rather shall be allocated and apportioned to the gross income generated by the receivable. In cases of transfers of receivables to a domestic international sales corporation described in § 1.994-1(c)(6)(v), the rule of this paragraph (b)(3) shall not apply for purposes of computing combined taxable income.

(B) *Example.*.—On October 1, X sells a widget to Y for $100 payable in 30 days, after which the receivable will bear stated interest at 13 percent. On October 4, X sells Y's obligation to Z for $98. Assume that the applicable federal rate for the month of October is 10 percent. Applying 120 percent of the applicable federal rate to the $98 received on the sale of the receivable, the obligation is discounted at a 12 percent rate for a period of 27 days. At this discount rate, the obligation would have sold for $99.22. Thus, 88 cents of the $2 loss on the sale is apportioned in the same manner as interest expense, and $1.22 of the $2 loss on the sale is directly allocated to the income generated on the widget sale.

(4) *Rent in certain leasing transactions.*—[Reserved.]

(5) *Treatment of bond premium.*—(i) *Treatment by the issuer.*—If a bond or other debt obligation is issued at a premium, an amount of interest expense incurred by the issuer on that bond or other debt obligation equal to the amortized portion of that premium that is included in gross income for the year shall be allocated and apportioned solely to the amortized portion of premium derived by the issuer for the year.

(ii) *Treatment by the holder.*—If a bond or debt obligation is purchased at a premium, the portion of that premium amortized during the year by the holder under section 171 and the regulations thereunder shall be allocated and apportioned solely to interest income derived from the bond by the holder for the year.

(6) *Financial products that alter effective cost of borrowing.*—(i) *In general.*—Various derivative financial products can be part of transactions or series of transactions described in paragraph (b)(1) of this section. Such derivative financial products, including interest rate swaps, options, forwards, caps, and collars, potentially alter a taxpayer's effective cost of borrowing with respect to an actual liability of the taxpayer. For example, a taxpayer that is obligated to pay interest at a fixed rate may, in effect, pay interest at a floating rate by entering into an interest rate swap. Similarly, a taxpayer that is obligated to pay interest at a floating rate may, in effect, limit its exposure to rising interest rates by purchasing a cap. Such a taxpayer may have gains or losses associated with such derivative financial products. This paragraph (b)(6) provides rules for the treatment of gains and losses from such derivative financial products ("financial products") that are part of transactions described in paragraph (b)(1) of this section and that are used by the taxpayer to alter its effective cost of borrowing with respect to an actual liability. This paragraph (b)(6) shall only apply where the hedge and the borrowing are in the same currency and shall not apply to the extent otherwise provided in section 988 and the regulations thereunder. The allocation and apportionment of a loss under this paragraph (b) shall not affect the characterization of such loss as capital or ordinary for other purposes of the Code and the regulations thereunder.

(ii) *Definition of gain and loss.*—For purposes of this paragraph (b)(6), the term "gain" refers to the excess of the amounts properly taken into income under a financial product that alters the effective cost of borrowing over the amounts properly allowed as a deduction thereunder within a given taxable year. *See, e.g.,* Notice 89-21. The term "loss" refers to the excess of the amounts properly allowed as a deduction under such a financial product over the amounts properly taken into income thereunder within a given taxable year.

(iii) *Treatment of gain or loss on the disposition of a financial product.*—[Reserved.]

(iv) *Entities that are not financial services entities.*—An entity that does not constitute a financial services entity within the meaning of § 1.904-4(e)(3) shall treat gains and losses on financial products described in paragraph (b)(6)(i) of this section as follows.

(A) *Losses.*—Losses on any financial product described in paragraph (b)(6)(i) of this section shall be apportioned in the same manner as interest expense whether or not such financial product is identified by the taxpayer under paragraph (b)(6)(iv)(C) of this section as a liability hedge.

(B) *Gains.*—Gains on any financial product described in paragraph (b)(6)(i) of this section shall reduce the taxpayer's total interest expense that is subject to apportionment, but only if such financial product is identified by the taxpayer under paragraph (b)(6)(iv)(C) of this section as a liability hedge. Such reduction is accomplished by directly allocating interest expense to the income derived from such a financial product.

(C) *Identification of financial products.*—A taxpayer can identify a financial product described in paragraph (b)(6)(i) of this section as hedging a particular interest-bearing liability (or any group of such liabilities) by clearly identifying on its books and records on the same day that it becomes a party to such arrangement that such arrangement hedges a given liability (or group of liabilities). In the case of a partial hedge, such identification shall apply to only that part of the liability that is hedged. If the taxpayer clearly identifies on its books and records a financial product as a hedge of an interest-bearing asset (or any group of such assets), it will create a rebuttable presumption that such financial product is not described in paragraph (b)(6)(i) of this section. A taxpayer may identify a hedge as relating to an anticipated liability, provided that such liability is in fact incurred within 120 days following the date of such identification. Gains and losses on such an anticipatory arrangement accruing prior to the time at which the liability is incurred shall constitute an adjustment to interest expense.

(v) *Financial services entities.*—[Reserved.]

(vi) *Dealers.*—The rule of paragraph (b)(6)(iv) of this section shall not apply to a person acting in its capacity as a regular dealer in the financial products described in paragraph (b)(6)(i) of this section. Instead, losses sustained by a regular dealer in connection with such financial products shall be allocated to the class of gross income from such arrangements. Gains of a regular dealer in notional principal contracts are governed by the rules of § 1.863-7T(b). Amounts received or accrued by any person from any financial product that is integrated as specified in Notice 89-90 with an asset shall not be treated as amounts received or accrued by a person acting in its capacity as a regular dealer in financial products.

(vii) *Examples.*—The principles of this paragraph (b)(6) may be illustrated by the following examples.

Example (1). X is not a financial services entity or regular dealer in the financial products described in paragraph (b)(6)(i) of this section and has a dollar functional currency. In 1990, X incurred a total of $200 of interest expense. On January 1, 1990, X entered into an interest rate swap agreement with Y, in order to hedge its interest rate exposure with respect to a pre-existing floating rate liability. On the same day, X properly identified the agreement as a hedge of such liability. Under the agreement, X is required to pay Y an amount equal to a fixed rate of 10 percent on a notional principal amount of $1,000. Y is required to pay X an amount equal to a floating rate of interest on the same notional principal amount. Under the agreement, X received from Y during 1990 a net payment of $25. Because X identified the swap agreement as a liability hedge under the rules of paragraph (b)(6)(iv)(C), X may effectively reduce its total allocable interest expense for 1990 to $175 by directly allocating $25 of interest expense to the swap income. Had X not properly identified the swap as a liability hedge, this swap payment would have been treated as domestic source income in accordance with the rule of § 1.863-7T(b).

Example (2). Assume the same facts as Example (1), except that X did not properly identify the agreement as a liability hedge on January 1, 1990. In 1990, X made a net payment of $25 to Y under the swap agreement. This swap payment is allocated and apportioned in the same manner as interest expense under the rules of paragraph (b)(6)(iv)(A).

(7) *Foreign currency gain or loss.*—In addition to the rules of paragraph (b)(1), (b)(2), and (b)(6) of this section, any foreign currency loss that is treated as an adjustment to interest expense under regulations issued under section 988 shall be allocated and apportioned in the same manner as interest expense. Any foreign currency gain that is treated as an adjustment to interest expense under regulations issued under section 988 shall offset apportionable interest expense.

(8) *Guaranteed payments.*—For further guidance, see § 1.861-9(b)(8).

(c) *Allowable deductions.*—In order for an interest expense to be allocated and apportioned, it must first be determined that the interest expense is currently deductible. A number of provisions in the Code disallow or suspend deductions of interest expense or require the capitalization thereof.

(1) *Disallowed deductions.*—A taxpayer does not allocate and apportion interest expense under this section that is permanently disallowed as a deduction by operation of section 163(h), section 265, or any other provision or rule that permanently disallows the deduction of interest expense.

(2) *Section 263A.*—Section 263A requires the capitalization of interest expense that is allocable to designated types of property. Any interest expense that is capitalized under section 263A does not constitute deductible interest expense for purposes of this section. Furthermore, interest expense capitalized in inventory or depreciable property is not separately allocated and apportioned when the inventory is sold or depreciation is allowed. Capitalized interest expense is effectively allocated and apportioned as part of, and in the same manner as, the cost of goods sold, amortization, or depreciation deduction.

(3) *Section 163(d).*—Section 163(d) suspends the deduction for interest expense to the extent that it exceeds net investment income. In the year that suspended investment interest expense becomes allowable under the rules of section 163(d), that interest expense is apportioned under rules set forth in paragraph (d)(1) of this section as though it were incurred in the taxable year in which the expense is deducted.

(4) *Section 469.*—(i) *General rule.*—Section 469 suspends the deduction of passive activity losses to the extent that they exceed passive activity income for the year. Passive activity losses may consist in part of interest expense properly allocable to passive activity. In the year that suspended interest expense becomes allowable as a deduction under the rules of section 469, that interest expense is apportioned under rules set forth in paragraph (d)(1) of this section as though it were incurred in the taxable year in which the expense is deducted.

(ii) *Identification of the interest component of a suspended passive loss.*—A suspended passive loss may consist of a variety of items of expense other than interest expense. Suspended interest expense for any taxable year is computed by multiplying the total suspended passive loss for the year by a fraction, the numerator of which is passive interest expense for the year (determined under regulations issued under section 163) and the denominator of which is total passive expenses for the year. The amount of the suspended interest expense that is considered to be deductible in a subsequent taxable year is computed by multiplying the amount of any cumulative suspended interest expense (reduced by suspended interest expense allowed as a deduction in prior taxable years) times a fraction, the numerator of which is the portion of cumulative suspended passive losses that become deductible in the taxable year and the denominator of which is the cumulative suspended passive losses for prior taxable years (reduced by suspended passive losses allowed as deductions in prior taxable years).

(iii) *Example.*—The rules of this paragraph (c)(4) may be illustrated by the following example.

Example. On January 1, 1987, A, a United States citizen, invested in a passive activity. In 1987, the passive activity generated no passive income and $100 in passive losses, all of which were suspended by operation of section 469. The suspended loss included $10 of suspended interest expense. In 1988, the passive activity generated $50 in passive income and $150 in passive expenses which included $30 of interest expense. The entire $100 passive loss was suspended in 1988 and included $20 of interest expense ($100 suspended passive loss × $30 passive interest expense / $150 total passive expenses). Thus, at the end of 1988, A had total suspended passive losses of $200, including $30 of suspended interest expense. In 1989, the passive activity generated $100 in passive income and no passive expenses. Thus, $100 of A's cumulative suspended passive loss was therefore allowed in 1989. The $100 of deductible passive loss includes $15 of suspended interest expense ($30 cumulative suspended interest expense × $100 of cumulative suspended passive losses allowable in 1989 / $200 of total cumulative suspended passive losses). The $15 of interest expense is apportioned under the rules of paragraph (d) of this section as though it were incurred in 1989.

(5) *Section 163(j).*—For further guidance, see § 1.861-9(c)(5).

(d) *Apportionment rules for individuals, estates, and certain trusts.*—(1) *United States individuals.*—In the case of taxable years beginning after December 31, 1986, individuals generally shall apportion interest expense under different rules according to the type of interest expense incurred. The interest expense of individuals shall be characterized under the regulations issued under section 163. However, in the case of an individual whose foreign source income (including income that is excluded under section 911) does not exceed a gross amount of $5,000, the apportionment of interest expense under this section is not required. Such an individual's interest expense may be allocated entirely to domestic source income.

(i) *Interest incurred in the conduct of a trade or business.*—An individual who incurs business interest described in section 163(h)(2)(A) shall apportion such interest expense using an asset method by reference to the individual's business assets.

(ii) *Investment interest.*—An individual who incurs investment interest described in section 163(h)(2)(B) shall apportion that interest expense on the basis of the individual's investment assets.

(iii) *Interest incurred in a passive activity.*—An individual who incurs passive activity interest described in section 163(h)(2)(C) shall apportion that interest expense on the basis of the individual's passive activity assets. Individuals who receive a distributive share of interest expense incurred in a partnership are subject to special rules set forth in paragraph (e) of this section.

(iv) *Qualified residence and deductible personal interest.*—Individuals who incur qualified residence interest described in section 163(h)(2)(D) shall apportion that interest expense under a gross income method, taking into account all income (including business, passive activity, and investment income) but excluding income that is exempt under section 911. For purposes of this section, any qualified residence that is rented shall be considered to be a business asset for the period in which it is rented, with the result that the interest on such a residence is not apportioned under this subdivision (iv) but instead under subdivisions (i) or (iii) of this paragraph (d)(1). To the extent that personal interest described in section 163(h)(2) remains deductible under transitional rules, individuals shall apportion such interest expense in the same manner as qualified residence interest.

(v) *Example.*—The following example illustrates the principles of this section.

Example—(i) *Facts.* A is a resident individual taxpayer engaged in the active conduct of a trade or business, which A operates as a sole proprietor. A's business generates only domestic source income. A's investment portfolio consists of several less than 10 percent stock investments. Certain stocks in which A's adjusted basis is $40,000 generate domestic source income and other stocks in which A's adjusted basis is $60,000 generate foreign source passive income. In addition, A owns his personal residence, which is subject to a mortgage in the amount of $100,000. All interest expense incurred with respect to A's mortgage is qualified residence interest for purposes of section 163(h)(2)(D). A's other indebtedness consists of a bank loan in the amount of $40,000. Under the regulations issued under section 163(h), it is determined that the proceeds of the $40,000 loan were divided equally between A's business and his investment portfolio. In 1987, the gross income of A's business, before the apportionment of interest expense, was $50,000. A's investment portfolio generated $4,000 in domestic source income and $6,000 in foreign source passive income. All of A's debt obligations bear interest at the annual rate of 10 percent.

(ii) *Analysis of business interest.* Under section 163(h) of the Code, $2,000 of A's interest expense is attributable to his business. Under the rules of paragraph (d)(1)(i), such interest must be apportioned on the basis of the business assets. Applying the asset method described in paragraph (g) of this section, it is determined that all of A's business assets generate domestic income and, therefore, constitute domestic assets. Thus, the $2,000 in interest expense on the business loan is allocable to domestic source income.

(iii) *Analysis of investment interest.* Under section 163(h) of the Code, $2,000 of A's interest expense is investment interest. Under the rules of paragraph (d)(1)(ii) of this section, such interest must be apportioned on the basis of investment assets. Applying the asset method, A's investment assets consist of stock generating domestic source income with an adjusted basis of $40,000 and stock generating foreign source passive income with an adjusted basis of $60,000. Thus, 40 percent ($800) of A's investment interest is apportioned to domestic source income and 60 percent ($1,200) of A's investment interest is apportioned to foreign source passive income for purposes of section 904.

(iv) *Analysis of qualified residence interest.* The $10,000 of qualified residence interest expense is apportioned under the rules of paragraph (d)(1)(iv) of this section on the basis of all of A's gross income. A's gross income consists of $60,000, $54,000 of which is domestic source and $6,000 of which is foreign source passive income. Thus, $9,000 of A's qualified residence interest is apportioned to domestic source income and $1,000 of A's qualified residence interest is apportioned to foreign source passive income.

(2) *Nonresident aliens.*—(i) *General rule.*—For taxable years beginning on or after January 1, 1988, interest expense incurred by a nonresident alien shall be considered to be connected with income effectively connected with a United States trade or business only to the extent that interest expense is incurred with respect to liabilities that—

(A) Are entered on the books and records of the United States trade or business when incurred, or

(B) Are secured by assets that generate such effectively connected income.

(ii) *Limitations.*—(A) *Maximum debt capitalization.*—Interest expense incurred by a nonresident alien is not considered to be connected with effectively connected income to the extent that it is incurred with respect to liabilities that exceed 80 percent of the gross assets of the United States trade or business.

(B) *Collateralization by other assets.*—Interest expense on indebtedness that is secured by specific assets (not including the general credit of the nonresident alien) other than the assets of the United States trade or business shall not be considered to be connected with effectively connected income.

(3) *Estates and trusts.*—Estates shall be treated in the same manner as individuals. In the case of a trust that is beneficially owned by individuals and is a complex trust, the trust shall be treated in the same manner as individuals under the rules of paragraph (d) of this section, except that no de minimis amount shall apply. In the case of a trust that is beneficially owned by one or more corporations, the trust shall be treated either as a partnership or as a corporation depending on how the trust is characterized under the rules of section 7701 and the regulations thereunder.

(e) *Partnerships.*—(1) *In general—aggregate rule.*—A partner's distributive share of the interest expense of a partnership that is directly allocable under § 1.861-10T to income from specific partnership property shall be treated as directly allocable to the income generated by such partnership property. Subject to the exceptions set forth in paragraph (e)(4), a partner's distributive share of the interest expense of a partnership that is not directly allocable under § 1.861-10T generally is considered related to all income producing activities and assets of the partner and shall be subject to apportionment under the rules described in this paragraph. For purposes of this section, a partner's percentage interest in a partnership shall be determined by reference to the partner's interest in partnership income for the year. Similarly, a partner's pro rata share of partnership assets shall be determined by reference to the partner's interest in partnership income for the year.

(e)(2) through (e)(3) [Reserved]. For further guidance see § 1.861-9(e)(2) through (e)(3).

(4) *Less than 10 percent limited partners and less than 10 percent corporate general partners—entity rule.*—(i) *Partnership interest expense.*—For further guidance, see § 1.861-9(e)(4)(i).

(ii) *Other interest expense of the partner.*—For purposes of apportioning other interest expense of the partner on an asset basis, the partner's interest in the partnership, and not the partner's pro rata share of partnership assets, is considered to be the relevant asset. The value of this asset for apportionment purposes is either the tax book value or fair market value of the partner's partnership interest, depending on the method of apportionment used by the taxpayer. This amount of a partner's interest in the partnership is allocated among various limitation categories in the same manner as partnership interest expense (that is not directly allocable under § 1.861-10T) is apportioned in subdivision (i) of this paragraph (e)(4). If the partner uses the tax book value method of apportionment, the partner's interest in the partnership must be reduced, for this purpose, to the extent that the partner's basis consists of liabilities that are taken into account under section 752. Under either the tax book value or fair market value method of apportionment, for purposes of this section only, the value of the partner's interest in the partnership must be reduced by the principal amount of any indebtedness of the partner the interest on which is directly allocated to its partnership interest under § 1.861-10T.

(5) *Tiered partnerships.*—If a partnership is a partner in another partnership, the distributive share of interest expense of a lower-tier partnership that is subject to the rules of paragraph (e)(4) shall not be reapportioned in the hands of any higher-tier partner. However, the distributive share of interest expense of lower-tier partnership that is subject to the rules of paragraph (e)(2) or (3) shall be apportioned by the partner of the higher-tier partnership or by any higher-tier partnership to which the rules of paragraph (e)(4) apply, taking into account the partner's indirect pro rata share of the lower-tier partnership's income or assets.

(6) *Example.*—(i) *Facts.*—A, B, and C are partners in a limited partnership. A is a corporate general partner, owns a 5 percent interest in the partnership, and has an adjusted basis in its partnership interest, determined without regard to section 752 of the Code, of $5. A's investment in the partnership is not held in the ordinary course of the taxpayer's active trade or business, as defined in § 1.904-7(i)(2). B, a corporate limited partner, owns a 70 percent interest in the partnership, and has an adjusted basis in its partnership interest, determined without regard to section 752 of the Code, of $70. C is an individual limited partner, owns a 25 percent interest in the partnership, and has an adjusted basis in the partnership interest, determined without regard to section 752 of the Code, of $25. The partners' interests in the profits and losses of the partnership conform to their respective interests. None of the interest expense incurred directly by any of the partners is directly allocable to their partnership interest under § 1.861-10T. The ABC partnership's sole assets are two apartment buildings, one domestic and the other foreign. The domestic building has an adjusted inside basis of $600 and the foreign building has an adjusted inside basis of $500. Each of the buildings is subject to a nonrecourse liability in the amount of $500. The ABC partnership's total interest expense for the taxable year is $120, both nonrecourse liabilities bearing interest at the rate of 12 percent. The indebtedness on the domestic building qualifies for direct allocation under the rules of § 1.861-10T. The indebtedness on the foreign building does not so qualify. The partnership incurred no foreign taxes. The partnership's gross income for the taxable year is $360, consisting of $100 in foreign source income and $260 in domestic source income. Under § 1.752-1(e), the nonrecourse liabilities of the partnership are allocated among the partners according to their share of the partnership profits. Accordingly, the adjusted basis of A, B, and C in their respective partnership interests (for other than apportionment purposes) is, respectively, $55, $770, and $275.

(ii) *Determination of the amount of partnership interest expense that is subject to allocation and apportionment.*—Interest on the nonrecourse loan on the domestic building is, under § 1.861-10T, directly allocable to income from that investment. The interest expense is therefore directly allocable to domestic income. Interest on the nonrecourse loan on the foreign building is not directly allocable. The interest expense is therefore subject to allocation and apportionment. Thus, $60 of interest expense is directly allocable to domestic income and $60 of interest expense is subject to allocation and apportionment.

(iii) *Analysis for Partner A.*—A's distributive share of the partnership's gross income is $18, which consists of $5 in foreign source income and $13 in domestic source income. A's distributive share of the ABC interest expense is $6, $3 of which is directly allocable to domestic income and $3 of which is subject to apportionment. After direct allocation of qualifying interest expense, A's distributive share of the partnership's gross income consists of $5 in foreign source income and $10 in domestic source income. Because A is a less than 10 percent corporate partner, A's distributive share of any foreign source partnership income is considered to be passive income. Accordingly, in apportioning the $3 of partnership interest expense that is subject to apportionment on a gross income method, one-third ($1) is apportioned to foreign source passive income and two-thirds ($2) is apportioned to domestic source income. In apportioning its other interest expense, A uses the tax book value method. A's adjusted basis in A's partnership interest ($55) includes A's share of the partnership's liabilities ($50), which are included in basis under section 752. For purposes of apportioning other interest expense, A's adjusted basis in the partnership must be reduced to the extent of such liabilities. Thus, A's adjusted basis in the partnership, for purposes of apportionment, is $5. For the purpose of apportioning A's other interest expense, this $5 in basis is characterized one-third as a foreign passive asset and two-thirds as a domestic asset, which is the ratio determined in paragraph (e)(4)(i).

(iv) *Analysis for Partner B.*—B's distributive share of the ABC interest expense is $84, $42 of which is directly allocable to domestic income and $42 of which is subject to apportionment. As a corporate limited partner whose interest in the partnership is 10 percent or more, B is subject to the rules of paragraph (e)(2) and paragraph (f) of this section. These rules require that a corporate partner apportion its distributive share of partnership interest expense at the partner level on the asset method described in paragraph (g) of this section by reference to its corporate assets, which include, for this purpose, 70 percent of the partnership's assets, adjusted in the manner described in § 1.861-10T(e) to reflect directly allocable interest expense.

(v) *Analysis for Partner C.*—C's distributive share of the ABC interest expense is $30, $15 of which is directly allocable to domestic income and $15 of which is subject to apportionment. As an individual limited partner whose interest in the partnership is 10 percent or more, C is subject to the rules of paragraph (e)(3) of this section. These rules require that an individual's share of partnership interest expense be classified under regulations issued under section 163(h) and then apportioned under the rules applicable to individuals, which are set forth in paragraph (d) of this section.

(7) *Foreign partners.*—The distributive share of partnership interest expense of a nonresident alien who is a partner in a partnership shall be considered to be connected with effectively connected income based on the percentage of the assets of the partnership that generate effectively connected income. No interest expense directly incurred by the partner may be allocated and apportioned to effectively connected income derived by the partnership.

(8) *Special rule for downstream partnership loans.*—For further guidance, see § 1.861-9(e)(8) through (10).

(9) and (10) [Reserved]

(f) *Corporations.*—(1) *Domestic corporations.*—Domestic corporations shall apportion interest expense using the asset method described in paragraph (g) of this section and the applicable rules of §§ 1.861-10T through 1.861-13T.

(2) *Section 987 QBUs of domestic corporations.*—For further guidance, see § 1.861-9(f)(2) through (f)(3)(i).

(3)(i) [Reserved]

(ii) *Manner of election.*—The election to use the asset method described in paragraph (g) of this section or the modified gross income method described in paragraph (j) of this section may be made either by the controlled foreign corporation or by the controlling United States shareholders on behalf of the controlled foreign corporation. The term "controlling United States shareholders" means those United States shareholders (as defined in section 951(b)) who, in aggregate, own (within the meaning of section 958(a)) greater than 50 percent of the total combined voting power of all classes of stock of the foreign corporation entitled to vote. In the case of a controlled foreign corporation in which the United States shareholders own stock representing more than 50 percent of the value of the stock in such corporation, but less than 50 percent of the combined voting power of all classes of stock in such corporation, the term "controlling United States shareholders" means all the United States shareholders (as defined in section 951(b)) who own (within the meaning of section 958(a)) stock of the controlled foreign corporation. All United States shareholders are bound by the election of either the controlled foreign corporation or the controlling United States shareholders. For guidance relating to the time and manner of this election, see § 1.861-9(f)(3)(ii).

(iii) *Consistency requirement.*—The same method of apportionment must be employed by all controlled foreign corporations in which a United States taxpayer and the members of its affiliated group (as defined in § 1.861-11T(d)) constitute controlling United States shareholders. A controlled foreign corporation that is required by this paragraph (f)(3)(iii) to utilize a particular method of apportionment must do so with respect to all United States shareholders.

(iv) *Stock characterization.*—Pursuant to § 1.861-12T(c)(2), the stock of a controlled foreign corporation shall be characterized in the hands of any United States shareholder using the same method that the controlled foreign corporation uses to apportion its interest expense.

(4) *Noncontrolled 10-percent owned foreign corporations.*—For further guidance, see § 1.861-9(f)(4).

(5) *Other relevant provisions.*—Affiliated groups of corporations are subject to special rules set forth in § 1.861-11T. Section 1.861-12T sets forth rules relating to basis adjustments for stock in nonaffiliated 10 percent owned corporations, special rules relating to the consideration and characterization of certain assets in the apportionment of interest expense, and to other special rules pertaining to the apportionment of interest expense. Section 1.861-13T contains transition rules limiting the application of the rules of §§ 1.861-8T through 1.861-12T, which are otherwise applicable to taxable years beginning after 1986. In the case of an affiliated group of corporations as defined in § 1.861-11T(d), any reference in §§ 1.861-8T through 1.861-13T to the "taxpayer" with respect to the allocation and apportionment of interest expense generally denotes the entire affiliated group of corporations and not the separate members thereof, unless the context otherwise requires.

(g) *Asset method.*—(1) *In general.*—(i) Under the asset method, the taxpayer apportions interest expense to the various statutory groupings based on the average total value of assets within each such grouping for the taxable year, as determined under the asset valuation rules of this paragraph (g)(1) and paragraph (g)(2) of this section and the asset characterization rules of paragraph (g)(3) of this section and § 1.861-12T. Except to the extent otherwise provided (*see, e.g.,* paragraph (d)(1)(iv) of this section), taxpayers must apportion interest expense only on the basis of asset values and may not apportion any interest deduction on the basis of gross income.

(ii) For further guidance, see § 1.861-9(g)(1)(ii) through (g)(2)(i).

(iii) through (v) [Reserved]

(2)(i) [Reserved]

(ii) *Special rule for qualified business units of domestic corporations with functional currency other than the U.S. dollar.*—(A) *Tax book value method.*—In the case of taxpayers using the tax book value method of apportionment, the following rules shall apply to determine the value of the assets of a qualified business unit (as defined in section 989(a)) of a domestic corporation with a functional currency other than the dollar.

(1) Section 987 QBU.—In the case of a section 987 QBU (as defined in § 1.987-1(b)(2)), the tax book value shall be determined by applying the rules of paragraphs (g)(2)(i) and (g)(3) of this section to the beginning-of-year and end-of-year functional currency amount of assets. The beginning-of-year functional currency amount of assets shall be determined by reference to the functional currency amount of assets computed under § 1.987-4(d)(1)(i)(B) and (e) on the last day of the preceding taxable year. The end-of-year functional currency amount of assets shall be determined by reference to the functional currency amount of assets computed under § 1.987-4(d)(1)(i)(A) and (e) on the last day of the current taxable year. The beginning-of-year and end-of-year functional currency amount of assets, as so determined within each grouping, must then be averaged as provided in paragraph (g)(2)(i) of this section.

(2) U.S. dollar approximate separate transactions method.—For further guidance, see § 1.861-9(g)(2)(ii)(A)(2).

(B) *Fair market value method.*—In the case of taxpayers using the fair market value method of apportionment, the beginning-of-year and end-of-year fair market values of branch assets within each grouping shall be computed in dollars and averaged as provided in this paragraph (g)(2).

(iii) *Adjustment for directly allocated interest.*—Prior to averaging, the year-end value of any asset to which interest expense is directly allocated during the current taxable year under the rules of § 1.861-10T(b) or (c) shall be reduced (but not below zero) by the percentage of the principal amount of indebtedness outstanding at year-end equal to the percentage of all interest on the debt for the taxable year that is directly allocated.

(iv) *Assets in intercompany transactions.*—In the application of the asset method described in this paragraph (g), the tax book value of assets transferred between affiliated corporations in intercompany transactions shall be determined without regard to the gain or loss that is deferred under the regulations issued under section 1502.

(v) [Reserved]

(vi) *Effective/applicability date*.—Generally, paragraph (g)(2)(ii)(A)*(1)* of this section shall apply to taxable years beginning on or after one year after the first day of the first taxable year following December 7, 2016. If pursuant to § 1.987-11(b) a taxpayer applies §§ 1.987-1 through 1.987-11 beginning in a taxable year prior to the earliest taxable year described in § 1.987-11(a), then paragraph (g)(2)(ii)(A)*(1)* of this section shall apply to taxable years beginning on or after the first day of such prior taxable year.

(3) *Characterization of assets*.—Assets are characterized for purposes of this section according to the source and type of the income that they generate, have generated, or may reasonably be expected to generate. The physical location of assets is not relevant to this determination. Subject to the special rules of paragraph (h) concerning the application of the fair market value method of apportionment, the value of assets within each statutory grouping and the residual grouping at the beginning and end of each year shall be determined by dividing the taxpayer's assets into three types—

(i) *Single category assets*.—Assets that generate income that is exclusively within a single statutory grouping or the residual grouping;

(ii) *Multiple category assets*.—Assets that generate income within more than one grouping of income (statutory or residual); and

(iii) *Assets without directly identifiable yield*.—Assets that produce no directly identifiable income yield or that contribute equally to the generation of all the income of the taxpayer (such as assets used in general and administrative functions).

Single category assets are directly attributable to the relevant statutory or residual grouping of income. In order to attribute multiple category assets to the relevant groupings of income, the income yield of each such asset for the taxable year must be analyzed to determine the proportion of gross income generated by it within each relevant grouping. The value of each asset is then prorated among the relevant groupings of income according to their respective proportions of gross income. The value of each asset without directly identifiable income yield must be identified. However, because prorating the value of such assets cannot alter the ratio of assets within the various groupings of income (as determined by reference to the single and multiple category assets), they are not taken into account in determining that ratio. Special asset characterization rules that are set forth in § 1.861-12T. An example demonstrating the application of the asset method is set forth in § 1.861-12T(d).

(h) *Fair market value method*.—For further guidance, see § 1.861-9(h).

(1) *Determination of values*.—(i) *Valuation of group assets*.—The taxpayer shall first determine the aggregate value of the assets of the taxpayer on the last day of its taxable year without excluding the value of stock in foreign subsidiaries or any other asset. In the case of a publicly traded corporation, this determination shall be equal to the aggregate trading value of the taxpayer's stock traded on established securities markets at year-end increased by the taxpayer's year-end liabilities to unrelated persons and its pro rata share of year-end liabilities of all related persons owed to unrelated persons. In determining whether persons are related, § 1.861-8T(c)(2) shall apply. In the case of a corporation that is not publicly traded, this determination shall be made by reference to the capitalization of corporate earnings, in accordance with the rules of Rev. Rul. 68-609. In either case, control premium shall not be taken into account.

(ii) *Valuation of tangible assets*.—The taxpayer shall determine the value of all assets held by the taxpayer and its pro rata share of assets held by other related persons on the last day of its taxable year, excluding stock or indebtedness in such persons, any intangible property as defined in section 936(h)(3)(B), or goodwill or going concern value intangibles. Such valuations shall be made using generally accepted valuation techniques. For this purpose, assets may be combined into reasonable groupings. Statistical methods of valuation may only be used in connection with fungible property, such as commodities. The value of stock in any corporation that is not a related person shall be determined under the rules of paragraph (h)(1)(i) of this section, except that no liabilities shall be taken into account.

(iii) *Computation of intangible asset value*.—The value of the intangible assets of the taxpayer and of intangible assets of all related persons attributable to the taxpayer's ownership in related persons is equal to the amount obtained by subtracting the amount determined under paragraph (h)(1)(ii) of this section from the amount determined under paragraph (h)(1)(i) of this section.

(2) *Apportionment of intangible asset value*.—The value of the intangible assets determined under paragraph (h)(1)(iii) of this section is apportioned among the taxpayer and all related persons in proportion to the net income before interest expense of the taxpayer and the taxpayer's pro rata share of the net income before interest expense of each related person held by the taxpayer, excluding income that is passive under § 1.904-4(b). For this purpose, net income is determined before reduction for income taxes. Net income of the taxpayer and of related persons shall be computed without regard to dividends or interest received from any person that is related to the taxpayer.

(3) *Characterization of affiliated group's portion of intangible asset value*.—The portion of the value of intangible assets of the taxpayer and related persons that is apportioned to the taxpayer under paragraph (h)(2) of this section is characterized on the basis of net income before interest expense, as determined under paragraph (h)(2) of this section, of the taxpayer within each statutory or residual grouping of income.

(4) [Reserved]. For further guidance see § 1.861-9(h)(4).

(5) [Reserved]. For further guidance, see § 1.861-9(h)(5).

(6) *Adjustments for apportioning related person expenses*.—For purposes of apportioning expenses of a related person, the value of stock in a second related person as otherwise determined under paragraph (h)(4) of this section (which is determined on the basis of the taxpayer's percentage ownership interest in the second related person) shall be increased to reflect the first related person's percentage ownership interest in the second related person to the extent it is larger.

Example. Assume that a taxpayer owns 80 percent of CFC1, which owns 100 percent of CFC2. The value of CFC1 is determined generally under paragraph (h)(4) on the basis of the taxpayer's 80 percent indirect interest in CFC2. For purposes of apportioning expenses of CFC1, 100 percent of the stock of CFC1 must be taken into account. Therefore, the value of CFC2 stock in the hands of CFC1 shall equal the value of CFC2 stock in the hands of CFC1 as determined under paragraph (h)(4) of this section, increased by 25 percent of such amount to reflect the fact that CFC1 owns 100 percent and not 80 percent of CFC2.

(i) [Reserved]. For further guidance, see § 1.861-9(i).

(j) *Modified gross income method*.—Subject to rules set forth in paragraph (f)(3) of this section, the interest expense of a controlled foreign corporation may be allocated according to the following rules.

(1) *Single-tier controlled foreign corporation*.—In the case of a controlled foreign corporation that does not hold stock in any lower-tier controlled foreign corporation, the interest expense of the controlled foreign corporation shall be apportioned based on its gross income.

(2) *Multiple vertically owned controlled foreign corporations*.—In the case of a controlled foreign corporation that holds stock in any lower-tier controlled foreign corporation, the interest expense of that controlled foreign corporation and each upper-tier controlled foreign corporation shall be apportioned based on the following methodology:

(i) *Step 1*.—Commencing with the lowest-tier controlled foreign corporation in the chain, allocate and apportion its interest expense based on its gross income as provided in paragraph (j)(1) of this section, yielding gross income in each grouping net of interest expense.

(ii) *Step 2*.—For further guidance, see § 1.861-9(j)(2)(ii).

(k) *Effective/applicability dates*.—In general, the rules of this section apply for taxable years beginning after December 31, 1986. Paragraphs (b)(2) (concerning the treatment of certain foreign currency) and (d)(2) (concerning the treatment of interest incurred by nonresident aliens) of this section are applicable for taxable years commencing after December 31, 1988. Paragraph (b)(6) of this section applies to losses on any transaction described in paragraph (b)(6)(i) of this section that was entered into after September 14, 1988. Paragraph (b)(6) of this section also applies to any gain that was realized on any transaction described in paragraph (b)(6)(i) of this section that was entered into after August 11, 1989. Taxpayers may also apply paragraph (b)(6) of this section to any gain that was realized on any transaction described in paragraph (b)(6)(i) of this section that was entered into after September 14, 1988, and on or before August 11, 1989, if the taxpayer can demonstrate to the satisfaction of the Commissioner that substantially all of the arrangements described in paragraph (b)(6)(i) of this section to which the taxpayer became a party during that interim period were identified on the taxpayer's books and records with the liabilities of the taxpayer in a substantially contemporaneous manner and that all losses and expenses that are subject to the rules of paragraph (b)(6) of this section were treated in the same manner as interest expense. For further guidance, see §1.861-9(k). [Temporary Reg. §1.861-9T.]

☐ [*T.D.* 8228, 9-9-88. *Amended by T.D.* 8257, 8-1-89; *T.D.* 8597, 7-12-95; *T.D.* 8658, 3-5-96; *T.D.* 8916, 12-29-2000; *T.D.* 9120, 3-25-2004; *T.D.* 9247, 1-27-2006; *T.D.* 9260, 4-20-2006; *T.D.* 9452, 6-10-2009; *T.D.* 9456, 7-31-2009; *T.D.* 9571, 1-13-2012 (*corrected* 2-17-2012), *T.D.* 9676, 7-15-2014; *T.D.* 9794, 12-7-2016, *T.D.* 9849, 3-11-2019, *T.D.* 9882, 12-16-2019 *and T.D.* 9922, 11-2-2020.]

§1.861-10. Special allocations of interest expense.—

* * *

(e) *Treatment of certain related group indebtedness.*—(1) *In general.*—If, for any taxable year beginning after December 31, 1991, a U.S. shareholder (as defined in paragraph (e)(5)(i) of this section) has both—

(i) Excess related group indebtedness (as determined under Step One in paragraph (e)(2) of this section) and

(ii) Excess U.S. shareholder indebtedness (as determined under Step Two in paragraph (e)(3) of this section),

the U.S. shareholder shall allocate, to its gross income in the various separate limitation categories described in section 904(d)(1), a portion of its interest expense paid or accrued to any obligee who is not a member of the affiliated group (as defined in §1.861-11T(d)) of the U.S. shareholder ("third party interest expense"), excluding amounts allocated under paragraphs (b) and (c) of §1.861-1OT. The amount of third party interest expense so allocated shall equal the total amount of interest income derived by the U.S. shareholder during the year from related group indebtedness, multiplied by the ratio of the lesser of the foregoing two amounts of excess indebtedness for the year to related group indebtedness for the year. This amount of third party interest expense is allocated as described in Step Three in paragraph (e)(4) of this section.

(2) *Step One: Excess related group indebtedness.*

(i) The excess related group indebtedness of a U.S. shareholder for the year equals the amount by which its related group indebtedness for the year exceeds its allowable related group indebtedness for the year.

(ii) The "related group indebtedness" of the U.S. shareholder is the average of the aggregate amounts at the beginning and end of the year of indebtedness owed to the U.S. shareholder by each controlled foreign corporation which is a related person (as defined in paragraph (e)(5)(ii) of this section) with respect to the U.S. shareholder.

(iii) The "allowable related group indebtedness" of a U.S. shareholder for the year equals—

(A) The average of the aggregate values at the beginning and end of the year of the assets (including stock holdings in and obligations of related persons, other than related controlled foreign corporations) of each related controlled foreign corporation, multiplied by

(B) The foreign base period ratio of the U.S. shareholder for the year.

(iv) The "foreign base period ratio" of the U.S. shareholder for the year is the average of the related group debt-to-asset ratios of the U.S. shareholder for each taxable year comprising the foreign base period for the current year (each a "base year"). For this purpose, however, the related group debt-to-asset ratio of the U.S. shareholder for any base year may not exceed 110 percent of the foreign base period ratio for that base year. This limitation shall not apply with respect to any of the five taxable years chosen as initial base years by the U.S. shareholder under paragraph (e)(2)(v) of this section or with respect to any base year for which the related group debt-to-asset ratio does not exceed 0.10.

(v)(A) The foreign base period for any current taxable year (except as described in paragraphs (e)(2)(v)(B) and (C) of this section) shall consist of the five taxable years immediately preceding the current year.

(B) The U.S. shareholder may choose as foreign base periods for all of its first five taxable years for which this paragraph (e) is effective the following alternative base periods:

(1) For the first effective taxable year, the 1982, 1983, 1984, 1985 and 1986 taxable years;

(2) For the second effective taxable year, the 1983, 1984, 1985 and 1986 taxable years and the first effective taxable year;

(3) For the third effective taxable year, the 1984, 1985 and 1986 taxable years and the first and second effective taxable years;

(4) For the fourth effective taxable year, the 1985 and 1986 taxable years and the first, second and third effective taxable years; and

(5) For the fifth effective taxable year, the 1986 taxable year and the first, second, third and fourth effective taxable years.

(C) If, however, the U.S. shareholder does not choose, under paragraph (e)(10) (ii) of this section, to apply this paragraph (e) to one or more taxable years beginning before January 1, 1992, the U.S. shareholder may not include within any foreign base period the taxable year immediately preceding the first effective taxable year. Thus, for example, a U.S. shareholder for which the first effective taxable year is the taxable year beginning on October 1, 1992, may not include the taxable year beginning on October 1, 1991, in any foreign base period. Assuming that the U.S. shareholder does not elect the alternative base periods described in paragraph (e)(2)(v)(B) of this section, the initial foreign base period for the U.S. shareholder will consist of the taxable years beginning on October 1 of 1986, 1987, 1988, 1989, and 1990. The foreign base period for the U.S. shareholder for the following taxable year, beginning on October 1, 1993, will consist of the taxable years beginning on October 1 of 1987, 1988, 1989, 1990, and 1992.

(D) If the U.S. shareholder chooses the base periods described in paragraph (e)(2)(v)(B) of this section as foreign base periods, it must make a similar election under paragraph (e)(3)(v)(B) of this section with respect to its U.S. base periods.

(vi) The "related group debt-to-asset ratio" of a U.S. shareholder for a year is the ratio between—

(A) The related group indebtedness of the U.S. shareholder for the year (as determined under paragraph (e)(2)(ii) of this section); and

(B) The average of the aggregate values at the beginning and end of the year of the assets (including stock holdings in and obligations of related persons, other than related controlled foreign corporations) of each related controlled foreign corporation.

(vii) Notwithstanding paragraph (e)(2)(i) of this section, a U.S. shareholder is considered to have no excess related group indebtedness for the year if—

(A) Its related group indebtedness for the year does not exceed its allowable related group indebtedness for the immediately preceding year (as determined under paragraph (e)(2)(iii) of this section); or

(B) Its related group debt-to-asset ratio (as determined under paragraph (e)(2)(vi) of this section) for the year does not exceed 0.10.

(3) *Step Two: Excess U.S. shareholder indebtedness.*

(i) The excess indebtedness of a U.S. shareholder for the year equals the amount by which its unaffiliated indebtedness for the year exceeds its allowable indebtedness for the year.

(ii) The "unaffiliated indebtedness" of the U.S. shareholder is the average of the aggregate amounts at the beginning and end of the year of indebtedness owed by the U.S. shareholder to any obligee, other than a member of the affiliated group (as defined in §1.861-11T(d)) of the U.S. shareholder.

(iii) The "allowable indebtedness" of a U.S. shareholder for the year equals—

(A) The average of the aggregate values at the beginning and end of the year of the assets of the U.S. shareholder (including stock holdings in and obligations of related controlled foreign corporations, but excluding stock holdings in and obligations of members of the affiliated group (as defined in §1.861-11T(d)) of the U.S. shareholder), reduced by the amount of the excess related group indebtedness of the U.S. shareholder for the year (as determined under Step One in paragraph (e)(2) of this section), multiplied by

(B) The U.S. base period ratio of the U.S. shareholder for the year.

(iv) The "U.S. base period ratio" of the U.S. shareholder for the year is the average of the debt-to-asset ratios of the U.S. shareholder for each taxable year comprising the U.S. base period for the current year (each a "base year"). For this purpose, however, the debt-to-asset ratio of the U.S. shareholder for any base year may not exceed 110 percent of the U.S. base period ratio for that base year. This limitation shall not apply with respect to any of the five taxable years chosen as initial base years by the U.S. shareholder under paragraph (e)(3)(v) of this section or with respect to any base year for which the debt-to-asset ratio does not exceed 0.10.

(v)(A) The U.S. base period for any current taxable year (except as described in paragraphs (e)(3)(v)(B) and (C) of this section) shall consist of the five taxable years immediately preceding the current year.

(B) The U.S. shareholder may choose as U.S. base periods for all of its first five taxable years for which this paragraph (e) is effective the following alternative base periods:

(1) For the first effective taxable year, the 1982, 1983, 1984, 1985 and 1986 taxable years;

(2) For the second effective taxable year, the 1983, 1984, 1985 and 1986 taxable years and the first effective taxable year;

(3) For the third effective taxable year, the 1984, 1985 and 1986 taxable years and the first and second effective taxable years;

(4) For the fourth effective taxable year, the 1985 and 1986 taxable years and the first, second and third effective taxable years; and

(5) For the fifth effective taxable year, the 1986 taxable year and the first, second, third and fourth effective taxable years.

(C) If, however, the U.S. shareholder does not choose, under paragraph (e)(10)(ii) of this section, to apply this paragraph (e) to one or more taxable years beginning before January 1, 1992, the U.S. shareholder may not include within any U.S. base period the taxable year immediately preceding the first effective taxable year. Thus, for example, a U.S. shareholder for which the first effective taxable year is the taxable year beginning on October 1, 1992, may not include the taxable year beginning on October 1, 1991, in any U.S. base period. Assuming that the U.S. shareholder does not elect the alternative base periods described in paragraph (e)(3)(v)(B) of this section, the initial U.S. base period for the U.S. shareholder will consist of the taxable years beginning on October 1 of 1986, 1987, 1988, 1989, and 1990. The U.S. base period for the U.S. shareholder for the following taxable year, beginning on October 1, 1993, will consist of the taxable years beginning on October 1, 1987, 1988, 1989, 1990, and 1992.

(D) If the U.S. shareholder chooses the base periods described in paragraph (e)(3)(v)(B) of this section as U.S. base periods, it must make a similar election under paragraph (e)(2)(v)(B) of this section with respect to its foreign base periods.

(vi) The "debt-to-asset ratio" of a U.S. shareholder for a year is the ratio between—

(A) The unaffiliated indebtedness of the U.S. shareholder for the year (as determined under paragraph (e)(3)(ii) of this section); and

(B) The average of the aggregate values at the beginning and end of the year of the assets of the U.S. shareholder. For this purpose, the assets of the U.S. shareholder include stock holdings in and obligations of related controlled foreign corporations but do not include stock holdings in and obligations of members of the affiliated group (as defined in § 1.861-11T(d)).

(vii) A U.S. shareholder is considered to have no excess indebtedness for the year if its debt-to-asset ratio (as determined under paragraph (e)(3)(vi) of this section) for the year does not exceed 0.10.

(4) *Step Three: Allocation of third party interest expense.*—(i) A U.S. shareholder shall allocate to its gross income in the various separate limitation categories described in section 904(d)(1) a portion of its third party interest expense incurred during the year equal in amount to the interest income derived by the U.S. shareholder during the year from allocable related group indebtedness.

(ii) The "allocable related group indebtedness" of a U.S. shareholder for any year is an amount of related group indebtedness equal to the lesser of—

(A) The excess related group indebtedness of the U.S. shareholder for the year (determined under Step One in paragraph (e)(2) of this section); or

(B) The excess U.S. shareholder indebtedness for the year (determined under Step Two in paragraph (e)(3) of this section).

(iii) The amount of interest income derived by a U.S. shareholder from allocable related group indebtedness during the year equals the total amount of interest income derived by the U.S. shareholder during the year with respect to related group indebtedness, multiplied by the ratio of allocable related group indebtedness for the year to the aggregate amount of related group indebtedness for the year.

(iv) The portion of third party interest expense described in paragraph (e)(4)(i) of this section shall be allocated in proportion to the relative average amounts of related group indebtedness held by the U.S. shareholder in each separate limitation category during the year. The remaining portion of third party interest expense of the U.S. shareholder for the year shall be apportioned as provided in §§ 1.861-8T through 1.861-13T, excluding paragraph (e) of § 1.861-10T and this paragraph (e).

(v) The average amount of related group indebtedness held by the U.S. shareholder in each separate limitation category during the year equals the average of the aggregate amounts of such indebtedness in each separate limitation category at the beginning and end of the year. Solely for purposes of this paragraph (e)(4), each debt obligation of a related controlled foreign corporation held by the U.S. shareholder at the beginning or end of the year is attributed to separate limitation categories in the same manner as the stock of the obligor would be attributed under the rules of § 1.861-12T(c)(3), whether or not such stock is held directly by the U.S. shareholder.

(vi) The amount of third party interest expense of a U.S. shareholder allocated pursuant to this paragraph (e)(4) shall not exceed the total amount of the third party interest expense of the U.S. shareholder for the year (excluding any third party interest expense allocated under paragraphs (b) and (c) of § 1.861-10T).

(5) *Definitions.*—For purposes of this paragraph (e), the following terms shall have the following meanings.

(i) *U.S. shareholder.*—The term "U.S. shareholder" has the same meaning as the term "United States shareholder" when used in section 957, except that, in the case of a United States shareholder that is a member of an affiliated group (as defined in § 1.861-11T(d)), the entire affiliated group is considered to constitute a single U.S. shareholder.

(ii) *Related person.*—For the definition of the term "related person", see § 1.861-8T(c)(2). A controlled foreign corporation is considered "related" to a U.S. shareholder if it is a related person with respect to the U.S. shareholder.

(6) *Determination of asset values.*—A U.S. shareholder shall determine the values of the assets of each related controlled foreign corporation (for purposes of Step One in paragraph (e)(2) of this section) and the assets of the U.S. shareholder (for purposes of Step Two in paragraph (e)(3) of this section) for any year in accordance with the valuation method (tax book value or fair market value) elected for that year pursuant to § 1.861-9T(g). However, solely for purposes of this paragraph (e), a U.S. shareholder may instead choose to determine the values of the assets of all related controlled foreign corporations by reference to their values as reflected on Forms 5471 (the annual information return with respect to each related controlled foreign corporation), subject to the translation rules of paragraph (e)(8)(i) of this section. This method of valuation may be used only if the taxable years of each of the related controlled foreign corporations begin with, or no more than one month earlier than, the taxable year of the U.S. shareholder. Once chosen for a taxable year, this method of valuation must be used in each subsequent taxable year and may be changed only with the consent of the Commissioner.

(7) *Adjustments to asset value.*—For purposes of apportioning remaining interest expense under § 1.861-9T, a U.S. shareholder shall reduce (but not below zero) the value of its assets for the year (as determined under § 1.861-9T(g)(3) or (h)) by an amount equal to the allocable related group indebtedness of the U.S. shareholder for the year (as determined under Step Three in paragraph (e)(4)(ii) of this section). This reduction is allocated among assets in each separate limitation category in proportion to the average amount of related group indebtedness held by the U.S. shareholder in each separate limitation category during the year (as determined under Step Three in paragraph(e)(4)(v) of this section).

(8) *Special rules.*—(i) *Exchange rates.*—All indebtedness amounts and asset values (including current year and base year amounts and values) denominated in a foreign currency shall be translated into U.S. dollars at the exchange rate for the current year. The exchange rate for the current year may be determined under any reasonable method (*e.g.*, average of month-end exchange rates for each month in the current year) if it is consistently applied to the current year and all base years. Once chosen for a taxable year, a method for determin-

ing an exchange rate must be used in each subsequent taxable year and will be treated as a method of accounting for purposes of section 446. A taxpayer may apply a different translation rule only with the prior consent of the Commissioner. In this regard, the Commissioner will be guided by the extent to which a different rule would reduce the comparability of dollar amounts of indebtedness and dollar asset values for the base years and the current year.

(ii) *Exempt assets.*—Solely for purposes of this paragraph (e), any exempt assets otherwise excluded under section 864(e)(3) and § 1.861-8T(d) shall be included as assets of the U.S. shareholder or related controlled foreign corporation.

(iii) *Exclusion of certain directly allocated indebtedness and assets.*—Qualified nonrecourse indebtedness (as defined in § 1.861-10T(b)(2)) and indebtedness incurred in connection with an integrated financial transaction (as defined in § 1.861-10T(c)(2)) shall be excluded from U.S. shareholder indebtedness and related group indebtedness. In addition, assets which are the subject of qualified nonrecourse indebtedness or integrated financial transactions shall be excluded from the assets of the U.S. shareholder and each related controlled foreign corporation.

(iv) *Exclusion of certain receivables.*—Receivables between related controlled foreign corporations (or between members of the affiliated group constituting the U.S. shareholder) shall be excluded from the assets of the related controlled foreign corporation (or affiliated group member) holding such receivables. See also § 1.861-11T(e)(1).

(v) *Classification of loans between controlled foreign corporations.*—In determining the amount of related group indebtedness for any taxable year, loans outstanding from one controlled foreign corporation to a related controlled foreign corporation are not treated as related group indebtedness. For purposes of determining the foreign base period ratio under paragraph (e)(2)(iv) of this section for a taxable year that ends on or after November 2, 2020, the rules of this paragraph (e)(8)(v) apply to determine the related group debt-to-asset ratio in each taxable year included in the foreign base period, including in taxable years that end before November 2, 2020.

(vi) *Classification of hybrid stock.*—In determining the amount of its related group indebtedness for any taxable year, a U.S. shareholder must not treat stock in a related controlled foreign corporation as related group indebtedness, regardless of whether the related controlled foreign corporation claims a deduction for interest under foreign law for distributions on such stock. For purposes of determining the foreign base period ratio under paragraph (e)(2)(iv) of this section for a taxable year that ends on or after December 4, 2018, the rules of this paragraph (e)(8)(vi) apply to determine the related group debt-to-asset ratio in each taxable year included in the foreign base period, including in taxable years that end before December 4, 2018.

(9) *Corporate events.*—(i) *Initial acquisition of a controlled foreign corporation.*—If the foreign base period of the U.S. shareholder for any year includes a base year in which the U.S. shareholder did not hold stock in any related controlled foreign corporation, then, in computing the foreign base period ratio, the related group debt-to-asset ratio of the U.S. shareholder for any such base year shall be deemed to be 0.10.

(ii) *Incorporation of U.S. shareholder.*

(A) *Nonapplication.*—This paragraph (e) does not apply to the first taxable year of the U.S. shareholder. However, this paragraph (e) does apply to all following years, including years in which later members of the affiliated group may be incorporated.

(B) *Foreign and U.S. base period ratios.*—In computing the foreign and U.S. base period ratios, the foreign and U.S. base periods of the U.S. shareholder shall be considered to be only the period prior to the current year that the U.S. shareholder was in existence if this prior period is less than five taxable years.

(iii) *Acquisition of additional corporations.*—(A) If a U.S. shareholder acquires (directly or indirectly) stock of a foreign or domestic corporation which, by reason of the acquisition, then becomes a related controlled foreign corporation or a member of the affiliated group, then in determining excess related group indebtedness or excess U.S. shareholder indebtedness, the indebtedness and assets of the acquired corporation shall be taken into account only at the end of the acquisition year and in following years. Thus, amounts of indebtedness and assets and the various debt-to-asset ratios of the U.S. shareholder existing at the beginning of the acquisition year or relating to preceding years are not recalculated to take account of indebtedness and assets of the acquired corporation existing as of dates before the end of the year. If, however, a major acquisition is made within the last three months of the year and a substantial distortion of values for the year would otherwise result, the taxpayer must take into account the average values of the acquired indebtedness and assets weighted to reflect the time such indebtedness is owed and such assets are held by the taxpayer during the year.

(B) In the case of a reverse acquisition subject to this paragraph (e)(9), the rules of § 1.1502-75(d)(3) apply in determining which corporations are the acquiring and acquired corporations. For this purpose, whether corporations are affiliated is determined under § 1.861-11T(d).

(C) If the stock of a U.S. shareholder is acquired by (and, by reason of such acquisition, the U.S. shareholder becomes affiliated with) a corporation described below, then such U.S. shareholder shall be considered to have acquired such corporation for purposes of the application of the rules of this paragraph (e). A corporation to which this paragraph (e)(9)(iii)(C) applies is—

(1) A corporation which is not affiliated with any other corporation (other than another similarly described corporation); and

(2) Substantially all of the assets of which consist of cash, securities and stock.

(iv) *Election to compute base period ratios by including acquired corporations.*—A U.S. shareholder may choose, solely for purposes of paragraph (e)(9)(i) and (iii) of this section, to compute its foreign and U.S. base period ratios for the acquisition year and all subsequent years by taking into account the indebtedness and asset values of the acquired corporation or corporations (including related group indebtedness owed to a former U.S. shareholder) at the beginning of the acquisition year and in each of the five base years preceding the acquisition year. This election, if made for an acquisition, must be made for all other acquisitions occurring during the same taxable year or initiated in that year and concluded in the following year.

(v) *Dispositions.*—If a U.S. shareholder disposes of stock of a foreign or domestic corporation which, by reason of the disposition, then ceases to be a related controlled foreign corporation or a member of the affiliated group (unless liquidated or merged into a related corporation), in determining excess related group indebtedness or excess U.S. shareholder indebtedness, the indebtedness and assets of the divested corporation shall be taken into account only at the beginning of the disposition year and for the relevant preceding years. Thus, amounts of indebtedness and assets and the various debt-to-asset ratios of the U.S. shareholder existing at the end of the year or relating to following years are not affected by indebtedness and assets of the divested corporation existing as of dates after the beginning of the year. If, however, a major disposition is made within the first three months of the year and a substantial distortion of values for the year would otherwise result, the taxpayer must take into account the average values of the divested indebtedness and assets weighted to reflect the time such indebtedness is owed and such assets are held by the taxpayer during the year.

(vi) *Election to compute base period ratios by excluding divested corporations.*—A U.S. shareholder may choose, solely for purposes of paragraph (e)(9)(v) and (vii) of this section, to compute its foreign and U.S. base period ratios for the disposition year and all subsequent years without taking into account the indebtedness and asset values of the divested corporation or corporations at the beginning of the disposition year and in each of the five base years preceding the disposition year. This election, if made for a disposition, must be made for all other dispositions occurring during the same taxable year or initiated in that year and concluded in the following year.

(vii) *Section 355 transactions.*—A U.S. corporation which becomes a separate U.S. shareholder as a result of a distribution of its stock to which section 355 applies shall be considered—

(A) As disposed of by the U.S. shareholder of the affiliated group of which the distributing corporation is a member, with this disposition subject to the rules of paragraphs (e)(9)(v) and (vi) of this section; and

(B) As having the same related group debt-to-asset ratio and debt-to-asset ratio as the distributing U.S. shareholder in each year preceding the year of distribution for purposes of applying this paragraph (e) to the year of distribution and subsequent years of the distributed corporation.

(10) [Reserved]

(11) The following example illustrates the provisions of this paragraph (e):

Example. (i) *Facts.* X, a domestic corporation, elects to apply this paragraph (e) to its 1990 tax year. X has a calendar taxable year and apportions its interest expense on the basis of the tax book value of its assets. In 1990, X incurred deductible third-party interest expense of $24,960 on an average amount of indebtedness (determined on the basis of beginning-of-year and end-of-year amounts) of $249,600. X manufactures widgets, all of which are sold in the United States. X owns all of the stock of Y, a controlled foreign corporation that also has a calendar taxable year and is also engaged in the manufacture and sale of widgets. Y has no earnings and profits or deficit of earnings and profits attributable to taxable years prior to 1987. X's total assets and their average tax book values (determined on the basis of beginning-of-year and end-of-year tax book values) for 1990 are:

Asset	*Average Tax Book Value*
Plant and equipment	$315,000
Corporate headquarters	60,000
Y stock	75,000
Y note	50,000
	$500,000

Y had $25,000 of income before the deduction of any interest expense. Of this total, $5,000 is high withholding tax interest income. The remaining $20,000 is derived from widget sales, and constitutes foreign source general limitation income. Assume that Y has no deductions from gross income other than interest expense. During 1990, Y paid $5,000 of interest expense to X on the Y note and $10,000 of interest expense to third parties, giving Y total interest expense of $15,000. X elects pursuant to § 1.861-9T to apportion Y's interest expense under the gross income method prescribed in section 1.861-9T(j).

(ii) *Step 1:* Using a beginning and end of year average, X (the U.S. shareholder) held the following average amounts of indebtedness of Y and Y had the following average asset values:

		1985	*1986-88*	*1989*	*1990*
(A)	Related group indebtedness	$11,000	24,000	26,000	50,000
(B)	Average Value of Assets of Related CFC	$100,000	200,000	200,000	250,000
(C)	Related Group Debt-to-Asset Ratio	.11	.12	.13	.20

(*1*) X's "foreign base period ratio" for 1990, an average of its ratios of related group indebtedness to related group assets for 1985 through 1989, is:

(.11 + .12 + .12 + .12 + .13)/5 = .12

(*2*) X's "allowable related group indebtedness" for 1990 is:

$250,000 × .12 = $30,000

(*3*) X's "excess related group indebtedness" for 1990 is:

$50,000 – $30,000 = $20,000

X's related group indebtedness of $50,000 for 1990 is greater than its allowable related group indebtedness of $24,000 for 1989 (assuming a foreign base period ratio in 1989 of .12), and X's related group debt-to-asset ratio for 1990 is .20, which is greater than the ratio of .10 described in paragraph (e)(2)(vii)(B) of this section. Therefore, X's excess related group indebtedness for 1990 remains at $20,000.

(iii) *Step 2:* Using a beginning and end of year average, X has the following average amounts of U.S. and foreign indebtedness and average asset values:

	1985	*1986*	*1987*	*1988*	*1989*	*1990*
(1)	$231,400	225,000	225,000	225,000	220,800	249,600
(2)	$445,000	450,000	450,000	450,000	460,000	480,000 (a)
(3)	.52	.50	.50	.50	.48	.52

(1) U.S. and foreign indebtedness
(2) Average value of assets of U.S. shareholder
(3) Debt-to-Asset ratio of U.S. shareholder
(a) [500,000 – 20,000 (excess related group indebtedness determined in Step 1)]

X's "U.S. base period ratio" for 1990 is:

(.52 + .50 + .50 + .50 + .48)/5 = .50

X's "allowable indebtedness" for 1990 is:

$480,000 × .50 = $240,000

X's "excess U.S. shareholder indebtedness" for 1990 is:

$249,600 – $240,000 = $9,600

X's debt-to-asset ratio for 1990 is .52, which is greater than the ratio of .10 described in paragraph (e)(3)(vii) of this section. Therefore, X's excess U.S. shareholder indebtedness for 1990 remains at $9,600.

(iv) *Step 3:* (a) Since X's excess U.S. shareholder indebtedness of $9,600 is less than its excess related group indebtedness of $20,000, X's allocable related group indebtedness for 1990 is $9,600. The amount of interest received by X during 1990 on allocable related group indebtedness is:

$$\$5,000 \times \frac{\$9,600}{\$50,000} = \$960$$

(b) Therefore, $960 of X's third party interest expense ($24,960) shall be allocated among various separate limitation categories in proportion to the relative average amounts of Y obligations held by X in each such category. The amount of Y obligations in each limitation category is determined in the same manner as the stock of Y would be attributed under the rules of § 1.861-12T(c)(3). Since Y's interest expense is apportioned under the gross income method prescribed in § 1.861-9T(j), the Y stock must be characterized under the gross income method described in § 1.861-12T(c)(3)(iii). Y's gross income net of interest expense is determined as follows:

Foreign source high withholding tax interest income = $5,000 – [($15,000) multiplied by ($5,000)/($5,000 + $20,000)]
= $2,000

and

Foreign source general limitation income = $20,000 – [($15,000) multiplied by ($20,000)/($5,000 + $20,000)]
= $8,000

(c) Therefore, $192 [($960 × $2,000/($2,000+$8,000)]of X's third party interest expense is allocated to foreign source high withholding tax interest income and $768 [$960 × $8,000/($2,000+$8,000)]is allocated to foreign source general limitation income.

(v) As a result of these direct allocations, for purposes of apportioning X's remaining interest expense under § 1.861-9T, the value of X's assets generating foreign source general limitation income is reduced by the principal amount of indebtedness the interest on which is directly allocated to foreign source general limitation income ($7,680), and the value of X's assets generating foreign source high withholding tax interest income is reduced by the principal amount of indebtedness the interest on which is directly allocated to foreign source high withholding tax interest income ($1,920), determined as follows:

Reduction of X's assets generating foreign source general limitation income:

$$\text{X's allocable related group indebtedness} \times \frac{\text{Y's Foreign source general limitation income}}{\text{Y's Foreign source income}}$$

$$\$9{,}600 \times \$8{,}000/(\$8{,}000 + \$2{,}000) = \$7{,}680$$

Reduction of X's assets generating foreign source high withholding tax interest income:

$$\text{X's allocable related group indebtedness} \times \frac{\text{Y's Foreign source high withholding tax interest income}}{\text{Y's Foreign source income}}$$

$$\$9{,}600 \times \$2{,}000/(\$8{,}000 + \$2{,}000) = \$1{,}920$$

(f) *Indebtedness of certain regulated utilities.*—If an automatically excepted regulated utility trade or business (as defined in § 1.163(j)-1(b)(15)(i)(A) has qualified nonrecourse indebtedness within the meaning of the second sentence in § 1.163(j)-10(d)(2), interest expense from the indebtedness is directly allocated to the taxpayer's assets in the manner and to the extent provided in § 1.861-10T(b).

(g) [Reserved]

(h) *Applicability dates.*—Except as provided in this paragraph (h), this section applies to taxable years ending on or after December 4, 2018. Paragraph (e)(8)(v) of this section applies to taxable years ending on or after November 2, 2020, and paragraph (f) of this section applies to taxable years beginning on or after December 28, 2021. [Reg. § 1.861-10.]

☐ [*T.D.* 8410, 4-14-92. *Amended by T.D.* 9882, 12-16-2019 *and T.D.* 9959, 12-28-2021.]

§ 1.861-10T. Special allocations of interest expense (temporary).—(a) *In general.*—This section applies to all taxpayers and provides three exceptions to the rules of § 1.861-9T that require the allocation and apportionment of interest expense on the basis of all assets of all members of the affiliated group. Paragraph (b) of this section describes the direct allocation of interest expense to the income generated by certain assets that are subject to qualified nonrecourse indebtedness. Paragraph (c) of this section describes the direct allocation of interest expense to income generated by certain assets that are acquired in integrated financial transactions. Paragraph (d) of this section provides special rules that are applicable to all transactions described in paragraphs (b) and (c) of this section. Paragraph (e) of this section requires the direct allocation of third party interest of an affiliated group to such group's investment in related controlled foreign corporations in cases involving excess related person indebtedness (as defined therein). See also § 1.861-9T(b)(5), which requires direct allocation of amortizable bond premium.

(b) *Qualified nonrecourse indebtedness.*—(1) *In general.*—In the case of qualified nonrecourse indebtedness (as defined in paragraph (b)(2) of this section), the deduction for interest shall be considered directly allocable solely to the gross income which the property acquired, constructed, or improved with the proceeds of the indebtedness generates, has generated, or could reasonably be expected to generate.

(2) *Qualified nonrecourse indebtedness defined.*—The term "qualified nonrecourse indebtedness" means any borrowing that is not excluded by paragraph (b)(4) of this section if:

(i) The borrowing is specifically incurred for the purpose of purchasing, constructing, or improving identified property that is either depreciable tangible personal property or real property with a useful life of more than one year or for the purpose of purchasing amortizable intangible personal property with a useful life of more than one year;

(ii) The proceeds are actually applied to purchase, construct, or improve the identified property;

(iii) Except as provided in paragraph (b)(7)(ii) (relating to certain third party guarantees in leveraged lease transactions), the creditor can look only to the identified property (or any lease or other interest therein) as security for payment of the principal and interest on the loan and, thus, cannot look to any other property, the borrower, or any third party with respect to repayment of principal or interest on the loan;

(iv) The cash flow from the property, as defined in paragraph (b)(3) of this section, is reasonably expected to be sufficient in the first year of ownership as well as in each subsequent year of ownership to fulfill the terms and conditions of the loan agreement with respect to the amount and timing of payments of interest and original issue discount and periodic payments of principal in each such year; and

(v) There are restrictions in the loan agreement on the disposal or use of the property consistent with the assumptions described in subdivisions (iii) and (iv) of this paragraph (b)(2).

(3) *Cash flow defined.*—(i) *In general.*—The term "cash flow from the property" as used in paragraph (b)(2)(iv) of this section means a stream of revenue (as computed under paragraph (b)(3)(ii) of this section) substantially all of which derives directly from the property. The phrase "cash flow from the property" does not include revenue if a significant portion thereof is derived from activities such as sales, labor, services, or the use of other property. Thus, revenue derived from the sale or lease of inventory or of similar property does not constitute cash flow from the property, including plant or equipment used in the manufacture and sale or lease, or purchase and sale or lease, of such inventory or similar property. In addition, revenue derived in part from the performance of services that are not ancillary and subsidiary to the use of property does not constitute cash flow from the property.

(ii) *Self-constructed assets.*—The activities associated with self-construction of assets shall be considered to constitute labor or services for purposes of paragraph (b)(3)(i) only if the self-constructed asset—

(A) Is constructed for the purposes of resale, or

(B) Without regard to purpose, is sold to an unrelated person within one year from the date that the property is placed in service for purposes of section 167.

(iii) *Computation of cash flow.*—Cash flow is computed by subtracting cash disbursements excluding debt service from cash receipts.

(iv) *Analysis of operating costs.*—[Reserved]

(v) *Examples.*—The principles of this paragraph may be demonstrated by the following examples.

Example (1). In 1987, X borrows $100,000 in order to purchase an apartment building, which X then purchases. The loan is secured only by the building and the leases thereon. Annual debt service on the loan is $12,000. Annual gross rents from the building are $20,000. Annual taxes on the building are $2,000. Other expenses deductible under section 162 are $2,000. Rents are reasonably expected to remain stable or increase in subsequent years, and taxes and expenses are reasonably expected to remain proportional to gross rents in subsequent years. X provides security, maintenance, and utilities to the tenants of the building. Based on facts and circumstances, it is determined that, although services are provided to tenants, these services are ancillary and subsidiary to the occupancy of the apartments. Accordingly, the cash flow of $16,000 is considered to constitute a return from the property. Furthermore, such cash flow is sufficient to fulfill the terms and conditions of the loan agreement as required by paragraph (b)(2)(iii).

Example (2). In 1987, X borrows funds in order to purchase a hotel, which X then purchases and operates. The loan is secured only by the hotel. Based on facts and circumstances, it is determined that the operation of the hotel involves services the value of which is significant in relation to amounts paid to occupy the rooms. Thus, a significant portion of the cash flow is derived from the performance of services incidental to the occupancy of hotel rooms. Accordingly, the cash flow from the hotel is considered not to constitute a return on or from the property.

Example (3). In 1987, X borrows funds in order to build a factory, which X then builds and operates. The loan is secured only by the factory and the equipment therein. Based on the facts and circumstances, it is determined that the operation of the factory involves significant expenditures for labor and raw materials. Thus, a significant portion of the cash flow is derived from labor and the processing of raw materials. Accordingly, the cash flow from the factory is considered not to constitute a return on or from the property.

(4) *Exclusions.*—The term "qualified nonrecourse indebtedness" shall not include any transaction that—

(i) Lacks economic significance within the meaning of paragraph (b)(5) of this section;

(ii) Involves cross collateralization within the meaning of paragraph (b)(6) of this section;

(iii) Except in the case of a leveraged lease described in paragraph (b)(7)(ii) of this section, involves credit enhancement within the meaning of paragraph (b)(7) of this section or, with respect to loans made on or after October 14, 1988, does not, under the terms of the loan documents, prohibit the acquisition by the holder of bond insurance or similar forms of credit enhancement;

(iv) Involves the purchase of inventory;

(v) Involves the purchase of any financial asset, including stock in a corporation, an interest in a partnership or a trust, or the debt obligation of any obligor (although interest incurred in order to purchase certain financial instruments may qualify for direct allocation under paragraph (c) of this section);

(vi) Involves interest expense that constitutes qualified residence interest as defined in section 163(h)(3); or

(vii) [Reserved].

(5) *Economic significance.*—Indebtedness that otherwise qualifies under paragraph (b)(2) shall nonetheless be subject to apportionment under § 1.861-9T if, taking into account all the facts and circumstances, the transaction (including the security arrangement) lacks economic significance.

(6) *Cross collateralization.*—The term "cross collateralization" refers to the pledge as security for a loan of—

(i) Any asset of the borrower other than the identified property described in paragraph (b)(2) of this section, or

(ii) Any asset belonging to any related person, as defined in § 1.861-8T(c)(2).

(7) *Credit enhancement.*—(i) *In general.*—Except as provided in paragraph (b)(7)(ii) of this section, the term "credit enhancement" refers to any device, including a contract, letter of credit, or guaranty, that expands the creditor's rights, directly or indirectly, beyond the identified property purchased, constructed, or improved with the funds advanced and, thus, effectively provides as security for a loan the assets of any person other than the borrower. The acquisition of bond insurance or any other contract of suretyship by an initial or subsequent holder of an obligation shall constitute credit enhancement.

(ii) *Special rule for leveraged leases.*—For purposes of this paragraph (b), the term "credit enhancement" shall not include any device under which any person that is not a related person within the meaning of § 1.861-8T(c)(2) agrees to guarantee, without recourse to the lessor or any person related to the lessor, a lessor's payment of principal and interest on indebtedness that was incurred in order to purchase or improve an asset that is depreciable tangible personal property or depreciable tangible real property (and the land on which such real property is situated) that is leased to a lessee that is not a related person in a transaction that constitutes a lease for federal income tax purposes.

(iii) *Syndication of credit risk and sale of loan participations.*—The term "syndication of credit risk" refers to an arrangement in which one primary lender secures the promise of a secondary lender to bear a portion of the primary lender's credit risk on a loan. The term "sale of loan participations" refers to an arrangement in which one primary lender divides a loan into several portions, sells and assigns all rights with respect to one or more portions to participating secondary lenders, and does not remain at risk in any manner with respect to the portion assigned. For purposes of this paragraph (b), the syndication of credit risk shall constitute credit enhancement because the primary lender can look to secondary lenders for payment of the loan, notwithstanding limitations on the amount of the secondary lender's liability. Conversely, the sale of loan participations does not constitute credit enhancement, because the holder of each portion of the loan can look solely to the asset securing the loan and not to the credit or other assets of any person.

(8) *Other arrangements that do not constitute cross collateralization or credit enhancement.*—For purposes of paragraphs (b)(6) and (7) of this section, the following arrangements do not constitute cross collateralization or credit enhancement:

(i) *Integrated projects.*—A taxpayer's pledge of multiple assets of an integrated project, provided that the integrated project. An integrated project consists of functionally related and geographically contiguous assets that, as to the taxpayer, are used in the same trade or business.

(ii) *Insurance.*—A taxpayer's purchase of third-party casualty and liability insurance on the collateral or, by contract, bearing the risk of loss associated with destruction of the collateral or with respect to the attachment of third party liability claims.

(iii) *After-acquired property.*—Extension of a creditor's security interest to improvements made to the collateral, provided that the extension does not constitute excess collateralization under paragraph (b)(6), determined by taking into account the value of improvements at the time the improvements are made and the value of the original property at the time the loan was made.

(iv) *Warranties of completion and maintenance.*—A taxpayer's warranty to a creditor that it will complete construction or manufacture of the collateral or that it will maintain the collateral in good condition.

(v) *Substitution of collateral.*—A taxpayer's right to substitute collateral under any loan contract. However, after the right is exercised, the loan shall no longer constitute qualified nonrecourse indebtedness.

(9) *Refinancings.*—If a taxpayer refinances qualified nonrecourse indebtedness (as defined in paragraph (b)(2) of this section) with new indebtedness, such new indebtedness shall continue to qualify only if—

(i) The principal amount of the new indebtedness does not exceed by more than five percent the remaining principal amount of the original indebtedness,

(ii) The term of the new indebtedness does not exceed by more than six months the remaining term of the original indebtedness, and

(iii) The requirements of this paragraph (other than those of paragraph (b)(2)(i) and (ii) of this section) are satisfied at the time of the refinancing, and the exclusions contained in this paragraph (b)(4) do not apply.

(10) *Post-construction permanent financing.*—Financing that is obtained after the completion of constructed property will be deemed to satisfy the requirements of paragraph (b)(2)(i) and (ii) of this section if—

(i) The financing is obtained within one year after the constructed property or substantially all of a constructed integrated project (as defined in paragraph (b)(9)(i) of this section) is placed in service for purposes of section 167; and

(ii) The financing does not exceed the cost of construction (including construction period interest).

(11) *Assumptions of pre-existing qualified nonrecourse indebtedness.*—If a transferee of property that is subject to qualified nonrecourse indebtedness assumes such indebtedness, the indebtedness shall continue to constitute qualified nonrecourse indebtedness, provided that the assumption in no way alters the qualified status of the debt.

(12) *Excess collateralization.*—[Reserved]

(c) *Direct allocations in the case of certain integrated financial transactions.*—(1) *General rule.*—Interest expense incurred on funds borrowed in connection with an integrated financial transaction (as defined in paragraph (c)(2) of this section) shall be directly allocated to the income generated by the investment funded with the borrowed amounts.

(2) *Definition.*—The term "integrated financial transaction" refers to any transaction in which—

(i) The taxpayer—

(A) Incurs indebtedness for the purpose of making an identified term investment,

(B) Identifies the indebtedness as incurred for such purpose at the time the indebtedness is incurred, and

(C) Makes the identified term investment within ten business days after incurring the indebtedness;

(ii) The return on the investment is reasonably expected to be sufficient throughout the term of the investment to fulfill the terms and conditions of the loan agreement with respect to the amount and timing of payments of principal and interest or original issue discount;

(iii) The income constitutes interest or original issue discount or would constitute income equivalent to interest if earned by a controlled foreign corporation (as described in § 1.954-2T(h));

(iv) The debt incurred and the investment mature within ten business days of each other;

(v) The investment does not relate in any way to the operation of, and is not made in the normal course of, the trade or business of the taxpayer or any related person, including the financing of the sale of goods or the performance of services by the taxpayer or any related person, or the compensation of the taxpayer's employees (including any contribution or loan to an employee stock ownership plan (as defined in section 4975(e)(7)) or other plan that is qualified under section 401(a)); and

(vi) The borrower does not constitute a financial services entity (as defined in section 904 and the regulations thereunder).

(3) *Roll-overs.*—In the event that a taxpayer sells or otherwise liquidates an investment described in paragraph (c)(2) of this section, the interest expense incurred on the borrowing shall, subsequent to that liquidation, no longer qualify for direct allocation under this paragraph (c).

(4) *Examples.*—The principles of this paragraph (c) may be demonstrated by the following examples.

Example (1). X is a manufacturer and does not constitute a financial services entity as defined in the regulations under section 904. On January 1, 1988, X borrows $100 for 6 months at an annual interest rate of 10 percent. X identifies on its books and records by the close of that day that the indebtedness is being incurred for the purpose of making an investment that is intended to qualify as an integrated financial transaction. On January 5, 1988, X uses the proceeds to purchase a portfolio of stock that approximates the composition of the Standard & Poor's 500 Index. On that day, X also enters into a forward sale contract that requires X to sell the stock on June 1, 1988 for $110. X identifies on its books and records by the close of January 5, 1988, that the portfolio stock purchases and the forward sale contract constitute part of the integrated financial transaction with respect to which the identified borrowing was incurred. Under § 1.954-2T(h), the income derived from the transaction would constitute income equivalent to interest. Assuming that the return on the investment to be derived on June 1, 1988, will be sufficient to pay the interest due on June 1, 1988, the interest on the borrowing is directly allocated to the gain from the investment.

Example (2). X does not constitute a financial services entity as defined in the regulations under section 904. X is in the business of, among other things, issuing credit cards to consumers and purchasing from merchants who accept the X card the receivables of consumers who make purchases with the X card. X borrows from Y in order to purchase X credit card receivables from Z, a merchant. Assuming that the Y borrowing satisfies the other requirements of paragraph (c)(2) of this section, the transaction nonetheless cannot constitute an integrated financial transaction because the purchase relates to the operation of X's trade or business.

Example (3). Assume the same facts as in Example 2, except that X borrows in order to purchase the receivables of A, a merchant who does not accept the X card and is not otherwise engaged directly or indirectly in any business transaction with X. Because the borrowing is not related to the operation of X's trade or business, the borrowing may qualify as an integrated financial transaction if the other requirements of paragraph (c)(2) of this section are satisfied.

(d) *Special rules.*—In applying paragraphs (b) and (c) of this section, the following special rules shall apply.

(1) *Related person transactions.*—The rules of this section shall not apply to the extent that any transaction—

(i) Involves either indebtedness between related persons (as defined in section § 1.861-8T(c)(2)) or indebtedness incurred from unrelated persons for the purpose of purchasing property from a related person; or

(ii) Involves the purchase of property that is leased to a related person (as defined in section § 1.861-8T(c)(2)) in a transaction described in paragraph (b) of this section. If a taxpayer purchases property and leases such property in whole or in part to a related person, a portion of the interest incurred in connection with such an acquisition, based on the ratio that the value of the property leased to the related person bears to the total value of the property, shall not qualify for direct allocation under this section.

(2) *Consideration of assets or income to which interest is directly allocated in apportioning other interest expense.*—In apportioning interest expense under § 1.861-9T, the year-end value of any asset to which interest expense is directly allocated under this section during the current taxable year shall be reduced to the extent provided in § 1.861-9T(g)(2)(iii) to reflect the portion of the principal amount of the indebtedness outstanding at year-end relating to the interest which is directly allocated. A similar adjustment shall be made to the end-of-year value of assets for the prior year for purposes of determining the beginning-of-year value of assets for the current year. These adjustments shall be made prior to averaging beginning-of-year and end-of-year values pursuant to § 1.861-9T(g)(2). In apportioning interest expense under the modified gross income method, gross income shall be reduced by the amount of income to which interest expense is directly allocated under this section.

(e) *Treatment of certain related group indebtedness.*—For further guidance, see § 1.861-10(e).

(f) *Effective/applicability date.*—(1) In general, the rules of this section apply for taxable years beginning after December 31, 1986.

(2) Paragraphs (b)(3)(ii) (providing an operating costs test for purposes of the nonrecourse indebtedness exception) and (b)(6) (concerning excess collateralization of nonrecourse borrowings) of this section are applicable for taxable years commencing after December 31, 1988.

(3) Paragraph (e) (concerning the treatment of related controlled foreign corporation indebtedness) of this section is applicable for taxable years commencing after December 31, 1987. For rules for taxable years beginning before January 1, 1987, and for later years to the extent permitted by § 1.861-13T, see § 1.861-8 (revised as of April 1, 1986). [Temporary Reg. § 1.861-10T.]

□ [*T.D. 8228, 9-9-88. Amended by T.D. 9456, 7-31-2009 and T.D. 9882, 12-16-2019.*]

§ 1.861-11. Special rules for allocating and apportioning interest expense of an affiliated group of corporations.—(a) *In general.*—For further guidance, see § 1.861-11T(a).

(b) *Scope of application.*—(1) *Application of section 864(e)(1) and (5) (concerning the definition and treatment of affiliated groups).*—Section 864(e)(1) and (5) and the portions of this section implementing section 864(e)(1) and (5) apply to the computation of foreign source taxable income for purposes of section 904 (relating to various limitations on the foreign tax credit). Section 864(e)(1) and (5) and the portions of this section implementing section 864(e)(1) and (5) also apply in connection with section 907 to determine reductions in the amount allowed as a foreign tax credit under section 901. Section 864(e)(1) and (5) and the portions of this section implementing section 864(e)(1) and (5) also apply to the computation of the combined taxable income of the related supplier and a foreign sales corporation (FSC) (under sections 921 through 927) as well as the combined taxable income of the related supplier and a domestic international sales corporation (DISC) (under sections 991 through 997).

(2) *Nonapplication of section 864(e)(1) and (5) (concerning the definition and treatment of affiliated groups).*—For further guidance, see § 1.861-11T(b)(2).

(c) *General rule for affiliated corporations.*—For further guidance, see § 1.861-11T(c).

(d) *Definition of affiliated group*.—(1) *General rule*.—For purposes of this section, in general, the term *affiliated group* has the same meaning as is given that term by section 1504. Section 1504(a) defines an affiliated group as one or more chains of includible corporations connected through 80-percent stock ownership with a common parent corporation which is an includible corporation (as defined in section 1504(b)). In the case of a corporation that either becomes or ceases to be a member of the group during the course of the corporation's taxable year, only the interest expense incurred by the group member during the period of membership shall be allocated and apportioned as if all members of the group were a single corporation. In this regard, assets held during the period of membership shall be taken into account. Other interest expense incurred by the group member during its taxable year but not during the period of membership shall be allocated and apportioned without regard to the other members of the group.

(2) [Reserved]

(d)(3) through (6)(i) [Reserved]. For further guidance see § 1.861-11T(d)(3) through (6)(i).

(ii) Any foreign corporation if more than 50 percent of the gross income of such foreign corporation for the taxable year is effectively connected with the conduct of a trade or business within the United States and at least 80 percent of either the vote or value of all outstanding stock of such foreign corporation is owned directly or indirectly by members of the affiliated group (determined with regard to this sentence). This paragraph (d)(6)(ii) applies to taxable years beginning on or after July 16, 2014. See 26 CFR 1.861-11T(d)(6)(ii) (revised as of April 1, 2014) for rules applicable to taxable years beginning after August 10, 2010, and before July 16, 2014. See 26 CFR 1.861-11T(d)(6)(ii) (revised as of April 1, 2010) for rules applicable to taxable years beginning on or before August 10, 2010.

(7) *Special rules for the application of § 1.861-11T(d)(6)*.—The attribution rules of section 1563(e) and the regulations under that section shall apply in determining indirect ownership under § 1.861-11T(d)(6). The Commissioner shall have the authority to disregard trusts, partnerships, and pass-through entities that break affiliated status. Corporations described in § 1.861-11T(d)(6) shall be considered to constitute members of an affiliated group that does not file a consolidated return and shall therefore be subject to the limitations imposed under § 1.861-11T(g). The affiliated group filing a consolidated return shall be considered to constitute a single corporation for purposes of applying the rules of § 1.861-11T(g). For taxable years beginning after December 31, 1989, § 1.861-11T(d)(6)(i) shall not apply in determining foreign source alternative minimum taxable income within each separate category and the alternative minimum tax foreign tax credit pursuant to section 59(a) to the extent that such application would result in the inclusion of a section 936 corporation within the affiliated group. This paragraph (d)(7) applies to taxable years beginning after December 31, 1986.

(e) through (g) [Reserved]. For further guidance, see § 1.861-11T(e) through (g).

(h) *Applicability dates*.—This section applies to taxable years that both begin after December 31, 2017, and end on or after December 4, 2018. [Reg. § 1.861-11.]

☐ [*T.D. 8916, 12-29-2000. Amended by T.D. 9676, 7-15-2014 and T.D.* 9882, 12-16-2019.]

§ 1.861-11T. Special rules for allocating and apportioning interest expense of an affiliated group of corporations (temporary).—(a) *In general*.—Sections 1.861-9T, 1.861-10T, 1.861-12T, and 1.861-13T provide rules that are generally applicable in apportioning interest expense. The rules of this section relate to affiliated groups of corporations and implement section 864(e)(1) and (5), which requires affiliated group allocation and apportionment of interest expense. The rules of this section apply to taxable years beginning after December 31, 1986, except as otherwise provided in § 1.861-13T. Paragraph (b) of this section describes the scope of the application of the rule for the allocation and apportionment of interest expense of affiliated groups of corporations, which is contained in paragraph (c) of this section. Paragraph (d) of this section sets forth the definition of the term "affiliated group" for purposes of this section. Paragraph (e) describes the treatment of loans between members of an affiliated group. Paragraph (f) of this section provides rules concerning the affiliated group allocation and apportionment of interest expense in computing the combined taxable income of a FSC or DISC and its related supplier. Paragraph (g) of this section describes the treatment of losses caused by apportionment of interest expense in the case of an affiliated group that does not file a consolidated return.

(b) *Scope of application*.—(1) *Application of section 864(e)(1) and (5) (concerning the definition and treatment of affiliated groups)*.—For further guidance, see § 1.861-11(b)(1).

(2) *Nonapplication of section 864(e)(1) and (5) (concerning the definition and treatment of affiliated groups)*.—Section 864(e)(1) and (5) and the portions of this section implementing section 864(e)(1) and (5) do not apply to the computation of subpart F income of controlled foreign corporations (under sections 951 through 964), the computation of combined taxable income of a possessions corporation and its affiliates (under section 936), or the computation of effectively connected taxable income of foreign corporations. For the rules with respect to the allocation and apportionment of interest expenses of foreign corporations other than controlled foreign corporations, see §§ 1.882-4 and 1.882-5.

(c) *General rule for affiliated corporations*.—Except as otherwise provided in this section, the taxable income of each member of an affiliated group within each statutory grouping shall be determined by allocating and apportioning the interest expense of each member according to apportionment fractions which are computed as if all members of such group were a single corporation. For purposes of determining these apportionment fractions, stock in corporations within the affiliated group (as defined in section 864(e)(5) and the rules of this section) shall not be taken into account. In the case of an affiliated group of corporations that files a consolidated return, consolidated foreign tax credit limitations are computed for the group in accordance with the rules of § 1.1502-4. Except as otherwise provided, all the interest expense of all members of the group will be treated as definitely related and therefore allocable to all the gross income of the members of the group and all the assets of all the members of the group shall be taken into account in apportioning this interest expense. For purposes of this section, the term "taxpayer" refers to the affiliated group (regardless of whether the group files a consolidated return), rather than to the separate members thereof.

(d)(1) and (2) [Reserved]. For further guidance, see § 1.861-11(d)(1) and (2).

(3) *Treatment of life insurance companies subject to taxation under section 801*.—(i) *General rule*.—A life insurance company that is subject to taxation under section 801 shall be considered to constitute a member of the affiliated group composed of companies not taxable under section 801 only if a parent corporation so elects under section 1504(c)(2)(A) of the Code. If a parent does not so elect, no adjustments shall be required with respect to such an insurance company under paragraph (g) of this section.

(ii) *Treatment of stock*.—Stock of a life insurance company that is subject to taxation under section 801 that is not included in an affiliated group shall be disregarded in the allocation and apportionment of the interest expense of such affiliated group.

(4) *Treatment of certain financial corporations*.—(i) *In general*.—In the case of an affiliated group (as defined in paragraph (d)(1) of this section), any members that constitute financial corporations as defined in paragraph (d)(4)(ii) of this section shall be treated as a separate affiliated group consisting of financial corporations (the "financial group"). The members of the group that do not constitute financial corporations shall be treated as members of a separate affiliated group consisting of nonfinancial corporations ("the nonfinancial group").

(ii) *Financial corporation defined*.—The term "financial corporation" means any corporation which meets all of the following conditions:

(A) It is described in section 581 (relating to the definition of a bank) or section 591 (relating to the deduction for dividends paid on deposits by mutual savings banks, cooperative banks, domestic building and loan associations, and other savings institutions chartered and supervised as savings and loan or similar associations);

(B) Its business is predominantly with persons other than related persons (within the meaning of section 864(d)(4) and the regulations thereunder) or their customers; and

(C) It is required by state or Federal law to be operated separately from any other entity which is not such an institution.

(iii) *Treatment of bank holding companies*.—The total aggregate interest expense of any member of an affiliated group that constitutes a bank holding company subject to regulation under the Bank Holding Company Act of 1956 shall be prorated between the financial group and the nonfinancial group on the basis of the assets in the financial and nonfinancial groups. For purposes of making this proration, the assets of each member of each group, and not the stock basis in each member, shall be taken into account. Any direct or indirect subsidiary of a bank holding company that is predominantly engaged in the active conduct of a banking, financing, or similar business shall be considered to be a financial corporation for purposes of this paragraph (d)(4). The interest expense of the bank holding company must be further apportioned in accordance with § 1.861-9T(f) to the various section 904(d) categories of income contained in both the financial group and the nonfinancial group on the basis of the assets owned by each group. For purposes of computing the apportionment fractions for each group, the assets owned directly by a bank holding company within each limitation category described in section 904(d)(1) (other than stock in affiliates or assets described in § 1.861-9T(f)) shall be treated as owned pro rata by the nonfinancial group and the financial group based on the relative amounts of investment of the bank holding company in the nonfinancial group and financial group.

(iv) *Consideration of stock of the members of one group held by members of the other group.*—In apportioning interest expense, the nonfinancial group shall not take into account the stock of any lower-tier corporation that is treated as a member of the financial group under paragraph (d)(4)(i) of this section. Conversely, in apportioning interest expense, the financial group shall not take into account the stock of any lower-tier corporation that is treated as a member of the nonfinancial group under paragraph (d)(4)(i) of this section. For the treatment of loans between members of the financial group and members of the nonfinancial group, see paragraph (e)(1) of this section.

(5) *Example.*—(i) *Facts.*—X, a domestic corporation which is not a bank holding company, is the parent of domestic corporations Y and Z. Z owns 100 percent of the stock Z1, which is also a domestic corporation. X, Y, Z, and Z1 were organized after January 1, 1987, and constitute an affiliated group within the meaning of paragraph (d)(1) of this section. Y and Z are financial corporations described in paragraph (d)(4) of this section. X also owns 25 percent of the stock of A, a domestic corporation. Y owns 25 percent of the voting stock of B, a foreign corporation that is not a controlled foreign corporation. Z owns less than 10 percent of the voting stock of C, another foreign corporation. The foreign source income generated by Y's or Z's direct assets is exclusively financial services income. The foreign source income generated by X's or Z1's direct assets is exclusively general limitation income. X and Z1 are not financial corporations described in paragraph (d)(4)(ii) of this section. Y and Z, therefore, constitute a separate affiliated group apart from X and Z1 for purposes of section 864(e). The combined interest expense of Y and Z of $100,000 ($50,000 each) is apportioned separately on the basis of their assets. The combined interest expense of X and Z1 of $50,000 ($25,000 each) is allocated on the basis of the assets of the XZ1 group.

Analysis of the YZ group assets

Adjusted basis of assets of the YZ group that generate foreign source financial services income (excluding stock of foreign subsidiaries not included in the YZ affiliated group)	$200,000
Z's basis in the C stock (not adjusted by the allocable amount of C's earnings and profits because Z owns less than 10 percent of the stock) which would be considered to generate passive income in the hands of a nonfinancial services entity but is considered to generate financial services income when in the hands of Z, a financial services entity	$100,000
Y's basis in the B stock (adjusted by the allocable amount of B's earnings and profits) which generates dividends subject to a separate limitation for B dividends	$100,000
Adjusted basis of assets of the YZ group that generate U.S. source income	$600,000
Total assets	$1,000,000

Analysis of the XZ1 group assets

Adjusted basis of assets of the XZ1 group that generate foreign source general limitation income	$500,000
Adjusted basis of assets of the XZ1 group other than A stock that generate domestic source income	$1,900,000
X's basis in the A stock adjusted by the allocable amount of A's earnings and profits	$100,000
Total domestic assets	$2,000,000
Total assets	$2,500,000

(ii) *Allocation.*—No portion of the $50,000 deduction of the YZ group is definitely related solely to specific property within the meaning of § 1.861-10T. Thus, the YZ group's deduction for interest is related to all its activities and properties. Similarly, no portion of the $50,000 deduction of the XZ1 group is definitely related solely to specific property within the meaning of § 1.861-10T. Thus, the XZ1 group's deduction for interest is related to all its activities and properties.

(iii) *Apportionment.*—The YZ group would apportion its interest expense as follows:

To gross financial services income from sources outside the United States:

$$\$50{,}000 \times \frac{\$300{,}000}{\$1{,}000{,}000} \quad \$15{,}000$$

To gross income subject to a separate limitation for dividends from B:

$$\$50{,}000 \times \frac{\$100{,}000}{\$1{,}000{,}000} \quad \$5{,}000$$

To gross income from sources inside the United States:

$$\$50{,}000 \times \frac{\$600{,}000}{\$1{,}000{,}000} \quad \$30{,}000$$

The XZ1 group would apportion its interest expense as follows:

To gross general limitation income from sources outside the United States:

$$\$50{,}000 \times \frac{\$500{,}000}{\$2{,}500{,}000} \quad \$10{,}000$$

To gross income from sources inside the United States:

$$\$50{,}000 \times \frac{\$2{,}000{,}000}{\$2{,}500{,}000} \quad \$40{,}000$$

(6) *Certain unaffiliated corporations.*—Certain corporations that are not described in paragraph (d)(1) of this section will nonetheless be considered to constitute affiliated corporations for purposes of §§ 1.861-9T through 1.861-13T. These corporations include:

(i) Any includible corporation (as defined in section 1504(b) without regard to section 1504(b)(4)) if 80 percent of either the vote or value of all outstanding stock of such corporation is owned directly or indirectly by an includible corporation or by members of an affiliated group, and

(ii) [Reserved]. For further guidance see § 1.861-11(d)(6)(ii).

(7) *Special rules for the application of § 1.861-11T(d)(6).*—[Reserved]. For special rules for the application of § 1.861-11T(d)(6), see § 1.861-11(d)(7).

(e) *Loans between members of an affiliated group.*—(1) *General rule.*—In the case of loans (including any receivable) between members of an affiliated group, as defined in paragraph (d) of this section, for purposes of apportioning interest expense, the indebtedness of the member borrower shall not be considered an asset of the member lender. However, in the case of members of separate financial and nonfinancial groups under paragraph (d)(4) of this section, the indebtedness of the member borrower shall be considered an asset of the member lender and such asset shall be characterized by reference to the member lender's income from the asset as determined under paragraph (e)(2)(ii) of this section. For purposes of this paragraph (e), the terms "related person interest income" and "related person interest payment" refer to interest paid and received by members of the same affiliated group as defined in paragraph (d) of this section.

(2) *Treatment of interest expense within the affiliated group.*—(i) *General rule.*—A member borrower shall deduct related person interest payments in the same manner as unrelated person interest expense using group apportionment fractions computed under § 1.861-9T(f). A member lender shall include related person interest income in the same class of gross income as the class of gross income from which the member borrower deducts the related person interest payment.

(ii) *Special rule for loans between financial and nonfinancial affiliated corporations.*—In the case of a loan between two affiliated corporations only one of which constitutes a financial corporation under paragraph (d)(4) of this section, the member borrower shall allocate and apportion related person interest payments in the same manner as unrelated person interest expense using group apportionment fractions computed under § 1.861-9T(f). The source of the related person interest income to the member lender shall be determined under section 861(a)(1).

(iii) *Special rule for high withholding tax interest.*—In the case of an affiliated corporation that pays interest that is high withholding tax interest under § 1.904-5(f)(1) to another affiliated corporation, the interest expense of the payor shall be allocated to high withholding tax interest.

(3) *Back-to-back loans.*—If a member of the affiliated group makes a loan to a nonmember who makes a loan to a member borrower, the rule of paragraph (e)(1) and (2) of this section shall apply, in the Commissioner's discretion, as if the member lender made the loan directly to the member borrower, provided that the loans constitute a back-to-back loan transaction. Such loans will constitute a back-to-back loan for purposes of this paragraph (e) if the loan by the nonmember would not have been made or maintained on substantially the same terms irrespective of the loan of funds by the lending member to the nonmember or other intermediary party.

(4) *Examples.*—The rules of this paragraph (e) may be illustrated by the following examples.

Example (1). X, a domestic corporation, is the parent of Y, a domestic corporation. X and Y were organized after January 1, 1987, and constitute an affiliated group within the meaning of paragraph (d)(1) of this section. Among X's assets is the note of Y for the amount of $100,000. Because X and Y are members of an affiliated group, Y's note does not constitute an asset for purposes of apportionment. The apportionment fractions for the relevant tax year of the XY group are 50 percent domestic, 40 percent foreign general, and 10 percent foreign passive. Y deducts its related person interest payment using those apportionment fractions. Of the $10,000 in related person interest income received by X, $5,000 consists of domestic source income, $4,000 consists of foreign general limitation income, and $1,000 consists of foreign passive income.

Example (2). X is a domestic corporation organized after January 1, 1987. X owns all the stock of Y, a domestic corporation. On June 1, 1987, X loans $100,000 to Z, an unrelated person. On June 2, 1987, Z makes a loan to Y with terms substantially similar to those of the loan from X to Z. Based on the facts and circumstances of the transaction, it is determined that Z would not have made the loan to Y on the same terms if X had not made the loan to Z. Because the transaction constitutes a back-to-back loan, as defined in paragraph (e)(3) of this section, the Commissioner may require, in his discretion, that neither the note of Y nor the note of Z may be considered an asset of X for purposes of this section.

(f) *Computations of combined taxable income.*—In the computation of the combined taxable income of any FSC or DISC and its related supplier which is a member of an affiliated group under the pricing rules of sections 925 or 994, the combined taxable income of such FSC or DISC and its related supplier shall be reduced by the portion of the total interest expense of the affiliated group that is incurred in connection with those assets of the group used in connection with export sales involving that FSC or DISC. This amount shall be computed by multiplying the total interest expense of the affiliated group and interest expense of the FSC or DISC by a fraction the numerator of which is the assets of the affiliated group and of the FSC or DISC generating foreign trade income or gross income attributable to qualified export receipts, as the case may be, and the denominator of which is the total assets of the affiliated group and the FSC or DISC. Under this rule, interest of other group members may be attributed to the combined taxable income of a FSC or DISC and its related supplier without affecting the amount of interest otherwise deductible by the FSC or DISC, the related supplier or other member of the affiliated group. The FSC or DISC is entitled to only the statutory portion of the combined taxable income, net of any deemed interest expense, which determines the commission paid to the FSC or DISC or the transfer price of qualifying export property sold to the FSC or DISC.

(g) *Losses created through apportionment.*—(1) *General rules.*—In the case of an affiliated group that is eligible to file, but does not file, a consolidated return and in the case of any corporation described in paragraph (d)(6) of this section, the foreign tax credits in any separate limitation category are limited to the credits computed under the rules of this paragraph (g). As a consequence of the affiliated group allocation and apportionment of interest expense required by section 864(e)(1) and this section, interest expense of a group member may be apportioned for section 904 purposes to a limitation category in which that member has no gross income, resulting in a loss in that limitation category. The same is true in connection with any expense other than interest that is subject to apportionment under the rules of section 864(e)(6) of the Code. Any reference to "interest expense" in this paragraph (g) shall be treated as including such expenses. For purposes of this paragraph, the term "limitation category" includes domestic source income, as well as the types of income described in section 904(d)(1)(A) through (I). A loss of one affiliate in a limitation category will reduce the income of another member in the same limitation category if a consolidated return is filed. (See § 1.1502-4.) If a consolidated return is not filed, this netting does not occur. Accordingly, in such a case, the following adjustments among members are required in order to give effect to the group allocation of interest expense:

(i) Losses created through group apportionment of interest expense in one or more limitation categories within a given member must be eliminated; and

(ii) A corresponding amount of income of other members in the same limitation category must be recharacterized.

Such adjustments shall be accomplished, in accordance with paragraph (g)(2) of this section, without changing the total taxable income of any member and before the application of section 904(f). Section 904(f) (including section 904(f)(5)) does not apply to a loss created through the apportionment of interest expense to the extent that the loss is eliminated pursuant to paragraph (g)(2)(ii) of this section. For purposes of this section, the terms "limitation adjustment" and "recharacterization" mean the recharacterization of income in one limitation category as income in another limitation category.

(2) *Mechanics of computation.*—(i) *Step 1: Computation of consolidated taxable income.*—The members of an affiliated group must first allocate and apportion all other deductible expenses other than interest. The members must then deduct from their respective gross incomes within each limitation category interest expense apportioned under the rules of § 1.861-9T(f). The taxable income of the entire affiliated group within each limitation category is then totalled.

(ii) *Step 2: Loss offset adjustments.*—If, after step 1, a member has losses in a given limitation category or limitation categories created through apportionment of interest expense, any such loss (*i.e.*, the portion of such loss equal to interest expense) shall be eliminated by offsetting that loss against taxable income in other limitation categories of that member to the extent of the taxable income of other members within the same limitation category as the loss. If the member has taxable income in more than one limitation category, then the loss shall offset taxable income in all such limitation categories on a pro rata basis. If there is insufficient domestic income of the member to offset the net losses in all foreign limitation categories caused by the apportionment of interest expense, the losses in each limitation category shall be recharacterized as domestic losses to the extent of the taxable income of other members in the same respective limitation categories. After these adjustments are made, the income of the entire affiliated group within each limitation category is totalled again.

(iii) *Step 3: Determination of amount subject to recharacterization.*—In order to determine the amount of income to be recharacterized in step 4, the income totals computed under step 1 in each limitation category shall be subtracted from the income totals computed under step 2 in each limitation category.

(iv) *Step 4: Recharacterization.*—Because any differences determined under step 3 represent deviations from the consolidated totals computed under step 1, such differences (in any limitation category) must be eliminated.

(A) *Limitation categories to be reduced.*—In the case of any limitation category in which there is a positive change, the income of group members with income in that limitation category must be reduced on a pro rata basis (by reference to net income figures as determined under Step 2) to the extent of such positive change ("limitation reductions"). Each member shall separately compute the sum of the limitation reductions.

(B) *Limitation categories to be increased.*—In any case in which only one limitation category has a negative change in Step 3, the sum of the limitation reductions within each member is added to that limitation category. In the case in which multiple limitation categories have negative changes in Step 3, the sum of the limitation reductions within each member is prorated among the negative change limitation categories based on the ratio that the negative change for the entire group in each limitation category bears to the total of all negative changes for the entire group in all limitation categories.

(3) *Examples.*—The following examples illustrate the principles of this paragraph.

Example (1)—(i) *Facts.* X, a domestic corporation, is the parent of domestic corporations Y and Z. X, Y, and Z were organized after January 1, 1987, constitute an affiliated group within the meaning of paragraph (d)(1) of this section, but do not file a consolidated return. The XYZ group apportions its interest expense on the basis of the fair market value of its assets. X, Y, and Z have the following assets, interest expense, and taxable income before apportioning interest expense:

Assets	X	Y	Z	Total
Domestic	2,000.00	0.00	1,000.00	3,000.00
Foreign Passive	0.00	50.00	50.00	100.00
Foreign General	0.00	700.00	200.00	900.00
Interest expense	48.00	12.00	80.00	140.00
Taxable Income (pre-interest)				
Domestic	100.00	0.00	63.00	163.00
Foreign Passive	0.00	5.00	5.00	10.00
Foreign General	0.00	60.00	35.00	95.00

(ii) *Step 1: Computation of consolidated taxable income.* Each member of the XYZ group apportions its interest expense according to group apportionment ratios determined under the asset method described in § 1.861-9T(f), yielding the following results:

Apportioned interest expense	X	Y	Z	Total
Domestic	36.00	9.00	60.00	105.00
Foreign Passive	1.20	0.30	2.00	3.50
Foreign General	10.80	2.70	18.00	31.50
Total	48.00	12.00	80.00	140.00

The members of the group then compute taxable income within each category by deducting the apportioned interest expense from the amounts of pre-interest taxable income specified in the facts in paragraph (i), yielding the following results:

Taxable Income	X	Y	Z	Total
Domestic	64.00	-9.00	3.00	58.00
Foreign Passive	-1.20	4.70	3.00	6.50
Foreign General	-10.80	57.30	17.00	63.50
Total	52.00	53.00	23.00	128.00

(iii) *Step 2: Loss offset adjustments.* Because X and Y have losses created through apportionment, these losses must be eliminated by reducing taxable income of the member in other limitation categories. Because X has a total of $12 in apportionment losses and because it has only one limitation category with income (*i.e.*, domestic), domestic income must be reduced by $12, thus eliminating its apportionment losses. Because Y has a total of $9 in apportionment losses and because it has two limitation categories with income (*i.e.*, foreign passive and foreign general limitation), the income in these two limitation categories must be reduced on a pro rata basis in order to eliminate its apportionment losses. In summary, the following adjustments are required:

Loss Offset Adjustments	X	Y	Z	Total
Domestic	-12.00	+9.00	0	-3.00
Foreign Passive	+1.20	-0.68	0	+0.52
Foreign General	+10.80	-8.32	0	+2.48

These adjustments yield the following adjusted taxable income figures:

Adjusted Taxable Income	X	Y	Z	Total
Domestic	52.00	0.00	3.00	55.00
Foreign Passive	0.00	4.02	3.00	7.02
Foreign General	0.00	48.98	17.00	65.98
Total	52.00	53.00	23.00	128.00

(iv) *Step 3: Determination of amount subject to recharacterization.* The adjustments performed under Step 2 led to a change in the group's taxable income within each limitation category. The total loss offset adjustments column shown in paragraph (iii) above shows the net deviations between Steps 1 and 2.

(v) *Step 4: Recharacterization.* The loss offset adjustments yield a positive change in the foreign passive and the foreign general limitation categories. Y and Z both have income in these limitation categories. Accordingly, the income of Y and Z in each of these limitation categories must be reduced on a pro rata basis (by reference to the adjusted taxable income figures) to the extent of the positive change in each limitation category. The total positive change in the foreign passive limitation category is $0.52. The adjusted taxable income of Y in the foreign passive limitation category is $4.02 and the adjusted taxable income of Z in the foreign passive limitation category is $3. Therefore, $0.30 is drawn from Y and $0.22 is drawn from Z. The total positive change in the foreign general limitation category is $2.48. The adjusted taxable income of Y in the foreign general limitation category is $48.98, and the adjusted taxable income of Z in the foreign general limitation category is $17. Therefore, $1.84 is drawn from Y and $.64 is drawn from Z.

The members must then separately compute the sum of the limitation reductions. Y has limitation reductions of $0.30 in the foreign passive limitation category and $1.84 in the foreign general limitation category, yielding total limitation reduction of $2.14. Under these facts, domestic income is the only limitation category requiring a positive adjustment. Accordingly, Y's domestic income is increased by $2.14. Z has limitation reductions of $0.22 in the foreign passive limitation category and $0.64 in the foreign general limitation category, yielding total limitation reductions of $0.86. Under these facts, domestic income is the only limitation category of Z requiring a positive adjustment. Accordingly, Z's domestic income is increased by $0.86.

Recharacterization Adjustments	X	Y	Z	Total
Domestic	0	+2.14	+0.86	+3.00
Foreign Passive	0	−0.30	−0.22	−0.52
Foreign General	0	−1.84	−0.64	−2.48

These recharacterization adjustments yield the following final taxable income figures:

Final Taxable Income	X	Y	Z	Total
Domestic	52.00	2.14	3.86	58.00
Foreign Passive	0.00	3.72	2.78	6.50
Foreign General	0.00	47.14	16.36	63.50
Total	52.00	53.00	23.00	128.00

Example (2)—(i) *Facts.* X, a domestic corporation, is the parent of domestic corporations Y and Z. X, Y, and Z were organized after January 1, 1987, constitute an affiliated group within the meaning of paragraph (d)(1) of this section, but do not file a consolidated return. Moreover, X has served as the sole borrower in the group and, as a result, has sustained an overall loss. The XYZ group apportions its interest expense on the basis of the fair market value of its assets. X, Y, and Z have the following assets, interest expense, and taxable income before interest expense:

	X	Y	Z	Total
Assets				
Domestic	2,000.00	0.00	1,000.00	3,000.00
Foreign Passive	0.00	50.00	50.00	100.00
Foreign General	0.00	700.00	200.00	900.00
Interest Expense	140.00	0.00	0.00	140.00
Taxable Income (pre-interest)				
Domestic	100.00	0.00	100.00	200.00
Foreign Passive	0.00	5.00	5.00	10.00
Foreign General	0.00	70.00	35.00	105.00

(ii) *Step 1: Computation of consolidated taxable income.* Each member of the XYZ group apportions its interest expense according to group apportionment ratios determined under the asset method described in § 1.861-9T(g), yielding the following results:

Apportioned Interest Expense	X	Y	Z	Total
Domestic	105.00	0	0	105.00
Foreign Passive	3.50	0	0	3.50
Foreign General	31.50	0	0	31.50
Total	140.00	0	0	140.00

The members of the group then compute taxable income within each category by deducting the apportioned interest expense from the amounts of pre-interest taxable income specified in the facts in paragraph (i), yielding the following results:

Taxable Income	X	Y	Z	Total
Domestic	−5.00	0.00	100.00	95.00
Foreign Passive	−3.50	5.00	5.00	6.50
Foreign General	−31.50	70.00	35.00	73.50
Total	−40.00	75.00	140.00	175.00

(iii) *Step 2: Loss offset adjustment.* Because X has insufficient domestic income to offset the sum of the losses in the foreign limitation categories caused by apportionment, the amount of apportionment losses in each limitation category shall be recharacterized as domestic losses to the extent of taxable income of other members in the same limitation category. This is accomplished by adding to each foreign limitation categories an amount equal to the loss therein and by subtracting the sum of such foreign losses from domestic income, as follows:

Loss Offset Adjustments	X	Y	Z	Total
Domestic	−35.00	0	0	−35.00
Foreign Passive	+3.50	0	0	+3.50
Foreign General	+31.50	0	0	+31.50

These adjustments yield the following adjusted taxable income figures:

Adjusted Taxable Income	X	Y	Z	Total
Domestic	−40.00	0.00	100.00	60.00
Foreign Passive	0.00	5.00	5.00	10.00
Foreign General	0.00	70.00	35.00	105.00
Total	−40.00	75.00	140.00	175.00

(iv) *Step 3: Determination of amount subject to recharacterization.* The adjustments performed under Step 2 led to a change in the group's taxable income within each limitation category. The total loss offset adjustments column shown in paragraph (iii) above shows the net deviations between Steps 1 and 2.

(v) *Step 4: Recharacterization.* The loss offset adjustments yield a positive change in the foreign passive and the foreign general limitation categories. Y and Z both have income in these limitation categories. Accordingly, the income of Y and Z in each of these limitation categories must be reduced on a pro rata basis (by reference to the adjusted taxable income figures) to the extent of the positive change in each limitation category. The total positive change in the foreign passive limitation category is $3.50. The adjusted taxable income of Y in the foreign passive limitation category is $5, and the adjusted taxable income of Z in the foreign passive limitation category is $5. Therefore, $1.75 is drawn from Y and $1.75 is drawn from Z. The total positive change in the foreign general limitation category is $31.50. The adjusted taxable income of Y in the foreign general limitation category is $70, and the adjusted taxable income of Z in the foreign general limitation category is $35. Therefore, $21 is drawn from Y and $10.50 is drawn from Z.

The members must then separately compute the sum of the limitation reductions. Y has limitation reductions of $1.75 in the foreign passive limitation category and $21 in the foreign general limitation category, yielding total limitation reductions of $22.75. Under these facts, domestic income is the only limitation category requiring a positive adjustment. Accordingly, Y's domestic income is increased by $22.75. Z has limitation reductions of $1.75 in the foreign passive limitation category and $10.50 in the foreign general limitation category, yielding total limitation reductions of $12.25. Under these facts, domestic income is the only limitation category requiring a positive adjustment. Accordingly, Z's domestic income is increased by $12.25.

Recharacterization Adjustments	X	Y	Z	*Total*
Domestic	0	+22.75	+12.25	+35.00
Foreign Passive	0	−1.75	−1.75	−3.50
Foreign General	0	−21.00	−10.50	−31.50

These recharacterization adjustments yield the following final taxable income figures:

Final Taxable Income	X	Y	Z	*Total*
Domestic	−40.00	22.75	112.25	95.00
Foreign Passive	0.00	3.25	3.25	6.50
Foreign General	0.00	49.00	24.50	73.50
Total	−40.00	75.00	140.00	175.00

(h) *Effective/applicability date.*—In general, the rules of this section apply for taxable years beginning after December 31, 1986. [Temporary Reg. § 1.861-11T.]

[*T.D.* 8228, 9-9-88. *Amended by T.D.* 8916, 12-29-2000; *T.D.* 9456, 7-31-2009; *T.D.* 9571, 1-13-2012 (*corrected* 2-17-2012), *T.D.* 9676, 7-15-2014 *and T.D.* 9882, 12-16-2019.]

§ 1.861-12. Characterization rules and adjustments for certain assets.—(a) *In general.*—The rules in this section apply to taxpayers apportioning expenses under an asset method to income in the various separate categories described in § 1.904-5(a)(4)(v), and supplement other rules provided in §§ 1.861-9 through 1.861-11T. The principles of the rules in this section also apply in apportioning expenses among statutory and residual groupings for any other operative section. See also § 1.861-8(f)(2)(i) for a rule requiring conformity of allocation methods and apportionment principles for all operative sections. Paragraph (b) of this section describes the treatment of inventories. Paragraph (c)(1) of this section concerns the treatment of various stock assets. Paragraph (c)(2) of this section describes a basis adjustment for stock in 10 percent owned corporations. Paragraph (c)(3) of this section sets forth rules for characterizing the stock in controlled foreign corporations. Paragraph (c)(4) of this section describes the treatment of stock of noncontrolled 10-percent owned foreign corporations. Paragraph (d)(1) of this section concerns the treatment of notes. Paragraph (d)(2) of this section concerns the treatment of notes of controlled foreign corporations. Paragraph (e) of this section describes the treatment of certain portfolio securities that constitute inventory or generate income primarily in the form of gains. Paragraph (f) of this section describes the treatment of assets that are funded by interest that is capitalized, deferred, or disallowed. Paragraph (g) of this section concerns the treatment of FSC stock and of assets of the related supplier generating foreign trade income. Paragraph (h) of this section concerns the treatment of DISC stock and of assets of the related supplier generating qualified export receipts.

(b) *Inventories.*—For further guidance, see § 1.861-12T(b).

(c) *Treatment of stock.*—(1) *In general.*—For further guidance, see § 1.861-12T(c)(1).

(2) *Basis adjustment for stock in 10 percent owned corporations.*—(i) *Taxpayers using the tax book value method.*—(A) *General rule.*—For purposes of apportioning expenses on the basis of the tax book value of assets, the adjusted basis of any stock in a 10 percent owned corporation owned by the taxpayer either directly or indirectly through a partnership or other pass-through entity (after taking into account the adjustments described in paragraph (c)(2)(i)(B)(*1*) of this section) shall be—

(*1*) Increased by the amount of the earnings and profits of such corporation (and of lower-tier 10 percent owned corporations) attributable to such stock and accumulated during the period the taxpayer or other members of its affiliated group held 10 percent or more of such stock; or

(*2*) Reduced by any deficit in earnings and profits of such corporation (and of lower-tier 10 percent owned corporations) attributable to such stock for such period; or

(*3*) Zero, if after application of paragraphs (c)(2)(i)(A)(*1*) and (*2*) of this section, the adjusted basis of the stock is less than zero.

(B) *Computational rules.*—(*1*) *Adjustments to basis.*—(*i*) *Application of section 961 or 1293(d).*—For purposes of this section, a taxpayer's adjusted basis in the stock of a foreign corporation does not include any amount included in basis under section 961 or 1293(d) of the Code.

(*ii*) *Application of section 965(b).*—For purposes of this section, if a taxpayer owned the stock of a specified foreign corporation (as defined in § 1.965-1(f)(45)) as of the close of the last taxable year of the specified foreign corporation that began before January 1, 2018, the taxpayer's adjusted basis in the stock of the specified foreign corporation for that taxable year and any subsequent taxable year is determined as if the taxpayer did not make the election described in § 1.965-2(f)(2)(i) (regardless of whether the election was actually made) and is further adjusted as described in this paragraph (c)(2)(i)(B)(*1*)(*ii*). If § 1.965-2(f)(2)(ii)(B) applied (or would have applied if the election had been made) with respect to the stock of a specified foreign corporation, the taxpayer's adjusted basis in the stock of the specified foreign corporation is reduced by the amount described in § 1.965-2(f)(2)(ii)(B)(*1*) (without regard to the rule for limited basis adjustments in § 1.965-2(f)(2)(ii)(B)(*2*) and the limitation in § 1.965-2(f)(2)(ii)(C), and without regard to the rules regarding the netting of basis adjustments in § 1.965-2(h)(2)). The reduction in the taxpayer's adjusted basis in the stock may reduce the taxpayer's adjusted basis in the stock below zero prior to the application of paragraphs (c)(2)(i)(A)(*1*) and (*2*) of this section. No adjustment is made in the taxpayer's adjusted basis in the stock of a specified foreign corporation for an amount described in § 1.965-2(f)(2)(ii)(A). To the extent that, in an exchange described in section 351, 354, or 356, a taxpayer receives stock of a foreign corporation in exchange for stock of a specified foreign corporation described in this paragraph (c)(2)(i)(B)(*1*)(*ii*), this paragraph (c)(2)(i)(B)(*1*)(*ii*) applies to such stock received.

(*2*) *Amount of earnings and profits.*—For purposes of this paragraph (c)(2), earnings and profits (or deficits) are computed under the rules of section 312 and, in the case of a foreign corporation, sections 964(a) and 986 for taxable years of the 10 percent owned corporation ending on or before the close of the taxable year of the taxpayer. Accordingly, the earnings and profits of a controlled foreign corporation include all earnings and profits described in section 959(c). The amount of the earnings and profits with respect to stock of a foreign corporation held by the taxpayer is determined according to the attribution principles of section 1248 and the regulations under section 1248. The attribution principles of section 1248 apply without regard to the requirements of section 1248 that are not relevant to the determination of a shareholder's pro rata portion of earnings and profits, such as whether earnings and profits (or deficits) were derived (or incurred) during taxable years beginning before or after December 31, 1962.

(*3*) *Annual noncumulative adjustment.*—The adjustment required by paragraph (c)(2)(i)(A) of this section is made annually and is noncumulative. Thus, the adjusted basis of the stock (determined without regard to prior years' adjustments under paragraph (c)(2)(i)(A) of this section) is adjusted annually by the amount of accumulated earnings and profits (or deficits) attributable to the stock as of the end of each year.

(4) *Translation of non-dollar functional currency earnings and profits*.—Earnings and profits (or deficits) of a qualified business unit that has a functional currency other than the dollar must be computed under this paragraph (c)(2) in functional currency and translated into dollars using the exchange rate at the end of the taxpayer's current taxable year (and not the exchange rates for the years in which the earnings and profits or deficits were derived or incurred).

(C) *Examples*.—The following examples illustrate the application of paragraph (c)(2)(i) of this section.

(1) *Example 1: No election described in § 1.965-2(f)(2)(i)*—(i) *Facts*. USP, a domestic corporation, owns all of the stock of CFC1 and CFC2, both controlled foreign corporations. USP, CFC1, and CFC2 all use the calendar year as their U.S. taxable year. USP owned CFC1 and CFC2 as of December 31, 2017, and CFC1 and CFC2 were specified foreign corporations with respect to USP. USP's basis in each share of stock of each of CFC1 and CFC2 is identical. USP did not make the election described in § 1.965-2(f)(2)(i), but if USP had made the election, § 1.965-2(f)(2)(ii)(B) would have applied to the stock of CFC2 and the amount described in § 1.965-2(f)(2)(ii)(B)(*1*) (without regard to the rule for limited basis adjustments in § 1.965-2(f)(2)(ii)(B)(*2*) and without regard to the rules regarding the netting of basis adjustments in § 1.965-2(h)(2)) with respect to the stock of CFC2, in aggregate, is $75x. For purposes of determining the value of the stock of CFC1 and CFC2 at the beginning of the 2019 taxable year, without regard to amounts included in basis under section 961 or 1293(d), USP's adjusted basis in the stock of CFC1 is $100x and its adjusted basis in the stock of CFC2 is $350x (before the application of paragraph (c)(2)(i)(B) of this section).

(*ii*) *Analysis*. Under paragraph (c)(2)(i)(B)(*1*)(*ii*) of this section, USP's adjusted basis in the stock of CFC1 is determined as if USP did not make the election described in § 1.965-2(f)(2)(i). USP's adjusted basis in the stock of CFC2 is then reduced by $75x, the amount described in § 1.965-2(f)(2)(ii)(B)(*1*), without regard to the rule for limited basis adjustments in § 1.965-2(f)(2)(ii)(B)(*2*) and without regard to the rules regarding the netting of basis adjustments in § 1.965-2(h)(2). No adjustment is made to USP's adjusted basis in the stock in CFC1. Accordingly, for purposes of determining the value of stock of CFC1 and CFC2 at the beginning of the 2019 taxable year, USP's adjusted basis in the stock of CFC1 is $100x and USP's adjusted basis in the stock of CFC2 is $275x ($350x – $75x).

(2) *Example 2: Election described in § 1.965-2(f)(2)(i)*—(*i*) *Facts*. USP, a domestic corporation, owns all of the stock of CFC1, which owns all of the stock of CFC2, both controlled foreign corporations. USP, CFC1, and CFC2 all use the calendar year as their U.S. taxable year. USP owned CFC1, and CFC1 owned CFC2 as of December 31, 2017, and CFC1 and CFC2 were specified foreign corporations with respect to USP. USP's basis in each share of stock of CFC1 is identical. USP made the election described in § 1.965-2(f)(2)(i). As a result of the election, USP was required to increase its basis in the stock of CFC1 by $90x under § 1.965-2(f)(2)(ii)(A)(*1*), and to decrease its basis in the stock of CFC1 by $90x under § 1.965-2(f)(2)(ii)(B)(*1*). Pursuant to § 1.965-2(h)(2), USP netted the increase of $90x against the decrease of $90x and made no net adjustment to the basis in the stock of CFC1. For purposes of determining the value of the stock of CFC1 at the beginning of the 2019 taxable year, without regard to amounts included in basis under section 961 or 1293(d), USP's adjusted basis in the stock of CFC1 is $600x (before the application of paragraph (c)(2)(i)(B) of this section).

(*ii*) *Analysis*. Under paragraph (c)(2)(i)(B)(*1*)(*ii*) of this section, USP's adjusted basis in the stock of CFC1 is determined as if USP did not make the election described in § 1.965-2(f)(2)(i). While USP made the election, no adjustment was made to the stock of CFC1 as a result of the election. However, USP's adjusted basis in the stock of CFC1 is then reduced by $90x, the amount described in § 1.965-2(f)(2)(ii)(B)(*1*), without regard to the rules regarding the netting of basis described in § 1.965-2(h)(2). No adjustment is made to USP's basis in the stock of CFC1 for the amount described in § 1.965-2(f)(2)(ii)(A)(*1*). Accordingly, for purposes of determining the value of stock of CFC1 at the beginning of the 2019 taxable year, USP's adjusted basis in the stock of CFC1 is $510x ($600x – $90x).

(3) *Example 3: Adjusted basis below zero*—(*i*) *Facts*. The facts are the same as in paragraph (c)(2)(i)(C)(*1*)(*i*) of this section (the facts in *Example 1*), except that for purposes of determining the value of the stock of CFC2 at the beginning of the 2019 taxable year, without regard to amounts included in basis under section 961 or 1293(d), USP's adjusted basis in the stock of CFC2 is $0 (before the application of paragraph (c)(2)(i)(B) of this section). Additionally, the adjusted basis of USP in the stock of CFC1 and CFC2 at the end of the 2019 taxable year is the same as at the beginning of that year, and as of the end of the 2019 taxable year, CFC1 has earnings and profits of $25x and CFC2 has earnings and profits of $50x that are attributable to the stock owned by USP and accumulated during the period that USP held the stock of CFC1 and CFC2.

(*ii*) *Analysis*. The analysis is the same as in paragraph (c)(2)(i)(C)(*1*)(*ii*) of this section (the analysis in *Example 1*) except that for purposes of determining the value of stock of CFC1 and CFC2 at the beginning of the 2019 taxable year, USP's adjusted basis in the stock of CFC2 is -$75x ($0 – $75x). Because USP's basis in the stock of CFC1 and CFC2 is the same at the end of the 2019 taxable year, prior to the application of the adjustments in paragraphs (c)(2)(i)(A)(*1*) and (*2*) of this section, USP's adjusted basis in the stock of CFC1 is $100x and USP's adjusted basis in the stock of CFC2 is - $75x. Under paragraph (c)(2)(i)(A)(*1*) of this section, for purposes of apportioning expenses on the basis of the tax book value of assets, USP's adjusted basis in the stock of CFC1 is $125x ($100x + $25x). Under paragraph (c)(2)(i)(A)(*3*) of this section, for purposes of apportioning expenses on the basis of the tax book value of assets, USP's adjusted basis in the stock of CFC2 is $0 because after applying paragraph (c)(2)(i)(A)(*1*) of this section, USP's adjusted basis in the stock of CFC2 is less than zero (-$75x + $50x).

(4) *Example 4: Election described in § 1.965-2(f)(2)(i) and adjusted basis below zero*—(*i*) *Facts*. The facts are the same as in paragraph (c)(2)(i)(C)(*3*)(*i*) of this section (the facts in *Example 3*), except that USP made the election described in § 1.965-2(f)(2)(i) and, as result, recognized $75x of gain under § 1.965-2(h)(3).

(*ii*) *Analysis*. The analysis is the same as in paragraph (c)(2)(i)(C)(*3*)(*ii*) of this section (the analysis in *Example 3*).

(c)(2)(ii) through (c)(2)(vi) [Reserved]. For further guidance, see § 1.861-12T(c)(2)(ii) through (c)(2)(vi).

(3) *Characterization of stock of controlled foreign corporations*.—(i) *Operative sections*.—(A) *Operative sections other than section 904*.—For purposes of applying this section to an operative section other than section 904, stock in a controlled foreign corporation (as defined in section 957) is characterized as an asset in the relevant groupings on the basis of the asset method described in paragraph (c)(3)(ii) of this section, or the modified gross income method described in paragraph (c)(3)(iii) of this section. Stock in a controlled foreign corporation whose interest expense is apportioned on the basis of assets is characterized in the hands of its United States shareholders under the asset method described in paragraph (c)(3)(ii) of this section. Stock in a controlled foreign corporation whose interest expense is apportioned on the basis of modified gross income is characterized in the hands of its United States shareholders under the modified gross income method described in paragraph (c)(3)(iii) of this section.

(B) *Section 904 as operative section*.—For purposes of applying this section to section 904 as the operative section, § 1.861-13 applies to characterize the stock of a controlled foreign corporation as an asset producing foreign source income in the separate categories described in § 1.904-5(a)(4)(v), or as an asset producing U.S. source income in the residual grouping, in the hands of the United States shareholder, and to determine the portion of the stock that gives rise to an inclusion under section 951A(a) that is treated as an exempt asset under § 1.861-8(d)(2)(ii)(C). Section 1.861-13 also provides rules for subdividing the stock in the various separate categories and the residual grouping into a section 245A subgroup and a non-section 245A subgroup in order to determine the amount of the adjustments required by section 904(b)(4) and § 1.904(b)-3(c) with respect to the section 245A subgroup, and provides rules for determining the portion of the stock that gives rise to a dividend eligible for a deduction under section 245(a)(5) that is treated as an exempt asset under § 1.861-8(d)(2)(ii)(B).

(ii) *Asset method*.—For further guidance, see § 1.861-12T(c)(3)(ii).

(iii) *Modified gross income method*.—Under the modified gross income method, the taxpayer characterizes the tax book value of the stock of the first-tier controlled foreign corporation based on the gross income, net of interest expense, of the controlled foreign corporation (as computed under § 1.861-9T(j) to include certain gross income, net of interest expense, of lower-tier controlled foreign corporations) within each relevant category for the taxable year of the controlled foreign corporation ending with or within the taxable year of the taxpayer. For purposes of this paragraph (c)(3)(iii), however, the gross income, net of interest expense, of the first-tier controlled foreign corporation includes the total amount of gross subpart F income, net of interest expense, of any lower-tier controlled foreign corporation that was excluded under the rules of § 1.861-9(j)(2)(ii)(B).

(4) *Characterization of stock of noncontrolled 10-percent owned foreign corporations.*—(i) *In general.*—Except in the case of a nonqualifying shareholder described in paragraph (c)(4)(ii) of this section, the principles of § 1.861-12(c)(3), including the relevant rules of § 1.861-13 when section 904 is the operative section, apply to characterize stock in a noncontrolled 10-percent owned foreign corporation (as defined in section 904(d)(2)(E)). Accordingly, stock in a noncontrolled 10-percent owned foreign corporation is characterized as an asset in the various separate categories on the basis of either the asset method described in § 1.861-12T(c)(3)(ii) or the modified gross income method described in § 1.861-12(c)(3)(iii). Stock in a noncontrolled 10-percent owned foreign corporation the interest expense of which is apportioned on the basis of assets is characterized in the hands of its shareholders under the asset method described in § 1.861-12T(c)(3)(ii). Stock in a noncontrolled 10-percent owned foreign corporation the interest expense of which is apportioned on the basis of gross income is characterized in the hands of its shareholders under the modified gross income method described in § 1.861-12(c)(3)(iii).

(ii) *Nonqualifying shareholders.*—Stock in a noncontrolled 10-percent owned foreign corporation is characterized as a passive category asset in the hands of a shareholder that either is not a domestic corporation or is not a United States shareholder with respect to the noncontrolled 10-percent owned foreign corporation for the taxable year. Stock in a noncontrolled 10-percent owned foreign corporation is characterized as in the separate category described in section 904(d)(4)(C)(ii) in the hands of any shareholder with respect to whom look-through treatment is not substantiated. *See also* § 1.904-5(c)(4)(iii)(B). In the case of a noncontrolled 10-percent owned foreign corporation that is a passive foreign investment company with respect to a shareholder, stock in the noncontrolled 10-percent owned foreign corporation is characterized as a passive category asset in the hands of the shareholder if such shareholder does not meet the ownership requirements described in section 904(d)(2)(E)(i)(II).

(d) *Treatment of notes.*—(1) *General rule.*—For further guidance, see § 1.861-12T(d)(1).

(2) *Characterization of related controlled foreign corporation notes.*—The debt of a controlled foreign corporation is characterized in the same manner as the interest income derived from that debt obligation. See §§ 1.904-4 and 1.904-5(c)(2) for rules treating interest income as income in a separate category.

(e) *Portfolio securities that constitute inventory or generate primarily gains.*—For further guidance, see § 1.861-12T(e).

(f) *Assets connected with capitalized, deferred, or disallowed interest.*—(1) *In general.*—In the case of any asset in connection with which interest expense accruing during a taxable year is capitalized, deferred, or disallowed under any provision of the Code, the value of the asset for allocation and apportionment purposes is reduced by the principal amount of indebtedness the interest on which is so capitalized, deferred, or disallowed. Assets are connected with debt (the interest on which is capitalized, deferred, or disallowed) only if using the debt proceeds to acquire or produce the asset causes the interest to be capitalized, deferred, or disallowed.

(2) *Examples.*—The following examples illustrate the application of paragraph (f)(1) of this section.

(i) *Example 1: Capitalized interest under section 263A.*—(A) *Facts.* X is a domestic corporation that uses the tax book value method of apportionment. X has $1,000x of indebtedness and incurs $100x of interest expense. Using $800x of the $1,000x debt proceeds to produce tangible property, X capitalizes $80x of interest expense under the rules of section 263A. X deducts the remaining $20x of interest expense.

(B) *Analysis.* Because interest on $800x of debt is capitalized under section 263A by reason of the use of debt proceeds to produce the tangible property, $800x of the principal amount of X's debt is connected to the tangible property under paragraph (f)(1) of this section. Therefore, for purposes of apportioning the remaining $20x of X's interest expense, the adjusted basis of the tangible property is reduced by $800x.

(ii) *Example 2: Disallowed interest under section 163(l).*—(A) *Facts.* X, a domestic corporation, owns 100% of the stock of Y, a domestic corporation. X and Y file a consolidated return and use the tax book value method of apportionment. In Year 1, X makes a loan of $1,000x to Y (Loan A) and Y then uses the Loan A proceeds to acquire in a cash purchase all the stock of a foreign corporation, Z. Interest on Loan A is payable in U.S. dollars or, at the option of Y, in stock of Z.

(B) *Analysis.* Under section 163(l), Loan A is a disqualified debt instrument because interest on Loan A is payable at the option of Y in stock of a related party to Y. Because Loan A is a disqualified debt instrument, section 163(l)(1) disallows Y's interest deduction for interest payable on Loan A. However, the value of the Z stock is not reduced under paragraph (f)(1) of this section because the use of the Loan A proceeds to acquire the stock of Z is not the cause of Y's interest deduction being disallowed. Rather, the Loan A terms allowing interest to be paid in stock of Z is the cause of Y's interest deduction being disallowed under section 163(l). Therefore, no adjustment is made to Y's adjusted basis in the stock of Z for purposes of allocating the interest expense of X and Y.

(g) *Special rules for FSCs.*—For further guidance, see § 1.861-12T(g) through (j).

(h) [Reserved]

(i) [Reserved]

(j) [Reserved]

(k) *Applicability date.*—(1) Except as provided in paragraph (k)(2) of this section, this section applies to taxable years that both begin after December 31, 2017, and end on or after December 4, 2018.

(2) Paragraph (f) of this section applies to taxable years that end on or after December 16, 2019. For taxable years that both begin after December 31, 2017, and end on or after December 4, 2018, and before December 16, 2019, see § 1.861-12T(f) as contained in 26 CFR part 1 revised as of April 1, 2019. [Reg. § 1.861-12.]

□ [*T.D. 9452, 6-10-2009. Amended by T.D. 9866, 6-14-2019, T.D. 9882, 12-16-2019 and T.D. 9922, 11-2-2020.*]

§ 1.861-12T. Characterization rules and adjustments for certain assets (temporary).—(a) *In general.*—For further guidance, see § 1.861-12(a).

(b) *Inventories.*—Inventory must be characterized by reference to the source and character of sales income, or sales receipts in the case of LIFO inventory, from that inventory during the taxable year. If a taxpayer maintains separate inventories for any federal tax purpose, including the rules for establishing pools of inventory items under sections 472 and 474 of the Code, each separate inventory shall be separately characterized in accordance with the previous sentence.

(c) *Treatment of stock.*—(1) *In general.*—Subject to the adjustment and special rules of paragraphs (c) and (e) of this section, stock in a corporation is taken into account in the application of the asset method described in § 1.861-9T(g). However, an affiliated group (as defined in § 1.861-11T(d)) does not take into account the stock of any member in the application of the asset method.

(c)(2)(i)(A) through (C) [Reserved]. For further guidance, see § 1.861-12(c)(2)(i)(A) through (c)(2)(i)(C).

(ii) *10 percent owned corporation defined.*—(A) *In general.*—The term "10 percent owned corporation" means any corporation (domestic or foreign)—

(1) Which is not included within the taxpayer's affiliated group as defined in § 1.861-11T(d)(1) or (6),

(2) In which the members of the taxpayer's affiliated group own directly or indirectly 10 percent or more of the total combined voting power of all classes of the stock entitled to vote, and

(3) Which is taken into account for purposes of apportionment.

(B) *Rule of attribution.*—Stock that is owned by a corporation, partnership, or trust shall be treated as being indirectly owned proportionately by its shareholders, partners, or beneficiaries. For this purpose, a partner's interest in stock held by a partnership shall be determined by reference to the partner's distributive share of partnership income.

(iii) *Earnings and profits of lower-tier corporations taken into account.*—For purposes of the adjustment to the basis of the stock of the 10 percent owned corporation owned by the taxpayer under paragraph (c)(2)(i) of this section, the earnings and profits of that corporation shall include its pro rata share of the earnings and profits (or any deficit therein) of each succeeding lower-tier 10 percent owned corporation. Thus, a first-tier 10 percent owned corporation shall combine with its own earnings and profits its pro rata share of the earnings and profits of all such lower-tier corporations. The affiliated group shall then adjust its basis in the stock of the first-tier corporation by its pro rata share of the total combined earnings and profits of the first-tier and the lower-tier corporations. In the case of a 10 percent owned corporation whose tax year does not conform to that of the taxpayer, the taxpayer shall include the annual earnings and profits of such 10 percent owned corporation for the tax year ending within the tax year of the taxpayer, whether or not such 10 percent owned corporation is owned directly by the taxpayer.

(iv) *Special rules for foreign corporations in pre-effective date tax years.*—Solely for purposes of determining the adjustment required under paragraph (c)(2)(i) of this section, for tax years beginning after 1912 and before 1987, financial earnings (or losses) of a foreign corporation computed using United States generally accepted accounting principles may be substituted for earnings and profits in making the adjustment required by paragraph (c)(2)(i) of this section. A taxpayer is not required to isolate the financial earnings of a foreign corporation derived or incurred during its period of 10 percent ownership or during the post-1912 taxable years and determine earnings and profits (or deficits) attributable under section 1248 principles to the taxpayer's stock in a 10 percent owned corporation. Instead, the taxpayer may include all historic financial earnings for purposes of this adjustment. If the affiliated group elects to use financial earnings with respect to any foreign corporation, financial earnings must be used by that group with respect to all foreign corporations, except that earnings and profits may in any event be used for controlled foreign corporations for taxable years beginning after 1962 and before 1987. However, if the affiliated group elects to use earnings and profits with respect to any single controlled foreign corporation for the 1963 through 1986 period, such election shall apply with respect to all its controlled foreign corporations.

(v) *Taxpayers using the fair market value method.*—Because the fair market value of any asset which is stock will reflect retained earnings and profits, taxpayers who use the fair market value method shall not adjust stock basis by the amount of retained earnings and profits, as otherwise required by paragraph (c)(2)(i) of this section.

(3) *Characterization of stock of controlled foreign corporations.*—(i) *Operative sections.*—For further guidance, see § 1.861-12(c)(3)(i).

(ii) *Asset method.*—Under the asset method, the taxpayer characterizes the tax book value or fair market value of the stock of a controlled foreign corporation based on an analysis of the assets owned by the controlled foreign corporation during the foreign corporation's taxable year that ends with or within the taxpayer's taxable year. This process is based on the application of § 1.861-9T(g) at the level of the controlled foreign corporation. In the case of a controlled foreign corporation that owns stock in one or more lower-tier controlled foreign corporations in which the United States taxpayer is a United States shareholder, the characterization of the tax book value or the fair market value of the stock of the first-tier controlled foreign corporation to the various separate limitation categories of the affiliated group must take into account the stock in lower-tier corporations. For this purpose, the stock of each such lower-tier corporation shall be characterized by reference to the assets owned during the lower-tier corporation's taxable year that ends during the taxpayer's taxable year. The analysis of assets within a chain of controlled foreign corporations must begin at the lowest-tier controlled foreign corporation and proceed up the chain to the first-tier controlled foreign corporation. For purposes of this paragraph (c), the value of any passive asset to which related person interest is allocated under § 1.904-5(c)(2)(ii) must be reduced by the principal amount of indebtedness on which such interest is incurred. Furthermore, the value of any asset to which interest expense is directly allocated under § 1.861-10T must be reduced as provided in § 1.861-9T(g)(2)(iii). See § 1.861-9T(h)(5) for further guidance concerning characterization of stock in a related person under the fair market value method.

(iii) *Modified gross income method.*—For further guidance, see § 1.861-12(c)(3)(iii).

(4) *[Reserved].*—For further guidance, see § 1.861-12(c)(4).

(d) *Treatment of notes.*—(1) *General rule.*—Subject to the adjustments and special rules of this paragraph (d) and paragraph (e) of this section, all notes held by a taxpayer are taken into account in the application of the asset method described in § 1.861-9T(g). However, the notes of an affiliated corporation are subject to special rules set forth in § 1.861-11T(e). For purposes of this section, the term notes means all interest bearing debt, including debt bearing original issue discount.

(2) *Characterization of related controlled foreign corporation notes.*—For further guidance, see § 1.861(d)(2).

(e) *Portfolio securities that constitute inventory or generate primarily gains.*—Because gain on the sale of securities is sourced by reference to the residence of the seller, a resident of the United States will generally receive domestic source income (and a foreign resident will generally receive foreign source income) upon sale or disposition of securities that otherwise generate foreign source dividends and interest (or domestic source dividends and interest in the case of a foreign resident). Although under paragraphs (c) and (d) of this section securities are characterized by reference to the source and character of dividends and interest, the source and character of income on gain or disposition must also be taken into account for purposes of characterizing portfolio securities if:

(1) The securities constitute inventory in the hands of the holder, or

(2) 80 percent or more of the gross income generated by a taxpayer's entire portfolio of such securities during a taxable year consists of gains.

For this purpose, a portfolio security is a security in any entity other than a controlled foreign corporation with respect to which the taxpayer is a United States shareholder under section 957, a noncontrolled section 902 corporation with respect to the taxpayer, or a 10 percent owned corporation as defined in § 1.861-12(c)(2)(ii). In taking gains into account, a taxpayer must treat all portfolio securities generating foreign source dividends and interest as a single asset and all portfolio securities generating domestic source dividends as a single asset and shall characterize the total value of that asset based on the source of all income and gain generated by those securities in the taxable year.

(f) *Assets connected with capitalized, deferred, or disallowed interest.*—For further guidance, see § 1.861-12(f).

(g) *Special rules for FSCs.*—(1) *Treatment of FSC stock.*—No interest expense shall be allocated or apportioned to stock of a foreign sales corporation ("FSC") to the extent that the FSC stock is attributable to the separate limitation for certain FSC distributions described in section 904(d)(1)(H). FSC stock is considered to be attributable solely to the separate limitation category described in section 904(d)(1)(H) unless the taxpayer can demonstrate that more than 20 percent of the FSC's gross income for the taxable year consists of income other than foreign trading income.

(2) *Treatment of assets that generate foreign trade income.*—Assets of the related supplier that generate foreign trade income must be prorated between assets attributable to foreign source general limitation income and assets attributable to domestic source income in proportion to foreign source general limitation income and domestic source income derived from transactions generating foreign trade income.

(i) *Value of assets attributable to foreign source income.*—The value of assets attributable to foreign source general limitation income is computed by multiplying the value of assets for the taxable year generating foreign trading gross receipts by a fraction:

(A) The numerator of which is foreign source general limitation income for the taxable year derived from transactions giving rise to foreign trading gross receipts, after the application of the limitation provided in section 927(e)(1), and

(B) The denominator of which is total income for the taxable year derived from the transactions giving rise to foreign trading gross receipts.

(ii) *Value of assets attributable to domestic source income.*—The value of assets attributable to domestic source income is computed by subtracting from the total value of assets for the taxable year generating foreign trading gross receipts the value of assets attributable to foreign source general limitation income as computed under paragraph (g)(2)(i) of this section.

(h) *Special rules for DISCs.*—(1) *Treatment of DISC stock.*—No interest shall be allocated or apportioned to stock in a DISC (or stock in a former DISC to the extent that the stock in the former DISC is attributable to the separate limitation category described in section 904(d)(1)(F)).

(2) *Treatment of assets that generate qualified export receipts.*—Assets of the related supplier that generate qualified export receipts must be prorated between assets attributable to foreign source general limitation income and assets attributable to domestic source income in proportion to foreign source general limitation income and domestic source income derived from transactions during the taxable year from transactions generating qualified export receipts.

(i) [Reserved.]

(j) [Reserved]

(k) *Effective/applicability date.*—The rules of this section apply for taxable years beginning after December 31, 1986. [Temporary Reg. § 1.861-12T.]

□ [*T.D.* 8228, 9-9-88. *Amended by T.D.* 9260, 4-20-2006, *T.D.* 9452, 6-10-2009, *T.D.* 9456, 7-31-2009, *T.D.* 9866, 6-14-2019, *T.D.* 9882, 12-16-2019 *and T.D.* 9922, 11-2-2020.]

§ 1.861-13. Special rules for characterization of controlled foreign corporation stock.—(a) *Methodology.*—For purposes of allocating and apportioning deductions for purposes of sections 245A or 904 as the operative section, stock in a controlled foreign corporation owned directly or indirectly through a partnership or other pass-through entity by a United States shareholder is characterized by the United States shareholder under the rules described in this section. In general, paragraphs (a)(1) through (5) of this section characterize the stock of the controlled foreign corporation as an asset in the various statutory groupings and residual grouping based on the type of income that the stock of the controlled foreign corporation generates, has generated, or may reasonably be expected to generate when the income is included by the United States shareholder.

(1) *Step 1: Characterize stock as generating income in statutory groupings under the asset or modified gross income method.*—(i) *Asset method.*—A United States shareholder of a controlled foreign corporation that apportions its interest expense on the basis of assets must characterize stock of the controlled foreign corporation using the asset method described in § 1.861-12T(c)(3)(ii) to assign the assets of the controlled foreign corporation to the statutory groupings described in paragraphs (a)(1)(i)(A)(*1*) through (*10*) and (a)(1)(i)(B) of this section. If the controlled foreign corporation owns stock in a lower-tier noncontrolled 10-percent owned foreign corporation, the assets of the lower-tier noncontrolled 10-percent owned foreign corporation are assigned to a gross subpart F income grouping to the extent such assets generate income that, if distributed to the controlled foreign corporation, would be gross subpart F income of the controlled foreign corporation. *See also* § 1.861-12(c)(4).

(A) *General and passive categories.*—Within each of the controlled foreign corporation's general category and passive category, each of the following subgroups within each category is a separate statutory grouping—

(*1*) Foreign source gross tested income;

(*2*) For each applicable treaty, U.S. source gross tested income that, when taken into account by a United States shareholder under section 951A, is resourced in the hands of the United States shareholder (*resourced gross tested income*);

(*3*) U.S. source gross tested income not described in paragraph (a)(1)(i)(A)(2) of this section;

(*4*) Foreign source gross subpart F income;

(*5*) For each applicable treaty, U.S. source gross subpart F income that, when included by a United States shareholder under section 951(a)(1), is resourced in the hands of the United States shareholder (*resourced gross subpart F income*);

(*6*) U.S. source gross subpart F income not described in paragraph (a)(1)(i)(A)(5) of this section;

(*7*) Foreign source gross section 245(a)(5) income;

(*8*) U.S. source gross section 245(a)(5) income;

(*9*) Any other foreign source gross income (*specified foreign source general category gross income* or *specified foreign source passive category gross income*, as the case may be); and

(*10*) Any other U.S. source gross income (*specified U.S. source general category gross income* or *specified U.S. source passive category gross income*, as the case may be).

(B) *Section 901(j) income.*—For each country described in section 901(j), all gross income from sources in that country.

(ii) *Modified gross income method.*—A United States shareholder of a controlled foreign corporation that apportions its interest expense on the basis of modified gross income must characterize stock of the controlled foreign corporation using the modified gross income method under § 1.861-12(c)(3)(iii) to assign the modified gross income of the controlled foreign corporation to the statutory groupings described in paragraphs (a)(1)(i)(A)(*1*) through (*10*) and (a)(1)(i)(B) of this section. For purposes of this paragraph (a)(1)(ii), the rules described in §§ 1.861-12(c)(3)(iii) and 1.861-9T(j)(2) apply to combine gross income in a statutory grouping that is earned by the controlled foreign corporation with gross income of lower-tier controlled foreign corporations that is in the same statutory grouping. For example, foreign source general category gross tested income (net of interest expense) earned by the controlled foreign corporation is combined with its pro rata share of the foreign source general category gross tested income (net of interest expense) of lower-tier controlled foreign corporations. If the controlled foreign corporation owns stock in a lower-tier noncontrolled 10-percent owned foreign corporation, gross income of the lower-tier noncontrolled 10-percent owned foreign corporation is assigned to a gross subpart F income grouping to the extent that the income, if distributed to the upper-tier controlled foreign corporation, would be gross subpart F income of the upper-tier controlled foreign corporation. *See also* § 1.861-12(c)(4).

(2) *Step 2: Assign stock to the section 951A category.*—A controlled foreign corporation is not treated as earning section 951A category income. The portion of the value of the stock of the controlled foreign corporation that is assigned to the section 951A category (as defined in § 1.904-4(g)) equals the value of the portion of the stock of the controlled foreign corporation that is assigned to the foreign source gross tested income statutory groupings within the general category (*general category gross tested income stock*) multiplied by the United States shareholder's inclusion percentage. Under § 1.861-8(d)(2)(ii)(C)(*2*)(*ii*), a portion of the value of stock assigned to the section 951A category may be treated as an exempt asset. The portion of the general category gross tested income stock that is not characterized as a section 951A category asset remains a general category asset and may result in expenses being disregarded under section 904(b)(4). *See* paragraph (a)(5)(ii) of this section and § 1.904(b)-3. No portion of the passive category gross tested income stock or U.S. source gross tested income stock is assigned to the section 951A category.

(3) *Step 3: Assign stock to a treaty category.*—(i) *Inclusions under section 951A(a).*—The portion of the value of the stock of the controlled foreign corporation that is assigned to a particular treaty category due to an inclusion of U.S. source income under section 951A(a) that was resourced under a particular treaty equals the value of the portion of the stock of the controlled foreign corporation that is assigned to the resourced gross tested income statutory grouping within each of the controlled foreign corporation's general or passive categories (*resourced gross tested income stock*) multiplied by the United States shareholder's inclusion percentage. Under § 1.861-8(d)(2)(ii)(C)(*2*)(*ii*), a portion of the value of stock assigned to a particular treaty category by reason of this paragraph (a)(3)(i) may be treated as an exempt asset. The portion of the resourced gross tested income stock that is not characterized as a treaty category asset remains a U.S. source general or passive category asset, as the case may be, that is in the residual grouping and may result in expenses being disregarded under section 904(b)(4) for purposes of determining entire taxable income under section 904(a). *See* paragraph (a)(5)(iv) of this section and § 1.904(b)-3.

(ii) *Inclusions under section 951(a)(1).*—The portion of the value of the stock of the controlled foreign corporation that is assigned to a particular treaty category due to an inclusion of U.S. source income under section 951(a)(1) that was resourced under a treaty equals the value of the portion of the stock of the controlled foreign corporation that is assigned to the resourced gross subpart F income statutory grouping within each of the controlled foreign corporation's general category or passive category.

(4) *Step 4: Aggregate stock within each separate category and assign stock to the residual grouping.*—The portions of the value of stock of the controlled foreign corporation assigned to foreign source statutory groupings that were not specifically assigned to the section 951A category under paragraph (a)(2) of this section (Step 2) are aggregated within the general category and the passive category to characterize the stock as general category stock and passive category stock, respectively. The portions of the value of stock of the controlled foreign corporation assigned to U.S. source statutory groupings that were not specifically assigned to a particular treaty category under

paragraph (a)(3) of this section (Step 3) are aggregated to characterize the stock as U.S. source category stock, which is in the residual grouping. Stock assigned to the separate category for income described in section 901(j)(1) remains in that category.

(5) *Step 5: Determine section 245A and non-section 245A subgroups for each separate category and U.S. source category.*—(i) *In general.*—In the case of stock of a controlled foreign corporation that is held directly or indirectly through a partnership or other pass-through entity by a United States shareholder that is a domestic corporation, stock of the controlled foreign corporation that is general category stock, passive category stock, and U.S. source category stock is subdivided between a section 245A subgroup and a non-section 245A subgroup under paragraphs (a)(5)(ii) through (v) of this section for purposes of applying section 904(b)(4) and § 1.904(b)-3(c). Each subgroup is treated as a statutory grouping under § 1.861-8(a)(4) for purposes of allocating and apportioning deductions under §§ 1.861-8 through 1.861-14T and 1.861-17 in applying section 904 as the operative section. Deductions apportioned to each section 245A subgroup are disregarded under section 904(b)(4). *See* § 1.904(b)-3. Deductions apportioned to the statutory groupings for gross section 245(a)(5) income are not disregarded under section 904(b)(4); however, a portion of the stock assigned to those groupings is treated as exempt under § 1.861-8T(d)(2)(ii)(B).

(ii) *Section 245A subgroup of general category stock.*—The portion of the general category stock of the controlled foreign corporation that is assigned to the section 245A subgroup of the general category equals the value of the general category gross tested income stock of the controlled foreign corporation that is not assigned to the section 951A category under paragraph (a)(2) of this section (Step 2), plus the value of the portion of the stock of the controlled foreign corporation that is assigned to the specified foreign source general category gross income statutory grouping.

(iii) *Section 245A subgroup of passive category stock.*—The portion of passive category stock of the controlled foreign corporation that is assigned to the section 245A subcategory of the passive category equals the sum of—

(A) The value of the portion of the stock of the controlled foreign corporation that is assigned to the gross tested income statutory grouping within foreign source passive category income multiplied by a percentage equal to 100 percent minus the United States shareholder's inclusion percentage for passive category gross tested income; and

(B) The value of the portion of the stock of the controlled foreign corporation that was assigned to the specified foreign source passive category gross income statutory grouping.

(iv) *Section 245A subgroup of U.S. source category stock.*—The portion of U.S. source category stock of the controlled foreign corporation that is assigned to the section 245A subgroup of the U.S. source category equals the sum of—

(A) The value of the portion of the stock of the controlled foreign corporation that is assigned to the U.S. source general category gross tested income statutory grouping multiplied by a percentage equal to 100 percent minus the United States shareholder's inclusion percentage for the general category;

(B) The value of the portion of the stock of the controlled foreign corporation that is assigned to the U.S. source passive category gross tested income statutory grouping multiplied by a percentage equal to 100 percent minus the United States shareholder's inclusion percentage for the passive category;

(C) The value of the resourced gross tested income stock of the controlled foreign corporation that is not assigned to a particular treaty category under paragraph (a)(3)(i) of this section (Step 3);

(D) The value of the portion of the stock of the controlled foreign corporation that is assigned to the specified U.S. source general category gross income statutory grouping; and

(E) The value of the portion of the stock of the controlled foreign corporation that is assigned to the specified U.S. source passive category gross income statutory grouping.

(v) *Non-section 245A subgroup.*—The value of stock of a controlled foreign corporation that is not assigned to the section 245A subgroup within the general or passive category or the residual grouping is assigned to the non-section 245A subgroup within such category or grouping. The value of stock of a controlled foreign corporation that is assigned to the section 951A category, the separate category for income described in section 901(j)(1), or a particular treaty category is always assigned to a non-section 245A subgroup.

(b) *Definitions.*—This paragraph (b) provides definitions that apply for purposes of this section.

(1) *Gross section 245(a)(5) income.*—The term *gross section 245(a)(5) income* means all items of gross income described in section 245(a)(5)(A) and (B).

(2) *Gross subpart F income.*—The term *gross subpart F income* means all items of gross income that are taken into account by a controlled foreign corporation in determining its subpart F income under section 952, except for items of gross income described in section 952(a)(5).

(3) *Gross tested income.*—The term *gross tested income* has the meaning provided in § 1.951A-2(c)(1).

(4) *Inclusion percentage.*—The term *inclusion percentage* has the meaning provided in § 1.960-2(c)(2).

(5) *Separate category.*—The term *separate category* has the meaning provided in § 1.904-5(a)(4)(v).

(6) *Treaty category.*—The term *treaty category* means a category of income earned by a controlled foreign corporation for which section 904(a), (b), and (c) are applied separately as a result of income being resourced under a treaty. See, for example, section 245(a)(10), 865(h), or 904(h)(10). A United States shareholder may have multiple treaty categories for amounts of income resourced by the United States shareholder under a treaty. *See* § 1.904-5(m)(7).

(7) *U.S. source category.*—The term *U.S. source category* means the aggregate of U.S. source income in each separate category listed in section 904(d)(1).

(c) *Examples.*—The following examples illustrate the application of the rules in this section.

(1) *Example 1: Asset method*—(i) *Facts*—(A) USP, a domestic corporation, directly owns all of the stock of a controlled foreign corporation, CFC1. The tax book value of CFC1's stock is $20,000x. USP uses the asset method described in § 1.861-12T(c)(3)(ii) to characterize the stock of CFC1. USP's inclusion percentage is 70%.

(B) CFC1 owns the following assets with the following values as determined under §§ 1.861-9(g)(2) and 1.861-9T(g)(3): assets that generate income described in the foreign source gross tested income statutory grouping within the general category ($4,000x), assets that generate income described in the foreign source gross subpart F income statutory grouping within the general category ($1,000x), assets that generate specified foreign source general category gross income ($3,000x), and assets that generate income described in the foreign source gross subpart F income statutory grouping within the passive category ($2,000x).

(C) CFC1 also owns all of the stock of CFC2, a controlled foreign corporation. The tax book value of CFC1's stock in CFC2 is $6,000x. CFC2 owns the following assets with the following values as determined under §§ 1.861-9(g)(2) and 1.861-9T(g)(3): assets that generate income described in the foreign source gross subpart F income statutory grouping within the general category ($2,250x) and assets that generate specified foreign source general category gross income ($750x).

(ii) *Analysis*—(A) *Step 1*—(*1*) *Characterization of CFC2 stock.* CFC2 has total assets of $3,000x, $2,250x of which are in the foreign source gross subpart F income statutory grouping within the general category and $750x of which are in the specified foreign source general category gross income statutory grouping. Accordingly, CFC2's stock is characterized as $4,500x ($2,250x/$3,000x x $6,000x) in the foreign source gross subpart F income statutory grouping within the general category and $1,500x ($750x/$3,000x x $6,000x) in the specified foreign source general category gross income statutory grouping.

(*2*) *Characterization of CFC1 stock.* CFC1 has total assets of $16,000x, $4,000x of which are in the foreign source gross tested income statutory grouping within the general category, $5,500x of which are in the foreign source gross subpart F income statutory grouping within the general category (including the portion of CFC2 stock assigned to that statutory grouping), $4,500x of which are in the specified foreign source gross general category income statutory grouping (including the portion of CFC2 stock assigned to that statutory grouping), and $2,000x of which are in the foreign source gross subpart F income statutory grouping within the passive category. Accordingly, CFC1's stock is characterized as $5,000x ($4,000x/$16,000x x $20,000x) in the foreign source gross tested income statutory grouping within the general category, $6,875x ($5,500x/$16,000x x $20,000x) in the foreign source gross subpart F income statutory grouping within the general category, $5,625x ($4,500x/$16,000x x $20,000x) in the specified foreign source gross general category income statutory grouping, and $2,500x ($2,000x/$16,000x x $20,000x) in the foreign source gross subpart F income statutory grouping within the passive category.

(B) *Step 2*. The value of the portion of the stock of CFC1 that is general category gross tested income stock is $5,000x. USP's inclusion percentage is 70%. Accordingly, under paragraph (a)(2) of this section, $3,500x of the stock of CFC1 is assigned to the section 951A category and a portion thereof may be treated as an exempt asset under § 1.861-8(d)(2)(ii)(C)(2)(*ii*). The remainder, $1,500x, remains a general category asset.

(C) *Step 3*. No portion of the stock of CFC1 is resourced gross tested income stock or assigned to the resourced gross subpart F income statutory grouping in any treaty category. Accordingly, no portion of the stock of CFC1 is assigned to a treaty category under paragraph (a)(3) of this section.

(D) *Step 4—(1) General category stock*. The total value of the portion of the stock of CFC1 that is general category stock is $14,000x, which is equal to $1,500x (the value of the portion of the general category stock of CFC1 that was not assigned to the section 951A category in paragraph (c)(1)(ii)(B) of this section (Step 2)) plus $6,875x (the value of the portion of the stock of CFC1 assigned to the foreign source gross subpart F income statutory grouping within the general category) plus $5,625x (the value of the portion of the stock of CFC1 assigned to the specified foreign source gross income statutory grouping within the general category).

(2) *Passive category stock*. The total value of the portion of the stock of CFC1 that is passive category stock is $2,500x.

(3) *U.S source category stock*. No value of the portion of the stock of CFC1 is U.S. source category stock.

(E) *Step 5—(1) General category stock*. Under paragraph (a)(5)(ii) of this section, the value of the portion of the stock of CFC1 assigned to the section 245A subgroup of general category stock is $7,125x, which is equal to $1,500x (the value of the portion of the general category stock of CFC1 that was not assigned to the section 951A category in paragraph (c)(1)(ii)(B) of this section (Step 2)) plus $5,625x (the value of the portion of the stock of CFC1 assigned to the specified foreign source general category gross income statutory grouping). Under paragraph (a)(5)(v) of this section, the remainder of the general category stock of CFC1, $6,875x, is assigned to the non-section 245A subgroup of general category stock.

(2) *Passive category stock*. No portion of the passive category stock of CFC1 is in the foreign source gross tested income statutory grouping or the specified foreign source passive category gross income statutory grouping. Accordingly, under paragraph (a)(5)(iii) of this section, no value of the portion of the stock of CFC1 is assigned to the section 245A subgroup of passive category stock. Under paragraph (a)(5)(v) of this section, the passive category stock of CFC1, $2,500x is assigned to the non-section 245A subgroup of passive category stock.

(3) *Section 951A category stock*. Under paragraph (a)(5)(v) of this section, all of the section 951A category stock, $3,500x, is assigned to the non-section 245A subgroup of section 951A category stock.

(F) *Summary*. For purpose of the allocation and apportionment of expenses, $14,000x of the stock of CFC1 is characterized as general category stock, $7,125x of which is in the section 245A subgroup and $6,875x of which is in the non-section 245A subgroup; $2,500x of the stock of CFC1 is characterized as passive category stock, all of which is in the non-section 245A subgroup; and $3,500x of the stock of CFC1 is characterized as section 951A category stock, all of which is in the non-section 245A subgroup.

(2) *Example 2: Asset method with noncontrolled 10-percent owned foreign corporation*—(i) *Facts*. The facts are the same as in paragraph (c)(1)(i) of this section (the facts in *Example 1*), except that CFC1 does not own CFC2 and instead owns 20% of the stock of FC2, a foreign corporation that is a noncontrolled 10-percent owned foreign corporation. The tax book value of CFC1's stock in FC2 is $6,000x. FC2 owns assets with the following values as determined under §§ 1.861-9(g)(2) and 1.861-9T(g)(3): assets that generate specified foreign source general category gross income ($3,000x). All of the assets of FC2 generate income that, if distributed to CFC1 as a dividend, would be foreign source gross subpart F income in the general category to CFC1.

(ii) *Analysis*—(A) *Step 1—(1) Characterization of FC2 stock*. All of the assets of FC2 generate income that, if distributed to CFC1, would be foreign source gross subpart F income in the general category to CFC1. Accordingly, under paragraph (a)(1)(i) of this section, all of CFC1's stock in FC2 ($6,000x) is characterized as in the foreign source gross subpart F income statutory grouping within the general category.

(2) *Characterization of CFC1 stock*. CFC1 has total assets of $16,000x, $4,000x of which are in the foreign source gross tested income statutory grouping within the general category, $7,000x of which are in the foreign source gross subpart F income statutory grouping within the general category (including the FC2 stock assigned to that statutory grouping), $3,000x of which are in the specified foreign source general category gross income statutory grouping, and $2,000x of which are in the foreign source gross subpart F income statutory grouping within the passive category. Accordingly, CFC1's stock is characterized as $5,000x ($4,000x/$16,000x x $20,000x) in the foreign source gross tested income statutory grouping within the general category, $8,750x ($7,000x/$16,000x x $20,000x) in the foreign source gross subpart F income statutory grouping within the general category, $3,750x ($3,000x/$16,000x x $20,000x) in the specified foreign source general category gross income statutory grouping, and $2,500x ($2,000x/$16,000x x $20,000x) in the foreign source gross subpart F income statutory grouping within the passive category.

(B) *Step 2*. The analysis is the same as in paragraph (c)(1)(ii)(B) of this section (the analysis of Step 2 in *Example 1*).

(C) *Step 3*. The analysis is the same as in paragraph (c)(1)(ii)(C) of this section (the analysis of Step 3 in *Example 1*).

(D) *Step 4—(1) General category stock*. The total value of the portion of the stock of CFC1 that is general category stock is $14,000x, which is equal to $1,500x (the value of the portion of the general category stock of CFC1 that was not assigned to the section 951A category in paragraph (c)(2)(ii)(B) of this section (Step 2)) plus $3,750x (the value of the portion of the stock of CFC1 assigned to the specified foreign source gross income statutory grouping within the general category general category) plus $8,750x (the value of the portion of the stock of CFC1 assigned to the foreign source gross subpart F income statutory grouping within the general category).

(2) *Passive category stock*. The analysis is the same as in paragraph (c)(1)(ii)(D)(2) of this section (the analysis of Step 4 in *Example 1*).

(E) *Step 5—(1) General category stock*. Under paragraph (a)(5)(ii) of this section, the value of the stock of CFC1 assigned to the section 245A subgroup of general category stock is $5,250x, which is equal to $1,500x (the value of the portion of the general category stock of CFC1 that was not assigned to the section 951A category in paragraph (c)(2)(ii)(B) of this section (Step 2)) plus $3,750x (the value of the portion of the stock of CFC1 assigned to the specified foreign source general category gross income statutory grouping). Under paragraph (a)(5)(v) of this section, the remainder of the general category stock of CFC1, $8,750x, is assigned to the non-section 245A subgroup of general category stock.

(2) *Passive category stock*. The analysis is the same as in paragraph (c)(1)(ii)(E)(2) of this section (the analysis of Step 5 in *Example 1*).

(3) *Section 951A category stock*. The analysis is the same as in paragraph (c)(1)(ii)(E)(3) of this section (the analysis of Step 5 in *Example 1*).

(F) *Summary*. For purpose of the allocation and apportionment of expenses, $14,000x of the stock of CFC1 is characterized as general category stock, $5,250x of which is in the section 245A subgroup and $8,750x of which is in the non-section 245A subgroup; $2,500x of the stock of CFC1 is characterized as passive category stock, all of which is in the non-section 245A subgroup; and $3,500x of the stock of CFC1 is characterized as section 951A category stock, all of which is in the non-section 245A subgroup.

(3) *Example 3: Modified gross income method*—(i) *Facts*—(A) USP, a domestic corporation, directly owns all of the stock of a controlled foreign corporation, CFC1. The tax book value of CFC1's stock is $100,000x. CFC1 owns all of the stock of CFC2, a controlled foreign corporation. USP uses the modified gross income method described in § 1.861-12(c)(3)(iii) to characterize the stock in CFC1. USP's inclusion percentage is 100%.

(B) CFC1 earns $1,500x of foreign source gross tested income within the general category and $500x of foreign source gross subpart F income within the passive category. CFC1 incurs $1,000x of interest expense.

(C) CFC2 earns $3,000x of foreign source gross tested income within the general category, $2,000x of foreign source gross subpart F income within the general category, and $1,000x of specified foreign source general category gross income. CFC2 incurs $3,000x of interest expense.

(ii) *Analysis*—(A) *Step 1—(1) Determination of CFC2 gross income (net of interest expense)*. CFC2 has total gross income of $6,000x. CFC2's $3,000x of interest expense is apportioned among the statutory groupings of gross income based on the gross income of CFC2 to determine the gross income (net of interest expense) of CFC2 in each statutory grouping. As a result, $1,500x ($3,000x/$6,000x x $3,000x) of interest expense is apportioned to foreign source gross tested income within the general category, $1,000x ($2,000x/$6,000x x

$3,000x) of interest expense is apportioned to foreign source gross subpart F income within the general category, and $500x ($1,000x/ $6,000x x $3,000x) of interest expense is apportioned to specified foreign source general category gross income. Accordingly, CFC2 has the following amounts of gross income (net of interest expense): $1,500x ($3,000x – $1,500x) of foreign source gross tested income within the general category, $1,000x ($2,000x – $1,000x) of foreign source gross subpart F income within the general category, and $500x ($1,000x – $500x) of specified foreign source general category gross income.

(2) *Determination of CFC1 gross income (net of interest expense).* Before including the gross income consisting of subpart F income (net of interest expense) of CFC2, CFC1 has total gross income of $4,000x, including $1500x of CFC2's foreign source gross tested income within the general category and $500x of CFC2's specified foreign source general category gross income which are combined with CFC1's items of gross income under § 1.861-9(j)(2)(ii). CFC1's $1,000x of interest expense is apportioned among the statutory groupings of gross income of CFC1 to determine the gross income (net of interest expense) of CFC1 in each statutory grouping. As a result, $750x ($3,000x/$4,000x x $1,000x) of interest expense is apportioned to foreign source gross tested income within the general category, $125x ($500x/$4,000 x $1,000x) to foreign source gross subpart F income within the passive category, and $125x ($500x/$4,000x x $1,000x) to specified foreign source general category gross income. Accordingly, CFC1 has the following amounts of gross income (net of interest expense) before including the gross income consisting of subpart F income (net of interest expense) of CFC2: $2,250x ($3,000x – $750x) of foreign source gross tested income within the general category, $375x ($500x – $125x) of foreign source gross subpart F income within the passive category, and $375x ($500 – $125x) of specified foreign source general category gross income. After including the gross income consisting of subpart F income (net of interest expense) of CFC2, CFC1 has the following amounts of gross income (net of interest expense): $2,250x of foreign source gross tested income within the general category, $1,000x of foreign source gross subpart F income within the general category, $375x of specified foreign source general category gross income, and $375x of foreign source gross subpart F income within the passive category.

(3) *Characterization of CFC1 stock.* CFC1 is considered to have a total of $4,000x of gross income (net of interest expense) for purposes of characterizing the stock of CFC1. Accordingly, CFC1's stock is characterized as $56,250x ($2,250x/$4,000x x $100,000x) in the foreign source gross tested income statutory grouping within the general category, $25,000x ($1,000x/$4,000x x $100,000x) in the foreign source gross subpart F income statutory grouping within the general category, $9,375x ($375x/$4,000x x $100,000x) in the specified foreign source general category gross income statutory grouping, and $9,375x ($375x/$4,000x x $100,000x) in the foreign source gross subpart F income statutory grouping within the passive category.

(B) *Step 2.* The value of the portion of the stock of CFC1 that is general category gross tested income stock is $56,250x. USP's inclusion percentage is 100%. Accordingly, under paragraph (a)(2) of this section, all of the $56,250x of the stock of CFC1 is assigned to the section 951A category and a portion thereof may be treated as an exempt asset under § 1.861-8(d)(2)(ii)(C)(2)(*ii*).

(C) *Step 3.* No portion of the stock of CFC1 is resourced gross tested income or assigned to the resourced gross subpart F income statutory group in any treaty category. Accordingly, no portion of the stock of CFC1 is assigned to a treaty category under paragraph (a)(3) of this section.

(D) *Step 4*—(1) *General category stock.* The total value of the portion of the stock of CFC1 that is general category stock is $34,375x, which is equal to $25,000x (the value of the portion of the stock of CFC1 assigned to the subpart F income statutory grouping within the general category income statutory grouping) plus $9,375x (the value of the portion of the stock of CFC1 assigned to the specified foreign source general category gross income statutory grouping).

(2) *Passive category stock.* The total value of the portion of the stock of CFC1 that is passive category stock is $9,375x.

(3) *U.S. source category stock.* No value of the portion of the stock of CFC1 is U.S. source category stock.

(E) *Step 5*—(1) *General category stock.* All of the value of the general category gross tested income stock of CFC1 was assigned to the section 951A category in paragraph (c)(3)(ii)(B) of this section (Step 2). Accordingly, under paragraph (a)(5)(ii) of this section, the value of the stock of CFC1 assigned to the section 245A subgroup of general category stock is $9,375x, which is equal to the value of the portion assigned to the specified foreign source general category gross income statutory grouping. Under paragraph (a)(5)(v) of this section, the remainder of the general category stock of CFC1, $25,000x, is assigned to the non-section 245A subgroup of general category stock.

(2) *Passive category stock.* No portion of the passive category stock of CFC1 is in the foreign source gross tested income statutory grouping or the specified foreign source passive category gross income statutory grouping. Accordingly, under paragraph (a)(5)(iii) of this section, no value of the portion of the stock of CFC1 is assigned to the section 245A subgroup. Under paragraph (a)(5)(v) of this section, the passive category stock of CFC1, $9,375x, is assigned to the non-section 245A subgroup of passive category stock.

(3) *Section 951A category stock.* Under paragraph (a)(5)(v) of this section, all of the section 951A category stock, $56,250x, is assigned to the non-section 245A subgroup of section 951A category stock.

(F) *Summary.* For purposes of the allocation and apportionment of expenses, $56,250x of the stock of CFC1 is characterized as section 951A category stock, all of which is in the non-section 245A subgroup; $34,375x of the stock of CFC1 is characterized as general category stock, $9,375x of which is in the section 245A subgroup and $25,000x of which is in the non-section 245A subgroup; and $9,375x of the stock of CFC1 is characterized as passive category stock, all of which is in the non-section 245A subgroup.

(d) *Applicability dates.*—This section applies for taxable years that both begin after December 31, 2017, and end on or after December 4, 2018. [Reg. § 1.861-13.]

☐ [*T.D. 9882, 12-16-2019. Amended by T.D. 9959, 12-28-2021.*]

§ 1.861-14. Special rules for allocating and apportioning certain expenses (other than interest expense) of an affiliated group of corporations.—(a) through (c) [Reserved]. For further guidance, see § 1.861-14T(a) through (c).

(d) *Definition of affiliated group.*—(1) *General rule.*—For purposes of this section, the term *affiliated group* has the same meaning as is given that term by section 1504. Section 1504(a) defines an affiliated group as one or more chains of includible corporations connected through 80% stock ownership with a common parent corporation which is an includible corporation (as defined in section 1504(b)). In the case of a corporation that either becomes or ceases to be a member of the group during the course of the corporation's taxable year, only the expenses incurred by the group member during the period of membership shall be allocated and apportioned as if all members of the group were a single corporation. In this regard, the apportionment factor chosen shall relate only to the period of membership. For example, if apportionment on the basis of assets is chosen, the average amount of assets (tax book value or fair market value) for the taxable year shall be multiplied by a fraction, the numerator of which is the number of months of the corporation's taxable year during which the corporation was a member of the affiliated group, and the denominator of which is the number of months within the corporation's taxable year. If apportionment on the basis of gross income is chosen, only gross income generated during the period of membership shall be taken into account. If apportionment on the basis of units sold or sales receipts is chosen, only units sold or sales receipts during the period of membership shall be taken into account. Expenses incurred by the group member during its taxable year, but not during the period of membership, shall be allocated and apportioned without regard to other members of the group.

(2) [Reserved]

(3) *Inclusion of financial corporations.*—For further guidance, see § 1.861-14T(d)(3) through (4).

(4) [Reserved]

(e) *Expenses to be allocated and apportioned under this section.*—(1) *Expenses not directly allocable to specific income-producing activities or property.*—(i) The expenses that are required to be allocated and apportioned under the rules of this section are expenses that are not directly allocable to specific income-producing activities or property solely of the member of the affiliated group that incurred the expense, including (but not limited to) certain expenses related to research and experimental expenses, supportive functions, deductions under section 250, legal and accounting expenses, and litigation damages awards, prejudgment interest, and settlement payments. Interest expense of members of an affiliated group of corporations is allocated and apportioned under § 1.861-11T and not under the rules of this section. Expenses that are included in inventory costs or that are capitalized are not subject to allocation and apportionment under the rules of this section. In addition, stewardship expenses are not subject to allocation and apportionment under the rules of this section; instead, stewardship expenses of a taxpayer are allocated and apportioned on a separate entity basis without treating members of the affiliated group as a single taxpayer. See § 1.861-8(e)(4)(ii)(A).

(ii) For further guidance, see § 1.861-14T(e)(1)(ii).

(2) *Research and experimental expenditures.*—R&E expenditures (as defined in § 1.861-17(a)) in the case of an affiliated group are allocated and apportioned under the rules of § 1.861-17 as if all members of the affiliated group were a single taxpayer. Thus, R&E expenditures are allocated to all gross intangible income of all members of the affiliated group reasonably connected with the relevant broad SIC code category. If fewer than all members of the affiliated group derive gross intangible income reasonably connected with that relevant broad SIC code category, then such expenditures are apportioned under the rules of this paragraph (e)(2) only among those members, as if those members were a single taxpayer.

(3) *Expenses related to supportive functions.*—For further guidance, see § 1.861-14T(e)(3).

(4) *Section 250 deduction.*—Except as provided in this paragraph (e)(4), the deduction allowed under section 250(a) (the section 250 deduction) to a member of an affiliated group is allocated and apportioned on a separate entity basis under the rules of § 1.861-8(e)(13) and (14). However, the section 250 deduction of a member of a consolidated group is not directly allocable to specific income-producing activities or property solely of the member of the affiliated group that is allowed the deduction. See § 1.1502-50 for rules on applying section 250 and §§ 1.250-1 through 1.250(b)-6 to a member of a consolidated group. In such case, the section 250 deduction is allocated and apportioned as if all members of the consolidated group are treated as a single corporation.

(5) *Legal and accounting fees and expenses; damages awards, prejudgment interest, and settlement payments.*—Legal and accounting fees and expenses, as well as litigation or arbitral damages awards, prejudgment interest, and settlement payments, are allocated and apportioned under the rules of § 1.861-8(e)(5). To the extent that under § 1.861-14T(c)(2) and (e)(1)(ii) such expenses are not directly allocable to specific income-producing activities or property of one or more members of the affiliated group, such expenses must be allocated and apportioned as if all members of the affiliated group were a single corporation. Specifically, such expenses must be allocated to a class of gross income that takes into account the gross income which is generated, has been generated, or is reasonably expected to be generated by the other members of the affiliated group. If the expenses relate to the gross income of fewer than all members of the affiliated group as determined under § 1.861-14T(c)(2), then those expenses must be apportioned under the rules of § 1.861-14T(c)(2), as if those fewer members were a single corporation. Such expenses must be apportioned taking into account the apportionment factors contributed by the members of the group that are treated as a single corporation.

(6) *Charitable contribution expenses.*—A deduction for a charitable contribution by a member of an affiliated group shall be allocated and apportioned under the rules of §§ 1.861-8(e)(12) and 1.861-14T(c)(1).

(f) *Computation of FSC or DISC combined taxable income.*—For further guidance, see § 1.861-14T(f) through (g).

(g) [Reserved]

(h) *Special rule for the allocation and apportionment of section 818(f)(1) items of a life insurance company.*—(1) *In general.*—Except as provided in paragraph (h)(2) of this section, life insurance company items specified in section 818(f)(1) ("section 818(f)(1) items") are allocated and apportioned as if all members of the life subgroup (as defined in § 1.1502-47(b)(8)) were a single corporation ("life subgroup method"). See also § 1.861-8(e)(16) for rules on the allocation of reserve expenses with respect to dividends received by a life insurance company.

(2) *Alternative separate entity treatment.*—A consolidated group may choose not to apply the life subgroup method and may instead allocate and apportion section 818(f)(1) items solely among items of the life insurance company that generated the section 818(f)(1) items ("separate entity method"). A consolidated group indicates its choice to apply the separate entity method by applying this paragraph (h)(2) for purposes of the allocation and apportionment of section 818(f)(1) items on its Federal income tax return filed for its first taxable year to which this section applies. A consolidated group's use of the separate entity method constitutes a binding choice to use the method chosen for that year for all members of the consolidated group and all taxable years of such members thereafter. The choice to use the separate entity method may not be revoked without the prior consent of the Commissioner.

(i) through (j) [Reserved]

(k) *Applicability dates.*—Except as provided in this paragraph (k), this section applies to taxable years beginning after December 31, 2019. Paragraph (h) of this section applies to taxable years beginning on or after December 28, 2021. [Reg. § 1.861-14.]

□ [*T.D.* 8916, 12-29-2000. *Amended by T.D.* 9211, 7-13-2005 *T.D.* 9882, 12-16-2019, *T.D.* 9922, 11-2-2020 *and T.D.* 9959, 12-28-2021.]

§ 1.861-14T. Special rules for allocating and apportioning certain expenses (other than interest expense) of an affiliated group of corporations (temporary).—(a) *In general.*—Section 1.861-11T provides special rules for allocating and apportioning interest expense of an affiliated group of corporations. The rules of this § 1.861-14T also relate to affiliated groups of corporations and implement section 864(e)(6), which requires affiliated group allocation and apportionment of expenses other than interest which are not directly allocable and apportionable to any specific income producing activity or property. In general, the rules of this section apply to taxable years beginning after December 31, 1986. Paragraph (b) of this section describes the scope of the application of the rule for the allocation and apportionment of such expenses of affiliated groups of corporations. Such rule is then set forth in paragraph (c) of this section. Paragraph (d) of this section contains the definition of the term "affiliated group" for purposes of this section. Paragraph (e) of this section describes the expenses subject to allocation and apportionment under the rules of this section. Paragraph (f) of this section provides rules concerning the affiliated group allocation and apportionment of such expenses in computing the combined taxable income of a FSC or DISC and its related supplier. Paragraph (g) of this section describes the treatment of losses caused by apportionment of such expenses in the case of an affiliated group that does not file a consolidated return. Paragraph (h) of this section provides rules concerning the treatment of the reserve expenses of a life insurance company. Paragraph (j) of this section provides examples illustrating the application of this section.

(b) *Scope.*—(1) *Application of section 864(e)(6).*—Section 864(e)(6) and this section apply to the computation of taxable income for purposes of computing separate limitations on the foreign tax credit under section 904. Section 864(e)(6) and this section also apply in connection with section 907 to determine reductions in the amount allowed as a foreign tax credit under section 901. Section 864(e)(6) and this section also apply to the computation of the combined taxable income of the related supplier and a foreign sales corporation (FSC) (under sections 921 through 927) as well as the combined taxable income of the related supplier and a domestic international sales corporation (DISC) (under sections 991 through 997).

(2) *Nonapplication of section 864(e)(6).*—Section 864(e)(6) and this section do not apply to the computation of subpart F income of controlled foreign corporations (under sections 951 through 964) or the computation of effectively connected taxable income of foreign corporations.

(3) *Application of section 864(e)(6) to the computation of combined taxable income of a possessions corporation and its affiliates.*—[Reserved.]

(c) *General rule for affiliated corporations.*—(1) *General rule.*—(i) Except as otherwise provided in paragraph (c)(2) of this section, the taxable income of each member of an affiliated group within each statutory grouping shall be determined by allocating and apportioning the expenses described in paragraph (e) of this section of each member according to apportionment fractions which are computed as if all members of such group were a single corporation. For purposes of determining these apportionment fractions, any interaffiliate transactions or property that are duplicative with respect to the measure of apportionment chosen shall be eliminated. For example, in the application of an asset method of apportionment, stock in affiliated corporations shall not be taken into account, and loans between members of an affiliated group shall be treated in accordance with the rules of § 1.861-11T(e). Similarly, in the application of a gross income method of apportionment, interaffiliate dividends and interest, gross income from sales or services, and other interaffiliate gross income shall be eliminated. Likewise, in the application of a method of apportionment based on units sold or sales receipts, interaffiliate sales shall be eliminated.

(ii) Except as otherwise provided in this section, the rules of § 1.861-8T apply to the allocation and apportionment of the expenses described in paragraph (e) of this section. Thus, allocation under this paragraph (c) is accomplished by determining, with respect to each expense described in paragraph (e), the class of gross income to which the expense is definitely related and then allocating the deduction to such class of gross income. For this purpose, the gross income of all members of the affiliated group must be taken in account. Then, the expense is apportioned by attributing the expense to gross income (within the class to which the expense has been allocated) which is in the statutory grouping and to gross income (within the class) which is in the residual grouping. Section 1.861-8T(c)(1) identifies a number of factors upon which apportionment may be based, such as comparison of units sold, gross sales or receipts, assets used, or gross income. The apportionment method chosen must be applied consistently by each member of the affiliated group in apportioning the expense when more than one member incurred the expense or when members incurred separate portions of the expense. The apportionment fraction must take into account the apportionment factors contributed by all members of the affiliated group. In the case of an affiliated group of corporations that files a consolidated return, consolidated foreign tax credit limitations are computed for the group in accordance with the rules of § 1.1502-4. For purposes of this section the term "taxpayer" refers to the affiliated group (regardless of whether the group files a consolidated return), rather than to the separate members thereof.

(2) *Expenses relating to fewer than all members.*—An expense relates to fewer than all members of an affiliated group if the expense is allocable under paragraph (e)(1) of this section to gross income of at least one member other than the member that incurred the expense but fewer than all members of the affiliated group. The taxable income of the member that incurred the expense shall be determined by apportioning that expense under the rules of paragraph (c)(1) of this section as if the members of the affiliated group that derive gross income to which such expense is allocable under paragraph (e)(1) were treated as a single corporation.

(3) *Prior application of section 482.*—The rules of this section do not supersede the application of section 482 and the regulations thereunder. Section 482 may be applied effectively to deny a deduction for an expense to one member of an affiliated group and to allow a deduction for that expense to another member of the affiliated group. In cases to which section 482 is applied, expenses shall be reallocated and reapportioned under section 864(e)(6) and this section after taking into account the application of section 482.

(d)(1) and (2) [Reserved]. For further guidance, see § 1.861-14(d)(1) and (2).

(3) *Inclusion of financial corporations.*—For purposes of this section, in the case of an affiliated group (as defined in paragraph (d)(1) of this section), any members that constitute financial corporations as defined in § 1.861-11T(d)(4)(ii) shall be treated as members of the affiliated group. The rule of § 1.861-11T(d)(4)(i), which treats such financial corporations as a separate affiliated group, applies only for purposes of allocation and apportionment of interest expense and does not apply to the allocation and apportionment of other expenses under this section.

(4) *Treatment of life insurance companies subject to taxation under section 801.*—A life insurance company that is subject to taxation under section 801 shall be considered to constitute a member of the affiliated group composed of companies not taxable under section 801 only if a parent corporation so elects under section 1504(c)(2)(A) of the Code.

(e) *Expenses to be allocated and apportioned under this section.*—(1) *Expenses not directly traceable to specific income producing activities or property.*—(i) For further guidance, see § 1.861-14(e)(1)(i).

(ii) An item of expense is not considered to be directly allocable to specific income producing activities or property solely of the member incurring the expense if, were all members of the affiliated group treated as a single corporation, the expense would not be considered definitely related, within the meaning of § 1.861-8T(b)(2), only to a class of gross income derived solely by the member which actually incurred the expense. Furthermore, the expense is presumed not to be definitely related only to a class of gross income derived solely by the member incurring the expense (and is, therefore, presumed not to be directly allocable to specific income producing activities or property of that member) unless the taxpayer is able affirmatively to establish otherwise. As provided in paragraph (c)(1) of this section, expenses described in this paragraph (e)(1) generally shall be apportioned by the member incurring the expense according to apportionment fractions computed as if all members of the affiliated group were a single corporation. Under paragraph (c)(2) of this section, however, an expense shall be apportioned according to apportionment fractions computed as if only some (but fewer than all) members of the affiliated group were a single corporation, if the expense is considered allocable to gross income of at least one member other than the member incurring the expense but fewer than all members of the affiliated group. An item of expense shall be considered to be allocable to gross income of fewer than all members of the group if, were all members of the affiliated group treated as a single corporation, the expense would not be considered definitely related within the meaning of § 1.861-8T(b)(2) to gross income derived by all members of the group. In such case, the expense shall be considered allocable, for purposes of paragraph (c)(2) of this section, to gross income of those members of the group that generated (or could reasonably be expected to generate) the gross income to which the expense would be considered definitely related if the group were treated as a single corporation.

(2) *Research and experimental expenses.*—(i) For further guidance, see § 1.861-14(e)(2)(i) and (ii).

(ii) [Reserved]

(3) *Expenses related to supportive functions.*—Expenses which are supportive in nature (such as overhead, general and administrative, supervisory expenses, advertising, marketing, and other sales expenses) are to be allocated and apportioned in accordance with the rules of § 1.861-8T(b)(3). To the extent that such expenses are not directly allocable under paragraph (e)(1)(ii) of this section to specific income producing activities or property of the member of the affiliated group that incurred the expense, such expenses must be allocated and apportioned as if all members of the affiliated group were a single corporation in accordance with the rules of paragraph (c) of this section. Specifically, such expenses must be allocated to a class of gross income that takes into account gross income that is generated, has been generated, or could reasonably have been expected to have been generated by the members of the affiliated group. If the expenses relate to the gross income of fewer than all members of the affiliated group as determined under paragraph (c)(2) of this section, then those expenses must be apportioned under the rules of paragraph (c)(2) of this section, as if those fewer members were a single corporation. See *Example* (3) of paragraph (j) of this section. Such expenses must be apportioned between statutory and residual groupings of income within the appropriate class of gross income by reference to the apportionment factors contributed by the members of the affiliated group that are treated as a single corporation.

(4) *Section 250 deduction.*—For further guidance, see § 1.861-14(e)(4).

(5) *Legal and accounting fees and expenses; damages awards, prejudgment interest, and settlement payments.*—For further guidance, see § 1.861-14(e)(5).

(f) *Computation of FSC or DISC combined taxable income.*—In the computation under the pricing rules of sections 925 and 994 of the combined taxable income of any FSC or DISC and its related supplier which are members of an affiliated group, the combined taxable income of such FSC or DISC and its related supplier shall be reduced by the portion of the expenses of the affiliated group described in paragraph (e) of this section that is incurred in connection with export sales involving that FSC or DISC. In order to determine the portion of the expenses of the affiliated group that is incurred in connection with export sales by or through a FSC or DISC, the portion of the total of the apportionment factor chosen that relates to the generation of that export income must be determined. Thus, if gross income is the apportionment factor chosen, the portion of total gross income of the affiliated group that consists of combined gross income derived from transactions involving the FSC or DISC and related supplier must be determined. Similarly, if units sold or sales receipts is the apportionment factor chosen, the portion of total units sold or sales receipts that generated export income of the FSC or DISC and related supplier must be determined. The amount of the expense shall then be multiplied by a fraction, the numerator of which is the export related apportionment factor as determined above, and the denominator of which is the total apportionment factor. Thus, if gross income is the apportionment factor chosen, apportionment is based on a fraction, the numerator of which is export related combined gross income of the FSC or DISC and related supplier and the denominator of which is the total gross income of the affiliated group. Similarly, if units sold or sales receipts is the apportionment factor chosen, the fraction is the units sold or sales receipts that generated export income of the FSC or DISC and related supplier over the total units sold or sales receipts of the affiliated group. Under this rule, expenses of other group members may be attributed to the combined gross income of a FSC or DISC and its related supplier without affecting the amount of expenses (other than any commission payable by the related supplier to the FSC or DISC) otherwise deductible by the FSC or DISC, the related supplier, or other members of the affiliated group. The FSC or DISC must calculate combined taxable income, taking into account any reduction by expenses attributed from other members of the affiliated group to determine the commission derived by the FSC or DISC or the transfer price of qualifying export property sold to the FSC or DISC.

(g) *Losses created through apportionment.*—In the case of an affiliated group that does not file a consolidated return, the taxable income in any separate limitation category must be adjusted under this paragraph (g) for purposes of computing the separate foreign tax credit limitations under section 904(d). As a consequence of the affiliated group allocation and apportionment of expenses required by section 864(e)(6) and this section, expenses of a group member may be apportioned for section 904 purposes to a limitation category with a consequent loss in that limitation category. For purposes of this paragraph, the term "limitation category" includes domestic source income, as well as the types of income described in section 904(d)(1)(A) through (I). A loss of one affiliate in a limitation category will reduce the income of another member in the same limitation category if a consolidated return is filed. (*See* § 1.1502-4.) If a consolidated return is not filed, this netting does not occur. Accordingly, in such a case, the following adjustments among members are required, in order to give effect to the group allocation of expense:

(1) Losses created through group apportionment of expense in one or more limitation categories within a given member must be eliminated; and

(2) A corresponding amount of income of other members in the same limitation category must be recharacterized.

Such adjustments shall be accomplished in accordance with the rules of § 1.861-11T(g).

(h) *Special rule for allocation of reserve expenses of life insurance companies.*—For further guidance, see § 1.861-14(h).

(i) [Reserved]

(j) *Examples.*—The rules of this section may be illustrated by the following examples. All of these examples assume that section 482 has not been applied by the Commissioner.[1]

Example (1)—(i) *Facts.* P owns all of the stock of X and all of the stock of Y. P, X and Y are domestic corporations. P is a holding company for the stock of X and Y. Both X and Y manufacture and sell a product which is included in a broad product category listed in § 1.861-8(e)(3)(i). During 1988, X incurred $100,000 on research connected with that product. All of the research was performed in the United States. In 1988, the domestic sales by X of the product totalled $400,000 and the foreign sales of the product totalled $200,000; Y's domestic sales of the product totalled $200,000 and Y's foreign sales of the product totalled $200,000. In 1988, X's gross income is $300,000, of which $200,000 is from domestic sales and $100,000 is from foreign sales; Y's gross income is $200,000 of which $100,000 is from domestic sales and $100,000 is from foreign sales.

(ii) P, X and Y are affiliated corporations within the meaning of section 864(e)(5) and this section. The research expenses incurred by X are allocable to all income connected with the relevant broad category listed in § 1.861-8T(e)(3)(i). Both X and Y have gross income includible within the class of gross income related to that product category. Accordingly, the research and experimental expenses incurred by X are to be allocated and apportioned as if X and Y were a single corporation. The apportionment for 1988 is as follows:

Tentative Apportionment on the Basis of Sales

Research expenses to be apportioned	$100,000
Exclusive apportionment to United States source gross income	$30,000
Research expense to be apportioned on the basis of sales	$70,000

Apportionment of research expense to foreign source general limitation income:

$$\$70,000 \times \frac{\$200,000 + \$200,000}{\$600,000 + \$400,000} \ldots \$28,000$$

Apportionment of research expense to United States source gross income:

$$\$70,000 \times \frac{\$400,000 + \$200,000}{\$600,000 + \$400,000} \ldots \$42,000$$

Total apportioned deduction for research	$100,000
Of which—	
Apportioned to foreign source gross income	$28,000
Apportioned to U.S. source gross income ($30,000 + $42,000)	$72,000

Tentative Apportionment on the Basis of Gross Income

Research expense apportioned to foreign source gross income:

$$\$100,000 \times \frac{\$100,000 + \$100,000}{\$300,000 + \$200,000} \ldots \$40,000$$

Research expense apportioned to United States source gross income:

$$\$100,000 \times \frac{\$200,000 + \$100,000}{\$300,000 + \$200,000} \ldots \$60,000$$

Example (2)—(i) *Facts.* P owns all of the stock of X, which owns all of the stock of Y. P, X and Y are all domestic corporations. P has incurred general training program expenses of $100,000 in 1987. Employees of P, X and Y participate in the training program. In 1987, P had United States source gross income of $200,000 and foreign source general limitation income of $200,000; X had U.S. source gross income of $100,000 and foreign source general limitation income of $100,000; and Y had U.S. source gross income of $300,000 and foreign source general limitation income of $100,000.

(ii) *Analysis.* P, X and Y are an affiliated group of corporations within the meaning of section 864(e)(5). The training expenses incurred by P are not definitely related solely to specific income producing activities or property of P. The employees of X and Y also participate in the training program. Thus, this expense relates to gross income generated by P, X and Y. This expense is definitely related and allocable to all of the gross income from foreign and domestic sources of P, X and Y. It is assumed that apportionment on the basis of gross income is reasonable. The apportionment of the expense is as follows:

Apportionment of $100,000 expense to foreign source general limitation income:

$$\$100,000 \times \frac{\$200,000 + \$100,000 + \$100,000}{\$400,000 + \$200,000 + \$400,000} \ldots \$40,000$$

[1] Examples 1 and 4 of this paragraph (j) apply to taxable years beginning before January 1, 2018.

Apportionment of $100,000 expense to United States source gross income:

$$\$100{,}000 \times \frac{\$200{,}000 + \$100{,}000 + \$300{,}000}{\$400{,}000 + \$200{,}000 + \$400{,}000} \quad \ldots\ldots \quad \$60{,}000$$

Total apportioned expense $100,000

Example (3)—(i) *Facts.* The facts are the same as in *Example* (2) above, except that only employees of P and X participate in the training program.

(ii) *Analysis.* Because only the employees of P and X participate in the training program and they perform no services for Y, the expense relates only to gross income generated by P and X. Accordingly, the $100,000 expense must be allocated and apportioned as if P and X were a single corporation. The apportionment of the $100,000 expense is as follows:

Apportionment of $100,000 expense to foreign source general limitation income:

$$\$100{,}000 \times \frac{\$200{,}000 + \$100{,}000}{\$400{,}000 + \$200{,}000} \quad \ldots\ldots \quad \$50{,}000$$

Apportionment of $100,000 expense to United States source gross income:

$$\$100{,}000 \times \frac{\$200{,}000 + \$100{,}000}{\$400{,}000 + \$200{,}000} \quad \ldots\ldots \quad \$50{,}000$$

Example (4)—(i) *Facts.* P owns all of the stock of X which owns all of the stock of Y. P and X are domestic corporations; Y is a foreign corporation. In 1987 P incurred $10,000 of stewardship expenses relating to an audit of Y.

(ii) *Analysis.* The stewardship expenses incurred by P are not directly allocable to specific income producing activities or property of P. The expense is definitely related and allocable to dividends received or to be received by X. Accordingly, the expense of P is allocated and apportioned as if P and X were a single corporation. The expense is definitely related to dividends received or to be received by X from Y, a foreign corporation. Such dividends are foreign source general limitation income. Thus, the entire amount of the expense must be allocated to foreign source dividend income.

Example (5)—(i) *Facts.* P owns all of the stock of X which owns all of the stock of Y. P, X and Y are all domestic corporations. In 1987, P incurred $10,000 legal expense relating to the testimony of certain employees of P in connection with litigation to which Y is a party. This expense is not allocable to specific income of Y. In 1987, Y had $100,000 foreign source general limitation income and $300,000 U.S. source gross income.

(ii) *Analysis.* The legal expenses incurred by P are not definitely related solely to specific income producing activities or property of P. The expense is definitely related and allocable to the class of gross income which includes only gross income generated by Y. Accordingly, the expense of P is allocated and apportioned as if Y were the only member of the affiliated group, as follows:

Apportionment of legal expenses to foreign source general limitation income:

$$\$10{,}000 \times \frac{\$100{,}000}{\$400{,}000} \quad \ldots\ldots \quad \$2{,}500$$

Apportionment of legal expenses to U.S. source gross income:

$$\$10{,}000 \times \frac{\$300{,}000}{\$400{,}000} \quad \ldots\ldots \quad \$7{,}500$$

Example (6)—(i) *Facts.* P owns all of the stock of R, which owns all of the stock of F. P and R are domestic corporations, and F is a foreign sales corporation under section 922 of the Code. R and F have entered into an agreement whereby F is paid a commission with respect to sales of product A. In 1987, P had gross receipts of $1,000,000 from domestic sales of product A, and gross receipts of $1,000,000 from foreign sales of product A. R had gross receipts of $1,000,000 from domestic sales of product A, and $1,000,000 from export sales of product A. R's cost of goods sold attributable to export sales is $500,000. R has deductible expenses of $100,000 directly related to its export sales, and F has such deductible expenses of $100,000. During 1987, P incurred an expense of $100,000 for marketing studies involving the worldwide market for product A.

(ii) *Analysis.* P and R are an affiliated group of corporations within the meaning of section 864(e)(5) and this section. The expense incurred by P for marketing studies regarding the worldwide market for product A is an expense that is not directly related solely to the activities of P, but also to the activities of R. This expense must be allocated and apportioned under the rules of paragraph (c)(1) of this section, as if P and R were a single corporation. The expense is allocable to the class of gross income that includes all gross income generated by sales of product A. Apportionment on the basis of gross receipts is reasonable under these facts. F, a foreign corporation, is not a member of the affiliated group. However, for purposes of determining F's commission on its sales, the combined gross income of F and R must be reduced by the portion of the marketing studies expense of P that is incurred in connection with export sales involving F under the rules of paragraph (f) of this section. The computation of the combined taxable income of R and F is as follows:

Combined Taxable Income of R and F

R's gross receipts from export sales	$1,000,000
R's cost of goods sold	$500,000
Combined Gross Income	$500,000
Less:	
R's other deductible expenses	$100,000
F's other deductible expenses	$100,000
Apportionment of P's expense:	
$\$100{,}000 \times \frac{\$1{,}000{,}000}{\$2{,}000{,}000 + \$2{,}000{,}000}$	$25,000
Total	$225,000
Combined Taxable Income	$275,000

(k) *Effective/applicability date.*—The rules of this section apply for taxable years beginning after December 31, 1986. [Temporary Reg. § 1.861-14T.]

☐ [*T.D.* 8228, 9-9-88. *Amended by T.D.* 8916, 12-29-2000; *T.D.* 9143, 7-27-2004; *T.D.* 9211, 7-13-2005, *T.D.* 9456, 7-31-2009 *and T.D.* 9922, 11-2-2020.]

§ 1.861-17. Allocation and apportionment of research and experimental expenditures.—(a) *Scope.*—This section provides rules for the allocation and apportionment of research and experimental expenditures that a taxpayer deducts, or amortizes and deducts, in a taxable year under section 174 or section 59(e) (applicable to expenditures that are allowable as a deduction under section 174(a)) (*R&E expenditures*). R&E expenditures do not include any expenditures that are not deductible expenses by reason of the second sentence under § 1.482-7(j)(3)(i) (relating to CST Payments (as defined in § 1.482-7(b)(1)) owed to a controlled participant in a cost sharing arrangement).

(b) *Allocation.*—(1) *In general.*—The method of allocation and apportionment of R&E expenditures set forth in this section recognizes that research and experimentation is an inherently speculative activity, that findings may contribute unexpected benefits, and that the gross income derived from successful research and experimentation must bear the cost of unsuccessful research and experimentation. In addition, the method set forth in this section recognizes that successful R&E expenditures ultimately result in the creation of intangible property that will be used to generate income. Therefore, R&E expenditures ordinarily are considered deductions that are definitely related to gross intangible income (as defined in paragraph (b)(2) of this section) reasonably connected with the relevant SIC code category (or categories) of the taxpayer and therefore allocable to gross intangible income as a class related to the SIC code category (or categories) and apportioned under the rules in this section. For purposes of the allocation under this paragraph (b)(1), a taxpayer's SIC code category (or categories) are determined in accordance with the provisions of paragraph (b)(3) of this section. For purposes of this section, the term *intangible property* means intangible property (as defined in section 367(d)(4)), including intangible property either created or acquired by the taxpayer, that is derived from R&E expenditures.

(2) *Definition of gross intangible income.*—The term *gross intangible income* means all gross income earned by a taxpayer that is attributable to a sale or license of intangible property (including income from platform contribution transactions described in § 1.482-7(b)(1)(ii), royalty income from the licensing of intangible property, or amounts taken into account under section 367(d) by reason of a transfer of intangible property), and the full amount of gross income from sales or leases of products or services if the income is derived directly or indirectly (in whole or in part) from intangible property. Gross intangible income also includes a distributive share of any amounts described in the previous sentence, but does not include dividends or any amounts included in income under section 951, 951A, or 1293. See § 1.904-4(f)(2)(vi) for rules addressing the assignment of gross income, including gross intangible income, to a separate category by reason of certain disregarded payments to or from a taxpayer's foreign branch.

(3) *SIC code categories.*—(i) *Allocation based on SIC code categories.*—Ordinarily, a taxpayer's R&E expenditures are incurred to produce gross intangible income that is reasonably connected with one or more relevant SIC code categories. Except as provided in paragraph (b)(3)(iv) of this section, where research and experimentation is conducted with respect to more than one SIC code category, the taxpayer may aggregate the categories for purposes of allocation and apportionment, provided the categories are in the same Major Group. However, the taxpayer may not subdivide any categories. Where research and experimentation is not clearly related to any SIC code category (or categories), it will be considered conducted with respect to all of the taxpayer's SIC code categories.

(ii) *Use of three digit standard industrial classification codes.*—A taxpayer determines the relevant Major Groups and SIC code categories by reference to the two digit and three digit classification, respectively, of the Standard Industrial Classification Manual (SIC code). The SIC Manual is available at https://www.osha.gov/pls/imis/sic_manual.html.

(iii) *Consistency.*—Once a taxpayer selects a SIC code category or Major Group for the first taxable year for which this section applies to the taxpayer, it must continue to use that category in following years unless the taxpayer establishes to the satisfaction of the Commissioner that, due to changes in the relevant facts, a change in the category is appropriate. Therefore, once a taxpayer elects a permissible aggregation of three digit SIC code categories into a two digit Major Group, it must continue to use that two digit category in following years unless the taxpayer establishes to the satisfaction of the Commissioner that, due to changes in the relevant facts, a change is appropriate.

(iv) *Wholesale trade and retail trade categories.*—A taxpayer must use a SIC code category within the divisions of "wholesale trade" or "retail trade" if it is engaged solely in sales-related activities with respect to a particular category of products. In the case of a taxpayer that conducts material non-sales-related activities with respect to a particular category of products, all R&E expenditures related to sales of the products must be allocated and apportioned as if the expenditures were reasonably connected to the most closely related three digit SIC code category other than those within the wholesale and retail trade divisions. For example, if a taxpayer engages in both the manufacturing and assembling of cars and trucks (SIC code 371) and in a wholesaling activity related to motor vehicles and motor vehicle parts and supplies (SIC code 501), the taxpayer must allocate and apportion all R&E expenditures related to both activities as if they relate solely to the manufacturing SIC code 371. By contrast, if the taxpayer engages only in the wholesaling activity related to motor vehicles and motor vehicle parts and supplies, the taxpayer must allocate and apportion all R&E expenditures to the wholesaling SIC code 501.

(c) *Exclusive apportionment.*—Solely for purposes of applying this section to section 904 as the operative section, an amount equal to fifty percent of a taxpayer's R&E expenditures in a SIC code category (or categories) is apportioned exclusively to the residual grouping of U.S. source gross intangible income if research and experimentation that accounts for at least fifty percent of such R&E expenditures was performed in the United States. Similarly, an amount equal to fifty percent of a taxpayer's R&E expenditures in a SIC code category (or categories) is apportioned exclusively to the statutory grouping (or groupings) of foreign source gross intangible income in that SIC code category if research and experimentation that accounts for more than fifty percent of such R&E expenditures was performed outside the United States. If there are multiple separate categories with foreign source gross intangible income in the SIC code category, the fifty percent of R&E expenditures apportioned under the previous sentence is apportioned ratably to foreign source gross intangible income based on the relative amounts of gross receipts from gross intangible income in the SIC code category in each separate category, as determined under paragraph (d) of this section. Solely for purposes of determining whether fifty percent or more of R&E expenditures in a year are performed within or without the United States under this paragraph (c), a taxpayer's R&E expenditures with respect to a taxable year are determined by taking into account only the R&E expenditures incurred in such taxable year (without regard to whether such expenditures are capitalized under section 59(e) or any other provision in the Code), and do not include amounts that were capitalized in a prior taxable year and are deducted in such taxable year.

(d) *Apportionment based on gross receipts from sales of products or services.*—(1) *In general.*—A taxpayer's R&E expenditures not apportioned under paragraph (c) of this section are apportioned between the statutory grouping (or among the statutory groupings) within the class of gross intangible income and the residual grouping within such class according to the rules in paragraphs (d)(1)(i) through (iv) of this section. See paragraph (b) of this section for defining the class of gross intangible income in relation to SIC code categories.

(i) A taxpayer's R&E expenditures not apportioned under paragraph (c) of this section are apportioned in the same proportions that:

(A) The amounts of the taxpayer's gross receipts from sales and leases of products (as measured by gross receipts without regard to cost of goods sold) or services that are related to gross intangible income within the statutory grouping (or statutory groupings) and in the residual grouping bear, respectively; to

(B) The total amount of such gross receipts in the class.

(ii) For purposes of this paragraph (d), gross receipts from sales and leases of products are related to gross intangible income if intangible property is embedded or used in connection with the manufacture or sale of such products, and gross income from services is related to gross intangible income if intangible property is incorporated in or directly or indirectly benefits such services. See paragraph (g)(7) of this section (*Example 7*). The amount of the gross receipts used to apportion R&E expenditures also includes gross receipts from sales and leases of products or services of any controlled or uncontrolled party to the extent described in paragraphs (d)(3) and (4) of this section. A royalty or other amount paid to the taxpayer for intangible property constitutes gross intangible income, but is not considered part of gross receipts arising from the sale or lease of a product or service, and so is not taken into account in apportioning the taxpayer's R&E expenditures to its gross intangible income.

(iii) The statutory grouping (or groupings) or residual grouping to which the gross receipts are assigned is the grouping to which the gross intangible income related to the sale, lease, or service is assigned. In cases where the gross intangible income of the taxpayer is income not described in paragraph (d)(3) or (4) of this section, the grouping to which the taxpayer's gross receipts and the gross intangible income are assigned is the same. In cases where the taxpayer's gross intangible income is related to sales, leases, or services described in paragraph (d)(3) or (4) of this section, the gross receipts that will be used for purposes of this paragraph (d) are the gross receipts of the controlled and uncontrolled parties that are taken into account under paragraphs (d)(3) and (4) of this section. The grouping to which the controlled or uncontrolled parties' gross receipts are assigned is determined based on the grouping of the taxpayer's gross intangible income attributable to the license, sale, or other transfer of intangible property to such controlled or uncontrolled party as described in paragraph (d)(3)(i) or (d)(4)(i) of this section, and not the grouping to which the gross receipts would be assigned if the assignment were based on the income earned by the controlled or uncontrolled party. See paragraph (g)(1) of this section (*Example 1*). For purposes of applying this paragraph (d)(1)(iii) to section 250 or section 904 as the operative section, the assignment of gross receipts to the general and foreign branch categories is made after taking into account the assignment of gross intangible income to those categories as adjusted by reason of disregarded payments under the rules of § 1.904-4(f)(2)(vi), and by making similar adjustments to gross receipts under the principles of § 1.904-4(f)(2)(vi).

(iv) For purposes of applying this section to section 904 as the operative section, because a United States person's gross intangible income cannot include income assigned to the section 951A category, no R&E expenditures of a United States person are apportioned to foreign source income in the section 951A category.

(2) *Apportionment in excess of gross income.*—Amounts apportioned under this section may exceed the amount of gross income related to the SIC code category within the statutory or residual grouping. In such case, the excess is applied against other gross income within the statutory or residual grouping. See § 1.861-8(d)(1) for applicable rules where the apportionment results in an excess of deductions over gross income within the statutory or residual grouping.

(3) *Sales or services of uncontrolled parties.*—(i) *In general.*—For purposes of the apportionment within a class under paragraph (d)(1) of this section, if a taxpayer reasonably expects an uncontrolled party to (through a license, purchase, or transfer): acquire intangible property that would arise from the taxpayer's current R&E expenditures; acquire products in which such intangible property is embedded or used in connection with the manufacture or sale of such products; or receive services that incorporate or directly or indirectly benefit from such intangible property, then the gross receipts of the uncontrolled party from sales, licenses, leases, or services of the particular products or services in which the taxpayer's intangible property is embedded or incorporated or which the taxpayer's intangible property directly or indirectly benefitted are taken into account. If the taxpayer has previously licensed, sold, or transferred intangible property related to a SIC code category to an uncontrolled party, the taxpayer is presumed to expect to license, sell, or transfer to that uncontrolled party all future intangible property related to the same SIC code category. The presumption described in the preceding sentence may be rebutted by the taxpayer with facts that demonstrate that the taxpayer reasonably expects not to license, sell, or transfer future intangible property to the uncontrolled party.

(ii) *Definition of uncontrolled party.*—For purposes of this paragraph (d)(3), the term *uncontrolled party* means a person that is not a controlled party as defined in paragraph (d)(4)(ii) of this section.

(iii) *Sales of components.*—In the case of a sale or lease of a product by an uncontrolled party that is derived from the taxpayer's intangible property but is incorporated as a component of a larger product (for example, where the product incorporating the intangible property is a component of a large machine), only the portion of the gross receipts from the larger product that are attributable to the component derived from the intangible property is included. For purposes of the preceding sentence, a reasonable estimate based on the principles of section 482 must be made. See paragraph (g)(4)(ii)(B)(*3*) of this section (*Example 4*).

(iv) *Reasonable estimates of gross receipts.*—If the amount of gross receipts of an uncontrolled party is unknown, a reasonable estimate of gross receipts must be made annually. Appropriate economic analyses, based on the principles of section 482, must be used to estimate gross receipts. See paragraph (g)(5)(ii)(B)(*3*)(*ii*) of this section (*Example 5*).

(4) *Sales or services of controlled parties.*—(i) *In general.*—For purposes of the apportionment within a class under paragraph (d)(1) of this section, if the controlled party is reasonably expected to (through a license, sale, or transfer): acquire intangible property that would arise from the taxpayer's current R&E expenditures; acquire products in which such intangible property is embedded or used in connection with the manufacture or sale of such products; or receive services that incorporate or directly or indirectly benefit from such intangible property, then the gross receipts of the controlled party from all of its sales, licenses, leases, or services are taken into account. Except to the extent provided in paragraph (d)(4)(iv) of this section, if the taxpayer has previously licensed, sold, or transferred intangible property related to a SIC code category to a controlled party, the taxpayer is presumed to expect to license, sell, or transfer to that controlled party all future intangible property related to the same SIC code category. The presumption described in the preceding sentence may be rebutted by the taxpayer with facts that demonstrate that the taxpayer will not license, sell, or transfer future intangible property to the controlled party.

(ii) *Definition of a controlled party.*—For purposes of this paragraph (d)(4), the term *controlled party* means any person that has a relationship to the taxpayer specified in section 267(b) or 707(b), or is a member of a controlled group of corporations (within the meaning of section 267(f)) to which the taxpayer belongs. Because an affiliated group is treated as a single taxpayer, a member of an affiliated group is not a controlled party. See paragraph (e) of this section.

(iii) *Gross receipts not to be taken into account more than once.*—Sales, licenses, leases, or services among the taxpayer, controlled parties, and uncontrolled parties are not taken into account more than once; in such a situation, the amount of gross receipts of the selling person must be subtracted from the gross receipts of the buying person. Therefore, the gross receipts taken into account under paragraph (d)(4)(i) of this section generally reflect the gross receipts from sales made to end users.

(iv) *Effect of cost sharing arrangements.*—If the controlled party has entered into a cost sharing arrangement, in accordance with the provisions of § 1.482-7, with the taxpayer for the purpose of developing intangible property, then ordinarily the controlled party is not reasonably expected to acquire rights in intangible property that would arise from the taxpayer's share of the R&E expenditures with respect to the cost shared intangibles as defined in § 1.482-7(j)(1)(i); acquire products in which such intangible property is embedded or used in connection with the manufacture or sale of such products; or receive services that incorporate or directly or indirectly benefit from such intangible property. Therefore, solely for purposes of apportioning a taxpayer's R&E expenditures (which do not include the amount of CST Payments received by the taxpayer; see paragraph (a) of this section) that are intangible development costs (as defined in § 1.482-7(d)) with respect to a cost sharing arrangement, the controlled party's gross receipts are not taken into account for purposes of paragraphs (d)(1) and (d)(4)(i) of this section. However, the rule in this paragraph (d)(4)(iv) does not apply, and the controlled party's sales are taken into account, to the extent the taxpayer licenses, or has licensed, to the controlled party intangible property resulting from a cost sharing arrangement with the controlled party.

(5) *Application of section 864(e)(3).* Section 864(e)(3) and § 1.861-8(d)(2) do not apply for purposes of this section.

(e) *Affiliated groups.*—See § 1.861-14(e)(2) for rules on allocating and apportioning R&E expenditures of an affiliated group (as defined in § 1.861-14(d)).

(f) *Special rules for partnerships.*—(1) *R&E expenditures.*—For purposes of applying this section, if R&E expenditures are incurred by a partnership in which the taxpayer is a partner, the taxpayer's R&E expenditures include the taxpayer's distributive share of the partnership's R&E expenditures.

(2) *Purpose and location of expenditures.*—In applying exclusive apportionment under paragraph (c) of this section, a partner's distributive share of R&E expenditures incurred by a partnership is

treated as incurred by the partner for the same purpose and in the same location as incurred by the partnership.

(3) *Apportionment based on gross receipts.*—In applying the remaining apportionment under paragraph (d) of this section, if a taxpayer is a partner in a partnership that incurs R&E expenditures described in paragraph (f)(1) of this section and the taxpayer is not reasonably expected to license, sell, or transfer to the partnership (directly or indirectly) intangible property that would arise from the taxpayer's current R&E expenditures, in the manner described in paragraph (d)(3)(i) or (d)(4)(i) of this section, then the taxpayer's gross receipts in a SIC code category include only the taxpayer's share of any gross receipts in the SIC code category of the partnership. For purposes of the preceding sentence, the taxpayer's share of gross receipts is proportionate to the taxpayer's distributive share of the partnership's gross income in the product category. However, if the taxpayer is reasonably expected to license, sell, or transfer to the partnership (directly or indirectly) intangible property that would arise from the taxpayer current R&E expenditures, in the manner described in paragraph (d)(3)(i) or (d)(4)(i) of this section, then the taxpayer's gross receipts in a SIC code category include the full amount of any gross receipts in the SIC code category of the partnership as provided in paragraph (d)(3)(i) or (d)(4)(i) of this section.

(g) *Examples.*—The following examples illustrate the application of the rules in this section.

(1) *Example 1: Controlled party and single product.*—(i) *Facts.* X, a domestic corporation, is a manufacturer and distributor of small gasoline engines for lawnmowers. Gasoline engines are a product within the category, Engines and Turbines (SIC Industry Group 351). Y, a wholly owned foreign subsidiary of X, also manufactures and sells these engines abroad. X owns no other foreign subsidiaries. During Year 1, X incurred R&E expenditures of $60,000x, which it deducts under section 174 as a current expense, to invent and patent a new and improved gasoline engine. All of the research and experimentation was performed in the United States. Also in Year 1, the domestic gross receipts of X from sales of gasoline engines total $500,000x and foreign gross receipts of Y from sales of gasoline engines total $300,000x. X provides technology for the manufacture of engines to Y through a license that requires the payment of an arm's length royalty. Because X has licensed its intangible property to Y related to the SIC code, it is presumed to reasonably expect to license the intangible property that would be developed from the current research and experimentation. In Year 1, X's gross income is $210,000x, of which $140,000x is U.S. source income from domestic sales of gasoline engines, $40,000x is income included under section 951A, all of which relates to Y's foreign source income from sales of gasoline engines, $20,000x is foreign source royalties from Y, and $10,000x is U.S. source interest income. None of the foreign source royalties are allocable to passive category income of Y, and therefore, under § § 1.904-4(d) and 1.904-5(c)(3), the foreign source royalties are general category income to X.

(ii) *Analysis*—(A) *Allocation.* The R&E expenditures were incurred in connection with developing intangible property related to small gasoline engines and they are definitely related to X's items of gross intangible income related to the SIC code category 351, namely gross income from the sale of small gasoline engines in the United States and royalties received from subsidiary Y, a foreign manufacturer of gasoline engines. Accordingly, under paragraph (b) of this section, the R&E expenditures are allocable to the class of gross intangible income related to SIC code category 351, all of which is general category income of X. X's U.S. source interest income and income included under section 951A are not within this class of gross intangible income and, therefore, no portion of the R&E expenditures are allocated to the U.S. source interest income or foreign source income in the section 951A category.

(B) *Apportionment*—(*1*) *In general.* For purposes of applying this section to section 904 as the operative section, the statutory grouping of gross intangible income is foreign source general category income and the residual grouping of gross intangible income is U.S. source income.

(*2*) *Exclusive apportionment.* Under paragraph (c) of this section, because at least 50% of X's research and experimental activity was performed in the United States, 50% of the R&E expenditures, or $30,000x ($60,000x x 50%), is apportioned exclusively to the residual grouping of U.S. source gross intangible income. The remaining 50% of the R&E expenditures is then apportioned between the statutory and residual groupings on the basis of the relative amounts of gross receipts from sales of small gasoline engines by X and Y that are related to the U.S. source sales income and foreign source royalty income, respectively.

(*3*) *Apportionment based on gross receipts.* After taking into account exclusive apportionment, X has $30,000x ($60,000x − $30,000x) of R&E expenditures that must be apportioned between the statutory and residual groupings. Under paragraph (d)(4) of this section, Y's gross receipts within the SIC code are taken into account in apportioning X's R&E expenditures. Although X has gross intangible income of $140,000x from domestic sales and $20,000x in royalties from Y, X's R&E expenditures are apportioned to that gross intangible income on the basis of the relative amounts of gross receipts arising from the sale of products by X and Y (and not the relative amounts of X's gross intangible income) in the statutory and residual groupings. Therefore, under paragraphs (d)(1) and (4) of this section $11,250x ($30,000x x $300,000x / ($500,000x + $300,000x)) is apportioned to the statutory grouping of X's gross intangible income attributable to its license of intangible property to Y, or foreign source general category income. No portion of the gross receipts by X or Y are disregarded under section 864(e)(3), regardless of whether the income related to those sales is eligible for a deduction under section 250(a)(1)(A). The remaining $18,750x ($30,000x x $500,000x / ($500,000x + $300,000x)) is apportioned to the residual grouping of gross intangible income, or U.S. source income.

(*4*) *Summary.* Accordingly, for purposes of the foreign tax credit limitation, $11,250x of X's R&E expenditures are apportioned to foreign source general category income, and $48,750x ($30,000x + $18,750x) of X's R&E expenditures are apportioned to U.S. source income.

(2) *Example 2: Controlled party and two products in same SIC code category.*—(i) *Facts.* The facts are the same as in paragraph (g)(1)(i) of this section (the facts in *Example 1*), except that X also spends $30,000x in Year 1 for research on steam turbines, all of which is performed in the United States, and X has steam turbine gross receipts in the United States of $400,000x. X's foreign subsidiary Y neither manufactures nor sells steam turbines. The steam turbine research is in addition to the $60,000x in R&E expenditures incurred by X on gasoline engines for lawnmowers. X thus has $90,000x of R&E expenditures. X's gross income is $260,000x, of which $140,000x is U.S. source income from domestic sales of gasoline engines, $50,000x is U.S. source income from domestic sales of steam turbines, $40,000x is income included under section 951A all of which relates to foreign source income derived from Y's sales of gasoline engines, $20,000x is foreign source royalties from Y, and $10,000x is U.S. source interest income.

(ii) *Analysis*—(A) *Allocation.* X's R&E expenditures generate gross intangible income from sales of small gasoline engines and steam turbines. Both of these products are in the same three digit SIC code category, Engines and Turbines (SIC Industry Group 351). Therefore, under paragraph (a) of this section, X's R&E expenditures are definitely related to all items of gross intangible income attributable to SIC code category 351. These items of X's gross intangible income are gross income from the sale of small gasoline engines and steam turbines in the United States and royalties from foreign subsidiary Y, a foreign manufacturer and seller of small gasoline engines. X's U.S. source interest income and income included under section 951A is not within this class of gross intangible income and, therefore, no portion of X's R&E expenditures are allocated to the U.S. source interest income or income in the section 951A category.

(B) *Apportionment*—(*1*) *In general.* For purposes of applying this section to section 904 as the operative section, the statutory grouping of gross intangible income is foreign source general category income and the residual grouping of gross intangible income is U.S. source income.

(*2*) *Exclusive apportionment.* Under paragraph (c) of this section, because at least 50% of X's research and experimental activity was performed in the United States, 50% of the R&E expenditures, or $45,000x ($90,000x x 50%), are apportioned exclusively to the residual grouping of U.S. source gross intangible income. The remaining 50% of the R&E expenditures is then apportioned between the statutory and residual groupings on the basis of the relative amounts of gross receipts of small gasoline engines and steam turbines by X and Y with respect to which gross intangible income is foreign source general category income and U.S. source income.

(*3*) *Apportionment based on gross receipts.* After taking into account exclusive apportionment, X has $45,000x ($90,000x − $45,000x) of R&E expenditures that must be apportioned between the statutory and residual groupings. Although X has gross intangible income of $190,000x from domestic sales and $20,000x in royalties from Y, X's R&E expenditures are apportioned to that gross intangible income on the basis of the relative amounts of gross receipts arising from the sale of products by X and Y (and not the relative amounts of X's gross intangible income) in the statutory and residual groupings. Even though a portion of the R&E expenditures that must be apportioned are attributable to research performed with respect to steam turbines, and Y does not sell steam turbines, because Y is reasonably expected to license all intangible property related to SIC code category 351 from X, including intangible property related to steam turbines, under paragraphs (d)(1) and (4) of this section $11,250x ($45,000x x $300,000x / ($500,000x + $400,000x + $300,000x)) is apportioned to the statutory grouping of gross intangible income, or foreign source general category income attributable to the royalty income to which the gross receipts of Y are related. The remaining $33,750x ($45,000x x ($500,000x + $400,000x) / ($500,000x + $400,000x + $300,000x)) is apportioned to the residual grouping of gross intangible income, or U.S. source gross income.

(4) *Summary*. Accordingly, for purposes of the foreign tax credit limitation, $11,250x of X's R&E expenditures are apportioned to foreign source general category income and $78,750x ($45,000x + $33,750x) of X's R&E expenditures are apportioned to U.S. source income.

(3) *Example 3: Cost sharing arrangement.*—(i) *Facts*—(A) *Acquisitions and transfers by* X. The facts are the same as in paragraph (g)(1)(i) of this section (the facts in *Example 1*) except that, in Year 2, X and Y terminate the license for the manufacture of engines that was in place in Year 1 and enter into a cost sharing arrangement, in accordance with the provisions of § 1.482-7, to share the costs and risks of developing the intangible property related to the engines. Pursuant to the cost sharing arrangement, X has the exclusive rights to exploit the cost shared intangibles within the United States, and Y has the exclusive rights to exploit the cost shared intangibles outside the United States. X's and Y's shares of the reasonably anticipated benefits from the cost shared intangibles are 70% and 30%, respectively. In Year 2, Y makes a PCT Payment (as defined in § 1.482-7(b)(1)(ii)) of $50,000x that is characterized and sourced as a royalty for a license of small gasoline engine technology.

(B) *Gross receipts and R&E expenditures*. In Year 2, X and Y continue to sell gasoline engines, with gross receipts of $600,000x in the United States by X and $400,000x abroad by Y. X incurs intangible development costs associated with the cost shared intangibles of $100,000x in Year 2, which consist exclusively of research activities conducted in the United States. Y also makes a $30,000x CST Payment (as defined in § 1.482-7(b)(1)(i)) under the cost sharing arrangement. X is entitled to deduct $70,000x of its intangible development costs ($100,000x less the $30,000x CST Payment by Y) by reason of the second sentence under § 1.482-7(j)(3)(i) (relating to CST Payments).

(C) *Gross income of* X. In Year 2, X's gross income is $360,000x, of which $200,000x is U.S. source income from domestic sales of small gasoline engines, $50,000x is foreign source general category income attributable to the PCT Payment, $100,000x is income included under section 951A (all of which relates to foreign source income derived from engine sales by Y), and $10,000x is U.S. source interest income.

(ii) *Analysis*—(A) *Allocation*. The $70,000x of R&E expenditures incurred in Year 2 by X in connection with small gasoline engines are definitely related to the items of gross intangible income related to the SIC code category, namely gross income from the sale of small gasoline engines in the United States and PCT Payments from Y. Accordingly, under paragraph (a) of this section, the R&E expenditures are allocable to this class of gross intangible income. X's U.S. source interest income and income included under section 951A are not within this class of gross intangible income and, therefore, no portion of X's R&E expenditures is allocated to X's U.S. source interest income or section 951A category income.

(B) *Apportionment*—(*1*) *In general*. For purposes of applying this section to section 904 as the operative section, the statutory grouping of gross intangible income is foreign source general category income, and the residual grouping of gross intangible income is U.S. source income.

(*2*) *Exclusive apportionment*. Under paragraph (c) of this section, because at least 50% of X's research and experimentation in Year 2 was performed in the United States, 50% of the R&E expenditures, or $35,000x ($70,000x x 50%), is apportioned exclusively to the residual grouping of gross intangible income, U.S. source income.

(*3*) *Apportionment based on gross receipts*. Although X has gross intangible income of $200,000x from domestic sales and $50,000x as a PCT Payment from Y, X's R&E expenditures are apportioned to its gross intangible income on the basis of the relative amounts of gross receipts arising from the sale of products by X (and not the relative amounts of X's gross intangible income) in the statutory and residual groupings. Under paragraph (d)(4)(iv) of this section, because of the cost sharing arrangement, Y's gross receipts from sales are not taken into account in apportioning X's R&E expenditures that are intangible development costs with respect to the cost sharing arrangement. Because all of the gross receipts from sales that are taken into account under paragraph (d)(1) of this section relate to gross intangible income that is included in the residual grouping, $35,000x is apportioned to the residual grouping of gross intangible income, or U.S. source income.

(*4*) *Summary*. Accordingly, for purposes of the foreign tax credit limitation, $70,000x of X's R&E expenditures are apportioned to U.S. source income.

(4) *Example 4: Uncontrolled party.*—(i) *Facts*—(A) *X's R&E expenditures*. X, a domestic corporation, is engaged in continuous research and experimentation to improve the quality of the products that it manufactures and sells, which are floodlights, flashlights, fuse boxes, and solderless connectors. All of these products are in the same three digit SIC code category, Electric Lighting and Wiring Equipment (SIC Industry Group 364). X incurs $100,000x of R&E expenditures in Year 1 that is performed exclusively in the United States. As a result of this research activity, X acquires patents that it uses in its own manufacturing activity.

(B) *License to Y and Z*. In Year 1, X licenses its floodlight patent to Y and Z, uncontrolled parties, for use in their own territories, Countries Y and Z, respectively. Y pays X a royalty of $3,000x plus $0.20x for each unit sold. Gross receipts from sales of floodlights by Y for the taxable year are $135,000x (30,000 units at $4.50x per unit), and the royalty is $9,000x ($3,000x + $0.20x/unit × 30,000 units). Y has sales of other products of $500,000x. Z pays X a royalty of $3,000x plus $0.30x for each unit sold. Z manufactures 30,000 floodlights in the taxable year, and the royalty is $12,000x ($3,000x + $0.30x/unit × 30,000 units). The dollar value of Z's gross receipts from floodlight sales is not known to X because, in this case, the floodlights are not sold separately by Z but are instead used as a component in Z's manufacture of lighting equipment for theaters. However, a reasonable estimate of Z's gross receipts attributable to the floodlights, based on the principles of section 482, is $120,000x. The gross receipts from sales of all Z's products, including the lighting equipment for theaters, are $1,000,000x. Because X has licensed its intangible property to Y and Z related to the SIC code, it is presumed to reasonably expect to license the intangible property that would be developed from the current research and experimentation.

(C) *X's gross receipts and gross income*. X's gross receipts from sales of floodlights for the taxable year are $500,000x and its sales of its other products (flashlights, fuse boxes, and solderless connectors) are $400,000x. X has gross income of $500,000x, consisting of U.S. source gross income from domestic sales of floodlights, flashlights, fuse boxes, and solderless connectors of $479,000x, and foreign source gross income from royalties of $9,000x and $12,000x from foreign corporations Y and Z, respectively. The royalty income is general category income to X under § 1.904-4(b)(2)(ii).

(ii) *Analysis*—(A) *Allocation*. X's R&E expenditures are definitely related to all of the gross intangible income from the products that it produces, which are floodlights, flashlights, fuse boxes, and solderless connectors. All of these products are in SIC code category 364. Therefore, under paragraph (b) of this section, X's R&E expenditures are definitely related to the class of gross intangible income related to SIC code category 364 and to all items of gross intangible income attributable to the class. These items of X's gross intangible income are gross income from the sale of floodlights, flashlights, fuse boxes, and solderless connectors in the United States and royalties from Corporations Y and Z.

(B) *Apportionment*—(*1*) *In general*. For purposes of applying this section to section 904 as the operative section, the statutory grouping of gross intangible income is foreign source general category income, and the residual grouping of gross intangible income is U.S. source income.

(*2*) *Exclusive apportionment*. Under paragraph (c) of this section, because at least 50% of X's research and experimentation was performed in the United States, 50% of the R&E expenditures, or $50,000x ($100,000x x 50%), is apportioned exclusively to the residual grouping of U.S. source gross intangible income.

(*3*) *Apportionment based on gross receipts*. After taking into account exclusive apportionment, X has $50,000x ($100,000x − $50,000x) of R&E expenditures that must be apportioned between the statutory and residual groupings. Under paragraph (d)(3)(i) of this section, gross receipts from sales of Y and Z are taken into account in apportioning X's R&E expenditures. Although X has gross intangible income of $479,000x from domestic sales and $21,000x in royalties from Y and Z, X's R&E expenditures are apportioned to its gross intangible income on the basis of the relative amounts of gross receipts arising from the sale of products by X, Y and Z (and not the relative amounts of X's gross intangible income) in the statutory and residual groupings. In addition, under paragraph (d)(3)(iii) of this section only the portion of Z's gross receipts that are attributable to the floodlights that incorporate the intangible property licensed from X, rather than Z's total gross receipts, are used for purposes of apportionment. All of X's gross receipts from sales in the entire SIC code category are included for purposes of apportionment on the basis of gross intangible income attributable to those sales. Under paragraph (d)(1) of this section, $11,039x ($50,000x × ($135,000x + $120,000x) / ($900,000x + $135,000x + $120,000x)) is apportioned to the statutory grouping of gross intangible income, or foreign source general category income. The remaining $38,961x ($50,000x × $900,000x / ($900,000x + $135,000x + $120,000x)) is apportioned to the residual grouping of gross intangible income, or U.S. source income.

(4) *Summary*. Accordingly, for purposes of the foreign tax credit limitation, $11,039x of X's R&E expenditures are apportioned to foreign source general category income and $88,961x ($50,000x + $38,961x) of X's R&E expenditures are apportioned to U.S. source income.

(5) *Example 5: Uncontrolled party and sublicense*.—(i) *Facts*. X, a domestic corporation, is a cloud storage service provider. Cloud storage services are a service within the category, Computer Programming, Data Processing, and other Computer Related Services (SIC Industry Group 737). During Year 1, X incurs R&E expenditures of $50,000x to invent and copyright new storage monitoring and management software. All of the research and experimentation is performed in the United States. X uses this software in its own business to provide services to customers. X also licenses a version of the software that can be used by other businesses that provide cloud storage services. X licenses the software to uncontrolled party U, which sub-licenses the software to other businesses that provide cloud storage services to customers. U does not use the software except to sublicense it. As a part of the licensing agreement with U, U and its sub-licensees are only permitted to use the software in certain countries outside of the United States. Under the contract with U, U pays X a royalty of 50% on the amount it receives from its sub-licensees that use the software to provide services to customers. Because X has licensed its intangible property to U related to the SIC code and U has sublicensed it to other businesses, it is presumed that X is reasonably expected to license the intangible property that would be developed from its current research and experimentation to U and that U would sublicense it to other businesses. In Year 1, X earns $300,000x of gross receipts from providing cloud storage services within the United States. Further, in Year 1 U receives $10,000x of royalty income from its sub-licensees and pays a royalty of $5,000x to X. Thus, X earns $300,000x of U.S. source general category gross income and also earns $5,000x of foreign source general category royalty income from licensing its software to U for use outside of the United States.

(ii) *Analysis*—(A) *Allocation*. The R&E expenditures were incurred in connection with the development of cloud computing software and they are definitely related to the items of gross intangible income related to the SIC Code category, namely gross income from the storage monitoring and management software in the United States and royalties received from U. Accordingly, under paragraph (b) of this section, the R&E expenditures are allocable to this class of gross intangible income.

(B) *Apportionment*—(*1*) *In general*. For purposes of applying this section to section 904 as the operative section, the statutory grouping of gross intangible income is foreign source general category income, and the residual grouping of gross intangible income is U.S. source income.

(*2*) *Exclusive apportionment*. Under paragraph (c) of this section, because at least 50% of X's research and experimental activity was performed in the United States, 50% of the R&E expenditures, or $25,000x ($50,000x x 50%), is apportioned exclusively to the residual grouping of U.S. source gross intangible income.

(*3*) *Apportionment based on gross receipts*—(*i*) *In general*. After taking into account exclusive apportionment, X has $25,000x ($50,000x – $25,000x) of R&E expenditures that must be apportioned between the statutory and residual groupings. Because X has licensed its intangible property related to the SIC code to U and U has licensed it to the sub-licensees, under paragraph (d)(3)(i) of this section, gross receipts from sales of U's sublicensees are taken into account in apportioning X's R&E expenditures. Although X has gross intangible income of $300,000x from domestic sales of services and $5,000x in royalties from U, X's R&E expenditures are apportioned to its gross intangible income on the basis of the relative amounts of gross receipts arising from the sale of services by X and U's sub-licensees (and not the relative amounts of X's gross intangible income) in the statutory and residual groupings.

(*ii*) *Determination of U's sub-licensee's gross receipts*. Under paragraph (d)(3)(iv) of this section, X can make a reasonable estimate of the gross receipts of U's sub-licensees from services incorporating the intangible property licensed by X by estimating, after an appropriate economic analysis, that U would charge a royalty of 5% of the sub-licensee's sales. U received a royalty of $10,000x from the sub-licensees. X then determines U's sub-licensees' foreign sales by dividing the total royalty payments received by U by the royalty estimated rate ($10,000x / .05 = $200,000x).

(*iii*) *Results of apportionment based on gross receipts*. Therefore, under paragraphs (d)(1) and (3) of this section, $10,000x ($25,000x x $200,000x / ($300,000x + $200,000x)) is apportioned to the statutory grouping of gross intangible income, or foreign source general category income. The remaining $15,000x ($25,000x x $300,000x / ($300,000x + $200,000x)) is apportioned to the residual grouping of gross intangible income, or U.S. source income.

(*4*) *Summary*. Accordingly, for purposes of the foreign tax credit limitation, $10,000x of X's R&E expenditures are apportioned to foreign source general category income and $40,000x ($25,000x + $15,000x) of X's R&E expenditures are apportioned to U.S. source income.

(6) *Example 6: Foreign branch*.—(i) *Facts*—(A) *Overview for X*. X, a domestic corporation, owns FDE, a disregarded entity that is a foreign branch within the meaning of § 1.904-4(f)(3)(vii). FDE conducts activities solely in Country Y. FDE's functional currency is the U.S. dollar. X is a manufacturer and distributor of small gasoline engines for lawnmowers in the United States. Gasoline engines are a product within the category, Engines and Turbines (SIC Industry Group 351). FDE also manufactures and distributes small gasoline engines but only in Country Y. During Year 1, X incurred R&E expenditures of $60,000x, which it deducts under section 174 as a current expense, to invent and patent a new and improved gasoline engine. All of the research and experimentation was performed in the United States. Also in Year 1, the domestic gross receipts of X from gasoline engines total $500,000x. X provides technology for the manufacture of engines to FDE through a license. FDE compensates X for the technology with an arm's length royalty payment of $10,000x, which is disregarded for Federal income tax purposes.

(B) *Overview for FDE*. FDE accrues and records on its books and records $100,000x of gross income from sales of gasoline engines to unrelated persons. FDE's gross income is non-passive category income and is foreign source income. In Year 1, the foreign gross receipts of FDE from sales of gasoline engines total $300,000x. The disregarded royalty payment from FDE to X is not recorded on FDE's separate books and records (as adjusted to conform to Federal income tax principles) within the meaning of paragraph § 1.904-4(f)(2)(i) because it is disregarded for Federal income tax purposes. However, the $10,000x disregarded royalty payment would be allocable to foreign source gross income attributable to FDE under § 1.904-4(f)(2)(vi)(B)(*1*)(*ii*). Therefore, under § 1.904-4(f)(2)(vi)(A) the amount of foreign source gross income attributable to FDE is adjusted downwards and the amount of foreign source gross income attributable to X is adjusted upward to take the $10,000x disregarded royalty payment into account.

(C) *Assignment of X's gross income to separate categories*. In Year 1, X has U.S. source general category gross income of $140,000x from domestic sales of gasoline engines. After application of § 1.904-4(f)(2)(vi)(A) to the disregarded payment made by FDE, X has $10,000x of foreign source general category gross income and X also has $90,000x of foreign source foreign branch category gross income.

(ii) *Analysis*—(A) *Allocation*. The R&E expenditures were incurred in connection with developing intangible property related to small gasoline engines and are definitely related to the items of gross intangible income related to the SIC code category 351, namely gross income from the sale of small gasoline engines in both the United States and Country Y.

(B) *Apportionment*—(*1*) *In general*. For purposes of applying this section to section 904 as the operative section, the statutory groupings of gross intangible income are foreign source general category income and foreign source foreign branch category income, and the residual grouping of gross intangible income is U.S. source income.

(*2*) *Exclusive apportionment*. Under paragraph (c) of this section, because at least 50% of X's research and experimental activity was performed in the United States, 50% of the R&E expenditures, or $30,000 ($60,000x x 50%), is apportioned exclusively to the residual grouping of U.S. source gross intangible income. The remaining 50% of the R&E expenditures is then apportioned between the statutory and residual groupings on the basis of the relative amounts of gross receipts from sales of small gasoline engines that are related to U.S.

source income, foreign source general category income, and foreign source foreign branch category income.

(3) *Apportionment based on gross receipts.* After taking into account exclusive apportionment, X has $30,000x ($60,000x − $30,000x) of R&E expenditures that must be apportioned between the statutory and residual groupings. Because X's gross intangible income is not described in paragraph (d)(3) or (4) of this section (that is, there is no gross intangible income related to sales, leases or services from controlled or uncontrolled parties that are incorporating intangible property that was licensed, sold, or transferred to controlled or uncontrolled parties), the groupings to which the taxpayer's gross receipts and gross intangible income are assigned is the same. However, because the assignment of X's gross income to the foreign branch and general categories is made by taking into account disregarded payments under § 1.904-4(f)(2)(vi), the assignment of gross receipts between the general category and foreign branch category must be determined by making similar adjustments to X's gross receipts under the principles of § 1.904-4(f)(2)(vi). See paragraph (d)(1)(iii) of this section. Foreign gross receipts of FDE from gasoline engines total $300,000x. However, those gross receipts are adjusted under the principles of § 1.904-4(f)(2)(vi) for purposes of apportioning the remaining R&E expenditures by reducing the gross receipts initially assigned to the foreign branch category by an amount equal to the ratio of the royalty income to FDE's gross income that is initially assigned to the foreign branch category. Accordingly, since the disregarded royalty payment of $10,000x caused an adjustment equal to 10% of FDE's initial gross income of $100,000x, 10% of the gross receipts or $30,000x (10% x $300,000x) are similarly assigned to the grouping of foreign source general category income, and the remaining $270,000x of gross receipts are assigned to the grouping of foreign source foreign branch category income. Therefore, under paragraph (d)(1) of this section, $1,125x ($30,000x x $30,000x / ($500,000x + $270,000x + $30,000x)) is apportioned to the statutory grouping of X's gross intangible income attributable to foreign source general category income. $10,125x ($30,000x x $270,000x / ($500,000x + $270,000x + $30,000x)) is apportioned to the statutory grouping of X's foreign source foreign branch category income. The remaining $18,750x ($30,000x x $500,000x / ($500,000x + $270,000x + $30,000x)) is apportioned to the residual grouping of gross intangible income or U.S. source income.

(7) *Example 7: Indirectly derived gross intangible income.*—(i) *Facts.* P, a domestic corporation, develops and publishes an internet website that persons use (referred to as "users" and collectively referred to as "user base") without a fee. P incurs R&E expenditures to update software code and write new software code to maintain the website and develop new products that are incorporated into the website. P's activities consist of services that fall within SIC code category 737 (computer programming, data processing, and other computer related services). P sells space on its website for businesses to advertise to its user base in exchange for a fee. P's technology allows it to collect data on users and to use that data to effectively target advertisements. P does not grant rights to the technology or other intangible property to the businesses advertising on its website. In Year 1, P incurs R&E expenditures of $60,000x, which it deducts under section 174. All the research and experimentation is performed in the United States. Also in Year 1, P earns gross receipts of $200,000x from the sale of advertisements, all of which gives rise to U.S. source gross income.

(ii) *Analysis*—(A) *Allocation.* The R&E expenditures were incurred in connection with developing intangible property used for P's website. Accordingly, they are definitely related and allocable to gross intangible income derived directly or indirectly (in whole or in part) from that intangible property. Because P's advertising sales are dependent on the users attracted to its website, P's gross income from advertising is indirectly derived from intangible property and is included in gross intangible income. Accordingly, under paragraph (b) of this section, the R&E expenditures are allocable to the class of gross intangible income related to SIC code category 737, which consists of U.S. source income.

(B) *Apportionment.* Because all gross receipts from services that the intangible property directly or indirectly benefits result in U.S. source income, no apportionment is required.

(h) *Applicability date.*—This section applies to taxable years beginning after December 31, 2019. However, taxpayers may choose to apply this section to taxable years beginning on or after January 1, 2018, and before January 1, 2020, provided they apply this section in its entirety and for any subsequent year beginning before January 1, 2020. [Reg. § 1.861-17.]

☐ [*T.D.* 8646, 12-21-95. *Amended by T.D.* 9441, 12-31-2008, *T.D.* 9568, 12-16-2011, *T.D.* 9882, 12-16-2019 (*corrected* 5-14-2020) *and T.D.* 9922, 11-2-2020 (*corrected* 9-30-2021).]

§ 1.861-18. Classification of transactions involving computer programs.—(a) *General.*—(1) *Scope.*—This section provides rules for classifying transactions relating to computer programs for purposes of subchapter N of chapter 1 of the Internal Revenue Code, sections 367, 404A, 482, 551, 679, 1059A, chapter 3, chapter 5, sections 842 and 845 (to the extent involving a foreign person), and transfers to foreign trusts not covered by section 679.

(2) *Categories of transactions.*—This section generally requires that such transactions be treated as being solely within one of four categories (described in paragraph (b)(1) of this section) and provides certain rules for categorizing such transactions. In the case of a transfer of a copyright right, this section provides rules for determining whether the transaction should be classified as either a sale or exchange, or a license generating royalty income. In the case of a transfer of a copyrighted article, this section provides rules for determining whether the transaction should be classified as either a sale or exchange, or a lease generating rental income.

(3) *Computer program.*—For purposes of this section, a computer program is a set of statements or instructions to be used directly or indirectly in a computer in order to bring about a certain result. For purposes of this paragraph (a)(3), a computer program includes any media, user manuals, documentation, data base or similar item if the media, user manuals, documentation, data base or similar item is incidental to the operation of the computer program.

(b) *Categories of transactions.*—(1) *General.*—Except as provided in paragraph (b)(2) of this section, a transaction involving the transfer of a computer program, or the provision of services or of know-how with respect to a computer program (collectively, a transfer of a computer program) is treated as being solely one of the following—

(i) A transfer of a copyright right in the computer program;

(ii) A transfer of a copy of the computer program (a copyrighted article);

(iii) The provision of services for the development or modification of the computer program; or

(iv) The provision of know-how relating to computer programming techniques.

(2) *Transactions consisting of more than one category.*—Any transaction involving computer programs which consists of more than one of the transactions described in paragraph (b)(1) of this section shall be treated as separate transactions, with the appropriate provisions of this section being applied to each such transaction. However, any transaction that is de minimis, taking into account the overall transaction and the surrounding facts and circumstances, shall not be treated as a separate transaction, but as part of another transaction.

(c) *Transfers involving copyright rights and copyrighted articles.*—(1) *Classification.*—(i) *Transfers treated as transfers of copyright rights.*—A transfer of a computer program is classified as a transfer of a copyright right if, as a result of the transaction, a person acquires any one or more of the rights described in paragraphs (c)(2)(i) through (iv) of this section. Whether the transaction is treated as being solely the transfer of a copyright right or is treated as separate transactions is determined pursuant to paragraph (b)(1) and (b)(2) of this section. For example, if a person receives a disk containing a copy of a computer program which enables it to exercise, in relation to that program, a non-de minimis right described in paragraphs (c)(2)(i) through (iv) of this section (and the transaction does not involve, or involves only a de minimis provision of services as described in paragraph (d) of this section or of know-how as described in paragraph (e) of this section), then, under paragraph (b)(2) of this section, the transfer is classified solely as a transfer of a copyright right.

(ii) *Transfers treated solely as transfers of copyrighted articles.*—If a person acquires a copy of a computer program but does not acquire any of the rights described in paragraphs (c)(2)(i) through (iv) of this section (or only acquires a de minimis grant of such rights), and the transaction does not involve, or involves only a de minimis, provision of services as described in paragraph (d) of this section or of know-how as described in paragraph (e) of this section, the transfer of the copy of the computer program is classified solely as a transfer of a copyrighted article.

(2) *Copyright rights.*—The copyright rights referred to in paragraph (c)(1) of this section are as follows—

(i) The right to make copies of the computer program for purposes of distribution to the public by sale or other transfer of ownership, or by rental, lease or lending;

(ii) The right to prepare derivative computer programs based upon the copyrighted computer program;

(iii) The right to make a public performance of the computer program; or

(iv) The right to publicly display the computer program.

(3) *Copyrighted article.*—A copyrighted article includes a copy of a computer program from which the work can be perceived, reproduced, or otherwise communicated, either directly or with the aid of a machine or device. The copy of the program may be fixed in the magnetic medium of a floppy disk, or in the main memory or hard drive of a computer, or in any other medium.

(d) *Provision of services.*—The determination of whether a transaction involving a newly developed or modified computer program is treated as either the provision of services or another transaction described in paragraph (b)(1) of this section is based on all the facts and circumstances of the transaction, including, as appropriate, the intent of the parties (as evidenced by their agreement and conduct) as to which party is to own the copyright rights in the computer program and how the risks of loss are allocated between the parties.

(e) *Provision of know-how.*—The provision of information with respect to a computer program will be treated as the provision of know-how for purposes of this section only if the information is—

(1) Information relating to computer programming techniques;

(2) Furnished under conditions preventing unauthorized disclosure, specifically contracted for between the parties; and

(3) Considered property subject to trade secret protection.

(f) *Further classification of transfers involving copyright rights and copyrighted articles.*—(1) *Transfers of copyright rights.*—The determination of whether a transfer of a copyright right is a sale or exchange of property is made on the basis of whether, taking into account all facts and circumstances, there has been a transfer of all substantial rights in the copyright. A transaction that does not constitute a sale or exchange because not all substantial rights have been transferred will be classified as a license generating royalty income. For this purpose, the principles of sections 1222 and 1235 may be applied. Income derived from the sale or exchange of a copyright right will be sourced under section 865(a), (c), (d), (e), or (h), as appropriate. Income derived from the licensing of a copyright right will be sourced under section 861(a)(4) or 862(a)(4), as appropriate.

(2) *Transfers of copyrighted articles.*—The determination of whether a transfer of a copyrighted article is a sale or exchange is made on the basis of whether, taking into account all facts and circumstances, the benefits and burdens of ownership have been transferred. A transaction that does not constitute a sale or exchange because insufficient benefits and burdens of ownership of the copyrighted article have been transferred, such that a person other than the transferee is properly treated as the owner of the copyrighted article, will be classified as a lease generating rental income. Income from transactions that are classified as sales or exchanges of copyrighted articles will be sourced under sections 861(a)(6), 862(a)(6), 863, 865(a), (b), (c), or (e), as appropriate. Income derived from the leasing of a copyrighted article will be sourced under section 861(a)(4) or section 862(a)(4), as appropriate.

(3) *Special circumstances of computer programs.*—In connection with determinations under this paragraph (f), consideration must be given as appropriate to the special characteristics of computer programs in transactions that take advantage of these characteristics (such as the ability to make perfect copies at minimal cost). For example, a transaction in which a person acquires a copy of a computer program on disk subject to a requirement that the disk be destroyed after a specified period is generally the equivalent of a transaction subject to a requirement that the disk be returned after such period. Similarly, a transaction in which the program deactivates itself after a specified period is generally the equivalent of returning the copy.

(g) *Rules of operation.*—(1) *Term applied to transaction by parties.*—Neither the form adopted by the parties to a transaction, nor the classification of the transaction under copyright law, shall be determinative. Therefore, for example, if there is a transfer of a computer program on a single disk for a one-time payment with restrictions on transfer and reverse engineering, which the parties characterize as a license (including, but not limited to, agreements commonly referred to as shrink-wrap licenses), application of the rules of paragraphs (c) and (f) of this section may nevertheless result in the transaction being classified as the sale of a copyrighted article.

(2) *Means of transfer not to be taken into account.*—The rules of this section shall be applied irrespective of the physical or electronic or other medium used to effectuate a transfer of a computer program.

(3) *To the public.*—(i) *In general.*—For purposes of paragraph (c)(2)(i) of this section, a transferee of a computer program shall not be considered to have the right to distribute copies of the program to the public if it is permitted to distribute copies of the software to only either a related person, or to identified persons who may be identified by either name or by legal relationship to the original transferee. For purposes of this subparagraph, a related person is a person who bears a relationship to the transferee specified in section 267(b)(3), (10), (11), or (12), or section 707(b)(1)(B). In applying section 267(b), 267(f), 707(b)(1)(B), or 1563(a), "10 percent" shall be substituted for "50 percent."

(ii) *Use by individuals.*—The number of employees of a transferee of a computer program who are permitted to use the program in connection with their employment is not relevant for purposes of this paragraph (g)(3). In addition, the number of individuals with a contractual agreement to provide services to the transferee of a computer program who are permitted to use the program in connection with the performance of those services is not relevant for purposes of this paragraph (g)(3).

(h) *Examples.*—The provisions of this section may be illustrated by the following examples:

Example 1. (i) *Facts.* Corp A, a U.S. corporation, owns the copyright in a computer program, Program X. It copies Program X onto disks. The disks are placed in boxes covered with a wrapper on which is printed what is generally referred to as a shrink-wrap license. The license is stated to be perpetual. Under the license no reverse engineering, decompilation, or disassembly of the computer program is permitted. The transferee receives, first, the right to use the program on two of its own computers (for example, a laptop and a desktop) provided that only one copy is in use at any one time, and, second, the right to make one copy of the program on each machine as an essential step in the utilization of the program. The transferee is permitted by the shrink-wrap license to sell the copy so long as it destroys any other copies it has made and imposes the same terms and conditions of the license on the purchaser of its copy. These disks are made available for sale to the general public in Country Z. In return for valuable consideration, P, a Country Z resident, receives one such disk.

(ii) *Analysis.* (A) Under paragraph (g)(1) of this section, the label license is not determinative. None of the copyright rights described in paragraph (c)(2) of this section have been transferred in this transaction. P has received a copy of the program, however, and, therefore, under paragraph (c)(1)(ii) of this section, P has acquired solely a copyrighted article.

(B) Taking into account all of the facts and circumstances, P is properly treated as the owner of a copyrighted article. Therefore, under paragraph (f)(2) of this section, there has been a sale of a copyrighted article rather than the grant of a lease.

Example 2. (i) *Facts.* The facts are the same as those in *Example 1,* except that instead of selling disks, Corp A, the U.S. corporation, decides to make Program X available, for a fee, on a World Wide Web home page on the Internet. P, the Country Z resident, in return for payment made to Corp A, downloads Program X (via modem) onto the hard drive of his computer. As part of the electronic communication, P signifies his assent to a license agreement with terms identical to those in *Example 1,* except that in this case P may make a back-up copy of the program on to a disk.

(ii) *Analysis.* (A) None of the copyright rights described in paragraph (c)(2) of this section have passed to P. Although P did not buy a physical copy of the disk with the program on it, paragraph (g)(2) of this section provides that the means of transferring the program is irrelevant. Therefore, P has acquired a copyrighted article.

(B) As in *Example 1,* P is properly treated as the owner of a copyrighted article. Therefore, under paragraph (f)(2) of this section, there has been a sale of a copyrighted article rather than the grant of a lease.

Example 3. (i) *Facts.* The facts are the same as those in *Example 1,* except that Corp A only allows P, the Country Z resident, to use

Program X for one week. At the end of that week, P must return the disk with Program X on it to Corp A. P must also destroy any copies made of Program X. If P wishes to use Program X for a further period he must enter into a new agreement to use the program for an additional charge.

(ii) *Analysis.* (A) Under paragraph (c)(2) of this section, P has received no copyright rights. Because P has received a copy of the program under paragraph (c)(1)(ii) of this section, he has, therefore, received a copyrighted article.

(B) Taking into account all of the facts and circumstances, P is not properly treated as the owner of a copyrighted article. Therefore, under paragraph (f)(2) of this section, there has been a lease of a copyrighted article rather than a sale. Taking into account the special characteristics of computer programs as provided in paragraph (f)(3) of this section, the result would be the same if P were required to destroy the disk at the end of the one week period instead of returning it since Corp A can make additional copies of the program at minimal cost.

Example 4. (i) *Facts.* The facts are the same as those in *Example 2*, where P, the Country Z resident, receives Program X from Corp A's home page on the Internet, except that P may only use Program X for a period of one week at the end of which an electronic lock is activated and the program can no longer be accessed. Thereafter, if P wishes to use Program X, it must return to the home page and pay Corp A to send an electronic key to reactivate the program for another week.

(ii) *Analysis.* (A) As in *Example 3*, under paragraph (c)(2) of this section, P has not received any copyright rights. P has received a copy of the program, and under paragraph (g)(2) of this section, the means of transmission is irrelevant. P has, therefore, under paragraph (c)(1)(ii) of this section, received a copyrighted article.

(B) As in *Example 3*, P is not properly treated as the owner of a copyrighted article. Therefore, under paragraph (f)(2) of this section, there has been a lease of a copyrighted article rather than a sale. While P does retain Program X on its computer at the end of the one week period, as a legal matter P no longer has the right to use the program (without further payment) and, indeed, cannot use the program without the electronic key. Functionally, Program X is no longer on the hard drive of P=s computer. Instead, the hard drive contains only a series of numbers which no longer perform the function of Program X. Although in *Example 3*, P was required to physically return the disk, taking into account the special characteristics of computer programs as provided in paragraph (f)(3) of this section, the result in this *Example 4* is the same as in *Example 3*.

Example 5. (i) *Facts.* Corp A, a U.S. corporation, transfers a disk containing Program X to Corp B, a Country Z corporation, and grants Corp B an exclusive license for the remaining term of the copyright to copy and distribute an unlimited number of copies of Program X in the geographic area of Country Z, prepare derivative works based upon Program X, make public performances of Program X, and publicly display Program X. Corp B will pay Corp A a royalty of $y a year for three years, which is the expected period during which Program X will have commercially exploitable value.

(ii) *Analysis.* (A) Although Corp A has transferred a disk with a copy of Program X on it to Corp B, under paragraph (c)(1)(i) of this section because this transfer is accompanied by a copyright right identified in paragraph (c)(2)(i) of this section, this transaction is a transfer solely of copyright rights, not of copyrighted articles. For purposes of paragraph (b)(2) of this section, the disk containing a copy of Program X is a de minimis component of the transaction.

(B) Applying the all substantial rights test under paragraph (f)(1) of this section, Corp A will be treated as having sold copyright rights to Corp B. Corp B has acquired all of the copyright rights in Program X, has received the right to use them exclusively within Country Z, and has received the rights for the remaining life of the copyright in Program X. The fact the payments cease before the copyright term expires is not controlling. Under paragraph (g)(1) of this section, the fact that the agreement is labelled a license is not controlling (nor is the fact that Corp A receives a sum labelled a royalty). (The result in this case would be the same if the copy of Program X to be used for the purposes of reproduction were transmitted electronically to Corp B, as a result of the application of the rule of paragraph (g)(2) of this section.)

Example 6. (i) *Facts.* Corp A, a U.S. corporation, transfers a disk containing Program X to Corp B, a Country Z corporation, and grants Corp B the non exclusive right to reproduce (either directly or by contracting with either Corp A or another person to do so) and distribute for sale to the public an unlimited number of disks at its factory in Country Z in return for a payment related to the number of disks copied and sold. The term of the agreement is two years, which is less than the remaining life of the copyright.

(ii) *Analysis.* (A) As in *Example 5*, the transfer of the disk containing the copy of the program does not constitute the transfer of a copyrighted article under paragraph (c)(1) of this section because Corp B has also acquired a copyright right under paragraph (c)(2)(i) of this section, the right to reproduce and distribute to the public. For purposes of paragraph (b)(2) of this section, the disk containing Program X is a de minimis component of the transaction.

(B) Taking into account all of the facts and circumstances, there has been a license of Program X to Corp B, and the payments made by Corp B are royalties. Under paragraph (f)(1) of this section, there has not been a transfer of all substantial rights in the copyright to Program X because Corp A has the right to enter into other licenses with respect to the copyright of Program X, including licenses in Country Z (or even to sell that copyright, subject to Corp B's interest). Corp B has acquired no right itself to license the copyright rights in Program X. Finally, the term of the license is for less than the remaining life of the copyright in Program X.

Example 7. (i) *Facts.* Corp C, a distributor in Country Z, enters into an agreement with Corp A, a U.S. corporation, to purchase as many copies of Program X on disk as it may from time-to-time request. Corp C will then sell these disks to retailers. The disks are shipped in boxes covered by shrink-wrap licenses (identical to the license described in *Example 1*).

(ii) *Analysis.* (A) Corp C has not acquired any copyright rights under paragraph (c)(2) of this section with respect to Program X. It has acquired individual copies of Program X, which it may sell to others. The use of the term license is not dispositive under paragraph (g)(1) of this section. Under paragraph (c)(1)(ii) of this section, Corp C has acquired copyrighted articles.

(B) Taking into account all of the facts and circumstances, Corp C is properly treated as the owner of copyrighted articles. Therefore, under paragraph (f)(2) of this section, there has been a sale of copyrighted articles.

Example 8. (i) *Facts.* Corp A, a U.S. corporation, transfers a disk containing Program X to Corp D, a foreign corporation engaged in the manufacture and sale of personal computers in Country Z. Corp A grants Corp D the non-exclusive right to copy Program X onto the hard drive of an unlimited number of computers, which Corp D manufactures, and to distribute those copies (on the hard drive) to the public. The term of the agreement is two years, which is less than the remaining life of the copyright in Program X. Corp D pays Corp A an amount based on the number of copies of Program X it loads on to computers.

(ii) *Analysis.* The analysis is the same as in *Example 6*. Under paragraph (c)(2)(i) of this section, Corp D has acquired a copyright right enabling it to exploit Program X by copying it on to the hard drives of the computers that it manufactures and then sells. For purposes of paragraph (b)(2) of this section, the disk containing Program X is a de minimis component of the transaction. Taking into account all of the facts and circumstances, Corp D has not, however, acquired all substantial rights in the copyright to Program X (for example, the term of the agreement is less than the remaining life of the copyright). Under paragraph (f)(1) of this section, this transaction is, therefore, a license of Program X to Corp D rather than a sale and the payments made by Corp D are royalties. (The result would be the same if Corp D included with the computers it sells an archival copy of Program X on a floppy disk.)

Example 9. (i) *Facts.* The facts are the same as in *Example 8*, except that Corp D, the Country Z corporation, receives physical disks. The disks are shipped in boxes covered by shrink-wrap licenses (identical to the licenses described in *Example 1*). The terms of these licenses do not permit Corp D to make additional copies of Program X. Corp D uses each individual disk only once to load a single copy of Program X onto each separate computer. Corp D transfers the disk with the computer when it is sold.

(ii) *Analysis.* (A) As in *Example 7* (unlike *Example 8*) no copyright right identified in paragraph (c)(2) of this section has been transferred. Corp D acquires the disks without the right to reproduce and distribute publicly further copies of Program X. This is therefore the transfer of copyrighted articles under paragraph (c)(1)(ii) of this section.

(B) Taking into account all of the facts and circumstances, Corp D is properly treated as the owner of copyrighted articles. Therefore, under paragraph (f)(2) of this section, the transaction is classified as the sale of a copyrighted article. (The result would be the same if Corp D used a single physical disk to copy Program X onto each computer, and transferred an unopened box containing Program X with each computer, if Corp D were not permitted to copy Program X onto more computers than the number of individual copies purchased.)

Example 10. (i) *Facts.* Corp A, a U.S. corporation, transfers a disk containing Program X to Corp E, a Country Z corporation, and grants Corp E the right to load Program X onto 50 individual workstations for use only by Corp E employees at one location in return for a one-time per-user fee (generally referred to as a site license or enterprise license). If additional workstations are subsequently introduced, Program X may be loaded onto those machines for additional one-time per-user fees. The license which grants the rights to operate Program X on 50 workstations also prohibits Corp E from selling the disk (or any of the 50 copies) or reverse engineering the program. The term of the license is stated to be perpetual.

(ii) *Analysis.* (A) The grant of a right to copy, unaccompanied by the right to distribute those copies to the public, is not the transfer of a copyright right under paragraph (c)(2) of this section. Therefore, under paragraph (c)(1)(ii) of this section, this transaction is a transfer of copyrighted articles (50 copies of Program X).

(B) Taking into account all of the facts and circumstances, P is properly treated as the owner of copyrighted articles. Therefore, under paragraph (f)(2) of this section, there has been a sale of copyrighted articles rather than the grant of a lease. Notwithstanding the restriction on sale, other factors such as, for example, the risk of loss and the right to use the copies in perpetuity outweigh, in this case, the restrictions placed on the right of alienation.

(C) The result would be the same if Corp E were permitted to copy Program X onto an unlimited number of workstations used by employees of either Corp E or corporations that had a relationship to Corp E specified in paragraph (g)(3) of this section.

Example 11. (i) *Facts.* The facts are the same as in *Example 10*, except that Corp E, the Country Z corporation, acquires the right to make Program X available to workstation users who are Corp E employees by way of a local area network (LAN). The number of users that can use Program X on the LAN at any one time is limited to 50. Corp E pays a one-time fee for the right to have up to 50 employees use the program at the same time.

(ii) *Analysis.* Under paragraph (g)(2) of this section the mode of utilization is irrelevant. Therefore, as in *Example 10*, under paragraph (c)(2) of this section, no copyright right has been transferred, and, thus, under paragraph (c)(1)(ii) of this section, this transaction will be classified as the transfer of a copyrighted article. Under the benefits and burdens test of paragraph (f)(2) of this section, this transaction is a sale of copyrighted articles. The result would be the same if an unlimited number of Corp E employees were permitted to use Program X on the LAN or if Corp E were permitted to copy Program X onto LANs maintained by corporations that had a relationship to Corp E specified in paragraph (g)(3) of this section.

Example 12. (i) *Facts.* The facts are the same as in *Example 11*, except that Corp E pays a monthly fee to Corp A, the U.S. corporation, calculated with reference to the permitted maximum number of users (which can be changed) and the computing power of Corp E's server. In return for this monthly fee, Corp E receives the right to receive upgrades of Program X when they become available. The agreement may be terminated by either party at the end of any month. When the disk containing the upgrade is received, Corp E must return the disk containing the earlier version of Program X to Corp A. If the contract is terminated, Corp E must delete (or otherwise destroy) all copies made of the current version of Program X. The agreement also requires Corp A to provide technical support to Corp E but the agreement does not allocate the monthly fee between the right to receive upgrades of Program X and the technical support services. The amount of technical support that Corp A will provide to Corp E is not foreseeable at the time the contract is entered into but is expected to be de minimis. The agreement specifically provides that Corp E has not thereby been granted an option to purchase Program X.

(ii) *Analysis.* (A) Corp E has received no copyright rights under paragraph (c)(2) of this section. Corp A has not provided any services described in paragraph (d) of this section. Based on all the facts and circumstances of the transaction, Corp A has provided de minimis technical services to Corp E. Therefore, under paragraph (c)(1)(ii) of this section, the transaction is a transfer of a copyrighted article.

(B) Taking into account all facts and circumstances, under the benefits and burdens test Corp E is not properly treated as the owner of the copyrighted article. Corp E does not receive the right to use Program X in perpetuity, but only for so long as it continues to make payments. Corp E does not have the right to purchase Program X on advantageous (or, indeed, any) terms once a certain amount of money has been paid to Corp A or a certain period of time has elapsed (which might indicate a sale). Once the agreement is terminated, Corp E will no longer possess any copies of Program X, current or superseded. Therefore under paragraph (f)(2) of this section there has been a lease of a copyrighted article.

Example 13. (i) *Facts.* The facts are the same as in *Example 12*, except that, while Corp E must return copies of Program X as new upgrades are received, if the agreement terminates, Corp E may keep the latest version of Program X (although Corp E is still prohibited from selling or otherwise transferring any copy of Program X).

(ii) *Analysis.* For the reasons stated in *Example 10*, paragraph (ii)(B), the transfer of the program will be treated as a sale of a copyrighted article rather than as a lease.

Example 14. (i) *Facts.* Corp G, a Country Z corporation, enters into a contract with Corp A, a U.S. corporation, for Corp A to modify Program X so that it can be used at Corp G's facility in Country Z. Under the contract, Corp G is to acquire one copy of the program on a disk and the right to use the program on 5,000 workstations. The contract requires Corp A to rewrite elements of Program X so that it will conform to Country Z accounting standards and states that Corp A retains all copyright rights in the modified Program X. The agreement between Corp A and Corp G is otherwise identical as to rights and payment terms as the agreement described in *Example 10*.

(ii) *Analysis.* (A) As in *Example 10*, no copyright rights are being transferred under paragraph (c)(2) of this section. In addition, since no copyright rights are being transferred to Corp G, this transaction does not involve the provision of services by Corp A under paragraph (d) of this section. This transaction will be classified, therefore, as a transfer of copyrighted articles under paragraph (c)(1)(ii) of this section.

(B) Taking into account all facts and circumstances, Corp G is properly treated as the owner of copyrighted articles. Therefore, under paragraph (f)(2) of this section, there has been the sale of a copyrighted article rather than the grant of a lease.

Example 15. (i) *Facts.* Corp H, a Country Z corporation, enters into a license agreement for a new computer program. Program Q is to be written by Corp A, a U.S. corporation. Corp A and Corp H agree that Corp A is writing Program Q for Corp H and that, when Program Q is completed, the copyright in Program Q will belong to Corp H. Corp H gives instructions to Corp A programmers regarding program specifications. Corp H agrees to pay Corp A a fixed monthly sum during development of the program. If Corp H is dissatisfied with the development of the program, it may cancel the contract at the end of any month. In the event of termination, Corp A will retain all payments, while any procedures, techniques or copyrightable interests will be the property of Corp H. All of the payments are labelled royalties. There is no provision in the agreement for any continuing relationship between Corp A and Corp H, such as the furnishing of updates of the program, after completion of the modification work.

(ii) *Analysis.* Taking into account all of the facts and circumstances, Corp A is treated as providing services to Corp H. Under paragraph (d) of this section, Corp A is treated as providing services to Corp H because Corp H bears all of the risks of loss associated with the development of Program Q and is the owner of all copyright rights in Program Q. Under paragraph (g)(1) of this section, the fact that the agreement is labelled a license is not controlling (nor is the fact that Corp A receives a sum labelled a royalty).

Example 16. (i) *Facts.* Corp A, a U.S. corporation, and Corp I, a Country Z corporation, agree that a development engineer employed by Corp A will travel to Country Z to provide know-how relating to certain techniques not generally known to computer programmers, which will enable Corp I to more efficiently create computer programs. These techniques represent the product of experience gained by Corp A from working on many computer programming projects, and are furnished to Corp I under nondisclosure conditions. Such information is property subject to trade secret protection.

(ii) *Analysis.* This transaction contains the elements of know-how specified in paragraph (e) of this section. Therefore, this transaction will be treated as the provision of know-how.

Example 17. (i) *Facts.* Corp A, a U.S. corporation, transfers a disk containing Program Y to Corp E, a Country Z corporation, in exchange for a single fixed payment. Program Y is a computer program development program, which is used to create other computer programs, consisting of several components, including libraries of reusable software components that serve as general building blocks in new software applications. No element of these libraries is a significant component of any overall new program. Because a computer program created with the use of Program Y will not operate unless the libraries are also present, the license agreement between Corp A and Corp E grants Corp E the right to distribute copies of the libraries with any program developed using Program Y. The license agreement is otherwise identical to the license agreement in *Example 1*.

(ii) *Analysis.* (A) No non-de minimis copyright rights described in paragraph (c)(2) of this section have passed to Corp E. For purposes of paragraph (b)(2) of this section, the right to distribute the libraries in conjunction with the programs created using Program Y is a de minimis component of the transaction. Because Corp E has received a copy of the program under paragraph (c)(1)(ii) of this section, it has received a copyrighted article.

(B) Taking into account all the facts and circumstances, Corp E is properly treated as the owner of a copyrighted article. Therefore, under paragraph (f)(2) of this section, there has been the sale of a copyrighted article rather than the grant of a lease.

Example 18. (i) *Facts.* (A) Corp A, a U.S. corporation, transfers a disk containing Program X to Corp E, a country Z Corporation. The disk contains both the object code and the source code to Program X and the license agreement grants Corp E the right to—

(*1*) Modify the source code in order to correct minor errors and make minor adaptations to Program X so it will function on Corp E=s computer; and

(*2*) Recompile the modified source code.

(B) The license does not grant Corp E the right to distribute the modified Program X to the public. The license is otherwise identical to the license agreement in *Example 1.*

(ii) *Analysis.* (A) No non-de minimis copyright rights described in paragraph (c)(2) of this section have passed to Corp E. For purposes of paragraph (b)(2) of this section, the right to modify the source code and recompile the source code in order to create new code to correct minor errors and make minor adaptations is a de minimis component of the transaction. Because Corp E has received a copy of the program under paragraph (c)(1)(ii) of this section, it has received a copyrighted article.

(B) Taking into account all the facts and circumstances, Corp E is properly treated as the owner of a copyrighted article. Therefore, under paragraph (f)(2) of this section, there has been the sale of a copyrighted article rather than the grant of a lease.

(i) *Effective date.*—(1) *General.*—This section applies to transactions occurring pursuant to contracts entered into on or after December 1, 1998.

(2) *Elective transition rules.*—(i) *Contracts entered into in taxable years ending on or after October 2, 1998.*—A taxpayer may elect to apply this section to transactions occurring pursuant to contracts entered into in taxable years ending on or after October 2, 1998. A taxpayer that makes an election under this paragraph (i)(2)(i) must apply this section to all contracts entered into in taxable years ending on or after October 2, 1998.

(ii) *Contracts entered into before October 2, 1998.*—A taxpayer may elect to apply this section to transactions occurring in taxable years ending on or after October 2, 1998, pursuant to contracts entered into before October 2, 1998, provided the taxpayer would not be required under this section to change its method of accounting as a result of such election, or the taxpayer would be required to change its method of accounting but the resulting section 481(a) adjustment would be zero. A taxpayer that makes an election under this paragraph (i)(2)(ii) must apply this section to all transactions occurring in taxable years ending on or after October 2, 1998, pursuant to contracts entered into before October 2, 1998.

(3) *Manner of making election.*—Taxpayers may elect, under paragraph (i)(2)(i) or (i)(2)(ii) of this section, to apply this section, by treating the transactions in accordance with these regulations on their original tax return.

(4) *Examples.*—The following examples illustrate application of the transition rule of paragraph (i)(2)(ii) of this section:

(i) *Example 1.* Corp A develops computer programs for sale to third parties. Corp A uses an overall accrual method of accounting and files its tax return on a calendar-year basis. In year 1, Corp A enters into a contract to deliver a computer program in that year, and to provide updates for each of the following four years. Under the contract, the computer program and the updates are priced separately, and Corp A is entitled to receive payments for the computer program and each of the updates upon delivery. Assume Corp A properly accounts for the contract as a contract for the provision of services. Corp A properly includes the payments under the contract in gross income in the taxable year the payments are received and the computer program or updates are delivered. Corp A properly deducts the cost of developing the computer program and updates when the costs are incurred. Year 3 includes October 2, 1998. Assume under the rules of this section, the provision of updates would properly be accounted for as the transfer of copyrighted articles. If Corp A made an election under paragraph (i)(2)(ii) of this section, Corp A would not be required to change its method of accounting for income under the contract as a result of the election. Corp A would also not be required to change its method of accounting for the cost of developing the computer program and the updates under the contract as a result of the election. Therefore, under paragraph (i)(2)(ii) of this section, Corp A may elect to apply the provisions of this section to the updates provided in years 3, 4, and 5, because Corp A is not required to change from its method of accounting for the contract as a result of the election.

(ii) *Example 2.* Assume the same facts as in *Example 1* except that Corp A is entitled to receive payments for the computer program and each of the updates 30 days after delivery. Corp A properly includes the amounts due under the contract in gross income in the taxable year the computer program or updates are provided. Assume that Corp A properly uses the nonaccrual-experience method described in section 448(d)(5) and § 1.448-2T to account for income on its contracts. If Corp A made an election under paragraph (i)(2)(ii) of this section, Corp A would be required to change from the nonaccrual-experience method for income as a result of the election, because the method is only available with respect to amounts to be received for the performance of services. Therefore, Corp A may not elect to apply the provisions of this section to the updates provided in years 3, 4, and 5, under paragraph (i)(2)(ii) of this section, because Corp A would be required to change from the nonaccrual-experience method of accounting for income on the contract as a result of the election.

(j) *Change in method of accounting required by this section.*—(1) *Consent.*—A taxpayer is granted consent to change its method of accounting for contracts involving computer programs, to conform with the classification prescribed in this section. The consent is granted for contracts entered into on or after December 1, 1998, or in the case of a taxpayer making an election under paragraph (i)(2)(i) of this section, the consent is granted for contracts entered into in taxable years ending on or after October 2, 1998. In addition, a taxpayer that makes an election under paragraph (i)(2)(ii) of this section is granted consent to change its method of accounting for any contract with transactions subject to the election, if the taxpayer is required to change its method of accounting as a result of the election.

(2) *Year of change.*—The year of change is the taxable year that includes December 1, 1998, or in the case of a taxpayer making an election under paragraph (i)(2)(i) or (i)(2)(ii) of this section, the taxable year that includes October 2, 1998.

(k) *Time and manner of making change in method of accounting.*—(1) *General.*—A taxpayer changing its method of accounting in accordance with this section must file a Form 3115, Application for Change in Method of Accounting, in duplicate. The taxpayer must type or print the following statement at the top of page 1 of the Form 3115: "FILED UNDER TREASURY REGULATION § 1.861-18." The original Form 3115 must be attached to the taxpayers original return for the year of change. A copy of the Form 3115 must be filed with the National Office no later than when the original Form 3115 is filed for the year of change.

(2) *Copy of Form 3115.*—The copy required by this paragraph (k)(l) to be sent to the national office should be sent to the Commissioner of Internal Revenue, Attention: CC:DOM:IT&A, P.O. Box 7604, Benjamin Franklin Station, Washington DC 20044 (or in the case of a designated private delivery service: Commissioner of Internal Revenue, Attention: CC:DOM:IT&A, 1111 Constitution Avenue, NW., Washington, DC 20224).

(3) *Effect of consent and Internal Revenue Service review.*—A change in method of accounting granted under this section is subject to review by the district director and the national office and may be modified or revoked in accordance with the provisions of Rev. Proc. 97-37 (1997-33 IRB 18) (or its successors) (see § 601.601(d)(2) of this chapter). [Reg. § 1.861-18.]

☐ [*T.D.* 8785, 9-30-98 (*corrected* 11-24-98). *Amended by T.D.* 9870, 7-11-2019.]

Proposed Amendments to Regulation

§ 1.861-18. Classification of transactions involving digital content.

* * *

(a) * * *

(3) *Digital content.*—For purposes of this section, digital content means a computer program or any other content in digital format that is either protected by copyright law or no longer protected by

copyright law solely due to the passage of time. For example, digital content includes books in digital format, movies in digital format, and music in digital format. For purposes of this section, a computer program is a set of statements or instructions to be used directly or indirectly in a computer in order to bring about a certain result and includes any media, user manuals, documentation, data base, or similar item if the media, user manuals, documentation, data base, or other similar item is incidental to the operation of the computer program.

* * *

(c) * * *

(2) * * *

(iii) The right to make a public performance of digital content, other than a right to publicly perform digital content for the purpose of advertising the sale of the digital content performed; or

(iv) The right to publicly display digital content, other than a right to publicly display digital content for the purpose of advertising the sale of the digital content displayed.

* * *

(f) * * *

(2) *Transfers of copyrighted articles.*—(i) *Classification.*—The determination of whether a transfer of a copyrighted article is a sale or exchange is made on the basis of whether, taking into account all facts and circumstances, the benefits and burdens of ownership have been transferred. A transaction that does not constitute a sale or exchange because insufficient benefits and burdens of ownership of the copyrighted article have been transferred, such that a person other than the transferee is properly treated as the owner of the copyrighted article, will be classified as a lease generating rental income.

(ii) *Source.*—Income from transactions that are classified as sales or exchanges of copyrighted articles will be sourced under section 861(a)(6), 862(a)(6), 863, or 865(a), (b), (c), or (e), as appropriate. When a copyrighted article is sold and transferred through an electronic medium, the sale is deemed to have occurred at the location of download or installation onto the end-user's device used to access the digital content for purposes of § 1.861-7(c), subject to the tax avoidance provisions in § 1.861-7(c). However, in the absence of information about the location of download or installation onto the end-user's device used to access the digital content, the sale will be deemed to have occurred at the location of the customer, which is determined based on the taxpayer's recorded sales data for business or financial reporting purposes. Income derived from leasing a copyrighted article will be sourced under section 861(a)(4) or 862(a)(4), as appropriate.

* * *

(h) * * *

(19) *Example 19*—(i) *Facts.* Corp A operates a website that offers electronic books for download onto end-users' computers or other electronic devices. The books offered by Corp A are protected by copyright law. Under the agreements between content owners and Corp A, Corp A receives from the content owners a digital master copy of each book, which Corp A downloads onto its server, in addition to the nonexclusive right to distribute for sale to the public an unlimited number of copies in return for paying each content owner a specified amount for each copy sold. Corp A may not transfer any of the distribution rights it receives from the content owners. The term of each agreement Corp A has with a content owner is shorter than the remaining life of the copyright. Corp A charges each end-user a fixed fee for each book purchased. When purchasing a book on Corp A's website, the end-user must acknowledge the terms of a license agreement with the content owner that states that the end-user may view the electronic book but may not reproduce or distribute copies of it. In addition, the agreement provides that the end-user may download the book onto a limited number of its devices. Once the end-user downloads the book from Corp A's server onto a device, the end-user may access and view the book from that device, which does not need to be connected to the Internet in order for the end-user to view the book. The end-user owes no additional payment to Corp A for the ability to view the book in the future.

(ii) *Analysis.* (A) Notwithstanding the license agreement between each end-user and content owner granting the end-user rights to use the book, the relevant transactions are the transfer of a master copy of the book and rights to sell copies from the content owner to Corp A, and the transfers of copies of books by Corp A to end-users. Although the content owner is identified as a party to the license agreement memorializing the end-user's rights with respect to the book, each end-user obtains those rights directly from Corp A, not from the content owner. Because the end-user receives only a copy of each book and does not receive any of the copyright rights described in paragraph (c)(2) of this section, the transaction between Corp A and the end-user is classified as the transfer of a copyrighted article under paragraph (c)(1)(ii) of this section. See paragraphs (h)(1) and (2) of this section (*Example 1* and *Example 2*). Under the benefits and burdens test of paragraph (f)(2) of this section, the transaction is classified as a sale and not a lease, because the end-user receives the right to view the book in perpetuity on its device.

(B) The transaction between each content owner and Corp A is a transfer of copyright rights. In obtaining a master copy of the book along with the right to sell an unlimited number of copies to customers, Corp A receives a copyright right described in paragraph (c)(2)(i) of this section. For purposes of paragraph (b)(2) of this section, the digital master copy is de minimis. Under paragraph (f)(1) of this section, there has not been a transfer of all substantial rights in the copyright rights to the content because each content owner retains the right to further license or sell the copyrights, subject to Corp A's interest; Corp A has acquired no right itself to transfer the copyright rights to any of the content; and the grant of distribution rights is for less than the remaining life of the copyright to each book. Therefore, the transaction between each content owner and Corp A is classified as a license, and not a sale, of copyright rights.

(20) *Example 20*—(i) *Facts.* Corp A offers end-users memberships that provide them with unlimited access to Corp A's catalog of copyrighted music in exchange for a monthly fee. In order to access the music, an end-user must download each song onto a computer or other electronic device. The end-user may download songs onto a limited number of its devices. Under the membership agreement terms, an end-user may listen to the songs but may not reproduce or distribute copies of them. Once the end-user stops paying Corp A the monthly membership fee, an electronic lock is activated so that the end-user can no longer access the music.

(ii) *Analysis.* The end-users receive none of the copyright rights described in paragraph (c)(2) of this section and instead receive only copies of the digital content. Therefore, under paragraph (c)(1)(ii) of this section, each download is classified as the transfer of a copyrighted article. Although an end-user will retain a copy of the content at the end of the payment term, the end-user cannot access the content after the electronic lock is activated. Taking into account the special characteristics of digital content as provided in paragraph (f)(3) of this section, the activation of the electronic lock is the equivalent of having to return the copy. Therefore, under paragraph (f)(2) of this section, each transaction is classified as a lease of a copyrighted article because the right to access the music is limited.

(21) *Example 21*—(i) *Facts.* Corp A offers a catalog of movies and TV shows, all of which are subject to copyright protection. Corp A gives end-users several options for viewing the content, each of which has a separate price. A "streaming" option allows an end-user to view the video, which is hosted on Corp A's servers, while connected to the Internet for as many times as the end-user wants during a limited period. A "rent" option allows an end-user to download the video to its computer or other electronic device (which does not need to be connected to the Internet for viewing) and watch the video as many times as the end-user wants for a limited period, after which an electronic lock is activated and the end-user may no longer view the content. A "purchase" option allows an end-user to download the video and view it as many times as the end-user chooses with no end date. Under all three options, the end-user may view the video but may not reproduce or distribute copies of it. Under the "rent" and "purchase" options, the end-user may download the video onto a limited number of its devices.

(ii) *Analysis.* (A) With respect to the "rent" and "purchase" options, the end-user receives none of the copyright rights described in paragraph (c)(2) of this section but, rather, receives only copies of the digital content. Therefore, transactions under those two options are transfers of copyrighted articles. Transactions for which the end-user chooses the "purchase" option are classified as sales of copyrighted articles under the benefits and burdens test of paragraph (f)(2) of this section because the end-user receives the right to view the videos in perpetuity. Transactions under the "rent" option are classified as leases of copyrighted articles under paragraph (f)(2) of this section because the end-user's right to view the videos is for a limited period.

(B) For transactions under the "streaming" option, there is no transfer of any copyright rights described in paragraph (c)(2) of this section. There is also no transfer of a copyrighted article, because the content is not downloaded by an end-user, but rather is accessed through an on-demand network. The transaction also does not constitute the provision of services for the development of digital content or the provision of know-how under paragraph (b)(1) of this section. Therefore, paragraph (b)(1) of this section does not apply to such transaction. Instead, the transaction is a cloud transaction that is classified under § 1.861-19. See § 1.861-19(d)(9).

(i) *Effective date.*—This section applies to transactions not subject to § 1.861-19 involving the transfer of digital content, or the provision of services or of know-how in connection with digital content, pursuant to contracts entered into in taxable years beginning on or after the date of publication of a Treasury decision adopting these rules as final regulations in the **Federal Register**. For transactions involving computer programs occurring pursuant to contracts entered into in taxable years beginning before the date of publication of a Treasury decision adopting these rules as final regulations in the **Federal Register**, see § 1.861-18(i) as contained in T.D. 8785 and T.D. 9870.

(j) *Change in method of accounting required by this section.*—In order to comply with this section, a taxpayer engaging in a transaction involving digital content pursuant to a contract entered into in taxable years beginning on or after the date described in paragraph (i) of this section may be required to change its method of accounting. If so required, the taxpayer must secure the consent of the Commissioner in accordance with the requirements of § 1.446-1(e) and the applicable administrative procedures for obtaining the Commissioner's consent under section 446(e) for voluntary changes in methods of accounting. [Prop. Reg. § 1.861-18.]

[Proposed 8-14-2019 (*corrected* 10-2-2019).]

Proposed Regulation

§ 1.861-19. Classification of cloud transactions.—(a) *In general.*—This section provides rules for classifying a cloud transaction (as defined in paragraph (b) of this section) either as a provision of services or as a lease of property. The rules of this section apply for purposes of Internal Revenue Code sections 59A, 245A, 250, 267A, 367, 404A, 482, 679, and 1059A; subchapter N of chapter 1; chapters 3 and 4; and sections 842 and 845 (to the extent involving a foreign person), and apply with respect to transfers to foreign trusts not covered by section 679.

(b) *Cloud transaction defined.*—A cloud transaction is a transaction through which a person obtains on-demand network access to computer hardware, digital content (as defined in § 1.861-18(a)(3)), or other similar resources, other than on-demand network access that is de minimis taking into account the overall arrangement and the surrounding facts and circumstances. A cloud transaction does not include network access to download digital content for storage and use on a person's computer or other electronic device.

(c) *Classification of transactions.*—(1) *In general.*—A cloud transaction is classified solely as either a lease of computer hardware, digital content (as defined in § 1.861-18(a)(3)), or other similar resources, or the provision of services, taking into account all relevant factors, including the factors set forth in paragraph (c)(2) of this section. The relevance of any factor varies depending on the factual situation, and one or more of the factors set forth in paragraph (c)(2) of this section may not be relevant in a given instance. For purposes of this paragraph (c), computer hardware, digital content, or other similar resources are referred to as "the property," and the party to the transaction making such property available to customers for use is referred to as "the provider."

(2) *Factors demonstrating classification as the provision of services.*—Factors demonstrating that a cloud transaction is classified as the provision of services rather than a lease of property include the following factors—

(i) The customer is not in physical possession of the property;

(ii) The customer does not control the property, beyond the customer's network access and use of the property;

(iii) The provider has the right to determine the specific property used in the cloud transaction and replace such property with comparable property;

(iv) The property is a component of an integrated operation in which the provider has other responsibilities, including ensuring the property is maintained and updated;

(v) The customer does not have a significant economic or possessory interest in the property;

(vi) The provider bears any risk of substantially diminished receipts or substantially increased expenditures if there is nonperformance under the contract;

(vii) The provider uses the property concurrently to provide significant services to entities unrelated to the customer;

(viii) The provider's fee is primarily based on a measure of work performed or the level of the customer's use rather than the mere passage of time; and

(ix) The total contract price substantially exceeds the rental value of the property for the contract period.

(3) *Application to arrangements comprised of multiple transactions.*—An arrangement comprised of multiple transactions generally requires separate classification for each transaction. If at least one of the transactions is a cloud transaction, but not all of the transactions are cloud transactions, this section applies only to classify the cloud transactions. However, any transaction that is de minimis, taking into account the overall arrangement and the surrounding facts and circumstances, will not be treated as a separate transaction, but as part of another transaction.

(d) *Examples.*—The provisions of this section may be illustrated by the examples in this paragraph (d). For purposes of this paragraph, unless otherwise indicated, Corp A is a domestic corporation; Corp B is a foreign corporation; end-users are individuals; and no rights described in § 1.861-18(c)(2) (copyright rights) are transferred as part of the transactions described.

(1) *Example 1: Computing capacity*—(i) *Facts.* Corp A operates data centers on its premises in various locations. Corp A provides Corp B computing capacity on Corp A's servers in exchange for a monthly fee based on the amount of computing power made available to Corp B. Corp B provides its own software to run on Corp A's servers. Depending on utilization levels, the servers accessed by Corp B may also be used simultaneously by other customers. The computing capacity provided to Corp B can be sourced from a variety of servers in one or more of Corp A's data centers, and Corp A determines how its computing resources are allocated among customers. Corp A agrees to keep the servers operational, including by performing physical maintenance and repair, and may replace any server with another server of comparable functionality. Corp A agrees to provide Corp B with a payment credit for server downtime. Corp B has no ability to physically alter any server.

(ii) *Analysis.* (A) The computing capacity transaction between Corp A and Corp B is a cloud transaction described in paragraph (b) of this section because Corp B obtains a non-de minimis right to on-demand network access to computer hardware of Corp A.

(B) Corp B has neither physical possession of nor control of the servers, beyond Corp B's right to access and use the servers. Corp A may replace any server with a functionally comparable server. The servers are a component of an integrated operation in which Corp A has other responsibilities, including maintaining the servers. The transaction does not provide Corp B with a significant economic or possessory interest in the servers. The agreement provides that Corp A will provide Corp B with a payment credit for server downtime, such that Corp A bears risk of substantially diminished receipts in the event of contract nonperformance. The servers may, depending on utilization levels, be used by Corp A to provide significant computing capacity to entities unrelated to Corp B. Corp A is compensated according to the level of Corp B's use (that is, the amount of computing power made available) and not solely based on the passage of time. Taking into account all of the relevant factors, the transaction between Corp A and Corp B is classified as the provision of services under paragraph (c) of this section.

(2) *Example 2: Computing capacity on dedicated servers*—(i) *Facts.* The facts are the same as in paragraph (d)(1)(i) of this section (the facts in *Example 1*), except that, in order to offer more security to Corp B, Corp A provides Corp B computing capacity exclusively through designated servers, which are owned by Corp A and located at Corp A's facilities. Corp A agrees not to use a designated server for any other customer for the duration of its arrangement with Corp B. Corp A's compensation reflects a substantial return for maintaining the servers in addition to the rental value of the servers.

(ii) *Analysis.* (A) As in paragraph (d)(1) of this section, the transaction between Corp A and Corp B is a cloud transaction described in paragraph (b) of this section because Corp B obtains a non-de minimis right to on-demand network access to computer hardware resources of Corp A.

(B) The fact that Corp A provides computing capacity to Corp B through designated servers indicates that such servers are not used concurrently by other Corp A customers. However, Corp A retains physical possession of the servers. In addition, Corp A's sole responsibility for maintaining the servers, and its sole right to replace or physically alter the servers, indicate that Corp A controls the servers. Although Corp B obtains the exclusive right to use certain servers, Corp B does not have a significant economic or possessory interest in the servers because, among other things, Corp A retains the right to replace the servers, Corp A bears the risk of damage to the servers, and Corp B does not share in cost savings associated with the servers because the fee paid by Corp B to Corp A does not vary based on Corp A's costs. The compensation to Corp A substantially exceeds the rental value of the servers. The other relevant factors are analyzed in the same manner as paragraph (d)(1) of this section. Taking into account all of these factors, the transaction between Corp A and Corp B is classified as a provision of services under paragraph (c) of this section.

(3) *Example 3: Access to software development platform and website hosting*—(i) *Facts.* Corp A provides Corp B a software platform that Corp B uses to develop and deploy websites with a range of features, including blogs, message boards, and other collaborative knowledge bases. The software development platform consists of an operating system, web server software, scripting languages, libraries, tools, and back-end relational database software and allows Corp B to use in its websites certain visual elements subject to copyrights held by Corp A. The software development platform is hosted on servers owned by Corp A and located at Corp A's facilities. Corp B's finished websites are also hosted on Corp A's servers. The software development platform and servers are also used concurrently to provide similar functionality to Corp A customers unrelated to Corp B. Corp B accesses the software development platform via a standard web browser. Corp B has no ability to alter the software code. A small amount of scripting code is downloaded onto Corp B's computers to facilitate secure logins and access to the software development platform. All other functions of the software development platform execute on Corp A's servers, and no portion of the core software code is ever downloaded by Corp B or Corp B's customers. Corp A is solely responsible for maintaining the servers and software development platform, including ensuring continued functionality and compatibility with Corp B's browser, providing updates and fixes to the software for the duration of the contract with Corp B, and replacing or upgrading the servers or software at any time with a functionally similar version. Corp B pays Corp A a monthly fee for the platform and website hosting that takes into account the storage requirements of Corp B's websites and the amount of website traffic supported, but there is no stand-alone fee for use of the software development platform. Corp B agrees to pay for Corp A's website hosting services for a minimum period, after which Corp B may continue to pay for Corp A's website hosting services or transfer its developed websites to a different hosting provider. Corp A agrees to provide Corp B with a payment credit for server downtime.

(ii) *Analysis.* (A) Corp A's provision to Corp B of access to the software platform is a cloud transaction described in paragraph (b) of this section because Corp B obtains a non-de minimis right to on-demand network access to computer hardware and software resources of Corp A. Corp A's hosting of Corp B's finished websites is part of the provision of access to the software platform and hardware.

(B) Corp B does not have physical possession of the software platform or servers. Although Corp B uses Corp A's platform to develop and deploy websites, Corp B does not maintain the software platform or the servers on which it is hosted, and Corp B cannot alter the software platform. Accordingly, Corp B does not control the software platform or the servers. Corp A maintains the right to replace or upgrade the software platform and servers with functionally similar versions. The servers and software platform are components of an integrated operation in which Corp A has various responsibilities, including maintaining the servers and updating the software. Corp B does not have a significant economic or possessory interest in Corp A's software platform or servers. Corp B may lose revenue with respect to the websites that it deploys on Corp A's servers when the servers are down; nonetheless, Corp A bears the risk of substantially diminished receipts in the event of contract nonperformance because Corp A will provide Corp B with a payment credit for server downtime. Corp A provides access to the servers and platform to Corp B and other customers concurrently. Corp A is compensated based on Corp B's level of use (that is, the amount of computing resources provided) and not solely by the passage of time. Taking into account all of the factors, the transaction between Corp A and Corp B is classified as a provision of services under paragraph (c) of this section.

(C) Although the download of a small amount of scripting code to facilitate logins and access to the software platform would otherwise constitute a transfer of a computer program, instead of a cloud transaction under paragraph (b) of this section, the download is de minimis in the context of the overall arrangement, and therefore, under paragraph (c)(3) of this section, there is no separate classification of the download. Similarly, the fact that Corp B receives rights to publicly display certain copyrighted visual elements resulting from Corp A's software development platform on Corp B's own websites, which would otherwise constitute a transfer of copyright rights under § 1.861-18, instead of a cloud transaction under paragraph (b) of this section, does not require separate classification because the right to use such elements is also de minimis. Thus, under paragraph (c) of this section, the entire arrangement is classified as a service.

(4) *Example 4: Access to software*—(i) *Facts.* The facts are the same as in paragraph (d)(3)(i) of this section (the facts in *Example 3*), except that, instead of providing website development software, Corp A provides Corp B access to customer relationship management software under several options such as "entry-level," "mid-level," and "advanced-level," via a standard web browser, which Corp A hosts on its servers for a monthly subscription fee. Corp B has no ability to alter the software code, and Corp A agrees to make available new versions of the software as they are developed for the duration of Corp B's contract, and to ensure servers' uptime in accordance with the service level agreement.

(ii) *Analysis.* (A) As in paragraph (d)(3) of this section, the transaction between Corp A and Corp B is a cloud transaction described in paragraph (b) of this section because Corp B obtains a non-de minimis right to on-demand network access to computer hardware and software resources of Corp A.

(B) The relevant factors are analyzed in the same manner as in paragraph (d)(3) of this section, except that compensation due to Corp A is determined based on the option chosen and the passage of time rather than a measure of computing resources utilized. Although as a general matter compensation based on the passage of time is more indicative of a lease than a service transaction, that factor is outweighed by the other factors, which support classification as a service transaction. Taking into account all of the factors, the transaction between Corp A and Corp B is classified as a provision of services under paragraph (c) of this section.

(5) *Example 5: Downloaded software subject to § 1.861-18*—(i) *Facts.* Corp A provides software for download to Corp B that enables Corp B to create a scalable, shared pool of computing resources over Corp B's own network for use by Corp B's employees. Corp B downloads the software, which runs solely on Corp B's servers. Corp A provides Corp B with free updates for download as they become available. Corp B pays Corp A an annual fee, and, upon termination of the arrangement, an electronic lock is activated that prevents Corp B from further using the software.

(ii) *Analysis.* Under paragraph (b) of this section, the download of software for use with Corp B's computer hardware does not constitute on-demand network access by Corp B to Corp A's software. Accordingly, the transaction between Corp A and Corp B is not a cloud transaction described in paragraph (b) of this section. Because the transaction involves the transfer of digital content as defined in § 1.861-18(a)(3), it is classified under § 1.861-18.

(6) *Example 6: Access to online software via an application*—(i) *Facts.* Corp A provides Corp B word processing, spreadsheet, and presentation software and allows employees of Corp B to access the software over the Internet through a web browser or an application ("app"). In order to access the software from a mobile device, Corp B's employees usually download Corp A's app onto their devices. To access the full functionality of the app, the device must be connected to the Internet. Only a limited number of features on the app are available without an Internet connection. Corp B has no ability to alter the software code. The software is hosted on servers owned by Corp A and located at Corp A's facilities and is used concurrently by other Corp A customers. Corp A is solely responsible for maintaining and repairing the servers and software, and ensuring continued functionality and compatibility with Corp B's employees' devices and providing updates and fixes to the software (including the app) for the duration of the contract with Corp B. Corp B pays a monthly fee based on the number of employees with access to the software. Upon termination of the arrangement, Corp A activates an electronic lock preventing Corp B's employees from further utilizing the app, and Corp B's employees are no longer able to access the software via a web browser.

(ii) *Analysis.* (A) Corp A's provision to Corp B of a non-de minimis right to on-demand network access to Corp A's computer hardware and software resources for the purpose of fully utilizing Corp A's software is a cloud transaction described in paragraph (b) of this section.

(B) Corp B has neither physical possession of nor control over Corp A's word processing, spreadsheet, and presentation software or computer hardware. Additionally, the servers and software are part of an integrated operation in which Corp A maintains the servers and updates the software. Corp A makes available its word processing, spreadsheet, and presentation software and servers to Corp B and other customers concurrently. Corp A's compensation, though based in part on the passage of time, is also determined by reference to Corp B's level of use (that is, the number of Corp B employees with access to the software). Taking into account all of the factors, the transaction between Corp A and Corp B is classified as the provision of services under paragraph (c) of this section.

(C) The provision of the app to Corp B's employees by download onto their devices would be a transfer of a computer program rather than a cloud transaction subject to paragraph (b) of this section. However, under paragraph (c)(3) of this section, it is necessary to consider whether that transfer is de minimis in the context of the overall arrangement and in light of the surrounding facts and circumstances. Here, the significance of the download of the app by Corp B's employees is limited by the fact that the device running the app must be connected to Corp A's servers via the Internet to enable most of the app's core functions. The software that enables such functionality remains on Corp A's servers and is accessed through an on-demand network by Corp B's employees. Therefore, the download of the app is de minimis, and under paragraph (c)(3) of this section, the entire arrangement is classified as a service.

(7) *Example 7: Access to offline software with limited online functions*—(i) *Facts.* Corp A provides Corp B word processing, spreadsheet, and presentation software that is functionally similar to the software in paragraph (d)(6) of this section (*Example 6*). The software is made available for access over the Internet but only to download the software onto a computer or onto a mobile device in the form of an app. The downloaded software contains all the core functions of the software. Employees of Corp B can use the software on their computers or mobile devices regardless of whether their computer or mobile device is online. When online, the software provides a few ancillary functions that are not available offline, such as access to document templates and data collection for diagnosing problems with the software. Whether working online or offline, Corp B employees can store their files only on their own computer or mobile device, and not on Corp A's data storage servers. Because the software provides near full functionality without access to Corp A's servers, it requires more computing resources on employees' computers and devices than the app in paragraph (d)(6) of this section. Corp B's employees can also download updates to the software as part of the monthly fee arrangement. Upon termination of the arrangement, an electronic lock is activated so that the software can no longer be accessed.

(ii) *Analysis.* The provision of the software constitutes a lease of a copyrighted article under §1.861-18. See §1.861-18(h)(4). The access to the online ancillary functions otherwise would constitute a cloud transaction under paragraph (b) of this section, but the access to these functions is de minimis in the context of the overall arrangement, considering that the core functions are available offline through the downloaded software. Because there is no cloud transaction described in paragraph (b) of this section, this section does not apply.

(8) *Example 8: Data storage, separate from access to offline software*—(i) *Facts.* The facts are the same as in paragraph (d)(7)(i) of this section (the facts in *Example 7*), except that Corp A also provides data storage to Corp B on Corp A's server systems in exchange for a monthly fee based on the amount of data storage used by Corp B. Under the data storage terms, Corp B employees may store files created by Corp B employees using Corp A's software or other software. Although Corp A's word processing software is compatible with Corp A's data storage systems, the core functionality of Corp A's software is not dependent on Corp B's purchase of the storage plan. Depending on utilization levels, the server systems providing data storage to Corp B may also be used simultaneously for other customers. The data storage provided to Corp B can be sourced from a variety of server systems in one or more of Corp A's data centers, and Corp A determines how its computing resources are allocated among customers. Corp A agrees to keep the server systems operational, including by performing physical maintenance and repair, and may replace any server system with another one of comparable functionality. Corp A agrees to provide Corp B with a payment credit for server downtime. Corp B has no ability to physically alter the server systems.

(ii) *Analysis.* (A) Corp A's provision of software and data storage capacity constitute separate transactions, and neither is de minimis. Therefore, under paragraph (c)(3) of this section, the transactions are classified separately.

(B) As in paragraph (d)(7), Corp B's download of fully functional software, along with on-demand network access to certain limited online features, does not constitute a cloud transaction, but rather constitutes a lease of a copyrighted article under §1.861-18.

(C) Corp A's provision of data storage constitutes a cloud transaction because Corp B obtains a non-de minimis right to on-demand network access to computer hardware of Corp A.

(D) Corp B has neither physical possession of nor control of the server systems, beyond Corp B's right to access and use the servers. Corp A may replace any server with a functionally comparable server. The server systems are a component of an integrated operation in which Corp A has other responsibilities, including maintaining the server systems. The transaction does not provide Corp B with a significant economic or possessory interest in the servers. The servers may, depending on utilization levels, be used by Corp A to provide significant services to entities unrelated to Corp B. Corp A is compensated according to the level of Corp B's use (that is, the amount of data storage used by Corp B) and not solely based on the passage of time. Because Corp A will provide Corp B with a payment credit for server downtime, Corp A bears risk of substantially diminished receipts in the event of contract nonperformance. Taking into account all of these factors, the transaction for data storage is classified as a provision of services under paragraph (c) of this section.

(9) *Example 9: Streaming digital content using third-party servers*—(i) *Facts.* Corp A streams digital content in the form of videos and music to end-users from servers located in data centers owned and operated by Data Center Operator. Data Center Operator's content delivery network facility services multiple customers. Each end-user uses a computer or other electronic device to access unlimited streaming video and music in exchange for payment of a flat monthly fee to Corp A. The end-user may select from among the available content the particular video or song to be streamed. Corp A continually updates its content catalog, replacing content with higher quality versions and adding new content at no additional charge to the end-user. Content that is streamed to the end-user is not stored locally on the end-user's computer or other electronic device and therefore can be played only while the end-user's computer or other electronic device is connected to the Internet. Corp A pays Data Center Operator a fee based on the amount of data storage used and computing power made available in connection with Corp A's content streaming. The storage and computing power provided to Corp A can be sourced from a variety of servers in one or more of Data Center Operator's facilities, and Data Center Operator determines how computing resources are allocated among its customers. Data Center Operator covenants to keep the servers operational, including performing physical maintenance and repair. Corp A has no right or ability to physically alter the servers.

(ii) *Analysis.* (A) The relevant factors for classifying the transaction between Corp A and Data Center Operator are analyzed in the same manner as the computing capacity and data storage transactions in paragraphs (d)(1) and (8) of this section (*Example 1* and *Example 8*), respectively, such that the transaction between Corp A and Data Center Operator is classified as a provision of services by Data Center Operator to Corp A under paragraph (c) of this section.

(B) A transaction between Corp A and an end-user is a cloud transaction described in paragraph (b) of this section because the end-user obtains a non-de minimis right to on-demand network access to digital content of Corp A.

(C) An end-user has neither physical possession of nor control of the digital content. Additionally, Corp A has the right to determine the digital content used in the cloud transaction and retains the right to modify its selection of digital content. Digital content accessed by end-users is a component of an integrated operation in which Corp A's other responsibilities include maintaining and updating its content catalog. Corp A's end-users do not obtain a significant economic or possessory interest in any of the digital content in Corp A's catalog. The digital content provided by Corp A may be accessed concurrently by multiple unrelated end-users. Although, as a general matter, compensation based on the passage of time is more indicative of a lease than a service transaction, that factor is outweighed by the other factors, which support a services classification. Taking into account all of the factors, a transaction between an end-user and Corp A is classified as a provision of services under paragraph (c) of this section.

(10) *Example 10: Downloaded digital content subject to §1.861-18*—(i) *Facts.* Corp A offers digital content in the form of videos and music solely for download onto end-users' computers or other electronic devices for a fee. Once downloaded, the end-user accesses the videos and songs from the end-user's computer or other electronic device, which does not need to be connected to the Internet in order to play the content. The end-user owes no additional payment to Corp A for the ability to play the content in the future.

(ii) *Analysis.* Under paragraph (b) of this section, the download of digital content onto an end-user's computer for storage and use on that computer does not constitute on-demand network access by the end-user to the digital content of Corp A. Accordingly, the transaction between the end-user and Corp A is not a cloud transaction described in paragraph (b) of this section, and this section does not apply to the transaction. Because the transaction involves the transfer of digital content as defined in §1.861-18(a)(3), it will be classified under §1.861-18. See §1.861-18(h)(21).

(11) *Example 11: Access to online database*—(i) *Facts.* Corp A offers an online database of industry-specific materials. End-users access the materials through Corp A's website, which aggregates and organizes information topically and hosts a proprietary search engine. Corp A hosts the website and database on its own servers and provides multiple end-users access to the website and database concurrently. Corp A is solely responsible for maintaining and replacing the servers, website, and database (including adding or updating materials in the database). End-users have no ability to alter the servers, website, or database. Most materials in Corp A's database are publicly available by other means, but Corp A's website offers an efficient way to locate and obtain the information on demand. Certain materials in Corp A's database constitute digital content within the meaning of §1.861-18(a)(3), and Corp A pays the copyright owners a license fee for using them. Each end-user may download any of the materials to its own computer and keep such materials without further payment. The end-user pays Corp A a fee based on the number of searches or the amount of time spent on the website, and such fee is not dependent on the amount of materials the end-user downloads. The fee that the end-user pays is substantially higher than the stand-alone charge for accessing the same digital content outside of Corp A's system.

(ii) *Analysis.* (A) Corp A's provision to an end-user of access to Corp A's website and online database is a cloud transaction described in paragraph (b) of this section because the end-user obtains a non-de minimis right to on-demand access to Corp A's computer hardware and software resources.

(B) An end-user's downloading of the digital content would be classified as a sale of copyrighted articles under §1.861-18. Nonetheless, taking into account the entire arrangement, including that the primary benefit to the end-user is access to Corp A's database and its proprietary search engine, and that the stand-alone charge for accessing the digital content would be substantially less than the fee Corp A charges, the downloads are de minimis. Accordingly, under paragraph (c)(3) of this section, there is no separate classification of the downloads.

(C) The end-user has neither physical possession of nor control of the database, software, or the servers that host the database or software. Corp A retains the right to replace its servers and update its software and database. The database, software, and servers are part of an integrated operation in which Corp A is responsible for curating the database, updating the software, and maintaining the servers. Corp A provides each end-user on-demand network access to its software and online database concurrently with other end-users. Certain end-users pay Corp A a fee based on time spent on Corp A's website, which could be construed as compensation based on the passage of time and thus be more indicative of a lease than a service transaction. However, the fee that the end-user pays is substantially higher than the stand-alone charge for accessing the same digital content outside of Corp A's system. Accordingly, on balance, the fee arrangement supports the classification of the transaction as a service transaction. Taking into account all of these factors, the arrangement between end-users and Corp A is treated as the provision of services under paragraph (c) of this section.

(e) *Effective/applicability date.*—This section applies to cloud transactions occurring pursuant to contracts entered into in taxable years beginning on or after the date of publication of a Treasury decision adopting these rules as final regulations in the **Federal Register**.

(f) *Change in method of accounting required by this section.*—In order to comply with this section, a taxpayer engaging in a cloud transaction pursuant to a contract entered into on or after the date described in paragraph (e) of this section may be required to change its method of accounting. If so required, the taxpayer must secure the consent of the Commissioner in accordance with the requirements of §1.446-1(e) and the applicable administrative procedures for obtaining the Commissioner's consent under section 446(e) for voluntary changes in methods of accounting. [Prop. Reg. §1.861-19.]

[Proposed 8-14-2019.]

§1.861-20. Allocation and apportionment of foreign income taxes.—(a) *Scope.*—This section provides rules for the allocation and apportionment of foreign income taxes, including allocating and apportioning foreign income taxes to separate categories for purposes of the foreign tax credit. The rules of this section apply except as modified under the rules for an operative section (as described in §1.861-8(f)(1)). See, for example, §§1.704-1(b)(4)(viii)(*d*)(*1*), 1.904-6, 1.960-1(d)(3)(ii), and 1.965-5(b)(2). Paragraph (b) of this section provides definitions for the purposes of this section. Paragraph (c) of this section provides the general rule for allocation and apportionment of foreign income taxes. Paragraph (d) of this section provides rules for assigning foreign gross income to statutory and residual groupings. Paragraph (e) of this section provides rules for allocating and apportioning foreign law deductions to foreign gross income in the statutory and residual groupings. Paragraph (f) of this section provides rules for apportioning foreign income taxes among statutory and residual groupings. Paragraph (g) of this section provides examples that illustrate the application of this section. Paragraph (h) of this section provides the applicability date for this section.

(b) *Definitions.*—The following definitions apply for purposes of this section.

(1) *Corporation.*—The term *corporation* has the same meaning as set forth in §301.7701-2(b) of this chapter, and so includes a reverse hybrid.

(2) *Corresponding U.S. item.*—The term *corresponding U.S. item* means the item of U.S. gross income or U.S. loss, if any, that arises from the same transaction or other realization event from which an item of foreign gross income also arises. An item of U.S. gross income or U.S. loss is a corresponding U.S. item even if the item of foreign gross income that arises from the same transaction or realization event differs in amount from the item of U.S. gross income or U.S. loss. A corresponding U.S. item does not include an item of gross income that is exempt, excluded, or eliminated from U.S. gross income, nor does it include an item of U.S. gross income or U.S. loss that is not realized, recognized or taken into account by the taxpayer in the U.S. taxable year in which the taxpayer paid or accrued the foreign income tax, except as provided in the next sentence. If a taxpayer pays or accrues a foreign income tax that is imposed on foreign taxable income that includes an item of foreign gross income by reason of a transaction or other realization event that also gave rise to an item of U.S. gross income or U.S. loss, but the U.S. and foreign taxable years end on different dates and the event occurred in the last U.S. taxable year that ends before the end of the foreign taxable year, then the item of U.S. gross income or U.S. loss is a corresponding U.S. item.

(3) *Disregarded entity.*—The term *disregarded entity* means an entity described in §301.7701-2(c)(2) of this chapter that is disregarded as an entity separate from its owner for Federal income tax purposes.

(4) *Foreign capital gain amount.*—The term *foreign capital gain amount* means the portion of a distribution that under foreign law gives rise to gross income of a type described in section 301(c)(3)(A) or section 731(a).

(5) *Foreign dividend amount.*—The term *foreign dividend amount* means the portion of a distribution that is taxable as a dividend under foreign law.

(6) *Foreign gross income.*—The term *foreign gross income* means the items of gross income included in the base upon which a foreign income tax is imposed. This includes all items of foreign gross income included in the foreign tax base, even if the foreign taxable year begins in the U.S. taxable year that precedes the U.S. taxable year in which the taxpayer pays or accrues the foreign income tax.

(7) *Foreign income tax.*—The term *foreign income tax* has the meaning provided in §1.901-2(a).

(8) *Foreign law CFC.*—The term *foreign law CFC* means an entity that is a body corporate under foreign law, certain of the earnings of which are taxable to its shareholder under a foreign law inclusion regime.

(9) *Foreign law disposition.*—The term *foreign law disposition* means an event that foreign law treats as a taxable disposition or deemed disposition of property but that Federal income tax law does not treat as a disposition causing the recognition of gain or loss (for example, marking property to market under foreign law).

(10) *Foreign law distribution*.—The term *foreign law distribution* means an event that foreign law treats as a taxable distribution (other than by reason of a foreign law inclusion regime) but that Federal income tax law does not treat as a distribution of property within the meaning of section 317(a) (for example, a stock dividend described in section 305 or a foreign law consent dividend).

(11) *Foreign law inclusion regime*.—A *foreign law inclusion regime* is a foreign law tax regime similar to the subpart F or GILTI regime described in sections 951 through 959, or the PFIC regime described in sections 1293 through 1295 (relating to qualified electing funds), that imposes a tax on a shareholder of an entity based on an inclusion in the shareholder's taxable income of certain of the entity's current earnings, whether or not the foreign law deems the entity's earnings to be distributed.

(12) *Foreign law inclusion regime income*.—The term *foreign law inclusion regime income* means the items of foreign gross income included by a taxpayer with respect to a foreign law CFC by reason of a foreign law inclusion regime.

(13) *Foreign law pass-through income*.—The term *foreign law pass-through income* means the items of a reverse hybrid, computed under foreign law, that give rise to an inclusion in a taxpayer's foreign gross income under the laws of a foreign country imposing tax by reason of the taxpayer's ownership of the reverse hybrid.

(14) *Foreign taxable income*.—The term *foreign taxable income* means foreign gross income reduced by the deductions that are allowed under foreign law.

(15) *Foreign taxable year*.—The term *foreign taxable year* has the meaning set forth in section 7701(a)(23), applied by substituting "under foreign law" for the phrase "under subtitle A."

(16) *Partnership*.—The term *partnership* has the same meaning as set forth in § 301.7701-2(c)(1) of this chapter.

(17) *Previously taxed earnings and profits*.—The term *previously taxed earnings and profits* has the meaning provided in § 1.960-1(b).

(18) *Reverse hybrid*.—The term *reverse hybrid* means a corporation that is a fiscally transparent entity (under the principles of § 1.894-1(d)(3)) or a branch under the laws of a foreign country imposing tax on the income of the entity.

(19) *Taxpayer*.—The term *taxpayer* has the meaning described in § 1.901-2(f)(1).

(20) *U.S. capital gain amount*.—The term *U.S. capital gain amount* means gain recognized by a taxpayer on the sale, exchange, or other disposition of stock or an interest in a partnership or, in the case of a distribution with respect to stock or a partnership interest, the portion of the distribution to which section 301(c)(3)(A) or 731(a)(1), respectively, applies. A U.S. capital gain amount includes gain that is subject to section 751 and § 1.751-1, but does not include the portion of any gain recognized by a taxpayer that is included in gross income as a dividend under section 964(e) or 1248.

(21) *U.S. dividend amount*.—The term *U.S. dividend amount* means the portion of a distribution that is made out of earnings and profits under Federal income tax law, including distributions out of previously taxed earnings and profits described in section 959(a) or (b). It also includes amounts included in gross income as a dividend by reason of section 1248 or section 964(e).

(22) *U.S. equity hybrid instrument*.—The term *U.S. equity hybrid instrument* means an instrument that is treated as stock or a partnership interest for Federal income tax purposes but for foreign income tax purposes is treated as indebtedness or otherwise gives rise to the accrual of income to the holder with respect to such instrument that is not characterized as a dividend or distributive share of partnership income for foreign tax law purposes.

(23) *U.S. gross income*.—The term *U.S. gross income* means the items of gross income that a taxpayer recognizes and includes in taxable income under Federal income tax law for its U.S. taxable year.

(24) *U.S. loss*.—The term *U.S. loss* means the item of loss that a taxpayer recognizes and includes in taxable income under Federal income tax law for its U.S. taxable year.

(25) *U.S. return of capital amount*.—The term *U.S. return of capital amount* means, in the case of the sale, exchange, or other disposition of stock, the taxpayer's adjusted basis of the stock, or in the case of a distribution with respect to stock, the portion of the distribution to which section 301(c)(2) applies.

(26) *U.S. taxable year*.—The term *U.S. taxable year* has the same meaning as that of the term *taxable year* set forth in section 7701(a)(23).

(c) *General rule*.—A foreign income tax (other than certain in lieu of taxes described in paragraph (h) of this section) is allocated and apportioned to the statutory and residual groupings that include the items of foreign gross income included in the base on which the tax is imposed. Each such foreign income tax (that is, each separate levy) is allocated and apportioned separately under the rules in paragraphs (c) through (f) of this section. A foreign income tax is allocated and apportioned to or among the statutory and residual groupings under the following steps:

(1) First, by assigning the items of foreign gross income to the groupings under the rules of paragraph (d) of this section;

(2) Second, by allocating and apportioning the deductions that are allowed under foreign law to the foreign gross income in the groupings under the rules of paragraph (e) of this section; and

(3) Third, by allocating and apportioning the foreign income tax by reference to the foreign taxable income in the groupings under the rules of paragraph (f) of this section.

(d) *Assigning items of foreign gross income to the statutory and residual groupings*.—(1) *In general*.—Each item of foreign gross income is assigned to a statutory or residual grouping. The amount of the item is determined under foreign law. However, Federal income tax law applies to characterize the item and the transaction or other realization event from which the item arose, and to assign it to a grouping. Except as provided in paragraph (d)(3) of this section, if a taxpayer pays or accrues a foreign income tax that is imposed on foreign taxable income that includes an item of foreign gross income with respect to which the taxpayer also realizes, recognizes, or takes into account a corresponding U.S. item, then the item of foreign gross income is assigned to the grouping to which the corresponding U.S. item is assigned. See paragraph (g)(2) of this section (*Example 1*). If the corresponding U.S. item is a U.S. loss (or zero), the foreign gross income is assigned to the grouping to which a gain would be assigned had the transaction or other realization event given rise to a gain, rather than a U.S. loss (or zero), for Federal income tax purposes, and not (if different) to the grouping to which the U.S. loss is allocated and apportioned in computing U.S. taxable income. Paragraph (d)(3) of this section provides special rules regarding the assignment of the item of foreign gross income in particular circumstances.

(2) *Items of foreign gross income with no corresponding U.S. item*.—(i) *In general*.—The rules in paragraphs (d)(2)(ii) and (iii) of this section apply for purposes of characterizing an item of foreign gross income and assigning it to a grouping if the taxpayer does not realize, recognize, or take into account a corresponding U.S. item. But see paragraphs (d)(3)(i)(C) and (d)(3)(iii) of this section for special rules with respect to items of foreign gross income attributable to foreign law pass-through income and foreign law inclusion regime income.

(ii) *Foreign gross income from U.S. nonrecognition event, or U.S. recognition event that falls in a different U.S. taxable year*.—(A) *In general*.—If a taxpayer recognizes an item of foreign gross income arising from a transaction or other foreign realization event that does not result in the recognition of gross income or loss under Federal income tax law in the same U.S. taxable year in which the foreign income tax is paid or accrued or (in the circumstance described in the last sentence of paragraph (b)(2) of this section) in the immediately preceding U.S. taxable year, then the item of foreign gross income is characterized and assigned to the grouping to which the corresponding U.S. item (or the items described in paragraph (d)(3) of this section that are used to assign certain items of foreign gross income to the statutory and residual groupings) would be assigned if the event giving rise to the foreign gross income resulted in the recognition of gross income or loss under Federal income tax law in the U.S. taxable year in which the foreign income tax is paid or accrued.

(B) *Foreign law distributions.*—An item of foreign gross income that a taxpayer includes as a result of a foreign law distribution with respect to either stock or a partnership interest is assigned to the same statutory or residual groupings to which the foreign gross income would be assigned if a distribution of property in the amount of the taxable distribution under foreign law were made for Federal income tax purposes on the date on which the foreign law distribution occurred. See paragraph (g)(6) of this section (*Example 5*). See paragraph (d)(3)(i)(B) of this section for rules regarding the assignment of foreign gross income arising from a distribution with respect to stock. For purposes of applying paragraph (d)(3)(i)(B) of this section to a foreign law distribution, the U.S. dividend amount, U.S. capital gain amount, and U.S. return of capital amount are computed as if the distribution occurred on the date the distribution occurs for foreign law purposes. See § 1.960-1(d)(3)(ii) for rules for assigning foreign gross income arising from a foreign law distribution to income groups or PTEP groups for purposes of section 960 as the operative section, and paragraph (d)(3)(ii)(B) of this section for rules regarding the assignment of foreign gross income arising from a distribution by a partnership.

(C) *Foreign law dispositions.*—A foreign gross income item of gain that a taxpayer includes as a result of a foreign law disposition of property is assigned to the grouping to which a corresponding U.S. item of gain or loss would be assigned on a taxable disposition of the property under Federal income tax law in exchange for an amount equal to the gross receipts or other value used under foreign law to determine the amount of the items of foreign gross income arising from the foreign law disposition in the U.S. taxable year in which the taxpayer paid or accrued the foreign income tax. For example, an item of foreign gross income that results from a deemed disposition of stock under a foreign law mark-to-market regime is assigned under the rules of this paragraph (d)(2)(ii)(C) as though a taxable disposition of the stock occurred under Federal income tax law for an amount equal to the fair market value determined under foreign law for purposes of marking the stock to market. See paragraph (g)(3) of this section (*Example 2*).

(D) *Foreign law transfers between taxable units.*—This paragraph (d)(2)(ii) applies to an item of foreign gross income arising from an event that foreign law treats as a transfer of property, or as giving rise to an item of accrued income, gain, deduction, or loss with respect to a transaction, between taxable units (as defined in paragraph (d)(3)(v)(E) of this section) of the same taxpayer, and that would be treated as a disregarded payment (as defined in paragraph (d)(3)(v)(E) of this section) if the transfer of property occurred, or the item accrued, for Federal income tax purposes in the same U.S. taxable year in which the foreign income tax is paid or accrued. An item of foreign gross income to which this paragraph (d)(2)(ii) applies is characterized and assigned to the grouping to which a disregarded payment in the amount of the item of foreign gross income (or the gross receipts giving rise to the item of foreign gross income) would be assigned under the rules of paragraph (d)(3)(v) of this section if the event giving rise to the foreign gross income resulted in a disregarded payment in the U.S. taxable year in which the foreign income tax is paid or accrued. For example, an item of foreign gross income that a taxpayer recognizes by reason of a foreign law distribution (such as a stock dividend or a consent dividend) from a disregarded entity is assigned to the same statutory or residual groupings to which the foreign gross income would be assigned if a distribution of property in the amount of the taxable distribution under foreign law were made for Federal income tax purposes on the date on which the foreign law distribution occurred.

(iii) *Foreign gross income of a type that is recognized but excluded from U.S. gross income.*—(A) *In general.*—If a taxpayer recognizes an item of foreign gross income that is a type of recognized gross income that Federal income tax law excludes from U.S. gross income, then the item of foreign gross income is assigned to the grouping to which the item of gross income would be assigned if it were included in U.S. gross income. See paragraph (g)(4) of this section (*Example 3*). Notwithstanding the first sentence of this paragraph (d)(2)(iii)(A), foreign gross income that is attributable to a base difference is assigned under paragraph (d)(2)(iii)(B) of this section.

(B) *Base differences.*—If a taxpayer recognizes an item of foreign gross income that is attributable to a base difference, then the item of foreign gross income is assigned to the residual grouping. But see § 1.904-6(b)(1) (assigning foreign gross income attributable to a base difference to foreign source income in the separate category described in section 904(d)(2)(H)(i)) for purposes of applying section 904 as the operative section). An item of foreign gross income is attributable to a base difference under this paragraph (d)(2)(iii)(B) only if the item results from the receipt of one of the following items:

(*1*) Death benefits described in section 101;

(*2*) Gifts and inheritances described in section 102;

(*3*) Contributions to capital described in section 118;

(*4*) Money or other property in exchange for stock described in section 1032 (including by reason of a transfer described in section 351(a)); or

(*5*) Money or other property in exchange for a partnership interest described in section 721.

(3) *Special rules for assigning certain items of foreign gross income to a statutory or residual grouping.*—(i) *Items of foreign gross income that a taxpayer includes by reason of its ownership of an interest in a corporation.*—(A) *Scope.*—The rules of this paragraph (d)(3)(i) apply to characterize and assign to a statutory or residual grouping an item of foreign gross income that a taxpayer includes in foreign taxable income as a result of its ownership of an interest in a corporation with respect to which there is a distribution under both foreign law and Federal income tax law, an inclusion of foreign law pass-through income, or a disposition under both foreign law and Federal income tax law.

(B) *Foreign gross income items arising from a distribution with respect to a corporation.*—(*1*) *In general.*—If there is a distribution by a corporation that is treated as a distribution of property for both foreign law and Federal income tax purposes, a taxpayer first applies the rules of paragraph (d)(3)(i)(B)(*2*) of this section, and then (if necessary) applies the rules of paragraph (d)(3)(i)(B)(*3*) of this section to characterize and assign to the statutory and residual groupings the items of foreign gross income that constitute the foreign dividend amount and the foreign capital gain amount, if any, that arise from the distribution. See paragraph (g)(5) of this section (*Example 4*). For purposes of this paragraph (d)(3)(i)(B), the U.S. dividend amount, U.S. capital gain amount, and U.S. return of capital amount that result from a distribution (including a distribution that occurs on the same date, but in different taxable years, for foreign law purposes and Federal income tax purposes) are computed on the date the distribution occurred for Federal income tax purposes. See paragraph (d)(2)(ii)(B) of this section for rules for assigning foreign gross income arising from any portion of a distribution that is a foreign law distribution. See § 1.960-1(d)(3)(ii) for rules for assigning foreign gross income arising from a distribution described in this paragraph (d)(3)(i)(B) to income groups or PTEP groups for purposes of section 960 as the operative section.

(*2*) *Foreign dividend amounts.*—The foreign dividend amount is, to the extent of the U.S. dividend amount, assigned to the same statutory and residual grouping (or ratably to the groupings) to which a distribution of the U.S. dividend amount is assigned under Federal income tax law. If the foreign dividend amount exceeds the U.S. dividend amount, the excess foreign dividend amount is an item of foreign gross income that is, to the extent of the U.S. return of capital amount, assigned to the same statutory and residual grouping (or ratably to the groupings) to which earnings of the distributing corporation would be assigned if they were recognized for Federal income tax purposes in the U.S. taxable year in which the distribution is made. These earnings are deemed to arise in the statutory and residual groupings in the same proportions as the proportions in which the tax book value of the stock of the distributing corporation is (or would be if the taxpayer were a United States person) assigned to the groupings under the asset method in § 1.861-9 in the U.S. taxable year in which the distribution is made. Any additional excess of the foreign dividend amount over the sum of the U.S. dividend amount and the U.S. return of capital amount is an item of foreign gross income that is assigned to the statutory or residual grouping (or ratably to the groupings) to which the U.S. capital gain amount is assigned.

(*3*) *Foreign capital gain amounts.*—The foreign capital gain amount is, to the extent of the U.S. capital gain amount, assigned to the statutory and residual groupings to which the U.S. capital gain amount is assigned under Federal income tax law. If the foreign capital gain amount exceeds the U.S. capital gain amount, the excess is, to the extent of the U.S. return of capital amount, assigned to the statutory and residual groupings to which earnings equal to the U.S. return of capital amount would be assigned if they were recognized in the U.S. taxable year in which the distribution is made. These earnings are deemed to arise in the statutory and residual groupings in the same proportions as the proportions in which the tax book value of the stock of the distributing corporation is (or would be if the taxpayer were a United States person) assigned under the asset method in § 1.861-9 in the U.S. taxable year in which the distribution is made. Any excess of the foreign capital gain amount over the sum of the U.S. capital gain amount and the U.S. return of capital amount is assigned ratably to the statutory and residual groupings to which the U.S. dividend amount is assigned.

(C) *Foreign law pass-through income from a reverse hybrid.*—An item of foreign law pass-through income that a taxpayer includes in its foreign taxable income as a result of its direct or indirect ownership of a reverse hybrid is assigned to a statutory or residual grouping by treating the taxpayer's items of foreign law pass-through income as the foreign gross income of the reverse hybrid, and applying the rules in this paragraph (d) by treating the reverse hybrid as the taxpayer in the reverse hybrid's U.S. taxable year with or within which its foreign taxable year (under the law of the foreign jurisdiction imposing the owner-level tax) ends. See § 1.904-6(f) for special rules that apply for purposes of section 904 with respect to items of foreign gross income that under this paragraph (d)(3)(iii) would be assigned to a separate category that includes income that gives rise to inclusions under section 951A.

(D) *Foreign gross income items arising from a disposition of stock.*—An item of foreign gross income that arises from a transaction that is treated as a sale, exchange, or other disposition for both foreign law and Federal income tax purposes of an interest that is stock in a corporation for Federal income tax purposes is assigned first, to the extent of any U.S. dividend amount that results from the disposition, to the same statutory or residual grouping (or ratably to the groupings) to which the U.S. dividend amount is assigned under Federal income tax law. If the foreign gross income item exceeds the U.S. dividend amount, the foreign gross income item is next assigned, to the extent of the U.S. capital gain amount, to the statutory or residual grouping (or ratably to the groupings) to which the U.S. capital gain amount is assigned under Federal income tax law. Any excess of the foreign gross income item over the sum of the U.S. dividend amount and the U.S. capital gain amount is assigned to the same statutory or residual grouping (or ratably to the groupings) to which earnings equal to such excess amount would be assigned if they were recognized for Federal income tax purposes in the U.S. taxable year in which the disposition occurred. These earnings are deemed to arise in the statutory and residual groupings in the same proportions as the proportions in which the tax book value of the stock is (or would be if the taxpayer were a United States person) assigned to the groupings under the asset method in § 1.861-9 in the U.S. taxable year in which the disposition occurs. See paragraph (g)(10) of this section (*Example 9*).

(ii) *Items of foreign gross income included by a taxpayer by reason of its ownership of an interest in a partnership.*—(A) *Scope.*—The rules of this paragraph (d)(3)(ii) apply to assign to a statutory or residual grouping certain items of foreign gross income that a taxpayer includes in foreign taxable income by reason of its ownership of an interest in a partnership. See paragraphs (d)(1) and (2) of this section for rules that apply in characterizing items of foreign gross income that are attributable to a partner's distributive share of income of a partnership. See paragraph (d)(3)(iii) of this section for rules that apply in characterizing items of foreign gross income that are attributable to an inclusion under a foreign law inclusion regime.

(B) *Foreign gross income items arising from a distribution with respect to an interest in a partnership.*—If a partnership makes a distribution that is treated as a distribution of property for both foreign law and Federal income tax purposes, any foreign gross income item arising from the distribution (including foreign gross income attributable to a distribution from a partnership that foreign law classifies as a dividend from a corporation) is, to the extent of the U.S. capital gain amount arising from the distribution, assigned to the statutory and residual groupings to which the U.S. capital gain amount is assigned under Federal income tax law. If the foreign gross income item arising from the distribution exceeds the U.S. capital gain amount, such excess amount is assigned to the statutory and residual groupings to which a distributive share of income of the partnership in the amount of such excess would be assigned if such income were recognized for Federal income tax purposes in the U.S. taxable year in which the distribution is made. The items constituting this distributive share of income are deemed to arise in the statutory and residual groupings in the same proportions as the proportions in which the tax book value of the partnership interest or the partner's pro rata share of the partnership assets, as applicable, is assigned (or would be assigned if the partner were a United States person) for purposes of apportioning the partner's interest expense under § 1.861-9(e) in the U.S. taxable year in which the distribution is made.

(C) *Foreign gross income items arising from the disposition of an interest in a partnership.*—An item of foreign gross income arising from a transaction that is treated as a sale, exchange, or other disposition for both foreign law and Federal income tax purposes of an interest that is an interest in a partnership for Federal income tax purposes is assigned first, to the extent of the U.S. capital gain amount arising from the disposition, to the statutory or residual grouping (or ratably to the groupings) to which the U.S. capital gain amount is assigned. If the foreign gross income item arising from the disposition exceeds the U.S. capital gain amount, such excess amount is assigned to the statutory and residual grouping (or ratably to the groupings) to which a distributive share of income of the partnership in the amount of such excess would be assigned if such income were recognized for Federal income tax purposes in the U.S. taxable year in which the disposition occurred. The items constituting this distributive share of income are deemed to arise in the statutory and residual groupings in the same proportions as the proportions in which the tax book value of the partnership interest, or the partner's pro rata share of the partnership assets, as applicable, is assigned (or would be assigned if the partner were a United States person) for purposes of apportioning the partner's interest expense under § 1.861-9(e) in the U.S. taxable year in which the disposition occurred.

(iii) *Foreign law inclusion regime income.*—A gross item of foreign law inclusion regime income that a taxpayer includes in its capacity as a shareholder under foreign law of a foreign law CFC under a foreign law inclusion regime is assigned to the same statutory and residual groupings as the item of foreign gross income of the foreign law CFC that gives rise to the item of foreign law inclusion regime income of the taxpayer. The assignment is made by treating the gross items of foreign law inclusion regime income of the taxpayer as the items of foreign gross income of the foreign law CFC and applying the rules in this paragraph (d) by treating the foreign law CFC as the taxpayer in its U.S. taxable year with or within which its foreign taxable year (under the law of the foreign jurisdiction imposing the shareholder-level tax) ends. See paragraphs (g)(7) and (8) of this section (*Examples 6* and *7*). See § 1.904-6(f) for special rules with respect to items of foreign gross income relating to items of the foreign law CFC that give rise to inclusions under section 951A for purposes of applying section 904 as the operative section.

(iv) *Gain on sale of disregarded entity.*—An item of foreign gross income arising from gain recognized on the sale, exchange, or other disposition of a disregarded entity that is characterized as a disposition of assets for Federal income tax purposes is assigned to statutory and residual groupings in the same proportion as the gain that would be treated as foreign gross income in each grouping if the transaction were treated as a disposition of assets for foreign tax law purposes. See paragraph (g)(9) of this section (*Example 8*).

(v) *Disregarded payments.*—(A) *In general.*—This paragraph (d)(3)(v) applies to assign to a statutory or residual grouping a foreign gross income item that a taxpayer includes by reason of the receipt of a disregarded payment. In the case of a taxpayer that is an individual or a domestic corporation, this paragraph (d)(3)(v) applies to a disregarded payment made between a taxable unit that is a foreign branch, a foreign branch owner, or a non-branch taxable unit, and another such taxable unit of the same taxpayer. In the case of a taxpayer that is a foreign corporation, this paragraph (d)(3)(v) applies to a disregarded payment made between taxable units that are tested units of the same taxpayer. For purposes of this paragraph (d)(3)(v), an individual or corporation is treated as the taxpayer with respect to its distributive share of foreign income taxes paid or accrued by a partnership, estate, trust or other pass-through entity. The rules of paragraph (d)(3)(v)(B) of this section apply to attribute U.S. gross income comprising the portion of a disregarded payment that is a reattribution payment to a taxable unit, and to associate the foreign gross income item arising from the receipt of the reattribution payment with the statutory and residual groupings to which that U.S. gross income is assigned. The rules of paragraph (d)(3)(v)(C) of this section apply to assign to statutory and residual groupings items of foreign gross income arising from the receipt of the portion of a disregarded payment that is a remittance or a contribution. The rules of paragraph (d)(3)(v)(D) of this section apply to assign to statutory and residual groupings items of foreign gross income arising from disregarded payments, other than the portions of disregarded payments that are reattribution payments, in connection with disregarded sales or exchanges of property. Paragraph (d)(3)(v)(E) of this section provides definitions that apply for purposes of this paragraph (d)(3)(v) and paragraph (g) of this section.

(B) *Reattribution payments.—(1) In general.*—This paragraph (d)(3)(v)(B) assigns to a statutory or residual grouping a foreign gross income item that a taxpayer includes by reason of the receipt by a taxable unit of the portion of a disregarded payment that is a reattribution payment. The foreign gross income item is assigned to the statutory or residual groupings to which one or more reattribution amounts that constitute the reattribution payment are assigned upon receipt by the taxable unit. If a reattribution payment comprises multiple reattribution amounts and the amount of the foreign gross income item that is attributable to the reattribution payment differs from the amount of the reattribution payment, foreign gross income is apportioned among the statutory and residual groupings in proportion to the reattribution amounts in each statutory and residual grouping. The statutory or residual grouping of a reattribution amount received by a taxable unit is the grouping that includes the U.S. gross income attributed to the taxable unit by reason of its receipt of the gross reattribution amount, regardless of whether, after taking into account disregarded payments made by the taxable unit, the taxable unit has an attribution item as a result of its receipt of the reattribution amount. See paragraph (g)(13) of this section (*Example 12*).

(2) Attribution of U.S. gross income to a taxable unit.—This paragraph (d)(3)(v)(B)(2) provides attribution rules to determine the reattribution amounts received by a taxable unit in the statutory and residual groupings in order to apply paragraph (d)(3)(v)(B)(*1*) of this section to assign foreign gross income items arising from a reattribution payment to the groupings. In the case of a taxpayer that is an individual or a domestic corporation, the attribution rules in § 1.904-4(f)(2) apply to determine the reattribution amounts received by a taxable unit in the separate categories (as defined in § 1.904-5(a)(4)(v)) in order to apply paragraph (d)(3)(v)(B)(*1*) of this section for purposes of § 1.904-6(b)(2)(i). In the case of a taxpayer that is a foreign corporation, the attribution rules in § 1.951A-2(c)(7)(ii)(B) apply to determine the reattribution amounts received by a taxable unit in the statutory and residual groupings in order to apply paragraph (d)(3)(v)(B)(*1*) of this section for purposes of § § 1.951A-2(c)(3), 1.951A-2(c)(7), and 1.960-1(d)(3)(ii). For purposes of other operative sections (as described in § 1.861-8(f)(1)), the principles of § 1.904-4(f)(2)(vi) or § 1.951A-2(c)(7)(ii)(B), as applicable, apply to determine the reattribution amounts received by a taxable unit in the statutory and residual groupings. The rules and principles of § 1.904-4(f)(2)(vi) or § 1.951A-2(c)(7)(ii)(B), as applicable, apply to determine the extent to which a disregarded payment made by the taxable unit is a reattribution payment and the reattribution amounts that constitute a reattribution payment, and to adjust the U.S. gross income initially attributed to each taxable unit to reflect the reattribution payments that the taxable unit makes and receives. The rules in this paragraph (d)(3)(v)(B)(2) limit the amount of a disregarded payment that is a reattribution payment to the U.S. gross income of the payor taxable unit that is recognized in the U.S. taxable year in which the disregarded payment is made.

(3) Effect of reattribution payment on foreign gross income items of payor taxable unit.—The statutory or residual grouping to which an item of foreign gross income of a taxable unit is assigned is determined without regard to reattribution payments made by the taxable unit, and without regard to whether the taxable unit has one or more attribution items after taking into account such reattribution payments. No portion of the foreign gross income of the payor taxable unit is treated as foreign gross income of the payee taxable unit by reason of the reattribution payment, notwithstanding that U.S. gross income of the payor taxable unit that is used to assign foreign gross income of the payor taxable unit to statutory and residual groupings is reattributed to the payee taxable unit under paragraph (d)(3)(v)(B)(*1*) of this section by reason of the reattribution payment. See paragraph (e) of this section for rules reducing the amount of a foreign gross income item of a taxable unit by deductions allowed under foreign law, including deductions by reason of disregarded payments made by a taxable unit that are included in the foreign gross income of the payee taxable unit.

(C) *Remittances and contributions.—(1) Remittances.—(i) In general.*—An item of foreign gross income that a taxpayer includes by reason of the receipt of a remittance by a taxable unit is assigned to the statutory or residual groupings of the recipient taxable unit that correspond to the groupings out of which the payor taxable unit made the remittance under the rules of this paragraph (d)(3)(v)(C)(*1*)(*i*). A remittance paid by a taxable unit is considered to be made ratably out of all of the accumulated after-tax income of the taxable unit. The accumulated after-tax income of the taxable unit that pays the remittance is deemed to have arisen in the statutory and residual groupings in the same proportions as the proportions in which the tax book value of the assets of the taxable unit are (or would be if the owner of the taxable unit were a United States person) assigned for purposes of apportioning interest expense under the asset method in § 1.861-9 in the taxable year in which the remittance is made. See paragraph (g)(11) and (12) of this section (*Examples 10* and *11*). If the payor taxable unit is determined to have no assets under paragraph (d)(3)(v)(C)(*1*)(*ii*) of this section, then the foreign gross income that is included by reason of the receipt of the remittance is assigned to the residual grouping.

(ii) Assets of a taxable unit.—The assets of a taxable unit are determined in accordance with § 1.987-6(b), except that for purposes of applying § 1.987-6(b)(2) under this paragraph (d)(3)(v)(C)(*1*)(*ii*), a taxable unit is deemed to be a section 987 QBU (within the meaning of § 1.987-1(b)(2)) and assets of the taxable unit include stock held by the taxable unit, the portion of the tax book value of a reattribution asset that is assigned to the taxable unit, and the taxable unit's pro rata share of the assets of another taxable unit (other than a corporation or a partnership), including the portion of any reattribution assets assigned to the other taxable unit, in which it owns an interest. If a taxable unit owns an interest in a taxable unit that is a partnership, the assets of the taxable unit that is the owner include its interest in the partnership or its pro rata share of the partnership assets, as applicable, determined under the principles of § 1.861-9(e). The portion of the tax book value of a reattribution asset that is assigned to a taxable unit is an amount that bears the same ratio to the total tax book value of the reattribution asset as the sum of the attribution items of that taxable unit arising from gross income produced by the reattribution asset bears to the total gross income produced by the reattribution asset. The portion of a reattribution asset that is assigned to a taxable unit under this paragraph (d)(3)(v)(C)(*1*)(*ii*) is not treated as an asset of the taxable unit making the reattribution payment for purposes of applying paragraph (d)(3)(v)(C)(*1*)(*i*) of this section.

(2) Contributions.—An item of foreign gross income that a taxpayer includes by reason of the receipt of a contribution by a taxable unit is assigned to the residual grouping. See, however, § 1.904-6(b)(2)(ii) (assigning certain items of foreign gross income to the foreign branch category for purposes of applying section 904 as the operative section).

(3) Disregarded payment that comprises both a reattribution payment and a remittance or contribution.—If both a reattribution payment and either a remittance or a contribution result from a single disregarded payment, the foreign gross income is first attributed to the portion of the disregarded payment that is a reattribution payment to the extent of the amount of the reattribution payment, and any excess of the foreign gross income item over the amount of the reattribution payment is then to attributed to the portion of the disregarded payment that is a remittance or contribution.

(D) *Disregarded payments in connection with disregarded sales or exchanges of property.*—An item of foreign gross income that is attributable to gain recognized under foreign law by reason of a disregarded payment, other than the portion of the disregarded payment that is a reattribution payment, received in exchange for property is characterized and assigned under the rules of paragraph (d)(2) of this section. See paragraph (d)(3)(v)(B) of this section for rules for assigning an item of foreign gross income attributable to the portion of a disregarded payment that is a reattribution payment, including a reattribution payment received in exchange for property.

(E) *Definitions.*—The following definitions apply for purposes of this paragraph (d)(3)(v) and paragraph (g) of this section.

(1) Attribution item.—The term *attribution item* means the portion of an item of gross income, computed under Federal income tax law, that is attributed to a taxable unit after taking into account all reattribution payments made and received by the taxable unit.

(2) Contribution.—The term *contribution* means the excess amount of a disregarded payment, other than a disregarded payment received in exchange for property, made by a taxable unit to another taxable unit that the first taxable unit owns over the portion of the disregarded payment, if any, that is a reattribution payment.

(3) *Disregarded entity.*—The term *disregarded entity* means an entity described in § 301.7701-2(c)(2) of this chapter that is disregarded as an entity separate from its owner for Federal income tax purposes.

(4) *Disregarded payment.*—The term *disregarded payment* means an amount of property (within the meaning of section 317(a)) that is transferred to or from a taxable unit, including a transfer of property that would be a contribution to capital described in section 118 or a transfer described in section 351 if the taxable unit were a corporation under Federal income tax law, a transfer of property that would be a distribution by a corporation to a shareholder with respect to its stock if the taxable unit were a corporation under Federal income tax law, or a payment in exchange for property or in satisfaction of an account payable, in connection with a transaction that is disregarded for Federal income tax purposes and that is reflected on the separate set of books and records of the taxable unit. A disregarded payment also includes any other amount that is reflected on the separate set of books and records of a taxable unit in connection with a transaction that is disregarded for Federal income tax purposes and that would constitute an item of accrued income, gain, deduction, or loss of the taxable unit if the transaction to which the amount is attributable were regarded for Federal income tax purposes.

(5) *Reattribution amount.*—The term *reattribution amount* means an amount of gross income, computed under Federal income tax law, that is initially assigned to a single statutory or residual grouping that includes gross income of a taxable unit but that is, by reason of a disregarded payment made by that taxable unit, attributed to another taxable unit under paragraph (d)(3)(v)(B)(2) of this section.

(6) *Reattribution asset.*—The term *reattribution asset* means an asset that produces one or more items of gross income, computed under Federal income tax law, to which a disregarded payment is allocated under the rules of paragraph (d)(3)(v)(B)(2) of this section.

(7) *Reattribution payment.*—The term *reattribution payment* means the portion of a disregarded payment equal to the sum of all reattribution amounts that are attributed to the recipient of the disregarded payment.

(8) *Remittance.*—The term *remittance* means the excess amount, other than an amount that is treated as a contribution under paragraph (d)(3)(v)(E)(2) of this section, of a disregarded payment, other than a disregarded payment received in exchange for property, made by a taxable unit to a second taxable unit (including a second taxable unit that shares the same owner as the payor taxable unit) over the portion of the disregarded payment, if any, that is a reattribution payment.

(9) *Taxable unit.*—In the case of a taxpayer that is an individual or a domestic corporation, the term *taxable unit* means a foreign branch, a foreign branch owner, or a non-branch taxable unit, as defined in § 1.904-6(b)(2)(i)(B). In the case of a taxpayer that is a foreign corporation, the term *taxable unit* means a tested unit, as defined in § 1.951A-2(c)(7)(iv)(A).

(vi) *Foreign gross income included by reason of U.S. equity hybrid instrument ownership.*—(A) *Foreign gross income included by reason of an accrual.*—Foreign gross income included by reason of an accrual under foreign law with respect to a U.S. equity hybrid instrument is considered to arise from the same transaction or realization event as a distribution of property described in paragraph (d)(3)(i) or (ii) of this section and is assigned to the statutory and residual groupings by treating each amount accrued as a foreign law distribution made on the date of the accrual under foreign law.

(B) *Foreign gross income included by reason of a payment.*—Foreign gross income included by reason of a payment of interest under foreign law with respect to a U.S. equity hybrid instrument is considered to arise from the same transaction or realization event as a distribution of property described in paragraph (d)(3)(i) or (ii) of this section and is assigned to the statutory and residual groupings by treating each payment as a distribution made on the date of the payment.

(e) *Allocating and apportioning deductions (allowed under foreign law) to foreign gross income in a grouping.*—(1) *Application of foreign law expense allocation rules.*—In order to determine foreign taxable income in each statutory grouping, or the residual grouping, foreign gross income in each grouping is reduced by deducting any expenses, losses, or other amounts that are deductible under foreign law that are specifically allocable to the items of foreign gross income in the grouping under the laws of that foreign country. If expenses are not specifically allocated under foreign law, then the expenses are allocated and apportioned among the groupings under the principles of foreign law. Thus, for example, if foreign law provides that expenses will be apportioned on a gross income basis, the foreign law deduc tions are apportioned on the basis of the relative amounts of foreign gross income assigned to each grouping.

(2) *Application of U.S. expense allocation rules in the absence of foreign law rules.*—If foreign law does not provide rules for the allocation or apportionment of expenses, losses or other deductions to particular items of foreign gross income, then the principles of the section 861 regulations (as defined in § 1.861-8(a)(1)) apply in allocating and apportioning such expenses, losses, or other deductions to foreign gross income. For example, in the absence of foreign law expense allocation rules, the principles of the section 861 regulations apply to allocate definitely related expenses to particular categories of foreign gross income and provide the methods for apportioning foreign law expenses that are definitely related to more than one statutory grouping or that are not definitely related to any statutory grouping. For purposes of this paragraph (e)(2), the apportionment of expenses required to be made under the principles of the section 861 regulations need not be made on other than a separate company basis. If the taxpayer applies the principles of the section 861 regulations for purposes of allocating foreign law deductions under this paragraph (e), the taxpayer must apply the principles in the same manner as the taxpayer applies such principles in determining the income or earnings and profits for Federal income tax purposes of the taxpayer (or of the foreign branch, controlled foreign corporation, or other entity that paid or accrued the foreign taxes, as the case may be). For example, a taxpayer must use the modified gross income method under § 1.861-9T when applying the principles of that section for purposes of this paragraph (e) to determine the amount of foreign taxable income in each grouping if the taxpayer applies the modified gross income method in determining the income and earnings and profits of a controlled foreign corporation for Federal income tax purposes.

(f) *Allocation and apportionment of foreign income tax.*—Foreign income tax is allocated to the statutory or residual grouping or groupings to which the items of foreign gross income are assigned under the rules of paragraph (d) of this section. If foreign gross income is assigned to more than one grouping, then the foreign income tax is apportioned among the statutory and residual groupings by multiplying the foreign income tax by a fraction, the numerator of which is the foreign taxable income in a grouping and the denominator of which is all foreign taxable income on which the foreign income tax is imposed. If foreign law, including by reason of an income tax convention, exempts certain types of income from tax, or if foreign taxable income is reduced to or below zero by foreign law deductions, then no foreign income tax is allocated and apportioned to that income. A withholding tax (as defined in section 901(k)(1)(B)) is allocated and apportioned to the foreign gross income from which it is withheld. If foreign law, including by reason of an income tax convention, provides for a specific rate of tax with respect to certain types of income (for example, capital gains), or allows credits only against tax on particular items or types of income (for example, credit for foreign withholding taxes), then such provisions are taken into account in determining the amount of foreign tax imposed on such foreign taxable income.

(g) *Examples.*—The following examples illustrate the application of this section and § 1.904-6.

(1) *Presumed facts.*—Except as otherwise provided in this paragraph (g), the following facts are assumed for purposes of the examples inparagraphs (g)(2) through (9) of this section:

(i) USP and US2 are domestic corporations, which are unrelated;

(ii) USP elects to claim a foreign tax credit under section 901;

(iii) CFC, CFC1, and CFC2 are controlled foreign corporations organized in Country A, and are not reverse hybrids;

(iv) All parties have a U.S. dollar functional currency and a U.S. taxable year and foreign taxable year that correspond to the calendar year;

(v) No party has expenses for Country A tax purposes or expenses for U.S. tax purposes (other than foreign income tax expense); and

(vi) Section 904 is the operative section, and terms have the meaning provided in this section or §§1.904-4 and 1.904-5.

(2) *Example 1: Corresponding U.S. item.*—(i) *Facts.* USP conducts business in Country A that gives rise to a foreign branch (as defined in §1.904-4(f)(3)). In Year 1, in a transaction that is a sale for purposes of the laws of Country A and Federal income tax law, the foreign branch transfers Asset X to US2 for $1,000x. For Country A tax purposes, USP earns $600x of gross income from the sale of Asset X and incurs foreign income tax of $80x. For Federal income tax purposes, USP earns $800x of foreign branch category income from the sale of Asset X.

(ii) *Analysis.* For purposes of allocating and apportioning the $80x of Country A foreign income tax, the $600x of Country A gross income from the sale of Asset X is first assigned to separate categories. The $800x of foreign branch category income from the sale of Asset X is the corresponding U.S. item to the Country A item of gross income. Under paragraph (d)(1) of this section, because USP recognizes a corresponding U.S. item with respect to the Country A item of gross income in the same U.S. taxable year, the $600x of Country A gross income is assigned to the same separate category as the corresponding U.S. item. This is the case even though the amount of gross income recognized for Federal income tax purposes differs from the amount recognized for Country A tax purposes. Accordingly, the $600x of Country A gross income is assigned to the foreign branch category. Additionally, because all of the Country A taxable income is assigned to a single separate category, the $80x of Country A tax is also allocated to the foreign branch category. No apportionment of the $80x is necessary because the class of gross income to which the tax is allocated consists entirely of a single statutory grouping, foreign branch category income.

(3) *Example 2: Foreign law disposition.*—(i) *Facts.* USP owns all of the outstanding stock of CFC, which conducts business in Country A. CFC sells Asset X for $1,000x. For Country A tax purposes, CFC's basis in Asset X is $600x, the sale of Asset X occurs in Year 1, and CFC recognizes $400x of foreign gross income and incurs $80x of foreign income tax. For Federal income tax purposes, CFC's basis in Asset X is $500x, the sale of Asset X occurs in Year 2, and CFC recognizes $500x of general category income.

(ii) *Analysis.* For purposes of allocating and apportioning the $80x of Country A foreign income tax in Year 1, the $400x of Country A gross income from the sale of Asset X is first assigned to separate categories. There is no corresponding U.S. item because the sale occurs on a different date and in a different U.S. taxable year for U.S. and foreign tax purposes. Under paragraph (d)(2)(ii)(C) of this section, the item of foreign gross income (the $400x from the sale of Asset X) is characterized and assigned to the groupings to which the corresponding U.S. item would be assigned if for Federal income tax purposes Asset X were sold for $1,000x in Year 1, the same U.S. taxable year in which the foreign income tax accrued. This is the case even though the amount of gross income that would be recognized for Federal income tax purposes differs from the amount recognized for Country A tax purposes. Accordingly, the $400x of Country A gross income is assigned to the general category. Additionally, because all of the Country A taxable income is assigned to a single separate category, the $80x of Country A tax is also allocated to the general category. No apportionment of the $80x is necessary because the class of gross income to which the deduction is allocated consists entirely of a single statutory grouping, general category income.

(4) *Example 3: Foreign gross income excluded from U.S. gross income.*—(i) *Facts.* USP conducts business in Country A. In Year 1, USP earns $200x of interest income on a State or local bond. For Country A tax purposes, the $200x of income is included in gross income and incurs $10x of foreign income tax. For Federal income tax purposes, the $200x is excluded from gross income under section 103.

(ii) *Analysis.* For purposes of allocating and apportioning the $10x of Country A foreign income tax, the $200x of Country A gross income is first assigned to separate categories. There is no corresponding U.S. item because the interest income is excluded from U.S. gross income. Thus, the rules of paragraph (d)(2) of this section apply to characterize and assign the foreign gross income to the groupings to which a corresponding U.S. item would be assigned if it were recognized under Federal income tax law in that U.S. taxable year. The interest income is excluded from U.S. gross income but is otherwise described or identified by section 103. Accordingly, under paragraph (d)(2)(iii)(A) of this section, the $200x of Country A gross income is assigned to the separate category to which the interest income would be assigned under Federal income tax law if the income were included in gross income. Under section 904(d)(2)(B)(i), the interest income would be passive category income. Accordingly, the $200x of Country A gross income is assigned to the passive category. Additionally, because all of the Country A taxable income is assigned to a single separate category, the $10x of Country A tax is also allocated to the passive category (subject to the rules in §1.904-4(c)). No apportionment of the $10x is necessary because the class of gross income to which the deduction is allocated consists entirely of a single statutory grouping, passive category income.

(5) *Example 4: Actual distribution.*—(1) *Facts.* USP owns all of the outstanding stock of CFC1, which in turn owns all of the outstanding stock of CFC2. CFC1 and CFC2 conduct business in Country A. In Year 1, CFC2 distributes $300x to CFC1. For Country A tax purposes, $100x of the distribution is the foreign dividend amount, $160x is treated as a nontaxable return of capital, and the remaining $40x is the foreign capital gain amount. CFC1 incurs $20x of foreign income tax with respect to the foreign dividend amount and $4x of foreign income tax with respect to the foreign capital gain amount. The $20x and $4x of foreign income tax are each a separate levy within the meaning of §1.901-2(d). For Federal income tax purposes, $150x of the distribution is the U.S. dividend amount, $100x is the U.S. return of capital amount, and the remaining $50x is the U.S. capital gain amount. Under section 904(d)(3)(D) and §§1.904-4(d) and 1.904-5(c)(4), the $150x of U.S. dividend amount consists solely of general category income in the hands of CFC1. Under section 904(d)(2)(B)(i) and §1.904-4(b)(2)(i)(A), the $50x of U.S. capital gain amount is passive category income to CFC1.

(ii) *Analysis*—(A) *In general.* Because the $20x of Country A foreign income tax and the $4x of Country A foreign income tax are separate levies, the taxes are allocated and apportioned separately. For purposes of allocating and apportioning each foreign income tax, the relevant item of Country A gross income (the foreign dividend amount or foreign capital gain amount) is first assigned to separate categories. The U.S. dividend amount and U.S. capital gain amount are corresponding U.S. items. However, paragraph (d)(3)(i)(B) of this section (and not paragraph (d)(1) of this section) applies to assign the items of foreign gross income arising from the distribution.

(B) *Foreign dividend amount.* Under paragraph (d)(3)(i)(B)(2) of this section, the foreign dividend amount ($100x) is, to the extent of the U.S. dividend amount ($150x), assigned to the same separate category from which the distribution of the U.S. dividend amount is made under Federal income tax law. Thus, $100x of foreign gross income that is the foreign dividend amount is assigned to the general category. Additionally, because all of the Country A taxable income included in the base on which the $20x of foreign income tax is imposed is assigned to a single separate category, the $20x of Country A tax on the foreign dividend amount is also allocated to the general category. No apportionment of the $20x is necessary because the class of gross income to which the deduction for foreign income tax is allocated consists entirely of a single statutory grouping, general category income. See also section 245A(d) for rules that may apply to disallow a credit or deduction for certain foreign taxes.

(C) *Foreign capital gain amount.* Under paragraph (d)(3)(i)(B)(3) of this section, the foreign capital gain amount ($40x) is, to the extent of the U.S. capital gain amount ($50x), assigned to the same separate category to which the U.S. capital gain is assigned under Federal income tax law. Thus, the $40x of foreign gross income that is the foreign capital gain amount is assigned to the passive category. Additionally, because all of the Country A taxable income in the base on which the $4x of foreign income tax is imposed is assigned to a single separate category, the $4x of Country A tax on the foreign dividend amount is also allocated to the passive category. No apportionment of the $4x is necessary because the class of gross income to which the deduction is allocated consists entirely of a single statutory grouping, passive category income.

(6) *Example 5: Foreign law distribution.*—(i) *Facts.* USP owns all of the outstanding stock of CFC. In Year 1, for Country A tax purposes, CFC distributes $1,000x of its stock that is treated entirely as a dividend to USP, and Country A imposes a withholding tax on USP of $150x with respect to the $1,000x of foreign gross income. For Federal income tax purposes, the distribution is treated as a stock dividend described in section 305(a) and USP recognizes no U.S. gross income. At the time of the distribution, CFC has $800x of section 965(a) PTEP (as defined in §1.960-3(c)(2)(vi)) in a single annual PTEP account (as defined in §1.960-3(c)(1)), and $500x of earnings and profits described in section 959(c)(3). Section 965(g) is the operative section for purposes of this paragraph (g)(6). See §1.965-5(b)(2). Section 904 is also a relevant operative section, but is not addressed in this paragraph (g)(6).

(ii) *Analysis.* For purposes of allocating and apportioning the $150x of Country A foreign income tax, the $1,000x of Country A gross income is first assigned to the relevant statutory and residual groupings for purposes of applying section 965(g) as the operative section. Under § 1.965-5(b)(2), the statutory grouping is the portion of the distribution that is attributable to section 965(a) previously taxed earnings and profits and the residual grouping is the portion of the distribution attributable to other earnings and profits. There is no corresponding U.S. item because under section 305(a) USP recognizes no U.S. gross income with respect to the distribution. Under paragraph (d)(2)(ii)(B) of this section, the item of foreign gross income (the $1,000x distribution) is assigned under the rules of paragraph (d)(3)(i)(B) of this section to the same statutory or residual groupings to which the foreign gross income would be assigned if a distribution of the same amount were made for Federal income tax purposes in Year 1 on the date the distribution occurs for foreign law purposes. If recognized for Federal income tax purposes, a $1,000x distribution in Year 1 would result in a U.S. dividend amount of $1,000x. Under paragraph (d)(3)(i)(B)(2) of this section, the foreign dividend amount ($1,000x) is, to the extent of the U.S. dividend amount ($1,000x), assigned to the same statutory or residual groupings from which a distribution of the U.S. dividend amount would be made under Federal income tax law. Thus, $800x of foreign gross income related to the foreign dividend amount is assigned to the statutory grouping for the portion of the distribution attributable to section 965(a) previously taxed earnings and profits and $200x of foreign gross income is assigned to the residual grouping. Under paragraph (f) of this section, $120x ($150x x $800x / $1,000x) of the Country A foreign income tax is apportioned to the statutory grouping and $30x ($150x x $200x / $1,000x) of the Country A foreign income tax is apportioned to the residual grouping. See section 965(g)(2) and § 1.965-5(b) for application of the applicable percentage (as defined in § 1.965-5(d)) to the foreign income tax allocated and apportioned to the statutory grouping.

(7) *Example 6: Foreign law inclusion regime, CFC shareholder*.—(i) *Facts*. USP owns all of the outstanding stock of CFC1, which in turn owns all of the outstanding stock of CFC2. CFC2 is organized and conducts business in Country B. Country A has a foreign law inclusion regime that imposes a tax on CFC1 for certain earnings of CFC2, a foreign law CFC. In Year 1, CFC2 earns $400x of interest income and $200x of royalty income. CFC2 incurs no foreign income tax. For Country A tax purposes, the $400x of interest income and $200x of royalty income are each an item of foreign law inclusion regime income of CFC2 that are included in the gross income of CFC1. CFC1 incurs $150x of Country A foreign income tax with respect to the foreign law inclusion regime income. For Federal income tax purposes, with respect to CFC2, the $400x of interest income is passive category income under section 904(d)(2)(B)(i) and the $200x of royalty income is general category income under § 1.904-4(b)(2)(iii).

(ii) *Analysis*. For purposes of allocating and apportioning CFC1's $150x of Country A foreign income tax, the $600x of Country A gross income is first assigned to separate categories. The $600x of foreign gross income is not included in the U.S. gross income of CFC1, and thus, there is no corresponding U.S. item. Under paragraph (d)(3)(iii) of this section, each item of foreign law inclusion regime income that is included in CFC1's foreign gross income is assigned to the same separate category as the items of foreign gross income of CFC2 that give rise to the foreign law inclusion regime income of CFC1. With respect to CFC2, the $400x of interest income and the $200x of royalty income would be corresponding U.S. items if CFC2 were the taxpayer. Accordingly, $400x of CFC1's foreign gross income is assigned to the passive category and $200x of CFC1's foreign gross income is assigned to the general category. Under paragraph (f) of this section, $100x ($150x x $400x / $600x) of the Country A foreign income tax is apportioned to the passive category and $50x ($150x x $200x / $600x) of the Country A foreign income tax is apportioned to the general category.

(8) *Example 7: Foreign law inclusion regime, U.S. shareholder*.—(i) *Facts*. The facts are the same as in paragraph (g)(7)(i) of this section (the facts in *Example 6*), except that both CFC1 and CFC2 are organized and conduct business in Country B, all of the outstanding stock of CFC1 is owned by Individual X, a U.S. citizen resident in Country A, and Country A imposes tax of $150x on foreign gross income of $600x under its foreign law inclusion regime on Individual X, rather than on CFC1. For Federal income tax purposes, in the hands of CFC2, the $400x of interest income is passive category subpart F income and the $200x of royalty income is general category tested income (as defined in § 1.951A-2(b)(1)). CFC2's $400x of interest income gives rise to a passive category subpart F inclusion under section 951(a)(1)(A), and its $200x of tested income gives rise to a GILTI inclusion amount (as defined in § 1.951A-1(c)(1)) of $200x, with respect to Individual X.

(ii) *Analysis*. The analysis is the same as in paragraph (g)(7)(ii) of this section (the analysis in *Example 6*) except that under § 1.904-6(f), because $50x of the Country A foreign income tax is allocated and apportioned under paragraph (d)(3)(iii) of this section to CFC2's general category tested income group to which Individual X's inclusion under section 951A is attributable, the $50x of Country A foreign income tax is allocated and apportioned in the hands of Individual X to the section 951A category.

(9) *Example 8: Sale of disregarded entity*.—(i) *Facts*. USP sells FDE, a disregarded entity that is organized and operates a trade or business in Country A, for $500x. FDE owns Asset X and Asset Y in Country A, each having a fair market value of $250x. For Country A tax purposes, FDE has a basis in Asset X of $100x and a basis in Asset Y of $200x, USP's basis in FDE is $100x, and the sale is treated as a sale of stock. Country A imposes foreign income tax of $40x on USP on the Country A gross income of $400x resulting from the sale of FDE, based on its rules for taxing capital gains of nonresidents selling stock of companies operating a trade or business in Country A. For Federal income tax purposes, USP has a basis of $150x in each of Assets X and Y, and so the sale of FDE results in $100x of passive category income with respect to the sale of Asset X and $100x of general category income with respect to the sale of Asset Y.

(ii) *Analysis*. For purposes of allocating and apportioning USP's $40x of Country A foreign income tax, the $400x of Country A gross income resulting from the sale of FDE is first assigned to separate categories. Under paragraph (d)(3)(iv) of this section, USP's $400x of Country A gross income is assigned among the statutory groupings in the same percentages as the foreign gross income in each grouping that would have resulted if the sale of FDE were treated as an asset sale for Country A tax purposes. Because for Country A tax purposes Asset X had a built-in gain of $150x and Asset Y had a built-in gain of $50x, $300x ($400x x $150x / $200x) of the Country A gross income is assigned to the passive category and $100x ($400x x $50x / $200x) is assigned to the general category. Under paragraph (f) of this section, $30x ($40x x $300x / $400x) of the Country A foreign income tax is apportioned to the passive category, and $10x ($40x x $100x / $400x) of the Country A foreign income tax is apportioned to the general category.

(10) *Example 9: Gain on disposition of stock*.—(i) *Facts*. USP owns all of the outstanding stock of CFC, which conducts business in Country A. In Year 1, USP sells all of the stock of CFC to US2 for $1,000x. For Country A tax purposes, USP's basis in the stock of CFC is $200x. Accordingly, USP recognizes $800x of gain on which Country A imposes $80x of foreign income tax based on its rules for taxing capital gains of nonresidents, which satisfy the requirement in § 1.901-2(b)(5)(i)(C). For Federal income tax purposes, USP's basis in the stock of CFC is $400x. Accordingly, USP recognizes $600x of gain on the sale of the stock of CFC, of which $150x is included in the gross income of USP as a dividend under section 1248(a) that, as provided in section 1248(j), is treated as a dividend eligible for the deduction under section 245A(a). Under paragraphs (b)(20) and (21) of this section, respectively, the sale of CFC stock by USP gives rise to a $450x U.S. capital gain amount and a $150x U.S. dividend amount. Under §§ 1.904-4(d) and 1.904-5(c)(4), the $150x U.S. dividend amount is general category section 245A subgroup income, and the $450x U.S. capital gain amount is passive category income to USP. For purposes of allocating and apportioning its interest expense under §§ 1.861-9(g)(2)(i)(B) and 1.861-13, USP's stock in CFC is characterized as general category stock in the section 245A subgroup.

(ii) *Analysis*. For purposes of allocating and apportioning the $80x of Country A foreign income tax, the $800x of Country A gross income from the sale of the stock of CFC is first assigned to separate categories. Under paragraph (d)(3)(i)(D) of this section, the $800x of Country A gross income is first assigned to the separate category to which the $150x U.S. dividend amount is assigned, to the extent thereof, and is next assigned to the separate category to which the $450x U.S. capital gain amount is assigned, to the extent thereof. Accordingly, $150x of Country A gross income is assigned to the general category in the section 245A subgroup, and $450x of Country A gross income is assigned to the passive category. Under paragraph (d)(3)(i)(D) of this section, the remaining $200x of Country A gross income is assigned to the statutory and residual groupings to which earnings of CFC in that amount would be assigned if they were recognized for Federal income tax purposes in the U.S. taxable year in which the disposition occurred. These earnings are all deemed to arise in the section 245A subgroup of the general category, based on USP's characterization of its stock in CFC. Thus, under paragraph (d)(3)(i)(D) of this section the $800x of foreign gross income, and therefore the foreign taxable income, is characterized as $350x ($150x + $200x) of income in the general category section 245A subgroup and $450x of income in the passive category. This is the result even though for Country A tax purposes all $800x of Country A gross income is characterized as gain from the sale of stock, which would be passive category income under section 904(d)(2)(B)(i), because the income is assigned to a separate category based on the characterization of the gain under Federal income tax law. Under paragraph (f) of this section, the $80x of Country A tax is ratably apportioned between the general category section 245A subgroup and the passive category based on the relative amounts of foreign taxable income in each grouping. Accordingly, $35x ($80x × $350x/$800x) of the Country A tax is apportioned to the general category section 245A subgroup, and $45x ($80x × $450x/$800x) of the Country A tax is apportioned to the passive category. See also § 1.245A(d)-1 for rules that may disallow a credit or deduction for the $35x of Country A tax apportioned to the general category section 245A subgroup.

(11) *Example 10: Disregarded transfer of built-in gain property.*—(i) *Facts.* USP owns FDE, a disregarded entity that is treated for Federal income tax purposes as a foreign branch operating in Country A. FDE transfers Asset F, equipment used in FDE's trade or business in Country A, for no consideration to USP in a transaction that is a remittance described in paragraph (d)(3)(v)(E) of this section for Federal income tax purposes but is treated as a distribution of Asset F from a corporation to its shareholder, USP, for Country A tax purposes. At the time of the transfer, Asset F has a fair market value of $250x and an adjusted basis of $100x for both Federal and Country A income tax purposes. Country A imposes $30x of tax on FDE with respect to the $150x of built-in gain on a deemed sale of Asset F, which is recognized for Country A tax purposes by reason of the transfer to USP. If FDE had sold Asset F for $250x in a transaction that was regarded for Federal income tax purposes, FDE would also have recognized gain of $150x for Federal income tax purposes, and that gain would have been characterized as foreign branch category income under § 1.904-4(f). Country A also imposes $25x of withholding tax, a separate levy, on USP by reason of the distribution of Asset F to USP.

(ii) *Analysis*—(A) *Net income tax on built-in gain.* For purposes of allocating and apportioning the $30x of Country A foreign income tax imposed on FDE by reason of the transfer of Asset F to USP for Country A tax purposes, under paragraph (c)(1) of this section the $150x of Country A gross income is first assigned to a separate category. Because the transfer does not result in a deemed sale for Federal income tax purposes, there is no corresponding U.S. item. However, FDE would have recognized gain of $150x, which would have been the corresponding U.S. item, if the deemed sale had been recognized for Federal income tax purposes. Therefore, under paragraph (d)(2)(ii) of this section, the $150x item of foreign gross income is characterized and assigned to the grouping to which such corresponding U.S. item would have been assigned if the deemed sale were recognized under Federal income tax law. Because the sale of Asset F in a regarded transaction would have resulted in foreign branch category income, the foreign gross income is characterized as foreign branch category income. Under paragraph (f) of this section, the $30x of Country A tax is also allocated to the foreign branch category, the statutory grouping to which the $150x of Country A gross income is assigned. No apportionment of the $30x of Country A tax is necessary because the class of gross income to which the foreign gross income is allocated consists entirely of a single statutory grouping.

(B) *Withholding tax on distribution.* For purposes of allocating and apportioning the $25x of Country A withholding tax imposed on USP by reason of the transfer of Asset F, under paragraph (c)(1) of this section the $250x of Country A gross income arising from the transfer of Asset F is first assigned to a separate category. For Federal income tax purposes, the transfer of Asset F is a remittance from FDE to USP, and thus there is no corresponding U.S. item. Under paragraph (d)(3)(v)(C)(*1*)(*i*) of this section, the item of foreign gross income is assigned to the groupings to which the income out of which the payment is made is assigned; the payment is considered to be made ratably out of all of the accumulated after-tax income of FDE, as computed for Federal income tax purposes; and the accumulated after-tax income of FDE is deemed to have arisen in the statutory and residual groupings in the same proportions as those in which the tax book value of FDE's assets in the groupings, determined in accordance with paragraph (d)(3)(v)(C)(*1*)(*ii*) of this section, are assigned for purposes of apportioning USP's interest expense. Because all of FDE's assets produce foreign branch category income, under paragraph (d)(3)(v)(C)(*1*) of this section the foreign gross income is characterized as foreign branch category income. Under paragraph (f) of this section, the $25x of Country A withholding tax is also allocated entirely to the foreign branch category, the statutory grouping to which the $250x of Country A gross income is assigned. No apportionment of the $25x is necessary because the class of gross income to which the foreign gross income is allocated consists entirely of a single statutory grouping.

(12) *Example 11: Disregarded payment that is a remittance.*—(i) *Facts.* USP wholly owns CFC1, which is a tested unit within the meaning of § 1.951A-2(c)(7)(iv)(A) (the "CFC1 tested unit"). CFC1 wholly owns FDE, a disregarded entity that is organized in Country B, which is a tested unit within the meaning of § 1.951A-2(c)(7)(iv)(A) (the "FDE tested unit"). The sole assets of FDE (determined in accordance with paragraph (d)(3)(v)(C)(*1*)(*ii*) of this section) are all the outstanding stock of CFC3, a controlled foreign corporation organized in Country B. In Year 1, CFC3 pays a $400x dividend to FDE that is excluded from CFC1's foreign personal holding company income ("FPHCI") by reason of section 954(c)(6). FDE makes no payments to CFC1 and pays no Country B tax in Year 1. In Year 2, FDE makes a $400x remittance to CFC1 as defined in paragraph (d)(3)(v)(E) of this section. Under the laws of Country B, the remittance gives rise to a $400x dividend. Country B imposes a 5% ($20x) withholding tax (which is an eligible current year tax as defined in § 1.960-1(b) on CFC1 on the dividend. In Year 2, CFC3 pays no dividends to FDE, and FDE earns no income. For Federal income tax purposes, the $400x payment from FDE to CFC1 is a disregarded payment and results in no income to CFC1. For purposes of this paragraph (g)(12) (*Example 11*), section 960(a) is the operative section and the income groups described in § 1.960-1(d)(2) are the statutory and residual groupings. See § 1.960-1(d)(3)(ii)(A) (applying § 1.960-1 to allocate and apportion current year taxes to income groups). For Federal income tax purposes, in Year 2 the stock of CFC3 owned by FDE has a tax book value of $1,000x, $750x of which is assigned under the asset method in § 1.861-9 (as applied by treating CFC1 as a United States person) to the general category tested income group described in § 1.960-1(d)(2)(ii)(C), and $250x of which is assigned to a passive category FPHCI group described in § 1.960-1(d)(2)(ii)(B)(*2*)(*i*).

(ii) *Analysis.* (A) The $20x Country B withholding tax on the Year 2 remittance from FDE is imposed on a $400x item of foreign gross income that CFC1 includes in foreign gross income by reason of its receipt of a disregarded payment. In order to allocate and apportion the $20x of Country B withholding tax under paragraph (c) of this section for purposes of § 1.960-1(d)(3)(ii)(A), paragraph (d)(3)(v) of this section applies to assign the $400x item of foreign gross dividend income to a statutory or residual grouping. Under paragraph (d)(3)(v)(C)(*1*) of this section, the $400x item of foreign gross income is assigned to the statutory or residual groupings of the CFC1 tested unit that correspond to the statutory and residual groupings out of which FDE made the remittance.

(B) Under paragraph (d)(3)(v)(C)(*1*)(*i*) of this section, FDE is considered to have made the remittance ratably out of all of its accumulated after-tax income, which is deemed to have arisen in the statutory and residual groupings in the same proportions as the proportions in which the tax book value of FDE's assets would be assigned (if CFC1 were a United States person) for purposes of apportioning interest expense under the asset method in Year 2, the taxable year in which FDE made the remittance. Accordingly, $300x ($400x × $750x/$1,000x) of the remittance is deemed made out of the general category tested income of the FDE tested unit, and $100x ($400x × $250x/$1,000x) of the remittance is deemed made out of the passive category FPHCI of the FDE tested unit.

(C) Under paragraph (d)(3)(v)(C)(*1*)(*i*) of this section, $300x of the $400x item of foreign gross income from the remittance, and therefore an equal amount of foreign taxable income, is assigned to the income group that includes general category tested income attributable to the CFC1 tested unit, and $100x of this foreign gross income item, and therefore an equal amount of foreign taxable income, is assigned to the income group that includes passive category FPHCI attributable to the CFC1 tested unit. Under paragraph (f) of this section, the $20x of Country B withholding tax is ratably apportioned between the income groups based on the relative amounts of foreign taxable income in each grouping. Accordingly, $15x ($20x × $300x/$400x) of the Country B withholding tax is apportioned to the CFC1 tested unit's general category tested income group, and $5x ($20x × $100x/$400x) of the Country B withholding tax is apportioned to the CFC1 tested unit's passive category FPHCI income group. See § 1.960-2 for rules on determining the amount of such taxes that may be deemed paid under section 960(a) and (d).

(13) *Example 12: Disregarded payment that is a reattribution payment.*—(i) *Facts.* (A) USP wholly owns CFC1, a tested unit within the meaning of § 1.951A-2(c)(7)(iv)(A)(*1*) (the "CFC1 tested unit"). CFC1 wholly owns FDE1, a disregarded entity organized in Country B, that is a tested unit within the meaning of § 1.951A-2(c)(7)(iv)(A)(*2*) (the "FDE1 tested unit"). Country B imposes a 20 percent net income tax

on its residents. CFC1 also wholly owns FDE2, a disregarded entity organized in Country C, that is a tested unit within the meaning of §1.951A-2(c)(7)(iv)(A)(2) (the "FDE2 tested unit"). Country C imposes a 15 percent net income tax on its residents. The net income tax imposed by each of Country B and Country C on their tax residents is a foreign income tax within the meaning of §1.901-2(a) and a separate levy within the meaning of §1.901-2(d). For purposes of this paragraph (g)(13) (*Example 12*), the operative section is the high-tax exclusion of section 951A(c)(2)(A)(i)(III) and §1.951A-2(c)(7), and the statutory groupings are the tested income groups of each tested unit, as defined in §1.951A-2(c)(7)(iv)(A).

(B) FDE2 owns Asset A, which is intangible property with a tax book value of $12,000x that is properly reflected on the separate set of books and records of FDE2. In Year 1, pursuant to a license agreement between FDE1 and FDE2 for the use of Asset A, FDE1 makes a disregarded royalty payment to FDE2 of $1,000x that would be deductible if regarded for Federal income tax purposes. Because it is disregarded for Federal income tax purposes, the $1,000x disregarded royalty payment by FDE1 to FDE2 results in no income to CFC1 for Federal income tax purposes. Also, in Year 1, pursuant to a sublicense agreement between FDE1 and an unrelated third party for the use of Asset A, FDE1 earns $1,200x of royalty income for Federal income tax purposes (the "U.S. gross royalty") for the use of Asset A. The $1,200 of royalty income received by FDE1 from the unrelated third party is excluded from CFC1's foreign personal holding company income by reason of the active business exception in section 954(c)(2) because CFC1 satisfies the requirements of §1.954-2(d)(1). As a result, the $1,200x of royalty income that FDE1 earns from the sub-license agreement is gross tested income (as defined in §1.951A-2(c)(1)), which is properly reflected on the separate set of books and records of FDE1.

(C) Under the laws of Country B, the transaction that gives rise to the $1,200x item of U.S. gross royalty income causes FDE1 to include a $1,200x item of gross royalty income in its Country B taxable income (the "Country B gross royalty"). In addition, FDE1 deducts its $1,000x disregarded royalty payment to FDE2 for Country B tax purposes. For Country B tax purposes, FDE1 therefore has $200x ($1,200x–$1,000x) of taxable income on which Country B imposes $40x (20% × $200x) of net income tax.

(D) Under the laws of Country C, the $1,000x disregarded royalty payment from FDE1 to FDE2 causes FDE2 to include a $1,000x item of gross royalty income in its Country C taxable income (the "Country C gross royalty"). FDE2 therefore has $1,000x of taxable income for Country C tax purposes, on which Country C imposes $150x (15% × $1,000x) of net income tax.

(ii) *Analysis*—(A) *Country B net income tax*—(*1*) The Country B net income tax is imposed on foreign taxable income of FDE1 that consists of a $1,200x item of Country B gross royalty income and a $1,000x item of royalty expense. For Federal income tax purposes, the FDE1 tested unit has a $1,200x item of U.S. gross royalty income that is initially attributable to it under paragraph (d)(3)(v)(B)(2) of this section and §1.951A-2(c)(7)(ii)(B). The transaction that produced the $1,200x item of U.S. gross royalty income also produced the $1,200x item of Country B gross royalty income. Under paragraph (b)(2) of this section, the $1,200x item of U.S. gross royalty income is therefore the corresponding U.S. item for the $1,200x item of Country B gross royalty income of FDE1.

(*2*) The $1,000x disregarded royalty payment from FDE1 to FDE2 is allocated under paragraph (d)(3)(v)(B)(2) of this section and §1.951A-2(c)(7)(ii)(B) to the $1,200x of U.S. gross income of the FDE1 tested unit to the extent of that gross income. As a result, the $1,000x disregarded royalty payment causes $1,000x of the $1,200x item of U.S. gross royalty income to be reattributed from the FDE1 tested unit to the FDE2 tested unit, and results in a $1,000x reattribution amount that is also a reattribution payment.

(*3*) The $1,200x Country B gross royalty item that is included in the Country B taxable income of FDE1 is assigned under paragraph (d)(1) of this section to the statutory or residual grouping to which the $1,200x corresponding U.S. item is initially assigned under §1.951A-2(c)(7)(ii), namely, the FDE1 income group. This assignment is made without regard to the $1,000x reattribution payment from the FDE1 tested unit to the FDE2 tested unit; none of the FDE1 tested unit's $1,200x Country B gross royalty income is reattributed to the FDE2 tested unit for this purpose. See paragraph (d)(3)(v)(B)(*3*) of this section. Under paragraph (f) of this section, all of the $40x of Country B net income tax on the $200x of Country B taxable income is allocated to the FDE1 income group, the statutory grouping to which the $1,200x item of Country B gross royalty income of FDE1 is assigned. No apportionment of the $40x is necessary because the class of gross income to which the foreign gross income is allocated consists entirely of a single statutory grouping.

(B) *Country C net income tax*. The Country C net income tax is imposed on foreign taxable income of FDE2 that consists of a $1,000x item of Country C gross royalty income. For Federal income tax purposes, under paragraph (d)(3)(v)(B)(*2*) of this section and §1.951A-2(c)(7)(ii)(B), the FDE2 tested unit has a reattribution amount of $1,000x of U.S. gross royalty income by reason of its receipt of the $1,000x reattribution payment from FDE1. The $1,000x item of U.S. gross royalty income that is included in the taxable income of the FDE2 tested unit by reason of the $1,000x reattribution payment is assigned under paragraph (d)(3)(v)(B)(*1*) of this section to the statutory or residual grouping to which the $1,000x reattribution amount of U.S. gross royalty income that constitutes the reattribution payment is assigned upon receipt by the FDE2 tested unit under §1.951A-2(c)(7)(ii), namely, the FDE2 income group. Under paragraph (d)(3)(v)(B)(*1*) of this section, the $1,000x item of Country C gross royalty income is assigned to the statutory grouping to which the $1,000x corresponding U.S. item is assigned. Accordingly, under paragraph (f) of this section, all of the $150x of Country C net income tax is allocated to the FDE2 income group, the statutory grouping to which the $1,000x item of Country C gross royalty income of FDE2 is assigned. No apportionment of the $150x is necessary because the class of gross income to which the foreign gross income is allocated consists entirely of a single statutory grouping.

(14) *Example 13: Assets of a taxable unit that owns an interest in a lower-tier taxable unit*.—(i) *Facts*. USP wholly owns CFC1, a tested unit within the meaning of §1.951A-2(c)(7)(iv)(A) (the "CFC1 tested unit"). CFC1 wholly owns FDE1, a disregarded entity that is organized in Country A, and FDE2, a disregarded entity that is organized in Country B. CFC1's interests in FDE1 and FDE2 are each tested units within the meaning of §1.951A-2(c)(7)(iv)(A) (the "FDE1 tested unit" and "FDE2 tested unit," respectively). The FDE1 tested unit and FDE2 tested unit each own 50% of the interests in FDE3, a disregarded entity that is organized in Country C. CFC1's indirect interests in FDE3 are also a tested unit within the meaning of §1.951A-2(c)(7)(iv)(A) (the "FDE3 tested unit"). The FDE2 tested unit owns Asset A with a tax book value of $10,000x, and makes a reattribution payment to FDE3 that causes $5,000x of the tax book value of Asset A to be assigned to FDE3 under paragraph (d)(3)(v)(C)(*1*)(*ii*) of this section. FDE3 owns Asset B, which has a tax book value of $5,000x.

(ii) *Analysis*—(A) *Assets of the FDE3 tested unit*. The assets of the FDE3 tested unit consist of the portion of Asset A that is assigned to it under paragraph (d)(3)(v)(C)(*1*)(*ii*) of this section and any other assets determined in accordance with §1.987-6(b). The assets of the FDE3 tested unit thus consist of $5,000x of the tax book value of Asset A and all $5,000x of the tax book value of Asset B.

(B) *Assets of the FDE2 tested unit*. The assets of the FDE2 tested unit consist of the tax book value of any assets that it owns directly plus its pro rata share of the assets of the FDE3 tested unit, including the portion of reattribution assets assigned to the FDE3 tested unit. Asset A is a reattribution asset under paragraphs (d)(3)(v)(C)(*1*)(*ii*) and (d)(3)(v)(E) of this section. The assets of the FDE2 tested unit therefore consist of the portion of Asset A that it owns directly and that was not assigned to the FDE3 tested unit (or $5,000x) plus its pro rata share of the portion of Asset A that was assigned to the FDE3 tested unit, or $2,500x (50% of $5,000x). In addition, the assets of the FDE2 tested unit include its pro rata share of the tax book value of Asset B, or $2,500x (50% of $5,000x).

(C) *Assets of the FDE1 tested unit*. The assets of the FDE1 tested unit consist of its pro rata share of the assets of the FDE3 tested unit, including the portion of reattribution assets assigned to the FDE3 tested unit. Asset A is a reattribution asset under paragraphs (d)(3)(v)(C)(*1*)(*ii*) and (d)(3)(v)(E) of this section. The assets of the FDE1 tested unit therefore consist of its pro rata share of the portion of Asset A that was reattributed to the FDE3 tested unit, or $2,500x (50% of $5,000x), plus its pro rata share of the tax book value of Asset B, or $2,500x (50% of $5,000x).

(h) *Allocation and apportionment of certain foreign in lieu of taxes described in section 903*.—A tax that is a foreign income tax by reason of §1.903-1(c)(1) is allocated and apportioned to statutory and residual groupings in the same proportions as the foreign taxable income that comprises the excluded income (as defined in §1.903-1(c)(1)). See paragraph (f) of this section for rules on allocating and apportioning certain withholding taxes described in §1.903-1(c)(2).

(i) *Applicability dates*.—Except as provided in this paragraph (i), this section applies to taxable years beginning after December 31, 2019. Paragraphs (b)(19) and (23) and (d)(3)(i), (ii), and (v) of this section apply to taxable years that begin after December 31, 2019, and end on or after November 2, 2020. Paragraph (h) of this section applies to taxable years beginning after December 28, 2021. [Reg. § 1.861-20.]

□ [*T.D. 9922, 11-2-2020* (*corrected 9-30-2021*). *Amended by T.D. 9959, 12-28-2021* (*corrected 7-26-2022*).]

Proposed Amendments to Regulation

§ 1.861-20. Allocation and apportionment of foreign income taxes.—

* * *

(d) * * *

(3) * * *

(v) * * *

(E) * * *

(6) *Reattribution asset.*—The term *reattribution asset* means an asset thatproduces one or more items of gross income, computed under Federal income tax law, to which a disregarded payment, other than a disregarded payment received in exchange for property, is allocated under the rules of paragraph (d)(3)(v)(B)(2) of this section.

* * *

(i) *Applicability dates.*—(1) Except as provided in paragraphs (i)(2) through (4) of this section, this section applies to taxable years beginning after December 31, 2019.

(2) Paragraphs (b)(19) and (23) and (d)(3)(i), (ii), and (v) of this section apply to taxable years that begin after December 31, 2019, and end on or after November 2, 2020.

(3) Paragraph (d)(3)(v)(E)(*6*) of this section applies to taxable years that end on or after [date the final rule is filed with the **Federal Register**]. Taxpayers may choose to apply the rules in paragraph (d)(3)(v)(E)(*6*) of this section to taxable years beginning after December 31, 2019, and ending before [date the final rule is filed with the **Federal Register**], provided they apply paragraph (d)(3)(v)(E)(*6*) of this section consistently to their first taxable year beginning after December 31, 2019, and any subsequent taxable year beginning before [date the final rule is filed with the **Federal Register**]. Otherwise, for taxable years beginning after December 31, 2019, and ending before [date the final rule is filed with the **Federal Register**], see § 1.861-20(d)(3)(v)(E)(*6*) as contained in 26 CFR part 1 revised as of July 27, 2022.

(4) Paragraph (h) of this section applies to taxable years beginning after December 28, 2021. [Prop. Reg. § 1.861-20.]

[Proposed 11-22-2022.]

§ 1.862-1. Income specifically from sources without the United States.—(a) *Gross income.*—(1) The following items of gross income shall be treated as income from sources without the United States:

(i) Interest other than that specified in section 861(a)(1) and § 1.861-2 as being derived from sources within the United States;

(ii) Dividends other than those derived from sources within the United States as provided in section 861(a)(2) and § 1.861-3;

(iii) Compensation for labor or personal services performed without the United States;

(iv) Rentals or royalties from property located without the United States or from any interest in such property, including rentals or royalties for the use of, or for the privilege of using, without the United States, patents, copyrights, secret processes and formulas, goodwill, trademarks, trade brands, franchises, and other like property;

(v) Gains, profits, and income from the sale of real property located without the United States; and

(vi) Gains, profits, and income derived from the purchase of personal property within the United States and its sale without the United States.

For rules treating certain interest as income from sources without the United States, see paragraph (b) of § 1.861-2. For the treatment of compensation for labor or personal services performed partly within the United States and partly without the United States, see paragraph (b) of § 1.861-4.

(2) In applying subparagraph (1)(iv) of this paragraph for taxable years beginning after December 31, 1966, gains described in section 871 (a)(1)(D) and section 881(a)(4) from the sale or exchange after October 4, 1966, of patents, copyrights, and other like property shall be treated, as provided in section 871(e)(2), as rentals or royalties for the use of, or privilege of using, property or an interest in property. See paragraph (e) of § 1.871-11.

(3) For determining the time and place of sale of personal property for purposes of subparagraph (1)(vi) of this paragraph, see paragraph (c) of § 1.861-7.

(4) Income derived from the purchase of personal property within the United States and its sale within a possession of the United States shall be treated as derived entirely from within that possession.

(5) If interest is paid on an obligation of a nonresident of the United States by a resident of the United States acting in the resident's capacity as a guarantor of the obligation of the nonresident, the interest will be treated as income from sources without the United States.

(6) For rules treating certain interest as income from sources without the United States, see paragraph (b) of § 1.861-2.

(7) For the treatment of compensation for labor or personal services performed partly within the United States and partly without the United States, see paragraph (b) of § 1.861-4.

(b) *Taxable income.*—The taxable income from sources without the United States, in the case of the items of gross income specified in paragraph (a) of this section, shall be determined on the same basis as that used in § 1.861-8 for determining the taxable income from sources within the United States.

(c) *Income from certain property.*—For provisions permitting a taxpayer to elect to treat amounts of gross income attributable to certain aircraft or vessels first leased on or before December 28, 1980, as income from sources within the United States which would otherwise be treated as income from sources without the United States under paragraph (a) of this section, see § 1.861-9. For provisions requiring amounts of gross income attributable to certain aircraft, vessels, or spacecraft first leased by the taxpayer after December 28, 1980, to be treated as income from sources within the United States which would otherwise be treated as income from sources without the United States under paragraph (a) of this section, see § 1.861-9A. [Reg. § 1.862-1.]

□ [*T.D. 6258, 10-23-57. Amended by T.D. 7378, 9-29-75; T.D. 7635, 8-7-79 and T.D. 7928, 12-15-83.*]

§ 1.863-1. Allocation of gross income under section 863(a).—(a) *In general.*—Items of gross income other than those specified in section 861(a) and section 862(a) will generally be separately allocated to sources within or without the United States. See § 1.863-2 for alternate methods to determine the income from sources within or without the United States in the case of items specified in § 1.863-2(a). See also section 865(b) for rules for sourcing income from the sale of inventory property, within the meaning of section 865(i)(1) (inventory), generally, and section 865(e)(2) and § 1.865-3 for sourcing income from the sale of personal property (including inventory) by a nonresident that is attributable to the nonresident's office or other fixed place of business in the United States. In the case of sales of property involving partners and partnerships, the rules of § 1.863-3(f) apply.

(b) *Natural resources.*—(1) *In general.*—Notwithstanding any other provision of this part, except to the extent provided in paragraph (b)(2) of this section or § 1.865-3, gross receipts from the sale outside the United States of products derived from the ownership or operation of any farm, mine, oil or gas well, other natural deposit, or uncut timber within the United States shall be treated as from sources within the United States, and gross receipts from the sale within the United States of products derived from the ownership or operation of any farm, mine, oil or gas well, other natural deposit, or uncut timber outside the United States shall be treated as from sources without the United States.

(2) *Additional production activities.*—Notwithstanding any other provision of this section, gross receipts from the sale of products derived by a taxpayer who performs additional production activities as defined in paragraph (b) (3) (ii) of this section are allocated between sources within and without the United States based on the fair market value of the product immediately prior to the additional production activities. The source of gross receipts equal to the fair market value of the product immediately prior to the additional production activities will be from sources where the farm, mine, oil or gas well, other natural deposit, or uncut timber is located. The source of gross receipts from the sale of the product in excess of the fair market value immediately prior to the additional production activities must be determined under § 1.863-3. For purposes of applying § 1.863-3, only production assets used in the additional production activities are taken into account.

(3) *Definitions.*—(i) *Production activity.*—For purposes of this section, production activity means an activity that creates, fabricates, manufactures, extracts, processes, cures, or ages inventory. See § 1.864-1. Except as otherwise provided in § 1.1502-13 or 1.863-3(f)(2), only production activities conducted directly by the taxpayer are taken into account.

(ii) *Additional production activities.*—For purposes of this section, additional production activities are substantial production activities performed directly by the taxpayer in addition to activities from the ownership or operation of any farm, mine, oil or gas well, other natural deposit, or uncut timber. Whether a taxpayer's activities constitute additional production activities will be determined under the principles of § 1.954-3(a)(4) (except for § 1.954-3(a)(4)(iv)). However, in no case will activities that prepare the natural resource itself for export, including those that are designed to facilitate the transportation of the natural resource, be considered additional production activities for purposes of this section.

(4) *Determination of fair market value.*—For purposes of this section, fair market value depends on all of the facts and circumstances as they exist relative to a party in any particular case. Where the products are sold to a related party in a transaction subject to section 482, the determination of fair market value under this section must be consistent with the arm's length price determined under section 482.

(5) *Determination of gross income.*—To determine the amount of a taxpayer's gross income from sources within or without the United States, the taxpayer's gross receipts from sources within or without the United States determined under this paragraph (b) must be reduced by the cost of goods sold properly attributable to gross receipts from sources within or without the United States.

(6) *Tax return disclosure.*—A taxpayer that determines the source of its income under paragraph (b)(2) shall attach a statement to its return explaining the methodology used to determine fair market value under paragraph (b)(4) of this section, and explaining any additional production activities (as defined in paragraph (b)(3)(ii) of this section) performed by the taxpayer. In addition, the taxpayer must provide such other information as is required by § 1.863-3.

(7) *Examples.*—The following examples illustrate the rules of this paragraph (b):

(i) *Example 1. No additional production, foreign source gross receipts.*—U.S. Mines, a domestic corporation, operates a copper mine and mill in Country X. U.S. Mines extracts copper-bearing rocks from the ground and transports the rocks to the mill where the rocks are ground and processed to produce copper-bearing concentrate. The concentrate is transported to a port where it is dried in preparation for export, stored, and then shipped to purchasers in the United States. Because, under the facts and circumstances, none of U.S. Mines' activities constitute additional production activities, within the meaning of paragraph (b)(3)(ii) of this section, paragraph (b)(2) of this section does not apply, and under paragraph (b)(1) of this section, gross receipts from the sale of the concentrate will be treated as from sources without the United States.

(ii) *Example 2. No additional production, U.S. source gross receipts.*—U.S. Gas, a domestic corporation, extracts natural gas within the United States, and transports the natural gas to a Country X port where it is liquefied in preparation for shipment. The liquefied natural gas is then transported via freighter and sold without additional production activities in a foreign country. Under paragraph (b)(3)(ii) of this section, liquefaction of natural gas is not an additional production activity because liquefaction prepares the natural gas for transportation. Therefore, under paragraph (b)(1) of this section, gross receipts from the sale of the liquefied natural gas will be treated as from sources within the United States.

(iii) *Example 3. Production in United States, foreign sales.*—U.S. Gold, a domestic corporation, mines gold in Country X, produces gold jewelry using production assets located in the United States, and sells the jewelry in Country Y. Assume that the fair market value of the gold before the additional production activities in the United States is $40x and that U.S. Gold ultimately sells the gold jewelry in Country Y for $100x. Under paragraph (b)(2) of this section, $40x of U.S. Gold's gross receipts will be treated as from sources without the United States, and the remaining $60x of gross receipts will be treated as from sources within the United States under § 1.863-3.

(iv) *Example 4. Production and sales in United States.*—U.S. Oil, a domestic corporation, extracts oil in Country X, transports the oil via a pipeline to the United States, refines the oil using production assets located in the United States, and sells the refined product in the United States to unrelated persons. Assume that the fair market value of the oil before refinement in the United States is $80x and U.S. Oil ultimately sells the refined product for $100x. Under paragraph (b)(2) of this section, $80x of gross receipts will be treated as from sources without the United States, and the remaining $20x of gross receipts will be treated as from sources within the United States under § 1.863-3.

(v) *Example 5. Additional production.*—The facts are the same as in paragraph (b)(7)(i) of this section (the facts in *Example 1*), except that U.S. Mines also operates a smelter in Country X. The concentrate output from the mill is transported to the smelter where it is transformed into smelted copper. The smelted copper is exported to purchasers in the United States. Under the facts and circumstances, all the processes applied to make copper concentrate are considered mining. Therefore, under paragraph (b)(2) of this section, gross receipts equal to the fair market value of the concentrate at the smelter will be treated as from sources without the United States. Under the facts and circumstances, the conversion of the concentrate into smelted copper is an additional production activity in a foreign country within the meaning of paragraph (b)(3)(ii) of this section. Therefore, the source of U.S. Mines's excess gross receipts will be determined under § 1.863-3, pursuant to paragraph (b)(2) of this section.

(c) *Determination of taxable income.*—The taxpayer's taxable income from sources within or without the United States will be determined under the rules of §§ 1.861-8 through 1.861-14T for determining taxable income from sources within the United States.

(d) *Scholarships, fellowship grants, grants, prizes and awards.*—(1) *In general.*—This paragraph (d) applies to scholarships, fellowship grants, grants, prizes and awards. The provisions of this paragraph (d) do not apply to amounts paid as salary or other compensation for services.

(2) *Source of income.*—The source of income from scholarships, fellowship grants, grants, prizes and awards is determined as follows:

(i) *United States source income.*—Except as provided in paragraph (d)(2)(iii) of this section, scholarships, fellowship grants, grants, prizes and awards made by a U.S. citizen or resident, a domestic partnership, a domestic corporation, an estate or trust (other than a foreign estate or trust within the meaning of section 7701(a)(31)), the United States (or an instrumentality or agency thereof), a State (or any political subdivision thereof), or the District of Columbia shall be treated as income from sources within the United States.

(ii) *Foreign source income.*—Scholarships, fellowship grants, grants, prizes and awards made by a foreign government (or an instrumentality, agency, or any political subdivision thereof), an international organization (as defined in section 7701(a)(18)), or a person other than a U.S. person (as defined in section 7701(a)(30)) shall be treated as income from sources without the United States.

(iii) *Certain activities conducted outside the United States.*—Scholarships, fellowship grants, targeted grants, and achievement awards received by a person other than a U.S. person (as defined in section 7701(a)(30)) with respect to activities previously conducted (in the case of achievement awards) or to be conducted (in the case of scholarships, fellowships grants, and targeted grants) outside the United States shall be treated as income from sources without the United States.

(3) *Definitions.*—The following definitions apply for purposes of this paragraph (d):

(i) *Scholarships* are defined in section 117 and the regulations thereunder.

(ii) *Fellowship grants* are defined in section 117 and the regulations thereunder.

(iii) *Prizes and awards* are defined in section 74 and the regulations thereunder.

(iv) *Grants* are amounts described in subparagraph (3) of section 4945(g) and the regulations thereunder, and are not amounts otherwise described in paragraphs (d)(3)(i), (ii), or (iii) of this section.

For purposes of this paragraph (d), the reference to section 4945(g)(3) is applied without regard to the identity of the payor or recipient and without the application of the objective and nondiscriminatory basis test and the requirement of a procedure approved in advance.

(v) *Targeted grants* are grants—

(A) Issued by an organization described in section 501(c)(3), the United States (or an instrumentality or agency thereof), a State (or any political subdivision thereof), or the District of Columbia; and

(B) For an activity undertaken in the public interest and not primarily for the private financial benefit of a specific person or persons or organization.

(vi) *Achievement awards* are awards—

(A) Issued by an organization described in section 501(c)(3), the United States (or an instrumentality or agency thereof), a State (or political subdivision thereof), or the District of Columbia; and

(B) For a past activity undertaken in the public interest and not primarily for the private financial benefit of a specific person or persons or organization.

(4) *Effective dates.*—The following are the effective dates concerning this paragraph (d):

(i) *Scholarships and fellowship grants.*—This paragraph (d) is effective for scholarship and fellowship grant payments made after December 31, 1986. However, for scholarship and fellowship grant payments made after May 14, 1989, and before June 16, 1993, the residence of the payor rule of paragraph (d)(2)(i) and (ii) of this section may be applied without applying paragraph (d)(2)(iii) of this section.

(ii) *Grants, prizes and awards.*—This paragraph (d) is effective for payments made for grants, prizes and awards, targeted grants, and achievement awards after September 25, 1995. However, the taxpayer may elect to apply the provisions of this paragraph (d) to payments made for grants, prizes and awards, targeted grants, and achievement awards after December 31, 1986, and before September 26, 1995.

(e) *Residual interest in a REMIC.*—(1) *REMIC inducement fees.*—An inducement fee (as defined in § 1.446-6(b)(2)) shall be treated as income from sources within the United States.

(2) *Excess inclusion income and net losses.*—An excess inclusion (as defined in section 860E(c)) shall be treated as income from sources within the United States. To the extent of excess inclusion income previously taken into account with respect to a residual interest (reduced by net losses previously taken into account under this paragraph), a net loss (described in section 860C(b)(2)) with respect to the residual interest shall be allocated to the class of gross income and apportioned to the statutory grouping(s) or residual grouping of gross income to which the excess inclusion income was assigned.

(f) *Applicability date.*—Paragraph (b) of this section applies to taxable years ending on or after December 23, 2019. However, a taxpayer may apply paragraph (b) of this section in its entirety for taxable years beginning after December 31, 2017, and ending before December 23, 2019, provided that the taxpayer and all persons related to the taxpayer (within the meaning of section 267 or 707) apply paragraph (b) of this section and §§ 1.863-2(b), 1.863-3, 1.863-8(b)(3)(ii), 1.864-5(a) and (b), 1.864-6(c)(2), and 1.865-3 in their entirety for the taxable year, and once applied, the taxpayer and all persons related to the taxpayer (within the meaning of section 267 or 707) continue to apply these regulations in their entirety for all subsequent taxable years. For regulations generally applicable to taxable years ending before December 23, 2019, see § 1.863-1 as contained in 26 CFR part 1 revised as of April 1, 2020. Paragraph (e)(2) of this section applies for taxable years ending after August 1, 2006. [Reg. § 1.863-1.]

☐ [*T.D.* 6258, 10-23-57. *Amended by T.D.* 6348, 12-21-58; *T.D.* 8615, 8-24-95; *T.D.* 8687, 11-27-96; *T.D.* 9128, 5-7-2004; *T.D.* 9272, 7-31-2006, *T.D.* 9415, 7-11-2008 *and T.D.* 9921, 12-10-2020.]

§ 1.863-2. Allocation and apportionment of taxable income.—(a) *Determination of taxable income.*—Section 863(b) provides an alternate method for determining taxable income from sources within the United States in the case of gross income derived from sources partly within and partly without the United States. Under this method, taxable income is determined by deducting from such gross income the expenses, losses, or other deductions properly apportioned or allocated thereto and a ratable part of any other expenses, losses, or deductions that cannot definitely be allocated to some item or class of gross income. The income to which this section applies will consist of gains, profits, and income:

(1) From certain transportation or other services rendered partly within and partly without the United States to the extent not within the scope of section 863(c) or other specific provisions of this title;

(2) From the sale of inventory property (within the meaning of section 865(i)) produced (in whole or in part) by the taxpayer in the United States and sold outside the United States or produced (in whole or in part) by the taxpayer outside the United States and sold in the United States; or

(3) Derived from the purchase of personal property within a possession of the United States and its sale within the United States, to the extent not excluded from the scope of these regulations under § 1.936-6(a)(5), Q&A 7.

(b) *Determination of source of taxable income.*—Income treated as derived from sources partly within and partly without the United States under paragraph (a) of this section may be allocated or apportioned to sources within and without the United States pursuant to §§ 1.863-1, 1.863-3, 1.863-4, 1.863-8, and 1.863-9. To determine the source of certain types of income described in paragraph (a)(1) of this section, see § 1.863-4. To determine the source of gross income described in paragraph (a)(2) of this section, see § 1.863-1 for natural resources, § 1.863-3 for other sales of inventory property, and § 1.863-8 for source of gross income from space and ocean activity. Section 1.865-3 may apply instead of the provisions in this section to source gross income from sales of personal property (including inventory property) by nonresidents attributable to an office or other fixed place of business in the United States. To determine the source of income partly from sources within a possession of the United States, including income described in paragraph (a)(3) of this section, see § 1.863-3(e).

(c) *Applicability date.*—Except as provided in this paragraph (c), this section applies to taxable years beginning after December 30, 1996. Paragraph (b) of this section applies to taxable years ending on or after December 23, 2019. However, a taxpayer may apply paragraph (b) of this section in its entirety for taxable years beginning after December 31, 2017, and ending before December 23, 2019, provided that the taxpayer and all persons related to the taxpayer (within the meaning of section 267 or 707) apply paragraph (b) of this section and §§ 1.863-1(b), 1.863-3, 1.863-8(b)(3)(ii), 1.864-5(a) and (b), 1.864-6(c)(2), and 1.865-3 in their entirety for the taxable year, and once applied, the taxpayer and all persons related to the taxpayer (within the meaning of section 267 or 707) continue to apply these regulations in their entirety for all subsequent taxable years. For regulations generally applicable to taxable years ending before December 23, 2019, see § 1.863-2 as contained in 26 CFR part 1 revised as of April 1, 2020. [Reg. § 1.863-2.]

☐ [*T.D.* 6258, 10-23-57. *Amended by T.D.* 8687, 11-27-96 *and T.D.* 9921, 12-10-2020.]

§ 1.863-3. Allocation and apportionment of income from certain sales of inventory.—(a) *In general.*—(1) *Scope.*—Subject to the rules of § 1.865-3, paragraphs (a) through (d) of this section apply to determine the source of income derived from the sale of inventory property (inventory) that a taxpayer produces (in whole or in part) within the United States and sells without the United States, or that a taxpayer produces (in whole or in part) without the United States and sells within the United States (collectively, Section 863(b)(2) Sales). See section 865(i)(1) for the definition of inventory. Paragraph (b) of this section provides that the source of gross income from Section 863(b)(2) Sales is based solely on the production activities with respect to the inventory. Paragraph (c) of this section describes how to determine source based on production activity, including when inventory is produced partly within the United States and partly without the United States. Paragraph (d) of this section determines taxable income from Section 863(b)(2) Sales. Paragraph (e) of this section applies to determine the source of certain income derived from a possession of the United States. Paragraph (f) of this section provides special rules for partnerships for all sales subject to §§ 1.863-1 through 1.863-3. Paragraph (g) of this section provides applicability dates for the rules in this section.

(2) *Cross references.*—To determine the source of income derived from the sale of personal property (including inventory) by a nonresident that is attributable to the nonresident's office or other fixed place of business in the United States under section 865(e)(2) and § 1.865-3(c), the rules of § 1.865-3 apply, and the rules of this section do not apply except to the extent provided in § 1.865-3. To determine the source of income from sales of property produced by the tax-

payer, when the property is either produced in whole or in part in space, as defined in § 1.863-8(d)(1)(i), or international water, as defined in § 1.863-8(d)(1)(ii), or is sold in space or international water, the rules of § 1.863-8 apply, and the rules of this section do not apply except to the extent provided in § 1.863-8.

(b) *Sourcing based solely on production activities.*—Subject to the rules of § 1.865-3, all income, gain, or loss derived from Section 863(b)(2) Sales is allocated and apportioned solely on the basis of the production activities with respect to the inventory.

(c) *Determination of the source of gross income from production activity.*—(1) *Production only within the United States or only within foreign countries.*—(i) *Source of income.*—For purposes of this section, production activity means an activity that creates, fabricates, manufactures, extracts, processes, cures, or ages inventory. See § 1.864-1. Whether a taxpayer's activities constitute production activity is determined under the principles of § 1.954-3(a)(4) (except for § 1.954-3(a)(4)(iv)). Subject to the provisions in § 1.1502-13 or paragraph (f)(2)(ii) of this section, the only production activities that are taken into account for purposes of §§ 1.863-1, 1.863-2, and this section are those conducted directly by the taxpayer. Where the taxpayer's production assets are located only within the United States or only outside the United States, gross income is sourced where the taxpayer's production assets are located. For rules regarding the source of income when production assets are located both within the United States and without the United States, see paragraph (c)(2) of this section. For rules regarding the source of income when production takes place, in whole or in part, in space or international water, the rules of § 1.863-8 apply, and the rules of this section do not apply except to the extent provided in § 1.863-8.

(ii) *Definition of production assets.*—Subject to the provisions of § 1.1502-13 and paragraph (f)(2)(ii) of this section, production assets include only tangible and intangible assets owned directly by the taxpayer that are directly used by the taxpayer to produce inventory described in paragraph (a) of this section. Production assets do not include assets that are not directly used to produce inventory described in paragraph (a) of this section. Thus, production assets do not include such assets as accounts receivables, intangibles not related to production of inventory (e.g., marketing intangibles, including trademarks and customer lists), transportation assets, warehouses, the inventory itself, raw materials, or work-in-process. In addition, production assets do not include cash or other liquid assets (including working capital), investment assets, prepaid expenses, or stock of a subsidiary.

(iii) *Location of production assets.*—For purposes of this section, a tangible production asset will be considered located where the asset is physically located. An intangible production asset will be considered located where the tangible production assets owned by the taxpayer to which it relates are located.

(2) *Production both within and without the United States.*—(i) *Source of income.*—Where the taxpayer's production assets are located both within and without the United States, income from sources without the United States will be determined by multiplying the gross income by a fraction, the numerator of which is the average adjusted basis of production assets that are located outside the United States and the denominator of which is the average adjusted basis of all production assets within and without the United States. The remaining income is treated as from sources within the United States.

(ii) *Adjusted basis of production assets.*—(A) *In general.*—For purposes of paragraph (c)(2)(i) of this section, the adjusted basis of an asset is determined by using the alternative depreciation system under section 168(g)(2). The adjusted basis of all production assets for purposes of paragraph (c)(2)(i) of this section is determined as though the production assets were subject to the alternative depreciation system set forth in section 168(g)(2) for the entire period that such property has been in service. The adjusted basis of the production assets is determined without regard to the election to expense certain depreciable assets under section 179 and without regard to any additional first-year depreciation provision (for example, section 168(k), (l), and (m), and former sections 1400L(b) and 1400N(d)). The average adjusted basis of assets is computed by averaging the adjusted basis at the beginning and end of the taxable year, unless by reason of changes during the taxable year, as might be the case in the event of a major acquisition or disposition of assets, the average would materially distort the calculation in paragraph (c)(2)(i) of this section. In this event, the average adjusted basis is determined upon a more appropriate basis that is weighted to reasonably reflect the period for which the assets are held by the taxpayer during the taxable year.

(B) *Production assets used to produce other property.*—If a production asset is used to produce inventory sold in Section 863(b)(2) Sales and also used to produce other property during the taxable year, the portion of its adjusted basis that is included in the fraction described in paragraph (c)(2)(i) of this section will be determined under any method that reasonably reflects the portion of the asset that produces inventory sold in Section 863(b)(2) Sales. For example, the portion of such an asset that is included in the formula may be determined by multiplying the asset's average adjusted basis by a fraction, the numerator of which is the gross receipts from sales of inventory from Section 863(b)(2) Sales produced by the asset, and the denominator of which is the gross receipts from all property produced by that asset.

(3) *Anti-abuse rule.*—The purpose of paragraph (b) of this section and this paragraph (c) is to attribute the source of the taxpayer's gross income from certain sales of inventory property to the location of the taxpayer's production activity. Therefore, if the taxpayer has entered into or structured one or more transactions with a principal purpose of reducing its U.S. tax liability in a manner inconsistent with the purpose of paragraph (b) of this section or this paragraph (c), the Commissioner may make appropriate adjustments so that the source of the taxpayer's gross income more clearly reflects the location of production activity. For example, a taxpayer may be subject to the rule in this paragraph (c)(3) if domestic production assets are acquired by a related partnership (or a subsidiary of a related partnership) with a principal purpose of reducing its U.S. tax liability by claiming that the taxpayer's income from sales of inventory is subject to section 862(a)(6) rather than section 863(b).

(4) *Examples.*—The following examples illustrate the rules of this paragraph (c):

(i) *Example 1. Source of gross income.*—(A) *Facts.* A, a U.S. corporation, produces widgets that are sold both within the United States and within a foreign country. The initial manufacture of all widgets occurs in the United States. The second stage of production of widgets that are sold within a foreign country is completed within the country of sale. A's U.S. plant and machinery which is involved in the initial manufacture of the widgets has an average adjusted basis of $200, as determined using the alternative depreciation system under section 168(g)(2). A also owns warehouses used to store work-in-process. A owns foreign equipment with an average adjusted basis of $25. A's gross receipts from all sales of widgets is $100, and its gross receipts from export sales of widgets is $25. Assume that apportioning average adjusted basis using gross receipts is reasonable. Assume A's cost of goods sold from the sale of widgets in the foreign countries is $13 and thus, its gross income from widgets sold in foreign countries is $12.

(B) *Analysis.* A determines its gross income from sources without the United States by multiplying A's $12 of gross income from sales of widgets in foreign countries by a fraction, the numerator of which is all relevant foreign production assets, or $25, and the denominator of which is all relevant production assets, or $75 ($25 foreign assets + ($200 U.S. assets × $25 gross receipts from export sales/$100 gross receipts from all sales)). Therefore, A's gross income from sources without the United States is $4 ($12 × ($25/$75)).

(ii) *Example 2. Location of intangible property.*—Assume the same facts as in paragraph (c)(4)(i)(A) of this section (the facts in *Example 1*), except that A employs a patented process that applies only to the initial production of widgets. In computing the formula used to determine the source of gross income, A's patent, if it has an average adjusted basis, would be located in the United States.

(iii) *Example 3. Anti-abuse rule.*—(A) *Facts.* Assume the same facts as in paragraph (c)(4)(i)(A) of this section (the facts in *Example 1*). A sells its U.S. assets to B, an unrelated U.S. corporation, with a principal purpose of reducing its U.S. tax liability by manipulating the property fraction. A then leases these assets from B. After this transaction, under the general rule of paragraph (c)(2) of this section, all of A's gross income would be considered from sources without the United States, because all of A's relevant production assets are located within a foreign country. Since the leased property is not owned by the taxpayer, it is not included in the fraction.

(B) *Analysis.* Because A has entered into a transaction with a principal purpose of reducing its U.S. tax liability by manipulating the formula described in paragraph (c)(2)(i) of this section, A's income must be adjusted to more clearly reflect the source of that income. In this case, the Commissioner may redetermine the source of A's gross income by ignoring the sale-leaseback transactions.

(d) *Determination of source of taxable income.*—Once the source of gross income has been determined under paragraph (c) of this section, the taxpayer must properly allocate and apportion its expenses, losses, and other deductions to its respective amounts of gross income from sources within and without the United States from its Section 863(b)(2) Sales. See §§1.861-8 through 1.861-14T and 1.861-17.

(e) *Income partly from sources within a possession of the United States.*—(1) *In general.*—This paragraph (e) relates to certain sales that give rise to income, gain, or loss that is treated as derived partly from sources within the United States and partly from sources within a possession of the United States (Section 863 Possession Sales). This paragraph (e) applies to determine the source of income derived from the sale of inventory produced (in whole or in part) by a taxpayer within the United States and sold within a possession of the United States, or produced (in whole or in part) by a taxpayer in a possession of the United States and sold within the United States (collectively, Possession Production Sales). It also applies to determine the source of income derived from the purchase of personal property within a possession of the United States and its sale within the United States (Possession Purchase Sales). A taxpayer subject to this paragraph (e) must apportion gross income from Section 863 Possession Sales under paragraph (e)(2) of this section (in the case of Possession Production Sales) or under paragraph (e)(3) of this section (in the case of Possession Purchase Sales). The source of taxable income from Section 863 Possession Sales is determined under paragraph (d) of this section.

(2) *Allocation or apportionment for Possession Production Sales.*—The source of gross income from Possession Production Sales is determined under the rules of paragraph (c) of this section, except that the term *possession of the United States* is substituted for *foreign country* wherever it appears.

(3) *Allocation or apportionment for Possession Purchase Sales.*—(i) *Determination of source of gross income from Possession Purchase Sales.*—Gross income from Possession Purchase Sales is allocated in its entirety to the taxpayer's business activity, and is then apportioned between sources within the United States and sources within a possession of the United States under paragraph (e)(3)(ii) of this section.

(ii) *Determination of source of gross income from business activity.*—(A) *Source of gross income.*—Gross income from the taxpayer's business activity is sourced in the possession in the same proportion that the amount of the taxpayer's business activity for the taxable year within the possession bears to the amount of the taxpayer's business activity for the taxable year both within the possession and outside the possession, with respect to Possession Purchase Sales. The remaining income is sourced in the United States.

(B) *Business activity.*—For purposes of this paragraph (e)(3)(ii), the taxpayer's business activity is equal to the sum of—

(1) The amounts for the taxable period paid for wages, salaries, and other compensation of employees, and other expenses attributable to Possession Purchase Sales (other than amounts that are nondeductible under section 263A, interest, and research and development);

(2) Cost of goods sold attributable to Possession Purchase Sales during the taxable period; and

(3) Possession Purchase Sales for the taxable period.

(C) *Location of business activity.*—For purposes of determining the location of the taxpayer's business activity within a possession, the following rules apply:

(1) Sales activity.—Receipts from gross sales will be attributed to a possession in accordance with the principles of §1.861-7(c).

(2) Cost of goods sold.—Payments for cost of goods sold will be properly attributable to gross receipts from sources within the possession only to the extent that the property purchased was manufactured, produced, grown, or extracted in the possession (within the meaning of section 954(d)(1)(A)).

(3) Expenses.—Expenses will be attributed to a possession under the rules of §§1.861-8 through 1.861-14T.

(4) *Examples.*—The following examples illustrate the rules of paragraph (e)(3)(ii) of this section relating to the determination of source of gross income from business activity:

(i) *Example 1. Purchase of goods manufactured in possession.*—(A) *Facts.* U.S. Co. purchases in a possession product X for $80 from A. A manufactures X in the possession. Without further production, U.S. Co. sells X in the United States for $100. Assume U.S. Co. has sales and administrative expenses in the possession of $10.

(B) *Analysis.* To determine the source of U.S. Co.'s gross income, the $100 gross income from sales of X is allocated entirely to U.S. Co.'s business activity. Forty-seven dollars of U.S. Co.'s gross income is sourced in the possession. [Possession expenses ($10) plus possession purchases (i.e., cost of goods sold) ($80) plus possessions sales ($0), divided by total expenses ($10) plus total purchases ($80) plus total sales ($100).] The remaining $53 is sourced in the United States.

(ii) *Example 2. Purchase of goods manufactured outside possession.*—(A) *Facts.* Assume the same facts as in paragraph (e)(4)(i)(A) of this section (the facts in *Example 1*), except that A manufactures X outside the possession.

(B) *Analysis.* To determine the source of U.S. Co.'s gross income, the $100 gross income is allocated entirely to U.S. Co.'s business activity. Five dollars of U.S. Co.'s gross income is sourced in the possession. [Possession expenses ($10) plus possession purchases ($0) plus possession sales ($0), divided by total expenses ($10) plus total purchases ($80) plus total sales ($100).] The $80 purchase is not included in the numerator used to determine U.S. Co.'s business activity in the possession, since product X was not manufactured in the possession. The remaining $95 is sourced in the United States.

(5) *Special rules for partnerships.*—In applying the rules of this paragraph (e) to transactions involving partners and partnerships, the rules of paragraph (f) of this section apply.

(f) *Special rules for partnerships.*—(1) *General rule.*—For purposes of §1.863-1 and this section, a taxpayer's production activity does not include production activities conducted by a partnership of which the taxpayer is a partner either directly or through one or more partnerships, except as otherwise provided in paragraphs (c)(3) or (f)(2) of this section.

(2) *Exceptions.*—(i) *In general.*—For purposes of determining the source of the partner's distributive share of partnership income or determining the source of the partner's income from the sale of inventory property which the partnership distributes to the partner in kind, the partner's production activity includes an activity conducted by the partnership. In addition, the production activity of a partnership includes the production activity of a taxpayer that is a partner either directly or through one or more partnerships, to the extent that the partner's production activity is related to inventory that the partner contributes to the partnership in a transaction described under section 721.

(ii) *Attribution of production assets to or from a partnership.*—A partner will be treated as owning its proportionate share of the partnership's production assets only to the extent that, under paragraph (f)(2)(i) of this section, the partner's activity includes production activity conducted through a partnership. A partner's share of partnership assets will be determined by reference to the partner's distributive share of partnership income for the year attributable to such production assets. Similarly, to the extent a partnership's activities include the production activities of a partner, the partnership will be treated as owning the partner's production assets related to the inventory that is contributed in kind to the partnership. See paragraph (c)(2)(ii) of this section for rules apportioning the basis of assets to Section 863 Sales.

(iii) *Basis.*—For purposes of this section, in those cases where the partner is treated as owning its proportionate share of the partnership's production assets, the partner's basis in production assets held through a partnership shall be determined by reference to the partnership's adjusted basis in its assets (including a partner's special basis adjustment, if any, under section 743). Similarly, a partnership's basis in a partner's production assets is determined with reference to the partner's adjusted basis in its assets.

(3) *Examples.*—The following examples illustrate the rules of this paragraph (f):

(i) *Example 1. Distributive share of partnership income.*—A, a U.S. corporation, forms a partnership in the United States with B, a country X corporation. A and B each have a 50 percent interest in the income, gains, losses, deductions and credits of the partnership. The partnership is engaged in the manufacture and sale of widgets. The widgets are manufactured in the partnership's plant located in the United States and are sold by the partnership outside the United States. The partnership owns the manufacturing facility and all other production assets used to produce the widgets. A's distributive share of partnership income includes 50 percent of the sales income from these sales. In applying the rules of section 863 to determine the source of its distributive share of partnership income from the export sales of widgets, A is treated as carrying on the activity of the partnership related to production of these widgets and as owning a proportionate share of the partnership's assets related to production of the widgets, based upon its distributive share of partnership income.

(ii) *Example 2. Distribution in kind.*—Assume the same facts as in paragraph (f)(3)(i) of this section (the facts in *Example 1*) except that the partnership, instead of selling the widgets, distributes the widgets to A and B. A then further processes the widgets and then sells them outside the United States. In determining the source of the income earned by A on the sales outside the United States, A is treated as conducting the activities of the partnership related to production of the distributed widgets. Thus, the source of gross income on the sale of the widgets is determined under section 863 and this section. In applying paragraph (c) of this section, A is treated as owning its proportionate share of the partnership's production assets based upon its distributive share of partnership income.

(g) *Applicability dates.*—This section applies to taxable years ending on or after December 23, 2019. However, a taxpayer may apply this section in its entirety for taxable years beginning after December 31, 2017, and ending before December 23, 2019, provided that the taxpayer and all persons related to the taxpayer (within the meaning of section 267 or 707) apply this section and §§1.863-1(b), 1.863-2(b), 1.863-8(b)(3)(ii), 1.864-5(a) and (b), 1.864-6(c)(2), and 1.865-3 in their entirety for the taxable year, and once applied, the taxpayer and all persons related to the taxpayer (within the meaning of section 267 or 707) continue to apply these regulations in their entirety for all subsequent taxable years. For regulations generally applicable to taxable years ending before December 23, 2019, see §1.863-3 as contained in 26 CFR part 1 revised as of April 1, 2020. [Reg. §1.863-3.]

☐ [*T.D.* 8687, 11-27-96. *Amended by T.D.* 8786, 10-13-98 *T.D.* 9305, 12-26-2006 *and T.D.* 9921, 12-10-2020.]

Proposed Amendments to Regulation

☐ Paragraph (h) is redesignated as paragraph (i) and a new paragraph (h) is added to read as follows:

§1.863-3. Allocation and apportionment of income from certain sales of inventory.

* * *

(h) *Income from a global dealing operation.*—(1) *Purpose and scope.*—This paragraph (h) provides rules for sourcing income, gain and loss from a global dealing operation that, under the rules of §1.482-8, is earned by or allocated to a controlled taxpayer qualifying as a participant in a global dealing operation under §1.482-8(a)(2)(ii). This paragraph (h) does not apply to income earned by or allocated to a controlled taxpayer qualifying as a participant in a global dealing operation that is specifically sourced under sections 861, 862 or 865, or to substitute payments earned by a participant in a global dealing operation that are sourced under §1.861-2(a)(7) or §1.861-3(a)(6).

(2) *In general.*—The source of any income, gain or loss to which this section applies shall be determined by reference to the residence of the participant. For purposes of this paragraph (h), the residence of a participant shall be determined under section 988(a)(3)(B).

(3) *Qualified business units as participants in global dealing operations.*—(i) *In general.*—Except as otherwise provided in this paragraph (h), where a single controlled taxpayer conducts a global dealing operation through one or more qualified business units (QBUs), as defined in section 989(a) and §1.989(a)-1, the source of income, gain or loss generated by the global dealing operation and earned by or allocated to the controlled taxpayer shall be determined by applying the rules of §1.482-8 as if each QBU that performs activities of a regular dealer in securities as defined in §1.482-8(a)(2)(ii)(A) or the related activities described in §1.482-8(a)(2)(ii)(B) were a separate controlled taxpayer qualifying as a participant in the global dealing operation within the meaning of §1.482-8(a)(2)(ii). Accordingly, the amount of income sourced in the United States and outside of the United States shall be determined by treating the QBU as a participant in the global dealing operation, allocating income to each participant under §1.482-8, as modified by paragraph (h)(3)(ii) of this section, and sourcing the income to the United States or outside of the United States under §1.863-3(h)(2).

(ii) *Economic effects of a single legal entity.*—In applying the principles of §1.482-8, the taxpayer shall take into account the economic effects of conducting a global dealing operation through a single entity instead of multiple legal entities. For example, since the entire capital of a corporation supports all of the entity's transactions, regardless of where those transactions may be booked, the payment of a guarantee fee within the entity is inappropriate and will be disregarded.

(iii) *Treatment of interbranch and interdesk amounts.*—An agreement among QBUs of the same taxpayer to allocate income, gain or loss from transactions with third parties is not a transaction because a taxpayer cannot enter into a contract with itself. For purposes of this paragraph (h)(3), however, such an agreement, including a risk transfer agreement (as defined in §1.475(g)-2(b)) may be used to determine the source of global dealing income from transactions with third parties in the same manner and to the same extent that transactions between controlled taxpayers in a global dealing operation may be used to allocate income, gain or loss from the global dealing operation under the rules of §1.482-8.

(iv) *Deemed QBU.*—For purposes of this paragraph (h)(3), a QBU shall include a U.S. trade or business that is deemed to exist because of the activities of a dependent agent in the United States, without regard to the books and records requirement of §1.989(a)-1(b).

(v) *Examples.*—The following examples illustrate this paragraph (h)(3).

Example 1. Use of comparable uncontrolled financial transactions method to source global dealing income between branches. (i) F is a foreign bank that acts as a market maker in foreign currency through branch offices in London, New York, and Tokyo. In a typical business day, the foreign exchange desk in F's U.S. branch (USFX) enters into several hundred spot and forward contracts on the interbank market to purchase and sell Deutsche marks (DM) with unrelated third parties. Each of F's branches, including USFX, employs both marketers and traders for their foreign currency dealing. In addition, USFX occasionally transfers risk with respect to its third party DM contracts to F's London and Tokyo branches. These interbranch transfers are entered into in the same manner as trades with unrelated third parties. On a typical day, risk management responsibility for no more than 10% of USFX's DM trades are transferred interbranch. F records these transfers by making notations on the books of each branch that is a party to the transfers. The accounting procedures are nearly identical to those followed when a branch enters into an offsetting hedge with a third party. USFX maintains contemporaneous records of its interbranch transfers and third party transactions, separated according to type of trade and counterparty. Moreover, the volume of USFX's DM spot purchases and sales each day consistently provides USFX with third party transactions that are contemporaneous with the transfers between the branches.

(ii) As provided in paragraph (h)(3)(i) of this section, USFX and F's other branches that trade DM are participants in a global dealing operation. Accordingly, the principles of §1.482-8 apply in determining the source of income earned by F's qualified business units that are participants in a global dealing operation. Applying the comparability factors in §1.482-8(a)(3) shows that USFX's interbranch transfers and uncontrolled DM-denominated spot and forward contracts have no material differences. Because USFX sells DM in uncontrolled transactions and transfers risk management responsibility for DM-denominated contracts, and the uncontrolled transactions and interbranch transfers are consistently entered into contemporaneously, the interbranch transfers provide a reliable measure of an arm's length allocation of third party income from F's global dealing operation in DM-denominated contracts. This allocation of third party income is treated as U.S. source in accordance with §§1.863-3(h) and 1.988-4(h) and accordingly will be treated as income effectively connected with F's U.S. trade or business under §1.864-4.

Example 2. Residual profit split between branches. (i) F is a bank organized in country X that has a AAA credit rating and engages in a global dealing operation in foreign currency options through branch offices in London, New York, and Tokyo. F has dedicated marketers and traders in each branch who work closely together to design and sell foreign currency options that meet the particular needs of customers. Each branch also employs general salespeople who sell standardized foreign currency options, as well as other financial products and foreign currency offered by F. F's traders work from a common book of transactions that is risk managed at each branch during local business hours. Accordingly, all three branches share the responsibility for risk managing the book of products. Personnel in the home office of F process and confirm trades, reconcile trade tickets, and provide ongoing administrative support (back office services) for the other branches. The global dealing operation has generated $223 of operating profit for the period.

(ii) Under § 1.863-3(h), F applies § 1.482-8 to allocate global dealing income among its branches, because F's London, New York, and Tokyo branches are treated as participants in a global dealing operation that deals in foreign currency options under § 1.482-8(a)(2). After analyzing the foreign currency options business, F has determined that the residual profit split method is the best method to determine an arm's length amount of compensation allocable to each participant in the global dealing operation.

(iii) Under the first step of the residual profit split method (§ 1.482-8(e)(6)(ii)), F identifies and compensates the routine contributions performed by each participant. F determines that an arm's length compensation for general salespeople is $3, $4, and $5 in New York, London, and Tokyo, respectively, and that the home office incurred $11 of expenses in providing the back office services. Since F's capital legally supports all of the obligations of the branches, no amount is allocated to the home office of F for the provision of capital.

(iv) The second step of the residual profit split method (§ 1.482-8(e)(6)(iii)) requires that the residual profit be allocated to participants according to their nonroutine contributions. F determines that a multi-factor formula best reflects these contributions. After a detailed functional analysis, and applying the comparability factors in § 1.482-8(a)(3), 40% of the residual profit is allocated to the London branch, 35% to the New York branch, and the remaining 25% to the Tokyo branch. Thus, the residual profit of $200 ($223 operating profit minus $12 general salesperson commissions minus $11 back office allocation) is allocated $80 to London (40% allocation × $200), $70 to New York (35% × $200) and $50 to Tokyo (25% × $200).

Example 3. Residual profit split—deemed branches. (i) P, a U.K. corporation, conducts a global dealing operation in notional principal contracts, directly and through a U.S. subsidiary (USsub) and a Japanese subsidiary (Jsub). P is the counterparty to all transactions entered into with third parties. P, USsub, and Jsub each employ marketers and traders who work closely together to design and sell derivative products to meet the particular needs of customers. USsub also employs personnel who process and confirm trades, reconcile trade tickets and provide ongoing administrative support (back office services) for the global dealing operation. The global dealing operation maintains a single common book for each type of risk, and the book is maintained where the head trader for that type of risk is located. However, P, USsub, and Jsub have authorized a trader located in each of the other affiliates to risk manage its books during periods when the primary trading location is closed. This grant of authority is necessary because marketers, regardless of their location, are expected to sell all of the group's products, and need to receive pricing information with respect to products during their clients' business hours, even if the booking location is closed. The global dealing operation has generated $180 of operating profit for the period.

(ii) Because employees of USsub have authority to enter into contracts in the name of P, P is treated as being engaged in a trade or business in the United States through a deemed QBU. § 1.863-3(h)(3)(iv). Similarly, under U.S. principles, P would be treated as being engaged in business in Japan through a QBU. Under § 1.482-8(a)(2), P, USsub, and Jsub are participants in the global dealing operation relating to notional principal contracts. Additionally, under § 1.863-3(h)(3), the U.S. and Japanese QBUs are treated as participants in a global dealing operation for purposes of sourcing the income from that operation. Under § 1.863-3(h), P applies the methods in § 1.482-8 to determine the source of income allocated to the U.S. and non-U.S. QBUs of P.

(iii) After analyzing the notional principal contract business, P has concluded that the residual profit split method is the best method to allocate income under § 1.482-8 and to source income under § 1.863-3(h).

(iv) Under the first step of the residual profit split method (§ 1.482-8(e)(6)(ii)), P identifies and compensates the routine contributions performed by each participant. Although the back office function does not give rise to participant status, in the context of a residual profit split allocation, the back office function is relevant for purposes of receiving remuneration for a routine contribution to a global dealing operation. P determines that an arm's length compensation for the back office is $20. Since the back office services constitute a routine contribution, $20 of income is allocated to USsub under step 1 of the residual profit split method. Similarly, as the arm's length compensation for the risk to which P is subject as counterparty is $40, $40 is allocated to P as compensation for acting as counterparty.

(v) The second step of the residual profit split method (§ 1.482-8(e)(6)(iii)) requires that the residual profit be allocated to participants according to the relative value of their nonroutine contributions. Under P's transfer pricing method, P allocates the residual profit of $120 ($180 gross income minus $20 for back office services minus $40 compensation for the routine contribution of acting as counterparty) using a multi-factor formula that reflects the relative value of the nonroutine contributions. Applying the comparability factors set out in § 1.482-8(a)(3), P allocates 40% of the residual profit to P, 35% of the residual profit to USsub, and the remaining 25% of residual profit to Jsub. Accordingly, under step 2, $48 is allocated to P, $42 is allocated to USsub, and $30 is allocated to Jsub. Under § 1.863-3(h), the amounts allocated under the residual profit split is sourced according to the residence of each participant to which it is allocated.

(vi) Because the $40 allocated to P consists of compensation for the use of capital, the allocation is sourced according to where the capital is employed. Accordingly, the $40 is sourced 35% to P's deemed QBU in the United States under § 1.863-3(h)(3)(iv) and 65% to non-U.S. sources.

* * *

[Prop. Reg. § 1.863-3.]

[Proposed 3-6-98.]

§ 1.863-4. Certain transportation services.—(a) *General.*—A taxpayer carrying on the business of transportation service (other than an activity giving rise to transportation income described in section 863(c) or to income subject to other specific provisions of this title) between points in the United States and points outside the United States derives income partly from sources within and partly from sources without the United States.

(b) *Gross income.*—The gross income from sources within the United States derived from such services shall be determined by taking such a portion of the total gross revenues therefrom as (1) the sum of the costs or expenses of such transportation business carried on by the taxpayer within the United States and a reasonable return upon the property used in its transportation business while within the United States bears to (2) the sum of the total costs or expenses of such transportation business carried on by the taxpayer and a reasonable return upon the total property used in such transportation business. Revenues from operations incidental to transportation services, such as the sale of money orders, shall be apportioned on the same basis as direct revenues from transportation services.

(c) *Allocation of costs or expenses.*—In allocating the total costs or expenses incurred in such transportation business, costs or expenses incurred in connection with that part of the services which was wholly rendered in the United States shall be assigned to the cost of transportation business within the United States. For example, expenses of loading and unloading in the United States, rentals, office expenses, salaries, and wages wholly incurred for services rendered to the taxpayer in the United States belong to this class. Costs and expenses incurred in connection with services rendered partly within and partly without the United States may be prorated on a reasonable basis between such services. For example, ship wages, charter money, insurance, and supplies chargeable to voyage expenses shall ordinarily be prorated for each voyage on the basis of the proportion which the number of days the ship was within the territorial limits of the United States bears to the total number of days on the voyage; and fuel consumed on each voyage may be prorated on the basis of the proportion which the number of miles sailed within the territorial limits of the United States bears to the total number of miles sailed on the voyage. For other expenses entering into the cost of services, only such expenses as are allowable deductions under the internal revenue laws shall be taken into account.

(d) *Items not included as costs or expenses.*—(1) *Taxes and interest.*—Income, war profits, and excess profits taxes shall not be regarded as costs or expenses for the purpose of determining the proportion of gross income from sources within the United States; and, for such purpose, interest and other expenses for the use of borrowed capital shall not be taken into the cost of services rendered, for the reason that the return upon the property used measures the extent to which such borrowed capital is the source of the income. See paragraph (f)(2) of this section.

(2) *Other business activity and general expenses.*—If a taxpayer subject to this section is also engaged in a business other than that of providing transportation service between points in the United States and points outside the United States, the costs and expenses, including taxes, properly apportioned or allocated to such other business shall be excluded both from the deductions and from the apportionment process prescribed in paragraph (c) of this section; but, for the purpose of determining taxable income, a ratable part of any general expenses, losses, or deductions, which cannot definitely be allocated to some item or class of gross income, may be deducted from the gross income from sources within the United States after the amount of such gross income has been determined. Such ratable part shall ordinarily be based upon the ratio of gross income from sources within the United States to the total gross income. See paragraph (f)(3) of this section.

(3) *Personal exemptions and special deductions.*—The deductions for the personal exemptions, and the special deductions described in paragraph (c) of § 1.861-8, shall not be taken into account for purposes of paragraph (c) of this section.

(e) *Property used while within the United States.*—(1) *General.*—The value of the property used shall be determined upon the basis of cost less depreciation. Eight percent may ordinarily be taken as a reasonable rate of return to apply to such property. The property taken shall be the average property employed in the transportation service between points in the United States and points outside the United States during the taxable year.

(2) *Average property.*—For ships, the average shall be determined upon a daily basis for each ship, and the amount to be apportioned for each ship as assets employed within the United States shall be computed upon the proportion which the number of days the ship was within the territorial limits of the United States bears to the total number of days the ship was in service during the taxable period. For other assets employed in the transportation business, the average of the assets at the beginning and end of the taxable period ordinarily may be taken, but if the average so obtained does not, by reason of material changes during the taxable year, fairly represent the average for such year either for the assets employed in the transportation business in the United States or in total, the average must be determined upon a monthly or daily basis.

(3) *Current assets.*—Current assets shall be decreased by current liabilities and allocated to services between the United States and foreign countries and to other services. The part allocated to services between the United States and foreign countries shall be based on the proportion which the gross receipts from such services bear to the gross receipts from all services. The amount so allocated to services between the United States and foreign countries shall be further allocated to services rendered within the United States and to services rendered without the United States. The portion allocable to services rendered within the United States shall be based on the proportion which the expenses incurred within the territorial limits of the United States bear to the total expenses incurred in services between the United States and foreign countries.

(f) *Taxable income.*—(1) *General.*—In computing taxable income from sources within the United States there shall be allowed as deductions from the gross income from such sources, determined in accordance with paragraph (b) of this section, (i) the expenses of the transportation business carried on within the United States (as determined under paragraphs (c) and (d) of this section) and (ii) the expenses and deductions determined in accordance with this paragraph.

(2) *Interest and taxes.*—Interest and income, war-profits, and excess profits taxes shall be excluded from the apportionment process, as indicated in paragraph (d) of this section; but, for the purpose of computing taxable income, there may be deducted from the gross income from sources within the United States, after the amount of such gross income has been determined, a ratable part of all interest deductible under section 163 and of all income, war-profits, and excess profits taxes deductible under section 164, paid or accrued in respect of the business of transportation service between points in the United States and points outside the United States. The ratable part shall ordinarily be based upon the ratio of gross income from sources within the United States to the total gross income, from such transportation service.

(3) *General expenses.*—General expenses, losses, or deductions shall be deducted under this paragraph to the extent indicated in paragraph (d)(2) of this section.

(4) *Personal exemptions.*—The deductions for the personal exemptions shall be allowed under this paragraph to the same extent as provided by paragraph (b) of § 1.861-8.

(5) *Special deductions.*—The special deductions allowed in the case of a corporation by sections 241, 922, and 941 shall be allowed under this paragraph to the same extent as provided by paragraph (c) of § 1.861-8.

(g) *Allocation based on books of account.*—Application for permission to base the return upon the taxpayer's books of account will be considered by the district director (or, if applicable, the Director of International Operations) in the case of any taxpayer subject to this section, who, in good faith and unaffected by considerations of tax liability, regularly employs in his books of account a detailed allocation of receipts and expenditures which more clearly reflects the income derived from sources within the United States than does the process prescribed by paragraphs (b) to (f), inclusive, of this section. [Reg. § 1.863-4.]

☐ [*T.D. 6258, 10-23-57. Amended by T.D. 8687, 11-27-96.*]

§ 1.863-7. Allocation of income attributable to certain notional principal contracts under section 863(a).—(a) *Scope.*—(1) *Introduction.*—This section provides rules relating to the source and, in certain cases, the character of notional principal contract income. However, this section does not apply to income from a section 988 transaction within the meaning of section 988 and the regulations thereunder, relating to the treatment of certain nonfunctional currency transactions. Further, this section does not apply to a dividend equivalent described in section 871(m) and the regulations thereunder. Notional principal contract income is income attributable to a notional principal contract as defined in § 1.446-3(c). An agreement between a taxpayer and a qualified business unit (as defined in section 989(a)) of the taxpayer, or among qualified business units of the same taxpayer, is not a notional principal contract, because a taxpayer cannot enter into a contract with itself.

(2) *Effective/applicability date.*—This section applies to notional principal contract income includible in income on or after February 13, 1991. However, any taxpayer desiring to apply paragraph (b)(2)(iv) of this section to notional principal contract income includible in income prior to February 13, 1991 in lieu of temporary Income Tax Regulations § 1.863-7T(b)(2)(iv) may (on a consistent basis) so choose. See paragraph (c) of this section for an election to apply the rules of this section to notional principal contract income includible in income before December 24, 1986. With respect to a dividend equivalent described in section 871(m) and the regulations thereunder, this section applies to payments made on or after January 23, 2012.

(b) *Source of notional principal contract income.*—(1) *General rule.*—Unless paragraph (b)(2) or (3) of this section applies, the source of notional principal contract income shall be determined by reference to the residence of the taxpayer as determined under section 988(a)(3)(B)(i).

(2) *Qualified business unit exception.*—The source of notional principal contract income shall be determined by reference to the residence of a qualified business unit of a taxpayer if—

(i) The taxpayer's residence, determined under section 988(a)(3)(B)(i), is the United States;

(ii) The qualified business unit's residence, determined under section 988(a)(3)(B)(ii), is outside the United States;

(iii) The qualified business unit is engaged in the conduct of a trade or business where it is a resident as determined under section 988(a)(3)(B) (ii); and

(iv) The notional principal contract is properly reflected on the books of the qualified business unit. Whether a notional principal contract is properly reflected on the books of such qualified business unit is a question of fact. The degree of participation in the negotiation and acquisition of a notional principal contract shall be considered in this determination. Participation in connection with the negotiation or acquisition of a notional principal contract may be disregarded if the district director determines that a purpose for such participation was to affect the source of notional principal contract income.

(3) *Effectively connected notional principal contract income.*—Notional principal contract income that under principles similar to those set forth in § 1.864-4(c) arises from the conduct of a United States trade or business shall be sourced in the United States and such income shall be treated as effectively connected to the conduct of a United States trade or business for purposes of sections 871(b) and 882(a)(1).

(c) *Election.*—(1) *Eligibility and effect.*—A taxpayer described in paragraph (b)(2)(i) of this section may make an election to apply the rules of this section to all, but not part, of the taxpayer's income attributable to notional principal contracts for all taxable years (or portion thereof) beginning before December 24, 1986, for which the period of limitations for filing a claim for refund under section 6511(a) has not expired. A taxpayer not described in paragraph (b)(2)(i) of this section that is engaged in trade or business within the United States may make an election to apply the rules of this section to all, but not part, of the taxpayer's income described in paragraph (b)(3) of this section for all taxable years (or portion thereof) beginning before December 24, 1986, for which the period of limitations for filing a claim for refund under section 6511(a) has not expired. If a taxpayer makes an election pursuant to this paragraph (c)(1) in the time and manner provided in paragraph (c)(2) and (3) of this section, then, with respect to such taxable years (or portion thereof), no tax shall be deducted or withheld under sections 1441 and 1442 with respect to payments made by the taxpayer pursuant to a notional principal contract the income attributable to which is subject to such election. The election may be revoked only with the consent of the Commissioner.

(2) *Time for making election.*—The election specified in paragraph (c)(1) of this section shall be made by May 15, 1991.

(3) *Manner of making election.*—The election described in paragraph (c)(1) of this section shall be made by attaching a statement to the tax return or an amended tax return for each taxable year beginning before December 24, 1986, in which the taxpayer accrued or received notional principal contract income. The statement shall—

(i) Contain the name, address, and taxpayer identifying number of the electing taxpayer;

(ii) Identify the election as a "Notional Principal Contract Election under § 1.863-7"; and

(iii) Specify each taxable year described in paragraph (c)(1) of this section in which payments were made.

(d) *Example.*—The operation of this section is illustrated by the following example:

(1) On January 1, 1990, X, a calendar year domestic corporation, entered into an interest rate swap contract with FZ, an unrelated foreign corporation. X does not have a qualified business unit outside the United States. Under the contract, X is required to pay FZ fixed rate dollar amounts, and FZ is required to pay X floating rate dollar amounts, each determined solely by reference to a notional dollar denominated principal amount specified under the contract. The contract is a notional principal contract under § 1.863-7(a) because the contract provides for the payment of amounts at specified intervals calculated by reference to a specified index upon a notional principal amount in exchange for a promise to pay similar amounts.

(2) Assume that during 1990 X had notional principal contract income of $100 in connection with the notional principal contract described in (1) above. Also assume that the contract provides that payments more than 30 days late give rise to a $5 fee, and that X receives such a fee in 1990. Under paragraph (b)(1) of this section, the source of X's $100 of income attributable to the swap agreement is domestic. The $5 fee is not notional principal contract income.

(e) *Cross references.*—See § 1.861-9T(b) for the allocation of expense to certain notional principal contracts. For rules relating to the source of income from nonfunctional currency notional principal contracts, see § 1.988-4T. For rules relating to the taxable amount of notional principal contract income allocable under this section to sources inside or outside the United States, see § 1.863-1(c). [Reg. § 1.863-7.]

☐ [*T.D.* 8330, 1-11-91. *Amended by T.D.* 9572, 1-19-2012 *and T.D.* 9648, 12-4-2013.]

§ 1.863-8. Source of income derived from space and ocean activity under section 863(d).—(a) *In general.*—Income of a United States or a foreign person derived from space and ocean activity (space and ocean income) is sourced under the rules of this section, notwithstanding any other provision, including sections 861, 862, 863, and 865. A taxpayer will not be considered to derive income from space or ocean activity, as defined in paragraph (d) of this section, if such activity is performed by another person, subject to the rules for the treatment of consolidated groups in § 1.1502-13.

(b) *Source of gross income from space and ocean activity.*—(1) *Space and ocean income derived by a United States person.*—Space and ocean income derived by a United States person is income from sources within the United States. However, space and ocean income derived by a United States person is income from sources without the United States to the extent the income, based on all the facts and circumstances, is attributable to functions performed, resources employed, or risks assumed in a foreign country or countries.

(2) *Space and ocean income derived by a foreign person.*—(i) *In general.*—Space and ocean income derived by a person other than a United States person is income from sources without the United States, except as otherwise provided in this paragraph (b)(2).

(ii) *Space and ocean income derived by a controlled foreign corporation.*—Space and ocean income derived by a controlled foreign corporation (CFC) is income from sources within the United States. However, space and ocean income derived by a CFC is income from sources without the United States to the extent the income, based on all the facts and circumstances, is attributable to functions performed, resources employed, or risks assumed in a foreign country or countries. For purposes of this section, a CFC has the meaning provided in section 957, determined without applying section 318(a)(3)(A), (B), and (C) so as to consider a United States person as owning stock which is owned by a person who is not a United States person.

(iii) *Space and ocean income derived by foreign persons engaged in a trade or business within the United States.*—Space and ocean income derived by a foreign person (other than a CFC) engaged in a trade or business within the United States is income from sources within the United States to the extent the income, based on all the facts and circumstances, is attributable to functions performed, resources employed, or risks assumed within the United States.

(3) *Source rules for income from certain sales of property.*—(i) *Sales of purchased property.*—When a taxpayer sells purchased property in space or international water, the source of gross income from the sale generally will be determined under paragraph (b)(1) or (2) of this section, as applicable. However, if such property is inventory property within the meaning of section 1221(a)(1) (inventory property) and is sold for use, consumption, or disposition outside space and international water, the source of income from the sale will be determined under § 1.861-7(c).

(ii) *Sales of property produced by the taxpayer.*—(A) *General.*—If the taxpayer both produces property and sells such property and either the production (in whole or in part) or the sale takes place in space or international water, the taxpayer must allocate and apportion all income, gain, or loss derived from sales of such property solely on the basis of the production activities with respect to such property, and the source of that income will be determined under paragraph (b)(3)(ii)(B) or (C) of this section. To determine the source of income derived from the sale of personal property (including inventory) by a nonresident that is attributable to the nonresident's office or other fixed place of business in the United States under section 865(e)(2), the rules of § 1.865-3 apply, and the rules of this section do not apply.

(B) *Production only in space or international water, or only outside space and international water.*—When production occurs only in space or international water, gross income is sourced under paragraph (b)(1) or (2) of this section, as applicable. When production occurs only outside space and international water, gross income is sourced under § 1.863-3(c).

(C) *Production both in space or international water and outside space and international water.*—When property is produced both in space or international water and outside space and international water, gross income must be allocated to production occurring in space or international water and production occurring outside space and international water. Such gross income is allocated to production activity occurring in space or international water to the extent the income, based on all the facts and circumstances, is attributable to functions performed, resources employed, or risks assumed in space or international water. The balance of such gross income is allocated to production activity occurring outside space and international water. The source of gross income in space or international water is determined under paragraph (b)(1) or (2) of this section, as applicable. The source of gross income occurring outside space and international water is determined under § 1.863-3(c).

(4) *Special rule for determining the source of gross income from services.*—To the extent a transaction characterized as the performance of a service constitutes a space or ocean activity, as determined under paragraph (d)(2)(ii) of this section, the source of gross income derived from such transaction is determined under paragraph (b)(1) or (2) of this section.

(5) *Special rule for determining source of income from communications activity (other than income from international communications activity).*—Space and ocean activity, as defined in paragraph (d) of this section, includes activity that occurs in space or international water that is characterized as a communications activity as defined in § 1.863-9(h)(1) (other than international communications activity). The source of space and ocean income that is also communications income as defined in § 1.863-9(h)(2) (but not space/ocean communications income as defined in § 1.863-9(h)(3)(v)) is determined under the rules of § 1.863-9(c), (d), and (f), as applicable, rather than under paragraph (b) of this section. The source of space and ocean income that is also space/ocean communications income as defined in § 1.863-9(h)(3)(v) is determined under the rules of paragraph (b) of this section. See § 1.863-9(e).

(c) *Taxable income.*—When a taxpayer allocates gross income under paragraph (b)(1), (b)(2), (b)(3)(ii), or (b)(4) of this section, the taxpayer must allocate expenses, losses, and other deductions as prescribed in §§ 1.861-8 through 1.861-14T to the class or classes of gross income that include the income so allocated in each case. A taxpayer must then apply the rules of §§ 1.861-8 through 1.861-14T to apportion properly amounts of expenses, losses, and other deductions so allocated to such gross income between gross income from sources within the United States and gross income from sources without the United States.

(d) *Space and ocean activity.*—(1) *Definition.*—(i) *Space activity.*—In general, space activity is any activity conducted in space. For purposes of this section, space means any area not within the jurisdiction (as recognized by the United States) of a foreign country, possession of the United States, or the United States, and not in international water. For purposes of determining space activity, the Commissioner may separate parts of a single transaction into separate transactions or combine separate transactions as part of a single transaction. Paragraph (d)(3) of this section lists specific exceptions to the general definition of space activity. Activities that constitute space activity include but are not limited to—

(A) Performance and provision of services in space, as defined in paragraph (d)(2)(ii) of this section;

(B) Leasing of equipment located in space, including spacecraft (for example, satellites) or transponders located in space;

(C) Licensing of technology or other intangibles for use in space;

(D) Production, processing, or creation of property in space, as defined in paragraph (d)(2)(i) of this section;

(E) Activity occurring in space that is characterized as communications activity (other than international communications activity) under § 1.863-9(h)(1);

(F) Underwriting income from the insurance of risks on activities that produce space income; and

(G) Sales of property in space (See § 1.861-7(c)).

(ii) *Ocean activity.*—In general, ocean activity is any activity conducted on or under water not within the jurisdiction (as recognized by the United States) of a foreign country, possession of the United States, or the United States (collectively, in international water). For purposes of determining ocean activity, the Commissioner may separate parts of a single transaction into separate transactions or combine separate transactions as part of a single transaction. Paragraph (d)(3) of this section lists specific exceptions to the general definition of ocean activity. Activities that constitute ocean activity include but are not limited to—

(A) Performance and provision of services in international water, as defined in paragraph (d)(2)(ii) of this section;

(B) Leasing of equipment located in international water, including underwater cables;

(C) Licensing of technology or other intangibles for use in international water;

(D) Production, processing, or creation of property in international water, as defined in paragraph (d)(2)(i) of this section;

(E) Activity occurring in international water that is characterized as communications activity (other than international communications activity) under § 1.863-9(h)(1);

(F) Underwriting income from the insurance of risks on activities that produce ocean income;

(G) Sales of property in international water (see § 1.861-7(c));

(H) Any activity performed in Antarctica;

(I) The leasing of a vessel that does not transport cargo or persons for hire between ports-of-call (for example, the leasing of a vessel to engage in research activities in international water); and

(J) The leasing of drilling rigs, extraction of minerals, and performance and provision of services related thereto, except as provided in paragraph (d)(3)(ii) of this section.

(2) *Determining a space or ocean activity.*—(i) *Production of property in space or international water.*—For purposes of this section, production activity means an activity that creates, fabricates, manufactures, extracts, processes, cures, or ages property within the meaning of section 864(a) and § 1.864-1.

(ii) *Special rule for performance of services.*—(A) *General.*—Except as provided in paragraph (d)(2)(ii)(B) of this section, if a transaction is characterized as the performance of a service, then such service will be treated as a space or ocean activity in its entirety when any part of the service is performed in space or international water. Services are performed in space or international water if functions are performed, resources are employed, or risks are assumed in space or international water, regardless of whether performed by personnel, equipment, or otherwise.

(B) *Exception to the general rule.*—If the taxpayer can demonstrate the value of the service attributable to performance occurring in space or international water, and the value of the service attributable to performance occurring outside space and international water, then such service will be treated as space or ocean activity only to the extent of the activity performed in space or international water. The value of the service is attributable to performance occurring in space or international water to the extent the performance of the service, based on all the facts and circumstances, is attributable to functions performed, resources employed, or risks assumed in space or international water. In addition, if the taxpayer can demonstrate, based on all the facts and circumstances, that the value of the service attributable to performance in space and international water is de minimis, such service will not be treated as space or ocean activity.

(3) *Exceptions to space or ocean activity.*—Space or ocean activity does not include the following types of activities:

(i) Any activity giving rise to transportation income as defined in section 863(c).

(ii) Any activity with respect to mines, oil and gas wells, or other natural deposits, to the extent the mines, wells, or natural deposits are located within the jurisdiction (as recognized by the United States) of any country, including the United States and its possessions.

(iii) Any activity giving rise to international communications income as defined in § 1.863-9(h)(3)(ii).

(e) *Treatment of partnerships.*—This section is applied at the partner level.

(f) *Examples.*—The following examples illustrate the rules of this section:

(1) *Example 1. Space activity—activity occurring on land and in space.*—(i) *Facts.* S, a United States person, owns satellites in orbit. S leases one of its satellites to A. S, as lessor, will not operate the satellite. Part of S's performance as lessor in this transaction occurs on land. Assume that the combination of S's activities is characterized as the lease of equipment.

(ii) *Analysis.* Because the leased equipment is located in space, the transaction is defined in its entirety as space activity under paragraph (d)(1)(i) of this section. Income derived from the lease will be sourced under paragraph (b)(1) of this section. Under paragraph (b)(1) of this section, S's space income is sourced outside the United States to the extent the income, based on all the facts and circumstances, is attributable to functions performed, resources employed, or risks assumed in a foreign country or countries.

(2) *Example 2. Space activity.*—(i) *Facts.* X is an Internet service provider. X offers a service that permits a customer (C) to connect to the Internet via a telephone call, initiated by the modem of C's personal computer, to a control center. X transmits information requested by C to C's personal computer, in part using satellite capacity leased by X from S. X performs the uplink and downlink functions. X charges its customers a flat monthly fee. Assume that neither X nor S derive international communications income within the meaning of § 1.863-9(h)(3)(ii). In addition, assume that X is able to demonstrate, pursuant to paragraph (d)(2)(ii)(B) of this section, the extent to which the value of the service is attributable to functions performed, resources employed, and risks assumed in space.

(ii) *Analysis.* Under paragraph (d)(2)(ii) of this section, the service performed by X constitutes space activity to the extent the value of the service is attributable to functions performed, resources employed, and risks assumed in space. To the extent the service performed by X constitutes space activity, the source of X's income from the service transaction is determined under paragraph (b) of this section. To the extent the service performed by X does not constitute space or ocean activity, the source of X's income from the service is determined under sections 861, 862, and 863, as applicable. To the extent that X derives space and ocean income that is also communications income within the meaning of § 1.863-9(h)(2), the source of X's income is determined under paragraph (b) of this section and § 1.863-9(c), (d), and (f), as applicable, as provided in paragraph (b)(5) of this section. S derives space and ocean income that is also communications income within the meaning of § 1.863-9(h)(2), and the source of S's income is therefore determined under paragraph (b) of this section and § 1.863-9(c), (d), and (f), as applicable, as provided in paragraph (b)(5) of this section.

(3) *Example 3. Services as space activity—de minimis value attributable to performance occurring in space.*—(i) *Facts.* R owns a retail outlet in the United States. R engages S to provide a security system for R's premises. S operates its security system by transmitting images from R's premises directly to a satellite, and from the satellite to a group of S employees located in Country B, who monitor the premises by viewing the transmitted images. The satellite is used as a medium of delivery and not as a method of surveillance. O provides S with transponder capacity on O's satellite, which S uses to transmit those images. Assume that S's transaction with R is characterized as the performance of a service. Assume that O's provision of transponder capacity is also viewed as the provision of a service. Assume also that S is able to demonstrate, pursuant to § 1.863-9(h)(1), that the value of the transaction with R attributable to communications activities is de minimis.

(ii) *Analysis.* S derives income from providing monitoring services. S can demonstrate, pursuant to paragraph (d)(2)(ii) of this section, that based on all the facts and circumstances, the value of S's service transaction attributable to performance in space is de minimis. Thus, S is not treated as engaged in a space activity, and none of S's income from the service transaction is space income. In addition, because S demonstrates that the value of the transaction with R attributable to communications activities is de minimis, S is not required under § 1.863-9(h)(1)(ii) to treat the transaction as separate communications and non-communications transactions, and none of S's gross income from the transaction is treated as communications income within the meaning of § 1.863-9(h)(2). O's provision of transponder capacity is viewed as the provision of a service. Based on all the facts and circumstances, the value of O's service transaction attributable to performance in space is not de minimis. Thus, O's activity will be considered space activity, pursuant to paragraph (d)(2)(ii) of this section, to the extent the value of the services transaction is attributable to performance in space (unless O's activity in space is international communications activity). To the extent that O derives communications income, the source of such income is determined under paragraph (b) of this section and § 1.863-9(b), (c), (d), and (f), as applicable, as provided in paragraph (b)(5) of this section. R does not derive any income from space activity.

(4) *Example 4. Space activity.*—(i) *Facts.* L, a domestic corporation, offers programming and certain other services to customers located both in the United States and in foreign countries. Assume that L's provision of programming and other services in paragraph (f)(4)(i) (*Example 4*) is characterized as the provision of a service, and that no part of the service transaction occurs in space or international water. Assume that the delivery of the programming constitutes a separate transaction also characterized as the performance of a service. L uses satellite capacity acquired from S to deliver the programming service directly to customers' television sets. L performs the uplink and downlink functions, so that part of the value of the delivery transaction derives from functions performed and resources employed in space. Assume that these contributions to the value of the delivery transaction occurring in space are not considered de minimis under paragraph (d)(2)(ii)(B) of this section. Customer C pays L to provide and deliver programming to C's residence in the United States. Assume S's provision of satellite capacity in paragraph (f)(4)(i) (*Example 4*) is viewed as the provision of a service, and also that S does not derive international communications income within the meaning of § 1.863-9(h)(3)(ii).

(ii) *Analysis.* S's activity will be considered space activity. To the extent that S derives space and ocean income that is also communications income under § 1.863-9(h)(2), the source of S's income is determined under paragraph (b) of this section and § 1.863-9(c), (d), and (f), as applicable, as provided in paragraph (b)(5) of this section. On these facts, L's activities are treated as two separate service transactions: the provision of programming (and other services), and the delivery of programming. L's income derived from provision of programming and other services is not income derived from space activity. L's delivery of programming and other services is considered space activity, pursuant to paragraph (d)(2)(ii) of this section, to the extent the value of the delivery transaction is attributable to performance in space. To the extent that the delivery of programming is treated as a space activity, the source of L's income derived from the delivery transaction is determined under paragraph (b)(1) of this section, as provided in paragraph (b)(4) of this section. To the extent that L derives space and ocean income that is also communications income within the meaning of § 1.863-9(h)(2), the source of such income is determined under paragraph (b) of this section and § 1.863-9(b), (c), (d), (e), and (f), as applicable, as provided in paragraph (b)(5) of this section.

(5) *Example 5. Space activity.*—(i) *Facts.* The facts are the same as in paragraph (f)(4)(i) of this section (the facts in *Example 4*), except that L does not deliver the programming service directly but instead engages R, a domestic corporation specializing in content delivery, to deliver by transmission its programming. For all portions of a transmission which require satellite capacity, R, in turn, contracts out such functions to S. S performs the uplink and downlink functions, so that part of the value of the delivery transaction derives from functions performed and resources employed in space.

(ii) *Analysis.* L's activity will not be considered space activity because none of L's activity occurs in space. Thus, L does not derive any space and ocean income. L does, however, derive communications income within the meaning of § 1.863-9(h)(2). This is the case even though L does not perform the transmission function because L is paid by Customer C to transmit, and bears the risk of transmitting, the communications or data. To the extent that L's activity consists in part of non-de minimis communications and non-de minimis non-communications activity, each part of the transaction must be treated as a separate transaction and gross income is allocated accordingly under § 1.863-9(h)(1)(ii). In addition, L must also allocate expenses, losses, and other deductions, for example, payments to R, to the class or classes of gross income that include the income so allocated. R's activity will not be considered space activity. Since R contracts out all of the functions involving satellite capacity to S, no part of R's activity occurs in space. Thus, R does not derive any space and ocean income. R does, however, derive communications income within the meaning of § 1.863-9(h)(2). This is the case even though R does not perform the transmission function because R is paid by L to transmit, and bears the risk of transmitting, the communications or data. S's activity will be considered space activity. To the extent that S derives space and ocean income that is also communications income within the meaning of § 1.863-9(h)(2), the source of such income is determined under paragraph (b) of this section and § 1.863-9(b), (c), (d), (e), and (f), as applicable, as provided in paragraph (b)(5) of this section.

(6) *Example 6. Space activity—treatment of land activity.*—(i) *Facts.* S, a United States person, offers remote imaging products and services to its customers. In year 1, S uses its satellite's remote sensors to gather data on certain geographical terrain. In year 3, C, a construction development company, contracts with S to obtain a satellite image of an area for site development work. S pulls data from its archives and transfers to C the images gathered in year 1, in a transaction that is characterized as a sale of the data. S's rights, title, and interest in the data pass to C in the United States. Before

transferring the images to C, S uses computer software in its land-based office to enhance the images so that the images can be used.

(ii) *Analysis*. The collection of data and creation of images in space is characterized as the creation of property in space. Because S both produces and sells the data, the source of the gross income from the sale of the data is determined under paragraph (b)(3)(ii) of this section solely on the basis of the production activities. The source of S's gross income is determined under paragraph (b)(3)(ii)(C) of this section because production activities occur both in space and on land.

(7) *Example 7. Use of intangible property in space.*—(i) *Facts*. X acquires a license to use a particular satellite slot or orbit, which X sublicenses to C. C pays X a royalty.

(ii) *Analysis*. Because the royalty is paid for the right to use intangible property in space, the source of the royalty paid by C to X is determined under paragraph (b) of this section.

(8) *Example 8. Performance of services.*—(i) *Facts*. E, a domestic corporation, operates satellites with sensing equipment that can determine how much heat and light particular plants emit and reflect. Based on the data, E will provide F, a U.S. farmer, a report analyzing the data, which F will use in growing crops. E analyzes the data from offices located in the United States. Assume that E's combined activities are characterized as the performance of services.

(ii) *Analysis*. Based on all the facts and circumstances, the value of E's service transaction attributable to performance in space is not de minimis. Thus, E's activities will be considered space activities, pursuant to paragraph (d)(2)(ii) of this section, to the extent the value of E's service transaction is attributable to performance in space. To the extent E's service transaction constitutes a space activity, the source of E's income derived from the service transaction will be determined under paragraph (b)(4) of this section, by reference to paragraph (b)(1) of this section. To the extent that E's service transaction does not constitute a space or ocean activity, the source of E's income derived from the service transaction is determined under sections 861, 862, and 863, as applicable.

(9) *Example 9. Separate transactions.*—(i) *Facts*. The same facts as in paragraph (f)(8)(i) of this section (the facts in *Example 8*), except that E provides the raw data to F in a transaction characterized as a sale of a copyrighted article. In addition, E provides an analysis in the form of a report to F. The price F pays E for the raw data is separately stated.

(ii) *Analysis*. To the extent that the provision of raw data and the analysis of the data are each treated as separate transactions, the source of income from the production and sale of data is determined under paragraph (b)(3)(ii) of this section. The provision of services would be analyzed in the same manner as in paragraph (f)(8)(ii) of this section (the analysis in *Example 8*).

(10) *Example 10. Sale of property in international water.*—(i) *Facts*. T purchased and owns transatlantic cable that lies in international water. T sells the cable to B, with T's rights, title, and interest in the cable passing to B in international water. Assume that the transatlantic cable is not inventory property within the meaning of section 1221(a)(1).

(ii) *Analysis*. Because T's rights, title, and interest in the property pass to B in international water, the sale takes place in international water under § 1.861-7(c), and the sale transaction is ocean activity under paragraph (d)(1)(ii) of this section. The source of T's sales income is determined under paragraph (b)(3)(i) of this section, by reference to paragraph (b)(1) or (2) of this section.

(11) *Example 11. Sale of property in space.*—(i) *Facts*. S, a United States person, manufactures a satellite in the United States and sells it to a customer who is not a United States person. S's rights, title, and interest in the satellite pass to the customer in space.

(ii) *Analysis*. Because S's rights, title, and interest in the satellite pass to the customer in space, the sale takes place in space under § 1.861-7(c), and the sale transaction is space activity under paragraph (d)(1)(i) of this section. The source of income derived from the sale of the satellite manufactured in the United States and sold in space is determined under paragraph (b)(3)(ii) of this section solely on the basis of the production activities with respect to the satellite.

(12) *Example 12. Sale of property in space.*—(i) *Facts*. S has a right to operate from a particular position (satellite slot or orbit) in space. S sells the right to operate from that position to P. Assume that the sale of the satellite slot is characterized as a sale of property and that S's rights, title, and interest in the satellite slot pass to P in space.

(ii) *Analysis*. The sale of the satellite slot takes place in space under § 1.861-7(c) because S's rights, title, and interest in the satellite slot pass to P in space. The sale of the satellite slot is space activity under paragraph (d)(1)(i) of this section, and income or gain from the sale is sourced under paragraph (b)(3)(i) of this section, by reference to paragraph (b)(1) or (2) of this section.

(13) *Example 13. Source of income of a foreign person.*—(i) *Facts*. FP, a foreign corporation that is not a CFC, derives income from the operation of satellites. FP operates ground stations in the United States and in foreign Country FC. Assume that FP is considered engaged in a trade or business within the United States based on FP's operation of the ground station in the United States.

(ii) *Analysis*. Under paragraph (b)(2)(iii) of this section, FP's space income is sourced in the United States to the extent the income, based on all the facts and circumstances, is attributable to functions performed, resources employed, or risks assumed within the United States.

(14) *Example 14. Source of income of a foreign person.*—(i) *Facts*. FP, a foreign corporation that is not a CFC, operates remote sensing satellites in space to collect data and images for its customers. FP uses an independent agent, A, in the United States who provides marketing, order-taking, and other customer service functions. Assume that FP is considered engaged in a trade or business within the United States based on A's activities on FP's behalf in the United States.

(ii) *Analysis*. Under paragraph (b)(2)(iii) of this section, FP's space income is sourced in the United States to the extent the income, based on all the facts and circumstances, is attributable to functions performed, resources employed, or risks assumed within the United States.

(g) *Reporting and documentation requirements.*—(1) *In general.*—A taxpayer making an allocation of gross income under paragraph (b)(1), (b)(2), (b)(3)(ii), or (b)(4) of this section must satisfy the requirements in paragraphs (g)(2), (3), and (4) of this section.

(2) *Required documentation.*—In all cases, a taxpayer must prepare and maintain documentation in existence when its return is filed regarding the allocation of gross income and allocation and apportionment of expenses, losses, and other deductions, the methodologies used, and the circumstances justifying use of those methodologies. The taxpayer must make available such documentation within 30 days upon request.

(3) *Access to software.*—If the taxpayer or any third party used any computer software, within the meaning of section 7612(d), to allocate gross income, or to allocate or apportion expenses, losses, and other deductions, the taxpayer must make available upon request—

(i) Any computer software executable code, within the meaning of section 7612(d), used for such purposes, including an executable copy of the version of the software used in the preparation of the taxpayer's return (including any plug-ins, supplements, etc.) and a copy of all related electronic data files. Thus, if software subsequently is upgraded or supplemented, a separate executable copy of the version used in preparing the taxpayer's return must be retained;

(ii) Any related computer software source code, within the meaning of section 7612(d), acquired or developed by the taxpayer or a related person, or primarily for internal use by the taxpayer or such person rather than for commercial distribution; and

(iii) In the case of any spreadsheet software or similar software, any formulae or links to supporting worksheets.

(4) *Use of allocation methodology.*—In general, when a taxpayer allocates gross income under paragraph (b)(1), (b)(2), (b)(3)(ii), or (b)(4) of this section, it does so by making the allocation on a timely filed original return (including extensions). However, a taxpayer will be permitted to make changes to such allocations made on its original return with respect to any taxable year for which the statute of limitations has not closed as follows:

(i) In the case of a taxpayer that has made a change to such allocations prior to the opening conference for the audit of the taxable year to which the allocation relates or who makes such a change within 90 days of such opening conference, if the IRS issues a written information document request asking the taxpayer to provide the documents and such other information described in paragraphs (g)(2) and (3) of this section with respect to the changed allocations and the taxpayer complies with such request within 30 days of the request, then the IRS will complete its examination, if any, with respect to the allocations for that year as part of the current examination cycle. If the taxpayer does not provide the documents and information described in paragraphs (g)(2) and (3) of this section within 30 days of the request, then the procedures described in paragraph (g)(4)(ii) of this section shall apply.

(ii) If the taxpayer changes such allocations more than 90 days after the opening conference for the audit of the taxable year to which the allocations relate or the taxpayer does not provide the documents and information with respect to the changed allocations as requested in accordance with paragraphs (g)(2) and (3) of this section, then the IRS will, in a separate cycle, determine whether an examination of the taxpayer's allocations is warranted and complete any such examination. The separate cycle will be worked as resources are available and may not have the same estimated completion date as the other issues under examination for the taxable year. The IRS may ask the taxpayer to extend the statute of limitations on assessment and collection for the taxable year to permit examination of the taxpayer's method of allocation, including an extension limited, where appropriate, to the taxpayer's method of allocation.

(h) *Applicability dates.*—Except as provided in this paragraph (h), this section applies to taxable years beginning on or after December 27, 2006. The provisions in paragraph (b)(2)(ii) of this section relating to the meaning of a CFC apply to taxable years of foreign corporations ending on or after October 1, 2019. For taxable years of foreign corporations ending before October 1, 2019, a taxpayer may apply such provisions to the last taxable year of a foreign corporation beginning before January 1, 2018, and each subsequent taxable year of the foreign corporation, provided that the taxpayer and United States persons that are related (within the meaning of section 267 or 707) to the taxpayer consistently apply such provisions with respect to all foreign corporations. For taxable years of foreign corporations ending before October 1, 2019, where the taxpayer does not apply the provisions of paragraph (b)(2)(ii) of this section relating to the meaning of a CFC, see paragraph (b)(2)(ii) of this section as in effect and contained in 26 CFR part 1, as revised April 1, 2020. Paragraph (b)(3)(ii) of this section applies to taxable years ending on or after December 23, 2019. However, a taxpayer may apply paragraph (b)(3)(ii) of this section in its entirety for taxable years beginning after December 31, 2017, and ending before December 23, 2019, provided that the taxpayer and all persons related to the taxpayer (within the meaning of section 267 or 707) apply paragraph (b)(3)(ii) of this section and §§1.863-1(b), 1.863-2(b), 1.863-3, 1.864-5(a) and (b), 1.864-6(c)(2), and 1.865-3 in their entirety for the taxable year, and once applied, the taxpayer and all persons related to the taxpayer (within the meaning of section 267 or 707) continue to apply these regulations in their entirety for all subsequent taxable years. For regulations generally applicable to taxable years ending before December 23, 2019, see §1.863-8 as contained in 26 CFR part 1 revised as of April 1, 2020. [Reg. §1.863-8.]

☐ [*T.D. 9305, 12-26-2006. Amended by T.D. 9908, 9-21-2020 and T.D. 9921, 12-10-2020.*]

§1.863-9. Source of income derived from communications activity under section 863(a), (d), and (e).—(a) *In general.*—Income of a United States or a foreign person derived from each type of communications activity, as defined in paragraph (h)(3) of this section, is sourced under the rules of this section, notwithstanding any other provision including sections 861, 862, 863, and 865. Notwithstanding that a communications activity would qualify as space or ocean activity under section 863(d) and the regulations thereunder, the source of income derived from such communications activity is determined under this section, and not under section 863(d) and the regulations thereunder, except to the extent provided in §1.863-8(b)(5).

(b) *Source of international communications income.*—(1) *International communications income derived by a United States person.*—Income derived from international communications activity (international communications income) by a United States person is one-half from sources within the United States and one-half from sources without the United States.

(2) *International communications income derived by foreign persons.*—(i) *In general.*—International communications income derived by a person other than a United States person is, except as otherwise provided in this paragraph (b)(2), wholly from sources without the United States.

(ii) *International communications income derived by a controlled foreign corporation.*—International communications income derived by a controlled foreign corporation (CFC) is one-half from sources within the United States and one-half from sources without the United States. For purposes of this section, a CFC has the meaning provided in section 957, determined without applying section 318(a)(3)(A), (B), and (C) so as to consider a United States person as owning stock which is owned by a person who is not a United States person.

(iii) *International communications income derived by foreign persons with a fixed place of business in the United States.*—International communications income derived by a foreign person, other than a CFC, that is attributable to an office or other fixed place of business of the foreign person in the United States is from sources within the United States. The principles of section 864(c)(5) apply in determining whether a foreign person has an office or fixed place of business in the United States. See §1.864-7. International communications income is attributable to an office or other fixed place of business to the extent of functions performed, resources employed, or risks assumed by the office or other fixed place of business.

(iv) *International communications income derived by foreign persons engaged in a trade or business within the United States.*—International communications income derived by a foreign person (other than a CFC) engaged in a trade or business within the United States is income from sources within the United States to the extent the income, based on all the facts and circumstances, is attributable to functions performed, resources employed, or risks assumed within the United States.

(c) *Source of U.S. communications income.*—Income derived by a United States or foreign person from U.S. communications activity is from sources within the United States.

(d) *Source of foreign communications income.*—Income derived by a United States or foreign person from foreign communications activity is from sources without the United States.

(e) *Source of space/ocean communications income.*—The source of income derived by a United States or foreign person from space/ocean communications activity is determined under section 863(d) and the regulations thereunder.

(f) *Source of communications income when taxpayer cannot establish the two points between which the taxpayer is paid to transmit the communication.*—Income derived by a United States or foreign person from communications activity, when the taxpayer cannot establish the two points between which the taxpayer is paid to transmit the communication as required in paragraph (h)(3)(i) of this section, is from sources within the United States.

(g) *Taxable income.*—When a taxpayer allocates gross income under paragraph (b)(2)(iii), (b)(2)(iv), or (h)(1)(ii) of this section, the taxpayer must allocate expenses, losses, and other deductions as prescribed in §§1.861-8 through 1.861-14T to the class or classes of gross income that include the income so allocated in each case. A taxpayer must then apply the rules of §§1.861-8 through 1.861-14T properly to apportion amounts of expenses, losses, and other deductions so allocated to such gross income between gross income from sources within the United States and gross income from sources without the United States. For amounts of expenses, losses, and other deductions allocated to gross income derived from international communications activity, when the source of income is determined under the 50/50 method of paragraph (b)(1) or (b)(2)(ii) of this section, taxpayers generally must apportion expenses, losses, and other deductions between sources within the United States and sources without the United States pro rata based on the relative amounts of gross income from sources within the United States and gross income from sources without the United States. However, the preceding sentence shall not apply to research and experimental expenditures qualifying under §1.861-17, which are to be allocated and apportioned under the rules of that section.

(h) *Communications activity and income derived from communications activity.*—(1) *Communications activity.*—(i) *General rule.*—For purposes of this part, communications activity consists solely of the delivery by transmission of communications or data (communications). Delivery of communications other than by transmission (for example, by delivery of physical packages and letters) is not communications activity within the meaning of this section. Communications activity also includes the provision of capacity to transmit communications. Provision of content or any other additional service provided along with, or in connection with, a non-de minimis communications activity must be treated as a separate non-communications activity unless de minimis. Communications activity or non-communications activity will be treated as de minimis to the extent, based on the facts and circumstances, the value attributable to such activity is de minimis.

(ii) *Separate transaction.*—To the extent that a taxpayer's transaction consists in part of non-de minimis communications activity and in part of non-de minimis non-communications activity, each such part of the transaction must be treated as a separate transaction. Gross income is allocated to each such communications activity transaction and non-communications activity transaction to the extent the income, based on all the facts and circumstances, is attributable to functions performed, resources employed, or risks assumed in each such activity.

(2) *Income derived from communications activity.*—Income derived from communications activity (communications income) is income derived from the delivery by transmission of communications, including income derived from the provision of capacity to transmit communications. Income may be considered derived from a communications activity even if the taxpayer itself does not perform the transmission function, but in all cases, the taxpayer derives communications income only if the taxpayer is paid to transmit, and bears the risk of transmitting, the communications.

(3) *Determining the type of communications activity.*—(i) *In general.*—Whether income is derived from international communications activity, U.S. communications activity, foreign communications activity, or space/ocean communications activity is determined by identifying the two points between which the taxpayer is paid to transmit the communication. The taxpayer must establish the two points between which the taxpayer is paid to transmit, and bears the risk of transmitting, the communication. Whether the taxpayer contracts out part or all of the transmission function is not relevant. A taxpayer may satisfy the requirement that the taxpayer establish the two points between which the taxpayer is paid to transmit, and bears the risk of transmitting, the communication by using any consistently applied reasonable method to establish one or both endpoints. In evaluating the reasonableness of such method, consideration will be given to all the facts and circumstances, including whether the endpoints would otherwise be identifiable absent this reasonable method provision and the reliability of the data. Depending on the facts and circumstances, methods based on, for example, records of port or transport charges, customer billing records, a satellite footprint, or records of termination fees made pursuant to an international settlement agreement may be reasonable. In addition, practices used by taxpayers to classify or categorize certain communications activity in connection with preparation of statements and analyses for the use of management, creditors, minority shareholders, joint ventures, or other parties or governmental agencies in interest may be reliable indicators of the reasonableness of the method chosen, but need not be accorded conclusive weight by the Commissioner. In all cases, the method chosen to establish the two points between which the taxpayer is paid to transmit, and bears the risk of transmitting, the communication must be supported by sufficient documentation to permit verification by the Commissioner.

(ii) *Income derived from international communications activity.*—Income derived by a taxpayer from international communications activity (international communications income) is income derived from communications activity, as defined in paragraph (h)(2) of this section, when the taxpayer is paid to transmit—

(A) Between a point in the United States and a point in a foreign country (or a possession of the United States); or

(B) Foreign-originating communications (communications with a beginning point in a foreign country or a possession of the United States) from a point in space or international water to a point in the United States.

(iii) *Income derived from U.S. communications activity.*—Income derived by a taxpayer from U.S. communications activity (U.S. communications income) is income derived from communications activity, as defined in paragraph (h)(2) of this section, when the taxpayer is paid to transmit—

(A) Between two points in the United States; or

(B) Between the United States and a point in space or international water, except as provided in paragraph (h)(3)(ii)(B) of this section.

(iv) *Income derived from foreign communications activity.*—Income derived by a taxpayer from foreign communications activity (foreign communications income) is income derived from communications activity, as defined in paragraph (h)(2) of this section, when the taxpayer is paid to transmit—

(A) Between two points in a foreign country or countries (or a possession or possessions of the United States);

(B) Between a foreign country and a possession of the United States; or

(C) Between a foreign country (or a possession of the United States) and a point in space or international water.

(v) *Income derived from space/ocean communications activity.*—Income derived by a taxpayer from space/ocean communications activity (space/ocean communications income) is income derived from communications activity, as defined in paragraph (h)(2) of this section, when the taxpayer is paid to transmit between a point in space or international water and another point in space or international water.

(i) *Treatment of partnerships.*—This section is applied at the partner level.

(j) *Examples.*—The following examples illustrate the rules of this section:

Example 1. Income derived from non-communications activity—remote data base access—(i) *Facts.* D provides its customers in various foreign countries with access to its data base, which contains information on certain individuals' health care insurance coverage. Customer C obtains access to D's data base by placing a call to D's telephone number. Assume that C's telephone service, used to access D's data base, is provided by a third party, and that D assumes no responsibility for the transmission of the information via telephone.

(ii) *Analysis.* D is not paid to transmit communications and does not derive income from communications activity within the meaning of paragraph (h)(2) of this section. Rather, D derives income from provision of content or provision of services to its customers. Therefore, the rules of this section do not apply to determine the source of D's income.

Example 2. Income derived from U.S. communications activity—U.S. portion of international communication—(i) *Facts.* TC, a local telephone company, receives an access fee from an international carrier for picking up a call from a local telephone customer and delivering the call to a U.S. point of presence (POP) of the international carrier. The international carrier picks up the call from its U.S. POP and delivers the call to a foreign country.

(ii) *Analysis.* TC is not paid to carry the transmission between the United States and a foreign country. TC is paid to transmit a communication between two points in the United States. TC derives U.S. communications income as defined in paragraph (h)(3)(iii) of this section, which is sourced under paragraph (c) of this section as U.S. source income.

Example 3. Income derived from international communications activity—underwater cable—(i) *Facts.* TC, a domestic corporation, owns an underwater fiber optic cable. Pursuant to contracts, TC makes available to its customers capacity to transmit communications via the cable. TC's customers then solicit telephone customers and arrange to transmit the telephone customers' calls. The cable runs in part through U.S. waters, in part through international waters, and in part through foreign country waters.

(ii) *Analysis.* TC derives international communications income as defined in paragraph (h)(3)(ii) of this section because TC is paid to make available capacity to transmit communications between the United States and a foreign country. Because TC is a United States person, TC's international communications income is sourced under paragraph (b)(1) of this section as one-half from sources within the United States and one-half from sources without the United States.

Example 4. Income derived from international communications activity—satellite—(i) *Facts.* S, a United States person, owns satellites in orbit and uplink facilities in Country X, a foreign country. B, a resident of Country X, pays S to deliver B's programming from S's uplink facility, located in Country X, to a downlink facility in the United States owned by C, a customer of B.

(ii) *Analysis.* S derives international communications income under paragraph (h)(3)(ii) of this section because S is paid to transmit the communications between a beginning point in a foreign country and an endpoint in the United States. Because S is a United States person, the source of S's international communications income is determined under paragraph (b)(1) of this section as one-half from sources within the United States and one-half from sources without the United States.

Example 5. The paid-to-do rule—foreign communications via domestic route—(i) *Facts*. TC is paid to transmit communications from Toronto, Canada, to Paris, France. TC transmits the communications from Toronto to New York. TC pays another communications company, IC, to transmit the communications from New York to Paris.

(ii) *Analysis*. Under the paid-to-do rule of paragraph (h)(3)(i) of this section, TC derives foreign communications income under paragraph (h)(3)(iv) of this section because TC is paid to transmit communications between two points in foreign countries, Toronto and Paris. Under paragraph (h)(3)(i) of this section, the character of TC's communications activity is determined without regard to the fact that TC pays IC to transmit the communications for some portion of the delivery path. IC has international communications income under paragraph (h)(3)(ii) of this section because IC is paid to transmit the communications between a point in the United States and a point in a foreign country.

Example 6. The paid-to-do rule—domestic communication via foreign route—(i) *Facts*. TC is paid to transmit a call between two points in the United States, but routes the call through Canada.

(ii) *Analysis*. Under paragraph (h)(3)(i) of this section, the character of income derived from communications activity is determined by the two points between which the taxpayer is paid to transmit, and bears the risk of transmitting, the communications, without regard to the path of the transmission between those two points. Thus, under paragraph (h)(3)(iii) of this section, TC derives income from U.S. communications activity because it is paid to transmit the communications between two U.S. points.

Example 7. The paid-to-do rule—foreign-originating communications—(i) *Facts*. Under an international settlement agreement, G, a Country X international carrier, pays T to receive all calls originating in Country X that are bound for the United States and to terminate such calls in the United States. Due to Country X legal restrictions, the international settlement agreement specifies that G carries the transmission to a point outside the territory of Country X and that T carries the foreign-originating transmission from such point to the destined point in the United States. T, in turn, contracts out with another communications company, S, to transmit the U.S. portion of the communications. Tracing and identifying the endpoints of each transmission is not possible or practical. T does, however, keep records of termination fees received from G for terminating the foreign-originating calls.

(ii) *Analysis*. T derives communications income as defined in paragraph (h)(2) of this section. Based on all the facts and circumstances, T can establish that T is paid to transmit, and bears the risk of transmitting, foreign-originating calls from a point in space or international water to a point in the United States using a reasonable method to establish the endpoints, assuming that this method is consistently applied. In this case, T can reasonably establish that T is paid to receive foreign-originating calls and terminate such calls in the United States based on the records of termination fees pursuant to an international settlement agreement. Under paragraph (h)(3)(ii)(B) of this section, a taxpayer derives income from international communications activity when the taxpayer is paid to transmit foreign-originating communications from space or international water to the United States. Thus, under paragraph (h)(3)(ii)(B) of this section, T derives income from international communications. If, based on all the facts and circumstances, T could reasonably trace and identify the endpoints, then T would have to directly establish that each call originated in a foreign country. Assuming T is able to do so, the rest of the analysis in this *Example 7* remains the same. Under paragraph (h)(3)(iii) of this section, S derives income from U.S. communications activity because S is paid to transmit the communications between two U.S. points.

Example 8. Indeterminate endpoints—prepaid telephone calling cards—(i) *Facts*. S purchases capacity from TC to transmit telephone calls. S sells prepaid telephone calling cards that give customers access to TC's telephone lines for a certain number of minutes. Assume that S cannot establish the endpoints of its customers' telephone calls, even under the reasonable method rule of paragraph (h)(3) of this section.

(ii) *Analysis*. S derives communications income as defined in paragraph (h)(2) of this section because S makes capacity to transmit communications available to its customers. In this case, S cannot establish the two points between which the communications are transmitted. Therefore, S's communications income is U.S. source income, as provided by paragraph (f) of this section.

Example 9. Reasonable methods—minutes of use data on long distance calling plans—(i) *Facts*. B provides both domestic and international long distance services in a calling plan for a limited number of minutes for a set amount each month. Tracing and identifying the endpoints of each transmission is not possible or practical. B is, however, able to establish that the calling plan generated $10,000 of revenue for 25,000 minutes based on reports derived from customer billing records. Based on minutes of use data in these reports, B is able to establish that of the total 25,000 minutes, 60 percent or 15,000 minutes were for U.S. long distance calls and 40 percent or 10,000 minutes were for international calls.

(ii) *Analysis*. B derives communications income as defined in paragraph (h)(2) of this section. Based on all the facts and circumstances, B can establish the two points between which B is paid to transmit, and bears the risk of transmitting, the communications using a reasonable method to establish the endpoints, assuming that this method is consistently applied. In this case, B can reasonably establish that 60 percent of the income derived from the long distance calling plan is U.S. communications income and 40 percent is international communications income based on the minutes of use data derived from customer billing records to establish the endpoints of the communications. If, based on all the facts and circumstances, B could reasonably trace and identify the endpoints, then B would have to directly identify the endpoints between which B is paid to transmit the communications.

Example 10. Reasonable methods—system design—(i) *Facts*. D operates satellites which are designed to transmit signals through two separate ranges of signal frequencies (bands). Due to technological limitations, requirements, and practicalities, one band is designed to only transmit signals within the United States. The other band is designed to transmit signals between foreign countries and the United States. D cannot trace and identify the endpoints of each individual transmission. D does, however, track the total transmission through each band and the total income derived from transmitting signals through each band.

(ii) *Analysis*. D derives communications income as defined in paragraph (h)(2) of this section. Based on all the facts and circumstances, D can establish the two points between which D is paid to transmit, and bears the risk of transmitting, the communications using a reasonable method to establish endpoints, assuming that this method is consistently applied. In this case, D can reasonably establish that income derived from transmissions through the first band is U.S. communications income and income derived from transmissions through the second band is international communications income based on the design of the bands to establish the endpoints of the communications.

Example 11. Reasonable methods—port locations—(i) *Facts*. X provides its customer, C, with a virtual private network (VPN) so that C's U.S. headquarter office can connect and communicate with offices in the United States, Country X, Country Y, and Country Z. Assume that the VPN is only for communications with the U.S. headquarter office. X cannot trace and identify the endpoints of each transmission. C pays X a set amount each month for the entire service, regardless of the magnitude of the usage or the geographic points between which C uses the service.

(ii) *Analysis*. X derives communications income as defined in paragraph (h)(2) of this section. Based on the facts and circumstances, X can establish the two points between which X is paid to transmit, and bears the risk of transmitting, the communications using a reasonable method to establish endpoints, assuming that this method is consistently applied. In this case, X can reasonably establish that one-fourth of the income derived from the VPN service is U.S. communications income and three-fourths is international communications income based on the location of the VPN ports to establish the endpoints of the communications.

Example 12. Indeterminate endpoints—Internet access—(i) *Facts*. B, a domestic corporation, is an Internet service provider. B charges its customer, C, a monthly lump sum for Internet access. C accesses the Internet via a telephone call, initiated by the modem of C's personal computer, to one of B's control centers, which serves as C's portal to the Internet. B transmits data sent by C from B's control center in France to a recipient in England, over the Internet. B does not maintain records as to the beginning and endpoints of the transmission.

(ii) *Analysis*. B derives communications income as defined in paragraph (h)(2) of this section. The source of B's communications income is determined under paragraph (f) of this section as income from sources within the United States because B cannot establish the two points between which it is paid to transmit the communications.

Example 13. De minimis non-communications activity—(i) *Facts*. The same facts as in *Example 12*. Assume in addition that B replicates frequently requested sites on B's own servers, solely to speed up response time. Assume that B's replication of frequently requested sites would be considered a de minimis non-communications activity under this section.

(ii) *Analysis*. On these facts, because B's replication of frequently requested sites would be considered a de minimis non-communications activity, B is not required to treat the replication activity as a separate non-communications activity transaction under paragraph (h)(1) of this section. B derives communications income under paragraph (h)(2) of this section. The character and source of B's communications income are determined by demonstrating the points between which B is paid to transmit the communications, under paragraph (h)(3)(i) of this section.

Example 14. Income derived from communications and non-communications activity—bundled services—(i) *Facts*. A, a domestic corporation, offers customers local and long distance phone service, video, and Internet services. Customers pay a flat monthly fee plus 10 cents a minute for all long-distance calls, including international calls.

(ii) *Analysis*. Under paragraph (h)(1)(ii) of this section, to the extent that A's transaction with its customer consists in part of non-de minimis communications activity and in part of non-de minimis non-communications activity, each such part of the transaction must be treated as a separate transaction. A's gross income from the transaction is allocated to each such communications activity transaction and non-communications activity transaction in accordance with paragraph (h)(1)(ii) of this section. To the extent A can establish that it derives international communications income as defined in paragraph (h)(3)(ii) of this section, A would determine the source of such income under paragraph (b)(1) of this section. If A cannot establish the points between which it is paid to transmit communications, as required by paragraph (h)(3)(i) of this section, A's communications income is from sources within the United States, as provided by paragraph (f) of this section.

Example 15. Income derived from communications and non-communications activity—(i) *Facts*. B, a domestic corporation, is paid by D, a cable system operator in Foreign Country, to provide television programs and to transmit the television programs to Foreign Country. Using its own satellite transponder, B transmits the television programs from the United States to downlink facilities owned by D in Foreign Country. D receives the transmission, unscrambles the signals, and distributes the broadcast to D's customers in Foreign Country. Assume that B's provision of television programs is a non-de minimis non-communications activity, and that B's transmission of television programs is a non-de minimis communications activity.

(ii) *Analysis*. Under paragraph (h)(1)(ii) of this section, B must treat its communications and non-communications activities as separate transactions. B's gross income is allocated to each such separate communications and non-communications activity transaction in accordance with paragraph (h)(1)(ii) of this section. Income derived by B from the transmission of television programs to D's Foreign Country downlink facility is international communications income as defined in paragraph (h)(3)(ii) of this section because B is paid to transmit communications from the United States to a foreign country.

Example 16. Income derived from foreign communications activity—(i) *Facts*. S provides satellite capacity to B, a broadcaster located in Australia. B beams programming from Australia to the satellite. S's satellite picks the communications up in space and beams the programming over a footprint covering Southeast Asia.

(ii) *Analysis*. S derives communications income as defined in paragraph (h)(2) of this section. S's income is characterized as foreign communications income under paragraph (h)(3)(iv) of this section because S picks up the communication in space, and beams it to a footprint entirely covering a foreign area. Under paragraph (d) of this section, S's foreign communications income is from sources without the United States. If S were beaming the programming over a satellite footprint that covered area both in the United States and outside the United States, S would be required to allocate the income derived from the different types of communications activity.

(k) *Reporting and documentation requirements*.—(1) *In general*.—A taxpayer making an allocation of gross income under paragraph (b)(2)(iii), (b)(2)(iv), or (h)(1)(ii) of this section must satisfy the requirements in paragraphs (k)(2), (3), and (4) of this section.

(2) *Required documentation*.—In all cases, a taxpayer must prepare and maintain documentation in existence when its return is filed regarding the allocation of gross income, and allocation and apportionment of expenses, losses, and other deductions, the methodologies used, and the circumstances justifying use of those methodologies. The taxpayer must make available such documentation within 30 days upon request.

(3) *Access to software*.—If the taxpayer or any third party used any computer software, within the meaning of section 7612(d), to allocate gross income, or to allocate or apportion expenses, losses, and other deductions, the taxpayer must make available upon request—

(i) Any computer software executable code, within the meaning of section 7612(d), used for such purposes, including an executable copy of the version of the software used in the preparation of the taxpayer's return (including any plug-ins, supplements, etc.) and a copy of all related electronic data files. Thus, if software subsequently is upgraded or supplemented, a separate executable copy of the version used in preparing the taxpayer's return must be retained;

(ii) Any related computer software source code, within the meaning of section 7612(d), acquired or developed by the taxpayer or a related person, or primarily for internal use by the taxpayer or such person rather than for commercial distribution; and

(iii) In the case of any spreadsheet software or similar software, any formulae or links to supporting worksheets.

(4) *Use of allocation methodology*.—In general, when a taxpayer allocates gross income under paragraph (b)(2)(iii), (b)(2)(iv), or (h)(1)(ii) of this section, it does so by making the allocation on a timely filed original return (including extensions). However, a taxpayer will be permitted to make changes to such allocations made on its original return with respect to any taxable year for which the statute of limitations has not closed as follows:

(i) In the case of a taxpayer that has made a change to such allocations prior to the opening conference for the audit of the taxable year to which the allocation relates or who makes such a change within 90 days of such opening conference, if the IRS issues a written information document request asking the taxpayer to provide the documents and such other information described in paragraphs (k)(2) and (3) of this section with respect to the changed allocations and the taxpayer complies with such request within 30 days of the request, then the IRS will complete its examination, if any, with respect to the allocations for that year as part of the current examination cycle. If the taxpayer does not provide the documents and information described in paragraphs (k)(2) and (3) of this section within 30 days of the request, then the procedures described in paragraph (k)(4)(ii) of this section shall apply.

(ii) If the taxpayer changes such allocations more than 90 days after the opening conference for the audit of the taxable year to which the allocations relate or the taxpayer does not provide the documents and information with respect to the changed allocations as requested in accordance with paragraphs (k)(2) and (3) of this section, then the IRS will, in a separate cycle, determine whether an examination of the taxpayer's allocations is warranted and complete any such examination. The separate cycle will be worked as resources are available and may not have the same estimated completion date as the other issues under examination for the taxable year. The IRS may ask the taxpayer to extend the statute of limitations on assessment and collection for the taxable year to permit examination of the taxpayer's method of allocation, including an extension limited, where appropriate, to the taxpayer's method of allocation.

(l) *Applicability dates*.—Except as otherwise provided in this paragraph (l), this section applies to taxable years beginning on or after December 27, 2006. The provisions in paragraph (b)(2)(ii) of this section relating to the meaning of a CFC apply to taxable years of foreign corporations ending on or after October 1, 2019. For taxable years of foreign corporations ending before October 1, 2019, a taxpayer may apply such provisions to the last taxable year of a foreign corporation beginning before January 1, 2018, and each subsequent taxable year of the foreign corporation, provided that the taxpayer and United States persons that are related (within the meaning of section 267 or 707) to the taxpayer consistently apply such provisions with respect to all foreign corporations. For taxable years of foreign corporations ending before October 1, 2019, where the taxpayer does not apply the provisions of paragraph (b)(2)(ii) of this section relating to the meaning of a CFC, see paragraph (b)(2)(ii) of this section as in effect and contained in 26 CFR part 1, as revised April 1, 2020. [Reg. § 1.863-9.]

☐ [*T.D. 9305, 12-26-2006. Amended by T.D. 9908, 9-21-2020.*]

§ 1.863-10. Source of income from a qualified fails charge.—(a) *In general*.—Except as provided in paragraphs (b) and (c) of this section, the source of income from a qualified fails charge shall be determined by reference to the residence of the taxpayer as determined under section 988(a)(3)(B)(i).

(b) *Qualified business unit exception*.—The source of income from a qualified fails charge shall be determined by reference to the residence of a qualified business unit (as defined in section 989) of a taxpayer if—

(1) The taxpayer's residence, determined under section 988(a)(3)(B)(i), is the United States;

(2) The qualified business unit's residence, determined under section 988(a)(3)(B)(ii), is outside the United States;

(3) The qualified business unit is engaged in the conduct of a trade or business in the country where it is a resident; and

(4) The transaction to which the qualified fails charge relates is attributable to the qualified business unit. A transaction will be treated as attributable to a qualified business unit if it satisfies the principles of § 1.864-4(c)(5)(iii) (substituting "qualified business unit" for "U.S. office").

(c) *Effectively connected income exception.*—Qualified fails charge income that arises from a transaction any income from which is (or would be if the transaction produced income) effectively connected with a United States trade or business pursuant to § 1.864-4(c) is treated as from sources within the United States, and the income from the qualified fails charge is treated as effectively connected to the conduct of a United States trade or business.

(d) *Qualified fails charge.*—For purposes of this section, a qualified fails charge is a payment that—

(1) Compensates a party to a transaction that provides for delivery of a designated security (as defined in paragraph (e) of this section) in exchange for the payment of cash (delivery-versus-payment settlement) for another party's failure to deliver the specified designated security on the settlement date specified in the relevant agreement; and

(2) Is made pursuant to—

(i) A trading practice or similar guidance approved or adopted by either an agency of the United States government or the Treasury Market Practices Group, or

(ii) Any trading practice, program, policy or procedure approved by the Commissioner in guidance published in the Internal Revenue Bulletin.

(e) *Designated security.*—For purposes of this section, a *designated security* means any—

(i) Debt instrument (as defined in § 1.1275-1(d)) issued by the United States Treasury Department, the Federal National Mortgage Association, the Federal Home Loan Mortgage Corporation, or any Federal Home Loan Bank; or

(ii) Pass-through mortgage-backed security guaranteed by the Federal National Mortgage Association, the Federal Home Loan Mortgage Corporation, or the Government National Mortgage Association.

(g) *Effective/applicability date.*—This section is effective on February 21, 2012. This section applies to a qualified fails charge paid or accrued on or after December 8, 2010. [Reg. § 1.863-10.]

□ [*T.D. 9579, 2-17-2012.*]

§ 1.864-1. Meaning of sale, etc.—For purposes of §§ 1.861 through 1.864-7, the word "sale" includes "exchange"; the word "sold" includes "exchanged"; and the word "produced" includes "created", "fabricated", "manufactured", "extracted", "processed", "cured", and "aged". [Reg. § 1.864-1.]

□ [*T.D. 6948, 3-27-68.*]

§ 1.864-2. Trade or business within the United States.—(a) *In general.*—As used in part I (section 861 and following) and part II (section 871 and following), subchapter N, chapter 1 of the Code, and chapter 3 (section 1441 and following) of the Code, and the regulations thereunder, the term "engaged in trade or business within the United States" does not include the activities described in paragraphs (c) and (d) of this section, but includes the performance of personal services within the United States at any time within the taxable year except to the extent otherwise provided in this section.

(b) *Performance of personal services for foreign employer.*—(1) *Excepted services.*—For purposes of paragraph (a) of this section, the term "engaged in trade or business within the United States" does not include the performance of personal services—

(i) For a nonresident alien individual, foreign partnership, or foreign corporation, not engaged in trade or business within the United States at any time during the taxable year, or

(ii) For an office or place of business maintained in a foreign country or in a possession of the United States by an individual who is a citizen or resident of the United States or by a domestic partnership or a domestic corporation,

by a nonresident alien individual who is temporarily present in the United States for a period or periods not exceeding a total of 90 days during the taxable year and whose compensation for such services does not exceed in the aggregate a gross amount of $3,000.

(2) *Rules of application.*—(i) As a general rule, the term "day", as used in subparagraph (1) of this paragraph, means a calendar day during any portion of which the nonresident alien individual is physically present in the United States.

(ii) Solely for purposes of applying this paragraph, the nonresident alien individual, foreign partnership, or foreign corporation for which the nonresident alien individual is performing personal services in the United States shall not be considered to be engaged in trade or business in the United States by reason of the performance of such services by such individual.

(iii) In applying subparagraph (1) of this paragraph it is immaterial whether the services performed by the nonresident alien individual are performed as an employee for his employer or under any form of contract with the person for whom the services are performed.

(iv) In determining for purposes of subparagraph (1) of this paragraph whether compensation received by the nonresident alien individual exceeds in the aggregate a gross amount of $3,000, any amounts received by the individual from an employer as advances or reimbursements for travel expenses incurred on behalf of the employer shall be omitted from the compensation received by the individual, to the extent of expenses incurred, where he was required to account and did account to his employer for such expenses and has met the tests for such accounting provided in § 1.162-17 and paragraph (e)(4) of § 1.274-5. If advances or reimbursements exceed such expenses, the amount of the excess shall be included as compensation for personal services for purposes of such subparagraph. Pensions and retirement pay attributable to personal services performed in the United States are not to be taken into account for purposes of subparagraph (1) of this paragraph.

(v) See section 7701(a)(5) and § 301.7701-5 of this chapter (Procedure and Administration Regulations) for the meaning of "foreign" when applied to a corporation or partnership.

(vi) As to the source of compensation for personal services, see §§ 1.861-4 and 1.862-1.

(3) *Illustrations.*—The application of this paragraph may be illustrated by the following examples:

Example (1). During 1967, A, a nonresident alien individual, is employed by the London office of a domestic partnership. A, who uses the calendar year as his taxable year, is temporarily present in the United States during 1967 for 60 days performing personal service in the United States for the London office of the partnership and is paid by that office a total gross salary of $2,600 for such services. During 1967, A is not engaged in trade or business in the United States solely by reason of his performing such personal services for the London office of the domestic partnership.

Example (2). The facts are the same as in example (1), except that A's total gross salary for the services performed in the United States during 1967 amounts to $3,500, of which $2,625 is received in 1967 and $875 is received in 1968. During 1967, A is engaged in trade or business in the United States by reason of his performance of personal services in the United States.

(c) *Trading in stocks or securities.*—For purposes of paragraph (a) of this section—

(1) *In general.*—The term "engaged in trade or business within the United States" does not include the effecting of transactions in the United States in stocks or securities through a resident broker, commission agent, custodian, or other independent agent. This subparagraph shall apply to any taxpayer, including a broker or dealer in stocks or securities, except that it shall not apply if at any time during the taxable year the taxpayer has an office or other fixed place of business in the United States through which, or by the direction of which, the transactions in stocks or securities are effected. The volume of stock or security transactions effected during the taxable year shall not be taken into account in determining under this subparagraph whether the taxpayer is engaged in trade or business within the United States.

(2) *Trading for taxpayer's own account.*—(i) *In general.*—The term "engaged in trade or business within the United States" does not include the effecting of transactions in the United States in stocks or securities for the taxpayer's own account, irrespective of whether such transactions are effected by or through—

(*a*) The taxpayer himself while present in the United States, *(b)* Employees of the taxpayer, whether or not such employees are present in the United States while effecting the transactions, or

(c) A broker, commission agent, custodian, or other agent of the taxpayer, whether or not such agent while effecting the transactions is *(1)* dependent or independent, or *(2)* resident, nonresident, or present, in the United States,

and irrespective of whether any such employee or agent has discretionary authority to make decisions in effecting such transactions. For purposes of this paragraph, the term "securities" means any note, bond, debenture, or other evidence of indebtedness, or any evidence of an interest in or right to subscribe to or purchase any of the foregoing; and the effecting of transactions in stocks or securities includes buying, selling (whether or not by entering into short sales), or trading in stocks, securities, or contracts or options to buy or sell stocks or securities, on margin or otherwise, for the account and risk of the taxpayer, and any other activity closely related thereto (such as obtaining credit for the purpose of effectuating such buying, selling, or trading). The volume of stock or security transactions effected during the taxable year shall not be taken into account in determining under this subparagraph whether the taxpayer is engaged in trade or business within the United States. The application of this subdivision may be illustrated by the following example:

Example. A, a nonresident alien individual who is not a dealer in stocks or securities, authorizes B, an individual resident of the United States, as his agent to effect transactions in the United States in stocks and securities for the account of A. B is empowered with complete authority to trade in stocks and securities for the account of A and to use his own discretion as to when to buy or sell for A's account. This grant of discretionary authority from A to B is also communicated in writing by A to various domestic brokerage firms through which A ordinarily effects transactions in the United States in stocks or securities. Under the agency arrangement B has the authority to place orders with the brokers, and all confirmations are to be made by the brokers to B, subject to his approval. The brokers are authorized by A to make payments to B and to charge such payments to the account of A. In addition, B is authorized to obtain and advance the necessary funds, if any, to maintain credits with the brokerage firms. Pursuant to his authority B carries on extensive trading transactions in the United States during the taxable year through the various brokerage firms for the account of A. During the taxable year A makes several visits to the United States in order to discuss with B various aspects of his trading activities and to make necessary changes in his trading policy. A is not engaged in trade or business within the United States during the taxable year solely because of the effecting by B of transactions in the United States in stocks or securities during such year for the account of A.

(ii) *Partnerships.*—A nonresident alien individual, foreign partnership, foreign estate, foreign trust, or foreign corporation shall not be considered to be engaged in trade or business within the United States solely because such person is a member of a partnership (whether domestic or foreign) which, pursuant to discretionary authority granted to such partnership by such person, effects transactions in the United States in stock or securities for the partnership's own account or solely because an employee of such partnership, or a broker, commission agent, custodian, or other agent, pursuant to discretionary authority granted by such partnership, effects transactions in the United States in stocks or securities for the account of such partnership. This subdivision shall not apply, however, to any member of *(a)* a partnership which is a dealer in stocks or securities or *(b)* a partnership (other than a partnership in which, at any time during the last half of its taxable year, more than 50 percent of either the capital interest or the profits interest is owned, directly or indirectly, by five or fewer partners who are individuals) the principal business of which is trading in stocks or securities for its own account, if the principal office of such partnership is in the United States at any time during the taxable year. The principles of subdivision (iii) of this subparagraph for determining whether a foreign corporation has its principal office in the United States shall apply in determining under this subdivision whether a partnership has its principal office in the United States. See section 707(b)(3) and paragraph (b)(3) of §1.707-1 for rules for determining the extent of the ownership by a partner of a capital interest or profits interest in a partnership. The application of this subdivision may be illustrated by the following examples:

Example (1). B, a nonresident alien individual, is a member of partnership X, the members of which are U.S. citizens, nonresident alien individuals, and foreign corporations. The principal business of partnership X is trading in stocks or securities for its own account. Pursuant to discretionary authority granted by B, partnership X effects transactions in the United States in stock or securities for its own account. Partnership X is not a dealer in stocks or securities, and more than 50 percent of either the capital interest or the profits interest in partnership X is owned throughout its taxable year by five or fewer partners who are individuals. B is not engaged in trade or business within the United States solely by reason of such effecting of transactions in the United States in stocks or securities by partnership X for its own account.

Example (2). The facts are the same as in example (1), except that not more than 50 percent of either the capital interest or the profits interest in partnership X is owned throughout the taxable year by five or fewer partners who are individuals. However, partnership X does not maintain its principal office in the United States at any time during the taxable year. B is not engaged in trade or business within the United States solely by reason of the trading in stocks or securities by partnership X for its own account.

Example (3). The facts are the same as in example (1), except that, pursuant to discretionary authority granted by partnership X, domestic broker D effects transactions in the United States in stocks or securities for the account of partnership X. B is not engaged in trade or business in the United States solely by reason of such trading in stocks or securities for the account of partnership X.

(iii) *Dealers in stocks or securities and certain foreign corporations.*—This subparagraph shall not apply to the effecting of transactions in the United States for the account of *(a)* a dealer in stocks or securities or *(b)* a foreign corporation (other than a corporation which is, or but for section 542(c)(7) or 543(b)(1)(C) would be, a personal holding company) the principal business of which is trading in stocks or securities for its own account, if the principal office of such corporation is in the United States at any time during the taxable year. Whether a foreign corporation's principal office is in the United States for this purpose is to be determined by comparing the activities (other than trading in stocks or securities) which the corporation conducts from its office or other fixed place of business located in the United States with the activities it conducts from its offices or other fixed places of business located outside the United States. For purposes of this subdivision, a foreign corporation is considered to have only one principal office, and an office of such corporation will not be considered to be its principal office merely because it is a statutory office of such corporation. For example, a foreign corporation which carries on most or all of its investment activities in the United States but maintains a general business office or offices outside the United States in which its management is located will not be considered as having its principal office in the United States if all or a substantial portion of the following functions is carried on at or from an office or offices located outside the United States:

(1) Communicating with its shareholders (including the furnishing of financial reports),

(2) Communicating with the general public,

(3) Soliciting sales of its own stock,

(4) Accepting the subscriptions of new stockholders,

(5) Maintaining its principal corporate records and books of account,

(6) Auditing its books of account,

(7) Disbursing payments of dividends, legal fees, accounting fees, and officers' and directors' salaries,

(8) Publishing or furnishing the offering and redemption price of the shares of stock issued by it,

(9) Conducting meetings of its shareholders and board of directors, and

(10) Making redemptions of its own stock.

The application of this subdivision may be illustrated by the following examples:

Example (1). (a) Foreign corporation X (not a corporation which is, or but for section 542(c)(7) or 543(b)(1)(C) would be, a personal holding company) was organized to sell its shares to nonresident alien individuals and foreign corporations and to invest the proceeds from the sale of such shares in stocks or securities in the United States. Foreign corporation X is engaged primarily in the business of investing, reinvesting, and trading in stocks or securities for its own account.

(b) For a period of three years, foreign corporation X irrevocably authorizes domestic corporation Y to exercise its discretion in effecting transactions in the United States in stocks or securities for the account and risk of foreign corporation X. Foreign corporation X issues a prospectus in which it is stated that its funds will be invested pursuant to an investment advisory contract with domestic corporation Y and otherwise advertises its services. Shares of foreign corporation X are sold to nonresident aliens and foreign corporations who are customers of United States brokerage firms unrelated to domestic corporation Y or foreign corporation X. The principal functions performed for foreign corporation X by domestic corporation Y are the rendering of investment advice and the effecting of transactions in the United States in stocks or securities for the account of foreign corporation X. Moreover, domestic corporation Y occasionally communicates with prospective foreign investors in foreign corporation X (through speaking engagements abroad by management of domestic corporation Y, and otherwise) for the purpose of explaining the investment techniques and policies used by domestic corporation Y in investing the funds of foreign corporation X. However, domestic corporation Y does not participate in the day-to-day conduct of other business activities of foreign corporation X.

(c) Foreign corporation X maintains a general business office or offices outside the United States in which its management is permanently located and from which it carries on, except to the extent noted heretofore, the functions enumerated in *(b)(1)* through *(10)* of this subdivision. The management of foreign corporation X at all times retains the independent power to cancel the investment advisory contract with domestic corporation Y subject to the contractual limitations contained therein and is in all other respects independent of the management of domestic corporation Y. The managing personnel of foreign corporation X communicate on a regular basis with domestic corporation Y, and periodically visit the offices of domestic corporation Y, in connection with the business activities of foreign corporation X.

(d) The principal office of foreign corporation X will not be considered to be in the United States; and, therefore, foreign corporation X is not engaged in trade or business within the United States solely by reason of its relationship with domestic corporation Y.

Example (2). The facts are the same as in example (1) except that, in lieu of having the investment advisory contract with domestic corporation Y, foreign corporation X has an office in the United States in which its employees perform the same functions as are performed by domestic corporation Y in example (1). Foreign corporation X is not engaged in trade or business within the United States during the taxable year solely because the employees located in its United States office effect transactions in the United States in stocks or securities for the account of that corporation.

(iv) *Definition of dealer in stocks or securities.—(a) In general.—* For purposes of this subparagraph, a dealer in stocks or securities is a merchant of stocks or securities, with an established place of business, regularly engaged as a merchant in purchasing stocks or securities and selling them to customers with a view to the gains and profits that may be derived therefrom. Persons who buy and sell, or hold, stocks or securities for investment or speculation, irrespective of whether such buying or selling constitutes the carrying on of a trade or business, and offices of corporations, members of partnerships, or fiduciaries, who in their individual capacities buy and sell, or hold, stocks or securities for investment or speculation are not dealers in stocks or securities within the meaning of this subdivision whether a person is a dealer in stocks or securities such person's transactions in stocks or securities effected both in and outside the United States shall be taken into account.

(b) Underwriting syndicates and dealers trading for others.—A foreign person who otherwise may be considered a dealer in stocks or securities under *(a)* of this subdivision shall not be considered a dealer in stocks or securities for purposes of this subparagraph—

(1) Solely because he acts as an underwriter, or as a selling group member, for the purpose of making a distribution of stocks or securities of a domestic issuer to foreign purchasers of such stocks or securities, irrespective of whether other members of the selling group distribute the stocks or securities of the domestic issuer to domestic purchasers, or

(2) Solely because of transactions effected in the United States in stocks or securities pursuant to his grant of discretionary authority to make decisions in effecting those transactions, if he can demonstrate to the satisfaction of the Commissioner that the broker, commission agent, custodian, or other agent through whom the transactions were effected acted pursuant to his written representation that the funds in respect of which such discretion was granted were the funds of a customer who is neither a dealer in stocks or securities, a partnership described in subdivision (ii)*(b)* of this subparagraph, or a foreign corporation described in subdivision (iii)*(b)* of this subparagraph.

For purposes of this *(b)*, a foreign person includes a nonresident alien individual, a foreign corporation, or a partnership any member of which is a nonresident alien individual or a foreign corporation. This *(b)* shall apply only if the foreign person at no time during the taxable year has an office or other fixed place of business in the United States through which, or by the direction of which, the transaction in stocks or securities are effected.

(c) Illustrations.—The application of this subdivision may be illustrated by the following examples:

Example (1). Foreign corporation X is a member of an underwriting syndicate organized to distribute stock issued by domestic corporation Y. Foreign corporation X distributes the stock of domestic corporation Y to foreign purchasers only. Domestic corporation M is syndicate manager of the underwriting syndicate and, pursuant to the terms of the underwriting agreement, reserves the right to sell certain quantities of the underwritten stock on behalf of all the members of the syndicate so as to engage in stabilizing transactions and to take certain other actions which may result in the realization of profit by all members of the underwriting syndicate. Foreign corporation X is not engaged in trade or business within the United States solely by reason of its participation as a member of such underwriting syndicate for the purpose of distributing the stock of domestic corporation Y to foreign purchasers or by reason of the exercise by M corporation of its discretionary authority as manager of such syndicate.

Example (2). Foreign corporation Y, a calendar year taxpayer, is a bank which trades in stocks or securities both for its own account and for the account of others. During 1967 foreign corporation Y authorizes domestic corporation M, a broker, to exercise its discretion in effecting transactions in the United States in stocks or securities for the account of B, a nonresident alien individual who has a trading account with foreign corporation Y. Foreign corporation Y furnishes a written representation to domestic corporation M to the effect that the funds in respect of which foreign corporation Y has authorized domestic corporation M to use its discretion in trading in the United States in stocks or securities are not funds in respect of which foreign corporation Y is trading for its own account but are the funds of one of its customers who is neither a dealer in stocks or securities, a partnership described in subdivision (ii)*(b)* of this subparagraph, or a foreign corporation described in subdivision (iii)*(b)* of this subparagraph. Pursuant to the discretionary authority so granted, domestic corporation M effects transactions in the United States during 1967 in stocks or securities for the account of the customer of foreign corporation Y. At no time during 1967 does foreign corporation Y have an office or other fixed place of business in the United States through which, or by the direction of which, such transactions in stocks or securities are effected by domestic corportion M. During 1967 foreign corporation Y is not engaged in trade or business within the United States solely by reason of such trading in stocks or securities during such year by domestic corporation M for the account of the customer of foreign corporation Y. Copies of the written representations furnished to domestic corporation M should be retained by foreign corporation Y for inspection by the Commissioner, if inspection is requested.

(d) *Trading in commodities.*—For purposes of paragraph (a) of this section—

(1) *In general.*—The term "engaged in trade or business within the United States" does not include the effecting of transactions in the United States in commodities (including hedging transactions) through a resident broker, commission agent, custodian, or other independent agent if (i) the commodities are of a kind customarily dealt in on an organized commodity exchange, such as a grain futures or a cotton futures market, (ii) the transaction is of a kind customarily consummated at such place, and (iii) the taxpayer at no time during the taxable year has an office or other fixed place of business in the United States through which, or by the direction of which, the transactions in commodities are effected. The volume of commodity transactions effected during the taxable year shall not be taken into account in determining under this subparagraph whether the taxpayer is engaged in trade or business in the United States.

(2) *Trading for taxpayer's own account.*—(i) *In general.*—The term "engaged in trade or business within the United States" does not include the effecting of transactions in the United States in commodities (including hedging transactions) for the taxpayer's own account if the commodities are of a kind customarily dealt in on an organized commodity exchange and if the transaction is of a kind customarily consummated at such place. This rule shall apply irrespective of whether such transactions are effected by or through—

(a) The taxpayer himself while present in the United States,

(b) Employees of the taxpayer, whether or not such employees are present in the United States while effecting the transactions, or

(c) A broker, commission agent, custodian, or other agent of the taxpayer, whether or not such agent while effecting the transactions is (1) dependent or independent, or (2) resident, nonresident, or present, in the United States,

and irrespective of whether any such employee or agent has discretionary authority to make decisions in effecting such transactions. The volume of commodity transactions effected during the taxable year shall not be taken into account in determining under this subparagraph whether the taxpayer is engaged in trade or business within the United States. This subparagraph shall not apply to the effecting of transactions in the United States for the account of a dealer in commodities.

(ii) *Partnerships.*—A nonresident alien individual, foreign partnership, foreign estate, foreign trust, or foreign corporation shall not be considered to be engaged in trade or business within the United States solely because such person is a member of a partnership (whether domestic or foreign) which, pursuant to discretionary authority granted to such partnership by such person, effects transactions in the United States in commodities for the partnership's account or solely because an employee of such partnership, or a broker, commission agent, custodian, or other agent, pursuant to discretionary authority granted by such partnership, effects transactions in the United States in commodities for the account of such partnership. This subdivision shall not apply to any member of a partnership which is a dealer in commodities.

(iii) *Illustration.*—The application of this subparagraph may be illustrated by the following example:

Example. Foreign corporation X, a calendar year taxpayer, is engaged as a merchant in the business of purchasing grain in South America and selling such cash grain outside the United States under long-term contracts for delivery in foreign countries. Foreign corporation X consummates a sale of 100,000 bushels of cash grain in February 1967 for July delivery to Sweden. Because foreign corporation X does not actually own such grain at the time of the sales transaction, such corporation buys as a hedge a July "futures contract" for delivery of 100,000 bushels of grain, in order to protect itself from loss by reason of a possible rise in the price of grain between February and July. The "futures contract" is ordered through domestic corporation Y, a futures commission merchant registered under the Commodity Exchange Act. Foreign corporation X is not engaged in trade or business within the United States during 1967 solely by reason of its effecting of such futures contract for its own account through domestic corporation Y.

(3) *Definition of commodity.*—For purposes of section 864(b)(2)(B) and this paragraph the term "commodities" does not include goods or merchandise in the ordinary channels of commerce.

(e) *Other rules.*—The fact that a person is not determined by reason of this section to be not engaged in trade or business with the United States is not to be considered a determination that such person is engaged in trade or business within the United States. Whether or not such person is engaged in trade or business within the United States shall be determined on the basis of the facts and circumstances in each case. For other rules relating to the determination of whether a taxpayer is engaged in trade or business in the United States see section 875 and the regulations thereunder.

(f) *Effective date.*—The provisions of this section shall apply only in the case of taxable years beginning after December 31, 1966. [Reg. § 1.864-2.]

☐ [*T.D. 6948, 3-27-68. Amended by T.D. 7378, 9-29-75.*]

§ 1.864-3. Rules for determining income effectively connected with U.S. business of nonresident aliens or foreign corporations.—(a) *In general.*—For purposes of the Income Revenue Code, in the case of a nonresident alien individual or a foreign corporation that is engaged in a trade or business in the United States at any time during the taxable year, the rules set forth in §§ 1.864-4 through 1.864-7 and this section shall apply in determining whether income, gain, or loss shall be treated as effectively connected for a taxable year beginning after December 31, 1966, with the conduct of a trade or business in the United States. Except as provided in sections 871(c) and (d) and 882(d) and (e), and the regulations thereunder, in the case of a nonresident alien individual or a foreign corporation that is at no time during the taxable year engaged in a trade or business in the United States, no income, gain, or loss shall be treated as effectively connected for the taxable year with the conduct of a trade or business in the United States. The general rule prescribed by the preceding sentence shall apply even though the income, gain, or loss would have been treated as effectively connected with the conduct of a trade or business in the United States if such income or gain had been received or accrued, or such loss had been sustained, in an earlier taxable year when the taxpayer was engaged in a trade or business in the United States. In applying §§ 1.864-4 through 1.864-7 and this section, the determination whether an item of income, gain, or loss is effectively connected with the conduct of a trade or business in the United States shall not be controlled by any administrative, judicial, or other interpretation made under the laws of any foreign country.

(b) *Illustrations.*—The application of this section may be illustrated by the following examples:

Example (1). During 1967 foreign corporation N, which uses the calendar year as the taxable year, is engaged in the business of purchasing and selling household equipment on the installment plan. During 1967 N is engaged in business in the United States by reason of the sales activities it carries on in the United States for the purpose of selling therein some of the equipment which it has purchased. During 1967 N receives installment payments of $800,000 on sales it makes that year in the United States, and the income from sources within the United States for 1967 attributable to such payments is $200,000. By reason of section 864(c)(3) and paragraph (b) of § 1.864-4 this income of $200,000 is effectively connected for 1967 with the conduct of a trade or business in the United States by N. In December of 1967, N discontinues its efforts to make any further sales of household equipment in the United States, and at no time during 1968 is N engaged in a trade or business in the United States. During 1968 N receives installment payments of $500,000 on the sales it made in the United States during 1967, and the income from sources within the United States for 1968 attributable to such payments is $125,000. By reason of section 864(c)(1)(B) and this section, this income of $125,000 is not effectively connected for 1968 with the conduct of a trade or business in the United States by N, even though such amount, if it had been received by N during 1967, would have been effectively connected for 1967 with the conduct of a trade or business in the United States by that corporation.

Example (2). R, a foreign holding company, owns all of the voting stock in five corporations, two of which are domestic corporations. All of the subsidiary corporations are engaged in the active conduct of a trade or business. R has an office in the United States where its chief executive officer, who is also the chief executive officer of one of the domestic corporations, spends a substantial portion of the taxable year supervising R's investment in its operating subsidiaries and performing his function as chief executive officer of the domestic operating subsidiary. R is not considered to be engaged in a trade or business in the United States during the taxable year by reason of the activities carried on in the United States by its chief executive officer in the supervision of its investment in its operating subsidiary corporations. Accordingly, the dividends from sources within the United States received by R during the taxable year from its domestic subsidiary corporations are not effectively connected for that year with the conduct of a trade or business in the United States by R.

Example (3). During the months of June through December 1971, B, a nonresident alien individual who uses the calendar year as the taxable year and the cash receipts and disbursements method of accounting, is employed in the United States by domestic corporation M for a salary of $2,000 per month, payable semimonthly. During 1971, B receives from M salary payments totaling $13,000, all of which income by reason of section 864(c)(2) and paragraph (c)(6)(ii) of § 1.864-4, is effectively connected for 1971 with the conduct of a trade or business in the United States by B. On December 31, 1971, B terminates his employment with M and departs from the United States. At no time during 1972 is B engaged in a trade or business in the United States. In January of 1972, B receives from M salary of $1,000 for the last half of December 1971, and a bonus of $1,000 in consideration of the services B performed in the United States during 1971 for that corporation. By reason of section 864(c)(1)(B) and this section, the $2,000 received by B during 1972 from sources within the United States is not effectively connected for that year with the conduct of a trade or business in the United States, even though such amount, if it had been received by B during 1971, would have been effectively connected for 1971 with the conduct of a trade or business in the United States by B. [Reg. § 1.864-3.]

☐ [*T.D. 7216, 11-2-72.*]

§ 1.864-4. U.S. source income effectively connected with U.S. business.—(a) *In general.*—This section applies only to a nonresident alien individual or a foreign corporation that is engaged in a trade or business in the United States at some time during a taxable year beginning after December 31, 1966, and to the income, gain, or loss of such person from sources within the United States. If the income, gain, or loss of such person for the taxable year from sources within the United States consists of (1) gain or loss from the sale or exchange of capital assets or (2) fixed or determinable annual or periodical gains, profits, and income or certain other gains described in section 871(a)(1) or 881(a), certain factors must be taken into account, as prescribed by section 864(c)(2) and paragraph (c) of this section, in order to determine whether the income, gain, or loss is effectively connected for the taxable year with the conduct of a trade or business in the United States by that person. All other income, gain, or loss of such person for the taxable year from sources within the United States shall be treated as effectively connected for the taxable year with the conduct of a trade or business in the United States by that person, as prescribed by section 864(c)(3) and paragraph (b) of this section.

(b) *Income other than fixed or determinable income and capital gains.*—All income, gain, or loss for the taxable year derived by a nonresident alien individual or foreign corporation engaged in a trade or business in the United States from sources within the United States which does not consist of income, gain, or loss described in section 871(a)(1) or 881(a), or of gain or loss from the sale or exchange of capital assets, shall, for purposes of paragraph (a) of this section, be treated as effectively connected for the taxable year with the conduct of a trade or business in the United States. This income, gain, or loss shall be treated as effectively connected for the taxable year with the conduct of a trade or business in the United States, whether or not the income, gain, or loss is derived from the trade or business being carried on in the United States during the taxable year. The application of this paragraph may be illustrated by the following examples:

Example (1). M, a foreign corporation which uses the calendar year as the taxable year, is engaged in the business of manufacturing machine tools in a foreign country. It establishes a branch office in the United States during 1968 which solicits orders from customers in the United States for the machine tools manufactured by that corporation. All negotiations with respect to such sales are carried on in the United States. By reason of its activity in the United States M is engaged in business in the United States during 1968. The income or loss from sources within the United States from such sales during 1968 is treated as effectively connected for that year with the conduct of a business in the United States by M. Occasionally, during 1968 the customers in the United States write directly to the home office of M, and the home office makes sales directly to such customers without routing the transactions through its branch office in the United States. The income or loss from sources within the United States for 1968 from these occasional direct sales by the home office is also treated as effectively connected for that year with the conduct of a business in the United States by M.

Example (2). The facts are the same as in example (1) except that during 1967 M was also engaged in the business of purchasing and selling office machines and that it used the installment method of accounting for the sales made in this separate business. During 1967 M was engaged in business in the United States by reason of the sales activities it carried on in the United States for the purpose of selling therein a number of the office machines which it had purchased. Although M discontinued this business activity in the United States in December of 1967, it received in 1968 some installment payments on the sales which it had made in the United States during 1967. The income of M for 1968 from sources within the United States which is attributable to such installment payments is effectively connected for 1968 with the conduct of a business in the United States, even though such income is not connected with the business carried on in the United States during 1968 through its sales office located in the United States for the solicitation of orders for the machine tools it manufactures.

Example (3). Foreign corporation S, which uses the calendar year as the taxable year, is engaged in the business of purchasing and selling electronic equipment. The home office of such corporation is also engaged in the business of purchasing and selling vintage wines. During 1968, S establishes a branch office in the United States to sell electronic equipment to customers, some of whom are located in the United States and the balance, in foreign countries. This branch office is not equipped to sell, and does not participate in sale of, wine purchased by the home office. Negotiations for the sales of the electronic equipment take place in the United States. By reason of the activity of its branch office in the United States, S is engaged in business in the United States during 1968. As a result of advertisements which the home office of S places in periodicals sold in the United States, customers in the United States frequently place orders for the purchase of wines with the home office in the foreign country, and the home office makes sales of wine in 1968 directly to such customers without routing the transactions through its branch office in the United States. The income or loss from sources within the United States for 1968 from sales of electronic equipment by the branch office, together with the income or loss from sources within the United States for that year from sales of wine by the home office, is treated as effectively connected for that year with the conduct of a business in the United States by S.

(c) *Fixed or determinable income and capital gains.*—(1) *Principal factors to be taken into account.*—(i) *In general.*—In determining for purposes of paragraph (a) of this section whether any income for the taxable year from sources within the United States which is described in section 871(a)(1) or 881(a), relating to fixed or determinable annual or periodical gains, profits, and income and certain other gains, or whether gain or loss from sources within the United States for the taxable year from the sale or exchange of capital assets, is effectively connected for the taxable year with the conduct of a trade or business in the United States, the principal tests to be applied are *(a)* the asset-use test, that is, whether the income, gain, or loss is derived from assets used in, or held for use in, the conduct of the trade or business in the United States, and *(b)* the business-activities test, that is, whether the activities of the trade or business conducted in the United States were a material factor in the realization of the income, gain, or loss.

(ii) *Special rule relating to interest on certain deposits.*—For purposes of determining under section 861(a)(1)(A) (relating to interest on deposits with banks, savings and loan associations, and insurance companies paid or creditied before Jan. 1, 1976) whether the interest described therein is effectively connected for the taxable year with the conduct of a trade or business in the United States, such interest shall be treated as income from sources within the United States for purposes of applying this paragraph and § 1.864-5. If by reason of the application of this paragraph such interest is determined to be income which is not effectively connected for the taxable year with the conduct of a trade or business in the United States, it shall then be treated as interest from sources without the United States which is not subject to the application of § 1.864-5.

(2) *Application of the asset-use test.*—(i) *In general.*—For purposes of subparagraph (1) of this paragraph, the asset-use test ordinarily shall apply in making a determination with respect to income, gain, or loss of a passive type where the trade or business activities as such do not give rise directly to the realization of the income, gain, or loss. However, even in the case of such income, gain, or loss, any activities of the trade or business which materially contribute to the realization of such income, gain, or loss shall also be taken into account as a factor in determining whether the income, gain, or loss is effectively connected with the conduct of a trade or business in the United States. The asset-use test is of primary significance where, for example, interest income is derived from sources within the United States by a nonresident alien individual or foreign corporation that is engaged in the business of manufacturing or selling goods in the United States. See also subparagraph (5) of this paragraph for rules applicable to taxpayers conducting a banking, financing, or similar business in the United States.

(ii) *Cases where applicable.*—Ordinarily, an asset shall be treated as used in, or held for use in, the conduct of a trade or business in the United States if the asset is—

(a) Held for the principal purpose of promoting the present conduct of the trade or business in the United States; or

(b) Acquired and held in the ordinary course of the trade or business conducted in the United States, as, for example, in the case of an account or note receivable arising from that trade or business; or

(c) Otherwise held in a direct relationship to the trade or business conducted in the United States, as determined under paragraph (c)(2)(iv) of this section.

(iii) *Application of asset-use test to stock.*—*(a) In general.*—Except as provided in paragraph (c)(2)(iii)*(b)* of this section, stock of a corporation (whether domestic or foreign) shall not be treated as an asset used in, or held for use in, the conduct of a trade or business in the United States.

(b) Stock held by foreign insurance companies.—This paragraph (c)(2)(iii) shall not apply to stock of a corporation (whether domestic or foreign) held by a foreign insurance company unless the foreign insurance company owns 10 percent or more of the total voting power or value of all classes of stock of such corporation. For

purposes of this section, section 318(a) shall be applied in determining ownership, except that in applying section 318(a)(2)(C), the phrase "10 percent" is used instead of the phrase "50 percent."

(iv) *Direct relationship between holding of asset and trade or business.*—*(a) In general.*—In determining whether an asset is held in a direct relationship to the trade or business conducted in the United States, principal consideration shall be given to whether the asset is needed in that trade or business. An asset shall be considered needed in a trade or business, for this purpose, only if the asset is held to meet the present needs of that trade or business and not its anticipated future needs. An asset shall be considered as needed in the trade or business conducted in the United States if, for example, the asset is held to meet the operating expenses of that trade or business. Conversely, an asset shall be considered as not needed in the trade or business conducted in the United States if, for example, the asset is held for the purpose of providing for *(1)* future diversification into a new trade or business, *(2)* expansion of trade or business activities conducted outside of the United States, *(3)* future plant replacement, or *(4)* future business contingencies.

(b) Presumption of direct relationship.—Generally, an asset will be treated as held in a direct relationship to the trade or business if *(1)* the asset was acquired with funds generated by that trade or business, *(2)* the income from the asset is retained or reinvested in that trade or business, and *(3)* personnel who are present in the United States and actively involved in the conduct of that trade or business exercise significant management and control over the investment of such asset.

(v) *Illustration.*—The application of paragraph (iv) may be illustrated by the following examples:

Example (1). M, a foreign corporation which uses the calendar year as the taxable year, is engaged in industrial manufacturing in a foreign country. M maintains a branch in the United States which acts as importer and distributor of the merchandise it manufactures abroad; by reason of these branch activities, M is engaged in business in the United States during 1968. The branch in the United States is required to hold a large current cash balance for business purposes, but the amount of the cash balance so required varies because of the fluctuating seasonal nature of the branch's business. During 1968 at a time when large cash balances are not required the branch invests the surplus amount in U.S. Treasury bills. Since these Treasury bills are held to meet the present needs of the business conducted in the United States they are held in a direct relationship to that business, and the interest for 1968 on these bills is effectively connected for that year with the conduct of the business in the United States by M.

Example (2). Foreign corporation M, which uses the calendar year as the taxable year, has a branch office in the United States where it sells to customers located in the United States various products which are manufactured by that corporation in a foreign country. By reason of this activity M is engaged in business in the United States during 1997. The U.S. branch establishes in 1997 a fund to which are periodically credited various amounts which are derived from the business carried on at such branch. The amounts in this fund are invested in various securities issued by domestic corporations by the managing officers of the U.S. branch, who have the responsibility for maintaining proper investment diversification and investment of the fund. During 1997, the branch office derives from sources within the United States interest on these securities, and gains and losses resulting from the sale or exchange of such securities. Since the securities were acquired with amounts generated by the business conducted in the United States, the interest is retained in that business, and the portfolio is managed by personnel actively involved in the conduct of that business, the securities are presumed under paragraph (c)(2)(iv)*(b)* of this section to be held in a direct relationship to that business. However, M is able to rebut this presumption by demonstrating that the fund was established to carry out a program of future expansion and not to meet the present needs of the business conducted in the United States. Consequently, the income, gains, and losses from the securities for 1997 are not effectively connected for that year with the conduct of a trade or business in the United States by M.

(3) *Application of the business-activities test.*—(i) *In general.*—For purposes of subparagraph (1) of this paragraph, the business-activities test shall ordinarily apply in making a determination with respect to income, gain, or loss which, even though generally of the passive type, arises directly from the active conduct of the taxpayer's trade or business in the United States. The business-activities test is of primary significance, for example, where *(a)* dividends or interest are derived by a dealer in stocks or securities, *(b)* gain or loss is derived from the sale or exchange of capital assets in the active conduct of a trade or business by an investment company, *(c)* royalties are derived in the active conduct of a business consisting of the licensing of patents or similar intangible property, or *(d)* service fees are derived in the active conduct of a servicing business. In applying the business-activities test, activities relating to the management of investment portfolios shall not be treated as activities of the trade or business conducted in the United States unless the maintenance of the investments constitutes the principal activity of that trade or business. See also subparagraph (5) of this paragraph for rules applicable to taxpayers conducting a banking, financing, or similar business in the United States.

(ii) *Illustrations.*—The application of this subparagraph may be illustrated by the following examples:

Example (1). Foreign corporation S is a foreign investment company organized for the purpose of investing in stocks and securities. S is not a personal holding company or a corporation which would be a personal holding company but for section 542(c)(7) or 543(b)(1)(C). Its investment portfolios consist of common stocks issued by both foreign and domestic corporations and a substantial amount of high grade bonds. The business activity of S consists of the management of its portfolios for the purpose of investing, reinvesting, or trading in stocks and securities. During the taxable year 1968, S has its principal office in the United States within the meaning of paragraph (c)(2)(iii) of § 1.864-2 and, by reason of its trading in the United States in stocks and securities, is engaged in business in the United States. The dividends and interest derived by S during 1968 from sources within the United States, and the gains and losses from sources within the United States for such year from the sale of stocks and securities from its investment portfolios, are effectively connected for 1968 with the conduct of the business in the United States by that corporation, since its activities in connection with the management of its investment portfolios are activities of that business and such activities are a material factor in the realization of such income, gains, and losses.

Example (2). N, a foreign corporation which uses the calendar year as the taxable year, has a branch in the United States which acts as an importer and distributor of merchandise: by reason of the activities of that branch, *N* is engaged in business in the United States during 1968. *N* also carries on a business in which it licenses patents to unrelated persons in the United States for use in the United States. The businesses of the licensees in which these patents are used have no direct relationship to the business carried on in N's branch in the United States, although the merchandise marketed by the branch is similar in type to that manufactured under the patents. The negotiations and other activities leading up to the consummation of these licenses are conducted by employees of N who are not connected with the U.S. branch of that corporation, and the U.S. branch does not otherwise participate in arranging for the licenses. Royalties received by N during 1968 from these licenses are not effectively connected for that year with the conduct of its business in the United States because the activities of that business are not a material factor in the realization of such income.

(4) *Method of accounting as a factor.*—In applying the asset-use test or the business-activities test described in subparagraph (1) of this paragraph, due regard shall be given to whether or not the asset, or the income, gain, or loss, is accounted for through the trade or business conducted in the United States, that is, whether or not the asset, or the income, gain, or loss, is carried on books of account separately kept for that trade or business, but this accounting test shall not by itself be controlling. In applying this subparagraph, consideration shall be given to whether the accounting treatment of an item reflects the consistent application of generally accepted accounting principles in a particular trade or business in accordance with accepted conditions or practices in that trade or business and whether there is a consistent accounting treatment of that item from year to year by the taxpayer.

(5) *Special rules relating to banking, financing, or similar business activity.*—(i) *Definition of banking, financing or similar business.*—A nonresident alien individual or a foreign corporation shall be considered for purposes of this section and paragraph (b)(2) of § 1.864-5 to be engaged in the active conduct of a banking, financing, or similar business in the United States if at some time during the taxable year the taxpayer is engaged in business in the United States and the activities of such business consist of any one or more of the following activities carried on, in whole or in part, in the United States in transactions with persons situated within or without the United States:

(a) Receiving deposits of funds from the public,

(b) Making personal, mortgage, industrial, or other loans to the public,

(c) Purchasing, selling, discounting, or negotiating for the public on a regular basis, notes, drafts, checks, bills of exchange, acceptances, or other evidences of indebtedness,

(d) Issuing letters of credit to the public and negotiating drafts drawn thereunder,

(e) Providing trust services for the public, or

(f) Financing foreign exchange transactions for the public.

Although the fact that the taxpayer is subjected to the banking and credit laws of a foreign country shall be taken into account in determining whether he is engaged in the active conduct of a banking, financing, or similar business, the character of the business actually carried on during the taxable year in the United States shall determine whether the taxpayer is actively conducting a banking, financing, or similar business in the United States. A foreign corporation which acts merely as a financing vehicle for borrowing funds for its parent corporation or any other person who would be a related person within the meaning of section 954(d) (3) if such foreign corporation were a controlled foreign corporation shall not be considered to be engaged in the active conduct of a banking, financing, or similar business in the United States.

(ii) *Effective connection of income from stocks or securities with active conduct of a banking, financing, or similar business.*—Notwithstanding the rules in subparagraphs (2) and (3) of this paragraph with respect to the asset-use test and the business-activities test, any dividends or interest from stocks or securities, or any gain or loss from the sale or exchange of stocks or securities which are capital assets, which is from sources within the United States and derived by a nonresident alien individual or a foreign corporation in the active conduct during the taxable year of a banking, financing, or similar business in the United States shall be treated as effectively connected for such year with the conduct of that business only if the stocks or securities giving rise to such income, gain, or loss are attributable to the U.S. office through which such business is carried on and—

(a) Were acquired—

(1) As a result of, or in the course of making loans to the public,

(2) In the course of distributing such stocks or securities to the public, or

(3) For the purpose of being used to satisfy the reserve requirements, or other requirements similar to reserve requirements, established by a duly constituted banking authority in the United States, or

(b) Consist of securities (as defined in subdivision (v) of this subparagraph) which are—

(1) Payable on demand or at a fixed maturity date not exceeding 1 year from the date of acquisition,

(2) Issued by the United States, or any agency or instrumentality thereof, or

(3) Not described in *(a)* or in *(1)* or *(2)* of this *(b)*.

However, the amount of interest from securities described in *(b)(3)* of this subdivision (ii) which shall be treated as effectively connected for the taxable year with the active conduct of a banking, financing, or similar business in the United States shall be an amount (but not in excess of the entire interest for the taxable year from sources within the United States from such securities) determined by multiplying the entire interest for the taxable year from sources within the United States from such securities by a fraction the numerator of which is 10 percent and the denominator of which is the same percentage, determined on the basis of a monthly average for the taxable year, as the book value of the total of such securities held by the U.S. office through which such business is carried on bears to the book value of the total assets of such office. The amount of gain or loss, if any, for the taxable year from the sale or exchange of such securities which shall be treated as effectively connected for the taxable year with the active conduct of a banking, financing, or similar business in the United States shall be an amount (but not in excess of the entire gain or loss for the taxable year from sources within the United States from the sale or exchange of such securities) determined by multiplying the entire gain or loss for the taxable year from sources within the United States from the sale or exchange of such securities by the fraction described in the immediately preceding sentence. The percentage of the denominator of the limiting fraction for such purposes shall be the percentage obtained by separately adding the book value of such securities and such total assets held at the close of each month in the taxable year, dividing each such sum by 12, and then dividing the amount of securities so obtained by the amount of assets so obtained. This subdivision does not apply to dividends from stock owned by a foreign corporation in a domestic corporation of which more than 50 percent of the total combined voting power of all classes of stock entitled to vote is owned by such foreign corporation and which is engaged in the active conduct of a banking business in the United States. The application of this subdivision may be illustrated by the following example:

Example. Foreign corporation M, created under the laws of foreign country Y, has in the United States a branch, B, which during the taxable year is engaged in the active conduct of the banking business in the United States within the meaning of subdivision (i) of this subparagraph. During the taxable year M derives from sources within the United States through the activities carried on through B, \$7,500,000 interest from securities described in subdivision *(b)(3)* of this subdivision (ii) and \$7,500,000 gain from the sale or exchange of such securities. The monthly average, determined as of the last day of each month in the taxable year, of such securities held by B divided by the monthly average, as so determined, of the total assets held by B equals 15 percent. Under this subdivision, the amount of interest income from such securities that shall be treated as effectively connected for the taxable year with the active conduct by M of a banking business in the United States is \$5 million (\$7,500,000 interest × 10%/15%), and the amount of gain from the sale or exchange of such securities that shall be treated as effectively connected for such year with the active conduct of such business is \$5 million (\$7,500,000 gain × 10%/15%).

(iii) *Stocks or securities attributable to U.S. office.*—*(a) In general.*—For purposes of paragraph (c)(5)(ii) of this section, a stock or security shall be deemed to be attributable to a U.S. office only if such office actively and materially participated in soliciting, negotiating, or performing other activities required to arrange the acquisition of the stock or security. The U.S. office need not have been the only active participant in arranging the acquisition of the stock or security.

(b) Exceptions.—A stock or security shall not be deemed to be attributable to a U.S. office merely because such office conducts one or more of the following activities:

(1) Collects or accounts for the dividends, interest, gain, or loss from such stock or security,

(2) Exercises general supervision over the activities of the persons directly responsible for carrying on the activities described in paragraph (c)(5)(iii)*(a)* of this section,

(3) Performs merely clerical functions incident to the acquisition of such stock or security,

(4) Exercises final approval over the execution of the acquisition of such stock or security, or

(5) Holds such stock or security in the United States or records such stock or security on its books or records as having been acquired by such office or for its account.

(c) Effective date.—This paragraph (c)(5)(iii) shall be effective for income includible in taxable years beginning on or after June 18, 1984, except that 26 CFR § 1.864-4(c)(5)(iii) as it appeared in the Code of Federal Regulations revised as of April 1, 1983, shall apply to income received or accrued under a loan made by the taxpayer on or before May 18, 1984 or pursuant to a written binding commitment entered into on or before May 18, 1984.

(iv) *Acquisitions in course of making loans to the public.*—For purposes of subdivision (ii) of this subparagraph—

(a) A stock or security shall be considered to have been acquired in the course of making a loan to the public where, for example, such stock or security was acquired as additional consideration for the making of the loan,

(b) A stock or security shall be considered to have been acquired as a result of making a loan to the public if, for example, such stock or security was acquired by foreclosure upon a bona fide default of the loan and is held as an ordinary and necessary incident to the active conduct of the banking, financing, or similar business in the United States, and

(c) A stock or security acquired on a stock exchange or organized over-the-counter market shall be considered not to have been acquired as a result of, or in the course of, making loans to the public.

(v) *Security defined.*—For purposes of this subparagraph, a security is any bill, note, bond, debenture, or other evidence of indebtedness, or any evidence of an interest in, or right to subscribe to or purchase, any of the foregoing items.

(vi) *Limitations on application of subparagraph.—(a) Other business activity.*—This subparagraph provides rules for determining when certain income from stocks or securities is effectively connected with the active conduct of a banking, financing, or similar business in the United States. Any dividends, interest, gain, or loss from sources within the United States which by reason of the application of subdivision (ii) of this subparagraph is not effectively connected with the active conduct by a nonresident alien individual or a foreign corporation of a banking, financing, or similar business in the United States may be effectively connected for the taxable year, under subparagraph (2) or (3) of this paragraph with the conduct by such taxpayer of another trade or business in the United States, such as, for example, the business of selling or manufacturing goods or merchandise or of trading in stocks or securities for the taxpayer's own account.

(b) Other income.—For rules relating to income, gain, or loss from sources within the United States (other than dividends or interest from, or gain or loss from the sale or exchange of, stocks or securities referred to in subdivision (ii) of this subparagraph) derived in the active conduct of a banking, financing, or similar business in the United States, see subparagraphs (2) and (3) of this paragraph and paragraph (b) of this section.

(vii) *Illustrations.*—The application of this subparagraph may be illustrated by the following examples:

Example (1). Foreign Corporation F, which is created under the laws of foreign country X and engaged in the active conduct of the banking business in country X and a number of other foreign countries, has in the United States a branch, B, which during the taxable year is engaged in the active conduct of the banking business in the United States within the meaning of subdivision (i) of this subparagraph. In the course of its banking business in foreign countries, F receives at its branches located in country X and other foreign countries substantial deposits in U.S. dollars which are transferred to the accounts of B in the United States. During the taxable year, B actively participates in negotiating loans to residents of the United States, such as call loans to U.S. brokers, which are financed from the U.S. dollar deposits transferred to B by F. In addition, B actively participates in purchasing on the New York Stock Exchange and over-the-counter markets long-term bonds and notes issued by the U.S. Government, U.S. Treasury bills, and long-term interest-bearing bonds issued by domestic corporations and having a maturity date of less than 1 year from the date of acquisition, all of which are purchased from the deposits transferred to B by F. All of the securities so acquired are held by B and recorded on its books in the United States. Pursuant to subdivision (ii) of this subparagraph, the interest received by F during the taxable year on these loans, bonds, notes, and bills is effectively connected for such year with the active conduct by F of a banking business in the United States.

Example (2). The facts are the same as in example (1) except that B also actively participates in using part of the U.S. dollar deposits, which are transferred to it by F, to purchase on the New York Stock Exchange shares of common stock issued by various domestic corporations. All of the shares so purchased are considered to be capital assets within the meaning of section 1221 and are recorded on B's books in the United States. None of the shares so purchased were acquired for the purpose of meeting reserve or other similar requirements. During the taxable year some of the shares are sold by B on the stock exchange. Pursuant to subdivision (ii) of this subparagraph, the dividends and gains received by F during the taxable year on these shares of stock are not effectively connected with the active conduct by F of a banking, financing, or similar business in the United States.

Example (3). The facts are the same as in example (1) except that B also uses part of the U.S. dollar deposits, which are transferred to it by F, to make a loan to domestic corporation M. As part of the consideration for the loan, M gives to B a number of shares of common stock issued by M. All of these shares of stock are considered to be capital assets within the meaning of section 1221 and are recorded on B's books in the United States. During the taxable year one-half of these shares of stock is sold by B on the New York Stock Exchange. Pursuant to subdivision (ii) of this subparagraph, the dividends and gains received by F during the taxable year on these shares of stock are effectively connected for such year with the active conduct by F of a banking business in the United States.

Example (4). The facts are the same as in example (1) except that during the taxable year the home office of F in country X actively participates in negotiating loans to residents of the United States, such as call loans to U.S. brokers, which are financed by the U.S. dollar deposits received at the home office and are recorded on the books of the home office. B does not participate in negotiating these loans. Pursuant to subdivision (ii) of this subparagraph the interest received by F during the taxable year on these loans made by the home office in country X is not effectively connected with the active conduct by F of a banking, financing, or similar business in the United States.

Example (5). Foreign corporation *Y*, which is created under the laws of foreign country X and is engaged in the active conduct of a banking business in country X and other foreign countries, has a branch, *C*, in the United States that is engaged in the active conduct of a banking business in the United States, within the meaning of paragraph (c)(5)(i) of this section, during the taxable year. *C* handles the negotiation and acquisition of securities involved in loans made by *Y* to U.S. persons. *C* also presents interest coupons with respect to such securities for payment, presents all such securities for payment at maturity, and maintains complete photocopy files with respect to such securities. The activities of the office of *Y* in country X with respect to these securities consist of giving pro forma approval of the loans, storing the original securities, and recording the securities on the books of the country X office. Pursuant to paragraphs (c)(5)(ii) and (c)(5)(iii) of this section, the U.S. source interest income received by *Y* during the taxable year on these securities is effectively connected for such year with the active conduct by *Y* of a banking business in the United States.

(6) *Income related to personal services of an individual.—(i) Income, gain, or loss from assets.*—Income or gains from sources within the United States described in section 871(a)(1) and derived from an asset, and gain or loss from sources within the United States from the sale or exchange of capital assets realized by a nonresident alien individual engaged in a trade or business in the United States during the taxable year solely by reason of his performing personal services in the United States shall not be treated as income, gain, or loss which is effectively connected for the taxable year with the conduct of a trade or business in the United States, unless there is a direct economic relationship between his holding of the asset from which the income, gain, or loss results and his trade or business of performing the personal services.

(ii) *Wages, salaries, and pensions.*—Wages, salaries, fees, compensations, emoluments, or other remunerations, including bonuses, received by a nonresident alien individual for performing personal services in the United States which, under paragraph (a) of § 1.864-2, constitute engaging in a trade or business in the United States, and pensions and retirement pay attributable to such personal services, constitute income which is effectively connected for the taxable year with the conduct of a trade or business in the United States by that individual if he is engaged in a trade or business in the United States at some time during the taxable year in which such income is received.

(7) *Effective date.*—Paragraphs (c)(2) and (c)(6)(i) of this section are effective for taxable years beginning on or after June 6, 1996. [Reg. § 1.864-4.]

☐ [*T.D. 7216, 11-2-72. Amended by T.D. 7332, 12-30-74; T.D. 7958, 5-17-84, T.D. 8657, 3-5-96 and T.D. 9226, 9-30-2005.*]

Proposed Amendments to Regulation

§ 1.864-4. U.S. source income effectively connected with U.S. business.

* * *

(c) * * *

(2) * * *

(iv) *Special rule relating to a global dealing operation.*—An asset used in a global dealing operation, as defined in § 1.482-8(a)(2)(i), will be treated as an asset used in a U.S. trade or business only if and to the extent that the U.S. trade or business is a participant in the global dealing operation under § 1.863-3(h)(3), and income, gain or loss produced by the asset is U.S. source under § 1.863-3(h) or would be treated as U.S. source if § 1.863-3(h) were to apply to such amounts.

* * *

(3) * * *

(ii) *Special rule relating to a global dealing operation.*—A U.S. trade or business shall be treated as a material factor in the realization of income, gain or loss derived in a global dealing operation, as defined in § 1.482-8(a)(2)(i), only if and to the extent that the U.S. trade or business is a participant in the global dealing operation under § 1.863-3(h)(3), and income, gain or loss realized by the U.S.

trade or business is U.S. source under § 1.863-3(h) or would be treated as U.S. source if § 1.863-3(h) were to apply to such amounts.

* * *

(5) * * *

(vi) * * *

(a) *Certain income earned by a global dealing operation.*—Notwithstanding paragraph (c)(5)(ii) of this section, U.S. source interest, including substitute interest as defined in § 1.861-2(a)(7), and dividend income, including substitute dividends as defined in § 1.861-3(a)(6), derived by a participant in a global dealing operation, as defined in § 1.482-8(a)(2)(i), shall be treated as attributable to the foreign corporation's U.S. trade or business, only if and to the extent that the income would be treated as U.S. source if § 1.863-3(h) were to apply to such amounts.

[Prop. Reg. § 1.864-4.]

[Proposed 3-6-98.]

§ 1.864-5. Foreign source income effectively connected with U.S. business.—(a) *In general.*—This section applies only to a nonresident alien individual or a foreign corporation that is engaged in a trade or business in the United States at some time during a taxable year beginning after December 31, 1966, and to the income, gain, or loss of such person from sources without the United States. The income, gain, or loss of such person for the taxable year from sources without the United States which is specified in paragraph (b) of this section shall be treated as effectively connected for the taxable year with the conduct of a trade or business in the United States, only if he also has in the United States at some time during the taxable year, but not necessarily at the time the income, gain, or loss is realized, an office or other fixed place of business, as defined in § 1.864-7, to which such income, gain, or loss is attributable in accordance with § 1.864-6. The income of such person for the taxable year from sources without the United States which is specified in paragraph (c) of this section shall be treated as effectively connected for the taxable year with the conduct of a trade or business in the United States when derived by a foreign corporation carrying on a life insurance business in the United States. Except as provided in paragraphs (b) and (c) of this section, no income, gain, or loss of a nonresident alien individual or a foreign corporation for the taxable year from sources without the United States shall be treated as effectively connected for the taxable year with the conduct of a trade or business in the United States by that person. Any income, gain, or loss described in paragraph (b) or (c) of this section which, if it were derived by the taxpayer from sources within the United States for the taxable year, would not be treated under § 1.864-4 as effectively connected for the taxable year with the conduct of a trade or business in the United States shall not be treated under this section as effectively connected for the taxable year with the conduct of a trade or business in the United States. To determine the source of income, gain or loss from the sale of personal property (including inventory property) attributable to an office or other fixed place of business in the United States by nonresidents, as defined in section 865(g)(1)(B), see § 1.865-3.

(b) *Income other than income attributable to U.S. life insurance business.*—Income, gain, or loss from sources without the United States other than income described in paragraph (c) of this section or income from section 865(e)(2) sales, as defined in § 1.865-3(c), shall be taken into account pursuant to paragraph (a) of this section in applying §§ 1.864-6 and 1.864-7 only if it consists of—

(1) *Rents, royalties, or gains on sales of intangible property.*—(i) Rents or royalties for the use of, or for the privilege of using, intangible personal property located outside the United States or from any interest in such property, including rents or royalties for the use, or for the privilege of using, outside the United States, patents, copyrights, secret processes and formulas, good will, trademarks, trade brands, franchises, and other like properties, if such rents or royalties are derived in the active conduct of the trade or business in the United States.

(ii) Gains or losses on the sale or exchange of intangible personal property located outside the United States or from any interest in such property, including gains or losses on the sale or exchange of the privilege of using, outside the United States, patents, copyrights, secret processes and formulas, good will, trademarks, trade brands, franchises, and other like properties, if such gains or losses are derived in the active conduct of the trade or business in the United States.

(iii) Whether or not such an item of income, gain, or loss is derived in the active conduct of a trade or business in the United States shall be determined from the facts and circumstances of each case. The frequency with which a nonresident alien individual or a foreign corporation enters into transactions of the type from which the income, gain, or loss is derived shall not of itself determine that the income, gain, or loss is derived in the active conduct of a trade or business.

(iv) This subparagraph shall not apply to rents or royalties for the use of, or for the privilege of using, real property or tangible personal property, or to gain or loss from the sale or exchange of such property.

(2) *Dividends or interest, or gains or loss from sales of stocks or securities.*—(i) *In general.*—Dividends or interest from any transaction, or gains or losses on the sale or exchange of stocks or securities, realized by *(a)* a nonresident alien individual or a foreign corporation in the active conduct of a banking, financing, or similar business in the United States or *(b)* a foreign corporation engaged in business in the United States whose principal business is trading in stocks or securities for its own account. Whether the taxpayer is engaged in the active conduct of a banking, financing, or similar business in the United States for purposes of this subparagraph shall be determined in accordance with the principles of paragraph (c)(5)(i) of § 1.864-4.

(ii) *Substitute payments.*—For purposes of this paragraph (b)(2), a substitute interest payment (as defined in § 1.861-2(a)(7)) received by a foreign person subject to tax under this paragraph (b) pursuant to a securities lending transaction or a sale-repurchase transaction (as defined in § 1.861-2(a)(7)) with respect to a security (as defined in § 1.864-6(b)(2)(ii)(*c*)) shall have the same character as interest income paid or accrued with respect to the terms of the transferred security. Similarly, for purposes of this paragraph (b)(2), a substitute dividend payment (as defined in § 1.861-3(a)(6)) received by a foreign person pursuant to a securities lending transaction or a sale-repurchase transaction (as defined in § 1.861-3(a)(6)) with respect to a stock shall have the same character as a distribution received with respect to the transferred security. This paragraph (b)(2)(ii) is applicable to payments made after November 13, 1997.

(iii) *Incidental investment activity.*—This subparagraph shall not apply to income, gain, or loss realized by a nonresident alien individual or foreign corporation on stocks or securities held, sold, or exchanged in connection with incidental investment activities carried on by that person. Thus, a foreign corporation which is primarily a holding company owning significant percentages of the stocks or securities issued by other corporations shall not be treated under this subparagraph as a corporation the principal business of which is trading in stocks or securities for its own account, solely because it engages in sporadic purchases or sales of stocks or securities to adjust its portfolio. The application of this subdivision may be illustrated by the following example:

Example. F, a foreign corporation, owns voting stock in foreign corporations M, N, and P, its holdings in such corporations constituting 15, 20, and 100 percent, respectively, of all classes of their outstanding voting stock. Each of such stock holdings by F represents approximately 20 percent of its total assets. The remaining 40 percent of F's assets consist of other investments, 20 percent being invested in securities issued by foreign governments and in stocks and bonds issued by other corporations in which F does not own a significant percentage of their outstanding voting stock, and 20 percent being invested in bonds issued by N. None of the assets of F are held primarily for sale; but, if the officers of that corporation were to decide that other investments would be preferable to its holding of such assets, F would sell the stocks and securities and reinvest the proceeds therefrom in other holdings. Any income, gain, or loss which F may derive from this investment activity is not considered to be realized by a foreign corporation described in subdivision (i) of this subparagraph.

(3) *Sale of goods or merchandise through U.S. office.*—(i) Income, gain, or loss from the sale of inventory items or of property held primarily for sale to customers in the ordinary course of business, as described in section 1221 (1), where the sale is outside the United States but through the office or other fixed place of business which the nonresident alien or foreign corporation has in the United States, irrespective of the destination to which such property is sent for use, consumption, or disposition.

(ii) This subparagraph shall not apply to income, gain, or loss resulting from a sales contract entered into on or before February 24, 1966. See section 102(e)(1) of the Foreign Investors Tax Act of 1966 (80 Stat. 1547). Thus, for example, the sales office in the United States of a foreign corporation enters into negotiations for the sale of 500,000 industrial bearings which the corporation produces in a foreign country for consumption in the Western Hemisphere. These negotiations culminate in a binding agreement entered into on January 1, 1966. By its terms delivery under the contract is to be made over a period of 3 years beginning in March of 1966. Payment is due upon delivery. The income from sources without the United States resulting from this sale negotiated by the U.S. sales office of the foreign corporation shall not be taken into account under this subparagraph for any taxable year.

(iii) This subparagraph shall not apply to gains or losses on the sale or exchange of intangible personal property to which subparagraph (1) of this paragraph applies or of stocks or securities to which subparagraph (2) of this paragraph applies.

(c) *Income attributable to U.S. life insurance business.*—(1) All of the income for the taxable year of a foreign corporation described in subparagraph (2) of this paragraph from sources without the United States, which is attributable to its U.S. life insurance business, shall be treated as effectively connected for the taxable year with the conduct of a trade or business in the United States by that corporation. Thus, in determining its life insurance company taxable income from its U.S. business for purposes of section 802, the foreign corporation shall include all of its items of income from sources without the United States which would appropriately be taken into account in determining the life insurance company taxable income of a domestic corporation. The income to which this subparagraph applies shall be taken into account for purposes of paragraph (a) of this section without reference to §§1.864-6 and 1.864-7.

(2) A foreign corporation to which subparagraph (1) of this paragraph applies is a foreign corporation carrying on an insurance business in the United States during the taxable year which—

(i) Without taking into account its income not effectively connected for that year with the conduct of any trade or business in the United States, would qualify as a life insurance company under part I (section 801 and following) of subchapter L, chapter 1 of the Code, if it were a domestic corporation, and

(ii) By reason of section 842 is taxable under that part on its income which is effectively connected for that year with its conduct of any trade or business in the United States.

(d) *Excluded foreign source income.*—Notwithstanding paragraphs (b) and (c) of this section, no income from sources without the United States shall be treated as effectively connected for any taxable year with the conduct of a trade or business in the United States by a nonresident alien individual or a foreign corporation if the income consists of—

(1) *Dividends, interest, or royalties paid by a related foreign corporation.*—Dividends, interest, or royalties paid by a foreign corporation in which the nonresident alien individual or the foreign corporation described in paragraph (a) of this section owns, within the meaning of section 958(a), or is considered as owning, by applying the ownership rules of section 958(b), at the time such items are paid more than 50 percent of the total combined voting power of all classes of stock entitled to vote.

(2) *Subpart F income of a controlled foreign corporation.*—Any income of the foreign corporation described in paragraph (a) of this section which is subpart F income for the taxable year, as determined under section 952(a), even though part of the income is attributable to amounts which, if distributed by the foreign corporation, would be distributed with respect to its stock which is owned by shareholders who are not U.S. shareholders within the meaning of section 951(b). This subparagraph shall not apply to any income of the foreign corporation which is excluded in determining its subpart F income for the taxable year for purposes of section 952(a). Thus, for example, this subparagraph shall not apply to—

(i) Foreign base company shipping income which is excluded under section 954(b)(2),

(ii) Foreign base company income amounting to less than 10 percent (30 percent in the case of taxable years of foreign corporations ending before January 1, 1976) of gross income which by reason of section 954(b)(3)(A) does not become subpart F income for the taxable year,

(iii) Any income excluded from foreign base company income under section 954(b)(4), relating to exception for foreign corporations not availed of to reduce taxes,

(iv) Any income derived in the active conduct of a trade or business which is excluded under section 954(c)(3), or

(v) Any income received from related persons which is excluded under section 954(c)(4).

This subparagraph shall apply to the foreign corporation's entire subpart F income for the taxable year determined under section 952(a), even though no amount is included in the gross income of a U.S. shareholder under section 951(a) with respect to that subpart F income because of the minimum distribution provisions of section 963(a) or because of the reduction under section 970(a) with respect to an export trade corporation. This subparagraph shall apply only to a foreign corporation which is a controlled foreign corporation within the meaning of section 957 and the regulations thereunder. The application of this subparagraph may be illustrated by the following examples:

Example (1). Controlled foreign corporation M, incorporated under the laws of foreign country X, is engaged in the business of purchasing and selling merchandise manufactured in foreign country Y by an unrelated person. M negotiates sales, through its sales office in the United States, of its merchandise for use outside of country X. These sales are made outside the United States, and the merchandise is sold for use outside the United States. No office maintained by M outside the United States participates materially in the sales made through its U.S. sales office. These activities constitute the only activities of M. During the taxable year M derives $100,000 income from these sales made through its U.S. sales office, and all of such income is foreign base company sales income by reason of section 954(d)(2) and paragraph (b) of §1.954-3. The entire $100,000 is also subpart F income, determined under section 952(a). In addition, all of this income would, without reference to section 864(c)(4)(D)(ii) and this subparagraph, be treated as effectively connected for the taxable year with the conduct of a trade or business in the United States by M. Through its entire taxable year 60 percent of the one class of stock of M is owned within the meaning of section 958(a) by U.S. shareholders, as defined in section 951(b), and 40 percent of its one class of stock is owned within the meaning of section 958(a) by persons who are not U.S. shareholders, as defined in section 951(b). Although only $60,000 of the subpart F income of M for the taxable year is includible in the income of the U.S. shareholders under section 951(a), the entire subpart F income of $100,000 constitutes income which, by reason of section 864(c)(4)(D)(ii) and this subparagraph, is not effectively connected for the taxable year with the conduct of a trade or business in the United States by M.

Example (2). The facts are the same as in example (1) except that the foreign base company sales income amounts to $150,000 determined in accordance with paragraph (d)(3)(i) of §1.954-1, and that M also has gross income from sources without the United States of $50,000 from sales, through its sales office in the United States, of merchandise for use in country X. These sales are made outside the United States. All of this income would, without reference to section 864(c)(4)(D)(ii) and this subparagraph, be treated as effectively connected for the taxable year with the conduct of a trade or business in the United States by M. Since the foreign base company income of $150,000 amounts to 75 percent of the entire gross income of $200,000, determined as provided in paragraph (d)(3)(ii) of §1.954-1, the entire $200,000 constitutes foreign base company income under section 954(b)(3)(B). Assuming that M has no amounts to be taken into account under paragraphs (1), (2), (4), and (5) of section 954(b), the $200,000 is also subpart F income, determined under section 952(a). This subpart F income of $200,000 constitutes income which, by reason of section 864(c)(4)(D)(ii) and this subparagraph, is not effectively connected for the taxable year with the conduct of a trade or business in the United States by M.

(3) *Interest on certain deposits.*—Interest which, by reason of section 861(a)(1)(A) (relating to interest on deposits with banks, savings and loan associations, and insurance companies paid or credited before January 1, 1976) and paragraph (c) of §1.864-4, is determined to be income from sources without the United States because it is not effectively connected for the taxable year with the conduct of a trade or business in the United States by the nonresident alien individual or foreign corporation.

(e) *Applicability dates.*—Paragraphs (a) and (b) of this section apply to taxable years ending on or after December 23, 2019. However, a taxpayer may apply paragraphs (a) and (b) of this section in their entirety for taxable years beginning after December 31, 2017, and ending before December 23, 2019, provided that the taxpayer and all persons related to the taxpayer (within the meaning of section 267 or 707) apply paragraphs (a) and (b) of this section and §§1.863-1(b), 1.863-2(b), 1.863-3, 1.863-8(b)(3)(ii), 1.864-6(c)(2), and 1.865-3 in their entirety for the taxable year, and once applied, the taxpayer and all persons related to the taxpayer (within the meaning of section 267 or 707) continue to apply these regulations in their entirety for all subsequent taxable years. For regulations generally applicable to taxable years ending before December 23, 2019, see §1.864-5 as contained in 26 CFR part 1 revised as of April 1, 2020. [Reg. §1.864-5.]

☐ [*T.D. 7216*, 11-2-72. *Amended by T.D.* 7893, 5-11-83, *T.D.* 8735, 10-6-97 *and T.D.* 9921, 12-10-2020.]

§1.864-6. Income, gain, or loss attributable to an office or other fixed place of business in the United States.—(a) *In general.*—Income, gain, or loss from sources without the United States which is specified in paragraph (b) of §1.864-5 and received by a nonresident alien individual or a foreign corporation engaged in a trade or business in the United States at some time during a taxable year beginning after December 31, 1966, shall be treated as effectively connected for the taxable year with the conduct of a trade or business in the United States only if the income, gain, or loss is attributable under paragraphs (b) and (c) of this section to an office or other fixed place of business, as defined in §1.864-7, which the taxpayer has in the United States at some time during the taxable year.

(b) *Material factor test.*—(1) *In general.*—For purposes of paragraph (a) of this section, income, gain, or loss is attributable to an office or other fixed place of business which a nonresident alien individual or a foreign corporation has in the United States only if such office or other fixed place of business is a material factor in the realization of the income, gain, or loss, and if the income, gain, or loss is realized in the ordinary course of the trade or business carried on through that office or other fixed place of business. For this purpose, the activities of the office or other fixed place of business shall not be considered to be a material factor in the realization of the income, gain, or loss unless they provide a significant contribution to, by being an essential economic element in, the realization of the income, gain, or loss. Thus, for example, meetings in the United States of the board of directors of a foreign corporation do not of themselves constitute a material factor in the realization of income, gain, or loss. It is not necessary that the activities of the office or other fixed place of business in the United States be a major factor in the realization of income, gain, or loss. An office or other fixed place of business located in the United States at some time during a taxable year may be a material factor in the realization of an item of income, gain, or loss for that year even though the office or other fixed place of business is not present in the United States when the income, gain, or loss is realized.

(2) *Application of material factor test to specific classes of income.*—For purposes of paragraph (a) of this section, an office or other fixed place of business which a nonresident alien individual or a foreign corporation, engaged in a trade or business in the United States at some time during the taxable year, had in the United States, shall be considered a material factor in the realization of income, gain, or loss consisting of—

(i) *Rents, royalties, or gains on sales of intangible property.*—Rents, royalties, or gains or losses, from intangible personal property specified in paragraph (b)(1) of §1.864-5, if the office or other fixed place of business either actively participates in soliciting, negotiating, or performing other activities required to arrange, the lease, license, sale, or exchange from which such income, gain, or loss is derived or performs significant services incident to such lease, license, sale, or exchange. An office or other fixed place of business in the United States shall not be considered to be a material factor in the realization of income, gain, or loss for purposes of this subdivision merely because the office or other fixed place of business conducts one or more of the following activities: (*a*) develops, creates, produces, or acquires and adds substantial value to, the property which is leased, licensed, or sold, or exchanged, (*b*) collects or accounts for the rents, royalties, gains, or losses, (*c*) exercises general supervision over the activities of the persons directly responsible for carrying on the activities or services described in the immediately preceding sentence, (*d*) performs merely clerical functions incident to the lease, license, sale or exchange or (*e*) exercises final approval over the execution of the lease, license, sale, or exchange. The application of this subdivision may be illustrated by the following examples:

Example (1). F, a foreign corporation, is engaged in the active conduct of the business of licensing patents which it has either purchased or developed in the United States. F has a business office in the United States. Licenses for the use of such patents outside the United States are negotiated by offices of F located outside the United States, subject to approval by an officer of such corporation located in the U.S. office. All services which are rendered to F's foreign licensees are performed by employees of F's offices located outside the United States. None of the income, gain, or loss resulting from the foreign licenses so negotiated by F is attributable to its business office in the United States.

Example (2). N, a foreign corporation, is engaged in the active conduct of the business of distributing motion picture films and television programs. N does not distribute such films or programs in the United States. The foreign distribution rights to these films and programs are acquired by N's U.S. business office from the U.S. owners of these films and programs. Employees of N's offices located in various foreign countries carry on in such countries all the solicitations and negotiations for the licensing of these films and programs to licensees located in such countries and provide the necessary incidental services to the licensees. N's U.S. office collects the rentals from the foreign licensees and maintains the necessary records of income and expense. Officers of N located in the United States also maintain general supervision over the employees of the foreign offices, but the foreign employees conduct the day to day business of N outside the United States of soliciting, negotiating, or performing other activities required to arrange the foreign licenses. None of the income, gain, or loss resulting from the foreign licenses so negotiated by N is attributable to N's U.S. office.

(ii) *Dividends or interest, or gains or losses from sales of stock or securities.*—*(a) In general.*—Dividends or interest from any transaction, or gains or losses on the sale or exchange of stocks or securities, specified in paragraph (b)(2) of §1.864-5, if the office or other fixed place of business either actively participates in soliciting, negotiating, or performing other activities required to arrange, the issue, acquisition, sale, or exchange, of the asset from which such income, gain, or loss is derived or performs significant services incident to such issue, acquisition, sale, or exchange. An office or other fixed place of business in the United States shall not be considered to be a material factor in the realization of income, gain, or loss for purposes of this subdivision merely because the office or other fixed place of business conducts one or more of the following activities: (*1*) collects or accounts for the dividends, interest, gains, or losses, (*2*) exercises general supervision over the activities of the persons directly responsible for carrying on the activities or services described in the immediately preceding sentence, (*3*) performs merely clerical functions incident to the issue, acquisition, sale, or exchange, or (*4*) exercises final approval over the execution of the issue, acquisition, sale, or exchange.

(b) Effective connection of income from stocks or securities with active conduct of a banking, financing, or similar business.—Notwithstanding (*a*) of this subdivision (ii), the determination as to whether any dividends or interest from stocks or securities, or gain or loss from the sale or exchange of stocks or securities which are capital assets, which is from sources without the United States and derived by a nonresident alien individual or a foreign corporation in the active conduct during the taxable year of a banking, financing, or similar business in the United States, shall be treated as effectively connected for such year with the active conduct of that business shall be made by applying the principles of paragraph (c)(5)(ii) of §1.864-4 for determining whether income, gain, or loss of such type from sources within the United States is effectively connected for such year with the active conduct of that business.

(c) Security defined.—For purposes of this subdivision (ii), a security is any bill, note, bond, debenture, or other evidence of indebtedness, or any evidence of an interest in, or right to subscribe to or purchase, any of the foregoing items.

(d) Limitations on application of rules on banking, financing, or similar business.—*(1) Trading for taxpayer's own account.*—The provisions of (*b*) of this subdivision (ii) apply for purposes of determining when certain income, gain, or loss from stocks or securities is effectively connected with the active conduct of a banking, financing, or similar business in the United States. Any dividends, interest, gain, or loss from sources without the United States which by reason of the application of (*b*) of this subdivision (ii) is not effectively connected with the active conduct by a foreign corporation of a banking, financing, or similar business in the United States may be effectively connected for the taxable year, under (*a*) of this subdivision (ii), with the conduct by such taxpayer of a trade or business in the United States which consists of trading in stocks or securities for the taxpayer's own account.

(2) Other income.—For rules relating to dividends or interest from sources without the United States (other than dividends or interest from, or gain or loss from the sale or exchange of, stocks or securities referred to in (*b*) of this subdivision (ii)) derived in the active conduct of a banking, financing, or similar business in the United States, see (*a*) of this subdivision (ii).

(iii) *Sale of goods or merchandise through U.S. office.*—Income, gain, or loss from sales of goods or merchandise specified in paragraph (b)(3) of § 1.864-5, if the office or other fixed place of business actively participates in soliciting the order, negotiating the contract of sale, or performing other significant services necessary for the consummation of the sale which are not the subject of a separate agreement between the seller and the buyer. The office or other fixed place of business in the United States shall be considered a material factor in the realization of income, gain, or loss from a sale made as a result of a sales order received in such office or other fixed place of business except where the sales order is received unsolicited and that office or other fixed place of business is not held out to potential customers as the place to which such sales orders should be sent. The income, gain, or loss must be realized in the ordinary course of the trade or business carried on through the office or other fixed place of business in the United States. Thus, if a foreign corporation is engaged solely in a manufacturing business in the United States, the income derived by its office in the United States as a result of an occasional sale outside the United States is not attributable to the U.S. office if the sales office of the manufacturing business is located outside the United States. On the other hand, if a foreign corporation establishes a sales office in the United States to sell for consumption in the Western Hemisphere merchandise which the corporation produces in Africa, the income derived by the sales office in the United States as a result of an occasional sale made by it in Europe shall be attributable to the U.S. sales office. An office or other fixed place of business in the United States shall not be considered to be a material factor in the realization of income, gain, or loss for purposes of this subdivision merely because of one or more of the following activities: (*a*) the sale is made subject to the final approval of such office or other fixed place of business, (*b*) the property sold is held in, and distributed from, such office or other fixed place of business, (*c*) samples of the property sold are displayed (but not otherwise promoted or sold) in such office or other fixed place of business, or (*d*) such office or other fixed place of business performs merely clerical functions incident to the sale. Activities carried on by employees of an office or other fixed place of business constitute activities of that office or other fixed place of business.

(3) *Limitation where foreign office is a material factor in realization of income.*—(i) *Goods or merchandise destined for foreign use, consumption, or disposition.*—Notwithstanding subparagraphs (1) and (2) of this paragraph, an office or other fixed place of business which a nonresident alien individual or a foreign corporation has in the United States shall not be considered, for purposes of paragraph (a) of this section, to be a material factor in the realization of income, gain or loss from sales of goods or merchandise specified in paragraph (b)(3) of § 1.864-5 if the property is sold for use, consumption, or disposition outside the United States and an office or other fixed place of business, as defined in § 1.864-7, which such nonresident alien individual or foreign corporation has outside the United States participates materially in the sale. For this purpose an office or other fixed place of business which the taxpayer has outside the United States shall be considered to have participated materially in a sale made through the office or other fixed place of business in the United States if the office or other fixed place of business outside the United States actively participates in soliciting the order resulting in the sale, negotiating the contract of sale, or performing other significant services necessary for the consummation of the sale which are not the subject of a separate agreement between the seller and buyer. An office or other fixed place of business which the taxpayer has outside the United States shall not be considered to have participated materially in a sale merely because of one or more of the following activities: (*a*) The sale is made subject to the final approval of such office or other fixed place of business, (*b*) the property sold is held in, and distributed from, such office or other fixed place of business, (*c*) samples of the property sold are displayed (but not otherwise promoted or sold) in such office or other fixed place of business, (*d*) such office or other fixed place of business is used for purposes of having title to the property pass outside the United States, or (*e*) such office or other fixed place of business performs merely clerical functions incident to the sale.

(ii) *Rules for determining country of use, consumption, or disposition.*—(*a*) *In general.*—As a general rule, personal property which is sold to an unrelated person shall be presumed for purposes of this subparagraph to have been sold for use, consumption, or disposition in the country of destination of the property sold; for such purpose, the occurrence in a country of a temporary interruption in shipment of property shall not cause that country to be considered the country of destination. However, if at the time of a sale of personal property to an unrelated person the taxpayer knew, or should have known from the facts and circumstances surrounding the transaction, that the property probably would not be used, consumed, or disposed of in the country of destination, the taxpayer must determine the country of ultimate use, consumption, or disposition of the property or the property shall be presumed to have been sold for use, consumption, or disposition in the United States. A taxpayer who sells personal property to a related person shall be presumed to have sold the property for use, consumption, or disposition in the United States unless the taxpayer establishes the use made of the property by the related person; once he has established that the related person has disposed of the property, the rules in the two immediately preceding sentences relating to sales to an unrelated person shall apply at the first stage in the chain of distribution at which a sale is made by a related person to an unrelated person. Notwithstanding the preceding provisions of this subdivision (*a*), a taxpayer who sells personal property to any person whose principal business consists of selling from inventory to retail customers at retail outlets outside the United States may assume at the time of the sale to that person that the property will be used, consumed, or disposed of outside the United States. For purposes of this (*a*), a person is related to another person if either person owns or controls directly or indirectly the other, or if any third person or persons own or control directly or indirectly both. For this purpose, the term "control" includes any kind of control, whether or not legally enforceable, and however exercised or exercisable. For illustrations of the principles of this subdivision, see paragraph (a)(3)(iv) of § 1.954-3.

(*b*) *Fungible goods.*—For purposes of this subparagraph, a taxpayer who sells to a purchaser personal property which because of its fungible nature cannot reasonably be specifically traced to other purchasers and to the countries of ultimate use, consumption, or disposition shall, unless the taxpayer establishes a different disposition as being proper, treat that property as being sold, for ultimate use, consumption, or disposition in those countries, and to those other purchasers, in the same proportions in which property from the fungible mass of the first purchaser is sold in the ordinary course of business by such first purchaser. No apportionment is required to be made, however, on the basis of sporadic sales by the first purchaser. This (*b*) shall apply only in a case where the taxpayer knew, or should have known from the facts and circumstances surrounding the transaction, the manner in which the first purchaser disposes of property from the fungible mass.

(iii) *Illustration.*—The application of this subparagraph may be illustrated by the following example:

Example. Foreign corporation M has a sales office in the United States during the taxable year through which it sells outside the United States for use in foreign countries industrial electrical generators which such corporation manufactures in a foreign country. M is not a controlled foreign corporation within the meaning of section 957 and the regulations thereunder, and, by reason of its activities in the United States, is engaged in business in the United States during the taxable year. The generators require specialized installation and continuous adjustment and maintenance services. M has an office in foreign country X which is the only organization qualified to perform these installation, adjustment, and maintenance services. During the taxable year M sells several generators through its U.S. office for use in foreign country Y under sales contracts which also provide for installation, adjustment, and maintenance by its office in country X. The generators are installed in country Y by employees of M's office in country X, who also are responsible for the servicing of the equipment. Since the office of M in country X performs significant services incident to these sales which are necessary for their consummation and are not subject of a separate agreement between M and the purchaser, the U.S. office of M is not considered to be a material factor in the realization of the income from the sales and, for purposes of paragraph (a) of this section, such income is not attributable to the U.S. office of that corporation.

(c) *Amount of income, gain, or loss allocable to U.S. office.*—(1) *In general.*—If, in accordance with paragraph (b) of this section, an office or other fixed place of business which a nonresident alien individual or a foreign corporation has in the United States at some time during the taxable year is a material factor in the realization for that year of an item of income, gain, or loss specified in paragraph (b) of § 1.864-5, such item of income, gain, or loss shall be considered to be allocable in its entirety to that office or other fixed place of business. In no case may any income, gain, or loss for the taxable year from sources without the United States, or part thereof, be allocable under this paragraph to an office or other fixed place of business which a nonresident alien individual or a foreign corporation has in the United States if the taxpayer is at no time during the taxable year engaged in a trade or business in the United States.

(2) *Special limitation in case of sales of goods or merchandise through U.S. office.*—Notwithstanding paragraph (c)(1) of this section, the special rules described in this paragraph (c)(2) apply with respect to a sale of goods or merchandise specified in § 1.864-5(b)(3), to which paragraph (b)(3)(i) of this section does not apply. In the case of a nonresident alien with a tax home within the United States, as defined in section 911(d)(3), the amount of income from the sale of goods or merchandise that is properly allocable to the individual's U.S. office is determined under § 1.865-3(d).

(3) *Examples.*—The application of this paragraph (c) may be illustrated by the following examples—

(i) *Example 1. Sales of produced inventory through a U.S. sales office.*—Individual A, who is a nonresident alien within the meaning of section 7701(b)(1)(B) and has a tax home in the United States, manufactures machinery in a foreign country and sells the machinery outside the United States through A's sales office in the United States for use in foreign countries. A is not a nonresident within the meaning of section 865(g)(1)(B). Therefore, § 1.865-3 does not apply to A's sale of the machinery, except to the extent provided in paragraph (c)(2) of this section. Title to the property sold is transferred to the foreign purchaser outside the United States, but no office or other fixed place of business of A in a foreign country materially participates in the sale made through A's U.S. office. By reason of its sales activities in the United States, A is engaged in business in the United States during the taxable year. During the taxable year, A derives a total income of $250,000x from these sales. Under paragraph (c)(2) of this section, the amount of income that is allocable to A's U.S. office is determined under § 1.865-3(d)(2). The taxpayer does not allocate income from the sale under the books and records method described in § 1.865-3(d)(2)(ii). Thus, 50 percent of A's foreign source income of $250,000x, plus any additional income allocable based on the location of production activities under § § 1.865-3(d)(2)(i) and 1.863-3 (in this case, $0x), is effectively connected for the taxable year with the conduct of A's U.S. trade or business, or $125,000x.

(ii) *Example 2. Sales of inventory purchased and resold through a U.S. sales office by a nonresident alien with a tax home in the United States.*—Individual B, who is a nonresident alien within the meaning of section 7701(b)(1)(B) and has a tax home in the United States, has an office in a foreign country that purchases merchandise and sells it through B's sales office in the United States for use in various foreign countries, with title to the property passing outside the United States. B is not a nonresident within the meaning of section 865(g)(1)(B). Therefore, § 1.865-3 does not apply to B's sale of the merchandise, except to the extent provided in paragraph (c)(2) of this section. No other office of B materially participates in these sales made through its U.S. office. By reason of its sales activities in the United States, B is engaged in business in the United States during the taxable year. During the taxable year, B derives income of $300,000x from these sales made through its U.S. sales office. All of B's income from these sales is foreign source as B purchases the merchandise outside the United States and title to the merchandise also passes outside the United States. The amount of income properly allocable to B's U.S. office determined under § 1.865-3(d)(3) is $300,000x, and thus $300,000x is effectively connected for the taxable year with the conduct of B's U.S. trade or business.

(iii) *Example 3. Foreign sales office also materially participates in sale.*—The facts are the same as in paragraph (c)(3)(ii) of this section (the facts in *Example 2*), except that B also has an office in a foreign country that is a material factor in the realization of income from the sales made through B's U.S. office. No income from the sale of merchandise is allocable to B's U.S. sales office for the taxable year, by reason of paragraph (b)(3)(i) of this section, and thus none of the $300,000x is effectively connected for the taxable year with the conduct of B's U.S. trade or business.

(iv) *Example 4. Sales of inventory purchased and resold through a U.S. sales office by a foreign corporation.*—The facts are the same as in paragraph (c)(3)(ii) of this section (the facts in *Example 2*), except that B is a foreign corporation. B is a nonresident within the meaning of section 865(g)(1)(B). The income from such sales will be sourced in accordance with § 1.865-3(a) and (d)(3).

(4) *Applicability date.*—Paragraph (c)(2) of this section applies to taxable years ending on or after December 23, 2019. However, a taxpayer may apply paragraph (c)(2) of this section in its entirety for taxable years beginning after December 31, 2017, and ending before December 23, 2019, provided that the taxpayer and all persons related to the taxpayer (within the meaning of section 267 or 707) apply paragraph (c)(2) of this section and § § 1.863-1(b), 1.863-2(b), 1.863-3, 1.863-8(b)(3)(ii), 1.864-5(a) and (b), and 1.865-3 in their entirety for the taxable year, and once applied, the taxpayer and all persons related to the taxpayer (within the meaning of section 267 or 707) continue to apply these regulations in their entirety for all subsequent taxable years. For regulations generally applicable to taxable years ending before December 23, 2019, see § 1.864-6 as contained in 26 CFR part 1 revised as of April 1, 2020. [Reg. § 1.864-6.]

□ [*T.D. 7216, 11-2-72. Amended by T.D. 9921, 12-10-2020.*]

§ 1.864-7. Definition of office or other fixed place of business.—(a) *In general.*—(1) This section applies for purposes of determining whether a nonresident alien individual or a foreign corporation that is engaged in a trade or business in the United States at some time during a taxable year beginning after December 31, 1966, has an office or other fixed place of business in the United States for purposes of applying section 864(c)(4)(B) and § 1.864-6 to income, gain, or loss specified in paragraph (b) of § 1.864-5 from sources without the United States or has an office or other fixed place of business outside the United States for purposes of applying section 864(c)(4)(B)(iii) and paragraph (b)(3)(i) of § 1.864-6 to sales of goods or merchandise for use, consumption, or disposition outside the United States.

(2) In making a determination under this section due regard shall be given to the facts and circumstances of each case, particularly to the nature of the taxpayer's trade or business and the physical facilities actually required by the taxpayer in the ordinary course of the conduct of his trade or business.

(3) The law of a foreign country shall not be controlling in determining whether a nonresident alien individual or a foreign corporation has an office or other fixed place of business.

(b) *Fixed facilities.*—(1) *In general.*—As a general rule, an office or other fixed place of business is a fixed facility, that is, a place, site, structure, or other similar facility, through which a nonresident alien individual or a foreign corporation engages in a trade or business. For this purpose an office or other fixed place of business shall include, but shall not be limited to, a factory; a store or other sales outlet; a workshop; or a mine, quarry, or other place of extraction of natural resources. A fixed facility may be considered an office or other fixed place of business whether or not the facility is continuously used by a nonresident alien individual or foreign corporation.

(2) *Use of another person's office or other fixed place of business.*—A nonresident alien individual or a foreign corporation shall not be considered to have an office or other fixed place of business merely because such alien individual or foreign corporation uses another person's office or other fixed place of business, whether or not the office or place of business of a related person, through which to transact a trade or business, if the trade or business activities of the alien individual or foreign corporation in that office or other fixed place of business are relatively sporadic or infrequent, taking into account the overall needs and conduct of that trade or business.

(c) *Management activity.*—A foreign corporation shall not be considered to have an office or other fixed place of business merely because a person controlling that corporation has an office or other fixed place of business from which general supervision and control over the policies of the foreign corporation are exercised. The fact that top management decisions affecting the foreign corporation are made in a country shall not of itself mean that the foreign corporation has an office or other fixed place of business in that country. For example, a foreign sales corporation which is a wholly owned subsidiary of a domestic corporation shall not be considered to have an office or other fixed place of business in the United States merely because of the presence in the United States of officers of the domestic parent corporation who are generally responsible only for the policy decisions affecting the foreign sales corporation, provided that the foreign corporation has a chief executive officer, whether or not he is also an officer of the domestic parent corporation, who conducts the day-to-day trade or business of the foreign corporation from a foreign office. The result in this example would be the same even if the executive officer should (1) regularly confer with the officers of the domestic parent corporation, (2) occasionally visit the U.S. office of the domestic parent corporation, and (3) during such visits to the United States temporarily conduct the business of the foreign subsidiary corporation out of the domestic parent corporation's office in the United States.

(d) *Agent activity.*—(1) *Dependent agents.*—(i) *In general.*—In determining whether a nonresident alien individual or a foreign corporation has an office or other fixed place of business, the office or other fixed place of business of an agent who is not an independent agent, as defined in subparagraph (3) of this paragraph, shall be disregarded unless such agent (*a*) has the authority to negotiate and conclude contracts in the name of the nonresident alien individual or foreign corporation, and regularly exercises that authority, or (*b*) has a stock of merchandise belonging to the nonresident alien individual or foreign corporation from which orders are regularly filed on behalf of such alien individual or foreign corporation. A person who purchases goods from a nonresident alien individual or a foreign corporation shall not be considered to be an agent for such alien individual or foreign corporation for purposes of this paragraph where such person is carrying on such purchasing activities in the ordinary course of its own business, even though such person is related in some manner to the nonresident alien individual or foreign corporation. For example, a wholly owned domestic subsidiary corporation of a foreign corporation shall not be treated as an agent of the foreign parent corporation merely because the subsidiary corporation purchases goods from the foreign parent corporation and resells them in its own name. However, if the domestic subsidiary corporation regularly negotiates and concludes contracts in the name of its foreign parent corporation or maintains a stock of merchandise from which it regularly fills orders on behalf of the foreign parent corporation, the office or other fixed place of business of the domestic subsidiary corporation shall be treated as the office or other fixed place of business of the foreign parent corporation unless the domestic subsidiary corporation is an independent agent within the meaning of subparagraph (3) of this paragraph.

(ii) *Authority to conclude contracts or fill orders.*—For purposes of subdivision (i) of this subparagraph, an agent shall be considered regularly to exercise authority to negotiate and conclude contracts or regularly to fill orders on behalf of his foreign principal only if the authority is exercised, or the orders are filled, with some frequency over a continuous period of time. This determination shall be made on the basis of the facts and circumstances in each case, taking into account the nature of the business of the principal; but, in all cases, the frequency and continuity tests are to be applied conjunctively. Regularity shall not be evidenced by occasional or incidental activity. An agent shall not be considered regularly to negotiate and conclude contracts on behalf of his foreign principal if the agent's authority to negotiate and conclude contracts is limited only to unusual cases or such authority must be separately secured by the agent from his principal with respect to each transaction effected.

(2) *Independent agents.*—The office or other fixed place of business of an independent agent, as defined in subparagraph (3) of this paragraph, shall not be treated as the office or other fixed place of business of his principal who is a nonresident alien individual or a foreign corporation, irrespective of whether such agent has authority to negotiate and conclude contracts in the name of his principal, and regularly exercises that authority, or maintains a stock of goods from which he regularly fills orders on behalf of his principal.

(3) *Definition of independent agent.*—(i) *In general.*—For purposes of this paragraph, the term "independent agent" means a general commission agent, broker, or other agent of an independent status acting in the ordinary course of his business in that capacity. Thus, for example, an agent who, in pursuance of his usual trade or business, and for compensation, sell goods or merchandise consigned or entrusted to his possession, management, and control for that purpose by or for the owner of such goods or merchandise is an independent agent.

(ii) *Related persons.*—The determination of whether an agent is an independent agent for purposes of this paragraph shall be made without regard to facts indicating that either the agent or the principal owns or controls directly or indirectly the other or that a third person or persons own or control directly or indirectly both. For example, a wholly owned domestic subsidiary corporation of a foreign corporation which acts as an agent for the foreign parent corporation may be treated as acting in the capacity of independent agent for the foreign parent corporation. The facts and circumstances of a specific case shall determine whether the agent, while acting for his principal, is acting in pursuance of his usual trade or business and in such manner as to constitute him an independent agent in his relations with the nonresident alien individual or foreign corporation.

(iii) *Exclusive agents.*—Where an agent who is otherwise an independent agent within the meaning of subdivision (i) of this subparagraph acts in such capacity exclusively, or almost exclusively, for one principal who is a nonresident alien individual or a foreign corporation, the facts and circumstances of a particular case shall be taken into account in determining whether the agent, while acting in that capacity, may be classified as an independent agent.

(e) *Employee activity.*—Ordinarily, an employee of a nonresident alien individual or a foreign corporation shall be treated as a dependent agent to whom the rules of paragraph (d)(1) of this section apply if such employer does not in and of itself have a fixed facility (as defined in paragraph (b) of this section) in the United States or outside the United States, as the case may be. However, where the employee, in the ordinary course of his duties, carries on the trade or business of his employer in or through a fixed facility of such employer which is regularly used by the employee in the course of carrying out such duties, such fixed facility shall be considered the office or other fixed place of business of the employer, irrespective of the rules of paragraph (d)(1) of this section. The application of this paragraph may be illustrated by the following example:

Example. M, a foreign corporation, opens a showroom office in the United States for the purpose of promoting its sales of merchandise which it purchases in foreign country X. The employees of the U.S. office, consisting of salesmen and general clerks, are empowered only to run the office, to arrange for the appointment of distributing agents for the merchandise offered by M, and to solicit orders generally. These employees do not have the authority to negotiate and conclude contracts in the name of M, nor do they have a stock of merchandise from which to fill orders on behalf of M. Any negotiations entered into by these employees are under M's instructions and subject to its approval as to any decision reached. The only independent authority which the employees have is in the appointment of distributors to whom M is to sell merchandise, but even this authority is subject to the right of M to approve or disapprove these buyers on receipt of information as to their business standing. Under the circumstances, this office used by a group of salesmen for sales promotion is a fixed place of business which M has in the United States.

(f) *Office or other fixed place of business of a related person.*—The fact that a nonresident alien individual or a foreign corporation is related in some manner to another person who has an office or other fixed place of business shall not of itself mean that such office or other fixed place of business of the other person is the office or other fixed place of business of the nonresident alien individual or foreign corporation. Thus, for example, the U.S. office of foreign corporation M, a wholly owned subsidiary corporation of foreign corporation N, shall not be considered the office or other fixed place of business of N unless the facts and circumstances show that N is engaged in trade or business in the United States through that office or other fixed place of business. However, see paragraph (b)(2) of this section.

(g) *Illustrations.*—The application of this section may be illustrated by the following examples:

Example (1). S, a foreign corporation, is engaged in the business of buying and selling tangible personal property. S is a wholly owned subsidiary of P, a domestic corporation engaged in the business of buying and selling similar property, which has an office in the United States. Officers of P are generally responsible for the policies followed by S and are directors of S, but S has an independent group of officers, none of whom are regularly employed in the United States. In addition to this group of officers, S has a chief executive officer, D, who is also an officer of P but who is permanently stationed outside the United States. The day-to-day conduct of S's business is handled by D and the other officers of such corporation, but they regularly confer with the officers of P and on occasion temporarily visit P's offices in the United States, at which time they continue to conduct the business of S. S does not have an office or other fixed place of business in the United States for purposes of this section.

Example (2). The facts are the same as in example (1) except that, on rare occasions, an employee of P receives an order which he, after consultation with officials of S and because P cannot fill the order, accepts on behalf of S rather than on behalf of P. P does not hold itself out as a person which those wishing to do business with S should contact. Assuming that orders for S are seldom handled in this manner and that they do not constitute a significant part of that corporation's business, S shall not be considered to have an office or other fixed place of business in the United States because of these activities of an employee of P.

Example (3). The facts are the same as in example (1) except that all orders received by S are subject to review by an officer of P before acceptance. S has a business office in the United States.

Example (4). S, a foreign corporation organized under the laws of Puerto Rico, is engaged in the business of manufacturing dresses in Puerto Rico and is entitled to an income tax exemption under the Puerto Rico Industrial Incentive Act of 1963. S is a wholly owned subsidiary of P, a domestic corporation engaged in the business of buying and selling dresses to customers in the United States. S sells most of the dresses it produces to P, the assumption being made that the income from these sales is derived from sources without the United States. P in turn sells these dresses in the United States in its name and through the efforts of its own employees and of distributors appointed by it. S does not have a fixed facility in the United States, and none of its employees are stationed in the United States. On occasion, employees of S visit the office of P in the United States, and executives of P visit the office of S in Puerto Rico, to discuss with one another matters of mutual business interest involving both corporations, including the strategy for marketing the dresses produced by S. These matters are also regularly discussed by such persons by telephone calls between the United States and Puerto Rico. S's employees do not otherwise participate in P's marketing activities. Officers of P are generally responsible for the policies followed by S and are directors of S, but S has a chief executive officer in Puerto Rico who, from its office therein, handles the day-to-day conduct of S's business. Based upon the facts presented, and assuming there are no other facts which would lead to a different determination, S shall not be considered to have an office or other fixed place of business in the United States for purposes of this section.

Example (5). The facts are the same as in example (4) except that the dresses are manufactured by S in styles and designs furnished by P and out of goods and raw materials purchased by P and sold to S. Based upon the facts presented, and assuming there are no other facts which would lead to a different determination, S shall not be considered to have an office or other fixed place of business in the United States for purposes of this section.

Example (6). The facts are the same as in example (5) except that pursuant to the instructions of P, the dresses sold by P are shipped by S directly to P's customers in the United States. Based upon the facts presented, and assuming there are no other facts which would lead to a different determination, S shall not be considered to have an office or other fixed place of business in the United States for purposes of this section. [Reg. § 1.864-7.]

☐ [*T.D.* 7216, 11-2-72.]

§ 1.864-8T. Treatment of related person factoring income (temporary).—(a) *Applicability.*—(1) *General rule.*—This section applies for purposes of determining the treatment of income derived by a person from a trade or service receivable acquired from a related person. Except as provided in paragraph (d) of this section, if a person acquires (directly or indirectly) a trade or service receivable from a related person, any income (including any stated interest, discount or service fee) derived from the trade or service receivable shall be treated as if it were interest received on a loan to the obligor under the receivable. The characterization of income as interest pursuant to this section shall apply only for purposes of sections 551-558 (relating to foreign personal holding companies), sections 951-964 (relating to controlled foreign corporations), and section 904 (relating to the limitation on the foreign tax credit) of the Code and the regulations thereunder. The principles of sections 861 through 863 and the regulations thereunder shall be applied to determine the source of such interest income for purposes of section 904.

(2) *Override.*—With respect to income characterized as interest under this section, the special rules of section 864(d) and this section override any conflicting provisions of the Code and regulations relating to foreign personal holding companies, controlled foreign corporations, and the foreign tax credit limitation. Thus, for example, pursuant to section 864(d)(5) and paragraph (e) of this section, stated interest derived from a factored trade or service receivable is not eligible for the subpart F de minimis rule of section 954(b)(3), the same country exception of section 954(c)(3)(A)(i), or the special rules for export financing interest of sections 904(d)(2) and 954(c)(2)(B), even if in the absence of this section the treatment of such stated interest would be governed by those sections.

(3) *Limitation.*—Section 864(d) and this section apply only with respect to the tax treatment of income derived from a trade or service receivable acquired from a related person. Therefore, neither section 864(d) nor this section affects the characterization of an expense or loss of either the seller of a receivable or the obligor under a receivable. Accordingly, the obligor under a trade or service receivable shall not be allowed to treat any part of the purchase price of property or services as interest (other than amounts treated as interest under provisions other than section 864(d)).

(b) *Definitions.*—The following definitions apply for purposes of this section and § 1.956-3T.

(1) *Trade or service receivable.*—The term "trade or service receivable" means any account receivable or evidence of indebtedness, whether or not issued at a discount and whether or not bearing stated interest, arising out of the disposition by a related person of property described in section 1221(l) (hereinafter referred to as "inventory property") or the performance of services by a related person.

(2) *Related person.*—A "related person" is:

(i) A person who is a related person within the meaning of section 267(b) and the regulations thereunder;

(ii) A United States shareholder (as defined in section 951(b)); or

(iii) A person who is related (within the meaning of section 267(b) and the regulations thereunder) to a United States shareholder.

(c) *Acquisition of a trade or service receivable.*—(1) *General rule.*—A trade or service receivable is considered to be acquired by a person at the time when that person is entitled to receive all or a portion of the income from the trade or service receivable. A person who acquires a trade or service receivable (hereinafter referred to as the "factor") is considered to have acquired a trade or service receivable regardless of whether:

(i) The acquisition is characterized for federal income tax purposes as a sale, a pledge of collateral for a loan, an assignment, a capital contribution, or otherwise;

(ii) The factor takes title to or obtains physical possession of the trade or service receivable;

(iii) The related person assigns the trade or service receivable with or without recourse;

(iv) The factor or some other person is obligated to collect the payments due under the trade or service receivable;

(v) The factor is liable for all property, excise, sales, or similar taxes due upon collection of the receivable;

(vi) The factor advances the entire face amount of the trade or service receivable transferred;

(vii) All trade or service receivables assigned by the related person are assigned to one factor; and

(viii) The obligor under the trade or service receivable is notified of the assignment.

(2) *Example.*—The following example illustrates the application of paragraphs (a), (b), and (c)(1) of this section.

Example. P, a domestic corporation, owns all of the outstanding stock of FS, a controlled foreign corporation. P manufactures and sells paper products to customers, including X, an unrelated domestic corporation. As part of a sales transaction, P takes back a trade receivable from X and sells the receivable to FS. Because FS has acquired a trade or service receivable from a related person, the income derived by FS from P's receivable is interest income described in paragraph (a)(1) of this section.

(3) *Indirect acquisitions.*—(i) *Acquisition through unrelated person.*—A trade or service receivable will be considered to be acquired from a related person if it is acquired from an unrelated person who acquired (directly or indirectly) such receivable from a person who is a related person to the factor. The following example illustrates the application of this paragraph (c)(3)(i).

Example. A, a United States citizen, owns all of the outstanding stock of FPHC, a foreign personal holding company. A performs engineering services within and without the United States for customers, including X, an unrelated corporation. A performs engineering services for X and takes back a service receivable. A sells the receivable to Y, an unrelated corporation engaged in the factoring business. Y resells the receivable to FPHC. Because FPHC has indirectly acquired a service receivable from a related person, the income derived by FPHC from A's receivable is interest income described in paragraph (a)(1) of this section.

(ii) *Acquisition by nominee or pass-through entity.*—A factor will be considered to have acquired a trade or service receivable held on its behalf by a nominee or by a partnership, simple trust, S corporation or other pass-through entity to the extent the factor owns (directly or indirectly) a beneficial interest in such partnership or other pass-through entity. The rule of this paragraph (c)(3)(ii) does not limit the application of paragraph (c)(3)(iii) of this section regarding the characterization of trade or service receivables of unrelated persons acquired pursuant to certain swap or pooling arrangements. The following example illustrates the application of this paragraph (c)(3)(ii).

Example. FS1, a controlled foreign corporation, acquires a 20 percent limited partnership interest in PS, a partnership. PS purchases trade or service receivables resulting from the sale of inventory property by FS1's domestic parent, P. PS does not purchase receivables of any person who is related to any other partner in PS. FS1 is considered to have acquired a 20 percent interest in the receivables acquired by PS. Thus, FS1's distributive share of the income derived by PS from the receivables of P is considered to be interest income described in paragraph (a)(1) of this section.

(iii) *Swap or pooling arrangements.*—A trade or service receivable of a person unrelated to the factor will be considered to be a trade or service receivable acquired from a related person and subject to the rules of this section if it is acquired in accordance with an arrangement that involves two or more groups of related persons that are unrelated to each other and the effect of the arrangement is that one or more related persons in each group acquire (directly or indirectly) trade or service receivables of one or more unrelated persons who are also parties to the arrangement, in exchange for reciprocal purchases of the first group's receivables. The following example illustrates the application of this paragraph (c)(3)(iii).

Example. Controlled foreign corporations A, B, C, and D are wholly-owned subsidiaries of domestic corporations M, N, O, and P, respectively. M, N, O, and P are not related persons. According to a prearranged plan, A, B, C, and D each acquire trade or service receivables of M, N, O, and/or P, except that neither A, B, C nor D acquires receivables of its own parent corporation. Because the effect of this arrangement is that the unrelated groups acquire each other's trade or service receivables pursuant to the arrangement, income derived by A, B, C, and D from the receivables acquired from M, N, O, and P is interest income described in paragraph (a)(1) of this section.

(iv) *Financing arrangements.*—If a controlled foreign corporation (as defined in section 957(a)) participates (directly or indirectly) in a lending transaction that results in a loan to the purchaser of inventory property, services, or trade or service receivables of a related person (or a loan to a person who is related to the purchaser), and if the loan would not have been made or maintained on the same terms but for the corresponding purchase, then the controlled foreign corporation shall be considered to have indirectly acquired a trade or service receivable, and income derived by the controlled foreign corporation from such a loan shall be considered to be income described in paragraph (a)(1) of this section. For purposes of this paragraph (c)(3)(iv), it is immaterial that the sums lent are not, in fact, the sums used to finance the purchase of a related person's inventory property, services, or trade or service receivables. The amount of income derived by the controlled foreign corporation to be taken into account shall be the total amount of income derived from a lending transaction described in this paragraph (c)(3)(iv), if the amount lent is less than or equal to the purchase price of the inventory property, services, or trade or service receivables. If the amount lent is greater than the purchase price of the inventory property, services or receivables, the amount to be taken into account shall be the proportion of the interest charge (including original issue discount) that the purchase price bears to the total amount lent pursuant to the lending transaction. The following examples illustrate the application of this paragraph (c)(3)(iv).

Example (1). P, a domestic corporation, owns all of the outstanding stock of FS1, a controlled foreign corporation engaged in the financing business in Country X. P manufactures and sells toys, including sales to C, an unrelated corporation. Prior to P's sale of toys to C for $2,000, D, a wholly-owned Country X subsidiary of C, borrows $3,000 from FS1. The loan from FS1 to D would not have been made or maintained on the same terms but for C's purchase of toys from P. Two-thirds of the income derived by FS1 from the loan to D is interest income described in paragraph (a)(1) of this section.

Example (2). P, a domestic corporation, owns all of the outstanding stock of FS1, a controlled foreign corporation organized under the laws of Country X. FS1 has accumulated cash reserves. P has uncollected trade and service receivables of foreign obligors. FS1 makes a $1,000 loan to U, a foreign corporation that is unrelated to P or FS1. U purchases P's trade and service receivables for $2,000. The loan would not have been made or maintained on the same terms but for U's purchase of P's receivables. The income derived by U from the receivables is not interest income within the meaning of paragraph (a) of this section. However, the interest paid by U to FS1 is interest income described in paragraph (a)(1) of this section.

Example (3). The facts are the same as in Example (2), except that U is a wholly-owned Country Y subsidiary of FS1. Because U is related to P within the meaning of paragraph (b)(2) of this section, under paragraph (c)(1) of this section, income derived by U from P's receivables is interest income described in paragraph (a)(1) of this section. In addition, the income derived by FS1 from the loan to U is interest income described in paragraph (a)(1) of this section.

(d) *Same country exception.*—(1) *Income from trade or service receivables.*—Income derived from a trade or service receivable acquired from a related person shall not be treated as interest income described in paragraph (a)(1) of this section if:

(i) The person acquiring the trade or service receivable and the related person are created or organized under the laws of the same foreign country;

(ii) The related person has a substantial part of its assets used in its trade or business located in such foreign country; and

(iii) The related person would not have derived foreign base company income, as defined in section 954(a) and the regulations thereunder, or income effectively connected with a United States trade or business from such receivable if the related person had collected the receivable.

For purposes of paragraph (d)(1)(ii) of this section, the standards contained in § 1.954-2(e) shall apply in determining the location of a substantial part of the assets of a related person. For purposes of paragraph (d)(1)(iii) of this section, a determination of whether the related person would have derived foreign base company income shall be made without regard to the de minimis test described in section 954(b)(3)(A). The following examples illustrate the application of this paragraph (d)(1).

Example (1). FS1, a controlled foreign corporation incorporated under the laws of Country X, owns all of the outstanding stock of FS2, which is also incorporated under the laws of Country X. FS1 has a substantial part of its assets used in its business in Country X. FS1 manufactures and sells toys for use in Country Y. The toys sold are considered to be manufactured in Country X under § 1.954-3(a)(2). FS1 is not considered to have a branch or similar establishment in Country Y that is treated as a separate corporation under section 954(d)(2) and § 1.954-3(b). Thus, gross income derived by FS1 from the toy sales is not foreign base company sales income. FS1 takes back receivables without stated interest from its customers. FS1 assigns those receivables to FS2. The income derived by FS2 from the receivables of FS1 is not interest income described in paragraph (a)(1) of this section, because it satisfies the same country exception under paragraph (d)(1) of this section.

Example (2). The facts are the same as in Example (1), except that the toys sold by FS1 are purchased from FS1's U.S. parent and are sold for use outside of Country X. Thus, any income derived by FS1 from the sale of the toys would be foreign base company sales income. Therefore, income derived by FS2 from the receivables of FS1 is interest income described in paragraph (a)(1) of this section. FS2 is considered to derive interest income from the receivable even if, solely by reason of the de minimis rule of section 954(b)(3)(A), FS1 would not have derived foreign base company income if FS1 had collected the receivable.

(2) *Income from financing arrangements.*—Income derived by a controlled foreign corporation from a loan to a person that purchases inventory property or services of a person that is related to the controlled foreign corporation, or from other loans described in paragraph (c)(3)(iv) of this section, shall not be treated as interest income described in paragraph (a)(1) of this section if:

(i) The person providing the financing and the related person are created or organized under the laws of the same foreign country;

(ii) The related person has a substantial part of its assets used in its trade or business located in such foreign country; and

(iii) The related person would not have derived foreign base company income or income effectively connected with a United States trade or business:

(A) From the sale of inventory property or services to the borrower or from financing the borrower's purchase of inventory property or services, in the case of a loan to the purchaser of inventory property or services of a related person; or

(B) From collecting amounts due under the receivable or from financing the purchase of the receivable, in the case of a loan to the purchaser of a trade or service receivable of a related person.

For purposes of paragraph (d)(2)(ii) of this section, the standards contained in § 1.954-2(e) shall apply in determining the location of a substantial part of the assets of a related person. For purposes of paragraph (d)(2)(iii) of this section, a determination of whether the related person would have derived foreign base company income shall be made without regard to the de minimis test described in section 954(b)(3)(A). The following examples illustrate the application of this paragraph (d)(2).

Example (1). FS1, a controlled foreign corporation incorporated under the laws of Country X, owns all of the outstanding stock of FS2, which is also incorporated under the laws of Country X. FS1, which has a substantial part of its assets used in its business located in Country X, manufactures and sells toys for use in Country Y. The toys sold are considered to be manufactured in Country X under § 1.954-3(a)(2). FS1 is not considered to have a branch or similar establishment in Country Y that is treated as a separate corporation under section 954(d)(2) and § 1.954-3(b). Thus, the gross income derived by FS1 from the toy sales is not foreign base company sales income. FS2 makes a loan to FS3, a wholly-owned subsidiary of FS1 which is also incorporated under the laws of Country X, in connection with FS3's purchase of toys from FS1. FS3 does not earn any subpart F gross income. Thus, FS1 would not have derived foreign personal holding company interest income if FS1 had made the loan to FS3, because the interest would be covered by the same country exception of section 954(c)(3). Therefore, the income derived by FS2 from its loan to FS3 is not treated as interest income described in paragraph (a)(1) of this section, because it satisfies the same country exception under paragraph (d)(2) of this section. Such income is also not treated as foreign personal holding company income described in section 954(c)(1)(A) because the same country exception of section 954(c)(3) also applies to the interest actually derived by FS2 from its loan to FS3.

Example (2). FS1, a controlled foreign corporation incorporated under the laws of Country X, owns all of the outstanding stock of FS2, which is also incorporated under the laws of Country X. FS1 purchases toys from its U.S. parent and resells them for use outside of Country X. As part of a sales transaction, FS1 takes back trade receivables. FS2 makes a loan to U, an unrelated corporation, to finance U's purchase of FS1's trade receivables. Because FS1 would have derived foreign base company income if FS1 had collected the receivables or made the loan itself, the same country exception of paragraph (d)(2) of this section does not apply. Accordingly, under paragraph (c)(3)(iv) of this section, the income derived by FS2 from its loan to U is treated as interest income described in paragraph (a)(1) of this section.

(e) *Special rules.*—(1) *Foreign personal holding companies and controlled foreign corporations.*—For purposes of sections 551-558 (relating to foreign personal holding companies), the exclusion provided by section 552(c) for interest described in section 954(c)(3)(A) shall not apply to income described in paragraph (a)(1) of this section. For purposes of the sections 951-964 (relating to controlled foreign corporations), income described in paragraph (a)(1) of this section shall be included in a United States shareholder's pro rata share of a controlled foreign corporation's subpart F income without regard to the de minimis rule under section 954(b)(3)(A). However, income described in paragraph (a)(1) of this section shall be included in the computation of a controlled foreign corporation's foreign base company income for purposes of applying the de minimis rule under section 954(b)(3)(A) and the more than 70 percent of gross income test under section 954(b)(3)(B). In addition, income described in paragraph (a)(1) of this section shall be considered to be subpart F income without regard to the exclusions from foreign base company income provided by section 954(c)(2)(B) (relating to export financing interest derived in the conduct of a banking business) and section 954(c)(3)(A)(i) (relating to certain interest income received from related persons).

(2) *Foreign tax credit.*—Income described in paragraph (a)(1) of this section shall be considered to be interest income for purposes of the section 904 foreign tax credit limitation and is not eligible for the exceptions for export financing interest provided in section 904(d)(2)(A)(iii)(II), (B)(ii), and (C)(iii). In addition, such income will be subject to the look-through rule for subpart F income set forth in section 904(d)(3) without regard to the de minimis exception provided in section 904(d)(3)(E).

(3) *Possessions corporations.*—(i) *Limitation on credit.*—Income described in paragraph (a)(1) of this section shall not be treated as income described in section 936(a)(1)(A) or (B) unless the income is considered under the principles of § 1.863-6 to be derived from sources within the possessions. Thus, the credit provided by section 936 is not available for income described in paragraph (a)(1) of this section unless the obligor under the receivable is a resident of a possession. In the case of a loan described in section 864(d)(6), the credit provided by section 936 is not available for income described in paragraph (a)(1) of this section unless the purchaser of the inventory property or services is a resident of a possession.

(ii) *Eligibility determination.*—Notwithstanding the limitation on the availability of the section 936 credit for income described in paragraph (a)(1) of this section, if income treated as interest income under paragraph (a)(1) of this section is derived from sources within a possession (determined without regard to this section), such income shall be eligible for inclusion in a corporation's gross income for purposes of section 936(a)(2)(A). If such income is derived from the active conduct of a trade or business within a possession (determined without regard to this section), such income shall be eligible for inclusion in a corporation's gross income for purposes of section 936(a)(2)(B). (These rules apply for purposes of determining whether a corporation is eligible to elect the credit provided under section 936(a)).

(iii) *Example.*—The following example illustrates the application of paragraph (e)(3) of this section.

Example. Corporation X is operating in a possession as a possessions corporation. In 1985, X earned $50,000 from the active conduct of a business in the possession, including $5,000 from trade or service receivables acquired from a related party. Obligors under the receivables acquired by X are not residents of the possession. Corporation X also earned $20,000 from activities other than its active conduct of business in the possession. The $5,000 derived by X from the receivables is not eligible for the section 936 credit. However, the $5,000 may be used by X to meet the percentage tests under section 936(a)(2) to the extent that such income is considered to be derived from sources within the possession (for purposes of section 936(a)(2)(A)) or is considered to be derived from the active conduct of a trade or business in the possession (for purposes of section 936(a)(2)(B)), in either case determined without regard to the characterization of such income under this section.

(f) *Effective date.*—The provisions of this section shall apply with respect to accounts receivable and evidences of indebtedness transferred after March 1, 1984 and are effective June 14, 1988. [Temporary Reg. § 1.864-8T.]

[*T.D.* 8209, 6-13-88.]

§ 1.864(c)(8)-1. Gain or loss by foreign persons on the disposition of certain partnership interests.—(a) *Overview.*—This section provides rules and definitions under section 864(c)(8). Paragraph (b) of this section provides the general rule treating gain or loss recognized by a nonresident alien individual or foreign corporation from the sale or exchange of a partnership interest as effectively connected gain or effectively connected loss. Paragraph (c) of this section provides rules for determining the limitations on the amount of effectively connected gain or effectively connected loss under section 864(c)(8) and paragraph (b) of this section. Paragraph (d) of this section provides rules regarding coordination with section 897. Paragraph (e) of this section provides rules regarding certain tiered partnerships. Paragraph (f) of this section provides rules regarding U.S. income tax treaties. Paragraph (g) of this section provides definitions. Paragraph (h) of this section provides a rule regarding certain contributions of property to a partnership. Paragraph (i) of this section contains examples illustrating the rules set forth in this section. Paragraph (j) of this section provides the applicability date.

(b) *Gain or loss treated as effectively connected gain or loss.*—(1) *In general.*—Notwithstanding any other provision of subtitle A of the Internal Revenue Code, if a foreign transferor owns, directly or indirectly, an interest in a partnership that is engaged in the conduct of a trade or business within the United States, outside capital gain, outside capital loss, outside ordinary gain, or outside ordinary loss (each as defined in paragraph (b)(2) of this section) recognized by the foreign transferor on the transfer of all (or any portion) of the interest is treated as effectively connected gain or effectively connected loss, subject to the limitations described in paragraph (b)(3) of this section. Except as provided in paragraph (d) of this section, this section does not apply to prevent any portion of the gain or loss that is otherwise treated as effectively connected gain or effectively connected loss under provisions of the Internal Revenue Code other than section 864(c)(8) from being so treated.

(2) *Determination of outside gain and loss.*—(i) *In general.*—The amount of gain or loss recognized by the foreign transferor in connection with the transfer of its partnership interest is determined under all relevant provisions of the Internal Revenue Code and the regulations thereunder. See, e.g., §§1.741-1(a) and 1.751-1(a)(2). For purposes of this section, the amount of gain or loss that is treated as capital gain or capital loss under sections 741 and 751 is referred to as *outside capital gain* or *outside capital loss*, respectively. The amount of gain or loss that is treated as ordinary gain or ordinary loss under sections 741 and 751 is referred to as *outside ordinary gain* or *outside ordinary loss*, respectively.

(ii) *Nonrecognition provisions.*—A foreign transferor's gain or loss recognized in connection with the transfer of its partnership interest does not include gain or loss to the extent that the gain or loss is not recognized by reason of one or more nonrecognition provisions of the Internal Revenue Code.

(3) *Limitations.*—For purposes of applying this section, this paragraph (b)(3) limits the amount of gain or loss recognized by a foreign transferor that may be treated as effectively connected gain or effectively connected loss.

(i) *Capital gain limitation.*—Outside capital gain recognized by a foreign transferor is treated as effectively connected gain to the extent it does not exceed aggregate deemed sale EC capital gain determined under paragraph (c)(3)(ii)(B) of this section.

(ii) *Capital loss limitation.*—Outside capital loss recognized by a foreign transferor is treated as effectively connected loss to the extent it does not exceed aggregate deemed sale EC capital loss determined under paragraph (c)(3)(ii)(B) of this section.

(iii) *Ordinary gain limitation.*—Outside ordinary gain recognized by a foreign transferor is treated as effectively connected gain to the extent it does not exceed aggregate deemed sale EC ordinary gain determined under paragraph (c)(3)(ii)(A) of this section.

(iv) *Ordinary loss limitation.*—Outside ordinary loss recognized by a foreign transferor is treated as effectively connected loss to the extent it does not exceed aggregate deemed sale EC ordinary loss determined under paragraph (c)(3)(ii)(A) of this section.

(c) *Amount treated as effectively connected with the conduct of a trade or business within the United States.*—This paragraph (c) describes the steps to be followed in computing the limitations described in paragraph (b)(3) of this section.

(1) *Step 1: Determine deemed sale gain and loss.*—Determine the amount of gain or loss that the partnership would recognize with respect to each of its assets (other than interests in partnerships described in paragraph (e) of this section) upon a deemed sale of all of the partnership's assets on the date of the transfer of the partnership interest described in paragraph (b)(1) of this section (deemed sale). For this purpose, a deemed sale is treated as a sale by the partnership to an unrelated person of each of its assets (tangible and intangible) in a fully taxable transaction for cash in an amount equal to the fair market value of each asset (taking into account section 7701(g)) immediately before the partner's transfer of the interest in the partnership. For rules concerning the deemed sale of certain partnership interests, see paragraph (e) of this section.

(2) *Step 2: Determine deemed sale EC gain and loss.*—(i) *In general.*—(A) *Effectively connected determination.*—With respect to each asset deemed sold in paragraph (c)(1) of this section, determine the amount of gain or loss from the deemed sale that would be treated as effectively connected gain or effectively connected loss (including by reason of section 897). Gain described in this paragraph (c)(2) is referred to as *deemed sale EC gain*, and loss described in this paragraph (c)(2) is referred to as *deemed sale EC loss*. Section 864 and the regulations thereunder apply for purposes of determining whether deemed sale gain or loss would be treated as effectively connected gain or loss. See paragraph (c)(2)(ii) of this section for sourcing rules that apply for purposes of determining deemed sale EC gain and deemed sale EC loss.

(B) *10-year exception.*—For purposes of applying paragraph (c)(2)(i)(A) of this section, gain or loss from the deemed sale of an asset (other than a United States real property interest within the meaning of section 897(c)) will not be treated as deemed sale EC gain or deemed sale EC loss if—

(*1*) No income or gain produced by the asset was taxable as income that was effectively connected with the conduct of a trade or business within the United States by the partnership (or the foreign transferor, a predecessor of the foreign transferor, or a predecessor of the partnership) during the lesser of the ten-year period ending on the date of the transfer or the period for which the partnership (and, if applicable, the foreign transferor, a predecessor of the foreign transferor, and a predecessor of the held the asset; and

(*2*) The asset has not been used, or held for use, in the conduct of a trade or business within the United States by the partnership (or the foreign transferor, a predecessor of the foreign transferor, or a predecessor of the partnership) during that same period.

(ii) *Sourcing rules for determining deemed sale EC gain and deemed sale EC loss.*—(A) *In general.*—For purposes of applying section 865(e)(2)(A) in connection with the determination of deemed sale EC gain and deemed sale EC loss under this paragraph (c)(2)(ii)(A), except to the extent provided in paragraphs (c)(2)(ii)(B) through (E) of this section, the deemed sale of an asset will be treated as attributable to an office or other fixed place of business maintained by the partnership in the United States. However, if the partnership does not maintain an office or other fixed place of business in the United States (within the meaning of section 864(c)(5)(A) and §1.864-7), neither the office attribution described in this paragraph (c)(2)(ii)(A), nor the rules of paragraphs (c)(2)(ii)(B) through (E) of this section, will apply.

(B) *Look-back rule for sale of inventory property.*—The deemed sale of inventory property (as defined in section 865(i)(1)) will not be treated as attributable to an office or other fixed place of business maintained by the partnership in the United States to the extent of *foreign source inventory gain or loss*. Foreign source inventory gain or loss is determined by multiplying the deemed sale gain or deemed sale loss attributable to inventory property by the foreign source inventory ratio. The foreign source inventory ratio cannot exceed one. If the amount in paragraph (c)(2)(ii)(B)(*1*) of this section is not positive, the foreign source inventory ratio is zero. If the amount in paragraph (c)(2)(ii)(B)(*1*) of this section is positive, but the amount in in paragraph (c)(2)(ii)(B)(2) of this section is not positive, the foreign source inventory ratio is one. The foreign source inventory ratio is—

(*1*) The gross income of the partnership from sources without the United States (as determined under sections 865(b) and 865(e)(2)) that was attributable to inventory property sold during the lesser of—

(*i*) The period comprised of the partnership's three taxable years immediately preceding the date of the deemed sale, or

(*ii*) The period beginning on the date the partnership (or any of its predecessors) was formed and ending on the last day of the partnership's taxable year immediately preceding the date of the deemed sale; over

(*2*) The total gross income of the partnership that was attributable to inventory property sold during that same period.

(C) *Look-back rule for intangibles.*—The deemed sale of an intangible (as defined in section 865(d)(2), including going concern value) will not be treated as attributable to an office or other fixed place of business maintained by the partnership in the United States to the extent of *foreign source intangible gain or loss*. Foreign source intangible gain or loss is determined by multiplying the deemed sale gain or deemed sale loss from an intangible, without regard to any gain described in section 865(d)(4)(A), by the foreign source intangible ratio. The foreign source intangible ratio cannot exceed one. If the amount in paragraph (c)(2)(ii)(C)(*1*) of this section is not positive, the foreign source intangible ratio is zero. If the amount in paragraph (c)(2)(ii)(C)(*1*) of this section is positive, but the amount in in paragraph (c)(2)(ii)(C)(2) of this section is not positive, the foreign source inventory ratio is one. The foreign source intangible ratio is–

(*1*) The gross ordinary income (other than from dispositions of depreciable or amortizable property) of the partnership from sources without the United States that was not effectively connected with the conduct of a trade or business within the United States, during the lesser of—

(*i*) The period comprised of the partnership's three taxable years immediately preceding the date of the deemed sale, or

(*ii*) The period beginning on the date the partnership (or any of its predecessors) is formed and ending on the last day of the partnership's taxable year immediately preceding the year in which the deemed sale occurs; over

(2) The total gross ordinary income (other than from dispositions of depreciable or amortizable property) of the partnership during that period.

(D) *Depreciable personal property.*—(*1*) *Depreciation recapture.*—The deemed sale of depreciable personal property (as defined in section 865(c)(4)(A)), including from the sale of an amortizable intangible (as defined in section 865(d)(2)), will not be treated as attributable to an office or other fixed place of business maintained by the partnership in the United States to the extent the deemed sale gain would be treated as from sources outside the United States after applying section 865(c)(1) at the time of the deemed sale.

(*2*) *Gain in excess of depreciation or loss with respect to depreciable personal property.*—For purposes of this section, if the deemed sale of depreciable personal property (other than an amortizable intangible) results in deemed sale gain in excess of the property's depreciation adjustments (as defined in section 865(c)(4)(B)), or results in deemed sale loss, attribution to an office or other fixed place of business maintained by the partnership in the United States with respect to the excess deemed sale gain, or deemed sale loss, will be determined based on where the property is located: if the property is located outside the United States, the excess deemed sale gain, or the deemed sale loss, will not be treated as attributable to an office or other fixed place of business maintained by the partnership in the United States; if the property is located within the United States, the excess deemed sale gain, or the deemed sale loss, will be treated as attributable to an office or other fixed place of business maintained by the partnership in the United States.

(E) *Material change in circumstances rule.*—If a material change in circumstances occurred that causes the applicable rule provided in paragraph (c)(2)(ii)(B) or (C) of this section to provide a sourcing result that is materially different from the sourcing result that would occur if the applicable period described in paragraph (c)(2)(ii)(B)(*1*) or (c)(2)(ii)(C)(*1*) of this section began on the date on which the material change in circumstance occurred and ended on the last day of the partnership's taxable year immediately preceding the year in which the deemed sale occurs (the *modified look-back period*), the applicable rule provided in paragraph (c)(2)(ii)(B) or (C) of this section may be applied by reference to the modified look-back period. The difference between the sourcing results is determined by comparing the foreign source inventory ratio (as described in paragraph (c)(2)(ii)(B) of this section) or the foreign source intangible ratio (as described in paragraph (c)(2)(ii)(C) of this section), as applicable, with the foreign source inventory ratio or foreign source intangible ratio, as applicable, if that ratio were determined by reference to the modified look-back period. For purposes of this paragraph (c)(2)(ii)(E), the sourcing results will not be materially different unless the percentage point difference between the ratios described in the preceding sentence is at least 30 percentage points.

(iii) *Examples.*—This paragraph (c)(2)(iii) provides examples that illustrate the rules of paragraph (c)(2)(ii) of this section. Except as otherwise provided, the following facts apply for purposes of this paragraph (c)(2)(iii). FP is a foreign corporation and a partner in PRS, a partnership that is engaged in the conduct of a trade or business within the United States (the U.S. Business) and a business in Country A (the Country A Business). Both businesses purchase inventory property and sell the purchased inventory property to unrelated customers; this is the only income-generating activity carried on by the businesses. PRS maintains an office or fixed place of business within the U.S. (within the meaning of section 864(c)(5)(A) and § 1.864-7) and, for its U.S. business, PRS sells its inventory property through its U.S. office. For the Country A business, PRS sells its inventory property through its Country A office for consumption in Country A; PRS's Country A office materially participates in each sale. The gain or loss from the inventory sold through PRS's Country A office is treated as from sources without the United States and is not effectively connected with PRS's U.S. Business. In year 4, FP sells its entire interest in PRS, thereby triggering the deemed sale described in paragraph (c)(1) of this section. In the deemed sale, PRS recognizes $10x of gain on the sale of its inventory property (the only asset PRS holds other than goodwill and going concern value). The 10-year exception provided in paragraph (c)(2)(i)(B) of this section does not apply.

(A) *Example 1: Determining foreign source inventory gain.*—(*1*) *Facts.* Based on PRS's sales records for the three taxable years immediately preceding the date of the deemed sale, PRS's gross income from sources without the United States that is attributable to sales of inventory property is $12x and PRS's total gross income attributable to sales of inventory property during that period is $30x.

(*2*) *Analysis.* To determine foreign source inventory gain or loss described in paragraph (c)(2)(ii)(B) of this section, the $10x deemed sale gain attributable to inventory property is multiplied by PRS's foreign source inventory ratio. PRS's foreign source inventory ratio is PRS's gross income from sources without the United States that are attributable to sales of inventory property within PRS's three taxable years preceding the date of the deemed sale, over PRS's total gross income attributable to sales of inventory property during the same period. Thus, based on PRS's sales records from the three taxable years preceding the date of the deemed sale, the foreign source inventory gain for PRS's inventory is $4x (the $10x deemed sale gain attributable to inventory multiplied by the foreign source inventory ratio of $12x over $30x).

(B) *Example 2: Determining deemed sale EC gain attributable to inventory property under the material change in circumstances rule.*—(*1*) *Facts.* The facts are the same as in paragraph (c)(2)(iii)(A)(*1*) of this section (the facts of *Example 1* in this paragraph (c)(2)(iii)), except that at the beginning of year 3 (PRS's taxable year immediately preceding the date of the deemed sale), PRS started a new business in Country B (the Country B Business) to take advantage of favorable market prospects for its products in Country B. For the Country B Business, PRS sells its inventory property through its Country B office for consumption in Country B; PRS's Country B office materially participates in each such sale. The gain or loss from the inventory sold through PRS's Country B office is foreign source gain or loss. Also, at the beginning of year 3, PRS substantially reduced its U.S. Business as a result of market factors. As a result of these changes in year 3, 95% of PRS's inventory property is sold in its Country A Business and Country B Business (collectively, the Foreign Businesses) beginning on the date in which these changes occurred; accordingly, 5% of PRS' inventory property is sold in its U.S. Business after these changes. Based on PRS's sales records for the three taxable years preceding the date of the deemed sale, PRS's gross income from sources without the United States that are attributable to sales of inventory property is $15x and PRS's total gross income attributable to sales of inventory property during that period is $30x; for year 3, PRS's gross income from sources without the United States that are attributable to sales of inventory property is $9.5x, and PRS's total gross income attributable to sales of inventory property in Year 3 is $10x.

(*2*) *Analysis.* The material change in circumstances rule described in paragraph (c)(2)(ii)(E) of this section applies if due to a material change in circumstances, the sourcing rule provided in paragraph (c)(2)(ii)(B) of this section provides a sourcing result that is materially different from the sourcing result that would occur if that sourcing rule was applied by reference to the modified look-back period; that is, the period beginning on the date in which a material chance in circumstances occurred and ending on the last day of the PRS's taxable year immediately preceding the date of the deemed sale. For this purpose, the reduction in PRS's U.S. business in year 3, coupled with the creation of the Country B Business in the same year, qualifies as a material change in circumstances. Thus, the modified look-back period consists of year 3; that is, the period starting at the beginning of year 3, the date in which the material change in circumstances occurred, and ending of the last day of year 3, the last day of PRS's taxable year immediately preceding the date of the deemed sale. Based on PRS's sales records for the three taxable years preceding the deemed sale, the foreign source inventory ratio, expressed as a percentage, is 50% ($15x attributable to PRS's gross income from sources without the United States with respect to sales of its inventory property, over $30x attributable to PRS's total gross income with respect to sales of its inventory property). Due to the material change in circumstances, however, 95% of PRS's inventory property is sold in its Foreign Businesses. ($9.5x attributable to PRS's gross income from sources without the United States with respect to sales of its inventory property, over $10x attributable to PRS's total gross income with respect to sales of its inventory property.) Accordingly, if PRS applied the sourcing rule provided in paragraph (c)(2)(ii)(B) of this section by reference to the modified look-back period, 95% ($9.5x/$10x), or $9.5x, of the gain would be attributable to sales for PRS's Foreign Businesses (gain from sources without the United States), and only 5% ($.5x/$10x), or $0.5x, of the gain would be attributable to sales for PRS's U.S. Business (gain from United States sources). The excess of the foreign source inventory ratio determined by reference to the modified look-back period (expressed as a percentage), over the foreign source inventory ratio (also expressed as a percentage) is 45%; that is 95% (as determined under the modified look-back period) minus 50% (as determined under the foreign source inventory ratio). Accordingly, the sourcing results are materially different because the 45 percentage point difference is greater than the 30 percentage point threshold provided in paragraph (c)(2)(ii)(E) of this section. Thus, the material change in circumstances rule of paragraph (c)(2)(ii)(E) of this section applies and the foreign source inventory gain determined under paragraph (c)(2)(ii)(B) of this section, determined by reference to the modified look-back period, is $9.5x; that is, the deemed sale gain attributable to inventory property ($10x), multiplied by the foreign source inventory ratio determined by reference to the modified look-back period ($9.5x/$10x).

(3) *Step 3: Determine the foreign transferor's distributive share of deemed sale EC gain or deemed sale EC loss.*—(i) *In general.*—A foreign transferor's distributive share of deemed sale EC gain or deemed sale EC loss with respect to each asset is the amount of the deemed sale EC gain and deemed sale EC loss determined under paragraph (c)(2) of this section that would have been allocated to the foreign transferor by the partnership under all applicable Internal Revenue Code sections (including section 704) upon the deemed sale described in paragraph (c)(1) of this section, taking into account allocations of tax items applying the principles of section 704(c), including any remedial allocations (see § 1.704-3(d)), and any section 743(b) basis adjustments (see § 1.743-1(j)(3)). For this purpose, a foreign transferor's distributive share of deemed sale EC gain or deemed sale EC loss does not include any amount that is excluded from the foreign transferor's gross income or otherwise exempt from U.S. Federal income tax by reason of an applicable provision of the Internal Revenue Code (including, for example, by reason of section 864(b)(2), 872(b), or 883). Similarly, a foreign transferor's distributive share of deemed sale EC gain or deemed sale EC loss does not include any amount to which an exception under section 897 applies, such as section 897(k) or section 897(l), if that amount is not otherwise treated as effectively connected under a provision of the Code. For rules regarding the determination of a foreign transferor's distributive share of deemed sale EC gain and deemed sale EC loss under an applicable U.S. income tax treaty, see paragraph (f) of this section.

(ii) *Aggregate deemed sale EC items.*—(A) *Ordinary gain or loss.*—A foreign transferor's *aggregate deemed sale EC ordinary gain* (if the net aggregate of the foreign transferor's distributive share of the deemed sale EC ordinary gain and loss is a gain) or *aggregate deemed sale EC ordinary loss* (if the net aggregate of the foreign transferor's distributive share of the deemed sale EC ordinary gain and loss is a loss) is determined by taking into account—

(1) The portion of the foreign transferor's distributive share of deemed sale EC gain and deemed sale EC loss that is attributable to the deemed sale of the partnership's assets that are section 751(a) property; and

(2) Deemed sale EC gain and deemed sale EC loss from the deemed sale of assets that are section 751(a) property that would be allocated to the foreign transferor with respect to interests in partnerships that are engaged in the conduct of a trade or business within the United States under paragraph (e)(1)(ii) of this section upon the deemed asset sales described in paragraph (e)(1)(i) of this section.

(B) *Capital gain or loss.*—A foreign transferor's *aggregate deemed sale EC capital gain* (if the net aggregate of the foreign transferor's distributive share of the deemed sale EC capital gain and loss is a gain) or *aggregate deemed sale EC capital loss* (if the net aggregate of the foreign transferor's distributive share of the deemed sale EC capital gain and loss is a loss) is determined by taking into account—

(1) The portion of the foreign transferor's distributive share of deemed sale EC gain and deemed sale EC loss that is attributable to the deemed sale of assets that are not section 751(a) property; and

(2) Deemed sale EC gain and deemed sale EC loss from the sale of assets that are not section 751(a) property and that would be allocated to the foreign transferor with respect to all interests in partnerships that are engaged in the conduct of a trade or business within the United States under paragraph (e)(1)(ii) of this section upon the deemed asset sales described in paragraph (e)(1)(i) of this section.

(iii) *Partial transfers.*—If a foreign transferor transfers less than all of its interest in a partnership, then for purposes of paragraph (c)(3)(i) of this section, the foreign transferor's distributive share of deemed sale EC gain and deemed sale EC loss is determined by reference to the amount of deemed sale EC gain or deemed sale EC loss determined under paragraph (c)(3)(i) of this section that is attributable to the portion of the foreign transferor's partnership interest that was transferred.

(d) *Coordination with section 897.*—If a foreign transferor transfers an interest in a partnership in a transfer that is subject to section 864(c)(8) and the partnership owns one or more United States real property interests (as defined in section 897(c)), then the foreign transferor determines its effectively connected gain and effectively connected loss under this section, and not pursuant to section 897(g). Accordingly, with respect to a transfer that is subject to section 864(c)(8), section 864(c)(8)(C) does not reduce the amount of gain or loss treated as effectively connected gain or loss under this section. For rules regarding a transfer not subject to section 864(c)(8) of an interest in a partnership that owns one or more United States real property interests, see section 897(g) and the regulations thereunder. If a foreign transferor transfers an interest in a partnership in the manner described in paragraph (b)(2)(ii) of this section, the transfer is treated as not subject to section 864(c)(8) to the extent of the gain or loss that is not recognized; instead, if the partnership owns one or more United States real property interests at the time of transfer, the rules of section 897(g) and the regulations thereunder apply to the unrecognized gain or loss.

(e) *Tiered partnerships.*—(1) *Transfers of upper-tier partnerships.*—Assets sold in a deemed sale described in paragraph (c)(1) of this section do not include interests in partnerships that are engaged in the conduct of a trade or business within the United States or interests in partnerships that hold, directly or indirectly, partnerships that are engaged in the conduct of a trade or business within the United States. Rather, if a foreign transferor transfers an interest in a partnership (upper-tier partnership) that owns, directly or indirectly, an interest in one or more partnerships that are engaged in the conduct of a trade or business within the United States, then—

(i) Beginning with the lowest-tier partnership that is engaged in the conduct of a trade or business within the United States in a chain of partnerships and going up the chain, each partnership that is engaged in the conduct of a trade or business within the United States is treated as selling its assets in a deemed sale in accordance with the principles of paragraph (c)(1) of this section; and

(ii) Each partnership must determine its deemed sale EC gain and deemed sale EC loss in accordance with the principles of paragraph (c)(2) of this section, and determine the distributive share of deemed sale EC gain and deemed sale EC loss for each partner that is either a partnership (in which the foreign transferor is a direct or indirect partner) or a foreign transferor, in accordance with the principles of paragraph (c)(3)(i) of this section.

(2) *Transfers by upper-tier partnerships.*—If a foreign transferor is a direct or indirect partner in an upper-tier partnership and the upper-tier partnership transfers an interest in a partnership that is engaged in the conduct of a trade or business within the United States (including a partnership held indirectly through one or more partnerships), then the principles of this section (including paragraph (e)(1) of this section) apply with respect to the gain or loss on the transfer that is allocated to the foreign transferor by the upper-tier partnership.

(3) *Coordination with section 897.*—For purposes of this paragraph (e), a lower-tier partnership that holds one or more United States real property interests is treated as engaged in the conduct of a trade or business within the United States.

(f) *Treaty coordination.*—This paragraph (f) describes how paragraph (c)(3) of this section applies in the case of a transfer of an interest in a partnership by a foreign transferor that is eligible for benefits under an applicable U.S. income tax treaty. As a general matter, a foreign transferor must satisfy the requirements of the limitation on benefits article, if any, in the treaty between the jurisdiction in which the transferor is resident and the United States to be eligible for treaty benefits. In the case of a foreign transferor that is entitled to treaty benefits, in determining the foreign transferor's distributive share of deemed sale EC gain and deemed sale EC loss, gain or loss derived by the foreign transferor attributable to assets deemed sold that would be exempt from tax under an applicable U.S. income tax treaty if disposed of by the partnership are not taken into account under paragraph (c)(3) of this section. In general, gain or loss on the alienation of a partnership interest will be treated as effectively connected gain or loss under section 864(c)(8) to the extent that the gain or loss is either attributable to assets forming part of a U.S. permanent establishment or fixed place of business, or taxable under a provision governing the disposition of United States real property interests. Gain or loss from the alienation of a partnership interest will be considered gain or loss attributable to the alienation of assets forming part of a permanent establishment or fixed place of business in the United States to the extent the assets deemed sold under section 864(c)(8) form a part of the U.S. permanent establishment or fixed place of business of the partnership. If, however, after applying treaty benefits in paragraph (c)(3) of this section, the only gains or losses that would be taken into account are gains or losses attributable to United States real property interests, the foreign transferor determines its effectively connected gain and effectively connected loss pursuant to section 897 and not under this section.

(g) *Definitions.*—The following definitions apply for purposes of this section.

(1) *Effectively connected gain.*—The term *effectively connected gain* means gain that is treated as effectively connected with the conduct of a trade or business within the United States.

(2) *Effectively connected loss.*—The term *effectively connected loss* means loss treated as effectively connected with the conduct of a trade or business within the United States.

(3) *Foreign transferor.*—The term *foreign transferor* means a nonresident alien individual or foreign corporation.

(4) *Section 751(a) property.*—The term *section 751(a) property* means unrealized receivables described in section 751(c) and inventory items described in section 751(d).

(5) *Transfer.*—The term *transfer* means a sale, exchange, or other disposition, and includes a distribution from a partnership to a partner to the extent that gain or loss is recognized on the distribution, as well as a transfer treated as a sale or exchange under section 707(a)(2)(B).

(h) *Anti-stuffing rule.*—If a foreign transferor (or a person that is related to a foreign transferor within the meaning of section 267(b) or 707(b)) transfers property (including another partnership interest) to a partnership in a transaction with a principal purpose of reducing the amount of gain treated as effectively connected gain, or increasing the amount of loss treated as effectively connected loss, under section 864(c)(8) or section 897, the transfer is disregarded for purposes of section 864(c)(8) or section 897, as appropriate.

(i) *Examples.*—This paragraph (i) provides examples that illustrate the rules of this section. Except as otherwise provided, the following facts are presumed for purposes of this paragraph (i). FP is a foreign corporation. USP is a domestic corporation. PRS is a partnership that was formed on January 1, 2018, when FP and USP each contributed $100x in cash. PRS has made no distributions and received no contributions other than those described in the preceding sentence. FP's adjusted basis in its interest in PRS is $100x. X is a foreign corporation that is unrelated to FP, USP, or PRS. Upon the formation of PRS, FP and USP entered into an agreement providing that all income, gain, loss, and deduction of PRS will be allocated equally between FP and USP. PRS is engaged in the conduct of a trade or business within the United States (the U.S. Business) and an unrelated business in Country A (the Country A Business). In a deemed sale described in paragraph (c)(1) of this section, gain or loss on assets of the U.S. Business would be treated as effectively connected gain or effectively connected loss, and gain or loss on assets of the Country A Business would not be so treated (including by reason of paragraph (c)(2)(i)(B) of this section). PRS has no liabilities.

(1) *Example 1. Deemed sale limitation.*—(i) *Facts.* On January 1, 2019, FP sells its entire interest in PRS to X for $105x. FP does not qualify for the benefits of an income tax treaty between the United States and another country. Immediately before the sale, PRS's balance sheet appears as follows:

	Adjusted Basis	*Fair Market Value*
U.S. Business section 1231 asset	$100x	$104x
Country A Business capital asset	100x	106x
Total	$200x	$210x

(ii) *Analysis*—(A) *Outside gain or loss.* FP is a foreign transferor (within the meaning of paragraph (g)(3) of this section) and transfers (within the meaning of paragraph (g)(5) of this section) its interest in PRS to X. For purposes of this example, for simplicity, PRS is assumed to hold no section 751(a) property and depreciation recapture is assumed to be zero. FP recognizes a $5x capital gain under section 741, which is an outside capital gain within the meaning of paragraph (b)(2)(i) of this section. Under paragraph (b)(1) of this section, FP's $5x capital gain is treated as effectively connected gain to the extent that it does not exceed the limitation described in paragraph (b)(3)(i) of this section, which is FP's aggregate deemed sale EC capital gain.

(B) *Deemed sale.* FP's aggregate deemed sale EC capital gain is determined according to the three-step process set forth in paragraph (c) of this section. First, the amount of gain or loss that PRS would recognize with respect to each of its assets upon a deemed sale described in paragraph (c)(1) of this section is a $4x gain with respect to the U.S. Business section 1231 asset and a $6x gain with respect to the Country A Business capital asset. Second, under paragraph (c)(2) of this section, PRS's deemed sale EC gain is $4x. Third, under paragraph (c)(3)(ii)(B) of this section, FP's aggregate deemed sale EC capital gain is $2x (that is, the aggregate of its distributive share of deemed sale EC gain attributable to the deemed sale of assets that are not section 751(a) property, which is 50% of $4x).

(C) *Limitation.* Under paragraph (b)(3)(i) of this section, the $5x outside capital gain recognized by FP is treated as effectively connected gain to the extent that it does not exceed FP's $2x aggregate deemed sale EC capital gain. Accordingly, FP recognizes $2x of capital gain that is treated as effectively connected gain.

(2) *Example 2. Outside gain limitation.*—(i) *Facts.* On January 1, 2019, FP sells its entire interest in PRS to X for $110x. FP does not qualify for the benefits of an income tax treaty between the United States and another country. Immediately before the sale, PRS's balance sheet appears as follows:

	Adjusted Basis	Fair Market Value
U.S. Business section 1231 asset	$100x	$150x
Country A Business capital asset	100x	70x
Total	$200x	$220x

(ii) *Analysis*— (A) *Outside gain or loss.* FP is a foreign transferor (within the meaning of paragraph (g)(3) of this section) and transfers (within the meaning of paragraph (g)(5) of this section) its interest in PRS to X. For purposes of this example, for simplicity, PRS is assumed to hold no section 751(a) property and depreciation recapture is assumed to be zero. FP recognizes a $10x capital gain under section 741, which is an outside capital gain within the meaning of paragraph (b)(2)(i) of this section. Under paragraph (b)(1) of this section, FP's $10x capital gain is treated as effectively connected gain to the extent that it does not exceed the limitation described in paragraph (b)(3)(i) of this section, which is FP's aggregate deemed sale EC capital gain.

(B) *Deemed sale.* FP's aggregate deemed sale EC capital gain is determined according to the three-step process set forth in paragraph (c) of this section. First, the amount of gain or loss that PRS would recognize with respect to each of its assets upon a deemed sale described in paragraph (c)(1) of this section is a $50x gain with respect to the U.S. Business section 1231 asset and a $30x loss with respect to the Country A Business capital asset. Second, under paragraph (c)(2) of this section, PRS's deemed sale EC gain is $50x. Third, under paragraph (c)(3)(ii)(B) of this section, FP's aggregate deemed sale EC capital gain is $25x (that is, the aggregate of its distributive share of deemed sale EC gain attributable to the deemed sale of assets that are not section 751(a) property, which is 50% of $50x).

(C) *Limitation.* Under paragraph (b)(3)(i) of this section, the $10x outside capital gain recognized by FP is treated as effectively connected gain to the extent that it does not exceed FP's $25x aggregate deemed sale EC capital gain. Accordingly, FP recognizes $10x of capital gain that is treated as effectively connected gain.

(3) *Example 3. Interaction with section 751(a).*—(i) *Facts.* On January 1, 2019, FP sells its entire interest in PRS to X for $95x. FP does not qualify for the benefits of an income tax treaty between the United States and another country. Through both its U.S. Business and its Country A Business, PRS holds inventory items and receivables that are section 751 property (as defined in § 1.751-1(a)). Immediately before the sale, PRS's balance sheet appears as follows:

	Adjusted Basis	Fair Market Value
U.S. Business section 1231 asset	$20x	$50x
U.S. Business inventory and receivables	30x	50x
Country A Business capital asset	100x	80x
Country A Business inventory	50x	10x
Total	$200x	$190x

(ii) *Analysis*—(A) *Outside gain or loss.* FP is a foreign transferor (within the meaning of paragraph (g)(3) of this section) and transfers (within the meaning of paragraph (g)(5) of this section) its interest in PRS to X. Under sections 741 and sections 751, FP recognizes a $10x ordinary loss and a $5x capital gain. See § 1.751-1(a). Under paragraph (b)(2)(i) of this section, FP has outside ordinary loss equal to $10x and outside capital gain equal to $5x. Under paragraph (b)(1) of this section, FP's outside ordinary loss and outside capital gain are treated as effectively connected loss and effectively connected gain to the extent that each does not exceed the applicable limitation described in paragraph (b)(3) of this section. In the case of FP's outside ordinary loss, the applicable limitation is FP's aggregate deemed sale EC ordinary loss. In the case of FP's outside capital gain, the applicable limitation is FP's aggregate deemed sale EC capital gain.

(B) *Deemed sale.* FP's aggregate deemed sale EC ordinary loss and aggregate deemed sale EC capital gain are determined according to the three-step process set forth in paragraph (c) of this section.

(*1*) *Step 1.* The amount of gain or loss that PRS would recognize with respect to each of its assets upon a deemed sale described in paragraph (c)(1) of this section is as follows:

Asset	Gain/(Loss)
U.S. Business section 1231 asset	$30x
U.S. Business inventory and receivables	20x
Country A Business capital asset	(20x)
Country A Business inventory	(40x)

(*2*) *Step 2.* Under paragraph (c)(2) of this section, PRS's deemed sale EC gain and deemed sale EC loss must be determined with respect to each asset. The amounts determined under paragraph (c)(2) of this section are as follows:

Asset	Deemed Sale EC Gain/(Loss)
U.S. Business section 1231 asset	$30x
U.S. Business inventory and receivables	20x
Country A Business capital asset	0
Country A Business inventory	0

(*3*) *Step 3.* Under paragraph (c)(3)(ii)(B) of this section, FP's aggregate deemed sale EC capital gain is $15x (that is, the aggregate of its distributive share of deemed sale EC gain that is attributable to the deemed sale of assets that are not section 751(a) property, which is 50% of $30x) and FP's aggregate deemed sale EC ordinary loss is $0 (that is, the aggregate of its distributive share of deemed sale EC loss that is attributable to the deemed sale of assets that are section 751(a) property).

(C) *Limitation*— (i) *Capital gain.* Under paragraph (b)(3)(i) of this section, the $5x outside capital gain recognized by FP is treated as effectively connected gain to the extent that it does not exceed FP's $15x aggregate deemed sale EC capital gain. Accordingly, the amount of FP's capital gain that is treated as effectively connected gain is $5x.

(ii) *Ordinary loss.* Under paragraph (b)(3)(iv) of this section, the $10x outside ordinary loss recognized by FP is treated as effectively connected loss to the extent that it does not exceed FP's $0 aggregate deemed sale EC ordinary loss. Accordingly, the amount of FP's ordinary loss that is treated as effectively connected loss is $0.

(4) *Example 4. Coordination with income tax treaties.*—(i) *Facts*—(A) *Sale of interest.* On January 1, 2019, FP sells its entire interest in PRS to X for $105x. Immediately before the sale, PRS's balance sheet appears as follows:

	Adjusted Basis	Fair Market Value
U.S. Business section 1231 asset	$100x	$104x
Country A Business capital asset	100x	106x
Total	$200x	$210x

(B) *Treaty benefits.* FP is a qualified resident of Country A under a U.S. income tax treaty between the United States and Country A that is similar or identical in all material respects to the 2006 U.S. Model Income Tax Convention (the Treaty). PRS is treated as fiscally transparent for purposes of Country A tax law. PRS does not carry on its U.S. Business through a U.S. permanent establishment (PE).

(ii) *Analysis*— (A) *Outside gain or loss.* FP is a foreign transferor (within the meaning of paragraph (g)(3) of this section) and transfers (within the meaning of paragraph (g)(5) of this section) its interest in PRS to X. For purposes of this example, for simplicity, PRS is assumed to hold no section 751(a) property and depreciation recapture is assumed to be zero. FP recognizes a $5x capital gain under section 741, which is an outside capital gain within the meaning of paragraph (b)(2)(i) of this section. Under paragraph (b)(1) of this section, FP's $5x capital gain is treated as effectively connected gain to the extent that it does not exceed the limitation described in paragraph (b)(3)(i) of this section, which is FP's aggregate deemed sale EC capital gain.

(B) *Deemed sale.* FP's aggregate deemed sale EC capital gain is determined according to the three-step process set forth in paragraph (c) of this section by taking into account the treaty coordination rule under paragraph (f) of this section.

(*1*) *Step 1.* The amount of gain or loss that PRS would recognize with respect to each of its assets upon a deemed sale described in paragraph (c)(1) of this section is as follows:

Asset	Gain/(Loss)
U.S. Business section 1231 asset	$4x
Country A Business capital asset	6x

(*2*) *Step 2.* Under paragraph (c)(2) of this section, PRS's deemed sale EC gain is as follows:

Asset	Gain/(Loss)
U.S. Business section 1231 asset	$4x
Country A Business capital asset	0x

(*3*) *Step 3.* FP is eligible for benefits under the Treaty and derives the gain on the deemed sale of U.S. Business section 1231 asset. Under paragraph (c)(3)(i) and paragraph (f) of this section, because gain from the disposition of the U.S. Business section 1231 asset does not form part of a U.S. PE, the gain is exempt from U.S. tax under the Treaty, and is not taken into account in determining FP's distributive share of deemed sale EC gain under paragraphs (c)(3)(i) and paragraph (f) of this section. Therefore, FP's aggregate deemed sale EC capital gain is $0x under paragraph (c)(3)(ii)(B) of this section.

(C) *Limitation.* Under paragraph (b)(3)(i) of this section, the $5x outside capital gain recognized by FP is not treated as effectively connected gain since all of it would exceed FP's $0x aggregate deemed sale EC capital gain.

(j) *Applicability date.*—This section applies to transfers occurring on or after December 26, 2018, and to amounts received on or after December 26, 2018, pursuant to an installment sale (as defined in section 453(b)) occurring on or after November 27, 2017. [Reg. § 1.864(c)(8)-1.]

☐ [*T.D.* 9919, 11-5-2020.]

§ 1.864(c)(8)-2. Notification and reporting requirements.—(a) *Notification by foreign transferor.*—(1) *In general.*—Except as provided in paragraph (a)(2) of this section, a notifying transferor that transfers an interest in a specified partnership must notify the partnership of the transfer in writing within 30 days after the transfer. The notification must include—

(i) The names and addresses of the notifying transferor and the transferee or transferees;

(ii) The U.S. taxpayer identification number (TIN) of the notifying transferor and, if known, of the transferee or transferees; and

(iii) The date of the transfer.

(2) *Exceptions.*—(i) *Certain interests in publicly traded partnerships.*—Paragraph (a)(1) of this section does not apply to a notifying transferor that transfers an interest in a publicly traded partnership if the interest is publicly traded on an established securities market or is readily tradable on a secondary market (or the substantial equivalent thereof).

(ii) *Certain distributions.*—Paragraph (a)(1) of this section does not apply to a notifying transferor that is treated as transferring an interest in a specified partnership because it received a distribution from that specified partnership.

(3) *Section 6050K.*—The notification described in paragraph (a)(1) of this section may be combined with or provided at the same time as the notification described in § 1.6050K-1(d), provided that it satisfies the requirements of both sections.

(4) *Other guidance.*—The notification described in paragraph (a)(1) of this section must also include any information prescribed by the Commissioner in forms or instructions or in publications or guidance published in the Internal Revenue Bulletin (see §§ 601.601(d)(2) and 601.602 of this chapter).

(b) *Reporting by specified partnerships with notifying transferor.*—(1) *In general.*—(i) *Requirement to provide statement.*—A specified partnership must provide to a notifying transferor the statement described in paragraph (b)(2) of this section if—

(A) The partnership receives the notice described in paragraph (a) of this section, or otherwise has actual knowledge that there has been a transfer of an interest in the partnership by a notifying transferor; and

(B) At the time of the transfer, the notifying transferor would have had a distributive share of deemed sale EC gain or deemed sale EC loss within the meaning of § 1.864(c)(8)-1(c).

(ii) *Distributions.*—For purposes of paragraph (b)(1)(i)(B) of this section, a specified partnership that is a transferee because it makes a distribution is treated as having actual knowledge of that transfer.

(2) *Contents of statement.*—The statement required to be furnished by the specified partnership under paragraph (b)(1) of this section must include—

(i) The items described in § 1.864(c)(8)-1(c)(3)(ii) (foreign transferor's aggregate deemed sale EC items, which includes items derived from lower-tier partnerships);

(ii) Whether the items described in paragraph (b)(2)(i) of this section were determined (in whole or in part) under § 1.864(c)(8)-1(c)(2)(ii)(E) (material change in circumstances rule for determining deemed sale EC gain or deemed sale EC loss from a deemed sale of the partnership's inventory property or intangibles); and

(iii) Any other information as may be prescribed by the Commissioner in forms, instructions, publications, or guidance published in the Internal Revenue Bulletin (see §§ 601.601(d)(2) and 601.602 of this chapter).

(3) *Time for furnishing statement.*—The specified partnership must furnish the required information on or before the due date (with extensions) for issuing Schedule K-1 (Form 1065), *Partner's Share of Income, Deductions, Credits, etc.*, or other statement required to be furnished under § 1.6031(b)-1T, to the notifying transferor for the year of the transfer. *See* § 1.6031(b)-1T(b).

(4) *Manner of furnishing statement.*—The statement required to be furnished under paragraph (b)(1) of this section must be provided on Schedule K-1 (Form 1065), *Partner's Share of Income, Deductions, Credits, etc.*, or other statement required to be furnished under § 1.6031(b)-1T.

(5) *Partnership notifying transferor.*—For purposes of this paragraph (b), a specified partnership must treat a notifying transferor that is a partnership as a nonresident alien individual.

(c) *Statement may be provided to agent.*—A specified partnership may provide a statement required under paragraph (b)(2) of this section to a person other than the notifying transferor if the person is described in § 1.6031(b)-1T(c).

(d) *Definitions.*—The following definitions apply for purposes of this section.

(1) *Notifying transferor.*—The term *notifying transferor* means any foreign person, any domestic partnership that has a foreign person as a direct partner, and any domestic partnership that has actual knowledge that a foreign person indirectly holds, through one or more partnerships, an interest in the domestic partnership.

(2) *Specified partnership.*—The term *specified partnership* means a partnership that is engaged in a trade or business within the United States or that owns (directly or indirectly) an interest in a partnership that is engaged in a trade or business within the United States.

(3) *Transfer.*—The term *transfer* has the meaning provided in § 1.864(c)(8)-1(g)(5).

(e) *Applicability dates.*—Paragraph (a) of this section applies to transfers that occur on or after November 30, 2020. Paragraphs (b) and (c) of this section apply to returns filed on or after November 30, 2020. Paragraph (d) of this section applies beginning on November 30, 2020. [Reg. § 1.864(c)(8)-2.]

☐ [*T.D.* 9926, 11-27-2020.]

§ 1.865-1. Loss with respect to personal property other than stock.—(a) *General rules for allocation of loss.*—(1) *Allocation against gain.*—Except as otherwise provided in § 1.865-2 and paragraph (c) of this section, loss recognized with respect to personal property shall be allocated to the class of gross income and, if necessary, apportioned between the statutory grouping of gross income (or among the statutory groupings) and the residual grouping of gross income, with respect to which gain from a sale of such property would give rise in the hands of the seller. For purposes of this section, loss includes bad debt deductions under section 166 and loss on property that is marked-to-market (such as under section 475) and subject to the rules of this section. Thus, for example, loss recognized by a United States resident on the sale or worthlessness of a bond generally is allocated to reduce United States source income.

(2) *Loss attributable to foreign office.*—Except as otherwise provided in § 1.865-2 and paragraph (c) of this section, and except with respect to loss subject to paragraph (b) of this section, in the case of loss recognized by a United States resident with respect to property that is attributable to an office or other fixed place of business in a foreign country within the meaning of section 865(e)(3), the loss shall be allocated to reduce foreign source income if a gain on the sale of the property would have been taxable by the foreign country and the highest marginal rate of tax imposed on such gains in the foreign country is at least 10 percent. However, paragraph (a)(1) of this section and not this paragraph (a)(2) will apply if gain on the sale of such property would be sourced under section 865(c), (d)(1)(B), or (d)(3).

(3) *Loss recognized by United States citizen or resident alien with foreign tax home.*—Except as otherwise provided in § 1.865-2 and paragraph (c) of this section, and except with respect to loss subject to paragraph (b) of this section, in the case of loss with respect to property recognized by a United States citizen or resident alien that has a tax home (as defined in section 911(d)(3)) in a foreign country,

the loss shall be allocated to reduce foreign source income if a gain on the sale of such property would have been taxable by a foreign country and the highest marginal rate of tax imposed on such gains in the foreign country is at least 10 percent.

(4) *Allocation for purposes of section 904.*—For purposes of section 904, loss recognized with respect to property that is allocated to foreign source income under this paragraph (a) shall be allocated to the separate category under section 904(d) to which gain on the sale of the property would have been assigned (without regard to section 904(d)(2)(A)(iii)(III)). For purposes of § 1.904-4(c)(2)(ii)(A), any such loss allocated to passive income shall be allocated (prior to the application of § 1.904-4(c)(2)(ii)(B)) to the group of passive income to which gain on a sale of the property would have been assigned had a sale of the property resulted in the recognition of a gain under the law of the relevant foreign jurisdiction or jurisdictions.

(5) *Loss recognized by partnership.*—A partner's distributive share of loss recognized by a partnership with respect to personal property shall be allocated and apportioned in accordance with this section as if the partner had recognized the loss. If loss is attributable to an office or other fixed place of business of the partnership within the meaning of section 865(e)(3), such office or fixed place of business shall be considered to be an office of the partner for purposes of this section.

(b) *Special rules of application.*—(1) *Depreciable property.*—In the case of a loss recognized with respect to depreciable personal property, the gain referred to in paragraph (a)(1) of this section is the gain that would be sourced under section 865(c)(1) (depreciation recapture).

(2) *Contingent payment debt instrument.*—Loss described in the last sentence of § 1.1275-4(b)(9)(iv)(A) that is recognized with respect to a contingent payment debt instrument to which § 1.1275-4(b) applies (instruments issued for money or publicly traded property) shall be allocated to the class of gross income and, if necessary, apportioned between the statutory grouping of gross income (or among the statutory groupings) and the residual grouping of gross income, with respect to which interest income from the instrument (in the amount of the loss subject to this paragraph (b)(2)) would give rise.

(c) *Exceptions.*—(1) *Foreign currency and certain financial instruments.*—This section does not apply to loss governed by section 988 and loss recognized with respect to options contracts or derivative financial instruments, including futures contracts, forward contracts, notional principal contracts, or evidence of an interest in any of the foregoing.

(2) *Inventory.*—This section does not apply to loss recognized with respect to property described in section 1221(a)(1).

(3) *Interest equivalents and trade receivables.*—Loss subject to § 1.861-9T(b) (loss equivalent to interest expense and loss on trade receivables) shall be allocated and apportioned under the rules of § 1.861-9T and not under the rules of this section.

(4) *Unamortized bond premium.*—If a taxpayer recognizing loss with respect to a bond (within the meaning of § 1.171-1(b)) did not amortize bond premium to the full extent permitted by section 171 and the regulations thereunder, then, to the extent of the amount of bond premium that could have been, but was not, amortized by the taxpayer, loss recognized with respect to the bond shall be allocated to the class of gross income and, if necessary, apportioned between the statutory grouping of gross income (or among the statutory groupings) and the residual grouping of gross income, with respect to which interest income from the bond was assigned.

(5) *Accrued interest.*—Loss attributable to accrued but unpaid interest on a debt obligation shall be allocated to the class of gross income and, if necessary, apportioned between the statutory grouping of gross income (or among the statutory groupings) and the residual grouping of gross income, with respect to which interest income from the obligation was assigned. For purposes of this section, whether loss is attributable to accrued but unpaid interest (rather than to principal) shall be determined under the principles of §§ 1.61-7(d) and 1.446-2(e).

(6) *Anti-abuse rules.*—(i) *Transactions involving built-in losses.*—If one of the principal purposes of a transaction is to change the allocation of a built-in loss with respect to personal property by transferring the property to another person, qualified business unit, office or other fixed place of business, or branch that subsequently recognizes the loss, the loss shall be allocated by the transferee as if it were recognized by the transferor immediately prior to the transaction. If one of the principal purposes of a change of residence is to change the allocation of a built-in loss with respect to personal property, the loss shall be allocated as if the change of residence had not occurred. If one of the principal purposes of a transaction is to change the allocation of a built-in loss on the disposition of personal property by converting the original property into other property and subsequently recognizing loss with respect to such other property, the loss shall be allocated as if it were recognized with respect to the original property immediately prior to the transaction. Transactions subject to this paragraph shall include, without limitation, reorganizations within the meaning of section 368(a), liquidations under section 332, transfers to a corporation under section 351, transfers to a partnership under section 721, transfers to a trust, distributions by a partnership, distributions by a trust, transfers to or from a qualified business unit, office or other fixed place of business, or branch, or exchanges under section 1031. A person may have a principal purpose of affecting loss allocation even though this purpose is outweighed by other purposes (taken together or separately).

(ii) *Offsetting positions.*—If a taxpayer recognizes loss with respect to personal property and the taxpayer (or any person described in section 267(b) (after application of section 267(c)), 267(e), 318 or 482 with respect to the taxpayer) holds (or held) offsetting positions with respect to such property with a principal purpose of recognizing foreign source income and United States source loss, the loss shall be allocated and apportioned against such foreign source income. For purposes of this paragraph (c)(6)(ii), positions are offsetting if the risk of loss of holding one or more positions is substantially diminished by holding one or more other positions.

(iii) *Matching rule.*—If a taxpayer (or a person described in section 1059(c)(3)(C) with respect to the taxpayer) engages in a transaction or series of transactions with a principal purpose of recognizing foreign source income that results in the creation of a corresponding loss with respect to personal property (as a consequence of the rules regarding the timing of recognition of income, for example), the loss shall be allocated and apportioned against such income to the extent of the recognized foreign source income. For an example illustrating a similar rule with respect to stock loss, see § 1.865-2(b)(4)(iv) *Example 3.*

(d) *Definitions.*—(1) *Contingent payment debt instrument.*—A contingent payment debt instrument is any debt instrument that is subject to § 1.1275-4.

(2) *Depreciable personal property.*—Depreciable personal property is any property described in section 865(c)(4)(A).

(3) *Terms defined in § 1.861-8.*—See § 1.861-8 for the meaning of *class of gross income, statutory grouping of gross income,* and *residual grouping of gross income.*

(e) *Examples.*—The application of this section may be illustrated by the following examples:

Example 1. On January 1, 2000, *A*, a domestic corporation, purchases for $1,000 a machine that produces widgets, which *A* sells in the United States and throughout the world. Throughout *A*'s holding period, the machine is located and used in Country *X*. During *A*'s holding period, *A* incurs depreciation deductions of $400 with respect to the machine. Under § 1.861-8, *A* allocates and apportions depreciation deductions of $250 against foreign source general limitation income and $150 against U.S. source income. On December 12, 2002, *A* sells the machine for $100 and recognizes a loss of $500. Because the machine was used predominantly outside the United States, under sections 865(c)(1)(B) and 865(c)(3)(B)(ii) gain on the disposition of the machine would be foreign source general limitation income to the extent of the depreciation adjustments. Therefore, under paragraph (b)(1) of this section, the entire $500 loss is allocated against foreign source general limitation income.

Example 2. On January 1, 2002, *A*, a domestic corporation, loans $2,000 to *N*, its wholly-owned controlled foreign corporation, in exchange for a contingent payment debt instrument subject to § 1.1275-4(b). During 2002 through 2004, *A* accrues and receives interest income of $630, $150 of which is foreign source general limitation income and $480 of which is foreign source passive income under section 904(d)(3). Assume there are no positive or negative adjustments pursuant to § 1.1275-4(b)(6) in 2002 through 2004. On January 1, 2005, *A* disposes of the debt instrument and recognizes a $770 loss. Under § 1.1275-4(b)(8)(ii), $630 of the loss is treated as ordinary loss and $140 is treated as capital loss. Assume that $140 of interest income earned in 2005 with respect to the debt instrument would be foreign source passive income under section 904(d)(3). Under § 1.1275-4(b)(9)(iv), $150 of the ordinary loss is allocated against foreign source general limitation income and $480 of the ordinary loss is allocated against foreign source passive income. Under paragraph (b)(2) of this section, the $140 capital loss is allocated against foreign source passive income.

Example 3. (i) On January 1, 2003, *A*, a domestic corporation, purchases for $1,200 a taxable bond maturing on December 31, 2008, with a stated principal amount of $1,000, payable at maturity. The bond provides for unconditional payments of interest of $100, payable December 31 of each year. The issuer of the bond is a foreign corporation and interest on the bond is thus foreign source. Interest payments for 2003 and 2004 are timely made. *A* does not elect to amortize its bond premium under section 171 and the regulations thereunder, which would have permitted *A* to offset the $100 of interest income by $28.72 of bond premium in 2003, and by $30.42 in 2004. On January 1, 2005, *A* sells the bond and recognizes a $100 loss. Under paragraph (c)(4) of this section, $59.14 of the loss is allocated against foreign source income. Under paragraph (a)(1) of this section, the remaining $40.86 of the loss is allocated against U.S. source income.

(ii) The facts are the same as in paragraph (i) of this *Example 3*, except that *A* made the election to amortize its bond premium effective for taxable year 2004 (see § 1.171-4(c)). Under paragraph (c)(4) of this section, $28.72 of the loss is allocated against foreign source income. Under paragraph (a)(1) of this section, the remaining $71.28 of the loss is allocated against U.S. source income.

Example 4. On January 1, 2002, *A*, a domestic corporation, purchases for $1,000 a bond maturing December 31, 2014, with a stated principal amount of $1,000, payable at maturity. The bond provides for unconditional payments of interest of $100, payable December 31 of each year. The issuer of the bond is a foreign corporation and interest on the bond is thus foreign source. Between 2002 and 2006, *A* accrues and receives foreign source interest income of $500 with respect to the bond. On January 1, 2007, *A* sells the bond and recognizes a $500 loss. Under paragraph (a)(1) of this section, the $500 loss is allocated against U.S. source income.

Example 5. On January 1, 2002, *A*, a domestic corporation on the accrual method of accounting, purchases for $1,000 a bond maturing December 31, 2012, with a stated principal amount of $1,000, payable at maturity. The bond provides for unconditional payments of interest of $100, payable December 31 of each year. The issuer of the bond is a foreign corporation and interest on the bond is thus foreign source. On June 10, 2002, after *A* has accrued $44 of interest income, but before any interest has been paid, the issuer suddenly becomes insolvent and declares bankruptcy. *A* sells the bond (including the accrued interest) for $20. Assuming that *A* properly accrued $44 of interest income, *A* treats the $20 proceeds from the sale of the bond as payment of interest previously accrued and recognizes a $1,000 loss with respect to the bond principal and a $24 loss with respect to the accrued interest. See § 1.61-7(d). Under paragraph (a)(1) of this section, the $1,000 loss with respect to the principal is allocated against U.S. source income. Under paragraph (c)(5) of this section, the $24 loss with respect to accrued but unpaid interest is allocated against foreign source interest income.

(f) *Effective date.*—(1) *In general.*—Except as provided in paragraph (f)(2) of this section, this section is applicable to loss recognized on or after January 8, 2002. For purposes of this paragraph (f), loss that is recognized but deferred (for example, under section 267 or 1092) shall be treated as recognized at the time the loss is taken into account.

(2) *Application to prior periods.*—A taxpayer may apply the rules of this section to losses recognized in any taxable year beginning on or after January 1, 1987, and all subsequent years, provided that—

(i) The taxpayer's tax liability as shown on an original or amended tax return is consistent with the rules of this section for each such year for which the statute of limitations does not preclude the filing of an amended return on June 30, 2002; and

(ii) The taxpayer makes appropriate adjustments to eliminate any double benefit arising from the application of this section to years that are not open for assessment.

(3) *Examples.*—See § 1.865-2(e)(3) for examples illustrating an applicability date provision similar to the applicability date provided in this paragraph (f). [Reg. § 1.865-1.]

□ [*T.D.* 8973, 12-27-2001.]

§ 1.865-2. Loss with respect to stock.—(a) *General rules for allocation of loss with respect to stock.*—(1) *Allocation against gain.*—Except as otherwise provided in paragraph (b) of this section, loss recognized with respect to stock shall be allocated to the class of gross income and, if necessary, apportioned between the statutory grouping of gross income (or among the statutory groupings) and the residual grouping of gross income, with respect to which gain (other than gain treated as a dividend under section 964(e)(1) or 1248) from a sale of such stock would give rise in the hands of the seller (without regard to section 865(f)). For purposes of this section, loss includes loss on property that is marked-to-market (such as under section 475) and subject to the rules of this section. Thus, for example, loss recognized by a United States resident on the sale of stock generally is allocated to reduce United States source income.

(2) *Stock attributable to foreign office.*—Except as otherwise provided in paragraph (b) of this section, in the case of loss recognized by a United States resident with respect to stock that is attributable to an office or other fixed place of business in a foreign country within the meaning of section 865(e)(3), the loss shall be allocated to reduce foreign source income if a gain on the sale of the stock would have been taxable by the foreign country and the highest marginal rate of tax imposed on such gains in the foreign country is at least 10 percent.

(3) *Loss recognized by United States citizen or resident alien with foreign tax home.*—(i) *In general.*—Except as otherwise provided in paragraph (b) of this section, in the case of loss with respect to stock that is recognized by a United States citizen or resident alien that has a tax home (as defined in section 911(d)(3)) in a foreign country, the loss shall be allocated to reduce foreign source income if a gain on the sale of the stock would have been taxable by a foreign country and the highest marginal rate of tax imposed on such gains in the foreign country is at least 10 percent.

(ii) *Bona fide residents of Puerto Rico.*—Except as otherwise provided in paragraph (b) of this section, in the case of loss with respect to stock in a corporation described in section 865(g)(3) recognized by a United States citizen or resident alien that is a bona fide resident of Puerto Rico during the entire taxable year, the loss shall be allocated to reduce foreign source income. If gain from a sale of such stock would give rise to income exempt from tax under section 933, the loss with respect to such stock shall be allocated to amounts that are excluded from gross income under section 933(1) and therefore shall not be allowed as a deduction from gross income. See section 933(1) and § 1.933-1(c).

(4) *Stock constituting a United States real property interest.*—Loss recognized by a nonresident alien individual or a foreign corporation with respect to stock that constitutes a United States real property interest shall be allocated to reduce United States source income. For additional rules governing the treatment of such loss, see section 897 and the regulations thereunder.

(5) *Allocation for purposes of section 904.*—For purposes of section 904, loss recognized with respect to stock that is allocated to foreign source income under this paragraph (a) shall be allocated to the separate category under section 904(d) to which gain on a sale of the stock would have been assigned (without regard to section 904(d)(2)(A)(iii)(III)). For purposes of § 1.904-4(c)(2)(ii)(A), any such loss allocated to passive income shall be allocated (prior to the application of § 1.904-4(c)(2)(ii)(B)) to the group of passive income to which gain on a sale of the stock would have been assigned had a sale of the stock resulted in the recognition of a gain under the law of the relevant foreign jurisdiction or jurisdictions.

(b) *Exceptions.*—(1) *Dividend recapture exception.*—(i) *In general.*—If a taxpayer recognizes a loss with respect to shares of stock, and the taxpayer (or a person described in section 1059(c)(3)(C) with respect to such shares) included in income a dividend recapture amount (or amounts) with respect to such shares at any time during the recapture period, then, to the extent of the dividend recapture amount (or amounts), the loss shall be allocated and apportioned on a proportionate basis to the class or classes of gross income or the statutory or residual grouping or groupings of gross income to which the dividend recapture amount was assigned.

(ii) *Exception for de minimis amounts.*—Paragraph (b)(1)(i) of this section shall not apply to a loss recognized by a taxpayer on the disposition of stock if the sum of all dividend recapture amounts (other than dividend recapture amounts eligible for the exception described in paragraph (b)(1)(iii) of this section (passive limitation dividends)) included in income by the taxpayer (or a person described in section 1059(c)(3)(C)) with respect to such stock during the recapture period is less than 10 percent of the recognized loss.

(iii) *Exception for passive limitation dividends.*—Paragraph (b)(1)(i) of this section shall not apply to the extent of a dividend recapture amount that is treated as income in the separate category for passive income described in section 904(d)(2)(A) (without regard to section 904(d)(2)(A)(iii)(III)). The exception provided for in this paragraph (b)(1)(iii) shall not apply to any dividend recapture amount that is treated as income in the separate category for financial services income described in section 904(d)(2)(C).

(iv) *Examples.*—The application of this paragraph (b)(1) may be illustrated by the following examples:

Example 1. (i) *P*, a domestic corporation, is a United States shareholder of *N*, a controlled foreign corporation. *N* has never had any subpart F income and all of its earnings and profits are described in section 959(c)(3). On May 5, 1998, *N* distributes a dividend to *P* in the amount of $100. The dividend gives rise to a $5 foreign withholding tax, and *P* is deemed to have paid an additional $45 of foreign income tax with respect to the dividend under section 902. Under the look-through rules of section 904(d)(3) the dividend is general limitation income described in section 904(d)(1)(I).

(ii) On February 6, 2000, *P* sells its shares of *N* and recognizes a $110 loss. In 2000, *P* has the following taxable income, excluding the loss on the sale of *N*:

(A) $1,000 of foreign source income that is general limitation income described in section 904(d)(1)(I);

(B) $1,000 of foreign source capital gain from the sale of stock in a foreign affiliate that is sourced under section 865(f) and is passive income described in section 904(d)(1)(A); and

(C) $1,000 of U.S. source income.

(iii) The $100 dividend paid in 1998 is a dividend recapture amount that was included in *P*'s income within the recapture period preceding the disposition of the *N* stock. The de minimis exception of paragraph (b)(1)(ii) of this section does not apply because the $100 dividend recapture amount exceeds 10 percent of the $110 loss. Therefore, to the extent of the $100 dividend recapture amount, the loss must be allocated under paragraph (b)(1)(i) of this section to the separate limitation category to which the dividend was assigned (general limitation income).

(iv) *P*'s remaining $10 loss on the disposition of the *N* stock is allocated to U.S. source income under paragraph (a)(1) of this section.

(v) After allocation of the stock loss, *P*'s foreign source taxable income in 2000 consists of $900 of foreign source general limitation income and $1,000 of foreign source passive income.

Example 2. (i) *P*, a domestic corporation, owns all of the stock of *N1*, which owns all of the stock of *N2*, which owns all of the stock of *N3*. *N1*, *N2*, and *N3* are controlled foreign corporations. All of the corporations use the calendar year as their taxable year. On February 5, 1997, *N3* distributes a dividend to *N2*. The dividend is foreign personal holding company income of *N2* under section 954(c)(1)(A) that results in an inclusion of $100 in *P*'s income under section 951(a)(1)(A)(i) as of December 31, 1997. Under section 904(d)(3)(B) the inclusion is general limitation income described in section 904(d)(1)(I). The income inclusion to *P* results in a corresponding increase in *P*'s basis in the stock of *N1* under section 961(a).

(ii) On March 5, 1999, *P* sells its shares of *N1* and recognizes a $110 loss. The $100 1997 subpart F inclusion is a dividend recapture amount that was included in *P*'s income within the recapture period preceding the disposition of the *N1* stock. The de minimis exception of paragraph (b)(1)(ii) of this section does not apply because the $100 dividend recapture amount exceeds 10 percent of the $110 loss. Therefore, to the extent of the $100 dividend recapture amount, the loss must be allocated under paragraph (b)(1)(i) of this section to the separate limitation category to which the dividend recapture amount was assigned (general limitation income). The remaining $10 loss is allocated to U.S. source income under paragraph (a)(1) of this section.

Example 3. (i) *P*, a domestic corporation, owns all of the stock of *N1*, which owns all of the stock of *N2*. *N1* and *N2* are controlled foreign corporations. All the corporations use the calendar year as their taxable year and the U.S. dollar as their functional currency. On May 5, 1998, *N2* pays a dividend of $100 to *N1* out of general limitation earnings and profits.

(ii) On February 5, 2000, *N1* sells its *N2* stock to an unrelated purchaser. The sale results in a loss to *N1* of $110 for U.S. tax purposes. In 2000, *N1* has the following current earnings and profits, excluding the loss on the sale of *N2*:

(A) $1,000 of non-subpart F foreign source general limitation earnings and profits described in section 904(d)(1)(I);

(B) $1,000 of foreign source gain from the sale of stock that is taken into account in determining foreign personal holding company income under section 954(c)(1)(B)(i) and which is passive limitation earnings and profits described in section 904(d)(1)(A);

(C) $1,000 of foreign source interest income received from an unrelated person that is foreign personal holding company income under section 954(c)(1)(A) and which is passive limitation earnings and profits described in section 904(d)(1)(A).

(iii) The $100 dividend paid in 1998 is a dividend recapture amount that was included in *N1*'s income within the recapture period preceding the disposition of the *N2* stock. The de minimis exception of paragraph (b)(1)(ii) of this section does not apply because the $100 dividend recapture amount exceeds 10 percent of the $110 loss. Therefore, to the extent of the $100 dividend recapture amount, the loss must be allocated under paragraph (b)(1)(i) of this section to the separate limitation category to which the dividend was assigned (general limitation earnings and profits).

(iv) *N1*'s remaining $10 loss on the disposition of the *N2* stock is allocated to foreign source passive limitation earnings and profits under paragraph (a)(1) of this section.

(v) After allocation of the stock loss, *N1*'s current earnings and profits for 1998 consist of $900 of foreign source general limitation earnings and profits and $1,990 of foreign source passive limitation earnings and profits.

(vi) After allocation of the stock loss, *N1*'s subpart F income for 2000 consists of $1,000 of foreign source interest income that is foreign personal holding company income under section 954(c)(1)(A) and $890 of foreign source net gain that is foreign personal holding company income under section 954(c)(1)(B)(i). *P* includes $1,890 in income under section 951(a)(1)(A)(i) as passive income under sections 904(d)(1)(A) and 904(d)(3)(B).

Example 4. *P*, a foreign corporation, has two wholly-owned subsidiaries, *S*, a domestic corporation, and *B*, a foreign corporation. On January 1, 2000, *S* purchases a one-percent interest in *N*, a foreign corporation, for $100. On January 2, 2000, *N* distributes a $20 dividend to *S*. The $20 dividend is foreign source financial services income. On January 3, 2000, *S* sells its *N* stock to *B* for $80 and recognizes a $20 loss that is deferred under section 267(f). On June 10, 2008, *B* sells its *N* stock to an unrelated person for $55. Under section 267(f) and § 1.267(f)-1(c)(1), *S*'s $20 loss is deferred until 2008. Under this paragraph (b)(1), the $20 loss is allocated to reduce foreign source financial services income in 2008 because the loss was recognized (albeit deferred) within the 24-month recapture period following the receipt of the dividend. See §§ 1.267(f)-1(a)(2)(i)(B) and 1.267(f)-1(c)(2).

Example 5. The facts are the same as in *Example 4*, except *P*, *S*, and *B* are domestic corporations and members of the *P* consolidated group. Under the matching rule of § 1.1502-13(c)(1), the separate entity attributes of *S*'s intercompany items and *B*'s corresponding items are redetermined to the extent necessary to produce the same effect on consolidated taxable income as if *S* and *B* were divisions of a single corporation and the intercompany transaction was a transaction between divisions. If *S* and *B* were divisions of a single corporation, the transfer of *N* stock on January 3, 2000 would be ignored for tax purposes, and the corporation would be treated as selling that stock only in 2008. Thus, the corporation's entire $45 loss would have been allocated against U.S. source income under paragraph (a)(1) of this section because a dividend recapture amount was not received during the corporation's recapture period. Accordingly, *S*'s $20 loss and *B*'s $25 loss are allocated to reduce U.S. source income.

Example 6. (i) On January 1, 1998, *P*, a domestic corporation, purchases *N*, a foreign corporation, for $1,000. On March 1, 1998, *P* causes *N* to sell its operating assets, distribute a $400 general limitation dividend to *P*, and invest its remaining $600 in short-term government securities. *P* converted the *N* assets into low-risk investments with a principal purpose of holding the *N* stock without significant risk of loss until the recapture period expired. *N* earns interest income from the securities. The income constitutes subpart F income that is included in *P*'s income under section 951, increasing *P*'s basis in the *N* stock under section 961(a). On March 1, 2002, *P* sells *N* and recognizes a $400 loss.

(ii) Pursuant to paragraph (d)(3) of this section, the recapture period is increased by the period in which *N*'s assets were held as low-risk investments because *P* caused *N*'s assets to be converted into and held as low-risk investments with a principal purpose of enabling *P* to hold the *N* stock without significant risk of loss. Accordingly, under paragraph (b)(1)(i) of this section the $400 loss is allocated against foreign source general limitation income.

(2) *Exception for inventory.*—This section does not apply to loss recognized with respect to stock described in section 1221(1).

(3) *Exception for stock in an S corporation.*—This section does not apply to loss recognized with respect to stock in an S corporation (as defined in section 1361).

(4) *Anti-abuse rules.*—(i) *Transactions involving built-in losses.*—If one of the principal purposes of a transaction is to change the allocation of a built-in loss with respect to stock by transferring the stock to another person, qualified business unit (within the meaning of section 989(a)), office or other fixed place of business, or branch that subsequently recognizes the loss, the loss shall be allocated by the transferee as if it were recognized with respect to the stock by the transferor immediately prior to the transaction. If one of the principal purposes of a change of residence is to change the allocation of a built-in loss with respect to stock, the loss shall be allocated as if the change of residence had not occurred. If one of the principal purposes of a transaction is to change the allocation of a built-in loss with respect to stock (or other personal property) by converting the original property into other property and subsequently recognizing loss with respect to such other property, the loss shall be allocated as if it were recognized with respect to the original property immediately prior to the transaction. Transactions subject to this paragraph shall include, without limitation, reorganizations within the meaning of section 368(a), liquidations under section 332, transfers to a corporation under section 351, transfers to a partnership under section 721, transfers to a trust, distributions by a partnership, distributions by a trust, or transfers to or from a qualified business unit, office or other fixed place of business. A person may have a principal purpose of affecting loss allocation even though this purpose is outweighed by other purposes (taken together or separately).

(ii) *Offsetting positions.*—If a taxpayer recognizes loss with respect to stock and the taxpayer (or any person described in section 267(b) (after application of section 267(c)), 267(e), 318 or 482 with respect to the taxpayer) holds (or held) offsetting positions with respect to such stock with a principal purpose of recognizing foreign source income and United States source loss, the loss will be allocated and apportioned against such foreign source income. For purposes of this paragraph (b)(4)(ii), positions are offsetting if the risk of loss of holding one or more positions is substantially diminished by holding one or more other positions.

(iii) *Matching rule.*—If a taxpayer (or a person described in section 1059(c)(3)(C) with respect to the taxpayer) engages in a transaction or series of transactions with a principal purpose of recognizing foreign source income that results in the creation of a corresponding loss with respect to stock (as a consequence of the rules regarding the timing of recognition of income, for example), the loss shall be allocated and apportioned against such income to the extent of the recognized foreign source income. This paragraph (b)(4)(iii) applies to any portion of a loss that is not allocated under paragraph (b)(1)(i) of this section (dividend recapture rule), including a loss in excess of the dividend recapture amount and a loss that is related to a dividend recapture amount described in paragraph (b)(1)(ii) (de minimis exception) or (b)(1)(iii) (passive dividend exception) of this section.

(iv) *Examples.*—The application of this paragraph (b)(4) may be illustrated by the following examples. No inference is intended regarding the application of any other Internal Revenue Code section or judicial doctrine that may apply to disallow or defer the recognition of loss. The examples are as follows:

Example 1. (i) *Facts.* On January 1, 2000, *P*, a domestic corporation, owns all of the stock of *N1*, a controlled foreign corporation, which owns all of the stock of *N2*, a controlled foreign corporation. *N1*'s basis in the stock of *N2* exceeds its fair market value, and any loss recognized by *N1* on the sale of *N2* would be allocated under paragraph (a)(1) of this section to reduce foreign source passive limitation earnings and profits of *N1*. In contemplation of the sale of *N2* to an unrelated purchaser, *P* causes *N1* to liquidate with principal purposes of recognizing the loss on the *N2* stock and allocating the loss against U.S. source income. *P* sells the *N2* stock and *P* recognizes a loss.

(ii) *Loss allocation.* Because one of the principal purposes of the liquidation was to transfer the stock to *P* in order to change the allocation of the built-in loss on the *N2* stock, under paragraph (b)(4)(i) of this section the loss is allocated against *P*'s foreign source passive limitation income.

Example 2. (i) *Facts.* On January 1, 2000, *P*, a domestic corporation, forms *N* and *F*, foreign corporations, and contributes $1,000 to the capital of each. *N* and *F* enter into offsetting positions in financial instruments that produce financial services income. Holding the *N* stock substantially diminishes *P*'s risk of loss with respect to the *F* stock (and vice versa). *P* holds *N* and *F* with a principal purpose of recognizing foreign source income and U.S. source loss. On March 31, 2000, when the financial instrument held by *N* is worth $1,200 and the financial instrument held by *F* is worth $800, *P* sells its *F* stock and recognizes a $200 loss.

(ii) *Loss allocation.* Because *P* held an offsetting position with respect to the *F* stock with a principal purpose of recognizing foreign source income and U.S. source loss, the $200 loss is allocated against foreign source financial services income under paragraph (b)(4)(ii) of this section.

Example 3. (i) *Facts.* On January 1, 2002, *P* and *Q*, domestic corporations, form *R*, a domestic partnership. The corporations and partnership use the calendar year as their taxable year. *P* contributes $900 to *R* in exchange for a 90-percent partnership interest and *Q* contributes $100 to *R* in exchange for a 10-percent partnership interest. *R* purchases a dance studio in Country *X* for $1,000. On January 2, 2002, *R* enters into contracts to provide dance lessons in Country *x* for a 5-year period beginning January 1, 2003. These contracts are prepaid by the dance studio customers on December 31, 2002, and *R* recognizes foreign source taxable income of $500 from the prepayments (*R*'s only income in 2002). *P* takes into income its $450 distributive share of partnership taxable income. On January 1, 2003, *P*'s basis in its partnership interest is $1,350 ($900 from its contribution under section 722, increased by its $450 distributive share of partnership income under section 705). On September 22, 2003, *P* contributes its *R* partnership interest to *S*, a newly-formed domestic corporation, in exchange for all the stock of *S*. Under section 358, *P*'s basis in *S* is $1,350. On December 1, 2003, *P* sells *S* to an unrelated party for $1050 and recognizes a $300 loss.

(ii) *Loss allocation. P* recognized foreign source income for tax purposes before the income had economically accrued, and the accelerated recognition of income increased *P*'s basis in *R* without increasing its value by a corresponding amount, which resulted in the creation of a built-in loss with respect to the *S* stock. Under paragraph (b)(4)(iii) of this section the $300 loss is allocated against foreign source income if *P* had a principal purpose of recognizing foreign source income and corresponding loss.

(c) *Loss recognized by partnership.*—A partner's distributive share of loss recognized by a partnership shall be allocated and apportioned in accordance with this section as if the partner had recognized the loss. If loss is attributable to an office or other fixed place of business of the partnership within the meaning of section 865(e)(3), such office or fixed place of business shall be considered to be an office of the partner for purposes of this section.

(d) *Definitions.*—(1) *Terms defined in §1.861-8.*—See §1.861-8 for the meaning of *class of gross income, statutory grouping of gross income,* and *residual grouping of gross income.*

(2) *Dividend recapture amount.*—A dividend recapture amount is a dividend (except for an amount treated as a dividend under section 78), an inclusion described in section 951(a)(1)(A)(i) (but only to the extent attributable to a dividend (including a dividend under section 964(e)(1)) included in the earnings of a controlled foreign corporation (held directly or indirectly by the person recognizing the loss) that is included in foreign personal holding company income under section 954(c)(1)(A)) and an inclusion described in section 951(a)(1)(B).

(3) *Recapture period.*—A recapture period is the 24-month period ending on the date on which a taxpayer recognized a loss with respect to stock. For example, if a taxpayer recognizes a loss on March 15, 2002, the recapture period begins on and includes March 16, 2000, and ends on and includes March 15, 2002. A recapture period is increased by any period of time in which the taxpayer has diminished its risk of loss in a manner described in section 246(c)(4) and the regulations thereunder and by any period in which the assets of the corporation are hedged against risk of loss (or are converted into and held as low-risk investments) with a principal purpose of enabling the taxpayer to hold the stock without significant risk of loss until the recapture period has expired. In the case of a loss recognized after a dividend is declared but before such dividend is paid, the recapture period is extended through the date on which the dividend is paid.

(4) *United States resident.*—See section 865(g) and the regulations thereunder for the definition of United States resident.

(e) *Effective date.*—(1) *In general.*—This section is applicable to loss recognized on or after January 11, 1999, except that paragraphs (a)(3)(ii), (b)(1)(iv) *Example 6*, (b)(4)(iii), (b)(4)(iv) *Example 3*, and (d)(3) of this section are applicable to loss recognized on or after January 8, 2002. For purposes of this paragraph (e), loss that is recognized but deferred (for example, under section 267 or 1092) shall be treated as recognized at the time the loss is taken into account.

(2) *Application to prior periods.*—A taxpayer may apply the rules of this section to losses recognized in any taxable year beginning on or after January 1, 1987, and all subsequent years, provided that—

(i) The taxpayer's tax liability as shown on an original or amended tax return is consistent with the rules of this section for each such year for which the statute of limitations does not preclude the filing of an amended return on June 30, 2002; and

(ii) The taxpayer makes appropriate adjustments to eliminate any double benefit arising from the application of this section to years that are not open for assessment.

(3) *Examples.*—The rules of this paragraph (e) may be illustrated by the following examples:

Example 1. (i) *P*, a domestic corporation, has a calendar taxable year. On March 10, 1985, *P* recognizes a $100 capital loss on the sale of *N*, a foreign corporation. Pursuant to sections 1211(a) and 1212(a), the loss is not allowed in 1985 and is carried over to the 1990 taxable year. The loss is allocated against foreign source income under § 1.861-8(e)(7). In 1999, *P* chooses to apply this section to all losses recognized in its 1987 taxable year and in all subsequent years.

(ii) Allocation of the loss on the sale of *N* is not affected by the rules of this section because the loss was recognized in a taxable year that did not begin after December 31, 1986.

Example 2. (i) *P*, a domestic corporation, has a calendar taxable year. On March 10, 1988, *P* recognizes a $100 capital loss on the sale of *N*, a foreign corporation. Pursuant to sections 1211(a) and 1212(a), the loss is not allowed in 1988 and is carried back to the 1985 taxable year. The loss is allocated against foreign source income under § 1.861-8(e)(7) on *P*'s federal income tax return for 1985 and increases an overall foreign loss account under § 1.904(f)-1.

(ii) In 1999, *P* chooses to apply this section to all losses recognized in its 1987 taxable year and in all subsequent years. Consequently, the loss on the sale of *N* is allocated against U.S. source income under paragraph (a)(1) of this section. Allocation of the loss against U.S. source income reduces *P*'s overall foreign loss account and increases *P*'s tax liability in 2 years: 1990, a year that will not be open for assessment on June 30, 1999, and 1997, a year that will be open for assessment on June 30, 1999. Pursuant to paragraph (e)(2)(i) of this section, *P* must file an amended federal income tax return that reflects the rules of this section for 1997, but not for 1990.

Example 3. (i) *P*, a domestic corporation, has a calendar taxable year. On March 10, 1989, *P* recognizes a $100 capital loss on the sale of *N*, a foreign corporation. The loss is allocated against foreign source income under § 1.861-8(e)(7) on *P*'s federal income tax return for 1989 and results in excess foreign tax credits for that year. The excess credit is carried back to 1988, pursuant to section 904(c). In 1999, *P* chooses to apply this section to all losses recognized in its 1989 taxable year and in all subsequent years. On June 30, 1999, *P*'s 1988 taxable year is closed for assessment, but *P*'s 1989 taxable year is open with respect to claims for refund.

(ii) Because *P* chooses to apply this section to its 1989 taxable year, the loss on the sale of *N* is allocated against U.S. source income under paragraph (a)(1) of this section. Allocation of the loss against U.S. source income would have permitted the foreign tax credit to be used in 1989, reducing *P*'s tax liability in 1989. Nevertheless, under paragraph (e)(2)(ii) of this section, because the credit was carried back to 1988, *P* may not claim the foreign tax credit in 1989.

[Reg. § 1.865-2.]

☐ [*T.D. 8805, 1-8-99. Amended by T.D. 8973, 12-27-2001.*]

§ 1.865-3. Source of gross income from sales of personal property (including inventory property) by a nonresident attributable to an office or other fixed place of business in the United States.—(a) *In general.*—Notwithstanding any provision of section 861 through 865 or other regulations in this part, this section provides the sole sourcing rules for gross income, gain, or loss from section 865(e)(2) sales. Gross income, gain, or loss from a section 865(e)(2) sale is U.S. source income to the extent that the gross income, gain, or loss is properly allocable to an office or other fixed place of business in the United States under paragraph (d) of this section.

(b) *Exception for certain inventory sales for use, disposition or consumption outside the United States.*—A section 865(e)(2) sale does not include any sale of inventory property that is sold for use, disposition, or consumption outside the United States if an office or other fixed place of business of the nonresident in a foreign country materially participates in the sale. See § 1.864-6(b)(3) to determine whether a foreign office materially participates in the sale and whether the property was destined for foreign use.

(c) *Section 865(e)(2) sales.*—For purposes of this section, a "section 865(e)(2) sale" is a sale of personal property by a nonresident, including inventory property, other than a sale described in paragraph (b) of this section, that is attributable to an office or other fixed place of business in the United States under the principles of section 864(c)(5)(B) as prescribed in § 1.864-6(b)(1) and (2). In determining whether a nonresident maintains an office or other fixed place of business in the United States, the principles of section 864(c)(5)(A) as prescribed in § 1.864-7 apply, including the rules of paragraph (d) of that section regarding the office or other fixed place of business of a dependent agent of the nonresident. For purposes of this section, "inventory property" has the meaning provided in section 865(i)(1), and "nonresident" has the meaning provided in section 865(g)(1)(B).

(d) *Amount of gross income, gain, or loss on sale of personal property properly allocable to a U.S. office.*—(1) *In general.*—Except as otherwise provided in paragraphs (d)(2) through (4) of this section, the amount of gross income, gain, or loss from a section 865(e)(2) sale that is properly allocable to an office or other fixed place of business in the United States is determined under the principles of § 1.864-6(c)(1).

(2) *Produced inventory property.*—Gross income, gain, or loss from a section 865(e)(2) sale of inventory property that is produced by the nonresident seller is properly allocable to an office or other fixed place of business in the United States or to production activities in accordance with the "50/50 method" described in paragraph (d)(2)(i) of this section. However, in lieu of the 50/50 method, the nonresident seller may elect to allocate the gross income, gain, or loss under the "books and records method" described in paragraph (d)(2)(ii)(A) of this section, provided that the nonresident satisfies all of the requirements described in paragraph (d)(2)(ii)(B) of this section to the satisfaction of the Commissioner. Gross income allocable to production activities under this paragraph (d)(2) is sourced in accordance with § 1.863-3. For purposes of this paragraph (d)(2), the term "produced" includes created, fabricated, manufactured, extracted, processed, cured, and aged, as determined under the principles of § 1.954-3(a)(4) (except for § 1.954-3(a)(4)(iv)). See section 864(a) and § 1.864-1.

(i) *The 50/50 method.*—Fifty percent of the gross income, gain, or loss from a section 865(e)(2) sale of inventory property that is produced by the nonresident seller is properly allocable to an office or other fixed place of business in the United States, and the remaining 50 percent of the gross income, gain, or loss is properly allocable to production activities (the "50/50 method").

(ii) *Books and records method.*—(A) *Method.*—Subject to paragraph (d)(2)(ii)(B) of this section, a nonresident may elect to determine the amount of its gross income, gain, or loss from the sale of inventory property produced by the nonresident seller that is properly allocable to production activities and sales activities for the taxable year based upon its books of account (the "books and records method"). The gross income, gain, or loss allocable to sales activities under this method is treated as properly allocable to an office or other fixed place of business in the United States and the remaining gross income, gain, or loss is treated as properly allocable to production activities.

(B) *Election and reporting rules.*—(*1*) *In general.*—A nonresident may not make the election described in paragraph (d)(2)(ii)(A) of this section unless the requirements of paragraphs (d)(2)(ii)(B)(*2*) through (*4*) of this section are satisfied. Once the election is made, the nonresident must continue to satisfy the requirements of paragraphs (d)(2)(ii)(B)(*2*) through (*4*) of this section until the election is revoked. If the nonresident fails to satisfy the requirements in paragraphs (d)(2)(ii)(B)(*2*) through (*4*) of this section to the satisfaction of the Commissioner, the Commissioner may, in its sole discretion, apply the 50/50 method described in paragraph (d)(2)(i) of this section.

(2) *Books of account.*—The nonresident must establish that it, in good faith and unaffected by considerations of tax liability, regularly employs in its books of account a detailed allocation of receipts and expenditures that, under the principles of section 482, clearly reflects both the amount of the nonresident's gross income, gain, or loss from its inventory sales that are attributable to its sales activities, and the amount of its gross income, gain, or loss from its inventory sales that are attributable to its production activities. For purposes of this paragraph (d)(2)(ii)(B)(2), section 482 principles apply as if the office or other fixed place of business in the United States were a separate organization, trade, or business (and, thus, a separate controlled taxpayer) from the nonresident (whether or not payments are made between the United States office or other fixed place of business and the nonresident's other offices, and whether or not the nonresident itself would otherwise constitute an organization, trade, or business).

(3) *Required records.*—The nonresident must prepare and maintain the records described in paragraph (d)(2)(ii)(B)(2) of this section, which must be in existence when its return is filed. The nonresident must also prepare an explanation of how the allocation clearly reflects the nonresident's gross income, gain, or loss from production and sales activities under the principles of section 482. The nonresident must make available the explanation and records of the nonresident (including for the office or other fixed place of business in the United States and the offices or branches that perform the production activities) upon request of the Commissioner, within 30 days, unless some other period is agreed upon between the Commissioner and the nonresident.

(4) *Making and revoking the books and records method election; disclosure of election.*—Except as otherwise provided in publications, forms, instructions, or other guidance, a nonresident makes or revokes the election to apply the books and records method by attaching a statement to its original timely filed Federal income tax return (including extensions) providing that it elects, or revokes the election, to apply the books and records method described in paragraph (d)(2)(ii)(A) of this section. For nonresidents making the election, the statement must provide that the nonresident has prepared the records described in paragraph (d)(2)(ii)(B)(2) and (3) of this section.

(5) *Limitation on revoking the books and records method election.*—Once made, the books and records method election continues until revoked. An election cannot be revoked, without the consent of the Commissioner, for any taxable year beginning within 48 months of the last day of the taxable year for which the election was made.

(3) *Purchased inventory property.*—All gross income, gain, or loss from a section 865(e)(2) sale of inventory property that is both purchased and sold by a nonresident is properly allocable to an office or other fixed place of business in the United States.

(4) *Depreciable personal property.*—Gain from a section 865(e)(2) sale of depreciable personal property (as defined in section 865(c)(4)) is allocated under paragraphs (d)(4)(i) and (ii) of this section.

(i) The gain not in excess of the depreciation adjustments, if any, is properly allocable to an office or other fixed place of business in the United States to the same extent that the gain would be allocated to sources within the United States under the rules of section 865(c)(1). The remaining gain not in excess of the depreciation adjustments, if any, is allocated to sources without the United States in accordance with section 865(c)(1). However, notwithstanding the preceding sentences, if the property was predominantly used in the United States, within the meaning of section 865(c)(3)(B)(i), for a particular taxable year, all of the gain not in excess of depreciation for that year is properly allocable to the office or other fixed place of business in the United States.

(ii) The gain in excess of the depreciation adjustments, if any, is treated as if such gain was from the sale of inventory and the amount allocable to an office or fixed place of business in the United States is determined under paragraph (d)(2) or (3) of this section, as applicable.

(e) *Determination of source of taxable income.*—For rules allocating and apportioning expenses to gross income effectively connected with the conduct of a trade or business of a foreign corporation in the United States (including gross income, gain, or loss sourced under this section), see section 882(c)(1). For rules allocating and apportioning expenses to gross income, gain, or loss effectively connected with the conduct of a trade or business of a nonresident alien in the United States (including gross income, gain, or loss sourced under this section), see section 873(a).

(f) *Export trade corporations.*—This section does not apply for purposes of defining an export trade corporation under section 971(a).

(g) *Applicability date.*—This section applies to taxable years ending on or after December 23, 2019. However, a nonresident may apply this section in its entirety for taxable years beginning after December 31, 2017, and ending before December 23, 2019, provided that the nonresident and all persons related to the nonresident (within the meaning of section 267 or 707) apply this section and §§1.863-1(b), 1.863-2(b), 1.863-3, 1.863-8(b)(3)(ii), 1.864-5(a) and (b), and 1.864-6(c)(2) in their entirety for the taxable year, and once applied, the nonresident and all persons related to the nonresident (within the meaning of section 267 or 707) continue to apply these regulations in their entirety for all subsequent taxable years. [Reg. §1.865-3.]

□ [*T.D. 9921, 12-10-2020.*]

Nonresident Aliens and Foreign Corporations

§1.871-1. Classification and manner of taxing alien individuals.—(a) *Classes of aliens.*—For purposes of the income tax, alien individuals are divided generally into two classes, namely, resident aliens and nonresident aliens. Resident alien individuals are, in general, taxable the same as citizens of the United States; that is, a resident alien is taxable on income derived from all sources, including sources without the United States. See §1.1-1(b). Nonresident alien individuals are taxable only on certain income from sources within the United States and on the income described in section 864(c)(4) from sources without the United States which is effectively connected for the taxable year with the conduct of a trade or business in the United States. However, nonresident alien individuals may elect, under section 6013(g) or (h), to be treated as U.S. residents for purposes of determining their income tax liability under Chapters 1 and 24 of the Code. Accordingly, any reference in §§1.1-1 through 1.1388-1 to nonresident alien individuals does not include those with respect to whom an election under section 6013(g) or (h) is in effect, unless otherwise specifically provided. Similarly, any reference to resident aliens or U.S. residents includes those with respect to whom an election is in effect, unless otherwise specifically provided.

(b) *Classes of nonresident aliens.*—(1) *In general.*—For purposes of the income tax, nonresident alien individuals are divided into the following three classes:

(i) Nonresident alien individuals who at no time during the taxable year are engaged in a trade or business in the United States,

(ii) Nonresident alien individuals who at any time during the taxable year are, or are deemed under §1.871-9 to be, engaged in a trade or business in the United States, and

(iii) Nonresident alien individuals who are bona fide residents of a section 931 possession (as defined in §1.931-1(c)(1) of this chapter) or Puerto Rico during the entire taxable year. An individual described in paragraph (b)(1)(i) or (ii) of this section is subject to tax pursuant to the provisions of subpart A (section 871 and following), part II, subchapter N, chapter 1 of the Code, and the regulations under those provisions. The provisions of subpart A do not apply to individuals described in this paragraph (b)(1)(iii), but such individuals, except as provided in section 931 or 933, are subject to the tax imposed by section 1 or 55. See §1.876-1.

(2) *Treaty income.*—If the gross income of a nonresident alien individual described in subparagraph (1)(i) or (ii) of this paragraph includes income on which the tax is limited by tax convention, see §1.871-12.

(3) *Exclusions from gross income.*—For rules relating to the exclusion of certain items from the gross income of a nonresident alien individual, including annuities excluded under section 871(f), see §§1.872-2 and 1.894-1.

(4) *Expatriation to avoid tax.*—For special rules applicable in determining the tax of a nonresident alien individual who has lost United States citizenship with a principal purpose of avoiding certain taxes, see section 877.

(5) *Adjustment of tax of certain nonresident aliens.*—For the application of pre-1967 income tax provisions to residents of a foreign country which imposes a more burdensome income tax than the United States, and for the adjustment of the income tax of a national or resident of a foreign country which imposes a discriminatory income tax on the income of citizens of the United States or domestic corporations, see section 896.

(6) *Conduit financing arrangements.*—For rules regarding conduit financing arrangements, see §§881-3 and 1.881-4.

(c) *Effective/applicability date.*—This section shall apply for taxable years beginning after December 31, 1966. For corresponding rules applicable to taxable years beginning before January 1, 1967, see 26 CFR 1.871-1 and 1.871-7(a) (Rev. as of Jan. 1, 1971). Paragraph (b)(1)(iii) of this section applies to taxable years ending after April 9, 2008. [Reg. §1.871-1.]

☐ [*T.D.* 6258, 10-23-57. *Amended by T.D.* 7332, 12-20-74, *T.D.* 7670, 1-30-80; *T.D.* 8611, 8-10-95; *T.D.* 9194, 4-6-2005, *T.D.* 9391, 4-4-2008 *and T.D.* 9849, 3-11-2019.]

§1.871-2. Determining residence of alien individuals.—(a) *General.*—The term "nonresident alien individual" means an individual whose residence is not within the United States, and who is not a citizen of the United States. The term includes a nonresident alien fiduciary. For such purpose the term "fiduciary" shall have the meaning assigned to it by section 7701(a)(6) and the regulations in Part 301 of this chapter (Regulations on Procedure and Administration). For presumption as to an alien's nonresidence, see paragraph (b) of §1.871-4.

(b) *Residence defined.*—An alien actually present in the United States who is not a mere transient or sojourner is a resident of the United States for purposes of the income tax. Whether he is a transient is determined by his intentions with regard to the length and nature of his stay. A mere floating intention, indefinite as to time, to return to another country is not sufficient to constitute him a transient. If he lives in the United States and has no definite intention as to his stay, he is a resident. One who comes to the United States for a definite purpose which in its nature may be promptly accomplished is a transient; but, if his purpose is of such a nature that an extended stay may be necessary for its accomplishment, and to that end the alien makes his home temporarily in the United States, he becomes a resident, though it may be his intention at all times to return to his domicile abroad when the purpose for which he came has been consummated or abandoned. An alien whose stay in the United States is limited to a definite period by the immigration laws is not a resident of the United States within the meaning of this section, in the absence of exceptional circumstances.

(c) *Application and effective dates.*—Unless the context indicates otherwise, §§1.871-2 through 1.871-5 apply to determine the residence of aliens for taxable years beginning before January 1, 1985. To determine the residence of aliens for taxable years beginning after December 31, 1984, see section 7701(b) and §§301.7701(b)-1 through 301.7701(b)-9 of this chapter. However, for purposes of determining whether an individual is a qualified individual under section 911(d)(1)(A), the rules of §§1.871-2 and 1.871-5 shall continue to apply for taxable years beginning after December 31, 1984. For purposes of determining whether an individual is a resident of the United States for estate and gift tax purposes, see §20.0-1(b)(1) and (2) and §25.2501-1(b) of this chapter, respectively. [Reg. §1.871-2.]

☐ [*T.D.* 6258, 10-23-57. *Amended by T.D.* 8411, 4-24-92.]

§1.871-3. Residence of alien seamen.—In order to determine whether an alien seaman is a resident of the United States for purposes of the income tax, it is necessary to decide whether the presumption of nonresidence (as prescribed by paragraph (b) of §1.871-4) is overcome by facts showing that he has established a residence in the United States. Residence may be established on a vessel regularly engaged in coastwise trade, but the mere fact that a sailor makes his home on a vessel which is flying the United States flag and is engaged in foreign trade is not sufficient to establish residence in the United States, even though the vessel, while carrying on foreign trade, touches at American ports. An alien seaman may acquire an actual residence in the United States within the rules laid down in §1.871-4, although the nature of his calling requires him to be absent for a long period from the place where his residence is established. An alien seaman may acquire such a residence at a sailors' boarding house or hotel, but such a claim should be carefully scrutinized in order to make sure that such residence is bona fide. The filing of Form 1078 or taking out first citizenship papers is proof of residence in the United States from the time the form is filed or the papers taken out, unless rebutted by other evidence showing an intention to be a transient. [Reg. §1.871-3.]

☐ [*T.D.* 6258, 10-23-57.]

§1.871-4. Proof of residence of aliens.—(a) *Rules of evidence.*—The following rules of evidence shall govern in determining whether or not an alien within the United States has acquired residence therein for purposes of the income tax.

(b) *Nonresidence presumed.*—An alien, by reason of his alienage, is presumed to be a nonresident alien.

(c) *Presumption rebutted.*—(1) *Departing alien.*—In the case of an alien who presents himself for determination of tax liability before departure from the United States, the presumption as to the alien's nonresidence may be overcome by proof—

(i) That the alien, at least six months before the date he so presents himself, has filed a declaration of his intention to become a citizen of the United States under the naturalization laws; or

(ii) That the alien, at least six months before the date he so presents himself, has filed Form 1078 or its equivalent; or

(iii) Of acts and statements of the alien showing a definite intention to acquire residence in the United States or showing that his stay in the United States has been of such an extended nature as to constitute him a resident.

(2) *Other aliens.*—In the case of other aliens, the presumption as to the alien's nonresidence may be overcome by proof—

(i) That the alien has filed a declaration of his intention to become a citizen of the United States under the naturalization laws; or

(ii) That the alien has filed Form 1078 or its equivalent; or

(iii) Of acts and statements of the alien showing definite intention to acquire residence in the United States or showing that his stay in the United States has been of such an extended nature as to constitute him a resident.

(d) *Certificate.*—If, in the application of paragraphs (c)(1)(iii) or (2)(iii) of this section, the internal revenue officer or employee who examines the alien is in doubt as to the facts, such officer or employee may, to assist him in determining the facts, require a certificate or certificates setting forth the facts relied upon by the alien seeking to overcome the presumption. Each such certificate, which shall contain, or be verified by, a written declaration that it is made under the penalties of perjury, shall be executed by some credible person or persons, other than the alien and members of his family, who have known the alien at least six months before the date of execution of the certificate or certificates. [Reg. §1.871-4.]

☐ [*T.D.* 6258, 10-23-57.]

§1.871-5. Loss of residence by an alien.—An alien who has acquired residence in the United States retains his status as a resident until he abandons the same and actually departs from the United States. An intention to change his residence does not change his status as a resident alien to that of a nonresident alien. Thus, an alien who has acquired a residence in the United States is taxable as a resident for the remainder of his stay in the United States. [Reg. §1.871-5.]

☐ [*T.D.* 6258, 10-23-57.]

§1.871-6. Duty of withholding agent to determine status of alien payees.—For the obligation of a withholding agent to withhold the tax imposed by this section, see chapter 3 of the Internal Revenue Code and the regulations thereunder. [Reg. §1.871-6.]

☐ [*T.D.* 6258, 10-23-57. *Amended by T.D.* 7332, 12-20-74; *T.D.* 7977, 9-19-84 *and T.D.* 8734, 10-6-97 (T.D. 8804 extended the effective date of T.D. 8734 from January 1, 1999, to January 1, 2000; T.D. 8856 further delayed the effective date of T.D. 8734 until January 1, 2001).]

§1.871-7. Taxation of nonresident alien individuals not engaged in U.S. business.—(a) *Imposition of tax.*—(1) This section applies for purposes of determining the tax of a nonresident alien individual who at no time during the taxable year is engaged in trade or business in the United States. However, see also §1.871-8 where such individual is a student or trainee deemed to be engaged in trade or business in the United States or where he has an election in effect for the taxable year in respect to real property income. Except as otherwise provided in §1.871-12, a nonresident alien individual to whom this section applies is not subject to the tax imposed by section 1 or section 1201(b) but, pursuant to the provisions of section 871(a), is liable to a flat tax of 30 percent upon the aggregate of the amounts determined under paragraphs (b), (c), and (d) of this section which are received during the taxable year from sources within the United States. Except as specifically provided in such paragraphs, such amounts do not include gains from the sale or exchange of property. To determine the source of such amounts, see sections 861 through 863, and the regulations thereunder.

(2) The tax of 30 percent is imposed by section 871(a) upon an amount only to the extent the amount constitutes gross income. Thus, for example, the amount of an annuity which is subject to such tax shall be determined in accordance with section 72.

(3) Deductions shall not be allowed in determining the amount subject to tax under this section except that losses from sales or exchanges of capital assets shall be allowed to the extent provided in section 871(a)(2) and paragraph (d) of this section.

(4) Except as provided in §§1.871-9 and 1.871-10, a nonresident alien individual not engaged in trade or business in the United States during the taxable year has no income, gain, or loss for the taxable year which is effectively connected for the taxable year with the conduct of a trade or business in the United States. See section 864(c)(1)(B) and §1.864-3.

(5) Gains and losses which, by reason of section 871(d) and §1.871-10, are treated as gains or losses which are effectively connected for the taxable year with the conduct of a trade or business in the United States by the nonresident alien individual shall not be taken into account in determining the tax under this section. See, for example, paragraph (c)(2) of §1.871-10.

(6) For special rules applicable in determining the tax of certain nonresident alien individuals, see paragraph (b) of §1.871-1.

(b) *Fixed or determinable annual or periodical income.*—(1) *General rule.*—The tax of 30 percent imposed by section 871(a)(1) applies to the gross amount received from sources within the United States as fixed or determinable annual or periodical gains, profits, or income. Specific items of fixed or determinable annual or periodical income are enumerated in section 871(a)(1)(A) as interest, dividends, rents, salaries, wages, premiums, annuities, compensations, remunerations, and emoluments, but other items of fixed or determinable annual or periodical gains, profits, or income are also subject to the tax, as, for instance, royalties, including royalties for the use of patents, copyrights, secret processes and formulas, and other like property. As to the determination of fixed or determinable annual or periodical income, see §1.1441-2(b). For special rules treating gain on the disposition of section 306 stock as fixed or determinable annual or periodical income for purposes of section 871(a), see section 306(f) and paragraph (h) of §1.306-3.

(2) *Substitute payments.*—For purposes of this section, a substitute interest payment (as defined in §1.861-2(a)(7)) received by a foreign person pursuant to a securities lending transaction or a sale-repurchase transaction (as defined in §1.861-2(a)(7)) shall have the same character as interest income paid or accrued with respect to the terms of the transferred security. Similarly, for purposes of this section, a substitute dividend payment (as defined in §1.861-3(a)(6)) received by a foreign person pursuant to a securities lending transaction or a sale-repurchase transaction (as defined in §1.861-3(a)(6)) shall have the same character as a distribution received with respect to the transferred security. Where, pursuant to a securities lending transaction or a sale-repurchase transaction, a foreign person transfers to another person a security the interest on which would qualify as portfolio interest under section 871(h) in the hands of the lender, substitute interest payments made with respect to the transferred security will be treated as portfolio interest, provided that in the case of interest on an obligation in registered form (as defined in §1.871-14(c)(1)(i)), the transferor complies with the documentation requirement described in §1.871-14(c)(1)(ii)(C) with respect to the payment of the substitute interest and none of the exceptions to the portfolio interest exemption in sections 871(h)(3) and (4) apply. See also §§1.861-2(b)(2) and 1.894-1(c).

(c) *Other income and gains.*—(1) *Items subject to tax.*—The tax of 30 percent imposed by section 871(a)(1) also applies to the following gains received during the taxable year from sources within the United States:

(i) Gains described in section 402(a)(2), relating to the treatment of total distributions from certain employees' trusts; section 403(a)(2), relating to treatment of certain payments under certain employee annuity plans; and section 631(b) or (c), relating to treatment of gain on the disposal of timber, coal, or iron ore with a retained economic interest;

(ii) [Reserved]

(iii) Gains on transfers described in section 1235, relating to certain transfers of patent rights, made on or before October 4, 1966; and

(iv) Gains from the sale or exchange after October 4, 1966, of patents, copyrights, secret processes and formulas, good will, trademarks, trade brands, franchises, or other like property, or of any interest in any such property, to the extent the gains are from payments (whether in a lump sum or in installments) which are contingent on the productivity, use, or disposition of the property or interest sold or exchanged, or from payments which are treated under section 871(e) and §1.871-11 as being so contingent.

(2) *Nonapplication of 183-day rule.*—The provisions of section 871(a)(2), relating to gains from the sale or exchange of capital assets, and paragraph (d)(2) of this section do not apply to the gains described in this paragraph; as a consequence, the taxpayer receiving gains described in subparagraph (1) of this paragraph during a taxable year is subject to the tax of 30 percent thereon without regard to the 183-day rule contained in such provisions.

(3) *Determination of amount of gain.*—The tax of 30 percent imposed upon the gains described in subparagraph (1) of this paragraph applies to the full amount of the gains and is determined (i) without regard to the alternative tax imposed by section 1201(b) upon the excess of the net long-term capital gain over the net short-term capital loss; (ii) without regard to the deduction allowed by section 1202 in respect of capital gains; (iii) without regard to section 1231, relating to property used in the trade or business and involuntary conversions; and (iv), except in the case of gains described in subparagraph (1)(ii) of this paragraph, whether or not the gains are considered to be gains from the sale or exchange of property which is a capital asset.

(d) *Gains from sale or exchange of capital assets.*—(1) *Gains subject to tax.*—The tax of 30 percent imposed by section 871(a)(2) applies to the excess of gains derived from sources within the United States over losses allocable to sources within the United States, which are derived from the sale or exchange of capital assets, determined in accordance with the provisions of subparagraphs (2) through (4) of this paragraph.

(2) *Presence in the United States 183 days or more.*—(i) If the nonresident alien individual has been present in the United States for a period or periods aggregating 183 days or more during the taxable year, he is liable to a tax of 30 percent upon the amount by which his gains, derived from sources within the United States, from sales or exchanges of capital assets effected at any time during the year exceed his losses, allocable to sources within the United States, from sales or exchanges of capital assets effected at any time during that year. Gains and losses from sales or exchanges effected at any time during such taxable year are to be taken into account for this purpose even though the nonresident alien individual is not present in the United States at the time the sales or exchanges are effected. In addition, if the nonresident alien individual has been present in the United States for a period or periods aggregating 183 days or more during the taxable year, gains and losses for such taxable year from sales or exchanges of capital assets effected during a previous taxable year beginning after December 31, 1966, are to be taken into account, but only if he was also present in the United States during such previous taxable year for a period or periods aggregating 183 days or more.

(ii) If the nonresident alien individual has not been present in the United States during the taxable year, or if he has been present in the United States for a period or periods aggregating less than 183 days during the taxable year, gains and losses from sales or exchanges of capital assets effected during the year are not to be taken into account, except as required by paragraph (c) of this section, in determining the tax of such individual even though the sales or exchanges are effected during his presence in the United States. Moreover, gains and losses for such taxable year from sales or exchanges of capital assets effected during a previous taxable year beginning after December 31, 1966, are not to be taken into account, even though the nonresident alien individual was present in the United States during such previous year for a period or periods aggregating 183 days or more.

(iii) For purposes of this subparagraph, a nonresident alien individual is not considered to be present in the United States by reason of the presence in the United States of a person who is an agent or partner of such individual or who is a fiduciary of an estate or trust of which such individual is a beneficiary or a grantor-owner to whom section 671 applies.

(iv) The application of this subparagraph may be illustrated by the following examples:

Example (1). B, a nonresident alien individual not engaged in trade or business in the United States and using the calendar year as the taxable year, is present in the United States from May 1, 1971, to November 15, 1971, a period of more than 182 days. While present in the United States, B effects for his own account on various dates a number of transactions in stocks and securities on the stock exchange, as a result of which he has recognized capital gains of $10,000. During the period from January 1, 1971, to April 30, 1971, he carries out similar transactions through an agent in the United States, as a result of which B has recognized capital gains of $5,000. On December 15, 1971, through an agent in the United States B sells a capital asset on the installment plan, no payments being made by the purchaser in 1971. During 1972, B receives installment payments of $50,000 on the installment sale made in 1971, and the capital gain from sources within the United States for 1972 attributable to such payments is $12,500. In addition, during the period from January 1, 1972, to May 31, 1972, B effects for his own account, through an agent in the United States, a number of transactions in stocks and securities on the stock exchange, as a result of which B has recognized capital gains of $20,000. At no time during 1972 is B present in the United States or engaged in trade or business in the United States. Accordingly, for 1971, B is subject to tax under section 871(a)(2) on his capital gains of $15,000 from the transactions in that year on the stock exchange. For 1972, B is not subject to tax on the capital gain of $12,500 from the installment sale in 1971 or on the capital gains of $20,000 from the transactions in 1972 on the stock exchange.

Example (2). The facts are the same as in example (1) except that B is present in the United States from June 15, 1972, to December 31, 1972, a period of more than 182 days. Accordingly, B is subject to tax under section 871(a)(2) for 1971 on his capital gains of $15,000 from the transactions in that year on the stock exchange. He is also subject to tax under section 871(a)(2) for 1972 on his capital gains of $32,500 ($12,500 from the installment sale in 1971 plus $20,000 from the transactions in 1972 on the stock exchange).

Example (3). D, a nonresident alien individual not engaged in trade or business in the United States and using the calendar year as the taxable year, is present in the United States from April 1, 1971, to August 31, 1971, a period of less than 183 days. While present in the United States, D effects for his own account on various dates a number of transactions in stocks and securities on the stock exchange, as a result of which he has recognized capital gains of $15,000. During the period from January 1, 1971, to March 31, 1971, he carries out similar transactions through an agent in the United States, as a result of which D has recognized capital gains of $8,000. On December 20, 1971, through an agent in the United States, D sells a capital asset on the installment plan, no payments being made by the purchaser in 1971. During 1972, D receives installment payments of $200,000 on the installment sale made in 1971, and the capital gain from sources within the United States for 1972 attributable to such payments is $50,000. In addition, during the period from February 1, 1972, to August 15, 1972, a period of more than 182 days, D effects for his own account, through an agent in the United States, a number of transactions in stocks and securities on the stock exchange, as a result of which D has recognized capital gains of $25,000. At no time during 1972 is D present in the United States or engaged in trade or business in the United States. Accordingly, D is not subject to tax for 1971 or 1972 on any of his recognized capital gains.

Example (4). The facts are the same as in example (3) except that D is present in the United States from February 1, 1972, to August 15, 1972, a period of more than 182 days. Accordingly, D is not subject to tax for 1971 on his capital gains of $23,000 from the transactions in that year on the stock exchange. For 1972 he is subject to tax under section 871(a)(2) on his capital gains of $25,000 from the transactions in that year on the stock exchange, but he is not subject to the tax on the capital gain of $50,000 from the installment sale in 1971.

(3) *Determination of 183-day period.*—(i) *In general.*—In determining the total period of presence in the United States for a taxable year for purposes of subparagraph (2) of this paragraph, all separate periods of presence in the United States during the taxable year are to be aggregated. If the nonresident alien individual has not previously established a taxable year, as defined in section 441(b), he shall be treated as having a taxable year which is the calendar year, as defined in section 441(d). Subsequent adoption by such individual of a fiscal year as the taxable year will be treated as a change in the taxpayer's annual accounting period to which section 442 applies, and the change must be authorized under this part (Income Tax Regulations) or prior approval must be obtained by filing an application on Form 1128 in accordance with paragraph (b) of § 1.442-1. If in the course of his taxable year the nonresident alien individual changes his status from that of a citizen or resident of the United States to that of a nonresident alien individual, or vice versa, the determination of whether the individual has been present in the United States for 183 days or more during the taxable year shall be made by taking into account the entire taxable year, and not just that part of the taxable year during which he has the status of a nonresident alien individual.

(ii) *Definition of "day"*.—The term "day", as used in subparagraph (2) of this paragraph, means a calendar day during any portion of which the nonresident alien individual is physically present in the United States (within the meaning of sections 7701(a)(9) and 638) except that, in the case of an individual who is a resident of Canada or Mexico and, in the normal course of his employment in transportation service touching points within both Canada or Mexico and the United States, performs personal services in both the foreign country and the United States, the following rules shall apply:

(a) The performance of labor or personal services during eight hours or more in any one day within the United States shall be considered as one day in the United States, except that if a period of more or less than eight hours is considered a full work day in the transportation job involved, such period shall be considered as one day within the United States.

(b) The performance of labor or personal services during less than eight hours in any day in the United States shall, except as provided in *(a)*, be considered as a fractional part of a day in the United States. The total number of hours during which such services are performed in the United States during the taxable year, when divided by eight, shall be the number of days during which such individual shall be considered present in the United States during the taxable year.

(c) The aggregate number of days determined under *(a)* and *(b)* shall be considered the total number of days during which such individual is present in the United States during the taxable year.

(4) *Determination of amount of excess gains.*—(i) *In general.*—For the purpose of determining the excess of gains over losses subject to tax under this paragraph, gains and losses shall be taken into account only if, and to the extent that, they would be recognized and taken into account if the nonresident alien individual were engaged in trade or business in the United States during the taxable year and such gains and losses were effectively connected for such year with the conduct of a trade or business in the United States by such individual. However, in determining such excess of gains over losses no deduction may be taken under section 1202, relating to the deduction for capital gains, or section 1212, relating to the capital loss carryover. Thus, for example, in determining such excess gains all amounts considered under chapter 1 of the Code as gains or losses from the sale or exchange of capital assets shall be taken into account, except those gains which are described in section 871(a)(1)(B) or (D) and taken into account under paragraph (c) of this section and are considered to be gains from the sale or exchange of capital assets. Also, for example, a loss described in section 631(b) or (c) which is considered to be a loss from the sale of a capital asset shall be taken into account in determining the excess gains which are subject to tax under this paragraph. In further illustration, in determining such excess gains no deduction shall be allowed, pursuant to the provisions of section 267, for losses from sales or exchanges of property between related taxpayers. Any gains which are taken into account under section 871(a)(1) and paragraph (c) of this section shall not be taken into account in applying section 1231 for purposes of this paragraph. Gains and losses are to be taken into account under this paragraph whether they are short-term or long-term capital gains or losses within the meaning of section 1222.

(ii) *Gains not included.*—The provisions of this paragraph do not apply to any gains described in section 871(a)(1)(B) or (D), and in subdivision (i), (iii), or (iv) of paragraph (c)(1) of this section, which are considered to be gains from the sale or exchange of capital assets.

(iii) *Allowance of losses.*—In determining the excess of gains over losses subject to tax under this paragraph losses shall be allowed only to the extent provided by section 165(c). Losses from sales or exchanges of capital assets in excess of gains from sales or exchanges of capital assets shall not be taken into account.

(e) *Credits against tax.*—The credits allowed by section 31 (relating to tax withheld on wages), by section 32 (relating to tax withheld at source on nonresident aliens), by section 39 (relating to certain uses of gasoline and lubricating oil), and by section 6402 (relating to overpayments of tax) shall be allowed against the tax of a nonresident alien individual determined in accordance with this section.

(f) *Effective date.*—Except as otherwise provided in this paragraph, this section shall apply for taxable years beginning after December 31, 1966. Paragraph (b)(2) of this section is applicable to payments made after November 13, 1997. For corresponding rules applicable to taxable years beginning before January 1, 1967, see 26 CFR 1.871-7(b) and (c) (Rev. as of Jan. 1, 1971). [Reg. § 1.871-7.]

☐ [*T.D.* 6258, 10-23-57. *Amended by T.D.* 6464, 5-11-60; *T.D.* 6782, 12-23-64; *T.D.* 6823, 5-5-65; *T.D.* 6841, 7-26-65; *T.D.* 7332, 12-20-74; *T.D.* 8734, 10-6-97 (T.D. 8804 extended the effective date of T.D. 8734 from January 1, 1999, to January 1, 2000; T.D. 8856 further delayed the effective date of T.D. 8734 until January 1, 2001) *and T.D.* 8735, 10-6-97.]

§ 1.871-8. Taxation of nonresident alien individuals engaged in U.S. business or treated as having effectively connected income.—(a) *Segregation of income.*—This section applies for purposes of determining the tax of a nonresident alien individual who at any time during the taxable year is engaged in trade or business in the United States. It also applies for purposes of determining the tax of a nonresident alien student or trainee who is deemed under section 871(c) and § 1.871-9 to be engaged in trade or business in the United States or of a nonresident alien individual who at no time during the taxable year is engaged in trade or business in the United States but has an election in effect for the taxable year under section 871(d) and § 1.871-10 in respect to real property income. A nonresident alien individual to whom this section applies must segregate his gross income for the taxable year into two categories, namely, (1) the income which is effectively connected for the taxable year with the conduct of a trade or business in the United States by that individual and (2) the income which is not effectively connected for the taxable year with the conduct of a trade or business in the United States by that individual. A separate tax shall then be determined upon each such category of income, as provided in paragraph (b) of this section. The determination of whether income or gain is or is not effectively connected for the taxable year with the conduct of a trade or business in the United States by the nonresident alien individual shall be made in accordance with section 864(c) and §§ 1.864-3 through 1.864-7. For purposes of this section income which is effectively connected for the taxable year with the conduct of a trade or business in the United States includes all income which is treated under section 871(c) or (d) and § 1.871-9 or § 1.871-10 as income which is effectively connected for such year with the conduct of a trade or business in the United States by the nonresident alien individual.

(b) *Imposition of tax.*—(1) *Income not effectively connected with the conduct of a trade or business in the United States.*—If a nonresident alien individual who is engaged in trade or business in the United States at any time during the taxable year derives during such year from sources within the United States income or gains described in section 871(a)(1) and paragraph (b) or (c) of § 1.871-7 or gains from the sale or exchange of capital assets determined as provided in section 871(a)(2) and paragraph (d) of § 1.871-7, which are not effectively connected for the taxable year with the conduct of a trade or business in the United States by that individual, such income or gains shall be subject to a flat tax of 30 percent of the aggregate amount of such items. This tax shall be determined in the manner, and subject to the same conditions, set forth in § 1.871-7 as though the income or gains were derived by a nonresident alien individual not engaged in trade or business in the United States during the taxable year, except that (i) the rule in paragraph (d)(3) of such section for treating the calendar year as the taxable year shall not apply and (ii) in applying paragraph (c) and (d)(4) of such section, there shall not be taken into account any gains or losses which are taken into account in determining the tax under section 871(b) and subparagraph (2) of this paragraph. A nonresident alien individual who has an election in effect for the taxable year under section 871(d) and § 1.871-10 and who at no time during the taxable year is engaged in trade or business in the United States must determine his tax under § 1.871-7 on his income which is not treated as effectively connected with the conduct of a trade or business in the United States, subject to the exception contained in subdivision (ii) of this subparagraph.

(2) *Income effectively connected with the conduct of a trade or business in the United States.*—(i) *In general.*—If a nonresident alien to whom this section applies derives income or gains which are effectively connected for the taxable year with the conduct of a trade or business in the United States by that individual, the taxable income or gains shall, except as provided in § 1.871-12, be taxed in accordance with section 1 or, in the alternative, section 1201(b). See section 871(b)(1). Any income of the nonresident alien individual which is not effectively connected for the taxable year with the conduct of a trade or business in the United States by that individual shall not be taken into account in determining either the rate or amount of such tax. See paragraph (b) of § 1.872-1.

(ii) *Determination of taxable income.*—The taxable income for any taxable year for purposes of this subparagraph consists only of the nonresident alien individual's taxable income which is effectively connected for the taxable year with the conduct of a trade or business in the United States by that individual; and, for this purpose, it is immaterial that the trade or business with which that income is effectively connected is not the same as the trade or business carried on in the United States by that individual during the taxable year. See example (2) in § 1.864-4(b). In determining such taxable income all amounts constituting, or considered to be, gains or losses for the taxable year from the sale or exchange of capital assets shall be taken into account if such gains or losses are effectively connected for the taxable year with the conduct of a trade or business in the United States by that individual, and, for such purpose, the 183-day rule set forth in section 871(a)(2) and paragraph (d)(2) of § 1.871-7 shall not apply. Losses which are not effectively connected for the taxable year with the conduct of a trade or business in the United States by that individual shall not be taken into account in determining taxable income under this subdivision, except as provided in section 873(b)(1).

(iii) *Cross references.*—For rules for determining the gross income and deductions for the taxable year, see sections 872 and 873, and the regulations thereunder.

(c) *Change in trade or business status.*—(1) *In general.*—The determination as to whether a nonresident alien individual is engaged in trade or business within the United States during the taxable year is to be made for each taxable year. If at any time during the taxable year he is engaged in a trade or business in the United States, he is considered to be engaged in trade or business within the United States during the taxable year for purposes of sections 864(c)(1) and 871(b), and the regulations thereunder. Income, gain, or loss of a nonresident alien individual is not treated as being effectively connected for the taxable year with the conduct of a trade or business in the United States if he is not engaged in trade or business within the United States during such year, even though such income, gain, or loss may have been effectively connected for a previous taxable year with the conduct of a trade or business in the United States. See § 1.864-3. However, income, gain, or loss which is treated as effectively connected for the taxable year with the conduct of a trade or business in the United States by a nonresident alien individual will generally be treated as effectively connected for a subsequent taxable year if he is engaged in a trade or business in the United States during such subsequent year, even though such income, gain, or loss is not effectively connected with the conduct of the trade or business carried on in the United States during such subsequent year. This subparagraph does not apply to income described in section 871(c) or (d). It may not apply to a nonresident alien individual who for the taxable year uses an accrual method of accounting or to income which is constructively received in the taxable year within the meaning of § 1.451-2.

(2) *Illustrations.*—The application of this paragraph may be illustrated by the following examples:

Example (1). B, a nonresident alien individual using the calendar year as the taxable year and the cash receipts and disbursements method of accounting, is engaged in business (business R) in the United States from January 1, 1971, to August 31, 1971. During the period of September 1, 1971, to December 31, 1971, B receives installment payments of $30,000 on sales made in the United States by business R during that year, and the income from sources within the United States for that year attributable to such payments is $7,500. On September 15, 1971, another business (business S) which is carried on by B only in a foreign country sells to U.S. customers on the installment plan several pieces of equipment from inventory. During the period of September 16, 1971, to December 31, 1971, B receives installment payments of $50,000 on these sales by business S, and the income from sources within the United States for that year attributable to such payments is $10,000. Under section 864(c)(3) and paragraph (b) of § 1.864-4 the entire income of $17,500 is effectively connected for 1971 with the conduct of a business in the United

States by B. Accordingly, such income is taxable to B under paragraph (b)(2) of this section.

Example (2). Assume the same facts as in Example (1), except that during 1972 B receives installment payments of $20,000 from the sales made during 1971 in the United States by business R, and of $80,000 from the sales made in 1971 to U.S. customers by business S, the total income from sources within the United States for 1972 attributable to such payments being $13,000. At no time during 1972 is B engaged in a trade or business in the United States. Under section 864(c)(1)(B) the income of $13,000 for 1972 is not effectively connected with the conduct of a trade or business in the United States by B. Moreover, such income is not fixed or determinable annual or periodical income. Accordingly, no amount of such income is taxable to B under section 871.

Example (3). Assume the same facts as in Example (2), except that during 1972 B is engaged in a new business (business T) in the United States from July 1, 1972, to December 31, 1972. Under section 864(c)(3) and paragraph (b) of §1.864-4, the income of $13,000 is effectively connected for 1972 with the conduct of a business in the United States by B. Accordingly, such income is taxable to B under paragraph (b)(2) of this section.

Example (4). Assume the same facts as in Example (2), except that the installment payments of $20,000 from the sales made during 1971 in the United States by business R and not received by B until 1972 could have been received by B in 1971 if he had so desired. Under §1.451-2, B is deemed to have constructively received the payments of $20,000 in 1971. Accordingly, the income attributable to such payments is effectively connected for 1971 with the conduct of a business in the United States by B and is taxable to B in 1971 under paragraph (b)(2) of this section.

(d) *Credits against tax.*—The credits allowed by section 31 (relating to tax withheld on wages), section 32 (relating to tax withheld at source on nonresident aliens), section 33 (relating to the foreign tax credit), section 35 (relating to partially tax-exempt interest), section 38 (relating to investment in certain depreciable property), section 39 (relating to certain uses of gasoline and lubricating oil), section 40 (relating to expenses of work incentive programs), and section 6402 (relating to overpayments of tax) shall be allowed against the tax determined in accordance with this section. However, the credits allowed by sections 33, 38 and 40 shall not be allowed against the flat tax of 30 percent imposed by section 871(a) and paragraph (b)(1) of this section. Moreover, no credit shall be allowed under section 35 to a nonresident alien individual with respect to whom a tax is imposed for the taxable year under section 871(a) and paragraph (b)(1) of this section, even though such individual has income for such year upon which tax is imposed under section 871(b) and paragraph (b)(2) of this section. For special rules applicable in determining the foreign tax credit, see section 906(b) and the regulations thereunder. For the disallowance of certain credits where a return is not filed for the taxable year, see section 874 and §1.874-1.

(e) *Effective date.*—This section shall apply for taxable years beginning after December 31, 1966. For corresponding rules applicable to taxable years beginning before January 1, 1967, see 26 CFR 1.871-7(d) (Rev. as of Jan. 1, 1971). [Reg. §1.871-8.]

☐ [*T.D. 6258, 10-23-57. Amended by T.D. 6782, 12-23-64 and T.D.* 7332, 12-20-74.]

§1.871-9. Nonresident alien students or trainees deemed to be engaged in U.S. business.—(a) *Participants in certain exchange or training programs.*—For purposes of §§1.871-7 and 1.871-8 a nonresident alien individual who is temporarily present in the United States during the taxable year as a nonimmigrant under subparagraph (F) (relating to the admission of students into the United States) or subparagraph (J) (relating to the admission of teachers, trainees, specialists, etc., into the United States) of section 101(a)(15) of the Immigration and Nationality Act (8 U.S.C. 1101(a)(15)(F) or (J)), and who without regard to this paragraph is not engaged in trade or business in the United States during such year, shall be deemed to be engaged in trade or business in the United States during the taxable year. For purposes of determining whether an alien who is present in the United States on an F visa or a J visa is a resident of the United States, see §§301.7701(b)-1 through 301.7701(b)-9 of this chapter.

(b) *Income treated as effectively connected with U.S. business.*—Any income described in paragraph (1) (relating to the nonexcluded portion of certain scholarship or fellowship grants) or paragraph (2) (relating to certain nonexcluded expenses incident to such grants) of section 1441(b) which is received during the taxable year from sources within the United States by a nonresident alien individual described in paragraph (a) of this section is to be treated for purposes of §§1.871-7, 1.871-8, 1.872-1, and 1.873-1 as income which is effectively connected for the taxable year with the conduct of a trade or business in the United States by that individual. However, such income is not to be treated as effectively connected for the taxable year with the conduct of a trade or business in the United States for purposes of section 1441(c)(1) and paragraph (a) of §1.1441-4. For exclusion relating to compensation paid to such individual by a foreign employer, see paragraph (b) of §1.872-2.

(c) *Exchange visitors.*—For purposes of paragraph (a) of this section a nonresident alien individual who is temporarily present in the United States during the taxable year as a nonimmigrant under subparagraph (J) of section 101(a)(15) of the Immigration and Nationality Act includes a nonresident alien individual admitted to the United States as an "exchange visitor" under section 201 of the United States Information and Educational Exchange Act of 1948 (22 U.S.C. 1446), which section was repealed by section 111 of the Mutual Educational and Cultural Exchange Act of 1961 (75 Stat. 538).

(d) *Mandatory application of rule.*—The application of this section is mandatory and not subject to an election by the taxpayer.

(e) *Effective date.*—This section shall apply for taxable years beginning after December 31, 1966. For corresponding rules applicable to taxable years beginning before January 1, 1967, see 26 CFR 1.871-7(a)(3) (Rev. as of Jan. 1, 1971). [Reg. §1.871-9.]

☐ [*T.D. 7332, 12-20-74. Amended by T.D.* 8411, 4-24-92.]

§1.871-10. Election to treat real property income as effectively connected with U.S. business.—(a) *When election may be made.*—A nonresident alien individual or foreign corporation which during the taxable year derives any income from real property which is located in the United States and, in the case of a nonresident alien individual, held for the production of income, or derives income from any interest in any such property, may elect, pursuant to section 871(d) or 882(d) and this section, to treat all such income as income which is effectively connected for the taxable year with the conduct of a trade or business in the United States by that taxpayer. The election may be made whether or not the taxpayer is engaged in trade or business in the United States during the taxable year for which the election is made or whether or not the taxpayer has income from real property which for the taxable year is effectively connected with the conduct of a trade or business in the United States, but it may be made only with respect to that income from sources within the United States which, without regard to this section, is not effectively connected for the taxable year with the conduct of a trade or business in the United States by the taxpayer. If for the taxable year the taxpayer has no income from real property located in the United States, or from any interest in such property, which is subject to the tax imposed by section 871(a) or 881(a), the election may not be made. But if an election has been properly made under this section for a taxable year, the election remains in effect, unless properly revoked, for subsequent taxable years even though during any such subsequent taxable year there is no income from the real property, or interest therein, in respect of which the election applies.

(b) *Income to which the election applies.*—(1) *Included income.*—An election under this section shall apply to all income from real property which is located in the United States and, in the case of a nonresident alien individual, held for the production of income, and to all income derived from any interest in such property, including (i) gains from the sale or exchange of such property or an interest therein, (ii) rents or royalties from mines, oil or gas wells, or other natural resources, and (iii) gains described in section 631(b) or (c), relating to treatment of gain on the disposal of timber, coal, or iron ore with a retained economic interest. The election may not be made with respect to only one class of such income. For purposes of the election, income from real property, or from any interest in real property, includes any amount included under section 652 or 662 in the gross income of a nonresident alien individual or foreign corporation that is the beneficiary of an estate or trust if, by reason of the application of section 652(b) or 662(b), and the regulations thereunder, such amount has the character in the hands of that beneficiary of income from real property, or from any interest in real property. It is immaterial that no tax would be imposed on the income by section 871(a) and paragraph (a) of §1.871-7, or by section 881(a) and paragraph (a) of §1.881-2, if the election were not in effect. Thus, for example, if an election under this section has been made by a nonresident alien individual not engaged in trade or business in the United States during the taxable year, the tax imposed by section

871(b)(1) and paragraph (b)(2) of § 1.871-8 applies to his gains derived from the sale of real property located in the United States and held for the production of income, even though such income would not be subject to tax under section 871(a) if the election had not been made. In further illustration, assume that a nonresident alien individual not engaged in trade or business, or present, in the United States during the taxable year has income from sources within the United States consisting of oil royalties, rentals from a former personal residence, and capital gain from the sale of another residence held for the production of income. If he makes an election under this section, it will apply with respect to his royalties, rentals, and capital gain, even though such capital gain would not be subject to tax under section 871(a) if the election had not been made.

(2) *Income not included.*—For purposes of subparagraph (1) of this paragraph, income from real property, or from any interest in real property, does not include (i) interest on a debt obligation secured by a mortgage of real property, (ii) any portion of a dividend, within the meaning of section 316, which is paid by a corporation or a trust, such as a real estate investment trust described in section 857, which derives income from real property, (iii) in the case of a nonresident alien individual, income from real property, such as a personal residence, which is not held for the production of income or from any transaction in such property which was not entered into for profit, (iv) rentals from personal property, or royalties from intangible personal property, within the meaning of subparagraph (3) of this paragraph, or (v) income which, without regard to section 871(d) or 882(d) and this section, is treated as income which is effectively connected for the taxable year with the conduct of a trade or business in the United States.

(3) *Rules applicable to personal property.*—For purposes of subparagraph (2) of this paragraph, in the case of a sales agreement, or rental or royalty agreement, affecting both real and personal property, the income from the transaction is to be allocated between the real property and the personal property in proportion to their respective fair market values unless the agreement specifically provides otherwise. In the case of such a rental or royalty agreement, the respective fair market values are to be determined as of the time the agreement is signed. In making determinations under this subparagraph, the principles of paragraph (c) of § 1.48-1, relating to the definition of "section 38 property", apply for purposes of determining whether property is tangible or intangible personal property and of paragraph (a)(5) of § 1.1245-1 apply for purposes of making the allocation of income between real and personal property.

(c) *Effect of the election.*—(1) *Determination of tax.*—The income to which, in accordance with paragraph (b) of this section, an election under this section applies shall be subject to tax in the manner, and subject to the same conditions, provided by section 871(b)(1) and paragraph (b)(2) of § 1.871-8, or by section 882(a)(1) and paragraph (b)(2) of § 1.882-1. For purposes of determining such tax for the taxable year, income to which the election applies shall be aggregated with all other income of the nonresident alien individual or foreign corporation which is effectively connected for the taxable year with the conduct of a trade or business in the United States by that taxpayer. To the extent that deductions are connected with income from real property to which the election applies, they shall be treated for purposes of section 873(a) or section 882(c)(1) as connected with income which is effectively connected for the taxable year with the conduct of a trade or business in the United States by the nonresident alien individual or foreign corporation. An election under this section does not cause a nonresident alien individual or foreign corporation, which is not engaged in trade or business in the United States during the taxable year, to be treated as though such taxpayer were engaged in trade or business in the United States during the taxable year. Thus, for example, the compensation received during the taxable year for services performed in the United States in a previous taxable year by a nonresident alien individual, who has an election in effect for the taxable year under this section but is engaged in trade or business in the United States at no time during the taxable year, is not effectively connected for the taxable year with the conduct of a trade or business in the United States. In further illustration, gain for the taxable year from the casual sale of personal property described in section 1221(1) derived by a nonresident alien individual who is not engaged in trade or business in the United States during the taxable year but has an election in effect for such year under this section is not effectively connected with the conduct of a trade or business in the United States. See § 1.864-3. If an election under this section is in effect for the taxable year, the income to which the election applies shall be treated, for purposes of section 871(b)(1) or section 882(a)(1), section 1441(c)(1), and paragraph (a) of § 1.441-4, as income which is effectively connected for the taxable year with the conduct of a trade or business in the United States by the taxpayer.

(2) *Treatment of property to which election applies.*—Any real property, or interest in real property, with respect to which an election under this section applies shall be treated as a capital asset which, if depreciable, is subject to the allowance for depreciation provided in section 167 and the regulations thereunder. Such property, or interest in property, shall be treated as property not used in a trade or business for purposes of applying any provisions of the Code, such as section 172(d)(4)(A), relating to gain or loss attributable to a trade or business for purposes of determining a net operating loss; section 1221(2), relating to property not constituting a capital asset; or section 1231(b), relating to special rules for treatment of gains and losses. For example, if a nonresident alien individual makes the election under this section and, while the election is in effect, sells unimproved land which is located in the United States and held for investment purposes, any gain or loss from the sale shall be considered gain or loss from the sale of a capital asset and shall be treated, for purposes of determining the tax under section 871(b)(1) and paragraph (b)(2) of § 1.871-8, as a gain or loss which is effectively connected for the taxable year with the conduct of a trade or business in the United States.

(d) *Manner of making or revoking an election.*—(1) *Election, or revocation, without consent of Commissioner.*—(i) *In general.*—A nonresident alien individual or foreign corporation may, for the first taxable year for which the election under this section is to apply, make the initial election at any time before the expiration of the period prescribed by section 6511(a), or by section 6511(c) if the period for assessment is extended by agreement, for filing a claim for credit or refund of the tax imposed by chapter 1 of the Code for such taxable year. This election may be made without the consent of the Commissioner. Having made the initial election, the taxpayer may, within the time prescribed for making the election for such taxable year, revoke the election without the consent of the Commissioner. If the revocation is timely and properly made, the taxpayer may make his initial election under this section for a later taxable year without the consent of the Commissioner. If the taxpayer revokes the initial election without the consent of the Commissioner, he must file amended income tax returns, or claims for credit or refund, where applicable, for the taxable years to which the revocation applies.

(ii) *Statement to be filed with return.*—An election made under this section without the consent of the Commissioner shall be made for a taxable year by filing with the income tax return required under section 6012 and the regulations thereunder for such taxable year a statement to the effect that the election is being made. This statement shall include (*a*) a complete schedule of all real property, or any interest in real property, of which the taxpayer is titular or beneficial owner, which is located in the United States, (*b*) an indication of the extent to which the taxpayer has direct or beneficial ownership in each such item of real property, or interest in real property, (*c*) the location of the real property or interest therein, (*d*) a description of any substantial improvements on any such property, and (*e*) an identification of any taxable year or years in respect of which a revocation or new election under this section has previously occurred. This statement may not be filed with any return under section 6851 and the regulations thereunder.

(iii) *Exemption from withholding of tax.*—For statement to be filed with a withholding agent at the beginning of a taxable year in respect of which an election under this section is to be made, see paragraph (a) of § 1.1441-4.

(2) *Revocation, or election, with consent of Commissioner.*—(i) *In general.*—If the nonresident alien individual or foreign corporation makes the initial election under this section for any taxable year and the period prescribed by subparagraph (1)(i) of this paragraph for making the election for such taxable year has expired, the election shall remain in effect for all subsequent taxable years, including taxable years for which the taxpayer realizes no income from real property, or from any interest therein, or for which he is not required under section 6012 and the regulations thereunder to file an income tax return. However, the election may be revoked in accordance with subdivision (iii) of this subparagraph for any subsequent taxable year with the consent of the Commissioner. If the election for any such taxable year is revoked with the consent of the Commissioner, the taxpayer may not make a new election before his fifth taxable year which begins after the first taxable year for which the revocation is effective unless consent is given to such new election by the Commissioner in accordance with subdivision (iii) of this subparagraph.

(ii) *Effect of new election.*—A new election made for the fifth taxable year, or taxable year thereafter, without the consent of the Commissioner, and a new election made with the consent of the Commissioner, shall be treated as an initial election to which subparagraph (1) of this paragraph applies.

(iii) *Written request required.*—A request to revoke an election made under this section when such revocation requires the consent of the Commissioner, or to make a new election when such election requires the consent of the Commissioner, shall be made in writing and shall be addressed to the Director of International Operations, Internal Revenue Service, Washington, D.C. 20225. The request shall include the name and address of the taxpayer and shall be signed by the taxpayer or his duly authorized representative. It must specify the taxable year for which the revocation or new election is to be effective and shall be filed within 75 days after the close of the first taxable year for which it is desired to make the change. The request must specify the grounds which are considered to justify the revocation or new election. The Director of International Operations may require such other information as may be necessary in order to determine whether the proposed change will be permitted. A copy of the consent by the Director of International Operations shall be attached to the taxpayer's return required under section 6012 and the regulations thereunder for the taxable year for which the revocation or new election is effective. A copy of such consent may not be filed with any return under section 6851 and the regulations thereunder.

(3) *Election by partnership.*—If a nonresident alien individual or foreign corporation is a member of a partnership which has income described in paragraph (b)(1) of this section from real property, any election to be made under this section in respect of such income shall be made by the partners and not by the partnership. A nonresident alien or foreign corporation that makes an election generally must provide the partnership a Form W-8ECI, "Certificate of Foreign Person's Claim for Exemption from Withholding on Income Effectively Connected with the Conduct of a Trade or Business in the United States," and attach to such form a copy of the election (or a statement that indicates that the nonresident alien or foreign corporation will make the election). However, if the nonresident alien or foreign corporation has already submitted a valid form to the partnership that establishes such partner's foreign status, the partner shall furnish the partnership a copy of the election (or a statement that indicates that the nonresident alien or foreign corporation will make the election). To the extent the partnership has income to which the election pertains, the partnership shall treat such income as effectively connected income subject to withholding under section 1446. See also § 1.1446-2.

(e) *Effective date.*—This section shall apply for taxable years beginning after December 31, 1966, except the last four sentences of paragraph (d)(3) of this section shall apply to partnership taxable years beginning after May 18, 2005, or such earlier time as the regulations under § § 1.1446-1 through 1.1446-5 apply by reason of an election under § 1.1446-7. There are no corresponding rules in this part for taxable years beginning before January 1, 1967. [Reg. § 1.871-10.]

☐ [*T.D. 7332, 12-20-74. Amended by T.D. 9200, 5-13-2005.*]

§ 1.871-11. Gains from sale or exchange of patents, copyrights, or similar property.—(a) *Contingent payment defined.*—For purposes of section 871(a)(1)(D), section 881(a)(4), § 1.871-7(c)(1)(iv), § 1.881-2(c)(1)(iii), and this section, payments which are contingent on the productivity, use, or disposition of property or of an interest therein include continuing payments measured by a percentage of the selling price of the products marketed, or based on the number of units manufactured or sold, or based in a similar manner upon production, sale or use, or disposition of the property or interest transferred. A payment which is certain as to the amount to be received, but contingent as to the time of payment, or an installment payment of a principal sum agreed upon in a transfer agreement, shall not be treated as a contingent payment for purposes of this paragraph. For the inapplication of section 1253 to certain amounts described in this paragraph, see paragraph (a) of § 1.1253-1.

(b) *Payments treated as contingent on use.*—Pursuant to section 871(e), if more than 50 percent of the gain of a nonresident alien individual or foreign corporation for any taxable year from the sale or exchange after October 4, 1966, of any patent, copyright, secret process or formula, goodwill, trademark, trade brand, franchise, or other like property, or of any interest in any such property, is from payments which are contingent on the productivity, use, or disposition of such property or interest, all of the gain of such individual or corporation for the taxable year from the sale or exchange of such property or interest are, for purposes of section 871(a)(1)(D), section 881(a)(4), section 1441(b), or section 1442(a), and the regulations thereunder, to be treated as being from payments which are contingent on the productivity, use, or disposition of such property or interest. This paragraph does not apply for purposes of determining under section 871(b)(1) or 882(a)(1) the tax of a nonresident alien individual or foreign corporation on income which is effectively connected for the taxable year with the conduct of a trade or business in the United States.

(c) *Sale or exchange.*—A sale or exchange for purposes of this section includes, but is not limited to, a transfer by an individual which by reason of section 1235, relating to the sale or exchange of patents, is considered the sale or exchange of a capital asset. The provisions of section 1253, relating to transfers of franchises, trademarks, and trade names, do not apply in determining whether a transfer is a sale or exchange for purposes of this section.

(d) *Recovery of adjusted basis.*—For purposes of determining for any taxable year the amount of gains which are subject to tax under section 871(a)(1)(D) or 881(a)(4), payments received by the nonresident alien individual or foreign corporation during such year must be reduced by amounts representing recovery of the taxpayer's adjusted basis of the property or interest which is sold or exchanged. Where the taxpayer receives in the same taxable year payments which, without reference to section 871(e) and this section, are not contingent on the productivity, use, or disposition of the property or interest which is sold or exchanged and payments which are contingent on the productivity, use, or disposition of the property or interest which is sold or exchanged, the taxpayer's unrecovered adjusted basis in the property or interest which is sold or exchanged must be allocated for the taxable year between such payments on the basis of the gross amount of each such type of payments. Where the taxpayer receives in the taxable year only payments which are not so contingent or only payments which are so contingent, the taxpayer's unrecovered basis must be allocated in its entirety to such payments for the taxable year.

(e) *Source rule.*—In determining whether gains described in section 871(a)(1)(D) or 881(a)(4) and paragraph (b) of this section are received from sources within the United States, such gains shall be treated, for purposes of section 871(a)(1)(D), section 881(a)(4), section 1441(b), and section 1442(a), as rentals or royalties for the use of, or privilege of using, property or an interest in property. See section 861(a)(4), § 1.861-5, and paragraph (a) of § 1.862-1.

(f) *Illustrations.*—The application of this section may be illustrated by the following examples:

Example (1). (a) A, a nonresident alien individual who uses the cash receipts and disbursements method of accounting and the calendar year as the taxable year, holds a United States patent which he developed through his own effort. On December 15, 1967, A enters into an agreement of sale with M Corporation, a domestic corporation, whereby A assigns to M Corporation all of his United States rights in the patent. In consideration of the sale, M Corporation is obligated to pay a fixed sum of $60,000, $20,000 being payable on execution of the contract and the balance payable in four annual installments of $10,000 each. As additional consideration, M Corporation agrees to pay to A a royalty in the amount of 2 percent of the gross sales of the products manufactured by M Corporation under the patent. A is not engaged in trade or business in the United States at any time during 1967 and 1968. His adjusted basis in the patent at the time of sale is $28,800.

(b) In 1967, A receives only the $20,000 paid by M Corporation on the execution of the contract of sale. No gain is realized by A upon receipt of this amount, and his unrecovered adjusted basis in the patent is reduced to $8,800 ($28,800 less $20,000).

(c) In 1968, M Corporation has gross sales of $600,000 from products manufactured under the patent. Consequently, for 1968, M Corporation pays $22,000 to A, $10,000 being the annual installment on the fixed payment and $12,000 being payments under the terms of the royalty provision. A's recognized gain for 1968 is $13,200 ($22,000 reduced by the unrecovered adjusted basis of $8,800). Of the total gain of $13,200, gain in the amount of $6,000 ($10,000 − [$8,800 × $10,000/$22,000]) is considered to be from the fixed installment payment and of $7,200 ($12,000 − [$8,800 × $12,000/$22,000]) is considered to be from the royalty payment. Since 54.5 percent ($7,200/$13,200) of the gain recognized in 1968 from the sale of the patent is from payments which are contingent on the productivity, use, or disposition of the patent, all of the $13,200 gain recognized in

1968 is treated, for purposes of section 871(a)(1)(D) and section 1441(b), as being from payments which are contingent on the productivity, use, or disposition of the patent.

Example (2). (a) F, a foreign corporation using the calendar year as the taxable year and not engaged in trade or business in the United States, holds a U.S. patent on certain property which it developed through its own efforts. Corporation F uses the cash receipts and disbursements method of accounting. On December 1, 1966, F Corporation enters into an agreement of sale with D Corporation, a domestic corporation, whereby D Corporation purchases the exclusive right and license, and the right to sublicense to others, to manufacture, use, and/or sell certain devices under the patent in the United States during the term of the patent. The agreement grants D Corporation the right to dispose, anywhere in the world, of machinery manufactured in the United States and equipped with such devices. Corporation D is granted the right, at its own expense, to prosecute infringers in its own name or in the name of F Corporation, or both, and to retain any damages recovered.

(b) Corporation D agrees to pay to F Corporation annually $5 for each device manufactured under the patent during the year but in no case less than $5,000 per year. In 1967, D Corporation manufactures 2,500 devices under the patent; and, in 1968, 1,500 devices. Under the terms of the contract D Corporation pays to F Corporation in 1967 $12,500 with respect to production in that year and $7,500 in 1968 with respect to production in that year. F Corporation's basis in the patent at the time of the sale is $17,000.

(c) With respect to the payments received by F Corporation in 1967, no gain is realized by that corporation and its unrecovered adjusted basis in the patent is reduced to $4,500 ($17,000 less $12,500).

(d) With respect to the payments received by F Corporation in 1968, such corporation has recognized gain of $3,000 ($7,500 reduced by unrecovered adjusted basis of $4,500). Of the total gain of $3,000, gain in the amount of $2,000 ($5,000 − [$4,500 × $5,000/$7,500]) is considered to be from the fixed installment payment and of $1,000 ($2,500 − [$4,500 × $2,500/$7,500]) is considered to be from payments which are contingent on the productivity, use, or disposition of the patent. Since 33.3 percent ($1,000/$3,000) of the gain recognized in 1968 from the sale of the patent is from payments which are contingent on the productivity, use, or disposition of the patent, only $1,000 of the $3,000 gain for that year constitutes gains which, for purposes of section 881(a)(4) and section 1442(a), are from payments which are contingent on the productivity, use, or disposition of the patent. The balance of $2,000 is gain from the sale of property and is not subject to tax under section 881(a).

(g) *Effective date.*—This section shall apply for taxable years beginning after December 31, 1966, but only in respect of gains from sales or exchanges occurring after October 4, 1966. There are no corresponding rules in this part for taxable years beginning before January 1, 1967. [Reg. § 1.871-11.]

□ [*T.D. 7332, 12-20-74.*]

§ 1.871-12. Determination of tax on treaty income.—(a) *In general.*—This section applies for purposes of determining under § 1.871-7 or § 1.871-8 the tax on a nonresident alien individual, or under § 1.881-2 or § 1.882-1 the tax of a foreign corporation, which for the taxable year has income described in section 872(a) or 882(b) upon which the tax is limited by an income tax convention to which the United States is a party. Income for such purposes does not include income of any kind which is exempt from tax under the provisions of an income tax convention to which the United States is a party. See §§ 1.872-2(c) and 1.883-1(b). This section shall not apply to a nonresident alien individual who is a bona fide resident of Puerto Rico during the entire taxable year.

(b) *Definition of treaty and nontreaty income.*—(1) *In general.*—(i) For purposes of this section the term "treaty income" shall be construed to mean the gross income of a nonresident alien individual or foreign corporation, as the case may be, the tax on which is limited by a tax convention. The term "nontreaty income" shall be construed, for such purposes, to mean the gross income of the nonresident alien individual or foreign corporation other than the treaty income. Neither term includes income of any kind which is exempt from the tax imposed by chapter 1 of the Code.

(ii) In determining either the treaty or nontreaty income the gross income shall be determined in accordance with §§ 1.872-1 and 1.872-2, or with §§ 1.882-3 and 1.883-1, except that in determining the treaty income the exclusion granted by section 116(a) for dividends shall not be taken into account. Thus, for example, treaty income includes the total amount of dividends paid by a domestic corporation not disqualified by section 116(b) and received from sources within the United States if, in accordance with a tax convention, the dividends are subject to the income tax at a rate not to exceed 15 percent but does not include interest which, in accordance with a tax convention, is exempt from the income tax. In further illustration, neither the treaty nor the nontreaty income includes interest on certain governmental obligations which by reason of section 103 is excluded from gross income, or interest which by reason of a tax convention is exempt from the tax imposed by chapter 1 of the Code.

(iii) For purposes of applying any income tax convention to which the United States is a party, original issue discount which is subject to tax under section 871(a)(1)(C) or 881 (a)(3) is to be treated as interest, and gains which are subject to tax under section 871(a)(1)(D) or 881(a)(4) are to be treated as royalty income. This subdivision shall not apply, however, where its application would be contrary to any treaty obligation of the United States.

(2) *Application of permanent establishment rule of treaties.*—In applying this section with respect to income which is not effectively connected for the taxable year with the conduct of a trade or business in the United States by a nonresident alien individual or foreign corporation, see section 894(b), which provides that with respect to such income the nonresident alien individual or foreign corporation shall be deemed not to have a permanent establishment in the United States at any time during the taxable year for purposes of applying any exemption from, or reduction in rate of, tax provided by any tax convention.

(c) *Determination of tax.*—(1) *In general.*—If the gross income of a nonresident alien individual or foreign corporation, as the case may be, consists of both treaty and nontreaty income, the tax liability for the taxable year shall be the sum of the amounts determined in accordance with subparagraphs (2) and (3) of this paragraph. In no case, however, may the tax liability so determined exceed the tax liability (tax reduced by allowable credits) with respect to the taxpayer's entire income, determined in accordance with § 1.871-7 or § 1.871-8, or with § 1.881-2 or § 1.882-1, as though the tax convention had not come into effect and without reference to the provisions of this section. Determinations under this paragraph shall be made without taking into account any credits allowed by sections 31, 32, 39, and 6402, but such credits shall be allowed against the tax liability determined in accordance with this subparagraph.

(2) *Tax on nontreaty income.*—For purposes of subparagraph (1) of this paragraph, compute a partial tax (determined without the allowance of any credit) upon only the nontreaty income in accordance with § 1.871-7 or § 1.871-8, or with § 1.881-2 or § 1.882-1, whichever applies, as though the tax convention had not come into effect. To the extent allowed by paragraph (d) of § 1.871-8, or paragraph (c) of § 1.882-1, the credits allowed by sections 33, 35, 38, and 40 shall then be allowed, without taking into account any item included in the treaty income, against the tax determined under this subparagraph.

(3) *Tax on treaty income.*—For purposes of subparagraph (1) of this paragraph, compute a tax upon the gross amount, determined without the allowance of any deduction, of each separate item of treaty income at the reduced rate applicable to that item under the tax convention. No credits shall be allowed against the tax determined under this subparagraph.

(d) *Illustration.*—The application of this section may be illustrated by the following example:

Example. (a) A nonresident alien individual who is a resident of a foreign country with which the United States has entered into a tax convention receives during the taxable year 1967 from sources within the United States total gross income of $22,000, consisting of the following items:

Compensation for personal services the tax on which is not limited by the tax convention (effectively connected income under § 1.864-4(c)(6)(ii))	$20,000
Oil royalties the tax on which is limited by the tax convention to 15 percent of the gross amount thereof (effectively connected income by reason of election under § 1.871-10)	2,000
Total gross income	$22,000

(b) The taxpayer is engaged in business in the United States during the taxable year but does not have a permanent establishment therein. There are no allowable deductions, other than the deductions allowed by sections 613 and 873(b)(3).

(c) The tax liability for the taxable year is $6,100, determined as follows:

Nontreaty gross income	$20,000
Less: Deduction for personal exemption	600
Nontreaty taxable income	$19,400
Tax under section 1 of the Code on nontreaty taxable income ($5,170 plus 45% of $1,400)	$ 5,800
Plus: Tax on treaty income (Gross oil royalties) ($2,000 × 15%)	300
Total tax (determined as provided in paragraph (c)(2) and (3) of this section)	$6,100

(d) If the tax had been determined under paragraph (b)(2) of § 1.871-8 as though the tax convention had not come into effect, the tax liability would have been $6,478, determined as follows and by taking into account the election under § 1.871-10:

Total gross income		$22,000
Less: Deduction under section 613 for percentage depletion ($2,000 × 27½%)	$550	
Deduction for personal exemption	600	1,150
Taxable income		$20,850
Tax under section 1 of the Code on taxable income ($6,070 plus 48% of $850)		$ 6,478

(e) *Effective date.*—This section shall apply for taxable years beginning after December 31, 1966. For corresponding rules applicable to taxable years beginning before January 1, 1967, see 26 CFR 1.871-7(e) (Rev. as of Jan. 1, 1971). [Reg. § 1.871-12.]

☐ [*T.D. 7332, 12-20-74. Amended by T.D. 8657, 3-5-96.*]

§ 1.871-13. Taxation of individuals for taxable year of change of U.S. citizenship or residence.—(a) *In general.*—(1) An individual who is a citizen or resident of the United States at the beginning of the taxable year but a nonresident alien at the end of the taxable year, or a nonresident alien at the beginning of the taxable year but a citizen or resident of the United States at the end of the taxable year, is taxable for such year as though his taxable year were comprised of two separate periods, one consisting of the time during which he is a citizen or resident of the United States and the other consisting of the time during which he is not a citizen or resident of the United States. Thus, for example, the income tax liability of an alien individual under chapter 1 of the Code for the taxable year in which he changes his residence will be computed under two different sets of rules, one relating to resident aliens for the period of residence and the other relating to nonresident aliens for the period of nonresidence. However, in determining the taxable income for such year which is subject to the graduated rate of tax imposed by section 1 or 1201 of the Code, all income for the period of U.S. citizenship or residence must be aggregated with the income for the period of nonresidence which is effectively connected for such year with the conduct of a trade or business in the United States. This section does not apply to alien individuals treated as residents for the entire taxable year under section 6013(g) or (h). These individuals are taxed under the rules in § 1.1-1(b).

(2) For purposes of this section, an individual is deemed to be a citizen or resident of the United States for the day on which he becomes a citizen or resident of the United States, a nonresident of the United States for the day on which he abandons his U.S. residence, and an alien for the day on which he gives up his U.S. citizenship.

(b) *Acquisition of U.S. citizenship or residence.*—Income from sources without the United States which is not effectively connected with the conduct by the taxpayer of a trade or business in the United States is not taxable if received by an alien individual while he is not a resident of the United States even though he becomes a citizen or resident of the United States after its receipt and before the close of the taxable year. However, income from sources without the United States which is not effectively connected with the conduct by the taxpayer of a trade or business in the United States is taxable if received by an individual while he is a citizen or resident of the United States, even though he earns the income earlier in the taxable year while he is neither a citizen nor resident of the United States.

(c) *Abandonment of U.S. citizenship or residence.*—Income from sources without the United States which is not effectively connected with the conduct by the taxpayer of a trade or business in the United States is not taxable if received by an alien individual while he is not a resident of the United States, even though he earns the income earlier in the taxable year while he is a citizen or resident of the United States. However, income from sources without the United States which is not effectively connected with the conduct by the taxpayer of a trade or business in the United States is taxable if received by an individual while he is a citizen or resident of the United States, even though he abandons his U.S. citizenship or residence after its receipt and before the close of the taxable year.

(d) *Special rules.*—(1) *Method of accounting.*—Paragraphs (b) and (c) of this section may not apply to an individual who for the taxable year uses an accrual method of accounting.

(2) *Deductions for personal exemptions.*—An alien individual to whom this section applies is entitled to deduct one personal exemption for the taxable year under section 151. In addition, he is entitled to such additional exemptions as are allowed as a deduction under section 151 but only to the extent the amount of such additional exemptions do not exceed his taxable income (determined without regard to any deduction for personal exemptions) for the period in the taxable year during which he is a citizen or resident of the United States. This subparagraph does not apply to the extent it is inconsistent with section 873, and the regulations thereunder, or with the provisions of an income tax convention to which the United States is a party.

(3) *Exclusion of dividends received.*—In determining the $100 exclusion for the taxable year provided by section 116 in respect of certain dividends, only those dividends for the period during which the individual is neither a citizen nor resident of the United States may be taken into account as are effectively connected for the taxable year with the conduct of a trade or business in the United States. See § 1.116-1(e)(1).

(e) *Illustrations.*—The application of this section may be illustrated by the following examples:

Example (1). A, a married alien individual who uses the calendar year as the taxable year and the cash receipts and disbursements method of accounting, becomes a resident of the United States on June 1, 1971. During the period of nonresidence from January 1, 1971, to May 31, 1971, inclusive, A receives $15,000 income from sources without the United States which is not effectively connected with the conduct of a trade or business in the United States. During the period of residence from June 1, 1971, to December 31, 1971, A receives wages of $10,000, dividends of $200 from a foreign corporation, and dividends of $75 from a domestic corporation qualifying under section 116(a). Of the amount of wages so received, $2,000 is for services performed by A outside the United States during the period of nonresidence. Total allowable deductions (other than for personal exemptions) amount to $700, none of which are deductible under section 62 in computing adjusted gross income. For 1971 A's spouse has no gross income and is not the dependent of another taxpayer. For 1971, A's taxable income is $8,200, all of which is subject to tax under section 1, as follows:

Wages		$10,000
Dividends from foreign corporation		200
Dividends from domestic corporation ($75 less $75 exclusion)		0
Adjusted gross income		$10,200
Less deductions:		
Personal exemptions (2 × $650)	$1,300	
Other allowable deductions	700	2,000
Taxable income		$ 8,200

Example (2). The facts are the same as in example (1) except that during the period of nonresidence from January 1, 1971, to May 31, 1971, A receives from sources within the United States income of $1,850 which is effectively connected with the conduct by A of a business in the United States and $350 in dividends from domestic corporations qualifying under section 116(a). Only $50 of these dividends are effectively connected with the conduct by A of a business in the United States. The assumption is made that there are no allowable deductions connected with such effectively connected income. For 1971, A has taxable income of $10,075 subject to tax under section 1 and $300 income subject to tax under section 871(a)(1)(A), as follows:

Wages	$10,000
Business income	1,850
Dividends from foreign corporation	200
Dividends from domestic corporation ($125 less $100 exclusion)	25
Adjusted gross income	$12,075

Less deductions:		
Personal exemptions (2 × $650) . . .	$1,300	
Other allowable deductions	700	2,000
Taxable income subject to tax under section 1		$10,075
Income subject to tax under section 871(a)(1)(A)		$ 300

Example (3). A, a married alien individual with three children, uses the calendar year as the taxable year and the cash receipts and disbursements method of accounting. On October 1, 1971, A and his family become residents of the United States. During the period of nonresidence from January 1, 1971, to September 30, 1971, A receives income of $18,000 from sources without the United States which is not effectively connected with the conduct of a trade or business in the United States and of $2,500 from sources within the United States which is effectively connected with the conduct of a business in the United States. It is assumed there are no allowable deductions connected with such effectively connected income. During the period of residence from October 1, 1971, to December 31, 1971, A receives wages of $2,000, of which $400 is for services performed outside the United States during the period of nonresidence. Total allowable deductions (other than for personal exemptions) amount to $250, none of which are deductible under section 62 in computing adjusted gross income. Neither the spouse nor any of the children has any gross income for 1971, and the spouse is not the dependent of another taxpayer for such year. For 1971, A's taxable income is $1,850, all of which is subject to tax under section 1, as follows:

Wages (residence period)	$2,000	
Less: Allowable deductions	250	
Taxable income (without deduction for personal exemptions) (residence period)		$1,750
Business income (nonresidence period)		2,500
Total taxable income (without deduction for personal exemptions)		$4,250
Less deduction for personal exemptions:		
Taxpayer	$ 650	
Wife and 3 children (4 × $650, but not to exceed $1,750)	1,750	2,400
Taxable income		$1,850

(f) *Effective date.*—This section shall apply for taxable years beginning after December 31, 1966. There are no corresponding rules in this part for taxable years beginning before January 1, 1967. [Reg. § 1.871-13.]

□ [*T.D. 7332, 12-20-74. Amended by T.D. 7670, 1-30-80.*]

§ 1.871-14. Rules relating to repeal of tax on interest of nonresident alien individuals and foreign corporations received from certain portfolio debt investments.—(a) *General rule.*—No tax shall be imposed under section 871(a)(1)(A), 871(a)(1)(C), 881(a)(1) or 881(a)(3) on any portfolio interest as defined in sections 871(h)(2) and 881(c)(2) received by a foreign person. But see section 871(b) or 882(a) if such interest is effectively connected with the conduct of a trade or business within the United States.

(b) *Rules concerning obligations in bearer form before March 19, 2012.*—(1) *In general.*—Interest (including original issue discount) with respect to an obligation in bearer form is portfolio interest within the meaning of section 871(h)(2)(A) or 881(c)(2)(A) only if it is paid with respect to an obligation issued after July 18, 1984, and issued before March 19, 2012, that is described in section 163(f)(2)(B), as in effect before the amendment by section 502 of the Hiring Incentives to Restore Employment Act of 2010 (HIRE Act), Public Law 111-147, and the regulations under that section and an exception under section 871(h) or 881(c) does not apply. Any obligation that is not in registered form as defined in paragraph (c)(1)(i) of this section is an obligation in bearer form.

(2) *Coordination with withholding and reporting rules.*—For an exemption from withholding under section 1441 with respect to obligations described in this paragraph (b), see § 1.1441-1(b)(4)(i). See § 1.1471-2 for rules relating to withholding under chapter 4 of the Code that may apply to withholdable payments (as defined in § 1.1471-4(b)(145)) made on or after July 1, 2014, with respect to an agreement or instrument that is not treated as an obligation outstanding before March 19, 2012. For purposes of the preceding sentence, the terms *obligation* and *outstanding* are described in § 1.1471-2(b)). See also § 1.1471-4(d)(6) for the reporting requirements of participating foreign financial institutions (as defined in § 1.1471-1(b)(91)) with respect to accounts held by recalcitrant account holders (as defined in § 1.1471-5(g)). For rules relating to an exemption from Form 1099 reporting and backup withholding under section 3406, see section 6049 and § 1.6049-5(b)(8) for the payment of interest and § 1.6045-1(g)(1)(ii) for the redemption, retirement, or sale of an obligation in bearer form.

(c) *Rules concerning obligations in registered form.*—(1) *In general.*—(i) *Obligation in registered form.*—For purposes of this section, an obligation is in registered form only as provided in this paragraph (c)(1)(i). The conditions for an obligation to be considered in registered form are identical to the conditions described in § 5f.103-1 of this chapter. Therefore, an obligation that would be an obligation in registered form except for the fact that it can be converted at any time in the future into an obligation that is not in registered form shall not be an obligation in registered form. An obligation that is not in registered form by reason of the preceding sentence may nevertheless be in registered form, but only after the possibility of conversion is terminated. An obligation that is not in registered form and can be converted into an obligation that would meet the requirements of this paragraph (c)(1)(i) for being in registered form shall be considered in registered form only after the conversion is effected. For purposes of this section, an obligation is convertible if the obligation can be transferred by any means not described in § 5f.103-1(c) of this chapter. An obligation is treated as an obligation in registered form if—

(A) The obligation is registered as to both principal and any stated interest with the issuer (or its agent) and transfer of the obligation may be effected only by surrender of the old instrument, and either the reissuance by the issuer of the old instrument to the new holder or the issuance by the issuer of a new instrument to the new holder;

(B) The right to the principal of, and stated interest on, the obligation may be transferred only through a book entry system maintained by the issuer (or its agent) described in this paragraph (c)(1)(i)(B). An obligation shall be considered transferable through a book entry system if the ownership of an interest in the obligation, is required to be reflected in a book entry, whether or not physical securities are issued. A book entry is a record of ownership that identifies the owner of an interest in the obligation; or

(C) It is registered as to both principal and any stated interest with the issuer (or its agent) and may be transferred by way of either of the methods described in paragraph (c)(1)(i)(A) or (B) of this section.

(ii) *Requirements for portfolio interest qualification in the case of an obligation in registered form.*—Interest (including original issue discount) received on an obligation that is in registered form qualifies as portfolio interest only if—

(A) The interest is paid on an obligation issued after July 18, 1984;

(B) The interest would be subject to tax under section 871(a)(1)(A), 871(a)(1)(C), 881(a)(1) or 881(a)(3) but for section 871(h) or 881(c);

(C) A United States (U.S.) person otherwise required to deduct and withhold tax under chapter 3 of the Internal Revenue Code (Code) receives a statement that meets the requirements of section 871(h)(5) that the beneficial owner of the obligation is not a U.S. person; and

(D) An exception under section 871(h) or 881(c) does not apply.

(2) *Required statement.*—For purposes of paragraph (c)(1)(ii)(C) of this section, a U.S. person will be considered to have received a statement that meets the requirements of section 871(h)(5) if either it complies with one of the procedures described in this paragraph (c)(2) and does not have actual knowledge or reason to know that the beneficial owner is a U.S. person or it complies with the procedures described in paragraph (d) or (e) of this section (to the extent applicable).

(i) The U.S. person (or its authorized agent described in § 1.1441-7(c)(2)) can reliably associate the payment with documentation upon which it can rely to treat the payment as made to a foreign beneficial owner in accordance with § 1.1441-1(e)(1)(ii). See § 1.1441-1(b)(2)(vii) for rules regarding reliable association with documentation.

(ii) The U.S. person (or its authorized agent described in § 1.1441-7(c)(2)) can reliably associate the payment with a withholding certificate described in § 1.1441-5(c)(2)(iv) from a person claiming to be a withholding foreign partnership or § 1.1441-5(e)(v) for a person claiming to be a withholding foreign trust.

(iii) The U.S. person (or its authorized agent described in § 1.1441-7(c)(2)) can reliably associate the payment with a withholding certificate described in § 1.1441-1(e)(3)(ii) from a person representing to be a qualified intermediary that has assumed primary withholding responsibility for the payment in accordance with §1.1441-1(e)(5)(iv) or a qualified intermediary that has provided a withholding statement that meets the requirements of §1.1441-1(e)(5)(v)(C) or that includes the payment in a withholding rate pool for payments excepted from withholding.

(iv) The U.S. person (or its authorized agent described in §1.1441-7(c)(2)) can reliably associate the payment with a withholding certificate described in §1.1441-1(e)(3)(v) from a person claiming to be a U.S. branch of a foreign bank or of a foreign insurance company that is described in §1.1441-1(b)(2)(iv)(A) or a U.S. branch designated in accordance with §1.1441-1(b)(2)(iv)(E).

(v) The U.S. person receives a statement from a securities clearing organization, a bank, or another financial institution that holds customers' securities in the ordinary course of its trade or business. In such case the statement must be signed under penalties of perjury by an authorized representative of the financial institution and must state that the institution has received from the beneficial owner a withholding certificate described in §1.1441-1(e)(2)(i) (a Form W-8 or an acceptable substitute form as defined §1.1441-1(e)(4)(vi)) or that it has received from another financial institution a similar statement that it, or another financial institution acting on behalf of the beneficial owner, has received the Form W-8 from the beneficial owner. In the case of multiple financial institutions between the beneficial owner and the U.S. person, this statement must be given by each financial institution to the one above it in the chain. No particular form is required for the statement provided by the financial institutions. However, the statement must provide the name and address of the beneficial owner, and a copy of the Form W-8 provided by the beneficial owner must be attached. The statement is subject to the same rules described in §1.1441-1(e)(4) that apply to intermediary Forms W-8 described in §1.1441-1(e)(3)(iii). If the information on the Form W-8 changes, the beneficial owner must so notify the financial institution acting on its behalf within 30 days of such changes, and the financial institution must promptly so inform the U.S. person. This notice also must be given if the financial institution has actual knowledge that the information has changed but has not been so informed by the beneficial owner. In the case of multiple financial institutions between the beneficial owner and the U.S. person, this notice must be given by each financial institution to the institution above it in the chain.

(vi) The U.S. person complies with procedures that the U.S. competent authority may agree to with the competent authority of a country with which the United States has an income tax treaty in effect.

(3) *Time for providing certificate or documentary evidence.*—(i) *General rule.*—Interest on a registered obligation shall qualify as portfolio interest if the withholding certificate or documentary evidence that must be provided is furnished before expiration of the beneficial owner's period of limitation for claiming a refund of tax with respect to such interest. See, however, §1.1441-1(b)(7) for consequences to a withholding agent that makes a payment without withholding even though it cannot reliably associate the payment with the documentation prior to the payment. If a withholding agent withholds an amount under chapter 3 of the Code because it cannot reliably associate the payment with the documentation for the beneficial owner on the date of payment, the beneficial owner may nevertheless claim the benefit of an exemption from tax under this section by claiming a refund or credit for the amount withheld based upon the procedures described in §§1.1464-1 and 301.6402-3(e) of this chapter. See §§1.1474-5 and 301.6402-3(e) of this chapter for the allowance and requirements for a refund with respect to an amount (including a payment of interest) that was withheld upon under chapter 4 of the Code. In the alternative, adjustments to any amount of overwithheld tax may be made under the procedures described in §1.1461-2(a) for a payment withheld upon under chapter 3 of the Code or in §1.1474-2 for a payment withheld upon under chapter 4 of the Code.

(ii) *Example.*—The following example illustrates the rules of this paragraph (c)(3) and their coordination with §1.1441-1(b)(7):

Example. A is a withholding agent who, on October 12, 2001, pays interest on a registered obligation to B, a foreign corporation. B is a calendar year taxpayer, engaged in the conduct of a trade or business in the United States, and is, therefore, required to file an annual income tax return on Form 1120F. The interest, however, is not effectively connected with B's U.S. trade or business. On the date of payment, B has not furnished, and A cannot associate the payment with documentation for B. However, A does not withhold under section 1442, even though, under §1.1441-1(b)(3)(iii)(A), A should presume that B is a foreign person, because A's communications with B are mailed to an address in a foreign country. Assuming that B files a return for its taxable year ending December 31, 2001, and that its statute of limitations period with regard to that year expires on June 15, 2005, the interest paid on October 12, 2001, may qualify as portfolio interest only if B provides appropriate documentation to A on or before June 15, 2005. If B does not provide the documentation on or before June 15, 2005, and does not pay the tax, A is liable for the tax under section 1463, even if B provides the documentation to A after June 15, 2005. Therefore, the provisions in §1.1441-1(b)(7), regarding late-received documentation would not help A avoid liability for tax under section 1463 even if the documentation is furnished within the statute of limitations period of A. This is because, in a case involving interest, the documentation received within the limitations period of the beneficial owner serves as a condition for the interest to qualify as portfolio interest. When documentation is received after the expiration of the beneficial owner's limitations period, the interest can no longer qualify as portfolio interest. On the other hand, A could rely on documentation that it receives after the expiration of B's limitations period to establish B's right to a reduced rate of withholding under an applicable income tax treaty (since, in such a case, a claim of treaty benefits is not conditioned upon providing documentation prior to the expiration of the beneficial owner's limitations period).

(4) *Coordination with withholding and reporting rules.*—For an exemption from withholding under section 1441 with respect to obligations described in this paragraph (c)(4), see §1.1441-1(b)(4)(i). For rules applicable to withholding certificates, see §1.1441-1(e)(4). For rules regarding documentary evidence, see §1.6049-5(c)(1). For application of presumptions when the U.S. person cannot reliably associate the payment with documentation, see §1.1441-1(b)(3). For standards of knowledge applicable to withholding agents, see §1.1441-7(b). For rules relating to reporting on Forms 1042 and 1042-S, see §1.1461-1(b) and (c). For rules relating to an exemption from Form 1099 reporting and backup withholding under section 3406, see section 6049 and §1.6049-5(b)(8) for the payment of interest and §1.6045-1(g)(1)(i) for the redemption, retirement, or sale of an obligation in registered form. For rules relating to withholding under sections 1471 and 1472 that may apply notwithstanding the exemption for payments of portfolio interest under section 1441, see §§1.1471-2(a), 1.1471-4(b), and 1.1472-1(b).

(d) *Application of repeal of 30-percent withholding to pass-through certificates.*—(1) *In general.*—Interest received on a pass-through certificate qualifies as portfolio interest under section 871(h)(2) or 881(c)(2) if the interest satisfies the conditions described in paragraph (b)(1), (c)(1), or (e) of this section without regard to whether any obligation held by the fund or trust to which the pass-through certificate relates is described in paragraph (b)(1), (c)(1)(ii), or (e) of this section. This paragraph (d)(1) applies only to payments made to the holder of the pass-through certificate from the trustee of the pass-through trust and does not apply to payments made to the trustee of the pass-through trust. For example, a mortgage pass-through certificate in bearer form must meet the requirements set forth in paragraph (b)(1) of this section, but the obligations held by the fund or trust to which the mortgage pass-through certificate relates need not meet the requirements set forth in paragraph (b)(1), (c)(1)(ii), or (e) of this section. However, for purposes of paragraphs (b)(1), (c)(1)(ii), and (e) of this section and section 127 of the Tax Reform Act of 1984, a pass-through certificate will be considered as issued after July 18, 1984, only to the extent that the obligations held by the fund or trust to which the pass-through certificate relates are issued after July 18, 1984.

(2) *Interest in REMICs.*—Interest received on a regular or residual interest in a REMIC qualifies as portfolio interest under section 871(h)(2) or 881(c)(2) if the interest satisfies the conditions described in paragraph (b)(1), (c)(1)(ii), or (e) of this section. For purposes of paragraph (b)(1), (c)(1)(ii), or (e) of this section, interest on a regular interest in a REMIC is not considered interest on any mortgage obligations held by the REMIC. The foregoing rule, however, applies only to payments made to the holder of the regular interest from the REMIC and does not apply to payments made to the REMIC. For purposes of paragraph (b)(1), (c)(1)(ii), or (e) of this section, interest on a residual interest in a REMIC is considered to be interest on or with respect to the obligations held by the REMIC, and not on or with respect to the residual interest. For purposes of paragraphs (b)(1), (c)(1)(ii), and (e) of this section and section 127 of the Tax Reform Act of 1984, a residual interest in a REMIC will be considered as issued after July 18, 1984, only to the extent that the obligations held by the REMIC are issued after July 18, 1984, but a regular interest in a REMIC will be considered as issued after July 18, 1984, if the regular interest was issued after July 18, 1984, without

regard to the date on which the mortgage obligations held by the REMIC were issued.

(3) *Date of issuance.*—In general, a mortgage pass-through certificate will be considered to have been issued after July 18, 1984, if all of the mortgages held by the fund or trust were issued after July 18, 1984. If some of the mortgages held by the fund or trust were issued before July 19, 1984, then the portion of any interest payment which represents interest on those mortgages shall not be considered to be portfolio interest. The preceding sentence shall not apply, however, if all of the following conditions are satisfied:

(i) The mortgage pass-through certificate is issued after December 31, 1986;

(ii) Payment of the mortgage pass-through certificate is guaranteed by, and a guarantee commitment has been issued by, an entity that is independent from the issuer of the underlying obligation;

(iii) The guarantee commitment with respect to the mortgage pass-through certificate cannot have been issued more than 14 months prior to the date on which the mortgage pass-through certificate is issued; and

(iv) The fund or trust to which the mortgage pass-through certificate relates cannot contain mortgage obligations on which the first scheduled monthly payment of principal and interest was made more than twelve months before the date on which the guarantee commitment was made.

(e) *Foreign-targeted registered obligations.*—(1) *General rule.*—The statement described in paragraph (c)(1)(ii) of this section is not required with respect to interest paid on an obligation issued before January 1, 2016, that is a registered obligation targeting foreign markets in accordance with the provisions of paragraph (e)(2) of this section if the interest is paid by a U.S. person, a withholding foreign partnership, or a U.S. branch described in §1.1441-1(b)(2)(iv)(A) or (E) to a registered owner at an address outside the United States, provided that the registered owner is a financial institution described in section 871(h)(5)(B). In that case, the U.S. person otherwise required to deduct and withhold tax may treat the interest as portfolio interest if it does not have actual knowledge that the beneficial owner is a United States person and if it receives the certificate described in paragraph (e)(3)(i) of this section from a financial institution or member of a clearing organization, which member is the beneficial owner of the obligation, or the documentary evidence or statement described in paragraph (e)(3)(ii) of this section from the beneficial owner, in accordance with the procedures described in paragraph (e)(4) of this section.

(2) *Definition of a foreign-targeted registered obligation.*—An obligation is considered to be targeted to foreign markets for purposes of paragraph (e)(1) of this section if it is sold (or resold in connection with its original issuance) only to foreign persons (or to foreign branches of United States financial institutions described in section 871(h)(5)(B)) in accordance with procedures similar to those prescribed in §1.163-5(c)(2)(i)(A), (B), or (D). However, the provisions of that section that require an obligation to be offered for sale or resale in connection with its original issuance only outside the United States do not apply with respect to registered obligations offered for sale through a public auction. Similarly, the provisions of that section that require delivery to be made outside the United States do not apply to registered obligations offered for sale through a public auction if the obligations are considered to be in registered form by virtue of the fact that they may be transferred only through a book entry system. The obligation, if evidenced by a physical document other than a confirmation receipt, must contain on its face a legend indicating that it has been sold (or resold in connection with its original issuance) in accordance with those procedures.

(3) *Documentation.*—A certificate described in paragraph (e)(3)(i) of this section is required if the United States person otherwise required to deduct and withhold tax (the withholding agent) pays interest to a financial institution described in section 871(h)(5)(B) or to a member of a clearing organization, which member is the beneficial owner of the obligation. The documentation described in paragraph (e)(3)(ii) of this section is required if a withholding agent pays interest to a beneficial owner that is neither a financial institution described in section 871(h)(5)(B) nor a member of a clearing organization.

(i) *Interest paid to a financial institution or a member of a clearing organization.*—(A) *Requirement of a certificate.*—*(1)* If the withholding agent pays interest to a financial institution described in section 871(h)(5)(B) or to a member of a clearing organization, which member is the beneficial owner of the obligation, the withholding agent must receive a certificate which states that, beginning at the time the last preceding certificate under this paragraph (e)(3)(i) was provided and while the financial institution or clearing organization member has held the obligation, with respect to each foreign-targeted registered obligation which has been held by the person providing the certificate at any time since the provision of such last preceding certificate, either—

(i) The beneficial owner of the obligation has not been a United States person on each interest payment date; or

(ii) If the person providing the certificate is a financial institution which is holding or has held an obligation on behalf of the beneficial owner, the beneficial owner of the obligation has been a United States person on one or more interest payment dates (identifying such date or dates), and the person making the certification has forwarded or will forward the appropriate United States beneficial ownership notification to the withholding agent in accordance with the provisions of paragraph (e)(4) of this section.

(2) The person providing the certificate need not state the foregoing where no previous certificate has been required to be provided by the payee to the withholding agent under this paragraph (e)(3)(i).

(B) *Additional representations.*—Whether or not a previous certificate has been required to be provided with respect to the obligation, each certificate furnished pursuant to the provisions in this paragraph (e)(3)(i) must further state that, for each foreign-targeted registered obligation held and every other such obligation to be acquired and held by the person providing the certificate during the period beginning on the date of the certificate and ending on the date the next certificate is required to be provided, the beneficial owner of the obligation will not be a United States person on each interest payment date while the financial institution or clearing organization member holds the obligation and that, if the person providing the certificate is a financial institution which is holding or will be holding the obligation on behalf of a beneficial owner, such person will provide a United States beneficial ownership notification to the withholding agent (and a clearing organization that is not a withholding agent where a member organization is required by this paragraph (e)(3) to furnish the clearing organization with a statement) in accordance with paragraph (e)(4) of this section in the event such certificate (or statement in the case of a statement provided by a member organization to a clearing organization that is not a withholding agent) is or becomes untrue with respect to any obligation. A clearing organization is an entity which is in the business of holding obligations for member organizations and transferring obligations among such members by credit or debit to the account of a member without the necessity of physical delivery of the obligation.

(C) *Obligation must be identified.*—The certificate described in paragraph (e)(3)(ii)(A) of this section must identify the obligation or obligations with respect to which it is given, except where the certification is given with respect to an obligation that has not been acquired at the time the certification is made. An obligation is identified if it or the larger issuance of which it is a part is described on a list (e.g., $5 million principal amount of 12% debentures of ABC Savings and Loan Association due February 25, 1995, $3 million principal amount of 10% U.S. Treasury notes due May 28, 1990) of all registered obligations targeted to foreign markets held by or on behalf of the person providing the certificate and the list is attached to, and incorporated by reference into, the certificate. The certificate must identify and provide the address of the person furnishing the certificate.

(D) *Payment to a depository of a clearing organization.*—If the withholding agent pays interest to a depository of a clearing organization, then the clearing organization must provide the certificate described in this paragraph (e)(3)(i) to the withholding agent. Any certificate that is provided by a clearing organization must state that the clearing organization has received a statement from each member which complies with the provisions of this paragraph (e)(3)(i) and of paragraph (e)(4) of this section (as if the clearing organization were the withholding agent and regardless of whether the member is a financial institution described in section 871(h)(5)(B)).

(E) *Statement in lieu of Form W-8.*—Subject to the requirements set out in paragraph (e)(4) of this section, a certificate or statement in the form described in this paragraph (e)(3)(i), in conjunction with the next annual certificate or statement, will serve as the certificate that may be provided in lieu of a Form W-8 with respect to interest on all foreign-targeted registered obligations held by the person making the certification or statement and which is paid to such person within the period beginning on the date of the certificate and ending on the date the next certificate is required to be provided.

(F) *Electronic transmission.*—The certificate described in this paragraph (e)(3)(i) may be provided electronically under the terms and conditions of § 1.163-5(c)(2)(i)(D)(*3*)(*ii*).

(ii) *Payment to a person other than a financial institution or member of a clearing organization.*—If the withholding agent pays interest to the beneficial owner of an obligation that is neither a financial institution described in section 871(h)(5)(B) nor a member of a clearing organization, then such owner must provide the withholding agent a statement described in paragraph (c)(1)(ii)(C) of this section.

(4) *Applicable procedures regarding documentation.*—(i) *Procedures applicable to certificates required under paragraph (e)(3)(i) of this section.*—(A) *Time for providing certificate.*—Where no previous certificate for foreign-targeted registered obligations has been provided to the withholding agent by the person providing the certificate under paragraph (e)(3)(i) of this section, such certificate must be provided within the period beginning 90 days prior to the first interest payment date on which the person holds a foreign-targeted registered obligation. The withholding agent may, in its discretion, withhold under section 1441(a), 1442(a), or 1443 if the certificate is not received by the date 30 days prior to the interest payment. Thereafter the certificate must be filed within the period beginning on January 15 and ending January 31 of each year. If a certificate provided pursuant to the first sentence of this paragraph (e)(4)(i)(A) is provided during the period beginning on January 15 and ending on January 31 of any year, then no other certificate need be provided during such period in such year.

(B) *Change of status notification on Form W-9.*—If, on any interest payment date after the obligation was acquired by the person making the certification, the beneficial owner of the obligation is a U.S. person, then the person to whom the withholding agent pays interest must furnish the withholding agent with a U.S. beneficial ownership notification within 30 days after such interest payment date. A U.S. beneficial ownership notification must include a statement that the beneficial owner of the obligation has been a U.S. person on an interest payment date (identifying such date), that such owner has provided to the person providing the notification a Form W-9 (or a substitute form that is substantially similar to Form W-9 and completed under penalties of perjury), and that the person providing the notification has been and will be complying with the information reporting requirements of section 6049, if applicable.

(C) *Alternative notification statement.*—Where the person providing the notification described in paragraph (e)(4)(i)(B) of this section is neither a controlled foreign corporation within the meaning of section 957(a), nor a foreign corporation 50-percent or more of the gross income of which from all sources for the three-year period ending with the close of the taxable year preceding the date of the statement was effectively connected with the conduct of trade or business in the United States, such person must attach to the notification a copy of the Form W-9 (or substitute form that is substantially similar to Form W-9 and completed under penalties of perjury) provided by the beneficial owner. When a person that provides the U.S. beneficial ownership notification does not attach to it a copy of such Form W-9 (or substitute form that is substantially similar to Form W-9 and completed under penalties of perjury), such person must state that it is either a controlled foreign corporation within the meaning of section 957(a), or a foreign corporation 50-percent or more of the gross income of which from all sources for the three-year period ending with the close of its taxable year preceding the date of the statement was effectively connected with the conduct of a trade or business in the United States. A withholding agent that receives a Form W-9 (or a substitute form that is substantially similar to Form W-9 and completed under penalties of perjury) must send a copy of such form to the IRS, at such address as the IRS shall indicate, within 30 days after receiving it and must attach a statement that the Form W-9 or substitute form was provided pursuant to this paragraph (e)(4) with respect to a U.S. person that has owned a foreign-targeted registered obligation on one or more interest payment dates.

(D) *Failure to provide notification.*—If either a Form W-9 (or a substitute form that is substantially similar to a Form W-9 and completed under penalties of perjury) or the statement described in paragraph (e)(4)(i)(C) of this section is not attached to the U.S. beneficial ownership notification provided pursuant to paragraph (e)(4)(i)(B) of this section, the withholding agent is required to withhold under section 1441, 1442, or 1443 on a payment of interest made after the withholding agent has received the notification unless such form or statement (or a statement that the beneficial owner of the obligation is no longer a U.S. person) is received before the interest payment date from the person who provided the notification (or transferee). If, during the period beginning on the next January 15 and ending on the next January 31, such person certifies as set out in paragraph (e)(3)(i) of this section (subject to paragraph (e)(3)(i)(A)(2) of this section) then the withholding agent is not required to withhold during the year following such certification (unless such person again provides a U.S. beneficial ownership notification without attaching a Form W-9 or substitute form that is substantially similar to Form W-9 and completed under penalties of perjury or the statement described in paragraph (e)(4)(i)(C) of this section).

(E) *Procedures for clearing organizations.*—Within the period beginning 10 days before the end of the calendar quarter and ending on the last day of each calendar quarter, any clearing organization (including a clearing organization that is a withholding agent) relying on annual certificates or statements from its member organizations, as set forth in paragraph (e)(3)(i) of this section, must send each member organization having submitted such certificate or statement a reminder that the member organization must give the clearing organization a U.S. beneficial ownership notification in the circumstances described in paragraph (e)(4)(i)(B) of this section.

(F) *Retention of certificates.*—The certificate described in paragraph (e)(3)(i) of this section must be retained in the records of the withholding agent for four years from the end of the calendar year in which it was received. The statement described in paragraph (e)(3)(i) of this section that is received by a clearing organization from a member organization must be retained in the records of the clearing organization for four years from the end of the calendar year in which it was received.

(G) *No reporting requirement.*—The withholding agent who receives the certificate described in paragraph (e)(3)(i) of this section is not required to file Form 1042S to report payments under § 1.1461-1(b) or (c) of interest that are made with respect to foreign-targeted registered obligations held by the person providing the certificate and are made within the period beginning with the certificate date and ending on the last date for filing the next certificate.

(ii) *Procedures regarding certificates required under paragraph (e)(3)(ii) of this section.*—(A) *Time for providing certificate.*—The statement described in paragraph (e)(3)(ii) of this section must be provided to the withholding agent within the period beginning 90 days prior to and ending on the first interest payment date on which the withholding agent pays interest to the beneficial owner. The withholding agent may, in its discretion, withhold under section 1441(a), 1442(a), or 1443 if the statement is not received by the date 30 days prior to the interest payment. The beneficial owner must confirm to the withholding agent the continuing validity of the documentary evidence within the period beginning 90 days prior to the first day of the third calendar year following the provision of such evidence and during the same period every three years thereafter while the owner still owns the obligation. The withholding agent who receives the statement described in paragraph (e)(3)(ii) of this section is not required to report payments of interest under § 1.1461-1(b) or (c) if the payments are made with respect to foreign-targeted registered obligations held by the person who provides the statement and are made within the period beginning with the date on which the statement is provided and ending on the last date for confirming the validity of the statement. The statement received for purposes of paragraph (e)(3)(ii) of this section is subject to the applicable procedures set forth in § 1.1441-1(e)(4).

(B) *Change of status notification on Form W-9.*—If on any interest payment date after the obligation was acquired by the person providing the statement described in paragraph (e)(3)(ii) of this section, the beneficial owner of the obligation is a U.S. person, then the beneficial owner must so inform the withholding agent within 30 days after such interest payment date and must provide a Form W-9 (or substitute form that is substantially similar completed under penalties of perjury) to the withholding agent. However, the beneficial owner is not required to provide another Form W-9 (or substitute form that is substantially similar and completed under penalties of perjury) if such person has already provided it to the withholding agent within the same calendar year.

(iii) *Disqualification of documentation.*—In accordance with the provisions of section 871(h)(4), the Secretary may make a determination in appropriate cases that a certificate or statement by any person, or class of persons, does not satisfy the requirements of that section. Should that determination be made, all payments of interest that otherwise qualify as portfolio interest to that person would become subject to 30-percent withholding under section 1441(a), 1442(a), or 1443.

(5) *Information reporting.*—See § 1.6049-5(b)(7) for special information reporting rules applicable to interest on foreign-targeted registered obligations. See § 1.6045-1(g)(1)(ii) for information reporting rules applicable to the redemption, retirement, or sale of foreign-targeted registered obligations.

(f) *Securities lending transactions.*—For applicable rules regarding substitute interest payments received pursuant to a securities lending transaction or a sale-repurchase transaction, see § § 1.871-7(b)(2) and 1.881-2(b)(2).

(g) *Portfolio interest not to include interest received by 10-percent shareholders.*—(1) *In general.*—For purposes of section 871(h), the term portfolio interest shall not include any interest received by a 10-percent shareholder.

(2) *Ten-percent shareholder.*—(i) *In general.*—The term *10-percent shareholder* means—

(A) In the case of an obligation issued by a corporation, any person who owns 10-percent or more of the total combined voting power of all classes of stock of such corporation entitled to vote; or

(B) In the case of an obligation issued by a partnership, any person who owns 10-percent or more of the capital or profits interest in such partnership.

(ii) *Ownership.*—(A) *Stock ownership.*—For purposes of paragraph (g)(2)(i)(A) of this section, *stock owned* means stock directly or indirectly owned and stock owned by reason of the attribution rules of section 318(a), as modified by section 871(h)(3)(C).

(B) *Ownership of partnership interest.*—For purposes of paragraph (g)(2)(i)(B) of this section, rules similar to the rules in paragraph (g)(2)(ii)(A) of this section shall be applied in determining the ownership of a capital or profits interest in a partnership.

(3) *Application of 10-percent shareholder test to partners receiving interest through a partnership.*—(i) *Partner level test.*—Whether interest paid to a partnership and included in the distributive share of a partner that is a nonresident alien individual or foreign corporation is received by a 10 percent shareholder shall be determined by applying the rules of this paragraph (g) only at the partner level.

(ii) *Time at which 10-percent shareholder test is applied.*—The determination of whether a nonresident alien individual or foreign corporation that is a partner in a partnership is a 10-percent shareholder under the rules of section 871(h)(3), section 881(c)(3), and this paragraph (g) with respect to interest paid to such partnership shall be made at the time that the withholding agent, absent the provisions of section 871(h), 881(c) and the rules of this paragraph, would otherwise be required to withhold under sections 1441 and 1442 with respect to such interest. For example, in the case of U.S. source interest paid by a domestic corporation to a domestic partnership or withholding foreign partnership (as defined in § 1.1441-5(c)(2)), the 10-percent shareholder test is applied when any distributions that include the interest are made to a foreign partner and, to the extent that a foreign partner's distributive share of the interest has not actually been distributed, on the earlier of the date that the statement required under section 6031(b) is mailed or otherwise provided to such partner, or the due date for furnishing such statement. See § 1.1441-5(b)(2) and (c)(2)(iii).

(4) *Application of 10-percent shareholder test to interest paid to a simple trust or grantor trust.*—Whether interest paid to a simple trust or grantor trust and distributed to or included in the gross income of a nonresident alien individual or foreign corporation that is a beneficiary or owner of such trust, as the case may be, is received by a 10-percent shareholder shall be determined by applying the rules of this paragraph (g) only at the beneficiary or owner level. The 10-percent shareholder test is applied with respect to a nonresident alien individual or foreign corporation that is a beneficiary of a simple trust or an owner of a grantor trust at the time that a withholding agent, absent any exceptions, would otherwise be required to withhold under sections 1441 and 1442 with respect to such interest.

(h) *Portfolio interest not to include certain contingent interest.*—(1) *Dividend equivalents.*—Contingent interest does not qualify as portfolio interest to the extent that the interest is a dividend equivalent within the meaning of section 871(m).

(2) *Amount of dividend equivalent that is not portfolio interest.*—The amount that does not qualify as portfolio interest because it is a dividend equivalent equals the amount of the dividend equivalent determined pursuant to § 1.871-15(j). Unless otherwise excluded pursuant to section 871(h), any other interest paid on an obligation that is not a dividend equivalent may qualify as portfolio interest.

(i) *Definitions.*—For purposes of this section, the terms *U.S. person* and *foreign person* have the meaning set forth in § 1.1441-1(c)(2), the term *beneficial owner* has the meaning set forth in § 1.1441-1(c)(6), the term *withholding agent* has the meaning set forth in § 1.1441-7(a); the term *payee* has the meaning set forth in § 1.1441-1(b)(2); and the term *payment* has the meaning set forth in § 1.1441-2(e).

(j) *Effective/applicability date.*—(1) *In general.*—Except as otherwise provided in paragraph (j)(2) and (3) of this section, this section applies to payments of interest made on or after January 6, 2017. (For the rules that apply after June 30, 2014, and before January 6, 2017, see this section as in effect and contained in 26 CFR part 1, as revised April 1, 2016. For payments of interest made after December 31, 2000, and before July 1, 2014, see this section as in effect and contained in 26 CFR part 1, as revised April 1, 2013.)

(2) *Portfolio interest not to include interest received by 10-percent shareholders.*—Paragraph (g) applies to interest paid after April 12, 2007. Taxpayers may choose to apply the rules of paragraph (g) to interest paid in any taxable year not closed by the period of limitations as of April 12, 2007, provided they do so consistently for all relevant partnerships during such years.

(3) *Portfolio interest not to include certain contingent interest.*—The rules of paragraph (h) of this section apply beginning September 18, 2015. [Reg. § 1.871-14.]

☐ *[T.D. 8734, 10-6-97. Amended by T.D. 8804, 12-30-98; T.D. 8856, 12-29-99; T.D. 9323, 4-11-2007 (corrected 5-9-2007), T.D. 9658, 2-28-2014 (corrected 6-30-2014), T.D. 9734, 9-17-2015 and T.D. 9808, 12-30-2016.]*

§ 1.871-15. Treatment of dividend equivalents.—(a) *Definitions.*—For purposes of this section, the following terms have the meanings described in this paragraph (a).

(1) *Broker.*—A *broker* is a broker within the meaning provided in section 6045(c), except that the term does not include any corporation that is a broker solely because it regularly redeems its own shares.

(2) *Dealer.*—A *dealer* is a dealer in securities within the meaning of section 475(c)(1).

(3) *Dividend.*—A *dividend* is a dividend as described in section 316 (even if there is no actual distribution of cash or property).

(4) *Equity-linked instrument.*—An *equity-linked instrument* (*ELI*) is a financial transaction, other than a securities lending or sale-repurchase transaction or an NPC, that references the value of one or more underlying securities. For example, a futures contract, forward contract, option, debt instrument, or other contractual arrangement that references the value of one or more underlying securities is an ELI.

(5) *Initial hedge.*—An *initial hedge* is the number of underlying security shares that a short party would need to fully hedge an NPC or ELI (whether the NPC or ELI is a complex contract or a simple contract benchmark (within the meaning of paragraph (h)(2) of this section), as appropriate) with respect to an underlying security at the calculation time for the NPC or ELI, even if the short party does not in fact fully hedge the NPC or ELI.

(6) *Issue.*—An NPC or ELI is treated as issued at inception, original issuance, or at the time of an issuance as a result of a deemed exchange pursuant to section 1001.

(7) *Notional principal contract.*—A *notional principal contract* (*NPC*) is a notional principal contract as defined in § 1.446-3(c).

(8) *Option.*—An *option* includes an option embedded in any debt instrument, forward contract, NPC, or other potential section 871(m) transaction.

(9) *Parties to the transaction.*—(i) *Long party.*—A *long party* is the party to a potential section 871(m) transaction with respect to an underlying security that would be entitled to receive a payment of a dividend equivalent (within the meaning of paragraph (i) of this section) described in paragraph (c) of this section.

(ii) *Short party.*—A *short party* is the party to a potential section 871(m) transaction with respect to an underlying security that would be obligated to make a payment of a dividend equivalent (within the meaning of paragraph (i) of this section) described in paragraph (c) of this section.

(iii) *Party to the transaction.*—A *party to the transaction* is any person that is a long party or a short party to a potential section 871(m) transaction, any agent acting on behalf of the long party or short party, or any person acting as an intermediary with respect to the potential section 871(m) transaction.

(iv) *Party to the transaction that is both a long party and a short party.*—(A) *In general.*—If a potential section 871(m) transaction references more than one underlying security, the long party and short party are determined separately with respect to each underlying security. A party to a potential section 871(m) transaction is both a long party and a short party when the party is entitled to a payment that references a dividend payment on an underlying security and the same party is obligated to make a payment that references a dividend payment on another underlying security pursuant to the potential section 871(m) transaction.

(B) *Example.*—The following example illustrates the definitions in paragraph (a)(9) of this section:

Example. (i) Stock X and Stock Y are underlying securities. A and B enter into an NPC that entitles A to receive payments from B based on any appreciation in the value of Stock X and dividends paid on Stock X during the term of the contract and obligates A to make payments to B based on any depreciation in the value of Stock X during the term of the contract. In return, the NPC entitles B to receive payments from A based on any appreciation in the value of Stock Y and dividends paid on Stock Y during the term of the contract and obligates B to make payments to A based on any depreciation in the value of Stock Y during the term of the contract.

(ii) A is the long party with respect to Stock X, and the short party with respect to Stock Y. B is the long party with respect to Stock Y, and the short party with respect to Stock X.

(10) *Payment.*—A *payment* has the meaning provided in paragraph (i) of this section.

(11) *Reference.*—To *reference* means to be contingent upon or determined by reference to, directly or indirectly, whether in whole or in part.

(12) *Section 871(m) transaction and potential section 871(m) transaction.*—A *section 871(m) transaction* is any securities lending or sale-repurchase transaction, specified NPC, or specified ELI. A *potential section 871(m) transaction* is any securities lending or sale-repurchase transaction, NPC, or ELI that references one or more underlying securities.

(13) *Securities lending or sale-repurchase transaction.*—A *securities lending or sale-repurchase transaction* is any securities lending transaction, sale-repurchase transaction, or substantially similar transaction that references an underlying security. *Securities lending transaction* and *sale-repurchase transaction* have the same meaning as provided in § 1.861-3(a)(6).

(14) *Simple contracts and complex contracts.*—(i) *Simple contract.*—A *simple contract* is an NPC or ELI for which, with respect to each underlying security, all amounts to be paid or received on maturity, exercise, or any other payment determination date are calculated by reference to a single, fixed number of shares (as determined in paragraph (j)(3) of this section) of the underlying security, provided that the number of shares can be ascertained at the calculation time for the contract, and there is a single maturity or exercise date with respect to which all amounts (other than any upfront payment or any periodic payments) are required to be calculated with respect to the underlying security. For purposes of this section, a contract that provides an adjustment to the number of shares of the underlying security for a merger, stock split, cash dividend, or similar corporate action that affects all holders of the underlying securities proportionately will not cease to be treated as referencing a single, fixed number of shares solely as a result of that provision. A contract has a single exercise date even though it may be exercised by the holder at any time on or before the stated expiration of the contract. An NPC or ELI that includes a term that discontinuously increases or decreases the amount paid or received (such as a digital option), or that accelerates or extends the maturity is not a simple contract. A simple contract that is an NPC is a *simple NPC*. A simple contract that is an ELI is a *simple ELI*.

(ii) *Complex contract.*—(A) *In general.*—A *complex contract* is any NPC or ELI that is not a simple contract. A complex contract that is an NPC is a *complex NPC*. A complex contract that is an ELI is a *complex ELI*.

(B) *Example.*—An ELI entitles the long party to a return equal to 200 percent of the appreciation on 100 shares of Stock X, and obligates the long party to pay an amount equal to the actual depreciation on 100 shares of Stock X. Pursuant to paragraph (j)(3) of the section, the ELI references 200 shares when Stock X appreciates, but only 100 shares when Stock X depreciates. Because the ELI does not provide the long party with an amount that is calculated by reference to a single, fixed number of shares of Stock X on the maturity date that can be ascertained at the calculation time, it is not a simple ELI. More specifically, upon maturity the ELI will either entitle the long party to receive a payment that is, in substance, measured by reference to 200 shares of stock or obligate the long party to make a payment measured by reference to 100 shares of stock. The ELI is a complex ELI because it is not a simple ELI.

(15) *Underlying security.*—An *underlying security* is any interest in an entity if that interest could give rise to a U.S. source dividend pursuant to § 1.861-3, where applicable taking into account paragraph (m) of this section. Except as provided in paragraph (l) of this section, if a potential section 871(m) transaction references an interest in more than one entity described in the preceding sentence or different interests in the same entity, each referenced interest is a separate underlying security for purposes of applying the rules of this section.

(b) *Source of a dividend equivalent.*—A dividend equivalent is treated as a dividend from sources within the United States for purposes of sections 871(a), 881, 892, 894, and 4948(a), and chapters 3 and 4 of subtitle A of the Internal Revenue Code.

(c) *Dividend equivalent.*—(1) *In general.*—Except as provided in paragraph (c)(2) of this section, *dividend equivalent* means—

(i) Any payment that references a dividend from an underlying security pursuant to a securities lending or sale-repurchase transaction;

(ii) Any payment that references a dividend from an underlying security pursuant to a specified NPC described in paragraph (d) of this section;

(iii) Any payment that references a dividend from an underlying security pursuant to a specified ELI described in paragraph (e) of this section; and

(iv) Any other substantially similar payment as described in paragraph (f) of this section.

(2) *Exceptions.*—(i) *Not a dividend.*—A payment that references a distribution with respect to an underlying security is not a dividend equivalent to the extent that the distribution would not be subject to tax pursuant to section 871(a) or section 881 if the long party owned the underlying security. For example, if an NPC references stock in a regulated investment company that pays a dividend that includes a capital gains dividend described in section 852(b)(3)(C) that would not be subject to tax under section 871(a) or section 881 if paid directly to the long party, then an NPC payment is not a dividend equivalent to the extent that it is determined by reference to the capital gains dividend.

(ii) *Section 305 coordination.*—A dividend equivalent received by a long party, who is a shareholder as defined in § 1.305-1(d) of an instrument that gives rise to a dividend pursuant to sections 305(b) and (c) (including a debt instrument that is convertible into shares of stock and stock that is convertible into shares of another class of stock) that is also a section 871(m) transaction, is reduced by any amount treated as a dividend by sections 305(b) and (c) to the long party. For other section 871(m) transactions that reference an underlying security that is an instrument treated as paying a dividend pursuant to sections 305(b) and (c) and for which the long party is not a shareholder as defined in § 1.305-1(d), the dividend equivalent received by the long party with respect to the section 871(m) transaction includes (and is not reduced by) any amount treated as a dividend pursuant to sections 305(b) and (c).

(iii) *Due bills.*—A dividend equivalent does not include a payment made pursuant to a due bill arising from the actions of a securities exchange that apply to all transactions in the stock with respect to the dividend. For purposes of this section, a stock will be considered to trade with a due bill only when the relevant securities exchange has set an ex-dividend date with respect to a dividend that occurs after the record date.

(iv) *Payments made pursuant to annuity, endowment, and life insurance contracts.*—(A) *Insurance contracts issued by domestic insurance companies.*—A payment made pursuant to a contract that is an annuity, endowment, or life insurance contract issued by a domestic corporation (including its foreign or U.S. possession branch) that is a life insurance company described in section 816(a) does not include a dividend equivalent if the payment is subject to tax under section 871(a) or section 881.

(B) *Insurance contracts issued by foreign insurance companies.*—A payment does not include a dividend equivalent if it is made pursuant to a contract that is an annuity, endowment, or life insurance contract issued by a foreign corporation that would be subject to tax under subchapter L if it were a domestic corporation.

(C) *Insurance contracts held by foreign insurance companies.*—A payment made pursuant to a policy of insurance (including a policy of reinsurance) does not include a dividend equivalent if it is made to a foreign corporation that would be subject to tax under subchapter L if it were a domestic corporation.

(v) *Certain payments pursuant to employee compensation arrangements.*—A dividend equivalent does not include the portion of equity-based compensation for personal services of a nonresident alien individual that is—

(A) Wages subject to withholding under section 3402 and the regulations under that section;

(B) Excluded from the definition of wages under § 31.3401(a)(6)-1; or

(C) Exempt from withholding under § 1.1441-4(b).

(d) *Specified NPCs.*—(1) *Specified NPCs entered into before January 1, 2017.*—(i) *In general.*—For payments made after March 18, 2012, and before January 1, 2017, a specified NPC is any NPC if—

(A) In connection with entering into the contract, any long party to the contract transfers the underlying security to any short party to the contract;

(B) In connection with the termination of the contract, any short party to the contract transfers the underlying security to any long party to the contract;

(C) The underlying security is not readily tradable on an established securities market; or

(D) In connection with entering into the contract, the underlying security is posted as collateral by any short party to the contract with any long party to the contract.

(ii) *Specified NPC status as of January 1, 2017.*—An NPC that is treated as a specified NPC pursuant to paragraph (d)(1)(i) of this section will remain a specified NPC on or after January 1, 2017.

(2) *Specified NPCs on or after January 1, 2017.*—(i) *Simple NPCs.*—A simple NPC that has a delta of 0.8 or greater with respect to an underlying security at the calculation time for the NPC is a specified NPC.

(ii) *Complex NPCs.*—A complex NPC that meets the substantial equivalence test described in paragraph (h) of this section with respect to an underlying security at the calculation time for the NPC is a specified NPC.

(e) *Specified ELIs.*—(1) *Simple ELIs.*—A simple ELI that has a delta of 0.8 or greater with respect to an underlying security at the calculation time for the ELI is a specified ELI.

(2) *Complex ELIs.*—A complex ELI that meets the substantial equivalence test described in paragraph (h) of this section with respect to an underlying security at the calculation time for the ELI is a specified ELI.

(f) *Other substantially similar payments.*—For purposes of this section, any payment made in satisfaction of a tax liability of the long party with respect to a dividend equivalent by a withholding agent is a dividend equivalent received by the long party. The amount of that dividend equivalent constitutes additional income to the payee to the extent provided in § 1.1441-3(f)(1).

(g) *Delta.*—(1) *In general.*—Delta is the ratio of the change in the fair market value of an NPC or ELI to a small change in the fair market value of the number of shares of the underlying security (as determined under paragraph (j)(3) of this section) referenced by the NPC or ELI. If an NPC or ELI contains more than one reference to a single underlying security, all references to that underlying security are taken into account in determining the delta with respect to that underlying security. If an NPC or ELI references more than one underlying security or other property, the delta with respect to each underlying security must be determined without taking into account any other underlying security or property. The delta of an equity derivative that is embedded in a debt instrument or other derivative is determined without taking into account changes in the market value of the debt instrument or other derivative that are not directly related to the equity element of the instrument. Thus, for example, the delta of an option embedded in a convertible note is determined without regard to the debt component of the convertible note. For purposes of this section, delta must be determined in a commercially reasonable manner. If a taxpayer calculates delta for non-tax business purposes, that delta ordinarily is the delta used for purposes of this section.

(2) *Time for determining delta.*—(i) *In general.*—Except as provided in paragraph (g)(4) of this section, the delta of a potential section 871(m) transaction is determined at the calculation time for the potential section 871(m) transaction.

(ii) *Calculation time.*—The calculation time for a potential section 871(m) transaction is the earlier of when the potential section 871(m) transaction is priced and when the potential section 871(m) transaction is issued. Notwithstanding the preceding sentence, if the pricing time is more than 14 calendar days before the potential section 871(m) transaction is issued, the calculation time is when the potential section 871(m) transaction is issued.

(iii) *Pricing time.*—A potential section 871(m) transaction is priced when all material economic terms for the transaction have been agreed upon, including the price at which the transaction is sold.

(3) *Simplified delta calculation for certain simple contracts that reference multiple underlying securities.*—If an NPC or ELI references 10 or more underlying securities and an exchange-traded security (for example, an exchange-traded fund) is available that would fully hedge the NPC or ELI at the calculation time, the delta of the NPC or ELI may be calculated by determining the ratio of the change in the fair market value of the simple contract to a small change in the fair market value of the exchange-traded security. A delta determined under this paragraph (g)(3) must be used as the delta for each underlying security for purposes of calculating the amount of a dividend equivalent as provided in paragraph (j)(1)(ii) of this section.

(4) *Delta calculation for listed options.*—(i) *In general.*—The delta of an option contract that is listed on a regulated exchange described in paragraph (g)(4)(ii) of this section is the delta of that option at the close of business on the business day before the date of issuance. On the date an option contract is listed for the first time, the delta is the delta of that option at the close of business on the date of issuance. Notwithstanding the preceding two sentences, the delta of a listed option that is also a customized option is determined under the rules of paragraphs (g)(2) and (g)(3) of this section.

(ii) *Regulated exchange.*—For purposes of paragraph (g)(4)(i) of this section, a regulated exchange is any exchange that is either:

(A) Described in paragraph (l)(3)(vii) of this section; or

(B) *Foreign securities exchange.*—*(1) In general.*—A foreign securities exchange that:

(i) Is regulated or supervised by a governmental authority of the country in which the market is located;

(ii) Has trading volume, listing, financial disclosure, surveillance, and other requirements designed to prevent fraudulent and manipulative acts and practices, to remove impediments to and perfect the mechanism of a free and open, fair and orderly market, and to protect investors, and the laws of the country in which the exchange is located and the rules of the exchange ensure that those requirements are actually enforced;

(iii) Has rules that effectively promote active trading of listed options on the exchange; and

(iv) Has an average daily trading volume on the exchange exceeding $10 billion notional amount during the immediately preceding calendar year.

(2) *Application to an exchange with more than one tier or market.*—If an exchange in a foreign country has more than one tier or market level on which listed options may be separately listed or traded, each tier or market level is treated as a separate exchange.

(5) *Examples.*—The following examples illustrate the rules of this paragraph (g). For purposes of these examples, Stock X and Stock Y are common stock of domestic corporations X and Y. LP is the long party to the transaction.

Example 1. Delta calculation for an NPC. The terms of an NPC require LP to pay the short party an amount equal to all of the depreciation in the value of 100 shares of Stock X and an interest-rate based return. In return, the NPC requires the short party to pay LP an amount equal to all of the appreciation in the value of 100 shares of Stock X and any dividends paid by X on those shares. The value of the NPC will change by $1 for each $0.01 change in the price of a share of Stock X. When LP entered into the NPC, Stock X had a fair market value of $50 per share. The NPC therefore has a delta of 1.0 ($1.00 / ($0.01 x 100)).

Example 2. Delta calculation for an option. LP purchases a call option that references 100 shares of Stock Y. At the time LP purchases the call option, the value of the option is expected to change by $0.30 for a $0.01 change in the price of a share of Stock Y. When LP purchases the option, Stock Y has a fair market value of $100 per share. The call option has a delta of 0.3 ($0.30 / ($0.01 x 100)).

(h) *Substantial equivalence test.*—(1) *In general.*—The substantial equivalence test described in this paragraph (h) applies to determine whether a complex contract is a section 871(m) transaction. The substantial equivalence test assesses whether a complex contract substantially replicates the economic performance of the underlying security by comparing, at various testing prices for the underlying security, the differences between the expected changes in value of that complex contract and its initial hedge with the differences between the expected changes in value of a simple contract benchmark (as described in paragraph (h)(2) of this section) and its initial hedge. If the complex contract contains more than one reference to a single underlying security, all references to that underlying security are taken into account for purposes of applying the substantial equivalence test with respect to that underlying security. With respect to an equity derivative that is embedded in a debt instrument or other derivative, the substantial equivalence test is applied to the complex contract without taking into account changes in the market value of the debt instrument or other derivative that are not directly related to the equity element of the instrument. The complex contract is a section 871(m) transaction with respect to an underlying security if, for that underlying security, the expected change in value of the complex contract and its initial hedge is equal to or less than the expected change in value of the simple contract benchmark and its initial hedge when the substantial equivalence test described in this paragraph (h) is calculated at the calculation time for the complex contract. To the extent that the steps of the substantial equivalence test set out in this paragraph (h) cannot be applied to a particular complex contract, a taxpayer must use the principles of the substantial equivalence test to reasonably determine whether the complex contract is a section 871(m) transaction with respect to each underlying security. For purposes of this section, the test must be applied and the inputs must be determined in a commercially reasonable manner. The term of the simple contract benchmark must be, and the inputs must use, a reasonable time period, consistently applied (for example, in determining the standard deviation and probability). If a taxpayer calculates any relevant input for non-tax business purposes, that input ordinarily is the input used for purposes of this section.

(2) *Simple contract benchmark.*—The simple contract benchmark is an actual or hypothetical simple contract that, at the calculation time for the complex contract, has a delta of 0.8, references the applicable underlying security referenced by the complex contract, and has terms that are consistent with all the material terms of the complex contract, including the maturity date. If an actual simple contract does not exist, the taxpayer must create a hypothetical simple contract. Depending on the complex contract, the simple contract benchmark might be, for example, a call option, a put option, or a collar.

(3) *Substantial equivalence.*—A complex contract is a section 871(m) transaction with respect to an underlying security if the complex contract calculation described in paragraph (h)(4) of this section results in an amount that is equal to or less than the amount of the benchmark calculation described in paragraph (h)(5) of this section.

(4) *Complex contract calculation.*—(i) *In general.*—The complex contract calculation for each underlying security referenced by a potential section 871(m) transaction that is a complex contract is computed by:

(A) Determining the change in value (as described in paragraph (h)(4)(ii) of this section) of the complex contract with respect to the underlying security at each testing price (as described in paragraph (h)(4)(iii) of this section);

(B) Determining the change in value of the initial hedge for the complex contract at each testing price;

(C) Determining the absolute value of the difference between the change in value of the complex contract determined in paragraph (h)(4)(i)(A) of this section and the change in value of the initial hedge determined in paragraph (h)(4)(i)(B) of this section at each testing price;

(D) Determining the probability (as described in paragraph (h)(4)(iv) of this section) associated with each testing price;

(E) Multiplying the absolute value for each testing price determined in paragraph (h)(4)(i)(C) of this section by the corresponding probability for that testing price determined in paragraph (h)(4)(i)(D) of this section;

(F) Adding the product of each calculation determined in paragraph (h)(4)(i)(E) of this section; and

(G) Dividing the sum determined in paragraph (h)(4)(i)(F) of this section by the initial hedge for the complex contract.

(ii) *Determining the change in value.*—The change in value of a complex contract is the difference between the value of the complex contract with respect to the underlying security at the calculation time for the complex contract and the value of the complex contract with respect to the underlying security if the price of the underlying security were equal to the testing price at the calculation time for the complex contract. The change in value of the initial hedge of a complex contract with respect to the underlying security is the difference between the value of the initial hedge at the calculation time for the complex contract and the value of the initial hedge if the price of the underlying security were equal to the testing price at the calculation time for the complex contract.

(iii) *Testing price.*—The testing prices must include the prices of the underlying security if the price of the underlying security at the calculation time for the complex contract were alternatively increased by one standard deviation and decreased by one standard deviation, each of which is a separate testing price. In circumstances where using only two testing prices is reasonably likely to provide an inaccurate measure of substantial equivalence, a taxpayer must use additional testing prices as necessary to determine whether a complex contract satisfies the substantial equivalence test. If additional testing prices are used for the substantial equivalence test, the probabilities as described in paragraph (h)(4)(iv) of this section must be adjusted accordingly.

(iv) *Probability.*—For purposes of paragraphs (h)(4)(i)(D) and (E) of this section, the probability of an increase by one standard deviation is the measure of the likelihood that the price of the underlying security will increase by any amount from its price at the calculation time for the complex contract. For purposes of paragraphs (h)(4)(i)(D) and (E) of this section, the probability of a decrease by one standard deviation is the measure of the likelihood that the price of the underlying security will decrease by any amount from its price at the calculation time for the complex contract.

(5) *Benchmark calculation.*—The benchmark calculation with respect to each underlying security referenced by the potential section 871(m) transaction is determined by using the computation method-

ology described in paragraph (h)(4) of this section with respect to a simple contract benchmark for the underlying security.

(6) *Substantial equivalence calculation for certain complex contracts that reference multiple underlying securities.*—If a complex contract references 10 or more underlying securities and an exchange-traded security (for example, an exchange-traded fund) is available that would fully hedge the complex contract at its calculation time, the substantial equivalence calculations for the complex contract may be calculated by treating the exchange-traded security as the underlying security. When the exchange-traded security is used for the substantial equivalence calculation pursuant to this paragraph (h)(6), the initial hedge is the number of shares of the exchange-traded security for purposes of calculating the amount of a dividend equivalent as provided in paragraph (j)(1)(iii) of this section.

(7) *Example.*—The following example illustrates the rules of paragraph (h) of this section. For purposes of this example, Stock X is common stock of domestic corporation X. FI is the financial institution that structures the transaction described in the example, and is the short party to the transaction. Investor is a nonresident alien individual.

Example. Complex contract that is not substantially equivalent. (i) FI issues an investment contract (the Contract) that has a stated maturity of one year, and Investor purchases the Contract from FI at issuance for $10,000. At maturity, the Contract entitles Investor to a return of $10,000 (i) plus 200 percent of any appreciation in Stock X above $100 per share, capped at $110, on 100 shares or (ii) minus 100 percent of any depreciation in Stock X below $90 on 100 shares. At the calculation time for the Contract, the price of Stock X is $100 per share. Thus, for example, Investor will receive $11,000 if the price of Stock X is $105 per share at maturity of the Contract, but Investor will receive $9,000 if the price of Stock X is $80 per share when the Contract matures. At issuance, FI acquires 64 shares of Stock X to fully hedge the Contract issued to Investor. The calculation time for this example is the issuance.

(ii) The Contract references an underlying security and is not an NPC, so it is classified as an ELI under paragraph (a)(4) of this section. At the calculation time for the Contract, the Contract does not provide for an amount paid at maturity that is calculated by reference to a single, fixed number of shares of Stock X. When the Contract matures, the amount paid is effectively calculated based on either 200 shares of Stock X (if the price of Stock X has appreciated up to $110) or 100 shares of Stock X (if the price of Stock X has declined below $90). Consequently, the Contract is a complex contract described in paragraph (a)(14) of this section.

(iii) Because it is a complex ELI, FI applies the substantial equivalence test described in paragraph (h) of this section to determine whether the Contract is a specified *ELI. FI* determines that the price of Stock X would be $120 if the price of Stock X were increased by one standard deviation, and $79 if the price of Stock X were decreased by one standard deviation. Based on these results, FI next determines the change in value of the Contract to be $2000 at the testing price that represents an increase by one standard deviation ($12,000 testing price minus $10,000 issue price) and a negative $1,100 at the testing price that represents a decrease by one standard deviation ($10,000 issue price minus $8,900 testing price). FI performs the same calculations for the 64 shares of Stock X that constitute the initial hedge, determining that the change in value of the initial hedge is $1,280 at the testing price that represents an increase by one standard deviation ($6,400 at issuance compared to $7,680 at the testing price) and negative $1,344 at the testing price that represents a decrease by one standard deviation ($6,400 at issuance compared to $5,056 at the testing price).

(iv) FI then determines the absolute value of the difference between the change in value of the initial hedge and the Contract at the testing price that represents an increase by one standard deviation and a decrease by one standard deviation. Increased by one standard deviation, the absolute value of the difference is $720 ($2,000-$1,280); decreased by one standard deviation, the absolute value of the difference is $244 (negative $1,100 minus negative $1,344). FI determines that there is a 52% chance that the price of Stock X will have increased in value when the Contract matures and a 48% chance that the price of Stock X will have decreased in value at that time. FI multiplies the absolute value of the difference between the change in value of the initial hedge and the Contract at the testing price that represents an increase by one standard deviation by 52%, which equals $374.40. FI multiplies the absolute value of the difference between the change in value of the initial hedge and the Contract at the testing price that represents a decrease by one standard deviation by 48%, which equals $117.12. FI adds these two numbers and divides by the number of shares that constitute the initial hedge to determine that the transaction calculation is 7.68 ((374.40 plus 117.12) divided by 64).

(v) FI then performs the same calculation with respect to the simple contract benchmark, which is a one-year call option that references one share of Stock X, settles on the same date as the Contract, and has a delta of 0.8. The one-year call option has a strike price of $79 and has a cost (the purchase premium) of $22. The initial hedge for the one-year call option is 0.8 shares of Stock X.

(vi) FI first determines that the change in value of the simple contract benchmark is $19.05 if the testing price is increased by one standard deviation ($22.00 at issuance to $41.05 at the testing price) and negative $20.95 if the testing price is decreased by one standard deviation ($22.00 at issuance to $1.05 at the testing price). Second, FI determines that the change in value of the initial hedge is $16.00 at the testing price that represents an increase by one standard deviation ($80 at issuance to $96 at the testing price) and negative $16.80 at the testing price that represents a decrease by one standard deviation ($80.00 at issuance to $63.20 at the testing price).

(vii) FI determines the absolute value of the difference between the change in value of the initial hedge and the one-year call option at the testing price that represents an increase by one standard deviation is $3.05 ($16.00 minus $19.05). FI next determines the absolute value of the difference between the change in value of the initial hedge and the option at the testing price that represents a decrease by one standard deviation is $4.15 (negative $16.80 minus negative $20.95). FI multiplies the absolute value of the difference between the change in value of the initial hedge and the option at the testing price that represents an increase by one standard deviation by 52%, which equals $1.586. FI multiplies the absolute value of the difference between the change in value of the initial hedge and the option at the testing price that represents a decrease by one standard deviation by 48%, which equals $1.992. FI adds these two numbers and divides by the number of shares that constitute the initial hedge to determine that the benchmark calculation is 4.473 ((1.586 plus 1.992) divided by .8).

(viii) FI concludes that the Contract is not a section 871(m) transaction because the transaction calculation of 7.68 exceeds the benchmark calculation of 4.473.

(i) *Payment of a dividend equivalent.*—(1) *Payments determined on gross basis.*—For purposes of this section, a payment includes any gross amount that references a dividend and that is used in computing any net amount transferred to or from the long party even if the long party makes a net payment to the short party or no amount is paid because the net amount is zero.

(2) *Actual and estimated dividends.*—(i) *In general.*—A payment includes any amount that references an actual or estimated dividend, whether the reference is explicit or implicit. If a potential section 871(m) transaction provides for a payment based on an estimated dividend that adjusts to account for the amount of an actual dividend paid, the payment is treated as referencing the actual dividend amount and not an estimated dividend amount.

(ii) *Implicit dividends.*—A payment includes an actual or estimated dividend that is implicitly taken into account in computing one or more of the terms of a potential section 871(m) transaction, including interest rate, notional amount, purchase price, premium, upfront payment, strike price, or any other amount paid or received pursuant to the potential section 871(m) transaction.

(iii) *Actual dividend presumption.*—A short party to a section 871(m) transaction is treated as paying a per-share dividend amount equal to the actual dividend amount unless the short party to the section 871(m) transaction identifies a reasonable estimated dividend amount in writing at the calculation time. For this purpose, a reasonable estimated dividend amount stated in an offering document or the documents governing the terms at the calculation time will establish the estimated dividend amount. To qualify as an estimated dividend amount, the written estimated dividend amount must separately state the amount estimated for each anticipated dividend or state a formula that allows each dividend to be determined. If an underlying security is not expected to have a dividend, a reasonable estimate of the dividend amount may be zero.

(iv) *Additions to estimated payments.*—If a section 871(m) transaction provides for any payment in addition to an estimated dividend and that additional payment is determined by reference to a dividend (for example, a special dividend), both the estimated dividend and the additional payment are used to determine the per-share dividend amount.

(3) *Dividends for certain baskets.*—(i) *In general.*—If a section 871(m) transaction references long positions in more than 25 underlying securities, the short party may treat the dividends with respect to the referenced underlying securities as paid at the end of the applicable calendar quarter to compute the per share dividend amount.

(ii) *Publicly available dividend amount.*—For purposes of paragraph (i)(3)(i) of this section, if a section 871(m) transaction references the same underlying securities as a security (for example, stock in an exchange-traded fund) or index for which there is a publicly available quarterly dividend amount, the publicly available dividend amount may be used to determine the per-share dividend amount for the section 871(m) transaction with any adjustment for special dividends.

(iii) *Dividend amount for a section 871(m) transaction using the simplified delta calculation.*—When the delta of a section 871(m) transaction is determined under paragraph (g)(3) of this section, the per-share dividend amount for that section 871(m) transaction must be determined using the dividend amount for the exchange-traded security that would fully hedge the section 871(m) transaction (whether or not the exchange-traded security is actually acquired).

(4) *Examples.*—The following examples illustrate the rules of this paragraph (i). For purposes of these examples, Stock X is common stock of Corporation X, a domestic corporation, that historically pays quarterly dividends on Stock X. The parties anticipate that Corporation X will continue to pay quarterly dividends.

Example 1. Forward contract to purchase domestic stock. (i) When Stock X is trading at $50 per share, Foreign Investor enters into a forward contract to purchase 100 shares of Stock X in one year. Reasonable estimates of the quarterly dividend are specified in the transaction documents. The price in the forward contract is determined by multiplying the number of shares referenced in the contract by the current price of the shares and an interest rate, and subtracting the value of any dividends expected to be paid during the term of the contract. Assuming that the forward contract is priced using an interest rate of 4 percent and total estimated dividends with a future value of $1 per share during the term of the forward contract, the purchase price set in the forward contract is $5,100 (100 shares x $50 per share x 1.04 - ($1 x 100)).

(ii) Subject to paragraph (i)(2)(iv) of this section, the estimated dividend amounts are the per-share dividend amounts because the estimates are reasonable and specified in accordance with paragraph (i)(2)(iii) of this section. The estimated per-share dividend amounts are dividend equivalents for purposes of this section.

Example 2. Price return only swap contract. (i) Foreign Investor enters into a price return swap contract that entitles Foreign Investor to receive payments based on the appreciation in the value of 100 shares of Stock X and requires Foreign Investor to pay an amount based on LIBOR plus any depreciation in the value of Stock X. The swap contract neither explicitly entitles Foreign Investor to payments based on dividends paid on Stock X during the term of the contract nor references an estimated dividend amount. The LIBOR rate in the swap contract, however, is reduced to reflect expected annual dividends on Stock X.

(ii) Because the LIBOR leg of the swap contract is reduced to reflect estimated dividends and the estimated dividend amounts are not specified, Foreign Investor is treated as receiving the actual dividend amounts are in accordance with paragraph (i)(2) of this section. The actual per-share dividend amounts are dividend equivalents for purposes of this section.

(j) *Amount of dividend equivalent.*—(1) *Calculation of the amount of a dividend equivalent.*—The long party is liable for tax on any dividend equivalents required to be determined pursuant to paragraph (j)(2) of this section only with respect to dividend equivalents that arise while the long party is a party to the transaction. The amount of any dividend equivalent is determined as follows:

(i) *Securities lending or sale-repurchase transactions.*—For a securities lending or sale-repurchase transaction, the amount of the dividend equivalent for each dividend on an underlying security equals the amount of the actual per-share dividend paid on the underlying security multiplied by the number of shares of the underlying security.

(ii) *Simple contracts.*—For a simple contract that is a section 871(m) transaction, the amount of the dividend equivalent for each dividend on an underlying security equals:

(A) The per-share dividend amount (as determined under either paragraph (i)(2) or (i)(3) of this section) with respect to the underlying security multiplied by;

(B) The number of shares of the underlying security multiplied by;

(C) The delta of the section 871(m) transaction with respect to the underlying security.

(iii) *Complex contracts.*—For a complex contract that is a section 871(m) transaction, the amount of the dividend equivalent for each dividend on an underlying security equals:

(A) The per-share dividend amount (as determined under paragraph (i)(2) or (i)(3) of this section) with respect to the underlying security multiplied by;

(B) The initial hedge for the underlying security.

(iv) *Other substantially similar payments.*—In addition to any amount determined pursuant to paragraph (j)(1)(i), (ii), or (iii), the amount of a dividend equivalent includes the amount of any payment described in paragraph (f) of this section.

(2) *Time for determining the amount of a dividend equivalent.*—The amount of a dividend equivalent is determined on the earlier of the date that is the record date of the dividend and the day prior to the ex-dividend date with respect to the dividend. For example, if a specified NPC provides for a payment at settlement that takes into account an earlier dividend payment, the amount of the dividend equivalent is determined on the earlier of the record date or the day prior to the ex-dividend date for that dividend.

(3) *Number of shares.*—The number of shares of an underlying security generally is the number of shares of the underlying security stated in the contract. If the transaction modifies that number by a factor or fraction or otherwise alters the amount of any payment, the number of shares is adjusted to take into account the factor, fraction, or other modification. For example, in a transaction in which the long party receives or makes payments based on 200 percent of the appreciation or depreciation (as applicable) of 100 shares of stock, the number of shares of the underlying security is 200 shares of the stock.

(4) *Taxable year of a dividend equivalent.*—A long party is liable for tax on a dividend equivalent in the year the dividend equivalent is subject to withholding pursuant to § 1.1441-2(e)(7). Notwithstanding the preceding sentence, a long party that is a qualified derivatives dealer is liable for tax on a dividend equivalent when the applicable dividend on the underlying security would be subject to withholding pursuant to § 1.1441-2(e)(4). The amount of the long party's tax liability, however, is determined by reference to the amount that would have been due at the time the dividend equivalent amount is determined pursuant to paragraph (j)(2) of this section based on the beneficial owners at that time (for example, based on the tax rate at that time, whether the long party qualified for a treaty benefit at that time, and in the case of a partnership, based on the partners at that time).

(k) *Limitation on the treatment of certain corporate acquisitions as section 871(m) transactions.*—A potential section 871(m) transaction is not a section 871(m) transaction with respect to an underlying security if the transaction obligates the long party to acquire ownership of the underlying security as part of a plan pursuant to which one or more persons (including the long party) are obligated to acquire underlying securities representing more than 50 percent of the value of the entity issuing the underlying securities.

(l) *Rules relating to indices.*—(1) *Purpose.*—The purpose of this paragraph (l) is to provide a safe harbor for potential section 871(m) transactions that reference certain passive indices that are based on a diverse basket of publicly-traded securities and that are widely used by numerous market participants. Notwithstanding any other provision in this paragraph (l), an index is not a qualified index if treating the index as a qualified index would be contrary to the purpose described in this paragraph (l)(1).

(2) *Qualified index not treated as an underlying security.*—(i) *In general.*—For purposes of this section, a qualified index is treated as a single security that is not an underlying security. The determination of whether an index referenced in a potential section 871(m) transaction is a qualified index is made at the calculation time for the transaction based on whether the index is a qualified index on the first business day of the calendar year containing the calculation time.

(ii) *Rule for the first year of an index.*—In the case of an index that was not in existence on the first business day of the calendar year containing the calculation time for the transaction, paragraph (l)(2) of this section is applied by testing the index on the first business day it is created, and the dividend yield calculation required by paragraph (l)(3)(vi) of this section is determined by using the dividend yield that the index would have had in the immediately preceding year if it had the same components throughout that year that it has on the day it is created.

(3) *Qualified index.*—A *qualified index* means an index that—

(i) References 25 or more component securities (whether or not the security is an underlying security);

(ii) Except as provided in paragraph (l)(6)(ii) of this section, references only long positions in component securities;

(iii) References no component underlying security that represents more than 15 percent of the weighting of the component securities in the index;

(iv) References no five or fewer component underlying securities that together represent more than 40 percent of the weighting of the component securities in the index;

(v) Is modified or rebalanced only according to publicly stated, predefined criteria, which may require interpretation by the index provider or a board or committee responsible for maintaining the index;

(vi) Did not provide an annual dividend yield in the immediately preceding calendar year from component underlying securities that is greater than 1.5 times the annual dividend yield of the S&P 500 Index as reported for the immediately preceding calendar year; and

(vii) Is traded through futures contracts or option contracts (regardless of whether the contracts provide price only or total return exposure to the index or provide for dividend reinvestment in the index) on—

(A) A national securities exchange that is registered with the Securities and Exchange Commission or a domestic board of trade designated as a contract market by the Commodity Futures Trading Commission; or

(B) A foreign exchange or board of trade that is a qualified board or exchange as determined by the Secretary pursuant to section 1256(g)(7)(C) or that has a staff no action letter from the CFTC permitting direct access from the United States that is effective on the applicable testing date, provided that the referenced component underlying securities, in the aggregate, comprise less than 50 percent of the weighting of the component securities in the index.

(4) *Safe harbor for certain indices that reference assets other than underlying securities.*—Notwithstanding paragraph (l)(3) of this section, an index is a qualified index if the index is widely traded, the referenced component underlying securities in the aggregate comprise 10 percent or less of the weighting of the component securities in the index, and the index was not formed or availed of with a principal purpose of avoiding U.S. withholding tax.

(5) *Weighting of component securities.*—For purposes of this paragraph (l), the weighting of a component security of an index is the percentage of the index's value represented, or accounted for, by the component security.

(6) *Transactions that reference a qualified index and one or more component securities or indices.*—(i) *In general.*—When a potential section 871(m) transaction references a qualified index and one or more component securities or other indices, the qualified index remains a qualified index only if the potential section 871(m) transaction does not reference a short position in any referenced component security of the qualified index, other than a short position with respect to the entire qualified index (for example, a cap or floor) or a de minimis short position described in paragraph (l)(6)(ii) of this section. If, in connection with a potential section 871(m) transaction that references a qualified index, a taxpayer (or a related person within the meaning of section 267(b) or section 707(b)) enters into one or more transactions that reduce exposure to any referenced component security of the index, other than transactions that reduce exposure to the entire index, then the potential section 871(m) transaction is not treated as referencing a qualified index.

(ii) *Safe harbor for de minimis short positions.*—Notwithstanding paragraphs (l)(3)(ii) and (l)(6)(i) of this section, an index may be a qualified index if the short position (whether part of the index or entered into separately by the taxpayer or related person within the meaning of section 267(b) or section 707(b)) reduces exposure to referenced component securities of a qualified index (excluding any short positions with respect to the entire qualified index) by five percent or less of the value of the long positions in component securities in the qualified index.

(7) *Transactions that indirectly reference a qualified index.*—If a potential section 871(m) transaction references an exchange-traded fund that tracks a qualified index, the potential section 871(m) transaction will be treated as referencing a qualified index.

(m) *Rules relating to derivatives that reference partnerships.*—(1) *In general.*—When a potential section 871(m) transaction references a partnership interest, the assets of the partnership will be treated as referenced by the potential section 871(m) transaction only if the partnership carries on a trade or business of dealing or trading in securities, holds significant investments in securities (either of which is a covered partnership), or directly or indirectly holds an interest in a lower-tier partnership that is a covered partnership. For purposes of this section, if a covered partnership directly or indirectly holds assets that are underlying securities or potential section 871(m) transactions, any potential section 871(m) transaction that references an interest in the covered partnership is treated as referencing the shares of the underlying securities, including underlying securities of potential section 871(m) transactions, directly or indirectly allocable to that partnership interest. For purposes of this paragraph (m), a security is defined in section 475(c).

(2) *Significant investments in securities.*—(i) *In general.*—For purposes of this paragraph (m), a partnership holds significant investments in securities if either—

(A) 25 percent or more of the value of the partnership's assets consist of underlying securities or potential section 871(m) transactions; or

(B) The value of the underlying securities or potential section 871(m) transactions equals or exceeds $25 million.

(ii) *Determining the value of the partnership's assets.*—For purposes of this paragraph (m)(2), the value of a partnership's assets is determined at the calculation time for the potential section 871(m) transaction referencing that partnership interest based on the value of the assets held by the partnership on the last day of the partnership's prior taxable year unless the long party or the short party has actual knowledge that a subsequent transaction has caused the partnership to cross either of the thresholds described in paragraph (m)(2)(i) of this section. The value of a partnership's assets is equal to their fair market value, except that the value of any NPC, futures contract, forward contract, option, and any similar financial instrument held by the partnership is deemed to be the value of the notional securities referenced by the transaction.

(n) *Combined transactions.*—(1) *In general.*—For purposes of determining whether a potential section 871(m) transaction is a section 871(m) transaction, two or more potential section 871(m) transactions are treated as a single transaction with respect to an underlying security when—

(i) A person (or a related person within the meaning of section 267(b) or section 707(b)) is the long party with respect to the underlying security for each potential section 871(m) transaction;

(ii) The potential section 871(m) transactions reference the same underlying security;

(iii) The potential section 871(m) transactions, when combined, replicate the economics of a transaction that would be a section 871(m) transaction if the transactions had been entered into as a single transaction; and

(iv) The potential section 871(m) transactions are entered into in connection with each other (regardless of whether the transactions are entered into simultaneously or with the same counterparty).

(2) *Section 871(m) transactions.*—If a potential section 871(m) transaction is a section 871(m) transaction, either by itself or as a result of a combination with one or more other potential section 871(m) transactions, it does not cease to be a section 871(m) transaction as a result of applying paragraph (n) of this section or disposing of one or more of the potential section 871(m) transaction with which it is combined.

(3) *Short party presumptions regarding combined transactions.*—(i) *In general.*—If a short party relies on the presumption provided in paragraph (n)(3)(ii) of this section or in paragraph (n)(3)(iii) of this section, the short party is not required to treat those potential section

871(m) transactions as part of a single transaction pursuant to paragraph (n)(1) of this section.

(ii) *Transactions in separate accounts.*—A short party that is a broker may presume that transactions are not entered into in connection with each other for purposes of paragraph (n)(1) of this section if a long party holds or reflects the transactions in separate accounts maintained by the short party, unless the short party has actual knowledge that the transactions held or reflected in separate accounts by the long party were entered into in connection with each other or that separate accounts were created or used to avoid section 871(m).

(iii) *Transactions separated by at least two business days.*—A short party that is a broker may presume that transactions entered into two or more business days apart are not entered into in connection with each other for purposes of paragraph (n)(1) of this section unless the short party has actual knowledge that the transactions were entered into in connection with each other.

(4) *Presumptions Commissioner will apply to long party.*—(i) *Transactions in separate trading books.*—The Commissioner will presume that a long party did not enter into two or more transactions in connection with each other for purposes of paragraph (n)(1) of this section if the long party properly reflected those transactions on separate trading books. The Commissioner may rebut this presumption with facts and circumstances showing that transactions reflected on separate trading books were entered into in connection with each other or that separate trading books were created or used to avoid section 871(m).

(ii) *Transactions separated by at least two days.*—The Commissioner will presume that a long party did not enter into two or more transactions in connection with each other for purposes of paragraph (n)(1) of this section if the long party entered into the transactions two or more business days apart. The Commissioner may rebut this presumption with facts and circumstances showing that the transactions entered into two or more business days apart were entered into in connection with each other.

(iii) *Transactions separated by fewer than two days and reflected in the same trading book.*—The Commissioner will presume that transactions that are entered into fewer than two business days apart and reflected on the same trading book are entered into in connection with each other. A long party can rebut this presumption with facts and circumstances showing that the transactions were not entered into in connection with each other.

(5) *Rules of application.*—(i) *Two business days rule.*—For the purpose of determining the number of business days between transactions, the short party may, and the Commissioner will, assume that all transactions are entered into at 4:00 pm on the date the transaction becomes effective in the jurisdiction of the long party.

(ii) *No long party presumptions.*—Notwithstanding the presumptions described in paragraphs (n)(3) and (n)(4) of this section, the long party must treat two or more transactions as combined transactions if the transactions are described in paragraph (n)(1) of section.

(6) *Ordering rule for transactions entered into in connection with each other.*—If a long party enters into more than two potential section 871(m) transactions that could be combined under this paragraph (n), a short party is required to apply paragraph (n)(1) of this section by combining transactions in a manner that results in the most transactions with a delta of 0.8 or higher with respect to the referenced underlying security. Thus, for example, if a taxpayer has sold one at-the-money put and purchased two at-the-money calls, each with respect to 100 shares of the same underlying security, the put and one call are combined. Similarly, a purchased call on 100 shares and a sold put on 200 shares of the same underlying security can be combined for 100 shares with 100 shares of the put remaining separate. The two calls are not combined because they do not provide the long party with economic exposure to depreciation in the underlying security. Similarly, if a long party enters into more than two potential section 871(m) transactions that could be combined under this paragraph (n), but have not been combined by a short party, the long party is required to apply paragraph (n)(1) of this section by combining transactions in a manner that results in the most transactions with a delta of 0.8 or higher with respect to the referenced underlying security.

(7) *More than one underlying security referenced.*—If potential section 871(m) transactions reference more than one underlying security, paragraph (n)(1) of this section applies separately with respect to each underlying security.

(o) *Anti-abuse rule.*—If a taxpayer (directly or through the use of a related person within the meaning of section 267(b) or section 707(b)) acquires (whether by entering into, purchasing, accepting by transfer, by exchange, or by conversion, or otherwise acquiring) or disposes of (whether by sale, offset, exercise, termination, expiration, maturity, or other means) a transaction or transactions with a principal purpose of avoiding the application of this section, the Commissioner may treat any payment (as described in paragraph (i) of this section) made with respect to that transaction or transactions as a dividend equivalent to the extent necessary to prevent the avoidance of this section. Therefore, notwithstanding any other provision of this section, the Commissioner may, for example, adjust the delta of a transaction, change the number of shares, adjust an estimated dividend amount, change the maturity, adjust the timing of payments, treat a transaction that references a partnership interest as referencing the assets of the partnership, combine, separate, or disregard transactions, indices, or components of indices to reflect the substance of the transaction or transactions, or otherwise depart from the rules of this section as necessary to determine whether the transaction includes a dividend equivalent or the amount or timing of a dividend equivalent. A purpose may be a principal purpose even though it is outweighed by other purposes (taken together or separately). When a withholding agent knows that the taxpayer acquired or disposed of a transaction or transactions with a principal purpose of avoiding the application of this section and the Commissioner treats a payment made with respect to any transaction as a dividend equivalent, the withholding agent may be liable for any tax pursuant to section 1461.

(p) *Information required to be reported regarding a potential section 871(m) transaction.*—(1) *Responsible party.*—(i) *In general.*—If a broker or dealer is a party to a potential section 871(m) transaction with a counterparty or customer that is not a broker or dealer, the broker or dealer is required to determine whether the potential section 871(m) transaction is a section 871(m) transaction. If both parties to a potential section 871(m) transaction are brokers or dealers, or neither party to a potential section 871(m) transaction is a broker or dealer, the short party must determine whether the potential section 871(m) transaction is a section 871(m) transaction.

(ii) *Transactions with multiple brokers.*—For a potential section 871(m) transaction in which both the short party and an agent or intermediary acting on behalf of the short party are a broker or dealer, the short party must determine whether the potential section 871(m) transaction is a section 871(m) transaction. For a potential section 871(m) transaction in which the short party is not a broker or dealer and more than one agent or intermediary acting on behalf of the short party is a broker or dealer, the broker or dealer that is a party to the transaction and closest to the short party in the payment chain must determine whether the potential section 871(m) transaction is a section 871(m) transaction. For a potential section 871(m) transaction in which neither the short party nor any agent or intermediary acting on behalf of the short party is a broker or dealer, and the long party and an agent or intermediary acting on behalf of the long party are a broker or dealer, or more than one agent or intermediary acting on behalf of the long party is a broker or dealer, the broker or dealer that is a party to the transaction and closest to the long party in the payment chain must determine whether the potential section 871(m) transaction is a section 871(m) transaction.

(iii) *Responsible party for transactions traded on an exchange and cleared by a clearing organization.*—Except as provided in paragraph (p)(1)(iv) of this section, for a potential section 871(m) transaction that is traded on an exchange and cleared by a clearing organization, and for which more than one broker-dealer acts as an agent or intermediary between the short party and a foreign payee, the broker or dealer that has an ongoing customer relationship with the foreign payee with respect to that transaction (generally the clearing firm) must determine whether the potential section 871(m) transaction is a section 871(m) transaction.

(iv) *Responsible party for certain structured notes, warrants, and convertible instruments.*—When a potential section 871(m) transaction is a structured note, warrant, convertible stock, or convertible debt, the issuer is the party responsible for determining whether a potential section 871(m) transaction is a section 871(m) transaction.

(v) *Obligations of the responsible party.*—The party to the transaction that is required to determine whether a transaction is a section 871(m) transaction must also determine and report to the counterparty or customer the timing and amount of any dividend equivalent (as described in paragraphs (i) and (j) of this section). Except as otherwise provided in paragraph (n)(3) of this section, the party required to make the determinations described in this paragraph is required to exercise reasonable diligence to determine whether a transaction is a section 871(m) transaction, the amount of any dividend equivalents, and any other information necessary to apply the rules of this section. The information must be provided in the manner prescribed in paragraphs (p)(2) and (p)(3) of this section. The determinations required by paragraph (p) of this section are binding on the parties to the potential section 871(m) transaction and on any person who is a withholding agent with respect to the potential section 871(m) transaction unless the person knows or has reason to know that the information received is incorrect. The determinations are not binding on the Commissioner.

(2) *Reporting requirements.*—For rules regarding the reporting requirements of withholding agents with respect to dividend equivalents described in this section, see §§1.1461-1(b) and (c) and 1.1474-1(c) and (d).

(3) *Additional information available to a party to a potential section 871(m) transaction.*—(i) *In general.*—Upon request by any person described in paragraph (p)(3)(ii) of this section, the party required to report information pursuant to paragraph (p)(1) of this section must provide the requester with information regarding the amount of each dividend equivalent, the delta of the potential section 871(m) transaction, the amount of any tax withheld and deposited, the estimated dividend amount if specified in accordance with paragraph (i)(2)(iii) of this section, the identity of any transactions combined pursuant to paragraph (n) of this section, and any other information necessary to apply the rules of this section. The information requested must be provided within a reasonable time, not to exceed 10 business days, and communicated in one or more of the following ways:

(A) By telephone, and confirmed in writing;

(B) By written statement sent by first class mail to the address provided by the requesting party;

(C) By electronic publication available to all persons entitled to request information; or

(D) By any other method agreed to by the parties, and confirmed in writing.

(ii) *Persons entitled to request information.*—Any party to the transaction described in paragraph (a)(9) of this section may request the information specified in paragraph (p) of this section with respect to a potential section 871(m) transaction from the party required by paragraph (p)(3)(i) of this section to provide the information.

(iii) *Reliance on information received.*—A person described in paragraph (p)(1) or (p)(3)(ii) of this section that receives information described in paragraph (p)(1) or (p)(3)(i) of this section may rely on that information to provide information to any other person unless the recipient knows or has reason to know that the information received is incorrect. When the recipient knows or has reason to know that the information received is incorrect, the recipient must make a reasonable effort to determine and provide the information described in paragraph (p)(1) or (p)(3)(i) of this section to any person described in paragraph (p)(1) or (p)(3)(ii) of this section that requests information from the recipient.

(4) *Recordkeeping rules.*—(i) *In general.*—For rules regarding recordkeeping requirements sufficient to establish whether a transaction is a section 871(m) transaction and whether a payment is a dividend equivalent and the amount of gross income treated as a dividend equivalent, see §1.6001-1.

(ii) *Records sufficient to establish whether a transaction is a section 871(m) transaction and any dividend equivalent amount.*—Any person required to retain records must keep sufficient information to establish whether a transaction is a section 871(m) transaction and the amount of a dividend equivalent (if any), including documentation and work papers supporting the delta calculation or the substantial equivalence test (including the number of shares of the initial hedge), as applicable, and written estimated dividends (if any). The records and documentation must be created substantially contemporaneously. A record will be considered to have been created substantially contemporaneously if it was created within 10 business days of the date containing the calculation time for the potential section 871(m) transaction.

(iii) *Recordkeeping required for certain options.*—With respect to any option to which paragraph (g)(4) of this section applies, contemporaneous documentation is not required to be retained provided that there is a pre-existing documented methodology that is sufficient to permit the delta for the transaction to be verified at a later time.

(5) *Example.*—The following example illustrates the rules of paragraph (p) of this section.

(i) *Example 1: Responsible party for a transaction with multiple broker-dealers.* (A) *Facts.* CO is a domestic clearing organization and is not a broker as defined in paragraph (a)(1) of this section. CO serves as a central counterparty clearing and settlement service provider for derivatives exchanges in the United States. EB and CB are brokers organized in the United States and members of CO. FC, a foreign corporation, instructs EB to execute the purchase of a call option that is a specified ELI (as described in paragraph (e) of this section). EB effects the trade for FC on the exchange and then, as instructed by FC, transfers the option to CB to be cleared with CO. The exchange matches FC's order with an order for a written call option with the same terms and then sends the matched trade to CO, which clears the trade. CB and the clearing member representing the person who sold the call option settle the trade with CO. Upon receiving the matched trade, the option contracts are novated and CO becomes the counterparty to CB and the counterparty to the clearing member representing the person who sold the call option.

(B) *Analysis.* Both EB and CB are broker-dealers acting on behalf of FC for a potential section 871(m) transaction. Under paragraph (p)(1)(iii) of this section, however, only CB is required to make the determinations described in paragraph (p) of this section because CB has the ongoing customer relationship with FC with respect to the call option.

(ii) [Reserved]

(q) *Dividend and dividend equivalent payments to a qualified derivatives dealer.*—(1) *In general.*—Except as otherwise provided in this paragraph (q), a qualified derivatives dealer described in §1.1441-1(e)(6) that receives a payment (within the meaning of paragraph (i) of this section) of a dividend equivalent in its equity derivatives dealer capacity will not be liable for tax under section 881 on that dividend equivalent, provided that the qualified derivatives dealer complies with its obligations under the qualified intermediary withholding agreement described in §§1.1441-1(e)(5) and 1.1441-1(e)(6). A qualified derivatives dealer is liable for tax under section 881(a)(1) on its section 871(m) amount for each dividend on each underlying security. This tax liability is reduced (but not below zero) by the amount of tax paid by the qualified derivatives dealer under section 881(a)(1) on dividends it receives with respect to that underlying security on that same dividend in its capacity as an equity derivatives dealer. In addition, a qualified derivatives dealer is liable for tax under section 881(a)(1) for all dividend equivalents it receives that are not received in its equity derivatives dealer capacity. A qualified derivatives dealer also is liable for tax under section 881(a)(1) for all dividends it receives, other than dividends received in 2017 in its equity derivatives dealer capacity. This paragraph does not apply for a qualified derivatives dealer that is a foreign branch of a United States financial institution (within the meaning of §1.1471-5(e)).

(2) *Transactions on the books of an equity derivatives dealer.*—Transactions properly reflected in a qualified derivatives dealer's equity derivatives dealer book are presumed to be held by the dealer in its equity derivatives dealer capacity for purposes of determining the qualified derivatives dealer's tax liability. For purposes of determining whether a dealer is acting in its equity derivatives dealer capacity, only the dealer's activities as an equity derivatives dealer are taken into account. Accordingly, for purposes of this paragraph (q), a dividend or dividend equivalent is treated as received by a qualified derivatives dealer acting in its non-equity derivatives dealer capacity if the dividend or dividend equivalent is received by a qualified derivatives dealer acting as a proprietary trader.

(3) *Section 871(m) amount.*—For each dividend on each underlying security, the section 871(m) amount is the product of:

(i) The qualified derivatives dealer's net delta exposure to the underlying security for the applicable dividend, multiplied by;

(ii) The applicable dividend amount per share.

(4) *Net delta exposure.*—The net delta exposure to an underlying security is the amount (measured in number of shares) by which (A)

the aggregate number of shares of an underlying security that the qualified derivatives dealer has exposure to as a result of positions in the underlying security (including as a result of owning the underlying security) with values that move in the same direction as the underlying security (the long positions) exceeds (B) the aggregate number of shares of an underlying security that the qualified derivatives dealer has exposure to as a result of positions in the underlying security with values that move in the opposite direction from the underlying security (the short positions). The net delta exposure calculation only includes long positions and short positions that the qualified derivatives dealer holds in its equity derivatives dealer capacity (as described in paragraph (q)(2) of this section). Any long positions or short positions that are treated as effectively connected with the qualified derivatives dealer's conduct of a trade or business in the United States for U.S. federal income tax purposes are excluded from the net delta exposure computation. The net delta exposure to an underlying security is determined at the end of the day on the date provided in § 1.871-15(j)(2) for the applicable dividend. For purposes of this calculation, net delta must be determined in a commercially reasonable manner. If a qualified derivatives dealer calculates net delta for non-tax business purposes, the net delta ordinarily will be the delta used for that purpose, subject to the modifications required by this definition. Each qualified derivatives dealer must determine its net delta exposure separately only taking into account transactions that are recognized and are attributable to that qualified derivatives dealer for U.S. federal income tax purposes.

(5) *Examples.*—The following examples illustrate the rules of this paragraph (q):

Example 1. Forward contract entered into by a foreign equity derivatives dealer. (i) *Facts.* FB is a foreign bank that is a qualified intermediary that acts as a qualified derivatives dealer. On April 1, Year 1, FB enters into a cash settled forward contract initiated by a foreign customer (Customer) that entitles Customer to receive from FB all of the appreciation and dividends on 100 shares of Stock X, and obligates Customer to pay FB any depreciation on 100 shares of Stock X, at the end of three years. FB hedges the forward contract by entering into a total return swap contract with a domestic broker (U.S. Broker) and maintains the swap contract as a hedge for the duration of the forward contract. The swap contract entitles FB to receive an amount equal to all of the dividends on 100 shares of Stock X and obligates FB to pay an amount referenced to a floating interest rate each quarter, and also entitles FB to receive from or pay to U.S. Broker, as the case may be, the difference between the value of 100 shares of Stock X at the inception of the swap and the value of 100 shares of Stock X at the end of 3 years. Stock X pays a quarterly dividend of $0.25 per share. At the end of the day on the date provided in paragraph (j)(2) of this section for the dividend, FB owns the forward contract and total return swap; FB does not own any shares of Stock X or any other transactions that reference Stock X. FB provides valid documentation to U.S. Broker that FB will receive payments under the swap contract in its capacity as a qualified derivatives dealer, and FB contemporaneously enters both the swap contract with U.S. Broker and the forward contract with Customer on its equity derivatives dealer books.

(ii) *Application of rules.* At the end of the day on the date provided in paragraph (j)(2) of this section for the dividend, FB is a long party on a delta one contract (the total return swap) and a short party on a delta one contract (the forward contract with Customer). Pursuant to § 1.1441-1(b)(4)(xxii), U.S. Broker is not obligated to withhold on the dividend equivalent payments to FB on the swap contract that are referenced to Stock X dividends because U.S. Broker has received valid documentation that it may rely upon to treat the payment as made to FB acting as a qualified derivatives dealer. Pursuant to paragraph (q)(1) of this section, FB is not liable for tax under sections 871(m) and 881 on the payments it receives from U.S. Broker referenced to Stock X dividends because FB's net delta exposure with respect to 100 shares of Stock X is zero at the end of the day on the date provided in paragraph (j)(2) of this section for the dividend. The net delta exposure is zero because the taxpayer has 100 shares of Stock X long position exposure as a result of the total return swap that is reduced by 100 shares of Stock X short position exposure as a result of the forward contract. FB is required to withhold on dividend equivalent payments to Customer on the forward contract in accordance with § 1.1441-2(e)(7).

Example 2. At-the-money option contract entered into by a foreign equity derivatives dealer. (i) *Facts.* The facts are the same as Example 1, but Customer purchases from FB an at-the-money call option on 100 shares of Stock X with a term of one year. The call option has a delta of 0.5, and FB hedges the call option by entering into a total return swap that references 50 shares of Stock X with U.S. Broker. At the end of the day on the date provided in paragraph (j)(2) of this section for the dividend, the call option has a delta of 0.6, FB hedges the call option with a total return swap that references 60 shares of Stock X with U.S. Broker, and FB has no shares of Stock X or other transactions that reference Stock X.

(ii) *Application of rules.* At the end of the day on the date provided in paragraph (j)(2) of this section for the dividend, FB is a long party on 60 shares of Stock X through the total return swap and a short party on an option. Because the option has a delta of less than 0.8 at the calculation time, it is not a section 871(m) transaction. Therefore, there will be no dividend equivalent payments made by FB to Customer that are subject to withholding. Pursuant to § 1.1441-1(b)(4)(xxii), U.S. Broker is not obligated to withhold on the dividend equivalents with respect to Stock X paid to FB because U.S. Broker has received valid documentation that it may rely upon to treat the dividend equivalents as paid to FB acting as a qualified derivatives dealer. The net delta exposure is zero at the end of the day on the date provided in paragraph (j)(2) of this section for the dividend because FB has a long position of 60 shares as a result of the total return swap, which is reduced by FB's short position of 60 shares as a result of the option.

Example 3. In-the-money option contract entered into by a foreign equity derivatives dealer. (i) *Facts.* The facts are the same as Example 2, but Customer purchases from FB an in-the-money call option on 100 shares of Stock X with a term of one year. The call option has a delta of 0.8 and FB hedges the call option by purchasing 80 shares of Stock X, which are held in an account with U.S. Broker, who also acts as paying agent. The price of Stock X declines substantially and the option lapses unexercised. At the end of the day on the date provided in paragraph (j)(2) of this section for the dividend, the call option has a delta of 0.48 and FB has reduced its hedge to 50 shares of Stock X with U.S. Broker. In addition, on that date, FB owns no other shares of Stock X or any other transactions that reference Stock X in its equity derivatives dealer capacity.

(ii) *Application of rules.* At the end of the day on the date provided in paragraph (j)(2) of this section for the dividend, FB is a long party on 50 shares of Stock X and a short party on an option. Because the option has a delta of 0.8 at the calculation time, it is a section 871(m) transaction. Therefore, FB is required to withhold on dividend equivalent payments to Customer on the option contract in accordance with § 1.1441-2(e)(7). U.S. Broker is required to withhold on the Stock X dividends paid to FB. Assuming that FB is a qualified resident of a country with a treaty that provides withholding on dividends at a 15 percent rate, U.S. Broker is required withhold on the dividends with respect to the 50 shares of stock held by FB. FB's net delta exposure is two shares of Stock X at the end of the day on the date provided in paragraph (j)(2) of this section because FB has a long position of 50 shares, reduced by FB's short position of 48 shares as a result of the option. FB's section 881 tax on the $0.50 (two shares multiplied by a dividend of $0.25 per share) is reduced (but not below zero) by the section 881 tax amount paid by the qualified derivatives dealer on the 50 shares. Therefore, FB's section 871(m) amount is zero.

(r) *Effective/applicability date.*—(1) *In general.*—This section applies to payments made on or after January 19, 2017 except as provided in paragraphs (r)(2) and (3) of this section.

(2) *Effective/applicability date for paragraphs (d)(2) and (e).*—Paragraphs (d)(2) and (e) of this section apply to any payment made on or after January 1, 2017, with respect to any transaction with a delta of one issued on or after January 1, 2017. Paragraphs (d)(2) and (e) of this section apply to any payment made on or after January 1, 2018, with respect to any other transaction issued on or after January 1, 2018. Notwithstanding the prior sentence, paragraphs (d)(2) and (e) of this section will apply to any payments made on or after January 1, 2020, with respect to the exchange-traded notes issued on or after January 1, 2017, that are identified in a separate notice, and not payments made before January 1, 2020, with respect to those notes. Notwithstanding the first sentence of this paragraph (r)(3), paragraphs (d)(2) and (e) of this section do not apply to payments made in 2017 to a qualified derivatives dealer in its equity derivatives dealer capacity to hedge transactions that have a delta of less than one.

(3) *Effective/applicability date for paragraphs (g)(4)(ii)(B), (p)(1)(ii) through (iv), and (p)(5) of this section.*—Paragraphs (c)(2)(iv), (h), and (q) of this section apply to payments made on or after January 1, 2017. [Reg. § 1.871-15.]

☐ [*T.D.* 9648, 12-4-2013. *Amended by T.D.* 9734, 9-17-2015 (*corrected* 12-4-2015), *T.D.* 9815, 1-19-2017 (*corrected* 10-25-2017) *and T.D.* 9887, 12-16-2019.]

§ 1.872-1. Gross income of nonresident alien individuals.—(a) *In general.*—(1) *Inclusions.*—The gross income of a nonresident alien individual for any taxable year includes only (i) the gross income which is derived from sources within the United States and which is not effectively connected for the taxable year with the conduct of a trade or business in the United States by that individual and (ii) the gross income, irrespective of whether such income is derived from sources within or without the United States, which is effectively connected for the taxable year with the conduct of a trade or business in the United States by that individual. For the determination of the sources of income, see sections 861 through 863 and the regulations thereunder. For the determination of whether income from sources within or without the United States is effectively connected for the taxable year with the conduct of a trade or business in the United States, see sections 864(c) and 871(c) and (d), §§ 1.864-3 through 1.864-7, and §§ 1.871-9 and 1.871-10. For special rules for determining the income of an alien individual who changes his residence during the taxable year, see § 1.871-13.

(2) *Exchange transactions.*—Even though a nonresident alien individual who effects certain transactions in the United States in stocks, securities, or commodities during the taxable year may not, by reason of section 864(b)(2) and paragraph (c) or (d) of § 1.864-2, be engaged in trade or business in the United States during the taxable year through the effecting of such transactions, nevertheless he shall be required to include in gross income for the taxable year the gains and profits from those transactions to the extent required by § 1.871-7 or § 1.871-8.

(3) *Exclusions.*—For exclusions from gross income, see § 1.872-2.

(b) *Individuals not engaged in U.S. business.*—In the case of a nonresident alien individual who at no time during the taxable year is engaged in trade or business in the United States, the gross income shall include only (1) the gross income from sources within the United States which is described in section 871(a) and paragraphs (b), (c), and (d) of § 1.871-7 and (2) the gross income from sources within the United States which, by reason of section 871(c) or (d) and § 1.871-9 or § 1.871-10, is treated as effectively connected for the taxable year with the conduct of a trade or business in the United States by that individual.

(c) *Individuals engaged in U.S. business.*—In the case of a nonresident alien individual who is engaged in trade or business in the United States at any time during the taxable year, the gross income shall include (1) the gross income from sources within and without the United States which is effectively connected for the taxable year with the conduct of a trade or business in the United States by that individual, (2) the gross income from sources within the United States which, by reason of the election provided in section 871(d) and § 1.871-10, is treated as effectively connected for the taxable year with the conduct of a trade or business in the United States by that individual, and (3) the gross income from sources within the United States which is described in section 871(a) and paragraphs (b), (c), and (d) of § 1.871-7 and is not effectively connected for the taxable year with the conduct of a trade or business in the United States by the individual.

(d) *Special rules applicable to certain expatriates.*—For special rules for determining the gross income of a nonresident alien individual who has lost United States citizenship with a principal purpose of avoiding certain taxes, see section 877(b)(1).

(e) *Alien resident of Puerto Rico.*—This section shall not apply in the case of a nonresident alien individual who is a bona fide resident of Puerto Rico during the entire taxable year. See section 876 and § 1.876-1.

(f) *Effective date.*—This section shall apply for taxable years beginning after December 31, 1966. For corresponding rules applicable to taxable years beginning before January 1, 1967, see 26 CFR 1.872-1 (Rev. as of Jan. 1, 1971). [Reg. § 1.872-1.]

☐ [*T.D. 6528, 10-23-57. Amended by T.D.* 7332, 12-20-74.]

§ 1.872-2. Exclusions from gross income of nonresident alien individuals.—(a) *Earnings of foreign ships or aircraft.*—(1) *Basic rule.*—So much of the income from sources within the United States of a nonresident alien individual as consists of earnings derived from the operation of a ship or ships documented, or of aircraft registered, under the laws of a foreign country which grants an equivalent exemption to citizens of the United States nonresident in that foreign country and to corporations organized in the United States shall not be included in gross income.

(2) *Equivalent exemption.*—(i) *Ships.*—A foreign country which either imposes no income tax, or, in imposing an income tax, exempts from taxation so much of the income of a citizen of the United States nonresident in that foreign country and of a corporation organized in the United States as consists of earnings derived from the operation of a ship or ships documented under the laws of the United States is considered as granting an equivalent exemption for purposes of the exclusion from gross income of the earnings of a foreign ship or ships.

(ii) *Aircraft.*—A foreign country which either imposes no income tax, or, in imposing an income tax, exempts from taxation so much of the income of a citizen of the United States nonresident in that foreign country and of a corporation organized in the United States as consists of earnings derived from the operation of aircraft registered under the laws of the United States is considered as granting an equivalent exemption for purposes of the exclusion from gross income of the earnings of foreign aircraft.

(3) *Definition of earnings.*—For purposes of subparagraphs (1) and (2) of this paragraph, compensation for personal services performed by an individual aboard a ship or aircraft does not constitute earnings derived by such individual from the operation of ships or aircraft.

(b) *Compensation paid by foreign employer to participants in certain exchange or training programs.*—(1) *Exclusion from income.*—Compensation paid to a nonresident alien individual for the period that the nonresident alien individual is temporarily present in the United States as a nonimmigrant under subparagraph (F) (relating to the admission of students into the United States) or subparagraph (J) (relating to the admission of teachers, trainees, specialists, etc., into the United States) of section 101(a)(15) of the Immigration and Nationality Act (8 U.S.C. 1101(a)(15)(F) or (J)) shall be excluded from gross income if the compensation is paid to such alien by his foreign employer. Compensation paid to a nonresident alien individual by the United States office of a domestic bank which is acting as paymaster on behalf of a foreign employer constitutes compensation paid by a foreign employer for purposes of this paragraph if the domestic bank is reimbursed by the foreign employer for such payment. A nonresident alien individual who is temporarily present in the United States as a nonimmigrant under such subparagraph (J) includes a nonresident alien individual admitted to the United States as an "exchange visitor" under section 201 of the United States Information and Educational Exchange Act of 1948 (22 U.S.C. 1446), which section was repealed by section 111 of the Mutual Education and Cultural Exchange Act of 1961 (75 Stat. 538).

(2) *Definition of foreign employer.*—For purposes of this paragraph, the term "foreign employer" means a nonresident alien individual, a foreign partnership, a foreign corporation, or an office or place of business maintained in a foreign country or in a possession of the United States by a domestic corporation, a domestic partnership, or an individual who is a citizen or resident of the United States. The term does not include a foreign government. However, see section 893 and § 1.893-1. Thus, if a French citizen employed in the Paris branch of a banking company incorporated in the State of New York were admitted to the United States under section 101(a)(15)(J) of the Immigration and Nationality Act to study monetary theory and continued to receive a salary from such foreign branch while studying in the United States, such salary would not be includible in his gross income.

(c) *Tax convention.*—Income of any kind which is exempt from tax under the provisions of a tax convention or treaty to which the United States is a party shall not be included in the gross income of a nonresident alien individual. Income on which tax is limited by tax convention shall be included in the gross income of a nonresident alien individual if it is not otherwise excluded from gross income. See §§ 1.871-12 and 1.894-1.

(d) *Certain bond income of residents of the Ryukyu Islands or the Trust Territory of the Pacific Islands.*—Income derived by a nonresident alien individual from a series E or series H United States savings bond shall not be included in gross income if such individual acquired the bond while he was a resident of the Ryukyu Islands or the Trust Territory of the Pacific Islands. It is not necessary that the individual continue to be a resident of such Islands or Trust Territory for the period when, without regard to section 872(b)(4) and this paragraph, the income from the bond would otherwise be includible in his gross income under the provisions of section 446 or 454.

(e) *Certain annuities received under qualified plans.*—Pursuant to section 871(f), income received by a nonresident alien individual as an annuity under a qualified annuity plan described in section 403(a)(1) (relating to taxation of employee annuities), or from a qualified trust described in section 401(a) (relating to qualified pension, profit-sharing, and stock bonus plans) which is exempt from tax under section 501(a) (relating to exemption from tax on corporations, certain trusts, etc.), shall not be included in gross income, and shall be exempt from tax, for purposes of section 871 and §§1.871-7 and 1.871-8, if—

(1) All of the personal services by reason of which the annuity is payable were either—

(i) Personal services performed outside the United States by an individual (whether or not the annuitant) who, at the time of performance of the services, was a nonresident alien individual, or

(ii) Personal services performed in the United States by a nonresident alien individual (whether or not the annuitant) which, by reason of section 864(b)(1) (or corresponding provision of any prior law), were not personal services causing such individual to be engaged in trade or business in the United States during the taxable year, and

(2) At the time the first amount is paid (even though paid in a taxable year beginning before January 1, 1967) as such annuity under such annuity plan, or by such trust, to (i) the individual described in subparagraph (1) of this paragraph, or (ii) his nonresident alien beneficiary if such beneficiary is entitled to receive such first amount, 90 percent or more of the employees or annuitants for whom contributions or benefits are provided under the annuity plan, or under the plan or plans of which the trust is a part, are citizens or residents of the United States.

This paragraph shall apply whether or not the taxpayer is engaged in trade or business in the United States at any time during the taxable year in which the annuity is received. This paragraph shall not apply to distributions by an employees' trust or from an annuity plan which give rise to gains described in section 402(a)(2) or 403(a)(2), whichever applies. See section 871(a)(1)(B) and paragraph (c)(1)(i) of §1.871-7. For exemption from withholding of tax at source on an annuity which is exempt from tax under section 871(f) and this paragraph, see paragraph (g) of §1.1441-4.

(f) *Other exclusions.*—Income which is from sources without the United States, as determined under the provisions of sections 861 through 863, and the regulations thereunder, is not included in the gross income of a nonresident alien individual unless such income is effectively connected for the taxable year with the conduct of a trade or business in the United States by that individual. To determine specific exclusions in the case of other items which are from sources within the United States, see the applicable sections of the Code. For special rules under a tax convention for determining the sources of income and for excluding, from gross income, income from sources without the United States which is effectively connected with the conduct of a trade or business in the United States, see the applicable tax convention. For determining which income from sources without the United States is effectively connected with the conduct of a trade or business in the United States, see section 864(c)(4) and §1.864-5.

(g) *Effective date.*—This section shall apply for taxable years beginning after December 31, 1966. For corresponding rules applicable to taxable years beginning before January 1, 1967, see 26 CFR 1.872-2 (Rev. as of Jan. 1, 1971). [Reg. §1.872-2.]

☐ [*T.D.* 6258, 10-23-57. *Amended by T.D.* 6782, 12-12-64 *and T.D.* 7332, 12-20-74.]

§1.873-1. Deductions allowed nonresident alien individuals.—(a) *General provisions.*—(1) *Allocation of deductions.*—In computing the taxable income of a nonresident alien individual the deductions otherwise allowable shall be allowed only if, and to the extent that, they are connected with income from sources within the United States. No deduction shall be allowed in respect of any item, or portion thereof, which is not connected with income from such sources. For this purpose, the proper apportionment and allocation of the deductions with respect to sources of income within and without the United States shall be determined as provided in Part I (section 861 and following), subchapter N, chapter 1 of the Code, and the regulations thereunder, except as may otherwise be provided by tax convention. Thus, from the items of gross income specifically from sources within the United States and from the items allocated thereto under the provisions of section 863(a), there shall be deducted (i) the expenses, losses, and other deductions which are connected with those items of income and are properly apportioned or allocated thereto, and (ii) a ratable part of any other expenses, losses, or deductions which are connected with those items of income but cannot definitely be allocated to some item or class of gross income. The ratable part shall be based upon the ratio of gross income from sources within the United States to the total gross income. See §§1.861-8 and 1.863-1. In the case of income partly from within and partly from without the United States the expenses, losses, and other deductions connected with income from sources within the United States shall also be deducted in the manner prescribed by §§1.863-2 through 1.863-5 in order to ascertain under section 863 the portion of the taxable income attributable to sources within the United States.

(2) *Personal exemptions.*—The deductions for the personal exemptions allowed by section 151 or 642(b) shall not be taken into account for purposes of subparagraph (1) of this paragraph but shall be allowed to the extent provided by paragraphs (b) and (c) of this section.

(3) *Adjusted gross income.*—The adjusted gross income of a nonresident alien individual shall be the gross income from sources within the United States, determined in accordance with §1.871-7, minus the deductions prescribed by section 62 to the extent such deductions are allowed under this section in computing taxable income.

(4) *Standard deduction.*—The standard deduction shall not be allowed in computing the taxable income of a nonresident alien individual. See section 142(b)(1) and the regulations thereunder.

(5) *Exempt income.*—No deduction shall be allowed under this section for the amount of any item or part thereof allocable to a class or classes of exempt income, including income exempt by tax convention. See section 265 and the regulations thereunder.

(b) *No United States business.*—(1) *Income of not more than $15,400.*—(i) *Deduction for losses only.*—A nonresident alien individual within class 1 shall not be allowed any deductions other than the deduction for losses from sales or exchanges of capital assets determined in the manner prescribed by paragraph (b)(4)(vii) of §1.871-7. Thus, an individual within this class shall not be allowed any deductions for the personal exemptions otherwise allowed by section 151 or 642(b).

(ii) *Source of losses.*—Notwithstanding the provisions of section 873(b)(1), losses from sales or exchanges of capital assets shall be allowed under this subparagraph only if allocable to sources within the United States. See paragraph (b)(4)(i) of §1.871-7.

(2) *Aggregate more than $15,400.*—(i) *Deductions allowed.*—In computing the income subject to tax under section 1 or section 1201(b), a nonresident alien individual within class 2 shall be allowed deductions to the extent prescribed by paragraph (c)(3) of §1.871-7, but subject to the limitations of this section. For this purpose, the deduction for the personal exemptions shall be allowed in accordance with subdivision (iii) of this subparagraph.

(ii) *Deductions disallowed.*—In computing the minimum tax prescribed by section 871(b)(3), that individual shall not be allowed any deductions other than the deduction for losses from sales or exchanges of capital assets determined in the manner prescribed by paragraph (b)(4)(vii) of §1.871-7. For this purpose, the deductions for the personal exemptions shall not be allowed. See paragraph (c)(4) of §1.871-7.

(iii) *Personal exemptions.*—When the deductions for personal exemptions are allowed under this subparagraph, only one exemption under section 151 shall be allowed in the case of an individual who is not a resident of Canada or Mexico. A resident of either of those countries shall be allowed all the exemptions granted by section 151 to the extent prescribed therein. An estate or trust, whether or not a resident of Canada or Mexico, shall determine its deduction for the personal exemption in accordance with section 642(b) and the regulations thereunder.

(iv) *Source of losses.*—Notwithstanding the provisions of section 873(b), losses from sales or exchanges of capital assets shall be allowed under this subparagraph only if allocable to sources within the United States. See paragraph (c)(3)(i) of §1.871-7.

(3) *Election to be taxed on a net basis.*—Notwithstanding the other provisions of this paragraph, a nonresident alien individual within class 1 or 2 shall be allowed the deductions allowed by paragraph (c) of this section, if pursuant to a tax convention he is entitled, and does elect, to be subject to United States tax on a net basis as though he were engaged in trade or business within the United States through a permanent establishment situated therein.

(c) *United States business.*—(1) *Deductions in general.*—For purposes of computing the income subject to tax, a nonresident alien individual within class 3 shall be allowed deductions to the extent prescribed by paragraph (d) of § 1.871-7, but subject to the limitations of this section. For this purpose, the deductions for the personal exemptions shall be allowed in accordance with subparagraph (3) of this paragraph.

(2) *Special deductions.*—Notwithstanding the rule of source prescribed in paragraph (a) of this section, an individual within class 3 shall be allowed the following deductions whether or not they are connected with income from sources within the United States:

(i) *Losses on transactions for profit.*—Any loss sustained during the taxable year and not compensated for by insurance or otherwise, if incurred in any transaction entered into for profit, though not connected with a trade or business, shall be allowed to the extent allowed by section 165(c)(2), but only if and to the extent that the profit, if the transaction had resulted in a profit, would be taxable to such individual. Losses allowed under this subdivision shall be deducted in full, as provided in §§ 1.861-8 and 1.863-1, when the profit from the transaction, if it had resulted in a profit, would, under the provisions of section 861(a) or 863(a), have been taxable in full as income from sources within the United States; but shall be deducted under the provisions of § 1.863-3 when the profit from the transaction, if it had resulted in profit, would have been taxable only in part.

(ii) *Casualty losses.*—Any loss of property not connected with a trade or business, sustained during the taxable year and not compensated for by insurance or otherwise, if the loss arises from fire, storm, shipwreck, or other casualty, or from theft, shall be allowed to the extent allowed by section 165(c)(3), but only if the loss is of property within the United States. Losses allowed under this subdivision shall be deducted in full, as provided in §§ 1.861-8 and 1.863-1, from the items of gross income specified under sections 861(a) and 863(a) as being derived in full from sources within the United States; but, if greater than the sum of those items, the unabsorbed loss shall be deducted from the income apportioned under the provisions of § 1.863-3 to sources within the United States.

(iii) *Charitable contributions.*—The deduction for charitable contributions and gifts, to the extent allowed by section 170, shall be allowed under this subparagraph, but only as to contributions or gifts made to domestic corporations, or to community chests, funds, or foundations, created in the United States.

(3) *Personal exemptions.*—Only one exemption under section 151 shall be allowed in the case of an individual who is not a resident of Canada or Mexico. A resident of either of those countries shall be allowed all the exemptions granted by section 151 to the extent prescribed therein. An estate or trust, whether or not a resident of Canada or Mexico, shall determine its deduction for the personal exemption in accordance with section 642(b) and the regulations thereunder. [Reg. § 1.873-1.]

☐ [*T.D. 6258, 10-23-57.*]

§ 1.874-1. Allowance of deductions and credits to nonresident alien individuals.—(a) *Return required.*—A nonresident alien individual shall receive the benefit of the deductions and credits otherwise allowable with respect to the income tax, only if the nonresident alien individual timely files or causes to be filed with the Philadelphia Service Center, in the manner prescribed in subtitle F, a true and accurate return of the income which is effectively connected, or treated as effectively connected, with the conduct of a trade or business within the United States by the nonresident alien individual. No provision of this section (other than paragraph (c)(2)) shall be construed, however, to deny the credits provided by sections 31, 32, 33, 34 and 852(b)(3)(D)(ii). In addition, notwithstanding the requirement that a nonresident alien must file a timely return in order to receive the benefit of the deductions and credits otherwise allowable with respect to the income tax, the nonresident alien individual may, for purposes of determining the amount of tax to be withheld under section 1441 from remuneration paid for labor or personal services performed within the United States, receive the benefit of the deduction for personal exemptions provided in section 151, to the extent allowable under section 873(b)(3) and paragraph (c)(3) of § 1.873-1, or any applicable tax convention, by filing a claim therefor with the withholding agent. The amount of the deduction for the personal exemptions and the amount of the tax to be withheld under those circumstances shall be determined in accordance with paragraph (e)(2) of § 1.1441-3. The deductions and credits allowed such a nonresident alien individual electing under a tax convention to be subject to tax on a net basis may be obtained by filing a return of income in the manner prescribed in the regulations (if any) under the tax convention or under any other guidance issued by the Commissioner.

(b) *Filing deadline for return.*—(1) *General rule.*—As provided in paragraph (a) of this section, for purposes of computing the nonresident alien individual's taxable income for any taxable year, otherwise allowable deductions and credits will be allowed only if a true and accurate return for that taxable year is filed by the nonresident alien individual on a timely basis. For taxable years of a nonresident alien individual ending after July 31, 1990, whether a return for the current taxable year has been filed on a timely basis is dependent upon whether the nonresident alien individual filed a return for the taxable year immediately preceding the current taxable year. If a return was filed for that immediately preceding taxable year, or if the current taxable year is the first taxable year of the nonresident alien individual for which a return is required to be filed, the required return for the current taxable year must be filed within 16 months of the due date, as set forth in section 6072 and the regulations under that section, for filing the return for the current taxable year. If no return for the taxable year immediately preceding the current taxable year has been filed, the required return for the current taxable year (other than the first taxable year of the nonresident alien individual for which a return is required to be filed) must have been filed no later than the earlier of the date which is 16 months after the due date, as set forth in section 6072, for filing the return for the current taxable year or the date the Internal Revenue Service mails a notice to the nonresident alien individual advising the nonresident alien individual that the current year tax return has not been filed and that no deductions or credits (other than those provided in sections 31, 32, 33, 34 and 852(b)(3)(D)(ii)) may be claimed by the nonresident alien individual.

(2) *Waiver.*—The filing deadlines set forth in paragraph (b)(1) of this section may be waived if the nonresident alien individual establishes to the satisfaction of the Commissioner or his or her delegate that the individual, based on the facts and circumstances, acted reasonably and in good faith in failing to file a U.S. income tax return (including a protective return (as described in paragraph (b)(6) of this section)). For this purpose, a nonresident alien individual shall not be considered to have acted reasonably and in good faith if the individual knew that he or she was required to file the return and chose not to do so. In addition, a nonresident alien individual shall not be granted a waiver unless the individual cooperates in determining his or her U.S. income tax liability for the taxable year for which the return was not filed. The Commissioner or his or her delegate shall consider the following factors in determining whether the nonresident alien individual, based on the facts and circumstances, acted reasonably and in good faith in failing to file a U.S. income tax return—

(i) Whether the individual voluntarily identifies himself or herself to the Internal Revenue Service as having failed to file a U.S. income tax return before the Internal Revenue Service discovers the failure to file;

(ii) Whether the individual did not become aware of his or her ability to file a protective return (as described in paragraph (b)(6) of this section) by the deadline for filing the protective return;

(iii) Whether the individual had not previously filed a U.S. income tax return;

(iv) Whether the individual failed to file a U.S. income tax return because, after exercising reasonable diligence (taking into account his or her relevant experience and level of sophistication), the individual was unaware of the necessity for filing the return;

(v) Whether the individual failed to file a U.S. income tax return because of intervening events beyond the individual's control; and

(vi) Whether other mitigating or exacerbating factors existed.

(3) *Examples.*—The following examples illustrate the provisions of paragraph (b). In all examples, A is a nonresident alien individual

and uses the calendar year as A's taxable year. The examples are as follows:

Example 1. Nonresident alien individual discloses own failure to file. In Year 1, A became a limited partner with a passive investment in a U.S. limited partnership that was engaged in a U.S. trade or business. During Year 1 through Year 4, A incurred losses with respect to A's U.S. partnership interest. A's foreign tax advisor incorrectly concluded that because A was a limited partner and had only losses from A's partnership interest, A was not required to file a U.S. income tax return. A was aware neither of A's obligation to file a U.S. income tax return for those years nor of A's ability to file a protective return for those years. A had never filed a U.S. income tax return before. In Year 5, A began realizing a profit rather than a loss with respect to the partnership interest and, for this reason, engaged a U.S. tax advisor to handle A's responsibility to file U.S. income tax returns. In preparing A's U.S. income tax return for Year 5, A's U.S. tax advisor discovered that returns were not filed for Year 1 through Year 4. Therefore, with respect to those years for which applicable filing deadlines in paragraph (b)(1) of this section were not met, A would be barred by paragraph (a) of this section from claiming any deductions that otherwise would have given rise to net operating losses on returns for these years, and that would have been available as loss carryforwards in subsequent years. At A's direction, A's U.S. tax advisor promptly contacted the appropriate examining personnel and cooperated with the Internal Revenue Service in determining A's income tax liability, for example, by preparing and filing the appropriate income tax returns for Year 1 through Year 4 and by making A's books and records available to an Internal Revenue Service examiner. A has met the standard described in paragraph (b)(2) of this section for waiver of any applicable filing deadlines in paragraph (b)(1) of this section.

Example 2. Nonresident alien individual refuses to cooperate. Same facts as in *Example 1*, except that while A's U.S. tax advisor contacted the appropriate examining personnel and filed the appropriate income tax returns for Year 1 through Year 4, A refused all requests by the Internal Revenue Service to provide supporting information (for example, books and records) with respect to those returns. Because A did not cooperate in determining A's U.S. tax liability for the taxable years for which an income tax return was not timely filed, A is not granted a waiver as described in paragraph (b)(2) of this section of any applicable filing deadlines in paragraph (b)(1) of this section.

Example 3. Nonresident alien individual fails to file a protective return. Same facts as in *Example 1*, except that in Year 1 through Year 4, A also consulted a U.S. tax advisor, who advised A that it was uncertain whether U.S. income tax returns were necessary for those years and that A could protect A's right subsequently to claim the loss carryforwards by filing protective returns under paragraph (b)(6) of this section. A did not file U.S. income tax returns or protective returns for those years. A did not present evidence that intervening events beyond A's control prevented A from filing an income tax return, and there were no other mitigating factors. A has not met the standard described in paragraph (b)(2) of this section for waiver of any applicable filing deadlines in paragraph (b)(1) of this section.

Example 4. Nonresident alien with effectively connected income. In Year 1, A, a computer programmer, opened an office in the United States to market and sell a software program that A had developed outside the United States. A had minimal business or tax experience internationally, and no such experience in the United States. Through A's personal efforts, U.S. sales of the software produced income effectively connected with a U.S. trade or business. A, however, did not file U.S. income tax returns for Year 1 or Year 2. A was aware neither of A's obligation to file a U.S. income tax return for those years, nor of A's ability to file a protective return for those years. A had never filed a U.S. income tax return before. In November of Year 3, A engaged U.S. counsel in connection with licensing software to an unrelated U.S. company. U.S. counsel reviewed A's U.S. activities and advised A that A should have filed U.S. income tax returns for Year 1 and Year 2. A immediately engaged a U.S. tax advisor who, at A's direction, promptly contacted the appropriate examining personnel and cooperated with the Internal Revenue Service in determining A's income tax liability, for example, by preparing and filing the appropriate income tax returns for Year 1 and Year 2 and by making A's books and records available to an Internal Revenue Service examiner. A has met the standard described in paragraph (b)(2) of this section for waiver of any applicable filing deadlines in paragraph (b)(1) of this section.

Example 5. IRS discovers nonresident alien's failure to file. In Year 1, A, a computer programmer, opened an office in the United States to market and sell a software program that A had developed outside the United States. Through A's personal efforts, U.S. sales of the software produced income effectively connected with a U.S. trade or business. A had extensive experience conducting similar business activities in other countries, including making the appropriate tax filings. A, however, was aware neither of A's obligation to file a U.S. income tax return for those years, nor of A's ability to file a protective return for those years. A had never filed a U.S. income tax return before. Despite A's extensive experience conducting similar business activities in other countries, A made no effort to seek advice in connection with A's U.S. tax obligations. A failed to file either U.S. income tax returns or protective returns for Year 1 and Year 2. In November of Year 3, an Internal Revenue Service examiner asked A for an explanation of A's failure to file U.S. income tax returns. A immediately engaged a U.S. tax advisor, and cooperated with the Internal Revenue Service in determining A's income tax liability, for example, by preparing and filing the appropriate income tax returns for Year 1 and Year 2 and by making A's books and records available to the examiner. A did not present evidence that intervening events beyond A's control prevented A from filing a return, and there were no other mitigating factors. A has not met the standard described in paragraph (b)(2) of this section for waiver of any applicable filing deadlines in paragraph (b)(1) of this section.

Example 6. Nonresident alien with prior filing history. A began a U.S. trade or business in Year 1 as a sole proprietorship. A's tax advisor filed the appropriate U.S. income tax returns for Year 1 through Year 6, reporting income effectively connected with A's U.S. trade or business. In Year 7, A replaced this tax advisor with a tax advisor unfamiliar with U.S. tax law. A did not file a U.S. income tax return for any year from Year 7 through Year 10, although A had effectively connected income for those years. A was aware of A's ability to file a protective return for those years. In Year 11, an Internal Revenue Service examiner contacted A and asked for an explanation of A's failure to file income tax returns after Year 6. A immediately engaged a U.S. tax advisor and cooperated with the Internal Revenue Service in determining A's income tax liability, for example, by preparing and filing the appropriate income tax returns for Year 7 through Year 10 and by making A's books and records available to the examiner. A did not present evidence that intervening events beyond A's control prevented A from filing a return, and there were no other mitigating factors. A has not met the standard described in paragraph (b)(2) of this section for waiver of any applicable filing deadlines in paragraph (b)(1) of this section.

(4) *Effective date.*—Paragraphs (b)(2) and (3) of this section are applicable to open years for which a request for a waiver is filed on or after January 29, 2002.

(5) *Income tax treaties.*—A nonresident alien individual who has a permanent establishment or fixed base, as defined in an income tax treaty between the United States and the country of residence of the nonresident alien individual, in the United States is subject to the filing deadlines as set forth in paragraph (b)(1) of this section.

(6) *Protective return.*—If a nonresident alien individual conducts limited activities in the United States in a taxable year which the nonresident alien individual determines does not give rise to gross income which is effectively connected with the conduct of a trade or business within the United States as defined in sections 871(b) and 864(b) and (c) and the regulations under those sections, the nonresident alien individual may nonetheless file a return for that taxable year on a timely basis under paragraph (b)(1) of this section and thereby protect the right to receive the benefit of the deductions and credits attributable to that gross income if it is later determined, after the return was filed, that the original determination was incorrect. On that timely filed return, the nonresident alien individual is not required to report any gross income as effectively connected with a United States trade or business or any deductions or credits but should attach a statement indicating that the return is being filed for the reason set forth in this paragraph (b)(4). If the nonresident alien individual determines that part of the activities which he or she conducts in the United States in a taxable year gives rise to gross income which is effectively connected with the conduct of a trade or business and part does not, the nonresident alien individual must timely file a return for that taxable year to report the gross income determined to be effectively connected, or treated as effectively connected, with the conduct of that trade or business within the United States and the deductions and credits attributable to the gross income. In addition, the nonresident alien individual should attach to that return the statement described in this paragraph (b)(4) with regard to the other activities. The nonresident alien individual may follow the same procedure if the nonresident alien individual determines initially that he or she has no United States tax liability under the provisions of an applicable income tax treaty. In the event the nonresident alien individual relies on the provisions of an income tax treaty to reduce or eliminate the income subject to taxation, or to

reduce the rate of tax to which that income is subject, disclosure may be required pursuant to section 6114.

(c) *Allowed deductions and credits.*—(1) *In general.*—Except for losses of property located within the United States, charitable contributions and personal exemptions (see section 873(b)), deductions are allowed to a nonresident alien individual only to the extent they are connected with gross income which is effectively connected, or treated as effectively connected, with the conduct of the nonresident alien individual's trade or business in the United States. Other than credits allowed by sections 31, 32, 33, 34 and 852(b)(3)(D)(ii), the nonresident alien individual is entitled to credits only if they are attributable to effectively connected income. See paragraph (a) of this section for the requirement that a return be timely filed. Except as provided by section 906, a nonresident alien individual shall not be allowed the credit against the tax for taxes of foreign countries and possessions of the United States allowed by section 901.

(2) *Verification.*—At the request of the Internal Revenue Service, a nonresident alien individual claiming deductions from gross income which is effectively connected or treated as effectively connected with the conduct of a trade or business in the United States and credits attributable to that income must furnish at the place designated pursuant to § 301.7605-1(a) information sufficient to establish that the nonresident alien individual is entitled to the deductions and credits in the amounts claimed. All information must be furnished in a form suitable to permit verification of the claimed deductions and credits. The Internal Revenue Service may require, as appropriate, that an English translation be provided with any information in a foreign language. If a nonresident alien individual fails to furnish sufficient information, the Internal Revenue Service may in its discretion disallow any claimed deductions and credits in full or in part.

(d) *Return by Internal Revenue Service.*—If a nonresident alien individual has various sources of income within the United States, so that from any one source, or from all sources combined, the amount of income shall call for the assessment of a tax greater than that withheld at the source in the case of that individual, and a return of income has not been filed in the manner prescribed by subtitle F, including the filing deadlines set forth in paragraph (b)(1) of this section, the Internal Revenue Service shall:

(1) Cause a return of income to be made,

(2) Include on the return the income described in § 1.871-7 or § 1.871-8 of that individual from all sources concerning which it has information, and

(3) *Assess the tax.*—If the nonresident alien individual is not engaged in, or does not receive income that is treated as being effectively connected with, a United States trade or business and § 1.871-7 is applicable, the tax shall be assessed on the basis of gross income without allowance for deductions or credits (other than the credits provided by sections 31, 32, 33, 34 and 852(b)(3)(D)(ii)) and collected from one or more sources of income within the United States. If the nonresident alien individual is engaged in a United States trade or business or is treated as having effectively connected income and § 1.871-8 applies, the tax on the income of the nonresident alien individual that is not effectively connected, or treated as effectively connected with the conduct of a United States trade or business shall be assessed on the basis of gross income, determined in accordance with the rules of § 1.871-7, without allowance for deductions or credits (other than the credits provided by sections 31, 32, 33, 34 and 852(b)(3)(D)(ii)) and collected from one or more of the sources of income within the United States. Tax on income that is effectively connected, or treated as effectively connected, with the conduct of a United States trade or business shall be assessed in accordance with either section 1, 55 or 402(e)(1) without allowance for deductions or credits (other than the credits provided by sections 31, 32, 33, 34 and 852(b)(3)(D)(ii)) and collected from one or more of the sources of income within the United States.

(e) *Alien resident of Puerto Rico, Guam, American Samoa, or the Commonwealth of the Northern Mariana Islands.*—This section shall not apply to a nonresident alien individual who is a bona fide resident of Puerto Rico, Guam, American Samoa, or the Commonwealth of the Northern Mariana Islands during the entire taxable year. *See* section 876 and § 1.876-1. [Reg. § 1.874-1.]

☐ [*T.D.* 6258, 10-23-57. *Amended by T.D.* 6462, 5-5-60; *T.D.* 6669, 8-26-63; *T.D.* 8322, 12-10-90; *T.D.* 8981, 1-28-2002 *and T.D.* 9043, 3-7-2003.]

§ 1.881-1. Manner of taxing foreign corporations.—(a) *Classes of foreign corporations.*—For purposes of the income tax, foreign corporations are divided into two classes, namely, foreign corporations which at no time during the taxable year are engaged in trade or business in the United States and foreign corporations which, at any time during the taxable year, are engaged in trade or business in the United States.

(b) *Manner of taxing.*—(1) *Foreign corporations not engaged in U.S. business.*—A foreign corporation which at no time during the taxable year is engaged in trade or business in the United States is taxable, as provided in § 1.881-2, on all income received from sources within the United States which is fixed or determinable annual or periodical income and on other items of income enumerated under section 881(a). Such a foreign corporation is also taxable on certain income from sources within the United States which, pursuant to § 1.882-2, is treated as effectively connected for the taxable year with the conduct of a trade or business in the United States.

(2) *Foreign corporations engaged in U.S. business.*—A foreign corporation which at any time during the taxable year is engaged in trade or business in the United States is taxable, as provided in § 1.882-1, on all income from whatever source derived, whether or not fixed or determinable annual or periodical income, which is effectively connected for the taxable year with the conduct of a trade or business in the United States. Such a foreign corporation is also taxable, as provided in § 1.882-1, on income received from sources within the United States which is not effectively connected for the taxable year with the conduct of a trade or business in the United States and consists of (i) fixed or determinable annual or periodical income, or (ii) other items of income enumerated in section 881(a). A foreign corporation which at any time during the taxable year is engaged in trade or business in the United States is also taxable on certain income from sources within the United States which, pursuant to § 1.882-2, is treated as effectively connected for the taxable year with the conduct of a trade or business in the United States.

(c) *Meaning of terms.*—For the meaning of the term "engaged in trade or business within the United States," as used in section 881 and this section, see section 864(b) and the regulations thereunder. For determining when income, gain, or loss of a foreign corporation for a taxable year is effectively connected for that year with the conduct of a trade or business in the United States, see section 864(c), the regulations thereunder, and § 1.882-2. The term *foreign corporation* has the meaning assigned to it by section 7701(a)(3) and (5) and the regulations thereunder. However, for special rules relating to possessions of the United States, see § 1.881-5.

(d) *Rules applicable to foreign insurance companies.*—(1) *Corporations qualifying under subchapter L.*—A foreign corporation carrying on an insurance business in the United States at any time during the taxable year, which, without taking into account its income not effectively connected for the taxable year with the conduct of a trade or business in the United States, would qualify for the taxable year under part I, II, or III of subchapter L if it were a domestic corporation, shall be taxable for such year under that part on its entire taxable income (whether derived from sources within or without the United States) which is, or which pursuant to section 882(d) or (e) and § 1.882-2 is treated as, effectively connected for the taxable year with the conduct of a trade or business (whether or not its insurance business) in the United States. Any income derived by that foreign corporation from sources within the United States which is not effectively connected for the taxable year with the conduct of a trade or business in the United States is taxable as provided in section 881(a) an § 1.882-1. See sections 842 and 861 through 864, and the regulations thereunder.

(2) *Corporations not qualifying under subchapter L.*—A foreign corporation which carries on an insurance business in the United States at any time during the taxable year, and which, without taking into account its income not effectively connected for the taxable year with the conduct of a trade or business in the United States, would not qualify for the taxable year under part I, II, or III of subchapter L if it were a domestic corporation, and a foreign insurance company which does not carry on an insurance business in the United States at any time during the taxable year, shall be taxable—

(i) Under section 881(a) and § 1.881-2 or § 1.882-1 on its income from sources within the United States which is not effectively connected for the taxable year with the conduct of a trade or business in the United States,

(ii) Under section 882(a)(1) and § 1.882-1 on its income (whether derived from sources within or without the United States) which is effectively connected for the taxable year with the conduct of a trade or business in the United States, and

(iii) Under section 882(a)(1) and § 1.882-1 on its income from sources within the United States which pursuant to section 882(d) or (e) and § 1.882-2, is treated as effectively connected for the taxable year with the conduct of a trade or business in the United States.

(e) *Other provisions applicable to foreign corporations.*—(1) *Accumulated earnings tax.*—For the imposition of the accumulated earnings tax upon the accumulated taxable income of a foreign corporation formed or availed of for tax avoidance purposes, whether or not such corporation is engaged in trade or business in the United States, see section 532 and the regulations thereunder.

(2) *Personal holding company tax.*—For the imposition of the personal holding company tax upon the undistributed personal holding company income of a foreign corporation which is a personal holding company, whether or not such corporation is engaged in trade or business in the United States, see sections 541 through 547, and the regulations thereunder. Except in the case of a foreign corporation having personal service contract income to which section 543(a)(7) applies, a foreign corporation is not a personal holding company if all of its stock outstanding during the last half of the taxable year is owned by nonresident alien individuals, whether directly or indirectly through foreign estates, foreign trusts, foreign partnerships, or other foreign corporations. See section 542(c)(7).

(3) *Foreign personal holding companies.*—For the mandatory inclusion in the gross income of the United States shareholders of the undistributed foreign personal holding company income of a foreign personal holding company, see section 551 and the regulations thereunder.

(4) *Controlled foreign corporations.*—(i) *Subpart F income and increase of earnings invested in U.S. property.*—For the mandatory inclusion in the gross income of the U.S. shareholders of the subpart F income, of the previously excluded subpart F income withdrawn from investment in less developed countries, of the previously excluded subpart F income withdrawn from investment in foreign base company shipping operations, and of the increase in earnings invested in U.S. property, of a controlled foreign corporation, see sections 951 through 964, and the regulations thereunder.

(ii) *Certain accumulations of earnings and profits.*—For the inclusion in the gross income of U.S. persons as a dividend of the gain recognized on certain sales or exchanges of stock in a foreign corporation, to the extent of certain earnings and profits attributable to the stock which were accumulated while the corporation was a controlled foreign corporation, see section 1248 and the regulations thereunder.

(5) *Changes in tax rate.*—For provisions respecting the effect of any change in rate of tax during the taxable year on the income of a foreign corporation, see section 21 and the regulations thereunder.

(6) *Consolidated returns.*—Except in the case of certain corporations organized under the laws of Canada or Mexico and maintained solely for the purpose of complying with the laws of that country as to title and operation of property, a foreign corporation is not an includible corporation for purposes of the privilege of making a consolidated return by an affiliated group of corporations. See section 1504 and the regulations thereunder.

(7) *Adjustment of tax of certain foreign corporations.*—For the application of pre-1967 income tax provisions to corporations of a foreign country which imposes a more burdensome income tax than the United States, and for the adjustment of the income tax of a corporation of a foreign country which imposes a discriminatory income tax on the income of citizens of the United States or domestic corporations, see section 896.

(f) *Effective/applicability date.*—This section applies for taxable years beginning after December 31, 1966. For corresponding rules applicable to taxable years beginning before January 1, 1967, see 26 CFR 1.881-1 (Rev. as of Jan. 1, 1971). [Reg. § 1.881-1.]

☐ [*T.D.* 6258, 10-23-57. *Amended by T.D.* 7293, 11-27-73, *T.D.* 7385, 10-28-75; *T.D.* 7893, 5-11-83; *T.D.* 9194, 4-6-2005 *and T.D.* 9391, 4-4-2008.]

§ 1.881-2. Taxation of foreign corporations not engaged in U.S. business.—(a) *Imposition of tax.*—(1) This section applies for purposes of determining the tax of a foreign corporation which at no time during the taxable year is engaged in trade or business in the United States. However, see also § 1.882-2 where such corporation has an election in effect for the taxable year in respect to real property income or receives interest on obligations of the United States. Except as otherwise provided in § 1.871-12, a foreign corporation to which this section applies is not subject to the tax imposed by section 11 or section 1201(a) but, pursuant to the provisions of section 881(a), is liable to a flat tax of 30 percent upon the aggregate of the amounts determined under paragraphs (b) and (c) of this section which are received during the taxable year from sources within the United States. Except as specifically provided in such paragraphs, such amounts do not include gains from the sale or exchange of property. To determine the source of such amounts, see sections 861 through 863, and the regulations thereunder.

(2) The tax of 30 percent is imposed by section 881(a) upon an amount only to the extent the amount constitutes gross income.

(3) Deductions shall not be allowed in determining the amount subject to tax under this section.

(4) Except as provided in § 1.882-2, a foreign corporation which at no time during the taxable year is engaged in trade or business in the United States has no income, gain, or loss for the taxable year which is effectively connected for the taxable year with the conduct of a trade or business in the United States. See section 864(c)(1)(B) and § 1.864-3.

(5) Gains and losses which, by reason of section 882(d) and § 1.882-2, are treated as gains or losses which are effectively connected for the taxable year with the conduct of a trade or business in the United States by such a foreign corporation shall not be taken into account in determining the tax under this section. See, for example, paragraph (c)(2) of § 1.871-10.

(6) Interest received by a foreign corporation pursuant to certain portfolio debt instruments is not subject to the flat tax of 30 percent described in paragraph (a)(1) of this section. For rules applicable to a foreign corporation's receipt of interest on certain portfolio debt instruments, see sections 871(h), 881(c), and § 1.871-14.

(b) *Fixed or determinable annual or periodical income.*—(1) *General rule.*—The tax of 30 percent imposed by section 881(a) applies to the gross amount received from sources within the United States as fixed or determinable annual or periodical gains, profits, or income. Specific items of fixed or determinable annual or periodical income are enumerated in section 881(a)(1) as interest, dividends, rents, salaries, wages, premiums, annuities, compensations, remunerations, and emoluments, but other items of fixed or determinable annual or periodical gains, profits, or income are also subject to the tax as, for instance, royalties, including royalties for the use of patents, copyrights, secret processes and formulas, and other like property. As to the determination of fixed or determinable annual or periodical income, see paragraph (a) of § 1.441-2. For special rules treating gain on the disposition of section 306 stock as fixed or determinable annual or periodical income for purposes of section 881(a), see section 306(f) and paragraph (h) of § 1.306-3.

(2) *Substitute payments.*—For purposes of this section, a substitute interest payment (as defined in § 1.861-2(a)(7)) received by a foreign person pursuant to a securities lending transaction or a sale-repurchase transaction (as defined in § 1.861-2(a)(7)) shall have the same character as interest income received pursuant to the terms of the transferred security. Similarly, for purposes of this section, a substitute dividend payment (as defined in § 1.861-3(a)(6)) received by a foreign person pursuant to a securities lending transaction or a sale-repurchase transaction (as defined in § 1.861-2(a)(7)) shall have the same character as a distribution received with respect to the transferred security. Where, pursuant to a securities lending transaction or a sale-repurchase transaction, a foreign person transfers to another person a security the interest on which would qualify as portfolio interest under section 881(c) in the hands of the lender, substitute interest payments made with respect to the transferred security will be treated as portfolio interest, provided that in the case of interest on an obligation in registered form (as defined in § 1.871-14(c)(1)(i)), the transferor complies with the documentation requirement described in § 1.871-14(c)(1)(ii)(C) with respect to the payment of substitute interest and none of the exceptions to the portfolio interest exemption in sections 881(c)(3) and (4) apply. See also § § 1.871-7(b)(2) and 1.894-1(c).

(3) *Dividend Equivalents.*—For rules applicable to a foreign corporation's receipt of a dividend equivalent, see section 871(m) and the regulations thereunder.

(c) *Other income and gains.*—(1) *Items subject to tax.*—The tax of 30 percent imposed by section 881(a) also applies to the following gains received during the taxable year from sources within the United States:

(i) Gains described in section 631(b) or (c), relating to the treatment of gain on the disposal of timber, coal, or iron ore with a retained economic interest;

(ii) [Reserved]

(iii) Gains from the sale or exchange after October 4, 1966, of patents, copyrights, secret processes and formulas, goodwill, trademarks, trade brands, franchises, or other like property, or of any interest in any such property, to the extent the gains are from payments (whether in a lump sum or in installments) which are contingent on the productivity, use, or disposition of the property or interest sold or exchanged, or from payments which are treated under section 871(e) and § 1.871-11 as being so contingent.

(2) *Determination of amount of gain.*—The tax of 30 percent imposed upon the gains described in subparagraph (1) of this paragraph applies to the full amount of the gains and is determined (i) without regard to the alternative tax imposed by section 1201(a) upon the excess of net long-term capital gain over the net short-term capital loss; (ii) without regard to section 1231, relating to property used in the trade or business and involuntary conversions; and (iii) except in the case of gains described in subparagraph (1)(ii) of this paragraph, whether or not the gains are considered to be gains from the sale or exchange of property which is a capital asset.

(d) *Credits against tax.*—The credits allowed by section 32 (relating to tax withheld at source on foreign corporations), by section 39 (relating to certain uses of gasoline and lubricating oil), and by section 6402 (relating to overpayments of tax) shall be allowed against the tax of a foreign corporation determined in accordance with this section.

(e) *Effective/applicability date.*—Except as otherwise provided in this paragraph, this section applies for taxable years beginning after December 31, 1966. Paragraph (b)(2) of this section is applicable to payments made after November 13, 1997. For corresponding rules applicable to taxable years beginning before January 1, 1967, see 26 CFR 1.881-2 (Rev. as of Jan. 1, 1971). Paragraph (b)(3) of this section applies to payments made on or after January 23, 2012. [Reg. § 1.881-2.]

☐ [*T.D. 6258, 10-23-57. Amended by T.D. 6841, 7-26-65; T.D. 7293, 11-27-73; T.D. 8735, 10-6-97; T.D. 9323, 4-11-2007; T.D. 9572, 1-19-2012 and T.D. 9648, 12-4-2013.*]

§ 1.881-3. Conduit financing arrangements.—(a) *General rules and definitions.*—(1) *Purpose and scope.*—Pursuant to the authority of section 7701(l), this section provides rules that permit the director of field operations to disregard, for purposes of section 881, the participation of one or more intermediate entities in a financing arrangement where such entities are acting as conduit entities. For purposes of this section, any reference to tax imposed under section 881 includes, except as otherwise provided and as the context may require, a reference to tax imposed under sections 871 or 884(f)(1)(A) or required to be withheld under section 1441 or 1442. See § 1.881-4 for recordkeeping requirements concerning financing arrangements. See § § § 1.1441-3(g) and § 1.1441-7(f) for withholding rules applicable to conduit financing arrangements. See § 1.1471-3(e)(5) for withholding rules applicable to conduit financing arrangements for purposes of sections 1471 and 1472. See also § § 1.267A-1 and 1.267A-4 (disallowing a deduction for certain interest or royalty payments to the extent the income attributable to the payment is offset by a hybrid deduction).

(2) *Definitions.*—The following definitions apply for purposes of this section and § § 1.881-4, § 1.1441-3(g) and § 1.1441-7(f).

(i) *Financing arrangement.*—(A) *In general.*—Financing arrangement means a series of transactions by which one person (the financing entity) advances money or other property, or grants rights to use property, and another person (the financed entity) receives money or other property, or rights to use property, if the advance and receipt are effected through one or more other persons (intermediate entities) and, except in cases to which paragraph (a)(2)(i)(B) of this section applies, there are financing transactions linking the financing entity, each of the intermediate entities, and the financed entity. A transfer of money or other property in satisfaction of a repayment obligation is not an advance of money or other property. A financing arrangement exists regardless of the order in which the transactions are entered into, but only for the period during which all of the financing transactions coexist. See paragraphs (e)(1) through (5) of this section (*Examples 1* through *5*) for illustrations of the term financing arrangement.

(B) *Special rule for related parties.*—If two (or more) financing transactions involving two (or more) related persons would form part of a financing arrangement but for the absence of a financing transaction between the related persons, the director of field operations may treat the related persons as a single intermediate entity if he determines that one of the principal purposes for the structure of the financing transactions is to prevent the characterization of such arrangement as a financing arrangement. This determination shall be based upon all of the facts and circumstances, including, without limitation, the factors set forth in paragraph (b)(2) of this section. See paragraphs (e)(6) and (7) of this section (*Examples 6 and 7*) for illustrations of this paragraph (a)(2)(i)(B).

(C) *Treatment of disregarded entities.*—For purposes of this section, the term person includes a business entity that is disregarded as an entity separate from its single member owner under § § 301.7701-1 through 301.7701-3 of this chapter and, therefore, such entity may, for example, be treated as a party to a financing transaction with its owner. See paragraph (e)(3) of this section (*Example 3*).

(ii) *Financing transaction.*—(A) *In general.*—Financing transaction means—

(1) Debt;

(2) Stock in a corporation (or a similar interest in a partnership, trust, or other person) that meets the requirements of paragraph (a)(2)(ii)(B) of this section;

(3) Any lease or license; or

(4) Any other transaction (including an interest in a trust described in sections 671 through 679) pursuant to which a person makes an advance of money or other property or grants rights to use property to a transferee who is obligated to repay or return a substantial portion of the money or other property advanced, or the equivalent in value. This paragraph (a)(2)(ii)(A)(4) shall not apply to the posting of collateral unless the collateral consists of cash or the person holding the collateral is permitted to reduce the collateral to cash (through a transfer, grant of a security interest or similar transaction) prior to default on the financing transaction secured by the collateral.

(B) *Limitation on inclusion of stock or similar.*—interests

(1) In general.—Stock in a corporation (or a similar interest in a partnership, trust, or other person) will constitute a financing transaction only if one or more of the following conditions is satisfied—

(i) The issuer is required to redeem the stock or similar interest at a specified time or the holder has the right to require the issuer to redeem the stock or similar interest or to make any other payment with respect to the stock or similar interest;

(ii) The issuer has the right to redeem the stock or similar interest, but only if, based on all of the facts and circumstances as of the issue date, redemption pursuant to that right is more likely than not to occur;

(iii) The owner of the stock or similar interest has the right to require a person related to the issuer (or any other person who is acting pursuant to a plan or arrangement with the issuer) to acquire the stock or similar interest or make a payment with respect to the stock or similar interest; or

(iv) The stock or similar interest is treated as debt under the tax law of the issuer's country of residence or, if the issuer is not a tax resident of any country, such as a partnership, the tax law of the country in which the issuer is created, organized, or otherwise established.

(v) [Reserved]

(2) Rules of special application.—*(i) Existence of a right.*—For purposes of this paragraph (a)(2)(ii)(B), a person will be considered to have a right to cause a redemption or payment if the person has the right (other than rights arising, in the ordinary course, between the date that a payment is declared and the date that a payment is made) to enforce the payment through a legal proceeding or to cause the issuer to be liquidated if it fails to redeem the interest or to make a payment. A person will not be considered to have a right to force a redemption or a payment if the right is derived solely from ownership of a controlling interest in the issuer in cases where the control does not arise from a default or similar contingency under

the instrument. The person is considered to have such a right if the person has the right as of the issue date or, as of the issue date, it is more likely than not that the person will receive such a right, whether through the occurrence of a contingency or otherwise.

(ii) Restrictions on payment.—The fact that the issuer does not have the legally available funds to redeem the stock or similar interest, or that the payments are to be made in a blocked currency, will not affect the determinations made pursuant to this paragraph (a)(2)(ii)(B).

(iii) *Conduit entity.*—means an intermediate entity whose participation in the financing arrangement may be disregarded in whole or in part pursuant to this section, whether or not the director of field operations has made a determination that the intermediate entity should be disregarded under paragraph (a)(3)(i) of this section.

(iv) *Conduit financing arrangement.*—means a financing arrangement that is effected through one or more conduit entities.

(v) *Related.*—means related within the meaning of sections 267(b) or 707(b)(1), or controlled within the meaning of section 482, and the regulations under those sections. For purposes of determining whether a person is related to another person, the constructive ownership rules of section 318 shall apply, and the attribution rules of section 267(c) also shall apply to the extent they attribute ownership to persons to whom section 318 does not attribute ownership.

(3) *Disregard of participation of conduit entity.*—(i) *Authority of director of field operations.*—The director of field operations may determine that the participation of a conduit entity in a conduit financing arrangement should be disregarded for purposes of section 881. For this purpose, an intermediate entity will constitute a conduit entity if it meets the standards of paragraph (a)(4) of this section. The director of field operations has discretion to determine the manner in which the standards of paragraph (a)(4) of this section apply, including the financing transactions and parties composing the financing arrangement.

(ii) *Effect of disregarding conduit entity.*—(A) *In general.*—If the director of field operations determines that the participation of a conduit entity in a financing arrangement should be disregarded, the financing arrangement is recharacterized as a transaction directly between the remaining parties to the financing arrangement (in most cases, the financed entity and the financing entity) for purposes of section 881. To the extent that a disregarded conduit entity actually receives or makes payments pursuant to a conduit financing arrangement, it is treated as an agent of the financing entity. Except as otherwise provided, the recharacterization of the conduit financing arrangement also applies for purposes of sections 871, 884(f)(1)(A), 1441, and 1442 and other procedural provisions relating to those sections. This recharacterization will not otherwise affect a taxpayer's Federal income tax liability under any substantive provisions of the Internal Revenue Code. Thus, for example, the recharacterization generally applies for purposes of section 1461, in order to impose liability on a withholding agent who fails to withhold as required under §§1.1441-3(g), but not for purposes of §1.882-5.

(B) *Character of payments made by the financed entity.*—If the participation of a conduit financing arrangement is disregarded under this paragraph (a)(3), payments made by the financed entity generally shall be characterized by reference to the character (e.g., interest or rent) of the payments made to the financing entity. However, if the financing transaction to which the financing entity is a party is a transaction described in paragraph (a)(2)(ii)(A)(2) or (4) of this section that gives rise to payments that would not be deductible if paid by the financed entity, the character of the payments made by the financed entity will not be affected by the disregard of the participation of a conduit entity. The characterization provided by this paragraph (a)(3)(ii)(B) does not, however, extend to qualification of a payment for any exemption from withholding tax under the Internal Revenue Code or a provision of any applicable tax treaty if such qualification depends on the terms of, or other similar facts or circumstances relating to, the financing transaction to which the financing entity is a party that do not apply to the financing transaction to which the financed entity is a party. Thus, for example, payments made by a financed entity that is not a bank cannot qualify for the exemption provided by section 881(i) of the Code even if the loan between the financing entity and the conduit entity is a bank deposit.

(C) *Effect of income tax treaties.*—Where the participation of a conduit entity in a conduit financing arrangement is disregarded pursuant to this section, it is disregarded for all purposes of section 881, including for purposes of applying any relevant income tax treaties. Accordingly, the conduit entity may not claim the benefits of a tax treaty between its country of residence and the United States to reduce the amount of tax due under section 881 with respect to payments made pursuant to the conduit financing arrangement. The financing entity may, however, claim the benefits of any income tax treaty under which it is entitled to benefits in order to reduce the rate of tax on payments made pursuant to the conduit financing arrangement that are recharacterized in accordance with paragraph (a)(3)(ii)(B) of this section.

(D) *Effect on withholding tax.*—For the effect of recharacterization on withholding obligations, see §§§1.1441-3(g) and §1.1441-7(f).

(E) *Special rule for a financing entity that is unrelated to both intermediate entity and financed entity.*—*(1) Liability of financing entity.*—Notwithstanding the fact that a financing arrangement is a conduit financing arrangement, a financing entity that is unrelated to the financed entity and the conduit entity (or entities) shall not itself be liable for tax under section 881 unless the financing entity knows or has reason to know that the financing arrangement is a conduit financing arrangement. But see §§1.1441-3(g) for the withholding agent's withholding obligations.

(2) Financing entity's knowledge.—*(i) In general.*—A financing entity knows or has reason to know that the financing arrangement is a conduit financing arrangement only if the financing entity knows or has reason to know of facts sufficient to establish that the financing arrangement is a conduit financing arrangement, including facts sufficient to establish that the participation of the intermediate entity in the financing arrangement is pursuant to a tax avoidance plan. A person that knows only of the financing transactions that comprise the financing arrangement will not be considered to know or have reason to know of facts sufficient to establish that the financing arrangement is a conduit financing arrangement.

(ii) Presumption regarding financing entity's knowledge.—It shall be presumed that the financing entity does not know or have reason to know that the financing arrangement is a conduit financing arrangement if the financing entity is unrelated to all other parties to the financing arrangement and the financing entity establishes that the intermediate entity who is a party to the financing transaction with the financing entity is actively engaged in a substantial trade or business. An intermediate entity will not be considered to be engaged in a trade or business if its business is making or managing investments, unless the intermediate entity is actively engaged in a banking, insurance, financing or similar trade or business and such business consists predominantly of transactions with customers who are not related persons. An intermediate entity's trade or business is substantial if it is reasonable for the financing entity to expect that the intermediate entity will be able to make payments under the financing transaction out of the cash flow of that trade or business. This presumption may be rebutted if the director of field operations establishes that the financing entity knew or had reason to know that the financing arrangement is a conduit financing arrangement. See paragraph (e)(8) of this section (*Example 8*) for an illustration of the rules of this paragraph (a)(3)(ii)(E).

(iii) *Limitation on taxpayer's use of this section.*—A taxpayer may not apply this section to reduce the amount of its Federal income tax liability by disregarding the form of its financing transactions for Federal income tax purposes or by compelling the director of field operations to do so. See, however, paragraph (b)(2)(i) of this section for rules regarding the taxpayer's ability to show that the participation of one or more intermediate entities results in no significant reduction in tax.

(4) *Standard for treatment as a conduit entity.*—(i) *In general.*—An intermediate entity is a conduit entity with respect to a financing arrangement if—

(A) The participation of the intermediate entity (or entities) in the financing arrangement reduces the tax imposed by section 881 (determined by comparing the aggregate tax imposed under section 881 on payments made on financing transactions making up the financing arrangement with the tax that would have been imposed under paragraph (d) of this section);

(B) The participation of the intermediate entity in the financing arrangement is pursuant to a tax avoidance plan; and

(C) Either—

(1) The intermediate entity is related to the financing entity or the financed entity; or

(2) The intermediate entity would not have participated in the financing arrangement on substantially the same terms but for the fact that the financing entity engaged in the financing transaction with the intermediate entity.

(ii) *Multiple intermediate entities.*—(A) *In general.*—If a financing arrangement involves multiple intermediate entities, the director of field operations will determine whether each of the intermediate entities is a conduit entity. The director of field operations will make the determination by applying the special rules for multiple intermediate entities provided in this section or, if no special rules are provided, applying principles consistent with those of paragraph (a)(4)(i) of this section to each of the intermediate entities in the financing arrangement.

(B) *Special rule for related persons.*—The director of field operations may treat related intermediate entities as a single intermediate entity if he determines that one of the principal purposes for the involvement of multiple intermediate entities in the financing arrangement is to prevent the characterization of an intermediate entity as a conduit entity, to reduce the portion of a payment that is subject to withholding tax or otherwise to circumvent the provisions of this section. This determination shall be based upon all of the facts and circumstances, including, but not limited to, the factors set forth in paragraph (b)(2) of this section. If a director of field operations determines that related persons are to be treated as a single intermediate entity, financing transactions between such related parties that are part of the conduit financing arrangement shall be disregarded for purposes of applying this section. See paragraphs (e)(9) and (10) of this section (*Examples 9 and 10*) for illustrations of the rules of this paragraph (a)(4)(ii).

(b) *Determination of whether participation of intermediate entity is pursuant to a tax avoidance plan.*—(1) *In general.*—A tax avoidance plan is a plan one of the principal purposes of which is the avoidance of tax imposed by section 881. Avoidance of the tax imposed by section 881 may be one of the principal purposes for such a plan even though it is outweighed by other purposes (taken together or separately). In this regard, the only relevant purposes are those pertaining to the participation of the intermediate entity in the financing arrangement and not those pertaining to the existence of a financing arrangement as a whole. The plan may be formal or informal, written or oral, and may involve any one or more of the parties to the financing arrangement. The plan must be in existence no later than the last date that any of the financing transactions comprising the financing arrangement is entered into. The director of field operations may infer the existence of a tax avoidance plan from the facts and circumstances. In determining whether there is a tax avoidance plan, the director of field operations will weigh all relevant evidence regarding the purposes for the intermediate entity's participation in the financing arrangement. See paragraphs (e)(13) and (14) of this section (*Examples 13 and 14*) for illustrations of the rule of this paragraph (b)(1).

(2) *Factors taken into account in determining the presence or absence of a tax avoidance purpose.*—The factors described in paragraphs (b)(2)(i) through (iv) of this section are among the facts and circumstances taken into account in determining whether the participation of an intermediate entity in a financing arrangement has as one of its principal purposes the avoidance of tax imposed by section 881.

(i) *Significant reduction in tax.*—The director of field operations will consider whether the participation of the intermediate entity (or entities) in the financing arrangement significantly reduces the tax that otherwise would have been imposed under section 881. The fact that an intermediate entity is a resident of a country that has an income tax treaty with the United States that significantly reduces the tax that otherwise would have been imposed under section 881 is not sufficient, by itself, to establish the existence of a tax avoidance plan. The determination of whether the participation of an intermediate entity significantly reduces the tax generally is made by comparing the aggregate tax imposed under section 881 on payments made on financing transactions making up the financing arrangement with the tax that would be imposed under paragraph (d) of this section. However, the taxpayer is not barred from presenting evidence that the financing entity, as determined by the director of field operations, was itself an intermediate entity and another entity should be treated as the financing entity for purposes of applying this test. A reduction in the absolute amount of tax may be significant even if the reduction in rate is not. A reduction in the amount of tax may be significant if the reduction is large in absolute terms or in relative terms. See paragraphs (e)(15) through (17) of this section (*Examples 15* through *17*) for illustrations of this factor.

(ii) *Ability to make the advance.*—The director of field operations will consider whether the intermediate entity had sufficient available money or other property of its own to have made the advance to the financed entity without the advance of money or other property to it by the financing entity (or in the case of multiple intermediate entities, whether each of the intermediate entities had sufficient available money or other property of its own to have made the advance to either the financed entity or another intermediate entity without the advance of money or other property to it by either the financing entity or another intermediate entity).

(iii) *Time period between financing transactions.*—The director of field operations will consider the length of the period of time that separates the advances of money or other property, or the grants of rights to use property, by the financing entity to the intermediate entity (in the case of multiple intermediate entities, from one intermediate entity to another), and ultimately by the intermediate entity to the financed entity. A short period of time is evidence of the existence of a tax avoidance plan while a long period of time is evidence that there is not a tax avoidance plan. See paragraph (e)(18) of this section (*Example 18*) for an illustration of this factor.

(iv) *Financing transactions in the ordinary course of business.*—If the parties to the financing transaction are related, the director of field operations will consider whether the financing transaction occurs in the ordinary course of the active conduct of complementary or integrated trades or businesses engaged in by these entities. The fact that a financing transaction is described in this paragraph (b)(2)(iv) is evidence that the participation of the parties to that transaction in the financing arrangement is not pursuant to a tax avoidance plan. A loan will not be considered to occur in the ordinary course of the active conduct of complementary or integrated trades or businesses unless the loan is a trade receivable or the parties to the transaction are actively engaged in a banking, insurance, financing or similar trade or business and such business consists predominantly of transactions with customers who are not related persons. See paragraph (e)(19) of this section (*Example 19*) for an illustration of this factor.

(3) *Presumption if significant financing activities performed by a related intermediate entity.*—(i) *General rule.*—It shall be presumed that the participation of an intermediate entity (or entities) in a financing arrangement is not pursuant to a tax avoidance plan if the intermediate entity is related to either or both the financing entity or the financed entity and the intermediate entity performs significant financing activities with respect to the financing transactions forming part of the financing arrangement to which it is a party. This presumption may be rebutted if the director of field operations establishes that the participation of the intermediate entity in the financing arrangement is pursuant to a tax avoidance plan. See paragraphs (e)(23) through (25) of this section (*Examples 23* through *25*) for illustrations of this presumption.

(ii) *Significant financing activities.*—For purposes of this paragraph (b)(3), an intermediate entity performs significant financing activities with respect to such financing transactions only if the financing transactions satisfy the requirements of either paragraph (b)(3)(ii)(A) or (B) of this section.

(A) *Active rents or royalties.*—An intermediate entity performs significant financing activities with respect to leases or licenses if rents or royalties earned with respect to such leases or licenses are derived in the active conduct of a trade or business within the meaning of section 954(c)(2)(A), to be applied by substituting the term *intermediate entity* for the term *controlled foreign corporation.*

(B) *Active risk management.*—*(1) In general.*—An intermediate entity is considered to perform significant financing activities with respect to financing transactions only if officers and employees of the intermediate entity participate actively and materially in arranging the intermediate entity's participation in such financing transactions (other than financing transactions described in paragraph (b)(3)(ii)(*B*)(*3*) of this section) and perform the business activity and risk management activities described in paragraph (b)(3)(ii)(*B*)(*2*) of this section with respect to such financing transactions, and the participation of the intermediate entity in the financing transactions produces (or reasonably can be expected to produce) efficiency savings by reducing transaction costs and overhead and other fixed costs.

(2) Business activity and risk management requirements.—An intermediate entity will be considered to perform significant financing activities only if, within the country in which the intermediate entity is organized (or, if different, within the country with respect to which the intermediate entity is claiming the benefits of a tax treaty), its officers and employees—

(i) Exercise management over, and actively conduct, the day-to-day operations of the intermediate entity. Such operations must consist of a substantial trade or business or the supervision, administration and financing for a substantial group of related persons; and

(ii) Actively manage, on an ongoing basis, material market risks arising from such financing transactions as an integral part of the management of the intermediate entity's financial and capital requirements (including management of risks of currency and interest rate fluctuations) and management of the intermediate entity's short-term investments of working capital by entering into transactions with unrelated persons.

(3) Special rule for trade receivables and payables entered into in the ordinary course of business.—If the activities of the intermediate entity consist in whole or in part of cash management for a controlled group of which the intermediate entity is a member, then employees of the intermediate entity need not have participated in arranging any such financing transactions that arise in the ordinary course of a substantial trade or business of either the financed entity or the financing entity. Officers or employees of the financing entity or financed entity, however, must have participated actively and materially in arranging the transaction that gave rise to the trade receivable or trade payable. Cash management includes the operation of a sweep account whereby the intermediate entity nets intercompany trade payables and receivables arising from transactions among the other members of the controlled group and between members of the controlled group and unrelated persons.

(4) Activities of officers and employees of related persons.—Except as provided in paragraph (b)(3)(ii)(B)(3) of this section, in applying this paragraph (b)(3)(ii)(B), the activities of an officer or employee of an intermediate entity will not constitute significant financing activities if any officer or employee of a related person participated materially in any of the activities described in this paragraph, other than to approve any guarantee of a financing transaction or to exercise general supervision and control over the policies of the intermediate entity.

(c) *Determination of whether an unrelated intermediate entity would not have participated in financing arrangement on substantially the same terms.*—(1) *In general.*—The determination of whether an intermediate entity would not have participated in a financing arrangement on substantially the same terms but for the financing transaction between the financing entity and the intermediate entity shall be based upon all of the facts and circumstances.

(2) *Effect of guarantee.*—(i) *In general.*—The director of field operations may presume that the intermediate entity would not have participated in the financing arrangement on substantially the same terms if there is a guarantee of the financed entity's liability to the intermediate entity (or in the case of multiple intermediate entities, a guarantee of the intermediate entity's liability to the intermediate entity that advanced money or property, or granted rights to use other property). However, a guarantee that was neither in existence nor contemplated on the last date that any of the financing transactions comprising the financing arrangement is entered into does not give rise to this presumption. A taxpayer may rebut this presumption by producing clear and convincing evidence that the intermediate entity would have participated in the financing transaction with the financed entity on substantially the same terms even if the financing entity had not entered into a financing transaction with the intermediate entity.

(ii) *Definition of guarantee.*—For the purposes of this paragraph (c)(2), a guarantee is any arrangement under which a person, directly or indirectly, assures, on a conditional or unconditional basis, the payment of another person's obligation with respect to a financing transaction. The term shall be interpreted in accordance with the definition of the term in section 163(j)(6)(D)(iii) (as in effect for taxable years beginning before January 1, 2018).

(d) *Determination of amount of tax liability.*—(1) *Amount of payment subject to recharacterization.*—(i) *In general.*—If a financing arrangement is a conduit financing arrangement, a portion of each payment made by the financed entity with respect to the financing transactions that comprise the conduit financing arrangement shall be recharacterized as a transaction directly between the financed entity and the financing entity. If the aggregate principal amount of the financing transaction(s) to which the financed entity is a party is less than or equal to the aggregate principal amount of the financing transaction(s) linking any of the parties to the financing arrangement, the entire amount of the payment shall be so recharacterized. If the aggregate principal amount of the financing transaction(s) to which the financed entity is a party is greater than the aggregate principal amount of the financing transaction(s) linking any of the parties to the financing arrangement, then the recharacterized portion shall be determined by multiplying the payment by a fraction the numerator of which is equal to the lowest aggregate principal amount of the financing transaction(s) linking any of the parties to the financing arrangement (other than financing transactions that are disregarded pursuant to paragraphs (a)(2)(i)(B) and (a)(4)(ii)(B) of this section) and the denominator of which is the aggregate principal amount of the financing transaction(s) to which the financed entity is a party. In the case of financing transactions the principal amount of which is subject to adjustment, the fraction shall be determined using the average outstanding principal amounts for the period to which the payment relates. The average principal amount may be computed using any method applied consistently that reflects with reasonable accuracy the amount outstanding for the period. See paragraph (e)(26) of this section (*Example 26*) for an illustration of the calculation of the amount of tax liability.

(ii) *Determination of principal amount.*—(A) *In general.*—Unless otherwise provided in this paragraph (d)(1)(ii), the principal amount equals the amount of money advanced, or the fair market value of other property advanced or subject to a lease or license, in the financing transaction. In general, fair market value is calculated in U.S. dollars as of the close of business on the day on which the financing transaction is entered into. However, if the property advanced, or the right to use property granted, by the financing entity is the same as the property or rights received by the financed entity, the fair market value of the property or right shall be determined as of the close of business on the last date that any of the financing transactions comprising the financing arrangement is entered into. In the case of fungible property, property of the same type shall be considered to be the same property. See paragraph (e)(27) of this section (*Example 27*) for an illustration of the calculation of the principal amount in the case of financing transactions involving fungible property. The principal amount of a financing transaction shall be subject to adjustments, as set forth in this paragraph (d)(1)(ii).

(B) *Debt instruments and certain stock.*—In the case of a debt instrument or of stock that is subject to the current inclusion rules of sections 305(c)(3) or (e), the principal amount generally will be equal to the issue price. However, if the fair market value on the issue date differs materially from the issue price, the fair market value of the debt instrument shall be used in lieu of the instrument's issue price. Appropriate adjustments will be made for accruals of original issue discount and repayments of principal (including accrued original issue discount).

(C) *Partnership and trust interests.*—In the case of a partnership interest or an interest in a trust, the principal amount is equal to the fair market value of the money or property contributed to the partnership or trust in return for that partnership or trust interest.

(D) *Leases or licenses.*—In the case of a lease or license, the principal amount is equal to the fair market value of the property subject to the lease or license on the date on which the lease or license is entered into. The principal amount shall be adjusted for depreciation or amortization, calculated on a basis that accurately reflects the anticipated decline in the value of the property over its life.

(iii) [Reserved]

(2) *Rate of tax.*—The rate at which tax is imposed under section 881 on the portion of the payment that is recharacterized pursuant to paragraph (d)(1) of this section is determined by reference to the nature of the recharacterized transaction, as determined under paragraphs (a)(3)(ii)(B) and (C) of this section.

(e) *Examples.*—The following examples illustrate this section. For purposes of the examples in this paragraph (e), unless otherwise indicated, it is assumed that FP, a corporation organized in country N, owns all of the stock of FS, a corporation organized in country T, and DS, a corporation organized in the United States. Country T, but not country N, has an income tax treaty with the United States. The treaty exempts interest, rents and royalties paid by a resident of one state (the source state) to a resident of the other state from tax in the source state. For purposes of these examples, unless otherwise indicated, it is assumed that no stock is of the type described in paragraph (a)(2)(ii)(B)(*1*)(*iv*) of this section.

(1) *Example 1. Financing arrangement.*—(i) On January 1, 1996, BK, a bank organized in country T, lends $1,000,000 to DS in exchange for a note issued by DS. FP guarantees to BK that DS will satisfy its repayment obligation on the loan. There are no other transactions between FP and BK.

(ii) BK's loan to DS is a financing transaction within the meaning of paragraph (a)(4)(ii)(A)(*1*) of this section. FP's guarantee of DS's repayment obligation is not a financing transaction as described in paragraphs (a)(2)(ii)(A)(*1*) through (*4*) of this section. Therefore, these transactions do not constitute a financing arrangement as defined in paragraph (a)(2)(i) of this section.

(2) *Example 2. Financing arrangement.*—(i) On January 1, 1996, FP lends $1,000,000 to DS in exchange for a note issued by DS. On January 1, 1997, FP assigns the DS note to FS in exchange for a note issued by FS. After receiving notice of the assignment, DS remits payments due under its note to FS.

(ii) The DS note held by FS and the FS note held by FP are financing transactions within the meaning of paragraph (a)(2)(ii)(A)(*1*) of this section, and together constitute a financing arrangement within the meaning of paragraph (a)(2)(i) of this section.

(3) *Example 3. Participation of a disregarded intermediate entity.*—The facts are the same as in paragraph (e)(2) of this section (the facts in *Example 2*), except that FS is an entity that is disregarded as an entity separate from its owner, FP, under § 301.7701-3 of this chapter. Under paragraph (a)(2)(i)(C) of this section, FS is a person and, therefore, may itself be an intermediate entity that is linked by financing transactions to other persons in a financing arrangement. The DS note held by FS and the FS note held by FP are financing transactions within the meaning of paragraph (a)(2)(ii) of this section, and together constitute a financing arrangement within the meaning of paragraph (a)(2)(i) of this section.

(4) *Example 4. Hybrid instrument as financing arrangement.*—The facts are the same as in paragraph (e)(2) of this section (the facts in *Example 2*), except that FP assigns the DS note to FS in exchange for stock issued by FS. The stock issued by FS is in form convertible debt with a 49-year term that is treated as debt under the tax law of Country T. The FS stock is not subject to any of the redemption, acquisition, or payment rights or requirements specified in paragraphs (a)(2)(ii)(B)(*1*)(*i*) through (iii) of this section. However, because the FS stock is treated as debt under the tax law of Country T, the FS stock is a financing transaction under paragraph (a)(2)(ii)(B)(*1*)(*iv*) of this section. Therefore, the DS note held by FS and the FS stock held by FP are financing transactions within the meaning of paragraphs (a)(2)(ii)(A)(*1*) and (*2*) of this section, respectively, and together constitute a financing arrangement within the meaning of paragraph (a)(2)(i) of this section. See also § 1.267A-4 for rules applicable to disqualified imported mismatch amounts.

(5) *Example 5. Financing arrangement.*—(i) On December 1, 1994 FP creates a special purposes subsidiary, FS. On that date FP capitalizes FS with $1,000,000 in cash and $10,000,000 in debt from BK, a Country N bank. On January 1, 1995, C, a U.S. person, purchases an automobile from DS in return for an installment note. On August 1, 1995, DS sells a number of installment notes, including C's, to FS in exchange for $10,000,000. DS continues to service the installment notes for FS.

(ii) The C installment note now held by FS (as well as all of the other installment notes now held by FS) and the FS note held by BK are financing transactions within the meaning of paragraph (a)(2)(ii)(A)(*1*) of this section, and together constitute a financing arrangement within the meaning of paragraph (a)(2)(i) of this section.

(6) *Example 6. Related persons treated as a single intermediate entity.*—(i) On January 1, 1996, FP deposits $1,000,000 with BK, a bank that is organized in country N and is unrelated to FP and its subsidiaries. M, a corporation also organized in country N, is wholly-owned by the sole shareholder of BK but is not a bank within the meaning of section 881(c)(3)(A). On July 1, 1996, M lends $1,000,000 to DS in exchange for a note maturing on July 1, 2006. The note is in registered form within the meaning of section 881(c)(2)(B)(i) and DS has received from M the statement required by section 881(c)(2)(B)(ii). One of the principal purposes for the absence of a financing transaction between BK and M is the avoidance of the application of this section.

(ii) The transactions described above would form a financing arrangement but for the absence of a financing transaction between BK and M. However, because one of the principal purposes for the structuring of these financing transactions is to prevent characterization of such arrangement as a financing arrangement, the director of field operations may treat the financing transactions between FP and BK, and between M and DS as a financing arrangement under paragraphs (a)(2)(i)(B) of this section. In such a case, BK and M would be considered a single intermediate entity for purposes of this section. See also paragraph (a)(4)(ii)(B) of this section for the authority to treat BK and M as a single intermediate entity.

(7) *Example 7. Related persons treated as a single intermediate entity.*—(i) On January 1, 1995, FP lends $10,000,000 to FS in exchange for a 10-year note that pays interest annually at a rate of 8 percent per annum. On January 2, 1995, FS contributes $10,000,000 to FS2, a wholly-owned subsidiary of FS organized in country T, in exchange for common stock of FS2. On January 1, 1996, FS2 lends $10,000,000 to DS in exchange for an 8-year note that pays interest annually at a rate of 10 percent per annum. FS is a holding company whose most significant asset is the stock of FS2. Throughout the period that the FP-FS loan is outstanding, FS causes FS2 to make distributions to FS, most of which are used to make interest and principal payments on the FP-FS loan. Without the distributions from FS2, FS would not have had the funds with which to make payments on the FP-FS loan. One of the principal purposes for the absence of a financing transaction between FS and FS2 is the avoidance of the application of this section.

(ii) The conditions of paragraph (a)(4)(i)(A) of this section would be satisfied with respect to the financing transactions between FP, FS, FS2 and DS but for the absence of a financing transaction between FS and FS2. However, because one of the principal purposes for the structuring of these financing transactions is to prevent characterization of an entity as a conduit, the director of field operations may treat the financing transactions between FP and FS, and between FS2 and DS as a financing arrangement. See paragraph (a)(4)(ii)(B) of this section. In such a case, FS and FS2 would be considered a single intermediate entity for purposes of this section. See also paragraph (a)(2)(i)(B) of this section for the authority to treat FS and FS2 as a single intermediate entity.

(8) *Example 8. Presumption with respect to unrelated financing entity.*—(i) FP is a corporation organized in country T that is actively engaged in a substantial manufacturing business. FP has a revolving credit facility with a syndicate of banks, none of which is related to FP and FP's subsidiaries, which provides that FP may borrow up to a maximum of $100,000,000 at a time. The revolving credit facility provides that DS and certain other subsidiaries of FP may borrow directly from the syndicate at the same interest rates as FP, but each subsidiary is required to indemnify the syndicate banks for any withholding taxes imposed on interest payments by the country in which the subsidiary is organized. BK, a bank that is organized in country N, is the agent for the syndicate. Some of the syndicate banks are organized in country N, but others are residents of country O, a country that has an income tax treaty with the United States which allows the United States to impose a tax on interest at a maximum rate of 10 percent. It is reasonable for BK and the syndicate banks to have determined that FP will be able to meet its payment obligations on a maximum principal amount of $100,000,000 out of the cash flow of its manufacturing business. At various times throughout 1995, FP borrows under the revolving credit facility until the outstanding principal amount reaches the maximum amount of $100,000,000. On December 31, 1995, FP receives $100,000,000 from a public offering of its equity. On January 1, 1996, FP pays BK $90,000,000 to reduce the outstanding principal amount under the revolving credit facility and lends $10,000,000 to DS. FP would have repaid the entire principal amount, and DS would have borrowed directly from the syndicate, but for the fact that DS did not want to incur the U.S. withholding tax that would have applied to payments made directly by DS to the syndicate banks.

(ii) Pursuant to paragraph (a)(3)(ii)(E)(*1*) of this section, even though the financing arrangement is a conduit financing arrangement (because the financing arrangement meets the standards for recharacterization in paragraph (a)(4)(i)) of this section, BK and the other syndicate banks have no section 881 liability unless they know or have reason to know that the financing arrangement is a conduit financing arrangement. Moreover, pursuant to paragraph (a)(3)(ii)(E)(*2*)(*ii*) of this section, BK and the syndicate banks are presumed not to know that the financing arrangement is a conduit financing arrangement. The syndicate banks are unrelated to both FP and DS, and FP is actively engaged in a substantial trade or business—that is, the cash flow from FP's manufacturing business is sufficient for the banks to expect that FP will be able to make the payments required under the financing transaction. See § 1.1441-3(g) for the withholding obligations of the withholding agents.

(9) *Example 9. Multiple intermediate entities—special rule for related persons.*—(i) On January 1, 1995, FP lends $10,000,000 to FS in exchange for a 10-year note that pays interest annually at a rate of 8 percent per annum. On January 2, 1995, FS contributes $9,900,000 to FS2, a wholly-owned subsidiary of FS organized in country T, in exchange for common stock and lends $100,000 to FS2. On January 1, 1996, FS2 lends $10,000,000 to DS in exchange for an 8-year note that pays interest annually at a rate of 10 percent per annum. FS is a holding company that has no significant assets other than the stock of FS2. Throughout the period that the FP-FS loan is outstanding, FS causes FS2 to make distributions to FS, most of which are used to make interest and principal payments on the FP-FS loan. Without the distributions from FS2, FS would not have had the funds with which to make payments on the FP-FS loan. One of the principal purposes for structuring the transactions between FS and FS2 as primarily a contribution of capital is to the amount of the payment that would be recharacterized under paragraph (d) of this section.

(ii) Pursuant to paragraph (a)(4)(ii)(B) of this section, the director of field operations may treat FS and FS2 as a single intermediate entity for purposes of this section since one of the principal purposes for the participation of multiple intermediate entities is to reduce the amount of the tax liability on any recharacterized payment by inserting a financing transaction with a low principal amount.

(10) *Example 10. Multiple intermediate entities.*—(i) On January 1, 1995, FP deposits $1,000,000 with BK, a bank that is organized in country T and is unrelated to FP and its subsidiaries, FS and DS. On January 1, 1996, at a time when the FP-BK deposit is still outstanding, BK lends $500,000 to BK2, a bank that is wholly-owned by BK and is organized in country T. On the same date, BK2 lends $500,000 to FS. On July 1, 1996, FS lends $500,000 to DS. FP pledges its deposit with BK to BK2 in support of FS' obligation to repay the BK2 loan. FS', BK's and BK2's participation in the financing arrangement is pursuant to a tax avoidance plan.

(ii) The conditions of paragraphs (a)(4)(i)(A) and (B) of this section are satisfied because the participation of BK, BK2 and FS in the financing arrangement reduces the tax imposed by section 881, and FS', BK's and BK2's participation in the financing arrangement is pursuant to a tax avoidance plan. However, since BK and BK2 are unrelated to FP and DS, under paragraph (a)(4)(i)(C)(*2*) of this section, BK and BK2 will be treated as conduit entities only if BK and BK2 would not have participated in the financing arrangement on substantially the same terms but for the financing transaction between FP and BK.

(iii) It is presumed that BK2 would not have participated in the financing arrangement on substantially the same terms but for the BK-BK2 financing transaction because FP's pledge of an asset in support of FS' obligation to repay the BK2 loan is a guarantee within the meaning of paragraph (c)(2)(ii) of this section. If the taxpayer does not rebut this presumption by clear and convincing evidence, then BK2 will be a conduit entity.

(iv) Because BK and BK2 are related intermediate entities, the director of field operations must determine whether one of the principal purposes for the involvement of multiple intermediate entities was to prevent characterization of an entity as a conduit entity. In making this determination, the director of field operations may consider the fact that the involvement of two related intermediate entities prevents the presumption regarding guarantees from applying to BK. In the absence of evidence showing a business purpose for the involvement of both BK and BK2, the director of field operations may treat BK and BK2 as a single intermediate entity for purposes of determining whether they would have participated in the financing arrangement on substantially the same terms but for the financing transaction between FP and BK. The presumption that applies to BK2 therefore will apply to BK. If the taxpayer does not rebut this presumption by clear and convincing evidence, then BK will be a conduit entity.

(11) *Example 11. Reduction of tax.*—(i) On February 1, 1995, FP issues debt to the public that would satisfy the requirements of section 871(h)(2)(A) (relating to obligations that are not in registered form) if issued by a U.S. person. FP lends the proceeds of the debt offering to DS in exchange for a note.

(ii) The debt issued by FP and the DS note are financing transactions within the meaning of paragraph (a)(2)(ii)(A)(*1*) of this section and together constitute a financing arrangement within the meaning of paragraph (a)(2)(i) of this section. The holders of the FP debt are the financing entities, FP is the intermediate entity and DS is the financed entity. Because interest payments on the debt issued by FP would not have been subject to withholding tax if the debt had been issued by DS, there is no reduction in tax under paragraph (a)(4)(i)(A) of this section. Accordingly, FP is not a conduit entity.

(12) *Example 12. Reduction of tax.*—(i) On January 1, 1995, FP licenses to FS the rights to use a patent in the United States to manufacture product A. FS agrees to pay FP a fixed amount in royalties each year under the license. On January 1, 1996, FS sublicenses to DS the rights to use the patent in the United States. Under the sublicense, DS agrees to pay FS royalties based upon the units of product A manufactured by DS each year. Although the formula for computing the amount of royalties paid by DS to FS differs from the formula for computing the amount of royalties paid by FS to FP, each represents an arm's length rate.

(ii) Although the royalties paid by DS to FS are exempt from U.S. withholding tax, the royalty payments between FS and FP are income from U.S. sources under section 861(a)(4) subject to the 30 percent gross tax imposed by § 1.881-2(b) and subject to withholding under § 1.1441-2(a). Because the rate of tax imposed on royalties paid by FS to FP is the same as the rate that would have been imposed on royalties paid by DS to FP, the participation of FS in the FP-FS-DS financing arrangement does not reduce the tax imposed by section 881 within the meaning of paragraph (a)(4)(i)(A) of this section. Accordingly, FP is not a conduit entity.

(13) *Example 13. A principal purpose.*—(i) On January 1, 1995, FS lends $10,000,000 to DS in exchange for a 10-year note that pays interest annually at a rate of 8 percent per annum. As was intended at the time of the loan from FS to DS, on July 1, 1995, FP makes an interest-free demand loan of $10,000,000 to FS. A principal purpose for FS' participation in the FP-FS-DS financing arrangement is that FS generally coordinates the financing for all of FP's subsidiaries (although FS does not engage in significant financing activities with respect to such financing transactions). However, another principal purpose for FS' participation is to allow the parties to benefit from the lower withholding tax rate provided under the income tax treaty between country T and the United States.

(ii) The financing arrangement satisfies the tax avoidance purpose requirement of paragraph (a)(4)(i)(B) of this section because FS participated in the financing arrangement pursuant to a plan one of the principal purposes of which is to allow the parties to benefit from the country T-U.S. treaty.

(14) *Example 14. A principal purpose.*—(i) DX is a U.S. corporation that intends to purchase property to use in its manufacturing business. FX is a partnership organized in country N that is owned in equal parts by LC1 and LC2, leasing companies that are unrelated to DX. BK, a bank organized in country N and unrelated to DX, LC1 and LC2, lends $100,000,000 to FX to enable FX to purchase the property. On the same day, FX purchases the property and engages in a transaction with DX which is treated as a lease of the property for country N tax purposes but a loan for U.S. tax purposes. Accordingly, DX is treated as the owner of the property for U.S. tax purposes. The parties comply with the requirements of section 881(c) with respect to the debt obligation of DX to FX. FX and DX structured these transactions in this manner so that LC1 and LC2 would be entitled to accelerated depreciation deductions with respect to the property in country N and DX would be entitled to accelerated depreciation deductions in the United States. None of the parties would have participated in the transaction if the payments made by DX were subject to U.S. withholding tax.

(ii) The loan[s] from BK to FX and from FX to DX are financing transactions and, together constitute a financing arrangement. The participation of FX in the financing arrangement reduces the tax imposed by section 881 because payments made to FX, but not BK, qualify for the portfolio interest exemption of section 881(c) because BK is a bank making an extension of credit in the ordinary course of its trade or business within the meaning of section 881(c)(3)(A). Moreover, because DX borrowed the money from FX instead of borrowing the money directly from BK to avoid the tax imposed by section 881, one of the principal purposes of the participation of FX was to avoid that tax (even though another principal purpose of the participation of FX was to allow LC1 and LC2 to take advantage of accelerated depreciation deductions in country N). Assuming that FX would not have participated in the financing arrangement on substantially the same terms but for the fact that BK loaned it $100,000,000, FX is a conduit entity and the financing arrangement is a conduit financing arrangement.

(15) *Example 15. Significant reduction of tax.*—(i) FS owns all of the stock of FS1, which also is a resident of country T. FS1 owns all of the stock of DS. On January 1, 1995, FP contributes $10,000,000 to the capital of FS in return for perpetual preferred stock. On July 1, 1995, FS lends $10,000,000 to FS1. On January 1, 1996, FS1 lends $10,000,000 to DS. Under the terms of the country T-U.S. income tax treaty, a country T resident is not entitled to the reduced withholding rate on interest income provided by the treaty if the resident is entitled to specified tax benefits under country T law. Although FS1 may deduct interest paid on the loan from FS, these deductions are not pursuant to any special tax benefits provided by country T law. However, FS qualifies for one of the enumerated tax benefits pursuant to which it may deduct dividends paid with respect to the stock held by FP. Therefore, if FS had made a loan directly to DS, FS would not have been entitled to the benefits of the country T-U.S. tax treaty with respect to payments it received from DS, and such payments would have been subject to tax under section 881 at a 30 percent rate.

(ii) The FS-FS1 loan and the FS1-DS loan are financing transactions within the meaning of paragraph (a)(2)(ii)(A)(*1*) of this section and together constitute a financing arrangement within the meaning of paragraph (a)(2)(i) of this section. Pursuant to paragraph (b)(2)(i) of this section, the significant reduction in tax resulting from the participation of FS1 in the financing arrangement is evidence that the participation of FS1 in the financing arrangement is pursuant to a tax avoidance plan. However, other facts relevant to the presence of such a plan must also be taken into account.

(16) *Example 16. Significant reduction of tax.*—(i) FP owns 90 percent of the voting stock of FX, an unlimited liability company organized in country T. The other 10 percent of the common stock of FX is owned by FP1, a subsidiary of FP that is organized in country N. Although FX is a partnership for U.S. tax purposes, FX is entitled to the benefits of the U.S.-country T income tax treaty because FX is subject to tax in country T as a resident corporation. On January 1, 1996, FP contributes $10,000,000 to FX in exchange for an instrument denominated as preferred stock that pays a dividend of 7 percent and that must be redeemed by FX in seven years. For U.S. tax purposes, the preferred stock is a partnership interest. On July 1, 1996, FX makes a loan of $10,000,000 to DS in exchange for a 7-year note paying interest at 6 percent.

(ii) Because FX is required to redeem the partnership interest at a specified time, the partnership interest constitutes a financing transaction within the meaning of paragraph (a)(2)(ii)(A)(*2*) of this section. Moreover, because the FX-DS note is a financing transaction within the meaning of paragraph (a)(2)(ii)(A)(*1*) of this section, together the transactions constitute a financing arrangement within the meaning of (a)(2)(i) of this section. Payments of interest made directly by DS to FP and FP1 would not be eligible for the portfolio interest exemption and would not be entitled to a reduction in withholding tax pursuant to a tax treaty. Therefore, there is a significant reduction in tax resulting from the participation of FX in the financing arrangement, which is evidence that the participation of FX in the financing arrangement is pursuant to a tax avoidance plan. However, other facts relevant to the existence of such a plan must also be taken into account.

(17) *Example 17. Significant reduction of tax.*—(i) FP owns a 10 percent interest in the profits and capital of FX, a partnership organized in country N. The other 90 percent interest in FX is owned by G, an unrelated corporation that is organized in country T. FX is not engaged in business in the United States. On January 1, 1996, FP contributes $10,000,000 to FX in exchange for an instrument documented as perpetual subordinated debt that provides for quarterly interest payments at 9 percent per annum. Under the terms of the instrument, payments on the perpetual subordinated debt do not otherwise affect the allocation of income between the partners. FP has the right to require the liquidation of FX if FX fails to make an interest payment. For U.S. tax purposes, the perpetual subordinated debt is treated as a partnership interest in FX and the payments on the perpetual subordinated debt constitute guaranteed payments within the meaning of section 707(c). On July 1, 1996, FX makes a loan of $10,000,000 to DS in exchange for a 7-year note paying interest at 8 percent per annum.

(ii) Because FP has the effective right to force payment of the "interest" on the perpetual subordinated debt, the instrument constitutes a financing transaction within the meaning of paragraph (a)(2)(ii)(A)(*2*) of this section. Moreover, because the note between FX and DS is a financing transaction within the meaning of paragraph (a)(2)(ii)(A)(*1*) of this section, together the transactions are a financing arrangement within the meaning of (a)(2)(i) of this section. Without regard to this section, 90 percent of each interest payment received by FX would be treated as exempt from U.S. withholding tax because it is beneficially owned by G, while 10 percent would be subject to a 30 percent withholding tax because beneficially owned by FP. If FP held directly the note issued by DS, 100 percent of the interest payments on the note would have been subject to the 30 percent withholding tax. The significant reduction in the tax imposed by section 881 resulting from the participation of FX in the financing arrangement is evidence that the participation of FX in the financing arrangement is pursuant to a tax avoidance plan. However, other facts relevant to the presence of such a plan must also be taken into account.

(18) *Example 18. Time period between transactions.*—(i) On January 1, 1995, FP lends $10,000,000 to FS in exchange for a 10-year note that pays no interest annually. When the note matures, FS is obligated to pay $24,000,000 to FP. On January 1, 1996, FS lends $10,000,000 to DS in exchange for a 10-year note that pays interest annually at a rate of 10 percent per annum.

(ii) The FS note held by FP and the DS note held by FS are financing transactions within the meaning of paragraph (a)(2)(ii)(A)(*1*) of this section and together constitute a financing arrangement within the meaning of (a)(2)(i) of this section. Pursuant to paragraph (b)(2)(iii) of this section, the short period of time (twelve months) between the loan by FP to FS and the loan by FS to DS is evidence that the participation of FS in the financing arrangement is pursuant to a tax avoidance plan. However, other facts relevant to the presence of such a plan must also be taken into account.

(19) *Example 19. Financing transactions in the ordinary course of business.*—(i) FP is a holding company. FS is actively engaged in country T in the business of manufacturing and selling product A. DS manufactures product B, a principal component in which is product A. FS' business activity is substantial. On January 1, 1995, FP lends $100,000,000 to FS to finance FS' business operations. On January 1, 1996, FS ships $30,000,000 of product A to DS. In return, FS creates an interest-bearing account receivable on its books. FS' shipment is in the ordinary course of the active conduct of its trade or business (which is complementary to DS' trade or business.)

(ii) The loan from FP to FS and the accounts receivable opened by FS for a payment owed by DS are financing transactions within the meaning of paragraph (a)(2)(ii)(A)(*1*) of this section and together constitute a financing arrangement within the meaning of paragraph (a)(2)(i) of this section. Pursuant to paragraph (b)(2)(iv) of this section, the fact that DS' liability to FS is created in the ordinary course of the active conduct of DS' trade or business that is complementary to a business actively engaged in by DS is evidence that the participation of FS in the financing arrangement is not pursuant to a tax avoidance plan. However, other facts relevant to the presence of such a plan must also be taken into account.

(20) *Example 20. Tax avoidance plan—other factors.*—(i) On February 1, 1995, FP issues debt in Country N that is in registered form within the meaning of section 881(c)(3)(A). The FP debt would satisfy the requirements of section 881(c) if the debt were issued by a U.S. person and the withholding agent received the certification required by section 871(h)(2)(B)(ii). The purchasers of the debt are financial institutions and there is no reason to believe that they would not furnish Forms W-8. On March 1, 1995, FP lends a portion of the proceeds of the offering to DS.

(ii) The FP debt and the loan to DS are financing transactions within the meaning of paragraph (a)(2)(ii)(A)(*1*) of this section and together constitute a financing arrangement within the meaning of paragraph (a)(2)(i) of this section. The owners of the FP debt are the financing entities, FP is the intermediate entity and DS is the financed entity. Interest payments on the debt issued by FP would be subject to withholding tax if the debt were issued by DS, unless DS received all necessary Forms W-8. Therefore, the participation of FP in the financing arrangement potentially reduces the tax imposed by section 881(a). However, because it is reasonable to assume that the purchasers of the FP debt would have provided certifications in order to avoid the withholding tax imposed by section 881, there is not a tax avoidance plan. Accordingly, FP is not a conduit entity.

(21) *Example 21. Tax avoidance plan—other factor.*—(i) Over a period of years, FP has maintained a deposit with BK, a bank organized in the United States, that is unrelated to FP and its subsidiaries. FP often sells goods and purchases raw materials in the United States.

FP opened the bank account with BK in order to facilitate this business and the amounts it maintains in the account are reasonably related to its dollar-denominated working capital needs. On January 1, 1995, BK lends $5,000,000 to DS. After the loan is made, the balance in FP's bank account remains within a range appropriate to meet FP's working capital needs.

(ii) FP's deposit with BK and BK's loan to DS are financing transactions within the meaning of paragraph (a)(2)(ii)(A)(*1*) of this section and together constitute a financing arrangement within the meaning of paragraph (a)(2)(i) of this section. Pursuant to section 881(i), interest paid by BK to FP with respect to the bank deposit is exempt from withholding tax. Interest paid directly by DS to FP would not be exempt from withholding tax under section 881(i) and therefore would be subject to a 30% withholding tax. Accordingly, there is a significant reduction in the tax imposed by section 881, which is evidence of the existence of a tax avoidance plan. See paragraph (b)(2)(i) of this section. However, the director of field operations also will consider the fact that FP historically has maintained an account with BK to meet its working capital needs and that, prior to and after BK's loan to DS, the balance within the account remains within a range appropriate to meet those business needs as evidence that the participation of BK in the FP-BK-DS financing arrangement is not pursuant to a tax avoidance plan. In determining the presence or absence of a tax avoidance plan, all relevant facts will be taken into account.

(22) *Example 22. Tax avoidance plan—other factor.*—(i) Assume the same facts as in paragraph (e)(21) of this section (the facts in *Example 21*), except that on January 1, 2000, FP's deposit with BK substantially exceeds FP's expected working capital needs and on January 2, 2000, BK lends additional funds to DS. Assume also that BK's loan to DS provides BK with a right of offset against FP's deposit. Finally, assume that FP would have lent the funds to DS directly but for the imposition of the withholding tax on payments made directly to FP by DS.

(ii) As in paragraph (e)(20) of this section (*Example 20*) the transactions in paragraph (e)(22)(i) of this section (this *Example 22*) are a financing arrangement within the meaning of paragraph (a)(2)(i) and the participation of the BK reduces the section 881 tax. In this case, the presence of funds substantially in excess of FP's working capital needs and the fact that FP would have been willing to lend funds directly to DS if not for the withholding tax are evidence that the participation of BK in the FP-BK-FS financing arrangement is pursuant to a tax avoidance plan. However, other facts relevant to the presence of such a plan must also be taken into account. Even if the director of field operations determines that the participation of BK in the financing arrangement is pursuant to a tax avoidance plan, BK may not be treated as a conduit entity unless BK would not have participated in the financing arrangement on substantially the same terms in the absence of FP's deposit with BK. BK's right of offset against FP's deposit (a form of guarantee of BK's loan to DS) creates a presumption that BK would not have made the loan to DS on substantially the same terms in the absence of FP's deposit with BK. If the taxpayer overcomes the presumption by clear and convincing evidence, BK will not be a conduit entity.

(23) *Example 23. Significant financing activities.*—(i) FS is responsible for coordinating the financing of all of the subsidiaries of FP, which are engaged in substantial trades or businesses and are located in country T, country N, and the United States. FS maintains a centralized cash management accounting system for FP and its subsidiaries in which it records all intercompany payables and receivables; these payables and receivables ultimately are reduced to a single balance either due from or owing to FS and each of FP's subsidiaries. FS is responsible for disbursing or receiving any cash payments required by transactions between its affiliates and unrelated parties. FS must borrow any cash necessary to meet those external obligations and invests any excess cash for the benefit of the FP group. FS enters into interest rate and foreign exchange contracts as necessary to manage the risks arising from mismatches in incoming and outgoing cash flows. The activities of FS are intended (and reasonably can be expected) to reduce transaction costs and overhead and other fixed costs. FS has 50 employees, including clerical and other back office personnel, located in country T. At the request of DS, on January 1, 1995, FS pays a supplier $1,000,000 for materials delivered to DS and charges DS an open account receivable for this amount. On February 3, 1995, FS reverses the account receivable from DS to FS when DS delivers to FP goods with a value of $1,000,000.

(ii) The accounts payable from DS to FS and from FS to other subsidiaries of FP constitute financing transactions within the meaning of paragraph (a)(2)(ii)(A)(*1*) of this section, and the transactions together constitute a financing arrangement within the meaning of paragraph (a)(2)(i) of this section. FS's activities constitute significant financing activities with respect to the financing transactions even though FS did not actively and materially participate in arranging the financing transactions because the financing transactions consisted of trade receivables and trade payables that were ordinary and necessary to carry on the trades or businesses of DS and the other subsidiaries of FP. Accordingly, pursuant to paragraph (b)(3)(i) of this section, FS' participation in the financing arrangement is presumed not to be pursuant to a tax avoidance plan.

(24) *Example 24. Significant financing activities—active risk management.*—(i) The facts are the same as in paragraph (e)(23) of this section (the facts in *Example 23*), except that, in addition to its short-term funding needs, DS needs long-term financing to fund an acquisition of another U.S. company; the acquisition is scheduled to close on January 15, 1995. FS has a revolving credit agreement with a syndicate of banks located in Country N. On January 14, 1995, FS borrows ¥10 billion for 10 years under the revolving credit agreement, paying yen LIBOR plus 50 basis points on a quarterly basis. FS enters into a currency swap with BK, an unrelated bank that is not a member of the syndicate, under which FS will pay BK ¥10 billion and will receive $100 million on January 15, 1995; these payments will be reversed on January 15, 2004. FS will pay BK U.S. dollar LIBOR plus 50 basis points on a notional principal amount of $100 million semi-annually and will receive yen LIBOR plus 50 basis points on a notional principal amount of ¥10 billion quarterly. Upon the closing of the acquisition on January 15, 1995, DS borrows $100 million from FS for 10 years, paying U.S. dollar LIBOR plus 50 basis points semiannually.

(ii) Although FS performs significant financing activities with respect to certain financing transactions to which it is a party, FS does not perform significant financing activities with respect to the financing transactions between FS and the syndicate of banks and between FS and DS because FS has eliminated all material market risks arising from those financing transactions through its currency swap with BK. Accordingly, the financing arrangement does not benefit from the presumption of paragraph (b)(3)(i) of this section and the director of field operations must determine whether the participation of FS in the financing arrangement is pursuant to a tax avoidance plan on the basis of all the facts and circumstances. However, if additional facts indicated that FS reviews its currency swaps daily to determine whether they are the most cost efficient way of managing their currency risk and, as a result, frequently terminates swaps in favor of entering into more cost efficient hedging arrangements with unrelated parties, FS would be considered to perform significant financing activities and FS' participation in the financing arrangements would not be pursuant to a tax avoidance plan.

(25) *Example 25. Significant financing activities—presumption rebutted.*—(i) The facts are the same as in paragraph (e)(23) of this section (the facts in *Example 23*), except that, on January 1, 1995, FP lends to FS DM 15,000,000 (worth $10,000,000) in exchange for a 10 year note that pays interest annually at a rate of 5 percent per annum. Also, on March 15, 1995, FS lends $10,000,000 to DS in exchange for a 10-year note that pays interest annually at a rate of 8 percent per annum. FS would not have had sufficient funds to make the loan to DS without the loan from FP. FS does not enter into any long-term hedging transaction with respect to these financing transactions, but manages the interest rate and currency risk arising from the transactions on a daily, weekly or quarterly basis by entering into forward currency contracts.

(ii) Because FS performs significant financing activities with respect to the financing transactions between FS, DS and FP, the participation of FS in the financing arrangement is presumed not to be pursuant to a tax avoidance plan. The director of field operations may rebut this presumption by establishing that the participation of FS is pursuant to a tax avoidance plan, based on all the facts and circumstances. The mere fact that FS is a resident of country T is not sufficient to establish the existence of a tax avoidance plan. However, the existence of a plan can be inferred from other factors in addition to the fact that FS is a resident of country T. For example, the loans are made within a short time period and FS would not have been able to make the loan to DS without the loan from FP.

(26) *Example 26. Determination of amount of tax liability.*—(i) On January 1, 1996, FP makes two three-year installment loans of $250,000 each to FS that pay interest at a rate of 9 percent per annum. The loans are self-amortizing with payments on each loan of $7,950 per month. On the same date, FS lends $1,000,000 to DS in exchange for a two-year note that pays interest semi-annually at a rate of 10 percent per annum, beginning on June 30, 1996. The FS-DS loan is not self-amortizing. Assume that for the period of January 1, 1996

through June 30, 1996, the average principal amount of the financing transactions between FP and FS that comprise the financing arrangement is $469,319. Further, assume that for the period of July 1, 1996 through December 31, 1996, the average principal amount of the financing transactions between FP and FS is $393,632. The average principal amount of the financing transaction between FS and DS for the same periods is $1,000,000. The director of field operations determines that the financing transactions between FP and FS, and FS and DS, are a conduit financing arrangement.

(ii) Pursuant to paragraph (d)(1)(i) of this section, the portion of the $50,000 interest payment made by DS to FS on June 30, 1996, that is recharacterized as a payment to FP is $23,450 computed as follows: ($50,000 × $469,319/$1,000,000) = $23,450. The portion of the interest payment made on December 31, 1996 that is recharacterized as a payment to FP is $19,650, computed as follows: ($50,000 × $393,632/$1,000,000) = $19,650. Furthermore, under § 1.1441-3(g), DS is liable for withholding tax at a 30 percent rate on the portion of the $50,000 payment to FS that is recharacterized as a payment to FP, i.e., $7,035 with respect to the June 30, 1996 payment and $5,895 with respect to the December 31, 1996 payment.

(27) *Example 27. Determination of principal amount.*—(i) FP lends DM 5,000,000 to FS in exchange for a ten year note that pays interest semi-annually at a rate of 8 percent per annum. Six months later, pursuant to a tax avoidance plan, FS lends DM 10,000,000 to DS in exchange for a 10 year note that pays interest semi-annually at a rate of 10 percent per annum. At the time FP make[s] its loan to FS, the exchange rate is DM 1.5/$1. At the time FS makes its loan to DS the exchange rate is DM 1.4/$1.

(ii) FP's loan to FS and FS' loan to DS are financing transactions and together constitute a financing arrangement. Furthermore, because the participation of FS reduces the tax imposed under section 881 and FS' participation is pursuant to a tax avoidance plan, the financing arrangement is a conduit financing arrangement.

(iii) Pursuant to paragraph (d)(1)(i) of this section, the amount subject to recharacterization is a fraction the numerator of which is the 10 west aggregate principal amount advanced and the denominator of which is the principal amount advanced from FS to DS. Because the property advanced in these financing transactions is the same type of fungible property, under paragraph (d)(1)(ii)(A) of this section, both are valued on the date of the last financing transaction. Accordingly, the portion of the payments of interest that is recharacterized is ((DM 5,000,000 × DM 1.4/$1)/(DM 10,000,000 × DM 1.4/$1) or 0.5.

(f) *Applicability date.*—This section is effective for payments made by financed entities on or after September 11, 1995. This section shall not apply to interest payments covered by section 127(g)(3) of the Tax Reform Act of 1984, and to interest payments with respect to other debt obligations issued prior to October 15, 1984 (whether or not such debt was issued by a Netherlands Antilles corporation). Paragraphs (a)(2)(i)(C) and (e)(3) (*Example* 3) of this section apply to payments made on or after December 9, 2011. Paragraph (a)(2)(ii)(B)(*1*)(*iv*) of this section applies to payments made on or after November 12, 2020. [Reg. § 1.881-3.]

☐ [*T.D.* 8611, 8-10-95. Amended by *T.D.* 9562, 12-8-2011 (*corrected* 4-13-2012) *and T.D.* 9922, 11-2-2020 (*corrected* 9-30-2021).]

§ 1.881-4. Recordkeeping requirements concerning conduit financing arrangements.—(a) *Scope.*—This section provides rules for the maintenance of records concerning certain financing arrangements to which the provisions of § 1.881-3 apply.

(b) *Recordkeeping requirements.*—(1) *In general.*—Any person subject to the general recordkeeping requirements of section 6001 must keep the permanent books of account or records, as required by section 6001, that may be relevant to determining whether that person is a party to a financing arrangement and whether that financing arrangement is a conduit financing arrangement.

(2) *Application of Sections 6038 and 6038A.*—A financed entity that is a reporting corporation within the meaning of section 6038A(a) and the regulations under that section, and any other person that is subject to the recordkeeping requirements of § 1.6038A-3, must comply with those recordkeeping requirements with respect to records that may be relevant to determining whether the financed entity is a party to a financing arrangement and whether that financing arrangement is a conduit financing arrangement. Such records, including records that a person is required to maintain pursuant to paragraph (c) of this section, shall be considered records that are required to be maintained pursuant to section 6038 or 6038A. Accordingly, the provisions of sections 6038 and 6038A (including, without limitation, the penalty provisions thereof), and the regulations under those sections, shall apply to any records required to be maintained pursuant to this section.

(c) *Records to be maintained.*—(1) *In general.*—An entity described in paragraph (b) of this section shall be required to retain any records containing the following information concerning each financing transaction that the entity knows or has reason to know comprises the financing arrangement—

(i) The nature (e.g., loan, stock, lease, license) of each financing transaction;

(ii) The name, address, taxpayer identification number (if any) and country of residence of—

(A) Each person that advanced money or other property, or granted rights to use property;

(B) Each person that was the recipient of the advance or rights; and

(C) Each person to whom a payment was made pursuant to the financing transaction (to the extent that person is a different person than the person who made the advance or granted the rights);

(iii) The date and amount of—

(A) Each advance of money or other property or grant of rights; and

(B) Each payment made in return for the advance or grant of rights;

(iv) The terms of any guarantee provided in conjunction with a financing transaction, including the name of the guarantor; and

(v) In cases where one or both of the parties to a financing transaction are related to each other or another entity in the financing arrangement, the manner in which these persons are related.

(2) *Additional documents.*—An entity described in paragraph (b) of this section must also retain all records relating to the circumstances surrounding its participation in the financing transactions and financing arrangements. Such documents may include, but are not limited to—

(i) Minutes of board of directors meetings;

(ii) Board resolutions or other authorizations for the financing transactions;

(iii) Private letter rulings;

(iv) Financial reports (audited or unaudited);

(v) Notes to financial statements;

(vi) Bank statements;

(vii) Copies of wire transfers;

(viii) Offering documents;

(ix) Materials from investment advisors, bankers and tax advisors; and

(x) Evidences of indebtedness.

(3) *Effect of record maintenance requirement.*—Record maintenance in accordance with paragraph (b) of this section generally does not require the original creation of records that are ordinarily not created by affected entities. If, however, a document that is actually created is described in this paragraph (c), it is to be retained even if the document is not of a type ordinarily created by the affected entity.

(d) *Effective date.*—This section is effective September 11, 1995. This section shall not apply to interest payments covered by section 127(g)(3) of the Tax Reform Act of 1984, and to interest payments with respect to other debt obligations issued prior to October 15, 1984 (whether or not such debt was issued by a Netherlands Antilles corporation). [Reg. § 1.881-4.]

☐ [*T.D.* 8611, 8-10-95].

§ 1.881-5. Exception for certain possessions corporations.—(a) *Scope.*—Section 881(b) and this section provide special rules for the application of sections 881 and 884 to certain corporations created or organized in possessions of the United States. Paragraph (g) of this section provides special rules for the application of sections 881 and 884 to corporations created or organized in the United States for purposes of determining tax liability incurred to certain possessions that administer income tax laws that are identical (except for the substitution of the name of the possession for the term "United States" where appropriate) to those in force in the United States. See § 1.884-0(b) for special rules relating to the application of section 884 with respect to possessions of the United States.

(b) *Operative rules.*—(1) Corporations described in paragraphs (c) and (d) of this section are not treated as foreign corporations for purposes of section 881. Accordingly, they are exempt from the tax imposed by section 881(a).

(2) For corporations described in paragraph (c) of this section, the rate of tax imposed by section 881(a) on U.S. source dividends received is 10 percent (rather than the generally applicable 30 percent).

(c) *U.S. Virgin Islands and section 931 possessions.*—A corporation created or organized in, or under the law of, the U.S. Virgin Islands or a section 931 possession is described in this paragraph (c) for a taxable year when the following conditions are satisfied—

(1) At all times during such taxable year, less than 25 percent in value of the stock of such corporation is beneficially owned (directly or indirectly) by foreign persons;

(2) At least 65 percent of the gross income of such corporation is shown to the satisfaction of the Commissioner upon examination to be effectively connected with the conduct of a trade or business in such a possession or the United States for the 3-year period ending with the close of the taxable year of such corporation (or for such part of such period as the corporation or any predecessor has been in existence); and

(3) No substantial part of the income of such corporation for the taxable year is used (directly or indirectly) to satisfy obligations to persons who are not bona fide residents of such a possession or the United States.

(d) *Section 935 possessions.*—A corporation created or organized in, or under the law of, a section 935 possession is described in this paragraph (d) for a taxable year when the following conditions are satisfied—

(1) At all times during such taxable year, less than 25 percent in value of the stock of such corporation is owned (directly or indirectly) by foreign persons; and

(2) At least 20 percent of the gross income of such corporation is shown to the satisfaction of the Commissioner upon examination to have been derived from sources within such possession for the 3-year period ending with the close of the preceding taxable year of such corporation (or for such part of such period as the corporation has been in existence).

(e) *Puerto Rico.*—A corporation created or organized in, or under the law of, Puerto Rico is described in this paragraph (e) for a taxable year when the conditions of paragraphs (c)(1) through (c)(3) of this section are satisfied (using the language "Puerto Rico" instead of "such a possession").

(f) *Definitions and other rules.*—For purposes of this section—

(1) "Section 931 possession" is defined in § 1.931-1(c)(1); and

(2) "Section 935 possession" is defined in § 1.935-1(a)(3)(i).

(3) *Foreign person* means any person other than—

(i) A United States person (as defined in section 7701(a)(30) and the regulations under that section); or

(ii) A person who would be a United States person if references to the United States in section 7701 included references to a possession of the United States.

(4) *Bona fide resident*—

(i) With respect to a particular possession, means—

(A) An individual who is a bona resident of the possession as defined in § 1.937-1; or

(B) A business entity organized under the laws of the possession and taxable as a corporation in the possession; and

(ii) With respect to the United States, means—

(A) An individual who is a citizen or resident of the United States (as defined under section 7701(b)(1)(A)); or

(B) A business entity organized under the laws of the United States or any State that is classified as a corporation for federal tax purposes under § 301.7701-2(b) of this chapter.

(5) *Source.*—The rules of § 1.937-2 will apply for determining whether income is from sources within a possession.

(6) *Effectively connected income.*—The rules of § 1.937-3 (other than paragraph (c) of that section) will apply for determining whether income is effectively connected with the conduct of a trade or business in a possession.

(7) *Indirect ownership.*—The rules of section 318(a)(2) will apply except that the language "5 percent" will be used instead of "50 percent" in section 318(a)(2)(C).

(g) *Mirror code jurisdictions.*—For purposes of applying mirrored section 881 to determine tax liability incurred to a section 935 possession or the U.S. Virgin Islands—

(1) The rules of paragraphs (b) through (d) of this section will not apply; and

(2) A corporation created or organized in, or under the law of, such possession or the United States will not be considered a foreign corporation.

(h) *Example.*—The principles of this section are illustrated by the following example:

Example. X is a corporation organized under the law of the U.S. Virgin Islands with a branch located in State F. At least 65 percent of the gross income of X is effectively connected with the conduct of a trade or business in the U.S. Virgin Islands and no substantial part of the income of X for the taxable year is used to satisfy obligations to persons who are not bona fide residents of the United States or the U.S. Virgin Islands. Seventy-four percent of the stock of X is owned by unrelated individuals who are residents of the United States or the U.S. Virgin Islands. Y, a corporation organized under the law of State D, and Z, a partnership organized under the law of State F, each own 13 percent of the stock of X. A, an unrelated foreign individual, owns 100 percent of the stock of corporation Y. B and C, unrelated foreign individuals, each own a 50 percent interest in partnership Z. Thus, the condition of paragraph (c)(1) of this section is not satisfied, because 26 percent of X is owned indirectly by foreign persons (A, B, and C). Accordingly, X is treated as a foreign corporation for purposes of section 881.

(i) *Effective/applicability dates.*—Except as otherwise provided in this paragraph (i), this section applies to payments made in taxable years ending after April 9, 2008. If, on or after April 9, 2008, there takes effect an increase in the Commonwealth of Puerto Rico's withholding tax generally applicable to dividends paid to United States corporations not engaged in a trade or business in the Commonwealth to a rate greater than 10 percent, the rules of paragraphs (b)(2) and (e) of this section will not apply to dividends received on or after the effective date of the increase. Paragraph (f)(4) of this section applies to payments made after January 31, 2006. Taxpayers may choose to apply paragraph (f)(4) of this section to payments made after October 22, 2004. [Reg. § 1.881-5.]

☐ [*T.D. 9248, 1-30-2006. Amended by T.D. 9391, 4-4-2008 (corrected 5-13-2008).*]

§ 1.882-1. Taxation of foreign corporations engaged in U.S. business or of foreign corporations treated as having effectively connected income.—(a) *Segregation of income.*—This section applies for purposes of determining the tax of a foreign corporation which at any time during the taxable year is engaged in trade or business in the United States. It also applies for purposes of determining the tax of a foreign corporation which at no time during the taxable year is engaged in trade or business in the United States but has for the taxable year real property income or interest on obligations of the United States which, by reason of section 882(d) or (e) and § 1.882-2, is treated as effectively connected for the taxable year with the conduct of a trade or business in the United States by that corporation. A foreign corporation to which this section applies must segregate its gross income for the taxable year into two categories, namely, the income which is effectively connected for the taxable year with the conduct of a trade or business in the United States by that corporation and the income which is not effectively connected for the taxable year with the conduct of a trade or business in the United States by that corporation. A separate tax shall then be determined upon each such category of income, as provided in paragraph (b) of this section. The determination of whether income or gain is or is not effectively connected for the taxable year with the conduct of a trade or business in the United States by the foreign corporation shall be made in accordance with section 864(c) and §§ 1.864-3 through 1.864-7. For purposes of this section income which is effectively connected for the taxable year with the conduct of a trade or business in the United States includes all income which is treated under section 882(d) or (e) and § 1.882-2 as income which is effectively connected for the taxable year with the conduct of a trade or business in the United States by the foreign corporation.

(b) *Imposition of tax.*—(1) *Income not effectively connected with the conduct of a trade or business in the United States.*—If a foreign corporation to which this section applies derives during the taxable year from sources within the United States income or gains described in section 881(a) and paragraph (b) or (c) of §1.881-2 which are not effectively connected for the taxable year with the conduct of a trade or business in the United States by that corporation, such income or gains shall be subject to a flat tax of 30 percent of the aggregate amount of such items. This tax shall be determined in the manner, and subject to the same conditions, set forth in §1.881-2 as though the income or gains were derived by a foreign corporation not engaged in trade or business in the United States during the taxable year, except that in applying paragraph (c) of such section there shall not be taken into account any gains which are taken into account in determining the tax under section 882(a)(1) and subparagraph (2) of this paragraph.

(2) *Income effectively connected with the conduct of a trade or business in the United States.*—(i) *In general.*—If a foreign corporation to which this section applies derives income or gains which are effectively connected for the taxable year with the conduct of a trade or business in the United States by that corporation, the taxable income or gains shall, except as provided in §1.871-12, be taxed in accordance with section 11 or, in the alternative, section 1201(a). See sections 11(f) and 882(a)(1). Any income of the foreign corporation which is not effectively connected for the taxable year with the conduct of a trade or business in the United States by that corporation shall not be taken into account in determining either the rate or amount of such tax.

(ii) *Determination of taxable income.*—The taxable income for any taxable year for purposes of this subparagraph consists only of the foreign corporation's taxable income which is effectively connected for the taxable year with the conduct of a trade or business in the United States by that corporation; and, for this purpose, it is immaterial that the trade or business with which that income is effectively connected is not the same as the trade or business carried on in the United States by that corporation during the taxable year. See example (2) in §1.864-4(b). In determining such taxable income all amounts constituting, or considered to be, gains or losses for the taxable year from the sale or exchange of capital assets shall be taken into account if such gains or losses are effectively connected for the taxable year with the conduct of a trade or business in the United States by that corporation.

(iii) *Cross references.*—For rules for determining the gross income and deductions for the taxable year, see section 882(b) and (c)(1) and the regulations thereunder.

(c) *Change in trade or business status.*—The principles of paragraph (c) of §1.871-8 shall apply to cases where there has been a change in the trade or business status of a foreign corporation.

(d) *Credits against tax.*—The credits allowed by section 32 (relating to tax withheld at source on foreign corporations), section 33 (relating to the foreign tax credit), section 38 (relating to investment in certain depreciable property), section 39 (relating to certain uses of gasoline and lubricating oil), section 40 (relating to expenses of work incentive programs), and section 6042 (relating to overpayments of a tax) shall be allowed against the tax determined in accordance with this section. However, the credits allowed by sections 33, 38, and 40 shall not be allowed against the flat tax of 30 percent imposed by section 881(a) and paragraph (b)(1) of this section. For special rules applicable in determining the foreign tax credit, see section 906(b) and the regulations thereunder. For the disallowance of certain credits where a return is not filed for the taxable year see section 882(c)(2) and the regulations thereunder.

(e) *Payment of estimated tax.*—Every foreign corporation which for the taxable year is subject to tax under section 11 or 1201(a) and this section must make payment of its estimated tax in accordance with section 6154 and the regulations thereunder. In determining the amount of the estimated tax the foreign corporation must treat the tax imposed by section 881(a) and paragraph (b)(1) of this section as though it were a tax imposed by section 11.

(f) *Effective date.*—This section applies for taxable years beginning after December 31, 1966. For corresponding rules applicable to taxable years beginning before January 1, 1967, see 26 CFR 1.882-1 (Rev. as of Jan. 1, 1971). [Reg. §1.882-1.]

☐ [*T.D. 6258, 10-23-57. Amended by T.D. 7244, 12-29-72 and T.D. 7293, 11-27-73.*]

§1.882-2. Income of foreign corporation treated as effectively connected with U.S. business.—(a) *Election as to real property income.*—A foreign corporation which during the taxable year derives any income from real property which is located in the United States, or derives income from any interest in any such real property, may elect, pursuant to section 882(d) and §1.871-10, to treat all such income as income which is effectively connected for the taxable year with the conduct of a trade or business in the United States by that corporation. The election may be made whether or not the foreign corporation is engaged in trade or business in the United States during the taxable year for which the election is made or whether or not the corporation has income from real property which for the taxable year is effectively connected with the conduct of a trade or business in the United States, but it may be made only with respect to income from sources within the United States which, without regard to section 882(d) and §1.871-10, is not effectively connected for the taxable year with the conduct of a trade or business in the United States by that corporation. The income to which the election applies shall be determined as provided in paragraph (b) of §1.871-10 and shall be subject to tax in the manner, and subject to the same conditions, provided by section 882(a)(1) and paragraph (b)(2) of §1.882-1. Section 871(d)(2) and (3) and the provisions of §1.871-10 thereunder shall apply in respect of an election under section 882(d) in the same manner and to the same extent as they apply in respect of elections under section 871(d).

(b) *Interest on U.S. obligations received by banks organized in possessions.*—Interest received from sources within the United States during the taxable year on obligations of the United States by a foreign corporation created or organized in, or under the law of, a possession of the United States and carrying on the banking business in a possession of the United States during the taxable year shall be treated, pursuant to section 882(e) and this paragraph, as income which is effectively connected for the taxable year with the conduct of a trade or business in the United States by that corporation. This paragraph applies whether or not the foreign corporation is engaged in trade or business in the United States at any time during the taxable year but only with respect to income which, without regard to this paragraph, is not effectively connected for the taxable year with the conduct of a trade or business in the United States by that corporation. Any interest to which this paragraph applies shall be subject to tax in the manner, and subject to the same conditions, provided by section 882(a)(1) and paragraph (b)(2) of §1.882-1. To the extent that deductions are connected with interest to which this paragraph applies, they shall be treated for purposes of section 882(c)(1) and the regulations thereunder as connected with income which is effectively connected for the taxable year with the conduct of a trade or business in the United States by the foreign corporation. An election by the taxpayer is not required in respect of the income to which this paragraph applies. For purposes of this paragraph the term "possession of the United States" includes Guam, the Midway Islands, the Panama Canal Zone, the Commonwealth of Puerto Rico, American Samoa, the Virgin Islands, and Wake Island.

(c) *Treatment of income.*—Any income in respect of which an election described in paragraph (a) of this section is in effect, and any interest to which paragraph (b) of this section applies, shall be treated, for purposes of paragraph (b)(2) of §1.882-1 and paragraph (a) of §1.441-4, as income which is effectively connected for the taxable year with the conduct of a trade or business in the United States by the foreign corporation. A foreign corporation shall not be treated as being engaged in trade or business in the United States merely by reason of having such income for the taxable year.

(d) *Effective date.*—This section applies for taxable years beginning after December 31, 1966. There are no corresponding rules in this part for taxable years beginning before January 1, 1967. [Reg. §1.882-2.]

☐ [*T.D. 6258, 10-23-57. Amended by T.D. 7293, 11-27-73.*]

§1.882-3. Gross income of a foreign corporation.—(a) *In general.*—(1) *Inclusions.*—The gross income of a foreign corporation for any taxable year includes only (i) the gross income which is derived from sources within the United States and which is not effectively connected for the taxable year with the conduct of a trade or business in the United States by that corporation, and (ii) the gross income, irrespective of whether such income is derived from sources within or without the United States, which is effectively connected for the taxable year with the conduct of a trade or business in the United States by that corporation. For the determination of the sources of income, see sections 861 through 863, and the regulations thereunder. For the determination of whether income from sources within or without the United States is effectively connected for the taxable year with the conduct of a trade or business in the United States, see sections 864(c) and 882(d) and (e), §§1.864-3 through 1.864-7, and §1.882-2.

(2) *Exchange transactions.* Even though a foreign corporation which effects certain transactions in the United States in stocks, securities, or commodities during the taxable year may not, by reason of section 864(b)(2) and paragraph (c) or (d) of §1.864-2, be engaged in trade or business in the United States during the taxable year through the effecting of such transactions, nevertheless it shall be required to include in gross income for the taxable year the gains and profits from those transactions to the extent required by paragraph (c) of §1.881-2 or by paragraph (a) of §1.882-1.

(3) *Exclusions.*—For exclusions from gross income of a foreign corporation, see §1.883-1.

(b) *Foreign corporations not engaged in U.S. business.*—In the case of a foreign corporation which at no time during the taxable year is engaged in trade or business in the United States the gross income shall include only (1) the gross income from sources within the United States which is described in section 881(a) and paragraphs (b) and (c) of §1.881-2, and (2) the gross income from sources within the United States which, by reason of section 882(d) or (e) and §1.882-2, is treated as effectively connected for the taxable year with the conduct of a trade or business in the United States by that corporation.

(c) *Foreign corporations engaged in U.S. business.*—In the case of a foreign corporation which is engaged in trade or business in the United States at any time during the taxable year, the gross income shall include (1) the gross income from sources within and without the United States which is effectively connected for the taxable year with the conduct of a trade or business in the United States by that corporation, (2) the gross income from sources within the United States which, by reason of section 882(d) or (e) and §1.882-2, is treated as effectively connected for the taxable year with the conduct of a trade or business in the United States by that corporation, and (3) the gross income from sources within the United States which is described in section 881(a) and paragraphs (b) and (c) of §1.881-2 and is not effectively connected for the taxable year with the conduct of a trade or business in the United States by that corporation.

(d) *Effective date.*—This section applies for taxable years beginning after December 31, 1966. For corresponding rules applicable to taxable years beginning before January 1, 1967, see 26 CFR 1.882-2 (Rev. as of Jan. 1, 1971). [Reg. §1.882-3.]

□ [*T.D. 6258, 10-23-57. Amended by T.D. 7293, 11-27-73.*]

§1.882-4. Allowance of deductions and credits to foreign corporations.—(a) *Foreign corporations.*—(1) *In general.*—A foreign corporation that is engaged in, or receives income treated as effectively connected with, a trade or business within the United States is allowed the deductions which are properly allocated and apportioned to the foreign corporation's gross income which is effectively connected, or treated as effectively connected, with its conduct of a trade or business within the United States. The foreign corporation is entitled to credits which are attributable to that effectively connected income. No provision of this section (other than paragraph (b)(2)) shall be construed to deny the credits provided by sections 33, 34 and 852(b)(3)(D)(ii) or the deduction allowed by section 170.

(2) *Return necessary.*—A foreign corporation shall receive the benefit of the deductions and credits otherwise allowed to it with respect to the income tax, only if it timely files or causes to be filed with the Philadelphia Service Center, in the manner prescribed in subtitle F, a true and accurate return of its taxable income which is effectively connected, or treated as effectively connected, for the taxable year with the conduct of a trade or business in the United States by that corporation. The deductions and credits allowed such a corporation electing under a tax convention to be subject to tax on a net basis may be obtained by filing a return of income in the manner prescribed in the regulations (if any) under the tax convention or under any other guidance issued by the Commissioner.

(3) *Filing deadline for return.*—(i) As provided in paragraph (a)(2) of this section, for purposes of computing the foreign corporation's taxable income for any taxable year, otherwise allowable deductions (other than that allowed by section 170) and credits (other than those allowed by sections 33, 34 and 852(b)(3)(D)(ii)) will be allowed only if a return for that taxable year is filed by the foreign corporation on a timely basis. For taxable years of a foreign corporation ending after July 31, 1990, whether a return for the current taxable year has been filed on a timely basis is dependent upon whether the foreign corporation filed a return for the taxable year immediately preceding the current taxable year. If a return was filed for that immediately preceding taxable year, or if the current taxable year is the first taxable year of the foreign corporation for which a return is required to be filed, the required return for the current taxable year must be filed within 18 months of the due date as set forth in section 6072 and the regulations under that section, for filing the return for the current taxable year. If no return for the taxable year immediately preceding the current taxable year has been filed, the required return for the current taxable year (other than the first taxable year of the foreign corporation for which a return is required to be filed) must have been filed no later than the earlier of the date which is 18 months after the due date, as set forth in section 6072, for filing the return for the current taxable year or the date the Internal Revenue Service mails a notice to the foreign corporation advising the corporation that the current year tax return has not been filed and that no deductions (other than that allowed under section 170) or credits (other than those allowed under sections 33, 34 and 852(b)(3)(D)(ii)) may be claimed by the taxpayer.

(ii) The filing deadlines set forth in paragraph (a)(3)(i) of this section may be waived if the foreign corporation establishes to the satisfaction of the Commissioner or his or her delegate that the corporation, based on the facts and circumstances, acted reasonably and in good faith in failing to file a U.S. income tax return (including a protective return (as described in paragraph (a)(3)(vi) of this section)). For this purpose, a foreign corporation shall not be considered to have acted reasonably and in good faith if it knew that it was required to file the return and chose not to do so. In addition, a foreign corporation shall not be granted a waiver unless it cooperates in the process of determining its income tax liability for the taxable year for which the return was not filed. The Commissioner or his or her delegate shall consider the following factors in determining whether the foreign corporation, based on the facts and circumstances, acted reasonably and in good faith in failing to file a U.S. income tax return—

(A) Whether the corporation voluntarily identifies itself to the Internal Revenue Service as having failed to file a U.S. income tax return before the Internal Revenue Service discovers the failure to file;

(B) Whether the corporation did not become aware of its ability to file a protective return (as described in paragraph (a)(3)(vi) of this section) by the deadline for filing a protective return;

(C) Whether the corporation had not previously filed a U.S. income tax return;

(D) Whether the corporation failed to file a U.S. income tax return because, after exercising reasonable diligence (taking into account its relevant experience and level of sophistication), the corporation was unaware of the necessity for filing the return;

(E) Whether the corporation failed to file a U.S. income tax return because of intervening events beyond its control; and

(F) Whether other mitigating or exacerbating factors existed.

(iii) The following examples illustrate the provisions of this section. In all examples, FC is a foreign corporation and uses the calendar year as its taxable year. The examples are as follows:

Example 1. Foreign corporation discloses own failure to file. In Year 1, FC became a limited partner with a passive investment in a U.S. limited partnership that was engaged in a U.S. trade or business. During Year 1 through Year 4, FC incurred losses with respect to its U.S. partnership interest. FC's foreign tax director incorrectly concluded that because it was a limited partner and had only losses from its partnership interest, FC was not required to file a U.S. income tax return. FC's management was aware neither of FC's obligation to file a U.S. income tax return for those years, nor of its ability to file a protective return for those years. FC had never filed a U.S. income tax return before. In Year 5, FC began realizing a profit rather than a loss with respect to its partnership interest and, for this reason, engaged a U.S. tax advisor to handle its responsibility to file U.S. income tax returns. In preparing FC's income tax return for Year 5, FC's U.S. tax advisor discovered that returns were not filed for Year 1 through Year 4. Therefore, with respect to those years for which applicable filing deadlines in paragraph (a)(3)(i) of this section were not met, FC would be barred by paragraph (a)(2) of this section from claiming any deductions that otherwise would have given rise to net operating losses on returns for those years, and that would have been available as loss carryforwards in subsequent years. At FC's direction, its U.S. tax advisor promptly contacted the appropriate examining personnel and cooperated with the Internal Revenue Service in determining FC's income tax liability, for example, by preparing and filing the appropriate income tax returns for Year 1 through Year 4 and by making FC's books and records available to an Internal Revenue Service examiner. FC has met the standard described in paragraph (a)(3)(ii) of this section for waiver of any applicable filing deadlines in paragraph (a)(3)(i) of this section.

Example 2. Foreign corporation refuses to cooperate. Same facts as in *Example 1*, except that while FC's U.S. tax advisor contacted the appropriate examining personnel and filed the appropriate income tax returns for Year 1 through Year 4, FC refused all requests by the Internal Revenue Service to provide supporting information (for example, books and records) with respect to those returns. Because FC did not cooperate in determining its U.S. tax liability for the taxable years for which an income tax return was not timely filed, FC is not granted a waiver as described in paragraph (a)(3)(ii) of this section of any applicable filing deadlines in paragraph (a)(3)(i) of this section.

Example 3. Foreign corporation fails to file a protective return. Same facts as in *Example 1*, except that in Year 1 through Year 4, FC's tax director also consulted a U.S. tax advisor, who advised FC's tax director that it was uncertain whether U.S. income tax returns were necessary for those years and that FC could protect its right subsequently to claim the loss carryforwards by filing protective returns under paragraph (a)(3)(vi) of this section. FC did not file U.S. income tax returns or protective returns for those years. FC did not present evidence that intervening events beyond FC's control prevented it from filing an income tax return, and there were no other mitigating factors. FC has not met the standard described in paragraph (a)(3)(ii) of this section for waiver of any applicable filing deadlines in paragraph (a)(3)(i) of this section.

Example 4. Foreign corporation with effectively connected income. In Year 1, FC, a technology company, opened an office in the United States to market and sell a software program that FC had developed outside the United States. FC had minimal business or tax experience internationally, and no such experience in the United States. Through FC's direct efforts, U.S. sales of the software produced income effectively connected with a U.S. trade or business. FC, however, did not file U.S. income tax returns for Year 1 or Year 2. FC's management was aware neither of FC's obligation to file a U.S. income tax return for those years, nor of its ability to file a protective return for those years. FC had never filed a U.S. income tax return before. In January of Year 4, FC engaged U.S. counsel in connection with licensing software to an unrelated U.S. company. U.S. counsel reviewed FC's U.S. activities and advised FC that it should have filed U.S. income tax returns for Year 1 and Year 2. FC immediately engaged a U.S. tax advisor who, at FC's direction, promptly contacted the appropriate examining personnel and cooperated with the Internal Revenue Service in determining FC's income tax liability, for example, by preparing and filing the appropriate income tax returns for Year 1 and Year 2 and by making FC's books and records available to an Internal Revenue Service examiner. FC has met the standard described in paragraph (a)(3)(ii) of this section for waiver of any applicable filing deadlines in paragraph (a)(3)(i) of this section.

Example 5. IRS discovers foreign corporation's failure to file. In Year 1, FC, a technology company, opened an office in the United States to market and sell a software program that FC had developed outside the United States. Through FC's direct efforts, U.S. sales of the software produced income effectively connected with a U.S. trade or business. FC had extensive experience conducting similar business activities in other countries, including making the appropriate tax filings. However, FC's management was aware neither of FC's obligation to file a U.S. income tax return for those years, nor of its ability to file a protective return for those years. FC had never filed a U.S. income tax return before. Despite FC's extensive experience conducting similar business activities in other countries, it made no effort to seek advice in connection with its U.S. tax obligations. FC failed to file either U.S. income tax returns or protective returns for Year 1 and Year 2. In January of Year 4, an Internal Revenue Service examiner asked FC for an explanation of FC's failure to file U.S. income tax returns. FC immediately engaged a U.S. tax advisor, and cooperated with the Internal Revenue Service in determining FC's income tax liability, for example, by preparing and filing the appropriate income tax returns for Year 1 and Year 2 and by making FC's books and records available to the examiner. FC did not present evidence that intervening events beyond its control prevented it from filing a return, and there were no other mitigating factors. FC has not met the standard described in paragraph (a)(3)(ii) of this section for waiver of any applicable filing deadlines in paragraph (a)(3)(i) of this section.

Example 6. Foreign corporation with prior filing history. FC began a U.S. trade or business in Year 1. FC's tax advisor filed the appropriate U.S. income tax returns for Year 1 through Year 6, reporting income effectively connected with FC's U.S. trade or business. In Year 7, FC replaced its tax advisor with a tax advisor unfamiliar with U.S. tax law. FC did not file a U.S. income tax return for any year from Year 7 through Year 10, although it had effectively connected income for those years. FC's management was aware of FC's ability to file a protective return for those years. In Year 11, an Internal Revenue Service examiner contacted FC and asked its chief financial officer for an explanation of FC's failure to file U.S. income tax returns after Year 6. FC immediately engaged a U.S. tax advisor and cooperated with the Internal Revenue Service in determining FC's income tax liability, for example, by preparing and filing the appropriate income tax returns for Year 7 through Year 10 and by making FC's books and records available to the examiner. FC did not present evidence that intervening events beyond its control prevented it from filing a return, and there were no other mitigating factors. FC has not met the standard described in paragraph (a)(3)(ii) of this section for waiver of any applicable filing deadlines in paragraph (a)(3)(i) of this section.

(iv) Paragraphs (a)(3)(ii) and (iii) of this section are applicable to open years for which a request for a waiver is filed on or after January 29, 2002.

(v) A foreign corporation which has a permanent establishment, as defined in an income tax treaty between the United States and the foreign corporation's country of residence, in the United States is subject to the filing deadlines set forth in paragraph (a)(3)(i) of this section.

(vi) If a foreign corporation conducts limited activities in the United States in a taxable year which the foreign corporation determines does not give rise to gross income which is effectively connected with the conduct of a trade or business within the United States as defined in sections 882(b) and 864(b) and (c) and the regulations under those sections, the foreign corporation may nonetheless file a return for that taxable year on a timely basis under paragraph (a)(3)(i) of this section and thereby protect the right to receive the benefit of the deductions and credits attributable to that gross income if it is later determined, after the return was filed, that the original determination was incorrect. On that timely filed return, the foreign corporation is not required to report any gross income as effectively connected with a United States trade or business or any deductions or credits but should attach a statement indicating that the return is being filed for the reason set forth in this paragraph (a)(3). If the foreign corporation determines that part of the activities which it conducts in the United States in a taxable year gives rise to gross income which is effectively connected with the conduct of a trade or business and part does not, the foreign corporation must timely file a return for that taxable year to report the gross income determined to be effectively connected, or treated as effectively connected, with the conduct of the trade or business within the United States and the deductions and credits attributable to the gross income. In addition, the foreign corporation should attach to that return the statement described in this paragraph (b)(3) with regard to the other activities. The foreign corporation may follow the same procedure if it determines initially that it has no United States tax liability under the provisions of an applicable income tax treaty. In the event the foreign corporation relies on the provisions of an income tax treaty to reduce or eliminate the income subject to taxation, or to reduce the rate of tax, disclosure may be required pursuant to section 6114.

(vii) In order to be eligible for any deductions and credits for purposes of computing the accumulated earnings tax of section 531, a foreign corporation must file a true and accurate return, on a timely basis, in the manner as set forth in paragraph (a)(2) and (3) of this section.

(4) *Return by Internal Revenue Service.*—If a foreign corporation has various sources of income within the United States and a return of income has not been filed, in the manner prescribed by subtitle F, including the filing deadlines set forth in paragraph (a)(3) of this section, the Internal Revenue Service shall:

(i) Cause a return of income to be made,

(ii) Include on the return the income described in § 1.882-1 of that corporation from all sources concerning which it has information, and

(iii) Assess the tax and collect it from one or more of those sources of income within the United States, without allowance for any deductions (other than that allowed by section 170) or credits (other than those allowed by sections 33, 34 and 852(b)(3)(D)(ii)).

If the income of the corporation is not effectively connected with, or if the corporation did not receive income that is treated as being effectively connected with, the conduct of a United States trade or business, the tax will be assessed under § 1.882-1(b)(1) on a gross basis, without allowance for any deduction (other than that allowed by section 170) or credit (other than the credits allowed by sections 33, 34 and 852(b)(3)(d)(ii)). If the income is effectively connected, or treated as effectively connected, with the conduct of a United States trade or business, tax will be assessed in accordance with either section 11, 55 or 1201(a) without allowance for any deduction (other than that allowed by section 170) or credit (other than the credits allowed by sections 33, 34 and 852(b)(3)(D)(ii)).

(b) *Allowed deductions and credits.*—(1) *In general.*—Except for the deduction allowed under section 170 for charitable contributions and gifts (see section 882(c)(1)(B)), deductions are allowed to a foreign corporation only to the extent they are connected with gross income which is effectively connected, or treated as effectively connected, with the conduct of a trade or business in the United States. Deductible expenses (other than interest expense) are properly allocated and apportioned to effectively connected gross income in accordance with the rules of §1.861-8. For the method of determining the interest deduction allowed to a foreign corporation, see §1.882-5. Other than the credits allowed by sections 33, 34 and 852(b)(3)(D)(ii), the foreign corporation is entitled to credits only if they are attributable to effectively connected income. See paragraph (a)(2) of this section for the requirement that a return be filed. Except as provided by section 906, a foreign corporation shall not be allowed the credit against the tax for taxes of foreign countries and possessions of the United States allowed by section 901.

(2) *Verification.*—At the request of the Internal Revenue Service, a foreign corporation claiming deductions from gross income which is effectively connected, or treated as effectively connected, with the conduct of a trade or business in the United States or credits which are attributable to that income must furnish at the place designated pursuant to §301.7605-1(a) information sufficient to establish that the corporation is entitled to the deductions and credits in the amounts claimed. All information must be furnished in a form suitable to permit verification of claimed deductions and credits. The Internal Revenue Service may require, as appropriate, that an English translation be provided with any information in a foreign language. If a foreign corporation fails to furnish sufficient information, the Internal Revenue Service may in its discretion disallow any claimed deductions and credits in full or in part. For additional filing requirements and for penalties for failure to provide information, see also section 6038A. [Reg. §1.882-4.]

☐ [*T.D.* 6258, 10-23-57. *Amended by T.D.* 7749, 12-30-80; *T.D.* 8322, 12-10-90; *T.D.* 8981, 1-28-2002 *and T.D.* 9043, 3-7-2003.]

§1.882-5. Determination of interest deduction.—(a)(1) *Overview.*—(i) *In general.*—The amount of interest expense of a foreign corporation that is allocable under section 882(c) to income which is (or is treated as) effectively connected with the conduct of a trade or business within the United States (ECI) is the sum of the interest allocable by the foreign corporation under the three-step process set forth in paragraphs (b), (c), and (d) of this section and the specially allocated interest expense determined under paragraph (a)(1)(ii) of this section. The provisions of this section provide the exclusive rules for allocating interest expense to the ECI of a foreign corporation under section 882(c). Under the three-step process, the total value of the U.S. assets of a foreign corporation is first determined under paragraph (b) of this section (Step 1). Next, the amount of U.S.-connected liabilities is determined under paragraph (c) of this section (Step 2). Finally, the amount of interest paid or accrued on U.S.-booked liabilities, as determined under paragraph (d)(2) of this section, is adjusted for interest expense attributable to the difference between U.S.-connected liabilities and U.S.-booked liabilities (Step 3). Alternatively, a foreign corporation may elect to determine its interest rate on U.S.-connected liabilities by reference to its U.S. assets, using the separate currency pools method described in paragraph (e) of this section.

(ii) *Direct allocations.*—(A) *In general.*—A foreign corporation that has a U.S. asset and indebtedness that meet the requirements of §1.861-10T (b) or (c), as limited by §1.861-10T(d)(1), shall directly allocate interest expense from such indebtedness to income from such asset in the manner and to the extent provided in §1.861-10T. For purposes of paragraph (b)(1) or (c)(2) of this section, a foreign corporation that allocates its interest expense under the direct allocation rule of this paragraph (a)(1)(ii)(A) shall reduce the basis of the asset that meets the requirements of §1.861-10T (b) or (c) by the principal amount of the indebtedness that meets the requirements of §1.861- 10T (b) or (c). The foreign corporation shall also disregard any indebtedness that meets the requirements of §1.861-10T (b) or (c) in determining the amount of the foreign corporation's liabilities under paragraphs (c)(2) and (d)(2) of this section and shall not take into account any interest expense paid or accrued with respect to such a liability for purposes of paragraph (d) or (e) of this section.

(B) *Partnership interest.*—A foreign corporation that is a partner in a partnership that has a U.S. asset and indebtedness that meet the requirements of §1.861-10T (b) or (c), as limited by §1.861-10T(d)(1), shall directly allocate its distributive share of interest expense from that indebtedness to its distributive share of income from that asset in the manner and to the extent provided in §1.861-10T. A foreign corporation that allocates its distributive share of interest expense under the direct allocation rule of this paragraph (a)(1)(ii)(B) shall disregard any partnership indebtedness that meets the requirements of §1.861-10T (b) or (c) in determining the amount of its distributive share of partnership liabilities for purposes of paragraphs (b)(1), (c)(2)(vi), and (d)(2)(vii) or (e)(1)(ii) of this section, and shall not take into account any partnership interest expense paid or accrued with respect to such a liability for purposes of paragraph (d) or (e) of this section. For purposes of paragraph (b)(1) of this section, a foreign corporation that directly allocates its distributive share of interest expense under this paragraph (a)(1)(ii)(B) shall—

(1) Reduce the partnership's basis in such asset by the amount of such indebtedness in allocating its basis in the partnership under §1.884-1(d)(3)(ii); or

(2) Reduce the partnership's income from such asset by the partnership's interest expense from such indebtedness under §1.884-1(d)(3)(iii).

(2) *Coordination with tax treaties.*—Except as expressly provided by or pursuant to a U.S. income tax treaty or accompanying documents (such as an exchange of notes), the provisions of this section provide the exclusive rules for determining the interest expense attributable to the business profits of a permanent establishment under a U.S. income tax treaty.

(3) *Limitation on interest expense.*—In no event may the amount of interest expense computed under this section exceed the amount of interest on indebtedness paid or accrued by the taxpayer within the taxable year (translated into U.S. dollars at the weighted average exchange rate for each currency prescribed by §1.989(b)-1 for the taxable year).

(4) *Translation convention for foreign currency.*—For each computation required by this section, the taxpayer shall translate values and amounts into the relevant currency at a spot rate or a weighted average exchange rate consistent with the method such taxpayer uses for financial reporting purposes, provided such method is applied consistently from year to year. Interest expense paid or accrued, however, shall be translated under the rules of §1.988-2. The district director or the Assistant Commissioner (International) may require that any or all computations required by this section be made in U.S. dollars if the functional currency of the taxpayer's home office is a hyperinflationary currency, as defined in §1.985-1, and the computation in U.S. dollars is necessary to prevent distortions.

(5) *Coordination with other sections.*—Any provision that disallows, defers, or capitalizes interest expense applies after determining the amount of interest expense allocated to ECI under this section. For example, in determining the amount of interest expense that is disallowed as a deduction under section 265 or 163(j), deferred under section 163(e)(3) or 267(a)(3), or capitalized under section 263A with respect to a United States trade or business, a taxpayer takes into account only the amount of interest expense allocable to ECI under this section.

(6) *Special rule for foreign governments.*—The amount of interest expense of a foreign government, as defined in §1.892-2T(a), that is allocable to ECI is the total amount of interest paid or accrued within the taxable year by the United States trade or business on U.S. booked liabilities (as defined in paragraph (d)(2) of this section). Interest expense of a foreign government, however, is not allocable to ECI to the extent that it is incurred with respect to U.S. booked liabilities that exceed 80 percent of the total value of U.S. assets for the taxable year (determined under paragraph (b) of this section). This paragraph (a)(6) does not apply to controlled commercial entities within the meaning of §1.892-5T.

(7) *Elections under §1.882-5.*—(i) *In general.*—A corporation must make each election provided in this section on the corporation's original timely filed Federal income tax return for the first taxable year it is subject to the rules of this section. An amended return does not qualify for this purpose, nor shall the provisions of §301.9100-1

of this chapter and any guidance promulgated thereunder apply. Except as provided elsewhere in this section, each election under this section, whether an election for the first taxable year or a subsequent change of election, shall be made by indicating the method used on Schedule I (Form 1120-F) attached to the corporation's timely filed return. An elected method (other than the fair market value method under paragraph (b)(2)(ii) of this section, or the annual 30-day London Interbank Offered Rate (LIBOR) election in paragraph (d)(5)(ii) of this section) must be used for a minimum period of five years before the taxpayer may elect a different method. To change an election before the end of the requisite five-year period, a taxpayer must obtain the consent of the Commissioner or his delegate. The Commissioner or his delegate will generally consent to a taxpayer's request to change its election only in rare and unusual circumstances. After the five-year minimum period, an elected method may be changed for any subsequent year on the foreign corporation's original timely filed tax return for the first year to which the changed election applies.

(ii) *Failure to make the proper election*.—If a taxpayer, for any reason, fails to make an election provided in this section in a timely fashion, the Director of Field Operations may make any or all of the elections provided in this section on behalf of the taxpayer, and such elections shall be binding as if made by the taxpayer.

(iii) *Step 2 special election for banks*.—For the first taxable year for which an original income tax return is due (including extensions) after August 17, 2006, in which a taxpayer that is a bank as described in paragraph (c)(4) of this section is subject to the requirements of this section, a taxpayer may make a new election to use the fixed ratio on an original timely filed return. A new fixed ratio election may be made in any subsequent year subject to the timely filing and five-year minimum period requirements of paragraph (a)(7)(i) of this section. A new fixed ratio election under this paragraph (a)(7)(iii) is subject to the adjusted basis or fair market value conforming election requirements of paragraph (b)(2)(ii)(A)(2) of this section and may not be made if a taxpayer elects or maintains a fair market value election for purposes of paragraph (b) of this section. Taxpayers that already use the fixed ratio method under an existing election may continue to use the new fixed ratio at the higher percentage without having to make a new five-year election in the first year that the higher percentage is effective.

(8) *Examples*.—The following examples illustrate the application of paragraph (a) of this section:

Example 1. Direct allocations. (i) *Facts*: *FC* is a foreign corporation that conducts business through a branch, *B*, in the United States. Among *B's* U.S. assets is an interest in a partnership, *P*, that is engaged in airplane leasing solely in the U.S. *FC* contributes 200x to *P* in exchange for its partnership interest. *P* incurs qualified nonrecourse indebtedness within the meaning of § 1.861-10T to purchase an airplane. *FC's* share of the liability of *P*, as determined under section 752, is 800x.

(ii) *Analysis*: Pursuant to paragraph (a)(1)(ii)(B) of this section, *FC* is permitted to directly allocate its distributive share of the interest incurred with respect to the qualified nonrecourse indebtedness to *FC's* distributive share of the rental income generated by the airplane. A liability the interest on which is allocated directly to the income from a particular asset under paragraph (a)(1)(ii)(B) of this section is disregarded for purposes of paragraphs (b)(1), (c)(2)(vi), and (d)(2)(vii) or (e)(1)(ii) of this section. Consequently, for purposes of determining the value of *FC's* assets under paragraphs (b)(1) and (c)(2)(vi) of this section, *FC's* basis in *P* is reduced by the 800x liability as determined under section 752, but is not increased by the 800x liability that is directly allocated under paragraph (a)(1)(ii)(B) of this section. Similarly, pursuant to paragraph (a)(1)(ii)(B) of this section, the 800x liability is disregarded for purposes of determining *FC's* liabilities under paragraphs (c)(2)(vi) and (d)(2)(vii) of this section.

Example 2. Limitation on interest expense—(i) *FC* is a foreign corporation that conducts a real estate business in the United States. In its 1997 tax year, *FC* has no outstanding indebtedness, and therefore incurs no interest expense. *FC* elects to use the 50% fixed ratio under paragraph (c)(4) of this section.

(ii) Under paragraph (a)(3) of this section, *FC* is not allowed to deduct any interest expense that exceeds the amount of interest on indebtedness paid or accrued in that taxable year. Since *FC* incurred no interest expense in taxable year 1997, *FC* will not be entitled to any interest deduction for that year under § 1.882-5, notwithstanding the fact that *FC* has elected to use the 50% fixed ratio.

Example 3. Coordination with other sections—(i) *FC* is a foreign corporation that is a bank under section 585(a)(2) and a financial institution under section 265(b)(5). *FC* is a calendar year taxpayer, and operates a U.S. branch, *B*. Throughout its taxable year 1997, *B* holds only two assets that are U.S. assets within the meaning of paragraph (b)(1) of this section. *FC* does not make a fair-market value election under paragraph (b)(2)(ii) of this section, and, therefore, values its U.S. assets according to their bases under paragraph (b)(2)(i) of this section. The first asset is a taxable security with an adjusted basis of $100. The second asset is an obligation the interest on which is exempt from federal taxation under section 103, with an adjusted basis of $50. The tax-exempt obligation is not a qualified taxexempt obligation as defined by section 265(b)(3)(B).

(ii) *FC* calculates its interest expense under § 1.882-5 to be $12. Under paragraph (a)(5) of this section, however, a portion of the interest expense that is allocated to *FC's* effectively connected income under § 1.882-5 is disallowed in accordance with the provisions of section 265(b). Using the methodology prescribed under section 265, the amount of disallowed interest expense is $4, calculated as follows:

$$\$12 \times \frac{\$50 \text{ Tax-exempt U.S. assets}}{\$150 \text{ Total U.S. assets}} = \$4$$

(iii) Therefore, *FC* deducts a total of $8 ($12 - $4) of interest expense attributable to its effectively connected income in 1997.

Example 4. Treaty exempt asset—(i) *FC* is a foreign corporation, resident in Country X, that is actively engaged in the banking business in the United States through a permanent establishment, *B*. The income tax treaty in effect between Country X and the United States provides that *FC* is not taxable on foreign source income earned by its U.S. permanent establishment. In its 1997 tax year, *B* earns $90 of U.S. source income from U.S. assets with an adjusted tax basis of $900, and $12 of foreign source interest income from U.S. assets with an adjusted tax basis of $100. *FC's* U.S. interest expense deduction, computed in accordance with § 1.882-5, is $500.

(ii) Under paragraph (a)(5) of this section, *FC* is required to apply any provision that disallows, defers, or capitalizes interest expense after determining the interest expense allocated to ECI under § 1.882-5. Section 265(a)(2) disallows interest expense that is allocable to one or more classes of income that are wholly exempt from taxation under subtitle A of the Internal Revenue Code. Section 1.265-1(b) provides that income wholly exempt from taxes includes both income excluded from tax under any provision of subtitle A and income wholly exempt from taxes under any other law. Section 894 specifies that the provisions of subtitle A are applied with due regard to any relevant treaty obligation of the United States. Because the treaty between the United States and Country X exempts foreign source income earned by *B* from U.S. tax, *FC* has assets that produce income wholly exempt from taxes under subtitle A, and must therefore allocate a portion of its § 1.882-5 interest expense to its exempt income. Using the methodology prescribed under section 265, the amount of disallowed interest expense is $50, calculated as follows:

$$\$500 \times \frac{\$100 \text{ Treaty-exempt U.S. assets}}{\$1000 \text{ Total U.S. assets}} = \$50$$

(iii) Therefore, *FC* deducts a total of $450 ($500 $50) of interest expense attributable to its effectively connected income in 1997.

(b) *Step 1: Determination of total value of U.S. assets for the taxable year*.—(1) *Classification of an asset as a U.S. asset*.—(i) *General rule*.—Except as otherwise provided in this paragraph (b)(1), an asset is a U.S. asset for purposes of this section to the extent that it is a U.S. asset under § 1.884-1(d). For purposes of this section, the term *determination date*, as used in § 1.884-1(d), means each day for which the total value of U.S. assets is computed under paragraph (b)(3) of this section.

(ii) *Items excluded from the definition of U.S. asset*.—For purposes of this section, the term *U.S. asset* excludes an asset to the extent it produces income or gain described in sections 883(a)(3) and (b).

(iii) *Items included in the definition of U.S. asset*.—For purposes of this section, the term *U.S. asset* includes—

(A) U.S. real property held in a whollyo-wned domestic subsidiary of a foreign corporation that qualifies as a bank under section 585(a)(2)(B) (without regard to the second sentence thereof), provided that the real property would qualify as used in the foreign corporation's trade or business within the meaning of § 1.864-4(c)(2) or (3) if held directly by the foreign corporation and either was initially acquired through foreclosure or similar proceedings or is U.S. real property occupied by the foreign corporation (the value of which shall be adjusted by the amount of any indebtedness that is reflected in the value of the property);

(B) An asset that produces income treated as ECI under section 921(d) or 926(b) (relating to certain income of a FSC and certain dividends paid by a FSC to a foreign corporation);

(C) An asset that produces income treated as ECI under section 953(c)(3)(C) (relating to certain income of a captive insurance company that a corporation elects to treat as ECI) that is not otherwise ECI; and

(D) An asset that produces income treated as ECI under section 882(e) (relating to certain interest income of possessions banks).

(iv) *Interbranch transactions.*—A transaction of any type between separate offices or branches of the same taxpayer does not create a U.S. asset.

(v) *Assets acquired to increase U.S. assets artificially.*—An asset shall not be treated as a U.S. asset if one of the principal purposes for acquiring or using that asset is to increase artificially the U.S. assets of a foreign corporation on the determination date. Whether an asset is acquired or used for such purpose will depend upon all the facts and circumstances of each case. Factors to be considered in determining whether one of the principal purposes in acquiring or using an asset is to increase artificially the U.S. assets of a foreign corporation include the length of time during which the asset was used in a U.S. trade or business, whether the asset was acquired from a related person, and whether the aggregate value of the U.S. assets of the foreign corporation increased temporarily on or around the determination date. A purpose may be a principal purpose even though it is outweighed by other purposes (taken together or separately).

(2) *Determination of the value of a U.S. asset.*—(i) *General rule.*— The value of a U.S. asset is the adjusted basis of the asset for determining gain or loss from the sale or other disposition of that item, further adjusted as provided in paragraph (b)(2)(iii) of this section.

(ii) *Fair-market value election.*—(A) *In general.*—*(1) Fair market value conformity requirement.*—A taxpayer may elect to value all of its U.S. assets on the basis of fair market value, subject to the requirements of § 1.861-9T(g)(1)(iii), and provided the taxpayer is eligible and uses the actual ratio method under paragraph (c)(2) of this section and the methodology prescribed in § 1.861-9T(h). Once elected, the fair market value must be used by the taxpayer for both Step 1 and Step 2 described in paragraphs (b) and (c) of this section, and must be used in all subsequent taxable years unless the Commissioner or his delegate consents to a change.

(2) Conforming election requirement.—Taxpayers that as of the effective date of this paragraph (b)(2)(ii)(A)(2) have elected and currently use both the fair market value method for purposes of paragraph (b) of this section and a fixed ratio for purposes of paragraph (c)(4) of this section must conform either the adjusted basis or fair market value methods in Step 1 and Step 2 of the allocation formula by making an adjusted basis election for paragraph (b) of this section purposes while continuing the fixed ratio for Step 2, or by making an actual ratio election under paragraph (c)(2) of this section while remaining on the fair market value method under paragraph (b) of this section. Taxpayers who elect to conform Step 1 and Step 2 of the formula to the adjusted basis method must remain on both methods for the minimum five-year period in accordance with the provisions of paragraph (a)(7) of this section. Taxpayers that elect to conform Step 1 and Step 2 of the formula to the fair market value method must remain on the actual ratio method until the consent of the Commissioner or his delegate is obtained to switch to the adjusted basis method. If consent to use the adjusted basis method in Step 1 is granted in a later year, the taxpayer must remain on the actual ratio method for the minimum five-year period unless consent to use the fixed ratio is independently obtained under the requirements of paragraph (a)(7) of this section. For the first taxable year for which an original income tax return is due (including extensions) after August 17, 2006, taxpayers that are required to make a conforming election under this paragraph (b)(2)(ii)(A)(2), may do so on an original timely filed return. If a conforming election is not made within the timeframe provided in this paragraph, the Director of Field Operations or his delegate may make the conforming elections in accordance with the provisions of paragraph (a)(7)(ii) of this section.

(B) *Adjustment to partnership basis.*—If a partner makes a fair market value election under paragraph (b)(2)(ii) of this section, the value of the partner's interest in a partnership that is treated as an asset shall be the fair market value of his partnership interest, increased by the fair market value of the partner's share of the liabilities determined under paragraph (c)(2)(vi) of this section. See § 1.884-1(d)(3).

(iii) *Reduction of total value of U.S. assets by amount of bad debt reserves under section 585.*—(A) *In general.*—The total value of loans that qualify as U.S. assets shall be reduced by the amount of any reserve for bad debts additions to which are allowed as deductions under section 585.

(B) *Example.*—The following example illustrates the provisions of paragraph (b)(2)(iii)(A) of this section:

Example. Foreign banks; bad debt reserves. FC is a foreign corporation that qualifies as a bank under section 585(a)(2)(B) (without regard to the second sentence thereof), but is not a large bank as defined in section 585(c)(2). *FC* conducts business through a branch, *B*, in the United States. Among *B*'s U.S. assets are a portfolio of loans with an adjusted basis of $500. *FC* accounts for its bad debts for U.S. federal income tax purposes under the reserve method, and *B* maintains a deductible reserve for bad debts of $50. Under paragraph (b)(2)(iii) of this section, the total value of *FC*'s portfolio of loans is $450 ($500 $50).

(3) *Computation of total value of U.S. assets.*—(i) *General rule.*— The total value of U.S. assets for the taxable year is the average of the sums of the values (determined under paragraph (b)(2) of this section) of U.S. assets. For each U.S. asset, value shall be computed at the most frequent regular intervals for which data are reasonably available. In no event shall the value of any U.S. asset be computed less frequently than monthly (beginning of taxable year and monthly thereafter) by a large bank (as defined in section 585(c)(2)) or a dealer in securities (within the meaning of section 475) and semi-annually (beginning, middle and end of taxable year) by any other taxpayer.

(ii) *Adjustment to basis of financial instruments.*—For purposes of determining the total average value of U.S. assets in this paragraph (b)(3), the value of a security or contract that is marked to market pursuant to section 475 or section 1256 shall be determined as if each determination date is the most frequent regular interval for which data are reasonably available that reflects the taxpayer's consistent business practices for reflecting mark-to-market valuations on its books and records.

(c) *Step 2: Determination of total amount of U.S.-connected liabilities for the taxable year.*—(1) *General rule.*—The amount of U.S.-connected liabilities for the taxable year equals the total value of U.S. assets for the taxable year (as determined under paragraph (b)(3) of this section) multiplied by the actual ratio for the taxable year (as determined under paragraph (c)(2) of this section) or, if the taxpayer has made an election in accordance with paragraph (c)(4) of this section, by the fixed ratio.

(2) *Computation of the actual ratio.*—(i) *In general.*—A taxpayer's actual ratio for the taxable year is the total amount of its worldwide liabilities for the taxable year divided by the total value of its worldwide assets for the taxable year. The total amount of worldwide liabilities and the total value of worldwide assets for the taxable year is the average of the sums of the amounts of the taxpayer's worldwide liabilities and the values of its worldwide assets (determined under paragraphs (c)(2)(iii) and (iv) of this section). In each case, the sums must be computed semi-annually (beginning, middle and end of taxable year) by a large bank (as defined in section 585(c)(2)) and annually (beginning and end of taxable year) by any other taxpayer.

(ii) *Classification of items.*—The classification of an item as a liability or an asset must be consistent from year to year and in accordance with U.S. tax principles.

(iii) *Determination of amount of worldwide liabilities.*—The amount of a liability must be determined consistently from year to year and must be substantially in accordance with U.S. tax principles. To be substantially in accordance with U.S. tax principles, the principles used to determine the amount of a liability must not differ from U.S. tax principles to a degree that will materially affect the value of taxpayer's worldwide liabilities or the taxpayer's actual ratio.

(iv) *Determination of value of worldwide assets*.—The value of an asset must be determined consistently from year to year and must be substantially in accordance with U.S. tax principles. To be substantially in accordance with U.S. tax principles, the principles used to determine the value of an asset must not differ from U.S. tax principles to a degree that will materially affect the value of the taxpayer's worldwide assets or the taxpayer's actual ratio. The value of an asset is the adjusted basis of that asset for determining the gain or loss from the sale or other disposition of that asset, adjusted in the same manner as the basis of U.S. assets are adjusted under paragraphs (b)(2) (ii) through (iv) of this section. The rules of paragraph (b)(3) of this section apply in determining the total value of applicable worldwide assets for the taxable year, except that the minimum number of determination dates are those stated in paragraph (c)(2)(i) of this section.

(v) *Hedging transactions*.—[Reserved]

(vi) *Treatment of partnership interests and liabilities*.—For purposes of computing the actual ratio, the value of a partner's interest in a partnership that will be treated as an asset is the partner's adjusted basis in its partnership interest, reduced by the partner's share of liabilities of the partnership as determined under section 752 and increased by the partner's share of liabilities determined under this paragraph (c)(2)(vi). If the partner has made a fair market value election under paragraph (b)(2)(ii) of this section, the value of its interest in the partnership shall be increased by the fair market value of the partner's share of the liabilities determined under this paragraph (c)(2)(vi). For purposes of this section a partner shares in any liability of a partnership in the same proportion that it shares, for income tax purposes, in the expense attributable to that liability for the taxable year. A partner's adjusted basis in a partnership interest cannot be less than zero.

(vii) *Computation of actual ratio of insurance companies*.—[Reserved]

(viii) *Interbranch transactions*.—A transaction of any type between separate offices or branches of the same taxpayer does not create an asset or a liability.

(ix) *Amounts must be expressed in a single currency*.—The actual ratio must be computed in either U.S. dollars or the functional currency of the home office of the taxpayer, and that currency must be used consistently from year to year. For example, a taxpayer that determines the actual ratio annually using British pounds converted at the spot rate for financial reporting purposes must translate the U.S. dollar values of assets and amounts of liabilities of the U.S. trade or business into pounds using the spot rate on the last day of its taxable year. The district director or the Assistant Commissioner (International) may require that the actual ratio be computed in dollars if the functional currency of the taxpayer's home office is a hyperinflationary currency, as defined in §1.985-1, that materially distorts the actual ratio.

(3) *Adjustments*.—The district director or the Assistant Commissioner (International) may make appropriate adjustments to prevent a foreign corporation from intentionally and artificially increasing its actual ratio. For example, the district director or the Assistant Commissioner (International) may offset a loan made from or to one person with a loan made to or from another person if any of the parties to the loans are related persons, within the meaning of section 267(b) or 707(b)(1), and one of the principal purposes for entering into the loans was to increase artificially the actual ratio of a foreign corporation. A purpose may be a principal purpose even though it is outweighed by other purposes (taken together or separately).

(4) *Elective fixed ratio method of determining U.S. liabilities*.—A taxpayer that is a bank as defined in section 585(a)(2)(B) (without regard to the second sentence thereof or whether any such activities are effectively connected with a trade or business within the United States) may elect to use a fixed ratio of 95 percent in lieu of the actual ratio. A taxpayer that is neither a bank nor an insurance company may elect to use a fixed ratio of 50 percent in lieu of the actual ratio.

(5) *Examples*.—The following examples illustrate the application of paragraph (c) of this section:

Example 1. Classification of item not in accordance with U.S. tax principles. Bank Z, a resident of country X, has a branch in the United States through which it conducts its banking business. In preparing its financial statements in country X, Z treats an instrument documented as perpetual subordinated debt as a liability. Under U.S. tax principles, however, this instrument is treated as equity. Consequently, the classification of this instrument as a liability for purposes of paragraph (c)(2)(iii) of this section is not in accordance with U.S. tax principles.

Example 2. Valuation of item not substantially in accordance with U.S. tax principles. Bank Z, a resident of country X, has a branch in the United States through which it conducts its banking business. Bank Z is a large bank as defined in section 585(c)(2). The tax rules of country X allow Bank Z to take deductions for additions to certain reserves. Bank Z decreases the value of the assets on its financial statements by the amounts of the reserves. The additions to the reserves under country X tax rules cause the value of Bank Z's assets to differ from the value of those assets determined under U.S. tax principles to a degree that materially affects the value of taxpayer's worldwide assets. Consequently, the valuation of Bank Z's worldwide assets under country X tax principles is not substantially in accordance with U.S. tax principles. Bank Z must increase the value of its worldwide assets under paragraph (c)(2)(iii) of this section by the amount of its country X reserves.

Example 3. Valuation of item substantially in accordance with U.S. tax principles. Bank Z, a resident of country X, has a branch in the United States through which it conducts its banking business. In determining the value of its worldwide assets, Bank Z computes the adjusted basis of certain non-U.S. assets according to the depreciation methodology provided under country X tax laws, which is different than the depreciation methodology provided under U.S. tax law. If the depreciation methodology provided under country X tax laws does not differ from U.S. tax principles to a degree that materially affects the value of Bank Z's worldwide assets or Bank Z's actual ratio as computed under paragraph (c)(2) of this section, then the valuation of Bank Z's worldwide assets under paragraph (c)(2)(iv) of this section is substantially in accordance with U.S. tax principles.

Example 4. [Reserved]

Example 5. Adjustments. *FC* is a foreign corporation engaged in the active conduct of a banking business through a branch, *B*, in the United States. *P*, an unrelated foreign corporation, deposits $100,000 in the home office of *FC*. Shortly thereafter, in a transaction arranged by the home office of *FC*, *B* lends $80,000 bearing interest at an arm's length rate to *S*, a wholly owned U.S. subsidiary of *P*. The district director or the Assistant Commissioner (International) determines that one of the principal purposes for making and incurring such loans is to increase *FC*'s actual ratio. For purposes of this section, therefore, *P* is treated as having directly lent $80,000 to *S*. Thus, for purposes of paragraph (c) of this section (Step 2), the district director or the Assistant Commissioner (International) may offset *FC*'s liability and asset arising from this transaction, resulting in a net liability of $20,000 that is not a booked liability of *B*. Because the loan to *S* from *B* was initiated and arranged by the home office of *FC*, with no material participation by *B*, the loan to *S* will not be treated as a U.S. asset.

(d) *Step 3: Determination of amount of interest expense allocable to ECI under the adjusted U.S. booked liabilities method*.—(1) *General rule*.—The adjustment to the amount of interest expense paid or accrued on U.S. booked liabilities is determined by comparing the amount of U.S.-connected liabilities for the taxable year, as determined under paragraph (c) of this section, with the average total amount of U.S. booked liabilities, as determined under paragraphs (d)(2) and (3) of this section. If the average total amount of U.S. booked liabilities equals or exceeds the amount of U.S.-connected liabilities, the adjustment to the interest expense on U.S. booked liabilities is determined under paragraph (d)(4) of this section. If the amount of U.S.-connected liabilities exceeds the average total amount of U.S. booked liabilities, the adjustment to the amount of interest expense paid or accrued on U.S. booked liabilities is determined under paragraph (d)(5) of this section.

(2) *U.S. booked liabilities*.—(i) *In general*.—A liability is a *U.S. booked liability* if it is properly reflected on the books of the U.S. trade or business, within the meaning of paragraph (d)(2)(ii) or (iii) of this section.

(ii) *Properly reflected on the books of the U.S. trade or business of a foreign corporation that is not a bank*.—(A) *In general*.—A liability, whether interest bearing or non-interest bearing, is properly reflected on the books of the U.S. trade or business of a foreign corporation that is not a bank as described in section 585(a)(2)(B) (without regard to the second sentence thereof) if—

(1) The liability is secured predominantly by a U.S. asset of the foreign corporation;

(2) The foreign corporation enters the liability on a set of books reasonably contemporaneously with the time at which the liability is incurred and the liability relates to an activity that produces ECI.

(3) The foreign corporation maintains a set of books and records relating to an activity that produces ECI and the Director of Field Operations determines that there is a direct connection or relationship between the liability and that activity. Whether there is a direct connection between the liability and an activity that produces ECI depends on the facts and circumstances of each case.

(B) *Identified liabilities not properly reflected.*—A liability is not properly reflected on the books of the U.S. trade or business merely because a foreign corporation identifies the liability pursuant to § 1.884-4(b)(1)(ii) and (b)(3).

(iii) *Properly reflected on the books of the U.S. trade or business of a foreign corporation that is a bank.*—(A) *In general.*—A liability, whether interest bearing or non-interest bearing, is properly reflected on the books of the U.S. trade or business of a foreign corporation that is a bank as described in section 585(a)(2)(B) (without regard to the second sentence thereof) if—

(1) The bank enters the liability on a set of books before the close of the day on which the liability is incurred, and the liability relates to an activity that produces ECI; and

(2) There is a direct connection or relationship between the liability and that activity. Whether there is a direct connection between the liability and an activity that produces ECI depends on the facts and circumstances of each case. For example, a liability that is used to fund an interbranch or other asset that produces non-ECI may have a direct connection to an ECI producing activity and may constitute a U.S.-booked liability if both the interbranch or non-ECI activity is the same type of activity in which ECI assets are also reflected on the set of books (for example, lending or money market interbank placements), and such ECI activities are not de minimis. Such U.S. booked liabilities may still be subject to paragraph (d)(2)(v) of this section.

(B) *Inadvertent error.*—If a bank fails to enter a liability in the books of the activity that produces ECI before the close of the day on which the liability was incurred, the liability may be treated as a U.S. booked liability only if, under the facts and circumstances, the taxpayer demonstrates a direct connection or relationship between the liability and the activity that produces ECI and the failure to enter the liability in those books was due to inadvertent error.

(iv) *Liabilities of insurance companies.*—[Reserved]

(v) *Liabilities used to increase artificially interest expense on U.S. booked liabilities.*—U.S. booked liabilities shall not include a liability if one of the principal purposes for incurring or holding the liability is to increase artificially the interest expense on the U.S. booked liabilities of a foreign corporation. Whether a liability is incurred or held for the purpose of artificially increasing interest expense will depend upon all the facts and circumstances of each case. Factors to be considered in determining whether one of the principal purposes for incurring or holding a liability is to increase artificially the interest expense on U.S. booked liabilities of a foreign corporation include whether the interest expense on the liability is excessive when compared to other liabilities of the foreign corporation denominated in the same currency and whether the currency denomination of the liabilities of the U.S. branch substantially matches the currency denomination of the U.S. branch's assets. A purpose may be a principal purpose even though it is outweighed by other purposes (taken together or separately).

(vi) *Hedging transactions.*—[Reserved]

(vii) *Amount of U.S. booked liabilities of a partner.*—A partner's share of liabilities of a partnership is considered a booked liability of the partner provided that it is properly reflected on the books (within the meaning of paragraph (d)(2)(ii) of this section) of the U.S. trade or business of the partnership.

(viii) *Interbranch transactions.*—A transaction of any type between separate offices or branches of the same taxpayer does not result in the creation of a liability.

(3) *Average total amount of U.S. booked liabilities.*—The *average total amount* of U.S. booked liabilities for the taxable year is the average of the sums of the amounts (determined under paragraph (d)(2) of this section) of U.S. booked liabilities. The amount of U.S. booked liabilities shall be computed at the most frequent, regular intervals for which data are reasonably available. In no event shall the amount of U.S. booked liabilities be computed less frequently than monthly by a large bank (as defined in section 585(c)(2)) and semi-annually by any other taxpayer.

(4) *Interest expense where U.S. booked liabilities equal or exceed U.S. liabilities.*—(i) *In general.*—If the average total amount of U.S. booked liabilities (as determined in paragraphs (d)(2) and (3) of this section) exceeds the amount of U.S.-connected liabilities (as determined under paragraph (c) of this section (Step 2)), the interest expense allocable to ECI is the product of the total amount of interest paid or accrued within the taxable year by the U.S. trade or business on U.S. booked liabilities and the scaling ratio set out in paragraph (d)(4)(ii) of this section. For purposes of this section, the reduction resulting from the application of the scaling ratio is applied pro-rata to all interest expense paid or accrued by the foreign corporation. A similar reduction in income, expense, gain, or loss from a hedging transaction (as described in paragraph (d)(2)(vi) of this section) must also be determined by multiplying such income, expense, gain, or loss by the scaling ratio. If the average total amount of U.S. booked liabilities (as determined in paragraph (d)(3) of this section) equals the amount of U.S.-connected liabilities (as determined under *Step 2*), the interest expense allocable to ECI is the total amount of interest paid or accrued within the taxable year by the U.S. trade or business on U.S. booked liabilities.

(ii) *Scaling ratio.*—For purposes of this section, the scaling ratio is a fraction the numerator of which is the amount of U.S.-connected liabilities and the denominator of which is the average total amount of U.S. booked liabilities.

(iii) *Special rules for insurance companies.*—[Reserved]

(5) *U.S.-connected interest rate where U.S. booked liabilities are less than U.S.-connected liabilities.*—(i) *In general.*—If the amount of U.S.-connected liabilities (as determined under paragraph (c) of this section (Step 2)) exceeds the average total amount of U.S. booked liabilities, the interest expense allocable to ECI is the total amount of interest paid or accrued within the taxable year by the U.S. trade or business on U.S. booked liabilities, plus the excess of the amount of U.S.-connected liabilities over the average total amount of U.S. booked liabilities multiplied by the interest rate determined under paragraph (d)(5)(ii) of this section.

(ii) *Interest rate on excess U.S.-connected liabilities.*—(A) *General rule.*—The applicable interest rate on excess U.S.-connected liabilities is determined by dividing the total interest expense paid or accrued for the taxable year on U.S.-dollar liabilities that are not U.S.-booked liabilities (as defined in paragraph (d)(2) of this section) and that are shown on the books of the offices or branches of the foreign corporation outside the United States by the average U.S.-dollar denominated liabilities (whether interest-bearing or not) that are not U.S.-booked liabilities and that are shown on the books of the offices or branches of the foreign corporation outside the United States for the taxable year.

(B) *Annual published rate election.*—For each taxable year beginning with the first year end for which the original tax return due date (including extensions) is after August 17, 2006, in which a taxpayer is a bank within the meaning of section 585(a)(2)(B) (without regard to the second sentence thereof or whether any such activities are effectively connected with a trade or business within the United States), such taxpayer may elect to compute its excess interest by reference to a published average 30-day London Interbank Offering Rate (LIBOR) for the year. The election may be made for any eligible year by indicating the rate used on Schedule I (Form 1120-F) attached to the timely filed return. Once selected, the rate may not be changed by the taxpayer. If a taxpayer that is eligible to make the 30-day LIBOR election either does not file a timely return or files a calculation that allocates interest expense under the scaling ratio in paragraph (d)(4) of this section and it is determined by the Director of Field Operations that the taxpayer's U.S.-connected liabilities exceed its U.S.-booked liabilities, then the Director of Field Operations, and not the taxpayer, may choose whether to determine the taxpayer's excess interest rate under paragraph (d)(5)(ii)(A) or (B) of this section and may select the published 30-day LIBOR rate.

(6) *Examples.*—The following examples illustrate the rules of this section:

Example 1. Computation of interest expense; actual ratio—(i) *Facts.* (A) *FC* is a foreign corporation that is not a bank and that actively conducts a real estate business through a branch, *B*, in the United States. For the taxable year, *FC*'s balance sheet and income statement is as follows (assume amounts are in U.S. dollars and computed in accordance with paragraphs (b)(2) and (b)(3) of this section):

	Value
Asset 1	$2,000
Asset 2	$2,500
Asset 3	$5,500

	Amount	*Interest Expense*
Liability 1	$800	56
Liability 2	$3,200	256
Capital	$6,000	0

(B) Asset 1 is the stock of *FC*'s wholly-owned domestic subsidiary that is also actively engaged in the real estate business. Asset 2 is a building in the United States producing rental income that is entirely ECI to *FC*. Asset 3 is a building in the home country of *FC* that produces rental income. Liabilities 1 and 2 are loans that bear interest at the rates of 7% and 8%, respectively. Liability 1 is a booked liability of B, and Liability 2 is booked in *FC*'s home country. Assume that *FC* has not elected to use the fixed ratio in Step 2.

(ii) *Step 1.* Under paragraph (b)(1) of this section, Assets 1 and 3 are not U.S. assets, while Asset 2 qualifies as a U.S. asset. Thus, under paragraph (b)(3) of this section, the total value of U.S. assets for the taxable year is $2,500, the value of Asset 2.

(iii) *Step 2.* Under paragraph (c)(1) of this section, the amount of *FC*'s U.S.-connected liabilities for the taxable year is determined by multiplying $2,500 (the value of U.S. assets determined under Step 1) by the actual ratio for the taxable year. The actual ratio is the average amount of *FC*'s worldwide liabilities divided by the average value of *FC*'s worldwide assets. The amount of Liability 1 is $800, and the amount of Liability 2 is $3,200. Thus, the numerator of the actual ratio is $4,000. The average value of worldwide assets is $10,000 (Asset 1 + Asset 2 + Asset 3). The actual ratio, therefore, is 40% ($4,000/$10,000), and the amount of U.S.-connected liabilities for the taxable year is $1,000 ($2,500 U.S. assets × 40%).

(iv) *Step 3.* Because the amount of *FC*'s U.S.-connected liabilities ($1,000) exceeds the average total amount of U.S. booked liabilities of *B* ($800), *FC* determines its interest expense in accordance with paragraph (d)(5) of this section by adding the interest paid or accrued on U.S. booked liabilities, and the interest expense associated with the excess of its U.S.-connected liabilities over its average total amount of U.S. booked liabilities. Under paragraph (d)(5)(ii) of this section, *FC* determines the interest rate attributable to its excess U.S.-connected liabilities by dividing the interest expense paid or accrued by the average amount of U.S.-dollar denominated liabilities, which produces an interest rate of 8% ($256/$3200). Therefore, *FC*'s allocable interest expense is $72 ($56 of interest expense from U.S. booked liabilities plus $16 ($200 × 8%) of interest expense attributable to its excess U.S.-connected liabilities).

Example 2. Computation of interest expense; fixed ratio—(i) The facts are the same as in *Example 1*, except that *FC* makes a fixed ratio election under paragraph (c)(4) of this section. The conclusions under Step 1 are the same as in *Example 1*.

(ii) *Step 2.* Under paragraph (c)(1) of this section, the amount of U.S.-connected liabilities for the taxable year is determined by multiplying $2,500 (the value of U.S. assets determined under Step 1) by the fixed ratio for the taxable year, which, under paragraph (c)(4) of this section is 50 percent. Thus, the amount of U.S.-connected liabilities for the taxable year is $1,250 ($2,500 U.S. assets × 50%).

(iii) *Step 3.* As in *Example 1*, the amount of *FC*'s U.S.-connected liabilities exceed the average total amount of U.S. booked liabilities of *B*, requiring *FC* to determine its interest expense under paragraph (d)(5) of this section. In this case, however, *FC* has excess U.S.-connected liabilities of $450 ($1,250 of U.S.-connected liabilities $800 U.S. booked liabilities). *FC* therefore has allocable interest expense of $92 ($56 of interest expense from U.S. booked liabilities plus $36 ($450 × 8%) of interest expense attributable to its excess U.S.-connected liabilities).

Example 3. Scaling ratio.—(i) *Facts.* Bank Z, a resident of country *X*, has a branch in the United States through which it conducts its banking business. For the taxable year, *Z* has U.S.-connected liabilities, determined under paragraph (c) of this section, equal to $300. *Z*, however, has U.S. booked liabilities of $300 and *U* 500. Therefore, assuming an exchange rate of the *U* to the U.S. dollar of 5:1, Z has U.S. booked liabilities of $400 ($300 + (*U* 500 ÷5)).

(ii) *U.S.-connected liabilities.* Because *Z*'s U.S. booked liabilities of $400 exceed its U.S.-connected liabilities by $100, all of *Z*'s interest expense allocable to its U.S. trade or business must be scaled back pro-rata. To determine the scaling ratio, Z divides its U.S.-connected liabilities by its U.S. booked liabilities, as required by paragraph (d)(4) of this section. *Z*'s interest expense is scaled back pro rata by the resulting ratio of 3/4 ($300 ÷ $400). *Z*'s income, expense, gain or loss from hedging transactions described in paragraph (d)(2)(vi) of this section must be similarly reduced.

Example 4. [Reserved]

Example 5. U.S. booked liabilities - direct relationship. (i) *Facts.* Bank A, a resident of Country X maintains a banking office in the U.S. that records transactions on three sets of books for State A, an International Banking Facility (IBF) for its bank regulatory approved international transactions, and a shell branch licensed operation in Country C. Bank A records substantial ECI assets from its bank lending and placement activities and a mix of interbranch and non-ECI producing assets from the same or similar activities on the books of State A branch and on its IBF. Bank A's Country C branch borrows substantially from third parties, as well as from its home office, and lends all of its funding to its State A branch and IBF to fund the mix of ECI, interbranch and non-ECI activities on those two books. The consolidated books of State A branch and IBF indicate that a substantial amount of the total book assets constitute U.S. assets under paragraph (b) of this section. Some of the third-party borrowings on the books of the State A branch are used to lend directly to Bank A's home office in Country X. These borrowings reflect the average borrowing rate of the State A branch, IBF and Country C branches as a whole. All third-party borrowings reflected on the books of State A branch, the IBF and Country C branch were recorded on such books before the close of business on the day the liabilities were acquired by Bank A.

(ii) *U.S. booked liabilities.* The facts demonstrate that the separate State A branch, IBF and Country C branch books taken together, constitute a set of books within the meaning of paragraph (d)(2)(iii)(A)(1) of this section. Such set of books as a whole has a direct relationship to an ECI activity under paragraph (d)(2)(iii)(A)(2) of this section even though the Country C branch books standing alone would not. The third-party liabilities recorded on the books of Country C constitute U.S. booked liabilities because they were timely recorded and the overall set of books on which they were reflected has a direct relationship to a bank lending and interbank placement ECI producing activity. The third-party liabilities that were recorded on the books of State A branch that were used to lend funds to Bank A's home office also constitute U.S. booked liabilities because the interbranch activity the funds were used for is a lending activity of a type that also gives rise to a substantial amount of ECI that is properly reflected on the same set of books as the interbranch loans. Accordingly, the liabilities are not traced to their specific interbranch use but to the overall activity of bank lending and interbank placements which gives rise to substantial ECI. The facts show that the liabilities were not acquired to increase artificially the interest expense of Bank A's U.S. booked liabilities as a whole under paragraph (d)(2)(v) of this section. The third-party liabilities also constitute U.S. booked liabilities for purposes of determining Bank A's branch interest under § 1.884-4(b)(1)(i)(A) regardless of whether Bank A uses the Adjusted U.S. booked liability method, or the Separate Currency Pool method to allocate its interest expense under paragraph 5(e) of this section.

(e) *Separate currency pools method.*—(1) *General rule.*—If a foreign corporation elects to use the method in this paragraph, its total interest expense allocable to ECI is the sum of the separate interest deductions for each of the currencies in which the foreign corporation has U.S. assets. The separate interest deductions are determined under the following three-step process.

(i) *Determine the value of U.S. assets in each currency pool.*—First, the foreign corporation must determine the amount of its U.S. assets, using the methodology in paragraph (b) of this section, in each currency pool. The foreign corporation may convert into U.S. dollars any currency pool in which the foreign corporation holds less than 3% of its U.S. assets. A transaction (or transactions) that hedges a U.S. asset shall be taken into account for purposes of determining the currency denomination and the value of the U.S. asset.

(ii) *Determine the U.S.-connected liabilities in each currency pool.*—Second, the foreign corporation must determine the amount of its U.S.-connected liabilities in each currency pool by multiplying the amount of U.S. assets (as determined under paragraph (b)(3) of this section) in the currency pool by the foreign corporation's actual ratio (as determined under paragraph (c)(2) of this section) for the taxable year or, if the taxpayer has made an election in accordance with paragraph (c)(4) of this section, by the fixed ratio.

(iii) *Determine the interest expense attributable to each currency pool.*—Third, the foreign corporation must determine the interest expense attributable to each currency pool by multiplying the U.S.-connected liabilities in each currency pool by the prescribed interest rate as defined in paragraph (e)(2) of this section.

(2) *Prescribed interest rate.*—For each currency pool, the prescribed interest rate is determined by dividing the total interest expense that is paid or accrued for the taxable year with respect to the foreign corporation's worldwide liabilities denominated in that currency, by the foreign corporation's average worldwide liabilities (whether interest bearing or not) denominated in that currency. The interest expense and liabilities are to be stated in that currency.

(3) *Hedging transactions.*—[Reserved]

(4) *Election not available if excessive hyperinflationary assets.*—The election to use the separate currency pools method of this paragraph (e) is not available if the value of the foreign corporation's U.S. assets denominated in a hyperinflationary currency, as defined in § 1.985-1, exceeds ten percent of the value of the foreign corporation's total U.S. assets. If a foreign corporation made a valid election to use the separate currency pools method in a prior year but no longer qualifies to use such method pursuant to this paragraph (e)(4), the taxpayer must use the method provided by paragraphs (b) through (d) of this section.

(5) *Examples.*—The separate currency pools method of this paragraph (e) is illustrated by the following examples:

Example 1. Separate currency pools method—(i) *Facts.* (A) Bank Z, a resident of country *X*, has a branch in the United States through which it conducts its banking business. For its 1997 taxable year, Z has U.S. assets, as defined in paragraph (b) of this section, that are denominated in U.S. dollars and in *U*, the country *X* currency. Accordingly, Z's U.S. assets are as follows:

	Average Value
U.S. Dollar Assets	$20,000
U Assets	*U* 5,000

(B) Z's worldwide liabilities are also denominated in U.S. Dollars and in *U*. The average interest rates on Z's worldwide liabilities, including those in the United States, are 6% on its U.S. dollar liabilities, and 12% on its liabilities denominated in *U*. Assume that Z has properly elected to use its actual ratio of 95% to determine its U.S.-connected liabilities in Step 2, and has also properly elected to use the separate currency pools method provided in paragraph (e) of this section.

(ii) *Determination of interest expense.* Z determines the interest expense attributable to its U.S.-connected liabilities according to the steps described below.

(A) First, Z separates its U.S. assets into two currency pools, one denominated in U.S. dollars ($20,000) and the other denominated in *U* (*U* 5,000).

(B) Second, Z multiplies each pool of assets by the applicable ratio of worldwide liabilities to assets, which in this case is 95%. Thus, Z has U.S.-connected liabilities of $19,000 ($20,000 × 95%), and *U* 4750 (*U* 5000 × 95%).

(C) Third, Z calculates its interest expense by multiplying each pool of its U.S.-connected liabilities by the relevant interest rates. Accordingly, Z's allocable interest expense for the year is $1140 ($19,000 × 6%), the sum of the expense associated with its U.S. dollar liabilities, plus *U* 570 (*U* 4750 × 12%), the interest expense associated with its liabilities denominated in *U*. Z must translate its interest expense denominated in *U* in accordance with the rules provided in section 988, and then must determine whether it is subject to any other provision of the Code that would disallow or defer any portion of its interest expense so determined.

Example 2. [Reserved]

(f) *Effective/applicability date.*—(1) *General rule.*—This section is applicable for taxable years ending on or after August 15, 2009. A taxpayer, however, may choose to apply § 1.882-5T, rather than applying the final regulations, for any taxable year beginning on or after August 16, 2008 but before August 15, 2009.

(2) *Special rules for financial products.*—[Reserved] [Reg. § 1.882-5.]

☐ [*T.D. 7749, 12-30-80. Amended by T.D. 7939, 2-2-84; T.D. 8658, 3-5-96; T.D. 9281, 8-15-2006 (corrected 9-27-2006) and T.D. 9465, 9-25-2009.*]

Proposed Amendments to Regulation

§ 1.882-5. Determination of interest deduction.—(a) * * *

(7) * * *

(i) * * * An elected method (other than the fair market value method under paragraph (b)(2)(ii) of this section, or the published rate election in paragraph (d)(5)(ii) of this section) must be used for a minimum period of five years before the taxpayer may elect a different method. * * *

* * *

(d) * * *

(5) * * *

(ii) * * *

(B) *Published rate election.*—For each taxable year in which a taxpayer is a bank within the meaning of section 585(a)(2)(B) (without regard to the second sentence thereof or whether any activities are effectively connected with a trade or business within the United States), the taxpayer may elect to compute the interest expense attributable to excess U.S.-connected liabilities by using the yearly average Secured Overnight Financing Rate (SOFR) published by the Federal Bank of New York for the taxable year rather than the interest rate provided in paragraph (d)(5)(ii)(A) of this section. A taxpayer may elect to apply the rate provided in paragraph (d)(5)(ii)(A) of this section or in this paragraph (d)(5)(ii)(B) on an annual basis and the taxpayer does not need the consent of the Commissioner to change this election in a subsequent taxable year. If a taxpayer that is eligible to make the published rate election either does not file a timely return or files a calculation with no excess U.S.-connected liabilities and it is later determined by the Director of Field Operations that the taxpayer has excess U.S.- connected liabilities, then the Director of Field Operations, and not the taxpayer, may choose whether to apply the interest rate provided under either paragraph (d)(5)(ii)(A) or (B) of this section to the taxpayer's excess U.S.-connected liabilities in determining interest expense.

* * *

(f) * * *—

(1) *General rule.*—* * *

* * *

(3) *Applicability date for published rate election.*—Paragraph (d)(5)(ii)(B) of this section applies to taxable years ending after the date of publication of a Treasury decision adopting these rules as final regulations is published in the **Federal Register**. [Prop. Reg. § 1.882-5.]

[Proposed 10-9-2019.]

§ 1.883-1. Exclusion of income from the international operation of ships or aircraft.—(a) *General rule.*—Qualified income derived by a qualified foreign corporation from its international operation of ships or aircraft is excluded from gross income and exempt from United States Federal income tax. Paragraph (b) of this section defines the term *qualified income.* Paragraph (c) of this section defines the term *qualified foreign corporation.* Paragraph (f) of this section defines the term *international operation of ships or aircraft.*

(b) *Qualified income.*—Qualified income is income derived from the international operation of ships or aircraft that—

(1) Is properly includible in any of the income categories described in paragraph (h)(2) of this section; and

(2) Is the subject of an equivalent exemption, as defined in paragraph (h) of this section, granted by the qualified foreign country, as defined in paragraph (d) of this section, in which the foreign corporation seeking qualified foreign corporation status is organized.

(c) *Qualified foreign corporation.*—(1) *General rule.*—A qualified foreign corporation is a corporation that is organized in a qualified foreign country and considered engaged in the international operation of ships or aircraft. The term *corporation* is defined in section 7701(a)(3) and the regulations thereunder. Paragraph (d) of this section defines the term *qualified foreign country.* Paragraph (e) of this section defines the term *operation of ships or aircraft*, and paragraph (f) of this section defines the term *international operation of ships or aircraft.* To be a qualified foreign corporation, the corporation must satisfy the stock ownership test of paragraph (c)(2) of this section and satisfy the substantiation and reporting requirements described in paragraph (c)(3) of this section. A corporation may be a qualified foreign corporation with respect to one category of qualified income but not with respect to another such category. See paragraph (h)(2) of this section for a discussion of the categories of qualified income.

(2) *Stock ownership test.*—To be a qualified foreign corporation, a foreign corporation must satisfy the publicly-traded test of § 1.883-2(a), the CFC stock ownership test of § 1.883-3(a), or the qualified shareholder stock ownership test of § 1.883-4(a).

(3) *Substantiation and reporting requirements.*—(i) *General rule.*—To be a qualified foreign corporation, a foreign corporation must include the following information in its Form 1120-F, "U.S. Income Tax Return of a Foreign Corporation," in the manner prescribed by such form and its accompanying instructions—

(A) The corporation's name and address (including mailing code);

(B) The corporation's U.S. taxpayer identification number;

(C) The foreign country in which the corporation is organized;

(D) The applicable authority for an equivalent exemption, for example, the citation of a statute in the country where the corporation is organized, a diplomatic note between the United States and such country, or an income tax convention between the United States and such country in the case of a corporation described in paragraphs (h)(3)(i), (ii) and (iii) of this section;

(E) The category or categories of qualified income for which an exemption is being claimed;

(F) A reasonable estimate of the gross amount of income in each category of qualified income for which the exemption is claimed, to the extent such amounts are readily determinable;

(G) A statement as to whether any shares of the foreign corporation or of any intermediary corporation that are relied on to satisfy any stock ownership test described in paragraph (c)(2) of this section are issued in bearer form and whether the bearer shares are maintained in a dematerialized book-entry system in which the bearer shares are represented only by book entries and no physical certificates are issued or transferred, or in an immobilized book-entry system in which evidence of ownership is maintained on the books and records of the corporate issuer or by a broker or financial institution;

(H) Any other information required under § 1.883-2(f), § 1.883-3(d), or § 1.883-4(e), as applicable; and

(I) Any other relevant information specified in Form 1120-F, "U.S. Income Tax Return of a Foreign Corporation," and its accompanying instructions.

(ii) *Further documentation.*—(A) *General rule.*—Except as provided in paragraph (c)(3)(ii)(B) of this section, if the Commissioner requests in writing that the foreign corporation provide documentation or substantiate any representations made under paragraph (c)(3)(i) of this section, or under § 1.883-2(f), § 1.883-3(d), or § 1.883-4(e), as applicable, the foreign corporation must provide the requested documentation or substantiation within 60 days of receiving the written request. If the foreign corporation does not provide the requested documentation or substantiation within the 60-day period, but demonstrates that the failure was due to reasonable cause and not willful neglect, the Commissioner may grant the foreign corporation a 30-day extension to provide the requested documentation or substantiation. Whether a failure to provide the documentation or substantiation in a timely manner was due to reasonable cause and not willful neglect shall be determined by the Commissioner based on all the facts and circumstances.

(B) *Names and permanent addresses of certain shareholders.*—If the Commissioner requests the names and permanent addresses of individual qualified shareholders of a foreign corporation, as represented on each individual's ownership statement, to substantiate the requirements of the exception to the closely-held test in the publicly-traded test in § 1.883-2(e), the qualified shareholder stock ownership test in § 1.883-4(a), or the qualified U.S. person ownership test in § 1.883-3(b), the foreign corporation must provide the requested information within 30 days of receiving the written request. If the foreign corporation does not provide the requested information within the 30-day period, but demonstrates that the failure was due to reasonable cause and not willful neglect, the Commissioner may grant the foreign corporation a 30-day extension to provide the requested information. Whether a failure to provide the requested information was due to reasonable cause and not willful neglect shall be determined by the Commissioner based on all the facts and circumstances.

(4) *Commissioner's discretion to cure defects in documentation.*—The Commissioner retains the discretion to cure any defects in the documentation where the Commissioner is satisfied that the foreign corporation would otherwise be a qualified foreign corporation.

(d) *Qualified foreign country.*—A qualified foreign country is a foreign country that grants to corporations organized in the United States an equivalent exemption, as described in paragraph (h) of this section, for the category of qualified income, as described in paragraph (h)(2) of this section, derived by the foreign corporation seeking qualified foreign corporation status. A foreign country may be a qualified foreign country with respect to one category of qualified income but not with respect to another such category.

(e) *Operation of ships or aircraft.*—(1) *General rule.*—Except as provided in paragraph (e)(2) of this section, a foreign corporation is considered engaged in the operation of ships or aircraft only during the time it is an owner or lessee of one or more entire ships or aircraft and uses such ships or aircraft in one or more of the following activities—

(i) Carriage of passengers or cargo for hire;

(ii) In the case of a ship, the leasing out of the ship under a time or voyage charter (full charter), space or slot charter, or bareboat charter, as those terms are defined in paragraph (e)(5) of this section, provided the ship is used to carry passengers or cargo for hire; and

(iii) In the case of aircraft, the leasing out of the aircraft under a wet lease (full charter), space, slot, or block-seat charter, or dry lease, as those terms are defined in paragraph (e)(5) of this section, provided the aircraft is used to carry passengers or cargo for hire.

(2) *Pool, partnership, strategic alliance, joint operating agreement, code-sharing arrangement or other joint venture.*—A foreign corporation is considered engaged in the operation of ships or aircraft within the meaning of paragraph (e)(1) of this section with respect to its participation in a pool, partnership, strategic alliance, joint operating agreement, code-sharing arrangement or other joint venture if it directly, or indirectly through one or more fiscally transparent entities under the income tax laws of the United States, as defined in paragraph (e)(5)(v) of this section—

(i) Owns an interest in a partnership, disregarded entity, or other fiscally transparent entity under the income tax laws of the United States that itself would be considered engaged in the operation of ships or aircraft under paragraph (e)(1) of this section if it were a foreign corporation; or

(ii) Participates in a pool, strategic alliance, joint operating agreement, code-sharing arrangement, or other joint venture that is not an entity, as defined in paragraph (e)(5)(iv) of this section, involving one or more activities described in paragraphs (e)(1)(i) through (iii) of this section, but only if—

(A) In the case of a direct interest, the foreign corporation is otherwise engaged in the operation of ships or aircraft under paragraph (e)(1) of this section; or

(B) In the case of an indirect interest, either the foreign corporation is otherwise engaged, or one of the fiscally transparent entities would be considered engaged if it were a foreign corporation, in the operation of ships or aircraft under paragraph (e)(1) of this section.

(3) *Activities not considered operation of ships or aircraft.*—Activities that do not constitute operation of ships or aircraft include, but are not limited to—

(i) The activities of a nonvessel operating common carrier, as defined in paragraph (e)(5)(vii) of this section;

(ii) Ship or aircraft management;

(iii) Obtaining crews for ships or aircraft operated by another party;

(iv) Acting as a ship's agent;

(v) Ship or aircraft brokering;

(vi) Freight forwarding;

(vii) The activities of travel agents and tour operators;

(viii) Rental by a container leasing company of containers and related equipment; and

(ix) The activities of a concessionaire.

(4) *Examples.*—The rules of paragraphs (e)(1) through (3) of this section are illustrated by the following examples:

Example 1. Three tiers of charters—(i) *Facts.* A, B, and C are foreign corporations. A purchases a ship. A and B enter into a bareboat charter of the ship for a term of 20 years, and B, in turn, enters into a time charter of the ship with C for a term of 5 years. Under the time charter, B is responsible for the complete operation of the ship, including providing the crew and maintenance. C uses the ship during the term of the time charter to carry its customers' freight between U.S. and foreign ports. C owns no ships.

(ii) *Analysis.* Because A is the owner of the entire ship and leases out the ship under a bareboat charter to B, and because the sublessor, C, uses the ship to carry cargo for hire, A is considered engaged in the operation of a ship under paragraph (e)(1) of this section during the term of the time charter. B leases in the entire ship from A and leases out the ship under a time charter to C, who uses the ship to carry cargo for hire. Therefore, B is considered engaged in the operation of a ship under paragraph (e)(1) of this section during the term of the time charter. C time charters the entire ship from B and uses the ship to carry its customers' freight during the term of the charter. Therefore, C is also engaged in the operation of a ship under paragraph (e)(1) of this section during the term of the time charter.

Example 2. Partnership with contributed shipping assets—(i) *Facts.* X, Y, and Z, each a foreign corporation, enter into a partnership, P. P is a fiscally transparent entity under the income tax laws of the United States, as defined in paragraph (e)(5)(v) of this section. Under the terms of the partnership agreement, each partner contributes all of the ships in its fleet to P in exchange for interests in the partnership and shares in the P profits from the international carriage of cargo. The partners share in the overall management of P, but each partner, acting in its capacity as partner, continues to crew and manage all ships previously in its fleet.

(ii) *Analysis.* P owns the ships contributed by the partners and uses these ships to carry cargo for hire. Therefore, if P were a foreign corporation, it would be considered engaged in the operation of ships within the meaning of paragraph (e)(1) of this section. Accordingly, because P is a fiscally transparent entity under the income tax laws of the United States, as defined in paragraph (e)(5)(v) of this section, X, Y, and Z are each considered engaged in the operation of ships through P, within the meaning of paragraph (e)(2)(i) of this section, with respect to their distributive share of income from P's international carriage of cargo.

Example 3. Joint venture with chartered in ships—(i) *Facts.* Foreign corporation A owns a number of foreign subsidiaries involved in various aspects of the shipping business, including S1, S2, S3, and S4. S4 is a foreign corporation that provides cruises but does not own any ships. S1, S2, and S3 are foreign corporations that own cruise ships. S1, S2, S3, and S4 form joint venture JV, in which they are all interest holders, to conduct cruises. JV is a fiscally transparent entity under the income tax laws of the United States, as defined in paragraph (e)(5)(v) of this section. Under the terms of the joint venture, S1, S2, and S3 each enter into time charter agreements with JV, pursuant to which S1, S2, and S3 retain control of the navigation and management of the individual ships, and JV will use the ships to carry passengers for hire. The overall management of the cruise line will be provided by S4.

(ii) *Analysis.* S1, S2, and S3 each owns ships and time charters those ships to JV, which uses the ships to carry passengers for hire. Accordingly, S1, S2, and S3 are each considered engaged in the operation of ships under paragraph (e)(1) of this section. JV leases in entire ships by means of the time charters, and JV uses those ships to carry passengers on cruises. Thus, JV would be engaged in the operation of ships within the meaning of paragraph (e)(1) of this section if it were a foreign corporation. Therefore, although S4 does not directly own or lease in a ship, S4 also is engaged in the operation of ships, within the meaning of paragraph (e)(2)(i) of this section, with respect to its participation in JV.

Example 4. Tiered partnerships—(i) *Facts.* Foreign corporations A, B, and C enter into a partnership, P1. P1 is one of several shareholders of Poolco, a foreign limited liability company that makes an election pursuant to § 301.7701-3 of this chapter to be treated as a partnership for U.S. tax purposes. P1 acquires several ships and time charters them out to Poolco. Poolco slot or voyage charters such ships out to third parties for use in the carriage of cargo for hire. P1 and Poolco are fiscally transparent entities under the income tax laws of the United States, as defined in paragraph (e)(5)(v) of this section.

(ii) *Analysis.* A, B, and C are considered engaged in the operation of ships under paragraph (e)(2)(i) of this section with respect to their direct interest in P1 and with respect to their indirect interest in Poolco because both P1 and Poolco are fiscally transparent entities under the income tax laws of the United States and would be considered engaged in the operation of ships under paragraph (e)(1) of this section if they were foreign corporations. The result would be the same if Poolco were a single-member disregarded entity owned solely by P1.

(5) *Definitions.*—(i) *Bareboat charter.*—A bareboat charter is a contract for the use of a ship or aircraft whereby the lessee is in complete possession, control, and command of the ship or aircraft. For example, in a bareboat charter, the lessee is responsible for the navigation and management of the ship or aircraft, the crew, supplies, repairs and maintenance, fees, insurance, charges, commissions and other expenses connected with the use of the ship or aircraft. The lessor of the ship bears none of the expense or responsibility of operation of the ship or aircraft.

(ii) *Code-sharing arrangement.*—A code-sharing arrangement is an arrangement in which one air carrier puts its identification code on the flight of another carrier. This arrangement allows the first carrier to hold itself out as providing service in markets where it does not otherwise operate or where it operates infrequently. Code-sharing arrangements can range from a very limited agreement between two carriers involving only one market to agreements involving multiple markets and alliances between or among international carriers which also include joint marketing, baggage handling, one-stop check-in service, sharing of frequent flyer awards, and other services. For rules involving the sale of code-sharing tickets, see paragraph (g)(1)(vi) of this section.

(iii) *Dry lease.*—A dry lease is the bareboat charter of an aircraft.

(iv) *Entity.*—For purposes of this paragraph (e), an entity is any person that is treated by the United States as other than an individual for U.S. Federal income tax purposes. The term includes disregarded entities.

(v) *Fiscally transparent entity under the income tax laws of the United States.*—For purposes of this paragraph (e), an entity is fiscally transparent under the income tax laws of the United States if the entity would be considered fiscally transparent under the income tax laws of the United States under the principles of § 1.894-1(d)(3).

(vi) *Full charter.*—Full charter (or full rental) means a time charter or a voyage charter of a ship or a wet lease of an aircraft but during which the full crew and management are provided by the lessor.

(vii) *Nonvessel operating common carrier.*—A nonvessel operating common carrier is an entity that does not exercise control over any part of a vessel, but holds itself out to the public as providing transportation for hire, issues bills of lading, assumes responsibility or is liable by law as a common carrier for safe transportation of shipments, and arranges in its own name with other common carriers, including those engaged in the operation of ships, for the performance of such transportation.

(viii) *Space or slot charter.*—A space or slot charter is a contract for use of a certain amount of space (but less than all of the space) on a ship or aircraft, and may be on a time or voyage basis. When used in connection with passenger aircraft this sort of charter may be referred to as the sale of block seats.

(ix) *Time charter.*—A time charter is a contract for the use of a ship or aircraft for a specific period of time, during which the lessor of the ship or aircraft retains control of the navigation and management of the ship or aircraft (i.e., the lessor continues to be responsible for the crew, supplies, repairs and maintenance, fees and insurance, charges, commissions and other expenses connected with the use of the ship or aircraft).

(x) *Voyage charter.*—A voyage charter is a contract similar to a time charter except that the ship or aircraft is chartered for a specific voyage or flight rather than for a specific period of time.

(xi) *Wet lease.*—A wet lease is the time or voyage charter of an aircraft.

(f) *International operation of ships or aircraft.*—(1) *General rule.*—The term *international operation of ships or aircraft* means the operation of ships or aircraft, as defined in paragraph (e) of this section, with respect to the carriage of passengers or cargo on voyages or flights that begin or end in the United States, as determined under paragraph (f)(2) of this section. The term does not include the carriage of passengers or cargo on a voyage or flight that begins and ends in the United States, even if the voyage or flight contains a segment extending beyond the territorial limits of the United States, unless the passenger disembarks or the cargo is unloaded outside the United States. Operation of ships or aircraft beyond the territorial limits of the United States does not constitute in itself international operation of ships or aircraft.

(2) *Determining whether income is derived from international operation of ships or aircraft.*—Whether income is derived from international operation of ships or aircraft is determined on a passenger by passenger basis (as provided in paragraph (f)(2)(i) of this section) and on an item-of-cargo by item-of-cargo basis (as provided in paragraph (f)(2)(ii) of this section). In the case of the bareboat charter of a ship or the dry lease of an aircraft, whether the charter income for a particular period is derived from international operation of ships or aircraft is determined by reference to how the ship or aircraft is used by the lowest-tier lessee in the chain of lessees (as provided in paragraph (f)(2)(iii) of this section).

(i) *International carriage of passengers.*—(A) *General rule.*—Except in the case of a round trip described in paragraph (f)(2)(i)(B) of this section, income derived from the carriage of a passenger will be income from international operation of ships or aircraft if the passenger is carried between a beginning point in the United States and an ending point outside the United States, or vice versa. Carriage of a passenger will be treated as ending at the passenger's final destination even if, en route to the passenger's final destination, a stop is made at an intermediate point for refueling, maintenance, or other business reasons, provided the passenger does not change ships or aircraft at the intermediate point. Similarly, carriage of a passenger will be treated as beginning at the passenger's point of origin even if, en route to the passenger's final destination, a stop is made at an intermediate point, provided the passenger does not change ships or aircraft at the intermediate point. Carriage of a passenger will be treated as beginning or ending at a U.S. or foreign intermediate point if the passenger changes ships or aircraft at that intermediate point. Income derived from the sale of a ticket for international carriage of a passenger will be treated as income derived from international operation of ships or aircraft even if the passenger does not begin or complete an international journey because of unanticipated circumstances.

(B) *Round trip travel on ships.*—In the case of income from the carriage of a passenger on a ship that begins its voyage in the United States, calls on one or more foreign intermediate ports, and returns to the same or another U.S. port, such income from carriage of a passenger on the entire voyage will be treated as income derived from international operation of ships or aircraft under paragraph (f)(2)(i)(A) of this section. This result obtains even if such carriage includes one or more intermediate stops at a U.S. port or ports and even if the passenger does not disembark at the foreign intermediate point.

(ii) *International carriage of cargo.*—Income from the carriage of cargo will be income derived from international operation of ships or aircraft if the cargo is carried between a beginning point in the United States and an ending point outside the United States, or vice versa. Carriage of cargo will be treated as ending at the final destination of the cargo even if, en route to that final destination, a stop is made at a U.S. intermediate point, provided the cargo is transported to its ultimate destination on the same ship or aircraft. If the cargo is transferred to another ship or aircraft, the carriage of the cargo may nevertheless be treated as ending at its final destination, if the same taxpayer transports the cargo to and from the U.S. intermediate point and the cargo does not pass through customs at the U.S. intermediate point. Similarly, carriage of cargo will be treated as beginning at the cargo's point of origin, even if en route to its final destination a stop is made at a U.S. intermediate point, provided the cargo is transported to its ultimate destination on the same ship or aircraft. If the cargo is transferred to another ship or aircraft at the U.S. intermediate point, the carriage of the cargo may nevertheless be treated as beginning at the point of origin, if the same taxpayer transports the cargo to and from the U.S. intermediate point and the cargo does not pass through customs at the U.S. intermediate point. Repackaging, recontainerization, or any other activity involving the unloading of the cargo at the U.S. intermediate point does not change these results, provided the same taxpayer transports the cargo to and from the U.S. intermediate point and the cargo does not pass through customs at the U.S. intermediate point. A lighter vessel that carries cargo to, or picks up cargo from, a vessel located beyond the territorial limits of the United States and correspondingly loads or unloads that cargo at a U.S. port, carries cargo between a point in the United States and a point outside the United States. However, a lighter vessel that carries cargo to, or picks up cargo from, a vessel located within the territorial limits of the United States, and correspondingly loads or unloads that cargo at a U.S. port, is not engaged in international operation of ships or aircraft. Income from the carriage of military cargo on a voyage that begins in the United States, stops at a foreign intermediate port or a military prepositioning location, and returns to the same or another U.S. port without unloading its cargo at the foreign intermediate point, will nevertheless be treated as derived from international operation of ships or aircraft.

(iii) *Bareboat charter of ships or dry lease of aircraft used in international operation of ships or aircraft.*—If a qualified foreign corporation bareboat charters a ship or dry leases an aircraft to a lessee, and the lowest tier lessee in the chain of ownership uses such ship or aircraft for the international carriage of passengers or cargo for hire, as described in paragraphs (f)(2)(i) and (ii) of this section, then the amount of charter income attributable to the period the ship or aircraft is used by the lowest tier lessee is income from international operation of ships or aircraft. The foreign corporation generally must determine the amount of the charter income that is attributable to such international operation of ships or aircraft by multiplying the amount of charter income by a fraction, the numerator of which is the total number of days of uninterrupted travel on voyages or flights of such ship or aircraft between the United States and the farthest point or points where cargo or passengers are loaded en route to, or discharged en route from, the United States during the smaller of the taxable year or the particular charter period, and the denominator of which is the total number of days in the smaller of the taxable year or the particular charter period. For this purpose, the number of days during which the ship or aircraft is not generating transportation income, within the meaning of section 863(c)(2), are not included in the numerator or denominator of the fraction. However, the foreign corporation may adopt an alternative method for determining the amount of the charter income that is attributable to the international operation of ships or aircraft if it can establish that the alternative method more accurately reflects the amount of such income.

(iv) *Charter of ships or aircraft for hire.*—For purposes of this section, if a foreign corporation time, voyage, or bareboat charters out a ship or aircraft, and the lowest-tier lessee uses the ship or aircraft to carry passengers or cargo on a fee basis, the ship or aircraft is considered used to carry passengers or cargo for hire, regardless of whether the ship or aircraft may be empty during a portion of the charter period due to a backhaul voyage or flight or for purposes of repositioning. If a foreign corporation time, voyage, or bareboat charters out a ship or aircraft, and the lowest-tier lessee uses the ship or aircraft for the carriage of proprietary goods, including an empty backhaul voyage or flight or repositioning related to such carriage of proprietary goods, the ship or aircraft similarly will be treated as used to carry cargo for hire.

(g) *Activities incidental to the international operation of ships or aircraft.*—(1) *General rule.*—Certain activities of a foreign corporation engaged in the international operation of ships or aircraft are so closely related to the international operation of ships or aircraft that they are considered incidental to such operation, and income derived by the foreign corporation from its performance of these incidental activities is deemed to be income derived from the international operation of ships or aircraft. Examples of such activities include—

(i) Temporary investment of working capital funds to be used in the international operation of ships or aircraft by the foreign corporation;

(ii) Sale of tickets by the foreign corporation engaged in the international operation of ships for the international carriage of passengers by ship on behalf of another corporation engaged in the international operation of ships;

(iii) Sale of tickets by the foreign corporation engaged in the international operation of aircraft for the international carriage of passengers by air on behalf of another corporation engaged in the international operation of aircraft;

(iv) Contracting with concessionaires for performance of services onboard during the international operation of the foreign corporation's ships or aircraft;

(v) Providing (either by subcontracting or otherwise) for the carriage of cargo preceding or following the international carriage of cargo under a through bill of lading, airway bill or similar document through a related corporation or through an unrelated person (and the rules of section 267(b) shall apply for purposes of determining whether a corporation or other person is related to the foreign corporation);

(vi) To the extent not described in paragraph (g)(1)(iii) of this section, the sale or issuance by the foreign corporation engaged in the international operation of aircraft of intraline, interline, or code-sharing tickets for the carriage of persons by air between a U.S. gateway and another U.S. city preceding or following international carriage of passengers, provided that all such flight segments are provided pursuant to the passenger's original invoice, ticket or itinerary and in the case of intraline tickets are a part of uninterrupted international air transportation (within the meaning of section 4262(c)(3));

(vii) Arranging for port city hotel accommodations within the United States for a passenger for the one night before or after the international carriage of that passenger by the foreign corporation engaged in the international operation of ships;

(viii) Bareboat charter of ships or dry lease of aircraft normally used by the foreign corporation in international operation of ships or aircraft but currently not needed, if the ship or aircraft is used by the lessee for international carriage of cargo or passengers;

(ix) Arranging by means of a space or slot charter for the carriage of cargo listed on a bill of lading or airway bill or similar document issued by the foreign corporation on the ship or aircraft of another corporation engaged in the international operation of ships or aircraft;

(x) The provision of containers and related equipment by the foreign corporation in connection with the international carriage of cargo for use by its customers, including short-term use within the United States immediately preceding or following the international carriage of cargo (for this purpose, a period of five days or less shall be presumed to be short-term); and

(xi) The provision of goods and services by engineers, ground and equipment maintenance staff, cargo handlers, catering staff, and customer services personnel, and the provision of facilities such as passenger lounges, counter space, ground handling equipment, and hangars.

(2) *Activities not considered incidental to the international operation of ships or aircraft.*—Examples of activities that are not considered incidental to the international operation of ships or aircraft include—

(i) The sale of or arranging for train travel, bus transfers, single day shore excursions, or land tour packages;

(ii) Arranging for hotel accommodations within the United States other than as provided in paragraph (g)(1)(vii) of this section;

(iii) The sale of airline tickets or cruise tickets other than as provided in paragraph (g)(1)(ii), (iii), or (vi) of this section;

(iv) The sale or rental of real property;

(v) Treasury activities involving the investment of excess funds or funds awaiting repatriation, even if derived from the international operation of ships or aircraft;

(vi) The carriage of passengers or cargo on ships or aircraft on domestic legs of transportation not treated as either international operation of ships or aircraft under paragraph (f) of this section or as an activity that is incidental to such operation under paragraph (g)(1) of this section;

(vii) The carriage of cargo by bus, truck or rail by a foreign corporation between a U.S. inland point and a U.S. gateway port or airport preceding or following the international carriage of such cargo by the foreign corporation; and

(viii) The provision of containers or other related equipment by the foreign corporation within the United States other than as provided in paragraph (g)(1)(x) of this section, including warehousing.

(3) *Other services.*—[Reserved].

(4) *Activities involved in a pool, partnership, strategic alliance, joint operating agreement, code-sharing arrangement or other joint venture.*—Notwithstanding paragraph (g)(1) of this section, an activity is considered incidental to the international operation of ships or aircraft by a foreign corporation, and income derived by the foreign corporation with respect to such activity is deemed to be income derived from the international operation of ships or aircraft, if the activity is performed by or pursuant to a pool, partnership, strategic alliance, joint operating agreement, code-sharing arrangement or other joint venture in which such foreign corporation participates directly, or indirectly through a fiscally transparent entity under the income tax laws of the United States, provided that—

(i) Such activity is incidental to the international operation of ships or aircraft by the pool, partnership, strategic alliance, joint operating agreement, code-sharing arrangement or other joint venture, and provided that it is described in paragraph (e)(2)(i) of this section; or

(ii) Such activity would be incidental to the international operation of ships or aircraft by the foreign corporation, or fiscally transparent entity if it performed such activity itself, and provided the foreign corporation is engaged or the fiscally transparent entity would be considered engaged if it were a foreign corporation in the operation of ships or aircraft under paragraph (e)(1) of this section.

(h) *Equivalent exemption.*—(1) *General rule.*—A foreign country grants an equivalent exemption when it exempts from taxation income from the international operation of ships or aircraft derived by corporations organized in the United States. Whether a foreign country provides an equivalent exemption must be determined separately with respect to each category of income, as provided in paragraph (h)(2) of this section. An equivalent exemption may be available for income derived from the international operation of ships even though income derived from the international operation of aircraft may not be exempt, and vice versa. For rules regarding foreign corporations organized in countries that provide exemptions only through an income tax convention, see paragraph (h)(3) of this section. An equivalent exemption may exist where the foreign country—

(i) Generally imposes no tax on income, including income from the international operation of ships or aircraft;

(ii) Provides an exemption from tax for income derived from the international operation of ships or aircraft, either by statute, decree, income tax convention, or otherwise; or

(iii) Exchanges diplomatic notes with the United States, or enters into an agreement with the United States, that provides for a reciprocal exemption for purposes of section 883.

(2) *Determining equivalent exemptions for each category of income.*—Whether a foreign country grants an equivalent exemption must be determined separately with respect to income from the international operation of ships and income from the international operation of aircraft for each category of income listed in paragraphs (h)(2)(i) through (v), (vii), and (viii) of this section. If an exemption is unavailable in the foreign country for a particular category of income, the foreign country is not considered to grant an equivalent exemption with respect to that category of income. Income in that category is not considered to be the subject of an equivalent exemption and, thus, is not eligible for exemption from income tax in the United States, even though the foreign country may grant an equivalent exemption for other categories of income. With respect to paragraph (h)(2)(vi) of this section, a foreign country may be considered to grant an equivalent exemption for one or more types of income described in paragraph (g)(1) of this section. The following categories of income derived from the international operation of ships or aircraft may be exempt from United States income tax if an equivalent exemption is available—

(i) Income from the carriage of passengers and cargo;

(ii) Time or voyage (full) charter income of a ship or wet lease income of an aircraft;

(iii) Bareboat charter income of a ship or dry charter income of an aircraft;

(iv) Incidental bareboat charter income or incidental dry lease income;

(v) Incidental container-related income;

(vi) Income incidental to the international operation of ships or aircraft other than incidental income described in paragraphs (h)(2)(iv) and (v) of this section;

(vii) Capital gains derived by a qualified foreign corporation engaged in the international operation of ships or aircraft from the sale, exchange or other disposition of a ship, aircraft, container or related equipment or other moveable property used by that qualified foreign corporation in the international operation of ships or aircraft; and

(viii) Income from participation in a pool, partnership, strategic alliance, joint operating agreement, code-sharing arrangement, international operating agency, or other joint venture described in paragraph (e)(2) of this section.

(3) *Special rules with respect to income tax conventions.*—(i) *Countries with only an income tax convention.*—If a foreign country grants an exemption from tax for profits from the international operation of ships or aircraft only under an income tax convention with the United States, that exemption shall constitute an equivalent exemption with respect to a foreign corporation organized in that country only if—

(A) The foreign corporation satisfies the conditions for claiming benefits with respect to such profits under the income tax convention; and

(B) The profits that are exempt from tax pursuant to the shipping and air transport or gains article of the income tax convention and are described within a category of income included in paragraphs (h)(2)(i) through (viii) of this section.

(ii) *Countries with both an income tax convention and an equivalent exemption.*—(A) *General rule.*—If a foreign country grants an exemption from tax for profits from the international operation of ships or aircraft under the shipping and air transport or gains article of an income tax convention with the United States and also by some other means (for example, by diplomatic note or domestic law of the foreign country), a foreign corporation may elect annually whether to claim an exemption from tax under section 883 or the income tax convention. Except as provided in paragraph (h)(3)(ii)(B) of this section, the foreign corporation must apply the elected exemption (section 883 or the income tax convention) to all categories of income described in paragraph (h)(2) of this section. If the foreign corporation elects to claim the exemption under section 883, it must satisfy all of the requirements for claiming the exemption under section 883. If the foreign corporation elects to claim the exemption under the income tax convention, it must satisfy all of the requirements and conditions for claiming benefits under the income tax convention. See § 1.883-4(b)(3) for rules concerning relying on shareholders resident in a foreign country that grants an equivalent exemption under an income tax convention to satisfy the stock ownership test of paragraph (c)(2) of this section.

(B) *Special rule for claiming simultaneous benefits under section 883 and an income tax convention.*—If a foreign corporation that is organized in a country that grants an exemption from tax under an income tax convention and also by some other means (such as by diplomatic note or domestic law of the foreign country) with respect to a specific category of income described in paragraph (h)(2) of this section, and the foreign corporation elects to claim the exemption under the income tax convention, the foreign corporation may nonetheless simultaneously claim an exemption under section 883 with respect to a category of income exempt from tax by such other means if the foreign corporation—

(1) Satisfies the requirements of paragraphs (h)(3)(i)(A) and (B) of this section for each category of income;

(2) Satisfies one of the stock ownership tests of paragraph (c)(2) of this section; and

(3) Complies with the substantiation and reporting requirements in paragraph (c)(3) of this section.

(iii) *Participation in certain joint ventures.*—If a foreign country grants an exemption for a category of income only through an income tax convention, a foreign corporation that is organized in that country and that derives income, directly or indirectly, through a participation in a pool, partnership, strategic alliance, joint operating agreement, code-sharing arrangement, or other joint venture described in paragraph (e)(2) of this section, may treat that exemption as an equivalent exemption even if the foreign corporation would not be eligible to claim benefits under the income tax convention for that category of income solely because the joint venture was not fiscally transparent, within the meaning of § 1.894-1(d)(3)(iii)(A), with respect to that category of income under the income tax laws of the foreign corporation's country of residence.

(iv) *Independent interpretation of income tax conventions.*—Nothing in this section nor §§ 1.883-2 through 1.883-5 affects the rights or obligations under any income tax convention between the United States and a foreign country. The definitions provided in this section and §§ 1.883-2 through 1.883-5 shall not give meaning to similar or identical terms used in an income tax convention, or provide guidance regarding the scope of any exemption provided by such convention, unless the income tax convention entered into force after August 26, 2003, and it, or its legislative history, explicitly refers to section 883 and guidance promulgated under that section for its meaning.

(4) *Exemptions not qualifying as equivalent exemptions.*—(i) *General rule.*—Certain types of exemptions provided to corporations organized in the United States by foreign countries do not satisfy the equivalent exemption requirements of this section. Paragraphs (h)(4)(ii) through (vii) of this section provide descriptions of some of the types of exemptions that do not qualify as equivalent exemptions for purposes of this section.

(ii) *Reduced tax rate or time limited exemption.*—The exemption granted by the foreign country's law or income tax convention must be a complete exemption. The exemption may not constitute merely a reduction to a nonzero rate of tax levied against the income of corporations organized in the United States derived from the international operation of ships or aircraft or a temporary reduction to a zero rate of tax, such as in the case of a tax holiday.

(iii) *Inbound or outbound freight tax.*—With respect to the carriage of cargo, the foreign country must provide an exemption from tax for income from transporting freight both inbound and outbound. For example, a foreign country that imposes tax only on outbound freight will not be treated as granting an equivalent exemption for income from transporting freight inbound into that country.

(iv) *Exemptions for limited types of cargo.*—A foreign country must provide an exemption from tax for income from transporting all types of cargo. For example, if a foreign country were generally to impose tax on income from the international carriage of cargo but were to provide a statutory exemption for income from transporting agricultural products, the foreign country would not be considered to grant an equivalent exemption with respect to income from the international carriage of cargo, including agricultural products.

(v) *Territorial tax systems.*—A foreign country with a territorial tax system will be treated as granting an equivalent exemption if it treats all income derived from the international operation of ships or aircraft derived by a U.S. corporation as entirely foreign source and therefore not subject to tax, including income derived from a voyage or flight that begins or ends in that foreign country.

(vi) *Countries that tax on a residence basis.*—A foreign country that provides an equivalent exemption to corporations organized in the United States but also imposes a residencebased tax on certain corporations organized in the United States may nevertheless be considered to grant an equivalent exemption if the residence-based tax is imposed only on a corporation organized in the United States that maintains its center of management and control or other comparable attributes in that foreign country. If the residence-based tax is imposed on corporations organized in the United States and engaged in the international operation of ships or aircraft that are not managed and controlled in that foreign country, the foreign country shall not be treated as a qualified foreign country and shall not be considered to grant an equivalent exemption for purposes of this section.

(vii) *Exemptions within categories of income.*—With respect to paragraphs (h)(2)(i) through (v), (vii), and (viii) of this section, a foreign country must provide an exemption from tax for all income in a category of income, as defined in paragraph (h)(2) of this section. For example, a country that exempts income from the bareboat charter of passenger aircraft but not the bareboat charter of cargo aircraft does not provide an equivalent exemption. However, an equivalent exemption may be available for income derived from the international operation of ships even though income derived from the international operation of aircraft may not be exempt, and vice versa. With respect to paragraph (h)(2)(vi) of this section, a foreign country may be considered to grant an equivalent exemption for one or more types of income described in paragraph (g)(1) of this section.

(i) *Treatment of possessions.*—For purposes of this section, a possession of the United States will be treated as a foreign country. A possession of the United States will be considered to grant an equivalent exemption and will be treated as a qualified foreign country if it applies a mirror system of taxation. If a possession does not apply a mirror system of taxation, the possession may nevertheless be a qualified foreign country if, for example, it provides for an equivalent exemption through its internal law. A possession applies the mirror system of taxation if the U.S. Internal Revenue Code of 1986, as amended, applies in the possession with the name of the possession used instead of "United States" where appropriate.

(j) *Expenses related to qualified income.*—If a qualified foreign corporation derives qualified income from the international operation of ships or aircraft as well as income that is not qualified income, and the nonqualified income is effectively connected with the conduct of a trade or business within the United States, the foreign corporation may not deduct from such nonqualified income any amount otherwise allowable as a deduction from qualified income, if that qualified income is excluded under this section. See section 265(a)(1). [Reg. § 1.883-1.]

☐ [*T.D.* 6258, 10-23-57. *Amended by T.D.* 7293, 11-27-73; *T.D.* 9087, 8-25-2003; *T.D.* 9332, 6-22-2007 (*corrected* 8-10-2007) *and T.D.* 9502, 9-16-2010.]

§ 1.883-2. Treatment of publicly-traded corporations.—(a) *General rule.*—A foreign corporation satisfies the stock ownership test of § 1.883-1(c)(2) if it is considered a publicly-traded corporation and satisfies the substantiation and reporting requirements of paragraphs (e) and (f) of this section. To be considered a publicly-traded corporation, the stock of the foreign corporation must be primarily traded and regularly traded, as defined in paragraphs (c) and (d) of this section, respectively, on one or more established securities markets, as defined in paragraph (b) of this section, in either the United States or any qualified foreign country.

(b) *Established securities market.*—(1) *General rule.*—For purposes of this section, the term *established securities market* means, for any taxable year—

(i) A foreign securities exchange that is officially recognized, sanctioned, or supervised by a governmental authority of the qualified foreign country in which the market is located, and has an annual value of shares traded on the exchange exceeding $1 billion during each of the three calendar years immediately preceding the beginning of the taxable year;

(ii) A national securities exchange that is registered under section 6 of the Securities Act of 1934 (15 U.S.C. 78f);

(iii) A United States over-the-counter market, as defined in paragraph (b)(4) of this section;

(iv) Any exchange designated under a Limitation on Benefits article in a United States income tax convention; and

(v) Any other exchange that the Secretary may designate by regulation or otherwise.

(2) *Exchanges with multiple tiers.*—If an exchange in a foreign country has more than one tier or market level on which stock may be separately listed or traded, each such tier shall be treated as a separate exchange.

(3) *Computation of dollar value of stock traded.*—For purposes of paragraph (b)(1)(i) of this section, the value in U.S. dollars of shares traded during a calendar year shall be determined on the basis of the dollar value of such shares traded as reported by the International Federation of Stock Exchanges located in Paris, or, if not so reported, then by converting into U.S. dollars the aggregate value in local currency of the shares traded using an exchange rate equal to the average of the spot rates on the last day of each month of the calendar year.

(4) *Over-the-counter market.*—An over-the-counter market is any market reflected by the existence of an interdealer quotation system. An interdealer quotation system is any system of general circulation to brokers and dealers that regularly disseminates quotations of stocks and securities by identified brokers or dealers, other than by quotation sheets that are prepared and distributed by a broker or dealer in the regular course of business and that contain only quotations of such broker or dealer.

(5) *Discretion to determine that an exchange does not qualify as an established securities market.*—The Commissioner may determine that a securities exchange that otherwise meets the requirements of paragraph (b) of this section does not qualify as an established securities market, if—

(i) The exchange does not have adequate listing, financial disclosure, or trading requirements (or does not adequately enforce such requirements); or

(ii) There is not clear and convincing evidence that the exchange ensures the active trading of listed stocks.

(c) *Primarily traded.*—For purposes of this section, stock of a corporation is primarily traded in a country on one or more established securities markets, as defined in paragraph (b) of this section, if, with respect to each class of stock described in paragraph (d)(1)(i) of this section (relating to classes of stock relied on to meet the regularly traded test)—

(1) The number of shares in each such class that are traded during the taxable year on all established securities markets in that country exceeds

(2) The number of shares in each such class that are traded during that year on established securities markets in any other single country.

(d) *Regularly traded.*—(1) *General rule.*—For purposes of this section, stock of a corporation is regularly traded on one or more established securities markets, as defined in paragraph (b) of this section, if—

(i) One or more classes of stock of the corporation that, in the aggregate, represent more than 50 percent of the total combined voting power of all classes of stock of such corporation entitled to vote and of the total value of the stock of such corporation are listed on such market or markets during the taxable year, and

(ii) With respect to each class relied on to meet the more than 50 percent requirement of paragraph (d)(1)(i) of this section—

(A) Trades in each such class are effected, other than in de minimis quantities, on such market or markets on at least 60 days during the taxable year (or 1/6 of the number of days in a short taxable year); and

(B) The aggregate number of shares in each such class that are traded on such market or markets during the taxable year are at least 10 percent of the average number of shares outstanding in that class during the taxable year (or, in the case of a short taxable year, a percentage that equals at least 10 percent of the average number of shares outstanding in that class during the taxable year multiplied by the number of days in the short taxable year, divided by 365).

(2) *Classes of stock traded on a domestic established securities market treated as meeting trading requirements.*—A class of stock that is traded during the taxable year on an established securities market located in the United States shall be considered to meet the trading requirements of paragraph (d)(1)(ii) of this section if the stock is regularly quoted by dealers making a market in the stock. A dealer makes a market in a stock only if the dealer regularly and actively offers to, and in fact does, purchase the stock from, and sell the stock to, customers who are not related persons (as defined in section 954(d)(3)) with respect to the dealer in the ordinary course of a trade or business.

(3) *Closely-held classes of stock not treated as meeting trading requirements.*—(i) *General rule.*—Except as provided in paragraph (d)(3)(ii) of this section, a class of stock of a foreign corporation that otherwise meets the requirements of paragraph (d)(1) or (2) of this section shall not be treated as meeting such requirements for a taxable year if, for more than half the number of days during the taxable year, one or more persons who own at least 5 percent of the vote and value of the outstanding shares of the class of stock, as determined under paragraph (d)(3)(iii) of this section (each a 5-percent shareholder), own, in the aggregate, 50 percent or more of the vote and value of the outstanding shares of the class of stock. If one or more 5-percent shareholders own, in the aggregate, 50 percent or more of the vote and value of the outstanding shares of the class of stock, such shares held by the 5-percent shareholders will constitute a closely-held block of stock.

(ii) *Exception.*—Paragraph (d)(3)(i) of this section shall not apply to a class of stock if the foreign corporation can establish that qualified shareholders, as defined in § 1.883-4(b), applying the attribution rules of § 1.883-4(c), own sufficient shares in the closely-held block of stock to preclude nonqualified shareholders in the closelyheld block of stock from owning 50 percent or more of the total value of the class of stock of which the closely-held block is a part for more than half the number of days during the taxable year. Any shares that are owned, after application of the attribution rules in § 1.883-4(c), by a qualified shareholder shall not also be treated as owned by a nonqualified shareholder in the chain of ownership for purposes of the preceding sentence. A foreign corporation must obtain the documentation described in § 1.883-4(d) from the qualified shareholders relied upon to satisfy this exception. However, no person otherwise treated as a qualified shareholder under § 1.883-4(b) may be treated for purposes of this paragraph (d)(3) as a qualified shareholder if such person's interest in the foreign corporation, or in any intermediary corporation, is held through bearer shares that are not maintained during the relevant period in a dematerialized or immobilized book-entry system, as described in § 1.883-1(c)(3)(i)(G).

(iii) *Five-percent shareholders.*—(A) *Related persons.*—Solely for purposes of determining whether a person is a 5-percent shareholder, persons related within the meaning of section 267(b) shall be treated as one person. In determining whether two or more corporations are members of the same controlled group under section 267(b)(3), a person is considered to own stock owned directly by such person, stock owned through the application of section 1563(e)(1), and stock owned through the application of section 267(c). In determining whether a corporation is related to a partnership under section

267(b)(10), a person is considered to own the partnership interest owned directly by such person and the partnership interest owned through the application of section 267(e)(3).

(B) *Investment companies.*—For purposes of this paragraph (d)(3), an investment company registered under the Investment Company Act of 1940, as amended (54 Stat. 789), shall not be treated as a 5-percent shareholder.

(4) *Anti-abuse rule.*—Trades between or among related persons described in section 267(b), as modified by paragraph (d)(3)(iii) of this section, and trades conducted in order to meet the requirements of paragraph (d)(1) of this section shall be disregarded. A class of stock shall not be treated as meeting the trading requirements of paragraph (d)(1) of this section if there is a pattern of trades conducted to meet the requirements of that paragraph. For example, trades between two persons that occur several times during the taxable year may be treated as an arrangement or a pattern of trades conducted to meet the trading requirements of paragraph (d)(1)(ii) of this section.

(5) *Example.*—The closely-held test in paragraph (d)(3) of this section is illustrated by the following example:

Example. Closely-held exception—(i) *Facts.* X is a foreign corporation organized in a qualified foreign country and engaged in the international operation of ships. X has one class of stock, which is primarily traded on an established securities market in the qualified foreign country. The stock of X meets the regularly traded requirements of paragraph (d)(1)(ii) of this section without regard to paragraph (d)(3)(i) of this section. A, B, C and D are four members of the corporation's founding family who each own, during the entire taxable year, 25 percent of the stock of Hold Co, a company that issues registered shares. Hold Co, in turn, owns 60 percent of the stock of X during the entire taxable year. The remaining 40 percent of the stock of X is not owned by any 5-percent shareholder, as determined under paragraph (d)(3)(iii) of this section. A, B, and C are not residents of a qualified foreign country, but D is a resident of a qualified foreign country.

(ii) *Analysis.* Because Hold Co owns 60 percent of the stock of X for more than half the number of days during the taxable year, Hold Co is a 5-percent shareholder that owns 50 percent or more of the value of the stock of X. Thus, the shares owned by Hold Co constitute a closely-held block of stock. Under paragraph (d)(3)(i) of this section, the stock of X will not be regularly traded within the meaning of paragraph (d)(1) of this section unless X can establish, under paragraph (d)(3)(ii) of this section, that qualified shareholders within the closely-held block of stock own sufficient shares in the closely-held block of stock to preclude nonqualified shareholders in the closely-held block of stock from owning 50 percent or more of the value of the outstanding shares in the class of stock for more than half the number of days during the taxable year. A, B, and C are not qualified shareholders within the meaning of § 1.883-4(b) because they are not residents of a qualified foreign country, but D is a resident of a qualified foreign country and therefore is a qualified shareholder. D owns 15 percent of the outstanding shares of X through Hold Co (25 percent × 60 percent = 15 percent) while A, B, and C in the aggregate own 45 percent of the outstanding shares of X through Hold Co. D, therefore, owns sufficient shares in the closely-held block of stock to preclude the nonqualified shareholders in the closely-held block of stock, A, B and C, from owning 50 percent or more of the value of the class of stock (60 percent − 15 percent = 45 percent) of which the closely-held block is a part. Provided that X obtains from D the documentation described in § 1.883-4(d), X's sole class of stock meets the exception in paragraph (d)(3)(ii) of this section and will not be disqualified from the regularly traded test by virtue of paragraph (d)(3)(i) of this section.

(e) *Substantiation that a foreign corporation is publicly traded.*—(1) *General rule.*—A foreign corporation that relies on the publicly traded test of this section to meet the stock ownership test of § 1.883-1(c)(2) must substantiate that the stock of the foreign corporation is primarily and regularly traded on one or more established securities markets, as that term is defined in paragraph (b) of this section. If one of the classes of stock on which the foreign corporation relies to meet this test is closely-held within the meaning of paragraph (d)(3)(i) of this section, the foreign corporation must obtain an ownership statement described in § 1.883-4(d) from each qualified shareholder and intermediary that it relies upon to satisfy the exception to the closely-held test, but only to the extent such statement would be required if the foreign corporation were relying on the qualified shareholder stock ownership test of § 1.883-4 with respect to those shares of stock. The foreign corporation must also maintain and provide to the Commissioner upon request a list of its shareholders of record and any other relevant information known to the foreign corporation supporting its entitlement to an exemption under this section.

(2) *Availability and retention of documents for inspection.*—A foreign corporation seeking qualified foreign corporation status must retain the documentation described in paragraph (e)(1) of this section until the expiration of the statute of limitations for its taxable year to which the documentation relates. The foreign corporation must make such documentation available for inspection at such time and such place as the Commissioner requests in writing under § 1.883-1(c)(3)(ii)(A) or (B).

(f) *Reporting requirements.*—A foreign corporation relying on this section to satisfy the stock ownership test of § 1.883-1(c)(2) must provide the following information in addition to the information required in § 1.883-1(c)(3) to be included in its Form 1120-F, "U.S. Income Tax Return of a Foreign Corporation," for the taxable year. The information must be current as of the end of the corporation's taxable year and must include the following—

(1) The name of the country in which the stock is primarily traded;

(2) The name of the established securities market or markets on which the stock is listed;

(3) A description of each class of stock relied upon to meet the requirements of paragraph (d) of this section, including whether the class is issued in registered or bearer form and whether any such bearer shares are maintained in a dematerialized or immobilized book-entry system, as described in § 1.883-1(c)(3)(i)(G), the number of shares issued and outstanding in that class as of the close of the taxable year, and the relative value of each class in relation to the total value of all shares of stock of the corporation that are outstanding as of the close of the taxable year;

(4) For each class of stock relied upon to meet the requirements of paragraph (d) of this section, if one or more 5-percent shareholders, as defined in paragraph (d)(3)(i) of this section, own in the aggregate 50 percent or more of the vote and value of the outstanding shares of that class of stock for more than half the number of days during the taxable year—

(i) The days during the taxable year of the corporation in which the stock was closely-held without regard to the exception in paragraph (d)(3)(ii) of this section and the percentage of the vote and value of the class of stock that is owned by 5-percent shareholders during such days;

(ii) With respect to all qualified shareholders that own directly, or by application of the attribution rules in § 1.883-4(c), shares of the closely-held block of stock and that the foreign corporation relies on to satisfy the exception provided by paragraph (d)(3)(ii) of this section—

(A) The number of such qualified shareholders;

(B) The total percentage of the value of the shares owned, directly or indirectly, by such qualified shareholders by country of residence, determined under § 1.883-4(b)(2) (residence of individual shareholders) or § 1.883-4(d)(3) (special rules for residence of certain shareholders); and

(C) The number of days during the taxable year of the foreign corporation that such qualified shareholders owned, directly or indirectly, their shares in the closely held block of stock.

(5) Any other relevant information specified by Form 1120-F and its accompanying instructions. [Reg. § 1.883-2.]

[*T.D. 9087, 8-25-2003. Amended by T.D. 9332, 6-22-2007 and T.D.* 9502, 9-16-2010 (corrected 10-14-2010).]

§ 1.883-3. Treatment of controlled foreign corporations.—(a) *General rule.*—A foreign corporation satisfies the stock ownership test of § 1.883-1(c)(2) if it satisfies the qualified U.S. person ownership test in paragraph (b) of this section and the substantiation and reporting requirements of paragraphs (c) and (d) of this section, respectively. A foreign corporation that fails the qualified U.S. person ownership test of paragraph (b) of this section can satisfy the stock ownership test of § 1.883-1(c)(2) if it meets either the publicly-traded test of § 1.883-2(a) or the qualified shareholder stock ownership test of § 1.883-4(a).

(b) *Qualified U.S. person ownership test.*—(1) *General rule.*—A foreign corporation satisfies the qualified U.S. person ownership test only if the following two conditions are satisfied concurrently during more than half the days in its taxable year:

(i) The foreign corporation is a controlled foreign corporation (within the meaning of section 957(a)).

(ii) One or more qualified U.S. persons own more than 50 percent of the total value of all the outstanding stock of the foreign corporation (within the meaning of section 958(a) and paragraph (b)(4) of this section).

(2) *Qualified U.S. person.*—For purposes of this section, a *qualified U.S. person* is a United States citizen or resident alien, a domestic corporation, or a domestic trust described in section 501(a), but only if the person provides the controlled foreign corporation an ownership statement described in paragraph (c)(2) of this section, and the controlled foreign corporation meets the reporting requirements of paragraph (d) of this section with respect to that person.

(3) *Treatment of bearer shares.*—For purposes of paragraph (b)(1)(ii) of this section, any shares of the foreign corporation or of any intermediary corporation that are issued in bearer form, shall be treated as not owned by qualified U.S. persons if the bearer shares are not maintained in a dematerialized or immobilized book-entry system, as described in § 1.883-1(c)(3)(i)(G).

(4) *Ownership attribution through certain domestic entities.*—For purposes of paragraph (b)(1)(ii) of this section, stock owned, directly or indirectly, by or for a domestic partnership, a domestic trust not described in section 501(a), or a domestic estate, shall be treated as owned proportionately by the partners, beneficiaries, grantors, or other interest holders, respectively, under the rules of section 958(a), which shall be applied by treating each domestic entity as a foreign entity. Stock that is considered owned by a person under this paragraph (b)(4) shall, for purposes of applying this paragraph (b)(4) to such person, be treated as actually owned by such person.

(5) *Examples.*—The following examples illustrate the qualified U.S. person ownership test of paragraph (b)(1) of this section:

Example 1. Ship Co is a controlled foreign corporation (within the meaning of section 957(a)) for more than half the days of its taxable year and is organized in a qualified foreign country. A domestic partnership owns all of the outstanding stock of Ship Co for the entire taxable year. All of the partners in the domestic partnership are residents of foreign countries and not citizens of the United States. Ship Co does not satisfy the qualified U.S. person ownership test of paragraph (b)(1) of this section because qualified U.S. persons do not own shares of Ship Co stock with a value that is greater than 50 percent of the total value of the outstanding stock of the corporation for at least half the days of Ship Co's taxable year. Therefore, to satisfy the stock ownership test of § 1.883-1(c)(2) and constitute a qualified foreign corporation, Ship Co must meet the qualified shareholder stock ownership test of § 1.883-4(a).

Example 2. Ship Co is a controlled foreign corporation (within the meaning of section 957(a)) for more than half the days of its taxable year and is organized in a qualified foreign country. Ship Co has a single class of stock outstanding. For Ship Co's entire taxable year, a foreign corporation (Corp A), that is wholly owned by a resident of a foreign country who is not a U.S. citizen, owns 40 percent of the outstanding Ship Co stock. During that same period, a domestic partnership owns the remaining 60 percent of the outstanding Ship Co stock. The domestic partnership is wholly owned by 20 United States citizens, each of whom owns a 5-percent partnership interest for Ship Co's entire taxable year. Ship Co meets the qualified U.S. person ownership test of paragraph (b)(1) of this section because during more than half the days in its taxable year it was a controlled foreign corporation within the meaning of section 957(a), and, applying the ownership attribution rules of paragraph (b)(4) of this section, qualified U.S. persons (the partners in the domestic partnership) owned Ship Co stock with a value that is greater than 50 percent of the total value of all the outstanding Ship Co shares. Therefore, Ship Co will meet the stock ownership test of § 1.883-1(c)(2) if it satisfies the substantiation and reporting requirements of paragraphs (c) and (d) of this section with respect to the partners in the domestic partnership. Alternatively, if four or more partners in the domestic partnership were not qualified U.S. persons, Ship Co would not meet the qualified U.S. person ownership test of paragraph (b)(1) of this section because, even though during more than half the days in its taxable year it would have been a controlled foreign corporation within the meaning of section 957(a), qualified U.S. persons would not have owned Ship Co stock with a value that is greater than 50 percent of the total value of all the outstanding Ship Co shares during that period.

Example 3. Ship Co is a controlled foreign corporation (within the meaning of section 957(a)) and is organized in a qualified foreign country. Ship Co has two classes of stock outstanding, Class A representing 60 percent of the vote and value and Class B representing the remaining 40 percent of the vote and value of all the shares outstanding of Ship Co. The Class A stock is issued in bearer form and is maintained in a dematerialized book-entry system, as described in § 1.883-1(c)(3)(i)(G). The Class B stock is also issued in bearer form, but is not maintained in a dematerialized or immobilized book-entry system. For Ship Co's entire taxable year, a United States citizen A holds all the Class A stock and nonresident alien individual B owns all the Class B stock. Although the Class A stock is issued in bearer form, Ship Co will satisfy the qualified U.S. person ownership test of paragraph (b)(1) of this section because the Class A stock is maintained in a dematerialized book-entry system on behalf of A. The Class B stock is not owned by a qualified U.S. person but is taken into account in determining the total value of Ship Co's outstanding stock. Alternatively, if the Class B stock were owned by a qualified U.S. person, the results would be similar. Class B stock would not be taken into account in determining if the qualified U.S. person ownership test were satisfied, but would be taken into account in determining the total value of Ship Co's outstanding stock.

(c) *Substantiation of CFC stock ownership.*—(1) *In general.*—A controlled foreign corporation must establish all of the facts necessary to demonstrate to the Commissioner that it satisfies the qualified U.S. person ownership test of paragraph (b)(1) of this section by obtaining a written ownership statement (described in paragraph (c)(2) or (3) of this section, as applicable), signed under penalties of perjury by an individual authorized to sign that person's Federal tax or information return, from—

(i) Each qualified U.S. person whose ownership of stock of the controlled foreign corporation is taken into account for purposes of meeting the qualified U.S. person ownership test; and

(ii) Each domestic intermediary described in paragraph (b)(4) of this section, each foreign intermediary (including a foreign corporation, partnership, trust, or estate), and mere legal owners or record holders acting as nominees in the chain of ownership between each such qualified U.S. person and the controlled foreign corporation, if any.

(2) *Ownership statements from qualified U.S. persons.*—An ownership statement from a qualified U.S. person must include—

(i) The qualified U.S. person's name, permanent address, and taxpayer identification number;

(ii) If the qualified U.S. person directly owns shares in the controlled foreign corporation, the number of shares of each class of stock of the controlled foreign corporation owned by the qualified U.S. person, whether any shares are issued in bearer form, whether any bearer shares are maintained in a dematerialized or immobilized book-entry system, as described in § 1.883-1(c)(3)(i)(G), and the period (or periods) in the taxable year of the controlled foreign corporation during which the qualified U.S. person owned the shares;

(iii) If the qualified U.S. person indirectly owns shares in the controlled foreign corporation through a foreign or domestic intermediary described in paragraph (c)(1)(ii) of this section, the name of each intermediary, the amount and nature of the qualified U.S. person's interest in each intermediary, the period (or periods) in the taxable year of the controlled foreign corporation during which the qualified U.S. person held such interest, and, with respect to any intermediary foreign corporation, whether any shares are issued in bearer form and whether any such bearer shares are maintained in a dematerialized or immobilized book-entry system, as described in § 1.883-1(c)(3)(i)(G); and

(iv) Any other information specified in published guidance by the Internal Revenue Service (see § 601.601(d)(2) of this chapter).

(3) *Ownership statements from intermediaries.*—An ownership statement from a domestic or foreign intermediary must include:

(i) The intermediary's name, permanent address, and taxpayer identification number, if any.

(ii) If the intermediary directly owns stock in the controlled foreign corporation, the number of shares of each class of stock of the controlled foreign corporation owned by the intermediary, whether such shares are issued in bearer form and maintained in a dematerialized or immobilized book-entry system, as described in § 1.883-1(c)(3)(i)(G), and the period (or periods) in the taxable year of the controlled foreign corporation during which the intermediary owned the shares.

(iii) If the intermediary indirectly owns the stock of the controlled foreign corporation, the name and address of each intermediary in the chain of ownership between it and the controlled foreign corporation, the period (or periods) in the taxable year of the controlled foreign corporation during which the intermediary owned the shares, the percentage of its indirect ownership interest in the controlled foreign corporation, and, if any intermediary in the chain of ownership is a foreign corporation, whether any shares of such intermediary are issued in bearer form and if any such bearer shares are maintained in a dematerialized or immobilized book-entry system, as described in § 1.883-1(c)(3)(i)(G).

(iv) Any other information specified in published guidance by the Internal Revenue Service (see § 601.601(d)(2) of this chapter).

(4) *Three-year period of validity.*—The rules of § 1.883-4(d)(2)(ii) shall apply for determining the validity of the ownership statements required under paragraph (c)(2) of this section.

(5) *Availability and retention of documents for inspection.*—The foreign corporation seeking qualified foreign corporation status must retain the ownership statements described in this paragraph (c) until the expiration of the statute of limitations for its taxable year to which the ownership statements relate. The ownership statements must be made available for inspection at such time and place as the Commissioner may request in writing in accordance with § 1.883-1(c)(3)(ii).

(d) *Reporting requirements.*—A controlled foreign corporation that relies on this section to satisfy the stock ownership test of § 1.883-1(c)(2) must include the following information (in addition to the information required by § 1.883-1(c)(3)) with its Form 1120-F, "U.S. Income Tax Return of a Foreign Corporation", filed for its taxable year. This information must be consistent with the ownership statements obtained by the controlled foreign corporation pursuant to paragraph (c) of this section and must be current as of the end of the corporation's taxable year—

(1) The relative value of the shares of the controlled foreign corporation that are owned (directly, and indirectly applying the rules of paragraph (b)(4) of this section) by all qualified U.S. persons identified in paragraph (c)(2) of this section as compared to the value of all outstanding shares of the corporation;

(2) The period (or periods) in the taxable year during which such qualified U.S. persons held such shares;

(3) The period (or periods) in the taxable year during which the foreign corporation was a controlled foreign corporation;

(4) A statement as to whether the controlled foreign corporation or any intermediary corporation had bearer shares outstanding during the taxable year, and whether any such bearer shares taken into account for purposes of satisfying the qualified U.S. person ownership test are maintained in a dematerialized or immobilized book-entry system, as described in § 1.883-1(c)(3)(i)(G); and

(5) Any other information specified by Form 1120-F, and its accompanying instructions, or in published guidance by the Internal Revenue Service (see § 601.601(d)(2) of this chapter). [Reg. § 1.883-3.]

☐ [*T.D. 9087, 8-25-2003. Amended by T.D. 9332, 6-22-2007 and T.D. 9502, 9-16-2010.*]

§ 1.883-4. Qualified shareholder stock ownership test.—(a) *General rule.*—A foreign corporation satisfies the stock ownership test of § 1.883-1(c)(2) if more than 50 percent of the value of its outstanding shares is owned, or treated as owned by applying the attribution rules of paragraph (c) of this section, for at least half of the number of days in the foreign corporation's taxable year by one or more qualified shareholders, as defined in paragraph (b) of this section. A shareholder may be a qualified shareholder with respect to one category of income while not being a qualified shareholder with respect to another. A foreign corporation will not be considered to satisfy the stock ownership test of § 1.883-1(c)(2) pursuant to this section unless the foreign corporation meets the substantiation and reporting requirements of paragraphs (d) and (e) of this section.

(b) *Qualified shareholder.*—(1) *General rule.*—A shareholder is a qualified shareholder only if the shareholder—

(i) With respect to the category of income for which the foreign corporation is seeking an exemption, is—

(A) An individual who is a resident, as described in paragraph (b)(2) of this section, of a qualified foreign country;

(B) The government of a qualified foreign country (or a political subdivision or local authority of such country);

(C) A foreign corporation that is organized in a qualified foreign country and meets the publicly traded test of § 1.883-2(a);

(D) A not-for-profit organization described in paragraph (b)(4) of this section that is not a pension fund as defined in paragraph (b)(5) of this section and that is organized in a qualified foreign country;

(E) An individual beneficiary of a pension fund (as defined in paragraph (b)(5)(iv) of this section) that is administered in or by a qualified foreign country, who is treated as a resident under paragraph (d)(3)(iii) of this section, of a qualified foreign country; or

(F) A shareholder of a foreign corporation that is an airline covered by a bilateral Air Services Agreement in force between the United States and the qualified foreign country in which the airline is organized, provided the United States has not waived the ownership requirement in the Air Services Agreement, or that the ownership requirement has not otherwise been made ineffective;

(ii) Does not own its interest in the foreign corporation through bearer shares, either directly or by applying the attribution rules of paragraph (c) of this section, unless such bearer shares are maintained in a dematerialized or immobilized bookentry system, as described in § 1.883-1(c)(3)(i)(G); and

(iii) Provides to the foreign corporation the documentation required in paragraph (d) of this section and the foreign corporation meets the reporting requirements of paragraph (e) of this section with respect to such shareholder.

(2) *Residence of individual shareholders.*—(i) *General rule.*—An individual described in paragraph (b)(1)(i)(A) of this section is a resident of a qualified foreign country only if the individual is fully liable to tax as a resident in such country (e.g., an individual who is liable to tax on a remittance basis in a foreign country will not be treated as a resident of that country unless all residents of that country are taxed on a remittance basis only) and, in addition—

(A) The individual has a tax home, within the meaning of paragraph (b)(2)(ii) of this section, in that qualified foreign country for 183 days or more of the taxable year; or

(B) The individual is treated as a resident of a qualified foreign country based on special rules pursuant to paragraph (d)(3) of this section.

(ii) *Tax home.*—For purposes of this section, an individual's tax home is considered to be located at the individual's regular or principal (if more than one regular) place of business. If the individual has no regular or principal place of business because of the nature of his business (or lack of a business), then the individual's tax home is located at his regular place of abode in a real and substantial sense. If an individual has no regular or principal place of business and no regular place of abode in a real and substantial sense in a qualified foreign country for 183 days or more of the taxable year, that individual does not have a tax home for purposes of this section. A foreign estate or trust, as defined in section 7701(a)(31), does not have a tax home for purposes of this section. See paragraph (c)(3) of this section for alternative rules in the case of trusts or estates.

(3) *Certain income tax convention restrictions applied to shareholders.*—For purposes of paragraph (b)(1) of this section, a shareholder described in paragraph (b)(1) of this section may be considered a resident of, or organized in, a qualified foreign country if that foreign country provides an exemption by means of an income tax convention with the United States, but only if the shareholder demonstrates that it is treated as a resident of that country under the convention and qualifies for benefits under any Limitation on Benefits article, and that the convention provides an exemption for the relevant category of income. If the convention has a requirement in the shipping and air transport article other than residence, such as place of registration or documentation of the ship or aircraft, the shareholder is not required to demonstrate that the corporation seeking qualified foreign corporation status could satisfy any such additional requirement.

(4) *Not-for-profit organizations.*—The term *not-for-profit organization* means an organization that meets the following requirements—

(i) It is a corporation, association taxable as a corporation, trust, fund, foundation, league or other entity operated exclusively for religious, charitable, educational, or recreational purposes, and not organized for profit;

(ii) It is generally exempt from tax in its country of organization by virtue of its not-for-profit status; and

(iii) Either—

(A) More than 50 percent of its annual support is expended on behalf of individuals described in paragraph (b)(1)(i)(A) of this section (see paragraph (d)(3)(v) of this section for special rules to substantiate the residence of individual beneficiaries of not-for-profit organizations) and on behalf of U.S. exempt organizations that have received determination letters under section 501(c)(3); or

(B) More than 50 percent of its annual support is derived from individuals described in paragraph (b)(1)(i)(A) of this section (see paragraph (d)(3)(v) of this section for special rules to substantiate the residence of individual supporters of not-for-profit organizations).

(5) *Pension funds.*—(i) *Pension fund defined.*—The term *pension fund* shall mean a government pension fund or a nongovernment pension fund, as those terms are defined, respectively, in paragraphs (b)(5)(ii) and (iii) of this section, that is a trust, fund, foundation, or other entity that is established exclusively for the benefit of employees or former employees of one or more employers, the principal purpose of which is to provide retirement, disability, and death benefits to beneficiaries of such entity and persons designated by such beneficiaries in consideration for prior services rendered.

(ii) *Government pension funds.*—A government pension fund is a pension fund that is a controlled entity of a foreign sovereign within the principles of § 1.892-2T(c)(1) (relating to pension funds established for the benefit of employees or former employees of a foreign government).

(iii) *Nongovernment pension funds.*—A nongovernment pension fund is a pension fund that—

(A) Is administered in a foreign country and is subject to supervision or regulation by a governmental authority (or other authority delegated to perform such supervision or regulation by a governmental authority) in such country;

(B) Is generally exempt from income taxation in its country of administration;

(C) Has 100 or more beneficiaries; and

(D) The trustees, directors or other administrators of which pension fund provide the documentation required in paragraph (d) of this section.

(iv) *Beneficiary of a pension fund.*—The term *beneficiary of a pension fund* shall mean any person who has made contributions to a pension fund, as that term is defined in paragraph (b)(5)(i) of this section, or on whose behalf contributions have been made, and who is currently receiving retirement, disability, or death benefits from the pension fund or can reasonably be expected to receive such benefits in the future, whether or not the person's right to receive benefits from the fund has vested. See paragraph (c)(7) of this section for rules regarding the computation of stock ownership through nongovernment pension funds.

(c) *Rules for determining constructive ownership.*—(1) *General rules for attribution.*—For purposes of applying paragraph (a) of this section and the exception to the closely-held test in § 1.883-1(d)(3)(ii), stock owned by or for a corporation, partnership, trust, estate, or mutual insurance company or similar entity shall be treated as owned proportionately by its shareholders, partners, beneficiaries, grantors, or other interest holders, as provided in paragraphs (c)(2) through (7) of this section. The proportionate interest rules of this paragraph (c) shall apply successively upward through the chain of ownership, and a person's proportionate interest shall be computed for the relevant days or period taken into account in determining whether a foreign corporation satisfies the requirements of paragraph (a) of this section. Stock treated as owned by a person by reason of this paragraph (c) shall be treated as actually owned by such person for purposes of this section. An owner of an interest in an association taxable as a corporation shall be treated as a shareholder of such association for purposes of this paragraph (c). Stock issued in bearer form will not be treated as owned proportionately by its shareholders unless the shares are maintained in a dematerialized or immobilized book-entry system, as described in § 1.883-1(c)(3)(i)(G).

(2) *Partnerships.*—(i) *General rule.*—A partner shall be treated as having an interest in stock of a foreign corporation owned by a partnership in proportion to the least of—

(A) The partner's percentage distributive share of the partnership's dividend income from the stock;

(B) The partner's percentage distributive share of gain from disposition of the stock by the partnership; or

(C) The partner's percentage distributive share of the stock (or proceeds from the disposition of the stock) upon liquidation of the partnership.

(ii) *Partners resident in the same country.*—For purposes of this paragraph, all qualified shareholders that are partners in a partnership and that are residents of, or organized in, the same qualified foreign country shall be treated as one partner. Thus, the percentage distributive shares of dividend income, gain and liquidation rights of all qualified shareholders that are partners in a partnership and that are residents of, or organized in, the same qualified foreign country are aggregated prior to determining the least of the three percentages set out in paragraph (c)(2)(i) of this section. For the meaning of the term *resident*, see paragraph (b)(2) of this section.

(iii) *Examples.*—The rules of paragraph (c)(2)(ii) of this section are illustrated by the following examples:

Example 1. Stock held solely by qualified shareholders through a partnership. Country X grants an equivalent exemption. A and B are individual residents of Country X and are qualified shareholders within the meaning of paragraph (b)(1) of this section. A and B are the sole partners of Partnership P. P's only asset is the stock of Corporation Z, a Country X corporation seeking a reciprocal exemption under this section. A's distributive share of P's income and gain on the disposition of P's assets is 80 percent, but A's distributive share of P's assets (or the proceeds therefrom) on P's liquidation is 20 percent. B's distributive share of P's income and gain is 20 percent and B is entitled to 80 percent of the assets (or proceeds therefrom) on P's liquidation. Under the attribution rules of paragraph (c)(2)(ii) of this section, A and B will be treated as a single partner owning in the aggregate 100 percent of the stock of Z owned by P.

Example 2. Stock held by both qualified and nonqualified shareholders through a partnership. Assume the same facts as in *Example 1* except that C, an individual who is not a resident of a qualified foreign country, is also a partner in P and that C's distributive share of P's income is 60 percent. The distributive shares of A and B are the same as in *Example 1*, except that A's distributive share of income is 20 percent. Under the attribution rules of paragraph (c)(2)(ii) of this section, qualified shareholders A and B will be treated as a single partner owning in the aggregate 40 percent of the stock of Z owned by P (i.e., the lowest aggregate percentage of A and B's distributive shares of dividend income (40 percent), gain (100 percent), and liquidation rights (100 percent) with respect to the Z stock). Thus, only 40 percent of the Z stock is treated as owned by qualified shareholders.

Example 3. Stock held through tiered partnerships. Country X grants an equivalent exemption. A and B are individual residents of Country X and are qualified shareholders within the meaning of paragraph (b)(1) of this section. A and B are the sole partners of Partnership P. P is a partner in Partnership P1, which owns the stock of Corporation Z, a Country X corporation seeking a reciprocal exemption under this section. Assume that P's distributive share of the dividend income, gain and liquidation rights with respect to the Z stock held by P1 is 40 percent. Assume that of the remaining partners of P1 only D is a qualified shareholder. D's distributive share of P1's dividend income and gain is 15 percent; D's distributive share of P1's assets on liquidation is 25 percent. Under the attribution rules of paragraph (c)(2)(ii) of this section, A and B, treated as a single partner, will own 40 percent of the Z stock owned by P1 (100 percent × 40 percent) and D will be treated as owning 15 percent of the Z stock owned by P1 (the least of D's dividend income (15 percent), gain (15 percent), and liquidation rights (25 percent) with respect to the Z stock). Thus, 55 percent of the Z stock owned by P1 is treated as owned by qualified shareholders.

(3) *Trusts and estates.*—(i) *Beneficiaries.*—In general, an individual shall be treated as having an interest in stock of a foreign corporation owned by a trust or estate in proportion to the individual's actuarial interest in the trust or estate, as provided in section 318(a)(2)(B)(i), except that an income beneficiary's actuarial interest in the trust will be determined as if the trust's only asset were the stock. The interest of a remainder beneficiary in stock will be equal to 100 percent minus the sum of the percentages of any interest in the stock held by income beneficiaries. The ownership of an interest in stock owned by a trust shall not be attributed to any beneficiary whose interest cannot be determined under the preceding sentence, and any such interest, to the extent not attributed by reason of this paragraph (c)(3)(i), shall not be considered owned by a beneficiary unless all potential beneficiaries with respect to the stock are qualified shareholders. In addition, a beneficiary's actuarial interest will be treated as zero to the extent that someone other than the beneficiary is treated as owning the stock under paragraph (c)(3)(ii) of this section. A substantially separate and independent share of a trust, within the meaning of section 663(c), shall be treated as a separate trust for purposes of this paragraph (c)(3)(i), provided that payment of income, accumulated income or corpus of a share of one beneficiary (or group of beneficiaries) cannot affect the proportionate share

of income, accumulated income or corpus of another beneficiary (or group of beneficiaries).

(ii) *Grantor trusts.*—A person is treated as the owner of stock of a foreign corporation owned by a trust to the extent that the stock is included in the portion of the trust that is treated as owned by the person under sections 671 through 679 (relating to grantors and others treated as substantial owners).

(4) *Corporations that issue stock.*—A shareholder of a corporation that issues stock shall be treated as owning stock of a foreign corporation that is owned by such corporation on any day in a proportion that equals the value of the stock owned by such shareholder to the value of all stock of such corporation. If, however, there is an agreement, express or implied, that a shareholder of a corporation will not receive distributions from the earnings of stock owned by the corporation, the shareholder will not be treated as owning that stock owned by the corporation.

(5) *Taxable nonstock corporations.*—A taxable nonstock corporation that is entitled in its country of organization to deduct from its taxable income amounts distributed for charitable purposes may deem a recipient of such charitable distributions to be a shareholder of such taxable nonstock corporation in the same proportion as the amount that such beneficiary receives in the taxable year bears to the total income of such taxable nonstock corporation in the taxable year. Whether each such recipient is a qualified shareholder may then be determined under paragraph (b) of this section or under the special rules of paragraph (d)(3)(vii) of this section.

(6) *Mutual insurance companies and similar entities.*—Stock held by a mutual insurance company, mutual savings bank, or similar entity (including an association taxable as a corporation that does not issue stock interests) shall be considered owned proportionately by the policyholders, depositors, or other owners in the same proportion that such persons share in the surplus of such entity upon liquidation or dissolution.

(7) *Computation of beneficial interests in nongovernment pension funds.*—Stock held by a pension fund shall be considered owned by the beneficiaries of the fund equally on a pro-rata basis if—

(i) The pension fund meets the requirements of paragraph (b)(5)(iii) of this section;

(ii) The trustees, directors or other administrators of the pension fund have no knowledge, and no reason to know, that a pro-rata allocation of interests of the fund to all beneficiaries would differ significantly from an actuarial allocation of interests in the fund (or, if the beneficiaries' actuarial interest in the stock held directly or indirectly by the pension fund differs from the beneficiaries' actuarial interest in the pension fund, the actuarial interests computed by reference to the beneficiaries' actuarial interest in the stock);

(iii) Either—

(A) Any overfunding of the pension fund would be payable, pursuant to the governing instrument or the laws of the foreign country in which the pension fund is administered, only to, or for the benefit of, one or more corporations that are organized in the country in which the pension fund is administered, individual beneficiaries of the pension fund or their designated beneficiaries, or social or charitable causes (the reduction of the obligation of the sponsoring company or companies to make future contributions to the pension fund by reason of overfunding shall not itself result in such overfunding being deemed to be payable to or for the benefit of such company or companies); or

(B) The foreign country in which the pension fund is administered has laws that are designed to prevent overfunding of a pension fund and the funding of the pension fund is within the guidelines of such laws; or

(C) The pension fund is maintained to provide benefits to employees in a particular industry, profession, or group of industries or professions and employees of at least 10 companies (other than companies that are owned or controlled, directly or indirectly, by the same interests) contribute to the pension fund or receive benefits from the pension fund; and

(iv) The trustees, directors or other administrators provide the relevant documentation as required in paragraph (d) of this section.

(d) *Substantiation of stock ownership.*—(1) *General rule.*—A foreign corporation that relies on this section to satisfy the stock ownership test of § 1.883-1(c)(2), must establish all the facts necessary to satisfy the Commissioner that more than 50 percent of the value of its shares is owned, or treated as owned applying paragraph (c) of this section, by qualified shareholders for the relevant period. If a foreign corporation relies upon bearer shares in the chain of ownership to satisfy one of the stock ownership tests, the foreign corporation must also establish all of the facts necessary to satisfy the Commissioner that such shares are maintained in a dematerialized book-entry system, as described in § 1.883-1(c)(3)(i)(G), for the benefit of the relevant shareholder.

(2) *Application of general rule.*—(i) *Ownership statements.*—Except as provided in paragraph (d)(3) of this section, a person shall only be treated as a qualified shareholder of a foreign corporation if—

(A) For the relevant period, the person completes an ownership statement described in paragraph (d)(4) of this section or has a valid ownership statement in effect under paragraph (d)(2)(ii) of this section;

(B) In the case of a person owning stock in the foreign corporation indirectly through one or more intermediaries (including mere legal owners or recordholders acting as nominees), each intermediary in the chain of ownership between that person and the foreign corporation seeking qualified foreign corporation status completes an intermediary ownership statement described in paragraph (d)(4)(v) of this section or has a valid intermediary ownership statement in effect under paragraph (d)(2)(ii) of this section; and

(C) The foreign corporation seeking qualified foreign corporation status obtains the statements described in paragraphs (d)(2)(i)(A) and (B) of this section.

(ii) *Three-year period of validity.*—The ownership statements required in paragraph (d)(2)(i) of this section shall remain valid until the earlier of the last day of the third calendar year following the year in which the ownership statement is signed, or the day that a change of circumstance occurs that makes any information on the ownership statement incorrect. For example, an ownership statement signed on September 30, 2000, remains valid through December 31, 2003, unless a change of circumstance occurs that makes any information on the ownership statement incorrect.

(3) *Special rules.*—(i) *Substantiating residence of certain shareholders.*—A foreign corporation seeking qualified foreign corporation status or an intermediary that is a direct or indirect shareholder of such foreign corporation may substantiate the residence of certain shareholders, for purposes of paragraph (b)(2)(i)(B) of this section, under one of the following special rules in paragraphs (d)(3)(ii) through (viii) of this section, in lieu of obtaining the ownership statements required in paragraph (d)(2)(i) of this section from such shareholders.

(ii) *Special rule for registered shareholders owning less than one percent of widely-held corporations.*—A foreign corporation with at least 250 registered shareholders, that is not a publicly-traded corporation, as described in § 1.883-2 (a widely-held corporation), is not required to obtain an ownership statement from an individual shareholder owning less than one percent of the widely- held corporation at all times during the taxable year if the requirements of paragraphs (d)(3)(ii)(A) and (B) of this section are satisfied. If the widely-held foreign corporation is the foreign corporation seeking qualified foreign corporation status, or an intermediary that meets the documentation requirements of paragraphs (d)(4)(v)(A) and (B) of this section, the widely-held foreign corporation may treat the address of record in its ownership records as the residence of any less than one percent individual shareholder if—

(A) The individual's address of record is a specific street address and not a nonresidential address, such as a post office box or in care of a financial intermediary or stock transfer agent; and

(B) The officers and directors of the widely-held corporation neither know nor have reason to know that the individual does not reside at that address.

(iii) *Special rule for beneficiaries of pension funds.*—(A) *Government pension fund.*—An individual who is a beneficiary of a government pension fund, as defined in paragraph (b)(5)(ii) of this section, may be treated as a resident of the country in which the pension fund is administered if the pension fund satisfies the documentation requirements of paragraphs (d)(4)(v)(A) and (C)(*1*) of this section.

(B) *Nongovernment pension fund.*—An individual who is a beneficiary of a nongovernment pension fund, as described in paragraph (b)(5)(iii) of this section, may be treated as a resident of the country of the beneficiary's address as it appears on the records of the fund, provided it is not a nonresidential address, such as a post office box or an address in care of a financial intermediary, and provided none of the trustees, directors or other administrators of the pension fund know, or have reason to know, that the beneficiary is not an individual resident of such foreign country. The rules of this paragraph (d)(3)(iii)(B) shall apply only if the nongovernment pension fund satisfies the documentation requirements of paragraphs (d)(4)(v)(A) and (C)(2) of this section.

(iv) *Special rule for stock owned by publicly-traded corporations.*—Any stock in a foreign corporation seeking qualified foreign corporation status that is owned by a publicly-traded corporation will be treated as owned by an individual resident in the country where the publicly-traded corporation is organized if the foreign corporation receives the statement described in paragraph (d)(4)(iii) of this section from the publicly-traded corporation and copies of any relevant ownership statements from shareholders of the publicly-traded corporation relied on to satisfy the exception to the closely-held test of § 1.883-2(d)(3)(ii), as required in paragraph (d)(2)(i) of this section.

(v) *Special rule for not-for-profit organizations.*—For purposes of meeting the ownership requirements of paragraph (a) of this section, a not-for-profit organization may rely on the addresses of record of its individual beneficiaries and supporters to determine the residence of an individual beneficiary or supporter, within the meaning of paragraph (b)(2)(i)(B) of this section, to the extent required under paragraph (b)(4) of this section, provided that—

(A) The addresses of record are not nonresidential addresses such as a post office box or in care of a financial intermediary;

(B) The officers, directors or administrators of the organization do not know or have reason to know that the individual beneficiaries or supporters do not reside at that address; and

(C) The foreign corporation seeking qualified foreign corporation status receives the statement required in paragraph (d)(4)(iv) of this section from the not-for-profit organization.

(vi) *Special rule for a foreign airline covered by an air services agreement.*—A foreign airline that is covered by a bilateral Air Services Agreement in force between the United States and the qualified foreign country in which the airline is organized may rely exclusively on the Air Services Agreement currently in effect and will not have to otherwise substantiate its ownership under this section, provided that the United States has not waived the ownership requirements in the agreement or that the ownership requirements have not otherwise been made ineffective. Such an airline will be treated as owned by qualified shareholders resident in the country where the foreign airline is organized.

(vii) *Special rule for taxable nonstock corporations.*—Any stock in a foreign corporation seeking qualified foreign corporation status that is owned by a taxable nonstock corporation will be treated as owned, in any taxable year, by the recipients of distributions made during that taxable year, as set out in paragraph (c)(5) of this section. The taxable nonstock corporation may treat the address of record in its distribution records as the residence of any recipient if—

(A) An individual recipient's address is in a qualified foreign country and is a specific street address and not a nonresidential address, such as a post office box or in care of a financial intermediary or stock transfer agent;

(B) The address of a nonindividual recipient's principal place of business is in a qualified foreign country;

(C) The officers and directors of the taxable nonstock corporation neither know nor have reason to know that the recipients do not reside or have their principal place of business at such addresses; and

(D) The foreign corporation receives the statement described in paragraph (d)(4)(v)(D) of this section from the taxable nonstock corporation intermediary.

(viii) *Special rule for closely-held corporations traded in the United States.*—To demonstrate that a class of stock is not closely-held for purposes of § 1.883-2(d)(3)(i), a foreign corporation whose stock is traded on an established securities market in the United States may rely on current Schedule 13D and Schedule 13G filings with the Securities and Exchange Commission to identify its 5-percent shareholders in each class of stock relied upon to meet the regularly traded test, without having to make any independent investigation to determine the identity of the 5-percent shareholder. However, if any class of stock is determined to be closely-held within the meaning of § 1.883-2(d)(3)(i), the publicly traded corporation cannot satisfy the requirements of § 1.883-2(e) unless it obtains sufficient documentation described in this paragraph (d) to demonstrate that the requirements of § 1.883-2(d)(3)(ii) are met with respect to the 5-percent shareholders.

(4) *Ownership statements from shareholders.*—(i) *Ownership statements from individuals.*—An ownership statement from an individual is a written statement signed by the individual under penalties of perjury stating—

(A) The individual's name, permanent address and country where the individual is fully liable to tax as a resident, if any;

(B) If the individual was not a resident of the country for the entire taxable year of the foreign corporation seeking qualified foreign corporation status, each of the foreign countries in which the individual resided and the dates of such residence during the taxable year of such foreign corporation;

(C) If the individual directly owns shares of stock in the corporation seeking qualified foreign corporation status, the name of the corporation, the number of shares in each class of stock of the corporation owned by the individual, whether any such shares are issued in bearer form and maintained in a dematerialized or immobilized book-entry system, as described in § 1.883-1(c)(3)(i)(G), and the period (or periods) in the taxable year of the foreign corporation during which the individual owned the shares;

(D) If the individual directly owns an interest in a corporation, partnership, trust, estate, or other intermediary that directly or indirectly owns stock in the corporation seeking qualified foreign corporation status, the name of the intermediary, the number and class of shares or the amount and nature of the interest that the individual holds in such intermediary, and, if the intermediary is a corporation, whether any such shares are issued in bearer form and maintained in a dematerialized or immobilized book-entry system, as described in § 1.883-1(c)(3)(i)(G), and the period (or periods) in the taxable year of the foreign corporation seeking qualified foreign corporation status during which the individual held such interest;

(E) To the extent known by the individual, a description of the chain of ownership through which the individual owns stock in the corporation seeking qualified foreign corporation status, including the name and address of each intermediary standing between the intermediary described in paragraph (d)(4)(i)(D) of this section and the foreign corporation and whether this interest is owned either directly or indirectly through bearer shares; and

(F) Any other information as specified in guidance published by the Internal Revenue Service (see § 601.601(d)(2) of this chapter).

(ii) *Ownership statements from foreign governments.*—An ownership statement from a foreign government that is a qualified shareholder is a written statement—

(A) Signed by any one of the following—

(1) An official of the governmental authority, agency or office who has supervisory authority with respect to the government's ownership interest and who is authorized to sign such a statement on behalf of the authority, agency or office; or

(2) The competent authority of the foreign country (as defined in the income tax convention between the United States and the foreign country); or

(3) An income tax return preparer that, for purposes of this paragraph (d)(4)(ii) only, shall mean a firm of licensed or certified public accountants, a law firm whose principals or members are admitted to practice in one or more states, territories or possessions of the United States or the country of such government, or a bank or other financial institution licensed to do business in such foreign country and having assets at least equivalent to 50 million U.S. dollars and who is authorized to represent the government or governmental authority; and

(B) That provides—

(1) The title of the official or other person signing the statement;

(2) The name and address of the government authority, agency or office that has supervisory authority and, if applicable, the income tax preparer which has prepared such ownership statement;

(3) The information described in paragraphs (d)(4)(i)(C) through (E) of this section (as if the language applied "government" instead of "individual") with respect to the government's direct or indirect ownership of stock in the corporation seeking qualified resident status;

(4) In the case of an ownership statement prepared by an income tax return preparer, a statement under penalties of perjury identifying the documentation relied upon in the conduct of due diligence for the taxable year to determine the aggregate government investment in the stock of the shipping or aircraft company in

preparation of such ownership statement attached to a valid power of attorney to represent the taxpayer for the taxable year; and

(5) Any other information as specified in guidance published by the Internal Revenue Service (see § 601.601(d)(2) of this chapter).

(iii) *Ownership statements from publicly-traded corporate shareholders.*—An ownership statement from a publicly-traded corporation that is a direct or indirect owner of the corporation seeking qualified foreign corporation status is a written statement, signed under penalties of perjury by a person that would be authorized to sign a tax return on behalf of the shareholder corporation containing the following information—

(A) The name of the country in which the stock is primarily traded;

(B) The name of the established securities market or markets on which the stock is listed;

(C) A description of each class of stock relied upon to meet the requirements of § 1.883-2(d)(1), including the number of shares issued and outstanding as of the close of the taxable year;

(D) For each class of stock relied upon to meet the requirements of § 1.883-2(d)(1), if one or more 5-percent shareholders, as defined in § 1.883-2(d)(3)(i), own in the aggregate 50 percent or more of the vote and value of the outstanding shares of that class of stock for more than half the number of days during the taxable year—

(1) The days during the taxable year of the corporation in which the stock was closely-held without regard to the exception in paragraph (d)(3)(ii) of this section and the percentage of the vote and value of the class of stock that is owned by 5-percent shareholders during such days;

(2) For each qualified shareholder who owns or is treated as owning stock in the closely-held block upon whom the corporation intends to rely to satisfy the exception to the closely-held test of § 1.883-2(d)(3)(ii)—

(i) The name of each such shareholder;

(ii) The percentage of the total value of the class of stock held by each such shareholder and the days during which the stock was held;

(iii) The address of record of each such shareholder; and

(iv) The country of residence of each such shareholder, determined under paragraph (b)(2) or (d)(3) of this section;

(E) The information described in paragraphs (d)(4)(i)(C) through (E) of this section (as if the language applied "publicly-traded corporation" instead of "individual") with respect to the publicly-traded corporation's direct or indirect ownership of stock in the corporation seeking qualified resident status; and

(F) Any other information as specified in guidance published by the Internal Revenue Service (see § 601.601(d)(2) of this chapter).

(iv) *Ownership statements from not-for-profit organizations.*—An ownership statement from a not-for-profit organization (other than a pension fund as defined in paragraph (b)(5) of this section) is a written statement signed by a person authorized to sign a tax return on behalf of the organization under penalties of perjury stating—

(A) The name, permanent address, and principal location of the activities of the organization (if different from its permanent address);

(B) The information described in paragraphs (d)(4)(i)(C) through (E) of this section (as if the language applied "not-for-profit organization" instead of "individual");

(C) A representation that the not-for-profit organization satisfies the requirements of paragraph (b)(4) of this section; and

(D) Any other information as specified in guidance published by the Internal Revenue Service (see § 601.601(d)(2) of this chapter).

(v) *Ownership statements from intermediaries.*—(A) *General rule.*—The foreign corporation seeking qualified foreign corporation status under the shareholder stock ownership test must obtain an intermediary ownership statement from each intermediary standing in the chain of ownership between it and the qualified shareholders on whom it relies to meet this test. An intermediary ownership statement is a written statement signed under penalties of perjury by the intermediary (if the intermediary is an individual) or a person who would be authorized to sign a tax return on behalf of the intermediary (if the intermediary is not an individual) containing the following information—

(1) The name, address, country of residence, and principal place of business (in the case of a corporation or partnership) of the intermediary, and, if the intermediary is a trust or estate, the name and permanent address of all trustees or executors (or equivalent under foreign law), or if the intermediary is a pension fund, the name and permanent address of place of administration of the intermediary;

(2) The information described in paragraphs (d)(4)(i)(C) through (E) of this section (as if the language applied "intermediary" instead of "individual");

(3) If the intermediary is a nominee for a shareholder or another intermediary, the name and permanent address of the shareholder, or the name and principal place of business of such other intermediary;

(4) If the intermediary is not a nominee for a shareholder or another intermediary, the name and country of residence (within the meaning of paragraph (b)(2) of this section) and the proportionate interest in the intermediary of each direct shareholder, partner, beneficiary, grantor, or other interest holder (or if the direct holder is a nominee, of its beneficial shareholder, partner, beneficiary, grantor, or other interest holder), on which the foreign corporation seeking qualified foreign corporation status intends to rely to satisfy the requirements of paragraph (a) of this section. In addition, such intermediary must obtain from all such persons an ownership statement that includes the period of time during the taxable year for which the interest in the intermediary was owned by the shareholder, partner, beneficiary, grantor or other interest holder. For purposes of this paragraph (d)(4)(v)(A), the proportionate interest of a person in an intermediary is the percentage interest (by value) held by such person, determined using the principles for attributing ownership in paragraph (c) of this section;

(5) If the intermediary is a widely-held corporation with registered shareholders owning less than one percent of the stock of such widely-held corporation, the statement set out in paragraph (d)(4)(v)(B) of this section, relating to ownership statements from widely-held intermediaries with registered shareholders owning less than one percent of such widely-held intermediaries;

(6) If the intermediary is a pension fund, within the meaning of paragraph (b)(5) of this section, the statement set out in paragraph (d)(4)(v)(C) of this section, relating to ownership statements from pension funds;

(7) If the intermediary is a taxable nonstock corporation, within the meaning of paragraph (c)(5) of this section, the statement set out in paragraph (d)(4)(v)(D) of this section, relating to ownership statements from intermediaries that are taxable nonstock corporations; and

(8) Any other information as specified in guidance published by the Internal Revenue Service (see § 601.601(d)(2) of this chapter).

(B) *Ownership statements from widely-held intermediaries with registered shareholders owning less than one percent of such widely-held intermediary.*—An ownership statement from an intermediary that is a corporation with at least 250 registered shareholders, but that is not a publicly-traded corporation within the meaning of § 1.883-2, and that relies on paragraph (d)(3)(ii) of this section, relating to the special rule for registered shareholders owning less than one percent of widely-held corporations, must provide the following information in addition to the information required in paragraph (d)(4)(v)(A) of this section—

(1) The aggregate proportionate interest by country of residence in the widely-held corporation of such registered shareholders or other interest holders whose address of record is a specific street address and not a nonresidential address, such as a post office box or in care of a financial intermediary or stock transfer agent; and

(2) A representation that the officers and directors of the widely-held intermediary neither know nor have reason to know that the individual shareholder does not reside at his or her address of record in the corporate records; and

(3) Any other information as specified in guidance published by the Internal Revenue Service (see § 601.601(d)(2) of this chapter).

(C) *Ownership statements from pension funds.*—*(1) Ownership statements from government pension funds.*—A government pension fund (as defined in paragraph (b)(5)(ii) of this section) that relies on paragraph (d)(3)(iii) of this section (relating to the special rules for pension funds) generally must provide the documentation required in paragraph (d)(4)(v)(A) of this section, and, in addition, the government pension fund must also provide the following information—

(i) The name of the country in which the plan is administered;

(ii) A representation that the fund is established exclusively for the benefit of employees or former employees of a foreign government, or employees or former employees of a foreign government and nongovernmental employees or former employees that perform or performed governmental or social services;

(iii) A representation that the funds that comprise the trust are managed by trustees who are employees of, or persons appointed by, the foreign government;

(iv) A representation that the trust forming part of the pension plan provides for retirement, disability, or death benefits in consideration for prior services rendered;

(v) A representation that the income of the trust satisfies the obligations of the foreign government to the participants under the plan, rather than inuring to the benefit of a private person; and

(vi) Any other information as specified in guidance published by the Internal Revenue Service (see § 601.601(d)(2) of this chapter).

(2) *Ownership statements from nongovernment pension funds.*—The trustees, directors, or other administrators of the nongovernment pension fund, as defined in paragraph (b)(5)(iii) of this section, that rely on paragraph (d)(3)(iii) of this section, relating to the special rules for pension funds, generally must provide the pension fund's intermediary ownership statement described in paragraph (d)(4)(v)(A) of this section. In addition, the nongovernment pension fund must also provide the following information—

(i) The name of the country in which the pension fund is administered;

(ii) A representation that the pension fund is subject to supervision or regulation by a governmental authority (or other authority delegated to perform such supervision or regulation by a governmental authority) in such country, and, if so, the name of the governmental authority (or other authority delegated to perform such supervision or regulation);

(iii) A representation that the pension fund is generally exempt from income taxation in its country of administration;

(iv) The number of beneficiaries in the pension plan;

(v) The aggregate percentage interest of beneficiaries by country of residence based on addresses shown on the books and records of the fund, provided the addresses are not nonresidential addresses, such as a post office box or an address in care of a financial intermediary, and provided none of the trustees, directors or other administrators of the pension fund know, or have reason to know, that the beneficiary is not a resident of such foreign country;

(vi) A representation that the pension fund meets the requirements of paragraph (b)(5)(iii) of this section;

(vii) A representation that the trustees, directors or other administrators of the pension fund have no knowledge, and no reason to know, that a pro-rata allocation of interests of the fund to all beneficiaries would differ significantly from an actuarial allocation of interests in the fund (or, if the beneficiaries' actuarial interest in the stock held directly or indirectly by the pension fund differs from the beneficiaries' actuarial interest in the pension fund, the actuarial interests computed by reference to the beneficiaries' actuarial interest in the stock);

(viii) A representation that any overfunding of the pension fund would be payable, pursuant to the governing instrument or the laws of the foreign country in which the pension fund is administered, only to, or for the benefit of, one or more corporations that are organized in the country in which the pension fund is administered, individual beneficiaries of the pension fund or their designated beneficiaries, or social or charitable causes (the reduction of the obligation of the sponsoring company or companies to make future contributions to the pension fund by reason of overfunding shall not itself result in such overfunding being deemed to be payable to or for the benefit of such company or companies); or that the foreign country in which the pension fund is administered has laws that are designed to prevent overfunding of a pension fund and the funding of the pension fund is within the guidelines of such laws; or that the pension fund is maintained to provide benefits to employees in a particular industry, profession, or group of industries or professions, and that employees of at least 10 companies (other than companies that are owned or controlled, directly or indirectly, by the same interests) contribute to the pension fund or receive benefits from the pension fund; and

(ix) Any other information as specified in guidance published by the Internal Revenue Service (see § 601.601(d)(2) of this chapter).

(3) *Time for making determinations.*—The determinations required to be made under this paragraph (d)(4)(v)(C) shall be made using information shown on the records of the pension fund for a date during the foreign corporation's taxable year to which the determination is relevant.

(D) *Ownership statements from taxable nonstock corporations.*—An ownership statement from an intermediary that is a taxable nonstock corporation must provide the following information in addition to the information required in paragraph (d)(4)(v)(A) of this section—

(1) With respect to paragraph (d)(4)(v)(A)(7) of this section, for each beneficiary that is treated as a qualified shareholder, the name, address of residence (in the case of an individual beneficiary, the address must be a specific street address and not a nonresidential address, such as a post office box or in care of a financial intermediary; in the case of a nonindividual beneficiary, the address of the principal place of business) and percentage that is the same proportion as the amount that the beneficiary receives in the tax year bears to the total net income of the taxable nonstock corporation in the tax year;

(2) A representation that the officers and directors of the taxable nonstock corporation neither know nor have reason to know that the individual beneficiaries do not reside at the address listed in paragraph (d)(4)(v)(D)(1) of this section or that any other nonindividual beneficiary does not conduct its primary activities at such address or in such country of residence; and

(3) Any other information as specified in guidance published by the Internal Revenue Service (see § 601.601(d)(2) of this chapter).

(5) *Availability and retention of documents for inspection.*—The documentation described in paragraphs (d)(3) and (4) of this section must be retained by the corporation seeking qualified foreign corporation status (the foreign corporation) until the expiration of the statute of limitations for the taxable year of the foreign corporation to which the documentation relates. Such documentation must be made available for inspection by the Commissioner at such time and place as the Commissioner may request in writing.

(e) *Reporting requirements.*—A foreign corporation relying on the qualified shareholder stock ownership test of this section to meet the stock ownership test of § 1.883-1(c)(2) must provide the following information in addition to the information required in § 1.883-1(c)(3) to be included in its Form 1120-F, "U.S. Income Tax Return of a Foreign Corporation," for each taxable year. The information should be current as of the end of the corporation's taxable year. The information must include the following—

(1) A representation that more than 50 percent of the value of the outstanding shares of the corporation is owned (or treated as owned by reason of paragraph (c) of this section) by qualified shareholders for each category of income for which the exemption is claimed;

(2) With respect to all qualified shareholders relied upon to satisfy the 50 percent ownership test of paragraph (a) of this section, the total number of such qualified shareholders as defined in paragraph (b)(1) of this section; the total percentage of the value of the outstanding shares owned, applying the attribution rules of paragraph (c) of this section, by such qualified shareholders by country of residence or organization, whichever is applicable; and the period during the taxable year of the foreign corporation that such stock was held by qualified shareholders; and

(3) Any other relevant information specified by the Form 1120-F, "U.S. Income Tax Return of a Foreign Corporation," and its accompanying instructions, or in published guidance by the Internal Revenue Service (see § 601.601(d)(2) of this chapter). [Reg. § 1.883-4.]

☐ [*T.D. 9087, 8-25-2003. Amended by T.D. 9332, 6-22-2007 and T.D. 9502, 9-16-2010.*]

§ 1.883-5. Effective/applicability dates.—Effective/applicability dates.—(a) *General rule.*—Sections 1.883-1 through 1.883-4 apply to taxable years of a foreign corporation seeking qualified foreign corporation status beginning after September 24, 2004.

(b) *Election for retroactive application.*—Taxpayers may elect to apply §§ 1.883-1 through 1.883-4 for any open taxable year of the foreign corporation beginning after December 31, 1986, except that the substantiation and reporting requirements of § 1.883-1(c)(3) (relating to the substantiation and reporting required to be treated as a qualified foreign corporation) or §§ 1.883-2(f), 1.883-3(d) and 1.883-4(e) (relating to additional information to be included in the return to demonstrate whether the foreign corporation satisfies the stock ownership test) will not apply to any year beginning before September 25, 2004. Such election shall apply to the taxable year of the election and to all subsequent taxable years beginning before September 25, 2004.

(c) *Transitional information reporting rule.*—For taxable years of the foreign corporation beginning after September 24, 2004, and until such time as the Form 1120-F, "U.S. Income Tax Return of a Foreign Corporation," or its instructions are revised to provide otherwise, the information required in § 1.883-1(c)(3) and § 1.883-2(f), § 1.883-3(d) or § 1.883-4(e), as applicable, must be included on a written statement attached to the Form 1120-F and filed with the return.

(d) *Effective/applicability dates.*—Except as otherwise provided in this paragraph (d), §§ 1.883-1, 1.883-2, 1.883-3, and 1.883-4 apply to taxable years of the foreign corporation beginning after June 25, 2007, and may be applied to any open taxable years of the foreign corporation beginning on or after December 31, 2004. The portion of any provision concerning bearer shares maintained in a dematerialized or immobilized book-entry system, as described in § 1.883-1(c)(3)(i)(G), applies to taxable years of a foreign corporation beginning on or after September 17, 2010. [Reg. § 1.883-5.]

☐ [*T.D.* 9087, 8-25-2003. Amended by T.D. 9218, 8-5-2005; *T.D.* 9332, 6-22-2007 *and T.D.* 9502, 9-16-2010 (corrected 10-14-2010).]

§ 1.884-0. Overview of regulation provisions for section 884.—(a) *Introduction.*—Section 884 consists of three main parts: a branch profits tax on certain earnings of a foreign corporation's U.S. trade or business; a branch-level interest tax on interest paid, or deemed paid, by a foreign corporation's U.S. trade or business; and an anti-treaty shopping rule. A foreign corporation is subject to section 884 by virtue of owning an interest in a partnership, trust, or estate that is engaged in a U.S. trade or business or has income treated as effectively connected with the conduct of a trade or business in the United States. An international organization (as defined in section 7701(a)(18)) is not subject to the branch profits tax by reason of section 884(e)(5). A foreign government treated as a corporate resident of its country of residence under section 892(a)(3) shall be treated as a corporation for purposes of section 884. The preceding sentence shall be effective for taxable years ending on or after September 11, 1992, except that, for the first taxable year ending on or after that date, the branch profits tax shall not apply to effectively connected earnings and profits of the foreign government earned prior to that date nor to decreases in the U.S. net equity of a foreign government occurring after the close of the preceding taxable year and before that date. Similarly, § 1.884-4 shall apply, in the case of branch interest, only with respect to amounts of interest accrued and paid by a foreign government on or after that date, or, in the case of excess interest, only with respect to amounts attributable to interest accrued by a foreign government on or after that date and apportioned to ECI, as defined in § 1.884-1(d)(1)(iii). Except as otherwise provided, for purposes of the regulations under section 884, the term "U.S. trade or business" includes all the U.S. trades or businesses of a foreign corporation.

(1) *The branch profits tax.*—Section 1.884-1 provides rules for computing the branch profits tax and defines various terms that affect the computation of the tax. In general, section 884(a) imposes a 30-percent branch profits tax on the after-tax earnings of a foreign corporation's U.S. trade or business that are not reinvested in a U.S. trade or business by the close of the taxable year, or are disinvested in a later taxable year. Changes in the value of the equity of the foreign corporation's U.S. trade or business are used as the measure of whether earnings have been reinvested in, or disinvested from, a U.S. trade or business. An increase in the equity during the taxable year is generally treated as a reinvestment of the earnings for the current taxable year; a decrease in the equity during the taxable year is generally treated as a disinvestment of prior years' earnings that have not previously been subject to the branch profits tax. The amount subject to the branch profits tax for the taxable year is the dividend equivalent amount. Section 1.884-2T contains special rules relating to the effect on the branch profits tax of the termination or incorporation of a U.S. trade or business or the liquidation or reorganization of a foreign corporation or its domestic subsidiary.

(2) *The branch-level interest tax.*—Section 1.884-4 provides rules for computing the branch-level interest tax. In general, interest paid by a U.S. trade or business of a foreign corporation ("branch interest", as defined in § 1.884-4(b)) is treated as if it were paid by a domestic corporation and may be subject to tax under section 871(a) or 881, and to withholding under section 1441 or 1442. In addition, if the interest apportioned to ECI exceeds branch interest, the excess is treated as interest paid to the foreign corporation by a wholly-owned domestic corporation and is subject to tax under section 881(a).

(3) *Qualified resident.*—Section 1.884-5 provides rules for determining whether a foreign corporation is a qualified resident of a foreign country. In general, a foreign corporation must be a qualified resident of a foreign country with which the United States has an income tax treaty in order to claim an exemption or rate reduction with respect to the branch profits tax, the branch-level interest tax, and the tax on dividends paid by the foreign corporation.

(b) *Special rules for U.S. possessions.*—(1) Section 884 does not apply to a corporation created or organized in, or under the law of, American Samoa, Guam, the Northern Mariana Islands, or the U.S. Virgin Islands, provided that the conditions of § 1.881-5(c)(1) through (c)(3) are satisfied with respect to such corporation. The preceding sentence applies for taxable years ending after April 9, 2008.

(2) Section 884 does not apply for purposes of determining tax liability incurred to a section 935 possession or the U.S. Virgin Islands by a corporation created or organized in, or under the law of, such possession or the United States. The preceding sentence applies for taxable years ending after April 9, 2008.

* * *

[Reg. § 1.884-0.]

☐ [*T.D.* 8432, 9-10-92. *Amended by T.D.* 8657, 3-5-96; *T.D.* 9194, 4-6-2005 *and T.D.* 9391, 4-4-2008 (*corrected* 5-13-2008).]

§ 1.884-1. Branch profits tax.—(a) *General rule.*—A foreign corporation shall be liable for a branch profits tax in an amount equal to 30 percent of the foreign corporation's dividend equivalent amount for the taxable year. The branch profits tax shall be in addition to the tax imposed by section 882 and shall be reported on a foreign corporation's income tax return for the taxable year. The tax shall be due and payable as provided in section 6151 and such other provisions of Subtitle F of the Internal Revenue Code as apply to the income tax liability of corporations. However, no estimated tax payments shall be due with respect to a foreign corporation's liability for the branch profits tax. See paragraph (g) of this section for the application of the branch profits tax to corporations that are residents of countries with which the United States has an income tax treaty, and § 1.884-2T for the effect on the branch profits tax of the termination or incorporation of a U.S. trade or business, or the liquidation or reorganization of a foreign corporation or its domestic subsidiary.

(b) *Dividend equivalent amount.*—(1) *Definition.*—The term "dividend equivalent amount" means a foreign corporation's effectively connected earnings and profits ("ECEP", as defined in paragraph (f)(1) of this section) for the taxable year, adjusted pursuant to paragraph (b)(2) or (3) of this section, as applicable. The dividend equivalent amount cannot be less than zero.

(2) *Adjustment for increase in U.S. net equity.*—If a foreign corporation's U.S. net equity (as defined in paragraph (c) of this section) as of the close of the taxable year exceeds the foreign corporation's U.S. net equity as of the close of the preceding taxable year, then, for purposes of computing the foreign corporation's dividend equivalent amount for the taxable year, the foreign corporation's ECEP for the taxable year shall be reduced (but not below zero) by the amount of such excess.

(3) *Adjustment for decrease in U.S. net equity.*—(i) *In general.*—Except as provided in paragraph (b)(3)(ii) of this section, if a foreign corporation's U.S. net equity as of the close of the taxable year is less than the foreign corporation's U.S. net equity as of the close of the preceding taxable year, then, for purposes of computing the foreign corporation's dividend equivalent amount for the taxable year, the foreign corporation's ECEP for the taxable year shall be increased by the amount of such difference.

(ii) *Limitation based on accumulated ECEP.*—The increase of a foreign corporation's ECEP under paragraph (b)(3)(i) of this section shall not exceed the accumulated ECEP of the foreign corporation as of the beginning of the taxable year. The term "accumulated ECEP" means the aggregate amount of ECEP of a foreign corporation for preceding taxable years beginning after December 31, 1986, minus the aggregate dividend equivalent amounts for such preceding taxable years. Accumulated ECEP may be less than zero.

(4) *Examples.*—The principles of paragraph (b)(2) and (3) of this section are illustrated by the following examples.

Example 1. Reinvestment of all ECEP. Foreign corporation A, a calendar year taxpayer, had $1,000 U.S. net equity as of the close of 1986 and $100 of ECEP for 1987. A acquires $100 of additional U.S. assets during 1987 and its U.S. net equity as of the close of 1987 is $1,100. In computing A's dividend equivalent amount for 1987, A's ECEP of $100 is reduced under paragraph (b)(2) of this section by the $100 increase in U.S. net equity between the close of 1986 and the close of 1987. A has no dividend equivalent amount for 1987.

Example 2. Partial reinvestment of ECEP. Assume the same facts as in *Example 1* except that A acquires $40 (rather than $100) of U.S. assets during 1987 and its U.S. net equity as of the close of 1987 is $1,040. In computing A's dividend equivalent amount for 1987, A's ECEP of $100 is reduced under paragraph (b)(2) of this section by the $40 increase in U.S. net equity between the close of 1986 and the close of 1987. A has a dividend equivalent amount of $60 for 1987.

Example 3. Disinvestment of prior year's ECEP. Assume the same facts as in *Example 1* for 1987. A has no ECEP for 1988. A's U.S. net equity decreases by $40 (to $1,060) as of the close of 1988. A has a dividend equivalent amount of $40 for 1988, even though it has no ECEP for 1988. A's ECEP of $0 for 1988 is increased under paragraph (b)(3)(i) of this section by the $40 reduction in U.S. net equity (subject to the limitation in paragraph (b)(3)(ii) of this section of $100 of accumulated ECEP).

Example 4. Accumulated ECEP limitation. Assume the same facts as in *Example 2* for 1987. For 1988, A has $125 of ECEP and its U.S. net equity decreases by $50. A's U.S. net equity as of the close of 1988 is $990 ($1,040-$50). In computing A's dividend equivalent amount for 1988, the $125 of ECEP for 1988 is not increased under paragraph (b)(3)(i) of this section by the full amount of the $50 decrease in U.S. net equity during 1988. Rather, the increase in ECEP resulting from the decrease in U.S. net equity is limited to A's accumulated ECEP as of the beginning of 1988. A had $100 of ECEP for 1987 and a dividend equivalent amount of $60 for that year, so A had $40 of accumulated ECEP as of the beginning of 1988. The increase in ECEP resulting from a decrease in U.S. net equity is thus limited to $40, and the dividend equivalent amount for 1988 is $165 ($125 ECEP + $40 decrease in U.S. net equity).

Example 5. Effect of deficits in ECEP. Foreign corporation A, a calendar year taxpayer, has $150 of accumulated ECEP as of the beginning of 1991 ($200 aggregate ECEP less $50 aggregate dividend equivalent amounts for years preceding 1991). A has U.S. net equity of $450 as of the close of 1990, U.S. net equity of $350 as of the close of 1991 (*i.e.,* a $100 decrease in U.S. net equity) and a $90 deficit in ECEP for 1991. A's dividend equivalent amount is $10 for 1991, *i.e.,* A's deficit of $90 in ECEP for 1991 increased by $100, the decrease in A's U.S. net equity during 1991. A portion of the reduction in U.S. net equity in 1991 ($90) is attributable to A's deficit in ECEP for that year. The reduction in U.S. net equity in 1991 ($100) triggers a dividend equivalent amount only to the extent it exceeds the $90 current year deficit in ECEP for 1991. As of the beginning of 1992, A has $50 of accumulated ECEP (*i.e.,* $110 aggregate ECEP less $60 aggregate dividend equivalent amounts for years preceding 1992).

Example 6. Nimble dividend equivalent amount. Foreign corporation A, a calendar year taxpayer, had a deficit in ECEP of $100 for 1987 and $100 for 1988, and has $90 of ECEP for 1989. A had $2,000 U.S. net equity as of the close of 1988 and has $2,000 U.S. net equity as of the close of 1989. A has a dividend equivalent amount of $90 for 1989, its ECEP for the year, even though it has a net deficit of $110 in ECEP for the period 1987-1989.

(c) *U.S. net equity.*—(1) *Definition.*—The term "U.S. net equity" means the aggregate amount of the U.S. assets (as defined in paragraphs (c)(2) and (d)(1) of this section) of a foreign corporation as of the determination date (as defined in paragraph (c)(3) of this section), reduced (including below zero) by the U.S. liabilities (as defined in paragraph (e) of this section) of the foreign corporation as of the determination date.

(2) *Definition of the amount of a U.S. asset.*—(i) *In general.*—For purposes of this section, the term "amount of a U.S. asset" means the U.S. asset's adjusted basis for purposes of computing earnings and profits ("E&P basis") multiplied by the proportion of the asset that is treated as a U.S. asset under paragraphs (d)(1) through (4) of this section. The amount of a U.S. asset that is money shall be its face value. See paragraph (d)(6) of this section for rules concerning the computation of the E&P basis of a U.S. asset.

(ii) *Bad debt reserves.*—A bank described in section 585(a)(2)(B) (without regard to the second sentence thereof) that uses the reserve method of accounting for bad debts for U.S. federal income tax purposes shall decrease the amount of loans that qualify as U.S. assets by any reserve that is permitted under section 585.

(3) *Definition of determination date.*—For purposes of this section, the term "determination date" means the close of the day on which the amount of U.S. net equity is required to be determined. Unless otherwise provided, the U.S. net equity of a foreign corporation is required to be determined as of the close of the foreign corporation's taxable year.

(d) *U.S. assets.*—(1) *Definition of a U.S. asset.*—(i) *General rule.*—Except as provided in paragraph (d)(5) of this section, the term "U.S. asset" means an asset of a foreign corporation (other than an interest in a partnership, trust, or estate) that is held by the corporation as of the determination date if—

(A) All income produced by the asset on the determination date is ECI (as defined in paragraph (d)(1)(iii) of this section) (or would be ECI if the asset produced income on that date); and

(B) All gain from the disposition of the asset would be ECI if the asset were disposed of on that date and the disposition produced gain.

For purposes of determining whether income or gain from an asset would be ECI under this paragraph (d)(1)(i), it is immaterial whether the asset is of a type that is unlikely to, or cannot, produce income or gain. For example, money may be a U.S. asset although it does not produce income or gain. In the case of an asset that does not produce income, however, the determination of whether income from the asset would be ECI shall be made under the principles of section 864 and the regulations thereunder, but without regard to § 1.864-4(c)(2)(iii)(*b*). For purposes of determining whether an asset is a U.S. asset under this paragraph (d)(1), a foreign corporation may presume, unless it has reason to know otherwise, that gain from the sale of personal property (including inventory property) would be U.S. source if gain from the sale of that type of property would ordinarily be attributable to an office or other fixed place of business of the foreign corporation within the United States (within the meaning of section 865(e)(2)).

(ii) *Special rules for assets not described in paragraph (d)(1)(i) of this section.*—An asset of a foreign corporation that is held by the corporation as of the determination date and is not described in paragraph (d)(1)(i) of this section shall be treated as a U.S. asset to the extent provided in paragraph (d)(2) of this section (relating to special rules for certain assets, including assets that produce income or gain at least a portion of which is ECI), and in paragraphs (d)(3) and (4) of this section (relating to special rules for interests in a partnership, trust, and estate).

(iii) *Definition of ECI.*—For purposes of the regulations under section 884, the term "ECI" means income that is effectively connected with the conduct of a trade or business in the United States and income that is treated as effectively connected with the conduct of a trade or business in the United States under any provision of the Code. The term "ECI" also includes all income that is or is treated as effectively connected with the conduct of a U.S. trade or business whether or not the income is included in gross income (for example, interest income earned with respect to tax-exempt bonds).

(2) *Special rules for certain assets.*—(i) *Depreciable and amortizable property.*—An item of depreciable personal property or an item of amortizable intangible property shall be treated as a U.S. asset of a foreign corporation in the same proportion that the amount of the depreciation or amortization with respect to the item of property that is allowable as a deduction, or is includible in cost of goods sold, for the taxable year in computing the effectively connected taxable income of the foreign corporation bears to the total amount of depreciation or amortization computed for the taxable year with respect to the item of property.

(ii) *Inventory.*—An item or pool of inventory property (as defined in section 865(i)(1)) shall be treated as a U.S. asset in the same proportion as the amount of gross receipts from the sale or exchange of such property for the three preceding taxable years (or for such part of the three-year period as the corporation has been in existence) that is effectively connected with the conduct of a U.S. trade or business bears to the total amount of gross receipts from the sale or exchange of such property during such period (or part thereof). If a foreign corporation has not sold or exchanged such property during such three-year period (or part thereof), then the property shall be treated as a U.S. asset in the same proportion that the anticipated amount of gross receipts from the sale or exchange of the property that is reasonably anticipated to be ECI bears to the anticipated total amount of gross receipts from the sale or exchange of the property.

(iii) *Installment obligations.*—An installment obligation received in connection with an installment sale (as defined in section 453(b)) for which an election under section 453(d) has not been made shall be treated as a U.S. asset to the extent that it is received in connection with the sale of a U.S. asset. If an obligation is received in connection with the sale of an asset that is wholly a U.S. asset, it shall be treated as a U.S. asset in its entirety. If a single obligation is received in connection with the sale of an asset that is in part a U.S. asset under the rules of paragraphs (d)(2) through (4) of this section, or in connection with the sale of several assets including one or more non-U.S. assets, the obligation shall be treated as U.S. asset in the same proportion as—

(A) The sum of the amount of gain from the installment sale that would be ECI if the obligation were satisfied in full on the determination date and the adjusted basis of the obligation on such date (as determined under section 453B) attributable to the amount of gain that would be ECI bears to

(B) The sum of the total amount of gain from the sale if the obligation were satisfied in full and the adjusted basis of the obligation on such date (as determined under section 453B).

However, the obligation will only be treated as a U.S. asset if the interest income or original issue discount with respect to the obligation is ECI or the foreign corporation elects to treat the interest or original issue discount as ECI in the same proportion that the obligation is treated as a U.S. asset. A foreign corporation may elect to treat interest income or original issue discount as ECI by reporting such interest income or original issue discount as ECI on its income tax return or an amended return for the taxable year. See paragraph (d)(6)(ii) of this section to determine the E&P basis of an installment obligation for purposes of this paragraph (d)(2)(iii).

(iv) *Receivables.*—(A) *Receivables arising from the sale or exchange of inventory property.*—An account or note receivable (whether or not bearing stated interest) with a maturity not exceeding six months that arises from the sale or exchange of inventory property (as defined in section 865(i)(1)) shall be treated as a U.S. asset in the proportion determined under paragraph (d)(2)(iii) of this section as if the receivable were an installment obligation.

(B) *Receivables arising from the performance of services or leasing of property.*—An account or note receivable (whether or not bearing stated interest) with a maturity not exceeding six months that arises from the performance of services or the leasing of property in the ordinary course of a foreign corporation's trade or business shall be treated as a U.S. asset in the same proportion that the amount of gross income represented by the receivable that is ECI bears to the total amount of gross income represented by the receivable. For purposes of this paragraph (d)(2)(iv)(B), the amount of income represented by a receivable shall not include interest income or original issue discount.

(v) *Bank and other deposits.*—A deposit or credit balance with a person described in section 871(i)(3) or a Federal Reserve Bank that is interest-bearing shall be treated as a U.S. asset if all income derived by the foreign corporation with respect to the deposit or credit balance during the taxable year is ECI. Any other deposit or credit balance shall only be treated as a U.S. asset if the deposit or credit balance is needed in a U.S. trade or business within the meaning of § 1.864-4(c)(2)(iii)(*a*).

(vi) *Debt instruments.*—A debt instrument, as defined in section 1275(a)(1) (other than an asset treated as a U.S. asset under any other subdivision of this paragraph (d)) shall be treated as a U.S. asset, notwithstanding the fact that gain from the sale or exchange of the obligation on the determination date would not be ECI, if—

(A) All income derived by the foreign corporation from such obligation during the taxable year is ECI; and

(B) The yield for the period that the instrument was held during the taxable year equals or exceeds the Applicable Federal Rate for instruments of similar type and maturity.

Shares in a regulated investment company that purchases solely instruments that, under this paragraph (d)(2)(vi), would be U.S. assets if held directly by the foreign corporation shall also be treated as a U.S. asset.

(vii) *Securities held by a foreign corporation engaged in a banking, financing or similar business.*—Securities described in § 1.864-4(c)(5)(ii)(*b*)(3) held by a foreign corporation engaged in the active conduct of a banking, financing, or similar business in the United States during the taxable year shall be treated as U.S. assets in the same proportion that income, gain, or loss from such securities is ECI for the taxable year under § 1.864-4(c)(5)(ii).

(viii) *Federal income taxes.*—An overpayment of Federal income taxes shall be treated as a U.S. asset to the extent that the tax would reduce a foreign corporation's ECEP for the taxable year but for the fact that the tax does not accrue during the taxable year.

(ix) *Losses involving U.S. assets.*—A foreign corporation that sustains, with respect to a U.S. asset, a loss for which a deduction is not allowed under section 165 (in whole or in part) because there exists a reasonable prospect of recovering compensation for the loss shall be treated as having a U.S. asset ("loss property") from the date of the loss in the same proportion that the asset was treated as a U.S. asset immediately before the loss. See paragraph (d)(6)(iv) of this section to determine the E&P basis of the loss property.

(x) *Ruling for involuntary conversion.*—If property that is a U.S. asset of a foreign corporation is compulsorily or involuntarily converted into property not similar or related in service or use (within the meaning of section 1033), the foreign corporation may apply to the Commissioner for a ruling to determine its U.S. assets for the taxable year of the involuntary conversion.

(xi) *Examples.*—The principles of paragraphs (c) and (d)(1) and (2) of this section are illustrated by the following examples.

Example 1. Depreciable property. Foreign corporation A, a calendar year taxpayer, is engaged in a trade or business in the United States. A owns equipment that is used in its manufacturing business in country X and in the United States. Under § 1.861-8, A's depreciation deduction with respect to the equipment is allocated to sales income and is apportioned 70 percent to ECI and 30 percent to income that is not ECI. Under paragraph (d)(2)(ii) of this section, the equipment is 70 percent a U.S. asset. The equipment has an E&P basis of $100 at the beginning of 1993. A's depreciation deduction (for purposes of computing earnings and profits) with respect to the equipment is $10 for 1993. To determine the amount of A's U.S. asset at the close of 1993, the equipment's $90 E&P basis at the close of 1993 is multiplied by 70 percent (the proportion of the asset that is a U.S. asset). The amount of the U.S. asset as of the close of 1993 is $63.

Example 2. U.S. real property interest connected to a U.S. business. FC is a foreign corporation that is a bank, within the meaning of section 585(a)(2)(B) (without regard to the second sentence thereof), and is engaged in the business of taking deposits and making loans through its branch in the United States. In 1996, FC makes a loan in the ordinary course of its lending business in the United States, securing the loan with a mortgage on the U.S. real property being financed by the borrower. In 1997, after the borrower has defaulted on the loan, FC takes title to the real property that secures the loan. On December 31, 1997, FC continues to hold the property, classifying it on its financial statement as *Other Real Estate Owned*. Because all income and gain from the property would be ECI to FC under the principles of section 864(c)(2), the U.S. real property constitutes a U.S. asset within the meaning of paragraph (d) of this section.

Example 3. U.S. real property interest not connected to a U.S. business. Foreign corporation A owns a condominium apartment in the United States. Assume that holding the apartment does not constitute a U.S. trade or business and the foreign corporation has not made an election under section 882(d) to treat income with respect to the property as ECI. The condominium apartment is not a U.S. asset of A because the income, if any, from the asset would not be ECI. However, the disposition by A of the condominium apartment at a gain will give rise to ECEP.

Example 4. Stock in a domestically-controlled REIT. As an investment, foreign corporation A owns stock in a domestically-controlled REIT, within the meaning of section 897(h)(4)(B). Under section 897(h)(2), gain on disposition of stock in the REIT is not treated as ECI. For this reason the stock does not qualify as a U.S. asset under paragraph (d)(1) of this section even if dividend distributions from the REIT are treated as ECI. Thus, A will have a dividend equivalent amount based on the ECEP attributable to a distribution of ECI from the REIT, even if A invests the proceeds from the dividend in additional stock of the REIT. (Stock in a REIT that is not a domestically-controlled REIT is also not a U.S. asset. See § 1.884-1(d)(5)).

Example 5. Section 864(c)(7) property. Foreign corporation A is engaged in the equipment leasing business in the United States and

Canada. A transfers the equipment leased by its U.S. trade or business to its Canadian business after the equipment is fully depreciated in the United States. The Canadian business sells the equipment two years later. Section 864(c)(7) would treat the gain on the disposition of the equipment by A as taxable under section 882 as if the sale occurred immediately before the equipment was transferred to the Canadian business. The equipment would not be treated as a U.S. asset even if the gain was ECI because the income from the equipment in the year of the sale in Canada would not be ECI.

(3) *Interest in a partnership.*—(i) *In general.*—A foreign corporation that is a partner in a partnership must take into account its interest in the partnership (and not the partnership assets) in determining its U.S. assets. For purposes of determining the proportion of the partnership interest that is a U.S. asset, a foreign corporation may elect to use either the asset method described in paragraph (d)(3)(ii) of this section or the income method described in paragraph (d)(3)(iii) of this section.

(ii) *Asset method.*—(A) *In general.*—A partner's interest in a partnership shall be treated as a U.S. asset in the same proportion that the sum of the partner's proportionate share of the adjusted bases of all partnership assets as of the determination date, to the extent that the assets would be treated as U.S. assets if the partnership were a foreign corporation, bears to the sum of the partner's proportionate share of the adjusted bases of all partnership assets as of the determination date. Generally a partner's proportionate share of a partnership asset is the same as its proportionate share of all items of income, gain, loss, and deduction that may be generated by the asset.

(B) *Non-uniform proportionate shares.*—If a partner's proportionate share of all items of income, gain, loss, and deduction that may be generated by a single asset of the partnership throughout the period that includes the taxable year of the partner is not uniform, then, for purposes of determining the partner's proportionate share of the adjusted basis of that asset, a partner must take into account the portion of the adjusted basis of the asset that reflects the partner's economic interest in that asset. A partner's economic interest in an asset of the partnership must be determined by applying the following presumptions. These presumptions may, however, be rebutted if the partner or the Internal Revenue Service shows that the presumption is inconsistent with the partner's true economic interest in the asset during the corporation's taxable year.

(1) If a partnership asset ordinarily generates directly identifiable income, a partner's economic interest in the asset is determined by reference to its proportionate share of income that may be generated by the asset for the partnership's taxable year ending with or within the partner's taxable year.

(2) If a partnership asset ordinarily generates current deductions and ordinarily generates no directly identifiable income, for example because the asset contributes equally to the generation of all the income of the partnership (such as an asset used in general and administrative functions), a partner's economic interest in the asset is determined by reference to its proportionate share of the total deductions that may be generated by the asset for the partnership's taxable year ending with or within the partner's taxable year.

(3) For other partnership assets not described in paragraph (d)(3)(ii)(B)*(1)* or *(2)* of this section, a partner's economic interest in the asset is determined by reference to its proportionate share of the total gain or loss to which it would be entitled if the asset were sold at a gain or loss in the partnership's taxable year ending with or within the partner's taxable year.

(C) *Partnership election under section 754.*—If a partnership files an election in accordance with section 754, then for purposes of this paragraph (d)(3)(ii), the basis of partnership property shall reflect adjustments made pursuant to sections 734 (relating to distributions of property to a partner) and 743 (relating to the transfer of an interest in a partnership). However, adjustments made pursuant to section 743 may be made with respect to a transferee partner only.

(iii) *Income method.*—Under the income method, a partner's interest in a partnership shall be treated as a U.S. asset in the same proportion that its distributive share of partnership ECI for the partnership's taxable year that ends with or within the partner's taxable year bears to its distributive share of all partnership income for that taxable year.

(iv) *Manner of election.*—(A) *In general.*—In determining the proportion of a foreign corporation's interest in a partnership that is a U.S. asset, a foreign corporation must elect one of the methods described in paragraph (d)(3) of this section on a timely filed return for the first taxable year beginning on or after the effective date of this section. An amended return does not qualify for this purpose, nor shall the provisions of § 301.9100-1 of this chapter and any guidance promulgated thereunder apply. An election shall be made by the foreign corporation calculating its U.S. assets in accordance with the method elected. An elected method must be used for a minimum period of five years before the foreign corporation may elect a different method. To change an election before the end of the requisite five-year period, a foreign corporation must obtain the consent of the Commissioner or her delegate. The Commissioner or her delegate will generally consent to a foreign corporation's request to change its election only in rare and unusual circumstances. A foreign corporation that is a partner in more than one partnership is not required to elect to use the same method for each partnership interest.

(B) *Elections with tiered partnerships.*—If a foreign corporation elects to use the asset method with respect to an interest in a partnership, and that partnership is a partner in a lower-tier partnership, the foreign corporation may apply either the asset method or the income method to determine the proportion of the upper-tier partnership's interest in the lower-tier partnership that is a U.S. asset.

(v) *Failure to make proper election.*—If a foreign corporation, for any reason, fails to make an election to use one of the methods required by paragraph (d)(3) of this section in a timely fashion, the district director or the Assistant Commissioner (International) may make the election on behalf of the foreign corporation and such election shall be binding as if made by that corporation.

(vi) *Special rule for determining a partner's adjusted basis in a partnership interest.*—For purposes of paragraphs (d)(3) and (6) of this section, a partner's adjusted basis in a partnership interest shall be the partner's basis in such interest (determined under section 705) reduced by the partner's share of the liabilities of the partnership determined under section 752 and increased by a proportionate share of each liability of the partnership equal to the partner's proportionate share of the expense, for income tax purposes, attributable to such liability for the taxable year. A partner's adjusted basis in a partnership interest cannot be less than zero.

(vii) *E&P basis of a partnership interest.*—See paragraph (d)(6)(iii) of this section for special rules governing the calculation of a foreign corporation's E&P basis in a partnership interest.

(viii) The application of this paragraph (d)(3) is illustrated by the following examples:

Example 1. General rule—(i) *Facts.* Foreign corporation, FC, is a partner in partnership ABC, which is engaged in a trade or business within the United States. FC and ABC are both calendar year taxpayers. ABC owns and manages two office buildings located in the United States, each with an adjusted basis of $50. ABC also owns a non-U.S. asset with an adjusted basis of $100. ABC has no liabilities. Under the partnership agreement, FC has a 50 percent interest in the capital of ABC and a 50 percent interest in all items of income, gain, loss, and deduction that may be generated by the partnership's assets. FC's adjusted basis in ABC is $100. In determining the proportion of its interest in ABC that is a U.S. asset, FC elects to use the asset method described in paragraph (d)(3)(ii) of this section.

(ii) *Analysis.* FC's interest in ABC is treated as a U.S. asset in the same proportion that the sum of FC's proportionate share of the adjusted bases of all ABC's U.S. assets (50% of $100), bears to the sum of FC's proportionate share of the adjusted bases of all of ABC's assets (50% of $200). Under the asset method, the amount of FC's interest in ABC that is a U.S. asset is $50 ($100 × $50/$100).

Example 2. Special allocation of gain with respect to real property—(i) *Facts.* The facts are the same as in *Example 1,* except that under the partnership agreement, FC is allocated 20 percent of the income from the partnership property but 80 percent of the gain on disposition of the partnership property.

(ii) *Analysis.* Assuming that the buildings ordinarily generate directly identifiable income, there is a rebuttable presumption under paragraph (d)(3)(ii)(B)*(1)* of this section that FC's proportionate share of the adjusted basis of the buildings is FC's proportionate share of the income generated by the buildings (20%) rather than the total gain that it would be entitled to under the partnership agreement (80%) if the buildings were sold at a gain on the determination date. Thus, the sum of FC's proportionate share of the adjusted bases in ABC's U.S. assets (the buildings) is presumed to be $20 [(20% of $50) + (20% of $50)]. Assuming that the non-U.S. asset is not income-producing and does not generate current deductions, there is a rebuttable presumption under paragraph (d)(3)(ii)(B)(3) of this section that FC's proportionate share of the adjusted basis of that asset is FC's interest in the gain on the disposition of the asset (80%) rather than its proportionate share of the income that may be generated by the asset (20%). Thus, FC's proportionate share of the adjusted basis of ABC's non-U.S. asset is presumed to be $80 (80% of $100). FC's proportionate share of the adjusted bases of all of the assets of ABC is $100 ($20 + $80). The amount of FC's interest in ABC that is a U.S. asset is $20 ($100 x $20/$100).

Example 3. Tiered partnerships (asset method)—(i) *Facts.* The facts are the same as in *Example 1,* except that FC's adjusted basis in ABC is $175 and ABC also has a 50 percent interest in the capital of partnership DEF. DEF owns and operates a commercial shopping center in the United States with an adjusted basis of $200 and also owns non-U.S. assets with an adjusted basis of $100. DEF has no liabilities. ABC's adjusted basis in its interest in DEF is $150 and ABC has a 50 percent interest in all the items of income, gain, loss and deduction that may be generated by the assets of DEF.

(ii) *Analysis.* Because FC has elected to use the asset method described in paragraph (d)(3)(ii) of this section, it must determine what proportion of ABC's partnership interest in DEF is a U.S. asset. As permitted by paragraph (d)(3)(iv)(B) of this section, FC also elects to use the asset method with respect to ABC's interest in DEF. ABC's interest in DEF is treated as a U.S. asset in the same proportion that the sum of ABC's proportionate share of the adjusted bases of all DEF's U.S. assets (50% of $200), bears to the sum of ABC's proportionate share of the adjusted bases of all of DEF's assets (50% of $300). Thus, the amount of ABC's interest in DEF that is a U.S. asset is $100 ($150 × $100/$150). FC must then apply the rules of paragraph (d)(3)(ii) of this section to all the assets of ABC, including ABC's interest in DEF that is treated in part as a U.S. asset ($100) and in part as a non-U.S. asset ($50). FC's interest in ABC is treated as a U.S. asset in the same proportion that the sum of FC's proportionate share of the adjusted bases of the U.S. assets of ABC (including ABC's interest in DEF), bears to the sum of FC's proportionate share of the adjusted bases of all ABC's assets (including ABC's interest in DEF). Thus, the amount of FC's interest in ABC that is a U.S. asset is $100 (FC's adjusted basis in ABC ($175) multiplied by FC's proportionate share of the sum of the adjusted bases of ABC's U.S. assets ($100)) over FC's proportionate share of the sum of the adjusted bases of ABC's assets ($175)).

Example 4. Tiered partnerships (income method)—(i) *Facts.* The facts are the same as in *Example 3,* except that FC has elected to use the income method described in paragraph (d)(3)(iii) of this section to determine the proportion of its interest in ABC that is a U.S. asset. The two office buildings located in the United States generate $60 of income that is ECI for the taxable year. The non-U.S. asset is not-income producing. In addition ABC's distributive share of income from DEF consists of $40 of income that is ECI and $140 of income that is not ECI.

(ii) *Analysis.* Because FC has elected to use the income method it does need to determine what proportion of ABC's partnership interest in DEF is a U.S. asset. FC's interest in ABC is treated as a U.S. asset in the same proportion that its distributive share of ABC's income for the taxable year that is ECI ($50) ($30 earned directly by ABC + $20 distributive share from DEF) bears to its distributive share of all ABC's income for the taxable year ($55) ($30 earned directly by ABC + $25 distributive share from DEF). Thus, FC's interest in ABC that is a U.S. asset is $159 ($175 × $50/$55).

(4) *Interest in a trust or estate.*—(i) *Estates and non-grantor trusts.*—A foreign corporation that is a beneficiary of a trust or estate shall not be treated as having a U.S. asset by virtue of its interest in the trust or estate.

(ii) *Grantor trusts.*—If, under sections 671 through 678, a foreign corporation is treated as owning a portion of a trust that includes all the income and gain that may be generated by a trust asset (or pro rata portion of a trust asset), the foreign corporation will be treated as owning the trust asset (or pro rata portion thereof) for purposes of determining its U.S. assets under this section.

(5) *Property that is not a U.S. asset.*—(i) *Property that does not give rise to ECEP.*—Property described in paragraphs (d)(1) through (4) of this section shall not be treated as a U.S. asset of a foreign corporation if, on the determination date, income from the use of the property, or gain or loss from the disposition of the property, would be described in paragraph (f)(2) of this section (relating to certain income that does not produce ECEP).

(ii) *Assets acquired to increase U.S. net equity artificially.*—U.S. assets shall not include assets acquired or used by a foreign corporation if one of the principal purposes of such acquisition or use is to increase artificially the U.S. assets of a foreign corporation on the determination date. Whether assets are acquired or used for such purpose will depend upon all the facts and circumstances of each case. Factors to be considered in determining whether one of the principal purposes in acquiring or using an asset is to increase artificially the U.S. assets of a foreign corporation include the length of time during which the asset was used in a U.S. trade or business, whether the asset was acquired from, or disposed of to, a related person, and whether the aggregate value of the U.S. assets of the foreign corporation increased temporarily on the determination date. For purposes of this paragraph (d)(5)(ii), to be one of the principal purposes, a purpose must be important, but it is not necessary that it be the primary purpose.

(iii) *Interbranch transactions.*—A transaction of any type between separate offices or branches of the same taxpayer does not create a U.S. asset.

(6) *E&P basis of a U.S. asset.*—(i) *General rule.*—The E&P basis of a U.S. asset for purposes of this section is its adjusted basis for purposes of computing the foreign corporation's earnings and profits. In determining the E&P basis of a U.S. asset, the adjusted basis of the asset (for purposes of computing taxable income) must be increased or decreased to take into account inclusions of income or gain, and deductions or similar charges, that affect the basis of the asset where such items are taken into account in a different manner for purposes of computing earnings and profits than for purposes of computing taxable income. For example, if section 312(k) requires that depreciation with respect to a U.S. asset be determined using the straight line method for purposes of computing earnings and profits, but depreciation with respect to the asset is determined using a different method for purposes of computing taxable income, the E&P basis of the property for purposes of this section must be computed using the straight line method of depreciation.

(ii) *Installment obligations.*—(A) *Sales in taxable year beginning on or after January 1, 1987.*—For purposes of this section, the E&P basis of an installment obligation described in paragraph (d)(2)(iii) of this section that arises in connection with an installment sale occurring in a taxable year beginning on or after January 1, 1987, shall equal the sum of the total amount of gain from the sale if the obligation were satisfied in full and the adjusted basis of the property sold as of the date of sale, reduced by payments received with respect to the obligation that are not interest or original issue discount. See paragraph (j)(2)(ii) of this section, however, for a special E&P basis rule for an installment obligation arising in connection with a sale of a U.S. asset by a foreign corporation described in section 312(k)(4), where such sale occurs in a taxable year beginning in 1987.

(B) *Sales in taxable year prior to January 1, 1987.*—For purposes of this section, the E&P basis of an installment obligation described in paragraph (d)(2)(iii) of this section that arises in connection with an installment sale occurring in a taxable year beginning before January 1, 1987, shall equal zero.

(iii) *Computation of E&P basis in a partnership.*—For purposes of this section, a foreign corporation's E&P basis in a partnership interest shall be the foreign corporation's adjusted basis in such interest (as determined under paragraph (d)(3)(vi) of this section), further adjusted to take into account any differences between the foreign corporation's distributive share of items of partnership income, gain, loss, and deduction for purposes of computing the taxable income of the foreign corporation and the foreign corporation's distributive share of items of partnership income, gain, loss, and deduction for purposes of computing the earnings and profits of the foreign corporation.

(iv) *Computation of E&P basis of a loss property.*—The E&P basis of a loss property (as defined in paragraph (d)(2)(ix) of this section) shall equal the E&P basis, immediately before the loss, of the U.S. asset with respect to which the loss was sustained, reduced (but not below zero) by—

(A) The amount of any deduction claimed under section 165 by the foreign corporation with respect to the loss for earnings and profits purposes; and

(B) Any compensation received with respect to the loss.

(v) *Computation of E&P basis of financial instruments.*—[Reserved]

(vi) *Example.*—The application of paragraph (d)(6)(ii) of this section is illustrated by the following example.

Example. Sale in taxable year beginning on or after January 1, 1987. Foreign corporation A, a calendar year taxpayer, sells a U.S. asset on the installment method in 1993. Under the terms of the sale, A is to receive $100, payable in ten annual installments of $10 beginning in 1994, plus an arm's-length rate of interest on the unpaid balance of the sales price. A's adjusted basis in the property sold is $70. The obligation received in connection with the installment sale is treated as a U.S. asset with an E&P basis of $100 ($30 (the amount of gain from the sale if the obligation were satisfied in full) + $70 (the adjusted basis of the property sold)). If A receives a payment of $10 (not including interest) in 1994 with respect to the obligation, the obligation is treated as a U.S. asset with an E&P basis of $90 ($100 – $10) as of the close of 1994.

(e) *U.S. liabilities.*—The term "U.S. liabilities" means the amount of liabilities determined under paragraph (e)(1) of this section decreased by the amount of liabilities determined under paragraph (e)(3) of this section, and increased by the amount of liabilities determined under paragraph (e)(2) of this section.

(1) *Liabilities based on § 1.882-5.*—The amount of liabilities determined under this paragraph (e)(1) is the amount of U.S.-connected liabilities of a foreign corporation under § 1.882-5 if the U.S.-connected liabilities were computed using the assets and liabilities of the foreign corporation as of the determination date (rather than the average of such assets and liabilities for the taxable year) and without regard to paragraph (e)(3) of this section.

(2) *Additional liabilities—Insurance reserves.*—(i) The amount of liabilities determined under this paragraph (e)(2)(i) is the amount (as of the determination date) of the total insurance liabilities on United States business (within the meaning of section 842 (b)(2)(B)) of a foreign corporation described in section 842(a) (relating to foreign corporations carrying on an insurance business in the United States) to the extent that such liabilities are not otherwise treated as U.S. liabilities by reason of paragraph (e)(1) of this section.

(ii) *Liabilities described in § 1.882-5(a)(1)(ii).*—The amount of liabilities determined under this paragraph (e)(2)(ii) is the amount (as of the determination date) of liabilities described in § 1.882-5(a)(1)(ii) (relating to liabilities giving rise to interest expense that is directly allocated to income from a U.S. asset).

(3) *Election to reduce liabilities.*—(i) *General rule.*—The amount of liabilities determined under this paragraph (e)(3) is the amount by which a foreign corporation elects to reduce its liabilities under paragraph (e)(1) of this section.

(ii) *Limitation.*—For any taxable year, a foreign corporation may elect to reduce the amount of its liabilities determined under paragraph (e)(1) of this section by an amount that does not exceed the lesser of the amount of U.S. liabilities as of the determination date, or the amount of U.S. liability reduction needed to reduce a dividend equivalent amount as of the determination date to zero.

(iii) *Effect of election on interest deduction and branch-level interest tax.*—A foreign corporation that elects to reduce its liabilities under this paragraph (e)(3) must, for purposes of computing the amount of its interest apportioned to ECI under § 1.882-5, reduce its U.S.-connected liabilities for the taxable year of the election by the amount of the reduction in liabilities under this paragraph (e)(3). The reduction of its U.S.-connected liabilities will also require a corresponding decrease in the amount of its interest apportioned to ECI under § 1.882-5 for purposes of § 1.884-4(a) and for all other Code sections for which the amount of interest apportioned under § 1.882-5 is relevant.

(iv) *Method of election.*—A foreign corporation that elects the benefits of this paragraph (e)(3) for a taxable year shall attach a statement to its return for the taxable year that it has elected to reduce its liabilities for the taxable year under this paragraph (e)(3) and that it has reduced the amount of its U.S.-connected liabilities as provided in paragraph (e)(3)(iii) of this section and shall indicate the amount of such reductions on such attachment. The cumulative amount of all U.S. liability reductions is shown on Schedule I (Form 1120-F) in addition to the separate elections attached to the timely filed return. An election under this paragraph (e)(3) must be made before the due date (including extensions) for the foreign corporation's income tax return for the taxable year.

(v) *Effect of election on complete termination.*—If a foreign corporation completely terminates its U.S. trade or business (within the meaning of § 1.884-2T (a)(2)), notwithstanding § 1.884-2T(a), the foreign corporation will be subject to tax on a dividend equivalent amount that equals the lesser of—

(A) The foreign corporation's accumulated ECEP that is attributable to an election to reduce liabilities; or

(B) The amount by which the corporation elected to reduce liabilities at the end of the taxable year preceding the year of complete termination.

For purposes of the preceding sentence, accumulated ECEP is attributable to an election to reduce liabilities to the extent that the ECEP was accumulated because of such an election rather than because of an increase in U.S. assets. For example, if a foreign corporation did not have positive ECEP in any year for which an election was made, it would not be required to include an amount as a dividend equivalent amount under this paragraph (e)(3)(v) because any accumulated ECEP that it may have is not attributable to an election to reduce liabilities.

(4) *Artificial decrease in U.S. liabilities.*—If a foreign corporation repays or otherwise decreases its U.S. liabilities and one of the principal purposes of such decrease is to decrease artificially its U.S. liabilities on the determination date, then such decrease shall not be taken into account for purposes of computing the foreign corporation's U.S. net equity. Whether the U.S. liabilities of a foreign corporation are artificially decreased will depend on all the facts and circumstances of each case. Factors to be considered in determining whether one of the principal purposes for the repayment or decrease of the liabilities is to decrease artificially the U.S. liabilities of a foreign corporation shall include whether the aggregate liabilities are temporarily decreased on or before the determination date by, for example, the repayment of liabilities, or U.S. liabilities are temporarily decreased on or before the determination date by the acquisition with contributed funds of passive-type assets that are not U.S. assets. For purposes of this paragraph (e)(4), to be one of the principal purposes, a purpose must be important, but it is not necessary that it be the primary purpose.

(5) *Examples.* The application of this paragraph (e) is illustrated by the following examples.

Example 1. General rule for computation of U.S. liabilities. As of the close of 1997, foreign corporation A, a calendar year taxpayer computes its U.S.-connected liabilities under § 1.882-5(c) using its actual ratio of liabilities to assets. For purposes of computing its U.S. connected liabilities under § 1.882-5(c), A must determine the average total value of its assets that are U.S. assets. Assume that the average value of such assets is $100, while the amount of such assets as of the close of 1997 is $125. For purposes of § 1.882-5(c)(2), A must determine the ratio of the average of its worldwide liabilities for the year to the average total value of worldwide assets for the taxable year. Assume that A's average liabilities-to-assets ratio under § 1.882-5(c)(2) is 55 percent, while its liabilities-to-assets ratio at the close of 1997 is only 50 percent. Thus, assuming no further adjustments under paragraph (e)(3) of this section, A's U.S.-connected liabilities for purposes of § 1.882-5 are $55 ($100 x 55%). However, A's U.S. liabilities are $62.50 for purposes of this section, the value of its assets determined under § 1.882-5(b)(2) as of the close of December ($125) multiplied by the liabilities-to-assets ratio (50%) as of such date.

Example 2. Election made to reduce liabilities. (i) As of the close of 2007, foreign corporation A, a real estate company, owns U.S. assets with an E&P basis of $1000. A has $800 of liabilities under paragraph (e)(1) of this section. A has accumulated ECEP of $500 and in 2008, A has $60 of ECEP that it intends to retain for future expansion of its U.S. trade or business. A elects under paragraph (e)(3) of this section to reduce its liabilities by $60 from $800 to $740. As a result of the election, assuming A's U.S. assets and U.S. liabilities would otherwise have remained constant, A's U.S. net equity as of the close of 2007 will increase by the amount of the decrease in liabilities ($60) from $200 to $260 and its ECEP will be reduced to zero. Under paragraph (e)(3)(iii) of this section, A's interest expense for the taxable year is reduced by the amount of interest attributable to $60 of liabilities and A's excess interest is reduced by the same amount. A's taxable income and ECEP are increased by the amount of the reduction in interest expense attributable to the liabilities, and A may make an election under paragraph (e)(3) of this section to further reduce its liabilities, thus increasing its U.S. net equity and reducing the amount of additional ECEP created for the election.

(ii) In 2009, assuming A again has $60 of ECEP, A may again make the election under paragraph (e)(3) to reduce its liabilities. However, assuming A's U.S. assets and liabilities under paragraph (e)(1) of this section remain constant, A will need to make an election to reduce its liabilities by $120 to reduce to zero its ECEP in 2009 and to continue to retain for expansion (without the payment of the branch profits tax) the $60 of ECEP earned in 2008. Without an election to reduce liabilities, A's dividend equivalent amount for 2009 would be $120 ($60 of ECEP plus the $60 reduction in U.S. net equity from $260 to $200). If A makes the election to reduce liabilities by $120 (from $800 to $680), A's U.S. net equity will increase by $60 (from $260 at the end of the previous year to $320), the amount necessary to reduce its ECEP to $0. However, the reduction of liabilities will itself create additional ECEP subject to section 884 because of the reduction in interest expense attributable to the $120 of liabilities. A can make the election to reduce liabilities by $120 without exceeding the limitation on the election provided in paragraph (e)(3)(ii) of this section because the $120 reduction does not exceed the amount needed to treat the 2009 and 2008 ECEP as reinvested in the net equity of the trade or business within the United States.

(iii) If A terminates its U.S. trade or business in 2009 in accordance with the rules in § 1.884-2T(a), A would not be subject to the branch profits tax on the $60 of ECEP earned in that year. Under paragraph (e)(3)(v) of this section, however, it would be subject to the branch profits tax on the portion of the $60 of ECEP that it earned in 2008 that became accumulated ECEP because of an election to reduce liabilities.

(f) *Effectively connected earnings and profits—.*—(1) *In general.*—Except as provided in paragraph (f)(2) of this section and as modified by § 1.884-2T (relating to the incorporation or complete termination of a U.S. trade or business or the reorganization or liquidation of a foreign corporation or its domestic subsidiary), the term "effectively connected earnings and profits" ("ECEP") means the earnings and profits (or deficits therein) determined under section 312 and this paragraph (f) that are attributable to ECI (within the meaning of paragraph (d)(1)(iii) of this section). Because the term "ECI" includes income treated as effectively connected, income that is ECI under section 842(b) (relating to minimum net investment income of an insurance business) or 864(c)(7) (relating to gain from property formerly held for use in a U.S. trade or business) gives rise to ECEP. ECEP also includes earnings and profits attributable to ECI of a foreign corporation earned through a partnership, and through a trust or estate. For purposes of section 884, gain on the sale of a U.S. real property interest by a foreign corporation that has made an election to be treated as a domestic corporation under section 897(i) will also give rise to ECEP. ECEP is not reduced by distributions made by the foreign corporation during any taxable year or by the amount of branch profits tax or tax on excess interest (as defined in § 1.884-4(a)(2)) paid by the foreign corporation. Earnings and profits are treated as attributable to ECI even if the earnings and profits are taken into account under section 312 in an earlier or later taxable year than the taxable year in which the ECI is taken into account.

(2) *Income that does not produce ECEP.*—The term "ECEP" does not include any earnings and profits attributable to—

(i) Income excluded from gross income under section 883(a)(1) or 883(a)(2) (relating to certain income derived from the operation of ships or aircraft);

(ii) Income that is ECI by reason of section 921(d) or 926(b) (relating to certain income of a FSC and certain dividends paid by a FSC to a foreign corporation or nonresident alien) that is not otherwise ECI;

(iii) Gain on the disposition of a U.S. real property interest described in section 897(c)(1)(A)(ii) (relating to certain interests in a domestic corporation);

(iv) Income that is ECI by reason of section 953(c)(3)(C) (relating to certain income of a captive insurance company that a corporation elects to treat as ECI) that is not otherwise ECI;

(v) Income that is exempt from tax under section 892 (relating to certain income of foreign governments); and

(vi) Income that is ECI by reason of section 882(e) (relating to certain interest income of banks organized under the laws of a possession of the United States) that is not otherwise ECI.

(3) *Allocation of deductions attributable to income that does not produce ECEP.*—In determining the amount of a foreign corporation's ECEP for the taxable year, deductions and other adjustments shall be allocated and apportioned under the principles of § 1.861-8 between ECI that gives rise to ECEP and income described in paragraph (f)(2) of this section (relating to income that is ECI but does not give rise to ECEP).

(4) *Examples.*—The principles of paragraph (f) of this section are illustrated by the following examples.

Example 1. Tax-exempt income. Foreign corporation A owns a tax-exempt municipal bond that is a U.S. asset as of the close of its 1989 taxable year. The municipal bond gives rise in 1989 to ECI (even though the income is excluded from gross income under section 103(a) and is not gross income of a foreign corporation by reason of section 882(b)), and therefore gives rise to ECEP in 1989.

Example 2. Income exempt under a treaty. Foreign corporation A derives ECI that constitutes business profits that are not attributable to a permanent establishment maintained by A in the United States. The ECI is exempt from taxation under section 882(a) by reason of an income tax treaty and section 894(a). The income nevertheless gives rise to ECEP under this paragraph (f). However, a dividend equivalent amount attributable to such ECEP may be exempt from the branch profits tax by reason of paragraph (g) of this section (relating to the application of the branch profits tax to corporations that are residents of countries with which the United States has an income tax treaty).

(g) *Corporations resident in countries with which the United States has an income tax treaty.*—(1) *General rule.*—Except as provided in paragraph (g)(2) of this section, a foreign corporation that is a resident of a country with which the United States has an income tax treaty in effect for a taxable year in which it has a dividend equivalent amount and that meets the requirements, if any, of the limitation on benefits provisions of such treaty with respect to the dividend equivalent amount shall not be subject to the branch profits tax on such amount (or will qualify for a reduction in the amount of tax with respect to such amount) only if—

(i) The foreign corporation is a qualified resident of such country for the taxable year, within the meaning of § 1.884-5(a); or

(ii) The limitation on benefits provision, or an amendment to that provision, entered into force after December 31, 1986.

If, after application of § 1.884-5(e)(4)(iv), a foreign corporation is a qualified resident under § 1.884-5(e) (relating to the active trade or business test) only with respect to one of its trades or businesses in the United States, *i.e.*, the trade or business that is an integral part of its business conducted in its country of residence, and not with respect to another, the rules of this paragraph shall apply only to that portion of its dividend equivalent amount attributable to the trade or business for which the foreign corporation is a qualified resident.

(2) *Special rules for foreign corporations that are qualified residents on the basis of their ownership.*—(i) *General rule.*—A foreign corporation that, in any taxable year, is a qualified resident of a country with which the United States has an income tax treaty in effect solely by reason of meeting the requirements of § 1.884-5(b) and (c) (relating, respectively, to stock ownership and base erosion) shall be exempt from the branch profits tax or subject to a reduced rate of branch profits tax under paragraph (g)(1) of this section with respect to the portion of its dividend equivalent amount for the taxable year attributable to accumulated ECEP only if the foreign corporation is a qualified resident of such country within the meaning of § 1.884-5(a) for the taxable years includible, in whole or in part, in a consecutive 36-month period that includes the taxable year of the dividend equivalent amount. A foreign corporation that fails the 36-month test described in the preceding sentence shall be exempt from the branch profits tax or subject to the branch profits tax at a reduced rate under paragraph (g)(1) of this section with respect to accumulated ECEP (determined on a last-in-first-out basis) accumulated only during prior years in which the foreign corporation was a qualified resident of such country within the meaning of § 1.884-5(a).

(ii) *Rules of application.*—A foreign corporation that has not satisfied the 36-month test as of the close of the taxable year of the dividend equivalent amount but satisfies the test with respect to such dividend equivalent amount by meeting the 36-month test by the close of the second taxable year succeeding the taxable year of the dividend equivalent amount shall be subject to the branch profits tax for the year of the dividend equivalent amount without regard to paragraph (g)(1) of this section on the portion of the dividend equivalent amount attributable to accumulated ECEP derived in a taxable year in which the foreign corporation was not a qualified resident within the meaning of § 1.884-5(a). Upon meeting the 36-month test, the foreign corporation shall be entitled to claim by amended return a refund of the tax paid with respect to the dividend equivalent amount in excess of the branch profits tax calculated by taking into account paragraph (g)(2)(i) of this section, provided the foreign corporation establishes in the amended return for the taxable year that it has met the requirements of such paragraph. For purposes of section 6611 (dealing with interest on overpayments), any overpayment of branch profits tax by reason of this paragraph (g)(2)(ii) shall be deemed not to have been made before the filing date for the taxable year in which the foreign corporation establishes that it has met the 36-month test.

(iii) *Example.*—The application of this paragraph (g)(2) is illustrated by the following example.

Example. (i) Foreign corporation A, a calendar year taxpayer, is a resident of the United Kingdom. A has a dividend equivalent amount for its taxable year 1991 of $300, of which $100 is attributable to 1991 ECEP and $200 to accumulated ECEP. A is a qualified resident for its taxable year 1991 because for that year it meets the requirements of § 1.884-5(b) and (c), relating, respectively, to stock ownership and base erosion. For 1991 A does not meet the requirements of § 1.884-5(d), (e), or (f) for qualified residence. A is not a qualified resident of the United Kingdom for any taxable year prior to 1990 but is a qualified resident for its taxable years 1990 and 1992.

(ii) Because A is a qualified resident for the 3-year period (1990, 1991, and 1992) that includes the taxable year of the dividend equivalent amount (1991), A satisfies the 36-month test of this paragraph (g)(2) and no branch profits tax is imposed on the total $300 dividend equivalent amount. However, since A was not a qualified resident for any taxable year prior to 1990 and therefore cannot establish that it has satisfied the 36-month test until the taxable year following the year of the dividend equivalent amount, A must pay the branch profits tax for its taxable year 1991 with respect to the portion of the dividend equivalent amount attributable to accumulated ECEP relating to years prior to 1990 without regard to paragraph (g)(1) of this section. A may file for a refund of the branch profits tax paid with respect to its 1991 taxable year at any time after it establishes that it is a qualified resident for its 1992 taxable year.

(3) *Exemptions for foreign corporations resident in certain countries with income tax treaties in effect on January 1, 1987.*—The branch profits tax shall not be imposed on the portion of the dividend equivalent amount with respect to which a foreign corporation satisfies the requirements of paragraphs (g)(1) and (2) of this section for a country listed below, so long as the income tax treaty between the United States and that country, as in effect on January 1, 1987, remains in effect, except to the extent the treaty is modified on or after January 1, 1987, to expressly provide for the imposition of the branch profits tax:

Aruba
Austria
Belgium
People's Republic of China
Cyprus
Denmark
Egypt
Finland
Germany
Greece
Hungary
Iceland
Ireland
Italy
Jamaica
Japan
Korea
Luxembourg
Malta
Morocco
Netherlands
Netherlands Antilles
Norway
Pakistan
Philippines
Sweden
Switzerland
United Kingdom

(4) *Modifications with respect to other income tax treaties.*—(i) *Limitation on rate of tax.*—(A) *General rule.*—If, under paragraphs (g)(1) and (2) of this section, a corporation qualifies for a reduction in the amount of the branch profits tax and paragraph (g)(3) of this section does not apply, the rate of tax shall be the rate of tax on branch profits specified in the treaty between the United States and the corporation's country of residence or, if no rate of tax on branch profits is specified, the rate of tax that would apply under such treaty to dividends paid to the foreign corporation by a wholly-owned domestic corporation.

(B) *Certain treaties in effect on January 1, 1987.*—The branch profits tax shall generally be imposed at the following rates on the portion of the dividend equivalent amount with respect to which a foreign corporation satisfies the requirements of paragraphs (g)(1) and (2) of this section for a country listed below, for as long as the relevant provisions of those income tax treaties remain in effect and are not modified or superseded by subsequent agreement:

Australia (15%)
Barbados (5%)
Canada (10%)
France (5%)
New Zealand (5%)
Poland (5%)
Romania (10%)
South Africa (30%)
Trinidad & Tobago (10%)
U.S.S.R. (30%)

However, for special rates imposed on corporations resident in France and Trinidad & Tobago that have certain amounts of dividend and interest income, see the dividend articles of the income tax treaties with those countries.

(ii) *Limitations other than rate of tax.*—If, under paragraphs (g)(1) and (2) of this section, a foreign corporation qualifies for a reduction in the amount of branch profits tax and paragraph (g)(3) of this section does not apply, then—

(A) The foreign corporation shall be entitled to the benefit of any limitations on imposition of a tax on branch profits (in addition to any limitations on the rate of tax) contained in the treaty; and

(B) No branch profits tax shall be imposed with respect to a dividend equivalent amount out of ECEP or accumulated ECEP of the foreign corporation unless the ECEP or accumulated ECEP is attributable to a permanent establishment in the United States or, if not otherwise prohibited under the treaty, to gain from the disposition of a U.S. real property interest described in section 897(c)(1)(A)(i), except to the extent the treaty specifically permits the imposition of the branch profits tax on such earnings and profits.

No article in such treaty shall be construed to provide any limitations on imposition of the branch profits tax other than as provided in this paragraph (g)(4).

(iii) *Computation of the dividend equivalent amount if a foreign corporation has both ECEP attributable to a permanent establishment and not attributable to a permanent establishment.*—To determine the dividend equivalent amount of a foreign corporation out of ECEP that is attributable to a permanent establishment, the foreign corporation may only take into account its U.S. assets, U.S. liabilities, U.S. net equity and ECEP attributable to its permanent establishment. Thus, a foreign corporation may not reduce the amount of its ECEP attributable to its permanent establishment by reinvesting all or a portion of that amount in U.S. assets not attributable to the permanent establishment.

(iv) *Limitations under the Canadian treaty.*—The limitations on the imposition of the branch profits tax under the Canadian treaty include, but are not limited to, those described in paragraphs (g)(4)(iv)(A) and (B).

(A) *Effect of deficits in earnings and profits.*—In the case of a foreign corporation that is a qualified resident of Canada, the dividend equivalent amount for any taxable year shall not exceed the foreign corporation's accumulated ECEP as of the beginning of the taxable year plus the corporation's ECEP for the taxable year. Thus, for example, if a foreign corporation that is a qualified resident of Canada has a deficit in accumulated ECEP of $200 as of the beginning of the taxable year and ECEP of $100 for the taxable year, it will have no dividend equivalent amount for the taxable year because it would have a cumulative deficit in ECEP of $100 as of the close of the taxable year. For purposes of this paragraph (g)(4)(iii)(A), any net deficit in accumulated earnings and profits attributable to taxable years beginning before January 1, 1987, shall be includible in determining accumulated ECEP.

(B) *One-time exemption of Canadian $500,000.*—*(1) General rule.*—In the case of a foreign corporation that is a qualified resident of Canada, the branch profits tax shall be imposed only with respect to that portion of the dividend equivalent amount for the taxable year that, when translated into Canadian dollars and added to the dividend equivalent amounts for preceding taxable years translated into Canadian dollars, exceeds Canadian $500,000. The value of the dividend equivalent amount in Canadian currency shall be determined by translating the ECEP for each taxable year that is includible in the dividend equivalent amount (as determined in U.S. dollars under the currency translation method used in determining the foreign corporation's taxable income for U.S. tax purposes) by the weighted average exchange rate for the taxable year (determined under the rules of section 989(b)(3)) during which the earnings and profits were derived.

(2) Reduction in amount of exemption in the case of related corporations.—The amount of a foreign corporation's exemption under this paragraph (g)(4)(iii)(B) shall be reduced by the amount of any exemption that reduced the dividend equivalent amount of an associated foreign corporation with respect to the same or a similar business. For purposes of this paragraph (g)(4)(iii)(B), a foreign corporation is an associated foreign corporation if it is related to the foreign corporation for purposes of section 267(b) or it and the foreign corporation are stapled entities (within the meaning of section 269B(c)(2)) or are effectively stapled entities. A business is the same as or similar to another business if it involves the sale, lease, or manufacture of the same or a similar type of property or the provision of the same or a similar type of services. A U.S. real property interest described in section 897(c)(1)(A)(i) shall be treated as a business and all such U.S. real property interests shall be treated as businesses that are the same or similar.

(3) Coordination with second-tier withholding tax.—The value of the dividend equivalent amount that is exempt from the branch profits tax by reason of paragraph (g)(4)(iii)(B)(*1*) of this section shall not be subject to tax under section 871(a) or 881, or to withholding under section 1441 or 1442, when distributed by the foreign corporation.

(5) *Benefits under treaties other than income tax treaties.*—A treaty that is not an income tax treaty does not exempt a foreign corporation from the branch profits tax or reduce the amount of the tax.

(h) *Stapled entities.*—Any foreign corporation that is treated as a domestic corporation by reason of section 269B (relating to stapled entities) shall continue to be treated as a foreign corporation for purposes of section 884 and the regulations thereunder, notwithstanding section 269B or the regulations thereunder. Dividends paid by such foreign corporation shall be treated as paid by a domestic corporation and shall be subject to the tax imposed by section 871(a) or 881(a), and to withholding under section 1441 or 1442, as applicable, to the extent paid out of earnings and profits that are not subject to tax under section 884(a). Dividends paid by such foreign corporation out of earnings and profits subject to tax under section 884(a) shall be exempt from the tax imposed by sections 871(a) and 881(a) and shall not be subject to withholding under section 1441 or 1442. Whether dividends are paid out of earnings and profits that are subject to tax under section 884(a) shall be determined under section 884(e)(3)(A) and the regulations thereunder. The limitation on the application of treaty benefits in section 884(e)(3)(B) (relating to qualified residents) shall apply to a foreign corporation described in this paragraph (h).

(i) *Effective date.*—(1) *General rule.*—This section is effective for taxable years beginning on or after [*the date that is 30 days after these regulations are published in the Federal Register*]. With respect to a taxable year beginning before [*the date that is 30 days after these regulations are published in the Federal Register*] and after December 31, 1986, a foreign corporation may elect to apply this section in lieu of § 1.884-1T of the temporary regulations (as contained in the CFR edition revised as of April 1, 1992), but only if the foreign corporation also makes an election under § 1.884-4(e) to apply § 1.884-4 in lieu of § 1.884-4T (as contained in the CFR edition revised as of April 1, 1992) for that taxable year, and the statute of limitations for assessment of a deficiency has not expired for that taxable year. Once an election has been made, an election under this section shall apply to all subsequent taxable years. However, paragraph (f)(2)(vi) of this section (relating to certain interest income of Possessions banks) shall not apply for taxable years beginning before January 1, 1990.

(2) *Election to reduce liabilities.*—A foreign corporation may make an election to reduce its liabilities under paragraph (e)(3) of this section with respect to a taxable year for which an election under paragraph (i)(1) of this section is in effect by filing an amended return for the taxable year and recomputing its interest deduction and any other item affected by the election on an amended Form 1120F to take into account the reduction in liabilities for such year.

(3) *Separate election for installment obligations.*—A foreign corporation may make a separate election to apply paragraphs (d)(2)(iii) and (d)(6)(ii) of this section (relating to installment obligations treated as U.S. assets) to any prior taxable year without making an election under paragraph (i)(1) of this section, provided the statute of limitations for assessment of a deficiency has not expired for that taxable year and each succeeding taxable year. Once an election under this paragraph (i)(3) has been made, it shall apply to all subsequent taxable years.

(4) *Special rules for certain U.S. assets and liabilities.*—Paragraphs (c)(2)(i) and (ii), (d)(3), (d)(4), (d)(5)(iii), (d)(6)(iii), (d)(6)(vi), (e)(2), and (e)(3)(ii), of this section are effective for taxable years beginning on or after June 6, 1996.

(j) *Transition rules.*—(1) *General rule.*—Except as provided in paragraph (j)(2) of this section, in order to compute its dividend equivalent amount in the first taxable year to which this section applies (whether or not such year begins before [*the date that is 30 days after these regulations are published in the Federal Register*]), a foreign corporation must recompute its U.S. net equity as of close of the preceding taxable year using the rules of this section and use such recomputed amount, rather than the amount computed under § 1.884-1T (as contained in the CFR edition revised as of April 1, 1992), to determine the amount of any increase or decrease in the U.S. net equity as of the close of that taxable year.

(2) *Installment obligations.*—(i) *Interest election.*—In recomputing its U.S. net equity as of the close of the preceding taxable year, a foreign corporation that holds an installment obligation treated as a U.S. asset under § 1.884-1T(d)(7) (as contained in the CFR edition revised as of April 1, 1992) as of such date may apply the rules of paragraph (d)(2)(iii) of this section without regard to the rule in that paragraph that requires interest or original issue discount on the obligation to be treated as ECI in order for such obligation to be treated as a U.S. asset.

(ii) *1987 sales by certain foreign corporations.*—The E&P basis of an installment obligation arising in connection with a sale of property by a foreign corporation described in section 312(k)(4), where such sale occurs in a taxable year beginning in 1987, shall equal the E&P basis of the property sold as of the determination date reduced by payments received with respect to the obligation that do not represent gain for earnings and profits purposes, interest or original issue discount. [Reg. § 1.884-1.]

☐ [*T.D.* 8432, 9-10-92. *Amended by T.D.* 8657, 3-5-96; *T.D.* 9281, 8-15-2006 *and T.D.* 9465, 9-25-2009 (*corrected* 11-4-2009).]

§ 1.884-2. Special rules for termination or incorporation of a U.S. trade or business or liquidation or reorganization of a foreign corporation or its domestic subsidiary.—(a) through (a)(2)(i) [Reserved]. For further information, see § 1.884-2T(a) through (a)(2)(ii).

(a)(2)(ii) *Waiver of period of limitations.*—The waiver referred to in § 1.884-2T(a)(2)(i)(D) shall be executed on Form 8848, or substitute form, and shall extend the period for assessment of the branch profits tax for the year of complete termination to a date not earlier than the close of the sixth taxable year following that taxable year. This form shall include such information as is required by the form and accompanying instructions. The waiver must be signed by the person authorized to sign the income tax returns for the foreign corporation (including an agent authorized to do so under a general or specific power of attorney). The waiver must be filed on or before the date (including extensions) prescribed for filing the foreign corporation's income tax return for the year of complete termination. With respect to a complete termination occurring in a taxable year ending prior to June 6, 1996, a foreign corporation may also satisfy the requirements of this paragraph (a)(2)(ii) by applying § 1.884-2T(a)(2)(ii) of the temporary regulations (as contained in the CFR edition revised as of April 1, 1995). A properly executed Form 8848, substitute form, or other form of waiver authorized by this paragraph (a)(2)(ii) shall be deemed to be consented to and signed by a Service Center Director or the Assistant Commissioner (International) for purposes of § 301.6501(c)-1(d) of this chapter.

(a)(3) through (a)(4) [Reserved]. For further information, see § 1.884-2T(a)(3) through (a)(4).

(a)(5) *Special rule if a foreign corporation terminates an interest in a trust.*—A foreign corporation whose beneficial interest in a trust terminates (by disposition or otherwise) in any taxable year shall be subject to the branch profits tax on ECEP attributable to amounts (including distributions of accumulated income or gain) treated as ECI to such beneficiary in such taxable year notwithstanding any other provision of § 1.884-2T(a).

(b) through (c)(2)(ii) [Reserved]. For further information, see § 1.884-2T(b) through (c)(2)(ii).

(c)(2)(iii) *Waiver of period of limitations and transferee agreement.*—In the case of a transferee that is a domestic corporation, the provisions of § 1.884-2T(c)(2)(i) shall not apply unless, as part of the section 381(a) transaction, the transferee executes a Form 2045 (Transferee Agreement) and a waiver of period of limitations as described in this paragraph (c)(2)(iii), and files both documents with its timely filed (including extensions) income tax return for the taxable year in which the section 381(a) transaction occurs. The waiver shall be executed on Form 8848, or substitute form, and shall extend the period for assessment of any additional branch profits tax for the taxable year in which the section 381(a) transaction occurs to a date not earlier than the close of the sixth taxable year following the taxable year in which such transaction occurs. This form shall include such information as is required by the form and accompanying instructions. The waiver must be signed by the person authorized to sign Form 2045. With respect to a complete termination occurring in a taxable year ending prior to June 6, 1996, a foreign corporation may also satisfy the requirements of this paragraph (c)(2)(iii) by applying § 1.884-2T(c)(2)(iii) of the temporary regulations (as contained in the CFR edition revised as of April 1, 1995). A properly executed Form 8848, substitute form, or other form of waiver authorized by this paragraph (c)(2)(iii) shall be deemed to be consented to and signed by a Service Center Director or the Assistant Commissioner (International) for purposes of § 301.6501(c)-1(d) of this chapter.

(c)(3) through (c)(6)(i)(A) [Reserved]. For further guidance, see § 1.884-2T(c)(3) through (c)(6)(i)(A).

(B) Shareholders of the transferee (or of the transferee's parent in the case of a triangular reorganization described in section 368(a)(1)(C) or a reorganization described in sections 368(a)(1)(A) and 368(a)(2)(D) or (E)) who in the aggregate owned more than 25 percent of the value of the stock of the transferor at any time within the 12-month period preceding the close of the year in which the section 381(a) transaction occurs sell, exchange or otherwise dispose of their stock or securities in the transferee at any time during a period of three years from the close of the taxable year in which the section 381(a) transaction occurs.

(C) In the case of a triangular reorganization described in section 368(a)(1)(C) or a reorganization described in sections 368(a)(1)(A) and 368(a)(2)(D) or (E), the transferee's parent sells, exchanges, or otherwise disposes of its stock or securities in the transferee at any time during a period of three years from the close of the taxable year in which the section 381(a) transaction occurs.

(D) A corporation related to any such shareholder or the shareholder itself if it is a corporation (subsequent to an event described in paragraph (c)(6)(i)(A) or (B) of this section) or the transferee's parent (subsequent to an event described in paragraph (c)(6)(i)(C) of this section), uses, directly or indirectly, the proceeds or property received in such sale, exchange or disposition, or property attributable thereto, in the conduct of a trade or business in the United States at any time during a period of three years from the date of sale in the case of a disposition of stock in the transferor, or from the close of the taxable year in which the section 381(a) transaction occurs in the case of a disposition of the stock or securities in the transferee (or the transferee's parent in the case of a triangular reorganization described in section 368(a)(1)(C) or a reorganization described in sections 368(a)(1)(A) and (a)(2)(D) or (E)). Where this paragraph (c)(6)(i) applies, the transferor's branch profits tax liability for the taxable year in which the section 381(a) transaction occurs shall be determined under § 1.884-1, taking into account all the adjustments in U.S. net equity that result from the transfer of U.S. assets and liabilities to the transferee pursuant to the section 381(a) transaction, without regard to any provisions in this paragraph (c). If an event described in paragraph (c)(6)(i)(A), (B), or (C) of this section occurs after the close of the taxable year in which the section 381(a) transaction occurs, and if additional branch profits tax is required to be paid by reason of the application of this paragraph (c)(6)(i), then interest must be paid on that amount at the underpayment rates determined under section 6621(a)(2), with respect to the period between the date that was prescribed for filing the transferor's income tax return for the year in which the section 381(a) transaction occurs and the date on which the additional tax for that year is paid. Any such additional tax liability together with interest thereon shall be the liability of the transferee within the meaning of section 6901 pursuant to section 6901 and the regulations there under.

(c)(6)(ii) through (f) [Reserved]. For further guidance, see § 1.884-2T(c)(6)(ii) through (f).

(g) *Effective dates.*—Paragraphs (a)(2)(ii) and (c)(2)(iii) of this section are effective for taxable years beginning after December 31, 1986. Paragraph (a)(5) of this section is effective for taxable years beginning on or after June 6, 1996. Paragraphs (c)(6)(i)(B), (C), and (D), are applicable for tax years beginning after December 31, 1986, except that such paragraphs are applicable to transactions occurring on or after January 23, 2006 in the case of reorganizations described in sections 368(a)(1)(A) and 368(a)(2)(D) or (E). [Reg. § 1.884-2.]

☐ [*T.D. 8657, 3-5-96. Amended by T.D. 9243, 1-23-2006.*]

§ 1.884-2T. Special rules for termination or incorporation of a U.S. trade or business or liquidation or reorganization of a foreign corporation or its domestic subsidiary (Temporary).—(a) *Complete termination of a U.S. trade or business.*—(1) *General rule.*—A foreign corporation shall not be subject to the branch profits tax for the taxable year in which it completely terminates all of its U.S. trade or business within the meaning of paragraph (a)(2) of this section. A foreign corporation's non-previously taxed accumulated effectively connected earnings and profits as of the close of the taxable year of complete termination shall be extinguished for purposes of section 884 and the regulations thereunder, but not for other purposes (for example, sections 312, 316 and 381).

(2) *Operating rules.*—(i) *Definition of complete termination.*—A foreign corporation shall have completely terminated all of its U.S. trade or business for any taxable year ("the year of complete termination") only if—

(A) As of the close of that taxable year, the foreign corporation either has no U.S. assets, or its shareholders have adopted an irrevocable resolution in that taxable year to completely liquidate and dissolve the corporation and, before the close of the immediately succeeding taxable year (also a "year of complete termination" for purposes of applying this paragraph (a)(2)), all of its U.S. assets are either distributed, used to pay off liabilities, or cease to be U.S. assets;

(B) Neither the foreign corporation nor a related corporation uses, directly or indirectly, any of the U.S. assets or the terminated U.S. trade or business, or property attributable thereto or to effectively connected earnings and profits earned by the foreign corporation in the year of complete termination, in the conduct of a trade or business in the United States at any time during a period of three years from the close of the year of complete termination;

(C) The foreign corporation has no income that is, or is treated as, effectively connected with the conduct of a trade or business in the United States (other than solely by reason of section 864(c)(6) or (c)(7)) during the period of three years from the close of the year of complete termination; and

(D) The foreign corporation attaches to its income tax return for each year of complete termination a waiver of the period of limitations, as described in paragraph (a)(2)(ii) of this section.

If a foreign corporation fails to completely terminate all of its U.S. trade or business because of the failure to meet any of the requirements of this paragraph (a)(2), then its branch profits tax liability for the taxable year and all subsequent taxable years shall be determined under the provisions of § 1.884-1, without regard to any provisions in this paragraph (a), taking into account any reduction in U.S. net equity that results from a U.S. trade or business of the foreign corporation ceasing to have U.S. assets. Any additional branch profits tax liability that may result, together with interest thereon (charged at the underpayment rates determined under section 6621(a)(2) with respect to the period between the date that was prescribed for filing the foreign corporation's income tax return for the taxable year with respect to which the branch profits tax liability arises and the date on which the additional tax for that year is paid), and applicable penalties, if any, shall be the liability of the foreign corporation (or of any person who is a transferee of the foreign corporation within the meaning of section 6901).

(ii) *Waiver of period of limitations.*—[Reserved] See § 1.884-2(a)(2)(ii) for rules relating to this paragraph.

(iii) *Property subject to reinvestment prohibition rule.*—For purposes of paragraph (a)(2)(i)(B) of this section—

(A) The term "U.S. assets of the terminated U.S. trade or business" shall mean all the money and other property that qualified as U.S. assets of the foreign corporation as of the close of the taxable year immediately preceding the year of complete termination; and

(B) Property attributable to U.S. assets or to effectively connected earnings and profits earned by the foreign corporation in the year of complete termination shall mean money or other property into which any part or all of such assets or effectively connected earnings and profits are converted at any time before the expiration of the three-year period specified in paragraph (a)(2)(i)(B) of this section by way of sale, exchange, or other disposition, as well as any money or other property attributable to the sale by a shareholder of the foreign corporation of its interest in the foreign corporation (or a successor corporation) at any time after a date which is 12 months before the close of the year of complete termination (24 months in the case of a foreign corporation that makes an election under paragraph (b) of this section).

(iv) *Related corporation.*—For purposes of paragraph (a)(2)(i)(B) of this section, a corporation shall be related to a foreign corporation if either corporation is a 10-percent shareholder of the other corporation or, where the foreign corporation completely liquidates, if either corporation would have been a 10-percent shareholder of the other corporation had the foreign corporation remained in existence. For this purpose, the term "10-percent shareholder" means any person described in section 871(h)(3)(B) as well as any person who owns 10 percent or more of the total value of the stock of the corporation, and stock ownership shall be determined on the basis of the attribution rules described in section 871(h)(3)(C).

(v) *Direct or indirect use of U.S. assets.*—The use of any part or all of the property referred to in paragraph (a)(2)(i)(B) of this section shall include the loan thereof to a related corporation or the use thereof as security (as a pledge, mortgage, or otherwise) for any indebtedness of a related corporation.

(3) *Complete termination in the case of a section 338 election.*—A foreign corporation whose stock is acquired by another corporation that makes (or is deemed to make) an election under section 338 with respect to the stock of the foreign corporation shall be treated as having completely liquidated as of the close of the acquisition date (as defined in section 338(h)(2)) and to have completely terminated all of its U.S. trade or business with respect to the taxable year ending on such acquisition date provided the foreign corporation that exists prior to the section 338 transactions complies with the requirements of paragraph (a)(2)(i)(B) and (D) of this section. For purposes of the preceding sentence, any of the money or other property paid as consideration for the acquisition of the stock in the foreign corporation (and for any debt claim against the foreign corporation) shall be treated as property attributable to the U.S. assets of the terminated U.S. trade or business and to the effectively connected earnings and profits of the foreign corporation earned in the year of complete termination.

(4) *Complete termination in the case of a foreign corporation with income under section 864(c)(6) or 864(c)(7).*—No branch profits tax shall be imposed on effectively connected earnings and profits attributable to income that is treated as effectively connected with the conduct of a trade or business in the United States solely by reason of section 864(c)(6) or 864(c)(7) if—

(i) No income of the foreign corporation for the taxable year is, or is treated as, effectively connected with the conduct of a trade or business in the United States, without regard to section 864(c)(6) or 864(c)(7),

(ii) The foreign corporation has no U.S. assets as of the close of the taxable year, and

(iii) Such effectively connected earnings and profits would not have been subject to branch profits tax pursuant to the complete termination provisions of paragraph (a)(1) of this section if income or gain subject to section 864(c)(6) had not been deferred or if property subject to section 864(c)(7) had been sold immediately prior to the date the property ceased to have been used in the conduct of a trade or business in the United States.

(5) *Special rule if a foreign corporation terminates an interest in a trust.*—[Reserved]See § 1.884-2(a)(5) for rules relating to this paragraph.

(6) *Coordination with second-level withholding tax.*—Effectively connected earnings and profits and non-previously taxed accumulated effectively connected earnings and profits of a foreign corporation that are exempt from branch profits tax by reason of the provisions of paragraph (a)(1) of this section shall not be subject to tax under section 871(a), 881(a), 1441 or 1442 when paid as a dividend by such foreign corporation (or a successor-in-interest).

(b) *Election to remain engaged in a U.S. trade or business.*—(1) *General rule.*—A foreign corporation that would be considered to have completely terminated all of its U.S. trade or business for the taxable year under the provisions of paragraph (a)(2)(i) of this section, but for the provisions of paragraph (a)(2)(i)(B) of this section that prohibit reinvestment within a three-year period, may make an election under this paragraph (b) for the taxable year in which it completely terminates all its U.S. trade or business (as determined without regard to paragraph (a)(2)(i)(B) of this section) and, if it so chooses, for the following taxable year (but not for any succeeding taxable year). The election under this paragraph (b) is an election by the foreign corporation to designate an amount of marketable securities as U.S. assets for purposes of § 1.884-1. The marketable securities identified pursuant to the election under paragraph (b)(3) of this section shall be treated as being U.S. assets in an amount equal, in the aggregate, to the lesser of the adjusted basis of the U.S. assets that ceased to be U.S. assets during the taxable year in which the election is made (determined on the date or dates the U.S. assets ceased to be U.S. assets) or the adjusted basis of the marketable securities as of the end of the taxable year. The securities must be held from the date that they are identified until the end of the taxable year for which the election is made, or if disposed of during the taxable year, must be replaced on the date of disposition with other marketable securities that are acquired on or before that date and that have a fair market value as of the date of substitution not less than their adjusted basis.

(2) *Marketable security.*—For purposes of this paragraph (b), the term "marketable security" means a security (including stock) that is part of an issue any portion of which is regularly traded on an established securities market (within the meaning of § 1.884-5(d)(2) and (4)) and a deposit described in section 871(i)(3)(A) or (B).

(3) *Identification requirements.*—In order to qualify for this election—

(i) The marketable securities must be identified on the books and records of the U.S. trade or business within 30 days of the date an equivalent amount of U.S. assets ceases to be U.S. assets; and

(ii) On the date a marketable security is identified, its adjusted basis must not exceed its fair market value.

(4) *Treatment of income from deemed U.S. assets.*—The income or gain from the marketable securities (or replacement securities) subject to an election under this paragraph (b) that arises in a taxable year for which an election is made shall be treated as ECI (other than for purposes of section 864(c)(7)), and losses from the disposition of such marketable securities shall be allocated entirely to income that is ECI. In addition, all such securities shall be treated as if they had been sold for their fair market value on the earlier of the last business day of a taxable year for which an election is in effect or the day immediately prior to the date of substitution by the foreign corporation of a U.S. asset for the marketable security, and any gain (but not loss) and accrued interest on the securities shall also be treated as ECI. The adjusted basis of such property shall be increased by the amount of any gain recognized by reason of this paragraph (b).

(5) *Method of election.*—A foreign corporation may make an election under this paragraph (b) by attaching to its income tax return for the taxable year a statement—

(i) Identifying the marketable securities treated as U.S. assets under this paragraph (b);

(ii) Setting forth the E&P bases of such securities; and

(iii) Agreeing to treat any income, gain or loss as provided in paragraph (b)(4) of this section.

Such statement must be filed on or before the due date (including extensions) of the foreign corporation's income tax return for the taxable year. A foreign corporation shall not be permitted to make an election under this paragraph (b) more than once.

(6) *Effective date.*—This paragraph (b) is effective for taxable years beginning on or after October 13, 1992. However, if a foreign corporation has made a valid election under § 1.884-1 (i) to apply that section with respect to a taxable year beginning before October 13, 1992, and after December 31, 1986, this paragraph (b) shall be effective beginning with such taxable year.

(c) *Liquidation, reorganization, etc., of a foreign corporation.*—The following rules apply to the transfer by a foreign corporation engaged (or deemed engaged) in the conduct of a U.S. trade or business (the "transferor") of its U.S. assets to another corporation (the "transferee") in a complete liquidation or reorganization described in section 381(a) (a "section 381(a) transaction") if the transferor is engaged (or deemed engaged) in the conduct of a U.S. trade or business immediately prior to the section 381(a) transaction. For purposes of this paragraph (c), a section 381(a) transaction is considered to occur in the taxable year that ends on the date of distribution or transfer (as defined in § 1.381(b)-1(b)) pursuant to the section 381(a) transaction.

(1) *Inapplicability of paragraph (a)(1) of this section to section 381(a) transactions.*—Paragraph (a)(1) of this section (relating to the complete termination of a U.S. trade or business of a foreign corporation) does not apply to exempt the transferor from branch profits tax liability for the taxable year in which the section 381(a) transaction occurs or in any succeeding taxable year.

(2) *Transferor's dividend equivalent amount for the taxable year in which a section 381(a) transaction occurs.*—The dividend equivalent amount for the taxable year, including a short taxable year, in which a section 381(a) transaction occurs shall be determined under the provisions of § 1.884-1, as modified under the provisions of this paragraph (c)(2).

(i) *U.S. net equity.*—The transferor's U.S. net equity as of the close of the taxable year shall be determined without regard to any transfer in that taxable year of U.S. assets to or from the transferee pursuant to a section 381(a) transaction, and without regard to any U.S. liabilities assumed or acquired by the transferee from the transferor in that taxable year pursuant to a section 381(a) transaction. The transferor's adjusted basis (for earnings and profits purposes) in U.S. assets transferred to the transferee pursuant to a section 381(a) transaction shall be the adjusted basis of those assets (for earnings and profits purposes) immediately prior to the section 381(a) transaction, adjusted as provided under section 362(b), treating the transferor, for that purpose, as though it were the transferee and treating the gain taken into account for earnings and profits purposes as gain recognized.

(ii) *Effectively connected earnings and profits.*—The transferor's effectively connected earnings and profits for the taxable year in which the section 381(a) transaction occurs and its non-previously taxed accumulated effectively connected earnings and profits shall be determined without regard to the carryover to the transferee of the transferor's earnings and profits under section 381(a) and (c)(2) of paragraph (c)(4) of this section. Effectively connected earnings and profits for the taxable year in which a section 381(a) transaction occurs shall be adjusted by the amount of any gain recognized to the transferor in that year pursuant to the section 381(a) transaction (to the extent taken into account for earnings and profits purposes).

(iii) *Waiver of period of limitations and transferee agreement.*—[Reserved] See § 1.884-2(c)(2)(iii) for rules relating to this paragraph.

(3) *Transferor's dividend equivalent amount for any taxable year succeeding the taxable year in which the section 381(a) transaction occurs.*—Any decrease in U.S. net equity in any taxable year succeeding the taxable year in which the section 381(a) transaction occurs shall increase the transferor's dividend equivalent amount for those years without regard to the limitation in § 1.884-1(b)(3)(ii), to the extent such decrease in U.S. net equity does not exceed the balance of effectively connected earnings and profits and non-previously taxed accumulated effectively connected earnings and profits carried over to the transferee pursuant to section 381(a) and (c)(2), as determined under paragraph (c)(4) of this section.

(4) *Earnings and profits of the transferor carried over to the transferee pursuant to the section 381(a) transaction.*—(i) *Amount.*—The amount of effectively connected earnings and profits and non-previously taxed accumulated effectively connected earnings and profits of the transferor that carry over to the transferee under section 381(a) and (c)(2) shall be the effectively connected earnings and profits and the non-previously taxed accumulated effectively connected earnings and profits of the transferor immediately before the close of the taxable year in which the section 381(a) transaction occurs. For this purpose, the provisions in § 1.381(c)(2)-1 shall generally apply with proper adjustments to reflect the fact that effectively connected earnings and profits and non-previously taxed accumulated effectively connected earnings and profits are not affected by distributions to shareholders but, rather, by dividend equivalent amounts. Therefore, the amounts of effectively connected earnings and profits and non-previously taxed accumulated effectively connected earnings and profits that carry over to the transferee pursuant to those provisions are reduced by the transferor's dividend equivalent amount for the taxable year in which the section 381(a) transaction occurs. Such amounts are also reduced to the extent of any dividend equivalent amount determined for any succeeding taxable year solely as a result of the provisions of paragraph (c)(3) of this section. For purposes of this paragraph (c)(4)(i), if the transferor accumulates non-previously taxed effectively connected earnings and profits, or incurs a deficit in effectively connected earnings and profits, attributable to a period that is after the close of the taxable year in which the section 381(a) transaction occurs and before the liquidation of the transferor, then such effectively connected earnings and profits, or deficits therein, shall be deemed to have been accumulated or incurred on or before the close of the taxable year in which the section 381(a) transaction occurs.

(ii) *Retention of character.*—All of the transferor's effectively connected earnings and profits and non-previously taxed accumulated effectively connected earnings and profits that carry over to the transferee shall constitute non-previously taxed accumulated effectively connected earnings and profits of the transferee. In the case of a domestic transferee, such non-previously taxed accumulated effectively connected earnings and profits shall also constitute accumulated earnings and profits of the transferee for purposes of section 316(a)(2).

(iii) *Treatment of distributions by a domestic transferee out of non-previously taxed accumulated effectively connected earnings and profits.*—In the event the transferee is a domestic corporation, distributions out of the transferee's non-previously taxed accumulated effectively connected earnings and profits that are received by a foreign distributee shall qualify for benefits under an applicable income tax treaty only (A) if the distributee qualifies for the benefits under such treaty and (B) to the extent that the transferor foreign corporation would have qualified under the principles of § 1.884-1(g)(1) and (2)(i) for an exemption or reduction in rate with respect to the branch profits tax if the non-previously taxed accumulated effectively connected earnings and profits had been reflected in a dividend equivalent amount for the taxable year in which the section 381(a) transaction occurs. (The tax rate on dividends specified in the treaty between the distributee's country of residence and the United States shall apply to any dividends received by a distributee who qualifies for a treaty benefit under the preceding sentence.) In addition, distributions out of such non-previously taxed accumulated effectively connected earnings and profits shall retain their character in the hands of any domestic distributee up a chain of corporate shareholders for purposes of applying this paragraph (c)(4)(iii) to distributions made by any such person to a foreign distributee. If a domestic transferee has non-previously taxed accumulated effectively connected earnings and profits carried over from the transferor as well as accumulated earnings and profits, then each category of earnings and profits shall be accounted for in two separate pools, and any distribution of earnings and profits shall be treated as a distribution out of each pool in proportion to the respective amount of undistributed earnings and profits in each pool. Section 871(i) (relating, in part, to dividends paid by a domestic corporation meeting the 80-percent foreign business requirements of section 861(c)(1)) shall not apply to any dividends paid by a domestic transferee out of its non-previously taxed accumulated effectively connected earnings and profits.

(5) *Determination of U.S. net equity of a transferee that is a foreign corporation.*—In the event the transferee is a foreign corporation, then for purposes of determining the transferee's increase or decrease in U.S. net equity under § 1.884-1 for its taxable year during which the section 381(a) transaction occurs, its U.S. net equity as of the close of its immediately preceding taxable year shall be increased by the amount of U.S. net equity acquired by the transferee from the transferor pursuant to the section 381(a) transaction, taking into account the adjustments to the basis (for earnings and profits purposes) of U.S. assets under the principles of section 362(b).

(6) *Special rules in the case of the disposition of stock or securities in a domestic transferee or in the transferor.*—(i) *General rule.*—This paragraph (c)(6)(i) shall apply where the transferee is a domestic corporation, subdivision (A), (B), or (C) of this paragraph applies and subdivision (D) of this paragraph applies.

(A) Shareholders of the transferor sell, exchange or otherwise dispose of stock in the transferor at any time during a 12-month period before the date of distribution or transfer (as defined in § 1.381(b)-1(b)) and the aggregate amount of such stock sold, exchanged or otherwise disposed of exceeds 25 percent of the value of the stock of the transferor, determined on a date that is 12 months before the date of distribution or transfer.

(B), (C) and (D) [Reserved]. For further guidance, see §1.884-2(c)(6)(i)(B), (C), and (D).

(ii) *Operating rule.*—For purposes of paragraph (c)(6)(i) of this section paragraph (a)(2)(iii)(B), (iv) and (v) of this section shall apply for purposes of making the determinations under paragraph (c)(6)(i)(D) of this section.

(d) *Incorporation under section 351.*—(1) *In general.*—The following rules apply to the transfer by a foreign corporation engaged (or deemed engaged) in the conduct of a U.S. trade or business (the "transferor") of part or all of its U.S. assets to a U.S. corporation (the "transferee") in exchange for stock or securities in the transferee in a transaction that qualifies under section 351(a) (a "section 351 transaction"), provided that immediately after the transaction, the transferor is in control (as defined in section 368(c)) of the transferee, without regard to other transferors.

(2) *Inapplicability of paragraph (a)(1) of this section to section 351 transactions.*—Paragraph (a)(1) of this section does not apply to exempt the transferor from branch profits tax liability for the taxable year in which a section 351 transaction described in paragraph (d)(1) of this section occurs and shall not apply for any subsequent taxable year of the transferor in which it, or a successor-in-interest, owns stock or securities of a transferee as of the close of the transferor's taxable year.

(3) *Transferor's dividend equivalent amount for the taxable year in which a section 351 transaction occurs.*—The dividend equivalent amount of the transferor for the taxable year in which a section 351 transaction described in paragraph (d)(1) of this section occurs shall be determined under the provisions of §1.884-1, as modified by the provisions of this paragraph (d)(3) provided that the transferee elects under paragraph (d)(4) of this section to be allocated a proportionate amount of the transferor's effectively connected earnings and profits and non-previously taxed accumulated effectively connected earnings and profits and the foreign corporation files a statement as provided in paragraph (d)(5)(i) of this section and complies with the agreement included in such statement with respect to a subsequent disposition of the transferee's stock.

(i) *U.S. net equity.*—The transferor's U.S. net equity as of the close of the taxable year shall be determined without regard to any transfer in that taxable year of U.S. assets to or from the transferee pursuant to a section 351 transaction, and without regard to any U.S. liabilities assumed or acquired by the transferee from the transferor in that taxable year pursuant to a section 351 transaction. The transferor's adjusted basis for earnings and profits purposes in U.S. assets transferred to the transferee pursuant to a section 351 transaction shall be the adjusted basis of those assets for earnings and profits purposes immediately prior to the section 351 transaction, increased by the amount of any gain recognized by the transferor on the transfer of such assets in the section 351 transaction to the extent taken into account for earnings and profits purposes.

(ii) *Effectively connected earnings and profits.*—Subject to the limitation in paragraph (d)(3)(iii) of this section, the calculation of the transferor's dividend equivalent amount shall take into account the transferor's effectively connected earnings and profits for the taxable year in which a section 351 transaction occurs (including any amount of gain recognized to the transferor pursuant to the section 351 transaction to the extent the gain is taken into account for earnings and profits purposes) and, for purposes of applying the limitation of §1.884-1(b)(3)(ii), its non-previously taxed accumulated effectively connected earnings and profits, determined without regard to the allocation to the transferee of the transferor's effectively connected earnings and profits and non-previously taxed accumulated effectively connected earnings and profits pursuant to the election under paragraph (d)(4)(i) of this section.

(iii) *Limitation on dividend equivalent amount.*—The dividend equivalent amount determined under this paragraph (d)(3) shall not exceed the sum of the transferor's effectively connected earnings and profits and non-previously taxed accumulated effectively connected earnings and profits determined after taking into account the allocation to the transferee of the transferor's earnings pursuant to an election under paragraph (d)(4)(i) of this section.

(4) *Election to increase earnings and profits.*—(i) *General rule.*—The election referred to in paragraph (d)(3) of this section is an election by the transferee to increase its earnings and profits by the amount determined under paragraph (d)(4)(ii) of this section. An election under this paragraph (d)(4)(i) shall be effective only if the transferee attaches a statement to its timely filed (including extensions) income tax return for the taxable year in which the section 351 transaction occurs, in which—

(A) It agrees to be subject to the rules of paragraph (c)(4)(ii) and (iii) of this section with respect to the transferor's effectively connected earnings and profits and non-previously taxed accumulated effectively connected earnings and profits allocated to the transferee pursuant to the election under this paragraph (d)(4)(i) in the same manner as if such earnings and profits had been carried over to the transferee pursuant to section 381(a) and (c)(2), and

(B) It identifies the amount of effectively connected earnings and profits and non-previously taxed accumulated effectively connected earnings and profits that are allocated from the transferor. An election with respect to a taxable year ending on or before December 1, 1988, may be made by filing an amended Form 1120F on or before January 3, 1989, to which the statement described in this paragraph (d)(4)(i) shall be attached.

(ii) *Amount of the transferor's effectively connected earnings and profits and non-previously taxed accumulated effectively connected earnings and profits allocated to the transferee.*—The amount referred to in paragraph (d)(4)(i) of this section is equal to the same proportion of the transferor's effectively connected earnings and profits and non-previously taxed accumulated effectively connected earnings and profits (determined immediately prior to the section 351 transaction and without regard to this paragraph (d)(4) or any dividend equivalent amount for the taxable year) that the adjusted bases for purposes of computing earnings and profits in all the U.S. assets transferred to the transferee by the transferor pursuant to the section 351 transaction bear to the adjusted bases for purposes of computing earnings and profits in all the U.S. assets of the transferor, determined immediately prior to the section 351 transaction.

(iii) *Effect of election on transferor.*—For purposes of computing the transferor's dividend equivalent amount for the taxable year succeeding the taxable year in which a section 351 transaction occurs, the transferor's effectively connected earnings and profits and non-previously taxed accumulated effectively connected earnings and profits as of the close of the taxable year in which the section 351 transaction occurs shall be reduced by the amount of its effectively connected earnings and profits and non-previously taxed accumulated effectively connected earnings and profits allocated to the transferee pursuant to the election under paragraph (d)(4)(i) of this section (and by its dividend equivalent amount for the taxable year in which the section 351 transaction occurs).

(5) *Dispositions of stock or securities of the transferee by the transferor.*—(i) *General rule.*—The statement referred to in paragraph (d)(3) of this section is a statement executed by the transferor stating the transferor's agreement that, upon the disposition of part or all of the stock or securities it owns in the transferee (or a successor-in-interest), it shall treat as a dividend equivalent amount for the taxable year in which the disposition occurs an amount equal to the lesser of (A) the amount realized upon such disposition or (B) the total amount of effectively connected earnings and profits and non-previously taxed accumulated effectively connected earnings and profits that was allocated from the transferor to that transferee pursuant to an election under paragraph (d)(4)(i) of this section, which amount shall be reduced to the extent previously taken into account by the transferor as dividends or dividend equivalent amounts for tax or branch profits tax purposes. The extent and manner in which such dividend equivalent amount may be subject to the branch profits tax in the taxable year of disposition shall be determined under the provisions of section 884 and the regulations thereunder, including the provisions of paragraph (a) of this section (relating to complete terminations), as limited under paragraph (d)(2) of this section. Except as otherwise provided in paragraph (d)(5)(ii) of this section, the term "disposition" means any transfer that would constitute a disposition by the transferor for any purpose of the Internal Revenue Code and the regulations thereunder. This paragraph (d)(5)(i) shall apply regardless of whether the stock or securities of the transferee are U.S. assets in the hands of the transferor at the time of sale, exchange or disposition.

(ii) *Exception for certain tax-free dispositions.*—For purposes of paragraph (d)(5)(i) of this section, a disposition does not include a transfer of stock or securities of the transferee by the transferor in a transaction that qualifies as a transfer pursuant to a complete liquidation described in section 332(b) or a transfer pursuant to a reorganization described in section 368(a)(1)(F). Any other transfer that qualifies for non-recognition of gain or loss shall be treated as a disposition for purposes of paragraph (d)(5)(i) of this section, unless the Commissioner has, by published guidance or by prior ruling issued to the taxpayer upon its request, determined such transfer not to be a disposition for purposes of paragraph (d)(5)(i) of this section.

(iii) *Distributions governed by section 355.*—In the case of a distribution or exchange of stock or securities of a transferee to which section 355 applies (or so much of section 356 as relates to section 355) and that is not in pursuance of a plan meeting the requirements of a reorganization as defined in section 368(a)(1)(D), § 1.312-10(b) (relating to the allocation of earnings and profits in certain corporate separations) shall not apply to reduce the transferor's effectively connected earnings and profits or non-previously taxed accumulated effectively connected earnings and profits.

(iv) *Filing of statement.*—The statement referred to in paragraph (d)(5)(i) of this section shall be attached to a timely filed (including extensions) income tax return of the transferor for the taxable year in which the section 351 transaction occurs. An election with respect to a taxable year ending on or before December 1, 1988, may be made by filing an amended Form 1120F on or before January 3, 1989, to which the statement described in this paragraph (d)(5)(iv) shall be attached.

(6) *Example.*—The provisions of this paragraph (d) are illustrated by the following example.

Example. Foreign corporation X has a calendar taxable year. X's only assets are U.S. assets and X computes its interest deduction using the actual ratio of liabilities to assets under § 1.882-5(b)(2)(ii). X's U.S. net equity as of the close of its 1988 taxable year is $2,000, resulting from the following amounts of U.S. assets and liabilities:

U.S. assets		*U.S. liabilities*	
U.S. building A	$1,000	Mortgage A	$800
U.S. building B	$2,500	Mortgage B	$1,500
Other U.S. assets	$800		
Total	$4,300		$2,300

Assume that X's adjusted basis in its assets is equal to X's adjusted basis in its assets for earnings and profits purposes. On September 30, 1989, X transfers building A, which has a fair market value of $1,800, to a newly created U.S. corporation Y under section 351 in exchange for 100% of the stock of Y with a fair market value of $800, other property with a fair market value of $200, and the assumption of Mortgage A. Assume that under sections 11 and 351(b), tax of $30 is imposed with respect to the $200 of other property received by X. X's non-previously taxed accumulated effectively connected earnings and profits as of the close of its 1988 taxable year are $200 and its effectively connected earnings and profits for its 1989 taxable year are $330, including $170 of gain recognized to X on the transfer as adjusted for earnings and profits purposes (*i.e.*, $200 of gain recognized minus $30 of tax paid with respect to the gain). Y takes a $1,200 basis in the building transferred from X, equal to the basis in the hands of X ($1,000) increased by the amount of gain recognized to X in the section 351 transaction ($200). Y makes an election in the manner described in paragraph (d)(4)(i) of this section to increase its earnings and profits by the amount described in paragraph (d)(4)(ii) of this section and X files a statement as provided in paragraph (d)(5)(i) of this section. The branch profits tax consequences to X and Y in the taxable year in which the section 351 transaction occurs and in subsequent taxable years are as follows:

(i) *X's dividend equivalent amount for 1989.* The determination of X's dividend equivalent amount for 1989 is a three-step process: determining X's U.S. net equity as of the close of its 1989 taxable year under paragraph (d)(3)(i) of this section; determining the amount of X's effectively connected earnings and profits and non-previously taxed accumulated effectively connected earnings and profits for its 1989 taxable year under paragraph (d)(3)(ii) of this section; and applying the limitation in paragraph (d)(3)(iii) of this section.

Step one: Pursuant to paragraph (d)(3)(i) of this section, X's U.S. net equity as of the close of its 1989 taxable year is calculated without regard to the section 351 transaction except that X's basis in its U.S. assets is increased by the $170 amount of gain it has recognized for earnings and profits in connection with the section 351 transaction. Thus, X's U.S. net equity as of the close of its 1989 taxable year is $1,870, consisting of the following U.S. assets and liabilities, taking into account the fact that X's other U.S. assets have decreased to $500:

U.S. assets		*U.S. liabilities*	
Building A	$1,170	Mortgage A	$800
Building B	$2,500	Mortgage B	$1,500
Other U.S. assets	$500		
Total	$4,170		$2,300

Thus, X's U.S. net equity as of the close of its 1989 taxable year has decreased by $130 relative to its U.S. net equity as of the close of its 1988 taxable year.

Step two: Pursuant to paragraph (d)(3)(ii) of this section, X's effectively connected earnings and profits and non-previously taxed accumulated effectively connected earnings and profits for the taxable year are determined without taking into account the allocation to Y of X's effectively connected earnings and profits and non-previously taxed accumulated effectively connected earnings and profits pursuant to the election under paragraph (d)(4)(i) of this section. Thus, X's effectively connected earnings and profits for its 1989 taxable year are $330 and X's non-previously taxed accumulated effectively connected earnings and profits are $200. Thus, but for the limitation in paragraph (d)(3)(iii) of this section, X's dividend equivalent amount for the taxable year would be $460, equal to X's effectively connected earnings and profits for the taxable year ($330), increased by the decrease in X's U.S. net equity ($130).

Step three: Pursuant to paragraph (d)(3)(iii) of this section, X's dividend equivalent amount for its 1989 taxable year may not exceed the sum of the transferor's effectively connected earnings and profits and non-previously taxed accumulated effectively connected earnings and profits, determined as of the close of its 1989 taxable year, after taking into account the allocation of the transferor's earnings and profits pursuant to the election under paragraph (d)(4)(i) of this section. Based upon subdivision (ii) of this example, X's dividend equivalent amount for 1989 cannot exceed $423, which is equal to the total amount of X's effectively connected earnings and profits and non-previously taxed accumulated effectively connected earnings and profits, determined as of the close of its 1989 taxable year without regard to the allocation of earnings and profits to Y pursuant to Y's election under paragraph (d)(4)(i) of this section ($530), reduced by the amount of X's effectively connected earnings and profits and non-previously taxed accumulated effectively connected earnings and profits allocated to Y pursuant to Y's election under paragraph (d)(4)(i) of this section ($107). Thus, X's dividend equivalent amount for its 1989 taxable year is limited to $423.

(ii) *Amount of X's effectively connected earnings and profits and non-previously taxed accumulated effectively connected earnings and profits transferred to Y.* Pursuant to Y's election under paragraph (d)(4)(i) of this section, Y increases its earnings and profits by the amount prescribed in paragraph (d)(4)(ii) of this section. This amount is equal to the sum of X's effectively connected earnings and profits and non-previously taxed accumulated effectively connected earnings and profits determined immediately before the section 351 transaction, without regard to X's dividend equivalent amount for the year, allocated in the same proportion that X's basis in the U.S. assets transferred to Y bears to the bases of all of X's U.S. assets, which bases are determined immediately prior to the section 351(a) transaction. The amount of X's effectively connected earnings and profits immediately before the section 351 transaction is assumed to be $260. The total amount of effectively connected earnings and profits ($260) and non-previously taxed accumulated effectively connected earnings and profits ($200) determined immediately before the section 351 transaction is, therefore, $460. The portion of $460 that is allocated to Y pursuant to Y's election under paragraph (d)(4)(i) of this section is $107, calculated as $460 multiplied by a fraction, the numerator of which is the basis of the U.S. assets transferred to Y pursuant to the section 351 transaction ($1,000), and the denominator of which is the bases of X's U.S. assets determined immediately before the section 351 transaction ($4,300). Pursuant to paragraph (d)(4)(i) of this section, the amount of $107 of X's effectively connected earnings and profits and non-previously taxed accumulated effectively connected earnings and profits allocated to Y pursuant to paragraph (d)(4)(i) of this section constitutes non-previously taxed accumulated effectively connected earnings and profits of Y.

(iii) *X's non-previously taxed accumulated effectively connected earnings and profits for 1990.* Pursuant to paragraph (d)(4)(iii) of this section, X's non-previously taxed accumulated effectively connected earnings and profits as of the close of its 1989 taxable year for purposes of computing its dividend equivalent amount for its taxable year 1990 are zero, *i.e.,* $530 of effectively connected earnings and profits and non-previously taxed accumulated effectively connected earnings and profits reduced by $107 of effectively connected earnings and profits and non-previously taxed accumulated effectively connected earnings and profits allocated to Y, and further reduced by X's $423 dividend equivalent amount for its 1989 taxable year.

U.S. assets	
Building B	$2,500
Other U.S. assets	500
	$3,000

(iv) *X's U.S. net equity for purposes of determining the dividend equivalent amount for succeeding taxable years.* For 1990, X must determine its U.S. net equity as of December 31, 1989, in order to determine whether there has been an increase or decrease in its U.S. net equity as of December 31, 1990. For this purpose, X's U.S. net equity as of December 31, 1989 is determined under the provisions of § 1.884-1 without regard to the special rules in paragraph (d)(3)(i) of this section. Thus, X's U.S. net equity as of December 31, 1989 is $1,500, consisting of the following U.S. assets and liabilities:

U.S. liabilities	
Mortgage B	$1,500
	$1,500

(e) *Certain transactions with respect to a domestic subsidiary.*—In the case of a section 381(a) transaction in which a domestic subsidiary of a foreign corporation transfers assets to that foreign corporation or to another foreign corporation with respect to which the first foreign corporation owns stock (directly or indirectly) meeting the requirements of section 1504(a)(2), the transferee's non-previously taxed accumulated effectively connected earnings and profits for the taxable year in which the section 381(a) transaction occurs shall be increased by all of the domestic subsidiary's current earnings and profits and earnings and profits accumulated after December 31, 1986, that carry over to the transferee under sections 381(a) and (c)(1) (including non-previously taxed accumulated effectively connected earnings and profits, if any, transferred to the domestic subsidiary under paragraphs (c)(4) and (d)(4) of this section and treated as earnings and profits under paragraphs (c)(4)(ii) and (d)(4)(ii) of this section). For purposes of determining the transferee's dividend equivalent amount for the taxable year in which the section 381(a) transaction occurs, the transferee's U.S. net equity as of the close of its taxable year immediately preceding the taxable year during which the section 381(a) transaction occurs shall be increased by the greater of (1) the amount by which the transferee's U.S. net equity computed immediately prior to the transfer would have increased due to the transfer of the subsidiary's assets and liabilities if U.S. net equity were computed immediately prior to the transfer and immediately after the transfer (taking into account in the earnings and profits basis of the assets transferred any gain recognized on the transfer to the extent reflected in earnings and profits), or (2) the total amount of U.S. net equity transferred (directly or indirectly) by the foreign parent to the domestic subsidiary in one or more prior section 351 or 381(a) transactions.

(f) *Effective date.*—This section is effective for taxable years beginning after December 31, 1986. [Temporary Reg. § 1.884-2T.]

☐ [*T.D.* 8223, 8-29-88. *Amended by T.D.* 8432, 9-10-92; *T.D.* 8657, 3-5-96 *and T.D.* 9243, 1-23-2006.]

§ 1.884-4. Branch-level interest tax.—(a) *General rule.*—(1) *Tax on branch interest.*—In the case of a foreign corporation that, during the taxable year, is engaged in trade or business in the United States or has gross income that is ECI (as defined in § 1.884-1(d)(1)(iii)), any interest paid by such trade or business (hereinafter "branch interest," as defined in paragraph (b) of this section) shall, for purposes of subtitle A (Income Taxes), be treated as if it were paid by a domestic corporation (other than a corporation described in section 861(c)(1), relating to a domestic corporation that meets the 80 percent foreign business requirement). Thus, for example, whether such interest is treated as income from sources within the United States by the person who receives the interest shall be determined in the same manner as if such interest were paid by a domestic corporation (other than a corporation described in section 861(c)(1)). Such interest shall be subject to tax under section 871(a) or 881, and to withholding under section 1441 or 1442, in the same manner as interest paid by a domestic corporation (other than a corporation described in section 861(c)(1)) if received by a foreign person and not effectively connected with the conduct by the foreign person of a trade or business in the United States, unless the interest, if paid by a domestic corporation, would be exempt under section 871(h) or 881(c) (relating to exemption for certain portfolio interest received by a foreign person), section 871(i) or 881(d) (relating, in part, to exemption for certain bank deposit interest received by a foreign person), or another provision of the Code. Such interest shall also be treated as interest paid by a domestic corporation (other than a corporation described in section 861(c)(1)) for purposes of sections 864(c), 871(b) and 882(a) (relating to income that is effectively connected with the conduct of a trade or business within the United States) and section 904 (relating to the limitation on the foreign tax credit). For purposes of this section, a foreign corporation also shall be treated as engaged in trade or business in the United States if, at any time during the taxable year, it owns an asset taken into account under § 1.882-5(a)(1)(ii) or (b)(1) for purposes of determining the amount of the foreign corporation's interest expense allocated or apportioned to ECI. See paragraph (b)(8) of this section for the effect of income tax treaties on branch interest.

(2) *Tax on excess interest.*—(i) *Definition of excess interest.*—For purposes of this section, the term "excess interest" means—

(A) The amount of interest allocated or apportioned to ECI of the foreign corporation under § 1.882-5 for the taxable year, after application of § 1.884-1(e)(3); minus

(B) The foreign corporation's branch interest (as defined in paragraph (b) of this section) for the taxable year, but not including interest accruing in a taxable year beginning before January 1, 1987; minus

(C) The amount of interest determined under paragraph (c)(2) of this section (relating to interest paid by a partnership).

(ii) *Imposition of tax.*—A foreign corporation shall be liable for tax on excess interest under section 881(a) in the same manner as if such excess interest were interest paid to the foreign corporation by a wholly-owned domestic corporation (other than a corporation described in section 861(c)(1)) on the last day of the foreign corporation's taxable year. Excess interest shall be exempt from tax under section 881(a) only as provided in paragraph (a)(2)(iii) of this section (relating to treatment of certain excess interest of banks as interest on deposits) or paragraph (c)(3) of this section (relating to income tax treaties).

(iii) *Treatment of a portion of the excess interest of banks as interest on deposits.*—A portion of the excess interest of a foreign corporation that is a bank (as defined in section 585(a)(2)(B) without regard to the second sentence thereof) provided that a substantial part of its business in the United States, as well as all other countries in which it operates, consists of receiving deposits and making loans and discounts, shall be treated as interest on deposits (as described in section 871(i)(3)), and shall be exempt from the tax imposed by section 881(a) as provided in such section. The portion of the excess interest of the foreign corporation that is treated as interest on deposits shall equal the product of the foreign corporation's excess interest and the greater of—

(A) The ratio of the amount of interest bearing deposits, within the meaning of section 871(i)(3)(A), of the foreign corporation as of the close of the taxable year to the amount of all interest bearing liabilities of the foreign corporation on such date; or

(B) 85 percent.

(iv) *Reporting and payment of tax on excess interest.*—The amount of tax due under section 884(f) and this section with respect to excess interest of a foreign corporation shall be reported on the foreign corporation's income tax return for the taxable year in which the excess interest is treated as paid to the foreign corporation under section 884(f)(1)(B) and paragraph (a)(2) of this section, and shall not be subject to withholding under section 1441 or 1442. The tax shall be due and payable as provided in section 6151 and such other sections of Subtitle F of the Internal Revenue Code as apply, and estimated tax payments shall be due with respect to a foreign corporation's liability for the tax on excess interest as provided in section 6655.

(3) *Original issue discount.*—For purposes of this section, the term "interest" includes original issue discount, as defined in section 1273(a)(1).

(4) *Examples.*—The application of this paragraph (a) is illustrated by the following examples.

Example 1. Taxation of branch interest and excess interest. Foreign corporation A, a calendar year taxpayer that is not a corporation described in paragraph (a)(2)(iii) of this section (relating to banks), has $120 of interest allocated or apportioned to ECI under § 1.882-5 for 1997. A's branch interest (as defined in paragraph (b) of this section) for 1997 is as follows: $55 of portfolio interest (as defined in section 871(h)(2)) to B, a nonresident alien; $25 of interest to foreign corporation C, which owns 15 percent of the combined voting power of A's stock, with respect to bonds issued by A; and $20 to D, a domestic corporation. B and C are not engaged in the conduct of a trade or business in the United States. A, B and C are residents of countries with which the United States does not have an income tax treaty. The interest payments made to B and D are not subject to tax under section 871(a) or 881 and are not subject to withholding under section 1441 or 1442. The payment to C, which does not qualify as portfolio interest because C owns at least 10 percent of the combined voting power of A's stock, is subject to withholding of $7.50 ($25 × 30%). In addition, because A's interest allocated or apportioned to ECI under § 1.882-5 ($120) exceeds its branch interest ($100), A has excess interest of $20, which is subject to a tax of $6 ($20 × 30%) under section 881. The tax on A's excess interest must be reported on A's income tax return for 1997.

Example 2. Taxation of excess interest of a bank. Foreign corporation A, a calendar year taxpayer, is a corporation described in paragraph (a)(2)(iii) of this section (relating to banks) and is a resident of a country with which the United States does not have an income tax treaty. A has excess interest of $100 for 1997. At the close of 1997, A has $10,000 of interest-bearing liabilities (including liabilities that give rise to branch interest), of which $8,700 are interest-bearing deposits. For purposes of computing the tax on A's excess interest, $87 of the excess interest ($100 excess interest × ($8,700 interest-bearing deposits/$10,000 interest-bearing liabilities)) is treated as interest on deposits. Thus, $87 of A's excess interest is exempt from tax under section 881(a) and the remaining $13 of excess interest is subject to a tax of $3.90 ($13 × 30%) under section 881(a).

(b) *Branch interest.*—(1) *Definition of branch interest.*—For purposes of this section, the term "branch interest" means interest that is—

(i) Paid by a foreign corporation with respect to a liability that is—

(A) A U.S. booked liability within the meaning of § 1.882-5(d)(2) (other than a U.S. booked liability of a partner within the meaning of § 1.882-5(d)(2)(vii)); or

(B) Described in § 1.884-1(e)(2) (relating to insurance liabilities on U.S. business and liabilities giving rise to interest expense that is directly allocated to income from a U.S. asset); or

(ii) In the case of a foreign corporation other than a corporation described in paragraph (a)(2)(iii) of this section, a liability specifically identified (as provided in paragraph (b)(3)(i) of this section) as a liability of a U.S. trade or business of the foreign corporation on or before the earlier of the date on which the first payment of interest is made with respect to the liability or the due date (including extensions) of the foreign corporation's income tax return for the taxable year, provided that—

(A) The amount of such interest does not exceed 85 percent of the amount of interest of the foreign corporation that would be excess interest before taking into account interest treated as branch interest by reason of this paragraph (b)(1)(ii);

(B) The requirements of paragraph (b)(3)(ii) of this section (relating to notification of recipient of interest) are satisfied; and

(C) The liability is not described in paragraph (b)(3)(iii) of this section (relating to liabilities incurred in the ordinary course of a foreign business or secured by foreign assets) or paragraph (b)(1)(i) of this section.

(2) [Reserved]

(3) *Requirements relating to specifically identified liabilities.*—(i) *Method of identification.*—A liability described in paragraph (b)(1)(ii) of this section is identified as a liability of a U.S. trade or business only if the liability is shown on the records of the U.S. trade or business, or is identified as a liability of the U.S. trade or business on other records of the foreign corporation or on a schedule established for the purpose of identifying the liabilities of the U.S. trade or business. Each such liability must be identified with sufficient specificity so that the amount of branch interest attributable to the liability, and the name and address of the recipient, can be readily identified from such records or schedule. However, with respect to liabilities that give rise to portfolio interest (as defined in sections 871(h) and 881(c)) or that are payable 183 days or less from the date of original issue, and form part of a larger debt issue, such liabilities may be identified by reference to the issue and maturity date, principal amount and interest payable with respect to the entire debt issue. Records or schedules described in this paragraph that identify liabilities that give rise to branch interest must be maintained in the United States by the foreign corporation or an agent of the foreign corporation for the entire period commencing with the due date (including extensions) of the income tax return for the taxable year to which the records or schedules relate and ending with the expiration of the period of limitations for assessment of tax for such taxable year. A foreign corporation that is subject to this section may identify a liability under paragraph (b)(1)(ii) of this section whether or not it is actually engaged in the conduct of a trade or business in the United States.

(ii) *Notification to recipient.*—Interest with respect to a liability described in paragraph (b)(1)(ii) of this section shall not be treated as branch interest unless the foreign corporation paying the interest either—

(A) Makes a return, pursuant to section 6049, with respect to the interest payment; or

(B) Sends a notice to the person who receives such interest in a confirmation of the transaction, a statement of account, or a separate notice, within two months of the end of the calendar year in which the interest was paid, stating that the interest paid with respect to the liability is from sources within the United States.

(iii) *Liabilities that do not give rise to branch interest under paragraph (b)(1)(ii) of this section.*—A liability is described in this paragraph (b)(3)(iii) (and interest with respect to the liability may not be treated as branch interest of a foreign corporation by reason of paragraph (b)(1)(ii) of this section) if—

(A) The liability is directly incurred in the ordinary course of the profit-making activities of a trade or business of the foreign corporation conducted outside the United States, as, for example, an account or note payable arising from the purchase of inventory or receipt of services by such trade or business; or

(B) The liability is secured (during more than half the days during the portion of the taxable year in which the interest accrues) predominantly by property that is not a U.S. asset (as defined in § 1.884-1(d)) unless such liability is secured by substantially all the property of the foreign corporation.

(4) [Reserved]

(5) *Increase in branch interest where U.S. assets constitute 80 percent or more of a foreign corporation's assets.*—(i) *General rule.*—If a foreign corporation would have excess interest before application of this paragraph (b)(5) and the amount of the foreign corporation's U.S. assets as of the close of the taxable year equals or exceeds 80 percent of all money and the aggregate E&P basis of all property of the foreign corporation on such date, then all interest paid and accrued by the foreign corporation during the taxable year that was not treated as branch interest before application of this paragraph (b)(5) and that is not paid with respect to a liability described in paragraph (b)(3)(iii) of this section (relating to liabilities incurred in the ordinary course of a foreign business or secured by non-U.S. assets) shall be treated as branch interest. However, if application of the preceding sentence would cause the amount of the foreign corporation's branch interest to exceed the amount permitted by paragraph (b)(6)(i) of this section (relating to branch interest in excess of a foreign corporation's interest allocated or apportioned to ECI under § 1.882-5) the amount of branch interest arising by reason of this paragraph shall be reduced as provided in paragraphs (b)(6)(ii) and (iii) of this section, as applicable.

(ii) *Example.*—The application of this paragraph (b)(5) is illustrated by the following example.

Example. Application of 80 percent test. Foreign corporation A, a calendar year taxpayer, has $90 of interest allocated or apportioned to ECI under § 1.882-5 for 1993. Before application of this paragraph (b)(5), A has $40 of branch interest in 1993. A pays $60 of other interest during 1993, none of which is attributable to a liability described in paragraph (b)(3)(iii) of this section (relating to liabilities incurred in the ordinary course of a foreign business and liabilities predominantly secured by foreign assets). As of the close of 1993, A has an amount of U.S. assets that exceeds 80 percent of the money and E&P bases of all A's property. Before application of this paragraph (b)(5), A would have $50 of excess interest (*i.e.*, the $90 interest allocated or apportioned to its ECI under § 1.882-5 less $40 of branch interest). Under this paragraph (b)(5), the $60 of additional interest paid by A is also treated as branch interest. However, to the extent that treating the $60 of additional interest as branch interest would create an amount of branch interest that would exceed the amount of branch interest permitted under paragraph (b)(6) of this section (relating to branch interest that exceeds a foreign corporation's interest allocated or apportioned to ECI under § 1.882-5) the amount of the additional branch interest is reduced under paragraph (b)(6)(iii) of this section, which generally allows a foreign corporation to specify certain liabilities that do not give rise to branch interest or paragraph (b)(6)(ii) of this section, which generally specifies liabilities that do not give rise to branch interest beginning with the most-recently incurred liability.

(6) *Special rule where branch interest exceeds interest allocated or apportioned to ECI of a foreign corporation.*—(i) *General rule.*—If the amount of branch interest that is both paid and accrued by a foreign corporation during the taxable year (including interest that the foreign corporation elects under paragraph (c)(1) of this section to treat as paid during the taxable year) exceeds the amount of interest allocated or apportioned to ECI of a foreign corporation under § 1.882-5 for the taxable year, then the amount of the foreign corporation's branch interest shall be reduced by the amount of such excess as provided in paragraphs (b)(6)(ii) and (iii) of this section, as applicable. The rules of paragraphs (b)(6)(ii) and (iii) of this section shall also apply where the amount of branch interest with respect to liabilities identified under paragraph (b)(1)(ii) of this section exceeds the maximum amount that may be treated as branch interest under that paragraph. This paragraph (b)(6) shall apply whether or not a reduction in the amount of branch interest occurs as a result of adjustments made during the examination of the foreign corporation's income tax return, such as a reduction in the amount of interest allocated or apportioned to ECI of the foreign corporation under § 1.882-5.

(ii) *Reduction of branch interest beginning with most-recently incurred liability.*—Except as provided in paragraph (b)(6)(iii) of this section (relating to an election to specify liabilities that do not give rise to branch interest), the amount of the excess in paragraph (b)(6)(i) of this section shall first reduce branch interest attributable to liabilities described in paragraph (b)(1)(ii) of this section (relating to liabilities identified as giving rise to branch interest) and then, if such excess has not been reduced to zero, branch interest attributable to the group of liabilities described in paragraph (b)(1)(i) of this section. The reduction of branch interest attributable to each group of liabilities (*i.e.*, liabilities described in paragraph (b)(1)(ii) of this section and liabilities described in paragraph (b)(1)(i) of this section) shall be made beginning with interest attributable to the latest-incurred liability and continuing, in reverse chronological order, with branch interest attributable to the next-latest incurred liability. The branch interest attributable to a liability must be reduced to zero before a reduction is made with respect to branch interest attributable to the next-latest incurred liability. Where only a portion of the branch interest attributable to a liability is reduced by reason of this paragraph (b)(6)(ii), the reduction shall be made beginning with the last interest payment made with respect to the liability during the taxable year and continuing, in reverse chronological order, with the next-latest payment until the amount of branch interest has been reduced by the amount specified in paragraph (b)(6)(i) of this section. The amount of interest that is not treated as branch interest by reason of this paragraph (b)(6)(ii) shall not be treated as paid by a domestic corporation and thus shall not be subject to tax under section 871(a) or 881(a).

(iii) *Election to specify liabilities that do not give rise to branch interest.*—For purposes of reducing the amount of branch interest under paragraph (b)(6)(i) of this section, a foreign corporation may, instead of using the method described in paragraph (b)(6)(ii) of this section, elect for any taxable year to specify which liabilities will not be treated as giving rise to branch interest or will be treated as giving rise only in part to branch interest. Branch interest paid during the taxable year with respect to a liability specified under this paragraph (b)(6)(iii) must be reduced to zero before a reduction is made with respect to branch interest attributable to the next-specified liability. If all interest payments with respect to a specified liability, when added to all interest payments with respect to other liabilities specified under this paragraph (b)(6)(iii), would exceed the amount of the reduction under paragraph (b)(6)(i) of this section, then only a portion of the branch interest attributable to that specified liability shall be reduced under this paragraph (b)(6)(iii), and the reduction shall be made beginning with the last interest payment made with respect to the liability during the taxable year and continuing, in reverse chronological order, with the next-latest payment until the amount of branch interest has been reduced by the amount of the reduction under paragraph (b)(6)(i) of this section. A foreign corporation that elects to have this paragraph (b)(6)(iii) apply shall note on its books and records maintained in the United States that the liability is not to be treated as giving rise to branch interest, or is to be treated as giving rise to branch interest only in part. Such notation must be made after the close of the taxable year in which the foreign corporation pays the interest and prior to the due date (with extensions) of the foreign corporation's income tax return for the taxable year. However, if the excess interest in paragraph (b)(6)(i) of this section occurs as a result of adjustments made during the examination of the foreign corporation's income tax return, the election and notation may be made at the time of examination. The amount of interest that is not treated as branch interest by reason of this paragraph (b)(6)(iii) shall not be treated as paid by a domestic corporation and thus shall not be subject to tax under section 871(a) or 881(a).

(iv) *Examples.*—The application of this paragraph (b)(6) is illustrated by the following examples.

Example 1. Branch interest exceeds interest apportioned to ECI with no election in effect. Foreign corporation A, a calendar year, accrual method taxpayer, has interest expense apportioned to ECI under § 1.882-5 of $230 for 1997. A's branch interest for 1997 is as follows:

(i) $130 paid to B, a domestic corporation, with respect to a note issued on March 10, 1997, and secured by real property located in the United States;

(ii) $60 paid to C, an individual resident of country X who is entitled to a 10 percent rate of withholding on interest payments under the income tax treaty between the United States and X, with respect to a note issued on October 15, 1996, which gives rise to interest subject to tax under section 871(a);

(iii) $80 paid to D, an individual resident of country Y who is entitled to a 15 percent rate of withholding on interest payments under the income tax treaty between the United States and Y, with respect to a note issued on February 15, 1997, which gives rise to interest subject to tax under section 871(a); and

(iv) $70 of portfolio interest (as defined in section 871(h)(2)) paid to E, a nonresident alien, with respect to a bond issued on March 1, 1997.

A's branch interest accrues during 1997 for purposes of calculating the amount of A's interest apportioned to ECI under § 1.882-5. A has identified under paragraph (b)(1)(ii) of this section the liabilities described in paragraphs (ii), (iii) and (iv) of this example. A has not made an election under paragraph (b)(6)(iii) of this section to specify liabilities that do not give rise to branch interest. The amount of A's branch interest in 1997 is limited under paragraph (b)(6)(i) of this section to $230, the amount of the interest apportioned to A's ECI for 1997. The amount of A's branch interest must thus be reduced by $110 ($340 − $230) under paragraph (b)(6)(ii) of this section. The reduction is first made with respect to interest attributable to liabilities described in paragraph (b)(1)(ii) of this section (*i.e.*, liabilities identified as giving rise to branch interest) and, within the group of liabilities described in paragraph (b)(1)(ii) of this section, is first made with respect to the latest-incurred liability. Thus, the $70 of interest paid to E with respect to the bond issued on March 1, 1997, and $40 of the $80 of interest paid to D with respect to the note issued on February 15, 1997, are not treated as branch interest. The interest paid to D is no longer subject to tax under section 871(a), and D may claim a refund of amounts withheld with respect to the interest payments. There is no change in the tax consequences to E because the interest received by E was portfolio interest and was not subject to tax when it was treated as branch interest.

Example 2. Effect of election to specify liabilities. Assume the same facts as in *Example 1* except that A makes an election under paragraph (b)(6)(iii) of this section to specify which liabilities are not to be treated as giving rise to branch interest. A specifies the liability to D, who would be taxable at a rate of 15 percent on interest paid with respect to the liability, as a liability that does not give rise to branch interest, and D is therefore not subject to tax under section 871(a) and is entitled to a refund of amounts withheld with respect to the interest payments. A also specifies the liability to C as a liability that gives rise to branch interest only in part. As a result, $30 of the $60 of interest paid to C is not treated as branch interest, and C is entitled to a refund with respect to the $30 of interest that is not treated as branch interest.

(7) *Effect of election under paragraph (c)(1) of this section to treat interest as if paid in year of accrual.*—If a foreign corporation accrues an interest expense in a taxable year earlier than the taxable year of payment and elects under paragraph (c)(1) of this section to compute its excess interest as if the interest expense were branch interest paid in the year of accrual, the interest expense shall be treated as branch

interest that is paid at the close of such year (and not in the actual year of payment) for all purposes of this section. Such interest shall thus be subject to tax under section 871(a) or 881(a) and withholding under section 1441 or section 1442, as if paid on the last day of the taxable year of accrual. Interest that is treated under paragraph (c)(1) of this section as paid in a later year for purposes of computing excess interest shall be treated as paid only in the actual year of payment for all purposes of this section other than paragraphs (a)(2) and (c)(1) of this section (relating to excess interest).

(8) *Effect of treaties.*—(i) *Payor's treaty.*—In the case of a foreign corporation's branch interest, relief shall be available under an article of an income tax treaty between the United States and the foreign corporation's country of residence relating to interest paid by the foreign corporation only if, for the taxable year in which the branch interest is paid (or if the branch interest is treated as paid in an earlier taxable year under paragraph (b)(7) of this section, for the earlier taxable year)—

(A) The foreign corporation meets the requirements of the limitation on benefits provision, if any, in the treaty, and either—

(1) The corporation is a qualified resident (as defined in § 1.884-5(a)) of that foreign country in such year; or

(2) The corporation meets the requirements of paragraph (b)(8)(iii) of this section in such year; or

(B) The limitation on benefits provision, or an amendment to that provision, entered into force after December 31, 1986.

(ii) *Recipient's treaty.*—A foreign person (other than a foreign corporation) that derives branch interest is entitled to claim benefits under provisions of an income tax treaty between the United States and its country of residence relating to interest derived by the foreign person. A foreign corporation may claim such benefits if it meets, with respect to the branch interest, the requirements of the limitation on benefits provision, if any, in the treaty and—

(A) The foreign corporation meets the requirements of paragraphs (b)(8)(i)(A) or (B) of this section; and

(B) In the case of interest paid in a taxable year beginning after December 31, 1988, with respect to an obligation with a maturity not exceeding one year, each foreign corporation that beneficially owned the obligation prior to maturity was a qualified resident (for the period specified in paragraph (b)(8)(i) of this section) of a foreign country with which the United States has an income tax treaty or met the requirements of the limitation on benefits provision in a treaty with respect to the interest payment and such provision entered into force after December 31, 1986.

(iii) *Presumption that a foreign corporation continues to be a qualified resident.*—For purposes of this paragraph (b)(8), a foreign corporation that was a qualified resident for the prior taxable year because it fulfills the requirements of § 1.884-5 shall be considered a qualified resident with respect to branch interest that is paid or received during the current taxable year if—

(A) In the case of a foreign corporation that met the stock ownership and base erosion tests in § 1.884-5(b) and (c) for the preceding taxable year, the foreign corporation does not know, or have reason to know, that either 50 percent of its stock (by value) is not beneficially owned (or treated as beneficially owned by reason of § 1.884-5(b)(2)) by qualifying shareholders at any time during the portion of the taxable year that ends with the date on which the interest is paid, or that the base erosion test is not met during the portion of the taxable year that ends with the date on which the interest is paid;

(B) In the case of a foreign corporation that met the requirements of § 1.884-5(d) (relating to publicly-traded corporations) for the preceding taxable year, the foreign corporation is listed on an established securities exchange in the United States or its country of residence at all times during the portion of the taxable year that ends with the date on which the interest is paid and does not fail the requirements of § 1.884-5(d)(4)(iii) (relating to certain closely-held corporations) at any time during such period; or

(C) In the case of a foreign corporation that met the requirements of § 1.884-5(e) (relating to the active trade or business test) for the preceding taxable year, the foreign corporation continues to operate (other than in a nominal degree), at all times during the portion of the taxable year that ends with the date on which the interest is paid, the same business in the U.S. and its country of residence that caused it to meet such requirements for the preceding taxable year.

(iv) *Treaties other than income tax treaties.*—A treaty that is not an income tax treaty does not provide any benefits with respect to branch interest.

(v) *Effect of income tax treaties on interest paid by a partnership.*—If a foreign corporation is a partner (directly or indirectly) in a partnership that is engaged in a trade or business in the United States and owns an interest of 10 percent or more (as determined under the attribution rules of section 318) in the capital, profits, or losses of the partnership at any time during the partner's taxable year, the relief that may be claimed under an income tax treaty with respect to the foreign corporation's distributive share of interest paid or treated as paid by the partnership shall not exceed the relief that would be available under paragraphs (b)(8)(i) and (ii) of this section if such interest were branch interest of the foreign corporation. See paragraph (c)(2) of this section for the effect on a foreign corporation's excess interest of interest paid by a partnership of which the foreign corporation is a partner.

(vi) *Examples.*—The following examples illustrate the application of this paragraph (b)(8).

Example 1. Payor's treaty. The income tax treaty between the United States and country X provides that the United States may not impose a tax on interest paid by a corporation that is a resident of that country (and that is not a domestic corporation) if the recipient of the interest is a nonresident alien or a foreign corporation. Corp A is a qualified resident of country X and meets the limitation on benefits provision in the treaty. A's branch interest is not subject to tax under section 871(a) or 881(a) regardless of whether the recipient is entitled to benefits under an income tax treaty.

Example 2. Recipient's treaty and interest received from a partnership. A, a foreign corporation, and B, a nonresident alien, are partners in a partnership that owns and operates U.S. real estate and each has a distributive share of partnership interest deductions equal to 50 percent of the interest deductions of the partnership. There is no income tax treaty between the United States and the countries of residence of A and B. The partnership pays $1,000 of interest to a bank that is a resident of a foreign country, Y, and that qualifies under an income tax treaty in effect with the United States for a 5 percent rate of tax on U.S. source interest paid to a resident of country Y. However, the bank is not a qualified resident of country Y and the limitation on benefits provision of the treaty has not been amended since December 31, 1986. The partnership is required to withhold at a rate of 30 percent on $500 of the interest paid to the bank (*i.e.*, A's 50 percent distributive share of interest paid by the partnership) because the bank cannot, under paragraph (b)(8)(iv) of this section, claim greater treaty benefits by lending money to the partnership than it could claim if it lent money to A directly and the $500 were branch interest of A.

(c) *Rules relating to excess interest.*—(1) *Election to compute excess interest by treating branch interest that is paid and accrued in different years as if paid in year of accrual.*—(i) *General rule.*—If branch interest is paid in one or more taxable years before or after the year in which the interest accrues, a foreign corporation may elect to compute its excess interest as if such branch interest were paid on the last day of the taxable year in which it accrues, and not in the taxable year in which it is actually paid. The interest expense will thus reduce the amount of the foreign corporation's excess interest in the year of accrual rather than in the year of actual payment. Except as provided in paragraph (c)(1)(ii) of this section, if an election is made for a taxable year, this paragraph (c)(1)(i) shall apply to all branch interest that is paid or accrued during that year. See paragraph (b)(7) of this section for the effect of an election under this paragraph (c)(1) on branch interest that accrues in a taxable year after the year of payment.

(ii) *Election not to apply in certain cases.*—An election under this paragraph (c)(1) shall not apply to an interest expense that accrued in a taxable year beginning before January 1, 1987, and shall not apply to an interest expense that was paid in a taxable year beginning before such date unless the interest was income from sources within the United States. An election under this paragraph (c)(1) shall not apply to branch interest that accrues during the taxable year and is paid in an earlier taxable year if the branch interest reduced excess interest in such earlier year. However, a foreign corporation may amend its income tax return for such earlier taxable year so that the branch interest does not reduce excess interest in such year.

(iii) *Requirements for election.*—A foreign corporation that elects to apply this paragraph (c)(1) shall attach to its income tax return (or to an amended income tax return) a statement that it elects to have the provisions of this paragraph (c)(1) apply, or shall provide written notice to the Commissioner during an examination that it elects to apply this paragraph (c)(1). The election shall be effective for the taxable year to which the return relates and for all subsequent taxable years unless the Commissioner consents to revocation of the election.

(iv) *Examples.*—The following examples illustrate the application of this paragraph (c)(1).

Example 1. Interest accrued before paid. Foreign corporation A, a calendar year, accrual method taxpayer, has $100 of interest allocated or apportioned to ECI under § 1.882-5 for 1997. A has $60 of branch interest in 1997 before application of this paragraph (c)(1). A has an interest expense of $20 that properly accrues for tax purposes in 1997 but is not paid until 1998. When the interest is paid in 1998 it will meet the requirements for branch interest under paragraph (b)(1) of this section. A makes a timely election under this paragraph (c)(1) to treat the accrued interest as if it were paid in 1997. A will be treated as having branch interest of $80 for 1997 and excess interest of $20 in 1997. The $20 of interest treated as branch interest of A in 1997 will not again be treated as branch interest in 1998.

Example 2. Interest paid before accrued. Foreign corporation A, a calendar year, accrual method taxpayer, has $60 of branch interest in 1997. The interest expense does not accrue until 1998 and the amount of interest allocated or apportioned to A's ECI under § 1.882-5 is zero for 1997 and $60 for 1998. A makes an election under this paragraph (c)(1) with respect to 1997. As a result of the election, A's $60 of branch interest in 1997 reduces the amount of A's excess interest for 1998 rather than in 1997.

(2) *Interest paid by a partnership.*—(i) *General rule.*—Except as otherwise provided in paragraphs (c)(2)(i) and (ii) of this section, if a foreign corporation is a partner in a partnership that is engaged in trade or business in the United States, the amount of the foreign corporation's distributive share of interest paid or accrued by the partnership shall reduce (but not below zero) the amount of the foreign corporation's excess interest for the year to the extent such interest is taken into account by the foreign corporation in that year for purposes of calculating the interest allocated or apportioned to the ECI of the foreign corporation under § 1.882-5. A foreign corporation's excess interest shall not be reduced by its distributive share of partnership interest that is attributable to a liability described in paragraph (b)(3)(iii) of this section (relating to interest on liabilities incurred in the ordinary course of a foreign business or secured predominantly by assets that are not U.S. assets) or would be described in paragraph (b)(3)(iii) of this section if entered on the partner's books. See paragraph (b)(8)(v) of this section for the effect of income tax treaties on interest paid by a partnership.

(ii) *Special rule for interest that is paid and accrued in different years.*—Paragraph (c)(2)(i) of this section shall not apply to any portion of a foreign corporation's distributive share of partnership interest that is paid and accrued in different taxable years unless the foreign corporation has an election in effect under paragraph (c)(1) of this section that is effective with respect to such interest and any tax due under section 871(a) or 881(a) with respect to such interest has been deducted and withheld at source in the earlier of the taxable year of payment or accrual.

(3) *Effect of treaties.*—(i) *General rule.*—The rate of tax imposed on the excess interest of a foreign corporation that is a resident of a country with which the United States has an income tax treaty shall not exceed the rate provided under such treaty that would apply with respect to interest paid by a domestic corporation to that foreign corporation if the foreign corporation meets, with respect to the excess interest, the requirements of the limitation on benefits provision, if any, in the treaty and either—

(A) The corporation is a qualified resident (as defined in § 1.884-5(a)) of that foreign country for the taxable year in which the excess interest is subject to tax; or

(B) The limitation on benefits provision, or an amendment to that provision, entered into force after December 31, 1986.

(ii) *Provisions relating to interest paid by a foreign corporation.*—Any provision in an income tax treaty that exempts or reduces the rate of tax on interest paid by a foreign corporation does not prevent imposition of the tax on excess interest or reduce the rate of such tax.

(4) *Example.*—The application of paragraphs (c)(2) and (3) of this section is illustrated by the following example.

Example. Interest paid by a partnership. Foreign corporation A, a calendar year taxpayer, is not a resident of a foreign country with which the United States has an income tax treaty. A is engaged in the conduct of a trade or business both in the United States and in foreign countries, and owns a 50 percent interest in X, a calendar year partnership engaged in the conduct of a trade or business in the United States. For 1997, all of X's liabilities are of a type described in paragraph (b)(1) of this section (relating to liabilities on U.S. books) and none are described in paragraph (b)(3)(iii) of this section (relating to liabilities that may not give rise to branch interest). A's distributive share of interest paid by X in 1997 is $20. For 1997, A has $150 of interest allocated or apportioned to its ECI under § 1.882-5, $120 of which is attributable to branch interest. Thus, the amount of A's excess interest for 1997, before application of paragraph (c)(2)(i) of this section, is $30. Under paragraph (c)(2)(i) of this section, A's $30 of excess interest is reduced by $20, representing A's share of interest paid by X. Thus, the amount of A's excess interest for 1997 is reduced to $10. A is subject to a tax of 30 percent on its $10 of excess interest.

(d) *Stapled entities.*—A foreign corporation that is treated as a domestic corporation by reason of section 269B (relating to stapled entities) shall continue to be treated as a foreign corporation for purposes of section 884(f) and this section, notwithstanding section 269B and the regulations thereunder. Interest paid by such foreign corporation shall be treated as paid by a domestic corporation and shall be subject to the tax imposed by section 871(a) or 881(a), and to withholding under sections 1441 and 1442, as applicable, to the extent such interest is not subject to tax by reason of section 884(f) and this section.

(e) *Effective dates.*—(1) *General rule.*—Except as provided in paragraph (e)(2) of this section, this section is effective for taxable years beginning October 13, 1992, and for payments of interest described in section 884(f)(1)(A) made (or treated as made under paragraph (b)(7) of this section) during taxable years of the payor beginning after such date. With respect to taxable years beginning before October 13, 1992 and after December 31, 1986, a foreign corporation may elect to apply this section in lieu of § 1.884-4T of the temporary regulations (as contained in the CFR edition revised as of April 1, 1992) as they applied to the foreign corporation after issuance of Notice 89-80, 1989-2 C.B. 394, but only if the foreign corporation has made an election under § 1.884-1(i) to apply § 1.884-1 in lieu of § 1.884-1T (as contained in the CFR edition revised as of April 1, 1992) for that year, and the statute of limitations for assessment of a deficiency has not expired for that taxable year. Once an election has been made, an election under this section shall apply to all subsequent taxable years.

(2) *Special rule.*—Paragraphs (a)(1), (a)(2)(i)(A), (a)(2)(iii), (b)(1), (b)(3), (b)(5)(i), (b)(6)(i), (b)(6)(ii), and (c)(2)(i) of this section are effective for taxable years beginning on or after June 6, 1996.

(f) *Transition rules.*—(1) *Election under paragraph (c)(1) of this section.*—If a foreign corporation has made an election described in § 1.884-4T(b)(7) (as contained in the CFR edition revised as of April 1, 1992) with respect to interest that has accrued and been paid in different taxable years, such election shall be effective for purposes of paragraph (c)(1) of this section as if the corporation had made the election under paragraph (c)(1) of this section of these regulations.

(2) *Waiver of notification requirement for non-banks under Notice 89-80.*—If a foreign corporation that is not a bank has made an election under Notice 89-80 to apply the rules in Part 2 of Section I of the Notice in lieu of the rules in § 1.884-4T(b) (as contained in the CFR edition revised as of April 1, 1992) to determine the amount of its interest paid and excess interest in taxable years beginning prior to 1990, the requirement that the foreign corporation satisfy the notification requirements described in paragraph (b)(3)(ii) of this section is waived with respect to interest paid in taxable years ending on or before the date the Notice was issued.

(3) *Waiver of legending requirement for certain debt issued prior to January 3, 1989.*—For purposes of sections 871(h), 881(c), and this section, branch interest of a foreign corporation that would be treated as portfolio interest under section 871(h) or 881(c) but for the fact that it fails to meet the requirements of section 163 (f)(2)(B)(ii)(II) (relating to the legend requirement), shall nevertheless be treated as portfolio interest provided the interest arises with respect to a liability incurred by the foreign corporation before January 3, 1989, and interest with respect to the liability was treated as branch interest in a taxable year beginning before January 1, 1990. [Reg. § 1.884-4.]

☐ [*T.D. 8432, 9-10-92. Amended by T.D. 8657, 3-5-96.*]

§1.884-5. Qualified resident.—(a) *Definition of qualified resident.*—A foreign corporation is a qualified resident of a foreign country with which the United States has an income tax treaty in effect if, for the taxable year, the foreign corporation is a resident of that country (within the meaning of such treaty) and either—

(1) Meets the requirements of paragraphs (b) and (c) of this section (relating to stock ownership and base erosion);

(2) Meets the requirements of paragraph (d) of this section (relating to publicly-traded corporations);

(3) Meets the requirements of paragraph (e) of this section (relating to the conduct of an active trade or business); or

(4) Obtains a ruling as provided in paragraph (f) of this section that it shall be treated as a qualified resident of its country of residence.

(b) *Stock ownership requirement.*—(1) *General rule.*—(i) *Ownership by qualifying shareholders.*—A foreign corporation satisfies the stock ownership requirement of this paragraph (b) for the taxable year if more than 50 percent of its stock (by value) is beneficially owned (or is treated as beneficially owned by reason of paragraph (b)(2) of this section) during at least half of the number of days in the foreign corporation's taxable year by one or more qualifying shareholders. A person shall be treated as a qualifying shareholder only if such person meets the requirements of paragraph (b)(3) of this section and is either—

(A) An individual who is either a resident of the foreign country of which the foreign corporation is a resident or a citizen or resident of the United States;

(B) The government of the country of which the foreign corporation is a resident (or a political subdivision or local authority of such country), or the United States, a State, the District of Columbia, or a political subdivision or local authority of a State;

(C) A corporation that is a resident of the foreign country of which the foreign corporation is a resident and whose stock is primarily and regularly traded on an established securities market (within the meaning of paragraph (d) of this section) in that country or the United States or a domestic corporation whose stock is primarily and regularly traded on an established securities market (within the meaning of paragraph (d) of this section) in the United States;

(D) A not-for-profit organization described in paragraph (b)(1)(iv) of this section that is not a pension fund as defined in paragraph (b)(8)(i)(A) of this section and that is organized under the laws of the foreign country of which the foreign corporation is a resident or the United States; or

(E) A beneficiary of certain pension funds (as defined in paragraph (b)(8)(i)(A) of this section) administered in or by the country in which the foreign corporation is a resident to the extent provided in paragraph (b)(8) of this section.

Beneficial owners of an association taxable as a corporation shall be treated as shareholders of such association for purposes of this paragraph (b)(1). If stock of a foreign corporation is owned by a corporation that is treated as a qualifying shareholder under paragraph (b)(1)(i)(C) of this section, such stock shall not also be treated as owned, directly or indirectly, by any qualifying shareholders of such corporation for purposes of this paragraph (b). Notwithstanding the above, a foreign corporation will not be treated as a qualified resident unless it obtains the documentation described in paragraph (b)(3) of this section to show that the requirements of this paragraph (b)(1)(i) have been met and maintains the documentation as provided in paragraph (b)(9) of this section. See also paragraph (b)(1)(iii) of this section, which treats certain publicly-traded classes of stock as owned by qualifying shareholders.

(ii) *Special rules relating to qualifying shareholders.*—For purposes of applying paragraph (b)(1)(i) of this section—

(A) Stock owned on any day shall be taken into account only if the beneficial owner is a qualifying shareholder on that day or, in the case of a corporation or not-for-profit organization that is a qualifying shareholder under paragraph (b)(1)(i)(C) or (D) of this section, for a one-year period that includes such day; and

(B) An individual, corporation or not-for-profit organization is a resident of a foreign country if it is a resident of that country for purposes of the income tax treaty between the United States and that country.

(iii) *Publicly-traded class of stock treated as owned by qualifying shareholders.*—A class of stock of a foreign corporation shall be treated as owned by qualifying shareholders if—

(A) The class of stock is listed on an established securities market in the United States or in the country of residence of the foreign corporation seeking qualified resident status; and

(B) The class of stock is primarily and regularly traded on such market (within the meaning of paragraphs (d)(3) and (4) of this section, applied as if the class of stock were the sole class of stock relied on to meet the requirements of paragraph (d)(4)(i)(A)).

For purposes of this paragraph (b), stock in such class shall not also be treated as owned by any qualifying shareholders who own such stock, either directly or indirectly.

(iv) *Special rule for not-for-profit organizations.*—A not-for-profit organization is described in paragraph (b)(1)(iv) of this section if it meets the following requirements—

(A) It is a corporation, association taxable as a corporation, trust, fund, foundation, league or other entity operated exclusively for religious, charitable, educational, or recreational purposes, and it is not organized for profit;

(B) It is generally exempt from tax in its country of organization by virtue of its not-for-profit status; and

(C) Either—

(1) More than 50 percent of its annual support is expended on behalf of persons described in paragraphs (b)(1)(i)(A) through (E) of this section or on qualified residents of the country in which the organization is organized; or

(2) More than 50 percent of its annual support is derived from persons described in paragraphs (b)(1)(i)(A) through (E) of this section or from persons who are qualified residents of the country in which the organization is organized.

For purposes of meeting the requirements of paragraph (b)(1)(iv)(C) of this section, a not-for-profit organization may rely on the addresses of record of its individual beneficiaries and supporters to determine if such persons are resident in the country in which the not-for-profit organization is organized, provided that the addresses of record are not nonresidential addresses such as a post office box or in care of a financial intermediary, and the officers, directors or administrators of the organization do not know or have reason to know that the individual beneficiaries or supporters do not reside at that address.

(2) *Rules for determining constructive ownership.*—(i) *General rules for attribution.*—For purposes of this section, stock owned by a corporation, partnership, trust, estate, or mutual insurance company or similar entity shall be treated as owned proportionately by its shareholders, partners, beneficiaries, grantors or other interest holders as provided in paragraph (b)(2)(ii) through (v) of this section. The proportionate interest rules of this paragraph (b)(2) shall apply successively upward through a chain of ownership, and a person's proportionate interest shall be computed for the relevant days or period that is taken into account in determining whether a foreign corporation is a qualified resident. Except as otherwise provided, stock treated as owned by a person by reason of this paragraph (b)(2) shall, for purposes of applying this paragraph (b)(2), be treated as actually owned by such person.

(ii) *Partnerships.*—A partner shall be treated as having an interest in stock of a foreign corporation owned by a partnership in proportion to the least of—

(A) The partner's percentage distributive share of the partnership's dividend income from the stock;

(B) The partner's percentage distributive share of gain from disposition of the stock by the partnership;

(C) The partner's percentage distributive share of the stock (or proceeds from the disposition of the stock) upon liquidation of the partnership.

For purposes of this paragraph (b)(2)(ii), however, all qualifying shareholders that are partners of a partnership shall be treated as one partner. Thus, the percentage distributive shares of dividend income, gain and liquidation rights of all qualifying shareholders that are partners in a partnership are aggregated prior to determining the least of the three percentages.

(iii) *Trusts and estates.*—(A) *Beneficiaries.*—In general, a person shall be treated as having an interest in stock of a foreign corporation owned by a trust or estate in proportion to the person's actuarial interest in the trust or estate, as provided in section 318(a)(2)(B)(i), except that an income beneficiary's actuarial interest in the trust will be determined as if the trust's only asset were the stock. The interest of a remainder beneficiary in stock will be equal to 100 percent minus the sum of the percentages of any interest in the stock held by income beneficiaries. The ownership of an interest in stock owned by a trust shall not be attributed to any beneficiary whose interest cannot be determined under the preceding sentence, and any such interest, to the extent not attributed by reason of this paragraph (b)(2)(iii)(A), shall not be considered owned by a beneficiary unless all potential beneficiaries with respect to the stock are qualifying shareholders. In addition, a beneficiary's actuarial interest will be treated as zero to the extent that a grantor is treated as owning the stock under paragraph (b)(2)(iii)(B) of this section. A substantially separate and independent share of a trust, within the meaning of section 663(c), shall be treated as a separate trust for purposes of this paragraph (b)(2)(iii)(A), provided that payment of income, accumulated income or corpus of a share of one beneficiary (or group of beneficiaries) cannot affect the proportionate share of income, accumulated income or corpus of another beneficiary (or group of beneficiaries).

(B) *Grantor trusts.*—A person is treated as the owner of stock of a foreign corporation owned by a trust to the extent that the stock is included in the portion of the trust that is treated as owned by the person under sections 671 to 679 (relating to grantors and others treated as substantial owners).

(iv) *Corporations that issue stock.*—A shareholder of a corporation that issues stock shall be treated as owning stock of a foreign corporation that is owned by such corporation on any day in a proportion that equals the value of the stock owned by such shareholder to the value of all stock of such corporation. If there is an agreement, express or implied, that a shareholder of a corporation will not receive distributions from the earnings of stock owned by the corporation, the shareholder will not be treated as owning that stock owned by the corporation.

(v) *Mutual insurance companies and similar entities.*—Stock held by a mutual insurance company, mutual savings bank, or similar entity (including an association taxable as a corporation that does not issue stock interests) shall be considered owned proportionately by the policy holders, depositors, or other owners in the same proportion that such persons share in the surplus of such entity upon liquidation or dissolution.

(vi) *Pension funds.*—See paragraphs (b)(8)(ii) and (iii) of this section for the attribution of stock owned by a pension fund (as defined in paragraph (b)(8)(i)(A)) to beneficiaries of the fund.

(vii) *Examples.*—The rules of paragraph (b)(2)(ii) of this section are illustrated by the following examples.

Example 1. Stock held solely by qualifying shareholders through a partnership. A and B, residents of country X, are qualifying shareholders, within the meaning of paragraphs (b)(1)(i)(A) through (E) of this section, and the sole partners of partnership P. P's only asset is the stock of foreign corporation Z, a country X corporation seeking qualified resident status under this section. A's distributive share of P's income and gain on the disposition of P's assets is 80 percent, but A's distributive share of P's assets (or the proceeds therefrom) on P's liquidation is 20 percent. B's distributive share of P's income and gain is 20 percent and S is entitled to 80 percent of the assets (or proceeds therefrom) on P's liquidation. Under the attribution rules of paragraph (b)(2)(ii) of this section, A and B will be treated as a single partner owning in the aggregate 100 percent of the stock of Z owned by P.

Example 2. Stock held by both qualifying and nonqualifying shareholders through a partnership. Assume the same facts as in *Example 1* except that C, an individual who is not a qualifying shareholder, is also a partner in P and that C's distributive share of P's income is 60 percent. The distributive shares of A and B are the same as in *Example 1* except that A's distributive share of income is 20 percent. Under the attribution rules of paragraph (b)(2) (ii) of this section, A and B will be treated as a single partner owning in the aggregate 40 percent of the stock of Z owned by P (*i.e.*, the least of A and B's aggregate distributive shares of dividend income (40 percent), gain (100 percent), and liquidation rights (100 percent) with respect to the Z stock).

Example 3. Stock held through tiered partnerships. Assume the same facts as in *Example 1*, except that P does not own the stock of Z directly, but rather is a partner in partnership PI, which owns the stock of Z. Assume that P's distributive share of the dividend income, gain and liquidation rights with respect to the Z stock held by PI is 40 percent. Assume that of the remaining partners of PI only D is a qualifying shareholder. D's distributive share of P1's dividend income and gain is 15 percent; D's distributive share of P1's assets on liquidation is 25 percent. Under the attribution rules of paragraph (b)(2)(ii) of this section, A and B, treated as a single partner, will own 40 percent of the Z stock owned by P1 (100 percent × 40 percent) and D will be treated as owning 15 percent of the Z stock owned by P1 (the least of D's dividend income (15 percent), gain (15 percent), and liquidation rights (25 percent) with respect to the Z stock). Thus, 55 percent of the Z stock owned by P1 is treated as owned by qualifying shareholders under paragraph (b)(2)(ii) of this section.

(3) *Required documentation.*—(i) *Ownership statements, certificates of residency and intermediary ownership statements.*—Except as provided in paragraphs (b)(3)(ii), (iii) and (iv) and paragraph (b)(8) of this section, a person shall only be treated as a qualifying shareholder of a foreign corporation if—

(A) For the relevant period, the person completes an ownership statement described in paragraph (b)(4) of this section and, in the case of an individual who is not a U.S. citizen or resident, also obtains a certificate of residency described in paragraph (b)(5) of this section;

(B) In the case of a person owning stock in the foreign corporation indirectly through one or more intermediaries (including mere legal owners or recordholders acting as nominees), each intermediary completes an intermediary ownership statement described in paragraph (b) (6) of this section; and

(C) Such ownership statements and certificates of residency are received by the foreign corporation on or before the earlier of the date it files its income tax return for the taxable year to which the statements relate or the due date (including extensions) for filing such return or, in the case of a foreign corporation claiming treaty benefits under § 1.884-4(b)(8)(i) or (ii) (relating to branch interest) on or before the date on which such interest is paid.

(ii) *Substitution of intermediary verification statement for ownership statements and certificates of residency.*—If a qualifying shareholder owns stock through an intermediary that is either a domestic corporation, a resident of the United States, or a resident (for treaty purposes) of a country with which the United States has an income tax treaty in effect, the intermediary may provide an intermediary verification statement (as described in paragraph (b)(7) of this section) in place of any relevant ownership statements and certificates of residency from qualifying shareholders, and in place of intermediary ownership statements (or, where applicable, intermediary verification statements) from all intermediaries standing in the chain of ownership between the qualifying shareholders and the intermediary issuing the intermediary verification statement. An intermediary verification statement generally certifies that the verifying intermediary holds the documentation described in the preceding sentence and agrees to make it available to the District Director on request. Such intermediary verification statements, along with an intermediary ownership statement from the verifying intermediary, must be received by the foreign corporation on or before the earlier of the date it files its income tax return for the taxable year to which the statements relate or the due date (including extensions) for filing such return. An indirect owner of a foreign corporation is thus treated as a qualifying shareholder of a foreign corporation if the foreign corporation receives, on or before the time specified above, an intermediary verification statement and an intermediary ownership statement from the verifying intermediary and an intermediary ownership statement from all intermediaries standing in the chain of the verifying intermediary's ownership of its interest in the foreign corporation.

(iii) *Special rule for registered shareholders of widely-held corporations.*—An ownership statement and a certificate of residency shall not be required in the case of an individual who is a shareholder of record of a corporation that has at least 250 shareholders if—

(A) The individual owns less than one percent of the stock (by value) (applying the attribution rules of section 318) of the corporation at all times during the taxable year;

(B) The individual's address of record is in the corporation's country of residence and is not a nonresidential address such as a post office box or in care of a financial intermediary or stock transfer agent; and

(C) The officers and directors of the corporation do not know or have reason to know that the individual does not reside at that address.

The rule in this paragraph (b)(3)(iii) may also be applied with respect to individual owners of mutual insurance companies, mutual savings banks or similar entities, provided that the same conditions set forth in this paragraph (b)(3)(iii) are met with respect to such individuals.

(iv) *Special rule for pension funds.*—See paragraphs (b)(8)(ii) through (v) of this section for special documentation rules applicable to pension funds (as defined in paragraph (b)(8)(i)(A) of this section).

(v) *Reasonable cause exception.*—If a foreign corporation does not obtain the documentation described in this paragraph (b)(3) or (b)(8) of this section in a timely manner but is able to show prior to notification of an examination of the return for the taxable year that the failure was due to reasonable cause and not willful neglect, the foreign corporation may perfect the documentation after the deadlines specified in this paragraph (b)(3) or (b)(8) of this section. It may make such a showing by providing a written statement to the District Director having jurisdiction over the taxpayer's return or the Office of the Assistant Commissioner (International), as applicable, setting forth the reasons for the failure to obtain the documentation in a timely manner and describing the documentation that was received after the deadline had passed. Whether a failure to obtain the documentation in a timely manner was due to reasonable cause shall be determined by the District Director or the Office of the Assistant Commissioner (International), as applicable, under all the facts and circumstances.

(4) *Ownership statements from qualifying shareholders.*—(i) *Ownership statements from individuals.*—An ownership statement from an individual is a written statement signed by the individual under penalties of perjury stating—

(A) The name, permanent address, and country of residence of the individual and, if the individual was not a resident of the country for the entire taxable year of the foreign corporation seeking qualified resident status, the period during which it was a resident of the foreign corporation's country of residence;

(B) If the individual is a direct beneficial owner of stock in the foreign corporation, the name of the corporation, the number of shares in each class of stock of the corporation that are so owned, and the period of time during the taxable year of the foreign corporation during which the individual owned the stock (or, in the case of an association taxable as a corporation, the amount and nature of the owner's interest in such association);

(C) If the individual directly owns an interest in a corporation, partnership, trust, estate or other intermediary that owns (directly or indirectly) stock in the foreign corporation, the name of the intermediary, the number and class of shares or amount and nature of the interest of the individual in such intermediary (that is relevant for purposes of attributing ownership in paragraph (b)(2) of this section), and the period of time during the taxable year of the foreign corporation during which the individual held such interest; and

(D) To the extent known by the individual, a description of the chain of ownership through which the individual owns stock in the foreign corporation, including the name and address of each intermediary standing between the intermediary described in paragraph (b)(4)(i)(C) of this section and the foreign corporation.

(ii) *Ownership statements from governments.*—An ownership statement from a government that is a qualifying shareholder is a written statement signed by either—

(A) An official of the governmental authority, agency or office that has supervisory authority with respect to the government's ownership interest who is authorized to sign such a statement on behalf of the authority, agency or office; or

(B) The competent authority of the foreign country (as defined in the income tax treaty between the United States and the foreign country).

Such statement shall provide the title of the official signing the statement and the name and address of the government agency, and shall provide the information described in paragraphs (b)(4)(i)(B) through (D) of this section (substituting "government" for "individual") with respect to the government's direct or indirect ownership of stock in the foreign corporation seeking qualified resident status.

(iii) *Ownership statements from publicly-traded corporations.*—An ownership statement from a corporation that is a qualifying shareholder under paragraph (b)(1)(i)(C) of this section is a written statement signed by a person authorized to sign a tax return on behalf of the corporation under penalties of perjury stating—

(A) The name, permanent address, and principal place of business of the corporation (if different from its permanent address);

(B) The information described in paragraphs (b)(4)(i)(B) through (D) of this section (substituting "corporation" for "individual"); and

(C) That the corporation's stock is primarily and regularly traded on an established securities exchange (within the meaning of paragraph (d) of this section) in the United States or its country of residence.

(iv) *Ownership statements from not-for-profit organizations.*—An ownership statement from a not-for-profit organization (other than a pension fund as defined in paragraph (b)(8)(i)(A) of this section) is a written statement signed by a person authorized to sign a tax return on behalf of the organization under penalties of perjury stating—

(A) The name, permanent address, and principal location of the activities of the organization (if different from its permanent address);

(B) The information described in paragraphs (b)(4)(i)(B) through (D) of this section (substituting "not-for-profit organization" for "individual") with respect to the not-for-profit organization's direct or indirect ownership of stock in the foreign corporation seeking qualified resident status; and

(C) That the not-for-profit organization satisfies the requirements of paragraph (b)(1)(iv) of this section.

(v) *Ownership through a nominee.*—For purposes of this paragraph (b)(4) and paragraph (b)(6) of this section, a person who owns either stock in a foreign corporation seeking qualified resident status or an interest in an intermediary described in paragraph (b)(4)(i)(C) of this section through a nominee shall be treated as owning such stock or interest directly and must, therefore, provide the information described in paragraphs (b)(4)(i) through (iv) of this section, as applicable. Such person must also provide the name and address of the nominee.

(5) *Certificate of residency.*—A certificate of residency must be signed by the relevant authorities (as described below) of the country of residence of the individual shareholder and must state that the individual is a resident of that country for purposes of its income tax laws or, if the authorities do not customarily make such a determination, that the individual has filed a tax return claiming resident status and subjecting the individual's income to tax on a resident basis for the taxable year or period that ends with or within the taxable year for which the corporation is seeking qualified resident status. In the case of an individual who is not legally required to file a tax return in his or her country of residence or in any other country, a certificate of residency of a parent or guardian residing at such individual's address shall be considered sufficient to meet that individual's obligation under this paragraph (b)(5). The relevant authorities shall be the competent authority of the foreign country of which the foreign corporation is a resident, as defined in the income tax treaty between the foreign country and the United States, or such other governmental office of the foreign country (or political subdivision thereof) that customarily provides statements of residence. Notwithstanding the foregoing, the Commissioner may consult with the competent authority of a country regarding the procedures set forth in this paragraph (b)(5) and if necessary agree on additional or alternative procedures under which these certificates may be issued.

(6) *Intermediary ownership statement.*—An intermediary ownership statement is a written statement signed under penalties of perjury by the intermediary (if the intermediary is an individual) or a person that would be authorized to sign a tax return on behalf of the intermediary (if the intermediary is not an individual) containing the following information:

(i) The name, address, country of residence, and principal place of business (in the case of a corporation or partnership) of the intermediary and, if the intermediary is a trust or estate, the name and permanent address of all trustees or executors (or equivalent under foreign law);

(ii) The information described in paragraphs (b)(4)(i)(B) through (D) (substituting "intermediary making the ownership statement" for "individual") with respect to the intermediary's direct or indirect ownership in the stock in the foreign corporation seeking qualified resident status;

(iii) If the intermediary is a nominee for a qualifying shareholder or another intermediary, the name and permanent address of the qualifying shareholder, or the name and principal place of business of such other intermediary;

(iv) If the intermediary is not a nominee for a qualifying shareholder or another intermediary, the proportionate interest in the intermediary of each direct shareholder, partner, beneficiary, grantor, or other interest holder (or if the direct holder is a nominee, of its beneficial shareholder, partner, beneficiary, grantor, or other interest holder) from which the intermediary received an ownership statement and the period of time during the taxable year for which the interest in the intermediary was owned by such shareholder, partner, beneficiary, grantor or other interest holder. For purposes of this paragraph (b)(6)(iv), the proportionate interest of a person in an intermediary is the percentage interest (by value) held by such person, determined using the principles for attributing ownership in paragraph (b)(2) of this section. If an intermediary is not required to receive an ownership statement from its individual registered shareholders or other interest holders by reason of paragraph (b)(3)(iii) of this section, then it must provide a list of the names and addresses of such registered shareholders or other interest holders and the aggregate proportionate interest in the intermediary of such registered shareholders or other interest holders.

(7) *Intermediary verification statement.*—An intermediary verification statement that may be substituted for certain documentation under paragraph (b)(3)(ii) of this section is a written statement signed under penalties of perjury by the intermediary (if the intermediary is an individual) or by a person that would be authorized to sign a tax return on behalf of the intermediary (if the verifying intermediary is not an individual) containing the following information—

(i) The name, principal place of business, and country of residence of the verifying intermediary;

(ii) A statement that the verifying intermediary has obtained either—

(A) An ownership statement and, if applicable, a certificate of residency from a qualifying shareholder with respect to the foreign corporation seeking qualified resident status, and an intermediary ownership statement from each intermediary standing in the chain of ownership between the verifying intermediary and the qualifying shareholder; or

(B) An intermediary verification statement substituting for the documentation described in paragraph (b)(7)(ii)(A) and an intermediary ownership statement from such intermediary and each intermediary standing in the chain of ownership between such intermediary and the verifying intermediary;

(iii) The proportionate interest (as computed using the documentation described in paragraph (b)(7)(ii) of this section) in the intermediary owned directly or indirectly by qualifying shareholders;

(iv) An agreement to make available to the Commissioner at such time and place as the Commissioner may request the underlying documentation described in paragraph (b)(7)(ii) of this section; and

(v) A specific and valid waiver of any right to bank secrecy or other secrecy under the laws of the country in which the verifying intermediary is located, with respect to any qualifying shareholder ownership statements, certificates of residency, intermediary ownership statements or intermediary verification statements that the verifying intermediary has obtained pursuant to paragraph (b)(7)(ii) of this section.

A foreign corporation may combine, in a single statement, the information in an intermediary ownership statement and the information in an intermediary verification statement.

(8) *Special rules for pension funds.*—(i) *Definitions.*—(A) *Pension fund.*—For purposes of this section, the term "pension fund" shall mean a trust, fund, foundation, or other entity that is established exclusively for the benefit of employees or former employees of one or more employers, the principal purpose of which is to provide retirement, disability, and death benefits to beneficiaries of such entity and persons designated by such beneficiaries in consideration for prior services rendered.

(B) *Beneficiary.*—For purposes of this section, the term "beneficiary" of a pension fund shall mean any person who has made contributions to the pension fund, or on whose behalf contributions have been made, and who is currently receiving retirement, disability, or death benefits from the pension fund or can reasonably be expected to receive such benefits in the future, whether or not the person's right to receive benefits from the fund has vested.

(ii) *Government pension funds.*—An individual who is a beneficiary of a pension fund that would be a controlled entity of a foreign sovereign within the principles of § 1.892-2T(c)(1) of the regulations (relating to pension funds established for the benefit of employees or former employees of a foreign government) shall be treated as a qualifying shareholder of a foreign corporation in which the pension fund owns a direct or indirect interest without having to meet the documentation requirements under paragraph (b)(3)(i)(A) of this section, if the foreign corporation is resident in the country of the foreign sovereign and the trustees, directors, or other administrators of the pension fund provide, with the pension fund's intermediary ownership statement described in paragraph (b)(6) of this section, a written statement that the fund is a controlled entity described in this paragraph (b)(8)(ii). See paragraph (b)(4)(ii) of this section regarding an ownership statement from a pension fund that is an integral part of a foreign government.

(iii) *Non-government pension funds.*—For purposes of this section, an individual who is a beneficiary of a pension fund not described in paragraph (b)(8)(ii) of this section shall be treated as a qualifying shareholder of a foreign corporation owned directly or indirectly by such pension fund without having to meet the documentation requirements under paragraph (b)(3)(i)(A) of this section, if—

(A) The pension fund is administered in the foreign corporation's country of residence and is subject to supervision or regulation by a governmental authority (or other authority delegated to perform such supervision or regulation by a governmental authority) in such country;

(B) The pension fund is generally exempt from income taxation in its country of administration;

(C) The pension fund has 100 or more beneficiaries;

(D) The beneficiary's address, as it appears on the records of the fund, is in the foreign corporation's country of residence or the United States and is not a nonresidential address, such as a post office box or in care of a financial intermediary, and none of the trustees, directors or other administrators of the pension fund know, or have reason to know, that the beneficiary is not an individual resident of such foreign country or the United States;

(E) In the case of a pension fund that has fewer than 500 beneficiaries, the beneficiary's employer provides (if the beneficiary is currently contributing to the fund) to the trustees, directors or other administrators a written statement that the beneficiary is currently employed in the country in which the fund is administered or is usually employed in such country but is temporarily employed by the company outside of the country; and

(F) The trustees, directors or other administrators of the pension fund provide, with the pension fund's intermediary ownership statement described in paragraph (b)(6) of this section, a written statement signed under penalties of perjury declaring that the pension fund meets the requirements in paragraphs (b)(8)(iii)(A), (B) and (C) of this section and giving the number of beneficiaries who meet the requirements of paragraph (b)(8)(iii) (D) of this section, and, if applicable, paragraph (b)(8)(iii)(E) of this section.

(iv) *Computation of beneficial interests in nongovernment pension funds.*—The number of shares in a foreign corporation that are held indirectly by beneficiaries of a pension fund who are qualifying shareholders may be computed based on the ratio of the number of such beneficiaries to all beneficiaries of the pension fund (rather than on the basis of the rules in paragraph (b)(2) of this section) if—

(A) The pension fund meets the requirements of paragraphs (b)(8)(iii) (A), (B) and (C) of this section;

(B) The trustees, directors or other administrators of the pension fund have no knowledge, and no reason to know, that the ratio of the pension fund's beneficiaries who are residents of either the country in which the pension fund is administered or of the United States to all beneficiaries of the pension fund would differ significantly from the ratio of the sum of the actuarial interests of such residents in the pension fund to the actuarial interests of all beneficiaries in the pension fund (or, if the beneficiaries' actuarial interest in the stock held directly or indirectly by the pension fund differs from the beneficiaries's actuarial interest in the pension fund, the ratio of actuarial interests computed by reference to the beneficiaries' actuarial interest in the stock);

(C) Either—

(1) Any overfunding of the pension fund would be payable, pursuant to the governing instrument or the laws of the foreign country in which the pension fund is administered, only to, or for the benefit of, one or more corporations that are qualified residents of the country in which the pension fund is administered, individual beneficiaries of the pension fund or their designated beneficiaries, or social or charitable causes (the reduction of the obligation of the sponsoring company or companies to make future contributions to the pension fund by reason of overfunding shall not itself result in such overfunding being deemed to be payable to or for the benefit of such company or companies); or

(2) The foreign country in which the pension fund is administered has laws that are designed to prevent overfunding of a pension fund and the funding of the pension fund is within the guidelines of such laws; or

(3) The pension fund is maintained to provide benefits to employees in a particular industry, profession, or group of industries or professions and employees of at least 10 companies (other than companies that are owned or controlled, directly or indirectly, by the same interests) contribute to the pension fund or receive benefits from the pension fund; and

(D) The trustees, directors or other administrators provide, with the pension fund's intermediary ownership statement described in paragraph (b)(6) of this section, a written statement signed under penalties of perjury certifying that the requirements in paragraphs (b)(8)(iv)(A), (B), and either (C)(*1*), (C)(*2*) or (C)(*3*) of this section have been met.

The statement described in paragraph (b)(8)(iv)(D) of this section may be combined, in a single statement, with the information required in paragraph (b)(8)(iii)(F) of this section.

(v) *Time for making determinations.*—The determinations required to be made under this paragraph (b)(8) shall be made using information shown on the records of the pension fund for a date on or after the beginning of the foreign corporation's taxable year to which the determination is relevant.

(9) *Availability of documents for inspection.*—(i) *Retention of documents by the foreign corporation.*—The documentation described in paragraphs (b)(3) and (b)(8) of this section must be retained by the foreign corporation until expiration of the period of limitations for the taxable year to which the documentation relates and must be made available for inspection by the District Director at such time and place as the District Director may request.

(ii) *Retention of documents by an intermediary issuing an intermediary verification statement.*—The documentation upon which an intermediary relies to issue an intermediary verification statement under paragraph (b)(7) of this section must be retained by the intermediary for a period of six years from the date of issuance of the intermediary verification statement and must be made available for inspection by the District Director at such time and place as the District Director may request.

(10) *Examples.*—The application of this paragraph (b) is illustrated by the following examples.

Example 1. Foreign corporation A is a resident of country L, which has an income tax treaty in effect with the United States. Foreign corporation A has one class of stock issued and outstanding consisting of 1,000 shares, which are beneficially owned by the following alien individuals, directly or by application of paragraph (b)(2) of this section:

Individual	*Shares owned, directly or indirectly by application of paragraph (b) (2) of this section*	*Percentage*
T —resident of the U.S.	200	20%
U—resident of country L	400	40%
V —resident of country M	100	10%
W—resident of country L	210	21%
X —resident of country N	90	9%
Total	1,000	100%

(i) T owns his 200 shares directly and is a beneficial owner.

(ii) U and V own, respectively, an 80 percent and a 20 percent actuarial interest in foreign trust FT, (which interest does not differ from their respective interests in the stock owned by FT), which beneficially owns 100 percent of the stock of a foreign corporation B with bearer shares, which beneficially owns 500 shares of foreign corporation A. Foreign corporation B is incorporated in a country that does not have an income tax treaty with the United States. The foreign trust has deposited the bearer shares it owns in B with a bank in a foreign country that has an income tax treaty with the United States.

(iii) W beneficially owns all the shares of foreign corporation C, which are registered in the name of individual Z, a nominee, who resides in country L; foreign corporation C beneficially owns a 70 percent interest in foreign corporation D, which beneficially owns 300 shares of A. D's shares are bearer shares that C (not a resident of a country with which the United States has an income tax treaty) has deposited with a bank in a foreign country that has an income tax treaty with the United States.

(iv) X beneficially owns a 30 percent interest in foreign corporation D.

(v) A is a qualified resident of country L if it obtains the applicable documentation described in paragraph (b)(3) of this section either with respect to ownership by individuals U and W or with respect to ownership by individuals T and U, since either combination of qualifying shareholders of foreign corporation A will exceed 50 percent.

Example 2. Assume the same facts as in *Example 1* and assume that foreign corporation A chooses to obtain documentation with respect to individuals T and U.

(i) A must obtain, pursuant to paragraph (b)(3)(i) of this section, an ownership statement (as described in paragraph (b)(4)(i) of this section) signed by T. T is not required to furnish a certificate of residency because T is a U.S. resident.

(ii) U must provide foreign trust FT with an ownership statement and certificate of residency, as described in paragraphs (b)(4) and (b)(5) of this section. The trustees of FT must provide the depository bank holding foreign corporation B's bearer shares with an intermediary ownership statement concerning its beneficial ownership of B's shares and must attach to it the documentation provided by U. The depository bank must provide B with an intermediary ownership statement regarding its holding of B shares on behalf of FT and has the choice of attaching—

(A) The documentation from U and the intermediary ownership statement from FT; or

(B) An intermediary verification statement described in paragraph (b)(7) of this section, in which case foreign corporation B would not be provided with U's individual documentation or FT's intermediary ownership statement, both of which are retained by the depository bank.

(iii) In either case, B must then provide foreign corporation A with an intermediary ownership statement regarding its direct beneficial ownership of shares in A and, as the case may be, either—

(A) U's documentation and the intermediary ownership statements by FT and the depository bank; or

(B) The depository bank's intermediary ownership and verification statements.

(iv) Thus, with respect to U, A must obtain under paragraph (b)(3)(i) of this section the individual documentation regarding U and an intermediary ownership statement from each intermediary standing in the chain of U's indirect beneficial ownership of shares in A, *i.e.*, from FT, the depository bank and B. In the alternative, A must obtain under paragraph (b)(3)(ii) of this section an intermediary verification statement issued by the depository bank and an intermediary ownership statement from the bank and from B, which, in this example, are the only intermediaries standing in the chain of ownership of the verifying intermediary (*i.e.*, the depository bank).

Example 3. Assume the same facts as in *Example 1*. In addition, assume that foreign corporation A chooses to obtain documentation with respect to individuals U and W. With respect to U, A must obtain the same documentation that is described in *Example 2*. With respect to W, A must obtain, under paragraph (b)(3)(i) of this section, individual documentation regarding W and an intermediary ownership statement from each intermediary standing in the chain of W's indirect beneficial ownership of shares in A, *i.e.*, from individual Z, foreign corporation C, the depository bank in the foreign treaty country, and foreign corporation D. In the alternative, A must obtain, under paragraph (b)(3)(ii) of this section, either—

(i) An intermediary verification statement by the depository bank in the foreign treaty country and an intermediary ownership statement from the bank and from D; or

(ii) An intermediary verification statement from Z and an intermediary ownership statement from Z and from each intermediary standing in the chain of ownership of shares in foreign corporation A, *i.e.*, from C, the depository bank in the foreign treaty country and D. C may not issue an intermediary verification statement because it is not a resident of a country with which the United States has an income tax treaty.

(c) *Base erosion.*—A foreign corporation satisfies the requirement relating to base erosion for a taxable year if it establishes that less than 50 percent of its income for the taxable year is used (directly or indirectly) to make deductible payments in the current taxable year to persons who are not residents (or, in the case of foreign corporations, qualified residents) of the foreign country of which the foreign corporation is a resident and who are not citizens or residents (or, in the case of domestic corporations, qualified residents) of the United States. Whether a domestic corporation is a qualified resident of the United States shall be determined under the principles of this section. For purposes of this paragraph (c), the term "deductible payments" includes payments that would be ordinarily deductible under U.S. income tax principles without regard to other provisions of the Code that may require the capitalization of the expense, or disallow or defer the deduction. Such payments include, for example, interest, rents, royalties and reinsurance premiums. For purposes of this paragraph (c), the income of a foreign corporation means the corporation's gross income for the taxable year (or, if the foreign corporation has no gross income for the taxable year, the average of its gross income for the three previous taxable years) under U.S. tax principles, but not excluding items of income otherwise excluded from gross income under U.S. tax principles.

(d) *Publicly-traded corporations.*—(1) *General rule.*—A foreign corporation that is a resident of a foreign country shall be treated as a qualified resident of that country for any taxable year in which—

(i) Its stock is primarily and regularly traded (as defined in paragraphs (d)(3) and (4) of this section) on one or more established securities markets (as defined in paragraph (d)(2) of this section) in that country, or in the United States, or both; or

(ii) At least 90 percent of the total combined voting power of all classes of stock of such foreign corporation entitled to vote and at least 90 percent of the total value of the stock of such foreign corporation is owned, directly or by application of paragraph (b)(2) of this section, by a foreign corporation that is a resident of the same foreign country or a domestic corporation and the stock of such parent corporation is primarily and regularly traded on an established securities market in that foreign country or in the United States, or both.

(2) *Established securities market.*—(i) *General rule.*—For purposes of section 884, the term "established securities market" means, for any taxable year—

(A) A foreign securities exchange that is officially recognized, sanctioned, or supervised by a governmental authority of the country in which the market is located, is the principal exchange in that country, and has an annual value of shares traded on the exchange exceeding $1 billion during each of the three calendar years immediately preceding the beginning of the taxable year;

(B) A national securities exchange that is registered under section 6 of the Securities Act of 1934 (15 U.S.C. 78f); and

(C) A domestic over-the-counter market (as defined in paragraph (d)(2)(iv) of this section).

(ii) *Exchanges with multiple tiers.*—If a principal exchange in a foreign country has more than one tier or market level on which stock may be separately listed or traded, each such tier shall be treated as a separate exchange.

(iii) *Computation of dollar value of stock traded.*—For purposes of paragraph (d)(2)(i)(A) of this section, the value in U.S. dollars of shares traded during a calendar year shall be determined on the basis of the dollar value of such shares traded as reported by the International Federation of Stock Exchanges, located in Paris, or, if not so reported, then by converting into U.S. dollars the aggregate value in local currency of the shares traded using an exchange rate equal to the average of the spot rates on the last day of each month of the calendar year.

(iv) *Definition of over-the-counter market.*—An over-the-counter market is any market reflected by the existence of an interdealer quotation system. An interdealer quotation system is any system of general circulation to brokers and dealers that regularly disseminates quotations of stocks and securities by identified brokers or dealers, other than by quotation sheets that are prepared and distributed by a broker or dealer in the regular course of business and that contain only quotations of such broker or dealer.

(v) *Discretion to determine that an exchange qualifies as an established securities market.*—The Commissioner may, in his sole discretion, determine in a published document that a securities exchange that does not meet the requirements of paragraph (d)(2)(i)(A) of this section qualifies as an established securities market. Such a determination will be made only if it is established that—

(A) The exchange, in substance, has the attributes of an established securities market (including adequate trading volume, and comparable listing and financial disclosure requirements);

(B) The rules of the exchange ensure active trading of listed stocks; and

(C) The exchange is a member of the International Federation of Stock Exchanges.

(vi) *Discretion to determine that an exchange does not qualify as an established securities market.*—The Commissioner may, in his sole discretion, determine in a published document that a securities exchange that meets the requirements of paragraph (d)(2)(i) of this section does not qualify as an established securities market. Such determination shall be made if, in the view of the Commissioner—

(A) The exchange does not have adequate listing, financial disclosure, or trading requirements (or does not adequately enforce such requirements); or

(B) There is not clear and convincing evidence that the exchange ensures the active trading of listed stocks.

(3) *Primarily traded.*—For purposes of this section, stock of a corporation is "primarily traded" on one or more established securities markets in the corporation's country of residence or in the United States in any taxable year if, with respect to each class described in paragraph (d)(4)(i)(A) of this section (relating to classes of stock relied on to meet the regularly traded test)—

(i) The number of shares in each such class that are traded during the taxable year on all established securities markets in the corporation's country of residence or in the United States during the taxable year exceeds

(ii) The number of shares in each such class that are traded during that year on established securities markets in any other single foreign country.

(4) *Regularly traded.*—(i) *General rule.*—For purposes of this section, stock of a corporation is "regularly traded" on one or more established securities markets in the foreign corporation's country of residence or in the United States for the taxable year if—

(A) One or more classes of stock of the corporation that, in the aggregate, represent 80 percent or more of the total combined voting power of all classes of stock of such corporation entitled to vote and of the total value of the stock of such corporation are listed on such market or markets during the taxable year;

(B) With respect to each class relied on to meet the 80 percent requirement of paragraph (d)(4)(i)(A) of this section—

(1) Trades in each such class are effected, other than in *de minimis* quantities, on such market or markets on at least 60 days during the taxable year (or 1/6 of the number of days in a short taxable year); and

(2) The aggregate number of shares in each such class that is traded on such market or markets during the taxable year is at least 10 percent of the average number of shares outstanding in that class during the taxable year (or, in the case of a short taxable year, a percentage that equals at least 10 percent of the number of days in the short taxable year divided by 365).

If stock of a foreign corporation fails the 80 percent requirement of paragraph (d)(4)(i)(A) of this section, but a class of such stock meets the trading requirements of paragraph (d)(4)(i)(B) of this section, such class of stock may be taken into account under paragraph (b)(1)(iii) of this section as owned by qualifying shareholders for purposes of meeting the ownership test of paragraph (b)(1) of this section.

(ii) *Classes of stock traded on a domestic established securities market treated as meeting trading requirements.*—A class of stock that is traded during the taxable year on an established securities market located in the United States shall be treated as meeting the trading requirements of paragraph (d)(4)(i)(B) of this section if the stock is regularly quoted by brokers or dealers making a market in the stock. A broker or dealer makes a market in a stock only if the broker or dealer holds himself out to buy or sell the stock at the quoted price.

(iii) *Closely-held classes of stock not treated as meeting trading requirement.*—(A) *General rule.*—A class of stock shall not be treated as meeting the trading requirements of paragraph (d)(4)(i)(B) of this section (or the requirements of paragraph (d)(4)(ii) of this section) for a taxable year if, at any time during the taxable year, one or more persons who are not qualifying shareholders (as defined in paragraph (b)(1) of this section) and who each beneficially own 5 percent or more of the value of the outstanding shares of the class of stock own, in the aggregate, 50 percent or more of the outstanding shares of the class of stock for more than 30 days during the taxable year. For purposes of the preceding sentence, shares shall not be treated as owned by a qualifying shareholder unless such shareholder provides to the foreign corporation, by the time prescribed in paragraph (b)(3) of this section, the documentation described in paragraph (b)(3) of this section necessary to establish that it is a qualifying shareholder. For purposes of this paragraph (d)(4)(iii)(A), shares of stock owned by a pension fund, as defined in paragraph (b)(8)(i)(A) of this section, shall be treated as beneficially owned by the beneficiaries of such fund, as defined in paragraph (b)(8)(i)(B) of this section.

(B) *Treatment of related persons.*—Persons related within the meaning of section 267(b) shall be treated as one person for purposes of this paragraph (d)(4)(iii). In determining whether two or more corporations are members of the same controlled group under section 267(b)(3), a person is considered to own stock owned directly by such person, stock owned with the application of section 1563(e)(1), and stock owned with the application of section 267(c). Further, in determining whether a corporation is related to a partnership under section 267(b)(10), a person is considered to own the partnership interest owned directly by such person and the partnership interest owned with the application of section 267(e)(3).

(iv) *Anti-abuse rule.*—Trades between persons described in section 267(b)(as modified in paragraph (d)(4)(iii)(B) of this section) and trades conducted in order to meet the requirements of paragraph (d)(4)(i)(B) of this section shall be disregarded. A class of stock shall not be treated as meeting the trading requirements of paragraph (d)(4)(i)(B) of this section if there is a pattern of trades conducted to meet the requirements of that paragraph. For example, trades between two persons that occur several times during the taxable year may be treated as an arrangement or a pattern of trades conducted to meet the trading requirements of paragraph (d)(4)(i)(B) of this section.

(5) *Burden of proof for publicly-traded corporations.*—A foreign corporation that relies on this paragraph (d) to establish that it is a qualified resident of a country with which the United States has an income tax treaty shall have the burden of proving all the facts necessary for the corporation to be treated as a qualified resident, except that with respect to paragraphs (d)(4)(iii) and (iv) of this section, a foreign corporation, with either registered or bearer shares, will meet the burden of proof if it has no reason to know and no actual knowledge of facts that would cause the corporation's stock not to be treated as regularly traded under such paragraphs. A foreign corporation that has shareholders of record must also maintain a list of such shareholders and, on request, make available to the District Director such list and any other relevant information known to the foreign corporation.

(e) *Active trade or business.*—(1) *General rule.*—A foreign corporation that is a resident of a foreign country shall be treated as a qualified resident of that country with respect to any U.S. trade or business if, during the taxable year—

(i) It is engaged in the active conduct of a trade or business (as defined in paragraph (e)(2) of this section) in its country of residence;

(ii) It has a substantial presence (within the meaning of paragraph (e)(3) of this section) in its country of residence; and

(iii) Either—

(A) Such U.S. trade or business is an integral part (as defined in paragraph (e)(4) of this section) of an active trade or business conducted by the foreign corporation in its country of residence; or

(B) In the case of interest received by the foreign corporation for which a treaty exemption or rate reduction is claimed pursuant to § 1.884-4(b)(8)(ii), the interest is derived in connection with, or is incidental to, a trade or business described in paragraph (e)(1)(i) of this section.

A foreign corporation may determine whether it is a qualified resident under this paragraph (e) by applying the rules of this paragraph (e) to the entire affiliated group (as defined in section 1504(a) without regard to section 1504(b)(2) or (3)) of which the foreign corporation is a member rather than to the foreign corporation separately. If a foreign corporation chooses to apply the rules of this paragraph (e) to its entire affiliated group as provided in the preceding sentence, then it must apply such rules consistently to all of its U.S. trades or businesses conducted during the taxable year.

(2) *Active conduct of a trade or business.*—A foreign corporation is engaged in the active conduct of a trade or business only if either—

(i) It is engaged in the active conduct of a trade or business within the meaning of section 367(a)(3) and the regulations thereunder; or

(ii) It qualifies as a banking or financing institution under the laws of the foreign country of which it is a resident, it is licensed to do business with residents of its country of residence, and it is engaged in the active conduct of a banking, financing, or similar business within the meaning of § 1.864-4(c)(5)(i) in its country of residence.

A foreign corporation that is an insurance company within the meaning of § 1.801-3(a) or (b) is engaged in the active conduct of a trade or business only if it is predominantly engaged in the active conduct of an insurance business within the meaning of section 952(c)(1)(B)(v) and the regulations thereunder.

(3) *Substantial presence test.*—(i) *General rule.*—Except as provided in paragraph (e)(3)(ii) of this section, a foreign corporation that is engaged in the active conduct of a trade or business in its country of residence has a substantial presence in that country if, for the taxable year, the average of the following three ratios exceeds 25 percent and each ratio is at least equal to 20 percent—

(A) The ratio of the value of the assets of the foreign corporation used or held for use in the active conduct of a trade or business in its country of residence at the close of the taxable year to the value of all assets of the foreign corporation at the close of the taxable year;

(B) The ratio of gross income from the active conduct of the foreign corporation's trade or business in its country of residence that is derived from sources within such country for the taxable year to the worldwide gross income of the foreign corporation for the taxable year; and

(C) The ratio of the payroll expenses in the foreign corporation's country of residence for the taxable year to the foreign corporation's worldwide payroll expenses for the taxable year.

(ii) *Special rules.*—(A) *Asset ratio.*—For purposes of paragraph (e)(3)(i)(A) of this section, the value of an asset shall be determined using the method used by the taxpayer in keeping its books for purposes of financial reporting in its country of residence. An asset shall be treated as used or held for use in a foreign corporation's trade or business if it meets the requirements of § 1.367(a)-2(d)(5). Stock held by a foreign corporation shall not be treated as an asset of the foreign corporation for purposes of paragraph (e)(3)(i)(A) of this section if the foreign corporation owns 10 percent or more of the total combined voting power of all classes of stock of such corporation entitled to vote. The rules of § 1.954-2T(b)(3) (other than § 1.954-2T(b)(3)(x)) shall apply to determine the location of assets used or held for use in a trade or business. Loans originated or acquired in the course of the normal customer loan activities of a banking, financing or similar institution, and securities and derivative financial instruments held by dealers, traders and insurance companies for use in a trade or business shall be treated as located in the country in which an office or other fixed place of business is primarily responsible for the acquisition of the asset and the realization of income, gain or loss with respect to the asset.

(B) *Gross income ratio.*—*(1) General rule.*—For purposes of paragraph (e)(3)(i)(B) of this section, the term "gross income" means the gross income of a foreign corporation for purposes of financial reporting in its country of residence. Gross income shall not include, however, dividends, interest, rents, or royalties unless such corporation derives such dividends, interest, rents, or royalties in the active conduct of its trade or business. Gross income shall also not include gain from the disposition of stock if the foreign corporation owns 10 percent or more of the total combined voting power of all classes of stock of such corporation entitled to vote. Except as provided in this paragraph (e)(3)(ii)(B), the principles of sections 861 through 865 shall apply to determine the amount of gross income of a foreign corporation derived within its country of residence.

(2) Banks, dealers and traders.—Dividend income and gain from the sale of securities, or from entering into or disposing of derivative financial instruments by dealers and traders in such securities or derivative financial instruments shall be treated as derived within the country where the assets are located under paragraph (e)(3)(ii)(A) of this section. Other income, including interest and fees, earned in the active conduct of a banking, financing or similar business shall be treated as derived within the country where the payor of such interest or other income resides. For purposes of the

preceding sentence, if a branch or similar establishment outside the country in which the payor resides makes a payment of interest or other income, such amounts shall be treated as derived within the country in which the branch or similar establishment is located.

(3) *Insurance companies.*—The gross income of a foreign insurance company shall include only gross premiums received by the company.

(4) *Other corporations.*—Gross income from the performance of services, including transportation services, shall be treated as derived within the country of residence of the person for whom the services are performed. Gross income from the sale of property by a foreign corporation shall be treated as derived within the country in which the purchaser resides.

(5) *Anti-abuse rule.*—The Commissioner may disregard the source of income from a transaction determined under this paragraph (e)(3)(ii)(B) if it is determined that one of the principal purposes of the transaction was to increase the source of income derived within the country of residence of the foreign corporation for purposes of this section.

(C) *Payroll ratio.*—For purposes of paragraph (e)(3)(i)(C) of this section, the payroll expenses of a foreign corporation shall include expenses for "leased employees" (within the meaning of section 414(n)(2) but without regard to subdivision (B) of that section) and commission expenses paid to employees and agents for services performed for or on behalf of the corporation. Payroll expense for an employee, agent or a "leased employee" shall be treated as incurred where the employee, agent or "leased employee" performs services on behalf of the corporation.

(iii) *Exception to gross income test for foreign corporations engaged in certain trades or businesses.*—In determining whether a foreign corporation engaged primarily in selling tangible property or in manufacturing, producing, growing, or extracting tangible property has a substantial presence in its country of residence for purposes of paragraph (e)(3)(i) of this section, the foreign corporation may apply the ratio provided in this paragraph (e)(3)(iii) instead of the ratio described in paragraph (e)(3)(i)(B) of this section (relating to the ratio of gross income derived from its country of residence). This ratio shall be the ratio of the direct material costs of the foreign corporation with respect to tangible property manufactured, produced, grown, or extracted in the foreign corporation's country of residence to the total direct material costs of the foreign corporation.

(4) *Integral part of an active trade or business in a foreign corporation's country of residence.*—(i) *In general.*—A U.S. trade or business of a foreign corporation is an integral part of an active trade or business conducted by a foreign corporation in its country of residence if the active trade or business conducted by the foreign corporation in both its country of residence and in the United States comprise, in principal part, complementary and mutually interdependent steps in the United States and its country of residence in the production and sale or lease of goods or in the provision of services. Subject to the presumption and de minimis rule in paragraphs (e)(4)(iii) and (iv) of this section, if a U.S. trade or business of a foreign corporation sells goods that are not, in principal part, manufactured, produced, grown, or extracted by the foreign corporation in its country of residence, such business shall not be treated as an integral part of an active trade or business conducted in the foreign corporation's country of residence unless the foreign corporation takes physical possession of the goods in a warehouse or other storage facility that is located in its country of residence and in which goods of such type are normally stored prior to sale to customers in such country.

(ii) *Presumption for banks.*—A U.S. trade or business of a foreign corporation that is described in § 1.884-4(a)(2)(iii) shall be presumed to be an integral part of an active banking business conducted by the foreign corporation in its country of residence provided that a substantial part of the business of the foreign corporation in both its country of residence and the United States consists of receiving deposits and making loans and discounts. This paragraph shall be effective for taxable years beginning on or after June 6, 1996.

(iii) *Presumption if business principally conducted in country of residence.*—A U.S. trade or business of a foreign corporation shall be treated as an integral part of an active trade or business of a foreign corporation in its country of residence with respect to the sale or lease of property (or the performance of services) if at least 50 percent of the foreign corporation's worldwide gross income from the sale or lease of property of the type sold in the United States (or from the performance of services of the type performed in the United States) is derived from the sale or lease of such property for consumption, use, or disposition in the foreign corporation's country of residence (or from the performance of such services in the foreign corporation's country of residence). In determining whether property or services are of the same type, a foreign corporation shall follow recognized industry or trade usage or the three-digit major groups (or any narrower classification) of the Standard Industrial Classification as prepared by the Statistical Policy Division of the Office of Management and Budget, Executive Office of the President. The determination of whether income is of the same kind must be made in a consistent manner from year to year.

(iv) *De minimis rule.*—If a foreign corporation is engaged in more than one U.S. trade or business and if at least 80 percent of the sum of the ECEP from the current year and the preceding two years is attributable to one or more trades or businesses that meet the integral part test of this paragraph (e)(4), all of the U.S. trades or businesses of the foreign corporation shall be treated as an integral part of an active trade or business conducted by the foreign corporation. If a foreign corporation has more than one U.S. trade or business and does not meet the requirements of the preceding sentence but otherwise meets the requirements of this paragraph (e)(4) with regard to one or more trade or business, see § 1.884-1(g)(1) to determine the extent to which treaty benefits apply to such corporation.

(f) *Qualified resident ruling.*—(1) *Basis for ruling.*—In his or her sole discretion, the Commissioner may rule that a foreign corporation is a qualified resident of its country of residence if the Commissioner determines that individuals who are not residents of the foreign country of which the foreign corporation is a resident do not use the treaty between that country and the United States in a manner inconsistent with the purposes of section 884. The purposes of section 884 include, but are not limited to, the prevention of treaty shopping by an individual with respect to any article of an income tax treaty between the country of residence of the foreign corporation and the United States.

(2) *Factors.*—In order to make this determination, the Commissioner may take into account the following factors, including, but not limited to:

(i) The business reasons for establishing and maintaining the foreign corporation in its country of residence;

(ii) The date of incorporation of the foreign corporation in relation to the date that an income tax treaty between the United States and the foreign corporation's country of residence entered into force;

(iii) The continuity of the historical business and ownership of the foreign corporation;

(iv) The extent to which the foreign corporation meets the requirements of one or more of the tests described in paragraphs (b) through (e) of this section;

(v) The extent to which the U.S. trade or business is dependent on capital, assets, or personnel of the foreign trade or business;

(vi) The extent to which the foreign corporation receives special tax benefits in its country of residence;

(vii) Whether the foreign corporation is a member of an affiliated group (as defined in section 1504(a) without regard to section 1504(b)(2) or (3)), that has no members resident outside the country of residence of the foreign corporation; and

(viii) The extent to which the foreign corporation would be entitled to comparable treaty benefits with respect to all articles of an income tax treaty that would apply to that corporation if it had been incorporated in the country or countries of residence of the majority of its shareholders. For purposes of the preceding sentence, shareholders taken into account shall generally be limited to persons described in paragraph (b)(1)(i) of this section but for the fact that they are not residents of the foreign corporation's country of residence.

(3) *Procedural requirements.*—A request for a ruling under this paragraph (f) must be submitted on or before the due date (including extensions) of the foreign corporation's income tax return for the taxable year for which the ruling is requested. A foreign corporation receiving a ruling will be treated as a qualified resident of its country of residence for the taxable year for which the ruling is requested and for the succeeding two taxable years. If there is a material change in any fact that formed the basis of the ruling, such as the ownership or the nature of the trade or business of the foreign corporation, the foreign corporation must notify the Secretary within 90 days of such

change and submit a new private letter ruling request. The Commissioner will then rule whether the change affects the foreign corporation's status as a qualified resident, and such ruling will be valid for the taxable year in which the material change occurred and the two succeeding taxable years, subject to the requirement in the preceding sentence to notify the Commissioner of a material change.

(g) *Effective dates.*—Except as provided in paragraph (e)(4)(ii) of this section, this section is effective for taxable years beginning on or after October 13, 1992.

(h) *Transition rule.*—If a foreign corporation elects to apply this section in lieu of § 1.884-5T (as contained in the CFR edition revised as of April 1, 1992) as provided in paragraph (g) of this section, and the application of paragraph (b) of this section results in additional documentation requirements in order for the foreign corporation to be treated as a qualified resident, the foreign corporation must obtain the documentation required under that paragraph on or before March 11, 1993. [Reg. § 1.884-5.]

☐ [*T.D.* 8432, 9-10-92. *Amended by T.D.* 8657, 3-5-96 *and T.D.* 9803, 12-15-2016.]

§ 1.892-1T. Purpose and scope of regulations (Temporary).—(a) *In general.*—These regulations provide guidance with respect to the taxation of income derived by foreign governments and international organizations from sources within the United States. Under section 892, certain specific types of income received by foreign governments are excluded from gross income and are exempt, unless derived from the conduct of a commercial activity or received from or by a controlled commercial entity. This section sets forth the effective date of the regulations. Section 1.892-2T defines a foreign government. In particular it describes the extent to which either an integral part of a foreign sovereign or an entity which is not an integral part of a foreign sovereign will be treated as a foreign government for purposes of section 892. Section 1.892-3T describes the types of income that generally qualify for exemption and certain limitations on the exemption. Section 1.892-4T provides rules concerning the characterization of activities as commercial activities. Section 1.892-5T defines a controlled commercial entity. Section 1.892-6T sets forth the extent to which income of international organizations from sources within the United States is excluded from gross income and is exempt from taxation. Section 1.892-7T sets forth the relationship of section 892 to other Internal Revenue Code sections.

(b) *Effective date.*—The regulations set forth in §§ 1.892-1T through 1.892-7T apply to income received by a foreign government on or after July 1, 1986. No amount of income shall be required to be deducted and withheld, by reason of the amendment of section 892 by section 1247 of the Tax Reform Act of 1986 (Pub.L. 99-514, 100 Stat. 2085, 2583) from any payment made before October 22, 1986. [Temporary Reg. § 1.892-1T.]

☐ [*T.D.* 8211, 6-24-88.]

§ 1.892-2T. Foreign government defined (Temporary).—(a) *Foreign government.*—(1) *Definition.*—The term "foreign government" means only the integral parts or controlled entities of a foreign sovereign.

(2) *Integral part.*—An "integral part" of a foreign sovereign is any person, body of persons, organization, agency, bureau, fund, instrumentality, or other body, however designated, that constitutes a governing authority of a foreign country. The net earnings of the governing authority must be credited to its own account or to other accounts of the foreign sovereign, with no portion inuring to the benefit of any private person. An integral part does not include any individual who is a sovereign, official, or administrator acting in a private or personal capacity. Consideration of all the facts and circumstances will determine whether an individual is acting in a private or personal capacity.

(3) *Controlled entity.*—The term "controlled entity" means an entity that is separate in form from a foreign sovereign or otherwise constitutes a separate juridical entity if it satisfies the following requirements:

(i) It is wholly owned and controlled by a foreign sovereign directly or indirectly through one or more controlled entities;

(ii) It is organized under the laws of the foreign sovereign by which owned;

(iii) Its net earnings are credited to its own account or to other accounts of the foreign sovereign, with no portion of its income inuring to the benefit of any private person; and

(iv) Its assets vest in the foreign sovereign upon dissolution.

A controlled entity does not include partnerships or any other entity owned and controlled by more than one foreign sovereign. Thus, a foreign financial organization organized and wholly owned and controlled by several foreign sovereigns to foster economic, financial, and technical cooperation between various foreign nations is not a controlled entity for purposes of this section.

(b) *Inurement to the benefit of private persons.*—For purposes of this section, income will be presumed not to inure to the benefit of private persons if such persons (within the meaning of section 7701(a)(1)) are the intended beneficiaries of a governmental program which is carried on by the foreign sovereign and the activities of which constitute governmental functions (within the meaning of § 1.892-4T (c)(4)). Income will be considered to inure to the benefit of private persons if such income benefits:

(1) Private persons through the use of a governmental entity as a conduit for personal investment; or

(2) Private persons who divert such income from its intended use by the exertion of influence or control through means explicitly or implicitly approved of by the foreign sovereign.

(c) *Pension trusts.*—(1) *In general.*—A controlled entity includes a separately organized pension trust if it meets the following requirements:

(i) The trust is established exclusively for the benefit of (A) employees or former employees of a foreign government or (B) employees or former employees of a foreign government and non-governmental employees or former employees that perform or performed governmental or social services;

(ii) The funds that comprise the trust are managed by trustees who are employees of, or persons appointed by, the foreign government;

(iii) The trust forming a part of the pension plan provides for retirement, disability, or death benefits in consideration for prior services rendered; and

(iv) Income of the trust satisfies the obligations of the foreign government to participants under the plan, rather than inuring to the benefit of a private person.

Income of a pension trust is subject to the rules of § 1.892-5T(b)(3) regarding the application of the rules for controlled commercial entities to pension trusts. Income of a superannuation or similar pension fund of an integral part or controlled entity (which is not a separate pension trust as defined in this paragraph (c)(1)) is subject to the rules that generally apply to a foreign sovereign. Such a pension fund may also benefit non-governmental employees or former employees that perform or performed governmental or social services.

(2) *Illustrations.*—The following examples illustrate the application of paragraph (c)(1).

Example (1). The Ministry of Welfare (MW), an integral part of foreign sovereign FC, instituted a retirement plan for FC's employees and former employees. Retirement benefits under the plan are based on a percentage of the final year's salary paid to an individual, times the number of years of government service. Pursuant to the plan, contributions are made by MW to a pension trust managed by persons appointed by MW to the extent actuarially necessary to fund accrued pension liabilities. The pension trust in turn invests such contributions partially in United States Treasury obligations. The income of the trust is credited to the trust's account and subsequently used to satisfy the pension plan's obligations to retired employees. Under these circumstances, the income of the trust is not deemed to inure to the benefit of private persons. Accordingly, the trust is considered a controlled entity of FC.

Example (2). The facts are the same as in *Example* (1), except that the retirement plan also benefits employees performing governmental or social services for the following non-government institutions: (i) a university in a local jurisdiction; (ii) a harbor commission; and (iii) a library system. The retirement benefits under the plan are based on the total amounts credited to an individual's account over the term of his or her employment. MW makes annual contributions to each covered employee's account equal to a percentage of annual compensation. In addition, the income derived from investment of the annual contributions is credited annually to individual accounts. The annual contributions do not exceed an amount that is determined to be actuarially necessary to provide the employee with reasonable retirement benefits. Notwithstanding that retirement benefits vary depending upon the investment experience of the trust, no portion of the income of the trust is deemed to inure to the benefit of private persons. Accordingly, the trust is considered a controlled entity of FC.

Example (3). The facts are the same as in *Example* (1), except that employees are allowed to make unlimited contributions to the trust, and such contributions are credited to the employee's account as well as interest accrued on such contributions. Retirement benefits will reflect the amounts credited to the individual accounts in addition to the usual annuity computation based on the final year's salary and years of service. A pension plan established under these rules is in part acting as an investment conduit. As a result, the income of the trust is deemed to inure to the benefit of private persons. Accordingly, the trust is not considered a controlled entity of FC.

Example (4). (a) The facts are the same as in *Example* (2), except that MW establishes a pension fund rather than a separate pension trust. A pension fund is merely assets of an integral part or controlled entity allocated to a separate account and held and invested for purposes of providing retirement benefits. Under these circumstances, the income of the pension fund is not deemed to inure to the benefit of private persons. Accordingly, income earned from the United States Treasury obligations by the pension fund is considered to be received by a foreign government and is exempt from taxation under section 892.

(b) The facts are the same as in *Example* (4)(a), except that MW is a controlled entity of foreign sovereign FC. The result is the same as in *Example* (4)(a). However, should MW engage in commercial activities (whether within or outside the United States), the income from the Treasury obligations earned by the pension fund will not be exempt from taxation under section 892 since MW will be considered a controlled commercial entity within the meaning of § 1.892-5T(a).

(d) *Political subdivision and transnational entity.*—The rules that apply to a foreign sovereign apply to political subdivisions of a foreign country and to transnational entities. A transnational entity is an organization created by more than one foreign sovereign that has broad powers over external and domestic affairs of all participating foreign countries stretching beyond economic subjects to those concerning legal relations and transcending state or political boundaries. [Temporary Reg. § 1.892-2T.]

☐ [*T.D.* 8211, 6-24-88.]

§ 1.892-3. Income of foreign governments.—(a)(1) through (a)(5) [Reserved]. For further information, see § 1.892-3T(a)(1) through (a)(5).

(6) *Dividend equivalents.*—Income from investments in stocks includes the payment of a dividend equivalent described in section 871(m) and the regulations thereunder.

(b) [Reserved].—For further information, see § 1.892-3T(b).

(c) *Effective/applicability date.*—Paragraph (a)(6) of this section applies to payments made on or after December 5, 2013. [Reg. § 1.892-3.]

☐ [*T.D.* 9648, 12-4-2013.]

§ 1.892-3T. Income of foreign governments (Temporary).—(a) *Types of income exempt.*—(1) *In general.*—Subject to the exceptions contained in §§ 1.892-4T and 1.892-5T for income derived from the conduct of a commercial activity or received from or by a controlled commercial entity, the following types of income derived by a foreign government (as defined in § 1.892-2T) are not included in gross income and are exempt:

(i) Income from investments in the United States in stocks, bonds, or other securities;

(ii) Income from investments in the United States in financial instruments held in the execution of governmental financial or monetary policy; and

(iii) Interest on deposits in banks in the United States of moneys belonging to such foreign government.

Income derived from sources other than described in this paragraph (such as income earned from a U.S. real property interest described in section 897(c)(1)(A)(i)) is not exempt from taxation under section 892. Furthermore, any gain derived from the disposition of a U.S. real property interest defined in section 897(c)(1)(A)(i) shall in no event qualify for exemption under section 892.

(2) *Income from investments.*—For purposes of paragraph (a) of this section, income from investments in stocks, bonds or other securities includes gain from their disposition and income earned from engaging in section 1058 securities lending transactions. Gain on the disposition of an interest in a partnership or a trust is not exempt from taxation under section 892.

(3) *Securities.*—For purposes of paragraph (a) of this section, the term "other securities" includes any note or other evidence of indebtedness. Thus, an annuity contract, a mortgage, a banker's acceptance or a loan are securities for purposes of this section. However, the term "other securities" does not include partnership interests (with the exception of publicly traded partnerships within the meaning of section 7704) or trust interests. The term also does not include commodity forward or futures contracts and commodity options unless they constitute securities for purposes of section 864(b)(2)(A).

(4) *Financial instrument.*—For purposes of paragraph (a) of this section, the term "financial instrument" includes any forward, futures, options contract, swap agreement or similar instrument in a functional or nonfunctional currency (see section 985(b) for the definition of functional currency) or in precious metals when held by a foreign government or central bank of issue (as defined in § 1.895-1(b)). Nonfunctional currency or gold shall be considered a "financial instrument" also when physically held by a central bank of issue.

(5) *Execution of financial or monetary policy.*—(i) *Rule.*—A financial instrument shall be deemed held in the execution of governmental financial or monetary policy if the primary purpose for holding the instrument is to implement or effectuate such policy.

(ii) *Illustration.*—The following example illustrates the application of this paragraph (a)(5).

Example. In order to ensure sufficient currency reserves, the monetary authority of foreign country FC issues short-term government obligations. The amount received from the obligations is invested in U.S. financial instruments. Since the primary purpose for obtaining the U.S. financial instruments is to implement FC's monetary policy, the income received from the financial instruments is exempt from taxation under section 892.

(b) *Illustrations.*—The principles of paragraph (a) of this section may be illustrated by the following examples.

Example (1). X, a foreign corporation not engaged in commercial activity anywhere in the world, is a controlled entity of a foreign sovereign within the meaning of § 1.892-2T(a)(3). X is not a central bank of issue as defined in § 1.895-1(b). In 1987, X received the following items of income from investments in the United States: (i) dividends from a portfolio of publicly traded stocks in U.S. corporations in which X owns less than 50 percent of the stock; (ii) dividends from BTB Corporation, an automobile manufacturer, in which X owns 50 percent of the stock; (iii) interest from bonds issued by noncontrolled entities and from interest bearing bank deposits in noncontrolled entities; (iv) rents from a net lease on real property; (v) gains from silver futures contracts; (vi) gains from wheat futures contracts; (vii) gains from spot sales of nonfunctional foreign currency in X's possession; (viii) gains from the disposition of a publicly traded partnership interest, and (ix) gains from the disposition of the stock of Z Corporation, a United States real property holding company as defined in section 897, of which X owns 12 percent of the stock. Only income derived from sources described in paragraph (a)(1) of this section is treated as income of a foreign government eligible for exemption from taxation. Accordingly, only income received by X from items (i), (iii), (v) provided that the silver futures contracts are held in the execution of governmental financial or monetary policy, and (ix) is exempt from taxation under section 892.

Example (2). The facts are the same as in *Example (1)*, except that X is also a central bank of issue within the meaning of section 895. Since physical possession of nonfunctional foreign currency when held by a central bank of issue is considered a financial instrument, the item (vii) gains from spot sales of nonfunctional foreign currency are exempt from taxation under paragraph (a)(1) of this section, if physical possession of the currency was an essential part of X's reserve policy in the execution of its governmental financial or monetary policy.

Example (3). State Concert Bureau, an integral part of a foreign sovereign within the meaning of § 1.892-2T(a)(2), entered into an agreement with a U.S. corporation engaged in the business of promoting international cultural programs. Under the agreement the State Concert Bureau agreed to send a ballet troupe on tour for 5 weeks in the United States. The Bureau received approximately $60,000 from the performances. Regardless of whether the performances themselves constitute commercial activities under § 1.892-4T, the income received by the Bureau is not exempt from taxation under section 892 since the income is from sources other than described in paragraph (a)(1) of this section. [Temporary Reg. § 1.892-3T.]

☐ [*T.D.* 8211, 6-24-88.]

§1.892-4T. Commercial activities (Temporary).—(a) *Purpose.*—The exemption generally applicable to a foreign government (as defined in §1.892-2T) for income described in §1.892-3T does not apply to income derived from the conduct of a commercial activity or income received by a controlled commercial entity or received (directly or indirectly) from a controlled commercial entity. This section provides rules for determining whether income is derived from the conduct of a commercial activity. These rules also apply in determining under §1.892-5T whether an entity is a controlled commercial entity.

(b) *In general.*—Except as provided in paragraph (c) of this section, all activities (whether conducted within or outside the United States) which are ordinarily conducted by the taxpayer or by other persons with a view towards the current or future production of income or gain are commercial activities. An activity may be considered a commercial activity even if such activity does not constitute the conduct of a trade or business in the United States under section 864(b).

(c) *Activities that are not commercial.*—(1) *Investments.*—(i) *In general.*—Subject to the provisions of paragraphs (ii) and (iii) of this paragraph (c)(1), the following are not commercial activities: investments in stock, bonds, and other securities; loans; investments in financial instruments held in the execution of governmental financial or monetary policy; the holding of net leases on real property or land which is not producing income (other than on its sale or from an investment in net leases on real property); and the holding of bank deposits in banks. Transferring securities under a loan agreement which meets the requirements of section 1058 is an investment for purposes of this paragraph (c)(1)(i). An activity will not cease to be an investment solely because of the volume of transactions of that activity or because of other unrelated activities.

(ii) *Trading.*—Effecting transactions in stocks, securities, or commodities for a foreign government's own account does not constitute a commercial activity regardless of whether such activities constitute a trade or business for purposes of section 162 or a U.S. trade or business for purposes of section 864. Such transactions are not commercial activities regardless of whether they are effected by the foreign government through its employees or through a broker, commission agent, custodian, or other independent agent and regardless of whether or not any such employee or agent has discretionary authority to make decisions in effecting the transactions. An activity undertaken as a dealer, however as defined in §1.864-2(c)(2)(iv)(*a*) will not be an investment for purposes of this paragraph (c)(1)(i). For purposes of this paragraph (c)(1)(ii), the term "commodities" means commodities of a kind customarily dealt in on an organized commodity exchange but only if the transaction is of a kind customarily consummated at such place.

(iii) *Banking, financing, etc.*—Investments (including loans) made by a banking, financing, or similar business constitute commercial activities, even if the income derived from such investments is not considered to be income effectively connected to the active conduct of a banking, financing, or similar business in the U.S. by reason of the application of §1.864-4(c)(5).

(2) *Cultural events.*—Performances and exhibitions within or outside the United States of amateur athletic events and events devoted to the promotion of the arts by cultural organizations are not commercial activities.

(3) *Non-profit activities.*—Activities that are not customarily attributable to or carried on by private enterprise for profit are not commercial activities. The fact that in some instances Federal, State, or local governments of the United States also are engaged in the same or similar activity does not mean necessarily that it is a non-profit activity. For example, even though the United States Government may be engaged in the activity of operating a railroad, operating a railroad is not a non-profit activity.

(4) *Governmental functions.*—Governmental functions are not commercial activities. The term "governmental functions" shall be determined under U.S. standards. In general, activities performed for the general public with respect to the common welfare or which relate to the administration of some phase of government will be considered governmental functions. For example, the operation of libraries, toll bridges, or local transportation services and activities substantially equivalent to the Federal Aviation Authority, Interstate Commerce Commission, or United States Postal Service will all be considered governmental functions for purposes of this section.

(5) *Purchasing.*—The mere purchasing of goods for the use of a foreign government is not a commercial activity. [Temporary Reg. §1.892-4T.]

□ [*T.D.* 8211, 6-24-88.]

Proposed Regulation

§1.892-4. Commercial activities.—(a) through (c) [Reserved]. For further guidance, see §1.892-4T(a) through (c).

(d) *In general.*—Except as provided in paragraph (e) of this section, all activities (whether conducted within or outside the United States) which are ordinarily conducted for the current or future production of income or gain are commercial activities. Only the nature of the activity, not the purpose or motivation for conducting the activity, is determinative of whether the activity is commercial in character. An activity may be considered a commercial activity even if such activity does not constitute a trade or business for purposes of section 162 or does not constitute (or would not constitute if undertaken in the United States) the conduct of a trade or business in the United States for purposes of section 864(b).

(e) *Activities that are not commercial.*—(1) *Investments.*—(i) *In general.*—Subject to the provisions of paragraphs (e)(1)(ii) and (iii) of this section, the following are not commercial activities: investments in stocks, bonds, and other securities (as defined in §1.892-3T(a)(3)); loans; investments in financial instruments (as defined in §1.892-3T(a)(4)); the holding of net leases on real property; the holding of real property which is not producing income (other than on its sale or from an investment in net leases on real property); and the holding of bank deposits in banks. Transferring securities under a loan agreement which meets the requirements of section 1058 is an investment for purposes of this paragraph (e)(1)(i). An activity will not cease to be an investment solely because of the volume of transactions of that activity or because of other unrelated activities.

(ii) *Trading.*—Effecting transactions in stocks, bonds, other securities (as defined in §1.892-3T(a)(3)), commodities, or financial instruments (as defined in §1.892-3T(a)(4)) for a foreign government's own account does not constitute a commercial activity regardless of whether such activity constitutes a trade or business for purposes of section 162 or constitutes (or would constitute if undertaken within the United States) the conduct of a trade or business in the United States for purposes of section 864(b). Such transactions are not commercial activities regardless of whether they are effected by the foreign government through its employees or through a broker, commission agent, custodian, or other independent agent and regardless of whether or not any such employee or agent has discretionary authority to make decisions in effecting the transactions. Such transactions undertaken as a dealer (as determined under the principles of §1.864-2(c)(2)(iv)(a)), however, constitute commercial activity. For purposes of this paragraph (e)(1)(ii), the term *commodities* means commodities of a kind customarily dealt in on an organized commodity exchange but only if the transaction is of a kind customarily consummated at such place.

(iii) *Banking, financing, etc.*—Investments (including loans) made by a banking, financing, or similar business constitute commercial activities, even if the income derived from such investments is not considered to be income effectively connected with the active conduct of a banking, financing, or similar business in the U.S. by reason of the application of §1.864-4(c)(5).

(iv) *Disposition of a U.S. real property interest.*—A disposition (including a deemed disposition under section 897(h)(1)) of a U.S. real property interest (as defined in section 897(c)), by itself, does not constitute the conduct of a commercial activity. As described in §1.892-3T(a), however, gain derived from a disposition of a U.S. real property interest defined in section 897(c)(1)(A)(i) will not qualify for exemption from tax under section 892.

(2) through (5) [Reserved]. For further guidance, see §1.892-4T(c)(2) through (c)(5).

(f) *Effective/applicability date.*—This section applies on the date the regulations are published as final regulations in the **FEDERAL REGISTER**. See §1.892-4T for the rules that apply before the date the regulations are published as final regulations in the **FEDERAL REGISTER**.

[Prop. Reg. §1.892-4.]

[Proposed 11-3-2011 (corrected 11-23-2011).]

§1.892-5. Controlled commercial entity.—(a) through (a)(2) [Reserved]. For further information, see §1.892-5T(a) through (a)(2).

(3) For purposes of section 892(a)(2)(B), the term *entity* means and includes a corporation, a partnership, a trust (including a pension trust described in §1.892-2T(c)) and an estate.

(4) *Effective date.*—This section applies on or after January 14, 2002. See §1.892-5T(a) for the rules that apply before January 14, 2002.

(b) through (d) [Reserved]. For further information, see §1.892-5T(b) through (d). [Reg. §1.892-5.]

☐ [*T.D. 9012, 7-31-2002.*]

§1.892-5T. Controlled commercial entity (Temporary).—(a) *In general.*—The exemption generally applicable to a foreign government (as defined in §1.892-2T) for income described in §1.892-3T does not apply to income received by a controlled commercial entity or received (directly or indirectly) from a controlled commercial entity. The term "controlled commercial entity" means any entity engaged in commercial activities as defined in §1.892-4T (whether conducted within or outside the United States) if the government—

(1) holds (directly or indirectly) any interest in such entity which (by value or voting power) is 50 percent or more of the total of such interests in such entity, or

(2) holds (directly or indirectly) a sufficient interest (by value or voting power) or any other interest in such entity which provides the foreign government with effective practical control of such entity.

(3) [Reserved]. For further information, see §1.892-5(a)(3).

(b) *Entities treated as engaged in commercial activity.*—(1) *U.S. real property holding corporations.*—A United States real property holding corporation, as defined in section 897(c)(2) or a foreign corporation that would be a United States real property holding corporation if it was a United States corporation, shall be treated as engaged in commercial activity and, therefore, is a controlled commercial entity if the requirements of paragraph (a)(1) or (a)(2) of this section are satisfied.

(2) *Central banks.*—Notwithstanding paragraph (a) of this section, a central bank of issue (as defined in §1.895-1(b)) shall be treated as a controlled commercial entity only if it engages in commercial activities within the United States.

(3) *Pension trusts.*—A pension trust, described in §1.892-2T(c), which engages in commercial activities within or outside the United States, shall be treated as a controlled commercial entity. Income derived by such a pension trust is not income of a foreign government for purposes of the exemption from taxation provided in section 892. A pension trust described in §1.892-2T(c) shall not be treated as a controlled commercial entity if such trust solely earns income which would not be unrelated business taxable income (as defined in section 512(a)(1)) if the trust were a qualified trust described in section 401(a). However, only income derived by a pension trust that is described in §1.892-3T and which is not from commercial activities as defined in §1.892-4T is exempt from taxation under section 892.

(c) *Control.*—(1) *Attribution.*—(i) *Rule.*—In determining for purposes of paragraph (a) of this section the interest held by a foreign government, any interest in an entity (whether or not engaged in commercial activity) owned directly or indirectly by an integral part or controlled entity of a foreign sovereign shall be treated as actually owned by such foreign sovereign.

(ii) *Illustration.*—The following example illustrates the application of paragraph (c)(1)(i) above.

Example. FX, a controlled entity of foreign sovereign FC, owns 20 percent of the stock of Corp 1. Neither FX nor Corp 1 is engaged in commercial activity anywhere in the world. Corp 1 owns 60 percent of the stock of Corp 2, which is engaged in commercial activity. The remaining 40 percent of Corp 2's stock is owned by Bureau, an integral part of foreign sovereign FC. For purposes of determining whether Corp 2 is a controlled commercial entity of FC, Bureau will be treated as actually owning the 12 percent of Corp 2's stock indirectly owned by FX. Therefore, since Bureau directly and indirectly owns 52 percent of the stock of Corp 2, Corp 2 is a controlled commercial entity of FC within the meaning of paragraph (a) of this section. Accordingly, dividends or other income received, directly or indirectly, from Corp 2 by either Bureau or FX will not be exempt from taxation under section 892. Furthermore, dividends from Corp 1 to the extent attributable to dividends from Corp 2 will not be exempt from taxation. Thus, a distribution from Corp 1 to FX shall be exempt only to the extent such distribution exceeds Corp 1's earnings and profits attributable to the Corp 2 dividend amount received by Corp 1.

(2) *Effective practical control.*—An entity engaged in commercial activity may be treated as a controlled commercial entity if a foreign government holds sufficient interests in such entity to give it "effective practical control" over the entity. Effective practical control may be achieved through a minority interest which is sufficiently large to achieve effective control, or through creditor, contractual or regulatory relationships which, together with ownership interests held by the foreign government, achieve effective control. For example, an entity engaged in commercial activity may be treated as a controlled commercial entity if a foreign government, in addition to holding a small minority interest (by value or voting power), is also a substantial creditor of the entity or controls a strategic natural resource which such entity uses in the conduct of its trade or business, giving the foreign government effective practical control over the entity.

(d) *Related controlled entities.*—(1) *Brother/sister entities.*—Commercial activities of a controlled entity are not attributed to such entity's other brother/sister related entities. Thus, investment income described in §1.892-2T that is derived by a controlled entity that is not itself engaged in commercial activity within or outside the United States is exempt from taxation notwithstanding the fact that such entity's brother/sister related entity is a controlled commercial entity.

(2) *Parent/subsidiary entities.*—(i) *Subsidiary to parent attribution.*—Commercial activities of a subsidiary controlled entity are not attributed to its parent. Thus, investment income described in §1.892-3T that is derived by a parent controlled entity that is not itself engaged in commercial activity within or outside the United States is exempt from taxation notwithstanding the fact that its subsidiary is a controlled commercial entity. Dividends or other payments of income received by the parent controlled entity from the subsidiary are not exempt under section 892, because it constitutes income received from a controlled commercial entity. Furthermore, dividends paid by the parent are not exempt to the extent attributable to the dividends received by the parent from the subsidiary. Thus, a distribution by the parent shall be exempt only to the extent such distribution exceeds earnings and profits attributable to the dividend received from its subsidiary.

(ii) *Parent to subsidiary attribution.*—Commercial activities of a parent controlled entity are attributed to its subsidiary. Thus, investment income described in §1.892-3T that is derived by a subsidiary controlled entity (not engaged in commercial activity within or outside the United States) is not exempt from taxation under section 892 if its parent is a controlled commercial entity.

(3) *Partnerships.*—Except for partners of publicly traded partnerships, commercial activities of a partnership are attributable to its general and limited partners for purposes of section 892. For example, where a controlled entity is a general partner in a partnership engaged in commercial activities, the controlled entity's distributive share of partnership income (including income described in §1.892-3T) will not be exempt from taxation under section 892.

(4) *Illustrations.*—The principles of this section may be illustrated by the following examples.

Example (1). (a) The Ministry of Industry and Development is an integral part of a foreign sovereign under §1.892-2T(a)(2). The Ministry is engaged in commercial activity within the United States. In addition, the Ministry receives income from various publicly traded stocks and bonds, soybean futures contracts and net leases on U.S. real property. Since the Ministry is an integral part, and not a controlled entity, of a foreign sovereign, it is not a controlled commercial entity within the meaning of paragraph (a) of this section. Therefore, income described in §1.892-3T is ineligible for exemption under section 892 only to the extent derived from the conduct of commercial activities. Accordingly, the Ministry's income from the stocks and bonds is exempt from U.S. tax.

(b) The facts are the same as in *Example* (1)(a), except that the Ministry also owns 75 percent of the stock of R, a U.S. holding company that owns all the stock of S, a U.S. operating company engaged in commercial activity. Ministry's dividend income from R is income received indirectly from a controlled commercial entity. The Ministry's income from the stocks and bonds, with the exception of dividend income from R, is exempt from U.S. tax.

(c) The facts are the same as in *Example* (1)(a), except that the Ministry is a controlled entity of a foreign sovereign. Since the Ministry is a controlled entity and is engaged in commercial activity, it is a controlled commercial entity within the meaning of paragraph (a) of this section, and none of its income is eligible for exemption.

Example (2). (a) Z, a controlled entity of a foreign sovereign, has established a pension trust as part of a pension plan for the benefit of its employees and former employees. The pension trust (T), which meets the requirements of §1.892-2T(c), has investments in the U.S. in various stocks, bonds, annuity contracts, and a shopping center which is leased and managed by an independent real estate management firm. T also makes securities loans in transactions that qualify under section 1058. T's investment in the shopping center is not considered an unrelated trade or business within the meaning of section 513(b). Accordingly, T will not be treated as engaged in commercial activity. Since T is not a controlled commercial entity, its investment income described in §1.892-3T, with the exception of income received from the operations of the shopping center, is exempt from taxation under section 892.

(b) The facts are the same as *Example* (2)(a), except that T has an interest in a limited partnership which owns the shopping center. The shopping center is leased and managed by the partnership rather than by an independent management firm. Managing a shopping center, directly or indirectly through a partnership of which a trust is a member, would be considered an unrelated trade or business within the meaning of section 513(b) giving rise to unrelated business taxable income. Since the commercial activities of a partnership are attributable to its partners, T will be treated as engaged in commercial activity and thus will be considered a controlled commercial entity. Accordingly, none of T's income will be exempt from taxation under section 892.

(c) The facts are the same as *Example* (2)(a), except that Z is a controlled commercial entity. The result is the same as in *Example* (2)(a).

Example (3). (a) The Department of Interior, an integral part of foreign sovereign FC, wholly owns corporations G and H. G, in turn, wholly owns S. G, H and S are each controlled entities. G, which is not engaged in commercial activity anywhere in the world, receives interest income from deposits in banks in the United States. Both H and S do not have any investments in the U.S. but are both engaged in commercial activities. However, only S is engaged in commercial activities within the United States. Because neither the commercial activities of H nor the commercial activities of S are attributable to the Department of Interior or G, G's interest income is exempt from taxation under section 892.

(b) The facts are the same as *Example* (3)(a), except that G rather than S is engaged in commercial activities and S rather than G receives the interest income from the United States. Since the commercial activities of G are attributable to S, S's interest income is not exempt from taxation.

Example (4). (a) K, a controlled entity of a foreign sovereign, is a general partner in the Daj partnership. The Daj partnership has investments in the U.S. in various stocks and bonds and also owns and manages an office building in New York. K will be deemed to be engaged in commercial activity by being a general partner in Daj even if K does not actually make management decisions with regard to the partnership's commercial activity, the operation of the office building. Accordingly, K's distributive share of partnership income (including income derived from stocks and bonds) will not be exempt from taxation under section 892.

(b) The facts are the same as in *Example* (4)(a), except that the Daj partnership has hired a real estate management firm to lease offices and manage the building. Notwithstanding the fact that an independent contractor is performing the activities, the partnership shall still be deemed to be engaged in commercial activity. Accordingly, K's distributive share of partnership income (including income derived from stocks and bonds) will not be exempt from taxation under section 892.

(c) The facts are the same as in *Example* (4)(a), except that K is a partner whose partnership interest is considered a publicly traded partnership interest within the meaning of section 7704. Under paragraph (d)(3) of this section, the partnership's commercial activity will not be attributed to K. Since K will not be deemed to be engaged in commercial activity, K's distributive share of partnership income derived from stocks and bonds will be exempt from taxation under section 892. [Temporary Reg. §1.892-5T.]

☐ [*T.D. 8211, 6-24-88. Amended by T.D. 9012, 7-31-2002.*]

Proposed Amendments to Regulation

§1.892-5. Controlled commercial entity. (a) *In general.*—(1) *General rule and definition of the term "controlled commercial entity".*—Under section 892(a)(2)(A)(ii) and (a)(2)(A)(iii), the exemption generally applicable to a foreign government (as defined in §1.892-2T) for income described in §1.892-3T does not apply to income received by a controlled commercial entity or received (directly or indirectly) from a controlled commercial entity, or to income derived from the disposition of any interest in a controlled commercial entity. For purposes of section 892 and the regulations thereunder, the term *entity* means and includes a corporation, a partnership, a trust (including a pension trust described in §1.892-2T(c)), and an estate, and the term *controlled commercial entity* means any entity (including a controlled entity as defined in §1.892-2T(a)(3)) engaged in commercial activities (as defined in §§1.892-4 and 1.892-4T) (whether conducted within or outside the United States) if the government—

(i) Holds (directly or indirectly) any interest in such entity which (by value or voting power) is 50 percent or more of the total of such interests in such entity, or

(ii) Holds (directly or indirectly) any other interest in such entity which provides the foreign government with effective practical control of such entity.

(2) *Inadvertent commercial activity.*—(i) *General rule.*—For purposes of determining whether an entity is a controlled commercial entity for purposes of section 892(a)(2)(B) and paragraph (a)(1) of this section, an entity that conducts only inadvertent commercial activity will not be considered to be engaged in commercial activities. However, any income derived from such inadvertent commercial activity will not qualify for exemption from tax under section 892. Commercial activity of an entity will be treated as inadvertent commercial activity only if:

(A) Failure to avoid conducting the commercial activity is reasonable as described in paragraph (a)(2)(ii) of this section;

(B) The commercial activity is promptly cured as described in paragraph (a)(2)(iii) of this section; and

(C) The record maintenance requirements described in paragraph (a)(2)(iv) of this section are met.

(ii) *Reasonable failure to avoid commercial activity.*—(A) *In general.*—Subject to paragraphs (a)(2)(ii)(B) and (C) of this section, whether an entity's failure to prevent its worldwide activities from resulting in commercial activity is reasonable will be determined in light of all the facts and circumstances. Due regard will be given to the number of commercial activities conducted during the taxable year and in prior taxable years, as well as the amount of income earned from, and assets used in, the conduct of the commercial activities in relationship to the entity's total income and assets, respectively. For purposes of this paragraph (a)(2)(ii)(A) and paragraph (a)(2)(ii)(C) of this section, where a commercial activity conducted by a partnership is attributed under paragraph (d)(5)(i) of this section to an entity owning an interest in the partnership—

(1) Assets used in the conduct of the commercial activity by the partnership are treated as assets used in the conduct of commercial activity by the entity in proportion to the entity's interest in the partnership; and

(2) The entity's distributive share of the partnership's income from the conduct of the commercial activity shall be treated as income earned by the entity from the conduct of commercial activities.

(B) *Continuing due diligence requirement.*—A failure to avoid commercial activity will not be considered reasonable unless there is continuing due diligence to prevent the entity from engaging in commercial activities within or outside the United States as evidenced by having adequate written policies and operational procedures in place to monitor the entity's worldwide activities. A failure to avoid commercial activity will not be considered reasonable if the management-level employees of the entity have not undertaken reasonable efforts to establish, follow, and enforce such written policies and operational procedures.

(C) *Safe Harbor.*—Provided that adequate written policies and operational procedures are in place to monitor the entity's worldwide activities as required in paragraph (a)(2)(ii)(B) of this section, the entity's failure to avoid commercial activity during the taxable year will be considered reasonable if:

(1) The value of the assets used in, or held for use in, all commercial activity does not exceed five percent of the total value of

the assets reflected on the entity's balance sheet for the taxable year as prepared for financial accounting purposes, and

(2) The income earned by the entity from commercial activity does not exceed five percent of the entity's gross income as reflected on its income statement for the taxable year as prepared for financial accounting purposes.

(iii) *Cure requirement.*—A timely cure shall be considered to have been made if the entity discontinues the conduct of the commercial activity within 120 days of discovering the commercial activity. For example, if an entity that holds an interest as a general partner in a partnership discovers that the partnership is conducting commercial activity, the entity will satisfy the cure requirement if, within 120 days of discovering the commercial activity, the entity discontinues the conduct of the activity by divesting itself of its interest in the partnership (including by transferring its interest in the partnership to a related entity), or the partnership discontinues its conduct of commercial activity.

(iv) *Record maintenance.*—Adequate records of each discovered commercial activity and the remedial action taken to cure that activity must be maintained. The records shall be retained so long as the contents thereof may become material in the administration of section 892.

(3) *Annual determination of controlled commercial entity status.*—If an entity described in paragraph (a)(1)(i) or (ii) of this section engages in commercial activities at any time during a taxable year, the entity will be considered a controlled commercial entity for the entire taxable year. An entity not otherwise engaged in commercial activities during a taxable year will not be considered a controlled commercial entity for a taxable year even if the entity engaged in commercial activities in a prior taxable year.

(b) through (d)(4) [Reserved]. For further guidance, see § 1.892-5T(b) through (d)(4).

(5) *Partnerships.*—(i) *General rule.*—Except as provided in paragraph (d)(5)(ii) or paragraph (d)(5)(iii) of this section, the commercial activities of an entity classified as a partnership for federal tax purposes will be attributable to its partners for purposes of section 892. For example, if an entity described in paragraph (a)(1)(i) or (ii) of this section holds an interest as a general partner in a partnership that is engaged in commercial activities, the partnership's commercial activities will be attributed to that entity for purposes of determining if the entity is a controlled commercial entity within the meaning of section 892(a)(2)(B) and paragraph (a) of this section.

(ii) *Trading activity exception.*—An entity not otherwise engaged in commercial activities will not be considered to be engaged in commercial activities solely because the entity is a member of a partnership (whether domestic or foreign) that effects transactions in stocks, bonds, other securities (as defined in § 1.892-3T(a)(3)), commodities (as defined in § 1.892-4(e)(1)(ii)), or financial instruments (as defined in § 1.892-3T(a)(4)) for the partnership's own account or solely because an employee of such partnership, or a broker, commission agent, custodian, or other agent, pursuant to discretionary authority granted by such partnership, effects such transactions for the account of the partnership. This exception shall not apply to any member in the case of a partnership that is a dealer in stocks, bonds, other securities, commodities, or financial instruments, as determined under the principles of § 1.864-2(c)(2)(iv)(a).

(iii) *Limited partner exception.*—(A) *General rule.*—An entity that is not otherwise engaged in commercial activities (including, for example, performing services for a partnership as described in section 707(a) or section 707(c)) will not be deemed to be engaged in commercial activities solely because it holds an interest as a limited partner in a limited partnership. Nevertheless, pursuant to sections 875, 882, and 892(a)(2)(A)(i), a foreign government member's distributive share of partnership income will not be exempt from taxation under section 892 to the extent that the partnership derived such income from the conduct of a commercial activity. For example, where a controlled entity described in § 1.892-2T(a)(3) that is not otherwise engaged in commercial activities holds an interest as a limited partner in a limited partnership that is a dealer in stocks, bonds, other securities, commodities, or financial instruments in the United States, although the controlled entity partner will not be deemed to be engaged in commercial activities solely because of its interest in the limited partnership, its distributive share of partnership income derived from the partnership's activity as a dealer will not be exempt from tax under section 892 because it was derived from the conduct of a commercial activity.

(B) *Interest as a limited partner in a limited partnership.*—Solely for purposes of paragraph (d)(5)(iii) of this section, an interest in an entity classified as a partnership for federal tax purposes shall be treated as an interest as a limited partner in a limited partnership if the holder of such interest does not have rights to participate in the management and conduct of the partnership's business at any time during the partnership's taxable year under the law of the jurisdiction in which the partnership is organized or under the governing agreement. Rights to participate in the management and conduct of a partnership's business do not include consent rights in the case of extraordinary events such as admission or expulsion of a general or limited partner, amendment of the partnership agreement, dissolution of the partnership, disposition of all or substantially all of the partnership's property outside of the ordinary course of the partnership's activities, merger, or conversion.

(iv) *Illustration.*—The following example illustrates the application of this paragraph (d)(5):

Example 1. K, a controlled entity of a foreign sovereign, has investments in various stocks and bonds of United States corporations and in a 20% interest in Opco, a limited liability company that is classified as a partnership for federal tax purposes. Under the governing agreement of Opco, K has the authority to participate in the management and conduct of Opco's business. Opco has investments in various stocks and bonds of United States corporations and also owns and manages an office building in New York. Because K has authority to participate in the management and conduct of Opco's business, its interest in Opco is not a limited partner interest. Therefore, K will be deemed to be engaged in commercial activities because of attribution of Opco's commercial activity, even if K does not actually make management decisions with regard to Opco's commercial activity, the operation of the office building. Accordingly, K is a controlled commercial entity, and all of its income, including its distributive share of partnership income from its interest in Opco and its income from the stocks and bonds it owns directly, will not be exempt from tax under section 892.

Example 2. The facts are the same as in *Example 1*, except that Opco has hired a real estate management firm to lease offices and manage the office building. Notwithstanding the fact that an independent contractor is performing the activities, Opco will still be deemed to be engaged in commercial activities. Accordingly, K is a controlled commercial entity, and all of its income, including its distributive share of partnership income from its interest in Opco and its income from the stocks and bonds it owns directly, will not be exempt from tax under section 892.

Example 3. The facts are the same as in *Example 1*, except that K is a member that has no right to participate in the management and conduct of Opco's business. Assume further that K is not otherwise engaged in commercial activities. Under paragraph (d)(5)(iii) of this section, Opco's commercial activities will not be attributed to K. Accordingly, K will not be a controlled commercial entity, and its income derived from the stocks and bonds it owns directly and the portion of its distributive share of partnership income from its interest in Opco that is derived from stocks and bonds will be exempt from tax under section 892. The portion of K's distributive share of partnership income from its interest in Opco that is derived from the operation of the office building will not be exempt from tax under section 892 and § 1.892-3T(a)(1).

(e) *Effective/applicability date.*—This section applies on the date these regulations are published as final regulations in the **FEDERAL REGISTER**. See § 1.892-5(a) as issued under TD 9012 (August 1, 2002) for rules that apply on or after January 14, 2002, and before the date these regulations are published as final regulations in the **FEDERAL REGISTER**. See § 1.892-5T(a) for rules that apply before January 14, 2002, and § 1.892-5T(b) through (d) for rules that apply before the date these regulations are published as final regulations in the **FEDERAL REGISTER**.

[Prop. Reg. § 1.892-5.]

[Proposed 11-3-2011 (corrected 11-23-2011).]

Proposed Amendments to Regulation

§ 1.892-5. Controlled commercial entity.—

* * *

(b) *Entities treated as engaged in commercial activity.*—(1) *United States real property holding corporations.*—(i) *General rule.*—Except as provided in paragraph (b)(1)(ii) of this section, a United States real property holding corporation as defined in section 897(c)(2), which may include a foreign corporation, is treated as engaged in commercial activity and, therefore, is a controlled commercial entity if the requirements of § 1.892-5T(a)(1) or (2) are satisfied.

(ii) *Exceptions.*—Paragraph (b)(1)(i) of this section does not apply to the following—

(A) A foreign corporation that is a qualified holder under § 1.897(l)-1(d); or

(B) A corporation that is a United States real property holding corporation, as defined in section 897(c)(2), solely by reason of its direct or indirect ownership interest in one or more other corporations that are not controlled by the foreign government (as determined under § 1.892-5T(a)).

(iii) *Applicability date.*—This paragraph (b)(1) applies to taxable years ending on or after December 28, 2022. For rules that apply to taxable years ending before December 28, 2022, see § 1.892-5T(b)(1), as contained in 26 CFR part 1, revised as of April 1, 2022.

(b)(2) through (d)(4). For further guidance, see § 1.892-5T(b)(2) through (d)(4).

* * *

[Prop. Reg. § 1.892-5.]

[Proposed 12-29-2022.]

Proposed Amendments to Regulation

§ 1.892-5T. Controlled commercial entity (temporary regulations).—

* * *

(b) * * *

(1)(i) For further guidance, see § 1.892-5(b)(1)(i).

(ii) For further guidance, see § 1.892-5(b)(1)(ii).

* * *

[Prop. Reg. § 1.892-5T.]

[Proposed 12-29-2022.]

§ 1.892-6T. Income of international organizations (Temporary).— (a) *Exempt from tax.*—Subject to the provisions of section 1 of the International Organizations Immunities Act (22 U.S.C. 288) (the provisions of which are set forth in paragraph (b)(3) of § 1.893-1), the income of an international organization (as defined in section 7701(a)(18)) received from investments in the United States in stocks, bonds, or other domestic securities, owned by such international organization, or from interest on deposits in banks in the United States of moneys belonging to such international organization, or from any other source within the United States, is exempt from Federal income tax.

(b) *Income received prior to Presidential designation.*—An organization designated by the President through appropriate Executive order as entitled to enjoy the privileges, exemptions, and immunities provided in the International Organizations Immunities Act may enjoy the benefits of the exemption with respect to income of the prescribed character received by such organization prior to the date of the issuance of such Executive order, if (i) the Executive order does not provide otherwise and (ii) the organization is a public international organization in which the United States participates, pursuant to a treaty or under the authority of an act of Congress authorizing such participation or making an appropriation for such participation, at the time such income is received. [Temporary Reg. § 1.892-6T.]

☐ [*T.D.* 8211, 6-24-88.]

§ 1.892-7T. Relationship to other Internal Revenue Code sections (Temporary).—(a) *Section 893.*—The term "foreign government" referred to in section 893 (relating to the exemption for compensation of employees of foreign governments) has the same meaning as given such term in § 1.892-2T.

(b) *Section 895.*—A foreign central bank of issue (as defined in § 1.895-1(b)) that fails to qualify for the exemption from tax provided by this section (for example, it is not wholly owned by a foreign sovereign) may nevertheless be exempt from tax on the items of income described in section 895.

(c) *Section 883(b).*—Nothing in section 892 or these regulations shall limit the exemption provided under section 883(b) relating generally to the exemption of earnings derived by foreign participants from the ownership or operation of communications satellite systems.

(d) *Section 884.*—Earnings and profits attributable to income of a controlled entity of a foreign sovereign which is exempt from taxation under section 892 shall not be subject to the tax imposed by section 884(a).

(e) *Sections 1441 and 1442.*—No withholding is required under sections 1441 and 1442 in the case of income exempt from taxation under section 892. [Temporary Reg. § 1.892-7T.]

☐ [*T.D.* 8211, 6-24-88.]

§ 1.893-1. Compensation of employees of foreign governments or international organizations.—(a) *Employees of foreign governments.*—(1) *Exempt from tax.*—Except to the extent that the exemption is limited by the execution and filing of the waiver provided for in section 247(b) of the Immigration and Nationality Act (8 U.S.C. 1257(b)), all employees of a foreign government (including consular or other officers, or nondiplomatic representatives) who are not citizens of the United States, or are citizens of the Republic of the Philippines (whether or not citizens of the United States), are exempt from Federal income tax with respect to wages, fees, or salaries received by them as compensation for official services rendered to such foreign government, provided (i) the services are of a character similar to those performed by employees of the Government of the United States in that foreign country and (ii) the foreign government whose employees are claiming exemption grants an equivalent exemption to employees of the Government of the United States performing similar services in that foreign country.

(2) *Certificate by Secretary of State.*—Section 893(b) provides that the Secretary of State shall certify to the Secretary of the Treasury the names of the foreign countries which grant an equivalent exemption to the employees of the Government of the United States performing services in such foreign countries, and the character of the services performed by employees of the Government of the United States in foreign countries.

(3) *Items not exempt.*—The income received by employees of foreign governments from sources other than their salaries, fees, or wages, referred to in subparagraph (1) of this paragraph, is subject to Federal income tax.

(4) *Immigration and Nationality Act.*—Section 247(b) of the Immigration and Nationality Act provides as follows:

Sec. 247. Adjustment of status of certain resident aliens. * * *

(b) The adjustment of status required by subsection (a) [of section 247 of the Immigration and Nationality Act] shall not be applicable in the case of any alien who requests that he be permitted to retain his status as an immigrant and who, in such form as the Attorney General may require, executes and files with the Attorney General a written waiver of all rights, privileges, exemptions, and immunities under any law or any executive order which would otherwise accrue to him because of the acquisition of an occupational status entitling him to a nonimmigrant status under paragraph (15)(A), (15)(E), or (15)(G) of section 101(a).

(5) *Effect of waiver.*—An employee of a foreign government who executes and files with the Attorney General the waiver provided for in section 247(b) of the Immigration and Nationality Act thereby waives the exemption conferred by section 893 of the Code. As a consequence, that exemption does not apply to income received by that alien after the date of filing of the waiver.

(6) *Citizens of the United States.*—The compensation of citizens of the United States (other than those who are also citizens of the Republic of the Philippines) who are officers or employees of a foreign government is not exempt from income tax pursuant to this paragraph. But see section 911 and the regulations thereunder.

(b) *Employees of international organizations.*—(1) *Exempt from tax.*—Except to the extent that the exemption is limited by the execution and filing of the waiver provided for in section 247(b) of the Immigration and Nationality Act and subject to the provisions of sections 1, 8, and 9 of the International Organizations Immunities Act (22 U.S.C. 288, 288e, 288f), wages, fees, or salary of any officer or employee of an international organization (as defined in section 7701(a)(18)) received as compensation for official services to that international organization is exempt from Federal income tax, if that officer or employee (i) is not a citizen of the United States or (ii) is a citizen of the Republic of the Philippines (whether or not a citizen of the United States).

(2) *Income earned prior to executive action.*—An individual of the prescribed class who receives wages, fees, or salary as compensation for official services to an organization designated by the President through appropriate Executive order as entitled to enjoy the privileges, exemptions, and immunities provided in the International Organizations Immunities Act and who has been duly notified to, and accepted by, the Secretary of State as an officer or employee of that organization, or who has been designated by the Secretary of State, prior to formal notification and acceptance, as a prospective officer or employee of that organization, may enjoy the benefits of the exemption with respect to compensation of the prescribed character earned by that individual, either prior to the date of the issuance of the Executive order, or prior to the date of the acceptance or designation by the Secretary of State, for official services to that organization, if (i) the Executive order does not provide otherwise, (ii) the organization is a public international organization in which the United States participates, pursuant to a treaty or under the authority of an act of Congress authorizing such participation or making an appropriation for such participation, at the time the compensation is earned, and (iii) the individual is an officer or employee of that organization at that time.

(3) *International Organizations Immunities Act.*—Sections 1, 8, and 9 of the International Organizations Immunities Act (22 U.S.C. 288, 288e, 288f) provide in part as follows:

Section 1. For the purposes of this title [International Organizations Immunities Act], the term "international organization" means a public international organization in which the United States participates pursuant to any treaty or under the authority of any Act of Congress authorizing such participation or making an appropriation for such participation, and which shall have been designated by the President through appropriate Executive order as being entitled to enjoy the privileges, exemptions, and immunities herein provided. The President shall be authorized, in the light of the functions performed by any such international organization, by appropriate Executive order to withhold or withdraw from any such organization or its officers or employees any of the privileges, exemptions, and immunities provided for in this title (including the amendments made by this title) or to condition or limit the enjoyment by any such organization or its officers or employees of any such privilege, exemption, or immunity. The President shall be authorized, if in his judgment such action should be justified by reason of the abuse by an international organization or its officers and employees of the privileges, exemptions, and immunities herein provided or for any other reason, at any time to revoke the designation of any international organization under this section, whereupon the international organization in question shall cease to be classed as an international organization for the purposes of this title.

* * *

Sec. 8. (a) No person shall be entitled to the benefits of this title [International Organizations Immunities Act] unless he (1) shall have been duly notified to and accepted by the Secretary of State as a * * * officer, or employee; or (2) shall have been designated by the Secretary of State, prior to formal notification and acceptance, as a prospective * * * officer, or employee; * * *

(b) Should the Secretary of State determine that the continued presence in the United States of any person entitled to the benefits of this title is not desirable, he shall so inform the * * * international organization concerned * * * and after such person shall have had a reasonable length of time, to be determined by the Secretary of State, to depart from the United States, he shall cease to be entitled to such benefits.

(c) No person shall, by reason of the provisions of this title, be considered as receiving diplomatic status or as receiving any of the privileges incident thereto other than such as are specifically set forth herein.

Sec. 9. The privileges, exemptions, and immunities of international organizations and of their officers and employees * * * provided for in this title [International Organizations Immunities Act], shall be granted notwithstanding the fact that the similar privileges, exemptions, and immunities granted to a foreign government, its officers, or employees, may be conditioned upon the existence of reciprocity by that foreign government: *Provided,* That nothing contained in this title shall be construed as precluding the Secretary of State from withdrawing the privileges, exemptions, and immunities herein provided from persons who are nationals of any foreign country on the ground that such country is failing to accord corresponding privileges, exemptions, and immunities to citizens of the United States.

(4) *Effect of waiver.*—An officer or employee of an international organization who executes and files with the Attorney General the waiver provided for in section 247(b) of the Immigration and Nationality Act (8 U.S.C. 1257(b)) thereby waives the exemption conferred by section 893 of the Code. As a consequence, that exemption does not apply to income received by that individual after the date of filing of the waiver.

(5) *Citizens of the United States.*—The compensation of citizens of the United States (other than those who are also citizens of the Republic of the Philippines) who are officers or employees of an international organization is not exempt from income tax pursuant to this paragraph. But see section 911 and the regulations thereunder.

(c) *Tax conventions, consular conventions, and international agreements.*—(1) *Exemption dependent upon internal revenue laws.*—A tax convention or consular convention between the United States and a foreign country, which provides that the United States may include in the tax base of its residents all income taxable under the internal revenue laws, and which makes no specific exception for the income of the employees of that foreign government, does not provide any exemption (with respect to residents of the United States) beyond that which is provided by the internal revenue laws. Accordingly, the effect of the execution and filing of a waiver under section 247(b) of the Immigration and Nationality Act by an employee of a foreign government which is a party to such a convention is to subject the employee to tax to the same extent as provided in paragraph (a)(5) of this section with respect to the waiver of exemption under section 893.

(2) *Exemption not dependent upon internal revenue laws.*—If a tax convention, consular convention, or international agreement provides that compensation paid by the foreign government or international organization to its employees is exempt from Federal income tax, and the application of this exemption is not dependent upon the provisions of the internal revenue laws, the exemption so conferred is not affected by the execution and filing of a waiver under section 247(b) of the Immigration and Nationality Act. For examples of exemptions which are not affected by the Immigration and Nationality Act, see article X of the income tax convention between the United States and the United Kingdom (60 Stat. 1383); article IX, section 9(b), of the Articles of Agreement of the International Monetary Fund (60 Stat. 1414); and article VII, section 9(b), of the Articles of Agreement of the International Bank for Reconstruction and Development (60 Stat. 1458). [Reg. § 1.893-1.]

☐ [*T.D. 6258, 10-23-57.*]

§ 1.894-1. Income affected by treaty.—(a) *Income exempt under treaty.*—Income of any kind is not included in gross income and is exempt from tax under subtitle A (relating to income taxes), to the extent required by any income tax convention to which the United States is a party. However, unless otherwise provided by an income tax convention, the exclusion from gross income under section 894(a) and this paragraph does not apply in determining the accumulated taxable income of a foreign corporation under section 535 and the regulations thereunder or the undistributed personal holding company income of a foreign corporation under section 545 and the regulations thereunder. Moreover, the distributable net income of a foreign trust is determined without regard to section 894 and this paragraph, to the extent provided by section 643(a)(6)(B). Further, the compensating tax adjustment required by section 819(a)(3) in the case of a foreign life insurance company is to be determined without regard to section 894 and this paragraph, to the extent required by section 819(a)(3)(A). See § 1.871-12 for the manner of determining the tax liability of a nonresident alien individual or foreign corporation whose gross income includes income on which the tax is reduced under a tax convention.

(b) *Taxpayer treated as having no permanent establishment in the United States.*—(1) *In general.*—A nonresident alien individual or a foreign corporation, that is engaged in trade or business in the United States through a permanent establishment located therein at any time during a taxable year beginning after December 31, 1966, shall be deemed not to have a permanent establishment in the United States at any time during that year for purposes of applying any exemption from, or reduction in the rate of, any tax under subtitle A of the Code which is provided by any income tax convention with respect to income which is not effectively connected for that year with the conduct of a trade or business in the United States by the taxpayer. This paragraph applies to all treaties or conventions entered into by the United States, whether entered into before, on, or after November

13, 1966, the date of enactment of the Foreign Investors Tax Act of 1966 (80 Stat. 1539). This paragraph is not considered to be contrary to any obligation of the United States under an income tax convention to which it is a party. The benefit granted under section 894(b) and this paragraph applies only to those items of income derived from sources within the United States which are subject to the tax imposed by section 871(a) or 881(a), and section 1441, 1442, or 1451, on the noneffectively connected income received from sources within the United States by a nonresident alien individual or a foreign corporation. The benefit does not apply to any income from real property in respect of which an election is in effect for the taxable year under § 1.871-10 or in determining under section 877(b) the tax of a nonresident alien individual who has lost United States citizenship at any time after March 8, 1965. The benefit granted by section 894(b) and this paragraph is not elective.

(2) *Illustrations.*—The application of this paragraph may be illustrated by the following examples:

Example (1). M, a corporation organized in foreign country X, uses the calendar year as the taxable year. The United States and country X are parties to an income tax convention which provides in part that dividends received from sources within the United States by a corporation of country X not having a permanent establishment in the United States are subject to tax under chapter 1 of the Code at a rate not to exceed 15 percent. During 1967, M is engaged in business in the United States through a permanent establishment located therein and receives $100,000 in dividends from domestic corporation B, which under section 861(a)(2)(A) constitute income from sources within the United States. Under section 864(c)(2) and § 1.864-4(c), the dividends received from B are not effectively connected for 1967 with the conduct of a trade or business in the United States by M. Although M has a permanent establishment in the United States during 1967, it is deemed, under section 894(b) and this paragraph, not to have a permanent establishment in the United States during that year with respect to the dividends. Accordingly, in accordance with paragraph (c)(3) of § 1.871-12 the tax on the dividends is $15,000, that is, 15 percent of $100,000, determined without the allowance of any deductions.

Example (2). T, a corporation organized in foreign country X, uses the calendar year as the taxable year. The United States and country X are parties to an income tax convention which provides in part that an enterprise of country X is not subject to tax under chapter 1 of the Code in respect of its industrial or commercial profits unless it is engaged in trade or business in the United States during the taxable year through a permanent establishment located therein and that, if it is so engaged, the tax may be imposed upon the entire income of that enterprise from sources within the United States. The convention also provides that the tax imposed by chapter 1 of the Code on dividends received from sources within the United States by a corporation of X which is not engaged in trade or business in the United States through a permanent establishment located therein shall not exceed 15 percent of the dividend. During 1967, T is engaged in a business (business A) in the United States which is carried on through a permanent establishment in the United States; in addition, T is engaged in a business (business B) in the United States which is not carried on through a permanent establishment. During 1967, T receives from sources within the United States $60,000 in service fees through the operation of business A and $10,000 in dividends through the operation of business B, both of which amounts are, under section 864(c)(2)(B), and § 1.864-4(c)(3), effectively connected for that year with the conduct of a trade or business in the United States by that corporation. The service fees are considered to be industrial or commercial profits under the tax convention with country X. Since T has no income for 1967 which is not effectively connected for that year with the conduct of a trade or business in the United States by that corporation, section 894(b), this paragraph, and § 1.871-12 do not apply. Accordingly, for 1967 T's entire income of $70,000 from sources within the United States is subject to tax, after allowance of deductions, in accordance with section 882(a)(1) and paragraph (b)(2) of § 1.882-1.

Example (3). S, a corporation organized in foreign country W, uses the calendar year as the taxable year. The United States and country W are parties to an income tax convention which provides in part that a corporation of country W is not subject to tax under chapter 1 of the Code in respect of its industrial or commercial profits unless it is engaged in trade or business in the United States during the taxable year through a permanent establishment located therein and that, if it is so engaged, the tax may be imposed upon the entire income of that corporation from sources within the United States. The convention also provides that the tax imposed by chapter 1 of the Code on dividends received from sources within the United States by a corporation of country W which is not engaged in trade or business in the United States through a permanent establishment located therein shall not exceed 15 percent of the dividend. During 1967, S is engaged in business in the United States through a permanent establishment located therein and derives from sources within the United States $100,000 in service fees which, under section 864(c)(2)(B) and § 1.864-4(c)(3), are effectively connected for that year with the conduct of a trade or business in the United States by S and which are considered to be industrial or commercial profits under the tax convention with country W. During 1967, S also derives from sources within the United States, through another business it carries on in foreign country X, $10,000 in sales income which, under section 864(c)(3) and § 1.864-4(b), is effectively connected for that year with the conduct of a trade or business in the United States by S and $5,000 in dividends which, under section 864(c)(2)(A) and § 1.864-4(c)(2), are not effectively connected for that year with the conduct of a trade or business in the United States by S. The sales income is considered to be industrial or commercial profits under the tax convention with country W. Although S is engaged in a trade or business in the United States during 1967 through a permanent establishment located therein, it is deemed, under section 894(b) and this paragraph, not to have a permanent establishment therein with respect to the $5,000 in dividends. Accordingly, in accordance with paragraph (c) of § 1.871-12, for 1967 S is subject to a tax of $750 on the dividends ($5,000 × .15) and a tax, determined under section 882(a) and § 1.882-1, on its $110,000 industrial or commercial profits.

Example (4). (a) N, a corporation organized in foreign country Z, uses the calendar year as the taxable year. The United States and country Z are parties to an income tax convention which provides in part that the tax imposed by chapter 1 of the Code on dividends received from sources within the United States by a corporation of country Z shall not exceed 15 percent of the amount distributed if the recipient does not have a permanent establishment in the United States or, where the recipient does have a permanent establishment in the United States, if the shares giving rise to the dividends are not effectively connected with the permanent establishment. The tax convention also provides that if a corporation of country Z is engaged in industrial or commercial activity in the United States through a permanent establishment in the United States, income tax may be imposed by the United States on so much of the industrial or commercial profits of such corporation as are attributable to the permanent establishment in the United States.

(b) During 1967, N is engaged in a business (business A) in the United States which is not carried on through a permanent establishment in the United States. In addition, N has a permanent establishment in the United States through which it carries on another business (business B) in the United States. During 1967, N holds shares of stock in domestic corporation D which are not effectively connected with N's permanent establishment in the United States. During 1967, N receives $100,000 in dividends from D which, pursuant to section 864(c)(2)(A) and § 1.864-4(c)(2), are effectively connected for that year with the conduct of business A. Under section 861(a)(2)(A) these dividends are treated as income from sources within the United States. In addition, during 1967, N receives from sources within the United States $150,000 in sales income which, pursuant to section 864(c)(3) and § 1.864-4(b), is effectively connected with the conduct of a trade or business in the United States and which is considered to be industrial or commercial profits under the tax convention with country Z. Of these total profits, $70,000 is from business A and $80,000 is from business B. Only the $80,000 of industrial or commercial profits is attributable to N's permanent establishment in the United States.

(c) Since N has no income for 1967 which is not effectively connected for that year with the conduct of a trade or business in the United States by that corporation, section 894(b) and this paragraph do not apply. However, N is entitled to the reduced rate of tax under the tax convention with country Z with respect to the dividends because the shares of stock are not effectively connected with N's permanent establishment in the United States. Accordingly, assuming that there are no deductions connected with N's industrial or commercial profits, the tax for 1967, determined as provided in paragraph (c) of § 1.871-12, is $46,900 as follows:

Tax on nontreaty income:	
$80,000 × .48	$38,400
Less $25,000 × .26	6,500
	31,900
Tax on treaty income:	
$100,000 (gross dividends) × .15	15,000
Total tax	$46,900

Example (5). M, a corporation organized in foreign country Z, uses the calendar year as the taxable year. The United States and country Z are parties to an income tax convention which provides in part that a corporation of country Z is not subject to tax under chapter 1 of the Code in respect of its commercial and industrial profits except such profits as are allocable to its permanent establishment in the United States. The regulations in this chapter under the tax convention with country Z provide that a corporation of country Z having a permanent establishment in the United States is subject to U.S. tax upon its industrial and commercial profits from sources within the United States and that its industrial and commercial profits from such sources are deemed to be allocable to the permanent establishment in the United States. During 1967, M is engaged in a business (business A) in the United States, which is carried on through a permanent establishment in the United States; in addition, M is engaged in a business (business B) in foreign country X and none of such business is carried on in the United States. During 1967, M receives from sources within the United States $40,000 in sales income through the operation of business A and $10,000 in sales income through the operation of business B, both of which amounts are, under section 864(c)(3) and § 1.864-4(b), effectively connected for that year with the conduct of a trade or business in the United States by that corporation. The sales income is considered to be industrial and commercial profits under the tax convention with country Z. Since M has no income for 1967 which is not effectively connected for that year with the conduct of a trade or business in the United States by that corporation, section 894(b) and this paragraph do not apply. Accordingly, for 1967 M's entire income of $50,000 from sources within the United States is subject to tax, after allowance of deductions, in accordance with section 882(a)(1) and paragraph (b)(2) of § 1.882-1.

(c)(1) *Substitute interest and dividend payments.*—The provisions of an income tax convention dealing with interest or dividends paid to or derived by a foreign person include substitute interest or dividend payments that have the same character as interest or dividends under § 1.864-5(b)(2)(ii), 1.871-7(b)(2) or 1.881-2(b)(2). The provisions of this paragraph (c) shall apply for purposes of securities lending transactions or sale-repurchase transactions as defined in § 1.861-2(a)(7) and § 1.861-3(a)(6).

(2) *Dividend equivalents.*—The provisions of an income tax convention relating to dividends paid to or derived by a foreign person apply to the payment of a dividend equivalent described in section 871(m) and the regulations thereunder.

(d) *Special rule for items of income received by entities.*—(1) *In general.*—The tax imposed by sections 871(a), 881(a), 1443, 1461, and 4948(a) on an item of income received by an entity, wherever organized, that is fiscally transparent under the laws of the United States and/or any other jurisdiction with respect to an item of income shall be eligible for reduction under the terms of an income tax treaty to which the United States is a party only if the item of income is derived by a resident of the applicable treaty jurisdiction. For this purpose, an item of income may be derived by either the entity receiving the item of income or by the interest holders in the entity or, in certain circumstances, both. An item of income paid to an entity shall be considered to be derived by the entity only if the entity is not fiscally transparent under the laws of the entity's jurisdiction, as defined in paragraph (d)(3)(ii) of this section, with respect to the item of income. An item of income paid to an entity shall be considered to be derived by the interest holder in the entity only if the interest holder is not fiscally transparent in its jurisdiction with respect to the item of income and if the entity is considered to be fiscally transparent under the laws of the interest holder's jurisdiction with respect to the item of income, as defined in paragraph (d)(3)(iii) of this section. Notwithstanding the preceding two sentences, an item of income paid directly to a type of entity specifically identified in a treaty as a resident of a treaty jurisdiction shall be treated as derived by a resident of that treaty jurisdiction.

(2) *Application to domestic reverse hybrid entities.*—(i) *In general.*—An income tax treaty may not apply to reduce the amount of federal income tax on U.S. source payments received by a domestic reverse hybrid entity. Further, notwithstanding paragraph (d)(1) of this section, the foreign interest holders of a domestic reverse hybrid entity are not entitled to the benefits of a reduction of U.S. income tax under an income tax treaty on items of income received from U.S. sources by such entity. A domestic reverse hybrid entity is a domestic entity that is treated as not fiscally transparent for U.S. tax purposes and as fiscally transparent under the laws of the interest holder's jurisdiction, with respect to the item of income received by the domestic entity.

(ii) *Payments by domestic reverse hybrid entities.*—(A) *General rule.*—Except as otherwise provided in paragraph (d)(2)(ii)(B) of this section, an item of income paid by a domestic reverse hybrid entity to an interest holder in such entity shall have the character of such item of income under U.S. law and shall be considered to be derived by the interest holder, provided the interest holder is not fiscally transparent in its jurisdiction, as defined in paragraph (d)(3)(iii) of this section, with respect to the item of income. In determining whether the interest holder is fiscally transparent with respect to the item of income under this paragraph (d)(2)(ii)(A), the determination under paragraph (d)(3)(ii) of this section shall be made based on the treatment that would have resulted had the item of income been paid by an entity that is not fiscally transparent under the laws of the interest holder's jurisdiction with respect to any item of income.

(B) *Payment made to related foreign interest holder.*—(*1*) *General rule.*—If—

(*i*) A domestic entity makes a payment to a related domestic reverse hybrid entity that is treated as a dividend under either the laws of the United States or the laws of the jurisdiction of a related foreign interest holder in the domestic reverse hybrid entity, and under the laws of the jurisdiction of the related foreign interest holder in the domestic reverse hybrid entity, the related foreign interest holder is treated as deriving its proportionate share of the payment under the principles of paragraph (d)(1) of this section; and

(*ii*) The domestic reverse hybrid entity makes a payment of a type that is deductible for U.S. tax purposes to the related foreign interest holder or to a person, wherever organized, the income and losses of which are available, under the laws of the jurisdiction of the related foreign interest holder, to offset the income and losses of the related foreign interest holder, and for which a reduction in U.S. withholding tax would be allowed under an applicable income tax treaty; then

(*iii*) To the extent the amount of the payment described in paragraph (d)(2)(ii)(B)(*1*)(*ii*) of this section does not exceed the sum of the portion of the payment described in paragraph (d)(2)(ii)(B)(*1*)(*i*) of this section treated as derived by the related foreign interest holder and the portion of any other prior payments described in paragraph (d)(2)(ii)(B)(*1*)(*i*) of this section treated as derived by the related foreign interest holder, the amount of the payment described in (d)(2)(ii)(B)(*1*)(*ii*) of this section will be treated for all purposes of the Internal Revenue Code and any applicable income tax treaty as a distribution within the meaning of section 301(a) of the Internal Revenue Code, and the tax to be withheld from the payment described in paragraph (d)(2)(ii)(B)(*1*)(*ii*) of this section (assuming the payment is a dividend under section 301(c)(1) of the Internal Revenue Code) shall be determined based on the appropriate rate of withholding that would be applicable to dividends paid from the domestic reverse hybrid entity to the related foreign interest holder in accordance with the principles of paragraph (d)(2)(ii)(A) of this section.

(*2*) *Determining amount to be recharacterized under paragraph (d)(2)(ii)(B)(1)(iii).*—For purposes of determining the amount to be recharacterized under paragraph (d)(2)(ii)(B)(*1*)(*iii*) of this section, the portion of the payment described in paragraph (d)(2)(ii)(B)(*1*)(*i*) of this section treated as derived by the related foreign interest holder shall be increased by the portion of the payment derived by any other person described in paragraph (d)(2)(ii)(B)(*1*)(*ii*), and shall be reduced by the amount of any prior section 301(c) distributions made by the domestic reverse hybrid entity to the related foreign interest holder or any other person described in paragraph (d)(2)(ii)(B)(*1*)(*ii*) and by the amount of any payments from the domestic reverse hybrid entity previously recharacterized under paragraph (d)(2)(ii)(B)(*1*)(*iii*) of this section.

(*3*) *Tiered entities.*—The principles of this paragraph (d)(2)(ii)(B) also shall apply to payments referred to in this paragraph (d)(2)(ii)(B) made among related entities when there is more than one domestic reverse hybrid entity or other fiscally transparent entity involved.

(*4*) *Definition of related.*—For purposes of this section, a person shall be treated as related to a domestic reverse hybrid entity if it is related by reason of the ownership requirements of section 267(b) or 707(b)(1), except that the language "at least 80 percent" applies instead of "more than 50 percent," where applicable. For purposes of determining whether a person is related by reason of the ownership requirements of section 267(b) or 707(b)(1), the constructive ownership rules of section 318 shall apply, and the attribution rules of section 267(c) also shall apply to the extent they attribute ownership to persons to whom section 318 does not attribute ownership.

(C) *Payments to persons not described in paragraph (d)(2)(ii)(B)(1)(ii).* (1) *Related persons.*—The Commissioner may treat a payment by a domestic reverse hybrid entity to a related person (who is neither the related foreign interest holder nor otherwise described in paragraph (d)(2)(ii)(B)(*1*)(*ii*) of this section), in whole or in part, as being made to a related foreign interest holder for purposes of applying paragraph (d)(2)(ii)(B) of this section, if—

(*i*) The payment to the related person is of a type that is deductible by the domestic reverse hybrid entity; and

(*ii*) The payment is made in connection with one or more transactions the effect of which is to avoid the application of paragraph (d)(2)(ii)(B) of this section.

(*2*) *Unrelated persons.*—The Commissioner may treat a payment by a domestic reverse hybrid entity to an unrelated person, in whole or in part, as being made to a related foreign interest holder for purposes of applying paragraph (d)(2)(ii)(B) of this section, if—

(*i*) The payment to the unrelated person is of a type that is deductible by the domestic reverse hybrid entity;

(*ii*) The unrelated person (or other person (whether related or not) which receives a payment in a series of transactions that includes a transaction involving such unrelated person) makes a payment to the related foreign interest holder (or other person described in paragraph (d)(2)(ii)(B)(*1*)(*ii*));

(*iii*) The foregoing payments are made in connection with a series of transactions which constitute a financing arrangement, as defined in § 1.881-3(a)(2)(i); and

(*iv*) The transactions have the effect of avoiding the application of paragraph (d)(2)(ii)(B) of this section.

(iii) *Examples.*—The rules of this paragraph (d)(2) are illustrated by the following examples:

Example 1. Dividend paid by unrelated entity to domestic reverse hybrid entity. (i) *Facts.* Entity A is a domestic reverse hybrid entity, as defined in paragraph (d)(2)(i) of this section, with respect to the U.S. source dividends it receives from B, a domestic corporation to which A is not related within the meaning of paragraph (d)(2)(ii)(B)(*4*) of this section. A's 85-percent shareholder, FC, is a corporation organized under the laws of Country X, which has an income tax treaty in effect with the United States. A's remaining 15-percent shareholder is an unrelated domestic corporation. Under Country X law, FC is not fiscally transparent with respect to the dividend, as defined in paragraph (d)(3)(ii) of this section. In year 1, A receives $100 of dividend income from B. Under Country X law, FC is treated as deriving $85 of the $100 dividend payment received by A. The applicable rate of tax on dividends under the U.S.-Country X income tax treaty is 5 percent with respect to a 10-percent or more corporate shareholder.

(ii) *Analysis.* Under paragraph (d)(2)(i) of this section, the U.S.-Country X income tax treaty does not apply to the dividend income received by A because the payment is made by B, a domestic corporation, to A, another domestic corporation. A remains fully taxable under the U.S. tax laws as a domestic corporation with regard to that item of income. Further, pursuant to paragraph (d)(2)(i) of this section, notwithstanding the fact that A is treated as fiscally transparent with respect to the dividend income under the laws of Country X, FC may not claim a reduced rate of taxation on its share of the U.S. source dividend income received by A.

Example 2. Interest paid by domestic reverse hybrid entity to related foreign interest holder where dividend is paid by unrelated entity. (i) *Facts.* The facts are the same as in *Example 1*. Both the United States and Country X characterize the payment by B in year 1 as a dividend. In addition, in year 2, A makes a payment of $25 to FC that is characterized under the Internal Revenue Code as interest on a loan from FC to A. Under the U.S.-Country X income tax treaty, the rate of tax on interest is zero. Under Country X laws, had the interest been paid by an entity that is not fiscally transparent under Country X's laws with respect to any item of income, FC would not be fiscally transparent as defined in paragraph (d)(2)(ii) of this section with respect to the interest.

(ii) *Analysis.* The analysis is the same as in *Example 1* with respect to the $100 payment from B to A. With respect to the $25 payment from A to FC, paragraph (d)(2)(ii)(B) of this section will not apply because, although FC is a related foreign interest holder in A, A is not related to B, the payor of the dividend income it received. Under paragraph (d)(2)(ii)(A) of this section, the $25 of interest paid by A to FC in year 2 is characterized under U.S. law as interest. Accordingly, in year 2, A is entitled to an interest deduction with respect to the $25 interest payment from A to FC, and FC is entitled to the reduced rate of withholding applicable to interest under the U.S.-Country X income tax treaty, assuming all other requirements for claiming treaty benefits are met.

Example 3. Interest paid by domestic reverse hybrid entity to related foreign interest holder where dividend is paid by a related entity. (i) *Facts.* The facts are the same as in *Example 2*, except the $100 dividend income received by A in year 1 is from A's wholly-owned subsidiary, S.

(ii) *Analysis.* The analysis is the same as in *Example 1* with respect to the $100 dividend payment from S to A. However, the $25 interest payment in year 2 by A to FC will be treated as a dividend for all purposes of the Internal Revenue Code and the U.S.-Country X income tax treaty because $25 does not exceed FC's share of the $100 dividend payment made by S to A ($85). Since FC is not fiscally transparent with respect to the payment as determined under paragraph (d)(2)(ii)(A) of this section, FC is entitled to the reduced rate applicable to dividends under the U.S.-Country X income tax treaty with respect to the $25 payment. Because the $25 payment in year 2 is recharacterized as a dividend for all purposes of the Internal Revenue Code and the U.S.-Country X income tax treaty, A is not entitled to an interest deduction with respect to that payment and FC is not entitled to claim the reduced rate of withholding applicable to interest.

Example 4. Definition of related foreign interest holder. (i) *Facts.* The facts are the same as in *Example 3*, except that A has two 50-percent shareholders, FC1 and FC2. In year 2, A makes an interest payment of $25 to both FC1 and FC2. FC1 is a corporation organized under the laws of Country X, which has an income tax treaty in effect with the United States. FC2 is a corporation organized under the laws of Country Y, which also has an income tax treaty in effect with the United States. FP owns 100-percent of both FC1 and FC2, and is organized under the laws of Country X. Under Country X law, FC1 is not fiscally transparent with respect to the dividend, as defined in paragraph (d)(3)(ii) of this section. Under Country X law, FC1 is treated as deriving $50 of the $100 dividend payment received by A because A is fiscally transparent under the laws of Country X, as determined under paragraph (d)(3)(iii) of this section. The applicable rate of tax on dividends under the U.S.-Country X income tax treaty is 5-percent with respect to a 10-percent or more corporate shareholder. Under Country Y law, FC2 is not treated as deriving any of the $100 dividend payment received by A because, under the laws of Country Y, A is not a fiscally transparent entity.

(ii) *Analysis.* The analysis is the same as in *Example 1* with respect to the $100 dividend payment from S to A. With respect to the $25 payment in year 2 by A to FC1, the payment will be treated as a dividend for all purposes of the Internal Revenue Code and the U.S.-Country X income tax treaty because FC1 is a related foreign interest holder as determined under paragraph (d)(2)(ii)(B)(*4*) of this section, and because $25 does not exceed FC1's share of the dividend payment made by S to A ($50). FC1 is a related foreign interest holder because FC1 is treated as owning the stock of A owned by FC2 under section 267(b)(3). Since FC1 is not fiscally transparent with respect to the payment as determined under paragraph (d)(2)(ii)(A) of this section, FC1 is entitled to the 5-percent reduced rate applicable to dividends under the U.S.-Country X income tax treaty with respect to the $25 payment. Because the $25 payment in year 2 is recharacterized as a dividend for all purposes of the Internal Revenue Code and the U.S.-Country X income tax treaty, A is not entitled to an interest deduction with respect to that payment. Even though FC2 is also a related foreign interest holder, the $25 interest payment by A to FC2 in year 2 is not recharacterized because A is not fiscally transparent under the laws of Country Y, and FC2 is not treated as deriving any of the $100 dividend payment received by A. Thus, the U.S.-Country Y income tax treaty is not implicated.

Example 5. Higher treaty withholding rate on dividends. (i) *Facts.* The facts are the same as in *Example 3*, except that under the U.S.-Country X income tax treaty, the rate of tax on interest is 10-percent and the rate of tax on dividends is 5-percent.

(ii) *Analysis.* The analysis is the same as in *Example 1* with respect to the $100 dividend payment from S to A. The analysis is the same as in *Example 3* with respect to the $25 interest payment in year 2 from A to FC.

Example 6. Foreign sister corporation the income and losses of which may offset the income and losses of related foreign interest holder. (i) *Facts.* The facts are the same as *Example 3*, except that in year 2, A makes the interest payment of $25 to FS, a subsidiary of FC also organized in Country X. Under the laws of Country X, FS is not fiscally transparent with respect to the interest payment, and the income and losses of FS may be used to offset the income and losses of FC.

(ii) *Analysis.* The analysis is the same as in *Example 1* with respect to the $100 dividend payment from S to A. With respect to the

$25 interest payment from A to FS in year 2, FS is a person described in paragraph (d)(2)(ii)(B)(*1*)(*ii*) of this section because the income and losses of FS may be used under the laws of Country X to offset the income and losses of FC, the related foreign interest holder that derived its proportionate share of the payment from S to A. Therefore, paragraph (d)(2)(ii)(B) of this section applies, and the $25 interest payment in year 2 by A to FS is treated as a dividend for all purposes of the Internal Revenue Code and the U.S.-Country X income tax treaty because the $25 payment does not exceed FC's share of the $100 dividend payment made by S to A ($85). Since FS is not fiscally transparent with respect to the payment as determined under paragraph (d)(2)(ii)(A) of this section, FS is entitled to obtain the rate applicable to dividends under the U.S.-Country X income tax treaty with respect to the $25 payment. Because the $25 payment in year 2 is recharacterized as a dividend for all purposes of the Internal Revenue Code and the U.S.-Country X income tax treaty, A is not entitled to an interest deduction with respect to the payment and FS is not entitled to claim the reduced rate of withholding applicable to interest under the U.S.-Country X income tax treaty.

Example 7. Interest paid by domestic reverse hybrid entity to unrelated foreign bank. (i) *Facts.* The facts are the same as in *Example 3*, except that in year 2, A makes the interest payment of $25 to FB, a Country Y unrelated foreign bank, on a loan from FB to A.

(ii) *Analysis.* The analysis is the same as in *Example 1* with respect to the $100 dividend payment from S to A. With respect to the payment from A to FB, paragraph (d)(2)(ii)(B) of this section will not apply because, although A is related to S, the payor of the dividend income it received, A is not related to FB under paragraph (d)(2)(ii)(B)(*4*) of this section. Under paragraph (d)(2)(ii)(A) of this section, the $25 interest payment made from A to FB in year 2 is characterized as interest under the Internal Revenue Code.

Example 8. Interest paid by domestic reverse hybrid to an unrelated entity pursuant to a financing arrangement. (i) *Facts.* The facts are the same as in *Example 7*, except that in year 3, FB makes an interest payment of $25 to FC on a deposit made by FC with FB.

(ii) *Analysis.* The analysis is the same as in *Example 1* with respect to the $100 dividend payment from S to A. With respect to the $25 payment from A to FB in year 2, because the payment is made in connection with a transaction that constitutes a financing arrangement within the meaning of paragraph (d)(2)(ii)(C)(*2*) of this section, the payment may be treated by the Commissioner as being made directly to FC. If the Commissioner disregards FB, then the analysis is the same as in *Example 3* with respect to the $25 interest payment in year 2 from A to FC.

Example 9. Royalty paid by related entity to domestic reverse hybrid entity. (i) *Facts.* The facts are the same as in *Example 3*, except the $100 income received by A from S in year 1 is a royalty payment under both the laws of the United States and the laws of Country X. The royalty rate under the treaty is 10 percent and the interest rate is 0 percent.

(ii) *Analysis.* The analysis as to the royalty payment from S to A is the same as in *Example 1* with respect to the $100 dividend payment from S to A. With respect to the $25 payment from A to FC, paragraph (d)(2)(ii)(B) of this section will not apply because the payment from S to A is not treated as a dividend under the Internal Revenue Code or the laws of Country X. Under paragraph (d)(2)(ii)(A) of this section, the $25 of interest paid by A to FC in year 2 is characterized as interest under the Internal Revenue Code. Accordingly, in year 2, FC may obtain the reduced rate of withholding applicable to interest under the U.S.-Country X income tax treaty, assuming all other requirements for claiming treaty benefits are met.

(3) *Definitions.*—(i) *Entity.*—For purposes of this paragraph (d), the term *entity* shall mean any person that is treated by the United States or the applicable treaty jurisdiction as other than an individual. The term *entity* includes disregarded entities, including single member disregarded entities with individual owners.

(ii) *Fiscally transparent under the law of the entity's jurisdiction.*—(A) *General rule.*—For purposes of this paragraph (d), an entity is fiscally transparent under the laws of the entity's jurisdiction with respect to an item of income to the extent that the laws of that jurisdiction require the interest holder in the entity, wherever resident, to separately take into account on a current basis the interest holder's respective share of the item of income paid to the entity, whether or not distributed to the interest holder, and the character and source of the item in the hands of the interest holder are determined as if such item were realized directly from the source from which realized by the entity. However, the entity will be fiscally transparent with respect to the item of income even if the item of income is not separately taken into account by the interest holder, provided the item of income, if separately taken into account by the interest holder, would not result in an income tax liability for that interest holder different from that which would result if the interest holder did not take the item into account separately, and provided the interest holder is required to take into account on a current basis the interest holder's share of all such nonseparately stated items of income paid to the entity, whether or not distributed to the interest holder. In determining whether an entity is fiscally transparent with respect to an item of income in the entity's jurisdiction, it is irrelevant that, under the laws of the entity's jurisdiction, the entity is permitted to exclude such item from gross income or that the entity is required to include such item in gross income but is entitled to a deduction for distributions to its interest holders.

(B) *Special definitions.*—For purposes of this paragraph (d)(3)(ii), an entity's jurisdiction is the jurisdiction where the entity is organized or incorporated or may otherwise be considered a resident under the laws of that jurisdiction. An interest holder will be treated as taking into account that person's share of income paid to an entity on a current basis even if such amount is taken into account by the interest holder in a taxable year other than the taxable year of the entity if the difference is due solely to differing taxable years.

(iii) *Fiscally transparent under the law of an interest holder's jurisdiction.*—(A) *General rule.*—For purposes of this paragraph (d), an entity is treated as fiscally transparent under the law of an interest holder's jurisdiction with respect to an item of income to the extent that the laws of the interest holder's jurisdiction require the interest holder resident in that jurisdiction to separately take into account on a current basis the interest holder's respective share of the item of income paid to the entity, whether or not distributed to the interest holder, and the character and source of the item in the hands of the interest holder are determined as if such item were realized directly from the source from which realized by the entity. However, an entity will be fiscally transparent with respect to the item of income even if the item of income is not separately taken into account by the interest holder, provided the item of income, if separately taken into account by the interest holder, would not result in an income tax liability for that interest holder different from that which would result if the interest holder did not take the item into account separately, and provided the interest holder is required to take into account on a current basis the interest holder's share of all such nonseparately stated items of income paid to the entity, whether or not distributed to the interest holder. An entity will not be treated as fiscally transparent with respect to an item of income under the laws of the interest holder's jurisdiction, however, if, under the laws of the interest holder's jurisdiction, the interest holder in the entity is required to include in gross income a share of all or a part of the entity's income on a current basis year under any type of anti-deferral or comparable mechanism. In determining whether an entity is fiscally transparent with respect to an item of income under the laws of an interest holder's jurisdiction, it is irrelevant how the entity is treated under the laws of the entity's jurisdiction.

(B) *Special definitions.*—For purposes of this paragraph (d)(3)(iii), an interest holder's jurisdiction is the jurisdiction where the interest holder is organized or incorporated or may otherwise be considered a resident under the laws of that jurisdiction. An interest holder will be treated as taking into account that person's share of income paid to an entity on a current basis even if such amount is taken into account by such person in a taxable year other than the taxable year of the entity if the difference is due solely to differing taxable years.

(iv) *Applicable treaty jurisdiction.*—The term *applicable treaty jurisdiction* means the jurisdiction whose income tax treaty with the United States is invoked for purposes of reducing the rate of tax imposed under sections 871(a), 881(a), 1461, and 4948(a).

(v) *Resident.*—The term *resident* shall have the meaning assigned to such term in the applicable income tax treaty.

(4) *Application to all income tax treaties.*—Unless otherwise explicitly agreed upon in the text of an income tax treaty, the rules contained in this paragraph (d) shall apply in respect of all income tax treaties to which the United States is a party. Notwithstanding the foregoing sentence, the competent authorities may agree on a mutual basis to depart from the rules contained in this paragraph (d) in appropriate circumstances. However, a reduced rate under a tax treaty for an item of U.S. source income paid will not be available irrespective of the provisions in this paragraph (d) to the extent that the applicable treaty jurisdiction would not grant a reduced rate

under the tax treaty to a U.S. resident in similar circumstances, as evidenced by a mutual agreement between the relevant competent authorities or by a public notice of the treaty jurisdiction. The Internal Revenue Service shall announce the terms of any such mutual agreement or public notice of the treaty jurisdiction. Any denial of tax treaty benefits as a consequence of such a mutual agreement or notice shall affect only payment of U.S. source items of income made after announcement of the terms of the agreement or of the notice.

(5) *Examples.*—This paragraph (d) is illustrated by the following examples.

Example 1. Treatment of entity treated as partnership by U.S. and country of organization. (i) *Facts.* Entity A is a business organization formed under the laws of Country X that has an income tax treaty in effect with the United States. A is treated as a partnership for U.S. federal income tax purposes. A is also treated as a partnership under the laws of Country X, and therefore Country X requires the interest holders in A to separately take into account on a current basis their respective shares of the items of income paid to A, whether or not distributed to the interest holders, and the character and source of the items in the hands of the interest holders are determined as if such items were realized directly from the source from which realized by A. A receives royalty income from U.S. sources that is not effectively connected with the conduct of a trade or business in the United States.

(ii) *Analysis.* A is fiscally transparent in its jurisdiction within the meaning of paragraph (d)(3)(ii) of this section with respect to the U.S. source royalty income in Country X and, thus, A does not derive such income for purposes of the U.S.-X income tax treaty.

Example 2. Treatment of interest holders in entity treated as partnership by U.S. and country of organization. (i) *Facts.* The facts are the same as under *Example 1.* A's partners are M, a corporation organized under the laws of Country Y that has an income tax treaty in effect with the United States, and T, a corporation organized under the laws of Country Z that has an income tax treaty in effect with the United States. M and T are not fiscally transparent under the laws of their respective countries of incorporation. Country Y requires M to separately take into account on a current basis M's respective share of the items of income paid to A, whether or not distributed to M, and the character and source of the items of income in M's hands are determined as if such items were realized directly from the source from which realized by A. Country Z treats A as a corporation and does not require T to take its share of A's income into account on a current basis whether or not distributed.

(ii) *Analysis.* M is treated as deriving its share of the U.S. source royalty income for purposes of the U.S.-Y income tax treaty because A is fiscally transparent under paragraph (d)(3)(iii) with respect to that income under the laws of Country Y. Under Country Z law, however, because T is not required to take into account its share of the U.S. source royalty income received by A on a current basis whether or not distributed, A is not treated as fiscally transparent. Accordingly, T is not treated as deriving its share of the U.S. source royalty income for purposes of the U.S.-Z income tax treaty.

Example 3. Dual benefits to entity and interest holder. (i) *Facts.* The facts are the same as under *Example 2*, except that A is taxable as a corporation under the laws of Country X. Article 12 of the U.S.-X income tax treaty provides for a source country reduced rate of taxation on royalties of 5-percent. Article 12 of the U.S.-Y income tax treaty provides that royalty income may only be taxed by the beneficial owner's country of residence.

(ii) *Analysis.* A is treated as deriving the U.S. source royalty income for purposes of the U.S.-X income tax treaty because it is not fiscally transparent with respect to the item of income within the meaning of paragraph (d)(3)(ii) of this section in Country X, its country of organization. M is also treated as deriving its share of the U.S. source royalty income for purposes of the U.S.-Y income tax treaty because A is fiscally transparent under paragraph (d)(3)(iii) of this section with respect to that income under the laws of Country Y. T is not treated as deriving the U.S. source royalty income for purposes of the U.S.-Z income tax treaty because under Country Z law A is not fiscally transparent. Assuming all other requirements for eligibility for treaty benefits have been satisfied, A is entitled to the 5-percent treaty reduced rate on royalties under the U.S.-X income tax treaty with respect to the entire royalty payment. Assuming all other requirements for treaty benefits have been satisfied, M is also entitled to a zero rate under the U.S.-Y income tax treaty with respect to its share of the royalty income.

Example 4. Treatment of grantor trust. (i) *Facts.* Entity A is a trust organized under the laws of Country X, which does not have an income tax treaty in effect with the United States. M, the grantor and owner of A for U.S. income tax purposes, is a resident of Country Y, which has an income tax treaty in effect with the United States. M is also treated as the grantor and owner of the trust under the laws of Country Y. Thus, Country Y requires M to take into account all items of A's income in the taxable year, whether or not distributed to M, and determines the character of each item in M's hands as if such item was realized directly from the source from which realized by A. Country X does not treat M as the owner of A and does not require M to account for A's income on a current basis whether or not distributed to M. A receives interest income from U.S. sources that is neither portfolio interest nor effectively connected with the conduct of a trade or business in the United States.

(ii) *Analysis.* A is not fiscally transparent under the laws of Country X within the meaning of paragraph (d)(3)(ii) of this section with respect to the U.S. source interest income, but A may not claim treaty benefits because there is no U.S.-X income tax treaty. M, however, does derive the income for purposes of the U.S.-Y income tax treaty because under the laws of Country Y, A is fiscally transparent.

Example 5. Treatment of complex trust. (i) *Facts.* The facts are the same as in *Example 4* except that M is treated as the owner of the trust only under U.S. tax law, after application of section 672(f), but not under the law of Country Y. Although the trust document governing A does not require that A distribute any of its income on a current basis, some distributions are made currently to M. There is no requirement under Country Y law that M take into account A's income on a current basis whether or not distributed to him in that year. Under the laws of Country Y, with respect to current distributions, the character of the item of income in the hands of the interest holder is determined as if such item were realized directly from the source from which realized by A. Accordingly, upon a current distribution of interest income to M, the interest income retains its source as U.S. source income.

(ii) *Analysis.* M does not derive the U.S. source interest income because A is not fiscally transparent under paragraph (d)(3)(ii) of this section with respect to the U.S. source interest income under the laws of Country Y. Although the character of the interest in the hands of M is determined as if realized directly from the source from which realized by A, under the laws of Country Y, M is not required to take into account his share of A's interest income on a current basis whether or not distributed. Accordingly, neither A nor M is entitled to claim treaty benefits, since A is a resident of a non-treaty jurisdiction and M does not derive the U.S. source interest income for purposes of the U.S.-Y income tax treaty.

Example 6. Treatment of interest holders required to include passive income under anti-deferral regime. (i) *Facts.* The facts are the same as under *Example 2.* However, Country Z does require T, who is treated as owning 60-percent of the stock of A, to take into account its respective share of the royalty income of A under an anti-deferral regime applicable to certain passive income of controlled foreign corporations.

(ii) *Analysis.* T is still not eligible to claim treaty benefits with respect to the royalty income. T is not treated as deriving the U.S. source royalty income for purposes of the U.S.-Z income tax treaty under paragraph (d)(3)(iii) of this section because T is only required to take into account its pro rata share of the U.S. source royalty income by reason of Country Z's anti-deferral regime.

Example 7. Treatment of contractual arrangements operating as collective investment vehicles. (i) *Facts.* A is a contractual arrangement without legal personality for all purposes under the laws of Country X providing for joint ownership of securities. Country X has an income tax treaty in effect with the United States. A is a collective investment fund which is of a type known as a Common Fund under Country X law. Because of the absence of legal personality in Country X of the arrangement, A is not liable to tax as a person at the entity level in Country X and is thus not a resident within the meaning of the Residence Article of the U.S.-X income tax treaty. A is treated as a partnership for U.S. income tax purposes and receives U.S. source dividend income. Under the laws of Country X, however, investors in A only take into account their respective share of A's income upon distribution from the Common Fund. Some of A's interest holders are residents of Country X and some of Country Y. Country Y has no income tax treaty in effect with the United States.

(ii) *Analysis.* A is not fiscally transparent under paragraph (d)(3)(ii) of this section with respect to the U.S. source dividend income because the interest holders in A are not required to take into account their respective shares of such income in the taxable year whether or not distributed. Because A is an arrangement without a legal personality that is not considered a person in Country X and thus not a resident of Country X under the Residence Article of the U.S.-X income tax treaty, however, A does not derive the income as a resident of Country X for purposes of the U.S.-X income tax treaty.

Further, because A is not fiscally transparent under paragraph (d)(3)(iii) of this section with respect to the U.S. source dividend income, A's interest holders that are residents of Country X do not derive the income as residents of Country X for purposes of the U.S.-X income tax treaty.

Example 8. Treatment of person specifically listed as resident in applicable treaty. (i) *Facts.* The facts are the same as in *Example 7* except that A (the Common Fund) is organized in Country Z and the Residence Article of the U.S.-Z income tax treaty provides that "the term 'resident of a Contracting State' includes, in the case of Country Z, Common Funds . . . "

(ii) *Analysis.* A is treated, for purposes of the U.S.-Z income tax treaty as deriving the dividend income as a resident of Country Z under paragraph (d)(1) of this section because the item of income is paid directly to A, A is a Common Fund under the laws of Country Z, and Common Funds are specifically identified as residents of Country Z in the U.S.-Z treaty. There is no need to determine whether A meets the definition of fiscally transparent under paragraph (d)(3)(ii) of this section.

Example 9. Treatment of investment company when entity receives distribution deductions, and all distributions sourced by residence of entity. (i) *Facts.* Entity A is a business organization formed under the laws of Country X, which has an income tax treaty in effect with the United States. A is treated as a partnership for U.S. income tax purposes. Under the laws of Country X, A is an investment company taxable at the entity level and a resident of Country X. It is also entitled to a distribution deduction for amounts distributed to its interest holders on a current basis. A distributes all its net income on a current basis to its interest holders and, thus, in fact, has no income tax liability to Country X. A receives U.S. source dividend income. Under Country X law, all amounts distributed to interest holders of this type of business entity are treated as dividends from sources within Country X and Country X imposes a withholding tax on all payments by A to foreign persons. Under Country X laws, the interest holders in A do not have to separately take into account their respective shares of A's income on a current basis if such income is not, in fact, distributed.

(ii) *Analysis.* A is not fiscally transparent under paragraph (d)(3)(ii) of this section with respect to the U.S. source dividends because the interest holders in A do not have to take into account their respective share of the U.S. source dividends on a current basis whether or not distributed. A is also not fiscally transparent under paragraph (d)(3)(ii) of this section because there is a change in source of the income received by A when A distributes the income to its interest holders and, thus, the character and source of the income in the hands of A's interest holder are not determined as if such income were realized directly from the source from which realized by A. Accordingly, A is treated as deriving the U.S. source dividends for purposes of the U.S.-Country X treaty.

Example 10. Item by item determination of fiscal transparency. (i) *Facts.* Entity A is a business organization formed under the laws of Country X, which has an income tax treaty in effect with the United States. A is treated as a partnership for U.S. income tax purposes. Under the laws of Country X, A is an investment company taxable at the entity level and a resident of Country X. It is also entitled to a distribution deduction for amounts distributed to its interest holders on a current basis. A receives both U.S. source dividend income and interest income from U.S. sources that is neither portfolio interest nor effectively connected with the conduct of a trade or business in the United States. Country X law sources all distributions attributable to dividend income based on the residence of the investment company. In contrast, Country X law sources all distributions attributable to interest income based on the residence of the payor of the interest. No withholding applies with respect to distributions attributable to U.S. source interest and the character of the distributions attributable to the interest income remains the same in the hands of A's interest holders as if such items were realized directly from the source from which realized by A. However, under Country X law the interest holders in A do not have to take into account their respective share of the interest income received by A on a current basis whether or not distributed.

(ii) *Analysis.* An item by item analysis is required under paragraph (d) of this section. The analysis is the same as *Example 9* with respect to the dividend income. A is also not fiscally transparent under paragraph (d)(3)(ii) of this section with respect to the interest income because, although the character of the distributions attributable to the interest income in the hands of A's interest holders is determined as if realized directly from the source from which realized by A, under Country X law the interest holders in A do not have to take into account their respective share of the interest income received by A on a current basis whether or not distributed. Accordingly, A derives the U.S. source interest income for purpose of the U.S.-X treaty.

Example 11. Treatment of charitable organizations. (i) *Facts.* Entity A is a corporation organized under the laws of Country X that has an income tax treaty in effect with the United States. Entity A is established and operated exclusively for religious, charitable, scientific, artistic, cultural, or educational purposes. Entity A receives U.S. source dividend income from U.S. sources. A provision of Country X law generally exempts Entity A's income from Country X tax due to the fact that Entity A is established and operated exclusively for religious, charitable, scientific, artistic, cultural, or educational purposes. But for such provision, Entity A's income would be taxed by Country X.

(ii) *Analysis.* Entity A is not fiscally transparent under paragraph (d)(3)(ii) of this section with respect to the U.S. source dividend income because, under Country X law, the dividend income is treated as an item of income of A and no other persons are required to take into account their respective share of the item of income on a current basis, whether or not distributed. Accordingly, Entity A is treated as deriving the U.S. source dividend income.

Example 12. Treatment of pension trusts. (i) *Facts.* Entity A is a trust established and operated in Country X exclusively to provide pension or other similar benefits to employees pursuant to a plan. Entity A receives U.S. source dividend income. A provision of Country X law generally exempts Entity A's income from Country X tax due to the fact that Entity A is established and operated exclusively to provide pension or other similar benefits to employees pursuant to a plan. Under the laws of Country X, the beneficiaries of the trust are not required to take into account their respective share of A's income on a current basis, whether or not distributed and the character and source of the income in the hands of A's interest holders are not determined as if realized directly from the source from which realized by A.

(ii) *Analysis.* A is not fiscally transparent under paragraph (d)(3)(ii) of this section with respect to the U.S. source dividend income because under the laws of Country X, the beneficiaries of A are not required to take into account their respective share of A's income on a current basis, whether or not distributed. A is also not fiscally transparent under paragraph (d)(3)(ii) of this section with respect to the U.S. source dividend income because under the laws of Country X, the character and source of the income in the hands of A's interest holders are not determined as if realized directly from the source from which realized by A. Accordingly, A derives the U.S. source dividend income for purposes of the U.S.-X income tax treaty.

(6) *Effective dates.*—This paragraph (d) applies to items of income paid on or after June 30, 2000, except paragraphs (d)(2)(ii) and (d)(2)(iii) of this section apply to items of income paid by a domestic reverse hybrid entity on or after June 12, 2002 with respect to amounts received by the domestic reverse hybrid entity on or after June 12, 2002.

(e) *Effective/applicability date.*—Paragraphs (a) and (b) of this section apply for taxable years beginning after December 31, 1966. For corresponding rules applicable to taxable years beginning before January 1, 1967, (see 26 CFR part 1 revised April 1, 1971). Paragraph (c)(1) of this section applies to payments made after November 13, 1997. Paragraph (c)(2) of this section applies to payments made on or after December 5, 2013. See paragraph (d)(6) of this section for applicability dates for paragraph (d) of this section. [Reg. § 1.894-1.]

☐ [*T.D.* 6258, 10-23-57. *Amended by T.D.* 7293, 11-27-73; *T.D.* 8735, 10-6-97; *T.D.* 8889, 6-30-2000 (*corrected* 12-7-2000); *T.D.* 8999, 6-11-2002 *and T.D.* 9648, 12-4-2013.]

Proposed Amendments to Regulation

§ 1.894-1. Income affected by treaty.

* * *

(d) *Income from a global dealing operation.*—If a taxpayer that is engaged in a global dealing operation, as defined in § 1.482-8(a)(2)(i), has a permanent establishment in the United States under the principles of an applicable U.S. income tax treaty, the principles of § 1.863-3(h), § 1.864-4(c)(2)(iv), § 1.864-4(c)(3)(ii), § 1.864-4(c)(5)(vi)(a) or § 1.864-6(b)(2)(ii)(*d*)(3) shall apply for purposes of determining the income attributable to that U.S. permanent establishment.

* * *

[Prop. Reg. § 1.894-1.]

[Proposed 3-6-98.]

§1.897-1. Taxation of foreign investment in United States real property interests, definition of terms.—(a) *In general.*—(1) *Purpose and scope of regulations.*—These regulations provide guidance with respect to the taxation of foreign investment in U.S. real property interests and related matters. This section defines various terms for purposes of sections 897, 1445, and 6039C and the regulations thereunder. Section 1.897-2 provides rules regarding the definition of, and consequences of, U.S. real property holding corporation status. Section 1.897-3 sets forth rules pursuant to which certain foreign corporations may elect under section 897(i) to be treated as domestic corporations for purposes of sections 897 and 6039C. Finally, §1.897-4 provides rules concerning the similar election under section 897(k) for certain foreign corporations in the process of liquidation.

(2) *Effective date.*—The regulations set forth in §§1.897-1 through 1.897-4 are effective for transactions occurring after June 18, 1980. However, with respect to all transactions occurring after June 18, 1980, and before January 30, 1985, taxpayers may at their option choose to apply the Temporary Regulations under section 897 (in their entirety). The Temporary Regulations are located at 26 CFR §§6a. 897-1 through 6a. 897-4 (Revised as of April 1, 1983), and were originally published in the *Federal Register* for September 21, 1982 (47 FR 41532) and amended by T.D. 7890, published in the *Federal Register* on April 28, 1983 (48 FR 19163).

(b) *Real property.*—(1) *In general.*—The term "real property" includes the following three categories of property: Land and unsevered natural products of the land, improvements, and personal property associated with the use of real property. The three categories of real property are defined in subparagraphs (2), (3), and (4) of this paragraph (b). Local law definitions will not be controlling for purposes of determining the meaning of the term "real property" as it is used in sections 897, 1445, and 6039C and the regulations thereunder.

(2) *Land and unsevered natural products of the land.*—The term "real property" includes land, growing crops and timber, and mines, wells, and other natural deposits. Crops and timber cease to be real property at the time that they are severed from the land. Ores, minerals, and other natural deposits cease to be real property when they are extracted from the ground. The storage of severed or extracted crops, timber, or minerals in or upon real property will not cause such property to be recharacterized as real property.

(3) *Improvements.*—(i) *In general.*—The term "real property" includes improvements on land. An improvement is a building, any other inherently permanent structure, or the structural components of either, as defined in subdivisions (ii) through (iv) of this paragraph (b)(3).

(ii) *Building.*—The term "building" generally means any structure or edifice enclosing a space within its walls, and usually covered by a roof, the purpose of which is, for example, to provide shelter or housing or to provide working, office, parking, display, or sales space. The term includes, for example, structures such as apartment houses, factory and office buildings, warehouses, barns, garages, railway or bus stations, and stores. Any structure that is classified as a building for purposes of section 48(a)(1)(B) and §1.48-1 shall be treated as such for purposes of this section.

(iii) *Inherently permanent structure.*—(A) *In general.*—The term "inherently permanent structure" means any property not otherwise described in this paragraph (b)(3) that is affixed to real property and that will ordinarily remain affixed for an indefinite period of time. Property that is not classified as a building for purposes of section 48(a)(1)(B) and §1.48-1 may nevertheless constitute an inherently permanent structure. For purposes of this section, affixation to real property may be accomplished by weight alone.

(B) *Use of precedents under section 48.*—Any property not otherwise described in this paragraph (b)(3) that constitutes "other tangible property" under the principles of section 48(a)(1)(B) and §1.48-1(c) and (d) shall be treated for purposes of this section as an inherently permanent structure. Thus, for example, the term includes swimming pools, paved parking areas and other pavements, special foundations for heavy equipment, wharves and docks, bridges, fences, inherently permanent advertising displays, inherently permanent outdoor lighting facilities, railroad tracks and signals, telephone poles, permanently installed telephone and television cables, broadcasting towers, oil derricks, oil and gas pipelines, oil and gas storage tanks, grain storage bins, and silos. However, property that is determined to be either property in the nature of machinery under §1.48-1(c) or property which is essentially an item of machinery or equipment under §1.48-1(e)(1)(i) shall not be treated as an inherently permanent structure.

(C) *Absence of precedents under section 48.*—Where precedents developed under the principles of section 48 fail to provide adequate guidance with respect to the classification of particular property, the determination of whether such property constitutes an inherently permanent structure shall be made in view of all the facts and circumstances. In particular, the following factors must be taken into account:

(1) The manner in which the property is affixed to real property;

(2) Whether the property was designed to be easily removable or to remain in place indefinitely;

(3) Whether the property has been moved since its initial installation;

(4) Any circumstances that suggest the expected period of affixation (e.g., a lease that requires removal of the property upon its expiration);

(5) The amount of damage that removal of the property would cause to the property itself or to the real property to which it is affixed; and

(6) The extent of the effort that would be required to remove the property, in terms of time and expense.

(iv) *Structural components of buildings and other inherently permanent structures.*—Structural components of buildings and other inherently permanent structures, as defined in §1.48-1(e)(2), themselves constitute improvements. Structural components include walls, partitions, floors, ceilings, windows, doors, wiring, plumbing, central heating and central air conditioning systems, lighting fixtures, pipes, ducts, elevators, escalators, sprinkler systems, fire escapes, and other components relating to the operation or maintenance of a building. However, the term "structural components" does not include machinery the sole justification for the installation of which is the fact that such machinery is required to meet temperature or humidity requirements which are essential for the operation of other machinery or the processing of materials or foodstuffs. Machinery may meet the "sole justification" test provided by the preceding sentence even though it incidentally provides for the comfort of employees or serves to an insubstantial degree areas where such temperature or humidity requirements are not essential.

(4) *Personal property associated with the use of the real property.*—(i) *In general.*—The term "real property" includes movable walls, furnishings, and other personal property associated with the use of the real property. Personal property is associated with the use of real property only if it is described in one of the categories set forth in subdivisions (A) through (D) of this paragraph (b)(4)(i). "Personal property" for purposes of this section means any property that constitutes "tangible personal property" under the principles of §1.48-1(c), without regard to whether such property qualifies as section 38 property. Such property will be associated with the use of the real property only where both the personal property and the United States real property interest with which it is associated are held by the same person or by related persons within the meaning of §1.897-1(i). For purposes of this paragraph (b)(4)(i), property is used "predominantly" in a named activity if it is devoted to that activity during at least half of the time in which it is in use during a calendar year.

(A) *Property used in mining, farming, and forestry.*—Personal property is associated with the use of real property if it is predominantly used to exploit unsevered natural products in or upon the land. Such property includes mining equipment used to extract ores, minerals, and other natural deposits from the ground. It also includes any property used to cultivate the soil and harvest its products, such as farm machinery, draft animals, and equipment used in the growing and cutting of timber. However, personal property used to process or transport minerals, crops, or timber after they are severed from the land is not associated personal property.

(B) *Property used in the improvement of real property.*—Personal property is associated with the use of real property if it is predominantly used to construct or otherwise carry out improvements to real property. Such property includes equipment used to alter the natural contours of the land, equipment used to clear and prepare raw land for construction, and equipment used to carry out the construction of improvements.

(C) *Property used in the operation of a lodging facility.*—Personal property is associated with the use of real property if it is predominantly used in connection with the operation of a lodging facility. Property that is used in connection with the operation of a lodging facility includes property used in the living quarters of such facility, such as beds and other furniture, refrigerators, ranges and other equipment, as well as property used in the common areas of such facility, such as lobby furniture and laundry equipment. Such property constitutes personal property associated with the use of real property in the hands of the owner or operator of the facility, not of the tenant or guest. A lodging facility is an apartment house or apartment, hotel, motel, dormitory, residence, or any other facility (or part of a facility) predominantly used to provide, at a charge, living and/or sleeping accommodations, whether on a daily, weekly, monthly, annual, or other basis. The term "lodging facility" does not include a personal residence occupied solely by its owner, or a facility used primarily as a means of transportation (such as an aircraft, vessel, or a railroad car) or used primarily to provide medical or convalescent services, even though sleeping accommodations are provided. Nor does the term include temporary living quarters provided by an employer due to the unavailability of lodgings within a reasonable distance of a worksite (such as a mine or construction project). The term "lodging facility" does not include any portion of a facility that constitutes a nonlodging commercial facility and that is available to persons not using the lodging facility on the same basis that it is available to tenants of the lodging facility. Examples of nonlodging commercial facilities include restaurants, drug stores, and grocery stores located in a lodging facility.

(D) *Property used in the rental of furnished office and other work space.*—Personal property is associated with the use of real property if it is predominantly used by a lessor to provide furnished office or other work space to lessees. Property that is so used includes office furniture and equipment included in the rental of furnished space. Such property constitutes personal property associated with the use of real property in the hands of the lessor, not of the lessee.

(ii) *Dispositions of associated personal property.*—(A) *In general.*—Personal property that has become associated with the use of a real property interest shall itself be treated as real property interest upon its disposition, unless either:

(1) The personal property is disposed of more than one year before the disposition of any present right to use or occupy the real property with which it was associated (and subject to the provisions of subdivision (B) of this paragraph (b)(4)(ii));

(2) The personal property is disposed of more than one year after the disposition of all present rights to use or occupy the real property with which it was associated (and subject to the provisions of subdivision (C) of this paragraph (b)(4)(ii)); or

(3) The personal property and the real property with which it was associated are separately sold to persons that are related neither to the transferor nor to one another (and subject to the provisions of subdivision (D) of this paragraph (b)(4)(ii)).

(B) *Personalty disposed of one year before realty.*—A transferor of personal property associated with the use of real property need not treat such property as a real property interest upon disposition if on the date of disposition the transferor does not expect or intend to dispose of the real property until more than one year later. However, if the real property is in fact disposed of within the following year, the transferor must treat the personal property as having been a real property interest as of the date on which the personalty was disposed of. If the transferor had not previously filed an income tax return, a return must be filed and tax paid, together with any interest due thereon, by the later of the date on which a tax return or payment is actually due (with extensions), or the 60th day following the date of disposition. If the transferor had previously filed an income tax return, an amended return must be filed and tax paid, together with any interest due thereon, by the later of the dates specified above. Such a transferor may be liable to penalties for failure to file, for late payment of tax, or for understatement of liability, but only if the transferor knew or had reason to anticipate that the real property would be disposed of within one year of the disposition of the associated personal property.

(C) *Personalty disposed of one year after realty.*—A disposition of real property shall be disregarded for purposes of subdivision (A)(2) of this paragraph (b)(4)(ii) if any right to use or occupy the real property is reacquired within the one-year period referred to in that subdivision. However, the disposition shall not be disregarded if such reacquisition is made in foreclosure of a mortgage or other security interest, in the exercise of a contractual remedy, or in the enforcement of a judgment. If, however, the reacquisition of the property is made pursuant to a plan the principal purpose of which is the avoidance of the provisions of section 897, 1445, or 6039C and the regulations thereunder, then the initial disposition shall be disregarded for purposes of subdivision (A)(2) of this paragraph (b)(4)(ii).

(D) *Separate dispositions of personalty and realty.*—A transferor of personal property associated with the use of real property need not treat such property as a real property interest upon disposition if within 90 days before or after such disposition the transferor separately disposes of the real property interest to persons that are related neither to the transferor nor to the purchaser of the personal property. A transferor may rely upon this rule unless the transferor knows or has reason to know that the purchasers of the real property and the personal property—

(1) Are related persons; or

(2) Intend to reassociate the personal property with the use of the real property within one year of the date of disposition of the personal property.

(E) *Status of property in hands of transferee.*—Personal property that has been associated with the use of real property and that is sold to an unrelated party will be treated as real property in the hands of the transferee only if the personal property becomes associated with the use of real property held or acquired by the transferee, in the manner described in paragraph (b)(4)(i) of this section.

(iii) *Determination dates.*—The determination of whether personal property is personal property associated with the use of real property as defined in this paragraph (b)(4) is to be made on the date the personal property is disposed of and on each applicable determination date. See § 1.897-2(c).

(c) *United States real property interest.*—(1) *In general.*—The term "United States real property interest" means any interest, other than an interest solely as a creditor, in either:

(i) Real property located in the United States or the Virgin Islands, or

(ii) A domestic corporation unless it is established that the corporation was not a U.S. real property holding corporation within the period described in section 897(c)(1)(A)(ii).

In addition, for the limited purpose of determining whether any corporation is a U.S. real property holding corporation, the term "United States real property interest" means an interest, other than an interest solely as a creditor, in a foreign corporation unless it is established that the foreign corporation is not a U.S. real property holding corporation within the period prescribed in section 897(c)(1)(A)(ii). See § 1.897-2 for rules regarding the manner of establishing that a corporation is not a United States real property holding corporation.

(2) *Exceptions and special rules.*—(i) *Domestically-controlled REIT.*—An interest in a domestically-controlled real estate investment trust (REIT) is not a U.S. real property interest. A domestically-controlled REIT is one in which less than 50 percent of the fair market value of the outstanding stock was directly or indirectly held by foreign persons during the five-year period ending on the applicable determination date (or the period since June 18, 1980, if shorter). For purposes of this determination the actual owners of stock, as determined under § 1.857-8, must be taken into account.

(ii) *Corporation that has disposed of all U.S. real property interests.*—The term "United States real property interest" does not include an interest in a corporation which has disposed of all its U.S. real property interests in transactions in which the full amount of gain, if any, was recognized, as provided in section 897(c)(1)(B). See § 1.897-2(f) for rules regarding the requirements of section 897(c)(1)(B).

(iii) *Publicly-traded corporations.*—If, at any time during the calendar year, any class of stock of a domestic corporation is regularly traded on an established securities market, an interest in such corporation shall be treated as a U.S. real property interest only in the case of:

(A) A regularly traded interest owned by a person who beneficially owned more than 5 percent of the total fair market value of that class of interests at any time during the five-year period ending either on the date of disposition of such interest or other applicable determination date (or the period since June 18, 1980, if shorter), or

(B) [Reserved]

(iv) *Publicly traded partnerships and trusts.*—If any class of interests in a partnership or trust is, within the meaning of § 1.897-1(m) and (n), regularly traded on an established securities market, then for purposes of sections 897(g) and 1445 and § 1.897-2(d) and (e) an interest in the entity shall not be treated as an interest in a partnership or trust. Instead, such an interest shall be subject to the rules applicable to interests in publicly traded corporations pursuant to paragraph (c)(2)(iii) of this section. Such interests can be real property interests in the hands of a person that holds a greater than 5 percent interest. Therefore, solely for purposes of determining whether greater than 5 percent interests in such an entity constitutes U.S. real property interests the disposition of which is subject to tax, the entity is required to determine pursuant to the provisions of § 1.897-2 whether the assets it holds would cause it to be classified as a U.S. real property holding corporation if it were a corporation. The treatment of dispositions of U.S. real property interests by publicly traded partnerships and trusts is not affected by the rules of this paragraph (c)(2)(iv); by reason of the operation of section 897(a), foreign partners or beneficiaries are subject to tax upon their distributive share of any gain recognized upon such dispositions by the partnership or trust. The rules of this paragraph (c)(2)(iv) are illustrated by the following example.

Example. PTP is a partnership one class of interests in which is regularly traded on an established securities market. A is a nonresident alien individual who owns 1 percent of a class of limited partnership interests in PTP. B is a nonresident alien individual who owns 10 percent of the same class of limited partnership interests in PTP. On July 1, 1986, A and B sell their interests in PTP. Pursuant to the rules of this paragraph (c)(2)(iv), neither disposition is treated as the disposition of a partnership interest subject to the provisions of section 897(g). Instead, A and B are treated as having disposed of interests in a publicly traded corporation. Therefore, pursuant to the rule of paragraph (c)(2)(iii) of this section, A's disposition of a 1 percent interest has no consequences under section 897. However, B's disposition of a 10 percent interest will constitute the disposition of a U.S. real property interest subject to tax by reason of the operation of section 897 unless it is established pursuant to the rules of § 1.897-2 that the interest is not a U.S. real property interest.

(d) *Interest other than an interest solely as a creditor.*—(1) *In general.*—This paragraph defines an interest other than an interest solely as a creditor, with respect to real property, and with respect to corporations, partnerships, trusts, and estates. An interest solely as a creditor either in real property or in a domestic corporation does not constitute a United States real property interest. Similarly, where one corporation holds an interest solely as a creditor in a second corporation or in a partnership, trust, or estate, that interest will be disregarded for purposes of determining whether the first corporation is a U.S. real property holding corporation (except to the extent that such interest constitutes an asset used or held for use in a trade or business, in accordance with the rules of § 1.897-1(f)). In addition, the disposition of an interest solely as a creditor in a partnership, trust, or estate is not subject to sections 897, 1445, and 6039C. Whether an interest is considered debt under any provisions of the Code is not determinative of whether it constitutes an interest solely as a creditor for purpose of sections 897, 1445, and 6039C and the regulations thereunder.

(2) *Interests in real property other than solely as creditor.*—(i) *In general.*—An interest in real property other than an interest solely as a creditor includes a fee ownership, co-ownership, or leasehold interest in real property, a time sharing interest in real property, and a life estate, remainder, or reversionary interest in such property. The term also includes any direct or indirect right to share in the appreciation in the value, or in the gross or net proceeds or profits generated by, the real property. A loan to an individual or entity under the terms of which a holder of the indebtedness has any direct or indirect right to share in the appreciation in value of, or the gross or net proceeds or profits generated by, an interest in real property of the debtor or of a related person is, in its entirety, an interest in real property other than solely as a creditor. An interest in production payments described in section 636 does not generally constitute an interest in real property other than solely as a creditor. However, a right to production payments shall constitute an interest in real property other than solely as a creditor if it conveys a right to share in the appreciation in value of the mineral property. A production payment that is limited to a quantum of mineral (including a percentage of recoverable reserves produced) or a period of time will be considered to convey a right to share in the appreciation in value of the mineral property. The rules of this paragraph (d)(2)(i) are illustrated by the following example.

Example. A, a U.S. citizen, purchases a condominium unit located in the United States for $500,000. A makes a $100,000 down payment and borrows $400,000 from B, a foreign person, to pay the balance of the purchase price. Under the terms of the loan, A is to pay B 13 percent annual interest each year for 10 years and 35 percent of the appreciation in the fair market value of the condominium at the end of the 10-year period. Because B has a right to share in the appreciation in value of the condominium, B has an interest other than solely as a creditor in the condominium. B's entire interest in the obligation from A, therefore, is a United States real property interest.

(ii) *Special rules.*—(A) *Installment obligations.*—A right to installment or other deferred payments from the disposition of an interest in real property will constitute an interest solely as a creditor if the transferor elects not to have the installment method of section 453(a) apply, any gain or loss is recognized in the year of disposition, and all tax due is timely paid. See section 1445 and regulations thereunder for further guidance concerning the availability of installment sale treatment under section 453. If an agreement for the payment of tax with respect to an installment sale is entered into with the Internal Revenue Service pursuant to section 1445, that agreement may specify whether or not the installment obligation will constitute an interest solely as a creditor. If an installment obligation constitutes an interest other than solely as a creditor then the receipt of each payment shall be treated as the disposition of an interest in real property that is subject to section 897(a) to the extent of any gain required to be taken into account pursuant to section 453. If the original holder of an installment obligation that constitutes an interest other than solely as a creditor subsequently disposes of the obligation to an unrelated party and recognizes gain or loss pursuant to section 453B, the obligation will constitute an interest in real property solely as a creditor in the hands of the subsequent holder. However, if the obligation is disposed of to a related person and the full amount of gain realized upon the disposition of the real property has not been recognized upon such disposition of the installment obligation, then the obligation shall continue to be an interest in real property other than solely as a creditor in the hands of the subsequent holder subject to the rules of this paragraph (d)(2)(ii)(A). In addition, if the obligation is disposed of to any person for a principal purpose of avoiding the provisions of section 897, 1445, or 6039C, then the obligation shall continue to be an interest in real property other than solely as a creditor in the hands of the subsequent holder subject to the rules of this paragraph (d)(2)(ii)(A). However, rights to payments arising from dispositions that took place before June 19, 1980, shall in no event constitute interests in real property other than solely as a creditor, even if such payments are received after June 18, 1980. In addition, rights to payments arising from dispositions to unrelated parties that took place before January 1, 1985, and that were not subject to U.S. tax pursuant to the provisions of a U.S. income tax treaty, shall not constitute interests in real property other than solely as a creditor, even if such payments are received after December 31, 1984.

(B) *Options.*—An option, a contract, or a right of first refusal to acquire any interest in real property (other than an interest solely as a creditor) will itself constitute an interest in real property other than solely as a creditor.

(C) *Security interests.*—A right to repossess or foreclose on real property under a mortgage, security agreement, financing statement, or other collateral instrument securing a debt will not be considered a reversionary interest in, or a right to share in the appreciation in value of or gross or net proceeds or profits generated by, an interest in real property. Thus, no such right of repossession or foreclosure will of itself cause an interest in real property which is otherwise an interest solely as a creditor to become an interest other than solely as a creditor. In addition, a person acting as mortgagee in possession shall not be considered to hold an interest in real property other than solely as a creditor, if the mortgagee's interest in the property otherwise constitutes an interest solely as a creditor.

(D) *Indexed interest rates.*—An interest will not constitute a right to share in the appreciation in the value of, or gross or net proceeds or profits generated by, real property solely because it bears a rate of interest that is tied to an index of any kind that is intended to reflect general inflation or deflation of prices and interest rates (e.g., the Consumer Price Index). However, where an interest in real property bears a rate of interest that is tied to an index the principal purpose of which is to reflect changes in real property values, the real property interest will be considered an indirect right to share in the appreciation in value of, or gross or net proceeds or profits generated by, real property. Such an indirect right constitutes an interest in real property other than solely as a creditor.

(E) *Commissions.*—A right to payment of a commission, brokerage fee, or similar charge for professional services rendered in connection with the arrangement or financing of a purchase, sale, or lease of real property does not constitute a right to share in the appreciation in value of, or gross or net proceeds or profits of, real property solely because it is based upon a percentage of the purchase price or rent. Thus, a right to a commission earned by a real estate agent based on a percentage of the sales price does not constitute an interest in real property other than solely as a creditor. However, a right to a commission, brokerage fee, or similar charge will constitute an interest other than solely as a creditor if the total amount of the payment is contingent upon appreciation, proceeds, or profits of the real property occurring or arising after the date of the transaction with respect to which the professional services were rendered. For example, a commission earned in connection with the purchase of a real property interest that is contingent upon the amount of gain ultimately realized by the purchaser will constitute an interest in real property other than solely as a creditor.

(F) *Trustees' fees, etc.*—A right to payment of reasonable compensation for services rendered as a trustee, as an administrator of an estate, or in a similar capacity does not constitute a right to share in the appreciation in the value of, or gross or net proceeds or profits of, real property solely because the assets of the trust or estate include U.S. real property interests.

(3) *Interest in an entity other than solely as a creditor.*—(i) *In general.*—For purposes of sections 897, 1445, and 6039C, an interest in an entity other than an interest solely as a creditor is—

(A) Stock of a corporation;

(B) An interest in a partnership as a partner within the meaning of section 761(b) and the regulations thereunder;

(C) An interest in a trust or estate as a beneficiary within the meaning of section 643(c) and the regulations thereunder or an ownership interest in any portion of a trust as provided in section 671 through 679 and the regulations thereunder;

(D) An interest which is, in whole or in part, a direct or indirect right to share in the appreciation in value of an interest in an entity described in subdivision (A), (B), or (C) of this paragraph (d)(3)(i) or a direct or indirect right to share in the appreciation in value of assets of, or gross or net proceeds or profits derived by, the entity; or

(E) A right (whether or not presently exercisable) directly or indirectly to acquire, by purchase, conversion, exchange, or in any other manner, an interest described in subdivision (A), (B), (C), or (D) of this paragraph (d)(3)(i).

(ii) *Special rules.*—(A) *Installment obligations.*—A right to installment or other deferred payments from the disposition of an interest in an entity will constitute an interest solely as a creditor if the transferor elects not to have the installment method of section 453(a) apply, any gain or loss is recognized in the year of disposition, and tax due is timely paid. See section 1445 and regulations thereunder for further guidance concerning the availability of installment sale treatment under section 453. If an agreement for the payment of tax with respect to an installment sale is entered into with the Internal Revenue Service pursuant to section 1445, that agreement may specify whether or not the installment obligation will constitute an interest solely as a creditor. If an installment obligation constitutes an interest other than solely as a creditor then the receipt of each payment shall be treated as the disposition of such an interest and shall be subject to section 897(a) to the extent that: (*1*) It constitutes the disposition of a U.S. real property interest and (*2*) Gain or loss is required to be taken into account pursuant to section 453. Such treatment shall apply to payments arising from dispositions of interests in a corporation any class of the stock of which is regularly traded on an established securities market, but only in the case of a disposition of any portion of an interest described in paragraph (c)(2)(iii)(A) or (B) of this section. If the original holder of an installment obligation that constitutes an interest other than solely as a creditor subsequently disposes of the obligation to an unrelated party and recognizes gain or loss pursuant to section 453B, the obligation will constitute an interest in the entity solely as a creditor in the hands of the subsequent holder. However, if the obligation is disposed of to a related person and the full amount of gain realized upon the disposition of the interest in the entity has not been recognized upon such disposition of the installment obligation, then the obligation shall continue to be an interest in the entity other than solely as a creditor in the hands of the subsequent holder subject to the rules of this paragraph (d)(3)(ii)(A). In addition, if the obligation is disposed of to any person for a principal purpose of avoiding the provisions of section 897, 1445, or 6039C, then the obligation shall continue to be an interest in the entity other than solely as a creditor in the hands of the subsequent holder subject to the rules of this paragraph (d)(3)(ii)(A). However, rights to payments arising from dispositions that took place before June 19, 1980, shall in no event constitute interests in an entity other than solely as a creditor, even if such payments are received after June 18, 1980. In addition, such treatment shall not apply to payments arising from dispositions to unrelated parties that took place before January 1, 1985, and that were not subject to U.S. tax pursuant to the provisions of a U.S. income tax treaty, regardless of when such payments are received.

(B) *Contingent interests.*—The interests described in subdivision (D) of paragraph (d)(3)(i) of this section include any right to a payment from an entity the amount of which is contingent on the appreciation in value of an interest described in subdivision (A), (B), or (C) or paragraph (d)(3)(i) of this section or which is contingent on the appreciation in value of assets of, or the general gross or net proceeds or profits derived by, such entity. The right to such a payment is itself an interest in the entity other than solely as a creditor, regardless of whether the holder of such right actually holds an interest in the entity described in subdivision (A), (B), or (C) of paragraph (d)(3)(i) of this section. For example, a stock appreciation right constitutes an interest in a corporation other than solely as a creditor even if the holder of such right actually holds no stock in the corporation. However, the interests described in subdivision (D) of paragraph (d)(3)(i) of this section do not include any right to a payment that is (*1*) exclusively contingent upon and exclusively paid out of revenues from sales of personal property (whether tangible or intangible) or from services, or (*2*) exclusively contingent upon the resolution of a claim asserted against the entity by a person related neither to the entity nor to the holder of the interest.

(C) *Security interests.*—A right to repossess or foreclose on an interest in an entity under a mortgage, security agreement, financing statement, or other collateral instrument securing a debt will not of itself cause an interest in an entity which is otherwise an interest solely as a creditor to become an interest other than solely as a creditor.

(D) *Royalties.*—The interests described in subdivision (D) of paragraph (d)(3)(i) of this section do not include rights to payments representing royalties, license fees, or similar charges for the use of patents, inventions, formulas, copyrights, literary, musical or artistic compositions, trademarks, trade names, franchises, licenses, or similar intangible property.

(E) *Commissions.*—The interests described in subdivision (D) of paragraph (d)(3)(i) of this section do not include a right to a commission, brokerage fee or similar charge for professional services rendered in connection with the purchase or sale of an interest in an entity. However, a right to such a payment will constitute an interest other than solely as a creditor if the total amount of the payment is contingent upon appreciation in value of assets of, or proceeds or profits derived by, the entity after the date of the transaction with respect to which the payment was earned.

(F) *Trustee's fees.*—The interests described in subdivision (D) of paragraph (d)(3)(i) of this section do not include a right to payment representing reasonable compensation for services rendered as a trustee, as an administrator of an estate, or in a similar capacity.

(4) *Aggregation of interests.*—If a person holds both interests solely as a creditor and interests other than solely as a creditor in real property or in an entity, those interests will generally be treated as separate and distinct interests. However, such interests shall be aggregated and treated as interests other than solely as a creditor in their entirety if the interest solely as a creditor has been separated from, or acquired separately from, the interest other than solely as a creditor, for a principal purpose of avoiding the provisions of section 897, 1445, or 6039C by causing one or more of such interests to be an interest solely as a creditor. The existence of such a purpose will be determined with reference to all the facts and circumstances. Where an interest solely as a creditor has arm's-length interest and repayment terms it shall in no event be aggregated with and treated as an interest other than solely as a creditor. For purposes of this paragraph (d)(4), an interest rate that does not exceed 120 percent of the applicable Federal rate (as defined in section 1274(d)) shall be presumed to be an arm's-length interest rate. For purposes of applying

the rules of this paragraph (d)(4), a person shall be treated as holding any interests held by a related person within the meaning of § 1.897-1(i).

(5) *"Interest" means "interest other than solely as a creditor".*—Unless otherwise stated, the term "interest" as used with regard to real property or with regard to an entity hereafter in the regulations under sections 897, 1445, and 6039C, means an interest in such real property or entity other than an interest solely as a creditor

(e) *Proportionate share of assets held by an entity.*—(1) *In general.*—A person that holds an interest in an entity is for certain purposes treated as holding a proportionate or pro rata share of the assets held by the entity. Such proportionate share must be calculated, in accordance with the rules of this paragraph, for the following purposes.

(i) In determining whether a corporation is a U.S. real property holding corporation—

(A) A person holding an interest in a partnership, trust, or estate is treated as holding a proportionate share of the assets held by the partnership, trust, or estate (see § 1.897-2(e)(2)), and

(B) A corporation that holds a controlling interest in a second corporation is treated as holding a proportionate share of the assets held by the second corporation (see § 1.897-2(e)(3)).

(ii) In determining reporting obligations that may be imposed under section 6039C, the holder of an interest in a partnership, trust, or estate is treated as owning a proportionate share of the U.S. real property interests held by the partnership, trust, or estate.

(2) *Proportionate share of assets held by a corporation or partnership.*—(i) *In general.*—A person's proportionate or pro rata share of assets held by a corporation or partnership is determined by multiplying—

(A) The person's percentage ownership interest in the entity, by

(B) The fair market value of the assets held by the entity (or the book value of such assets, in the case of a determination pursuant to § 1.897-2(b)(2)).

(ii) *Percentage ownership interest.*—A person's percentage ownership interest in a corporation or partnership is the percentage equal to the ratio of (A) the sum of the liquidation values of all interests in the entity held by the person to (B) the sum of the liquidation values of all outstanding interests in the entity. The liquidation value of an interest in an entity is the amount of cash and the fair market value of any property that would be distributed with respect to such interest upon the liquidation of the entity after satisfaction of liabilities to persons having interests in the entity solely as creditors. With respect to an entity that has interests outstanding that grant a presently-exercisable option to acquire or right to convert into or otherwise acquire an interest in the entity other than solely as a creditor, the liquidation value of all interests in such entity shall be calculated as though such option or right had been exercised, giving effect both to the payment of any consideration required to exercise the option or right and to the issuance of the additional interest.
The fair market value of the assets of the entity, the amount of cash held by the entity, and the amount of liabilities to persons having interests solely as creditors is determined for this purpose on the date with respect to which the percentage ownership interest is determined.

(iii) *Examples.*—The rules of this paragraph (e)(2) are illustrated by the following examples.

Example (1). Corporation K's only assets are stock and securities with a fair market value as of the applicable determination date of $20,000,000. K's assets are subject to liabilities of $10,000,000. Among K's liabilities are a $1,000,000 loan from L, under the terms of which L is entitled, upon payment of the loan principal, to a profit share equal to 10 percent of the excess of the fair market value of K's assets over $18,000,000, but only if all other corporate liabilities have been paid. K has two classes of stock, common and preferred. PS1 and PS2 each own 100 of the 200 outstanding shares of preferred stock. CS1 and CS2 each own 500 of the 1,000 outstanding shares of common stock. Each preferred shareholder is entitled to $10,000 per share of preferred stock upon liquidation, subject to payment of all corporate liabilities and to any amount owed to L, but before any common shareholder is paid. The liquidation value of L's interest in K, which constitutes an interest other than an interest solely as a creditor, is $1,200,000 ($1,000,000 principal of the loan to K plus $200,000 (10 percent of the excess of $20,000,000 over $18,000,000). The liquidation value of each of PS1's and PS2's blocks of preferred stock is $1,000,000 ($10,000 times 100 shares each). The liquidation value of each of CS1's and CS2's blocks of common stock is $3,900,000 [$20,000,000 (the total fair market value of K's assets) – $9,000,000 (liabilities to creditors other than L) – $1,200,000 (L's liquidation value) – $2,000,000 (PS1's and PS2's liquidation value)) times 50 percent (the percentage of common stock owned by each)]. The sum of the liquidation values of all of the outstanding interests in K (i.e., interests other than solely as a creditor) is $11,000,000 [$1,200,000 (L's liquidation value) + $2,000,000 (PS1's and PS2's liquidation values) + $7,800,000 (CS1's and CS2's liquidation values)]. Each of CS1's and CS2's percentage ownership interests in K is 35.5 percent ($3,900,000 divided by $11,000,000). Each of PS1's and PS2's percentage ownership interests in K is 9 percent ($1,000,000 divided by $11,000,000). L's percentage ownership interest in K is 11 percent ($1,200,000 divided by $11,000,000).

Example (2). A, a U.S. person, and B, a foreign person are partners in a partnership the only asset of which is a parcel of undeveloped land located in the United States that was purchased by the partnership in 1980 for $300,000. The partnership has no liabilities, and its capital is $300,000. A's and B's interests in the capital of the partnership are 25 percent and 75 percent, respectively, and A and B each has a 50 percent profit interest in the partnership. The partnership agreement provides that upon liquidation any unrealized gain will be distributed in accordance with the partners' profit interests. In 1984 the partnership has no items of income or deduction, and the fair market value of its parcel of undeveloped land is $500,000. In 1984 the percentage ownership interest of A in the partnership is 35 percent [the ratio of $100,000 (the liquidation value of A's profit interest in 1984) plus $75,000 (the liquidation value of A's 25 percent interest in the partnership's $300,000 capital) to $500,000 (the sum of the liquidation values of all outstanding interests in the partnership)]. The percentage ownership interest of B in the partnership in 1984 is 65 percent [the ratio of $325,000 (B's $100,000 profit interest plus his $225,000 capital interest) to $500,000].

(3) *Proportionate share of assets held by trusts and estates.*—(i) *In general.*—A person's proportionate or pro rata share of assets held by a trust or estate is determined by multiplying—

(A) The person's percentage ownership interest in the trust or estate, by

(B) The fair market value of the assets held by the trust or estate (or the book value of such assets, in the case of a determination pursuant to § 1.897-2(b)(2)).

(ii) *Percentage ownership interest.*—(A) *General rule.*—A person's percentage ownership interest in a trust or an estate—is the percentage equal to the ratio of: *(1)* The sum of the actuarial values of such person's interests in the cash and other assets held by the trust or estate after satisfaction of the liabilities of the trust or estate to persons holding interests in the trust or estate solely as creditors, to *(2)* the entire amount of such cash and other assets after satisfaction of liabilities to persons holding interests in the trust or estate solely as creditors. For purposes of calculating this ratio, the fair market value of the trust's or estate's assets, the amount of cash held by the trust or estate, and the amount of the liabilities to persons having interests solely as creditors is determined on the date with respect to which the percentage ownership interest is determined. With respect to a trust or estate that has interests outstanding that grant a presently-exercisable option to acquire or right to convert into or otherwise acquire an interest in the trust or estate other than solely as a creditor, the liquidation value of all interests in such entity shall be calculated as though such option or right had been exercised, giving effect both to the payment of any consideration required to exercise the option or right and to the issuance of the additional interest. With respect to a trust or estate that has interests outstanding that entitle any person to a distribution of U.S. real property interests upon liquidation that is disproportionate to such person's interest in the total assets of the trust or estate, such disproportionate right shall be disregarded in the calculation of the interest-holders' proportionate share of the U.S. real property interests held by the entity. For purposes of determining his own percentage ownership interest in a trust, a grantor or other person will be treated as owning any portion of the trust's cash and other assets which such person is treated as owning under sections 671 through 679.

(B) *Discretionary trusts and estates.*—In determining percentage ownership interest in a trust or an estate, the sum of the definitely ascertainable actuarial values of interests in the cash and the other assets of the trust or estate held by persons in existence on the date with respect to which such determination is made must equal the amount in paragraph (e)(3)(ii)(A)(2) of this section. If the amount in paragraph (e)(3)(ii)(A)(2) of this section exceeds the sum of the definitely ascertainable actuarial values of the interests held by persons in existence on the determination date, the excess will be considered to be owned in total by each beneficiary who is in existence on such date, whose interest in the excess is not definitely ascertainable and who is potentially entitled to such excess. However, such excess shall not be considered to be owned in total by each beneficiary if the discretionary terms of the trust or estate were included for a principal purpose of avoiding the provisions of section 897, 1445, or 6039C by causing assets other than U.S. real property interests to be attributed in total to each beneficiary. The rules of this paragraph (e)(3) are illustrated by the following example.

Example. A, a U.S. person, established a trust on December 31, 1984, and contributed real property with a fair market value of $10,000 to the trust. The terms of that trust provided that the trustee, a bank that is unrelated to A, at its discretion may retain trust income or may distribute it to X, a foreign person, or to the head of state of any country other than the United States. The remainder upon the death of X is to go in equal shares to such of Y and Z, both foreign persons, as survive X. On December 31, 1984, the total value of the trust's assets is $10,000. On the same date, the actuarial values of the remainder interests of Y and Z in the corpus of the trust are definitely ascertainable. They are $1,000 and $500, respectively. Neither the income interest of X nor of the head of state of any country other than the United States has a definitely ascertainable actuarial value on December 31, 1984. The interests of Y and Z in the income portion of the trust similarly have no definitely ascertainable actuarial values on such date since the income may be distributed rather than retained by the trust. Since the sum of the actuarial values of definitely ascertainable interests of persons in existence ($1,500) is less than $10,000, the difference ($8,500) is treated as owned by each beneficiary who is in existence on December 31, 1984, and who is potentially entitled to such excess. Therefore, X, Y, Z, and the head of state of any country other than the United States are each considered as owning the entire $8,500 income interest in the trust. On December 31, 1984, the total actuarial value of X's interest is $8,500, and his percentage ownership interest is 85 percent. The total actuarial value of Y's interest in the trust is $9,500 ($1,000 plus $8,500), and his percentage ownership interest is 95 percent. The total actuarial value of Z's interest is $9,000 ($500 plus $8,500), and his percentage ownership interest is 90 percent. The actuarial value of the interest of the head of state of each country other than the United States is $8,500, and his percentage ownership interest is 85 percent.

(4) *Dates with respect to which percentage ownership interests are determined.*—The dates with respect to which percentage ownership interests are determined are the applicable determination dates outlined in § 1.897-2 or in regulations under section 6039C.

(f) *Asset used or held for use in a trade or business.*—(1) *In general.*—The term "asset used or held for use in a trade or business" means—

(i) Property, other than a U.S. real property interest, that is—

(A) Stock in trade of an entity or other property of a kind which would properly be included in the inventory of the entity if on hand at the close of the taxable year, or property held by the entity primarily for sale to customers in the ordinary course of its trade or business, or

(B) Depreciable property used or held for use in the trade or business, as described in section 1231(b)(1) but without regard to the holding period limitations of section 1231(b), or

(C) Livestock, including poultry, used or held for use in a trade or business for draft, breeding, dairy, or sporting purposes, and

(ii) Goodwill and going concern value, patents, inventions, formulas, copyrights, literary, musical, or artistic compositions, trademarks, trade names, franchises, licenses, customer lists, and similar intangible property, but only to the extent that such property is used or held for use in the entity's trade or business and subject to the valuation rules of § 1.897-1(o)(4), and

(iii) Cash, stock, securities, receivables of all kinds, options or contracts to acquire any of the foregoing, and options or contracts to acquire commodities, but only to the extent that such assets are used or held for use in the corporation's trade or business and do not constitute U.S. real property interests.

(2) *Used or held for use in a trade or business.*—An asset is used or held for use in an entity's trade or business if it is, under the principles of § 1.864-4(c)(2)—

(i) Held for the principal purpose of promoting the present conduct of the trade or business,

(ii) Acquired and held in the ordinary course of the trade or business, as, for example, in the case of an account or note receivable arising from that trade or business (including the performance of services), or

(iii) Otherwise held in a direct relationship to the trade or business.

In determining whether an asset is held in a direct relationship to the trade or business, consideration shall be given to whether the asset is needed in that trade or business. An asset shall be considered to be needed in a trade or business only if the asset is held to meet the present needs of that trade or business and not its anticipated future needs. An asset shall be considered as needed in the trade or business if, for example, the asset is held to meet the operating expenses of that trade or business. Conversely, an asset shall be considered as not needed in the trade or business if, for example, the asset is held for the purpose of providing for future diversification into a new trade or business, future expansion of trade or business activities, future plant replacement, or future business contingencies. An asset that is held to meet reserve or capitalization requirements imposed by applicable law shall be presumed to be held in a direct relationship to the trade or business.

(3) *Special rules concerning liquid assets.*—(i) *Safe harbor amount.*—Assets described in paragraph (f)(1)(iii) of this section shall be presumed to be used or held for use in a trade or business, in an amount up to 5 percent of the fair market value of other assets used or held for use in the trade or business. However, the rule of this paragraph (f)(3)(i) shall not apply with respect to any assets described in paragraph (f)(1)(iii) of this section that are held or acquired for the principal purpose of avoiding the provisions of section 897 or 1445.

(ii) *Investment companies.*—Assets described in paragraph (f)(1)(iii) of this section shall be presumed to be used or held for use in an entity's trade or business if the principal business of the entity is trading or investing in such assets for its own account. An entity's principal business shall be presumed to be trading or investing in assets, described in paragraph (f)(1)(iii) of this section if the fair market value of such assets held by the entity equals or exceeds 90 percent of the sum of the fair market values of the entity's U.S. real property interests, interests in real property located outside the United States, assets otherwise used or held for use in a trade or business, and assets described in paragraph (f)(1)(iii) of this section.

(4) *Examples.*—The application of this paragraph (f) may be illustrated by the following examples:

Example (1). M, a domestic corporation engaged in industrial manufacturing, is required to hold a large current cash balance for the purposes of purchasing materials and meeting its payroll. The amount of the cash balance so required varies because of the fluctuating seasonal nature of the corporation's business. In months when large cash balances are not required, the corporation invests the surplus amount in U.S. Treasury bills. Since both the cash and the Treasury bills are held to meet the present needs of the business, they are held in a direct relationship to that business, and, therefore, constitute assets used or held for use in the trade or business.

Example (2). R, a domestic corporation engaged in the manufacture of goods, engages a stock brokerage firm to manage securities which were purchased with funds from R's general surplus reserves. The funds invested in these securities are intended to provide for the future expansion of R into a new trade or business. Thus, the funds are not necessary for the present needs of the business; they are accordingly not held in a direct relationship to the business and do not constitute assets used or held for use in the trade or business.

Example (3). B, a federally chartered and regulated bank, is required by law to hold substantial reserves of cash, stock, and securities. Pursuant to the rule of paragraph (f)(2) of this section, such assets are presumed to be held in a direct relationship to B's business, and thus constitute assets used or held for use in the trade or business. In addition, B holds substantial loan receivables which are acquired and held in the ordinary course of its banking business. Pursuant to the rule of paragraph (f)(1)(iii) of this section, such receivables constitute assets used or held for use in the trade or business.

(g) *Disposition:* For purposes of sections 897, 1445, and 6039C, the term "disposition" means any transfer that would constitute a disposition by the transferor for any purpose of the Internal Revenue Code and regulations thereunder. The severance of crops or timber and the extraction of minerals do not alone constitute the disposition of a U.S. real property interest.

(h) *Gain or loss,* the amount of gain or loss arising from the disposition of the U.S. real property interest shall be determined as provided in section 1001(a) and (b). Such gain or loss shall be subject to the provisions of section 897(a) and (b), unless a nonrecognition provision is applicable pursuant to section 897(d) or (e) and regulations thereunder. Amounts otherwise treated for Federal income tax purposes as principal and interest payments on debt obligations of all kinds (including obligations that are interests other than solely as a creditor) do not give rise to gain or loss that is subject to section 897(a). However, principal payments on installment obligations described in §§1.897-1(d)(2)(ii)(A) and 1.897-1(d)(3)(ii)(A) do give rise to gain or loss that is subject to section 897(a), to the extent such gain or loss is required to be recognized pursuant to section 453. The rules of paragraphs (g) and (h) are illustrated by the following examples.

Example (1). Foreign individual C has an undivided fee interest in a parcel of real property located in the United States. The fair market value of C's interest is $70,000, and C's basis in such interest is $50,000. The only liability to which the real property is subject is the liability of $65,000 secured by a mortgage in the same amount. C transfers his fee interest in the property subject to the mortgage by gift to D. C realizes $15,000 of gain upon such transfer. As a transfer by gift constitutes a disposition for purposes of the Code, and as gain is realized upon that transfer, the gift is a disposition for purposes of sections 897, 1445, and 6039C and is subject to section 897(a) to the extent of the gain realized. However, section 897(a) would not be applicable to the transfer if the mortgage on the U.S. real property were equal to or less than C's $50,000 basis, since the transfer then would not give rise to the realization of gain or loss under the Internal Revenue Code.

Example (2). Foreign corporation Y makes a loan of $1 million to domestic individual Z, secured by a mortgage on residential real property purchased with the loan proceeds. The loan agreement provides that Y is entitled to receive fixed monthly payments from Z, constituting repayment of principal plus interest at a fixed rate. In addition, the agreement provides that Y is entitled to receive a percentage of the appreciation in value of the real property as of the time that the loan is retired. The obligation in its entirety is considered debt for Federal income tax purposes. However, because of Y's right to share in the appreciation in value of the real property, the debt obligation gives Y an interest in the real property other than solely as a creditor. Nevertheless, as principal and interest payments do not constitute gain under section 1001 and paragraph (h) of this section, and both the monthly and final payments received by Y are considered to consist solely of principal and interest for Federal income tax purposes, section 897(a) shall not apply to Y's receipt of such payments. However, Y's sale of the debt obligation to foreign corporation A would give rise to gain that is subject to section 897(a).

(i) *Related person.*—For purposes of sections 897, 1445, and 6039C, persons are considered to be related if they are partners or partnerships described in section 707(b)(1) of the Code or if they are related within the meaning of section 267(b) and (c) of the Code (except that section 267(f) shall apply without regard to section 1563(b)(2)).

(j) *Domestic corporation.*—The term "domestic corporation" has the same meaning as set forth in section 7701(a)(3) and (4) and §301.7701-5. For purposes of sections 897 and 6039C, it also includes a foreign corporation with respect to which an election under section 897(i) and §1.897-3 or section 897(k) and §1.897-4 to be treated as domestic corporation is in effect.

(k) *Foreign person.*—[Reserved]

(l) *Foreign corporation.*—The term "foreign corporation" has the meaning ascribed to such term in section 7701(a)(3) and (5) and §301.7701-5. For purposes of sections 897 and 6039C, however, the term does not include a foreign corporation with respect to which there is in effect an election under section 897(i) and §1.897-3 or section 897(k) and § 1.897-4 to be treated as a domestic corporation.

(m) *Established securities market.*—For purposes of sections 897, 1445, and 6039C, the term "established securities market" means—

(1) A national securities exchange which is registered under section 6 of the Securities Exchange Act of 1934 (15 U.S.C. 78f),

(2) A foreign national securities exchange which is officially recognized, sanctioned, or supervised by governmental authority, and

(3) Any over-the-counter market.

An over-the-counter market is any market reflected by the existence of an interdealer quotation system. An interdealer quotation system is any system of general circulation to brokers and dealers which regularly disseminates quotations of stocks and securities by identified brokers or dealers, other than by quotation sheets which are prepared and distributed by a broker or dealer in the regular course of business and which contain only quotations of such broker or dealer.

(n) *Regularly traded.*—[Reserved]

(o) *Fair market value.*—(1) *In general.*—For purposes of sections 897, 1445, and 6039C only, the term "fair market value" means the value of the property determined in accordance with the rules, contained in this paragraph (o). The definition of fair market value provided herein is not to be used in the calculation of gain or loss from the disposition of a U.S. real property interest pursuant to section 1001. An independent professional appraisal of the value of property must be submitted only if such an appraisal is specifically requested in connection with the negotiation of a security agreement pursuant to section 1445.

(2) *Method of calculating fair market value.*—(i) *In general.*—The fair market value of property is its gross value (as defined in paragraph (o)(2)(ii) of this section) reduced by the outstanding balance of any debts secured by the property which are described in paragraph (o)(2)(iii) of this section. See §1.897-2(b) for the alternative use of book values in certain limited circumstances.

(ii) *Gross value.*—Gross value is the price at which the property would change hands between an unrelated willing buyer and willing seller, neither being under any compulsion to buy or sell and both having reasonable knowledge of all relevant facts. Generally, with respect to trade or business assets, going concern value should be used as it will provide the most accurate reflection of such a price. However, taxpayers may use other methods of valuation if they can establish that such method will provide a more accurate determination of gross value and if they consistently apply such method to all assets to be valued. See subdivisions (3) and (4) of this paragraph (o) for special rules with respect to the valuation of leases and of intangible assets.

(iii) *Debts secured by the property.*—The gross value of property shall be reduced by the outstanding balance of debts that are:

(A) Secured by a mortgage or other security interest in the property that is valid and enforceable under the law of the jurisdiction in which the property is located, and

(B) Either (*1*) incurred to acquire the property (including long-term financing obtained in replacement of construction loans or other short-term debt within one year of the acquisition or completion of the property), or (*2*) otherwise incurred in direct connection with the property, such as property tax liens upon real property or debts incurred to maintain or improve property.

In addition, if any debt described in this paragraph (o)(2)(iii) is refinanced for a valid business purpose (such as obtaining a more favorable rate of interest), the principal amount of the replacement debt does not exceed the outstanding balance of the original debt, and the replacement debt is secured by the property, then the gross value of the property shall be reduced by the replacement debt. Obligations to related persons shall not be taken into account for purposes of this paragraph (o)(2)(iii) unless such obligations constitute interests, solely as a creditor pursuant to the provisions of paragraph (d)(4) of this section and unless the related person has made similar loans to unrelated persons on similar terms and conditions.

(iv) *Anti-abuse rule.*—The gross value of real property located outside the United States and of assets used or held for use in a trade or business shall be reduced by the outstanding balance of any debt that was entered into for the principal purpose of avoiding the provisions of section 897, 1445, or 6039C by enabling the corporation to acquire such assets. The existence of such a purpose shall be determined with reference to all the facts and circumstances. Debts that a particular corporation routinely enters into the ordinary course of its acquisition of assets used or held for use in its trade or business will not be considered to be entered into for the principal purpose of avoiding the provisions of section 897, 1445, or 6039C.

(3) *Fair market value of leases and options.*—For purposes of sections 897, 1445, and 6039C, the fair market value of a leasehold interest in real property is the price at which the lease could be assigned or the property sublet, neither party to such transaction being under any compulsion to enter into the transaction and both having reasonable knowledge of all relevant facts. Thus, the value of a leasehold interest will generally consist of the present value, over the period of the lease remaining, of the difference between the rental provided for in the lease and the current rental value of the real property. A leasehold interest bearing restrictions on its assignment or sublease has a fair market value of zero, but only if those restrictions in practical effect preclude (rather than merely condition) the

lessee's ability to transfer, at a gain, the benefits of a favorable lease. The normal commercial practice of lessors may be used to determine whether restrictions in a lease have the practical effect of precluding transfer at a gain. The fair market value of an option to purchase any property is, similarly, the price at which the option could be sold, consisting generally of the difference between the option price and the fair market value of the property, taking proper account of any restrictions upon the transfer of the option.

(4) *Fair market value of intangible assets.*—For purposes of determining whether a corporation is a U.S. real property holding corporation, the fair market value of intangible assets described in § 1.897-1(f)(1)(ii) may be determined in accordance with the following rules.

(i) *Purchase price.*—Intangible assets described in § 1.897-1(f)(1)(ii) that were acquired by purchase from a person not related to the purchaser within the meaning of § 1.897-1(i) may be valued at their purchase price. However, such purchase price must be adjusted to reflect any amortization required by generally accepted accounting principles applied in the United States. Intangible assets acquired by purchase shall include any amounts allocated to goodwill or going concern value pursuant to section 338(b)(3) and regulations thereunder. Intangible assets acquired by purchase shall not include assets that were acquired indirectly through an acquisition of stock to which section 338 does not apply. Such assets must be valued pursuant to a method described in subdivision (ii) or (iii) of this paragraph (o)(4).

(ii) *Book value.*—Intangible assets described in § 1.897-1(f)(1)(ii) (other than goodwill and going concern value) may be valued at the amount at which such assets are carried on the financial accounting records of the holder of such assets, provided that such amount is determined in accordance with generally accepted accounting principles applied in the United States. However, this method may not be used with respect to assets acquired by purchase from a related person within the meaning of § 1.897-1(i).

(iii) *Other methods.*—Intangible assets described in § 1.897-1(f)(1)(ii) may be valued pursuant to any other reasonable method at an amount reflecting the price at which the asset would change hands between an unrelated willing buyer and willing seller, neither being under any compulsion to buy or to sell and both having reasonable knowledge of all relevant facts. However, a corporation that uses a method of valuation other than the purchase price or book value methods may be required to comply with the special notification requirements of § 1.897-2(h)(1)(iii)(A).

(p) *Identifying number.*—The "identifying number" of an individual is the individual's United States social security number or the identification number assigned by the Internal Revenue Service (see § 301.6109-1 of this chapter). The "identifying number" of any other person is its United States employer identification number. [Reg. § 1.897-1.]

□ [*T.D. 7999, 12-26-84. Amended by T.D. 8113, 12-18-86; T.D. 8198, 5-4-88; T.D. 8657, 3-5-96 and T.D. 9082, 8-4-2003.*]

Proposed Amendments to Regulation

§ 1.897-1. Taxation of foreign investment in United States real property interests, definition of terms.—(a) * * *

(2) *Effective date.*—Except as otherwise provided in this paragraph (a)(2), the regulations set forth in §§ 1.897-1 through 1.897-4 are effective for transactions occurring after June 18, 1980. Paragraphs (c)(3) and (4), (k), and (l) of this section apply to transactions occurring on or after [the date these regulations are published as final regulations in the Federal Register] and transactions occurring before [the date these regulations are published as final regulations in the Federal Register] resulting from an entity classification election under § 301.7701-3 of this chapter that was effective on or before [the date these regulations are published as final regulations in the Federal Register] but was filed on or after [DATE OF PUBLICATION OF FINAL RULE]. For transactions occurring before [DATE OF PUBLICATION OF FINAL RULE], see paragraphs (c)(2)(i) and (l) of this section and § 1.897-9T(c) as in effect and contained in 26 CFR part 1, as revised April 1, 2022.

* * *

(c) * * *

(3) *Domestically controlled QIE.*—(i) *In general.*—An interest in a domestically controlled QIE is not a United States real property interest. A QIE is domestically controlled if foreign persons hold directly or indirectly less than 50 percent of the fair market value of the QIE's outstanding stock at all times during the testing period. For rules that apply to distributions by a QIE (including a domestically controlled QIE) attributable to gain from the sale or exchange of a United States real property interest, see section 897(h)(1).

(ii) *Look-through approach for determining QIE stock held directly or indirectly.*—The following rules apply for purposes of determining whether a QIE is domestically controlled:

(A) *Non-look-through persons considered holders.*—Only a non-look-through person is considered to hold directly or indirectly stock of the QIE.

(B) *Attribution from look-through persons.*—Stock of a QIE that, but for the application of paragraph (c)(3)(ii)(A) of this section, would be considered held by a look-through person, is instead considered held directly or indirectly by the look-through person's shareholders, partners, or beneficiaries, as applicable, that are non-look-through persons based on the non-look-through person's proportionate interest in the look-through person. To the extent the shareholders, partners, or beneficiaries, as applicable, of the look-through person are also look-through persons, this paragraph applies to such shareholders, partners, or beneficiaries as if they held, but for the application of paragraph (c)(3)(ii)(A) of this section, their proportionate share of the stock of the QIE.

(C) *No attribution from non-look-through persons.*—Stock of a QIE considered held directly or indirectly by a non-look-through person is not considered held directly or indirectly by any other person.

(iii) *Special rules for applying look-through approach.*—(A) *Certain holders of U.S. publicly traded QIE stock.*—Notwithstanding any other provision of paragraph (c)(3) of this section, a person holding less than five percent of U.S. publicly traded QIE stock at all times during the testing period, determined without regard to paragraph (c)(3)(ii)(A) of this section, is treated as a United States person that is a non-look-through person with respect to that stock, unless the QIE has actual knowledge that such person is not a United States person. For an example illustrating the application of this paragraph (c)(3)(iii)(A), *see* paragraph (c)(3)(vi)(C) of this section.

(B) *Certain foreign-owned domestic C corporations.*—A non-public domestic C corporation is treated as a look-through-person if it is a foreign-owned domestic corporation. For an example illustrating the application of this paragraph (c)(3)(iii)(B), *see* paragraph (c)(3)(vi)(B) of this section.

(C) *Public QIEs.*—A public QIE is treated as a foreign person that is a non-look-through person. The preceding sentence does not apply, however, if the public QIE is a domestically controlled QIE as defined in paragraph (c)(3) of this section, determined after the application of this paragraph (c)(3)(iii)(C), in which case the public QIE is treated as a United States person that is a non-look-through person. For an example illustrating the application of this paragraph (c)(3)(iii)(C), *see* paragraph (c)(3)(vi)(C) of this section (*Example 3*).

(iv) *Treatment of certain persons as foreign persons.*—(A) *Qualified foreign pension fund or qualified controlled entity.*—For purposes of paragraph (c)(3) of this section, a qualified foreign pension fund (including any part of a qualified foreign pension fund) or a qualified controlled entity is treated as a foreign person, irrespective of whether the fund or entity qualifies for the exception from section 897 provided in § 1.897(l)-1(b)(1). For an example illustrating the application of this paragraph (c)(3)(iv)(A), *see* paragraph (c)(3)(vi)(A) of this section (*Example 1*). *See* also paragraph (k) of this section for a definition of foreign person that applies for purposes of sections 897, 1445, and 6039C.

(B) *International organization.*—For purposes of paragraph (c)(3) of this section, an international organization (as defined in section 7701(a)(18)) is treated as a foreign person. *See* § 1.897-9T(e) regarding the treatment of international organizations under sections 897, 1445, and 6039C, which provides that an international organization is not a foreign person with respect to United States real property interests, and is not subject to sections 897, 1445, and 6039C on the disposition of a United States real property interest.

(v) *Definitions.*—The following definitions apply for purposes of paragraph (c)(3) of this section:

(A) A *domestic C corporation* is any domestic corporation other than a regulated investment company ("RIC") as defined in section 851, a real estate investment trust ("REIT") as defined in section 856, or an S corporation as defined in section 1361.

(B) A *foreign-owned domestic corporation* is any non-public domestic C corporation if foreign persons hold directly or indirectly 25 percent or more of the fair market value of the non-public domestic C corporation's outstanding stock. For purposes of determining whether a non-public domestic C corporation is a foreign-owned domestic corporation, the rules of paragraphs (c)(3)(ii)(A) through (C) and (c)(3)(iii)(C) of this section apply with the following modifications—

(1) In paragraphs (c)(3)(ii)(A) through (C) of this section, treating references to "QIE" as references to "non-public domestic C corporation"; and

(2) A non-public domestic C corporation that is a foreign-owned domestic corporation under paragraph (c)(3)(v)(B) of this section is treated as a look-through person for purposes of determining whether any other non-public domestic C corporation is a foreign-owned domestic corporation.

(C) A *look-through person* is any person other than a non-look-through person. Thus, for example, a look-through person includes a RIC, a REIT, an S corporation, a non-publicly traded partnership (domestic or foreign), and a trust (domestic or foreign, whether or not the trust is described in sections 671 through 679). For a special rule that treats certain non-public domestic C corporations as look-through persons, see paragraph (c)(3)(iii)(B) of this section.

(D) A *non-look-through person* is an individual, a domestic C corporation (other than a foreign-owned domestic corporation), a nontaxable holder, a foreign corporation (including a foreign government pursuant to section 892(a)(3)), a publicly traded partnership (domestic or foreign), an estate (domestic or foreign), an international organization (as defined in section 7701(a)(18)), a qualified foreign pension fund (including any part of a qualified foreign pension fund), or a qualified controlled entity. For special rules that treat certain holders of QIE stock as non-look-through persons, see paragraphs (c)(3)(iii)(A) and (C) of this section.

(E) A *non-public domestic C corporation* is any domestic C corporation that is not a public domestic C corporation.

(F) A *nontaxable holder* is—

(1) Any organization that is exempt from taxation by reason of section 501(a);

(2) The United States, any State (as defined in section 7701(a)(10)), any territory of the United States, or a political subdivision of any State or any territory of the United States; or

(3) Any Indian tribal government (as defined in section 7701(a)(40)) or its subdivision (determined in accordance with section 7871(d)).

(G) A *public domestic C corporation* is a domestic C corporation any class of stock of which is regularly traded on an established securities market within the meaning of §§1.897-1(m) and 1.897-9T(d).

(H) A *public QIE* is a QIE any class of stock of which is regularly traded on an established securities market within the meaning of §§1.897-1(m) and 1.897-9T(d), or that is a RIC that issues redeemable securities within the meaning of section 2 of the Investment Company Act of 1940.

(I) A *publicly traded partnership* is a partnership any class of interest of which is regularly traded on an established securities market within the meaning of §§1.897-1(m) and 1.897-9T(d).

(J) A *qualified controlled entity* has the meaning set forth in §1.897(l)-1(e)(9).

(K) A *qualified foreign pension fund* has the meaning set forth in §1.897(l)-1(c).

(L) A *QIE* is a qualified investment entity, as defined in section 897(h)(4)(A).

(M) *Testing period* has the meaning set forth in section 897(h)(4)(D).

(N) *U.S. publicly traded QIE stock* is any class of stock of a QIE that is regularly traded on an established securities market within the meaning of §§1.897-1(m) and 1.897-9T(d), but only if the established securities market is in the United States.

(vi) *Examples.*—The rules of this paragraph (c)(3) are illustrated by the following examples. It is presumed that each entity has a single class of stock or other ownership interests, that the ownership described existed throughout the relevant testing period and that, unless otherwise stated, a QIE is not a public QIE as defined under paragraph (c)(3)(v)(H) of this section.

(A) *Example 1: QIE stock held by public domestic C corporation.*—*(1) Facts.*—USR is a REIT, 51 percent of the stock of which is held by X, a public domestic C corporation as defined in paragraph (c)(3)(v)(G) of this section, and 49 percent of the stock of which is held by nonresident alien individuals, which are foreign persons as defined in paragraph (k) of this section.

(2) Analysis.—Under paragraph (c)(3)(v)(L) of this section, USR is a QIE. X is a non-look-through person as defined under paragraph (c)(3)(v)(D) of this section. Thus, under paragraph (c)(3)(ii)(A) of this section X is considered as holding directly or indirectly stock of USR for purposes of determining whether USR is a domestically controlled QIE. Under paragraph (c)(3)(ii)(C) of this section, the USR stock held directly or indirectly by X is not considered held directly or indirectly by any other person, including the shareholders of X. Because X is not a foreign person as defined in paragraph (k) of this section and holds directly or indirectly 51 percent of the single class of outstanding stock of USR, foreign persons hold directly or indirectly less than 50 percent of the fair market value of the stock of USR, and USR therefore is a domestically controlled QIE under paragraph (c)(3)(i) of this section.

(3) Alternative facts: QIE stock held by domestic partnership.—The facts are the same as in paragraph (c)(3)(vi)(A)(1) of this section (*Example 1*), except that, instead of being a public domestic C corporation, X is a domestic partnership that is not a publicly traded partnership as defined in paragraph (c)(3)(v)(I) of this section. In addition, FC1, a foreign corporation, holds a 50 percent interest in X, and the remaining interests in X are held by U.S. citizens. X is a look-through person as defined in paragraph (c)(3)(v)(C) of this section and, therefore, under paragraph (c)(3)(ii)(A) of this section is not considered as holding directly or indirectly stock of USR for purposes of determining whether USR is a domestically controlled QIE. Under paragraph (c)(3)(ii)(B) of this section, the stock of USR that, but for paragraph (c)(3)(ii)(A) of this section, is considered held by X, a look-through person, is instead considered held proportionately by X's partners that are non-look-through persons. Accordingly, because FC1 and the U.S. citizen partners in X are non-look-through persons as defined in paragraph (c)(3)(v)(D) of this section, 25.5 percent of the stock of USR is considered as held directly or indirectly by FC1 (50% x 51%), a foreign person as defined in paragraph (k) of this section, and 25.5 percent (in the aggregate) of the stock of USR is considered as held directly or indirectly by the U.S. citizen partners in X (50% x 51%), who are not foreign persons as defined in paragraph (k) of this section. Foreign persons therefore hold directly or indirectly 74.5 percent of the stock of USR (49 percent of the stock of USR held directly or indirectly by nonresident alien individuals, who are non-look-through persons as defined in paragraph (c)(3)(v)(D) of this section, plus the 25.5 percent held directly or indirectly by FC1), and USR is not a domestically controlled QIE under paragraph (c)(3)(i) of this section. The result described in this paragraph (c)(3)(vi)(A)(3) would be the same if, instead of being a domestic partnership, X were a foreign partnership.

(4) Alternative facts: QIE stock held by a qualified foreign pension fund.—The facts are the same as in paragraph (c)(3)(vi)(A)(3) of this section (*Example 1*), except that, instead of being a foreign corporation, FC1 is a qualified foreign pension fund. The analysis is the same as in paragraph (c)(3)(vi)(A)(3) of this section regarding the treatment of X as a look-through person as defined in paragraph (c)(3)(v)(C) of this section. FC1, a foreign person under paragraph (c)(3)(iv)(A) of this section, is a non-look-through person as defined in paragraph (c)(3)(v)(D) of this section. Because FC1 and the U.S. citizen partners in X are non-look-through persons, 25.5 percent of the stock of USR is considered as held directly or indirectly by FC1 (50% x 51%), and 25.5 percent (in the aggregate) of the stock of USR is considered as held directly or indirectly by the U.S. citizen partners in X (50% x 51%). Foreign persons therefore hold directly or indirectly 74.5 percent of the stock of USR (49 percent of the stock of USR held directly or indirectly by nonresident alien individuals, who are foreign persons and non-look-through persons as defined in paragraph (c)(3)(v)(D) of this section, plus the 25.5 percent held directly or indirectly by FC1), and USR is not a domestically controlled QIE under paragraph (c)(3)(i) of this section.

(B) *Example 2: QIE stock held by non-public domestic C corporation that is a foreign-owned domestic corporation.*—*(1) Facts.*—USR is a REIT, 51 percent of the stock of which is held by X, a non-public domestic C corporation as defined in paragraph (c)(3)(v)(E) of this section, and 49 percent of the stock of which is held by nonresident alien individuals, which are foreign persons as defined in paragraph (k) of this section. FC1, a foreign corporation, holds 20 percent of the stock of X, and Y, a nonresident alien individual, holds 5 percent of the stock of X. The remaining 75 percent of the stock of X is held by U.S. citizens.

(2) *Analysis.*—Under paragraph (c)(3)(v)(L) of this section, USR is a QIE. X is a non-look-through person as defined under paragraph (c)(3)(v)(D) of this section, unless paragraph (c)(3)(iii)(B) of this section applies to treat X as a look-through person because X is a foreign-owned domestic corporation. FC1, Y, and the U.S. citizen shareholders of X are non-look-through persons as defined under paragraph (c)(3)(v)(D) of this section. Under paragraph (c)(3)(v)(B)(1) of this section, FC1, Y, and the U.S. citizen shareholders are all considered as holding directly or indirectly stock of X for purposes of determining whether X is a foreign-owned domestic corporation. Under paragraph (c)(3)(v)(B)(1) of this section, the stock held directly or indirectly by FC1, Y, and the U.S. citizen shareholders is not considered held directly or indirectly by any other person. Because FC1 and Y, both foreign persons as defined in paragraph (k) of this section, hold directly or indirectly 20 percent and 5 percent of the stock of X, respectively, foreign persons hold directly or indirectly 25 percent of the fair market value of the stock of X, and X is a foreign-owned domestic corporation under paragraph (c)(3)(v)(B) of this section. Accordingly, under paragraph (c)(3)(iii)(B) of this section, X is a look-through person as defined in paragraph (c)(3)(v)(C) of this section and, therefore, under paragraph (c)(3)(ii)(A) of this section is not considered as holding directly or indirectly stock of USR for purposes of determining whether USR is a domestically controlled QIE. Under paragraph (c)(3)(ii)(B) of this section, the stock of USR that, but for paragraph (c)(3)(ii)(A) of this section, is considered held by X, a look-through person, is instead considered held proportionately by X's shareholders that are non-look-through persons. Accordingly, because FC1, Y, and the U.S. citizen shareholders of X are non-look-through persons, 10.2 percent of the stock of USR is considered as held directly or indirectly by FC1 (20% x 51%), 2.55 percent of the stock of USR is considered as held directly or indirectly by Y (50% x 51%), and 38.25 percent (in the aggregate) of the stock of USR is considered as held directly or indirectly by the U.S. citizen shareholders (75% x 51%). Foreign persons therefore hold directly or indirectly 61.75 percent of the stock of USR (49 percent of the stock of USR held directly by nonresident alien individuals, who are foreign persons and non-look-through persons as defined in paragraph (c)(3)(v)(D) of this section, plus the 10.2 percent and 2.55 percent held indirectly by FC1 and Y, respectively), and USR is not a domestically controlled QIE under paragraph (c)(3)(i) of this section. The result described in this paragraph (c)(3)(vi)(B)(2) would be different if Y were a U.S. citizen instead of a nonresident alien individual, in which case X would be a non-look-through person because it is not a foreign-owned domestic corporation under paragraph (c)(3)(v)(B) of this section and, consequently, USR would be a domestically controlled QIE under paragraph (c)(3)(i) of this section.

(C) *Example 3: QIE stock held by public QIE that is a domestically controlled QIE.—(1) Facts.*—USR2 is a REIT, 51 percent of the stock of which is held by USR1, a REIT that is a public QIE as defined in paragraph (c)(3)(v)(H) of this section, and 49 percent of the stock of which is held by nonresident alien individuals, which are foreign persons as defined in paragraph (k) of this section. The stock of USR1 is U.S. publicly traded QIE stock as defined in paragraph (c)(3)(v)(N) of this section. FC1 and FC2, both foreign corporations, each hold 20 percent of the stock of USR1. The remaining 60 percent of the stock of USR1 is held by persons that each hold less than 5 percent of the stock of USR1 and with respect to which USR1 has no actual knowledge that such person is not a United States person ("USR1 small public shareholders").

(2) *Analysis.*—Under paragraph (c)(3)(v)(L) of this section, USR2 and USR1 are QIEs. Under paragraph (c)(3)(iii)(A) of this section, each of the USR1 small public shareholders is treated as a United States person that is a non-look-through person. Consequently, under paragraph (c)(3)(i) of this section USR1 is a domestically controlled QIE because FC1 and FC2, each a foreign person as defined in paragraph (k) of this section, together hold directly or indirectly only 40 percent of the stock of USR1 and, thus, foreign persons hold directly or indirectly less than 50 percent of the fair market value of the stock of USR1. In addition, the USR2 stock held by USR1 is treated as held directly or indirectly by a United States person that is a non-look-through person under paragraph (c)(3)(iii)(C) of this section. Because USR1 holds directly or indirectly 51 percent of the stock of USR2, foreign persons hold directly or indirectly less than 50 percent of the fair market value of the stock of USR2, and USR2 is a domestically controlled QIE under paragraph (c)(3)(i) of this section.

(3) *Alternative facts: QIE stock held by public QIE that is not a domestically controlled QIE.*—The facts are the same as in paragraph (c)(3)(vi)(C)(1) of this section (*Example 3*), except that 25 percent of the stock of USR1 is held by each of FC1 and FC2, with the remaining 50 percent of the stock of USR1 held by the USR1 small public shareholders. Regardless of the treatment of the USR1 small public shareholders, USR1 is not a domestically controlled QIE under paragraph (c)(3)(i) of this section because FC1 and FC2, each a foreign person as defined in paragraph (k) of this section, together hold directly or indirectly 50 percent of the stock of USR1 and, thus, foreign persons do not hold directly or indirectly less than 50 percent of the fair market value of the stock of USR1. In addition, the USR2 stock held by USR1 is treated as held by a foreign person that is a non-look-through person under paragraph (c)(3)(iii)(C) of this section. Because USR1 holds directly or indirectly 51 percent of the stock of USR2, foreign persons do not hold directly or indirectly less than 50 percent of the fair market value of the stock of USR2, and USR2 is not a domestically controlled QIE under paragraph (c)(3)(i) of this section.

(D) *Example 4: QIE stock held by non-public QIE.—(1) Facts.*—USR2 is a REIT, 49 percent of the stock of which is held by nonresident alien individuals, and 51 percent of the stock of which is held by USR1, a REIT. U.S. citizens hold 50 percent of the stock of USR1. The remaining 50 percent of the stock of USR1 is held by PRS, a domestic partnership, 50 percent of the interests in which are held by DC, a public domestic C corporation as defined in paragraph (c)(3)(v)(G) of this section, and 50 percent of the interests in which are held by nonresident alien individuals.

(2) *Analysis.*—Under paragraph (c)(3)(v)(L) of this section, USR2 and USR1 are QIEs. USR1 is not treated as a non-look-through person under paragraph (c)(3)(iii)(C) of this section because USR1 is not a public QIE as defined in paragraph (c)(3)(v)(H) of this section. Each of USR1 and PRS is a look-through person as defined in paragraph (c)(3)(v)(C) of this section that is not treated as holding directly or indirectly stock in USR2 for purposes of determining whether USR2 is a domestically controlled QIE under paragraph (c)(3)(ii)(A) of this section. Under paragraph (c)(3)(ii)(B) of this section, stock of a QIE that would be considered held by a look-through person but for the application of paragraph (c)(3)(ii)(A) of this section is considered held directly or indirectly proportionately by the look-through person's direct or indirect owners that are non-look-through persons. Because the U.S. citizens who hold USR1 stock are non-look-through persons as defined in paragraph (c)(3)(v)(D) of this section, those U.S. citizens are treated as holding directly or indirectly 25.5 percent of the stock of USR2 through their USR1 stock interest (50% x 51%) in accordance with paragraph (c)(3)(ii)(A) of this section. Similarly, because DC and the nonresident alien partners in PRS are non-look-through persons, each is treated as holding directly or indirectly the stock of USR2 through its interest in PRS and PRS's interest in USR1. Thus, DC is treated as holding directly or indirectly 12.75 percent of the stock of USR2 (50% x 50% x 51%) and the nonresident alien individual partners, which are foreign persons as defined in paragraph (k) of this section, are treated as directly or indirectly holding a 12.75 percent aggregate interest in the stock of USR2 (50% x 50% x 51%). Foreign persons therefore hold directly or indirectly 63.25 percent of the stock of USR2 (the 49 percent stock in USR2 directly held by nonresident alien individuals, who are foreign persons and non-look-through persons as defined in paragraph (c)(3)(v)(D) of this section, plus the 12.75 percent in stock indirectly held by the nonresident alien individual partners in PRS), and USR2 is not a domestically controlled QIE under paragraph (c)(3)(i) of this section.

(4) *Foreign ownership percentage.*—For purposes of calculating the foreign ownership percentage under section 897(h)(4)(C), the determination of the QIE stock that was held directly or indirectly by foreign persons is made under the rules of paragraphs (c)(3)(ii) through (vi) of this section.

* * *

(k) *Foreign person.*—The term *foreign person* means a nonresident alien individual (including an individual subject to the provisions of section 877), a foreign corporation as defined in paragraph (l) of this section, a foreign partnership, a foreign trust or a foreign estate, as such persons are defined by section 7701 and the regulations in this chapter under section 7701. A resident alien individual, including a nonresident alien individual with respect to whom there is in effect an election under section 6013(g) or 6013(h) to be treated as United States resident, is not a foreign person. With respect to the status of foreign governments and international organizations, see §1.897-9T(e). See paragraph (c)(3)(iv)(A) of this section regarding the treatment of qualified foreign pension funds and qualified controlled entities as foreign persons for purposes of section 897(h)(4)(B).

(l) * * * For purposes of sections 897 and 6013(h), however, the term does not include a foreign corporation with respect to which there is in effect an election under section 897(i) and §1.897-3 to be treated as a domestic corporation. For purposes of section 897, the term does not include a qualified holder described in §1.897(l)-1(d); see paragraph (c)(3)(iv)(A) of this section regarding the treatment of qualified foreign pension funds and qualified controlled entities as foreign persons for purposes of section 897(h)(4)(B).

* * *

(n) See §1.897-9T(d) for a definition of regularly traded for purposes of sections 897, 1445, and 6039C.

* * *

[Prop. Reg. §1.897-1.]

[Proposed 12-29-2022.]

§1.897-2. United States real property holding corporations.—(a) *Purpose and scope.*—This section provides rules regarding the definition and consequences of U.S. real property holding corporation status. U.S. real property holding corporation status is important for determining whether gain from the disposition by a foreign person of an interest in a domestic corporation is taxable. Such status is also important for purposes of the withholding and reporting requirements of sections 1445 and 6039C. For example, a person that buys stock of a U.S. real property holding corporation from a foreign person is required to withhold under section 1445. In addition, for purposes of determining whether another corporation is a U.S. real property holding corporation, an interest in a foreign corporation is a U.S. real property interest unless it is established that the foreign corporation is not a U.S. real property holding corporation. The general definition of a U.S. real property holding corporation is provided in paragraph (b) of this section. Paragraph (c) provides rules regarding the dates on which U.S. real property holding corporation status must be determined. The assets that must be included in making the determination of a corporation's status are set forth in paragraph (d), while paragraph (e) provides special rules regarding the treatment of interests held by a corporation in partnerships, trusts, estates, and other corporations. Rules regarding the termination of U.S. real property holding corporation status are set forth in paragraph (f). Paragraph (g) explains the manner in which an interest-holder can establish that a corporation is not a U.S. real property holding corporation, and paragraph (h) provides rules regarding certain notification requirements applicable to corporations.

(b) *U.S. real property holding corporation.*—(1) *In general.*—A corporation is a U.S. real property holding corporation if the fair market value of the U.S. real property interests held by the corporation on any applicable determination date equals or exceeds 50 percent of the sum of the fair market values of its—

(i) U.S. real property interests;

(ii) Interests in real property located outside the United States; and

(iii) Assets other than those described in subdivision (i) or (ii) of this paragraph (b)(1) that are used or held for use in its trade or business.

See paragraphs (d) and (e) of this section for rules regarding the directly and indirectly held assets that must be included in the determination of whether a corporation is a U.S. real property holding corporation. The term "interest in real property located outside the United States" means an interest other than solely as a creditor (as defined in §1.897-1(d)) in real property (as defined in §1.897-1(b)) that is located outside the United States or the Virgin Islands. If a corporation qualifies as a U.S. real property holding corporation on any applicable determination date after June 18, 1980, any interest in it shall be treated as a U.S. real property interest for a period of five years from that date, unless the provisions of paragraph (f)(2) of this section are applicable.

(2) *Alternative test.*—(i) *In general.*—The fair market value of a corporation's U.S. real property interests shall be presumed to be less than 50 percent of the fair market value of the aggregate of its assets described in paragraphs (d) and (e) of this section if on an applicable determination date the total book value of the U.S. real property interests held by the corporation is 25 percent or less of the book value of the aggregate of the corporation's assets described in paragraphs (d) and (e) of this section.

(ii) *Definition of book value.*—For purposes of this section and §1.897-1(e) the term "book value" shall be defined as follows. In the case of assets that are held directly by the corporation, the term means the value at which an item is carried on the financial accounting records of the corporation, if such value is determined in accordance with generally accepted accounting principles applied in the United States. In the case of assets of which a corporation is treated as holding a pro rata share pursuant to paragraphs (e)(2) and (3) of this section and §1.897-1(e), the term "book value" means the corporation's share of the value at which the asset is carried on the financial accounting records of the entity that directly holds the asset, if such value is determined in accordance with generally accepted accounting principles applied in the United States. For purposes of this paragraph (b)(2)(ii), an entity need not keep all of its books in accordance with U.S. accounting principles, so long as the value of the relevant assets is determined in accordance therewith.

(iii) *Denial of presumption.*—If the Internal Revenue Service determines, on the basis of information as to the fair market values of a corporation's assets, that the presumption allowed by this paragraph (b)(2) may not accurately reflect the status of the corporation, the Service will notify the corporation that it may not rely upon the presumption. The Service will provide a written notice to the corporation that sets forth the general grounds for the Service's conclusion that the presumption may be inaccurate. By the 90th day following the date on which the corporation receives the Service's notification, the corporation must determine whether on its most recent determination date it was a U.S. real property holding corporation pursuant to the general rule set forth in paragraph (b)(1) of this section and must notify the Service of its determination. If the corporation determines that it was not a U.S. real property holding corporation pursuant to the general rule, then the corporation may upon future determination dates rely upon the presumption allowed by this paragraph (b)(2), unless on the basis of additional information the Service again requests that the determination be made pursuant to the general rule. If the corporation determines that it was a U.S. real property holding corporation on its most recent determination date, then by the 180th day following the date on which the corporation received the Service's notification the corporation (if a domestic corporation) must notify each holder of an interest in it that contrary to any prior representations it was a U.S. real property holding corporation as of its most recent determination date.

(iv) *Applicability of penalties.*—A corporation that had previously relied upon the presumption allowed by this paragraph (b)(2) but that is determined to be a U.S. real property holding corporation shall not be subject to penalties for any incorrect notice previously given pursuant to the requirements of paragraph (h) of this section, if:

(A) The corporation in fact carried out the necessary calculations enabling it to rely upon the presumption allowed by this paragraph (b)(2); and

(B) The corporation complies with the provisions of paragraph (b)(2)(iii) of this section.

However, a corporation shall remain subject to any applicable penalties if at the time of its reliance on the presumption allowed by this paragraph (b)(2) the corporation knew that the book values of relevant assets was substantially higher or lower than the fair market value of those assets and therefore had reason to believe that under the general test of paragraph (b)(1) of this section the corporation would probably be a U.S. real property holding corporation. Information with respect to the fair market value of its assets is known by a corporation if such information is included on any books and records of the corporation or its agent, is known by its directors or officers, or is known by employees who in the course of their employment have reason to know such information. A corporation relying upon the presumption allowed by this paragraph (b)(2) has no affirmative duty to determine the fair market value of assets if such values are not otherwise known to it in accordance with the preceding sentence. The rules of this paragraph (b)(2)(iv) may be illustrated by the following examples.

Example 1. DC is a domestic corporation engaged in light manufacturing that knows that it has foreign shareholders. On its December 31, 1985 determination date DC held assets used in its trade or business, consisting largely of recently-purchased equipment, with a book value of $500,000. DC's only real property interest was a factory that it had occupied for over 50 years, which had a book value of $200,000. The factory was located in a deteriorated downtown area, and DC had no knowledge of any facts indicating that the fair market value of the property was substantially higher than its book value. Therefore, DC was entitled to rely upon the presumption allowed by §1.897-2(b)(2) and any incorrect statement pursuant to § 1.897-2(h) that arose out of such reliance would not give rise to penalties.

Example 2. The facts are the same as in Example 1, except as follows. By the time of DC's December 31, 1989 determination date, the downtown area in which DC's factory was located had become the subject of an extensive urban renewal program. On December 1, 1989, the president of DC was offered $750,000 for the factory by a developer who planned to convert the property into condominiums. Because DC thus had knowledge of the fair market value of its assets which made it clear that the corporation would probably be a U.S. real property holding corporation under the general rule of § 1.897-2(b)(1), DC was not entitled to rely upon the presumption allowed by § 1.897-2(b)(2) after December 1, 1989, and any false statements arising out of such reliance thereafter would give rise to penalties.

(v) *Effect on interestholders and related persons.*—For the effect on interestholders and related persons of reliance on a statement issued by a corporation that made a determination as to whether it was a U.S. real property holding corporation under the provisions of § 1.897-2(b), see § 1.897-2(g)(1)(ii)(A) and 1.897-2(g)(2)(ii).

(c) *Determination dates for applying U.S. real property holding corporation test.*—(1) *In general.*—Whether a corporation is a U.S. real property holding corporation is to be determined as of the following dates:

(i) The last day of the corporation's taxable year;

(ii) The date on which the corporation acquires any U.S. real property interest;

(iii) The date on which the corporation disposes of an interest in real property located outside the United States or disposes of other assets used or held for use in a trade or business during the calendar year, subject to the provisions of paragraph (c)(2)(i) of this section; and

(iv) In the case of a corporation that is treated pursuant to paragraph (d)(4) or (5) of this section as owning a portion of the assets held by an entity in which the corporation directly or indirectly holds an interest, the date on which that entity either (A) acquires a U.S. real property interest, (B) disposes of an interest in real property located outside the United States or (C) disposes of other assets used or held for use in a trade or business during the calendar year, subject to the provisions of paragraph (c)(2)(ii) of this section. A determination that is triggered by a transaction described in subdivision (ii), (iii), or (iv) of this paragraph (c)(1) must take such transaction into account. However, the first determination of a corporation's status need not be made until the 120th day after the later of the date of incorporation or of the date on which the corporation first acquires a shareholder. In addition, no determination of a corporation's status need be made during the 12-month period beginning on the date on which a corporation adopts a plan of complete liquidation, provided that all the assets of the corporation (other than assets retained to meet claims) are distributed within such period.

(2) *Transactions not requiring a determination.*—(i) *Transactions by corporation.*—Notwithstanding the provisions of paragraph (c)(1) of this section, a determination of U.S. real property holding corporation status need not be made on the date of:

(A) A corporation's disposition of inventory or livestock (as described in § 1.897-1(f)(1)(i)(A) and (C));

(B) The satisfaction of accounts receivable arising from the disposition of inventory or livestock or from the performance of services;

(C) The disbursement of cash to meet the regular operating needs of the business (e.g., to acquire inventory or to pay wages and salaries);

(D) A corporation's disposition of assets used or held for use in a trade or business (other than inventory or livestock) not in excess of a limitation amount determined in accordance with the rules of subdivision (iii) of this paragraph (c)(2); or

(E) A corporation's acquisition of U.S. real property interests not in excess of a limitation amount determined in accordance with the rules of subdivision (iii) of this paragraph (c)(2).

(ii) *Transactions by entity other than corporation.*—Notwithstanding the provisions of paragraph (c)(1)(iv) or (c)(2)(v) of this section, in the case of a corporation that is treated as owning a portion of the assets held by an entity in which the corporation directly or indirectly holds an interest, a determination of U.S. real property holding corporation status need not be made on the date of:

(A) The entity's disposition of inventory or livestock (as described in § 1.897-1(f)(1)(i)(A) and (C));

(B) The satisfaction of accounts receivable arising from the entity's disposition of inventory or livestock or from the performance of personal services;

(C) The entity's disbursement of cash to meet the regular operating needs of its business (e.g. to acquire inventory or to pay wages and salaries);

(D) The entity's disposition of assets used or held for use in a trade or business (other than inventory or livestock) not in excess of a limitation amount determined in accordance with the rules of subdivision (iii) of this paragraph (c)(2); or

(E) The entity's acquisition of U.S. real property interests not in excess of a limitation amount determined in accordance with the rules of subdivision (iii) of this paragraph (c)(2).

(iii) *Calculation of limitation amount.*—The amount of assets used or held for use in a trade or business that may be disposed of, and the amount of U.S. real property interests that may be acquired, by a corporation or other entity without triggering a determination date shall be calculated in accordance with the following rules.

(A) If, in accordance with the provisions of paragraphs (d) and (e) of this section, a corporation on its most recent determination date was considered to hold U.S. real property interests having a fair market value that was less than 25 percent of the aggregate fair market value of all the assets it was considered to hold, then the applicable limitation amount shall be 10 percent of the fair market value of all trade or business assets or all U.S. real property interests (as applicable) held directly by the corporation or by another entity described in paragraph (c)(1)(iv) of this section on that determination date.

(B) If, in accordance with the provisions of paragraphs (d) and (e) of this section, a corporation on its most recent determination date was considered to hold U.S. real property interests having a fair market value that was equal to or greater than 25 and less than 35 percent of the aggregate fair market value of all the assets it was considered to hold, then the applicable limitation amount shall be 5 percent of the fair market value of all trade or business assets or all U.S. real property interests (as applicable) held directly by the corporation or by another entity described in paragraph (c)(1)(iv) of this section on that determination date.

(C) If, in accordance with the provisions of paragraphs (d) and (e) of this section, a corporation on its most recent determination date was considered to hold U.S. real property interests having a fair market value that was equal to or greater than 35 percent of the aggregate fair market value of all the assets it was considered to hold, then the applicable limitation amount shall be 2 percent of the fair market value of all trade or business assets or all U.S. real property interests (as applicable) held directly by the corporation or by another entity described in paragraph (c)(1)(iv) of this section on that determination date.

(D) If a corporation is not a U.S. real property holding corporation under the alternative test of paragraph (b)(2) of this section (relating to the book value of the corporation's assets), then the applicable limitation shall be 10 percent of the book value of all trade or business assets or all U.S. real property interests (as applicable) held directly by the corporation or by another entity described in paragraph (c)(1)(iv) of this section on the most recent determination date.

Dispositions or acquisitions by the corporation or other entity of assets having a value less than the applicable limitation amount must be cumulated by the corporation or entity making such dispositions or acquisitions, and a determination must be made on the date of a transaction that causes the total of either type to exceed the applicable limitation. Once a determination is triggered by a transaction that causes the applicable limitation to be exceeded, the computation of the amount of trade or business assets disposed of or real property interests acquired after that date shall begin again at zero.

The rules of this paragraph (c)(2) may be illustrated by the following examples.

Example (1). DC is a domestic corporation, no class of stock of which is regularly traded on an established securities market, that knows that it has several foreign shareholders. As of December 31, 1984, DC holds U.S. real property interests with a fair market value of $500,000, no real property interests located outside the U.S., and other assets used in its trade or business with a fair market value of $1,600,000. Thus, the fair market value of DC's U.S. real property interests ($500,000) is less than 25% ($525,000) of the total ($2,100,000) of DC's U.S. real property interests ($500,000), interests in real property located outside the United States (zero), and assets used or held for use in a trade or business ($1,600,000). DC is not a U.S. real property holding corporation, and under the rule of paragraph (c)(2)(i) of this section it may dispose of trade or business assets with a fair market value equal to 10 percent ($160,000) of the total fair market value ($1,600,000) of such assets held by it on its most recent determination date (December 31, 1984), without triggering a determination of its U.S. real property holding corporation status. Therefore, when DC disposes of $60,000 worth of trade or business assets (other than inventory or livestock) on March 1, 1985, and again on April 1, 1985, no determination of its status is required on either date. However, when DC disposes of a further $60,000 worth of such trade or business assets on May 1, its total disposition of such assets ($180,000) exceeds its applicable limitation amount, and DC is therefore required to determine its U.S. real property holding corporation status. On May 1, 1985, the fair market value of DC's U.S. real property interests ($500,000) is greater than 25 percent or ($480,000) and less than 35 percent ($672,000) of the total ($1,920,000) of DC's U.S. real property interests ($500,000), interests in real property located outside the United States (zero), and assets used or held for use in a trade or business ($1,420,000). DC is still not a U.S. real property holding corporation, but must now compute its applicable limitation amount as of the May 1 determination date. Under the rule of paragraph (c)(2)(iii)(B) of this section, DC could now dispose of trade or business assets other than inventory or livestock with a total fair market value equal to 5 percent of the fair market value of all trade or business assets held by DC on the May 1 determination date. Therefore, disposition of such trade or business assets with a fair market value of more than $71,000 (5 percent of $1,420,000) will trigger a further determination date for DC.

Example (2). DC is a domestic corporation, no class of stock of which is regularly traded on an established securities market, that knows that it has several foreign shareholders. As of December 31, 1986, DC's only assets are a U.S. real property interest with a fair market value of $300,000 other assets used or held for use in its trade or business with a fair market value of $600,000, and a 50 percent partnership interest in domestic partnership DP. DC's interest in DP constitutes a percentage ownership interest in the partnership of 50 percent, and pursuant to the rules of paragraph (e)(2) of this section DC is treated as owning a portion of the assets of DP determined by multiplying that percentage by the fair market value of DP's assets. As of December 31, 1986, DP's only assets are U.S. real property interests with a fair market value of $120,000 and other assets used in its trade or business with a fair market value of $380,000. As of its December 31, 1986, determination date, the fair market value ($360,000) of the U.S. real property interests DC holds ($300,000) and is treated as holding ($60,000 [The fair market value of DP's U.S. real property interest ($120,000) multiplied by DC's percentage ownership interest in DP (50 percent)]), is equal to 31 percent of the sum of the fair market values ($1,150,000) of the U.S. real property interests DC holds and is treated as holding ($360,000) DC's interest in real property located outside the United States (zero), and assets used or held for use in a trade or business that DC holds or is treated as holding ($790,000 [$600,000 (held directly) plus $190,000 (DC's 50 percent share of assets used or held for use in a trade or business by DP)]). Thus, under the rules of paragraph (c)(2)(i) and (iii)(B) of this section DC may dispose of assets used or held for use in its trade or business with a fair market value equal to 5 percent ($30,000) of the total fair market value ($600,000) of such assets held directly by it on its most recent determination date (December 31, 1986), without triggering a determination of its U.S. real property holding corporation status. In addition, under the rules of paragraph (c)(2)(ii) and (iii)(A) of this section, a determination date for DC would not be triggered by DP's disposition of trade or business assets (other than inventory or livestock) with a fair market value equal to 5 percent ($19,000) of the total fair market value ($380,000) of such assets held by it as of DC's most recent determination date (December 31, 1986). However, any disposition of such assets by DP exceeding that limitation would trigger a determination of DC's U.S. real property holding corporation status. In addition, under the rule of paragraph (c)(1)(iv) of this section, any disposition of a U.S. real property interest by DP would trigger a determination date for DC, while under the rule of paragraph (c)(2)(ii) of this section no disposition of inventory or livestock by DP would trigger a determination for DC.

(3) *Alternative monthly determination dates.*—(i) *In general.*—Notwithstanding the provisions of paragraph (c)(1) and (2) of this section, a corporation may choose to determine its U.S. real property holding corporation status in accordance with the rules of this paragraph (c)(3). In the case of a corporation that has determined that it is not a U.S. real property holding corporation pursuant to the alternative test of paragraph (b)(2) of this section (relating to the book value of the corporation's assets), the rules of this paragraph (c)(3) may be applied by using book values rather than fair market values in all relevant calculations.

(ii) *Monthly determinations.*—A corporation that determines its U.S. real property holding corporation status in accordance with the rules of this paragraph (c)(3) must make a determination at the end of each calendar month.

(iii) *Transactional determinations.*—A corporation that determines its U.S. real property holding corporation status in accordance with the rules of this paragraph (c)(3) must make a determination as of the date on which, pursuant to a single transaction (consisting of one or more transfers):

(A) U.S. real property interests are acquired, and/or

(B) Interests in real property located outside the U.S. and/or assets used or held for use in a trade or business are disposed of,

if the total fair market value of the assets acquired and/or disposed of exceeds 5 percent of the sum of the fair market values of the U.S. real property interests, interests in real property located outside the U.S., and assets used or held for use in a trade or business held by the corporation.

(iv) *Exceptions.*—Notwithstanding any other provision of this paragraph (c)(3), the first determination of a corporation's status need not be made until the 120th day after the later of the date of incorporation or the date on which the corporation first acquires a shareholder. In addition, no determination of a corporation's status need be made during the 12-month period beginning on the date on which a corporation adopts a plan of complete liquidation, if all the assets of the corporation (other than assets retained to meet claims) are distributed within such period.

(4) *Valuation date methods.*—(i) *In general.*—For purposes of determining whether a corporation is a U.S. real property holding corporation on any applicable determination date, the fair market value of the assets held by the corporation (in accordance with § 1.897-2(d)) as of that determination date must be used.

(ii) *Alternative valuation date method for determination dates other than the last day of the taxable year.*—For purposes of paragraph (c)(4)(i) of this section, if an applicable determination date under paragraph (c)(1), (2), or (3) of this section is other than the last day of the taxable year, property may be valued as of the later of the last day of the previous taxable year or the date such property was acquired. For purposes of the determination date that falls on the last day of the taxable year, fair market value as of that date must always be used.

(iii) *Consistent methods.*—The valuation date method selected under this paragraph (c)(4) for the first determination date in a taxable year must be used for all subsequent determination dates for such year. In addition, the valuation date method selected must be used for all property with respect to which the determination is made. The use of one method for one taxable year does not preclude the use of the other method for any other taxable year.

(5) *Illustrations.*—The rules of this paragraph (c) are illustrated by the following examples:

Example (1). Nonresident alien individual C purchased 100 shares of stock of domestic corporation K on July 26, 1985. Although K has additional shares of common stock outstanding, its stock has never been traded on an established securities market. At all times during calendar year 1985, K's only assets were a parcel of U.S. real estate (parcel A) and a parcel of country Z real estate (parcel B). On December 31, 1985, the fair market value of parcel A was $1,000,000 and the fair market value of parcel B was $2,000,000. For purposes of determining whether K was a U.S. real property holding corporation during 1985, the only applicable determination date was December 31, 1985, because K did not make any acquisitions or dispositions described in paragraph (c)(1) of this section during the year. The test of paragraph (b) of this section is applied using the fair market value of the property held on that date. K was not a U.S. real property holding corporation during 1985 because as of December 31, 1985, the fair market value ($1,000,000) of the U.S. real property interests held by K did not equal or exceed 50 percent ($1,500,000) of the sum ($3,000,000) of the fair market value of K's U.S. real property interest ($1,000,000), the interests in real property located outside the United States ($2,000,000), plus other assets used or held for use by K in a trade or business (zero).

Example (2). The facts are the same as in example (1), except that on April 7, 1986, K purchased another parcel of U.S. real estate for $2,000,000. K's purchase of real property on April 7 triggered a determination on that date. As provided in paragraph (c)(3)(ii) of this section, K chooses to use the value of parcels A and B as of the previous December 31, while newly acquired parcel C must be valued as of its acquisition on April 7, 1986. On that date, K qualifies as a U.S. real property holding corporation, since the fair market value of its U.S. real property interests ($3,000,000) exceeds 50 percent ($2,500,000) of the sum ($5,000,000) of the fair market value of K's U.S. real property interests ($3,000,000), its interests in real property located outside the U.S. ($2,000,000), and its other assets used or held for use in a trade or business (zero).

(d) *Assets held by a corporation.*—The assets that must be included in the determination of whether a corporation is a U.S. real property holding corporation are the following:

(1) U.S. real property interests that are held directly by the corporation (including directly-held interests in foreign corporations that are treated as U.S. real property interests pursuant to the rules of paragraph (e)(1) of this section);

(2) Interests in real property located outside the United States that are held directly by the corporation;

(3) Assets used or held for use in a trade or business that are held directly by the corporation;

(4) A proportionate share of assets held through a partnership, trust, or estate pursuant to the rules of paragraph (e)(2) of this section; and

(5) A proportionate share of assets held through a domestic or foreign corporation in which a corporation holds a controlling interest, pursuant to the rules of paragraph (e)(3) of this section.

(e) *Special rules regarding assets held by a corporation.*—(1) *Interests in foreign corporations.*—For purposes only of determining whether any corporation is a U.S. real property holding corporation, an interest in a foreign corporation shall be treated as a U.S. real property interest unless it is established that the interest was not a U.S. real property interest under the rules of this section on the applicable determination date. The rules of paragraph (g)(2) of this section must be complied with to establish that the interest is not a U.S. real property interest. However, regardless of whether an interest in a foreign corporation is treated as a U.S. real property interest for this purpose, gain or loss from the disposition of an interest in such corporation will not be treated as effectively connected with the conduct of a U.S. trade or business by reason of section 897(a). The rules of this paragraph (e)(1) are illustrated by the following examples. In each example, fair market value is determined as of the applicable determination dates under paragraph (c)(4)(i) of this section.

Example (1). Nonresident alien individual F holds all of the stock of domestic corporation DC. DC's only assets are 40 percent of the stock of foreign corporation FC, with a fair market value of $500,000, and a parcel of country W real estate, with a fair market value of $400,000. Foreign corporation FP, unrelated to DC, holds the other 60 percent of the stock of FC. FC's only asset is a parcel of U.S. real estate with a fair market value of $1,250,000. FC is a U.S. real property holding corporation because the fair market value of its U.S. real property interests ($1,250,000) exceeds 50 percent ($625,000) of the sum of the fair market values of its U.S. real property interests ($1,250,000), its interests in real property located outside the United States (zero), plus its other assets used or held for use in a trade or business (zero). Consequently DC's interest in FC is treated as a U.S. real property interest under the rules of this paragraph (e)(1). DC is a U.S. real property holding corporation because the fair market value ($500,000) of its U.S. real property interest (the stock of FC) exceeds 50 percent ($450,000) of the sum ($900,000) of the fair market value of its U.S. real property interests ($500,000), its interests in real property located outside the United States ($400,000), plus its other assets used or held for use in a trade or business (zero). If F disposes of her stock within 5 years of the current determination date, her gain or loss on the disposition of her stock in DC will be treated as effectively connected with a U.S. trade or business under section 897(a). However, FP's gain on the disposition of its FC stock would not be subject to the provisions of section 897(a) because the stock of FC is a U.S. real property interest only for purposes of determining whether DC is a U.S. real property holding corporation.

Example (2). Nonresident alien individual B holds all of the stock of domestic corporation US. US's only assets are 40 percent of the stock of foreign corporation FC1. Nonresident alien individual N, unrelated to US, holds the other 60 percent of FC1's stock. FC1's only assets are 40 percent of the stock of foreign corporation FC2. The remaining 60 percent of the stock of FC2 is owned by nonresident alien individual X, who is unrelated to FC1. FC2's only asset is a parcel of U.S. real estate with fair market value of $1,000,000. FC2, therefore, is a U.S. real property holding corporation, and the stock of FC2 held by FC1 is a U.S. real property interest for purposes of determining whether FC1 is a U.S. real property holding corporation (but not for purposes of treating FC1's gain from the disposition of FC2 stock as effectively connected with a U.S. trade or business under section 897(a)). As all of FC1's assets are U.S. real property interests, the stock of FC1 held by US is a U.S. real property interest for purposes of determining whether US is a U.S. real property holding corporation (but not for purposes of subjecting N's gain on the disposition of FC1 stock to the provisions of section 897(a)). As US is a domestic corporation and as all of its assets are U.S. real property interests, US is a U.S. real property holding corporation, and the stock of US held by B is a U.S. real property interest for purposes of section 897(a). Therefore, B's gain or loss upon the disposition of the stock of US within 5 years of the most recent determination date is subject to the provisions of section 897(a).

(2) *Proportionate ownership of assets held by partnerships, trusts, and estates.*—For purposes of determining whether a corporation is a U.S. real property holding corporation, a holder of an interest in a partnership, a trust, or an estate (whether domestic or foreign) shall be treated pursuant to section 897(c)(4)(B) as holding a proportionate share of the assets held by the entity. However, a holder of an interest shall not be treated as holding a proportionate share of assets that in the hands of the entity are subject to the rule of § 1.897-1(f)(3)(ii) (concerning the trade or business assets of investment companies). Such proportionate share is to be determined in accordance with the rules of § 1.897-1(e) on each applicable determination date. The interest in the entity shall itself be disregarded when a proportionate share of the entity's assets is attributed to the interest-holder pursuant to the rule of this paragraph (e)(2). Any asset treated as held by a holder of an interest by reason of this paragraph (e)(2) which is used or held for use in a trade or business by the partnership, trust, or estate shall be treated as so used or held for use by the holder of the interest. The proportionate ownership rule of this paragraph (e)(2) applies successively upward through a chain of ownership. The proportionate ownership rule of this paragraph (e)(2) is illustrated by the following examples. In each example fair market value is determined as of the applicable determination date under paragraph (c)(4)(i) of this section.

Example (1). Nonresident alien individual F holds all of the stock of domestic corporation DC. DC is a partner in foreign partnership FP, and DC's percentage ownership interest in FP is 50 percent. DC's other assets are a parcel of country F real estate with a fair market value of $500,000 and other assets which it uses in its business with a fair market value of $100,000. FP's assets are a parcel of country Z real estate with a fair market value of $300,000 and a parcel of U.S. real estate with a fair market value of $2,000,000. For purposes of determining whether DC is a U.S. real property holding corporation, DC is treated as holding its pro rata share of the assets held by FP. DC's pro rata share of the U.S. real estate held by FP is $1,000,000, determined by multiplying the fair market value ($2,000,000) of the U.S. real property interests held by FP by DC's percentage ownership interest in FP (50 percent). DC's pro rata share of the country Z real estate held by FP is $150,000, determined in the same manner. DC is a U.S. real property holding corporation because the fair market value ($1,000,000) of its U.S. real property interests (the U.S. real estate it is treated as holding proportionately) exceeds 50 percent ($875,000) of the sum ($1,750,000) of the fair market value of its U.S. real property interests ($1,000,000), its interests in real property located outside the United States [($650,000) (its country F real estate and its pro rata share of the country Z real estate)], plus its other assets which are used or held for use in a trade or business ($100,000). Because DC is a domestic U.S. real property holding corporation, the stock of DC is a U.S. real property interest and F's gain or loss on the disposition of his DC stock within 5 years of the current determination date will be treated as effectively connected with a U.S. trade or business under section 897(a).

Example (2). Nonresident alien individual B holds all of the stock of domestic corporation US. US is a beneficiary of foreign trust FT. US's percentage ownership interest in FT is 90 percent. US has no other assets. FT is a partner in domestic partnership DP. FT's percentage ownership interest in DP is 30 percent. FT has no other assets. DP's only asset is a parcel of U.S. real estate with a fair market value of $1,000,000. FT is treated as holding U.S. real estate with a fair market value of $300,000 (30 percent of the U.S. real estate held by DP with a fair market value of $1,000,000). For purposes of determining whether US is a U.S. real property holding corporation, the proportionate ownership rule is applied successively upward through the chain of ownership. Thus, US is treated as holding 90 percent of FT's $300,000 pro rata share of the U.S. real estate held by DP. US is a U.S. real property holding corporation because the fair market value ($270,000) of its U.S. real property interests (its pro rata share of the U.S. real estate held by DP) exceeds 50 percent ($135,000) of the sum of the fair market values of its U.S. real property interests

($270,000), its interests in real property located outside the United States (zero), plus its other assets used or held for use in a trade or business (zero). Because US is a domestic U.S. real property holding corporation, the stock of US is a U.S. real property interest, and B's gain or loss from the disposition of US stock within 5 years of the current determination date will be treated as effectively connected with a U.S. trade or business under section 897(a).

(3) *Controlling interests in corporations.*—For purposes only of determining whether a corporation is a U.S. real property holding corporation, if the corporation (the "first corporation") holds a controlling interest in a second corporation—

(i) The first corporation is treated as holding a proportionate share of each asset (i.e., U.S. real property interests, interests in real property located outside the United States, and assets used or held for use in a trade or business) held by the second corporation, determined in accordance with the rules of § 1.897-1(e);

(ii) Any asset so treated as held proportionately by the first corporation which is used or held for use by the second corporation in a trade or business shall be treated as so used or held for use by the first corporation; and

(iii) Interests in the second corporation held by the first corporation are not themselves taken into account as U.S. real property interests (regardless of whether the second corporation is a U.S. real property holding corporation) or as trade or business assets.

However, the first corporation shall not be treated as holding a proportionate share of assets that in the hands of the second corporation are subject to the rule of § 1.897-1(f)(3)(ii) (concerning the trade or business assets of investment companies). A determination of what portion of the assets of the second corporation are considered to be held by the first corporation shall be made as of the applicable dates for determining whether the first corporation is a U.S. real property holding corporation. A "controlling interest" means 50 percent or more of the fair market value of all classes of stock of the corporation, determined as of the applicable determination date. In determining whether a corporation holds a controlling interest in another corporation, section 318(a) shall apply (except that sections 318(a)(2)(C) and (3)(C) are applied by substituting the phrase "5 percent" for "50 percent"). However, a corporation that does not directly hold any interest in a second corporation shall not be treated as holding a controlling interest in the second corporation by reason of the application of section 318(a)(3)(C). The rules of this paragraph (e)(3) apply successively upward through a chain of ownership. For example, if the second corporation owns a controlling interest in a third corporation, the rules of this paragraph shall be applied first to determine the portion of the assets of the third corporation that is considered to be held by the second corporation and then to determine the portion of the assets held and considered to be held by the second corporation that is considered to be held by the first corporation. The controlling interest rules of this paragraph (e)(3) apply, regardless of whether a corporation is domestic or foreign, whenever it is necessary to determine whether a corporation is a U.S. real property holding corporation. The rules of this paragraph (e)(3) are illustrated by the following examples. In each example fair market value is determined as of the applicable determination date under paragraph (c)(4)(i) of this section and no corporation holds constructively any interest not specified in the example.

Example (1). Nonresident alien individual N owns all of the stock of domestic corporation DC. DC's only assets are 60 percent of the fair market value of all classes of stock of foreign corporation FS and 60 percent of the fair market value of all classes of stock of domestic corporation DS. The percentage ownership interest of DC in each of FS and DS is 60 percent. The balance of the stock in FS and DS is held by nonresident alien individual B, who is unrelated to DC. FS's only asset is a parcel of country F real estate with a fair market value of $1,000,000. DS's only asset is a parcel of U.S. real estate with a fair market value of $2,000,000. The value of DC stock in FS and DS is not taken into account for purposes of determining whether DC is a U.S. real property holding corporation. Rather, because DC holds a controlling interest (60 percent) in each of FS and DS, DC is treated as holding a portion of each asset held by FS and DS. DC's portion of the country F real estate held by FS is $600,000, determined by multiplying the fair market value ($1,000,000) of the country F real estate by DC's percentage ownership interest (60 percent). Similarly, DC's portion of the U.S. real estate held by DS is $1,200,000 (60 percent of $2,000,000). DC is a U.S. real property holding corporation, because the fair market value ($1,200,000) of its U.S. real property interests (its portion of the U.S. real estate) exceeds 50 percent ($900,000) of the sum ($1,800,000) of the fair market values of its U.S. real property interests ($1,200,000), its interests in real property located outside the United States (the $600,000 portion of country F real estate), plus its other assets used or held for use in a trade or business (zero). Because DC is a domestic U.S. real property holding corporation, the stock of DC is a U.S. real property interest, and N's gain or loss on the disposition of DC stock within 5 years of the current determination date would be treated as effectively connected with a U.S. trade or business under section 897(a).

Example (2). (i) Nonresident alien individual F owns all of the stock of domestic corporation US1. US1's only asset is 85 percent of the fair market value of all classes of stock of domestic corporation US2. US2's only assets are 60 percent of the fair market value of all classes of stock of domestic corporation US3, with a fair market value of $800,000, and a parcel of country D real estate with a fair market value of $800,000. US3's only asset is a parcel of U.S. real estate with a fair market value of $2,000,000. The percentage ownership interest of F in US1 is 100 percent. Although US1 owns 85 percent of the stock of US2, US1's percentage ownership interest in US2 is 75 percent, because US2 has other interests other than solely as a creditor outstanding. US2's percentage ownership interest in US3 is 60 percent.

(ii) US2 holds a controlling interest in US3, since it holds more than 50 percent of the fair market value of all classes of stock of US3. Consequently, the value of US2's stock in US3 is not taken into account in determining whether US2 is a U.S. real property holding corporation, even though US3 is a U.S. real property holding corporation. Instead, US2 is treated as holding a portion of the U.S. real estate held by US3. US2's portion of the U.S. real estate is $1,200,000, determined by multiplying US2's percentage ownership interest (60 percent) by the fair market value ($2,000,000) of the U.S. real estate. US1 holds a controlling interest in US2 (75 percent). By reapplying the rules of paragraph (e)(3) of this section successively upward through the chain of ownership, US1's stock in US2 is not taken into account, and US1 is treated as holding a portion of the country D real estate held by US2 and the U.S. real estate which US2 is treated as holding proportionately. US1's portion of the country D real estate is $800,000, determined by multiplying US1's percentage ownership interest (75 percent) by the fair market value ($800,000) of the country D real estate. US1's portion of the U.S. real estate which US2 is treated as owning is $900,000, determined by multiplying US1's percentage ownership interest (75 percent) by the fair market value ($1,200,000) of US2's portion of U.S. real estate held by US3. US1 is a U.S. real property holding corporation, because the fair market value ($900,000) of its U.S. real property interests (its portion of US2's portion of U.S. real estate) is more than 50 percent ($750,000) of the sum ($1,500,000) of fair market values of its U.S. real property interests ($900,000), its interests in real property located outside the United States ($800,000), plus its other assets used or held for use in a trade or business (zero). Because US1 is a U.S. real property holding corporation and is a domestic corporation, the stock of US1 is a U.S. real property interest, and F's gain or loss on the disposition of US1 stock within 5 years of the current determination date will be treated as effectively connected with a U.S. trade or business under section 897(a).

Example (3). Nonresident alien individual B holds all of the stock of domestic corporation DC. DC's only assets are 40 percent of the fair market value of all classes of stock of foreign corporation FC and a parcel of country R real estate with a fair market value of $100,000. FC's only asset is one parcel of U.S. real estate with a fair market value of $1,000,000. The fair market value of the FC stock held by DC is $200,000. FC is a U.S. real property holding corporation. Since DC does not hold a controlling interest in FC, the controlling interest rules of paragraph (e)(3) of this section do not apply to treat DC as holding a portion of the U.S. real estate held by FC. However, because FC is a U.S. real property holding corporation, the stock of FC is a U.S. real property interest for purposes of determining whether DC is a U.S. real property holding corporation. DC is a U.S. real property holding corporation because the fair market value ($200,000) of its U.S. real property interest (the stock of FC) exceeds 50 percent ($150,000) of the sum ($300,000) of the fair market values of its U.S. real property interest ($200,000), its interests in real property located outside the United States ($100,000), plus its other assets used or held for use in a trade or business (zero). Because DC is a U.S. real property holding corporation and is a domestic corporation, its stock is a U.S. real property interest, and B's gain or loss on the disposition of DC stock within 5 years of the current determination date would be subject to the provisions of section 897(a).

Example (4). Nonresident alien individual C owns all of the stock of domestic corporation DC1. DC1's only assets are 25 percent of the fair market value of all classes of stock of domestic corporation DC2, and a parcel of U.S. real estate with a fair market value of $100,000. The stock of DC2 is not an asset used or held for use in DC1's trade or business. DC2's only assets are a building located in the U.S. with a fair market value of $100,000 and manufacturing equipment and inventory with a fair market value of $200,000. DC2 is not a U.S. real property holding corporation. Since DC1 does not hold a controlling interest in DC2, the rules of this paragraph (e)(3) do not apply to treat DC1 as holding a portion of the assets held by DC2. In addition, since DC2 is not a U.S. real property holding corporation, its stock does not constitute a U.S. real property interest. Therefore, for purposes of determining whether DC1 is a U.S. real property holding corporation, its interest in DC2 is not taken into account. Since DC1's only other asset is a parcel of U.S. real estate, DC1 is a U.S. real property holding corporation, and C's gain or loss on the disposition of DC1 stock within 5 years of the current determination date would be subject to the provisions of section 897(a).

(4) *Co-application of rules of this paragraph (e).*—The rules of this paragraph (e) apply in conjunction with one another for purposes of determining whether a corporation is a U.S. real property holding corporation. The rule of this paragraph (e)(4) is illustrated by the following example. In the example fair market value is determined as of the applicable determination date in accordance with paragraph (c)(4)(i) of this section.

Example. Nonresident alien individual B holds 100 percent of the stock of domestic corporation US. US's only asset is 10 percent of the stock of foreign corporation FC1. FC1's only asset is 100 percent of the stock of foreign corporation FC2. FC2's only asset is a 50 percent interest in domestic partnership DP. FC2's percentage ownership interest in DP is 50 percent. DP's only asset is a parcel of U.S. real estate with a fair market value of $10,000,000. In determining whether US is a U.S. real property holding corporation, the rules of this paragraph (e) apply in conjunction with one another. Consequently, under paragraph (e)(2) of this section FC2 is treated as holding U.S. real estate with a fair market value of $5,000,000 (50 percent of $10,000,000, its pro rata share of real estate held by DP). Under paragraph (e)(3) of this section, FC1 is treated as holding 100 percent of the assets of FC2 (U.S. real estate with a fair market value of $5,000,000). FC1, therefore, is a U.S. real property holding corporation. Under paragraph (e)(1) of this section, the stock of FC1 is treated as U.S. real property interest. US is a U.S. real property holding corporation because 100 percent of its assets (the stock of FC1) are U.S. real property interests. As US is a U.S. real property holding corporation and is a domestic corporation, the stock of US is a U.S. real property interest, and B's gain or loss from the disposition of stock of US within 5 years of the current determination date will be subject to the provisions of section 897(a).

(f) *Termination of U.S. real property holding corporation status.*—(1) *In general.*—A U.S. real property holding corporation may voluntarily determine its status as of the date of any acquisition or disposition of assets. If the fair market value of its U.S. real property interests on such date no longer equals or exceeds 50 percent of the fair market value of all assets described in paragraphs (d) and (e) of this section, such corporation shall cease to be U.S. real property holding corporation as of such date, and on the day that is five years after such date interests in such corporation shall cease to be treated as U.S. real property interests (unless subsequent transactions within the five-year period have caused the fair market value of the corporation's U.S. real property interests to equal or exceed 50 percent of the fair market value of assets described in paragraphs (d) and (e) of this section). A corporation that determines that interests in it have ceased to be U.S. real property interests pursuant to the rules of this paragraph (f) may so inform the Internal Revenue Service, as provided in paragraph (h) of this section.

(2) *Early termination.*—Interests in a U.S. real property holding corporation shall immediately cease to be U.S. real property interests as of the first date on which the following conditions are met—

(i) The corporation does not hold any U.S. real property interests;

(ii) All of the U.S. real property interests directly or indirectly held by such corporation at any time during the previous five years (but disregarding any disposed of before June 19, 1980) either (A) were directly or indirectly disposed of in transactions in which the full amount of the gain (if any) was recognized or (B) ceased to be U.S. real property interests by reason of the application of this paragraph (f) to one or more other corporations; and

(iii) If the disposition occurs on or after December 18, 2015, neither the corporation nor any predecessor of the corporation was a regulated investment company or a real estate investment trust at any time during the shorter of the periods described in section 897(c)(1)(A)(ii).

For purposes of this paragraph (f)(2), a corporation that disposes of all U.S. real property interests other than a lease that has a fair market value of zero will be considered to have disposed of all of its U.S. real property interests, provided that the leased property is used in the conduct by the corporation of a trade or business in the United States. Such a lease may include an option to renew, but only if such option is for a renewal at fair market rental rates prevailing at the time of renewal.

(g) *Establishing that a corporation is not a U.S. real property holding corporation.*—(1) *Foreign persons disposing of interests.*—(i) *In general.*—A foreign person disposing of an interest in a domestic corporation (other than an interest solely as a creditor) must establish that the interest was not a U.S. real property interest as of the date of disposition, either by:

(A) Obtaining a statement from the corporation pursuant to the provisions of subdivision (ii) of this paragraph (g)(1), or

(B) Obtaining a determination by the Commissioner, Small Business/Self Employed Division (SB/SE) pursuant to the provisions of subdivision (iii) of this paragraph (g)(1).

If the foreign person does not establish by either method that the interest disposed of was not a U.S. real property interest then the interest shall be presumed to have been a U.S. real property interest the disposition of which is subject to section 897(a). See paragraph (g)(3) of this section for certain exceptions to this rule. It should be noted that the rules of this section relate solely to interests in a corporation that are interests other than solely as a creditor. Therefore, a statement by a corporation or a determination by the Commissioner (under paragraphs (g) and (h) of this section) that an interest is not a U.S. real property interest depends solely upon whether or not the corporation was a U.S. real property holding corporation during the period described in section 897(c)(1)(A)(ii) (subject to certain special rules). The determination of whether an interest is one solely as a creditor is made under the rules of § 1.897-1(d).

(ii) *Statement from corporation.*—(A) *In general.*—A foreign person disposing of an interest in a domestic corporation may establish that the interest was not a U.S. real property interest as of the date of the disposition by requesting and obtaining from the corporation a statement that the interest was not a U.S. real property interest as of that date. However, a corporation's statement shall not be valid for purposes of this rule, and thus may not be relied upon for purposes of establishing that an interest was not a U.S. real property interest, unless the corporation complies with the notice requirements of paragraph (h)(2) or (h)(4) of this section.

A foreign person that requests and obtains such a statement is not required to forward the statement to the Internal Revenue Service and is not required to take any further action to establish that the interest disposed of was not a U.S. real property interest. To qualify under this rule, the foreign person must obtain the corporation's statement no later than the date, including any extensions, on which a tax return would otherwise be due with respect to a disposition. A foreign person that relies in good faith upon a statement from the corporation is not thereby excused from filing a return and paying any taxes and interest due thereon if the corporation's statement is later found to have been incorrect. However, such reliance shall be taken into account in determining whether the foreign person shall be subject to any penalty for the previous failure to file. However, a foreign person that knew or had reason to know that a corporation's statement was incorrect is not entitled to rely upon such statement and shall remain liable for all applicable penalties.

(B) *Coordination with section 1445.*—Pursuant to section 1445 and regulations thereunder, withholding of tax is not required with respect to a foreign person's disposition of an interest in a domestic corporation, if the transferee is furnished with a statement by the corporation under paragraph (h) of this section that the interest is not a U.S. real property interest. A foreign person that obtains a corporation's statement for that purpose prior to the date of disposition may also rely upon the statement for purposes of this paragraph (g)(1)(ii), unless the corporation informs the foreign person (pursuant to paragraph (h)(1)(iv)(C) of this section) that it became a U.S. real property holding corporation after the date of the notice but prior to the actual date of disposition.

(iii) *Determination by Commissioner.*—(A) *In general.*—A foreign person disposing of an interest in a domestic corporation may establish that the interest was not a U.S. real property interest as of the date of disposition by requesting and obtaining a determination to that effect from the Commissioner. Such a determination may be requested pursuant to the provisions of subdivision (B) or (C) of this paragraph (g)(1)(iii). A request for a determination should be addressed to: Commissioner, Small Business/Self Employed Division (SB/SE); S C3-413 NCFB, 500 Ellin Road, Lanham, MD 20706. A foreign transferor who has requested a determination by the Commissioner pursuant to the rules of this paragraph (g)(1)(iii) is not thereby excused from filing a return and paying any tax due by the date, including any extensions, on which such return and payment would otherwise be due with respect to a disposition. If the Commissioner subsequently determines and notifies the foreign transferor that the interest was not a U.S. real property interest, the foreign transferor shall be entitled to a refund of any taxes, penalties, and interest paid by reason of the application of section 897(a) pursuant to the rules of paragraph (g)(1)(i) of this section, together with any interest otherwise due on such refund, if a claim for refund is made within the applicable time limits.

(B) *Determination based on Commissioner's information.*—A foreign person may request that the Commissioner make a determination based on information contained in the Commissioner's records, if:

(1) The foreign person made a request to the corporation for information as to the status of its interest no later than the 90th day before the date, including any extensions, on which a tax return would otherwise be due with respect to a disposition, and

(2) The corporation failed to respond to such request by the 30th day following the date the request was delivered to the corporation.

If the Commissioner is unable to make a determination based on information available to him, he shall inform the foreign person that the interest must be treated as a U.S. real property interest unless the person subsequently obtains either the necessary statement from the corporation or a determination pursuant to subdivision (C) of this paragraph (g)(1)(iii).

(C) *Determination based on information supplied by foreign person.*—A foreign person may request that the Commissioner make a determination based on information supplied by the foreign person. Such information may be drawn, for example, from annual reports, financial statements, or records of the corporation, and must establish to the satisfaction of the Commissioner that the foreign person's interest was not a U.S. real property interest as of the date of disposition.

(D) *Determination by Commissioner on his own motion.*—Notwithstanding any other provision of this section, a foreign person shall not treat the disposition of an interest in a domestic corporation as a disposition of a U.S. real property interest if such person is notified that the Commissioner has upon his own motion determined that the interest was not a U.S. real property interest as of the date of disposition.

(2) *Corporations determining U.S. real property holding corporation status.*—(i) *In general.*—A corporation that must determine whether it is a U.S. real property holding corporation, and that holds an interest in another corporation (other than a controlling interest as defined in paragraph (e)(3) of this section), must determine whether or not that interest was a U.S. real property interest as of its own determination date, by either:

(A) Obtaining a statement from the second corporation pursuant to the provisions of subdivision (ii) of this paragraph (g)(2);

(B) Obtaining a determination by the Commissioner pursuant to the provisions of subdivision (iii) of this paragraph (g)(2); or

(C) Making an independent determination pursuant to the provisions of subdivision (iv) of this paragraph (g)(2).

A corporation that is unable to determine by any of the above methods whether its interest in a second corporation is a U.S. real property interest must presume that such interest is a U.S. real property interest.

(ii) *Statement from corporation.*—A corporation may determine whether or not an interest in a second corporation was a U.S. real property interest as of its own determination date by obtaining from the second corporation a statement that the interest was not a U.S. real property interest as of that date. However, the second corporation's statement shall not be valid for purposes of this rule, and thus may not be relied upon for purposes of establishing that an interest was not a U.S. real property interest, unless such corporation complies with the notice requirements of paragraph (h)(2) or (h)(4) of this section.

A corporation that requests and obtains such a statement is not required to forward the statement to the Internal Revenue Service and is not required to take any further action to establish that the interest in the second corporation was not a U.S. real property interest. If the second corporation's statement is later found to have been incorrect, the first corporation shall not be subject to penalties arising out of past failures to comply with the requirements of section 897 or 1445, if such failures were attributable to reliance upon the second corporation's statement. By the 90th day following receipt of a notification from the Service or from the second corporation that a prior statement was incorrect, the first corporation must redetermine its status (as of its most recent determination date) and if appropriate notify the Internal Revenue Service that it is a U.S. real property holding corporation in accordance with paragraph (h)(1)(ii)(C) of this section. However, a corporation that knew or had reason to know that a second corporation's statement was incorrect is not entitled to rely upon such statement and shall remain liable for all applicable taxes, penalties, and interest arising out of the second corporation's status as a U.S. real property holding corporation.

(iii) *Determination by Commissioner.*—(A) *In general.*—A corporation may determine whether or not an interest in a second corporation was a U.S. real property interest as of its own determination date by requesting and obtaining a determination to that effect from the Commissioner. Such a determination may be requested pursuant to the provisions of subdivision (B) or (C) of this paragraph (g)(2)(iii). A request for a determination must be addressed to: Commissioner, Small Business/Self Employed Division (SB/SE); S C3-413 NCFB, 500 Ellin Road, Lanham, MD 20706. A corporation that has requested a determination by the Commissioner pursuant to the provisions of this paragraph is not thereby excused from taking any action required by section 897 or 1445 by the date on which such action would otherwise be due. However, the Commissioner may grant a reasonable extension of time for the satisfaction of any requirement if the Commissioner is satisfied that the corporation has not sought a determination pursuant to this paragraph (g)(2)(iii) for a principal purpose of delay.

(B) *Determination based on Commissioner's information.*—A corporation may request that the Commissioner make a determination based on information contained in the Commissioner's records, if:

(1) The corporation made a request to the second corporation for information as to the status of its interest no later than the fifth day following the first corporation's determination date, and

(2) The second corporation failed to respond to such request by the 30th day following the date the request was delivered to the second corporation.

Pending his resolution of such a request, the Commissioner will generally grant an extension with respect to the change-of-status notification that may otherwise be required pursuant to paragraph (h)(1)(ii) of this section. If the Commissioner is unable to make a determination based on information available to him, he shall inform the corporation that the interest must be treated as a U.S. real property interest unless the corporation subsequently obtains either the necessary statement from the second corporation or a determination pursuant to paragraph (g)(2)(iii)(C) or (g)(2)(iv) of this section.

(C) *Determination based on information supplied by corporation.*—A corporation may request that the Commissioner make a determination based on information supplied by the corporation. Such information may be drawn, for example, from annual reports, financial statements, or records of the second corporation, and must establish to the satisfaction of the Commissioner that the interest in the second corporation was not a U.S. real property interest as of the first corporation's determination date.

(D) *Determination by Commissioner on his own motion.*—Notwithstanding any other provision of this section, a corporation shall not treat an interest in a second corporation as a U.S. real property interest if the corporation is notified that the Commissioner has upon his own motion determined that the interest in the second corporation is not a U.S. real property interest.

(iv) *Independent determination by corporation.*—A corporation may independently determine whether or not an interest in a second corporation was a U.S. real property interest as of the first corporation's own determination date. Such determination must be based upon the best evidence available, drawn from annual reports, financial statements, records of the second corporation, or from any other source, that demonstrates to a reasonable certainty that the interest in the second corporation was not a U.S. real property interest. A corporation that makes an independent determination pursuant to this paragraph (g)(2)(iv) shall be subject to the special notification rule of paragraph (h)(1)(iii)(D) of this section. If the Commissioner subsequently determines that the corporation's independent determination was incorrect, the corporation shall be subject to penalties for any past failure to comply with the requirements of section 897 or 1445 only if the corporation's determination was unreasonable in view of facts that the corporation knew or had reason to know.

(3) *Requirements not applicable.*—If at any time during the calendar year any class of stock of a corporation is regularly traded on an established securities market, the requirements of this paragraph (g) shall not apply with respect to any holder of an interest in such corporation other than a person who holds an interest described in § 1.897-1(c)(2)(iii)(A) or (B). For example, a corporation determining whether it is a U.S. real property holding corporation need not ascertain from a regularly traded corporation in which it neither holds, nor has held during the period described in section 897(c)(1)(A)(ii), more than a 5 percent interest whether that regularly traded corporation is itself a U.S. real property holding corporation. In addition, the requirements of this paragraph (g) do not apply to any holder of an interest in a domestically-controlled REIT, as defined in section 897(h)(4)(B).

(h) *Notice requirements applicable to corporations.*—(1) *Statement to foreign interest-holder.*—(i) *In general.*—A domestic corporation must, within a reasonable period after receipt of a request from a foreign person holding an interest in it, inform that person whether the interest constitutes a U.S. real property interest. No particular form is required for this statement, which need only indicate the corporation's determination. The statement must be dated and signed by a responsible corporate officer who must verify under penalties of perjury that the statement is correct to his knowledge and belief.

(ii) *Required determination.*—For purposes of the statement required by paragraph (h)(1)(i) of this section, an interest in a corporation is a U.S. real property interest if the corporation was a U.S. real property holding corporation on any determination date during the 5-year period ending on the date specified in the interest-holder's request, or on the date such request was received if no date is specified (or during such shorter period ending on the date that is applicable pursuant to section 897(c)(1)(A)(ii)). However, an interest in a corporation is not a U.S. real property interest if such interest is excluded under section 897(c)(1)(B).

(2) *Notice to the Internal Revenue Service.*—If a foreign interest holder requests that a domestic corporation provide a statement described in paragraph (h)(1) of this section, then such corporation must provide a notice to the Internal Revenue Service in accordance with this paragraph (h)(2). No particular form is required for such notice, but the following must be provided:

(i) A statement that the notice is provided pursuant to the requirements of § 1.897-2(h)(2);

(ii) The name, address, and identifying number of the corporation providing the notice;

(iii) The name, address, and identifying number (if any) of the foreign interest holder that requested the statement (this information may be omitted from the notice if fully set forth in the statement to the foreign interest holder attached to the notice);

(iv) Whether the interest in question is a U.S. real property interest;

(v) A statement signed by a responsible corporate officer verifying under penalties of perjury that the notice (including any attachments thereto) is correct to his knowledge and belief. A copy of any statement provided to the foreign interest holder must be attached to the notice. The notice must be mailed to the address specified in the Instructions for Form 8288 under the heading "Where To File" on or before the 30th day after the statement referred to in § 1.897-2(h)(1) is mailed to the interest holder that requested it. Failure to mail such notice within the time period set forth in the preceding sentence will cause the statement provided pursuant to § 1.897-2(h)(1) to become an invalid statement.

(3) *Requirements not applicable.*—The requirements of this paragraph (h) do not apply to domestically-controlled REITS, as defined in section 897(h)(4)(B). These requirements also do not apply to a corporation any class of stock in which is regularly traded on an established securities market at any time during the calendar year. However, such a corporation may voluntarily choose to comply with the requirements of paragraph (h)(4) of this section.

(4) *Voluntary notice to Internal Revenue Service.*—(i) *In general.*—A domestic corporation which determines that it is not a U.S. real property holding corporation—

(A) on each of the applicable determination dates in a taxable year, or

(B) pursuant to section 897(c)(1)(B),

may attach to its income tax return for that year a statement informing the Internal Revenue Service of its determination. A corporation that has provided a voluntary notice described in this § 1.897-2(h)(4)(i) for the immediately preceding taxable year and that does not have an event described in § 1.897-2(c)(1)(ii), (iii) or (iv) prior to receiving a request from a foreign person under § 1.897-2(h)(1), is exempt from the notice requirement of § 1.897-2(h)(2).

(ii) *Early termination of real property holding corporation status.*—A corporation that determines during the course of its taxable year that interests in it have ceased to be U.S. real property interests pursuant to the rules of section 897(c)(1)(B) may, on the day of its determination or thereafter, provide a statement to the address specified in the Instructions for Form 8288 under the heading "Where To File", informing the Service of its determination. No particular form is required but the statement must set forth the corporation's name, address, identification number, a brief statement regarding its determination and the date such determination was made. Such statement will enable foreign interest-holders to dispose of their interests without being subject to section 897(a), as provided in paragraph (g) of this section.

(5) *Supplemental statements.*—(i) *By corporations with substantial intangible assets.*—A corporation that is subject to the requirements of paragraph (h)(2) of this section (or that voluntarily complies with the requirements of paragraph (h)(4) of this section) must submit a supplemental statement to the Internal Revenue Service if—

(A) Such corporation values any of the intangible assets described in § 1.897-1(f)(1)(ii) (other than goodwill or going concern value) by a method other than the purchase price or book value methods described in § 1.897-1(o)(4); and

(B) The fair market value of such intangible assets equals or exceeds 25 percent of the total of the fair market values of the assets the corporation is considered to hold in accordance with the provisions of paragraphs (d) and (e) of this section.

The supplemental statement must inform the Internal Revenue Service that the corporation meets the criteria of subdivisions (A) and (B) of this paragraph (h)(5)(i), and must summarize the methods and calculations upon which the corporation's determination of the fair market value of its intangible assets is based. In addition, the supplemental statement must list any intangible assets that were purchased from any person that have been valued by the corporation at an amount other than their purchase price, and must provide a justification for such a departure from the purchase price. The supplemental statement must be attached to or incorporated in the statement provided under paragraph (h)(2) or (h)(4) of this section.

(ii) *Corporation not valuing goodwill or going concern value at purchase price.*—A corporation that is subject to the requirements of paragraph (h)(2) of this section (or that voluntarily complies with the requirements of paragraph (h)(4) of this section) must submit a supplemental statement to the Internal Revenue Service if such corporation values goodwill or going concern value pursuant to § 1.897-1(o)(4)(iii). The supplemental statement must set forth that it is made pursuant to this paragraph (h)(5)(ii), and must summarize the methods and calculations upon which the corporation's determination of the fair market value of such intangible assets is based. In addition, the supplemental statement must list any such assets that were purchased from any person that have been valued by the corporation at an amount other than their purchase price, and must provide a justification for such a departure from the purchase price. The supplemental statement must be attached to or incorporated in the statement provided under paragraph (h)(2) or (h)(4) of this section.

(iii) *Corporation using alternative U.S. real property holding corporation test.*—A corporation that is subject to the requirements of paragraph (h)(2) of this section (or that voluntarily complies with the requirements of paragraph (h)(4) of this section) must submit a supplemental statement to the Internal Revenue Service if—

(A) Such corporation utilizes the rule of paragraph (b)(2) of this section (regarding the book values of assets held by the corporation) to presume that it is not a U.S. real property holding corporation; and

(B) Such corporation is engaged in or is planning to engage in a trade or business of mining, farming, or forestry, or of buying and selling or developing real property, or of leasing real property to tenants.

The supplemental statement must inform the Internal Revenue Service that the corporation meets the criteria of subdivisions (A) and (B) of this paragraph (h)(5)(iii), and must be attached to or incorporated in the statement provided under paragraph (h)(2) or (h)(4) of this section.

(iv) *Corporation determining real property holding corporation status of second corporation.*—A corporation that is subject to the requirements of paragraph (h)(2) of this section (or that voluntarily complies with the requirements of paragraph (h)(4) of this section) must submit a supplemental statement to the Internal Revenue Service if such corporation independently determines whether or not an interest in a second corporation is a U.S. real property interest, pursuant to paragraph (g)(2)(iv) of this section. The supplemental statement must set forth that it is made pursuant to this paragraph (h)(5)(iv) and must briefly summarize the facts upon which the corporation's determination is based and the sources of the information relied upon by the corporation. The supplemental statement must be attached to or incorporated in the statement provided under paragraph (h)(2) or (h)(4) of this section.

(i) *Transition rules.*—(1) *General waiver of penalties for failure to file.*—If a foreign person disposed of an interest in a domestic corporation between June 18, 1980 and January 23, 1987, and such person establishes under the rules of paragraph (g) of this section at any time that the interest disposed of was not a U.S. real property interest, then such person shall not be subject to tax under section 897 and shall not be subject to penalties (or interest) for failure to file an income tax return with respect to such disposition.

(2) *Foreign persons that met the requirements of prior regulations.*—A foreign person that disposed of an interest in a domestic corporation between June 18, 1980 and January 23, 1987, shall be deemed to have satisfied the requirements of paragraph (g) of this section with respect to such disposition if such person established under prior temporary or prior final regulations issued under section 897 that the interest disposed of was not a U.S. real property interest. [Reg. § 1.897-2.]

☐ [*T.D.* 7999, 12-26-84. *Amended by T.D.* 8113, 12-18-86, *T.D.* 9082, 8-4-2003 *and T.D.* 9751, 2-17-2016.]

§ 1.897-3. Election by foreign corporation to be treated as a domestic corporation under section 897(i).—(a) *Purpose and scope.*—This section provides rules pursuant to which a foreign corporation may elect under section 897(i) to be treated as a domestic corporation for purposes of sections 897, 1445, and 6039C and the regulations thereunder. A foreign corporation with respect to which an election under section 897(i) is in effect is subject to all rules under sections 897 and 1445 that apply to domestic corporations. Thus, for example, if a foreign corporation that has made an election under section 897(i) is a U.S. real property holding corporation, interests in it are U.S. real property interests that are subject to withholding under section 1445, and any gain or loss from the disposition of such interests by a foreign person will be treated as effectively connected with a U.S. trade or business under section 897(a). Similarly, if a foreign corporation makes an election under section 897(i), its distribution of a U.S. real property interest pursuant to section 301 will be subject to the carryover basis rule of section 897(f). However, an interest in an electing corporation is not a U.S. real property interest if following the election the interest is described in section 897(c)(1)(B) or § 1.897-1(c)(2) (subject to the exceptions of subdivisions (i) and (ii) of that section). In addition, section 897(d) will not apply to any distribution of a U.S. real property interest by such corporation or to any sale or exchange of such interest pursuant to a plan of complete liquidation under section 337. A foreign corporation that makes an election under section 897(i) shall not be treated as a domestic corporation for purposes of any other provision of the Code or regulations, except to the extent that it is required to consent to such treatment as a condition to making the election. For further information concerning the effect of an election under section 897(i) upon the withholding requirements of section 1445, see § 1.1445-7. An election under section 897(i) is the exclusive remedy of any foreign person claiming discriminatory treatment under any treaty with respect to the application of sections 897, 1445, and 6039C to a foreign corporation. Therefore, if a corporation does not make an effective election, relief under a nondiscrimination article of any treaty shall not be otherwise available with respect to the application of sections 897, 1445, and 6039C to such corporation.

(b) *General conditions.*—A foreign corporation may make an election under section 897(i) only if it meets all three of the following conditions.

(1) *Holding a U.S. real property interest.*—The foreign corporation must hold a U.S. real property interest at the time of the election. This condition is satisfied when a U.S. real property interest is acquired simultaneously with the effective date of an election. For example, this condition is satisfied when real property is acquired in an exchange described in section 351 that is carried out simultaneously with the effective date of the election. This condition is also satisfied by a corporation that indirectly holds a U.S. real property interest through a partnership, trust, or estate.

(2) *Entitlement to nondiscriminatory treatment.*—The foreign corporation must be entitled to nondiscriminatory treatment with respect to its U.S. real property interest under any treaty to which the United States is a party. Where the corporation indirectly holds a U.S. real property interest through a partnership, trust, or estate, the corporation itself must be entitled to nondiscriminatory treatment with respect to such property interest.

(3) *Submission of election in proper form.*—The foreign corporation must comply with the requirements of paragraph (c) of this section respecting the manner and form in which an election must be submitted.

(c) *Manner and form of election.*—An election under section 897(i) is made by filing the documents described in subparagraphs (1) through (5) of this paragraph (c) at the address specified in the Instructions for Form 8288 under the heading "Where To File". The required items may be incorporated in a single document.

(1) *General statement.*—The foreign corporation must supply a general statement indicating that an election under section 897(i) is being made. The general statement must be signed by a responsible corporate officer, who must verify under penalty of perjury that the statement and all other documents submitted pursuant to the requirements of this paragraph (c) are true and correct to his knowledge and belief. No particular form is required for the statement, which must contain all the following information—

(i) The name, address, identifying number, and place and date of incorporation of the foreign corporation;

(ii) The treaty and article under which the foreign corporation is seeking nondiscriminatory treatment;

(iii) A description of the U.S. real property interests held by the corporation, either directly or through a partnership, trust, or estate, including the dates such interests were acquired, the corporation's adjusted bases in such interests, and their fair market values as of the date of the election (or book values if the corporation is not a U.S. real property holding corporation under the alternative test of § 1.897-2(b)(2)); and

(iv) A list of all dispositions of any interests in the foreign corporation after December 31, 1979, and before June 19, 1980, between related persons (as defined in section 453(f)(1)), giving the type and the amount of any interest transferred, the name and address of the related person to whom the interest was transferred, the transferor's basis in the interest transferred, and the amount of any nontaxed gain as defined in section 1125(d) of Pub. L. 96-499.

(2) *Waiver of treaty benefits.*—The foreign corporation must submit a binding waiver of the benefits of any U.S. treaty with respect to any gain or loss from the disposition of a U.S. real property interest during the period in which the election is in effect.

(3) *Consent to be taxed.*—The foreign corporation must submit a binding agreement to treat as though it were a domestic corporation any gain or loss, that is recognized upon—

(i) The disposition of any U.S. real property interest during the period in which the election is in effect, and

(ii) The disposition of any property that it acquired in exchange for a U.S. real property interest in a nonrecognition transaction (as defined under section 897(e)) during the period in which the election is in effect.

(4) *Interest-holders' consent to election.*—(i) *In general.*—The foreign corporation must submit both a signed consent to the making of the election and a waiver of U.S. treaty benefits with respect to any gain or loss from the disposition of an interest in the corporation from each person who holds an interest in the corporation on the date the election is made. In the case of a corporation any class of

stock of which is regularly traded on an established securities market at any time during the calendar year, the signed consent and waiver need only be provided by a person who holds an interest described in § 1.897-1(c)(2)(iii)(A) or (B) (determined after application of the constructive ownership rules of section 897(c)(6)(C)). The foreign corporation must also include with the signed consents and waivers a list that identifies and describes the interest in the corporation held by each interest holder, including the type and amount of such interest and its fair market value as of the date of the election.

(ii) *Corporation's retention of interest-holders' consents.*—A corporation need not file the consents and waivers of its interest-holders as required by paragraph (c)(4)(i) of this section, if it instead complies with the requirements of subdivisions (A) through (D) of this paragraph (c)(4)(ii).

(A) The corporation must place a legend on each outstanding certificate for shares of its stock that reads substantially as follows: "[Name of corporation] has made an election under section 897(i) of the United States Internal Revenue Code to be treated as a U.S. corporation for certain tax purposes, and any purchaser of this interest may therefore be required to withhold tax at the time of the purchase." The corporation must certify that the foregoing requirement has been met and that it will place an equivalent legend on every stock certificate that is issued while the election under section 897(i) is in effect and the corporation retains the consents and waivers of its interest-holders under the rules of this paragraph (c)(4)(ii). However, with respect to any registered certificate issued prior to January 30, 1985, in lieu of placing a legend on the certificate the corporation may certify that it will provide the purchaser of the interest with a copy of the legend at the time the certificate is surrendered for issuance of a new certificate.

(B) The corporation must include with its election a statement that the corporation has received both a signed consent to the making of the election and a waiver of U.S. treaty benefits with respect to any gain or loss from the disposition of an interest in the corporation from each person who holds an interest in the corporation on the date the election is made. In the case of a corporation any class of stock of which is regularly traded on an established securities market at any time during the calendar year, the signed consent and waiver need only be provided by a person who holds or has held an interest described in § 1.897-1(c)(2)(iii)(A) or (B) (determined after application of the constructive ownership rules of section 897(c)(6)(C)).

(C) The corporation must include with its election a list that describes the interests in the corporation held by each interest-holder. The list need not identify the interest-holders by name, but must set forth the type, amount, and fair market value of the interests held by each.

(D) The corporation must include with its election an agreement that the corporation will retain all signed consents and waivers for a period of three years from the date of the election and supply such documents to the Director within 30 days of his request for production thereof. The Director's review of the signed consents and waivers pursuant to this provision shall not constitute an examination for purposes of section 7605(b).

(5) *Statement regarding prior dispositions.*—The foreign corporation must state that no interest in the corporation was disposed of during the shortest of (A) the period from June 19, 1980, through the date of the election, (B) the period from the date on which the corporation first holds a U.S. real property interest through the date of the election, or (C) the five-year period ending on the date of the election. If the corporation cannot state that no such dispositions have been made, it may make the section 897(i) election only if it states that it has complied with the requirements of paragraph (d)(2) of this section.

(d) *Time and duration of election.*—(1) *In general.*—A foreign corporation that meets the conditions of paragraph (b) of this section may make an election under section 897(i) at any time before the first disposition of an interest in the corporation which would be subject to section 897(a) if the election had been made before that disposition, except as otherwise provided in paragraph (d)(2) of this section. The period to which the election applies begins on the date on which the election is made, or such earlier date as is specified in the election, but not earlier than June 19, 1980. Unless revoked, an election applies for the duration of the time for which the corporation remains in existence. An election is made on the date that the statements described in paragraph (c) of this section are delivered to the address specified in the Instructions for Form 8288 under the heading "Where To File". If the election is delivered by United States mail, the provisions of section 7502 and the regulations thereunder shall apply in determining the date of delivery.

(2) *Election after disposition of stock.*—An election under section 897(i) may be made after any disposition of an interest in the corporation which would have been subject to section 897(a) if the election had been made before that disposition, but only if the requirements of either subdivision (i) or (ii) of this paragraph (d)(2) are met with respect to all dispositions of interests during the period described in paragraph (c)(5) of this section.

(i) There is a payment of an amount equal to any taxes which would have been imposed by reason of the application of section 897 upon all persons who had disposed of interests in the corporation during the period described in paragraph (c)(5) of this section had the corporation made the election prior to such dispositions. Such payment must be made by the later of the date the election is made, or the date on which payment of such taxes would otherwise have been due, and must include any interest that would have accrued had tax actually been due with respect to the disposition. As an election made prior to any disposition of interests in the corporation would have been conditioned on a waiver of treaty benefits by the interest-holders, payment of an amount equal to tax and any interest with respect to such prior disposition is required as a condition to making a subsequent election under this subdivision (i) irrespective of the application of any treaty provision. For this purpose, it is not necessary that the payment be made by the person who would have owed the tax if the election under this section had been made prior to the disposition, and that person is under no obligation to supply any information to the present holders of interests in the electing corporation. The payment shall be made to the U.S. Treasury. Where the payment is made by a present holder of an interest, the basis of the person's interest in the corporation shall be increased to the extent of the amount paid.

(ii) Each person that acquired an interest in the electing corporation took a basis in the interest that was equal to the basis of the interest in the hands of the person from which the interest was acquired, increased by the sum of any gain recognized by the transferor of the interest and any tax paid under chapter 1 by the person that acquired the interest, if such interest was acquired after June 18, 1980.

(3) *Adequate proof of basis.*—For purposes of meeting the conditions of paragraph (d)(2)(i) or (ii) of this section, a corporation must establish the bases of and amount of gain realized by all persons who disposed of interests in the corporation during the period described in paragraph (c)(5) of this section. See paragraph (g)(3) of this section for an exception to this rule.

(4) *Acknowledgment of receipt.*—Within 60 days after its receipt of an election under section 897(i), the Internal Revenue Service will acknowledge receipt of the election. Such acknowledgment either will indicate that the information submitted with the election is complete or will specify any documents that remain to be submitted pursuant to the requirements of paragraph (c) of this section respecting the manner and form in which an election must be made.

(e) *Anti-abuse rule.*—(1) *In general.*—A corporation that is otherwise eligible to make an election under section 897(i) may do so only by complying with the requirements of subdivision (2) of this paragraph, if during the period described in paragraph (c)(5) of this section—

(i) Prior to receipt of a U.S. real property interest by the corporation seeking to make the election, stock in such corporation (or in any corporation controlled by such corporation) was acquired in a transaction in which the person acquiring such stock obtained an increase in basis in the stock over the adjusted basis of the stock in the hands of the person from whom it was acquired;

(ii) The full amount of gain realized by the person from whom the stock was acquired was not subject to U.S. tax; and

(iii) The corporation seeking to make the election received the U.S. real property interest in a transaction or series of transactions to which section 897(d)(1)(B) or (e)(1) applies to allow for nonrecognition of gain.

(2) *Recognition of gain.*—A corporation described in subparagraph (1) of this paragraph (e) may make an election under section 897(i) only if it pays an amount equal to the tax on the full amount of gain realized by the transferors of the stock of such corporation (or of any corporation controlled by it) in the transaction described in paragraph (e)(1)(i) of this section. However, such amount must be paid only if the stock of the corporation seeking to make the election

(or the stock of a corporation controlled by it) would have constituted a U.S. real property interest had it (or a corporation controlled by it) made the election before that acquisition. Such amount must be paid by the later of the date of the election or the date on which such tax would otherwise be due, and must include any interest that would have accrued had tax actually been due with respect to the disposition.

(3) *Definition of control.*—For purposes of this paragraph, a corporation controls a second corporation if it holds 80 percent or more of the total combined voting power of all classes of stock entitled to vote, and 80 percent or more of the total number of shares of all other classes of stock of the second corporation. In a chain of corporations where each succeeding corporation is controlled within the meaning of this subparagraph (3) by the corporation immediately above it in the chain, each corporation in the chain shall be considered to be controlled by all corporations that preceded it in the chain.

(4) *Examples.*—The rules of this paragraph (e) are illustrated by the following examples.

Example 1. Nonresident alien individual X owns 100 percent of the stock of foreign corporation L which was organized in 1981. L's only asset is a parcel of U.S. real property which it has held since 1981. The fair market value of the U.S. real property held by L on January 1, 1984, is $1,000,000. L's basis in the property is $200,000. X's basis in the L stock is $500,000. On June 1, 1984, M corporation, a foreign corporation owned by foreign persons who are unrelated to X, purchases the stock of L from X for $1,000,000 with title passing outside of the United States. Since the stock of L is not a U.S. real property interest, X's gain from the disposition of the L stock ($500,000) is not treated as effectively connected with a U.S. trade or business under section 897(a). In addition, since X was neither engaged in a U.S. trade or business nor present in the U.S. at any time during 1984, such gain is not subject to U.S. tax under section 871. On January 1, 1987, M liquidates L under a plan of liquidation adopted on that same date. Under section 332 of the Code M recognizes no gain on receipt of the parcel of U.S. real property distributed by L in liquidation. Under section 334 (b)(1) M takes $200,000 as its basis in the U.S. real property received from L. Under section 897(d)(1)(B) no gain would be recognized to L under section 897(d)(1)(A) on the liquidating distribution. As a consequence, no gain is recognized to L under section 336 of the Code. After its receipt of the U.S. real property from L, M seeks to make an election to be treated as a domestic corporation. Thus, M acquired the L stock in a transaction in which it obtained a basis in such stock in excess of the adjusted basis of X in the stock, U.S. tax was not paid on the full amount of the gain realized by X, and M has received the property in a distribution in which section 897(d)(1)(B) applied to provide for nonrecognition of gain to L. Therefore, M may make the election only if it pays an amount equal to the tax on the full amount of X's gain, pursuant to the rule of subparagraph (e)(2) of this section.

Example 2. Nonresident alien individual X owns 100 percent of the stock of foreign corporation A which owns 100 percent of the stock of foreign corporation B. X's basis in the A stock is $500,000. A's basis in the B stock is $500,000. B owns U.S. real property with a fair market value of $1,000,000. B's basis in the U.S. real property is $500,000. On January 1, 1985, X sells the stock of A to Y, an unrelated individual, for $1,000,000 with title passing outside of the United States. In addition, X was neither engaged in a U.S. trade or business nor present in the U.S. at any time during 1985. Since the A stock is not a U.S. real property interest, X's gain on such disposition is not treated as effectively connected with a U.S. trade or business under section 897(a) and is therefore not subject to U.S. tax under section 871. On July 1, 1987, a plan of liquidation is adopted, and B is liquidated into A. Under sections 332, 334(b)(1), 336, and 897(d)(1)(B), there is no tax to A on receipt of U.S. real property from B and no tax to B on the distribution of the U.S. real property interest to A. After receipt of the property A seeks to make an election under section 897(i). Under the rules of paragraph (e) of this section, A may make the election only if it pays an amount equal to the tax on the full amount of X's gain. (Assuming that A is a U.S. real property holding corporation, the same result would be required by the rule of paragraph (d)(2) of this section.)

(f) *Revocation of election.*—(1) *In general.*—An election under section 897(i) may be revoked only with the consent of the Commissioner. A request for revocation shall be in writing and shall be delivered to the address specified in the Instructions for Form 8288 under the heading "Where To File". The request shall include the name, address, and identifying number of the corporation seeking to revoke the election, and a description of all U.S. real property interests held by the corporation on the date of the request for revocation, including the dates such interests were acquired, the corporation's adjusted bases in such interests, and their fair market values as of the date of the request (or book value if the corporation is not a U.S. real property holding corporation under the alternative test of § 1.897-2(b)(2)). The request shall be signed by a responsible officer of the corporation under penalty of perjury and shall contain a statement either that the corporation has made no distributions described in subparagraph (2) of this paragraph (f) or that the conditions of that subparagraph have been satisfied. A revocation will be effective as of the date the request is delivered to the address specified in the Instructions for Form 8288 under the heading "Where To File" (unless the Commissioner provides otherwise in his consent to the revocation. If the request is delivered by United States mail, the provisions of section 7502 and the regulations thereunder shall apply in determining the date of delivery. The Commissioner will generally consent to a revocation, provided either that there have been no distributions described in subparagraph (2) of this paragraph (f), or that the conditions of that subparagraph have been satisfied. Within 90 days after its receipt of a request to revoke an election under section 897(i), the Internal Revenue Service will acknowledge receipt of the request. Such acknowledgement either will indicate that the information submitted with the request is complete or will specify any information that remains to be submitted pursuant to the requirements of this paragraph (f).

(2) *Revocation after distribution.*—If there have been any distributions of U.S. real property interests by the corporation during the period to which an election made under section 897(i) applies, the Commissioner shall consent to the revocation of such election only if one of the following conditions is met.

(i) The full amount of gain realized by the corporation upon the distribution was subject to U.S. income tax.

(ii) There is a payment of an amount equal to the taxes that would have been imposed upon the corporation by reason of the application of section 897 if the election had not been in effect on the date of the distribution. Such payment must be made by the later of the date of the request for revocation or the date on which payment of such tax would otherwise have been due, and must include any interest that would have accrued had tax actually been due with respect to the distribution. If under the terms of any treaty to which the United States is a party such distribution would not have been subject to U.S. income tax notwithstanding the provisions of section 897, then this condition may be satisfied by providing a statement with the request for revocation setting forth the treaty and article which would have exempted the distribution from U.S. tax had the election under section 897(i) not been in effect on the date thereof.

(iii) At the time of the receipt of the distributed property, the distributee would be subject to taxation under chapter 1 of the Code on a subsequent disposition of the distributed property, and the basis of the distributed property in the hands of the distributee is no greater than the adjusted basis of such property before the distribution, increased by the amount of gain (if any) recognized by the distributing corporation. For purposes of this paragraph (f)(2)(i)(C), a distributee shall be considered to be subject to taxation upon a subsequent disposition of distributed property only if such distributee waives the benefits of any U.S. treaty that would otherwise render such disposition not taxable by the United States. Such waiver must be attached to the corporation's request for revocation.

(g) *Transitional rules.*—(1) *In general.*—An election under section 897(i) that was made at any time after June 18, 1980, must be amended to comply with the requirements of paragraphs (b), (c), and (d) of this section. Such amendment must be delivered in writing to the Director, Philadelphia Service Center by April 1, 1985. If the amendment is delivered by United States mail, the provisions of section 7502 and the regulations thereunder shall apply in determining the date of delivery. An election that is properly amended pursuant to the requirements of this section shall be effective as of the date of the original election.

(2) *Corporations previously entitled to make election.*—A foreign corporation that would have been entitled under the rules of this section to make a section 897(i) election at any time between June 19, 1980, and January 30, 1985, may retroactively make such an election pursuant to the requirements of this section. Such election must be delivered to the Director, Foreign Operations District, by March 1, 1985.

(3) *Interests in corporation disposed of prior to publication.*—Where interests in a corporation were disposed of before January 3, 1984, the requirement of paragraph (d)(2) of this section may be met, notwithstanding the requirement of paragraph (d)(3), by paying a tax that is

based upon a reasonable estimate of the gain upon the prior dispositions. Such estimate must be based on all facts and circumstances known to, and ascertainable through the exercise of reasonable diligence by, the corporation seeking to make the election.

(h) *Effective date.*—The requirement in paragraph (c)(1)(i) of this section that the statement making the section 897(i) election contain the identifying number of the foreign corporation (in all cases) is applicable November 3, 2003. [Reg. § 1.897-3.]

□ [*T.D.* 7999, 12-26-84. *Amended by T.D.* 8115, 12-16-86, *T.D.* 9082, 8-4-2003 *and T.D.* 9751, 2-17-2016.]

§ 1.897-5. Corporate distributions.—(a) through (d)(1)(iii)(E) [Reserved]. For further guidance, see § 1.897-5T(a) through (d)(1)(iii)(E).

(d)(1)(iii)(F) Identification by name and address of the distributee or transferee, including the distributee's or transferee's taxpayer identification number;

(d)(1)(iii)(G) through (d)(4) [Reserved]. For further guidance, see § 1.897-5T(d)(1)(iii)(G) through (d)(4).

(e) *Effective date.*—This section is applicable to transfers and distributions after November 3, 2003. [Reg. § 1.897-5.]

□ [*T.D.* 9082, 8-4-2003.]

§ 1.897-5T. Corporate distributions (Temporary).—(a) *Purpose and scope.*—This section provides rules concerning the recognition of gain or loss and adjustments to basis required with respect to certain corporate distributions that are subject to section 897. Paragraph (b) of this section provides rules concerning such distributions by domestic corporations, including distributions under section 301, distributions in redemption of stock, and distributions in liquidation. Paragraph (c) sets forth rules concerning distributions by foreign corporations, including distributions under sections 301 and 355, distributions in redemption of stock, and distributions in liquidation. Finally, various rules generally applicable to distributions subject to this section, as well as to transfers subject to § 1.897-6T, are set forth in paragraph (d). The rules contained in this section are also subject to the tax avoidance rules of § 1.897-6T(c).

(b) *Distributions by domestic corporations.*—(1) *Limitation of basis upon dividend distribution of U.S. real property interest.*—Under section 897(f), if any domestic corporation (distributing corporation) distributes a U.S. real property interest to a shareholder that is a foreign person (distributee) in a distribution to which section 301 applies, then the basis of the distributed U.S. real property interest in the hands of the foreign distributee shall be determined in accordance with the provisions of section 301(d), and shall not exceed—

(i) The adjusted basis of the property before the distribution in the hands of the distributing corporation, increased by

(ii) The sum of—

(A) Any gain recognized by the distributing corporation on the distribution, and

(B) Any U.S. tax paid by or on behalf of the distributee with respect to the distribution.

(2) *Distributions by U.S. real property holding corporations which are taxable exchanges of stock under generally applicable rules.*—If a domestic corporation, stock in which is treated as a U.S. real property interest, distributes property with respect to such stock to a foreign shareholder, the distributee shall be treated as having disposed of a U.S. real property interest, and shall recognize gain or loss on the stock of such domestic corporation to the extent that, with respect to the distributees—

(i) Part or all of the distribution is treated pursuant to section 301(c)(3)(A) as a sale or exchange of stock;

(ii) Part or all of the distribution is treated pursuant to section 302(a) as made in part or full payment in exchange for stock; or

(iii) Part or all of the distribution is treated pursuant to section 331(a) as made in full payment in exchange for stock.

Stock in a domestic corporation shall not be considered a U.S. real property interest pursuant to the provisions of § 1.897-2(f)(2) if the corporation does not hold any U.S. real property interests and has disposed of all of its U.S. real property interests owned within the previous five years in transactions in which the full amount of gain was recognized under the rules of § 1.897-2(f)(2). If gain is recognized at the corporate level on either a distribution of a U.S. real property interest or a sale of a U.S. real property interest in a liquidation, such distribution or sale shall be considered a disposition for purposes of § 1.897-2(f)(2). With regard to the consequences of a distribution from a U.S. real property holding corporation under section 355(a), see § 1.897-6T(a)(1) and (4).

(3) *Section 332 liquidations of U.S. real property holding corporations.*—(i) *General rules.*—Exchanges that are subject to section 897(e) are normally covered by § 1.897-6T(a)(1), (2) and (3). This paragraph (b)(3) provides rules concerning the application of section 897(e) and the general principles of § 1.897-6T(a)(1), (2) and (3) to section 332 liquidations of U.S. real property holding corporations.

(ii) *Distribution to a foreign corporation under section 332 after June 18, 1980, and before the repeal of the General Utilities doctrine.*—Except for distributions under paragraph (b)(3)(iii) of this section (relating to section 332 and former section 334(b)(2)), the rules of this paragraph (b)(3)(ii) shall apply to section 332 distributions after June 18, 1980, and before January 1, 1990, pursuant to section 336(a) as in effect prior to the effective dates of the amendments made by section 631 of the Tax Reform Act of 1986. A foreign corporation that meets the stock ownership requirements of section 332(b) with respect to stock in a domestic corporation that is a U.S. real property interest shall not, after December 31, 1984, be subject to taxation by reason of section 367(a). The foreign corporation shall recognize gain pursuant to section 897(e)(1) on such stock upon the receipt of property in a section 332(a) liquidation from such domestic corporation, but only to the extent that the property received constitutes property other than a U.S. real property interest. The gain on the stock in the domestic corporation to be recognized by the foreign corporation pursuant to section 897(e)(1) shall be determined by multiplying the gain realized on the distribution by a fraction. The numerator of the fraction shall be the fair market value of the property other than U.S. real property interests received by the foreign corporation on the distribution, and the denominator shall be the fair market value of all property received by the foreign corporation on the distribution. The bases of the distributed U.S. real property interests in the hands of the foreign corporation shall be the same as the bases in the hands of the domestic corporation. The bases of the property other than U.S. real property interests in the hands of the foreign corporation shall be the same as the bases in the hands of the domestic corporation, plus any gain recognized by the foreign corporation on the distribution allocated among such assets in proportion to the potential gain inherent in each such asset at the time of distribution. However, the basis of each asset is limited to its fair market value. Property, other than a U.S. real property interest that is distributed by the domestic corporation, shall not be considered to be distributed by the domestic corporation pursuant to a section 332 liquidation (that is, the foreign corporation shall not be considered to be a corporation for purposes of section 332) if the requirements of section 367(a) are not satisfied. *See,* for example, sections 1245(b)(3) and 1250(d)(3) regarding the consequences to the distributing domestic corporation if the requirements of section 367(a) are not satisfied.

(iii) *Distribution to a foreign corporation under section 332 and former section 334(b)(2) after June 18, 1980.*—The rules of this paragraph (b)(2)(iii) shall apply to section 332 distributions after June 18, 1980 where the basis of the distributed property in the hands of the foreign corporation is determined under section 334(b)(2) as in effect prior to the Tax Equity and Fiscal Responsibility Act of 1982. A foreign corporation that meets the stock ownership requirements of section 332(b) with respect to stock in a domestic corporation that is a U.S. real property interest shall recognize gain on the receipt of property in a section 332(a) liquidation where section 334(b)(2) applies to the extent that the fair market value of the distributed assets that are not U.S. real property interests exceeds the basis of such assets determined under section 334(b)(2) (for example, if the liquidation does not occur immediately upon the purchase of stock in the domestic corporation). The gain recognized shall not exceed the excess of the fair market value of the stock of the domestic corporation in the hands of the foreign corporation at the time of the distribution over the shareholder's adjusted basis in such stock. The basis of the distributed U.S. real property interests in the hands of the foreign corporation shall be determined under section 334(b)(2), by reference to the adjusted basis of the stock with respect to which the distribution was made. The basis of such property other than U.S. real property interests shall be tentatively determined under section 334(b)(2), and then increased by any gain recognized by the foreign corporation on the distribution allocated among such assets in proportion to the potential gain inherent in each such asset at the time of distribution (computed using the tentative basis as determined under section 334(b)(2)). The basis of each asset is limited, however, to its fair market value.

(iv) *Distribution to a foreign corporation under section 332 after July 31, 1986 and after the repeal of the General Utilities doctrine.*—The rules of this subdivision (iv) shall apply to section 332 distributions after July 31, 1986, pursuant to section 337(a) as in effect after the effective dates of the amendments of section 631 of the Tax Reform Act of 1986.

(A) *Liquidation of domestic corporation.*—A foreign corporation that meets the stock ownership requirements of section 332(b) with respect to stock in a domestic corporation that is a U.S. real property interest (except a foreign corporation that has made an effective election under section 897(i) and the stock of which is treated as a U.S. real property interest) shall not recognize any gain under sections 367(a) or 897(e)(1) on the receipt of property in a section 332(a) liquidation. The domestic corporation shall not recognize gain under section 367(e)(2) on the distribution of U.S. real property interests (other than stock in a former U.S. real property holding corporation which is treated as a U.S. real property interest) to the foreign corporation. The domestic corporation shall recognize gain under section 367(e)(2) on the distribution of stock in a former U.S. real property holding corporation which is treated as a U.S. real property interest. With respect to the recognition of gain or loss by the domestic corporation under section 367(e)(2) on the distribution of property other than U.S. real property interests, see the regulations under section 367(e)(2). The basis of the distributed U.S. real property interests (other than stock in a former U.S. real property holding corporation) in the hands of the foreign corporation shall be the same as it was in the hands of the domestic corporation. The basis of any property (other than U.S. real property interests) and stock in a former U.S. real property holding corporation that is a U.S. real property interest in the hands of the foreign corporation shall be the same as it was in the hands of the domestic corporation increased by any gain recognized by the distributing corporation on the distribution that was subject to U.S. taxation.

(B) *Liquidation of certain foreign corporations making a section 897(i) election.*—A foreign corporation that meets the stock ownership requirements of section 332(b) with respect to stock in another foreign corporation, that has made an effective election under section 897(i) and the stock of which is treated as a U.S. real property interest, shall recognize gain pursuant to section 897(e)(1) on such stock upon the receipt from the distributing foreign corporation of property that is not a U.S. real property interest, and that is not used by the distributee foreign corporation in the conduct of a trade or business within the United States (if the distributee foreign corporation is not a resident of a country with which the United States maintains an income tax treaty) or in a permanent establishment within the United States (if the distributee foreign corporation is a resident of a country with which the United States maintains an income tax treaty). The gain on the stock in the foreign corporation (making an effective election under section 897(i)) to be recognized by the distributee foreign corporation pursuant to section 897(e)(1) shall be determined by multiplying the gain realized on the distribution by a fraction. The numerator of the fraction shall be the fair market value of the property received by the distributee foreign corporation upon which it must recognize gain, and the denominator of the fraction shall be the fair market value of all property received by the distributee foreign corporation on the distribution. The distributing foreign corporation shall not recognize gain under section 367(e)(2) on the distribution of U.S. real property interests to the distributee foreign corporation. With respect to the recognition of gain or loss under section 367(e)(2) on the distribution of property other than U.S. real property interests, see the regulations under section 367(e)(2). The basis of the distributed U.S. real property interests in the hands of the distributee foreign corporation shall be the same as it was in the hands of the distributing foreign corporation. The basis of the property upon which the distributee foreign corporation recognized gain in the hands of the distributee foreign corporation shall be the same as the basis in the hands of the distributing foreign corporation, plus any gain recognized by the distributee foreign corporation on the receipt of such property allocated among such property in proportion to the potential gain inherent in each such property at the time of the distribution. In regard to the basis of any other property received by the distributee foreign corporation in the liquidation, see the regulations under section 367(e)(2). However, the basis of each asset is limited to its fair market value.

(v) *Transfer of foreign corporation stock followed by a section 332 liquidation treated as a reorganization.*—If a nonresident alien or foreign corporation transfers the stock of a foreign corporation that owns a U.S. real property interest to a domestic corporation in exchange for stock of the domestic corporation (or its domestic or foreign parent corporation) in a reorganization under section 368(a)(1)(B) or in an exchange under section 351(a), and if the foreign corporation then distributes the U.S. real property interest to the domestic corporation in a liquidation described in section 332(a) within five years of the transfer of the stock of the foreign corporation to the domestic corporation, then the transfer of the foreign corporation stock and the liquidation shall be treated as a reorganization described in section 368(a)(1)(C) or (D). The rules of § 1.897-6T(a)(1) shall apply to the transfer of the U.S. real property interest to the domestic corporation in exchange for domestic corporation stock, and the rules of § 1.897-5T(c)(4) shall apply to the distribution of domestic corporation stock by the foreign corporation. However, the rules of this paragraph (b)(3)(v) shall not apply if the transfer of the foreign corporation stock and the liquidation under section 332(a) are separate and independent transactions justified by substantial and verifiable business purposes.

(4) *Section 897 (i) companies.*—Except as otherwise provided herein for purposes of this section and § 1.897-6T, a foreign corporation that has made a valid election under section 897(i) shall be treated as a domestic corporation and not as a foreign corporation in determining the application of section 897. For rules concerning the making of a section 897(i) election, see §§ 1.897-3 and 1.897-8T. In regard to section 367(e)(2) and foreign corporations that have made an effective election under section 897(i), see paragraph (b)(3)(iv) of this section.

(5) *Examples.*—The following examples illustrate the rules of this paragraph (b). In each example there is no applicable income tax treaty to which the United States is a party.

Example (1). (i) A is a nonresident alien who owns 100 percent of the stock of DC, a U.S. real property holding corporation. DC's only asset is Parcel P, a U.S. real property interest, with a fair market value of $500,000 and an adjusted basis of $300,000. DC completely liquidates in 1987 and distributes Parcel P to A in exchange for the DC stock held by A.

(ii) Under section 336(a), DC must recognize gain to the extent of the excess of the fair market value ($500,000) over the adjusted basis ($300,000), or $200,000.

(iii) A does not recognize any gain under section 897(a) because the DC stock in the hands of A is no longer a U.S. real property interest under paragraph (b)(2) of this section and paragraph 2(f) of § 1.897-2. A does recognize gain (if any) under section 331(a); however, the gain is not subject to taxation under section 871(a). A's adjusted basis in Parcel P is $500,000.

(iv) If DC did not recognize all of the gain on the disposition under a transitional rule to section 631 of the Tax Reform Act of 1986, then paragraph (b)(2) of this section and paragraph 2(f) of § 1.897-2 would not apply to A. A would recognize gain (if any) under paragraph (b)(2) because the distribution is treated as in full payment in exchange for the DC stock under section 897(a).

Example (2). (i) FC, a Country F corporation, owns 100 percent of the stock of DC, a U.S. real property holding corporation. FC's basis in the stock of DC is $400,000, and the fair market value of the DC stock is $800,000. DC owns a U.S. real property interest with an adjusted basis of $350,000 and a fair market value of $600,000. DC also owns other assets that are not U.S. real property interests that have an adjusted basis of $125,000 and a fair market value of $200,000. DC completely liquidates in 1985 and distributes all of its property to FC in exchange for the DC stock held by FC.

(ii) Under paragraph (b)(3)(ii) of this section, FC recognizes $100,000 of gain under section 897(a) on the disposition of the DC stock. This is determined by multiplying FC's gain realized ($400,000) by a fraction. The numerator of the fraction is the fair market value of the property other than U.S. real property interests ($200,000), and the denominator of the fraction is the fair market value of all property received ($800,000). FC takes a carryover adjusted basis in the U.S. real property interest ($350,000). FC's adjusted basis in the assets that are not U.S. real property interests ($200,000) is the basis of those assets in the hands of DC ($125,000) plus the gain recognized by FC on the distribution ($100,000) not to exceed the fair market value ($200,000).

Example (3). (i) FC, a Country F corporation, owns 100 percent of the stock of DC, a U.S. real property holding corporation. FC's basis in the stock of DC is $300,000, and the fair market value of the DC stock is $500,000. DC owns Parcel P, a U.S. real property interest, with an adjusted basis of $250,000 and a fair market value of $400,000. DC also owns all of the stock of DX, a former U.S. real property holding corporation whose stock is a U.S. real property interest, with an adjusted basis of $50,000 and a fair market value of

$100,000. DC completely liquidates in 1987 and distributes all of its property to FC in exchange for the DC stock held by FC.

(ii) Under paragraph (b)(3)(iv)(A) of this section, DC recognizes $50,000 of gain on the distribution to FC of the DX stock. DC does not recognize any gain for purposes of section 367(e)(2) on the distribution to FC of Parcel P.

(iii) Under paragraph (b)(3)(iv)(A) of this section, FC's disposition of its DC stock is not treated as a disposition of a U.S. real property interest. Under section 334(b)(1), FC takes a carryover adjusted basis of $250,000 in Parcel P. FC takes an increased basis of $100,000 in the DX stock which is equal to DC's basis ($50,000) increased by the gain recognized by DC ($50,000).

(iv) The result would be the same if FC had made an effective election under section 897(i).

(6) *Section 333 elections.*—(i) *General rule.*—A foreign shareholder that elects section 333 as in effect prior to its repeal by the Tax Reform Act of 1986 upon the distribution of property in a liquidation by a domestic corporation whose stock is treated as a U.S. real property interest shall recognize gain on such stock to the extent that—

(A) The property received by the foreign shareholder constitutes property other than U.S. real property interests subject to U.S. taxation upon its disposition as specified by paragraph (a)(1) of this section, or

(B) The basis of a U.S. real property interest subject to U.S. taxation upon its disposition in the hands of the recipient foreign shareholder exceeds the basis of the U.S. real property interest in the hands of the liquidating domestic corporation.

In determining the amount of gain recognized by the foreign shareholder, the foreign shareholder shall be considered to have exchanged the domestic corporation stock for all the property distributed on a proportionate fair market value basis. The gain recognized on a respective portion of domestic corporation stock shall not exceed the gain realized on that portion. Property other than U.S. real property interests subject to U.S. taxation upon disposition shall have a fair market value basis in the hands of the foreign shareholder. The basis of U.S. real property interests subject to U.S. taxation upon disposition shall be the basis of the proportionate part of the domestic corporation stock cancelled or redeemed in the liquidation, increased in the amount of gain recognized (other than gain recognized under this section) by the shareholder in respect to that proportionate part of the domestic corporation stock.

(ii) *Example.*—The rules of paragraph (b)(6)(i) of this section may be illustrated by the following example.

Example. (i) A is a citizen and resident of Country F with which the U.S. does not have an income tax treaty. A owns all of the stock of DC, a U.S. real property holding corporation. The DC stock has a fair market value of $1,000,000. A acquired the DC stock in two purchases. The basis of one lot of the DC stock is $150,000, and the basis of the other lot is $650,000.

(ii) DC owns Parcel P, a U.S. real property interest, with a fair market value of $750,000 and an adjusted basis of $400,000. DC's only other property is equipment with a fair market value of $250,000 and an adjusted basis of $100,000. DC does not have any earnings and profits.

(iii) DC completely liquidates in 1985 in accordance with section 333 by distributing Parcel P and the equipment to A. A elects section 333 treatment.

(iv) A is considered as having exchanged 75 percent (fair market value of Parcel P/fair market value of all property distributed) of the DC stock for Parcel P. A realized gain of $150,000 on that portion of the DC stock ($750,000 – $600,000). All of the gain of $150,000 is recognized under section 897(a) because A's basis in Parcel P under section 334(c) ($600,000) would exceed DC's basis in Parcel P ($400,000) by at least the amount of realized gain. A takes a basis of $750,000 in Parcel P.

(v) A is considered as having exchanged 25 percent (fair market value of equipment/fair market value of all property distributed) of the DC stock for the equipment. A realized gain of $50,000 on that portion of the DC stock ($250,000 – $200,000). All of the gain of $50,000 is recognized under section 897(a). A takes a basis of $250,000 in the equipment.

(c) *Distributions of U.S. real property interests by foreign corporations.*—(1) *Recognition of gain required.*—If a foreign corporation makes a distribution (including a distribution in liquidation or redemption) of a U.S. real property interest to a shareholder (whether foreign or domestic), then, except as provided in paragraph (c)(2), (3) or (4) of this section, the distributing corporation shall recognize gain (but not loss) on the distribution under section 897(d)(1). The gain recognized shall be equal to the excess of the fair market value of the U.S. real property interest (as of the time of the distribution) over its adjusted basis. Except as otherwise provided, the distributee's basis in the distributed U.S. real property interest shall be determined under the otherwise applicable sections of the Code. The distributee (whether domestic or foreign) of a foreign corporation in a liquidation under section 332 shall take the foreign corporation's basis in the distributed U.S. real property interest increased by any gain recognized (and subject to U.S. income taxation) by the foreign corporation on the distribution of such U.S. real property interest.

(2) *Recognition of gain not required.*—(i) *Statutory exception rule.*—Under section 897(d)(2)(A), gain shall not be recognized by a distributing foreign corporation if—

(A) At the time of the receipt of the distributed U.S. real property interest, the distributee would be subject to U.S. income taxation on a subsequent disposition of the U.S. real property interest, determined in accordance with the rules of paragraph (d)(1) of this section;

(B) The basis of the distributed U.S. real property interest in the hands of the distributee is no greater than the adjusted basis of such property before the distribution, increased by the amount of gain (if any) recognized by the distributing corporation upon the distribution and added to the adjusted basis under the otherwise applicable provisions; and

(C) The distributing corporation complies with the filing requirements of paragraph (d)(1)(iii) of this section.

(ii) *Section 332 liquidations.*—(A) *In general.*—A distributing foreign corporation that meets the requirements of paragraph (c)(2)(i) in a section 332(a) liquidation shall not recognize gain on the distribution of U.S. real property interests to a foreign corporation meeting the stock ownership requirements of section 332(b) if the distributing corporation complies with the procedural requirements of paragraph (d)(1)(iii). Whether a foreign corporation recognizes gain on the distribution of U.S. real property interests to a U.S. corporation meeting the stock ownership requirements of section 332(b) depends upon whether the U.S. corporation satisfies the subject to tax requirement provided in paragraph (d)(1)(i) (in addition to the procedural requirements of paragraph (d)(1)(iii)). With respect to section 332 distributions by a foreign corporation occurring after July 31, 1986, section 367(e)(2) shall not affect the application of section 337(a) (as in effect after the Tax Reform Act of 1986) and paragraph (c)(2)(i) of this section to the distribution of a U.S. real property interest.

(B) *Recognition of gain required in certain section 332 liquidations.*—Notwithstanding the other rules of this paragraph (c), a foreign corporation shall, pursuant to the authority conferred by section 897(e)(2), recognize gain on its distribution after May 5, 1988 of a U.S. real property interest to a domestic corporation meeting the stock ownership requirements of section 332(b) if—

(1) the foreign corporation has not made an election under section 897(i), and any gain on the stock in the foreign corporation would be subject to U.S. taxation if an election were made on the date of the liquidation; and

(2) The distribution of the U.S. real property interest by the foreign corporation to the domestic corporation pursuant to section 332(a) occurs less than five years after the date of the last gain from the disposition of stock of the foreign corporation that would be subject to payment of tax under section 1.897-3(d)(2)(i) if an election under section 897(i) were made by the foreign corporation on the date of its liquidation.

With regard to the treatment of certain foreign corporations as domestic corporations under section 897(i), however, see §§1.897-3 and 1.897-8T.

(iii) *Examples.*—The rules of this paragraph (c)(2) may be illustrated by the following examples.

Example (1). (i) DC, a domestic corporation, owns 100 percent of the stock of FC, a Country F corporation. FC's only asset is Parcel P, a U.S. real property interest, with a fair market value of $500x and an adjusted basis of $100x. In September 1987, FC liquidates under section 332(a) and transfers Parcel P to DC. The transitional rules contained in section 633 of the Tax Reform Act of 1986 concerning the repeal of the *General Utilities* doctrine would not be applicable to a subsequent distribution or disposition of assets by DC.

(ii) Assume that FC complies with the filing requirements of paragraph (d)(1)(iii). DC will be subject to U.S. income taxation on a subsequent disposition of Parcel P under the rules of paragraph (d)(1). The basis of Parcel P in the hands of DC will be $100x under section 334(b)(1), and thus no greater than the basis of Parcel P in the hands of FC. FC does not recognize any gain under the rules of paragraph (c)(1) of this section on the distribution because the exception of paragraph (d)(2)(i) applies.

Example (2). If in *Example (1)* the distribution by FC to DC occurred in September 1985, and DC sold or exchanged Parcel P under sections 336(a) or 337(a) as in effect prior to the Tax Reform Act of 1986, then FC must recognize gain of $400x on the distribution of Parcel P. The gain must be recognized because Parcel P in the hands of DC is not considered subject to U.S. income taxation on a subsequent disposition under the rules of paragraph (d)(1) of this section.

(3) *Limitation of gain recognized under paragraph (c)(1) of this section for certain section 355 distributions.*—(i) *In general.*—Under paragraph (c)(1) of this section, a foreign corporation that distributes stock in a domestic corporation that constitutes a U.S. real property interest in a distribution to which section 355 applies shall recognize gain on the distribution to the extent that the fair market value of the distributed stock exceeds its adjusted basis in the hands of the distributing foreign corporation. The gain recognized shall be limited under this paragraph (c)(3), however, to the amount by which the aggregate basis of the distributed stock in the hands of the distributees exceeds the aggregate adjusted basis of the distributed stock in the hands of the distributing corporation. The distributees' basis in the distributed U.S. real property interest shall be determined under the otherwise applicable provisions of section 358. (Thus, the distributees' basis in the distributed U.S. real property interest shall be determined without any increase for any gain recognized by the foreign corporation).

(ii) *Example.*—The rules of paragraph (c)(3)(i) of this section may be illustrated by the following example.

Example. (i) C is a citizen and resident of Country F. C owns all of the stock of FC, a Country F corporation. The fair market value of the FC stock is 1000x, and C has a basis of 600x in the FC stock. Country F does not have an income tax treaty with the United States.

(ii) In a transaction qualifying as a distribution of stock of a controlled corporation under section 355(a), FC distributes to C all of the stock of DC, a U.S. real property holding corporation. C does not surrender any of the FC stock. The DC stock has a fair market value of 600x, and FC has an adjusted basis of 200x in the DC stock. After the distribution, the FC stock has a fair market value of 400x.

(iii) Under paragraph (c)(3)(i) of this section, FC must recognize gain on the distribution of the DC stock to C equal to the difference between the fair market value of the DC stock (600x) and FC's adjusted basis in the DC stock (200x). This results in a potential gain of 400x. Under section 358, C takes a 360x adjusted basis in the DC stock. Provided that FC complies with the filing requirements of paragraph (d)(1)(iii) of this section, the gain recognized by FC is limited under paragraph (c)(3)(i) to 160x because (A) this is the amount by which the basis of the DC stock in the hands of C (360x) exceeds the adjusted basis of the DC stock in the hands of FC (200x), and (B) at the time of receipt of the DC stock, C would be subject to U.S. taxation on a subsequent disposition of the stock.

(iv) C's adjusted basis in the DC stock is not increased by the 160x recognized by FC.

(4) *Distribution by a foreign corporation in certain reorganizations.*—(i) *In general.*—Under paragraph (c)(1) of this section, a foreign corporation that transfers property to another corporation in an exchange under section 361(a) for stock of a domestic corporation which is a United States real property holding corporation immediately after the transfer in a reorganization under section 368(a)(1)(C), (D) or (F) shall recognize gain under section 897(d)(1) on the distribution (whether actual or deemed) of the stock of the domestic corporation received by the foreign corporation to its shareholders (whether domestic or foreign). See § 1.897-6T(a) of the regulations for the consequences to the foreign corporation of the exchange of its property for the domestic corporation stock.

(ii) *Statutory exception.*—Pursuant to the exception provided in section 897(d)(2)(A), no gain shall be recognized by the foreign corporation on its distribution of the domestic corporation stock if—

(A) At the time of the distribution, the distributee (*i.e.*, the exchanging shareholder in the section 354 exchange) would be subject to U.S. taxation on a subsequent disposition of the stock of the domestic corporation, determined in accordance with the rules of paragraph (d)(1) of this section;

(B) The distributee's adjusted basis in the stock of the foreign corporation immediately before the distribution was no greater than the foreign corporation's basis in the stock of the domestic corporation determined under section 358; and

(C) The distributing corporation complies with the filing requirements of paragraph (d)(1)(iii) of this section.

(iii) *Regulatory limitation on gain recognized.*—If the requirements of subdivisions (A) and (C) of paragraph (c)(4)(ii) are met, the amount of any gain recognized by the foreign corporation shall not exceed the excess of the distributee's adjusted basis in the stock of the foreign corporation immediately before the distribution over the foreign corporation's basis in the stock of the domestic corporation immediately before the distribution as determined under section 358.

(iv) *Examples.*—The rules of paragraph (c)(4) of this section may be illustrated by the following examples.

Example (1). (i) A, a nonresident alien, organized FC, a Country W corporation, in September 1980 to invest in U.S. real estate. In 1986, FC's only asset is Parcel P, a U.S. real property interest with a fair market value of $600,000 and an adjusted basis to FC of $200,000. Parcel P is subject to a mortgage with an outstanding balance of $100,000. The fair market value of the FC stock is $500,000, and A's adjusted basis in the stock is $100,000. FC does not have liabilities in excess of the adjusted basis in Parcel P. The United States does not have a treaty with Country W that entitles FC to nondiscriminatory treatment as described in section 1.897-3(b)(2) of the regulations.

(ii) Pursuant to a plan of reorganization under section 368(a)(1)(D), FC transfers Parcel P to DC, a newly formed domestic corporation, in exchange for DC stock. FC distributes the DC stock to A in exchange for A's FC stock.

(iii) FC's exchange of Parcel P for the DC stock is a disposition of a U.S. real property interest. Under § 1.897-6T(a)(1), there is an exchange of a U.S. real property interest (Parcel P) for another U.S. real property interest (DC stock) so that no gain is recognized on the exchange under section 897(e). DC takes FC's basis of $200,000 in Parcel P under section 362(b). Under section 358(a)(1), FC takes a $100,000 basis in the DC stock because FC's substituted basis of $200,000 in the DC stock is reduced by the $100,000 of liabilities to which Parcel P is subject.

(iv) Under section 897(d)(1) and paragraph (c)(4)(i) of this section, FC generally must recognize gain on the distribution of the DC stock received in exchange for FC's assets equal to the difference between the fair market value of the DC stock ($500,000) and FC's adjusted basis in the DC stock prior to the distribution ($100,000). This results in a potential gain of $400,000. Under section 358(a)(1), A takes a basis in the DC stock equal to the its basis in the FC stock of $100,000. Provided that FC complies with the filing requirements of paragraph (d)(1)(iii) of this section, no gain is recognized by FC on the distribution of the DC stock under the statutory exception to the general rule of section 897(d)(1) provided in section 897(d)(2)(A) and paragraph (c)(4)(ii) of this section because (*1*) A's basis in the DC stock ($100,000) does not exceed FC's adjusted basis in the DC stock ($100,000) immediately prior to the distribution and (*2*) A, at the time of receipt of the DC stock, would be subject to U.S. taxation on a subsequent disposition of the stock.

(v) The FC stock in the hands of A is not a U.S. real property interest because FC is a foreign corporation that has not elected to be treated as a domestic corporation under section 897(i). Accordingly, the exchange of the FC stock by A for DC stock is not a disposition of a U.S. real property interest under section 897(a).

Example (2). The facts are the same as in *Example* (1), except that A purchased the FC stock in September 1983 for $100,000 from S, a nonresident alien, and that S had a basis of $40,000 in the FC stock at the time of the sale to A. The results are the same as in Example 1.

Example (3). (i) The facts are the same as in *Example* 1, except that A's adjusted basis in the FC stock prior to the reorganization is $300,000. Following the distribution, A takes its basis of $300,000 in the FC stock as its basis in the DC stock pursuant to section 358(a)(1).

(ii) FC does not qualify under the statutory exception of paragraph (c)(4)(ii) to the general recognition rule of section 897(d)(1) and paragraph (c)(4)(i) of this section because A's basis in the DC stock ($300,000) exceeds FC's adjusted basis in the DC stock ($100,000) immediately prior to the distribution. However, provided that FC complies with the filing requirements of paragraph (d)(1)(iii) of this section, the gain recognized by FC is limited to $200,000 under the regulatory limitation of gain provided by paragraph (c)(4)(iii). This is the excess of A's basis in the FC stock immediately before the distribution ($300,000) over A's adjusted basis in the DC stock immediately before the distribution ($100,000).

(iii) A takes a basis of $300,000 in the DC stock under section 358(a)(1). A's basis in the DC stock is not increased by the gain recognized by FC. DC takes a basis of $200,000 in Parcel P under section 362(b).

Example (4). (i) The facts are the same as in *Example* (3), except that the United States has an income tax treaty with Country W entitling FC to nondiscriminatory treatment under section 1.897-3(b)(2) of the regulations. A valid election under section 897(i) is made to treat FC as a U.S. corporation.

(ii) FC is treated as a domestic corporation for purposes of section 897 and is not required to recognize gain under section 897(d)(1) and paragraph (c)(4)(i) of this section on the distribution of the DC stock as described in *Example* 3. (If a valid section 897(i) election were not made, the result would be same as in *Example* (3).)

(iii) The FC stock in the hands of A is a U.S. real property interest because an election was made under section 897(i) to treat FC as a U.S. corporation. The exchange of the FC stock for DC stock by A is a disposition of a U.S. real property interest. Under section 897(e)(1) and paragraph (a) of § 1.897-6T, A does not recognize gain on the exchange because there is an exchange of a U.S. real property interest (the FC stock) for another U.S. real property interest (the DC stock). Under section 358(a)(1), A takes as its basis in the DC stock A's basis in the FC stock ($300,000).

(5) *Sales of U.S. real property interests by foreign corporations under section 337.*—Section 337 as in effect prior to the Tax Reform Act of 1986 shall not apply to any sale or exchange (including a deemed section 337 sale pursuant to an election under section 338(a) to treat a stock purchase as an asset acquisition) of a U.S. real property interest by a foreign corporation.

(6) *Section 897(l) credit.*—If a foreign corporation adopts a plan of complete liquidation and if, solely by reason of section 897(d) and this section, section 337(a)(as in effect before the Tax Reform Act of 1986) does not apply to sales or exchanges of, or section 336 (as in effect before the Tax Reform Act of 1986) does not apply to distributions of, United States real property interests by the liquidating corporation, then—

(i) The amount realized by the shareholder on the distribution shall be increased by its proportionate share of the amount by which the tax imposed by chapter 1 of the Code, as modified by the provisions of any applicable U.S. income tax treaty, on the liquidating corporation would have been reduced if section 897(d) and this section had not been applicable, and

(ii) For purposes of the Code, the shareholder shall be deemed to have paid, on the last day prescribed by law for the payment of the tax imposed by subtitle A of the Code on the shareholder for the taxable year, an amount of tax equal to the amount of increase in the amount realized described in subdivision (i) of this paragraph (c).

The special rule provided by this paragraph (c)(5) applies only to shareholders who are United States citizens or residents, and who have held stock in the liquidating corporation continuously since June 18, 1980. This special rule also only applies for the first taxable year of any such shareholder in which the shareholder receives a distribution in complete liquidation from the foreign corporation.

(7) *Other applicable rules.*—For rules concerning exemption of gain pursuant to a U.S. income tax treaty, withholding of tax from distributions, and other applicable rules, see paragraph (d) of this section. For the treatment of liquidations described in section 334(b)(2)(A) of certain foreign corporations acquired before November 6, 1980, see § 1.897-4.

(d) *Rules of general application.*—(1) *Interests subject to taxation upon later disposition.*—(i) *In general.*—Pursuant to the otherwise applicable rules of this section and § 1.897-6T, nonrecognition of gain or loss may apply with respect to certain distributions or exchanges of U.S. real property interests if any gain from a subsequent disposition of the interests that are distributed or received by the transferor in the exchange would be included in the gross income of the distributee or transferor and be subject to U.S. taxation. Gain is considered subject to U.S. taxation if the gain is included on the income tax return of a U.S. tax paying entity even if there is no U.S. tax liability (for example, because of net operating losses or an investment tax credit). Gain is not considered subject to U.S. taxation if the gain is derived by a tax exempt entity. A real estate investment trust is considered to be a pass-through entity for purposes of the rule of taxability of this paragraph (d)(1)(i). Thus, for example, a tax exempt entity holding an interest in a real estate investment trust is not subject to tax. A domestic corporation (including a foreign corporation that makes an effective section 897(i) election after receipt of the U.S. real property interest) shall not be considered subject to U.S. taxation on a subsequent disposition of a U.S. real property interest if it received the U.S. real property interest prior to the effective date of the repeal of sections 336(a) or 337(a) as in effect prior to the Tax Reform Act of 1986, unless the U.S. real property interest has not been sold or exchanged by the domestic corporation prior to such effective date in a transaction to which either section 336(a) or section 337(a)(as in effect prior to such effective date) applied. In addition, an interest shall be considered to be subject to U.S. taxation upon its subsequent disposition only if the requirements set forth in subdivision (iii) of this paragraph (d)(1) are met.

(ii) *Effects of income tax treaties.*—(A) *Effect of treaty exemption from tax.*—Except as otherwise provided in subdivision (C) of this paragraph (d)(1)(ii), a U.S. real property interest shall not be considered to be subject to U.S. taxation upon a subsequent disposition if, at the time of its distribution or exchange, the recipient is entitled pursuant to the provisions of a U.S. income tax treaty to an exemption from U.S. taxation upon a disposition of the interest.

(B) *Effect of treaty reduction of tax.*—If, at the time of a distribution or exchange, a distributee of a U.S. real property interest in a distribution or a transferor who receives a U.S. real property interest in an exchange would be entitled pursuant to the provisions of a U.S. income tax treaty to reduced U.S. taxation upon the disposition of the interest, then a portion of the interest received shall be treated as an interest subject to U.S. taxation upon its disposition, and, therefore, that portion shall be entitled to nonrecognition treatment under the rules of this section or § 1.897-6T. The portion of the interest that is treated as subject to U.S. taxation is determined by multiplying the fair market value of the interest by a fraction. The numerator of the fraction is the amount of tax that would be due pursuant to the provisions of the applicable U.S. income tax treaty upon the recipient's disposition of the interest, determined as of the date of the distribution or transfer. The denominator of the fraction is the amount of tax that would be due upon such disposition but for the provisions of the treaty. However, nonrecognition treatment may be preserved in accordance with the provisions of subdivision (C) of this paragraph (d)(1)(ii). With regard to the provisions of this paragraph, see Article XIII (9) of the United States-Canada Income Tax Convention.

(C) *Waiver of treaty benefits to preserve nonrecognition.*—Notwithstanding the provisions of subdivisions (A) and (B) of this paragraph (d)(1)(ii), an interest shall be considered to be subject to U.S. taxation upon its subsequent disposition if, in accordance with paragraph (d)(1)(iii)(F) of this section, the recipient waives the benefits of a U.S. income tax treaty that would otherwise entitle the recipient to an exemption from (or reduction of) U.S. tax upon a disposition of the interest.

(iii) *Procedural requirements.*—If a U.S. real property interest is distributed or transferred after December 31, 1987, the transferor or distributor (that is a nonresident alien individual or a foreign corporation) shall file an income tax return for the taxable year of the distribution or transfer. Also, if a U.S. real property interest is distributed or transferred in a transaction before January 1, 1988, with respect to which nonrecognition treatment would not have been available under the express provisions of section 897(d) or (e) of the Code but is available under the provisions of this section or § 1.897-6T, then the person that would otherwise be subject to tax by reason of the operation of section 897 must file an income tax return for the taxable year of the distribution or transfer. This requirement is satisfied by filing a tax return or an amended tax return for the year of the distribution or transfer by May 5, 1989, or by the date that the filing of the return is otherwise required. The person filing the return must attach thereto a document setting forth the following:

(A) A statement that the distribution or transfer is one to which section 897 applies;

(B) A description of the U.S. real property interest distributed or transferred, including its location, its adjusted basis in the hands of the distributor or transferor immediately before the distribution or transfer, and the date of the distribution or transfer;

(C) A description of the U.S. real property interest received in an exchange;

(D) A declaration signed by an officer of the corporation that the distributing foreign corporation has substantiated the adjusted basis of the shareholder in its stock if the distributing corporation has nonrecognition or recognition limitation under paragraph (c)(3) or (4) of this section;

(E) The amount of any gain recognized and tax withheld by any person with respect to the distribution or transfer;

(F) [Reserved]. For further guidance, see § 1.897-5(d)(1)(iii)(F).

(G) The treaty and article (if any) under which the distributee or transferor would be exempt from U.S. taxation on a sale of the distributed U.S. real property interest or the U.S. real property interest received in the transfer; and

(H) A declaration, signed by the distributee or transferor or its authorized legal representative, that the distributee or transferor shall treat any subsequent sale, exchange, or other disposition of the U.S. real property interest as a disposition that is subject to U.S. taxation, notwithstanding the provisions of any U.S. income tax treaty or intervening change in circumstance.

A person who has provided or filed a notice described in § 1.1445-2(d)(2)(iii) or § 1.1445-5(b)(2)(ii) in connection with a transaction may satisfy the requirement of this paragraph (d)(1)(iii) by attaching to his return a copy of that notice together with any information or declaration required by this subdivision not contained in that notice.

(2) *Treaty exception to imposition of tax.*—If gain that would be currently recognized pursuant to the provisions of this section or § 1.897-6T is subject to an exemption from (or reduction of) U.S. tax pursuant to a U.S. income tax treaty, then gain shall be recognized only as provided by that treaty, for dispositions occurring before January 1, 1985. For dispositions occurring after December 31, 1984, all gain shall be recognized as provided in section 897 and the regulations thereunder, except as provided by Articles XIII (9) and XXX (5) of the United States-Canada Income Tax Convention or other income tax treaty entered into force after June 6, 1988. With regard to Article XXX (5) of the Income Tax Treaty with Canada, see, Rev. Rul. 85-76, 1985-1 C.B. 409. With regard to basis adjustments for certain related person transactions, see, § 1.897-6T (c)(3).

(3) *Withholding.*—Under sections 1441 and 1442, as modified by the provisions of any applicable U.S. income tax treaty, a corporation must withhold tax from a dividend distribution to which section 301 applies to a shareholder that is a foreign person, if the dividend is considered to be from sources inside the United States. For a description of dividends that are considered to be from sources inside the United States, see section 861(a)(2). Under section 1445, withholding is required with respect to certain dispositions and distributions of U.S. real property interests.

(4) *Effect on earnings and profits.*—With respect to adjustments to earnings and profits for gain recognized to a distributing corporation on a distribution, see section 312 and the regulations thereunder.

(e) *Effective date.*—Except as otherwise specifically provided in the text of these regulations, this section shall be effective for transfers, exchanges, distributions and other dispositions occurring after June 18, 1980. [Temporary Reg. § 1.897-5T.]

☐ [*T.D. 8198, 5-4-88. Amended by T.D. 9082, 8-4-2003.*]

§ 1.897-6T. Nonrecognition exchanges applicable to corporations, their shareholders, and other taxpayers, and certain transfers of property in corporate reorganizations (Temporary).—(a) *Nonrecognition exchanges.*—(1) *In general.*—Except as otherwise provided in this section and in § 1.897-5T, for purposes of section 897(e) any nonrecognition provision shall apply to a transfer by a foreign person of a U.S. real property interest on which gain is realized only to the extent that the transferred U.S. real property interest is exchanged for a U.S. real property interest which, immediately following the exchange, would be subject to U.S. taxation upon its disposition, and the transferor complies with the filing requirements of paragraph (d)(1)(iii) of § 1.897-5T. No loss shall be recognized pursuant to section 897(e) or the rules of this section unless such loss is otherwise permitted to be recognized. In the case of an exchange of a U.S. real property interest for stock in a domestic corporation (that is otherwise treated as a U.S. real property interest), such stock shall not be considered a U.S. real property interest unless the domestic corporation is a U.S. real property holding corporation immediately after the exchange. Whether an interest would be subject to U.S. taxation in the hands of the transferor upon its disposition shall be determined in accordance with the rules of § 1.897-5T (d)(1).

(2) *Definition of "nonrecognition" provision.*—A "nonrecognition provision" is any provision of the Code which provides that gain or loss shall not be recognized if the requirements of that provision are met. Nonrecognition provisions relevant to this section include, but are not limited to, sections 332, 351, 354, 355, 361, 721, 731, 1031, 1033 and 1036. For purposes of section 897(e), sections 121 and 453 are not nonrecognition provisions.

(3) *Consequence of nonapplication of nonrecognition provisions.*—If a nonrecognition provision does not apply to a transaction, then the U.S. real property interest transferred shall be considered exchanged pursuant to a transaction that is subject to U.S. taxation by reason of the operation of section 897. See, however, § 1.897-5T (d)(2) with respect to the treaty exceptions to the imposition of tax. If a U.S. real property interest is exchanged for an interest the disposition of which is only partially subject to taxation under chapter 1 of the Code (as modified by the provisions of any applicable U.S. income tax treaty), then any nonrecognition provision shall apply only to the extent that the interest received in the exchange would be subject to taxation under chapter 1 of the Code, as modified. For example, the exchange of a U.S. real property interest for an interest in a partnership will receive nonrecognition treatment pursuant to section 721 only to the extent that a disposition of the partnership interest will be subject to U.S. taxation by reason of the operation of section 897(g).

(4) *Section 355 distributions treated as exchanges.*—If a domestic corporation, stock in which is treated as a U.S. real property interest, distributes stock in a foreign corporation or stock in a domestic corporation that is not a U.S. real property holding corporation to a foreign person under section 355(a), then the foreign person shall be considered as having exchanged a proportionate part of the stock in the domestic corporation that is treated as a U.S. real property interest for stock that is not treated as a U.S. real property interest.

(5) [Reserved]

(6) *Determination of basis.*—If a nonrecognition provision applies to the transfer of a U.S. real property interest pursuant to the provisions of this section, then the basis of the property received in the exchange shall be determined in accordance with the rules generally applicable with respect to such nonrecognition provision. Similarly, the basis of the exchanged property in the hands of the transferee shall be determined in accordance with the rules that generally apply to such transfer.

(7) *Examples.*—The rules of paragraph (a)(1) through (6) of this section may be illustrated by the following examples. In each instance, the filing requirements of paragraph (d)(1)(iii) of § 1.897-5T have been satisfied.

Example (1). (i) A is a citizen and resident of Country F with which the U.S. does not have an income tax treaty. A owns Parcel P, a U.S. real property interest, with a fair market value of $500,000 and an adjusted basis of $300,000. A transfers Parcel P to DC, a newly formed U.S. real property holding corporation wholly owned by A, in exchange for DC stock.

(ii) Under paragraph (a)(1) of this section, A has exchanged a U.S. real property interest (Parcel P) for another U.S. real property interest (DC stock) which is subject to U.S. taxation upon its disposition. The nonrecognition provisions of section 351(a) apply to A's transfer of Parcel P.

(iii) Under paragraph (a)(6) of this section, the basis of the DC stock received by A is determined in accordance with the rules generally applicable to the transfer. A takes a $300,000 adjusted basis in the DC stock under the rules of section 358(a)(1).

Example (2). [Reserved]

Example (3). [Reserved]

Example (4). (i) B is a citizen and resident of Country F with which the U.S. does not have an income tax treaty. B owns stock in DC1, a U.S. real property holding corporation. In a reorganization qualifying for nonrecognition under section 368(a)(1)(B), B exchanges the DC1 stock under section 354(a) for stock in DC2, a U.S. real property holding corporation.

(ii) A does not recognize any gain under paragraph (a)(1) of this section on the exchange of the DC1 stock for DC2 stock because there is an exchange of a U.S. real property interest (the DC1 stock) for another U.S. real property interest (the DC2 stock) which is subject to U.S. taxation upon its disposition.

Example (5). (i) C is a citizen and resident of Country F with which the U.S. does not have an income tax treaty. C owns all of the stock of DC, a U.S. real property holding corporation. The fair market value of the DC stock is 500x, and C has a basis of 100x in the DC stock.

(ii) In a transaction qualifying as a distribution of stock of a controlled corporation under section 355(a), DC distributes to C all of the stock of FC, a foreign corporation that has not made a section 897(i) election. C does not surrender any of the DC stock. The FC stock has a fair market value of 200x. After the distribution, the DC stock has a fair market value of 300x.

(iii) Under the rules of paragraph (a)(4) of this section, C is considered to have exchanged DC stock with a fair market value of 200x and an adjusted basis of 40x for FC stock with a fair market value of 200x. Because the FC stock is not a U.S. real property interest, C must recognize gain of 160x under section 897(a) on the distribution. C takes a basis of 200x in the FC stock. C's basis in the DC stock is reduced to 60x pursuant to section 358(c).

Example (6). (i) A is an individual citizen and resident of Country F. F has an income tax treaty with the United States that exempts gain from the sale of stock, but not real property, by a resident of F from U.S. taxation. In 1981, A transferred Parcel P, an appreciated U.S. real property interest, to DC, a U.S. real property holding corporation, in exchange for DC stock. A owned all of the stock of DC.

(ii) Under the rules of paragraph (a)(1) of this section, A must recognize gain on the transfer of Parcel P. Even though there is an exchange of a U.S. real property interest for another U.S. real property interest, there is gain recognition because the U.S. real property interest received (the DC stock) would not have been subject to U.S. taxation upon a disposition immediately following the exchange. A may not convert a U.S. real property interest that was subject to taxation under section 897 into a U.S. real property interest that could be sold without taxation under section 897 due to a treaty exemption.

Example (7). (i) A, a nonresident alien, organized FC1, a Country W corporation in September 1980 to invest in U.S. real property. FC1's only asset is Parcel P, a U.S. real property interest with a fair market value of $500,000 and an adjusted basis of $200,000. The FC1 stock has a fair market value of $500,000 and A's basis in the FC1 stock is $100,000. The United States does not have a treaty with Country W.

(ii) A, organized FC2, a Country W corporation in July 1987. FC2 organized DC in August 1987. Pursuant to a plan of reorganization under section 368(a)(1)(C), FC1 transfers Parcel P to DC in exchange for FC2 voting stock. As a result of the transfer, DC is a U.S. real property holding corporation wholly owned by FC2. The FC2 stock used by DC in the acquisition had been transferred by FC2 to DC as part of the plan of reorganization. FC1 distributes the FC2 stock to A in exchange for A's FC1 stock.

(iii) FC1's exchange of Parcel P for the FC2 stock under section 361(a) is a disposition of a U.S. real property interest. FC1 must recognize gain of $300,000 under section 897(e) and paragraph (a)(1) of this section on the exchange because the FC2 stock received in exchange for Parcel P is not a U.S. real property interest.

(iv) Under section 362(b), DC takes a basis of $500,000 in Parcel P. FC2 takes a basis of $500,000 in the DC stock. A takes a basis of $100,000 in the FC2 stock under section 358(a)(1). Section 897(d) and paragraph (c)(1) of § 1.897-5T do not apply to FC1's distribution of the FC2 stock because the FC2 stock is not a U.S. real property interest.

Example (8). The facts are the same as in *Example* 7, except that the United States has a treaty with Country W that entitles FC1 and FC2 to nondiscriminatory treatment as described in § 1.897-3(b)(2). FC1, but not FC2, makes a valid section 897(i) election prior to the transaction.

(ii) FC1's transfer of Parcel P to DC in exchange for FC2 stock is not subject to section 897(e) and paragraph (a)(1) of this section because FC1 made an election under section 897(i). DC takes a basis of $200,000 in Parcel P under section 362(b).

(iii) FC1's distribution of the FC2 stock to A in exchange for the FC1 stock is not subject to the section 897(d) and paragraph (c)(1) of § 1.897-5T because FC1 made an election under section 897(i).

(iv) A must recognize gain on the exchange under section 354(a) of the FC1 stock for the FC2 stock. A exchanged a U.S. real property interest (the FC1 stock) for an interest which is not a U.S. real property interest (the FC2 stock). A recognizes gain of $400,000. Under section 1012, A takes a $500,000 basis in the FC2 stock.

Example (9). (i) The facts are the same as in *Example* 7 except that the United States has a treaty with Country W that entitles FC1 and FC2 to nondiscriminatory treatment as described in § 1.897-3(b)(2). FC2, but not FC1, makes a valid section 897(i) election prior to the transaction.

(ii) FC1's exchange of Parcel P for the FC2 stock under section 361(a) is a disposition of a U.S. real property interest. FC1 does not recognize any gain under section 897(e) and paragraph (a)(1) of this section because there is an exchange of a U.S. real property interest (Parcel P) for another U.S. real property interest (the FC2 stock). DC takes a basis of $200,000 in Parcel P under section 362(b). FC2 takes a basis of $200,000 in the DC stock.

(iii) FC1's distribution of the FC2 stock to A in exchange for the FC1 stock is subject to section 897(d) and paragraph (c)(1) of § 1.897-5T. Because A takes a basis of $100,000 in the FC2 stock under section 358(a) (which is less than the $200,000 basis of the FC2 stock in the hands of FC1), and A would be subject to U.S. taxation under section 897(a) on a subsequent disposition of the FC2 stock, FC1 does not recognize any gain under paragraph (c)(1) of § 1.897-5T due to the statutory exception of paragraph (c)(2)(i) of that section, provided that FC1 complies with the filing requirements of paragraph (d)(1)(C) of § 1.897-5T.

(iv) Since the FC1 stock was not a U.S. real property interest, its disposition by A in the section 354(a) exchange for FC2 stock is not subject to section 897(e) and paragraph (a)(1) of this section.

Example (10). The facts are the same as in *Example* 7, except that the United States has a treaty with Country W that entitles FC1 and FC2 to nondiscriminatory treatment as described in § 1.897-3(b)(2). FC1 and FC2 made valid section 897(i) elections prior to the transactions.

(ii) FC1's transfer of Parcel P to DC in exchange for FC2 stock is not subject to section 897(e) and paragraph (a)(1) of this section because FC1 made an election under section 897(i). DC takes a basis of $200,000 in Parcel P under section 362(a). FC2 takes a basis of $200,000 in the DC stock.

(iii) FC1's distribution of the FC2 stock to A in exchange for the FC1 stock is not subject to section 897(d) and paragraph (c)(1) of § 1.897-5T because FC1 made an election under section 897(i).

(iv) A does not recognize any gain on the exchange of the FC1 stock for the FC2 stock under section 354(a). Under paragraph (a)(1) of this section, there is an exchange of a U.S. real property interest (FC1 stock) for another U.S. real property interest (FC2 stock). A takes a basis of $100,000 in the FC2 stock under section 358(a).

(8) *Treatment of nonqualifying property.*—(i) *In general.*—If, under paragraph (a)(1) of this section, a nonrecognition provision would apply to an exchange but for the fact that nonqualifying property (cash or property other than U.S. real property interests) is received in addition to property (U.S. real property interests) that is permitted to be received under paragraph (a)(1) of this section, then the transferor shall recognize gain under this section equal to the lesser of—

(A) The sum of the cash received plus the fair market value of the nonqualifying property received, or

(B) The gain realized with respect to the U.S. real property interest transferred.

However, no loss shall be recognized pursuant to this paragraph (a)(8) unless such loss is otherwise permitted to be recognized.

(ii) *Treatment of mixed exchanges.*—In a mixed exchange where both a U.S. real property interest and other property (including cash) is transferred in exchange both for property the receipt of which would qualify for nonrecognition treatment pursuant to paragraph (a)(1) of this section and for other property (including cash) which would not so qualify, the transferor will recognize gain in accordance with the rules set forth in subdivisions (A) through (C) of this paragraph (a)(8)(ii).

(A) *Allocation of nonqualifying property.*—The amount of nonqualifying property (including cash) considered to be received in exchange for U.S. real property interests shall be determined by multiplying the fair market value of the nonqualifying property received by a fraction ("real property fraction"). The numerator of the fraction is the fair market value of the U.S. real property interest transferred in the exchange. The denominator of the fraction is the fair market value of all property transferred in the exchange.

(B) *Recognition of gain.*—The amount of gain that must be recognized, and that shall be subject to U.S. taxation by reason of the operation of section 897, shall be equal to the lesser of:

(1) The amount determined under subdivision (A) of this paragraph (a)(8)(ii), or

(2) The gain or loss realized with respect to the U.S. real property interest exchanged.

(C) *Treatment of other amounts.*—The treatment of other amounts received in a mixed exchange shall be determined as follows:

(1) The amount of nonqualifying property (including cash) considered to be received in exchange for property (including cash) other than U.S. real property interests shall be treated in the manner provided in the relevant nonrecognition provision. Such amounts shall be determined by subtracting the amount determined

under subdivision (A) of this paragraph (a)(8)(ii) from the total amount of nonqualifying property received in the exchange.

(2) The amount of qualifying property considered to be received in exchange for U.S. real property interests shall be treated in the manner provided in paragraph (a)(1) of this section. Such amount shall be determined by multiplying the total fair market value of qualifying property received in the exchange by the real property fraction described in subdivision (A) of this paragraph (a)(8)(ii).

(3) The amount of qualifying property considered to be received in exchange for property other than U.S. real property interests shall be treated in the manner provided in the relevant nonrecognition provision. Such amount shall be determined by subtracting the amount determined under subdivision (2) of this paragraph (a)(8)(ii)(C) from the total fair market value of qualifying property received in the exchange.

(iii) *Example.*—The rules of paragraph (a)(8)(ii) of this section may be illustrated by the following example.

Example. (i) A is an individual citizen and resident of country F. Country F does not have an income tax treaty with the United States. A is the sole proprietor of a business located in the United States, the assets of which consist of a U.S. real property interest with a fair market value of $1,000,000 and an adjusted basis of $700 000, and equipment used in the business with a fair market value of $500,000 and an adjusted basis of $250,000. A decides to incorporate the business, and on January 1, 1987, A transfers his assets to domestic corporation DC in exchange for 100 percent of the stock of DC, with a fair market value of $900,000. In addition, A receives a long term note (constituting a security) from DC for $600,000, bearing arm's length interest and repayment terms. DC has no assets other than those received in the exchange with A. Pursuant to section 897(c)(2) and § 1.897-2, DC is a U.S. real property holding corporation. Therefore, the stock of DC is a U.S. real property interest. Assume that the note from DC constitutes an interest in the corporation solely as a creditor as provided by § 1.897-1(d)(4) of the regulation. A complies with the filing requirements of paragraph (d)(1)(iii) of § 1.897-5T.

(ii) Because the note from DC would not be subject to U.S. taxation upon its disposition, it is nonqualifying property for purposes of determining whether A is entitled to receive nonrecognition treatment pursuant to section 351 with respect to his exchange of the U.S. real property interest. Thus, A must recognize gain in the manner provided in paragraph (a)(8)(ii) of this section. Pursuant to paragraph (a)(8)(ii)(A), the amount of nonqualifying property received in exchange for the real property interests is determined by multiplying the fair market value of such property ($600,000) by the real property fraction. The numerator of the fraction is $1,000,000, the fair market value of the real property transferred by A. The denominator is $1,500,000, the fair market value of all property transferred by A. Thus, A is considered to have received $400,000 of the note in exchange for the real property ($600,000 × $1,000,000/$1,500,000). Pursuant to paragraph (a)(8)(ii)(B), A must recognize the lesser of the amount initially determined or the gain realized with respect to the U.S. real property interest. Therefore, A must recognize the $300,000 gain realized with respect to the real property.

(iii) Pursuant to paragraph (a)(8)(ii)(C) of this section, A is considered to have received $200,000 of the note in exchange for equipment ($600,000 [total value of note received] minus $400,000 [portion of note received in exchange for real property]), $600,000 of the stock in exchange for real property ($900,000 [total value of stock received] times $1,000,000/1,500,000 [proportion of property exchanged consisting of real property]), and $300,000 of the stock in exchange for equipment ($900,000 [total value of stock received]minus $600,000 [portion of stock received in exchange for real property]). All three amounts are entitled to nonrecognition treatment pursuant to section 351.

(iv) Pursuant to paragraph (a)(2) of this section, A's basis in the stock and note received and DC's basis in the U.S. real property interest and equipment will be determined in accordance with the generally applicable rules. The $400,000 portion of the note received in exchange for the real property interest is other property. Pursuant to section 358(a)(2), A takes a fair market value ($400,000) basis for that portion of the note. Pursuant to section 358(a)(1), A's basis in the property received without the recognition of gain (the DC stock and the other portion of the note) will be equal to the basis of the property transferred ($950,000 [$700,000 basis of U.S. real property interest plus $250,000 basis of equipment]), decreased by the fair market value of the other property received ($400,000 portion of the note), and increased by the amount of gain recognized to A on the transaction ($300,000). Thus, A's basis in the stock and the nonrecognition portion of the note is $850,000 ($950,000 – $400,000 + $300,000). Under § 1.358-2(b)(2) of the regulations, the $850,000 is allocated between the stock and the nonrecognition portion of the note in proportion to their fair market values. A takes a basis of $697,000 in the DC stock ($850,000 × 900,000/1,100,000). A takes a basis of $153,000 in the nonrecognition portion of the note ($850,000 × 200,000/1,100,000). A's basis in the note is $553,000 ($400,000 + $153,000). DC's basis in the property received from A will be determined under section 362(a). DC takes a basis of $1,000,000 in the real property interest (A's basis of $700,000 increased by the $300,000 of gain recognized by A on it). DC takes a basis of $250,000 in the equipment (A's basis of $250,000).

(9) *Treaty exception to imposition of tax.*—If gain that would be currently recognized pursuant to the provisions of this section is subject to an exemption from, or reduction of, U.S. tax pursuant to a U.S. income tax treaty, then gain shall be recognized only as provided by that treaty for dispositions occurring before January 1, 1985. For dispositions occurring after December 31, 1984, all gain shall be recognized as provided in section 897 and the regulations thereunder, except as provided by Articles XII (9) and XXX (5) of the United States-Canada Income Tax Convention or other income tax treaty entered into after June 6, 1988. In regard to Article XXX (5) the Income Tax Treaty with Canada, see, Rev. Rul. 85-76, 1985-1 C.B. 409.

(b) *Certain foreign to foreign exchanges.*—(1) *Exceptions to the general rule.*—Notwithstanding the provisions of paragraph (a)(1) of this section and pursuant to authority conferred by section 897(e)(2), a foreign person shall not recognize gain, in the instances described in paragraph (b)(2) of this section, on the transfer of a U.S. real property interest to a foreign corporation in exchange for stock in a foreign corporation, but only if the transferee's subsequent disposition of the transferred U.S. real property interest would be subject to U.S. taxation, as determined in accordance with the provisions of § 1.897-5T (d)(1), if the filing requirements of paragraph (d)(1)(iii) of § 1.897-5T have been satisfied, if one of the five conditions set forth in paragraph (b)(2) exists, and if one of the following three forms of exchange takes place.

(i) The exchange is made by a foreign corporation pursuant to section 361(a) in a reorganization described in section 368(a)(1)(D) or (F) and there is an exchange of the transferor corporation stock for the transferee corporation stock under section 354(a); or

(ii) The exchange is made by a foreign corporation pursuant to section 361(a) in a reorganization described in section 368(a)(1)(C); there is an exchange of the transferor corporation stock for the transferee corporation stock (or stock of the transferee corporation's parent in the case of a parenthetical C reorganization) under section 354(a); and the transferor corporation's shareholders own more than fifty percent of the voting stock of the transferee corporation (or stock of the transferee corporation's parent in the case of a parenthetical C reorganization) immediately after the reorganization; or

(iii) The U.S. real property interest exchanged is stock in a U.S. real property holding corporation; the exchange qualifies under section 351(a) or section 354(a) in a reorganization described in section 368(a)(1)(B); and immediately after the exchange, all of the outstanding stock of the transferee corporation (or stock of the transferee corporation's parent in the case of a parenthetical B reorganization) is owned in the same proportions by the same nonresident alien individuals and foreign corporations that, immediately before the exchange, owned the stock of the U.S. real property holding corporation.

If, however, a nonresident alien individual or foreign corporation which received stock in an exchange described in subdivision (iii) of this paragraph (b)(1) (or the transferee corporation's parent) disposes of any of such foreign stock within three years from the date of its receipt, then that individual or corporation shall recognize that portion of the gain realized with respect to the stock in the U.S. real property holding corporation for which foreign stock disposed of was received.

(2) *Applicability of exception.*—The exception to the provisions of paragraph (a)(1) provided by paragraph (b)(1) shall apply only if one of the following five conditions exists.

(i) Each of the interests exchanged or received in a transferor corporation or transferee corporation would not be a U.S. real property interest as defined in § 1.897-1(c)(1) if such corporations were domestic corporations; or

(ii) The transferee corporation (and the transferee corporation's parent in the case of a parenthetical B or C reorganization) is incorporated in a foreign country that maintains an income tax treaty with the United States that contains an information exchange provision; the transfer occurs after May 5, 1988; and the transferee corporation (and the transferee corporation's parent in the case of a parenthetical B or C reorganization) submit a binding waiver of all benefits of the respective income tax treaty (including the opportunity to make an election under section 897(i)), which must be attached to each of the transferor and transferee corporation's income tax returns for the year of the transfer; or

(iii) The transferee foreign corporation (and the transferee corporation's parent in the case of a parenthetical B or C reorganization) is a qualified resident as defined in section 884(e) and any regulations thereunder of the foreign country in which it is incorporated; or

(iv) The transferee foreign corporation (and the transferee corporation's parent in the case of a parenthetical B or C reorganization) is incorporated in the same foreign country as the transferor foreign corporation; and there is an income tax treaty in force between that foreign country and the United States at the time of the transfer that contains an exchange of information provision; or

(v) The transferee foreign corporation is incorporated in the same foreign country as the transferor foreign corporation; and the transfer is incident to a mere change in identity, form, or place of organization of one corporation under section 368(a)(1)(F).

For purposes of any election by a transferee foreign corporation (or the transferee corporation's parent in the case of a parenthetical C reorganization) to be treated as a domestic corporation under section 897(i) and § 1.897-3 where the exchange was described in subdivisions (i) or (ii) of paragraph (b)(1) of this section, any prior dispositions of the transferor foreign corporation stock will be subject to the requirements of § 1.897-3(d)(2) upon an election under section 897(i) by the transferee foreign corporation (or the transferee corporation's parent in the case of a parenthetical C reorganization).

(3) *No exceptions.*—No exception to recognition of gain under paragraph (a)(1) of this section is provided for the transfer of a U.S. real property interest by a foreign person to a foreign corporation in exchange for stock in a foreign corporation other than as provided in this paragraph (b). Thus, no exception is provided where—

(i) Such exchange is made pursuant to section 351 and the U.S. real property interest transferred is not stock in a U.S. real property holding corporation; or

(ii) Such exchange is made pursuant to section 361(a) in a reorganization described in section 368 (a)(1) that does not qualify for nonrecognition of gain under this paragraph (b). With regard to the treatment of certain foreign corporations as domestic corporations under section 897(i), see §§ 1.897-3 and 1.897-8T.

(4) *Examples.*—The rules of paragraph (b)(1) and (2) of this section may be illustrated by the following examples. In each instance, the filing requirements of paragraph (d)(1)(iii) of § 1.897-5T have been satisfied.

Example (1). (i) FC is a Country F corporation that has not made a section 897(i) election. FC owns Parcel P, a U.S. real property interest, with a fair market value of $450x and an adjusted basis of 100x.

(ii) FC transfers Parcel P to FS, its wholly owned Country F subsidiary, in exchange for FS stock under section 351(a). FS has not made a section 897 (i) election. Under the rules of paragraph (a)(1) of this section, FC must recognize gain of 350x under section 897(a) because the FS stock received in the exchange is not a U.S. real property interest. No exception to the recognition rule of paragraph (a)(1) is provided under this paragraph (b) for a transfer under section 351(a) of a U.S. real property interest (that is not stock in a U.S. real property holding corporation) by a foreign corporation to another foreign corporation in exchange for stock of the transferee corporation.

Example (2). (i) FC is a Country F corporation that has not made a section 897(i) election. FC owns several U.S. real property interests that have appreciated in value since FC purchased the interests. FP, a Country F corporation, owns all of the outstanding stock of FC. Country F maintains an income tax treaty with the United States.

(ii) For valid business purposes, FC transferred substantially all of its assets including all of its U.S. real property interests to FS in 1989 under section 361(a) in a reorganization in exchange for FS stock. FS is a newly formed Country F corporation that is owned by FC. The transfer qualifies as a reorganization under section 368(a)(1)(D). FC immediately distributes the FS stock to FP in exchange for the FC stock and FC dissolves. FP has no gain or loss on the exchange of the FC stock for the FS stock under section 354(a).

(iii) Under the rules of paragraph (b)(1)(i) of this section, FC does not recognize any gain on the transfer of the U.S. real property interests to FS under section 361(a) in the reorganization under section 368(a)(1)(D) because FS would be subject to U.S. taxation on a subsequent disposition of the interests, as required by paragraph (b)(1) of this section; there is an exchange of stock under section 354(a), as required by paragraph (b)(1)(i); and FC and FS are incorporated in Country F which maintains an income tax treaty with the United States, as required by paragraph (b)(2)(iv).

(5) *Contributions of property.*—A foreign person that contributes a U.S. real property interest to a foreign corporation as paid in surplus or as a contribution to capital (including a contribution provided in section 304(a)) shall be treated, for purposes of section 897(j) and this section, as exchanging the U.S. real property interest for stock in the foreign corporation.

(c) *Denial of nonrecognition with respect to certain tax avoidance transfers.*—(1) *In general.*—The provisions of § 1.897-5T and paragraphs (a) and (b) of this section are subject to the rules of this paragraph (c).

(2) *Certain transfers to domestic corporations.*—(i) *General rule.*—If a foreign person transfers property, that is not a U.S. real property interest, to a domestic corporation in a nonrecognition exchange, where—

(A) The adjusted basis of such property transferred exceeded its fair market value on the date of the transfer to the domestic corporation;

(B) The property transferred will not immediately be used in, or held by the domestic corporation for use in, the conduct of a trade or business as defined in § 1.897-1(f); and

(C) Within two years of the transfer to the domestic corporation, the property transferred is sold at a loss;

then, it will be presumed, absent clear and convincing evidence to the contrary, that the purpose for transferring the loss property was the avoidance of taxation on the disposition of U.S. real property interests by the domestic corporation. Any loss recognized by the domestic corporation on the sale or exchange of such property shall not be used by the domestic corporation, either by direct offset or as part of a net operating loss or capital loss carryback or carryover, to offset any gain recognized from the sale or exchange of a U.S. real property interest by the domestic corporation.

(ii) *Example.*—The rules of paragraph (e)(2)(i) of this section may be illustrated by the following example.

Example. A is an individual citizen and resident of country F, which does not have an income tax treaty with the U.S. On January 1, 1987, A transfers a U.S. real property interest with a basis of $100,000 and a fair market value of $600,000 to domestic corporation DC in exchange for all of the stock of DC. On October 20, 1987, A transfers stock of a publicly traded domestic corporation with a basis in his hands of $900,000 and a fair market value of $500,000, in exchange for additional stock of DC. The stock of the publicly traded domestic corporation does not constitute an asset used or held for use in DC's trade or business. If DC sells the stock of the publicly traded domestic corporation before October 20, 1989 and recognizes a loss, the loss may not be used to offset any gain recognized on the sale of the U.S. real property interests by DC.

(3) *Basis adjustment for certain related person transactions.*—In the case of any disposition after December 31, 1979, of a U.S. real property interest to a related person (within the meaning of section 453(f)(1)), the basis of the interest in the hands of the person acquiring such interest shall be reduced by the amount of any gain which is not subject to taxation under section 871(b)(1) or 882(a)(1) because the disposition occurred before June 19, 1980 or because of any treaty obligation of the United States. If a foreign corporation makes an election under section 897 (i), and the stock of such corporation was transferred between related persons after December 31, 1979 and before June 19, 1980, then such stock shall be treated as a U.S. real property interest solely for purposes of this paragraph (c)(3).

(4) *Rearrangement of ownership to gain treaty benefit.*—A foreign person who directly or indirectly owns a U.S. real property interest may not directly or indirectly rearrange the incidents of ownership of the U.S. real property interest through the use of nonrecognition provisions in order to gain the benefit of a treaty exemption from taxation. Such nonrecognition will not apply to the foreign transferor. The transferor will recognize gain but not loss on the transfer under section 897(a).

(d) *Effective date.*—Except as specifically provided otherwise in the text of the regulations, paragraphs (a) through (c) shall be effective for transfers, exchanges and other dispositions occurring after June

18, 1980. Paragraph (a)(5)(ii) of this section shall be effective for exchanges and elections occurring after June 6, 1988. [Temporary Reg. § 1.897-6T.]

☐ [*T.D. 8198, 5-4-88. Amended by T.D. 9082, 8-4-2003.*]

§ 1.897-7. Treatment of certain partnership interests, trusts and estates under section 897(g).—(a) through (b) [Reserved]. For further guidance, see § 1.897-7T(a) through (b).

(c) *Coordination with section 864(c)(8).*—Except as provided in § 1.864(c)(8)-1, the amount of any money, and the fair market value of any property, received by a nonresident alien individual or foreign corporation in exchange for all or part of its interest in a partnership, trust, or estate will, to the extent attributable to United States real property interests, be considered as an amount received from the sale or exchange in the United States of such property. See also § 1.864(c)(8)-1(h) for an anti-stuffing rule that may apply to transactions subject to section 897. This paragraph applies to transfers occurring on or after December 26, 2018, and to amounts received on or after December 26, 2018, pursuant to an installment sale (as defined in section 453(b)) occurring on or after November 27, 2017. [Reg. § 1.897-7.]

☐ [*T.D. 9919, 11-5-2020.*]

§ 1.897-7T. Treatment of certain partnership interests as entirely U.S. real property interests under sections 897(g) and 1445(e) (Temporary).—(a) *Rule.*—Pursuant to section 897(g), an interest in a partnership in which, directly or indirectly, fifty percent or more of the value of the gross assets consist of U.S. real property interests, and ninety percent or more of the value of the gross assets consist of U.S. real property interests plus any cash or cash equivalents shall, for purposes of section 1445, be treated as entirely a U.S. real property interest. For purposes of section 897(g), such interest shall be treated as a U.S. real property interest only to the extent that the gain on the disposition is attributable to U.S. real property interests (and not cash, cash equivalents or other property). Consequently, a disposition of any portion of such partnership interest shall be subject to partial taxation under section 897(a) and full withholding under section 1445(a). For purposes of this paragraph, cash equivalent means any asset readily convertible into cash (whether or not denominated in U.S. dollars) including, but not limited to, bank accounts, certificates of deposit, money market accounts, commercial paper, U.S. and foreign treasury obligations and bonds, corporate obligations and bonds, precious metals or commodities, and publicly traded instruments.

(b) *Effective date.*—Section 1.897-7T shall be effective for transfers, exchanges, distributions and other dispositions occurring after June 6, 1988.

(c) *Coordination with section 864(c)(8).*—[Reserved]. For further guidance, see § 1.897-7(c). [Temporary Reg. § 1.897-7T.]

☐ [*T.D. 8198, 5-4-88. Amended by T.D. 9919, 11-5-2020.*]

§ 1.897-9T. Treatment of certain interest in publicly traded corporations, definition of foreign person, and foreign governments and international organizations (Temporary).—(a) *Purpose and scope.*—This section provides a temporary regulation that, if and when adopted as a final regulation, will be added as new paragraphs (c)(2)(iii)(B), (k), (n) and (q) of § 1.897-1. Paragraph (b) of this section would then appear as paragraph (c)(2)(iii)(B) of § 1.897-1. Paragraph (c) of this section would then appear as paragraph (k) of § 1.897-1. Paragraph (d) of this section would then appear as paragraph (n) of § 1.897-1. Paragraph (e) of this section would then appear as paragraph (q) of § 1.897-1.

(b) Any other interest in the corporation (other than an interest solely as a creditor) if on the date such interest was acquired by its present holder it had a fair market value greater than the fair market value on that date of 5 percent of the regularly traded class of the corporation's stock with the lowest fair market value. However, if a non-regularly traded class of interests in the corporation is convertible into a regularly traded class of interests in the corporation, an interest in such non-regularly traded class shall be treated as a U.S. real property interest if on the date it was acquired by its present holder it had a fair market value greater than the fair market value on that date of 5 percent of the regularly traded class of the corporation's stock into which it is convertible. If a person holds interests in a corporation of a class that is not regularly traded, and subsequently acquires additional interests of the same class, then all such interests must be aggregated and valued as of the date of the subsequent acquisition. If the subsequent acquisition causes that person's interests to exceed the applicable limitation, then all such interests shall be treated as U.S. real property interests, regardless of when acquired. In addition, if a person holds interests in a corporation of separate classes that are not regularly traded, and if such interests were separately acquired for a principal purpose of avoiding the applicable 5 percent limitation of this paragraph, then such interests shall be aggregated for purposes of applying that limitation. This rule shall not apply to interests of separate classes acquired in transactions more than three years apart. For purposes of paragraph (c)(2)(iii) of § 1.897-1, section 318(a) shall apply (except that section 318(a)(2)(C) and (3)(C) shall each be applied by substituting "5 percent" for "50 percent").

(c) *Foreign person.*—The term "foreign person" means a nonresident alien individual (including an individual subject to the provisions of section 877), a foreign corporation as defined in paragraph (1) of this section, a foreign partnership, a foreign trust or a foreign estate, as such persons are defined respectively by § 1.871-2 and by 7701 and the regulations thereunder. A resident alien individual, including a nonresident alien with respect to whom there is in effect an election under section 6013(g) or (h) to be treated as United States resident, is not a foreign person. With respect to the status of foreign governments and international organizations, see paragraph (e) of this section.

(d) *Regularly traded.*—(1) *General rule.*—(i) *Trading requirements.*—A class of interests that is traded on one or more established securities markets is considered to be regularly traded on such market or markets for any calendar quarter during which—

(A) Trades in such class are effected, other than in *de minimis* quantities, on at least 15 days during the calendar quarter;

(B) The aggregate number of the interests in such class traded is at least 7.5 percent or more of the average number of interests in such class outstanding during the calendar quarter; and

(C) The requirements of paragraph (d)(3) of this section are met.

(ii) *Exceptions.*—(A) In the case of the class of interests which is held by 2,500 or more record shareholders, the requirements of paragraph (d)(1)(i)(B) of this section shall be applied by substituting "2.5 percent" for "7.5 percent".

(B) If at any time during the calendar quarter 100 or fewer persons own 50 percent or more of the outstanding shares of a class of interests, such class shall not be considered to be regularly traded for purposes of sections 897, 1445 and 6039C. Related persons shall be treated as one person for purposes of this paragraph (d)(1)(ii)(B).

(iii) *Anti-abuse rule.*—Trades between related persons shall be disregarded. In addition, a class of interests shall not be treated as regularly traded if there is an arrangement or a pattern of trades designed to meet the requirements of this paragraph (d)(1). For example, trades between two persons that occur several times during the calendar quarter may be treated as an arrangement or a pattern of trades designed to meet the requirements of this paragraph (d)(1).

(2) *Interests traded on domestic established securities markets.*—For purposes of sections 897, 1445 and 6039C, a class of interests that is traded on an established securities market located in the United States is considered to be regularly traded for any calendar quarter during which it is regularly quoted by brokers or dealers making a market in such interests. A broker or dealer makes a market in a class of interests only if the broker or dealer holds himself out to buy or sell interests in such class at the quoted price. Stock of a corporation that is described in section 851(a)(1) and units of a unit investment trust registered under the Investment Company Act of 1940 (15 U.S.C. sections 80a-1 to 80a-2) shall be treated as regularly traded within the meaning of this paragraph.

(3) *Reporting requirement for interests traded on foreign securities markets.*—A class of interests in a domestic corporation that is traded on one or more established securities markets located outside the United States shall not be considered to be regularly traded on such market or markets unless such class is traded in registered form, and—

(i) The corporation registers such class of interests pursuant to section 12 of the Securities Exchange Act of 1934, 15 U.S.C. sec. 78, or

(ii) The corporation attaches to its federal income tax return a statement providing the following:

(A) A caption which states "The following information concerning certain shareholders of this corporation is provided in accordance with the requirements of § 1.897-9T."

(B) The name under which the corporation is incorporated, the state in which such corporation is incorporated, the principal place of business of the corporation, and its employer identification number, if any;

(C) The identity of each person who, at any time during the corporation's taxable year, was the beneficial owner of more than 5 percent of any class of interests of the corporation to which this paragraph (d)(3) applies;

(D) The title, and the total number of shares issued, of any class of interests so owned; and

(E) With respect to each beneficial owner of more than 5 percent of any class of interests of the corporation, the number of shares owned, the percentage of the class represented thereby, and the nature of the beneficial ownership of each class of shares so owned.

Interests in a domestic corporation which has filed a report pursuant to this paragraph (d)(3)(ii) shall be considered to be regularly traded on an established securities market only for the taxable year of the corporation with respect to which such a report is filed.

(4) *Coordination with section 1445.*—For purposes of section 1445, a class of interests in a corporation shall be presumed to be regularly traded during a calendar quarter if such interests were regularly traded within the meaning of this paragraph during the previous calendar quarter.

(e) *Foreign governments and international organizations.*—A foreign government shall be treated as a foreign person with respect to U.S. real property interests, and shall be subject to sections 897, 1445, and 6039C on the disposition of a U.S. real property interest except to the extent specifically otherwise provided in the regulations issued under section 892. An international organization (as defined in section 7701(a)(18)) is not a foreign person with respect to U.S. real property interests, and is not subject to sections 897, 1445, and 6039C on the disposition of a U.S. real property interest. Buildings or parts of buildings and the land ancillary thereto (including the residence of the head of the diplomatic mission) used by the foreign government for a diplomatic mission shall not be a U.S. real property interest in the hands of the respective foreign government.

(f) *Effective date.*—Section 1.897-9T with the exception of paragraph (e) shall be effective for transfers, exchanges, distributions and other dispositions occurring on or after June 6, 1988. Paragraph (e) of this section shall be effective for transfers, exchanges, distributions and other dispositions occurring on or after July 1, 1986. [Temporary Reg. § 1.897-9T.]

☐ [*T.D. 8198, 5-4-88.*]

Proposed Amendments to Regulation

§ 1.897-9T. Treatment of certain interest in publicly traded corporations, definition of foreign person, and foreign governments and international organizations (temporary).—

* * *

(e) * * * See § 1.897-1(c)(3)(iv)(B) regarding the treatment of international organizations as foreign persons for purposes of section 897(h)(4)(B). * * *

* * *

[Prop. Reg. § 1.897-9T.]

[Proposed 12-29-2022.]

§ 1.897(l)-1. Exception for interests held by foreign pension funds.—(a) *Scope and overview.*—This section provides rules regarding the exception from section 897 for qualified holders. The definitions and requirements in this section apply only for purposes of this section (including as applicable by cross-reference from other sections), and no inference is to be drawn with respect to the definitions and requirements in this section, including with respect to the meaning of a pension fund, for any other purpose. Paragraph (b) of this section provides the general rule excepting qualified holders from section 897. Paragraph (c) of this section provides the requirements that an eligible fund must satisfy to be treated as a qualified foreign pension fund. Paragraph (d) of this section provides the requirements that a qualified foreign pension fund or a qualified controlled entity must satisfy to be treated as a qualified holder. Paragraph (e) of this section provides definitions. Paragraph (f) of this section provides examples illustrating the application of the rules of this section. Paragraph (g) of this section provides applicability dates. For rules applicable to a qualified foreign pension fund or qualified controlled entity claiming an exemption from withholding under chapter 3, see generally § § 1.1441-3, 1.1445-2, 1.1445-5, 1.1445-8, 1.1445-8, and 1.1446-2.

(b) *Exception from section 897.*—(1) *In general.*—Gain or loss of a qualified holder from the disposition of a United States real property interest, including gain from a distribution described in section 897(h), is not subject to section 897(a).

(2) *Limitation.*—Paragraph (b)(1) of this section applies solely with respect to gain or loss that is attributable to one or more qualified segregated accounts maintained by a qualified holder.

(c) *Qualified foreign pension fund requirements.*—(1) *In general.*—An eligible fund is a qualified foreign pension fund if it satisfies the requirements of this paragraph (c). Paragraph (c)(2) of this section provides rules regarding the application of the requirements of section 897(l)(2) to an eligible fund. Paragraph (c)(3) of this section provides rules on the application of the requirements in paragraph (c)(2) of this section, including rules regarding the application of those requirements to an eligible fund that is an organization or arrangement and rules regarding recordkeeping.

(2) *Applicable requirements.*—(i) *Created or organized.*—An eligible fund must be created, organized, or established under the laws of a foreign jurisdiction. For purposes of this paragraph (c)(2)(i), a governmental unit is treated as created or organized in the foreign jurisdiction with respect to which it is, or is a part of, the foreign government

(ii) *Establishment of eligible fund.*—(A) *General requirement.*—*(1) Purpose of and parties establishing eligible fund.*—An eligible fund must be established —

(i) By, or at the direction of, the foreign jurisdiction in which it is created or organized to provide retirement and pension benefits to participants or beneficiaries that are current or former employees or persons designated by such employees as a result of services rendered by such employees to their employers; or

(ii) By one or more employers (including a governmental unit in its capacity as an employer) to provide retirement and pension benefits to participants or beneficiaries that are current or former employees or persons designated by such employees in consideration for services rendered by such employees to such employers.

(2) Identification of type of eligible fund.—An eligible fund that is described in both paragraphs (c)(2)(ii)(A)(1)(i) and (ii) of this section shall be treated solely as described in the latter paragraph.

(3) Role of parties other than the foreign jurisdiction or employer.—For purposes of paragraph (c)(2)(ii)(A)(*1*) of this section, the determination of whether an eligible fund is established by, or at the direction of, a foreign jurisdiction or established by an employer is made without regard to whether one or more persons that are not the foreign jurisdiction or employer administer or otherwise provide services with regard to the eligible fund (including holding assets in a qualified segregated account as part of or on behalf of the eligible fund).

(B) *Established to provide retirement or pension benefits.*—An eligible fund is established to provide retirement or pension benefits for purposes of the general requirement in paragraph (c)(2)(ii)(A) of this section if—

(1) All of the benefits that an eligible fund provides are qualified benefits provided to qualified recipients;

(2) At least 85 percent of the present value of the qualified benefits that the eligible fund reasonably expects to provide to qualified recipients in the future are retirement and pension benefits; and

(3) No more than five percent of the present value of the qualified benefits the eligible fund reasonably expects to provide to qualified recipients in the future are non-ancillary benefits.

(C) *Present valuation.*—*(1) In general.*—For purposes of satisfying the requirements in paragraphs (c)(2)(ii)(B)(2) and (3) of this section, an eligible fund must determine, on at least an annual basis, the present value of the qualified benefits that the eligible fund reasonably expects to provide to qualified recipients during the entire period during which the eligible fund is expected to be in existence. An eligible fund may utilize any reasonable method for performing the present valuation.

(2) 48-month average alternative calculation.—An eligible fund that does not satisfy the requirements of paragraph (c)(2)(ii)(B)(*2*) or (*3*) of this section based on the present value determination under paragraph (c)(2)(ii)(C)(*1*) of this section may satisfy the requirements of paragraph (c)(2)(ii)(B)(*2*) or (*3*) of this section based on the alternative calculation in this paragraph (c)(2)(ii)(C)(*2*). The alternative calculation in this paragraph is satisfied if the average of the present values of the future qualified benefits that the eligible fund reasonably expected to provide, as determined during the 48-month period preceding (and including) the most recent present valuation determination, satisfies the requirements of paragraph (c)(2)(ii)(B)(*2*) or (*3*) of this section, respectively. The determination of such average must be based on the valuations described in paragraph (c)(2)(ii)(C)(*1*) of this section that were carried out during the 48-month period preceding (and including) the most recent present value determination, and must use the values (not percentages) of the qualified benefits the eligible fund reasonably expected to provide. The determination described in this paragraph must be calculated using a weighted average whereby values are adjusted if the relevant valuations are applicable for different periods (as described in paragraph (c)(2)(ii)(C)(*3*) of this section) because an eligible fund performs valulations more frequently than on an annual basis. If an eligible fund has been in existence for less than 48 months, this paragraph (c)(2)(ii)(C)(*2*) is applied to the period that the eligible fund has been in existence. The alternative calculation in this paragraph (c)(2)(ii)(C)(*2*) may be satisfied based on any reasonable determination of the present valuation described in paragraph (c)(2)(ii)(C)(*1*) of this section for any period that starts before the date that the requirements of paragraph (c)(2)(ii)(C) of this section first apply to an organization or arrangement and ends on or before December 29, 2022.

(3) Application of present valuation.—An eligible fund must use the present value determination made as of the most recent valuation under paragraph (c)(2)(ii)(C)(*1*) of this section or the alternative calculation provided in paragraph (c)(2)(ii)(C)(*2*) of this section (to the extent the eligible fund did not satisfy the requirements of paragraphs (c)(2)(ii)(B)(*2*) and (*3*) of this section in the most recent valuation) for purposes of meeting the requirements in paragraphs (c)(2)(ii)(B)(*2*) and (*3*) of this section with respect to dispositions of United States real property interests or distributions described in section 897(h) occurring in the twelve months succeeding the most recent valuation, or until a new present value determination is made, whichever occurs first.

(D) *Certain distributions from eligible funds.*—The following distributions are not taken into account for purposes of determining whether an eligible fund satisfies the requirements of paragraph (c)(2)(ii)(B) of this section—

(*1*) A loan to a qualified recipient pursuant to terms set by the eligible fund (other than a loan with respect to which a qualified recipient defaults and is not required to repay in whole or part, unless the default is subject to tax and penalty in such foreign jurisdiction);

(*2*) A distribution (as permitted by the laws of the foreign jurisdiction in which the eligible fund is established or operates) made before the participant or beneficiary reaches the retirement age (as determined under the relevant foreign laws), provided that the distribution is to a designee that is a qualified holder or to another arrangement subject to similar distribution or tax rules under the laws of the foreign jurisdiction; and

(*3*) A withdrawal of funds before the participant or beneficiary reaches the retirement age (as determined under the relevant foreign laws) to satisfy a financial need (under principles similar to the U.S. hardship distribution rules, see § 1.401(k)-1(d)(3)) as permitted under the laws of the foreign jurisdiction in which the eligible fund is established or operates, provided the distribution (or at least the portion of the distribution exceeding basis) is subject to tax and penalty in such foreign jurisdiction.

(E) *Certain employers and employees.*—For purposes of this section, the following rules apply—

(*1*) A self-employed individual is treated as both an employer and an employee;

(*2*) Employees of an individual, trust, corporation, or partnership that is a member of an employer group are treated as employees of each member of the employer group that includes the individual, trust, corporation, or partnership; and

(*3*) An eligible fund established by a trade union, professional association, or similar group, either alone or in combination with the employer or group of employers, is treated as established by any employer that funds, in whole or in part, the eligible fund.

(iii) *Single participant or beneficiary.*—(A) *In general.*—An eligible fund may not have a single qualified recipient that has a right to more than five percent of the assets or income of the eligible fund.

(B) *Constructive ownership.*—For purposes of paragraph (c)(2)(iii)(A) of this section, an individual is considered to have a right to the assets or income of an eligible fund to which any person who bears a relationship to the individual described in section 267(b) or 707(b) has a right.

(iv) *Regulation and information reporting.*—(A) *In general.*—The eligible fund must be subject to government regulation and annually provide to the relevant tax authorities (or other relevant governmental units) in the foreign jurisdiction in which the eligible fund is established or operates information about the amount of qualified benefits (if any) provided to each qualified recipient by the eligible fund, or such information must otherwise be available to the relevant tax authorities (or other relevant governmental units). An eligible fund is not treated as failing to satisfy the requirement of this paragraph (c)(2)(iv)(A) as a result of the eligible fund not being required to provide information to the relevant tax authorities (or other relevant governmental units) in a year in which no qualified benefits are provided to qualified recipients.

(B) *Treatment of certain eligible funds established by foreign jurisdictions.*—An eligible fund that is described in paragraph (c)(2)(ii)(A)(*1*)(*i*) of this section is deemed to satisfy the requirements of paragraph (c)(2)(iv)(A) of this section.

(v) *Tax treatment.*—(A) *In general.*—The tax laws of the foreign jurisdiction in which the eligible fund is established or operates must provide that, due to the status of the eligible fund as a retirement or pension fund, either—

(*1*) Contributions to the eligible fund that would otherwise be subject to tax under such laws are deductible or excluded from the gross income of the eligible fund or taxed at a reduced rate; or

(*2*) Taxation of any investment income of the eligible fund is deferred or excluded from the gross income of the eligible fund or such income is taxed at a reduced rate.

(B) *Income subject to preferential tax treatment.*—An eligible fund is treated as satisfying the requirement of paragraph (c)(2)(v)(A) of this section in a taxable year if, under the tax laws of the foreign jurisdiction in which the eligible fund is established or operates—

(*1*) At least 85 percent of the contributions to the eligible fund are subject to the tax treatment described in paragraph (c)(2)(v)(A)(*1*) of this section, or

(*2*) At least 85 percent of the investment income of the eligible fund is subject to the tax treatment described in paragraph (c)(2)(v)(A)(*2*) of this section.

(C) *Income not subject to tax.*—An eligible fund is treated as satisfying the requirement of paragraph (c)(2)(v)(A) of this section if the eligible fund is exempt from the income tax of the foreign jurisdiction in which it is established or operates or the foreign jurisdiction in which it is established or operates has no income tax.

(D) *Other preferential tax regimes.*—An eligible fund that does not receive the tax treatment described in either paragraph (c)(2)(v)(A)(*1*) or (*2*) of this section is nonetheless treated as satisfying the requirement of paragraph (c)(2)(v)(A) of this section if the eligible fund establishes that each of the conditions described in paragraphs (c)(2)(v)(D)(*1*) and (*2*) of this section is satisfied:

(*1*) Under the tax laws of the foreign jurisdiction in which the eligible fund is established or operates, the eligible fund is subject to a preferential tax regime due to its status as a retirement or pension fund; and

(*2*) The preferential tax regime described in paragraph (c)(2)(v)(D)(*1*) of this section has a substantially similar effect as the tax treatment described in paragraphs (c)(2)(v)(A)(*1*) or (*2*) of this section.

(E) *Tax law of subnational jurisdictions.*—Solely for purposes of this paragraph (c)(2)(v), a reference to the tax law of a foreign jurisdiction includes the tax law of a political subdivision or other local authority of a foreign jurisdiction, provided that income taxes imposed under the subnational tax law are treated as covered taxes under an income tax treaty between that foreign jurisdiction and the United States.

(3) *Operating rules.*—(i) *Rules on the application of the requirements in paragraph (c)(2) of this section.*—(A) *Organizations or arrangements.*—An organization or arrangement is treated as a single entity for purposes of determining whether the requirements of paragraph (c)(2) of this section are satisfied, except that each person or governmental unit that is part of or party to an organization or arrangement must satisfy the requirement of paragraph (c)(2)(i) of this section.

(B) *Relevant income, assets, and functions.*—The determination of whether an eligible fund satisfies the requirements of paragraph (c)(2) of this section is made solely with respect to the assets and income of the eligible fund held in one or more qualified segregated accounts, the qualified benefits funded by the qualified segregated accounts, the information reporting and regulation related to the qualified segregated accounts, and the qualified recipients whose benefits are funded by the qualified segregated accounts. For this purpose, all assets held by an eligible fund in qualified segregated accounts (within the meaning of paragraph (e)(13)(ii) of this section) are treated as a single qualified segregated account.

(ii) *Aggregate approach to partnerships.*—For purposes of this section, assets held by a partnership shall be treated as held proportionately by its partners, and activities conducted by a partnership shall be treated as conducted by its partners.

(iii) *Recordkeeping.*—An eligible fund that claims the exemption under section 897(l) must have records sufficient to establish that it satisfies the requirements of paragraph (c)(2) of this section. See section 6001 and § 1.6001-1, requiring records to be maintained.

(d) *Qualified holder requirements.*—(1) *In general.*—With respect to a disposition described in section 897(a) or a distribution described in section 897(h), a qualified foreign pension fund (including a part of a qualified foreign pension fund) or a qualified controlled entity is a qualified holder only if it satisfies the requirement of paragraph (d)(2) or (3) of this section.

(2) *Qualified holders that did not hold U.S. real property interests.*—The requirement of this paragraph (d)(2) is satisfied if the qualified foreign pension fund or qualified controlled entity owned no United States real property interests as of the earliest date during an uninterrupted period, ending on the date of the disposition or distribution, in which the qualified foreign pension fund or qualified controlled entity satisfied the requirements of paragraph (c)(2) of this section or paragraph (e)(9) of this section, as applicable.

(3) *Qualified holders that satisfy the testing period.*—(i) *In general.*—The requirement of this paragraph (d)(3) is satisfied if the qualified foreign pension fund or qualified controlled entity continuously satisfies the requirements of paragraph (c)(2) of this section or paragraph (e)(9) of this section, as applicable, for the duration of the testing period.

(ii) *Testing Period.*—The term testing period means whichever of the following periods is the shortest:

(A) The period beginning on December 18, 2015, and ending on the date of the disposition or the distribution;

(B) The ten-year period ending on the date of the disposition or the distribution; and,

(C) The period beginning on the date the entity (or its predecessor) was created or organized and ending on the date of the disposition or the distribution.

(4) *Transition Rules.*—(i) *Qualified foreign pension fund or qualified controlled entity requirements.*—With respect to any period from December 18, 2015, to the date when the requirements of paragraph (c)(2) or (e)(9) of this section first apply to a qualified foreign pension fund or qualified controlled entity under paragraph (g) of this section, as applicable (but in any event no later than December 29, 2022, in the case of paragraph (c)(2) of this section, and no later than June 6, 2019, in the case of paragraph (e)(9) of this section), the qualified foreign pension fund or qualified controlled entity is deemed to satisfy the requirements of paragraphs (c)(2) and (e)(9) of this section, as applicable, for purposes of paragraphs (d)(2) and (3) of this section if the qualified foreign pension fund or qualified controlled entity satisfies the requirements of section 897(l)(2) based on a reasonable interpretation of those requirements (including determining any applicable valuations using a consistent method).

(ii) *Ownership of qualified controlled entity by service providers.*—Solely for purposes of paragraphs (d)(2) and (3) of this section, the determination of whether a corporation or trust is a qualified controlled entity will not include stock or interests held directly or indirectly by any person that provides services to such corporation or trust, provided that such stock or interests are, in the aggregate, no more than five percent (by vote or value) of the stock or interests of such corporation or trust. This paragraph (d)(4)(ii) applies to interests held from December 18, 2015 until February 27, 2023.

(e) *Definitions.*—The following definitions apply for purposes of this section.

(1) *Ancillary benefits.*—(i) *In general.*—The term *ancillary benefits* means—

(A) Benefits payable upon the diagnosis of a terminal illness, incidental death benefits (for example, funeral expenses), short-term disability benefits, life insurance benefits, and medical benefits;

(B) Unemployment, shutdown, or layoff benefits that do not continue past retirement age and do not affect the payment of accrued retirement and pension benefits; and

(C) Other health-related or unemployment benefits that are similar to the benefits described in paragraphs (e)(1)(i) and (ii) of this section.

(ii) *Overlap with retirement and pension benefits.*—Ancillary benefits do not include any benefits that could also be defined as retirement and pension benefits within the meaning of paragraph (e)(14) of this section.

(2) *Eligible fund.*—The term *eligible fund* means a trust, corporation, or other organization or arrangement that maintains one or more qualified segregated accounts.

(3) *Employer group.*—The term *employer group* means all individuals, trusts, partnerships, and corporations with a relationship to each other specified in section 267(b) or section 707(b).

(4) *Foreign jurisdiction.*—The term *foreign jurisdiction* means a jurisdiction other than the United States, including a country, a state, province, or political subdivision of a foreign country, and a territory of the United States.

(5) *Governmental unit.*—The term *governmental unit* means any foreign government or part thereof, including any person, body, group of persons, organization, agency, bureau, fund, or instrumentality, however designated, of a foreign government.

(6) *Non-ancillary benefits.*—The term *non-ancillary benefits* means benefits that are neither ancillary benefits (within the meaning of paragraph (e)(1) of this section) nor retirement and pension benefits (within the meaning of paragraph (e)(14) of this section), and are provided by the eligible fund as permitted or required under the laws of the foreign jurisdiction in which the eligible fund is established or operates.

(7) *Organization or arrangement.*—The term *organization or arrangement* means one or more trusts, corporations, governmental units, or employers.

(8) *Qualified benefits.*—The term *qualified benefits* means retirement and pension benefits, ancillary benefits and non-ancillary benefits. However, the portions of qualified benefits consisting of ancillary benefits and non-ancillary benefits provided by a qualified foreign pension fund are limited as provided in paragraph (c)(2)(ii)(B) of this section.

(9) *Qualified controlled entity.*—The term *qualified controlled entity* means a trust or corporation created or organized under the laws of a foreign jurisdiction all of the interests of which are held by one or more qualified foreign pension funds directly or indirectly through one or more qualified controlled entities.

(10) *Qualified foreign pension fund.*—The term *qualified foreign pension fund* means an eligible fund that satisfies the requirements of paragraph (c) of this section.

(11) *Qualified holder.*—The term *qualified holder* means a qualified foreign pension fund or qualified controlled entity that satisfies the requirements of paragraph (d) of this section.

(12) *Qualified recipient.*—(i) *In general.*—The term *qualified recipient* means—

(A) With respect to an eligible fund described in paragraph (c)(2)(ii)(A)(*1*)(*i*) of this section, any person eligible to be treated as a participant or beneficiary of such eligible fund and any person designated by such participant or beneficiary to receive qualified benefits, and

(B) With respect to an eligible fund described in paragraph (c)(2)(ii)(A)(*1*)(*ii*) of this section, a current or former employee, a spouse of a current or former employee, and any person designated by such participants or beneficiaries to receive qualified benefits.

(C) To the extent not already described in paragraph (e)(12)(i)(B) of this section, with respect to an eligible fund described in paragraph (c)(2)(ii)(A)(*1*)(*ii*) of this section, any person eligible to be treated as a participant or beneficiary of such fund and any person designated by such participant or beneficiary to receive qualified benefits, so long as such recipients do not exceed five percent of the eligible fund's total qualified recipients or have a right to more than five percent of the assets or income of the eligible fund. An eligible fund must make a determination for purposes of this paragraph (e)(12)(i)(C) on at least an annual basis and may utilize any reasonable method in doing so. An eligible fund must use its most recent determination under this paragraph with respect to dispositions of United States real property interests or distributions described in section 897(h) occurring in the twelve months succeeding such determination, or until a new determination is made, whichever occurs first.

(ii) *Special rule regarding automatic designation.*—For purposes of paragraph (e)(12)(i) of this section, a person is treated as designating another person to receive qualified benefits if the other person is, by reason of such person's relationship or other status with respect to the first person, entitled to receive benefits pursuant to the terms applicable to the eligible fund or pursuant to the laws of the foreign jurisdiction in which the eligible fund is created or organized, whether or not the first person expressly designated such person as a beneficiary.

(13) *Qualified segregated account.*—(i) *In general.*—The term *qualified segregated account* means an identifiable pool of assets maintained by an eligible fund or a qualified controlled entity for the sole purpose of funding and providing qualified benefits to qualified recipients.

(ii) *Assets held by eligible funds.*—For purposes of paragraph (e)(13)(i) of this section, an identifiable pool of assets of an eligible fund is treated as maintained for the sole purpose of funding qualified benefits to qualified recipients, and hence as a qualified segregated account, only if the terms applicable to the eligible fund or the laws of the foreign jurisdiction in which the eligible fund is established or operates require that all the assets in the pool, and all the income earned with respect to such assets, be used exclusively to fund the provision of qualified benefits to qualified recipients or to satisfy necessary reasonable expenses of the eligible fund, and that such assets or income may not inure to the benefit of a person other than a qualified recipient. For purposes of this paragraph (e)(13)(ii), the fact that assets or income may inure to the benefit of a governmental unit by operation of escheat or similar laws, or may revert (such as upon plan termination or dissolution (after all obligations to qualified recipients and creditors have been satisfied) or the qualified recipients' benefits failing to vest) to the governmental unit or employer in accordance with applicable foreign law is ignored, so long as contributions to the plan are not more than reasonably necessary to fund the qualified benefits to be provided to qualified recipients.

(iii) *Assets held by qualified controlled entities.*—For purposes of paragraph (e)(13)(i) of this section, the assets of a qualified controlled entity are treated as an identifiable pool of assets maintained for the sole purpose of funding qualified benefits to qualified recipients only if both of the following requirements are satisfied:

(A) All of the net earnings of the qualified controlled entity are credited to its own account or to the qualified segregated account of a qualified foreign pension fund or another qualified controlled entity, with no portion of the net earnings of the qualified controlled entity inuring to the benefit of a person other than a qualified recipient; and

(B) Upon dissolution, all of the assets of the qualified controlled entity, after satisfaction of liabilities to persons having interests in the entity solely as creditors, vest in a qualified segregated account of a qualified foreign pension fund or another qualified controlled entity.

(14) *Retirement and pension benefits.*—The term *retirement and pension benefits* means distributions to qualified recipients that are made after the qualified recipient reaches retirement age as determined under or in accordance with the laws in the foreign jurisdiction in which the eligible fund is established or operates (including a benefit paid to a qualified recipient who retires on or after a stated early retirement age), or after a specified event that results in a qualified recipient being permanently unable to work, and includes any such distribution made to a surviving beneficiary of the qualifying recipient. Retirement and pension benefits may be based on one or more of the following factors: contributions, investment performance, years of service with an employer, or compensation received by the qualified recipient.

(f) *Examples.*—This paragraph (f) provides examples that illustrate the rules of this section. The examples do not illustrate the application of the applicable withholding rules, including sections 1445 and 1446 and the regulations thereunder. It is assumed that no person is entitled to more than five percent of any eligible fund's assets or income, taking into account the constructive ownership rules in paragraph (c)(2)(iii)(B) of this section, and that the eligible fund owns no United States real property interests other than as described.

(1) *Example 1: No legal entity.*—(i) *Facts.*—On January 1, 2023, Country A establishes Retirement Plan for the sole purpose of providing retirement and pension benefits to citizens of Country A aged 65 or older. Retirement Plan is composed of Asset Pool and Agency. Asset Pool is a group of accounts maintained on the balance sheet of the government of Country A. Pursuant to the laws of Country A, income and gain earned by Asset Pool is used solely to support the provision of retirement and pension benefits by Retirement Plan. Agency is a Country A agency that administers the provision of benefits by Retirement Plan and manages Asset Pool's investments. Under the laws of Country A, investment income earned by Retirement Plan is not subject to Country A's income tax. At the end of each calendar year, Retirement Plan performs a present valuation of the retirement and pension benefits it reasonably expects to provide in the future, and all of the benefits that Retirement Plan reasonably expects to provide are retirement and pension benefits. On January 1, 2024, Agency purchases Property, which is an interest in real property located in the United States owned by Asset Pool. On June 1, 2026, Agency sells Property, realizing $100x of gain with respect to Property that would be subject to tax under section 897(a) unless paragraph (b) of this section applies with respect to the gain.

(ii) *Analysis.*—(A) Retirement Plan, which is composed of Asset Pool and Agency, includes one or more governmental units described in paragraph (e)(5) of this section. Accordingly, Retirement Plan is an organization or arrangement described in paragraph (e)(7) of this section. Furthermore, Retirement Plan maintains a qualified segregated account in the form of Asset Pool, an identifiable pool of assets maintained for the sole purpose of funding retirement and pension benefits to beneficiaries of the Retirement Fund (qualified recipients as defined in paragraph (e)(12)(i)(A) of this section). Therefore, Retirement Plan is an eligible fund within the meaning of paragraph (e)(2) of this section.

(B) Paragraph (c)(3)(i) of this section applies for purposes of determining whether Retirement Plan is an eligible fund that satisfies the requirements of paragraph (c)(2) of this section and would therefore be treated as a qualified foreign pension fund. Accordingly, the activities of Asset Pool and Agency are integrated and treated as undertaken by a single entity to determine whether the requirements of paragraph (c)(2) of this section are met. However, Asset Pool and Agency must independently satisfy the requirement of paragraph (c)(2)(i) of this section.

(C) Retirement Plan is composed of Asset Pool and Agency, each of which is a governmental unit and treated as created or organized under the laws of Country A for purposes of paragraph (c)(2)(i) of this section. Accordingly, Retirement Plan satisfies the requirement of paragraph (c)(2)(i) of this section.

(D) Retirement Plan is established by Country A as an eligible fund described in paragraph (c)(2)(ii)(A)(*1*)(*i*) of this section to provide retirement and pension benefits, which are qualified benefits described in paragraph (e)(8) of this section, to citizens of Country A, who are qualified recipients described in paragraph (e)(12)(i)(A) of this section because they are eligible to be participants or beneficiaries of Retirement Plan. Accordingly, all of the benefits that Retirement Plan provides are qualified benefits provided to qualified recipients. In addition, Retirement Plan satisfies the requirements of the present valuation test as described in paragraphs (c)(2)(ii)(B) and (C) of this section. Accordingly, Retirement Plan satisfies the requirement of paragraph (c)(2)(ii) of this section.

(E) Retirement Plan provides retirement and pension benefits to citizens of Country A aged 65 or older, with no citizen entitled to more than five percent of Retirement Fund's assets or to more than five percent of the income of the eligible fund. Accordingly, Retirement Plan satisfies the requirement of paragraph (c)(2)(iii) of this section.

(F) Retirement Plan is composed solely of governmental units within the meaning of paragraph (e)(5) of this section. Accordingly, under paragraph (c)(2)(iv)(B) of this section, Retirement Plan is treated as satisfying the requirements of paragraph (c)(2)(iv)(A) of this section.

(G) Investment income earned by Retirement Plan is not subject to income tax in Country A. Accordingly, Retirement Plan satisfies the requirement of paragraph (c)(2)(v) of this section.

(H) Because Retirement Plan satisfies the requirements of paragraph (c)(2) of this section, Retirement Plan is a qualified foreign pension fund. Because Retirement Plan held no United States real property interests as of January 1, 2023, the earliest date during an uninterrupted period ending on June 1, 2026, the date of the disposition, in which it satisfied the requirements of paragraph (c)(2) of this section, Retirement Plan is a qualified holder under paragraph (d)(2) of this section. Retirement Plan's gain with respect to Property is attributable solely to Asset Pool, a qualified segregated account maintained by Retirement Plan. Accordingly, under paragraph (b) of this section, the $100x gain realized by Retirement Plan attributable to the disposition of Property is not subject to section 897(a).

(2) *Example 2: Fund established by an employer.*—(i) *Facts.*—Employer, a corporation organized in Country B, establishes Fund to provide retirement and pension benefits to current and former employees of Employer and S1, a Country B corporation that is wholly owned by Employer. On January 1, 2023, Fund is established as a trust under the laws of Country B, and Employer retains discretion to invest assets and to administer benefits on Fund's behalf. Fund receives contributions from Employer and S1 and contributions from employees of Employer and S1 who are beneficiaries of Fund. All contributions to Fund and all of Fund's earnings are separately accounted for on Fund's books and records and are required by Fund's organizational documents to exclusively fund the provision of benefits to Fund's beneficiaries, except as necessary to satisfy reasonable expenses of Fund. Fund currently has over 100 beneficiaries, a number that is reasonably expected to grow as Employer expands. Fund will pay benefits to employees upon retirement based on years of service and employee contributions, but, if a beneficiary dies before retirement, Fund will pay an incidental death benefit in addition to payment of any accrued retirement and pension benefits to the beneficiary's designee (or deemed designee under local laws if the beneficiary fails to identify a designee). Fund annually performs a present valuation of the benefits it reasonably expects to provide to Fund's beneficiaries, and the valuation concludes that more than 85 percent of the present value of the total benefits it reasonably expects to pay to its beneficiaries in the future are retirement and pension benefits. In addition, it is reasonably expected that the incidental death benefits paid by Fund will account for less than fifteen percent of the present value of the total benefits that Fund expects to provide in the future, and Fund does not reasonably expect to pay any other types of benefits to its beneficiaries in the future. Fund annually provides to the tax authorities of Country B the amount of benefits distributed to each participant (or designee). Country B's tax authorities prescribe rules and regulations governing Fund's operations. Under the laws of Country B, Fund is not taxed on its investment income. On January 1, 2024, Fund purchases Property, which is an interest in real property located in the United States. On June 1, 2026, Fund sells Property, realizing $100x of gain with respect to Property that would be subject to tax under section 897(a) unless paragraph (b) of this section applies with respect to the gain.

(ii) *Analysis.*—(A) Fund is a trust that maintains an identifiable pool of assets for the sole purpose of funding retirement and pension benefits and ancillary benefits to current and former employees of the employer group (within the meaning of paragraph (e)(3) of this section) that includes Employer and S1 (current and former employees of Employer and S1 constitute qualified recipients, as defined in paragraph (e)(12)(i)(B) of this section). All assets held by Fund and all income earned by Fund are used to provide such benefits. Therefore, Fund is a trust that maintains a qualified segregated account within the meaning of paragraph (e)(13) of this section. Accordingly, Fund is an eligible fund within the meaning of paragraph (e)(2) of this section.

(B) Because Fund is created or organized under the laws of Country B, Fund satisfies the requirement of paragraph (c)(2)(i) of this section.

(C) The only benefits that Fund provides are retirement and pension benefits described in paragraph (e)(14) of this section and ancillary benefits (that is, the incidental death benefits) described in paragraph (e)(1) of this section, both of which constitute qualified benefits described in paragraph (e)(8) of this section, to qualified recipients, described in paragraph (e)(12)(i)(B) of this section. Furthermore, Fund satisfies the requirements of the present valuation test as described in paragraphs (c)(2)(ii)(B) and (C) of this section. Accordingly, Fund is established by Employer to provide retirement and pension benefits to qualified recipients in consideration for services rendered by such qualified recipients to Employer and S1, and Fund satisfies the requirement of paragraph (c)(2)(ii) of this section.

(D) No single qualified recipient has a right to more than five percent of the assets or income of the eligible fund. Accordingly, Fund satisfies the requirement of paragraph (c)(2)(iii) of this section.

(E) Fund is regulated and annually provides to the relevant tax authorities in the foreign jurisdiction in which it is established or operates the amount of qualified benefits provided to each qualified recipient by the eligible fund. Accordingly, Fund satisfies the requirements of paragraph (c)(2)(iv) of this section.

(F) Fund is not subject to income tax on its investment income. Accordingly, Fund satisfies the requirement of paragraph (c)(2)(v) of this section.

(G) Because Fund meets the requirements of paragraph (c)(2) of this section, Fund is treated as a qualified foreign pension fund. Furthermore, because Fund held no United States real property interests as of January 1, 2023, the earliest date during an uninterrupted period ending on June 1, 2026, the date of the disposition, in which it satisfied the requirements of paragraph (c)(2) of this section, Fund is a qualified holder under paragraph (d)(2) of this section. All of Fund's assets are held in a qualified segregated account within the meaning of paragraph (e)(13) of this section. Accordingly, under paragraph (b) of this section, the $100x gain attributable to the disposition of Property is not subject to section 897(a).

(3) *Example 3: Fund established by an employer at the direction of a foreign jurisdiction.*—(i) *Facts.*—The facts are the same as in paragraph (f)(2) of this section (*Example 2*), except that Fund was established by Employer at the direction of Country B and, in addition to being established to provide retirement and pension benefits to current and former employees of Employer and S1, Fund was also established to provide retirement and pension benefits to other employees. All employees that are beneficiaries provide contributions to Fund. Fund makes a determination on at least an annual basis using a reasonable method to measure the number of participants in the Fund who are not current and former employees of Employer and S1. Each time such a determination is made, Fund finds that such employees constitute less than five percent of Fund's total qualified recipients and do not have a right to more than five percent of the assets or income of Fund.

(ii) *Analysis.*—Fund satisfies the requirements of paragraph (c)(2)(ii)(A)(1)(*i*) of this section because it was established by, or at the direction of, Country B to provide retirement and pension benefits to participants or beneficiaries that are current or former employees or persons designated by such employees as a result of services rendered by such employees to their employers. Fund also satisfies the requirements of paragraph (c)(2)(ii)(A)(1)(ii) of this section because it was established by Employer to provide retirement and pension benefits to participants or beneficiaries that are current or former employees or persons designated by such employees in consideration for services rendered by such employees to Employer and S1. Because it satisfies the requirements of both such provisions, under paragraph (c)(2)(ii)(A)(2) of this section, Fund will be treated solely as an eligible fund under paragraph (c)(2)(ii)(A)(*1*)(*ii*) of this section. As a result, Fund must meet the reporting requirements described in paragraph (c)(2)(iv)(A) of this section and must apply the definition of qualified recipient described in paragraphs (e)(12)(i)(B) and (C) of this section. Because Fund makes a determination on at least an annual basis using a reasonable method to measure the number of participants in the Fund who are not current and former employees of Employer and S1, finding that such employees constitute less than five percent of Fund's total qualified recipients and do not have a right to more than five percent of the assets or income of Fund, the requirement of paragraph (c)(2)(ii)(B)(1) of this section, requiring that all of the benefits that an eligible fund provides are provided to qualified recipients, is considered satisfied. Because Fund meets the requirements of paragraph (c)(2) of this section, Fund is treated as a qualified foreign pension fund under paragraph (b) of this section. Accordingly, the $100x gain attributable to the disposition of Property is not subject to section 897(a).

(4) *Example 4: Employer controlled organization or arrangement.*—(i) *Facts.*—The facts are the same as in paragraph (f)(2) of this section (*Example 2*), except that S2, a Country B corporation that is wholly owned by Employer, performs all tax compliance functions for Employer, S1, and S2, including information reporting with respect to Fund participants.

(ii) *Analysis.*—For purposes of the requirements of paragraph (c)(2) of this section, Fund and S2 are an organization or arrangement that is treated as a single entity under paragraph (c)(3)(i)(A) of this section and an eligible fund under paragraph (e)(2) of this section with respect to the qualified segregated account held by Fund. Because the eligible fund composed of Fund and S2 satisfies the requirements of paragraph (c)(2) of this section (including the rule under paragraph (c)(3)(i)(A) of this section that each entity satisfy the foreign organization requirement of paragraph (c)(2)(i) of this section) with respect to the qualified benefits provided to the qualified recipients out of the eligible fund's qualified segregated account (determined in accordance with paragraph (c)(3)(i)(B) of this section), the eligible fund that is composed of Fund and S2 constitutes a qualified foreign pension fund. Furthermore, the requirements for qualified holder status are satisfied, as described in paragraph (f)(2) of this section. Thus, under paragraph (b) of this section, the $100x gain attributable to the disposition of Property is not subject to section 897(a).

(5) *Example 5: Third-party assumption of pension liabilities.*—(i) *Facts.*—The facts are the same as in paragraph (f)(2) of this section (*Example 2*), except that Fund does not purchase Property on January 1, 2024. In addition, Fund anticipates $100x of qualified benefits will be paid each year beginning on January 1, 2028. Fund enters into an agreement with Guarantor, a privately held Country B corporation, which provides that Fund will, on January 30, 2023, cede a portion of its assets to Guarantor in exchange for annual payments of $100x beginning on January 1, 2028 and continuing until one or more previously identified participants (and their designees) ceases to be eligible to receive benefits. Guarantor has discretion to invest the ceded assets as it chooses, subject to certain agreed upon investment restrictions. Pursuant to its agreement with Fund, Guarantor must maintain Segregated Pool, a pool of assets securing its obligations under its agreement with Fund. The value of Segregated Pool must exceed a specified amount (determined based on an agreed upon formula) until Guarantor's payment obligations are completed, and any remaining assets in Segregated Pool (that is, assets exceeding the required payments to Fund) are retained by Guarantor. Guarantor bears all investment risk with respect to Segregated Pool. Accordingly, Guarantor is required to make annual payments of $100x to Fund regardless of the performance of Segregated Pool. On January 1, 2024, Guarantor purchases stock in Company A, a United States real property holding company that is a United States real property interest, and holds the Company A stock in Segregated Pool. On June 1, 2027, Guarantor sells the stock in Company A, realizing a gain of $100x.

(ii) *Analysis.*—The Segregated Pool is not a qualified segregated account, because it is not maintained for the sole purpose of funding qualified benefits to qualified recipients, and because income attributable to assets in the Segregated Pool (including the Company A stock) may inure to Guarantor, which is not a qualified recipient. Accordingly, Fund and Guarantor do not qualify as an organization or arrangement that is an eligible fund with respect to the Company A stock. Therefore, Guarantor is not exempt under paragraph (b) of this section with respect to the $100x of gain realized in connection with the sale of its shares in Company A.

(6) *Example 6: Asset manager.*—(i) *Facts.*—The facts are the same as in paragraph (f)(5) of this section (*Example 5*) except that instead of ceding legal ownership of a portion of its assets to Guarantor, Fund transfers the assets into Trust with respect to which Fund is the sole beneficiary on January 30, 2023, and Trust purchases stock in Company A on January 1, 2024. Guarantor has exclusive management authority over the Trust assets and is entitled to a reasonable fixed management fee which it withdraws annually from Trust's assets. On June 1, 2027, Trust sells the stock in Company A, realizing a gain of $100x.

(ii) *Analysis.*—For purposes of testing the requirements of paragraph (c)(2) of this section, Fund and Trust are an organization or arrangement that is treated as a single entity under paragraph (c)(3)(i)(A) of this section and an eligible fund under paragraph (e)(2) of this section. Assets held by Trust are held in a qualified segregated account, and those assets are the assets that are relevant for purposes of determining whether the eligible fund composed of Fund and Trust meets the requirements of paragraph (c)(2) of this section. The eligible fund that is composed of Fund and Trust is treated as established by Employer notwithstanding that Guarantor provides management services. See paragraph (c)(2)(ii)(A)(3) of this section. Paragraph (e)(13)(ii) of this section provides that the assets held by an eligible fund in a qualified segregated account may be used to satisfy reasonable expenses of the eligible fund, such that the reasonable fixed management fee paid to Guarantor does not cause the assets held in Trust to fail to be treated as held in a qualified segregated account. All of the other requirements for qualified foreign pension fund status are satisfied by the eligible fund that is composed of Fund and Trust, as described in paragraph (f)(2) of this section. The eligible fund that is composed of Fund and Trust is a qualified holder under paragraph (d)(2) of this section because it held no United States real property interests on January 1, 2023, the earliest date during an uninterrupted period ending on June 1, 2027, the date of the disposition of Company A stock, in which it satisfied the requirements of paragraph (c)(2) of this section. The eligible fund that is composed of Fund and Trust is therefore exempt under paragraph (b) of this section with respect to the $100x of gain realized in connection with the sale by Trust of the shares in Company A.

(7) *Example 7: Partnership.*—(i) *Facts.*—The facts are the same as in paragraph (f)(5) of this section (*Example 5*) except that instead of ceding legal ownership of the assets to Guarantor, Fund contributes the assets to a partnership (PRS) formed with Guarantor and PRS purchases stock in Company A on January 30, 2023. Guarantor receives a profits interest in the partnership that is reasonable in light of Guarantor's management activity. Guarantor has no direct or indirect ownership in PRS assets, and the partnership agreement provides that upon dissolution, PRS assets would be distributed to Fund. Guarantor serves as the general partner of PRS and has discretionary authority to buy and sell PRS assets without approval from Fund. On June 1, 2027, PRS sells the stock in Company A, realizing a gain of $100x.

(ii) *Analysis.*—All of Fund's assets, including the assets held by PRS that are treated as held proportionately by Fund under paragraph (c)(3)(ii) of this section, are held in a qualified segregated account within the meaning of paragraph (e)(13) of this section. See paragraph (f)(2)(ii)(A) of this section (*Example 2*). The eligible fund that is composed of Fund is treated as established by Employer notwithstanding that Guarantor provides management services to PRS. See paragraphs (c)(2)(ii)(A)(3) and (c)(3)(ii) of this section. All of the other requirements for qualified foreign pension fund status are satisfied by Fund as described in paragraphs (f)(2)(ii)(B) through (F) of this section, and Fund is a qualified holder as described in paragraph (f)(2)(ii)(G) of this section. Accordingly, Fund is exempt under paragraph (b) of this section with respect to its allocable share of the $100x of gain realized in connection with the sale by PRS of the shares in Company A. Guarantor is not exempt under paragraph (b) of this section with respect to its allocable share of the $100x of gain realized in connection with the sale by PRS of the shares in Company A because Guarantor is neither part of the organization or arrangement that forms Fund nor a qualified holder under paragraph (d) of this section that maintains qualified segregated accounts.

(8) *Example 8: Not a qualified holder.*—(i) *Facts.*—Fund is a qualified foreign pension fund organized in Country C that meets the requirements of paragraph (c)(2) of this section. Fund owns all the outstanding stock of OpCo, a manufacturing corporation organized in Country C, in a qualified segregated account maintained by Fund. OpCo was originally formed by a person other than Fund on January 1, 2023. Fund purchased all of the stock of OpCo on November 1, 2023 for the purpose of conducting the manufacturing business and utilizing the business profits to fund pension liabilities. During the period from January 1, 2023, through October 31, 2023, OpCo was not a qualified foreign pension fund, a part of a qualified foreign pension fund, or a qualified controlled entity. On January 30, 2023, OpCo purchased Property A, a United States real property interest, from a third party. For all periods after Fund acquired OpCo, OpCo must either retain or distribute to Fund all of its net earnings, and upon dissolution, must distribute all of its assets to its stockholder (that is, Fund) after satisfaction of liabilities to its creditors. On June 1, 2024, OpCo realizes $100x of gain on the disposition of Property A.

(ii) *Analysis.*—(A) A qualified controlled entity described in paragraph (e)(9) of this section includes any corporation organized under the laws of a foreign jurisdiction all the interests of which are owned by one or more qualified foreign pension funds directly or indirectly through one or more qualified controlled entities. Fund is a qualified foreign pension fund that wholly owns OpCo. Accordingly, OpCo is a qualified controlled entity for the period when it is owned by Fund beginning on November 1, 2023.

(B) Under paragraph (d)(1) of this section, a qualified controlled entity is a qualified holder only if either, under paragraph (d)(2) of this section, the qualified controlled entity owned no United States real property interests as of the earliest date during an uninterrupted period ending on the date of the disposition or distribution in which the qualified controlled entity satisfied the requirements of paragraph (e)(9) of this section, or, under paragraph (d)(3) of this section, the qualified controlled entity satisfies the requirements of paragraph (e)(9) of this section throughout the entire testing period. Because OpCo owned a United States real property interest as of November 1, 2023, the earliest date during an uninterrupted period ending on the date of the disposition during which it satisfied the requirements of paragraph (e)(9) of this section, OpCo cannot satisfy the requirements of paragraph (d)(2) of this section and must instead satisfy the requirements of paragraph (d)(3) of this section to be a qualified holder. Under paragraph (d)(3) of this section, a qualified holder does not include any entity that was not a qualified foreign pension fund, a part of a qualified foreign pension fund, or a qualified controlled entity at any time during the testing period. The testing period with respect to OpCo is the period from January 1, 2023 (the date of OpCo's formation), to June 1, 2024 (the date of the disposition). Because OpCo was not a qualified foreign pension fund, a part of a qualified foreign pension fund, or a qualified controlled entity from January 1, 2023, to October 31, 2023, OpCo was not a qualified foreign pension fund, a part of a qualified foreign pension fund, or a qualified controlled entity at all times during the testing period. Accordingly, OpCo is not a qualified holder with respect to the disposition of Property A, and the $100x of gain recognized by OpCo is not exempt from tax under section 897(l), regardless of the amount of unrealized gain in Property A as of November 1, 2023.

(9) *Example 9: 48-month alternative test.*—(i) *Facts.*—Fund is a qualified foreign pension fund organized in Country C that, except as otherwise noted, meets the requirements of paragraph (c)(2) of this section. Fund owns all the outstanding stock of OpCo, a manufacturing corporation organized in Country C and formed by Fund on January 1, 2023, in a qualified segregated account maintained by Fund. On January 30, 2023, OpCo purchased Property A, a United States real property interest, from a third party. OpCo either retains or distributes to Fund all of its net earnings, and upon dissolution, must distribute all of its assets to its stockholder (that is, Fund) after satisfaction of liabilities to its creditors. On June 1, 2027, OpCo realizes $100x of gain on the disposition of Property A. Fund reasonably expected to provide $90x of retirement and pension benefits and $100x of qualified benefits for the valuations that it performed pursuant to paragraph (c)(2)(ii)(C)(*1*) of this section on December 31, 2023, December 31, 2024, and December 31, 2025. Fund reasonably expected to provide $160x of retirement and pension benefits and $200x of qualified benefits for the valuation that it performed pursuant to paragraph (c)(2)(ii)(C)(*1*) of this section on December 31, 2026.

(ii) *Analysis.*—In each of the years ending on December 31, 2023, December 31, 2024, and December 31, 2025, the valuation performed pursuant to paragraph (c)(2)(ii)(C)(*1*) of this section demonstrates that that the requirements of paragraph (c)(2)(ii)(B)(*2*) of this section have been met because $90x of retirement and pension benefits constitutes 90 percent of the total $100x of qualified benefits. For the year ending on December 31, 2026, the valuation performed pursuant to paragraph (c)(2)(ii)(C)(*1*) of this section does not demonstrate that that the requirements of paragraph (c)(2)(ii)(B)(*2*) of this section have been met because $160x of retirement and pension benefits constitutes only 80 percent of the total $200x of qualified benefits. Thus, Fund does not meet the requirements of paragraph (c)(2)(ii)(C)(1) of this section for the year ending on December 31, 2026. However, under the 48-month alternative calculation in paragraph (c)(2)(ii)(C)(*2*) of this section, Fund satisfies the requirement that it reasonably expects to provide 85 percent retirement and pension benefits to qualified recipients as of December 31, 2026. This is because when averaging the values (not percentages) of the qualified benefits and retirement and pension benefits that Fund reasonably expected to provide from the valuations performed over the preceding 48 months (including the most recent valuation), Fund divides the total retirement and pension benefits of $430x ($90x + $90x + $90x + $160x) by the total qualified benefits that it reasonably expected to provide of $500x ($100x + $100x + $100x + $200x) for an average of 86 percent. Under paragraph (c)(2)(ii)(C)(*3*) of this section, Fund may rely on either the most recent present valuation described in paragraph (c)(2)(ii)(C)(*1*) of this section or the alternative calculation in paragraph (c)(2)(ii)(C)(*2*) of this section, both of which are determined as of December 31, 2026. Because Fund satisfies the requirements of paragraph (c)(2)(ii)(B)(*2*) of this section under the test in paragraph (c)(2)(ii)(C)(*2*) of this section, even though it does not do so under the test in paragraph (c)(2)(ii)(C)(*1*) of this section, Fund is a qualified foreign pension fund with respect to the disposition on June 1, 2027. Because OpCo is held by a qualified foreign pension fund as of the date of the disposition, OpCo is a qualified controlled entity within the meaning of paragraph (e)(9) of this section. Accordingly, the $100x of gain realized by OpCo is exempt from tax under section 897(l).

(10) *Example 10: 48-month alternative test with multiple valuations in the same year.*—(i) *Facts.*—The facts are the same as in paragraph (f)(9) of this section (Example 9), except that in the year ending December 31, 2023, Fund carried out two valuations pursuant to paragraph (c)(2)(ii)(C)(*1*) of this section, one on June 30, 2023 and the second on December 31, 2023. For each valuation, Fund reasonably expected to provide $90x of retirement and pension benefits and $100x of qualified benefits. In addition, in the year ending on December 31, 2026, pursuant to a valuation carried out under paragraph (c)(2)(ii)(C)(*1*) of this section, Fund reasonably expected to provide $150x retirement and pension benefits and $200x of qualified benefits.

(ii) *Analysis.*—In each of the years ending on December 31, 2023, December 31, 2024, and December 31, 2025 (including the two valuations performed in 2023), the valuation performed pursuant to paragraph (c)(2)(ii)(C)(*1*) of this section demonstrates that the requirements of paragraph (c)(2)(ii)(B)(*2*) of this section have been met because $90x of retirement and pension benefits constitutes 90 percent of the total $100x of qualified benefits. For the year ending on December 31, 2026, the valuation performed pursuant to paragraph (c)(2)(ii)(C)(*1*) of this section does not demonstrate that the requirements of paragraph (c)(2)(ii)(B)(*2*) of this section have been met because $150x of retirement and pension benefits constitutes 75 percent of the total $200x of qualified benefits. Thus, Fund does not meet the requirements of paragraph (c)(2)(ii)(C)(*1*) of this section for the year ending on December 31, 2026. Under the 48-month alternative calculation in paragraph (c)(2)(ii)(C)(*2*) of this section, Fund also does not satisfy the requirement that it reasonably expects to provide 85 percent retirement and pension benefits to qualified recipients as of December 31, 2026. This is because when averaging the values (not percentages) of the qualified benefits and retirement and pension benefits that Fund reasonably expected to provide from the valuations performed over the preceding 48 months (including the most recent valuation), Fund must use a weighted average whereby values are adjusted when the length of valuation periods differs. In this case, each of the two valuations in 2023 must be divided by two for a total weighted average for each valuation of $45x retirement and pension benefits and $50x of qualified benefits. When Fund then divides the total retirement and pension benefits that it reasonably expected to provide of $420x ($45x + $45x + $90x + $90x + $150x) by the total qualified benefits that it reasonably expected to provide of $500x ($50x + $50x + $100x + $100x + $200x), the average is 84 percent. Because Fund does not satisfy the requirements of paragraph (c)(2)(ii)(B)(*2*) of this section under the test in paragraph (c)(2)(ii)(C)(*2*) of this section or the test in paragraph (c)(2)(ii)(C)(1) of this section, Fund is not a qualified foreign pension fund with respect to the disposition on June 1, 2027. Because OpCo is not held by a qualified foreign pension fund as of the date of the disposition, OpCo is not a qualified controlled entity within the meaning of paragraph (e)(9) of this section. Accordingly, the $100x of gain realized by OpCo is not exempt from tax under section 897(l).

(11) *Example 11: Qualified foreign pension fund as qualified holder.*—(i) *Facts.*—The facts are the same as in paragraph (f)(10) of this section (Example 10), except that OpCo does not dispose of Property A on June 1, 2027 and Fund reasonably expects to provide 85 percent of retirement and pension benefits to qualified recipients in the future in each of the annual present valuations it performs as of December 31, 2027 through December 31, 2033. Fund also satisfies the other requirements of paragraph (c)(2) of this section during this period. On April 1, 2029, Fund purchases Property B, a United States real property interest, and holds it in a qualified segregated account. On June 1, 2034, Fund realizes $100x of gain on the disposition of Property B and OpCo realizes $100x of gain on the disposition of Property A. At least 85 percent and no more than five percent of the

actual value of the aggregate benefits provided by Fund before December 31, 2033, the most recent present value determination, were retirement and pension benefits and non-ancillary benefits, respectively.

(ii) *Analysis*.—(A) Because Fund reasonably expected to provide 85 percent of retirement and pension benefits to qualified recipients as of the valuation performed on December 31, 2033, and it met the other requirements of paragraph (c)(2) of this section, Fund is a qualified foreign pension fund under paragraph (c)(2)(ii)(C)(3) of this section for the twelve months succeeding the most recent valuation, which includes June 1, 2034, the date of the disposition of Property A and Property B.

(B) Fund is a qualified holder under paragraph (d)(2) of this section because Fund did not own any United States real property interests as of December 31, 2027, the earliest date during the uninterrupted period ending on the date of the disposition, June 1, 2034, during which it satisfied the requirements of paragraph (c)(2) of this section and therefore qualified as a qualified foreign pension fund. Fund is eligible for the exemption under section 897(l) with respect to the disposition of Property B because it held Property B in a qualified segregated account. Thus, the $100x of gain realized by Fund on the disposition of Property B is exempt from tax under section 897(l).

(C) Because OpCo owned Property A, a United States real property interest, as of December 31, 2027, the earliest date during an uninterrupted period ending on the date of the disposition, June 1, 2034, during which it was a qualified controlled entity, OpCo cannot satisfy the requirements of paragraph (d)(2) of this section and must instead satisfy the requirements of paragraph (d)(3) of this section to be a qualified holder. The testing period with respect to OpCo, determined under paragraph (d)(3)(ii) of this section, ends on June 1, 2034 (the date of the disposition) and begins on June 1, 2024 (the date that is ten years before the disposition date). Because Fund failed to qualify as a qualified foreign pension fund as of December 31, 2026, OpCo was not continuously owned by a qualified foreign pension fund for the duration of the testing period, and thus did not qualify as a qualified foreign pension fund, part of a qualified foreign pension fund, or a qualified controlled entity for the duration of the testing period. As a result, OpCo is not a qualified holder under paragraph (d)(3) of this section. Accordingly, the $100x of gain recognized by OpCo on the disposition of Property A is not exempt from tax under section 897(l).

(12) *Example 12: Qualified controlled entity as qualified holder*.—(i) *Facts*.—Fund is a qualified foreign pension fund organized in Country C that meets the requirements of paragraph (c)(2) of this section as of December 31, 2022 and December 31, 2023. Fund purchases an interest in Company A, a United States real property holding company, on June 1, 2024. As of December 31, 2024, Fund fails to satisfy the present valuation requirement of paragraph (c)(2)(ii)(B)(2) of this section and does not satisfy the alternative calculation under paragraph (c)(2)(ii)(C)(2) of this section. From December 31, 2025, through December 31, 2030, Fund satisfies the present valuation requirement of paragraph (c)(2)(ii)(B)(2) of this section and meets all other requirements in paragraph (c)(2) of this section to be treated as a qualified foreign pension fund. On June 1, 2026, Fund purchases all of the stock of Company B, a Country C corporation that owns no United States real property interests and is not a qualified foreign pension fund, a part of a qualified foreign pension fund, or a qualified controlled entity. On January 1, 2027, Company B purchases Property D, a United States real property interest. Company B retains or distributes to Fund all of its net earnings, and upon dissolution, must distribute all of its assets to its stockholders (that is, Fund) after satisfaction of liabilities to its creditors. On June 1, 2031, Fund realizes $100x of gain on the disposition of stock in Company A, and Company B realizes $100x of gain on the disposition of Property D.

(ii) *Analysis*.—(A) Fund owned Company A, a United States real property holding company, as of December 31, 2025, the earliest date during an uninterrupted period ending on the date of the disposition, June 1, 2031, during which Fund satisfied the requirements of paragraph (c)(2) of this section. Accordingly, to be a qualified holder, Fund must satisfy the requirements of paragraph (d)(3) of this section. The testing period with respect to Fund, determined under paragraph (d)(3) of this section, ends on June 1, 2031 (the date of disposition) and begins on June 1, 2021 (the date that is ten years before the disposition date). Fund is not a qualified holder because it failed to satisfy the requirements of paragraph (c)(2) of this section as of December 31, 2024 and, thus, has not satisfied the requirements of paragraph (c)(2) of this section continuously for the duration of the testing period. Accordingly, the $100x of gain realized by Fund on the disposition of the stock of Company A is not exempt from tax under section 897(l).

(B) Although Fund is not a qualified holder as of June 1, 2031, the date of Company B's disposition of Property D, Fund is still a qualified foreign pension fund because it satisfies the requirements of paragraph (c)(2) of this section. Company B is therefore a qualified controlled entity within the meaning of paragraph (e)(9) of this section as of June 1, 2031, because it is wholly owned by Fund, a qualified foreign pension fund. Notwithstanding that Fund is not a qualified holder under either paragraph (d)(2) or (3) of this section, Company B is a qualified holder under paragraph (d)(2) of this section because Company B did not own a United States real property interest as of June 1, 2026, the earliest date during an uninterrupted period ending on June 1, 2031 (the date of the disposition) during which Company B was a qualified controlled entity. Lastly, all of Company B's assets constitute a qualified segregated account. Accordingly, the $100x of gain realized by Company B on the disposition of Property D is exempt from tax under section 897(l).

(g) *Applicability date*.—(1) *In general*.—Except as otherwise provided in paragraph (g)(2) of this section, this section applies to dispositions of United States real property interests and distributions described in section 897(h) occurring on or after December 29, 2022.

(2) *Certain provisions*.—Paragraphs (b)(1), (d), (e)(5) and (e)(9) of this section apply with respect to dispositions of United States real property interests and distributions described in section 897(h) occurring on or after June 6, 2019.

(3) *Early application*.—An eligible fund may choose to apply this section with respect to dispositions and distributions occurring on or after December 18, 2015, and before December 29, 2022, provided that the eligible fund, and all persons bearing a relationship to the eligible fund described in section 267(b) or 707(b), consistently apply the rules in this section for all relevant years. An eligible fund that chooses to apply this section pursuant to this paragraph (g)(3) must apply the principles of paragraph (d)(4)(i) of this section to any valuation requirements with respect to dates preceding December 18, 2015. [Reg. § 1.897(l)-1.]

☐ [*T.D.* 9971, 12-28-2022.]

Foreign Tax Credits

§ 1.901-1. Allowance of credit for foreign income taxes.—(a) *In general*.—Citizens of the United States, domestic corporations, certain aliens resident in the United States or Puerto Rico, and certain estates and trusts may choose to claim a credit, as provided in section 901, against the tax imposed by chapter 1 of the Internal Revenue Code (Code) for certain taxes paid or accrued to foreign countries and possessions of the United States, subject to the conditions prescribed in this section.

(1) *Citizen of the United States*.—An individual who is a citizen of the United States, whether resident or nonresident, may claim a credit for—

(i) The amount of any foreign income taxes, as defined in § 1.901-2(a), paid or accrued (as the case may be, depending on the individual's method of accounting for such taxes) during the taxable year;

(ii) The individual's share of any such taxes of a partnership of which the individual is a member, or of an estate or trust of which the individual is a beneficiary; and

(iii) In the case of an individual who has made an election under section 962, the taxes deemed to have been paid under section 960 (see § 1.962-1(b)(2)).

(2) *Domestic corporation*.—A domestic corporation may claim a credit for—

(i) The amount of any foreign income taxes, as defined in § 1.901-2(a), paid or accrued (as the case may be, depending on the corporation's method of accounting for such taxes) during the taxable year;

(ii) The corporation's share of any such taxes of a partnership of which the corporation is a member, or of an estate or trust of which the corporation is a beneficiary; and

(iii) The taxes deemed to have been paid under section 960.

(3) *Alien resident of the United States or Puerto Rico.*—Except as provided in a Presidential proclamation described in section 901(c), an individual who is a resident alien of the United States (as defined in section 7701(b)), or an individual who is a bona fide resident of Puerto Rico (as defined in section 937(a)) during the entire taxable year, may claim a credit for—

(i) The amount of any foreign income taxes, as defined in § 1.901-2(a), paid or accrued (as the case may be, depending on the individual's method of accounting for such taxes) during the taxable year;

(ii) The individual's share of any such taxes of a partnership of which the individual is a member, or of an estate or trust of which the individual is a beneficiary; and

(iii) In the case of an individual who has made an election under section 962, the taxes deemed to have been paid under section 960 (see § 1.962-1(b)(2)).

(4) *Estates and trusts.*—An estate or trust may claim a credit for—

(i) The amount of any foreign income taxes, as defined in § 1.901-2(a), paid or accrued (as the case may be, depending on the estate or trust's method of accounting for such taxes) during the taxable year to the extent not allocable to and taken into account by its beneficiaries under paragraph (a)(1)(ii), (a)(2)(ii), or (a)(3)(ii) of this section (see section 642(a)); and

(ii) In the case of an estate or trust that has made an election under section 962, the taxes deemed to have been paid under section 960 (see § 1.962-1(b)(2)).

(b) *Limitations.*—Certain Code sections, including sections 245A(d) and (e)(3), section 814, section 901(e) through section (m), section 904, section 906, section 907, section 908, section 909, section 911, section 965(g), section 999, and section 6038, reduce, defer, or otherwise limit the credit against the tax imposed by chapter 1 of the Code for certain amounts of foreign income taxes.

(c) *Deduction denied if credit claimed.*—(1) *In general.*—Except as provided in paragraphs (c)(2) and (3) of this section, if a taxpayer chooses with respect to any taxable year to claim a credit under section 901 to any extent, such choice will apply to all of the foreign income taxes paid or accrued (as the case may be, depending on the taxpayer's method of accounting for such taxes) by the taxpayer in such taxable year, and no deduction from gross income is allowed for any portion of such taxes in any taxable year. See section 275(a)(4).

(2) *Exception for taxes not subject to section 275.*—A deduction may be allowed under section 164(a)(3) for foreign income tax for which a credit is disallowed under any Code section and to which section 275 does not apply. See, for example, sections 901(f), 901(j)(3), 901(k)(7), 901(l)(4), 901(m)(6), and 908(b). For rules on the taxable year in which a deduction for foreign income taxes is allowed under section 164(a)(3), see §§ 1.446-1(c)(1)(ii), 1.461-2(a)(2), and 1.461-4(g)(6)(iii)(B).

(3) *Exception for taxes paid by an accrual basis taxpayer that relate to a prior year in which the taxpayer deducted foreign income taxes.*—If a taxpayer claims a credit for foreign income taxes accrued in a taxable year (including a cash method taxpayer that elects under section 905(a) to claim a credit in the year the taxes accrue), a deduction may be claimed in that taxable year for additional foreign income taxes that are finally determined and paid as a result of a foreign tax redetermination in that taxable year if the additional foreign income taxes relate to a prior taxable year in which the taxpayer claimed a deduction, rather than a credit, for foreign income taxes paid or accrued (as the case may be, depending on the taxpayer's overall method of accounting) in that prior year.

(4) *Example.*—The following example illustrates the application of paragraph (c)(3) of this section.

(i) *Facts.*—U.S.C. is a domestic corporation that is engaged in a trade or business in Country X through a branch. U.S.C. uses the accrual method of accounting and a calendar year for U.S. and Country X tax purposes. For taxable Years 1 through 3, U.S.C. deducted foreign income taxes accrued in those years. In Years 4 through 6, U.S.C. claimed a credit for foreign income taxes accrued in those years. In Year 6, U.S.C. paid an additional $50x tax to Country X that relates to Year 1 because of the close of a Country X tax audit.

(ii) *Analysis.*—The additional $50x Country X tax paid by U.S.C. in Year 6 that relates to Year 1 cannot be claimed by U.S.C. as a deduction on an amended return for Year 1 because the additional tax accrued in Year 6. See section 461(f) (flush language); §§ 1.461-1(a)(2)(i) and 1.461-2(a)(2). In addition, because the additional $50x Country X tax relates to and is considered to accrue in Year 1 for foreign tax credit purposes, U.S.C. cannot claim a credit for the additional $50x Country X tax on its Federal income tax return for Year 6. See § 1.905-1(d)(1). However, pursuant to paragraph (c)(3) of this section, U.S.C. can claim a deduction for the additional $50x Country X tax that relates to Year 1 on its Federal income tax return for Year 6, even though it claims a credit for foreign income taxes that accrue in Year 6 and that relate to Year 6.

(d) *Period during which election can be made or changed.*—(1) *In general.*—The taxpayer may, for a particular taxable year, elect to claim a credit under section 901 (or claim a deduction in lieu of electing to claim a credit) at any time before the expiration of the period within which a claim for credit or refund of Federal income tax for such taxable year that is attributable to such credit or deduction, as the case may be, may be made (or, if longer, the period prescribed by section 6511(c) if the refund period for that taxable year is extended by an agreement to extend the assessment period under section 6501(c)(4)). Thus, an election to claim a credit for foreign income taxes paid or accrued (as the case may be, depending on the taxpayer's method of accounting for such taxes) in a particular taxable year can be made within the period prescribed by section 6511(d)(3)(A) for claiming a credit or refund of Federal income tax for that taxable year that is attributable to a credit for the foreign income taxes paid or accrued in that particular taxable year or, if longer, the period prescribed by section 6511(c) with respect to that particular taxable year. A choice to claim a deduction under section 164(a)(3), rather than a credit under section 901, for foreign income taxes paid or accrued in a particular taxable year can be made within the period prescribed by section 6511(a) or 6511(c), as applicable, for claiming a credit or refund of Federal income tax for that particular taxable year.

(2) *Manner in which election is made or changed.*—A taxpayer claims a deduction or a credit for foreign income taxes paid or accrued in a particular taxable year by filing an original or amended return for that taxable year within the relevant period specified in paragraph (d)(1) of this section. A claim for a credit shall be accompanied by Form 1116 in the case of an individual, estate or trust, and by Form 1118 in the case of a corporation (and an individual, estate or trust making an election under section 962). See §§ 1.905-3 and 1.905-4 for rules requiring the filing of amended returns for all affected years when a timely change in the taxpayer's election to claim a deduction or credit results in U.S. tax deficiencies.

(e) *Joint return.*—In the case of spouses making a joint return, credit for taxes paid or accrued to any foreign country or to any possession of the United States shall be computed upon the basis of the total taxes so paid by or accrued against the spouses.

(f) *Taxes against which credit is allowed.*—The credit for foreign income taxes is allowed only against the tax imposed by chapter 1 of the Code. The credit is not allowed against a tax that, under section 26(b)(2), is not treated as a tax imposed by such chapter.

(g) *Taxpayers to whom credit not allowed.*—Among those to whom the credit for taxes is not allowed are the following:

(1) Except as provided in section 906, a foreign corporation.

(2) Except as provided in section 906, a nonresident alien individual who is not described in section 876 (see sections 874(c) and 901(b)(4)).

(3) A nonresident alien individual described in section 876 other than a bona fide resident (as defined in section 937(a) and the regulations under that section) of Puerto Rico during the entire taxable year (see sections 901(b)(3) and (4)).

(4) A U.S. citizen or resident alien individual who is a bona fide resident of a section 931 possession (as defined in § 1.931-1(c)(1)), the U.S. Virgin Islands, or Puerto Rico, and who excludes certain income from U.S. gross income to the extent of taxes allocable to the income so excluded (see sections 931(b)(2), 933(1), and 932(c)(4)).

(h) *Taxpayers denied credit in a particular taxable year.*—Taxpayers who are denied the credit for taxes for particular taxable years are the following:

(1) Except as provided in paragraphs (c)(2) and (3) of this section, a taxpayer that claims a deduction for foreign income taxes paid or accrued (as the case may be, depending on the taxpayer's method of accounting for such taxes) for that taxable year (see sections 164 and 275); and

(2) A regulated investment company which has exercised the election under section 853.

(i) *Dividends from a DISC treated as foreign.*—For purposes of sections 901 through 906 and the regulations thereunder, any amount treated as a dividend from a corporation which is a DISC or former DISC (as defined in section 992(a)(1) or (3) as the case may be) will be treated as a dividend from a foreign corporation to the extent such dividend is treated under section 861(a)(2)(D) as income from sources without the United States.

(j) *Applicability date.*—Paragraph (g) of this section applies to taxable years ending after April 9, 2008. This section applies to foreign taxes paid or accrued in taxable years beginning on or after December 28, 2021. [Reg. § 1.901-1.]

☐ [*T.D. 6275, 12-2-57. Amended by T.D. 6466, 5-12-60; T.D. 6780, 12-21-64; T.D. 6798, 12-30-64; T.D. 6795, 1-28-65; T.D. 7283, 8-2-73; T.D. 7564, 9-11-78; T.D. 7636, 8-9-79; T.D. 7961, 6-20-84; T.D. 8160, 9-8-87; T.D. 9194, 4-6-2005; T.D. 9391, 4-4-2008; T.D. 9416, 7-15-2008; T.D. 9535, 7-13-2011 and T.D. 9959, 12-28-2021.*]

§ 1.901-2. Income, war profits, or excess profits tax paid or accrued.—(a) *Definition of foreign income tax.*—(1) *Overview and scope.*—Paragraphs (a) and (b) of this section define a foreign income tax for purposes of section 901. Paragraph (c) of this section is reserved. Paragraph (d) of this section contains rules describing what constitutes a separate levy. Paragraph (e) of this section provides rules for determining the amount of foreign income tax paid by a taxpayer. Paragraph (f) of this section contains rules for determining by whom foreign income tax is paid. Paragraph (g) of this section defines the terms used in this section, and in particular provides that the term "paid" means "paid" or "accrued," depending on the taxpayer's method of accounting for foreign income taxes. Paragraph (h) of this section provides the applicability date for this section.

(i) *In general.*—Section 901 allows a credit for the amount of income, war profits, and excess profits taxes paid during the taxable year to any foreign country, and section 903 provides that for purposes of Part III of subchapter N of the Code and sections 164(a) and 275(a), such taxes include a tax paid in lieu of a tax on income, war profits or excess profits that is otherwise generally imposed by a foreign country (collectively, for purposes of this section, a "foreign income tax"). Whether a foreign levy is a foreign income tax is determined independently for each separate levy. A foreign tax either is or is not a foreign income tax, in its entirety, for all persons subject to the foreign tax.

(ii) *Requirements.*—A foreign levy is a foreign income tax only if—

(A) It is a foreign tax; and

(B) Either:

(1) The foreign tax is a net income tax, as defined in paragraph (a)(3) of this section; or

(2) The foreign tax is a tax in lieu of an income tax, as defined in § 1.903-1(b).

(iii) *Coordination with treaties.*—A foreign levy that is treated as an income tax under the relief from double taxation article of an income tax treaty entered into by the United States and the foreign country imposing the levy is a foreign income tax if the levy is, as determined under such income tax treaty, paid by a citizen or resident of the United States that elects benefits under the treaty. In addition, a foreign levy (including a foreign levy paid by a controlled foreign corporation) that is modified by an applicable income tax treaty to which the foreign country imposing the levy is a party may qualify as a foreign income tax notwithstanding that the unmodified foreign levy does not satisfy the requirements in paragraph (b) of this section or the requirements of § 1.903-1(b) if the levy, as modified by such treaty, satisfies the requirements of paragraph (b) of this section or the requirements of § 1.903-1(b). See paragraph (d)(1)(iv) of this section for rules treating as a separate levy a foreign tax that is limited in its application or otherwise modified by the terms of an income tax treaty to which the foreign country imposing the tax is a party.

(2) *Tax.*—(i) *In general.*—A foreign levy is a tax if it requires a compulsory payment pursuant to the authority of a foreign country to levy taxes. A penalty, fine, interest, or similar obligation is not a tax, nor is a customs duty a tax. Whether a foreign levy requires a compulsory payment pursuant to a foreign country's authority to levy taxes is determined by principles of U.S. law and not by principles of law of the foreign country. Therefore, the assertion by a foreign country that a levy is pursuant to the foreign country's authority to levy taxes is not determinative that, under U.S. principles, it is pursuant thereto. Notwithstanding any assertion of a foreign country to the contrary, a foreign levy is not pursuant to a foreign country's authority to levy taxes, and thus is not a tax, to the extent a person subject to the levy receives (or will receive), directly or indirectly, a specific economic benefit (as defined in paragraph (a)(2)(ii)(B) of this section) from the foreign country in exchange for payment pursuant to the levy. Rather, to that extent, such levy requires a compulsory payment in exchange for such specific economic benefit. If, applying U.S. principles, a foreign levy requires a compulsory payment pursuant to the authority of a foreign country to levy taxes and also requires a compulsory payment in exchange for a specific economic benefit, the levy is considered to have two distinct elements: a tax and a requirement of compulsory payment in exchange for such specific economic benefit. In such a situation, these two distinct elements of the foreign levy (and the amount paid pursuant to each such element) must be separated. No credit is allowable for a payment pursuant to a foreign levy by a dual capacity taxpayer (as defined in paragraph (a)(2)(ii)(A) of this section) unless the person claiming such credit establishes the amount that is paid pursuant to the distinct element of the foreign levy that is a tax. See paragraph (a)(2)(ii) of this section and § 1.901-2A.

(ii) *Dual capacity taxpayers.*—(A) *In general.*—For purposes of this section and §§ 1.901-2A and 1.903-1, a person who is subject to a levy of a foreign state or of a possession of the United States or of a political subdivision of such a state or possession and who also, directly or indirectly (within the meaning of paragraph (a)(2)(ii)(E) of this section) receives (or will receive) a specific economic benefit from the state or possession or from a political subdivision of such state or possession or from an agency or instrumentality of any of the foregoing is referred to as a "dual capacity taxpayer." Dual capacity taxpayers are subject to the special rules of § 1.901-2A.

(B) *Specific economic benefit.*—For purposes of this section and §§ 1.901-2A and 1.903-1, the term "specific economic benefit" means an economic benefit that is not made available on substantially the same terms to substantially all persons who are subject to the income tax that is generally imposed by the foreign country, or, if there is no such generally imposed income tax, an economic benefit that is not made available on substantially the same terms to the population of the country in general. Thus, a concession to extract government-owned petroleum is a specific economic benefit, but the right to travel or to ship freight on a government-owned airline is not, because the latter, but not the former, is made generally available on substantially the same terms. An economic benefit includes property; a service; a fee or other payment; a right to use, acquire or extract resources, patents or other property that a foreign country owns or controls (within the meaning of paragraph (a)(2)(ii)(D) of this section); or a reduction or discharge of a contractual obligation. It does not include the right or privilege merely to engage in business generally or to engage in business in a particular form.

(C) *Pension, unemployment, and disability fund payments.*—A foreign levy imposed on individuals to finance retirement, old-age, death, survivor, unemployment, illness, or disability benefits, or for some substantially similar purpose, is not a requirement of compulsory payment in exchange for a specific economic benefit, as long as the amounts required to be paid by the individuals subject to the levy are not computed on a basis reflecting the respective ages, life expectancies or similar characteristics of such individuals.

(D) *Control of property.*—A foreign country controls property that it does not own if the country exhibits substantial indicia of ownership with respect to the property, for example, by both regulating the quantity of property that may be extracted and establishing the minimum price at which it may be disposed of.

(E) *Indirect receipt of a benefit.*—A person is considered to receive a specific economic benefit indirectly if another person receives a specific economic benefit and that other person—

(1) Owns or controls, directly or indirectly, the first person or is owned or controlled, directly or indirectly, by the first

person or by the same persons that own or control, directly or indirectly, the first person; or

(2) Engages in a transaction with the first person under terms and conditions such that the first person receives, directly or indirectly, all or part of the value of the specific economic benefit.

(3) *Net income tax.*—A foreign tax is a net income tax only if the foreign tax meets the net gain requirement in paragraph (b) of this section.

(b) *Net gain requirement.*—(1) *In general.*—A foreign tax satisfies the net gain requirement only if the tax satisfies the realization, gross receipts, cost recovery, and attribution requirements in paragraphs (b)(2), (3), (4), and (5) of this section, respectively, or if the foreign tax is a surtax described in paragraph (b)(6) of this section. Paragraphs (b)(2) through (6) of this section are applied with respect to a foreign tax solely on the basis of the foreign tax law governing the calculation of the foreign taxable base, unless otherwise provided, and without any consideration of the rate of tax imposed on the foreign taxable base.

(2) *Realization requirement.*—(i) *In general.*—A foreign tax satisfies the realization requirement if it is imposed upon one or more of the events described in paragraphs (b)(2)(i)(A) through (C) of this section. If a foreign tax meets the realization requirement in paragraphs (b)(2)(i)(A) through (C) of this section except with respect to one or more specific and defined classes of nonrealization events (such as, for example, imputed rental income from a personal residence used by the owner), and as judged based on the application of the foreign tax to all taxpayers subject to the foreign tax, the incidence and amounts of gross receipts attributable to such nonrealization events is insignificant relative to the incidence and amounts of gross receipts attributable to events covered by the foreign tax that do meet the realization requirement, then the foreign tax is treated as meeting the realization requirement in paragraph (b)(2) of this section (despite the fact that the foreign tax is also imposed on the basis of some nonrealization events, and that some persons subject to the foreign tax may only be taxed on nonrealization events).

(A) *Realization events.*—The foreign tax is imposed upon or after the occurrence of events ("realization events") that result in the realization of income under the income tax provisions of the Internal Revenue Code.

(B) *Pre-realization recapture events.*—The foreign tax is imposed upon the occurrence of an event before a realization event (a "pre-realization event") that results in the recapture (in whole or part) of a tax deduction, tax credit, or other tax allowance previously accorded to the taxpayer (for example, the recapture of an incentive tax credit if required investments are not completed within a specified period).

(C) *Pre-realization timing difference events.*—The foreign tax is imposed upon the occurrence of a pre-realization event, other than one described in paragraph (b)(2)(i)(B) of this section, but only if the foreign country does not, upon the occurrence of a later event, impose tax under the same or a separate levy (a "second tax") on the same taxpayer (for purposes of this paragraph (b)(2)(i)(C), treating a disregarded entity as defined in § 301.7701-3(b)(2)(i)(C) of this chapter as a taxpayer separate from its owner), with respect to the income on which tax is imposed by reason of such pre-realization event (or, if it does impose a second tax, a credit or other comparable relief is available against the liability for such a second tax for tax paid on the occurrence of the pre-realization event) and—

(1) The imposition of the tax upon such pre-realization event is based on the difference in the fair market value of property at the beginning and end of a period;

(2) The pre-realization event is the physical transfer, processing, or export of readily marketable property (as defined in paragraph (b)(2)(ii) of this section) and the imposition of the tax upon the pre-realization event is based on the fair market value of such property; or

(3) The pre-realization event relates to a deemed distribution (for example, by a corporation to a shareholder) or inclusion (for example, under a controlled foreign corporation inclusion regime) of amounts (such as earnings and profits) that meet the realization requirement in paragraph (b)(2) of this section in the hands of the person that, under foreign tax law, is deemed to distribute such amounts.

(ii) *Readily marketable property.*—Property is readily marketable if—

(A) It is stock in trade or other property of a kind that properly would be included in inventory if on hand at the close of the taxable year or if it is held primarily for sale to customers in the ordinary course of business, and

(B) It can be sold on the open market without further processing or it is exported from the foreign country.

(iii) *Examples.*—The following examples illustrate the rules of paragraph (b)(2) of this section:

(A) *Example 1.*—Residents of Country X are subject to a tax of 10 percent on the aggregate net appreciation in fair market value during the calendar year of all shares of stock held by them at the end of the year. In addition, all such residents are subject to a Country X tax that qualifies as a net income tax within the meaning of paragraph (a)(3) of this section. Included in the base of the net income tax are gains and losses realized on the sale of stock, and the basis of stock for purposes of determining such gain or loss is its cost. The operation of the stock appreciation tax and the net income tax as applied to sales of stock is exemplified as follows: A, a resident of Country X, purchases stock in June of Year 1 for 100u (units of Country X currency) and sells it in May of Year 3 for 160u. On December 31, Year 1, the stock is worth 120u and on December 31, Year 2, it is worth 155u. Pursuant to the stock appreciation tax, A pays 2u for Year 1 (10 percent of (120u–100u)), 3.5u for Year 2 (10 percent of (155u–120u)), and nothing for Year 3 because no stock was held at the end of that year. For purposes of the net income tax, A must include 60u (160u–100u) in his income for Year 3, the year of sale. Pursuant to paragraph (b)(2)(i)(C) of this section, the stock appreciation tax does not satisfy the realization requirement because Country X imposes a second tax upon the occurrence of a later event (that is, the sale of stock) with respect to the income that was taxed by the stock appreciation tax and no credit or comparable relief is available against such second tax for the stock appreciation tax paid.

(B) *Example 2.*—The facts are the same as those in paragraph (b)(2)(iii)(A) of this section (the facts in *Example 1*), except that if stock was held on the December 31 last preceding the date of its sale, the basis of such stock for purposes of computing gain or loss under the net income tax is the value of the stock on such December 31. Thus, in Year 3, A includes only 5u (160u–155u) as income from the sale for purposes of the net income tax. Because the net income tax imposed upon the occurrence of a later event (the sale) does not impose a tax with respect to the income that was taxed by the stock appreciation tax, under paragraph (b)(2)(i)(C) of this section, the stock appreciation tax satisfies the realization requirement. The result would be the same if, instead of a basis adjustment to reflect taxation pursuant to the stock appreciation tax, the Country X net income tax allowed a credit (or other comparable relief) to take account of the stock appreciation tax. If a credit mechanism is used, see also paragraph (e)(4)(i) of this section.

(C) *Example 3.*—Country X imposes a tax on the realized net income of corporations that do business in Country X. Country X also imposes a branch profits tax on corporations organized under the law of a country other than Country X that do business in Country X. The branch profits tax is imposed when realized net income is remitted or deemed to be remitted by branches in Country X to home offices outside of Country X. Because the branch profits tax is imposed subsequent to the occurrence of events that would result in realization of income by corporations subject to such tax under the income tax provisions of the Internal Revenue Code, under paragraph (b)(2)(i)(A) of this section the branch profits tax satisfies the realization requirement.

(D) *Example 4.*—Country X imposes a tax on the realized net income of corporations that do business in Country X (the "Country X corporate tax"). Country X also imposes a separate tax on shareholders of such corporations (the "Country X shareholder tax"). The Country X shareholder tax is imposed on the sum of the actual distributions received during the taxable year by such a shareholder from the corporation's realized net income for that year (that is, income from past years is not taxed in a later year when it is actually distributed) plus the distributions deemed to be received by such a shareholder. Deemed distributions are defined as a shareholder's pro rata share of the corporation's realized net income for the taxable year, less such shareholder's pro rata share of the corporation's Country X corporate tax for that year, less actual distributions made by such corporation to such shareholder from such net income. A shareholder's receipt of actual distributions is a realization event within the meaning of paragraph (b)(2)(i)(A) of this section. The deemed distributions are not realization events, but they are described in paragraph (b)(2)(i)(C)(*3*) of this section. Accordingly, the Country X shareholder tax satisfies the realization requirement.

(3) *Gross receipts requirement.*—(i) *Rule.*—A foreign tax satisfies the gross receipts requirement if it is imposed on the basis of the amounts described in paragraphs (b)(3)(i)(A) through (D) of this section.

(A) Actual gross receipts.

(B) In the case of either an insignificant nonrealization event described in the second sentence of paragraph (b)(2)(i) of this section or a realization event described in paragraph (b)(2)(i)(A) of this section that does not result in actual gross receipts, deemed gross receipts in an amount that is reasonably calculated to produce an amount that is not greater than fair market value.

(C) Deemed gross receipts in the amount of a tax deduction that is recaptured by reason of a pre-realization recapture event described in paragraph (b)(2)(i)(B) of this section.

(D) The amount of deemed gross receipts arising from pre-realization timing difference events described in paragraph (b)(2)(i)(C) of this section.

(ii) *Examples.*—The following examples illustrate the rules of paragraph (b)(3)(i) of this section.

(A) *Example 1: Cost-plus tax.*—(*1*) *Facts.* Country X imposes a "cost-plus tax" on Country X corporations that serve as regional headquarters companies for affiliated nonresident corporations, and this tax is a separate levy (within the meaning of paragraph (d)(1) of this section). A headquarters company for purposes of this tax is a corporation that performs administrative, management or coordination functions solely for nonresident affiliated entities. Due to the difficulty of determining on a case-by-case basis the arm's length gross receipts that headquarters companies would charge affiliates for such services, gross receipts of a headquarters company are deemed, for purposes of this tax, to equal 110 percent of the business expenses incurred by the headquarters company.

(*2*) *Analysis.* Because the cost-plus tax is based on costs and not on actual gross receipts, the cost-plus tax does not satisfy the gross receipts requirement of paragraph (b)(3)(i) of this section.

(B) *Example 2: Actual gross receipts determined under appropriate transfer pricing methodology.*—(*1*) *Facts.* Country X imposes a tax on resident corporations that meets the attribution requirement of paragraph (b)(5)(ii) of this section. The Country X tax is based on actual gross receipts, including gross receipts recorded on the taxpayer's books and records as due from related and unrelated persons. Corporation A, a resident of Country X, properly determines the arm's length transfer price for services provided to related persons using a cost-plus methodology, recording on its books and records receivables for the arm's length amounts due from those related persons and using those amounts to determine the realized gross receipts included in the base of the Country X tax.

(*2*) *Analysis.* Because the Country X tax is based on actual gross receipts, it satisfies the gross receipts requirement of paragraph (b)(3)(i) of this section.

(C) *Example 3: Petroleum taxed on extraction.*—(*1*) *Facts.* Country X imposes a tax that is a separate levy (within the meaning of paragraph (d)(1) of this section) on income from the extraction of petroleum. Under the terms of that tax, gross receipts from extraction income are deemed to equal 105 percent of the fair market value of petroleum extracted.

(*2*) *Analysis.* Because it is imposed on deemed gross receipts that exceed the fair market value of the petroleum extracted, the tax on extraction income does not satisfy the gross receipts requirement of paragraph (b)(3)(i) of this section.

(4) *Cost recovery requirement.*—(i) *Costs and expenses that must be recovered.*—(A) *In general.*—A foreign tax satisfies the cost recovery requirement if the base of the tax is computed by reducing gross receipts (as described in paragraph (b)(3) of this section) to permit recovery of the significant costs and expenses (including capital expenditures) described in paragraph (b)(4)(i)(C) of this section attributable, under reasonable principles, to such gross receipts. A foreign tax need not permit recovery of significant costs and expenses, such as certain personal expenses, that are not attributable, under reasonable principles, to gross receipts included in the foreign taxable base. A foreign tax whose base is gross receipts, with no reduction for costs and expenses, satisfies the cost recovery requirement only if there are no significant costs and expenses attributable to the gross receipts included in the foreign tax base that must be recovered under the rules of paragraph (b)(4)(i)(C)(*1*) of this section. See paragraph (b)(4)(iv)(A) of this section (*Example 1*). A foreign tax that provides an alternative cost allowance satisfies the cost recovery requirement only as provided in paragraph (b)(4)(i)(B) of this section. See paragraph (b)(4)(i)(D) of this section for rules regarding principles for attributing costs and expenses to gross receipts.

(B) *Alternative cost allowances.*—(*1*) *In general.*—Except as provided in paragraph (b)(4)(i)(B)(2) of this section, if foreign tax law does not permit recovery of one or more significant costs and expenses in computing the base of the foreign tax but provides an alternative cost allowance, the foreign tax satisfies the cost recovery requirement only if the alternative allowance permits recovery of an amount that by its terms may be greater, but can never be less, than the actual amounts of such significant costs and expenses (for example, under a provision identical to percentage depletion allowed under section 613). If foreign tax law provides an optional alternative cost allowance or an election to recover costs and expenses under an alternative method, the foreign tax satisfies the cost recovery requirement if the foreign tax law also expressly provides an option to recover actual costs and expenses. See § 1.901-2(e)(5) for rules limiting the amount of foreign income tax paid to the amount due under the option that minimizes the taxpayer's liability for foreign income tax over time. If foreign tax law provides an alternative cost allowance that does not by its terms permit recovery of an amount equal to or greater than the actual amounts of significant costs and expenses, the foreign tax does not satisfy the cost recovery requirement, even if, in practice, the amounts recovered under the alternative allowance equal or exceed the amount of actual costs and expenses.

(*2*) *Small business exception.*—If foreign tax law provides an alternative method for determining the amount of costs and expenses allowed in computing the taxable base of small business enterprises, the foreign tax satisfies the cost recovery requirement if the foreign tax law contains reasonable limits on the maximum size of business enterprises to which the alternative cost allowance applies (for example, business enterprises having asset values or annual gross revenues below specified thresholds). See paragraph (b)(4)(iv)(B) of this section (*Example 2*).

(C) *Significant costs and expenses.*—(*1*) *Amounts that must be recovered.*—Whether a cost or expense is significant for purposes of this paragraph (b)(4)(i) is determined based on whether, for all taxpayers in the aggregate to which the foreign tax applies, the item of cost or expense constitutes a significant portion of the taxpayers' total costs and expenses. Costs and expenses (as characterized under foreign law) related to capital expenditures, interest, rents, royalties, wages or other payments for services, and research and experimentation are always treated as significant costs or expenses for purposes of this paragraph (b)(4)(i). Significant costs and expenses (such as interest expense) are not considered to be recovered by reason of the time value of money attributable to the acceleration of a tax benefit or other economic benefit attributable to the timing of the recovery of other costs and expenses (such as the current expensing of debt-financed capital expenditures). Foreign tax law is considered to permit recovery of significant costs and expenses even if recovery of all or a portion of certain costs or expenses is disallowed, if such disallowance is consistent with any principle underlying the disallowances required under the Internal Revenue Code, including the principles of limiting base erosion or profit shifting and public policy concerns. For example, a foreign tax is considered to permit recovery of significant costs and expenses if the foreign tax law limits interest deductions based on a measure of taxable income (determined either before or after depreciation and amortization), disallows deductions in connection with hybrid transactions, disallows deductions attributable to gross receipts that in whole or in part are excluded, exempt or eliminated from taxable income, or disallows certain deductions based on public policy considerations similar to those underlying the disallowances contained in section 162. See paragraph (b)(4)(iv)(C) of this section (*Example 3*).

(*2*) *Amounts that need not be recovered.*—A foreign tax is considered to permit recovery of significant costs and expenses even if the foreign tax law does not permit recovery of any costs and expenses attributable to wage income or to investment income that is not derived from a trade or business. In addition, in determining whether a foreign tax (the "tested foreign tax") meets the cost recovery requirement, it is immaterial whether the tested foreign tax allows a deduction for other taxes that would qualify as foreign income taxes (determined without regard to whether such other tax allows a deduction for the tested foreign tax). See paragraph (b)(4)(iv)(D) and (E) of this section (*Examples 4* and *5*).

(*3*) *Timing of recovery.*—A foreign tax law permits recovery of significant costs and expenses even if such costs and expenses are recovered earlier or later than they are recovered under the Internal Revenue Code unless the time of recovery is so much later as effectively to constitute a denial of such recovery. The amount of costs and expenses that is recovered under the foreign tax law is neither discounted nor augmented by taking into account the time value of money attributable to any acceleration or deferral of a tax benefit resulting from the foreign law cost recovery method compared to when tax would be paid under the Internal Revenue Code. Therefore, a foreign tax satisfies the cost recovery requirement if items deductible under the Internal Revenue Code are capitalized under the foreign tax law and recovered either immediately, on a recurring basis over time, or upon the occurrence of some future event (for example, upon the property becoming worthless or being disposed of), or if the recovery of items capitalized under the Internal Revenue Code occurs more or less rapidly than under the foreign tax law.

(D) *Attribution of costs and expenses to gross receipts.*—Principles used in the foreign tax law to attribute costs and expenses to gross receipts may be reasonable even if they differ from principles that apply under the Internal Revenue Code (for example, principles that apply under section 265, 465 or 861(b) of the Internal Revenue Code). See also paragraph (b)(5) of this section for additional requirements relating to foreign tax law rules for attributing costs and expenses to gross receipts.

(ii) *Consolidation of profits and losses.*—In determining whether a foreign tax satisfies the cost recovery requirement, one of the factors to be taken into account is whether, in computing the base of the tax, a loss incurred in one activity (for example, a contract area in the case of oil and gas exploration) in a trade or business is allowed to offset profit earned by the same person in another activity (for example, a separate contract area) in the same trade or business. If such an offset is allowed, it is immaterial whether the offset may be made in the taxable period in which the loss is incurred or only in a different taxable period, unless the period is such that under the circumstances there is effectively a denial of the ability to offset the loss against profit. In determining whether a foreign tax satisfies the cost recovery requirement, it is immaterial that no such offset is allowed if a loss incurred in one such activity may be applied to offset profit earned in that activity in a different taxable period, unless the period is such that under the circumstances there is effectively a denial of the ability to offset such loss against profit. In determining whether a foreign tax satisfies the cost recovery requirement, it is immaterial whether a person's profits and losses from one trade or business (for example, oil and gas extraction) are allowed to offset its profits and losses from another trade or business (for example, oil and gas refining and processing), or whether a person's business profits and losses and its passive investment profits and losses are allowed to offset each other in computing the base of the foreign tax. Moreover, it is immaterial whether foreign tax law permits or prohibits consolidation of profits and losses of related persons, unless foreign tax law requires separate entities to be used to carry on separate activities in the same trade or business. If foreign tax law requires that separate entities carry on such separate activities, the determination whether the cost recovery requirement is satisfied is made by applying the same considerations as if such separate activities were carried on by a single entity.

(iii) *Carryovers.*—In determining whether a foreign tax satisfies the cost recovery requirement, it is immaterial, except as otherwise provided in paragraph (b)(4)(ii) of this section, whether losses incurred during one taxable period may be carried over to offset profits incurred in different taxable periods.

(iv) *Examples.*—The following examples illustrate the rules of paragraph (b)(4) of this section.

(A) *Example 1: Tax on gross interest income of certain residents; no deductions allowed.*—(*1*) *Facts.* Country X imposes a net income tax on corporations resident in Country X. Country X imposes a second tax (the "bank tax") of 1 percent on the gross amount of interest income derived by banks resident in Country X; no deductions are allowed in determining the base of the bank tax. Banks resident in Country X incur substantial costs and expenses, including interest expense, attributable to their interest income.

(*2*) *Analysis.* Because the terms of the bank tax do not permit recovery of significant costs and expenses attributable to the gross receipts included in the tax base, the bank tax does not satisfy the cost recovery requirement of paragraph (b)(4)(i) of this section.

(B) *Example 2: Small business alternative allowance.*—(*1*) *Facts.* Country X imposes a tax on the income of corporations resident in Country X. Under Country X tax law, corporations are generally allowed to deduct actual costs and expenses attributable to the realized gross receipts included in the Country X tax base. However, in lieu of deductions for actual costs and expenses, businesses with gross revenues of less than the Country X currency equivalent of $500,000 are allowed a flat cost allowance of 50 percent of gross revenues.

(*2*) *Analysis.* Under paragraph (b)(4)(i)(B)(*2*) of this section, the alternative cost allowance for small businesses provided under Country X tax law satisfies the cost recovery requirement.

(C) *Example 3: Permissible deduction disallowance.*—(*1*) *Facts.* Country X imposes a tax on the income of corporations resident in Country X. Under Country X tax law, deductions for the significant costs and expenses attributable to the gross receipts included in the Country X tax base are allowed, except that deductions for interest expense incurred by corporations are limited to 30 percent of the corporation's earnings before income taxes, depreciation, and amortization, and unused interest expense may be carried forward for a period of 5 years. In addition, Country X tax law contains anti-hybrid rules that deny deductions for interest, royalties, rents, and services payments made by a Country X resident to a related entity outside Country X that is treated as a transparent entity in the jurisdiction in which it is organized but as a separate entity in the jurisdiction of the entity's owners (a "reverse hybrid entity") to the extent that the payment is not included in the income of the reverse hybrid entity or its owners.

(*2*) *Analysis.* Under paragraph (b)(4)(i)(C)(*1*) of this section, costs and expenses related to interest, rents, royalties, and payments for services are treated as significant costs or expenses that must be recoverable under Country X tax law. However, because the interest expense limitation rule and the anti-hybrid rules in Country X tax law are consistent with the principles underlying the disallowances required under the Internal Revenue Code (namely, section 163(j) and section 267A), the Country X tax satisfies the cost recovery requirement.

(D) *Example 4: Gross basis tax on wages.*—(*1*) *Facts.* A foreign country imposes payroll tax on resident employees at the rate of 10 percent of the amount of gross wages; no deductions are allowed in computing the base of the payroll tax.

(*2*) *Analysis.* Although the foreign tax law does not allow for the recovery of any costs and expenses attributable to gross receipts included in the taxable base, under paragraph (b)(4)(i)(C)(2) of this section, because the only gross receipts included in the taxable base are from wages, the payroll tax satisfies the cost recovery requirement.

(E) *Example 5: No deduction for another net income tax.*—(*1*) *Facts.* Each of Country X and Province Y (a political subdivision of Country X) imposes a tax on resident corporations, called the "Country X income tax" and the "Province Y income tax," respectively. Each tax has an identical base, which is computed by reducing a corporation's realized gross receipts by deductions that, based on the laws of Country X and Province Y, generally permit recovery of the significant costs and expenses (including significant capital expenditures) that are attributable under reasonable principles to such gross receipts. However, the Country X income tax does not allow a deduction for the Province Y income tax for which a taxpayer is liable, nor does the Province Y income tax allow a deduction for the Country X income tax for which a taxpayer is liable.

(*2*) *Analysis.* Under paragraph (d)(1)(i) of this section, each of the Country X income tax and the Province Y income tax is a separate levy. Without regard to whether the Province Y income tax may allow a deduction for the Country X income tax, and without regard to whether the Country X income tax may allow a deduction for the Province Y income tax, both taxes would qualify as net income taxes under paragraph (a)(3) of this section. Therefore, under paragraph (b)(4)(i)(C)(2) of this section the fact that neither levy's base allows a deduction for the other levy is immaterial, and both levies satisfy the cost recovery requirement.

(5) *Attribution requirement.*—A foreign tax satisfies the attribution requirement if the amount of gross receipts and costs that are

included in the base of the foreign tax are determined based on rules described in paragraph (b)(5)(i) of this section (with respect to a separate levy imposed on nonresidents of the foreign country) or paragraph (b)(5)(ii) of this section (with respect to a separate levy imposed on residents of the foreign country).

(i) *Tax on nonresidents.*—The gross receipts and costs attributable to each of the items of income of nonresidents of a foreign country that is included in the base of the foreign tax must satisfy the requirements of paragraph (b)(5)(i)(A), (B), or (C) of this section.

(A) *Income attribution based on activities.*—The gross receipts and costs that are included in the base of the foreign tax are limited to gross receipts and costs that are attributable, under reasonable principles, to the nonresident's activities within the foreign country imposing the foreign tax (including the nonresident's functions, assets, and risks located in the foreign country). For purposes of the preceding sentence, attribution of gross receipts under reasonable principles includes rules similar to those for determining effectively connected income under section 864(c) but does not include rules that take into account as a significant factor the mere location of customers, users, or any other similar destination-based criterion, or the mere location of persons from whom the nonresident makes purchases in the foreign country. In addition, for purposes of the first sentence of this paragraph (b)(5)(i)(A), reasonable principles do not include rules that deem the existence of a trade or business or permanent establishment based on the activities of another person (other than an agent or other person acting on behalf of the nonresident or a pass-through entity of which the nonresident is an owner), or that attribute gross receipts or costs to a nonresident based upon the activities of another person (other than an agent or other person acting on behalf of the nonresident or a pass-through entity of which the nonresident is an owner).

(B) *Income attribution based on source.*—The amount of gross income arising from gross receipts (other than gross receipts from sales or other dispositions of property) that is included in the base of the foreign tax on the basis of source (instead of on the basis of activities or the situs of property as described in paragraphs (b)(5)(i)(A) and (C) of this section) is limited to gross income arising from sources within the foreign country that imposes the tax, and the sourcing rules of the foreign tax law are reasonably similar to the sourcing rules that apply under the Internal Revenue Code. A foreign tax law's application of such sourcing rules need not conform in all respects to the application of those sourcing rules for Federal income tax purposes. For purposes of determining whether the sourcing rules of the foreign tax law are reasonably similar to the sourcing rules that apply under the Internal Revenue Code, the character of gross income arising from gross receipts is determined under the foreign tax law (except as provided in paragraph (b)(5)(i)(B)(*3*) of this section), and the following rules apply:

(*1*) *Services.*—Under the foreign tax law, gross income from services must be sourced based on where the services are performed, as determined under reasonable principles (which do not include determining the place of performance of the services based on the location of the service recipient).

(*2*) *Royalties.*—A foreign tax on gross income from royalties must be sourced based on the place of use of, or the right to use, the intangible property.

(*3*) *Sales of property.*—Gross income arising from gross receipts from sales or other dispositions of property (including copyrighted articles sold through an electronic medium) must be included in the foreign tax base on the basis of the rules in paragraph (b)(5)(i)(A) or (C) of this section, and not on the basis of source. In the case of sales of copyrighted articles (as determined under rules similar to § 1.861-18), a foreign tax satisfies the attribution requirement of paragraph (b)(5) of this section only if the transaction is treated as a sale of tangible property and not as a license of intangible property.

(C) *Attribution based on situs of property.*—A foreign tax on gains of nonresidents from the sale or disposition of property, including shares in a corporation or an interest in a partnership or other pass-through entity, based on the situs of property satisfies the attribution requirement only as provided in this paragraph (b)(5)(i)(C). The amount of gross receipts from the sale or disposition of property that is included in the base of the foreign tax on the basis of the situs of real property (instead of on the basis of activities as described in paragraph (b)(5)(i)(A) of this section) may only include gross receipts that are attributable to the disposition of real property situated in the foreign country imposing the foreign tax (or an interest in a resident corporation or other entity that owns such real property) under rules reasonably similar to the rules in section 897. The amount of gross receipts from the sale or disposition of property other than shares in a corporation, including an interest in a partnership or other pass-through entity, that is included in the base of the foreign tax on the basis of the situs of property other than real property may only include gross receipts that are attributable to property forming part of the business property of a taxable presence in the foreign country imposing the foreign tax under rules that are reasonably similar to the rules in section 864(c).

(ii) *Tax on residents.*—The base of a foreign tax imposed on residents of the foreign country imposing the foreign tax may include all of the worldwide gross receipts of the resident. The foreign tax law must provide that any allocation to or from the resident of income, gain, deduction, or loss with respect to transactions between such resident and organizations, trades, or businesses owned or controlled directly or indirectly by the same interests (that is, any allocation made pursuant to the foreign country's transfer pricing rules) is determined under arm's length principles, without taking into account as a significant factor the location of customers, users, or any other similar destination-based criterion.

(iii) *Examples.*—The following examples illustrate the rules of paragraph (b)(5) of this section.

(A) *Example 1.*—(*1*) *Facts.* Country X imposes a separate levy on nonresident companies that furnish, from a location outside of Country X, specified types of electronically supplied services to users located in Country X (the "ESS tax"). The base of the ESS tax is computed by taking the nonresident company's overall net income related to supplying electronically supplied services, and deeming a portion of such net income to be attributable to a deemed permanent establishment of the nonresident company in Country X. The amount of the nonresident company's net income attributable to the deemed permanent establishment is determined on a formulary basis based on the percentage of the nonresident company's total users that are located in Country X.

(*2*) *Analysis.* The taxable base of the ESS tax is not computed based on a nonresident company's activities located in Country X, but instead takes into account the location of the nonresident company's users. Therefore, the ESS tax does not meet the requirement in paragraph (b)(5)(i)(A) of this section. The ESS tax also does not meet the requirement in paragraph (b)(5)(i)(B) of this section because it is not imposed on the basis of source, and it does not meet the requirement in paragraph (b)(5)(i)(C) of this section because it is not imposed on the sale or other disposition of property.

(B) *Example 2.*—(*1*) *Facts.* The facts are the same as those in paragraph (b)(5)(iii)(A)(*1*) of this section (the facts in *Example 1*), except that instead of imposing the ESS tax by deeming nonresident companies to have a permanent establishment in Country X, Country X treats gross income from electronically supplied services provided to users located in Country X as sourced in Country X. The gross income sourced to Country X is reduced by costs that are reasonably attributed to such gross income, to arrive at the taxable base of the ESS tax. The amount of the nonresident's gross income and costs that are sourced to Country X is determined by multiplying the nonresident's total gross income and costs by the percentage of its total users that are located in Country X.

(*2*) *Analysis.* Country X tax law's rule for sourcing electronically supplied services is not based on where the services are performed and is instead based on the location of the service recipient. Therefore, the ESS tax, which is imposed on the basis of source, does not meet the requirement in paragraph (b)(5)(i)(B) of this section. The ESS tax also does not meet the requirement in paragraph (b)(5)(i)(A) of this section because it is not imposed on the basis of a nonresident's activities located in Country X, and it does not meet the requirement in paragraph (b)(5)(i)(C) of this section because it is not imposed on the sale or other disposition of property.

(6) *Surtax on net income tax.*—A foreign tax satisfies the net gain requirement in this paragraph (b) if the base of the foreign tax is the amount of a net income tax. For example, if a tax (surtax) is computed as a percentage of a separate levy that is itself a net income tax, then such surtax is considered to satisfy the net gain requirement.

(c) [Reserved]

(d) *Separate levies.*—(1) *In general.*—Each foreign levy must be analyzed separately to determine whether it is a net income tax within the meaning of paragraph (a)(3) of this section and whether it is a tax in lieu of an income tax within the meaning of § 1.903-1(b)(2). Whether a single levy or separate levies are imposed by a foreign country depends on U.S. principles and not on whether foreign tax law imposes the levy or levies pursuant to a single or separate statutes. A foreign levy is a separate levy described in this paragraph (d)(1) if it is described in paragraph (d)(1)(i), (ii), (iii), or (iv) of this section. In the case of levies that apply to dual capacity taxpayers, see also § 1.901-2A(a).

(i) *Taxing authority.*—A levy imposed by one taxing authority (for example, the national government of a foreign country) is always separate from a levy imposed by another taxing authority (for example, a political subdivision of that foreign country), even if the base of the levy is the same.

(ii) *Different taxable base.*—Where the base of a foreign levy is computed differently for different classes of persons subject to the levy, the levy is considered to impose separate levies with respect to each such class of persons. For example, foreign levies identical to the taxes imposed by sections 1, 11, 541, 871(a), 871(b), 881, 882, 3101 and 3111 of the Internal Revenue Code are each separate levies, because the levies are imposed on different classes of taxpayers, and the base of each of those levies contains different items than the base of each of the others. A taxable base of a separate levy may consist of a particular type of income (for example, wage income, investment income, or income from self-employment). The taxable base of a separate levy may also consist of an amount unrelated to income (for example, wage expense or assets). A separate levy may provide that items included in the base of the tax are computed separately merely for purposes of a preliminary computation and are then combined as a single taxable base. Income included in the taxable base of a separate levy may also be included in the taxable base of another levy (which may or may not also include other items of income); separate levies are considered to be imposed if the taxable bases are not combined as a single taxable base, even if the taxable bases are determined using the same computational rules. For example, a foreign levy identical to the tax imposed by section 1 is a separate levy from a foreign levy identical to the tax imposed by section 1411, because tax is imposed under each levy on a separate taxable base that is not combined with the other as a single taxable base. Where foreign tax law imposes a levy that is the sum of two or more separately computed amounts of tax, and each such amount is computed by reference to a different base, separate levies are considered to be imposed. Levies are not separate merely because different rates apply to different classes of taxpayers that are subject to the same provisions in computing the base of the tax. For example, a foreign levy identical to the tax imposed on U.S. citizens and resident alien individuals by section 1 of the Internal Revenue Code is a single levy notwithstanding that the levy has graduated rates and applies different rate schedules to unmarried individuals, married individuals who file separate returns, and married individuals who file joint returns. In addition, in general, levies are not separate merely because some provisions determining the base of the levy apply, by their terms or in practice, to some, but not all, persons subject to the levy. For example, a foreign levy identical to the tax imposed by 861(b) of the Internal Revenue Code is a single levy even though some provisions apply by their terms to some but not all corporations subject to the section 11 tax (for example, section 465 is by its terms applicable to corporations described in sections 465(a)(1)(B), but not to other corporations), and even though some provisions apply in practice to some but not all corporations subject to the section 11 tax (for example, section 611 does not, in practice, apply to any corporation that does not have a qualifying interest in the type of property described in section 611(a)).

(iii) *Tax imposed on nonresidents.*—A foreign levy imposed on nonresidents is always treated as a separate levy from that imposed on residents, even if the base of the tax as applied to residents and nonresidents is the same, and even if the levies are treated as a single levy under foreign tax law. In addition, a withholding tax (as defined in section 901(k)(1)(B)) that is imposed on gross income of nonresidents is treated as a separate levy as to each separate class of income described in section 61 (for example, interest, dividends, rents, or royalties) subject to the withholding tax. If two or more subsets of a separate class of income are subject to a withholding tax based on different income attribution rules (for example, if technical services are subject to tax based on the residence of the payor and other services are subject to tax based on where the services are performed), separate levies are considered to be imposed with respect to each subset of that separate class of income.

(iv) *Foreign levy modified by an applicable income tax treaty.*—A foreign levy that is limited in its application by, or is otherwise modified by, an income tax treaty to which the foreign country imposing the levy is a party is a separate levy from the levy imposed under the domestic law (without regard to the treaty) of the foreign country, and is also a separate levy from the foreign levy as modified by a different income tax treaty to which the foreign country imposing the levy is a party, even if the two treaties modify the foreign levy in exactly the same manner. Accordingly, a foreign levy paid by taxpayers that qualify for and claim benefits under an income tax treaty is a separate levy from the levy as applied to taxpayers that are ineligible for, or that do not claim, benefits under that treaty, even if the two foreign levies would apply in the same manner to a particular taxpayer, and regardless of whether the unmodified foreign levy is a foreign income tax within the meaning of paragraph (a)(1)(ii) of this section.

(2) *Contractual modifications.*—Notwithstanding paragraph (d)(1) of this section, if foreign tax law imposing a levy is modified for one or more persons subject to the levy by a contract entered into by such person or persons and the foreign country, then the foreign tax law is considered for purposes of sections 901 and 903 to impose a separate levy for all persons to whom such contractual modification of the levy applies, as contrasted to the levy as applied to all persons to whom such contractual modification does not apply.

(3) *Examples.*—The following examples illustrate the rules of paragraph (d)(1) of this section.

(i) *Example 1: Separate taxable bases.*—(A) *Facts.* A foreign statute imposes a levy on corporations equal to the sum of 15% of the corporation's realized net income plus 3% of its net worth.

(B) *Analysis.* As the levy is the sum of two separately computed amounts, each of which is computed by reference to a separate base, under paragraph (d)(1)(ii) of this section each of the portion of the levy based on income and the portion of the levy based on net worth is considered, for purposes of sections 901 and 903, to be a separate levy.

(ii) *Example 2: Separate taxable bases.*—(A) *Facts.* A foreign statute imposes a levy on nonresident alien individuals analogous to the taxes imposed by section 871 of the Internal Revenue Code.

(B) *Analysis.* As the levy is imposed on separately computed amounts, each of which is computed by reference to a separate taxable base and portions of which comprise withholding tax on gross income of nonresidents, under paragraphs (d)(1)(ii) and (iii) of this section, each of the portions of the foreign levy imposed on each separate class of gross income analogous to the tax imposed by section 871(a) and the portion of the foreign levy analogous to the tax imposed by sections 871(b) and 1 is considered, for purposes of sections 901 and 903, to be a separate levy.

(iii) *Example 3: Separate taxable bases.*—(A) *Facts*—(*1*) A single foreign statute or separate foreign statutes impose a foreign levy that is the sum of the products of specified rates applied to specified bases, as follows:

Table 1 to paragraph (*d*)(3)(iii)(A)(*1*)

Base	Rate (percent)
Net income from mining	45
Net income from manufacturing	50
Net income from technical services	50
Net income from other services	45
Net income from investments	15
All other net income	50

(2) In computing each such base, deductible expenditures are allocated to the type of income they generate. If allocated deductible expenditures exceed the gross amount of a specified type of income, the excess may not be applied against income of a different specified type.

(B) *Analysis.* The levy is the sum of several separately computed amounts, each of which is computed by reference to a separate base. Accordingly, under paragraph (d)(1)(ii) of this section, each of the levies on mining net income, manufacturing net income, technical services net income, other services net income, investment net income and other net income is considered, for purposes of sections 901 and 903, to be a separate levy.

(iv) *Example 4: Combined taxable base after preliminary separate computation.*—(A) *Facts.* The facts are the same as those in paragraph (d)(3)(iii)(A) of this section (the facts in *Example 3*), except that excess deductible expenditures allocated to one type of income are applied against other types of income to which the same rate applies.

(B) *Analysis.* Under paragraph (d)(1)(ii) of this section, the levies on mining net income and other services net income together are considered, for purposes of sections 901 and 903, to be a single levy since, despite a separate preliminary computation of the bases, by reason of the permitted application of excess allocated deductible expenditures the bases are not separately computed. For the same reason, the levies on manufacturing net income, technical services net income and other net income together are considered, for purposes of sections 901 and 903, to be a single levy. The levy on investment net income is considered, for purposes of sections 901 and 903, to be a separate levy. These results are not dependent on whether the application of excess allocated deductible expenditures to a different type of income is permitted in the same taxable period in which the expenditures are taken into account for purposes of the preliminary computation, or only in a different (for example, later) taxable period.

(v) *Example 5: Combined taxable base with income subject to different rates.*—(A) *Facts.* The facts are the same as those in paragraph (d)(3)(iii)(A) of this section (the facts in *Example 3*), except that excess deductible expenditures allocated to any type of income other than investment income are applied against the other types of income (including investment income) according to a specified set of priorities of application. Excess deductible expenditures allocated to investment income are not applied against any other type of income.

(B) *Analysis.* For the same reasons as those set forth in paragraph (d)(3)(iv)(B) of this section (the analysis in *Example 4*), all of the levies are together considered, for purposes of sections 901 and 903, to be a single levy.

(vi) *Example 6: Minimum Tax.*—(A) *Facts.* Country X imposes a net income tax ("Income Tax") and a minimum tax ("Minimum Tax") on its residents. Under Country X tax law, alternative minimum taxable income for purposes of the Minimum Tax equals the taxable income under the Income Tax increased by certain disallowed deductions. The Minimum Tax equals the excess, if any, of the alternative minimum taxable income times the Minimum Tax rate over the amount of the Income Tax.

(B) *Analysis.* Under paragraph (d)(1)(ii) of this section, the Minimum Tax is a separate levy from the Income Tax, because the taxable base of each levy is separately computed and not combined as a single taxable base. The result would be the same if under Country X tax law the Minimum Tax equaled the alternative minimum taxable income times the Minimum Tax rate, and residents of Country X were required to pay the greater of the Income Tax or the Minimum Tax (rather than the Income Tax plus the excess, if any, of the Minimum Tax over the Income Tax).

(vii) *Example 7: Diverted Profits Tax.*—(A) *Facts.* Country X imposes a 20% net income tax ("Income Tax") and a 25% "Diverted Profits Tax" on nonresident corporations. Under Country X tax law, taxable income under the Diverted Profits Tax is determined first by attributing gross receipts of the nonresident corporation to a hypothetical permanent establishment in Country X. Country X applies the same computational rules that apply under the Income Tax to determine the taxable income attributable to a hypothetical permanent establishment under the Diverted Profits Tax.

(B) *Analysis.* Under paragraph (d)(1)(ii) of this section, the Diverted Profits Tax is a separate levy from the Income Tax, because the taxable income under the Diverted Profits Tax is not combined with the taxable income under the Income Tax as a single taxable base.

(viii) *Example 8: Modified Income Tax.*—(A) *Facts.* Country X imposes a net income tax ("Income Tax") on nonresident corporations that carry on a trade or business in Country X through a permanent establishment. Under Country X tax law, the taxable base of the Income Tax as initially enacted is determined by attributing profits of the nonresident corporation to its permanent establishment in Country X based upon rules similar to Articles 5 and 7 of the 2016 U.S. Model Income Tax Convention. However, Country X later amends the Income Tax to provide that nonresident corporations that are engaged in certain digital transactions in Country X and earning revenues above certain thresholds are deemed to have a permanent establishment; under the Income Tax as originally enacted, such activities would not have created a permanent establishment in Country X.

(B) *Analysis.* Under paragraph (d)(1)(ii) of this section, the Income Tax as applied to nonresident corporations engaged in digital transactions and deemed to have a permanent establishment under the modified Income Tax is not a separate levy from the Income Tax as applied to the same or other nonresident corporations that would have permanent establishments under the Income Tax as originally enacted, because income attributable to both actual and deemed permanent establishments is combined as a single taxable base.

(ix) *Example 9: Disallowed deductions.*—(A) *Facts.* Country X imposes a net income tax ("Income Tax") on resident corporations. In determining the taxable base for the Income Tax, Country X tax law has a cap on allowed interest deductions for companies engaged in the extraction, production, or refinement of oil or natural gas.

(B) *Analysis.* Under paragraph (d)(1)(ii) of this section, the Income Tax as applied to corporations engaged in the extraction, production, or refinement of oil or natural gas is not a separate levy from the Income Tax as applied to other corporations subject to the levy. The Income Tax is a single levy even though the cap on allowed interest expense deductions applies by its terms to some, but not all, corporations subject to the Income Tax.

(x) *Example 10: Different taxable base for class of taxpayers.*—(A) *Facts.* Country X imposes a net income tax ("Income Tax") and an oil tax. The oil tax applies only to resident corporations engaged in the extraction, production, or refinement of oil, and resident corporations subject to the oil tax are not subject to the Income Tax. The taxable base under the oil tax is the taxable income under the Income Tax increased by disallowed interest expense.

(B) *Analysis.* Under paragraph (d)(1)(ii) of this section, the oil tax is a separate levy from the Income Tax, because the taxable income under the oil tax is not combined with the taxable income under the Income Tax as a single taxable base. The levies are imposed on different classes of taxpayers (resident taxpayers engaged in the extraction, production, or refinement of oil, in the case of the oil tax, and all other resident corporations, in the case of the Income Tax), and the base of each of those levies contains different items.

(e) *Amount of foreign income tax that is creditable.*—(1) *In general.*—Credit is allowed under section 901 for the amount of foreign income tax that is paid by the taxpayer. Under paragraph (g) of this section, the term "paid" means "paid" or "accrued," depending on the taxpayer's method of accounting for such taxes. The amount of foreign income tax paid by the taxpayer is determined separately for each taxpayer under the rules in this paragraph (e).

(2) *Refunds and credits.*—(i) *Refundable amounts.*—An amount remitted to a foreign country is not an amount of foreign income tax paid to the extent that it is reasonably certain that the amount will be refunded, rebated, abated, or forgiven. It is reasonably certain that an amount will be refunded, rebated, abated, or forgiven to the extent the amount exceeds a reasonable approximation of final foreign income tax liability to the foreign country. See section 905(c) and § 1.905-3 for the required redeterminations if amounts claimed as a credit (on either the cash or accrual basis) exceed the amount of the final foreign income tax liability.

(ii) *Credits.*—Except as provided in paragraph (e)(2)(iii) of this section, an amount of foreign income tax liability is not an amount of foreign income tax paid to the extent the foreign income tax liability is reduced, satisfied, or otherwise offset by a tax credit, including a tax credit that under the foreign tax law is payable in cash only to the extent it exceeds the taxpayer's liability for foreign income tax or a tax credit acquired from another taxpayer.

(iii) *Exception for overpayments and other fully refundable credits.*—An amount of foreign income tax paid is not reduced (or treated as constructively refunded) solely by reason of the fact that a credit is allowed (or may be allowed) for the amount paid to reduce the amount of a different separate levy owed by the taxpayer. See paragraphs (e)(2)(ii) and (e)(4) of this section. However, under paragraph (e)(2)(i) of this section (and taking into account any redetermination required under section 905(c) and § 1.905-3), an amount remitted with respect to a separate levy for a foreign taxable period that constitutes an overpayment of the taxpayer's final liability for that levy for that period, and that is refundable in cash at the taxpayer's option, is not an amount of tax paid. Therefore, if such an overpayment of one tax is applied as a credit against a different foreign income tax liability of the taxpayer for the same or a different taxable period, the credited amount of the overpayment may qualify as an amount paid of that different foreign income tax, if the credited amount does not exceed a reasonable approximation of the taxpayer's final foreign income tax liability for the taxable period to which the overpayment is applied. Similarly, if under the foreign tax law, the full amount of a tax credit is payable in cash at the taxpayer's option, the taxpayer's choice to apply all or a portion of the tax credit in satisfaction of a foreign income tax liability of the taxpayer is treated as a constructive payment of cash to the taxpayer in the amount so applied, followed by a constructive payment of the foreign income tax liability against which the credit is applied. An overpayment or other tax credit that under the foreign tax law is otherwise fully payable in cash at the taxpayer's option and that is applied in part in satisfaction of a foreign income tax liability is treated as an amount of foreign income tax paid notwithstanding that a portion of the amount otherwise payable in cash to the taxpayer is subject to a lien or otherwise seized in order to satisfy a different, preexisting liability of the taxpayer to the foreign government or to a third party.

(iv) *Examples.*—The following examples illustrate the rules of paragraph (e)(2) of this section.

(A) *Example 1.*—The domestic law of Country X imposes a 25 percent tax described in § 1.903-1(b) on the gross amount of interest from sources in Country X that is received by a nonresident of Country X. Country X imposes the tax on the nonresident recipient and requires any resident of Country X that pays such interest to a nonresident to withhold and pay over to Country X 25 percent of such interest, which is applied to offset the recipient's liability for the 25 percent tax. A tax treaty between the United States and Country X modifies domestic law of Country X and provides that Country X may not tax interest received by a resident of the United States from a resident of Country X at a rate in excess of 10 percent of the gross amount of such interest. A resident of the United States may claim the benefit of the treaty only by applying for a refund of the excess withheld amount (15 percent of the gross amount of interest income) after the end of the taxable year. A, a resident of the United States, receives a gross amount of 100u (units of Country X currency) of interest income from a resident of Country X from sources in Country X in Year 1, from which 25u of Country X tax is withheld. A files a timely claim for refund of the 15u excess withheld amount. 15u of the amount withheld (25u - 10u) is reasonably certain to be refunded; therefore, under paragraph (e)(2)(i) of this section 15u is not considered an amount of foreign income tax paid to Country X.

(B) *Example 2.*—A's initial foreign income tax liability under Country X tax law is 100u (units of Country X currency). However, under Country X tax law A's initial income tax liability is reduced in order to compute A's final tax liability by an investment credit of 15u and a credit for charitable contributions of 5u. Under paragraph (e)(2)(ii) of this section, the amount of foreign income tax paid by A is 80u.

(C) *Example 3.*—A computes foreign income tax liability in Country X for Year 1 of 100u (units of Country X currency), files a tax return on that basis, and remits 100u of tax. The day after A files that return, A files a claim for refund of 90u. The difference between the 100u of liability reflected in A's original return and the 10u of liability reflected in A's refund claim depends on whether a particular expenditure made by A is nondeductible or deductible, respectively. Based on an analysis of the Country X tax law, A's Country X tax advisors have advised A that it is not clear whether or not that expenditure is deductible. In view of the uncertainty as to the proper treatment of the item in question under Country X tax law, no portion of the 100u paid by A is reasonably certain to be refunded. If A receives a refund, A must treat the refund as required by section 905(c) of the Internal Revenue Code.

(D) *Example 4.*—A levy of Country X, which qualifies as a foreign income tax within the meaning of paragraph (a)(1)(ii) of this section, provides that each person who makes payment to Country X pursuant to the levy will receive a bond to be issued by Country X with an amount payable at maturity equal to 10 percent of the amount paid pursuant to the levy. A remits 38,000u (units of Country X currency) to Country X and is entitled to receive a bond with an amount payable at maturity of 3,800u. It is reasonably certain that a refund in the form of property (the bond) will be made. The amount of that refund is equal to the fair market value of the bond. Therefore, only the portion of the 38,000u payment in excess of the fair market value of the bond is an amount of foreign income tax paid.

(3) *Subsidies.*—(i) *General rule.*—An amount of foreign income tax is not an amount of foreign income tax paid by a taxpayer to a foreign country to the extent that—

(A) The amount is used, directly or indirectly, by the foreign country imposing the tax to provide a subsidy by any means (including, but not limited to, a rebate, a refund, a credit, a deduction, a payment, a discharge of an obligation, or any other method) to the taxpayer, to a related person (within the meaning of section 482), to any party to the transaction, or to any party to a related transaction; and

(B) The subsidy is determined, directly or indirectly, by reference to the amount of the tax or by reference to the base used to compute the amount of the tax.

(ii) *Subsidy.*—The term "subsidy" includes any benefit conferred, directly or indirectly, by a foreign country to one of the parties enumerated in paragraph (e)(3)(i)(A) of this section. Substance and not form shall govern in determining whether a subsidy exists. The fact that the U.S. taxpayer may derive no demonstrable benefit from the subsidy is irrelevant in determining whether a subsidy exists.

(iii) *Official exchange rate.*—A subsidy described in paragraph (e)(3)(i)(B) of this section does not include the actual use of an official foreign government exchange rate converting foreign currency into dollars where a free exchange rate also exists if—

(A) The economic benefit represented by the use of the official exchange rate is not targeted to or tied to transactions that give rise to a claim for a foreign tax credit;

(B) The economic benefit of the official exchange rate applies to a broad range of international transactions, in all cases based on the total payment to be made without regard to whether the payment is a return of principal, gross income, or net income, and without regard to whether it is subject to tax; and

(C) Any reduction in the overall cost of the transaction is merely coincidental to the broad structure and operation of the official exchange rate.

(iv) *Examples.*—The following examples illustrate the rules of paragraph (e)(3) of this section.

(A) *Example 1.*—(1) *Facts.* Country X imposes a 30 percent tax on nonresident lenders with respect to interest which the nonresident lenders receive from borrowers who are residents of Country X, and it is established that this tax is a tax in lieu of an income tax within the meaning of § 1.903-1(b). Country X provides the nonresident lenders with receipts upon their payment of the 30 percent tax. Country X remits to resident borrowers an incentive payment for engaging in foreign loans, which payment is an amount equal to 20 percent of the interest paid to nonresident lenders.

(2) *Analysis.* Because the incentive payment is based on the interest paid, it is determined by reference to the base used to compute the tax that is imposed on the nonresident lender. The incentive payment is a subsidy under paragraph (e)(3)(i) of this section since it is provided to a party (the borrower) to the transaction and is based on the amount of tax that is imposed on the lender with respect to the transaction. Therefore, two-thirds (20 percent/30 percent) of the amount withheld by the resident borrower from interest payments to the nonresident lender is not an amount of foreign income tax paid.

(B) *Example 2.*—(1) *Facts.* A U.S. bank lends money to a development bank in Country X. The development bank relends the money to companies resident in Country X. A withholding tax is imposed by Country X on the U.S. bank with respect to the interest that the development bank pays to the U.S. bank, and appropriate receipts are provided. On the date that the tax is withheld, fifty percent of the tax is credited by Country X to an account of the development bank. Country X requires the development bank to transfer the amount credited to the borrowing companies.

(2) *Analysis.* The amount successively credited to the account of the development bank and then to the account of the borrowing companies is determined by reference to the amount of the tax and the tax base. Since the amount credited to the borrowing companies is a subsidy provided to a party (the borrowing companies) to a related transaction and is based on the amount of tax and the tax base, under paragraph (e)(3)(i) of this section it is not an amount of foreign income tax paid.

(C) *Example 3.*—(1) *Facts.* A U.S. bank lends dollars to a Country X borrower. Country X imposes a withholding tax on the lender with respect to the interest. The tax is to be paid in Country X currency, although the interest is payable in dollars. Country X has a dual exchange rate system, comprised of a controlled official exchange rate and a free exchange rate. Priority transactions such as exports of merchandise, imports of merchandise, and payments of principal and interest on foreign currency loans payable abroad to foreign lenders are governed by the official exchange rate which yields more dollars per unit of Country X currency than the free exchange rate. The Country X borrower remits the net amount of dollar interest due to the U.S. bank (interest due less withholding tax), pays the tax withheld in Country X currency to the Country X government, and provides to the U.S. bank a receipt for payment of the Country X taxes.

(2) *Analysis.* Under paragraph (e)(3)(iii) of this section, the use of the official exchange rate by the U.S. bank to determine foreign taxes with respect to interest is not a subsidy described in paragraph (e)(3)(i)(B) of this section. The official exchange rate is not targeted to or tied to transactions that give rise to a claim for a foreign tax credit. The use of the official exchange rate applies to the interest paid and to the principal paid. Any benefit derived by the U.S. bank through the use of the official exchange rate is merely coincidental to the broad structure and operation of the official exchange rate.

(D) *Example 4.*—(1) *Facts.* B, a U.S. corporation, is engaged in the production of oil and gas in Country X pursuant to a production sharing agreement among B, Country X, and the state petroleum authority of Country X. The agreement is approved and enacted into law by the Legislature of Country X. Both B and the petroleum authority are subject to the Country X income tax. Each entity files an annual income tax return and pays, to the tax authority of Country X, the amount of income tax due on its annual income. B is a dual capacity taxpayer as defined in § 1.901-2(a)(2)(ii)(A). Country X has agreed to return to the petroleum authority one-half of the income taxes paid by B by allowing it a credit in calculating its own tax liability to Country X.

(2) *Analysis.* The petroleum authority is a party to a transaction with B and the amount returned by Country X to the petroleum authority is determined by reference to the amount of the tax imposed on B. Therefore, under paragraph (e)(3)(i) of this section the amount returned is a subsidy, and one-half of the tax imposed on B is not an amount of foreign income tax paid.

(E) *Example 5.*—(1) *Facts.* The facts are the same as those in paragraph (e)(3)(iv)(D)(*1*) of this section (the facts in *Example 4*), except that the state petroleum authority of Country X does not receive amounts from Country X related to tax paid by B. Instead, the authority of Country X receives a general appropriation from Country X which is not calculated with reference to the amount of tax paid by B.

(2) *Analysis.* Because the general appropriation is not calculated with reference to the amount of tax paid by B, it is not a subsidy described in paragraph (e)(3)(i) of this section.

(4) *Multiple levies.*—(i) *In general.*—If, under foreign law, a taxpayer's tentative liability for one levy (the "reduced levy") is or can be reduced by the amount of the taxpayer's liability for a different levy (the "applied levy"), then the amount considered paid by the taxpayer to the foreign country pursuant to the applied levy is an amount equal to its entire liability for that applied levy (which is not considered to be reduced by the amount applied against the reduced levy), and the remainder of the total amount paid, if any, is considered paid pursuant to the reduced levy. See also paragraphs (e)(2)(ii) and (iii) of this section.

(ii) *Examples.*—The following examples illustrate the rules of paragraphs (e)(2)(ii) and (iii) and (e)(4)(i) of this section.

(A) *Example 1. Tax reduced by credits.*—(*1*) *Facts.* A's tentative liability for foreign income tax imposed by Country X is 100u (units of Country X currency). However, under Country X tax law, in determining A's final foreign income tax liability, its tentative liability is reduced by a 15u credit for a separate Country X levy that does not qualify as a foreign income tax and that A accrued and paid on its gross services income and is also reduced by a 5u credit for charitable contributions. Under Country X tax law, the amount of the charitable contributions credit is refundable in cash to the extent the credit exceeds the taxpayer's Country X income tax liability after applying the credit for the tax on gross services income. A timely remits the 80u due to Country X.

(2) *Analysis.* Under paragraphs (e)(2)(ii) and (e)(4) of this section, the amount of Country X income tax paid by A is 80u (100u tentative liability – 20u tax credits), and the amount of Country X tax on gross services income paid by A is 15u.

(B) *Example 2: Tax paid by credit for overpayment.*—(1) *Facts.* The facts are the same as those in paragraph (e)(4)(ii)(A)(*1*) of this section (the facts in *Example* 1), except that A's final Country X income tax liability of 80u is satisfied by applying a credit for an otherwise refundable 60u overpayment from the previous taxable year of A's liability for a separate levy imposed by Country X that is also a foreign income tax and remitting the balance due of 20u.

(2) *Analysis.* The result is the same as in paragraph (e)(4)(ii)(A)(*2*) of this section (the analysis in *Example 1*). Under paragraph (e)(2)(iii) of this section, the portion of A's Country X income tax liability that was satisfied by applying the 60u overpayment of A's different foreign income tax liability for the previous taxable year qualifies as an amount of Country X income tax paid, because that refundable overpayment exceeded (and so is not treated as a payment of) A's different foreign income tax liability for the previous taxable year.

(5) *Noncompulsory amounts.*—(i) *In general.*—An amount remitted to a foreign country (a "foreign payment") is not a compulsory payment, and thus is not an amount of foreign income tax paid, to the extent that the foreign payment exceeds the amount of liability for foreign income tax under the foreign tax law (as defined in paragraph (g) of this section). A foreign payment does not exceed the amount of such liability if the foreign payment is determined by the taxpayer in a manner that is consistent with a reasonable interpretation and application of the substantive and procedural provisions of foreign tax law (including applicable tax treaties) in such a way as to reduce, over time, the taxpayer's reasonably expected liability under foreign tax law for foreign income tax, and if the taxpayer exhausts all effective and practical remedies, including invocation of competent authority procedures available under applicable tax treaties, to reduce, over time, the taxpayer's liability for foreign income tax (including liability pursuant to a foreign tax audit adjustment). See paragraphs (e)(5)(ii) through (v) of this section. Whether a taxpayer has satisfied its obligation to minimize the aggregate amount of its liability for foreign income taxes over time is determined without regard to the present value of a deferred tax liability or other time value of money considerations. However, a taxpayer is not required to reduce its foreign income tax liability to the extent the reasonably expected, arm's length costs of reducing the liability would exceed the amount by which the liability could be reduced. For this purpose, such costs may include an additional liability for a different foreign tax (but not U.S. taxes) that is not a foreign income tax only to the extent the amount of the additional liability is determined in a manner consistent with the rules of this paragraph (e)(5). A taxpayer is not required to alter its form of doing business, its business conduct, or the form of any business transaction in order to reduce its liability under foreign law for foreign income tax.

(ii) *Reasonable application of foreign tax law.*—An interpretation or application of foreign tax law is not reasonable if there is actual notice or constructive notice (for example, a published court decision) to the taxpayer that the interpretation or application is likely to be erroneous. In interpreting foreign tax law, a taxpayer may generally rely on advice obtained in good faith from competent foreign tax advisors to whom the taxpayer has disclosed the relevant facts. Except as provided in paragraphs (e)(5)(i) and (e)(5)(iv) of this section, voluntarily forgoing a tax benefit to which a taxpayer is entitled under the foreign tax law results in a foreign payment in excess of the taxpayer's liability for foreign income tax.

(iii) *Effect of foreign tax law elections.*—(A) *In general.*—Where foreign tax law includes options or elections whereby a taxpayer's foreign income tax liability may be shifted, in whole or part, to a different year or years, the taxpayer's use or failure to use such options or elections does not result in a foreign payment in excess of the taxpayer's liability for foreign income tax. Except as provided in paragraph (e)(5)(iii)(B) of this section, where foreign tax law provides a taxpayer with options or elections in computing its liability for foreign income tax whereby a taxpayer's foreign income tax liability may be permanently decreased in the aggregate over time, the taxpayer's failure to use such options or elections results in a foreign payment in excess of the taxpayer's liability for foreign income tax.

(B) *Exception for certain options or elections.*—*(1) Entity classification elections.*—If foreign tax law provides an option or election to treat an entity as fiscally transparent or non-fiscally transparent, a taxpayer's decision to use or not use such option or election is not considered to increase the taxpayer's liability for foreign income tax over time for purposes of this paragraph (e)(5).

(2) Foreign consolidation, group relief, or other loss sharing regime.—If foreign tax law provides an option or election for one foreign entity to join in the filing of a consolidated return with another foreign entity, or to surrender its loss in order to offset the income of another foreign entity pursuant to a foreign group relief or other loss-sharing regime, a taxpayer's decision whether to file a consolidated return, whether to surrender a loss, or whether to use a surrendered loss, is not considered to increase the taxpayer's liability for foreign income tax over time for purposes of this paragraph (e)(5).

(C) *Alternative creditable levies.*—If under foreign tax law a taxpayer has the option to determine its foreign income tax liability under only one of multiple separate levies, each of which qualifies as a foreign income tax, then the amount of foreign income tax paid equals the smallest liability of the amounts that would be due under each of the alternative levies, regardless of which levy the taxpayer uses to determine its foreign income tax liability.

(iv) *Exception for increase in liability in connection with anti-hybrid rules.*—(A) *In general.*—If a taxpayer (the "first taxpayer") that makes a payment to another taxpayer (the "second taxpayer") is permitted to increase the first taxpayer's liability for foreign income tax (for example, by waiving an otherwise allowable deduction), and doing so results in a greater decrease in the amount of liability for foreign income tax of the second taxpayer by reason of the deactivation of a hybrid mismatch rule that would otherwise apply to the second taxpayer, then the increase in the first taxpayer's liability is not considered to result in a foreign payment in excess of the first taxpayer's liability for foreign income tax for purposes of this paragraph (e)(5).

(B) *Definition of hybrid mismatch rule.*—The term *hybrid mismatch rule* means foreign tax law rules substantially similar to sections 245A(e) and 267(a) and includes rules the purpose of which is to eliminate the deduction/no-inclusion outcome of hybrid and branch mismatch arrangements. Examples of such rules include rules based on, or substantially similar to, the recommendations contained in OECD/G-20, *Neutralising the Effects of Hybrid Mismatch Arrangements, Action 2: 2015 Final Report* (October 2015), and OECD/G-20, *Neutralising the Effects of Branch Mismatch Arrangements, Action 2: Inclusive Framework on BEPS* (July 2017).

(v) *Exhaustion of remedies.*—In determining whether a taxpayer has exhausted all effective and practical remedies, a remedy is effective and practical only if the cost of pursuing it (including the reasonably expected risk of incurring an offsetting or additional foreign income tax or other tax liability) is reasonable considering the amount at issue and the likelihood of success. An available remedy is considered effective and practical if an economically rational taxpayer would pursue it whether or not a compulsory payment of the amount at issue would be eligible for a U.S. foreign tax credit. A settlement by a taxpayer of two or more issues will be evaluated on an overall basis, not on an issue-by-issue basis, in determining whether an amount is a compulsory payment.

(vi) *Examples.*—The following examples illustrate the rules of paragraph (e)(5) of this section.

(A) *Example 1.*—A, a corporation organized and doing business solely in the United States, owns all of the stock of B, a corporation organized in Country X. In Year 1, A buys merchandise from unrelated persons for $1,000,000, and shortly thereafter resells that merchandise to B for $600,000. Later in Year 1, B resells the merchandise to unrelated persons for $1,200,000. Under the Country X income tax, which is a net income tax within the meaning of paragraph (a)(3) of this section, all corporations organized in Country X are subject to a tax equal to 3 percent of their net income. In computing its Year 1 Country X income tax liability, B reports $600,000 ($1,200,000 – $600,000) of profit from the purchase and resale of merchandise. The Country X tax law requires that transactions between related persons be reported at arm's length prices, and a reasonable interpretation of this requirement, as it has been applied in Country X, would consider B's arm's length purchase price of the merchandise purchased from A to be $1,050,000. When it computes its Country X tax liability B is aware that $600,000 is not an arm's length price (by Country X standards). B's knowing use of a non-arm's length price (by Country X standards) of $600,000, instead of a price of $1,050,000 (an arm's length price under Country X's law), is not consistent with a reasonable interpretation and application of Country X tax law, determined in such a way as to reduce over time B's reasonably expected liability for Country X income tax. Accordingly, $13,500 (3 percent of $450,000 ($1,050,000 – $600,000)), the amount of Country X income tax remitted by B to Country X that is attributable to the purchase of the merchandise from B's parent at less than an arm's length price, is in excess of the amount of B's liability for Country X income tax, and thus is not an amount of foreign income tax paid.

(B) *Example 2.*—A, a corporation organized and doing business solely in the United States, owns all of the stock of B, a corporation organized in Country X. Country X has in force an income tax treaty with the United States. The tax treaty provides that the profits of related persons shall be determined as if the persons were not related. A and B deal extensively with each other. A and B, with respect to a series of transactions involving both of them, treat A as having $300,000 of income and B as having $700,000 of income for purposes of A's United States income tax and B's Country X income tax, respectively. B has no actual or constructive notice that its treatment of these transactions under Country X tax law is likely to be erroneous. Subsequently, the Internal Revenue Service reallocates $200,000 of this income from B to A under the authority of section 482 and the tax treaty. This reallocation constitutes actual notice to A and constructive notice to B that B's interpretation and application of Country X's tax law and the tax treaty is likely to be erroneous. B does not exhaust all effective and practical remedies to obtain a refund of the amount remitted by B to Country X that is attributable to the reallocated $200,000 of income. Under paragraph (e)(5)(i) of this section, this amount is in excess of the amount of B's liability for Country X income tax and thus is not an amount of foreign income tax paid.

(C) *Example 3.*—The facts are the same as those in paragraph (e)(5)(vi)(B) of this section (the facts in *Example 2*), except that B files a claim for refund (an administrative proceeding) of Country X tax and A or B invokes the competent authority procedures of the tax treaty, the cost of which is reasonable in view of the amount at issue and the likelihood of success. Nevertheless, B does not obtain any refund of Country X income tax. The cost of pursuing any judicial remedy in Country X would be unreasonable in light of the amount at issue and the likelihood of B's success, and B does not pursue any such remedy. Under paragraph (e)(5)(i) of this section, the entire amount paid by B to Country X is a compulsory payment and thus is an amount of foreign income tax paid by B.

(D) *Example 4.*—The facts are the same as those in paragraph (e)(5)(vi)(B) of this section (the facts in *Example 2*), except that, when the Internal Revenue Service makes the reallocation, the Country X statute of limitations on refunds has expired, and neither the internal law of Country X nor the tax treaty authorizes the Country X tax authorities to pay a refund that is barred by the statute of limitations. B does not file a claim for refund, and neither A nor B invokes the competent authority procedures of the tax treaty. Because the Country X tax authorities would be barred by the statute of limitations from paying a refund, B has no effective and practical remedies. Under paragraph (e)(5)(i) of this section, the entire amount paid by B to Country X is a compulsory payment and thus is an amount of foreign income tax paid by B.

(E) *Example 5.*—A is a U.S. person doing business in Country X. In computing its income tax liability to Country X, A is permitted, at its election, to recover the cost of machinery used in its business either by deducting that cost in the year of acquisition or by depreciating that cost on the straight-line method over a period of 2, 4, 6 or 10 years. A elects to depreciate machinery over 10 years. This election merely shifts A's tax liability to different years (compared to the timing of A's tax liability under a different depreciation period); it does not result in a payment in excess of the amount of A's liability for Country X income tax in any year since the amount of Country X income tax paid by A is consistent with a reasonable interpretation of Country X tax law in such a way as to reduce over time A's reasonably expected liability for Country X income tax. Because the standard of paragraph (e)(5)(i) of this section refers to A's reasonably expected liability, not its actual liability, events actually occurring in subsequent years (for example, whether A has sufficient profit in such years so that such depreciation deductions actually reduce A's Country X tax liability or whether the Country X tax rates change) are immaterial.

(F) *Example 6*.—The domestic law of Country X imposes a 25 percent tax described in § 1.903-1(b) on the gross amount of interest from sources in Country X that is received by a nonresident of Country X. Country X tax law imposes the tax on the nonresident recipient and requires any resident of Country X that pays such interest to a nonresident to withhold and pay over to Country X 25 percent of such interest, which is applied to offset the recipient's liability for the 25 percent tax. A tax treaty between the United States and Country X overrides domestic law of Country X and provides that Country X may not tax interest received by a resident of the United States from a resident of Country X at a rate in excess of 10 percent of the gross amount of such interest. A resident of the United States may claim the benefit of the tax treaty only by applying for a refund of the excess withheld amount (15 percent of the gross amount of interest income) after the end of the taxable year. A, a resident of the United States, receives a gross amount of 100u (units of Country X currency) of interest income from a resident of Country X from sources in Country X in Year 1, from which 25u of Country X tax is withheld. A does not file a timely claim for refund. Under paragraph (e)(5)(i) of this section, 15u of the amount withheld (25u − 10u) is not a compulsory payment and thus is not an amount of foreign income tax paid.

(G) *Example 7: Reasonable steps to minimize creditable tax—larger noncreditable tax cost*.—(*1*) *Facts*. Corporations resident in Country X are subject to a 20% generally applicable net income tax, which qualifies as a foreign income tax under paragraph (a)(1)(ii) of this section ("Income Tax"), and a separate levy equal to 25% of certain deductible payments above a specified threshold made to related parties that are not residents of Country X, which does not qualify as a foreign income tax under paragraph (a)(1)(ii) of this section ("Base Erosion Tax"). CFC, a Country X corporation, makes payments to nonresident related parties that exceed the specified threshold of the Base Erosion Tax by 100u (units of Country X currency), which if claimed as deductions would result in a Base Erosion Tax of 25u (.25 × 100u), and would also result in 300u of taxable income for purposes of the Income Tax, thus resulting in Income Tax of 60u (.20 × 300u). If in computing its liability for Income Tax CFC does not claim deductions for the 100u of excess related party payments, its liability for the Base Erosion Tax would be zero, and its liability for Income Tax would be 80u (.20 × 400u).

(*2*) *Analysis*. If CFC chooses not to deduct the 100u of excess related party payments that would subject it to the Base Erosion Tax and pays 80u of Income Tax, the amount of foreign income tax paid under paragraph (e)(5) of this section is 80u. Under paragraph (e)(5)(i) of this section, although CFC could reduce its liability for Income Tax from 80u to 60u by claiming the deductions, no portion of the Income Tax remitted is a noncompulsory payment because reducing the Income Tax by 20u would incur a Base Erosion Tax of 25u, which exceeds the amount of the potential reduction.

(H) *Example 8: Reasonable steps to minimize creditable tax—smaller noncreditable tax cost*.—(*1*) *Facts*. The facts are the same as those in paragraph (e)(5)(vi)(G)(*1*) of this section (the facts in *Example 7*) except that the rate of the Base Erosion Tax is 20% and the rate of the Income Tax is 25%. Accordingly, if CFC claims the 100u of excess deductions its liability for Base Erosion Tax would be 20u (.20 × 100u), and its liability for Income Tax would be 75u (.25 × 300u). If CFC chooses not to claim the 100u of excess deductions its liability for Base Erosion Tax would be zero, and its liability for Income Tax would be 100u (.25 × 400u).

(*2*) *Analysis*. If CFC chooses not to claim the 100u of excess deductions in computing its liability for Income Tax and pays 100u of Income Tax, the amount of foreign income tax paid under paragraph (e)(5) of this section is 75u. CFC's additional payment of 25u is not an amount of Income Tax paid, because CFC could have reduced its Income Tax liability by 25u by claiming the excess deductions and paying 20u of Base Erosion Tax.

(I) *Example 9: Alternative creditable taxes*.—(*1*) *Facts*. The facts are the same as those in paragraph (e)(5)(vi)(G)(*1*) of this section (the facts in *Example 7*), except that Country X does not have a Base Erosion Tax, and it allows resident corporations to elect to pay either the Income Tax or a separate levy using an alternative cost allowance (the "Alternative Tax"), which qualifies as a tax in lieu of an income tax under § 1.903-1(b)(2). CFC's liability under the Income Tax is 80u, and its liability under the Alternative Tax is 100u. CFC chooses to pay the 100u of Alternative Tax rather than the 80u of Income Tax.

(*2*) *Analysis*. Under paragraph (e)(5)(iii)(C) of this section, the amount of foreign income tax paid by CFC is 80u, the smaller of the amounts due under the two alternative foreign income taxes.

(vii) *Structured passive investment arrangements*.—(A) *In general*.—Notwithstanding paragraph (e)(5)(i) of this section, an amount paid to a foreign country (a "foreign payment") is not a compulsory payment, and thus is not an amount of foreign income tax paid, if the foreign payment is attributable (within the meaning of paragraph (e)(5)(vii)(B)(*1*)(*ii*) of this section) to a structured passive investment arrangement (as described in paragraph (e)(5)(vii)(B) of this section).

(B) *Conditions*.—An arrangement is a structured passive investment arrangement if all of the following conditions are satisfied:

(*1*) *Special purpose vehicle (SPV)*.—An entity that is part of the arrangement meets the following requirements:

(*i*) Substantially all of the gross income (for U.S. tax purposes) of the entity, if any, is passive investment income, and substantially all of the assets of the entity are assets held to produce such passive investment income.

(*ii*) There is a foreign payment attributable to income of the entity (as determined under the laws of the foreign country to which such foreign payment is made), including the entity's share of income of a lower-tier entity that is a branch or pass-through entity under the laws of such foreign country, that, if the foreign payment were an amount of foreign income tax paid, would be paid in a U.S. taxable year in which the entity meets the requirements of paragraph (e)(5)(vii)(B)(*1*)(*i*) of this section. A foreign payment attributable to income of an entity includes a foreign payment attributable to income that is required to be taken into account by an owner of the entity, if the entity is a branch or pass-through entity under the laws of such foreign country. A foreign payment attributable to income of the entity also includes a withholding tax (within the meaning of section 901(k)(1)(B)) imposed on a dividend or other distribution (including distributions made by a pass-through entity or an entity that is disregarded as an entity separate from its owner for U.S. tax purposes) with respect to the equity of the entity.

(*2*) *U.S. party*.—A person would be eligible to claim a credit under section 901(a) (including a credit for foreign taxes deemed paid under section 960) for all or a portion of the foreign payment described in paragraph (e)(5)(vii)(B)(*1*)(*ii*) of this section if the foreign payment were an amount of foreign income tax paid.

(*3*) *Direct investment*.—The U.S. party's proportionate share of the foreign payment or payments described in paragraph (e)(5)(vii)(B)(*1*)(*ii*) of this section is (or is expected to be) substantially greater than the amount of credits, if any, that the U.S. party reasonably would expect to be eligible to claim under section 901(a) for foreign income taxes attributable to income generated by the U.S. party's proportionate share of the assets owned by the SPV if the U.S. party directly owned such assets. For this purpose, direct ownership shall not include ownership through a branch, a permanent establishment or any other arrangement (such as an agency arrangement or dual resident status) that would result in the income generated by the U.S. party's proportionate share of the assets being subject to tax on a net basis in the foreign country to which the payment is made. A U.S. party's proportionate share of the assets of the SPV shall be determined by reference to such U.S. party's proportionate share of the total value of all of the outstanding interests in the SPV that are held by its equity owners and creditors. A U.S. party's proportionate share of the assets of the SPV, however, shall not include any assets that produce income subject to gross basis withholding tax.

(*4*) *Foreign tax benefit*.—The arrangement is reasonably expected to result in a credit, deduction, loss, exemption, exclusion or other tax benefit under the laws of a foreign country that is available to a counterparty or to a person that is related to the counterparty (determined under the principles of paragraph (e)(5)(vii)(C)(*7*) of this section by applying the tax laws of a foreign country in which the counterparty is subject to tax on a net basis). However, a foreign tax benefit in the form of a credit is described in this paragraph (e)(5)(vii)(B)(*4*) only if the amount of any such credit corresponds to 10 percent or more of the amount of the U.S. party's share (for U.S. tax purposes) of the foreign payment referred to in paragraph (e)(5)(vii)(B)(*1*)(*ii*) of this section. In addition, a foreign tax benefit in the form of a deduction, loss, exemption, exclusion or other tax benefit is described in this paragraph (e)(5)(vii)(B)(*4*) only if such amount corresponds to 10 percent or more of the foreign base with respect to which the U.S. party's share (for U.S. tax purposes) of the foreign payment is imposed. For purposes of the preceding two sentences, if an arrangement involves more than one U.S. party or more than one counterparty or both, the aggregate amount of foreign tax benefits available to all of the counterparties and persons related to such counterparties is compared to the aggregate amount of all of the U.S. parties' shares of the foreign payment or foreign base, as the case may be. Where a U.S. party indirectly owns interests in an SPV that are treated as equity interests for both U.S. and foreign tax purposes, a foreign tax benefit available to a foreign entity in the chain of ownership that begins with the SPV and ends with the first-tier entity in the chain does not correspond to the U.S. party's share of the foreign payment attributable to income of the SPV to the extent that such benefit relates to earnings of the SPV that are distributed with respect to equity interests in the SPV that are owned directly or indirectly by the U.S. party for purposes of both U.S. and foreign tax law.

(*5*) *Counterparty.*—The arrangement involves a counterparty. A counterparty is a person that, under the tax laws of a foreign country in which the person is subject to tax on the basis of place of management, place of incorporation or similar criterion or otherwise subject to a net basis tax, directly or indirectly owns or acquires equity interests in, or assets of, the SPV. However, a counterparty does not include the SPV or a person with respect to which for U.S. tax purposes the same domestic corporation, U.S. citizen or resident alien individual directly or indirectly owns more than 80 percent of the total value of the stock (or equity interests) of each of the U.S. party and such person. A counterparty also does not include a person with respect to which for U.S. tax purposes the U.S. party directly or indirectly owns more than 80 percent of the total value of the stock (or equity interests), but only if the U.S. party is a domestic corporation, a U.S. citizen or a resident alien individual. In addition, a counterparty does not include an individual who is a U.S. citizen or resident alien.

(*6*) *Inconsistent treatment.*—The United States and an applicable foreign country treat one or more of the aspects of the arrangement listed in paragraph (e)(5)(vii)(B)(*6*)(*i*) through (*iv*) of this section differently under their respective tax systems, and for one or more tax years when the arrangement is in effect one or both of the following two conditions applies; either the amount of income attributable to the SPV that is recognized for U.S. tax purposes by the SPV, the U.S. party or parties, and persons related to a U.S. party or parties is materially less than the amount of income that would be recognized if the foreign tax treatment controlled for U.S. tax purposes; or the amount of credits claimed by the U.S. party or parties (if the foreign payment described in paragraph (e)(5)(vii)(B)(*1*)(*ii*) of this section were an amount of foreign income tax paid) is materially greater than it would be if the foreign tax treatment controlled for U.S. tax purposes:

(*i*) The classification of the SPV (or an entity that has a direct or indirect ownership interest in the SPV) as a corporation or other entity subject to an entity-level tax, a partnership or other flow-through entity or an entity that is disregarded for tax purposes.

(*ii*) The characterization as debt, equity or an instrument that is disregarded for tax purposes of an instrument issued by the SPV (or an entity that has a direct or indirect ownership interest in the SPV) to a U.S. party, a counterparty or a person related to a U.S. party or a counterparty.

(*iii*) The proportion of the equity of the SPV (or an entity that directly or indirectly owns the SPV) that is considered to be owned directly or indirectly by a U.S. party and a counterparty.

(*iv*) The amount of taxable income that is attributable to the SPV for one or more tax years during which the arrangement is in effect.

(C) *Definitions.*—The following definitions apply for purposes of paragraph (e)(5)(vii) of this section.

(*1*) *Applicable foreign country.*—An *applicable foreign country* means each foreign country to which a foreign payment described in paragraph (e)(5)(vii)(B)(*1*)(*ii*) of this section is made or which confers a foreign tax benefit described in paragraph (e)(5)(vii)(B)(*4*) of this section.

(*2*) *Counterparty.*—The term *counterparty* means a person described in paragraph (e)(5)(vii)(B)(*5*) of this section.

(*3*) *Entity.*—The term *entity* includes a corporation, trust, partnership or disregarded entity described in § 301.7701-2(c)(2)(i).

(*4*) *Indirect ownership. Indirect ownership* of stock or another equity interest (such as an interest in a partnership) shall be determined in accordance with the principles of section 958(a)(2), regardless of whether the interest is owned by a U.S. or foreign entity.

(*5*) *Passive investment income.*—(*i*) *In general.*—The term *passive investment income* means income described in section 954(c), as modified by this paragraph (e)(5)(vii)(C)(*5*)(*i*) and paragraph (e)(5)(vii)(C)(*5*)(*ii*) of this section. In determining whether income is described in section 954(c), paragraphs (c)(1)(H), (c)(3), and (c)(6) of section 954 shall be disregarded. Sections 954(c), 954(h), and 954(i) shall be applied at the entity level as if the entity (as defined in paragraph (e)(5)(vii)(C)(*3*) of this section) were a controlled foreign corporation (as defined in section 957(a)). For purposes of determining if sections 954(h) and 954(i) apply for purposes of this paragraph (e)(5)(vii)(C)(*5*)(*i*) and paragraph (e)(5)(vii)(C)(*5*)(*ii*) of this section, any income of an entity attributable to transactions that, assuming the entity is an SPV, are with a person that is a counterparty, or with persons that are related to a counterparty within the meaning of paragraph (e)(5)(vii)(B)(*4*) of this section, shall not be treated as qualified banking or financing income or as qualified insurance income, and shall not be taken into account in applying sections 954(h) and 954(i) for purposes of determining whether other income of the entity is excluded from section 954(c)(1) under section 954(h) or 954(i), but only if any such person (or a person that is related to such person within the meaning of paragraph (e)(5)(vii)(B)(*4*) of this section) is eligible for a foreign tax benefit described in paragraph (e)(5)(vii)(B)(*4*) of this section. In addition, in applying section 954(h) for purposes of this paragraph (e)(5)(vii)(C)(*5*)(*i*) and paragraph (e)(5)(vii)(C)(*5*)(*ii*) of this section, section 954(h)(3)(E) shall not apply, section 954(h)(2)(A)(ii) shall be satisfied only if the entity conducts substantial activity with respect to its business through its own employees, and the term "any foreign country" shall be substituted for "home country" wherever it appears in section 954(h).

(*ii*) *Income attributable to lower-tier entities; holding company exception.*—Income of an upper-tier entity that is attributable to an equity interest in a lower-tier entity, including dividends, an allocable share of partnership income, and income attributable to the ownership of an interest in an entity that is disregarded as an entity separate from its owner is passive investment income unless substantially all of the upper-tier entity's assets consist of qualified equity interests in one or more lower-tier entities, each of which is engaged in the active conduct of a trade or business and derives more than 50 percent of its gross income from such trade or business, and substantially all of the upper-tier entity's opportunity for gain and risk of loss with respect to each such interest in a lower-tier entity is shared by the U.S. party (or persons that are related to a U.S. party) and, assuming the entity is an SPV, a counterparty (or persons that are related to a counterparty) ("holding company exception"). If an arrangement involves more than one U.S. party or more than one counterparty or both, then substantially all of the upper-tier entity's opportunity for gain and risk of loss with respect to its interest in any lower-tier entity must be shared (directly or indirectly) by one or more U.S. parties (or persons related to such U.S. parties) and, assuming the upper-tier entity is an SPV, one or more counterparties (or persons related to such counterparties). Substantially all of the upper-tier entity's opportunity for gain and risk of loss with respect to its interest in any lower-tier entity is not shared if the opportunity for gain and risk of loss is borne (directly or indirectly) by one or more U.S. parties (or persons related to such U.S. party or parties) or, assuming the upper-tier entity is an SPV, by one or more counterparties (or persons related to such counterparty or counterparties). Whether and the extent to which a person is considered to share in an upper-tier entity's opportunity for gain and risk of loss is determined based on all the facts and circumstances, provided, however, that a person does not share in an upper-tier entity's opportunity for gain and risk of loss if its equity interest in the upper-tier entity was acquired in a sale-repurchase transaction or if its interest is treated as debt for U.S. tax purposes. If a U.S. party owns an interest in an entity indirectly through a chain of entities, the application of the holding company exception begins with the lowest-tier entity in the chain that may satisfy the holding company exception and proceeds upward; provided, however, that the opportunity for gain and risk of loss borne by any upper-tier entity in the chain that is a counterparty shall be disregarded to the extent borne indirectly by a U.S. party. An upper-tier entity that satisfies the holding company exception is itself considered to be engaged in the active conduct of a trade or business and to derive more than 50 percent of its gross income from such trade or business for purposes of applying the holding company exception to the owners of such entity. A lower-tier entity that is engaged in a banking, financing, or similar business shall not be considered to be engaged in the active conduct of a trade or business unless the income derived by such entity would be excluded from section 954(c)(1) under section 954(h) or 954(i) as modified by paragraph (e)(5)(vii)(C)(*5*)(*i*) of this section.

(*6*) *Qualified equity interest*.—With respect to an interest in a corporation, the term *qualified equity interest* means stock representing 10 percent or more of the total combined voting power of all classes of stock entitled to vote and 10 percent or more of the total value of the stock of the corporation or disregarded entity, but does not include any preferred stock (as defined in section 351(g)(3)). Similar rules shall apply to determine whether an interest in an entity other than a corporation is a qualified equity interest.

(*7*) *Related person*.—Two persons are related if—

(*i*) One person directly or indirectly owns stock (or an equity interest) possessing more than 50 percent of the total value of the other person; or

(*ii*) The same person directly or indirectly owns stock (or an equity interest) possessing more than 50 percent of the total value of both persons.

(*8*) *Special purpose vehicle (SPV)*.—The term *SPV* means the entity described in paragraph (e)(5)(vii)(B)(*1*) of this section.

(*9*) *U.S. party*.—The term *U.S. party* means a person described in paragraph (e)(5)(vii)(B)(*2*) of this section.

(D) *Examples*.—The following examples illustrate the rules of paragraph (e)(5)(vii) of this section. No inference is intended as to whether a taxpayer would be eligible to claim a credit under section 901(a) if a foreign payment were an amount of foreign income tax paid. The examples set forth below do not limit the application of other principles of existing law to determine the proper tax consequences of the structures or transactions addressed in the regulations.

(*1*) *Example 1: U.S. borrower transaction*.—(*i*) *Facts*. A domestic corporation (USP) forms a Country M corporation (Newco), contributing $1.5 billion in exchange for 100% of the stock of Newco. Newco, in turn, loans the $1.5 billion to a second Country M corporation (FSub) wholly owned by USP. USP then sells its entire interest in Newco to a Country M corporation (FP) for the original purchase price of $1.5 billion, subject to an obligation to repurchase the interest in five years for $1.5 billion. The sale has the effect of transferring ownership of the Newco stock to FP for Country M tax purposes. Assume the sale-repurchase transaction is structured in a way that qualifies as a collateralized loan for U.S. tax purposes. Therefore, USP remains the owner of the Newco stock for U.S. tax purposes. All of FSub's income is subpart F income. In Year 1, FSub pays Newco $120 million of interest. Newco pays $36 million to Country M with respect to such interest income and distributes the remaining $84 million to FP. Under Country M law, the $84 million distribution is excluded from FP's income. None of FP's stock is owned, directly or indirectly, by USP or any shareholders of USP that are domestic corporations, U.S. citizens, or resident alien individuals. Under an income tax treaty between Country M and the United States, Country M does not impose Country M tax on interest received by U.S. residents from sources in Country M.

(*ii*) *Result*. The $36 million payment by Newco to Country M is not a compulsory payment, and thus is not an amount of foreign income tax paid because the foreign payment is attributable to a structured passive investment arrangement. First, Newco is an SPV because all of Newco's income is passive investment income described in paragraph (e)(5)(iv)(C)(*5*) of this section; Newco's only asset, a note, is held to produce such income; the payment to Country M is attributable to such income; and if the payment were an amount of foreign income tax paid it would be paid in a U.S. taxable year in which Newco meets the requirements of paragraph (e)(5)(vii)(B)(*1*)(*i*) of this section. Second, if the foreign payment were treated as an amount of foreign income tax paid, USP would be deemed to pay the foreign payment under section 960(a) and, therefore, would be eligible to claim a credit for such payment under section 901(a). Third, USP would not pay any Country M tax if it directly owned Newco's loan receivable. Fourth, the distribution from Newco to FP is exempt from tax under Country M law, and the exempt amount corresponds to more than 10% of the foreign base with respect to which USP's share (which is 100% under U.S. tax law) of the foreign payment was imposed. Fifth, FP is a counterparty because FP owns stock of Newco under Country M law and none of FP's stock is owned by USP or shareholders of USP that are domestic corporations, U.S. citizens, or resident alien individuals. Sixth, FP is the owner of 100% of Newco's stock for Country M tax purposes, while USP is the owner of 100% of Newco's stock for U.S. tax purposes, and the amount of credits claimed by USP if the payment to Country M were an amount of foreign income tax paid is materially greater than it would be if Country M tax treatment controlled for U.S. tax purposes such that FP, rather than USP, owned 100% of Newco's stock. Because the payment to Country M is not an amount of foreign income tax paid, USP is not deemed to pay any Country M tax under section 960(a). USP includes $84 million in income under subpart F with respect to Newco and also has interest expense of $84 million. FSub's income and earnings and profits are reduced by $120 million of interest expense.

(*2*) *Example 2: U.S. borrower transaction*.—(*i*) *Facts*. The facts are the same as those in paragraph (e)(5)(vii)(D)(*1*)(*i*) of this section (the facts in *Example 1*), except that FSub is a wholly-owned subsidiary of Newco. In addition, assume FSub is engaged in the active conduct of manufacturing and selling widgets and derives more than 50% of its gross income from such business.

(*ii*) *Result*. The result is the same as in paragraph (e)(5)(vii)(D)(*1*)(*ii*) of this section (the result in *Example 1*), except that Newco's income is tested income rather than subpart F income, and if the $36 million foreign payment were an amount of foreign income tax paid USP would be deemed to pay a portion of the foreign payment under section 960(d), rather than section 960(a). Although Newco wholly owns FSub, which is engaged in the active conduct of manufacturing and selling widgets and derives more than 50% of its income from such business, Newco's income that is attributable to Newco's equity interest in FSub is passive investment income because the sale-repurchase transaction limits FP's interest in Newco and its assets to that of a creditor, so that substantially all of Newco's opportunity for gain and risk of loss with respect to its stock in FSub is borne by USP. See paragraph (e)(5)(vii)(C)(*5*)(*ii*) of this section. Accordingly, Newco's stock in FSub is held to produce passive investment income. Thus, Newco is an SPV because all of Newco's income is passive investment income described in paragraph (e)(5)(vii)(C)(*5*) of this section, Newco's assets are held to produce such income, the payment to Country M is attributable to such income, and if the payment were an amount of foreign income tax paid it would be paid in a U.S. taxable year in which Newco meets the requirements of paragraph (e)(5)(vii)(B)(*1*)(*i*) of this section.

(*3*) *Example 3: U.S. borrower transaction*.—(*i*) *Facts*. A domestic corporation (USP) loans $750 million to its wholly-owned domestic subsidiary (Sub). USP and Sub form a Country M partnership (Partnership) to which each contributes $750 million. Partnership loans all of its $1.5 billion of capital to Issuer, a wholly-owned Country M affiliate of USP, in exchange for a note and coupons providing for the payment of interest at a fixed rate over a five-year term. Partnership sells all of the coupons to Coupon Purchaser, a Country N partnership owned by a Country M corporation (Foreign Bank) and a wholly-owned Country M subsidiary of Foreign Bank, for $300 million. At the time of the coupon sale, the fair market value of the coupons sold is $290 million and, pursuant to section 1286(b)(3), Partnership's basis allocated to the coupons sold is $290 million. Several months later and prior to any interest payments on the note, Foreign Bank and its subsidiary sell all of their interests in Coupon Purchaser to an unrelated Country O corporation for $280 million. None of Foreign Bank's stock or its subsidiary's stock is owned, directly or indirectly, by USP or Sub or by any shareholders of USP or Sub that are domestic corporations, U.S. citizens, or resident alien individuals. Assume that both the United States and Country M respect the sale of the coupons for tax law purposes. In the year of the coupon sale, for Country M tax purposes USP's and Sub's shares of Partnership's profits total $300 million, a payment of $60 million to Country M is made with respect to those profits, and Foreign Bank and its subsidiary, as partners of Coupon Purchaser, are entitled to deduct the $300 million purchase price of the coupons from their taxable income. For U.S. tax purposes, USP and Sub recognize their distributive shares of the $10 million premium income and claim a direct foreign tax credit for their shares of the $60 million payment to Country M. Country M imposes no additional tax when Foreign Bank and its subsidiary sell their interests in Coupon Purchaser. Country M also does not impose Country M tax on interest received by U.S. residents from sources in Country M.

(*ii*) *Result.* The payment to Country M is not a compulsory payment, and thus is not an amount of foreign income tax paid, because the foreign payment is attributable to a structured passive investment arrangement. First, Partnership is an SPV because all of Partnership's income is passive investment income described in paragraph (e)(5)(vii)(C)(*5*) of this section; Partnership's only asset, Issuer's note, is held to produce such income; the payment to Country M is attributable to such income; and if the payment were an amount of foreign income tax paid, it would be paid in a U.S. taxable year in which Partnership meets the requirements of paragraph (e)(5)(vii)(B)(*1*)(*i*) of this section. Second, if the foreign payment were an amount of tax paid, USP and Sub would be eligible to claim a credit for such payment under section 901(a). Third, USP and Sub would not pay any Country M tax if they directly owned Issuer's note. Fourth, for Country M tax purposes, Foreign Bank and its subsidiary deduct the $300 million purchase price of the coupons and are exempt from Country M tax on the $280 million received upon the sale of Coupon Purchaser, and the deduction and exemption correspond to more than 10% of the $300 million base with respect to which USP's and Sub's 100% share of the foreign payments was imposed. Fifth, Foreign Bank and its subsidiary are counterparties because they indirectly acquired assets of Partnership, the interest coupons on Issuer's note, and are not directly or indirectly owned by USP or Sub or shareholders of USP or Sub that are domestic corporations, U.S. citizens, or resident alien individuals. Sixth, the amount of taxable income of Partnership for one or more years is different for U.S. and Country M tax purposes, and the amount of income attributable to USP and Sub for U.S. tax purposes is materially less than the amount of income they would recognize if the Country M tax treatment of the coupon sale controlled for U.S. tax purposes. Because the payment to Country M is not an amount of foreign income tax paid, USP and Sub are not considered to pay tax under section 901. USP and Sub have income of $10 million in the year of the coupon sale.

(4) *Example 4: Active business; no SPV.*—(*i*) *Facts.* A, a domestic corporation, wholly owns B, a Country X corporation engaged in the manufacture and sale of widgets. On January 1, Year 1, C, also a Country X corporation, loans $400 million to B in exchange for an instrument that is debt for U.S. tax purposes and equity in B for Country X tax purposes. As a result, C is considered to own stock of B for Country X tax purposes. B loans $55 million to D, a Country Y corporation wholly owned by A. In year 1, B has $166 million of net income attributable to its sales of widgets and $3.3 million of interest income attributable to the loan to D. Substantially all of B's assets are used in its widget business. Country Y does not impose tax on interest paid to nonresidents. B makes a payment of $50.8 million to Country X with respect to B's net income. Country X does not impose tax on dividend payments between Country X corporations. None of C's stock is owned, directly or indirectly, by A or by any shareholders of A that are domestic corporations, U.S. citizens, or resident alien individuals.

(*ii*) *Result.* B is not an SPV within the meaning of paragraph (e)(5)(vii)(B)(*1*) of this section because the amount of interest income received from D does not constitute substantially all of B's income and the $55 million note from D does not constitute substantially all of B's assets. Accordingly, the $50.8 million payment to Country X is not attributable to a structured passive investment arrangement.

(5) *Example 5: U.S. lender transaction.*—(*i*) *Facts.* A Country X corporation (Foreign Bank) contributes $2 billion to a newly-formed Country X company (Newco) in exchange for 90% of the common stock of Newco and securities that are treated as debt of Newco for U.S. tax purposes and preferred stock of Newco for Country X tax purposes. A domestic corporation (USP) contributes $1 billion to Newco in exchange for 10% of Newco's common stock and securities that are treated as preferred stock of Newco for U.S. tax purposes and debt of Newco for Country X tax purposes. Newco loans the $3 billion to a wholly-owned, Country X subsidiary of Foreign Bank (FSub) in return for a $3 billion, seven-year note paying interest currently. The Newco securities held by USP represent more than 50% of the voting power in Newco and more than 50% of the value of the securities in Newco that are treated as equity for U.S. tax purposes. The Newco securities held by USP entitle the holder to fixed distributions of $4 million per year, and the Newco securities held by Foreign Bank entitle the holder to receive $82 million per year, payable only on maturity of the $3 billion FSub note in Year 7. At the end of Year 5, pursuant to a prearranged plan, Foreign Bank acquires USP's Newco stock and securities for a prearranged price of $1 billion. Country X does not impose tax on dividends received by one Country X corporation from a second Country X corporation. Under an income tax treaty between Country X and the United States, Country X does not impose Country X tax on interest received by U.S. residents from sources in Country X. None of Foreign Bank's stock is owned, directly or indirectly, by USP or any shareholders of USP that are domestic corporations, U.S. citizens, or resident alien individuals. In each of Years 1 through 7, FSub pays Newco $124 million of interest on the $3 billion note. Newco distributes $4 million to USP in each of Years 1 through 5. The distributions are deductible for Country X tax purposes, and Newco pays Country X $36 million with respect to $120 million of taxable income from the FSub note in each year. For U.S. tax purposes, in each year Newco's subpart F income and earnings and profits are increased by $124 million of interest income and reduced by accrued interest expense with respect to the Newco securities held by Foreign Bank.

(*ii*) *Result.* The $36 million payment to Country X is not a compulsory payment, and thus is not an amount of foreign income tax paid, because the foreign payment is attributable to a structured passive investment arrangement. First, Newco is an SPV because all of Newco's income is passive investment income described in paragraph (e)(5)(vii)(C)(*5*) of this section; Newco's only asset, a note of FSub, is held to produce such income; the payment to Country X is attributable to such income; and if the payment were an amount of foreign income tax paid it would be paid in a U.S. taxable year in which Newco meets the requirements of paragraph (e)(5)(vii)(B)(*1*)(*i*) of this section. Second, if the foreign payment were an amount of foreign income tax paid, USP would be deemed to pay its pro rata share of the foreign payment under section 960(a) in each of Years 1 through 5 and, therefore, would be eligible to claim a credit under section 901(a). Third, USP would not pay any Country X tax if it directly owned its proportionate share of Newco's assets, a note of FSub. Fourth, for Country X tax purposes, Foreign Bank is eligible to receive a tax-free distribution of $82 million attributable to each of Years 1 through 5, and that amount corresponds to more than 10% of the foreign base with respect to which USP's share of the foreign payment was imposed. Fifth, Foreign Bank is a counterparty because it owns stock of Newco for Country X tax purposes and none of Foreign Bank's stock is owned, directly or indirectly, by USP or shareholders of USP that are domestic corporations, U.S. citizens, or resident alien individuals. Sixth, the United States and Country X treat various aspects of the arrangement differently, including whether the Newco securities held by Foreign Bank and USP are debt or equity. The amount of credits claimed by USP if the payment to Country X were an amount of foreign income tax paid is materially greater than it would be if the Country X tax treatment controlled for U.S. tax purposes such that the securities held by USP were treated as debt or the securities held by Foreign Bank were treated as equity, and the amount of income recognized by Newco for U.S. tax purposes is materially less than the amount of income recognized for Country X tax purposes. Because the payment to Country X is not an amount of foreign income tax paid, USP is not deemed to pay any Country X tax under section 960(a). USP has a subpart F inclusion of $4 million in each of Years 1 through 5.

(6) *Example 6: Holding company; no SPV.*—(*i*) *Facts.* A, a Country X corporation, and B, a domestic corporation, each contribute $1 billion to a newly-formed Country X entity (C) in exchange for 50% of the common stock of C. C is treated as a corporation for Country X purposes and a partnership for U.S. tax purposes. C contributes $1.95 billion to a newly-formed Country X corporation (D) in exchange for 100% of D's common stock. C loans its remaining $50 million to D. Accordingly, C's sole assets are stock and debt of D. D uses the entire $2 billion to engage in the business of manufacturing and selling widgets. In Year 1, D derives $300 million of income from its widget business and derives $2 million of interest income. Also in Year 1, C has dividend income of $200 million and interest income of $3.2 million with respect to its investment in D. Country X does not impose tax on dividends received by one Country X corporation from a second Country X corporation. C makes a payment of $960,000 to Country X with respect to C's net income.

(*ii*) *Result.* C qualifies for the holding company exception described in paragraph (e)(5)(vii)(C)(*5*)(*ii*) of this section because C holds a qualified equity interest in D, D is engaged in an active trade or business and derives more than 50% of its gross income from such trade or business, C's interest in D constitutes substantially all of C's assets, and A and B share in substantially all of C's opportunity for gain and risk of loss with respect to D. As a result, C's dividend income from D is not passive investment income and C's stock in D is not held to produce such income. Accordingly, C is not an SPV within the meaning of paragraph (e)(5)(vii)(B)(*1*) of this section, and the $960,000 payment to Country X is not attributable to a structured passive investment arrangement.

(7) *Example 7: Holding company; no SPV*.—(*i*) *Facts*. The facts are the same as those in paragraph (e)(5)(vii)(D)(*6*)(*i*) of this section (the facts in *Example 6*), except that instead of loaning $50 million to D, C contributes the $50 million to E in exchange for 10% of the stock of E. E is a Country Y corporation that is not engaged in the active conduct of a trade or business. Also in Year 1, D pays no dividends to C, E pays $3.2 million in dividends to C, and C makes a payment of $960,000 to Country X with respect to C's net income.

(*ii*) *Result*. C qualifies for the holding company exception described in paragraph (e)(5)(vii)(C)(*5*)(*ii*) of this section because C holds a qualified equity interest in D, D is engaged in an active trade or business and derives more than 50% of its gross income from such trade or business, C's interest in D constitutes substantially all of C's assets, and A and B share in substantially all of C's opportunity for gain and risk of loss with respect to D. As a result, less than substantially all of C's assets are held to produce passive investment income. Accordingly, C is not an SPV because it does not meet the requirements of paragraph (e)(5)(vii)(B)(*1*) of this section, and the $960,000 payment to Country X is not attributable to a structured passive investment arrangement.

(8) *Example 8: Holding company; no SPV*.—(*i*) *Facts*. The facts are the same as those in paragraph (e)(5)(vii)(D)(*6*)(*i*) of this section (the facts in *Example 6*), except that B's $1 billion investment in C consists of 30% of C's common stock and 100% of C's preferred stock. A's $1 billion investment in C consists of 70% of C's common stock. B sells its preferred stock to F, a Country X corporation, subject to a repurchase obligation. Assume that under Country X tax law, but not U.S. tax law, F is treated as the owner of the preferred shares and receives a distribution in Year 1 of $50 million. The remaining earnings are distributed 70% to A and 30% to B.

(*ii*) *Result*. C qualifies for the holding company exception described in paragraph (e)(5)(vii)(C)(*5*)(*ii*) of this section because C holds a qualified equity interest in D, D is engaged in an active trade or business and derives more than 50% of its gross income from such trade or business, and C's interest in D constitutes substantially all of C's assets. Additionally, although F does not share in C's opportunity for gain and risk of loss with respect to C's interest in D because F acquired its interest in C in a sale-repurchase transaction, B (the U.S. party) and in the aggregate A and F (who would be counterparties assuming C were an SPV) share in substantially all of C's opportunity for gain and risk of loss with respect to D and such opportunity for gain and risk of loss is not borne exclusively either by B or by A and F in the aggregate. Accordingly, C's shares in D are not held to produce passive investment income and the $200 million dividend from D is not passive investment income. C is not an SPV within the meaning of paragraph (e)(5)(vii)(B)(*1*) of this section, and the $960,000 payment to Country X is not attributable to a structured passive investment arrangement.

(9) *Example 9: Asset holding transaction*.—(*i*) *Facts*. A domestic corporation (USP) contributes $6 billion of Country Z debt obligations to a Country Z entity (DE) in exchange for all of the class A and class B stock of DE. DE is a disregarded entity for U.S. tax purposes and a corporation for Country Z tax purposes. A corporation unrelated to USP and organized in Country Z (FC) contributes $1.5 billion to DE in exchange for all of the class C stock of DE. DE uses the $1.5 billion contributed by FC to redeem USP's class B stock. The terms of the class C stock entitle its holder to all income from DE, but FC is obligated immediately to contribute back to DE all distributions on the class C stock. USP and FC enter into a contract under which USP agrees to buy after five years the class C stock for $1.5 billion and an agreement under which USP agrees to pay FC periodic payments on $1.5 billion. The transaction is structured in such a way that, for U.S. tax purposes, there is a loan of $1.5 billion from FC to USP, and USP is the owner of the class C stock and the class A stock. In Year 1, DE earns $400 million of interest income on the Country Z debt obligations. DE makes a payment to Country Z of $100 million with respect to such income and distributes the remaining $300 million to FC. FC contributes the $300 million back to DE. None of FC's stock is owned, directly or indirectly, by USP or shareholders of USP that are domestic corporations, U.S. citizens, or resident alien individuals. Assume that Country Z imposes a withholding tax on interest income derived by U.S. residents. Country Z treats FC as the owner of the class C stock. Pursuant to Country Z tax law, FC is required to report the $400 million of income with respect to the $300 million distribution from DE, but is allowed to claim credits for DE's $100 million payment to Country Z. For Country Z tax purposes, FC is entitled to current deductions equal to the $300 million contributed back to DE.

(*ii*) *Result*. The payment to Country Z is not a compulsory payment, and thus is not an amount of foreign income tax paid, because the payment is attributable to a structured passive investment arrangement. First, DE is an SPV because all of DE's income is passive investment income described in paragraph (e)(5)(vii)(C)(*5*) of this section; all of DE's assets are held to produce such income; the payment to Country Z is attributable to such income; and if the payment were an amount of tax paid it would be paid in a U.S. taxable year in which DE meets the requirements of paragraph (e)(5)(vii)(B)(*1*)(*i*) of this section. Second, if the payment were an amount of foreign income tax paid, USP would be eligible to claim a credit for such amount under section 901(a). Third, USP's proportionate share of DE's foreign payment of $100 million is substantially greater than the amount of credits USP would be eligible to claim if it directly held its proportionate share of DE's assets, excluding any assets that would produce income subject to gross basis withholding tax if directly held by USP. Fourth, FC is entitled to claim a credit under Country Z tax law for the payment and recognizes a deduction for the $300 million contributed to DE under Country Z law. The credit claimed by FC corresponds to more than 10% of USP's share (for U.S. tax purposes) of the foreign payment and the deductions claimed by FC correspond to more than 10% of the base with respect to which USP's share of the foreign payment was imposed. Fifth, FC is a counterparty because FC is considered to own equity of DE under Country Z law and none of FC's stock is owned, directly or indirectly, by USP or shareholders of USP that are domestic corporations, U.S. citizens, or resident alien individuals. Sixth, the United States and Country Z treat certain aspects of the transaction differently, including the proportion of equity owned in DE by USP and FC, and the amount of credits claimed by USP if the Country Z payment were an amount of tax paid is materially greater than it would be if the Country Z tax treatment controlled for U.S. tax purposes such that FC, rather than USP, owned the class C stock. Because the payment to Country Z is not an amount of foreign income tax paid, USP is not considered to pay tax under section 901. USP has $400 million of interest income.

(10) *Example 10: Loss surrender*.—(*i*) *Facts*. The facts are the same as those in paragraph (e)(5)(vii)(D)(*9*)(*i*) of this section (the facts in *Example 9*), except that the deductions attributable to the arrangement contribute to a loss recognized by FC for Country Z tax purposes, and pursuant to a group relief regime in Country Z FC elects to surrender the loss to its Country Z subsidiary.

(*ii*) *Result*. The results are the same as in paragraph (e)(5)(vii)(D)(*9*)(*ii*) of this section (the results in *Example 9*). The surrender of the loss to a related party is a foreign tax benefit that corresponds to the base with respect to which USP's share of the foreign payment was imposed.

(11) *Example 11: Joint venture; no foreign tax benefit*.—(*i*) *Facts*. FC, a Country X corporation, and USC, a domestic corporation, each contribute $1 billion to a newly-formed Country X entity (C) in exchange for stock of C. FC and USC are entitled to equal 50% shares of all of C's income, gain, expense and loss. C is treated as a corporation for Country X purposes and a partnership for U.S. tax purposes. In Year 1, C earns $200 million of net passive investment income, makes a payment to Country X of $60 million with respect to that income, and distributes $70 million to each of FC and USC. Country X does not impose tax on dividends received by one Country X corporation from a second Country X corporation.

(*ii*) *Result*. FC's tax-exempt receipt of $70 million, or its 50% share of C's profits, is not a foreign tax benefit within the meaning of paragraph (e)(5)(vii)(B)(*4*) of this section because it does not correspond to any part of the foreign base with respect to which USC's share of the foreign payment was imposed. Accordingly, the $60 million payment to Country X is not attributable to a structured passive investment arrangement.

(12) *Example 12: Joint venture; no foreign tax benefit*.—(*i*) *Facts*. The facts are the same as those in paragraph (e)(5)(vii)(D)(*11*)(*i*) of this section (the facts in *Example 11*), except that C in turn contributes $2 billion to a wholly-owned and newly-formed Country X entity (D) in exchange for stock of D. D is treated as a corporation for Country X purposes and disregarded as an entity separate from its owner for U.S. tax purposes. C has no other assets and earns no other income. In Year 1, D earns $200 million of passive investment income, makes a payment to Country X of $60 million with respect to that income, and distributes $140 million to C.

(*ii*) *Result*. C's tax-exempt receipt of $140 million is not a foreign tax benefit within the meaning of paragraph (e)(5)(vii)(B)(*4*) of this section because it does not correspond to any part of the foreign base with respect to which USC's share of the foreign payment was imposed. Fifty percent of C's foreign tax exemption is not a foreign tax benefit within the meaning of paragraph (e)(5)(vii)(B)(*4*) of this section because it relates to earnings of D that are distributed with respect to an equity interest in D that is owned indirectly by USC under both U.S. and foreign tax law. The remaining 50% of C's foreign tax exemption, as well as FC's tax-exempt receipt of $70 million from C, is also not a foreign tax benefit because it does not correspond to any part of the foreign base with respect to which USC's share of the foreign payment was imposed. Accordingly, the $60 million payment to Country X is not attributable to a structured passive investment arrangement.

(6) *Soak-up taxes*.—(i) *In general*.—An amount remitted to a foreign country is not an amount of foreign income tax paid to the extent that liability for the foreign income tax is dependent (by its terms or otherwise) on the availability of a credit for the tax against income tax liability to another country. Liability for foreign income tax is dependent on the availability of a credit for the foreign income tax against income tax liability to another country only if and to the extent that the foreign income tax would not be imposed but for the availability of such a credit.

(ii) *Examples*.—The following examples illustrate the application of paragraph (e)(6)(i) of this section.

(A) *Example 1: Tax rates dependent on availability of credit*.—(*1*) *Facts*. Country X imposes a tax on the receipt of royalties from sources in Country X by nonresidents of Country X. The tax is 15% of the gross amount of such royalties unless the recipient is a resident of the United States or of country A, B, C, or D, in which case the tax is 20% of the gross amount of such royalties. Like the United States, each of countries A, B, C, and D allows its residents a credit against the income tax otherwise payable to it for income taxes paid to other countries.

(*2*) *Analysis*. Because the 20% rate applies only to residents of countries that allow a credit for taxes paid to other countries and the 15% rate applies to residents of countries that do not allow such a credit, one-fourth of the Country X tax would not be imposed on residents of the United States but for the availability of such a credit. One-fourth of the Country X tax imposed on residents of the United States who receive royalties from sources in Country X is dependent on the availability of a credit for the Country X tax against income tax liability to another country and, accordingly, under paragraph (e)(6)(i) of this section that amount is not an amount of foreign income tax paid.

(B) *Example 2: Tax not dependent on availability of credit*.—(*1*) *Facts*. Country X imposes a net income tax on the realized net income of nonresidents of Country X from carrying on a trade or business in Country X. Although Country X tax law does not prohibit other nonresidents from carrying on business in Country X, United States persons are the only nonresidents of Country X that carry on business in Country X. The Country X tax would be imposed in its entirety on a nonresident of Country X irrespective of the availability of a credit for the Country X tax against income tax liability to another country.

(*2*) *Analysis*. Because no portion of the Country X tax liability is dependent on the availability of a credit for such tax in another country, under paragraph (e)(6)(i) of this section no portion of the Country X tax is a soak-up tax.

(C) *Example 3: Tax holiday denied to corporations with shareholders eligible for credit*.—(*1*) *Facts*. Country X imposes a net income tax on the realized net income of all corporations incorporated in Country X. Country X allows a tax holiday to qualifying corporations incorporated in Country X that are owned by nonresidents of Country X, pursuant to which no Country X tax is imposed on the net income of a qualifying corporation for the first 10 years of its operations in Country X. A corporation qualifies for the tax holiday if it meets certain minimum investment criteria and if the development office of Country X certifies that in its opinion the operations of the corporation will be consistent with specified development goals of Country X. The development office will not issue this certification to any corporation owned by persons resident in countries that allow a credit to shareholders (such as a deemed paid credit under section 960) for Country X tax paid by a corporation incorporated in Country X. In practice, tax holidays are granted to a large number of corporations, but the Country X net income tax is imposed on a significant number of other corporations incorporated in Country X (for example, those owned by Country X persons and those which have had operations for more than 10 years) in addition to corporations denied a tax holiday because their shareholders qualify for a credit for the Country X tax against income tax liability to another country.

(*2*) *Analysis*. Under paragraph (e)(6)(i) of this section, no portion of the Country X tax paid by Country X corporations denied a tax holiday because they have U.S. shareholders is dependent on the availability of a credit for the Country X tax against income tax liability to another country, because a significant number of other Country X corporations pay the Country X tax irrespective of the availability of a credit to their shareholders.

(D) *Example 4: Tax deferral allowed for corporations with shareholders eligible for credit*.—(*1*) *Facts*. The facts are the same as those in paragraph (e)(6)(ii)(C)(*1*) of this section (the facts of *Example 3*), except that Country X corporations owned by persons resident in countries that allow a credit for Country X tax when dividends are distributed by the corporations are granted a provisional tax holiday. Under the provisional tax holiday, instead of relieving such a corporation from Country X tax for 10 years, liability for such tax is deferred until the Country X corporation distributes dividends.

(*2*) *Analysis*. Because a significant number of other Country X corporations pay the Country X tax irrespective of the availability of a credit to their shareholders, the result is the same as in paragraph (e)(6)(ii)(C)(*2*) of this section.

(E) *Example 5: Tax based on greater of tax in lieu of income tax or amount eligible for credit*.—(*1*) *Facts*. Pursuant to a contract with Country X, A, a domestic corporation engaged in manufacturing activities in Country X, must pay tax to Country X equal to the greater of 5u (units of Country X currency) per item produced, or the maximum amount creditable by A against its U.S. income tax liability for that year with respect to income from its Country X operations. Also pursuant to the contract, A is exempted from Country X's otherwise generally-imposed net income tax. The contractual tax is a tax in lieu of income tax as defined in § 1.903-1(b). In Year 1, A produces 16 items, which would result in Country X tax of 16 × 5u = 80u, and taking into account the section 904 limitation, the maximum amount of Country X tax that A can claim as a credit against its U.S. income tax liability is 125u. Accordingly, A's contractual liability for Country X tax in lieu of income tax is 125u, the greater of the two amounts.

(*2*) *Analysis*. Under paragraph (e)(6)(i) of this section, the amount of tax paid by A that is dependent on the availability of a credit against income tax of another country is 125u–80u = 45u, the amount that would not be imposed but for the availability of a credit.

(f) *Taxpayer*.—(1) *In general*.—The person by whom tax is considered paid for purposes of sections 901 and 903 is the person on whom foreign law imposes legal liability for such tax, even if another person (*e.g.*, a withholding agent) remits such tax. For purposes of this section, § 1.901-2A and § 1.903-1, the person on whom foreign law imposes such liability is referred to as the "taxpayer." A foreign tax of a type described in paragraph (a)(2)(ii)(C) of this section is considered to be imposed on the recipients of wages if such tax is deducted from such wages under provisions that are comparable to section 3102(a) and (b) of the Internal Revenue Code.

(2) *Party undertaking tax obligation as part of transaction*.—(i) *In general*.—Tax is considered paid by the taxpayer even if another party to a direct or indirect transaction with the taxpayer agrees, as a part of the transaction, to assume the taxpayer's foreign tax liability. The rules of the foregoing sentence apply notwithstanding anything to the contrary in paragraph (e)(3) of this section. See § 1.901-2A for additional rules regarding dual capacity taxpayers.

(ii) *Examples*.—The following examples illustrate the rules of paragraphs (f)(1) and (2)(i) of this section.

(A) *Example 1*.—Under a loan agreement between A, a resident of Country X, and B, a United States person, A agrees to pay B a certain amount of interest net of any tax that Country X may impose on B with respect to its interest income. Country X imposes a 10 percent tax on the gross amount of interest income received by nonresidents of Country X from sources in Country X, and it is established that this tax is a tax in lieu of an income tax within the meaning of § 1.903-1(b). Under the law of Country X this tax is imposed on the nonresident recipient, and any resident of Country X that pays such interest to a nonresident is required to withhold and pay over to Country X 10 percent of the amount of such interest, which is applied to offset the recipient's liability for the tax. Because legal liability for the tax is imposed on the recipient of such interest income, B is the taxpayer with respect to the Country X tax imposed on B's interest income from B's loan to A. Accordingly, B's interest income for Federal income tax purposes includes the amount of Country X tax that is imposed on B with respect to such interest income and that is paid on B's behalf by A pursuant to the loan agreement, and, under paragraph (f)(2)(i) of this section, such tax is considered for purposes of section 903 to be paid by B.

(B) *Example 2.*—The facts are the same as those in paragraph (f)(2)(ii)(A) of this section (the facts in *Example 1*), except that in collecting and receiving the interest B is acting as a nominee for, or agent of, C, who is a United States person. Because C (not B) is the beneficial owner of the interest, legal liability for the tax is imposed on C, not B (C's nominee or agent). Thus, C is the taxpayer with respect to the Country X tax imposed on C's interest income from C's loan to A. Accordingly, C's interest income for Federal income tax purposes includes the amount of Country X tax that is imposed on C with respect to such interest income and that is paid on C's behalf by A pursuant to the loan agreement. Under paragraph (f)(2)(i) of this section, such tax is considered for purposes of section 903 to be paid by C. No such tax is considered paid by B.

(C) *Example 3.*—Country X imposes a tax called the "Country X income tax." A, a United States person engaged in construction activities in Country X, is subject to that tax. Country X has contracted with A for A to construct a naval base. A is a dual capacity taxpayer (as defined in paragraph (a)(2)(ii)(A) of this section) and, in accordance with paragraphs (a)(1) and (c)(1) of § 1.901-2A, A has established that the Country X income tax as applied to dual capacity persons and the Country X income tax as applied to persons other than dual capacity persons together constitute a single levy. A has also established that that levy is a net income tax within the meaning of paragraph (a)(3) of this section. Pursuant to the terms of the contract, Country X has agreed to assume any Country X tax liability that A may incur with respect to A's income from the contract. For Federal income tax purposes, A's income from the contract includes the amount of tax liability that is imposed by Country X on A with respect to its income from the contract and that is assumed by Country X; and for purposes of section 901 the amount of such tax liability assumed by Country X is considered to be paid by A. By reason of paragraph (f)(2)(i) of this section, Country X is not considered to provide a subsidy, within the meaning of paragraph (e)(3) of this section, to A.

(3) *Taxes imposed on combined income of two or more persons.*—(i) *In general.*—If foreign tax is imposed on the combined income of two or more persons (for example, a husband and wife or a corporation and one or more of its subsidiaries), foreign law is considered to impose legal liability on each such person for the amount of the tax that is attributable to such person's portion of the base of the tax. Therefore, if foreign tax is imposed on the combined income of two or more persons, such tax is allocated among, and considered paid by, such persons on a pro rata basis in proportion to each person's portion of the combined income, as determined under foreign law and paragraph (f)(3)(iii) of this section. Combined income with respect to each foreign tax that is imposed on a combined basis is computed separately, and the tax on that combined income is allocated separately under this paragraph (f)(3)(i). If foreign law exempts from tax, or provides for specific rates of tax with respect to, certain types of income, or if certain expenses, deductions or credits are taken into account only with respect to a particular type of income, combined income with respect to such portions of the combined income is also computed separately, and the tax on that combined income is allocated separately under this paragraph (f)(3)(i). The rules of this paragraph (f)(3) apply regardless of which person is obligated to remit the tax, which person actually remits the tax, or which person the foreign country could proceed against to collect the tax in the event all or a portion of the tax is not paid. For purposes of this paragraph (f)(3), the term *person* means an individual or an entity (including a disregarded entity described in § 301.7701-2(c)(2)(i) of this chapter) that is subject to tax in a foreign country as a corporation (or otherwise at the entity level). In determining the amount of tax paid by an owner of a partnership or a disregarded entity, this paragraph (f)(3) first applies to determine the amount of tax paid by the partnership or disregarded entity, and then paragraph (f)(4) of this section applies to allocate the amount of such tax to the owner.

(ii) *Combined income.*—For purposes of this paragraph (f)(3), foreign tax is imposed on the combined income of two or more persons if such persons compute their taxable income on a combined basis under foreign law and foreign tax would otherwise be imposed on each such person on its separate taxable income. For example, income is computed on a combined basis if two or more persons add their items of income, gain, deduction, and loss to compute a single consolidated taxable income amount for foreign tax purposes. Foreign tax is considered to be imposed on the combined income of two or more persons even if the combined income is computed under foreign law by attributing to one such person (for example, the foreign parent of a foreign consolidated group) the income of other such persons or by treating persons that would otherwise be subject to tax as separate entities as unincorporated branches of a single corporation for purposes of computing the foreign tax on the combined income of the group. However, foreign tax is not considered to be imposed on the combined income of two or more persons if, because one or more persons is a fiscally transparent entity (under the principles of § 1.894-1(d)(3)) under foreign law, only one of such persons is subject to tax under foreign law (even if two or more of such persons are corporations for U.S. Federal income tax purposes). Therefore, foreign tax is not considered to be imposed on the combined income of two or more persons solely because foreign law:

(A) Permits one person to surrender a loss to another person pursuant to a group relief or other loss-sharing regime described in § 1.909-2(b)(2)(vi);

(B) Requires a shareholder of a corporation to include in income amounts attributable to taxes imposed on the corporation with respect to distributed earnings, pursuant to an integrated tax system that allows the shareholder a credit for such taxes;

(C) Requires a shareholder to include, pursuant to an anti-deferral regime (similar to subpart F of the Internal Revenue Code (sections 951 through 965)), income attributable to the shareholder's interest in the corporation;

(D) Reallocates income from one person to a related person under foreign transfer pricing rules;

(E) Requires a person to take into account a distributive share of income of an entity that is a partnership or other fiscally transparent entity for foreign tax law purposes; or

(F) Requires a person to take all or part of the income of an entity that is a corporation for U.S. Federal income tax purposes into account because foreign law treats the entity as a branch or fiscally transparent entity (a reverse hybrid). A reverse hybrid does not include an entity that is treated under foreign law as a branch or fiscally transparent entity solely for purposes of calculating combined income of a foreign consolidated group.

(iii) *Portion of combined income.*—(A) *In general.*—Each person's portion of the combined income is determined by reference to any return, schedule or other document that must be filed or maintained with respect to a person showing such person's income for foreign tax purposes, as properly amended or adjusted for foreign tax purposes. If no such return, schedule or other document must be filed or maintained with respect to a person for foreign tax purposes, then, for purposes of this paragraph (f)(3), such person's income is determined from the books of account regularly maintained by or on behalf of the person for purposes of computing its income for foreign tax purposes. Each person's portion of the combined income is determined by adjusting such person's income determined under this paragraph (f)(3)(iii)(A) as provided in paragraph (f)(3)(iii)(B) and (f)(3)(iii)(C) of this section.

(B) *Effect of certain payments.*—*(1)* Each person's portion of the combined income is determined by giving effect to payments and accrued amounts of interest, rents, royalties, and other amounts between persons whose income is included in the combined base to the extent such amounts would be taken into account in computing the separate taxable incomes of such persons under foreign law if they did not compute their income on a combined basis. Each person's portion of the combined income is determined without taking into account any payments from other persons whose income is included in the combined base that are treated as dividends or other non-deductible distributions with respect to equity under foreign law, and without taking into account deemed dividends or any similar attribution of income made for purposes of computing the combined income under foreign law, regardless of whether any such deemed dividend or attribution of income results in a deduction or inclusion under foreign law.

(2) For purposes of determining each person's portion of the combined income, the treatment of a payment is determined under foreign law. Thus, for example, interest accrued by one group member with respect to an instrument held by another member that is treated as debt for foreign tax purposes but as equity for U.S. Federal income tax purposes would be considered income of the holder and would reduce the income of the issuer. See also

§ 1.909-2(b)(3)(i) for rules requiring suspension of foreign income taxes paid or accrued by the owner of a U.S. equity hybrid instrument.

(C) *Net losses.*—If tax is considered to be imposed on the combined income of three or more persons and one or more of such persons has a net loss for the taxable year for foreign tax purposes, the following rules apply. If foreign law provides mandatory rules for allocating the net loss among the other persons, then the rules that apply for foreign tax purposes apply for purposes of this paragraph (f)(3). If foreign law does not provide mandatory rules for allocating the net loss, the net loss is allocated among all other such persons on a pro rata basis in proportion to the amount of each person's income, as determined under paragraphs (f)(3)(iii)(A) and (f)(3)(iii)(B) of this section. For purposes of this paragraph (f)(3)(iii)(C), foreign law is not considered to provide mandatory rules for allocating a net loss solely because such loss is attributed from one person to a second person for purposes of computing combined income, as described in paragraph (f)(3)(ii) of this section.

(iv) *Collateral consequences.*—U.S. tax principles apply to determine the tax consequences if one person remits a tax that is the legal liability of, and thus is considered paid by, another person.

(4) *Taxes imposed on partnerships and disregarded entities.*—(i) *Partnerships.*—If foreign law imposes tax at the entity level on the income of a partnership, the partnership is considered to be legally liable for such tax under foreign law and therefore is considered to pay the tax for Federal income tax purposes. The rules of this paragraph (f)(4)(i) apply regardless of which person is obligated to remit the tax, which person actually remits the tax, or which person the foreign country could proceed against to collect the tax in the event all or a portion of the tax is not paid. See §§ 1.702-1(a)(6) and 1.704-1(b)(4)(viii) for rules relating to the determination of a partner's distributive share of such tax.

(ii) *Disregarded entities.*—If foreign law imposes tax at the entity level on the income of an entity described in § 301.7701-2(c)(2)(i) of this chapter (a *disregarded entity*), the person (as defined in section 7701(a)(1)) who is treated as owning the assets of the disregarded entity for Federal income tax purposes is considered to be legally liable for such tax under foreign law. Such person is considered to pay the tax for Federal income tax purposes. The rules of this paragraph (f)(4)(ii) apply regardless of which person is obligated to remit the tax, which person actually remits the tax, or which person the foreign country could proceed against to collect the tax in the event all or a portion of the tax is not paid.

(5) *Allocation of taxes in the case of certain ownership or classification changes.*—(i) *In general.*—If a partnership, disregarded entity, or corporation undergoes one or more covered events during its foreign taxable year that do not result in a closing of the foreign taxable year, then a portion of the foreign income tax (other than a withholding tax described in section 901(k)(1)(B)) paid by a person under paragraphs (f)(1) through (4) of this section with respect to the continuing foreign taxable year in which such covered event or events occur is allocated to and among all persons that were predecessor entities or prior owners during such foreign taxable year. The allocation is made based on the respective portions of the taxable income (as determined under foreign law) for the continuing foreign taxable year that are attributable under the principles of § 1.1502-76(b) to the period of existence or ownership of each predecessor entity or prior owner during the continuing foreign taxable year. Foreign income tax allocated to a person that is a predecessor entity is treated (other than for purposes of section 986) as paid by the person as of the close of the last day of its last U.S. taxable year. Foreign income tax allocated to a person that is a prior owner, for example a transferor of a disregarded entity, is treated (other than for purposes of section 986) as paid by the person as of the close of the last day of its U.S. taxable year in which the covered event occurred.

(ii) *Covered event.*—For purposes of this paragraph (f)(5), a covered event is a partnership termination under section 708(b)(1), a transfer of a disregarded entity, or a change in the entity classification of a disregarded entity or a corporation.

(iii) *Predecessor entity and prior owner.*—For purposes of this paragraph (f)(5), a predecessor entity is a partnership or a corporation that undergoes a covered event as described in paragraph (f)(5)(ii) of this section. A prior owner is a person that either transfers a disregarded entity or owns a disregarded entity immediately before a change in the entity classification of the disregarded entity as described in paragraph (f)(5)(ii) of this section.

(iv) *Partnership variances.*—In the case of a change in any partner's interest in the partnership (a variance), except as otherwise provided in section 706(d)(2) (relating to certain cash basis items) or 706(d)(3) (relating to tiered partnerships), foreign tax paid by the partnership during its U.S. taxable year in which the variance occurs is allocated between the portion of the U.S. taxable year ending on, and the portion of the U.S. taxable year beginning on the day after, the day of the variance. The allocation is made under the principles of this paragraph (f)(5) as if the variance were a covered event.

(6) *Allocation of foreign taxes in connection with elections under section 336(e) or 338 or § 1.245A-5(e).*—For rules relating to the allocation of foreign taxes in connection with elections made pursuant to section 336(e), see § 1.336-2(g)(3)(ii). For rules relating to the allocation of foreign taxes in connection with elections made pursuant to section 338, see § 1.338-9(d). For rules relating to the allocation of foreign taxes in connection with elections made pursuant to § 1.245A-5(e)(3)(i), see § 1.245A-5(e)(3)(i)(B).

(7) *Examples.*—The following examples illustrate the rules of paragraphs (f)(3) through (6) of this section.

(i) *Example 1.*—(A) *Facts.* A, a United States person, owns 100 percent of B, an entity organized in Country X. B owns 100 percent of C, also an entity organized in Country X. B and C are corporations for U.S. and foreign tax purposes that use the "u" as their functional currency. Pursuant to a consolidation regime, Country X imposes a net income tax described in paragraph (a)(3) of this section on the combined income of B and C within the meaning of paragraph (f)(3)(ii) of this section. In year 1, C pays 25u of interest to B. If B and C did not report their income on a combined basis for Country X tax purposes, the interest paid from C to B would result in 25u of interest income to B and 25u of deductible interest expense to C. For purposes of reporting the combined income of B and C, Country X first requires B and C to determine their own income (or loss) on a separate schedule. For this purpose, however, neither B nor C takes into account the 25u of interest paid from C to B because the income of B and C is included in the same combined base. The separate income of B and C reported on their Country X schedules for year 1, which do not reflect the 25u intercompany payment, is 100u and 200u, respectively. The combined income reported for Country X purposes is 300u (the sum of the 100u separate income of B and 200u separate income of C).

(B) *Result.* On the separate schedules described in paragraph (f)(3)(iii)(A) of this section, B's separate income is 100u and C's separate income is 200u. Under paragraph (f)(3)(iii)(B)(*1*) of this section, the 25u interest payment from C to B is taken into account for purposes of determining B's and C's portions of the combined income under paragraph (f)(3)(iii) of this section, because B and C would have taken the items into account if they did not compute their income on a combined basis. Thus, B's portion of the combined income is 125u (100u plus 25u) and C's portion of the combined income is 175u (200u less 25u). The result is the same regardless of whether the 25u interest payment from C to B is deductible for U.S. Federal income tax purposes. See paragraph (f)(3)(iii)(B)(*2*) of this section.

(ii) *Example 2.*—(A) *Facts.* A, a United States person, owns 100 percent of B, an entity organized in Country X. B is a corporation for Country X tax purposes, and a disregarded entity for U.S. income tax purposes. B owns 100 percent of C and D, entities organized in country X that are corporations for both U.S. and Country X tax purposes. B, C, and D use the "u" as their functional currency and file on a combined basis for Country X income tax purposes. Country X imposes a net income tax described in paragraph (a)(3) of this section at the rate of 30 percent on the taxable income of corporations organized in Country X. Under the Country X combined reporting regime, income (or loss) of C and D is attributed to, and treated as income (or loss) of, B. B has the sole obligation to pay Country X income tax imposed with respect to income of B and income of C and D that is attributed to, and treated as income of, B. Under Country X tax law, Country X may proceed against B, but not C or D, if B fails to pay over to Country X all or any portion of the Country X income tax imposed with respect to such income. In year 1, B has income of 100u, C has income of 200u, and D has a net loss of (60u). Under Country X tax law, B is considered to have 240u of taxable income with respect to which 72u of Country X income tax is imposed. Country X does not provide mandatory rules for allocating D's loss.

(B) *Result.* Under paragraph (f)(3)(ii) of this section, the 72u of Country X tax is considered to be imposed on the combined income of B, C, and D. Because Country X tax law does not provide mandatory rules for allocating D's loss between B and C, under paragraph (f)(3)(iii)(C) of this section D's (60u) loss is allocated pro rata: 20u to B ((100u/300u) × 60u) and 40u to C ((200u/300u) × 60u). Under paragraph (f)(3)(i) of this section, the 72u of Country X tax must be allocated pro rata among B, C, and D. Because D has no income for Country X tax purposes, no Country X tax is allocated to D. Accordingly, 24u (72u × (80u/240u)) of the Country X tax is allocated to B, and 48u (72u × (160u/240u)) of such tax is allocated to C. Under paragraph (f)(4)(ii) of this section, A is considered to have legal liability for the 24u of Country X tax allocated to B under paragraph (f)(3) of this section.

(g) *Definitions.*—For purposes of this section and §§1.901-2A and 1.903-1, the following definitions apply.

(1) *Foreign country and possession (territory) of the United States.*—The term *foreign country* means any foreign state, any possession (territory) of the United States, and any political subdivision of any foreign state or of any possession (territory) of the United States. The term *possession* (or *territory*) *of the United States* means American Samoa, Guam, the Commonwealth of the Northern Mariana Islands, the Commonwealth of Puerto Rico, and the U.S. Virgin Islands.

(2) *Foreign levy.*—The term *foreign levy* means a levy imposed by a foreign country.

(3) *Foreign tax.*—The term *foreign tax* means a foreign levy that is a tax as defined in paragraph (a)(2) of this section.

(4) *Foreign tax law.*—The term *foreign tax law* means the laws of the foreign country imposing a foreign tax, including a separate levy that is modified by an applicable income tax treaty. The foreign tax law is construed on the basis of the foreign country's statutes, regulations, case law, and administrative rulings or other official pronouncements, as modified by an applicable income tax treaty.

(5) *Paid, payment, and paid by.*—The term *paid* means "paid" or "accrued"; the term *payment* means "payment" or "accrual"; and the term *paid by* means "paid by" or "accrued by or on behalf of," depending on the taxpayer's method of accounting for foreign income taxes. In the case of a taxpayer that claims a foreign tax credit, the taxpayer's method of accounting for foreign income taxes refers to whether the taxpayer claims the foreign tax credit for taxes paid (that is, remitted) or taxes accrued (as determined under §1.905-1(d)) during the taxable year. The term *paid* does not include foreign taxes deemed paid under section 904(c) or section 960.

(6) *Resident and nonresident.*—The terms *resident* and *nonresident*, when used in the context of the foreign tax law of a foreign country, have the meaning provided in paragraphs (g)(6)(i) and (ii) of this section.

(i) *Resident.*—An individual is a resident of a foreign country if the individual is liable to income tax in such country by reason of the individual's residence, domicile, citizenship, or similar criterion under such country's foreign tax law. An entity (including a corporation, partnership, trust, estate, or an entity that is disregarded as an entity separate from its owner for Federal income tax purposes) is a resident of a foreign country if the entity is liable to tax on its income (regardless of whether tax is actually imposed) under the laws of the foreign country by reason of the entity's place of incorporation or place of management in that country (or in a political subdivision or local authority thereof), or by reason of a criterion of similar nature, or if the entity is of a type that is specifically identified as a resident in an income tax treaty with the United States to which the foreign country is a party.

(ii) *Nonresident.*—A nonresident with respect to a foreign country is any individual or entity that is not a resident of such foreign country.

(7) *Taxpayer.*—The term *taxpayer* has the meaning set forth in paragraph (f)(1) of this section.

(h) *Applicability dates.*—Except as otherwise provided in this paragraph (h), this section applies to foreign taxes paid (within the meaning of paragraph (g) of this section) in taxable years beginning on or after December 28, 2021. For foreign taxes that relate to (and if creditable are considered to accrue in) taxable years beginning before December 28, 2021, and that are remitted in taxable years beginning on or after December 28, 2021, by a taxpayer that accounts for foreign income taxes on the accrual basis, see §1.901-2 as contained in 26 CFR part 1 revised as of April 1, 2021. For foreign taxes paid to Puerto Rico by reason of section 1035.05 of the Puerto Rico Internal Revenue Code of 2011, as amended (13 L.P.R.A. §30155) (treating certain income, gain or loss as effectively connected with the active conduct of a trade or business with Puerto Rico) this section applies to foreign taxes paid (within the meaning of paragraph (g) of this section) in taxable years beginning on or after January 1, 2023. For foreign taxes described in the preceding sentence that are paid in taxable years beginning before January 1, 2023, see §1.901-2 as contained in 26 CFR part 1 revised as of April 1, 2021. [Reg. §1.901-2.]

□ [*T.D. 7918, 10-6-83. Amended by T.D.* 8372, 10-30-91; *T.D.* 9416, 7-15-2008; *T.D.* 9535, 7-13-2011; *T.D.* 9536, 7-14-2011 (*corrected* 8-29-2011); *T.D.* 9576, 2-9-2012; *T.D.* 9619, 5-10-2013; *T.D.* 9634, 9-3-2013 *and T.D.* 9959, 12-28-2021 (*corrected* 7-26-2022).]

Proposed Amendments to Regulation

§1.901-2. Income, war profits, or excess profits tax paid or accrued.

* * *

(e)(5) * * *

(iii) *U.S.-owned foreign entities.*—(A) *In general.*—If a U.S. person described in section 901(b) directly or indirectly owns stock possessing 80 percent or more of the total voting power and total value of one or more foreign corporations (or, in the case of a noncorporate foreign entity, directly or indirectly owns an interest in 80 percent or more of the income of one or more such foreign entities), the group comprising such foreign corporations and entities (the "U.S.-owned group") shall be treated as a single taxpayer for purposes of paragraph (e)(5) of this section. Therefore, if one member of such a U.S.-owned group transfers or surrenders a net loss for the taxable year to a second member of the U.S.-owned group and the loss reduces the foreign tax due from the second member pursuant to a foreign law group relief or similar regime, foreign tax paid by the first member in a different year does not fail to be a compulsory payment solely because such tax would not have been due had the member that transferred or surrendered the net loss instead carried over the loss to reduce its own income and foreign tax liability in that year. Similarly, if one or more members of the U.S.-owned group enter into a combined settlement under foreign law of two or more issues involving different members of the group, such settlement will be evaluated on an overall basis, not on an issue-by-issue or entity-by-entity basis, in determining whether an amount is a compulsory amount. The provisions of this paragraph (e)(5)(iii) apply solely for purposes of determining whether amounts paid are compulsory payments of foreign tax and do not, for example, modify the provisions of section 902 requiring separate pools of post-1986 undistributed earnings and post-1986 foreign income taxes for each member of a qualified group.

(B) *Special rules.*—All domestic corporations that are members of a consolidated group (as that term is defined in §1.1502-1(h)) shall be treated as one domestic corporation for purposes of this paragraph (e)(5)(iii). For purposes of this paragraph (e)(5)(iii), indirect ownership of stock or another equity interest (such as an interest in a partnership) shall be determined in accordance with the principles of section 958(a)(2), whether the interest is owned by a U.S. or foreign person.

(C) *Examples.*—The following examples illustrate the rules of this paragraph (e)(5)(iii):

Example 1. (i) *Facts.* A, a domestic corporation, wholly owns B, a country X corporation. B, in turn, wholly owns several country X corporations, including C and D. B, C, and D participate in group relief in country X. Under the country X group relief rules, a member with a net loss may choose to surrender the loss to another member of the group. In year 1, C has a net loss of (1,000x) and D has net income of 5,000x for country X tax purposes. Pursuant to the group relief rules in country X, C agrees to surrender its year 1 net loss to D and D agrees to claim the net loss. D uses the net loss to reduce its year 1 net income to 4,000x for country X tax purposes, which reduces the amount of country X tax D owes in year 1 by 300x. In year 2, C earns 3,000x with respect to which it pays 900x of country X tax. Country X permits a taxpayer to carry forward net losses for up to ten years.

(ii) *Result.* Paragraph (e)(5)(i) of this section provides, in part, that an amount paid to a foreign country does not exceed the amount of liability under foreign law for tax if the taxpayer determines such amount in a manner that is consistent with a reasonable interpretation and application of the substantive and procedural provisions of foreign law (including applicable tax treaties) in such a way as to reduce, over time, the taxpayer's reasonably expected liability under foreign law for tax. Under paragraph (e)(5)(iii)(A) of this section, B, C, and D are treated as a single taxpayer for purposes of testing whether the reasonably expected foreign tax liability has been minimized over time, because A directly and indirectly owns 100 percent of each of B, C, and D. Accordingly, none of the 900x paid by C in year 2 fails to be a compulsory payment solely because C could have reduced its year 2 country X tax liability by 300x by choosing to carry forward its year 1 net loss to year 2 instead of surrendering it to D to reduce D's country X liability in year 1.

Example 2. (i) *Facts.* L, M, and N are country Y corporations. L owns 100 percent of the common stock of M, which owns 100 percent of the stock of N. O, a domestic corporation, owns a security issued by M that is treated as debt for country Y tax purposes and as stock for U.S. tax purposes. As a result, L owns 100 percent of the stock of M for country Y purposes while O owns 99 percent of the stock of M for U.S. tax purposes. L, M, and N participate in group relief in country Y. Pursuant to the group relief rules in country Y, M may surrender its loss to any member of the group. In year 1, M has a net loss of $10 million, N has net income of $25 million, and L has net income of $15 million. M chooses to surrender its year 1 net loss to L. Country Y imposes tax of 30 percent on the net income of country Y corporations. Accordingly, in year 1, the loss surrender has the effect of reducing L's country Y tax by $3 million. In year 1, N makes a payment of $7.5 million to country Y with respect to its net income of $25 million. If M had surrendered its net loss to N instead of L, N would have had net income of $15 million, with respect to which it would have owed only $4.5 million of country Y tax.

(ii) *Result.* M and N, but not L, are treated as a single taxpayer for purposes of paragraph (e)(5) of this section because O directly and indirectly owns 99 percent of each of M and N, but owns no direct or indirect interest in L. Accordingly, in testing whether M and N's reasonably expected foreign tax liability has been minimized over time, L is not considered the same taxpayer as M and N, collectively, and the $3 million reduction in L's year 1 country Y tax liability through the surrender to L of M's $10 million country Y net loss in year 1 is not considered to reduce M and N's collective country Y tax liability.

* * *

(h) *Effective date.*—Paragraphs (a) through (e)(5)(ii) and paragraph (g) of this section, § 1.901-2A, and § 1.903-1 apply to taxable years beginning after November 14, 1983. Paragraphs (e)(5)(iii) and (iv) of this section are effective for foreign taxes paid or accrued during taxable years of the taxpayer ending on or after the date on which these regulations are published as final regulations in the Federal Register. [Prop. Reg. § 1.901–2.]

[Proposed 3-30-2007.]

Proposed Amendments to Regulation

§ 1.901-2. Income, war profits, or excess profits tax paid or accrued.—

* * *

(b) * * *

(4) * * *

(i) * * *

(A) *In general.*—A foreign tax satisfies the cost recovery requirement if the base of the tax is computed by reducing gross receipts (as described in paragraph (b)(3) of this section) to permit recovery of substantially all of each item of significant cost or expense (including each item of cost or expense related to the categories described in paragraph (b)(4)(i)(B)(2) of this section) attributable, under reasonable principles, to such gross receipts. See paragraph (b)(4)(i)(B) of this section for rules regarding the determination of what is a significant cost or expense, paragraph (b)(4)(i)(C) of this section for rules regarding the recovery of substantially all of an item, paragraph (b)(4)(i)(E) of this section for rules regarding principles for attributing costs and expenses to gross receipts, and paragraph (b)(4)(i)(F) of this section for exceptions to this rule. A foreign tax need not permit recovery of significant costs and expenses, such as certain personal expenses, that are not attributable, under reasonable principles, to gross receipts included in the foreign tax base. A foreign tax whose base is gross receipts, with no reduction for costs and expenses, satisfies the cost recovery requirement only if there are no significant costs and expenses described in paragraph (b)(4)(i)(B) of this section attributable to the gross receipts included in the foreign tax base. See paragraph (b)(4)(iv)(A) of this section (*Example 1*). A foreign tax that provides an alternative cost allowance satisfies the cost recovery requirement only as provided in paragraph (b)(4)(i)(G) of this section.

(B) *Significant costs and expenses.—(1) In general.*—Except as provided in paragraph (b)(4)(i)(B)(2) of this section, whether an item of cost or expense is significant for purposes of this paragraph (b)(4)(i) is determined based on whether, for all taxpayers in the aggregate to which the foreign tax applies, the item of cost or expense constitutes a significant portion of the taxpayers' total costs and expenses.

(2) Per se significant costs and expenses.—An item of cost or expense (as characterized under foreign law) related to capital expenditures, interest, rents, royalties, wages or other payments for services, and research and experimentation is always treated as an item of significant cost or expense for purposes of this paragraph (b)(4)(i).

(C) *Recovery of substantially all of each item.—(1) In general.*—Whether a foreign tax permits recovery of substantially all of each item of significant cost or expense is determined based solely on the terms of the foreign tax law.

(2) Safe harbor.—One or more disallowances of a stated portion of an item (or multiple items) of significant cost or expense does not prevent a foreign tax from being considered to permit recovery of substantially all of each item of significant cost or expense if the total portion of the item (or items) that is disallowed does not exceed 25 percent. A limitation that caps the recovery of an item of significant cost or expense, or multiple items of cost or expense that relate to a single category of significant costs and expenses described in paragraph (b)(4)(i)(B)(2) of this section does not prevent a foreign tax from being considered to permit recovery of substantially all of each item of significant cost or expense if the limitation is a qualifying cap. For such purpose, a limitation that caps the recovery at a stated portion of gross receipts, gross income, or a similar measure is a qualifying cap if the stated portion of such measure is not less than 15 percent. A limitation that caps the recovery at a stated portion of taxable income (determined without regard to the item at issue) or a similar measure is a qualifying cap if the stated portion of such measure is not less than 30 percent.

(3) Non-recovery of significant costs and expenses.—Significant costs and expenses (such as interest expense) are not considered to be recovered by reason of the time value of money attributable to the acceleration of a tax benefit or economic benefit attributable to the timing of the recovery of other costs and expenses (such as the current expensing of debt-financed capital expenditures).

(D) * * * A foreign tax law permits recovery of substantially all of each item of significant cost or expense even if such item of cost or expense is recovered earlier or later than it is recovered under the Internal Revenue Code unless the time of recovery is so much later as effectively to constitute a denial of such recovery. * * *

* * *

(F) *Exceptions.—(1) Disallowances consistent with U.S. principles.*—Notwithstanding paragraph (b)(4)(i)(A) of this section, a disallowance of all or a portion of an item of significant cost or expense does not prevent a foreign tax from satisfying the cost recovery requirement if such disallowance is consistent with any principle underlying the disallowances required under the income tax provisions of the Internal Revenue Code, including the principles of limiting base erosion or profit shifting and addressing non-tax public policy concerns similar to those reflected in the Internal Revenue Code. For example, a foreign tax may satisfy the cost recovery requirement even if the foreign tax law disallows deductions in connection with hybrid transactions, disallows deductions attributable to gross receipts that in whole or in part are excluded, exempt or eliminated from taxable income, or disallows certain deductions consistent with non-tax public policy considerations similar to those underlying the disallowances contained in section 162. See paragraphs (b)(4)(iv)(I) and (J) of this section (*Examples 9* and *10*).

(2) Amounts that need not be recovered.—A foreign tax law may satisfy the cost recovery requirement even if the foreign tax law does not permit recovery of costs and expenses attributable to wage

income or to investment income that is not derived from a trade or business. In addition, in determining whether a foreign tax (the "tested foreign tax") meets the cost recovery requirement, it is immaterial whether the tested foreign tax allows a deduction for other taxes that would qualify as foreign income taxes (determined without regard to whether such other tax allows a deduction for the tested foreign tax). See paragraphs (b)(4)(iv)(D) and (E) of this section (*Examples 4* and 5).

* * *

(iv) * * *

(F) *Example 6: Substantially all; application of the safe harbor.*—(*1*)*Facts.* Country X imposes a tax ("Country X tax") on the income of corporations that are resident in Country X. Under Country X tax law, full deductions are allowed for each item of significant cost or expense attributable under reasonable principles to the gross receipts included in the Country X tax base, except that Country X tax law disallows a deduction for 25 percent of a taxpayer's costs and expenses for royalties related to patents.

(*2*) *Analysis.* Under paragraph (b)(4)(i)(B)(*2*) of this section, an item of cost or expense related to royalties is always treated as a significant cost or expense, and therefore, under paragraph (b)(4)(i)(A) of this section, absent an exception, Country X tax law must permit recovery of substantially all of each item of cost or expense related to royalties, including the item of royalties related to patents. The stated percentage of costs and expenses from royalties related to patents (25 percent) that is disallowed under Country X tax law does not exceed 25 percent. Accordingly, under the safe harbor in paragraph (b)(4)(i)(C)(*2*) of this section, the disallowance does not prevent the Country X tax from being considered to permit recovery of substantially all of each item of cost or expense related to royalties, and therefore the Country X tax satisfies the cost recovery requirement.

(G) *Example 7: Substantially all; application of the safe harbor.*—(*1*) *Facts.* Country X imposes a tax ("Country X tax") on the income of corporations that are resident in Country X. Under Country X tax law, full deductions are allowed for each item of significant cost or expense attributable under reasonable principles to the gross receipts included in the Country X tax base, except that Country X tax law disallows a deduction for 15 percent of a taxpayer's costs and expenses for rents and 25 percent of a taxpayer's costs and expenses for interest.

(*2*) *Analysis.* Under paragraph (b)(4)(i)(B)(*2*) of this section, an item of cost or expense related to rents or interest is always treated as a significant cost or expense, and therefore, under paragraph (b)(4)(i)(A) of this section, absent an exception, Country X tax law must permit recovery of substantially all of each item of cost or expense related to royalties and interest. The stated percentage of the costs and expenses related to rents (15 percent) that is disallowed under Country X tax law does not exceed 25 percent. Additionally, the stated percentage of the costs and expenses related to interest (25 percent) that is disallowed under Country X law does not exceed 25 percent. Accordingly, under the safe harbor in paragraph (b)(4)(i)(C)(*2*) of this section, the disallowances do not prevent the Country X tax from being considered to permit recovery of substantially all of each item of cost or expense related to rents and interest, and therefore the Country X tax satisfies the cost recovery requirement.

(H) *Example 8: Substantially all; application of the safe harbor.*—(*1*) *Facts.* Country X imposes a tax ("Country X tax") on the income of corporations that are resident in Country X. Under Country X tax law, full deductions are allowed for each item of significant cost or expense attributable under reasonable principles to the gross receipts included in the Country X tax base, except that Country X tax law caps the recovery of the deduction of interest at 30 percent of the taxpayer's taxable income determined without regard to interest expense.

(*2*) *Analysis.* Under paragraph (b)(4)(i)(B)(*2*) of this section, an item of cost or expense related to interest is always treated as a significant cost or expense, and therefore, under paragraph (b)(4)(i)(A) of this section, absent an exception, Country X tax law must permit recovery of substantially all of each item of cost or expense related to interest. The stated cap on recovery in Country X tax law with respect to interest (30 percent of taxable income determined without regard to interest expense) is not less than 30 percent of taxable income determined without regard to interest expense. Additionally, the cap on recovery relates to a single category of significant costs and expenses described in paragraph (b)(4)(i)(B)(*2*) of this section. Accordingly, under the safe harbor in paragraph (b)(4)(i)(C)(*2*) of this section, the disallowance does not prevent the Country X tax from being considered to permit recovery of substantially all of each item of cost or expense related to interest, and therefore the Country X tax satisfies the cost recovery requirement.

(I) *Example 9: Permissible disallowance based on U.S. principles.*—(*1*) *Facts.* Country X imposes a tax on the income of corporations that are resident in Country X. Under Country X tax law, full deductions are allowed for each item of significant cost or expense attributable under reasonable principles to the gross receipts included in the Country X tax base, except that under Country X's anti-hybrid rules, a deduction is disallowed for any payment, including interest, royalties, rents, or payments for services, made by a Country X resident to a related entity located outside of Country X if the payment is not included in gross income by the payee or the payee is not subject to tax.

(*2*) *Analysis.* Under paragraph (b)(4)(i)(B)(*2*) of this section, each item of cost or expense related to interest, rents, royalties, and payments for services is always treated as a significant cost or expense, and therefore, under paragraph (b)(4)(i)(A) of this section, absent an exception, Country X tax law must permit recovery of substantially all of each item of cost or expense related to interest, rents, royalties, and payments for services. Country X tax law does not permit recovery of any portion of any item of significant cost or expense that is subject to the anti-hybrid rules. As a result, the safe harbor in paragraph (b)(4)(i)(C)(*2*) of this section does not apply to such item. Further, because a deduction is disallowed for any item of cost or expense that is subject to the Country X anti-hybrid rules, the Country X tax law completely disallows certain items of cost and expense related to interest, rents, royalties, and payments for services and thus does not permit recovery of substantially all of each item of significant cost or expense related to interest, rents, royalties, and payments for services. However, under paragraph (b)(4)(i)(F)(*1*) of this section, a disallowance of all or a portion of an item of significant cost or expense does not prevent a foreign tax from satisfying the cost recovery requirement if the disallowance is consistent with any principle underlying the disallowances required under the income tax provisions of the Internal Revenue Code. The income tax provisions of the Internal Revenue Code, specifically section 267A, contain disallowances of deductions based on the principle of limiting base erosion or profit shifting. Country X's disallowance of deductions for any payment, including interest, royalties, rents, or payments for services also reflects the principle of limiting base erosion or profit shifting. Accordingly, because Country X's anti-hybrid rules are consistent with the principle of limiting base erosion or profit shifting, the Country X tax satisfies the cost recovery requirement.

(J) *Example 10: Permissible disallowance based on U.S. principles.*—(*1*) *Facts.* Country X imposes a tax on the income of corporations that are resident in Country X. Under Country X tax law, full deductions are allowed for each item of significant cost or expense attributable to the gross receipts included in the Country X tax base, except that no deduction is permitted for any stock-based payments for services.

(*2*) *Analysis.* Under paragraph (b)(4)(i)(B)(*2*) of this section, each item of cost or expense related to wages or other payments for services is always treated as a significant cost or expense, and therefore, under paragraph (b)(4)(i)(A) of this section, absent an exception, Country X tax law must permit recovery of substantially all of each item of cost or expense related to wages or other payments for services. Country X tax law denies a deduction for any stock-based payments for services, and therefore the safe harbor in paragraph (b)(4)(i)(C)(*2*) of this section is not satisfied. Further, given that no deduction is allowed for stock-based payments for services, the Country X tax law completely disallows an item of cost or expense related to wages or other payments for services and thus does not permit recovery of substantially all of each item of significant cost or expense related to wages or other payments for services. However, under paragraph (b)(4)(i)(F)(*1*) of this section, a disallowance of all or a portion of an item of significant cost or expense does not prevent a foreign tax from satisfying the cost recovery requirement if such disallowance is consistent with any principle underlying the disallowances required under the income tax provisions of the Internal Revenue Code. The income tax provisions of the Internal Revenue Code contain targeted disallowances or limits on the deductibility of certain items of compensation in particular circumstances based on non-tax public policy reasons, including to influence the amount or use of a certain type of compensation in the labor market. For example, section 162(m) imposes limits on deductions for compensation of certain highly-paid employees, and section 280G limits the deductibility of certain "parachute payments" provided to individuals when an entity undergoes a change of control. Country X's targeted disallowance of deductions for the portion of payments for services attributable to stock-based compensation also reflects a principle of influencing the amount or use of a certain type of compensation (stock-based compensation) in the labor market. Accordingly, because the Country X tax law's disallowance is consistent with a principle underlying the disallowances required under the income tax provisions of the Internal Revenue Code, the Country X tax satisfies the cost recovery requirement.

(5) * * *

(i) * * *

(B) * * *

(2) Royalties.—Under the foreign tax law, gross income from royalties must be sourced based on the place of use of, or the right to use, the intangible property, as determined under reasonable principles (which do not include determining the place of use of, or the right to use, the intangible property based on the location of the payor).

* * *

(d) * * *

(1) * * *

(iii) *Tax imposed on nonresidents.*—(A) *In general.*—A foreign levy imposed on nonresidents is always treated as a separate levy from that imposed on residents, even if the base of the tax as applied to residents and nonresidents is the same, and even if the levies are treated as a single levy under foreign tax law.

(B) *Withholding tax.*—*(1) In general.*—Except as otherwise provided in this paragraph (d)(1)(iii)(B), a withholding tax (as defined in section 901(k)(1)(B)) that is imposed on a payment giving rise to gross income of nonresidents is treated as a separate levy as to each separate class of income described in section 61 (for example, interest, dividends, rents, or royalties) subject to the withholding tax.

(2) Subsets of income.—If two or more subsets of a separate class of income are subject to a withholding tax based on different income attribution rules (for example, if technical services are subject to tax based on the residence of the payor and other services are subject to tax based on where the services are performed), separate levies are considered to be imposed with respect to each subset of that separate class of income.

(3) Royalty income.—A withholding tax that is imposed on a payment giving rise to gross royalty income of a nonresident that is made pursuant to a single-country license (as determined under § 1.903-1(c)(2)(iv)) is treated as a separate levy from a withholding tax that is imposed on other gross royalty income of such nonresident and is also treated as a separate levy from any withholding tax imposed on other nonresidents.

* * *

(h) *Applicability dates.*—*(1) In general.*—Except as provided in paragraphs (h)(2) and (3) of this section, this section applies to foreign taxes paid (within the meaning of paragraph (g) of this section) in taxable years beginning on or after December 28, 2021. For foreign taxes that relate to (and if creditable are considered to accrue in) taxable years beginning before December 28, 2021, and that are remitted in taxable years beginning on or after December 28, 2021, by a taxpayer that accounts for foreign income taxes on the accrual basis, see § 1.901-2 as contained in 26 CFR part 1 revised as of April 1, 2021.

(2) Certain foreign taxes paid to Puerto Rico.—For foreign taxes paid to Puerto Rico by reason of section 1035.05 of the Puerto Rico Internal Revenue Code of 2011, as amended (13 L.P.R.A. 30155) (treating certain income, gain or loss as effectively connected with the active conduct of a trade or business with Puerto Rico), this section applies to foreign taxes paid (within the meaning of paragraph (g) of this section) in taxable years beginning on or after January 1, 2023. For foreign taxes described in the preceding sentence that are paid in taxable years beginning before January 1, 2023, see § 1.901-2 as contained in 26 CFR part 1 revised as of April 1, 2021.

(3) Modifications to cost recovery and royalty attribution rules.—Paragraphs (b)(4)(i) and (iv), (b)(5)(i)(B)(2), and (d)(1)(iii) of this section apply to foreign taxes paid (within the meaning of paragraph (g) of this section) in taxable years ending on or after November 18, 2022. For foreign taxes described in the preceding sentence that are paid in taxable years ending before November 18, 2022, see § 1.901-2(b)(4)(i) and (iv), (b)(5)(i)(B)(2), and (d)(1)(iii) as contained in 26 CFR part 1 revised as of July 27, 2022. Taxpayers may choose to apply the rules in paragraphs (b)(4)(i) and (iv) of this section to foreign taxes paid in taxable years beginning on or after December 28, 2021, and ending before November 18, 2022 provided that they consistently apply those rules to such taxable years. Additionally, taxpayers may choose to apply the rules of paragraphs (b)(5)(i)(B)(2) and (d)(1)(iii) of this section to foreign taxes paid in taxable years beginning on or after December 28, 2021, and ending before November 18, 2022, provided that they consistently apply those rules and the rules of § 1.903-1(c)(2) and (d)(3), (4), and (8) through (11) to such taxable years.

* * *

[Prop. Reg. § 1.901-2.]

[Proposed 11-22-2022.]

§ 1.901-2A. Dual capacity taxpayers.—(a) *Application of separate levy rules as applied to dual capacity taxpayers.*—(1) *In general.*—If the application of a foreign levy (as defined in § 1.901-2(g)(3)) is different, either by the terms of the levy or in practice, for dual capacity taxpayers (as defined in § 1.901-2(a)(2)(ii)(A)) from its application to other persons, then, unless the only such difference is that a lower rate (but the same base) applies to dual capacity taxpayers, such difference is considered to be related to the fact that dual capacity taxpayers receive, directly or indirectly, a specific economic benefit (as defined in § 1.901-2(a)(2)(ii)(B)) from the foreign country and thus to be a difference in kind, and not merely of degree. In such a case, notwithstanding any contrary provision of § 1.901-2(d), the levy as applicable to such dual capacity taxpayers is a separate levy (within the meaning of § 1.901-2(d)) from the levy as applicable to such other persons, regardless of whether such difference is in the base of the levy, in the rate of the levy, or both. In such a case, each of the levy as applied to dual capacity taxpayers and the levy as applied to other persons must be analyzed separately to determine whether it is an income tax within the meaning of § 1.901-2(a)(1) and whether it is a tax in lieu of an income tax within the meaning of § 1.903-1(a). However, if the application of the levy is neither different by its terms nor different in practice for dual capacity taxpayers from its application to other persons, or if the only difference is that a lower rate (but the same base) applies to dual capacity taxpayers, then, in accordance with § 1.901-2(d), such foreign levy as applicable to dual capacity taxpayers and such levy as applicable to other persons together constitute a single levy. In such a case, no amount paid (as defined in § 1.901-2(g)(1)) pursuant to such levy by any such dual capacity taxpayer is considered to be paid in exchange for a specific economic benefit, and such levy, as applicable in the aggregate to such dual capacity taxpayers and to such other persons, is analyzed to determine whether it is an income tax within the meaning of § 1.901-2(a)(1) or a tax in lieu of an income tax within the meaning of § 1.903-1(a). Application of a foreign levy to dual capacity taxpayers will be considered to be different in practice from application of that levy to other persons, even if no such difference is apparent from the terms of the levy, unless it is established that application of that levy to dual capacity taxpayers does not differ in practice from its application to other persons.

(2) *Examples.*—The provisions of paragraph (a)(1) of this section may be illustrated by the following examples:

Example (1). Under a levy of country X called the country X income tax, every corporation that does business in country X is required to pay to country X 40% of its income from its business in country X. Income for purposes of the country X income tax is computed by subtracting specified deductions from the corporation's gross income derived from its business in country X. The specified deductions include the corporation's expenses attributable to such gross income and allowances for recovery of the cost of capital expenditures attributable to such gross income, except that under the terms of the country X income tax a corporation engaged in the exploitation of minerals K, L or M in country X is not permitted to recover, currently or in the future, expenditures it incurs in exploring for those minerals. In practice, the only corporations that engage in exploitation of the specified minerals in country X are dual capacity taxpayers. Thus, the application of the country X income tax to dual capacity taxpayers is different from its application to other corporations. The country X income tax as applied to corporations that engage in the exploitation of minerals K, L or M (dual capacity taxpayers) is, therefore, a separate levy from the country X income tax as applied to other corporations. Accordingly, each of (i) the country X income tax as applied to such dual capacity taxpayers and (ii) the country X income tax as applied to such other persons, must be analyzed separately to determine whether it is an income tax within the meaning of § 1.901-2(a)(1) and whether it is a tax in lieu of an income tax within the meaning of § 1.903-1(a).

Example (2). The facts are the same as in example (1), except that it is demonstrated that corporations that engage in exploitation of the specified minerals in country X and that are subject to the levy include both dual capacity taxpayers and other persons. The country X income tax as applied to all corporations is, therefore, a single levy. Accordingly, no amount paid pursuant to the country X income tax by a dual capacity taxpayer is considered to be paid in exchange for a specific economic benefit; and, if the country X income tax is an income tax within the meaning of § 1.901-2(a)(1) or a tax in lieu of an income tax within the meaning of § 1.903-1(a), it will be so considered in its entirety for all corporations subject to it.

Example (3). Under a levy of country Y called the country Y income tax, each corporation incorporated in country Y is required to pay to country Y a percentage of its worldwide income. The applicable percentage is greater for such corporations that earn more than a specified amount of income than for such corporations that earn less than that amount. Income for purposes of the levy is computed by deducting from gross income specified types of expenses and specified allowances for capital expenditures. The expenses for which deductions are permitted differ depending on the type of business in which the corporation subject to the levy is engaged, *e.g.*, a deduction for interest paid to a related party is not allowed for corporations engaged in enumerated types of activities. In addition, carryover of losses from one taxable period to another is permitted for corporations engaged in specified types of activities, but not for corporations engaged in other activities. By its terms, the foreign levy makes no distinction between dual capacity taxpayers and other persons. It is established that in practice the higher rate of the country Y income tax applies to both dual capacity taxpayers and other persons and that in practice the differences in the base of the country Y income tax (*e.g.*, the lack of a deduction for interest paid to related parties for some corporations subject to the levy and the lack of a carryover provision for some corporations subject to the levy) apply to both dual capacity taxpayers and other persons. The country Y income tax as applied to all corporations incorporated in country Y is therefore a single levy. Accordingly, no amount paid pursuant to the country Y income tax by a dual capacity taxpayer is considered to be paid in exchange for a specific economic benefit; and if the country Y income tax is an income tax within the meaning of § 1.901-2(a)(1) or a tax in lieu of an income tax within the meaning of § 1.903-1(a), it will be so considered in its entirety for all persons subject to it.

Example (4). The facts are the same as in example (3), except that it is not established that in practice the higher rate does not apply only to dual capacity taxpayers. By reason of such higher rate, application of the country Y income tax to dual capacity taxpayers is different in practice from application of the country Y income tax to other persons subject to it. The country Y income tax as applied to dual capacity taxpayers is therefore a separate levy from the country Y income tax as applied to other corporations incorporated in country Y. Accordingly, each of (i) the country Y income tax as applied to dual capacity taxpayers and (ii) the country Y income tax as applied to other corporations incorporated in country Y, must be analyzed separately to determine whether it is an income tax within the meaning of § 1.901-2(a)(1) and whether it is a tax in lieu of an income tax within the meaning of § 1.903-1(a).

Example (5). Under a levy of country X called the country X tax, all persons who do not engage in business in country X and who receive interest income from residents of country X are required to pay to country X 25 percent of the gross amount of such interest income. It is established that the country X tax applies by its terms and in practice to certain banks that are dual capacity taxpayers and to persons who are not dual capacity taxpayers and that application to such dual capacity taxpayers does not differ by its terms or in practice from application to such other persons. The country X tax as applied to all such persons (both the dual capacity taxpayers and the other persons) is, therefore, a single levy. Accordingly, no amount paid pursuant to the country X tax by such a dual capacity taxpayer is considered to be paid in exchange for a specific economic benefit; and, if the country X tax is a tax in lieu of an income tax within the meaning of § 1.903-1(a), it will be so considered in its entirety for all persons subject to it.

Example (6). Under a levy of country X called the country X tax, every corporation incorporated outside of country X ("foreign corporation") that maintains a branch in country X is required annually to pay to country X 52 percent of its net income attributable to that branch. It is established that the application of the country X tax is neither different by its terms nor different in practice for certain banks that are dual capacity taxpayers from its application to persons (which may, but do not necessarily, include other banks) that are not dual capacity taxpayers. The country X tax as applied to all foreign corporations with branches in country X (*i.e.*, both those banks that are dual capacity taxpayers and the foreign corporations that are not dual capacity taxpayers) is, therefore, a single levy. Accordingly, no amount paid pursuant to the country X tax by a bank that is a dual capacity taxpayer is considered to be paid in exchange for a specific economic benefit, and, if the country X tax is an income tax within the meaning of § 1.901-2(a)(1) or a tax in lieu of an income tax within the meaning of § 1.903-1(a), it will be so considered in its entirety for all persons subject to it.

Example (7). Under a levy of country H called the country H tax, all corporations that are organized outside country H and that do not engage in business in country H are required to pay to country H a percentage of the gross amount of interest income derived from residents of country H. The percentage is 30 percent, except that it is 15 percent for a specified category of corporations. All corporations in that category are dual capacity taxpayers. It is established that the country H tax applies by its terms and in practice to dual capacity taxpayers and to persons that are not dual capacity taxpayers and that the only difference in application between such dual capacity taxpayers and such other persons is that a lower rate (but the same base) applies to such dual capacity taxpayers. The country H tax as applied to all such persons (both the dual capacity taxpayers and the other persons) is, therefore, a single levy. Accordingly, no amount paid pursuant to the country H tax by such a dual capacity taxpayer is considered to be paid in exchange for a specific economic benefit, and if the country H tax is a tax in lieu of an income tax within the meaning of § 1.903-1(a), it will be so considered in its entirety for all persons subject to it.

(b) *Burden of proof for dual capacity taxpayers.*—(1) *In general.*—For credit to be allowable under section 901 or 903, the person claiming credit must establish that the foreign levy with respect to which credit is claimed is an income tax within the meaning of § 1.901-2(a)(1) or a tax in lieu of an income tax within the meaning of § 1.903-1(a), respectively. Thus, such person must establish, among other things, that such levy is a tax. See § 1.901-2(a)(2)(i) and § 1.903-1(a). Where a person claims credit under section 901 or 903 for an amount paid by a dual capacity taxpayer pursuant to a foreign levy, § 1.901-2(a)(2)(i) and § 1.903-1(a), respectively, require such person to establish the amount, if any, that is paid pursuant to the distinct element of the levy that is a tax. If, pursuant to paragraph (a)(1) of this section and § 1.901-2(d), such levy as applicable to dual capacity taxpayers and such levy as applicable to other persons together constitute a single levy, then no amount paid pursuant to that levy by any such dual capacity taxpayer is considered to be paid in exchange for a specific economic benefit. Accordingly, such levy has only one distinct element, and the levy either is or is not, in its entirety, a tax. If, however, such levy as applicable to dual capacity taxpayers is a separate levy from such levy as applicable to other persons, then a person claiming credit under section 901 or 903 for an amount paid by a dual capacity taxpayer pursuant to such separate levy may establish the amount, if any, that is paid pursuant to the distinct element of the levy that is a tax only by the facts and circumstances method or the safe harbor method described in paragraph (c) of this section. If such person fails to so establish such amount, no portion of the amount that is paid pursuant to the separate levy by the dual capacity taxpayer to such foreign country shall be treated as an amount of tax. Any amount that, either by reason of application of the methods of paragraph (c) of this section or by reason of the immediately preceding sentence, is not treated as an amount of tax shall (i) be considered to have been paid in exchange for a specific economic benefit; (ii) be characterized (*e.g.*, as royalty, purchase price, cost of sales, reduction of the proceeds of a sale, or reduction of interest income) according to the nature of the transaction and of the specific economic benefit received; and (iii) be treated according to such characterization for all purposes of Chapter 1 of the Internal Revenue Code, except that any determination that an amount is not tax for purposes of section 901 or 903 by reason of application of the safe harbor method shall not be taken into account in determining whether or not such an amount is to be characterized and treated as tax for purposes of computing an allowance for percentage depletion under sections 611 and 613.

(2) *Effect of certain treaties.*—If, irrespective of whether such credit would be allowable under section 901 or 903 in the absence of a treaty, the United States has in force a treaty with a foreign country that treats a foreign levy as an income tax for purposes of allowing credit for United States tax and if the person claiming credit is entitled to the benefit of such treaty, then, unless such person claims credit not under the treaty but under section 901 or 903, and except to the extent the treaty provides otherwise and subject to all terms, conditions and limitations provided in the treaty, no portion of an

amount paid with respect to such levy by a dual capacity taxpayer shall be considered to be paid in exchange for a specific economic benefit. If, however, such person claims credit not under such treaty but rather under section 901 or 903 (*e.g.*, so as not to be subject to a limitation contained in such treaty), the provisions of this section apply to such levy.

(c) *Satisfaction of burden of proof.*—(1) *In general.*—This paragraph (c) sets out the methods by which a person who claims credit under section 901 or 903 for an amount paid by a dual capacity taxpayer pursuant to a foreign levy that satisfies all of the criteria of section 901 or 903 other than the determination of the distinct element of the levy that is a tax and of the amount that is paid pursuant to that distinct element (a "qualifying levy") may establish such distinct element and amount. Such person must establish the amount paid pursuant to a qualifying levy that is paid pursuant to the distinct element of the levy that is a tax (which amount therefore is an amount of income tax within the meaning of § 1.901-2(a)(1) or an amount of tax in lieu of income tax within the meaning of § 1.903-1(a) (a "qualifying amount")) only by the facts and circumstances method set forth in paragraph (c)(2) of this section or the safe harbor method set forth in paragraph (c)(3) of this section. A levy is not a qualifying levy, and neither the facts and circumstances method nor the safe harbor method applies to an amount paid by a dual capacity taxpayer pursuant to a foreign levy, if it has been established pursuant to § 1.901-2(d) and paragraph (a)(1) of this section that that levy as applied to that dual capacity taxpayer and that levy as applied to persons other than dual capacity taxpayers together constitute a single levy, or if it has been established in accordance with the first sentence of paragraph (b)(2) of this section that credit is allowable by reason of a treaty for an amount paid with respect to such levy.

(2) *Facts and circumstances method.*—(i) *In general.*—If the person claiming credit establishes, based on all of the relevant facts and circumstances, the amount, if any, paid by the dual capacity taxpayer pursuant to the qualifying levy that is not paid in exchange for a specific economic benefit, such amount is the qualifying amount with respect to such qualifying levy. In determining the qualifying amount with respect to a qualifying levy under the facts and circumstances method, neither the methodology nor the results that would have obtained if a person had elected to apply the safe harbor method to such qualifying levy is a relevant fact or circumstance. Accordingly, neither such methodology nor such results shall be taken into account in applying the facts and circumstances method.

(ii) *Examples.*—The application of the facts and circumstances method is illustrated by the following examples:

Example (1). Country A, which does not have a generally imposed income tax, imposes a levy, called the country A income tax, on corporations that carry on the banking business through a branch in country A. All such corporations lend money to the government of country A, and the consideration (interest) paid by the government of country A for the loans is not made available by the government on substantially the same terms to the population of country A in general. Thus, the country A income tax is imposed only on dual capacity taxpayers. *L*, a corporation that carries on the banking business through a branch in country A and that is a dual capacity taxpayer, establishes that all of the criteria of section 901 are satisfied by the country A income tax, except for the determination of the distinct element of the levy that is a tax and of *L*'s qualifying amount with respect thereto. The country A income tax is, therefore, a qualifying levy. *L* establishes that, although all persons subject to the country A income tax are dual capacity taxpayers, the country A income tax applies in the same manner to income from such persons' transactions with the government of country A as it does to income from their transactions with private persons; that there are significant transactions (either in volume or in amount) with private persons; and that the portion of such persons' income that is derived from transactions with the government of country A on the one hand or private persons on the other varies greatly among persons subject to the country A income tax. By making this showing, *L* has demonstrated that no portion of the amount paid by it to country A pursuant to the levy is paid in exchange for a specific economic benefit (the interest income). Accordingly, *L* has demonstrated under the facts and circumstances method that the entire amount it has paid pursuant to the country A income tax is a qualifying amount.

Example (2). *A*, a domestic corporation that is a dual capacity taxpayer subject to a qualifying levy of country X, pays 1000u (units of country X currency) to country X in 1986 pursuant to the qualifying levy. *A* does not elect to apply the safe harbor method to country X, but if it had so elected, 800u would have been *A*'s qualifying amount with respect to the levy. Based on all of the relevant facts and circumstances (which do not include either the methodology of the safe harbor method or the qualifying amount that would have obtained under that method), *A* establishes that 628u of such 1000u is not paid in exchange for a specific economic benefit. *A* has demonstrated under the facts and circumstances method that 628u is a qualifying amount. Pursuant to paragraph (b)(1) of this section, 372u (1000u – 628u) is considered to have been paid by *A* in exchange for a specific economic benefit. That amount is characterized and treated as provided in paragraph (b)(1) of this section.

Example (3). The facts are the same as in example (2), except that under the safe harbor method 580u would have been *A*'s qualifying amount with respect to the levy. That amount is not a relevant fact or circumstance and the result is the same as in example (2).

(3) *Safe harbor method.*—Under the safe harbor method, the person claiming credit makes an election as provided in paragraph (d) of this section and, pursuant to such election, applies the safe harbor formula described in paragraph (e) of this section to the qualifying levy or levies to which the election applies.

(d) *Election to use the safe harbor method.*—(1) *Scope of election.*—An election to use the safe harbor method is made with respect to one or more foreign states and possessions of the United States with respect to a taxable year of the person making the election (the "electing person"). Such election applies to such taxable year and to all subsequent taxable years of the electing person ("election years"), unless the election is revoked in accordance with paragraph (d)(4) of this section. If an election applies to a foreign state or possession of the United States ("elected country"), it applies to all qualifying levies of the elected country and to all qualifying levies of all political subdivisions of the elected country with respect to which the electing person claims credit for amounts paid (or deemed to be paid) by any dual capacity taxpayer. A member of an affiliated group that files a consolidated United States income tax return may use the safe harbor method for a foreign state or U.S. possession only if an election to use the safe harbor method for that state or possession has been made by the common parent of such affiliated group on behalf of all members of the group. Similarly, a member of an affiliated group that does not file a consolidated United States income tax return may elect to use the safe harbor method for a foreign state or U.S. possession only if an election to use the safe harbor method for that state or possession is made by each member of the affiliated group which claims credit for taxes paid to such state or possession or to any political subdivision thereof. An election to use the safe harbor method for an elected country does not apply to foreign taxes carried back or forward to any election year from any taxable year to which the election does not apply. Such election does apply to foreign taxes carried back or forward from any election year to any taxable year. A person who elects to use the safe harbor method for one or more foreign countries may, in a later taxable year, also elect to use that method for other foreign countries.

(2) *Effect of election.*—An election to use the safe harbor method described in paragraph (c)(3) of this section requires the electing person to apply the safe harbor formula of paragraph (e) of this section to all qualifying levies of all elected countries and their political subdivisions, and constitutes a specific waiver by such person of the right to use the facts and circumstances method described in paragraph (c)(2) of this section with respect to any levy of any elected country or any political subdivision thereof.

(3) *Time and manner of making election.*—(i) *In general.*—To elect to use the safe harbor method, an electing person must attach a statement to its United States income tax return for the taxable year for which the election is made and must file such return by the due date (including extensions) for the filing thereof. Such statement shall state that the electing person elects to use the safe harbor method for the foreign states and the possessions of the United States designated in the statement and their political subdivisions, and that the electing person waives the right, for any election year, to use the facts and circumstances method for any levy of the designated states, possessions and political subdivisions. Notwithstanding the foregoing, a person may, with the consent of the Commissioner, elect to use the safe harbor method for a taxable year for one or more foreign states or possessions of the United States, at a date later than that specified in the first sentence of this paragraph (d)(3)(i), *e.g.*, upon audit of such person's United States income tax return for such taxable year. The Commissioner will normally consent to such a later election if such person demonstrates that it failed to make a timely election for such a foreign state or possession for such taxable year because such person reasonably believed either that it was not a dual capacity taxpayer with respect to such state or possession or that no levy that

it paid to such state or possession or any political subdivision thereof was a qualifying levy (for example, because it reasonably, but incorrectly, believed that the levy it paid was not a separate levy from that applicable to persons other than dual capacity taxpayers). The Commissioner will not, however, consent to such a later election with respect to any state or possession for a taxable year if such person (or any other member of an affiliated group of which such person is a member) applied the facts and circumstances method to any levy of such state or possession or any political subdivision thereof for such taxable year.

(ii) *Certain retroactive elections.*—Notwithstanding the requirements of paragraph (d)(3)(i) of this section relating to the time and manner of making an election, an election may be made for a taxable year beginning on or before November 14, 1983, provided the electing person elects in accordance with § 1.901-2(h) to apply all of the provisions of this section, § 1.901-2 and § 1.903-1 to such taxable year and provided all of the requirements set forth in this paragraph (d)(3)(ii) are satisfied. Such an election shall be made by timely (including extensions) filing a federal income tax return or an amended federal income tax return for such taxable year; by attaching to such return a statement containing the statements and information set forth in paragraph (d)(3)(i) of this section; and by filing amended income tax returns for all subsequent election years for which income tax returns have previously been filed in which credit is claimed under section 901 or 903 and applying the safe harbor method in such amended returns. All amended returns referred to in the immediately preceding sentence must be filed on or before October 12, 1984 and at a time when neither assessment of a deficiency for any of such election years nor the filing of a claim for any refund claimed in any such amended return is barred.

(iii) *Election to credit taxes made in amended return.*—If a person has filed a United States income tax return for a taxable year to which this § 1.901-2A applies (including application by reason of the election provided in § 1.901-2(h)(2)) in which such person has deducted (instead of credited) qualifying foreign taxes and such person validly makes an election to credit (instead of deduct) such taxes in a timely filed amended return for such taxable year, an election to use the safe harbor method may be made in such amended return provided all of the requirements of paragraph (d)(3)(ii) of this section are satisfied other than the requirement that such amended return and the other amended returns referred to in that paragraph be filed on or before October 12, 1984.

(4) *Revocation of election.*—An election to use the safe harbor method described in paragraph (c)(3) of this section may not be revoked without the consent of the Commissioner. An application for consent to revoke such election with respect to one or more elected countries shall be made to the Commissioner of Internal Revenue, Washington, D.C. 20224. Such application shall be made not later than the 30th day before the due date (including extensions) for the filing of the income tax return for the first taxable year for which the revocation is sought to be effective, except in the case of an event described in (i), (ii), (iii) or (iv) below, in which case an application for revocation with retroactive effect may be made within a reasonable time after such event. The Commissioner may make his consent to any revocation conditioned upon adjustments being made in one or more taxable years so as to prevent the revocation from resulting in a distortion of the amount of any item relating to tax liability in any taxable year. The Commissioner will normally consent to a revocation (including, in the case of (i), (ii), (iii) or (iv) below, one with retroactive effect), if—

(i) An amendment to the Internal Revenue Code or the regulations thereunder is made which applies to the taxable year for which the revocation is to be effective and the amendment substantially affects the taxation of income from sources outside the United States under subchapter N of Chapter 1 of the Internal Revenue Code; or

(ii) After a safe harbor election is made with respect to a foreign state, a tax treaty between the United States and that state enters into force; that treaty covers a foreign tax to which the safe harbor election applies; and that treaty applies to the taxable year for which the revocation is to be effective; or

(iii) After a safe harbor election is made with respect to a foreign state or possession of the United States, a material change is made in the tax law of that state or possession or of a political subdivision of that state or possession; and the changed law applies to the taxable year for which the revocation is to be effective and has a material effect on the taxpayer; or

(iv) With respect to a foreign country to which a safe harbor election applies, the Internal Revenue Service issues a letter ruling to the electing person and that letter ruling (*A*) relates to the availability or application of the safe harbor method to one or more levies of such foreign country; (*B*) does not relate to the facts and circumstances method described in paragraph (c)(2) of this section; and (*C*) fails to include a ruling requested by the electing person or includes a ruling contrary to one requested by such person (in either case, other than one relating to the facts and circumstances method) and such failure or inclusion has a material adverse effect on the amount of such electing person's credit for taxes paid to such foreign country for the taxable year for which the revocation is to be effective; or

(v) A corporation ("new member") becomes a member of an affiliated group; the new member and one or more pre-existing members of such group are dual capacity taxpayers with respect to the same foreign country; and, with respect to such country, either the new member or the pre-existing members (but not both) have made a safe harbor election; and the Commissioner in his discretion determines that obtaining the benefit of the right to revoke the safe harbor election with respect to such foreign country was not the principal purpose of the affiliation between such new member and such group; or

(vi) The election has been in effect with respect to at least three taxable years prior to the taxable year for which the revocation is to be effective.

The Commissioner may, in his discretion, consent to a revocation even if none of the foregoing subdivisions (i) through (vi) is applicable. If an election has been revoked with respect to an elected country, a subsequent election to apply the safe harbor method with respect to such elected country may be made only with the consent of the Commissioner and upon such terms and conditions as the Commissioner in his discretion may require.

(e) *Safe harbor formula.*—(1) *In general.*—The safe harbor formula applies to determine the distinct element of a qualifying levy that is a tax and the amount paid by a dual capacity taxpayer pursuant to such qualifying levy that is the qualifying amount with respect to such levy. Under the safe harbor formula the amount paid in a taxable year pursuant to a qualifying levy that is the qualifying amount with respect to such levy is an amount equal to:

$$(A - B - C) \times D/(1 - D)$$

where (except as otherwise provided in paragraph (e)(5) of this section):

A = the amount of gross receipts as determined under paragraph (e)(2) of this section

B = the amount of costs and expenses as determined under paragraph (e)(2) of this section

C = the total amount paid in the taxable year by the dual capacity taxpayer pursuant to the qualifying levy (the "actual payment amount")

D = the tax rate as determined under paragraph (e)(3) of this section

In no case, however, shall the qualifying amount exceed the actual payment amount; and the qualifying amount is zero if the safe harbor formula yields a qualifying amount less than zero. The safe harbor formula is intended to yield a qualifying amount that is approximately equal to the amount of generally imposed income tax within the meaning of paragraphs (a) and (b)(1) of § 1.903-1 ("general tax") of the foreign country that would have been required to be paid in the taxable year by the dual capacity taxpayer if it had not been a dual capacity taxpayer and if the base of the general tax had allowed a deduction in such year for the amount ("specific economic benefit amount") by which the actual payment amount exceeds the qualifying amount. See, however, paragraph (e)(5) of this section if an elected country has no general tax. The specific economic benefit amount is considered to be the portion of the actual payment amount that is paid pursuant to the distinct portion of the qualifying levy that imposes an obligation in exchange for a specific economic benefit. The specific economic benefit amount is therefore considered to be an amount paid by the dual capacity taxpayer in exchange for such specific economic benefit, which amount must be treated for purposes of Chapter 1 of the Internal Revenue Code as provided in paragraph (b)(1) of this section.

(2) *Determination of gross receipts and costs and expenses.*—For purposes of the safe harbor formula, gross receipts and costs and expenses are, except as otherwise provided in this paragraph (e), the gross receipts and the deductions for costs and expenses, respectively, as determined under the foreign law applicable in computing the actual payment amount of the qualifying levy to which the safe

harbor formula applies. However, except as otherwise provided in this paragraph (e), if provisions of the qualifying levy increase or decrease the liability imposed on dual capacity taxpayers compared to the general tax liability of persons other than dual capacity taxpayers by reason of the determination or treatment of gross receipts or of costs or expenses, the provisions generally applicable in computing such other persons' tax base under the general tax shall apply to determine gross receipts and costs and expenses for purposes of computing the qualifying amount. If provisions of the qualifying levy relating to gross receipts meet the requirements of § 1.901-2(b)(3)(i), such provisions shall apply to determine gross receipts for purposes of computing the qualifying amount. If neither the general tax nor the qualifying levy permits recovery of one or more costs or expenses, and by reason of the failure to permit such recovery the qualifying levy does not satisfy the net income requirement of § 1.901-2(b)(4) (even though the general tax does satisfy that requirement), then such cost or expense shall be considered a cost or expense for purposes of computing the qualifying amount. If the qualifying levy does not permit recovery of one or more significant costs or expenses, but provides allowances that effectively compensate for nonrecovery of such significant costs or expenses, then, for purposes of computing the qualifying amount, costs and expenses shall not include the costs and expenses under the general tax whose nonrecovery under the qualifying levy is compensated for by such allowances but shall instead include such allowances. In determining costs and expenses for purposes of computing the qualifying amount with respect to a qualifying levy, the actual payment amount with respect to such levy shall not be considered a cost or expense. For purposes of this paragraph, the following differences in gross receipts and costs and expenses between the qualifying levy and the general tax shall not be considered to increase the liability imposed on dual capacity taxpayers compared to the general tax liability of persons other than dual capacity taxpayers, but only if the general tax would be an income tax within the meaning of § 1.901-2(a)(1) if such different treatment under the qualifying levy had also applied under the general tax:

(i) Differences in the time of realization or recognition of one or more items of income or in the time when recovery of one or more costs and expenses is allowed (unless the period of recovery of such costs and expenses pursuant to the qualifying levy is such that it effectively is a denial of recovery of such costs and expenses, as described in § 1.901-2(b)(4)(i)); and

(ii) Differences in consolidation or carryover provisions of the types described in paragraphs (b)(4)(ii) and (b)(4)(iii) of § 1.901-2.

(3) *Determination of tax rate.*—The tax rate for purposes of the safe harbor formula is the tax rate (expressed as a decimal) that is applicable in computing tax liability under the general tax. If the rate of the general tax varies according to the amount of the base of that tax, the rate to be applied in computing the qualifying amount is the rate that applies under the general tax to a person whose base is, using the terminology of paragraph (e)(1) of this section, "A" minus "B" minus the specific economic benefit amount paid by the dual capacity taxpayer pursuant to the qualifying levy, provided such rate applies in practice to persons other than dual capacity taxpayers, or, if such rate does not so apply in practice, the next lowest rate of the general tax that does so apply in practice.

(4) *Determination of applicable provisions of general tax.*—(i) *In general.*—If the general tax is a series of income taxes (*e.g.*, on different types of income), or if the application of the general tax differs by its terms for different classes of persons subject to the general tax (*e.g.*, for persons in different industries), then, except as otherwise provided in this paragraph (e), the qualifying amount shall be computed by reference to the income tax contained in such series of income taxes, or in the case of such different applications the application of the general tax, that by its terms and in practice imposes the highest tax burden on persons other than dual capacity taxpayers. Notwithstanding the preceding sentence, the general tax amount shall be computed by reference to the application of the general tax to entities of the same type (as determined under the general tax) as the dual capacity taxpayer and to persons of the same resident or nonresident status (as determined under the general tax) as the dual capacity taxpayer; and, if the general tax treats business income differently from non-business (*e.g.*, investment) income (as determined under the general tax), the dual capacity taxpayer's business and non-business income shall be treated as the general tax treats such income. If, for example, the dual capacity taxpayer would, under the general tax, be treated as a resident (*e.g.*, because the general tax treats an entity that is organized in the foreign country or managed or controlled there as a resident) and as a corporation (*i.e.*, because the rules of the general tax treat an entity like the dual capacity taxpayer as a corporation), and if some of the dual capacity taxpayer's income would, under the general tax, be treated as business income and some as non-business income, the dual capacity taxpayer and its income shall be so treated in computing the qualifying amount.

(ii) *Establishing that provisions apply in practice.*—For purposes of the safe harbor formula a provision (including tax rate) shall be considered a provision of the general tax only if it is reasonably likely that that provision applies by its terms and in practice to persons other than dual capacity taxpayers. In general, it will be assumed that a provision (including tax rate) that by its terms applies to persons other than dual capacity taxpayers is reasonably likely to apply in practice to such other persons, unless the person claiming credit knows or has reason to know otherwise. However, in cases of doubt, the person claiming credit may be required to demonstrate that such provision is reasonably likely so to apply in practice.

(5) *No general tax.*—If a foreign country does not impose a general tax (and thus a levy, in order to be a qualifying levy must satisfy all of the criteria of section 901 (because section 903 cannot apply, other than the determination of the distinct element of the levy that is a tax and of the amount that is paid pursuant to that distinct element), paragraphs (e)(2), (3) and (4) of this section to not apply to a qualifying levy of such country, and the terms of the safe harbor formula set forth in paragraph (e)(1) of this section are defined with respect to such levy as follows:

A = the amount of gross receipts as determined under the qualifying levy;

B = the amount of deductions for costs and expenses as determined under the qualifying levy;

C = the actual payment amount; and

D = the lower of the rate of the qualifying levy, or the rate of tax specified in section 11(b)(5) (or predecessor or successor section, as the case may be) of the Internal Revenue Code as applicable to the taxable year in which the actual payment amount is paid.

(6) *Certain taxes in lieu of an income tax.*—To the extent a tax in lieu of an income tax (within the meaning of § 1.903-1(a)) that applies in practice to persons other than dual capacity taxpayers would actually have been required to be paid in the taxable year by a dual capacity taxpayer if it had not been a dual capacity taxpayer (*e.g.*, in substitution for the general tax with respect to a type of income, such as interest income, dividend income, royalty income, insurance income), such tax in lieu of an income tax shall be treated as if it were an application of the general tax for purposes of applying the safe harbor formula of this paragraph (e) to such dual capacity taxpayer, and such formula shall be applied to yield a qualifying amount that is approximately equal to the general tax (so defined) that would have been required to be paid in the taxable year by such dual capacity taxpayer if the base of such general tax had allowed a deduction in such year for the specific economic benefit amount.

(7) *Multiple levies.*—If, in any election year of an electing person, with respect to any elected country and all of its political subdivisions,

(i) Amounts are paid by a dual capacity taxpayer pursuant to more than one qualifying levy or pursuant to one or more levies that are qualifying levies and one or more levies that are not qualifying levies by reason of the last sentence of paragraph (c)(1) of this section but with respect to which credit is allowable, or

(ii) More than one general tax (including a tax treated as if it were an application of the general tax under paragraph (e)(6)) would have been required to be paid by a dual capacity taxpayer (or taxpayers) if it (or they) had not been a dual capacity taxpayer (or taxpayers), or

(iii) Credit is claimed with respect to amounts paid by more than one dual capacity taxpayer,

the provisions of this paragraph (e) shall be applied such that the aggregate qualifying amount with respect to such qualifying levy or levies plus the aggregate amount paid with respect to levies referred to in (e)(7)(i) that are not qualifying levies shall be the aggregate amount that would have been required to be paid in the taxable year by such dual capacity taxpayer (or taxpayers) pursuant to such general tax or taxes if it (or they) had not been a dual capacity taxpayer (or taxpayers) and if the base of such general tax or taxes had allowed a deduction in such year for the aggregate specific economic benefit amount (except that, if paragraph (e)(5) applies to any levy of such elected country or any political subdivision thereof, the aggregate qualifying amount for qualifying levies of such elected country and all of its political subdivisions plus the aggregate amount paid with respect to levies referred to in paragraph (e)(7)(i) that are not qualifying levies shall not exceed the greater of the aggregate amount paid with respect to levies referred to in paragraph (e)(7)(i) that are not qualifying levies and the amount determined in accordance with paragraph (e)(5) where "D" is the rate of tax specified in section 11(b)(5) (or predecessor or successor section, as the case may be) of the Internal Revenue Code as applicable to the taxable year in which the actual payment amount is paid). However, in no event shall such aggregate amount exceed the aggregate actual payment amount plus the aggregate amount paid with respect to levies referred to in (e)(7)(i) that are not qualifying levies, nor be less than the aggregate amount paid with respect to levies referred to in (e)(7)(i) that are not qualifying levies. In applying (e)(7)(ii) a person who is not subject to a levy but who is considered to receive a specific economic benefit by reason of § 1.901-2(a)(2)(ii)(E) shall be treated as a dual capacity taxpayer. See example (12) in paragraph (e)(8) of this section.

(8) *Examples.*—The provisions of this paragraph (e) may be illustrated by the following examples:

Example (1). Under a levy of country X called the country X income tax, every corporation that does business in country X is required to pay to country X 40% of its income from its business in country X. Income for purposes of the country X income tax is computed by subtracting specified deductions from the corporation's gross income derived from its business in country X. The specified deductions include the corporation's expenses attributable to such gross income and allowances for recovery of the cost of capital expenditures attributable to such gross income, except that under the terms of the country X income tax a corporation engaged in the exploitation of minerals K, L or M in country X is not permitted to recover, currently or in the future, expenditures it incurs in exploring for those minerals. Under the terms of the country X income tax interest is not deductible to the extent it exceeds an arm's length amount (*e.g.*, if the loan to which the interest relates is not in accordance with normal commercial practice or to the extent the interest rate exceeds an arm's length rate). In practice, the only corporations that engage in exploitation of the specified minerals in country X are dual capacity taxpayers. Because no other persons subject to the levy engage in exploitation of minerals K, L or M in country X, the application of the country X income tax to dual capacity taxpayers is different from its application to other corporations. The country X income tax as applied to corporations that engage in the exploitation of minerals K, L or M (dual capacity taxpayers) is, therefore, a separate levy from the country X income tax as applied to other corporations.

A is a U.S. corporation that is engaged in country X in exploitation of mineral K. Natural deposits of mineral K in country X are owned by country X, and *A* has been allowed to extract mineral K in consideration of payment of a bonus and of royalties to an instrumentality of country X. Therefore, *A* is a dual capacity taxpayer. In 1984, *A* does business in country X within the meaning of the levy. *A* has validly elected the safe harbor method for country X for 1984. In 1984, as determined in accordance with the country X income tax as applied to *A*, *A* has gross receipts of 120u (units of country X currency), deducts 20u of costs and expenses, and pays 40u (40% of (120u – 20u)) to country X pursuant to the levy. *A* also incurs in 1984 10u of nondeductible expenditures for exploration for mineral K and 2u of nondeductible interest costs attributable to an advance of funds from a related party to finance an undertaking relating to the exploration for mineral K for which normal commercial financing was unavailable because of the substantial risk inherent in the undertaking. *A* establishes that the country X income tax as applied to persons other than dual capacity taxpayers is an income tax within the meaning of § 1.901-2(a)(1), that it is the generally imposed income tax of country X and hence the general tax, and that all of the criteria of section 903 are satisfied with respect to the country X income tax as applied to dual capacity taxpayers, except for the determination of the distinct element of the levy that is a tax and of *A*'s qualifying amount with respect thereto. (No conclusion is reached whether the country X income tax as applied to dual capacity taxpayers is an income tax within the meaning of § 1.901-2(a)(1). Such a determination would require, among other things, that the country X income tax as so applied, judged on the basis of its predominant character, meets the net income requirement of § 1.901-2(b)(4) notwithstanding its failure to permit recovery of exploration expenses.) *A* has therefore demonstrated that the country X income tax as applied to dual capacity taxpayers is a qualifying levy.

In applying the safe harbor formula, in accordance with paragraph (e)(2), the amount of *A*'s costs and expenses includes the 10u of nondeductible exploration expenses. The failure to permit recovery of interest in excess of arm's length amounts, a provision of both the general tax and the qualifying levy, does not cause the qualifying levy to fail to satisfy the net income requirement of § 1.901-2(b)(4); therefore, the amount of *A*'s cost and expenses does not include the 2u of nondeductible interest costs. Thus, under the safe harbor method, *A*'s qualifying amount with respect to the levy is 33.33u ((120u – 30u – 40u) × .40/(1 – .40)). *A*'s specific economic benefit amount is 6.67u (*A*'s actual payment amount (40u) less *A*'s qualifying amount (33.33u)). Under paragraph (a) of this section, this 6.67u is considered to be consideration paid by *A* for the right to extract mineral K. Pursuant to paragraph (b) of this section, this amount is characterized according to the nature of *A*'s transactions with country X and its instrumentality and of the specific economic benefit received (the right to extract mineral K), as an additional royalty or other business expense paid or accrued by *A* and is so treated for all purposes of Chapter 1 of the Internal Revenue Code, except that if an allowance for percentage depletion is allowable to *A* under sections 611 and 613 with respect to *A*'s interest in mineral K, the determination whether this 6.67u is tax or royalty for purposes of computing the amount of such allowance shall be made under sections 611 and 613 without regard to the determination that under the safe harbor formula such 6.67u is not tax for purposes of section 901 or 903.

Example (2). Under a levy of country Y called the country Y income tax, each corporation incorporated in country Y is required to pay to country Y a percentage of its worldwide income. The applicable percentage is 40 percent of the first 1,000u (units of country Y currency) of income and 50 percent of income in excess of 1,000u. Income for purposes of the levy is computed by deducting from gross income specified types of expenses and specified allowances for capital expenditures. The expenses for which deductions are permitted differ depending on the type of business in which the corporation subject to the levy is engaged, *e.g.*, a deduction for interest paid to a related party is not allowed for corporations engaged in enumerated types of activities. In addition, carryover of losses from one taxable period to another is permitted for corporations engaged in specified types of activities, but not for corporations engaged in other activities. By its terms, the foreign levy makes no distinction between dual capacity taxpayers and other persons. In practice the differences in the base of the country Y income tax (*e.g.*, the lack of a deduction for interest paid to related parties for some corporations subject to the levy and the lack of a carryover provision for some corporations subject to the levy) apply to both dual capacity taxpayers and other persons, but the 50 percent rate applies only to dual capacity taxpayers. By reason of such higher rate, application of the country Y income tax to dual capacity taxpayers is different in practice from application of the country Y income tax to other persons subject to it. The country Y income tax as applied to dual capacity taxpayers is therefore a separate levy from the country Y income tax as applied to other corporations incorporated in country Y.

B is a corporation incorporated in country Y that is engaged in construction activities in country Y. *B* has a contract with the government of country Y to build a hospital in country Y for a fee that is not made available on substantially the same terms to substantially all persons who are subject to the general tax of country X. Accordingly, *B* is a dual capacity taxpayer. *B* has validly elected the safe harbor method for country Y for 1985. In 1985, as determined in accordance with the country Y income tax as applied to *B*, *B* has gross receipts of 10,000u, deducts 6,000u of costs and expenses, and pays 1900u ((1,000u × 40%) + (3,000u × 50%)) to Country Y pursuant to the levy.

It is assumed that *B* has established that the country Y income tax as applied to persons other than dual capacity taxpayers is an income tax within the meaning of § 1.901-2(a)(1) and is the general tax. It is further assumed that *B* has demonstrated that all of the criteria of section 901 are satisfied with respect to the country Y income tax as applied to dual capacity taxpayers, except for the determination of the distinct element of such levy that is a tax and of *B*'s qualifying amount with respect to that levy, and therefore that the country Y income tax as applied to dual capacity taxpayers is a qualifying levy.

In applying the safe harbor formula, in accordance with paragraph (e)(3), the 50 percent rate is not used because it does not apply in practice to persons other than dual capacity taxpayers. The next lowest rate of the general tax that does apply in practice to such persons, 40 percent, is used. Accordingly, under the safe harbor formula, *B*'s qualifying amount with respect to the levy is 1400u ((10,000u – 6000u – 1900u) × .40/(1 – .40)). *B*'s specific economic benefit amount is 500u (*B*'s actual payment amount (1900u) less *B*'s qualifying amount (1400u)). Pursuant to paragraph (b) of this section, *B*'s specific economic benefit amount is characterized according to the nature of *B*'s transactions with country Y and of the specific economic benefit received, as a reduction of *B*'s proceeds of its contract with country Y; and this amount is so treated for all purposes of Chapter 1 of the Code, including the computation of *B*'s accumulated profits for purposes of section 902.

Example (3). The facts are the same as in example (2), with the following additional facts: The contract between *B* and country Y is a cost plus contract. One of the costs of the contract which country Y is required to pay or for which it is required to reimburse *B* is any tax of country Y on *B*'s income or receipts from the contract. Instead of reimbursing *B* therefor, country Y agrees with *B* to assume any such tax liability. Under country Y tax law, *B* is not considered to have additional income or receipts by reason of country Y's assumption of *B*'s country Y tax liability. In 1985, *B*'s gross receipts of 10,000u include 3000u from the contract, and its costs and expenses of 6000u include 2000u attributable to the contract. *B*'s other gross receipts and expenses do not relate to any transaction in which *B* receives a specific economic benefit. In accordance with the contract, country Y, and not *B*, is required to bear the amount of *B*'s country Y income tax liability on *B*'s 1000u (3000u − 2000u) income from the contract. In accordance with the contract *B* computes its country Y income tax without taking this 1000u into account and therefore pays 1400u ((1000u × 40%) + (2000u × 50%)) to country Y pursuant to the levy.

In accordance with § 1.901-2(f)(2)(i), the country Y income tax which country Y is, under the contract, required to bear is considered to be paid by country Y on behalf of *B*. *B*'s proceeds of its contract, for all purposes of Chapter 1 of the Code (including the computation of *B*'s accumulated profits for purposes of section 902), therefore, are increased by the additional 500u (1900u computed as in example (2) less 1400u as computed above) of *B*'s liability under the country Y income tax that is assumed by country Y and such 500u is considered to be paid pursuant to the levy by country Y on behalf of *B*. In applying the safe harbor formula, therefore, the computation is exactly as in example (2) and the results are the same as in example (2).

Example (4). Country L issues a decree (the "April 11 decree"), in which it states it is exercising its tax authority to impose a tax on all corporations on their "net income" from country L. "Net income" is defined as actual gross receipts less all expenses attributable thereto, except that in the case of income from extraction of petroleum, gross receipts are defined as 105% of actual gross receipts, and no deduction is allowed for interest incurred on loans whose proceeds are used for exploration for petroleum. Under the April 11 decree, wages paid by corporations subject to the decree are deductible in the year of payment, except that corporations engaged in the extraction of petroleum may deduct such wages only by amortization over a 5-year period and, to the extent such wages are paid to officers, they may be deducted only by amortization over a period of 50 years. The April 11 decree permits related corporations subject to the decree to file consolidated returns in which net income and net losses of related corporations offset each other in computing net income for purposes of the April 11 decree, except that corporations engaged in petroleum exploration or extraction activities are not eligible for inclusion in such a consolidated return. The law of country L does not require separate entities to carry on separate activities in connection with exploring for or extracting petroleum. Net losses of a taxable year may be carried over for 10 years to offset income, except that no more than 25% of net income (before deducting the loss carryover) in any such future year may be offset by a carryover of net loss, and, in the case of any corporation engaged in exploration or extraction of petroleum, losses incurred prior to such a corporation's having net income from production may be carried forward for only 8 years and no more than 15% of net income in any such future year may be offset by such a net loss. The rate to be paid under the April 11 decree is 50% of net income (as defined in the levy), except that if net income exceeds 10,000u (units of country L currency), the rate is 75% of the corporation's net income (including the first 10,000u thereof). In practice, no corporations other than corporations engaged in extraction of petroleum have net income in excess of 10,000u. All petroleum resources of country L are owned by the government of country L, whose petroleum ministry licenses corporations to explore for and extract petroleum in consideration for payment of royalties as petroleum is produced.

J is a U.S. corporation that is engaged in country L in the exploration and extraction of petroleum and therefore is a dual capacity taxpayer. *J* has validly elected the safe harbor method for country L for the year of 1983, the year that *J* commenced activities in country L, and has not revoked such election. For the years 1983 through 1986, *J*'s gross receipts, deductions and net income before application of the carryover provisions, determined in accordance with the April 11 decree, are as follows:

Year A.	*gross receipts (105% of actual gross receipts)* B.	*deductions other than wages* C.	*wages paid other than to officers (amortizable at 20%)* D.	*wages paid to officers (amortizable at 2%)* E.	*non-deductible exploration interest expense* F.	*net income (loss) (B-C-amortization of D-amortization of cumulative E)* G.
1983	0	13,000u	100u	50u	1,000u	(13,021u)
1984	0	17,000u	100u	50u	2,800u	(17,042u)
1985	42,000u	15,000u	100u	50u	2,800u	26,937u
1986	105,000u	20,000u	100u	50u	2,800u	84,916u

After application of the carryover provisions, *J*'s net income and actual payment amounts pursuant to the April 11 levy are as follows:

Year H.	*Net income (loss)* I.	*Actual payment amount (I × 75%)* J.
1983	(13,021u)	0
1984	(17,042u)	0
1985	22,896u	17,172u
1986	72,179u	54,134u

Pursuant to paragraph (a)(1) of this section, the April 11 decree as applied to corporations engaged in the exploration or extraction of petroleum in country L is a separate levy from the April 11 decree as applied to all other corporations. *J* establishes that the April 11 decree, as applied to such other corporations, is an income tax within the meaning of § 1.901-2(a)(1) and that the decree as so applied is the general tax.

The April 11 decree as applied to corporations engaged in the exploration or extraction of petroleum in country L does not meet the gross receipts requirement of § 1.901-2(b)(3); therefore, irrespective of whether it meets the other requirements of § 1.901-2(b)(1), it is not an income tax within the meaning of § 1.901-2(a)(1). However, the April 11 decree as applied to such corporations is a qualifying levy because *J* has demonstrated that all of the criteria of section 903 are satisfied with respect to the April 11 decree as applied to such corporations, except for the determination of the distinct element of such levy that imposes a tax and of *J*'s qualifying amount with respect thereto.

In applying the safe harbor formula, in accordance with paragraph (e)(2), gross receipts are computed by reference to the general levy, and thus are 100%, not 105%, of actual gross receipts. Similarly, costs and expenses include exploration interest expense. In accordance with paragraph (e)(2)(i) of this section the difference between the general tax and the qualifying levy in the timing of the deduction for wages, other than wages of officers, is not considered to increase the liability of dual capacity taxpayers because the general tax would not have failed to be an income tax within the meaning of § 1.901-2(a)(1) if it had provided for 5-year amortization of such wages instead of for current deduction. *See* § 1.901-2(b)(4)(i). However, amortization of wages paid to officers over a 50-year period is such a deferred recovery of such wages that it effectively is a denial of the deduction of the excess of such wages paid in any year over the amortization of such cumulative wages permitted in such year. See § 1.901-2(b)(4)(i). The different treatment of wages paid to officers under the general tax and the qualifying levy is thus not merely a difference in timing within the meaning of paragraph (e)(2)(i) of this section. Accordingly, the difference between the amount of wages paid by *J* to officers in any year and *J*'s deduction (in computing the actual payment amount) for amortization of such cumulative wages allowed in such year is, pursuant to paragraph (e)(2) of this section, treated as a cost and expense in computing *J*'s qualifying amount for such year with respect to the April 11 decree. The differences in the consolidation and carryover provisions between the general tax and the qualifying levy are of the types described in paragraph (e)(2)(ii) of this section and, pursuant to paragraphs (b)(4)(ii) and (b)(4)(iii) of §1.901-2, the general tax would not fail to be an income tax within the meaning of §1.901-2(a)(i) even if it contained the consolidation and carryover provisions of the qualifying levy. Thus, such differences are not considered to increase the liability of dual capacity taxpayers pursuant to the qualifying levy as compared to the general tax liability of persons other than dual capacity taxpayers.

Accordingly, in applying the safe harbor formula to the qualifying levy for 1985 and 1986, gross receipts and costs and expenses are computed as follows:

Gross receipts

1985: 42,000u × (100/105) = 40,000u
1986: 105,000u × (100/105) = 100,000u

Costs and expenses

	Item	*1985*	*1986*
1.	Deductions other than wages (column C in the preceding chart)	15,000u	20,000u
2.	Amortization of cumulative wages paid in 1983 and thereafter other than to officers	60u	80u
3.	Deduction of wages to officers paid in current year, instead of amortization allowed in current year of such cumulative wages paid in 1983 and thereafter	50u	50u
4.	Deduction of exploration interest expense	2,800u	2,800u
5.	Costs and expenses before carryover of net loss (sum of lines 1 through 4)	17,910u	22,930u
6.	Recalculation of loss carryover by recalculating 1983 and 1984 net income (loss) to reflect current deduction of wages to officers and exploration interest expense:		
	1983 adjusted net loss carryover: (13,021u) + (49u) + (1000u) = (14,070u)		
	1984 adjusted net loss carryover: (17,042u) + (48u) + (2800u) = (19,890u)		
7.	Recalculation of limitation on use of net loss carryover deduction:		

Item	*1985*	*1986*
gross receipts	40,000u	100,000u
less costs and expenses	(17,910u)	(22,930u)
	22,090u	77,070u

		1985	*1986*
	times 15% limitation	3,314u	11,561u
8.	Costs and expenses including net loss carryover deduction (line 5 plus line 7)	21,224u	34,491u

In years after 1986, costs and expenses for purposes of determining the qualifying amount would reflect net loss carryforward deductions based on the recomputed losses carried forward from 1983 and 1984 (14,070u and 19,890u, respectively) less the amounts thereof that were utilized in determining costs and expenses for 1985 and 1986 (3,314u and 11,561u, respectively). The 1983 and 1984 loss carryforwards would be considered utilized in accordance with the order of priority in which such losses are utilized under the terms of the qualifying levy.

In applying the safe harbor formula, the tax rate to be used, in accordance with paragraph (e)(3) of this section, is .50.

Accordingly, under the safe harbor method, *J*'s qualifying amounts with respect to the April 11 decree for 1985 and 1986 are computed as follows:

$$1985: (40{,}000u - 21{,}224u - 17{,}172u) \times .50 \,/\, (1 - .50) = 1604u$$
$$1986: (100{,}000u - 34{,}491u - 54{,}134u) \times .50 \,/\, (1 - .50) = 11{,}375u$$

Under the safe harbor method *J*'s qualifying amounts with respect to the April 11 decree for 1985 and 1986 are thus 1604u and 11,375u, respectively; and its specific economic benefit amounts are 15,568u (17,172u − 1604u) and 42,759u (54,134u − 11,375u), respectively. Pursuant to paragraph (b) of this section, *J*'s specific economic benefit amounts are characterized according to the nature of *J*'s transactions with country L and of the specific economic benefit received by *J* as additional royalties paid to country L with respect to the petroleum extracted by *J* in country L in 1985 and 1986, and these amounts are so treated for all purposes of Chapter 1 of the Code.

Example (5). Country E, which has no generally imposed income tax, imposes a levy called the country E income tax only on corporations carrying on the banking business through a branch in Country E and on corporations engaged in the extraction of petroleum in country E. All of the petroleum resources of country E are owned by the government of country E, whose petroleum ministry licenses corporations to explore for and extract petroleum in consideration of payment of royalties as petroleum is extracted. The base of the country E income tax is a corporation's actual gross receipts from sources in country E less all expenses attributable, on reasonable principles, to such gross receipts; the rate of tax is 29%.

A is a U.S. corporation that carries on the banking business through a branch in country E. *B* is a U.S. corporation (unrelated to *A*) that is engaged in the extraction of petroleum in country E. In 1984 *A* receives interest on loans it has made to 160 borrowers in country E, seven of which are agencies and instrumentalities of the government of country E. The economic benefits received by *A* and *B* (*i.e.*, the interest received by *A* from the government and *B*'s license to extract petroleum owned by the government) are not made available on substantially the same terms to the population of country E in general.

A and *B* are dual capacity taxpayers. Each of them has validly elected the safe harbor method for country E for 1984. *A* demonstrates that the country E income tax as applied to it (a dual capacity taxpayer) is not different by its terms or in practice from the country E income tax as applied to persons (in this case other banks) that are not dual capacity taxpayers. *A* has therefore established pursuant to paragraph (a)(1) of this section and §1.901-2(d) that the country E income tax as applied to it and the country E income tax as applied to persons other than dual capacity taxpayers are together a single levy. *A* establishes that such levy is an income tax within the meaning of §1.901-2(a)(1). In accordance with paragraph (a)(1) of this section, no portion of the amount paid by *A* pursuant to such levy is considered to be paid in exchange for a specific economic benefit. Thus, the entire amount paid by *A* pursuant to this levy is an amount of income tax paid.

B does not demonstrate that the country E income tax as applied to corporations engaged in the extraction of petroleum in country E (dual capacity taxpayers) is not different by its terms or in practice from the country E income tax as applied to persons other than dual capacity taxpayers (*i.e.*, banks that are not dual capacity taxpayers). Accordingly, pursuant to paragraph (a)(1) of this section and §1.901-2(d), the country E income tax as applied to corporations engaged in the extraction of petroleum in country E is a separate levy from the country E income tax as applied to other persons.

B demonstrates that all of the criteria of section 901 are satisfied with respect to the country E income tax as applied to corporations engaged in the exploration of petroleum in country E, except for the determination of the distinct element of such levy that imposes a tax and of *B*'s qualifying amount with respect to the levy. Pursuant to paragraph (e)(5) of this section, in applying the safe harbor formula to *B*, "A" is the amount of *B*'s gross receipts as determined under the country E income tax as applied to *B*; "B" is the amount of *B*'s costs and expenses as determined thereunder; "C" is *B*'s actual payment amount; and "D" is .29, the lower of the rate (29 percent) of the qualifying levy (the country E income tax as applied to corporations engaged in the extraction of petroleum in country E) or the rate (46 percent) of tax specified for 1984 in section 11(b)(5) of the Internal Revenue Code. Thus, *B*'s qualifying amount is equal to its actual payment amount.

Example (6). The facts are the same as in example (5), except that the rate of the country E income tax is 55 percent. For the reasons stated in example (5), the results with respect to *A* are the same as in example (5). In applying the safe harbor formula to *B*, "A," "B," and "C" are the same as in example (5), but "D" is .46, as that rate is less than .55. Thus, *B*'s qualifying amount is less than *B*'s actual payment amount, and the difference is *B*'s specific economic benefit amount.

Example (7). Country E imposes a tax (called the country E income tax) on the realized net income derived by corporations from sources in country E, except that, with respect to interest income received from sources in country E and certain insurance income, nonresident corporations are instead subject to other levies. With respect to such interest income a levy (called the country E interest tax) requires nonresident corporations to pay to country E 20 percent of such gross interest income unless the nonresident corporation falls within a specified category of corporations ("special corporations"), all of which are dual capacity taxpayers, in which case the rate is instead 25 percent. With respect to such insurance income nonresident corporations are subject to a levy (called the country E insurance tax), which is not an income tax within the meaning of § 1.901-2(a)(1).

The country E interest tax applies at the 20 percent rate by its terms and in practice to persons other than dual capacity taxpayers. The country E interest tax as applied at the 25 percent rate to special corporations applies only to dual capacity taxpayers; therefore, the country E interest tax as applied to special corporations is a separate levy from the country E interest tax as applied at the 20 percent rate.

A is a U.S. corporation which is a special corporation subject to the 25 percent rate of the country E interest tax. *A* does not have insurance income that is subject to the country E insurance tax. *A*, a dual capacity taxpayer, has validly elected the safe harbor formula for 1984. In 1984 *A* receives 100u (units of country E currency) of gross interest income subject to the country E interest tax and pays 25u to country E.

A establishes that the country E income tax is the generally imposed income tax of country E; that all of the criteria of section 903 are satisfied with respect to the country E interest tax as applied to special corporations except for the determination of the distinct element of the levy that is a tax and of *A*'s qualifying amount with respect thereto. *A* has therefore demonstrated that the country E interest tax as applied to special corporations is a qualifying levy. *A* establishes that the country E interest tax at the 20 percent rate is a tax in lieu of an income tax within the meaning of § 1.903-1(a). Pursuant to paragraph (e)(6) of this section the country E interest tax at the 20 percent rate is treated as if it were an application of the general tax for purposes of the safe harbor formula of this paragraph (e), since that tax would actually have been required to have been paid by *A* with respect to its interest income had *A* not been a dual capacity taxpayer (special corporation) instead subject to the qualifying levy (the country E interest tax at the 25 percent rate).

Even if the country E insurance tax is a tax in lieu of an income tax within the meaning of § 1.903-1(a), that tax is not treated as if it were an application of the general tax for purposes of applying the safe harbor formula to *A* since *A* had no insurance income in 1984 and hence such tax would not actually have been required to be paid by *A* had *A* not been a dual capacity taxpayer.

Example (8). Under a levy of country S called the country S income tax, each corporation operating in country S is required to pay country S 50 percent of its income from operations in country S. Income for purposes of the country S income tax is computed by subtracting all attributable costs and expenses from a corporation's gross receipts derived from its business in country S. Among corporations on which the country S income tax is imposed are corporations engaged in the exploitation of mineral K in country S. Natural deposits of mineral K in country S are owned by country S, and all corporations engaged in the exploitation thereof do so under concession agreements with an instrumentality of country S. Such corporations, in addition to the 50 percent country S income tax, are also subject to a levy called a surtax, which is equal to 60 percent of posted price net income less the amount of the country S income tax. The surtax is not deductible in computing the country S income tax of corporations engaged in the exploitation of mineral K in country S.

A is a U.S. corporation engaged in country S in the exploitation of mineral K, and *A* has been allowed to extract mineral K under a concession agreement with an instrumentality of country S. Therefore, *A* is a dual capacity taxpayer. In accordance with a term of the concession agreement, certain of *A*'s income (net of expenses attributable thereto) is exempted from the income tax and surtax.

The results for *A* in 1984 are as follows:

	Income Tax	*Surtax*
Gross Receipts		
Realized—Taxable	120u	—
Realized—Exempt	15u	—
Posted Price—Taxable	—	145u
Costs		
Attributable to Taxable Receipts	20u	20u
Attributable to Exempt Receipts	5u	—
Taxable Income	100u	125u
Tentative Surtax (60%)	—	75u
Petroleum Levy at 50%	50u	50u
Surtax	—	25u

Because of the difference (nondeductibility of the surtax) in the country S income tax as applied to dual capacity taxpayers from its application to other persons, the country S income tax as applied to dual capacity taxpayers and the country S income tax as applied to persons other than dual capacity taxpayers are separate levies. Moreover, because *A*'s concession agreement provides for a modification (exemption of certain income) of the country S income tax and surtax as they otherwise apply to other persons engaged in the exploitation of mineral K in country S, those levies (contractual levies) as applied to *A* are separate levies from those levies as applied to other persons engaged in the exploitation of mineral K in country S.

A establishes that the country S income tax as applied to persons other than dual capacity taxpayers is an income tax within the meaning of § 1.901-2(a)(1) and is the general tax. *A* demonstrates that all the criteria of section 903 are satisfied with respect to the country S income tax as applied to *A* and with respect to the surtax as applied to *A*, except for the determination of the distinct elements of such levies that are taxes and of *A*'s qualifying amounts with respect to such levies. Therefore, both the country S income tax as applied to *A* and the surtax as applied to *A* are qualifying levies.

In applying the safe harbor formula, in accordance with paragraph (e)(2), the amount of *A*'s gross receipts includes the exempt realized income, and the amount of *A*'s costs and expenses includes the costs attributable to such exempt income. In accordance with paragraph (e)(7)(i), the amount of the qualifying levy for purposes of the formula is the sum of *A*'s liability for the country S income tax and *A*'s liability for the surtax. Accordingly, under the safe harbor formula. *A*'s qualifying amount with respect to the country S income tax and the surtax is 35u ((135u − 25u − 75u) × .50/(1 − .50)). *A*'s specific economic benefit amount is 40u (*A*'s actual payment amount (75u) less *A*'s qualifying amount (35u)).

Example (9). Country T imposes a levy on corporations, called the country T income tax. The country T income tax is imposed at a rate of 50 percent on gross receipts less all costs and expenses, and affiliated corporations are allowed to consolidate their results in applying the country T income tax. Corporations engaged in the exploitation of mineral L in country T are subject to a levy that is identical to the country T income tax except that no consolidation among affiliated corporations is allowed. The levy allows unlimited loss carryforwards.

C and *D* are affiliated U.S. corporations engaged in country T in the exploitation of mineral L. Natural deposits of mineral L in country T are owned by country T, and *C* and *D* have been allowed to extract mineral L in consideration of certain payments to an instrumentality of country T. Therefore, *C* and *D* are dual capacity taxpayers.

The results for *C* and *D* in 1984 and 1985 are as follows:

	1984		*1985*	
	C	D	C	D
Gross Receipts	120u	0	120u	120u
Costs	20u	50u	20u	20u
Loss Carryforward				50u
Net Income (Loss)	100u	(50u)	100u	50u
Income Tax	50u	...	50u	25u

C and *D* establish that the country T income tax as applied to persons other than dual capacity taxpayers is an income tax within the meaning of § 1.901-2(a)(1) and is the general tax. *C* and *D* demonstrate that all of the criteria of section 901 are satisfied with respect to the country T income tax as applied to dual capacity taxpayers, except for the determination of the distinct element of such levy that is a tax and of *C* and *D*'s qualifying amounts with respect to that levy. Therefore, the country T income tax as applied to dual capacity taxpayers is a qualifying levy.

In applying the safe harbor formula, in accordance with paragraphs (e)(2)(ii) and (e)(7)(iii), the gross receipts, costs and expenses, and actual payment amounts of *C* and *D* are aggregated, except that in *D*'s loss year (1984) its gross receipts and costs and expenses are disregarded. The results of any loss year are disregarded since the country T income tax as applied to dual capacity taxpayers does not allow consolidation, and, pursuant to paragraph (e)(2)(ii), differences in consolidation provisions between such levy

an RFA in determining foreign income, regardless of whether the gain is deferred or otherwise not taken into account currently. Notwithstanding the foregoing, if after a section 743(b) CAA there is a disposition of an asset that is an RFA with respect to that section 743(b) CAA, foreign disposition gain has the meaning provided in § 1.901(m)-5(c)(2)(iii).

(24) The term *foreign disposition loss* means, with respect to a foreign income tax, the amount of loss recognized on a disposition of an RFA in determining foreign income, regardless of whether the loss is deferred or disallowed or otherwise not taken into account currently. Notwithstanding the foregoing, if after a section 743(b) CAA there is a disposition of an asset that is an RFA with respect to that section 743(b) CAA, foreign disposition loss has the meaning provided in § 1.901(m)-5(c)(2)(iii).

(25) The term *foreign income* means, with respect to a foreign income tax, the taxable income (or loss) reflected on a foreign tax return (as properly amended or adjusted), even if the taxable income (or loss) is reported by an entity that is a fiscally transparent entity for purposes of the foreign income tax. If, however, foreign law imposes tax on the combined income (within the meaning of § 1.901-2(f)(3)(ii)) of two or more foreign payors, foreign income means the combined taxable income (or loss) of such foreign payors, regardless of whether such income (or loss) is reflected on a single foreign tax return.

(26) The term *foreign income tax* means an income, war profits, or excess profits tax for which a credit is allowable under section 901 or section 903, except that it does not include any withholding tax determined on a gross basis as described in section 901(k)(1)(B).

(27) The term *foreign income tax amount* means, with respect to a foreign income tax, the amount of tax (including an amount of tax that is zero) reflected on a foreign tax return (as properly amended or adjusted). If foreign law imposes tax on the combined income (within the meaning of § 1.901-2(f)(3)(ii)) of two or more foreign payors, however, a foreign income tax amount means the amount of tax imposed on the combined income, regardless of whether the tax is reflected on a single foreign tax return.

(28) The term *foreign payor* means an individual or entity (including a disregarded entity) subject to a foreign income tax. If foreign law imposes tax on the combined income (within the meaning of § 1.901-2(f)(3)(ii)) of two or more individuals or entities, each such individual or entity is a foreign payor. An individual or entity may be a foreign payor with respect to more than one foreign income tax for purposes of applying section 901(m).

(29) The term *foreign taxable year* means a taxable year for purposes of a foreign income tax.

(30) The term *mid-year transaction* means a transaction in which a foreign payor that is a corporation or a disregarded entity has a change in ownership or makes an election pursuant to § 301.7701-3 to change its entity classification, or a transaction in which a foreign payor that is a partnership terminates under section 708(b)(1), provided in each case that the foreign payor's foreign taxable year does not close as a result of the transaction, and, if the foreign payor is a corporation or a partnership, the foreign payor's U.S. taxable year closes.

(31) The term *prior CAA* has the meaning provided in § 1.901(m)-6(b)(2).

(32) The term *prior section 743(b) CAA* has the meaning provided in § 1.901(m)-6(b)(4)(iii).

(33) The term *relevant foreign asset* (or *RFA*) has the meaning provided in § 1.901(m)-2.

(34) The term *reverse hybrid* has the meaning provided in § 1.909-2(b)(1)(iv).

(35) The term *RFA class exemption* has the meaning provided in § 1.901(m)-7(b)(3).

(36) The term *RFA exemption* has the meaning provided in § 1.901(m)-7(b)(4).

(37) The term *RFA owner (U.S.)* means a person that owns an RFA for U.S. income tax purposes.

(38) The term *RFA owner (foreign)* means an individual or entity (including a disregarded entity) that owns an RFA for purposes of a foreign income tax.

(39) The term *section 338 CAA* has the meaning provided in § 1.901(m)-2(b)(1).

(40) The term *section 743(b) CAA* has the meaning provided in § 1.901(m)-2(b)(3).

(41) The term *section 901(m) payor* means a person eligible to claim the foreign tax credit allowed under section 901(a), regardless of whether the person chooses to claim the foreign tax credit, as well as an applicable foreign corporation. Each member of a consolidated group is a separate section 901(m) payor. If individuals file a joint return, those individuals are treated as a single section 901(m) payor.

(42) The term *separate category* means each separate category described in § 1.904-5(a)(4)(v), and in the case of an applicable foreign corporation described in paragraph (a)(7)(ii) of this section, each income group described in § 1.960-1(d)(2)(ii).

(43) The term *subsequent CAA* has the meaning provided in § 1.901(m)-6(b)(4)(i).

(44) The term *subsequent section 743(b) CAA* has the meaning provided in § 1.901(m)-6(b)(4)(iii).

(45) The term *successor transaction* has the meaning provided in § 1.901(m)-6(b)(2).

(46) The term *tentative disqualified tax amount* has the meaning provided in § 1.901(m)-3(b)(2)(ii).

(47) The term *unallocated basis difference* means, with respect to an RFA and a foreign income tax, the basis difference reduced by the sum of the cost recovery amounts and the disposition amounts that have been computed under § 1.901(m)-5.

(48) The term *unallocated CAA gain* means, with respect to an RFA, the CAA gain reduced by the sum of the allocated basis difference adjustments that have been computed with respect to the RFA.

(49) The term *unallocated CAA loss* means, with respect to an RFA, the CAA loss reduced by the sum of the allocated basis difference adjustments that have been computed with respect to the RFA.

(50) The term *U.S. basis* means the adjusted basis of an asset determined for U.S. income tax purposes.

(51) The term *U.S. basis deduction* has the meaning provided in § 1.901(m)-5(b)(3).

(52) The term *U.S. disposition gain* means the amount of gain recognized for U.S. income tax purposes on a disposition of an RFA, regardless of whether the gain is deferred or otherwise not taken into account currently. Notwithstanding the foregoing, if after a section 743(b) CAA there is a disposition of an asset that is an RFA with respect to that section 743(b) CAA, U.S. disposition gain has the meaning provided in § 1.901(m)-5(c)(2)(iii).

(53) The term *U.S. disposition loss* means the amount of loss recognized for U.S. income tax purposes on a disposition of an RFA, regardless of whether the loss is deferred or disallowed or otherwise not taken into account currently. Notwithstanding the foregoing, if after a section 743(b) CAA there is a disposition of an asset that is an RFA with respect to that section 743(b) CAA, U.S. disposition loss has the meaning provided in § 1.901(m)-5(c)(2)(iii).

(54) The term *U.S. taxable year* means a taxable year as defined in section 7701(a)(23).

(b) *Applicability dates.*—(1) Except as provided in paragraph (b)(2) of this section, this section applies to CAAs occurring on or after March 23, 2020.

(2) Paragraphs (a)(8), (12), (13), (15), (16), (18), (19), (23) through (26), (31) through (33), (39), (40), (43) through (45), (47), (50), and (52) through (54) of this section apply to CAAs occurring on or after July 21, 2014, and to CAAs occurring before that date resulting from an entity classification election made under § 301.7701-3 that is filed on or after July 29, 2014, and that is effective on or before July 21, 2014. Paragraphs (a)(8), (12), (13), (15), (16), (18), (19), (23) through (26) through (33), (39), (40), (43) through (45), (47), (50), and (52) through (54) of this section also apply to CAAs occurring on or after January 1, 2011, and before July 21, 2014, other than CAAs occurring before July 21, 2014, resulting from an entity classification election made under § 301.7701-3 that is filed on or after July 29, 2014, and that is effective on or before July 21, 2014, but only if the basis difference (within the meaning of section 901(m)(3)(C)(i)) in one or more RFAs with respect to the CAA had not been fully taken into account under section 901(m)(3)(B) either as of July 21, 2014, or, in the case of an entity classification election made under § 301.7701-3 that is filed on or after July 29, 2014, and that is effective on or before July 21, 2014, before the transactions that are deemed to occur under § 301.7701-3(g) as a result of the change in classification.

(3) Taxpayers may, however, choose to apply provisions in this section before the date such provisions are applicable pursuant to paragraph (b)(1) or (2) of this section, provided that they (along with any persons that are related (within the meaning of section 267(b) or 707(b)) to the taxpayer)—

(i) Consistently apply this section, § 1.704-1(b)(4)(viii)(*c*)(*4*)(*v*) through (*vii*), and §§ 1.901(m)-3 through 1.901(m)-8 (excluding § 1.901(m)-4(e)) to all CAAs occurring on or after January 1, 2011, and consistently apply § 1.901(m)-2 (excluding § 1.901(m)-2(d)) to all CAAs occurring on or after December 7, 2016, on any original or amended tax return for each taxable year for which the application of the provisions listed in this paragraph (b)(3)(i) affects the tax liability and for which the statute of limitations does not preclude assessment or the filing of a claim for refund, as applicable;

(ii) File all tax returns described in paragraph (b)(3)(i) of this section for any taxable year ending on or before March 23, 2020, no later than March 23, 2021; and

(iii) Make appropriate adjustments to take into account deficiencies that would have resulted from the consistent application under paragraph (b)(3)(i) of this section for taxable years that are not open for assessment. [Reg. § 1.901(m)-1.]

□ [*T.D. 9895, 3-20-2020.*]

§ 1.901(m)-2. Covered asset acquisitions and relevant foreign assets.—(a) *In general.*—Paragraph (b) of this section sets forth the transactions that are covered asset acquisitions (or CAAs). Paragraph (c) of this section provides rules for identifying assets that are relevant foreign assets (or RFAs) with respect to a CAA. Paragraph (d) of this section provides special rules for identifying CAAs and RFAs with respect to transactions to which paragraphs (b) and (c) of this section do not apply. Paragraph (e) of this section provides examples illustrating the rules of this section, and paragraph (f) of this section provides applicability dates.

(b) *Covered asset acquisitions.*—Except as provided in paragraph (d) of this section, the transactions set forth in this paragraph (b) are CAAs.

(1) A qualified stock purchase (as defined in section 338(d)(3)) to which section 338(a) applies (*section 338 CAA*);

(2) Any transaction that is treated as an acquisition of assets for U.S. income tax purposes and treated as an acquisition of stock of a corporation (or disregarded) for foreign income tax purposes;

(3) Any acquisition of an interest in a partnership that has an election in effect under section 754 (*section 743(b) CAA*);

(4) Any transaction (or series of transactions occurring pursuant to a plan) to the extent it is treated as an acquisition of assets for purposes of U.S. income tax and as the acquisition of an interest in a fiscally transparent entity for purposes of a foreign income tax;

(5) Any transaction (or series of transactions occurring pursuant to a plan) to the extent it is treated as a partnership distribution of one or more assets the U.S. basis of which is determined by section 732(b) or 732(d) or to the extent it causes the U.S. basis of the partnership's remaining assets to be adjusted under section 734(b), provided the transaction results in an increase in the U.S. basis of one or more of the assets distributed by the partnership or retained by the partnership without a corresponding increase in the foreign basis of such assets; and

(6) Any transaction (or series of transactions occurring pursuant to a plan) to the extent it is treated as an acquisition of assets for purposes of both U.S. income tax and a foreign income tax, provided the transaction results in an increase in the U.S. basis without a corresponding increase in the foreign basis of one or more assets.

(c) *Relevant foreign asset.*—(1) *In general.*—Except as provided in paragraph (d) of this section, an RFA means, with respect to a foreign income tax and a CAA, any asset (including goodwill, going concern value, or other intangible) subject to the CAA that is relevant in determining foreign income for purposes of the foreign income tax.

(2) *RFA status with respect to a foreign income tax.*—An asset is relevant in determining foreign income if income, deduction, gain, or loss attributable to the asset is taken into account in determining foreign income immediately after the CAA, or would be taken into account in determining foreign income immediately after the CAA if the asset were to give rise to income, deduction, gain, or loss at such time.

(3) *Subsequent RFA status with respect to another foreign income tax.*—After a CAA, an asset will become an RFA with respect to another foreign income tax if, pursuant to a plan or series of related transactions that have a principal purpose of avoiding the application of section 901(m), an asset that was not relevant in determining foreign income for purposes of that foreign income tax immediately after the CAA becomes relevant in determining such foreign income. A principal purpose of avoiding section 901(m) will be deemed to exist if income, deduction, gain, or loss attributable to the asset is taken into account in determining such foreign income within the one-year period following the CAA, or would be taken into account in determining such foreign income during such time if the asset were to give rise to income, deduction, gain, or loss within the one-year period.

(d) *Identifying covered asset acquisitions and relevant foreign assets to which paragraphs (b) and (c) of this section do not apply.*—For transactions occurring on or after January 1, 2011, and before July 21, 2014, other than transactions occurring before July 21, 2014, resulting from an entity classification election made under § 301.7701-3 of this chapter that is filed on or after July 29, 2014, and that is effective on or before July 21, 2014, the transactions set forth under section 901(m)(2) are CAAs and the assets that are relevant foreign assets with respect to the CAA under section 901(m)(4) are RFAs.

(e) *Examples.*—The following examples illustrate the rules of this section:

(1) *Example 1: CAA involving an acquisition of a partnership interest for foreign income tax purposes.*—(i) *Facts.* (A) FPS is an entity organized in Country F that is treated as a partnership for both U.S. and Country F income tax purposes. FPS is owned equally by FC1 and FC2, each of which is a corporation organized in Country F and treated as a corporation for both U.S. and Country F income tax purposes. FPS has a single asset, Asset A. USP, a domestic corporation, owns all the interests in DE, a disregarded entity.

(B) Pursuant to the same transaction, USP acquires FC1's interest in FPS, and DE acquires FC2's interest in FPS. For U.S. income tax purposes, with respect to USP, the acquisition of the interests in FPS is treated as the acquisition of Asset A by USP. See Rev. Rul. 99-6, 1999-1 C.B. 432. For Country F tax purposes, the acquisitions of the interests of FPS by USP and DE are treated as acquisitions of partnership interests.

(ii) *Result.* The transaction is a CAA under paragraph (b)(4) of this section because it is treated as the acquisition of Asset A for U.S. income tax purposes and the acquisition of interests in a fiscally transparent entity for Country F tax purposes.

(2) *Example 2: CAA involving an asset acquisition for purposes of both U.S. income tax and a foreign income tax.*—(i) *Facts.* (A) USP, a domestic corporation, wholly owns CFC1, a foreign corporation, and CFC1 wholly owns CFC2, also a foreign corporation. CFC1 and CFC2 are organized in Country F. CFC1 owns Asset A.

(B) In an exchange described in section 351, CFC1 transfers Asset A to CFC2 in exchange for CFC2 common stock and cash. CFC1 recognizes gain on the exchange under section 351(b). Under section 362(a), CFC2's U.S. basis in Asset A is increased by the gain recognized by CFC1. For Country F tax purposes, gain or loss is not recognized on the transfer of Asset A to CFC2, and therefore there is no increase in the foreign basis in Asset A.

(ii) *Result.* The transaction is a CAA under paragraph (b)(6) of this section because it is treated as an acquisition of Asset A by CFC2 for both U.S. and Country F income tax purposes, and it results in an increase in the U.S. basis of Asset A without a corresponding increase in the foreign basis of Asset A.

(3) *Example 3: RFA status determined immediately after CAA; application of principal purpose rule.*—(i) *Facts.* (A) USP1 and USP2 are unrelated domestic corporations. USP1 wholly owns USSub, also a domestic corporation. On January 1 of Year 1, USP2 acquires all of the stock of USSub from USP1 in a qualified stock purchase (as defined in section 338(d)(3)) to which section 338(a) applies. Immediately after the acquisition, none of the income, deduction, gain, or loss attributable to any of the assets of USSub is taken into account in determining foreign income for purposes of a foreign income tax nor would such items be taken into account in determining foreign income for purposes of a foreign income tax immediately after the acquisition if such assets were to give rise to income, deduction, gain, or loss immediately after the acquisition.

(B) On December 1 of Year 1, USSub contributes all its assets to FSub, its wholly owned subsidiary, which is a corporation for both U.S. and Country X income tax purposes, in a transfer described in section 351 (subsequent transfer). USSub recognizes no gain or loss for U.S. or Country X income tax purposes as a result of the subsequent transfer. As a result of the subsequent transfer, income, deduction, gain, or loss attributable to the assets of USSub that were transferred to FSub is taken into account in determining foreign income of FSub for Country X tax purposes.

(ii) *Result.* (A) Under paragraph (b)(1) of this section, the acquisition by USP2 of the stock of USSub is a section 338 CAA. Under paragraph (c)(1) of this section, none of the assets of USSub are RFAs immediately after the CAA, because none of the income, deduction, gain, or loss attributable to such assets is taken into account for purposes of determining foreign income with respect to any foreign income tax immediately after the CAA (nor would such items be taken into account for purposes of determining foreign income immediately after the CAA if such assets were to give rise to income, deduction, gain, or loss at such time).

(B) Although the subsequent transfer is not a CAA under paragraph (b) of this section, the subsequent transfer causes the assets of USSub to become relevant in the hands of FSub in determining foreign income for Country X tax purposes. Because the subsequent transfer occurred within the one-year period following the CAA, it is presumed to have a principal purpose of avoiding section 901(m) under paragraph (c)(3) of this section. Accordingly, the assets of USSub with respect to the CAA occurring on January 1 of Year 1 become RFAs with respect to Country X tax as a result of the subsequent transfer. Thus, a basis difference with respect to Country X tax must be computed for the RFAs and taken into account under section 901(m).

(f) *Applicability dates.*—(1) Except as provided in paragraph (f)(2) of this section, this section applies to CAAs occurring on or after March 23, 2020.

(2) Paragraphs (a), (b)(1) through (3), and (c)(1) of this section apply to transactions occurring on or after July 21, 2014, and to transactions occurring before that date resulting from an entity classification election made under § 301.7701-3 of this chapter that is filed on or after July 29, 2014, and that is effective on or before July 21, 2014. Paragraph (d) of this section applies to transactions occurring on or after January 1, 2011, and before July 21, 2014, other than transactions occurring before July 21, 2014, resulting from an entity classification election made under § 301.7701-3 of this chapter that is filed on or after July 29, 2014, and that is effective on or before July 21, 2014.

(3) Taxpayers may, however, choose to apply provisions in this section before the date such provisions are applicable pursuant to paragraph (f)(1) or (2) of this section, provided that they (along with any persons that are related (within the meaning of section 267(b) or 707(b)) to the taxpayer)—

(i) Consistently apply this section (excluding paragraph (d) of this section) to all CAAs occurring on or after December 7, 2016 and consistently apply § 1.704-1(b)(4)(viii)(*c*)(*4*)(*v*) through (*vii*), § 1.901(m)-1, and §§ 1.901(m)-3 through 1.901(m)-8 (excluding § 1.901(m)-4(e)) to all CAAs occurring on or after January 1, 2011, on any original or amended tax return for each taxable year for which the application of the provisions listed in this paragraph (f)(3)(i) affects the tax liability and for which the statute of limitations does not preclude assessment or the filing of a claim for refund, as applicable;

(ii) File all tax returns described in paragraph (f)(3)(i) of this section for any taxable year ending on or before March 23, 2020, no later than March 23, 2021; and

(iii) Make appropriate adjustments to take into account deficiencies that would have resulted from the consistent application under paragraph (f)(3)(i) of this section for taxable years that are not open for assessment. [Reg. § 1.901(m)-2.]

☐ [*T.D. 9895, 3-20-2020.*]

§ 1.901(m)-3. Disqualified tax amount and aggregate basis difference carryover.—(a) *In general.*—If a section 901(m) payor has an aggregate basis difference, with respect to a foreign income tax and a foreign payor, for a U.S. taxable year, the section 901(m) payor must determine the portion of a foreign income tax amount that is disqualified under section 901(m) (*disqualified tax amount*). Paragraph (b) of this section provides rules for determining the disqualified tax amount. Paragraph (c) of this section provides rules for determining what portion, if any, of aggregate basis difference will be carried forward to the next U.S. taxable year (*aggregate basis difference carryover*). Paragraph (d) of this section provides applicability dates.

(b) *Disqualified tax amount.*—(1) *In general.*—A section 901(m) payor's disqualified tax amount is not taken into account in determining the credit allowed under section 901(a). If the section 901(m) payor is an applicable foreign corporation, the disqualified tax amount is not taken into account for purposes of section 902 (for tax years of foreign corporations beginning before January 1, 2018) or 960. Sections 78 and 275 do not apply to the disqualified tax amount. The disqualified tax amount is allowed as a deduction to the extent otherwise deductible. See sections 164, 212, and 964 and the regulations under those sections.

(2) *Determination of disqualified tax amount.*—(i) *In general.*—Except as provided in paragraph (b)(2)(iv) of this section, the disqualified tax amount is equal to the lesser of the foreign income tax amount that is paid or accrued by, or considered paid or accrued by, the section 901(m) payor for the U.S. taxable year or the tentative disqualified tax amount. All calculations are determined with respect to each separate category.

(ii) *Tentative disqualified tax amount.*—The tentative disqualified tax amount is equal to the amount determined under paragraph (b)(2)(ii)(A) of this section reduced (but not below zero) by the amount described in paragraph (b)(2)(ii)(B) of this section.

(A) The product of—

(*1*) The sum of the foreign income tax amount and the FCCTs that are paid or accrued by, or considered paid or accrued by, the section 901(m) payor, and

(*2*) A fraction, the numerator of which is the aggregate basis difference, but not in excess of the allocable foreign income, and the denominator of which is the allocable foreign income.

(B) The amount of the FCCT that is a disqualified tax amount of the section 901(m) payor with respect to another foreign income tax.

(iii) *Allocable foreign income.*—(A) *No allocation required.*—Except as provided in paragraph (b)(2)(iii)(D) of this section, if the entire foreign income tax amount is paid or accrued by, or considered paid or accrued by, a single section 901(m) payor, then the allocable foreign income is equal to the entire foreign income, determined with respect to each separate category.

(B) *Allocation required.*—Except as provided in paragraph (b)(2)(iii)(D) of this section, if the foreign income tax amount is allocated to, and considered paid or accrued by, more than one person, a section 901(m) payor's allocable foreign income is equal to the portion of the foreign income that relates to the foreign income tax amount allocated to that section 901(m) payor, determined with respect to each separate category.

(C) *Rules for allocations.*—This paragraph (b)(2)(iii)(C) provides allocation rules that apply to determine allocable foreign income in certain cases.

(*1*) If the foreign payor is involved in a mid-year transaction and the foreign income tax amount is allocated under § 1.336-2(g)(3)(ii), § 1.338-9(d), or § 1.901-2(f)(4), then, to the extent any portion of the foreign income tax amount is allocated to, and considered paid or accrued by, a section 901(m) payor, the allocable foreign income of the section 901(m) payor is determined in accordance with the principles of § 1.1502-76(b). To the extent the foreign income tax amount is allocated to an entity that is a partnership for U.S. income tax purposes, a portion of the foreign income is first allocated to the partnership in accordance with the principles of § 1.1502-76(b), which is then allocated under the rules of paragraph (b)(2)(iii)(C)(*2*) of this section to determine the allocable foreign income of a section 901(m) payor that owns an interest in the partnership directly or indirectly through one or more other partnerships for U.S. income tax purposes.

(*2*) If the foreign income tax amount is considered paid or accrued by a section 901(m) payor for a U.S. taxable year under § 1.702-1(a)(6), the determination of the allocable foreign income must be consistent with the allocation of the foreign income tax amount that relates to the foreign income. See § 1.704-1(b)(4)(viii).

(*3*) If the foreign income tax amount that is allocated to, and considered paid or accrued by, a section 901(m) payor for a U.S. taxable year is determined under § 1.901-2(f)(3)(i), the allocable foreign income is determined in accordance with § 1.901-2(f)(3)(iii).

(D) *Failure to substantiate allocable foreign income.*—If, pursuant to section 901(m)(3)(A), a section 901(m) payor fails to substantiate its allocable foreign income to the satisfaction of the Secretary, then allocable foreign income will equal the amount determined by dividing the sum of the foreign income tax amount and the FCCTs that are paid or accrued by, or considered paid or accrued by, the section 901(m) payor, by the highest marginal tax rate applicable to income of the foreign payor under foreign tax law.

(iv) *Special rule.*—A section 901(m) payor's disqualified tax amount is zero for a U.S. taxable year if:

(A) The section 901(m) payor's aggregate basis difference for the U.S. taxable year is a negative amount;

(B) Foreign income is less than or equal to zero for the foreign taxable year of the foreign payor; or

(C) The foreign income tax amount that is paid or accrued by, or considered paid or accrued by, the section 901(m) payor for the U.S. taxable year is zero.

(3) *Examples.*—The following examples illustrate the rules of paragraph (b)(2) of this section. For purposes of all the examples, unless otherwise specified: USP is a domestic corporation. CFC1, CFC2, DE1, and DE2 are organized in Country F and are treated as corporations for Country F tax purposes. CFC1 and CFC2 are applicable foreign corporations. DE1 and DE2 are disregarded entities. USP, CFC1, and CFC2 each have a calendar year for both U.S. and Country F income tax purposes, and DE1 and DE2 each have a calendar year for Country F tax purposes. Country F and Country G each impose a single tax that is a foreign income tax. CFC1, CFC2, DE1, and DE2 each have a functional currency of the u with respect to all activities. At all relevant times, 1u equals $1. All amounts are stated in millions. The examples assume that the applicable cost recovery method for property results in basis being recovered ratably over the life of the property beginning on the first day of the U.S. taxable year in which the property is acquired or placed into service; there is a single separate category with respect to a foreign income and foreign income tax amount; and a section 901(m) payor properly substantiates its allocable foreign income to the satisfaction of the Secretary.

(i) *Example 1: Determining aggregate basis difference; multiple foreign payors.*—(A) *Facts.* CFC1 wholly owns CFC2 and DE1. DE1 wholly owns DE2. Assume that the tax laws of Country F do not allow combined income reporting or the filing of consolidated income tax returns. Accordingly, CFC1, CFC2, DE1, and DE2 file separate tax returns for Country F tax purposes. USP acquires all of the stock of CFC1 in a qualified stock purchase (as defined in section 338(d)(3)) to which section 338(a) applies for both CFC1 and CFC2.

(B) *Result.* (*1*) The acquisition of CFC1 gives rise to four separate CAAs under § 1.901(m)-2(b). The acquisition of the stock of CFC1 and the deemed purchase of the stock of CFC2 under section 338(h)(3)(B) are each a section 338 CAA under § 1.901(m)-2(b)(1). Furthermore, because the deemed purchase of the assets of DE1 and DE2 for U.S. income tax purposes is disregarded for Country F tax purposes, each acquisition is a CAA under § 1.901(m)-2(b)(2). Because these four CAAs occur pursuant to a plan, under § 1.901(m)-1(a)(3) they are part of an aggregated CAA transaction. Under § 1.901(m)-1(a)(37), CFC1 is the RFA owner (U.S.) with respect to its assets and those of DE1 and DE2. CFC2 is the RFA owner (U.S.) with respect to its assets. Under § 1.901(m)-1(a)(28), CFC1, CFC2, DE1, and DE2 are each a foreign payor for Country F tax purposes. Under § 1.901(m)-1(a)(41), CFC1 is the section 901(m) payor with respect to foreign income tax amounts for which CFC1, DE1, and DE2 are the foreign payors (see § 1.901-2(f)(1) and (f)(4)(ii)). CFC2 is the section 901(m) payor with respect to foreign income tax amounts for which CFC2 is the foreign payor (see § 1.901-2(f)(1)).

(*2*) In determining aggregate basis difference under § 1.901(m)-1(a)(1) for a U.S. taxable year of CFC1, CFC1 has three computations with respect to Country F tax, because there are three foreign payors for Country F tax purposes whose foreign income tax amount, if any, is considered paid or accrued by CFC1 as the section 901(m) payor. Furthermore, for each U.S. taxable year, CFC1 will compute a separate disqualified tax amount and aggregate basis difference carryover (if any) under paragraph (b)(2) of this section, with respect to each foreign payor.

(*3*) In determining aggregate basis difference for a U.S. taxable year of CFC2 under § 1.901(m)-1(a)(1), CFC2 has a single computation with respect to Country F tax, because there is a single foreign payor (CFC2) for Country F tax purposes whose foreign income tax amount, if any, is considered paid or accrued by CFC2 as the section 901(m) payor. Furthermore, for each U.S. taxable year, CFC2 will compute a disqualified tax amount and aggregate basis difference carryover (if any) under paragraph (b)(2) of this section.

(C) *Alternative facts.* Assume the same facts as in paragraph (b)(3)(i)(A) of this section (paragraph (A) of this *Example 1*), except that foreign income for Country F tax purposes is based on combined income (within the meaning of § 1.901-2(f)(3)(ii)) of CFC1, CFC2, DE1, and DE2. For purposes of determining an aggregate basis difference for a U.S. taxable year of CFC1 under § 1.901(m)-1(a)(1), CFC1, DE1, and DE2 are treated as a single foreign payor because all of the items of income, deduction, gain, or loss with respect to CFC1, DE1, and DE2 are included in the earnings and profits of CFC1 for U.S. income tax purposes. For each U.S. taxable year, CFC1 will therefore compute a single aggregate basis difference, disqualified tax amount, and aggregate basis difference carryover. The result for CFC2 under the alternative facts is the same as in paragraph (b)(3)(i)(B)(*3*) (paragraph (B)(*3*) of this *Example 1*).

(ii) *Example 2: Computation of disqualified tax amount.*—(A) *Facts.* On December 31 of Year 0, USP acquires all of the stock of CFC1 in a qualified stock purchase (as defined in section 338(d)(3)) to which section 338(a) applies (Acquisition). CFC1 owns four assets (Asset A, Asset B, Asset C, and Asset D, and collectively, Assets) and conducts activities in Country F and in a Country G branch. The activities conducted by CFC1 in Country G are not subject to tax in Country F. The tax rate is 25% in Country F and 30% in Country G. For Country F tax purposes, CFC1's foreign income and foreign income tax amount for each foreign taxable year 1 through 15 is 100u and $25 (25u translated at the exchange rate of $1 = 1u), respectively. For Country G tax purposes, CFC1's foreign income and foreign income tax amount for each foreign taxable year 1 through 5 is 400u and $120 (120u translated at the exchange rate of $1 = 1u), respectively. No dispositions occur for any of the Assets during the applicable cost recovery period. Additional facts relevant to each of the Assets are summarized below.

Assets	Relevant foreign income tax	Basis Difference	Applicable Cost Recovery Period	Cost Recovery Amount
Asset A	Country F tax	150u	15 years	10u (150u / 15)
Asset B	Country F tax	50u	5 years	10u (50u / 5)
Asset C	Country G tax	300u	5 years	60u (300u / 5)
Asset D	Country G tax	(100u)	5 years	negative 20u (negative 100 / 5)

(B) *Result.* (*1*) Under § 1.901(m)-2(b)(1), the acquisition of the stock of CFC1 is a section 338 CAA. Under § 1.901(m)-2(c)(1), Assets A and B are RFAs with respect to Country F tax, because they are relevant in determining foreign income of CFC1 for Country F tax purposes and were owned by CFC1 when the Acquisition occurred. Assets C and D are RFAs with respect to Country G tax, because they are relevant in determining foreign income of CFC1 for Country G tax purposes and were owned by CFC1 when the Acquisition occurred. Under § 1.901(m)-1(a)(37), CFC1 is the RFA owner (U.S.) with respect to all of the RFAs. Under § 1.901(m)-1(a)(41) and (28), CFC1 is the section 901(m) payor and the foreign payor for Country F and Country G tax purposes.

(*2*) In determining aggregate basis difference for a U.S. taxable year of CFC1, CFC1 has two computations, one with respect to Country F tax and one with respect to Country G tax. Under § 1.901(m)-1(a)(1), the aggregate basis difference for a U.S. taxable year with respect to Country F tax is equal to the sum of the allocated basis differences and allocated basis difference adjustments with respect to Assets A and B for the U.S. taxable year. Under § 1.901(m)-1(a)(5), allocated basis differences are the sum of cost recovery amounts and disposition amounts. Because there are no dispositions, the only allocated basis differences taken into account in determining an aggregate basis difference are cost recovery amounts. Under § 1.901(m)-5(b), any cost recovery amounts are attributed to CFC1, because CFC1 is the section 901(m) payor and RFA owner (U.S.) with respect to all of the Assets. For each U.S. taxable year, CFC1 will compute a separate disqualified tax amount and aggregate basis difference carryover (if any) with respect to Country F tax and Country G tax under paragraph (b)(2) of this section. For purposes of both disqualified tax amount computations, because CFC1 is the section 901(m) payor and foreign payor, the foreign income tax amount paid or accrued by CFC1 with respect to Country F tax and Country G tax, respectively, will be the entire foreign income tax amount and CFC1's allocable foreign income will be the entire foreign income.

(*3*) With respect to Country F tax, in U.S. taxable years 1 through 5, CFC1 has an aggregate basis difference of 20u each year (10u cost recovery amount with respect to Asset A plus 10u cost recovery amount with respect to Asset B). For U.S. taxable years 1 through 5, under paragraph (b)(2) of this section, the disqualified tax amount each year is $5, the lesser of two amounts: the tentative disqualified tax amount, in this case, $5 ($25 foreign income tax amount x (20u aggregate basis difference / 100u allocable foreign income)), or the foreign income tax amount paid or accrued by CFC1, in this case, $25. After U.S. taxable year 5, Asset B has no unallocated basis difference with respect to Country F tax. Accordingly, in U.S. taxable years 6 through 15, CFC1 has an aggregate basis difference of 10u each year. Accordingly, for U.S. taxable years 6 through 15, the disqualified tax amount each year is $2.50, the lesser of two amounts: the tentative disqualified tax amount, in this case, $2.50 ($25 foreign income tax amount x (10u aggregate basis difference / 100u allocable foreign income)), or the foreign income tax amount paid or accrued by CFC1, in this case, $25. After U.S. taxable year 15, Asset A has no unallocated basis difference with respect to Country F tax and, therefore, CFC1 has no disqualified tax amount with respect to Country F Tax.

(4) With respect to Country G tax, in U.S. taxable years 1 through 5, CFC1 has an aggregate basis difference of 40u each year (60u cost recovery amount with respect to Asset C + (20u) cost recovery amount with respect to Asset D). For U.S. taxable years 1 through 5, under paragraph (b)(2) of this section, the disqualified tax amount each year is $12, the lesser of two amounts: the tentative disqualified tax amount, in this case, $12 ($120 foreign income tax amount x (40u aggregate basis difference / 400u allocable foreign income)), or the foreign income tax amount paid or accrued by CFC1, in this case, $120. After U.S. taxable year 5, Asset C and Asset D have no unallocated basis difference with respect to Country G tax. Accordingly, in U.S. taxable years 6 through 15, CFC1 has no disqualified tax amount with respect to Country G Tax.

(iii) *Example 3: FCCT.*—(A) *Facts.* In U.S. taxable year 1, USP acquires all of the interests in DE1 in a transaction (Transaction) that is treated as a stock acquisition for Country F tax purposes. Immediately after the Transaction, DE1 owns assets (Pre-Transaction Assets), all of which are used in a Country G branch and give rise to income that is taken into account for Country F tax and Country G tax purposes. After the Transaction, DE1 acquires additional assets (Post-Transaction Assets), which are not used by the Country G branch. Both Country F and Country G have a tax rate of 30%. Country F imposes worldwide tax on its residents and provides a foreign tax credit for taxes paid to other jurisdictions. In foreign taxable year 3, 100u of income is attributable to DE1's Post-Transaction Assets and 100u of income is attributable to DE1's Pre-Transaction Assets. For Country G tax purposes, the foreign income is 100u and foreign income tax amount is 30u (30% x 100u). For Country F tax purposes, the foreign income is 200u and the pre-foreign tax credit tax is 60u (30% x 200u). The 60u of Country F pre-foreign tax credit tax is reduced by the 30u foreign income tax amount imposed for Country G tax purposes. Thus, the foreign income tax amount for Country F tax purposes is $30 (30u translated into dollars at the exchange rate of $1 = 1u). Assume that for U.S. taxable year 3 USP has 100u aggregate basis difference with respect to Country F tax and 100u aggregate basis difference with respect to Country G tax. USP does not dispose of DE1 or any assets of DE1 in U.S. taxable year 3.

(B) *Result.* (*1*) Under § 1.901(m)-2(b)(2), the Transaction is a CAA. Under § 1.901(m)-2(c)(1), the Pre-Transaction Assets are RFAs with respect to both Country F tax and Country G tax, because they are relevant in determining the foreign income of DE1 for Country F tax and Country G tax purposes and were owned by DE1 when the Transaction occurred. Under § 1.901(m)-1(a)(37), USP is the RFA owner (U.S.) with respect to the RFAs. Under § 1.901(m)-1(a)(28), DE1 is a foreign payor for Country F tax and Country G tax purposes. Under § 1.901(m)-1(a)(41), USP is the section 901(m) payor with respect to foreign income tax amounts for which DE1 is the foreign payor (see § 1.901-2(f)(4)(ii)). Because the Country G foreign income tax amount is claimed as a credit for purposes of determining the Country F foreign income tax amount, the Country G foreign income tax amount is an FCCT under § 1.901(m)-1(a)(22).

(*2*) Under § 1.901(m)-1(a)(1), for each U.S. taxable year, USP will separately compute the aggregate basis difference with respect to Country F tax and with respect to Country G tax and will use those amounts to separately compute a disqualified tax amount and aggregate basis difference carryover (if any) with respect to each foreign income tax. Because DE1 is a disregarded entity owned by USP during the entire U.S. taxable year 3, the foreign income tax amount paid or accrued by DE1 is not subject to allocation. Accordingly, for purposes of each of the disqualified tax amount computations, the foreign income tax amount paid or accrued by USP with respect to Country F tax and Country G tax, respectively, is the entire foreign income tax amount paid or accrued by DE1, and, under paragraph (b)(2)(iii)(A) of this section, USP's allocable foreign income will be equal to DE1's entire foreign income.

(*3*) As stated in paragraph (b)(3)(iii)(A) of this section (paragraph (A) of this *Example 3*), for U.S. taxable year 3 USP has 100u aggregate basis difference with respect to Country F tax and 100u aggregate basis difference with respect to Country G tax. With respect to Country G tax, in U.S. taxable year 3, under paragraph (b)(2) of this section, the disqualified tax amount is $30, the lesser of the two amounts: the tentative disqualified tax amount, in this case, $30 ($30 foreign income tax amount x (100u aggregate basis difference / 100u allocable foreign income)), or the foreign income tax amount considered paid or accrued by USP, in this case, $30.

(*4*) With respect to Country F tax, in U.S. taxable year 3, under paragraph (b)(2) of this section, the disqualified tax amount is $0, the lesser of two amounts: the tentative disqualified tax amount, in this case $0 (($30 foreign income tax amount + $30 Country G FCCT) x (100u aggregate basis difference / 200u foreign income) = $30 reduced by $30 Country G FCCT that is a disqualified tax amount of USP), or the foreign income tax amount considered paid or accrued by USP, in this case, $30.

(c) *Aggregate basis difference carryover.*—(1) *In general.*—If a section 901(m) payor has an aggregate basis difference carryover for a U.S. taxable year, as determined under this paragraph (c), the aggregate basis difference carryover is taken into account in computing the section 901(m) payor's aggregate basis difference for the next U.S. taxable year. For successor rules that apply to an aggregate basis difference carryover, see § 1.901(m)-6(c).

(2) *Amount of aggregate basis difference carryover.*—(i) If a section 901(m) payor's disqualified tax amount is zero, all of the section 901(m) payor's aggregate basis difference (positive or negative) for the U.S. taxable year gives rise to an aggregate basis difference carryover to the next U.S. taxable year.

(ii) If a section 901(m) payor's disqualified tax amount is not zero, then aggregate basis difference carryover can arise in either or both of the following two situations:

(A) If a section 901(m) payor's aggregate basis difference for the U.S. taxable year exceeds its allocable foreign income, the excess gives rise to an aggregate basis difference carryover.

(B) If the tentative disqualified tax amount exceeds the disqualified tax amount, the excess tentative disqualified tax amount is converted into aggregate basis difference carryover by multiplying such excess by a fraction, the numerator of which is the allocable foreign income, and the denominator of which is the sum of the foreign income tax amount and the FCCTs that are paid or accrued by, or considered paid or accrued by, the section 901(m) payor.

(3) *Example.*—The following example illustrates the rules of paragraph (c) of this section.

(i) *Facts.* (A) On July 1 of Year 1, CFC1 acquires all of the interests of DE1 in a transaction (Transaction) that is treated as a stock acquisition for Country F tax purposes. CFC1 and DE1 are organized in Country F and are treated as corporations for Country F tax purposes. CFC1 is an applicable foreign corporation, and DE1 is a disregarded entity. CFC1 has a calendar year for U.S. income tax purposes, and DE1 has a June 30 year-end for Country F tax purposes. Country F imposes a single tax that is a foreign income tax. CFC1 and DE1 each have a functional currency of the u with respect to all activities. Immediately after the Transaction, DE1 owns one asset, Asset A, that gives rise to income that is taken into account for Country F tax purposes. For the first U.S. taxable year (U.S. taxable year 1) there is a cost recovery amount with respect to Asset A of 9u, and for each subsequent U.S. taxable year until the U.S. basis is fully recovered, there is a cost recovery amount with respect to Asset A of 18u. There is no disposition of Asset A.

(ii) *Result.* (A) Under § 1.901(m)-2(b)(2), the Transaction is a CAA. Under § 1.901(m)-2(c)(1), Asset A is an RFA with respect to Country F tax because it is relevant in determining the foreign income of DE1 for Country F tax purposes and was owned by DE1 when the Transaction occurred. Under § 1.901(m)-1(a)(37), CFC1 is the RFA owner (U.S.) with respect to Asset A. Under § 1.901(m)-1(a)(28), DE1 is a foreign payor for Country F tax purposes. Under § 1.901(m)-1(a)(41), CFC1 is the section 901(m) payor with respect to foreign income tax amounts for which DE1 is the foreign payor (see § 1.901-2(f)(4)(ii)).

(B) Under § 1.901(m)-1(a)(1), in determining the aggregate basis difference for U.S. taxable year 1, CFC1 has one computation with respect to Country F tax. Under § 1.901(m)-1(a)(1), aggregate basis difference with respect to Country F tax is equal to the sum of allocated basis differences and allocated basis difference adjustments with respect to all RFAs, which, in this case, is only Asset A. Under § 1.901(m)-1(a)(5), allocated basis differences are the sum of cost recovery amounts and disposition amounts. Because there is no disposition of Asset A, the only allocated basis difference taken into account in determining an aggregate basis difference are cost recovery amounts with respect to Asset A. Under § 1.901(m)-5(b), any cost recovery amounts are assigned to a U.S taxable year of CFC1, because CFC1 is the section 901(m) payor and RFA owner (U.S.) with respect to Asset A. Under paragraph (b)(2) of this section, for each U.S. taxable year, CFC1 will compute a disqualified tax amount and aggregate basis difference carryover with respect to the aggregate basis difference. Because DE1 is a disregarded entity owned by CFC1, the foreign income tax amount paid or accrued by DE1 is not subject to allocation. Accordingly, for purposes of the disqualified tax amount computation, the foreign income tax amount paid or accrued by CFC1 with respect to Country F tax is the entire foreign income tax amount paid or accrued by DE1, and under paragraph (b)(2)(iii)(A) of this section, CFC1's allocable foreign income will be equal to DE1's entire foreign income.

(C) In U.S. taxable year 1, CFC1 has an aggregate basis difference of 9u (the 9u cost recovery amount with respect to Asset A for U.S. taxable year 1). However, because the foreign taxable year of DE1, the foreign payor, will not end between July 1 and December 31, there will not be a foreign income tax amount for U.S. taxable year 1. Because the foreign income tax amount considered paid or accrued by CFC1 for U.S. taxable year 1 is zero, under paragraph (b)(2)(iv) of this section, the disqualified tax amount for U.S. taxable year 1 of CFC1 is also zero. Furthermore, because the disqualified tax amount is zero, under paragraph (c)(2)(i) of this section, CFC1 has an aggregate basis difference carryover equal to 9u, the entire amount of the aggregate basis difference for U.S. taxable year 1. Under paragraph (c)(1) of this section, the 9u aggregate basis difference carryover is taken into account in computing CFC1's aggregate basis difference for U.S. taxable year 2. Accordingly, in U.S. taxable year 2, CFC1 has an aggregate basis difference of 27u (18u cost recovery amount for U.S. taxable year 2, plus 9u aggregate basis difference carryover from U.S. taxable year 1).

(d) *Applicability dates.*—This section applies to CAAs occurring on or after March 23, 2020. Taxpayers may, however, choose to apply this section before the date this section is applicable provided that they (along with any persons that are related (within the meaning of section 267(b) or 707(b)) to the taxpayer)—

(1) Consistently apply this section, § 1.704-1(b)(4)(viii)(*c*)(*4*)(*v*) through (*vii*), § 1.901(m)-1, and §§ 1.901(m)-4 through 1.901(m)-8 (excluding § 1.901(m)-4(e)) to all CAAs occurring on or after January 1, 2011, and consistently apply § 1.901(m)-2 (excluding § 1.901(m)-2(d)) to all CAAs occurring on or after December 7, 2016, on any original or amended tax return for each taxable year for which the application of the provisions listed in this paragraph (d)(1) affects the tax liability and for which the statute of limitations does not preclude assessment or the filing of a claim for refund, as applicable

(2) File all tax returns described in paragraph (d)(1) of this section for any taxable year ending on or before March 23, 2020, no later than March 23, 2021; and

(3) Make appropriate adjustments to take into account deficiencies that would have resulted from the consistent application under paragraph (d)(1) of this section for taxable years that are not open for assessment. [Reg. § 1.901(m)-3.]

☐ [*T.D. 9895, 3-20-2020.*]

§ 1.901(m)-4. Determination of basis difference.—(a) *In general.*—This section provides rules for determining for each RFA the basis difference that arises as a result of a CAA. A basis difference is computed separately with respect to each foreign income tax for which an asset subject to a CAA is an RFA. Paragraph (b) of this section provides the general rule for determining basis difference that references only U.S. basis in the RFA. Paragraph (c) of this section provides for an election to determine basis difference by reference to foreign basis and sets forth the procedures for making the election. Paragraph (d) of this section provides special rules for determining basis difference in the case of a section 743(b) CAA. Paragraph (e) of this section provides a special rule for determining basis difference in an RFA with respect to a CAA to which paragraphs (b) through (d) of this section do not apply. Paragraph (f) of this section provides examples illustrating the rules of this section, and paragraph (g) of this section provides applicability dates.

(b) *General rule.*—Except as otherwise provided in paragraphs (c), (d), and (e) of this section, basis difference is the U.S. basis in the RFA immediately after the CAA, less the U.S. basis in the RFA immediately before the CAA. Basis difference is an attribute that attaches to an RFA.

(c) *Foreign basis election.*—(1) An election (*foreign basis election*) may be made to apply section 901(m)(3)(C)(i)(II) by reference to the foreign basis immediately after the CAA instead of the U.S. basis immediately before the CAA. Accordingly, if a foreign basis election is made, basis difference is the U.S. basis in the RFA immediately after the CAA, less the foreign basis in the RFA immediately after the CAA. For this purpose, the foreign basis immediately after the CAA takes into account any adjustment to that foreign basis resulting from the CAA for purposes of the foreign income tax.

(2) Except as otherwise provided in this paragraph (c), a foreign basis election is made by the RFA owner (U.S.). If, however, the RFA owner (U.S.) is a partnership, each partner in the partnership (and not the partnership) may independently make a foreign basis election. In the case of one or more tiered partnerships, the foreign basis election is made at the level at which a partner is not also a partnership.

(3) The foreign basis election may be made separately for each CAA, and with respect to each foreign income tax and each foreign payor. For purposes of making the foreign basis election, all CAAs that are part of an aggregated CAA transaction are treated as a single CAA. Furthermore, for purposes of making the foreign basis election, if foreign law imposes tax on the combined income (within the meaning of § 1.901-2(f)(3)(ii)) of two or more foreign payors, all foreign payors whose items of income, deduction, gain, or loss for U.S. income tax purposes are included in the U.S. taxable income or earnings and profits of a single section 901(m) payor are treated as a single foreign payor.

(4) A foreign basis election is made by using foreign basis to determine basis difference for purposes of computing a disqualified tax amount and an aggregate basis difference carryover for the U.S. taxable year, as provided under § 1.901(m)-3. A separate statement or form evidencing the foreign basis election need not be filed. Except as provided in paragraphs (c)(5) and (6) of this section, in order for a foreign basis election to be effective, the election must be reflected on a timely filed original federal income tax return (taking into account extensions) for the first U.S. taxable year that the foreign basis election is relevant to the computation of any amounts reported on such return, including on any required schedules.

(5) If the RFA owner (U.S.) is a partnership, a foreign basis election reflected on a partner's timely filed amended federal income tax return is also effective if all of the following conditions are satisfied:

(i) The partner's timely filed original federal income tax return (taking into account extensions) for the first U.S. taxable year of the partner in which a foreign basis election is relevant to the computation of any amounts reported on such return, including on any required schedules, does not reflect the application of section 901(m);

(ii) The information provided by the partnership to the partner for purposes of applying section 901(m) and any information required to be reported by the partnership is based solely on computations that use foreign basis to determine basis difference; and

(iii) Before the due date of the original federal income tax return described in paragraph (c)(5)(i) of this section, the partner delegated the authority to the partnership to choose whether to provide the partner with information to apply section 901(m) using foreign basis, either pursuant to a written partnership agreement (within the meaning of § 1.704-1(b)(2)(ii)(*h*)) or written notice provided by the partner to the partnership.

(6) If, pursuant to paragraph (g)(3) of this section, a taxpayer chooses to have this section apply to CAAs occurring on or after January 1, 2011, a foreign basis election will be effective if the election is reflected on a timely filed amended federal income tax return (or tax returns, as applicable) filed no later than March 23, 2021.

(7) The foreign basis election is irrevocable. Relief under § 301.9100-1 is not available for the foreign basis election.

(d) *Determination of basis difference in a section 743(b) CAA.*—(1) *In general.*—Except as provided in paragraphs (d)(2) and (e) of this section, if there is a section 743(b) CAA, basis difference is the resulting basis adjustment under section 743(b) that is allocated to the RFA under section 755.

(2) *Foreign basis election.*—If a foreign basis election is made with respect to a section 743(b) CAA, then, for purposes of paragraph (d)(1) of this section, the section 743(b) adjustment is determined by reference to the foreign basis of the RFA, determined immediately after the CAA.

(e) *Determination of basis difference in an RFA with respect to a CAA with respect to which paragraphs (b), (c), and (d) of this section do not apply.*—For CAAs occurring on or after January 1, 2011, and before July 21, 2014, other than CAAs occurring before July 21, 2014, resulting from an entity classification election made under § 301.7701-3 of this chapter that is filed on or after July 29, 2014, and that is effective on or before July 21, 2014, basis difference in an RFA with respect to the CAA is the amount of any basis difference (within the meaning of section 901(m)(3)(C)(i)) that had not been taken into account under section 901(m)(3)(B) either as of July 21, 2014, or, in the case of an entity classification election made under §301.7701-3 of this chapter that is filed on or after July 29, 2014, and that is effective on or before July 21, 2014, before the transactions that are deemed to occur under §301.7701-3(g) as a result of the change in classification.

(f) *Examples.*—The following examples illustrate the rules of this section:

(1) *Example 1: Scope of basis choice; identifying separate CAAs, RFA owners (U.S.), and foreign payors in an aggregated CAA transaction.*—(i) *Facts.* CFC1 wholly owns CFC2, both of which are applicable foreign corporations, organized in Country F, and treated as corporations for Country F tax purposes. CFC1 also wholly owns DE1, and DE1 wholly owns DE2. DE1 and DE2 are entities organized in Country F treated as corporations for Country F tax purposes and as disregarded entities for U.S. income tax purposes. Country F imposes a single tax that is a foreign income tax. All of the stock of CFC1 is acquired in a qualified stock purchase (within the meaning of section 338(d)(3)) to which section 338(a) applies for both CFC1 and CFC2. For Country F tax purposes, the transaction is treated as an acquisition of the stock of CFC1.

(*ii*) *Result.* (A) The acquisition of CFC1 gives rise to four separate CAAs described in §1.901(m)-2. Under §1.901(m)-2(b)(1), the acquisition of the stock of CFC1 and the deemed acquisition of the stock of CFC2 under section 338(h)(3)(B) are each a section 338 CAA. Furthermore, because the deemed acquisition of the assets of each of DE1 and DE2 for U.S. income tax purposes is disregarded for Country F tax purposes, the deemed acquisitions are CAAs under §1.901(m)-2(b)(2). Because the four CAAs occurred pursuant to a plan, under §1.901(m)-1(a)(3), all of the CAAs are part of an aggregated CAA transaction. Under §1.901(m)-1(a)(37), CFC1 is the RFA owner (U.S.) with respect to its assets and the assets of DE1 and DE2 that are RFAs. CFC2 is the RFA owner (U.S.) with respect to its assets that are RFAs. Under §1.901(m)-1(a)(28), CFC1, CFC2, DE1, and DE2 are each a foreign payor for Country F tax purposes.

(B) Under paragraph (c) of this section, a foreign basis election may be made by the RFA owner (U.S.). The election is made separately with respect to each CAA (for this purpose, treating all CAAs that are part of an aggregated CAA transaction as a single CAA) and with respect to each foreign income tax and foreign payor. Thus, in this case, CFC1 can make a separate foreign basis election for one or more of the following three groups of RFAs: RFAs that are relevant in determining foreign income of CFC1; RFAs that are relevant in determining foreign income of DE1; and RFAs that are relevant in determining foreign income of DE2. Furthermore, CFC2 can make a foreign basis election for all of its RFAs that are relevant in determining its foreign income.

(2) *Example 2: Scope of basis choice; RFA owner (U.S.) is a partnership.*—(i) *Facts.* USPS is a domestic partnership for which a section 754 election is in effect. USPS owns two assets, the stock of DE1 and DE2. DE1 is an entity organized in Country X and treated as a corporation for Country X tax purposes. DE2 is an entity organized in Country Y and treated as a corporation for Country Y tax purposes. DE1 and DE2 are disregarded entities. Country X and Country Y each impose a single tax that is a foreign income tax. US1 and US2, unrelated domestic corporations, and FP, a foreign person unrelated to US1 and US2, acquire partnership interests in USPS from existing partners of USPS pursuant to the same plan.

(ii) *Result.* Under §1.901(m)-2(b)(3), the acquisitions of the partnership interests in USPS by US1, US2, and FP each give rise to separate section 743(b) CAAs, but under §1.901(m)-1(a)(3), they are treated as an aggregated CAA transaction because they occur as part of a plan. Under §1.901(m)-1(a)(37), USPS is the RFA owner (U.S.) with respect to the assets of DE1 and DE2 that are RFAs. Under §1.901(m)-1(a)(28), DE1 is a foreign payor for Country X tax purposes, and DE2 is a foreign payor for Country Y tax purposes. Because the RFA owner (U.S.) is a partnership, paragraph (c)(2) of this section provides that US1, US2, and FP (the relevant partners in USPS) separately choose whether to make a foreign basis election for purposes of determining basis difference. Furthermore, under paragraph (c)(3) of this section, the choice to make the election is made separately by each partner with respect to each foreign payor. Thus, in this case, each partner may make separate elections for the RFAs that are relevant in determining foreign income of DE1 for Country X tax purposes and the RFAs that are relevant in determining foreign income of DE2 for Country Y tax purposes.

(g) *Applicability dates.*—(1) Except as provided in paragraph (g)(2) of this section, this section applies to CAAs occurring on or after March 23, 2020.

(2) Paragraphs (a), (b), and (d)(1) of this section apply to CAAs occurring on or after July 21, 2014, and to CAAs occurring before that date resulting from an entity classification election made under §301.7701-3 that is filed on or after July 29, 2014, and that is effective on or before July 21, 2014. Paragraph (e) of this section applies to CAAs occurring on or after January 1, 2011, and before July 21, 2014, other than CAAs occurring before July 21, 2014, resulting from an entity classification election made under §301.7701-3 of this chapter that is filed on or after July 29, 2014, and that is effective on or before July 21, 2014. Taxpayers may, however, consistently apply paragraph (d)(1) of this section to all section 743(b) CAAs occurring on or after January 1, 2011. For this purpose, persons that are related (within the meaning of section 267(b) or 707(b)) will be treated as a single taxpayer.

(3) Taxpayers may, however, choose to apply provisions in this section before the date such provisions are applicable pursuant to paragraph (g)(1) or (2) of this section, provided that they (along with any persons that are related (within the meaning of section 267(b) or 707(b)) to the taxpayer)—

(i) Consistently apply this section (excluding paragraph (e) of this section), §1.704-1(b)(4)(viii)(*c*)(*4*)(*v*) through (*vii*), §1.901(m)-1, §1.901(m)-3, and §§1.901(m)-5 through 1.901(m)-8 to all CAAs occurring on or after January 1, 2011, and consistently apply §1.901(m)-2 (excluding §1.901(m)-2(d)) to all CAAs occurring on or after December 7, 2016, on any original or amended tax return for each taxable year for which the application of the provisions listed in this paragraph (g)(3)(i) affects the tax liability and for which the statute of limitations does not preclude assessment or the filing of a claim for refund, as applicable;

(ii) File all tax returns described in paragraph (g)(3)(i) of this section for any taxable year ending on or before March 23, 2020, no later than March 23, 2021; and

(iii) Make appropriate adjustments to take into account deficiencies that would have resulted from the consistent application under paragraph (g)(3)(i) of this section for taxable years that are not open for assessment. [Reg. §1.901(m)-4.]

☐ [*T.D. 9895, 3-20-2020.*]

§1.901(m)-5. Basis difference taken into account.—(a) *In general.*—This section provides rules for determining the amount of basis difference with respect to an RFA that is taken into account in a U.S. taxable year for purposes of determining the disqualified portion of a foreign income tax amount. Paragraph (b) of this section provides rules for determining a cost recovery amount and assigning that amount to a U.S. taxable year of a single section 901(m) payor when the RFA owner (U.S.) is the section 901(m) payor. Paragraph (c) of this section provides rules for determining a disposition amount and assigning that amount to a U.S. taxable year of a single section 901(m) payor when the RFA owner (U.S.) is the section 901(m) payor. Paragraph (d) of this section provides rules for allocating cost recovery amounts and disposition amounts when the RFA owner (U.S.) is a fiscally transparent entity for U.S. income tax purposes. Paragraph (e) of this section provides special rules for allocating cost recovery amounts and disposition amounts with respect to certain section 743(b) CAAs. Paragraph (f) of this section provides special rules for allocating certain disposition amounts when a foreign payor is transferred in a mid-year transaction. Paragraph (g) of this section provides special rules for allocating both cost recovery amounts and disposition amounts in certain cases in which the RFA owner (U.S.) either is a reverse hybrid or a fiscally transparent entity for both U.S. and foreign income tax purposes that is directly or indirectly owned by a reverse hybrid. Paragraph (h) of this section provides examples illustrating the application of this section. Paragraph (i) of this section provides the applicability dates.

(b) *Basis difference taken into account under applicable cost recovery method.*—(1) *In general.*—When the RFA owner (U.S.) is a section 901(m) payor, all of a cost recovery amount is attributed to the section 901(m) payor and assigned to the U.S. taxable year of the section 901(m) payor in which the corresponding U.S. basis deduction is taken into account under the applicable cost recovery method. This is the case regardless of whether the deduction is deferred or disallowed for U.S. income tax purposes. If instead the RFA owner (U.S.) is a fiscally transparent entity for U.S. income tax purposes, a cost recovery amount is allocated to one or more section 901(m) payors under paragraph (d) of this section, except as provided in paragraphs (e) and (g) of this section. If a cost recovery amount arises from an RFA with respect to a section 743(b) CAA, in certain cases the cost recovery amount is allocated to a section 901(m) payor under paragraph (e) of this section. In certain cases in which the RFA owner (U.S.) either is a reverse hybrid or a fiscally transparent entity for both U.S. and foreign income tax purposes that is directly or indirectly owned by a reverse hybrid, a cost recovery amount is allocated to one or more section 901(m) payors under paragraph (g) of this section.

(2) *Determining a cost recovery amount.*—(i) *General rule.*—A cost recovery amount for an RFA is determined by applying the applicable cost recovery method to the basis difference rather than to the U.S. basis.

(ii) *U.S. basis subject to multiple cost recovery methods.*—If the entire U.S. basis is not subject to the same cost recovery method, the applicable cost recovery method for determining the cost recovery amount is the cost recovery method that applies to the portion of the U.S. basis that corresponds to the basis difference.

(3) *Applicable cost recovery method.*—For purposes of section 901(m), an applicable cost recovery method includes any method for recovering the cost of property over time for U.S. income tax purposes (each application of a method giving rise to a *U.S. basis deduction*). Such methods include depreciation, amortization, or depletion, as well as a method that allows the cost (or a portion of the cost) of property to be expensed in the year of acquisition or in the placed-in-service year, such as under section 179. Applicable cost recovery methods do not include any provision allowing the U.S. basis to be recovered upon a disposition of an RFA.

(c) *Basis difference taken into account as a result of a disposition.*—(1) *In general.*—Except as provided in paragraph (f) of this section, when the RFA owner (U.S.) is a section 901(m) payor, all of a disposition amount is attributed to the section 901(m) payor and assigned to the U.S. taxable year of the section 901(m) payor in which the disposition occurs. If instead the RFA owner (U.S.) is a fiscally transparent entity for U.S. income tax purposes, except as provided in paragraphs (e), (f), and (g) of this section, a disposition amount is allocated to one or more section 901(m) payors under paragraph (d) of this section. If a disposition amount arises from an RFA with respect to a section 743(b) CAA, in certain cases the disposition amount is allocated to a section 901(m) payor under paragraph (e) of this section. If there is a disposition of an RFA in a foreign taxable year of a foreign payor during which there is a mid-year transaction, in certain cases a disposition amount is allocated under paragraph (f) of this section. In certain cases in which the RFA owner (U.S.) either is a reverse hybrid or a fiscally transparent entity for both U.S. and foreign income tax purposes that is directly or indirectly owned by a reverse hybrid, a disposition amount is allocated to one or more section 901(m) payors under paragraph (g) of this section.

(2) *Determining a disposition amount.*—(i) *Disposition is fully taxable for purposes of both U.S. income tax and the foreign income tax.*—If a disposition of an RFA is fully taxable (that is, results in all gain or loss, if any, being recognized with respect to the RFA) for purposes of both U.S. income tax and the foreign income tax, the disposition amount is equal to the unallocated basis difference with respect to the RFA.

(ii) *Disposition is not fully taxable for purposes of U.S. income tax or the foreign income tax (or both).*—If the disposition of an RFA is not fully taxable for purposes of both U.S. income tax and the foreign income tax, the disposition amount is determined under this paragraph (c)(2)(ii). See § 1.901(m)-6 for rules regarding the continued application of section 901(m) if the RFA has any unallocated basis difference after determining the disposition amount under paragraph (c)(2)(ii)(A) or (B) of this section, as applicable.

(A) *Positive basis difference.*—If the disposition of an RFA is not fully taxable for purposes of both U.S. income tax and the foreign income tax, and the RFA has a positive basis difference, the disposition amount equals the lesser of:

(1) Any foreign disposition gain plus any U.S. disposition loss (for this purpose, expressed as a positive amount), or

(2) Unallocated basis difference with respect to the RFA.

(B) *Negative basis difference.*—If the disposition of an RFA is not fully taxable for purposes of both U.S. income tax and the foreign income tax, and the RFA has a negative basis difference, the disposition amount equals the greater of:

(1) Any U.S. disposition gain (for this purpose, expressed as a negative amount) plus any foreign disposition loss, or

(2) Unallocated basis difference with respect to the RFA.

(iii) *Disposition of an RFA after a section 743(b) CAA.*—If an RFA was subject to a section 743(b) CAA and subsequently there is a disposition of the RFA, then, for purposes of determining the disposition amount, foreign disposition gain or foreign disposition loss are specially defined to mean the amount of gain or loss recognized for purposes of the foreign income tax on the disposition of the RFA that is allocable to the partnership interest that was transferred in the section 743(b) CAA. In addition, U.S. disposition gain or U.S. disposition loss are specially defined to mean the amount of gain or loss recognized for U.S. income tax purposes on the disposition of the RFA that is allocable to the partnership interest that was transferred in the section 743(b) CAA, taking into account the basis adjustment under section 743(b) that was allocated to the RFA under section 755.

(d) *General rules for allocating and assigning a cost recovery amount or a disposition amount when the RFA owner (U.S.) is a fiscally transparent entity.*—(1) *In general.*—Except as provided in paragraphs (e), (f), and (g) of this section, this paragraph (d) provides rules for allocating a cost recovery amount or a disposition amount when the RFA owner (U.S.) is a fiscally transparent entity for U.S. income tax purposes in which a section 901(m) payor directly or indirectly owns an interest, as well as for assigning the allocated amount to a U.S. taxable year of the section 901(m) payor. For purposes of this paragraph (d), unless otherwise indicated, a reference to direct or indirect ownership in an entity means for U.S. income tax purposes. For purposes of this paragraph (d), a person indirectly owns an interest in an entity for U.S. income tax purposes if the person owns the interest through one or more fiscally transparent entities for U.S. income tax purposes, and at least one of the fiscally transparent entities is not a disregarded entity. For purposes of this paragraph (d), a person indirectly owns an interest in an entity for foreign income tax purposes if the person owns the interest through one or more fiscally transparent entities for foreign income tax purposes. If the RFA owner (U.S.) is a lower-tier fiscally transparent entity for U.S. income tax purposes in which the section 901(m) payor indirectly owns an interest, the rules of this section apply in a manner consistent with the application of these rules when the section 901(m) payor directly owns an interest in the RFA owner (U.S.).

(2) *Allocation of a cost recovery amount.*—A cost recovery amount is allocated to a section 901(m) payor that directly or indirectly owns an interest in the RFA owner (U.S.) to the extent the U.S. basis deduction that corresponds to the cost recovery amount is (or will be) included in the section 901(m) payor's distributive share of the income of the RFA owner (U.S.) for U.S. income tax purposes.

(3) *Allocation of a disposition amount attributable to foreign disposition gain or foreign disposition loss.*—(i) *In general.*—Except as provided in paragraph (f) of this section, a disposition amount attributable to foreign disposition gain or foreign disposition loss (as determined under paragraph (d)(5) of this section) is allocated under paragraph (d)(3)(ii) or (d)(3)(iii) of this section to a section 901(m) payor that directly or indirectly owns an interest in the RFA owner (U.S.).

(ii) *First allocation rule.*—This paragraph (d)(3)(ii) applies when a section 901(m) payor, or a disregarded entity directly owned by a section 901(m) payor, is the foreign payor whose foreign income includes a distributive share of the foreign income of the RFA owner (foreign) and, therefore, all of the foreign income tax amount of the foreign payor is paid or accrued by, or considered paid by, the section 901(m) payor. Thus, this paragraph (d)(3)(ii) applies when the RFA owner (U.S.) is a fiscally transparent entity for both U.S. and foreign income tax purposes and a section 901(m) payor either directly owns an interest in the RFA owner (U.S.) or directly owns an interest in another fiscally transparent entity for U.S. and foreign income tax purposes, which, in turn, directly or indirectly owns an interest in the RFA owner (U.S.) for both U.S. and foreign income tax purposes. In these cases, the section 901(m) payor is allocated the portion of a disposition amount that is equal to the product of the disposition amount attributable to foreign disposition gain or foreign disposition loss, as applicable, and a fraction, the numerator of which is the portion of the foreign disposition gain or foreign disposition loss recognized by the RFA owner (foreign) for foreign income tax purposes that is (or will be) included in the foreign payor's distributive share of the foreign income of the RFA owner (foreign), and the denominator of which is the foreign disposition gain or foreign disposition loss.

(iii) *Second allocation rule.*—This paragraph (d)(3)(iii) applies when neither a section 901(m) payor nor a disregarded entity directly owned by a section 901(m) payor is the foreign payor with respect to the foreign income of the RFA owner (foreign). Instead, a section

901(m) payor directly or indirectly owns an interest in the foreign payor, which is a fiscally transparent entity for U.S. income tax purposes (other than a disregarded entity directly owned by the section 901(m) payor), and, therefore, the section 901(m) payor is considered to pay or accrue only its allocated portion of the foreign income tax amount of the foreign payor. This will be the case when the foreign payor is either the RFA owner (U.S.), another fiscally transparent entity for U.S. income tax purposes (other than a disregarded entity directly owned by a section 901(m) payor) that directly or indirectly owns an interest in the RFA owner (U.S.) for both U.S. and foreign income tax purposes, or a disregarded entity directly owned by the RFA owner (U.S.). In these cases, the section 901(m) payor is allocated the portion of a disposition amount that is equal to the product of the disposition amount attributable to foreign disposition gain or foreign disposition loss, as applicable, and a fraction, the numerator of which is the portion of the foreign disposition gain or foreign disposition loss that is included in the allocable foreign income of the section 901(m) payor, and the denominator of which is the foreign disposition gain or foreign disposition loss. If allocable foreign income is not otherwise required to be determined because there is no foreign income tax amount, the numerator is the portion of the foreign disposition gain or foreign disposition loss that would be included in the allocable foreign income of the section 901(m) payor if there were a foreign income tax amount.

(4) *Allocation of a disposition amount attributable to U.S. disposition gain or U.S. disposition loss.*—A section 901(m) payor that directly or indirectly owns an interest in the RFA owner (U.S.) is allocated the portion of a disposition amount that is equal to the product of the disposition amount attributable to U.S. disposition gain or U.S. disposition loss (as determined under paragraph (d)(5) of this section), as applicable, and a fraction, the numerator of which is the portion of the U.S. disposition gain or U.S. disposition loss that is (or will be) included in the section 901(m) payor's distributive share of income of the RFA owner (U.S.) for U.S. income tax purposes, and the denominator of which is the U.S. disposition gain or U.S. disposition loss.

(5) *Determining the extent to which a disposition amount is attributable to foreign or U.S. disposition gain or loss.*—(i) *RFA with a positive basis difference.*—When there is a disposition of an RFA with a positive basis difference and the disposition results in either a foreign disposition gain or a U.S. disposition loss, but not both, the entire disposition amount is attributable to foreign disposition gain or U.S. disposition loss, as applicable, even if the disposition amount exceeds the foreign disposition gain or the absolute value of the U.S. disposition loss. If the disposition results in both a foreign disposition gain and a U.S. disposition loss, the disposition amount is attributable first to foreign disposition gain to the extent thereof, and the excess disposition amount, if any, is attributable to the U.S. disposition loss, even if the excess disposition amount exceeds the absolute value of the U.S. disposition loss.

(ii) *RFA with a negative basis difference.*—When there is a disposition of an RFA with a negative basis difference and the disposition results in either a foreign disposition loss or a U.S. disposition gain, but not both, the entire disposition amount is attributable to foreign disposition loss or U.S. disposition gain, as applicable, even if the absolute value of the disposition amount exceeds the absolute value of the foreign disposition loss or the U.S. disposition gain. If the disposition results in both a foreign disposition loss and a U.S. disposition gain, the disposition amount is attributable first to foreign disposition loss to the extent thereof, and the excess disposition amount, if any, is attributable to the U.S. disposition gain, even if the absolute value of the excess disposition amount exceeds the U.S. disposition gain.

(6) *U.S. taxable year of a section 901(m) payor to which an allocated cost recovery amount or disposition amount is assigned.*—A cost recovery amount or a disposition amount allocated to a section 901(m) payor under paragraph (d) of this section is assigned to the U.S. taxable year of the section 901(m) payor that includes the last day of the U.S. taxable year of the RFA owner (U.S.) in which, in the case of a cost recovery amount, the RFA owner (U.S.) takes into account the corresponding U.S. basis deduction (without regard to whether the deduction is deferred or disallowed for U.S. income tax purposes), or in the case of a disposition amount, the disposition occurs.

(e) *Special rules for certain section 743(b) CAAs.*—If a section 901(m) payor acquires a partnership interest in a section 743(b) CAA, including a section 743(b) CAA with respect to a lower-tier partnership that results from a direct acquisition by the section 901(m) payor of an interest in an upper-tier partnership, and subsequently there is a cost recovery amount or a disposition amount that arises from an RFA with respect to that section 743(b) CAA, all of the cost recovery amount or the disposition amount is allocated to that section 901(m) payor. The U.S. taxable year of the section 901(m) payor to which the cost recovery amount or the disposition amount is assigned is the U.S. taxable year in which, in the case of a cost recovery amount, the section 901(m) payor takes into account the corresponding U.S. basis deduction (without regard to whether the deduction is deferred or disallowed for U.S. income tax purposes), or in the case of a disposition amount, the disposition occurs.

(f) *Mid-year transactions.*—(1) *In general.*—When a disposition of an RFA occurs in the same foreign taxable year that a foreign payor is involved in a mid-year transaction, the portion of the disposition amount that is attributable to foreign disposition gain or foreign disposition loss (as determined under paragraph (d)(5) of this section) is allocated to a section 901(m) payor and assigned to a U.S. taxable year of the section 901(m) payor under this paragraph (f). To the extent the disposition amount is attributable to U.S. disposition gain or U.S. disposition loss (as determined under paragraph (d)(5) of this section), see paragraph (c)(1) or (d) of this section, as applicable.

(2) *Allocation rule.*—To the extent a disposition amount is attributable to foreign disposition gain or foreign disposition loss, a section 901(m) payor is allocated the portion of the disposition amount equal to the product of the disposition amount attributable to foreign disposition gain or foreign disposition loss, as applicable, and a fraction, the numerator of which is the portion of the foreign disposition gain or foreign disposition loss that is included in the allocable foreign income of the section 901(m) payor, and the denominator of which is the foreign disposition gain or foreign disposition loss. If allocable foreign income is not otherwise required to be determined because there is no foreign income tax amount, the numerator is the portion of the foreign disposition gain or foreign disposition loss that would be included in the allocable foreign income of the section 901(m) payor if there were a foreign income tax amount.

(3) *Assignment to a U.S. taxable year of a section 901(m) payor.*—A disposition amount allocated to a section 901(m) payor under paragraph (f)(2) of this section is assigned to the U.S. taxable year of the section 901(m) payor in which the foreign disposition gain or foreign disposition loss (or portion thereof) is included in allocable foreign income of the section 901(m) payor or, if allocable foreign income is not otherwise required to be determined because there is no foreign income tax amount, the U.S. taxable year in which the foreign disposition gain or foreign disposition loss would be included in allocable foreign income if there were a foreign income tax amount.

(g) *Reverse hybrids.*—(1) *In general.*—This paragraph (g) provides rules for allocating a cost recovery amount or a disposition amount when the RFA owner (U.S.) is either a reverse hybrid or a fiscally transparent entity for U.S. and foreign income tax purposes that is directly or indirectly owned by a reverse hybrid for U.S. and foreign income tax purposes, and in each case, the foreign payor whose foreign income includes a distributive share of the foreign income of the RFA owner (foreign) directly or indirectly owns an interest in the reverse hybrid for foreign income tax purposes. Application of the allocation rules under paragraphs (g)(2) and (g)(3) of this section depend upon whether a section 901(m) payor or a disregarded entity directly owned by a section 901(m) payor is the foreign payor, or, instead, a section 901(m) payor directly or indirectly owns an interest in the foreign payor. For purposes of this paragraph (g), unless otherwise indicated, a reference to direct or indirect ownership in an entity means for U.S. income tax purposes. For purposes of this paragraph (g), a person indirectly owns an interest in an entity for U.S. income tax purposes if the person owns the interest through one or more fiscally transparent entities for U.S. income tax purposes, and at least one of the fiscally transparent entities is not a disregarded entity. For purposes of this paragraph (g), a person indirectly owns an interest in an entity for foreign income tax purposes if the person owns the interest through one or more fiscally transparent entities for foreign income tax purposes. If the RFA owner (U.S.) is a lower-tier fiscally transparent entity for U.S. income tax purposes in which the reverse hybrid indirectly owns an interest, the rules of this section apply in a manner consistent with the application of these rules when the reverse hybrid directly owns an interest in the RFA owner (U.S.).

(2) *First allocation rule.*—(i) *Allocation to a section 901(m) payor.*—This paragraph (g)(2)(i) applies when a section 901(m) payor, or a disregarded entity directly owned by a section 901(m) payor, is the

foreign payor whose foreign income includes a distributive share of the foreign income of the RFA owner (foreign), and, therefore, all of the foreign income tax amount of the foreign payor is paid or accrued by, or considered paid or accrued by, the section 901(m) payor. Thus, this paragraph (g)(2)(i) applies when a section 901(m) payor either directly owns an interest in the reverse hybrid or directly owns an interest in a fiscally transparent entity for U.S. and foreign income tax purposes, which, in turn, directly or indirectly owns an interest in the reverse hybrid for both U.S. and foreign income tax purposes. In these cases, the section 901(m) payor is allocated the portions of cost recovery amounts or disposition amounts (or both) with respect to RFAs that are equal to the product of the sum of the cost recovery amounts and the disposition amounts and a fraction, the numerator of which is the portion of the foreign income of the RFA owner (foreign) that is included in the foreign income of the foreign payor, and the denominator of which is the foreign income of the RFA owner (foreign).

(ii) *Assignment to a U.S. taxable year of a section 901(m) payor.*—This paragraph (g)(2)(ii) applies when a cost recovery amount or a disposition amount, or portion thereof, is allocated to a section 901(m) payor under paragraph (g)(2)(i) of this section. If the reverse hybrid is the RFA owner (U.S.), a cost recovery amount or disposition amount, or portion thereof, is assigned to the U.S. taxable year of the section 901(m) payor that includes the last day of the U.S. taxable year of the reverse hybrid in which, in the case of a cost recovery amount, the reverse hybrid takes into account the corresponding U.S. basis deduction (without regard to whether the deduction is deferred or disallowed for U.S. income tax purposes), or, in the case of a disposition amount, the disposition occurs. If the reverse hybrid is not the RFA owner (U.S.) but instead the reverse hybrid directly or indirectly owns an interest in the RFA owner (U.S.) for both U.S. and foreign income tax purposes, a cost recovery amount or disposition amount, or portion thereof, is assigned to the U.S. taxable year of the section 901(m) payor that includes the last day of the U.S. taxable year of the reverse hybrid, which, in turn, includes the last day of the U.S. taxable year of the RFA owner (U.S.) in which, in the case of a cost recovery amount, the RFA owner (U.S.) takes into account the corresponding U.S. basis deduction (without regard to whether the deduction is deferred or disallowed for U.S. income tax purposes), or, in the case of a disposition amount, the disposition occurs.

(3) *Second allocation rule.*—(i) *Allocation to a section 901(m) payor.*—This paragraph (g)(3)(i) applies when neither a section 901(m) payor nor a disregarded entity directly owned by a section 901(m) payor is the foreign payor with respect to the foreign income of the RFA owner (foreign). Instead, a section 901(m) payor directly or indirectly owns an interest in the foreign payor, which is a fiscally transparent entity for U.S. income tax purposes (other than a disregarded entity directly owned by the section 901(m) payor), and, therefore, the section 901(m) payor is considered to pay or accrue only its allocated portion of the foreign income tax amount of the foreign payor. In these cases, the section 901(m) payor is allocated the portions of cost recovery amounts or disposition amounts (or both) with respect to RFAs that are equal to the product of the sum of the cost recovery amounts and the disposition amounts and a fraction, the numerator of which is the portion of the foreign income of the RFA owner (foreign) that is included in the foreign income of the foreign payor and included in the allocable foreign income of the section 901(m) payor, and the denominator of which is the foreign income of the RFA owner (foreign). If allocable foreign income is not otherwise required to be determined for a section 901(m) payor because there is no foreign income tax amount, the numerator is the foreign income of the RFA owner (foreign) that is included in the foreign income of the foreign payor and that would be included in allocable foreign income of the section 901(m) payor if there were a foreign income tax amount.

(ii) *Assignment to a U.S. taxable year of a section 901(m) payor.*—A cost recovery amount or a disposition amount, or portion thereof, that is allocated to a section 901(m) payor under paragraph (g)(3)(i) of this section is assigned to the U.S. taxable year of the section 901(m) payor in which the foreign income of the RFA owner (foreign) described in paragraph (g)(3)(i) of this section is included in the allocable foreign income of the section 901(m) payor, or, if there is no foreign income tax amount, the U.S. taxable year of the section 901(m) payor in which the foreign income of the RFA owner (foreign) described in paragraph (g)(3)(i) of this section would be included in allocable foreign income if there were a foreign income tax amount.

(h) *Examples.*—The following examples illustrate the rules of this section. In addition to any facts described in a particular example, the following facts apply to all the examples unless otherwise specified: CFC1, CFC2, and DE are organized in Country F and treated as corporations for Country F tax purposes. CFC1 and CFC2 are each an applicable foreign corporation that is wholly owned by the same U.S. corporation, and DE is a disregarded entity. CFC1 and CFC2 each have a U.S. taxable year that is a calendar year, and CFC1, CFC2, and DE each have a foreign taxable year that is a calendar year. Country F imposes a single tax that is a foreign income tax. CFC1, CFC2, and DE each have a functional currency of the u with respect to all activities. At all relevant times, 1u equals $1. All amounts are stated in millions. The examples assume that the applicable cost recovery method for property results in basis being recovered ratably over the life of the property beginning on the first day of the U.S. taxable year in which the property is acquired or placed into service.

(1) *Example 1: CAA followed by disposition: fully taxable for both U.S. income tax and foreign income tax purposes.*—(i) *Facts.* (A) On January 1, Year 1, USP acquires all of the stock of CFC1 in a qualified stock purchase (as defined in section 338(d)(3)) to which section 338(a) applies (Section 338 Acquisition). At the time of the Section 338 Acquisition, CFC1 owns a single asset (Asset A) that is located in Country F. Asset A gives rise to income that is taken into account for Country F tax purposes. Asset A is tangible personal property that, under the applicable cost recovery method in the hands of CFC1, is depreciable over 5 years. There are no cost recovery deductions available for Country F tax purposes with respect to Asset A. Immediately before the Section 338 Acquisition, Asset A has a U.S. basis of 10u and a foreign basis of 40u. Immediately after the Section 338 Acquisition, Asset A has a U.S. basis of 100u and foreign basis of 40u.

(B) On July 1, Year 2, Asset A is transferred to an unrelated third party in exchange for 120u in a transaction in which all realized gain is recognized for both U.S. income tax and Country F tax purposes (subsequent transaction). For U.S. income tax purposes, CFC1 recognizes U.S. disposition gain of 50u (amount realized of 120u, less U.S. basis of 70u (100u cost basis, less 30u of accumulated depreciation)) with respect to Asset A. The 30u of accumulated depreciation is the sum of 20u of depreciation in Year 1 (100u cost basis/5 years) and 10u of depreciation in Year 2 ((100u cost basis/5 years) x 6/12). For Country F tax purposes, CFC1 recognizes foreign disposition gain of 80u (amount realized of 120u, less foreign basis of 40u) with respect to Asset A. Immediately after the subsequent transaction, Asset A has a U.S. basis and a foreign basis of 120u.

(ii) *Result.* (A) Under § 1.901(m)-2(b)(1), USP's acquisition of the stock of CFC1 in the Section 338 Acquisition is a section 338 CAA. Under § 1.901(m)-2(c)(i), Asset A is an RFA with respect to Country F tax because it is relevant in determining the foreign income of CFC1 for Country F tax purposes. Under § 1.901(m)-4(b), the basis difference with respect to Asset A is 90u (100u – 10u). Under § 1.901(m)-1(a)(37), CFC1 is the RFA owner (U.S.) with respect to Asset A. Under § 1.901(m)-1(a)(28), CFC1 is a foreign payor for Country F tax purposes. Under § 1.901(m)-1(a)(41), CFC1 is the section 901(m) payor with respect to a foreign income tax amount for which CFC1 is the foreign payor (see § 1.901-2(f)(1)).

(B) Under § 1.901(m)-1(a)(5), allocated basis differences are the sum of cost recovery amounts and disposition amounts. In Year 1, Asset A has an allocated basis difference that includes only a cost recovery amount. Under paragraph (b)(2) of this section, the cost recovery amount for Year 1 is determined by applying the applicable cost recovery method of Asset A in the hands of CFC1 to the basis difference with respect to Asset A. Accordingly, the cost recovery amount is 18u (90u basis difference/5 years). Under paragraph (b)(1) of this section, all of the 18u cost recovery amount is attributed to CFC1 and assigned to Year 1, because CFC1 is a section 901(m) payor and RFA owner (U.S.) with respect to Asset A and Year 1 is the U.S. taxable year of CFC1 in which it takes into account the corresponding 20u of depreciation. Immediately after Year 1, under § 1.901(m)-1(a)(47), unallocated basis difference is 72u with respect to Asset A (90u – 18u).

(C) In Year 2, Asset A has an allocated basis difference that includes both a cost recovery amount and a disposition amount. Under paragraph (b)(2) of this section, the cost recovery amount for Year 2, as of the date of the subsequent transaction, is 9u ((90u basis difference/5 years) x 6/12). Under § 1.901(m)-1(a)(15), the subsequent transaction is a disposition of Asset A, because the subsequent transaction is an event that results in an amount of gain being recognized for U.S. income tax and Country F tax purposes. Because all realized gain in Asset A is recognized for U.S. income tax and Country F tax purposes, the rule in paragraph (c)(2)(i) of this section applies to determine the disposition amount. Under that rule, the disposition amount for Year 2 is the unallocated basis difference of 63u (90u basis difference, less total 27u taken into account as cost recovery amounts in Year 1 and Year 2). Accordingly, the allocated basis difference for Year 2 is 72u (9u of cost recovery amount, plus 63u of disposition amount). Under paragraphs (b)(1) and (c)(1) of this section, all of the 72u of allocated basis difference is attributed to CFC1 and assigned to Year 2, because CFC1 is a section 901(m) payor and the RFA owner (U.S.) with respect to Asset A and Year 2 is the U.S. taxable year of CFC1 in which it takes into account the corresponding 10u of depreciation and in which the disposition occurred.

(D) Unallocated basis difference with respect to Asset A, as determined immediately after the subsequent transaction, is 0u (90u basis difference less 90u basis difference taken into account as 27u total cost recovery amount in Year 1 and Year 2 and as a 63u disposition amount in Year 2). Accordingly, because there is no unallocated basis difference with respect to Asset A attributable to the Section 338 Acquisition, the subsequent transaction is not a successor transaction as defined in § 1.901(m)-6(b)(2). Furthermore, the subsequent transaction is not a CAA under § 1.901(m)-2(b). For these reasons, section 901(m) no longer applies to Asset A.

(2) *Example 2: CAA followed by disposition: nontaxable for U.S. income tax purposes and taxable for foreign income tax purposes.*—(i) *Facts.* The facts are the same as in paragraph (h)(1)(i)(A) of this section (paragraph (i)(A) of *Example 1*) but the facts in paragraph (h)(1)(i)(B) of this section (paragraph (i)(B) of *Example 1*) are instead that on July 1, Year 2, Asset A is transferred to CFC2, in exchange for 100u of stock of CFC2 (subsequent transaction). For U.S. income tax purposes, CFC1 does not recognize any U.S. disposition gain or U.S. disposition loss with respect to Asset A. For Country F tax purposes, CFC1 recognizes foreign disposition gain of 60u (amount realized of 100u, less foreign basis of 40u) with respect to Asset A. Immediately after the subsequent transaction, Asset A has a U.S. basis of 70u (100u cost basis less 30u accumulated depreciation) and a foreign basis of 100u. The 30u of accumulated depreciation is the sum of 20u of depreciation in Year 1 (100u cost basis/5 years) and 10u in Year 2 ((100u cost basis/5 years) x 6/12).

(ii) *Result.* (A) The results described in paragraph (h)(1)(ii)(A) of this section (paragraph (ii)(A) of *Example 1*) also apply to this paragraph (h)(2)(ii) (the results of this *Example 2*).

(B)The result for Year 1 is the same as in paragraph (h)(1)(ii)(B) of this section (paragraph (ii)(B) of *Example 1*).

(C) In Year 2, Asset A has an allocated basis difference that includes both a cost recovery amount and a disposition amount. Under paragraph (b)(2) of this section, the cost recovery amount for Year 2, as of the date of the subsequent transaction, is 9u ((90u basis difference/5 years) x 6/12). Under § 1.901(m)-1(a)(15), the subsequent transaction is a disposition of Asset A, because the subsequent transaction is an event that results in an amount of gain being recognized for Country F tax purposes. Because the disposition is not also fully taxable for U.S. income tax purposes, the rule in paragraph (c)(2)(ii) of this section applies to determine the disposition amount. Under that rule, the disposition amount is 60u, the lesser of (i) 60u (60u foreign disposition gain plus absolute value of 0u U.S. disposition loss), and (ii) 63u unallocated basis difference (90 basis difference less total 27u taken into account as cost recovery amounts, 18u in Year 1 and 9u in Year 2). Accordingly, the allocated basis difference for the first half of Year 2 is 69u (9u of cost recovery amount, plus 60u of disposition amount). Under paragraphs (b)(1) and (c)(1) of this section, all of the 69u of allocated basis difference is attributed to CFC1 and assigned to Year 2, because CFC1 is a section 901(m) payor and the RFA owner (U.S.) with respect to Asset A and Year 2 is the U.S. taxable year of CFC1 in which it takes into account the corresponding 10u of depreciation and in which the disposition occurred.

(D) Unallocated basis difference with respect to Asset A immediately after the subsequent transaction is 3u (90u basis difference less 87u basis difference taken into account as a 27u total cost recovery amount in Year 1 and Year 2 and as a 60u disposition amount in Year 2). Accordingly, because there is unallocated basis difference of 3u with respect to Asset A attributable to the Section 338 Acquisition, as determined immediately after the subsequent transaction, the subsequent transaction is a successor transaction as defined in § 1.901(m)-6(b)(2). Following the subsequent transaction, the unallocated basis difference of 3u must be taken into account as cost recovery amounts or disposition amounts (or both) by CFC2, the new section 901(m) payor and RFA owner (U.S.) of Asset A. See § 1.901(m)-6(b)(3)(ii). Because the subsequent transaction is not a CAA under § 1.901(m)-2(b), there is no additional basis difference with respect to Asset A as a result of the subsequent transaction.

(3) *Example 3: CAA followed by disposition: nontaxable for both U.S. income tax and foreign income tax purposes.*—(i) *Facts.* The facts are the same as in paragraph (h)(1)(i)(A) of this section (paragraph (i)(A) of *Example 1*) but the facts in paragraph (h)(1)(i)(B) of this section (paragraph (i)(B) of *Example 1*) are instead that on July 1, Year 2, CFC1 transfers Asset A to CFC2, in exchange for 110u of stock of CFC2 (subsequent transaction). For U.S. income tax purposes, CFC1 does not recognize any U.S. disposition gain or U.S. disposition loss with respect to Asset A as a result of the subsequent transaction. Furthermore, for Country F tax purposes, CFC1 recognizes no foreign disposition gain or foreign disposition loss with respect to Asset A as a result of the subsequent transaction. Immediately after the subsequent transaction, Asset A has a U.S. basis of 70u (100u cost basis less 30u accumulated depreciation) and a foreign basis of 40u. The 30u of accumulated depreciation is the sum of 20u of depreciation in Year 1 (100u cost basis/5 years) and 10u in Year 2 ((100u cost basis/5 years) x 6/12).

(ii) *Result.* (A) The result for Year 1 is the same as in paragraph (h)(1)(ii)(A) of this section (paragraph (ii)(A) of *Example 1*).

(B) The result for Year 1 is the same as in paragraph (h)(1)(ii)(B) of this section (paragraph (ii)(B) of *Example 1*).

(C) In Year 2, Asset A has an allocated basis difference that includes only a cost recovery amount. Under paragraph (b)(2) of this section, the cost recovery amount for Year 2, as of the date of the subsequent transaction, is 9u ((90u basis difference/5 years) x 6/12). Under § 1.901(m)-1(a)(15), the subsequent transaction does not constitute a disposition of Asset A, because the subsequent transaction is not an event that results in an amount of gain or loss being recognized for U.S. income tax or for Country F tax purposes. Therefore, no disposition amount is taken into account for Asset A in Year 2. Under paragraph (b)(1) of this section, all of the 9u of allocated basis difference is attributed to CFC1 and assigned to Year 2, because CFC1 is a section 901(m) payor and RFA owner (U.S.) with respect to Asset A and Year 2 is the U.S. taxable year of CFC1 in which it takes into account the corresponding 10u of depreciation.

(D) Unallocated basis difference with respect to Asset A immediately after the subsequent transaction is 63u (90u basis difference, less 27u total cost recovery amounts, 18u in Year 1 and 9u in Year 2). Accordingly, because there is unallocated basis difference of 63u with respect to Asset A attributable to the CAA, as determined immediately after the subsequent transaction, the subsequent transaction is a successor transaction as defined in § 1.901(m)-6(b)(2). Following the subsequent transaction, the unallocated basis difference of 63u must be taken into account as cost recovery amounts or disposition amounts (or both) by CFC2, the new section 901(m) payor and RFA owner (U.S.) of Asset A. See § 1.901(m)-6(b)(3)(ii). Because the subsequent transaction is not a CAA under § 1.901(m)-2(b), there is no additional basis difference with respect to Asset A as a result of the subsequent transaction.

(i) *Applicability dates.*—(1) Except as provided in paragraph (i)(2) of this section, this section applies to CAAs occurring on or after March 23, 2020.

(2) Paragraphs (b)(2)(i) and (c)(2) of this section apply to CAAs occurring on or after July 21, 2014, and to CAAs occurring before that date resulting from an entity classification election made under § 301.7701-3 of this chapter that is filed on or after July 29, 2014, and that is effective on or before July 21, 2014. Paragraphs (b)(2)(i) and (c)(2) of this section also apply to CAAs occurring on or after January 1, 2011, and before July 21, 2014, other than CAAs occurring before July 21, 2014, resulting from an entity classification election made under § 301.7701-3 that is filed on or after July 29, 2014, and that is effective on or before July 21, 2014, but only with respect to basis difference determined under § 1.901(m)-4T(e) with respect to the CAA.

(3) Taxpayers may, however, choose to apply provisions in this section before the date such provisions are applicable pursuant to paragraphs (i)(1) and (2) of this section, provided that they (along with any persons that are related (within the meaning of section 267(b) or 707(b)) to the taxpayer)—

(i) Consistently apply this section, § 1.704-1(b)(4)(viii)(*c*)(*4*)(*v*) through (*vii*), § 1.901(m)-1, § 1.901(m)-3, § 1.901(m)-4 (excluding § 1.901(m)-4(e)), § 1.901(m)-6, § 1.901(m)-7, and § 1.901(m)-8 to all CAAs occurring on or after January 1, 2011, and consistently apply § 1.901(m)-2 (excluding § 1.901(m)-2(d)) to all CAAs occurring on or after December 7, 2016, on any original or amended tax return for each taxable year for which the application of the provisions listed in this paragraph (i)(3)(i) affects the tax liability and for which the statute of limitations does not preclude assessment or the filing of a claim for refund, as applicable;

(ii) File all tax returns described in paragraph (i)(3)(i) of this section for any taxable year ending on or before March 23, 2020, no later than March 23, 2021; and

(iii) Make appropriate adjustments to take into account deficiencies that would have resulted from the consistent application under paragraph (i)(3)(i) of this section for taxable years that are not open for assessment. [Reg. § 1.901(m)-5.]

□ *[T.D. 9895, 3-20-2020.]*

§ 1.901(m)-6. Successor rules.—(a) *In general.*—This section provides successor rules applicable to section 901(m). Paragraph (b) of this section provides rules for the continued application of section 901(m) after an RFA that has unallocated basis difference has been transferred, including special rules applicable to successor transactions that are also CAAs or that involve partnerships. Paragraph (c) of this section provides rules for determining when an aggregate basis difference carryover of a section 901(m) payor either becomes an aggregate basis difference carryover of the section 901(m) payor with respect to another foreign payor or is transferred to another section 901(m) payor, and paragraph (d) of this section provides applicability dates.

(b) *Successor rules for unallocated basis difference.*—(1) *In general.*—Except as provided in paragraph (b)(4) of this section, section 901(m) continues to apply after a successor transaction to any unallocated basis difference attached to a transferred RFA until the entire basis difference has been taken into account as a cost recovery amount or a disposition amount (or both) under § 1.901(m)-5.

(2) *Definition of a successor transaction.*—A successor transaction occurs with respect to an RFA if, after a CAA (*prior CAA*), there is a transfer of the RFA for U.S. income tax purposes and the RFA has unallocated basis difference with respect to the prior CAA, determined immediately after the transfer. A successor transaction may occur regardless of whether the transfer of the RFA is a disposition, a CAA, or a nontaxable transaction for purposes of U.S. income tax. If the RFA was subject to multiple prior CAAs, a separate determination must be made with respect to each prior CAA as to whether the transfer is a successor transaction.

(3) *Special considerations.*—(i) If an asset is an RFA with respect to more than one foreign income tax, this paragraph (b) applies separately with respect to each foreign income tax.

(ii) Any subsequent cost recovery amount for an RFA transferred in a successor transaction is determined based on the post-transaction applicable cost recovery method, as described in § 1.901(m)-5(b)(3), that applies to the U.S. basis (or portion thereof) that corresponds to the unallocated basis difference.

(4) *Successor transaction is a CAA.*—(i) *In general.*—An asset may be an RFA with respect to multiple CAAs if a successor transaction is also a CAA (*subsequent CAA*). Except as otherwise provided in this paragraph (b)(4), if there is a subsequent CAA, unallocated basis difference with respect to any prior CAAs will continue to be taken into account under section 901(m) after the subsequent CAA. Furthermore, the subsequent CAA may give rise to additional basis difference subject to section 901(m).

(ii) *Foreign basis election.*—If a foreign basis election is made under § 1.901(m)-4(c) with respect to a foreign income tax in a subsequent CAA, any unallocated basis difference with respect to one or more prior CAAs will not be taken into account under section 901(m). The only basis difference that will be taken into account after the subsequent CAA with respect to that foreign income tax is the basis difference with respect to the subsequent CAA.

(iii) *Multiple section 743(b) CAAs.*—If an RFA is subject to two section 743(b) CAAs (*prior section 743(b) CAA* and *subsequent section 743(b) CAA*) and the same partnership interest is acquired in both the CAAs, the RFA will be treated as having no unallocated basis difference with respect to the prior section 743(b) CAA if the basis difference for the section 743(b) CAA is determined independently from the prior section 743(b) CAA. In this regard, see generally § 1.743-1(f). If the subsequent section 743(b) CAA results from the acquisition of only a portion of the partnership interest acquired in the prior section 743(b) CAA, then the transferor will be required to equitably apportion the unallocated basis difference attributable to the prior section 743(b) CAA between the portion retained by the transferor and the portion transferred. In this case, with respect to the portion transferred, the RFAs will be treated as having no unallocated basis difference with respect to the prior section 743(b) CAA if basis difference for the subsequent section 743(b) CAA is determined independently from the prior section 743(b) CAA.

(5) *Example.*—The following example illustrates the rules of paragraph (b) of this section.

(i) *Facts.* USP, a domestic corporation, wholly owns CFC, a foreign corporation organized in Country A and treated as a corporation for both U.S. and Country A tax purposes. FT is an unrelated foreign corporation organized in Country A and treated as a corporation for both U.S. and Country A tax purposes. FT owns one asset, a parcel of land (Asset). Country A imposes a single tax that is a foreign income tax. On January 1, Year 1, CFC acquires all of the stock of FT in exchange for 300u in a qualified stock purchase (as defined in section 338(d)(3)) to which section 338(a) applies (Acquisition). Immediately before the Acquisition, Asset had a U.S. basis of 100u, and immediately after the Acquisition, Asset had a U.S. basis of 300u. Effective on February 1, Year 1, FT elects to be a disregarded entity pursuant to § 301.7701-3. As a result of the election, FT is deemed, for U.S. income tax purposes, to distribute Asset to CFC in liquidation (Deemed Liquidation) immediately before the closing of the day before the election is effective pursuant to § 301.7701-3(g)(1)(iii) and (3)(ii). The Deemed Liquidation is disregarded for Country A tax purposes. No gain or loss is recognized on the Deemed Liquidation for either U.S. or Country A tax purposes.

(ii) *Result.* Under § 1.901(m)-2(b)(1), the acquisition by CFC of the stock of FT is a section 338 CAA. Under § 1.901(m)-2(c)(1), Asset is an RFA with respect to Country A tax and the Acquisition, because immediately after the Acquisition, Asset is relevant in determining foreign income of FT for Country A tax purposes, and FT owned Asset when the Acquisition occurred. Under § 1.901(m)-4(b), the basis difference with respect to Asset is 200u (300u − 100u). Under § 1.901(m)-2(b)(2), the Deemed Liquidation is a CAA (subsequent CAA) because the Deemed Liquidation is treated as an acquisition of assets for U.S. income tax purposes and is disregarded for Country A tax purposes. Because the U.S. basis in Asset is 300u immediately before and after the Deemed Liquidation, the subsequent CAA does not give rise to any additional basis difference. The Deemed Liquidation is not a disposition under § 1.901(m)-1(a)(15) because it did not result in gain or loss being recognized with respect to Asset for U.S. or Country A tax purposes. Accordingly, no basis difference with respect to Asset is taken into account under § 1.901(m)-5 as a result of the Deemed Liquidation, and the unallocated basis difference with respect to Asset immediately after the Deemed Liquidation is 200u (200u − 0u). Under paragraph (b)(2) of this section, the Deemed Liquidation is a successor transaction because there is a transfer of Asset for U.S. income tax purposes from FT to CFC and Asset has unallocated basis difference with respect to the Acquisition immediately after the Deemed Liquidation. Accordingly, under paragraph (b)(1) of this section, section 901(m) will continue to apply to the unallocated basis difference with respect to Asset until the entire 200u basis difference has been taken into account under § 1.901(m)-5.

(c) *Successor rules for aggregate basis difference carryover.*—(1) *Transfers of a section 901(m) payor's aggregate basis difference carryover to another person.*—If a corporation acquires the assets of a section 901(m) payor in a transaction to which section 381 applies, that corporation succeeds to any aggregate basis difference carryovers of the section 901(m) payor.

(2) *Transfers of a section 901(m) payor's aggregate basis difference carryover with respect to a foreign payor to another foreign payor.*—If a section 901(m) payor has an aggregate basis difference carryover, with respect to a foreign income tax and a foreign payor, and substantially all of the assets of the foreign payor are transferred to another foreign payor in which the section 901(m) payor owns an interest, the section 901(m) payor's aggregate basis difference carryover with respect to the first foreign payor is transferred to the section 901(m) payor's aggregate basis difference carryover with respect to the other foreign payor. In such a case, the section 901(m) payor's aggregate basis difference carryover with respect to the first foreign payor is reduced to zero.

(3) *Anti-abuse rule.*—If a section 901(m) payor has an aggregate basis difference carryover with respect to a foreign income tax and a foreign payor and, with a principal purpose of avoiding the application of section 901(m), assets of the foreign payor are transferred to another foreign payor in a transaction not described in paragraph (c)(1) or (2) of this section, then a portion of the aggregate basis difference carryover of the section 901(m) payor is transferred either to the aggregate basis difference carryover of the section 901(m) payor with respect to the other foreign payor or to another section 901(m) payor, as appropriate. The portion of the aggregate basis difference carryover transferred is determined based on the ratio of fair market value of the assets transferred to the fair market value of all of the assets of the foreign payor that transferred the assets. Similar principles apply when, with a principal purpose of avoiding the application of section 901(m), there is a change in the allocation of

foreign income for foreign income tax purposes or the allocation of foreign income tax amounts for U.S. income tax purposes that would otherwise separate foreign income tax amounts from the related aggregate basis difference carryover.

(4) *Ownership*.—For purposes of this paragraph (c), a section 901(m) payor owns an interest in a foreign payor if the section 901(m) payor owns the interest directly or indirectly through one or more fiscally transparent entities for U.S. income tax purposes.

(d) *Applicability dates*.—(1) Except as provided in paragraph (d)(2) of this section, this section applies to CAAs occurring on or after March 23, 2020.

(2) Paragraphs (a), (b)(1) and (2), (b)(4)(i) and (iii), and (b)(5) of this section apply to CAAs occurring on or after July 21, 2014, and to CAAs occurring before that date resulting from an entity classification election made under § 301.7701-3 of this chapter that is filed on or after July 29, 2014, and that is effective on or before July 21, 2014. Paragraphs (a), (b)(1) and (2), (b)(4)(i) and (iii), and (b)(5) of this section also apply to CAAs occurring on or after January 1, 2011, and before July 21, 2014, other than CAAs occurring before July 21, 2014, resulting from an entity classification election made under § 301.7701-3 that is filed on or after July 29, 2014, and that is effective on or before July 21, 2014, but only with respect to basis difference determined under § 1.901(m)-4T(e) with respect to the CAA.

(3) Taxpayers may, however, choose to apply provisions in this section before the date such provisions are applicable pursuant to paragraphs (d)(1) and (2) of this section, provided that they (along with any persons that are related (within the meaning of section 267(b) or 707(b)) to the taxpayer)—

(i) Consistently apply this section, § 1.704-1(b)(4)(viii)(*c*)(*4*)(*v*) through (*vii*), § 1.901(m)-1, §§ 1.901(m)-3 through 1.901(m)-5 (excluding § 1.901(m)-4(e)), § 1.901(m)-7, and § 1.901(m)-8 to all CAAs occurring on or after January 1, 2011, and consistently apply § 1.901(m)-2 (excluding § 1.901(m)-2(d)) to all CAAs occurring on or after December 7, 2016, on any original or amended tax return for each taxable year for which the application of the provisions listed in this paragraph (d)(3)(i) affects the tax liability and for which the statute of limitations does not preclude assessment or the filing of a claim for refund, as applicable;

(ii) File all tax returns described in paragraph (d)(3)(i) of this section for any taxable year ending on or before March 23, 2020, no later than March 23, 2021; and

(iii) Make appropriate adjustments to take into account deficiencies that would have resulted from the consistent application under paragraph (d)(3)(i) of this section for taxable years that are not open for assessment. [Reg. § 1.901(m)-6.]

☐ [*T.D.* 9895, 3-20-2020.]

§ 1.901(m)-7. De minimis rules.—(a) *In general*.—This section provides rules describing basis difference that is not taken into account under section 901(m) because a CAA results in a de minimis amount of basis difference. Paragraph (b) of this section sets forth the general rule for determining whether the de minimis threshold is met. Paragraph (c) of this section modifies the general rule in the case of CAAs that are part of an aggregated CAA transaction. Paragraph (d) of this section provides rules for applying this section, and paragraph (e) of this section provides an anti-abuse rule applicable to related persons. Paragraph (f) of this section provides examples that illustrate the application of this section. Paragraph (g) of this section provides applicability dates.

(b) *General rule*.—(1) *In general*.—A basis difference with respect to an RFA and a foreign income tax is not taken into account under section 901(m) if the requirements under the cumulative basis difference exemption, the RFA class exemption, or the RFA exemption are satisfied.

(2) *Cumulative basis difference exemption*.—Except as provided in paragraph (c) of this section, a basis difference, with respect to an RFA and a foreign income tax, is not taken into account under section 901(m) (*cumulative basis difference exemption*) if the sum of that basis difference and all other basis differences (including negative basis differences), with respect to a single CAA and a single RFA owner (U.S.), is less than the greater of:

(i) $10 million, or

(ii) 10 percent of the total U.S. basis of all the RFAs immediately after the CAA.

(3) *RFA class exemption*.—(i) Except as provided in paragraph (c) of this section, a basis difference, with respect to an RFA and a foreign income tax, is not taken into account under section 901(m) (*RFA class exemption*) if the RFA is part of a class of RFAs and the absolute value of the sum of the basis differences (including negative basis differences), with respect to a single CAA and a single RFA owner, for all the RFAs in that class is less than the greater of:

(A) $2 million, or

(B) 10 percent of the total U.S. basis of all the RFAs in that class of RFAs immediately after the CAA.

(ii) For purposes of this paragraph (b)(3), the classes of RFAs are the seven asset classes defined in § 1.338-6(b), regardless of whether the CAA is a section 338 CAA.

(4) *RFA exemption*.—A basis difference, with respect to an RFA and a foreign income tax, is not taken into account under section 901(m) (*RFA exemption*) if the absolute value of the basis difference with respect to the RFA is less than $20,000.

(c) *Special rule if a CAA is part of an aggregated CAA transaction*.—If a CAA is part of an aggregated CAA transaction and a single RFA owner (U.S.) does not own all the RFAs attributable to the CAAs that are part of the aggregated CAA transaction, the cumulative basis difference exemption and the RFA class exemption apply to such CAA only if, in addition to satisfying the requirements of paragraph (b)(2) or (b)(3) of this section, respectively, determined without regard to this paragraph (c), the cumulative basis difference exemption or the RFA class exemption, as modified by this paragraph (c), is satisfied. Solely for purposes of this paragraph (c), the cumulative basis difference exemption and the RFA class exemption are applied taking into account all the basis differences with respect to all the RFAs owned by all the RFA owners (U.S.) that are attributable to the CAAs that are part of the aggregated CAA transaction.

(d) *Rules of application*.—The following rules apply for purposes of this section.

(1) Whether a basis difference qualifies for the cumulative basis difference exemption, the RFA class exemption, or the RFA exemption is determined when an asset first becomes an RFA with respect to a CAA. In the case of a subsequent CAA described in § 1.901(m)-6(b)(4), the application of the cumulative basis difference exemption, the RFA class exemption, and the RFA exemption is based on basis difference, if any, that results from the subsequent CAA.

(2) If there is an aggregated CAA transaction, the cumulative basis difference exemption and each RFA class exemption are applied by treating all CAAs that are part of the aggregated CAA transaction as a single CAA.

(3) Basis difference is computed in accordance with § 1.901(m)-4 except that a foreign basis election need not be evidenced if the cumulative basis difference exemption, an RFA class exemption, or the RFA exemption apply to all RFAs with respect to the CAA.

(4) Basis difference is translated into U.S. dollars (if necessary) using the spot rate determined under the principles of § 1.988-1(d) on the date of the CAA.

(e) *Anti-abuse rule*.—The cumulative basis difference exemption, an RFA class exemption, and the RFA exemption are not available if the transferor and transferee in the CAA are related persons (as described in section 267(b) or 707(b)) and the CAA was entered into, or structured, with a principal purpose of avoiding the application of section 901(m). See also § 1.901(m)-8(c), which provides that certain built-in loss assets are not taken into account for purposes of applying this section.

(f) *Examples*.—The following examples illustrate the rules of this section:

(1) *Example 1: De minimis; cumulative basis difference exemption*.—(i) *Facts*. USP, a domestic corporation, as part of a plan, purchases all of the stock of CFC1 and CFC2 from a single seller. CFC1 and CFC2 are applicable foreign corporations, organized in Country F, and treated as corporations for Country F tax purposes. Country F imposes a single tax that is a foreign income tax. Each acquisition is a qualified stock purchase (as defined in section 338(d)(3)) to which section 338(a) applies. A foreign basis election is not made under § 1.901(m)-4(c). Immediately after the acquisition of the stock of CFC1 and CFC2, the assets of CFC1 and CFC2 give rise to income that is taken into account for Country F tax purposes, and those assets are in a single class, as defined in § 1.338-6(b). Assume that the absolute value of the basis difference with respect to any single RFA is greater than $20,000. At all relevant times, 1u equals $1. All amounts are stated in millions. The additional facts are summarized below.

Relevant Foreign Assets	Total U.S. Basis Immediately Before	Total U.S. Basis Immediately After	Total Basis Difference
Assets of CFC1	48u	60u	12u
Assets of CFC2	100u	96u	(4)u
Total	148u	156u	8u

(ii) *Result.* (A) Under § 1.901(m)-2(b)(1), USP's acquisitions of the stock of CFC1 and CFC2 are each a section 338 CAA. Under 1.901(m)-1(a)(3), the two section 338 CAAs constitute an aggregated CAA transaction because the acquisitions occur as part of a plan. Under § 1.901(m)-2(c)(1), the assets of CFC1 and CFC2 are RFAs for Country F tax purposes because they are relevant in determining foreign income of CFC1 and CFC 2, respectively, for Country F tax purposes. Under § 1.901(m)-1(a)(37), CFC1 is the RFA owner (U.S.) with respect to its assets, and CFC2 is the RFA owner (U.S.) with respect to its assets.

(B) Under paragraph (b)(2) of this section, the application of the cumulative basis difference exemption is based on a single CAA and a single RFA owner (U.S.), subject to the requirements under paragraph (c) of this section that apply when there is an aggregated CAA transaction. In the case of the section 338 CAA with respect to CFC1, without regard to paragraph (c) of this section, the requirements of the cumulative basis difference exemption are satisfied if the sum of the basis differences is less than the threshold of $10 million, the greater of $10 million or $6 million (10% of the total U.S. basis of $60 million (60 million u translated into dollars at the exchange rate of $1 = 1u)). In this case, the sum of the basis differences is $12 million (12 million u translated into dollars at the exchange rate of $1 = 1 u). Because the sum of the basis differences of $12 million is not less than the threshold of $10 million, the requirements of the cumulative basis difference exemption are not satisfied. Because the requirements of the cumulative basis difference exemption are not satisfied, without regard to paragraph (c) of this section, paragraph (c) of this section is not applicable. The RFA class exemption is not relevant because all of the RFAs of CFC1 are in a single class. Finally, because the absolute value with respect to each RFA is greater than $20,000, the RFA exemption does not apply. Accordingly, the basis differences with respect to all of the RFAs of CFC1 must be taken into account under section 901(m).

(C) In the case of the section 338 CAA with respect to CFC2, without regard to paragraph (c) of this section, the requirements of the cumulative basis difference exemption are satisfied if the sum of the basis differences is less than the threshold of $10 million, the greater of $10 million or $ 9.6 million (10% of the total U.S. basis of $96 million (96 million u translated into dollars at the exchange rate of $1 = 1u)) In this case, the sum of the basis differences is ($4) million ((4) million u translated into dollars at the exchange rate of $1 = 1 u). Because the sum of the basis differences of ($4) million is less than the threshold of $10 million, the requirements of the cumulative basis difference exemption are satisfied. However, because the section 338 CAA with respect to CFC2 is part of an aggregated CAA transaction that includes the section 338 CAA with respect to CFC1, paragraph (c) of this section is applicable. Under paragraph (c) of this section, the requirements of the cumulative basis difference exemption must also be satisfied taking into account all of the RFAs of both CFC2 and CFC1. In this case, the requirements of the cumulative basis difference exemption for purposes of paragraph (c) of this section are satisfied if the sum of the basis differences with respect to all of the RFAs of CFC2 and CFC1 is less than the threshold of $15.6 million, the greater of $10 million or $15.6 million (10% of the total U.S. basis of $156 million (156 million u translated into dollars at the exchange rate of $1 = 1u)). In this case, the sum of the basis differences is $8 million (8 million u translated into dollars at the exchange rate of $1 = 1 u). Because the sum of the basis differences of $8 million is less than the threshold of $15.6 million, the requirements of the cumulative basis difference exemption are satisfied in the case of the section 338 CAA with respect to CFC2. Accordingly, none of the basis differences with respect to the RFAs of CFC2 are taken into account under section 901(m).

(2) *Example 2: De minimis; RFA Class Exemption.*—(i) *Facts.* USP, a domestic corporation, acquires all the stock of CFC, an applicable foreign corporation organized in Country F and treated as a corporation for Country F tax purposes, in a qualified stock purchase (as defined in section 338(d)(3)) to which section 338(a) applies. Country F imposes a single tax that is a foreign income tax. A foreign basis election is not made under § 1.901(m)-4(c). Immediately after the acquisition of CFC, the assets of CFC give rise to income that is taken into account for Country F tax purposes. Assume that the absolute value of the basis difference with respect to any single RFA is greater than $20,000. At all relevant times, 1u equals $1. All amounts are stated in millions. The additional facts are summarized below.

Relevant Foreign Assets	Total U.S. Basis Immediately Before	Total U.S. Basis Immediately After	Total Basis Difference
Cash (Class I)	10u	10u	0u
Inventory (Class IV)	14u	15u	1u
Buildings (Class V)	19u	30u	11u
Total	43u	55u	12u

(ii) *Result.* (A) Under § 1.901(m)-2(b)(1), USP's acquisition of the stock of CFC is a section 338 CAA. Under § 1.901(m)-2(c)(1), the assets of CFC are RFAs for Country F tax purposes because they are relevant in determining foreign income of CFC for Country F tax purposes.

(B) Under paragraph (b)(2) of this section, the requirements of the cumulative basis difference exemption are satisfied if the sum of the basis differences is less than the threshold of $10 million, the greater of $10 million or $5.5 million (10% of the total U.S. basis of $55 million (55 million u translated into dollars at the exchange rate of $1 = 1u)). In this case, the sum of the basis differences is $12 million (12 million u translated into dollars at the exchange rate of $1 = 1 u). Because the sum of the basis differences of $12 million is not less than the threshold of $10 million, the requirements of the cumulative basis difference exemption are not satisfied.

(C) Under paragraph (b)(3) of this section, each of CFC's assets is allocated to its class under § 1.338-6(b) for purposes of the RFA class exemption. The requirements of the RFA class exemption with respect to the Class IV RFAs (in this case, inventory) are satisfied if the absolute value of the sum of the basis differences with respect to the Class IV RFAs is less than the threshold of $2 million, the greater of $2 million or $1.5 million (10% of the total U.S. basis of Class IV RFAs of $15 million (15 million u translated into dollars at the exchange rate of $1 = 1u)). In this case, the absolute value of the sum of the basis differences is $1 million (1 million u translated into dollars at the exchange rate of $1 = 1 u). Because the sum of the basis differences of $1 million is less than the threshold of $2 million, the requirements of the RFA class exemption are satisfied. Accordingly, the basis differences with respect to the Class IV RFAs are not taken into account under section 901(m).

(D) The requirements of the RFA class exemption with respect to the Class V RFAs (in this case, buildings) is satisfied if the absolute value of the sum of the basis differences with respect to the Class V RFAs is less than the threshold of $3 million, the greater of $2 million or $3 million (10% of the total U.S. basis of Class V RFAs of $30 million (30 million u translated into dollars at the exchange rate of $1 = 1u)). In this case, the absolute value of the sum of the basis differences is $11 million (11 million u translated into dollars at the exchange rate of $1 = 1 u). Because the sum of the basis differences of $11 million is not less than the threshold of $3 million, the requirements of the RFA class exemption are not satisfied. Finally, because the absolute value with respect to each RFA is greater than $20,000, the RFA exemption does not apply. Accordingly, the basis differences with respect to the Class V RFAs are taken into account under section 901(m).

(E) The Class I RFAs (in this case, cash) are irrelevant because there are no basis differences with respect to those RFAs.

(g) *Applicability dates.*—This section applies to CAAs occurring on or after March 23, 2020. Taxpayers may, however, choose to apply this section before the date this section is applicable provided that they (along with any persons that are related (within the meaning of section 267(b) or 707(b)) to the taxpayer)—

(1) Consistently apply this section, § 1.704-1(b)(4)(viii)(*c*)(*4*)(*v*) through (*vii*), § 1.901(m)-1, §§ 1.901(m)-3 through 1.901(m)-6 (excluding § 1.901(m)-4(e)), and § 1.901(m)-8 to all CAAs occurring on or after January 1, 2011, and consistently apply § 1.901(m)-2 (excluding § 1.901(m)-2(d)) to all CAAs occurring on or after December 7, 2016, on any original or amended tax return for each taxable year for which the application of the provisions listed in this paragraph (g)(1)

affects the tax liability and for which the statute of limitations does not preclude assessment or the filing of a claim for refund, as applicable;

(2) File all tax returns described in paragraph (g)(1) of this section for any taxable year ending on or before March 23, 2020, no later than March 23, 2021; and

(3) Make appropriate adjustments to take into account deficiencies that would have resulted from the consistent application under paragraph (g)(1) of this section for taxable years that are not open for assessment. [Reg. § 1.901(m)-7.]

☐ [*T.D.* 9895, 3-20-2020.]

§ 1.901(m)-8. Miscellaneous.—(a) *In general.*—This section provides guidance on other matters under section 901(m). Paragraph (b) of this section provides guidance on the application of section 901(m) to pre-1987 foreign income taxes. Paragraph (c) of this section provides anti-abuse rules relating to built-in loss assets. Paragraph (d) of this section provides guidance on the interaction of section 901(m) and section 909. Paragraph (e) of this section provides applicability dates.

(b) *Application of section 901(m) to pre-1987 foreign income taxes.*—Section 901(m) and §§ 1.901(m)-1 through 1.901-8 apply to pre-1987 foreign income taxes (as defined in § 1.902-1(a)(10)(iii)) of an applicable foreign corporation.

(c) *Anti-abuse rule for built-in loss RFAs.*—A basis difference with respect to an RFA described in section 901(m)(3)(C)(ii) (*built-in loss RFA*) will not be taken into account for purposes of computing an allocated basis difference for a U.S. taxable year of a section 901(m) payor if any RFA, including an RFA other than built-in loss RFAs, is acquired with a principal purpose of using one or more built-in loss RFAs to avoid the application of section 901(m). Furthermore, a basis difference with respect to a built-in loss RFA will not be taken into account for purposes of the cumulative basis difference exemption or the RFA class exemption under § 1.901(m)-7 if any RFAs, including RFAs other than built-in loss RFAs, are acquired with a principal purpose of avoiding the application of section 901(m).

(d) *Interaction with section 909.*—The amount of a foreign income tax that is disqualified under section 901(m) is determined before applying section 909. However, section 909 may apply to suspend a deduction for the amount of a foreign income tax that is disqualified under section 901(m).

(e) *Applicability dates.*—This section applies to CAAs occurring on or after March 23, 2020. Taxpayers may, however, choose to apply this section before the date this section is applicable provided that they (along with any persons that are related (within the meaning of section 267(b) or 707(b)) to the taxpayer)—

(1) Consistently apply this section, § 1.704-1(b)(4)(viii)(*c*)(*4*)(*v*) through (*vii*), § 1.901(m)-1, and §§ 1.901(m)-3 through 1.901(m)-7 (excluding § 1.901(m)-4(e)) to all CAAs occurring on or after January 1, 2011, and consistently apply § 1.901(m)-2 (excluding § 1.901(m)-2(d)) to all CAAs occurring on or after December 7, 2016, on any original or amended tax return for each taxable year for which the application of the provisions listed in this paragraph (e)(1) affects the tax liability and for which the statute of limitations does not preclude assessment or the filing of a claim for refund, as applicable;

(2) File all tax returns described in paragraph (e)(1) of this section for any taxable year ending on or before March 23, 2020, no later than March 23, 2021; and

(3) Make appropriate adjustments to take into account deficiencies that would have resulted from the consistent application under paragraph (e)(2) of this section for taxable years that are not open for assessment. [Reg. § 1.901(m)-8.]

☐ [*T.D.* 9895, 3-20-2020.]

§ 1.903-1. Taxes in lieu of income taxes.—(a) *Overview.*—Section 903 provides that the term "income, war profits, and excess profits taxes" includes a tax paid in lieu of a tax on income, war profits, or excess profits that is otherwise generally imposed by any foreign country. Paragraphs (b) and (c) of this section define a tax described in section 903. Paragraph (d) of this section provides examples illustrating the application of this section. Paragraph (e) of this section sets forth the applicability date of this section. For purposes of this section and §§ 1.901-2 and 1.901-2A, a tax described in section 903 is referred to as a "tax in lieu of an income tax" or an "in lieu of tax" and the definitions in § 1.901-2(g) apply for purposes of this section. Determinations of the amount of a tax in lieu of an income tax that is paid by a person and determinations of the person by whom such tax is paid are made under § 1.901-2(e) and (f), respectively. Section 1.901-2A contains additional rules applicable to dual capacity taxpayers (as defined in § 1.901-2(a)(2)(ii)(A)).

(b) *Definition of tax in lieu of an income tax.*—(1) *In general.*—Paragraphs (b)(2) and (c) of this section provide the requirements for a foreign levy to qualify as a tax in lieu of an income tax. The rules of this section are applied independently to each separate levy (within the meaning of §§ 1.901-2(d) and 1.901-2A(a)). A foreign tax either is or is not a tax in lieu of an income tax in its entirety for all persons subject to the tax. It is immaterial whether the base of the in lieu of tax bears any relation to realized net gain. The base of the foreign tax may, for example, be gross income, gross receipts or sales, or the number of units produced or exported. The foreign country's reason for imposing a foreign tax on a base other than net income (for example, because of administrative difficulty in determining the amount of income that would otherwise be subject to a net income tax) is immaterial, although paragraph (c)(1) of this section generally requires a showing that the foreign country made a deliberate and cognizant choice to impose the in lieu of tax instead of a net income tax (see paragraph (c)(1)(iii) of this section).

(2) *Requirements.*—A foreign levy is a tax in lieu of an income tax only if—

(i) It is a foreign tax; and

(ii) It satisfies the substitution requirement of paragraph (c) of this section.

(c) *Substitution requirement.*—(1) *In general.*—A foreign tax (the "tested foreign tax") satisfies the substitution requirement if, based on the foreign tax law, the requirements in paragraphs (c)(1)(i) through (iv) of this section are satisfied with respect to the tested foreign tax, or the tested foreign tax is a covered withholding tax described in paragraph (c)(2) of this section.

(i) *Existence of generally-imposed net income tax.*—A separate levy that is a net income tax (as described in § 1.901-2(a)(3)) is generally imposed by the same foreign country (the "generally-imposed net income tax") that imposes the tested foreign tax.

(ii) *Non-duplication.*—Neither the generally-imposed net income tax nor any other separate levy that is a net income tax is also imposed, in addition to the tested foreign tax, by the same foreign country on any persons with respect to any portion of the income to which the amounts (such as sales or units of production) that form the base of the tested foreign tax relate (the "excluded income"). Therefore, a tested foreign tax does not meet the requirement of this paragraph (c)(1)(ii) if a net income tax imposed by the same foreign country applies to the excluded income of any persons that are subject to the tested foreign tax, even if not all persons subject to the tested foreign tax are subject to the net income tax.

(iii) *Close connection to excluded income.*—But for the existence of the tested foreign tax, the generally-imposed net income tax would otherwise have been imposed on the excluded income. The requirement in the preceding sentence is met only if the imposition of such tested foreign tax bears a close connection to the failure to impose the generally-imposed net income tax on the excluded income; the relationship cannot be merely incidental, tangential, or minor. A close connection must be established with proof that the foreign country made a cognizant and deliberate choice to impose the tested foreign tax instead of the generally-imposed net income tax. Such proof must be based on foreign tax law, or the legislative history of either the tested foreign tax or the generally-imposed net income tax that describes the provisions excluding taxpayers subject to the tested foreign tax from the generally-imposed net income tax. Thus, a close connection exists if the generally-imposed net income tax would apply by its terms to the excluded income, but for the fact that the excluded income is expressly excluded, and the tested foreign tax is enacted contemporaneously with the generally-imposed net income tax. A close connection also exists if the generally-imposed net income tax by its terms does not apply to, but does not expressly exclude, the excluded income, and the tested foreign tax is enacted contemporaneously with the generally-imposed net income tax. Where the tested foreign tax is not enacted contemporaneously with the generally-imposed net income tax and the generally-imposed net income tax is not amended contemporaneously with the enactment of the tested foreign tax to exclude the excluded income or to narrow the scope of the generally-imposed net income tax so as not to apply to the excluded income, a close connection can be established only by reference to the legislative history of the tested foreign tax (or a predecessor in lieu of tax). Not all income derived by persons subject to the tested foreign tax need be excluded income, provided the tested foreign tax applies only to amounts that relate to the excluded income.

(iv) *Jurisdiction to tax excluded income.*—If the generally-imposed net income tax, or a hypothetical new tax that is a separate levy with respect to the generally-imposed net income tax, were applied to the excluded income, such generally-imposed net income tax or separate levy would meet the attribution requirement described in § 1.901-2(b)(5).

(2) *Covered withholding tax.*—A tested foreign tax is a covered withholding tax if, based on the foreign tax law, the requirements in paragraphs (c)(1)(i) and (c)(2)(i) through (iii) of this section are met with respect to the tested foreign tax. See also § 1.901-2(d)(1)(iii) for rules treating withholding taxes as separate levies with respect to each class of income subject to the tax or with respect to each subset of a class of income that is subject to different income attribution rules.

(i) *Withholding tax on nonresidents.*—The tested foreign tax is a withholding tax (as defined in section 901(k)(1)(B)) that is imposed on gross income of persons who are nonresidents of the foreign country imposing the tested foreign tax. It is immaterial whether the tested foreign tax is withheld by the payor or is imposed directly on the nonresident taxpayer.

(ii) *Non-duplication.*—The tested foreign tax is not in addition to any net income tax that is imposed by the foreign country on any portion of the net income attributable to the gross income that is subject to the tested foreign tax. Therefore, a tested foreign tax does not meet the requirement of this paragraph (c)(2)(ii) if by its terms it applies to gross income of nonresidents that are also subject to a net income tax imposed by the same foreign country on the same income, even if not all nonresidents subject to the tested foreign tax are also subject to the net income tax.

(iii) *Source-based attribution requirement.*—The income subject to the tested foreign tax satisfies the attribution requirement described in § 1.901-2(b)(5)(i)(B).

(d) *Examples.*—The following examples illustrate the rules of this section.

(1) *Example 1: Tax on gross income from services; non-duplication requirement.*—(i) *Facts.* Country X imposes a tax at the rate of 3 percent on the gross receipts of companies, wherever resident, from furnishing specified types of electronically supplied services to customers located in Country X (the "ESS tax"). No deductions are allowed in determining the taxable base of the ESS tax. In addition to the ESS tax, Country X imposes a net income tax within the meaning of § 1.901-2(a)(3) on resident companies (the "resident income tax") and also imposes a net income tax within the meaning of § 1.901-2(a)(3) on the income of nonresident companies that is attributable, under reasonable principles, to the nonresident's permanent establishment within Country X (the "nonresident income tax"). Under Country X tax law, a permanent establishment is defined in the same manner as under the 2016 U.S. Model Income Tax Convention. Both the resident income tax and the nonresident income tax, which are separate levies under § 1.901-2(d)(1)(iii), qualify as generally-imposed net income taxes. Under Country X tax law, the ESS tax applies to both resident and nonresident companies regardless of whether the company is also subject to the resident income tax or the nonresident income tax, respectively.

(ii) *Analysis.* Under § 1.901-2(d)(1)(iii), the ESS tax comprises two separate levies, one imposed on resident companies (the "resident ESS tax"), and one imposed on nonresident companies (the "nonresident ESS tax"). Under paragraph (c)(1)(ii) of this section, neither the resident ESS tax nor the nonresident ESS tax satisfies the substitution requirement, because by its terms the income to which the gross receipts subject to the ESS tax relate is also subject to one of the two generally-imposed net income taxes imposed by Country X. Similarly, under paragraph (c)(2)(ii) of this section, the nonresident ESS tax is not a covered withholding tax because by its terms it is imposed in addition to the nonresident income tax. The fact that nonresident taxpayers that do not have a permanent establishment in Country X are in practice subject to the nonresident ESS tax but not to the nonresident income tax on the gross receipts included in the base of the nonresident ESS tax is not relevant to the determination of whether the ESS tax meets the substitution requirement under paragraph (c)(1) of this section. Therefore, neither the resident ESS tax nor the nonresident ESS tax is a tax in lieu of an income tax.

(2) *Example 2: Tax on gross income from services; attribution of income.*—(i) *Facts.* The facts are the same as those in paragraph (d)(1)(i) of this section (the facts in *Example 1*), except that under Country X tax law, the nonresident ESS tax is imposed only if the nonresident company does not have a permanent establishment in Country X. If the nonresident company has a Country X permanent establishment, the nonresident income tax applies to the profits attributable to that permanent establishment. In addition, the statutory language and legislative history to the nonresident ESS tax demonstrate that Country X made a cognizant and deliberate choice to impose the nonresident ESS tax instead of the nonresident income tax with respect to the gross receipts that are subject to the nonresident ESS tax.

(ii) *Analysis*—(A) *General application of substitution requirement.* The nonresident ESS tax meets the requirements in paragraphs (c)(1)(i) and (ii) of this section because Country X has two generally-imposed net income taxes and neither generally-imposed net income tax nor any other separate levy that is a net income tax is imposed by Country X on a nonresident's income to which gross receipts that form the base of the nonresident ESS tax relate (which is the excluded income). The statutory language and legislative history to the nonresident ESS tax demonstrate that Country X made a cognizant and deliberate choice not to impose the nonresident income tax on the excluded income. Therefore, the nonresident ESS tax meets the requirement in paragraph (c)(1)(iii) of this section because, but for the existence of the tested foreign tax, the nonresident income tax would otherwise have been imposed on the excluded income. However, the nonresident ESS tax does not meet the requirement in paragraph (c)(1)(iv) of this section, because if Country X had chosen to apply the nonresident income tax (rather than the nonresident ESS tax) to the excluded income, the modified nonresident income tax would fail the attribution requirement in § 1.901-2(b)(5). First, the modified tax would not satisfy the requirement in § 1.901-2(b)(5)(i)(A) because the modified tax would not apply to income attributable under reasonable principles to the nonresident's activities within the foreign country, since the modified tax is determined by taking into account the location of customers. Second, the modified tax would not satisfy the requirement in § 1.901-2(b)(5)(i)(B) because the excluded income is from services performed outside of Country X. Third, the modified tax would not satisfy the requirement in § 1.901-2(b)(5)(i)(C) because the excluded income is not from sales or dispositions of real property located in Country X or from property forming part of the business property of a taxable presence in Country X. Because the Country X nonresident income tax as applied to the excluded income would fail to meet the attribution requirement in § 1.901-2(b)(5), as required by paragraph (c)(1)(iv) of this section, the nonresident ESS tax does not satisfy the substitution requirement in paragraph (c)(1) of this section.

(B) *Covered withholding tax analysis.* The nonresident ESS tax meets the requirement in paragraph (c)(1)(i) of this section because there exists a generally-imposed net income tax. It also meets the requirements in paragraphs (c)(2)(i) and (ii) of this section because it is a withholding tax on gross receipts of nonresidents and the income attributable to those gross receipts is not subject to a net income tax. However, the nonresident ESS tax does not meet the requirement in paragraph (c)(2)(iii) of this section because the services income subject to the nonresident ESS tax is from electronically supplied services performed outside of Country X. See § 1.901-2(b)(5)(i)(B). Therefore, the nonresident ESS tax is not a covered withholding tax under paragraph (c)(2) of this section. Because the nonresident ESS tax does not satisfy the substitution requirement of paragraph (c) of this section, it is not a tax in lieu of an income tax.

(3) *Example 3: Withholding tax on royalties; attribution requirement.*—(i) *Facts.* YCo, a resident of Country Y, is a controlled foreign corporation wholly-owned by USP, a domestic corporation. In Year 1, YCo grants a license to XCo, a resident of Country X unrelated to YCo or USP, for the right to use YCo's intangible property (IP) throughout the world, including in Country X. Under Country X's domestic tax law, all royalties paid by a resident of Country X to a nonresident are sourced in Country X and are subject to a 30% withholding tax on the gross income, regardless of whether the nonresident payee has a taxable presence in Country X. Country X's withholding tax on royalties is a separate levy under § 1.901-2(d)(1)(iii). In Year 1, XCo withholds 30u (units of Country X currency) tax from 100u of royalties owed and paid to YCo under the licensing arrangement, of which 50u is attributable to XCo's use of the YCo IP in Country X and 50u is attributable to use of the YCo IP outside Country X. The United States and Country X have an income

tax treaty (U.S.-Country X treaty); under the royalties article of the treaty, Country X agreed to impose its withholding tax on royalties paid to a U.S. resident only on royalties paid for IP used in Country X. Country X and Country Y do not have an income tax treaty.

(ii) *Analysis*. Under § 1.901-2(d)(1)(iv), the Country X withholding tax on royalties, as modified by the U.S.-Country X treaty, is a separate levy from the unmodified Country X withholding tax to which YCo was subject (because YCo is not a U.S. resident eligible for benefits under the U.S.-Country X treaty). The Country X withholding tax on royalties, unmodified by the U.S.-Country X treaty, does not meet the attribution requirement in § 1.901-2(b)(5)(i)(B) because Country X's source rule for royalties (based upon residence of the payor) is not reasonably similar to the sourcing rules that apply under the Internal Revenue Code. Thus, under paragraph (c)(2)(iii) of this section, the Country X withholding tax paid by YCo is not a covered withholding tax, and none of the 30u of Country X withholding tax paid by YCo with respect to the 100u of royalties for the use of the IP is a payment of foreign income tax.

(4) *Example 4: Withholding tax on royalties; attribution requirement*.—(i) *Facts*. The facts are the same as in paragraph (d)(3)(i) of this section (the facts of *Example 3*), except that XCo only uses the IP in Country X and the 100u of royalties paid to YCo in Year 1 is all attributable to XCo's use of the IP in Country X.

(ii) *Analysis*. The result is the same as in paragraph (d)(3) of this section (the analysis of *Example 3*). Because Country X's source rule for royalties (based upon residence of the payor) is not reasonably similar to the sourcing rules that apply under the Internal Revenue Code, the withholding tax paid by YCo does not meet the attribution requirement in § 1.901-2(b)(5)(i)(B). Under paragraph (c)(2)(iii) of this section, the Country X withholding tax paid by YCo is not a covered withholding tax, and none of the 30u of Country X withholding tax paid by YCo with respect to the 100u of royalties for IP used in Country X is a payment of foreign income tax.

(5) *Example 5: Multiple in-lieu-of taxes*.—(i) *Facts*. Country X imposes a net income tax within the meaning of § 1.901-2(a)(3) on the income of nonresident companies that is attributable, under reasonable principles, to the nonresident's activities within Country X (the "trade or business tax"). The trade or business tax applies to all nonresident corporations that engage in business in Country X except for nonresident corporations that engage in insurance activities, which are instead subject to two different taxes ("insurance taxes"). The insurance taxes apply to nonresident corporations that engage in insurance activities that are attributable, under reasonable principles, to the nonresident's activities within Country X. The insurance taxes do not satisfy the cost recovery requirement in § 1.901-2(b)(4). The trade or business tax and the two insurance taxes were enacted contemporaneously, and the statutory language of the trade or business tax expressly excludes gross income derived by nonresident corporations engaged in insurance activities from the trade or business tax.

(ii) *Analysis*. The insurance taxes meet the requirements in paragraphs (c)(1)(i) and (ii) of this section because Country X has a generally-imposed net income tax, the trade or business tax, and neither the trade or business tax nor any other separate levy that is a net income tax is imposed by Country X on a nonresident's gross income to which the amounts that form the base of the insurance taxes (the "excluded income") relate. The Country X tax law expressly provides that the trade or business tax does not apply to nonresident corporations engaged in insurance activities. In addition, the two insurance taxes were enacted contemporaneously with the trade or business tax. Therefore, it is demonstrated that Country X made a cognizant and deliberate choice to impose the insurance taxes in lieu of the generally-imposed trade or business tax, and the insurance taxes meet the requirement in paragraph (c)(1)(iii) of this section. If the trade or business tax also applied to the excluded income, the trade or business tax would meet the requirement in § 1.901-2(b)(5)(i)(A), because it would apply only to income attributable, under reasonable principles, to the nonresident's activities within the foreign country. Thus, the insurance taxes meet the requirement in paragraph (c)(1)(iv) of this section. Therefore, the insurance taxes satisfy the substitution requirement in paragraph (c)(1) of this section.

(6) *Example 6: Later-enacted in-lieu-of tax; close connection requirement*.—(i) *Facts*. The facts are the same as those in paragraph (d)(5)(i) of this section (the facts in *Example 5*), except that one of the two insurance taxes applies only to nonresident corporations engaged in the life insurance business in Country X and was enacted five years after the enactment of the trade or business tax and the other insurance tax enacted contemporaneously with the trade or business tax. The legislative history to the later-enacted insurance tax shows that Country X intended to increase the tax imposed on nonresident corporations engaged in life insurance activities and, instead of amending the first insurance tax to increase the rate applicable to life insurance companies, it enacted the second insurance tax that only applies to life insurance corporations.

(ii) *Analysis*. The later-enacted insurance tax meets the requirements in paragraphs (c)(1)(i) and (ii) of this section because Country X has a generally-imposed net income tax, the trade or business tax, and neither the trade or business tax nor any other separate levy that is a net income tax is imposed by Country X on the income attributable to the activities that form the base of the later-enacted insurance tax. The later-enacted insurance tax meets the requirement in paragraph (c)(1)(iii) of this section because the legislative history to the later-enacted insurance tax demonstrates that Country X made a cognizant and deliberate choice to impose the later-enacted insurance tax on life insurance companies instead of the trade or business tax. The later-enacted insurance tax also meets the requirement of paragraph (c)(1)(iv) of this section for the reasons set forth in paragraph (d)(5)(ii) of this section. Therefore, the later-enacted insurance tax satisfies the substitution requirement in paragraph (c)(1) of this section.

(7) *Example 7: Excise tax creditable against net income tax*.—(i) *Facts*. Country X imposes an excise tax that does not satisfy the cost recovery requirement in § 1.901-2(b)(4), and a net income tax within the meaning of § 1.901-2(a)(3). The excise tax, which is payable independently of the net income tax, is allowed as a credit against the net income tax. In Year 1, A has a tentative net income tax liability of 100u (units of Country X currency) but is allowed a credit for 30u of excise tax that it paid that year.

(ii) *Analysis*. Pursuant to § 1.901-2(e)(4), the amount of excise tax A has paid to Country X is 30u and the amount of net income tax A has paid to Country X is 70u. The excise tax paid by A does not satisfy the substitution requirement set forth in paragraph (c)(1) of this section because the excise tax is imposed in addition to, and not in substitution for, the generally-imposed net income tax.

(e) *Applicability dates*.—Except as otherwise provided in this paragraph (e), this section applies to foreign taxes paid (within the meaning of § 1.901-2(g)(5)) in taxable years beginning on or after December 28, 2021. For foreign taxes paid to Puerto Rico under section 3070.01 of the Puerto Rico Internal Revenue Code of 2011, as amended (13 L.P.R.A. § 31771) (imposing an excise tax on a controlled group member's acquisition from another group member of certain personal property manufactured or produced in Puerto Rico and certain services performed in Puerto Rico), this section applies to foreign taxes paid (within the meaning of § 1.901-2(g)(5)) in taxable years beginning on or after January 1, 2023. For foreign taxes described in the preceding sentence that are paid in taxable years beginning before January 1, 2023, see § 1.903-1 as contained in 26 CFR part 1 revised as of April 1, 2021. [Reg. § 1.903-1.]

☐ *[T.D. 7918, 10-6-83. Amended by T.D. 9959, 12-28-2021.]*

Proposed Amendments to Regulation

§ 1.903-1. Taxes in lieu of income taxes.—

* * *

(c) * * *

(2) *Covered withholding tax*.—A tested foreign tax is a covered withholding tax if, based on the foreign tax law (except as provided in paragraph (c)(2)(iii)(B) of this section), the requirements in paragraphs (c)(1)(i) and (c)(2)(i) through (iii) of this section are met with respect to the tested foreign tax. See also § 1.901-2(d)(1)(iii) for rules treating withholding taxes as separate levies with respect to each class of income subject to the tax, with respect to each subset of a class of income that is subject to different income attribution rules, or with respect to withholding tax that is imposed on a payment giving rise to gross royalty income of a nonresident that is made pursuant to a single-country license (as determined under paragraph (c)(2)(iv) of this section).

* * *

(iii) *Source-based attribution requirement*.—The income subject to the tested foreign tax satisfies the requirements in paragraph (c)(2)(iii)(A) or (B) of this section.

(A) The income subject to the tested foreign tax satisfies the attribution requirement described in § 1.901-2(b)(5)(i)(B).

(B) The income subject to the tested foreign tax is characterized as royalty income and the payment giving rise to such income is made pursuant to a single-country license as determined under paragraph (c)(2)(iv) of this section. For purposes of this paragraph (c)(2)(iii)(B) and paragraph (c)(2)(iv) of this section, whether the income is characterized as royalty income is determined under the foreign tax law, except that income from the sale of a copyrighted article (as determined under rules similar to §1.861-18) is not characterized as royalty income regardless of the characterization of the income under the foreign tax law.

(iv) *Single-country license.*—(A) *In general.*—Except as otherwise provided in this paragraph (c)(2)(iv), for purposes of paragraph (c)(2)(iii)(B) of this section, a payment is made pursuant to a single-country license if the terms of the license agreement pursuant to which the payment is made characterize the payment as a royalty and limit the territory of the license to the foreign country imposing the tested foreign tax.

(B) *Separately stated portions.*—If a written agreement that is not described in paragraph (c)(2)(iv)(A) of this section separately states a portion (whether as a specified amount or as a formula) of the payment subject to the tested foreign tax and such portion is both characterized as a royalty under the terms of the agreement and is attributable to the part of the territory of the license that is solely within the foreign country imposing the tested foreign tax, then that portion of the payment is treated as made pursuant to a single-country license.

(C) *Validity of agreement.*—A payment is considered not made pursuant to a single-country license if the taxpayer knows, or has reason to know, that the terms of the agreement pursuant to which the payment is made misstate the territory in which the relevant intangible property is used or overstate the amount of the royalty with respect to the part of the territory of the license that is solely within the foreign country imposing the tested foreign tax. A taxpayer is considered to have reason to know if its knowledge of relevant of facts or circumstances is such that a reasonably prudent person in the position of the taxpayer would question whether the terms of the agreement misstate the territory in which the relevant intangible property is used or overstate the amount of a royalty. For purposes of this section, the principles of sections 482 and 861 apply to determine whether the terms of the agreement misstate the territory in which the relevant intangible property is used or overstate the amount of a royalty. *See* paragraph (d)(11) of this section (*Example 11*).

(D) *Documentation.*—A taxpayer must provide the agreement described in paragraph (c)(2)(iv)(A) or (B) of this section, as applicable (the "required agreement"), within 30 days of a request by the Commissioner or another period as agreed between the Commissioner and the taxpayer. Except as provided in the next sentence, the required agreement pursuant to which the royalty is paid must be executed no later than the date of payment that gives rise to the gross royalty income that is subject to the tested foreign tax. In the case of a royalty that is paid before the date on which the required agreement is executed, in order to meet the requirement of this paragraph (c)(2)(iv)(D), the required agreement must be executed no later than May 17, 2023, and the agreement must state that royalties paid on or before the date of execution of the agreement are, for purposes of this paragraph (c)(2)(iv), considered paid pursuant to the terms of the agreement.

(d) * * *

(3) Example 3: Withholding tax on royalties; attribution requirement.—(i) *Facts.* YCo, a resident of Country Y, is a controlled foreign corporation wholly owned by USP, a domestic corporation. In Year 1, YCo enters into a written license agreement (the "Agreement") with XCo, a resident of Country X unrelated to YCo or USP, for the right to use YCo's intangible property ("IP") in a territory defined by the Agreement as the entire world, including Country X, in exchange for payments that the terms of the Agreement characterize as royalties. The payments made by XCo to YCo under the Agreement are also characterized as royalties under the laws of Country X. Under Country X's tax law, all gross royalty payments made by a Country X resident to a nonresident are treated as giving rise to Country X source income and are subject to a 20 percent withholding tax, regardless of whether the nonresident payee has a taxable presence in Country X. Country X has a generally-imposed net income tax within the meaning of paragraph (c)(1)(i) of this section, and nonresidents subject to the withholding tax on royalties are not also subject to a Country X net income tax on their royalty income. In Year 1, XCo withholds 20u (units of Country X currency) of tax on a 100u royalty paid to YCo under the Agreement.

(ii) *Analysis*—(A) *Separate levy.* Under §1.901-2(d)(1)(iii)(B)(*1*), Country X's withholding tax imposed on gross royalty income of nonresidents is treated as a separate levy. Under §1.901-2(d)(1)(iii)(B)(*3*), the 20u of Country X withholding tax imposed on the 100u of royalties paid by XCo to YCo is treated as a separate levy from the Country X withholding tax on royalties if the Agreement pursuant to which the royalties are paid is a single-country license under paragraph (c)(2)(iv) of this section. The Agreement does not meet the requirements of paragraph (c)(2)(iv) of this section because it neither limits the territory of the license to Country X nor separately states the portion of the payment that is with respect to the part of the territory of the license that is solely within Country X. Thus, the 20u of Country X withholding tax paid by YCo is not treated as a separate levy under §1.901-2(d)(1)(iii)(B)(3).

(B) *Covered withholding tax.* Under paragraph (c)(2) of this section, a tested foreign tax is a covered withholding tax if paragraphs (c)(1)(i) and (c)(2)(i) through (iii) of this section are met. Country X's withholding tax on royalties meets the requirements of paragraphs (c)(1)(i) and (c)(2)(i) and (ii) of this section because Country X has a generally-imposed net income tax, Country X's withholding tax on the royalties paid pursuant to the Agreement is imposed on the gross royalty income of persons who are nonresidents of Country X, and nonresidents subject to the withholding tax on royalties are not also subject to the Country X generally-imposed net income tax on their royalty income. However, the Country X withholding tax on royalties paid pursuant to the Agreement does not meet the requirements of §1.901-2(b)(5)(i)(B) and paragraph (c)(2)(iii)(A) of this section because Country X's sourcing rule for royalties (based on residence of the payor) is not based on the place of use of, or the right to use, the intangible property. Additionally, the payment that is subject to Country X's withholding tax is not made pursuant to a single-country license under paragraph (c)(2)(iv) of this section for the reasons described in paragraph (d)(3)(ii)(A) of this section (the separate levy analysis of this paragraph (d)(3) (*Example 3*)). Therefore, the requirement in paragraph (c)(2)(iii)(B) of this section is not met. Accordingly, the Country X withholding tax paid by YCo is not a covered withholding tax, and none of the 20u Country X withholding tax paid by YCo with respect to the 100u royalty payment made to XCo is a foreign income tax.

* * *

(8) Example 8: Withholding tax on royalties; single-country license.—(i) *Facts.* The facts are the same as in paragraph (d)(3)(i) of this section (the facts of *Example 3*) except that in Year 1, YCo enters into a written license agreement (the "Agreement") with XCo for the right to use YCo's IP in a territory defined by the Agreement as Country X, in exchange for payments that the terms of the Agreement characterize as royalties, and XCo in fact only uses the IP in Country X. In Year 1, XCo withholds 20u of tax from 100u of royalties paid to YCo under the Agreement.

(ii) *Analysis*—(A) *Separate levy.* Under §1.901-2(d)(1)(iii)(B)(*1*), Country X's withholding tax imposed on gross royalty income of nonresidents is treated as a separate levy. Under §1.901-2(d)(1)(iii)(B)(*3*), the 20u of Country X withholding tax imposed on the 100u of royalties paid by XCo to YCo is treated as a separate levy from the Country X withholding tax on royalties if the Agreement pursuant to which the royalties are paid is a single-country license under paragraph (c)(2)(iv) of this section. The Agreement meets the requirements of paragraph (c)(2)(iv)(A) of this section because it is a written license agreement that characterizes the payment as a royalty and limits the territory of the license to Country X. Thus, the 20u Country X withholding tax paid by YCo is treated as a separate levy under §1.901-2(d)(1)(iii)(B)(3).

(B) *Covered withholding tax.* Under paragraph (c)(2) of this section, a tested foreign tax is a covered withholding tax if paragraphs (c)(1)(i) and (c)(2)(i) through (iii) of this section are met. Country X has a generally-imposed net income tax, Country X's withholding tax on the royalties paid pursuant to the Agreement is a withholding tax that is imposed on the gross income of persons who are nonresidents of Country X, and nonresidents subject to the withholding tax on royalties paid pursuant to the Agreement are not also subject to a net income tax on their royalty income. Thus, the requirements of paragraphs (c)(1)(i) and (c)(2)(i) and (ii) of this section are met. The withholding tax paid by YCo does not meet the requirements of §1.901-2(b)(5)(i)(B) and paragraph (c)(2)(iii)(A) of this section because Country X's source rule for royalties (based on residence of the payor) is not based on the place of use of, or the right to use, the intangible property. However, the payment that is subject to Country X's withholding tax is made pursuant to a single-country license under paragraph (c)(2)(iv) of this section for the reasons described in paragraph (d)(8)(ii)(A) of this section (the separate levy analysis of this *Example 8*). Therefore, the requirement in paragraph (c)(2)(iii)(B) of this section is met. Accordingly, the Country X withholding tax on the payment made by XCo to YCo pursuant to the Agreement is a covered withholding tax and all of the 20u of Country X withholding tax paid by YCo with respect to the 100u of royalties under the Agreement is a foreign income tax.

(9) *Example 9: Withholding tax on royalties; separately stated portion.*—(i) *Facts.* The facts are the same as in paragraph (d)(3)(i) of this section (the facts of *Example 3*) except that in Year 1, YCo enters into a written agreement (the "Agreement") with XCo for the right to use YCo's IP in a territory defined by the Agreement as the entire world, as well as for YCo to provide certain services to XCo in Country Y, in exchange for a payment equal to 10 percent of XCo's annual revenue. The Agreement provides a formula for determining the amount of the payment that is characterized as a royalty and that is with respect to the part of the territory that is within Country X (the "separately stated formula"). The separately stated formula provides that the first 30u of the payment represents payment for services provided by YCo, and that 40 percent of the remainder of the payment represents payment of a royalty with respect to the part of the territory of the license that is solely within Country X. The portion of the payment by XCo to YCo that is characterized as services income under the Agreement is also characterized as services income under the laws of Country X. Additionally, all payments by a resident of Country X for services provided by a nonresident are treated as giving rise to Country X source income, regardless of where the services are performed, and gross income from services is subject to the same 20 percent withholding tax as gross royalty income. In Year 1, XCo earns gross income of 1,800u and pays YCo 180u under the Agreement. XCo withholds 12u of tax from the 60u of royalties attributable to the part of the territory of the license that is solely within Country X that are paid to YCo under the separately stated formula in the Agreement. The portion of the payment by XCo to YCo that is characterized as a royalty with respect to the part of the territory of the license that is solely within Country X under the separately stated formula in the Agreement is also characterized as a royalty under the laws of Country X. XCo withholds 24u of tax from the remaining 120u payment paid to YCo under the Agreement, consisting of 6u of tax on the 30u payment for services and 18u of tax on 90u of royalties. YCo does not know, or have reason to know, that the terms of the Agreement misstate the territory in which YCo's IP is used or overstate the amount of the royalty with respect to the part of the territory of the license that is solely within Country X.

(ii) *Analysis*—(A) *Separately stated portion.* The analysis is the same as in paragraph (d)(8)(ii) of this section (the analysis of *Example 8*), except that the portion of the payment that is a royalty with respect to the part of the territory of the license that is solely within Country X under the separately stated formula in the Agreement is treated as made pursuant to a single-country license under paragraph (c)(2)(iv) of this section because the Agreement is a written agreement that separately states the portion of the payment that is characterized as a royalty and that is with respect to the part of the territory of the license that is solely within Country X. Thus, the Country X withholding tax on the portion of the payment from XCo to YCo that is a payment of a royalty with respect to the part of the territory of the license that is solely within Country X under the separately stated formula under the Agreement is a separate levy and a covered withholding tax. Accordingly, the 12u Country X withholding tax paid by YCo from the 60u of royalties with respect to the part of the territory of the license that is solely within Country X is a foreign income tax.

(B) *Remaining portion of royalties.* The analysis is the same as paragraph (d)(3)(ii) of this section (the analysis of *Example 3*). Specifically, the 18u Country X withholding tax on the 90u royalty payment that is not with respect to the part of the territory that is within Country X is neither a separate levy nor a covered withholding tax. Accordingly, none of the 18u Country X withholding tax paid by YCo with respect to the remaining 90u royalty payment under the Agreement is a payment of foreign income tax.

(C) *Services portion.* Under § 1.901-2(d)(1)(iii)(B)(*1*), Country X's withholding tax imposed on gross services income of nonresidents is a separate levy. The Country X withholding tax of 6u on the 30u payment for services made by XCo to YCo under the Agreement is not a covered withholding tax. The withholding tax paid by YCo does not meet the requirements of § 1.901-2(b)(5)(i)(B) and paragraph (c)(2)(iii)(A) of this section because Country X's sourcing rule for services (based on residence of the payor) is not reasonably similar to the sourcing rule that applies under the Internal Revenue Code (based on where the services are performed). The special separate levy and covered withholding tax rules for single-country licenses under § 1.901-2(d)(1)(iii)(B)(*3*) and paragraph (c)(2)(iii)(B) of this section do not apply to withholding taxes on payments for services. Accordingly, none of the 6u of Country X withholding tax paid by YCo with respect to the 30u payment for services under the Agreement is a payment of foreign income tax.

(10) *Example 10: Characterization of payment.*—(i) *Facts.* The facts are the same as in paragraph (d)(3)(i) of this section (the facts of *Example 3*), except that in Year 1, YCo enters into a written license agreement (the "Agreement") with XCo for the right to use YCo's IP in a territory defined by the Agreement as Country X, in exchange for a payment that the terms of the Agreement characterize as a royalty, but that is characterized as a payment for services under the laws of Country X, and all payments of services paid by a resident of Country X to a nonresident are treated as giving rise to Country X source income, regardless of where the services are performed, and are subject to a 20 percent withholding tax.

(ii) *Analysis.* Under § 1.901-2(d)(1)(iii)(B)(*1*), Country X's withholding tax imposed on gross services income of nonresidents is a separate levy. The Country X withholding tax of 20u on the 100u payment for services made by XCo to YCo under the Agreement is not a covered withholding tax. The withholding tax paid by YCo does not meet the requirements of § 1.901-2(b)(5)(i)(B) and paragraph (c)(2)(iii)(A) of this section because Country X's sourcing rule for services (based on residence of the payor) is not reasonably similar to the sourcing rule that applies under the Internal Revenue Code (based on where the services are performed). The special separate levy and covered withholding tax rules for single-country licenses under § 1.901-2(d)(1)(iii)(B)(*3*) and paragraph (c)(2)(iii)(B) of this section do not apply to withholding taxes on income that is not characterized as royalty income under the foreign tax law. Accordingly, none of the 20u Country X withholding tax paid by YCo with respect to the 100u paid under the Agreement is a payment of foreign income tax.

(11) *Example 11: Withholding tax on royalties, validity of agreement.*—(i) *Facts.* The facts are the same as in paragraph (d)(3)(i) of this section (the facts of *Example 3*), except that XCo is a controlled foreign corporation wholly owned by USP. Additionally, in Year 2, XCo and YCo cancel the written license agreement entered into in Year 1 and YCo enters into two new written license agreements with XCo, one agreement which grants XCo the right to use certain YCo IP in a territory defined as Country X (the "Country X Agreement"), and one of which grants XCo the right to use the same YCo IP in a territory defined as the entire world except for Country X (the "Rest of World Agreement"). Both agreements characterize the payments under the agreements as royalties, and the payments are also characterized as royalties under the laws of Country X. In Year 2, XCo withholds a total of 20u of tax from a total of 100u of royalties paid to YCo under the Country X Agreement and the Rest of World Agreement. Based on the terms of each agreement, 18u of tax was withheld from 90u of royalties paid to YCo under the Country X Agreement, and 2u of tax from 10u of royalties paid to YCo under the Rest of World Agreement. YCo knew or had reason to know that under the principles of sections 482 and 861, with respect to the 100u of royalties paid by XCo to YCo, 40u is attributable to XCo's use of YCo IP in Country X and 60u is attributable to use of YCo IP outside Country X.

(ii) *Analysis*—(A) *Rest of World Agreement.* The analysis is the same as paragraph (d)(3)(ii) of this section (the analysis of *Example 3*). Specifically, the 2u Country X withholding tax on the 10u royalty payment under the Rest of World Agreement is neither a separate levy nor a covered withholding tax. Accordingly, none of the 2u Country X withholding tax paid by YCo with respect to the 10u royalty payment under the Rest of World Agreement is a payment of foreign income tax.

(B) *Country X Agreement.* The analysis is the same as paragraph (d)(3)(ii) of this section (the analysis of *Example 3*), except that the reason that the Country X Agreement does not meet the requirements of paragraph (c)(2)(iv) of this section is that YCo knew or had reason to know that the terms of the Country X Agreement overstate the amount of the royalty with respect to Country X. Thus, the 18u Country X withholding tax on the 90u royalty payment under the Country X Agreement is neither a separate levy nor a covered withholding tax. Accordingly, none of the 18u Country X withholding tax paid by YCo with respect to the 90u royalty payment under the Country X Agreement is a payment of foreign income tax.

(e) *Applicability dates.*—(1) *In general.*—Except as provided in paragraphs (e)(2) and (3) of this section, this section applies to foreign taxes paid (within the meaning of § 1.901-2(g)) in taxable years beginning on or after December 28, 2021. For foreign taxes that relate to (and if creditable are considered to accrue in) taxable years beginning before December 28, 2021, and that are remitted in taxable years beginning on or after December 28, 2021, by a taxpayer that accounts for foreign income taxes on the accrual basis, see § 1.903-1 as contained in 26 CFR part 1 revised as of April 1, 2021.

(2) *Certain foreign taxes paid to Puerto Rico.*—For foreign taxes paid to Puerto Rico under section 3070.01 of the Puerto Rico Internal Revenue Code of 2011, as amended (13 L.P.R.A. 31771) (imposing an excise tax on a controlled group member's acquisition from another group member of certain personal property manufactured or produced in Puerto Rico and certain services performed in Puerto Rico), this section applies to foreign taxes paid (within the meaning of § 1.901-2(g)) in taxable years beginning on or after January 1, 2023. For foreign taxes described in the preceding sentence that are paid in taxable years beginning before January 1, 2023, see § 1.903-1 as contained in 26 CFR part 1 revised as of April 1, 2021.

(3) *Modifications to the covered withholding tax rules.*—Paragraphs (c)(2) and (d)(3), (4), and (8) through (11) of this section apply to foreign taxes paid (within the meaning of § 1.901-2(g)) in taxable years ending on or after November 18, 2022. For foreign taxes that are paid in taxable years ending before November 18, 2022, see § 1.903-1(c)(2) and (d)(3) and (4) as contained in 26 CFR part 1 revised as of July 27, 2022. Taxpayers may choose to apply the rules in paragraphs (c)(2) and (d)(3), (4), and (8) through (11) of this section to foreign taxes paid in taxable years beginning on or after December 28, 2021, and ending before November 18, 2022, provided that they consistently apply those rules and the rules of § 1.901-2(b)(5)(i)(B)(2) and (d)(1)(iii) to such taxable years. [Prop. Reg. § 1.903-1.]

[Proposed 11-22-2022.]

§ 1.904-1. Limitation on credit for foreign income taxes.—(a) *In general.*—For each separate category described in § 1.904-5(a)(4)(v), the total credit for foreign income taxes (as defined in § 1.901-2(a)) paid or accrued (including those deemed to have been paid or accrued other than by reason of section 904(c)) to any foreign country (as defined in § 1.901-2(g)) does not exceed that proportion of the tax against which such credit is taken which the taxpayer's taxable income from foreign sources (but not in excess of the taxpayer's entire taxable income) in such separate category bears to the taxpayer's entire taxable income for the same taxable year.

(b) *Special computation of taxable income.*—For purposes of computing the limitation under paragraph (a) of this section, the taxable income in the case of an individual, estate, or trust is computed without any deduction for personal exemptions under section 151 or 642(b).

(c) *Joint return.*—In the case of spouses making a joint return, the applicable limitation prescribed by section 904(a) on the credit for taxes paid or accrued to foreign countries and possessions of the United States is applied with respect to the aggregate taxable income in each separate category from sources without the United States, and the aggregate taxable income from all sources, of the spouses.

(d) *Consolidated group.*—For rules relating to the computation of the foreign tax credit limitation for a consolidated group, see § 1.1502-4.

(e) *Applicability dates.*—This section applies to taxable years that both begin after December 31, 2017, and end on or after December 4, 2018. [Reg. § 1.904-1.]

☐ *[T.D. 6275, 12-2-57. Amended by T.D. 6789, 12-30-64, T.D. 7292, 11-30-73, T.D. 7294, 11-29-73, T.D. 7490, 6-10-77, T.D. 9882, 12-16-2019 and T.D. 9922, 11-2-2020.]*

§ 1.904-2. Carryback and carryover of unused foreign tax.—(a) *Credit for foreign tax carryback or carryover.*—A taxpayer who chooses to claim a credit under section 901 for a taxable year is allowed a credit under that section not only for taxes otherwise allowable as a credit but also for taxes deemed paid or accrued in that year as a result of a carryback or carryover of an unused foreign tax under section 904(c). However, the taxes so deemed paid or accrued are not allowed as a deduction under section 164(a). Foreign tax paid, accrued, or deemed paid under section 960 with respect to section 951A category income, including section 951A category income that is reassigned to a separate category for income resourced under a treaty, may not be carried back or carried forward or deemed paid or accrued under section 904(c). See § 1.904-6 for rules for allocating and apportioning taxes to separate categories. For special rules regarding these computations in case of taxes paid, accrued, or deemed paid with respect to foreign oil and gas extraction income or foreign oil related income, see section 907(f).

(b) *Years to which foreign taxes are carried.*—If the taxpayer chooses the benefits of section 901 for a taxable year, any unused foreign tax paid or accrued in that year is carried first to the immediately preceding taxable year and then, as applicable, to each of the ten succeeding taxable years, in chronological order, but only to the extent not absorbed as taxes deemed paid or accrued under paragraphs (a) and (d) of this section in a prior taxable year.

(c) *Definitions.*—This paragraph (c) provides definitions that apply for purposes of this section.

(1) *Unused foreign tax.*—The term *unused foreign tax* means, with respect to each separate category for any taxable year, the excess of the amount of creditable foreign tax paid or accrued, or deemed paid under section 902 (as in effect on December 21, 2017) or section 960, in such year, over the applicable foreign tax credit limitation under section 904 for the separate category in such year. Unused foreign tax does not include any amount for which a credit is disallowed, including foreign income taxes for which a credit is disallowed or reduced when the tax is paid, accrued, or deemed paid.

(2) *Separate category.*—The term *separate category* has the same meaning as provided in § 1.904-5(a)(4)(v).

(3) *Excess limitation.*—(i) *In general.*—The term *excess limitation* means, with respect to a separate category for any taxable year (the *excess limitation year*) and an unused foreign tax carried from another taxable year (the *excess credit year*), the amount (if any) by which the limitation for that separate category with respect to that excess limitation year exceeds the sum of—

(A) The creditable foreign tax actually paid or accrued or deemed paid under section 902 (as in effect on December 21, 2017) or section 960 with respect to the separate category in the excess limitation year; and

(B) The portion of any unused foreign tax for a taxable year preceding the excess credit year that is absorbed as taxes deemed paid or accrued in the excess limitation year under paragraphs (a) and (d) of this section.

(ii) *Deduction years.*—Excess limitation for a taxable year absorbs unused foreign tax, regardless of whether the taxpayer chooses to claim a credit under section 901 for the year. In such case, the amount of the excess limitation, if any, for the year is determined in the same manner as though the taxpayer had chosen to claim a credit under section 901 for that year. For purposes of this determination, if the taxpayer has an overall foreign loss account, the excess limitation in a deduction year is determined based on the amount of the overall foreign loss the taxpayer would have recaptured if the taxpayer had chosen to claim a credit under section 901 for that year and had not made an election under § 1.904(f)-2(c)(2) to recapture more of the overall foreign loss account than is required under § 1.904(f)-2(c)(1).

(d) *Taxes deemed paid or accrued.*—(1) *Amount deemed paid or accrued.*—The amount of unused foreign tax with respect to a separate category that is deemed paid or accrued in any taxable year to which such unused foreign tax may be carried under paragraph (b) of this section is equal to the smaller of—

(i) The portion of the unused foreign tax that may be carried to the taxable year under paragraph (b) of this section; or

(ii) The amount, if any, of the excess limitation for such taxable year with respect to the separate category of such unused foreign tax.

(2) *Carryback or carryover tax deemed paid or accrued in the same separate category.*—Any unused foreign tax, which is deemed to be paid or accrued under section 904(c) in the year to which it is carried, is deemed to be paid or accrued with respect to the same separate category as the category to which it was assigned in the year in which it was actually paid or accrued. However, see paragraphs (h) through (j) of this section for transition rules in the case of certain carrybacks and carryovers.

(3) *No duplicate disallowance of creditable foreign tax.*—Foreign income taxes for which a credit is partially disallowed, including when the tax is paid, accrued, or deemed paid, are not reduced again by

reason of the unused foreign tax being deemed to be paid or accrued in the year to which it is carried under section 904(c).

(e) *Periods of less than 12 months.*—A fractional part of a year which is a taxable year under sections 441(b) and 7701(a)(23) is a preceding or a succeeding taxable year for the purpose of determining under section 904(c) the years to which the unused foreign tax may be carried, and any unused foreign tax or excess limitation for such fractional part of a year is the unused foreign tax or excess limitation for a taxable year.

(f) *Statement with tax return.*—Every taxpayer claiming the benefit of a carryback or carryover of the unused foreign tax to any taxable year for which he chooses to claim a credit under section 901 shall file with his return (or with his claim for refund, if appropriate) for that year as an attachment to his Form 1116 or 1118, as the case may be, a statement setting forth the unused foreign tax deemed paid or accrued under this section and all material and pertinent facts relative thereto, including a detailed schedule showing the computation of the unused foreign tax so carried back or over.

(g) [Reserved]

(h) *Transition rules for carryovers of pre-2003 unused foreign tax and carrybacks of post-2002 unused foreign tax paid or accrued with respect to dividends from noncontrolled section 902 corporations.*—For transition rules for carryovers of pre-2003 unused foreign tax, and carrybacks of post-2002 unused foreign tax, paid or accrued with respect to dividends from noncontrolled section 902 corporations, see 26 CFR 1.904-2(h) (revised as of April 1, 2018).

(i) *Transition rules for carryovers of pre-2007 unused foreign tax and carrybacks of post-2006 unused foreign tax.*—For transition rules for carryovers of pre-2007 unused foreign tax, and carrybacks of post-2006 unused foreign tax, see 26 CFR 1.904-2(i) (revised as of April 1, 2018).

(j) *Transition rules for carryovers and carrybacks of pre-2018 and post-2017 unused foreign tax.*—(1) *Carryover of unused foreign tax.*—(i) *In general.*—For purposes of this paragraph (j), the terms *post-2017 separate category, pre-2018 separate category,* and *specified separate category* have the meanings set forth in § 1.904(f)-12(j)(1). The rules of this paragraph (j)(1) apply to reallocate to the taxpayer's post-2017 separate categories for foreign branch category income, general category income, passive category income, and specified separate categories of income, any unused foreign taxes (as defined in paragraph (c)(1) of this section) that were paid or accrued or deemed paid under sections 902 and 960 with respect to income in a pre-2018 separate category.

(ii) *Allocation to the same separate category.*—Except as provided in paragraph (j)(1)(iii) of this section, to the extent any unused foreign taxes paid or accrued or deemed paid with respect to a separate category of income are carried forward to a taxable year beginning after December 31, 2017, such taxes are allocated to the same post-2017 separate category as the pre-2018 separate category from which the unused foreign taxes are carried.

(iii) *Exception for certain general category unused foreign taxes.*—(A) *In general.*—To the extent any unused foreign taxes with respect to general category income are carried forward to a taxable year beginning after December 31, 2017, a taxpayer may choose to allocate those taxes to the taxpayer's post-2017 separate category for foreign branch category income to the extent the unused foreign taxes would have been allocated to the taxpayer's post-2017 separate category for foreign branch category income, and would have been unused foreign taxes with respect to foreign branch category income if that separate category had applied in the year or years the unused foreign taxes arose. Any remaining unused foreign taxes paid or accrued or deemed paid with respect to general category income carried forward to a taxable year beginning after December 31, 2017, are allocated to the taxpayer's post-2017 separate category for general category income.

(B) *Safe harbor.*—In lieu of applying paragraph (j)(1)(iii)(A) of this section, the taxpayer may choose to allocate the unused foreign taxes with respect to general category income in a taxable year beginning before January 1, 2018, to the taxpayer's post-2017 separate category for foreign branch category income based on a ratio equal to the amount of foreign income taxes assigned to the general category that were paid or accrued by the taxpayer's foreign branches (as defined in § 1.904-4(f)(3)(vii)) bears to all foreign income taxes assigned to the general category that were paid or accrued, or deemed paid by the taxpayer with respect to such taxable year. The amount of taxes paid or accrued by a foreign branch in a taxable year beginning before January1, 2018, means all foreign income taxes properly reflected on the separate set of books and records (as defined in § 1.989(a)-1(d)(1) and (2)) of the foreign branch as an expense (which does not include any taxes deemed paid under section 902 or 960).

(C) *Rules regarding the exception.*—A taxpayer applying the exception described in this paragraph (j)(1)(iii) (the *branch carryover exception*) must apply the exception to all of its unused foreign taxes paid or accrued with respect to general category income that are carried forward to all taxable years beginning after December 31, 2017. A taxpayer may apply the branch carryover exception on a timely filed original return (including extensions) or an amended return. A taxpayer that applies the exception on an amended return must make appropriate adjustments to eliminate any double benefit arising from application of the exception to years that are not open for assessment.

(D) *Coordination rule.*—See § 1.904(f)-12(j)(6) for coordination rule with respect to the exception described in paragraph (j)(1)(iii) of this section and the exceptions described in § 1.904(f)-12(j)(2) through (4).

(2) *Carryback of unused foreign tax.*—(i) *In general.*—The rules of this paragraph (j)(2) apply to any unused foreign taxes that were paid or accrued, or deemed paid under section 960, with respect to income in a post-2017 separate category.

(ii) *Passive category income and specified separate categories of income described in § 1.904-4(m).*—Any unused foreign taxes paid or accrued or deemed paid with respect to passive category income or a specified separate category of income in a taxable year beginning after December 31, 2017, that are carried back to a taxable year beginning before January 1, 2018, are allocated to the same pre-2018 separate category as the post-2017 separate category from which the unused foreign taxes are carried.

(iii) *General category income and foreign branch category income.*—Any unused foreign taxes paid or accrued or deemed paid with respect to general category income or foreign branch category income in a taxable year beginning after December 31, 2017, that are carried back to a taxable year beginning before January 1, 2018, are allocated to the taxpayer's pre-2018 separate category for general category income.

(k) *Applicability date.*—Paragraphs (a) through (i) of this section apply to taxable years that both begin after December 31, 2017, and end on or after December 4, 2018. Paragraph (j) of this section applies to taxable years beginning after December 31, 2017. Paragraph (j)(2) of this section also applies to the last taxable year beginning before January 1, 2018. [Reg. § 1.904-2.]

□ [*T.D. 6789, 12-30-64. Amended by T.D. 7292, 11-30-73, T.D. 7294, 11-29-73, T.D. 7490, 6-10-77; T.D. 7961, 6-27-84; T.D. 9260, 4-20-2006; T.D. 9368, 12-20-2007; T.D. 9452, 6-10-2009, T.D. 9521, 4-6-2011, T.D.* 9882, 12-16-2019 *and T.D.* 9956, 9-21-2021.]

§ 1.904-3. Carryback and carryover of unused foreign tax by spouses making a joint return.—(a) *In general.*—This section provides rules, in addition to those prescribed in § 1.904-2, for the carryback and carryover of the unused foreign tax paid or accrued to a foreign country or possession by spouses making a joint return for one or more of the taxable years involved in the computation of the carryback or carryover. The rules in this section apply separately with respect to each separate category as defined in § 1.904-5(a)(4)(v).

(b) *Joint unused foreign tax and joint excess limitation.*—In the case of spouses the joint unused foreign tax or the joint excess limitation for a taxable year for which a joint return is made shall be computed on the basis of the combined income, deductions, taxes, and credit of both spouses as if the combined income, deductions, taxes, and credit were those of one individual.

(c) *Continuous use of joint return.*—If spouses make a joint return for the current taxable year, and also make joint returns for each of the other taxable years involved in the computation of the carryback or carryover of the unused foreign tax to the current taxable year, the joint carryback or the joint carryover to the current taxable year shall be computed on the basis of the joint unused foreign tax and the joint excess limitations.

(d) *From separate to joint return.*—If spouses make a joint return for the current taxable year, but make separate returns for all of the other taxable years involved in the computation of the carryback or carryover of the unused foreign tax to the current taxable year, the separate carrybacks or separate carryovers shall be a joint carryback or a joint carryover to the current taxable year.

(e) *Amounts carried from or through a joint return year to or through a separate return year.*—(1) *In general.*—It is necessary to allocate to each spouse the spouse's share of an unused foreign tax or excess limitation for any taxable year for which the spouses filed a joint return if—

(i) The spouses file separate returns for the current taxable year and an unused foreign tax is carried thereto from a taxable year for which they filed a joint return;

(ii) The spouses file separate returns for the current taxable year and an unused foreign tax is carried to such taxable year from a year for which they filed separate returns but is first carried through a year for which they filed a joint return; or

(iii) The spouses file a joint return for the current taxable year and an unused foreign tax is carried from a taxable year for which they filed joint returns but is first carried through a year for which they filed separate returns.

(2) *Computation and adjustments.*—In the cases described in paragraph (e)(1) of this section, the separate carryback or carryover of each spouse to the current taxable year shall be computed in the manner described in § 1.904-2 but with the modifications set forth in paragraph (f) of this section. Where applicable, appropriate adjustments are made to take into account the fact that, for any taxable year involved in the computation of the carryback or the carryover, either spouse has combined foreign oil and gas income described in section 907(b) with respect to which the limitation in section 907(a) applies.

(f) *Allocation of unused foreign tax and excess limitation.*—(1) *Separate category limitation.*—The limitation in a separate category of a particular spouse for a taxable year for which a joint return is made shall be the portion of the limitation on the joint return which bears the same ratio to such limitation as such spouse's foreign source taxable income (with gross income and deductions taken into account to the same extent as taken into account on the joint return) in such separate category (but not in excess of the joint foreign source taxable income) bears to the joint foreign source taxable income in such separate category.

(2) *Unused foreign tax.*—For purposes of this section, the term *unused foreign tax* means, with respect to a particular spouse and separate category for a taxable year for which a joint return is made, the excess of the foreign tax paid or accrued by that spouse with respect to that separate category over that spouse's separate category limitation.

(3) *Excess limitation.*—For purposes of this section, the term *excess limitation* means, with respect to a particular spouse and separate category for a taxable year for which a joint return is made, the excess of that spouse's separate category limitation over the foreign taxes paid or accrued by such spouse with respect to such separate category for such taxable year.

(4) *Excess limitation to be applied.*—The excess limitation of the particular spouse for any taxable year which is applied against the unused foreign tax of that spouse for another taxable year in order to determine the amount of the unused foreign tax which shall be carried back or over to a third taxable year shall be, in a case in which the excess limitation is determined on a joint return, the sum of the following amounts:

(i) Such spouse's excess limitation determined under subparagraph (3) of this paragraph reduced as provided in subparagraph (5)(i) of this paragraph, and

(ii) The excess limitation of the other spouse determined under subparagraph (3) of this paragraph for that taxable year reduced as provided in subparagraph (5)(i) and (ii) of this paragraph.

(5) *Reduction of excess limitation.*—(i) The part of the excess limitation which is attributable to each spouse for the taxable year, as determined under subparagraph (3) of this paragraph, shall be reduced by absorbing as taxes deemed paid or accrued under section 904(c) in that year the unabsorbed separate unused foreign tax of such spouse, and the unabsorbed unused foreign tax determined under subparagraph (2) of this paragraph of such spouse, for taxable years which begin before the beginning of the year of origin of the unused foreign tax of the particular spouse against which the excess limitation so determined is being applied.

(ii) In addition, the part of the excess limitation which is attributable to the other spouse for the taxable year, as determined under subparagraph (3) of this paragraph, shall be reduced by absorbing as taxes deemed paid or accrued under section 904(c) in that year the unabsorbed unused foreign tax, if any, of such other spouse for the taxable year which begins on the same date as the beginning of the year of origin of the unused foreign tax of the particular spouse against which the excess limitation so determined is being applied.

(g) [Reserved]

(h) *Applicability date.*—This section is applicable for taxable years that both begin after December 31, 2017, and end on or after December 4, 2018. [Reg. § 1.904-3.]

□ [*T.D. 6789, 12-30-64. Amended by T.D. 7292, 11-30-73; T.D. 7490, 6-10-77, T.D. 7961, 6-27-84 and T.D. 9882, 12-16-2019.*]

§ 1.904-4. Separate application of section 904 with respect to certain categories of income.—(a) *In general.*—A taxpayer is required to compute a separate foreign tax credit limitation for income received or accrued in a taxable year that is described in section 904(d)(1)(A) (section 951A category income), 904(d)(1)(B) (foreign branch category income), 904(d)(1)(C) (passive category income), 904(d)(1)(D) (general category income), or paragraph (m) of this section (specified separate categories). For purposes of this section, the definitions in § 1.904-5(a)(4) apply.

(b) *Passive category income.*—(1) *In general.*—The term *passive category income* means passive income and specified passive category income.

(2) *Passive income.*—(i) *In general.*—The term *passive income* means any—

(A) Income received or accrued by any person that is of a kind that would be foreign personal holding company income (as defined in section 954(c), taking into account any exceptions or exclusions to section 954(c), including, for example, section 954(c)(3), (c)(6), (h), or (i)) if the taxpayer were a controlled foreign corporation, including any amount of gain on the sale or exchange of stock in excess of the amount treated as a dividend under section 1248;

(B) Amount includible in gross income under section 1293;

(C) Distributive shares of partnership income treated as passive category income under paragraph (n)(1) of this section, and income from the sale of a partnership interest treated as passive category income under paragraph (n)(2) of this section; or

(D) Income treated as passive category income under the look-through rules in § 1.904-5.

(ii) *Exceptions.*—Passive income does not include any export financing interest (as defined in paragraph (h) of this section), any high-taxed income (as defined in paragraph (c) of this section), financial services income (as defined in paragraph (e)(1)(ii) of this section), or any active rents and royalties (as defined in paragraph (b)(2)(iii) of this section). In addition, passive income does not include any income that would otherwise be passive but is excluded from passive category income under § 1.904-5(b)(1) or that is assigned to a separate category other than passive category income under § 1.904-5(c)(4)(iii). See also paragraph (k) of this section for rules relating to income resourced under a tax treaty. In determining whether any income is of a kind that would be foreign personal holding company income, the rules of section 864(d)(5)(A)(i) and (6) (treating related person factoring income of a controlled foreign corporation as foreign personal holding company income that is not eligible for the export financing income exception to the separate limitation for passive income) shall apply only in the case of income of a controlled foreign corporation (as defined in section 957). Thus, income earned directly by a United States person that is related person factoring income may be eligible for the exception for export financing interest.

(iii) *Active rents or royalties.*—(A) *In general.*—For rents and royalties paid or accrued after September 20, 2004, passive income does not include any rents or royalties that are derived in the active conduct of a trade or business, regardless of whether such rents or royalties are received from a related or an unrelated person. Except as provided in paragraph (b)(2)(iii)(B) of this section, the principles of section 954(c)(2)(A) and the regulations under that section shall apply in determining whether rents or royalties are derived in the active conduct of a trade or business. For this purpose, the term taxpayer shall be substituted for the term controlled foreign corporation if the recipient of the rents or royalties is not a controlled foreign corporation.

(B) Active conduct of trade or business. Rents and royalties are considered derived in the active conduct of a trade or business by a United States person or by a controlled foreign corporation (or other entity to which the look-through rules apply) for purposes of section 904 (but not for purposes of section 954) if the requirements of section 954(c)(2)(A) are satisfied by one or more corporations that are members of an affiliated group of corporations (within the meaning of section 1504(a), determined without regard to section 1504(b)(3)) of which the recipient is a member. For purposes of this paragraph (b)(2)(iii)(B), an affiliated group includes only domestic corporations and foreign corporations that are controlled foreign corporations in which domestic members of the affiliated group own, directly or indirectly, at least 80 percent of the total voting power and value of the stock. For purposes of this paragraph (b)(2)(iii)(B), indirect ownership shall be determined under section 318 and the regulations under that section.

(iv) *Examples.*—The following examples illustrate the application of this paragraph (b)(2).

(A) *Example 1.* For Year 1, USP, a domestic corporation, has a net foreign currency gain that would not constitute foreign personal holding company income if USP were a controlled foreign corporation because the gain is directly related to the business needs of USP. See section 954(c)(1)(D). Under paragraph (b)(2)(i)(A) of this section, the foreign currency gain is, therefore, not passive category income to USP because it is not income of a kind that would be foreign personal holding company income.

(B) *Example 2.* Controlled foreign corporation, CFC, is a wholly-owned subsidiary of USP, a domestic corporation. CFC is regularly engaged in the restaurant franchise business. USP licenses trademarks, tradenames, certain know-how, related services, and certain restaurant designs for which CFC pays USP an arm's length royalty. USP is regularly engaged in the development and licensing of such property. Some of the franchisees are unrelated to CFC and USP. Other franchisees are related to CFC or USP and use the licensed property outside of CFC's country of incorporation. CFC does not satisfy, but USP does satisfy, the active trade or business requirements of section 954(c)(2)(A). The royalty income earned by CFC from both its related and unrelated franchisees is foreign personal holding company income because CFC does not satisfy the active trade or business requirements of section 954(c)(2)(A) and, in addition, the royalty income from the related franchisees does not qualify for the same country exception of section 954(c)(3) or the look-through exception in section 954(c)(6). However, all of the royalty income earned by CFC is general category income to CFC under § 1.904-4(b)(2)(iii) because USP, a member of CFC's affiliated group, satisfies the active trade or business test (which is applied without regard to whether the royalties are paid by a related person). USP's inclusion under section 951(a)(1)(A) of CFC's royalty income is general category income to USP under § 1.904-5(c)(5) and paragraph (d) of this section. The royalties received by USP are general category income to USP under § 1.904-5(b)(1) and paragraph (d) of this section.

(3) *Specified passive category income* means—

(i) Dividends from a DISC or former DISC (as defined in section 992(a)) to the extent such dividends are treated as income from sources without the United States;

(ii) Taxable income attributable to foreign trade income (within the meaning of section 923(b)); or

(iii) Distributions from a FSC (or a former FSC) out of earnings and profits attributable to foreign trade income (within the meaning of section 923(b)) or interest or carrying charges (as defined in section 927(d)(1)) derived from a transaction which results in foreign trade income (as defined in section 923(b)).

(c) *High-taxed income.*—(1) *In general.*—Income received or accrued by a United States person that would otherwise be passive income is not treated as passive income if the income is determined to be high-taxed income. Income is considered to be high-taxed income if, after allocating expenses, losses, and other deductions of the United States person to that income under paragraph (c)(2) of this section, the sum of the foreign income taxes paid or accrued, and deemed paid under section 960, by the United States person with respect to such income (reduced by any portion of such taxes for which a credit is not allowed) exceeds the highest rate of tax specified in section 1 or 11, whichever applies (and with reference to section 15 if applicable), multiplied by the amount of such income (including the amount treated as a dividend under section 78). If, after application of this paragraph (c), income that would otherwise be passive income is determined to be high-taxed income, the income is treated as general category income, foreign branch category income, section 951A category income, or income in a specified separate category, as determined under the rules of this section, and any taxes imposed on that income are considered related to the same separate category of income under § 1.904-6. If, after application of this paragraph (c), passive income is zero or less than zero, any taxes imposed on the passive income are considered related to the same separate category of income to which the passive income (if not reduced to zero or less than zero) would have been assigned had the income been treated as high-taxed income (general category, foreign branch category, section 951A category, or a specified separate category). For additional rules regarding losses related to passive income, see paragraph (c)(2) of this section. Income and taxes shall be translated at the appropriate rates, as determined under sections 986, 987 and 989 and the regulations under those sections, before application of this paragraph (c). For purposes of allocating taxes to groups of income, United States source passive income is treated as any other passive income. In making the determination whether income is high-taxed, however, only foreign source income, as determined under United States tax principles, is relevant.

(2) *Grouping of items of income in order to determine whether passive income is high-taxed income.*—(i) *Initial allocation and apportionment of deductions and taxes.*—For purposes of determining whether passive income is high-taxed, expenses, losses and other deductions shall be allocated and apportioned initially to each of the groups of passive income (described in paragraphs (c)(3), (4), and (5) of this section) under the rules of §§ 1.861-8 through 1.861-17 and 1.865-1 and 1.865-2. Taxpayers that allocate and apportion interest expense on an asset basis may nevertheless apportion passive interest expense among the groups of passive income on a gross income basis. Foreign taxes are allocated to groups under the rules of § 1.904-6(a)(1)(iii). If a loss on a disposition of property gives rise to foreign tax (i.e., the transaction giving rise to the loss is treated under foreign law as having given rise to a gain), the foreign tax shall be allocated to the group of passive income to which gain on the sale would have been assigned under paragraph (c)(3) or (4) of this section. A determination of whether passive income is high-taxed shall be made only after application of paragraph (c)(2)(ii) of this section (if applicable).

(ii) *Reallocation of loss groups.*—If, after allocation and apportionment of expenses, losses and other deductions under paragraph (c)(2)(ii) of this section, the sum of the allocable deductions exceeds the gross income in one or more groups, the excess deductions shall proportionately reduce income in the other groups (but not below zero).

(iii) *Coordination with section 904(b), (f) and (g).*—The determination of whether foreign source passive income is high-taxed is made before taking into account any adjustments under section 904(b) or any allocation or recapture of a separate limitation loss, overall foreign loss, or overall domestic loss under section 904(f) and (g).

(3) *Amounts received or accrued by United States persons.*—Except as otherwise provided in paragraph (c)(5) of this section, all passive income received by a United States person are subject to the rules of this paragraph (c)(3). Paragraph (c)(4) of this section provides additional rules for inclusions under section 951(a)(1) or 951A(a) that are passive income, dividends from a controlled foreign corporation or noncontrolled 10-percent owned foreign corporation that are passive income, and income that is received or accrued by a United States person through a foreign QBU that is passive income. For purposes of this paragraph (c), a foreign QBU is a qualified business unit (as defined in section 989(a)), other than a controlled foreign corporation or noncontrolled 10-percent owned foreign corporation, that has its principal place of business outside the United States. The rules in this paragraph (c)(3) apply whether the income is received from a controlled foreign corporation of which the United States person is a United States shareholder, from a noncontrolled 10-percent owned foreign corporation of which the United States person is a United States shareholder that is a domestic corporation, or from any other person. In applying the rules in this paragraph (c)(3), passive income is not treated as subject to a withholding tax or other foreign tax when a credit is disallowed in full for such foreign tax, for example, under section 901(k). For purposes of determining whether passive income is high-taxed income, the following rules apply:

(i) All passive income received during the taxable year that is subject to a withholding tax of fifteen percent or greater shall be treated as one item of income.

(ii) All passive income received during the taxable year that is subject to a withholding tax of less than fifteen percent (but greater than zero) shall be treated as one item of income.

(iii) All passive income received during the taxable year that is subject to no withholding tax or other foreign tax shall be treated as one item of income.

(iv) All passive income received during the taxable year that is subject to no withholding tax but is subject to a foreign tax other than a withholding tax shall be treated as one item of income.

(4) *Dividends and inclusions from controlled foreign corporations, dividends from noncontrolled 10-percent owned foreign corporations, and income attributable to foreign QBUs.*—Except as provided in paragraph (c)(5) of this section, the rules of this paragraph (c)(4) apply to all dividends and all amounts included in gross income of a United States shareholder under section 951(a)(1) or 951A(a) with respect to the foreign corporation that (after application of the look-through rules of section 904(d)(3) and § 1.904-5) are attributable to passive income received or accrued by a controlled foreign corporation, all dividends from a noncontrolled 10-percent owned foreign corporation that are received or accrued by a United States shareholder that (after application of the look-through rules of section 904(d)(4) and § 1.904-5) are treated as passive income, and all amounts of passive income received or accrued by a United States person through a foreign QBU. The grouping rules of paragraphs (c)(3)(i) through (iv) of this section apply separately to dividends, to inclusions under section 951(a)(1) and to inclusions under section 951A(a) with respect to each controlled foreign corporation of which the taxpayer is a United States shareholder, and to dividends with respect to each noncontrolled 10-percent owned foreign corporation of which the taxpayer is a United States shareholder that is a domestic corporation. The grouping rules of paragraphs (c)(3)(i) through (iv) of this section also apply separately to income attributable to each tested unit, as defined in § 1.951A-2(c)(7)(iv), of a controlled foreign corporation, and to each foreign QBU of a noncontrolled 10-percent owned foreign corporation or any other look-through entity defined in § 1.904-5(i), or of any United States person.

(5) *Special rules.*—(i) *Certain rents and royalties.*—All items of rent or royalty income to which an item of rent or royalty expense is directly allocable shall be treated as a single item of income and shall not be grouped with other amounts.

(ii) *Treatment of partnership income.*—A partner's distributive share of income from a foreign or domestic partnership that is treated as passive income under paragraph (n)(1)(ii) of this section (generally providing that a less than 10 percent partner's distributive share of partnership income is passive income) is treated as a single item of income and is not grouped with other amounts. A distributive share of income from a partnership that is treated as passive income under paragraph (n)(1)(i) of this section is grouped according to the rules in paragraph (c)(3) of this section, except that the portion, if any, of the distributive share of income attributable to income earned by a domestic partnership through a foreign QBU is separately grouped under the rules of paragraph (c)(4) of this section.

(iii) *Currency gain or loss.*—(A) *Section 986(c).*—Any currency gain or loss with respect to a distribution received by a United States shareholder (other than a foreign QBU of that shareholder) of previously taxed earnings and profits that is recognized under section 986(c) and that is treated as an item of passive income shall be subject to the rules provided in paragraph (c)(3)(iii) of this section.

(B) *Section 987(3).*—Any currency gain or loss with respect to remittances or transfers of property between QBUs of a United States shareholder that is recognized under section 987(3)(B) and that is treated as an item of passive income shall be subject to the rules provided in paragraph (c)(3)(iii) of this section.

(C) *Example.*—The following example illustrates the application of this paragraph (c)(5)(iii).

(1) *Facts.* USP, a domestic corporation, owns all of the stock of CFC, a controlled foreign corporation organized and operating in Country X that uses the "u" as its functional currency. In Year 1, when the highest rate of U.S. tax in section 11 is 21%, CFC earns 100u of passive category foreign personal holding company income subject to no foreign tax. When included in USP's income under section 951(a), the applicable exchange rate is 1u=$1x. Therefore, USP's section 951(a) inclusion is $100x and no foreign taxes are deemed paid by USP with respect to the inclusion. At the end of Year 1, CFC has previously taxed earnings and profits of 100u and USP's basis in those earnings is $100x. In Year 2, CFC has no earnings and profits and distributes 100u to USP. The value of the earnings when distributed is $150x. Assume that under section 986(c), USP must recognize $50x of passive category income attributable to the appreciation of the previously taxed earnings and profits. Country X does not recognize any gain or loss on the distribution, but imposes a 10u withholding tax on USP with respect to the distribution.

(2) *Analysis.* Because the section 986(c) gain is not subject to any foreign withholding tax or other foreign tax, under paragraph (c)(3)(iii) of this section the section 986(c) gain is grouped with other items of USP's income that are subject to no withholding tax or other foreign tax. Under paragraph (c)(6)(iii) of this section, the 10u withholding tax is related to passive category income. See section 960(c) and § 1.960-4 for rules relating to the increase in limitation in the year of distribution of previously taxed earnings and profits.

(iv) *Coordination with section 954(b)(4).*—For rules relating to passive income of a controlled foreign corporation that is exempt from subpart F treatment because the income is subject to high foreign tax, see section 904(d)(3)(E), § 1.904-4(c)(7)(iii), and § 1.904-5(d)(2).

(6) *Application of this paragraph to additional taxes paid or deemed paid in the year of receipt of previously taxed income.*—(i) *Determination made in year of inclusion.*—The determination of whether an amount included in gross income under section 951(a)(1) or 951A(a) is high-taxed income is made in the taxable year the income is included in the gross income of the United States shareholder under section 951(a) or 951A(a) (for purposes of this paragraph (c), the *year of inclusion*). Any increase in foreign taxes paid or accrued, or deemed paid, when the taxpayer receives an amount that is excluded from gross income under section 959(a) and that is attributable to a controlled foreign corporation's earnings and profits relating to the amount previously included in gross income will not be considered in determining whether the amount included in income in the year of inclusion is high-taxed income.

(ii) *Exception.*—Paragraph (c)(6)(i) of this section shall not apply to an increase in tax in a case in which the taxpayer is required to adjust its foreign taxes in the year of inclusion under section 905(c).

(iii) *Allocation of foreign taxes imposed on distributions of previously taxed income.*—If an item of income is considered high-taxed income in the year of inclusion and paragraph (c)(6)(i) of this section applies, then any increase in foreign income taxes imposed with respect to that item are considered to be related to the same separate category to which the income was assigned in the taxable year of inclusion. If an item of income is not considered to be high-taxed income in the year of inclusion and paragraph (c)(6)(i) of this section applies, the following rules shall apply. The taxpayer shall treat an increase in taxes paid or accrued, or deemed paid, on any distribution of the earnings and profits attributable to the amount included in gross income in the year of inclusion as taxes related to passive income to the extent of the excess of the product of the highest rate of tax in section 11 (determined with regard to section 15 and determined as of the year of inclusion) and the amount of the inclusion (after allocation of parent expenses) over the taxes paid or accrued, or deemed paid, in the year of inclusion. The taxpayer shall treat any taxes paid or accrued, or deemed paid, on the distribution in excess of this amount as taxes related to the same category of income to which such inclusion would have been assigned had the income been treated as high-taxed income in the year of inclusion (general category income, section 951A category income, or income in a specified separate category). If these additional taxes are not creditable in the year of distribution, the carryover rules of section 904(c) apply (see section 904(c) and § 1.904-2(a) for rules disallowing carryovers in the section 951A category). For purposes of this paragraph (c)(6), the foreign tax on an inclusion under section 951(a)(1) or 951A(a) is considered increased on distribution of the earnings and profits associated with that inclusion if the total of taxes paid and deemed paid on the inclusion and the distribution (taking into account any reductions in tax and any withholding taxes) exceeds the total taxes deemed paid in the year of inclusion. Any foreign currency loss associated with the earnings and profits that are distributed with respect to the inclusion is not to be considered as giving rise to an increase in tax.

(iv) *Increase in taxes paid by successors.*—If passive earnings and profits previously included in income of a United States shareholder are distributed to a person that was not a United States shareholder of the distributing corporation in the year the earnings were included, any increase in foreign taxes paid or accrued, or deemed paid, on that distribution is treated as taxes related to general category income (or income in a specified separate category, if applicable) in the case of earnings and profits previously included under section 951(a)(1), and is treated as taxes related to section 951A category income (or income in a specified separate category, if applicable) in the case of earnings and profits previously included under section 951A(a), regardless of whether the previously-taxed income was considered high-taxed income under section 904(d)(2)(F) in the year of inclusion.

(7) *Application of this paragraph to certain reductions of tax on distributions of income.*—(i) *In general.*—If the effective rate of tax imposed by a foreign country on income of a foreign corporation that is included in a taxpayer's gross income is reduced under foreign law on distribution of such income, the rules of this paragraph (c) apply at the time that the income is included in the taxpayer's gross income, without regard to the possibility of a subsequent reduction of foreign tax on the distribution. If the inclusion is considered to be high-taxed income, then the taxpayer must initially treat the inclusion as general category income, section 951A category income, or income in a specified separate category as provided in paragraph (c)(1) of this section. When the foreign corporation distributes the earnings and profits to which the inclusion was attributable and the foreign tax on the inclusion is reduced, then if a redetermination of U.S. tax liability is required under § 1.905-3(b)(2), the taxpayer must redetermine whether the revised inclusion (if any) is considered to be high-taxed income. See § 1.905-3(b)(2)(ii) (requiring a redetermination of the amount of the inclusion, the application of the high-tax exception under section 954(b)(4), and the amount of foreign taxes deemed paid). If, taking into account the reduction in foreign tax, the inclusion is not considered high-taxed income, then the taxpayer, in redetermining its U.S. tax liability for the year or years affected, must treat the inclusion and the associated taxes (as reduced on the distribution) as passive category income and taxes. For purposes of this paragraph (c), the foreign tax on an inclusion under section 951(a)(1) or 951A(a) is considered reduced on distribution of the earnings and profits associated with the inclusion if the total taxes paid and deemed paid on the inclusion and the distribution (taking into account any reductions in tax and any withholding taxes) is less than the total taxes deemed paid in the year of inclusion. Therefore, any foreign currency gain associated with the earnings and profits that are distributed with respect to the inclusion is not taken into account in determining whether there is a reduction of tax requiring a redetermination of whether the inclusion is high-taxed income.

(ii) *Allocation of reductions of foreign tax.*—For purposes of paragraph (c)(7)(i) of this section, reductions in foreign tax shall be allocated among the separate categories under the same principles as those of § 1.904-6 for allocating taxes among the separate categories. Thus, for purposes of determining to which year's taxes the reduction in taxes relates, foreign law shall apply.If, however, foreign law does not attribute a reduction in taxes to a particular year or years, then the reduction in taxes shall be attributable, on an annual last in-first out (LIFO) basis, to foreign taxes potentially subject to reduction that are associated with previously taxed income, then on a LIFO basis to foreign taxes associated with income that under paragraph (c)(7)(iii) of this section remains as passive income but that was excluded from subpart F income or tested income under section 954(b)(4) or section 951A(c)(2)(A)(i)(III), and finally on a LIFO basis to foreign taxes associated with other earnings and profits. Furthermore, in applying the ordering rules of section 959(c), distributions shall be considered made on a LIFO basis first out of earnings described in section 959(c)(1) and (2), then on a LIFO basis out of earnings and profits associated with income that remains passive income under paragraph (c)(7)(iii) of this section but that was excluded from subpart F income or tested income under section 954(b)(4) or section 951A(c)(2)(A)(i)(III), and finally on a LIFO basis out of other earnings and profits. For purposes of this paragraph (c)(7)(ii), foreign law is not considered to attribute a reduction in tax to a particular year or years if foreign law attributes the tax reduction to a pool or group containing income from more than one taxable year and such pool or group is defined based on a characteristic of the income (for example, the rate of tax paid with respect to the income) rather than on the taxable year in which the income is derived.

(iii) *Treatment of income excluded under section 954(b)(4) or section 951A(c)(2)(A)(i)(III).*—If the effective rate of tax imposed by a foreign country on income of a foreign corporation is reduced under foreign law on distribution of that income, the rules of section 954(b)(4) (including for purposes of determining tested income under section 951A(c)(2)(A)(i)(III)) are applied in the year of inclusion without regard to the possibility of a subsequent reduction of foreign tax. See §§ 1.954-1(d)(3)(iii) and 1.951A-2(c)(6)(iv). If a taxpayer excludes passive income from a controlled foreign corporation's foreign personal holding company income or tested income under section 954(b)(4) or section 951A(c)(2)(A)(i)(III), then, notwithstanding the general rule of § 1.904-5(d)(2), the income is considered to be passive category income until distribution of that income. At that time, if after the redetermination of U.S. tax liability required under § 1.905-3(b)(2) the taxpayer still elects to exclude the passive income under section 954(b)(4) or section 951A(c)(2)(A)(i)(III), the rules of this paragraph (c)(7)(iii) apply to determine whether the income is high-taxed income upon distribution and, therefore, income in another separate category. For purposes of determining whether a reduction in tax is attributable to taxes on income excluded under section 954(b)(4) or section 951A(c)(2)(A)(i)(III), the rules of paragraph (c)(7)(ii) of this section apply. The rules of paragraph (c)(7)(ii) of this section also apply for purposes of ordering distributions to determine whether such distributions are out of earnings and profits associated with such excluded income. For an example illustrating the operation of this paragraph (c)(7)(iii), see paragraph (c)(8)(vi) of this section (*Example 6*).

(8) *Examples.*—The following examples illustrate the application of this paragraph (c). All of the examples assume that the highest tax rate under section 11 is 21%, unless otherwise noted.

(i) *Example 1.* CFC, a controlled foreign corporation, is a wholly-owned subsidiary of domestic corporation USP. CFC is a single qualified business unit (QBU) operating in foreign Country X. In Year 1, CFC earns $130x of gross royalty income that is passive income from Country X sources, and incurs $30x of expenses that do not include any payments to USP. CFC's $100x of pre-tax passive income from the royalty is subject to $30x of foreign tax, and is included under section 951(a)(1) in USP's gross income for the taxable year. USP allocates $50x of expenses to the $100x (consisting of the $70x section 951(a)(1) inclusion and $30x section 78 amount), resulting in net passive income of $50x. USP does not elect to exclude from subpart F under section 954(b)(4) the $70x of CFC's net passive income. After application of the high-tax kick-out rules of paragraph (c) of this section, the $50x of USP's net passive income is treated as general category income, and the $30x of taxes deemed paid are treated as taxes imposed on general category income, because the foreign taxes paid and deemed paid on the income exceed the highest U.S. tax rate multiplied by the $50x of net passive income ($30x > $10.5x (21% x $50x)).

(ii) *Example 2.* CFC, a controlled foreign corporation, is a wholly-owned subsidiary of domestic corporation USP. CFC is incorporated and operating in Country Y and has a branch in Country Z. CFC has two QBUs (QBU Y and QBU Z). In Year 1, CFC earns $65x of gross royalty income that is passive income in Country Y through QBU Y and $65x of gross royalty income that is passive income in Country Z through QBU Z. CFC allocates $15x of expenses to the gross royalty income earned by each QBU, resulting in pre-tax passive income of $50x in each QBU. Country Y imposes $5x of foreign tax on the royalty income earned in Y, and Country Z imposes $10x of tax on royalty income earned in Z. All of CFC's income constitutes foreign personal holding company income that is passive income and is included under section 951(a)(1) in USP's gross income for the taxable year. USP allocates $50x of expenses pro rata to the $100x section 951(a)(1) inclusion attributable to the QBUs (consisting of the $45x section 951(a)(1) inclusion derived through QBU Y, the $5x section 78 amount attributable to QBU Y, the $40x section 951(a)(1) inclusion derived through QBU Z, and the $10x section 78 amount attributable to QBU Z), resulting in net passive income of $50x. Pursuant to paragraph (c)(4) of this section, the high-tax kickout rules must be applied separately to the subpart F inclusion attributable to the income earned by QBU Y and the income earned by QBU Z. After application of the high-tax kickout rules, the $25x of net passive income attributable to QBU Y will be treated as passive category income because the foreign taxes paid and deemed paid on the income do not exceed the highest U.S. tax rate multiplied by the $25x of net passive income ($5x < $5.25x (21% x $25x)). The $25x of net passive income attributable to QBU Z will be treated as general category income because the foreign taxes paid and deemed paid on the income exceed the highest U.S. tax rate multiplied by the $25x of net passive income ($10x > $5.25x (21% x $25x)).

(iii) *Example 3.* Domestic corporation USP operates in branch form in foreign countries X and Y. The branches are qualified business units (QBUs), within the meaning of section 989(a). In Year 1, QBU X earns passive royalty income, interest income, and rental income. All of the QBU X passive income is from Country Z sources. The royalty income is not subject to a withholding tax, and is not taxed by Country X, and the interest and the rental income are subject to a 4% and 10% withholding tax, respectively. QBU Y earns interest income in Country Y that is not subject to foreign tax. For purposes of determining whether USP's foreign source passive income is high-taxed income, the rental income and the interest income earned in QBU X are treated as one item of income pursuant to paragraph (c)(3)(ii) of this section. The interest income earned in QBU Y and the royalty income earned in QBU X are each treated as a separate item of income under paragraphs (c)(4) and (c)(3)(iii) of this section. If, after allocation of expenses, QBU X's items of income composed of rental income and interest income are high-taxed income, the income may be treated as foreign branch category income.

(iv) *Example 4.* CFC, a controlled foreign corporation incorporated in foreign Country R, is a wholly-owned subsidiary of USP, a domestic corporation. USP and CFC have calendar year taxable years for both U.S. and Country R tax purposes. The highest tax rate under section 11 is 34% and 21% in Year 1 and Year 2, respectively. For Year 1, USP is required under section 951(a)(1) to include in gross income $80x (not including the section 78 amount) attributable to the earnings and profits of CFC for such year, all of which is foreign personal holding company income that is passive rent or royalty income. CFC does not make any distributions in Year 1. Foreign income taxes paid by CFC for Year 1 that are deemed paid by USP for such year under section 960(a) with respect to the section 951(a)(1) inclusion equal $20x. USP properly allocates $30x of expenses to the section 951(a)(1) inclusion. The foreign income tax paid with respect to the section 951(a)(1) inclusion does not exceed the highest U.S. tax rate multiplied by the amount of income after allocation of USP's expenses ($20x < $23.80x (34% x $70x)). Thus, USP's section 951(a)(1) inclusion for Year 1 is included in USP's passive category income and the $20x of taxes attributable to that inclusion are treated as taxes related to passive category income. In Year 2, CFC distributes $70x to USP, and under section 959 that distribution is treated as attributable to the earnings and profits with respect to the amount included in income by USP in Year 1 and is excluded from USP's gross income. Foreign Country R imposes a withholding tax of $14x on the distribution in Year 2. Under paragraph (c)(6)(i) of this section, the withholding tax in Year 2 does not affect the characterization of the Year 1 inclusion as passive category income, nor does it affect the characterization of the $20x of taxes paid in Year 1 as taxes paid with respect to passive category income. No further expenses of USP are allocable to the receipt of that distribution. In Year 2, the foreign taxes paid ($14x) exceed the product of the highest U.S. tax rate and the amount of the inclusion reduced by taxes deemed paid in the year of inclusion ($14x > $3.80x ((34% x $70x) – $20x)). Thus, under paragraph (c)(6)(iii) of this section, $3.80x ((34% x $70x) – $20x) of the $14x withholding tax paid in Year 2 is treated as taxes related to passive category income and the remaining $10.20x ($14x – $3.80x) of the withholding tax is treated as related to general category income.

(v) *Example 5.* CFC, a controlled foreign corporation, is a wholly-owned subsidiary of USP, a domestic corporation. USP and CFC are calendar year taxpayers. In Year 1, CFC's only earnings consist of $200x of pre-tax passive income that is foreign personal holding company income that is earned in foreign Country X. Under Country X's tax system, the corporate tax on particular earnings is reduced on distribution of those earnings and no withholding tax is imposed. In Year 1, CFC pays $100x of foreign tax with respect to its passive income. USP does not elect to exclude this income from subpart F under section 954(b)(4) and includes $200x in gross income ($100x of net foreign personal holding company income and $100x of the amount under section 78 (the "section 78 dividend")). At the time of the inclusion, the income is considered to be high-taxed income under paragraphs (c)(1) and (c)(6)(i) of this section and is general category income to USP ($100x > $42x (21% x $200x)). CFC does not distribute any of its earnings in Year 1. In Year 2, CFC has no additional earnings. On December 31, Year 2, CFC distributes the $100x of earnings from Year 1. At that time, CFC receives a $60x refund from Country X attributable to the reduction of the Country X corporate tax imposed on the Year 1 earnings. The refund is a foreign tax redetermination under § 1.905-3(a) that under § § 1.905-3(b)(2) and 1.954-1(d)(3)(iii) requires a redetermination of CFC's Year 1 subpart F income and the application of section 954(b)(4), as well as a redetermination of USP's Year 1 inclusion under section 951(a)(1), its deemed paid taxes under section 960(a), and its Year 1 U.S. tax liability. As recomputed taking into account the $60x refund, CFC's Year 1 passive category net foreign personal holding company income is increased by $60x to $160x, CFC's foreign income taxes attributable to that income are reduced from $100x to $40x, and the income still qualifies to be excluded from CFC's subpart F income under section 954(b)(4) ($40x > $37.80x (90% x 21% x $200x)). Assuming USP does not change its Year 1 election, USP's Year 1 inclusion under section 951(a)(1) is increased by $60x to $160x, and the associated deemed paid tax and section 78 dividend are reduced by $60x to $40x. Under paragraph (c)(7)(i) of this section, in connection with the adjustments required under section 905(c), USP must redetermine whether the adjusted Year 1 inclusion is high-taxed income of USP. Taking into account the $60x refund, the inclusion is not considered high-taxed income of USP ($40x < $42x (21% x $200x)). Therefore, USP must treat the $200x of income ($160x inclusion plus $40x section 78 amount) and the $40x of taxes associated with the inclusion in Year 1 as passive category income and taxes. USP must also follow the appropriate procedures under § 1.905-4.

(vi) *Example 6.* The facts are the same as in paragraph (c)(8)(v) of this section (the facts in *Example 5*), except that in Year 1, USP elects to apply section 954(b)(4) to exclude CFC's passive income from its subpart F income, both before and after the recomputation of CFC's Year 1 subpart F income and USP's Year 1 U.S. tax liability that is required by reason of the Year 2 $60x foreign tax redetermination. Although the income is not considered to be subpart F income, under paragraph (c)(7)(iii) of this section it remains passive category income until distribution. In Year 2, the $100x distribution is a dividend to USP, because CFC has $160x of accumulated earnings and profits described in section 959(c)(3) (the $100x of earnings in Year 1 increased by the $60x refund received in Year 2 that under § 1.905-3(b)(2) is taken into account in Year 1). Under paragraph (c)(7)(iii) of this section, USP must determine whether the dividend income is high-taxed income to USP in Year 2. The treatment of the dividend as passive category income may be relevant in determining deductions allocable or apportioned to such dividend income or related stock that are excluded in the computation of USP's foreign tax credit limitation under section 904(a) in Year 2. See section 904(b)(4). Under paragraph (c)(1) of this section, the dividend income is passive category income to USP because the foreign taxes paid and deemed paid by USP ($0x) with respect to the dividend income do not exceed the highest U.S. tax rate on that income.

(vii) *Example 7.* The facts are the same as in paragraph (c)(8)(v) of this section (the facts in *Example 5*), except that the distribution in Year 2 is subject to a withholding tax of $25x. Under paragraph (c)(7)(i) of this section, USP must redetermine whether its Year 1 inclusion should be considered high-taxed income of USP because there is a net $35x reduction ($60x refund of foreign corporate tax – $25x withholding tax) of foreign tax. By taking into account both the reduction in foreign corporate tax and the additional withholding tax, the inclusion continues to be considered high-taxed income of USP in Year 1 ($65x > $42x (21% x $200)). USP must follow the appropriate section 905(c) procedures. USP must redetermine its U.S. tax liability for Year 1, but the Year 1 inclusion and the $65x taxes ($40x of deemed paid tax in Year 1 and $25x withholding tax in Year 2) will continue to be treated as general category income and taxes.

(viii) *Example 8.* (A) CFC, a controlled foreign corporation operating in Country G, is a wholly-owned subsidiary of USP, a domestic corporation. USP and CFC are calendar year taxpayers. Country G imposes a tax of 50% on CFC's earnings. Under Country G's system, the foreign corporate tax on particular earnings is reduced on distribution of those earnings to 30% and no withholding tax is imposed. Under Country G's law, distributions are treated as made out of a pool of undistributed earnings subject to the 50% tax rate. For Year 1, CFC's only earnings consist of passive income that is foreign personal holding company income that is earned in foreign Country G. CFC has taxable income of $110x for Federal income tax purposes and $100x for Country G purposes. Country G, therefore, imposes a tax of $50x on the Year 1 earnings of CFC. USP does not elect to exclude this income from subpart F under section 954(b)(4) and includes $110x in gross income ($60x of net foreign personal holding company income under section 951(a) and $50x of the section 78 dividend). The highest rate of tax under section 11 in Year 1 is 34%. Therefore, at the time of the section 951(a) inclusion, the income is considered to be high-taxed income under paragraph (c) of this section ($50x > $37.4x (34% x $110x)) and is general category income to USP. CFC does not distribute any of its earnings in Year 1.

(B) In Year 2, CFC earns general category income that is not subpart F income or tested income. CFC again has $110x in taxable income for Federal income tax purposes and $100x in taxable income for Country G purposes, and CFC pays $50x of tax to foreign Country G. In Year 3, CFC has no taxable income or earnings. On December 31, Year 3, CFC distributes $60x of its total $120x of earnings and receives a refund of foreign tax of $24x. The $24x refund is a foreign tax redetermination under § 1.905-3(a) that under § 1.905-3(b)(2) requires a redetermination of CFC's Year 1 subpart F income and USP's deemed paid taxes and Year 1 U.S. tax liability. Country G treats the distribution of earnings as out of the 50% tax rate pool of $200x of earnings accumulated in Year 1 and Year 2, as calculated for Country G tax purposes. However, under paragraph (c)(7)(ii) of this section, the distribution, and, therefore, the reduction of tax is treated as first attributable to the $60x of passive category earnings attributable to income previously taxed in Year 1, and none of the distribution is treated as made out of the $60x of earnings accumulated in Year 2 (which is not previously taxed). Because 40 percent (the reduction in tax rates from 50 percent to 30 percent is a 40 percent reduction in the tax) of the $50x of foreign taxes attributable to the $60x of Year 1 passive income as calculated for Federal income tax purposes is refunded, $20x of the $24x foreign tax refund reduces foreign taxes on CFC's Year 1 passive income from $50x to $30x. The other $4x of the tax refund reduces the taxes imposed in Year 2 on CFC's general category income from $50x to $46x.

(C) Under paragraph (c)(7) of this section, in connection with the section 905(c) adjustment USP must redetermine whether its Year 1 subpart F inclusion is considered high-taxed income. By taking into account the reduction in foreign tax, the inclusion is increased by $20x to $80x, the deemed paid taxes are reduced by $20x to $30x, and the inclusion is not considered high-taxed income ($30x < 34% x $110x). Therefore, USP must treat the revised section 951(a) inclusion and the taxes associated with the section 951(a) inclusion as passive category income and taxes in Year 1. USP must follow the appropriate procedures under § 1.905-4.

(ix) *Example 9.* USP, a domestic corporation, earns $100x of passive royalty income from sources within the United States. Under the laws of Country X, however, that royalty is considered to be from sources within Country X, and Country X imposes a 5% withholding tax on the payment of the royalty. USP also earns $100x of foreign source passive dividend income from Country Y subject to a 10% withholding tax to which $15x of expenses are allocated. In determining whether USP's passive income is high-taxed, the $5x withholding tax on USP's royalty income is allocated to passive income, and to the group of passive income described in paragraph (c)(3)(ii) of this section (passive income subject to a withholding tax of less than 15% (but greater than zero)). For purposes of determining whether the income is high-taxed, however, only the $85x of foreign source dividend income (and not the $100x of U.S. source royalty income) is taken into account. The foreign source dividend income is treated as passive category income because the foreign taxes paid on the passive income in the group ($15x) do not exceed the highest U.S. tax rate multiplied by the $85x of net foreign source income in the group ($15x < $17.85x ($100x – $15x) x 21%).

(x) *Example 10.* In Year 1, P, a U.S. citizen with a tax home in Country X, earns the following items of gross income: $400x of foreign source, passive interest income not subject to foreign withholding tax but subject to Country X income tax of $100x, $200x of foreign source, passive royalty income subject to a 5% foreign withholding tax (foreign tax paid is $10x), $1,300x of foreign source, passive rental income subject to a 25% foreign withholding tax (foreign tax paid is $325x), $500x of foreign source, general category loss, and $2,000x of U.S. source capital gain that is not subject to any foreign tax. P has a $900x deduction allocable to its passive rental income. P's only other deduction is a $700x capital loss on the sale of stock that is allocated to foreign source passive category income under § 1.865-2(a)(3)(i). The $700x capital loss is initially allocated to the group of passive income described in paragraph (c)(3)(iv) of this section (passive income subject to no withholding tax but subject to foreign tax other than withholding tax). This group comprises the $400x of interest income not subject to foreign withholding tax but subject to Country X income tax. Under paragraph (c)(2)(ii) of this section, the $300x amount by which the capital loss exceeds the income in the group must be reallocated to the net income in the other groups described in paragraph (c)(3) of this section, but the $500x general category separate limitation loss is not allocated until the high-tax kickout rules are applied to determine whether the passive income is high-taxed income. P's $200x of royalty income subject to a 5% withholding tax is described in paragraph (c)(3)(i) of this section (passive income that is subject to a withholding tax of less than 15%, but greater than zero). P's $1,300x of rental income subject to a 25% withholding tax is described in paragraph (c)(3)(ii) of this section (passive income that is subject to a withholding tax of 15% or greater). The $1,300x of rental income is reduced by the $900x deduction allocable to such income. Therefore, the total net income in the other groups under paragraph (c)(3) is $600x, the $200x of royalty income and the $400x of rental income. The ($300x) net loss in the net basis tax group thus reduces the royalty income by $100x to $100x ($200x – ($300x x (200x/600x))) and the rental income by $200x to $200x ($400x – ($300x x (400x/600x))). The $100x of net royalty income is not high-taxed and remains passive category income because the foreign taxes of $10x do not exceed the highest U.S. rate of tax on that income, which is 37% for individuals ($10x < $37x (37% x $100x)). Under the high-tax kickout, the $200x of rental income and the $325x of associated foreign tax are assigned to the general category.

(xi) *Example 11.* The facts are the same as in paragraph (c)(8)(x) of this section (the facts in *Example 10*), except the amount of the capital loss that is allocated under § 1.865-2(a)(3)(i) and paragraph (c)(2) of this section to the group of foreign source passive income subject to no withholding tax but subject to foreign tax other than withholding tax is $1,200x. Under paragraph (c)(2)(ii) of this section, the excess deductions of $800x must be reallocated to the $200x of net royalty income subject to a 5% withholding tax and the $400x of net rental income subject to a 15% or greater withholding tax. The income in each of these groups is reduced to zero, and the foreign taxes imposed on the rental and royalty income are considered related to general category income. The remaining loss of $200x constitutes a separate limitation loss with respect to passive category income.

(xii) *Example 12.* In Year 1, USP, a domestic corporation, earns a $100x dividend that is foreign source passive income subject to a 30% withholding tax. The dividend is not paid by a specified 10-percent owned foreign corporation (as defined in section 245A(b)(1)). A foreign tax credit for the withholding tax on the dividend is disallowed under section 901(k). A deduction for the tax is allowed, however, under sections 164 and 901(k)(7). In determining whether USP's passive income is high-taxed, under paragraph (c)(3) of this section the $100x dividend and the $30x deduction are allocated to the group of income described in paragraph (c)(3)(iv) of this section (passive income subject to no withholding tax or other foreign tax).

(d) *General category income.*—The term *general category income* means all income other than passive category income, foreign branch category income, section 951A category income, and income in a specified separate category. Any item that is excluded from the passive category under paragraph (c) or (h) of this section or § 1.904-5(b)(1) is included in general category income only to the extent that such item does not meet the definition of another separate category. General category income also includes income treated as general category income under the look-through rules referenced in § 1.904-5(a)(2).

(e) *Financial services income.*—(1) *In general.*—(i) *Treatment of financial services income.*—Passive income that is characterized as financial services income is not assigned to the passive category but is assigned in accordance with this paragraph (e)(1)(i). Financial services income that meets the definition of foreign branch category income (see paragraph (f)(1) of this section) is treated as income in that category. Financial services income of a controlled foreign corporation that is included in gross income of a United States shareholder under section 951A(a) is treated as section 951A category income in the hands of the United States shareholder. Financial services income that is neither treated as foreign branch category income nor treated as section 951A category income is treated as general category income. Distributions, interest, rents, or royalties received from a related person that is a financial services entity that would be assigned to the passive category under the look-through rules in § 1.904-5, but for the fact such amounts are paid by a financial services entity (and, therefore, not attributable to passive category income of the payor), are assigned to separate categories (other than the passive category) under the rules in this section.

(ii) *Definition of financial services income.*—The term *financial services income* means income derived by a financial services entity, as defined in paragraph (e)(3) of this section, that is:

(A) Income derived in the active conduct of a banking, insurance, financing, or similar business (active financing income as defined in paragraph (e)(2) of this section);

(B) Passive income as defined in section 904(d)(2)(B) and paragraph (b) of this section as determined before the application of the exception for high-taxed income but after the application of the exception for export financing interest; or

(C) Incidental income as defined in paragraph (e)(4) of this section.

(2) *Active financing income.*—(i) *Income included.*—For purposes of paragraph (e)(1) and (e)(3) of this section, income is active financing income only if it is described in any of the following subdivisions.

(A) Income that is of a kind that would be insurance income as defined in section 953(a) (including related party insurance income as defined in section 953(c)(2)) and determined without regard to those provisions of section 953(a)(1)(A) that limit insurance income to income from countries other than the country in which the corporation was created or organized.

(B) Income from the investment by an insurance company of its unearned premiums or reserves ordinary and necessary to the proper conduct of the insurance business, income from providing services as an insurance underwriter, income from insurance brokerage or agency services, and income from loss adjuster and surveyor services.

(C) Income from investing funds in circumstances in which the taxpayer holds itself out as providing a financial service by the acceptance or the investment of such funds, including income from investing deposits of money and income earned investing funds received for the purchase of traveller's checks or face amount certificates.

(D) Income from making personal, mortgage, industrial, or other loans.

(E) Income from purchasing, selling, discounting, or negotiating on a regular basis, notes, drafts, checks, bills of exchange, acceptances, or other evidences of indebtedness.

(F) Income from issuing letters of credit and negotiating drafts drawn thereunder.

(G) Income from providing trust services.

(H) Income from arranging foreign exchange transactions, or engaging in foreign exchange transactions.

(I) Income from purchasing stock, debt obligations, or other securities from an issuer or holder with a view to the public distribution thereof or offering or selling stock, debt obligations, or other securities for an issuer or holder in connection with the public distribution thereof, or participating in any such undertaking.

(J) Income earned by broker-dealers in the ordinary course of business (such as commissions) from the purchase or sale of stock, debt obligations, commodities futures, or other securities or financial instruments and dividend and interest income earned by broker dealers on stock, debt obligations, or other financial instruments that are held for sale.

(K) Service fee income from investment and correspondent banking.

(L) Income from interest rate and currency swaps.

(M) Income from providing fiduciary services.

(N) Income from services with respect to the management of funds.

(O) Bank-to-bank participation income.

(P) Income from providing charge and credit card services or for factoring receivables obtained in the course of providing such services.

(Q) Income from financing purchases from third parties.

(R) Income from gains on the disposition of tangible or intangible personal property or real property that was used in the active financing business (as defined in paragraph (e)(3)(i) of this section) but only to the extent that the property was held to generate or generated active financing income prior to its disposition.

(S) Income from hedging gain with respect to other active financing income.

(T) Income from providing traveller's check services.

(U) Income from servicing mortgages.

(V) Income from a finance lease. For this purpose, a finance lease is any lease that is a direct financing lease or a leveraged lease for accounting purposes and is also a lease for tax purposes.

(W) [Reserved]

(X) Income from providing investment advisory services, custodial services, agency paying services, collection agency services, and stock transfer agency services.

(Y) Any similar item of income that is disclosed in the manner provided in the instructions to the Form 1118 or 1116 or that is designated as a similar item of income in guidance published by the Internal Revenue Service.

(3) *Financial services entities.*—(i) *In general.*—The term "financial services entity" means an individual or entity that is predominantly engaged in the active conduct of a banking, insurance, financing, or similar business (active financing business) for any taxable year. Except as provided in paragraph (e)(3)(ii) of this section, a determination of whether an entity is a financial services entity shall be done on an entity-by-entity basis. An individual or entity is predominantly engaged in the active financing business for any year if for that year at least 80 percent of its gross income is income described in paragraph (e)(2)(i) of this section. For this purpose, gross income includes all income realized by an individual or entity, whether includible or excludible from gross income under other operative provisions of the Code, but excludes gain from the disposition of stock of a corporation that prior to the disposition of its stock is related to the transferor within the meaning of section 267(b). For this purpose, income received from a related person that is a financial services entity shall be excluded if such income is characterized under the look-through rules of section 904(d)(3) and § 1.904-5. In addition, income received from a related person that is not a financial services entity but that is characterized as financial services income under the look-through rules shall be excluded. Any income received from a related person that is characterized under the look-through rules and that is not otherwise excluded by this paragraph will retain its character either as active financing income or other income in the hands of the recipient for purposes of determining if the recipient is a financial services entity and if the income is financial services income to the recipient. For purposes of this paragraph, related person is defined in § 1.904-5(i)(1).

(ii) *Special rule for affiliated groups.*—In the case of any corporation that is not a financial services entity under paragraph (e)(3)(i) of this section, but is a member of an affiliated group, such corporation will be deemed to be a financial services entity if the affiliated group as a whole meets the requirements of paragraph (e)(3)(i) of this section. For purposes of this paragraph (e)(3)(ii), affiliated group means an affiliated group as defined in section 1504(a), determined without regard to section 1504(b)(3). In counting the income of the group for purposes of determining whether the group meets the requirements of paragraph (e)(3)(i) of this section, the following rules apply. Only the income of group members that are United States corporations or foreign corporations that are controlled foreign corporations in which United States members of the affiliated group own, directly or indirectly, at least 80 percent of the total voting power and value of the stock shall be included. For purposes of this paragraph (e)(3)(ii), indirect ownership shall be determined under section 318 and the regulations under that section. The income of the group will not include any income from transactions with other members of the group. Passive income will not be considered to be active financing income merely because that income is earned by a member of the group that is a financial services entity without regard to the rule of this paragraph (e)(3)(ii).

(iii) *Treatment of partnerships and other pass-through entities.*—For purposes of determining whether a partner (including a partnership that is a partner in a second partnership) is a financial services entity, all of the partner's income shall be taken into account, except that income that is excluded under paragraph (e)(3)(i) of this section shall not be taken into account. Thus, if a partnership is determined to be a financial services entity none of the income of the partner received from the partnership that is characterized under the look-through rules shall be included for purpose of determining if the partner is a financial services entity. If a partnership is determined not to be a financial services entity, then income of the partner from the partnership that is characterized under the look-through rules will be taken into account (unless such income is financial services income) and such income will retain its character either as active financing income or as other income in the hands of the partner for purposes of determining if the partner is a financial service entity and if the income is financial services income to the partner. If a partnership is a financial services entity and the partner's income from the partnership is characterized as financial services income under the look-through rules, then, for purposes of determining a partner's foreign tax credit limitation, the income from the partnership shall be considered to be financial services income to the partner regardless of whether the partner is itself a financial services entity. The rules of this paragraph (e)(3)(iii) will apply for purposes of determining whether an owner of an interest in any other pass-through entity the character of the income of which is preserved when such income is included in the income of the owner of the interest is a financial services entity.

(iv) [Reserved]

(4) *Definition of incidental income.*—(i) *In general.*—(A) *Rule.*—Incidental income is income that is integrally related to active financing income of a financial services entity. Such income includes, for example, income from precious metals trading and commodity trading that is integrally related to futures income. If securities, shares of stock, or other types of property are acquired by a financial services entity as an ordinary and necessary incident to the conduct of a active financing business, the income from such property will be considered to be financial services income but only so long as the retention of such property remains an ordinary or necessary incident to the conduct of such business. Thus property, including stock, acquired as the result of, or in order to prevent, a loss in an active financing business upon a loan held by the taxpayer in the ordinary course of such business will be considered ordinary and necessary to the conduct of such business, but income from such property will be considered financial services income only so long as the holding of

such property remains an ordinary and necessary incident to the conduct of such business. If an entity holds such property for five years or less then the property is considered held incident to the financial services business. If an entity holds such property for more than five years, a presumption will be established that the entity is not holding such property incident to its financial services business. An entity will be able to rebut the presumption by demonstrating that under the facts and circumstances it is not holding the property as an investment. However, the fact that an entity holds the property for more than five years and is not able to rebut the presumption that it is not holding the property incident to its financial services business will not affect the characterization of any income received from the property during the first five years as financial services income.

(B) [Reserved]

(ii) *Income that is not incidental income.*—Income that is attributable to non-financial activity is not incidental income within the meaning of paragraph (e)(4)(i) and (ii) of this section solely because such income represents a relatively small proportion of the taxpayer's total income or that the taxpayer engages in non-financial activity on a sporadic basis. Thus, for example, income from data processing services provided to related or unrelated parties or income from the sale of goods or non-financial services (for example travel services) is not financial services income, even if the recipient is a financial services entity.

(f) *Foreign branch category income.*—(1) *Foreign branch category income.*—(i) *In general.*—Except as provided in paragraph (f)(1)(ii), (iii), or (iv) of this section, the term *foreign branch category income* means income of a United States person, other than a pass-through entity, that is—

(A) Income attributable to foreign branches of the United States person held directly or indirectly through disregarded entities;

(B) A distributive share of partnership income that is attributable to foreign branches held by the partnership directly or indirectly through disregarded entities, or held indirectly by the partnership through another partnership or other pass-through entity that holds the foreign branch directly or indirectly through disregarded entities; and

(C) Income from other pass-through entities determined under principles similar to those described in paragraph (f)(1)(i)(B) of this section.

(ii) *Passive category income excluded from foreign branch category income.*—Income assigned to the passive category under paragraph (b) of this section is not foreign branch category income, regardless of whether the income is described in paragraph (f)(1)(i) of this section. Income that is treated as passive category income under the look-through rules in § 1.904-5 is also excluded from foreign branch category income, regardless of whether the income is attributable to a foreign branch. However, income that would be passive category income but for the application of section 904(d)(2)(B)(iii) (export financing interest and high-taxed income) or 904(d)(2)(C) (financial services income) and also meets the definition of foreign branch category income is foreign branch category income.

(iii) *Income arising from U.S. activities excluded from foreign branch category income.*—Gross income that is attributable to a foreign branch and that arises from activities carried out in the United States by any foreign branch, including income that is reflected on a foreign branch's separate books and records, is not assigned to the foreign branch category. Instead, such income is assigned to the general category or a specified separate category under the rules of this section. However, under paragraph (f)(2)(vi) of this section, gross income (including U.S. source gross income) attributable to activities carried on outside the United States by the foreign branch may be assigned to the foreign branch category by reason of a disregarded payment to a foreign branch from a foreign branch owner or another foreign branch that is allocable to income recorded on the books and records of the payor foreign branch or foreign branch owner.

(iv) *Income arising from stock excluded from foreign branch category income.*—(A) *In general.*—Except as provided in paragraph (f)(1)(iv)(B) of this section, gross income that is attributable to a foreign branch and that comprises items of income arising from stock of a corporation (whether foreign or domestic), including gain from the disposition of such stock or any inclusion under section 951(a), 951A, 1248, or 1293(a), is not assigned to the foreign branch category. Instead, such income is assigned to the general category or a specified separate category under the rules of this section.

(B) *Exception for dealer property.*—Paragraph (f)(1)(iv)(A) of this section does not apply to gain recognized from dispositions of stock of a corporation, if the stock would be dealer property (as defined in § 1.954-2(a)(4)(v)) if the foreign branch were a controlled foreign corporation.

(2) *Gross income attributable to a foreign branch.*—(i) *In general.*—Except as provided in this paragraph (f)(2), gross income is attributable to a foreign branch to the extent the gross income (as adjusted to conform to Federal income tax principles) is reflected on the separate set of books and records (as defined in § 1.989(a)-1(d)(1) and (2)) of the foreign branch. Gross income that is not attributable to the foreign branch and is therefore attributable to the foreign branch owner is income in a separate category (other than the foreign branch category) under the other rules of this section.

(ii) [Reserved]

(iii) [Reserved]

(iv) *Disposition of interests in certain entities.*—(A) *In general.*—Except as provided in paragraph (f)(2)(iv)(B) of this section, gross income attributable to a foreign branch does not include gain from the disposition of an interest in a partnership or other pass-through entity or an interest in a disregarded entity. See also paragraph (n)(2) of this section for general rules relating to the sale of a partnership interest.

(B) *Exception for sales by a foreign branch in the ordinary course of business.*—The rule in paragraph (f)(2)(iv)(A) of this section does not apply to gain from the sale or exchange of an interest in a partnership or other pass-through entity or an interest in a disregarded entity if the gain is reflected on the books and records of a foreign branch and the interest is held by the foreign branch in the ordinary course of its active trade or business. An interest is considered to be held in the ordinary course of the foreign branch's active trade or business only if the foreign branch—

(1) Directly engages in the same, or a related, trade or business as that partnership, other pass-through entity, or disregarded entity; and

(2) In the case of a partnership or other pass-through entity, the foreign branch owns 10 percent or more of the capital or profits interests in the partnership or other pass-through entity.

(v) *Adjustments to items of gross income reflected on the books and records.*—If a principal purpose of recording or failing to record an item of gross income on the books and records of a foreign branch, or of making or not making a disregarded payment described in paragraph (f)(2)(vi) of this section, is the avoidance of Federal income tax, the purposes of section 904, or the purposes of section 250 (in connection with section 250(b)(3)(A)(i)(VI)), the item must be attributed to one or more foreign branches or the foreign branch owner in a manner that reflects the substance of the transaction. For purposes of this paragraph (f)(2)(v), interest received by a foreign branch from a related person is presumed to be attributable to the foreign branch owner (and not to the foreign branch) unless the interest income meets the definition of financial services income under paragraph (e)(1)(ii) of this section. For purposes of this paragraph (f)(2)(v), a related person is any person that bears a relationship to the foreign branch owner described in section 267(b) or 707.

(vi) *Attribution of gross income to which disregarded payments are allocable.*—(A) *In general.*—If a foreign branch makes a disregarded payment to its foreign branch owner or a second foreign branch, and the disregarded payment is allocable to gross income that would be attributable to the foreign branch under the rules in paragraphs (f)(2)(i) through (v) of this section, the gross income attributable to the foreign branch is adjusted downward (but not below zero) to reflect the allocable amount of the disregarded payment, and the gross income attributable to the foreign branch owner or the second foreign branch is adjusted upward by the same amount as the downward adjustment, translated (if necessary) from the foreign branch's functional currency to U.S. dollars (or the second foreign branch's functional currency, as applicable) at the spot rate (as defined in § 1.988-1(d)) on the date of the disregarded payment. For rules addressing multiple disregarded payments in a taxable year, see paragraph (f)(2)(vi)(F) of this section. Similarly, if a foreign branch owner makes a disregarded payment to its foreign branch and the disregarded payment is allocable to gross income attributable to the foreign branch owner, the gross income attributable to the foreign branch owner is adjusted downward (but not below zero) to reflect the allocable amount of the disregarded payment, and the gross income attributable to the foreign branch is adjusted upward by the same amount as the downward adjustment, translated (if necessary) from U.S. dollars to the foreign branch's functional currency at the spot rate on the date of the disregarded payment. An adjustment to the amount of attributable gross income under this paragraph (f)(2)(vi) does not change the total amount, character, or source of the United States person's gross income; does not change the amount of a United States person's income in any separate category other than the foreign branch and general categories (or a specified separate category associated with the foreign branch and general categories); and has no bearing on the analysis of whether an item of gross income is eligible to be resourced under an income tax treaty.

(B) *Allocation of disregarded payments.—(1) In general.*—Except as provided in paragraph (f)(2)(vi)(B)(2) of this section, whether a disregarded payment is allocable to gross income attributable to a foreign branch or gross income attributable to its foreign branch owner, and the source and separate category of the gross income to which the disregarded payment is allocable, is determined under the following rules:

(i) Disregarded payments from a foreign branch owner to its foreign branch are allocable to gross income attributable to the foreign branch owner to the extent a deduction for that payment or any disregarded cost recovery deduction relating to that payment, if regarded, would be allocated and apportioned to gross income attributable to the foreign branch owner under the principles of §§1.861-8 through 1.861-14T and 1.861-17 (without regard to exclusive apportionment) by treating foreign source gross income and U.S. source gross income in each separate category (determined prior to the application of this paragraph (f)(2)(vi) to the disregarded payment at issue) each as a statutory grouping; and

(ii) Disregarded payments from a foreign branch to its foreign branch owner or to another foreign branch are allocable to gross income attributable to the payor foreign branch to the extent a deduction for that payment or any disregarded cost recovery deduction relating to that payment, if regarded, would be allocated and apportioned to gross income attributable to the payor foreign branch under the principles of §§1.861-8 through 1.861-14T and 1.861-17 (without regard to exclusive apportionment) by treating foreign source gross income and U.S. source gross income in each separate category (determined before the application of this paragraph (f)(2)(vi) to the disregarded payment at issue) each as a statutory grouping.

(2) Special rule for certain disregarded payments.—Whether a disregarded payment made in connection with a sale or exchange of property is allocable to gross income attributable to a foreign branch or its foreign branch owner, and the source and separate category of the gross income to which the disregarded payment is allocable, is determined under the following rules:

(i) Except as provided in paragraph (f)(2)(vi)(D) of this section, disregarded payments from a foreign branch owner to its foreign branch in respect of non-inventory property are allocable to the gross income attributable to the foreign branch owner, if any, that is recognized with respect to a regarded sale or exchange of that property (including gross income arising in a later taxable year) to the extent of the adjusted disregarded gain with respect to the transferred property, and in the same proportions as the source and separate category of the gain recognized on the regarded sale or exchange of the transferred property;

(ii) Except as provided in paragraph (f)(2)(vi)(D) of this section, disregarded payments from a foreign branch to its foreign branch owner or to another foreign branch in respect of non-inventory property are allocable to the gross income attributable to the foreign branch, if any, that is recognized with respect to a regarded sale or exchange of that property (including gross income arising in a later taxable year) to the extent of the adjusted disregarded gain with respect to the transferred property, and in the same proportions as the source and separate category of the gain recognized on the regarded sale or exchange of the transferred property; and

(iii) The principles of paragraphs (f)(2)(vi)(B)(2)(*i*) and (*ii*) of this section apply in the case of disregarded payments in respect of inventory property between a foreign branch and its foreign branch owner or between foreign branches to the extent the disregarded payment, if regarded, would, for purposes of determining gross income, be subtracted from gross receipts that are regarded for Federal income tax purposes.

(3) Timing of reattribution.—(i) In general.—The gross income attributable to the foreign branch is adjusted under paragraph (f)(2)(vi)(B)(*1*) of this section only in the taxable year that a disregarded payment, if regarded, would be allowed as a deduction (including by giving rise to disregarded cost recovery deductions), or otherwise would be taken into account as an increase to cost of goods sold.

(ii) Disregarded sales of property.—The gross income attributable to a foreign branch is adjusted under paragraph (f)(2)(vi)(B)(2) of this section only in the taxable year or years in which gain is recognized by reason of the disposition of property with an adjusted disregarded basis in a transaction that is regarded for Federal income tax purposes.

(C) *Exclusion of certain disregarded payments.*—Paragraph (f)(2)(vi)(A) of this section does not apply to the following payments, accruals, or other transfers between a foreign branch and its foreign branch owner, or between foreign branches, that are disregarded for Federal income tax purposes:

(1) Interest, and interest equivalents that, if regarded, would be described in §§1.861-9(b) and 1.861-9T(b);

(2) Remittances from the foreign branch to its foreign branch owner, except as provided in paragraph (f)(2)(vi)(D) of this section;

(3) Contributions of money, securities, and other property from the foreign branch owner to its foreign branch, except as provided in paragraph (f)(2)(vi)(D) of this section; or

(4) Any disregarded payment that, if made to a foreign branch and regarded for Federal income tax purposes, could not result in the attribution of gross income to a foreign branch (for example, the sale of an interest in a partnership by a foreign branch to its foreign branch owner, unless the sale or exchange occurred in the ordinary course of business within the meaning of paragraph (f)(2)(iv)(B) of this section).

(D) *Certain transfers of intangible property.—(1) In general.*—For purposes of applying this paragraph (f)(2)(vi), the amount of gross income attributable to a foreign branch (and the amount of gross income attributable to its foreign branch owner) must be adjusted under the principles of paragraph (f)(2)(vi)(B) of this section to reflect all transactions that are disregarded for Federal income tax purposes in which property described in section 367(d)(4) is transferred to or from a foreign branch or between foreign branches, whether or not a disregarded payment is made in connection with the transfer. In determining the amount of gross income that is attributable to a foreign branch that must be adjusted by reason of this paragraph (f)(2)(vi)(D), the principles of sections 367(d) and 482 apply. For example, if a foreign branch owner transfers property described in section 367(d)(4) to a foreign branch, the principles of section 367(d) are applied by treating the foreign branch as a separate foreign corporation to which the property is transferred in exchange for stock of the corporation in a transaction described in section 351. Similarly, if a foreign branch remits property described in section 367(d)(4) to its foreign branch owner, the foreign branch is treated as having sold the transferred property to the foreign branch owner in exchange for annual payments contingent on the productivity or use of the property, the amounts of which are determined under the principles of section 367(d).

(2) Transactions occurring before December 7, 2018.—Paragraph (f)(2)(vi)(D)(*1*) of this section does not apply to a disregarded transfer of property that occurred before December 7, 2018.

(3) Transitory ownership.—(i) In general.—Paragraph (f)(2)(vi)(D)(*1*) of this section does not apply to disregarded transfers of property by a foreign branch or a foreign branch owner (such foreign branch or foreign branch owner, the *limited transferor*), if the conditions in paragraphs (f)(2)(vi)(D)(*3*)(*ii*) and (*iii*) of this section are met.

(ii) Transitory ownership period.—The limited transferor's ownership of the property is transitory.

(iii) Use of property.—The limited transferor does not develop, exploit, or otherwise employ the property in a trade or business, other than in the ordinary course of the limited transferor's business during the period of transitory ownership.

(iv) Predecessors.—For purposes of paragraphs (f)(2)(vi)(D)(*3*)(*ii*) and (*iii*) of this section, a reference to a limited

transferor that is a foreign branch owner includes any predecessor to the foreign branch owner. No person is a predecessor with respect to a foreign branch under this paragraph (f)(2)(vi)(D)(*3*)(*iv*).

(E) *Amount of disregarded payments.*—The amount of each disregarded payment used to make an adjustment under this paragraph (f)(2)(vi) (or the absence of any adjustment) must be determined in a manner that results in the attribution of the proper amount of gross income to each of a foreign branch and its foreign branch owner under the principles of section 482, applied as if the foreign branch were a corporation.

(F) *Multiple disregarded payments.*—In the case of multiple disregarded payments, this paragraph (f)(2)(vi) is applied with respect to each disregarded payment, and under the ordering rules specified in paragraphs (f)(2)(vi)(F)(*1*) and (*2*) of this section. For purposes of this paragraph (f)(2)(vi), paragraph (f)(2)(vi)(F)(*1*) of this section applies before paragraph (f)(2)(vi)(F)(*2*) of this section.

(*1*) *Income initially attributable to a foreign branch.*—In applying this paragraph (f)(2)(vi) to gross income that would, but for this paragraph (f)(2)(vi), be attributable to a foreign branch, adjustments related to disregarded payments from a foreign branch to another foreign branch are computed first, followed by adjustments related to disregarded payments from a foreign branch to its foreign branch owner, followed by adjustments related to disregarded payments from a foreign branch owner to its foreign branch.

(*2*) *Income initially attributable to a foreign branch owner.*—In applying this paragraph (f)(2)(vi) to gross income that would, but for this paragraph (f)(2)(vi), be attributable to a foreign branch owner, adjustments related to disregarded payments from a foreign branch owner to a foreign branch are computed first, followed by adjustments related to disregarded payments from a foreign branch to another foreign branch, followed by adjustments related to disregarded payments from a foreign branch to its foreign branch owner.

(G) *Effect of disregarded payments made and received by non-branch taxable units.*—(*1*) *In general.*—For purposes of determining the amount, source, and character of gross income attributable to a foreign branch and its foreign branch owner under paragraph (f)(2) of this section, the rules of paragraph (f)(2) of this section apply to a non-branch taxable unit as though the non-branch taxable unit were a foreign branch or a foreign branch owner, as appropriate, to attribute gross income to the non-branch taxable unit and to further attribute, under this paragraph (f)(2)(vi)(G), the income of a non-branch taxable unit to one or more foreign branches or to a foreign branch owner. See paragraph (f)(4)(xvi) of this section (*Example 16*).

(*2*) *Foreign branch group income.*—The income of a foreign branch group is attributed to the foreign branch that owns the group. The income of a foreign branch group is the aggregate of the U.S. gross income that is attributed, under the rules of this paragraph (f)(2), to each member of the foreign branch group, determined after accounting for all disregarded payments made and received by each member of the foreign branch group.

(*3*) *Foreign branch owner group income.*—The income of a foreign branch owner group is attributed to the foreign branch owner that owns the group. The income of a foreign branch owner group income is the aggregate of the U.S. gross income that is attributed, under the rules of this paragraph (f)(2), to each member of the foreign branch owner group, determined after accounting for all disregarded payments made and received by each member of the foreign branch owner group.

(3) *Definitions.*—The following definitions apply for purposes of this paragraph (f).

(i) *Adjusted disregarded basis.*—The term *adjusted disregarded basis* means, with respect to property transferred in a transaction that is disregarded for Federal income tax purposes, the tentative disregarded basis of the property—

(A) Reduced by any disregarded cost recovery deductions with respect to the property; and

(B) Increased by any disregarded section 1016(a)(1) expenditures with respect to the property.

(ii) *Adjusted disregarded gain.*—(A) *In general.*—The term *adjusted disregarded gain* means, with respect to property transferred in a transaction that is disregarded for Federal income tax purposes, the lesser of—

(*1*) The adjusted disregarded basis of the property, reduced by the adjusted basis of the property at the time the property was transferred in a transaction that is disregarded for Federal income tax purposes; and

(*2*) The gain (if any) attributable to a regarded sale or exchange of the transferred property.

(B) *Limitation.*—Adjusted disregarded gain may not be less than zero.

(iii) *Disregarded cost recovery deduction.*—For a taxable year, the term *disregarded cost recovery deduction* means, with respect to property transferred in a transaction that is disregarded for Federal income tax purposes—

(A) The amounts that would be allowed as a deduction, and that would give rise to an adjustment described in section 1016(a)(2), with respect to the transferred property if the transfer (and the foreign branch) were regarded for Federal income tax purposes, to the extent that, under paragraph (f)(2)(vi)(B)(*1*) of this section, the deduction would be allocable to—

(*1*) Gross income attributable to a foreign branch owner, in the case of property transferred to a foreign branch owner; or

(*2*) Gross income attributable to a foreign branch, in the case of property transferred to a foreign branch; reduced by

(B) The amounts that are allowed as a deduction, and that give rise to an adjustment described in section 1016(a)(2), with respect to the transferred property to the extent that, under the principles of paragraph (f)(2)(vi)(B)(*1*) of this section, the deduction would be allocable to—

(*1*) Gross income attributable to a foreign branch owner, in the case of property transferred to a foreign branch owner; or

(*2*) Gross income attributable to a foreign branch, in the case of property transferred to a foreign branch.

(iv) *Disregarded entity.*—The term *disregarded entity* means an entity described in § 301.7701-2(c)(2) of this chapter that is disregarded as an entity separate from its owner for Federal income tax purposes.

(v) *Disregarded payment.*—A disregarded payment includes an amount of property (within the meaning of section 317(a)) that is transferred to or from a non-branch taxable unit, foreign branch, or foreign branch owner, including a payment in exchange for property or in satisfaction of an account payable, or a remittance or contribution, in connection with a transaction that is disregarded for Federal income tax purposes and that is reflected on the separate set of books and records of a non-branch taxable unit (other than an individual or domestic corporation) or a foreign branch. A disregarded payment also includes any other amount that is reflected on the separate set of books and records of a non-branch taxable unit (other than an individual or a domestic corporation) or a foreign branch in connection with a transaction that is disregarded for Federal income tax purposes and that would constitute an item of accrued income, gain, deduction, or loss of the non-branch taxable unit (other than an individual or a domestic corporation) or the foreign branch if the transaction to which the amount is attributable were regarded for Federal income tax purposes.

(vi) *Disregarded section 1016(a)(1) expenditure.*—The term *disregarded section 1016(a)(1) expenditure* means a disregarded payment that, if regarded for Federal income tax purposes, would be described in section 1016(a)(1) and that, under the principles of paragraph (f)(2)(vi)(B)(*1*) of this section, would be allocable to—

(A) General category gross income, in the case of property held by a foreign branch owner; or

(B) Foreign branch category income, in the case of property held by a foreign branch.

(vii) *Foreign branch.*—(A) *In general.*—The term *foreign branch* means a qualified business unit (QBU), as defined in § 1.989(a)-1(b)(2)(ii) and (b)(3), that conducts a trade or business outside the United States. For an illustration of the principles of this paragraph (f)(3)(vii), see paragraph (f)(4)(i) of this section (Example 1).

(B) *Trade or business outside the United States.*—Activities carried out in the United States, whether or not such activities are described in § 1.989(a)-1(b)(3), do not constitute the conduct of a trade or business outside the United States. Activities carried out outside the United States that constitute a permanent establishment under the terms of an income tax treaty between the United States and the country in which the activities are carried out constitute a trade or business conducted outside the United States for purposes of this paragraph (f)(3)(vii)(B). In determining whether activities constitute a trade or business under § 1.989(a)-1(c), disregarded payments are taken into account and may give rise to a trade or business, provided that the activities (together with any other activities of the QBU) would otherwise satisfy the rule in § 1.989(a)-1(c).

(C) *Activities of a partnership, estate, trust, or corporation.—(1) Treatment as a foreign branch.*—For purposes of this paragraph (f)(3)(vii), the activities of a partnership, estate, trust, or corporation that conducts a trade or business that satisfies the requirements of § 1.989(a)-1(b)(2)(ii)(A) (as modified by paragraph (f)(3)(vii)(B) of this section) are—

(*i*) Deemed to satisfy the requirements of § 1.989(a)-1(b)(2)(ii)(B); and

(*ii*) Comprise a foreign branch.

(*2*) *Separate set of books and records.*—A foreign branch described in this paragraph (f)(3)(vii)(C) is treated as maintaining a separate set of books and records with respect to the activities described in paragraph (f)(3)(vii)(C)(*1*) of this section, and must determine, as the context requires, the items of gross income, disregarded payments, and any other items that would be reflected on those books and records in applying this paragraph (f) with respect to the foreign branch. The principles of § 1.1503(d)-5(c) apply for purposes of determining which items would be reflected on such books and records.

(viii) *Foreign branch group.*—The term *foreign branch group* means a foreign branch and any non-branch taxable units (other than an individual or a domestic corporation), to the extent that the foreign branch owns the non-branch taxable unit (if any) directly or indirectly through one or more other non-branch taxable units.

(ix) *Foreign branch owner.*—The term *foreign branch owner* means, with respect to a foreign branch, the person (including a foreign or domestic partnership or other pass-through entity) that owns the foreign branch, either directly or indirectly through one or more disregarded entities. For purposes of this paragraph (f)(3)(ix), the foreign branch owner does not include the foreign branch or another foreign branch of the person that owns the foreign branch.

(x) *Foreign branch owner group.*—The term *foreign branch owner group* means a foreign branch owner and any non-branch taxable units (other than an individual or a domestic corporation), to the extent that the foreign branch owner owns the non-branch taxable unit (if any) directly or indirectly through one or more other non-branch taxable units.

(xi) *Non-branch taxable unit.*—The term *non-branch taxable unit* has the meaning provided in § 1.904-6(b)(2)(i)(B).

(xii) *Remittance.*—The term *remittance* means a transfer of property (within the meaning of section 317(a)) by a foreign branch that would be treated as a distribution if the foreign branch were treated as a separate corporation.

(xiii) *Tentative disregarded basis.*—The term *tentative disregarded basis* means, in connection with the transfer of property in a transaction that is disregarded for Federal income tax purposes, the basis that property would have if the disregarded payment made in exchange for the transferred property were treated as the cost of such property under section 1012(a).

(4) *Examples.*—The following examples illustrate the application of this paragraph (f).

(i) *Example 1: Determination of foreign branches and foreign branch owner.*—(A) *Facts*—(*1*) P, a domestic corporation, is a partner in PRS, a domestic partnership. All other partners in PRS are unrelated to P. PRS conducts activities solely in Country A (the Country A Business), and those activities constitute a trade or business outside the United States within the meaning of paragraph (f)(3)(vii)(B) of this section. PRS reflects items of income, gain, loss, and expense of the Country A Business on the books and records of PRS's home office. PRS is in the business of manufacturing bicycles.

(*2*) PRS owns FDE1, a disregarded entity organized in Country B. FDE1 conducts activities in Country B (the Country B Business), and those activities constitute a trade or business outside the United States within the meaning of paragraph (f)(3)(vii)(B) of this section. FDE1 maintains a set of books and records that are separate from those of PRS, and the separate set of books and records reflects items of income, gain, loss, and expense with respect to the Country B Business. FDE1 is in the business of selling bicycles manufactured by PRS.

(*3*) FDE1 owns FDE2, a disregarded entity organized in Country C. FDE2 conducts activities in Country C (the Country C Business), and those activities constitute a trade or business outside the United States within the meaning of paragraph (f)(3)(vii)(B) of this section. FDE2 maintains a set of books and records that are separate from those of PRS and FDE1, and the separate set of books and records reflects items of income, gain, loss, and expense with respect to the Country C Business. FDE2's paper business is not related to FDE1's bicycle sales business, and FDE1 does not hold its interest in FDE2 in the ordinary course of its trade or business.

(B) *Analysis*—(*1*) Country A Business's activities comprise a trade or business conducted outside the United States within the meaning of § 1.989(a)-1(b)(2)(ii)(A) and (b)(3) (in each case, as modified by paragraph (f)(3)(vii) of this section). PRS does not maintain a separate set of books and records with respect to the Country A Business. However, under paragraph (f)(3)(vii)(C) of this section, the Country A Business's activities are deemed to satisfy the requirement of § 1.989(a)-1(b)(2)(ii)(B) that a QBU maintain a separate set of books and records with respect to the relevant activities. Thus, for purposes of this paragraph (f), the activities of the Country A Business constitute a QBU as defined in § 1.989-1(b)(2)(ii) and (b)(3), as modified by paragraph (f)(3)(vii) of this section, that conducts a trade or business outside the United States. Accordingly, the activities of the Country A Business constitute a foreign branch within the meaning of paragraph (f)(3)(vii) of this section. PRS, the person that owns the Country A Business, is the foreign branch owner, within the meaning of paragraph (f)(3)(ix) of this section, with respect to the Country A Business.

(*2*) Country B Business's activities comprise a trade or business outside the United States within the meaning of § 1.989(a)-1(b)(2)(ii)(A) and (b)(3) (in each case, as modified by paragraph (f)(3)(vii) of this section). PRS maintains a separate set of books and records with respect to the Country B Business, as described in § 1.989(a)-1(b)(2)(ii)(B). Thus, for purposes of this section, the activities of the Country B Business constitute a QBU as defined in § 1.989-1(b)(2)(ii) and (b)(3), as modified by paragraph (f)(3)(vii) of this section, that conducts a trade or business outside the United States. Accordingly, the activities of the Country B Business constitute a foreign branch within the meaning of paragraph (f)(3)(vii) of this section. Under paragraph (f)(3)(ix) of this section, PRS, the person that owns the Country B Business indirectly through FDE1 (a disregarded entity), is the foreign branch owner with respect to the Country B Business.

(*3*) The same analysis that applies to the Country B Business applies to the Country C Business. Accordingly, the activities of the Country C Business constitute a foreign branch within the meaning of paragraph (f)(3)(vii) of this section. PRS, the person that owns the Country C Business indirectly through FDE1 and FDE2 (disregarded entities), is the foreign branch owner with respect to the Country C Business.

(ii) *Example 2: Sale of foreign branch.*—(A) *Facts.* The facts are the same as in paragraph (f)(4)(i)(A) of this section (the facts in *Example 1*), except that in Year 1, FDE1 sells FDE2 to an unrelated person, recording gain from the sale on its books and records. In Year 2, PRS sells FDE1 to another unrelated person, recording gain from the sale on its books and records. In each year, PRS allocates a portion of the gain to P.

(B) *Analysis*—(*1*) *Sale of FDE2.* Under paragraph (f)(1)(i)(B) of this section, P's distributive share of gain recognized by PRS in connection with the sales of FDE1 and FDE2 constitutes foreign branch category income if it is attributable to a foreign branch held by PRS directly or indirectly through one or more disregarded entities. PRS's gross income from the Year 1 sale of FDE2 is reflected on the separate set of books and records maintained with respect to the Country B Business (a foreign branch) operated by FDE1. Therefore, absent an exception, under paragraph (f)(2)(i) of this section PRS's gross income from the sale of FDE2 would be attributable to the Country B Business, and would constitute foreign branch category income. However, under paragraph (f)(2)(iv) of this section, gross income attributable to the Country B Business does not include gain from the sale or exchange of an interest in FDE2, a disregarded entity, unless the interest in FDE2 is held by the Country B Business in the ordinary course of its active trade or business (within the meaning of paragraph (f)(2)(iv)(B) of this section). In this case, the Country B Business does not hold FDE2 in the ordinary course of its active trade or business within the meaning of paragraph (f)(2)(iv)(B) of this section. As a result, P's distributive share of gain from the sale of FDE2 is not attributable to a foreign branch, and is not foreign branch category income.

(2) *Sale of FDE1*. The analysis of PRS's sale of FDE1 in Year 2 is the same as the analysis for the sale of FDE2, except that PRS, through its Country A Business, holds FDE1 in the ordinary course of its active trade or business within the meaning of paragraph (f)(2)(iv)(B) of this section because the Country A Business engages in a trade or business that is related to the trade or business of FDE1. Therefore, P's distributive share of gain from the sale of FDE1 is attributable to a foreign branch, and is foreign branch category income.

(iii) *Example 3: Disregarded payment for services*.—(A) *Facts*. P, a domestic corporation, owns FDE, a disregarded entity that is a foreign branch within the meaning of paragraph (f)(3)(vii) of this section. FDE's functional currency is the U.S. dollar. In Year 1, P accrues and records on its books and records (and not FDE's books and records) $1,000x of gross income from the performance of services to unrelated parties that is not passive category income, $400x of which is foreign source income in respect of services performed outside the United States by employees of FDE and $600x of which is U.S. source income in respect of services performed in the United States. Absent the application of paragraph (f)(2)(vi) of this section, the $1,000x of gross income earned by P would be general category income that would not be attributable to FDE. FDE provides services in support of P's gross income from services. P compensates FDE for its services with an arm's length payment of $400x, which is disregarded for Federal income tax purposes. The deduction for the payment of $400x from P to FDE would be allocated to P's $1,000x of general category gross services income and apportioned entirely to the $400x of foreign source services income under §§1.861-8 and 1.861-8T principles (treating foreign source general category gross income and U.S. source general category gross income each as a statutory grouping) if the payment were regarded for Federal income tax purposes.

(B) *Analysis*. The disregarded payment from P, a United States person, to FDE, its foreign branch, is not recorded on FDE's separate books and records (as adjusted to conform to Federal income tax principles) within the meaning of paragraph (f)(2)(i) of this section because it is disregarded for Federal income tax purposes. However, the disregarded payment is allocable to gross income attributable to P because a deduction for the payment, if it were regarded, would be allocated and apportioned to the $400x of P's foreign source services income. Accordingly, under paragraphs (f)(2)(vi)(A) and (f)(2)(vi)(B)(*3*) of this section, the amount of gross income attributable to the FDE foreign branch (and the gross income attributable to P) is adjusted in Year 1 to take the disregarded payment into account. As such, $400x of P's foreign source gross income from the performance of services is attributable to the FDE foreign branch for purposes of this section. Therefore, $400x of the foreign source gross income that P earned with respect to its services in Year 1 constitutes gross income that is assigned to the foreign branch category.

(iv) *Example 4: Disregarded payment for non-inventory property*.—(A) *Facts*. P, a domestic corporation, owns FDE, a disregarded entity that is a foreign branch within the meaning of paragraph (f)(3)(vii) of this section. FDE's functional currency is the U.S. dollar. P holds Asset A, a non-depreciable asset, with an adjusted basis of $200x. In Year 1, P sells Asset A, which will be used in FDE's manufacturing business, to FDE for $500x. FDE makes no other disregarded payments with respect to Asset A. No adjustments described in section 1016(a) apply with respect to Asset A while FDE holds Asset A. In Year 3, FDE sells Asset A to a third party for $600x and reflects $400x of gross income on its separate set of books and records (that is, $600x amount realized less Asset A's $200x adjusted basis). Under sections 865(e)(1) and 904(d)(2)(B)(i), the income arising from the sale of Asset A is foreign source income that is not treated as passive category income. Asset A is not inventory property. Absent the application of paragraph (f)(2)(vi) of this section, the entire $400x of gross income earned by P by reason of FDE's sale of Asset A would be attributable to FDE and be treated as foreign branch category income.

(B) *Analysis*—(*1*) *Disregarded basis determinations*. If regarded, the $500x payment from FDE to P would result in FDE holding Asset A with a basis of $500x under section 1012. Accordingly, the tentative disregarded basis (within the meaning of paragraph (f)(3)(xiii) of this section) with respect to Asset A is $500x. Because there are no adjustments described in section 1016 with respect to Asset A (including any adjustments resulting from any disregarded payments made with respect to the transferred property), the adjusted disregarded basis (within the meaning of paragraph (f)(3)(i) of this section) with respect to Asset A is $500x.

(*2*) *Adjusted disregarded gain*. Under paragraph (f)(3)(ii) of this section, the adjusted disregarded gain with respect to Asset A is $300x, which is equal to the lesser of $300x (FDE's adjusted disregarded basis in Asset A ($500x) less the adjusted basis of Asset A at the time that Asset A was transferred to FDE ($200x)) and $400x (the gain (if any) attributable to the regarded sale or exchange of Asset A).

(*3*) *Attribution of gross income*. Under paragraph (f)(2)(vi)(A) of this section, the gross income attributable to FDE ($400x) is adjusted downward to the extent that the $500x disregarded payment from FDE to P is allocable to gross income of FDE that is reflected on FDE's separate set of books and records. Under paragraph (f)(2)(vi)(B)(*2*)(*ii*) of this section, the $500x payment from FDE to P is allocable to gross income attributable to FDE to the extent of FDE's adjusted disregarded gain ($300x) with respect to Asset A. The source and separate category of the gross income of FDE to which the payment is allocable is proportionate to the source and separate category of the gain recognized by FDE with respect to Asset A. Accordingly, $300x of the payment is allocable to foreign source income that would be foreign branch category income. Thus, under paragraphs (f)(2)(vi)(A) and (f)(2)(vi)(B)(*3*) of this section, foreign source gross income attributable to P is adjusted upward by $300x (increasing foreign source general category income by $300x) and foreign source gross income attributable to FDE is adjusted downward by $300x (decreasing foreign source foreign branch category income by $300x) in Year 3.

(v) *Example 5: Disregarded payment for depreciable non-inventory property*.—(A) *Facts*. The facts are the same as in paragraph (f)(4)(iv)(A) of this section (the facts in *Example 4*), except as set forth in this paragraph (f)(4)(v)(A). Asset A is depreciable property. In Year 2, P is entitled to a $20x depreciation deduction with respect to Asset A, $18x of which is allocated and apportioned to non-passive category gross income attributable to FDE under §§1.861-8 through 1.861-14T and $2x of which is allocated and apportioned to passive category gross income under §§1.861-8 through 1.861-14T. If the transfer of Asset A were regarded for Federal income tax purposes, FDE would be entitled to a $50x depreciation deduction, 90% of which would be allocated and apportioned to non-passive category gross income attributable to FDE under §§1.861-8 through 1.861-14T and 10% of which would be allocated and apportioned to passive category gross income under §§1.861-8 through 1.861-14T. In Year 2, FDE earns $315x of gross income that it reflects on its books and records that, in the absence of paragraph (f)(2)(vi) of this section, would be foreign branch category income. FDE also earns $35x of passive category income in Year 2 from the non-active rental of a portion of Asset A. In Year 3, FDE reflects $420x of gross income on its separate set of books and records by reason of the sale of Asset A (that is, $600x amount realized less Asset A's $180x adjusted basis), $42x of which is passive category income under paragraph (b) of this section.

(B) *Analysis*—(*1*) *Attribution of gross income in Year 2*. The disregarded payment from FDE to P in Year 1 is disregarded for Federal income tax purposes, and does not generate gross income. However, under paragraph (f)(2)(vi)(B)(*1*)(*ii*) of this section, the disregarded payment is allocable to gross income attributable to FDE to the extent of any disregarded cost recovery deduction relating to that payment in Year 2. Under paragraph (f)(3)(iii) of this section, the disregarded cost recovery deduction with respect to Asset A is $30x, which is $50x (the amount that would be allowed as a deduction, and that would give rise to an adjustment described in section 1016(a)(2), with respect to Asset A if the transfer of Asset A to FDE were regarded for Federal income tax purposes, to the extent that the deduction would be allocable to income attributable to a foreign branch), reduced by $20x (the amount allowed as a deduction, and that gives rise to an adjustment described in section 1016(a)(2), with respect to Asset A, to the extent allocable to income attributable to a foreign branch). If regarded, $27x (90% of $30x) of the disregarded cost recovery deduction would be allocated and apportioned to non-passive category gross income attributable to FDE under §§1.861-8 through 1.861-14T and $3x (10% of $30x) would be allocated and apportioned to passive category gross income under §§1.861-8 through 1.861-14T. Accordingly, under paragraphs (f)(2)(vi)(A) and (f)(2)(vi)(B)(*3*) of this section, the $315x of non-passive category gross income that would otherwise be attributed to FDE is reduced to $288x ($315x less $27x), and the non-passive category gross income attributable to P is increased by $27x in Year 2. As a result, in Year 2, P's foreign branch category gross income is $288x, and its general category gross income is increased by $27x. P's passive category gross income is $35x. *See* paragraphs (f)(1)(ii) and (f)(2)(vi)(A) of this section.

(2) *Attribution of gross income in Year 3*—(i) *Adjusted disregarded basis*. If regarded, the $500x payment from FDE to P would result in FDE holding Asset A with a basis of $500x under section 1012. Accordingly, the tentative disregarded basis (within the meaning of paragraph (f)(3)(xiii) of this section) with respect to Asset A is $500x. To determine FDE's adjusted disregarded basis with respect to Asset A under paragraph (f)(3)(i) of this section, FDE's tentative disregarded basis is reduced by $30x (the disregarded cost recovery deduction with respect to Asset A), resulting in an adjusted disregarded basis of $470x.

(*ii*) *Adjusted disregarded gain*. Under paragraph (f)(3)(ii) of this section, the adjusted disregarded gain with respect to Asset A is $270x, which is equal to the lesser of $270x (FDE's adjusted disregarded basis in Asset A ($470x) less the adjusted basis of Asset A at the time that Asset A was transferred to FDE ($200x)), and $420x (the gain attributable to the regarded sale or exchange of Asset A).

(*iii*) *Sale of Asset A*. Under paragraph (f)(2)(vi)(A) of this section, the gross income attributable to FDE ($420x) by reason of the sale of Asset A is adjusted downward to the extent that the $500x disregarded payment from FDE to P is allocable to gross income that would be attributable to FDE under paragraphs (f)(2)(i) through (v) of this section. Under paragraph (f)(2)(vi)(B)(2)(*ii*) of this section, the $500x payment from FDE to P is allocable to gross income attributable to FDE to the extent of the adjusted disregarded gain with respect to Asset A, which is $270x. The source and separate category of the gross income of FDE to which that amount is allocable is proportionate to the source and separate category of the $420x of gain recognized on the regarded sale of Asset A ($378x of foreign source non-passive category income and $42x of foreign source passive category income). Consequently, under paragraphs (f)(2)(vi)(A) and (f)(2)(vi)(B)(3) of this section, in Year 3, gross income attributable to P is adjusted upward by $270x (increasing P's foreign source general category gross income by $243x, which bears the same proportion to $270x as the foreign source non-passive gain ($378x) bears to P's overall gain with respect to Asset A ($420x)), and the foreign source gross income attributable to FDE is adjusted downward by $270x (with foreign source foreign branch category gross income reduced by $243x). P also has $42x of foreign source passive category income from the sale of Asset A. *See* paragraphs (f)(1)(ii) and (f)(2)(vi)(A) of this section.

(vi) *Example 6: Disregarded payment for non-depreciable non-inventory property — regarded gain limitation*.—(A) *Facts*. The facts are the same as in paragraph (f)(4)(iv)(A) of this section (the facts in *Example 4*), except that in Year 3, FDE sells Asset A to a third party for $340x and reflects $140x of gross income on its separate set of books and records (that is, $340x amount realized less Asset A's $200x adjusted basis), none of which is passive category income.

(B) *Analysis*. The analysis is the same as the analysis in paragraph (f)(4)(iv)(B) of this section (the analysis in *Example 4*), except that in Year 3, the adjusted disregarded gain with respect to Asset A is $140x, which is equal to the lesser of $300x (FDE's adjusted disregarded basis in Asset A ($500x) less the adjusted basis of Asset A at the time that Asset A was transferred to FDE ($200x)), and $140x (the gain attributable to the regarded sale or exchange of Asset A). Accordingly, under paragraphs (f)(2)(vi)(A) and (f)(2)(vi)(B)(3) of this section, gross income attributable to P is adjusted upward by $140x (increasing P's foreign source general category gross income by $140x) and gross income attributable to FDE is adjusted downward by $140x (decreasing P's foreign source foreign branch category gross income by $140x) in Year 3.

(vii) *Example 7: Disregarded payment for non-depreciable non-inventory property — loss*.—(A) *Facts*. The facts are the same as in paragraph (f)(4)(iv)(A) of this section (the facts in *Example 4*), except that in Year 3, FDE sells Asset A to a third party for $175x and reflects a $25x loss on its separate set of books and records (that is, $175x amount realized less Asset A's $200x adjusted basis).

(B) *Analysis*. The analysis is the same as the analysis in paragraph (f)(4)(iv)(B) of this section (the analysis in *Example 4*), except that in Year 3, the adjusted disregarded gain with respect to Asset A is $0x, which is equal to the lesser of $300x (FDE's adjusted disregarded basis in Asset A ($500x) less the adjusted basis of Asset A at the time that Asset A was transferred to FDE ($200x)), and $0x (the gain attributable to the regarded sale or exchange of Asset A). Accordingly, gross income amounts attributable to P and FDE are not adjusted under paragraph (f)(2)(vi)(A) of this section by reason of the transfer of Asset A from P to FDE.

(viii) *Example 8: Disregarded payment for non-depreciable non-inventory property — disregarded gain limitation*.—(A) *Facts*. The facts are the same as in paragraph (f)(4)(iv)(A) of this section (the facts in *Example 4*), except that in Year 1, P sells Asset A to FDE for $65x.

(B) *Analysis*. The analysis is the same as the analysis in paragraph (f)(4)(iv)(B) of this section (the analysis in *Example 4*), except that in Year 3, the tentative disregarded basis and the adjusted disregarded basis with respect to Asset A are $65x. Under paragraph (f)(3)(ii)(B) of this section, the adjusted disregarded gain with respect to Asset A is $0x. Accordingly, under paragraph (f)(2)(vi)(A) of this section, gross income amounts attributable to P and FDE are not adjusted under paragraph (f)(2)(vi)(A) of this section by reason of the transfer of Asset A from P to FDE.

(ix) *Example 9: Application of the rules to the sale of inventory from a foreign branch owner to a foreign branch for distribution*.—(A) *Facts*. P, a domestic corporation, owns FDE, a disregarded entity that is a foreign branch within the meaning of paragraph (f)(3)(vii) of this section. FDE's functional currency is the U.S. dollar. P manufactures portable electronic devices, which it sells to FDE for $1,500x during a taxable year in a transaction that is disregarded for Federal income tax purposes. In the same taxable year, FDE sells the portable electronic devices to its customers for $1,750x. P uses an overall accrual method of accounting and has $1,300x of cost of goods sold for the taxable year, $1,200x of which were incurred prior to the disregarded sale to FDE and recorded on P's separate set of books and records and $100x of which were incurred after the disregarded sale and recorded on the books and records of FDE. P reports $450x of gross income for the taxable year: $1,750x of gross receipts less cost of goods sold of $1,300x. The $450x of gross income from the sale of portable electronic devices is U.S. source income under section 863(b).

(B) *Analysis*—(*1*) *In general*. The gross receipts from the sale of portable electronic devices ($1,750x), which results in U.S. source gross income of $450x, is recorded on FDE's separate books and records (as adjusted to conform to Federal income tax principles). Therefore, the gross income ($450x) generally would be foreign branch category income under paragraph (f)(2)(i) of this section. However, under paragraph (f)(2)(vi)(A) of this section, the amount of gross income attributable to FDE (and the gross income attributable to P) is adjusted to take the disregarded payment for the portable electronic devices from FDE to P into account. If both FDE and the disregarded payment from FDE to P were recognized for Federal income tax purposes, the amount of the payment ($1,500x) would reduce FDE's gross income. Therefore, under paragraph (f)(2)(vi)(B)(2)(*iii*) of this section, the principles of paragraph (f)(2)(vi)(B)(2)(*ii*) of this section apply for purposes of determining whether, and to what extent, the disregarded payment is allocable to non-passive category income attributable to FDE for purposes of determining the extent of any adjustment.

(*2*) *Applying the principles of the fungible property rules to sales of inventory*. The principles of paragraph (f)(2)(vi)(B)(2)(*ii*) of this section are applied by treating the cost of goods sold with respect to expenses recorded on P's separate set of books and records ($1,200x) similarly to the adjusted basis at the time of the disregarded sale; the gross income ($450x) similarly to gain from the disposition of non-inventory property; and the lesser of the recognized gross income ($450x) and the disregarded payment less the cost of goods sold attributable to expenses reflected on P's separate set of books and records ($1,500x less $1,200x) similarly to disregarded gain ($300x). Accordingly, under paragraph (f)(2)(vi)(A) of this section, general category U.S. source gross income attributable to P is adjusted upward by $300x and the non-passive category U.S. source gross income attributable to FDE is adjusted downward by $300x.

(x) *Example 10: Gross income initially attributable to a foreign branch*.—(A) *Facts*-(*1*) *Overview*. P, a domestic corporation, owns FDE, which is a disregarded entity that is a foreign branch within the meaning of paragraph (f)(3)(vii) of this section that has the U.S. dollar as its functional currency. P, which is a foreign branch owner with respect to FDE, also conducts a trade or business in the United States. During a single taxable year, P and FDE engage in the transactions described in paragraphs (f)(4)(x)(A)(2) and (3) of this section.

(*2*) *Unrelated party transactions*. P, through its U.S. office, accrues and records on its books and records $5,000x of gross income from the performance of accounting services for Customer A, an unrelated party (the Customer A services). The gross income from the Customer A services performed by P is non-passive category income and, under section 861(a)(3), is U.S. source income. Absent the application of paragraph (f)(2)(vi) of this section, the gross income earned by P through its U.S. office would be general category income. FDE accrues and records on its books and records $3,400x of gross income from the performance of web design services for Customer B, an unrelated party (the Customer B services). The gross income from the Customer B services performed by FDE is non-passive category income and, under section 862(a)(3), is foreign source income. Absent the application of paragraph (f)(2)(vi) of this section, the $3,400x of gross income earned by FDE would be foreign branch category income.

(3) *Disregarded payments*. FDE provides web design services to P. As compensation for those services, P pays $300x to FDE. The deduction for P's payment to FDE (if regarded) would be allocable to the $5,000x of general category U.S. source gross income earned from P's performance of the Customer A services. P provides accounting services to FDE from P's U.S. office. As compensation for those services, FDE pays $300x to P. The deduction for FDE's payment to P (if regarded) would be allocable to the $3,400x of non-passive category foreign source gross income earned from FDE's performance of the Customer B services.

(B) *Analysis—(1) Application of multiple disregarded payments rule*. Under paragraph (f)(2)(vi)(F) of this section, paragraph (f)(2)(vi) of this section applies to determine the effects of the disregarded payments described in paragraph (f)(4)(x)(A)(3) of this section on gross income initially attributable to FDE before paragraph (f)(2)(vi) of this section is applied to gross income initially attributable to P.

(2) *Disregarded payment from FDE to P*. The disregarded payment from FDE to P is disregarded for Federal income tax purposes, and does not generate gross income. However, the disregarded payment is allocable to non-passive category gross income attributable to FDE because a deduction for the payment, if it were regarded, would be allocated to FDE's $3,400x of non-passive category foreign source gross services income under § 1.861-8. Under paragraph (f)(2)(vi)(A) of this section, the amount of non-passive category foreign source gross income attributable to FDE is adjusted downward, and the amount of general category foreign source gross income attributable to P (in its capacity as a foreign branch owner) is adjusted upward, to take the disregarded payment into account. Thus, $300x of FDE's foreign source gross income relating to the Customer B services is attributable to P for purposes of this section, and $3,100x of that income is attributable to FDE.

(3) *Disregarded payment from P to FDE*. The disregarded payment from P to FDE is not recorded on FDE's separate books and records (as adjusted to conform to Federal income tax principles) within the meaning of paragraph (f)(2)(i) of this section because it is disregarded for Federal income tax purposes. However, the disregarded payment is allocable to general category U.S. source gross income attributable to P because a deduction for the payment, if it were regarded, would be allocated to P's $5,000x of general category U.S. source gross services income under § 1.861-8. Accordingly, under paragraph (f)(2)(vi)(A) of this section, the amount of general category U.S. source gross income attributable to P is adjusted downward, and the amount of non-passive category U.S. source gross income attributable to FDE is adjusted upward, to take the disregarded payment into account. Thus, $300x of P's U.S. source gross income from the performance of Customer A services is attributable to FDE for purposes of this section, and $4,700x of that income is attributable to P.

(xi) *Example 11: Ordering rule*.—(A) *Facts—(1) Overview*. P, a domestic corporation, owns FDE1 and FDE2, each of which is a disregarded entity that is a foreign branch within the meaning of paragraph (f)(3)(vii) of this section that has the U.S. dollar as its functional currency. P, which is a foreign branch owner with respect to FDE1 and FDE2, also conducts a trade or business in the United States. During a single taxable year, P, FDE1, and FDE2 engage in the transactions described in paragraphs (f)(4)(xi)(A)(2) and (3) of this section.

(2) *Unrelated party transactions*. FDE1 accrues and records on its books and records $1,000x of gross income from the performance of services for Customer A, an unrelated party (the Customer A services). The gross income from the Customer A services performed by FDE is non-passive category income and, under section 862(a)(3), is foreign source income. Absent the application of paragraph (f)(2)(vi) of this section, the $1,000x of non-passive foreign source gross income earned by FDE1 would be foreign branch category income. FDE2 accrues and records on its books and records $1,100x of gross income from royalties received from Customer B, an unrelated party (the Customer B royalties) on licensed intangible property developed by FDE2 and used by Customer B in the United States. The gross income from the Customer B royalties is non-passive category income and under section 861(a)(4) is U.S. source income. Absent the application of paragraph (f)(2)(vi) of this section, the $1,100x of non-passive category U.S. source gross income earned by FDE2 would be foreign branch category income.

(3) *Disregarded payments*. FDE2 provides services to FDE1. As compensation for those services, FDE1 pays $200x to FDE2. The deduction for FDE1's payment to FDE2 (if regarded) would be allocable to the $1,000x of non-passive category foreign source gross income earned from the Customer A services. P provides services to FDE2 from P's U.S. office. As compensation for those services, FDE2 pays $50x to P. The deduction for FDE2's payment to P (if regarded) would be allocable to the non-passive category foreign source gross income attributable to FDE2 (see paragraph (f)(4)(xi)(B)(*1*) of this section) relating to gross income from the Customer A services.

(B) *Analysis—(1) Disregarded payment from FDE1 to FDE2*. The $1,000x of gross income earned by FDE1 from the Customer A services would, but for paragraph (f)(2)(vi) of this section, be attributable to FDE1 (a foreign branch). Accordingly, under paragraph (f)(2)(vi)(F)(*1*) of this section, adjustments related to disregarded payments from FDE1 to FDE2 are computed before adjustments related to disregarded payments from FDE2 to P (in its capacity as a foreign branch owner). The disregarded payment from FDE1 to FDE2 is not recorded on FDE2's separate books and records (as adjusted to conform to Federal income tax principles) within the meaning of paragraph (f)(2)(i) of this section because it is disregarded for Federal income tax purposes. However, the disregarded payment is allocable to gross income attributable to FDE1 because a deduction for the payment, if it were regarded, would be allocated to FDE1's $1,000x of non-passive category foreign source gross services income under § 1.861-8. Accordingly, under paragraph (f)(2)(vi)(A) of this section, the amount of non-passive category foreign source gross income attributable to FDE1 is adjusted downward, and the amount of non-passive category foreign source gross income attributable to FDE2 is adjusted upward, to take the disregarded payment into account. Thus, $200x of FDE1's non-passive category foreign source gross income from the performance of Customer A services is attributable to FDE2 for purposes of this section, and $800x of that income is attributable to FDE1.

(2) *Disregarded payment from FDE2 to P*. The disregarded payment from FDE2 to P is disregarded for Federal income tax purposes, and does not generate gross income. However, the disregarded payment is allocable to gross income attributable to FDE2 because a deduction for the payment, if it were regarded, would be allocated to FDE2's $200x of non-passive category foreign source gross services income under § 1.861-8. Under paragraph (f)(2)(vi)(A) of this section, the amount of non-passive category foreign source gross income attributable to FDE2 is adjusted downward, and the amount of general category foreign source gross income attributable to P is adjusted upward, to take the $50x disregarded payment into account. Thus, $50x of non-passive category foreign source gross income relating to the Customer A services is attributable to P for purposes of this section, $150x of that income is attributable to FDE2, and $800x of that income remains attributable to FDE1. FDE2's $1,100x of U.S. source royalty income is not adjusted under paragraph (f)(2)(vi) of this section and remains foreign branch category income.

(xii) *Example 12: Application of intangible property rules*.—(A) *Facts*. P, a domestic corporation that has a calendar taxable year, owns FDE, a disregarded entity that is a foreign branch within the meaning of paragraph (f)(3)(vii) of this section. FDE's functional currency is the U.S. dollar. Asset A, a patent with a useful life ending on December 31, Year 2, was obtained with respect to a discovery that was made by FDE in the course of its trade or business and was used in that trade or business until December 31, Year 1. On December 31, Year 1, FDE remits Asset A to P and receives no consideration. Asset A has an adjusted basis of $0. In Year 2, P uses Asset A to generate general category gross income. P earns $1,000x of general category U.S. source gross income in Year 2, including the income generated by its use of Asset A. If FDE were a domestic corporation, P were a foreign corporation, and Asset A had been transferred in exchange for stock in a transaction described in section 351, such that section 367(d) applied by its terms (but all other facts remained the same), the payment determined under section 367(d) for Year 2 would be $300x. A disregarded payment for the use of Asset A, if it were regarded, would be allocated to FDE's $1,000x of general category U.S. source gross income under § 1.861-8.

(B) *Analysis*. The remittance of Asset A by FDE to P is a transfer of intangible property described in section 367(d)(4) from a foreign branch to its foreign branch owner. The facts in paragraph (f)(4)(xii)(A) of this section do not implicate an exception in paragraph (f)(2)(vi)(D)(*2*) or (*3*) of this section. Therefore, this is a transaction to which paragraph (f)(2)(vi)(D)(*1*) of this section applies. The foreign branch is treated as having sold the transferred property to the foreign branch owner in exchange for annual payments contingent on the productivity or use of the property, the amount of which for Year 2 is determined under the principles of section 367(d) to be $300x. Thus, in Year 2, P is treated as making a $300x disregarded payment to FDE. The payment would be allocable to general category U.S. source income under paragraph (f)(2)(vi)(B)(*1*)(*i*) of this section. Therefore, $300x of P's non-passive category U.S. source gross income is attributable to FDE under paragraphs (f)(2)(vi)(A) and (f)(2)(vi)(B)(*3*) of this section. P has $700x of general category U.S. source gross income and $300x of foreign branch category U.S. source gross income in Year 2.

(xiii) *Example 13: Disregarded payment from domestic corporation to foreign branch.*—(A) *Facts.* P, a domestic corporation, owns FDE, a disregarded entity that is a foreign branch. FDE's functional currency is the U.S. dollar. In Year 1, P accrues and records on its books and records for Federal income tax purposes $400x of gross income from the license of intellectual property to unrelated parties that is not passive category income, all of which is U.S. source income. P also accrues $600x of foreign source passive category interest income. P compensates FDE for services that FDE performs in a foreign country with an arm's length payment of $350x, which FDE records on its books and records; the transaction is disregarded for Federal income tax purposes. Absent the application of paragraph (f)(2)(vi) of this section, the $400x of gross income earned by P from the license would be general category income that would not be attributable to FDE. If the $350x disregarded payment from P to FDE were regarded for Federal income tax purposes, the deduction for the payment would be allocated and apportioned entirely to P's $400x of general category gross licensing income under the principles of §§1.861-8 and 1.861-8T (treating U.S. source general category gross income and foreign source passive category gross income each as a statutory grouping). P and FDE incur no other expenses.

(B) *Analysis.* The $350x disregarded payment from P, a United States person, to FDE, its foreign branch, is not recorded on FDE's separate books and records (as adjusted to conform to Federal income tax principles) under paragraph (f)(2)(i) of this section because it is disregarded for Federal income tax purposes. The disregarded payment is allocable to gross income attributable to P because a deduction for the payment, if it were regarded, would be allocated and apportioned to the $400x of P's U.S. source licensing income. Accordingly, under paragraphs (f)(2)(vi)(A) and (f)(2)(vi)(B)(*3*) of this section, the amount of gross income attributable to the FDE foreign branch (and the gross income attributable to P) is adjusted in Year 1 to take the disregarded payment into account. Accordingly, $350x of P's $400x U.S. source general category gross income from the license is attributable to the FDE foreign branch for purposes of this section. Therefore, $350x of the U.S. source gross income that P earned with respect to its license in Year 1 constitutes U.S. source gross income that is assigned to the foreign branch category and $50x remains U.S. source general category income. P's $600x of foreign source passive category interest income is unchanged.

(xiv) *Example 14: Regarded payment from non-consolidated domestic corporation to a foreign branch.*—(A) *Facts.* The facts are the same as those in paragraph (f)(4)(xiii)(A) of this section (the facts in *Example 13*), except P wholly owns USS, and USS (rather than P) owns FDE. P and USS do not file a consolidated return. USS has no gross income other than the $350x foreign source services income from the $350x payment it receives from P, through FDE.

(B) *Analysis.* The $350x services payment from P, a United States person, to FDE, a foreign branch of USS, is not a disregarded payment because the transaction is regarded for Federal income tax purposes. Under §§1.861-8 and 1.861-8T, P's $350x deduction for the services payment is allocated and apportioned to its U.S. source general category gross income. The payment of $350x from P to USS is services income attributable to FDE, and foreign branch category income of USS under paragraph (f)(2)(i) of this section. Accordingly, USS has $350x of foreign source foreign branch category gross income. P has $600x of foreign source passive category income and $400x of U.S. source general category gross income and a $350x deduction for the services payment, resulting in $50x of U.S. source general category taxable income to P.

(xv) *Example 15: Regarded payment from a member of a consolidated group to a foreign branch of another member of the consolidated group.*—(A) *Facts.* The facts are the same as those in paragraph (f)(4)(xiv)(A) of this section (the facts in *Example 14*), except that P and USS are members of an affiliated group that files a consolidated return pursuant to section 1502 (P group).

(B) *Analysis*—(*1*) *Definitions under §1.1502-13.* Under §1.1502-13(b)(1), the $350x services payment from P to FDE, a foreign branch of USS, is an intercompany transaction between P and USS; USS is the selling member, P is the buying member, P has a deduction of $350x for the services payment that is a corresponding item, and USS has $350x of income that is an intercompany item. The payment is not a disregarded payment because the transaction is regarded for Federal income tax purposes.

(*2*) *Timing and attributes under §1.1502-13*—(*i*) *Separate entity versus single entity analysis.* Under a separate entity analysis, the result is the same as in paragraph (f)(4)(xiv)(B) of this section (the analysis in *Example 14*), whereby P has $600x of foreign source passive category income and $50x of U.S. source general category income, and USS has $350x of foreign source foreign branch category income. In contrast, under a single entity analysis, the result is the same as in paragraph (f)(4)(xiii)(B) of this section (the analysis in *Example 13*), whereby P has $600x of foreign source passive category income, $50x of U.S. source general category income, and $350x of U.S. source foreign branch category income.

(*ii*) *Application of the matching rule.* Under the matching rule in §1.1502-13(c), the timing, character, source, and other attributes of USS's $350x intercompany item and P's $350x corresponding item are redetermined to produce the effect of transactions between divisions of a single corporation, as if the services payment had been made to a foreign branch of that corporation. Accordingly, all of USS's foreign source income of $350x is redetermined to be U.S. source, rather than foreign source, income. Therefore, for purposes of §1.1502-4(c)(1), the P group has $600x of foreign passive category income, $50x of U.S. source general category income, and $350x of U.S. source foreign branch category income.

(xvi) *Example 16: Disregarded payment made from non-branch taxable unit.*—(A) *Facts.* The facts are the same as those in paragraph (f)(4)(xiii)(A) of this section (the facts in *Example 13*), except that P also wholly owns FDE1, a disregarded entity that is a non-branch taxable unit. In addition, FDE1 (rather than P) is the entity that properly accrues and records on its books and records the $400x of U.S. source general category income from the license of intellectual property and the $600x of foreign source passive category interest income, and FDE1 (rather than P) is the entity that makes the $350x payment, which is disregarded for Federal income tax purposes, to FDE in compensation for services.

(B) *Analysis.* Under paragraph (f)(2)(vi)(G) of this section, the rules of paragraph (f)(2) of this section apply to attribute gross income to FDE1, a non-branch taxable unit, as though FDE1 were a foreign branch. Under these rules, the $400x of licensing income and the $600 of interest income are initially attributable to FDE1. This income is adjusted in Year 1 to account for the $350x disregarded payment, which is allocable to the $400x of licensing income of FDE1. Accordingly, $50x of the $400x of U.S. source general category licensing income is attributable to FDE1 and $350x of this income is attributable to the FDE foreign branch. To determine the income that is attributable to P, the foreign branch owner, and FDE, the foreign branch, the income that is attributed to FDE1, after taking into account all of the disregarded payments that it makes and receives, must be further attributed to one or more foreign branches or a foreign branch owner under paragraph (f)(2)(vi)(G) of this section. Under paragraph (f)(2)(vi)(G) of this section, the income of FDE1 is attributed to the foreign branch group or foreign branch owner group of which it is a member. Because FDE1 is wholly owned by P, FDE is a member solely of the foreign branch owner group that is owned by P. See definition of "foreign branch owner group" in §1.904-4(f)(3). All the income that is attributed to FDE1 under paragraph (f)(2) of this section, namely, the $50x of U.S. source general category licensing income and the $600x of foreign source passive category interest income, is further attributed to P. See §1.904-4(f)(2)(vi)(G)(*3*). Therefore, the result is the same as in paragraph (f)(4)(xiii)(B) of this section (the analysis in *Example 13*).

(g) *Section 951A category income.*—(1) *In general.*—Except as provided in paragraph (g)(2) of this section, the term *section 951A category income* means amounts included (directly or indirectly through a pass-through entity) in gross income of a United States person under section 951A(a).

(2) *Exceptions for passive category income.*—Section 951A category income does not include any amounts included under section 951A(a) that are allocable to passive category income under §1.904-5(c)(6).

(h) *Export financing interest.*—(1) *Definitions.*—(i) *Export financing interest.*—The term "export financing interest" means any interest derived from financing the sale (or other disposition) for use or consumption outside the United States of any property that is manufactured, produced, grown, or extracted in the United States by the taxpayer or a related person, and not more than 50 percent of the fair market value of which is attributable to products imported into the United States. For purposes of this paragraph, the term "United States" includes the fifty States, the District of Columbia, and the Commonwealth of Puerto Rico.

(ii) *Fair market value.*—For purposes of this paragraph, the fair market value of any property imported into the United States shall be its appraised value, as determined by the Secretary under section 402 of the Tariff Act of 1930 (19 U.S.C. 1401a) in connection with its importation. For purposes of determining the foreign content of an item of property imported into the United States, see section 927 and the regulations thereunder.

(iii) *Related person.*—For purposes of this paragraph, the term "related person" has the meaning given it by section 954(d)(3) except that such section shall be applied by substituting "the person with respect to whom the determination is being made" for "controlled foreign corporation" each place it applies.

(2) *Treatment of export financing interest.*—Except as provided in paragraph (h)(3) of this section, if a taxpayer (including a financial services entity) receives or accrues export financing interest from an unrelated person, then that interest is not treated as passive category income. Instead, the interest income is treated as foreign branch category income, section 951A category income, general category income, or income in a specified separate category under the rules of this section.

(3) *Exception.*—Unless it is received or accrued by a financial services entity, export financing interest shall be treated as passive category income if that income is also related person factoring income. For this purpose, related person factoring income is—

(i) Income received or accrued by a controlled foreign corporation that is income described in section 864(d)(6) (income of a controlled foreign corporation from a loan for the purpose of financing the purchase of inventory property of a related person); or

(ii) Income received or accrued by any person that is income described in section 864(d)(1) (income from a trade receivable acquired from a related person).

(4) *Examples.*—The following examples illustrate the application of paragraph (h)(3) of this section.

(i) *Example 1.* Controlled foreign corporation CFC is a wholly-owned subsidiary of domestic corporation USP. CFC is not a financial services entity and has accumulated cash reserves. USP has uncollected trade and service receivables of foreign obligors. USP sells the receivables at a discount ("factors") to CFC. The income derived by CFC on the receivables is related person factoring income. The income is also export financing interest. Because the income is related person factoring income, the income is passive category income to CFC.

(ii) *Example 2.* Domestic corporation USS is a wholly-owned subsidiary of domestic corporation USP. USS is not a financial services entity, does not have any foreign qualified business entities, and has accumulated cash reserves. USP has uncollected trade and service receivables of foreign obligors. USP factors the receivables to USS. The income derived by USS on the receivables is related person factoring income. The income is also export financing interest. The income will be passive category income to USS.

(iii) *Example 3.* The facts are the same as in paragraph (h)(4)(ii) of this section (the facts in *Example 2*), except that instead of factoring USP's receivables, USS finances the sales of USP's goods by making loans to the purchasers of USP's goods. The interest derived by USS on these loans is export financing interest and is not related person factoring income. The income will be general category income to USS.

(5) *Income eligible for section 864(d)(7) exception (same country exception) from related person factoring treatment.*—(i) *Income other than interest.*—If any foreign person receives or accrues income that is described in section 864(d)(7) (income on a trade or service receivable acquired from a related person in the same foreign country as the recipient) and such income would also meet the definition of export financing interest if section 864(d)(1) applied to such income (income on a trade or service receivable acquired from a related person treated as interest), then the income is considered to be export financing interest and is not treated as passive category income. The income is treated as foreign branch category income, section 951A category income, general category income, or income in a specified separate category under the rules of this section.

(ii) *Interest income.*—If export financing interest is received or accrued by any foreign person and that income would otherwise be treated as related person factoring income of a controlled foreign corporation under section 864(d)(6) if section 864(d)(7) did not apply, section 904(d)(2)(B)(iii)(I) applies and the interest is not treated as passive category income. The income is treated as general category income in the hands of the controlled foreign corporation.

(iii) *Examples.*—The following examples illustrate the application of this paragraph (h)(5):

(A) *Example 1.* CFC1, a controlled foreign corporation, is a wholly-owned subsidiary of domestic corporation USP. CFC2, a controlled foreign corporation, is a wholly-owned subsidiary of CFC1. CFC1 and CFC2 are incorporated in Country M. In Year 1, USP sells tractors to CFC2, which CFC2 sells to X, an unrelated foreign corporation organized in Country M. The tractors are to be used in Country M. CFC2 uses a substantial part of its assets in its trade or business located in Country M. CFC2 has uncollected trade receivables from X that it factors to CFC1. The income is not related person factoring income because it is described in section 864(d)(7) (income eligible for the same country exception) and is tested income. If section 864(d)(1) applied, the income CFC1 derived from the receivables would meet the definition of export financing interest. The income, therefore, is considered to be export financing interest and is general category income to CFC1 and may be section 951A category income to USP.

(B) *Example 2.* CFC1, a controlled foreign corporation, is a wholly-owned subsidiary of domestic corporation, USP. CFC2, a controlled foreign corporation, is a wholly-owned subsidiary of CFC1. CFC1 and CFC2 are incorporated in Country M. In Year 1, USP sells tractors to CFC2, which CFC2 sells to X, a foreign partnership that is organized in Country M and is related to CFC1 and CFC2. CFC1 makes a loan to X to finance the tractor sales. The interest earned by CFC1 from financing the sales is described in section 864(d)(7) and is export financing interest and is tested income. Therefore, the income is general category income to CFC1 and may be section 951A category income to USP.

(i) *Interaction of section 907(c) and income described in this section.*—If a person receives or accrues income that is income described in section 907(c) (relating to oil and gas income), the rules of section 907(c) and the regulations thereunder, as well as the rules of this section, shall apply to the income. The reduction in amount allowed as foreign tax provided by section 907(a) shall therefore be calculated separately for income in each separate category.

(j) *Special rule for DASTM gain or loss.*—Any DASTM gain or loss computed under § 1.985-3(d) must be allocated among the categories of income under the rules of § 1.985-3(e)(2)(iv) or (e)(3). The rules of § 1.985-3(e) apply before the rules of section 904(d)(2)(B)(iii)(II) (the exception from passive income for high-taxed income).

(k) *Separate category under section 904(d)(6) or 865(h) for items resourced under treaties.*—(1) *Section 904(d)(6).*—(i) *In general.*—Except as provided in paragraph (k)(1)(iv)(A) of this section, sections 904(a), (b), (c), (d), (f), and (g) and sections 907 and 960 are applied separately to any item of income that, without regard to a treaty obligation of the United States, would be treated as derived from sources within the United States, but under a treaty obligation of the United States such item of income would be treated as arising from sources outside the United States, and the taxpayer chooses the benefits of such treaty obligation.

(ii) *Aggregation of items of income in each other separate category.*—For purposes of applying the general rule of paragraph (k)(1) of this section, items of income in each other separate category of income that are resourced under each applicable treaty are aggregated in a single separate category for income in that separate category that is resourced under that treaty. For example, all items of passive category income that would otherwise be treated as derived from sources within the United States but which the taxpayer chooses to treat as arising from sources outside the United States pursuant to a provision of a bilateral U.S. income tax treaty are treated as income in a separate category for passive category income resourced under the particular treaty, and the high-tax kickout grouping rules of paragraph (c) of this section are applied separately to the groups of passive income included in that separate category. Any items of resourced high-taxed passive income are assigned to a separate category for general (or other) category income resourced under a tax treaty. Items of income described in paragraph (k)(1) of this section are not combined with other income that is foreign source income under the Code, even if the other income arises from sources within the jurisdiction with which the United States has a bilateral income tax treaty ("treaty jurisdiction") and is included in the same separate category to which the resourced income would be assigned without regard to section 904(d)(6). Items of income described in paragraph (k)(1) of this section are also not combined with other items of resourced income that are subject to a separate limitation by reason of a Code provision other than section 904(d)(6).

(iii) *Related taxes.*—Foreign taxes, including foreign taxes paid to a foreign jurisdiction other than the treaty jurisdiction on an item of resourced income, are allocated to each separate category described in paragraph (k)(1)(ii) of this section in accordance with § 1.904-6.

(iv) *Coordination with certain income tax treaty provisions.*—(A) *Exception for special relief from double taxation for individual residents of treaty jurisdictions.*—Section 904(d)(6)(A) and paragraph (k)(1) of this section do not apply to any item of income deemed to be from foreign sources by reason of the relief from double taxation rules in any U.S. income tax treaty that is solely applicable to U.S. citizens who are residents of the other Contracting State.

(B) *U.S. competent authority assistance.*—For purposes of applying paragraph (k)(1) of this section, if, under the mutual agreement procedure provisions of an applicable income tax treaty, the U.S. competent authority agrees to allow a taxpayer to treat an item of income as foreign source income, where such item of income would otherwise be treated as derived from sources within the United States, then the taxpayer is considered to have chosen the benefits of such treaty obligation to treat the item as foreign source income.

(v) *Coordination with other Code provisions.*—Section 904(d)(6)(A) and paragraph (k)(1) of this section do not apply to any item of income to which any of section 245(a)(10), 865(h), or 904(h)(10) applies. *See also* paragraph (l) of this section.

(2) *Section 865(h).*—If any gain, as defined in section 865(h)(2)(A)(i), would be treated as derived from sources within the United States under section 865, but pursuant to a treaty obligation of the United States such gain would be treated as arising from sources outside the United States, and the taxpayer chooses the benefits of such treaty obligation, then that gain will be treated as foreign source income. However, sections 904(a), (b), (c), (d), (f), and (g) and sections 907 and 960 are applied separately to amounts described in the preceding sentence with respect to each treaty under which the taxpayer has claimed benefits and, within each treaty, to each separate category of income. The principles of the rules in paragraphs (k)(1)(ii) through (iv) of this section apply to gains, and foreign taxes on gains, that are subject to a separate limitation under section 865(h).

(l) *Priority rule.*—Income that meets the definitions of a specified separate category and another category of income described in section 904(d)(1) is subject to the separate limitation described in paragraph (m) of this section and is not treated as general category income, foreign branch category income, passive category income, or section 951A category income.

(m) *Income treated as allocable to an additional separate category.*—If section 904(a), (b), and (c) are applied separately to any category of income under the Internal Revenue Code (for example, under section 245(a)(10), 865(h), 901(j), 904(d)(6), or 904(h)(10)), that category of income is treated for all purposes of the Internal Revenue Code as if it were a separate category listed in section 904(d)(1). For purposes of this section, a separate category that is treated as if it were listed in section 904(d)(1) by reason of the first sentence in this paragraph (m) is referred to as a *specified separate category.*

(n) *Income from partnerships and other pass-through entities.*—(1) *Distributive shares of partnership income.*—(i) *In general.*—Except as provided in paragraph (n)(1)(ii) of this section, a partner's distributive share of partnership income is characterized as passive category income to the extent that the distributive share is a share of income earned or accrued by the partnership in the passive category. A partner's distributive share of partnership income that is not described in the first sentence of this paragraph (n) is treated as foreign branch category income, general category income, or income in a specified separate category under the rules of this section. The principles of the rules in this paragraph (n)(1)(i) also apply to characterize a person's share of income from any other pass-through entity.

(ii) *Less than 10 percent partners partnership interests.*—(A) *In general.*—Except as provided in paragraph (n)(1)(ii)(B) of this section, if any limited partner owns less than 10 percent of the value in a partnership, the partner's distributive share of partnership income from the partnership is passive income to the partner (subject to the exception for high-taxed income under section 904(d)(2)(B)(iii)(II) and paragraph (c) of this section), and the partner's distributive share of partnership deductions from the partnership is allocated and apportioned under the principles of § 1.861-8 only to the partner's passive income from that partnership. See also § 1.861-9(e)(4) for rules for apportioning partnership interest expense.

(B) *Exception for partnership interest held in the ordinary course of business.*—If a partnership interest described in paragraph (n)(1)(ii)(A) of this section is held in the ordinary course of a partner's active trade or business, the rules of paragraph (n)(1)(i) of this section apply for purposes of characterizing the partner's distributive share of the partnership income. A partnership interest is considered to be held in the ordinary course of a partner's active trade or business if the partner (or a member of the partner's affiliated group of corporations (within the meaning of section 1504(a) and without regard to section 1504(b)(3))) engages (other than through a less than 10 percent interest in a partnership) in the same or a related trade or business as the partnership.

(2) *Income from the sale of a partnership interest.*—(i) *In general.*—To the extent a partner recognizes gain on the sale of a partnership interest, that income shall be treated as passive income to the partner, subject to the exception for high-taxed income under section 904(d)(2)(B)(iii)(II) and paragraph (c) of this section.

(ii) *Exception for sale by 25-percent owner.*—Except as provided in paragraph (f)(2)(iv) of this section, in the case of a sale of an interest in a partnership by a partner that is a 25-percent owner of the partnership, determined by applying section 954(c)(4)(B) and substituting "partner" for "controlled foreign corporation" every place it appears, for purposes of determining the separate category to which the income recognized on the sale of the partnership interest is assigned such partner is treated as selling the proportionate share of the assets of the partnership attributable to such interest.

(3) *Value of a partnership interest.*—For purposes of paragraphs (n)(1) and (2) of this section, a partner will be considered as owning 10 percent of the value of a partnership for a particular year if the partner, together with any person that bears a relationship to the partner described in section 267(b) or 707, owns 10 percent of the capital and profits interest of the partnership. For purposes of this paragraph (n)(3), value will be determined at the end of the partnership's taxable year.

(4) *Example.*—The following example illustrates the application of this paragraph (n).

(i) *Facts.* PRS is a domestic partnership. PRS has two general partners, A and B. A and B each have a greater than 10% interest in PRS. PRS also has two limited partners, C and D. C has a 50% interest in the partnership and D has a 9% interest. D's partnership interest is not held in the ordinary course of business. A, B, C and D are all United States persons. In Year 1, PRS has $100x of general category non-subpart F income on which it pays no foreign tax.

(ii) *Analysis.* Under paragraph (n)(1)(i) of this section, A's, B's, and C's distributive shares of PRS's income are not passive category income. Under paragraph (n)(1)(ii)(A) of this section, because D is a limited partner with a less than 10% interest in PRS, D's distributive share of PRS's income is passive category income.

(o) *Separate category of section 78 gross up.*—The amount included in income under section 78 by reason of taxes deemed paid under section 960 is assigned to the separate category to which the taxes are allocated under 1.904-6(e).

(p) *Separate category of foreign currency gain or loss.*—Foreign currency gain or loss recognized under section 986(c) with respect to a distribution of previously taxed earnings and profits (as described in section 959 or 1293(c)) is assigned to the separate category or categories of the previously taxed earnings and profits from which the distribution is made. See § 1.987-6(b) for rules on assigning section 987 gain or loss on a remittance from a section 987 QBU to a separate category or categories.

(q) *Applicability date.*—(1) Except as provided in paragraphs (q)(2) and (3) of this section, this section applies for taxable years that both begin after December 31, 2017, and end on or after December 4, 2018.

(2) Paragraphs (c)(7)(i) and (iii) and (c)(8)(v) through (viii) apply to taxable years ending on or after December 16, 2019. For taxable years that both begin after December 31, 2017, and end on or after December 4, 2018, and also end before December 16, 2019, see § 1.904-4(c)(7)(i) and (iii) as in effect on December 17, 2019.

(3) Paragraphs (b)(2)(i)(A), (c)(4), and (f) of this section apply to taxable years that begin after December 31, 2019, and end on or after November 2, 2020. [Reg. § 1.904-4.]

☐ [*T.D. 8214, 7-15-88. Amended by T.D. 8412, 5-13-92; T.D. 8556, 7-22-94; T.D. 8805, 1-8-99 (corrected 6-16-99); T.D. 8916, 12-29-2000 (corrected 3-22-2001); T.D. 8973, 12-27-2001; T.D. 9141, 7-19-2004; T.D. 9260, 4-20-2006 (corrected 12-22-2006); T.D. 9368, 12-20-2007 (corrected 3-20-2008) T.D. 9452, 6-10-2009, T.D. 9521, 4-6-2011, T.D. 9882, 12-16-2019 (corrected 5-14-2020), T.D. 9922, 11-2-2020 (corrected 9-30-2021) and T.D. 9959, 12-28-2021 (corrected 7-26-2022).*]

Proposed Amendments to Regulation

§ 1.904-4. Separate application of section 904 with respect to certain categories of income.—

* * *

(f) * * *

(2) * * *

(vi) * * *

(D) * * *

(4) Multiple transfers of intangible property.—If the same intangible property is transferred in a series of transfers described in paragraph (f)(2)(vi)(D)(*1*) of this section, each successive transfer is separately subject to the provisions of paragraph (f)(2)(vi)(D)(*1*) and will not terminate or otherwise affect the application of paragraph (f)(2)(vi)(D)(*1*) to a prior transfer described in paragraph (f)(2)(vi)(D)(*1*).

* * *

(q) * * *

(3) Except as provided in the following sentence, paragraph (f) of this section applies to taxable years that begin after December 31, 2019, and end on or after November 2, 2020. Paragraph (f)(vi)(D)(4) of this section applies to taxable years that begin on or after [date of publication of final regulations in the **Federal Register**]. [Prop. Reg. § 1.904-4.]

[Proposed 5-3-2023.]

§ 1.904-5. Look-through rules as applied to controlled foreign corporations and other entities.—(a) *Scope and definitions.*—(1) *Look-through rules under section 904(d)(3) to passive category income.*—Paragraph (c) of this section provides rules for determining the extent to which dividends, interest, rents, and royalties received or accrued by certain eligible persons, and inclusions under sections 951(a)(1) and 951A(a), are treated as passive category income. Paragraph (g) of this section provides rules applying the principles of paragraph (c) of this section to foreign source interest, rents, and royalties paid by a domestic corporation to a related corporation. Paragraph (h) of this section provides rules for assigning a partnership payment to a partner described in section 707 to the passive category. Paragraph (i) of this section provides rules applying the principles of this section to assign distributions and payments from certain related entities to the passive category or to treat the distributions and payments as not in the passive category.

(2) *Other look-through rules under section 904(d).*—Under section 904(d)(4) and paragraph (c)(4)(iii) of this section, certain dividends from noncontrolled 10-percent owned foreign corporations are treated as income in a separate category. Under section 904(d)(3)(H) and paragraph (j) of this section, certain inclusions under section 1293 are treated as income in a separate category. Paragraph (i) of this section provides rules applying the principles of this section to assign distributions from certain related entities to separate categories.

(3) *Other rules provided in this section.*—Paragraph (b) of this section provides operative rules for this section. Paragraph (d) of this section provides rules addressing exceptions to passive category income for certain purposes in the case of controlled foreign corporations that meet the requirements of section 954(b)(3)(A) (de minimis rule) or section 954(b)(4) (high-tax exception). Paragraph (e) of this section provides rules for characterizing a controlled foreign corporation's foreign base company income and gross insurance income when section 954(b)(3)(B) (full inclusion rule) applies. Paragraph (f) of this section modifies the look-through rules for certain types of income. Paragraph (k) of this section provides ordering rules for applying the look-through rules. Paragraph (l) of this section provides examples illustrating the application of certain rules in this section. Paragraphs (m) and (n) of this section provide rules related to the resourcing rules described in section 904(h).

(4) *Definitions.*—For purposes of this section, the following definitions apply.

(i) The term *controlled foreign corporation* has the meaning given such term by section 957 (taking into account the special rule for certain captive insurance companies contained in section 953(c)), determined without applying section 318(a)(3)(A), (B), and (C) so as to consider a United States person as owning stock which is owned by a person who is not a United States person.

(ii) The term *look-through rules* means the rules described in this section that assign income to a separate category based on the separate category of the income to which it is allocable.

(iii) The term *noncontrolled 10-percent owned foreign corporation* has the meaning provided in section 904(d)(2)(E)(i).

(iv) The term *pass-through entity* means a partnership, S corporation, or any other person (whether domestic or foreign) other than a corporation to the extent that the income or deductions of the person are included in the income of one or more direct or indirect owners or beneficiaries of the person. For example, if a domestic trust is subject to Federal income tax on a portion of its income and its owners are subject to tax on the remaining portion, the domestic trust is treated as a domestic pass-through entity with respect to such remaining portion.

(v) The term *separate category* means, as the context requires, any category of income described in section 904(d)(1)(A), (B), (C), or (D), any specified separate category of income as defined in § 1.904-4(m), or any category of earnings and profits to which income described in such provisions is attributable.

(vi) The term *United States shareholder* has the meaning given such term by section 951(b) (taking into account the special rule for certain captive insurance companies contained in section 953(c)), determined without applying section 318(a)(3)(A), (B), and (C) so as to consider a United States person as owning stock which is owned by a person who is not a United States person, except that for purposes of this section, a United States shareholder includes any member of the controlled group of the United States shareholder. For purposes of this paragraph (a)(4)(vi), the controlled group is any member of the affiliated group within the meaning of section 1504(a)(1) except that "more than 50 percent" is substituted for "at least 80 percent" wherever it appears in section 1504(a)(2). When used in reference to a noncontrolled 10-percent owned foreign corporation described in section 904(d)(2)(E)(i)(II), the term *United States shareholder* also means a taxpayer that meets the stock ownership requirements described in section 904(d)(2)(E)(i)(II).

(b) *Operative rules.*—(1) *Assignment of income not assigned under the look-through rules.*—Except as provided by the look-through rules, dividends, interest, rents, and royalties received or accrued by a taxpayer from a controlled foreign corporation in which the taxpayer is a United States shareholder are excluded from passive category income. Income excluded from the passive category under this paragraph (b)(1) is assigned to another separate category (other than the passive category) under the rules in § 1.904-4.

(2) *Priority and ordering of look-through rules.*—Except as provided in this paragraph (b)(2), to the extent the look-through rules assign income to a separate category, the income is assigned to that separate category rather than the separate category to which the income would have been assigned under § 1.904-4 (not taking into account § 1.904-4(l)). See paragraph (k) of this section for ordering rules for applying the look-through rules. However, passive income that is financial services income is assigned to a separate category under the rules in § 1.904-4(e)(1), (f)(1), and (l), regardless of whether the look-through rules otherwise would have assigned such income to the passive category.

(c) *Rules for specific types of inclusions and payments.*—(1) *Scope.*—Subject to the exceptions in paragraph (f) of this section, paragraphs (c)(2) through (6) (other than paragraph (c)(4)(iii) of this section) of this section provide look-through rules with respect to interest, rents, royalties, dividends, and inclusions under sections 951(a)(1) and 951A(a) that are received or accrued from a controlled foreign corporation in which the taxpayer is a United States shareholder. Paragraph (c)(4)(iii) of this section provides a look-through rule for dividends received from a noncontrolled 10-percent owned foreign corporation by a domestic corporation that is a United States shareholder in the foreign corporation.

(2) *Interest.*—(i) *In general.*—For purposes of this paragraph, related person interest is any interest paid or accrued by a controlled foreign corporation to any United States shareholder in that corporation (or to any other related person) to which the look-through rules of section 904(d)(3) and this section apply. Unrelated person interest is all interest other than related person interest. Related person interest is treated as passive category income to the extent it is allocable to passive category income of the controlled foreign corporation. If related person interest is received or accrued from a controlled foreign corporation by two or more persons, the amount of interest received or accrued by each person that is allocable to passive category income is determined by multiplying the amount of related person interest allocable to passive category income by a fraction. The numerator of the fraction is the amount of related person interest received or accrued by that person and the denominator is the total amount of related person interest paid or accrued by the controlled foreign corporation. Solely for purposes of assigning interest income to a separate category under section 904(d)(3) and the look-through rule in this paragraph (c)(2), the rules in paragraph (c)(2)(ii) of this section for allocating and apportioning interest expense of a controlled foreign corporation apply for purposes of characterizing interest income in the hands of the recipient, even if a deduction for the interest expense is deferred or disallowed to the controlled foreign corporation.

(ii) *Allocating and apportioning expenses of a controlled foreign corporation including interest paid to a related person.*—Related person interest and other expenses of a controlled foreign corporation shall be allocated and apportioned in the following manner:

(A) Gross income in each separate category shall be determined;

(B) Any expenses that are definitely related to less than all of gross income as a class, including unrelated person interest that is directly allocated to income from a specific property, shall be allocated and apportioned under the principles of §§1.861-8 or 1.861-10T, as applicable, to income in each separate category;

(C) Related person interest shall be allocated to and shall reduce (but not below zero) the amount of passive foreign personal holding company income as determined after the application of paragraph (c)(2)(ii)(B) of this section;

(D) To the extent that related person interest exceeds passive foreign personal holding company income as determined after the application of paragraphs (c)(2)(ii)(B) and (C) of this section, the related person interest shall be apportioned under the rules of this paragraph to separate categories other than passive income.

(1) If under §1.861-9T, the modified gross income method of apportioning interest expense is elected, related person interest shall be apportioned as follows:

$$\left(\text{Related person interest} \;\text{minus}\; \begin{array}{c}\text{Related person interest allocated}\\ \text{under}\\ \text{paragraph}\\ \text{(c)(2)(ii)(C) of this section}\end{array}\right) \times \frac{\text{Gross income in a separate category (other than passive)}}{\text{Total gross income (other than passive).}}$$

(2) If under §1.861-9T, the asset method of apportioning interest expense is elected, related person interest shall be apportioned according to the following formula:

$$\left(\text{Related person interest} \;\text{minus}\; \begin{array}{c}\text{Related person interest allocated}\\ \text{under}\\ \text{paragraph}\\ \text{(c)(2)(ii)(C) of this section}\end{array}\right) \times \frac{\text{Value of assets in a separate category (other than passive)}}{\text{Value of total assets (other than passive).}}$$

(E) Any other expenses (including unrelated person interest that is not directly allocated to income from a specific property) that are not definitely related expenses or that are definitely related to all of gross income as a class shall be apportioned under the rules of this paragraph to reduce income in each separate category.

(1) If under §1.861-9T, the modified gross income method of apportioning interest expense is elected, the interest expense shall be apportioned as follows:

$$\text{Expense apportionable to a separate category} = \text{Expense} \times \frac{\text{Gross income in a separate category (minus related person interest allocated under paragraph (c)(2)(ii)(C) of this section if the category is passive)}}{\text{Total gross income minus related person interest allocated to passive income under paragraph (c)(2)(ii)(C) of this section}}$$

(2) If under §1.861-9T, the asset method of apportioning interest expense is elected, then the expense shall be apportioned as follows:

$$\text{Expense apportionable to a separate category} = \text{Expense} \times \frac{\text{Value of assets in a separate category (minus related person debt allocated to passive assets if the category is passive)}}{\text{Value of total assets minus related person debt allocated to passive assets}}$$

(3) Expenses other than interest shall be apportioned in a similar manner depending on the apportionment method used. *See* §1.861-8T(c)(1)(i)-(vi).

(iii) *Allocating and apportioning expenses of a noncontrolled 10-percent owned foreign corporation.*—Expenses of a noncontrolled 10-percent owned foreign corporation shall be allocated and apportioned in the same manner as expenses of a controlled foreign corporation under paragraph (c)(2)(ii) of this section, except that the related person interest rule of paragraphs (c)(2)(ii)(C) and (D) of this section shall not apply.

(iv) *Definitions.*—(A) *Value of assets and reduction in value of assets and gross income.*—For purposes of paragraph (c)(2)(ii)(D) and (E) of this section, the value of total assets is the value of assets in all categories (determined under the principles of §1.861-9T(g)). See §1.861-10T(d)(2) to determine the reduction in value of assets and gross income for purposes of apportioning additional third person interest expense that is not directly allocated when some interest expense has been directly allocated. For purposes of this paragraph and paragraph (c)(2)(ii)(E) of this section, any reduction in the value of assets for indebtedness that relates to interest allocated under paragraph (c)(2)(ii)(C) of this section is made before determining the average of asset values. For rules relating to the averaging of reduced asset values see §1.861-9T(g)(2).

(B) *Related person debt allocated to passive assets.*—For purposes of paragraph (c)(2)(ii)(E) of this section, related person debt allocated to passive assets is determined as follows:

Related person debt allocated to the passive category =

$$\text{Total related person debt} \times \frac{\text{Related person interest allocable to passive income under paragraph (c)(2)(ii)(C)}}{\text{All related person interest}}$$

For this purpose, the term "total related person debt" means the sum of the principal amounts of obligations of a controlled foreign corporation owed to any United States shareholder of such corporation or to any related entity (within the meaning of paragraph (g) of this section) determined at the end of the taxable year.

(v) *Examples*.—The following examples illustrate the application of this paragraph (c)(2)

(A) *Example 1*—(*1*) CFC, a controlled foreign corporation, is a wholly-owned subsidiary of USP, a domestic corporation. In Year 1, CFC earns $200x of foreign personal holding company income that is passive category income. CFC also earns $100x of foreign base company sales income that is general category income. CFC has $2,000x of passive category assets and $2,000x of general category assets. In Year 1, CFC makes a $150x interest payment to USP with respect to a $1,500x loan from USP. CFC also pays $100x of interest to an unrelated person on a $1,000x loan from that person. CFC has no other expenses. CFC uses the asset method to apportion interest expense.

(*2*) Under paragraph (c)(2)(ii)(C) of this section, the $150x related person interest payment is allocable to CFC's passive category foreign personal holding company income. Therefore, the $150x interest payment is passive category income to USP. Because the entire related person interest payment is allocated to passive category income under paragraph (c)(2)(ii)(C) of this section, none of the related person interest payment is apportioned to general category income under paragraph (c)(2)(ii)(D) of this section. Under paragraph (c)(2)(iv)(B) of this section, the entire amount of the related person debt is allocable to passive category assets ($1,500x = $1,500x x $150x/$150x). Under paragraph (c)(2)(ii)(E) of this section, $20x of the interest expense paid to an unrelated person is apportioned to passive category income ($20x = $100x x ($2,000x – $1,500x)/($4,000x – $1,500x)), and $80x of the interest expense paid to an unrelated person is apportioned to general category income ($80x = $100x x $2,000x/($4,000x – $1,500x)).

(B) *Example 2*. The facts are the same as in paragraph (c)(2)(v)(A) of this section (the facts in *Example 1*), except that CFC uses the modified gross income method to apportion interest expense. Under paragraph (c)(2)(ii)(E) of this section, the unrelated person interest expense is apportioned based on gross income. Therefore, $33x of interest expense paid to an unrelated person is apportioned to CFC's passive category income ($33x = $100x x ($200x – $150x)/($300x – $150x)) and $67x of interest expense paid to an unrelated person is apportioned to CFC's general category income ($67x = $100x x $100x/($300x – $150x)).

(C) *Example 3*—(*1*) The facts are the same as in paragraph (c)(2)(v)(A) of this section (the facts in *Example 1*), except that CFC has an additional $50x of third person interest expense that is directly allocated to income from a specific property that produces only passive category income. The principal amount of indebtedness to which the interest relates is $500x. CFC also has $50x of additional non-interest expenses that are not definitely related expenses and that are apportioned on an asset basis.

(*2*) Under paragraph (c)(2)(ii)(B) of this section, the $50x of directly allocated third person interest is first allocated to reduce the passive category income of CFC. Under paragraph (c)(2)(ii)(C) of this section, the $150x of related person interest is allocated to the remaining $150x of passive category income. Under paragraph (c)(2)(iv)(B) of this section, all of the related person debt is allocated to passive category assets ($1,500x = $1,500x x $150x/$150x).

(*3*) Under paragraph (c)(2)(ii)(E) of this section, the non-interest expenses that are not definitely related are apportioned on the basis of the asset values reduced by the allocated related person debt. Therefore, $10x of these expenses are apportioned to the passive category ($50x x ($2,000x – $1,500x)/($4,000x – $1,500x)) and $40x are apportioned to the general category ($50x x $2,000x/($4,000x – $1,500x)).

(*4*) In order to apportion third person interest (that was not directly allocated third person interest) between the categories of assets, the value of assets in a separate category must also be reduced under the principles of § 1.861-8 by the indebtedness relating to the specifically allocated interest. Therefore, under paragraph (c)(2)(iv)(B) of this section, the value of assets in the passive category for purposes of apportioning the additional third person interest = 0 ($2,000x minus $500x (the principal amount of the debt, the interest payment on which is directly allocated to specific interest-producing properties) minus $1,500x (the related person debt allocated to passive category assets)). Under paragraph (c)(2)(ii)(E) of this section, all $100x of the non-definitely related third person interest expense is apportioned to the general category ($100x = $100x x $2,000x/($4,000x – $500x – $1,500x)).

(D) *Example 4*—(*1*) CFC, a controlled foreign corporation, is a wholly-owned subsidiary of USP, a domestic corporation. In Year 1, CFC earns $100x of foreign personal holding company income that is passive category income. CFC also earns $100x of foreign base company sales income that is general category income. CFC has $1,000x of general category assets and $1,000x of passive category assets. In Year 1, CFC makes a $150x interest payment to USP on a $1,500x loan from USP and has $20x of general and administrative expenses (G & A) that under the principles of § § 1.861-8 through 1.861-14T is treated as directly allocable to all of CFC's gross income. CFC also makes a $25x interest payment to an unrelated person on a $250x loan from the unrelated person. CFC has no other expenses. CFC uses the asset method to apportion interest expense. CFC uses the modified gross income method to apportion G & A.

(*2*) Under paragraph (c)(2)(iv)(B) of this section, related person debt allocated to passive category assets equals $1,000x ($1,000x = $1,500x x $100x/$150x).Under paragraph (c)(2)(ii)(C) of this section, $100x of the interest payment to USP is allocable to CFC's passive category foreign personal holding company income. Under paragraph (c)(2)(ii)(D) of this section, the additional $50x of related person interest expense is apportioned to CFC's general category income ($50x = $50x x $1,000x/$1,000x).

(*3*) Under paragraph (c)(2)(ii)(E) of this section, none of the $25x of interest expense paid to an unrelated person is apportioned to passive category income ($0 = $25x x ($1,000x – $1,000x)/($2,000x – $1,000x)). All $25x of the interest expense paid to an unrelated person is apportioned to general category income ($25x = $25x x $1,000x/($2,000x – $1,000x)). Under paragraph (c)(2)(ii)(E) of this section, none of the G & A is allocable to CFC's passive category foreign personal holding company income ($0 = $20x x ($100x – $100x)/($200x – $100x)). All $20x of the G & A is apportioned to CFC's general category income ($20x = $20x x $100x/($200x – $100x)).

(E) *Example 5*. The facts are the same as in paragraph (c)(2)(v)(D) of this section (the facts in *Example 4*), except that CFC uses the modified gross income method to apportion interest expense. As in paragraph (c)(2)(v)(D) of this section (*Example 4*), $100x of the interest payment to USP is allocated to passive category income under paragraph (c)(2)(ii)(C) of this section. Under paragraph (c)(2)(ii)(D) of this section, the additional $50x of related person interest expense is apportioned to general category income ($150x – 100x x $100x/$100x). Under paragraph (c)(2)(ii)(E) of this section, none of the unrelated person interest expense and none of the G & A is apportioned to passive category income, because after the application of paragraph (c)(2)(ii)(C) of this section, no income remains in the passive category.

(F) *Example 6*. CFC2, a controlled foreign corporation, is a wholly-owned subsidiary of CFC1, a controlled foreign corporation. CFC1 is a wholly-owned subsidiary of USP, a domestic corporation. CFC1 and CFC2 are incorporated in the same country. In Year 1, USP sells tractors to CFC2, which CFC2 sells to X, a foreign corporation that is related to both CFC1 and CFC2 and is organized in the same country as CFC1 and CFC2. CFC1 makes a loan to X to finance the tractor sales. Assume that the interest earned by CFC1 from financing the sales is export financing interest that is neither related person factoring income nor foreign personal holding company income. Under § 1.904-4(h), the export financing interest earned by CFC1 is, therefore, general category income. CFC1 earns no other income. CFC1 makes a $100x interest payment to USP. The $100x of interest paid is not allocable under the look-through rules and paragraph (c)(2)(ii) of this section to passive category income of CFC1. The income is general category income to USP.

(3) *Rents and royalties*.—Any rents or royalties received or accrued from a controlled foreign corporation in which the taxpayer is a United States shareholder are treated as passive category income to the extent they are allocable to passive category income of the controlled foreign corporation under the principles of § § 1.861-8 through 1.861-14T.

(4) *Dividends*.—(i) *Look-through rule for controlled foreign corporations*.—Except as provided in paragraph (d)(2) of this section, any dividend paid or accrued out of the earnings and profits of any controlled foreign corporation is treated as passive category income in proportion to the ratio of the portion of earnings and profits attributable to passive category income to the total amount of earnings and profits of the controlled foreign corporation. For purposes of

this paragraph (c)(4), the term "dividend" includes any amount included in gross income under section 951(a)(1)(B) as a pro rata share of a controlled foreign corporation's increase in earnings invested in United States property.

(ii) *Special rule for dividends attributable to certain loans.*—If a dividend is distributed to a taxpayer by a controlled foreign corporation, that controlled foreign corporation is the recipient of loan proceeds from a related look-through entity (within the meaning of § 1.904-5 (i) of this section), and the purpose of such loan is to alter the characterization of the dividend for purposes of this section, then, to the extent of the principal amount of the loan, the dividend shall be characterized with respect to the earnings and profits of the related person lender rather than with respect to the earnings and profits of the dividend payor. A loan will not be considered made for the purpose of altering the characterization of a dividend if the loan would have been made or maintained on substantially the same terms irrespective of the dividend. The determination of whether a loan would have been made or maintained on substantially the same terms irrespective of the dividend will be made taking into account all the facts and circumstances of the relationship between the lender and the borrower. Thus, for example, a loan by a related party lender to a controlled foreign corporation that arises from the sale of inventory in the ordinary course of business will not be considered a loan made for the purpose of altering the character of any dividend paid by the borrower.

(iii) *Look-through rule for dividends from noncontrolled 10-percent owned foreign corporations.*—(A) *In general.*—Except as provided in paragraph (c)(4)(iii)(B) of this section, any dividend that is distributed by a noncontrolled 10-percent owned foreign corporation and received or accrued by a domestic corporation that is a United States shareholder of such foreign corporation is treated as income in a separate category in proportion to the ratio of the portion of earnings and profits attributable to income in such category to the total amount of earnings and profits of the noncontrolled 10-percent owned foreign corporation.

(B) *Inadequate substantiation.*—A dividend distributed by a noncontrolled 10-percent owned foreign corporation is treated as income in the separate category described in section 904(d)(4)(C)(ii) if the Commissioner determines that the look-through characterization of the dividend cannot reasonably be determined based on the available information.

(5) *Inclusions under section 951(a)(1)(A).*—Any amount included in gross income under section 951(a)(1)(A) is treated as passive category income to the extent the amount included is attributable to income received or accrued by the controlled foreign corporation that is passive category income. All other amounts included in gross income under section 951(a)(1)(A) are treated as general category income or income in a specified separate category under the rules in § 1.904-4. For rules concerning a distributive share of partnership income, see § 1.904-4(n). For rules concerning the gross up under section 78, see § 1.904-4(o). For rules concerning inclusions under section 951(a)(1)(B), see paragraph (c)(4)(i) of this section.

(6) *Inclusions under section 951A(a).*—Any amount included in gross income under section 951A(a) is treated as passive category income to the extent the amount included is attributable to income received or accrued by the controlled foreign corporation that is passive category income. All other amounts included in gross income under section 951A(a) are treated as section 951A category income or income in a specified separate category under the rules in § 1.904-4. For rules concerning a distributive share of partnership income, see § 1.904-4(n). For rules concerning the gross up under section 78, see § 1.904-4(o).

(7) *Examples.*—The following examples illustrate the application of paragraph (c) of this section.

(i) *Example 1*—(A) *Facts.* CFC, a controlled foreign corporation, is a wholly-owned subsidiary of USP, a domestic corporation. In Year 1, CFC earns $100x of net income, $85x of which is general category foreign base company sales income and $15x of which is passive category foreign personal holding company income. No foreign tax is imposed on the income. CFC's income of $100x is subpart F income taxed currently to USP under section 951(a)(1)(A).

(B) *Analysis.* Because $15x of the subpart F inclusion is attributable to passive category income of CFC, under section 904(d)(3)(B) and paragraph (c)(5) of this section $15x of the subpart F inclusion is passive category income to USP. The remaining $85x subpart F inclusion is general category income to USP.

(ii) *Example 2*—(A) *Facts.* CFC1, a controlled foreign corporation, is a wholly-owned subsidiary of USP, a domestic corporation. CFC2 is a controlled foreign corporation wholly owned by CFC1 and is incorporated and operates all of its business in the same country as CFC1. All of CFC2's earnings and profits are attributable to passive category foreign personal holding company income. USP elects to exclude CFC2's income from subpart F income under section 954(b)(4). In Year 1, CFC2 makes a distribution to CFC1 and CFC1 makes a distribution to USP, all of which is attributable to Year 1 earnings and profits. CFC1 has no earnings and profits in Year 1 other than those received from CFC2.

(B) *Analysis*—*(1)* With respect to the dividend from CFC2 to CFC1, such amount is not subpart F income. *See* section 954(c)(3). Under section 904(d)(3)(D) and (E) and paragraphs (c)(4) and (d)(2) of this section the dividend income is not passive category income and therefore under § 1.904-4 it is general category income to CFC1. Under section 951A(c)(2)(A)(i)(IV), such dividend income is not tested income.

(2) With respect to the dividend from CFC1 to USP, under section 904(d)(3)(D) and (E) and paragraphs (c)(4) and (d)(2) of this section, such dividend income is not passive category income and therefore under § 1.904-4 is general category income to USP.

(iii) *Example 3*—(A) *Facts.* The facts are the same as in paragraph (c)(7)(ii)(A) of this section (the facts in *Example 2*), except that CFC1 receives interest income from CFC2 instead of dividend income.

(B) *Analysis.* Under section 904(d)(3)(C) and paragraph (c)(2)(i) of this section, the interest income is passive category income to CFC1 because such interest is properly allocable to the passive category income of CFC2. The interest income from CFC2 is subpart F income of CFC1 taxable to USP because such income reduces the subpart F income of CFC2 or such interest is properly allocable to the subpart F income of CFC2. *See* section 954(c)(3) and (6). Under section 904(d)(3)(B) and paragraph (c)(5) of this section, the subpart F inclusion is passive category income to USP. Under section 959(a), the distribution from CFC1 to USP is excluded from USP's gross income.

(iv) *Example 4*—(A) *Facts.* The facts are the same as in paragraph (c)(7)(iii)(A) of this section (the facts in *Example 3*), except that USP elects to exclude CFC1's interest income from subpart F income under section 954(b)(4).

(B) *Analysis.* Under section 904(d)(3)(D) and (E) and paragraphs (c)(4) and (d)(2) of this section, the distribution from CFC1 to USP is not a passive category dividend and therefore under § 1.904-4 is general category income to USP.

(v) *Example 5*—(A) *Facts.* The facts are the same as in paragraph (c)(7)(iv)(A) of this section (the facts in *Example 4*), except that USP receives interest income from CFC1 instead of dividend income.

(B) *Analysis.* Under section 904(d)(3)(C) and paragraph (c)(2)(i) of this section, the interest income is passive category income to USP because such interest is properly allocable to passive category income of CFC1.

(d) *Effect of exclusions from subpart F income.*—(1) *De minimis amount of subpart F income.*—If the sum of a controlled foreign corporation's gross foreign base company income (determined under section 954(a) without regard to section 954(b)(5)) and gross insurance income (determined under section 953(a)) for the taxable year is less than the lesser of 5 percent of gross income or $1,000,000, then none of that income is treated as passive category income. In addition, if the test in the first sentence of this paragraph (d)(1) is satisfied, for purposes of paragraphs (c)(2)(ii)(D) and (E) of this section (apportionment of interest expense to passive income using the asset method), any passive assets are not treated as passive category assets but are treated as assets in the general category or a specified separate category. The determination in the first sentence of this paragraph (d)(1) is made before the application of the exception for certain income subject to a high rate of foreign tax described in paragraph (d)(2) of this section.

(2) *Exception for certain income subject to high foreign tax.*—Except as provided in § 1.904-4(c)(7)(iii) (relating to reductions in tax upon distribution), for purposes of the dividend look-through rule of paragraph (c)(4)(i) of this section, an item of net income that would otherwise be passive category income (after application of the priority rules of § 1.904-4(l)) and that is received or accrued by a controlled foreign corporation is not treated as passive category income, and the earnings and profits attributable to such income is not treated as passive category earnings and profits, if the taxpayer establishes to the satisfaction of the Secretary under section 954(b)(4) that the income was subject to an effective rate of income tax imposed by a foreign country greater than 90 percent of the maximum rate of tax

specified in section 11 (with reference to section 15, if applicable). Such income is treated as general category income or income in a specified separate category under the rules in § 1.904-4. The first sentence of this paragraph (d)(2) has no effect on amounts (other than dividends) paid or accrued by a controlled foreign corporation to a United States shareholder of such controlled foreign corporation to the extent those amounts are allocable to passive category income of the controlled foreign corporation.

(3) *Examples.*—The following example illustrates the application of this paragraph (d).

(i) *Facts.* CFC, a controlled foreign corporation, is a wholly-owned subsidiary of USP, a domestic corporation. In Year 1, CFC earns $100x of gross income, $4x of which is interest that is foreign personal holding company income and $96x of which is gross manufacturing income that is not subpart F income. CFC has no other earnings for Year 1. CFC has no expenses and pays no foreign taxes.

(ii) *Analysis.* Under the de minimis rule of section 954(b)(3)(A) and § 1.954-1(b)(1)(i), none of CFC's income is treated as foreign base company income. All of CFC's income, therefore, is treated as general category income and tested income. In Year 1, USP has a GILTI inclusion amount with respect to CFC. Such amount is section 951A category income to USP.

(e) *Treatment of subpart F income in excess of 70 percent of gross income.*—(1) *Rule.*—If the sum of a controlled foreign corporation's gross foreign base company income (determined without regard to section 954(b)(5)) and gross insurance income for the taxable year exceeds 70 percent of the gross income, then all of the controlled foreign corporation's gross income shall be treated as foreign base company income or gross insurance income (whichever is appropriate) and, thus, included in a United States shareholder's gross income. However, the inclusion in gross income of an amount that would not otherwise be subpart F income does not affect its character for purposes of determining whether the income is within a separate category. The determination of whether the controlled foreign corporation's gross foreign base company income and gross insurance income exceeds 70 percent of gross income is made before the exception for certain income subject to a high rate of foreign tax.

(2) *Example.*—The following example illustrates the application of this paragraph (e).

(i) *Facts.*—Controlled foreign corporation CFC is a wholly-owned subsidiary of USP, a domestic corporation. CFC earns $100x, $75x of which is foreign personal holding company income and $25x of which is non-subpart F services income. CFC's gross and net income are equal.

(ii) *Analysis.*—Under the 70 percent full inclusion rule of section 954(b)(3)(B), the entire $100x is foreign base company income currently taxable to USP under section 951. Because $75x of the $100x section 951 inclusion is attributable to CFC's passive category income, $75x of the inclusion is passive category income to USP. The remaining $25x of the inclusion is treated as general category income to USP.

(f) *Modification of look-through rules for certain income.*—(1) [Reserved]

(2) *Distributions from a FSC.*—Income received or accrued by a taxpayer that, under the rules of paragraph (c)(4) of this section (look-through rules for dividends), would be treated as foreign trade income or as passive income that is interest and carrying charges (as defined in section 927(d)(1)), and that is also a distribution from a FSC (or a former FSC), shall be treated as a distribution from a FSC (or a former FSC).

(g) *Application of look-through rules to certain domestic corporations.*—The principles of paragraph (c) of this section shall apply to any foreign source interest, rents and royalties paid by a domestic corporation to a related corporation. For this purpose, a domestic corporation and another corporation are considered to be related if one owns, directly or indirectly, stock possessing more than 50 percent of the total voting power of all classes of stock of the other corporation or more than 50 percent of the total value of the other corporation. In addition, a domestic corporation and another corporation shall be considered to be related if the same United States shareholders own, directly or indirectly, stock possessing more than 50 percent of the total voting power of all classes of stock or more than 50 percent of the total value of each corporation. For purposes of this paragraph, the constructive stock ownership rules of section 318 and the regulations under that section apply.

(h) *Application of look-through rules to payments from a partnership or other pass-through entity.*—Payments to a partner described in section 707 (e.g., payments to a partner not acting in capacity as a partner) are characterized as passive category income to the extent that the payment is attributable under the principles of § 1.861-8 and this section to passive category income of the partnership, if the payments are interest, rents, or royalties that would be characterized under the controlled foreign corporation look-through rules of paragraph (c) of this section if the partnership were a foreign corporation, and the partner who receives the payment owns 10 percent or more of the value of the partnership (as determined under § 1.904-4(n)(3)). A payment by a partnership to a member of the controlled group (as defined in paragraph (a)(4)(vi) of this section) of the partner is characterized under the look-through rules of this paragraph (h) if the payment would be a section 707 payment entitled to look-through treatment if it were made to the partner. The rules in this paragraph (h) do not apply with respect to interest to the extent the interest income is assigned to a separate category under the down-stream partnership loan rules described in § 1.861-9(e)(8). The principles of the rules in this paragraph (h) apply to characterize a payment from any other pass-through entity.

(i) *Application of look-through rules to related entities.*—(1) *In general.*—Except as provided in paragraphs (i)(2) and (3) of this section, the principles of this section shall apply to distributions and payments that are subject to the look-through rules of section 904(d)(3) and this section from a controlled foreign corporation or other entity otherwise entitled to look-through treatment (a "look-through entity") under this section to a related look-through entity. A noncontrolled 10-percent owned foreign corporation shall be considered a look-through entity only to the extent provided in paragraph (i)(3) of this section. Two look-through entities shall be considered to be related to each other if one owns, directly or indirectly, stock possessing more than 50 percent of the total voting power of all classes of voting stock of the other entity or more than 50 percent of the total value of such entity. In addition, two look-through entities are related if the same United States shareholders own, directly or indirectly, stock possessing more than 50 percent of the total voting power of all voting classes of stock (in the case of a corporation) or more than 50 percent of the total value of each look-through entity. In the case of a corporation, value shall be determined by taking into account all classes of stock. For purposes of this paragraph (i)(1), indirect ownership of stock is determined under section 318. In the case of a partnership or other pass-through entity, indirect ownership and value is determined under the rules in paragraph (i)(2) of this section.

(2) *Indirect ownership and value of a partnership interest.*—A person is considered as owning, directly or indirectly, more than 50 percent of the value of a partnership if the person, together with any other person that bears a relationship to the first person that is described in section 267(b) or 707, owns more than 50 percent of the capital and profits interests of the partnership. For purposes of this paragraph (i)(2), value will be determined at the end of the partnership's taxable year. The principles of this paragraph (i)(2) apply with respect to a person that owns a pass-through entity other than a partnership.

(3) *Special rule for dividends between certain foreign corporations.*—Solely for purposes of dividend payments between controlled foreign corporations, noncontrolled 10-percent owned foreign corporations, or a controlled foreign corporation and a noncontrolled 10-percent owned foreign corporation, the two foreign corporations are considered related look-through entities if the same person is a United States shareholder of both foreign corporations.

(4) [Reserved]

(5) *Examples.*—The following examples illustrate the application of this paragraph (i):

(i) *Example 1.* USP, a domestic corporation, owns all of the stock of CFC1, a controlled foreign corporation. CFC1 owns 40% of the stock of CFC2, a Country X corporation that is a controlled foreign corporation. The remaining 60% of the stock of CFC2 is owned by V, a domestic corporation, unrelated to USP. The percentages of value and voting power of CFC2 owned by CFC1 and V correspond to their percentages of stock ownership. CFC2 owns 40% (by vote and value) of the stock of CFC3, a Country Z corporation that is a controlled foreign corporation. The remaining 60% of CFC3 is owned by unrelated United States persons. CFC3 earns exclusively general category income that is neither subpart F income nor tested income.

In Year 1, CFC3 makes an interest payment of $100x to CFC2. Look-through principles do not apply because CFC2 and CFC3 are not related look-through entities under paragraph (i)(1) of this section (because CFC2 does not own more than 50% of the voting power or value of CFC3). The interest is passive category income to CFC2 and is subpart F income of CFC2 that is taxable to USP and V. Under paragraph (c)(5) of this section, USP and V's subpart F inclusion with respect to CFC2 is passive category income.

(ii) *Example 2.* The facts are the same as in paragraph (i)(5)(i) of this section (the facts in *Example 1*), except that instead of a $100x interest payment, CFC3 pays a $50x dividend to CFC2 in Year 1. USP and V each own, directly or indirectly, more than 10% of the voting power of all classes of stock of both CFC2 and CFC3, and, therefore, CFC2 and CFC3 have the same United States shareholders. Pursuant to paragraph (i)(3) of this section, because CFC2 and CFC3 have a common United States shareholder, for purposes of applying this section to the dividend from CFC2 to CFC3, CFC2 and CFC3 are treated as related look-through entities. Therefore, look-through principles apply. Because CFC3 has no passive category income or earnings and profits, the dividend income is characterized as general category income to CFC2. The dividend is subpart F income of CFC2 that is taxable to USP and V. Under paragraph (c)(5) of this section, the subpart F inclusions of USP and V are not passive category income to USP and V and therefore under § 1.904-4 the subpart F inclusions are general category income to USP and V.

(iii) *Example 3.* The facts are the same as in paragraph (i)(5)(i) of this section (the facts in *Example 1*), except that CFC3 pays both a $100x interest payment and a $50x dividend to CFC2, and CFC2 owns 80% (by vote and value) of CFC3. Under paragraph (i)(1) of this section, CFC2 and CFC3 are related look-through entities, because CFC2 owns more than 50% (by vote and value) of CFC3. Therefore, look-through principles apply to both the interest and dividend income paid or accrued by CFC3 to CFC2, and CFC2 treats both types of income as general category income because CFC3 does not have any passive category earnings. Under paragraph (c)(5) of this section and § 1.904-4, the resulting subpart F inclusions are general category income to USP and V.

(iv) *Example 4.* USP, a domestic corporation, owns 50% of the voting stock of CFC1, a controlled foreign corporation. CFC1 owns 10% of the voting stock of CFC2, a controlled foreign corporation. The remaining 50% of the stock of CFC1 is owned by X. The remaining 90% of the stock of CFC2 is owned by Y. X and Y are each United States shareholders of CFC2 but are not related to USP, CFC1, or each other. In Year 1, CFC2 pays a $100x dividend to CFC1. Under paragraph (i)(3) of this section because no person is a United States shareholder of both CFC1 and CFC2 (USP and X each own only 5% of CFC2), CFC1 and CFC2 are not related look-through entities. Because CFC2 is not a related person to CFC1 within the meaning of section 954(d)(3), section 954(c)(3) and (c)(6) are inapplicable, and the dividend is subpart F income of CFC1 that is taxable to USP and X. Therefore, under section 904(d)(2)(B)(i) and § 1.904-4(b)(2)(i)(A), because the dividend income is foreign personal holding company income, it is passive category income to CFC1.

(v) *Example 5.* The facts are the same as in paragraph (i)(5)(iv) of this section (the facts in *Example 4*), except that X owns 10% of the voting stock of CFC2 and Y owns only 80% of the voting stock of CFC2. Because CFC2 is not a related person to CFC1 within the meaning of section 954(d)(3), the dividend is subpart F income of CFC1 that is taxable to USP and X. In addition, because X is a United States shareholder of both CFC1 and CFC2, CFC2 and CFC1 are related look-through entities under paragraph (i)(3) of this section, the dividend income is general category income to CFC1 and the subpart F inclusion is general category income to USP and X.

(j) *Look-through rules applied to passive foreign investment company inclusions.*—If a passive foreign investment company is a controlled foreign corporation and the taxpayer is a United States shareholder in that passive foreign investment company, any amount included in gross income under section 1293 shall be treated as income in a separate category to the extent the amount so included is attributable to income received or accrued by that controlled foreign corporation that is described as income in the separate category.

(k) *Ordering rules.*—(1) *In general.*—Income received or accrued by a related person to which the look-through rules apply is characterized under § 1.904-4 before amounts included from, or paid or distributed by that person and received or accrued by a related person. For purposes of determining the character of income received or accrued by a person from a related person if the payor or another related person also receives or accrues income from the recipient and the look-through rules apply to the income in all cases, the rules of paragraph (k)(2) of this section apply.

(2) *Specific rules.*—For purposes of characterizing income under this paragraph, the following types of income are characterized in the order stated:

(i) Rents and royalties;

(ii) Interest;

(iii) Inclusions under sections 951(a)(1)(A) and 951A(a) and distributive shares of partnership income;

(iv) Dividend distributions.

If an entity is both a recipient and a payor of income described in any one of the categories described in (i) through (iv) of this paragraph, the income received will be characterized before the income that is paid. In addition, the amount of interest paid or accrued, directly or indirectly, by a person to a related person shall be offset against and eliminate any interest received or accrued, directly or indirectly, by a person from that related person before application of the ordering rules of this paragraph. In a case in which a person pays or accrues interest to a related person, and also receives or accrues interest indirectly from the related person, the smallest interest payment is eliminated and the amount of all other interest payments are reduced by the amount of the smallest interest payment.

(l) *Examples.*—The following examples illustrate the application of this section.

(1) *Example 1*—(i) *Facts.* CFC1 and CFC2, controlled foreign corporations, are wholly-owned subsidiaries of USP, a domestic corporation. CFC1 and CFC2 are incorporated in two different foreign countries and CFC2 is a financial services entity. In Year 1, CFC1 earns $100x of gross income that is passive category foreign personal holding company income. CFC1's only expense is a $50x interest payment to CFC2. CFC1's $50x of pre-tax income is subject to $20x of foreign income tax, and USP elects to exclude CFC1's $30x of net income from subpart F income under section 954(b)(4).

(ii) *Analysis.* The $50x of interest is foreign personal holding company income in CFC2's hands because section 954(c)(3)(A)(i) (same country exception for interest payments) and section 954(c)(6) do not apply, because the interest payment is allocable to and reduces CFC1's subpart F income. The $50x of interest income is also passive category income to CFC2 because CFC1 and CFC2 are related look-through entities within the meaning of paragraph (i)(1) of this section and, therefore the look-through rules of paragraph (c)(2)(i) of this section apply to characterize the interest payment. However, because CFC2 is a financial services entity, under § 1.904-4(e)(1) and paragraph (b)(2) of this section, the income is treated as financial services income and therefore as general category income in CFC2's hands. Thus, with respect to CFC2, under § 1.904-4(d) and paragraph (c)(5) of this section, USP includes in its gross income a $50x general category inclusion under section 951(a)(1)(A) attributable to the general category foreign personal holding company income.

(2) *Example 2*—(i) *Facts.* USP, a domestic corporation, owns 75% of USS, a domestic corporation. USP and USS are not financial services entities. In Year 1, USS's earnings consist of $100x of foreign source passive income. USS makes a $100x foreign source royalty payment to USP.

(ii) *Analysis.* Under paragraph (g) of this section, the royalty payment to USP is subject to the look-through rules of paragraph (c)(3) of this section and is characterized as passive category income the extent that it is allocable to such income in USS's hands.

(3) *Example 3*—(i) *Facts.* USP, a domestic corporation, owns 100% of the stock of CFC1, a controlled foreign corporation, and CFC1 owns 100% of the stock of CFC2, a controlled foreign corporation. CFC1 has $100x of passive foreign personal holding company income from unrelated persons and $100x of general category income. CFC1 also has $50x of interest income from CFC2. CFC1 pays CFC2 $100x of interest.

(ii) *Analysis.* Under paragraph (k)(2) of this section, the $100x interest payment from CFC1 to CFC2 is reduced for limitation purposes to the extent of the $50x interest payment from CFC2 to CFC1 before application of the rules in paragraph (c)(2)(ii) of this section. Therefore, the interest payment from CFC2 to CFC1 is disregarded. CFC1 is treated as if it paid $50x of interest to CFC2, all of which is allocable to CFC1's passive category foreign personal holding company income under paragraph (c)(2)(ii)(C) of this section. Therefore, under paragraph (c)(2)(i) of this section, the $50x interest payment from CFC1 to CFC2 is passive category income.

(4) *Example 4*—(i) *Facts.* USP, a domestic corporation, owns 100% of the stock of CFC1, a controlled foreign corporation. CFC1 owns 100% of the stock of CFC2, a controlled foreign corporation, and 100% of the stock of CFC3, a controlled foreign corporation. In Year 1, CFC2 pays CFC1 $5x of interest, CFC1 pays CFC3 $10x of interest, and CFC3 pays CFC2 $20x of interest.

(ii) *Analysis*. Under paragraph (k)(2) of this section, the interest payments from CFC1 to CFC3 must be offset by the amount of interest that CFC1 is considered as receiving indirectly from CFC3 and the interest payment from CFC3 to CFC2 is offset by the amount of the interest payment that CFC3 is considered as receiving indirectly from CFC2. The $10x payment by CFC1 to CFC3 is reduced by $5x, the amount of the interest payment from CFC2 to CFC1 that is treated as being paid indirectly by CFC3 to CFC1. Similarly, the $20x interest payment from CFC3 to CFC2 is reduced by $5x, the amount of the interest payment from CFC1 to CFC3 that is treated as being paid indirectly by CFC2 to CFC3. Therefore, under paragraph (k)(2) of this section, CFC2 is treated as having made no interest payment to CFC1, CFC1 is treated as having paid $5x of interest to CFC3, and CFC3 is treated as having paid $15x to CFC2.

(5) *Example 5*—(i) *Facts*. USP, a domestic corporation, owns 100% of the stock of CFC1, a controlled foreign corporation, and CFC1 owns 100% of the stock of CFC2, a controlled foreign corporation. In Year 1, CFC1 earns $100x of passive category foreign personal holding company income and $100x of general category non-subpart F sales income from unrelated persons and $100x of general category non-subpart F interest income from a related person. CFC1 pays $150x of interest to CFC2. CFC2 earns $200x of general category sales income from unrelated persons and the $150x interest payment from CFC1. CFC2 pays CFC1 $100x of interest. USP does not have an inclusion under section 951A.

(ii) *Analysis*—(A) Under paragraph (k)(2) of this section, the $100x interest payment from CFC2 to CFC1 reduces the $150x interest payment from CFC1 to CFC2. CFC1 is treated as though it paid $50x of interest to CFC2. CFC2 is treated as though it made no interest payment to CFC1.

(B) Under paragraph (k)(2)(ii) of this section, the remaining $50x interest payment from CFC1 to CFC2 is then characterized. The interest payment is first allocable under the rules of paragraph (c)(2)(ii)(C) of this section to CFC1's passive category income. Therefore, under paragraph (c)(2)(i) of this section, the $50x interest payment to CFC2 is passive category income. The interest income is foreign personal holding company income in CFC2's hands. CFC2, therefore, has $50x of passive category subpart F income and $200x of general category non-subpart F income.

(C) Under paragraph (k)(2)(iii) of this section, inclusions under section 951(a)(1)(A) are characterized next. USP has an inclusion under section 951(a)(1)(A) with respect to CFC1 of $50x that is attributable to passive category income of CFC1 and is treated as passive category income to USP. USP has an inclusion under section 951(a)(1)(A) with respect to CFC2 of $50x that is attributable to passive category income of CFC2 and is treated as passive category income to USP.

(6) *Example 6*—(i) *Facts*. USP, a domestic corporation, owns 100% of the stock of CFC1, a controlled foreign corporation, and CFC1 owns 100% of the stock of CFC2, a controlled foreign corporation. USP also owns 100% of the stock of CFC3, a controlled foreign corporation. CFC1, CFC2, and CFC3 are all incorporated in different foreign countries. In Year 1, CFC1 earns $100x of passive category foreign personal holding company income and $200x of general category non-subpart F income from unrelated persons. CFC1 also receives a $150x distribution from CFC2. CFC1 pays $100x of interest to CFC2 and $100x of interest to CFC3. CFC3 earns $300x of general category non-subpart F income and the $100x of interest received from CFC1. CFC3 pays a $100x royalty to CFC2. The royalty is directly allocable to CFC3's general category income and the royalty is not subpart F income to CFC2. CFC2 earns the $100x interest payment received from CFC1 and the $100x royalty received from CFC3. USP does not have an inclusion under section 951A.

(ii) *Analysis*—(A) Under paragraph (k)(2)(i) of this section, the royalty paid by CFC3 to CFC2 is characterized first. With respect to CFC2, the royalty is general category non-subpart F income.

(B) Under paragraph (k)(2)(ii) of this section, the interest payments from CFC1 to CFC2 and CFC3 are characterized next. Under paragraph (c)(2)(ii)(C) of this section, the interest payments are first allocable to CFC1's passive category income. Therefore, under paragraph (c)(2)(i) of this section, $50x of the interest payment to CFC2 is passive category income and $50x of the interest payment to CFC3 is passive category income. The remaining $50x paid to CFC2 is general category income and the remaining $50x paid to CFC3 is general category income. Because $100x of the interest income received or accrued from CFC1 is properly allocable to income of CFC1 which is not subpart F income, under section 954(c)(6) the general category interest income is not treated as foreign personal holding company income to CFC2 and CFC3. The remaining $100x of interest income received or accrued from CFC1 is passive category subpart F foreign personal holding company income to both recipients. Therefore, CFC3 and CFC2 each have $50x of passive category subpart F foreign personal holding company income related to the interest received from CFC1.

(C) Under paragraph (k)(2)(iii) of this section, USP's $50x inclusion under section 951(a)(1)(A) with respect to CFC2 is characterized next. Under paragraph (c)(5) of this section, USP's inclusion under section 951(a)(1)(A) is attributable to the passive category portion of the interest income received by CFC2 from CFC1 and is passive category income to USP. Under paragraph (k)(2)(iii) of this section, USP's $50x inclusion under section 951(a)(1)(A) with respect to CFC3 is also characterized next. Under paragraph (c)(5) of this section, USP's inclusion under section 951(a)(1)(A) is attributable to the passive category portion of the interest income received by CFC3 from CFC2 and is passive category income to USP.

(D) Under paragraph (k)(2)(iv) of this section, the $150x distribution from CFC2 to CFC1 is characterized next. The first $50x of the distribution is out of passive category earnings and profits described in section 959(c)(2). The remaining $100x of the distribution is a dividend that is not attributable to CFC2's passive category income, so under paragraph (c)(4)(i) of this section it is general category income to CFC1 in its entirety. Because $100x of the dividend received or accrued from CFC2 is attributable to income of CFC2 which is not subpart F income, under section 954(c)(6) such dividend income is not treated as foreign personal holding company income of CFC1.

(7) *Example 7*—(i) *Facts*. USP, a domestic corporation, owns 100% of the stock of CFC1, a controlled foreign corporation, and CFC1 owns 100% of the stock of CFC2, a controlled foreign corporation. USP also owns 100% of the stock of CFC3, a controlled foreign corporation. CFC1, CFC2, and CFC3 are all incorporated in different foreign countries. In Year 1, CFC2 earns $100x of general category income that is not subpart F income and distributes the entire amount to CFC1 as a dividend. CFC1 earns $100x of passive category foreign personal holding company income and the $100x dividend from CFC2. CFC1 pays $100x of interest to CFC3. CFC3 earns $200x of general category income that is foreign base company income and the $100x of interest income from CFC1. USP does not have an inclusion under section 951A.

(ii) *Analysis*. This transaction does not involve circular payments and, therefore, the ordering rules of paragraph (k)(2) of this section do not apply. Instead, pursuant to paragraph (k)(1) of this section, income received is characterized first. CFC2's earnings and, thus, the dividend from CFC2 to CFC1 are characterized first. Under paragraph (c)(4)(i) of this section, CFC1 includes the $100x dividend from CFC2 in gross income as general category income because none of CFC2's earnings are passive category income. CFC1 thus has $100x of passive category foreign personal holding company income and $100x of general category income that is excluded from subpart F income under section 954(c)(6)(A). The interest payment from CFC1 to CFC3 is then characterized as $100x passive category income under paragraph (c)(2)(ii)(C) of this section because it is allocable to passive foreign personal holding company income of CFC1. For Year 1, CFC3 thus has $200x of general category income that is subpart F income, and $100x of passive category foreign personal holding company income. For Year 1, under § 1.904-4(d) and paragraph (c)(5) of this section, USP includes in its gross income an inclusion under section 951(a)(1)(A) with respect to CFC3, $200x of which is general category income and $100x of which is passive category income.

(m) *Application of section 904(g)*.—(1) *In general*.—This paragraph (m) applies to certain amounts derived from controlled foreign corporations and noncontrolled 10-percent owned foreign corporations that are treated as United States-owned foreign corporations as defined in section 904(h)(6). For purposes of determining the portion of an interest payment that is allocable to income earned or accrued by a controlled foreign corporation or noncontrolled 10-percent owned foreign corporation from sources within the United States under section 904(h)(3), the rules in paragraph (m)(2) of this section apply. For purposes of determining the portion of a dividend (which, for purposes of this paragraph (m), includes amounts described in section 951(a)(1)(B)) paid or accrued by a controlled foreign corporation or noncontrolled 10-percent owned foreign corporation that is treated as from sources within the United States under section 904(h)(4), the rules in paragraph (m)(4) of this section apply. For purposes of determining the portion of an amount included in gross income under section 951(a)(1)(A), 951A(a) or 1293 that is attributable to income of the controlled foreign corporation or noncontrolled 10-percent owned foreign corporation from sources within the United States under section 904(h)(2), the rules in paragraph (m)(5) of this section apply. In order to determine whether section 904(h) applies, section 904(h)(5) (exception if a United States-owned foreign corporation has a de minimis amount of United States source income) shall be applied to the total amount of earnings and profits of a controlled foreign corporation or noncontrolled 10-percent owned foreign corporation for a taxable year without regard to the characterization of those earnings under section 904(d).

(2) *Treatment of interest payments.*—(i) *Interest payments from controlled foreign corporations.*—If interest is received or accrued by a United States shareholder or a person related to a United States shareholder (within the meaning of paragraph (c)(2)(ii) of this section) from a controlled foreign corporation, the interest shall be considered to be allocable to income of the controlled foreign corporation from sources within the United States for purposes of section 904(d) to the extent that the interest is allocable under paragraph (c)(2)(ii)(C) of this section to passive income that is from sources within the United States. If related person interest is less than or equal to passive income, the related person interest will be allocable to United States source passive income based on the ratio of United States source passive income to total passive income. To the extent that related person interest exceeds passive income, and, therefore, is allocated under paragraph (c)(2)(ii)(D) of this section to income in a separate category other than passive, the following formulas apply in determining the portion of the interest payment that is from sources within the United States. If the taxpayer uses the gross income method to allocate interest, the portion of the interest payment from sources within the United States is determined as follows:

$$\text{The amount of the interest payment allocated to the separate category under paragraph (c)(2)(ii)(D) of this section} \times \frac{\text{Gross income from United States sources in that category}}{\text{Gross income from all sources in that category}}$$

If the taxpayer uses the asset method to allocate interest, then the portion of the interest payment from sources within the United States is determined as follows:

$$\text{The amount of the interest payment allocated to the separate category under paragraph (c)(2)(ii)(D) of this section} \times \frac{\text{Value of domestic assets in that category}}{\text{Value of total assets in that category}}$$

For purposes of this paragraph, the value of assets in a separate category is the value of assets as determined under the principles of § 1.861-9T(g). See § 1.861-10T(d)(2) for purposes of determining the value of assets and gross income in a separate category as reduced for indebtedness the interest on which is directly allocated.

(ii) *Interest payments from noncontrolled 10-percent owned foreign corporations.*—If interest is received or accrued by a shareholder from a noncontrolled 10-percent owned foreign corporation (where the shareholder is a domestic corporation that is a United States shareholder of such noncontrolled 10-percent owned foreign corporation), the rules of paragraph (m)(2)(i) of this section apply in determining the portion of the interest payment that is from sources within the United States, except that the related party interest rules of paragraph (c)(2)(ii)(C) of this section do not apply.

(3) *Examples.*—The following examples illustrate the application of this paragraph (m).

(i) *Example 1*—(A) *Facts.* Controlled foreign corporation CFC is a wholly-owned subsidiary of USP, a domestic corporation. In Year 1, CFC pays USP $300x of interest. CFC has no other expenses. In Year 1, CFC has $3,000x of assets that generate $650x of foreign source general category income and a $1,000x loan to an unrelated foreign person that generates $20x of foreign source passive category interest income. CFC also has a $4,000x loan to an unrelated United States person that generates $70x of U.S. source passive category interest income and $4,000x of assets that generate $100x of U.S. source general category income. CFC uses the asset method to allocate interest expense. The following chart summarizes CFC's assets and income:

Table 1 to paragraph (m)(3)(i)(A)

	Foreign	U.S.	Totals
Assets:			
Passive	1,000x	4,000x	5,000x
General	3,000x	4,000x	7,000x
Total	4,000x	8,000x	12,000x
Income:			
Passive	20x	70x	90x
General	650x	100x	750x
Total	670x	170x	840x

(B) *Analysis.* Under paragraph (c)(2)(ii)(C) of this section, $90x of the related person interest payment is allocable to CFC's passive category income. Under paragraph (m)(2) of this section, $70x of USP's $90x of passive category interest income is from sources within the United States and $20x is from foreign sources. Under paragraph (c)(2)(ii)(D) of this section, the remaining $210x of the related person interest payment is allocated to general category income. Under paragraph (m)(2) of this section, $120x of the remaining $210x of USP's interest income is treated as general category income from sources within the United States ($120x = $210x x $4,000x/$7,000x) and $90x is treated as general category income from foreign sources ($90x = $210x x $3,000x/$7,000x).

(ii) *Example 2.* The facts are the same as in paragraph (m)(3)(i) of this section (the facts in *Example 1*), except that CFC uses the modified gross income method to allocate interest expense. The first $90x of related person interest expense is allocated to passive category income in the same manner as in paragraph (m)(3)(i) of this section (*Example 1*), $70x to U.S. sources and $20x to foreign sources. Under paragraph (c)(2)(ii)(D) of this section, the remaining $210x of the related person interest expense is allocated to CFC's general category income. Under paragraph (m)(2) of this section, $28x of the remaining $210x of USP's interest income is treated as general category income from U.S. sources ($28x = $210x x $100x/$750x) and $182x is treated as general category income from foreign sources ($182x = $210x x $650x/$750x).

(4) *Treatment of dividend payments.*—(i) *Rule.*—Any dividend or distribution treated as a dividend under this paragraph (m) (including an amount included in gross income under section 951(a)(1)(B)) that is received or accrued by a United States shareholder from a controlled foreign corporation, or any dividend that is received or accrued by a domestic corporation from a noncontrolled 10-percent owned foreign corporation with respect to which the shareholder is a United States shareholder, are treated as income in a separate category derived from sources within the United States in proportion to the ratio of the portion of the earnings and profits of the controlled foreign corporation or noncontrolled 10-percent owned foreign corporation in the corresponding separate category from U.S. sources to the total amount of earnings and profits of the controlled foreign corporation or noncontrolled 10-percent owned foreign corporation in that separate category.

(ii) *Determination of earnings and profits from United States sources.*—In order to determine the portions of earnings and profits from United States sources and from foreign sources within each separate category, related person interest shall be allocated to the United States source portion of income in a separate category by applying the rules of paragraph (m)(2) of this section. Other expenses shall be allocated by applying the rules of paragraph (c)(2)(ii) of this section separately to the United States source income and the foreign source income in each category. For example, unrelated person interest expense that is allocated among categories of income based upon the relative amounts of assets in a category must be allocated between United States and foreign source income within each category by applying the rules of paragraph (c)(2)(ii)(E) of this section separately to United States source and foreign source assets in the separate category.

(5) *Treatment of inclusions under sections 951(a)(1)(A), 951A and 1293.*—(i) *Rule.*—Any amount included in the gross income of a United States shareholder of a controlled foreign corporation under section 951(a)(1)(A), 951A, or in the gross income of a domestic corporation that is a United States shareholder of a noncontrolled 10-percent owned foreign corporation described in section 904(d)(2)(E)(i)(II) that is a qualified electing fund under section 1293 is treated as income subject to a separate category that is derived from sources within the United States to the extent the amount is attributable to income of the controlled foreign corporation or qualified electing fund, respectively, in the corresponding category of income from sources within the United States. In order to determine a controlled foreign corporation's taxable income and earnings and profits from sources within the United States in each separate category, the principles of paragraph (m)(4)(ii) of this section shall apply. In order to determine a qualified electing fund's earnings and profits from sources within the United States in each separate category, the principles of paragraph (m)(4)(ii) of this section shall apply, except that the related person interest rule of paragraph (m)(2) of this section shall not apply.

(ii) *Example.*—The following example illustrates the application of this paragraph (m)(5).

(A) *Facts.* Controlled foreign corporation CFC is a wholly-owned subsidiary of domestic corporation, USP. In Year 1, CFC earns $100x of subpart F foreign personal holding company income that is passive category income. Of this amount, $40x is derived from sources within the United States. CFC also earns $50x of subpart F general category income. None of this income is from sources within the United States. Assume that CFC pays no foreign taxes and has no expenses.

(B) *Analysis.* USP must include $150x in gross income under section 951(a). Of this amount, $60x is foreign source passive category income to USP, $40x is U.S. source passive category income to USP, and $50x is foreign source general category income to USP.

(6) *Treatment of section 78 amount.*—For purposes of treating taxes deemed paid by a taxpayer under section 960 as a dividend under section 78, taxes that are paid or accrued with respect to United States source income in a separate category shall be treated as United States source income in that separate category.

(7) *Coordination with treaties.*—(i) *Rule.*—If any amount of income derived from a United States-owned foreign corporation, as defined in section 904(h)(6), would be treated as derived from sources within the United States under section 904(h) and this paragraph (m) and, pursuant to an income tax convention with the United States, the taxpayer chooses to avail itself of benefits of the convention that treat that amount as arising from sources outside the United States under a rule explicitly treating the income as foreign source, then that amount will be treated as foreign source income. However, sections 904(a), (b), (c), (d), (f) and (g), 907, and 960 shall be applied separately to amounts described in the preceding sentence with respect to each treaty under which the taxpayer has claimed benefits and, within each treaty, to each separate category of income.

(ii) *Example.*—The following example illustrates the application of this paragraph (m)(7).

(A) *Facts.* Controlled foreign corporation CFC is incorporated in Country A and is a wholly-owned subsidiary of USP, a domestic corporation. In Year 1, CFC earns $80x of general category foreign base company sales income in Country A and $40x of passive category U.S. source interest income. CFC incurs $20x of expenses attributable to its sales business. CFC pays USP $40x of interest that is allocated to CFC's U.S. source passive category income under paragraph (c)(2)(ii)(C) of this section and so is U.S. source passive category income to USP under paragraphs (c)(2)(i) and (m)(2) of this section. Assume that earnings and profits equal net income. All of CFC's net income of $60x is subpart F income includible in USP's gross income under section 951(a)(1). For Year 1, USP also has $100x of foreign source passive category income derived from investments in Country B. Pursuant to section 904(h)(3) and paragraph (m)(2) of this section, the $40x interest payment from CFC is U.S. source income to USP because it is attributable to U.S. source interest income of CFC. The United States–Country A income tax treaty, however, treats all interest payments by residents of Country A as Country A sourced and USP elects to apply the treaty.

(B) *Analysis.* Pursuant to section 904(h)(10) and this paragraph (m)(7), the entire interest payment will be treated as foreign source income to USP. USP thus has $60x of foreign source general category income, $40x of foreign source Country A treaty category passive income from CFC, and $100x of foreign source passive category income.

(n) *Order of application of section 904(d) and (h).*—In order to apply the rules of this section, § 1.904-4 shall first be applied to the controlled foreign corporation or noncontrolled 10-percent owned foreign corporation to determine the amount of income and earnings and profits derived by the controlled foreign corporation or noncontrolled 10-percent owned foreign corporation in each separate category. The income and earnings and profits in each separate category that are from United States sources shall then be determined. Section 904(d)(3), (d)(4), and (h) and this section are then applied for purposes of characterizing and sourcing income received, accrued, or included by a United States shareholder of the foreign corporation that is attributable or allocable to income or earnings and profits of the foreign corporation.

(o) *Applicability dates.*—Except as otherwise provided in this paragraph (o), this section is applicable for taxable years that both begin after December 31, 2017, and end on or after December 4, 2018. Paragraphs (a)(4)(i) and (vi) of this section are applicable for taxable years of foreign corporations ending on or after October 1, 2019, and taxable years of United States persons ending on or after October 1, 2019. For taxable years of foreign corporations ending before October 1, 2019, and taxable years of United States persons ending before October 1, 2019, a taxpayer may apply such provisions to the last taxable year of a foreign corporation beginning before January 1, 2018, and each subsequent taxable year of the foreign corporation, and to taxable years of United States shareholders in which or with which such taxable years of the foreign corporation end, provided that the taxpayer and United States persons that are related (within the meaning of section 267 or 707) to the taxpayer consistently apply such provisions with respect to all foreign corporations. For taxable years of foreign corporations ending before October 1, 2019, and taxable years of United States persons ending before October 1, 2019, where the taxpayer does not apply the provisions of paragraphs (a)(4)(i) and (vi) of this section, see paragraphs (a)(4)(i) and (vi) of this section as in effect and contained in 26 CFR part 1, as revised April 1, 2020. [Reg. § 1.904-5.]

☐ [*T.D. 8214, 7-15-88. Amended by T.D. 8412, 5-13-92; T.D. 8767, 3-23-98; T.D. 8827, 7-12-99 (corrected 10-29-99); T.D. 8916, 12-29-2000; T.D. 9141, 7-19-2004; T.D. 9260, 4-20-2006 (corrected 12-22-2006); T.D. 9368, 12-20-2007; T.D. 9452, 6-10-2009, T.D. 9521, 4-6-2011, T.D. 9882, 12-16-2019 (corrected 5-14-2020) and T.D. 9908, 9-21-2020.*]

Proposed Amendments to Regulation

§ 1.904-5. Look-through rules as applied to controlled foreign corporations and other entities.

* * *

(k) *Ordering rules.*—(1) *In general.*—Income received or accrued by a related person to which the look-through rules apply is characterized before amounts included from, or paid or distributed by, that person and received or accrued by a related person. For purposes of determining the character of income received or accrued by a person from a related person if the payor or another related person also receives or accrues income from the recipient and the look-through rules apply to the income in all cases, the rules of paragraph (k)(2) of this section apply. Notwithstanding any other provision of this section, the principles of § 1.954-1(c)(1)(i) will apply to any expense subject to § 1.954-1(c)(1)(i).

* * *

[Prop. Reg. § 1.904-5.]

[Proposed 7-13-99.]

Proposed Amendments to Regulation

§1.904-5. Look-through rules as applied to controlled foreign corporations and other entities.—

* * *

(b) * * *

(2) *Priority and ordering of look-through rules.*—To the extent the look-through rules assign income to a separate category, the income is assigned to that separate category rather than the separate category to which the income would have been assigned under §1.904-4 (not taking into account §1.904-4(l)). See paragraph (k) of this section for ordering rules for applying the look-through rules.

* * *

(o) *Applicability dates.*—Except as provided in this paragraph (o), this section is applicable for taxable years that both begin after December 31, 2017, and end on or after December 4, 2018. Paragraph (b)(2) of this section applies to taxable years beginning on or after [the date final regulations are filed with the **Federal Register**]. [Prop. Reg. §1.904-5.]

[Proposed 11-12-2020.]

§1.904-6. Allocation and apportionment of foreign income taxes.—(a) *In general.*—The amount of foreign income taxes paid or accrued with respect to a separate category (as defined in §1.904-5(a)(4)(v)) of income (including U.S. source income assigned to the separate category) includes only those foreign income taxes that are allocated and apportioned to the separate category under the rules of §1.861-20 (as modified by this section). In applying the foreign tax credit limitation under sections 904(a) and (d) to general category income described in section 904(d)(2)(A)(ii) and §1.904-4(d), foreign source income in the general category is a statutory grouping. However, general category income is the residual grouping of income for purposes of assigning foreign income taxes to separate categories. In addition, in determining the numerator of the foreign tax credit limitation under sections 904(a) and (d), where U.S. source income is the residual grouping, the amount of foreign income taxes paid or accrued for which a deduction is allowed, for example, under section 901(k)(7), with respect to foreign source income in a separate category includes only those foreign income taxes that are allocated and apportioned to foreign source income in the separate category under the rules of §1.861-20 (as modified by this section). For purposes of this section, unless otherwise stated, terms have the same meaning as provided in §1.861-20(b). For examples illustrating the application of this section, see §1.861-20(g).

(b) *Assigning an item of foreign gross income to a separate category.*—For purposes of assigning an item of foreign gross income to a separate category or categories (or foreign source income in a separate category) under §1.861-20, the rules of this paragraph (b) apply.

(1) *Base differences.*—Any item of foreign gross income that is attributable to a base difference described in §1.861-20(d)(2)(ii)(B) is assigned to the separate category described in section 904(d)(2)(H)(i), and to foreign source income in that category.

(2) *Disregarded payments.*—(i) *In general.*—(A) *Assignment of foreign gross income.*—Except as provided in paragraph (b)(2)(ii) of this section, if a taxpayer that is an individual or a domestic corporation includes an item of foreign gross income by reason of the receipt of a disregarded payment by a foreign branch or foreign branch owner (as those terms are defined in §1.904-4(f)(3)), or a non-branch taxable unit, the foreign gross income item is assigned to a separate category under §1.861-20(d)(3)(v).

(B) *Definition of non-branch taxable unit.*—The term *non-branch taxable unit* means a person or interest that is described in paragraph (b)(2)(i)(B)(*1*) or (*2*) of this section, respectively.

(*1*) *Persons.*—A non-branch taxable unit described in this paragraph (b)(2)(i)(B)(*1*) means a person that is not otherwise a foreign branch owner and that is a U.S. individual, a domestic corporation, or a foreign or domestic partnership (or other pass-through entity, as defined in §1.904-5(a)(4)) an interest in which is owned, directly or indirectly through one or more other partnerships (or other pass-through entities), by a U.S. individual or a domestic corporation.

(*2*) *Interests.*—A non-branch taxable unit described in this paragraph (b)(2)(i)(B)(2) means an interest of a foreign branch owner or an interest of a person described in paragraph (b)(2)(i)(B)(*1*) of this section that is not otherwise a foreign branch, and that is either a disregarded entity or a branch, as defined in §1.267A-5(a)(2), including a branch described in §1.951A-2(c)(7)(iv)(A)(3) (modified by substituting the term "person" for "controlled foreign corporation").

(ii) *Foreign branch group contributions.*—(A) *In general.*—If a taxpayer includes an item of foreign gross income by reason of a foreign branch group contribution, the foreign gross income is assigned to the foreign branch category, or, in the case of a foreign branch owner that is a partnership, to the partnership's general category income that is attributable to the foreign branch. See, however, §§1.861 20(d)(3)(v)(C)(*7*), 1.960-1(d)(3)(ii)(A), and 1.960-1(e) for rules providing that foreign income tax on a disregarded payment that is a contribution from a controlled foreign corporation to a taxable unit is assigned to the residual grouping and cannot be deemed paid under section 960.

(B) *Foreign branch group contribution.*—A foreign branch group contribution is a contribution (as defined in §1.861-20(d)(3)(v)(E)) made by a member of a foreign branch owner group to a member of a foreign branch group that the payor owns, made by a member of a foreign branch group to another member of that group that the payor owns, or made by a member of a foreign branch group to a member of a different foreign branch group that the payor owns. For purposes of this paragraph (b)(2)(ii)(B), the terms *foreign branch group* and *foreign branch owner group* have the meanings provided in §1.904-4(f)(3).

(c) *Allocating and apportioning deductions.*—For purposes of applying §1.861-20(e) to allocate and apportion deductions allowed under foreign law to foreign gross income in the separate categories, before undertaking the steps outlined in §1.861-20(e), foreign gross income in the passive category is first reduced by any related person interest expense that is allocated to the income under the principles of section 954(b)(5) and §1.904-5(c)(2)(ii)(C). In allocating and apportioning expenses not specifically allocated under foreign law, the principles of foreign law are applied only after taking into account the reduction of passive income by the application of section 954(b)(5). In allocating and apportioning expenses when foreign law does not provide rules for the allocation or apportionment of expenses, losses or other deductions to particular items of foreign gross income, then the principles of section 954(b)(5), in addition to the principles of the section 861 regulations (as defined in §1.861-8(a)(1)), apply to allocate and apportion expenses, losses or other foreign law deductions to foreign gross income after reduction of passive income by the amount of related person interest expense allocated to passive income under section 954(b)(5) and §1.904-5(c)(2)(ii)(C).

(d) *Apportionment of taxes for purposes of applying the high-tax income tests.*—If taxes have been allocated and apportioned to passive income under the rules of paragraph (a) this section, the taxes must further be apportioned to the groups of income described in §1.904-4(c)(3) through (5) for purposes of determining if the group is high-taxed income that is recharacterized as income in another separate category under the rules of §1.904-4(c). See also §1.954-1(c)(1)(iii)(B) (defining a single item of passive category foreign personal holding company income by reference to the grouping rules under §1.904-4(c)(3) through (5)). Taxes are related to income in a particular group under the same rules as those in paragraph (a) of this section except that those rules are applied by apportioning foreign income taxes to the groups described in §1.904-4(c)(3) through (5) instead of separate categories.

(e) *Allocation and apportionment of deemed paid taxes and certain creditable foreign tax expenditures.*—(1) *Taxes deemed paid under section 960(a) or (d).*—If a domestic corporation that is a United States shareholder includes any amount in gross income under section 951(a)(1)(A) or 951A(a), any foreign tax deemed paid with respect to such amount under section 960(a) or (d) is allocated to the separate category to which the inclusion is assigned.

(2) *Taxes deemed paid under section 960(b)(1).*—If a domestic corporation that is a United States shareholder receives a distribution of previously taxed earnings and profits from a first-tier corporation that is excluded from the domestic corporation's income under section 959(a) and §1.959-1, any foreign tax deemed paid under section 960(b)(1) with respect to such distribution is allocated to the same separate category as the annual PTEP account and PTEP group (as defined in §1.960-3(c)) from which the distribution is made.

(3) *Taxes deemed paid under section 960(b)(2).*—If a controlled foreign corporation receives a distribution of previously taxed earnings and profits from an immediately lower-tier corporation that is excluded from such controlled foreign corporation's gross income

under section 959(b) and § 1.959-2, any foreign tax deemed paid under section 960(b)(2) with respect to such distribution is allocated to the same separate category as the annual PTEP account and PTEP group (as defined in § 1.960-3(c)) from which the distribution is made. *See also* § 1.960-3(c)(2).

(4) *Creditable foreign tax expenditures.*—(i) *In general.*—Except as provided in paragraph (e)(4)(ii) of this section, creditable foreign tax expenditures (CFTEs) allocated to a partner under § 1.704-1(b)(4)(viii)(*a*) are allocated for purposes of this section to the same separate category as the separate category to which the taxes were allocated in the hands of the partnership under the rules of paragraph (a) of this section.

(ii) *Foreign branch category.*—CFTEs allocated to a partner in a partnership under § 1.704-1(b)(4)(viii)(*a*) are allocated and apportioned to the foreign branch category of the partner to the extent that:

(A) The CFTEs are allocated and apportioned by the partnership under the rules of paragraph (a) of this section to the general category;

(B) In the hands of the partnership, the CFTEs are related to general category income attributable to a foreign branch (as described in § 1.904-4(f)(2)) under the principles of paragraph (a) of this section; and

(C) The partner's distributive share of the income described in paragraph (e)(4)(ii)(B) of this section is foreign branch category income of the partner under § 1.904-4(f)(1)(i)(B).

(f) *Treatment of certain foreign income taxes paid or accrued by United States shareholders.*—Some or all of the foreign gross income of a United States shareholder of a controlled foreign corporation, or of a U.S. person that owns the United States shareholder (the "U.S. owner"), that is attributable to foreign law inclusion regime income with respect to a foreign law CFC described in § 1.861-20(d)(3)(iii) or foreign law pass-through income from a reverse hybrid described in § 1.861-20(d)(3)(i)(C) is assigned to the section 951A category if, were the controlled foreign corporation the taxpayer that recognizes the foreign gross income, the foreign gross income would be assigned to the controlled foreign corporation's tested income group (as defined in § 1.960-1(b)(33)) within the general category to which an inclusion under section 951A is attributable. The amount of the United States shareholder's, or the U.S. owner's, foreign gross income that is assigned to the section 951A category (or a specified separate category associated with the section 951A category) is based on the inclusion percentage (as defined in § 1.960-2(c)(2)) of the United States shareholder. For example, if a United States shareholder has an inclusion percentage of 60 percent, then 60 percent of the foreign gross income of a United States shareholder that would be assigned (under § 1.861-20(d)(3)(iii)) to the tested income group within the general category income of a reverse hybrid that is a controlled foreign corporation to which an inclusion under section 951A is attributable is assigned to the section 951A category or the specified separate category for income resourced under a tax treaty, and not to the general category.

(g) *Applicability dates.*—Except as otherwise provided in this paragraph (g), this section applies to taxable years that begin after December 31, 2019. Paragraph (b)(2) of this section applies to taxable years that begin after December 31, 2019, and end on or after November 2, 2020. [Reg. § 1.904-6.]

☐ [*T.D.* 8214, 7-15-88. *Amended by T.D.* 8412, 5-13-92; *T.D.* 9141, 7-19-2004, *T.D.* 9260, 4-20-2006, *T.D.* 9882, 12-16-2019, *T.D.* 9922, 11-2-2020 (*corrected* 9-30-2021) *and T.D.* 9959, 12-28-2021.]

§ 1.904-7. Transition rules.—(a) *Characteriza-tion of distributions and section 951(a)(1)(A)(ii) and (iii) and (B) inclusions of earnings of a controlled foreign corporation accumulated in taxable years beginning before January 1, 1987, during taxable years of both the payor controlled foreign corporation and the recipient which begin after December 31, 1986.*—(1) *Distributions and section 951(a)(1)(A)(ii) and (iii) and (B) inclusions.*—Earnings accumulated in taxable years beginning before January 1, 1987, by a foreign corporation that was a controlled foreign corporation when such earnings were accumulated are characterized in that foreign corporation's hands under section 904(d)(1)(A) (separate limitation interest income) or section 904(d)(1)(E) (general limitation income) (prior to their amendment by the Tax Reform Act of 1986 (the Act)) after application of the de minimis rule of former section 904(d)(3)(C) (prior to its amendment by the Act). When, in a taxable year after the effective date of the Act, earnings and profits attributable to such income are distributed to, or included in the gross income of, a United States shareholder under section 951(a)(1)(A)(ii) or (iii) or (B) (hereinafter in this section "inclusions"), the ordering rules of section 904(d)(3)(D) and § 1.904-5(c)(4) shall be applied in determining initially the character of the income of the distributee or United States shareholder. Thus, a proportionate amount of a distribution described in this paragraph initially will be characterized as separate limitation interest income in the hands of the distributee based on the ratio of the separate limitation interest earnings and profits out of which the dividend was paid to the total earnings and profits out of which the dividend was paid. The distribution or inclusions must then be recharacterized in the hands of the distributee or United States shareholder on the basis of the following principles:

(i) Distributions and inclusions that are initially characterized as separate limitation interest income shall be treated as passive income;

(ii) Distributions and inclusions that initially are characterized as old general limitation income shall be treated as general limitation income, unless the taxpayer establishes to the satisfaction of the Commissioner that the distribution or inclusion is attributable to:

(A) Earnings and profits accumulated with respect to shipping income, as defined in section 904(d)(2)(D) and § 1.904-4(f); or

(B) In the case of a financial services entity, earnings and profits accumulated with respect to financial services income, as defined in section 904(d)(2)(C)(ii) and § 1.904-4(e)(1); or

(C) Earnings and profits accumulated with respect to high withholding tax interest, as defined in section 904(d)(2)(B) and § 1.904-4(d).

(2) *Limitation on establishing the character of earnings and profits.*—In order for a taxpayer to establish that distributions or inclusions that are attributable to general limitation earnings and profits of a particular taxable year beginning before January 1, 1987, are attributable to shipping, financial services or high withholding tax interest earnings and profits, the taxpayer must establish the amounts of foreign taxes paid or accrued with respect to income attributable to those earnings and profits that are to be treated as taxes paid or accrued with respect to shipping, financial services or high withholding tax interest income, as the case may be, under section 904(d)(2)(I). Conversely, in order for a taxpayer to establish the amounts of general limitation taxes paid or accrued in a taxable year beginning before January 1, 1987, that are to be treated as taxes paid or accrued with respect to shipping, financial services or high withholding tax interest income, as the case may be, the taxpayer must establish the amount of any distributions or inclusions that are attributable to shipping, financial services or high withholding tax interest earnings and profits. For purposes of establishing the amounts of general limitation taxes that are to be treated as taxes paid or accrued with respect to shipping, financial services or high withholding tax interest income, the principles of § 1.904-6 shall be applied.

(b) *Application of look-through rules to distributions (including deemed distributions) and payments by an entity to a recipient when one's taxable year begins before January 1, 1987 and the other's taxable year begins after December 31, 1986.*—(1) *In general.*—This paragraph provides rules relating to the application of section 904(d)(3) to payments made by a controlled foreign corporation or other entity to which the look-through rules apply during its taxable year beginning after December 31, 1986, but received in a taxable year of the recipient beginning before January 1, 1987. The paragraph also provides rules relating to distributions (including deemed distributions) or payments made by a controlled foreign corporation to which section 904(d)(3) (as in effect before the Act) applies during its taxable year beginning before January 1, 1987, and received in a taxable year of the recipient beginning after December 31, 1986.

(2) *Payor of interest, rents, or royalties is subject to the Act and recipient is not subject to the Act.*—If interest, rents, or royalties are paid or accrued on or after the start of the payor's first taxable year beginning on or after January 1, 1987, but prior to the start of the recipient's first taxable year beginning on or after January 1, 1987, such interest, rents, or royalties shall initially be characterized in accordance with section 904(d)(3) and § 1.904-5. To the extent that interest payments in the hands of the recipient are initially characterized as passive income under these rules, they will be treated as separate limitation interest in the hands of the recipient. To the extent that rents or royalties in the hands of the recipient are initially characterized as passive income under these rules, they will be recharacterized as general limitation income in the hands of the recipient.

(3) *Recipient of interest, rents, or royalties is subject to the Act and payor is not subject to the Act.*—If interest, rents, or royalties are paid or accrued before the start of the payor's first taxable year beginning on or after January 1, 1987, but on or after the start of the recipient's first taxable year beginning after January 1, 1987, the income in the recipient's hands shall be initially characterized in accordance with former section 904(d)(3) (prior to its amendment by the Act). To the extent interest income is characterized as separate limitation interest income under these rules, that income shall be recharacterized as passive income in the hands of the recipient. Rents or royalties will be characterized as general limitation income.

(4) *Recipient of dividends and subpart F inclusions is subject to the Act and payor is not subject to the Act.*—If dividends are paid or accrued or section 951(a)(1) inclusions occur before the start of the first taxable year of a controlled foreign corporation beginning on or after January 1, 1987, but on or after the start of the first taxable year of the distributee or United States shareholder beginning on or after January 1, 1987, the dividends or section 951(a)(1) inclusions in the hands of the distributee or United States shareholder shall be initially characterized in accordance with former section 904(d)(3) (including the ordering rules of section 904(d)(3)(A). Therefore, under former section 904(d)(3)(A), dividends are considered to be paid or derived first from earnings attributable to separate limitation interest income. To the extent the dividend or section 951(a)(1) inclusion is initially characterized under these rules as separate limitation interest income in the hands of the distributee or United States shareholder, the dividend or section 951(a)(1) inclusion shall be recharacterized as passive income in the hands of the distributee or United States shareholder. The portion, if any, of the dividend or section 951(a)(1) inclusion that is not characterized as passive income shall be characterized according to the rules in paragraph (a) of this section. Therefore, a taxpayer may establish that income that would otherwise be characterized as general limitation income is shipping or financial services income. Rules comparable to the rules contained in section 904(d)(2)(I) shall be applied for purposes of characterizing foreign taxes deemed paid with respect to distributions and section 951(a)(1) inclusions covered by this paragraph (b)(4).

(5) *Examples.*—The following examples illustrate the application of this paragraph (b).

Example (1). P is a domestic corporation that is a fiscal year taxpayer (July 1-June 30). S, a controlled foreign corporation, is a wholly-owned subsidiary of P and has a calendar taxable year. On June 1, 1987, S makes a $100 interest payment to P. Because the payment is made after January 1, 1987 (the first day of S's first taxable year beginning after December 31, 1986), the look-through rules of section 904(d)(3) apply to characterize the payment made by S. To the extent, however, that the interest payment to P is allocable to passive income earned by S, the payment will be included in P's separate limitation for interest as provided in former section 904(d)(1)(A).

Example (2). P is a domestic corporation that is a calendar year taxpayer. S, a controlled foreign corporation, is a wholly-owned subsidiary of P and has a July 1-June 30 taxable year. On June 1, 1987, S makes a $100 interest payment to P. Because the payment is made prior to July 1, 1987 (the first day of S's first taxable year beginning after December 31, 1986), the look-through rules of section 904(d)(3) do not apply. Assume that, under former section 904(d)(3), the interest payment would be characterized as separate limitation interest income. For purposes of determining P's foreign tax credit limitation, the interest payment will be passive income as provided in section 904(d)(1)(A).

Example (3). The facts are the same as in *Example (2)* except that on June 1, 1987, S makes a $100 dividend distribution to P. Because the dividend is paid prior to July 1, 1987 (the first day of S's first taxable year beginning after December 31, 1986), the look-through rules of section 904(d)(3) do not apply. Assume that, under former section 904(d)(3), S's earnings and profits for the taxable year ending June 30, 1987 consist of $200 of earnings attributable to general limitation income and $75 of earnings attributable to separate limitation interest income. The portion of the dividend that is attributable to S's separate limitation interest and is treated as separate limitation interest income under former section 904(d)(3) is $75. The remaining $25 of the dividend is treated as general limitation income under former section 904(d)(3). For purposes of determining P's foreign tax credit limitation, $75 of the dividend will be recharacterized as passive income. The remaining $25 of the dividend will be characterized as general limitation income, unless P can establish that the general limitation portion is attributable to shipping or financial services income.

(c) *Installment sales.*—If income is received or accrued by any person on or after the effective date of the Act (as applied to such person) that is attributable to a disposition of property by such person with regard to which section 453 or section 453A applies (installment sale treatment), and the disposition occurred prior to the effective date of the Act, that income shall be characterized according to the rules of §§1.904-4 through 1.904-7.

(d) *Special effective date for high withholding tax interest earned by persons with respect to qualified loans described in section 1201(e)(2) of the Act.*—For purposes of characterizing interest received or accrued by any person, the definition of high withholding tax interest in §1.904-4(d) shall apply to taxable years beginning after December 31, 1986 except as provided in section 1201(e)(2) of the Act.

(e) *Treatment of certain recapture income.*—Except as otherwise provided, if income is subject to recapture under section 585(c), the income shall be general limitation income. If the income is recaptured by a taxpayer that is a financial services entity, the entity may treat the income as financial services income if the taxpayer establishes to the satisfaction of the Secretary that the deduction to which the recapture amount is attributable is allocable to financial services income. If the taxpayer establishes to the satisfaction of the Secretary that the deduction to which the recapture amount is attributable is allocable to high-withholding tax interest income, the taxpayer may treat the income as high-withholding tax interest.

(f) *Treatment of non-look-through pools of a noncontrolled section 902 corporation or a controlled foreign corporation in post-2002 taxable years.*—(1) *Definition of non-look-through pools.*—The term *non-look-through pools* means the pools of post-1986 undistributed earnings (as defined in §1.902-1(a)(9)) that were accumulated, and post-1986 foreign income taxes (as defined in §1.902-1(a)(8)) paid, accrued, or deemed paid, in and after the first taxable year in which the foreign corporation had a domestic shareholder (as defined in §1.902-1(a)(1)) but before any such shareholder was eligible for look-through treatment with respect to dividends from the foreign corporation.

(2) *Treatment of non-look-through pools of a noncontrolled section 902 corporation.*—Any undistributed earnings in the non-look-through pool that were accumulated in taxable years beginning before January 1, 2003, by a noncontrolled section 902 corporation as of the last day of the corporation's last taxable year beginning before January 1, 2003, shall be treated in taxable years beginning after December 31, 2002, as if they were accumulated during a period when a dividend paid by the noncontrolled section 902 corporation to a domestic shareholder would have been eligible for look-through treatment under section 904(d)(4) and §1.904-5. Post-1986 foreign income taxes paid, accrued or deemed paid with respect to such earnings shall be treated as if they were paid, accrued or deemed paid during a period when the related earnings were eligible for look-through treatment. Any such earnings and taxes in the non-look-through pools shall constitute the opening balance of the noncontrolled section 902 corporation's pools of post-1986 undistributed earnings and post-1986 foreign income taxes on the first day of the foreign corporation's first taxable year beginning after December 31, 2002, in accordance with the rules of paragraph (f)(4) of this section.

(3) *Treatment of non-look-through pools of a controlled foreign corporation.*—A controlled foreign corporation may have non-look-through pools of post-1986 undistributed earnings and post-1986 foreign income taxes that were accumulated and paid in a taxable year beginning before January 1, 2003, in which it was a noncontrolled section 902 corporation. Any such undistributed earnings in the non-look-through pool as of the last day of the controlled foreign corporation's last taxable year beginning before January 1, 2003, shall be treated in taxable years beginning on or after January 1, 2003, as if they were accumulated during a period when a dividend paid by the controlled foreign corporation out of such earnings, or an amount included in the gross income of a United States shareholder under section 951 that is attributable to such earnings, would have been eligible for look-through treatment. Any post-1986 foreign income taxes paid, accrued, or deemed paid with respect to such earnings shall be treated in taxable years beginning on or after January 1, 2003, as if they were paid, accrued, or deemed paid during a period when a dividend or inclusion out of such earnings would have been eligible for look-through treatment. Any such undistributed earnings and taxes in the non-look-through pools shall be added to the pools of post-1986 undistributed earnings and post-1986 foreign income taxes of the controlled foreign corporation in the appropriate separate categories on the first day of the controlled foreign corporation's first taxable year beginning after December 31, 2002, in accordance with

the rules of paragraph (f)(4) of this section. Similar rules shall apply to characterize any previously-taxed earnings and profits described in section 959(c)(1)(A) that are attributable to earnings in the non-look-through pool.

(4) *Substantiation of look-through character of undistributed earnings and taxes in a non-look-through pool.*—(i) *Reconstruction of earnings and taxes pools.*—In order to substantiate the look-through characterization of undistributed earnings and taxes in a non-look-through pool under section 904(d)(4) and § 1.904-5, the taxpayer shall make a reasonable, good-faith effort to reconstruct the non-look-through pools of post-1986 undistributed earnings and post-1986 foreign income taxes (and previously-taxed earnings and profits, if any) on a look-through basis for each year in the non-lookthrough period, beginning with the first taxable year in which post-1986 undistributed earnings were accumulated in the non-look-through pool. Reconstruction shall be based on reasonably available books and records and other relevant information, and it must account for earnings distributed and taxes deemed paid in these years as if they were distributed and deemed paid pro rata from the amounts that were added to the non-look-through pools during the non-look-through period.

(ii) *Safe harbor method.*—A taxpayer that was eligible for look-through treatment with respect to a distribution from the foreign corporation in the taxpayer's first taxable year ending after the first day of the foreign corporation's first taxable year beginning after December 31, 2002, may allocate the undistributed earnings and taxes in the non-look-through pools to the foreign corporation's look-through pools of post-1986 undistributed earnings and post-1986 foreign income taxes in other separate categories on the first day of the foreign corporation's first taxable year beginning after December 31, 2002, in the same percentages as the taxpayer properly characterizes the stock of the foreign corporation in the separate categories for purposes of apportioning the taxpayer's interest expense in its first taxable year ending after the first day of the foreign corporation's first taxable year beginning after December 31, 2002, under § 1.861-12T(c)(3) or § 1.861-12(c)(4), as the case may be. If the modified gross income method described in § 1.861-9T(j) is used to apportion interest expense of the foreign corporation in its first taxable year beginning after December 31, 2002, the taxpayer must allocate the undistributed earnings and taxes in the non-look-through pools to the foreign corporation's look-through pools of post-1986 undistributed earnings and post-1986 foreign income taxes based on an average of the foreign corporation's modified gross income ratios for the foreign corporation's taxable years beginning in 2003 and 2004. A taxpayer may also use the safe harbor method described in this paragraph (f)(4)(ii) to allocate to separate categories any previously-taxed earnings and profits described in section 959(c)(1)(A) that are attributable to the non-look-through pool. A taxpayer may choose to use the safe harbor method on either a timely filed or amended tax return or during an audit. However, a taxpayer that uses the safe harbor method on an amended return or in the course of an audit must make appropriate adjustments to eliminate any duplicate benefits arising from application of the safe harbor method to taxable years that are not open for assessment. A taxpayer's choice to use the safe harbor method is evidenced by employing the method. The taxpayer need not file any separate statement.

(iii) *Inadequate substantiation.*—If a taxpayer does not use, or is ineligible to use, the safe harbor method described in paragraph (f)(4)(ii) of this section and the Commissioner determines that the look-through characterization of earnings and taxes in the non-look-through pools cannot reasonably be determined based on the available information, the Commissioner shall allocate the undistributed earnings and taxes in the non-look-through pools to the foreign corporation's passive category.

(iv) *Examples.*—The following examples illustrate the application of this paragraph (f)(4):

Example 1. P, a domestic corporation, has owned 50 percent of the voting stock of S, a foreign corporation, at all times since January 1, 1987, and S has been a noncontrolled section 902 corporation with respect to P since that date. P and S use the calendar year as their U.S. taxable year. The first year in which post-1986 undistributed earnings were accumulated in the non-look-through pool of S was 1987. As of December 31, 2002, S had 200u of post-1986 undistributed earnings and $100 of post-1986 foreign income taxes in its non-look-through pools. P does not use the safe harbor method under paragraph (f)(4)(ii) of this section to allocate the earnings and taxes in the non-look-through pools to S's other separate categories and does not attempt to substantiate the look-through characterization of S's non-look-through pools. The Commissioner, however, reasonably determines, based on information used to characterize S's stock for purposes of apportioning P's interest expense in P's 2003 and 2004 taxable years, that 100u of the earnings and all $100 of the taxes in the nonlook-through pools are properly assigned on a look-through basis to the general limitation category, and 100u of earnings and no taxes are properly assigned on a lookthrough basis to the passive category. Therefore, in accordance with the Commissioner's look-through characterization of the earnings and taxes in S's nonlook-through pools, on January 1, 2003, S has 100u of post-1986 undistributed earnings and $100 of post-1986 foreign income taxes in the general limitation category and 100u of post-1986 undistributed earnings and no post-1986 foreign income taxes in the passive category.

Example 2. The facts are the same as in *Example 1,* except that the Commissioner cannot reasonably determine, based on the available information, the proper look-through characterization of the 200u of undistributed earnings and $100 of taxes in S's non-look-through pools. Accordingly, the Commissioner will assign such earnings and taxes to the passive category, so that as of January 1, 2003, S has 200u of post-1986 undistributed earnings and $100 of post-1986 foreign income taxes in the passive category, and the Commissioner will treat S as a passive category asset for purposes of apportioning P's interest expense.

(5) *Treatment of a deficit accumulated in a non-look-through pool.*—Any deficit in the non-look-through pool of a noncontrolled section 902 corporation or a controlled foreign corporation as of the end of its last taxable year beginning before January 1, 2003, shall be treated in taxable years beginning after December 31, 2002, as if the deficit had been accumulated during a period in which a dividend paid by the foreign corporation would have been eligible for look-through treatment. In the case of a noncontrolled section 902 corporation, the deficit and taxes, if any, in the non-lookthrough pools shall constitute the opening balance of the look-through pools of post-1986 undistributed earnings and post-1986 foreign income taxes of the noncontrolled section 902 corporation in the appropriate separate categories on the first day of its first taxable year beginning after December 31, 2002. In the case of a controlled foreign corporation, the deficit and taxes, if any, in the non-look-through pools shall be added to the balance of the look-through pools of post-1986 undistributed earnings and post-1986 foreign income taxes of the controlled foreign corporation in the appropriate separate categories on the first day of its first taxable year beginning after December 31, 2002. The taxpayer must substantiate the look-through characterization of the deficit and taxes in accordance with the rules of paragraph (f)(4) of this section. If a taxpayer does not use the safe harbor method described in paragraph (f)(4)(ii) of this section and the Commissioner determines that the look-through characterization of the deficit and taxes cannot reasonably be determined based on the available information, the Commissioner shall allocate the deficit and taxes, if any, in the non-look-through pools to the foreign corporation's passive category. If, as of the end of a taxable year beginning after December 31, 2002, in which it pays a dividend, the foreign corporation has zero or a deficit in post-1986 undistributed earnings (taking into account any earnings or a deficit accumulated in taxable years beginning before January 1, 2003), the deficit in post-1986 undistributed earnings shall be carried back to reduce pre-1987 accumulated profits, if any, on a last-in first-out basis. See § 1.902-2(a)(1). If, as of the end of a taxable year beginning after December 31, 2002, in which the foreign corporation pays a dividend out of current earnings and profits, it has zero or a deficit in post-1986 undistributed earnings (taking into account any earnings or a deficit accumulated in taxable years beginning before January 1, 2003), and the sum of current plus accumulated earnings and profits is zero or less than zero, no foreign taxes shall be deemed paid with respect to the dividend. See § 1.902-1(b)(4).

(6) *Treatment of pre-1987 accumulated profits.*—Any pre-1987 accumulated profits (as defined in § 1.902-1(a)(10)) of a controlled foreign corporation or noncontrolled section 902 corporation shall be treated in taxable years beginning after December 31, 2002, as if they were accumulated during a period in which a dividend paid by the foreign corporation would have been eligible for look-through treatment. Any pre-1987 foreign income taxes (as defined in § 1.902-1(a)(10)(iii)) shall be treated as if they were paid, accrued or deemed paid during a year when a dividend out of the related pre-1987 accumulated profits would have been eligible for look-through treatment. The taxpayer must substantiate the look-through characterization of the pre-1987 accumulated profits and pre-1987 foreign income taxes in accordance with the rules of paragraph (f)(4) of this section. If a taxpayer does not use, or is ineligible to use, the safe harbor method described in paragraph (f)(4)(ii) of this section and the Commissioner determines that the look-through characterization of the pre-1987

accumulated profits and pre-1987 foreign income taxes cannot reasonably be determined based on the available information, the pre-1987 accumulated profits and pre-1987 foreign income taxes shall be allocated to the foreign corporation's passive category.

(7) *Treatment of post-1986 undistributed earnings or a deficit of a controlled foreign corporation attributable to dividends from a noncontrolled section 902 corporation paid in taxable years beginning before January 1, 2003.*—(i) *Look-through treatment of post-1986 undistributed earnings at controlled foreign corporation level.*—Dividends paid by a noncontrolled section 902 corporation to a controlled foreign corporation in post-1986 taxable years of the noncontrolled section 902 corporation beginning before January 1, 2003, were assigned to a separate category for dividends from that noncontrolled section 902 corporation. Beginning on the first day of the controlled foreign corporation's first taxable year beginning on or after the first day of the lower-tier corporation's first taxable year beginning after December 31, 2002, any post-1986 undistributed earnings, or previously-taxed earnings and profits described in section 959(c)(1) or (2), of the controlled foreign corporation in such a separate category shall be treated as if they were accumulated during a period when a dividend paid by the noncontrolled section 902 corporation would have been eligible for lookthrough treatment. Any post-1986 foreign income taxes in such a separate category shall also be treated as if they were paid, accrued or deemed paid during a period when such a dividend would have been eligible for look-through treatment. Any such post-1986 undistributed earnings and post-1986 foreign income taxes in a separate category for dividends from a noncontrolled section 902 corporation shall be added to the opening balance of the controlled foreign corporation's look-through pools of post-1986 undistributed earnings and post-1986 foreign income taxes in the appropriate separate categories on the first day of the controlled foreign corporation's first taxable year beginning on or after the first day of the lower-tier corporation's first taxable year beginning after December 31, 2002. Any section 952(c)(2) recapture account with respect to such a separate category shall be allocated in the same manner as the associated post-1986 undistributed earnings. The taxpayer must substantiate the lookthrough characterization of such earnings and taxes in accordance with the rules of paragraph (f)(7)(iii) of this section.

(ii) *Look-through treatment of deficit in post-1986 undistributed earnings at controlled foreign corporation level.*—If a controlled foreign corporation has a deficit in a separate category for dividends from a lower-tier noncontrolled section 902 corporation that is a member of the controlled foreign corporation's qualified group as defined in section 902(b)(2), such deficit shall be treated in taxable years of the upper-tier corporation beginning on or after the first day of the lower-tier corporation's first taxable year beginning after December 31, 2002, as if the deficit had been accumulated during a period in which a dividend from the lower-tier corporation would have been eligible for look-through treatment. Any post-1986 foreign income taxes in the separate category for dividends from the noncontrolled section 902 corporation shall also be treated as if they were paid, accrued or deemed paid during a period when the dividends were eligible for look-through treatment. The deficit and related post-1986 foreign income taxes, if any, shall be added to the opening balance of the controlled foreign corporation's look-through pools of post-1986 undistributed earnings and post-1986 foreign income taxes in the appropriate separate categories on the first day of the controlled foreign corporation's first taxable year beginning on or after the first day of the lower-tier corporation's first taxable year beginning after December 31, 2002. The taxpayer must substantiate the look-through characterization of the deficit and taxes in accordance with the rules of paragraph (f)(7)(iii) of this section.

(iii) *Substantiation required for look-through treatment.*—The taxpayer must substantiate the look-through characterization of post-1986 undistributed earnings, previously-taxed earnings and profits, or a deficit in post-1986 undistributed earnings in a separate category for dividends paid by a noncontrolled section 902 corporation in taxable years beginning before January 1, 2003, by making a reasonable, good-faith effort to reconstruct the earnings (or deficit) and taxes in the separate category at the level of the controlled foreign corporation on a look-through basis, in accordance with the principles of paragraph (f)(4)(i) of this section. Alternatively, the taxpayer may allocate the earnings (or deficit) and taxes to the controlled foreign corporation's lookthrough pools under the safe harbor method described in paragraph (f)(4)(ii) of this section at the level of the controlled foreign corporation. If the taxpayer uses the safe harbor method, the earnings (or deficit) and taxes shall be allocated to the controlled foreign corporation's look-through pools in the appropriate separate categories on the first day of the controlled foreign corporation's first taxable year beginning on or after the first day of the lower-tier corporation's first taxable year beginning after December 31, 2002. The allocation shall be made in the same percentages as the controlled foreign corporation would properly characterize the stock of the lower-tier noncontrolled section 902 corporation in the separate categories for purposes of apportioning the controlled foreign corporation's interest expense in its first taxable year ending after the first day of the noncontrolled section 902 corporation's first taxable year beginning after December 31, 2002. Under § 1.861-12T(c)(3), the apportionment ratios properly used by the controlled foreign corporation are in turn based on the apportionment ratios properly used by the noncontrolled section 902 corporation to apportion its interest expense in its first taxable year beginning after December 31, 2002. In the case of a taxpayer that uses the safe harbor method where the lower-tier noncontrolled section 902 corporation uses the modified gross income method described in § 1.861-9T(j) to apportion interest expense for its first taxable year beginning after December 31, 2002, earnings (or a deficit) and taxes in the separate category for dividends from the noncontrolled section 902 corporation shall be allocated to the look-through pools based on the average of the noncontrolled section 902 corporation's modified gross income ratios for its taxable years beginning in 2003 and 2004. In the case of a controlled foreign corporation that has in its qualified group a chain of lower-tier noncontrolled section 902 corporations, the safe harbor applies first to characterize the stock of the third-tier corporation and then to characterize the stock of the second-tier corporation. Where a taxpayer uses the safe harbor method with respect to a lower-tier noncontrolled section 902 corporation with respect to which the taxpayer did not meet the requirements of section 902(a) as of the end of the upper-tier controlled foreign corporation's last taxable year beginning before January 1, 2003, the earnings (or deficit) and taxes in the separate category for dividends from the lower-tier corporation shall be allocated to the upper-tier corporation's look-through pools in the separate categories in the same percentages as the stock of the lower-tier corporation would have been characterized for purposes of apportioning the upper-tier corporation's interest expense in the last year the taxpayer met the ownership requirements of section 902(a) with respect to the lower-tier corporation if the look-through rules had applied in that year. If a taxpayer does not use the safe harbor method described in this paragraph (f)(7)(iii), and the Commissioner determines that the look-through characterization of the earnings (or deficit) and taxes cannot reasonably be determined based on the available information, the Commissioner shall allocate the earnings (or deficit) and associated foreign income taxes to the controlled foreign corporation's passive category.

(8) *Treatment of distributions received by an upper-tier corporation from a lowertier noncontrolled section 902 corporation, including when the corporations do not have the same taxable years.*—(i) *Rule.*—In the case of dividends paid by a lower-tier noncontrolled section 902 corporation to an upper-tier corporation where both are members of the same qualified group as defined in section 902(b)(2), the following rules apply. Dividends paid by the lower-tier corporation in taxable years beginning before January 1, 2003, are assigned to a separate category for dividends from that corporation, regardless of whether the corresponding taxable year of the recipient corporation began after December 31, 2002. Post-1986 undistributed earnings, previously-taxed earnings and profits, and post-1986 foreign income taxes in such a separate category shall be treated, beginning on the first day of the upper-tier corporation's first taxable year beginning on or after the first day of the lower-tier corporation's first taxable year beginning after December 31, 2002, as if they were accumulated during a period when a dividend paid by the lower-tier corporation would have been eligible for look-through treatment under section 904(d)(4) and § 1.904-5. Dividends paid by a lower-tier corporation in taxable years beginning after December 31, 2002, are eligible for look-through treatment when paid, without regard to whether the corresponding taxable year of the recipient upper-tier corporation began after December 31, 2002.

(ii) *Example.*—The following example illustrates the application of paragraph (f) of this section:

Example. M, a domestic corporation, has directly owned 50 percent of the stock of foreign corporation X, and X has directly owned 50 percent of the stock of foreign corporation Y, at all times since X and Y were organized on January 1, 1990. Accordingly, X and Y are noncontrolled section 902 corporations with respect to M, and X and Y are members of the same qualified group. M and Y use the calendar year as their U.S. taxable year, and X uses a taxable year beginning on July 1. Under § 1.904-4(g) and paragraph (f)(10) of this section, a dividend paid to M by X on January 15, 2003 (during X's last pre-2003 taxable year) is not eligible for look-through treatment in 2003. However, under §1.861-12(c)(4), M will characterize the stock of X on a lookthrough basis for purposes of interest expense apportionment in its 2003 taxable year. Under §1.904-2(h)(1), any unused foreign taxes in M's separate category for dividends from X will be carried over to M's other separate categories on a look-through basis for M's taxable years beginning on and after January 1, 2004. Under paragraph (f)(2) of this section, any undistributed earnings and taxes in X's non-look-through pools will be allocated to X's other separate categories on July 1, 2003. Under §1.904-5(i)(4) and paragraphs (f)(8)(i) and (f)(10) of this section, a dividend paid to X by Y on January 15, 2003 (during Y's first post-2002 taxable year) is eligible for look-through treatment when paid, notwithstanding that it is received in a pre-2003 taxable year of X.

(9) *Election to apply pre-AJCA rules to 2003 and 2004 taxable years.*—(i) *Definition.*—The term *single category for dividends from all noncontrolled section 902 corporations* means the separate category described in section 904(d)(1)(E) as in effect for taxable years beginning after December 31, 2002, and prior to its repeal by the American Jobs Creation Act (AJCA), Public Law 108-357, 118 Stat. 1418 (October 22, 2004).

(ii) *Time, manner, and form of election.*—A taxpayer may elect not to apply the provisions of section 403 of the AJCA and to apply the rules of this paragraph (f)(9) to taxable years of noncontrolled section 902 corporations beginning after December 31, 2002, and before January 1, 2005, without regard to whether the corresponding taxable years of the taxpayer or any upper-tier corporation begin before or after such dates. A taxpayer shall be eligible to make such an election provided that—

(A) The taxpayer's tax liability as shown on an original or amended tax return for each of its affected taxable years is consistent with the rules of this paragraph (f)(9), the guidance set forth in Notice 2003-5 (2003-1 CB 294) (see §601.601(d)(2) of this chapter), and the principles of §1.861-12(c)(4) for each such year for which the statute of limitations does not preclude the filing of an amended return;

(B) The taxpayer makes appropriate adjustments to eliminate any duplicate benefits arising from the application of this paragraph (f)(9) to taxable years that are not open for assessment; and

(C) The taxpayer attaches a statement to its next tax return for which the due date (with extensions) is more than 90 days after April 25, 2006, indicating that the taxpayer elects not to apply the provisions of section 403 of the AJCA to taxable years of its noncontrolled section 902 corporations beginning in 2003 and 2004, and that the taxpayer has filed original returns or will file amended returns reflecting tax liabilities for each affected year that satisfy the requirements described in this paragraph (f)(9)(ii).

(iii) *Treatment of non-look-through pools in taxable years beginning after December 31, 2004.*—Undistributed earnings (or a deficit) and taxes in the non-lookthrough pools of a controlled foreign corporation or a noncontrolled section 902 corporation as of the end of its last taxable year beginning before January 1, 2005, shall be treated in taxable years beginning after December 31, 2004, as if they were accumulated and paid during a period in which a distribution out of earnings in the nonlook-through pool would have been eligible for look-through treatment. Such earnings (or deficit) and taxes shall be added to the foreign corporation's pools of post-1986 undistributed earnings and post-1986 foreign income taxes in the appropriate separate categories on the first day of the foreign corporation's first taxable year beginning after December 31, 2004. In accordance with the principles of paragraph (f)(4) of this section, the taxpayer must reconstruct the non-look-through pools or, if the taxpayer chooses to use the safe harbor method, allocate the earnings and taxes in the nonlook-through pools to the foreign corporation's look-through pools in the appropriate separate categories on the first day of the foreign corporation's first taxable year beginning after December 31, 2004. Under the safe harbor method, this allocation is made in the same percentages as the taxpayer properly characterized the stock of the foreign corporation for purposes of apportioning the taxpayer's interest expense in the taxpayer's first taxable year ending after the first day of the foreign corporation's first taxable year beginning after December 31, 2002. See §1.861-12T(c)(3) and §1.861-12(c)(4). If a taxpayer does not use the safe harbor method described in paragraph (f)(4)(ii) of this section and the Commissioner determines that the look-through characterization of the earnings (or deficit) and taxes cannot reasonably be determined based on the available information, the earnings (or deficit) and taxes shall be allocated to the foreign corporation's passive category.

(iv) *Carryover of unused foreign tax.*—To the extent that a taxpayer has unused foreign taxes in the single category for dividends from all noncontrolled section 902 corporations, such taxes shall be carried forward to the appropriate separate categories in the taxpayer's taxable years beginning on or after the first day of the relevant noncontrolled section 902 corporation's first taxable year beginning after December 31, 2004. Such unused taxes shall be carried forward in the same manner as §1.904-2(h)(1) provides that unused foreign taxes in the separate categories for dividends from each noncontrolled section 902 corporation are carried over to taxable years beginning on or after the first day of the noncontrolled section 902 corporation's first taxable year beginning after December 31, 2002, in the case of a taxpayer that does not make the election under this paragraph (f)(9). The electing taxpayer shall determine which noncontrolled section 902 corporations paid the dividends to which the unused foreign taxes are attributable and assign the taxes to the appropriate separate categories as if such dividends had been eligible for look-through treatment when paid. Accordingly, the taxpayer must substantiate the look-through characterization of the unused foreign taxes in accordance with paragraph (f)(4) of this section by reconstructing the non-lookthrough pools or, if the taxpayer uses the safe harbor method, by allocating the unused foreign taxes to other separate categories in the same percentages as the taxpayer properly characterized the stock of the noncontrolled section 902 corporation for purposes of apportioning the taxpayer's interest expense for its first taxable year ending after the first day of the noncontrolled section 902 corporation's first taxable year beginning after December 31, 2002. The rule described in this paragraph (f)(9)(iv) shall apply only to unused foreign taxes attributable to dividends out of earnings that were accumulated by noncontrolled section 902 corporations in taxable years of such corporations beginning before January 1, 2003, because only unused foreign taxes attributable to distributions out of pre-2003 earnings are included in the single category for dividends from all noncontrolled section 902 corporations. To the extent that unused foreign taxes carried forward to the single category for dividends from all noncontrolled section 902 corporations under the rules of Notice 2003-5 were either absorbed by low-taxed dividends paid by noncontrolled section 902 corporations out of the non-look-through pool in taxable years of such corporations beginning in 2003 or 2004, or expired unused, the amount of taxes carried forward to the separate categories on a look-through basis will be smaller than the aggregate amount of taxes initially carried forward to the single category for dividends from all noncontrolled section 902 corporations. In this case, the unused foreign taxes arising in each taxable year shall be deemed attributable to each noncontrolled section 902 corporation in the same ratio as the dividends included in the separate category that were paid by such corporation in such year bears to all such dividends paid by all noncontrolled section 902 corporations in such year. Unused foreign taxes carried forward from the separate categories for dividends from each noncontrolled section 902 corporation to the single category for dividends from all noncontrolled section 902 corporations will similarly be deemed to have been utilized on a pro rata basis. The remaining unused foreign taxes are then assigned to the appropriate separate categories under the rules of paragraph (f)(4) of this section. Unused foreign taxes shall be treated as allocable to general category income to the extent that such taxes would otherwise have been allocable to passive income (based on reconstructed pools or the safe harbor method), or to the extent that, under paragraph (f)(4)(iii) of this section, the Commissioner determines that the look-through characterization cannot reasonably be determined based on the available information.

(v) *Carryback of unused foreign tax.*—To the extent that a taxpayer has unused foreign taxes attributable to a dividend paid by a noncontrolled section 902 corporation that was eligible for look-through treatment under section 904(d)(4) and §1.904-5, any such unused foreign taxes shall be carried back to prior taxable years within the same separate category and not to the single category for dividends from all noncontrolled section 902 corporations or any separate category for dividends from a noncontrolled section 902 corporation. See Notice 2003-5 for rules relating to the carryback of unused foreign taxes in the single category for dividends from all noncontrolled section 902 corporations.

(vi) *Recapture of overall foreign loss or separate limitation loss in the single category for dividends from all noncontrolled section 902 corporations.*—To the extent that a taxpayer has a balance in a separate limitation loss or overall foreign loss account in the single category for dividends from all noncontrolled section 902 corporations under section 904(d)(1)(E) (prior to its repeal by the AJCA), at the end of the taxpayer's last taxable year beginning before January 1, 2005 (or a later taxable year in which the taxpayer received a dividend subject to the separate limitation for dividends from all noncontrolled section 902 corporations), the amount of such balance shall be allocated on the first day of the taxpayer's next taxable year to the taxpayer's other separate categories. The amount of such balance that is attributable to each noncontrolled section 902 corporation shall be allocated in the same percentages as the taxpayer properly characterized the stock of such corporation for purposes of apportioning the taxpayer's interest expense for its first taxable year ending after the first day of such corporation's first taxable year beginning after December 31, 2002, under § 1.861-12T(c)(3) or § 1.861-12(c)(4), as the case may be. To the extent that a taxpayer has a balance in a separate limitation loss account for the single category for dividends from all noncontrolled section 902 corporations with respect to another separate category, and the separate limitation loss account would otherwise be assigned to that other category under this paragraph (f)(9)(vi), such balance shall be eliminated.

(vii) *Recapture of separate limitation losses in other separate categories.*—To the extent that a taxpayer has a balance in any separate limitation loss account in a separate category with respect to the single category for dividends from all noncontrolled section 902 corporations at the end of the taxpayer's last taxable year with or within which ends the last taxable year of the relevant noncontrolled section 902 corporation beginning before January 1, 2005, such loss shall be recaptured in subsequent taxable years as income in the appropriate separate category. The separate limitation loss account shall be deemed attributable on a pro rata basis to those noncontrolled section 902 corporations that paid dividends out of earnings accumulated in taxable years beginning before January 1, 2003, in the years in which the separate limitation loss in the other separate category arose. The ratable portions of the separate limitation loss account shall be recaptured as income in the taxpayer's separate categories in the same percentages as the taxpayer properly characterized the stock of the relevant noncontrolled section 902 corporation for purposes of apportioning the taxpayer's interest expense in its first taxable year ending after the first day of such corporation's first taxable year beginning after December 31, 2002, under § 1.861-12T(c)(3) or § 1.861-12(c)(4), as the case may be. To the extent that a taxpayer has a balance in any separate limitation loss account in any separate category that would have been recaptured as income in that same category under this paragraph (f)(9)(vii), such balance shall be eliminated.

(viii) *Treatment of undistributed earnings in an upper-tier corporation-level single category for dividends from lower-tier noncontrolled section 902 corporations.*—Where a controlled foreign corporation or noncontrolled section 902 corporation has a single category for dividends from all noncontrolled section 902 corporations containing earnings attributable to dividends paid by one or more lower-tier corporations, the following rules apply. The post-1986 undistributed earnings, previously-taxed earnings and profits described in section 959(c)(1) or (2), if any, and associated post-1986 foreign income taxes shall be allocated to the upper-tier corporation's other separate categories in the same manner as earnings and taxes in a separate category for dividends from each noncontrolled section 902 corporation maintained by the upper-tier corporation are allocated under paragraph (f)(7) of this section. Accordingly, post-1986 undistributed earnings, previously-taxed earnings and profits, if any, and post-1986 foreign income taxes in the single category for dividends from all noncontrolled section 902 corporations shall be treated as if they were accumulated and paid, accrued or deemed paid during a period when a dividend paid by each lower-tier corporation that paid dividends included in the single category would have been eligible for look-through treatment. If the taxpayer uses the safe harbor method described in paragraph (f)(7)(iii) of this section, the earnings and taxes shall be allocated based on the apportionment ratios properly used by the lower-tier corporation to apportion its interest expense for its first taxable year beginning after December 31, 2002. Any section 952(c)(2) recapture account with respect to the single category shall be allocated in the same manner as the associated post-1986 undistributed earnings. The taxpayer must substantiate the look-through characterization of the earnings and taxes in accordance with the rules of paragraph (f)(7)(iii) of this section. If the taxpayer does not use the safe harbor method and the Commissioner determines that the look-through characterization of the earnings cannot reasonably be determined based on the available information, the earnings and taxes shall be assigned to the upper-tier corporation's passive category.

(ix) *Treatment of a deficit in the single category for dividends from lower-tier noncontrolled section 902 corporations.*—Where a controlled foreign corporation or noncontrolled section 902 corporation had an aggregate deficit in the single category for dividends from all noncontrolled section 902 corporations as of the end of the upper-tier corporation's last taxable year beginning before January 1, 2005, such deficit and the associated post-1986 foreign income taxes, if any, shall be allocated to the upper-tier corporation's other separate categories in the same percentages in which the non-lookthrough pools of each lower-tier corporation to which the deficit is attributable were assigned to such corporation's other separate categories in its first taxable year beginning after December 31, 2002. If the taxpayer uses the safe harbor method described in paragraph (f)(7)(iii) of this section, the deficit and taxes shall be allocated based on how the taxpayer properly characterized the stock of the lower-tier noncontrolled section 902 corporation for purposes of apportioning the upper-tier corporation's interest expense for the upper-tier corporation's first taxable year ending after the first day of the lower-tier corporation's first taxable year beginning after December 31, 2002. The taxpayer must substantiate the look-through characterization of the deficit and taxes in accordance with the rules of paragraph (f)(7)(iii) of this section. If the taxpayer does not use the safe harbor method and the Commissioner determines that the look-through characterization of the deficit cannot reasonably be determined based on the available information, the deficit and taxes shall be assigned to the upper-tier corporation's passive category.

(10) *Effective/applicability date.*—This paragraph (f) shall apply to dividends from a noncontrolled section 902 corporation that are paid in taxable years of the noncontrolled section 902 corporation ending on or after April 20, 2009. See 26 CFR § 1.904-7T(f) (revised as of April 1, 2009) for rules applicable, except in the case of a taxpayer that makes the election under paragraph (f)(9) of that section, to dividends from a noncontrolled section 902 corporation that are paid in taxable years of the noncontrolled section 902 corporation beginning after December 31, 2002, and ending before April 20, 2009. See 26 CFR § 1.904-7T(f) (revised as of April 1, 2009) for rules applicable, in the case of a taxpayer that makes the election under paragraph (f)(9) of that section, to dividends from a noncontrolled section 902 corporation that are paid in taxable years of the noncontrolled section 902 corporation beginning after December 31, 2004, and ending before April 20, 2009. However, taxpayers may choose to apply paragraph (f) of this section in its entirety in lieu of 26 CFR § 1.904-7T(f) to all dividends paid in periods covered by the temporary regulations, provided that appropriate adjustments are made to eliminate duplicate benefits arising from application of paragraph (f) to taxable years that are not open for assessment.

(g) *Treatment of earnings and foreign taxes of a controlled foreign corporation or a noncontrolled section 902 corporation accumulated in taxable years beginning before January 1, 2007.*—(1) *Definitions.*—(i) *Pre-2007 pools.*—means the pools in each separate category of post-1986 undistributed earnings (as defined in § 1.902-1(a)(9)) that were accumulated, and post 1986 foreign income taxes (as defined in § 1.902-1(a)(8)) paid, accrued, or deemed paid, in taxable years beginning before January 1, 2007.

(ii) *Pre-2007 separate categories.*—means the separate categories of income described in section 904(d) as applicable to taxable years beginning before January 1, 2007, and any other separate category of income described in § 1.904-4(m).

(iii) *Post-2006 separate categories.*—means the separate categories of income described in section 904(d) as applicable to taxable years beginning after December 31, 2006, and any other separate category of income described in § 1.904-4(m).

(2) *Treatment of pre-2007 pools of a controlled foreign corporation or a noncontrolled section 902 corporation.*—Any post-1986 undistributed earnings in a pre-2007 pool of a controlled foreign corporation or a noncontrolled section 902 corporation shall be treated in taxable years beginning after December 31, 2006, as if they were accumulated during a period in which the rules governing the determination of post-2006 separate categories applied. Post-1986 foreign income taxes paid, accrued, or deemed paid with respect to such earnings shall be treated as if they were paid, accrued, or deemed paid during a period in which the rules governing the determination of post-2006 separate categories (including the rules of section 904(d)(3)(E)) applied as well. Any such earnings and taxes in pre-2007 pools shall constitute the opening balance of the foreign corporation's post-1986 undistributed earnings and post-1986 foreign income taxes on the first day of the foreign corporation's first taxable year beginning after December 31, 2006, in accordance with the rules of paragraph (g)(3) of this section. Similar rules shall apply to characterize any deficits in the pre-2007 pools and previously-taxed earnings and profits described

in section 959(c)(1) and (2) that are attributable to earnings in the pre-2007 pools. Any section 952(c)(2) recapture account with respect to a separate category shall be allocated in the same manner as the post-1986 undistributed earnings in the associated pre-2007 pool.

(3) *Substantiation of post-2006 character of earnings and taxes in a pre-2007 pool.*—(i) *Reconstruction of earnings and taxes pools.*—In order to substantiate the post-2006 characterization of post-1986 undistributed earnings (as well as deficits and previously-taxed earnings, if any) and post-1986 foreign income taxes in pre-2007 pools of a controlled foreign corporation or a noncontrolled section 902 corporation, the taxpayer shall make a reasonable, good-faith effort to reconstruct the pre-2007 pools of post-1986 undistributed earnings (as well as deficits and previously-taxed earnings, if any) and post-1986 foreign income taxes following the rules governing the determination of post-2006 separate categories for each taxable year beginning before January 1, 2007, beginning with the first year in which post-1986 undistributed earnings were accumulated in the pre-2007 pool. Reconstruction shall be based on reasonably available books and records and other relevant information. To the extent any pre-2007 separate category includes earnings that would be allocated to more than one post-2006 separate category, the taxpayer must account for earnings distributed and taxes deemed paid in these years for such category as if they were distributed and deemed paid pro rata from the amounts that were added to that category during each taxable year beginning before January 1, 2007.

(ii) *Safe harbor method.*—(A) *In general.*—Subject to the rules of paragraph (g)(3)(iii) of this section, a taxpayer may allocate the post-1986 undistributed earnings and post-1986 foreign income taxes in pre-2007 pools of a controlled foreign corporation or a noncontrolled section 902 corporation (as well as deficits and previously-taxed earnings, if any) under one of the safe harbor methods described in paragraphs (g)(3)(ii)(B) and (g)(3)(ii)(C) of this section. A taxpayer may choose to use the safe harbor method on a timely filed (original or amended) tax return or during an audit. A taxpayer that uses the safe harbor method on an amended return or in the course of an audit must make appropriate adjustments to eliminate any double benefit arising from application of the safe harbor method to years that are not open for assessment. A taxpayer's choice to use the safe harbor method is evidenced by employing the method. The taxpayer need not file any separate statement.

(B) *General safe harbor method.*—*(1)* Any post-1986 undistributed earnings (as well as deficits and previously-taxed earnings, if any) and post-1986 foreign income taxes of a noncontrolled section 902 corporation or a controlled foreign corporation in a pre-2007 separate category for passive income, certain dividends from a DISC or former DISC, taxable income attributable to certain foreign trade income, or certain distributions from a FSC or former FSC shall be allocated to the post-2006 separate category for passive category income.

(2) Any post-1986 undistributed earnings (as well as deficits and previously-taxed earnings, if any) and post-1986 foreign income taxes of a noncontrolled section 902 corporation or a controlled foreign corporation in a pre-2007 separate category for financial services income, shipping income or general limitation income shall be allocated to the post-2006 separate category for general category income.

(3) Except as provided in paragraph (g)(3)(ii)(B)*(4)* of this section, any post-1986 undistributed earnings (as well as deficits and previously-taxed earnings, if any) and post-1986 foreign income taxes of a noncontrolled section 902 corporation or a controlled foreign corporation in a pre-2007 separate category for high withholding tax interest shall be allocated to the post-2006 separate category for passive category income.

(4) If a controlled foreign corporation has positive post-1986 undistributed earnings and post-1986 foreign income taxes in a pre-2007 separate category for high withholding tax interest, such earnings and taxes shall be allocated to the post-2006 separate category for general category income if the earnings would qualify as income subject to high foreign taxes under section 954(b)(4) if the entire amount of post-1986 undistributed earnings were treated as a net item of income subject to the rules of § 1.954-1(d). If the high withholding tax interest earnings would not qualify as income subject to high foreign taxes under section 954(b)(4), then the earnings and taxes shall be allocated to the post-2006 separate category for passive category income.

(C) *Interest apportionment safe harbor.*—A taxpayer may allocate the post-1986 undistributed earnings (as well as deficits and previously-taxed earnings, if any) and post-1986 foreign income taxes in pre-2007 pools of a controlled foreign corporation or a noncontrolled section 902 corporation following the principles of paragraph (f)(4)(ii) of this section.

(iii) *Consistency rule.*—The election to apply a safe harbor method under paragraph (g)(3)(ii) of this section in lieu of the rules described in paragraph (g)(3)(i) of this section may be made on a separate category by separate category basis. However, if a taxpayer elects to apply a safe harbor to allocate pre-2007 pools of more than one pre-2007 separate category of a controlled foreign corporation or a noncontrolled section 902 corporation, such safe harbor (the general safe harbor described in paragraph (g)(3)(ii)(B) of this section or the interest apportionment safe harbor described in paragraph (g)(3)(ii)(C) of this section) shall apply to allocate post-1986 undistributed earnings (as well as deficits and previously-taxed earnings, if any) and post-1986 foreign income taxes for the pre-2007 pools in each pre-2007 separate category of the foreign corporation for which the taxpayer elected to apply a safe harbor method in lieu of reconstructing the pre-2007 pools.

(4) *Treatment of pre-1987 accumulated profits.*—Any pre-1987 accumulated profits (as defined in § 1.902-1(a)(10)) of a noncontrolled section 902 corporation or a controlled foreign corporation shall be treated in taxable years beginning after December 31, 2006, as if they had been accumulated during a period in which the rules governing the determination of post-2006 separate categories applied. Foreign income taxes paid, accrued, or deemed paid with respect to such earnings shall be treated as if they were paid, accrued, or deemed paid during a period in which the rules governing the determination of post-2006 separate categories applied as well. The taxpayer must substantiate the post-2006 characterization of the pre-1987 accumulated profits and pre-1987 foreign income taxes in accordance with the rules of paragraph (g)(3) of this section, including the safe harbor provisions. Similar rules shall apply to characterize any deficits or previously-taxed earnings and profits described in section 959(c)(1) and (2) that are attributable to pre-1987 accumulated profits.

(5) *Treatment of earnings and foreign taxes in pre-2007 pools of a lower-tier controlled foreign corporation or noncontrolled section 902 corporation.*—The rules of paragraphs (g)(1) through (4) of this section apply to post-1986 undistributed earnings (as well as deficits and previously-taxed earnings, if any) and post-1986 foreign income taxes in pre-2007 pools, and pre-1987 accumulated profits and pre-1987 foreign income taxes, of a lower-tier controlled foreign corporation or noncontrolled section 902 corporation.

(6) *Effective/applicability date.*—This paragraph (g) shall apply to taxable years of United States persons and, for purposes of section 906, foreign persons beginning after December 31, 2006 and ending on or after December 21, 2007, and to taxable years of a foreign corporation which end with or within taxable years of its domestic corporate shareholder beginning after December 31, 2006 and ending on or after December 21, 2007. [Reg. § 1.904-7.]

□ [*T.D.* 8214, 7-15-88. *Amended by T.D.* 8412, 5-13-92; *T.D.* 9260, 4-20-2006; *T.D.* 9368, 12-20-2007; *T.D.* 9452, 6-10-2009 *and T.D.* 9521, 4-6-2011.]

§ 1.904(b)-1. Special rules for capital gains and losses.—(a) *Capital gains and losses included in taxable income from sources outside the United States.*—(1) *Limitation on capital gain from sources outside the United States when the taxpayer has net capital losses from sources within the United States.*—(i) *In general.*—Except as otherwise provided in this section, for purposes of section 904 and this section, taxable income from sources outside the United States (in all of the taxpayer's separate categories in the aggregate) shall include capital gain net income from sources outside the United States (determined by considering all of the capital gain and loss items in all of the taxpayer's separate categories in the aggregate) only to the extent of capital gain net income from all sources. Thus, capital gain net income from sources outside the United States (determined by considering all of the capital gain and loss items in all of the taxpayer's separate categories in the aggregate) shall be reduced to the extent such amount exceeds capital gain net income from all sources.

(ii) *Allocation of reduction to separate categories or rate groups.*—(A) *In general.*—If capital gain net income from sources outside the United States exceeds capital gain net income from all sources, and the taxpayer has capital gain net income from sources outside the United States in only one separate category, such excess is allocated as a reduction to that separate category. If a taxpayer has capital gain net income from foreign sources in two or more separate categories, such excess must be apportioned on a pro rata basis as a reduction to each such separate category. For purposes of the preceding sentence, pro rata means based on the relative amounts of the capital gain net income from sources outside the United States in each separate category.

(B) *Taxpayer with capital gain rate differential.*—If a taxpayer with a capital gain rate differential for the year (within the meaning of paragraph (b) of this section) has capital gain net income from foreign sources in only one rate group within a separate category, any reduction to such separate category pursuant to paragraph (a)(1)(ii)(A) of this section must be allocated to such rate group. If a taxpayer with a capital gain rate differential for the year (within the meaning of paragraph (b) of this section) has capital gain net income from foreign sources in two or more rate groups within a separate category, any reduction to such separate category pursuant to paragraph (a)(1)(ii)(A) of this section must be apportioned on a pro rata basis among such rate groups. For purposes of the preceding sentence, pro rata means based on the relative amounts of the capital gain net income from sources outside the United States in each rate group within the applicable separate category.

(2) *Exclusivity of rules; no reduction by reason of net capital losses from sources outside the United States in a different separate category.*—Capital gains from sources outside the United States in any separate category shall be limited by reason of section 904(b)(2)(A) and the comparable limitation of section 904(b)(2)(B)(i) only to the extent provided in paragraph (a)(1) of this section (relating to limitation on capital gain from sources outside the United States when taxpayer has net capital losses from sources within the United States).

(3) *Capital losses from sources outside the United States in the same separate category.*—Except as otherwise provided in paragraph (d) of this section, taxable income from sources outside the United States in each separate category shall be reduced by any capital loss that is allocable or apportionable to income from sources outside the United States in such separate category to the extent such loss is allowable in determining taxable income for the taxable year.

(4) *Examples.*—The following examples illustrate the application of this paragraph (a) to taxpayers that do not have a capital gain rate differential for the taxable year. See paragraph (g) of this section for examples that illustrate the application of this paragraph (a) to taxpayers that have a capital gain rate differential for the year. The examples are as follows:

Example 1. Taxpayer A, a corporation, has a $3,000 capital loss from sources outside the United States in the general limitation category, a $6,000 capital gain from sources outside the United States in the passive category, and a $2000 capital loss from sources within the United States. A's capital gain net income from sources outside the United States in the aggregate, from all separate categories, is $3000 ($6,000 - $3,000). A's capital gain net income from all sources is $1000 ($6000 – $3000 – $2000). Thus, for purposes of section 904, A's taxable income from sources outside the United States in all of A's separate categories in the aggregate includes only $1000 of capital gain net income from sources outside the United States. See paragraph (a)(1)(i) of this section. Pursuant to paragraphs (a)(1)(i) and (a)(1)(ii)(A) of this section, A must reduce the $6000 of capital gain net income from sources outside the United States in the passive category by $2000 ($3000 of capital gain net income from sources outside the United States - $1000 of capital gain net income from all sources). After the adjustment, A has $4000 of capital gain from sources outside the United States in the passive category and $3000 of capital loss from sources outside the United States in the general limitation category.

Example 2. Taxpayer B, a corporation, has a $300 capital gain from sources outside the United States in the general limitation category and a $200 capital gain from sources outside the United States in the passive category. B's capital gain net income from sources outside the United States is $500 ($300 + $200). B also has a $150 capital loss from sources within the United States and a $50 capital gain from sources within the United States. Thus, B's capital gain net income from all sources is $400 ($300 + $200 – $150 + $50). Pursuant to paragraph (a)(1)(ii)(A) of this section, the $100 excess of capital gain net income from sources outside the United States over capital gain net income from all sources ($500 – $400) must be apportioned, as a reduction, three-fifths ($300/$500 of $100, or $60) to the general limitation category and two-fifths ($200/$500 of $100, or $40) to the passive category. Therefore, for purposes of section 904, the general limitation category includes $240 ($300 – $60) of capital gain net income from sources outside the United States and the passive category includes $160 ($200 – $40) of capital gain net income from sources outside the United States.

Example 3. Taxpayer C, a corporation, has a $10,000 capital loss from sources outside the United States in the general limitation category, a $4,000 capital gain from sources outside the United States in the passive category, and a $2,000 capital gain from sources within the United States. C's capital gain net income from sources outside the United States is zero, since losses exceed gains. C's capital gain net income from all sources is also zero. C's capital gain net income from sources outside the United States does not exceed its capital gain net income from all sources, and therefore paragraph (a)(1) of this section does not require any reduction of C's passive category capital gain. For purposes of section 904, C's passive category includes $4,000 of capital gain net income. C's general limitation category includes a capital loss of $6,000 because only $6,000 of capital loss is allowable as a deduction in the current year. The entire $4,000 of capital loss in excess of the $6,000 of capital loss that offsets capital gain in the taxable year is carried back or forward under section 1212(a), and none of such $4,000 is taken into account under section 904(a) or (b) for the current taxable year.

(b) *Capital gain rate differential.*—(1) *Application of adjustments only if capital gain rate differential exists.*—Section 904(b)(2)(B) and paragraphs (c) and (d) of this section apply only for taxable years in which the taxpayer has a capital gain rate differential.

(2) *Determination of whether capital gain rate differential exists.*—For purposes of section 904(b) and this section, a capital gain rate differential is considered to exist for the taxable year only if the taxpayer has taxable income (excluding net capital gain and qualified dividend income) for the taxable year, a net capital gain for the taxable year and—

(i) In the case of a taxpayer other than a corporation, tax is imposed on the net capital gain at a reduced rate under section 1(h) for the taxable year; or

(ii) In the case of a corporation, tax is imposed under section 1201(a) on the taxpayer at a rate less than any rate of tax imposed on the taxpayer by section 11, 511, or 831(a) or (b), whichever applies (determined without regard to the last sentence of section 11(b)(1)), for the taxable year.

(3) *Special rule for certain noncorporate taxpayers.*—A taxpayer that has a capital gain rate differential for the taxable year under paragraph (b)(2)(i) of this section and is not subject to alternative minimum tax under section 55 for the taxable year may elect not to apply the rate differential adjustments contained in section 904(b)(2)(B) and paragraphs (c) and (d) of this section if the highest rate of tax imposed on such taxpayer's taxable income (excluding net capital gain and any qualified dividend income) for the taxable year under section 1 does not exceed the highest rate of tax in effect under section 1(h) for the taxable year and the amount of the taxpayer's net capital gain from sources outside the United States, plus the amount of the taxpayer's qualified dividend income from sources outside the United States, is less than $20,000. A taxpayer that has a capital gain rate differential for the taxable year under paragraph (b)(2)(i) of this section and is subject to alternative minimum tax under section 55 for the taxable year may make such election if the rate of tax imposed on such taxpayer's alternative minimum taxable income (excluding net capital gain and any qualified dividend income) under section 55 does not exceed 26 percent, the highest rate of tax imposed on such taxpayer's taxable income (excluding net capital gain and any qualified dividend income) for the taxable year under section 1 does not exceed the highest rate of tax in effect under section 1(h) for the taxable year and the amount of the taxpayer's net capital gain from sources outside the United States, plus the amount of the taxpayer's qualified dividend income from sources outside the United States, is less than $20,000. A taxpayer who makes this election shall apply paragraph (a) of this section as if such taxpayer does not have a capital gain rate differential for the taxable year. An eligible taxpayer shall be presumed to have elected not to apply the rate differential adjustments, unless such taxpayer applies the rate differential adjustments contained in section 904(b)(2)(B) and paragraphs (c) and (d) of this section in determining its foreign tax credit limitation for the taxable year.

(c) *Rate differential adjustment of capital gains.*—(1) *Rate differential adjustment of capital gains in foreign source taxable income.*—(i) *In general.*—Subject to paragraph (c)(1)(ii) of this section, in determining taxable income from sources outside the United States for purposes of section 904 and this section, capital gain net income from sources outside the United States in each long-term rate group in each separate category (separate category long-term rate group), shall be reduced by the rate differential portion of such capital gain net income. For purposes of paragraph (c)(1) of this section, references to capital gain net income are references to capital gain net income remaining after any reduction to such income pursuant to paragraph (a)(1) of this section (i.e., paragraph (a)(1) of this section applies before paragraphs (c) and (d) of this section).

(ii) *Special rule for taxpayers with a net long-term capital loss from sources within the United States.*—If a taxpayer has a net long-term capital loss from sources within the United States (i.e., the taxpayer's long-term capital losses from sources within the United States exceed the taxpayer's long-term capital gains from sources within the United States) and also has any short-term capital gains from sources within or without the United States, then capital gain net income from sources outside the United States in each separate category long-term rate group shall be reduced by the rate differential portion of the applicable rate differential amount. The applicable rate differential amount is determined as follows:

(A) *Step 1: Determine the U.S. long-term capital loss adjustment amount.*—The U.S. long-term capital loss adjustment amount is the excess, if any, of the net long-term capital loss from sources within the United States over the amount, if any, by which the taxpayer reduced long-term capital gains from sources without the United States pursuant to paragraph (a)(1) of this section.

(B) *Step 2: Determine the applicable rate differential amount.*—If a taxpayer has capital gain net income from sources outside the United States in only one separate category long-term rate group, the applicable rate differential amount is the excess of such capital gain net income over the U.S. long-term capital loss adjustment amount. If a taxpayer has capital gain net income from sources outside the United States in more than one separate category long-term rate group, the U.S. long-term capital loss adjustment amount shall be apportioned on a pro rata basis to each separate category long-term rate group with capital gain net income. For purposes of the preceding sentence, pro rata means based on the relative amounts of capital gain net income from sources outside the United States in each separate category long-term rate group. The applicable rate differential amount for each separate category long-term rate group with capital gain net income is the excess of such capital gain net income over the portion of the U.S. long-term capital loss adjustment amount apportioned to the separate category long-term rate group pursuant to this Step 2.

(iii) *Examples.*—The following examples illustrate the provisions of paragraph (c)(1)(ii) of this section. The taxpayers in the examples are assumed to have taxable income (excluding net capital gain and qualified dividend income) subject to a rate of tax under section 1 greater than the highest rate of tax in effect under section 1(h) for the applicable taxable year. The examples are as follows:

Example 1. (i) M, an individual, has $300 of long-term capital gain from foreign sources in the passive category, $200 of which is subject to tax at a rate of 15 percent under section 1(h) and $100 of which is subject to tax at a rate of 28% under section 1(h). M has $150 of short-term capital gain from sources within the United States. M has a $100 long-term capital loss from sources within the United States.

(ii) M's capital gain net income from sources outside the United States ($300) does not exceed M's capital gain net income from all sources ($350). Therefore, paragraph (a)(1) of this section does not require any reduction of M's capital gain net income in the passive category.

(iii) Because M has a net long-term capital loss from sources within the United States ($100) and also has a short-term capital gain from U.S. sources ($150), M must apply the provisions of paragraph (c)(1)(ii) of this section to determine the amount of the $300 of capital gain net income in the passive category that is subject to a rate differential adjustment. Under *Step 1*, the U.S. long-term capital loss adjustment amount is $100 ($100 - $0). Under *Step 2*, M must apportion this amount to each rate group in the passive category pro rata based on the amount of capital gain net income in each rate group. Thus, $66.67 ($200/$300 of $100) is apportioned to the 15 percent rate group and $33.33 ($100/$300 of $100) is apportioned to the 28 percent rate group. The applicable rate differential amount for the 15 percent rate group is $133.33 ($200 - $66.67). Thus, $133.33 of the $200 of capital gain net income in the 15 percent rate group is subject to a rate differential adjustment pursuant to paragraph (c)(1) of this section. The remaining $66.67 is not subject to a rate differential adjustment. The applicable rate differential amount for the 28 percent rate group is $66.67 ($100 - $33.33). Thus, $66.67 of the $100 of capital gain net income in the 28 percent rate group is subject to a rate differential adjustment pursuant to paragraph (c)(1) of this section. The remaining $33.33 is not subject to a rate differential adjustment.

Example 2. (i) N, an individual, has $300 of long-term capital gain from foreign sources in the passive category, all of which is subject to tax at a rate of 15 percent under section 1(h). N has $50 of short-term capital gain from sources within the United States. N has a $100 long-term capital loss from sources within the United States.

(ii) N's capital gain net income from sources outside the United States ($300) exceeds N's capital gain net income from all sources ($250). Pursuant to paragraph (a)(1) of this section, N must reduce the $300 capital gain in the passive category by $50. N has $250 of capital gain remaining in the passive category.

(iii) Because N has a net long-term capital loss from sources within the United States ($100) and also has a short-term capital gain from U.S. sources ($50), N must apply the provisions of paragraph (c)(1)(ii) of this section to determine the amount of the $250 of capital gain in the passive category that is subject to a rate differential adjustment. Under *Step 1*, the U.S. long-term capital loss adjustment amount is $50 ($100 - $50). Under *Step 2*, the applicable rate differential amount is $200 ($250 - $50). Thus, $200 of the capital gain in the passive category is subject to a rate differential adjustment under paragraph (c)(1) of this section. The remaining $50 is not subject to a rate differential adjustment.

Example 3. (i) O, an individual, has a $100 short-term capital gain from foreign sources in the passive category. O has $300 of long-term capital gain from foreign sources in the passive category, all of which is subject to tax at a rate of 15 percent under section 1(h). O has a $100 long-term capital loss from sources within the United States.

(ii) O's capital gain net income from sources outside the United States ($400) exceeds O's capital gain net income from all sources ($300). Pursuant to paragraph (a)(1) of this section, O must reduce the $400 capital gain net income in the passive category by $100. Because C has capital gain net income in two or more rate groups in the passive category, O must apportion such amount, as a reduction, to each rate group on a pro rata basis pursuant to paragraph (a)(1)(ii)(B) of this section. Thus, $25 ($100/$400 of $100) is apportioned to the short-term capital gain and $75 ($300/$400 of $100) is apportioned to the long-term capital gain in the 15 percent rate group. After application of paragraph (a)(1) of this section, O has $75 of short-term capital gain in the passive category and $225 of long-term capital gain in the 15 percent rate group in the passive category.

(iii) Because O has a net long-term capital loss from sources within the United States ($100) and also has a short-term capital gain from foreign sources ($100), O must apply the provisions of paragraph (c)(1)(ii) of this section to determine the amount of the $225 of long-term capital gain in the 15 percent rate group that is subject to a rate differential adjustment. Under *Step 1*, the U.S. long-term capital loss adjustment amount is $25 ($100 – $75). Under *Step 2*, the applicable rate differential amount is $200 ($225 – $25). Thus, $200 of the long-term capital gain is subject to a rate differential adjustment under paragraph (c)(1) of this section. The remaining $25 of long-term capital gain is not subject to a rate differential adjustment.

(2) *Rate differential adjustment of capital gains in entire taxable income.*—For purposes of section 904 and this section, entire taxable income shall include gains from the sale or exchange of capital assets only to the extent of capital gain net income reduced by the sum of the rate differential portions of each rate group of net capital gain.

(d) *Rate differential adjustment of capital losses from sources outside the United States.*—(1) *In general.*—In determining taxable income from sources outside the United States for purposes of section 904 and this section, a taxpayer with a net capital loss in a separate category rate group shall reduce such net capital loss by the sum of the rate differential portions of the capital gain net income in each long-term rate group offset by such net capital loss. A net capital loss in a separate category rate group is the amount, if any, by which capital losses in a rate group from sources outside the United States included in a separate category exceed capital gains from sources outside the United States in the same rate group and the same separate category.

(2) *Determination of which capital gains are offset by net capital losses from sources outside the United States.*—For purposes of paragraph (d)(1) of this section, in order to determine the capital gain net income offset by net capital losses from sources outside the United States, the following rules shall apply in the following order:

(i) Net capital losses from sources outside the United States in each separate category rate group shall be netted against capital gain net income from sources outside the United States from the same rate group in other separate categories.

(ii) Capital losses from sources within the United States shall be netted against capital gains from sources within the United States in the same rate group.

(iii) Net capital losses from sources outside the United States in excess of the amounts netted against capital gains under paragraph (d)(2)(i) of this section shall be netted against the taxpayer's remaining capital gains from sources within and outside the United States in the following order, and without regard to any net capital losses, from any rate group, from sources within the United States—

(A) First against capital gain net income from sources within the United States in the same rate group;

(B) Next, against capital gain net income in other rate groups, in the order in which capital losses offset capital gains for purposes of determining the taxpayer's taxable income and without regard to whether such capital gain net income derives from sources within or outside the United States, as follows:

(1) A net capital loss in the short-term rate group is used first to offset any capital gain net income in the 28 percent rate group, then to offset capital gain net income in the 25 percent rate group, then to offset capital gain net income in the 15 percent rate group, and finally to offset capital gain net income in the 5 percent rate group.

(2) A net capital loss in the 28 percent rate group is used first to offset capital gain net income in the 25 percent rate group, then to offset capital gain net income in the 15 percent rate group, and finally to offset capital gain net income in the 5 percent rate group.

(3) A net capital loss in the 15 percent rate group is used first to offset capital gain net income in the 5 percent rate group, and then to offset capital gain net income in the 28 percent rate group, and finally to offset capital gain net income in the 25 percent rate group.

(iv) Net capital losses from sources outside the United States in any rate group, to the extent netted against capital gains in any other separate category under paragraph (d)(2)(i) of this section or against capital gains in the same or any other rate group under paragraph (d)(2)(iii) of this section, shall be treated as coming pro rata from each separate category that contains a net capital loss from sources outside the United States in that rate group. For example, assume that the taxpayer has $20 of net capital losses in the 15 percent rate group in the passive category and $40 of net capital losses in the 15 percent rate group in the general limitation category, both from sources outside the United States. Further assume that $50 of the total $60 net capital losses from sources outside the United States are netted against capital gain net income in the 28 percent rate group (from other separate categories or from sources within the United States). One-third of the $50 of such capital losses would be treated as coming from the passive category, and two-thirds of such $50 would be treated as coming from the general limitation category.

(v) In determining the capital gain net income offset by a net capital loss from sources outside the United States pursuant to this paragraph (d)(2), a taxpayer shall take into account any reduction to capital gain net income from sources outside the United States pursuant to paragraph (a) of this section and shall disregard any adjustments to such capital gain net income pursuant to paragraph (c)(1) of this section.

(vi) If at any time during a taxable year, tax is imposed under section 1(h) at a rate other than a rate of tax specified in this paragraph (d)(2), the principles of this paragraph (d)(2) shall apply to determine the capital gain net income offset by any net capital loss in a separate category rate group.

(vii) The determination of which capital gains are offset by capital losses from sources outside the United States under this paragraph (d)(2) is made solely in order to determine the appropriate rate-differential-based adjustments to such capital losses under this section and section 904(b), and does not change the source, allocation, or separate category of any such capital gain or loss for purposes of computing taxable income from sources within or outside the United States or for any other purpose.

(e) *Qualified dividend income.*—(1) *In general.*—A taxpayer that has taxable income (excluding net capital gain and qualified dividend income) for the taxable year and that qualifies for a reduced rate of tax under section 1(h) on its qualified dividend income (as defined in section 1(h)(11)) for the taxable year shall adjust the amount of such qualified dividend income in a manner consistent with the rules of paragraphs (c)(1)(i) (first sentence) and (c)(2) of this section irrespective of whether such taxpayer has a net capital gain for the taxable year. For purposes of making adjustments pursuant to this paragraph (e), the special rule in paragraph (c)(1)(ii) of this section for taxpayers with a net long-term capital loss from sources within the United States shall be disregarded.

(2) *Exception.*—A taxpayer that makes the election provided for in paragraph (b)(3) of this section shall not make adjustments pursuant to paragraph (e)(1) of this section. Additionally, a taxpayer other than a corporation that does not have a capital gain rate differential for the taxable year within the meaning of paragraph (b)(2) of this section may elect not to apply paragraph (e)(1) of this section if such taxpayer would have qualified for the election provided for in paragraph (b)(3) of this section had such taxpayer had a capital gain rate differential for the taxable year. Such a taxpayer shall be presumed to make the election provided for in the preceding sentence unless such taxpayer applies the rate differential adjustments provided for in paragraph (e)(1) of this section to the qualified dividend income in determining its foreign tax credit limitation for the taxable year.

(f) *Definitions.*—For purposes of section 904(b) and this section, the following definitions apply:

(1) *Alternative tax rate.*—The term *alternative tax rate* means, with respect to any rate group, the rate applicable to that rate group under section 1(h) (for taxpayers other than corporations) or section 1201(a) (for corporations). For example, the alternative tax rate for unrecaptured section 1250 gain is 25 percent.

(2) *Net capital gain.*—For purposes of this section, net capital gain shall not include any qualified dividend income (as defined in section 1(h)(11)). See paragraph (e) of this section for rules relating to qualified dividend income.

(3) *Rate differential portion.*—The term *rate differential portion* with respect to capital gain net income from sources outside the United States in a separate category long-term rate group (or the applicable portion of such amount), net capital gain in a rate group, or capital gain net income in a long-term rate group, as the case may be, means the same proportion of such amount as—

(i) The excess of the highest applicable tax rate (as defined in section 904(b)(3)(E)(ii)) over the alternative tax rate; bears to

(ii) the highest applicable tax rate (as defined in section 904(b)(3)(E)(ii)).

(4) *Rate group.*—For purposes of this section, the term *rate group* means:

(i) *Short-term capital gains or losses.*—With respect to a short-term capital gain or loss, the rate group is the short-term rate group.

(ii) *Long-term capital gains.*—With respect to a long-term capital gain, the rate group is the particular rate of tax to which such gain is subject under section 1(h). Such a rate group is a long-term rate group. For example, the 28 percent rate group of capital gain net income from sources outside the United States consists of the capital gain net income from sources outside the United States that is subject to tax at a rate of 28 percent under section 1(h). Such 28 percent rate group is a long-term rate group. If a taxpayer has long-term capital gains that may be subject to tax at more than one rate under section 1(h) and the taxpayer's net capital gain attributable to such long-term capital gains and any qualified dividend income are taxed at one rate of tax under section 1(h), then all of such long-term capital gains shall be treated as long-term capital gains in that one rate group. If a taxpayer has long-term capital gains that may be subject to tax at more than one rate of tax under section 1(h) and the taxpayer's net capital gain attributable to such long-term capital gains and any qualified dividend income are taxed at more than one rate pursuant to section 1(h), the taxpayer shall determine the rate group for such long-term capital gains from sources within or outside the United States (and, to the extent from sources outside the United States, from each separate category) ratably based on the proportions of net capital gain and any qualified dividend income taxed at each applicable rate. For example, under the section 1(h) rates in effect for tax years beginning in 2004, a long-term capital gain (other than a long-term capital gain described in section 1(h)(4)(A) or (h)(6)) may be subject to tax at 5 percent or 15 percent.

(iii) *Long-term capital losses.*—With respect to a long-term capital loss, a loss described in section 1(h)(4)(B)(i) (collectibles loss) or (iii) (long-term capital loss carryover) is a loss in the 28 percent rate group. All other long-term capital losses shall be treated as losses in the highest rate group in effect under section 1(h) for the tax year with respect to long-term capital gains other than long-term capital gains described in section 1(h)(4)(A) or (h)(6). For example, under the section 1(h) rates in effect for tax years beginning in 2004, a long-term capital loss not described in section 1(h)(4)(B)(i) or (iii) shall be treated as a loss in the 15 percent rate group.

(5) *Terms used in sections 1(h), 904(b) or 1222.*—For purposes of this section, any term used in this section and also used in section 1(h), section 904(b) or section 1222 shall have the same meaning given such term by section 1(h), 904(b) or 1222, respectively, except as otherwise provided in this section.

(g) *Examples.*—The following examples illustrate the provisions of this section. In these examples, the rate differential adjustment is shown as a fraction, the numerator of which is the alternative tax rate percentage and the denominator of which is 35 percent (assumed to be the highest applicable tax rate for individuals under section 1). Finally, all dollar amounts in the examples are abbreviated from amounts in the thousands (for example, $50 represents $50,000). The examples are as follows:

Example 1. (i) AA, an individual, has items from sources outside the United States only in the passive category for the taxable year. AA has $1000 of long-term capital gains from sources outside the United States that are subject to tax at a rate of 15 percent under section 1(h). AA has $700 of long-term capital losses from sources outside the United States, which are not described in section 1(h)(4)(B)(i) or (iii). For the same taxable year, AA has $800 of long-term capital gains from sources within the United States that are taxed at a rate of 28 percent under section 1(h). AA also has $100 of long-term capital losses from sources within the United States, which are not described in section 1(h)(4)(B)(i) or (iii). AA also has $500 of ordinary income from sources within the United States. The highest tax rate in effect under section 1(h) for the taxable year with respect to long-term capital gains other than long-term capital gains described in section 1(h)(4)(A) or (h)(6) is 15 percent. Accordingly, AA's long-term capital losses are in the 15 percent rate group.

(ii) AA's items of ordinary income, capital gain and capital loss for the taxable year are summarized in the following table:

	U.S. source	foreign source: passive
15% rate group	($100)	$1,000 ($700)
28% rate group	$800	
Ordinary income	$500	

(iii) AA's capital gain net income from sources outside the United States ($300) does not exceed AA's capital gain net income from all sources ($1,000). Therefore, paragraph (a)(1) of this section does not require any reduction of AA's capital gain net income in the passive category.

(iv) In computing AA's taxable income from sources outside the United States in the numerator of the section 904(a) foreign tax credit limitation fraction for the passive category, AA's $300 of capital gain net income in the 15 rate group in the passive category must be adjusted as required under paragraph (c)(1) of this section. AA adjusts the $300 of capital gain net income using 15 percent as the alternative tax rate, as follows: $300(15%/35%).

(v) In computing AA's entire taxable income in the denominator of the section 904(a) foreign tax credit limitation fraction, AA combines the $300 of capital gain net income from sources outside the United States and the $100 net capital loss from sources within the United States in the same rate group (15 percent). AA must adjust the resulting $200 ($300 – $100) of net capital gain in the 15 percent rate group as required under paragraph (c)(2) of this section, using 15 percent as the alternative tax rate, as follows: $200(15% /35%). AA must also adjust the $800 of net capital gain in the 28 percent rate group, using 28 percent as the alternative tax rate, as follows: $800(28%/35%). AA must also include ordinary income from sources outside the United States in the numerator, and ordinary income from all sources in the denominator, of the foreign tax credit limitation fraction.

(vi) AA's passive category foreign tax credit limitation fraction is $128.58/$1225.72, computed as follows:

$$\frac{\$300(15\%/35\%)}{\$500 + \$200(15\%/35\%) + \$800(28\%/35\%)}$$

Example 2. (i) BB, an individual, has the following items of ordinary income, capital gain, and capital loss for the taxable year:

	U.S. source	foreign source: general	passive
15% rate group	$300	($500)	$100
25% rate group	$200		
28% rate group	$500	($300)	
Ordinary income	$1,000	$500	$500

(ii) BB's capital gain net income from sources outside the United States in the aggregate (zero, since losses exceed gains) does not exceed BB's capital gain net income from all sources ($300). Therefore, paragraph (a)(1) of this section does not require any reduction of BB's capital gain net income in the passive category.

(iii) In computing BB's taxable income from sources outside the United States in the numerators of the section 904(a) foreign tax credit limitation fractions for the passive and general limitation categories, BB must adjust capital gain net income from sources outside the United States in each separate category long-tem rate group and net capital losses from sources outside the United States in each separate category rate group as provided in paragraphs (c)(1) and (d) of this section.

(A) The $100 of capital gain net income in the 15 percent rate group in the passive category is adjusted under paragraph (c)(1) of this section as follows: $100(15%/35%).

(B) BB must adjust the net capital losses in the 15 percent and 28 percent rate groups in the general limitation category in accordance with the ordering rules contained in paragraph (d)(2) of this section. Under paragraph (d)(2)(i) of this section, BB's net capital loss in the 15 percent rate group is netted against capital gain net income from sources outside the United States in other separate categories in the same rate group. Thus, $100 of the $500 net capital loss in the 15 percent rate group in the general limitation category offsets $100 of capital gain net income in the 15 percent rate group in the passive category. Accordingly, $100 of the $500 net capital loss is adjusted under paragraph (d)(1) of this section as follows: $100(15% /35%).

(C) Next, under paragraph (d)(2)(iii)(A) of this section, BB's net capital losses from sources outside the United States in any separate category rate group are netted against capital gain net income in the same rate group from sources within the United States. Thus, $300 of the $500 net capital loss in the 15 percent rate group in the general limitation category offsets $300 of capital gain net income in the 15 percent rate group from sources within the United States. Accordingly, $300 of the $500 net capital loss is adjusted under paragraph (d)(1) of this section as follows: $300(15%/35%). Similarly, the $300 of net capital loss in the 28 percent rate group in the general limitation category offsets $300 of capital gain net income in the 28 percent rate group from sources within the United States. The $300 net capital loss is adjusted under paragraph (d)(1) of this section as follows: $300(28%/35%).

(D) Finally, under paragraph (d)(2)(iii)(B) of this section, the remaining net capital losses in a separate category rate group are netted against capital gain net income from other rate groups from sources within and outside the United States. Thus, the remaining $100 of the $500 net capital loss in the 15 percent rate group in the general limitation category offsets $100 of the remaining capital gain net income in the 28 percent rate group from sources within the United States. Accordingly, the remaining $100 of net capital loss is adjusted under paragraph (d)(1) of this section as follows: $100(28%/35%).

(iv) In computing BB's entire taxable income in the denominator of the section 904(a) foreign tax credit limitation fractions, BB must adjust net capital gain by netting all of BB's capital gains and losses, from sources within and outside the United States, and adjusting any remaining net capital gains, based on rate group, under paragraph (c)(2) of this section. BB must also include foreign source ordinary income in the numerators, and ordinary income from all sources in the denominator, of the foreign tax credit limitation fractions. The denominator of BB's foreign tax credit limitation fractions reflects $2,000 of ordinary income from all sources, $100 of net capital gain taxed at the 28% rate and adjusted as follows: $100(28% /35%), and $200 of net capital gain taxed at the 25% rate and adjusted as follows: $200(25%/35%).

(v) BB's foreign tax credit limitation fraction for the general limitation category is $8.56/$2222.86, computed as follows:

$$\frac{\$500 - \$100(15\%/35\%) - \$300(15\%/35\%) - \$300(28\%/35\%) - \$100(28\%/35\%)}{\$1,000 + \$500 + \$500 + \$100(28\%/35\%) + \$200(25\%/35\%)}$$

(vi) BB's foreign tax credit limitation fraction for the passive category is $542.86/$2222.86, computed as follows:

$$\frac{\$500 + \$100(15\%/35\%)}{\$1{,}000 + \$500 + \$500 + \$100(28\%/35\%) + \$200(25\%/35\%)}$$

Example 3. (i) CC, an individual, has the following items of ordinary income, capital gain, and capital loss for the taxable year:

	U.S. source	foreign source: general	passive
15% rate group	$300	($720)	($80)
25% rate group	$200		
28% rate group	$500	($150)	$50
Ordinary income	$1,000	$1,000	$500

(ii) CC's capital gain net income from sources outside the United States (zero, since losses exceed gains) does not exceed CC's capital gain net income from all sources ($100). Therefore, paragraph (a)(1) of this section does not require any adjustment.

(iii) In computing CC's taxable income from sources outside the United States in the numerators of the section 904(a) foreign tax credit limitation fractions for the passive and general limitation categories, CC must adjust capital gain net income from sources outside the United States in each separate category long-tem rate group and net capital losses from sources outside the United States in each separate category rate group as provided in paragraphs (c)(1) and (d) of this section.

(A) CC must adjust the $50 of capital gain net income in the 28 percent rate group in the passive category pursuant to paragraph (c)(1) of this section as follows: $50(28%/35%).

(B) Under paragraph (d)(2)(i) of this section, $50 of CC's $150 net capital loss in the 28 percent rate group in the general limitation category offsets $50 of capital gain net income in the 28 percent rate group in the passive category. Thus, $50 of the $150 net capital loss is adjusted as follows: $50(28%/35%). Next, under paragraph (d)(2)(iii)(A) of this section, the remaining $100 of net capital loss in the 28 percent rate group in the general limitation category offsets $100 of capital gain net income in the 28 percent rate group from sources within the United States. Thus, the remaining $100 of net capital loss is adjusted as follows: $100(28%/35%).

(C) Under paragraphs (d)(2)(iii)(A) and (d)(2)(iv) of this section, the net capital losses in the 15 percent rate group in the passive and general limitation categories offset on a pro rata basis the $300 of capital gain net income in the 15 percent rate group from sources within the United States. The proportionate amount of the $720 net capital loss ($720/$800 of $300, or $270) is adjusted as follows: $270(15%/35%). The proportionate amount of the $80 net capital loss ($80/$800 of $300, or $30) is adjusted as follows $30(15% /35%).

(D) Of the remaining $500 of net capital loss in the 15 percent rate group in the general limitation and passive categories, $400 offsets the remaining $400 of capital gain net income in the 28 percent rate group from sources within the United States under paragraph (d)(2)(iii)(B)(*3*) of this section. The proportionate amount of the $720 net capital loss ($720/$800 of $400, or $360) is adjusted as follows: $360(28%/35%). The proportionate amount of the $80 net capital loss ($80/$800 of $400, or $40) is adjusted as follows: $40(28% /35%).

(E) Under paragraph (d)(2)(iii)(B)(*3*) of this section, the remaining $100 of net capital loss in the 15 percent rate group in the general limitation and passive limitation categories offsets $100 of capital gain net income in the 25 percent rate group from sources within the United States. The proportionate amount of the $720 net capital loss ($720/$800 of $100, or $90) is adjusted as follows: $90(25% /35%). The proportionate amount of the $80 net capital loss ($80/$800 of $100 of $10) is adjusted as follows: $10(25%/35%).

(iv) In computing CC's entire taxable income in the denominator of the section 904(a) foreign tax credit limitation fractions, CC must adjust capital gain net income by netting all of CC's capital gains and losses, from sources within and outside the United States, and adjusting any remaining net capital gains, based on rate group, under paragraph (c)(2) of this section. The denominator of CC's foreign tax credit limitation fractions reflects $2,500 of ordinary income from all sources and $100 of net capital gain taxed at the 25% rate and adjusted as follows: $100(25%/35%).

(v) CC's foreign tax credit limitation fraction for the general limitation category is $412/$2571.42, computed as follows:

$$\frac{\$1{,}000 - \$50\,(28\%/35\%) - \$100(28\%/35\%) - \$270(15\%/35\%) - \$360(28\%/35\%) - \$90(25\%/35\%)}{\$1{,}000 + \$1{,}000 + \$500 + \$100(25\%/35\%)}$$

(vi) CC's foreign tax credit limitation fraction for the passive category is $488.00/$2571.42, computed as follows:

$$\frac{\$500 + \$50(28\%/35\%) - \$30(15\%/35\%) - \$40(28\%/35\%) - \$10(25\%/35\%)}{\$1{,}000 + \$1{,}000 + \$500 + \$100(25\%/35\%)}$$

Example 4. (i) DD, an individual, has the following items of ordinary income, capital gain and capital loss for the taxable year:

	U.S. source	foreign source: general	passive
15% rate group	($80)	($100)	$300
Short-term		$500	$100
Ordinary income	$500		

(ii) DD's capital gain net income from outside the United States ($800) exceeds DD's capital gain net income from all sources ($720). Pursuant to paragraph (a)(1)(ii)(A) of this section, DD must apportion the $80 of excess of capital gain net income from sources outside the United States between the general limitation and passive categories based on the amount of capital gain net income in each separate category. Thus, one-half ($400/$800 of $100, or $40) is apportioned to the general limitation category and one-half ($400/$800 of $80, or $40) is apportioned to the passive category. The $40 apportioned to the general limitation category reduces DD's $500 short-term capital gain in the general limitation category to $460. Pursuant to paragraph (a)(1)(ii)(B) of this section, the $40 apportioned to the passive category must be apportioned further between the capital gain net income in the short-term rate group and the 15 percent rate group based on the relative amounts of capital gain net income in each rate group. Thus, one-fourth ($100/$400 of $40 or $10) is apportioned to the short-term rate group and three-fourths ($300/$400 of $40 or $30) is apportioned to the 15 percent rate group. DD's passive category includes $90 of short-term capital gain and $270 of capital gain net income in the 15% rate group.

(iii) Because DD has a net long-term capital loss from sources within the United States ($80) and also has short-term capital gains, DD must apply the provisions of paragraph (c)(1)(ii) of this section to determine the amount of DD's $270 of capital gain net income in the 15% rate group that is subject to a rate differential adjustment under paragraph (c)(1) of this section. Under *Step 1*, the U.S. long-term capital loss adjustment amount is $50 ($80 – $30). Under *Step 2*, the applicable rate differential amount is the excess of the remaining capital gain net income over the U.S. long-term adjustment amount. Thus, the applicable rate differential amount is $220 ($270 – $50). In computing DD's taxable income from sources outside the United States in the numerator of the section 904(a) foreign tax credit limitation fraction for the passive category, DD must adjust this amount as/follows: $220(15%/35). DD does not adjust the remaining $50 of capital gain net income in the 15% rate group.

(iv) The amount of capital gain net income in the 15% rate group in the passive category, taking into account the adjustment pursuant to paragraph (a)(1) of this section and disregarding the adjustment pursuant to paragraph (c)(1) of this section, is $270. Under paragraphs (d)(2)(i) and (d)(2)(v) of this section, DD's $100 net capital loss in the 15% rate group in the general limitation category offsets capital gain net income in the 15% rate group in the passive category. Accordingly, the $100 of net capital loss is adjusted as follows: $100(15%/35%).

(v) In computing DD's entire taxable income in the denominator of the section 904(a) foreign tax credit limitation fractions, DD must adjust capital gain net income by netting all of DD's capital gains and losses from sources within and outside the United States, and adjusting the remaining net capital gain in each rate group pursuant to paragraph (c)(2) of this section. The denominator of DD's foreign tax credit limitation fraction reflects $500 of ordinary income from all sources, $600 of short-term capital gain and $120 of net capital gain in the 15 percent rate group adjusted as follows: $120(15%/35%).

(vi) DD's foreign tax credit limitation fraction for the general limitation category is $417.14/$1151.43, computed as follows:

$$\frac{\$460 - \$100(15\%/35\%)}{\$500 + \$600 + \$120(15\%/35\%)}$$

(vii) DD's foreign tax credit limitation fraction for the passive category is $234.29/$1151.43, computed as follows:

$$\frac{\$90 + \$220(15\%/35\%) + \$50}{\$500 + \$600 + \$120(15\%/35\%)}$$

Example 5. (i) EE, an individual, has the following items of ordinary income, capital gain and capital loss for the taxable year:

	U.S. source	foreign source: passive
15% rate group	($150)	$300
28% rate group		$200
Short-term	$30	$100
Ordinary income	$500	

(ii) EE's capital gain net income from sources outside the United States ($600) exceeds EE's capital gain net income from all sources ($480). Pursuant to paragraph (a)(1)(ii) of this section, the $120 of excess capital gain net income from sources outside the United States is allocated as a reduction to the passive category and must be apportioned pro rata to each rate group within the passive category with capital gain net income. Thus, $20 ($100/$600 of $120) is apportioned to the short-term rate group, $60 ($300/$600 of $120) is apportioned to the 15 percent rate group and $40($200/$600 of $120) is apportioned to the 28 percent rate group. After application of paragraph (a)(1) of this section, EE has $80 of capital gain net income in the short-term rate group, $240 of capital gain net income in the 15 percent rate group and $160 of capital gain net income in the 28 percent rate group.

(iii) Because EE has a net long-term capital loss from sources within the United States ($150) and also has short-term capital gains, EE must apply the provisions of paragraph (c)(1)(ii) of this section to determine the amount of EE's remaining $400 ($240 + $160) of capital gain net income in long-term rate groups in the passive category that is subject to a rate differential adjustment. Under *Step 1*, the U.S. long-term capital loss adjustment amount is $50 ($150 – $100). Under *Step 2*, EE must apportion this amount pro rata to each long-tem rate group within the passive category with capital gain net income. Thus, $30 ($240/$400 of $50) is apportioned to the 15 percent rate group and $20 ($160/$400 of $50) is apportioned to the 28 percent rate group. The applicable rate differential amount for the 15 percent rate group is $210 ($240 – $30). The applicable rate differential amount for the 28 percent rate group is $140 ($160 – $20).

(iv) Pursuant to paragraph (c)(1)(ii) of this section, EE must adjust $210 of the $240 capital gain in the 15 percent rate group as follows: $210 (15%/35%). EE does not adjust the remaining $30. Pursuant to paragraph (c)(1)(ii) of this section, EE must adjust $140 of the $160 capital gain in the 28 percent rate group as follows: $140 (28%/35%). EE does not adjust the remaining $20.

(v) In computing EE's entire taxable income in the denominator of the section 904(a) foreign tax credit limitation fractions, EE must adjust capital gain net income by netting all of EE's capital gains and losses from sources within and outside the United States, and adjusting the remaining net capital gain in each rate group pursuant to paragraph (c)(2) of this section. The denominator of EE's foreign tax credit limitation fraction reflects $500 of ordinary income from all sources, $130 of short-term capital gain, $150 of net capital gain in the 15 percent rate group adjusted as follows: $150(15%/35%), and $200 of net capital gain in the 28 percent rate group adjusted as follows: $200(28%/35%).

(vi) EE's foreign tax credit limitation fraction for the passive category is $332/$854.29, computed as follows:

$$\frac{\$80 + \$210(15\%/35\%) + \$30 + \$140(28\%/35\%) + \$20}{\$500 + \$130 + \$150(15\%/35\%) + \$200(28\%/35\%)}$$

(h) *Coordination with section 904(f).—*(1) *In general.—*Section 904(b) and this section shall apply before the provisions of section 904(f) as follows:

(i) The amount of a taxpayer's separate limitation income or loss in each separate category, the amount of overall foreign loss, and the amount of any additions to or recapture of separate limitation loss or overall foreign loss accounts pursuant to section 904(f) shall be determined after applying paragraphs (a), (c)(1), (d) and (e) of this section to adjust capital gains and losses and qualified dividend income from sources outside the United States in each separate category.

(ii) To the extent a capital loss from sources within the United States reduces a taxpayer's foreign source taxable income under paragraph (a)(1) of this section, such capital loss shall be disregarded in determining the amount of a taxpayer's taxable income from sources within the United States for purposes of computing the amount of any additions to the taxpayer's overall foreign loss accounts.

(iii) In determining the amount of a taxpayer's loss from sources in the United States under section 904(f)(5)(D) (section 904(f)(5)(D) amount), the taxpayer shall make appropriate adjustments to capital gains and losses from sources within the United States to reflect adjustments pursuant to section 904(b)(2) and this section. Therefore, for purposes of section 904, a taxpayer's section 904(f)(5)(D) amount shall be equal to the excess of the taxpayer's foreign source taxable income in all separate categories in the aggregate for the taxable year (taking into account any adjustments pursuant to paragraphs (a)(1), (c)(1), (d) and (e) of this section) over the taxpayer's entire taxable income for the taxable year (taking into account any adjustments pursuant to paragraphs (c)(2) and (e) of this section).

(2) *Examples.—*The following examples illustrate the application of paragraph (h) of this section:

Example 1. (i) W, an individual, has the following items of ordinary income, capital gain, and capital loss for the taxable year:

	U.S. source	foreign source: general	passive
15% rate group	$500	$100	($400)
Ordinary income	$900	$100	

(ii) In computing W's taxable income from sources outside the United States for purposes of section 904 and this section, W must adjust the capital gain net income and net capital loss in each separate category as provided in paragraphs (c)(1) and (d) of this section. Thus, W must adjust the $100 of capital gain net income in the general limitation category and the $400 of net capital loss in the passive category as follows: $100(15%/35%) and $400(15%/35%).

(iii) After the adjustment to W's net capital loss in the passive category, W has a $171.43 separate limitation loss in the passive category. After the adjustment to W's capital gain in the general limitation category, W has $142.86 of foreign source taxable income in the general limitation category. Thus, $142.86 of the separate limitation loss reduces foreign source taxable income in the general limitation category. See section 904(f)(5)(B). W adds $142.86 to the separate limitation loss account for the passive category. The remaining $28.57 of the separate limitation loss reduces income from sources within the United States. See section 904(f)(5)(A). Thus, W adds $28.57 to the overall foreign loss account for the passive category.

Example 2. (i) X, a corporation, has the following items of ordinary income, ordinary loss, capital gain and capital loss for the taxable year:

	U.S. source	foreign source: general
Capital gain	($500)	$700
Ordinary income	$1100	($1000)

(ii) X's capital gain net income from sources outside the United States ($700) exceeds X's capital gain net income from all sources ($200). Pursuant to paragraph (a)(1) of this section, X must reduce the $700 capital gain in the general limitation category by $500. After the adjustment, X has $200 of capital gain net income remaining in the general limitation category. Thus, X has an overall foreign loss attributable to the general limitation category of $800.

(iii) For purposes of computing the amount of the addition to X's overall foreign loss account for the general limitation category, the $500 capital loss from sources within the United States is disregarded and X's taxable income from sources within the United States is $1100. Accordingly, X must increase its overall foreign loss account for the general limitation category by $800.

Example 3. (i) Y, a corporation, has the following items of ordinary income, ordinary loss, capital gain and capital loss for the taxable year:

	U.S. source	foreign source: passive
Capital gain	($100)	$200
Ordinary income	($200)	$500

(ii) Y's capital gain net income from sources outside the United States ($200) exceeds Y's capital gain net income from all sources ($100). Pursuant to paragraph (a)(1) of this section, Y must reduce the

$200 capital gain in the passive category by $100. Y has $100 of capital gain net income remaining in the passive category.

(iii) Y is not required to make adjustments pursuant to paragraph (c), (d) or (e) of this section. See paragraphs (b) and (e) of this section. Y's foreign source taxable income in the passive category after the adjustment pursuant to paragraph (a)(1) of this section is $600. Y's entire taxable income for the taxable year is $400.

(iv) Y's section 904(f)(5)(D) amount is the excess of Y's foreign source taxable income in all separate categories in the aggregate for the taxable year after taking into account the adjustment pursuant to paragraph (a)(1) of this section ($600) over Y's entire taxable income for the taxable year ($400). Therefore, Y's section 904(f)(5)(D) amount is $200 and Y's foreign source taxable income in the passive category is reduced to $400. See section 904(f)(5)(D).

Example 4. (i) Z, an individual, has the following items of ordinary income, ordinary loss and capital gain for the taxable year:

	U.S. source	foreign source: general	passive
15% rate group	$100		
Ordinary income	($200)	$300	$300

(ii) Z's foreign source taxable income in all of Z's separate categories in the aggregate for the taxable year is $600. (There are no adjustments to Z's foreign source taxable income pursuant to paragraph (a)(1), (c)(1), (d) or (e) of this section.)

(iii) In computing Z's entire taxable income in the denominator of the section 904(d) foreign tax credit limitation fractions, Z must adjust the $100 of net capital gain in the 15 percent rate group pursuant to paragraph (c)(2) of this section as follows: $100(15%/35%). Thus, Z's entire taxable income for the taxable year, taking into account the adjustment pursuant to paragraph (c)(2) of this section, is $442.86.

(iv) Z's section 904(f)(5)(D) amount is the excess of Z's foreign source taxable income in all separate categories in the aggregate for the taxable year ($600) over Z's entire taxable income for the taxable year after the adjustment pursuant to paragraph (c)(2) of this section ($442.86). Therefore, Z's section 904(f)(5)(D) amount is $157.32. This amount must be allocated pro rata to the passive and general limitation categories in accordance with section 904(f)(5)(D).

Example 5. (i) O, an individual, has the following items of ordinary income, ordinary loss and capital gain for the taxable year:

	U.S. source	foreign source: general	passive
15% rate group	$1100	($500)	
Ordinary income	($1000)	$1000	$500

(ii) In determining O's taxable income from sources outside the United States, O must reduce the $500 capital loss in the general limitation category to $214.29 ($500 × 15%/35%) pursuant to paragraph (d) of this section. Taking this adjustment into account, O's foreign source taxable income in all of O's separate categories in the aggregate is $1285.71 ($1000 – $214.29 + $500).

(iii) In computing O's entire taxable income in the denominator of the section 904(a) foreign tax credit limitation fraction, O must reduce the $600 of net capital gain for the year to $257.14 ($600 × 15%/35%) pursuant to paragraph (c)(2) of this section. Taking this adjustment into account, O's entire taxable income for the year is $757.14 ($500 + $257.14).

(iv) Therefore, O's section 904(f)(5)(D) amount is $528.57 ($1285.71 – $757.14). This amount must be allocated pro rata to O's $500 of income in the passive category and O's $785.71 of adjusted income in the general limitation category in accordance with section 904(f)(5)(D).

(i) *Effective date.*—This section shall apply to taxable years beginning after July 20, 2004. Taxpayers may choose to apply this section and § 1.904(b)-2 to taxable years ending after July 20, 2004. [Reg. § 1.904(b)-1.]

□ [*T.D. 7914, 9-28-83. Amended by T.D. 9141, 7-19-2004 (corrected 10-20-2004).*]

§ 1.904(b)-2. Special rules for application of section 904(b) to alternative minimum tax foreign tax credit.—(a) *Application of section 904(b)(2)(B) adjustments.*—Section 904(b)(2)(B) shall apply for purposes of determining the alternative minimum tax foreign tax credit under section 59 (regardless of whether or not the taxpayer has made an election under section 59(a)(4)).

(b) *Use of alternative minimum tax rates.*—(1) *Taxpayers other than corporations.*—In the case of a taxpayer other than a corporation, for purposes of determining the alternative minimum tax foreign tax credit under section 59—

(i) Section 904(b)(3)(D)(i) shall be applied by using the language "section 55(b)(3)" instead of "subsection (h) of section 1";

(ii) Section 904(b)(3)(E)(ii)(I) shall be applied by using the language "section 55(b)(1)(A)(i)" instead of "subsection (a), (b), (c), (d), or (e) of section 1 (whichever applies)"; and

(iii) Section 904(b)(3)(E)(iii)(I) shall be applied by using the language "the alternative rate of tax determined under section 55(b)(3)" instead of "the alternative rate of tax determined under section 1(h)".

(2) *Corporate taxpayers.*—In the case of a corporation, for purposes of determining the alternative minimum tax foreign tax credit under section 59, section 904(b)(3)(E)(ii)(II) shall be applied by using the language "section 55(b)(1)(B)" instead of "section 11(b)".

(c) *Effective date.*—This section shall apply to taxable years beginning after July 20, 2004. See § 1.904(b)-1(i) for a rule permitting taxpayers to choose to apply § 1.904(b)-1 and this § 1.904(b)-2 to taxable years ending after July 20, 2004. [Reg. § 1.904(b)-2.]

□ [*T.D. 7914, 9-28-83. Amended by T.D. 9141, 7-19-2004 (corrected 10-20-2004).*]

§ 1.904(b)-3. Disregard of certain dividends and deductions under section 904(b)(4).—(a) *Disregard of certain dividends and deductions.*—(1) *In general.*—For purposes of section 904(a), in the case of a domestic corporation which is a United States shareholder with respect to a specified 10-percent owned foreign corporation (as defined in section 245A(b)), the domestic corporation's foreign source taxable income in a separate category and entire taxable income is determined without regard to the following items:

(i) Any dividend for which a deduction is allowed under section 245A;

(ii) Deductions properly allocable or apportioned to gross income in the section 245A subgroup as determined under paragraphs (b) and (c)(1) of this section; and

(iii) Deductions properly allocable or apportioned to stock of specified 10-percent owned foreign corporations in the section 245A subgroup as determined under paragraphs (b) and (c) of this section.

(2) *Deductions properly allocable or apportioned to the residual grouping.*—Deductions that are properly allocable or apportioned to gross income or stock in the section 245A subgroup of the residual grouping (consisting of U.S. source income) are disregarded solely for purposes of determining entire taxable income under section 904(a).

(b) *Determining properly allocable or apportioned deductions.*—The amount of deductions properly allocable or apportioned to gross income or stock described in paragraphs (a)(1)(ii) and (iii) of this section is determined by subdividing the United States shareholder's gross income and assets in each separate category described in § 1.904-5(a)(4)(v) into a section 245A subgroup and a non-section 245A subgroup. Gross income and assets in the residual grouping for U.S. source income are also subdivided into a section 245A subgroup and a non-section 245A subgroup. Each section 245A subgroup is treated as a statutory grouping under § 1.861-8(a)(4). Deductions properly allocable or apportioned to dividends or stock described in paragraphs (a)(1)(ii) and (iii) of this section only include those deductions that are allocated and apportioned under §§ 1.861-8 through 1.861-14T and 1.861-17 to the section 245A subgroups. The deduction allowed under section 245A(a) for dividends is allocated and apportioned solely among the section 245A subgroups on the basis of the relative amounts of gross income from such dividends in each section 245A subgroup.

(c) *Income and assets in the 245A subgroups.*—(1) *In general.*—For purposes of applying the section 861 regulations (as defined in § 1.861-8(a)) to the deductions of a United States shareholder, the only gross income included in a section 245A subgroup is dividend income for which a deduction is allowed under section 245A. The only asset included in a section 245A subgroup is the portion of the value of stock of each specified 10-percent owned foreign corporation that is assigned to the section 245A subgroup determined under paragraph (c)(2) of this section.

(2) *Assigning stock to a subgroup.*—The value of stock of a specified 10-percent owned foreign corporation is characterized as an asset in a separate category described in § 1.904-5(a)(4)(v) or the

residual grouping for U.S. source income under the rules of §1.861-12(c). If the specified 10-percent owned foreign corporation is not a controlled foreign corporation, all of the value of its stock (other than the portion of stock assigned to the statutory groupings for gross section 245(a)(5) income under §§1.861-12(c)(4) and 1.861-13) in each separate category and in the residual grouping for U.S. source income is assigned to the section 245A subgroup in such separate category or residual grouping. If the specified 10-percent owned foreign corporation is a controlled foreign corporation, a portion of the value of stock in each separate category and in the residual grouping for U.S. source income is subdivided between a section 245A and non-section 245A subgroup under §1.861-13(a)(5).

(d) *Coordination with OFL and ODL rules.*—(1) *In general.*—Section 904(b)(4) and this section apply before the operation of the overall foreign loss rules in section 904(f) and the overall domestic loss rules in section 904(g). *See* §1.904(g)-3(c).

(2) *Net operating losses.*—If the taxpayer has a net operating loss in the current taxable year, then solely for purposes of determining the source and separate category of the net operating loss, the overall foreign loss rules in section 904(f) and the overall domestic loss rules in section 904(g) are applied without taking into account the adjustments required under section 904(b) and this section.

(e) *Example.*—The following example illustrates the application of this section.

(1) *Facts*—(i) *Income and assets of USP.* USP is a domestic corporation. USP owns a factory in the United States with a tax book value of $27,000x. USP also directly owns all of the stock of each of the following three controlled foreign corporations: CFC1, CFC2, and CFC3. USP's tax book value in each of CFC1, CFC2, and CFC3 is $10,000x. USP incurs $1,500x of interest expense and earns $1,600x of U.S. source gross income. Under section 951A and the section 951A regulations (as defined in §1.951A-1(a)(1)), USP's GILTI inclusion amount is $2,200x. USP's deduction under section 250 is $1,100x ("section 250 deduction"), all of which is by reason of section 250(a)(1)(B)(i). No portion of USP's section 250 deduction is reduced by reason of section 250(a)(2)(B). None of the CFCs makes any distributions.

(ii) *Characterization of CFC stock.* After application of §1.861-13(a), USP determined that $8,000x of the stock of each of CFC1, CFC2, and CFC3 is assigned to the section 951A category ("section 951A category stock") in the non-section 245A subgroup and the remaining $2,000x of the stock of each of CFC1, CFC2, and CFC3 is assigned to the general category ("general category stock") in the section 245A subgroup. Additionally, under §1.861-8(d)(2)(ii)(C)(2), $4,000x of the stock of each of CFC1, CFC2, and CFC3 that is section 951A category stock is an exempt asset. Accordingly, with respect to the stock of its controlled foreign corporations in the aggregate, USP has $12,000x of section 951A category stock in a non-section 245A subgroup; $6,000x of general category stock in a section 245A subgroup; and $12,000x of stock that is an exempt asset.

(iii) *Apportioning of expenses.* Taking into account USP's factory and its stock in CFC1, CFC2, and CFC3, the tax book value of USP's assets for purposes of apportioning expenses is $45,000x (excluding the $12,000x of exempt assets). Under §1.861-9T(g), USP's $1,500 of interest expense is apportioned as follows: $400x ($1,500x x $12,000x/$45,000x) to section 951A category income, $200x ($1,500x x $6,000x/$45,000x) to general category income, and the remaining $900x ($1,500 x $27,000x/$45,000x) to the residual U.S. source grouping. Under §1.861-8(e)(14), all of USP's section 250 deduction is allocated and apportioned to section 951A category income.

(2) *Analysis*—(i) *USP's pre-credit U.S. tax.* USP's worldwide taxable income is $1,200x, which equals its GILTI inclusion amount of $2,200x plus its U.S. source gross income of $1,600x, less its deduction under section 250 of $1,100 and its interest expense of $1,500x. For purposes of applying section 904(a), before taking into account any foreign tax credit under section 901, USP's Federal income tax liability is 21% of $1,200x, or $252x.

(ii) *Application of section 904(b)(4).* Under section 904(d)(1), USP applies section 904(a) separately to each separate category of income.

(A) *General category income.* Before application of section 904(b)(4) and the rules in this section, USP's foreign source taxable income in the general category is a loss of $200x, which equals $0 (USP's foreign source general category income) less $200x (interest expense apportioned to general category income), and USP's worldwide taxable income is $1,200. Under paragraph (d) of this section, the rules in section 904(f) and (g) apply after section 904(b)(4) and the rules in this section. Under paragraphs (b) and (c)(1) of this section, USP has no deductions properly allocable or apportioned to gross income in the section 245A subgroup because USP has no dividend income in the general category for which a deduction is allowed under section 245A. Under paragraphs (b) and (c) of this section, USP has $200x of deductions for interest expense that are properly allocable or apportioned to stock of specified 10-percent owned foreign corporations in the section 245A subgroup because USP's only general category assets are the general category stock of CFC1, CFC2, and CFC3, all of which are in the section 245A subgroup. Therefore, under paragraph (a) of this section, USP's foreign source taxable income in the general category and its worldwide taxable income are determined without regard to the $200x of deductions for interest expense. Accordingly, USP's foreign source taxable income in the general category is $0 and its worldwide taxable income is $1,400x, and therefore, there is no separate limitation loss for purposes of section 904(f). Under section 904(a) and (d)(1) USP's foreign tax credit limitation for the general category is $0.

(B) *Section 951A category income.* Before application of section 904(b)(4) and the rules in this section, USP's foreign source taxable income in the section 951A category is $700x, which equals $2,200x (USP's GILTI inclusion amount) less $1,100x (USP's section 250 deduction) less $400x (interest apportioned to section 951A category income). Under paragraphs (b) and (c)(1) of this section, USP has no deductions properly allocable and apportioned to gross income in a section 245A subgroup of the section 951A category. Under paragraphs (b) and (c) of this section, USP has no deductions properly allocable and apportioned to stock of specified 10-percent owned foreign corporations in a section 245A subgroup of section 951A category stock because no portion of section 951A category stock is assigned to a section 245A subgroup. *See* §1.861-13(a)(5)(v). Therefore, under paragraph (a) of this section no adjustment is made to USP's foreign source taxable income in the section 951A category. However, the adjustments to USP's worldwide taxable income described in paragraph (e)(2)(ii)(A) of this section apply for purposes of calculating USP's foreign tax credit limitation for the section 951A category. Accordingly, USP's foreign source taxable income in the section 951A category is $700x and its worldwide taxable income is $1,400x. Under section 904(a) and (d)(1), USP's foreign tax credit limitation for the section 951A category is $126x ($252x x $700x/$1,400x).

(f) *Applicability dates.*—(1) Except as provided in paragraph (f)(2) of this section, this section applies to taxable years beginning after December 31, 2017.

(2) Paragraph (d)(2) of this section applies to taxable years ending on or after December 16, 2019. [Reg. §1.904(b)-3.]

□ [*T.D. 9882, 12-16-2019. Amended by T.D. 9922, 11-2-2020.*]

§1.904(f)-1. Overall foreign loss and the overall foreign loss account.—(a)(1) *Overview of regulations.*—In general, section 904(f) and these regulations apply to any taxpayer that sustains an overall foreign loss (as defined in paragraph (c)(1) of this section) in a taxable year beginning after December 31, 1975. For taxable years ending after December 31, 1984, and beginning before January 1, 1987, there can be five types of overall foreign losses: a loss under each of the five separate limitations contained in former section 904(d)(1)(A) (passive interest limitation), (d)(1)(B) (DISC dividend limitation), (d)(1)(C) (foreign trade income limitation), (d)(1)(D) (foreign sales corporation (FSC) distributions limitation), and (d)(1)(E) (general limitation). For taxable years beginning after December 31, 1982, and ending before January 1, 1985, there can be three types of overall foreign losses under former section 904(d)(1)(A) (passive interest limitation), former section 904(d)(1)(B) (DISC dividend limitation) and former section 904(d)(1)(C) (general limitation). For taxpayers subject to section 907, the post-1982 general limitation overall foreign loss account may be further subdivided, as provided in §1.904(f)-6. For taxable years beginning after December 31, 1975, and before January 1, 1983, taxpayers should have computed overall foreign losses separately under the passive interest limitation, the DISC dividend limitation, the general limitation, and the section 907(b) (FORI) limitation. However, for taxable years beginning after December 31, 1975, and before January 1, 1983, taxpayers may have computed only two types of overall foreign losses: a foreign oil related loss under the FORI limitation and an overall foreign loss computed on a combined basis for the passive interest limitation, the DISC dividend limitation, and the general limitation. A taxpayer that computed overall foreign losses for these years on a combined basis will not be required to amend its return to recompute such losses on a separate basis. If a taxpayer computed its overall foreign losses for these years separately under the passive interest limitation, the DISC dividend limitation, and the general limitation, on returns previously filed, a taxpayer may not amend those returns to compute such overall foreign losses on a combined basis. Section 1.904(f)-1 provides rules for determining a taxpayer's overall foreign losses, for establishing overall foreign loss accounts, and for making additions to and reductions of such accounts for purposes of section 904(f). Section 1.904(f)-2 provides rules for recapturing the balance in any overall foreign loss account under the general recapture rule of section 904(f)(1) and under the special recapture rule of section 904(f)(3) when the taxpayer disposes of property used predominantly outside the United States in a trade or business. Section 1.904(f)-3 provides rules for allocating overall foreign losses that are part of net operating losses or net capital losses to foreign source income in years to which such losses are carried. In addition, § 1.904(f)-3 provides transition rules for the treatment of net operating losses incurred in taxable years beginning after December 31, 1982, and carried back to taxable years beginning before January 1, 1983, and of net operating losses incurred in taxable years beginning before January 1, 1983, and carried forward to taxable years beginning after December 31, 1982. Section 1.904(f)-4 provides rules for recapture out of an accumulation distribution of a foreign trust. Section 1.904(f)-5 provides rules for recapture of overall foreign losses of domestic trusts. Section 1.904(f)-6 provides a transition rule for recapturing a taxpayer's pre-1983 overall foreign losses under the general limitation and the FORI limitation out of taxable income subject to the general limitation in taxable years beginning after December 31, 1982. Section § 1.1502-9 provides rules concerning the application of these regulations to corporations filing consolidated returns.

(2) *Application to post-1986 taxable years.*—The principles of § § 1.904(f)-1 through 1.904(f)-5 shall apply to any overall foreign loss sustained in taxable years beginning after December 31, 1986, modified so as to take into account the effect of statutory amendments.

(b) *Overall foreign loss accounts.*—Any taxpayer that sustains an overall foreign loss under paragraph (c) of this section must establish an account for such loss. Separate types of overall foreign losses must be kept in separate accounts. For taxable years beginning prior to January 1, 1983, taxpayers that computed losses on a combined basis in accordance with § 1.904(f)-1(c)(1) will keep one overall foreign loss account for such overall foreign loss. The balance in each overall foreign loss account represents the amount of such overall foreign loss subject to recapture by the taxpayer in a given year. From year to year, amounts may be added to or subtracted from the balances in such accounts as provided in paragraphs (d) and (e) of this section. The taxpayer must report the balances (if any) in its overall foreign loss accounts annually on a Form 1116 or 1118. Such forms must be filed for each taxable year ending after September 24, 1987. The balance in each account does not have to be attributed to the year or years in which the loss was incurred.

(c) *Determination of a taxpayer's overall foreign loss.*—(1) *Overall foreign loss defined.*—For taxable years beginning after December 31, 1982, and before January 1, 1987, a taxpayer sustains an overall foreign loss in any taxable year in which its gross income from sources without the United States subject to a separate limitation (as defined in paragraph (c)(2) of this section) is exceeded by the sum of the deductions properly allocated and apportioned thereto. Such losses are to be determined separately in accordance with the principles of the separate limitations. Accordingly, income and deductions subject to a separate limitation are not to be netted with income and deductions subject to another separate limitation for purposes of determining the amount of an overall foreign loss. A taxpayer may, for example, have an overall foreign loss under the general limitation in the same taxable year in which it has taxable income under the DISC dividend limitation. The same principles of calculating overall foreign losses on a separate limitation basis apply for taxable years beginning before January 1, 1983, except that a taxpayer shall determine its overall foreign losses on a combined basis, except for income subject to the FORI limitation, if the taxpayer filed its pre-1983 returns on such basis. Thus, for taxable years beginning prior to January 1, 1983, a taxpayer can net income and losses among the passive interest limitation, the DISC dividend limitation, and the general limitation if the taxpayer calculated its overall foreign losses that way at the time. Taxpayers that computed overall foreign losses separately under each of the separate limitations on their returns filed for taxable years beginning prior to January 1, 1983, may not amend such returns to compute their overall foreign losses for pre-1983 years on a combined basis.

(2) *Separate limitation defined.*—For purposes of paragraph (c)(1) of this section and these regulations, the term separate limitation means any of the separate limitations under former section 904(d)(1)(A) (passive interest limitation), (B) (DISC dividend limitation), (C) (foreign trade income limitation), (D) (FSC distributions limitation), and (E) (general limitation) and the separate limitation under section 907(b) (FORI limitation) (for taxable years ending after December 31, 1975, and beginning before January 1, 1983).

(3) *Method of allocation and apportionment of deductions.*—In determining its overall foreign loss, a taxpayer shall allocate and apportion expenses, losses, and other deductions to the appropriate category of gross income in accordance with section 862(b) and § 1.861-8 of the regulations. However, the following deductions shall not be taken into account:

(i) The amount of any net operating loss deduction for such year under section 172(a); and

(ii) To the extent such losses are not compensated for by insurance or otherwise, the amount of any—

(A) Expropriation losses for such year (as defined in section 172(h)), or

(B) Losses for such year which arise from fire, storm, shipwreck, or other casualty, or from theft.

(d) *Additions to the overall foreign loss account.*—(1) *General rule.*—A taxpayer's overall foreign loss as determined under paragraph (c) of this section shall be added to the applicable overall foreign loss account at the end of its taxable year to the extent that the overall foreign loss has reduced United States source income during the taxable year or during a year to which the loss has been carried back. For rules with respect to carryovers see paragraph (d)(3) of this section and § 1.904(f)-3.

(2) *Overall foreign losses of another taxpayer.*—If any portion of any overall foreign loss of another taxpayer is allocated to the taxpayer in accordance with § 1.904(f)-5 (relating to overall foreign losses of domestic trusts) or § 1.1502-9 (relating to consolidated overall foreign losses), the taxpayer shall add such amount to its applicable overall foreign loss account.

(3) *Additions to overall foreign loss account created by loss carryovers.*—Subject to the adjustments under § 1.904(f)-1(d)(4), the taxpayer shall add to each overall foreign loss account—

(i) All net operating loss carryovers to the current taxable year attributable to the same limitation to the extent that overall foreign losses included in the net operating loss carryovers reduced United States source income for the taxable year, and

(ii) All capital loss carryovers to the current taxable year attributable to the same limitation to the extent that foreign source capital loss carryovers reduced United States source capital gain net income for the taxable year.

(4) *Adjustments for capital gains and losses and qualified dividend income.*—If a taxpayer has capital gains or losses or qualified dividend income, as defined in section 1(h)(11), the taxpayer shall make adjustments to such capital gains and losses and qualified dividend income to the extent required under section 904(b)(2) and § 1.904(b)-1 before applying the provisions of § 1.904(f)-1. See § 1.904(b)-1(h).

(e) *Reductions of overall foreign loss accounts.*—The taxpayer shall subtract the following amounts from its overall foreign loss accounts at the end of its taxable year in the following order, if applicable:

(1) *Pre-recapture reduction for amounts allocated to other taxpayers.*—An overall foreign loss account is reduced by the amount of any overall foreign loss which is allocated to another taxpayer in accordance with § 1.904(f)-5 (relating to overall foreign losses of domestic trusts) or § 1.1502-9 (relating to consolidated overall foreign losses).

(2) *Reduction for amounts recaptured.*—An overall foreign loss account is reduced by the amount of any foreign source income that is subject to the same limitation as the loss that resulted in the account and that is recaptured in accordance with § § 1.904(f)-2(c) (relating to recapture under section 904(f)(1)); 1.904(f)-2(d) (relating to recapture when the taxpayer disposes of certain properties under section 904(f)(3)); and 1.904(f)-4 (relating to recapture when the taxpayer receives an accumulation distribution from a foreign trust under section 904(f)(4)).

(f) *Illustrations.*—The rules of this section are illustrated by the following examples.

Example (1). X Corporation is a domestic corporation with foreign branch operations in country C. X's taxable income and losses for its taxable year 1983 are as follows:

U.S. source taxable income	$1,000
Foreign source taxable income (loss) subject to general limitation	($500)
Foreign source taxable income subject to the passive interest limitation	$200

X has a general limitation overall foreign loss of $500 for 1983 in accordance with paragraph (c)(1) of this section. Since the general limitation overall foreign loss is not considered to of set income under the separate limitation for passive interest income, it therefore offsets $500 of United States source taxable income. This amount is added to X's general limitation overall foreign loss account at the end of 1983 in accordance with paragraphs (c)(1) and (d)(1) of this section.

Example (2). Y Corporation is a domestic corporation with foreign branch operations in Country C. Y's taxable income and losses for its taxable year 1982 are as follows:

U.S. source taxable income	$1,000
Foreign source taxable income (loss) subject to general limitation	($500)
Foreign source taxable income subject to the passive interest limitation	$250

For its pre-1983 taxable years, Y filed its returns determining its overall foreign losses on a combined basis. In accordance with paragraphs (a) and (c)(1) of this section, Y may net the foreign source income and loss before offsetting the United States source income. Y therefore has a section 904(d)(1)(A-C) overall foreign loss account of $250 at the end of 1982.

Example (3). X Corporation is a domestic corporation with foreign branch operations in Country C. For its taxable year 1985, X has taxable income (loss) determined as follows;

U.S. source taxable income	$200
Foreign source taxable income (loss) subject to general limitation	($1,000)
Foreign source taxable income (loss) subject to the passive limitation	$1,800

X has a general limitation overall foreign loss of $1,000 in accordance with paragraph (c)(1) of this section. The overall foreign loss offsets $200 of United States source taxable income in 1985 and therefore, X has a $200 general limitation overall foreign loss account at the end of 1985. The remaining $800 general limitation loss is offset by the passive interest limitation income in 1985 so that X has no net operating loss carryover that is attributable to the general limitation loss and no additional amount attributable to that loss will be added to the overall foreign loss account in 1985 or in any other year.

(g) *Effective/applicability date.*—Paragraphs (a)(2) and (d)(4) of this section shall apply to taxable years beginning on or after January 1, 2012. Taxpayers may choose to apply paragraphs (a)(2) and (d)(4) of this section to other taxable years beginning after December 21, 2007, including periods covered by 26 CFR 1.904(f)-1T (revised as of April 1, 2010). [Reg. § 1.904(f)-1.]

☐ [*T.D.* 8153, 8-21-87. *Amended by T.D.* 9371, 12-20-2007 *and T.D.* 9595, 6-21-2012.]

§ 1.904(f)-2. Recapture of overall foreign losses.—(a) *In general.*—A taxpayer shall be required to recapture an overall foreign loss as provided in this section. Recapture is accomplished by treating as United States source income a portion of the taxpayer's foreign source taxable income of the same limitation as the foreign source loss that resulted in an overall foreign loss account. As a result, if the taxpayer elects the benefits of section 901 or section 936, the taxpayer's foreign tax credit limitation with respect to such income is decreased. As provided in § 1.904(f)-1(e)(2), the balance in a taxpayer's overall foreign loss account is reduced by the amount of loss recaptured. Recapture continues until such time as the amount of foreign source taxable income recharacterized as United States source income equals the amount in the overall foreign loss account. As provided in § 1.904(f)-1(e)(2), the balance in an overall foreign loss account is reduced at the end of each taxable year by the amount of the loss recaptured during that taxable year. Regardless of whether recapture occurs in a year in which a taxpayer elects the benefits of section 901 or in a year in which a taxpayer deducts its foreign taxes under section 164, the overall foreign loss account is recaptured only to the extent of foreign source taxable income remaining after applying the appropriate section 904(b) adjustments, if any, as provided in paragraph (b) of this section.

(b) *Determination of taxable income from sources without the United States for purposes of recapture.*—(1) *In general.*—For purposes of determining the amount of an overall foreign loss subject to recapture, the taxpayer's taxable income from sources without the United States shall be computed with respect to each of the separate limitations described in § 1.904(f)-1(c)(2) in accordance with the rules set forth in § 1.904(f)-1(c)(1) and (3). This computation is made without taking into account foreign source taxable income (and deductions properly allocated and apportioned thereto) subject to other separate limitations. Before applying the recapture rules to foreign source taxable income, the following provisions shall be applied to such income in the following order:

(i) Former section 904(b)(3)(C) (prior to its removal by the Tax Reform Act of 1986) and the regulations thereunder shall be applied to treat certain foreign source gain as United States source gain; and

(ii) Section 904(b)(2) and the regulations thereunder shall be applied to make adjustments in the foreign tax credit limitation fraction for certain capital gains and losses.

(c) *Section 904(f)(1) recapture.*—(1) *In general.*—In a taxable year in which a taxpayer elects the benefits of section 901 or section 30A, the section 904(f)(1) recapture amount is the amount of foreign source taxable income subject to recharacterization in a taxable year in which recapture of an overall foreign loss is required under paragraph (a) of this section. The section 904(f)(1) recapture amount equals the lesser of the aggregate amount of maximum potential recapture in all overall foreign loss accounts or fifty percent of the taxpayer's total foreign source taxable income. If the aggregate amount of maximum potential recapture in all overall foreign loss accounts exceeds fifty percent of the taxpayer's total foreign source taxable income, foreign source taxable income in each separate category with an overall foreign loss account is recharacterized in an amount equal to the section 904(f)(1) recapture amount, multiplied by the maximum potential recapture in the overall foreign loss account, divided by the aggregate amount of maximum potential recapture in all overall foreign loss accounts. The maximum potential recapture in an overall foreign loss account in a separate category is the lesser of the balance in that overall foreign loss account or the foreign source taxable income for the year in the same separate category as the loss account. If, in any taxable year, in accordance with sections 164(a) and 275(a)(4)(A), a taxpayer deducts rather than credits its foreign taxes, recapture is applied to the extent of the lesser of—

(i) The balance in the overall foreign loss account in each separate category; or

(ii) Foreign source taxable income (net of foreign taxes) in each separate category.

(2) *Election to recapture more of the overall foreign loss than is required under paragraph (c)(1).*—In a year in which a taxpayer elects the benefits of sections 901 or 936, a taxpayer may make an annual revocable election to recapture a greater portion of the balance in an overall foreign loss account than is required to be recaptured under paragraph (c)(1) of this section. A taxpayer may make such an election or amend a prior election by attaching a statement to its annual Form 1116 or 1118. If an amendment is made to a prior year's election, an amended tax return should be filed. The statement attached to the Form 1116 or 1118 must indicate the percentage and dollar amount of the taxpayer's foreign source taxable income that is being recharacterized as United States source income and the percentage and dollar amount of the balance (both before and after recapture) in the overall foreign loss account that is being recaptured. Except for the special recapture rules for section 936 corporations and for recapture of pre-1983 overall foreign losses determined on a combined basis, the taxpayer that elects to credit its foreign taxes may not elect to recapture an amount in excess of the taxpayer's foreign source taxable income subject to the same limitation as the loss that resulted in the overall foreign loss account.

(3) *Special rule for recapture of losses incurred prior to section 936 election.*—If a corporation elects the application of section 936 and at the time of the election has a balance in any overall foreign loss account, such losses will be recaptured from the possessions source income of the electing section 936 corporation that qualifies for the section 936 credit, including qualified possession source investment income as defined in section 936(d)(2), even though the overall foreign loss to be recaptured may not be attributable to a loss in an income category of a type that would meet the definition of qualified possession source investment income. For purposes of recapturing an overall foreign loss incurred by a consolidated group including a corporation that subsequently elects to use section 936, the electing section 936 corporation's possession source income that qualifies for the section 936 credit, including qualified possession source invest-

ment income, shall be used to recapture the section 936 corporation's share of previously incurred overall foreign loss accounts. Rules for determining the section 936 corporation's share of the consolidated group's overall foreign loss accounts are provided in § 1.1502-9(c).

(4) *Recapture of pre-1983 overall foreign losses determined on a combined basis.*—If a taxpayer computed its overall foreign losses on a combined basis in accordance with § 1.904(f)-1(c)(1) for taxable years beginning before January 1, 1983, any losses recaptured in taxable years beginning after December 31, 1982, shall be recaptured from income subject to the general limitation, subject to the rules in § 1.904(f)-6(a) and (b). Ordering rules for recapture of these losses are provided in § 1.904(f)-6(c).

(5) *Illustrations.*—The rules of this paragraph (c) are illustrated by the following examples, all of which assume a United States corporate tax rate of 50 percent unless otherwise stated.

Example (1). X Corporation is a domestic corporation that does business in the United States and abroad. On December 31, 1983, the balance in X's general limitation overall foreign loss account is $600, all of which is attributable to a loss incurred in 1983. For 1984, X has United States source taxable income of $500 and foreign source taxable income subject to the general limitation of $500. For 1984, X pays $200 in foreign taxes and elects section 901. Under paragraph (c)(1) of this section, X is required to recapture $250 (the lesser of $600 or 50 percent of $500) of its overall foreign loss. As a consequence, X's foreign tax credit limitation under the general limitation is $250/$1,000 × $500, or $125, instead of $500/$1,000 × $500, or $250. The balance in X's general limitation overall foreign loss account is reduced by $250 in accordance with § 1.904(f)-1(e)(2).

Example (2). The facts are the same as in example (1) except that X makes an election to recapture its overall foreign loss to the extent of 80 percent of its foreign source taxable income subject to the general limitation (or $400) in accordance with paragraph (c)(2) of this section. As a result of recapture, X's 1984 foreign tax credit limitation for income subject to the general limitation is $100/$1,000 × $500, or $50, instead of $500/$1,000 × $500, or $250. X's general limitation overall foreign loss account is reduced by $400 in accordance with § 1.904(f)-1(e)(2).

Example (3). The facts are the same as in example (1) except that X does not elect the benefits of section 901 in 1984 and instead deducts its foreign taxes paid. In 1984, X recaptures $300 of its overall foreign loss, the difference between X's foreign source taxable income of $500 and $200 of foreign taxes paid. The balance in X's general limitation overall foreign loss account is reduced by $300 in accordance with § 1.904(f)-1(e)(2).

Example (4). Y Corporation is a domestic corporation that does business in the United States and abroad. On December 31, 2007, the balance in Y's general category overall foreign loss account is $500, all of which is attributable to a loss incurred in 2007. Y has no other loss accounts subject to recapture. For 2008, Y has U.S. source taxable income of $400 and foreign source taxable income of $300 in the general category and $900 in the passive category. Under paragraph (c)(1) of this section, the amount of Y's general category income subject to recharacterization is the lesser of the aggregate maximum potential recapture or 50% of the total foreign source taxable income. In this case, Y's aggregate maximum potential recapture is $300 (the lesser of the $500 balance in the general category overall foreign loss account or $300 foreign source income in the general category for the year), which is less than 50% of Y's total foreign source taxable income ($1200 × 50% = $600). Therefore, pursuant to paragraph (c) of this section, $300 of foreign source income in the general category is recharacterized as U.S. source income. The balance in Y's general category overall foreign loss account is reduced to $200 in accordance with § 1.904(f)-1(e)(2).

Example (5). On December 31, 1980, V, a domestic corporation that does business in the United States and abroad, has a balance in its section 904(d)(1)(A-C) overall foreign loss account of $600. V also has a balance in its FORI limitation overall foreign loss account of $900. For 1981, V has foreign source taxable income subject to the general limitation of $500 and $500 of United States source income. V also has foreign source taxable income subject to the FORI limitation of $800. V is required to recapture $250 of its section 904(d)(1)(A-C) overall foreign loss account (the lesser of $600 or 50% of $500) and its general limitation foreign tax credit limitation is $250/$1,800 × $900, or $125 instead of $500/$1,800 × $900, or $250. V is also required to recapture $400 of its FORI limitation overall foreign loss account (the lesser of $900 or 50% of $800). V's foreign tax credit limitation for FORI is $400/$1,800 × $900, or $200, instead of $800/$1,800 × $900, or $400. The balance in V's FORI limitation overall foreign loss account is reduced to $500 and the balance in V's section 904(d)(1)(A-C) account is reduced to $350, in accordance with § 1.904(f)-1(e)(2).

Example (6). This example assumes a United States corporate tax rate of 46 percent (under section 11(b)) and an alternative rate of tax under section 1201(a) of 28 percent. W is a domestic corporation that does business in the United States and abroad. On December 31, 1984, W has $350 in its general limitation overall foreign loss account. For 1985, W has $500 of United States source taxable income, and has foreign source income subject to the general limitation as follows:

Foreign source taxable income other than net capital gain . .	$720
Foreign source net capital gain	$460

Under paragraph (b)(2) of this section, foreign source taxable income for purposes of recapture includes foreign source capital gain net income, reduced, under section 904(b)(2), by the rate differential portion of foreign source net capital gain, which adjusts for the reduced tax rate for net capital gain under section 1201(a):

Foreign source capital gain net income	$460
Rate differential portion of foreign source net capital gain (18/46 of $460)	− 180
Foreign source capital gain included in foreign source taxable income	$280

The total foreign source taxable income of W for purposes of recapture in 1985 is $1,000 ($720 + $280). Under paragraph (c)(1) of this section, W is required to recapture $350 (the lesser of $350 or 50 percent of $1,000), and W's general limitation overall foreign loss account is reduced to zero. W's foreign tax credit limitation for income subject to the general limitation is $650/$1,500 × $690 ((.46) (500 + 720) + (.28) (460)), or $299, instead of $1,000/$1,500 × $690, or $460.

(d) *Recapture of overall foreign losses from dispositions under section 904(f)(3).*—(1) *In general.*—If a taxpayer disposes of property used or held for use predominantly without the United States in a trade or business during a taxable year and that property generates foreign source taxable income subject to a separate limitation to which paragraph (a) of this section applies, the applicable overall foreign loss account shall be recaptured as provided in paragraphs (d)(2), (d)(3), and (d)(4) of this section. See paragraph (d)(5) of this section for definitions. See the ordering rules under § 1.904(g)-3(f) and (i) for coordination with other loss recapture under section 904(f) and (g).

(2) *Treatment of net capital gain.*—If the gain from a disposition of property to which this paragraph (d) applies is treated as net capital gain, all references to such gain in paragraphs (d)(3) and (d)(4) of this section shall mean such gain as adjusted under paragraph (b) of this section. The amount by which the overall foreign loss account shall be reduced shall be determined from such adjusted gain.

(3) *Dispositions where gain is recognized irrespective of section 904 (f)(3).*—(i) *Foreign source gain.*—If a taxpayer recognizes foreign source gain in a separate category on the disposition of property described in paragraph (d)(1) of this section, and there is a balance in a taxpayer's overall foreign loss account that is attributable to a loss in such separate category after applying paragraph (c) of this section, an additional portion of such balance shall be recaptured in accordance with paragraphs (a) and (b) of this section. The amount recaptured shall be the lesser of such balance or the full amount of the foreign source gain recognized on the disposition that was not previously recharacterized.

(ii) *U.S. source gain.*—If a taxpayer recognizes U.S. source gain on the disposition of property described in paragraph (d)(1) of this section, and there is a balance in a taxpayer's overall foreign loss account that is attributable to a loss in the separate category to which the income generated by such property is assigned after applying paragraph (c) of this section, an amount of the gain shall be treated as foreign source and an additional portion of such balance equal to that amount shall be recaptured in accordance with paragraphs (a) and (b) of this section. The amount of gain treated as foreign source and the amount of overall foreign loss recaptured shall be the lesser of the balance in the overall foreign loss account or the full amount of the gain recognized on the disposition.

(4) *Dispositions in which gain would not otherwise be recognized.*—(i) *Recognition of gain to the extent of the overall foreign loss account.*—If a taxpayer makes a disposition of property described in paragraph (d)(1) of this section in which any amount of gain otherwise would not be recognized in the year of the disposition, and such property was used or held for use to generate foreign source taxable income subject to a separate limitation under which the taxpayer had a

balance in its overall foreign loss account (including a balance that arose in the year of the disposition), the taxpayer shall recognize foreign source taxable income in an amount equal to the lesser of:

(A) The sum of the balance in the applicable overall foreign loss account (but only after such balance has been increased by amounts added to the account for the year of the disposition or has been reduced by amounts recaptured for the year of the disposition under paragraph (c) and paragraph (d)(3) of this section) plus the amount of any overall foreign loss that would be part of a net operating loss for the year of the disposition if gain from the disposition were not recognized under section 904(f)(3), plus the amount of any overall foreign loss that is part of a net operating loss carryover from a prior year, or

(B) The excess of the fair market value of such property over the taxpayer's adjusted basis in such property.

The excess of the fair market value of such property over its adjusted basis shall be determined on an asset by asset basis. Losses from the disposition of an asset shall not be recognized. Any foreign source taxable income deemed received and recognized under this paragraph (d)(4)(i) will have the same character as if the property had been sold or exchanged in a taxable transaction and will constitute gain for all purposes.

(ii) *Basis adjustment.*—The basis of the property received in an exchange to which this paragraph (d)(4) applies shall be increased by the amount of gain deemed recognized, in accordance with applicable sections of subchapters C (relating to corporate distributions and adjustments), K (relating to partners and partnerships), O (relating to gain or loss on the disposition of property), and P (relating to capital gains and losses). If the property to which this paragraph (d)(4) applies was transferred by gift, the basis of such property in the hands of the donor immediately preceding such gift shall be increased by the amount of the gain deemed recognized.

(iii) *Recapture of overall foreign loss to the extent of amount recognized.*—The provisions of paragraphs (a) and (b) of this section shall be applied to the extent of 100 percent of the foreign source taxable income which is recognized under paragraph (d)(4)(i) of this section. However, amounts of foreign source gain that would not be recognized except by application of section 904(f)(3) and paragraph (d)(4)(i) of this section, and which are treated as United States source gain by application of section 904(b)(3)(C) (prior to its removal by the Tax Reform Act of 1986) and paragraph (b)(1) of this section, shall reduce the overall foreign loss account (subject to the adjustments described in paragraph (d)(2) of this section) if such gain is net capital gain, notwithstanding the fact that such amounts would otherwise not be recaptured under the ordering rules in paragraph (b) of this section.

(iv) *Priorities among dispositions in which gain is deemed to be recognized.*—If, in a single taxable year, a taxpayer makes more than one disposition to which this paragraph (d)(4) is applicable, the rules of this paragraph (d)(4) shall be applied to each disposition in succession starting with the disposition which occurred earliest, until the balance in the applicable overall foreign loss account is reduced to zero. If the taxpayer simultaneously makes more than one disposition to which this paragraph (d)(4) is applicable, the rules of paragraph (d)(4) shall be applied so that the balance in the applicable overall foreign loss account to be recaptured will be allocated pro rata among the assets in proportion to the excess of the fair market value of each asset over the adjusted basis of each asset.

(5) *Definitions.*—(i) *Disposition.*—A disposition to which this paragraph (d) applies includes a sale; exchange; distribution; gift; transfer upon the foreclosure of a security interest (but not a mere transfer of title to a creditor upon creation of a security interest or to a debtor upon termination of a security interest); involuntary conversion; contribution to a partnership, trust, or corporation; transfer at death; or any other transfer of property whether or not gain or loss is recognized under other provisions of the Code. However, a disposition to which this paragraph (d) applies does not include:

(A) A distribution or transfer of property to a domestic corporation described in section 381(a) (provided that paragraph (d)(6) of this section applies);

(B) A disposition of property which is not a material factor in the realization of income by the taxpayer (as defined in paragraph (d)(5)(iv) of this section);

(C) A transaction in which gross income is not realized; or

(D) The entering into of a unitization or pooling agreement (as defined in § 1.614-8(b)(6) of the regulations) containing a valid election under section 761(a)(2), and in which the source of the entire gain from any disposition of the interest created by the agreement would be determined to be foreign source under section 862(a)(5) if the disposition occurred presently.

(ii) *Property used in a trade or business.*—Property is used in a trade or business if it is held for the principal purpose of promoting the present or future conduct of the trade or business. This generally includes property acquired and held in the ordinary course of a trade or business or otherwise held in a direct relationship to a trade or business. In determining whether an asset is held in a direct relationship to a trade or business, principal consideration shall be given to whether the asset is used in the trade or business. Property will be treated as held in a direct relationship to a trade or business if the property was acquired with funds generated by that trade or business or if income generated from the asset is available for use in that trade or business. Property used in a trade or business may be tangible or intangible, real or personal property. It includes property, such as equipment, which is subject to an allowance for depreciation under section 167 or cost recovery under section 168. Property may be considered used in a trade or business even if it is a capital asset in the hands of the taxpayer. However, stock of another corporation shall not be considered property used in a trade or business if a substantial investment motive exists for acquiring and holding the stock. On the other hand, stock acquired or held to assure a source of supply for a trade or business shall be considered property used in that trade or business. Inventory is generally not considered property used in a trade or business. However, when disposed of in a manner not in the ordinary course of a trade or business, inventory will be considered property used in the trade or business. A partnership interest will be treated as property used in a trade or business if the underlying assets of the partnership would be property used in a trade or business. For purposes of section 904(f)(3) and §§ 1.904(f)-2(d)(1) and (5), a disposition of a partnership interest to which this section applies will be treated as a disposition of a proportionate share of each of the assets of the partnership. For purposes of allocating the purchase price of the interest and the seller's basis in the interest to those assets, the principles of § 1.751-1(a) will apply.

(iii) *Property used predominantly outside the United States.*—Property will be considered used predominantly outside the United States if for a 3-year period ending on the date of the disposition (or, if shorter, the period during which the property has been used in the trade or business) such property was located outside the United States more than 50 percent of the time. An aircraft, railroad rolling stock, vessel, motor vehicle, container, or other property used for transportation purposes is deemed to be used predominantly outside the United States if, during the 3-year (or shorter) period, either such propery is located outside the United States more than 50 percent of the time or more than 50 percent of the miles traversed in the use of such property are traversed outside the United States.

(iv) *Property which is a material factor in the realization of income.*—For purposes of this section, property used in a trade or business will be considered a material factor in the realization of income unless the taxpayer establishes that it is not (or, if the taxpayer did not realize income from the trade or business in the taxable year, would not be expected to be) necessary to the realization of income by the taxpayer.

(6) *Carryover of overall foreign loss accounts in a corporate acquisition to which section 381(a) applies.*—In the case of a distribution or transfer described in section 381(a), an overall foreign loss account of the distributing or transferor corporation shall be treated as an overall foreign loss account of the acquiring or transferee corporation as of the close of the date of the distribution or transfer. If the transferee corporation had an overall foreign loss account under the same separate limitation prior to the distribution or transfer, the balance in the transferor's account must be added to the transferee's account. If not, the transferee must adopt the transferor's overall foreign loss account. An overall foreign loss of the transferor will be treated as incurred by the transferee in the year prior to the year of the transfer.

(7) *Illustrations.*—The rules of this paragraph (d) are illustrated by the following examples which assume that the United States corporate tax rate is 50 percent (unless otherwise stated). For purposes of these examples, none of the foreign source gains are treated as net capital gains (unless so stated).

Example (1). X Corporation has a balance in its general limitation overall foreign loss account of $600 at the close of its taxable year ending December 31, 1984. In 1985, X sells assets used predominantly outside the United States in a trade or business and recognizes $1,000 of gain on the sale under section 1001. This gain is subject to the general limitation. This sale is a disposition within the meaning of paragraph (d)(5)(i) of this section, and to which this paragraph (d) applies. X has no other foreign source taxable income in 1985 and has $1,000 of United States source taxable income. Under paragraph (c), X is required to recapture $500 (the lesser of the balance in X's general limitation overall foreign loss account ($600) or 50 percent of $1,000) of its overall foreign loss account. The balance in X's general limitation overall foreign loss account is reduced to $100 in accordance with § 1.904(f)-1(e)(2). In addition, under paragraph (d)(3) of this section, X is required to recapture $100 (the lesser of the remaining balance in its general limitation overall foreign loss account ($100) or 100 percent of its foreign source taxable income recognized on such disposition that has not been previously recharacterized ($500)). The total amount recaptured is $600. X's foreign tax credit limitation for income subject to the general limitation in 1985 is $200 ($400/$2,000 × $1,000) instead of $500 ($1,000/$2,000 × $1,000). The balance in X's general limitation overall foreign loss account is reduced to zero in accordance with § 1.904(f)-1(e)(2).

Example (2). On December 31, 1984, Y Corporation has a balance in its general limitation overall foreign loss account of $1,500. In 1985, Y has $500 of United States source taxable income and $200 of foreign source taxable income subject to the general limitation. Y's foreign source taxable income is from the sale of property used predominantly outside of the United States in a trade or business. This sale is a disposition to which this paragraph (d) is applicable. In 1985, Y also transferred property used predominantly outside of the United States in a trade or business to another corporation. Under section 351, no gain was recognized on this transfer. Such property had been used to generate foreign source taxable income subject to the general limitation. The excess of the fair market value of the property transferred over Y's adjusted basis in such property was $2,000. In accordance with paragraph (c) of this section, Y is required to recapture $100 (the lesser of $1,500, the amount in Y's general limitation overall foreign loss account, or 50 percent of $200, the amount of general limitation foreign source taxable income for the current year) of its general limitation overall foreign loss. Y is then required to recapture an additional $100 of its general limitation overall foreign loss account under paragraph (d)(3) of this section out of the remaining gain recognized on the sale of assets, because 100 percent of such gain is subject to recapture. The balance in Y's general limitation overall foreign loss account is reduced to $1,300 in accordance with § 1.904(f)-1(e)(2). Y corporation is then required to recognize $1,300 of foreign source taxable income on its section 351 transfer under paragraph (d)(4) of this section. The remaining $700 of potential gain associated with the section 351 transfer is not recognized. Under paragraph (d)(4), 100 percent of the $1,300 is recharacterized as United States source taxable income, and Y's general limitation overall foreign loss account is reduced to zero. Y's entire taxable income for 1985 is:

U.S. source taxable income	$500
Foreign source taxable income subject to the general limitation that is recharacterized as U.S. source income by paragraphs (c) and (d)(3) of this section .	$200
Gain recognized under section 904(f)(3) and paragraph (d)(4) of this section, and recharacterized as U.S. source income	$1,300
Total	$2,000

Y's foreign tax credit limitation for 1985 for income subject to the general limitation is $0 ($0/$2,000 × $1,000) instead of $100 ($200/$700 × $350).

Example (3). W Corporation is a calendar year domestic corporation with foreign branch operations in country C. As of December 31, 1984, W has no overall foreign loss accounts and has no net operating loss carryovers. W's entire taxable income in 1985 is:

U.S. source taxable income	$800
Foreign source taxable income (loss) subject to the general limitation	($1,000)

W cannot carry back its 1985 NOL to any earlier year. As of December 31, 1985, W therefore has $800 in its general limitation overall foreign loss account. In 1986, W earns $400 United States source taxable income and has an additional $1,000 loss from the operations of the foreign branch. Income in the loss category would be subject to the general limitation. Also in 1986, W disposes of property used predominantly outside the United States in a trade or business. Such property generated income subject to the general limitation. The excess of the property's fair market value over its adjusted basis is $3,000. The disposition is of a type described in § 1.904(f)-2(d)(4)(i). W has no other income in 1986. Under § 1.904(f)-2(d)(4)(i), W is required to recognize foreign source taxable income on the disposition in an amount equal to the lesser of $2,000 ($800 (the balance in the general limitation overall foreign loss account as of 1985) + $400 (the increase in the general limitation overall foreign loss account attributable to the disposition year) + $600 (the general limitation overall foreign loss that is part of the NOL from 1986) + $200 (the general limitation overall foreign loss that is part of the NOL from 1985)) or $3,000. The $2,000 foreign source income required to be recognized under section 904(f)(3) is reduced to $1,200 by the remaining $600 loss in 1986 and the $200 net operating loss carried forward from 1985. This $1,200 of income is subject to the general limitation. In computing the foreign tax credit limitation for general limitation income, the $1,200 of foreign source income is treated as United States source income and, therefore, W's foreign tax credit limitation for income subject to the general limitation is zero. W's overall foreign loss account is reduced to zero.

Example (4). Z Corporation has a balance in its FORI overall foreign loss account of $1,500 at the end of its taxable year 1980. In 1981, Z has $1,600 of foreign oil related income subject to the separate limitation for FORI income and no United States source income. In addition, in 1981, Z makes two dispositions of property used predominantly outside the United States in a trade or business on which no gain was recognized. Such property generated foreign oil related income. The excess of the fair market value of the property transferred in the first disposition over Z's adjusted basis in such property is $575. The excess of the fair market value of the property transferred in the second disposition over Z's adjusted basis in such property is $1,000. Under paragraph (c) of this section, Z is required to recapture $800 (the lesser of 50 percent of its foreign oil related income of $1,600 or the balance ($1,500) in its FORI overall foreign loss account) of its foreign oil related loss. In accordance with paragraphs (d)(4)(i) and (iv) of this section, Z is required to recognize foreign oil related income in the amount of $575 on the first disposition and, since the foreign oil related loss account is now reduced by $1,375 (the $800 and $575 amounts previously recaptured), Z is required to recognize foreign oil related income in the amount of $125 on the second disposition. In accordance with paragraph (d)(4)(iii) of this section, the entire amount recognized is treated as United States source income and the balance in the FORI overall foreign loss account is reduced to zero under § 1.904(f)-1(e)(2). Z's foreign tax credit limitation for FORI is $400 ($800/$2,300 × $1,150) instead of $800 ($1,600/$1,600 × $800).

Example (5). The facts are the same as in example (4), except that the gain from the two dispositions of property is treated as net capital gain and the United States corporate tax rate is assumed to be 46 percent. As in example (4), Z is required to recapture $800 of its foreign oil related loss from its 1981 ordinary foreign oil related income. In accordance with paragraph (d)(4)(i) and (iv) of this section, Z is first required to recognize foreign oil related income (which is net capital gain) on the first disposition in the amount of $575. Under paragraphs (b) and (d)(2) of this section, this net capital gain is adjusted by subtracting the rate differential portion of such gain from the total amount of such gain to determine the amount by which the foreign oil related loss account is reduced, which is $350 ($575 – ($575 × 18/46)). The balance remaining in Z's foreign oil related loss account after this step is $350. Therefore, this process will be repeated, in accordance with paragraph (d)(4)(iv) of this section, to recapture that remaining balance out of the gain deemed recognized on the second disposition, resulting in reduction of the foreign oil related loss account to zero and net capital gain required to be recognized from the second disposition in the amount of $575, which must also be adjusted by subtracting the rate differential portion to determine the amount by which the foreign oil related loss account is reduced (which is $350). The $575 of net capital gain from each disposition is recharacterized as United States source net capital gain. Z's section 907(b) foreign tax credit limitation is the same as in example (4), and Z has $1,150 ($575 + $575) of United States source net capital gain.

(e) *Effective/applicability date.*—Paragraphs (c)(1), (c)(5) *Example 4*, (d)(1), and (d)(3) of this section shall apply to taxable years beginning on or after January 1, 2012. Taxpayers may choose to apply paragraphs (c)(1), (c)(5) *Example 4*, (d)(1), and (d)(3) of this section to other taxable years beginning after December 21, 2007, including periods covered by 26 CFR § 1.904(f)-2T (revised as of April 1, 2010). [Reg. § 1.904(f)-2.]

☐ [*T.D. 8153, 8-21-87. Amended by T.D.* 9371, 12-20-2007 *and T.D.* 9595, 6-21-2012.]

§ 1.904(f)-3. Allocation of net operating losses and net capital losses.—For rules relating to the allocation of net operating losses and net capital losses, see § 1.904(g)-3T.

☐ [*T.D.* 8153, 8-21-87. *Amended by T.D.* 8677, 6-26-96; *T.D.* 8823, 6-25-99 *and T.D.* 9371, 12-20-2007.]

§1.904(f)-7. Separate limitation loss and the separate limitation loss account.—(a) *Overview of regulations.*—This section provides rules for determining a taxpayer's separate limitation losses, for establishing separate limitation loss accounts, and for making additions to and reducing such accounts for purposes of section 904(f). Section 1.904(f)-8 provides rules for recharacterizing the balance in any separate limitation loss account under the general recharacterization rule of section 904(f)(5)(C).

(b) *Definitions.*—The definitions in paragraphs (b)(1) through (b)(4) of this section apply for purposes of this section and §§1.904(f)-8 and 1.904(g)-3.

(1) *Separate category* means each separate category of income described in section 904(d) and any other category of income described in §1.904-4(m). For example, income subject to section 901(j) or section 904(h)(10) is income in a separate category.

(2) *Separate limitation income* means, with respect to any separate category, the taxable income from sources outside the United States, separately computed for that category for the taxable year. Separate limitation income shall be determined by taking into account any adjustments for capital gains and losses and qualified dividend income, as defined in section 1(h)(11), under section 904(b)(2) and §1.904(b)-1. See §1.904(b)-1(h)(1)(i).

(3) *Separate limitation loss* means, with respect to any separate category, the amount by which the foreign source gross income in that category is exceeded by the sum of expenses, losses and other deductions (not including any net operating loss deduction under section 172(a) or any expropriation loss or casualty loss described in section 907(c)(4)(D)(iii)) properly apportioned or allocated to that separate category for the taxable year. Separate limitation losses shall be determined by taking into account any adjustments for capital gains and losses and qualified dividend income under section 904(b)(2) and §1.904(b)-1. See §1.904(b)-1(h)(1)(i).

(c) *Separate limitation loss account.*—Any taxpayer that sustains a separate limitation loss that is allocated to reduce separate limitation income in one or more other separate categories of the taxpayer under the rules of §1.904(g)-3 must establish a separate limitation loss account for the loss with respect to each such other separate category. The balance in any separate limitation loss account represents the amount of such separate limitation loss that is subject to recapture in a given taxable year pursuant to §1.904(f)-8 and section 904(f)(5)(F). From year to year, amounts may be added to or subtracted from the balance in such loss accounts, as provided in paragraphs (d) and (e) of this section.

(d) *Additions to separate limitation loss accounts.*—(1) *General rule.*—A taxpayer's separate limitation loss as defined in paragraph (b)(3) of this section shall be added to the applicable separate limitation loss accounts at the end of its taxable year to the extent that the separate limitation loss reduces separate limitation income in one or more other separate categories in that taxable year or in a year to which the loss has been carried back. For rules with respect to net operating loss carryovers, see paragraph (d)(3) of this section and §1.904(g)-3.

(2) *Separate limitation losses of another taxpayer.*—If any portion of any separate limitation loss account of another taxpayer is allocated to the taxpayer in accordance with §1.1502-9 (relating to consolidated separate limitation losses) the taxpayer shall add such amount to its applicable separate limitation loss account.

(3) *Additions to separate limitation loss account created by loss carryovers.*—The taxpayer shall add to each separate limitation loss account all net operating loss carryovers to the current taxable year to the extent that separate limitation losses included in the net operating loss carryovers reduced foreign source income in one or more other separate categories for the taxable year.

(e) *Reductions of separate limitation loss accounts.*—The taxpayer shall subtract the following amounts from its separate limitation loss accounts at the end of its taxable year in the following order as applicable:

(1) *Pre-recapture reduction for amounts allocated to other taxpayers.*—A separate limitation loss account is reduced by the amount of any separate limitation loss account that is allocated to another taxpayer in accordance with §1.1502-9 (relating to consolidated separate limitation losses).

(2) *Reduction for offsetting loss accounts.*—A separate limitation loss account is reduced to take into account any netting of separate limitation loss accounts under §1.904(g)-3(d)(1).

(3) *Reduction for amounts recaptured.*—A separate limitation loss account is reduced by the amount of any separate limitation income that is earned in the same separate category as the separate limitation loss and that is recharacterized in accordance with §1.904(f)-8 (relating to recapture of separate limitation losses) or section 904(f)(5)(F) (relating to recapture of separate limitation loss accounts out of gain realized from certain dispositions).

(f) *Effective/applicability date.*—This section applies to taxpayers that sustain separate limitation losses in taxable years beginning on or after January 1, 2012. Taxpayers may choose to apply this section to separate limitation losses sustained in other taxable years beginning after December 21, 2007, including periods covered by 26 CFR 1.904(f)-7T (revised as of April 1, 2010). For rules relating to taxable years beginning after December 31, 1986, and on or before December 21, 2007, see section 904(f)(5). [Reg. §1.904(f)-7.]

☐ [*T.D. 9371, 12-20-2007. Amended by T.D. 9595, 6-21-2012.*]

§1.904(f)-8. Recapture of separate limitation loss accounts.—(a) *In general.*—A taxpayer shall recapture a separate limitation loss account as provided in this section. If the taxpayer has a separate limitation loss account or accounts in any separate category (the "loss category") and the loss category has income in a subsequent taxable year, the income shall be recharacterized as income in that other category or categories. The amount of income recharacterized shall not exceed the aggregate balance in all separate limitation loss accounts for the loss category as determined under §1.904(f)-7. If the taxpayer has more than one separate limitation loss account in a loss category, and there is not enough income in the loss category to recapture all of the loss accounts, then separate limitation income in the loss category shall be recharacterized as separate limitation income in the other separate categories on a proportionate basis. This is determined by multiplying the total separate limitation income subject to recharacterization by a fraction, the numerator of which is the amount in a particular separate limitation loss account and the denominator of which is the total amount in all separate limitation loss accounts for the loss category.

(b) *Effect of recharacterization of separate limitation income on associated taxes.*—Recharacterization of income under paragraph (a) of this section shall not result in the recharacterization of any tax. The rules of §1.904-6, including the rules that the taxes are allocated on an annual basis and that foreign taxes paid on U.S. source income shall be allocated to the separate category that includes that U.S. source income (see §1.904-6(a)), shall apply for purposes of allocating taxes to separate categories. Allocation of taxes pursuant to §1.904-6 shall be made before the recapture of any separate limitation loss accounts of the taxpayer pursuant to the rules of this section.

(c) *Effective/applicability date.*—This section applies to taxpayers that sustain separate limitation losses in taxable years beginning on or after January 1, 2012. Taxpayers may choose to apply this section to separate limitation losses sustained in other taxable years beginning after December 21, 2007, including periods covered by 26 CFR §1.904(f)-8T (revised as of April 1, 2010). For rules relating to taxable years beginning after December 31, 1986, and on or before December 21, 2007, see section 904(f)(5). [Reg. §1.904(f)-8.]

☐ [*T.D. 9371, 12-20-2007. Amended by T.D. 9595, 6-21-2012.*]

§1.904(f)-12. Transition rules.—(a) *Recapture in years beginning after December 31, 1986, of overall foreign losses incurred in taxable years beginning before January 1, 1987.*—(1) *In general.*—If a taxpayer has a balance in an overall foreign loss account at the end of its last taxable year beginning before January 1, 1987 (pre-effective date years), the amount of that balance shall be recaptured in subsequent years by recharacterizing income received in the income category described in section 904(d) as in effect for taxable years beginning after December 31, 1986 (post-effective date years), that is analogous to the income category for which the overall foreign loss account was established, as follows:

(i) Interest income as defined in section 904(d)(1)(A) as in effect for pre-effective date taxable years is analogous to passive income as defined in section 904(d)(1)(A) as in effect for post-effective date years;

(ii) Dividends from a DISC or former DISC as defined in section 904(d)(1)(B) as in effect for pre-effective date taxable years is analogous to dividends from a DISC or former DISC as defined in section 904(d)(1)(F) as in effect for post-effective date taxable years;

(iii) Taxable income attributable to foreign trade income as defined in section 904(d)(1)(C) as in effect for pre-effective date taxable years is analogous to taxable income attributable to foreign trade income as defined in section 904(d)(1)(G) as in effect for post-effective date years;

(iv) Distributions from a FSC (or former FSC) as defined in section 904(d)(1)(D) as in effect for pre-effective date taxable years is analogous to distributions from a FSC (or former FSC) as defined in section 904(d)(1)(H) as in effect for post-effective date taxable years;

(v) For general limitation income as described in section 904(d)(1)(E) as in effect for pre-effective date taxable years, see the special rule in paragraph (a)(2) of this section.

(2) *Rule for general limitation losses.*—(i) *In general.*—Overall foreign losses incurred in the general limitation category of section 904(d)(1)(E), as in effect for pre-effective date taxable years, that are recaptured in post-effective date taxable years shall be recaptured from the taxpayer's general limitation income, financial services income, shipping income, and dividends from each noncontrolled section 902 corporation. If the sum of the taxpayer's general limitation income, financial services income, shipping income and dividends from each noncontrolled section 902 corporation for a taxable year subject to recapture exceeds the overall foreign loss to be recaptured, then the amount of each type of separate limitation income that will be treated as U.S. source income shall be determined as follows:

$$\text{Overall foreign loss subject to recapture} \times \frac{\text{Amount of income in each separate category from which the loss may be recaptured}}{\text{Sum of income in all separate categories from which the loss may be recaptured.}}$$

This recapture shall be made after the allocation of separate limitation losses pursuant to section 904(f)(5)(B) and before the recharacterization of post-effective date separate limitation income pursuant to section 904(f)(5)(C).

(ii) *Exception.*—If a taxpayer can demonstrate to the satisfaction of the district director that an overall foreign loss in the general limitation category of section 904(d)(1)(E), as in effect for pre-effective date taxable years, is attributable, in sums certain, to losses in one or more separate categories of section 904(d)(1) (including for this purpose the passive income category and the high withholding tax interest category), as in effect for post-effective date taxable years, then the taxpayer may recapture the loss (in the amounts demonstrated) from those separate categories only.

(3) *Priority of recapture of overall foreign losses incurred in pre-effective date taxable years.*—An overall foreign loss incurred by a taxpayer in pre-effective date taxable years shall be recaptured to the extent thereof before the taxpayer recaptures an overall foreign loss incurred in a post-effective date taxable year.

(4) *Examples.*—The following examples illustrate the application of this paragraph (a).

Example (1). X corporation is a domestic corporation which operates a branch in Country Y. For its taxable year ending December 31, 1988, X has $800 of financial services income, $100 of general limitation income and $100 of shipping income. X has a balance of $100 in its general limitation overall foreign loss account which resulted from an overall foreign loss incurred during its 1986 taxable year. X is unable to demonstrate to which of the income categories set forth in section 904(d)(1) as in effect for post-effective date taxable years the loss is attributable. In addition, X has a balance of $100 in its shipping overall foreign loss account attributable to a shipping loss incurred during its 1987 taxable year. X has no other overall foreign loss accounts. Pursuant to section 904(f)(1), the full amount in each of X corporation's overall foreign loss accounts is subject to recapture since $200 (the sum of those amounts) is less than 50% of X's foreign source taxable income for its 1988 taxable year, or $500. X's overall foreign loss incurred during its 1986 taxable year is recaptured before the overall foreign loss incurred during its 1987 taxable year, as follows: $80 ($100 × 800/1000) of X's financial services income, $10 ($100 × 100/1000) of X's general limitation income, and $10 ($100 × 100/1000) of X's shipping income will be treated as U.S. source income. The remaining $90 of X corporation's 1988 shipping income will be treated as U.S. source income for the purpose of recapturing X's $100 overall foreign loss attributable to the shipping loss incurred in 1987. $10 remains in X's shipping overall foreign loss account for recapture in subsequent taxable years.

Example (2). The facts are the same as in *Example* (1) except that X has $800 of financial services income, $100 of general limitation income, a $100 dividend from a noncontrolled section 902 corporation and a ($100) shipping loss for its taxable year ending December 31, 1988. Separate limitation losses are allocated pursuant to the rules of section 904(f)(5) before the recapture of overall foreign losses. Therefore, the ($100) shipping loss incurred by X will be allocated to its separate limitation income as follows: $80 ($100 × 800/1000) will be allocated to X's financial services income, $10 ($100 × 100/1000) will be allocated to its general limitation income and $10 ($100 × 100/1000) will be allocated to X's dividend from the noncontrolled section 902 corporation. Accordingly, after allocation of the 1988 shipping loss, X has $720 of financial services income, $90 of general limitation income, and a $90 dividend from the noncontrolled section 902 corporation. Pursuant to section 904(f)(1), the full amount in each of X corporation's overall foreign loss accounts is subject to recapture since $200 (the sum of those amounts) is less than 50% of X's net foreign source taxable income for its 1988 taxable year, or $450. X's overall foreign loss incurred during its 1986 taxable year is recaptured as follows: $80 ($100 × 720/900) of X's financial services income, $10 ($100 × 90/900) of its general limitation income and $10 ($100 × 90/900) of its dividend from the noncontrolled section 902 corporation will be treated as U.S. source income. Accordingly, after application of section 904(f), X has $100 of U.S. source income, $640 of financial services income, $80 of general limitation income and a $80 dividend from the noncontrolled section 902 corporation for its 1988 taxable year. X must establish a separate limitation loss account for each portion of the 1988 shipping loss that was allocated to its financial services income, general limitation income and dividends from the noncontrolled section 902 corporation. X's overall foreign loss account for the 1986 general limitation loss is reduced to zero. X still has a $100 balance in its overall foreign loss account that resulted from the 1987 shipping loss.

Example (3). Y is a domestic corporation which has a branch operation in Country Z. For its 1988 taxable year, Y has $5 of shipping income, $15 of general limitation income and $100 of financial services income. Y has a balance of $100 in its general limitation overall foreign loss account attributable to its 1986 taxable year. Y has no other overall foreign loss accounts. Pursuant to section 904(f)(1), $60 of the overall foreign loss is subject to recapture since 50% of Y's foreign source income for 1988 is less than the balance in its overall foreign loss account. Y can demonstrate that the entire $100 overall foreign loss was attributable to a shipping limitation loss incurred in 1986. Accordingly, only Y's $5 of shipping limitation income received in 1988 will be treated as U.S. source income. Because Y can demonstrate that the 1986 loss was entirely attributable to a shipping loss, none of Y's general limitation income or financial services income received in 1988 will be treated as U.S. source income.

Example (4). The facts are the same as in *Example* (3) except that Y can only demonstrate that $50 of the 1986 overall foreign loss account was attributable to a shipping loss incurred in 1986. Accordingly, Y's $5 of shipping limitation income received in 1988 will be treated as U.S. source income. The remaining $50 of the 1986 overall foreign loss that Y cannot trace to a particular separate limitation will be recaptured and treated as U.S. source income as follows: $43 ($50 × 100/115) of Y's financial services income will be treated as U.S. source income and $7 ($50 × 15/115) of Y's general limitation income will be treated as U.S. source income. Y has $45 remaining in its overall foreign loss account to be recaptured from shipping income in a future year.

(b) *Treatment of overall foreign losses that are part of net operating losses incurred in pre-effective date taxable years which are carried forward to post-effective date taxable years.*—(1) *Rule.*—An overall foreign loss that is part of a net operating loss incurred in a pre-effective date taxable year which is carried forward, pursuant to section 172, to a post-effective date taxable year will be carried forward under the rules of section 904(f)(5) and the regulations under that section. *See also* Notice 89-3, 1989-1 C.B. 623. For this purpose the loss must be allocated to income in the category analogous to the income category set forth in section 904(d) as in effect for pre-effective date taxable years in which the loss occurred. The analogous category shall be determined under the rules of paragraph (a) of this section.

(2) *Example*.—The following example illustrates the rule of paragraph (b)(1) of this section.

Example. Z is a domestic corporation which has a branch operation in Country D. For its taxable year ending December 31, 1988, Z has $100 of passive income and $200 of general limitation income. Z also has a $60 net operating loss which was carried forward pursuant to section 172 from its 1986 taxable year. The net operating loss resulted from an overall foreign loss attributable to the general limitation income category. Z can demonstrate that the loss is a shipping loss. Therefore, the net operating loss will be treated as a shipping loss for Z's 1988 taxable year. Pursuant to section 904(f)(5), the shipping loss will be allocated as follows: $20 ($60 × 100/300) will be allocated to Z's passive income and $40 ($60 × 200/300) will be allocated to Z's general limitation income. Accordingly, after application of section 904(f), Z has $80 of passive income and $160 of general limitation income for its 1988 taxable year. Although no addition to Z's overall foreign loss account for shipping income will result from the NOL carry forward, shipping income earned by Z in subsequent taxable years will be subject to recharacterization as passive income and general limitation income pursuant to the rules set forth in section 904(f)(5).

(c) *Treatment of overall foreign losses that are part of net operating losses incurred in post-effective date taxable years which are carried back to pre-effective date taxable years*.—(1) *Allocation to analogous income category*.—An overall foreign loss that is part of a net operating loss incurred by the taxpayer in a post-effective date taxable year which is carried back, pursuant to section 172, to a pre-effective date taxable year shall be allocated first to income in the pre-effective date income category analogous to the income category set forth in section 904(d) as in effect for post-effective date taxable years in which the loss occurred. Except for the general limitation income category, the pre-effective date income category that is analogous to a post-effective date income category shall be determined under paragraphs (a)(1)(i) through (iv) of this section. The general limitation income category for pre-effective date years shall be treated as the income category that is analogous to the post-effective date categories for general limitation income, financial services income, shipping income, dividends from each noncontrolled section 902 corporation and high withholding tax interest income. If the net operating loss resulted from separate limitation losses in more than one post-effective date income category and more than one loss is carried back to pre-effective date general limitation income, then the losses shall be allocated to the pre-effective date general limitation income based on the following formula:

$$\text{Pre-effective date general limitation income} \times \frac{\text{Loss in each post-effective date separate limitation category that is analogous to pre-effective date general limitation income}}{\text{Losses in all post-effective categories that are analogous to pre-effective date general limitation income.}}$$

(2) *Allocation to U.S. source income*.—If an overall foreign loss is carried back to a pre-effective date taxable year and the loss exceeds the foreign source income in the analogous category for the carry back year, the remaining loss shall be allocated against U.S. source income as set forth in § 1.904(f)-3. The amount of the loss that offsets U.S. source income must be added to the taxpayer's overall foreign loss account. An addition to an overall foreign loss account resulting from the carry back of a net operating loss incurred by a taxpayer in a post-effective date taxable year shall be treated as having been incurred by the taxpayer in the year in which the loss arose and shall be subject to recapture pursuant to section 904(f) as in effect for post-effective date taxable years.

(3) *Allocation to other separate limitation categories*.—To the extent that an overall foreign loss that is carried back as part of a net operating loss exceeds the separate limitation income to which it is allocated and the U.S. source income of the taxpayer for the taxable year to which the loss is carried, the loss shall be allocated pro rata to other separate limitation income of the taxpayer for the taxable year. However, there shall be no recharacterization of separate limitation income pursuant to section 904(f)(5) as a result of the allocation of such a net operating loss to other separate limitation income of the taxpayer.

(4) *Examples*.—The following examples illustrate the rules of paragraph (c) of this section.

Example (1). X is a domestic corporation which has a branch operation in Country A. For its taxable year ending December 31, 1987, X has a $60 net operating loss which is carried back pursuant to section 172 to its taxable year ending December 31, 1985. The net operating loss resulted from a shipping loss; X had no U.S. source income in 1987. X had $20 of general limitation income, $40 of DISC limitation income and $10 of U.S. source income for its 1985 taxable year. The $60 NOL is allocated first to X's 1985 general limitation income to the extent thereof ($20) since the general limitation income category of section 904(d) as in effect for pre-effective date taxable years is the income category that is analogous to shipping income for post-effective date taxable years. Therefore, X has no general limitation income for its 1985 taxable year. Next, pursuant to section 904(f) as in effect for pre-effective date taxable years, the remaining $40 of the NOL is allocated first to X's $10 of U.S. source income and then to $30 of X's DISC limitation income for its 1985 taxable year. Accordingly, X has no U.S. source income and $10 of DISC limitation income for its 1985 taxable year after allocation of the NOL. X has a $10 balance in its shipping overall foreign loss account which is subject to recapture pursuant to section 904(f) as in effect for post-effective date taxable years. X will not be required to recharacterize, pursuant to section 904(f)(5), subsequent shipping income as DISC limitation income.

Example (2). Y is a domestic corporation which has a branch operation in Country B. For its taxable year ending December 31, 1987, X has a $200 net operating loss which is carried back pursuant to section 172 to its taxable year ending December 31, 1986. The net operating loss resulted from a ($100) general limitation loss and a ($100) shipping loss. Y had $100 of general limitation income and $200 of U.S. source income for its taxable year ending December 31, 1986. The separate limitation losses for 1987 are allocated pro rata to Y's 1986 general limitation income as follows: $50 of the ($100) general limitation loss ($100 × 100/200) and $50 of the ($100) shipping loss ($100 × 100/200) is allocated to Y's $100 of 1986 general limitation income. The remaining $50 of Y's general limitation loss and the remaining $50 of Y's shipping loss are allocated to Y's 1986 U.S. source income. Accordingly, Y has no foreign source income and $100 of U.S. source income for its 1986 taxable year. Y has a $50 balance in its general limitation overall foreign loss account and a $50 balance in its shipping overall foreign loss account, both of which will be subject to recapture pursuant to section 904(f) as in effect for post-effective date taxable years.

(d) *Recapture of FORI and general limitation overall foreign losses incurred in taxable years beginning before January 1, 1983*.—For taxable years beginning after December 31, 1986, and before January 1, 1991, the rules set forth in § 1.904(f)-6 shall apply for purposes of recapturing general limitation and foreign oil related income (FORI) overall foreign losses incurred in taxable years beginning before January 1, 1983 (pre-1983). For taxable years beginning after December 31, 1990, the rules set forth in this section shall apply for purposes of recapturing pre-1983 general limitation and FORI overall foreign losses.

(e) *Recapture of pre-1983 overall foreign losses determined on a combined basis*.—The rules set forth in paragraph (a)(2) of this section shall apply for purposes of recapturing overall foreign losses incurred in taxable years beginning before January 1, 1983, that were computed on a combined basis in accordance with § 1.904(f)-1(c)(1).

(f) *Transition rules for taxable years beginning before December 31, 1990*.—For transition rules for taxable years beginning before January 1, 1990, see 26 CFR § 1.904(f)-13T as it appeared in the Code of Federal Regulations revised as of April 1, 1990.

(g) *Recapture in years beginning after December 31, 2002, of separate limitation losses and overall foreign losses incurred in years beginning before January 1, 2003, with respect to the separate category for dividends from a noncontrolled section 902 corporation*.—(1) *Recapture of separate limitation loss or overall foreign loss in a separate category for dividends from a noncontrolled section 902 corporation*.—To the extent that a taxpayer has a balance in any separate limitation loss or overall foreign loss account in a separate category for dividends from a noncontrolled section 902 corporation under section 904(d)(1)(E) (prior to its repeal by Public Law 108-357, 118 Stat. 1418 (October 22, 2004)) at the end of the taxpayer's last taxable year beginning before January 1, 2003 (or a later taxable year in which the taxpayer received a dividend subject to a separate limitation for dividends from that noncontrolled section 902 corporation), the amount of such balance shall be allocated on the first day of the taxpayer's next taxable year to the taxpayer's other separate categories. The amount of such balance shall be allocated in the same percentages as the taxpayer properly characterized the stock of the noncontrolled section 902 corporation for purposes of apportioning the taxpayer's interest expense for its first taxable year ending after the first day of such corporation's first taxable year beginning after December 31, 2002, under § 1.861-12T(c)(3) or § 1.861-12(c)(4), as the case may be. To the extent a taxpayer has a balance in any separate limitation loss account in a separate category for dividends from a noncontrolled section 902 corporation with respect to another separate category, and the separate limitation loss would otherwise be assigned to that other category under this paragraph (g)(1), such balance shall be eliminated.

(2) *Recapture of separate limitation loss in another separate category.*—To the extent that a taxpayer has a balance in any separate limitation loss account in a separate category with respect to a separate category for dividends from a noncontrolled section 902 corporation under section 904(d)(1)(E) (prior to its repeal by Public Law 108-357, 118 Stat. 1418 (October 22, 2004)) at the end of the taxpayer's last taxable year with or within which ends the last taxable year of the noncontrolled section 902 corporation beginning before January 1, 2003, such loss shall be recaptured in subsequent taxable years as income in the appropriate separate categories. The separate limitation loss shall be recaptured as income in other separate categories in the same percentages as the taxpayer properly characterizes the stock of the noncontrolled section 902 corporation for purposes of apportioning the taxpayer's interest expense in its first taxable year ending after the first day of the foreign corporation's first taxable year beginning after December 31, 2002, under § 1.861-12T(c)(3) or § 1.861-12(c)(4), as the case may be. To the extent a taxpayer has a balance in a separate limitation loss account in a separate category that would have been recaptured as income in that same category under this paragraph (g)(2), such balance shall be eliminated.

(3) *Exception.*—Where a taxpayer formerly met the stock ownership requirements of section 902(a) with respect to a foreign corporation, but did not meet the requirements of section 902(a) on December 20, 2002 (or on the first day of the taxpayer's first taxable year beginning after December 31, 2002, in the case of a transaction that was the subject of a binding contract in effect on December 20, 2002), if the taxpayer has a balance in any separate limitation loss or overall foreign loss account for a separate category for dividends from that foreign corporation under section 904(d)(1)(E) (prior to its repeal by Public Law 108-357, 118 Stat. 1418 (October 22, 2004)) at the end of the taxpayer's last taxable year beginning before January 1, 2003, then the amount of such balance shall not be subject to recapture under section 904(f) and this section. If a separate limitation loss or overall foreign loss account for such category is not subject to recapture under this paragraph (g)(3), the taxpayer cannot carry over any unused foreign taxes in such separate category to any other limitation category. However, a taxpayer may elect to recapture the balances of all separate limitation loss and overall foreign loss accounts for all separate categories for dividends from such formerly-owned noncontrolled section 902 corporations under the rules of paragraphs (g)(1) and (2) of this section. If a taxpayer so elects, it may carry over any unused foreign taxes in these separate categories to the appropriate separate categories as provided in § 1.904-2(h).

(4) *Examples.*—The following examples illustrate the application of this paragraph (g):

Example 1. X is a domestic corporation that meets the ownership requirements of section 902(a) with respect to Y, a foreign corporation the stock of which X owns 50 percent. Therefore, Y is a noncontrolled section 902 corporation with respect to X. Both X and Y use the calendar year as their taxable year. As of December 31, 2002, X had a $100 balance in its separate limitation loss account for the separate category for dividends from Y, of which $60 offset general limitation income and $40 offset passive income. For purposes of apportioning X's interest expense for its 2003 taxable year, X properly characterized the stock of Y as a multiple category asset (80% general and 20% passive). Under paragraph (g)(1) of this section, on January 1, 2003, $80 ($100 x 80/100) of the $100 balance in the separate limitation loss account is assigned to the general limitation category. Of this $80 balance, $32 ($80 × 40/100) is with respect to the passive category, and $48 ($80 × 60/100) is with respect to the general limitation category and therefore is eliminated. The remaining $20 balance ($100 × 20/100) of the $100 balance is assigned to the passive category. Of this $20 balance, $12 ($20 x 60/100) is with respect to the general limitation category, and $8 ($20 × 40/100) is with respect to the passive category and therefore is eliminated.

Example 2. The facts are the same as in *Example 1*, except that as of December 31, 2002, X had a $30 balance in its separate limitation loss account in the general limitation category, and a $20 balance in its separate limitation loss account in the passive category, both of which offset income in the separate category for dividends from Y. Under paragraph (g)(2) of this section, the separate limitation loss accounts in the general limitation and passive categories with respect to the separate category for dividends from Y will be recaptured on and after January 1, 2003, from income in other separate categories, as follows. Of the $30 balance in X's separate limitation loss account in the general category with respect to the separate category for dividends from Y, $6 ($30 × 20/100) is with respect to the passive category, and $24 ($30 × 80/100) is with respect to the general limitation category and therefore is eliminated. Of the $20 balance in X's separate limitation loss account in the passive category with respect to the separate category for dividends from Y, $16 ($20 × 80/100) will be recaptured out of general limitation income, and $4 ($20 × 20/100) would otherwise be recaptured out of passive income and therefore is eliminated.

(5) *Effective/applicability date.*—This paragraph (g) applies to taxable years ending on or after April 20, 2009. See 26 CFR § 1.904(f)-12T(g) (revised as of April 1, 2009) for rules applicable to taxable years beginning after December 31, 2002, and ending before April 20, 2009.

(h) *Recapture in years beginning after December 31, 2006, of separate limitation losses and overall foreign losses incurred in years beginning before January 1, 2007.*—(1) *Losses related to pre-2007 separate categories for passive income, certain dividends from a DISC or former DISC, taxable income attributable to certain foreign trade income or certain distributions from a FSC or former FSC.*—(i) *Recapture of separate limitation loss or overall foreign loss incurred in a pre-2007 separate category for passive income, certain dividends from a DISC or former DISC, taxable income attributable to certain foreign trade income or certain distributions from a FSC or former FSC.*—To the extent that a taxpayer has a balance in any separate limitation loss or overall foreign loss account in a pre-2007 separate category (as defined in § 1.904-7(g)(1)(ii)) for passive income, certain dividends from a DISC or former DISC, taxable income attributable to certain foreign trade income or certain distributions from a FSC or former FSC, at the end of the taxpayer's last taxable year beginning before January 1, 2007, the amount of such balance, or balances, shall be allocated on the first day of the taxpayer's next taxable year to the taxpayer's post-2006 separate category (as defined in § 1.904-7(g)(1)(iii)) for passive category income.

(ii) *Recapture of separate limitation loss with respect to a pre-2007 separate category for passive income, certain dividends from a DISC or former DISC, taxable income attributable to certain foreign trade income or certain distributions from a FSC or former FSC.*—To the extent that a taxpayer has a balance in any separate limitation loss account in any pre-2007 separate category with respect to a pre-2007 separate category for passive income, certain dividends from a DISC or former DISC, taxable income attributable to certain foreign trade income or certain distributions from a FSC or former FSC at the end of the taxpayer's last taxable year beginning before January 1, 2007, such loss shall be recaptured in subsequent taxable years as income in the post-2006 separate category for passive category income.

(2) *Losses related to pre-2007 separate categories for shipping, financial services income or general limitation income.*—(i) *Recapture of separate limitation loss or overall foreign loss incurred in a pre-2007 separate category for shipping income, financial services income or general limitation income.*—To the extent that a taxpayer has a balance in any separate limitation loss or overall foreign loss account in a pre-2007 separate category for shipping income, financial services income or general limitation income at the end of the taxpayer's last taxable year beginning before January 1, 2007, the amount of such balance, or balances, shall be allocated on the first day of the taxpayer's next taxable year to the taxpayer's post-2006 separate category for general category income.

(ii) *Recapture of separate limitation loss with respect to a pre-2007 separate category for shipping income, financial services income or general limitation income.*—To the extent that a taxpayer has a balance in any separate limitation loss account in any pre-2007 separate category with respect to a pre-2007 separate category for shipping income, financial services income or general limitation income at the end of the taxpayer's last taxable year beginning before January 1, 2007, such loss shall be recaptured in subsequent taxable years as income in the post-2006 separate category for general category income.

(3) *Losses related to a pre-2007 separate category for high withholding tax interest.*—(i) *Recapture of separate limitation loss or overall foreign loss incurred in a pre-2007 separate category for high withholding tax interest.*—To the extent that a taxpayer has a balance in any separate limitation loss or overall foreign loss account in a pre-2007 separate category for high withholding tax interest at the end of the taxpayer's last taxable year beginning before January 1, 2007, the amount of such balance shall be allocated on the first day of the taxpayer's next taxable year on a pro rata basis to the taxpayer's post-2006 separate categories for general category and passive category income, based on the proportion in which any unused foreign taxes in the same pre-2007 separate category for high withholding tax interest are allocated under § 1.904-2(i)(1). If the taxpayer, other than a financial services entity as defined in § 1.904-4(e)(3), has no unused foreign taxes in the pre-2007 separate category for high withholding tax interest, then any loss account balance in that category shall be allocated to the post-2006 separate category for passive category income. If the taxpayer is a financial services entity, as defined in § 1.904-4(e)(3), and has no unused foreign taxes in the pre-2007 separate category for high withholding tax interest, then any loss account balance in that category shall be allocated to the post-2006 separate category for general category income.

(ii) *Recapture of separate limitation loss with respect to a pre-2007 separate category for high withholding tax interest.*—To the extent that a taxpayer has a balance in a separate limitation loss account in any pre-2007 separate category with respect to a pre-2007 separate category for high withholding tax interest at the end of the taxpayer's last taxable year beginning before January 1, 2007, such loss shall be recaptured in subsequent taxable years on a pro rata basis as income in the post-2006 separate categories for general category and passive category income, based on the proportion in which any unused foreign taxes in the pre-2007 separate category for high withholding tax interest are allocated under § 1.904-2(i)(1). If the taxpayer, other than a financial services entity as defined in § 1.904-4(e)(3), has no unused foreign taxes in the pre-2007 separate category for high withholding tax interest, then the loss account balance shall be recaptured in subsequent taxable years solely as income in the post-2006 separate category for passive category income. If the taxpayer is a financial services entity, as defined in § 1.904-4(e)(3), and has no unused foreign taxes in the pre-2007 separate category for high withholding tax interest, then the loss account balance shall be recaptured in subsequent taxable years solely as income in the post-2006 separate category for general category income.

(4) *Elimination of certain separate limitation loss accounts.*—After application of paragraphs (h)(1) through (h)(3) of this section, any separate limitation loss account allocated to the post-2006 separate category for passive category income for which income is to be recaptured as passive category income, as determined under those same provisions, shall be eliminated. Similarly, after application of paragraphs (h)(1) through (h)(3) of this section, any separate limitation loss account allocated to the post-2006 separate category for general category income for which income is to be recaptured as general category income, as determined under those same provisions, shall be eliminated.

(5) *Alternative method.*—In lieu of applying the rules of paragraphs (h)(1) through (h)(3) of this section, a taxpayer may apply the principles of paragraphs (g)(1) and (g)(2) of this section to determine recapture in taxable years beginning after December 31, 2006, of separate limitation losses and overall foreign losses incurred in taxable years beginning before January 1, 2007. A taxpayer may choose to use the alternative method on a timely filed (original or amended) tax return or during an audit. A taxpayer that uses the alternative method on an amended return or in the course of an audit must make appropriate adjustments to eliminate any double benefit arising from application of the alternative method to years that are not open for assessment. A taxpayer's choice to use the alternative method is evidenced by employing the method. The taxpayer need not file any separate statement.

(6) *Effective/applicability date.*—This paragraph (h) shall apply to taxable years beginning after December 31, 2006, and ending on or after December 21, 2007. However, taxpayers may choose to apply 26 CFR 1.904(f)-12T(h) as it appeared in the Code of Federal Regulations as of April 1, 2010, in lieu of this paragraph (h) to taxable years beginning after December 31, 2006 and ending on or after December 21, 2007, but ending before April 7, 2011 provided that appropriate adjustments are made to eliminate duplicate benefits arising from application of 26 CFR 1.904(f)-12T(h) to taxable years that are not open for assessment. In addition, if a taxpayer that is a financial services entity (as defined in § 1.904-4(e)(3)) chooses to apply 26 CFR 1.904(f)-12T(h) to taxable years ending before April 7, 2011, then as of the beginning of the taxpayer's first taxable year ending on or after April 7, 2011 any remaining balance in a passive category loss account that is attributable to a loss account in a pre-2007 separate category for high withholding tax interest shall be allocated to the general category or eliminated pursuant to § 1.904(f)-12(h)(4), and any remaining balance in a separate limitation loss account with respect to passive category income that is attributable to a loss account with respect to a pre-2007 separate category for high withholding tax interest will be recaptured in such year and subsequent taxable years as general category income or eliminated pursuant to § 1.904(f)-12(h)(4).

(i) [Reserved]

(j) *Recapture in years beginning after December 31, 2017, of separate limitation losses, overall foreign losses, and overall domestic losses incurred in years beginning before January 1, 2018.*—(1) *Definitions.*—(i) The term *pre-2018 separate categories* means the separate categories of income described in section 904(d) and any specified separate categories of income, as applicable to taxable years beginning before January 1, 2018.

(ii) The term *post-2017 separate categories* means the separate categories of income described in section 904(d) and any specified separate categories of income, as applicable to taxable years beginning after December 31, 2017.

(iii) The term *specified separate category* has the meaning set forth in § 1.904-4(m)).

(2) *Allocation of separate limitation loss or overall foreign loss account incurred in a pre-2018 separate category.*—(i) *Allocation to the same category.*—To the extent that a taxpayer has a balance in any separate limitation loss or overall foreign loss account in a pre-2018 separate category at the end of the taxpayer's last taxable year beginning before January 1, 2018, the amount of such balance is allocated on the first day of the taxpayer's next taxable year to the same post-2017 separate category as the pre-2018 separate category of the separate limitation loss or overall foreign loss account.

(ii) *Exception for general category separate limitation loss or overall foreign loss account.*—(A) *In general.*—To the extent a taxpayer has a balance in any separate limitation loss or overall foreign loss account in the pre-2018 separate category for general category income at the end of the taxpayer's last taxable year beginning before January 1, 2018, a taxpayer may choose to allocate any such balance to the taxpayer's post-2017 separate category for foreign branch category income to the extent the balance in the loss account would have been allocated to the taxpayer's post-2017 separate category for foreign branch category income if that separate category applied in the year or years the losses giving rise to the account were incurred. Any remaining portion of the balance in the separate limitation loss or overall foreign loss account is allocated to the taxpayer's post-2017 separate category for general category income.

(B) *Safe harbor.*—In lieu of applying paragraph (j)(2)(ii)(A) of this section, the taxpayer may choose to recapture the balance in any loss account described in paragraph (j)(2)(ii)(A) of this section from the first available income in the taxpayer's post-2017 separate category for general category income or foreign branch category income. If the sum of taxpayer's general category income and foreign branch category income for a taxable year subject to recharacterization exceeds the amount of the loss account described in paragraph (j)(2)(ii)(A) of this section that is to be recaptured, then the amount of general category income and foreign branch category income that will be recharacterized under the relevant recapture provisions is determined on a proportionate basis. The recapture under this paragraph (j)(2)(ii)(B) of any loss account described in paragraph (j)(2)(ii)(A) of this section is made before the recapture of any amount by which the balance of the loss account is increased after the end of the taxpayer's last taxable year beginning before January 1, 2018.

(C) *Rules regarding the exception.*—A taxpayer applying the exception described in paragraph (j)(2)(ii)(A) or (B) of this section must apply the exception to all balances in any separate limitation loss or overall foreign loss account in a pre-2018 separate category for general category income at the end of the taxpayer's last taxable year beginning before January 1, 2018. A taxpayer may apply the exception on a timely filed original return (including extensions) or an amended return. A taxpayer that applies the exception on an amended return must make appropriate adjustments to eliminate any double benefit arising from application of the exception to years that are not open for assessment.

(3) *Recapture of separate limitation loss or overall domestic loss that reduced pre-2018 separate category income.*—(i) *Recapture as income in the same separate category.*—To the extent that at the end of the taxpayer's last taxable year beginning before January 1, 2018, a taxpayer has a balance in any separate limitation loss or overall domestic loss account which offset pre-2018 separate category income, such loss is recaptured in subsequent taxable years as income in the same post-2017 separate category as the pre-2018 separate category of income that was offset by the loss.

(ii) *Exception for separate limitation loss or overall domestic loss that reduced general category income.*—(A) *In general.*—To the extent that a taxpayer's separate limitation loss or overall domestic loss account offset pre-2018 separate category income that was general category income, a taxpayer may choose to recapture the balance in the loss account at the end of the taxpayer's last taxable year beginning before January 1, 2018, in subsequent taxable years as income in the post-2017 separate category for foreign branch category income to the extent the balance in the loss account would have offset foreign branch category income had that separate category applied in the year or years the losses were incurred. Any remaining portion of the balance in the loss account is recaptured as income in the taxpayer's post-2017 separate category for general category income.

(B) *Safe harbor.*—In lieu of applying paragraph (j)(3)(ii)(A) of this section, a taxpayer that had unused foreign income taxes in a pre-2018 taxable year that were allocated to the foreign branch category under § 1.904-2(j)(1)(iii)(A) or (B) may choose to recapture the balance in any loss account described in paragraph (j)(3)(ii)(A) of this section in subsequent taxable years ratably as income in the taxpayer's post-2017 separate categories for general category and foreign branch category income, based on the proportion in which any unused foreign taxes in the pre-2018 separate category for general category income are allocated under § 1.904-2(j)(1)(iii)(A) or (B).

(C) *Rules regarding the exception.*—A taxpayer applying the exception described in paragraph (j)(2)(ii)(A) or (B) of this section must apply the exception to the recapture of all balances at the end of the taxpayer's last taxable year beginning before January 1, 2018 in any separate limitation loss or overall domestic loss account which offset pre-2018 separate category income that was general category income. A taxpayer may apply the exception on a timely filed original return (including extensions) or an amended return. A taxpayer that applies the exception on an amended return must make appropriate adjustments to eliminate any double benefit arising from application of the exception to years that are not open for assessment.

(4) *Treatment of foreign losses that are part of net operating losses incurred in pre-2018 taxable years which are carried forward to post-2017 taxable years.*—(i) *Treatment as a loss in the same separate category.*—A foreign loss that is part of a net operating loss incurred in a taxable year beginning before January 1, 2018, which is carried forward, pursuant to section 172, to a taxable year beginning after December 31, 2017, will be carried forward under the rules of § 1.904(g)-3(b)(2). For purposes of applying the rules of § 1.904(g)-3(b)(2), the portion of a net operating loss carryforward that is attributable to a foreign loss from a pre-2018 separate category will be treated as a loss attributable to the same post-2017 separate category as the pre-2018 separate category.

(ii) *Exception for general category foreign losses that are part of net operating losses.*—(A) *In general.*—A taxpayer may choose to treat the portion of a net operating loss carryforward that is attributable to a foreign loss from the pre-2018 separate category for general category income as attributable to the post-2017 separate category for foreign branch category income to the extent the net operating loss would have been attributable to the taxpayer's post-2017 separate category for foreign branch category income had that separate category applied in the year or years the net operating loss arose. Any remaining portion of the net operating loss carryforward is treated as attributable to the taxpayer's post-2017 separate category for general category income.

(B) *Safe harbor.*—In lieu of applying paragraph (j)(4)(ii)(A) of this section, for the post-2017 taxable year in which a net operating loss carryforward described in paragraph (j)(4)(ii)(A) of this section is used, the taxpayer may choose to treat the net operating loss carryforward as attributable to the taxpayer's post-2017 separate categories for general category income and foreign branch category income to the extent of any general category income and foreign branch category income, respectively, that is available in the carryforward year to be offset by the net operating loss carryforward. To the extent the net operating loss carryforward offsets any other income in the carryforward year, it is treated as attributable to the taxpayer's post-2017 separate category for general category income. If the sum of taxpayer's general category income and foreign branch income in the carryforward year exceeds the amount of the net operating loss carryforward, then the amount of each type of separate income that is offset by the net operating loss carryforward, and therefore the separate category treatment of the net operating loss carryforward, is be determined on a proportionate basis. A general category net operating loss to which the exception is applied is absorbed before any general category net operating loss that is incurred after the end of the taxpayer's last taxable year beginning before January 1, 2018.

(C) *Rules regarding the exception.*—A taxpayer applying the exception described in paragraph (j)(4)(ii)(A) or (B) of this section must apply the exception to all of its net operating losses that are attributable to a foreign loss from the pre-2018 separate category for general category income. A taxpayer may apply the exception on a timely filed original return (including extensions) or an amended return. A taxpayer that applies the exception on an amended return must make appropriate adjustments to eliminate any double benefit arising from application of the exception to years that are not open for assessment.

(5) *Treatment of net operating losses incurred in post-2017 taxable years that are carried back to pre-2018 taxable years.*—(i) *In general.*—Except as provided in paragraph (j)(5)(ii) of this section, a net operating loss incurred in a taxable year beginning after December 31, 2017 (a "post-2017 taxable year"), which is carried back, pursuant to section 172, to a taxable year beginning before January 1, 2018 (a "pre-2018 carryback year"), will be carried back under the rules of § 1.904(g)-3(b). For purposes of applying the rules of § 1.904(g)-3(b), income in a pre-2018 separate category in the taxable year to which the net operating loss is carried back is treated as if it included only income that would be assigned to the post-2017 general category. Therefore, any separate limitation loss created by reason of a passive category component of a net operating loss from a post-2017 taxable year that is carried back to offset general category income in a pre-2018 carryback year will be recaptured in post-2017 taxable years as general category income, and not as a combination of general, foreign branch, and section 951A category income.

(ii) *Foreign source losses in the post-2017 separate categories for foreign branch category income and section 951A category income.*—Net operating losses attributable to a foreign source loss in the post-2017 separate categories for foreign branch category income and section 951A category income are treated as first offsetting general category income in a pre-2018 carryback year to the extent available to be offset by the net operating loss carryback. If the sum of foreign source losses in the taxpayer's separate categories for foreign branch category income and section 951A category income in the year the net operating loss is incurred exceeds the amount of general category income that is available to be offset in the carryback year, then the amount of foreign source loss in each of the foreign branch and section 951A categories that is treated as offsetting general category income under this paragraph (j)(5)(ii), is determined on a proportionate basis. General category income in the pre-2018 carryback year is first offset by foreign source loss in the taxpayer's post-2017 separate category for general category income in the year the net operating loss is incurred before any foreign source loss in that year in the separate categories for foreign branch category income and section 951A category income is carried back to reduce general category income. To the extent a foreign source loss in a post-2017 separate category for foreign branch category income or section 951A category income offsets general category income in a pre-2018 taxable year under the rules of this paragraph (j)(5)(ii), no separate limitation loss account is created.

(6) *Coordination rule with respect to exceptions.*—A taxpayer that applies any exception described in § 1.904-2(j)(1)(iii) or paragraph (j)(2)(ii), (j)(3)(ii), or (j)(4)(ii) of this section must apply all such exceptions and cannot apply any of the general rules described in § 1.904-2(j)(1)(ii) or paragraph (j)(2)(i), (j)(3)(i), (j)(4)(i) of this section. However, in applying each such exception, the taxpayer may choose to apply the safe harbor provision regardless of whether the safe harbor is applied for purposes of any other exception.

(7) *Applicability date.*—Except as otherwise provided in this paragraph (j)(7), this paragraph (j) applies to taxable years ending on

or after December 31, 2017. Paragraph (j)(5) of this section applies to carrybacks of net operating losses incurred in taxable years beginning on or after January 1, 2018. [Reg. § 1.904(f)-12.]

☐ [*T.D. 8306, 8-1-90. Amended by T.D. 9260, 4-20-2006; T.D. 9368, 12-20-2007; T.D. 9452, 6-10-2009, T.D. 9521, 4-6-2011, T.D. 9882, 12-16-2019 and T.D. 9956, 9-21-2021.*]

§ 1.904(g)-1. Overall domestic loss and the overall domestic loss account.—(a) *Overview of regulations.*—This section provides rules for determining a taxpayer's overall domestic losses, for establishing overall domestic loss accounts, and for making additions to and reducing such accounts for purposes of section 904(g). Section 1.904(g)-2 provides rules for recapturing the balance in any overall domestic loss account under the general recharacterization rule of section 904(g)(1). Section 1.904(g)-3 provides ordering rules for the allocation of net operating losses, net capital losses, U.S. source losses, and separate limitation losses, and the recapture of separate limitation losses, overall foreign losses and overall domestic losses.

(b) *Overall domestic loss accounts.*—(1) *In general.*—Any taxpayer that sustains an overall domestic loss under paragraph (c) of this section must establish an overall domestic loss account for such loss with respect to each separate category, as defined in § 1.904(f)-7(b)(1), of the taxpayer in which foreign source income is offset by the domestic loss. The balance in each overall domestic loss account represents the amount of such overall domestic loss subject to recapture in a given taxable year. From year to year, amounts may be added to or subtracted from the balances in such loss accounts as provided in paragraphs (d) and (e) of this section.

(2) *Taxable year in which overall domestic loss is sustained.*—When a domestic loss is carried back or carried forward as part of a net operating loss, and offsets foreign source income in a carryover year, the resulting overall domestic loss is treated as sustained in the later of the year in which the domestic loss was incurred or the year to which the loss was carried. Accordingly, when a taxpayer incurs a domestic loss that is carried back as part of a net operating loss to offset foreign source income in a qualified taxable year, as defined in paragraph (c)(3) of this section, the resulting overall domestic loss is treated as sustained in the later year in which the domestic loss was incurred and not in the earlier year in which the loss offset foreign source income. In addition, when a taxpayer incurs a domestic loss that is carried forward as part of a net operating loss and applied to offset foreign source income in a later taxable year, the resulting overall domestic loss is treated as sustained in the later year in which the domestic loss offsets foreign source income and not in the earlier year in which the loss was incurred. For example, if a taxpayer incurs a domestic loss in the 2007 taxable year that is carried back to the 2006 qualified taxable year and offsets foreign source income in 2006, the resulting overall domestic loss is treated as sustained in the 2007 taxable year. If a taxpayer incurs a domestic loss in a pre-2007 taxable year that is carried forward to a post-2006 qualified taxable year and offsets foreign source income in the post-2006 year, the resulting overall domestic loss is treated as sustained in the post-2006 year. An overall domestic loss account is established, or increased under paragraph (d) of this section, at the end of the taxable year in which the overall domestic loss is treated as sustained and will be recaptured from U.S. source income arising in subsequent taxable years.

(c) *Determination of a taxpayer's overall domestic loss.*—(1) *Overall domestic loss defined.*—For taxable years beginning after December 31, 2006, a taxpayer sustains an overall domestic loss—

(i) In any qualified taxable year in which its domestic loss for such taxable year offsets foreign source taxable income for the taxable year or for any preceding qualified taxable year by reason of a carryback; and

(ii) In any other taxable year in which the domestic loss for such taxable year offsets foreign source taxable income for any preceding qualified taxable year by reason of a carryback.

(2) *Domestic loss defined.*—For purposes of this section and §§ 1.904(g)-2 and 1.904(g)-3, the term *domestic loss* means the amount by which the U.S. source gross income for the taxable year is exceeded by the sum of the expenses, losses, and other deductions properly apportioned or allocated to such income, taking into account any net operating loss carried forward from a prior taxable year, but not any loss carried back. If a taxpayer has any capital gains or losses or qualified dividend income, as defined in section 1(h)(11), the amount of the taxpayer's domestic loss that offsets foreign source income must be determined taking into account adjustments under section 904(b)(2). See § 1.904(g)-1(d)(3) for further guidance.

(3) *Qualified taxable year defined.*—For purposes of this section and §§ 1.904(g)-2 and 1.904(g)-3, the term *qualified taxable year* means any taxable year for which the taxpayer chooses the benefits of section 901.

(4) *Method of allocation and apportionment of deductions.*—In determining its overall domestic loss, a taxpayer shall allocate and apportion expenses, losses, and other deductions to U.S. source gross income in accordance with sections 861(b) and 865 and the regulations thereunder, including §§ 1.861-8 through 1.861-14T.

(d) *Additions to overall domestic loss accounts.*—(1) *General rule.*—A taxpayer's overall domestic loss as determined under paragraph (c) of this section shall be added to the applicable overall domestic loss account at the end of its taxable year to the extent that the overall domestic loss either reduces foreign source income for the year (but only if such year is a qualified taxable year) or reduces foreign source income for a qualified taxable year to which the loss has been carried back.

(2) *Overall domestic loss of another taxpayer.*—If any portion of any overall domestic loss of another taxpayer is allocated to the taxpayer in accordance with § 1.1502-9 (relating to consolidated overall domestic losses) the taxpayer shall add such amount to its applicable overall domestic loss account.

(3) *Adjustments for capital gains and losses.*—If the taxpayer has capital gains or losses or qualified dividend income, the amount by which a domestic loss is considered to reduce foreign source income in a taxable year shall equal the section 904(f)(5)(D) amount determined under § 1.904(b)-1(h)(1)(iii), regardless of the amount of domestic loss that was determined before taking any section 904(b)(2) adjustments into account.

(e) *Reductions of overall domestic loss accounts.*—The taxpayer shall subtract the following amounts from its overall domestic loss accounts at the end of its taxable year in the following order, as applicable:

(1) *Pre-recapture reduction for amounts allocated to other taxpayers.*—An overall domestic loss account is reduced by the amount of any overall domestic loss which is allocated to another taxpayer in accordance with § 1.1502-9 (relating to consolidated overall domestic losses).

(2) *Reduction for amounts recaptured.*—An overall domestic loss account is reduced by the amount of any U.S. source income that is recharacterized in accordance with § 1.904(g)-2(c) (relating to recapture under section 904(g)(1)).

(f) *Effective/applicability date.*—This section applies to taxpayers that sustain an overall domestic loss for a taxable year beginning on or after January 1, 2012. Taxpayers may choose to apply this section to overall domestic losses sustained in other taxable years beginning after December 31, 2006, including periods covered by 26 CFR § 1.904(g)-1T (revised as of April 1, 2010). [Reg. § 1.904(g)-1.]

☐ [*T.D. 9371, 12-20-2007. Amended by T.D. 9595, 6-21-2012.*]

§ 1.904(g)-2. Recapture of overall domestic losses.—(a) *In general.*—A taxpayer shall recapture an overall domestic loss as provided in this section. Recapture is accomplished by treating a portion of the taxpayer's U.S. source taxable income as foreign source income. The recharacterized income is allocated among and increases foreign source income in separate categories in proportion to the balances of the overall domestic loss accounts with respect to those separate categories. As a result, if the taxpayer chooses the benefits of section 901, the taxpayer's foreign tax credit limitation is increased. As provided in § 1.904(g)-1(e)(2), the balance in a taxpayer's overall domestic loss account with respect to a separate category is reduced at the end of each taxable year by the amount of loss recaptured during that taxable year. Recapture continues until the amount of U.S. source income recharacterized as foreign source income equals the amount in the overall domestic loss account.

(b) *Determination of U.S. source taxable income for purposes of recapture.*—For purposes of determining the amount of an overall domestic loss subject to recapture, the taxpayer's taxable income from U.S. sources shall be computed in accordance with the rules set forth in § 1.904(g)-1(c)(4). U.S. source taxable income shall be determined by taking into account adjustments for capital gains and losses and qualified dividend income in a similar manner to the adjustments made to foreign source taxable income under section 904(b)(2) and § 1.904(b)-1, following the principles of § 1.904(b)-1(h)(1)(i).

(c) *Section 904(g)(1) recapture.*—The amount of any U.S. source taxable income subject to recharacterization in a taxable year in which paragraph (a) of this section applies is the lesser of the aggregate balance of the taxpayer's overall domestic loss accounts or 50 percent of the taxpayer's U.S. source taxable income (as determined under paragraph (b) of this section).

(d) *Effective/applicability date.*—This section applies to taxpayers that sustain an overall domestic loss for a taxable year beginning on or after January 1, 2012. Taxpayers may choose to apply this section to overall domestic losses sustained in other taxable years beginning after December 31, 2006, including periods covered by 26 CFR 1.904(g)-2T (revised as of April 1, 2010). [Reg. § 1.904(g)-2.]

□ [*T.D. 9371, 12-20-2007. Amended by T.D. 9595, 6-21-2012.*]

§ 1.904(g)-3. Ordering rules for the allocation of net operating losses, net capital losses, U.S. source losses, and separate limitation losses, and for the recapture of separate limitation losses, overall foreign losses, and overall domestic losses.—(a) *In general.*—This section provides ordering rules for the allocation of net operating losses, net capital losses, U.S. source losses, and separate limitation losses, and for the recapture of separate limitation losses, overall foreign losses, and overall domestic losses. The rules must be applied in the order set forth in paragraphs (b) through (j) of this section.

(b) *Step One: Allocation of net operating loss and net capital loss carryovers.*—(1) *In general.*—Net operating losses from a current taxable year are carried forward or back to a taxable year in the following manner. Net operating losses that are carried forward pursuant to section 172 are combined with income or loss in the carryover year in the manner described in this paragraph (b). The combined amounts are then subject to the ordering rules provided in paragraphs (c) through (i) of this section. Net operating losses that are carried back to a prior taxable year pursuant to section 172 are allocated to income in the carryback year in the manner set forth in paragraphs (b)(2), (b)(3), (c), (d), and (e) of this section. The income in the carryback year to which the net operating loss is allocated is the foreign source income in each separate category and the U.S. source income after the application of sections 904(f) and 904(g) to income and loss in that previous year, including as a result of net operating loss carryovers or carrybacks from taxable years prior to the current taxable year. See §§ 1.861-8(e)(8), 1.904(b)-3(d)(2), and 1.1502-4(c)(1)(iii) for rules to determine the source and separate category components of a net operating loss.

(2) *Full net operating loss deduction.*—If the full net operating loss (that remains after carryovers to other taxable years) is deducted in computing the taxable income in a particular year (carryover year), so that there is no remaining net operating loss that can be carried to other taxable years, U.S. source losses and foreign source losses in separate categories that comprise the net operating loss shall be combined with the U.S. source income or loss and the foreign source income or loss in the same separate categories in the carryover year.

(3) *Partial net operating loss deduction.*—If the full net operating loss (that remains after carryovers to other taxable years) is not deducted in computing the taxable income in a carryover year, so that there is remaining loss that can be carried to other taxable years, the following rules apply:

(i) Any U.S. source loss (not to exceed the amount of the net operating loss carryover deducted in computing the taxable income in the carryover year (the net operating loss deduction)) shall be carried over to the extent of any U.S. source income in the carryover year.

(ii) If the net operating loss deduction exceeds the U.S. source loss carryover determined under paragraph (b)(3)(i) of this section, then separate limitation losses that are part of the net operating loss shall be tentatively carried over to the extent of separate limitation income in the same separate category in the carryover year. If the sum of the potential separate limitation loss carryovers determined under the preceding sentence exceeds the amount of the net operating loss deduction reduced by any U.S. source loss carried over under paragraph (b)(3)(i) of this section, then the potential separate limitation loss carryovers shall be reduced pro rata so that their sum equals such amount.

(iii) If the net operating loss deduction exceeds the sum of the U.S. and separate limitation loss carryovers determined under paragraphs (b)(3)(i) and (ii) of this section, then a proportionate part of the remaining loss from each separate category shall be carried over to the extent of such excess and combined with the foreign source loss, if any, in the same separate categories in the carryover year.

(iv) If the net operating loss deduction exceeds the sum of all the loss carryovers determined under paragraphs (b)(3)(i), (ii), and (iii) of this section, then any U.S. source loss not carried over under paragraph (b)(3)(i) of this section shall be carried over to the extent of such excess and combined with the U.S. source loss, if any, in the carryover year.

(4) *Net capital loss carryovers.*—Rules similar to the rules of paragraphs (b)(1) through (3) of this section apply for purposes of determining the components of a net capital loss carryover to a taxable year.

(c) *Step Two: Section 904(b) adjustments.*—The taxpayer shall make any required adjustments to capital gains and losses and qualified dividend income under section 904(b)(2). The taxpayer also takes into account any adjustments required under section 904(b)(4) and § 1.904(b)-3.

(d) *Step Three: Allocation of separate limitation losses.*—The taxpayer shall allocate separate limitation losses sustained during the taxable year (increased, if appropriate, by any losses carried over under paragraph (b) of this section), in the following manner—

(1) The taxpayer shall allocate its separate limitation losses for the taxable year to reduce its separate limitation income in other separate categories on a proportionate basis, and increase its separate limitation loss accounts appropriately. To the extent a separate limitation loss in one separate category is allocated to reduce separate limitation income in a second separate category, and the second category has a separate limitation loss account from a prior taxable year with respect to the first category, the two separate limitation loss accounts shall be netted against each other.

(2) If the taxpayer's separate limitation losses for the taxable year exceed the taxpayer's separate limitation income for the year, so that the taxpayer has separate limitation losses remaining after the application of paragraph (d)(1) of this section, the taxpayer shall allocate those losses to its U.S. source income for the taxable year, to the extent thereof, and shall increase its overall foreign loss accounts to that extent in accordance with § 1.904(f)-1.

(e) *Step Four: Allocation of U.S. source losses.*—The taxpayer shall allocate U.S. source losses sustained during the taxable year (increased, if appropriate, by any losses carried over under paragraph (b) of this section) to separate limitation income on a proportionate basis, and shall increase its overall domestic loss accounts to the extent of such allocation in accordance with § 1.904(g)-1.

(f) *Step Five: Recapture of overall foreign loss accounts.*—If the taxpayer's separate limitation income for the taxable year (reduced by any losses carried over under paragraph (b) of this section) exceeds the sum of the taxpayer's U.S. source loss and separate limitation losses for the year, so that the taxpayer has separate limitation income remaining after the application of paragraphs (d)(1) and (e) of this section, then the taxpayer recaptures prior year overall foreign losses, if any, in accordance with § 1.904(f)-2, and reduces overall foreign loss accounts in accordance with § 1.904(f)-2. The recapture in this paragraph (f) includes amounts determined under § 1.904(f)-2(c) and (d)(3) but not § 1.904(f)-2(d)(4), which is covered in paragraph (i) of this section.

(g) *Step Six: Recapture of separate limitation loss accounts.*—To the extent the taxpayer has remaining separate limitation income for the year after the application of paragraph (f) of this section, then the taxpayer shall recapture prior year separate limitation losses, if any, in accordance with § 1.904(f)-8 and reduce separate limitation loss accounts in accordance with § 1.904(f)-7.

(h) *Step Seven: Recapture of overall domestic loss accounts.*—If the taxpayer's U.S. source income for the year (reduced by any losses carried over under paragraph (b) of this section or allocated under paragraph (d) of this section, but not increased by any recapture of overall foreign loss accounts under paragraph (f) of this section) exceeds the taxpayer's separate limitation losses for the year, so that the taxpayer has U.S. source income remaining after the application of paragraph (d)(2) of this section, then the taxpayer shall recapture its prior year overall domestic losses, if any, and reduce overall domestic loss accounts in accordance with § 1.904(g)-2.

(i) *Step Eight: Dispositions under section 904(f)(3) in which gain would not otherwise be recognized.*—The taxpayer determines the amount of gain that would otherwise not be recognized but that must be recognized in accordance with § 1.904(f)-2(d)(4) (not exceeding the taxpayer's applicable overall foreign loss account) and then applies § 1.904(f)-2(a) and (b) to recapture and reduce its overall foreign loss accounts in an amount equal to the gain recognized. To the extent this recognition of gain in a taxable year reduces the amount of a current year net operating loss or increases the amount of a net operating loss carryover to that taxable year, paragraphs (b) through (e) of this section are applied to determine the allocation of any additional net operating loss deduction and other deductions or losses and the applicable increases in the taxpayer's overall foreign loss, separate limitation loss, and overall domestic loss accounts, but only after the applicable overall foreign loss account has been recaptured as provided in this paragraph (i).

(j) *Step Nine: Dispositions that result in additional income recognition under the branch loss recapture and dual consolidated loss recapture rules.*—(1) *In general.*—If, after any gain is required to be recognized under section 904(f)(3) on a transaction that is otherwise a nonrecognition transaction, an additional amount of income is recognized under section 91(d), section 367(a)(3)(C) (as applicable to losses incurred before January 1, 2018), or § 1.1503(d)-6, and that additional income amount is determined by taking into account an offset for the amount of gain recognized under section 904(f)(3) and so is not initially taken into account in applying paragraph (b) of this section, then paragraphs (b) through (h) of this section are applied to determine the allocation of any additional net operating loss deduction and other deductions or losses and the applicable increases in the taxpayer's overall foreign loss, separate limitation loss, and overall domestic loss accounts, as well as any additional recapture and reduction of the taxpayer's separate limitation loss, overall foreign loss, and overall domestic loss accounts.

(2) *Rules for additional recapture of loss accounts.*—For the purpose of recapturing and reducing loss accounts under paragraph (j)(1) of this section, the taxpayer also takes into account any creation of or addition to loss accounts that result from the application of paragraphs (b) through (i) of this section in the current tax year. If any of the additional income described in paragraph (j)(1) of this section is foreign source income in a separate category for which there is a remaining balance in an overall foreign loss account after applying paragraph (i) of this section, the section 904(f)(1) recapture amount under § 1.904(f)-2(c) for that additional income is determined by first computing a hypothetical recapture amount as it would have been determined prior to the application of paragraph (i) of this section but taking into account the additional foreign source income described in this paragraph (j)(2) and then subtracting the actual overall foreign loss recapture determined prior to the application of paragraph (i) of this section (that did not take into account the additional foreign source income). The remainder is the overall foreign loss recapture amount with respect to the additional foreign source income described in this paragraph (j)(2).

(k) *Examples.*—The following examples illustrate the rules of this section. Unless otherwise noted, all corporations use the calendar year as the U.S. taxable year.

(1) *Example 1*—(i) *Facts*—(A) USC is a domestic corporation with foreign branch operations in Country X. For Year 1, USC had the following taxable income and losses after application of section 904(f) and (g) to income and loss in Year 1:

Table 1 to paragraph (k)(1)(i)(A)

Foreign Branch	Passive	US
$400x	$200x	$110x

(B) For Year 2, USC has a net operating loss of ($500x), determined as follows:

Table 2 to paragraph (k)(1)(i)(B)

Foreign Branch	Passive	US
($300x)	$0	($200x)

(ii) *Analysis*—(A) *Net operating loss allocation.* Because USC's taxable income for Year 1 exceeds its total net operating loss for Year 2, the full net operating loss is carried back. Under paragraph (b) of this section (Step 1), each component of the net operating loss is carried back and combined with its same category in Year 1. See paragraph (b)(2) of this section. After allocation of the net operating loss, USC has the following taxable income and losses for Year 1:

Table 3 to paragraph (k)(1)(ii)(A)

Foreign Branch	Passive	US
$100x	$200x	($90x)

(B) *Loss allocation.* Under paragraph (e) of this section (Step 4), the ($90x) of U.S. loss is allocated proportionately to reduce the foreign branch category and passive category income. Accordingly, $30x ($90x × $100x/$300x) of the U.S. loss is allocated to foreign branch category income and $60x ($90x × $200x/$300x) of the U.S. loss is allocated to passive category income, with a corresponding creation or increase to USC's overall domestic loss accounts.

(2) *Example 2*—(i) *Facts*—(A) USC is a domestic corporation with foreign branch operations in Country X. As of January 1, Year 1, USC has no loss accounts subject to recapture. For Year 1, USC has a net operating loss of ($1,400x), determined as follows:

Table 4 to paragraph (k)(2)(i)(A)

Foreign Branch	Passive	US
($400x)	($200x)	($800x)

(B) For Year 2, USC has the following taxable income and losses:

Table 5 to paragraph (k)(2)(i)(B)

Foreign Branch	Passive	US
$500x	($100x)	$1200x

(ii) *Analysis*—(A) *Net operating loss allocation.* Under paragraph (b) of this section (Step 1), because USC's total taxable income for Year 2 of $1600x ($1,200x + $500x − $100x) exceeds the total Year 1 net operating loss, the full $1,400x net operating loss is carried forward. Under paragraph (b)(2) of this section, each component of the net operating loss is carried forward and combined with its same category in Year 2. After allocation of the net operating loss, USC has the following taxable income and losses:

Table 6 to paragraph (k)(2)(ii)(A)

Foreign Branch	Passive	US
$100x	($300x)	$400x

(B) *Loss allocation.* Under paragraph (d) of this section (Step 3), $100x of the passive category loss offsets the $100x of foreign branch category income, resulting in a passive category separate limitation loss account with respect to foreign branch category income, and the other $200x of passive category loss offsets $200x of the U.S. source taxable income, resulting in the creation of an overall foreign loss account in the passive category.

(3) *Example 3*—(i) *Facts.* Assume the same facts as in paragraph (k)(2)(i) of this section (the facts in *Example 2*), except that in Year 2, USC had the following taxable income and losses:

Table 7 to paragraph (k)(3)(i)

Foreign Branch	Passive	US
$200x	($100x)	$1200x

(ii) *Analysis*—(A) *Net operating loss allocation.* Under paragraph (b) of this section (Step 1), because the total net operating loss for Year 1 of ($1,400x) exceeds total taxable income for Year 2 of $1,300x ($1,200x + $200x − $100x), USC has a partial net operating loss carryover to Year 2 of $1,300x. Under paragraph (b)(3)(i) of this section, first, the $800x U.S. source component of the net operating loss is allocated to U.S. income for Year 2. The tentative foreign branch category carryover under paragraph (b)(3)(ii) of this section ($200x) does not exceed the remaining net operating loss carryover amount ($500x). Therefore, $200x of the foreign branch category component of the net operating loss is next allocated to the foreign branch category income for Year 2. Under paragraph (b)(3)(iii) of this section, the remaining $300x of net operating loss carryover ($1300x − $800x − $200x) is carried over proportionally from the remaining net operating loss components in the foreign branch category ($200x, or $400x total foreign branch category loss − $200x foreign branch category loss already allocated) and passive category ($200x). Therefore, $150x ($300x × $200x/$400x) of the remaining net operating loss carryover is carried over from the foreign branch category for Year 1 and combined with the foreign branch category income for Year 2, and $150x ($300x × $200x/$400x) of the remaining net operating loss carryover is carried over from the passive category for Year 1 and combined with the passive category loss for Year 2. After allocation of the net operating loss carryover from Year 1 to the appropriate categories for Year 2, USC has the following taxable income and losses:

Table 8 to paragraph (k)(3)(ii)(A)

Foreign Branch	Passive	US
($150x)	($250x)	$400x

(B) *Loss allocation.* Under paragraph (d) of this section (Step 3), the losses in the foreign branch and passive categories fully offset the U.S. source income, resulting in the creation of foreign branch category and passive category overall foreign loss accounts.

(4) *Example 4*—(i) *Facts.* Assume the same facts as in paragraph (k)(2)(i) of this section (the facts in *Example 2*), except that in Year 2, USC has the following taxable income and losses:

Table 9 to paragraph (k)(4)(i)

Foreign Branch	Passive	US
$200x	$200x	($200x)

(ii) *Analysis*—(A) *Net operating loss allocation.* Under paragraph (b) of this section (Step 1), because the total net operating loss of ($1400x) exceeds total taxable income for Year 2 of $200x ($200x + $200x − $200x), USC has a partial net operating loss carryover to Year 2 of $200x. Because USC has no U.S. source income in Year 2, under paragraph (b)(3)(i) of this section no portion of the U.S. source component of the net operating loss is initially carried into Year 2. Because the total tentative carryover under paragraph (b)(3)(ii) of this section of $400x ($200x in each of the foreign branch and passive categories) exceeds the net operating loss carryover amount, the tentative carryover from each separate category is reduced proportionately by $100x ($200x × $200x/$400x). Accordingly, $100x ($200x − $100x) of the foreign branch category component of the net operating loss is carried forward and $100x ($200x − $100x) of the passive category component of the net operating loss is carried forward and combined with income in the same respective categories for Year 2. After allocation of the net operating loss carryover from Year 1, USC has the following taxable income and losses:

Table 10 to paragraph (k)(4)(ii)(A)

Foreign Branch	Passive	US
$100x	$100x	($200x)

(B) *Loss allocation.* Under paragraph (e) of this section (Step 4), the $200x U.S. source loss offsets the remaining $100x of foreign branch category income and $100x of passive category income, resulting in the creation of overall domestic loss accounts with respect to the foreign branch and passive categories.

(5) *Example 5*—(i) *Facts.* Assume the same facts as in paragraph (k)(2)(i) of this section (the facts in *Example 2*), except that in Year 2, USC has the following taxable income and losses:

Table 11 to paragraph (k)(5)(i)

Foreign Branch	Passive	US
$800x	($100x)	$100x

(ii) *Analysis*—(A) *Net operating loss allocation.* Under paragraph (b) of this section (Step 1), because USC's total net operating loss in Year 1 of ($1,400x) exceeds its total taxable income for Year 2 of $800x ($100x + $800x − $100x), USC has a partial net operating loss carryover to Year 2 of $800x. Under paragraph (b)(3)(i) of this section, $100x of the U.S. source component of the net operating loss is allocated to U.S. income for Year 2. The tentative foreign branch category carryover under paragraph (b)(3)(ii) of this section does not exceed the remaining net operating loss carryover amount. Therefore, $400x of the foreign branch category component of the net operating loss is allocated to reduce foreign branch category income in Year 2. Under paragraph (b)(3)(iii) of this section, of the remaining $300x of net operating loss carryover ($800x − $100x − $400x), $200x is carried forward from the passive category component of the net operating loss and combined with the passive category loss for Year 2. Under paragraph (b)(3)(iv) of this section, the remaining $100x ($300x − $200x) of net operating loss carryover is carried forward from the U.S. source component of the net operating loss and combined with the U.S. source income (and the previously allocated U.S. source component of the net operating loss) for Year 2. After allocation of the net operating loss carryover from Year 1, USC has the following taxable income and losses:

Table 12 to paragraph (k)(5)(ii)(A)

Foreign Branch	Passive	US
$400x	($300x)	($100x)

(B) *Loss allocation*—*(1)* Under paragraph (d) of this section (Step 3), the $300x passive category loss offsets the $300x of income in the foreign branch category, resulting in the creation of a passive category separate limitation loss account with respect to the foreign branch category.

(2) Under paragraph (e) of this section (Step 4), the $100x U.S. source loss offsets the remaining $100x of the foreign branch category income, resulting in the creation of an overall domestic loss account with respect to the foreign branch category.

(6) *Example 6*—(i) *Facts*—(A) USC is a domestic corporation with foreign branch operations in Country X. USC has no net operating

losses and does not make an election to recapture more than the required amount of overall foreign losses. As of January 1, Year 1, USC has a ($200x) foreign branch category overall foreign loss (OFL) account and a ($200x) foreign branch category separate limitation loss (SLL) account with respect to the passive category. For Year 1, USC has $400x of passive category income that is fully offset by a ($400x) domestic loss in that taxable year, giving rise to the creation of an overall domestic loss (ODL) account with respect to the passive category. As of January 1, Year 2, USC has the following balances in its OFL, SLL, and ODL accounts:

Table 13 to paragraph (k)(6)(i)(A)

Foreign Branch		US
OFL	SLL (Passive)	ODL (Passive)
$200x	$200x	$100x

(B) In Year 2, USC has the following taxable income and losses:

Table 14 to paragraph (k)(6)(i)(B)

Foreign Branch	Passive	US
$400x	($100x)	$600x

(ii) *Analysis*—(A) *Loss allocation.* Under paragraph (d) of this section (Step 3), the $100x of passive category loss offsets $100x of the foreign branch category income, creating a passive category SLL account of $100x with respect to the foreign branch category. Because there is an offsetting foreign branch category SLL account of $200x with respect to the passive category from a prior taxable year, the two accounts are netted against each other so that all that remains is a $100x foreign branch category SLL account with respect to the passive category.

(B) *OFL account recapture.* Under paragraph (f) of this section (Step 5), 50% of the remaining $300x, or $150x, of income in the foreign branch category is subject to recharacterization as U.S. source income as a recapture of part of the OFL account in the foreign branch category.

(C) *SLL account recapture.* Under paragraph (g) of this section (Step 6), $100x of the remaining $150x of income in the foreign branch category is recharacterized as passive category income as a recapture of the foreign branch category SLL account with respect to the passive category.

(D) *ODL account recapture.* Under paragraph (h) of this section (Step 7), 50% of the $600, or $300, of U.S. source income is subject to recharacterization as foreign source passive category income as a recapture of a part of the ODL account with respect to the passive category. None of the $150x of foreign branch category income that was recharacterized as U.S. source income under paragraph (f) of this section (Step 5) is included here as income subject to recharacterization in connection with recapture of the ODL account.

(E) *Results*—(*1*) After the allocation of loss and recapture of loss accounts, USC has the following taxable income and losses for Year 2:

Table 15 to paragraph (k)(6)(ii)(E)(*1*)

Foreign Branch	Passive	US
$50x	$400x	$450x

(*2*) As of January 1, Year 3, USC has the following balances in its OFL, SLL and ODL accounts:

Table 16 to paragraph (k)(6)(ii)(E)(*2*)

Foreign Branch		Passive	US
OFL	SLL (Passive)	SLL (Foreign Branch)	ODL (Passive)
$50x	$0	$0	$100x

(l) *Applicability date.*—This section applies to taxable years ending on or after November 2, 2020. [Reg. § 1.904(g)-3.]

☐ [*T.D.* 9371, 12-20-2007. *Amended by T.D.* 9595, 6-21-2012, *T.D.* 9882, 12-16-2019 *and T.D.* 9922, 11-2-2020 (*corrected* 9-30-2021).]

§ 1.904(i)-1. Limitation on use of deconsolidation to avoid foreign tax credit limitations.—(a) *General rule.*—If two or more includible corporations are affiliates, within the meaning of paragraph (b)(1) of this section, at any time during their taxable years, then, solely for purposes of applying the foreign tax credit provisions of section 59(a), sections 901 through 908, and section 960, the rules of this section will apply.

(1) *Determination of taxable income.*—(i) Each affiliate must compute its net taxable income or loss in each separate category (as defined in § 1.904-5(a)(4)(v), and treating U.S. source income or loss as a separate category) without regard to sections 904(f) and 907(c)(4). Only affiliates that are members of the same consolidated group use the consolidated return regulations (other than those under sections 904(f) and 907(c)(4)) in computing such net taxable income or loss. To the extent otherwise applicable, other provisions of the Internal Revenue Code and regulations must be used in the determination of an affiliate's net taxable income or loss in a separate category.

(ii) The net taxable income amounts in each separate category determined under paragraph (a)(1)(i) of this section are combined for all affiliates to determine one amount for the group of affiliates in each separate category. However, a net loss of an affiliate (first affiliate) in a separate category determined under paragraph (a)(1)(i) of this section will be combined under this paragraph (a) with net income or loss amounts of other affiliates in the same category only if, and to the extent that, the net loss offsets taxable income, whether U.S. or foreign source, of the first affiliate. The consolidated return regulations that apply the principles of sections 904(f) and 907(c)(4) to consolidated groups will then be applied to the combined amounts in each separate category as if all affiliates were members of a single consolidated group.

(2) *Allocation.*—Any net taxable income in a separate category calculated under paragraph (a)(1)(ii) of this section for purposes of the foreign tax credit provisions must then be allocated among the affiliates under any consistently applied reasonable method, taking into account all of the facts and circumstances. A method is consistently applied if used by all affiliates from year to year. Once chosen, an allocation method may be changed only with the consent of the Commissioner. This allocation will only affect the source and foreign tax credit separate limitation character of the income for purposes of the foreign tax credit separate limitation of each affiliate, and will not otherwise affect an affiliate's total net income or loss. This section applies whether the federal income tax consequences of its application favor, or are adverse to, the taxpayer.

(b) *Definitions and special rules.*—For purposes of this section only, the following terms will have the meanings specified.

(1) *Affiliate.*—(i) *Generally.*—Affiliates are includible corporations—

(A) That are members of the same affiliated group, as defined in section 1504(a); or

(B) That would be members of the same affiliated group, as defined in section 1504(a) if—

(*1*) Any non-includible corporation meeting the ownership test of section 1504(a)(2) with respect to any such includible corporation was itself an includible corporation; or

(*2*) The constructive ownership rules of section 1563(e) were applied for purposes of section 1504(a).

(ii) *Rules for consolidated groups.*—Affiliates that are members of the same consolidated group are treated as a single affiliate for purposes of this section. The provisions of paragraph (a) of this section shall not apply if the only affiliates under this definition are already members of the same consolidated group without operation of this section.

(iii) *Exception for newly acquired affiliates.*—(A) With respect to acquisitions after December 7, 1995, an includible corporation acquired from unrelated third parties (First Corporation) will not be considered an affiliate of another includible corporation (Second Corporation) during the taxable year of the First Corporation beginning before the date on which the First Corporation originally becomes an affiliate with respect to the Second Corporation.

(B) With respect to acquisitions on or before December 7, 1995, an includible corporation acquired from unrelated third parties will not be considered an affiliate of another includible corporation during its taxable year beginning before the date on which the first includible corporation first becomes an affiliate with respect to that other includible corporation.

(C) This exception does not apply where the acquisition of an includible corporation is used to avoid the application of this section.

(2) *Includible corporation.*—The term *includible corporation* has the same meaning it has in section 1504(b).

(c) *Taxable years.*—If all of the affiliates use the same U.S. taxable year, then that taxable year must be used for purposes of applying this section. If, however, the affiliates use more than one U.S. taxable year, then an appropriate taxable year must be used for applying this section. The determination whether a taxable year is appropriate must take into account all of the relevant facts and circumstances, including the U.S. taxable years used by the affiliates for general U.S. income tax purposes. The taxable year chosen by the affiliates for purposes of applying this section must be used consistently from year to year. The taxable year may be changed only with the prior consent of the Commissioner. Those affiliates that do not use the year determined under this paragraph (c) as their U.S. taxable year for general U.S. income tax purposes must, for purposes of this section, use their U.S. taxable year or years ending within the taxable year determined under this paragraph (c). If, however, the stock of an affiliate is disposed of so that it ceases to be an affiliate, then the taxable year of that affiliate will be considered to end on the disposition date for purposes of this section.

(d) *Consistent treatment of foreign taxes paid.*—All affiliates must consistently either elect under section 901(a) to claim a credit for foreign income taxes paid or accrued, or deemed paid or accrued, or deduct foreign taxes paid or accrued under section 164. See also § 1.1502-4(a); § 1.905-1(a).

(e) *Effective date.*—Except as provided in paragraph (b)(1)(iii) of this section (relating to newly acquired affiliates), this section is effective for taxable years of affiliates beginning after December 31, 1993. [Reg. § 1.904(i)-1.]

☐ [*T.D. 8627, 11-6-95. Amended by T.D. 9882, 12-16-2019.*]

§ 1.904(j)-1. Certain individuals exempt from foreign tax credit limitation.—(a) *Election available only if all foreign taxes are creditable foreign taxes.*—A taxpayer may elect to apply section 904(j) for a taxable year only if all of the taxes for which a credit is allowable to the taxpayer under section 901 for the taxable year (without regard to carryovers) are creditable foreign taxes (as defined in section 904(j)(3)(B)).

(b) *Coordination with carryover rules.*—(1) *No carryovers to or from election year.*—If the taxpayer elects to apply section 904(j) for any taxable year, then no taxes paid or accrued by the taxpayer during such taxable year may be deemed paid or accrued under section 904(c) in any other taxable year, and no taxes paid or accrued in any other taxable year may be deemed paid or accrued under section 904(c) in such taxable year.

(2) *Carryovers to and from other years determined without regard to election years.*—The amount of the foreign taxes paid or accrued, and the amount of the foreign source taxable income, in any year for which the taxpayer elects to apply section 904(j) shall not be taken into account in determining the amount of any carryover to or from any other taxable year. However, an election to apply section 904(j) to any year does not extend the number of taxable years to which unused foreign taxes may be carried under section 904(c) and § 1.904-2(b). Therefore, in determining the number of such carryover years, the taxpayer must take into account years to which a section 904(j) election applies.

(3) *Determination of amount of creditable foreign taxes.*—Otherwise allowable carryovers of foreign tax credits from other taxable years shall not be taken into account in determining whether the amount of creditable foreign taxes paid or accrued by an individual during a taxable year exceeds $300 ($600 in the case of a joint return) for purposes of section 904(j)(2)(B).

(c) *Examples.*—The following examples illustrate the provisions of this section:

Example 1. In 2006, X, a single individual using the cash basis method of accounting for income and foreign tax credits, pays $100 of foreign taxes with respect to general limitation income that was earned and included in income for United States tax purposes in 2005. The foreign taxes would be creditable under section 901 but are not shown on a payee statement furnished to X. X's only income for 2006 from sources outside the United States is qualified passive income, with respect to which X pays $200 of creditable foreign taxes shown on a payee statement. X may not elect to apply section 904(j) for 2006 because some of X's foreign taxes are not creditable foreign taxes within the meaning of section 904(j)(3)(B).

Example 2. (i) In 2009, A, a single individual using the cash basis method of accounting for income and foreign tax credits, pays creditable foreign taxes of $250 attributable to passive income. Under section 904(c), A may also carry forward to 2009 $100 of unused foreign taxes paid in 2005 with respect to passive income, $300 of unused foreign taxes paid in 2005 with respect to general limitation income, $400 of unused foreign taxes paid in 2006 with respect to passive income, and $200 of unused foreign taxes paid in 2006 with respect to general limitation income. In 2009, A's only foreign source income is passive income described in section 904(j)(3)(A)(i), and this income is reported to A on a payee statement (within the meaning of section 6724(d)(2)). If A elects to apply section 904(j) for the 2009 taxable year, the unused foreign taxes paid in 2005 and 2006 are not deemed paid in 2009, and A therefore cannot claim a foreign tax credit for those taxes in 2009.

(ii) In 2010, A again is eligible for and elects the application of section 904(j). The carryforwards from 2005 expire in 2010. The carryforward period established under section 904(c) is not extended by A's election under section 904(j). In 2011, A does not elect the application of section 904(j). The $600 of unused foreign taxes paid in 2006 on passive and general limitation income are deemed paid in 2011, under section 904(c), without any adjustment for any portion of those taxes that might have been used as a foreign tax credit in 2009 or 2010 if A had not elected to apply section 904(j) to those years.

(d) *Effective date.*—Section 1.904(j)-1 applies to taxable years beginning after July 20, 2004. [Reg. § 1.904(j)-1.]

☐ [*T.D. 9141, 7-19-2004.*]

§ 1.905-1. When credit for foreign income taxes may be taken.—(a) *Scope.*—This section provides rules regarding when the credit for foreign income taxes (as defined in § 1.901-2(a)) may be taken, based on a taxpayer's method of accounting for such taxes. Paragraph (b) of this section provides the general rule. Paragraph (c) of this section sets forth rules for determining the taxable year in which taxpayers using the cash receipts and disbursement method of accounting for income ("cash method") may claim a foreign tax credit. Paragraph (d) of this section sets forth rules for determining the taxable year in which taxpayers using the accrual method of accounting for income ("accrual method") may claim a foreign tax credit. Paragraph (e) of this section provides rules for taxpayers using the cash method to claim foreign tax credits on the accrual basis pursuant to the election provided under section 905(a). Paragraph (f) of this section provides rules for when foreign income tax expenditures of a pass-through entity can be taken as a credit by the entity's partners, shareholders, or owners. Paragraph (g) of this section provides rules for when a foreign tax credit can be taken with respect to blocked income. Paragraph (h) provides the applicability dates for this section.

(b) *General rule.*—The credit for foreign income taxes provided in subpart A, part III, subchapter N, chapter 1 of the Code (the "foreign tax credit") may be taken either on the return for the year in which the foreign income taxes accrued or on the return for the year in which the foreign income taxes were paid (that is, remitted), depending on whether the taxpayer uses the accrual or the cash receipts and disbursements method of accounting for purposes of computing taxable income and filing returns. However, regardless of the year in which the credit is claimed under the taxpayer's method of accounting for foreign income taxes, the foreign tax credit is allowed only to the extent the foreign income taxes are ultimately both owed and remitted to the foreign country (in the case of a taxpayer claiming the foreign tax credit on the accrual basis, within the time prescribed by section 905(c)(2)). See section 905(b) and §§1.901-1(a) and 1.901-2(e). Because the taxpayer's liability for foreign income tax may accrue (that is, become fixed and determinable) in a different taxable year than that in which the tax is paid (that is, remitted), the taxpayer's entitlement to the credit may be perfected, or become subject to adjustment, by reason of events that occur in a taxable year after the taxable year in which the credit is allowed. See section 905(c) and §1.905-3(a) for rules relating to changes to the taxpayer's foreign income tax liability that require a redetermination of the allowable foreign tax credit and the taxpayer's U.S. tax liability.

(c) *Rules for cash method taxpayers.*—(1) *Credit allowed in year paid.*—Except as provided in paragraph (e) of this section, a taxpayer who uses the cash method of accounting may claim a foreign tax credit only in the taxable year in which the foreign income taxes are paid. Generally, foreign income taxes are considered paid in the taxable year in which the taxes are remitted to the foreign country. However, foreign withholding taxes described in section 901(k)(1)(B), as well as foreign net income taxes described in §1.901-2(a)(3) that are withheld from the taxpayer's gross income by the payor, are treated as paid in the year in which they are withheld. Foreign income taxes that have been withheld or remitted but which are not considered an amount of tax paid for purposes of section 901 under the rules of §1.901-2(e) (for example, because the amount withheld or remitted was not a compulsory payment), however, are not eligible for a foreign tax credit. See §§1.901-2(e) and 1.905-3(b)(1)(ii)(B) (*Example* 2).

(2) *Payment of contested foreign tax liability.*—Under §1.901-2(e)(2)(i), a foreign income tax liability that is contested by the taxpayer is not a reasonable approximation of the taxpayer's final foreign income tax liability and, therefore, is not considered an amount of tax paid for purposes of section 901 until the contest is resolved. Thus, except as provided in paragraph (c)(3) of this section, a foreign tax credit for a contested foreign income tax liability (or portion thereof) that has been remitted to the foreign country cannot be claimed until such time as the contest is resolved and the tax is considered paid. Once the contest is resolved and the foreign income tax liability is finally determined, the tax liability is treated as paid in the taxable year in which the foreign tax was remitted. See paragraph (c)(1) of this section; see also section 6511(d)(3) and §301.6511(d)-3 of this chapter for a special 10-year period of limitations for claiming a credit or refund of U.S. tax that is attributable to foreign income taxes for which a credit is allowed under section 901, which for taxpayers claiming credits on the cash basis runs from the unextended due date of the return for the taxable year in which the foreign income taxes are paid (within the meaning of paragraph (c) of this section).

(3) *Election to claim a provisional credit for contested taxes remitted before contest is resolved.*—A taxpayer claiming foreign tax credits on the cash basis may, under the conditions provided in this paragraph (c)(3), elect to claim a foreign tax credit for a contested foreign income tax liability (or a portion thereof) in the year the contested amount (or a portion thereof) is remitted to the foreign country, notwithstanding that the liability is not finally determined and so is not considered an amount of tax paid. Such election applies only for contested foreign income taxes that are remitted in a taxable year in which the taxpayer elects under section 901(a) to claim a credit, instead of a deduction under section 164(a)(3), for taxes paid in such year. To make the election, a taxpayer must file a Form 1116 (Foreign Tax Credit (Individual, Estate, or Trust)) or Form 1118 (Foreign Tax Credit—Corporations), and the agreement described in paragraphs (d)(4)(ii) and (iii) of this section. In addition, the taxpayer must, for each subsequent taxable year up to and including the taxable year in which the contest is resolved, file the annual notice described in paragraph (d)(4)(iv) of this section. Any portion of a contested foreign income tax liability for which a provisional credit is claimed under this paragraph (c)(3) that is subsequently refunded by the foreign country results in a foreign tax redetermination under §1.905-3(a).

(4) *Adjustments to taxes claimed as a credit in the year paid.*—A refund of foreign income taxes for which a foreign tax credit has been claimed on the cash basis, or a subsequent determination that the amount paid exceeds the taxpayer's liability for foreign income tax, requires a redetermination of foreign income taxes paid and the taxpayer's U.S. tax liability pursuant to section 905(c) and §1.905-3. See §1.905-3(a) and 1.905-3(b)(1)(ii)(G) (*Example* 7). Additional foreign income taxes paid that relate back to a prior year in which foreign income taxes were claimed as a credit on the cash basis, including by reason of the settlement of a dispute with the foreign tax authority, may be claimed as a credit only in the year the additional taxes are paid (within the meaning of paragraph (c) of this section). The payment of such additional taxes does not result in a redetermination pursuant to section 905(c) or §1.905-3 of the foreign income taxes paid in any prior year, although a redetermination of U.S. tax liability may be required due, for example, to a carryback of unused foreign tax under section 904(c) and §1.904-2.

(d) *Rules for accrual method taxpayers.*—(1) *Credit allowed in year accrued.*—(i) *In general.*—A taxpayer who uses the accrual method of accounting may claim a foreign tax credit only in the taxable year in which the foreign income taxes are considered to accrue for foreign tax credit purposes under the rules of this paragraph (d). Foreign income taxes accrue in the taxable year in which all the events have occurred that establish the fact of the liability and the amount of the liability can be determined with reasonable accuracy. See §§1.446-1(c)(1)(ii)(A) and 1.461-4(g)(6)(iii)(B). For purposes of the preceding sentence, a foreign income tax that is contingent on a future distribution of earnings does not meet the all events test until the earnings are distributed. A foreign income tax liability determined on the basis of a foreign taxable year becomes fixed and determinable at the close of the taxpayer's foreign taxable year. Therefore, foreign income taxes that are computed based on items of income, deduction, and loss that arise in a foreign taxable year accrue in the United States taxable year with or within which the taxpayer's foreign taxable year ends. Foreign withholding taxes that are paid with respect to a foreign taxable year and that represent advance payments of a foreign net income tax liability determined on the basis of that foreign taxable year accrue at the close of the foreign taxable year. Foreign withholding taxes imposed on a payment giving rise to an item of foreign gross income accrue on the date the payment from which the tax is withheld is made (or treated as made under foreign tax law).

(ii) *Relation-back rule for adjustments to taxes claimed as a credit in year accrued.*—Additional tax paid as a result of a change in the foreign tax liability, including additional tax paid when a contest with a foreign tax authority is resolved, relates back and is considered to accrue at the end of the foreign taxable year with respect to which the tax is imposed (the "relation-back year"). Additional withholding tax paid as a result of a change in the amount of an item of foreign gross income (such as pursuant to a foreign transfer pricing adjustment) also relates back and is considered to accrue in the year in which the payment from which the additional tax is withheld is made (or considered to have been made under foreign tax law). Foreign income taxes that are not paid within 24 months after the close of the taxable year in which they were accrued are treated as refunded pursuant to §1.905-3(a); when subsequently paid, the foreign income taxes are allowed as a credit in the relation-back year. See §1.905-3(b)(1)(ii)(E) (*Example* 5). For special rules that apply to determine when foreign income tax is considered to accrue in the case of certain ownership and entity classification changes, see §§1.336-2(g)(3)(ii), 1.338-9(d), 1.901-2(f)(5), and 1.1502-76.

(2) *Special rule for 52-53 week U.S. taxable years.*—If a taxpayer has elected pursuant to section 441(f) to use a U.S. taxable year consisting of 52-53 weeks, and such U.S. taxable year closes within six calendar days of the end of the taxpayer's foreign taxable year, the determination of when foreign income taxes accrue under paragraph (d)(1) of this section is made by deeming the taxpayer's U.S. taxable year to end on the last day of its foreign taxable year.

(3) *Accrual of contested foreign tax liability.*—A contested foreign income tax liability is finally determined and accrues for purposes of paragraph (d)(1) of this section when the contest is resolved. However, pursuant to section 905(c)(2), no credit is allowed for any accrued tax that is not paid within 24 months of the close of the relation-back year until the tax is actually remitted and considered paid. Thus, except as provided in paragraph (d)(4) of this section, a foreign tax credit for a contested foreign income tax liability cannot be claimed until such time as both the contest is resolved and the tax is considered paid, even if the contested liability (or portion thereof) has previously been remitted to the foreign country. Once the contest is resolved and the foreign income tax liability is finally determined and paid, the tax liability accrues, and is considered to accrue in the relation-back year for purposes of the foreign tax credit. See paragraph (d)(1) of this section; see also section 6511(d)(3) and §301.6511(d)-3 of this chapter for a special 10-year period of limitations for claiming a credit or refund of U.S. tax that is attributable to foreign income taxes for which a credit is allowed under section 901,

which for taxpayers claiming credits on the accrual basis runs from the unextended due date of the return for the taxable year in which the foreign income taxes accrued (within the meaning of this paragraph (d)).

(4) *Election to claim a provisional credit for contested taxes remitted before accrual.*—(i) *Conditions of election.*—A taxpayer may, under the conditions provided in this paragraph (d)(4), elect to claim a foreign tax credit for a contested foreign income tax liability (or a portion thereof) in the relation-back year when the contested amount (or a portion thereof) is remitted to the foreign country, notwithstanding that the liability is not finally determined and so has not accrued. This election is available only for contested foreign income taxes that relate to a taxable year in which the taxpayer has elected under section 901(a) to claim a credit, instead of a deduction under section 164(a)(3), for foreign income taxes that accrue in such year. If the election is made by a taxpayer with respect to contested foreign income taxes of a controlled foreign corporation, such taxes are treated as deemed paid in the relation-back year and the controlled foreign corporation may deduct the taxes in computing its taxable income in the relation-back year. To make the election, a taxpayer must file an amended return for the taxable year to which the contested tax relates, together with a Form 1116 (Foreign Tax Credit (Individual, Estate, or Trust)) or Form 1118 (Foreign Tax Credit—Corporations), and the agreement described in paragraph (d)(4)(ii) of this section. In addition, the taxpayer must, for each subsequent taxable year up to and including the taxable year in which the contest is resolved, file the annual notice described in paragraph (d)(4)(iii) of this section. Any portion of a contested foreign income tax liability for which a provisional credit is claimed under this paragraph (d)(4) that is subsequently refunded by the foreign country results in a foreign tax redetermination under § 1.905-3(a).

(ii) *Contents of provisional foreign tax credit agreement.*—The provisional foreign tax credit agreement must contain the following:

(A) A statement that the document is an election and an agreement under the provisions of paragraph (d)(4) of this section;

(B) A description of the contested foreign income tax liability, including the name (or other identifier) of the foreign tax or taxes being contested, the name of the country imposing the tax, the name and identifying number of the payor of the contested tax, the amount of the contested tax, and the U.S. taxable year(s) and the income to which the contested foreign income tax liability relates;

(C) The amount of the contested foreign income tax liability in paragraph (d)(4)(ii)(B) of this section that has been remitted to the foreign country and the date of the remittance(s);

(D) An agreement by the taxpayer, for a period of three years from the later of the filing or the due date (with extensions) of the return for the taxable year in which the taxpayer notifies the Internal Revenue Service of the resolution of the contest, not to assert the statute of limitations on assessment as a defense to the assessment of additional taxes or interest related to the contested foreign income tax liability described in paragraph (d)(4)(ii)(B) of this section that may arise from a determination that the taxpayer failed to exhaust all effective and practical remedies to minimize its foreign income tax liability, so that the amount of the contested foreign income tax is not a compulsory payment and is not considered paid within the meaning of § 1.901-2(e)(5);

(E) A statement that the taxpayer agrees to comply with all the conditions and requirements of paragraph (d)(4) of this section, including to provide notice to the Internal Revenue Service upon the resolution of the contest; and

(F) Any additional information as may be prescribed by the Commissioner of Internal Revenue in Internal Revenue Service forms or instructions.

(iii) *Signatory.*—The provisional foreign tax credit agreement must be signed under penalties of perjury by a person authorized to sign the return of the taxpayer.

(iv) *Annual notice.*—For each taxable year following the year in which an election pursuant to paragraph (d)(4) of this section is made up to and including the taxable year in which the contest is resolved, the taxpayer must include with its timely-filed return the information described in paragraphs (d)(4)(iii)(A) through (C) of this section on Form 1116 or Form 1118 or in such other form or manner prescribed by the Commissioner of Internal Revenue in Internal Revenue Service forms or instructions.

(A) A description of the contested foreign income tax liability, including the name (or other identifier) of the foreign tax or taxes, the name of the country imposing the tax, the name and identifying number of the payor of the contested tax, the amount of the contested tax, and a description of the status of the contest.

(B) With the return for the taxable year in which the contest is resolved, notification that the contest has been resolved. Such notification must include the date of final resolution and the amount of the finally determined foreign income tax liability.

(C) Any additional information, which may include a copy of the final judgment, order, settlement, or other documentation of the contest resolution, as may be prescribed by the Commissioner of Internal Revenue in Internal Revenue Service forms or instructions.

(5) *Correction of improper accruals.*—(i) *In general.*—The accrual of a foreign income tax expense generally involves the determination of the proper timing for recognizing the expense for Federal income tax purposes. Thus, foreign income tax expense is a material item within the meaning of section 446. See § 1.446-1(e)(2)(ii). As a material item, a change in the timing of accruing a foreign income tax expense is generally a change in method of accounting. See section 446(e). A change from an improper method of accruing foreign income taxes to the proper method of accrual described in this paragraph (d) is treated as a change in a method of accounting, regardless of whether the taxpayer (or a partner or beneficiary taking into account a distributive share of foreign income taxes paid by a partnership or other pass-through entity) chooses to claim a deduction or a credit for such taxes in any taxable year. For purposes of this paragraph (d)(5), an improper method of accruing foreign income taxes includes a method under which foreign income tax is accrued in a taxable year other than the taxable year in which the requirements of the all events test in §§ 1.446-1(c)(1)(ii)(A) and 1.461-4(g)(6)(iii)(B) are met, or which fails to apply the relation-back rule in paragraph (d)(1) of this section that applies for purposes of the foreign tax credit, but does not include corrections to estimated accruals or errors in computing the amount of foreign income tax that is allowed as a deduction or credit in any taxable year. Taxpayers must file a Form 3115, Application for Change in Accounting Method, in accordance with Revenue Procedure 2015-13 (or any successor administrative procedure prescribed by the Commissioner) to obtain the Commissioner's permission to change from an improper method of accruing foreign income taxes to the proper method described in this paragraph (d). In order to prevent a duplication or omission of a benefit for foreign income taxes that accrue in any taxable year (whether through the double allowance or double disallowance of either a deduction or a credit, the allowance of both a deduction and a credit, or the disallowance of either a deduction or a credit, for the same amount of foreign income tax), the rules in paragraphs (d)(5)(ii) through (iv) of this section, describing a modified cut-off approach, apply if the Commissioner grants permission for the taxpayer to change to the proper method of accrual. Under the modified cut-off approach, a section 481(a) adjustment is neither required nor permitted with respect to the amounts of foreign income tax that were improperly accrued (or improperly not accrued) under the taxpayer's improper method in taxable years before the taxable year of change.

(ii) *Adjustments required to implement a change in method of accounting for accruing foreign income taxes.*—A change from an improper method of accruing foreign income taxes to the proper method described in this paragraph (d) is made under the modified cut-off approach described in this paragraph (d)(5)(ii). Under the modified cut-off approach, the amount of foreign income tax in a statutory or residual grouping (such as a separate category as defined in § 1.904-5(a)(4)) that properly accrues in the taxable year of change (accounted for in the currency in which the foreign tax liability is denominated) is first adjusted upward by the amount of foreign income tax in the same grouping that properly accrued in a taxable year before the taxable year of change but which, under the taxpayer's improper method of accounting, the taxpayer failed to accrue and claim as either a credit or a deduction in any taxable year before the taxable year of change, and next, adjusted downward (but not below zero) by the amount of foreign income tax in the same grouping that the taxpayer improperly accrued in a taxable year before the year of change and for which the taxpayer claimed a credit or a deduction in such prior taxable year, but only if the improperly-accrued amount of foreign income tax did not properly accrue in a taxable year before the taxable year of change. The modified cut-off approach is applied separately with respect to amounts of foreign income tax for which the foreign tax credit is disallowed and to which section 275 does not apply. See, for example, section 901(m)(6). For purposes of the foreign tax credit, the adjusted amounts of accrued foreign income taxes, including any upward adjustment, are translated into U.S. dollars under § 1.986(a)-1 as if those amounts properly accrued in the taxable year of change. To the extent that the downward adjustment in any grouping required under this modified cut-off approach exceeds the amount of foreign income tax properly accruing in that grouping in the year of change, as increased by the upward adjustment, if any, such excess will carry forward to each subsequent taxable year and reduce properly-accrued amounts of foreign income tax in the same grouping to the extent of those properly-accrued amounts, until all improperly-accrued amounts included in the downward adjustment are accounted for. See § 1.861-20 for rules that apply to assign foreign income taxes to statutory and residual groupings. See paragraphs (d)(6)(v) through (d)(6)(ix) of this section for examples illustrating the application of the modified cut-off approach.

(iii) *Application of section 905(c).*—(A) *Two-year rule.*—Except as otherwise provided in this paragraph (d)(5)(iii), if the taxpayer claimed a credit for improperly-accrued amounts in a taxable year before the taxable year of change, no adjustment is required under section 905(c)(2) and § 1.905-3(a) solely by reason of the improper accrual. For purposes of applying section 905(c)(2) and § 1.905-3(a) to improperly-accrued amounts of foreign income tax that were claimed as a credit in any taxable year before the taxable year of change, the 24-month period runs from the close of the U.S. taxable year(s) in which those amounts were accrued under the taxpayer's improper method and claimed as a credit. To the extent any improperly-accrued amounts remain unpaid as of the date 24 months after the close of the taxable year in which the amounts were improperly accrued and claimed as a credit, an adjustment is required under section 905(c)(2) and § 1.905-3(a) as if the improperly-accrued amounts were refunded as of the date 24 months after the close of such taxable year. See § 1.986(a)-1(c) (a refund or other downward adjustment to foreign income taxes paid or accrued on more than one date reduces the foreign income taxes paid or accrued on a last-in, first-out basis, starting with the amounts most recently paid or accrued).

(B) *Application of payments.*—Amounts of foreign income tax that a taxpayer accrued and claimed as a credit or a deduction in a taxable year before the taxable year of change under the taxpayer's improper method, but that had properly accrued either in the taxable year the credit or deduction was claimed or in a different taxable year before the taxable year of change, are not included in the downward adjustment required by paragraph (d)(5)(ii) of this section. Remittances to the foreign country of such amounts (accounted for in the currency in which the foreign tax liability is denominated) are treated first as payments of the amounts of tax that had properly accrued in the taxable year claimed as a credit or deduction to the extent thereof, and then as payments of the amounts of tax that were improperly accrued in a different taxable year, on a last-in, first-out basis, starting with the most recent improperly-accrued amounts. Remittances to the foreign country of amounts of foreign income tax that properly accrue in or after the taxable year of change (accounted for in the foreign currency in which the foreign tax liability is denominated) but that are offset by the amounts included in the downward adjustment required by paragraph (d)(5)(ii) of this section are treated as payments of the amounts of tax that were improperly accrued before the taxable year of change and included in the downward adjustment on a last-in, first-out basis, starting with the most recent improperly-accrued amounts. Additional amounts of foreign income tax that first accrue in or after the taxable year of change but that relate to a taxable year before the taxable year of change are taken into account in the earlier of the taxable year of change or the taxable year or years in which they would have been considered to accrue based upon the taxpayer's improper method. Additional amounts of foreign income tax that first accrue in or after the taxable year of change and that relate to the taxable year of change or a taxable year after the year of change are taken into account in the proper relation-back year, but may then be subject to the downward adjustment required by paragraph (d)(5)(ii) of this section.

(iv) *Foreign income tax expense improperly accrued by a foreign corporation, partnership, or other pass-through entity.*—Foreign income tax expense of a foreign corporation reduces both the corporation's taxable income and its earnings and profits, and may give rise to an amount of foreign taxes deemed paid under section 960 that may be claimed as a credit by a United States shareholder that is a domestic corporation or that is a person that makes an election under section 962. If the Commissioner grants permission for a foreign corporation to change its method of accounting for foreign income tax expense, the duplication or omission of those expenses (accounted for in the functional currency of the foreign corporation) and the associated foreign income taxes (translated into dollars in accordance with § 1.986(a)-1) are accounted for by applying the rules in paragraph (d)(5)(ii) of this section as if the foreign corporation were itself eligible to, and did, claim a credit under section 901 for such amounts. In the case of a partnership or other pass-through entity that is granted permission to change its method of accounting for accruing foreign income taxes to a proper method as described in this paragraph (d), such partnership or other pass-through entity must provide its partners or other owners with the information needed for the partners or other owners to properly account for the improperly-accrued or unaccrued amounts under the rules in paragraph (d)(5)(ii) of this section as if their proportionate shares of foreign income tax expense were directly paid or accrued by them.

(6) *Examples.*—The following examples illustrate the application of paragraph (d) of this section. Unless otherwise stated, the local currency of Country X and Country Y, and the functional currency of any foreign branch, is the Euro (€), and at all relevant times the exchange rate is $1:€1.

(i) *Example 1: Accrual of foreign income tax.*—(A) *Facts.* A, a U.S. citizen, resides and works in Country X. A uses the calendar year as the U.S. taxable year and has made an election under paragraph (e) of this section to claim foreign tax credits on an accrual basis. Country X has a tax year that begins on April 1 and ends on March 31. A's wages are subject to net income tax, at graduated rates, under Country X tax law and are subject to withholding on a monthly basis by A's employer in Country X. In the period between April 1, Year 1, and March 31, Year 2, A earns $50,000x in Country X wages, from which A's employer withholds $10,000x in tax. On December 1, Year 1, A receives a dividend distribution from a Country Y corporation, from which the corporation withheld $500x of tax. Country Y imposes withholding tax on dividends paid to nonresidents solely based on the gross amount of the dividend payment; A is not required to file a tax return in Country Y.

(B) *Analysis.* Under paragraph (d)(1) of this section, A's liability for Country X net income tax accrues on March 31, Year 2, the last day of the Country X taxable year. The Country X net income tax withheld by A's employer from A's wages is a reasonable approximation of, and represents an advance payment of, A's final net income tax liability for the year, which becomes fixed and determinable only at the close of the Country X taxable year. Thus, A cannot claim a credit for any portion of the Country X net income tax on A's Federal income tax return for Year 1, and may claim a credit for the entire Country X net income tax that accrues on March 31, Year 2, on A's Federal income tax return for Year 2. A may claim a credit for the Country Y withholding tax on A's Federal income tax return for Year 1, because the withholding tax accrued on December 1, Year 1.

(ii) *Example 2: 52-53 week taxable year.*—(A) *Facts.* U.S.C., an accrual method taxpayer, is a domestic corporation that operates in branch form in Country X. U.S.C. uses the calendar year for Country X tax purposes. For Federal income tax purposes, U.S.C. elects pursuant to § 1.441-2(a) to use a 52-53 week taxable year that ends on the last Friday of December. In Year 1, U.S.C.'s U.S. taxable year ends on Friday, December 25; in Year 2, U.S.C.'s U.S. taxable year ends Friday, December 31. For its foreign taxable year ending December 31, Year 1, U.S.C. earns $10,000x of foreign source income through its Country X branch and incurs Country X foreign income tax of $500x; for Year 2, U.S.C. earns $12,000x and incurs Country X foreign income tax of $600x.

(B) *Analysis.* Under paragraph (d)(1) of this section, the $500x of Country X foreign income tax becomes fixed and determinable at the close of U.S.C.'s foreign taxable year, on December 31, Year 1, which is after the close of its U.S. taxable year (December 25, Year 1). The $600x of Country X foreign income tax becomes fixed and determinable on December 31, Year 2. Thus, both the Year 1 and Year 2 Country X foreign income taxes accrue in U.S.C.'s U.S. taxable year ending December 31, Year 2. However, pursuant to paragraph (d)(2) of this section, for purposes of determining the amount of foreign income taxes accrued in each taxable year for foreign tax credit purposes, U.S.C.'s U.S. taxable year is deemed to end on December 31, the end of U.S.C.'s Country X taxable year. U.S.C. may therefore claim a foreign tax credit for $500x of Country X foreign income tax on its Federal income tax return for Year 1 and a credit for $600x of Country X foreign income tax on its Federal income tax return for Year 2.

(iii) *Example 3: Contested tax.*—(A) *Facts.* U.S.C. is a domestic corporation that operates in branch form in Country X. U.S.C. uses an accrual method of accounting and uses the calendar year as its U.S. and Country X taxable year. In Year 1, when the average exchange rate described in § 1.986(a)-1(a)(1) is $1:€1, U.S.C. earns €20,000x = $20,000x through its Country X branch for U.S. and Country X tax purposes and accrues Country X foreign income taxes of €500x = $500x, which U.S.C. claims as a credit on its Federal income tax return for Year 1. In Year 3, when the average exchange rate is $1:€1.2, Country X asserts that U.S.C. owes additional foreign income taxes of €100x with respect to U.S.C.'s Year 1 income. U.S.C. contests the liability but remits €40x to Country X with respect to the contested liability in Year 3. U.S.C. does not make an election under paragraph (d)(4) of this section to claim a provisional credit with respect to the €40x. In Year 6, after exhausting all effective and practical remedies, it is finally determined that U.S.C. is liable for €50x of additional Country X foreign income taxes with respect to its Year 1 income. U.S.C. pays an additional €10x to Country X on September 15, Year 6, when the spot rate described in §1.986(a)-1(a)(2)(i) is $1:€2.

(B) *Analysis.* Pursuant to paragraph (d)(3) of this section, the additional liability asserted by Country X with respect to U.S.C.'s Year 1 income does not accrue until the contest is resolved in Year 6. U.S.C.'s remittance of €40x of contested tax in Year 3 is not a payment of accrued tax, and so is not a foreign tax redetermination. Both the €40x of Country X taxes paid in Year 3 and the €10x of Country X taxes paid in Year 6 accrue in Year 6, when the contest is resolved. Once accrued and paid, the €50x relates back for foreign tax credit purposes to Year 1, and can be claimed as a credit by U.S.C. on a timely-filed amended return for Year 1. Under §1.986(a)-1(a), for foreign tax credit purposes the €40x paid in Year 3 is translated into dollars at the average exchange rate for Year 1 (€40x × $1/€1 = $40x), and the €10x paid in Year 6 is translated into dollars at the spot rate on the date paid (€10x × $1/€2 = $5x). Accordingly, after the €50x of Country X income tax is paid in Year 6 U.S.C. may claim an additional foreign tax credit of $45x for Year 1.

(iv) *Example 4: Provisional credit for contested tax.*—(A) *Facts.* The facts are the same as those in paragraph (d)(6)(iii)(A) of this section (the facts in *Example 3*), except that U.S.C. pays the entire contested tax liability of €100x to Country X in Year 3 and elects under paragraph (d)(4) of this section to claim a provisional foreign tax credit on an amended return for Year 1. In Year 6, upon resolution of the contest, U.S.C. receives a refund of €50x from Country X.

(B) *Analysis.* In Year 3, U.S.C. may claim a provisional foreign tax credit for $100x (€100x translated at the average exchange rate for Year 1) of contested foreign tax paid to Country X by filing an amended return for Year 1, with Form 1118 attached, and a provisional foreign tax credit agreement described in paragraph (d)(4)(ii) of this section. In each year for Years 4 through 6, U.S.C. must attach the certification described in paragraph (d)(4)(iii) of this section to its timely-filed Federal income tax return. In Year 6, as a result of the €50x refund, U.S.C. must redetermine its U.S. tax liability for Year 1 and for any other affected year pursuant to §1.905-3, reducing the Year 1 foreign tax credit by $50x (from $600x to $550x), and comply with the notification requirements in §1.905-4. See §1.986(a)-1(c) (refunds of foreign income tax translated into U.S. dollars at the rate used to claim the credit).

(v) *Example 5: Improperly accelerated accrual.*—(A) *Facts*—(1) *Foreign income tax accrued and paid.* U.S.C. is a domestic corporation that operates a foreign branch in Country X. All of U.S.C.'s gross and taxable income is foreign source foreign branch category income, and all of its foreign income taxes are properly allocated and apportioned under §1.861-20 to the foreign branch category. U.S.C. uses the accrual method of accounting and uses the calendar year as its U.S. taxable year. For Country X tax purposes, U.S.C. uses a fiscal year that ends on March 31. U.S.C. accrued €200x of Country X net income tax (as defined in §1.901-2(a)(3)) for its foreign taxable year ending March 31, Year 2, for which the average exchange rate was $1:€1. It timely filed its Country X tax return and paid the €200x on January 15, Year 3. U.S.C. accrued and paid with its timely filed Country X tax returns €280x and €240x of Country X net income tax for its foreign taxable years ending on March 31 of Year 3 and Year 4, respectively, on January 15 of Year 4 and Year 5, respectively.

(2) *Improper accrual.* On its Federal income tax return for Year 1, U.S.C. improperly pro-rated and accelerated the accrual of Country X net income tax and claimed a credit for $150x, equal to three-fourths of the Country X net income tax of $200x that relates to U.S.C.'s foreign taxable year ending March 31, Year 2. Continuing with this improper method of accruing foreign income taxes, U.S.C. claimed a foreign tax credit of $260x on its U.S. tax return for Year 2, comprising $50x (one-fourth of the $200x of net income tax relating to its foreign taxable year ending March 31, Year 2) plus $210x (three-fourths of the $280x of net income tax relating to its foreign taxable year ending March 31, Year 3). Similarly, U.S.C. improperly accrued and claimed a foreign tax credit on its U.S. tax return for Year 3 for $250x of Country X net income tax, comprising $70x (one-fourth of the $280x that properly accrued in Year 3) plus $180x (three-fourths of the $240x that properly accrued in Year 4). In Year 4, U.S.C. realizes its mistake and, as provided in paragraph (d)(5)(i) of this section, files Form 3115 with the IRS to seek permission to change from an improper method to a proper method of accruing foreign income taxes.

Table 1 to Paragraph (d)(6)(v)(A)(2)

Country X taxable year ending in U.S. calendar taxable year	Net income tax properly accrued ($1 = €1)	Net income tax accrued under improper method ($1 = €1)
3/31/Y1 ends in Year 1	0	3/4 (200x) = 150x.
3/31/Y2 ends in Year 2	200x	1/4 (200x) + 3/4 (280x) = 260x.
3/31/Y3 ends in Year 3	280x	1/4 (280x) + 3/4 (240x) = 250x.
3/31/Y4 ends in Year 4	240x	[year of change].

(B) *Analysis*—(1) *Downward adjustment.* Under paragraph (d)(5)(ii) of this section, in Year 4, the year of change, U.S.C. must reduce (but not below zero) the amount (in Euros) of Country X net income tax in the foreign branch category that properly accrues in Year 4, €240x, by the amount of foreign income tax that was accrued and claimed as either a deduction or a credit in a year before the year of change, and that had not properly accrued in either the year in which the tax was accrued under U.S.C.'s improper method or in any other taxable year before the taxable year of change. For all taxable years before the taxable year of change, under its improper method U.S.C. had accrued and claimed as a credit a total of €660x = $660x of foreign income tax, of which only €480x = $480x had properly accrued. Therefore, the downward adjustment required by paragraph (d)(5)(ii) of this section is €180x (€660x − €480x = €180x). In Year 4, U.S.C.'s foreign tax credit in the foreign branch category is reduced by $180x (€180x downward adjustment translated into dollars at $1:€1, the average exchange rate for Year 4), from $240x to $60x.

(2) *Application of section 905(c)*—(i) *Year 1.* Under paragraph (d)(5)(iii) of this section, the €200x U.S.C. paid on January 15, Year 3, that relates to its Country X taxable year ending on March 31, Year 2, is first treated as a payment of the €50x of that Country X net income tax liability that properly accrued and was claimed as a credit by U.S.C. in Year 2, and next as a payment of the €150x of that Country X net income tax liability that U.S.C. improperly accrued and claimed as a credit in Year 1. Because all €150x of the Country X net income tax that was improperly accrued and claimed as a credit in Year 1 was paid within 24 months of December 31, Year 1, no foreign tax redetermination occurs, and no redetermination of U.S. tax liability is required, for Year 1.

(ii) *Year 2.* Under paragraph (d)(5)(iii) of this section, the €280x U.S.C. paid on January 15, Year 4, that relates to its Country X taxable year ending on March 31, Year 3, is first treated as a payment of the €70x = $70x of that Country X net income tax liability that properly accrued and was claimed as a credit by U.S.C. in Year 3, and next as a payment of the €210x = $210x of that Country X net income tax liability that U.S.C. improperly accrued and claimed as a credit in Year 2. Together with the €50x = $50x of U.S.C.'s Country X net income tax liability that properly accrued and was claimed as a credit in Year 2, all €260x of the Country X net income tax that was accrued and claimed as a credit in Year 2 under U.S.C.'s improper method was paid within 24 months of December 31, Year 2. Accordingly, no foreign tax redetermination occurs, and no redetermination of U.S. tax liability is required, for Year 2.

(iii) *Year 3.* Under paragraph (d)(5)(iii) of this section, the €240x U.S.C. paid on January 15, Year 5, that relates to its Country X taxable year ending on March 31, Year 4, is first treated as a payment of the €60x = $60x of that Country X net income tax liability that properly accrued and was claimed as a credit by U.S.C. in Year 4, and next as a payment of the €180x = $180x of that Country X net income tax liability that U.S.C. improperly accrued and claimed as a credit in Year 3. Together with the €70x = $70x of U.S.C.'s Country X net income tax liability that properly accrued and was claimed as a credit by U.S.C. in Year 3, all €250x of the Country X net income tax that was accrued and claimed as a credit in Year 3 under U.S.C.'s improper method was paid within 24 months of December 31, Year 3.

Accordingly, no foreign tax redetermination occurs, and no redetermination of U.S. tax liability is required, for Year 3.

(*iv*) *Year 4*. Under paragraph (d)(5)(iii) of this section, €60x = $60x of U.S.C.'s January 15, Year 5 payment of €240x with respect to its Country X net income tax liability for Year 4 is treated as a payment of €60x = $60x of Country X net income tax that, after application of the downward adjustment required by paragraph (d)(5)(ii) of this section, was accrued and claimed as a credit in Year 4, the year of change.

(vi) *Example 6: Failure to pay improperly-accrued tax within 24 months*.—(A) *Facts*. The facts are the same as those in paragraph (d)(6)(v) of this section (the facts in *Example 5*), except that U.S.C. does not pay its €240x tax liability for its Country X taxable year ending on March 31, Year 4, until January 15 of Year 6, when the spot rate described in § 1.986(a)-1(a)(2)(i) is $1:€1.5.

(B) *Analysis*. The results are the same as in paragraphs (d)(6)(v)(B)(*2*)(*i*) and (*ii*) of this section (the analysis in *Example 5* for Year 1 and Year 2). With respect to Year 3, because the €180x = $180x of Year 4 foreign income tax that was improperly accrued and credited in Year 3 was not paid within 24 months of the end of Year 3, under section 905(c)(2) and § 1.905-3(a) that €180x = $180x is treated as refunded on December 31, Year 5, requiring a redetermination of U.S.C.'s Federal income tax liability for Year 3 (to reverse out the credit claimed). In Year 6, when U.S.C. pays the €240x of Country X income tax liability for Year 4, under paragraph (d)(5)(iii) of this section that payment is first treated as a payment of the €60x = $60x that was properly accrued and claimed as a credit in Year 4, and then as a payment of the €180x that was improperly accrued and claimed as a credit in Year 3 and that was treated as refunded in Year 5. Under section 905(c)(2)(B) and § 1.905-3(a), that Year 6 payment of accrued but unpaid tax is a second foreign tax redetermination for Year 3 that also requires a redetermination of U.S.C.'s U.S. tax liability. Under § 1.986(a)-1(a)(2), the €180x of redetermined tax for Year 3 is translated into dollars at the spot rate on January 15, Year 6, when the tax is paid (€180x × $1/€1.5 = $120x). Under § 1.905-4(b)(1)(iv), U.S.C. may file one amended return accounting for both foreign tax redeterminations (which occur in two consecutive taxable years) with respect to Year 3, which taken together result in a reduction in U.S.C.'s foreign tax credit for Year 3 from $250x to $190x ($250x originally accrued – $180x unpaid after 24 months + $120x paid in Year 6).

(vii) *Example 7: Additional payment of improperly-accrued tax*.—(A) *Facts*. The facts are the same as those in paragraph (d)(6)(v)(A) of this section (the facts in *Example 5*), except that in Year 6, Country X assessed additional net income tax of €100x with respect to U.S.C.'s Country X taxable year ending March 31, Year 3, and after exhausting all effective and practical remedies to reduce its liability for Country X income tax, U.S.C. pays the additional assessed tax on September 15, Year 7, when the spot rate described in § 1.986(a)-1(a)(2)(i) is $1:€0.5.

(B) *Analysis*. Under paragraph (d)(3) of this section, the additional €100x of Country X income tax U.S.C. paid in Year 7 with respect to its foreign taxable year that ended March 31, Year 3, relates back and is considered to accrue in Year 3. However, under its improper method of accounting U.S.C. had accrued and claimed foreign tax credits for Country X net income tax that related to Year 3 on its Federal income tax returns for both Year 2 and Year 3. Accordingly, under paragraph (d)(5)(iii)(B) of this section U.S.C. must redetermine its U.S. tax liability for both Year 2 and Year 3 (and any other affected years) to account for the additional €100x of Country X net income tax liability, using the improper method it used to accrue foreign income taxes before the year of change. Therefore, three-fourths of the €100x of additional tax, or €75x, is treated as if it accrued in Year 2, and one-fourth of the additional tax, or €25x, is treated as if it accrued in Year 3. Pursuant to § 1.986(a)-1(a)(2)(i), the €75x of tax treated as if it accrued in Year 2 and the €25x of tax treated as if it accrued in Year 3 are converted into dollars using the September 15, Year 7, spot rate of $1:€0.5, to $150x and $50x, respectively. Under § 1.905-4(b)(1)(iii), U.S.C. may claim a refund for any resulting overpayment of U.S. tax for Year 2 or Year 3 or any other affected year by filing an amended return within the period provided in section 6511.

(viii) *Example 8: Tax improperly accrued before year of change exceeds tax properly accrued in year of change*.—(A) *Facts*. U.S.C. owns all of the stock in CFC, a controlled foreign corporation organized in Country X. Country X imposes net income tax on Country X corporations at a rate of 10% only in the year its earnings are distributed to its shareholders, rather than in the year the income is earned. Both U.S.C. and CFC use the calendar year as their taxable year for both Federal and Country X income tax purposes and CFC uses the Euro as its functional currency. In each of Years 1-3, CFC earns €1,000x for both Federal and Country X income tax purposes of general category foreign base company sales income (before reduction for foreign income taxes). CFC improperly accrues €100x of Country X net income tax with respect to €1,000x of income at the end of each of Years 1 and 2, even though no distribution is made in those years. In Year 1, for which the average exchange rate is $1:€1, U.S.C. computes and includes in income with respect to CFC $900x of subpart F income, claims a deemed paid foreign tax credit of $100x under section 960(a), and has a section 78 dividend of $100x. In Year 2, for which the average exchange rate is $1:€0.5, U.S.C. computes and includes in income with respect to CFC $1,800x of subpart F income, claims a deemed paid foreign tax credit of $200x under section 960(a), and has a section 78 dividend of $200x. In Year 2, CFC makes a distribution to U.S.C. of €400x of earnings and pays €40x of net income tax to Country X. In Year 3, for which the average exchange rate is $1:€1, CFC makes another distribution to U.S.C. of €500x of earnings and pays €50x in net income tax to Country X. In Year 3, U.S.C. realizes its mistake and seeks permission from the IRS for CFC to change to a proper method of accruing foreign income taxes. In Year 4, for which the average exchange rate is $1:€2, CFC makes a distribution of €700x of earnings and pays €70x of net income tax to Country X.

Table 2 to Paragraph (d)(6)(viii)(A)

Taxable year ending	Foreign income tax properly accrued	Foreign income tax accrued under improper method
12/31/Y1 ($1:€1)	0	€100x = $100x.
12/31/Y2 ($1:€0.5)	€40x = $80x	€100x = $200x.
12/31/Y3 ($1:€1)	€50x = $50x	[year of change].
12/31/Y4 ($1:€2)	€70x = $35x	

(B) *Analysis*—(*1*) *Downward adjustment*. Under paragraph (d)(5)(iv) of this section, CFC applies the rules of paragraph (d)(5) of this section as if it claimed a foreign tax credit under section 901 for Country X taxes. Under paragraph (d)(5)(ii) of this section, in Year 3, the year of change, CFC must reduce (but not below zero) the amount (in Euros) of Country X net income tax allocated and apportioned to its general category foreign base company sales income group that properly accrues in Year 3, €50x, by the amount of foreign income tax (in Euros) that was improperly accrued in that statutory grouping in a year before the year of change, and that had not properly accrued in either the year accrued or in another taxable year before the year of change. For all taxable years before the year of change, under its improper method CFC had accrued a total of €200x of foreign income tax with respect to its general category foreign base company sales income group, of which only €40x had properly accrued. Therefore, the downward adjustment required by paragraph (d)(5)(ii) of this section is €160x (€200x—€40x = €160x). In Year 3, CFC's €50x of eligible foreign income taxes in the general category foreign base company sales income group is reduced by €50x to zero. The €110x balance of the downward adjustment carries forward to Year 4, and reduces CFC's €70x of eligible foreign income taxes in the general category foreign base company sales income group by €70x to zero. The remaining €40x balance of the downward adjustment carries forward to later years and will reduce CFC's eligible foreign income taxes in the general category foreign base company sales income group until all improperly-accrued amounts are accounted for.

(*2*) *Application of section 905(c)*—(*i*) *Year 2*. Under paragraph (d)(5)(iii) of this section, CFC's payment in Year 2 of the €40x of Country X net income tax that properly accrued in Year 2, before the year of change, is treated as a payment of €40x of foreign income tax that CFC properly accrued in Year 2. The €60x of foreign income tax that CFC improperly accrued in Year 2 that remains unpaid at the end of Year 2 is not adjusted in Year 2. Under paragraph (d)(5)(iii) of this section, CFC's payment in Year 3 of €50x of Country X net income tax that properly accrued but was offset by the downward adjustment in Year 3 is treated as a payment of €50x of the remaining €60x of Country X net income tax that CFC improperly accrued in Year 2, the most recent improper accrual. In addition, CFC's payment in Year 4 of €70x of Country X net income tax that properly accrued but was offset by the downward adjustment in Year 4 is treated first as a payment of the remaining €10x of Country X net income tax that CFC improperly accrued in Year 2. Because all €100x of foreign income tax accrued in Year 2 under CFC's improper method of accounting is treated as paid within 24 months of December 31, Year 2, no foreign tax redetermination occurs, and no redetermination of CFC's foreign base company sales income, earnings and profits, and eligible foreign income taxes or of U.S.C.'s $1,800x subpart F inclusion, $200x deemed paid credit, $200x section 78 dividend and U.S. tax liability is required, for Year 2.

(ii) *Year 1.* Because all €100x of the tax CFC improperly accrued in Year 1 remained unpaid as of December 31, Year 3, the date 24 months after the end of Year 1, under section 905(c)(2) and §1.905-3(a) that €100x is treated as refunded on December 31, Year 3. Under §1.905-3(b)(2)(ii), U.S.C. must redetermine its Federal income tax liability for Year 1 to account for the foreign tax redetermination, increasing CFC's foreign base company sales income and earnings and profits by €100x, and decreasing its eligible foreign income taxes by $100x. However, under paragraph (d)(5)(iii)(B) of this section €60x of CFC's payment in Year 4 of €70x of Country X net income tax that properly accrued but was offset by the downward adjustment in Year 4 is treated as a payment of €60x of the €100x of Country X net income tax that was improperly accrued in Year 1 and treated as refunded in Year 3. Under §1.905-4(b)(1)(iv), U.S.C. may account for the two foreign tax redeterminations that occurred in Years 3 and 4 on a single amended Federal income tax return for Year 1. CFC's foreign base company sales income (taking into account the reduction for foreign income taxes) and earnings and profits for Year 1 are recomputed as €1,000x of foreign base company sales income—€100x foreign income tax improperly accrued in Year 1 + €100x improperly accrued foreign income tax treated as refunded on December 31, Year 3—€60x improperly accrued foreign income tax treated as paid in Year 4 = €940x. CFC's eligible foreign income taxes for Year 1 are translated into dollars at the applicable exchange rate and recomputed as $100x foreign income tax improperly accrued in Year 1—$100x improperly accrued foreign income tax treated as refunded on December 31, Year 3 + $30x improperly accrued foreign income tax treated as paid in Year 4 = $30x. U.S.C.'s subpart F inclusion with respect to CFC for Year 1 (translated at the average exchange rate for Year 1 of $1:€1) is increased from $900x to $940x (€940x x $1/€1), and the amount of foreign taxes deemed paid under section 960(a) and the amount of the section 78 dividend are reduced from $100x to $30x.

(iii) *Summary.* As of the end of Year 4, CFC and U.S.C. have been allowed a $30x foreign tax credit for Year 1, and a $200x foreign tax credit for Year 2. If in a later taxable year CFC distributes additional earnings to U.S.C. and accrues €40x of additional Country X net income tax that is offset by the balance of the €40x downward adjustment, CFC's payment of that €40x Country X net income tax liability will be treated as a payment of the remaining €40x of Country X net income tax that was improperly accrued in Year 1 and treated as refunded as of the end of Year 3.

(ix) *Example 9: Improperly deferred accrual.*—(A) *Facts*—(1) *Foreign income tax accrued and paid.* U.S.C. is a domestic corporation that operates a foreign branch in Country X. All of U.S.C.'s gross and taxable income is foreign source foreign branch category income, and all of its foreign income taxes are properly allocated and apportioned under §1.861-20 to the foreign branch category. U.S.C. uses the accrual method of accounting and uses the calendar year as its taxable year for both Federal and Country X income tax purposes. U.S.C. accrued €160x of Country X net income tax (as defined in §1.901-2(a)(3)) with respect to Year 1. U.S.C. filed its Country X tax return and paid the €160x on June 30, Year 2. U.S.C. accrued €180x, €240x, and €150x of Country X tax for Years 2, 3, and 4, respectively, and paid with its timely filed Country X tax returns these tax liabilities on June 30 of Years 3, 4, and 5, respectively. The average exchange rate described in §1.986(a)-1(a)(1) is $1:€0.5 in Year 1, $1:€1 in Year 2, $1:€1.25 in Year 3, and $1:€1.5 in Year 4.

(2) *Improper accrual.* On its Federal income tax return for Year 1, U.S.C. claimed no foreign tax credit. On its Federal income tax return for Year 2, U.S.C. improperly accrued and claimed a credit for $160x (€160x of Country X tax for Year 1 that it paid in Year 2, translated into dollars at the average exchange rate for Year 2). Continuing with this improper method of accounting, U.S.C. improperly accrued and claimed a credit in Year 3 for $144x (€180x of Country X tax for Year 2 that it paid in Year 3, translated into dollars at the average exchange rate for Year 3). In Year 4, U.S.C. realizes its mistake and seeks permission from the IRS to change to a proper method of accruing foreign income taxes.

Table 3 to Paragraph (d)(6)(ix)(A)(2)

Taxable year ending	Foreign income tax properly accrued	Foreign income tax accrued under improper method
12/31/Y1 ($1:€0.5)	€160x = $320x	0.
12/31/Y2 ($1:€1)	€180x = $180x	€160x = $160x.
12/31/Y3 ($1:€1.25)	€240x = $192x	€180x = $144x.
12/31/Y4 ($1:€1.5)	€150x = $100x	[year of change]

(B) *Analysis*—(1) *Upward adjustment.* Under paragraph (d)(5)(ii) of this section, in Year 4, the year of change, U.S.C. increases the amount of Country X net income tax allocated and apportioned to its foreign branch category that properly accrues in Year 4, €150x, by the amount of foreign income tax in that same grouping that properly accrued in a taxable year before the taxable year of change, but which, under its improper method of accounting, U.S.C. failed to accrue and claim as either a credit or deduction before the taxable year of change. For all taxable years before the taxable year of change, under a proper method, U.S.C. would have accrued a total of €580x of foreign income tax, of which it accrued and claimed a credit for only €340x under its improper method. Thus, in Year 4, U.S.C. increases its €150x of properly accrued foreign income taxes in the foreign branch category by €240x (€580x – €340x), and may claim a credit in that year for the total, €390x, or $260x (translated into dollars at the average exchange rate for Year 4, as if the total amount properly accrued in Year 4).

(2) *Application of section 905(c).* Under paragraph (d)(5)(iii) of this section, U.S.C.'s payment in Year 2 of €160x of Country X net income tax that properly accrued in Year 1 but that U.S.C. accrued and claimed as a credit in Year 2 under its improper method of accounting is first treated as a payment of the amount of the Year 1 tax liability that properly accrued in Year 2. Since none of the €160x properly accrued in Year 2, the €160x is treated as a payment of the Year 1 tax liability that U.S.C. improperly accrued and claimed as a credit in Year 2, €160x. Because all €160x of the Country X net income tax that was improperly accrued and claimed as a credit in Year 2 was paid within 24 months of the end of Year 2, no foreign tax redetermination occurs, and no redetermination of U.S.C.'s $160x foreign tax credit and U.S. tax liability is required, for Year 2. Similarly, because all €180x of the Year 2 Country X net income tax that was improperly accrued and claimed as a credit in Year 3 was paid within 24 months of the end of Year 3, no foreign tax redetermination occurs, and no redetermination of U.S.C.'s $144x foreign tax credit and U.S. tax liability is required, for Year 3.

(e) *Election by cash method taxpayer to take credit on the accrual basis.*—(1) *In general.*—A taxpayer who uses the cash method of accounting for income may elect to take the foreign tax credit in the taxable year in which the taxes accrue in accordance with the rules in paragraph (d) of this section. Except as provided in paragraph (e)(2) of this section, an election pursuant to this paragraph (e)(1) must be made on a timely-filed original return, by checking the appropriate box on Form 1116 (Foreign Tax Credit (Individual, Estate, or Trust)) or Form 1118 (Foreign Tax Credit—Corporations) indicating the cash method taxpayer's choice to claim the foreign tax credit in the year the foreign income taxes accrue. Once made, the election is irrevocable and must be followed for purposes of claiming a foreign tax credit for all subsequent years. See section 905(a).

(2) *Exception for cash method taxpayers claiming a foreign tax credit for the first time.*—If the year with respect to which an election pursuant to paragraph (e)(1) of this section to claim the foreign tax credit on an accrual basis is made (the "election year") is the first year for which a taxpayer has ever claimed a foreign tax credit, the election to claim the foreign tax credit on an accrual basis can also be made on an amended return filed within the period permitted under §1.901-1(d)(1). The election is binding in the election year and all subsequent taxable years in which the taxpayer claims a foreign tax credit.

(3) *Treatment of taxes that accrued in a prior year.*—In the election year and subsequent taxable years, a cash method taxpayer that claimed foreign tax credits on the cash basis in a prior taxable year may claim a foreign tax credit not only for foreign income taxes that accrue in the election year, but also for foreign income taxes that accrued (or are considered to accrue) in a taxable year preceding the election year but that are paid in the election year or a subsequent taxable year, as applicable. Under paragraph (c) of this section, foreign income taxes paid with respect to a taxable year that precedes the election year may be claimed as a credit only in the year the taxes are paid and do not require a redetermination under section 905(c) or § 1.905-3 of U.S. tax liability in any prior year.

(4) *Examples.*—The following examples illustrate the application of paragraph (e) of this section.

(i) *Example 1.*—(A) *Facts.* A, a U.S. citizen who is a resident of Country X, is a cash method taxpayer who uses the calendar year as the taxable year for both U.S. and Country X tax purposes. In Year 1 through Year 5, A claims foreign tax credits for Country X foreign income taxes on the cash method, in the year the taxes are paid. For Year 6, A makes a timely election to claim foreign tax credits on the accrual basis. In Year 6, A accrues $100x of Country X foreign income taxes with respect to Year 6. Also in Year 6, A pays $80x in foreign income taxes that had accrued in Year 5.

(B) *Analysis.* Pursuant to paragraph (e)(3) of this section, A can claim a foreign tax credit in Year 6 for the $100x of Country X taxes that accrued in Year 6 and for the $80x of Country X taxes that accrued in Year 5 but that are paid in Year 6.

(ii) *Example 2.*—(A) *Facts.* The facts are the same as those in paragraph (e)(4)(i)(A) of this section (the facts in *Example 1*), except that in Year 7, A is assessed an additional $10x of foreign income tax by Country X with respect to A's income in Year 3. After exhausting all effective and practical remedies, A pays the additional $10x to Country X in Year 8.

(B) *Analysis.* Pursuant to paragraph (e)(3) of this section, A can claim a foreign tax credit in Year 8 for the additional $10x of foreign income tax paid to Country X in Year 8 with respect to Year 3.

(f) *Rules for creditable foreign tax expenditures of partners, shareholders, or beneficiaries of a pass-through entity.*—(1) *Effect of pass-through entity's method of accounting on when foreign tax credit or deduction can be claimed.*—Each partner that elects to claim the foreign tax credit for a particular taxable year may treat its distributive share of the creditable foreign tax expenditures (as defined in § 1.704-1(b)(4)(viii)(*b*)) of the partnership that are paid or accrued by the partnership, under the partnership's method of accounting, during the partnership's taxable year ending with or within the partner's taxable year, as foreign income taxes paid or accrued (as the case may be, according to the partner's method of accounting for such taxes) by the partner in that particular taxable year. See §§ 1.702-1(a)(6) and 1.703-1(b)(2). Under §§ 1.905-3(a) and 1.905-4(b)(2), additional creditable foreign tax expenditures of the partnership that result from a change in the partnership's foreign tax liability for a prior taxable year, including additional taxes paid when a contest with a foreign tax authority is resolved, must be identified by the partnership as a prior year creditable foreign tax expenditure in the information reported to its partners for its taxable year in which the additional tax is actually paid. Subject to the rules in paragraphs (c) and (e) of this section, a partner using the cash method of accounting for foreign income taxes may claim a credit (or a deduction) for its distributive share of such additional taxes in the partner's taxable year with or within which the partnership's taxable year ends. Subject to the rules in paragraph (d) of this section, a partner using the accrual method of accounting for foreign income taxes may claim a credit for the partner's distributive share of such additional taxes in the relation-back year, or may claim a deduction in its taxable year with or within which the partnership's taxable year ends. The principles of this paragraph (f)(1) apply to determine the year in which a shareholder of a S corporation, or the grantor or beneficiary of an estate or trust, may claim a foreign tax credit (or a deduction) for its proportionate share of foreign income taxes paid or accrued by the S corporation, estate or trust. See sections 642(a), 671, 901(b)(5), and 1373(a) and §§ 1.1363-1(c)(2)(iii) and 1.1366-1(a)(2)(iv). See §§ 1.905-3 and 1.905-4 for notifications and adjustments of U.S. tax liability that are required if creditable foreign tax expenditures of a partnership or S corporation, or foreign income taxes paid or accrued by a trust or estate, are refunded or otherwise reduced.

(2) *Provisional credit for contested taxes.*—Under paragraph (d)(3) of this section, a contested foreign tax liability does not accrue until the contest is resolved and the amount of the liability has been finally determined. In addition, under section 905(c)(2), a foreign income tax that is not paid within 24 months of the close of the taxable year to which the tax relates may not be claimed as a credit until the tax is actually paid. Thus, a partnership or other pass-through entity cannot take the contested tax into account as a creditable foreign tax expenditure until both the contest is resolved and the tax is actually paid. However, to the extent that a partnership or other pass-through entity remits a contested foreign tax liability to a foreign country, a partner or other owner of such pass-through entity that claims foreign tax credits may, by complying with the rules in paragraph (c)(3) or (d)(4) of this section, as applicable, elect to claim a provisional credit for its distributive share of such contested tax liability in the year the pass-through entity remits the tax (for owners claiming foreign tax credits on the cash basis) or in the relation-back year (for owners claiming foreign tax credits on the accrual basis).

(3) *Example.*—The following example illustrates the application of paragraph (f) of this section.

(i) *Facts.*—ABC is a U.S. partnership that is engaged in a trade or business in Country X. ABC has two U.S. partners, A and B. For Federal income tax purposes, ABC and partner A both use the accrual method of accounting and utilize a taxable year ending on September 30. ABC uses a taxable year ending on September 30 for Country X tax purposes. B is a calendar year taxpayer that uses the cash method of accounting. For its taxable year ending September 30, Year 1, ABC accrues $500x in foreign income tax to Country X; each partner's distributive share of the foreign income tax is $250x. In its taxable year ending September 30, Year 5, ABC settles a contest with Country X with respect to its Year 1 tax liability and, as a result of such settlement, accrues an additional $100x in foreign income tax for Year 1. ABC remits the additional tax to Country X in January of Year 6. A and B both elect to claim foreign tax credits for their respective taxable Years 1 through 6.

(ii) *Analysis.*—For its taxable year ending September 30, Year 1, A can claim a credit for its $250x distributive share of foreign income taxes paid by ABC with respect to ABC's taxable year ending September 30, Year 1. Pursuant to paragraph (f)(1) of this section, B can claim its distributive share of $250x of foreign income tax for its taxable year ending December 31, Year 1, even if ABC does not remit the Year 1 taxes to Country X until Year 2. Although the additional $100x of Country X foreign income tax owed by ABC with respect to Year 1 accrued in its taxable year ending September 30, Year 5, upon conclusion of the contest, because ABC uses the accrual method of accounting, it does not take the additional tax into account until the tax is actually paid, in its taxable year ending September 30, Year 6. See section 905(c)(2)(B) and paragraph (f)(1) of this section. Pursuant to § 1.905-4(b)(2), ABC is required to notify the IRS and its partners of the foreign tax redetermination. A's distributive share of the additional tax relates back, is considered to accrue, and may be claimed as a credit for Year 1; however, A cannot claim a credit for the additional tax until Year 6, when ABC remits the tax to Country X. See § 1.905-3(a). B's distributive share of the additional tax does not relate back to Year 1 and is creditable in B's taxable year ending December 31, Year 6.

(g) *Blocked income.*—If, under the provisions of the regulations under section 461, an amount otherwise constituting gross income for the taxable year from sources without the United States is, owing to monetary, exchange, or other restrictions imposed by a foreign country, not includible in gross income of the taxpayer for such year, the credit for foreign income taxes imposed by such foreign country with respect to such amount shall be taken proportionately in any subsequent taxable year in which such amount or portion thereof is includible in gross income.

(h) *Applicability dates.*—This section applies to foreign income taxes paid or accrued in taxable years beginning on or after December 28, 2021. In addition, the election described in paragraphs (c)(3) and (d)(4) of this section may be made (including by a partner or other owner of a pass-through entity described in paragraph (f)(2) of this section) with respect to amounts of contested tax that are remitted in taxable years beginning on or after December 28, 2021 and that relate to a taxable year beginning before December 28, 2021. [Reg. § 1.905-1.]

□ [*T.D. 6275, 12-2-57. Amended by T.D. 9959, 12-28-2021 (corrected 7-26-2022).*]

§1.905-2. Conditions of allowance of credit.—(a) *Forms and information.*—(1) Whenever the taxpayer chooses, in accordance with paragraph (d) of §1.901-1, to claim the benefits of the foreign tax credit, the claim for credit shall be accompanied by Form 1116 in the case of an individual or by Form 1118 in the case of a corporation.

(2) The form must be carefully filled in with all the information called for and with the calculations of credits indicated. Except where it is established to the satisfaction of the district director that it is impossible for the taxpayer to furnish such evidence, the taxpayer must provide upon request the receipt for each such tax payment if credit is sought for taxes already paid or the return on which each such accrued tax was based if credit is sought for taxes accrued. The receipt or return must be either the original, a duplicate original, or a duly certified or authenticated copy. The preceding two sentences are applicable for returns whose original due date falls on or after January 1, 1988. If the receipt or the return is in a foreign language, a certified translation thereof must be furnished by the taxpayer. Any additional information necessary for the determination under part I (section 861 and following), subchapter N, chapter 1 of the Code, of the amount of income derived from sources without the United States and from each foreign country shall, upon the request of the district director, be furnished by the taxpayer. If the taxpayer upon request fails without justification to furnish any such additional information which is significant, including any significant information which he is requested to furnish pursuant to §1.861-8(f)(5) as proposed in the Federal Register for November 8, 1976, the District Director may disallow the claim of the taxpayer to the benefits of the foreign tax credit.

(b) *Secondary evidence.*—Where it has been established to the satisfaction of the district director that it is impossible to furnish a receipt for such foreign tax payment, the foreign tax return, or direct evidence of the amount of tax withheld at the source, the district director, may, in his discretion, accept secondary evidence thereof as follows:

(1) *Receipt for payment.*—In the absence of a receipt for payment of foreign taxes there shall be submitted a photostatic copy of the check, draft, or other medium of payment showing the amount and date thereof, with certification identifying it with the tax claimed to have been paid, together with evidence establishing that the tax was paid for taxpayer's account as his own tax on his own income. If credit is claimed on an accrual method, it must be shown that the tax accrued in the taxable year.

(2) *Foreign tax return.*—If the foreign tax return is not available, the foreign tax has not been paid, and credit is claimed on an accrual method, there shall be submitted—

(i) A certified statement of the amount claimed to have accrued,

(ii) Excerpts from the taxpayer's accounts showing amounts of foreign income and tax thereon accrued on its books,

(iii) A computation of the foreign tax based on income from the foreign country carried on the books and at current rates of tax to be established by data such as excerpts from the foreign law, assessment notices, or other documentary evidence thereof,

(iv) A bond, if deemed necessary by the district director, filed in the manner provided in cases where the foreign return is available, and

(v) In case a bond is not required, a specific agreement wherein the taxpayer shall recognize its liability to report the correct amount of tax when ascertained, as required by the provisions of section 905(c).

If at any time the foreign tax receipts or foreign tax returns become available to the taxpayer, they shall be promptly submitted to the district director.

(3) *Tax withheld at source.*—In the case of taxes withheld at the source from dividends, interest, royalties, compensation, or other form of income, where evidence of withholding and of the amount withheld cannot be secured from those who have made the payments, the district director may, in his discretion, accept secondary evidence of such withholding and of the amount of the tax so withheld, having due regard to the taxpayer's books of account and to the rates of taxation prevailing in the particular foreign country during the period involved.

(c) In the case of a credit sought for a tax accrued but not paid, the district director may, as a condition precedent to the allowance of a credit, require a bond from the taxpayer, in addition to Form 1116 or 1118. If such a bond is required, Form 1117 shall be used by an individual or by a corporation. It shall be in such sum as the Commissioner may prescribe, and shall be conditioned for the payment by the taxpayer of any amount of tax found due upon any redetermination of the tax made necessary by such credit proving incorrect, with such further conditions as the district director may require. This bond shall be executed by the taxpayer, or the agent or representative of the taxpayer, as principal, and by sureties satisfactory to and approved by the Commissioner. See also 6 U.S.C. 15. [Reg. §1.905-2.]

☐ [*T.D. 6275, 12-2-57. Amended by T.D. 6789, 12-30-64; T.D. 7292, 11-30-74; T.D. 7456, 1-3-77; T.D. 8210, 6-22-88; T.D. 8412, 5-13-92, T.D. 8759, 1-26-98 and T.D. 9882, 12-16-2019.*]

§1.905-3. Adjustments to U.S. tax liability and to current earnings and profits as a result of a foreign tax redetermination.—(a) *Foreign tax redetermination.*—For purposes of this section and §1.905-4, the term *foreign tax redetermination* means a change in the liability for foreign income taxes (as defined in §1.901-2(a) or certain other changes described in this paragraph (a) that may affect a taxpayer's U.S. tax liability, including by reason of a change in the amount of its foreign tax credit, a change to claim a foreign tax credit for foreign income taxes that it previously deducted, a change to claim a deduction for foreign income taxes that it previously credited, a change in the amount of its distributions or inclusions under sections 951, 951(A), or 1293, a change in the application of the high-tax exception described in section 954(b)(4) (including for purposes of determining amounts excluded from gross tested income under section 951A(c)(2)(A)(i)(III) and §1.951A-2(c)(1)(iii)), or a change in the amount of tax determined under sections 1291(c)(2) and 1291(g)(1)(C)(ii). In the case of a taxpayer that claims the credit in the year the taxes are paid, a foreign tax redetermination occurs if any portion of the tax paid is subsequently refunded, or if the taxpayer's liability is subsequently determined to be less than the amount paid and claimed as a credit. In the case of a taxpayer that claims the credit in the year the taxes accrue, a foreign tax redetermination occurs if taxes that when paid or later adjusted differ from amounts accrued by the taxpayer and claimed as a credit or added to PTEP group taxes (as defined in §1.960-3(d)(1)). A foreign tax redetermination includes corrections and other adjustments to accrued amounts to reflect the final foreign tax liability, including additional payments of tax that accrue after the close of the taxable year to which the tax relates and, for foreign income taxes taken into account when accrued but translated into dollars on the date of payment, a payment of accrued tax if the value of the foreign currency relative to the dollar has changed between the date or taxable year of accrual and the date of payment. A foreign tax redetermination occurs if any tax claimed as a credit or added to PTEP group taxes is refunded in whole or in part, regardless of whether such tax was paid within the meaning of §1.901-2(e) at the time the tax was claimed as a credit or added to PTEP group taxes. A foreign tax redetermination also includes accrued foreign income taxes that are not paid on or before the date that is 24 months after the close of the taxable year of the section 901 taxpayer (as defined in §1.986(a)-1(a)(1)) to which such taxes relate, as well as a subsequent payment of any such accrued but unpaid taxes. If accrued foreign income taxes are not paid on or before the date that is 24 months after the close of the taxable year to which they relate, the resulting foreign tax redetermination is accounted for as if the unpaid portion of the foreign income taxes were refunded on such date. Foreign income taxes that first accrue after the date 24 months after the close of the taxable year to which such taxes relate may not be claimed as a credit or added to PTEP group taxes until paid. See section 905(b) and §1.461-4(g)(6)(iii)(B), which require the taxpayer to establish the amount of tax that was properly accrued.

(b) *Redetermination of U.S. tax liability.*—(1) *Foreign income taxes other than taxes deemed paid under section 960.*—(i) *In general.*—This paragraph (b)(1) applies to foreign income taxes claimed as a credit under section 901 other than foreign income taxes deemed paid under section 960. If a foreign tax redetermination occurs with respect to foreign income tax claimed as a credit under section 901 (other than a tax deemed paid under section 960), then a redetermination of U.S. tax liability is required for the taxable year in which the tax was claimed as a credit and any year to which unused foreign taxes from such year were carried under section 904(c). In the case of a taxpayer that claims the credit in the year the taxes are paid, the redetermination of U.S. tax liability is made by reducing the tax paid in such year by the amount refunded. In the case of a taxpayer that claims the credit in the year the taxes accrue, the redetermination of U.S. tax liability is made by treating the redetermined amount of foreign tax as the amount of tax that accrued in the year to which the redetermined tax relates. However, a redetermination of U.S. tax liability is not required (and a taxpayer need not notify the IRS) if the foreign income taxes are taken into account when accrued but translated into dollars on the date of payment, the difference between the dollar value of the accrued foreign income tax and the dollar value of the foreign income tax paid is solely attributable to fluctuations in the value of the foreign currency relative to the dollar between the date or taxable year of accrual and the date of payment, and the net dollar amount of the currency fluctuations attributable to the foreign tax redeterminations with respect to each and every foreign country is less than the lesser of $10,000 or two percent of the total dollar amount of the foreign income tax initially accrued with respect to that foreign country for the taxable year. In such case, if no redetermination of U.S. tax liability is made, an appropriate adjustment is made to the taxpayer's U.S. tax liability in the taxable year during which the foreign tax redeterminations occur.

(ii) *Examples.*—The following examples illustrate the application of this paragraph (b)(1) and § 1.986(a)-1. In all examples, assume that USC is a domestic corporation that uses the calendar year as its taxable year both for Federal income tax purposes and for foreign tax purposes and that it is doing business through a foreign branch operating in Country X, which is a qualified business unit (within the meaning of section 989 and § 1.989(a)-1) (QBU) the functional currency of which is the "u." Except as otherwise provided, the "u" is not an inflationary currency within the meaning of § 1.986(a)-1(a)(2)(iii). USC is an accrual basis taxpayer.

(A) *Example 1: Contested tax—(1) Facts.* In Year 1, USC earned 500u of foreign source foreign branch category income through its foreign branch in Country X and accrued and paid 50u of Country X foreign income tax on its earnings. The average exchange rate for Year 1 used to translate the foreign income taxes into dollars was $1x:1u. *See* § 1.986(a)-1(a)(1). On its Year 1 income tax return, USC claimed a foreign tax credit under section 901 of $50x (50u translated at the average exchange rate for Year 1, that is, $1x:1u). In Year 4, Country X assessed an additional 20u of tax with respect to USC's Year 1 earnings. USC did not pay or accrue the additional 20u of tax and contested the assessment. After exhausting all effective and practical remedies to reduce, over time, its liability for foreign tax, USC settled the contest with Country X in Year 6, paying 10u of additional tax on September 1, Year 6, when the spot rate was $1.10x:1u.

(2) *Analysis.* USC's payment in Year 6 of the 10u of additional tax accrued with respect to Year 1 is a foreign tax redetermination under paragraph (a) of this section. Under paragraph (b)(1)(i) of this section, the additional tax is taken into account in Year 1, the year to which the redetermined tax relates, irrespective of when the tax is paid. Under § 1.986(a)-1(a)(2)(i), because the tax was paid more than 24 months after the close of the year to which the redetermined tax relates, the 10u of tax is translated into dollars at the spot rate on the date of payment in Year 6 (10u at $1.10x:1u = $11x). If USC timely notifies the IRS, it may claim an increased foreign tax credit for Year 1. USC must also make corresponding adjustments in determining its taxable income and net unrecognized section 987 gain or loss in Year 1. See § § 1.987-3(c)(2)(v) and 1.987-4(d)(7).

(B) *Example 2: Refund of tax improperly claimed as a credit—(1) Facts.* USC holds a note issued by FC, an unrelated foreign corporation in Country Y. In Year 1, FC owed USC 500u of interest on the loan. The statutory rate of withholding on interest paid to a nonresident of Country Y is 20%. On December 1, Year 1, when the spot rate was $1x:1u, FC withheld and remitted to Country Y 100u of tax and paid 400u to USC. Effective for Year 1, USC elected under § 1.986(a)-1(a)(2)(iv) to translate its taxes denominated in nonfunctional currency into dollars at the spot rate on the date the taxes are paid. Under the United States – Country Y Income Tax Treaty (Treaty), USC was entitled to a reduced 15% rate of withholding that would result in a withholding tax of 75u. However, USC improperly claimed a foreign tax credit under section 901 for 100u = $100x on its Year 1 Federal income tax return. (See § 1.901-2(e)(2)(i) and (e)(5), providing that an amount is not tax paid to the extent it exceeds the taxpayer's liability for tax or is reasonably certain to be refunded.) In Year 4, USC filed a refund claim with Country Y for 25u, the difference between the amount actually withheld at the 20% statutory rate of tax and the amount owed by USC at the 15% Treaty rate. On March 15, Year 6, when the spot rate was $1.10x:1u, USC received a refund from Country Y of 25u. USC converted the 25u into dollars on the same day.

(2) *Analysis.* Notwithstanding that the 25u of refundable tax did not constitute an amount of tax paid within the meaning of § 1.901-2(e) at the time USC improperly claimed it as a credit, the 25u refund in Year 6 is a foreign tax redetermination under paragraph (a) of this section. Under paragraph (b)(1)(i) of this section, USC must redetermine its U.S. tax liability for Year 1, the taxable year to which the redetermined tax relates. Under § 1.986(a)-1(c), the refund is translated at the exchange rate that was used to translate such amount when originally claimed as a credit. Accordingly, if not previously adjusted by USC or the Internal Revenue Service, USC must file an amended return for Year 1, reducing the amount of foreign tax credit claimed for Year 1 by $25x (25u translated at the spot rate on December 1, Year 1; that is, $1x:1u). Under § 1.986(a)-1(e)(1), USC's basis in the 25u is the same dollar value of the refund as determined under § 1.986(a)-1(c), or $25x. When USC converted the 25u to $27.50x (translated at the spot rate on March 15, Year 6, that is, $1.10x:1u), it realized an exchange gain (within the meaning of § 1.988-1(e)) equal to $2.50x ($27.50x – $25x basis)

(C) *Example 3: Change in functional currency—(1) Facts.* In Year 1, USC earned 500u of foreign source foreign branch category income through its foreign branch in Country X and accrued 100u of Country X foreign income tax on its earnings. The average exchange rate for Year 1 used to translate the foreign income taxes into dollars was $1x:1u. *See* § 1.986(a)-1(a)(1). On its Federal income tax return for Year 1, USC claimed a foreign tax credit under section 901 of $100x (100u translated at the average exchange rate for Year 1, that is, $1x:1u). As of Year 2, the foreign branch changed its functional currency from the "u" to the dollar, and pursuant to § 1.985-5(d)(2), USC's foreign branch terminated and USC recognized section 987 gain or loss on December 31, Year 1 (the date of change). The rate of exchange, as determined under § 1.985-5(c), used to calculate the U.S. dollar basis in the foreign branch's property on the date of the change was $1.10x:1u, the spot rate on December 31, Year 1. On June 15, Year 3, when the spot rate was $1.30x:1u, USC's foreign branch received a refund from Country X of 10u. The foreign branch converted the 10u into $13x on the same day.

(2) *Analysis.* The 10u refund in Year 3 is a foreign tax redetermination under paragraph (a) of this section. Under paragraph (b)(1)(i) of this section, USC must redetermine its U.S. tax liability for Year 1, the taxable year to which the redetermined tax relates. Under § 1.986(a)-1(c), the refund is translated at the exchange rate that was used to translate such amount when originally claimed as a credit. Accordingly, USC must file an amended return, reducing the amount of foreign tax credit claimed for Year 1 by $10x (10u translated at the average exchange rate for Year 1, that is $1x:1u). USC must also make corresponding adjustments in determining its taxable income and net unrecognized section 987 gain or loss in Year 1. See § § 1.987-3(c)(2)(v) and 1.987-4(d)(8). Because the foreign branch changed its functional currency to the dollar in Year 2, the 10u it receives is a refund of nonfunctional currency tax that is denominated in a currency that was the functional currency of the foreign branch at the time USC originally claimed a credit for that foreign income tax. Under § § 1.985-5(d)(2) and 1.987-4(d), in Year 1 USC must recognize an additional $1x of section 987 gain (or $1x less of section 987 loss) by reason of the 10u being treated as an asset of the foreign branch at the time of the foreign branch's termination. Under § 1.986(a)-1(e)(2), USC's basis in the 10u refund is $11x, which is determined by using the exchange rate used under § 1.985-5(c) when the foreign branch changed its functional currency in Year 2 ($1.10x:1u). When the foreign branch converted the 10u to $13x (translated at the spot rate on June 15, Year 3, which is $1.30x:1u), it realized an exchange gain (within the meaning of § 1.988-1(e)) equal to $2x ($13x – $11x (10u translated at $1.10x:1u)).

(D) *Example 4: Inflationary currency—(1) Facts.* In Year 1, USC earned 500u of foreign source foreign branch category income through its foreign branch in Country X and accrued 100u of Country X foreign income tax on its earnings. The average exchange rate for Year 1 used to translate the foreign income taxes into dollars was $1x:1u. *See* § 1.986(a)-1(a)(1). On its Federal income tax return for Year 1, USC claimed a foreign tax credit under section 901 of $100x (100u translated at the average exchange rate for Year 1, that is, $1x:1u). USC paid the 100u of tax on April 15, Year 3, when the spot rate was $1x:2u. In Year 3, but not in Year 1, the u was an inflationary currency within the meaning of § 1.986(a)-1(a)(2)(iii).

(2) *Analysis.* Under § 1.986(a)-1(a)(2)(iii), because the u was an inflationary currency in the year the taxes were paid, USC must translate the 100u of Year 1 tax into dollars using the spot rate on the date of payment of the foreign taxes. Under paragraph (a) of this section, because the translated value of USC's Year 1 taxes when paid, that is, $50x (100u translated at the spot rate on April 15, Year 3, that is, $1x:2u), differs from the amount claimed as credits, that is, $100x (100u translated at the average exchange rate for Year 1, that is, $1x:1u), a foreign tax redetermination has occurred. Under paragraph (b)(1)(i) of this section, because the $50x foreign tax redetermination resulting from the currency fluctuation exceeds 2% of the $100x initially accrued, USC must redetermine its U.S. tax liability for Year 1, the taxable year to which the redetermined tax relates. Accordingly, USC must notify the IRS, reducing the amount of foreign tax credit claimed for Year 1 by $50x (the excess of the translated value of

the Year 1 taxes when accrued, that is, $100x, over the translated value of the Year 1 taxes when paid, that is, $50x).

(E) *Example 5: Two-year rule*—(1) *Facts.* In Year 1, USC earned 500u of foreign source foreign branch category income through its foreign branch in Country X and accrued 100u of Country X foreign income tax on its earnings. The average exchange rate used to translate the foreign income taxes into dollars for Year 1 was $1x:1u. See § 1.986(a)-1(a)(1). On its Federal income tax return for Year 1, USC claimed a foreign tax credit under section 901 of $100x (100u translated at the average exchange rate for Year 1, that is, $1x:1u). USC did not pay the Year 1 foreign income taxes until March 15, Year 6, when the spot rate was $0.8x:1u.

(2) *Analysis*—(i) *Result in Year 3.* USC's failure to pay the tax by the end of Year 3 results in a foreign tax redetermination under paragraph (a) of this section. Because the taxes were not paid on or before the date 24 months after the close of the taxable year to which the tax relates, USC must account for the redetermination as if the unpaid 100u of accrued taxes were refunded on the last day of Year 3. Under paragraph (b)(1)(i) of this section, USC must redetermine its U.S. tax liability for Year 1, the taxable year to which the redetermined tax relates. Under § 1.986(a)-1(c), the deemed refund is translated at the exchange rate that was used to translate such amount when originally claimed as a credit. Accordingly, USC must notify the IRS, reducing the amount of foreign tax credit claimed for Year 1 by $100x (100u translated at the average exchange rate for Year 1, that is, $1x:1u). USC must also make corresponding adjustments in determining its taxable income and net unrecognized section 987 gain or loss in Year 1. See § § 1.987-3(c)(2)(v) and 1.987-4(d)(8).

(*ii*) *Result in Year 6.* USC's payment of the Year 1 tax liability of 100u on March 15, Year 6, results in a second foreign tax redetermination under paragraph (a) of this section. Under paragraph (b)(1)(i) of this section, the additional tax is taken into account in Year 1, the year to which the redetermined tax relates, irrespective of when the tax is paid. Under § 1.986(a)-1(a)(2)(i), because the tax was paid more than 24 months after the close of the year to which the tax relates, USC must translate the 100u of tax at the spot rate on the date of payment of the foreign taxes in Year 6. If USC timely notifies the IRS, it may claim an increased foreign tax credit for Year 1. USC must also make corresponding adjustments in determining its taxable income and net unrecognized section 987 gain or loss in Year 1. See § § 1.987-3(c)(2)(v) and 1.987-4(d)(7).

(F) *Example 6: Cash basis taxpayer that pays additional foreign tax*—(1) *Facts.* Individual A, a U.S. citizen resident in Country X, is a cash basis taxpayer who has not made an election under section 905(a) to claim the foreign tax credit in the year the taxes accrue. A uses the calendar year as the taxable year for both U.S. and Country X tax purposes. In Year 2, A pays 100u of foreign income taxes to Country X with respect to Year 1. The exchange rate used to translate the foreign income taxes into dollars was $1x:1u, the spot rate on the date A paid the taxes in Year 2. *See* section 986(a)(2)(A) and § 1.986(a)-1(b). On A's Year 2 Federal income tax return, A claims a foreign tax credit under section 901 of $100x. In Year 4, Country X assesses an additional 20u of tax with respect to A's Year 1 income. A does not pay the additional 20u of tax and contests the assessment. After exhausting all effective and practical remedies to reduce, over time, A's liability for foreign tax, A settles the contest with Country X in Year 6, paying 10u of additional tax on September 1, Year 6, when the spot rate is $1.10x:1u.

(2) *Analysis.* Because A is a cash basis taxpayer that claims the foreign tax credit in the year the taxes are paid, A's payment in Year 6 of 10u of additional tax owed with respect to Year 1 is not a foreign tax redetermination requiring a redetermination of U.S. tax liability under paragraph (b)(1) of this section. Rather, A is eligible to claim the additional tax as a credit in Year 6, the year in which the tax is paid. Under § 1.986(a)-1(b), the 10u of tax is translated into dollars at the spot rate on the date of payment in Year 6 (10u at $1.10x:1u = $11x).

(G) *Example 7: Cash basis taxpayer that receives a refund of foreign tax*—(1) *Facts.* The facts are the same as paragraph (b)(1)(ii)(F) of this section (the facts in *Example 6*) except that instead of being assessed additional tax in Year 4, A receives a refund in Year 4 of 10u with respect to A's Year 1 tax that was claimed as a credit in Year 2.

(2) *Analysis.* Under paragraphs (a) and (b)(1) of this section, A must redetermine its U.S. tax liability for Year 2 and any year to which unused foreign taxes were carried from Year 2. Under § 1.986(a)-1(c), the amount of A's foreign tax credit for Year 2 is reduced by $10x, the 10u refund translated at the exchange rate used to translate the tax when claimed as a credit. Under § 1.986(a)-1(e)(1), A's basis in the 10u is $10x.

(2) *Foreign income taxes paid or accrued by foreign corporations.*—(i) *In general.*—A redetermination of U.S. tax liability is required to account for the effect of a redetermination of foreign income taxes taken into account by a foreign corporation in the year accrued, or a refund of foreign income taxes taken into account by the foreign corporation in the year paid.

(ii) *Required adjustments.*—If a redetermination of U.S. tax liability is required for any taxable year under paragraph (b)(2)(i) of this section, the foreign corporation's taxable income, earnings and profits, and current year taxes (as defined in § 1.960-1(b)(4)) must be adjusted in the year to which the redetermined tax relates (or, in the case of a foreign corporation that receives a refund of foreign income tax and uses the cash basis of accounting, in the year the tax was paid). The redetermination of U.S. tax liability is made by treating the redetermined amount of foreign tax as the amount of tax paid or accrued by the foreign corporation in such year. For example, in the case of a refund of foreign income taxes taken into account in the year accrued, the foreign corporation's subpart F income, tested income, and current earnings and profits are increased, as appropriate, in the year to which the foreign tax relates to reflect the functional currency amount of the foreign income tax refund. The required redetermination of U.S. tax liability must account for the effect of the foreign tax redetermination on the characterization and amount of distributions or inclusions under section 951, 951A, or 1293 taken into account by each of the foreign corporation's United States shareholders, on the application of the high-tax exception described in section 954(b)(4) (including for purposes of determining the exclusions from gross tested income under section 951A(c)(2)(A)(i)(III) and § 1.951A-2(c)(1)(iii)), and the amount of tax determined under sections 1291(c)(2) and 1291(g)(1)(C)(ii), as well as on the amount of foreign taxes deemed paid under section 960 in such year, regardless of whether any such shareholder chooses to deduct or credit its foreign income taxes in any taxable year. In addition, a redetermination of U.S. tax liability is required for any subsequent taxable year in which the characterization or amount of a United States shareholder's distribution or inclusion from the foreign corporation is affected by the foreign tax redetermination, up to and including the taxable year in which the foreign tax redetermination occurs, as well as any year to which unused foreign taxes from such year were carried under section 904(c).

(iii) *Reduction of corporate level tax on distribution of earnings and profits.*—If a United States shareholder of a controlled foreign corporation receives a distribution out of previously taxed earnings and profits described in section 959(c)(1) and (2) and a foreign country has imposed tax on the income of the controlled foreign corporation, which tax is reduced on distribution of the earnings and profits of the corporation (resulting in a foreign tax redetermination), then the United States shareholder must redetermine its U.S. tax liability for the year or years affected. See also § 1.904-4(c)(7)(i).

(iv) *Foreign tax redeterminations relating to taxable years beginning before January 1, 2018.*—In the case of a foreign tax redetermination of a foreign corporation that relates to a taxable year of the foreign corporation beginning before January 1, 2018, a redetermination of U.S. tax liability is required under the rules of § 1.905-5.

(v) *Examples.*—The following examples illustrate the application of this paragraph (b)(2).

(A) *Presumed Facts.*—Except as otherwise provided in this paragraph (b)(2)(v), the following facts are assumed for purposes of the examples in paragraphs (b)(2)(v)(B) through (E) of this section:

(*1*) All parties are accrual basis taxpayers that use the calendar year as their taxable year both for Federal income tax purposes and for foreign tax purposes and use the average exchange rate to translate accrued foreign income taxes;

(*2*) CFC, CFC1, and CFC2 are controlled foreign corporations organized in Country X that use the "u" as their functional currency;

(*3*) No income adjustment is required to reflect exchange gain or loss (within the meaning of § 1.988-1(e)) with respect to the disposition of nonfunctional currency attributable to a refund of foreign income taxes received by any CFC, because all foreign income taxes are denominated and paid in the CFC's functional currency;

(*4*) The highest rate of U.S. tax in section 11 and the rate applicable to USP in all years is 21 percent;

(5) No election to exclude high-taxed income under section 954(b)(4) or § 1.951A-2(c)(7) is made with respect to CFC, CFC1, or CFC2; and

(6) USP's foreign tax credit limitation under section 904(a) exceeds the amount of foreign income taxes it is deemed to pay.

(B) *Example 1: Refund of tested foreign income taxes.*—(1) *Facts.* CFC is a wholly-owned subsidiary of USP, a domestic corporation. In Year 1, CFC earns 3,660u of general category gross tested income and accrues and pays 300u of foreign income taxes with respect to that income. CFC has no allowable deductions other than the foreign income tax expense. Accordingly, CFC has tested income of 3,360u in Year 1. CFC has no qualified business asset investment (within the meaning of section 951A(d) and § 1.951A-3(b)). In Year 1, no portion of USP's deduction under section 250 ("section 250 deduction") is reduced by reason of section 250(a)(2)(B)(ii). USP's inclusion percentage (as defined in § 1.960-2(c)(2)) is 100%. In Year 1, USP earns no other income and has no other expenses. The average exchange rate used to translate USP's inclusion under section 951A and CFC's foreign income taxes into dollars for Year 1 is $1x:1u. See section 989(b)(3) and §§ 1.951A-1(d)(1) and 1.986(a)-1(a)(1). Accordingly, for Year 1, USP's tested foreign income taxes (as defined in § 1.960-2(c)(3)) with respect to CFC are $300x. In Year 3, CFC carries back a loss for foreign tax purposes and receives a refund of foreign tax of 100u that relates to Year 1.

(2) *Analysis*—(i) *Result in Year 1.* In Year 1, CFC has tested income of 3,360u and tested foreign income taxes of $300x. Under section 951A(a) and § 1.951A-1(c)(1), USP has a GILTI inclusion amount of $3,360x (3,360u translated at $1x:1u). Under section 960(d) and § 1.960-2(c), USP is deemed to have paid $240x (80% x 100% x $300x) of foreign income taxes. Under section 78 and § 1.78-1(a), USP is treated as receiving a dividend of $300x (a "section 78 dividend"). USP's section 250 deduction is $1,830x (50% x ($3,360x + $300x)). Accordingly, for Year 1, USP has taxable income of $1,830x ($3,360x + $300x – $1,830x) and pre-credit U.S. tax liability of $384.30x (21% x $1,830x). Accordingly, USP pays U.S. tax of $144.30x ($384.30x – $240x).

(ii) *Result in Year 3.* The refund of 100u to CFC in Year 3 is a foreign tax redetermination under paragraph (a) of this section. Under paragraph (b)(2)(ii) of this section, USP must account for the effect of the foreign tax redetermination on its GILTI inclusion amount and foreign taxes deemed paid in Year 1. In redetermining USP's U.S. tax liability for Year 1, USP must increase CFC's tested income and its earnings and profits in Year 1 by the refunded tax amount of 100u, must determine the effect of that increase on its GILTI inclusion amount, and must adjust the amount of foreign taxes deemed paid and the section 78 dividend to account for CFC's refund of foreign tax. Under § 1.986(a)-1(c), the refund is translated into dollars at the exchange rate that was used to translate such amount when initially accrued. As a result of the foreign tax redetermination, for Year 1, CFC has tested income of 3,460u (3,360u + 100u) and tested foreign income taxes of $200x ($300x – $100x). Under section 951A(a) and § 1.951A-1(c)(1), USP has a redetermined GILTI inclusion amount of $3,460x (3,460u translated at $1x:1u). Under section 960(d) and § 1.960-2(c), USP is deemed to have paid $160x (80% x 100% x $200x) of foreign income taxes. Under section 78 and § 1.78-1(a), USP's section 78 dividend is $200x. USP's redetermined section 250 deduction is $1,830x (50% x ($3,460x + $200x)). Accordingly, USP's redetermined taxable income is $1,830x ($3,460x + $200x – $1,830x) and its pre-credit U.S. tax liability is $384.30x (21% x $1,830x). Therefore, USP's redetermined U.S. tax liability is $224.3x ($384.30x – $160x), an increase of $80x ($224.30x – $144.30x).

(C) *Example 2: Additional payment of foreign income taxes.*—(1) *Facts.* CFC is a wholly-owned subsidiary of USP, a domestic corporation. In Year 1, CFC earns 1,000u of general category gross foreign base company sales income and accrues and pays 100u of foreign income taxes with respect to that income. CFC has no allowable deductions other than the foreign income tax expense. The average exchange rate used to translate USP's subpart F inclusion and CFC's foreign income taxes into dollars for Year 1 is $1x:1u. See section 989(b)(3) and § 1.986(a)-1(a)(1). In Year 1, USP earns no other income and has no other expenses. In Year 5, pursuant to a Country X audit CFC accrues and pays additional foreign income tax of 80u with respect to its 1,000u of general category foreign base company sales income earned in Year 1. The spot rate (as defined in § 1.988-1(d)) on the date of payment of the tax in Year 5 is $1x:0.8u. The foreign income taxes accrued and paid in Year 1 and Year 5 are properly attributable to CFC's foreign base company sales income that is included in income by USP under section 951(a)(1)(A) ("subpart F inclusion") in Year 1 with respect to CFC.

(2) *Analysis*—(i) *Result in Year 1.* In Year 1, CFC has subpart F income of 900u (1,000u – 100u). Accordingly, USP has a $900x (900u translated at $1x:1u) subpart F inclusion. Under section 960(a) and § 1.960-2(b), USP is deemed to have paid $100x (100u translated at $1x:1u) of foreign income taxes. Under section 78 and § 1.78-1(a), USP's section 78 dividend is $100x. Accordingly, for Year 1, USP has taxable income of $1,000x ($900x + $100x) and pre-credit U.S. tax liability of $210x (21% x $1,000x). Accordingly, USP's U.S. tax liability is $110x ($210x – $100x).

(ii) *Result in Year 5.* CFC's payment of 80u of additional foreign income tax in Year 5 with respect to Year 1 is a foreign tax redetermination as defined in paragraph (a) of this section. Under paragraph (b)(2)(ii) of this section, USP must reduce CFC's subpart F income and its earnings and profits in Year 1 by the additional tax amount of 80u. Further, USP must reduce its subpart F inclusion, adjust the amount of foreign taxes deemed paid, and adjust the amount of the section 78 dividend to account for CFC's additional payment of foreign tax. Under section 986(a)(1)(B)(i) and § 1.986(a)-1(a)(2)(i), because CFC's payment of additional tax occurs more than 24 months after the close of the taxable year to which it relates, the additional tax is translated into dollars at the spot rate on the date of payment ($1x:0.8u). Therefore, CFC has foreign income taxes of $200x (100u translated at $1x:1u plus 80u translated at $1x:0.8u) that are properly attributable to CFC's foreign base company sales income that gives rise to USP's subpart F inclusion in Year 1. As a result of the foreign tax redetermination, for Year 1, USP has a subpart F inclusion of $820x (1,000u – 180u = 820u translated at $1x:1u). Under section 960(a) and § 1.960-2(b), USP is deemed to have paid $200x of foreign income taxes. Under section 78 and § 1.78-1(a), USP's section 78 dividend is $200x. USP's redetermined U.S. taxable income is $1,020x ($820x + $200x) and its pre-credit U.S. tax liability is $214.20x (21% x $1,020x). Therefore, USP's redetermined U.S. tax liability is $14.20x ($214.20x – $200x), a decrease of $95.80x ($110x – $14.20x). If USP makes a timely refund claim within the period allowed by section 6511, USP will be entitled to a refund of any overpayment resulting from the redetermination of its U.S. tax liability.

(D) *Example 3: Two-year rule.*—(1) *Facts.* CFC is a wholly-owned subsidiary of USP, a domestic corporation. In Year 1, CFC earns 1,000u of general category gross foreign base company sales income and accrues 210u of foreign income taxes with respect to that income. In Year 1, USP earns no other income and has no other expenses. The average exchange rate used to translate USP's subpart F inclusion and CFC's foreign income taxes into dollars for Year 1 is $1x:1u. See sections 989(b)(3) and 986(a)(1)(A) and § 1.986(a)-1(a)(1). CFC does not pay its foreign income taxes for Year 1 until September 1, Year 5, when the spot rate is $0.8x:1u. The foreign income taxes accrued and paid in Year 1 and Year 5, respectively, are properly attributable to CFC's foreign base company sales income that gives rise to USP's subpart F inclusion in Year 1 with respect to CFC.

(2) *Analysis*—(i) *Result in Year 1.* In Year 1, CFC has subpart F income of 790u (1,000u – 210u). Accordingly, USP has a $790x (790u translated at $1x:1u) subpart F inclusion. Under section 960(a) and § 1.960-2(b), USP is deemed to have paid $210x (210u translated at $1x:1u) of foreign income taxes. Under section 78 and § 1.78-1(a), USP's section 78 dividend is $210x. Accordingly, for Year 1, USP has taxable income of $1,000x ($790x + $210x) and pre-credit U.S. tax liability of $210x (21% x $1,000x). Accordingly, USP owes no U.S. tax ($210x – $210x = 0).

(ii) *Result in Year 3.* CFC's failure to pay the tax by the end of Year 3 results in a foreign tax redetermination under paragraph (a) of this section. Because the taxes are not paid on or before the date 24 months after the close of the taxable year to which the tax relates, under paragraph (a) of this section CFC must account for the redetermination as if the unpaid 210u of taxes were refunded on the last day of Year 3. Under paragraph (b)(2)(ii) of this section, USP must increase CFC's subpart F income and its earnings and profits in Year 1 by the unpaid tax amount of 210u. Further, USP must increase its subpart F inclusion, and decrease the amount of foreign taxes deemed paid and the amount of the section 78 dividend to account for the unpaid taxes. As a result of the foreign tax redetermination, for Year 1, USP has a subpart F inclusion of $1,000x (1,000u translated at $1x:1u). Under section 960(a) and § 1.960-2(b), USP is deemed to have paid no foreign income taxes. Under section 78 and § 1.78-1(a), USP has no section 78 dividend. Accordingly, USP's redetermined taxable income is $1,000x and its pre-credit U.S. tax liability is unchanged at $210x (21% x $1,000x). However, USP has no foreign tax credits. Therefore, USP's redetermined U.S. tax liability for Year 1 is $210x, an increase of $210x.

(iii) *Result in Year 5.* CFC's payment of the Year 1 tax liability of 210u on September 1, Year 5, results in a second foreign tax redetermination under paragraph (a) of this section. Under paragraph (b)(2)(ii) of this section, USP must decrease CFC's subpart F income and its earnings and profits in Year 1 by the tax paid amount of 210u. Further, USP must reduce its subpart F inclusion, and adjust the amount of foreign taxes deemed paid and the amount of the section 78 dividend to account for CFC's payment of foreign tax. Under section 986(a)(1)(B)(i) and § 1.986(a)-1(a)(2)(i), because the tax was paid more than 24 months after the close of the year to which the tax relates, CFC must translate the 210u of tax at the spot rate on the date of payment of the foreign taxes in Year 5. Therefore, CFC has foreign income taxes of $168x (210u translated at $0.8x:1u) that are properly attributable to CFC's foreign base company sales income that gives rise to USP's subpart F inclusion in Year 1. As a result of the foreign tax redetermination, for Year 1, USP has a subpart F inclusion of $790x (1,000u – 210u = 790u translated at $1x:1u). Under section 960(a) and § 1.960-2(b), USP is deemed to have paid $168x of foreign income taxes. Under section 78 and § 1.78-1(a), USP's section 78 dividend is $168x. Accordingly, USP's redetermined taxable income is $958x ($790x + $168x), its pre-credit U.S. tax liability is $201.18x (21% x $958x), and its redetermined U.S. tax liability is $33.18 ($201.18x – $168x), a decrease of $176.82x ($210x – $33.18x). If USP makes a timely refund claim within the period allowed by section 6511, USP will be entitled to a refund of any overpayment resulting from the redetermination of its U.S. tax liability.

(E) *Example 4: Contested tax.*—(1) *Facts.* CFC is a wholly-owned subsidiary of USP, a domestic corporation. In Year 1, CFC earns 360u of general category gross tested income and accrues and pays 160u of current year taxes with respect to that income. CFC has no allowable deductions other than the foreign income tax expense. Accordingly, CFC has tested income of 200u in Year 1. CFC has no qualified business asset investment (within the meaning of section 951A(d) and § 1.951A-3(b)). In Year 1, no portion of USP's section 250 deduction is reduced by reason of section 250(a)(2)(B)(ii). USP's inclusion percentage (as defined in § 1.960-2(c)(2)) is 100%. In Year 1, USP earns no other income and has no other expenses. The average exchange rate used to translate USP's section 951A inclusion and CFC's foreign income taxes into dollars for Year 1 is $1x:1u. See section 989(b)(3) and §§ 1.951A-1(d)(1) and 1.986(a)-1(a)(1). Accordingly, for Year 1, CFC's tested foreign income taxes (as defined in § 1.960-2(c)(3) with respect to USP are $160x. In Year 3, Country X assessed an additional 30u of tax with respect to CFC's Year 1 income. CFC did not pay the additional 30u of tax and contested the assessment. After exhausting all effective and practical remedies to reduce, over time, its liability for foreign income tax, CFC settled the contest with Country X in Year 4 for 20u, which CFC did not pay until January 15, Year 5, when the spot rate was $1.1x:1u. CFC did not earn any other income or accrue any other foreign income taxes in Years 2 through 6 and made no distributions to USP. The additional taxes paid in Year 5 are also tested foreign income taxes of CFC with respect to USP.

(2) *Analysis*—(*i*) *Result in Year 1.* In Year 1, CFC has tested income of 200u and tested foreign income taxes of $160x. Under section 951A(a) and § 1.951A-1(c)(1), USP has a GILTI inclusion amount of $200x (200u translated at $1x:1u). Under section 960(d) and § 1.960-2(c), USP is deemed to have paid $128x (80% x 100% x $160x) of foreign income taxes. Under section 78 and § 1.78-1(a), USP's section 78 dividend is $160x. USP's section 250 deduction is $180x (50% x ($200x + $160x)). Accordingly, for Year 1, USP has taxable income of $180x ($200x + $160x – $180x) and a pre-credit U.S. tax liability of $37.80x (21% x $180x). Under section 904(a), because all of USP's income is section 951A category income (see § 1.904-4(g)), USP's foreign tax credit limitation is $37.80x ($37.80x x $180x / $180x), which is less than the $128x of foreign income tax that USP is deemed to have paid. Accordingly, USP owes no U.S. tax ($37.80x – $37.80x = 0).

(*ii*) *Result in Year 5.* CFC's accrual and payment of the additional 20u of foreign income tax with respect to Year 1 is a foreign tax redetermination under paragraph (a) of this section. Under § 1.461-4(g)(6)(iii)(B), the additional taxes accrue when the tax contest is resolved, that is, in Year 4. However, because the taxes, which relate to Year 1, were not paid on or before the date 24 months after close of CFC's taxable year to which the tax relates, that is, Year 1, under section 905(c)(2) and paragraph (a) of this section CFC cannot take these taxes into account when they accrue in Year 4. Instead, the taxes are taken into account when they are paid in Year 5. Under paragraph (b)(2)(ii) of this section, USP must decrease CFC's tested income and its earnings and profits in Year 1 by the additional tax amount of 20u. Further, USP must adjust its GILTI inclusion amount, the amount of foreign taxes deemed paid, and the amount of the section 78 dividend to account for CFC's additional payment of tax. Under section 986(a)(1)(B)(i) and § 1.986(a)-1(a)(2)(i), because CFC's payment of additional tax occurs more than 24 months after the close of the taxable year to which it relates, the additional tax is translated into dollars at the spot rate on the date of payment ($1.1x:1u). Therefore, CFC has tested foreign income taxes of $182x (160u translated at $1x:1u plus 20u translated at $1.1x:1u). As a result of the foreign tax redetermination, for Year 1, CFC has tested income of 180u (200u – 20u). Under section 951A(a) and § 1.951A-1(c)(1), USP has a redetermined GILTI inclusion amount of $180x (180u, translated at $1x:1u). Under section 960(d) and § 1.960-2(c), USP is deemed to have paid $145.60x (80% x 100% x $182x) of foreign income taxes. Under section 78 and § 1.78-1(a), USP's section 78 dividend is $182x. USP's redetermined section 250 deduction is $181x (50% x ($180x + $182x)). Accordingly, USP's redetermined taxable income is $181x ($180x + $182x – $181x), its pre-credit U.S. tax liability is $38.01x (21% x $181x), and its redetermined U.S. tax liability is zero ($38.01x – $38.01x).

(3) *Foreign tax redeterminations of successors or transferees.*—If at the time of a foreign tax redetermination the person with legal liability for the tax (or in the case of a refund, the legal right to such refund) (the "successor") is a different person than the person that had legal liability for the tax in the year to which the redetermined tax relates (the "original taxpayer"), the required redetermination of U.S. tax liability is made as if the foreign tax redetermination occurred in the hands of the original taxpayer. Federal income tax principles apply to determine the tax consequences if the successor remits (or receives a refund of) a tax that in the year to which the redetermined tax relates was the legal liability of, and thus under § 1.901-2(f) is considered paid by, the original taxpayer.

(4) *Change in election to claim a foreign tax credit.*—A redetermination of U.S. tax liability is required to account for the effect of a timely change by the taxpayer to claim a foreign tax credit or a deduction for foreign income taxes paid or accrued in any taxable year as permitted under § 1.901-1(d).

(c) *Foreign income tax imposed on foreign refund.*—If a redetermination of foreign income tax for a taxable year or years results from a refund to the section 901 taxpayer of foreign income taxes paid to a foreign country or possession of the United States and the foreign country or possession imposed foreign income tax on such refund, then, in accordance with section 905(c)(5), the amount of the refund is considered to be reduced by the amount of any foreign income tax described in section 901 imposed by the foreign country or possession of the United States with respect to such refund. In such case, no other credit under section 901, and no deduction under section 164, is allowed for any taxable year with respect to such tax imposed on such refund.

(d) *Applicability dates.*—Except as provided in this paragraph (d), this section applies to foreign tax redeterminations occurring in taxable years ending on or after December 16, 2019, and to foreign tax redeterminations of foreign corporations occurring in taxable years that end with or within a taxable year of a United States shareholder ending on or after December 16, 2019 and that relate to taxable years of foreign corporations beginning after December 31, 2017. The first two sentences of paragraph (a) of this section, and paragraph (b)(4) of this section, apply to foreign tax redeterminations occurring in taxable years beginning on or after December 28, 2021. [Reg. § 1.905-3.]

☐ [*T.D. 9882, 12-16-2019. Amended by T.D. 9922, 11-2-2020 and T.D. 9959, 12-28-2021.*]

§ 1.905-4. Notification of foreign tax redetermination.—(a) *Application of this section.*—The rules of this section apply if, as a result of a foreign tax redetermination (as defined in § 1.905-3(a)), a redetermination of U.S. tax liability is required under section 905(c) and § 1.905-3(b).

(b) *Time and manner of notification.*—(1) *Redetermination of U.S. tax liability.*—(i) *In general.*—Except as provided in paragraphs (b)(1)(v) and (b)(2) through (4) of this section, any taxpayer for which a redetermination of U.S. tax liability is required must notify the Internal Revenue Service (IRS) of the foreign tax redetermination by filing an amended return, Form 1118 (Foreign Tax Credit—Corporations) or Form 1116 (Foreign Tax Credit (Individual, Estate, or Trust)), and the statement described in paragraph (c) of this section for the taxable year with respect to which a redetermination of U.S. tax liability is required. Such notification must be filed within the time prescribed by this paragraph (b) and contain the information described in paragraph (c) of this section. If a foreign tax redetermination requires an individual to redetermine the individual's U.S. tax liability, and if, after taking into account such foreign tax redetermination, the amount of creditable foreign taxes (as defined in section 904(j)(3)(B)) that are paid or accrued by such individual during the taxable year does not exceed the applicable dollar limitation in section 904(j), the individual is not required to file Form 1116 with the amended return for such taxable year if the individual satisfies the requirements of section 904(j).

(ii) *Increase in amount of U.S. tax liability.*—Except as provided in paragraphs (b)(1)(iv) and (v) and (b)(2) through (4) of this section, for each taxable year of the taxpayer with respect to which a redetermination of U.S. tax liability is required by reason of a foreign tax redetermination that increases the amount of U.S. tax liability, for example, by reason of a downward adjustment to the amount of foreign income taxes paid or accrued by the taxpayer or a foreign corporation with respect to which the taxpayer computes an amount of foreign taxes deemed paid, the taxpayer must file a separate notification by the due date (with extensions) of the original return for the taxpayer's taxable year in which the foreign tax redetermination occurs.

(iii) *Decrease in amount of U.S. tax liability.*—Except as provided in paragraphs (b)(1)(iv) and (v) and (b)(2) through (4) of this section, for each taxable year of the taxpayer with respect to which a redetermination of U.S. tax liability is required by reason of a foreign tax redetermination that decreases the amount of U.S. tax liability and results in an overpayment, for example, by reason of an increase in the amount of foreign income taxes paid or accrued by the taxpayer or a foreign corporation with respect to which the taxpayer computes an amount of foreign taxes deemed paid, the taxpayer must file a claim for refund with the IRS within the period provided in section 6511. See section 6511(d)(3)(A) for the special refund period for refunds attributable to an increase in foreign tax credits.

(iv) *Multiple redeterminations of U.S. tax liability for same taxable year.*—The rules of this paragraph (b)(1)(iv) apply except as provided in paragraphs (b)(1)(v) and (b)(2) through (4) of this section. If more than one foreign tax redetermination requires a redetermination of U.S. tax liability for the same affected taxable year of the taxpayer and those foreign tax redeterminations occur within the same taxable year or within two consecutive taxable years of the taxpayer, the taxpayer may file for the affected taxable year one amended return, Form 1118 or Form 1116, and the statement described in paragraph (c) of this section that reflects all such foreign tax redeterminations. If the taxpayer chooses to file one notification for such redeterminations, one or more of such redeterminations would increase the U.S. tax liability, and the net effect of all such redeterminations is to increase the U.S. tax liability for the affected taxable year, the taxpayer must file such notification by the due date (with extensions) of the original return for the taxpayer's taxable year in which the first foreign tax redetermination that would result in an increased U.S. tax liability occurred. If the taxpayer chooses to file one notification for such redeterminations, one or more of such redeterminations would decrease the U.S. tax liability, and the net effect of all such redeterminations is to decrease the total amount of U.S. tax liability for the affected taxable year, the taxpayer must file such notification as provided in paragraph (b)(1)(iii) of this section, within the period provided by section 6511. If a foreign tax redetermination with respect to the taxable year for which a redetermination of U.S. tax liability is required occurs after the date for providing such notification, more than one amended return may be required with respect to that taxable year.

(v) *Amended return required only if there is a change in amount of U.S. tax due.*—If a redetermination of U.S. tax liability is required by reason of a foreign tax redetermination (or multiple foreign tax redeterminations, in the case of redeterminations described in paragraph (b)(1)(iv) of this section), but does not change the amount of U.S. tax due for any taxable year, the taxpayer may, in lieu of applying the applicable rules of paragraphs (b)(1)(i) through (iv) of this section, notify the IRS of such redetermination by attaching a statement to the original return for the taxpayer's taxable year in which the foreign tax redetermination occurs. The statement must be filed by the due date (with extensions) of the original return for the taxpayer's taxable year in which the foreign tax redetermination occurs and contain the information described in § 1.904-2(f). If a redetermination of U.S. tax liability is required by reason of a foreign tax redetermination (either alone, or if the taxpayer chooses to apply paragraph (b)(1)(iv) of this section, in combination with other foreign tax redeterminations, as provided therein) and the redetermination of U.S. tax liability results in a change to the amount of U.S. tax due for a taxable year, but does not change the amount of U.S. tax due for other taxable years, for example, because of a carryback or carryover of an unused foreign tax under section 904(c), the notification requirements for such other taxable years are deemed to be satisfied if the taxpayer complies with the applicable rules of paragraphs (b)(1)(i) through (iv) of this section with respect to each taxable year for which the foreign tax redetermination changes the amount of U.S. tax due.

(2) *Notification with respect to a change in the amount of foreign tax reported to an owner by a pass-through entity.*—(i) *In general.*—If a partnership, trust, or other pass-through entity that reports to its beneficial owners (or to any intermediary on behalf of its beneficial owners), including partners, shareholders, beneficiaries, or similar persons, an amount of creditable foreign tax expenditures, such pass-through entity must notify both the IRS and its owners of any foreign tax redetermination described in § 1.905-3(a) with respect to the foreign tax so reported. For purposes of this paragraph (b)(2), whether or not a redetermination has occurred within the meaning of § 1.905-3(a) is determined as if the pass-through entity were a domestic corporation which had elected to and claimed foreign tax credits in the amount reported for the year to which such foreign taxes relate. The notification required under this paragraph (b)(2) must include the statement described in paragraph (c) of this section along with any information necessary for the owners to redetermine their U.S. tax liability.

(ii) *Partnerships subject to subchapter C of chapter 63 of the Code.*—Except as provided in paragraph (b)(4) of this section, if a redetermination of U.S. tax liability that is required under § 1.905-3(b) by reason of a foreign tax redetermination described in § 1.905-3(a) would require a partnership adjustment as defined in § 301.6241-1(a)(6) of this chapter, the partnership must file an administrative adjustment request under section 6227 and make any adjustments required under section 6227. See § § 301.6227-2 and 301.6227-3 of this chapter for procedures for making adjustments with respect to an administrative adjustment request. An administrative adjustment request required under this paragraph (b)(2)(ii) must be filed by the due date (with extensions) of the original return for the partnership's taxable year in which the foreign tax redetermination occurs, and the restrictions in section 6227(c) do not apply to such filing. However, unless the administrative adjustment request may otherwise be filed after applying the limitations contained in section 6227(c), such a request is limited to adjustments that are required to be made under section 905(c). The requirements of paragraph (b)(2)(i) of this section are deemed to be satisfied with respect to any item taken into account in an administrative adjustment request filed under this paragraph (b)(2)(ii).

(3) *Alternative notification requirements.*—An amended return and Form 1118 (Foreign Tax Credit—Corporations) or Form 1116 (Foreign Tax Credit (Individual, Estate, or Trust)), is not required to notify the IRS of the foreign tax redetermination and redetermination of U.S. tax liability if the taxpayer satisfies alternative notification requirements that may be prescribed by the IRS through forms, instructions, publications, or other guidance.

(4) *Taxpayers under examination within the jurisdiction of the Large Business and International Division.*—(i) *In general.*—The alternative notification requirements of this paragraph (b)(4) apply if all of the conditions described in paragraphs (b)(4)(i)(A) through (E) of this section are satisfied.

(A) A foreign tax redetermination occurs while the taxpayer is under examination within the jurisdiction of the Large Business and International Division.

(B) The foreign tax redetermination results in an adjustment to the amount of foreign income taxes paid or accrued by the taxpayer or a foreign corporation with respect to which the taxpayer computes an amount of foreign income taxes deemed paid.

(C) The foreign tax redetermination requires a redetermination of U.S. tax liability that increases the amount of U.S. tax liability, and accordingly, but for this paragraph (b)(4), the taxpayer would be required to notify the IRS of such foreign tax redetermination under paragraph (b)(1)(ii) of this section (determined without regard to paragraphs (b)(1)(iv) and (v) of this section) or paragraph (b)(2)(ii) of this section. See paragraph (b)(4)(v) of this section regarding foreign tax redeterminations that decrease the amount of U.S. tax liability.

(D) The return for the taxable year for which a redetermination of U.S. tax liability is required is under examination.

(E) The due date specified in paragraph (b)(1)(ii) or (b)(2)(ii) of this section for providing notice of such foreign tax redetermination is not before the later of the opening conference or the hand-delivery or postmark date of the opening letter concerning an examination of the return for the taxable year for which a redetermination of U.S. tax liability is required by reason of such foreign tax redetermination.

(ii) *Notification requirements.*—(A) *Foreign tax redetermination occurring before commencement of the examination.*—If a foreign tax redetermination described in paragraphs (b)(4)(i)(B) and (C) of this section occurs before the later of the opening conference or the hand-delivery or postmark date of the opening letter and if the condition provided in paragraph (b)(4)(i)(E) of this section with respect to such foreign tax redetermination is met, the taxpayer, in lieu of applying the rules of paragraphs (b)(1)(i) and (ii) of this section (requiring the filing of an amended return, Form 1116 or 1118, and the statement described in paragraph (c) of this section) or paragraph (b)(2)(ii) of this section (requiring the filing of an administrative adjustment request), must notify the IRS of such redetermination by providing the statement described in paragraph (b)(4)(iii) of this section to the examiner no later than 120 days after the later of the date of the opening conference of the examination, or the hand-delivery or postmark date of the opening letter concerning the examination.

(B) *Foreign tax redetermination occurring within 180 days after commencement of the examination.*—If a foreign tax redetermination described in paragraphs (b)(4)(i)(B) and (C) of this section occurs on or after the latest of the opening conference or the hand-delivery or postmark date of the opening letter and on or before the date that is 180 days after the later of the opening conference or the hand-delivery or postmark date of the opening letter, the taxpayer, in lieu of applying the rules of paragraph (b)(1)(i) and (ii) of this section or paragraph (b)(2) of this section, must notify the IRS of such redetermination by providing the statement described in paragraph (b)(4)(iii) of this section to the examiner no later than 120 days after the date the foreign tax redetermination occurs.

(C) *Foreign tax redetermination occurring more than 180 days after commencement of the examination.*—If a foreign tax redetermination described in paragraphs (b)(4)(i)(B) and (C) of this section occurs after the date that is 180 days after the later of the opening conference or the hand-delivery or postmark date of the opening letter, the taxpayer must either apply the rules of paragraphs (b)(1)(i) and (ii) of this section or paragraph (b)(2) of this section, or, in lieu of applying paragraphs (b)(1)(i) and (ii) of this section or paragraph (b)(2) of this section, provide the statement described in paragraph (b)(4)(iii) of this section to the examiner within 120 days after the date the foreign tax redetermination occurs. However, the IRS, in its discretion, may either accept such statement or require the taxpayer to comply with the rules of paragraphs (b)(1)(i) and (ii) of this section or paragraph (b)(2) of this section, as applicable.

(iii) *Statement.*—The statement required by paragraphs (b)(4)(ii)(A) and (B) of this section must provide the original amount of foreign income taxes paid or accrued, the revised amount of foreign income taxes paid or accrued, and documentation with respect to the revisions, including exchange rates and dates of accrual or payment, and, if applicable, the information described in paragraph (c)(8) of this section. The statement must include the following declaration signed by a person authorized to sign the return of the taxpayer: "Under penalties of perjury, I declare that I have examined this written statement, and to the best of my knowledge and belief, this written statement is true, correct, and complete."

(iv) *Penalty for failure to file notice of a foreign tax redetermination.*—A taxpayer subject to the rules of this paragraph (b)(4) must satisfy the rules of paragraph (b)(4)(ii) of this section in order not to be subject to the penalty relating to the failure to file notice of a foreign tax redetermination under section 6689 and § 301.6689-1 of this chapter.

(v) *Notification of foreign tax redetermination that decreases U.S. tax liability in an affected year under audit.*—A taxpayer may (but is not required to) notify the IRS as provided in this paragraph (b)(4)(v) if the taxpayer has a foreign tax redetermination that meets the conditions in paragraphs (b)(4)(i)(A), (B), and (D) of this section and results in a decrease in the amount of U.S. tax liability that, but for this paragraph (b)(4), would require the taxpayer to notify the IRS of such foreign tax redetermination under paragraph (b)(1)(iii) or (b)(2)(ii) of this section (determined without regard to paragraphs (b)(1)(iv) and (v) of this section). The notification should be made in the time and manner specified in paragraph (b)(4)(ii) of this section. The IRS, in its discretion, may either accept such alternate notification or require the taxpayer to comply with the rules of paragraphs (b)(1)(i) and (iii) or paragraphs (b)(2) of this section, as applicable.

(5) *Examples.*—The following examples illustrate the application of paragraph (b) of this section.

(i) *Example 1.*—(A) X, a domestic corporation, is an accrual basis taxpayer and uses the calendar year as its U.S. taxable year. X conducts business through a branch in Country M, the currency of which is the m, and also conducts business through a branch in Country N, the currency of which is the n. X uses the average exchange rate to translate foreign income taxes. X is able to claim a credit under section 901 for all foreign income taxes paid or accrued.

(B) In Year 1, X accrued and paid 100m of Country M income taxes with respect to 400m of foreign source foreign branch category income. The average exchange rate for Year 1 was $1:1m. Also in Year 1, X accrued and paid 50n of Country N income taxes with respect to 150n of foreign source foreign branch category income. The average exchange rate for Year 1 was $1:1n. On its Year 1 Federal income tax return, X claimed a foreign tax credit under section 901 of $150 ($100 (100m translated at $1:1m) + $50 (50n translated at $1:1n)) with respect to its foreign source foreign branch category income. See § 1.986(a)-1(a)(1).

(C) In Year 2, X accrued and paid 100n of Country N income taxes with respect to 300n of foreign source foreign branch category income. The average exchange rate for Year 2 was $1.50:1n. On its Year 2 Federal income tax return, X claimed a foreign tax credit under section 901 of $150 (100n translated at $1.5:1n). See § 1.986(a)-1(a)(1).

(D) On June 15, Year 5, when the spot rate was $1.40:1n, X received a refund of 10n from Country N, and, on March 15, Year 6, when the spot rate was $1.20:1m, X was assessed by and paid Country M an additional 20m of tax. Both payments were with respect to X's foreign source foreign branch category income in Year 1. On May 15, Year 6, when the spot rate was $1.45:1n, X received a refund of 5n from Country N with respect to its foreign source foreign branch category income in Year 2.

(E) Both of the refunds and the assessment are foreign tax redeterminations under § 1.905-3(a). Under § 1.905-3(b)(1), X must redetermine its U.S. tax liability for both Year 1 and Year 2. With respect to Year 1, under paragraph (b)(1)(ii) of this section X must notify the IRS of the June 15, Year 5, refund of 10n from Country N that increased X's U.S. tax liability by filing an amended return, Form 1118, and the statement required by paragraph (c) of this section for Year 1 by the due date of the original return (with extensions) for Year 5. The amended return and Form 1118 would reflect the reduced amount of foreign income taxes claimed as a credit under section 901 and the increase in X's U.S. tax liability of $10 (10n refund translated at the average exchange rate for Year 1, or $1:1n (see § 1.986(a)-1(c)). With respect to the March 15, Year 6, additional assessment of 20m by Country M, under paragraph (b)(1)(iii) of this section X must notify the IRS within the time period provided by section 6511, increasing the foreign income taxes available as a credit and reducing X's U.S. tax liability by $24 (20m translated at the spot rate on the date of payment, or $1.20:1m). See sections 986(a)(1)(B)(i) and 986(a)(2)(A) and § 1.986(a)-1(a)(2)(i). X may so notify the IRS by filing a second amended return, Form 1118, and the statement described in paragraph (c) of this section for Year 1, within the time period provided by section 6511. Alternatively, under paragraph (b)(1)(iv) of this section, when X redetermines its U.S. tax liability for Year 1 to take into account the 10n refund from Country N that occurred in Year 5, X may also take into account the 20m additional assessment by Country M that occurred on March 15, Year 6. If X reflects both foreign tax redeterminations on the same amended return, Form 1118, and in the statement described in paragraph (c) of this section for Year 1, the amount of X's foreign income taxes available as a credit would be reduced by $10 (10n refund translated at $1:1n), and increased by $24 (20m additional assessment translated at the spot rate on the date of payment, March 15, Year 6, or $1.20:1m). The foreign income taxes available as a credit therefore would be increased by $14 ($24 (additional assessment) – $10 (refund)). Because the net effect of the foreign tax redeterminations is to increase the amount of foreign taxes paid or accrued and decrease X's U.S. tax liability for Year 1, under paragraph (b)(1)(iv) of this section the Year 1 amended return, Form 1118, and the statement required in paragraph (c) of this section reflecting foreign tax redeterminations in both years must be filed within the period provided by section 6511.

(F) With respect to Year 2, under paragraph (b)(1)(ii) of this section X must notify the IRS by filing an amended return, Form 1118, and the statement required by paragraph (c) of this section for Year 2, in addition to the amended return, Form 1118, and statement that are required by reason of the separate foreign tax redeterminations that affect Year 1. The amended return, Form 1118, and the statement required by paragraph (c) of this section for Year 2 must be filed by the due date (with extensions) of X's original return for Year 6. The amended return and Form 1118 must reflect the reduced amount of foreign income taxes claimed as a credit under section 901 and the increase in X's U.S. tax liability of $7.50 (5n refund translated at the average exchange rate for Year 2, or $1.50:1n).

(ii) *Example 2.*—X, a taxpayer within the jurisdiction of the Large Business and International Division, uses the calendar year as its U.S. taxable year. On November 15, Year 2, X receives a refund of foreign income taxes that constitutes a foreign tax redetermination and necessitates a redetermination of U.S. tax liability for X's Year 1 taxable year. Under paragraph (b)(1)(ii) of this section, X is required to notify the IRS of the foreign tax redetermination that increased its U.S. tax liability by filing an amended return, Form 1118, and the statement described in paragraph (c) of this section for its Year 1 taxable year by October 15, Year 3 (the due date (with extensions) of the original return for X's Year 2 taxable year). On December 15, Year 3, the IRS hand delivers an opening letter concerning the examination of the return for X's Year 1 taxable year, and the opening conference for such examination is scheduled for January 15, Year 4. Because the date for notifying the IRS of the foreign tax redetermination under paragraph (b)(1)(ii) of this section (October 15, Year 3) is before the date of the opening conference concerning the examination of the return for X's Year 1 taxable year (January 15, Year 4), the condition of paragraph (b)(4)(i)(E) of this section is not met, and so paragraph (b)(4)(i) of this section does not apply. Accordingly, X must notify the IRS of the foreign tax redetermination by filing an amended return, Form 1118, and the statement described in paragraph (c) of this section for the Year 1 taxable year by October 15, Year 3.

(6) *Transition rule for certain foreign tax redeterminations.*—In the case of foreign tax redeterminations occurring in taxable years ending on or after December 16, 2019, and before November 12, 2020, and foreign tax redeterminations of foreign corporations occurring in taxable years that end with or within a taxable year of a United States shareholder ending on or after December 16, 2019, and before November 12, 2020, any amended return or other notification that under paragraph (b)(1)(ii), (iv), or (v), or (b)(2)(ii) of this section must be filed by the due date (with extensions) of, or attached to, the original return for the taxpayer's taxable year in which the foreign tax redetermination occurs must instead be filed by the due date (with extensions) of, or attached to, the original return for the taxpayer's first taxable year ending on or after November 12, 2020. For purposes of paragraph (b)(4)(i)(E) of this section, the relevant due date is the due date specified in this paragraph (b)(6).

(c) *Notification contents.*—The statement required by paragraphs (b)(1)(i) through (iv) and (b)(2) of this section must contain information sufficient for the IRS to redetermine U.S. tax liability if such a redetermination is required under section 905(c). The information must be in a form that enables the IRS to verify and compare the original computation of U.S. tax liability, the revised computation resulting from the foreign tax redetermination, and the net changes resulting therefrom. The statement must include the following:

(1) The taxpayer's name, address, identifying number, the taxable year or years of the taxpayer that are affected by the foreign tax redetermination, and, in the case of foreign taxes deemed paid, the name and identifying number, if any, of the foreign corporation;

(2) The date or dates the foreign income taxes were accrued, if applicable; the date or dates the foreign income taxes were paid; the amount of foreign income taxes paid or accrued on each date (in foreign currency) and the exchange rate used to translate each such amount, as provided in § 1.986(a)-1(a) or (b);

(3) Information sufficient to determine any change to the characterization of a distribution, the amount of any inclusion under section 951(a), 951A, or 1293, or the deferred tax amount under section 1291;

(4) Information sufficient to determine any interest due from or owing to the taxpayer, including the amount of any interest paid by the foreign government to the taxpayer and the dates received;

(5) In the case of any foreign income tax that is refunded in whole or in part, the taxpayer must provide the date of each such refund; the amount of such refund (in foreign currency); and the exchange rate that was used to translate such amount when originally claimed as a credit (as provided in § 1.986(a)-1(c)) and the spot rate (as defined in § 1.988-1(d)) for the date the refund was received (for purposes of computing foreign currency gain or loss under section 988);

(6) In the case of any foreign income taxes that are not paid on or before the date that is 24 months after the close of the taxable year to which such taxes relate, the amount of such taxes in foreign currency, and the exchange rate that was used to translate such amount when originally claimed as a credit or added to PTEP group taxes (as defined in § 1.960-3(d)(1));

(7) If a redetermination of U.S. tax liability results in an amount of additional tax due, and the carryback or carryover of an unused foreign income tax under section 904(c) only partially eliminates such amount, the information required in § 1.904-2(f); and

(8) In the case of a pass-through entity, the name, address, and identifying number of each beneficial owner to which foreign taxes were reported for the taxable year or years to which the foreign tax redetermination relates, and the amount of foreign tax initially reported to each beneficial owner for each such year and the amount of foreign tax allocable to each beneficial owner for each such year after the foreign tax redetermination is taken into account.

(d) *Payment or refund of U.S. tax.*—The amount of tax, if any, due upon a redetermination of U.S. tax liability is paid by the taxpayer after notice and demand has been made by the IRS. Subchapter B of chapter 63 of the Internal Revenue Code (relating to deficiency procedures) does not apply with respect to the assessment of the amount due upon such redetermination. In accordance with sections 905(c) and 6501(c)(5), the amount of additional tax due is assessed and collected without regard to the provisions of section 6501(a) (relating to limitations on assessment and collection). The amount of tax, if any, shown by a redetermination of U.S. tax liability to have been overpaid is credited or refunded to the taxpayer in accordance with subchapter B of chapter 66 (sections 6511 through 6515).

(e) *Interest and penalties.*—(1) *In general.*—If a redetermination of U.S. tax liability is required by reason of a foreign tax redetermination, interest is computed on the underpayment or overpayment in accordance with sections 6601 and 6611. No interest is assessed or collected on any underpayment resulting from a refund of foreign income taxes for any period before the receipt of the refund, except to the extent interest was paid by the foreign country or possession of the United States on the refund for the period before the receipt of the refund. See section 905(c)(5). In no case, however, will interest assessed and collected pursuant to the preceding sentence for any period before receipt of the refund exceed the amount that otherwise would have been assessed and collected under section 6601 for that period. Interest is assessed from the time the taxpayer (or the foreign corporation, partnership, trust, or other pass-through entity of which the taxpayer is a shareholder, partner, or beneficiary) receives a refund until the taxpayer pays the additional tax due the United States.

(2) *Imposition of penalty.*—Failure to comply with the provisions of this section subjects the taxpayer to the penalty provisions of section 6689 and § 301.6689-1 of this chapter.

(f) *Applicability date.*—This section applies to foreign tax redeterminations (as defined in § 1.905-3(a)) occurring in taxable years ending on or after December 16, 2019, and to foreign tax redeterminations of foreign corporations occurring in taxable years that end with or within a taxable year of a United States shareholder ending on or after December 16, 2019. [Reg. § 1.905-4.]

☐ [*T.D. 9922, 11-2-2020.*]

§ 1.905-5. Foreign tax redeterminations of foreign corporations that relate to taxable years of the foreign corporation beginning before January 1, 2018.—(a) *In general.*—(1) *Effect of foreign tax redetermination of a foreign corporation.*—Except as provided in paragraph (e) of this section, a foreign tax redetermination (as defined in § 1.905-3(a)) of a foreign corporation that relates to a taxable year of the foreign corporation beginning before January 1, 2018, and that may affect a taxpayer's foreign tax credit in any taxable year, must be accounted for by adjusting the foreign corporation's taxable income and earnings and profits, post-1986 undistributed earnings as defined in § 1.902-1(a)(9), and post-1986 foreign income taxes as defined in § 1.902-1(a)(8) (or its pre-1987 accumulated profits as defined in § 1.902-1(a)(10)(i) and pre-1987 foreign income taxes as defined in § 1.902-1(a)(10)(iii), as applicable) in the taxable year of the foreign corporation to which the foreign taxes relate.

(2) *Required redetermination of U.S. tax liability.*—Except as provided in paragraph (e) of this section, a redetermination of U.S. tax

liability is required to account for the effect of the foreign tax redetermination on the earnings and profits and taxable income of the foreign corporation, the taxable income of a United States shareholder, and the amount of foreign taxes deemed paid by the United States shareholder under section 902 or section 960 (as in effect before December 22, 2017), in the year to which the redetermined foreign taxes relate. For example, in the case of a refund of foreign income taxes, the subpart F income, earnings and profits, and post-1986 undistributed earnings (or pre-1987 accumulated profits, as applicable) of the foreign corporation are increased in the year to which the foreign tax relates to reflect the functional currency amount of the foreign income tax refund. The required redetermination of U.S. tax liability must account for the effect of the foreign tax redetermination on the characterization and amount of distributions or inclusions under section 951 or 1293 taken into account by each of the foreign corporation's United States shareholders and on the application of the high-tax exception described in section 954(b)(4), as well as on the amount of foreign income taxes deemed paid in such year. In addition, a redetermination of U.S. tax liability is required for any subsequent taxable year in which the United States shareholder received or accrued a distribution or inclusion from the foreign corporation, up to and including the taxable year in which the foreign tax redetermination occurs, as well as any year to which unused foreign taxes from such year were carried under section 904(c).

(b) *Notification requirements.*—(1) *In general.*—The notification requirements of § 1.905-4, as modified by paragraphs (b)(2) and (3) of this section, apply if a redetermination of U.S. tax liability is required under paragraph (a) or (e) of this section.

(2) *Notification relating to post-1986 undistributed earnings and post-1986 foreign income taxes.*—In the case of foreign tax redeterminations with respect to taxes included in post-1986 foreign income taxes, in addition to the information required by § 1.905-4(c), the taxpayer must provide the balances of the pools of post-1986 undistributed earnings and post-1986 foreign income taxes before and after adjusting the pools, the dates and amounts of any dividend distributions or other inclusions made out of earnings and profits for the affected year or years, and the amount of earnings and profits from which such dividends were paid or such inclusions were made for the affected year or years.

(3) *Notification relating to pre-1987 accumulated profits and pre-1987 foreign income taxes.*—In the case of foreign tax redeterminations with respect to pre-1987 accumulated profits, in addition to the information required by § 1.905-4(c), the taxpayer must provide the following: the dates and amounts of any dividend distributions made out of earnings and profits for the affected year or years; the rate of exchange on the date of any such distribution; and the amount of earnings and profits from which such dividends were paid for the affected year or years.

(c) *Currency translation rules for adjustments to pre-1987 foreign income taxes.*—Foreign income taxes paid with respect to pre-1987 accumulated profits that are deemed paid under section 960 (or under section 902 in the case of an amount treated as a dividend under section 1248) are translated into dollars at the spot rate for the date of the payment of the foreign income taxes, and refunds of such taxes are translated into dollars at the spot rate for the date of the refund. Foreign income taxes deemed paid by a taxpayer under section 902 with respect to an actual distribution of pre-1987 accumulated profits and refunds of such taxes are translated into dollars at the spot rate for the date of the distribution of the earnings to which the foreign income taxes relate. See section 902(c)(6) (as in effect before December 22, 2017) and § 1.902-1(a)(10)(iii). For purposes of this section, the term *spot rate* has the meaning provided in § 1.988-1(d).

(d) *Timing and effect of pooling adjustments.*—The redetermination of U.S. tax liability required by paragraphs (a) and (e) of this section is made in accordance with section 905(c) as in effect for those taxable years, without regard (except as provided in paragraph (e) of this section) to rules that required adjustments to a foreign corporation's pools of post-1986 undistributed earnings and post-1986 foreign income taxes in the year of the foreign tax redetermination rather than in the year to which the redetermined foreign tax relates. No underpayment or overpayment of U.S. tax liability results from a foreign tax redetermination unless the required adjustments change the U.S. tax liability. Consequently, no interest is paid by or to a taxpayer as a result of adjustments, required by reason of a foreign tax redetermination, to a foreign corporation's pools of post-1986 undistributed earnings and post-1986 foreign income taxes in the year to which the redetermined foreign tax relates (or a subsequent year) that did not result in a change to U.S. tax liability, for example, because no foreign taxes were deemed paid in that year.

(e) *Election to account for certain foreign tax redeterminations with respect to pre-2018 taxable years in the foreign corporation's last pooling year.*—(1) *In general.*—A taxpayer may elect under the rules in paragraph (e)(2) of this section to account for foreign tax redeterminations of a foreign corporation that occur in the foreign corporation's taxable years ending with or within a taxable year of a United States shareholder of the foreign corporation ending on or after November 2, 2020, and that relate to taxable years of the foreign corporation beginning before January 1, 2018, by treating such foreign tax redeterminations as if they occurred in the foreign corporation's last taxable year beginning before January 1, 2018 (the "last pooling year"), and applying the rules in § § 1.905-3T(d) and 1.905-5T for purposes of determining whether the foreign tax redetermination is accounted for in the foreign corporation's last pooling year or must be accounted for in the year to which the redetermined foreign tax relates. Except with respect to determining under the preceding sentence whether the foreign tax redetermination is accounted for in the foreign corporation's last pooling year or in the year to which the redetermined foreign tax relates, the rules of this section apply to foreign tax redeterminations covered by an election under this paragraph (e). Therefore, unless an exception in § 1.905-3T(d)(3) applies, a foreign tax redetermination to which an election under this paragraph (e) applies is accounted for under paragraph (a)(2) of this section by adjusting the foreign corporation's pools of post-1986 undistributed earnings and post-1986 foreign income taxes in the last pooling year, rather than in the year to which the redetermined foreign tax relates. For purposes of this paragraph (e), references to § § 1.905-3T and 1.905-5T are to such provisions as contained in 26 CFR part 1, revised as of April 1, 2019.

(2) *Rules regarding the election.*—(i) *Time and manner of election.*—For a foreign corporation's first taxable year that ends with or within a taxable year of a United States shareholder of the foreign corporation ending on or after November 2, 2020 in which the foreign corporation has a foreign tax redetermination (the "first redetermination year"), the controlling domestic shareholders (as defined in § 1.964-1(c)(5)) of the foreign corporation make the election described in paragraph (e)(1) of this section by—

(A) Filing the statement required under § 1.964-1(c)(3)(ii) with a timely filed original income tax return for the taxable year of each controlling domestic shareholder of the foreign corporation in which or with which the foreign corporation's first redetermination year ends;

(B) Providing any notices required under § 1.964-1(c)(3)(iii);

(C) Filing amended returns as required under § 1.905-4 and this section for each controlling domestic shareholder's taxable year with or within which ends the foreign corporation's last pooling year and each other affected year before the controlling domestic shareholder's taxable year with or within which ends the foreign corporation's first redetermination year reflecting a redetermination of the controlling domestic shareholder's U.S. tax liability for each such taxable year, in cases where a redetermination of the shareholder's U.S. tax liability for taxable years ending before the foreign corporation's last pooling year ends is not required under the rules in § § 1.905-3T(d) and 1.905-5T;

(D) Filing amended returns as required under § 1.905-4 and this section with respect to each affected year before the controlling domestic shareholder's taxable year with or within which ends the foreign corporation's first redetermination year reflecting a redetermination of the controlling domestic shareholder's U.S. tax liability for each such taxable year, in cases where a redetermination of the shareholder's U.S. tax liability for taxable years ending before the foreign corporation's last pooling year ends is required under the rules in § § 1.905-3T(d) and 1.905-5T and this section; and

(E) Providing any additional information required by applicable administrative pronouncements.

(ii) *Scope, duration, and effect of election.*—An election under paragraph (e)(1) of this section with respect to the first redetermination year of a foreign corporation is binding on all persons who are, or were in a prior year to which the election applies, United States shareholders of the foreign corporation. In addition, such election applies to all foreign tax redeterminations in the first redetermination year and all subsequent taxable years of such foreign corporation and cannot be revoked. For foreign tax redeterminations that occur in taxable years after the first redetermination year, all United States shareholders of such foreign corporation must account for the foreign tax redeterminations under the rules in paragraph (e)(1) of this section by filing amended returns and providing other information as required by § 1.905-4 and paragraphs (e)(2)(i)(C) through (E) of this section.

(iii) *Requirements for valid election.*—An election under paragraph (e)(1) of this section is valid only if all of the requirements in paragraph (e)(2)(i) of this section, including the requirement to provide notice under paragraph (e)(2)(i)(B) of this section, are satisfied by each of the controlling domestic shareholders with respect to the first redetermination year.

(iv) *CFC group conformity requirement.*—(A) *In general.*—An election made under paragraph (e)(1) of this section applies to all controlled foreign corporations that are members of the same CFC group, and the rules in paragraphs (e)(1) and (e)(2)(i) through (iii) of this section apply by reference to the CFC group. Therefore, an election by the controlling domestic shareholders of any controlled foreign corporation with respect to that controlled foreign corporation's first redetermination year also applies to foreign tax redeterminations of all members of the CFC group that includes that controlled foreign corporation, determined as of the close of that controlled foreign corporation's first redetermination year. The election is binding on all persons who are, or were in a prior year to which the election applies, United States shareholders of any member of the CFC group, applies with respect to foreign tax redeterminations of each member that occur in and after that member's first taxable year with or within which ends such controlled foreign corporation's first redetermination year, and cannot be revoked.

(B) *Determination of the CFC group.*—*(1) Definition.*—Subject to the rules in paragraphs (b)(2)(iv)(B)(2) and (3) of this section, the term *CFC group* means an affiliated group as defined in section 1504(a) without regard to section 1504(b)(1) through (6), except that section 1504(a) is applied by substituting "more than 50 percent" for "at least 80 percent" each place it appears, and section 1504(a)(2)(A) is applied by substituting "or" for "and." For purposes of this paragraph (e)(2)(iv)(B)(*1*), stock ownership is determined by applying the constructive ownership rules of section 318(a), other than section 318(a)(3)(A) and (B), by applying section 318(a)(4) only to options (as defined in § 1.1504-4(d)) that are reasonably certain to be exercised as described in § 1.1504-4(g), and by substituting in section 318(a)(2)(C) "5 percent" for "50 percent."

(2) Member of a CFC group.—The determination of whether a controlled foreign corporation is included in a CFC group is made as of the close of the first redetermination year of any controlled foreign corporation for which an election is made under paragraph (e)(1) of this section. One or more controlled foreign corporations are members of a CFC group if the requirements of paragraph (e)(2)(iv)(B)(2) of this section are satisfied as of the end of the first redetermination year of at least one of the controlled foreign corporations, even if the requirements are not satisfied as of the end of the first redetermination year of all controlled foreign corporations. If the controlling domestic shareholders do not have the same taxable year, the determination of whether a controlled foreign corporation is a member of a CFC group is made with respect to the first redetermination year that ends with or within the taxable year of the majority of the controlling domestic shareholders (determined based on voting power) or, if no such majority taxable year exists, the calendar year.

(3) Controlled foreign corporations included in only one CFC group.—A controlled foreign corporation cannot be a member of more than one CFC group. If a controlled foreign corporation would be a member of more than one CFC group under paragraph (e)(2)(iv)(B)(2) of this section, then ownership of stock of the controlled foreign corporation is determined by applying paragraph (e)(2)(iv)(B)(2) of this section without regard to section 1504(a)(2)(B) or, if applicable, by reference to the ownership existing as of the end of the first redetermination year of a controlled foreign corporation that would cause a CFC group to exist.

(3) *Rules for successor entities.*—All of the United States persons that own equity interests in a successor entity to a foreign corporation ("U.S. owners") may elect under the principles of paragraph (e)(2) of this section to apply the rules in paragraph (e)(1) to foreign tax redeterminations of such foreign corporation that occur in taxable years of the successor entity that end with or within taxable years of its U.S. owners ending on or after November 2, 2020.

(f) *Applicability date.*—This section applies to foreign tax redeterminations (as defined in § 1.905-3(a)) of foreign corporation and successor entities that occur in taxable years that end with or within taxable years of a United States shareholder or other United States persons ending on or after November 2, 2020, and that relate to taxable years of such foreign corporations beginning before January 1, 2018. [Reg. § 1.905-5.]

☐ [*T.D.* 9922, 11-2-2020.]

§ 1.909-1 Definitions and special rules.—(a) *Definitions.*—For purposes of section 909, this section, and § § 1.909-2 through 1.909-5, the following definitions apply:

(1) The term *section 902 corporation* means any foreign corporation with respect to which one or more domestic corporations meet the ownership requirements of section 902(a) or (b).

(2) The term *section 902 shareholder* means any domestic corporation that meets the ownership requirements of section 902(a) or (b) with respect to a section 902 corporation.

(3) The term *payor* means a person that pays or accrues a foreign income tax within the meaning of § 1.901-2(f), and also includes a person that takes foreign income taxes paid or accrued by a partnership, S corporation, estate or trust into account pursuant to section 702(a)(6), section 901(b)(5) or section 1373(a).

(4) The term *covered person* means, with respect to a payor

(i) Any entity in which the payor holds, directly or indirectly, at least a 10 percent ownership interest (determined by vote or value);

(ii) Any person that holds, directly or indirectly, at least a 10 percent ownership interest (determined by vote or value) in the payor; or

(iii) Any person that bears a relationship that is described in section 267(b) or 707(b) to the payor.

(5) The term *foreign income tax* means any income, war profits, or excess profits tax paid or accrued to any foreign country or to any possession of the United States. A foreign income tax includes any tax paid or accrued in lieu of such a tax within the meaning of section 903.

(6) The term *post-1986 foreign income taxes* has the meaning provided in § 1.902-1(a)(8).

(7) The term *post-1986 undistributed earnings* has the meaning provided in § 1.902-1(a)(9).

(8) The term *disregarded entity* means an entity that is disregarded as an entity separate from its owner, as provided in § 301.7701-2(c)(2)(i) of this chapter.

(9) The term *hybrid partnership* means a partnership that is subject to income tax in a foreign country as a corporation (or otherwise at the entity level) on the basis of residence, place of incorporation, place of management or similar criteria.

(b) *Taxes paid or accrued by a partnership, S corporation or trust.*—Under section 909(c)(1), section 909 applies at the partner level, and similar rules apply in the case of an S corporation or trust. Accordingly, in the case of foreign income taxes paid or accrued by a partnership, S corporation or trust, taxes allocated to one or more partners, shareholders or beneficiaries (as the case may be) will be treated as split taxes to the extent such taxes would be split taxes if the partner, shareholder or beneficiary had paid or accrued the taxes directly on the date such taxes are taken into account by the partner under sections 702 and 706(a), by the shareholder under section 1373(a), or by the beneficiary under section 901(b)(5). Any such split taxes will be suspended in the hands of the partner, shareholder or beneficiary.

(c) *Related income of a partnership, S corporation or trust.*—For purposes of determining whether related income is taken into account by a covered person, related income of a partnership, S corporation or trust is considered to be taken into account by the partner, shareholder or beneficiary to whom the related income is allocated.

(d) *Application of section 909 to pre-1987 accumulated profits and pre-1987 foreign income taxes.*—Section 909 and § § 1.909-1 through 1.909-5 will apply to pre-1987 accumulated profits (as defined in § 1.902-1(a)(10)(i)) and pre-1987 foreign income taxes (as defined in § 1.902-1(a)(10)(iii)) of a section 902 corporation attributable to taxable years beginning on or after January 1, 2012.

(e) *Effective/applicability date.*—This section applies to taxable years ending after February 9, 2015. See 26 CFR 1.909-1T (revised as of April 1, 2014) for rules applicable to taxable years beginning on or after January 1, 2011, and ending on or before February 9, 2015. [Reg. §1.909-1.]

□ [*T.D. 9710, 2-9-2015.*]

§1.909-2. Splitter arrangements.—(a) *Foreign tax credit splitting event.*—(1) *In general.*—There is a foreign tax credit splitting event with respect to foreign income taxes paid or accrued if and only if, in connection with an arrangement described in paragraph (b) of this section (a *splitter arrangement*) the related income was, is or will be taken into account for U.S. Federal income tax purposes by a person that is a covered person with respect to the payor of the tax. Foreign income taxes that are paid or accrued in connection with a splitter arrangement are split taxes to the extent provided in paragraph (b) of this section. Income (or, as appropriate, earnings and profits) that was, is or will be taken into account by a covered person in connection with a splitter arrangement is related income to the extent provided in paragraph (b) of this section.

(2) *Split taxes not taken into account.*—Split taxes will not be taken into account for U.S. Federal income tax purposes before the taxable year in which the related income is taken into account by the payor or, in the case of split taxes paid or accrued by a section 902 corporation, by a section 902 shareholder of such section 902 corporation. Therefore, in the case of split taxes paid or accrued by a section 902 corporation, split taxes will not be taken into account for purposes of sections 902 or 960, or for purposes of determining earnings and profits under section 964(a), before the taxable year in which the related income is taken into account by the payor section 902 corporation, a section 902 shareholder of the section 902 corporation, or a member of the section 902 shareholder's consolidated group. See §1.909-3(a) for rules relating to when split taxes and related income are taken into account.

(b) *Splitter arrangements.*—The arrangements set forth in this paragraph (b) are splitter arrangements.

(1) *Reverse hybrid splitter arrangements.*—(i) *In general.*—A reverse hybrid is a splitter arrangement when a payor pays or accrues foreign income taxes with respect to income of a reverse hybrid. A reverse hybrid splitter arrangement exists even if the reverse hybrid has a loss or a deficit in earnings and profits for a particular year for U.S. Federal income tax purposes (for example, due to a timing difference).

(ii) *Split taxes from a reverse hybrid splitter arrangement.*—The foreign income taxes paid or accrued with respect to income of the reverse hybrid are split taxes.

(iii) *Related income from a reverse hybrid splitter arrangement.*—The related income with respect to split taxes from a reverse hybrid splitter arrangement is the earnings and profits (computed for U.S. Federal income tax purposes) of the reverse hybrid attributable to the activities of the reverse hybrid that gave rise to income included in the payor's foreign tax base with respect to which the split taxes were paid or accrued. Accordingly, related income of the reverse hybrid includes items of income or expense attributable to a disregarded entity owned by the reverse hybrid only to the extent that the income attributable to the activities of the disregarded entity is included in the payor's foreign tax base.

(iv) *Reverse hybrid.*—The term *reverse hybrid* means an entity that is a corporation for U.S. Federal income tax purposes but is a fiscally transparent entity (under the principles of §1.894-1(d)(3)) or a branch under the laws of a foreign country imposing tax on the income of the entity.

(v) *Examples.*—The following examples illustrate the rules of paragraph (b)(1) of this section.

Example 1. (i) *Facts.* USP, a domestic corporation, wholly owns DE, a disregarded entity for U.S. federal income tax purposes that is organized in country A and treated as a corporation for country A tax purposes. DE wholly owns RH, a corporation for U.S. Federal income tax purposes that is organized in country A and treated as a fiscally transparent entity for country A tax purposes. Country A imposes an income tax at the rate of 30% on DE with respect to the items of income earned by RH. Prior to year 1, RH had no income for country A purposes and had no post-1986 earnings and profits for U.S. Federal income tax purposes. In year 1, RH earns 200u of income on which DE pays 60u of country A tax. Pursuant to §1.901-2(f)(4)(ii), USP is treated as legally liable for the 60u of country A taxes paid by DE. DE has no other income. In year 2, RH earns no income and incurs no losses or expenses. At the end of year 2, RH distributes 100u to DE.

(ii) *Result.* (A) *Split taxes and related income.* Pursuant to §1.909-2(b)(1)(iv), RH is a reverse hybrid because it is a corporation for U.S. Federal income tax purposes and a fiscally transparent entity for country A purposes. Pursuant to §1.909-2(b)(1), RH is a covered person with respect to USP because USP wholly owns RH for U.S. Federal income tax purposes. Pursuant to §1.909-2(b)(1)(i), there is a splitter arrangement with respect to RH because USP paid country A tax with respect to the income of RH. All 60u of taxes paid by USP in year 1 with respect to the income of RH are split taxes pursuant to §1.909-2(b)(1)(ii). The post-1986 earnings and profits of RH are 200u as of the end of year 1. Pursuant to §1.909-2(b)(1)(iii), the related income in year 1 is the 200u of RH's earnings and profits that are attributable to the activities that gave rise to the split taxes. No additional split taxes or related income arise in year 2.

(B) *Distribution.* Because DE is a disregarded entity, the 100u distribution by RH at the end of year 2 is treated as a dividend to USP. Pursuant to §1.909-6(d)(7) and §1.909-3(a), 100u of the 200u of related income of RH, or 50%, is taken into account by USP by reason of the 100u dividend. Accordingly, pursuant to §1.909-6(e)(4) and §1.909-3(a), a ratable portion of the split taxes, or 30u of taxes (50% of 60u), is no longer treated as split taxes and is taken into account by USP for U.S. Federal income tax purposes.

Example 2. (i) *Facts.* The facts are the same as in *Example 1*, except that in year 2, RH has a 100u loss for U.S. Federal income tax purposes as well as for country A tax purposes. For country A tax purposes, DE takes the 100u loss into account in year 2 and may not carry back the 100u loss to offset its country A taxable income for year 1. At the end of year 2, RH distributes 100u to DE.

(ii) *Result.* (A) *Split taxes and related income.* The split taxes and related income for year 1 are the same as in *Example 1*. Pursuant to §1.909-2(b)(1)(iii), §1.909-6(d)(1) and §1.909-3(a), the total related income of RH is reduced to 100u (200u − 100u) in year 2 because RH incurred a 100u loss in year 2 attributable to the activities that are included in DE's country A tax base.

(B) *Distribution.* Because DE is a disregarded entity, the 100u distribution by RH at the end of year 2 is treated as a dividend to USP. Pursuant to §1.909-6(d)(7) and §1.909-3(a), 100u of the 100u of related income of RH, or 100%, is taken into account by USP by reason of the 100u dividend. Accordingly, pursuant to §1.909-6(e)(4) and §1.909-3(a), a ratable portion of the split taxes, or 60u of taxes (100% of 60u), is no longer treated as split taxes and is taken into account by USP for U.S. Federal income tax purposes.

(2) *Loss-sharing splitter arrangements.*—(i) *In general.*—A foreign group relief or other loss-sharing regime is a loss-sharing splitter arrangement to the extent that a shared loss of a U.S. combined income group could have been used to offset income of that group in the current or in a prior foreign taxable year (*usable shared loss*) but is used instead to offset income of another U.S. combined income group.

(ii) *U.S. combined income group.*—The term *U.S. combined income group* means an individual or a corporation and all entities (including entities that are fiscally transparent for U.S. Federal income tax purposes under the principles of §1.894-1(d)(3)) that for U.S. Federal income tax purposes combine any of their respective items of income, deduction, gain or loss with the income, deduction, gain or loss of such individual or corporation. A U.S. combined income group can arise, for example, as a result of an entity being disregarded or, in the case of a partnership or hybrid partnership and a partner, as a result of the allocation of income or any other item of the partnership to the partner. For purposes of this paragraph (b)(2)(ii), a branch is treated as an entity, all members of a U.S. affiliated group of corporations (as defined in section 1504) that file a consolidated return are treated as a single corporation, and two or more individuals that file a joint return are treated as a single individual. A U.S. combined income group may consist of a single individual or corporation and no other entities, but cannot include more than one individual or corporation. In addition, an entity may belong to more than one U.S. combined income group. For example, a hybrid partnership with two corporate partners that do not combine any of their items of income, deduction, gain or loss for U.S. Federal income tax purposes is in a separate U.S. combined income group with each of its partners.

(iii) *Income and shared loss of a U.S. combined income group.*—(A) *Income.*—Except as otherwise provided in this paragraph (b)(2)(iii)(A), the income of a U.S. combined income group is the aggregate amount of taxable income recognized or taken into account for foreign tax purposes by those members that have positive taxable income for foreign tax purposes. In the case of an entity that is fiscally transparent (under the principles of § 1.894-1(d)(3)) for foreign tax purposes and that is a member of more than one U.S. combined income group, the foreign taxable income of the entity is allocated between or among the groups under foreign tax law. In the case of an entity that is not fiscally transparent for foreign tax purposes and that is a member of more than one U.S. combined income group, the foreign taxable income of the entity is allocated between or among those groups based on U.S. Federal income tax principles. For example, in the case of a hybrid partnership, the foreign taxable income of the partnership is allocated between or among the groups in the manner the partnership allocates the income under section 704(b). To the extent the foreign taxable income would be income under U.S. Federal income tax principles in another year, the income is allocated between or among the groups based on how the hybrid partnership would allocate the income if the income were recognized for U.S. Federal income tax purposes in the year in which the income is recognized for foreign tax purposes. To the extent the foreign taxable income would not constitute income under U.S. Federal income tax principles in any year, the income is allocated between or among the groups in the same manner as the partnership items attributable to the activity giving rise to the foreign taxable income.

(B) *Shared loss.*—The term *shared loss* means a loss of one entity for foreign tax purposes that, in connection with a foreign group relief or other loss-sharing regime, is taken into account by one or more other entities. Except as otherwise provided in this paragraph (b)(2)(iii)(B), the amount of shared loss of a U.S. combined income group is the sum of the shared losses of all members of the U.S. combined income group. In the case of an entity that is fiscally transparent (under the principles of § 1.894-1(d)(3)) for foreign tax purposes and that is a member of more than one U.S. combined income group, the shared loss of the entity is allocated between or among the groups under foreign tax law. In the case of an entity that is not fiscally transparent for foreign tax purposes and that is a member of more than one U.S. combined income group, the shared loss of the entity will be allocated between or among those groups based on U.S. Federal income tax principles. For example, in the case of a hybrid partnership, the shared loss of the partnership will be allocated between or among the groups in the manner the partnership allocates the loss under section 704(b). To the extent the shared loss would be a loss under U.S. Federal income tax principles in another year, the loss is allocated between or among the groups based on how the partnership would allocate the loss if the loss were recognized for U.S. Federal income tax purposes in the year in which the loss is recognized for foreign tax purposes. To the extent the shared loss would not constitute a loss under U.S. Federal income tax principles in any year, the loss is allocated between or among the groups in the same manner as the partnership items attributable to the activity giving rise to the shared loss.

(iv) *Split taxes from a loss-sharing splitter arrangement.*—Split taxes from a loss-sharing splitter arrangement are foreign income taxes paid or accrued by a member of the U.S. combined income group with respect to income from the current foreign taxable year, or, in the case of a foregone carryback loss, from the prior foreign taxable year, equal to the amount of the usable shared loss of that group that offsets income of another U.S. combined income group.

(v) *Related income from a loss-sharing splitter arrangement.*—The related income with respect to split taxes from a loss-sharing splitter arrangement is an amount of income of the individual or corporate member of the U.S. combined income group equal to the amount of income under foreign tax law of that U.S. combined income group that is offset by the usable shared loss of another U.S. combined income group.

(vi) *Foreign group relief or other loss-sharing regime.*—A foreign group relief or other loss-sharing regime exists when an entity may surrender its loss to offset the income of one or more other entities. A foreign group relief or other loss-sharing regime does not include an allocation of loss of an entity that is a partnership or other fiscally transparent entity (under the principles of § 1.894-1(d)(3)) for foreign tax purposes or regimes in which foreign tax is imposed on combined income (such as a foreign consolidated regime), as described in § 1.901-2(f)(3).

(vii) *Examples.*—The following examples illustrate the rules of paragraph (b)(2) of this section.

Example 1. (i) *Facts.* USP, a domestic corporation, wholly owns CFC1, a corporation organized in country A. CFC1 wholly owns CFC2 and CFC3, both corporations organized in country A. CFC2 wholly owns DE, an entity organized in country A. DE is a corporation for country A tax purposes and a disregarded entity for U.S. Federal income tax purposes. Country A has a loss-sharing regime under which a loss of CFC1, CFC2, CFC3 or DE may be used to offset the income of one or more of the others. Country A imposes an income tax at the rate of 30% on the taxable income of corporations organized in country A. In year 1, before any loss sharing, CFC1 has no income, CFC2 has income of 50u, CFC3 has income of 200u, and DE has a loss of 100u. Under the provisions of country A's loss-sharing regime, the group decides to use DE's 100u loss to offset 100u of CFC3's income. After the loss is shared, for country A's tax purposes, CFC2 still has 50u of income on which it pays 15u of country A tax. CFC3 has income of 100u (200u less the 100u shared loss) on which it pays 30u of country A tax. For U.S. Federal income tax purposes, the loss sharing with CFC3 is not taken into account. Because DE is a disregarded entity, its 100u loss is taken into account by CFC2 and reduces its earnings and profits for U.S. Federal income tax purposes. Accordingly, before application of section 909, CFC2 has a loss for earnings and profits purposes of 65u (50u income less 15u taxes paid to country A less 100u loss of DE). CFC2 also has the U.S. dollar equivalent of 15u of foreign income taxes to add to its post-1986 foreign income taxes pool. CFC3 has earnings and profits of 170u (200u income less 30u of taxes) and the dollar equivalent of 30u of foreign income taxes to add to its post-1986 foreign income taxes pool.

(ii) *Result.* Pursuant to § 1.909-2(b)(2)(ii), CFC2 and DE constitute one U.S. combined income group, while CFC1 and CFC3 each constitute separate U.S. combined income groups. Pursuant to § 1.909-2(b)(2)(iii)(A), the income of the CFC2 U.S. combined income group is 50u (CFC2's country A taxable income of 50u). The income of the CFC3 U.S. combined income group is 200u (CFC3's country A taxable income of 200u). Pursuant to § 1.909-2(b)(2)(iii)(B), the shared loss of the CFC2 U.S. combined income group includes the 100u of shared loss incurred by DE. The usable shared loss of the CFC2 U.S. combined income group is 50u, the amount of the group's shared loss that could have otherwise offset CFC2's 50u of country A taxable income that is included in the income of the CFC2 U.S. combined income group. There is a splitter arrangement because the 50u usable shared loss of the CFC2 U.S. combined income group was used instead to offset income of CFC3, which is included in the CFC3 U.S. combined income group. Pursuant to § 1.909-2(b)(2)(iv), the split taxes are the 15u of country A income taxes paid by CFC2 on 50u of income, an amount of income of the CFC2 U.S. combined income group equal to the amount of usable shared loss of that group that was used to offset income of the CFC3 U.S. combined income group. Pursuant to § 1.909-2(b)(2)(v), the related income is the 50u of CFC3's income that equals the amount of income of the CFC3 U.S. combined income group that was offset by the usable shared loss of the CFC2 U.S. combined income group.

Example 2. (i) *Facts.* USP, a domestic corporation, wholly owns CFC1, a corporation organized in country B. CFC1 wholly owns CFC2 and CFC3, both corporations organized in country B. CFC2 wholly owns DE, an entity organized in country B. DE is a corporation for country B tax purposes and a disregarded entity for U.S. Federal income tax purposes. CFC2 and CFC3 each own 50% of HP1, an entity organized in country B. HP1 is a corporation for country B tax purposes and a partnership for U.S. Federal income tax purposes. All items of income and loss of HP1 are allocated for U.S. Federal income tax purposes equally between CFC2 and CFC3, and all entities use the country B currency "u" as their functional currency. Country B has a loss-sharing regime under which a loss of any of CFC1, CFC2, CFC3, DE, and HP1 may be used to offset the income of one or more of the others. Country B imposes an income tax at the rate of 30% on the taxable income of corporations organized in country B. In year 1, before any loss sharing, CFC2 has income of 100u, CFC1 and CFC3 have no income, DE has a loss of 100u, and HP1 has income of 200u. Under the provisions of country B's loss-sharing regime, the group decides to use DE's 100u loss to offset 100u of HP1's income. After the loss is shared, for country B tax purposes, CFC2 has 100u of income on which it pays 30u of country B income tax, and HP1 has 100u of income (200u less the 100u shared loss) on which it pays 30u of country B income tax. For U.S. Federal income tax purposes, the loss sharing with HP1 is not taken into account, and, because DE is a disregarded entity, its 100u loss is taken into account by CFC2 and reduces CFC2's earnings and profits for U.S. Federal income tax purposes. The 200u income of HP1 is allocated 50/50 to CFC2 and CFC3, as is the 30u of country B income tax paid by HP1. Accordingly, before application of section 909, for U.S. Federal income tax purposes, CFC2 has earnings and profits of 55u

(100u income plus 100u share of HP1's income less 100u loss of DE less 30u country B income tax paid by CFC2 less 15u share of HP1's country B income tax) and the dollar equivalent of 45u of country B income tax to add to its post-1986 foreign income taxes pool. CFC3 has earnings and profits of 85u (100u share of HP1's income less 15u share of HP1's country B income taxes) and the dollar equivalent of 15u of country B income tax to add to its post-1986 foreign income taxes pool.

(ii) *U.S. combined income groups*. Pursuant to § 1.909-2(b)(2)(ii), because the income and loss of HP1 are combined in part with the income and loss of both CFC2 and CFC3, it belongs to both of the separate CFC2 and CFC3 U.S. combined income groups. DE is a member of the CFC2 U.S. combined income group.

(iii) *Income of the U.S. combined income groups*. Pursuant to § 1.909-2(b)(2)(iii)(A), the income of the CFC2 U.S. combined income group is the 200u country B taxable income of the members of the group with positive taxable incomes (CFC2's country B taxable income of 100u plus 50% of HP1's country B taxable income of 200u, or 100u). Because DE does not have positive taxable income for country B tax purposes, its 100u loss is not included in the income of the CFC2 U.S. combined income group. The income of the CFC3 U.S. combined income group is 100u (50% of HP1's country B taxable income of 200u, or 100u).

(iv) *Shared loss of the U.S. combined income groups*. Pursuant to § 1.909-2(b)(2)(iii)(B), the shared loss of the CFC2 U.S. combined income group is the 100u loss incurred by DE that is used to offset 100u of HP1's income. The CFC3 U.S. combined income group has no shared loss. Pursuant to § 1.909-2(b)(2)(i), the usable shared loss of the CFC2 U.S. combined income group is 100u, the full amount of the group's 100u shared loss that could have been used to offset income of the CFC2 U.S. combined income group had the loss been used to offset 100u of CFC2's country B taxable income.

(v) *Income offset by shared loss*. The shared loss of the CFC2 combined income group is used to offset 100u country B taxable income of HP1. Because the taxable income of HP1 is allocated 50/50 between the CFC2 and CFC3 U.S. combined income groups, the shared loss is treated as offsetting 50u of the CFC2 U.S. combined income group's income and 50u of the CFC3 U.S. combined income group's income.

(vi) *Splitter arrangement*. There is a splitter arrangement because 50u of the 100u usable shared loss of the CFC2 U.S. combined income group was used to offset income of the CFC3 U.S. combined income group. Pursuant to § 1.909-2(b)(2)(iv), the split taxes are the 15u of country B income tax paid by CFC2 on 50u of its income, which is equal to the amount of the CFC2 U.S. combined income group's usable shared loss that was used to offset income of another U.S. combined income group. Pursuant to § 1.909-2(b)(2)(v), the related income is the 50u of CFC3's income that was offset by the usable shared loss of the CFC2 U.S. combined income group.

(3) *Hybrid instrument splitter arrangements.*—(i) *U.S. equity hybrid instrument splitter arrangement.*—(A) *In general.*—A U.S. equity hybrid instrument is a splitter arrangement if:

(1) Under the laws of a foreign jurisdiction in which the instrument owner is subject to tax, the instrument gives rise to income includible in the instrument owner's income and such inclusion results in foreign income taxes paid or accrued by the instrument owner;

(2) Under the laws of a foreign jurisdiction in which the issuer is subject to tax, the instrument gives rise to deductions that are incurred or otherwise taken into account by the issuer; and

(3) The events that give rise to income includible in the instrument owner's income for foreign tax purposes as described in paragraph (b)(3)(i)(A)(1) of this section, and to deductions for the issuer for foreign tax purposes as described in paragraph (b)(3)(i)(A)(2) of this section, do not result in an inclusion of income for the instrument owner for U.S. federal income tax purposes.

(B) *Split taxes from a U.S. equity hybrid instrument splitter arrangement.*—Split taxes from a U.S. equity hybrid instrument splitter arrangement equal the total amount of foreign income taxes paid or accrued by the owner of the hybrid instrument less the amount of foreign income taxes that would have been paid or accrued had the owner of the U.S. equity hybrid instrument not been subject to foreign tax on income from the instrument with respect to the events described in § 1.909-2(b)(3)(i)(A).

(C) *Related income from a U.S. equity hybrid instrument splitter arrangement.*—The related income with respect to split taxes from a U.S. equity hybrid instrument splitter arrangement is income of the issuer of the U.S. equity hybrid instrument in an amount equal to the amounts giving rise to the split taxes that are deductible by the issuer for foreign tax purposes, determined without regard to the actual amount of the issuer's income or earnings and profits for U.S. Federal income tax purposes.

(D) *U.S. equity hybrid instrument.*—The term *U.S. equity hybrid instrument* means an instrument that is treated as equity for U.S. Federal income tax purposes but for foreign income tax purposes either is treated as indebtedness or otherwise entitles the issuer to a deduction with respect to such instrument.

(E) *Example.*—(i) *Facts.* USP, a domestic corporation, wholly owns CFC1, which wholly owns CFC2. Both CFC1 and CFC2 are corporations organized in country A. CFC2 issues an instrument to CFC1 that is treated as indebtedness for country A tax purposes but equity for U.S. Federal income tax purposes. Under country A's income tax laws, the instrument accrues interest at the end of each month, which results in a deduction for CFC2 and an income inclusion and tax liability for CFC1 in country A. The accrual of interest does not result in an inclusion of income for CFC1 for U.S. Federal income tax purposes. Pursuant to the terms of the instrument, CFC2 makes a distribution at the end of the year equal to the amounts of interest that have accrued during the year, and such payment is treated as a dividend that is included in the income of CFC1 for U.S. Federal income tax purposes.

(ii) *Result.* Pursuant to § 1.909-2(b)(3)(i)(D), because the instrument is treated as equity for U.S. Federal income tax purposes but is treated as indebtedness for country A tax purposes, it is a U.S. equity hybrid instrument. Pursuant to § 1.909-2(b)(3)(i)(A)(*3*), because the accrual of interest under foreign law does not result in an inclusion of income of CFC1 for U.S. Federal income tax purposes, there is a splitter arrangement. The fact that the payment of the accrued amount at the end of the year pursuant to the terms of the instrument gives rise to a dividend that is included in income of CFC1 for U.S. Federal income tax purposes does not change the result because it is the accrual of interest and not the payment that gives rise to income or deductions under foreign law. The payments will be treated as a distribution of related income to the extent provided by § 1.909-3 and § 1.909-6(d).

(ii) *U.S. debt hybrid instrument splitter arrangement.*—(A) *In general.*—A U.S. debt hybrid instrument is a splitter arrangement if foreign income taxes are paid or accrued by the issuer of a U.S. debt hybrid instrument with respect to income in an amount equal to the interest (including original issue discount) paid or accrued on the instrument that is deductible for U.S. Federal income tax purposes but that does not give rise to a deduction under the laws of a foreign jurisdiction in which the issuer is subject to tax.

(B) *Split taxes from a U.S. debt hybrid instrument splitter arrangement.*—Split taxes from a U.S. debt hybrid instrument splitter arrangement are the foreign income taxes paid or accrued by the issuer on the income that would have been offset by the interest paid or accrued on the U.S. debt hybrid instrument had such interest been deductible for foreign tax purposes.

(C) *Related income from a U.S. debt hybrid instrument splitter arrangement.*—The related income from a U.S. debt hybrid instrument splitter arrangement is the gross amount of the interest income recognized for U.S. Federal income tax purposes by the owner of the U.S. debt hybrid instrument, determined without regard to the actual amount of the owner's income or earnings and profits for U.S. Federal income tax purposes.

(D) *U.S. debt hybrid instrument.*—The term *U.S. debt hybrid instrument* means an instrument that is treated as equity for foreign tax purposes but as indebtedness for U.S. Federal income tax purposes.

(4) *Partnership inter-branch payment splitter arrangements.*—(i) *In general.*—An allocation of foreign income tax paid or accrued by a partnership with respect to an inter-branch payment as described in § 1.704-1(b)(4)(viii)(*d*)(*3*) (revised as of April 1, 2011) (the *inter-branch payment tax*) is a splitter arrangement to the extent the interbranch payment tax is not allocated to the partners in the same proportion as the distributive shares of income in the CFTE category to which the inter-branch payment tax is or would be assigned under § 1.704-1(b)(4)(viii)(*d*) without regard to § 1.704-1(b)(4)(viii)(*d*)(*3*).

(ii) *Split taxes from a partnership inter-branch payment splitter arrangement.*—The split taxes from a partnership inter-branch splitter arrangement equal the excess of the amount of the inter-branch payment tax allocated to a partner under the partnership agreement over the amount of the inter-branch payment tax that would have been allocated to the partner if the inter-branch payment tax had been allocated to the partners in the same proportion as the distributive shares of income in the CFTE category referred to in paragraph (b)(4)(i) of this section.

(iii) *Related income from a partnership inter-branch payment splitter arrangement.*—The related income from a partnership inter-branch payment splitter arrangement equals the amount of income allocated to a partner that exceeds the amount of income that would have been allocated to the partner if income in the CFTE category referred to in paragraph (b)(4)(i) of this section in the amount of the inter-branch payment had been allocated to the partners in the same proportion as the inter-branch payment tax was allocated under the partnership agreement.

(c) *Effective/applicability date.*—This section applies to foreign income taxes paid or accrued in taxable years ending after February 9, 2015. However, a taxpayer may choose to apply the provisions of § 1.909-2T (as contained in 26 CFR part 1, revised as of April 1, 2014) in lieu of this section to foreign income taxes paid or accrued in its first taxable year ending after February 9, 2015, and in taxable years of foreign corporations with respect to which the taxpayer is a domestic shareholder (as defined in § 1.902-1(a)) that end with or within that first taxable year. See 26 CFR 1.909-2T (revised as of April 1, 2014) for rules applicable to foreign income taxes paid or accrued in taxable years beginning on or after January 1, 2012, and ending on or before February 9, 2015. [Reg. § 1.909-2.]

☐ [*T.D.* 9710, 2-9-2015.]

§ 1.909-3. Rules regarding related income and split taxes.—(a) *Interim rules for identifying related income and split taxes.*—The principles of paragraphs (d) through (f) of § 1.909-6 apply to related income and split taxes in taxable years beginning on or after January 1, 2011, except that the alternative method for identifying distributions of related income described in § 1.909-6(d)(4) applies only to identify the amount of pre-2011 split taxes of a section 902 corporation that are suspended as of the first day of the section 902 corporation's first taxable year beginning on or after January 1, 2011.

(b) *Split taxes on deductible disregarded payments.*—Split taxes include taxes paid or accrued in taxable years beginning on or after January 1, 2011, with respect to the amount of a disregarded payment that is deductible by the payor of the disregarded payment under the laws of a foreign jurisdiction in which the payor of the disregarded payment is subject to tax on related income from a splitter arrangement. The amount of the deductible disregarded payment to which this paragraph (b) applies is limited to the amount of related income from such splitter arrangement.

(c) *Effective/applicability date.*—This section applies to taxable years ending after February 9, 2015. See 26 CFR 1.909-3T (revised as of April 1, 2014) for rules applicable to taxable years beginning on or after January 1, 2011, and ending on or before February 9, 2015. [Reg. § 1.909-3.]

☐ [*T.D.* 9710, 2-9-2015.]

§ 1.909-4. Coordination rules.—(a) *Interim rules.*—The principles of paragraph (g) of § 1.909-6 apply to taxable years beginning on or after January 1, 2011.

(b) *Effective/applicability date.*—This section applies to taxable years ending after February 9, 2015. See 26 CFR 1.909-4T (revised as of April 1, 2014) for rules applicable to taxable years beginning on or after January 1, 2011, and ending on or before February 9, 2015. [Reg. § 1.909-4.]

☐ [*T.D.* 9710, 2-9-2015.]

§ 1.909-5. Coordination rules.—(a) *Taxes paid or accrued in taxable years beginning in 2011.*—(1) Foreign income taxes paid or accrued by any person in a taxable year beginning on or after January 1, 2011, and before January 1, 2012, in connection with a pre-2011 splitter arrangement (as defined in § 1.909-6(b)), are split taxes to the same extent that such taxes would have been treated as pre-2011 split taxes if such taxes were paid or accrued by a section 902 corporation in a taxable year beginning on or before December 31, 2010. The related income with respect to split taxes from such an arrangement is the related income described in § 1.909-6(b), determined as if the payor were a section 902 corporation.

(2) Foreign income taxes paid or accrued by any person in a taxable year beginning on or after January 1, 2011, and before January 1, 2012, in connection with a partnership inter-branch payment splitter arrangement described in § 1.909-2(b)(4) are split taxes to the extent that such taxes are identified as split taxes in § 1.909-2(b)(4)(ii). The related income with respect to the split taxes is the related income described in § 1.909-2(b)(4)(iii).

(b) *Taxes paid or accrued in certain taxable years beginning in 2012 with respect to a foreign consolidated group splitter arrangement.*—Foreign income taxes paid or accrued by any person in a taxable year beginning on or after January 1, 2012, and on or before February 14, 2012, in connection with a foreign consolidated group splitter arrangement described in § 1.909-6(b)(2) are split taxes to the same extent that such taxes would have been treated as pre-2011 split taxes if such taxes were paid or accrued by a section 902 corporation in a taxable year beginning on or before December 31, 2010. The related income with respect to split taxes from such an arrangement is the related income described in § 1.909-6(b)(2), determined as if the payor were a section 902 corporation.

(c) *Effective/applicability date.*—The rules of this section apply to foreign income taxes paid or accrued in taxable years beginning on or after January 1, 2011, and on or before February 14, 2012. [Reg. § 1.909-5.]

☐ [*T.D.* 9710, 2-9-2015.]

§ 1.909-6. Pre-2011 foreign tax credit splitting events.—(a) *Foreign tax credit splitting event.*—(1) *In general.*—This section provides rules for determining whether foreign income taxes paid or accrued by a section 902 corporation (as defined in section 909(d)(5)) in taxable years beginning on or before December 31, 2010 (*pre-2011 taxable years* and *pre-2011 taxes*) are suspended under section 909 in taxable years beginning after December 31, 2010, (*post-2010 taxable years*) of a section 902 corporation. Paragraph (b) of this section identifies an exclusive list of arrangements that will be treated as giving rise to foreign tax credit splitting events in pre-2011 taxable years (*pre-2011 splitter arrangements*). Paragraphs (c), (d), and (e) of this section provide rules for determining the related income and pre-2011 split taxes paid or accrued with respect to pre-2011 splitter arrangements. Paragraph (f) of this section provides rules concerning the application of section 909 to partnerships and trusts. Paragraph (g) of this section provides rules concerning the interaction between section 909 and other Internal Revenue Code (*Code*) provisions.

(2) *Taxes not subject to suspension under section 909.*—Pre-2011 taxes that will not be suspended under section 909 or paragraph (a) of this section are:

(i) Any pre-2011 taxes that were not paid or accrued in connection with a pre-2011 splitter arrangement identified in paragraph (b) of this section;

(ii) Any pre-2011 taxes that were paid or accrued in connection with a pre-2011 splitter arrangement identified in paragraph (b) of this section (*pre-2011 split taxes*) but that were deemed paid under section 902(a) or 960 on or before the last day of the section 902 corporation's last pre-2011 taxable year;

(iii) Any pre-2011 split taxes if either the payor section 902 corporation took the related income into account in a pre-2011 taxable year or a section 902 shareholder (as defined in § 1.909-1(a)(2)) of the relevant section 902 corporation took the related income into account on or before the last day of the section 902 corporation's last pre-2011 taxable year; and

(iv) Any pre-2011 split taxes paid or accrued by a section 902 corporation in taxable years of such section 902 corporation beginning before January 1, 1997.

(3) *Taxes subject to suspension under section 909.*—To the extent that the section 902 corporation paid or accrued pre-2011 split taxes that are not described in paragraph (a)(2) of this section, section 909 and the regulations under that section will apply to such pre-2011 split taxes for purposes of applying sections 902 and 960 in post-2010 taxable years of the section 902 corporation. Accordingly, these taxes will be removed from the section 902 corporation's pools of post-1986 foreign income taxes and suspended under section 909 as of the first day of the section 902 corporation's first post-2010 taxable year. There is no increase to a section 902 corporation's earnings and profits for the amount of any pre-2011 taxes to which section 909 applies that were previously deducted in computing earnings and profits in a pre-2011 taxable year.

(b) *Pre-2011 splitter arrangements.*—The arrangements set forth in this paragraph (b) are pre-2011 splitter arrangements.

(1) *Reverse hybrid structure splitter arrangements.*—A reverse hybrid structure exists when a section 902 corporation owns an interest in a reverse hybrid. A reverse hybrid is an entity that is a corporation for U.S. Federal income tax purposes but is a pass-through entity or a branch under the laws of a foreign country imposing tax on the income of the entity. As a result, the owner of the reverse hybrid is subject to tax on the income of the entity under foreign law. A pre-2011 splitter arrangement involving a reverse hybrid structure exists when pre-2011 taxes are paid or accrued by a section 902 corporation with respect to income of a reverse hybrid that is a covered person with respect to the section 902 corporation. A pre-2011 splitter arrangement involving a reverse hybrid structure may exist even if the reverse hybrid has a deficit in earnings and profits for a particular year (for example, due to a timing difference). Such taxes paid or accrued by the section 902 corporation are pre-2011 split taxes. The related income is the earnings and profits (computed for U.S. Federal income tax purposes) of the reverse hybrid attributable to the activities of the reverse hybrid that gave rise to income included in the foreign tax base with respect to which the pre-2011 split taxes were paid or accrued. Accordingly, related income of the reverse hybrid would not include any item of income or expense attributable to a disregarded entity (as defined in § 301.7701-2(c)(2)(i) of this chapter) owned by the reverse hybrid if income attributable to the activities of the disregarded entity is not included in the foreign tax base.

(2) *Foreign consolidated group splitter arrangements.*—A foreign consolidated group exists when a foreign country imposes tax on the combined income of two or more entities. Tax is considered imposed on the combined income of two or more entities even if the combined income is computed under foreign law by attributing to one such entity the income of one or more entities. A foreign consolidated group is a pre-2011 splitter arrangement to the extent that the taxpayer did not allocate the foreign consolidated tax liability among the members of the foreign consolidated group based on each member's share of the consolidated taxable income included in the foreign tax base under the principles of § 1.901-2(f)(3) (revised as of April 1, 2011). A pre-2011 splitter arrangement involving a foreign consolidated group may exist even if one or more members has a deficit in earnings and profits for a particular year (for example, due to a timing difference). Pre-2011 taxes paid or accrued with respect to the income of a foreign consolidated group are pre-2011 split taxes to the extent that taxes paid or accrued by one member of the foreign consolidated group are imposed on a covered person's share of the consolidated taxable income included in the foreign tax base. The related income is the earnings and profits (computed for U.S. Federal income tax purposes) of such other member attributable to the activities of that other member that gave rise to income included in the foreign tax base with respect to which the pre-2011 split taxes were paid or accrued. No inference should be drawn from the treatment of foreign consolidated groups under section 909 as to the determination of the person who paid the foreign income tax for U.S. Federal income tax purposes.

(3) *Group relief or other loss-sharing regime splitter arrangements.*—(i) *In general.*—A foreign group relief or other loss-sharing regime exists when one entity with a loss permits the loss to be used to offset the income of one or more entities (*shared loss*). A pre-2011 splitter arrangement involving a shared loss exists when the following three conditions are met:

(A) There is an instrument that is treated as indebtedness under the laws of the jurisdiction in which the issuer is subject to tax and that is disregarded for U.S. Federal income tax purposes (*disregarded debt instrument*). Examples of a disregarded debt instrument include a debt obligation between two disregarded entities that are owned by the same section 902 corporation, two disregarded entities that are owned by a partnership with one or more partners that are section 902 corporations, a section 902 corporation and a disregarded entity that is owned by that section 902 corporation, or a partnership in which the section 902 corporation is a partner and a disregarded entity that is owned by such partnership.

(B) The owner of the disregarded debt instrument pays a foreign income tax attributable to a payment or accrual on the instrument.

(C) The payment or accrual on the disregarded debt instrument gives rise to a deduction for foreign tax purposes and the issuer of the instrument incurs a shared loss that is taken into account under foreign law by one or more entities that are covered persons with respect to the owner of the instrument.

(ii) *Split taxes and related income.*—In situations described in paragraph (b)(3)(i) of this section, pre-2011 taxes paid or accrued by the owner of the disregarded debt instrument with respect to amounts paid or accrued on the instrument (up to the amount of the shared loss) are pre-2011 split taxes. The related income of a covered person is an amount equal to the shared loss, determined without regard to the actual amount of the covered person's earnings and profits.

(4) *Hybrid instrument splitter arrangements.*—(i) *In general.*—A hybrid instrument for purposes of this paragraph (b)(4) is an instrument that either is treated as equity for U.S. Federal income tax purposes but is treated as indebtedness for foreign tax purposes (*U.S. equity hybrid instrument*), or is treated as indebtedness for U.S. Federal income tax purposes but is treated as equity for foreign tax purposes (*U.S. debt hybrid instrument*).

(ii) *U.S. equity hybrid instrument splitter arrangement.*—If the issuer of a U.S. equity hybrid instrument is a covered person with respect to a section 902 corporation that is the owner of the U.S. equity hybrid instrument, there is a pre-2011 splitter arrangement with respect to the portion of the pre-2011 taxes paid or accrued by the owner section 902 corporation with respect to the amounts on the instrument that are deductible by the issuer as interest under the laws of a foreign jurisdiction in which the issuer is subject to tax but that do not give rise to income for U.S. Federal income tax purposes. Pre-2011 split taxes paid or accrued by the section 902 corporation equal the total amount of pre-2011 taxes paid or accrued by the section 902 corporation less the amount of pre-2011 taxes that would have been paid or accrued had the section 902 corporation not been subject to tax on income from the U.S. equity hybrid instrument. The related income of the issuer of the U.S. equity hybrid instrument is an amount equal to the amounts that are deductible by the issuer for foreign tax purposes, determined without regard to the actual amount of the issuer's earnings and profits.

(iii) *U.S. debt hybrid instrument splitter arrangement.*—If the owner of a U.S. debt hybrid instrument is a covered person with respect to a section 902 corporation that is the issuer of the U.S. debt hybrid instrument, there is a pre-2011 splitter arrangement with respect to the portion of the pre-2011 taxes paid or accrued by the section 902 corporation on income in an amount equal to the interest (including original issue discount) paid or accrued on the instrument that is deductible for U.S. Federal income tax purposes but that does not give rise to a deduction under the laws of a foreign jurisdiction in which the issuer is subject to tax. Pre-2011 split taxes are the pre-2011 taxes paid or accrued by the section 902 corporation on the income that would have been offset by the interest paid or accrued on the U.S. debt hybrid instrument had such interest been deductible for foreign tax purposes. The related income with respect to a U.S. debt hybrid instrument is the gross amount of the interest income recognized for U.S. Federal income tax purposes by the owner of the U.S. debt hybrid instrument, determined without regard to the actual amount of the owner's earnings and profits.

(c) *General rules for applying section 909 to pre-2011 split taxes and related income.*—(1) *Annual determination.*—The determination of related income, other income, pre-2011 split taxes, and other taxes, and the portion of these amounts that were distributed, deemed paid or otherwise transferred or eliminated must be made on an annual basis beginning with the first taxable year of the section 902 corporation beginning after December 31, 1996 (*post-1996 taxable year*) in which the section 902 corporation paid or accrued a pre-2011 tax with respect to a pre-2011 splitter arrangement and ending with the section 902 corporation's last pre-2011 taxable year. Annual amounts of related income and pre-2011 split taxes are aggregated for each separate pre-2011 splitter arrangement.

(2) *Separate categories.*—The determination of annual and aggregate amounts of related income and pre-2011 split taxes with respect to each pre-2011 splitter arrangement must be made for each separate category as defined in § 1.904-4(m) of the section 902 corporation, each covered person, and any other person that succeeds to the related income and pre-2011 split taxes. In the case of a pre-2011 splitter arrangement involving a shared loss (as described in paragraph (b)(3) of this section), the amount of the related income in each separate category of the covered person is equal to the amount of income in that separate category that was offset by the shared loss for foreign tax purposes. In the case of a pre-2011 splitter arrangement involving a U.S. equity hybrid instrument (as described in paragraph (b)(4)(ii) of this section), the related income is assigned to the issuer's separate categories in the same proportions as the pre-2011 split

taxes. Earnings and profits, including related income, are assigned to separate categories under the rules of §§1.904-4, 1.904-5, and 1.904-7. Foreign income taxes, including pre-2011 split taxes, are assigned to separate categories under the rules of §1.904-6. A section 902 shareholder must consistently apply methodologies for determining pre-2011 split taxes and related income with respect to all pre-2011 splitter arrangements.

(d) *Special rules regarding related income.*—(1) *Annual adjustments.*— In the case of each pre-2011 splitter arrangement involving a reverse hybrid or a foreign consolidated group (as described in paragraphs (b)(1) and (2) of this section, respectively), a covered person's aggregate amount of related income must be adjusted each year by the net amount of income and expense attributable to the activities of the covered person that give rise to income included in the foreign tax base, even if the net amount is negative and regardless of whether the section 902 corporation paid or accrued any pre-2011 split taxes in such year.

(2) *Effect of separate limitation losses and deficits.*—Related income is determined without regard to the application of §1.960-1(i)(4) (relating to the effect of separate limitation losses on earnings and profits in another separate category) or section 952(c)(1) (relating to certain earnings and profits deficits).

(3) *Pro rata method for distributions out of earnings and profits that include both related income and other income.*—If the earnings and profits of a covered person include amounts attributable to both related income and other income, including earnings and profits attributable to taxable years beginning before January 1, 1997, then distributions, deemed distributions, and inclusions out of earnings and profits (for example, under sections 301, 304, 367(b), 951(a), 964(e), 1248, or 1293) of the covered person are considered made out of related income and other income on a pro rata basis. Any reduction of a covered person's earnings and profits that results from a payment on stock that is not treated as a dividend for U.S. Federal income tax purposes (for example, pursuant to section 312(n)(7)) will also reduce related income and other income on a pro rata basis.

(4) *Alternative method for distributions out of earnings and profits that include both related income and other income.*—Solely for purposes of identifying the amount of pre-2011 split taxes of a section 902 corporation that are suspended as of the first day of the section 902 corporation's first post-2010 taxable year, in lieu of the rule set forth in paragraph (d)(3) of this section, a section 902 shareholder may choose to treat all distributions, deemed distributions, and inclusions out of earnings and profits of a covered person as attributable first to related income. A section 902 shareholder may choose to use this alternative method on a timely filed original income tax return for the first post-2010 taxable year in which the shareholder computes an amount of foreign income taxes deemed paid with respect to a section 902 corporation that paid or accrued pre-2011 split taxes. Such choice by a section 902 shareholder is evidenced by employing the method on its income tax return; the section 902 shareholder need not file a separate statement. A section 902 shareholder that chooses this alternative method must consistently apply it with respect to all pre-2011 splitter arrangements.

(5) *Distributions, deemed distributions, and inclusions of related income.*—Distributions, deemed distributions, and inclusions of related income (including indirectly through a partnership) to persons other than the payor section 902 corporation retain their character as related income with respect to the associated pre-2011 split taxes.

(6) *Carryover of related income.*—Related income carries over to other corporations in the same manner as earnings and profits carry over under section 381, §1.367(b)-7, or similar rules, and retains its character as related income with respect to the associated pre-2011 split taxes.

(7) *Related income taken into account by a section 902 shareholder.*— Related income will be considered taken into account by a section 902 shareholder to the extent that the related income is recognized as gross income by the section 902 shareholder, or by an affiliated corporation described in paragraph (d)(9) of this section, upon a distribution, deemed distribution, or inclusion (such as under section 951(a)) out of the earnings and profits of the covered person attributable to such related income.

(8) *Related income taken into account by a payor section 902 corporation.*—Related income will be considered taken into account by a payor section 902 corporation to the extent that:

(i) The related income is reflected in the earnings and profits of such section 902 corporation for U.S. Federal income tax purposes by reason of a distribution, deemed distribution, or inclusion out of the earnings and profits of the covered person attributable to such related income; or

(ii) The related income is reflected as a positive adjustment to the earnings and profits of such section 902 corporation for U.S. Federal income tax purposes by reason of the section 902 corporation and the covered person combining in a transaction described in section 381(a)(1) or (a)(2).

(9) *Related income taken into account by an affiliated group of corporations that includes a section 902 shareholder.*—A section 902 shareholder will be considered to have taken related income into account if one or more members of an affiliated group of corporations (as defined in section 1504) that files a consolidated Federal income tax return that includes the section 902 shareholder takes the related income into account.

(10) *Distributions of previously-taxed earnings and profits.*—Distributions and deemed distributions described in paragraph (d) of this section (including in the case of a section 902 shareholder that has chosen the alternative method described in paragraph (d)(4) of this section) do not include distributions of amounts described in section 959(c)(1) or (c)(2), which are distributed before amounts described in section 959(c)(3).

(e) *Special rules regarding pre-2011 split taxes.*—(1) *Taxes deemed paid pro-rata out of pre-2011 split taxes and other taxes.*—If the pre-2011 taxes of a section 902 corporation include both pre-2011 split taxes and other taxes, then foreign income taxes deemed paid under section 902 or 960 or otherwise removed from post-1986 foreign income taxes in pre-2011 taxable years will be treated as attributable to pre-2011 split taxes and other taxes on a pro-rata basis.

(2) *Pre-2011 split taxes deemed paid in pre-2011 taxable years.*— Pre-2011 split taxes deemed paid in pre-2011 taxable years in connection with a dividend paid to a shareholder described in section 902(b) retain their character as pre-2011 split taxes. The section 902(b) shareholder will be treated as the payor section 902 corporation with respect to those pre-2011 split taxes.

(3) *Carryover of pre-2011 split taxes.*—Pre-2011 split taxes that carry over to another foreign corporation, including under section 381, §1.367(b)-7 or similar rules, retain their character as pre-2011 split taxes. The transferee foreign corporation will be treated as the payor section 902 corporation with respect to those pre-2011 split taxes.

(4) *Determining when pre-2011 split taxes are no longer treated as pre-2011 split taxes.*—For each pre-2011 splitter arrangement, as related income is taken into account by the payor section 902 corporation or a section 902 shareholder as provided in paragraph (d) of this section, a ratable portion of the associated pre-2011 split taxes will no longer be treated as pre-2011 split taxes. In the case of a pre-2011 splitter arrangement involving a reverse hybrid or a foreign consolidated group (as described in paragraphs (b)(1) and (2) of this section, respectively), if aggregate related income is reduced to zero (other than as a result of a distribution, deemed distribution, or inclusion described in paragraph (d) of this section) or less than zero, pre-2011 split taxes will retain their character as pre-2011 split taxes until the amount of aggregate related income is positive and the related income is taken into account by the payor section 902 corporation or a section 902 shareholder as provided in paragraph (d) of this section.

(f) *Rules relating to partnerships and trusts.*—(1) *Taxes paid or accrued by partnerships.*—In the case of foreign income taxes paid or accrued by a partnership, the taxes will be treated as pre-2011 split taxes to the extent such taxes are allocated to one or more section 902 corporations and would be pre-2011 split taxes if the partner section 902 corporation had paid or accrued the taxes directly on the date such taxes are included by the section 902 corporation under sections 702 and 706(a). Further, any foreign income taxes subject to section 909 will be suspended in the hands of the partner section 902 corporation.

(2) *Section 704(b) allocations.*—Partnership allocations that satisfy the requirements of section 704(b) and the regulations thereunder will not constitute pre-2011 splitter arrangements except to the extent the arrangement is otherwise described in paragraph (b) of this section (for example, a payment or accrual on a disregarded debt instrument that gives rise to a shared loss).

(3) *Trusts.*—Rules similar to the rules of paragraph (f)(1) of this section will apply in the case of any trust with one or more beneficiaries that is a section 902 corporation.

(g) *Interaction between section 909 and other Code provisions.*—(1) *Section 904(c).*—Section 909 does not apply to excess foreign income taxes that were paid or accrued in pre-2011 taxable years and carried forward and deemed paid or accrued under section 904(c) in a post-2010 taxable year.

(2) *Section 905(a).*—For purposes of determining in post-2010 taxable years the allowable deduction for foreign income taxes paid or accrued under section 164(a), the carryover of excess foreign income taxes under section 904(c), and the extended period for claiming a credit or refund under section 6511(d)(3)(A), foreign income taxes to which section 909 applies are first taken into account and treated as paid or accrued in the year in which the related income is taken into account, and not in the earlier year to which the tax relates (determined without regard to section 909).

(3) *Section 905(c).*—If a redetermination of foreign income taxes claimed as a direct credit under section 901 occurs in a post-2010 taxable year and the foreign tax redetermination relates to a pre-2011 taxable year, to the extent such foreign tax redetermination increased the amount of foreign income taxes paid or accrued with respect to the pre-2011 taxable year (for example, due to an additional assessment of foreign tax or a payment of a previously accrued tax not paid within two years), section 909 will not apply to such taxes. If a redetermination of foreign tax paid or accrued by a section 902 corporation occurs in a post-2010 taxable year and increases the amount of foreign income taxes paid or accrued by the section 902 corporation with respect to a pre-2011 taxable year (for example, due to an additional assessment of foreign tax or a payment of a previously accrued tax not paid within two years), such taxes will be treated as pre-2011 taxes. Section 909 will apply to such taxes if they are pre-2011 split taxes and the taxes will be suspended in the post-2010 taxable year in which they would otherwise be taken into account as a prospective adjustment to the section 902 corporation's pools of post-1986 foreign income taxes.

(4) *Other foreign tax credit provisions.*—Section 909 does not affect the applicability of other restrictions or limitations on the foreign tax credit under existing law, including, for example, the substantiation requirements of section 905(b).

(h) *Effective/applicability date.*—This section applies to foreign income taxes paid or accrued by section 902 corporations in pre-2011 taxable years for purposes of computing foreign income taxes deemed paid with respect to distributions or inclusions out of earnings and profits of section 902 corporations in taxable years of the section 902 corporation ending after February 9, 2015. See 26 CFR 1.909-6T (revised as of April 1, 2014) for rules applicable to foreign income taxes paid or accrued by section 902 corporations in pre-2011 taxable years for purposes of computing foreign income taxes deemed paid with respect to distributions or inclusions out of earnings and profits of section 902 corporations in taxable years of the section 902 corporation beginning after December 31, 2010, and ending on or before February 9, 2015. [Reg. § 1.909-6.]

☐ [*T.D.* 9710, 2-9-2015.]

Foreign Earned Income Exclusion

§ 1.911-1. Partial exclusion for earned income from sources within a foreign country and foreign housing costs.—(a) *In general.*—Section 911 provides that a qualified individual may elect to exclude the individual's foreign earned income and the housing cost amount from the individual's gross income for the taxable year. Foreign earned income is excludable to the extent of the applicable limitation for the taxable year. The housing cost amount for the taxable year is excludable to the extent attributable to employer provided amounts. If a portion of the housing cost amount for the taxable year is attributable to non-employer provided amounts, such amount may be deductible by the qualified individual subject to a limitation. The amounts excluded under section 911(a) and the amount deducted under section 911(c)(3)(A) for the taxable year shall not exceed the individual's foreign earned income for such taxable year. Foreign earned income must be earned during a period for which the individual qualifies to make an election under section 911(d)(1). A housing cost amount that would be deductible except for the application of this limitation may be carried over to the next taxable year and is deductible to the extent of the limitation for that year. Except as otherwise provided, § § 1.911-1 through 1.911-7 apply to taxable years beginning after December 31, 1981. These sections do not apply to any item of income, expense, deduction, or credit arising before January 1, 1982, even if such item is attributable to services performed after December 31, 1981.

(b) *Scope.*—Section 1.911-2 provides rules for determining whether an individual qualifies to make an election under section 911. Section 1.911-3 provides rules for determining the amount of foreign earned income that is excludable under section 911(a)(1). Section 1.911-4 provides rules for determining the housing cost amount and the portions excludable under section 911(a)(2) or deductible under section 911(c)(3). Section 1.911-5 provides special rules applicable to married couples. Section 1.911-6 provides for the disallowance of deductions, exclusions, and credits attributable to amounts excluded under section 911. Section 1.911-7 provides procedural rules for making or revoking an election under section 911. Section 1.911-8 provides a reference to rules applicable to taxable years beginning before January 1, 1982. [Reg. § 1.911-1.]

☐ [*T.D.* 8006, 1-17-85. *Amended by* T.D. 8240, 1-19-89.]

§ 1.911-2. Qualified individuals.—(a) *In general.*—An individual is a qualified individual if:

(1) The individual's tax home is in a foreign country or countries throughout—

(i) The period of bona fide residence described in paragraph (a)(2)(i) of this section, or

(ii) The 330 full days of presence described in paragraph (a)(2)(ii) of this section; and

(2) The individual is either—

(i) A citizen of the United States who establishes to the satisfaction of the Commissioner or his delegate that the individual has been a bona fide resident of a foreign country or countries for an uninterrupted period which includes an entire taxable year, or

(ii) A citizen or resident of the United States who has been physically present in a foreign country or countries for at least 330 full days during any period of twelve consecutive months.

(b) *Tax home.*—For purposes of paragraph (a)(1) of this section, the term "tax home" has the same meaning which it has for purposes of section 162 (a)(2) (relating to travel expenses away from home). Thus, under section 911, an individual's tax home is considered to be located at his regular or principal (if more than one regular) place of business or, if the individual has no regular or principal place of business because of the nature of the business, then at his regular place of abode in a real and substantial sense. An individual shall not, however, be considered to have a tax home in a foreign country for any period for which the individual's abode is in the United States. Temporary presence of the individual in the United States does not necessarily mean that the individual's abode is in the United States during that time. Maintenance of a dwelling in the United States by an individual, whether or not that dwelling is used by the individual's spouse and dependents, does not necessarily mean that the individual's abode is in the United States.

(c) *Determination of bona fide residence.*—For purposes of paragraph (a)(2)(i) of this section, whether an individual is a bona fide resident of a foreign country shall be determined by applying, to the extent practical, the principles of section 871 and the regulations thereunder, relating to the determination of the residence of aliens. Bona fide residence in a foreign country or countries for an uninterrupted period may be established, even if temporary visits are made during the period to the United States or elsewhere on vacation or business. An individual with earned income from sources within a foreign country is not a bona fide resident of that country if:

(1) The individual claims to be a nonresident of that foreign country in a statement submitted to the authorities of that country, and

(2) The earned income of the individual is not subject, by reason of nonresidency in the foreign country, to the income tax of that country.

If an individual has submitted a statement of nonresidence to the authorities of a foreign country the accuracy of which has not been resolved as of any date when a determination of the individual's bona fide residence is being made, then the individual will not be considered a bona fide resident of the foreign country as of that date.

(d) *Determination of physical presence.*—For purposes of paragraph (a)(2)(ii) of this section, the following rules apply.

(1) *Twelve-month test.*—A period of twelve consecutive months may begin with any day but must end on the day before the corresponding day in the twelfth succeeding month. The twelve month period may begin before or after arrival in a foreign country and may end before or after departure.

(2) *330-day test.*—The 330 full days need not be consecutive but may be interrupted by periods during which the individual is not present in a foreign country. In computing the minimum 330 full days of presence in a foreign country or countries, all separate periods of such presence during the period of twelve consecutive months are aggregated. A full day is a continuous period of twenty-four hours beginning with midnight and ending with the following midnight. An individual who has been present in a foreign country and then travels over areas not within any foreign country for less than twenty-four hours shall not be deemed outside a foreign country during the period of travel. If an individual who is in transit between two points outside the United States is physically present in the United States for less than twenty-four hours, such individual shall not be treated as present in the United States during such transit but shall be treated as travelling over areas not within any foreign country. For purposes of this paragraph (d)(2), the term "transit between two points outside the United States" has the same meaning that it has when used in section 7701(b)(6)(C).

(3) *Illustrations of the physical presence requirement.*—The physical presence requirement of paragraph (a)(2)(ii) of this section is illustrated by the following examples:

Example (1). B, a U.S. citizen, arrives in Venezuela from New York at 12 noon on April 24, 1982. B remains in Venezuela until 2 p.m. on March 21, 1983, at which time B departs for the United States. Among other possible twelve month periods, B is present in a foreign country an aggregate of 330 full days during each of the following twelve month periods: March 21, 1982 through March 20, 1983; and April 25, 1982 through April 24, 1983.

Example (2). C, a U.S. citizen, travels extensively from the time C leaves the United States on March 5, 1982, until the time C departs the United Kingdom on January 1, 1984, to return to the United States permanently. The schedule of C's travel and the number of full days at each location are listed below:

Country	*Time and date of arrival*	*Time and date of departure*	*Full days in foreign country*
United States		10 p.m. (by air) Mar. 5, 1982	
United Kingdom	9 a.m. Mar. 6, 1982	10 p.m. (by ship) June 25, 1982	110
United States	11 a.m. June 30, 1982	1 p.m. (by ship) July 19, 1982	0
France	3 p.m. July 24, 1982	11 a.m. (by air) Aug. 22, 1983	393
United States	4 p.m. Aug. 22, 1983	9 a.m. (by air) Sept. 4, 1983	0
United Kingdom	9 a.m. Sept. 5, 1983	9 a.m. (by air) Jan. 1, 1984	117
United States	1 p.m. Jan. 1, 1984		

Among other possible twelve month periods, C is present in a foreign country or countries an aggregate of 330 full days during the following twelve month periods: March 2, 1982 through March 1, 1983; and January 21, 1983 through January 20, 1984. The computation of days with respect to each twelve month period may be illustrated as follows:

First twelve month period (March 2, 1982 through March 1, 1983):

	Full days in foreign country
Mar. 2, 1982 through Mar. 6, 1982	0
Mar. 7, 1982 through June 24, 1982	110
June 25, 1982 through July 24, 1982	0
July 25, 1982 through Mar. 1, 1983	220
Total full days	330

Second twelve month period (January 21, 1983 through January 20, 1984):

	Full days in foreign country
Jan. 21, 1983 through Aug. 21, 1983	213
Aug. 22, 1983 through Sept. 5, 1983	0
Sept. 6, 1983 through Dec. 31, 1983	117
Jan. 1, 1984 through Jan. 20, 1984	0
Total full days	330

(e) *Special rules.*—For purposes only of establishing that an individual is a qualified individual under paragraph (a) of this section, residence or presence in a foreign country while there employed by the U.S. government or any agency or instrumentality of the U.S. government counts towards satisfaction of the requirements of § 1.911-2(a). (But see section 911(b)(1)(B)(ii) and § 1.911-3(c)(3) for the rule excluding amounts paid by the U.S. government to an employee from the definition of foreign earned income.) Time spent in a foreign country prior to January 1, 1982, counts toward satisfaction of the bona fide residence and physical presence requirements, even though no exclusion or deduction may be allowed under section 911 for income attributable to services performed during that time. For purposes of paragraph (a)(2)(ii) of this section, the term "resident of the United States" includes an individual for whom a valid election is in effect under section 6013(g) or (h) for the taxable year or years during which the physical presence requirement is satisfied.

(f) *Waiver of period of stay in foreign country due to war or civil unrest.*—Notwithstanding the requirements of paragraph (a) of this section, an individual whose tax home is in a foreign country, and who is a bona fide resident of, or present in, a foreign country for any period, who leaves the foreign country after August 31, 1978, before meeting the requirements of paragraph (a) of this section, may, as provided in this paragraph, qualify to make an election under section 911(a) and § 1.911-7(a). If the Secretary determines, after consultation with the Secretary of State or his delegate, that war, civil unrest, or similar adverse conditions existed in a foreign country, then the Secretary shall publish the name of the foreign country and the dates between which such conditions were deemed to exist. In order to qualify to make an election under this paragraph, the individual must establish to the satisfaction of the Secretary that the individual left a foreign country, the name of which has been published by the Secretary, during the period when adverse conditions existed and that the individual could reasonably have expected to meet the requirements of paragraph (a) of this section but for the adverse conditions. The individual shall attach to his return for the taxable year a statement that the individual expected to meet the requirements of paragraph (a) of this section but for the conditions in the foreign country which precluded the normal conduct of business by the individual. Such individual shall be treated as a qualified individual, but only for the actual period of residence or presence. Thus, in determining the number of the individual's qualifying days, only days within the period of actual residence or presence shall be counted.

(g) *United States.*—The term "United States" when used in a geographical sense includes any territory under the sovereignty of the United States. It includes the states, the District of Columbia, the possessions and territories of the United States, the territorial waters of the United States, the air space over the United States, and the seabed and subsoil of those submarine areas which are adjacent to the territorial waters of the United States and over which the United States has exclusive rights, in accordance with international law, with respect to the exploration and exploitation of natural resources.

(h) *Foreign country.*—The term "foreign country" when used in a geographical sense includes any territory under the sovereignty of a government other than that of the United States. It includes the territorial waters of the foreign country (determined in accordance with the laws of the United States), the air space over the foreign country, and the seabed and subsoil of those submarine areas which are adjacent to the territorial waters of the foreign country and over which the foreign country has exclusive rights, in accordance with international law, with respect to the exploration and exploitation of natural resources. [Reg. § 1.911-2.]

☐ [*T.D.* 8006, 1-17-85.]

§ 1.911-3. Determination of amount of foreign earned income to be excluded.—(a) *Definition of foreign earned income.*—For purposes of section 911 and the regulations thereunder, the term "foreign earned income" means earned income (as defined in paragraph (b) of this section) from sources within a foreign country (as defined in § 1.911-2(h)) that is earned during a period for which the individual qualifies under § 1.911-2(a) to make an election. Earned income is from sources within a foreign country if it is attributable to services performed by an individual in a foreign country or countries. The place of receipt of earned income is immaterial in determining whether earned income is attributable to services performed in a foreign country or countries.

(b) *Definition of earned income.*—(1) *In general.*—The term "earned income" means wages, salaries, professional fees, and other amounts received as compensation for personal services actually rendered including the fair market value of all remuneration paid in any medium other than cash. Earned income does not include any portion of an amount paid by a corporation which represents a distribution of earnings and profits rather than a reasonable allowance as compensation for personal services actually rendered to the corporation.

(2) *Earned income from business in which capital is material.*—In the case of an individual engaged in a trade or business (other than in corporate form) in which both personal services and capital are material income producing factors, a reasonable allowance as compensation for the personal services actually rendered by the individual shall be considered earned income, but the total amount which shall be treated as the earned income of the individual from such trade or business shall in no case exceed thirty percent of the individual's share of the net profits of such trade or business.

(3) *Professional fees.*—Earned income includes all fees received by an individual engaged in a professional occupation (such as doctor or lawyer) in the performance of professional activities. Professional fees constitute earned income even though the individual employs assistants to perform part or all of the services, provided the patients or clients are those of the individual and look to the individual as the person responsible for the services rendered.

(c) *Amounts not included in foreign earned income.*—Foreign earned income does not include an amount:

(1) Excluded from gross income under section 119;

(2) Received as a pension or annuity (including social security benefits);

(3) Paid to an employee by an employer which is the U.S. government or any U.S. government agency or instrumentality;

(4) Included in the individual's gross income by reason of section 402(b) (relating to the taxability of a beneficiary of a nonexempt trust) or section 403(c) (relating to the taxability of a beneficiary under a nonqualified annuity or under annuities purchased by exempt organizations);

(5) Included in gross income by reason of § 1.911-6(b)(4)(ii); or

(6) Received after the close of the first taxable year following the taxable year in which the services giving rise to the amounts were performed. For treatment of amounts received after December 31, 1962, which are attributable to services performed on or before December 31, 1962, and with respect to which there existed on March 12, 1962, a right (whether forfeitable or nonforfeitable) to receive such amounts, see § 1.72-8.

(d) *Determination of the amount of foreign earned income that may be excluded under section 911(a)(1).*—(1) *In general.*—Foreign earned income described in this section may be excluded under section 911(a)(1) and this paragraph only to the extent of the limitation specified in paragraph (d)(2) of this section. Income is considered to be earned in the taxable year in which the services giving rise to the income are performed. The determination of the amount of excluded earned income in this manner does not affect the time for reporting any amounts included in gross income.

(2) *Limitation.*—(i) *In general.*—The term "section 911(a)(1) limitation" means the amount of foreign earned income for a taxable year which may be excluded under section 911(a)(1). The section 911(a)(1) limitation shall be equal to the lesser of the qualified individual's foreign earned income for the taxable year in excess of amounts that the individual elected to exclude from gross income under section 911(a)(2) or the product of the annual rate for the taxable year (as specified in paragraph (d)(2)(ii) of this section) multiplied by the following fraction:

$$\frac{\text{The number of qualifying days in the taxable year}}{\text{The number of days in the taxable year}}$$

(ii) *Annual rate for the taxable year.*—The annual rate for the taxable year is the rate set forth in section 911(b)(2)(A).

(3) *Number of qualifying days.*—For purposes of section 911 and the regulations thereunder, the number of qualifying days is the number of days in the taxable year within the period during which the individual met the tax home requirement and either the bona fide residence requirement or the physical presence requirement of § 1.911-2(a). Although the period of bona fide residence must include an entire taxable year, the entire uninterrupted period of residence may include fractional parts of a taxable year. For instance, if an individual who was a calendar year taxpayer established a tax home and a residence in a foreign country as of November 1, 1982, and maintained the tax home and the residence through March 31, 1984, then the uninterrupted period of bona fide residence includes fractional parts of the years 1982 and 1984, and all of 1983. The number of qualifying days in 1982 is sixty-one. The number of qualifying days in 1983 is 365. The number of qualifying days in 1984 is ninety-one. The period during which the physical presence requirement of § 1.911-2(a)(2)(ii) is met is any twelve consecutive month period during which the individual is physically present in one or more foreign countries for 330 days and the individual's tax home is in a foreign country during each day of such physical presence. Such period may include days when the individual is not physically present in a foreign country, and days when the individual does not maintain a tax home in a foreign country. Such period may include fractional parts of a taxable year. Thus, if an individual's period of physical presence is the twelve-month period beginning June 1, 1982, and ending May 31, 1983, the number of qualifying days in 1982 is 214 and the number of qualifying days in 1983 is 151.

(e) *Attribution rules.*—(1) *In general.*—Foreign earned income is considered to be earned in the taxable year in which the individual performed the services giving rise to the income. If income is earned in one taxable year and received in another taxable year, then, for purposes of determining the amount of foreign earned income that the individual may exclude under section 911(a), the individual must attribute the income to the taxable year in which the services giving rise to the income were performed. Thus, any reimbursement would be attributable to the taxable year in which the services giving rise to the obligation to pay the reimbursement were performed, not the taxable year in which the reimbursement was received. For example, tax equalization payments are normally received in the year after the year in which the services giving rise to the obligation to pay the tax equalization payment were performed. Therefore, such payments will almost always have to be attributed to the prior year. Foreign earned income attributable to services performed in a preceding taxable year shall be excludable from gross income in the year of receipt only to the extent such amount could have been excluded under paragraph (d)(1) in the preceding taxable year, had such amount been received in the preceding taxable year. The taxable year to which income is attributable will be determined on the basis of all the facts and circumstances.

(2) *Priority of use of the section 911(a)(1) limitation.*—Foreign earned income received in the year in which it is earned shall be applied to the section 911(a)(1) limitation for that year before applying income earned in that year that is received in any other year. Foreign earned income that is earned in one year and received in another year shall be applied to the section 911(a)(1) limitation for the year in which it was earned, on a year by year basis, in any order that the individual chooses. (But see section 911(b)(1)(B)(iv).) An individual may not amend his return to change the treatment of income with respect to the section 911(a)(1) exclusion after the period provided by section 6511(a). The special period of limitation provided by section 6511(d)(3) does not apply for this purpose. For example, C, a qualified individual, receives an advance bonus of $10,000 in 1982, salary of $70,000 in 1983, and a performance bonus of $10,000 in 1984, all of which are foreign earned income for 1983. C has a section 911(a)(1) limitation for 1983 of $80,000, and has no housing cost amount exclusion. On his income tax return for 1983, C elects to exclude foreign earned income of $70,000 received in 1983. C may also exclude his $10,000 advance bonus received in 1982 (by filing an amended return for 1982), or he may exclude the $10,000 performance bonus received in 1984 on his 1984 income tax return.

However, C may not exclude part of the 1982 bonus and part of the 1984 bonus.

(3) *Exception for year-end payroll period.*—Notwithstanding paragraph (e)(1) of this section, salary or wage payments of a cash basis taxpayer shall be attributed entirely to the year of receipt under the following circumstances:

(i) The period for which the payment is made is a normal payroll period of the employer which regularly applies to the employee;

(ii) The payroll period includes the last day of the employee's taxable year;

(iii) The payroll period does not exceed 16 days; and

(iv) The payment is part of a normal payroll of the employer that is distributed at the same time, in relation to the payroll period, that such payroll would normally be distributed, and is distributed before the end of the next succeeding payroll period.

(4) *Attribution of bonuses and substantially nonvested property to periods in which services were performed.*—(i) *In general.*—Bonuses and substantially nonvested property are attributable to all of the services giving rise to the income on the basis of all the facts and circumstances. If an individual receives a bonus or substantially nonvested property (as defined in § 1.83-3(b)) and it is determined to be attributable to services performed in more than one taxable year, then, for purposes of determining the amount eligible for exclusion from gross income in the year the bonus is received or the property vests, a portion of such amount shall be treated as attributable to services performed in each taxable year (or portion thereof) during the period when services giving rise to the bonus or the substantially nonvested property were performed. Such portion shall be determined by dividing the amount of the bonus or the excess of the fair market value of the vested property over the amount paid, if any, for the vested property, by the number of months in the period when services giving rise to such amount were performed, and multiplying the quotient by the number of months in such period in the taxable year. For purposes of this section, the term "month" means a calendar month. A fraction of a calendar month shall be deemed a month if it includes fifteen or more days.

(ii) *Examples.*—The following examples illustrate the application of this paragraph (e)(4).

Example (1). A, an employee of M Corporation during all of 1983 and 1984, worked in the United States from January 1 through April 30, 1983, and received $12,000 of salary for that period. A worked in country F from May 1, 1983 through the end of 1984, and is a qualified individual under § 1.911-2(a) for that period. For the period from May 1 through December 31, 1983, A received $32,000 of salary. M pays a bonus on December 20, 1983 to each of M's employees in an amount equal to 10 percent of the employee's regular wages or salary for the 1983 calendar year. The amount of A's bonus is $4,400 for 1983. The portion of A's bonus that is attributable to services performed in country F and is foreign earned income for 1983 is $3,200, or $32,000 × 10 percent. The remaining $1,200 of A's bonus is attributable to services performed in the United States, and is not foreign earned income.

Example (2). The facts are the same as in example (1), except that M determines bonuses separately for each country based on the productivity of the employees in that country. M pays a bonus to employees in country F, in the amount of 15 percent of each employee's wages or salary earned in country F. A's country F bonus is $4,800 for 1983 ($32,000 × 15 percent), and is foreign earned income for 1983. If A also receives a bonus (or if A's bonus is increased) for working in the United States during 1983, that amount is not foreign earned income.

Example (3). X corporation offers its employees a bonus of $40,000 if the employee accepts employment in a foreign country and remains in a foreign country for a period of at least four years. A, an employee of X, is a calendar year and cash basis taxpayer. A accepts employment with X in foreign country F. A begins work in F on July 1, 1983 and continues to work in F for X until June 30, 1987. In 1987 X pays A a $40,000 bonus. The bonus is attributable to services A performed from July 1, 1983 through June 30, 1987. The amount of the bonus attributable to 1987 is $5,000 (($40,000 ÷ 48) × 6). The amount of the bonus attributable to 1986 is $10,000 (($40,000 ÷ 48) × 12). A may exclude the $10,000 attributable to 1986 only to the extent that amount could have been excluded under section 911(a)(1) had A received it in 1986. The remaining $25,000 is attributable to services performed in taxable years before 1986. Such amounts may not be excluded under section 911 because they are received after the close of the taxable year following the taxable year in which the services giving rise to the income were performed.

(iii) *Special rule for elections under section 83(b).*—If an individual receives substantially nonvested property and makes an election under section 83(b) and § 1.83-2(a) to include in his gross income the amount determined under section 83(b)(1)(A) and (B) and § 1.83-2(a) for the taxable year in which the property is transferred (as defined in § 1.83-3(a)), then, for the purpose of determining the amount eligible for exclusion in the year of receipt, the individual may elect either of the following options.

(A) Substantially nonvested property may be treated as attributable entirely to services performed in the taxable year in which an election to include it in income is made. If so treated, then the amount otherwise included in gross income as determined under § 1.83-2(a) will be excludable under section 911(a) for such year subject to the limitation provided in § 1.911-3(d)(2) for such year.

(B) A portion of the substantially nonvested property may be treated as attributable to services performed or to be performed in each taxable year during which the substantial risk of forfeiture (as defined in section 83(c) and § 1.83-3(c)) exists. The portion treated as attributable to services performed or to be performed in each taxable year is determined by dividing the amount of the substantially nonvested property included in gross income as determined under § 1.83-2(a) by the number of months during the period when a substantial risk of forfeiture exists. The quotient is multiplied by the total number of months in the taxable year during which a substantial risk of forfeiture exists. The amount determined to be attributable to services performed in the year the election is made shall be excluded from gross income for such year as provided in paragraph (d)(2) of this section. Amounts treated as attributable to services performed in subsequent taxable years shall be excludable in the year of receipt only to the extent such amounts could be excluded under paragraph (d)(2) of this section in such subsequent year. An individual may obtain such additional exclusion by filing an amended return for the taxable year in which the property was transferred. The individual may only amend his or her return within the period provided by section 6511(a) and the regulations thereunder.

(5) *Moving expense reimbursements.*—(i) *Source of reimbursements.*—For the purpose of determining whether a moving expense reimbursement is attributable to services performed within a foreign country or within the United States, in the absence of evidence to the contrary, the reimbursement shall be attributable to future services to be performed at the new principal place of work. Thus, a reimbursement received by an employee from his employer for the expenses of a move to a foreign country will generally be attributable to services performed in the foreign country. A reimbursement received by an employee from his employer for the expenses of a move from a foreign country to the United States will generally be attributable to services performed in the United States. For purposes of this paragraph (e)(5), evidence to the contrary includes, but is not limited to, an agreement, between the employer and the employee, or a statement of company policy, which is reduced to writing before the move to the foreign country and which is entered into or established to induce the employee or employees to move to a foreign country. The writing must state that the employer will reimburse the employee for moving expenses incurred in returning to the United States regardless of whether the employee continues to work for the employer after the employee returns to the United States. The writing may contain conditions upon which the right to reimbursement is determined as long as the conditions set forth standards that are definitely ascertainable and the conditions can only be fulfilled prior to, or through completion of, the employee's return move to the United States that is the subject of the writing. In no case will an oral agreement or statement of company policy concerning moving expenses be considered evidence to the contrary. For the purpose of determining whether a storage expense reimbursement is attributable to services performed within a foreign country, in the case of storage expenses incurred after December 31, 1983, the reimbursement shall be attributable to services performed during the period of time for which the storage expenses are incurred.

(ii) *Attribution of foreign source reimbursements to taxable years in which services are performed.*—(A) *In general.*—If a reimbursement for moving expenses is determined to be from foreign sources under paragraph (e)(5)(i) of this section, then for the purpose of determining the amount eligible for exclusion in accordance with paragraphs (d)(2) and (e)(2) of this section, the reimbursement shall be considered attributable to services performed in the year of the move as long as the individual is a qualified individual for a period that includes 120 days in the year of the move. The period that is used in determining the number of qualifying days for purposes of the individual's section 911(a)(1) limitation (under paragraph (d)(2) of this section) must also be used in determining whether the individual is a qualified individual for a period that includes 120 days in the year of the move. If the individual is not a qualified individual for such period, then the individual shall treat a portion of the reimbursement as attributable to services performed in the year of the move, and a portion as attributable to services performed in the succeeding taxable year, if the move is from the United States to a foreign country, or to the prior taxable year, if the move is from a foreign country to the United States. The portion of the reimbursement treated as attributable to services performed in the year of the move shall be determined by multiplying the total reimbursement by the following fraction:

$$\frac{\text{The number of qualifying days (as defined in paragraph (d)(3) of this section) in the year of the move}}{\text{The number of days in the taxable year of the move.}}$$

The remaining portion of the reimbursement shall be treated as attributable to services performed in the year succeeding or preceding the year of the move. Amounts treated as attributable to services performed in a year succeeding or preceding the year of the move shall be excludable in the year of receipt only to the extent such amounts could be excluded under paragraph (d)(2) of this section in such succeeding or preceding year.

(B) *Moves beginning before January 1, 1984.*—Notwithstanding paragraph (e)(5)(ii)(A) of this section, this paragraph (e)(5)(ii)(B) shall apply for moves begun before January 1, 1984. If a reimbursement for moving expenses is determined to be from foreign sources under paragraph (e)(5)(i) of this section, then for the purpose of determining the amount eligible for exclusion in accordance with paragraphs (d)(2) and (e)(2) of this section, the reimbursement shall be considered attributable to services performed in the year of the move. However, if the individual does not qualify under section 911(d)(1) and § 1.911-2(a) for the entire taxable year of the move, then the individual shall treat a portion of the reimbursement as attributable to services performed in the succeeding taxable year, if the move is from the United States to a foreign country, or to the prior taxable year, if the move is from a foreign country to the United States. The portion of the reimbursement treated as attributable to services performed in the year succeeding or preceding the move shall be determined by multiplying the total reimbursement by the following fraction:

$$\frac{\text{The number of qualifying days (as defined in paragraph (d)(3) of this section) in the year of the move}}{\text{The number of days in the taxable year of the move.}}$$

and subtracting the product from the total reimbursement. Amounts treated as attributable to services performed in a year succeeding or preceding the year of the move shall be excludable in the year of receipt only to the extent such amounts could be excluded under paragraph (d)(2) of this section in such succeeding or preceding year.

(f) *Examples.*—The following examples illustrate the application of this section.

Example (1). A is a U.S. citizen and calendar year taxpayer. A's tax home was in foreign country F and A was physically present in F for 330 days during the period from July 4, 1982 through July 3, 1983. The number of A's qualifying days in 1982 as determined under paragraph (d)(2) of this section is 181. In 1982 A receives $40,000 attributable to services performed in foreign country F in 1982. Under paragraph (d)(2) of this section A's section 911(a)(1) limitation is $37,192, that is the lesser of $40,000 (foreign earned income) or

$$\$75{,}000 \text{ (annual rate)} \times \frac{181 \text{ (qualifying days)}}{365 \text{ (days in taxable year).}}$$

Example (2). The facts are the same as in example (1) except that in 1982 A receives $30,000 attributable to services performed in foreign country F. A excludes this amount from gross income under paragraph (d) of this section. In addition, in 1983 A receives $10,000 attributable to services performed in F in 1982 and $35,000 attributable to services performed in F in 1983. On his return for 1983, A must report $45,000 of income. A's section 911(a)(1) limitation for 1983 is the lesser of $35,000 (foreign earned income) or $40,329, the annual rate for the taxable year multiplied by a fraction the numerator of which is A's qualifying days in the taxable year and the denominator of which is the number of days in the taxable year ($80,000 × 184/365). On his tax return for 1983 A may exclude $35,000 attributable to services performed in 1983. A may only exclude $7,192 of the $10,000 received in 1983 attributable to services performed in 1982 because such amount is only excludable in 1983 to the extent such amount could have been excluded in 1982 subject to the section 911(a)(1) limitation for 1982 which is $37,192 ($75,000 × 181/365). No portion of amounts attributable to services performed in 1982 may be used in calculating A's section 911(a)(1) limitation for 1983. Thus, even though A could have excluded an additional $6,329 in 1983 if A had had more foreign earned income attributable to 1983, A may not exclude the $2,808 of remaining foreign earned income attributable to 1982.

Example (3). C is a U.S. citizen and calendar year taxpayer. C establishes a bona fide residence and a tax home in foreign country J on March 1, 1982, and maintains a tax home and a residence in J until December 31, 1986. In March of 1982 C's employer, Y corporation, transfers stock in Y to C. The stock is subject to forfeiture if C returns to the U.S. before January 1, 1985. C elects under section 83(b) to include $15,000, the amount determined with respect to such stock under section 83(b)(1), in gross income in 1982. C's other foreign earned income in 1982 is $58,000. C elects under paragraph (e)(4)(iii)(B) of this section to treat the stock as if earned over the period of the substantial risk of forfeiture. The number of months in the period of the substantial risk of forfeiture is thirty-four. The number of months in the taxable year 1982 within the period of foreign employment is ten. For purposes of determining C's section 911(a)(1) limitation, $4,412 (($15,000/34) × 10) of the amount included in gross income under section 83(b) is treated as attributable to services performed in 1982, $5,294 is treated as attributable to services to be performed in 1983, and $5,294 is treated as attributable to services to be performed in 1984. In 1982, C excludes $62,412 under section 911(a)(1). That is the lesser of foreign earned income for 1982 ($56,000 + $4,412) or the annual rate for the taxable year multiplied by a fraction the numerator of which is C's qualifying days in the taxable year and the denominator of which is the number of days in the taxable year ($75,000 × 306/365). C continues to perform services in foreign country J throughout 1983 and 1984. C would be able to exclude the remaining $5,294 attributable to services performed in 1983 and $5,294 attributable to services performed in 1984 if those amounts would be excludable if they had been received in 1983 or 1984 respectively. If C is entitled to exclude the additional amounts, C must claim the exclusion by filing an amended return for 1982.

Example (4). D is a U.S. citizen and calendar year taxpayer. In September, 1984 D moves to foreign country K. D is physically present in K, and D's tax home is in K, from September 15, 1984 through December 31, 1985. D receives $6,000 in April, 1985 from his employer, as a reimbursement for expenses of moving to K, pursuant to a written agreement that such moving expenses would be reimbursed to D upon successful completion of 6 months employment in K. Under paragraph (e)(5)(i) of this section, the reimbursement is attributable to services performed in K. Under the physical presence test of § 1.911-2(a)(2)(ii), among other periods D is a qualified individual for the period of August 10, 1984 through August 9, 1985, which includes 144 days in 1984. Under paragraph (e)(5)(ii)(A) of this section, for the purpose of determining the amount eligible for exclusion, the reimbursement is considered attributable to services performed in 1984 (the year of the move) because D is a qualified individual under § 1.911-2(a) for a period that includes 120 days in 1984. The reimbursement may be excluded under paragraphs (d)(2) and (c)(2) of this section, to the extent that D's foreign earned income for 1984 that was earned and received in 1984 was less than the annual rate for the taxable year multiplied by the number of D's qualifying days in the taxable year over the number of days in D's taxable year ($80,000 × 144/366), or $31,475.

Example (5). The facts are the same as in example (4) except that D is not a qualified individual under the physical presence test, but is a qualified individual under the bona fide residence test for the period of September 15, 1984 through December 31, 1985. Under paragraph (e)(5)(ii)(A) of this section, for the purpose of determining the amount eligible for exclusion, the reimbursement is considered attributable to services performed in 1984 and 1985 because D is not a qualified individual for a period that includes 120 days in 1984 (the year of the move). The portion of the reimbursement treated as attributable to services performed in 1984 is $6,000 × 108/366, or $1,770, and may be excluded, subject to D's 1984 section 911(a)(1) limitation. The balance of the reimbursement, $4,230, is treated as attributable to services performed in 1985, and may be excluded to the extent provided in paragraphs (d)(2) and (e)(2) of this section.

Example (6). The facts are the same as in Example (4), with the following additions. Before D moved to K, D and his employer signed a written agreement that D would perform services for the employer for at least one year, primarily in country K, and, if D did not voluntarily cease to work for the employer primarily in country K before one year had elapsed, the employer would reimburse D for one-half of D's expenses, up to a maximum of $4,000, of moving back to the United States. The agreement also stated that, if D did not voluntarily leave the employment in K before two years had elapsed, the employer would reimburse D for all of D's reasonable expenses of moving back to the United States. The agreement further stated that D's right to reimbursement would not be conditioned upon the performance of services after D ceased to work in K. D worked in country K for all of 1985. On January 1, 1986, D left K and moved to the United States. In February, 1986 the employer paid D $3,500 as reimbursement for one-half of D's expenses of moving to the United States. Although D did not fulfill the condition in the agreement to receive full reimbursement, all of the conditions in the agreement set forth definitely ascertainable standards and no condition could be fulfilled after D moved back to the United States. The agreement fulfills the requirements of paragraph (e)(5)(i) of this section, and therefore is evidence that the reimbursement should not be attributable to future services to be performed at D's new principal place of work. Under the facts and circumstances, the reimbursement is attributable to services performed in K. Under paragraph (e)(5)(ii)(A) of this section, the entire reimbursement is attributable to services performed in 1985. The amount attributable in 1985 may be excluded to the extent provided in paragraphs (d)(2) and (e)(2) of this section. [Reg. § 1.911-3.]

☐ [*T.D.* 8006, 1-17-85.]

§ 1.911-4. Determination of housing cost amount eligible for exclusion or deduction.—(a) *Definition of housing cost amount.*—The term "housing cost amount" means an amount equal to the reasonable expenses paid or incurred (as defined in section 7701(a)(25)) during the taxable year by or on behalf of the individual attributable to housing in a foreign country for the individual and any spouse or dependents who reside with the individual (or live in a second foreign household described in paragraph (b)(5) of this section) less the base housing amount as defined in paragraph (c) of this section. The housing cost amount must be reduced by the amount of any military or section 912 allowance or similar allowance excludable from gross income that is intended to compensate the individual or the individual's spouse in whole or in part for the expenses of housing during the same period for which the individual claims a housing cost amount exclusion or deduction.

(b) *Housing expenses.*—(1) *Included expenses.*—For purposes of paragraph (a) of this section, housing expenses include rent, the fair rental value of housing provided in kind by the employer, utilities (other than telephone charges), real and personal property insurance, occupancy taxes not described in paragraph (b)(2)(v) of this section, nonrefundable fees paid for securing a leasehold, rental of furniture and accessories, household repairs, and residential parking.

(2) *Excluded expenses.*—Housing expenses do not include:

(i) The cost of house purchase, improvements, and other costs that are capital expenditures;

(ii) The cost of purchased furniture or accessories or domestic labor (maids, gardeners, etc.);

(iii) Amortized payments of principal with respect to an evidence of indebtedness secured by a mortgage on the taxpayers housing;

(iv) Depreciation of housing owned by the taxpayer, or amortization or depreciation of capital improvements made to housing leased by the taxpayer;

(v) Interest and taxes deductible under section 163 or 164 or other amounts deductible under section 216(a) (relating to deduction of interest and taxes by cooperative housing corporation tenant);

(vi) The expenses of more than one foreign household except as provided in paragraph (b)(5) of this section;

(vii) Expenses excluded from gross income under section 119;

(viii) Expenses claimed as deductible moving expenses under section 217; or

(ix) The cost of a pay television subscription.

(3) *Limitation.* Housing expenses are taken into account for purposes of this section only to the extent attributable to housing for portions of the taxable year within the period during which the individual satisfies the requirements of § 1.911-2(a). Housing expenses are not taken into account for the period during which the value of the individual's housing is excluded from gross income under section 119, unless the individual maintains a second foreign household described in paragraph (b)(5) of this section. If an individual maintains two foreign households, only expenses incurred with respect to the abode which bears the closest relationship, not necessarily geographic, with respect to the individual's tax home shall be taken into account, unless one of the households is a second foreign household.

(4) *Reasonableness.*—An amount paid for housing shall not be treated as reasonable, for purposes of paragraph (a) of this section, to the extent that the expense is lavish or extravagant under the circumstances.

(5) *Expenses of a second foreign household.*—(i) *In general.*—The term "second foreign household" means a separate abode maintained by an individual outside of the U.S. for his or her spouse or dependents (who, if minors, are in the individual's legal custody or the joint custody of the individual and the individual's spouse) at a place other than the tax home of the individual because of adverse living conditions at the individual's tax home. If an individual maintains a second foreign household the expenses of the second foreign household may be included in the individual's housing expenses under paragraph (b)(1) of this section. Under no circumstances shall an individual be considered to maintain more than one second foreign household at the same time.

(ii) *Adverse living conditions.*—Solely for purposes of paragraph (b)(5)(i) of this section, adverse living conditions are living conditions which are dangerous, unhealthful, or otherwise adverse. Adverse living conditions include a state of warfare or civil insurrection in the general area of the individual's tax home. Adverse living conditions exist if the individual resides on the business premises of the employer for the convenience of the employer and, because of the nature of the business (for example, a construction site or drilling rig), it is not feasible for the employer to provide housing for the individual's spouse or dependents. The criteria used by the Department of State in granting a separate maintenance allowance are relevant, but not determinative, for purposes of determining whether a separate household is provided because of adverse living conditions.

(c) *Base housing amount.*—(1) *In general.*—The base housing amount is equal to the product of 16 percent of the annual salary of an employee of the United States who is compensated at a rate equal to the annual salary rate paid for step 1 of grade GS-14, multiplied by the following fraction:

$$\frac{\text{The number of qualifying days}}{\text{The number of days in the taxable year}}$$

For purposes of the above fraction, the number of qualifying days is determined in accordance with § 1.911-3(d)(3).

(2) *Annual salary of step 1 of grade GS-14.*—The annual salary rate for a step 1 of grade GS-14 is determined on January first of the calendar year in which the individual's taxable year begins.

(d) *Housing costs amount exclusion.*—(1) *Limitation.*—A qualified individual who has elected to exclude his or her housing cost amount may only exclude the lesser of the full amount of either the individual's housing cost amount attributable to employer provided amounts or the individual's foreign earned income for the taxable year. A qualified individual who elects to exclude his or her housing cost amount may not claim less than the full amount of the housing cost exclusion determined under this paragraph.

(2) *Employer provided amounts.*—For purposes of this section, the term "employer provided amounts" means any amounts paid or incurred on behalf of the individual by the individual's employer which are foreign earned income included in the individual's gross

income for the taxable year (without regard to section 911). Employer provided amounts include, but are not limited to, the following amounts: any salary paid by the employer to the employee; any reimbursement paid by the employer to the employee for housing expenses, educational expenses for the individual's dependents, or as part of a tax equalization plan; the fair market value of compensation provided in kind (including lodging, unless excluded under section 119, relating to meals and lodging furnished for the convenience of the employer); and any amount paid by the employer to any third party on behalf of the employee. An individual will only have earnings that are not employer provided amounts if the individual has earnings from self-employment.

(3) *Housing cost amount attributable to employer provided amounts.*—For the purpose of determining what portion of the housing cost amount is excludable and what portion is deductible the following rules apply. If the individual has no income from self-employment, then the entire housing cost amount is attributable to employer provided amounts and is, therefore, excludable to the extent of the limitation provided in paragraph (d)(1) of this section. If the individual only has income from self-employment, then the entire housing cost amount is attributable to non-employer provided amounts and is, therefore, deductible to the extent of the limitation provided in paragraph (e) of this section. In all other instances, the housing cost amount attributable to employer provided amounts shall be determined by multiplying the housing cost amount by the following fraction: employer provided amounts over foreign earned income for the taxable year. The housing cost amount attributable to non-employer provided amounts shall be determined by subtracting the portion of the housing cost amount attributable to employer provided amounts from the total housing cost amount.

(e) *Housing cost amount deduction.*—(1) *In general.*—If a portion of the individual's housing cost amount is determined under paragraph (d)(3) of this section to be attributable to non-employer provided amounts, the individual may deduct that amount from gross income for the taxable year but only to the extent of the individual's foreign earned income (as defined in § 1.911-3) for the taxable year in excess of foreign earned income excluded and the housing cost amount excluded from gross income for the taxable year under § 1.911-3 and this section.

(2) *Carryover.*—If any portion of the individual's housing cost amount deduction is disallowed for the taxable year under paragraph (e)(1) of this section, such portion shall be carried over and treated as a deduction from gross income for the succeeding taxable year (but only for the succeeding taxable year) to the extent of the excess, if any, of:

(i) The amount of foreign earned income for the succeeding taxable year less the foreign earned income and the housing cost amount excluded from gross income under § 1.911-3 and this section for the succeeding taxable year over,

(ii) The portion, if any, of the housing cost amount that is deductible under paragraph (e)(1) of this section for the succeeding taxable year.

(f) *Examples.*—The following examples illustrate the application of this section. In all examples the annual rate for a step 1 of GS-14 as of January first of the calendar year in which the individual's taxable year begins is $39,689.

Example (1). B, a U.S. citizen, is a calendar year taxpayer who was a bona fide resident of and whose tax home was located in foreign country G for the entire taxable year 1982. B receives an $80,000 salary from B's employer for services performed in G. B incurs no business expenses. B receives housing provided by B's employer with a fair rental value of $15,000. The value of the housing furnished by B's employer is not excluded from gross income under section 119. B pays $10,000 for housing expenses. B's gross income and foreign earned income for 1982 is $95,000. B elects the foreign earned income exclusion of section 911(a)(1) and the housing cost amount exclusion of section 911(a)(2). B must first compute his housing cost amount exclusion. B's housing cost amount is $18,650 determined by reducing B's housing expenses, $25,000 ($15,000 fair rental value of housing and $10,000 of other expenses), by the base housing amount of $6,350 (($39,689 × .16) × 365/365). Because B has no income from self-employment, the entire amount is attributable to employer provided amounts and, therefore, is excludable. B's section 911(a)(1) limitation is over $75,000. That is the lesser of $75,000 × 365/365 or $95,000 – 18,650. B's total exclusion for 1982 under section 911(a)(1) and (2) is $93,650.

Example (2). The facts are the same as in example (1) except that B's salary for 1982 is $70,000. B's foreign earned income for 1982 is $85,000. B's housing cost amount is $18,650, all of which is attributable to employer provided amounts. B's housing cost amount is excludable to the extent of the lesser of B's housing cost amount attributable to employer provided amounts, $18,650, or the foreign earned income for the taxable year, $85,000. Thus, B excludes $18,650 under section 911(a)(2). B's section 911(a)(1) limitation for 1982 is $66,350 (the lesser of $75,000 × 365/365 or $85,000 – 18,650). B's total exclusion for 1982 under section 911(a)(1) and (2) is $85,000.

Example (3). The facts are the same as in example (2) except that in 1983, B receives $5,000 attributable to services performed in 1982. B may exclude the entire $5,000 in 1983 because such amount would have been excludable under § 1.911-3(d)(1) had it been received in 1982.

Example (4). C is a U.S. citizen, self-employed, and a calendar year and cash basis taxpayer. C arrived in foreign country H on October 3, 1982, and departed from H on March 8, 1984. C's tax home was located in H throughout that period. C was physically present for 330 full days during the twelve consecutive month period August 30, 1982 through August 29, 1983. The number of C's qualifying days in 1982 is 124. During 1982 C had $35,000 of foreign earned income, none of which was attributable to employer provided amounts, and $8,000 of reasonable housing expenses. C's housing cost amount is $5,843 ($8,000 – ((39,689 × .16) × 124/365)). C elects to exclude her foreign earned income under § 1.911-3(d)(1). C's section 911(a)(1) limitation for 1982 is $25,479 (the lesser of C's foreign earned income for the taxable year ($35,000) or the annual rate for the taxable year multiplied by the number of C's qualifying days over the number of days in the taxable year ($75,000 × 124/365 = $25,479)). C may not claim the housing cost amount exclusion under section 911(a)(2) because no portion of the housing cost amount is attributable to employer provided amounts. C may deduct the lesser of her housing cost amount ($5,843) or her foreign earned income in excess of amounts excluded under section 911(a) ($35,000 – 25,479 = $9,521). Thus, C's housing cost amount deduction is $5,843.

Example (5). The facts are the same as in example (4) except that C had $30,000 of foreign earned income for 1982, none of which was attributable to employer provided amounts. C elects to exclude $25,479 under § 1.911-3(d)(1). C may only deduct $4,521 of her housing cost amount under paragraph (e)(1) of this section because her foreign earned income in excess of amounts excluded under section 911(a) is $4,521 ($30,000 – 25,479). The $1322 of unused housing cost amount deduction may be carried over to the subsequent taxable year.

Example (6). The facts are the same as in example (4) except that C had $15,000 of foreign earned income for 1982, none of which was attributable to employer provided amounts. C elects to exclude the entire $15,000 under § 1.911-3(d)(1). C is not entitled to a housing cost amount deduction for 1982 since she has no foreign earned income in excess of amounts excluded under section 911(a). C may carryover her entire housing cost amount deduction to 1983.

Example (7). The facts are the same as in example (6). In addition, during taxable year 1983 C had $115,000 of foreign earned income, none of which was attributable to employer provided amounts, and $40,000 of reasonable housing expenses. C elects to exclude her foreign earned income under § 1.911-3(d)(1). C's section 911(a)(1) limitation is the lesser of $115,000 or $80,000 ($80,000 × 365/365). C's housing cost amount for 1983 is $33,650 (40,000 – ($39,689 × .16) × 365/365). Since no portion of that amount is attributable to employer provided amounts, C may not claim a housing cost amount exclusion. C may deduct the lesser of her housing cost amount ($33,650) or her foreign earned income in excess of amounts excluded under section 911(a) ($115,000 – 80,000 = 35,000). Thus, C may deduct her $33,650 housing cost amount in 1983. In addition, C may deduct $1,350 of the housing cost amount deduction carried over from taxable year 1982 (($115,000 – 80,000) – 33,650 = $1,350). The remaining $4,493 ($5,843 – 1,350) of the housing cost amount deduction carried over from taxable year 1982 may not be deducted in 1983 or carried over to 1984.

Example (8). D is a U.S. citizen and a calendar year and cash basis taxpayer. D is a bona fide resident of and maintains his tax home in foreign country J for all of taxable year 1984. In 1984, D earns $80,000 of foreign earned income, $60,000 of which is an employer provided amount and $20,000 of which is a non-employer provided amount. D's total housing cost amount for 1984 is $25,000. D elects to exclude, under section 911(a)(2), the portion of his housing cost amount that is attributable to employer provided amounts. D's excludable housing cost amount is $18,750; that is the total housing cost amount ($25,000) multiplied by employer provided amounts for the taxable year ($60,000) over foreign earned income for the taxable year ($80,000). D also elects to exclude his foreign earned income under § 1.911-3(d)(1). D's section 911(a)(1) limitation for 1984 is $61,250 (the lesser of $80,000 – $18,750 or $80,000 × 366/366). D's total exclusion for 1984 under section 911(a)(1) and (2) is $80,000. D cannot claim a housing cost amount deduction in 1984 because D has no foreign earned income in excess of his foreign earned income and housing cost amount excluded from gross income for the taxable year under § 1.911-3 and this section. D may carry over his housing cost amount deduction of $6,250, the total housing cost amount less the portion attributable to employer provided amounts ($25,000 – 18,750), to taxable year 1985. [Reg. § 1.911-4.]

☐ [*T.D.* 8006, 1-17-85.]

§ 1.911-5. Special rules for married couples.—(a) *Married couples with two qualified individuals.*—(1) *In general.*—In the case in which a husband and wife both are qualified individuals under § 1.911-2(a), each individual may make one or more elections under § 1.911-7 and exclude from gross income foreign earned income and exclude or deduct housing cost amounts subject to the rules of paragraph (a)(2) and (3) of this section.

(2) *Computation of excluded foreign earned income.*—The amount of excludable foreign earned income is determined separately for each spouse under the rules of § 1.911-3 on the basis of the income attributable to the services of that spouse. If the spouses file separate returns each may exclude the amount of his or her foreign earned income attributable to his or her services subject to the limitations of § 1.911-3(d)(2). If the spouses file a joint return, the sum of these foreign earned income amounts so determined for each spouse may be excluded. For example, H and W both qualify under § 1.911-2(a)(2)(i) for the entire 1983 taxable year. During 1983 W earns $100,000 of foreign earned income and H earns $45,000 of foreign earned income. H and W file a joint return for 1983. On their joint return H and W may exclude from gross income a total of $125,000. That amount is determined by adding W's section 911(a)(1) limitation, $80,000 (the lesser of $80,000 × 365/365 or $100,000), and H's section 911(a)(1) limitation, $45,000 (the lesser of $80,000 × 365/365 or $45,000).

(3) *Computation of housing cost amount.*—(i) *Spouses residing together.*—If the spouses reside together, and file a joint return, they may compute their housing cost amount either jointly or separately. If the spouses reside together and file separate returns, they must compute their housing cost amounts separately. If the spouses compute their housing cost amounts separately, they may allocate the housing expenses to either of them or between them for the purpose of calculating separate housing cost amounts, but each spouse claiming a housing cost amount exclusion or deduction must use his or her full base housing amount in such computation. If the spouses compute their housing cost amount jointly, then only one of the spouses may claim the housing cost amount exclusion or deduction. Either spouse may claim the housing cost amount exclusion or deduction; however, if the spouses have different periods of residence or presence and the spouse with the shorter period of residence or presence claims the exclusion or deduction, then only the expenses incurred in that shorter period may be claimed as housing expenses. The spouse claiming the exclusion or deduction may aggregate the couple's housing expenses, and subtract his or her base housing amount. For example, H and W reside together and file a joint return. H was a bona fide resident of and maintained his tax home in foreign country M from August 17, 1982 through December 31, 1983. W was a bona fide resident of and maintained her tax home in foreign country M from September 15, 1982 through December 31, 1983. During 1982, H and W earn and receive, respectively, $25,000 and $10,000 of foreign earned income. H paid $10,000 for qualified housing expenses in 1982, $7,500 of that was for qualified housing expenses incurred from September 15, 1982 through December 31, 1982. W paid $3,000 for qualified housing expenses in 1982 all of which were incurred during her period of residence. H and W may choose to compute their housing cost amount jointly. If they do so and H claims the housing cost amount exclusion his exclusion would be $10,617. H's housing expenses would be $13,000 ($10,000 + $3,000) and his base housing amount would be $2,383 (($39,689 × .16) × 137/365 = $2,383). If instead W claims the housing cost amount exclusion her exclusion would be $8,621. W's housing expenses would be $10,500 ($7,500 + 3,000) and her base housing amount would be $1,879 (($39,689 × .16) × 108/365 = $1,879). If H and W file jointly and both claim a housing cost amount exclusion, then H's and W's housing cost amounts would be, respectively, $7,617 ($10,000 – 2,383) and $1,121 ($3,000 – 1,879).

(ii) *Spouses residing apart.*—If the spouses reside apart, both spouses may exclude or deduct their housing cost amount if the spouses have different tax homes that are not within reasonable commuting distance (as defined in § 1.119-(d)(4)) of each other and neither spouse's residence is within a reasonable commuting distance of the other spouse's tax home. If the spouses' tax homes, or one spouse's residence and the other spouse's tax home, are within a reasonable commuting distance of each other, only one spouse may exclude or deduct his or her housing cost amount. Regardless of whether the spouses file joint or separate returns, the amount of the housing cost amount exclusion or deduction must be determined separately for each spouse under the rules of § 1.911-4. If both spouses claim a housing cost amount exclusion or deduction directly as qualified individuals, neither may claim any such exclusion or deduction under section 911(c)(2)(B)(ii), relating to a second foreign household maintained for the other spouse. If one spouse fails to claim a housing cost amount exclusion or deduction which that spouse could claim directly, the other spouse may claim such exclusion or deduction under section 911(c)(2)(B)(ii), relating to a second foreign household maintained for the first spouse, provided that all the requirements of that section are met. Spouses may not claim more than one second foreign household and the expenses of such household may only be claimed by one spouse. For example, if both H and W are qualified individuals and H's tax home is in London and W's tax home is in Paris, then both H and W may exclude or deduct their housing cost amounts; however, H and W must compute these amounts separately regardless of whether they file joint or separate returns. If instead of living in Paris, W lives in an area where there are adverse living conditions and W maintains H's home in London, then W may add those housing expenses to her housing expenses and compute one base housing amount. In that case H may not claim a housing cost amount exclusion or deduction.

(iii) *Housing cost amount attributable to employer provided amounts.*—Each spouse claiming a housing cost amount exclusion or deduction shall compute the portion of the housing cost amount that is attributable to employer provided amounts separately, based on his or her separate foreign earned income, in accordance with § 1.911-4(d)(3).

(b) *Married couples with community income.*—The amount of excludable foreign earned income of a husband and wife with community income is determined separately for each spouse in accordance with paragraph (a) of this section on the basis of income attributable to that spouse's services without regard to community property laws. See sections 879 and 6013(g) and (h) for special rules regarding treatment of community income of a nonresident alien individual married to a U.S. citizen or resident. [Reg. § 1.911-5.]

☐ [*T.D.* 8006, 1-17-85.]

§ 1.911-6. Disallowance of deductions, exclusions, and credits.—(a) *In general.*—No deduction or exclusion from gross income under Subtitle A of the Code or credit against the tax imposed by chapter 1 of the Code shall be allowed to the extent the deduction, exclusion, or credit is properly allocable to or chargeable against amounts excluded from gross income under section 911(a). For purposes of the preceding sentence, deductions, exclusions, and credits which are definitely related (as provided in § 1.861-8), in whole or in part, to earned income shall be allocated and apportioned to foreign earned income and U.S. source earned income in accordance with the rules contained in § 1.861-8. Deductions, exclusions, and credits which are definitely related to all gross income under § 1.861-8, including deductions for interest described in § 1.861-8(e)(2)(ii), are definitely related, in whole or in part, to earned income. In the case of interest expense allocable, in whole or in part, to foreign earned income under § 1.861-8(e)(2)(ii), the expense shall normally be apportioned under option one of the optional gross income methods of apportionment (§ 1.861-8(e)(2)(vi)(A)), but without regard to conditions *(1)* and *(2)* of subdivision (vi)(A) (the fifty percent conditions). Such interest expense shall not normally be apportioned under the asset method of § 1.861-8(e)(2)(v). This is because, where section 911 is the operative section, the expense normally relates more closely to gross income generated from activities than to the amount of capital utilized or invested in activities or property. Deductions that are allocated and apportioned to foreign earned income must then be allocated and apportioned to foreign earned income that is excluded under section 911(a). If an individual has foreign earned income from both self-employment and other employment, the amount excluded under section 911(a)(1) shall be deemed to include a pro rata amount of the self-employment income and the income from other employment; thus, a pro rata portion of deductible expenses attributable to self-employment income must be disallowed. For purposes of section

911(d)(6) and this section only, deductions, exclusions, or credits which are not definitely related to any class of gross income shall not be allocable or chargeable to excluded amounts and are, therefore, deductible to the extent allowed by chapter 1 of the Code. Examples of deductions that are not definitely related to a class of gross income are personal and family medical expenses, qualified retirement contributions (but see section 219(b)(1)), real estate taxes and mortgage interest on a personal residence, charitable contributions, alimony payments, and deductions for personal exemptions. In addition, for purposes of this section, amounts excludable or deductible under section 911 or 119 shall not be allocable or chargeable to other amounts excluded under section 911(a). Thus, an individual's housing cost amount which is excludable or deductible under § 1.911-4(d) for a taxable year is not apportioned in part to the individual's foreign earned income which is excluded for such year under § 1.911-3(d). Therefore, the entire amount of such exclusion or deduction is allowed to the extent provided in § 1.911-4. This section does not affect the time for claiming any deduction, exclusion, or credit that is not allocated or apportioned to excluded amounts.

(b) *Moving expenses.*—(1) *In general.*—No deduction shall be allowed for moving expenses under section 217 to the extent the deduction is properly allocable to or chargeable against amounts of foreign earned income excluded from gross income under section 911(a). If an individual's new principal place of work is in a foreign country, deductible moving expenses will be allocable to foreign earned income. If an individual treats a reimbursement from his employer for the expenses of a move from a foreign country to the United States as attributable to services performed in a foreign country under § 1.911-3(e)(5)(i), then deductible moving expenses attributable to that move will be allocable to foreign earned income. If the individual is a qualified individual who elects to exclude foreign earned income under section 911(a), then some or all of such moving expenses must be disallowed as a deduction.

(2) *Attribution of moving expense deduction to taxable years in which services are performed.*—If a moving expense deduction is properly allocable to foreign earned income, the deduction shall be considered attributable to services performed in the year of the move as long as the individual is a qualified individual under § 1.911-2(a) for a period that includes 120 days in the year of the move. If the individual is not a qualified individual for such period, then the individual shall treat the deduction as attributable to services performed in both the year of the move and the succeeding taxable year, if the move is from the United States to the foreign country, or the prior taxable year, if the move is from a foreign country to the United States. Notwithstanding the preceding two sentences, storage expenses incurred after December 31, 1983 shall be treated as attributable to services performed in the year in which the expenses are incurred.

(3) *Formula for disallowance of moving expense deduction.*—The portion of the moving expense deduction that is disallowed shall be determined by multiplying the moving expense deduction by a fraction the numerator of which is all amounts excluded under section 911(a) for the year or years to which the deduction is attributable (under paragraph (b)(2) of this section) and the denominator of which is foreign earned income (as defined in § 1.911-3(a)) for that year or years.

(4) *Effect of disallowance based on attribution of deduction to subsequent year's income.*—An individual may claim a moving expense deduction in the taxable year in which the amount of the expense is paid or incurred even if attributable, in part, to the succeeding year. However, at such time as the individual excludes income under section 911(a) for the year or years to which the deduction is attributable, the individual shall either—

(i) file an amended return for the year in which the deduction was claimed that does not claim the portion of the deduction that is disallowed because it is chargeable against excluded income, or

(ii) include in income for the year following the year in which the deduction was claimed an amount equal to the amount of the deduction that is disallowed.

Any amount included in income under paragraph (b)(4)(ii) of this section is not foreign earned income.

(5) *Moves beginning before January 1, 1984.*—Notwithstanding paragraph (b)(1) through (3) of this section, the rules of this paragraph (b)(5) shall apply for moves beginning before January 1, 1984.

(i) *Individual qualifies for the entire taxable year of the move.*—If the individual is a qualified individual for the entire taxable year of the move, then the amount of moving expenses disallowed shall be determined by multiplying the moving expense deduction otherwise allowable by a fraction the numerator of which is the foreign earned income excluded under section 911(a) for the taxable year of the move and the denominator of which is the foreign earned income for the same taxable year.

(ii) *Individual qualifies for less than the entire taxable year of the move.*—If the individual is a qualified individual for less than the entire taxable year of the move, then, for the purpose of determining the portion of the otherwise allowable moving expense deduction that is disallowed, the individual must attribute a portion of the otherwise allowable moving expense deduction either to the succeeding taxable year, if the move is from the United States to a foreign country, or to the prior taxable year, if the move is from a foreign country to the United States. The portion of the moving expense deduction treated as attributable to services performed in the year of the move shall be determined by multiplying the otherwise allowable moving expense deduction by the following fraction:

$$\frac{\text{The number of qualifying days (as defined in § 1.911-3(d)(3)) in the year of the move}}{\text{The number of days in the taxable year of the move.}}$$

The portion of the moving expense deduction treated as attributable to the year succeeding or preceding the move shall be determined by subtracting the portion of the moving expense deduction that is attributable to the year of the move from the total moving expense deduction. The allocation of a portion of the moving expense deduction to a succeeding or preceding taxable year does not affect the time for claiming the allowable moving expense deduction. The portion of the moving expense deduction that is disallowed shall be determined by multiplying the moving expense deduction attributable to the year of the move or the succeeding or preceding year, as the case may be, by a fraction the numerator of which is amounts excluded under section 911(a) for that year and the denominator of which is foreign earned income for that year.

(c) *Foreign taxes.*—(1) *Amount disallowed.*—No deduction or credit is allowed for foreign income, war profits, or excess profits taxes paid or accrued with respect to amounts excluded from gross income under section 911. To determine the amount of disallowed foreign taxes, multiply the foreign tax imposed on foreign earned income (as defined in § 1.911-3(a)) received or accrued during the taxable year by a fraction, the numerator of which is amounts excluded under section 911(a) in such taxable year less deductible expenses properly allocated to such amounts (see paragraphs (a) and (b) of this section), and the denominator of which is foreign earned income (as defined in § 1.911-3(a)) received or accrued during the taxable year less deductible expenses properly allocated or apportioned thereto. For the purpose of determining the extent to which foreign taxes are disallowed, the housing cost amount deduction is treated as definitely related to foreign earned income that is not excluded. If the foreign tax is imposed on foreign earned income and some other income (for example, earned income from sources within the United States or an amount not subject to tax in the United States), and the taxes on the other amount cannot be segregated, then the denominator equals the total of the amounts subject to tax less deductible expenses allocable to all such amounts.

(2) *Definitions and special rules.*—(i) *Taxable year.*—For purposes of paragraph (c)(1) of this section, the term "taxable year" means the individual's taxable year for U.S. tax purposes. Such term includes the portion of any foreign taxable year within the individual's U.S. taxable year and excludes the portion of any foreign taxable year not within the individual's U.S. taxable year.

(ii) *Apportionment of foreign taxes.*—For purposes of this paragraph (c), foreign taxes imposed on foreign earned income shall be deemed to accrue, on a pro rata basis, to income as the income is received or accrued. The taxes so accrued shall be apportioned to the taxable year during which the income is received or accrued. This rule applies for all individuals, regardless of their method of accounting.

(iii) *Effect of disallowance.*—The disallowance of foreign taxes under this paragraph (c) shall not affect the time for claiming any deduction or credit for foreign taxes paid. Rather, the disallowance shall only affect the amount of taxes considered paid or accrued to any foreign country.

(iv) *Interest on foreign taxes.*—Any interest expense incurred on a liability for foreign taxes is allocated and apportioned not under this paragraph (c) but under paragraph (a) of this section to foreign earned income and then to excluded foreign earned income and to that extent disallowed as a deduction under paragraph (a). In that regard, see also § 1.861-8(e)(2) for the specific rules for allocation and apportionment of interest expense.

(d) *Examples.*—The following examples illustrate the application of this section.

Example (1). In 1982 A, an architect, operated his business as a sole proprietorship in which capital is not a material income producing factor. A receives $1,000,000 in gross receipts, all of which is foreign source earned income, and incurs $500,000 of otherwise deductible business expenses definitely related to the foreign earned income. A elects to exclude $75,000 under section 911(a)(1). The expenses must be apportioned to excluded earned income as follows: $500,000 × $75,000/1,000,000. Thus, $37,500 of the business expenses are not deductible.

Example (2). The facts are the same as in example (1), except that $100,000 of A's gross receipts is U.S. source earned income and $68,000 of A's business expenses are attributable to the U.S. source earned income. Thus, A has $900,000 of foreign earned income and $432,000 of deductions allocated to foreign earned income. The expenses apportioned to excluded earned income are $432,000 × $75,000/$900,000, or $36,000, which are not deductible.

Example (3). B is a U.S. citizen, calendar year and cash basis taxpayer. B moves to foreign country N and maintains a tax home and is physically present there from July 1, 1984 through May 26, 1985. Among other possible periods, B is a qualified individual for 219 days in the year of the move. B pays $6,000 of otherwise deductible moving expenses in 1984. For 1984, B's foreign earned income is $60,000 and B excludes $47,869 ($80,000 × 219/366) under section 911(a). Under paragraph (b)(2) of this section, B's moving expenses are attributable to services performed in 1984. Under paragraph (b)(3) of this section, $6,000 × $47,869/$60,000, or $4,789, of B's moving expense deduction is disallowed. B may deduct $1,211 of moving expenses on his 1984 return.

Example (4). The facts are the same as in example (3) except that B maintains a tax home and is physically present in foreign country N from October 9, 1984 through September 3, 1985. Among other possible periods, B is a qualified individual for no more than 119 days in 1984 and 281 days in 1985. B's foreign earned income for 1984 is $60,000. B's foreign earned income for 1985 is $150,000. Because B is a qualified individual for less than 120 days in the year of the move, under paragraph (b)(2) of this section, B's moving expenses are attributable to services performed in 1984 and 1985. At the close of 1984, B may either seek an extension of time to file under § 1.911-7(c) or may file an income tax return without claiming the exclusions or deduction under section 911. B does not seek an extension and files without excluding foreign earned income; thus B may deduct his moving expenses in full. B later amends his 1984 return and excludes foreign earned income for that year. B excludes foreign earned income for 1985. B must determine the portion of the moving expense deduction that is disallowed. The portion of the moving expense deduction that is disallowed is determined by multiplying the otherwise allowable moving expense deduction by a fraction. The numerator of the fraction is the sum of amounts excluded under section 911(a) for 1984 and 1985, that is, $26,082, or $80,000 × 119/365, plus $61,589, or $80,000 × 281/365, which totals $87,671. The denominator of the fraction is the sum of foreign earned income for 1984 and 1985, that is, $60,000 plus $150,000, or $210,000. B's allowable moving expense deduction is $3,495, or $6,000—($6,000 × $87,671/$210,000). If B does not file an amended 1984 return (and does not exclude foreign earned income for 1984), but excludes foreign earned income under section 911(a) for 1985, a portion of his moving expense deduction is disallowed, based on the same formula. The amount disallowed is $6,000 × $61,589/$210,000, or $1,760. This amount may be recaptured either by filing an amended return for 1984 or by including it in income for 1985 (in which case it is not foreign earned income).

Example (5). C is a U.S. citizen, a self-employed individual, and a cash basis and calendar year taxpayer. For the entire 1982 taxable year C maintained his tax home and his bona fide residence in foreign country P. During 1982 C earned and received $120,000 of foreign earned income, none of which was attributable to employer provided amounts. C paid $40,000 of business expenses. C elected to exclude foreign earned income under section 911(a)(1) and claimed a housing cost amount deduction of $15,000. C received $10,000 of foreign source interest income which was included with C's earned income in a single tax base and taxed at graduated rates. For 1982, C paid $30,000 in income tax to foreign country P. The amount of C's business expenses that is properly apportioned to excluded amounts (and therefore, not deductible) equals $25,000, which is determined by multiplying the otherwise allowable deductions by C's excluded amounts over C's foreign earned income ($40,000 × $75,000/$120,000). The amount of country P tax that is properly apportioned to excluded amounts (and therefore, not deductible or creditable) equals $20,000, which is determined by multiplying the tax of $30,000 by the following fraction:

$$\frac{\text{\$50,000 (\$75,000 excluded amounts less \$25,000 of deductible expenses allocable thereto)}}{\text{\$75,000 ((\$120,000 foreign earned income less \$40,000 of deductible expenses allocable thereto) less \$15,000 (housing cost amount deduction allocable thereto) plus \$10,000 other taxable income).}}$$

Example (6). D is a U.S. citizen and an accrual basis and calendar year taxpayer for U.S. tax purposes. For the entire period from January 1, 1982 through December 31, 1983, D maintains his tax home and his bona fide residence in foreign country R. For purposes of R's income tax, D is a cash basis taxpayer and uses a fiscal year that begins on April 1 and ends on the following March 31. During his entire period of residence in R, D receives foreign earned income of $10,000 each month, all of which is attributable to employer provided amounts. For his foreign taxable year ending March 31, 1982, D pays $10,000 of income tax to R. For his foreign taxable year ending March 31, 1983, D pays $54,000 of income tax to R. Under paragraph (c)(2)(ii) of this section, all of the $10,000 of tax paid for his foreign taxable year ending March 31, 1982 is imposed on foreign earned income received in 1982, as is $40,500 or 9/12 × $54,000, of tax paid for his foreign taxable year ending March 31, 1983. (D received $10,000 per month for the last 3 months of his foreign taxable year ending March 31, 1982, all of which are within his U.S. taxable year ending December 31, 1982 under paragraph (c)(2)(i) of this section, and $10,000 per month for each month of his foreign taxable year ending March 31, 1983, of which the first 9 months are within his U.S. taxable year ending December 31, 1982. Under paragraph (c)(2)(ii) of this section, foreign taxes are deemed to accrue on a pro rata basis to income as it is received or accrued. Thus, all of the $10,000 of foreign taxes imposed on the income received during D's foreign taxable year ending March 31, 1982 accrue to D's 1982 foreign earned income, as do 9/12 (or $90,000/$120,000) of foreign taxes imposed on income received during D's foreign taxable year ending March 31, 1983, for purposes of determining the amount of D's foreign taxes that is disallowed.) For 1982, D has no deductible expenses, and elects to exclude his housing cost amount of $21,000 under section 911(a)(2) and foreign earned income of $75,000 under section 911(a)(1). The amount of D's foreign taxes disallowed for deduction or credit purposes for 1982 is $8,000 (that is, $10,000 × $96,000/$120,000) of the taxes for his foreign taxable year ending March 31, 1982, plus $32,400 (that is, $40,500 × $96,000/$120,000) of the taxes for his foreign taxable year ending March 31, 1983, or $40,400. From 1982, D has $2,000 ($10,000 – $8,000) of deductible or creditable taxes accrued on March 31, 1982, and $8,100 ($40,500 – $32,400) of deductible or creditable taxes accrued on March 31, 1983, after the disallowance based on his 1982 excluded income.

Example (7). E is a United States citizen, calendar year and cash basis taxpayer. E is physically present in and establishes his tax home in foreign country S on May 1, 1981. For purposes of country S, E's taxable year begins on April 1 and ends the following March 31. E receives foreign earned income of $15,000 each month beginning May 1, 1981. At the end of his foreign taxable year ending on March 31, 1982, E pays $70,000 of income tax to S on $165,000 of foreign earned income. Under section 911, as in effect for taxable years beginning before January 1, 1982, E may not exclude any income that is earned or received during 1981. None of E's taxes paid in 1982 that are attributable to income earned or received in 1981 are subject to disallowance because, under paragraph (c)(2)(ii) of this section, the only taxes disallowed are those deemed to accrue on income earned and received after December 31, 1981, and excluded from gross income. The amount of E's taxes paid in 1982 that are attributable to 1981 is $50,909, or $70,000 × $120,000/$165,000. E elects to exclude foreign earned income for 1982. The amount of E's taxes paid to S in 1982 that accrue to 1982 foreign earned income, and are therefore subject to disallowance based on excluded income, is $19,091, or $70,000 × $45,000/$165,000. [Reg. § 1.911-6.]

☐ [*T.D. 8006, 1-17-85.*]

§1.911-7. Procedural rules.—(a) *Elections of a qualified individual.*—(1) *In general.*—In order to receive either exclusion provided by section 911(a), a qualified individual must elect, separately with respect to each exclusion, to exclude foreign earned income under section 911(a)(1) and the housing cost amount under section 911(a)(2). Any such elections may be made on Form 2555 or on a comparable form. Each election must be filed either with the income tax return, or with an amended return, for the first taxable year of the individual for which the election is to be effective. An election once made remains in effect for that year and all subsequent years unless revoked under paragraph (b) of this section. Each election shall contain information sufficient to determine whether the individual is a qualified individual as provided in §1.911-2. The statement shall include the following information:

(i) The individual's name, address, and social security number;

(ii) The name of the individual's employer;

(iii) Whether the individual claimed exclusions under section 911 for earlier years after 1981 and within the five preceding taxable years;

(iv) Whether the individual has revoked a previously made election and the taxable year for which such revocation was effective;

(v) The exclusion or exclusions the individual is electing;

(vi) The foreign country or countries in which the individual's tax home is located and the date when such tax home was established;

(vii) The status (either bona fide residence or physical presence) under which the individual claims the exclusion;

(viii) The individual's qualifying period of residence or presence;

(ix) The individual's foreign earned income for the taxable year including the fair market value of all noncash remuneration; and,

(x) If the individual elects to exclude the housing cost amount, the individual's housing expenses.

(2) *Requirement of a return.*—(i) *In general.*—In order to make a valid election under this paragraph (a), the election must be made:

(A) With an income tax return that is timely filed (including any extensions of time to file),

(B) With a later return filed within the period prescribed in section 6511(a) amending the foregoing timely filed income tax return,

(C) With an original income tax return that is filed within one year after the due date of the return (determined without regard to any extension of time to file); this one year period does not constitute an extension of time for any purpose—it is merely a period during which a valid election may be made on a late return, or

(D) With an income tax return filed after the period described in paragraphs (a)(2)(i)(A), (B), or (C) of this section provided—

(1) The taxpayer owes no federal income tax after taking into account the exclusion and files Form 1040 with Form 2555 or a comparable form attached either before or after the Internal Revenue Service discovers that the taxpayer failed to elect the exclusion; or

(2) The taxpayer owes federal income tax after taking into account the exclusion and files Form 1040 with Form 2555 or a comparable form attached before the Internal Revenue Service discovers that the taxpayer failed to elect the exclusion.

(3) A taxpayer filing an income tax return pursuant to paragraph (a)(2)(i)(D)(*1*) or (2) of this section must type or legibly print the following statement at the top of the first page of the Form 1040: "Filed Pursuant to Section 1.911-7(a)(2)(i)(D)."

(ii) *Election for 1982 and 1983 taxable years.*—Solely for purposes of paragraph (a)(2)(i)(A) of this section, an income tax return for any taxable year beginning before January 1, 1984 shall be considered timely filed if it is filed on or before July 23, 1985.

(3) *Housing cost amount deduction.*—An individual does not have to make an election in order to claim the housing cost amount deduction. However, such individual must provide the Commissioner with information sufficient to determine the individual's correct amount of tax. Such information shall include the following: the individual's name, address, and social security number; the name of the individual's employer; the foreign country in which the individual's tax home was established; the status under which the individual claims the deduction; the individual's qualifying period of residence or presence; the individual's foreign earned income for the taxable year; and the individual's housing expenses.

(4) *Effect of immaterial error or omission.*—An inadvertent error or omission of information required to be provided to make an election under this paragraph (a) shall not render the election invalid if the error or omission is not material in determining whether the individual is a qualified individual or whether the individual intends to make the election.

(b) *Revocation of election.*—(1) *In general.*—An individual may revoke any election made under paragraph (a) of this section for any taxable year. A revocation must be made separately with respect to each election. The individual may revoke an election for any taxable year, including the first taxable year for which an election was effective, by filing a statement that the individual is revoking one or more of the previously made elections. The statement must be filed with the income tax return, or with an amended return, for the first taxable year of individual for which the revocation is to be effective. A revocation once made is effective for that year and all subsequent years. If an election is revoked for any taxable year, including the first taxable year for which the election was effective, the individual may not, without the consent of the Commissioner, again make the same election until the sixth taxable year following the taxable year for which the revocation was first effective. For example, a qualified individual makes an election to exclude foreign earned income under section 911(a)(1) and files it with his 1982 income tax return. The individual files 1983 and 1984 income tax returns on which he excludes his foreign earned income. Then, within 3 years after filing his 1982 income tax return, the individual files an amended 1982 income tax return with a statement revoking his election to exclude foreign earned income under section 911(a)(1). The revocation of the election is effective for taxable years 1982, 1983, and 1984. The individual may not elect to exclude income under section 911(a)(1) for any taxable year before 1988, unless he obtains consent to reelect under paragraph (b)(2) of this section.

(2) *Reelection before sixth taxable year after revocation.*—If an individual revoked an election under paragraph (b)(1) of this section and within five taxable years the individual wishes to reelect the same exclusion, then the individual may apply for consent to the reelection. The application for consent shall be made by requesting a ruling from the Associate Chief Counsel (Technical), National Office, Internal Revenue Service, 1111 Constitution Avenue NW., Washington, D.C. 20224. In determining whether to consent to a reelection the Associate Chief Counsel or his delegate shall consider any facts and circumstances that may be relevant to the determination. Relevant facts and circumstances may include the following: a period of United States residence, a move from one foreign country to another foreign country with differing tax rates, a substantial change in the tax laws of the foreign country of residence or physical presence, and a change of employer.

(c) *Returns and extensions.*—(1) *In general.*—Any return filed before completion of the period necessary to qualify an individual for any exclusion or deduction provided by section 911 shall be filed without regard to any exclusion or deduction provided by that section. A claim for a credit or refund of any overpayment of tax may be filed, however, if the taxpayer subsequently qualifies for any exclusion or deduction under section 911. See section 6012(c) and §1.6012-1(a)(3), relating to returns to be filed and information to be furnished by individuals who qualify for any exclusion or deduction under section 911.

(2) *Extensions.*—An individual desiring an extension of time (in addition to the automatic extension of time granted by §1.6081-4) for filing a return until after the completion of the qualifying period described in paragraph (c)(1) of this section for claiming any exclusion or deduction under section 911 may apply for an extension. An individual whose moving expense deduction is attributable to services performed in two years may apply for an extension of time for filing a return until after the end of the second year. The individual may make such application on Form 2350, "Application for Extension of Time to File U.S. Income Tax Return" or in any other manner prescribed by the Commissioner. The application must be filed in accordance with the instructions to the form or as prescribed by the Commissioner. The application must set forth the facts relied on to justify the extension of time requested and must include a statement as to the earliest date the individual expects to become entitled to any

exclusion or deduction by reason of completion of the qualifying period.

(d) *Declaration of estimated tax.*—In estimating gross income for the purpose of determining whether a declaration of estimated tax must be made for any taxable year, an individual is not required to take into account income which the individual reasonably believes will be excluded from gross income under the provisions of section 911. In computing estimated tax, however, the individual must take into account, among other things, the denial of the foreign tax credit for foreign taxes allocable to the excluded income (see § 1.911-6(c)).

(e) *Effective/applicability date.*—This section applies to applications for extension of time to file returns filed after July 1, 2008. [Reg. § 1.911-7.]

☐ [*T.D. 8006, 1-17-85. Amended by T.D. 8480, 6-29-93 and T.D. 9407, 6-30-2008.*]

§ 1.911-8. Former deduction for certain expenses of living abroad.—For rules relating to the deduction for certain expenses of living abroad applicable to taxable years beginning before January 1, 1982, see 26 CFR §§ 1.913-1 through 1.913-13 as they appeared in the Code of Federal Regulations revised as of April 1, 1982. [Reg. § 1.911-8.]

☐ [*T.D. 8006, 1-17-85.*]

Controlled Foreign Corporations

§ 1.951-1. Amounts included in gross income of United States shareholders.—(a) *In general.*—If a foreign corporation is a controlled foreign corporation (within the meaning of section 957) at any time during any taxable year of such corporation, every person—

(1) Who is a United States shareholder (as defined in section 951(b) and paragraph (g) of this section) of such corporation at any time during such taxable year, and

(2) Who owns (within the meaning of section 958(a)) stock in such corporation on the last day, in such year, on which such corporation is a controlled foreign corporation shall include in his gross income for his taxable year in which or with which such taxable year of the corporation ends, the sum of—

(i) Such shareholder's pro rata share (determined under paragraph (b) of this section) of the corporation's subpart F income (as defined in section 952) for such taxable year of the corporation,

(ii) Such shareholder's pro rata share (determined under paragraph (c)(1) of this section) of the corporation's previously excluded subpart F income withdrawn from investment in less developed countries for such taxable year of the corporation,

(iii) Such shareholder's pro rata share (determined under paragraph (c)(2) of this section) of the corporation's previously excluded subpart F income withdrawn from investment in foreign base company shipping operations for such taxable year of the corporation, and

(iv) The amount determined under section 956 with respect to such shareholder for such taxable year of the corporation (but only to the extent not excluded from gross income under section 959(a)(2)).

(3) For purposes of determining whether a United States shareholder which is a domestic corporation is a personal holding company under section 542 and § 1.542-1, the character of the amount includible in gross income of such domestic corporation under this paragraph shall be determined as if such amount were realized directly by such corporation from the source from which it is realized by the controlled foreign corporation. See paragraph (a) of § 1.957-2 for special limitation on the amount of subpart F income in the case of a controlled foreign corporation described in section 957(b). See section 970(a) and § 1.970-1 which provides for the reduction of subpart F income of export trade corporations.

(4) See § 1.958-1(d) for rules regarding the ownership of stock of a foreign corporation through a domestic partnership for purposes of section 951 and for purposes of any provision that specifically applies by reference to section 951 or the regulations in this part under section 951.

(b) *Limitation on a United States shareholder's pro rata share of subpart F income.*—(1) *In general.*—For purposes of paragraph (a)(2)(i) of this section, a United States shareholder's pro rata share (determined in accordance with the rules of paragraph (e) of this section) of the foreign corporation's subpart F income for the taxable year of such corporation is—

(i) The amount which would have been distributed with respect to the stock which such shareholder owns (within the meaning of section 958(a)) in such corporation if on the last day, in such corporation's taxable year, on which such corporation is a controlled foreign corporation it had distributed pro rata to its shareholders an amount which bears the same ratio to its subpart F income for such taxable year as the part of such year during which such corporation is a controlled foreign corporation bears to the entire taxable year, reduced by—

(ii) The lesser of—

(A) The amount of distributions received by any other person during such taxable year as a dividend with respect to such stock multiplied by a fraction, the numerator of which is the subpart F income of such corporation for the taxable year and the denominator of which is the sum of the subpart F income and the tested income (as defined in section 951A(c)(2)(A) and § 1.951A-2(b)(1)) of such corporation for the taxable year, and

(B) The dividend which would have been received by such other person if the distributions by such corporation to all its shareholders had been the amount which bears the same ratio to the subpart F income of such corporation for the taxable year as the part of such year during which such shareholder did not own (within the meaning of section 958(a)) such stock bears to the entire taxable year.

(2) *Examples.*—The following examples illustrate the application of this paragraph (b).

(i) *Facts.*—The following facts are assumed for purposes of the examples.

(A) A is a United States shareholder.

(B) M is a foreign corporation that has only one class of stock outstanding.

(C) B is a nonresident alien individual, and stock owned by B is not considered owned by a domestic entity under section 958(b).

(D) P and R are foreign corporations.

(E) All persons use the calendar year as their taxable year.

(F) Year 1 ends on or after October 3, 2018, and has 365 days.

(ii) *Example 1*—(A) *Facts.* A owns 100% of the stock of M throughout Year 1. For Year 1, M derives $100x of subpart F income, has $100x of earnings and profits, and makes no distributions.

(B) *Analysis.* Under section 951(a)(2) and paragraph (b)(1) of this section, A's pro rata share of the subpart F income of M for Year 1 is $100x.

(iii) *Example 2*—(A) *Facts.* The facts are the same as in paragraph (b)(2)(ii)(A) of this section (the facts in *Example 1*), except that instead of holding 100% of the stock of M for the entire year, A sells 60% of such stock to B on May 26, Year 1. Thus, M is a controlled foreign corporation for the period January 1, Year 1, through May 26, Year 1.

(B) *Analysis.* Under section 951(a)(2)(A) and paragraph (b)(1)(i) of this section, A's pro rata share of the subpart F income of M is limited to the subpart F income of M which bears the same ratio to its subpart F income for such taxable year ($100x) as the part of such year during which M is a controlled foreign corporation bears to the entire taxable year (146/365). Accordingly, under section 951(a)(2) and paragraph (b)(1) of this section, A's pro rata share of the subpart F income of M for Year 1 is $40x ($100x x 146/365).

(iv) *Example 3*—(A) *Facts.* The facts are the same as in paragraph (b)(2)(ii)(A) of this section (the facts in *Example 1*), except that instead of holding 100% of the stock of M for the entire year, A holds 60% of such stock on December 31, Year 1, having acquired such stock on May 26, Year 1, from B, who owned such stock from January 1, Year 1. Before A's acquisition of the stock, M had distributed a dividend of $15x to B in Year 1 with respect to the stock so acquired by A. M has no tested income for Year 1.

(B) *Analysis.* Under section 951(a)(2) and paragraph (b)(1) of this section, A's pro rata share of the subpart F income of M for Year 1 is $21x, such amount being determined as follows:

Table 1 to paragraph (b)(2)(iv)(B):

M's subpart F income for Year 1		$100x
Less: Reduction under section 951(a)(2)(A) for period (1–1 through 5–26) during which M is not a controlled foreign corporation ($100x x 146/365)		40x
Subpart F income for Year 1 as limited by section 951(a)(2)(A)		60x
A's pro rata share of subpart F income as determined under section 951(a)(2)(A) (0.6 x $60x)		36x
Less: Reduction under section 951(a)(2)(B) for dividends received by B during Year 1 with respect to the stock of M acquired by A:		
(i) Dividend received by B ($15x), multiplied by a fraction ($100x/$100x), the numerator of which is the subpart F income of such corporation for the taxable year ($100x) and the denominator of which is the sum of the subpart F income and the tested income of such corporation for the taxable year ($100x) ($15x x ($100x/$100x))	15x	
(ii) B's pro rata share (60%) of the amount which bears the same ratio to the subpart F income of such corporation for the taxable year ($100x) as the part of such year during which A did not own (within the meaning of section 958(a)) such stock bears to the entire taxable year (146/365) (0.6 x $100x x (146/365))	24x	
(iii) Amount of reduction under section 951(a)(2)(B) (lesser of (i) or (ii))		15x
A's pro rata share of subpart F income as determined under section 951(a)(2)		21x

(v) *Example 4*—(A) *Facts*. A owns 100% of the only class of stock of P throughout Year 1, and P owns 100% of the only class of stock of R throughout Year 1. For Year 1, R derives $100x of subpart F income, has $100x of earnings and profits, and distributes a dividend of $20x to P. R has no gross tested income. P has no income for Year 1 other than the dividend received from R.

(B) *Analysis*. Under section 951(a)(2) and paragraph (b)(1) of this section, A's pro rata share of the subpart F income of R for Year 1 is $100x. A's pro rata share of the subpart F income of R is not reduced under section 951(a)(2)(B) and paragraph (b)(1)(ii) of this section for the dividend of $20x paid to P because there was no part of Year 1 during which A did not own (within the meaning of section 958(a)) the stock of R. Under section 959(b), the $20x distribution from R to P is not again includible in the gross income of A under section 951(a). The $20x distribution from R to P is not includible in the gross tested income of P.

(vi) *Example 5*—(A) *Facts*. The facts are the same as in paragraph (b)(2)(v)(A) of this section (the facts in *Example 4*), except that instead of holding 100% of the stock of R for the entire year, P holds 60% of such stock on December 31, Year 1, having acquired such stock on March 14, Year 1, from B. Before P's acquisition of the stock, R had distributed a dividend of $100x to B in Year 1 with respect to the stock so acquired by P. The stock interest so acquired by P was owned by B from January 1, Year 1, until acquired by P. R also has $300x of tested income for Year 1.

(B) *Analysis*—(1) *Limitation of pro rata share of subpart F income*. Under section 951(a)(2) and paragraph (b)(1) of this section, A's pro rata share of the subpart F income of M for Year 1 is $28x, such amount being determined as follows:

Table 1 to paragraph (b)(2)(vi)(B)(1):

R's subpart F income for Year 1		$100x
Less: Reduction under section 951(a)(2)(A) for period (1-1 through 3-14) during which R is not a controlled foreign corporation ($100x x 73/365)		20x
Subpart F income for Year 1 as limited by section 951(a)(2)(A)		80x
A's pro rata share of subpart F income as determined under section 951(a)(2)(A) (0.6 x $80x)		48x
Less: Reduction under section 951(a)(2)(B) for dividends received by B during Year 1 with respect to the stock of R indirectly acquired by A:		
(i) Dividend received by B ($100x) multiplied by a fraction ($100x/$400x), the numerator of which is the subpart F income of such corporation for the taxable year ($100x) and the denominator of which is the sum of the subpart F income and the tested income of such corporation for the taxable year ($400x) ($100x x ($100x/$400x))	25x	
(ii) B's pro rata share (60%) of the amount which bears the same ratio to the subpart F income of such corporation for the taxable year ($100x) as the part of such year during which A did not own (within the meaning of section 958(a)) such stock bears to the entire taxable year (73/365) (0.6 x $100x x (73/365))	12x	
(iii) Amount of reduction under section 951(a)(2)(B) (lesser of (i) or (ii))		12x
A's pro rata share of subpart F income as determined under section 951(a)(2)		36x

(2) *Limitation of pro rata share of tested income*. Under section 951A(e)(1) and §1.951A-1(d)(2), A's pro rata share of the tested income of M for Year 1 is $108x, such amount being determined as follows:

Table 1 to paragraph (b)(2)(vi)(B)(2):

R's tested income for Year 1		$300x
Less: Reduction under section 951(a)(2)(A) for period (1-1 through 3-14) during which R is not a controlled foreign corporation ($300x x 73/365)		60x
Tested income for Year 1 as limited by under section 951(a)(2)(A)		240x
A's pro rata share of tested income as determined under §1.951A-1 (d)(2) (0.6 x $240x)		144x
Less: Reduction under section 951(a)(2)(B for dividends received by B during Year 1 with respect to the stock of R indirectly acquired by A:		
(i) Dividend received by B ($100x) multiplied by a fraction ($300x/$400x), the numerator of which is the tested income of such corporation for the taxable year ($300x) and the denominator of which is the sum of the subpart F income and the tested income of such corporation for the taxable year ($400x) ($100x x ($300x/$400x))	75x	
(ii) B's pro rata share (60%) of the amount which bears the same ratio to the tested income of such corporation for the taxable year ($300x) as the part of such year during which A did not own (within the meaning of section 958(a)) such stock bears to the entire taxable year (73/365) (0.6 x $300x x (73/365))	36x	
(iii) Amount of reduction under section 951(a)(2)(B) (lesser of (i) or (ii))		36x
A's pro rata share of tested income under section 951A(e)(1)		108x

(c) [Reserved]
(d) [Reserved].

(e) *Pro rata share of subpart F income defined.*—(1) *In general.*—(i) *Hypothetical distribution.*—For purposes of paragraph (b) of this section, a United States shareholder's pro rata share of a controlled foreign corporation's subpart F income for a taxable year is the amount that bears the same ratio to the corporation's subpart F income for the taxable year as the amount of the corporation's allocable earnings and profits that would be distributed with respect to the stock of the corporation which the United States shareholder owns (within the meaning of section 958(a)) for the taxable year bears to the total amount of the corporation's allocable earnings and profits that would be distributed with respect to the stock owned by all the shareholders of the corporation if all the allocable earnings and profits of the corporation for the taxable year (not reduced by actual distributions during the year) were distributed (*hypothetical distribution*) on the last day of the corporation's taxable year on which such corporation is a controlled foreign corporation (*hypothetical distribution date*).

(ii) *Definition of allocable earnings and profits.*—For purposes of this paragraph (e), the term *allocable earnings and profits* means, with respect to a controlled foreign corporation for a taxable year, the amount that is the greater of—

(A) The earnings and profits of the corporation for the taxable year determined under section 964; and

(B) The sum of the subpart F income (as determined under section 952 after the application of section 951A(c)(2)(B)(ii) and §1.951A-6(b)) of the corporation for the taxable year and the tested income (as defined in section 951A(c)(2)(A) and §1.951A-2(b)(1)) of the corporation for the taxable year.

(2) *One class of stock.*—If a controlled foreign corporation for a taxable year has only one class of stock outstanding on the hypothetical distribution date, the amount of the corporation's allocable earnings and profits distributed in the hypothetical distribution with respect to each share in the class of stock is determined as if the hypothetical distribution were made pro rata with respect to each share in the class of stock.

(3) *More than one class of stock.*—If a controlled foreign corporation for a taxable year has more than one class of stock outstanding on the hypothetical distribution date, the amount of the corporation's allocable earnings and profits distributed in the hypothetical distribution with respect to each class of stock is determined based on the distribution rights of each class of stock on the hypothetical distribution date, which amount is then further distributed pro rata with respect to each share in the class of stock. Subject to paragraphs (e)(4) through (6) of this section, the distribution rights of a class of stock are determined taking into account all facts and circumstances related to the economic rights and interest in the allocable earnings and profits of the corporation of each class, including the terms of the class of stock, any agreement among the shareholders and, if and to the extent appropriate, the relative fair market value of shares of stock. For purposes of this paragraph (e)(3), facts and circumstances do not include actual distributions (including distributions by redemption) or any amount treated as a dividend under any other provision of subtitle A of the Internal Revenue Code (for example, under section 78, 356(a)(2), 367(b), or 1248) made during the taxable year that includes the hypothetical distribution date.

(4) *Special rules.*—(i) *Redemptions, liquidations, and returns of capital.*—No amount of allocable earnings and profits is distributed in the hypothetical distribution with respect to a particular class of stock based on the terms of the class of stock of the controlled foreign corporation or any agreement or arrangement with respect thereto that would result in a redemption (even if such redemption would be treated as a distribution of property to which section 301 applies pursuant to section 302(d)), a distribution in liquidation, or a return of capital.

(ii) *Certain cumulative preferred stock.*—If a controlled foreign corporation has outstanding a class of redeemable preferred stock with cumulative dividend rights and dividend arrearages on such stock do not compound at least annually at a rate that equals or exceeds the applicable Federal rate (as defined in section 1274(d)(1)) that applies on the date the stock is issued for the term from such issue date to the mandatory redemption date based on a comparable compounding assumption (the *relevant AFR*), the amount of the corporation's allocable earnings and profits distributed in the hypothetical distribution with respect to the class of stock may not exceed the amount of dividends actually paid during the taxable year with respect to the class of stock plus the present value at the end of the controlled foreign corporation's taxable year of the unpaid current dividends with respect to the class determined using the relevant AFR and assuming the dividends will be paid at the mandatory redemption date. For purposes of this paragraph (e)(4)(ii), if the class of preferred stock does not have a mandatory redemption date, the mandatory redemption date is the date that the class of preferred stock is expected to be redeemed based on all facts and circumstances.

(iii) *Dividend arrearages.* If there is an arrearage in dividends for prior taxable years with respect to a class of preferred stock of a controlled foreign corporation, an amount of the corporation's allocable earnings and profits is distributed in the hypothetical distribution to the class of preferred stock by reason of the arrearage only to the extent the arrearage exceeds the accumulated earnings and profits of the controlled foreign corporation remaining from prior taxable years beginning after December 31, 1962, as of the beginning of the taxable year, or the date on which such stock was issued, whichever is later (the *applicable date*). If there is an arrearage in dividends for prior taxable years with respect to more than one class of preferred stock, the previous sentence is applied to each class in order of priority, except that the accumulated earnings and profits remaining after the applicable date are reduced by the allocable earnings and profits necessary to satisfy arrearages with respect to classes of stock with a higher priority. For purposes of this paragraph (e)(4)(iii), the amount of any arrearage with respect to stock described in paragraph (e)(4)(ii) of this section is determined in the same manner as the present value of unpaid current dividends on such stock under paragraph (e)(4)(ii) of this section.

(5) *Restrictions or other limitations on distributions.*—(i) *In general.*—A restriction or other limitation on distributions of an amount of earnings and profits by a controlled foreign corporation is not taken into account in determining the amount of the corporation's allocable earnings and profits distributed in a hypothetical distribution to a class of stock of the controlled foreign corporation.

(ii) *Definition.*—For purposes of paragraph (e)(5)(i) of this section, a restriction or other limitation on distributions includes any limitation that has the effect of limiting the distribution of an amount of earnings and profits by a controlled foreign corporation with respect to a class of stock of the corporation, other than currency or other restrictions or limitations imposed under the laws of any foreign country as provided in section 964(b).

(iii) *Exception for certain preferred distributions.*—For purposes of paragraph (e)(5)(i) of this section, the right to receive periodically a fixed amount (whether determined by a percentage of par value, a reference to a floating coupon rate, a stated return expressed in terms of a certain amount of U.S. dollars or foreign currency, or otherwise) with respect to a class of stock the distribution of which is a condition precedent to a further distribution of earnings and profits that year with respect to any class of stock (not including a distribution in partial or complete liquidation) is not a restriction or other limitation on the distribution of earnings and profits by a controlled foreign corporation.

(iv) *Illustrative list of restrictions and limitations.*—Except as provided in paragraph (e)(5)(iii) of this section, restrictions or other limitations on distributions include, but are not limited to—

(A) An arrangement that restricts the ability of a controlled foreign corporation to pay dividends on a class of stock of the corporation until a condition or conditions are satisfied (for example, until another class of stock is redeemed);

(B) A loan agreement entered into by a controlled foreign corporation that restricts or otherwise affects the ability to make distributions on its stock until certain requirements are satisfied; or

(C) An arrangement that conditions the ability of a controlled foreign corporation to pay dividends to its shareholders on the financial condition of the corporation.

(6) *Transactions and arrangements with a principal purpose of changing pro rata shares.*—Appropriate adjustments must be made to the allocation of allocable earnings and profits that would be distributed (without regard to this paragraph (e)(6)) in a hypothetical distribution with respect to any share of stock outstanding as of the hypothetical distribution date to disregard the effect on the hypothetical distribution of any transaction or arrangement that is undertaken as part of a plan a principal purpose of which is the avoidance of Federal income taxation by changing the amount of allocable earnings and profits distributed in any hypothetical distribution with respect to such share. This paragraph (e)(6) also applies for purposes

of the pro rata share rules described in § 1.951A-1(d) that reference this paragraph (e), including the rules in § 1.951A-1(d)(3) that determine the pro rata share of qualified business asset investment based on the pro rata share of tested income.

(7) *Examples.*—The following examples illustrate the application of this paragraph (e).

(i) *Facts.*—Except as otherwise stated, the following facts are assumed for purposes of the examples:

(A) FC1 is a controlled foreign corporation.

(B) USP1 and USP2 are domestic corporations.

(C) Individual A is a foreign individual, and FC2 is a foreign corporation that is not a controlled foreign corporation.

(D) All persons use the calendar year as their taxable year.

(E) Any ownership of FC1 by any shareholder is for all of Year 1.

(F) The common shareholders of FC1 are entitled to dividends when declared by FC1's board of directors.

(G) There are no accrued but unpaid dividends with respect to preferred shares, the preferred stock is not described in paragraph (e)(4)(ii) of this section, and common shares have positive liquidation value.

(H) There are no other facts and circumstances related to the economic rights and interest of any class of stock in the allocable earnings and profits of a foreign corporation, and no transaction or arrangement was entered into as part of a plan a principal purpose of which is the avoidance of Federal income taxation.

(I) FC1 has neither tested income within the meaning of section 951A(c)(2)(A) and § 1.951A-2(b)(1) nor tested loss within the meaning of section 951A(c)(2)(B)(i) and § 1.951A-2(b)(2).

(ii) *Example 1: Single class of stock*—(A) *Facts.* FC1 has outstanding 100 shares of one class of stock. USP1 owns 60 shares of FC1. USP2 owns 40 shares of FC1. For Year 1, FC1 has $1,000x of earnings and profits and $100x of subpart F income within the meaning of section 952.

(B) *Analysis.* FC1 has one class of stock. Therefore, under paragraph (e)(2) of this section, FC1's allocable earnings and profits of $1,000x are distributed in the hypothetical distribution pro rata to each share of stock. Accordingly, under paragraph (e)(1) of this section, for Year 1, USP1's pro rata share of FC1's subpart F income is $60x ($100x x $600x/$1,000x) and USP2's pro rata share of FC1's subpart F income is $40x ($100x x $400x/$1,000x).

(iii) *Example 2: Common and preferred stock*—(A) *Facts.* FC1 has outstanding 70 shares of common stock and 30 shares of 4% nonparticipating, voting preferred stock with a par value of $10x per share. USP1 owns all of the common shares. Individual A owns all of the preferred shares. For Year 1, FC1 has $100x of earnings and profits and $50x of subpart F income within the meaning of section 952.

(B) *Analysis.* The distribution rights of the preferred shares are not a restriction or other limitation within the meaning of paragraph (e)(5) of this section. Under paragraph (e)(3) of this section, the amount of FC1's allocable earnings and profits distributed in the hypothetical distribution with respect to Individual A's preferred shares is $12x (0.04 x $10x x 30) and with respect to USP1's common shares is $88x ($100x - $12x). Accordingly, under paragraph (e)(1) of this section, USP1's pro rata share of FC1's subpart F income is $44x ($50x x $88x/$100x) for Year 1.

(iv) *Example 3: Restriction based on cumulative income*—(A) *Facts.* FC1 has outstanding 10 shares of common stock and 400 shares of 2% nonparticipating, voting preferred stock with a par value of $1x per share. USP1 owns all of the common shares. FC2 owns all of the preferred shares. USP1 and FC2 cause the governing documents of FC1 to provide that no dividends may be paid to the common shareholders until FC1 cumulatively earns $100,000x of income. For Year 1, FC1 has $50x of earnings and profits and $50x of subpart F income within the meaning of section 952.

(B) *Analysis.* The agreement restricting FC1's ability to pay dividends to common shareholders until FC1 cumulatively earns $100,000x of income is a restriction or other limitation within the meaning of paragraph (e)(5) of this section. Therefore, the restriction is disregarded for purposes of determining the amount of FC1's allocable earnings and profits distributed in the hypothetical distribution to a class of stock. The distribution rights of the preferred shares are not a restriction or other limitation within the meaning of paragraph (e)(5) of this section. Under paragraph (e)(3) of this section, the amount of FC1's allocable earnings and profits distributed in the hypothetical distribution with respect to FC2's preferred shares is $8x (0.02 x $1x x 400) and with respect to USP1's common shares is $42x ($50x - $8x). Accordingly, under paragraph (e)(1) of this section, USP1's pro rata share of FC1's subpart F income is $42x for Year 1.

(v) *Example 4: Redemption rights*—(A) *Facts.* FC1 has outstanding 40 shares of common stock and 10 shares of 4% nonparticipating, preferred stock with a par value of $50x per share. Pursuant to the terms of the preferred stock, FC1 has the right to redeem at any time, in whole or in part, the preferred stock. FC2 owns all of the preferred shares. USP1, wholly owned by FC2, owns all of the common shares. Pursuant to the governing documents of FC1, no dividends may be paid to the common shareholders while the preferred stock is outstanding. For Year 1, FC1 has $100x of earnings and profits and $100x of subpart F income within the meaning of section 952.

(B) *Analysis.* The agreement restricting FC1's ability to pay dividends to common shareholders while the preferred stock is outstanding is a restriction or other limitation within the meaning of paragraph (e)(5) of this section. Therefore, the restriction is disregarded for purposes of determining the amount of FC1's allocable earnings and profits distributed in the hypothetical distribution to a class of stock. Under paragraph (e)(4)(i) of this section, no amount of allocable earnings and profits is distributed in the hypothetical distribution to the preferred shareholders on the hypothetical distribution date as a result of FC1's right to redeem the preferred shares. This is the case regardless of the restriction on paying dividends to the common shareholders while the preferred stock is outstanding, and regardless of the fact that a redemption of FC2's preferred shares would be treated as a distribution to which section 301 applies under section 302(d) (due to FC2's constructive ownership of the common shares). Thus, neither the restriction on paying dividends to the common shareholders while the preferred stock is outstanding nor FC1's redemption rights with respect to the preferred shares affects the distribution of allocable earnings and profits in the hypothetical distribution to FC1's shareholders. However, the distribution rights of the preferred shares are not a restriction or other limitation within the meaning of paragraph (e)(5) of this section. As a result, the amount of FC1's allocable earnings and profits distributed in the hypothetical distribution with respect to FC2's preferred shares is $20x (0.04 x $50x x 10) and with respect to USP1's common shares is $80x ($100x - $20x). Accordingly, under paragraph (e)(1) of this section, USP1's pro rata share of FC1's subpart F income is $80x for Year 1.

(vi) *Example 5: Shareholder owns common and preferred stock*—(A) *Facts.* FC1 has outstanding 40 shares of common stock and 60 shares of 6% nonparticipating, nonvoting preferred stock with a par value of $100x per share. USP1 owns 30 shares of the common stock and 15 shares of the preferred stock during Year 1. The remaining 10 shares of common stock and 45 shares of preferred stock of FC1 are owned by Individual A. For Year 1, FC1 has $1,000x of earnings and profits and $500x of subpart F income within the meaning of section 952.

(B) *Analysis.* The right of the holder of the preferred stock to receive 6% of par value is not a restriction or other limitation within the meaning of paragraph (e)(5) of this section. The amount of FC1's allocable earnings and profits distributed in the hypothetical distribution with respect to FC1's preferred shares is $360x (0.06 x $100x x 60) and with respect to its common shares is $640x ($1,000x - $360x). As a result, the amount of FC1's allocable earnings and profits distributed in the hypothetical distribution to USP1 is $570x, the sum of $90x ($360x x 15/60) with respect to its preferred shares and $480x ($640x x 30/40) with respect to its common shares. Accordingly, under paragraph (e)(1) of this section, USP1's pro rata share of the subpart F income of FC1 is $285x ($500x x $570x/$1,000x).

(vii) *Example 6: Subpart F income and tested income*—(A) *Facts.* FC1 has outstanding 700 shares of common stock and 300 shares of 4% nonparticipating, voting preferred stock with a par value of $100x per share. USP1 owns all of the common shares. USP2 owns all of the preferred shares. For Year 1, FC1 has $10,000x of earnings and profits, $2,000x of subpart F income within the meaning of section 952, and $9,000x of tested income within the meaning of section 951A(c)(2)(A) and § 1.951A-2(b)(1).

(B) *Analysis*—(*1*) *Hypothetical distribution.* The allocable earnings and profits of FC1 determined under paragraph (e)(1)(ii) of this section are $11,000x, the greater of FC1's earnings and profits as determined under section 964 ($10,000x) or the sum of FC1's subpart F income and tested income ($2,000x + $9,000x). The amount of FC1's allocable earnings and profits distributed in the hypothetical distribution with respect to USP2's preferred shares is $1,200x (0.04 x $100x x 300) and with respect to USP1's common shares is $9,800x ($11,000x - $1,200x).

(*2*) *Pro rata share of subpart F income.* Accordingly, under paragraph (e)(1) of this section, USP1's pro rata share of FC1's subpart F income is $1,782x ($2,000x x $9,800x/$11,000x), and USP2's pro rata share of FC1's subpart F income is $218x ($2,000x x $1,200x/ $11,000x).

(*3*) *Pro rata share of tested income.* Accordingly, under § 1.951A-1(d)(2), USP1's pro rata share of FC1's tested income is

$8,018x ($9,000x x $9,800x/$11,000x), and USP2's pro rata share of FC1's tested income is $982x ($9,000x x $1,200x/$11,000x) for Year 1.

(viii) *Example 7: Subpart F income and tested loss*—(A) *Facts.* The facts are the same as in paragraph (e)(7)(vii)(A) of this section (the facts in *Example 6*), except that for Year 1, FC1 has $8,000x of earnings and profits, $10,000x of subpart F income within the meaning of section 952 (but without regard to the limitation in section 952(c)(1)(A)), and $2,000x of tested loss within the meaning of section 951A(c)(2)(B)(i) and § 1.951A-2(b)(2). Under section 951A(c)(2)(B)(ii) and § 1.951A-6(b), the earnings and profits of FC1 are increased for purposes of section 952(c)(1)(A) by the amount of FC1's tested loss. Accordingly, after the application of section 951A(c)(2)(B)(ii) and § 1.951A-6(b), the subpart F income of FC1 is $10,000x.

(B) *Analysis*—(*1*) *Pro rata share of subpart F income.* The allocable earnings and profits determined under paragraph (e)(1)(ii) of this section are $10,000x, the greater of the earnings and profits of FC1 determined under section 964 ($8,000x) or the sum of FC1's subpart F income and tested income ($10,000x + $0). The amount of FC1's allocable earnings and profits distributed in the hypothetical distribution with respect to USP2's preferred shares is $1,200x (.04 x $100x x 300) and with respect to USP1's common shares is $8,800x ($10,000x -$1,200x). Accordingly, under paragraph (e)(1) of this section, for Year 1, USP1's pro rata share of FC1's subpart F income is $8,800x and USP2's pro rata share of FC1's subpart F income is $1,200x.

(*2*) *Pro rata share of tested loss.* The allocable earnings and profits determined under § 1.951A-1(d)(4)(i)(B) are $2,000x, the amount of FC1's tested loss. Under § 1.951A-1(d)(4)(i)(C), the entire $2,000x of tested loss is allocated in the hypothetical distribution to USP1's common shares. Accordingly, USP1's pro rata share of the tested loss is $2,000x.

(f) *Determination of holding period.*—For purposes of sections 951 through 964, the holding period of an asset (including stock of a controlled foreign corporation) shall be determined by excluding the day on which such asset is acquired and including the day on which such asset is disposed of. The application of this paragraph may be illustrated by the following example:

Example. On June 30, 1963, United States person E acquires 70 of the 100 shares of the only class of stock of foreign corporation A from non-resident alien B, who until such time owns all such 100 shares. E sells 10 shares of stock of such corporation on November 30, 1963, and 60 shares on December 31, 1963, to nonresident alien F. Corporation A is a controlled foreign corporation for the period beginning with July 1, 1963, and extending through December 31, 1963. As to the 10 shares of stock sold on November 30, 1963, E is treated as not owning such shares at any time after November 30, 1963, nor before July 1, 1963. As to the remaining 60 shares of stock, E is treated as not owning them before July 1, 1963, or after December 31, 1963.

(g) *United States shareholder defined.*—(1) *In general.*—For purposes of sections 951 through 964, the term *United States shareholder* means, with respect to a foreign corporation, a United States person (as defined in section 957(c)) who owns within the meaning of section 958(a), or is considered as owning by applying the rules of ownership of section 958(b), 10 percent or more of the total combined voting power of all classes of stock entitled to vote of such foreign corporation, or 10 percent or more of the total value of shares of all classes of stock of such foreign corporation.

(2) *Percentage of total combined voting power owned by United States person.*—(i) *Meaning of combined voting power.*—In determining for purposes of subparagraph (1) of this paragraph whether a United States person owns the requisite percentage of voting power of all classes of stock entitled to vote, consideration will be given to all the facts and circumstances in each case. In any case where—

(*a*) A foreign corporation has more than one class of stock outstanding, and

(*b*) One or more United States persons own (within the meaning of section 958) shares of any one class of stock which possesses the power to elect, appoint, or replace a person, or persons, who with respect to such corporation, exercise the powers ordinarily exercised by a member of the board of directors of a domestic corporation,

the percentage of the total combined voting power with respect to such corporation owned by any such United States person shall be his proportionate share of the percentage of the persons exercising the powers ordinarily exercised by members of the board of directors of a domestic corporation (described in (*b*) of this subdivision) which such class of stock (as a class) possesses the power to elect, appoint, or replace. In all cases, however, a United States person will be deemed to own 10 percent or more of the total combined voting power with respect to a foreign corporation if such person owns (within the meaning of section 958) 20 percent or more of the total number of shares of a class of stock of such corporation possessing one or more powers enumerated in paragraph (b)(1) of § 1.957-1. Whether a foreign corporation is a controlled foreign corporation for purposes of sections 951 through 964 shall be determined by applying the rules of section 957 and §§ 1.957-1 through 1.957-4.

(ii) *Illustration.*—The application of this paragraph may be illustrated by the following examples:

Example (1). Foreign corporation S has two classes of capital stock outstanding, consisting of 60 shares of class A stock and 40 shares of class B stock. Each class of the outstanding stock is entitled to participate on a share for share basis in any dividend distributions by S Corporation. The owners of a majority of the class A stock are entitled to elect 7 of the 10 corporate directors, and the owners of a majority of the class B stock are entitled to elect the other 3 of the 10 directors. Thus, the class A stock (as a class) possesses 70 percent of the total combined voting power of all classes of stock entitled to vote of S Corporation, and the class B stock (as a class) possesses 30 percent of such voting power. D, a United States person, owns 31 shares of the class A stock and thus owns 36.167 percent (31/60 × 70 percent) of the total combined voting power of all classes of stock entitled to vote of S Corporation. By reason of the ownership of such voting power, D is a United States shareholder of S Corporation under section 951(b). For purposes of section 957, S Corporation is a controlled foreign corporation by reason of D's ownership of a majority of the class A stock, as illustrated in example (2) of paragraph (c) of § 1.957-1. E, a United States person, owns eight shares of the class A stock and thus owns 9.333 percent (8/60 × 70 percent) of the total combined voting power of all classes of stock entitled to vote of S Corporation. Since E owns only 9.333 percent of such voting power and less than 20 percent of the number of shares of the class A stock, he is not a United States shareholder of S Corporation under section 951(b). F, a United States person, owns 14 shares of the class B stock and thus owns 10.5 percent (14/40 × 30 percent) of the total combined voting power of all classes of stock entitled to vote of S Corporation. By reason of the ownership of such voting power, F is a United States shareholder of S Corporation under section 951(b).

Example (2). Foreign corporation R has three classes of stock outstanding, consisting of 10 shares of class A stock, 20 shares of class B stock, and 300 shares of class C stock. Each class of the outstanding stock is entitled to participate on a share for share basis in any distribution by R Corporation. The owners of a majority of the class A stock are entitled to elect 6 of the 10 corporate directors, and the owners of a majority of the class B stock are entitled to elect the other 4 of the 10 directors. The class C stock is not entitled to vote. D, E, and F, United States persons, each own 2 shares of the class A stock and 100 shares of the class C stock. As owners of a majority of the class A stock, D, E, and F elect 6 members of the board of directors. D, E, and F are United States shareholders of R Corporation under section 951(b) since each owns 20 percent of the total number of shares of the class A stock which possesses the power to elect a majority of the board of directors of R Corporation. For purposes of section 957, R Corporation is a controlled foreign corporation by reason of the ownership by D, E, and F of a majority of the class A stock, as illustrated in example (2) of paragraph (c) of § 1.957-1.

(h) *Applicability dates.*—Paragraphs (a), (b)(1)(ii), (b)(2), (e)(1)(ii)(B), and (g)(1) of this section apply to taxable years of foreign corporations beginning after December 31, 2017, and to taxable years of United States shareholders in which or with which such taxable years of foreign corporations end. Except for paragraph (e)(1)(ii)(B) of this section, paragraph (e) of this section applies to taxable years of United States shareholders ending on or after October 3, 2018. [Reg. § 1.951-1.]

☐ [*T.D.* 6795, 1-28-65. *Amended by T.D.* 7893, 5-11-83; *T.D.* 9222, 8-24-2005 (*corrected* 11-8-2005), *T.D.* 9251, 2-21-2006, *T.D.* 9866, 6-14-2019 (*corrected* 8-22-2019) *and T.D.* 9960, 1-24-2022.]

§ 1.951A-1. General provisions.—(a) *Overview.*—(1) *In general.*—This section and §§ 1.951A-2 through 1.951A-7 (collectively, the *section 951A regulations*) provide rules to determine a United States shareholder's income inclusion under section 951A, describe certain consequences of an income inclusion under section 951A with respect to controlled foreign corporations and their United States shareholders, and define certain terms for purposes of section 951A and the section 951A regulations. This section provides general rules for determining a United States shareholder's inclusion of global intangible low-taxed income, including a rule relating to the application of section 951A and the section 951A regulations to domestic partnerships and their partners. Section 1.951A-2 provides rules for determining a controlled foreign corporation's tested income or tested loss. Section 1.951A-3 provides rules for determining a controlled foreign corporation's qualified business asset investment. Section 1.951A-4 provides rules for determining a controlled foreign corporation's tested interest expense and tested interest income. Section 1.951A-5 provides rules relating to the treatment of the inclusion of global intangible low-taxed income for certain purposes. Section 1.951A-6 provides certain adjustments to earnings and profits and basis of a controlled foreign corporation related to a tested loss. Section 1.951A-7 provides dates of applicability.

(2) *Scope.*—Paragraph (b) of this section provides the general rule requiring a United States shareholder to include in gross income its global intangible low-taxed income for a U.S. shareholder inclusion year. Paragraph (c) of this section provides rules for determining the amount of a United States shareholder's global intangible low-taxed income for the U.S. shareholder inclusion year, including a rule for the application of section 951A and the section 951A regulations to consolidated groups. Paragraph (d) of this section provides rules for determining a United States shareholder's pro rata share of certain items for purposes of determining the United States shareholder's global intangible low-taxed income. Paragraph (e) of this section provides rules for the treatment of a domestic partnership and its partners for purposes of section 951A and the section 951A regulations. Paragraph (f) of this section provides additional definitions for purposes of this section and the section 951A regulations.

(b) *Inclusion of global intangible low-taxed income.*—Each person who is a United States shareholder of any controlled foreign corporation and owns section 958(a) stock of any such controlled foreign corporation includes in gross income in the U.S. shareholder inclusion year the shareholder's GILTI inclusion amount, if any, for the U.S. shareholder inclusion year.

(c) *Determination of GILTI inclusion amount.*—(1) *In general.*—Except as provided in paragraph (c)(4) of this section, the term *GILTI inclusion amount* means, with respect to a United States shareholder and a U.S. shareholder inclusion year, the excess (if any) of—

(i) The shareholder's net CFC tested income (as defined in paragraph (c)(2) of this section) for the year, over

(ii) The shareholder's net deemed tangible income return (as defined in paragraph (c)(3) of this section) for the year.

(2) *Definition of net CFC tested income.*—The term *net CFC tested income* means, with respect to a United States shareholder and a U.S. shareholder inclusion year, the excess (if any) of—

(i) The aggregate of the shareholder's pro rata share of the tested income of each tested income CFC (as defined in § 1.951A-2(b)(1)) for a CFC inclusion year that ends with or within the U.S. shareholder inclusion year, over

(ii) The aggregate of the shareholder's pro rata share of the tested loss of each tested loss CFC (as defined in § 1.951A-2(b)(2)) for a CFC inclusion year that ends with or within the U.S. shareholder inclusion year.

(3) *Definition of net deemed tangible income return.*—(i) *In general.*—The term *net deemed tangible income return* means, with respect to a United States shareholder and a U.S. shareholder inclusion year, the excess (if any) of—

(A) The shareholder's deemed tangible income return (as defined in paragraph (c)(3)(ii) of this section) for the U.S. shareholder inclusion year, over

(B) The shareholder's specified interest expense (as defined in paragraph (c)(3)(iii) of this section) for the U.S. shareholder inclusion year.

(ii) *Definition of deemed tangible income return.*—The term *deemed tangible income return* means, with respect to a United States shareholder and a U.S. shareholder inclusion year, 10 percent of the aggregate of the shareholder's pro rata share of the qualified business asset investment (as defined in § 1.951A-3(b)) of each tested income CFC for a CFC inclusion year that ends with or within the U.S. shareholder inclusion year.

(iii) *Definition of specified interest expense.*—The term *specified interest expense* means, with respect to a United States shareholder and a U.S. shareholder inclusion year, the excess (if any) of—

(A) The aggregate of the shareholder's pro rata share of the tested interest expense (as defined in § 1.951A-4(b)(1)) of each controlled foreign corporation for a CFC inclusion year that ends with or within the U.S. shareholder inclusion year, over

(B) The aggregate of the shareholder's pro rata share of the tested interest income (as defined in § 1.951A-4(b)(2)) of each controlled foreign corporation for a CFC inclusion year that ends with or within the U.S. shareholder inclusion year.

(4) *Determination of GILTI inclusion amount for consolidated groups.*—For purposes of section 951A and the section 951A regulations, a member of a consolidated group (as defined in § 1.1502-1(h)) determines its GILTI inclusion amount taking into account the rules provided in § 1.1502-51.

(d) *Determination of pro rata share.*—(1) *In general.*—For purposes of paragraph (c) of this section, each United States shareholder that owns section 958(a) stock of a controlled foreign corporation as of a hypothetical distribution date determines its pro rata share (if any) of each tested item of the controlled foreign corporation for the CFC inclusion year that includes the hypothetical distribution date and ends with or within the U.S. shareholder inclusion year. Except as otherwise provided in this paragraph (d), a United States shareholder's pro rata share of each tested item is determined independently of its pro rata share of each other tested item. In no case may the sum of the pro rata share of any tested item of a controlled foreign corporation for a CFC inclusion year allocated to stock under this paragraph (d) exceed the amount of such tested item of the controlled foreign corporation for the CFC inclusion year. Except as modified in this paragraph (d), a United States shareholder's pro rata share of any tested item is determined under the rules of section 951(a)(2) and § 1.951-1(b) and (e) in the same manner as those provisions apply to subpart F income. Under section 951(a)(2) and § 1.951-1(b) and (e), as modified by this paragraph (d), a United States shareholder's pro rata share of any tested item for a U.S. shareholder inclusion year is determined with respect to the section 958(a) stock of the controlled foreign corporation owned by the United States shareholder on a hypothetical distribution date with respect to a CFC inclusion year that ends with or within the U.S. shareholder inclusion year. A United States shareholder's pro rata share of any tested item is translated into United States dollars using the average exchange rate for the CFC inclusion year of the controlled foreign corporation. Paragraphs (d)(2) through (5) of this section provide rules for determining a United States shareholder's pro rata share of each tested item of a controlled foreign corporation.

(2) *Tested income.*—(i) *In general.*—Except as provided in paragraph (d)(2)(ii) of this section, a United States shareholder's pro rata share of the tested income of each tested income CFC for a U.S. shareholder inclusion year is determined under section 951(a)(2) and § 1.951-1(b) and (e), substituting "tested income" for "subpart F income" each place it appears, other than in § 1.951-1(e)(1)(ii)(B) and the denominator of the fraction described in § 1.951-1(b)(1)(ii)(A).

(ii) *Special rule for prior allocation of tested loss.*—In any case in which tested loss has been allocated to any class of stock in a prior CFC inclusion year under paragraph (d)(4)(iii) of this section, tested income is first allocated to each such class of stock in the order of its liquidation priority to the extent of the excess (if any) of the sum of the tested loss allocated to each such class of stock for each prior CFC inclusion year under paragraph (d)(4)(iii) of this section, over the sum of the tested income allocated to each such class of stock for each prior CFC inclusion year under this paragraph (d)(2)(ii). Paragraph (d)(2)(i) of this section applies for purposes of determining a United States shareholder's pro rata share of the remainder of the tested income, except that, for purposes of the hypothetical distribution of section 951(a)(2)(A) and § 1.951-1(b)(1)(i) and (e)(1)(i), the amount of allocable earnings and profits of the tested income CFC is reduced by the amount of tested income allocated under the first sentence of this paragraph (d)(2)(ii). For an example of the application of this paragraph (d)(2), see paragraph (d)(4)(iv)(B) of this section (*Example 2*).

(3) *Qualified business asset investment.*—(i) *In general.*—Except as provided in paragraphs (d)(3)(ii) of this section, a United States shareholder's pro rata share of the qualified business asset investment of a tested income CFC for a U.S. shareholder inclusion year bears the same ratio to the total qualified business asset investment of the tested income CFC for the CFC inclusion year as the United States shareholder's pro rata share of the tested income of the tested income CFC for the U.S. shareholder inclusion year bears to the total tested income of the tested income CFC for the CFC inclusion year.

(ii) *Special rule for excess hypothetical tangible return.*—(A) *In general.*—If the tested income of a tested income CFC for a CFC inclusion year is less than the hypothetical tangible return of the tested income CFC for the CFC inclusion year, a United States shareholder's pro rata share of the qualified business asset investment of the tested income CFC for a United States shareholder inclusion year bears the same ratio to the qualified business asset investment of the tested income CFC as the United States shareholder's pro rata share of the hypothetical tangible return of the CFC for the U.S. shareholder inclusion year bears to the total hypothetical tangible return of the CFC for the CFC inclusion year.

(B) *Determination of pro rata share of hypothetical tangible return.*—For purposes of paragraph (d)(3)(ii)(A) of this section, a United States shareholder's pro rata share of the hypothetical tangible return of a CFC for a CFC inclusion year is determined in the same manner as the United States shareholder's pro rata share of the tested income of the CFC for the CFC inclusion year under paragraph (d)(2) of this section by treating the amount of the hypothetical tangible return as the amount of tested income.

(C) *Definition of hypothetical tangible return.*—For purposes of this paragraph (d)(3)(ii), the term *hypothetical tangible return* means, with respect to a tested income CFC for a CFC inclusion year, 10 percent of the qualified business asset investment of the tested income CFC for the CFC inclusion year.

(iii) *Examples.*—The following examples illustrate the application of paragraphs (d)(2) and (3) of this section. See also § 1.951-1(e)(7)(vii) (*Example 6*) (illustrating a United States shareholder's pro rata share of tested income).

(A) *Example 1*—(*1*) *Facts.* FS, a controlled foreign corporation, has outstanding 70 shares of common stock and 30 shares of 4% nonparticipating, cumulative preferred stock with a par value of $10x per share. P Corp, a domestic corporation and a United States shareholder of FS, owns all of the common shares. Individual A, a United States citizen and a United States shareholder, owns all of the preferred shares. Individual A, FS, and P Corp use the calendar year as their taxable year. Individual A and P Corp are shareholders of FS for all of Year 4. At the beginning of Year 4, FS had no dividend arrearages with respect to its preferred stock. For Year 4, FS has $100x of earnings and profits, $120x of tested income, and no subpart F income within the meaning of section 952. FS also has $750x of qualified business asset investment for Year 4.

(*2*) *Analysis*—(*i*) *Determination of pro rata share of tested income.* For purposes of determining P Corp's pro rata share of FS's tested income under paragraph (d)(2) of this section, the amount of FS's allocable earnings and profits for purposes of the hypothetical distribution described in § 1.951-1(e)(1)(i) is $120x, the greater of its earnings and profits as determined under section 964 ($100x) and the sum of its subpart F income and tested income ($0 + $120x). Under paragraph (d)(2) of this section and § 1.951-1(e)(3), the amount of FS's allocable earnings and profits distributed in the hypothetical distribution with respect to Individual A's preferred shares is $12x (0.04 x $10x x 30) and the amount distributed with respect to P Corp's common shares is $108x ($120x - $12x). Accordingly, under paragraph (d)(2) of this section and § 1.951-1(e)(1), Individual A's pro rata share of FS's tested income is $12x, and P Corp's pro rata share of FS's tested income is $108x for Year 4.

(*ii*) *Determination of pro rata share of qualified business asset investment.* The special rule of paragraph (d)(3)(ii)(A) of this section does not apply because FS's tested income of $120x is not less than FS's hypothetical tangible return of $75x, which is 10% of FS's qualified business asset investment of $750x. Accordingly, under the general rule of paragraph (d)(3)(i) of this section, Individual A's and P Corp's respective pro rata shares of FS's qualified business asset investment bears the same ratio to FS's total qualified business asset investment as their respective pro rata shares of FS's tested income bears to FS's total tested income. Thus, Individual A's pro rata share of FS's qualified business asset investment is $75x ($750x x $12x/ $120x), and P Corp's pro rata share of FS's qualified business asset investment is $675x ($750x x $108x/$120x).

(B) *Example 2*—(*1*) *Facts.* The facts are the same as in paragraph (d)(3)(iv)(A)(*1*) of this section (the facts in *Example 1* of this section), except that FS has $1,500x of qualified business asset investment for Year 4.

(*2*) *Analysis*—(*i*) *Determination of pro rata share of tested income.* The analysis and the result are the same as in paragraph (d)(3)(iv)(A)(*2*)(*i*) of this section (paragraph (i) of the analysis in *Example 1* of this section).

(*ii*) *Determination of pro rata share of qualified business asset investment.* The special rule of paragraph (d)(3)(ii)(A) of this section applies because FS's tested income of $120x is less than FS's hypothetical tangible return of $150x, which is 10% of FS's qualified business asset investment of $1,500x. Under paragraph (d)(3)(ii)(A) of this section, Individual A's and P Corp's respective pro rata shares of FS's qualified business asset investment bears the same ratio to FS's qualified business asset investment as their respective pro rata shares of the hypothetical tangible return of FS bears to the total hypothetical tangible return of FS. Under paragraph (d)(3)(ii)(B) of this section, P Corp's and Individual A's respective pro rata share of FS's hypothetical tangible return is determined under paragraph (d)(2) of this section in the same manner as their respective pro rata shares of the tested income of FS by treating the hypothetical tangible return as the amount of tested income. The amount of FS's allocable earnings and profits for purposes of the hypothetical distribution described in § 1.951-1(e)(1)(i) is $150x, the greater of its earnings and profits as determined under section 964 ($100x) and the sum of its subpart F income and hypothetical tangible return ($0 + $150x). The amount of FS's allocable earnings and profits distributed in the hypothetical distribution is $12x (.04 x $10x x 30) with respect to Individual A's preferred shares and $138x ($150x - $12x) with respect to P Corp's common shares. Accordingly, Individual A's pro rata share of FS's qualified business asset investment is $120x ($1,500x x $12x/$150x), and P Corp's pro rata share of FS's qualified business asset investment is $1,380x ($1,500x x $138x/$150x).

(C) *Example 3*—(*1*) *Facts.* P Corp, a domestic corporation and a United States shareholder, owns 100% of the only class of stock of FS, a controlled foreign corporation, from January 1 of Year 1, until May 26 of Year 1. On May 26 of Year 1, P Corp sells all of its FS stock to R Corp, a domestic corporation that is not related to P Corp, and recognizes no gain or loss on the sale. R Corp, a United States shareholder of FS, owns 100% of the stock of FS from May 26 through December 31 of Year 1. For Year 1, FS has $50x of earnings and profits, $50x of tested income, and no subpart F income within the meaning of section 952. FS also has $1,500x of qualified business asset investment for Year 1. On May 1 of Year 1, FS distributes a $20x dividend to P Corp. P Corp, R Corp, and FS all use the calendar year as their taxable year.

(*2*) *Analysis*—(*i*) *Determination of pro rata share of tested income.* For purposes of determining R Corp's pro rata share of FS's tested income under paragraph (d)(2) of this section, the amount of FS's allocable earnings and profits for purposes of the hypothetical distribution described in § 1.951-1(e)(1)(i) is $50x, the greater of its earnings and profits as determined under section 964 ($50x) or the sum of its subpart F income and tested income ($0 + $50x). Under paragraph (d)(2) of this section and § 1.951-1(e)(1), FS's allocable earnings and profits of $50x are distributed in the hypothetical distribution pro rata to each share of stock. R Corp's pro rata share of FS's tested income for Year 1 is its pro rata share under section 951(a)(2)(A) and § 1.951-1(b)(1)(i) ($50x), reduced under section 951(a)(2)(B) and § 1.951-1(b)(1)(ii) by $20x, which is the lesser of $20x, the dividend received by P Corp during Year 1 with respect to the FS stock acquired by R Corp ($20x), multiplied by a fraction, the numerator of which is the tested income ($50x) of FS for Year 1 and the denominator of which is the sum of the subpart F income ($0) and the tested income ($50x) of FS for Year 1 ($20x x $50x/$50x), and $20x, which is P Corp's pro rata share (100%) of the amount which bears the same ratio to FS's tested income for Year 1 ($50x) as the period during which R Corp did not own (within the meaning of section 958(a)) the FS stock (146 days) bears to the entire taxable year (1 x $50x x 146/365). Accordingly, R Corp's pro rata share of tested income of FS for Year 1 is $30x ($50x - $20x).

(*ii*) *Determination of pro rata share of qualified business asset investment.* The special rule of paragraph (d)(3)(ii) of this section applies because FS's tested income of $50x is less than FS's hypothetical tangible return of $150x, which is 10% of FS's qualified business asset investment of $1,500x. Under paragraph (d)(3)(ii) of this section, R Corp's pro rata share of FS's qualified business asset investment is the amount that bears the same ratio to FS's qualified business asset investment as R Corp's pro rata share of the hypothetical tangible return of FS bears to the total hypothetical tangible return of FS. R Corp's pro rata share of FS's hypothetical tangible return is its pro rata share under section 951(a)(2)(A) and § 1.951-1(b)(1)(i) ($150x), reduced under section 951(a)(2)(B) and § 1.951-1(b)(1)(ii) by $20x, which is the lesser of $20x, the dividend received by P Corp during Year 1 with respect to the FS stock acquired by R Corp ($20x) multiplied by a fraction, the numerator of which is the hypothetical tangible return ($150x) of FS for Year 1 and the denominator of which is the sum of the subpart F income ($0) and the hypothetical tangible return ($150x) of FS for Year 1 ($20x x $150x/$150x), and $60x, which is P Corp's pro rata share (100%) of the amount which bears the same ratio to FS's hypothetical tangible return for Year 1 ($150x) as the period during which R Corp did not own (within the meaning of section 958(a)) the FS stock (146 days) bears to the entire taxable year (1 x $150x x 146/365). Accordingly, R Corp's pro rata share of the hypothetical tangible return of FS for Year 1 is $130x ($150x - $20x), and R Corp's pro rata share of FS's qualified business asset investment is $1,300x ($1,500x x $130x/$150x).

(4) *Tested loss.*—(i) *In general.*—A United States shareholder's pro rata share of the tested loss of each tested loss CFC for a U.S. shareholder inclusion year is determined under section 951(a)(2) and § 1.951-1(b) and (e) with the following modifications—

(A) "Tested loss" is substituted for "subpart F income" each place it appears;

(B) For purposes of the hypothetical distribution described in section 951(a)(2)(A) and § 1.951-1(b)(1)(i) and (e)(1)(i), the amount of allocable earnings and profits of a controlled foreign corporation for a CFC inclusion year is treated as being equal to the tested loss of the tested loss CFC for the CFC inclusion year;

(C) Except as provided in paragraphs (d)(4)(ii) and (iii) of this section, the hypothetical distribution described in section 951(a)(2)(A) and § 1.951-1(b)(1)(i) and (e)(1)(i) is treated as made solely with respect to the common stock of the tested loss CFC; and

(D) In lieu of applying section 951(a)(2)(B) and § 1.951-1(b)(1)(ii), the United States shareholder's pro rata share of the tested loss allocated to section 958(a) stock of the tested loss CFC is reduced by an amount that bears the same ratio to the amount of the tested loss as the part of such year during which such shareholder did not own (within the meaning of section 958(a)) such stock bears to the entire taxable year.

(ii) *Special rule in case of accrued but unpaid dividends.*—If a tested loss CFC's earnings and profits that have accumulated since the issuance of preferred shares are reduced below the amount necessary to satisfy any accrued but unpaid dividends with respect to such preferred shares, then the amount by which the tested loss reduces the earnings and profits below the amount necessary to satisfy the accrued but unpaid dividends is allocated in the hypothetical distribution described in section 951(a)(2)(A) and § 1.951-1(b)(1)(i) and (e)(1)(i) to the preferred stock of the tested loss CFC and the remainder of the tested loss is allocated in the hypothetical distribution to the common stock of the tested loss CFC.

(iii) *Special rule for stock with no liquidation value.*—If a tested loss CFC's common stock has a liquidation value of zero and there is at least one other class of equity with a liquidation preference relative to the common stock, then the tested loss is allocated in the hypothetical distribution described in section 951(a)(2)(A) and § 1.951-1(b)(1)(i) and (e)(1)(i) to the most junior class of equity with a positive liquidation value to the extent of such liquidation value. Thereafter, tested loss is allocated to the next most junior class of equity to the extent of its liquidation value and so on. All determinations of liquidation value are to be made as of the beginning of the CFC inclusion year of the tested loss CFC.

(iv) *Examples.*—The following examples illustrate the application of this paragraph (d)(4). See also § 1.951-1(e)(7)(viii) (*Example 7*) (illustrating a United States shareholder's pro rata share of subpart F income and tested loss).

(A) *Example 1*—(1) *Facts.* FS, a controlled foreign corporation, has outstanding 70 shares of common stock and 30 shares of 4% nonparticipating, cumulative preferred stock with a par value of $10x per share. P Corp, a domestic corporation and a United States shareholder of FS, owns all of the common shares. Individual A, a United States citizen and a United States shareholder, owns all of the preferred shares. FS, Individual A, and P Corp all use the calendar year as their taxable year. Individual A and P Corp are shareholders of FS for all of Year 5. At the beginning of Year 5, FS had earnings and profits of $120x, which accumulated after the issuance of the preferred stock. At the end of Year 5, the accrued but unpaid dividends with respect to the preferred stock are $36x. For Year 5, FS has a $100x tested loss, and no other items of income, gain, deduction or loss. At the end of Year 5, FS has earnings and profits of $20x.

(2) *Analysis.* FS is a tested loss CFC for Year 5. Before taking into account the tested loss in Year 5, FS had sufficient earnings and profits to satisfy the accrued but unpaid dividends of $36x. The amount of the reduction in earnings below the amount necessary to satisfy the accrued but unpaid dividends attributable to the tested loss is $16x ($36x - ($120x - $100x)). Accordingly, under paragraph (d)(4)(ii) of this section, $16x of the tested loss is allocated to Individual A's preferred stock in the hypothetical distribution described in section 951(a)(2)(A) and § 1.951-1(b)(1)(i) and (e)(1)(i), and $84x ($100x - $16x) of the tested loss is allocated to P Corp's common shares in the hypothetical distribution.

(B) *Example 2*—(1) *Facts.* FS, a controlled foreign corporation, has outstanding 100 shares of common stock and 50 shares of 4% nonparticipating, cumulative preferred stock with a par value of $100x per share. P Corp, a domestic corporation and a United States shareholder of FS, owns all of the common shares. Individual A, a United States citizen and a United States shareholder, owns all of the preferred shares. FS, Individual A, and P Corp all use the calendar year as their taxable year. Individual A and P Corp are shareholders of FS for all of Year 1 and Year 2. At the beginning of Year 1, the common stock has no liquidation value and the preferred stock has a liquidation value of $5,000x and no accrued but unpaid dividends. In Year 1, FS has a tested loss of $1,000x and no other items of income, gain, deduction, or loss. In Year 2, FS has tested income of $3,000x and no other items of income, gain, deduction, or loss. FS has earnings and profits of $3,000x for Year 2. At the end of Year 2, FS has accrued but unpaid dividends of $400x with respect to the preferred stock, the sum of $200x for Year 1 (0.04 x $100x x 50) and $200x for Year 2 (0.04 x $100x x 50).

(2) *Analysis*—(i) *Year 1.* FS is a tested loss CFC in Year 1. The common stock of FS has liquidation value of zero, and the preferred stock has a liquidation preference relative to the common stock. The tested loss ($1,000x) does not exceed the liquidation value of the preferred stock ($5,000x). Accordingly, under paragraph (d)(4)(iii) of this section, the tested loss is allocated to the preferred stock in the hypothetical distribution described in section 951(a)(2)(A) and § 1.951-1(b)(1)(i) and (e)(1)(i). Individual A's pro rata share of the tested loss is $1,000x, and P Corp's pro rata share of the tested loss is $0.

(ii) *Year 2.* FS is a tested income CFC in Year 2. Because $1,000x of tested loss was allocated to the preferred stock in Year 1 under paragraph (d)(4)(iii) of this section, the first $1,000x of tested income in Year 2 is allocated to the preferred stock under paragraph (d)(2)(ii) of this section. P Corp's and Individual A's pro rata shares of the remaining $2,000x of tested income are determined under the general rule of paragraph (d)(2)(i) of this section, except that for purposes of the hypothetical distribution the amount of FS's allocable earnings and profits is reduced by the tested income allocated under paragraph (d)(2)(ii) of this section to $2,000x ($3,000x - $1,000x). Accordingly, under paragraph (d)(2)(i) of this section and § 1.951-1(e), the amount of FS's allocable earnings and profits distributed in the hypothetical distribution with respect to Individual A's preferred stock is $400x ($400x of accrued but unpaid dividends) and with respect to P Corp's common stock is $1,600x ($2,000x - $400x). Individual A's pro rata share of the tested income is $1,400x ($1,000x + $400x), and P Corp's pro rata share of the tested income is $1,600x.

(5) *Tested interest expense.*—A United States shareholder's pro rata share of tested interest expense of a controlled foreign corporation for a U.S. shareholder inclusion year is equal to the amount by which the tested interest expense reduces the shareholder's pro rata share of tested income of the controlled foreign corporation for the U.S. shareholder inclusion year, increases the shareholder's pro rata share of tested loss of the controlled foreign corporation for the U.S. shareholder inclusion year, or both.

(6) *Tested interest income.*—A United States shareholder's pro rata share of tested interest income of a controlled foreign corporation for a U.S. shareholder inclusion year is equal to the amount by which the tested interest income increases the shareholder's pro rata share of tested income of the controlled foreign corporation for the U.S. shareholder inclusion year, reduces the shareholder's pro rata share of tested loss of the controlled foreign corporation for the U.S. shareholder inclusion year, or both.

(e) *Stock owned through domestic partnerships.*—See § 1.958-1(d) for rules regarding the ownership of stock of a foreign corporation through a domestic partnership for purposes of section 951A and for purposes of any provision that specifically applies by reference to section 951A or the section 951A regulations.

(f) *Definitions.*—This paragraph (f) provides additional definitions that apply for purposes of this section and the section 951A regulations. Other definitions relevant to the section 951A regulations are included in §§ 1.951A-2 through 1.951A-4.

(1) *CFC inclusion year.*—The term *CFC inclusion year* means any taxable year of a foreign corporation beginning after December 31, 2017, at any time during which the corporation is a controlled foreign corporation.

(2) *Controlled foreign corporation.*—The term *controlled foreign corporation* has the meaning set forth in section 957(a).

(3) *Hypothetical distribution date.*—The term *hypothetical distribution date* has the meaning set forth in § 1.951-1(e)(1)(i).

(4) *Section 958(a) stock.*—The term *section 958(a) stock* means stock of a controlled foreign corporation owned (directly or indirectly) by a United States shareholder within the meaning of section 958(a), as modified by paragraph (e)(1) of this section.

(5) *Tested item.*—The term *tested item* means tested income, tested loss, qualified business asset investment, tested interest expense, or tested interest income.

(6) *United States shareholder.*—The term *United States shareholder* has the meaning set forth in section 951(b).

(7) *U.S. shareholder inclusion year.*—The term *U.S. shareholder inclusion year* means any taxable year of a United States shareholder in which or with which a CFC inclusion year of a controlled foreign corporation ends. [Reg. § 1.951A-1.]

☐ [*T.D. 9866, 6-14-2019. Amended by T.D. 9960, 1-24-2022.*]

Proposed Amendments to Regulation

§ 1.951A-1. General provisions.—

* * *

(e) *Stock owned through domestic partnerships and S corporations.*—(1) *Cross-references.*—See § 1.958-1(d) for rules regarding the ownership of stock of a foreign corporation through a domestic partnership (or S corporation, as defined in section 1361(a)(1), by reason of section 1373(a)) for purposes of section 951A and for purposes of any provision that specifically applies by reference to section 951A or the section 951A regulations. See § 1.958-1(e) for rules regarding an election for certain S corporations to be treated as an entity for purposes of section 951A and the section 951A regulations.

(2) *Application of entity treatment for taxable years ending before June 22, 2019.*—(i) *General rule.*—If a domestic partnership or S corporation satisfies the notification and reporting requirements in paragraph (e)(2)(iii) of this section, the domestic partnership or S corporation may apply the rules in proposed § 1.951A-5 as if the amendments proposed on October 10, 2018, had been finalized in their entirety *(proposed GILTI rules)*, for taxable years ending before June 22, 2019.

(ii) *Inapplicability of penalties.*—If a domestic partnership or S corporation satisfies the requirements of paragraph (e)(2)(iii) of this section, penalties for failures described in sections 6698(a), 6699(a), 6722(a), or any similar provision will not apply to the domestic partnership or S corporation to the extent such failures arise from acting consistently with the proposed GILTI rules before June 22, 2019.

(iii) *Notification and reporting requirements.*—(A) *Notification.*—To be eligible for the rules described in paragraphs (e)(2)(i) and (ii) of this section, a domestic partnership or S corporation must provide the notification described in paragraphs (e)(2)(iii)(A)*(1)* through *(3)* of this section to each partner of the partnership or shareholder of the S corporation. Such notification must be provided no later than the due date (taking into account extensions, if any, or any additional time that would have been granted if the domestic partnership or S corporation had made an extension request) of the domestic partnership's or S corporation's tax return for the last taxable year ending before June 22, 2019, and may be provided through any reasonable method, including via mail, email, or posting on a website through which the domestic partnership or S corporation would ordinarily disseminate tax information to its partners or shareholders. The domestic partnership or S corporation must also attach the notification described in this paragraph (e)(2)(iii)(A) and Form 8992, "U.S. Shareholder Calculation of Global Intangible Low-Taxed Income (GILTI)," reflecting computations under the proposed GILTI rules to any tax return with respect to which the rules described in paragraph (e)(2)(i) or (ii) of this section are being applied if the tax return has not been filed as of September 9, 2019. The notification required under this paragraph (e)(2)(iii) must provide—

(1) That the Schedule K-1, "Partner's Share of Income, Deductions, Credits, etc.," or the Schedule K-1, "Shareholder's Share of Income, Deductions, Credits, etc.," provided to the partner or shareholder, respectively, is consistent with the proposed GILTI rules;

(2) Whether the domestic partnership or S corporation filed a Form 1065, "U.S. Return of Partnership Income," or Form 1120-S, "U.S. Income Tax Return for an S Corporation," consistent with the proposed GILTI rules or this paragraph (e); and

(3) That the notification is provided in accordance with Notice 2019-46, 2019-37 I.R.B. 695.

(B) *Schedule K-1 distribution reporting.*—If a domestic partnership or S corporation furnished a Schedule K-1 based on the proposed GILTI rules, the domestic partnership or S corporation must separately state on Schedules K-1 for subsequent taxable years the partner's or shareholder's distributive share or pro rata share of a foreign corporation's distributions to the domestic partnership or S corporation of earnings and profits that relate to the GILTI inclusion amount of the partnership or S corporation that was reflected on the initially provided Schedules K-1. This information must be provided for each taxable year of the domestic partnership or S corporation following the taxable year to which the first Schedule K-1 relates.

* * *

[Prop. Reg. § 1.951A-1.]

[Proposed 1-25-2022.]

§ 1.951A-2. Tested income and tested loss.—(a) *Scope.*—This section provides rules for determining the tested income or tested loss of a controlled foreign corporation for purposes of determining a United States shareholder's net CFC tested income under § 1.951A-1(c)(2). Paragraph (b) of this section provides definitions related to tested income and tested loss. Paragraph (c) of this section provides rules for determining the gross tested income of a controlled foreign corporation and the deductions that are properly allocable to gross tested income.

(b) *Definitions related to tested income and tested loss.*—(1) *Tested income and tested income CFC.*—The term *tested income* means the excess (if any) of a controlled foreign corporation's gross tested income for a CFC inclusion year, over the allowable deductions (including taxes) properly allocable to the gross tested income for the CFC inclusion year (a controlled foreign corporation with tested income for a CFC inclusion year, a *tested income CFC*).

(2) *Tested loss and tested loss CFC.*—The term *tested loss* means the excess (if any) of a controlled foreign corporation's allowable deductions (including taxes) properly allocable to gross tested income (or that would be allocable to gross tested income if there were gross tested income) for a CFC inclusion year, over the gross tested income of the controlled foreign corporation for the CFC inclusion year (a controlled foreign corporation without tested income for a CFC inclusion year, a *tested loss CFC*).

(c) *Rules relating to the determination of tested income and tested loss.*—(1) *Definition of gross tested income.*—The term *gross tested income* means the gross income of a controlled foreign corporation for a CFC inclusion year determined without regard to—

(i) Items of income described in section 952(b),

(ii) Gross income taken into account in determining the subpart F income of the corporation,

(iii) Gross income excluded from the foreign base company income (as defined in section 954) or the insurance income (as defined in section 953) of the corporation by reason of the exception described in section 954(b)(4) pursuant to an election under § 1.954-1(d)(5), or a tentative gross tested income item of the corporation that qualifies for the exception described in section 954(b)(4) pursuant to an election under paragraph (c)(7) of this section,

(iv) Dividends received by the corporation from related persons (as defined in section 954(d)(3)), and

(v) Foreign oil and gas extraction income (as defined in section 907(c)(1)) of the corporation.

(2) *Determination of gross income and allowable deductions.*—(i) *In general.*—For purposes of determining tested income and tested loss, the gross income and allowable deductions of a controlled foreign corporation for a CFC inclusion year are determined under the rules of § 1.952-2 for determining the subpart F income of the controlled foreign corporation, except, for a controlled foreign corporation which is engaged in the business of reinsuring or issuing insurance or annuity contracts and which, if it were a domestic corporation engaged only in such business, would be taxable as an insurance company to which subchapter L of chapter 1 of the Code applies, substituting "the rules of sections 953 and 954(i)" for "the principles of §§ 1.953-4 and 1.953-5" in § 1.952-2(b)(2).

(ii) *Deemed payment under section 367(d).*—The allowable deductions of a controlled foreign corporation include a deemed payment of the controlled foreign corporation under section 367(d)(2)(A).

(3) *Allocation of deductions to gross tested income.*—(i) *In general.*—Except as provided in paragraph (c)(5) of this section, any deductions of a controlled foreign corporation allowable under paragraph (c)(2) of this section are allocated and apportioned to gross tested income

under the principles of section 954(b)(5) and § 1.954-1(c), by treating gross tested income that falls within a single separate category (as defined in § 1.904-5(a)(4)(v)) as a single item of gross income, separate and in addition to the items set forth in § 1.954-1(c)(1)(iii). Losses in other separate categories of income resulting from the application of § 1.954-1(c)(1)(i) cannot reduce any separate category of gross tested income, and losses in a separate category of gross tested income cannot reduce income in a category of subpart F income. In addition, deductions of a controlled foreign corporation that are allocated and apportioned to gross tested income under this paragraph (c)(3) are not taken into account for purposes of determining a qualified deficit as defined in section 952(c)(1)(B)(ii).

(ii) *Coordination with the high-tax exclusion.*—(A) *In general.*—In the case of a taxpayer that has made an election under paragraph (c)(7) of this section, in allocating and apportioning deductions under this paragraph (c)(3), the taxpayer must apply the rules of sections 861 through 865 and 904(d) (taking into account the rules of section 954(b)(5) and § 1.954-1(c)) in a manner that achieves results consistent with those under paragraph (c)(7) of this section.

(B) *Application of consistency rule to deductions allocated and apportioned to the residual grouping in applying the high-tax exclusion.*—Deductions that are allocated and apportioned to the residual income group under paragraph (c)(7)(iii)(A) of this section for purposes of applying the high-tax exclusion to a controlled foreign corporation's tentative gross tested income items are allocated and apportioned for purposes of determining the controlled foreign corporation's net income in each relevant statutory grouping using a method that provides for a consistent allocation and apportionment of deductions to gross income in the relevant groupings. See §§ 1.954-1(c) and 1.960-1(d)(3) for rules relating to the allocation and apportionment of expenses for purposes of determining subpart F income, which is included in the residual grouping for purposes of applying the high-tax exclusion of sections 951A(c)(2)(A)(i)(III) and 954(b)(4) and paragraph (c)(7) of this section. Therefore, for example, interest expense that is apportioned under the modified gross income method to a tentative gross tested income item of a lower-tier corporation under paragraph (c)(7)(iii)(A) of this section may be allocated and apportioned to the tested income of the upper-tier corporation or to the residual grouping, depending on whether the lower-tier corporation's tentative gross tested income item is an item of gross tested income or is excluded from gross tested income under the high-tax exclusion. *See* paragraph (c)(8)(iii)(C) (Example 3) of this section for an example illustrating the rules of this paragraph (c)(3).

(4) *Gross income taken into account in determining subpart F income.*—(i) *In general.*—Except as provided in paragraph (c)(4)(iii) of this section, gross income of a controlled foreign corporation for a CFC inclusion year described in section 951A(c)(2)(A)(i)(II) and paragraph (c)(1)(ii) of this section is gross income described in paragraphs (c)(4)(ii)(A) through (E) of this section.

(ii) *Items of gross income included in subpart F income.*—(A) *Insurance income.*—Gross income described in this paragraph (c)(4)(ii)(A) is any item of gross income included in the insurance income (adjusted net insurance income as defined in § 1.954-1(a)(6)) of the controlled foreign corporation for the CFC inclusion year.

(B) *Foreign base company income.*—Gross income described in this paragraph (c)(4)(ii)(B) is any item of gross income included in the foreign base company income (adjusted net foreign base company income as defined in § 1.954-1(a)(5)) of the controlled foreign corporation for the CFC inclusion year.

(C) *International boycott income.*—Gross income described in this paragraph (c)(4)(ii)(C) is the product of the gross income of the controlled foreign corporation for the CFC inclusion year that gives rise to the income described in section 952(a)(3)(A) multiplied by the international boycott factor described in section 952(a)(3)(B).

(D) *Illegal bribes, kickbacks, or other payments.*—Gross income described in this paragraph (c)(4)(ii)(D) is the sum of the amounts of the controlled foreign corporation for the CFC inclusion year described in section 952(a)(4).

(E) *Income earned in certain foreign countries.*—Gross income described in this paragraph (c)(4)(ii)(E) is income of the controlled foreign corporation for the CFC inclusion year described in section 952(a)(5).

(iii) *Coordination rules.*—(A) *Coordination with E&P limitation.*—Gross income of a controlled foreign corporation for a CFC inclusion year described in section 951A(c)(2)(A)(i)(II) and paragraph (c)(1)(ii) of this section includes any item of gross income that is excluded from subpart F income of the controlled foreign corporation for the CFC inclusion year, or that is otherwise excluded from the amount included under section 951(a)(1)(A) in the gross income of a United States shareholder of the controlled foreign corporation for the U.S. shareholder inclusion year in which or with which the CFC inclusion year ends, under section 952(c)(1) and § 1.952-1(c), (d), or (e).

(B) *Coordination with E&P recapture.*—Gross income of a controlled foreign corporation for a CFC inclusion year described in section 951A(c)(2)(A)(i)(II) and paragraph (c)(1)(ii) of this section does not include any item of gross income that results in the recharacterization of earnings and profits as subpart F income of the controlled foreign corporation for the CFC inclusion year under section 952(c)(2) and § 1.952-1(f)(2).

(C) *Coordination with full inclusion rule and high tax exception.*—Gross income of a controlled foreign corporation for a CFC inclusion year described in section 951A(c)(2)(A)(i)(II) and paragraph (c)(1)(ii) of this section does not include full inclusion foreign base company income that is excluded from subpart F income under § 1.954-1(d)(6). Full inclusion foreign base company income that is excluded from subpart F income under § 1.954-1(d)(6) is also not included in gross income of a controlled foreign corporation for a CFC inclusion year described in section 951A(c)(2)(A)(i)(III) and paragraph (c)(1)(iii) of this section.

(iv) *Examples.*—The following examples illustrate the application of this paragraph (c)(4).

(A) *Example 1*—(*1*) *Facts.* A Corp, a domestic corporation, owns 100% of the single class of stock of FS, a controlled foreign corporation. Both A Corp and FS use the calendar year as their taxable year. In Year 1, FS has passive category foreign personal holding company income of $100x, a general category loss in foreign oil and gas extraction income of $100x, and earnings and profits of $0. FS has no other income. In Year 2, FS has general category gross income of $100x and earnings and profits of $100x. Without regard to section 952(c)(2), in Year 2 FS has no income described in any of the categories of income excluded from gross tested income in paragraphs (c)(1)(i) through (v) of this section. FS has no allowable deductions properly allocable to gross tested income for Year 2.

(*2*) *Analysis*—(*i*) *Year 1.* As a result of the earnings and profits limitation of section 952(c)(1)(A), FS has no subpart F income in Year 1, and A Corp has no inclusion with respect to FS under section 951(a)(1)(A). Under paragraph (c)(4)(iii)(A) of this section, gross income described in section 951A(c)(2)(A)(i)(II) and paragraph (c)(1)(ii) of this section includes any item of gross income excluded from the subpart F income of FS for Year 1 under section 952(c)(1)(A) and § 1.952-1(c). Therefore, the $100x foreign personal holding company income of FS in Year 1 is excluded from gross tested income by reason of section 951A(c)(2)(A)(i)(II) and paragraph (c)(1)(ii) of this section, and FS has no gross tested income in Year 1.

(*ii*) *Year 2.* In Year 2, under section 952(c)(2) and § 1.952-1(f)(2), FS's general category earnings and profits ($100x) in excess of its subpart F income ($0) give rise to the recharacterization of its passive category recapture account as subpart F income. Therefore, FS has passive category subpart F income of $100x in Year 2, and A Corp has an inclusion of $100x with respect to FS under section 951(a)(1)(A). Under paragraph (c)(4)(iii)(B) of this section, gross income described in section 951A(c)(2)(A)(i)(II) and paragraph (c)(1)(ii) of this section does not include any item of gross income that results in the recharacterization of earnings and profits as subpart F income in FS's taxable year under section 952(c)(2) and § 1.952-1(f)(2). Accordingly, the $100x of general category gross income of FS in Year 2 is not excluded from gross tested income by reason of section 951A(c)(2)(A)(i)(II) and paragraph (c)(1)(ii) of this section, and FS has $100x of general category gross tested income in Year 2.

(B) *Example 2*—(*1*) *Facts.* A Corp, a domestic corporation, owns 100% of the single class of stock of FC1 and FC2, controlled foreign corporations. A Corp, FC1, and FC2 use the calendar year as their taxable year. In Year 1, FC1 has gross income of $290x from product sales to unrelated persons within its country of incorporation, gross interest income of $10x (an amount that is less than $1,000,000) that does not qualify for an exception to foreign personal holding company income, and earnings and profits of $300x. In Year 1, FC2 has gross income of $45x for performing consulting services within its country of incorporation for unrelated persons, gross interest income of $150x (an amount that is not less than $1,000,000) that does not qualify for an exception to foreign personal holding company income, and earnings and profits of $195x.

(2) *Analysis*—(i) *FC1*. In Year 1, by application of the de minimis rule of section 954(b)(3)(A) and § 1.954-1(b)(1)(i), the $10x of gross interest income earned by FC1 is not treated as foreign base company income ($10x of gross foreign base company income is less than $15x, the lesser of 5% of $300x, FC's total gross income for Year 1, or $1,000,000). Accordingly, FC1 has no subpart F income in Year 1, and A Corp has no inclusion with respect to FC1 under section 951(a)(1)(A). Under paragraph (c)(1)(i) of this section, gross income described in section 951A(c)(2)(A)(i)(II) and paragraph (c)(1)(ii) of this section is any item of gross income included in foreign base company income, and thus gross income described in section 951A(c)(2)(A)(i)(II) and paragraph (c)(1)(ii) of this section does not include any item of gross income excluded from foreign base company income under the de minimis rule in section 954(b)(3)(A) and § 1.954-1(b)(1)(i). Accordingly, FS's $10x of gross interest income in Year 1 is not excluded from gross tested income by reason of section 951A(c)(2)(A)(i)(II) and paragraph (c)(1)(ii) of this section, and FC1 has $300x ($290x of gross sales income and $10x of gross interest income) of gross tested income in Year 1.

(*ii*) *FC2*. In Year 1, by application of the full inclusion rule in section 954(b)(3)(B) and § 1.954-1(b)(1)(ii), the $45x of gross income earned by FC2 for performing consulting services within its country of incorporation for unrelated persons is treated as foreign base company income ($150x of gross foreign base company income exceeds $136.5x, which is 70% of $195x, FC2's total gross income for Year 1). Therefore, FC2 has $195x of foreign base company income in Year 1, including $45x of full inclusion foreign base company income as defined in § 1.954-1(b)(2), and A Corp has an inclusion of $195x with respect to FC2 under section 951(a)(1)(A). Under paragraph (c)(4)(i) of this section, gross income described in section 951A(c)(2)(A)(i)(II) and paragraph (c)(1)(ii) of this section is any item of gross income included in foreign base company income, and thus gross income described in section 951A(c)(2)(A)(i)(II) and paragraph (c)(1)(ii) of this section includes any item of gross income included as foreign base company income under the full inclusion rule in section 954(b)(3)(B) and § 1.954-1(b)(1)(ii). Accordingly, FC2's $45x of gross services income and its $150x of gross interest income in Year 1 are excluded from gross tested income by reason of section 951A(c)(2)(A)(i)(II) and paragraph (c)(1)(ii) of this section, and FC2 has no gross tested income in Year 1.

(C) *Example 3*—(*1*) *Facts*. A Corp, a domestic corporation, owns 100% of the single class of stock of FS, a controlled foreign corporation. A Corp and FS use the calendar year as their taxable year. In Year 1, FS has gross income of $1,000x, of which $720x is general category foreign base company sales income and $280x is general category income from sales within its country of incorporation; FS has expenses of $650x (including creditable foreign income taxes), of which $500x are allocated and apportioned to foreign base company sales income and $150x are allocated and apportioned to sales income from sales within FS's country of incorporation; and FS has earnings and profits of $350x for Year 1. Foreign income tax of $55x is considered imposed on the $220x ($720x - $500x) of net foreign base company sales income, and $26x is considered imposed on the $130x ($280x - $150x) of net income from sales within FS's country of operation. The maximum rate of tax in section 11 for the taxable year is 21%, and FS elects the high tax exception of section 954(b)(4) under § 1.954-1(d)(1) for Year 1 for its foreign base company sales income. In a prior taxable year, FS had losses with respect to income other than foreign base company or insurance income that, by reason of the limitation in section 952(c)(1)(A), reduced the subpart F income of FS (consisting entirely of foreign source general category income) by $600x; as of the beginning of Year 1, such amount has not been recharacterized as subpart F income in a subsequent taxable year under section 952(c)(2).

(2) *Analysis*—(i) *Foreign base company income*. In Year 1, by application of the full inclusion rule in section 954(b)(3)(B) and § 1.954-1(b)(1)(ii), the $280x of gross income earned by FS for sales within its country of incorporation is treated as foreign base company income ($720x of gross foreign base company income exceeds $700x, which is 70% of $1,000x, FS's total gross income for the taxable year). However, the $220x of foreign base company sales income qualifies for the high tax exception of section 954(b)(4) and § 1.954-1(d)(1), because the effective rate of tax with respect to the net foreign base company sales income ($220x) is 20% ($55x/($220x + $55x)) which is greater than 18.9% (90% of 21%, the maximum rate of tax in section 11 for the taxable year). Because the $220x of net foreign base company sales income qualifies for the high tax exception of section 954(b)(4) and § 1.954-1(d)(1), the $130x of full inclusion foreign base company income is also excluded from subpart F income under § 1.954-1(d)(6).

(ii) *Recapture of subpart F income*. Under section 952(c)(2) and § 1.952-1(f)(2), FS's general category earnings and profits ($350x) in excess of its subpart F income ($0) give rise to the recharacterization of its general category recapture account ($600x) as subpart F income to the extent of current year earnings and profits. Therefore, FS has general category subpart F income of $350x in Year 1, and A Corp has an inclusion of $350x with respect to FS under section 951(a)(1)(A).

(iii) *Gross tested income*. The $720x of gross foreign base company income is excluded from gross tested income under section 951A(c)(2)(A)(i)(III) and paragraph (c)(1)(iii) of this section. However, the $280x of gross sales income earned from sales within FS's country of incorporation is not excluded from gross tested income under either section 951A(c)(2)(A)(i)(II) and paragraph (c)(1)(ii) of this section or section 951A(c)(2)(A)(i)(III) and paragraph (c)(1)(iii) of this section. Under paragraph (c)(4)(iii)(B) of this section, the $280x of gross sales income earned from sales within FS's country of incorporation is not excluded from gross tested income under section 951A(c)(2)(A)(i)(II) and paragraph (c)(1)(ii) of this section, because gross income described in paragraph (c)(1)(ii) of this section does not include any item of gross income that results in the recharacterization of earnings and profits as subpart F income under section 952(c)(2) and § 1.952-1(f)(2). Further, under paragraph (c)(4)(iii)(C) of this section, the $280x of gross sales income earned from sales within FS's country of incorporation is not excluded from gross tested income under either section 951A(c)(2)(A)(i)(II) and paragraph (c)(1)(ii) of this section or section 951A(c)(2)(A)(i)(III) and paragraph (c)(1)(iii) of this section, because gross income described in section 951A(c)(2)(A)(i)(II) and paragraph (c)(1)(ii) of this section or section 951A(c)(2)(A)(i)(III) and paragraph (c)(1)(iii) of this section does not include full inclusion foreign base company income that is excluded from subpart F income under § 1.954-1(d)(6). Accordingly, FS has $280x of gross tested income for Year 1.

(5) *Allocation of deduction or loss attributable to disqualified basis*.—(i) *In general*.—A deduction or loss attributable to disqualified basis is allocated and apportioned solely to residual CFC gross income, and any depreciation, amortization, or cost recovery allowances attributable to disqualified basis is not properly allocable to property produced or acquired for resale under section 263, 263A, or 471.

(ii) *Determination of deduction or loss attributable to disqualified basis*.—Except as otherwise provided in this paragraph (c)(5)(ii), in the case of a depreciation or amortization deduction with respect to property with disqualified basis and adjusted basis other than disqualified basis, the deduction or loss is treated as attributable to the disqualified basis in the same proportion that the disqualified basis bears to the total adjusted basis in the property. In the case of a loss from a taxable sale or exchange of property with disqualified basis and adjusted basis other than disqualified basis, the loss is treated as attributable to disqualified basis to the extent thereof.

(iii) *Definitions*.—The following definitions apply for purposes of this paragraph (c)(5).

(A) *Disqualified basis*.—The term *disqualified basis* has the meaning set forth in § 1.951A-3(h)(2)(ii).

(B) *Residual CFC gross income*.—The term *residual CFC gross income* means gross income other than gross tested income, gross income taken into account in determining subpart F income, or gross income that is effectively connected, or treated as effectively connected, with the conduct of a trade or business in the United States (as described in § 1.882-4(a)(1)).

(iv) *Reductions to disqualified basis pursuant to coordination rules*.—See § 1.245A-7(b) or § 1.245A-8(b), as applicable, for reductions to disqualified basis resulting from the application of § 1.245A-5.

(v) *Examples*.—The following examples illustrate the application of this paragraph (c)(5).

(A) *Example 1: Sale of intangible property during the disqualified period*—(*1*) *Facts*. USP, a domestic corporation, owns all of the stock in CFC1 and CFC2, each a controlled foreign corporation. Both USP and CFC2 use the calendar year as their taxable year. CFC1 uses a taxable year ending November 30. On November 1, 2018, before the start of its first CFC inclusion year, CFC1 sells Asset A to CFC2 in exchange for $100x of cash. Asset A is intangible property that is amortizable under section 197. Immediately before the sale, the adjusted basis in Asset A is $20x, and CFC1 recognizes $80x of gain as a result of the sale ($100x - $20x). CFC1's gain is not subject to U.S. tax or taken into account in determining an inclusion to USP under section 951(a)(1)(A).

(2) *Analysis.* The sale by CFC1 is a disqualified transfer (within the meaning of § 1.951A-3(h)(2)(ii)(C)(*2*)) because it is a transfer of property in which gain was recognized by CFC1, CFC1 and CFC2 are related persons, and the transfer occurs during the disqualified period (within the meaning of § 1.951A-3(h)(2)(ii)(C)(*1*)). The disqualified basis in Asset A is $80x, the excess of CFC2's adjusted basis in Asset A immediately after the disqualified transfer ($100x), over the sum of CFC1's basis in Asset A immediately before the transfer ($20x) and the qualified gain amount (as defined in § 1.951A-3(h)(2)(ii)(C)(*3*)) ($0). Accordingly, under paragraph (c)(5)(i) of this section, any deduction or loss of CFC2 attributable to the disqualified basis is allocated and apportioned solely to residual CFC gross income of CFC2 and, therefore, is not taken into account in determining the tested income, tested loss, subpart F income, or effectively connected income of CFC2 for any CFC inclusion year.

(B) *Example 2: Related party transfer after the disqualified period; gain recognition*—(*1*) *Facts.* The facts are the same as in paragraph (c)(5)(v)(A)(*1*) of this section (the facts in *Example 1*), except that, on November 30, 2020, CFC2 sells Asset A to CFC3, a controlled foreign corporation wholly-owned by CFC2, in exchange for $120x of cash. Immediately before the sale, the adjusted basis in Asset A is $90x, $72x of which is disqualified basis. The gain recognized by CFC2 on the sale of Asset A is not described in paragraphs (c)(1)(i) through (v) of this section.

(2) *Analysis.* Paragraph (c)(5)(i) of this section does not apply to the sale of Asset A from CFC2 to CFC3 because the sale does not give rise to a deduction or loss attributable to disqualified basis, but instead gives rise to gain. Therefore, CFC2 recognizes $30x ($120x - $90x) of gain that is included in gross tested income for its CFC inclusion year ending November 30, 2019. Under § 1.951A-3(h)(2)(ii)(B)(*1*)(ii), because CFC2 sold Asset A to CFC3, a related person, and CFC2 did not recognize a deduction or loss on the sale, the disqualified basis in Asset A is not reduced or eliminated by reason of the sale. Accordingly, under paragraph (c)(5)(i) of this section, any deduction or loss of CFC3 attributable to the $72x of disqualified basis in Asset A is allocated and apportioned solely to residual CFC gross income of CFC3.

(C) *Example 3: Related party transfer after the disqualified period; loss recognition*—(*1*) *Facts.* The facts are the same as in paragraph (c)(5)(v)(B)(*1*) of this section (the facts in *Example 2*), except that CFC2 sells Asset A to CFC3 in exchange for $70x of cash.

(2) *Analysis.* Under paragraph (c)(5)(ii) of this section, the $20x loss recognized by CFC2 on the sale is attributable to disqualified basis, to the extent thereof, notwithstanding that the loss may be deferred under section 267(f). Thus, under paragraph (c)(5)(i) of this section, the loss is allocated and apportioned solely to residual CFC gross income of CFC2 in the CFC inclusion year in which the loss is taken into account pursuant to section 267(f). Under § 1.951A-3(h)(2)(ii)(B)(*1*)(*ii*), the disqualified basis in Asset A is reduced by $20x, the loss of CFC2 that is attributable to disqualified basis under paragraph (c)(5)(ii) of this section. Accordingly, under paragraph (c)(5)(i) of this section, any deduction or loss of CFC3 attributable to the remaining $52x of disqualified basis in Asset A is allocated and apportioned solely to residual CFC gross income of CFC3.

(6) *Allocation of deductions attributable to disqualified payments.*—(i) *In general.*—A deduction related directly or indirectly to a disqualified payment is allocated and apportioned solely to residual CFC gross income, and any deduction related to a disqualified payment is not properly allocable to property produced or acquired for resale under section 263, 263A, or 471.

(ii) *Definitions.*—The following definitions apply for purposes of this paragraph (c)(6).

(A) *Disqualified payment.*—The term *disqualified payment* means a payment made by a person to a related recipient CFC during the disqualified period with respect to the related recipient CFC, to the extent the payment would constitute income described in section 951A(c)(2)(A)(i) and paragraph (c)(1) of this section without regard to whether section 951A applies.

(B) *Disqualified period.*—The term *disqualified period* has the meaning provided in § 1.951A-3(h)(2)(ii)(C)(*1*), substituting "related recipient CFC" for "transferor CFC."

(C) *Related recipient CFC.*—The term *related recipient CFC* means, with respect to a payment by a person, a recipient of the payment that is a controlled foreign corporation that bears a relationship to the payor described in section 267(b) or 707(b) immediately before or after the payment.

(iii) *Treatment of partnerships.*—For purposes of determining whether a payment is made by a person to a related recipient CFC for purposes of paragraph (c)(6)(ii)(A) of this section, a payment by or to a partnership is treated as made proportionately by or to its partners, as applicable.

(iv) *Reductions to disqualified payments pursuant to coordination rules.*—See § 1.245A-5(j)(8) and § 1.245A-7(b) or § 1.245A-8(b), as applicable, for reductions to disqualified payments resulting from the application of § 1.245A-5.

(v) *Examples.*—The following examples illustrate the application of this paragraph (c)(6).

(A) *Example 1: Deduction related directly to disqualified payment to related recipient CFC.*—(*1*) *Facts.* USP, a domestic corporation, owns all of the stock in CFC1 and CFC2, each a controlled foreign corporation. Both USP and CFC2 use the calendar year as their taxable year. CFC1 uses a taxable year ending November 30. On October 15, 2018, before the start of its first CFC inclusion year, CFC1 receives and accrues a payment from CFC2 of $100x of prepaid royalties with respect to a license. The $100x payment is excluded from subpart F income pursuant to section 954(c)(6) and would constitute income described in section 951A(c)(2)(A)(i) and paragraph (c)(1) of this section without regard to whether section 951A applies.

(2) *Analysis.* CFC1 is a related recipient CFC (within the meaning of paragraph (c)(6)(ii)(C) of this section) with respect to the royalty prepayment by CFC2 because it is related to CFC2 within the meaning of section 267(b). The royalty prepayment is received by CFC1 during its disqualified period (within the meaning of paragraph (c)(6)(ii)(B) of this section) because it is received during the period beginning January 1, 2018, and ending November 30, 2018. Because it would constitute income described in section 951A(c)(2)(A)(i) and paragraph (c)(1) of this section without regard to whether section 951A applies, the payment is a disqualified payment. Accordingly, CFC2's deductions related to such payment accrued during taxable years ending on or after April 7, 2020, are allocated and apportioned solely to residual CFC gross income under paragraph (c)(6)(i) of this section.

(B) *Example 2: Deduction related indirectly to disqualified payment to partnership in which related recipient CFC is a partner.*—(*1*) *Facts.* The facts are the same as in paragraph (c)(6)(v)(A)(*1*) of this section (the facts in *Example 1*), except that CFC1 and USP own 99% and 1%, respectively of FPS, a foreign partnership, which has a taxable year ending November 30. USP receives a prepayment of $110x from CFC2 for the performance of future services. USP subcontracts the performance of these future services to FPS for which FPS receives and accrues a $100x prepayment from USP. The services will be performed in the same country under the laws of which CFC1 and FPS are created or organized, and the $100x prepayment is not foreign base company services income under section 954(e) and § 1.954-4(a). The $100x prepayment would constitute income described in section 951A(c)(2)(A)(i) and paragraph (c)(1) of this section without regard to whether section 951A applies.

(2) *Analysis.* CFC1 is a related recipient CFC (within the meaning of paragraph (c)(6)(ii)(C) of this section) with respect to the services prepayment by USP because, under paragraph (c)(6)(iii) of this section, it is treated as receiving $99x (99% of $100x) of the services prepayment from USP, and it is related to USP within the meaning of section 267(b). The services prepayment is received by CFC1 during its disqualified period (within the meaning of paragraph (c)(6)(ii)(B) of this section) because it is received during the period beginning January 1, 2018, and ending November 30, 2018. Because it would constitute income described in section 951A(c)(2)(A)(i) and paragraph (c)(1) of this section without regard to whether section 951A applies, the prepayment is a disqualified payment. In addition, CFC2's deductions related to its prepayment to USP are indirectly related to the disqualified payment by USP. Accordingly, CFC2's deductions related to such payment accrued during taxable years ending on or after April 7, 2020 are allocated and apportioned solely to residual CFC gross income under paragraph (c)(6)(i) of this section.

(7) *Election to apply high-tax exception of section 954(b)(4).*—(i) *In general.*—For purposes of section 951A(c)(2)(A)(i)(III) and paragraph (c)(1)(iii) of this section, a tentative gross tested income item of a controlled foreign corporation for a CFC inclusion year qualifies for the exception described in section 954(b)(4) only if—

(A) An election made under paragraph (c)(7)(viii) of this section is effective with respect to the controlled foreign corporation for the CFC inclusion year; and

(B) The tentative tested income item with respect to the tentative gross tested income item was subject to an effective rate of foreign tax, as determined under paragraph (c)(7)(vi) of this section, that is greater than 90 percent of the maximum rate of tax specified in section 11.

(ii) *Calculation of tentative gross tested income item.*—(A) *In general.*—A tentative gross tested income item with respect to a controlled foreign corporation for a CFC inclusion year is the aggregate of all items of gross income of the controlled foreign corporation attributable to a tested unit (as defined in paragraph (c)(7)(iv) of this section) of the controlled foreign corporation in the CFC inclusion year that would be gross tested income without regard to this paragraph (c)(7) and would be in a single tested income group (as defined in §1.960-1(d)(2)(ii)(C)). A controlled foreign corporation may have multiple tentative gross tested income items. See paragraphs (c)(8)(iii)(A)(2)(*i*) (Example 1) and (c)(8)(iii)(B)(2)(*i*) (Example 2) of this section for illustrations of the application of the rule set forth in this paragraph (c)(7)(ii)(A).

(B) *Gross income attributable to a tested unit.*—(*1*) *Items properly reflected on separate set of books and records.*—Items of gross income of a controlled foreign corporation are attributable to a tested unit of the controlled foreign corporation to the extent they are properly reflected on the separate set of books and records of the tested unit, as modified under paragraph (c)(7)(ii)(B)(2) of this section. Each item of gross income of a controlled foreign corporation is attributable to a tested unit (and not to more than one tested unit) of the controlled foreign corporation. See paragraphs (c)(8)(iii)(D)(2) and (c)(8)(iii)(D)(*5*) (Example 4) of this section for illustrations of the application of the rule set forth in this paragraph (c)(7)(ii)(B).

(*2*) *Gross income determined under federal income tax principles, as adjusted for disregarded payments.*—For purposes of paragraph (c)(7)(ii)(B)(*1*) of this section, gross income must be determined under federal income tax principles, except that the principles of §1.904-4(f)(2)(vi) apply to adjust gross income of the tested unit, to the extent thereof, to reflect disregarded payments. For purposes of this paragraph (c)(7)(ii)(B)(2), the principles of §1.904-4(f)(2)(vi) are applied taking into account the rules in paragraphs (c)(7)(ii)(B)(2)(*i*) through (*v*) of this section.

(*i*) The controlled foreign corporation is treated as the foreign branch owner and any other tested units of the controlled foreign corporation are treated as foreign branches.

(*ii*) The principles of the rules in §1.904-4(f)(2)(vi)(A) apply in the case of disregarded payments between a foreign branch and another foreign branch without regard to whether either foreign branch makes a disregarded payment to, or receives a disregarded payment from, the foreign branch owner.

(*iii*) The exclusion for interest and interest equivalents described in §1.904-4(f)(2)(vi)(C)(*1*) does not apply to the extent of the amount of a disregarded payment that is deductible in the country of tax residence (or location, in the case of a branch) of the tested unit that is the payor.

(*iv*) In the case of an amount described in paragraph (c)(7)(ii)(B)(2)(*iii*) of this section, the rules for determining how a disregarded payment is allocated to gross income of a foreign branch or foreign branch owner in §1.904-4(f)(2)(vi)(B) are applied by treating the disregarded payment as allocated and apportioned ratably to all of the gross income attributable to the tested unit that is making the disregarded payment. If a tested unit is both a payor and payee of an amount described in paragraph (c)(7)(ii)(B)(2)(*iii*) of this section, gross income to which the disregarded payments are allocable include gross income allocated to the payor tested unit as a result of the receipt of amounts described in paragraph (c)(7)(ii)(B)(2)(*iii*) of this section, to the extent thereof. If a tested unit makes and receives payments described in paragraph (c)(7)(ii)(B)(2)(*iii*) of this section to and from the same tested unit, the payments are netted so that paragraph (c)(7)(ii)(B)(2)(*iii*) of this section and the principles of §1.904-4(f)(2)(vi) apply only to the net amount of such payments between the two tested units.

(*v*) In the case of multiple disregarded payments, in lieu of §1.904-4(f)(2)(vi)(F), disregarded payments are taken into account under paragraph (c)(7)(ii)(B)(2) of this section and the principles of §1.904-4(f)(2)(vi) under the rules provided in this paragraph (c)(7)(ii)(B)(2)(*v*). Adjustments are made with respect to a disregarded payment received by a tested unit before payments made by that tested unit. Except as provided in paragraph (c)(7)(ii)(B)(2)(*iv*) of this section, if a tested unit both makes and receives disregarded payments, adjustments are first made with respect to disregarded payments that would be definitely related to a single class of gross income under the principles of §1.861-8; second, adjustments are made with respect to disregarded payments that would be definitely related to multiple classes of gross income under the principles of §1.861-8, but that are not definitely related to all gross income of the tested unit; third, adjustments are made with respect to disregarded payments (other than interest described in paragraph (c)(7)(ii)(B)(2)(*iii*) of this section) that would be definitely related to all gross income under the principles of §1.861-8; and fourth, adjustments are made with respect to interest described in paragraph (c)(7)(ii)(B)(2)(*iii*) and disregarded payments that would not be definitely related to any gross income under the principles of §1.861-8.

(iii) *Calculation of tentative tested income item.*—(A) *In general.*—A tentative tested income item with respect to the tentative gross tested income item described in paragraph (c)(7)(ii)(A) of this section is determined by allocating and apportioning deductions for the CFC inclusion year (including expense for current year taxes (as defined in §1.960-1(b)(4)), and not including any items described in §1.951A-2(c)(5) or (c)(6)) to the tentative gross tested income item under the principles of §1.960-1(d)(3) and the rules of §1.861–20. For purposes of this paragraph (c)(7)(iii), each tentative gross tested income item (if any) is treated as assigned to a separate tested income group, as that term is described in §1.960-1(d)(2)(ii)(C), and all other income is treated as assigned to a residual income group. For purposes of applying §§1.861-9 and 1.861-9T under the principles of §1.960-1(d)(3), the amount of interest deductions that are allocated and apportioned to the assets (or gross income, in the case of a taxpayer that has elected the modified gross income method) of a lower-tier corporation, such as a corporation the stock of which is owned by the controlled foreign corporation indirectly through the tested unit, are allocated and apportioned to the residual income category and not to any tentative gross tested income item of the controlled foreign corporation. See paragraphs (c)(8)(iii)(A)(2)(*iii*) (Example 1), (c)(8)(iii)(B)(2)(*iv*) (Example 2), and (c)(8)(iii)(C)(2)(*iv*) (Example 3) of this section for illustrations of the application of the rules set forth in this paragraph (c)(7)(iii)(A).

(B) *Effect of potential and actual changes in taxes paid or accrued.*—Except as otherwise provided in this paragraph (c)(7)(iii)(B), the amount of current year taxes paid or accrued by a controlled foreign corporation for purposes of this paragraph (c)(7) does not take into account any potential reduction in foreign income taxes that may occur by reason of a future distribution to shareholders of all or part of such income. However, to the extent the foreign income taxes paid or accrued by the controlled foreign corporation are reasonably certain to be returned to a shareholder by the foreign country imposing such taxes, directly or indirectly, through any means (including, but not limited to, a refund, credit, payment, discharge of an obligation, or any other method) on a subsequent distribution to such shareholder, the foreign income taxes are not treated as paid or accrued for purposes of this paragraph (c)(7). In addition, foreign income taxes that have not been paid or accrued because they are contingent on a future distribution of earnings (or other similar transaction, such as a loan to a shareholder) are not taken into account for purposes of this paragraph (c)(7). If, pursuant to section 905(c) and §1.905-3, a redetermination of U.S. tax liability is required to account for the effect of a foreign tax redetermination (as defined in §1.905-3(a)), this paragraph (c)(7) is applied in the adjusted year taking into account the adjusted amount of the redetermined foreign tax.

(iv) *Tested unit rules.*—(A) *In general.*—Subject to the combination rule in paragraph (c)(7)(iv)(C) of this section, the term *tested unit* means any corporation, interest, or branch described in paragraphs (c)(7)(iv)(A)(*1*) through (*3*) of this section. See paragraph (c)(8)(iii)(D) (Example 4) of this section for an example that illustrates the application of the tested unit rules set forth in this paragraph (c)(7)(iv).

(*1*) A controlled foreign corporation (as defined in section 957(a)).

(*2*) An interest held directly or indirectly by a controlled foreign corporation in a pass-through entity that is—

(*i*) A tax resident (as described in §1.267A-5(a)(23)(i)) of any foreign country; or

(ii) Not treated as fiscally transparent (as determined under the principles of § 1.267A-5(a)(8)) for purposes of the tax law of the foreign country of which the controlled foreign corporation is a tax resident or, in the case of an interest in a pass-through entity held by a controlled foreign corporation indirectly through one or more other tested units, for purposes of the tax law of the foreign country of which the tested unit that directly (or indirectly through the fewest number of transparent interests) owns the interest is a tax resident.

(3) A branch (as described in § 1.267A-5(a)(2)) the activities of which are carried on directly or indirectly (through one or more pass-through entities) by a controlled foreign corporation. However, in the case of a branch that does not give rise to a taxable presence under the tax law of the foreign country where the branch is located, the branch is a tested unit only if, under the tax law of the foreign country of which the controlled foreign corporation is a tax resident (or, if applicable, under the tax law of a foreign country of which the tested unit that directly (or indirectly, through the fewest number of transparent interests) carries on the activities of the branch is a tax resident), an exclusion, exemption, or other similar relief (such as a preferential rate) applies with respect to income attributable to the branch. For purposes of this paragraph (c)(7)(iv)(A)(3), similar relief does not include a credit (for example, a foreign tax credit) against the tax imposed under such tax law. If a controlled foreign corporation carries on directly or indirectly (through one or more pass-through entities) less than all of the activities of a branch (for example, if the activities are carried on indirectly through an interest in a partnership), then the rules in this paragraph apply separately with respect to the portion (or portions, if carried on indirectly through more than one chain of pass-through entities) of the activities carried on by the controlled foreign corporation. See paragraphs (c)(8)(iii)(D)(3) and (c)(8)(iii)(D)(4) (Example 4) of this section for illustrations of the application of the rules set forth in this paragraph (c)(7)(iv)(A)(3).

(B) *Items attributable to only one tested unit.*—For purposes of paragraph (c)(7) of this section, if an item is attributable to more than one tested unit in a tier of tested units, the item is considered attributable only to the lowest-tier tested unit. Thus, for example, if a controlled foreign corporation directly owns a branch tested unit described in paragraph (c)(7)(iv)(A)(3) of this section, and an item of gross income is (under the rules of paragraph (c)(7)(ii)(B) of this section) attributable to both the branch tested unit and the controlled foreign corporation tested unit, then the item is considered attributable only to the branch tested unit.

(C) *Combination rule.*—*(1) In general.*—Except as provided in paragraph (c)(7)(iv)(C)(2) of this section, tested units of a controlled foreign corporation (including the controlled foreign corporation tested unit) are treated as a single tested unit if the tested units are tax residents of, or located in (in the case of a tested unit that is a branch, or a portion of the activities of a branch, that gives rise to a taxable presence under the tax law of a foreign country), the same foreign country. For purposes of this paragraph (c)(7)(iv)(C)(1), in the case of a tested unit that is an interest in a pass-through entity or a portion of the activities of a branch, a reference to the tax residency or location of the tested unit means the tax residency of the entity the interest in which is the tested unit or the location of the branch, as applicable. See paragraphs (c)(8)(iii)(D)(2) and (c)(8)(iii)(D)(5) (Example 4) of this section for illustrations of the application of the rule set forth in this paragraph (c)(7)(iv)(C)(1).

(2) Exception for nontaxed branches.—The rule in paragraph (c)(7)(iv)(C)(1) of this section does not apply to a tested unit that is described in paragraph (c)(7)(iv)(A)(3) of this section if the branch described in paragraph (c)(7)(iv)(A)(3) of this section does not give rise to a taxable presence under the tax law of the foreign country where the branch is located. See paragraph (c)(8)(iii)(D)(4) (Example 4) of this section for an illustration of the application of the rule set forth in this paragraph (c)(7)(v)(C)(2).

(3) Effect of combination rule.—If, pursuant to paragraph (c)(7)(iv)(C)(1) of this section, tested units are treated as a single tested unit, then, solely for purposes of paragraph (c)(7) of this section, items of gross income attributable to such tested units, and items of deduction and foreign taxes allocated and apportioned to such gross income, are aggregated for purposes of determining the combined tested unit's tentative gross tested income item, tentative tested income item, and foreign income taxes paid or accrued with respect to such tentative tested income item.

(v) *Separate set of books and records.*—(A) *In general.*—For purposes of this paragraph (c)(7), the term *separate set of books and records* has the meaning set forth in § 1.989(a)-1(d). In addition, for purposes of this paragraph (c)(7), in the case of a tested unit or a transparent interest that is an interest in a pass-through entity or a portion of the activities of a branch, a reference to the separate set of books and records of the tested unit or the transparent interest means the separate set of books and records of the entity or the branch, as applicable.

(B) *Failure to maintain separate set of books and records.*—If a separate set of books and records is not maintained for a tested unit or transparent interest, the items of gross income, disregarded payments, and any other items required to apply paragraph (c)(7) of this section that would be reflected on a separate set of books and records of the tested unit or transparent interest must be determined. Such items are treated as properly reflected on the separate set of books and records of the tested unit or transparent interest for purposes of applying paragraph (c)(7) of this section.

(C) *Transparent interests.*—If a tested unit of a controlled foreign corporation or an entity an interest in which is a tested unit of a controlled foreign corporation holds a transparent interest, either directly or indirectly through one or more other transparent interests, then, for purposes of paragraph (c)(7) of this section (and subject to the rule of paragraph (c)(7)(iv)(C) of this section), items of the controlled foreign corporation properly reflected on the separate set of books and records of the transparent interest are treated as being properly reflected on the separate set of books and records of the tested unit, as modified under paragraph (c)(7)(ii)(B)(2) of this section. See paragraph (c)(8)(iii)(D)(6) (Example 4) of this section for an illustration of the application of the rule set forth in this paragraph (c)(7)(v)(C).

(D) *Items not taken into account for financial accounting purposes.*—For purposes of this paragraph (c)(7), an item of gross income in a CFC inclusion year that is not taken into account in such year for financial accounting purposes, and therefore not properly reflected on a separate set of books and records of a tested unit or a transparent interest, or an entity an interest in which is a tested unit or a transparent interest, is treated as properly reflected on a separate set of books and records to the extent it would have been so reflected if the item were taken into account for financial accounting purposes in such CFC inclusion year.

(vi) *Effective rate at which foreign taxes are imposed.*—For a CFC inclusion year of a controlled foreign corporation, the effective rate of foreign tax with respect to the tentative tested income items of the controlled foreign corporation is determined separately for each such item. See paragraphs (c)(8)(iii)(A)(2)(*v*) (Example 1), (c)(8)(iii)(B)(2)(*vi*) (Example 2), and (c)(8)(iii)(C)(2)(*vi*) (Example 3) of this section for illustrations of the application of the rules set forth in this paragraph (c)(7)(vi). The effective rate at which foreign income taxes are imposed on a tentative tested income item is—

(A) The U.S. dollar amount of foreign income taxes paid or accrued with respect to the tentative tested income item, determined by applying paragraph (c)(7)(vii) of this section; divided by

(B) [Reserved]

(vii) *Foreign income taxes paid or accrued with respect to a tentative tested income item.*—For a CFC inclusion year, the amount of foreign income taxes paid or accrued by a controlled foreign corporation with respect to a tentative tested income item of the controlled foreign corporation for purposes of this paragraph (c)(7) is the U.S. dollar amount of the controlled foreign corporation's eligible current year taxes (as defined in § 1.960-1(b)(5)) that are allocated and apportioned to the related tentative gross tested income item under the rules of paragraph (c)(7)(iii) of this section. See paragraphs (c)(8)(iii)(A)(2)(*iv*) (Example 1), (c)(8)(iii)(B)(2)(*v*) (Example 2), and (c)(8)(iii)(C)(2)(*v*) (Example 3) of this section for illustrations of the application of the rule set forth in this paragraph (c)(7)(vii).

(viii) *Rules regarding the high-tax election.*—(A) *Manner.*—*(1)* An election is made under this paragraph (c)(7)(viii) by the controlling domestic shareholders (as defined in § 1.964-1(c)(5)) with respect to a controlled foreign corporation for a CFC inclusion year (a *high-tax election)* in accordance with the rules provided in forms or instructions and by—

(i) Filing the statement required under § 1.964-1(c)(3)(ii) with a timely filed original federal income tax return, or with an amended federal income tax return in accordance with paragraph (c)(7)(viii)(A)(2) of this section, for the U.S. shareholder inclusion

year of each controlling domestic shareholder in which or with which such CFC inclusion year ends;

(ii) Providing any notices required under § 1.964-1(c)(3)(iii); and

(iii) Providing any additional information required by applicable administrative pronouncements.

(2) In the case of an election (or revocation) made with an amended federal income tax return—

(i) The election (or revocation) must be made on an amended federal income tax return duly filed within 24 months of the unextended due date of the original federal income tax return for the U.S. shareholder inclusion year with or within which the CFC inclusion year ends;

(ii) Each United States shareholder that owns within the meaning of section 958(a) (including both domestic partnerships that are United States shareholders that own stock within the meaning of section 958(a) without regard to § 1.951A-1(e)(1) and partners of a domestic partnership that are United States shareholders that are treated as owning stock withing the meaning of section 958(a) by reason of § 1.951A-1(e)(1)) stock of the controlled foreign corporation as of the end of the CFC's taxable year to which the election relates must file amended Federal income tax returns (or timely original federal income tax returns if a return has not yet been filed) reflecting the effect of such election (or revocation) for the U.S. shareholder inclusion year with or within which the CFC inclusion year ends as well as for any other taxable year in which the U.S. tax liability of the United States shareholder would be increased by reason of the election (or revocation) (or in the case of a partnership if any item reported by the partnership or any partnership-related item would change as a result of the election (or revocation)) within a single period no greater than six months within the 24-month period described in paragraph (c)(7)(viii)(A)(2)(*i*) of this section; and

(iii) Each United States shareholder in the controlled foreign corporation as of the end of the controlled foreign corporation's taxable year to which the election relates must pay any tax due as a result of such adjustments within a single period no greater than six months within the 24-month period described in paragraph (c)(7)(viii)(A)(2)(*i*) of this section.

(3) In the case of a United States shareholder that is a partnership, paragraphs (c)(7)(viii)(A)(*1*) and (2) and (c)(7)(viii)(C) of this section are applied by substituting "Form 1065 (or successor form)" for "federal income tax return" and by substituting "amended Form 1065 (or successor form) or administrative adjustment request (as described in § 301.6227-1), as applicable," for "amended federal income tax return", each place that it appears.

(4) A United States shareholder that is a partner in a partnership that is also a United States shareholder in the controlled foreign corporation must generally file an amended return, as required under paragraph (c)(7)(viii)(A)(2)(*ii*) of this section, and must generally pay any additional tax owed as required under paragraph (c)(7)(viii)(A)(2)(*iii*) of this section. However, in the case of a United States shareholder that is a partner in a partnership that duly files an administrative adjustment request under paragraph (c)(7)(viii)(A)(2) of this section, the partner is treated as having satisfied the requirements of paragraphs (c)(7)(viii)(A)(2)(*ii*) and (*iii*) of this section with respect to the interest held through that partnership if:

(i) The partnership timely files an administrative adjustment request described in paragraph (c)(7)(viii)(A)(2)(*i*) or (*ii*) of this section, as applicable; and,

(ii) Both the partnership and its partners timely comply with the requirements of section 6227 with respect to the administrative adjustment request. See § § 301.6227-1 through -3for rules relating to administrative adjustment requests.

(B) *Scope.*—A high-tax election applies with respect to each tentative gross tested income item of the controlled foreign corporation for the CFC inclusion year and is binding on all United States shareholders of the controlled foreign corporation.

(C) *Revocation.*—A high-tax election may be revoked by the controlling domestic shareholders of the controlled foreign corporation in the same manner as prescribed for an election made on an amended return as described in paragraph (c)(7)(viii)(A) of this section.

(D) *Failure to satisfy election requirements.*—A high-tax election (or revocation) is valid only if all of the requirements in paragraph (c)(7)(viii)(A) of this section, including the requirement to provide notice under paragraph (c)(7)(viii)(A)(*1*)(*ii*) of this section, are satisfied.

(E) *Rules applicable to CFC groups.—(1) In general.*—In the case of a controlled foreign corporation that is a member of a CFC group, a high-tax election is made under paragraph (c)(7)(viii)(A) of this section, or revoked under paragraph (c)(7)(viii)(C) of this section, with respect to all controlled foreign corporations that are members of the CFC group and the rules in paragraphs (c)(7)(viii)(A) through (D) of this section apply by reference to the CFC group.

(2) Determination of the CFC group.—(i) Definition.—Subject to the rules in paragraphs (c)(7)(viii)(E)(2)(*ii*) and (*iii*) of this section, the term *CFC group* means an affiliated group as defined in section 1504(a) without regard to section 1504(b)(1) through (6), except that section 1504(a) is applied by substituting "more than 50 percent" for "at least 80 percent" each place it appears, and section 1504(a)(2)(A) is applied by substituting "or" for "and." For purposes of this paragraph (c)(7)(viii)(E)(2)(*i*), stock ownership is determined by applying the constructive ownership rules of section 318(a), other than section 318(a)(3)(A) and (B), by applying section 318(a)(4) only to options (as defined in § 1.1504-4(d)) that are reasonably certain to be exercised as described in § 1.1504-4(g), and by substituting in section 318(a)(2)(C) "5 percent" for "50 percent.

(ii) Member of a CFC group.—The determination of whether a controlled foreign corporation is included in a CFC group is made as of the close of the CFC inclusion year of the controlled foreign corporation that ends with or within the taxable years of the controlling domestic shareholders. One or more controlled foreign corporations are members of a CFC group if the requirements of paragraph (c)(7)(viii)(E)(2) of this section are satisfied as of the end of the CFC inclusion year of at least one of the controlled foreign corporations, even if the requirements are not satisfied as of the end of the CFC inclusion year of all controlled foreign corporations. If the controlling domestic shareholders do not have the same taxable year, the determination of whether a controlled foreign corporation is a member of a CFC group is made with respect to the CFC inclusion year that ends with or within the taxable year of the majority of the controlling domestic shareholders (determined based on voting power) or, if no such majority taxable year exists, the calendar year. See paragraph (c)(8)(iii)(E) (Example 5) of this section for an example that illustrates the application of the rule set forth in this paragraph (c)(7)(viii)(E)(2)(*ii*). Notwithstanding the rule set forth in this paragraph (c)(7)(viii)(E)(2)(*ii*), a controlled foreign corporation is not a member of a CFC group if, as of the close of its CFC inclusion year, the controlled foreign corporation does not have a controlling domestic shareholder.

(iii) Controlled foreign corporations included in only one CFC group.—A controlled foreign corporation cannot be a member of more than one CFC group. If a controlled foreign corporation would be a member of more than one CFC group under paragraph (c)(7)(viii)(E)(2) of this section, then ownership of stock of the controlled foreign corporation is determined by applying paragraph (c)(7)(viii)(E)(2) of this section without regard to section 1504(a)(2)(B) or, if applicable, by reference to the ownership existing as of the end of the first CFC inclusion year of a controlled foreign corporations that would cause a CFC group to exist.

(ix) *Definitions.*—The following definitions apply for purposes of this paragraph (c)(7).

(A) *Indirectly.*—The term *indirectly*, when used in reference to ownership, means ownership through one or more pass-through entities.

(B) *Pass-through entity.*—The term *pass-through entity* means a partnership, a disregarded entity, or any other person (whether domestic or foreign) other than a corporation to the extent that income, gain, deduction or loss of the person is taken into account in determining the income or loss of a controlled foreign corporation that owns, directly or indirectly, interests in the person.

(C) *Transparent interest.*—The term *transparent interest* means an interest in a pass-through entity (or the activities of a branch) that is not a tested unit.

(8) *Examples.*—(i) *Scope.*—This paragraph (c)(8) provides examples illustrating the application of the rules in paragraph (c)(7) of this section.

(ii) *Presumed facts.*—For purposes of the examples in paragraph (c)(8)(iii) of this section, except as otherwise stated, the following facts are presumed:

(A) USP is a domestic corporation.

(B) CFC1X and CFC2X are controlled foreign corporations organized in, and tax residents of, Country X.

(C) CFC3Z is a controlled foreign corporation organized in, and tax resident of, Country Z.

(D) FDEX is a disregarded entity that is a tax resident of Country X.

(E) FDE1Y and FDE2Y are disregarded entities that are tax residents of Country Y.

(F) FPSY is an entity that is organized in, and a tax resident of, Country Y but is classified as a partnership for federal income tax purposes.

(G) CFC1X, CFC2X, CFC3Z, and the interests in FDEX, FDE1Y, FDE2Y, and FPSY are tested units (the CFC1X tested unit, CFC2X tested unit, CFC3Z tested unit, FDEX tested unit, FDE1Y tested unit, FDE2Y tested unit, and FPSY tested unit, respectively).

(H) CFC1X, CFC2X, CFC3Z, FDEX, FDE1Y, and FDE2Y conduct activities in the foreign country in which they are tax resident, and properly reflect items of income, gain, deduction, and loss on separate sets of books and records.

(I) All entities have calendar taxable years (for both federal income tax purposes and for purposes of the relevant foreign country) and use the Euro (€) as their functional currency. At all relevant times €1 = $1.

(J) The maximum rate of tax specified in section 11 for the CFC inclusion year is 21 percent.

(K) Neither CFC1X, CFC2X, nor CFC3Z directly or indirectly earns income described in section 952(b), has any items of income, gain, deduction, or loss, or makes or receives disregarded payments. In addition, no tested unit of CFC1X, CFC2X, or CFC3Z makes or receives disregarded payments.

(L) An election made under section 954(b)(4) and paragraph (c)(7)(viii) of this section is effective with respect to CFC1X and CFC2X, as applicable, for the CFC inclusion year.

(M) The same amounts of regarded items of income and deduction that are accrued under federal income tax law are also accrued under foreign law.

(iii) *Examples.*—(A) *Example 1: Effect of disregarded interest.*—(1) *Facts*—(*i*) *Ownership.* USP owns all of the stock of CFC1X, and CFC1X owns all of the interests of FDE1Y.

(*ii*) *Gross income and deductions (other than for foreign income taxes).* In Year 1, CFC1X generates €100x of gross income from services to unrelated parties that would be gross tested income without regard to paragraph (c)(7) of this section and that is properly reflected on the books and records of FDE1Y. The €100x of services income is general category income under §1.904-4(d). In Year 1, FDE1Y accrues and pays €20x of interest to CFC1X that is deductible for Country Y tax purposes but is disregarded for federal income tax purposes. The €20x of disregarded interest income received by CFC1X from FDE1Y is properly reflected on CFC1X's books and records, and the €20x of disregarded interest expense paid from FDE1Y to CFC1X is properly reflected on FDE1Y's books and records.

(*iii*) *Foreign income taxes.* Country X imposes no tax on net income, and Country Y imposes a 25% tax on net income. For Country Y tax purposes, FDE1Y (which is not disregarded under Country Y tax law) has €80x of taxable income (€100x of services income from the unrelated parties, less a €20x deduction for the interest paid to CFC1X). Accordingly, FDE1Y incurs a Country Y income tax liability with respect to Year 1 of €20x (€80x x 25%), the U.S. dollar amount of which is $20x.

(2) *Analysis*—(*i*) *Tentative gross tested income items.* Under paragraph (c)(7)(ii)(A) of this section, the tentative gross tested income item with respect to each of the CFC1X tested unit and the FDE1Y tested unit is the aggregate of the gross income of CFC1X that is attributable to the tested unit, that would be gross tested income (without regard to this paragraph (c)(7)), and that would be in a single tested income group. Under paragraphs (c)(7)(ii)(B)(*1*) and (2) of this section, items of gross income of CFC1X are attributable to the CFC1X tested unit, or the FDE1Y tested unit, to the extent properly reflected on its separate set of books and records, as determined under federal income tax principles and adjusted to take into account disregarded payments. Without regard to the €20x disregarded interest payment from FDE1Y to CFC1X, gross income attributable to the CFC1X tested unit would be €0 (that is, the €20x of interest income reflected on the books and records of CFC1X would be reduced by €20x, the amount attributable to the payment that is disregarded for federal income tax purposes). Similarly, without regard to the €20x disregarded interest payment from FDE1Y to CFC1X, gross income attributable to the FDE1Y tested unit would be €100x (that is, €100x of services income reflected on the books and records of FDE1Y, unreduced by the €20x disregarded interest payment from FDE1Y to CFC1X). However, under paragraph (c)(7)(ii)(B)(2) of this section, the gross income attributable to each of the CFC1X tested unit and the FDE1Y tested unit is adjusted by €20x, the amount of the disregarded interest payment from FDE1Y to CFC1X that is deductible for Country Y tax purposes. Accordingly, the tentative gross tested income item attributable to the CFC1X tested unit (the "CFC1X tentative gross tested income item") is €20x (€0 + €20x), and the tentative gross tested income item attributable to the FDE1Y tested unit (the "FDE1Y tentative gross tested income item") is €80x (€100x - €20x).

(*ii*) *Foreign income tax deduction.* Under paragraph (c)(7)(iii)(A) of this section, CFC1X's tentative tested income items are computed by treating the CFC1X tentative gross tested income item and the FDE1Y tentative gross tested income item each as income in a separate tested income group (the "CFC1X income group" and the "FDE1Y income group") and by allocating and apportioning CFC1X's deductions for current year taxes under §1.861-20 (CFC1X has no other deductions to allocate and apportion). Under paragraph (c)(7)(iii)(A) of this section and §1.861-20(d)(3)(v), the €20x deduction for Country Y income taxes is allocated and apportioned solely to the FDE1Y income group (the "FDE1Y group tax") and none of the Country Y taxes are allocated and apportioned to the CFC1X income group.

(*iii*) *Tentative tested income items.* Under paragraph (c)(7)(iii) of this section, the tentative tested income item with respect to the CFC1X income group (the "CFC1X tentative tested item"), is €20x. The tentative tested income item with respect to the FDE1Y income group (the "CFC1X tentative tested item") is €60x (the FDE1Y tentative gross tested income item of €80x, less the €20x deduction for the FDE1Y group tax).

(*iv*) *Foreign income tax paid or accrued with respect to a tentative tested income item.* Under paragraph (c)(7)(vii) of this section, the foreign income taxes paid or accrued with respect to a tentative tested income item is the U.S. dollar amount of the eligible current year taxes that are allocated and apportioned to the related tentative gross tested income item under the rules of paragraph (c)(7)(iii) of this section. Therefore, the foreign income taxes paid or accrued with respect to the FDE1Y tentative tested income item is $20x, the U.S. dollar amount of the FDE1Y group tax. The foreign income tax paid or accrued with respect to the CFC1X tentative tested income item is $0, the U.S. dollar amount of the foreign tax allocated and apportioned to the CFC1X tentative gross tested income item under paragraph (c)(7)(iii) of this section.

(*v*) *Effective foreign tax rate.* The effective foreign tax rate is determined under paragraph (c)(7)(vi) of this section by dividing the U.S. dollar amount of foreign income taxes paid or accrued with respect to each respective tentative tested income item by the U.S. dollar amount of the tentative tested income item increased by the U.S. dollar amount of the relevant foreign income taxes. Therefore, the effective foreign tax rate with respect to the FDE1Y tentative tested income item is 25%, computed by dividing $20x (the U.S. dollar amount of the foreign income taxes paid or accrued with respect to the FDE1Y tentative tested income item under paragraph (c)(7)(vii) of this section) by $80x (the sum of $60x, the U.S. dollar amount of the FDE1Y tentative tested income item, and $20x, the U.S. dollar amount of the foreign income taxes paid or accrued with respect to the FDE1Y tentative tested income item). The CFC1X tentative tested income item is not subject to any foreign income tax, so is subject to an effective foreign tax rate of 0%, calculated as $0 (the U.S. dollar amount of the foreign income taxes paid or accrued with respect to the CFC1X tentative tested income item) divided by $20x (the U.S. dollar amount of the CFC1X tentative tested income item).

(*vi*) *Gross income items excluded under sections 954(b)(4) and 951A(c)(2)(A)(i)(III).* The FDE1Y tentative tested income item is subject to an effective foreign tax rate (25%) that is greater than 18.9% (90% of the maximum rate of tax specified in section 11). Therefore, the requirement of paragraph (c)(7)(i)(B) of this section is satisfied, and the FDE1Y tentative gross tested income item qualifies under paragraph (c)(7)(i) of this section for the high-tax exception of section 954(b)(4) and is excluded from tested income under sections 951A(c)(2)(A)(i)(III) and 954(b)(4) and paragraph (c)(1)(iii) of this section. The CFC1X tentative tested income item is subject to an effective foreign tax rate of 0%. Therefore, the CFC1X tentative tested income item does not satisfy the requirement of paragraph (c)(7)(i)(B) of this section, and the CFC1X tentative gross tested income item does not qualify under paragraph (c)(7)(i) of this section for the high-tax exception of section 954(b)(4) and is not excluded from tested income under sections 951A(c)(2)(A)(i)(III) and 954(b)(4) and paragraph (c)(1)(iii) of this section.

(B) [Reserved]

(C) *Example 3: Interest expense allocated and apportioned with respect to the income of a lower-tier CFC.*—(1) *Facts*—(*i*) *Ownership.* USP owns all of the stock of CFC1X. CFC1X directly owns all the interests of FDE1Y. FDE1Y owns all of the stock of CFC3Z. Pursuant to § 1.861-9(j) and § 1.861-9T(j), CFC1X uses the modified gross income method to allocate and apportion its interest expense.

(*ii*) *Gross income and deductions (including for foreign income taxes).* During Year 1, CFC1X generates € 4,000x of gross income from services that would be gross tested income without regard to paragraph (c)(7) of this section, € 3,000x of which is properly reflected on the books and records of the CFC1X tested unit and € 1,000x of which is properly reflected on the books and records of the FDE1Y tested unit. CFC1X also accrues € 1,000x of interest expense to an unrelated person. Country X imposes € 200x of income taxes with respect to the € 3,000x of gross income properly reflected on the books and records of the CFC1X tested unit, and Country Y imposes € 200x of income taxes with respect to the € 1,000x of gross income properly reflected on the books and records of the FDE1Y tested unit. CFC3Z generates € 1,000x of gross income from services that would be gross tested income without regard to paragraph (c)(7) of this section, and such gross income is properly reflected on the books and records of the CFC3Z tested unit. CFC3Z accrues no expenses, and Country Z imposes € 100x of income taxes with respect to the € 1,000x of gross income generated by CFC3Z.

(2) *Analysis*--(*i*) *Tentative gross tested income items.* Under paragraph (c)(7)(ii) of this section, the € 3,000x of gross income that is reflected on the books and records of the CFC1X tested unit, and the € 1,000x of gross income that is reflected on the books and records of the FDE1Y tested unit, are attributable to the CFC1X tested unit and the FDE1Y tested unit, respectively. Under paragraph (c)(7)(ii) of this section, each of these amounts is a separate tentative gross tested income item of CFC1X (the "CFC1X tentative gross tested income item" and the "FDE1Y tentative gross tested income item," respectively). Under paragraph (c)(7)(ii) of this section, the € 1,000x item of tentative gross tested income that is properly reflected on the books and records of the CFC3Z tested unit is attributable to the CFC3Z tested unit. Under paragraph (c)(7)(ii) of this section, the amount attributable to the CFC3Z tested unit is a tentative gross tested income item of CFC3Z (the "CFC3Z tentative gross tested income item").

(*ii*) *Allocation and apportionment of interest expense.* To compute CFC1X's tentative tested income items, the principles of § 1.960-1(d)(3) apply by treating each of CFC1X's tentative gross tested income items as income in a separate tested income group (the "CFC1X income group" and the "FDE1Y income group") and allocate and apportion its deductions among those income groups under federal income tax principles. Because CFC1X uses the modified gross income method under § 1.861-9(j) and § 1.861-9T(j) to allocate and apportion interest expense, it must allocate and apportion its interest expense between the CFC1X income group and the FDE1Y income group based on a combined gross income amount that includes both the gross income of CFC1X (including the gross income attributable to both the CFC1X tested unit and the FDE1Y tested unit) and the gross income of CFC3Z, adjusted as provided under § 1.861-9(j) and § 1.861-9T(j). Under § 1.861-9(j) and § 1.861-9T(j), the adjusted combined gross income of CFC1X comprises the CFC1X tentative gross tested income item (€ 3,000x), or 60% of the combined adjusted gross income amount, the FDE1Y tentative gross tested income item (€ 1,000x), or 20% of the combined adjusted gross income amount, and the CFC3Z gross tentative tested income item (€ 1,000x), or 20% of the combined adjusted gross income amount. Under paragraph (c)(7)(iii) of this section, interest expense of CFC1X that is allocated and apportioned to the gross income of CFC3Z under § 1.861-9(j) and § 1.861-9T(j) is not allocated and apportioned to either the CFC1X income group or the FDE1Y income group. Therefore, € 600x of interest expense (60% of the € 1,000x of interest expense) is allocated and apportioned to the CFC1X income group, and € 200x of interest expense (20% of the € 1,000x of interest expense) is allocated and apportioned to the FDE1Y income group. The € 200x of interest expense that is allocated and apportioned to the € 1,000x of gross tentative tested income of CFC3Z is allocated and apportioned to the residual income group for purposes of paragraph (c)(7) of this section, but can still be allocated and apportioned to a statutory grouping of tested income of CFC1X for purposes of paragraph (c)(3) of this section. *See* paragraph (c)(7)(iii) of this section.

(*iii*) *Foreign income tax deduction.* Under paragraph (c)(7)(iii) of this section, deductions for foreign income taxes paid or accrued by CFC1X are allocated and apportioned under § 1.861–20 to the CFC1X income group and the FDE1Y income group. Similarly, foreign income taxes paid or accrued by CFC3Z are allocated and apportioned under § 1.861–20 to the tentative gross tested income item of CFC3Z (the "CFC3Z income group"). Under § 1.861–20, € 200x of Country X income taxes are allocated and apportioned to the CFC1X income group (the "CFC1X group tax"), the € 200x of Country Y income taxes are allocated and apportioned to the FDE1Y income group (the "FDE1Y group tax"), and the € 100x of Country Z income taxes are allocated and apportioned to the CFC3Z income group (the "CFC3Z group tax").

(*iv*) *Tentative tested income items.* After the allocation and apportionment of deductions to reduce the tentative gross tested income in each income group, under paragraph (c)(7)(iii) of this section, CFC1X has a tentative tested income item with respect to the CFC1X tested unit of € 2,200x (€ 3,000x, less € 600x of interest expense and € 200x of foreign income tax expense, the "CFC1X tentative tested income item") and a tentative tested income item with respect to the FDE1Y tested unit of € 600x (€ 1,000x, less € 200x of interest expense and € 200x of foreign income tax expense, the "FDE1Y tentative tested income item"). CFC3Z has a tentative tested income item of € 900x (€ 1,000x, less € 100x of foreign income tax expense, the "CFC3Z tentative tested income item").

(*v*) *Foreign income taxes paid or accrued with respect to a tentative tested income item.* Under paragraph (c)(7)(vii) of this section, the foreign income taxes paid or accrued with respect to a tentative tested income item is the U.S. dollar amount of the eligible current year taxes that are allocated and apportioned to the related tentative gross tested income item under the rules of paragraph (c)(7)(iii) of this section. Therefore, the foreign income tax paid or accrued with respect to the CFC1X tentative tested income item is $200x, the U.S. dollar amount of the CFC1X group tax. Similarly, the foreign income tax paid or accrued with respect to the FDE1Y tentative tested income item is $200x, the U.S. dollar amount of the FDE1Y group tax, and the foreign income tax paid or accrued with respect to the CFC3Z tentative tested income item is $100x, the U.S. dollar amount of the CFC3Z group tax.

(*vi*) *Effective foreign tax rate.* The effective foreign tax rate is determined under paragraph (c)(7)(vi) of this section by dividing the U.S. dollar amount of foreign income taxes paid or accrued with respect to each respective tentative tested income item by the U.S. dollar amount of the tentative tested income item increased by the U.S. dollar amount of the relevant foreign income taxes. Therefore, the effective foreign tax rate for the CFC1X tentative tested income item is 8.3%, computed by dividing $200x (the U.S. dollar amount of the foreign income taxes paid or accrued with respect to the CFC1X tentative tested income item), by $2,400x (the sum of $2,200x, the U.S. dollar amount of the CFC1X tentative tested income item and $200x, the U.S. dollar amount of the foreign taxes paid or accrued with respect to the CFC1X tentative tested income item). The effective foreign tax rate for the FDE1Y tentative tested income item is 25%, computed by dividing $200x (the U.S. dollar amount of the foreign taxes paid or accrued with respect to the FDE1Y tentative tested income item) by $800x (the sum of $600x, the U.S. dollar amount of the FDE1Y tentative tested income item, and $200x, the U.S. dollar amount of the foreign taxes paid or accrued with respect to the FDE1Y tentative tested income item). The effective foreign tax rate for the CFC3Z tentative tested income item is 10%, computed by dividing $100x (the U.S. dollar amount of the foreign taxes paid or accrued with respect to the CFC3Z tentative tested income item) by $1,000x (the sum of $900x, the U.S. dollar amount of the CFC3Z tentative tested income item, and $100x, the U.S. dollar amount of the foreign taxes paid or accrued with respect to the CFC3Z tentative tested income item).

(*vii*) *Gross income items excluded under sections 954(b)(4) and 951A(c)(2)(A)(i)(III).* The FDE1Y tentative tested income item is subject to tax at an effective foreign tax rate (25%) that is greater than 18.9% (90% of the maximum rate of tax specified in section 11). Therefore, the requirement of paragraph (c)(7)(i)(B) of this section is satisfied, and the FDE1Y tentative gross tested income item qualifies under paragraph (c)(7)(i) of this section for the high-tax exception of section 954(b)(4) and is excluded from tested income under sections 951A(c)(2)(A)(i)(III) and 954(b)(4) and paragraph (c)(1)(iii) of this section. In computing the tested income of CFC1X under paragraph (c)(3) of this section, the deductions of CFC1X that were allocated and apportioned to the FDE1Y tentative gross tested income item (that is, the € 200x of interest expense and the € 200x of FDE1Y group taxes) are allocated and apportioned to this item of tentative gross tested income. As a result, the € 1,000x of tentative gross tested income excluded from tested income under section 954(b)(4), as well as the € 200x of interest expense and € 200x of foreign tax expense allocable to that gross income, are allocated and apportioned to the residual category under paragraph (c)(3) of this section for purposes of determining the tested income of CFC1X. Under § 1.960-1(d)(3), the $200x of foreign income taxes allocated and apportioned to the excluded gross income would also be assigned to the residual income group for purposes of determining CFC1X's tested taxes for purposes of section 960(d). The CFC1X tentative tested income item and CFC3Z tentative tested income item each have effective foreign tax rates (8.3% and 10%, respectively) that are not greater than 90% of the maximum rate of tax specified in section 11. Therefore, the CFC1X tentative gross tested income item and the CFC3Z tentative gross tested income item do not qualify under paragraph (c)(7)(i) of this section for the high-tax exception of section 954(b)(4), and are not excluded from tested income under sections 951A(c)(2)(A)(i)(III) and 954(b)(4) and paragraph (c)(1)(i) of this section. Under paragraph (c)(3) of this section, the corresponding deductions are allocated and apportioned to that gross tested income in a manner that achieves a result that is consistent the result of the allocation and apportionment of those deductions under paragraph (c)(7) of this section. Accordingly, because CFC3Z's tentative gross tested income is not excluded from gross tested income under sections 951A(c)(2)(A)(i)(III) and 954(b)(4) and paragraph (c)(1)(i) of this section, under paragraph (c)(3) of this section the €200x of CFC1X's interest expense that was apportioned to tentative gross tested income of CFC3Z under the modified gross income method in §1.861-9 is allocated and apportioned to gross tested income of CFC1X and therefore reduces CFC1X's tested income. In contrast, if the CFC3Z tentative gross tested item had been excluded from gross tested income under sections 951A(c)(2)(A)(i)(III) and 954(b)(4) and paragraph (c)(1)(i) of this section, then the €200x of CFC1X's interest expense that was allocated and apportioned to that income would be assigned to the residual category.

(D) *Example 4: Application of tested unit rules.—(1) Facts—(i) Ownership.* USP owns all of the stock of CFC1X. CFC1X directly owns all the interests of FDEX and FDE1Y. In addition, CFC1X directly carries on activities in Country Y that constitute a branch (as described in §1.267A-5(a)(2)) and that give rise to a taxable presence under Country Y tax law and Country X tax law (such branch, "FBY").

(ii) Items reflected on books and records. For the CFC inclusion year, CFC1X had a €20x item of gross income (Item A), which is properly reflected on the books and records of FBY, and a €30x item of gross income (Item B), which is properly reflected on the books and records of FDEX.

(2) *Analysis—(i) Identifying the tested units of CFC1X.* Without regard to the combination rule of paragraph (c)(7)(iv)(C) of this section, CFC1X, CFC1X's interest in FDEX, CFC1X's interest in FDE1Y, and FBY would each be a tested unit of CFC1X. *See* paragraph (c)(7)(iv)(A) of this section. Pursuant to the combination rule, however, the FDE1Y tested unit is combined with the FBY tested unit and treated as a single tested unit because FDE1Y is a tax resident of Country Y, the same country in which FBY is located (the "Country Y tested unit"). *See* paragraph (c)(7)(iv)(C)(*1*) of this section. The CFC1X tested unit (without regard to any items attributable to the FDEX, FDE1Y, or FBY tested units) is also combined with the FDEX tested unit and treated as a single tested unit because CFC1X and FDEX are both tax residents of County X (the "Country X tested unit"). *See* paragraph (c)(7)(iv)(C)(*1*) of this section.

(ii) Computing the items of CFC1X. Under paragraph (c)(7)(ii)(A) of this section, a tentative gross tested income item is determined with respect to each of the Country Y tested unit and the Country X tested unit. To determine the tentative gross tested income item of each tested unit, the item of gross income that is attributable to the tested unit is determined under paragraph (c)(7)(ii)(B) of this section. Under paragraph (c)(7)(ii)(B) of this section, only Item A is attributable to the Country Y tested unit. Item A is not attributable to the Country X tested unit because it is not reflected on the separate set of books and records of the CFC1X tested unit or the FDEX tested unit, and an item of gross income is only attributable to one tested unit. *See* paragraph (c)(7)(ii)(B)(*1*) of this section. Under paragraph (c)(7)(ii)(B) of this section, only Item B is attributable to the Country X tested unit.

(3) *Alternative facts – branch does not give rise to a taxable presence in country where located—(i) Facts.* The facts are the same as in paragraph (c)(8)(iii)(D)(*1*) of this section (the original facts in this *Example 4*), except that FBY does not give rise to a taxable presence under Country Y tax law; moreover, Country X tax law does not provide an exclusion, exemption, or other similar relief with respect to income attributable to FBY.

(ii) Analysis. FBY is not a tested unit but is a transparent interest. *See* paragraphs (c)(7)(iv)(A)(*3*) and (c)(7)(ix)(C) of this section. CFC1X has a tested unit in Country X that includes the CFC1X tested unit (without regard to any items related to the interest in FDEX or FDE1Y, but that includes FBY since it is a transparent interest and not a tested unit) and the interest in FDEX. *See* paragraph (c)(7)(iv)(C) of this section. CFC1X has another tested unit in Country Y, the interest in FDE1Y.

(4) *Alternative facts — branch is a tested unit but is not combined—(i) Facts.* The facts are the same as in paragraph (c)(8)(iii)(D)(*1*) of this section (the original facts in this *Example 4*), except that FBY does not give rise to a taxable presence under Country Y tax law but Country X tax law provides an exclusion, exemption, or other similar relief (such as a preferential rate) with respect to income attributable to FBY.

(ii) Analysis. FBY is a tested unit. *See* paragraph (c)(7)(iv)(A)(*3*) of this section. CFC1X has two tested units in Country Y, the interest in FDE1Y and FBY. The interest in FDE1Y and FBY tested units are not combined because FBY does not give rise to a taxable presence under the tax law of Country Y. *See* paragraph (c)(7)(iv)(C)(*2*) of this section. CFC1X also has a tested unit in Country X that includes the activities of CFC1X (without regard to any items related to the interest in FDEX, the interest in FDE1Y, or FBY) and the interest in FDEX.

(5) *Alternative facts – split ownership of tested unit—(i) Facts.* The facts are the same as in paragraph (c)(8)(iii)(D)(*1*) of this section (the original facts in this *Example 4*), except that USP also owns CFC2X, CFC1X does not own FDE1Y, and CFC1X and CFC2X own 60% and 40%, respectively, of the interests of FPSY.

(ii) Analysis for CFC1X. Under paragraph (c)(7)(iv)(C)(*1*) of this section, FBY and CFC1X's 60% interest in FPSY are combined and treated as a single tested unit of CFC1X ("CFC1X's Country Y tested unit"), and CFC1X's interest in FDEX and CFC1X's other activities are combined and treated as a single tested unit of CFC1X ("CFC1X's Country X tested unit"). CFC1X's Country Y tested unit is attributed any item of CFC1X that is derived through its interest in FPSY to the extent the item is properly reflected on the books and records of FPSY. *See* paragraph (c)(7)(ii)(B)(*1*) of this section.

(iii) Analysis for CFC2X. Under paragraphs (c)(7)(iv)(A)(*1*) and (c)(7)(iv)(A)(*2*)(*i*) of this section, CFC2X and CFC2X's 40% interest in FPSY are tested units of CFC2X. CFC2X's interest in FPSY is attributed any item of CFC2X that is derived through FPSY to the extent that it is properly reflected on the books and records of FPSY. *See* paragraph (c)(7)(ii)(B)(*1*) of this section.

(iv) Analysis for not combining CFC1X and CFC2X tested units. None of the tested units of CFC1X are combined with the tested units of CFC2X under paragraph (c)(7)(iv)(C)(*1*) of this section because they are tested units of different controlled foreign corporations, and the combination rule only combines tested units of the same controlled foreign corporation.

(6) *Alternative facts – split ownership of transparent interest—(i) Facts.* The facts are the same as in paragraph (c)(8)(iii)(D)(*1*) of this section (the original facts in this *Example 4*), except that USP also owns CFC2X, CFC1X does not own FDE1Y, and CFC1X and CFC2X own 60% and 40%, respectively, of the interests in FPSY, but FPSY is not a tax resident of any foreign country and is fiscally transparent for Country X tax law purposes.

(ii) Analysis for CFC1X. CFC1X's interest in FPSY is not a tested unit but is a transparent interest. *See* paragraphs (c)(7)(iv)(A)(2) and (c)(7)(ix)(C) of this section. Under paragraph (c)(7)(v)(C) of this section, any item of CFC1X that is derived through its interest in FPSY and is properly reflected on the books and records of FPSY is treated as properly reflected on the books and records of CFC1X.

(iii) Analysis for CFC2X. CFC2X's interest in FPSY is not a tested unit but is a transparent interest. *See* paragraphs (c)(7)(iv)(A)(2) and (c)(7)(ix)(C) of this section. Under paragraph (c)(7)(v)(C) of this section, any item of CFC2X that is derived through its interest in FPSY and is properly reflected on the books and records of FPSY is treated as properly reflected on the books and records of CFC2X.

(E) *Example 5: CFC group — Controlled foreign corporations with different taxable years.—(1) Facts.* USP owns all the stock of CFC1X and CFC2X. CFC2X has a taxable year ending November 30. On December 15, Year 1, USP sells all the stock of CFC2X to an unrelated party for cash.

(2) *Analysis.* The determination of whether CFC1X and CFC2X are in a CFC group is made as of the close of their CFC inclusion years that end with or within the taxable year ending December 31, Year 1, the taxable year of USP, the controlling domestic shareholder. *See* paragraph (c)(7)(viii)(E)(*2*)(*ii*) of this section. Under paragraph (c)(7)(viii)(E)(*2*)(*i*) of this section, USP directly owns more than 50% of the stock of CFC1X as of December 31, Year 1, the end of CFC1X's CFC inclusion year. USP also directly owns more

than 50% of the stock of CFC2X as of November 30, Year 1, the end of CFC2X's CFC inclusion year. Therefore, CFC1X and CFC2X are members of a CFC group, and USP must consistently make high-tax elections, or revocations, under paragraph (c)(7)(viii) of this section with respect to CFC1X's taxable year ending December 31, Year 1, and CFC2X's taxable year ending November 30, Year 1. This is the case notwithstanding that USP does not directly own more than 50% of the stock of CFC2X as of December 31, Year 1, the end of CFC1X's CFC inclusion year. *See* paragraph (c)(7)(viii)(E)(*2*)(*ii*) of this section.
[Reg. § 1.951A-2.]

☐ [*T.D. 9866, 6-14-2019 (corrected 8-26-2019). Amended by T.D. 9902, 12-16-2019, T.D. 9902, 7-20-2020 (corrected 10-8-2020 and 12-10-2020) T.D. 9922, 11-2-2020, T.D. 9934, 11-25-2020 and T.D. 9959, 12-28-2021 (corrected 7-26-2022).*]

Proposed Amendments to Regulation

§ 1.951A-2. Tested income and tested loss.—

***

(c) ***

(1) ***

(iii) Gross income described in section 951A(c)(2)(A)(i)(III) that is excluded from the foreign base company income (as defined in section 954) or insurance income (as defined in section 953) of the corporation by reason of the exception described in section 954(b)(4) and § 1.954-1(d)(1) pursuant to an election under § 1.954-1(d)(6),

***

[Prop. Reg. § 1.951A-2.]
[Proposed 7-23-2020.]

Proposed Amendments to Regulation

§ 1.951A-2. Tested income and tested loss.—

***

(c) ***

(2) *Determination of gross income and allowable deductions.*—For purposes of determining tested income and tested loss, the gross income and allowable deductions of a controlled foreign corporation for a CFC inclusion year are determined under the rules of § 1.952-2 for determining the subpart F income of the controlled foreign corporation, except, for a controlled foreign corporation which is engaged in the business of reinsuring or issuing insurance or annuity contracts and which, if it were a domestic corporation engaged only in such business, would be taxable as an insurance company to which subchapter L of chapter 1 of the Code applies, substituting "the rules of sections 953 and 954(i)" for "the principles of §§ 1.953-4 and 1.953-5" in § 1.952-2(b)(2).

***

[Prop. Reg. § 1.951A-2.]
[Proposed 5-3-2023.]

§ 1.951A-3. Qualified business asset investment.—(a) *Scope.*—This section provides rules for determining the qualified business asset investment of a controlled foreign corporation for purposes of determining a United States shareholder's deemed tangible income return under § 1.951A-1(c)(3)(ii). Paragraph (b) of this section defines qualified business asset investment. Paragraph (c) of this section defines tangible property and specified tangible property. Paragraph (d) of this section provides rules for determining the portion of tangible property that is specified tangible property when the property is used in the production of both gross tested income and gross income that is not gross tested income. Paragraph (e) of this section provides rules for determining the adjusted basis in specified tangible property. Paragraph (f) of this section provides rules for determining qualified business asset investment of a tested income CFC with a short taxable year. Paragraph (g) of this section provides rules for increasing the qualified business asset investment of a tested income CFC by reason of property owned by a partnership. Paragraph (h) of this section provides anti-avoidance rules that disregard the basis in property transferred in certain transactions when determining the qualified business asset investment of a tested income CFC.

(b) *Qualified business asset investment.*—The term *qualified business asset investment* means the average of a tested income CFC's aggregate adjusted bases as of the close of each quarter of a CFC inclusion year in specified tangible property that is used in a trade or business of the tested income CFC and is of a type with respect to which a deduction is allowable under section 167. In the case of partially depreciable property, only the depreciable portion of the property is of a type with respect to which a deduction is allowable under section 167. A tested loss CFC has no qualified business asset investment.

(c) *Specified tangible property.*—(1) *In general.*—The term *specified tangible property* means, with respect to a tested income CFC and a CFC inclusion year, tangible property of the tested income CFC used in the production of gross tested income for the CFC inclusion year. For purposes of the preceding sentence, tangible property of a tested income CFC is used in the production of gross tested income for a CFC inclusion year if some or all of the depreciation or cost recovery allowance with respect to the tangible property is either allocated and apportioned to the gross tested income of the tested income CFC for the CFC inclusion year under § 1.951A-2(c)(3) or capitalized to inventory or other property held for sale, some or all of the gross income or loss from the sale of which is taken into account in determining tested income of the tested income CFC for the CFC inclusion year. None of the tangible property of a tested loss CFC is specified tangible property.

(2) *Tangible property.*—The term *tangible property* means property for which the depreciation deduction provided by section 167(a) is eligible to be determined under section 168 without regard to section 168(f)(1), (2), or (5), section 168(k)(2)(A)(i)(II), (IV), or (V), and the date placed in service.

(d) *Dual use property.*—(1) *In general.*—The amount of the adjusted basis in dual use property of a tested income CFC for a CFC inclusion year that is treated as adjusted basis in specified tangible property for the CFC inclusion year is the average of the tested income CFC's adjusted basis in the property multiplied by the dual use ratio with respect to the property for the CFC inclusion year.

(2) *Definition of dual use property.*—The term *dual use property* means, with respect to a tested income CFC and a CFC inclusion year, specified tangible property of the tested income CFC that is used in both the production of gross tested income and the production of gross income that is not gross tested income for the CFC inclusion year. For purposes of the preceding sentence, specified tangible property of a tested income CFC is used in the production of gross tested income and the production of gross income that is not gross tested income for a CFC inclusion year if less than all of the depreciation or cost recovery allowance with respect to the property is either allocated and apportioned to the gross tested income of the tested income CFC for the CFC inclusion year under § 1.951A-2(c)(3) or capitalized to inventory or other property held for sale, the gross income or loss from the sale of which is taken into account in determining the tested income of the tested income CFC for the CFC inclusion year.

(3) *Dual use ratio.*—The term *dual use ratio* means, with respect to dual use property, a tested income CFC, and a CFC inclusion year, a ratio (expressed as a percentage) calculated as—

(i) The sum of—

(A) The depreciation deduction or cost recovery allowance with respect to the property that is allocated and apportioned to the gross tested income of the tested income CFC for the CFC inclusion year under § 1.951A-2(c)(3), and

(B) The depreciation or cost recovery allowance with respect to the property that is capitalized to inventory or other property held for sale, the gross income or loss from the sale of which is taken into account in determining the tested income of the tested income CFC for the CFC inclusion year, divided by

(ii) The sum of—

(A) The total amount of the tested income CFC's depreciation deduction or cost recovery allowance with respect to the property for the CFC inclusion year, and

(B) The total amount of the tested income CFC's depreciation or cost recovery allowance with respect to the property capitalized to inventory or other property held for sale, the gross income or loss from the sale of which is taken into account in determining the income or loss of the tested income CFC for the CFC inclusion year.

(4) *Example.*—The following example illustrates the application of this paragraph (d).

(i) *Facts.* FS is a tested income CFC and a wholesale distributor of Product A. FS owns a warehouse and trucks that store and deliver Product A, respectively. The warehouse has an average adjusted basis for Year 1 of $20,000x. The depreciation with respect to the warehouse for Year 1 is $2,000x, which is capitalized to inventory of

Product A. Of the $2,000x depreciation capitalized to inventory of Product A, $500x is capitalized to FS's ending inventory of Product A, $1,200x is capitalized to inventory of Product A, the gross income or loss from the sale of which is taken into account in determining FS's tested income for Year 1, and $300x is capitalized to inventory of Product A, the gross income or loss from the sale of which is taken into account in determining FS's foreign base company sales income for Year 1. The trucks have an average adjusted basis for Year 1 of $4,000x. FS does not capitalize depreciation with respect to the trucks to inventory or other property held for sale. FS's depreciation deduction with respect to the trucks is $20x for Year 1, $15x of which is allocated and apportioned to FS's gross tested income under § 1.951A-2(c)(3).

(ii) *Analysis*—(A) *Dual use property*. The warehouse and trucks are property for which the depreciation deduction provided by section 167(a) is eligible to be determined under section 168 (without regard to section 168(f)(1), (2), or (5), section 168(k)(2)(A)(i)(II), (IV), or (V), and the date placed in service). Therefore, under paragraph (c)(2) of this section, the warehouse and trucks are tangible property. Furthermore, because the warehouse and trucks are used in the production of gross tested income in Year 1 within the meaning of paragraph (c)(1) of this section, the warehouse and trucks are specified tangible property. Finally, because the warehouse and trucks are used in both the production of gross tested income and the production of gross income that is not gross tested income in Year 1 within the meaning of paragraph (d)(2) of this section, the warehouse and trucks are dual use property. Therefore, under paragraph (d)(1) of this section, the amount of FS's adjusted basis in the warehouse and trucks that is treated as adjusted basis in specified tangible property for Year 1 is determined by multiplying FS's adjusted basis in the warehouse and trucks by FS's dual use ratio with respect to the warehouse and trucks determined under paragraph (d)(3) of this section.

(B) *Depreciation not capitalized to inventory*. Because none of the depreciation with respect to the trucks is capitalized to inventory or other property held for sale, FS's dual use ratio with respect to the trucks is determined entirely by reference the depreciation deduction with respect to the trucks. Therefore, under paragraph (d)(3) of this section, FS's dual use ratio with respect to the trucks for Year 1 is 75%, which is FS's depreciation deduction with respect to the trucks that is allocated and apportioned to gross tested income under § 1.951A-2(c)(3) for Year 1 ($15x), divided by the total amount of FS's depreciation deduction with respect to the trucks for Year 1 ($20x). Accordingly, under paragraph (d)(1) of this section, $3,000x ($4,000x x 0.75) of FS's average adjusted bases in the trucks is taken into account under paragraph (b) of this section in determining FS's qualified business asset investment for Year 1.

(C) *Depreciation capitalized to inventory*. Because all of the depreciation with respect to the warehouse is capitalized to inventory, FS's dual use ratio with respect to the warehouse is determined entirely by reference to the depreciation with respect to the warehouse that is capitalized to inventory and included in cost of goods sold. Therefore, under paragraph (d)(3) of this section, FS's dual use ratio with respect to the warehouse for Year 1 is 80%, which is FS's depreciation with respect to the warehouse that is capitalized to inventory of Product A, the gross income or loss from the sale of which is taken into account in determining in FS's tested income for Year 1 ($1,200x), divided by FS's depreciation with respect to the warehouse that is capitalized to inventory of Product A, the gross income or loss from the sale of which is taken into account in determining FS's income for Year 1 ($1,500x). Accordingly, under paragraph (d)(1) of this section, $16,000x ($20,000x x 0.8) of FS's average adjusted basis in the warehouse is taken into account under paragraph (b) of this section in determining FS's qualified business asset investment for Year 1.

(e) *Determination of adjusted basis in specified tangible property*.—(1) *In general*.—Except as provided in paragraph (e)(3)(ii) of this section, the adjusted basis in specified tangible property for purposes of this section is determined by using the cost capitalization methods of accounting used by the controlled foreign corporation for purposes of determining the gross income and allowable deductions of the controlled foreign corporation under § 1.951A-2(c)(2) and the alternative depreciation system under section 168(g), and by allocating the depreciation deduction with respect to such property for a CFC inclusion year ratably to each day during the period in the CFC inclusion year to which such depreciation relates. For purposes of the preceding sentence, the period in the CFC inclusion year to which such depreciation relates is determined without regard to the applicable convention under section 168(d).

(2) *Effect of change in law*.—The adjusted basis in specified tangible property is determined without regard to any provision of law enacted after December 22, 2017, unless such later enacted law specifically and directly amends the definition of qualified business asset investment under section 951A. For purposes of applying section 951A(d)(3) and this paragraph (e), the technical amendment to section 168(g) (to provide a recovery period of 20 years for qualified improvement property for purposes of the alternative depreciation system) enacted in section 2307(a) of the Coronavirus Aid, Relief, and Economic Security Act, Pub. L. 116-136 (2020) is treated as enacted on December 22, 2017.

(3) *Specified tangible property placed in service before enactment of section 951A*.—(i) *In general*.—Except as provided in paragraph (e)(3)(ii) of this section, the adjusted basis in specified tangible property placed in service before December 22, 2017, is determined using the alternative depreciation system under section 168(g), as if this system had applied from the date that the property was placed in service.

(ii) *Election to use income and earnings and profits depreciation method for property placed in service before the first taxable year beginning after December 22, 2017*.—(A) *In general*.—If a controlled foreign corporation is not required to use, and does not in fact use, the alternative depreciation system under section 168(g) for purposes of determining income under § 1.952-2 and earnings and profits under § 1.964-1 with respect to property placed in service before the first taxable year beginning after December 22, 2017, and the controlling domestic shareholders (as defined in § 1.964-1(c)(5)) of the controlled foreign corporation make an election described in this paragraph (e)(3)(ii), the adjusted basis in specified tangible property of the controlled foreign corporation that was placed in service before the first taxable year of the controlled foreign corporation beginning after December 22, 2017, and the partner adjusted basis in partnership specified tangible property of any partnership of which the controlled foreign corporation is a partner that was placed in service before the first taxable year of the partnership beginning after December 22, 2017, is determined for purposes of this section based on the method of accounting for depreciation used by the controlled foreign corporation for purposes of determining income under § 1.952-2, subject to the modification described in this paragraph (e)(3)(ii)(A). If the controlled foreign corporation's method of accounting for depreciation takes into account salvage value of the property, the salvage value is reduced to zero by allocating the salvage value ratably to each day of the taxable year immediately after the last taxable year in which the method of accounting determined an amount of depreciation deduction for the property.

(B) *Manner of making the election*.—The controlling domestic shareholders making the election described in this paragraph (e)(3) must file a statement that meets the requirements of § 1.964-1(c)(3)(ii) with their income tax returns for the taxable year that includes the last day of the controlled foreign corporation's applicable taxable year and follow the notice requirements of § 1.964-1(c)(3)(iii). The controlled foreign corporation's applicable taxable year is the first CFC inclusion year that begins after December 31, 2017, and ends within the controlling domestic shareholder's taxable year. For purposes of § 301.9100-3 of this chapter (addressing requests for extensions of time for filing certain regulatory elections), a controlling domestic shareholder is qualified to make the election described in this paragraph (e)(3) only if the shareholder determined the adjusted basis in specified tangible property placed in service before the first taxable year beginning after December 22, 2017, by applying the method described in paragraph (e)(3)(ii)(A) of this section with respect to the first taxable year of the controlled foreign corporation beginning after December 22, 2017, and each subsequent taxable year. The election statement must be filed in accordance with the rules provided in forms or instructions.

(f) *Special rules for short taxable years*.—(1) *In general*.—In the case of a tested income CFC that has a CFC inclusion year that is less than twelve months (a *short taxable year*), the rules for determining the qualified business asset investment of the tested income CFC under this section are modified as provided in paragraphs (f)(2) and (3) of this section with respect to the CFC inclusion year.

(2) *Determination of quarter closes*.—For purposes of determining quarter closes, in determining the qualified business asset investment of a tested income CFC for a short taxable year, the quarters of the tested income CFC for purposes of this section are the full quarters beginning and ending within the short taxable year (if any), determining quarter length as if the tested income CFC did not have a short taxable year, plus one or more short quarters (if any).

(3) *Reduction of qualified business asset investment*.—The qualified business asset investment of a tested income CFC for a short taxable year is the sum of—

(i) The sum of the tested income CFC's aggregate adjusted bases in specified tangible property as of the close of each full quarter (if any) in the CFC inclusion year divided by four, plus

(ii) The tested income CFC's aggregate adjusted bases in specified tangible property as of the close of each short quarter (if any) in the CFC inclusion year multiplied by the sum of the number of days in each short quarter divided by 365.

(4) *Example*.—The following example illustrates the application of this paragraph (f).

(i) *Facts*. USP1, a domestic corporation, owns all of the stock of FS, a controlled foreign corporation. USP1 owns FS from the beginning of Year 1. On July 15, Year 1, USP1 sells FS to USP2, an unrelated person. USP2 makes a section 338(g) election with respect to the purchase of FS, as a result of which FS's taxable year is treated as ending on July 15. USP1, USP2, and FS all use the calendar year as their taxable year. FS's aggregate adjusted bases in specified tangible property is $250x as of March 31, $300x as of June 30, $275x as of July 15, $500x as of September 30, and $450x as of December 31.

(ii) *Analysis*—(A) *Determination of short taxable years and quarters*. FS has two short taxable years in Year 1. The first short taxable year is from January 1 to July 15, with two full quarters (January 1 through March 31 and April 1 through June 30) and one short quarter (July 1 through July 15). The second taxable year is from July 16 to December 31, with one short quarter (July 16 through September 30) and one full quarter (October 1 through December 31).

(B) *Calculation of qualified business asset investment for the first short taxable year*. Under paragraph (f)(2) of this section, for the first short taxable year in Year 1, FS has three quarter closes (March 31, June 30, and July 15). Under paragraph (f)(3) of this section, the qualified business asset investment of FS for the first short taxable year is $148.80x, the sum of $137.50x (($250x + $300x)/4) attributable to the two full quarters and $11.30x ($275x x 15/365) attributable to the short quarter.

(C) *Calculation of qualified business asset investment for the second short taxable year*. Under paragraph (f)(2) of this section, for the second short taxable year in Year 1, FS has two quarter closes (September 30 and December 31). Under paragraph (f)(3) of this section, the qualified business asset investment of FS for the second short taxable year is $217.98x, the sum of $112.50x ($450x/4) attributable to the one full quarter and $105.48x ($500x x 77/365) attributable to the short quarter.

(g) *Partnership property*.—(1) *In general*.—If a tested income CFC holds an interest in one or more partnerships during a CFC inclusion year (including indirectly through one or more partnerships that are partners in a lower-tier partnership), the qualified business asset investment of the tested income CFC for the CFC inclusion year (determined without regard to this paragraph (g)(1)) is increased by the sum of the tested income CFC's partnership QBAI with respect to each partnership for the CFC inclusion year. A tested loss CFC has no partnership QBAI for a CFC inclusion year.

(2) *Determination of partnership QBAI*.—For purposes of paragraph (g)(1) of this section, the term *partnership QBAI* means, with respect to a partnership, a tested income CFC, and a CFC inclusion year, the sum of the tested income CFC's partner adjusted basis in each partnership specified tangible property of the partnership for each partnership taxable year that ends with or within the CFC inclusion year. If a partnership taxable year is less than twelve months, the principles of paragraph (f) of this section apply in determining a tested income CFC's partnership QBAI with respect to the partnership.

(3) *Determination of partner adjusted basis*.—(i) *In general*.—For purposes of paragraph (g)(2) of this section, the term *partner adjusted basis* means the amount described in paragraph (g)(3)(ii) of this section with respect to sole use partnership property or paragraph (g)(3)(iii) of this section with respect to dual use partnership property. The principles of section 706(d) apply to this determination.

(ii) *Sole use partnership property*.—(A) *In general*.—The amount described in this paragraph (g)(3)(ii), with respect to sole use partnership property, a partnership taxable year, and a tested income CFC, is the sum of the tested income CFC's proportionate share of the partnership adjusted basis in the sole use partnership property for the partnership taxable year and the tested income CFC's partner-specific QBAI basis in the sole use partnership property for the partnership taxable year.

(B) *Definition of sole use partnership property*.—The term *sole use partnership property* means, with respect to a partnership, a partnership taxable year, and a tested income CFC, partnership specified tangible property of the partnership that is used in the production of only gross tested income of the tested income CFC for the CFC inclusion year in which or with which the partnership taxable year ends. For purposes of the preceding sentence, partnership specified tangible property of a partnership is used in the production of only gross tested income for a CFC inclusion year if all the tested income CFC's distributive share of the partnership's depreciation deduction or cost recovery allowance with respect to the property (if any) for the partnership taxable year that ends with or within the CFC inclusion year is allocated and apportioned to the tested income CFC's gross tested income for the CFC inclusion year under § 1.951A-2(c)(3) and, if any of the partnership's depreciation or cost recovery allowance with respect to the property is capitalized to inventory or other property held for sale, all the tested income CFC's distributive share of the partnership's gross income or loss from the sale of such inventory or other property for the partnership taxable year that ends with or within the CFC inclusion year is taken into account in determining the tested income of the tested income CFC for the CFC inclusion year.

(iii) *Dual use partnership property*.—(A) *In general*.—The amount described in this paragraph (g)(3)(iii), with respect to dual use partnership property, a partnership taxable year, and a tested income CFC, is the sum of the tested income CFC's proportionate share of the partnership adjusted basis in the property for the partnership taxable year and the tested income CFC's partner-specific QBAI basis in the property for the partnership taxable year, multiplied by the tested income CFC's dual use ratio with respect to the property for the partnership taxable year determined under the principles of paragraph (d)(3) of this section, except that the ratio described in paragraph (d)(3) of this section is determined by reference to the tested income CFC's distributive share of the amounts described in paragraph (d)(3) of this section.

(B) *Definition of dual use partnership property*.—The term *dual use partnership property* means partnership specified tangible property other than sole use partnership property.

(4) *Determination of proportionate share of the partnership's adjusted basis in partnership specified tangible property*.—(i) *In general*.—For purposes of paragraph (g)(3) of this section, the tested income CFC's proportionate share of the partnership adjusted basis in partnership specified tangible property for a partnership taxable year is the partnership adjusted basis in the property multiplied by the tested income CFC's proportionate share ratio with respect to the property for the partnership taxable year. Solely for purposes of determining the proportionate share ratio under paragraph (g)(4)(ii) of this section, the partnership's calculation of, and a partner's distributive share of, any income, loss, depreciation, or cost recovery allowance is determined under section 704(b).

(ii) *Proportionate share ratio*.—The term *proportionate share ratio* means, with respect to a partnership, a partnership taxable year, and a tested income CFC, the ratio (expressed as a percentage) calculated as—

(A) The sum of—

(1) The tested income CFC's distributive share of the partnership's depreciation deduction or cost recovery allowance with respect to the property for the partnership taxable year, and

(2) The amount of the partnership's depreciation or cost recovery allowance with respect to the property that is capitalized to inventory or other property held for sale, the gross income or loss from the sale of which is taken into account in determining the tested income CFC's distributive share of the partnership's income or loss for the partnership taxable year, divided by

(B) The sum of—

(1) The total amount of the partnership's depreciation deduction or cost recovery allowance with respect to the property for the partnership taxable year, and

(2) The total amount of the partnership's depreciation or cost recovery allowance with respect to the property capitalized to inventory or other property held for sale, the gross income or loss from the sale of which is taken into account in determining the partnership's income or loss for the partnership taxable year.

(5) *Definition of partnership specified tangible property*.—The term *partnership specified tangible property* means, with respect to a tested income CFC, tangible property (as defined in paragraph (c)(2) of this section) of a partnership that is—

(i) Used in the trade or business of the partnership,

(ii) Of a type with respect to which a deduction is allowable under section 167, and

(iii) Used in the production of gross income included in the tested income CFC's gross tested income.

(6) *Determination of partnership adjusted basis*.—For purposes of this paragraph (g), the term *partnership adjusted basis* means, with respect to a partnership, partnership specified tangible property, and a partnership taxable year, the amount equal to the average of the partnership's adjusted basis in the partnership specified tangible property as of the close of each quarter in the partnership taxable year determined without regard to any adjustments under section 734(b) except for adjustments under section 734(b)(1)(B) or section 734(b)(2)(B) that are attributable to distributions of tangible property (as defined in paragraph (c)(2) of this section) and for adjustments under section 734(b)(1)(A) or 734(b)(2)(A). The principles of paragraphs (e) and (h) of this section apply for purposes of determining a partnership's adjusted basis in partnership specified tangible property and the proportionate share of the partnership's adjusted basis in partnership specified tangible property.

(7) *Determination of partner-specific QBAI basis*.—For purposes of this paragraph (g), the term *partner-specific QBAI basis* means, with respect to a tested income CFC, a partnership, and partnership specified tangible property, the amount that is equal to the average of the basis adjustment under section 743(b) that is allocated to the partnership specified tangible property of the partnership with respect to the tested income CFC as of the close of each quarter in the partnership taxable year. For this purpose, a negative basis adjustment under section 743(b) is expressed as a negative number. The principles of paragraphs (e) and (h) of this section apply for purposes of determining the partner-specific QBAI basis with respect to partnership specified tangible property.

(8) *Examples*.—The following examples illustrate the rules of this paragraph (g).

(i) *Facts*.—Except as otherwise stated, the following facts are assumed for purposes of the examples:

(A) FC, FC1, FC2, and FC3 are tested income CFCs.

(B) PRS is a partnership and its allocations satisfy the requirements of section 704.

(C) All properties are partnership specified tangible property.

(D) All persons use the calendar year as their taxable year.

(E) There is neither disqualified basis nor partner-specific QBAI basis with respect to any property.

(ii) *Example 1: Sole use partnership property*—(A) *Facts*. FC is a partner in PRS. PRS owns two properties, Asset A and Asset B. The average of PRS's adjusted basis as of the close of each quarter of PRS's taxable year in Asset A is $100x and in Asset B is $500x. In Year 1, PRS's section 704(b) depreciation deduction is $10x with respect to Asset A and $5x with respect to Asset B, and FC's section 704(b) distributive share of the depreciation deduction is $8x with respect to Asset A and $1x with respect to Asset B. None of the depreciation with respect to Asset A or Asset B is capitalized to inventory or other property held for sale. FC's entire distributive share of the depreciation deduction with respect to Asset A and Asset B is allocated and apportioned to FC's gross tested income for Year 1 under § 1.951A-2(c)(3).

(B) *Analysis*—(*1*) *Sole use partnership property*. Because all of FC's distributive share of the depreciation deduction with respect to Asset A and B is allocated and apportioned to gross tested income for Year 1, Asset A and Asset B are sole use partnership property within the meaning of paragraph (g)(3)(ii)(B) of this section. Therefore, under paragraph (g)(3)(ii)(A) of this section, FC's partner adjusted basis in Asset A and Asset B is equal to the sum of FC's proportionate share of PRS's partnership adjusted basis in Asset A and Asset B for Year 1 and FC's partner-specific QBAI basis in Asset A and Asset B for Year 1, respectively.

(*2*) *Proportionate share*. Under paragraph (g)(4)(i) of this section, FC's proportionate share of PRS's partnership adjusted basis in Asset A and Asset B is PRS's partnership adjusted basis in Asset A and Asset B for Year 1, multiplied by FC's proportionate share ratio with respect to Asset A and Asset B for Year 1, respectively. Because none of the depreciation with respect to Asset A or Asset B is capitalized to inventory or other property held for sale, FC's proportionate share ratio with respect to Asset A and Asset B is determined entirely by reference to the depreciation deduction with respect to Asset A and Asset B. Therefore, FC's proportionate share ratio with respect to Asset A for Year 1 is 80%, which is the ratio of FC's section 704(b) distributive share of PRS's section 704(b) depreciation deduction with respect to Asset A for Year 1 ($8x), divided by the total amount of PRS's section 704(b) depreciation deduction with respect to Asset A for Year 1 ($10x). FC's proportionate share ratio with respect to Asset B for Year 1 is 20%, which is the ratio of FC's section 704(b) distributive share of PRS's section 704(b) depreciation deduction with respect to Asset B for Year 1 ($1x), divided by the total amount of PRS's section 704(b) depreciation deduction with respect to Asset B for Year 1 ($5x). Accordingly, under paragraph (g)(4)(i) of this section, FC's proportionate share of PRS's partnership adjusted basis in Asset A is $80x ($100x x 0.8), and FC's proportionate share of PRS's partnership adjusted basis in Asset B is $100x ($500x x 0.2).

(*3*) *Partner adjusted basis*. Because FC has no partner-specific QBAI basis with respect to Asset A and Asset B, FC's partner adjusted basis in Asset A and Asset B is determined entirely by reference to its proportionate share of PRS's partnership adjusted basis in Asset A and Asset B. Therefore, under paragraph (g)(3)(ii)(A) of this section, FC's partner adjusted basis in Asset A is $80x, FC's proportionate share of PRS's partnership adjusted basis in Asset A, and FC's partner adjusted basis in Asset B is $100x, FC's proportionate share of PRS's partnership adjusted basis in Asset A.

(*4*) *Partnership QBAI*. Under paragraph (g)(2) of this section, FC's partnership QBAI with respect to PRS is $180x, the sum of FC's partner adjusted basis in Asset A ($80x) and FC's partner adjusted basis in Asset B ($100x). Accordingly, under paragraph (g)(1) of this section, FC increases its qualified business asset investment for Year 1 by $180x.

(iii) *Example 2: Dual use partnership property*—(A) *Facts*. FC owns a 50% interest in PRS. All section 704(b) and tax items are identical and are allocated equally between FC and its other partner. PRS owns three properties, Asset C, Asset D, and Asset E. PRS sells two products, Product A and Product B. All of FC's distributive share of the gross income or loss from the sale of Product A is taken into account in determining FC's tested income, and none of FC's distributive share of the gross income or loss from the sale of Product B is taken into account in determining FC's tested income.

(*1*) *Asset C*. The average of PRS's adjusted basis as of the close of each quarter of PRS's taxable year in Asset C is $100x. In Year 1, PRS's depreciation is $10x with respect to Asset C, none of which is capitalized to inventory or other property held for sale. FC's distributive share of the depreciation deduction with respect to Asset C is $5x ($10x x 0.5), $3x of which is allocated and apportioned to FC's gross tested income under § 1.951A-2(c)(3).

(*2*) *Asset D*. The average of PRS's adjusted basis as of the close of each quarter of PRS's taxable year in Asset D is $500x. In Year 1, PRS's depreciation is $50x with respect to Asset D, $10x of which is capitalized to inventory of Product A and $40x is capitalized to inventory of Product B. None of the $10x depreciation with respect to Asset D capitalized to inventory of Product A is capitalized to ending inventory. However, of the $40x capitalized to inventory of Product B, $10x is capitalized to ending inventory. Therefore, the amount of depreciation with respect to Asset D capitalized to inventory of Product A that is taken into account in determining FC's distributive share of the income or loss of PRS for Year 1 is $5x ($10x x 0.5), and the amount of depreciation with respect to Asset D capitalized to inventory of Product B that is taken into account in determining FC's distributive share of the income or loss of PRS for Year 1 is $15x ($30x x 0.5).

(*3*) *Asset E*. The average of PRS's adjusted basis as of the close of each quarter of PRS's taxable year in Asset E is $600x. In Year 1, PRS's depreciation is $60x with respect to Asset E. Of the $60x depreciation with respect to Asset E, $20x is allowed as a deduction, $24x is capitalized to inventory of Product A, and $16x is capitalized to inventory of Product B. FC's distributive share of the depreciation deduction with respect to Asset E is $10x ($20x x 0.5), $8x of which is allocated and apportioned to FC's gross tested income under § 1.951A-2(c)(3). None of the $24x depreciation with respect to Asset E capitalized to inventory of Product A is capitalized to ending inventory. However, of the $16x depreciation with respect to Asset E capitalized to inventory of Product B, $10x is capitalized to ending inventory. Therefore, the amount of depreciation with respect to Asset E capitalized to inventory of Product A that is taken into account in determining FC's distributive share of the income or loss of PRS for Year 1 is $12x ($24x x 0.5), and the amount of depreciation with respect to Asset E capitalized to inventory of Product B that is taken into account in determining FC's distributive share of the income or loss of PRS for Year 1 is $3x ($6x x 0.5).

(B) *Analysis*. Because Asset C, Asset D, and Asset E are not used in the production of only gross tested income in Year 1 within the meaning of paragraph (g)(3)(ii)(B) of this section, Asset C, Asset D, and Asset E are partnership dual use property within the meaning of paragraph (g)(3)(iii)(B) of this section. Therefore, under paragraph (g)(3)(iii)(A) of this section, FC's partner adjusted basis in Asset C, Asset D, and Asset E is the sum of FC's proportionate share of PRS's partnership adjusted basis in Asset C, Asset D, and Asset E, respectively, for Year 1, and FC's partner-specific QBAI basis in Asset C, Asset D, and Asset E, respectively, for Year 1, multiplied by FC's dual use ratio with respect to Asset C, Asset D, and Asset E, respectively, for Year 1, determined under the principles of paragraph (d)(3) of this section, except that the ratio described in paragraph (d)(3) of this section is determined by reference to FC's distributive share of the amounts described in paragraph (d)(3) of this section.

(*1*) *Asset C*—(*i*) *Proportionate share.* Under paragraph (g)(4)(i) of this section, FC's proportionate share of PRS's partnership adjusted basis in Asset C is PRS's partnership adjusted basis in Asset C for Year 1, multiplied by FC's proportionate share ratio with respect to Asset C for Year 1. Because none of the depreciation with respect to Asset C is capitalized to inventory or other property held for sale, FC's proportionate share ratio with respect to Asset C is determined entirely by reference to the depreciation deduction with respect to Asset C. Therefore, FC's proportionate share ratio with respect to Asset C is 50%, which is the ratio calculated as the amount of FC's section 704(b) distributive share of PRS's section 704(b) depreciation deduction with respect to Asset C for Year 1 ($5x), divided by the total amount of PRS's section 704(b) depreciation deduction with respect to Asset C for Year 1 ($10x). Accordingly, under paragraph (g)(4)(i) of this section, FC's proportionate share of PRS's partnership adjusted basis in Asset C is $50x ($100x x 0.5).

(*ii*) *Dual use ratio.* Because none of the depreciation with respect to Asset C is capitalized to inventory or other property held for sale, FC's dual use ratio with respect to Asset C is determined entirely by reference to the depreciation deduction with respect to Asset C. Therefore, FC's dual use ratio with respect to Asset C is 60%, which is the ratio calculated as the amount of FC's distributive share of PRS's depreciation deduction with respect to Asset C that is allocated and apportioned to FC's gross tested income under §1.951A-2(c)(3) for Year 1 ($3x), divided by the total amount of FC's distributive share of PRS's depreciation deduction with respect to Asset C for Year 1 ($5x).

(*iii*) *Partner adjusted basis.* Because FC has no partner-specific QBAI basis with respect to Asset C, FC's partner adjusted basis in Asset C is determined entirely by reference to FC's proportionate share of PRS's partnership adjusted basis in Asset C, multiplied by FC's dual use ratio with respect to Asset C. Under paragraph (g)(3)(iii)(A) of this section, FC's partner adjusted basis in Asset C is $30x, FC's proportionate share of PRS's partnership adjusted basis in Asset C for Year 1 ($50x), multiplied by FC's dual use ratio with respect to Asset C for Year 1 (60%).

(*3*) *Asset D*—(*i*) *Proportionate share.* Under paragraph (g)(4)(i) of this section, FC's proportionate share of PRS's partnership adjusted basis in Asset D is PRS's partnership adjusted basis in Asset D for Year 1, multiplied by FC's proportionate share ratio with respect to Asset D for Year 1. Because all of the depreciation with respect to Asset D is capitalized to inventory, FC's proportionate share ratio with respect to Asset D is determined entirely by reference to the depreciation with respect to Asset D that is capitalized to inventory and included in cost of goods sold. Therefore, FC's proportionate share ratio with respect to Asset D is 50%, which is the ratio calculated as the amount of PRS's section 704(b) depreciation with respect to Asset D capitalized to Product A and Product B that is taken into account in determining FC's section 704(b) distributive share of PRS's income or loss for Year 1 ($20x), divided by the total amount of PRS's section 704(b) depreciation with respect to Asset D capitalized to Product A and Product B that is taken into account in determining PRS's section 704(b) income or loss for Year 1 ($40x). Accordingly, under paragraph (g)(4)(i) of this section, FC's proportionate share of PRS's partnership adjusted basis in Asset D is $250x ($500x x 0.5).

(*ii*) *Dual use ratio.* Because all of the depreciation with respect to Asset D is capitalized to inventory, FC's dual use ratio with respect to Asset D is determined entirely by reference to the depreciation with respect to Asset D that is capitalized to inventory and included in cost of goods sold. Therefore, FC's dual use ratio with respect to Asset D is 25%, which is the ratio calculated as the amount of depreciation with respect to Asset D capitalized to inventory of Product A and Product B that is taken into account in determining FC's tested income for Year 1 ($5x), divided by the total amount of depreciation with respect to Asset D capitalized to inventory of Product A and Product B that is taken into account in determining FC's income or loss for Year 1 ($20x).

(*iii*) *Partner adjusted basis.* Because FC has no partner-specific QBAI basis with respect to Asset D, FC's partner adjusted basis in Asset D is determined entirely by reference to FC's proportionate share of PRS's partnership adjusted basis in Asset D, multiplied by FC's dual use ratio with respect to Asset D. Under paragraph (g)(3)(iii)(A) of this section, FC's partner adjusted basis in Asset D is $62.50x, FC's proportionate share of PRS's partnership adjusted basis in Asset D for Year 1 ($250x), multiplied by FC's dual use ratio with respect to Asset D for Year 1 (25%).

(*4*) *Asset E*—(*i*) *Proportionate share.* Under paragraph (g)(4)(i) of this section, FC's proportionate share of PRS's partnership adjusted basis in Asset E is PRS's partnership adjusted basis in Asset E for Year 1, multiplied by FC's proportionate share ratio with respect to Asset E for Year 1. Because the depreciation with respect to Asset E is partly deducted and partly capitalized to inventory, FC's proportionate share ratio with respect to Asset E is determined by reference to both the depreciation that is deducted and the depreciation that is capitalized to inventory and included in cost of goods sold. Therefore, FC's proportionate share ratio with respect to Asset E is 50%, which is the ratio calculated as the sum ($25x) of the amount of FC's section 704(b) distributive share of PRS's section 704(b) depreciation deduction with respect to Asset E for Year 1 ($10x) and the amount of PRS's section 704(b) depreciation with respect to Asset E capitalized to inventory of Product A and Product B that is taken into account in determining FC's section 704(b) distributive share of PRS's income or loss for Year 1 ($15x), divided by the sum ($50x) of the total amount of PRS's section 704(b) depreciation deduction with respect to Asset E for Year 1 ($20x) and the total amount of PRS's section 704(b) depreciation with respect to Asset E capitalized to inventory of Product A and Product B that is taken into account in determining PRS's section 704(b) income or loss for Year 1 ($30x). Accordingly, under paragraph (g)(4)(i) of this section, FC's proportionate share of PRS's partnership adjusted basis in Asset E is $300x ($600x x 0.5).

(*ii*) *Dual use ratio.* Because the depreciation with respect to Asset E is partly deducted and partly capitalized to inventory, FC's dual use ratio with respect to Asset E is determined by reference to the depreciation that is deducted and the depreciation that is capitalized to inventory and included in cost of goods sold. Therefore, FC's dual use ratio with respect to Asset E is 80%, which is the ratio calculated as the sum ($20x) of the amount of FC's distributive share of PRS's depreciation deduction with respect to Asset E that is allocated and apportioned to FC's gross tested income under §1.951A-2(c)(3) for Year 1 ($8x) and the amount of depreciation with respect to Asset E capitalized to inventory of Product A and Product B that is taken into account in determining FC's tested income for Year 1 ($12x), divided by the sum ($25x) of the total amount of FC's distributive share of PRS's depreciation deduction with respect to Asset E for Year 1 ($10x) and the total amount of depreciation with respect to Asset E capitalized to inventory of Product A and Product B that is taken into account in determining FC's income or loss for Year 1 ($15x).

(*iii*) *Partner adjusted basis.* Because FC has no partner-specific QBAI basis with respect to Asset E, FC's partner adjusted basis in Asset E is determined entirely by reference to FC's proportionate share of PRS's partnership adjusted basis in Asset E, multiplied by FC's dual use ratio with respect to Asset E. Under paragraph (g)(3)(ii i)(A) of this section, FC's partner adjusted basis in Asset E is $240x, FC's proportionate share of PRS's partnership adjusted basis in Asset E for Year 1 ($300x), multiplied by FC's dual use ratio with respect to Asset E for Year 1 (80%).

(*5*) *Partnership QBAI.* Under paragraph (g)(2) of this section, FC's partnership QBAI with respect to PRS is $332.50x, the sum of FC's partner adjusted basis in Asset C ($30x), FC's partner adjusted basis in Asset D ($62.50x), and FC's partner adjusted basis in Asset E ($240x). Accordingly, under paragraph (g)(1) of this section, FC increases its qualified business asset investment for Year 1 by $332.50x.

(iv) *Example 3: Sole use partnership specified tangible property; section 743(b) adjustments*—(A) *Facts.* The facts are the same as in paragraph (g)(8)(ii)(A) of this section (the facts in *Example 1*), except that there is an average of $40x positive adjustment to the adjusted basis in Asset A as of the close of each quarter of PRS's taxable year with respect to FC under section 743(b) and an average of $20x negative adjustment to the adjusted basis in Asset B as of the close of each quarter of PRS's taxable year with respect to FC under section 743(b).

(B) *Analysis*. Under paragraph (g)(3)(ii)(A) of this section, FC's partner adjusted basis in Asset A is $120x, which is the sum of $80x

(FC's proportionate share of PRS's partnership adjusted basis in Asset A as illustrated in paragraph (g)(8)(ii)(B)(2) of this section (paragraph (B)(2) of the analysis in *Example 1*)) and $40x (FC's partner-specific QBAI basis in Asset A). Under paragraph (g)(3)(ii)(A) of this section, FC's partner adjusted basis in Asset B is $80x, the sum of $100x (FC's proportionate share of the partnership adjusted basis in the property as illustrated in paragraph (g)(8)(ii)(B)(2) of this section (paragraph (B)(2) of the analysis in *Example 1*)) and (-$20x) (FC's partner-specific QBAI basis in Asset B). Therefore, under paragraph (g)(2) of this section, FC's partnership QBAI with respect to PRS is $200x ($120x + $80x). Accordingly, under paragraph (g)(1) of this section, FC increases its qualified business asset investment for Year 1 by $200x.

(v) *Example 4: Tested income CFC with distributive share of loss from a partnership*—(A) *Facts.* FC owns a 50% interest in PRS. All section 704(b) and tax items are identical and are allocated equally between FC and its other partner. PRS owns Asset F. None of the depreciation with respect to Asset F is capitalized to inventory or other property held for sale. The average of PRS's adjusted basis as of the close of each quarter of PRS's taxable year in Asset F is $220x. PRS has $20x of gross income, a $22x depreciation deduction with respect to Asset F, and no other income or expense in Year 1. FC's distributive share of the gross income is $10x, all of which is includible in FC's gross tested income in Year 1, and FC's distributive share of PRS's depreciation deduction with respect to Asset F is $11x in Year 1, all of which is allocated and apportioned to FC's gross tested income under § 1.951A-2(c)(3). FC's distributive share of loss from PRS is $1x. FC also has $8x of gross tested income from other sources in Year 1 and no other deductions. Therefore, FC has tested income of $7x for Year 1.

(B) *Analysis.* FC's partner adjusted basis in Asset F is $110x, which is the sum of FC's proportionate share of the partnership adjusted basis in the property ($220x x 0.5) and FC's partnership-specific QBAI basis in Asset F ($0). Therefore, FC's partnership QBAI with respect to PRS is $110x. Accordingly, under paragraph (g)(1) of this section, FC increases its qualified business asset investment by $110x, notwithstanding that FC would not be a tested income CFC but for its $8x of gross tested income from other sources.

(vi) *Example 5: Tested income CFC sale of partnership interest before CFC inclusion date*—(A) *Facts.* FC1 owns a 50% interest in PRS on January 1 of Year 1. On July 1 of Year 1, FC1 sells its entire interest in PRS to FC2. PRS owns Asset G. The average of PRS's adjusted basis as of the close of each quarter of PRS's taxable year in Asset G is $100x. FC1's section 704(b) distributive share of the depreciation deduction with respect to Asset G is 25% with respect to PRS's entire year. FC2's section 704(b) distributive share of the depreciation deduction with respect to Asset G is also 25% with respect to PRS's entire year. Both FC1's and FC2's entire distributive shares of the depreciation deduction with respect to Asset G are allocated and apportioned under § 1.951A-2(c)(3) to FC1's and FC2's gross tested income, respectively, for Year 1. PRS's allocations satisfy section 706(d).

(B) *Analysis*—(*1*) *FC1.* Because FC1 owns an interest in PRS during FC1's CFC inclusion year and receives a distributive share of partnership items of the partnership under section 706(d), FC1 has partnership QBAI with respect to PRS in the amount determined under paragraph (g)(2) of this section. Under paragraph (g)(3)(i) of this section, FC1's partner adjusted basis in Asset G is $25x, the product of $100x (the partnership's adjusted basis in the property) and 25% (FC1's section 704(b) distributive share of depreciation deduction with respect to Asset G). Therefore, FC1's partnership QBAI with respect to PRS is $25x. Accordingly, under paragraph (g)(1) of this section, FC1 increases its qualified business asset investment by $25x for Year 1.

(*2*) *FC2.* FC2's partner adjusted basis in Asset G is also $25x, the product of $100x (the partnership's adjusted basis in the property) and 25% (FC2's section 704(b) distributive share of depreciation deduction with respect to Asset G). Therefore, FC2's partnership QBAI with respect to PRS is $25x. Accordingly, under paragraph (g)(1) of this section, FC2 increases its qualified business asset investment by $25x for Year 1.

(vii) *Example 6: Partnership adjusted basis; distribution of property in liquidation of partnership interest*—(A) *Facts.* FC1, FC2, and FC3 are equal partners in PRS, a partnership. FC1 and FC2 each has an adjusted basis of $100x in its partnership interest. FC3 has an adjusted basis of $50x in its partnership interest. PRS has a section 754 election in effect. PRS owns Asset H with a fair market value of $50x and an adjusted basis of $0, Asset I with a fair market value of $100x and an adjusted basis of $100x, and Asset J with a fair market value of $150x and an adjusted basis of $150x. Asset H and Asset J are tangible property, but Asset I is not tangible property. PRS distributes Asset I to FC3 in liquidation of FC3's interest in PRS. None of FC1, FC2, FC3, or PRS recognizes gain on the distribution. Under section 732(b), FC3's adjusted basis in Asset I is $50x. PRS's adjusted basis in Asset H is increased by $50x to $50x under section 734(b)(1)(B), which is the amount by which PRS's adjusted basis in Asset I immediately before the distribution exceeds FC3's adjusted basis in Asset I.

(B) *Analysis.* Under paragraph (g)(6) of this section, PRS's adjusted basis in Asset H is determined without regard to any adjustments under section 734(b) except for adjustments under section 734(b)(1)(B) or section 734(b)(2)(B) that are attributable to distributions of tangible property and for adjustments under section 734(b)(1)(A) or 734(b)(2)(A). The adjustment to the adjusted basis in Asset H is under section 734(b)(1)(B) and is attributable to the distribution of Asset I, which is not tangible property. Accordingly, for purposes of applying paragraph (g)(1) of this section, PRS's adjusted basis in Asset H is $0.

(h) *Anti-avoidance rules related to certain transfers of property.*—(*1*) *Disregard of adjusted basis in specified tangible property held temporarily.*—(i) *In general.*—For purposes of determining a controlled foreign corporation's aggregate adjusted bases in specified tangible property as of the close of a quarter (*tested quarter close*), the adjusted basis in specified tangible property is disregarded as of the tested quarter close if the controlled foreign corporation (*acquiring CFC*) acquires the property temporarily before the tested quarter close with a principal purpose of increasing the deemed tangible income return of a U.S. shareholder (*applicable U.S. shareholder*) for a U.S. shareholder year, and the holding of the property by the acquiring CFC as of the tested quarter close would, without regard to this paragraph (h)(1)(i), increase the deemed tangible income return of the applicable U.S. shareholder for the U.S. shareholder inclusion year.

(ii) *Disregard of first quarter close.*—The adjusted basis in specified tangible property may be disregarded under paragraph (h)(1)(i) of this section for purposes of multiple tested quarter closes that follow an acquisition and on which the acquiring CFC holds the property. However, if the holding of specified tangible property would, without regard to paragraph (h)(1)(i) of this section, increase the deemed tangible income return of an applicable U.S. shareholder because the adjusted basis in such property is taken into account for only one additional quarter close of a tested income CFC of the applicable U.S. shareholder in determining the deemed tangible income return of the applicable U.S. shareholder of the U.S. shareholder inclusion year, the adjusted basis in the property is disregarded for purposes of determining the acquiring CFC's aggregate adjusted bases in specified tangible property only as of the first tested quarter close that follows the acquisition.

(iii) *Safe harbor for certain transfers involving CFCs.*—The holding of specified tangible property as of a tested quarter close does not increase the deemed tangible income return of an applicable U.S. shareholder within the meaning of paragraph (h)(1)(i) of this section if each of the following conditions is satisfied with respect to the acquisition and subsequent transfer of property by the acquiring CFC—

(A) A controlled foreign corporation (*predecessor CFC*) holds the property on a quarter close of the predecessor CFC (*preceding quarter close*) that occurs on the same date as the last quarter close of the acquiring CFC preceding the acquisition.

(B) A controlled foreign corporation (*successor CFC*) holds the property on a quarter close of the successor CFC (*succeeding quarter close*) that occurs on the same date as the first quarter close of the acquiring CFC following the subsequent transfer.

(C) The proportion of the stock that the applicable U.S. shareholder owns (within the meaning of section 958(a)) of the acquiring CFC on the tested quarter close does not exceed the proportion of the stock that the applicable U.S. shareholder owns of either the predecessor CFC on the preceding quarter close or the successor CFC on the succeeding quarter close; and

(D) Each of the predecessor CFC and the successor CFC is a tested income CFC for its CFC inclusion year that includes the date of the tested quarter close.

(iv) *Determination of principal purpose and transitory holding.*—(A) *Presumption for ownership less than 12 months.*—For purposes of paragraph (h)(1)(i) of this section, specified tangible property is presumed to be acquired temporarily with a principal purpose of increasing the deemed tangible income return of an applicable U.S. shareholder for a U.S. shareholder inclusion year if the property is held by the acquiring CFC for less than 12 months and the holding of the property by the acquiring CFC as of the tested quarter close would have the effect of increasing the deemed tangible income return of the applicable U.S. shareholder for a U.S. shareholder inclusion year. The presumption described in the preceding sentence may be rebutted only if the facts and circumstances clearly establish that the subsequent transfer of the property by the acquiring CFC was not contemplated when the property was acquired by the acquiring CFC and that a principal purpose of the acquisition of the property was not to increase the deemed tangible income return of the applicable U.S. shareholder for a U.S. shareholder inclusion year. In order to rebut the presumption, a statement must be attached to the Form 5471 filed by the taxpayer for the taxable year of the CFC in which the subsequent transfer occurs and include any information required by applicable administrative announcements, forms or instructions. The statement must explain the facts and circumstances supporting the rebuttal and be in accordance with any rules provided in forms and instructions.

(B) *Presumption for ownership greater than 36 months.*—For purposes of paragraph (h)(1)(i) of this section, specified tangible property is presumed not to be acquired temporarily with a principal purpose of increasing the deemed tangible income return of an applicable U.S. shareholder for a U.S. shareholder inclusion year if the property is held by the acquiring CFC for more than 36 months. The presumption described in the preceding sentence may be rebutted only if the facts and circumstances clearly establish that the subsequent transfer of the property by the acquiring CFC was contemplated when the property was acquired by the acquiring CFC and that a principal purpose of the acquisition of the property was to increase the deemed tangible income return of the applicable U.S. shareholder for a U.S. shareholder inclusion year.

(v) *Determination of holding period.*—For purposes of this paragraph (h)(1), the period during which an acquiring CFC holds specified tangible property is determined without regard to section 1223.

(vi) *Treatment as single applicable U.S. shareholder.*—For purposes of this paragraph (h)(1), all U.S. persons that are related persons are treated as a single applicable U.S. shareholder. For purposes of the preceding sentence, U.S. persons are related if they bear a relationship described in section 267(b) or 707(b) immediately before or immediately after a transaction.

(vii) *Examples.*—The following examples illustrate the application of this paragraph (h)(1).

(A) *Facts.*—Except as otherwise stated, the following facts are assumed for purposes of the examples:

(1) USP is a domestic corporation.

(2) CFC1, CFC2 and CFC3 are tested income CFCs.

(3) R is unrelated to USP.

(4) All persons use the calendar year as their taxable year.

(5) Asset A is specified tangible property.

(6) Both Year 1 and Year 2 begin on or after January 1, 2018, and have 365 days.

(7) USP has no specified interest expense (as defined in § 1.951A-1(c)(3)(iii)).

(B) *Example 1: Qualification for safe harbor*—*(1) Facts.* USP owns all of the stock of CFC1, which owns all of the stock of CFC2, which owns all the stock of CFC3. As of January 1, Year 1, CFC1 owns Asset A, which is specified tangible property. On December 30, Year 1, CFC1 transfers Asset A to CFC2. On April 10, Year 2, CFC2 transfers Asset A to CFC3. CFC3 holds Asset A for the rest of Year 2.

(2) *Analysis.* Under the safe harbor of paragraph (h)(1)(iii) of this section, CFC2's holding of Asset A as of each of the December 31, Year 1 tested quarter close and the March 31, Year 2 tested quarter close does not increase the deemed tangible income return of USP, the applicable United States shareholder, for Year 1 or Year 2 because each of the requirements in paragraphs (h)(1)(iii)(A) through (D) of this section is satisfied. The requirement in paragraph (h)(1)(iii)(A) of this section is satisfied because CFC1, a predecessor CFC, held Asset A on September 30, Year 1, a quarter close of CFC1 that occurs on the same date as the last quarter close of CFC2, the acquiring CFC, preceding the December 30, Year 1 acquisition of Asset A. The requirement in paragraph (h)(1)(iii)(B) of this section is satisfied because CFC3, a successor CFC, holds Asset A on June 30, Year 2, a quarter close of CFC3 that occurs on the same date as the first quarter close of CFC2 following April 10, Year 2, the date of the subsequent transfer of Asset A. The requirement in paragraph (h)(1)(iii)(C) of this section is satisfied because the proportion of stock that USP, the applicable U.S. shareholder, owns (within the meaning of section 958(a)) of CFC2, the acquiring CFC, on each of the December 31, Year 1 tested quarter close and the March 31, Year 2 tested quarter close (100%), does not exceed the proportion of the stock that USP owns of either CFC1 (100%) on the preceding quarter close (September 30, Year 1) or of CFC3 (100%) on the succeeding quarter close (June 30, Year 2). Finally, the requirement in paragraph (h)(1)(iii)(D) of this section is satisfied because each of CFC1 and CFC3 is a tested income CFC for Year 1 and Year 2, the CFC inclusion years that include the December 31, Year 1 tested quarter close and the March 31, Year 2 tested quarter close. Accordingly, paragraph (h)(1)(i) of this section does not apply to disregard the adjusted basis in Asset A in determining CFC2's aggregate adjusted basis in specified tangible property as of December 31, Year 1, or March 30, Year 2.

(C) *Example 2: Transfers between CFCs with different taxable year ends*—*(1) Facts.* The facts are the same as in paragraph (h)(1)(vii)(B)*(1)* of this section (the facts in *Example 1*), except that CFC1 has a taxable year ending November 30, and the facts and circumstances do not clearly establish that the April 10, Year 2 transfer of Asset A by CFC2 was not contemplated when Asset A was acquired by CFC2 and that a principal purpose of the acquisition of the property was not to increase the deemed tangible income return of USP, the applicable U.S. shareholder.

(2) *Analysis.* CFC2's holding of Asset A as of each of the December 31, Year 1 tested quarter close and the March 31, Year 2 tested quarter close does not satisfy the safe harbor under paragraph (h)(1)(iii) of this section because CFC1, the predecessor CFC, does not hold Asset A on a quarter close of CFC1 that occurs on the same date as the September 30, Year 1, quarter close of CFC2, the acquiring CFC, which is the last quarter close of CFC2 preceding the December 30, Year 1 acquisition of Asset A. In addition, because CFC2 held Asset A for less than 12 months (from December 31, Year 1, until April 10, Year 2), the presumption in paragraph (h)(1)(iv)(A) of this section applies such that CFC2 is presumed to have acquired Asset A temporarily with a principal purpose of increasing the deemed tangible income return of USP for the shareholder inclusion year, and the facts and circumstances do not clearly establish that CFC2 did not acquire Asset A with such a principal purpose. Because CFC2 holds Asset A as of December 31, Year 1, the tested quarter close, the adjusted basis in Asset A would be, without regard to paragraph (h)(1)(i) of this section, taken into account for purposes of determining USP's deemed tangible income return for its Year 1 taxable year as of five quarter closes (CFC1's quarter closes on February 28, May 31, August 31, and November 30, and CFC2's quarter close on December 31). If instead CFC1 had retained Asset A during the period CFC2 temporarily held the asset and had transferred Asset A directly to CFC3 on January 10, Year 2, the adjusted basis in Asset A would have been taken into account for purposes of determining USP's deemed tangible income return for its Year 1 taxable year as of only four quarter closes (CFC1's quarter closes on February 28, May 30, August 30, and November 30). Under paragraph (h)(1)(ii) of this section, because the adjusted basis in Asset A would (without regard to paragraph (h)(1)(i) of this section) be taken into account for only one additional quarter close of a tested income CFC of USP in determining USP's deemed tangible income return for Year 1 and Year 2, the adjusted basis in Asset A is disregarded for purposes of determining CFC's aggregate adjusted bases in specified tangible property only as of December 31, Year 1, the first tested quarter close that follows the acquisition. Accordingly, under paragraph (h)(1)(i) of this section, the adjusted basis in Asset A is disregarded in determining CFC2's aggregate adjusted basis in specified tangible property as of December 31, Year 1.

(D) *Example 3: Acquisition from unrelated person*—*(1) Facts.* USP owns all of the stock of CFC1 and CFC2. CFC1 has a taxable year ending November 30. On October 30, Year 1, CFC1 acquires Asset B from R. On December 30, Year 1, CFC1 transfers Asset B to CFC2. The facts and circumstances do not clearly establish that the December 31, Year 1, transfer of Asset B by CFC1 was not contemplated when Asset B was acquired by CFC1 and that a principal purpose of the acquisition of the property was not to increase the deemed tangible income return of USP, the applicable U.S. shareholder.

(2) *Analysis.* CFC1's holding of Asset B as of the November 30, Year 1 tested quarter close does not satisfy the safe harbor under paragraph (h)(1)(iii) of this section because the requirements in paragraphs (h)(1)(iii)(A) through (D) of this section are not satisfied. Because CFC1 held Asset B for less than 12 months (from October 30, Year 1, until December 30, Year 1), the presumption in paragraph (h)(1)(iv)(A) of this section applies such that CFC1 is presumed to have held Asset B temporarily with a principal purpose of increasing the deemed tangible income return of USP for the taxable year, and the facts and circumstances do not clearly establish that CFC1 did not acquire Asset B with a principal purpose of increasing the deemed

tangible income return of USP. Because CFC1 holds Asset B as of November 30, Year 1, the adjusted basis in Asset B would be, without regard to paragraph (h)(1)(i) of this section, taken into account for purposes of determining USP's deemed tangible income return for its Year 1 taxable year as of two quarter closes (CFC1's quarter close on November 30, Year 1, and CFC2's quarter close on December 31, Year 1). If instead CFC2 had acquired Asset B directly from R, the adjusted basis in Asset B would have been taken into account for purposes of determining USP's deemed tangible income return for its Year 1 taxable year as of only one quarter close (CFC2's quarter close on December 31, Year 1). Accordingly, under paragraph (h)(1)(i) of this section, the adjusted basis in Asset B is disregarded in determining CFC1's aggregate adjusted basis in specified tangible property as of November 30, Year 1.

(E) *Example 4: Acquisitions from tested loss CFCs*—(*1*) *Facts.* USP owns all of the stock of CFC1 and CFC2. As of January 1, Year 1, CFC1 owns Asset C. On March 30, Year 1, CFC1 transfers Asset C to CFC2. For Year 1, CFC1 is a tested loss CFC and CFC2 is a tested income CFC. On March 30, Year 2, CFC2 transfers Asset C back to CFC1. For Year 2, both CFC1 and CFC2 are tested income CFCs. A principal purpose of CFC2 holding Asset C as of March 31, Year 1, June 30, Year 1, September 30, Year 1, and December 31, Year 1, was to increase USP's deemed tangible income return.

(*2*) *Analysis.* CFC2's holding of Asset C as of March 31, Year 1, June 30, Year 1, September 30, Year 1, and December 31, Year 1 does not satisfy the safe harbor under paragraph (h)(1)(iii) of this section because CFC1 is not a tested income CFC for Year 1 and thus the requirement in paragraph (h)(1)(iii)(D) of this section is not satisfied. Because CFC2 acquired Asset C before, and temporarily held as of, March 31, Year 1, June 30, Year 1, September 30, Year 1, December 31, Year 1 and the holding of the property by CFC2 as of each such tested quarter close would increase the deemed tangible income return of USP, under paragraph (h)(1)(i) of this section, the adjusted basis in Asset C is disregarded in determining CFC2's aggregate adjusted basis in specified tangible property as of each of March 31, Year 1, June 30, Year 1, September 30, Year 1, and December 31, Year 1.

(2) *Disregard of adjusted basis in property transferred during the disqualified period.*—(i) *Operative rules.*—(A) *In general.*—For purposes of determining the qualified business asset investment of a tested income CFC for any CFC inclusion year, disqualified basis in property is disregarded.

(B) *Application to dual use property.*—In the case of dual use property (as defined in paragraph (d)(2) of this section), paragraph (h)(2)(i)(A) of this section applies by reducing the amount of the adjusted basis in the property treated as adjusted basis in specified tangible property for the CFC inclusion year under paragraph (d)(1) of this section by the amount of the disqualified basis in the property. For purposes of determining the amount described in paragraph (d)(1) of this section, including for purposes of determining whether tangible property is dual use property within the meaning of paragraph (d)(2) of this section and for purposes of determining the dual use ratio with respect to dual use property under paragraph (d)(3) of this section, the rules of § 1.951A-2(c)(5) are not taken into account.

(C) *Application to partnership specified tangible property.*—In the case of partnership specified tangible property (as defined in paragraph (g)(5) of this section), paragraph (h)(2)(i)(A) of this section applies by reducing a tested income CFC's partner adjusted basis with respect to partnership specified tangible property under paragraph (g)(3)(i) of this section by the tested income CFC's share of the disqualified basis in the partnership specified tangible property. A tested income CFC's share of disqualified basis in partnership specified tangible property is the sum of the tested income CFC's proportionate share of the disqualified basis in the partnership specified tangible property determined under the principles of paragraph (g)(4) of this section and the tested income CFC's partner-specific QBAI basis in the property determined under the principles of paragraph (g)(7) of this section that is disqualified basis. For purposes of determining the amount described in paragraph (g)(3)(i) of this section, including for purposes of determining whether partnership specified tangible property is sole use partnership property within the meaning of paragraph (g)(3)(ii)(B) of this section or dual use partnership property within the meaning of paragraph (g)(3)(iii)(B) of this section and for purposes of determining the dual use ratio with respect to dual use partnership property under the principles of paragraph (d)(3) of this section, the rules of § 1.951A-2(c)(5) are not taken into account.

(ii) *Determination of disqualified basis.*—(A) *In general.*—Subject to the adjustments described in paragraph (h)(2)(ii)(B) of this section, the term *disqualified basis* means, with respect to property (other than property described in section 1221(a)(1)), the excess (if any) of the property's adjusted basis immediately after a disqualified transfer, over the sum of the property's adjusted basis immediately before the disqualified transfer and the qualified gain amount with respect to the disqualified transfer. For this purpose, the adjusted basis in property immediately after a disqualified transfer includes a positive adjustment to the adjusted basis in partnership property with respect to a partner under section 734(b)(1)(A) or 743(b).

(B) *Adjustments to disqualified basis.*—(*1*) *Reduction or elimination of disqualified basis.*—(*i*) *In general.*—Except to the extent provided in this paragraph (h)(2)(ii)(B)(*1*), disqualified basis in property is reduced or eliminated to the extent that such basis reduces taxable income through, for example, depreciation, amortization, and taxable sales or exchanges, or is otherwise reduced or eliminated, for example, through the application of section 362(e) or 732(a) or (b). In such circumstances, in the case of property with disqualified basis and adjusted basis other than disqualified basis, disqualified basis in the property is reduced or eliminated in the same proportion that the disqualified basis bears to the total adjusted basis in the property. However, in the case of a loss from a taxable sale or exchange, disqualified basis in the property is reduced or eliminated to the extent the loss is treated as attributable to disqualified basis under § 1.951A-2(c)(5)(ii).

(*ii*) *Exception for related party transfers.*—Disqualified basis in property is not reduced or eliminated by reason of any transfer of the property to a related person, except to the extent any loss recognized on the transfer of such property is treated as attributable to the disqualified basis under § 1.951A-2(c)(5)(ii), or the basis is reduced or eliminated in a nonrecognition transaction within the meaning of section 7701(a)(45), for example, through the application of section 362(e) or 732(a) or (b).

(*2*) *Increase to disqualified basis for nonrecognition transactions.*—(*i*) *Increase corresponding to adjustments in other property.*—If the adjusted basis in property is increased by reason of a nonrecognition transaction (as defined in section 7701(a)(45)), for example, through the application of section 732(b) or section 734(b)(1)(B), the disqualified basis in the property is increased by a proportionate share of the aggregate reduction to the disqualified basis (if any) in one or more other properties by reason of such nonrecognition transaction under paragraph (h)(2)(ii)(B)(*1*) of this section.

(*ii*) *Exchanged basis property.*—Disqualified basis in exchanged basis property (as defined in section 7701(a)(44)) includes the amount of the disqualified basis in any property by reference to which the adjusted basis in the exchanged basis property was determined, in whole or in part, provided that the nonrecognition transaction giving rise to such exchanged basis did not also increase the disqualified basis in the exchanged basis property under paragraph (h)(2)(ii)(B)(2)(*i*) of this section.

(*iii*) *Increase by reason of section 732(d).*—Disqualified basis in property is increased by the amount of a positive adjustment to the adjusted basis in property under section 732(d) to the extent that, if an election provided in section 754 were in effect at the time of the acquisition described in section 732(d), the adjusted basis in the property immediately after the acquisition would have been disqualified basis under paragraph (h)(2)(ii)(A) of this section.

(*3*) *Election to eliminate disqualified basis.*—(*i*) *In general.*—If an election made under this paragraph (h)(2)(ii)(B)(3) with respect to a controlled foreign corporation or a partnership is effective, the adjusted basis in each property with disqualified basis held by the controlled foreign corporation or the partnership is reduced by the amount of the disqualified basis and the disqualified basis in each property is eliminated. The reduction of the adjusted basis and the elimination of the disqualified basis described in the preceding sentence is treated as occurring immediately after the disqualified transfer of each property.

(*ii*) *Manner of making the election with respect to a controlled foreign corporation.*—The election described in this paragraph (h)(2)(ii)(B)(3) with respect to a controlled foreign corporation is made by each controlling domestic shareholder (as defined in § 1.964-1(c)(5)) of the controlled foreign corporation by filing a statement as described in § 1.964-1(c)(3)(ii) with its income tax return for its taxable year that includes the last day of the taxable year of the controlled foreign corporation that includes the disqualified transfer and follow the notice requirements of § 1.964-1(c)(3)(iii). If the return for the taxable year has been filed before July 22, 2019, the statement must be included with an amended return filed within 180 days of June 21, 2019. The election statement must be filed in accordance with the rules provided in forms or instructions.

(*iii*) *Manner of making the election with respect to a partnership.*—The election described in this paragraph (h)(2)(ii)(B)(*3*) with respect to a partnership is made by the partnership by filing a statement as described in § 1.754-1(b)(1) for the taxable year that includes the date of the disqualified transfer. If a return for the taxable year has been filed before July 22, 2019, the statement must be included with an amended return filed within 180 days of June 21, 2019. The election statement must be filed in accordance with the rules provided in forms or instructions.

(*iv*) *Conditions of making an election.*—An election under this paragraph (h)(2)(ii)(B)(*3*) with respect to a controlled foreign corporation or a partnership is not effective unless the election is made with respect to each controlled foreign corporation or partnership that holds property with disqualified basis and that is related (within the meaning of section 267(b) and 707(b)) to the controlled foreign corporation or partnership and unless any return that has been filed that is inconsistent with the elimination of the adjusted basis and disqualified basis immediately after the disqualified transfer by reason of this paragraph (h)(2)(ii)(B)(*3*) is amended to take into account the elimination of the adjusted basis and disqualified basis immediately after the disqualified transfer by reason of this paragraph (h)(2)(ii)(B)(*3*).

(C) *Definitions related to disqualified basis.*—The following definitions apply for purposes of this paragraph (h)(2).

(*1*) *Disqualified period.*—The term *disqualified period* means, with respect to a transferor CFC, the period beginning on January 1, 2018, and ending as of the close of the transferor CFC's last taxable year that is not a CFC inclusion year. A transferor CFC that has a CFC inclusion year beginning January 1, 2018, has no disqualified period.

(*2*) *Disqualified transfer.*—The term *disqualified transfer* means a transfer of property during a transferor CFC's disqualified period by the transferor CFC to a related person in which gain was recognized, in whole or in part, by the transferor CFC.

(*3*) *Qualified gain amount.*—The term *qualified gain amount* means, with respect to a disqualified transfer by a transferor CFC, the sum of the following amounts:

(*i*) The amount of gain recognized by the transferor CFC on the disqualified transfer of property that is subject to Federal income tax under section 882 (except to the extent the gain is exempt from tax pursuant to an applicable treaty obligation of the United States); and

(*ii*) Any United States shareholder's pro rata share of the gain recognized by the transferor CFC on the disqualified transfer of property (determined without regard to properly allocable deductions) taken into account in determining the United States shareholder's inclusion under section 951(a)(1)(A), excluding any amount that is described in paragraph (h)(2)(ii)(C)(*3*)(*i*) of this section.

(*4*) *Related person.*—The term *related person* means, with respect to a person that transfers property, any person that bears a relationship to such person described in section 267(b) or 707(b) immediately before or immediately after the transfer.

(*5*) *Transfer.*—The term *transfer* includes any disposition of property, including any sale, exchange, contribution, or distribution of property, and includes an indirect transfer. For example, a transfer of an interest in a partnership is treated as an indirect transfer of the property of the partnership and a transfer by or to a partnership is treated as an indirect transfer by or to its partners. In addition, a distribution of property to a partner with respect to which gain is recognized to the distributee partner under section 731(a)(1) is treated as an indirect transfer of the property of the partnership.

(*6*) *Transferor CFC.*—The term *transferor CFC* means any controlled foreign corporation that transfers property during the disqualified period of the controlled foreign corporation.

(iii) *Examples.*—The following examples illustrate the application of this paragraph (h)(2).

(A) *Example 1: Sale of asset; disqualified period*—(*1*) *Facts.* USP, a domestic corporation, owns all of the stock of CFC1 and CFC2, each a controlled foreign corporation. Both USP and CFC2 use the calendar year as their taxable year. CFC1 uses a taxable year ending November 30. On November 1, 2018, before the start of its first CFC inclusion year, CFC1 sells Asset A, which has an adjusted basis of $10x in the hands of CFC1, to CFC2 in exchange for $100x of cash. CFC1 recognizes $90x of gain as a result of the sale ($100x - $10x) $30x of which is foreign base company income. USP includes in gross income under section 951(a)(1)(A) its pro rata share of the subpart F income of $30x. CFC1's gain is not otherwise subject to U.S. tax or taken into account in determining USP's inclusion under section 951(a)(1)(A).

(*2*) *Analysis.* The transfer of Asset A is a disqualified transfer of Asset A because it is a transfer of property (other than property described in section 1221(a)(1)) by CFC1; CFC1 and CFC2 are related persons; and the transfer occurs during the disqualified period, the period that begins on January 1, 2018, and ends the last day before the first CFC inclusion year of CFC1 (November 30, 2018). Accordingly, under paragraph (h)(2)(ii)(A) of this section, the disqualified basis in Asset A immediately after the disqualified transfer is $60x, the excess of CFC2's adjusted basis in Asset A immediately after the disqualified transfer ($100x), over the sum of CFC1's adjusted basis in Asset A immediately before the transfer ($10x) and USP's pro rata share of the gain recognized by CFC1 on the transfer of the property taken into account by USP under section 951(a)(1)(A) ($30x).

(B) *Example 2: Sale of asset; no disqualified period*—(*1*) *Facts.* The facts are the same as in paragraph (h)(2)(iii)(A)(*1*) of this section (the facts in *Example 1*), except that CFC1 uses the calendar year as its taxable year.

(*2*) *Analysis.* Because CFC1 has a taxable year beginning January 1, 2018, CFC1 has no disqualified period. Accordingly, the property was not transferred during a disqualified period of CFC1, and there is no disqualified basis with respect to the property.

(C) *Example 3: Sale of partnership interest*—(*1*) *Facts.* USP, a domestic corporation, owns all of the stock of CFC1, CFC2, and CFC3, each a controlled foreign corporation. CFC1 and CFC2 are equal partners in PRS, a partnership. PRS owns Asset B with an adjusted basis of $20x and a fair market value of $100x. PRS has a section 754 election in effect. USP, CFC2, and CFC3 all use the calendar year as their taxable year. CFC1 uses a taxable year ending November 30. On November 1, 2018, before the start of its first CFC inclusion year, CFC1 sells its interest in the partnership to CFC3 for $50x of cash. CFC1 has an adjusted basis of $10x in its partnership interest, and thus CFC1 recognizes $40x of gain as a result of the sale ($50x - $10x), none of which is foreign base company income or otherwise subject to U.S. tax. As a result of the sale, there is a $40x adjustment to the adjusted basis in Asset B with respect to CFC3 under section 743(b).

(*2*) *Analysis.* The transfer of the PRS partnership interest is a disqualified transfer of Asset B because it is an indirect transfer of property (other than property described in section 1221(a)(1)) by CFC1; CFC1 and CFC3 are related persons; and the transfer occurs during the disqualified period, the period that begins on January 1, 2018, and ends the last day before the first CFC inclusion year of CFC1 (November 30, 2018). Accordingly, under paragraph (h)(2)(ii)(A) of this section, the disqualified basis in Asset B immediately after the disqualified transfer is $40x, the excess of CFC3's share of adjusted basis in Asset B immediately after the disqualified transfer ($50x), taking into account the basis adjustment with respect to CFC3 under section 743(b), over CFC1's share of adjusted basis in the property immediately before the transfer ($10x).

(D) *Example 4: Distribution of property in liquidation of partnership interest*—(*1*) *Facts.* FC1, FC2, and FC3 are controlled foreign corporations that are equal partners in PRS, a partnership. FC1's adjusted basis in its partnership interest in PRS is $0, FC2's basis is $50x, and FC3's basis is $50x. PRS has a section 754 election in effect. PRS owns Asset C with a fair market value of $50x and an adjusted basis of $0, Asset D with a fair market value of $50x and an adjusted basis of $50x, and Asset E with a fair market value of $50x and an adjusted basis of $50x, and all the adjusted basis in Asset D and Asset E is disqualified basis. PRS distributes Asset C to FC3 in liquidation of FC3's interest in PRS. None of FC1, FC2, FC3, or PRS recognizes gain on the distribution. Under section 732(b), FC3's adjusted basis in Asset C is $50x. PRS's adjusted bases in Asset D and Asset E are decreased, in the aggregate, by $50x under section 734(b)(2)(B), which is the amount by which FC3's adjusted basis in Asset C exceeds PRS's adjusted basis in Asset C immediately before the distribution.

(2) *Analysis.* The distribution of Asset C is a nonrecognition transaction under section 7701(a)(45). Under paragraph (h)(2)(ii)(B)(*1*)(*i*) of this section, the disqualified bases in Asset D and Asset E are reduced, in the aggregate, by $50x. Further, under paragraph (h)(2)(ii)(B)(*2*)(*i*) of this section, the disqualified basis in Asset C is increased by $50x, the aggregate reduction to the disqualified basis in Asset D and Asset E.

(E) *Example 5: Distribution of property to a partner in basis reduction transaction* —(*1*) *Facts.* The facts are the same as in paragraph (h)(2)(iii)(D)(*1*) of this section (the facts in *Example 4*), except PRS distributes Asset D to FC1. Under section 732(a), FC1's adjusted basis in Asset D is $0. PRS's adjusted basis in Asset C is increased by $50x under section 734(b)(1)(B), which is the amount by which PRS's adjusted basis in Asset D immediately before the distribution exceeds FC1's adjusted basis in Asset D under section 732(a).

(2) *Analysis.* The distribution of Asset D is a nonrecognition transaction under section 7701(a)(45). Under paragraph (h)(2)(ii)(B)(*1*)(*i*) of this section, the disqualified basis in Asset D is reduced by $50x. Further, under paragraph (h)(2)(ii)(B)(*2*)(*i*) of this section, the disqualified basis in Asset C is increased by $50x, the reduction to the disqualified basis in Asset D.

(F) *Example 6: Dual use property with disqualified basis*—(*1*) *Facts.* FS is a tested income CFC and a wholesale distributor of Product A. FS owns trucks that deliver Product A. The trucks are specified tangible property. In Year 1, FS earns $250x in total gross income from inventory sales of Product A, $200x of which is included in gross tested income. The trucks have an average adjusted basis for Year 1 of $4,000x, of which $2,500x is disqualified basis. FS does not capitalize depreciation with respect to the trucks to inventory or other property held for sale. The depreciation deduction with respect to the trucks is $20x, $15x of which would be allocated and apportioned to gross tested income under § 1.951A-2(c)(3) without regard to § 1.951A-2(c)(5).

(2) *Analysis.* Because the trucks are used in both the production of gross tested income and the production of gross income that is not gross tested income in Year 1, the trucks are dual use property within the meaning of paragraph (d)(2) of this section. Under paragraph (h)(2)(i)(A) of this section, the disqualified basis in the trucks is disregarded for purposes of determining FS's qualified business asset investment for Year 1. Under paragraph (h)(2)(i)(B) of this section, paragraph (h)(2)(i)(A) of this section applies by reducing the amount of FS's adjusted basis in the trucks treated as adjusted basis in specified tangible property for Year 1 under paragraph (d)(1) of this section (determined without regard to § 1.951A-2(c)(5)) by the amount of the disqualified basis in the trucks. Without regard to § 1.951A-2(c)(5), FS's adjusted basis in the trucks treated as adjusted basis in specified tangible property for Year 1 under paragraph (d)(1) of this section is FS's adjusted basis in the trucks multiplied by FS's dual use ratio with respect to the trucks for Year 1. Because none of the depreciation with respect to the trucks is capitalized into inventory or other property held for sale, FS's dual use ratio with respect to the trucks is determined entirely by reference to the depreciation deduction with respect to the trucks. Therefore, under paragraph (d)(3) of this section, without regard to § 1.951A-2(c)(5), FS's dual use ratio with respect to the trucks for Year 1 is 75%, which is FS's depreciation deduction with respect to the trucks that is allocated and apportioned to gross tested income under § 1.951A-2(c)(3) for Year 1 ($15x), divided by FS's depreciation deduction with respect to the trucks for Year 1 ($20x). Accordingly, paragraph (d)(1) of this section, without regard to paragraph (h)(2)(i)(A) of this section, FS's adjusted basis in the trucks treated as adjusted basis in specified tangible property is $3,000x ($4,000x x 0.75). Under paragraph (h)(2)(i)(A) and (B) of this section, the amount of the adjusted basis in the trucks treated as adjusted basis in specified tangible property is reduced by the $2,500x of disqualified basis in the trucks. Accordingly, $500x ($3,000x - $2,500x) of FS's average adjusted basis in the trucks is taken into account under paragraph (b) of this section in determining FS's qualified business asset investment for Year 1. [Reg. § 1.951A-3.]

☐ [*T.D. 9866, 6-14-2019. Amended by T.D. 9956, 9-21-2021.*]

§ 1.951A-4. Tested interest expense and tested interest income.—(a) *Scope.*—This section provides rules for determining the tested interest expense and tested interest income of a controlled foreign corporation for purposes of determining a United States shareholder's specified interest expense under § 1.951A-1(c)(3)(iii). Paragraph (b) of this section provides definitions related to tested interest expense and tested interest income. Paragraph (c) of this section provides examples illustrating these definitions and the application of § 1.951A-1(c)(3)(iii). The amount of specified interest expense determined under § 1.951A-1(c)(3)(iii) and this section is the amount of interest expense described in section 951A(b)(2)(B).

(b) *Definitions related to specified interest expense.*—(1) *Tested interest expense.*—(i) *In general.*—The term *tested interest expense* means, with respect to a controlled foreign corporation for a CFC inclusion year, interest expense paid or accrued by the controlled foreign corporation that is allocated and apportioned to gross tested income of the controlled foreign corporation for the CFC inclusion year under § 1.951A-2(c)(3), reduced (but not below zero) by the sum of the qualified interest expense of the controlled foreign corporation for the CFC inclusion year and the tested loss QBAI amount of the controlled foreign corporation for the CFC inclusion year.

(ii) *Interest expense.*—The term *interest expense* means any expense or loss that is treated as interest expense under section 163(j).

(iii) *Qualified interest expense.*—(A) *In general.*—The term *qualified interest expense* means, with respect to a controlled foreign corporation for a CFC inclusion year, to the extent established by the controlled foreign corporation, the interest expense paid or accrued by the controlled foreign corporation that is allocated and apportioned to gross tested income of the controlled foreign corporation for the CFC inclusion year under § 1.951A-2(c)(3), multiplied by a fraction, the numerator of which is the average of the aggregate adjusted bases as of the close of each quarter of the CFC inclusion year of qualified assets held by the controlled foreign corporation, and the denominator of which is the average of the aggregate adjusted bases as of the close of each quarter of the CFC inclusion year of all assets held by the controlled foreign corporation.

(B) *Qualified asset.*—(*1*) *In general.*—Except as provided in paragraph (b)(1)(iii)(B)(*2*) of this section, the term *qualified asset* means, with respect to a controlled foreign corporation for a CFC inclusion year, any obligation or financial instrument held by the controlled foreign corporation that gives rise to income included in the gross tested income of the controlled foreign corporation for the CFC inclusion year that is excluded from foreign personal holding company income (as defined in section 954(c)(1)) by reason of section 954(c)(2)(C)(ii) or section 954(h) or (i).

(*2*) *Exclusion for related party receivables.*—A qualified asset does not include an asset that gives rise to interest income that is also excludible from foreign personal holding company income by reason of section 954(c)(3) or (6).

(*3*) *Look-through rule for subsidiary stock.*—For purposes of paragraph (b)(1)(iii)(A) of this section, the adjusted basis in the stock of another controlled foreign corporation held by a controlled foreign corporation is treated as adjusted basis in a qualified asset in an amount equal to the adjusted basis in the stock multiplied by the fraction described in paragraph (b)(1)(iii)(A) of this section determined with respect to the assets of such other controlled foreign corporation.

(*4*) *Look-through rule for certain partnership interests.*—For purposes of paragraph (b)(1)(iii)(A) of this section, if a controlled foreign corporation owns 25 percent or more of the capital or profits interest in a partnership the controlled foreign corporation is treated as holding its attributable share of any property held by the partnership, as determined under the principles of § 1.956-4(b), and the controlled foreign corporation's basis in the partnership interest is not taken into account.

(iv) *Tested loss QBAI amount.*—The term *tested loss QBAI amount* means, with respect to a tested loss CFC for a CFC inclusion year, 10 percent of the amount that would be the qualified business asset investment of the tested loss CFC for the CFC inclusion year under section 951A(d) and § 1.951A-3 if the tested loss CFC were a tested income CFC for the CFC inclusion year.

(2) *Tested interest income.*—(i) *In general.*—The term *tested interest income* means, with respect to a controlled foreign corporation for a CFC inclusion year, interest income included in gross tested income of the controlled foreign corporation for the CFC inclusion year, reduced by qualified interest income of the controlled foreign corporation for the CFC inclusion year.

(ii) *Interest income.*—The term *interest income* means any income or gain that is treated as interest income under section 163(j).

(iii) *Qualified interest income.*—(A) *In general.*—Except as provided in paragraph (b)(2)(iii)(B) of this section, the term *qualified interest income* means, with respect to a controlled foreign corporation for a CFC inclusion year, interest income of the controlled foreign corporation for the CFC inclusion year included in the gross tested income of the controlled foreign corporation for the CFC inclusion year that is excluded from foreign personal holding company income (as defined in section 954(c)(1)) by reason of section 954(c)(2)(C)(ii) or section 954(h) or (i).

(B) *Exclusion for related party interest.*—Qualified interest income does not include interest income that is also excludible from foreign personal holding company income by reason of section 954(c)(3) or (6).

(c) *Examples.*—The following examples illustrate the application of this section.

(1) *Example 1: Wholly-owned CFCs*—(i) *Facts.* A Corp, a domestic corporation, owns 100% of the single class of stock of each of FS1 and FS2, each a controlled foreign corporation. A Corp, FS1, and FS2 all use the calendar year as their taxable year. For Year 1, FS1 and FS2 are both tested income CFCs. In Year 1, FS1 pays $100x of interest to FS2. The interest expense of FS1 is allocated and apportioned to its gross tested income under § 1.951A-2(c)(3). The interest income of FS2 is excluded from its foreign personal holding company income under section 954(c)(6). Also, in Year 1, FS2 pays $100x of interest to a bank that is not related to FS2, which interest expense is allocated and apportioned to FS2's gross tested income under § 1.951A-2(c)(3). Neither FS1 nor FS2 holds qualified assets or owns stock of another controlled foreign corporation.

(ii) *Analysis*—(A) *CFC-level determination; tested interest expense and tested interest income*—(*1*) *Tested interest expense and tested interest income of FS1.* FS1 has $100x of interest expense that is allocated and apportioned to its gross tested income under § 1.951A-2(c)(3). FS1 has no interest income. Accordingly, FS1 has $100x of tested interest expense and no tested interest income for Year 1.

(*2*) *Tested interest expense and tested interest income of FS2.* FS2 has $100x of interest expense that is allocated and apportioned to its gross tested income under § 1.951A-2(c)(3) and $100x of interest income that is included in its gross tested income. Accordingly, FS2 has $100x of tested interest expense and $100x of tested interest income for Year 1.

(B) *United States shareholder-level determination; pro rata share and specified interest expense.* Under § 1.951A-1(d)(5) and (6), A Corp's pro rata share of FS1's tested interest expense is $100x, its pro rata share of FS2's tested interest expense is $100x, and its pro rata share of FS2's tested interest income is $100x. For Year 1, A Corp's aggregate pro rata share of tested interest expense is $200x and its aggregate pro rata share of tested interest income is $100x. Accordingly, under § 1.951A-1(c)(3)(iii), A Corp's specified interest expense is $100x ($200x - $100x) for Year 1.

(2) *Example 2: Less than wholly-owned CFCs*—(i) *Facts.* The facts are the same as in paragraph (c)(1)(i) of this section (the facts in *Example 1*), except that A Corp owns 50% of the single class of stock of FS1 and 80% of the single class of stock of FS2.

(ii) *Analysis*—(A) *CFC-level determination; tested interest expense and tested interest income.* The analysis is the same as in paragraph (c)(1)(ii)(A) of this section (paragraph (A) of the analysis in *Example 1*).

(B) *United States shareholder-level determination; pro rata share and specified interest expense.* Under § 1.951A-1(d)(5) and (6), A Corp's pro rata share of FS1's tested interest expense is $50x ($100x x 0.50), its pro rata share of FS2's tested interest expense is $80x ($100x x 0.80), and its pro rata share of FS2's tested interest income is $80x ($100x x 0.80). For Year 1, A Corp's aggregate pro rata share of the tested interest expense is $130x ($50x + $80x) and its aggregate pro rata share of the tested interest income is $80x ($0 + $80x). Accordingly, under § 1.951A-1(c)(3)(iii), A Corp's specified interest expense is $50x ($130x - $80x) for Year 1.

(3) *Example 3: Operating company; qualified interest expense*—(i) *Facts.* B Corp, a domestic corporation, owns 100% of the single class of stock of each of FS1 and FS2, each a controlled foreign corporation. For Year 1, FS1 and FS2 are both tested income CFCs. B Corp, FS1, and FS2 all use the calendar year as their taxable year. FS2 is an eligible controlled foreign corporation within the meaning of section 954(h)(2). In Year 1, FS1 pays $100x of interest to FS2. The interest expense of FS1 is allocated and apportioned to its gross tested income under § 1.951A-2(c)(3). The interest income of FS2 is excluded from its foreign personal holding company income by reason of section 954(c)(6). In addition, in Year 1, FS2 receives $300x of interest from customers that are not related to FS2, which interest income is excluded from FS2's foreign personal holding company income by reason of section 954(h), and FS2 pays $300x of interest to a bank, which interest expense is allocated and apportioned to FS2's gross tested income under § 1.951A-2(c)(3). Neither FS1 nor FS2 owns stock of another controlled foreign corporation. FS1 does not hold qualified assets. FS2's average adjusted bases in qualified assets is $8,000x, and FS2's average adjusted bases in all its assets is $12,000x.

(ii) *Analysis*—(A) *CFC-level determination; tested interest expense and tested interest income*—(*1*) *Tested interest expense and tested interest income of FS1.* FS1 has $100x of interest expense that is allocated and apportioned to its gross tested income under § 1.951A-2(c)(3). FS1 has no interest income. Accordingly, FS1 has $100x of tested interest expense and no tested interest income for Year 1.

(*2*) *Tested interest expense and tested interest income of FS2.* FS2 has $300x of interest expense that is allocated and apportioned to its gross tested income under § 1.951A-2(c)(3) and $400x of interest income that is included in gross tested income. However, a portion of FS2's interest income is excluded from foreign personal holding company income by reason of section 954(h), and a portion of FS2's assets are qualified assets. As a result, in determining the tested interest income and tested interest expense of FS2, the qualified interest income and qualified interest expense of FS2 are excluded. FS2 has qualified interest income of $300x, the amount of FS2's interest income that is excluded from foreign personal holding company income by reason of section 954(h). In addition, FS2 has qualified interest expense of $200x, the amount of FS2's interest expense that is allocated and apportioned to its gross tested income under § 1.951A-2(c)(3) ($300x), multiplied by a fraction, the numerator of which is FS2's average adjusted bases in qualified assets ($8,000x), and the denominator of which is FS2's average adjusted bases in all its assets ($12,000x). Accordingly, FS2 has tested interest income of $100x ($400x - $300x) and tested interest expense of $100x ($300x - $200x) for Year 1.

(B) *United States shareholder-level determination; pro rata share and specified interest expense.* Under § 1.951A-1(d)(5) and (6), B Corp's pro rata share of FS1's tested interest expense is $100x, its pro rata share of FS2's tested interest expense is $100x, and its pro rata share of FS2's tested interest income is $100x. For Year 1, B Corp's aggregate pro rata share of tested interest expense is $200x ($100x + $100x) and its aggregate pro rata share of tested interest income is $100x ($0 + $100x). Accordingly, under § 1.951A-1(c)(3)(iii), B Corp's specified interest expense is $100x ($200x - $100x) for Year 1.

(4) *Example 4: Holding company; qualified interest expense*—(i) *Facts.* C Corp, a domestic corporation, owns 100% of the single class of stock of each of FS1 and FS2, each a controlled foreign corporation. FS2 owns 100% of the single class of stock of FS3, a qualifying insurance company within the meaning of section 953(e)(3). For Year 1, FS1, FS2, and FS3 are all tested income CFCs. C Corp, FS1, FS2, and FS3 all use the calendar year as their taxable year. In Year 1, FS1 pays $100x of interest to FS3. The interest expense of FS1 is allocated and apportioned to its gross tested income under § 1.951A-2(c)(3). The interest income of FS3 is excluded from its foreign personal holding company income by reason of section 954(c)(6). In addition, FS3 receives $300x of interest from persons that are not related to FS3, which interest income is excluded from FS's foreign personal holding company income by reason of section 954(i). Also in Year 1, FS2 pays $300x of interest to a bank, which interest expense is allocated and apportioned to FS2's gross tested income under § 1.951A-2(c)(3). None of FS1, FS2, or FS3 owns stock of another controlled foreign corporation, except for the stock of FS3 owned by FS2. FS2 has no assets other than the stock of FS3. Neither FS1 nor FS2 hold qualified assets directly. FS2's average adjusted bases in the FS3 stock is $6,000x. FS3's average adjusted bases in qualified assets is $8,000x, and FS3's average adjusted bases in all its assets is $12,000x.

(ii) *Analysis*—(A) *CFC-level determination; tested interest expense and tested interest income*—(*1*) *Tested interest expense and tested interest income of FS1.* In Year 1, FS1 has $100x of interest expense allocated and apportioned to its gross tested income under § 1.951A-2(c)(3). FS1 has no interest income. Accordingly, FS1 has $100x of tested interest expense and no tested interest income for Year 1.

(*2*) *Tested interest expense and tested interest income of FS2.* FS2 has $300x of interest expense that is allocated and apportioned to its gross tested income under § 1.951A-2(c)(3). FS2 has no interest income. While FS2 holds no qualified assets directly, $4,000x of FS3's average adjusted basis in FS3 stock is treated as adjusted basis in a qualified asset, which is equal to FS3's average adjusted basis in FS3 stock ($6,000x) multiplied by a fraction, the numerator of which is FS3's average adjusted bases in qualified assets ($8,000x), and the denominator of which is FS3's average adjusted bases in all its assets ($12,000x). Accordingly, FS2 has qualified interest expense of $200x, the amount of FS2's interest expense allocated and apportioned to

FS2's gross tested income under § 1.951A-2(c)(3) ($300x), multiplied by a fraction, the numerator of which is FS2's average adjusted bases in qualified assets ($4,000x), and the denominator of which is FS2's average adjusted bases in all its assets ($6,000x). Therefore, FS2 has tested interest expense of $100x ($300x - $200x) and no tested interest income for Year 1.

(3) *Tested interest expense and tested interest income of FS3.* In Year 1, FS3 has no interest expense, but FS3 has $400x of interest income that is included in gross tested income. However, a portion of FS3's interest income is excluded from foreign personal holding company income by reason of section 954(i). As a result, in determining the tested interest income of FS3, the qualified interest income of FS3 is excluded. FS3 has qualified interest income of $300x, the amount of FS3's interest income that is excluded from foreign personal holding company income by reason of section 954(i). Therefore, FS2 has tested interest income of $100x ($400x - $300x) and no tested interest expense for Year 1.

(B) *United States shareholder-level determination; pro rata share and specified interest expense.* Under § 1.951A-1(d)(5) and (6), C Corp's pro rata share of FS1's tested interest expense is $100x, its pro rata share of FS2's tested interest expense is $100x, and its pro rata share of FS3's tested interest income is $100x. For Year 1, C Corp's aggregate pro rata share of tested interest expense is $200x ($100x + $100x + $0) and its aggregate pro rata share of tested interest income is $100x ($0 + $0 + $100x). Accordingly, under § 1.951A-1(c)(3)(iii), C Corp's specified interest expense is $100x ($200x - $100x) for Year 1.

(5) *Example 5: Specified interest expense and tested loss QBAI amount*—(i) *Facts.* D Corp, a domestic corporation, owns 100% of a single class of stock of each of FS1 and FS2, each a controlled foreign corporation. For Year 1, FS1 is a tested income CFC and FS2 is a tested loss CFC. D Corp, FS1, and FS2 all use the calendar year as their taxable year. In Year 1, FS1 pays $100x of interest to FS2. The interest expense of FS1 is allocated and apportioned to its gross tested income under § 1.951A-2(c)(3). The interest income of FS2 is excluded from its foreign personal holding company income by reason of section 954(c)(6). Also, in Year 1, FS2 pays $100x of interest to a bank that is not related to FS2, which interest expense is allocated and apportioned to FS2's gross tested income under § 1.951A-2(c)(3). Neither FS1 nor FS2 holds qualified assets or owns stock of another controlled foreign corporation. Because FS2 is a tested loss CFC, FS2 has no QBAI. See § 1.951A-3(b). However, if FS2 were a tested income CFC, FS2 would have QBAI of $1,000x.

(ii) *Analysis*—(A) *CFC-level determination; tested interest expense and tested interest income*—(1) *Tested interest expense and tested interest income of FS1.* In Year 1, FS1 has $100x of interest expense that is allocated and apportioned to its gross tested income under § 1.951A-2(c)(3). FS1 has no interest income. Accordingly, FS1 has $100x of tested interest expense and no tested interest income for Year 1.

(2) *Tested interest expense and tested interest income of FS2.* FS2 has $100x of interest income that is included in gross tested income. Accordingly, FS2 has $100x of tested interest income. FS2 also has 100x of interest expense that is allocated and apportioned to its gross tested income. However, because FS2 is a tested loss CFC, FS2's tested interest expense is reduced by its tested loss QBAI amount. FS2's tested loss QBAI amount is $100x (10% of $1,000x, the amount that would be QBAI if FS2 were a tested income CFC). Accordingly, FS2's tested interest expense is $0 ($100x interest expense - $100x tested loss QBAI amount) for Year 1.

(B) *United States shareholder-level determination; pro rata share and specified interest expense.* Under § 1.951A-1(d)(5) and (6), D Corp's pro rata share of FS1's tested interest expense is $100x, its pro rata share of FS2's tested interest expense is $0, and its pro rata share of FS2's tested interest income is $100x. For Year 1, D Corp's aggregate pro rata share of tested interest expense is $100x, and its aggregate pro rata share of tested interest income is $100x. Accordingly, under § 1.951A-1(c)(3)(iii), D Corp's specified interest expense is $0 ($100x - $100x) for Year 1. [Reg. § 1.951A-4.]

☐ [*T.D. 9866, 6-14-2019.*]

§ 1.951A-5. Treatment of GILTI inclusion amounts.—(a) *Scope.*—This section provides rules relating to the treatment of GILTI inclusion amounts and adjustments to earnings and profits to account for tested losses. Paragraph (b) of this section provides that a GILTI inclusion amount is treated in the same manner as an amount included under section 951(a)(1)(A) for purposes of applying certain Code sections. Paragraph (c) of this section provides rules for the treatment of amounts taken into account in determining the net CFC tested income of a United States shareholder when applying sections 163(e)(3)(B)(i) and 267(a)(3)(B). Paragraph (d) of this section provides a rule for the treatment of a GILTI inclusion amount for purposes of determining the personal holding company income of a United States shareholder that is a domestic corporation under section 543.

(b) *Treatment as subpart F income for certain purposes.*—(1) *In general.*—A GILTI inclusion amount is treated in the same manner as an amount included under section 951(a)(1)(A) for purposes of applying sections 168(h)(2)(B), 535(b)(10), 851(b), 904(h)(1), 959, 961, 962, 993(a)(1)(E), 996(f)(1), 1248(b)(1), 1248(d)(1), 1411, 6501(e)(1)(C), 6654(d)(2)(D), and 6655(e)(4).

(2) *Allocation of GILTI inclusion amount to tested income CFCs.*—(i) *In general.*—For purposes of the sections referred to in paragraph (b)(1) of this section, the portion of the GILTI inclusion amount of a United States shareholder for a U.S. shareholder inclusion year treated as being with respect to each controlled foreign corporation of the United States shareholder for the U.S. shareholder inclusion year is—

(A) In the case of a tested loss CFC, zero, and

(B) In the case of a tested income CFC, the portion of the GILTI inclusion amount of the United States shareholder which bears the same ratio to such amount as the United States shareholder's pro rata share of the tested income of the tested income CFC for the U.S. shareholder inclusion year bears to the aggregate amount of the United States shareholder's pro rata share of the tested income of each tested income CFC for the U.S. shareholder inclusion year.

(ii) *Example.*—The following example illustrates the application of paragraph (b)(2)(i) of this section.

(A) *Facts.* USP, a domestic corporation, owns all of the stock of three controlled foreign corporations, CFC1, CFC2, and CFC3. USP, CFC1, CFC2, and CFC3 all use the calendar year as their taxable year. In Year 1, CFC1 has tested income of $100x, CFC2 has tested income of $300x, and CFC3 has tested loss of $50x. USP has no net deemed tangible income return for Year 1.

(B) *Analysis.* In Year 1, USP has net CFC tested income (as defined in § 1.951A-1(c)(2)) of $350x ($100x + $300x - $50x) and, because USP has no net deemed tangible income return, a GILTI inclusion amount (as defined in § 1.951A-1(c)(1)) of $350x ($350x - $0). The aggregate amount of USP's pro rata share of tested income is $400x ($100x from CFC1 + $300x from CFC2). Therefore, under paragraph (b)(2)(i) of this section, the portion of USP's GILTI inclusion amount treated as being with respect to CFC1 is $87.50x ($350x x $100x/$400x). The portion of USP's GILTI inclusion amount treated as being with respect to CFC2 is $262.50x ($350x x $300x/$400x). The portion of USP's GILTI inclusion amount treated as being with respect to CFC3 is $0 because CFC3 is a tested loss CFC.

(3) *Translation of portion of GILTI inclusion amount allocated to tested income CFC.*—The portion of the GILTI inclusion amount of a United States shareholder allocated to a tested income CFC under section 951A(f)(2) and paragraph (b)(2)(i) of this section is translated into the functional currency of the tested income CFC using the average exchange rate for the CFC inclusion year of the tested income CFC.

(c) *Treatment as an amount includible in the gross income of a United States person.*—For purposes of sections 163(e)(3)(B)(i) and 267(a)(3)(B), an item (including original issue discount) is treated as includible in the gross income of a United States person to the extent that the item increases a United States shareholder's pro rata share of tested income of a controlled foreign corporation for a U.S. shareholder inclusion year, reduces the shareholder's pro rata share of tested loss of a controlled foreign corporation for the U.S. shareholder inclusion year, or both.

(d) *Treatment for purposes of personal holding company rules.*—For purposes of determining whether a United States shareholder that is a domestic corporation is a personal holding company under section 542, no portion of the adjusted ordinary gross income of such domestic corporation that consists of its GILTI inclusion amount for the U.S. shareholder inclusion year is personal holding company income (as defined in section 543(a)). [Reg. § 1.951A-5.]

☐ [*T.D. 9866, 6-14-2019.*]

§ 1.951A-6. Adjustments related to tested losses.—(a) *Scope.*—This section provides rules relating to adjustments related to tested losses. Paragraph (b) of this section provides rules that increase the earnings and profits of a tested loss CFC for purposes of section 952(c)(1)(A). Paragraph (c) of this section is reserved for a rule for tested loss adjustments.

(b) *Increase of earnings and profits of tested loss CFC for purposes of section 952(c)(1)(A).*—For purposes of section 952(c)(1)(A) with respect to a CFC inclusion year, the earnings and profits of a tested loss CFC are increased by an amount equal to the tested loss of the tested loss CFC for the CFC inclusion year.

(c) [Reserved]

[Reg. § 1.951A-6.]

☐ [*T.D.* 9866, 6-14-2019.]

§ 1.951A-7. Applicability dates.—(a) *In general.*—Except as otherwise provided in this section, sections 1.951A-1 through 1.951A-6 apply to taxable years of foreign corporations beginning after December 31, 2017, and to taxable years of United States shareholders in which or with which such taxable years of foreign corporations end.

(b) *High-tax exception.*—Except as otherwise provided in this paragraph (b), section, 1.951A-2(c)(1)(iii), (c)(3)(ii), and (c)(7) and (8) apply to taxable years of foreign corporations beginning on or after July 23, 2020, and to taxable years of United States shareholders in which or with which such taxable years of foreign corporations end. In addition, taxpayers may choose to apply the rules in § 1.951A-2(c)(1)(iii), (c)(3)(ii), and (c)(7) and (8) to taxable years of foreign corporations that begin after December 31, 2017, and before July 23, 2020, and to taxable years of U.S. shareholders in which or with which such taxable years of the foreign corporations end, provided that they consistently apply those rules and the rules in § 1.954-1(c)(1)(iii)(A)*(3)*, § 1.954-1(c)(1)(iv), and the first sentence of § 1.954-1(d)(3)(i) to such taxable years. Section 1.951A-2(c)(7)(iii)(B), (c)(8)(ii), (c)(8)(iii)(A)*(2)*(*ii*), and (c)(8)(iii)(B) apply to taxable years of foreign corporations beginning on or after December 28, 2021, and to taxable years of United States shareholders in which or with which such taxable years of the foreign corporations end. In addition, taxpayers may choose to apply the rules in § 1.951A-2(c)(7)(iii)(B), (c)(8)(iii)(A)*(2)*(*ii*), and (c)(8)(iii)(B)*(2)*(*iii*) to taxable years of foreign corporations that begin after December 31, 2019, and before December 28, 2021, and to taxable years of U.S. shareholders in which or with which such taxable years of the foreign corporations end. For taxable years of foreign corporations beginning before December 28, 2021, see § 1.951A-2(c)(7)(iii)(B), (c)(8)(iii)(A)*(2)*(*ii*), and (c)(8)(iii)(B)*(2)*(*iii*) as contained in 26 CFR part 1 revised as of April 1, 2021.

(c) [Reserved]

(d) *Deduction for disqualified payments.*—Section 1.951A-2(c)(6) applies to taxable years of foreign corporations ending on or after April 7, 2020, and to taxable years of United States shareholders in which or with which such taxable years end. [Reg. § 1.951A-7.]

☐ [*T.D.* 9866, 6-14-2019. *Amended by T.D.* 9902, 7-20-2020; *T.D.* 9922, 11-2-2020 *and T.D.* 9959, 12-28-2021.]

Proposed Amendments to Regulation

§ 1.951A-7. Applicability dates.—

* * *

(c) *Domestic partnerships.*—Section 1.951A-1(e) applies to taxable years of foreign corporations beginning after December 31, 2017, and before the date of publication of the Treasury decision adopting these rules as final regulations in the **Federal Register**, and to taxable years of United States persons in which or with which such taxable years of foreign corporations end. [Prop. Reg. § 1.951A-7.]

[Proposed 6-21-2019.]

Proposed Amendments to Regulation

§ 1.951A-7. Applicability dates.—

* * *

(b) *High-tax exception.*—Section 1.951A-2(c)(1)(iii) applies to taxable years of foreign corporations beginning after [the date that final regulations are filed for public inspection], and to taxable years of United States shareholders in which or with which such taxable years of foreign corporations end. For the application of § 1.951A-2(c)(1)(iii) to taxable years of controlled foreign corporations beginning on or after September 21, 2020, and before [the date final regulations are filed with the **Federal Register**] and to taxable years of United States shareholders in which or with which such taxable years of foreign corporations end, see § 1.951A-2(c)(1)(iii), as in effect on September 21, 2020. [Prop. Reg. § 1.951A-7.]

[Proposed 7-23-2020.]

Proposed Amendments to Regulation

§ 1.951A-7. Applicability dates.—

* * *

(e) *Entity treatment of domestic partnerships and S corporations.*—Section 1.951A-1(e)(2) applies to taxable years of foreign corporations ending before June 22, 2019, and to taxable years of United States shareholders in which or with which such taxable years end. [Prop. Reg. § 1.951A-7.]

[Proposed 1-25-2022.]

Proposed Amendments to Regulation

§ 1.951A-7. Applicability dates.—

* * *

(e) *Determination of gross income and allowable deductions.*—Section 1.951A-2(c)(2) applies to taxable years of foreign corporations ending on or after [date of publication of final regulations in the **Federal Register**], and to taxable years of United States shareholders in which or with which such taxable years end. For taxable years of foreign corporations ending before [date of publication of final regulations in the **Federal Register**], and to taxable years of United States shareholders in which or with which such taxable years end, see § 1.951A-2(c)(2)(i) and (ii) as contained in 26 CFR part 1, revised as of April 1, 2022. [Prop. Reg. § 1.951A-7.]

[Proposed 5-3-2023.]

§ 1.952-1. Subpart F income defined.—(a) *In general.*—For purposes of sections 951 through 964, a controlled foreign corporation's subpart F income for any taxable year shall, except as provided in paragraph (b) of this section and subject to the limitations of paragraphs (c) and (d) of this section, consist of the sum of—

(1) The income derived by such corporation for such year from the insurance of United States risks (determined in accordance with the provisions of section 953 and §§ 1.953-1 through 1.953-6),

(2) The income derived by such corporation for such year which constitutes foreign base company income (determined in accordance with the provisions of section 954 and §§ 1.954-1 through 1.954-8),

(3)(i) An amount equal to the product of—

(A) The income of such corporation other than income which—

(1) Is attributable to earnings and profits of the foreign corporation included in the gross income of a United States person under section 951 (other than by reason of this paragraph) (determined in accordance with the provisions of section 951 and § 1.951-1), or

(2) Is described in section 952(b),

multiplied by

(B) The international boycott factor determined in accordance with the provisions of section 999(c)(1), or

(ii) In lieu of the amount determined under paragraph (a)(3)(i) of this section, the amount described under section 999(c)(2) of such international boycott income, and

(4) The sum of the amount of any illegal bribes, kickbacks, or other payments paid after November 3, 1976, by or on behalf of the corporation during the taxable year of the corporation directly or indirectly to an official, employee, or agent in fact of a government. An amount is paid by a controlled foreign corporation where it is paid by an officer, director, employee, shareholder or agent of such corporation for the benefit of such corporation. For purposes of this section, the principles of section 162(c) and the regulations thereunder shall apply. In the case of payments made after September 3, 1982, a payment is illegal if the payment would be unlawful under the Foreign Corrupt Practices Act of 1977 if the payor were a United States person. The fair market value of an illegal payment made in the form of property or services shall be considered the amount of such illegal payment.

Pursuant to section 951(a)(1)(A)(i) and § 1.951-1, a United States shareholder of such controlled foreign corporation must include his pro rata share of such subpart F income in his gross income for his taxable year in which or with which such taxable year of the foreign corporation ends. See section 952(a). However, see paragraph (a) of § 1.957-2 for special rule limiting the subpart F income to the income derived from the insurance of United States risks in the case of certain controlled foreign corporations described in section 957(b).

(b) *Exclusion of U.S. income.*—(1) *Taxable years beginning before January 1, 1967.*—For rules applicable to taxable years beginning before January 1, 1967, see 26 CFR § 1.952-1(b)(1) (Rev. as of April 1, 1975).

(2) *Taxable years beginning after December 31, 1966.*—Notwithstanding paragraph (a) of this section, a controlled foreign corporation's subpart F income for any taxable year beginning after December 31, 1966, shall not include any item of income from sources within the United States which is effectively connected for that year with the conduct by such corporation of a trade or business in the United States unless, pursuant to a treaty to which the United States is a party, such item of income either is exempt from the income tax imposed by chapter 1 (relating to normal taxes and surtaxes) of the Code or is subject to such tax at a reduced rate. Thus, for example, dividends received from sources within the United States by a foreign corporation engaged in business in the United States during the taxable year, which are not effectively connected for that year with the conduct of a trade or business in the United States by that corporation, shall not be excluded from subpart F income under section 952(b) and this subparagraph even though such dividends are subject to the tax of 30 percent imposed by section 881(a). Also, for example, if, by reason of an income tax convention to which the United States is a party, an amount of interest from sources within the United States which is effectively connected for the taxable year with the conduct of a business in the United States by a foreign corporation is subject to tax under chapter 1 at a flat rate of 15 percent, as provided in § 1.871-12, such interest is not excluded from subpart F income under section 952(b) and this subparagraph. The deductions attributable to items of income which are excluded from subpart F income under this subparagraph shall not be taken into account for purposes of section 952.

(3) *Rule applicable under section 956(b)(2).*—For purposes only of paragraph (b)(1)(viii) of § 1.956-2, an item of income derived by a controlled foreign corporation from sources within the United States with respect to which for the taxable year a tax is imposed in accordance with section 882(a) shall be considered described in section 952(b) whether or not such item of income would have constituted subpart F income for such year.

(c) *Limitation on a controlled foreign corporation's subpart F income.*—(1) *In general.*—A United States shareholder's pro rata share (determined in accordance with the rules of paragraph (e) of § 1.951-1) of a controlled foreign corporation's subpart F income for any taxable year shall not exceed his pro rata share of the earnings and profits (as defined in section 964(a) and § 1.964-1) of such corporation for such taxable year, computed as of the close of such taxable year without diminution by reason of any distributions made during such taxable year, minus the sum of—

(i) The amount, if any, by which such shareholder's pro rata share of—

(a) The sum of such corporation's deficits in earnings and profits for prior taxable years beginning after December 31, 1962, plus

(b) The sum of such corporation's deficits in earnings and profits for taxable years beginning after December 31, 1959, and before January 1, 1963 (reduced by the sum of the earnings and profits (as so defined) of such corporation for any of such taxable years) exceeds

(c) The sum of such corporation's earnings and profits for prior taxable years beginning after December 31, 1962, which, with respect to such shareholder, are allocated to other earnings and profits under section 959(c)(3) and § 1.959-3; and

(ii) Such shareholder's pro rata share of any deficits in earnings and profits of other foreign corporations for a taxable year beginning after December 31, 1962, which are attributable to stock of such other foreign corporations owned by such shareholder within the meaning of section 958(a) and which, in accordance with section 952(d) and paragraph (d) of this section, are taken into account as a reduction in the controlled foreign corporation's earnings and profits for such taxable year.

For purposes of applying this subparagraph, the reduction (if any) provided by subdivision (i) of this subparagraph in a United States shareholder's pro rata share of the earnings and profits of a controlled foreign corporation shall be taken into account before the reduction provided by subdivision (ii) of this subparagraph. See section 952(c).

(2) *Special rules.*—For purposes only of determining the limitation under subparagraph (1) of this paragraph on a United States shareholder's pro rata share of a controlled foreign corporation's subpart F income for any taxable year—

(i) *Status of foreign corporation.*—The earnings and profits, or deficit in earnings and profits, of a foreign corporation for any taxable year shall be taken into account whether or not such foreign corporation is a controlled foreign corporation at the time such earnings and profits are derived or such deficit in earnings and profits is incurred.

(ii) *Deficits in earnings and profits taken into account only once.*—A controlled foreign corporation's deficit in earnings and profits for any taxable year preceding the taxable year shall be taken into account for the taxable year only to the extent such deficit has not been taken into account under this paragraph, paragraph (d) of this section, or paragraph (d)(2)(ii) of § 1.963-2 (applied as if section 963 had not been repealed by the Tax Reduction Act of 1975) in computing a minimum distribution, for any taxable year preceding the taxable year, to reduce earnings and profits of such preceding year of such controlled foreign corporation or of any other controlled foreign corporation. To the extent a controlled foreign corporation's (the "first corporation") excess foreign base company shipping deductions for any taxable year (determined under § 1.955A-3(c)(2)(i)) reduce the foreign base company shipping income of another member of a related group (as defined in § 1.955A-2(b)), such deductions shall not be taken into account in determining the earnings and profits or deficit in earnings and profits of such first corporation for such taxable year for purposes of this paragraph (c) and paragraph (d) of this section. The rule of the preceding sentence shall not apply to the extent the excess foreign base company shipping deductions of the first corporation reduce the foreign base company shipping income of another member of a related group below zero.

(iii) *Determination of pro rata share.*—A United States shareholder's pro rata share of a controlled foreign corporation's earnings and profits, or deficit in earnings and profits, for any taxable year shall be determined in accordance with the principles of paragraph (e) of § 1.951-1 and paragraph (d)(2)(ii) of § 1.963-2.

(3) *Illustrations.*—The application of this paragraph may be illustrated by the following examples:

Example (1). (a) A is a United States shareholder who owns 100 percent of the only class of stock of M Corporation, a controlled foreign corporation organized on January 1, 1963. Both A and M Corporation use the calendar year as a taxable year.

(b) During 1963, M Corporation derives $20,000 of subpart F income and has earnings and profits of $30,000. Corporation M makes no distributions to A during such year. The limitation under section 952(c) on M Corporation's subpart F income for 1963 is $30,000; and $20,000 is includible in A's gross income for such year under section 951(a)(1)(A)(i).

(c) On January 1, 1964, M Corporation acquires 100 percent of the only class of stock of N Corporation, a controlled foreign corporation which uses the calendar year as a taxable year. During 1964, N Corporation derives $6,000 of subpart F income, has $7,000 of earnings and profits, and distributes $5,000 to M Corporation. The limitation under section 952(c) on N Corporation's subpart F income for 1964 is $7,000; and $6,000 of subpart F income is includible in A's gross income for such year under section 951(a)(1)(A)(i).

(d) During 1964, M Corporation derives $8,000 of rents which constitute subpart F income, makes a $10,000 distribution to A, and has earnings and profits of $12,000 (including the $5,000 dividend received from N Corporation). The limitation under section 952(c) on M Corporation's subpart F income for 1964 is $7,000, determined as follows:

Corporation M's earnings and profits for 1964 (determined under section 964(a) and § 1.964-1 as of the close of such year without diminution for any distributions made during such year)	$12,000
Less: Corporation M's earnings and profits for 1964 described in section 959(b)	5,000
Limitation on M Corporation's subpart F income for 1964	$7,000

Thus, for 1964 with respect to A's interest in M Corporation, $7,000 of subpart F income is includible in his gross income under section 951(a)(1)(A)(i). The $10,000 dividend received from M Corporation is excludable from A's gross income for 1964 under section 959(a)(1) and paragraph (b) of § 1.959-1.

Example (2). A is a United States shareholder who owns 100 percent of the only class of stock of R Corporation which was organized on January 1, 1961. R Corporation is a controlled foreign corporation for the entire period after December 31, 1962, here involved. Both A and R Corporation use the calendar year as a taxable year. During 1963, R Corporation derives $25,000 of subpart F income and has $50,000 of earnings and profits. Corporation R has $15,000 of earnings and profits for 1961, and a deficit in earnings and profits of $45,000 for 1962. Thus, R Corporation has as of December 31, 1963, a net deficit in earnings and profits of $30,000 for the years 1961 and 1962. Corporation R makes no distributions to A during 1963. The limitation under section 952(c) on R Corporation's subpart F income for 1963 is $20,000 ($50,000 minus $30,000), and $20,000 of subpart F income is includible in A's gross income for 1963 under section 951(a)(1)(A)(i). During 1964, R Corporation derives $18,000 of subpart F income and has $30,000 of earnings and profits. Corporation R makes no distributions to A during 1964. The entire $18,000 of subpart F income is includible in A's gross income for 1964 under section 951(a)(1)(A)(i).

(d) *Treatment of deficits in earnings and profits attributable to stock of other foreign corporations indirectly owned by a United States shareholder.*—(1) *In general.*—For purposes of paragraph (c)(1)(ii) of this section, if—

(i) A United States shareholder owns (within the meaning of section 958(a)) stock in two or more foreign corporations in a chain of foreign corporations (as defined in subparagraph (2)(ii) of this paragraph), and

(ii) Any of the corporations in such chain has a deficit in earnings and profits for taxable year beginning after December 31, 1962,

then, with respect to such shareholder and only for purposes of determining the limitation on subpart F income under paragraph (c) of this section, the earnings and profits for the taxable year of each such foreign corporation which is a controlled foreign corporation shall, in accordance with the rules of subparagraph (2) of this paragraph, be reduced to take into account any deficit in earnings and profits referred to in subdivision (ii) of this subparagraph. See section 952(d).

(2) *Special rules.*—For purposes of this paragraph—

(i) *Applicable rules.*—The special rules set forth in paragraph (c)(2) of this section shall apply.

(ii) *"Chain" defined.*—A chain of foreign corporations shall, with respect to a United States shareholder, include—

(a) Any foreign corporation in which such shareholder owns (within the meaning of section 958(a)(1)(A)) stock, but only to the extent of the stock so owned, and

(b) All foreign corporations in which such shareholder owns (within the meaning of section 958(a)(2)) stock, but only to the extent of the stock so owned by reason of his ownership of the stock referred to in *(a)* of this subdivision.

(iii) *Allocation of deficit.*—If one or more foreign corporations (whether or not a controlled foreign corporation) includible in a chain of foreign corporations has a deficit in earnings and profits (determined under section 964(a) and § 1.964-1) for the taxable year, the amount of deficit taken into account under section 952(d) with respect to a United States shareholder in such chain as a reduction in earnings and profits for the taxable year of a controlled foreign corporation includible in such chain shall be an amount which bears the same ratio to such shareholder's pro rata share of the total deficits in earnings and profits for the taxable year of all includible foreign corporations as his pro rata share of the earnings and profits (determined under paragraph (c) of this section but without regard to the provisions of subparagraph (1)(ii) of such paragraph) for the taxable year of such includible controlled foreign corporation bears to his pro rata share of the total earnings and profits (as so determined under paragraph (c) of this section) for the taxable year of all includible controlled foreign corporations. The amount of deficit taken into account under this subdivision with respect to any controlled foreign corporation includible in a chain of foreign corporations shall not exceed the United States shareholder's pro rata share of the controlled foreign corporation's earnings and profits for the taxable year.

(iv) *Taxable year.*—The taxable year from which a deficit is allocated under this paragraph, and the taxable year to which such deficit is allocated to reduce earnings and profits, shall be the taxable year of the foreign corporation ending with or within the taxable year of the United States shareholder described in subparagraph (1)(i) of this paragraph.

(3) *Illustration.*—The application of this paragraph may be illustrated by the following examples:

Example (1). (a) Domestic corporation M owns 100 percent, 20 percent, and 100 percent, respectively, of the only class of stock of foreign corporations A, B, and F, respectively. Corporation A owns 80 percent of the only class of stock of each of foreign corporations B and C, respectively. Corporation F owns 20 percent of such stock of C Corporation. Corporation B owns 75 percent of the only class of stock of foreign corporation D, and 50 percent of the only class of stock of each of foreign corporations G and H, respectively. C Corporation owns 75 percent of the only class of stock of foreign corporation E. All the corporations use the calendar year as a taxable year, and all of the foreign corporations, except corporations G and H, are controlled foreign corporations throughout the period here involved.

(b) The subpart F income, and the earnings and profits (determined under paragraph (c) of this section but without regard to subparagraph (1)(ii) of such paragraph) or deficit in earnings and profits (determined under section 964(a) and § 1.964-1), of each of the foreign corporations for 1963 are as follows, the deficits being set forth in parentheses:

	Subpart F income	Earnings and profits (deficits)
A Corporation	$6,000	$18,000
B Corporation	...	(7,500)
C Corporation	...	(2,500)
D Corporation	4,000	5,000
E Corporation	12,000	15,000
F Corporation	8,000	20,250
G Corporation	...	(10,000)
H Corporation	...	7,000

(c) The chains of foreign corporations (within the meaning of subparagraph (2)(ii) of this paragraph) for 1963 are the "A" chain, consisting of corporations A, B, C, D, E, G, and H, but only to the extent of M Corporation's stock interest in such corporations under section 958(a) by reason of its ownership of stock in A Corporation; the "B" chain, consisting of corporations B, D, G, and H, but only to the extent of M Corporation's stock interest in such corporations under section 958(a) by reason of its ownership of stock in B Corporation; and the "F" chain, consisting of corporations F, C, and E, but only to the extent of M Corporation's stock interest in such corporations under section 958(a) by reason of its ownership of stock in F Corporation.

(d) Corporation M's stock interest under section 958(a) in each of the chains of foreign corporations is as follows for 1963:

	A %	B %	C %	D %	E %	F %	G %	H %
A chain:								
Direct interest	100							
(100% × 80%)		80						
(100% × 80%)			80					
(80% × 75%)				60				
(80% × 75%)					60			
(80% × 50%)							40	
(80% × 50%)								40
B chain:								
Direct interest		20						
(20% × 75%)				15				
(20% × 50%)							10	
(20% × 50%)								10

	A %	B %	C %	D %	E %	F %	G %	H %
F chain:								
Direct interest						100		
(100% × 20%)			20					
(20% × 75%)					15			
Total interests	100	100	100	75	75	100	50	50

(e) Corporation M's pro rata share of the earnings and profits (determined under paragraph (c) of this section but without regard to subparagraph (1)(ii) of such paragraph), or of the deficit, of each controlled foreign corporation or each foreign corporation, respectively, includible in the respective chains for 1963 is as follows:

	Earnings and profits	Deficit
A chain:		
A Corporation (100%)	$18,000	...
B Corporation (80%)	...	($6,000)
C Corporation (80%)	...	(2,000)
D Corporation (60%)	3,000	...
E Corporation (60%)	9,000	...
G Corporation (40%)	...	(4,000)
H Corporation (40%)	*	...
Total	$30,000	($12,000)
B chain:		
B Corporation (20%)	...	($1,500)
D Corporation (15%)	$750	...
G Corporation (10%)	...	(1,000)
H Corporation (10%)	*	...
Total	$750	($2,500)
F chain:		
F Corporation (100%)	$20,250	...
C Corporation (20%)	...	($500)
E Corporation (15%)	2,250	...
Total	$22,500	($500)

* The earnings and profits of H Corporation are not included in the total earnings and profits for the chain because H Corporation is not a controlled foreign corporation.

(f) The amount by which M Corporation's pro rata share of the earnings and profits for 1963 of the controlled foreign corporations in each respective chain shall be reduced under section 952(d) by M Corporation's pro rata share of the deficits of corporations B, C, and G for 1963 is determined as follows:

			Amount of reduction
A chain:			
A Corporation ($12,000 × $18,000/$30,000)			$7,200
D Corporation ($12,000 × $3,000/$30,000)			1,200
E Corporation ($12,000 × $9,000/$30,000)			3,600
Total			$12,000
B chain:			
D Corporation ($2,500 × $750/$750)		$2,500	
Limitation: M Corporation's pro rata share of D Corporation's earnings and profits		750	
Allocation of used deficit ($750) to M Corporation's pro rata share of the deficits of corporations B and G:			
B Corporation ($750 × ($1,500/$2,500))	$ 450		
G Corporation ($750 × ($1,000/$2,500))	300		
Total	$ 750		$ 750
F chain:			
F Corporation ($500 × $20,250/$22,500)			$ 450
E Corporation ($500 × $2,250/$22,500)			50
Total			$ 500

(g) Corporation M's pro rata share of the earnings and profits (determined after reduction for deficits under section 952(d)) for 1963 of each controlled foreign corporation in the respective chains, determined on a chain-by-chain basis, is determined as follows:

	Earnings and profits before reduction	Reduction (sec. 952(d))	Reduced earnings and profits
A chain:			
A Corporation	$18,000	$7,200	$10,800
D Corporation	3,000	1,200	1,800
E Corporation	9,000	3,600	5,400
B chain:			
D Corporation	750	750	......
F chain:			
F Corporation	20,250	450	19,800
E Corporation	2,250	50	2,200

(h) Corporation M's pro rata share of each controlled foreign corporation's subpart F income, limited as provided by section 952(c) and paragraph (c) of this section, for 1963 which is includible in its gross income for such year under section 951(a)(1)(A)(i) and § 1.951-1 is determined as follows:

	Subpart F income (before limitation)	*Earnings and profits (sec. 952(c))*	*Amount includible in income*
A Corporation (100%)	$6,000	$10,800	$6,000
D Corporation (75%)	3,000	1,800	1,800
E Corporation (75%)	9,000	7,600	7,600
F Corporation (100%)	8,000	19,800	8,000
Total includible under section 951(a)(1)(A)(i)			$23,400

Example (2). The facts are the same as in example (1) except that, in addition, for 1964, foreign corporations C, D, and E have no subpart F income and no earnings and profits and foreign corporations G and H have no earnings and profits. For 1964, B Corporation has subpart F income of $1,000 and earnings and profits (determined in accordance with section 964(a) and § 1.964-1) of $1,500; A Corporation has subpart F income of $800 and earnings and profits of $1,000; and F Corporation has subpart F income of $500 and earnings and profits of $1,000. Such earnings and profits are determined without regard to distributions for 1964. Corporation B has an unused deficit in earnings and profits of $1,050 for 1963 ($1,500 minus $450) applicable to M Corporation's interest in such corporation (paragraph (f) of example (1)), and, under paragraph (c)(1)(i)(*a*) of this section, with respect to M Corporation, such deficit reduces B Corporation's earnings and profits for 1964 to $450. Inasmuch as G Corporation is not a controlled foreign corporation for 1964, such corporation's unused deficit in earnings and profits of $700 for 1963 ($1,000 minus $300) applicable to M Corporation's interest in such corporation (paragraph (f) of example (1)) may be used under paragraph (c)(1)(i)(*a*) of this section to reduce M Corporation's interest in G Corporation's earnings and profits in a later year or years for which G Corporation is a controlled foreign corporation. Corporation M's pro rata share of each controlled foreign corporation's subpart F income, limited as provided by section 952(c) and paragraph (c) of this section, for 1964 which is includible in its gross income for such year under section 951(a)(1)(A)(i) and § 1.951-1 is determined as follows:

	Subpart F income (before limitation)	*Earnings and profits (sec. 952(c))*	*Amount includible in income*
A Corporation	$800	$1,000	$800
B Corporation	1,000	450	450
F Corporation	500	1,000	500

Example (3). The facts are the same as in example (2), except that for 1964 B Corporation has subpart F income of $550 and earnings and profits (determined in accordance with section 964(a) and § 1.964-1) of $550; such earnings and profits are determined without regard to distributions for 1964. Under paragraph (c)(1)(i)(*a*) of this section, B Corporation's unused deficit of $1,050 for 1963 reduces its earnings and profits for 1964 with respect to M Corporation to zero. The remaining $500 of the unused deficit for 1963 applicable to M Corporation's interest in B Corporation may be used under paragraph (c)(1)(i)(*a*) of this section in later years to reduce M Corporation's interest in B Corporation's earnings and profits.

(e) *Application of current earnings and profits limitation.*—(1) *In general.*—If the subpart F income (as defined in section 952(a)) of a controlled foreign corporation exceeds the foreign corporation's earnings and profits for the taxable year, the subpart F income includible in the income of the corporation's United States shareholders is reduced under section 952(c)(1)(A) in accordance with the following rules. The excess of subpart F income over current year earnings and profits shall—

(i) First, proportionately reduce subpart F income in each separate category of the controlled foreign corporation, as defined in § 1.904-5(a)(4)(v), in which current earnings and profits are zero or less than zero;

(ii) Second, proportionately reduce subpart F income in each separate category in which subpart F income exceeds current earnings and profits; and

(iii) Third, proportionately reduce subpart F income in other separate categories.

(2) *Allocation to a category of subpart F income.*—An excess amount that is allocated under paragraph (e)(1) of this section to a separate category must be further allocated to a category of subpart F income if the separate category contains more than one category of subpart F income described in section 952(a) or, in the case of foreign base company income, described in § 1.954-1(c)(1)(iii)(A)(*1*) or (2). In such case, the excess amount that is allocated to the separate category must be allocated to the various categories of subpart F income within that separate category on a proportionate basis.

(3) *Recapture of subpart F income reduced by operation of earnings and profits limitation.*—Any amount in a category of subpart F income described in section 952(a) or, in the case of foreign base company income, described in § 1.954-1(c)(1)(iii)(A)(*1*) or (2) that is reduced by operation of the current year earnings and profits limitation of section 952(c)(1)(A) and this paragraph (e) shall be subject to recapture in a subsequent year under the rules of section 952(c)(2) and paragraph (f) of this section.

(4) *Coordination with sections 953 and 954.*—The rules of this paragraph (e) shall be applied after the application of sections 953 and 954 and the regulations under those sections, except as provided in § 1.954-1(d)(4)(ii).

(5) *Earnings and deficits retain separate limitation character.*—The income reduction rules of paragraph (e)(1) of this section shall apply only for purposes of determining the amount of an inclusion under section 951(a)(1)(A) from each separate category as defined in § 1.904-5(a)(4)(v) and the separate categories in which recapture accounts are established under section 952(c)(2) and paragraph (f) of this section. For rules applicable in computing post-1986 undistributed earnings, see generally section 902 and the regulations under that section. For rules relating to the allocation of deficits for purposes of computing foreign taxes deemed paid under section 960 with respect to an inclusion under section 951(a)(1)(A), see § 1.960-1(i).

(f) *Recapture of subpart F income in subsequent taxable year.*—(1) *In general.*—If a controlled foreign corporation's subpart F income for a taxable year is reduced under the current year earnings and profits limitation of section 952(c)(1)(A) and paragraph (e) of this section, recapture accounts will be established and subject to recharacterization in any subsequent taxable year to the extent the recapture accounts were not previously recharacterized or distributed, as provided in paragraphs (f)(2) and (3) of this section.

(2) *Rules of recapture.*—(i) *Recapture account.*—If a category of subpart F income described in section 952(a) or, in the case of foreign base company income, described in § 1.954-1(c)(1)(iii)(A)(*1*) or (*2*) is reduced under the current year earnings and profits limitation of section 952(c)(1)(A) and paragraph (e) of this section for a taxable year, the amount of such reduction shall constitute a recapture account.

(ii) *Recapture.*—Each recapture account of the controlled foreign corporation will be recharacterized, on a proportionate basis, as subpart F income in the same separate category (as defined in § 1.904-5(a)(4)(v)) as the recapture account to the extent that current year earnings and profits exceed subpart F income in a taxable year. The United States shareholder must include his pro rata share (determined under the rules of § 1.951-1(e)) of each recharacterized amount in income as subpart F income in such separate category for the taxable year.

(iii) *Reduction of recapture account and corresponding earnings.*—Each recapture account, and post-1986 undistributed earnings in the separate category containing the recapture account, will be reduced in any taxable year by the amount which is recharacterized under paragraph (f)(2)(ii) of this section. In addition, each recapture account, and post-1986 undistributed earnings in the separate category containing the recapture account, will be reduced in the amount of any distribution out of that account (as determined under the ordering rules of section 959(c) and paragraph (f)(3)(ii) of this section).

(3) *Distribution ordering rules.*—(i) *Coordination of recapture and distribution rules.*—If a controlled foreign corporation distributes an amount out of earnings and profits described in section 959(c)(3) in a year in which current year earnings and profits exceed subpart F income and there is an amount in a recapture account for such year, the recapture rules will apply first.

(ii) *Distributions reduce recapture accounts first.*—Any distribution made by a controlled foreign corporation out of earnings and profits described in section 959(c)(3) shall be treated as made first on a proportionate basis out of the recapture accounts in each separate category to the extent thereof (even if the amount in the recapture account exceeds post-1986 undistributed earnings in the separate category containing the recapture account). Any remaining distribution shall be treated as made on a proportionate basis out of the remaining earnings and profits of the controlled foreign corporation in each separate category. See section 904(d)(3)(D).

(4) *Examples.*—The application of paragraphs (e) and (f) of this section may be illustrated by the following examples:

Example 1. (i) A, a U.S. person, is the sole shareholder of CFC, a controlled foreign corporation formed on January 1, 1998, whose functional currency is the u. In 1998, CFC earns 100u of foreign base company sales income that is general limitation income described in section 904(d)(1)(I) and incurs a (200u) loss attributable to activities that would have produced general limitation income that is not subpart F income. In 1998 CFC also earns 100u of foreign personal holding company income that is passive income described in section 904(d)(1)(A), and 100u of foreign personal holding company income that is dividend income subject to a separate limitation described in section 904(d)(1)(E) for dividends from a noncontrolled section 902 corporation. CFC's subpart F income for 1998, 300u, exceeds CFC's current earnings and profits, 100u, by 200u. Under section 952(c)(1)(A) and paragraph (e) of this section, subpart F income is limited to CFC's current earnings and profits of 100u, all of which is included in A's gross income under section 951(a)(1)(A). The 200u of CFC's 1998 subpart F income that is not included in A's income in 1998 by reason of section 952(c)(1)(A) is subject to recapture under section 952(c)(2) and paragraph (f) of this section.

(ii) For purposes of determining the amount and type of income included in A's gross income and the amount and type of income in CFC's recapture account, the rules of paragraphs (e)(1) and (2) of this section apply. Under paragraph (e)(1)(i) of this section, the amount by which CFC's subpart F income exceeds its earnings and profits for 1998, 200u, first reduces from 100u to 0 CFC's subpart F income in the general limitation category, which has a current year deficit of (100u) in earnings and profits. Next, under paragraph (e)(1)(iii) of this section, the remaining 100u by which CFC's 1998 subpart F income exceeds earnings and profits is applied proportionately to reduce CFC's subpart F income in the separate categories for passive income (100u) and dividends from the noncontrolled section 902 corporation (100u). Thus, A includes 50u of passive limitation/foreign personal holding company income and 50u of dividends from the noncontrolled section 902 corporation/foreign personal holding company income in gross income in 1998. CFC has 100u in its general limitation/foreign base company sales income recapture account attributable to the 100u of foreign base company sales income that is not included in A's income by reason of the earnings and profits limitation of section 952(c)(1)(A). CFC also has 50u in its passive limitation recapture account, all of which is attributable to foreign personal holding company income, and 50u in its recapture account for dividends from the noncontrolled section 902 corporation, all of which is attributable to foreign personal holding company income.

(iii) For purposes of computing post-1986 undistributed earnings, the rules of sections 902 and 960, including the rules of § 1.960-1(i), apply. Under § 1.960-1(i), the general limitation deficit of (100u) is allocated proportionately to reduce passive limitation earnings of 100u and noncontrolled section 902 dividend earnings of 100u. Thus, passive limitation earnings are reduced by 50u to 50u (100u passive limitation earnings/200u total earnings in positive separate categories x (100u) general limitation deficit = 50u reduction), and the noncontrolled section 902 corporation earnings are reduced by 50u to 50u (100u noncontrolled section 902 corporation earnings/200u total earnings in positive separate categories x (100u) general limitation deficit = 50u reduction). All of CFC's post-1986 foreign income taxes with respect to passive limitation income and dividends from the noncontrolled section 902 corporation are deemed paid by A under section 960 with respect to the subpart F inclusions (50u inclusion/50u earnings in each separate category). After the inclusion and deemed-paid taxes are computed, at the close of 1998 CFC has a (100u) deficit in general limitation earnings (100u subpart F earnings + (200u) nonsubpart F loss), 50u of passive limitation earnings (100u of earnings attributable to foreign personal holding company income – 50u inclusion) with a corresponding passive limitation/foreign personal holding company income recapture account of 50u, and 50u of earnings subject to a separate limitation for dividends from the noncontrolled section 902 corporation (100u earnings – 50u inclusion) with a corresponding noncontrolled section 902 corporation/foreign personal holding company income recapture account of 50u.

Example 2. (i) The facts are the same as in *Example 1* with the addition of the following facts. In 1999, CFC earns 100u of foreign base company sales income that is general limitation income and 100u of foreign personal holding company income that is passive limitation income. In addition, CFC incurs (10u) of expenses that are allocable to its separate limitation for dividends from the noncontrolled section 902 corporation. Thus, CFC's subpart F income for 1999, 200u, exceeds CFC's current earnings and profits, 190u, by 10u. Under section 952(c)(1)(A) and paragraph (e) of this section, subpart F income is limited to CFC's current earnings and profits of 190u, all of which is included in A's gross income under section 951(a)(1)(A).

(ii) For purposes of determining the amount and type of income included in A's gross income and the amount and type of income in CFC's recapture accounts, the rules of paragraphs (e)(1) and (2) of this section apply. While CFC's general limitation post-1986 undistributed earnings for 1999 are 0 ((100u) opening balance + 100u subpart F income), CFC's general limitation subpart F income (100u) does not exceed its general limitation current earnings and profits (100u) for 1999. Accordingly, under paragraph (e)(1)(iii) of this section, the amount by which CFC's subpart F income exceeds its earnings and profits for 1999, 10u, is applied proportionately to reduce CFC's subpart F income in the separate categories for general limitation income, 100u, and passive income, 100u. Thus, A includes 95u of general limitation foreign base company sales income and 95u of passive limitation foreign personal holding company income in gross income in 1999. At the close of 1999 CFC has 105u in its general limitation/foreign base company sales income recapture account (100u from 1998 + 5u from 1999), 55u in its passive limitation/foreign personal holding company income recapture account (50u from 1998 + 5u from 1999), and 50u in its dividends from the noncontrolled section 902 corporation/foreign personal holding company income recapture account (all from 1998).

(iii) For purposes of computing post-1986 undistributed earnings in each separate category, the rules of sections 902 and 960, including the rules of § 1.960-1(i), apply. Thus, post-1986 undistributed earnings (or an accumulated deficit) in each separate category are increased (or reduced) by current earnings and profits or current deficits in each separate category. The accumulated deficit in CFC's general limitation earnings and profits (100u) is reduced to 0 by the addition of 100u of 1999 earnings and profits. CFC's passive limitation earnings of 50u are increased by 100u to 150u, and CFC's noncontrolled section 902 corporation earnings of 50u are decreased by (10u) to 40u. After the addition of current year earnings and profits and deficits to the separate categories there are no deficits remaining in any separate category. Thus, the allocation rules of § 1.960-1(i)(4) do not apply in 1999. Accordingly, in determining the post-1986 foreign income taxes deemed paid by A, post-1986 undistributed earnings in each separate category are unaffected by earnings in the other categories. Foreign taxes deemed paid under section 960 for 1999 would be determined as follows for each separate category: with respect to the inclusion of 95u of foreign base company sales income out of general limitation earnings, the section 960 fraction is 95u inclusion/0 total earnings; with respect to the inclusion of 95u of passive limitation income the section 960 fraction is 95u inclusion/150u passive earnings. Thus, no general limitation taxes would be associated with the inclusion of the general limitation earnings because there are no accumulated earnings in the general limitation category. After the deemed-paid taxes are computed, at the close of 1999 CFC has a (95u) deficit in general limitation earnings and profits ((100u) opening balance + 100u current earnings – 95u inclusion), 55u of passive limitation earnings and profits (50u opening balance + 100u current foreign personal holding company income – 95u inclusion), and 40u of earnings and profits subject to the separate limitation for dividends from the noncontrolled section 902 corporation (50u opening balance + (10u) expense).

Example 3. (i) A, a U.S. person, is the sole shareholder of CFC, a controlled foreign corporation whose functional currency is the u. At the beginning of 1998, CFC has post-1986 undistributed earnings of

275u, all of which are general limitation earnings described in section 904(d)(1)(I). CFC has no previously-taxed earnings and profits described in section 959(c)(1) or (c)(2). In 1998, CFC has a (200u) loss in the shipping category described in section 904(d)(1)(D), 100u of foreign personal holding company income that is passive income described in section 904(d)(1)(A), and 125u of general limitation manufacturing earnings that are not subpart F income. CFC's subpart F income for 1998, 100u, exceeds CFC's current earnings and profits, 25u, by 75u. Under section 952(c)(1)(A) and paragraph (e) of this section, subpart F income is limited to CFC's current earnings and profits of 25u, all of which is included in A's gross income under section 951(a)(1)(A). The 75u of CFC's 1998 subpart F income that is not included in A's income in 1998 by reason of section 952(c)(1)(A) is subject to recapture under section 952(c)(2) and paragraph (f) of this section.

(ii) For purposes of determining the amount and type of income included in A's gross income and the amount and type of income in CFC's recapture account, the rules of paragraphs (e)(1) and (2) of this section apply. Under paragraph (e)(1) of this section, the amount of CFC's subpart F income in excess of earnings and profits for 1998, 75u, reduces the 100u of passive limitation foreign personal holding company income. Thus, A includes 25u of passive limitation foreign personal holding company income in gross income, and CFC has 75u in its passive limitation/foreign personal holding company income recapture account.

(iii) For purposes of computing post-1986 undistributed earnings in each separate category the rules of sections 902 and 960, including the rules of § 1.960-1(i), apply. Under § 1.960-1(i), the shipping limitation deficit of (200u) is allocated proportionately to reduce general limitation earnings of 400u and passive limitation earnings of 100u. Thus, general limitation earnings are reduced by 160u to 240u (400u general limitation earnings/500u total earnings in positive separate categories x (200u) shipping deficit = 160u reduction), and passive limitation earnings are reduced by 40u to 60u (100u passive earnings/500u total earnings in positive separate categories x (200u) shipping deficit = 40u reduction). Five-twelfths of CFC's post-1986 foreign income taxes with respect to passive limitation earnings are deemed paid by A under section 960 with respect to the subpart F inclusion (25u inclusion/60u passive earnings). After the inclusion and deemed-paid taxes are computed, at the close of 1998 CFC has 400u of general limitation earnings (275u opening balance + 125u current earnings), 75u of passive limitation earnings (100u of foreign personal holding company income − 25u inclusion), and a (200u) deficit in shipping limitation earnings.

Example 4. (i) The facts are the same as in *Example 3* with the addition of the following facts. In 1999, CFC earns 50u of general limitation earnings that are not subpart F income and 75u of passive limitation income that is foreign personal holding company income. Thus, CFC has 125u of current earnings and profits. CFC distributes 200u to A. Under paragraph (f)(3)(i) of this section, the recapture rules are applied first. Thus, the amount by which 1999 current earnings and profits exceed subpart F income, 50u, is recharacterized as passive limitation foreign personal holding company income. CFC's total subpart F income for 1999 is 125u of passive limitation foreign personal holding company income (75u current earnings plus 50u recapture account), and the passive limitation/foreign personal holding company income recapture account is reduced from 75u to 25u.

(ii) CFC has 150u of previously-taxed earnings and profits described in section 959(c)(2) (25u attributable to 1998 and 125u attributable to 1999), all of which is passive limitation earnings and profits. Under section 959(c), 150u of the 200u distribution is deemed to be made from earnings and profits described in section 959(c)(2). The remaining 50u is deemed to be made from earnings and profits described in section 959(c)(3). Under paragraph (f)(3)(ii) of this section, the dividend distribution is deemed to be made first out of the passive limitation recapture account to the extent thereof (25u). Under paragraph (f)(2)(iii) of this section, the passive limitation recapture account is reduced from 25u to 0. The remaining distribution of 25u is treated as made out of CFC's general limitation earnings and profits.

(iii) For purposes of computing post-1986 undistributed earnings, the rules of section 902 and 960, including the rules of § 1.960-1(i), apply. Thus, the shipping limitation accumulated deficit of (200u) reduces general limitation earnings and profits of 450u and passive limitation earnings and profits of 150u on a proportionate basis. Thus, 100% of CFC's post-1986 foreign income taxes with respect to passive limitation earnings are deemed paid by A under section 960 with respect to the 1999 subpart F inclusion of 125u (100u inclusion (numerator limited to denominator)/100u passive earnings). No post-1986 foreign income taxes remain to be deemed paid under section 902 in connection with the 25u distribution from the passive limitation/foreign personal holding company income recapture account. One-twelfth of CFC's post-1986 foreign income taxes with respect to general limitation earnings are deemed paid by A under section 902 with respect to the distribution of 25u general limitation earnings and profits described in section 959(c)(3) (25u inclusion/300u general limitation earnings). After the deemed-paid taxes are computed, at the close of 1999 CFC has 425u of general limitation earnings and profits (400u opening balance + 50u current earnings − 25u distribution), 0 of passive limitation earnings (75u recapture account + 75u current foreign personal holding company income − 125u inclusion − 25u distribution), and a (200u) deficit in shipping limitation earnings.

(5) *Effective date.*—Paragraph (e) of this section and this paragraph (f) apply to taxable years of a controlled foreign corporation beginning after March 3, 1997.

(g) *Treatment of distributive share of partnership income.*—(1) *In general.*—A controlled foreign corporation's distributive share of any item of income of a partnership is income that falls within a category of subpart F income described in section 952(a) to the extent the item of income would have been income in such category if received by the controlled foreign corporation directly. For specific rules regarding the treatment of a distributive share of partnership income under certain provisions of subpart F, see §§ 1.954-1(g), 1.954-2(a)(5), 1.954-3(a)(6), and 1.954-4(b)(2)(iii).

(2) *Example.*—The application of this paragraph (g) may be illustrated by the following example:

Example. CFC, a controlled foreign corporation, is an 80- percent partner in PRS, a foreign partnership. PRS earns $100 of interest income that is not export financing interest as defined in section 954(c)(2)(B), or qualified banking or financing income as defined in section 954(h)(3)(A), from a person unrelated to CFC. This interest income would have been foreign personal holding company income to CFC, under section 954(c), if it had received this income directly. Accordingly, CFC's distributive share of this interest income, $80, is foreign personal holding company income.

(3) *Effective date.*—This paragraph (g) applies to taxable years of a controlled foreign corporation beginning on or after July 23, 2002. [Reg. § 1.952-1.]

☐ [*T.D.* 6795, 1-28-65. *Amended by T.D.* 6892, 8-22-66; *T.D.* 7293, 11-27-73; *T.D.* 7545, 5-5-78; *T.D.* 7862, 12-16-82; *T.D.* 7893, 5-11-83; *T.D.* 7894, 5-11-83; T.D. 8331, 1-24-91; *T.D.* 8704, 12-31-96, *T.D.* 9008, 7-22-2002 *and T.D.* 9882, 12-16-2019.]

Proposed Amendments to Regulation

§ 1.952-1. Subpart F income defined.—

***

(e) ***

(4) *Coordination with sections 953 and 954.*—The rules of this paragraph (e) apply after the determination of net foreign base company income, as provided in § 1.954-1(a)(5). This paragraph (e)(4) applies to taxable years of controlled foreign corporations beginning after [the date that final regulations are filed for public inspection], and to taxable years of United States shareholders in which or with which such taxable years of foreign corporations end. For taxable years before those described in the preceding sentence, see § 1.952-1(e)(4), as contained in 26 CFR part 1 revised as of April 1, 2020.

***

(f) ***

(4) *Carryover of recapture accounts in transactions to which section 381(a) applies.*—In the case of a distribution or transfer described in section 381(a), any recapture accounts (as described in paragraph (f)(2)(i) of this section) of the distributor or transferor corporation are treated as recapture accounts of the acquiring corporation as of the close of the date of the distribution or transfer. If the acquiring corporation has recapture accounts in the same separate category (as defined in § 1.904-5(a)(4)(v) and § 1.954-1(c)(1)(iii)(*1*) or (2)), the recapture accounts of the distributor or transferor corporation are added to the recapture accounts of the acquiring corporation in such category; if not, the acquiring corporation adopts the recapture accounts of the distributor or transferor corporation in such category.

***

(6) *Effective date.*—(i) *Paragraphs (e) and (f).*—Except as provided in paragraphs (e)(4) and (f)(6)(ii) of this section, paragraph (e) of this section and this paragraph (f) apply to taxable years of a controlled foreign corporation beginning after March 3, 1997.

(ii) *Paragraph (f)(4).*—Paragraph (f)(4) of this section applies to taxable years of a corporation ending on or after July 20, 2020 (even if the distribution or transfer described in section 381(a) occurred in a taxable year ending before July 20, 2020).

* * *

[Prop. Reg. § 1.952-1.]

[Proposed 7-23-2020.]

§ 1.952-2. Determination of gross income and taxable income of a foreign corporation.—(a) *Determination of gross income.*—(1) *In general.*—Except as provided in subparagraph (2) of this paragraph, the gross income of a foreign corporation for any taxable year shall, subject to the special rules of paragraph (c) of this section, be determined by treating such foreign corporation as a domestic corporation taxable under section 11 and by applying the principles of section 61 and the regulations thereunder.

(2) *Insurance gross income.*—(i) *Life insurance gross income.*—The gross income for any taxable year of a controlled foreign corporation which is engaged in the business of reinsuring or issuing insurance or annuity contracts and which, if it were a domestic corporation engaged only in such business, would be taxable as a life insurance company to which part I (sections 801 through 820) of subchapter L of chapter 1 of the Code applies, shall, subject to the special rules of paragraph (c) of this section, be the sum of—

(*a*) The gross investment income, as defined under section 804(b), except that interest which is excluded from gross income under section 103 shall not be taken into account;

(*b*) The sum of the items taken into account under section 809(c), except that advance premiums shall not be taken into account; and

(*c*) The amount by which the net long-term capital gain exceeds the net short-term capital loss.

(ii) *Mutual and other insurance gross income.*—The gross income for any taxable year of a controlled foreign corporation which is engaged in the business of reinsuring or issuing insurance or annuity contracts and which, if it were a domestic corporation engaged only in such business, would be taxable as a mutual insurance company to which part II (sections 821 through 826) of subchapter L of chapter 1 of the Code applies or as a mutual marine insurance or other insurance company to which part III (sections 831 and 832) of subchapter L of chapter 1 of the Code applies, shall, subject to the special rules of paragraph (c) of this section, be—

(*a*) The sum of—

(*1*) The gross income, as defined in section 832(b)(1);

(*2*) The amount of losses incurred, as defined in section 832(b)(5); and

(*3*) The amount of expenses incurred, as defined in section 832(b)(6); reduced by

(*b*) The amount of interest which under section 103 is excluded from gross income.

(b) *Determination of taxable income.*—(1) *In general.*—Except as provided in subparagraph (2) of this paragraph, the taxable income of a foreign corporation for any taxable year shall, subject to the special rules of paragraph (c) of this section, be determined by treating such foreign corporation as a domestic corporation taxable under section 11 and by applying the principles of section 63.

(2) *Insurance taxable income.*—The taxable income for any taxable year of a controlled foreign corporation which is engaged in the business of reinsuring or issuing insurance or annuity contracts and which, if it were a domestic corporation engaged only in such business, would be taxable as an insurance company to which subchapter L of chapter 1 of the Code applies shall, subject to the special rules of paragraph (c) of this section, be determined by treating such corporation as a domestic corporation taxable under subchapter L of chapter 1 of the Code and by applying the principles of §§ 1.953-4 and 1.953-5 for determining taxable income.

(c) *Special rules for purposes of this section.*—(1) *Nonapplication of certain provisions.*—Except where otherwise distinctly expressed, the provisions of subchapters F, G, H, L, M, N, S, and T of chapter 1 of the Internal Revenue Code shall not apply and, for taxable years of a controlled foreign corporation beginning after March 3, 1997, the provisions of section 103 of the Internal Revenue Code shall not apply.

(2) *Application of principles of § 1.964-1.*—The determinations with respect to a foreign corporation shall be made as follows:

(i) *Books of account.*—The books of account to be used shall be those regularly maintained by the corporation for the purpose of accounting to its shareholders.

(ii) *Accounting principles.*—Except as provided in subparagraphs (3) and (4) of this paragraph, the accounting principles to be employed are those described in paragraph (b) of § 1.964-1. Thus, in applying accounting principles generally accepted in the United States for purposes of reflecting in the financial statements of a domestic corporation the operations of foreign affiliates, no adjustment need be made unless such adjustment will have a material effect, within the meaning of paragraph (a) of § 1.964-1.

(iii) *Translation into United States dollars.*—(*a*) *In general.*—Except as provided in (*b*) of this subdivision, the amounts determined in accordance with subdivision (ii) of this subparagraph shall be translated into United States dollars in accordance with the principles of paragraph (d) of § 1.964-1.

(*b*) *Special rule.*—In any case in which the value of the foreign currency in relation to the United States dollar fluctuates more than 10 percent during any translation period (within the meaning of paragraph (d)(6) of § 1.964-1), the subpart F income and non-subpart F income shall be separately translated as if each constituted all the income of the controlled foreign corporation for the translation period.

(iv) *Tax accounting methods.*—The tax accounting methods to be employed as those established or adopted by or on behalf of the foreign corporation under paragraph (c) of § 1.964-1. Thus, such accounting methods must be consistent with the manner of treating inventories, depreciation, and elections referred to in subdivisions (ii), (iii), and (iv) of paragraph (c)(1) of § 1.964-1 and used for purposes of such paragraph; however, if, in accordance with paragraph (c)(6) of § 1.964-1, a foreign corporation receives foreign base company income before any elections are made or before an accounting method is adopted by or on behalf of such corporation under paragraph (c)(3) of § 1.964-1, the determinations of whether an exclusion set forth in section 954(b) applies shall be made as if no elections had been made and no accounting method had been adopted.

(v) *Exchange gain or loss.*—(*a*) Exchange gain or loss, determined in accordance with the principles of § 1.964-1(e), shall be taken into account for purposes of determining gross income and taxable income.

(*b*) Exchange gain or loss shall be treated as foreign base company shipping income (or as a deduction allocable thereto) to the extent that it is attributable to foreign base company shipping operations. The extent to which exchange gain or loss is attributable to foreign base company shipping operations may be determined under any reasonable method which is consistently applied from year to year. For example, the extent to which the exchange gain or loss is attributable to foreign base company shipping operations may be determined on the basis of the ratio which the foreign base company shipping income of the corporation for the taxable year bears to its total gross income for the taxable year, such ratio to be determined without regard to this subdivision (v).

(*c*) The remainder of the exchange gain or loss shall be allocated between subpart F income and non-subpart F income under any reasonable method which is consistently applied from year to year. For example, such remainder may be allocated to subpart F income in the same ratio that the gross subpart F income (exclusive of foreign base company shipping income) of the corporation for the taxable year bears to its total gross income (exclusive of foreign base company shipping income) for the taxable year, such ratio to be determined without regard to this subdivision (v).

(3) *Necessity for recognition of gain or loss.*—Gross income of a foreign corporation (including an insurance company) includes gain or loss only if such gain or loss would be recognized under the provisions of the Internal Revenue Code if the foreign corporation were a domestic corporation taxable under section 11 (subject to the modifications of subparagraph (1) of this paragraph). See section 1002. However, a foreign corporation shall not be treated as a domes-

tic corporation for purposes of determining whether section 367 applies.

(4) *Gross income and gross receipts.*—The term "gross income" may not have the same meaning as the term "gross receipts". For example, in a manufacturing, merchandising, or mining business, gross income means the total sales less the cost of goods sold, plus any income from investments and from incidental or outside operations or sources.

(5) *Treatment of capital loss and net operating loss.*—In determining taxable income of a foreign corporation for any taxable year—

(i) *Capital loss carryback and carryover.*—The capital loss carryback and carryover provided by section 1212(a) shall not be allowed.

(ii) *Net operating loss deduction.*—The net operating loss deduction under section 172(a) or the operations loss deduction under section 812 shall not be allowed.

(6) *Corporations which have insurance income.*—For purposes of paragraphs (a)(2) and (b)(2) of this section, in determining whether a controlled foreign corporation which is engaged in the business of reinsuring or issuing insurance or annuity contracts and which, if it were a domestic corporation engaged only in such business, would be taxable as an insurance company to which subchapter L of chapter 1 of the Code applies, it is immaterial that—

(i) The corporation would be exempt from taxation as an organization described in section 501(a),

(ii) The corporation would not be taxable as an insurance company to which subchapter L of the Code applies, or

(iii) The corporation would be subject to the alternative tax for small mutual insurance companies provided by section 821(c). [Reg. § 1.952-2.]

□ [*T.D. 6795, 1-28-65. Amended by T.D. 7893, 5-11-83; T.D. 7894, 5-11-83 and T.D. 8704, 12-31-96.*]

§ 1.954-0. Introduction.—(a) *Effective dates.*—(1) *Final regulations.*—(i) *In general.*—Except as otherwise specifically provided, the provisions of §§ 1.954-1 and 1.954-2 apply to taxable years of a controlled foreign corporation beginning after November 6, 1995. If any of the rules described in §§ 1.954-1 and 1.954-2 are inconsistent with provisions of other regulations under subpart F, these final regulations are intended to apply instead of such other regulations.

(ii) *Election to apply final regulations retroactively.*—(A) *Scope of election.*—An election may be made to apply the final regulations retroactively with respect to any taxable year of the controlled foreign corporation beginning on or after January 1, 1987. If such an election is made, these final regulations must be applied in their entirety for such taxable year and all subsequent taxable years. All references to section 11 in the final regulations shall be deemed to include section 15, where applicable.

(B) *Manner of making election.*—An election under this paragraph (a)(1)(ii) is binding on all United States shareholders of the controlled foreign corporation and must be made—

(*1*) By the controlling United States shareholders, as defined in § 1.964-1(c)(5), by attaching a statement to such effect with their original or amended income tax returns for the taxable year of such United States shareholders in which or with which the taxable year of the CFC ends, and including any additional information required by applicable administrative pronouncements, or

(*2*) In such other manner as may be prescribed in applicable administrative pronouncements.

(C) *Time for making election.*—An election may be made under this paragraph (a)(1)(ii) with respect to a taxable year of the controlled foreign corporation beginning on or after January 1, 1987 only if the time for filing a return or claim for refund has not expired for the taxable year of any United States shareholder of the controlled foreign corporation in which or with which such taxable year of the controlled foreign corporation ends.

(D) *Revocation of election.*—An election made under this paragraph (a)(1)(ii) may not be revoked.

(2) *Temporary regulations.*—The provisions of §§ 4.954-1 and 4.954-2 of this chapter apply to taxable years of a controlled foreign corporation beginning after December 31, 1986 and on or before November 6, 1995. However, the provisions of § 4.954-2(b)(6) of this chapter continue to apply. For transactions entered into on or before October 9, 1995, taxpayers may rely on Notice 89-90, 1989-2 C.B. 407, in applying the temporary regulations.

(3) *§§ 1.954A-1 and 1.954A-2.*—The provisions of §§ 1.954A-1 and 1.954A-2 (as contained in 26 CFR part 1 edition revised April 1, 1995) apply to taxable years of a controlled foreign corporation beginning before January 1, 1987. All references therein to sections of the Code are to the Internal Revenue Code of 1954 prior to the amendments made by the Tax Reform Act of 1986.

* * *

[Reg. § 1.954-0.]

□ [*T.D. 8618, 9-6-95. Amended by T.D. 8767, 3-23-98; T.D. 9039, 1-30-2003; T.D. 9883, 11-18-2019 and T.D. 9902, 7-20-2020.*]

§ 1.954-1. Foreign base company income.—(a) *In general.*—(1) *Purpose and scope.*—Section 954 and §§ 1.954-1 and 1.954-2 provide rules for computing the foreign base company income of a controlled foreign corporation. Foreign base company income is included in the subpart F income of a controlled foreign corporation under the rules of section 952. Subpart F income is included in the gross income of a United States shareholder of a controlled foreign corporation under the rules of section 951 and thus is subject to current taxation under section 1, 11 or 55 of the Internal Revenue Code. The determination of whether a foreign corporation is a controlled foreign corporation, the subpart F income of which is included currently in the gross income of its United States shareholders, is made under the rules of section 957.

(2) *Gross foreign base company income.*—The gross foreign base company income of a controlled foreign corporation consists of the following categories of gross income (determined after the application of section 952(b))—

(i) Foreign personal holding company income, as defined in section 954(c);

(ii) Foreign base company sales income, as defined in section 954(d);

(iii) Foreign base company services income, as defined in section 954(e);

(iv) Foreign base company shipping income, as defined in section 954(f); and

(v) Foreign base company oil related income, as defined in section 954(g).

(3) *Adjusted gross foreign base company income.*—The term *adjusted gross foreign base company income* means the gross foreign base company income of a controlled foreign corporation as adjusted by the de minimis and full inclusion rules of paragraph (b) of this section.

(4) *Net foreign base company income.*—The term *net foreign base company income* means the adjusted gross foreign base company income of a controlled foreign corporation reduced so as to take account of deductions (including taxes) properly allocable or apportionable to such income under the rules of section 954(b)(5) and paragraph (c) of this section.

(5) *Adjusted net foreign base company income.*—The term *adjusted net foreign base company income* means the net foreign base company income of a controlled foreign corporation reduced, first, by any items of net foreign base company income excluded from subpart F income pursuant to section 952(c) and, second, by any items excluded from subpart F income pursuant to the high tax exception of section 954(b). See paragraph (d)(4)(ii) of this section. The term *foreign base company income* as used in the Internal Revenue Code and elsewhere in the Income Tax Regulations means adjusted net foreign base company income, unless otherwise provided.

(6) *Insurance income.*—The term *gross insurance income* includes all gross income taken into account in determining insurance income under section 953. The term *adjusted gross insurance income* means gross insurance income as adjusted by the de minimis and full inclusion rules of paragraph (b) of this section. The term *net insurance income* means adjusted gross insurance income reduced under section 953 so as to take into account deductions (including taxes) properly allocable or apportionable to such income. The term *adjusted net insurance income* means net insurance income reduced by any items of net insurance income that are excluded from subpart F income pursuant to section 952(b) or pursuant to the high tax exception of section 954(b). The term *insurance income* as used in subpart F of the

Internal Revenue Code and in the regulations under that subpart means adjusted net insurance income, unless otherwise provided.

(7) *Additional items of adjusted net foreign base company income or adjusted net insurance income by reason of section 952(c).*—Earnings and profits of the controlled foreign corporation that are recharacterized as foreign base company income or insurance income under section 952(c) are items of adjusted net foreign base company income or adjusted net insurance income, respectively. Amounts subject to recharacterization under section 952(c) are determined after adjusted net foreign base company income and adjusted net insurance income are otherwise determined under subpart F and are not again subject to any exceptions or special rules that would affect the amount of subpart F income. Thus, for example, items of gross foreign base company income or gross insurance income that are excluded from adjusted gross foreign base company income or adjusted gross insurance income because the de minimis test is met are subject to recharacterization under section 952(c). Further, the de minimis and full inclusion tests of paragraph (b) of this section, and the high tax exception of paragraph (d) of this section, for example, do not apply to such amounts.

(b) *Computation of adjusted gross foreign base company income and adjusted gross insurance income.*—(1) *De minimis and full inclusion tests.*—(i) *De minimis test.*—(A) *In general.*—Except as provided in paragraph (b)(1)(i)(C) of this section, adjusted gross foreign base company income and adjusted gross insurance income are equal to zero if the sum of the gross foreign base company income and the gross insurance income of a controlled foreign corporation is less than the lesser of—

(1) 5 percent of gross income; or

(2) $1,000,000.

(B) *Currency translation.*—Controlled foreign corporations having a functional currency other than the United States dollar shall translate the $1,000,000 threshold using the exchange rate provided under section 989(b)(3) for amounts included in income under section 951(a).

(C) *Coordination with sections 864(d) and 881(c).*—Adjusted gross foreign base company income or adjusted gross insurance income of a controlled foreign corporation always includes income from trade or service receivables described in section 864(d)(1) or (6), and portfolio interest described in section 881(c), even if the de minimis test of this paragraph (b)(1)(i) is otherwise satisfied.

(ii) *Seventy percent full inclusion test.*—Except as provided in section 953, adjusted gross foreign base company income consists of all gross income of the controlled foreign corporation other than gross insurance income and amounts described in section 952(b), and adjusted gross insurance income consists of all gross insurance income other than amounts described in section 952(b), if the sum of the gross foreign base company income and the gross insurance income for the taxable year exceeds 70 percent of gross income. See paragraph (d)(6) of this section, under which certain items of full inclusion foreign base company income may nevertheless be excluded from subpart F income.

(2) *Character of gross income included in adjusted gross foreign base company income.*—The gross income included in the adjusted gross foreign base company income of a controlled foreign corporation generally retains its character as foreign personal holding company income, foreign base company sales income, foreign base company services income, foreign base company shipping income, or foreign base company oil related income. However, gross income included in adjusted gross foreign base company income because the full inclusion test of paragraph (b)(1)(ii) of this section is met is termed *full inclusion foreign base company income,* and constitutes a separate category of adjusted gross foreign base company income for purposes of allocating and apportioning deductions under paragraph (c) of this section.

(3) *Coordination with section 952(c).*—Income that is included in subpart F income because the full inclusion test of paragraph (b)(1)(ii) of this section is met does not reduce amounts that, under section 952(c), are subject to recharacterization.

(4) *Anti-abuse rule.*—(i) *In general.*—For purposes of applying the de minimis test of paragraph (b)(1)(i) of this section, the income of two or more controlled foreign corporations shall be aggregated and treated as the income of a single corporation if a principal purpose for separately organizing, acquiring, or maintaining such multiple corporations is to prevent income from being treated as foreign base company income or insurance income under the de minimis test. A purpose may be a principal purpose even though it is outweighed by other purposes (taken together or separately).

(ii) *Presumption.*—Two or more controlled foreign corporations are presumed to have been organized, acquired or maintained to prevent income from being treated as foreign base company income or insurance income under the de minimis test of paragraph (b)(1)(i) of this section if the corporations are related persons, as defined in paragraph (b)(4)(iii) of this section, and the corporations are described in paragraph (b)(4)(ii)(A), (B), or (C) of this section. This presumption may be rebutted by proof to the contrary.

(A) The activities carried on by the controlled foreign corporations, or the assets used in those activities, are substantially the same activities that were previously carried on, or assets that were previously held, by a single controlled foreign corporation. Further, the United States shareholders of the controlled foreign corporations or related persons (as determined under paragraph (b)(4)(iii) of this section) are substantially the same as the United States shareholders of the one controlled foreign corporation in a prior taxable year. A presumption made in connection with the requirements of this paragraph (b)(4)(ii)(A) may be rebutted by proof that the activities carried on by each controlled foreign corporation would constitute a separate branch under the principles of § 1.367(a)-6T(g)(2) if carried on directly by a United States person.

(B) The controlled foreign corporations carry on a business, financial operation, or venture as partners directly or indirectly in a partnership (as defined in section 7701(a)(2) and § 301.7701-3 of this chapter) that is a related person (as defined in paragraph (b)(4)(iii) of this section) with respect to each such controlled foreign corporation.

(C) The activities carried on by the controlled foreign corporations would constitute a single branch operation under § 1.367(a)-6T(g)(2) if carried on directly by a United States person.

(iii) *Related persons.*—For purposes of this paragraph (b), two or more persons are related persons if they are in a relationship described in section 267(b). In determining for purposes of this paragraph (b) whether two or more corporations are members of the same controlled group under section 267(b)(3), a person is considered to own stock owned directly by such person, stock owned with the application of section 1563(e)(1), and stock owned with the application of section 267(c). In determining for purposes of this paragraph (b) whether a corporation is related to a partnership under section 267(b)(10), a person is considered to own the partnership interest owned directly by such person and the partnership interest owned with the application of section 267(e)(3).

(iv) *Example.*—The following example illustrates the application of this paragraph (b)(4).

Example. (i)(1) *USP* is the sole United States shareholder of three controlled foreign corporations: *CFC1, CFC2* and *CFC3.* The three controlled foreign corporations all have the same taxable year. The three controlled foreign corporations are partners in *FP,* a foreign entity classified as a partnership under section 7701(a)(2) and § 301.7701-3 of the regulations. For their current taxable years, each of the controlled foreign corporations derives all of its income other than foreign base company income from activities conducted through *FP,* and its foreign base company income from activities conducted both jointly through *FP* and separately without *FP.* Based on the facts in the table below, the foreign base company income derived by each controlled foreign corporation for its current taxable year, including income derived from *FP,* is less than five percent of the gross income of each controlled foreign corporation and is less than $1,000,000:

	CFC1	*CFC2*	*CFC3*
Gross income	$4,000,000	$8,000,000	$12,000,000
Five percent of gross income	200,000	400,000	600,000
Foreign base company income	199,000	398,000	597,000

(2) Thus, without the application of the anti-abuse rule of this paragraph (b)(4), each controlled foreign corporation would be treated as having no foreign base company income after the applica-

tion of the de minimis test of section 954(b)(3)(A) and paragraph (b)(1)(i) of this section.

(ii) However, under these facts, the requirements of paragraph (b)(4)(i) of this section are met unless the presumption of paragraph (b)(4)(ii) of this section is successfully rebutted. The sum of the foreign base company income of the controlled foreign corporations is $1,194,000. Thus, the amount of gross foreign base company income of each controlled foreign corporation will not be reduced by reason of the de minimis rule of section 954(b)(3)(A) and this paragraph (b).

(c) *Computation of net foreign base company income.*—(1) *General rule.*—The net foreign base company income of a controlled foreign corporation (as defined in paragraph (a)(4) of this section) is computed under the rules of this paragraph (c)(1). The principles of § 1.904-5(k) shall apply where payments are made between controlled foreign corporations that are related persons (within the meaning of section 954(d)(3)). Consistent with these principles, only payments described in § 1.954-2(b)(4)(ii)(B)(2) may be offset as provided in § 1.904-5(k)(2).

(i) *Deductions against gross foreign base company income.*—The net foreign base company income of a controlled foreign corporation is computed first by taking into account deductions in the following manner:

(A) First, the gross amount of each item of income described in paragraph (c)(1)(iii) of this section is determined.

(B) Second, any expenses definitely related to less than all gross income as a class shall be allocated and apportioned under the principles of sections 861, 864 and 904(d) to the gross income described in paragraph (c)(1)(i)(A) of this section.

(C) Third, foreign personal holding company income that is passive within the meaning of section 904 (determined before the application of the high-taxed income rule of § 1.904-4(c)) is reduced (but not below zero) by related person interest expense allocable to passive income under § 1.904-5(c)(2); such interest must be further allocated and apportioned to items described in paragraph (c)(1)(iii)(B) of this section.

(D) Fourth, the amount of each item of income described in paragraph (c)(1)(iii) of this section is reduced by other expenses allocable and apportionable to such income under the principles of sections 861, 864 and 904(d).

(ii) *Losses reduce subpart F income by operation of earnings and profits limitation.*—Except as otherwise provided in § 1.954-2(g)(4), if after applying the rules of paragraph (c)(1)(i) of this section, the amount remaining in any category of foreign base company income or foreign personal holding company income is less than zero, the loss in that category may not reduce any other category of foreign base company income or foreign personal holding company income except by operation of the earnings and profits limitation of section 952(c)(1).

(iii) *Items of income.*—(A) *Income other than passive foreign personal holding company income.*—A single item of income (other than foreign personal holding company income that is passive) is the aggregate amount from all transactions that falls within a single separate category (as defined in § 1.904-5(a)(4)(v)), and either—

(*1*) Falls within a single category of foreign personal holding company income as—

(*i*) Dividends, interest, rents, royalties and annuities;

(*ii*) Gain from certain property transactions;

(*iii*) Gain from commodities transactions;

(*iv*) Foreign currency gain; or

(*v*) Income equivalent to interest; or

(*2*) Falls within a single category of foreign base company income, other than foreign personal holding company income, as—

(*i*) Foreign base company sales income;

(*ii*) Foreign base company services income; or

(*iii*) [Reserved]

(*iv*) [Reserved]

(*v*) Full inclusion foreign base company income.

(*3*) For purposes of paragraph (c)(1)(iii)(A) of this section, the aggregate amount from all transactions that falls within a single separate category (as defined in § 1.904-5(a)(4)(v)) and is described in paragraph (c)(1)(iii)(A)(*1*)(*i*) of this section is a single item of income. Similarly, the aggregate amount from all transactions that falls within a single separate category (as defined in § 1.904-5(a)(4)(v)) and is described in each one of paragraphs (c)(1)(iii)(A)(*1*)(*ii*) through (c)(1)(iii)(A)(*1*)(*v*) of this section is in each case a separate single item of income. The same principles apply for transactions described in each one of paragraphs (c)(1)(iii)(A)(*2*)(*i*) through (*v*) of this section.

(B) *Passive foreign personal holding company income.*—A single item of foreign personal holding company income that is passive is an amount of income that falls within a single group of passive income under the grouping rules of § 1.904-4(c)(3), (4) and (5) and a single category of foreign personal holding company income described in paragraphs (c)(1)(iii)(A)(*1*)(*i*) through (*v*).

(iv) *Treatment of deductions or loss attributable to disqualified basis.*—For purposes of paragraph (c)(1)(i) of this section (and in the case of insurance income, paragraph (a)(6) of this section), in determining the amount of a net item of foreign base company income or insurance income, deductions or loss described in § 1.951A-2(c)(5) or (c)(6) are not allocated and apportioned to gross foreign base company income or gross insurance income.

(2) *Computation of net foreign base company income derived from same country insurance income.*—Deductions relating to foreign base company income attributable to the issuing (or reinsuring) of any insurance or annuity contract in connection with risks located in the country under the laws of which the controlled foreign corporation is created or organized shall be allocated and apportioned in accordance with the rules set forth in section 953.

(d) *Computation of adjusted net foreign base company income or adjusted net insurance income.*—(1) *Application of high tax exception.*—Adjusted net foreign base company income (or adjusted net insurance income) equals the net foreign base company income (or net insurance income) of a controlled foreign corporation, reduced by any net item of such income that qualifies for the high tax exception provided by section 954(b)(4) and this paragraph (d). Any item of income that is portfolio interest, as described in section 881(c), does not qualify for the high tax exception. See paragraph (c)(1)(iii) of this section for the definition of the term *item of income.* For rules concerning the treatment for foreign tax credit purposes of amounts excluded from subpart F under section 954(b)(4), see § 1.904-4(c). For rules concerning the application of the high-tax exception of sections 954(b)(4) and 951A(c)(2)(A)(i)(III) to tentative gross tested income items, see § 1.951A-2(c)(1)(iii), (c)(3)(ii), and (c)(7) and (8). A net item of income qualifies for the high tax exception only if—

(i) An election is made under section 954(b)(4) and paragraph (d)(5) of this section to exclude the income from the computation of subpart F income; and

(ii) It is established that the net item of income was subject to foreign income taxes at an effective rate that is greater than 90 percent of the maximum rate of tax specified in section 11 for the taxable year of the controlled foreign corporation.

(2) *Effective rate at which taxes are imposed.*—The effective rate with respect to a net item of income shall be determined separately for each controlled foreign corporation. The effective rate at which taxes are imposed on a net item of income is—

(i) The United States dollar amount of foreign income taxes paid or accrued with respect to the net item of income, determined under paragraph (d)(3) of this section; divided by

(ii) The United States dollar amount of the net item of foreign base company income or insurance income, described in paragraph (c)(1)(iii) of this section, increased by the amount of foreign income taxes referred to in paragraph (d)(2)(i) of this section.

(3) *Taxes paid or accrued with respect to an item of income.*—(i) *In general.*—The amount of foreign income taxes paid or accrued by a controlled foreign corporation with respect to a net item of income for purposes of section 954(b)(4) and this paragraph (d) is the U.S. dollar amount of the controlled foreign corporation's current year taxes (as defined in § 1.960-1(b)(4)) that are allocated and apportioned under § 1.960-1(d)(3)(ii) to the subpart F income group (as defined in § 1.960-1(d)(2)(ii)(B)) that corresponds with the net item of income.

(ii) [Reserved]

(iii) *Effect of potential and actual changes in taxes paid or accrued.*—Except as otherwise provided in this paragraph (d)(3)(iii), the amount of foreign income taxes paid or accrued with respect to a net item of income, determined in the manner provided in this paragraph (d), does not take into account any potential reduction in foreign income taxes that may occur by reason of a future distribution to shareholders of all or part of such income. However, to the extent the foreign income taxes paid or accrued by the controlled foreign corporation are reasonably certain to be returned by the foreign jurisdiction imposing such taxes to a shareholder, directly or indirectly, through any means (including, but not limited to, a refund, credit, payment, discharge of an obligation, or any other method) on a subsequent distribution to such shareholder, the foreign income taxes are not treated as paid or accrued for purposes of this paragraph (d)(3). In addition, foreign income taxes that have not been paid or accrued because they are contingent on a future distribution of earnings are not taken into account for purposes of this paragraph (d)(3). If, pursuant to section 905(c) and § 1.905-3(b)(2), a redetermination of U.S. tax liability is required to account for the effect of a foreign tax redetermination (as defined in § 1.905-3(a)), this paragraph (d) is applied in the adjusted year taking into account the adjusted amount of the redetermined foreign tax.

(4) *Special rules.*—(i) *Consistency rule.*—An election to exclude income from the computation of subpart F income for a taxable year must be made consistently with respect to all items of passive foreign personal holding company income eligible to be excluded for the taxable year. Thus, high-taxed passive foreign personal holding company income of a controlled foreign corporation must either be excluded in its entirety, or remain subject to subpart F in its entirety.

(ii) *Coordination with earnings and profits limitation.*—If the amount of income included in subpart F income for the taxable year is reduced by the earnings and profits limitation of section 952(c)(1), the amount of income that is a net item of income, within the meaning of paragraph (c)(1)(iii) of this section, is determined after the application of the rules of section 952(c)(1).

(iii) *Example.*—The following example illustrates the provisions of paragraph (d)(4)(ii) of this section. All of the taxes referred to in the following example are foreign income taxes. For simplicity, this example assumes that the amount of taxes that are taken into account as a deduction under section 954(b)(5) and the amount of the gross-up required under sections 960 and 78 are equal. Therefore, this example does not separately illustrate the deduction for taxes and gross-up.

Example. During its 1995 taxable year, CFC, a controlled foreign corporation, earns royalty income, net of taxes, of $100 that is foreign personal holding company income. CFC has no expenses associated with this royalty income. CFC pays $50 of foreign income taxes with respect to the royalty income. For 1995, CFC has current earnings and profits of $50. CFC's subpart F income, as determined prior to the application of this paragraph (d), exceeds its current earnings and profits. Thus, under paragraph (d)(4)(ii) of this section, the amount of CFC's only net item of income, the royalty income, will be limited to $50. The remaining $50 will be subject to recharacterization in a subsequent taxable year under section 952(c)(2). Because the amount of foreign income taxes paid with respect to this net item of income is $50, the effective rate of tax on the item, for purposes of this paragraph (d), is 50 percent ($50 of taxes/$50 net item + $50 of taxes). Accordingly, an election under paragraph (d)(5) of this section may be made to exclude the item of income from the computation of subpart F income.

(5) *Procedure.*—An election made under the procedure provided by this paragraph (d)(5) is binding on all United States shareholders of the controlled foreign corporation and must be made—

(i) By the controlling United States shareholders, as defined in § 1.964-1(c)(5), by attaching a statement to such effect with their original or amended income tax returns, and including any additional information required by applicable administrative pronouncements; or

(ii) In such other manner as may be prescribed in applicable administrative pronouncements.

(6) *Coordination of full inclusion and high tax exception rules.*—Notwithstanding paragraph (b)(1)(ii) of this section, full inclusion foreign base company income will be excluded from subpart F income if more than 90 percent of the adjusted gross foreign base company income and adjusted gross insurance company income of a controlled foreign corporation (determined without regard to the full inclusion test of paragraph (b)(1) of this section) is attributable to net amounts excluded from subpart F income pursuant to an election to have the high tax exception described in section 954(b)(4) and this paragraph (d) apply.

(e) *Character of income.*—(1) *Substance of the transaction.*—For purposes of section 954, income shall be characterized in accordance with the substance of the transaction, and not in accordance with the designation applied by the parties to the transaction. For example, an amount that is designated as rent by the taxpayer but actually constitutes income from the sale of property, royalties, or income from services shall not be characterized as rent but shall be characterized as income from the sale of property, royalties or income from services, as the case may be. Local law shall not be controlling in characterizing income.

(2) *Separable character.*—To the extent the definitional provisions of section 953 or 954 describe the income or gain derived from a transaction, or any portion or portions thereof, that income or gain, or portion or portions thereof, is so characterized for purposes of subpart F. Thus, a single transaction may give rise to income in more than one category of foreign base company income described in paragraph (a)(2) of this section. For example, if a controlled foreign corporation, in its business of purchasing personal property and selling it to related persons outside its country of incorporation, also performs services outside its country of incorporation with respect to the property it sells, the sales income will be treated as foreign base company sales income and the services income will be treated as foreign base company services income for purposes of these rules.

(3) *Predominant character.*—The portion of income or gain derived from a transaction that is included in the computation of foreign personal holding company income is always separately determinable and thus must always be segregated from other income and separately classified under paragraph (e)(2) of this section. However, the portion of income or gain derived from a transaction that would meet a particular definitional provision under section 954 or 953 (other than the definition of foreign personal holding company income) in unusual circumstances may not be separately determinable. If such portion is not separately determinable, it must be classified in accordance with the predominant character of the transaction. For example, if a controlled foreign corporation engineers, fabricates, and installs a fixed offshore drilling platform as part of an integrated transaction, and the portion of income that relates to services is not accounted for separately from the portion that relates to sales, and is otherwise not separately determinable, then the classification of income from the transaction shall be made in accordance with the predominant character of the arrangement.

(4) *Coordination of categories of gross foreign base company income or gross insurance income.*—(i) *In general.*—The computations of gross foreign base company income and gross insurance income are limited by the following rules:

(A) If income is foreign base company shipping income, pursuant to section 954(f), it shall not be considered insurance income or income in any other category of foreign base company income.

(B) If income is foreign base company oil related income, pursuant to section 954(g), it shall not be considered insurance income or income in any other category of foreign base company income, except as provided in paragraph (e)(4)(i)(A) of this section.

(C) If income is insurance income, pursuant to section 953, it shall not be considered income in any category of foreign base company income except as provided in paragraph (e)(4)(i)(A) or (B) of this section.

(D) If income is foreign personal holding company income, pursuant to section 954(c), it shall not be considered income in any other category of foreign base company income, other than as provided in paragraph (e)(4)(i)(A), (B) or (C) of this section.

(ii) *Income excluded from other categories of gross foreign base company income.*—Income shall not be excluded from a category of gross foreign base company income or gross insurance income under this paragraph (e)(4) by reason of being included in another category of gross foreign base company income or gross insurance income, if the income is excluded from that other category by a more specific provision of section 953 or 954. For example, income derived from a commodity transaction that is excluded from foreign personal holding company income under § 1.954-2(f) as income from a qualified active sale may be included in gross foreign base company income if it also meets the definition of foreign base company sales income. See § 1.954-2(a)(2) for the coordination of overlapping categories within the definition of foreign personal holding company income.

(f) *Definition of related person.*—(1) *Persons related to controlled foreign corporation.*—Unless otherwise provided, for purposes of section 954 and §§ 1.954-1 through 1.954-8 inclusive, the following persons are considered under section 954(d)(3) to be related persons with respect to a controlled foreign corporation:

(i) *Individuals.*—An individual, whether or not a citizen or resident of the United States, who controls the controlled foreign corporation.

(ii) *Other persons.*—A foreign or domestic corporation, partnership, trust or estate that controls or is controlled by the controlled foreign corporation, or is controlled by the same person or persons that control the controlled foreign corporation.

(2) *Control.*—(i) *Corporations.*—With respect to a corporation, control means the ownership, directly or indirectly, of stock possessing more than 50 percent of the total voting power of all classes of stock entitled to vote or of the total value of the stock of the corporation.

(ii) *Partnerships.*—With respect to a partnership, control means the ownership, directly or indirectly, of more than 50 percent (by value) of the capital or profits interest in the partnership.

(iii) *Trusts and estates.*—With respect to a trust or estate, control means the ownership, directly, or indirectly, of more than 50 percent (by value) of the beneficial interest in the trust or estate.

(iv) *Direct or indirect ownership.*—For purposes of section 954(d)(3) and this paragraph (f), to determine direct or indirect ownership—

(A) The principles of § 1.958-1 and section 958(a) apply without regard to whether a corporation, partnership, trust, or estate is foreign or domestic or whether an individual is a citizen or resident of the United States; and

(B) The principles of § 1.958-2 and section 958(b) apply, except that—

(1) Neither section 318(a)(3), nor § 1.958-2(d) or the principles thereof, applies to attribute stock or other interests to a corporation, partnership, estate, or trust; and

(2) Neither section 318(a)(4), nor § 1.958-2(e) or the principles thereof, applies to treat dividends, interest, rents, or royalties received or accrued from a foreign corporation as received or accrued from a controlled foreign corporation payor if a principal purpose of the use of an option to acquire stock or an equity interest, or an interest similar to such an option, that causes the foreign corporation to be a controlled foreign corporation payor is to qualify dividends, interest, rents, or royalties paid by the foreign corporation for the section 954(c)(6) exception. For purposes of this paragraph (f)(2)(iv)(B)(2), an interest that is similar to an option to acquire stock or an equity interest includes, but is not limited to, a warrant, a convertible debt instrument, an instrument other than debt that is convertible into stock or an equity interest, a put, a stock or equity interest subject to risk of forfeiture, and a contract to acquire or sell stock or an equity interest.

(3) Neither section 318(a)(4), nor § 1.958-2(e) or the principles thereof, applies to treat a person that has an option to acquire stock or an equity interest, or an interest similar to such an option, as owning the stock or equity interest if a principal purpose for the use of the option or similar interest is to treat a person as a related person with respect to a controlled foreign corporation under this paragraph (f). For purposes of this paragraph (f)(2)(iv)(B)(3), an interest that is similar to an option to acquire stock or an equity interest includes, but is not limited to, a warrant, a convertible debt instrument, an instrument other than debt that is convertible into stock or an equity interest, a put, a stock or equity interest subject to risk of forfeiture, and a contract to acquire or sell stock or an equity interest.

(3) *Applicability dates.*—(i) *General rule.*—Except as otherwise provided in this paragraph (f)(3), paragraph (f)(2)(iv) of this section applies to taxable years of controlled foreign corporations ending on or after November 19, 2019, and taxable years of United States shareholders in which or with which such taxable years end.

(ii) *Option rule in paragraph (f)(2)(iv)(B)(2) of this section.*—Paragraph (f)(2)(iv)(B)(2) of this section applies to taxable years of controlled foreign corporations beginning after December 31, 2006, and ending before November 19, 2019, and taxable years of United States shareholders in which or with which such taxable years end.

(iii) *Anti-abuse rule.*—Paragraphs (f)(2)(iv)(B)*(1)* and *(3)* of this section apply to taxable years of controlled foreign corporations ending on or after May 17, 2019, and to taxable years of United States shareholders in which or with which such taxable years end, with respect to amounts that are received or accrued by a controlled foreign corporation on or after May 17, 2019 to the extent the amounts are received or accrued in advance of the period to which such amounts are attributable with a principal purpose of avoiding the application of paragraph (f)(2)(iv)(B)*(1)* or *(3)* of this section with respect to such amounts.

(g) *Distributive share of partnership income.*—(1) *Application of related person and country of organization tests.*—Unless otherwise provided, to determine the extent to which a controlled foreign corporation's distributive share of any item of gross income of a partnership would have been subpart F income if received by it directly, under § 1.952-1(g), if a provision of subpart F requires a determination of whether an entity is a related person, within the meaning of section 954(d)(3), or whether an activity occurred within or outside the country under the laws of which the controlled foreign corporation is created or organized, this determination shall be made by reference to such controlled foreign corporation and not by reference to the partnership.

(2) *Application of related person test for sales and purchase transactions between a partnership and its controlled foreign corporation partner.*—For purposes of determining whether a controlled foreign corporation's distributive share of any item of gross income of a partnership is foreign base company sales income under section 954(d)(1) when the item of income is derived from the sale by the partnership of personal property purchased by the partnership from (or sold by the partnership on behalf of) the controlled foreign corporation; or the sale by the partnership of personal property to (or the purchase of personal property by the partnership on behalf of) the controlled foreign corporation (CFC-partnership transaction), the CFC-partnership transaction will be treated as a transaction with an entity that is a related person, within the meaning of section 954(d)(3), under paragraph (g)(1) of this section, if—

(i) The controlled foreign corporation purchased such personal property from (or sold it to the partnership on behalf of), or sells such personal property to (or purchases it from the partnership on behalf of), a related person with respect to the controlled foreign corporation (other than the partnership), within the meaning of section 954(d)(3); or

(ii) The branch rule of section 954(d)(2) applies to treat as foreign base company sales income the income of the controlled foreign corporation from selling to the partnership (or a third party) personal property that the controlled foreign corporation has manufactured, in the case where the partnership purchases personal property from (or sells personal property on behalf of) the controlled foreign corporation.

(3) *Examples.*—The application of this paragraph (g) is illustrated by the following examples:

Example 1. CFC, a controlled foreign corporation organized in Country A, is an 80-percent partner in Partnership, a partnership organized in Country A. All of the stock of CFC is owned by USP, a U.S. corporation. Partnership earns commission income from purchasing Product O on behalf of USP, from unrelated manufacturers in Country B, for sale in the United States. To determine whether CFC's distributive share of Partnership's commission income is foreign base company sales income under section 954(d), CFC is treated as if it purchased Product O on behalf of USP. Under section 954(d)(3), USP is a related person with respect to CFC. Thus, with respect to CFC, the sales income is deemed to be derived from the purchase of personal property on behalf of a related person. Because the property purchased is both manufactured and sold for use outside of Country A, CFC's country of organization, CFC's distributive share of the sales income is foreign base company sales income.

Example 2. (i) CFC 1, a controlled foreign corporation organized in Country A, is an 80-percent partner in Partnership, a partnership organized in Country B. CFC2, a controlled foreign corporation organized in Country B, owns the remaining 20 percent interest in Partnership. CFC1 and CFC2 are owned by a common U.S. parent, USP. CFC2 manufactures Product A in Country B. Partnership earns sales income from purchasing Product A from CFC2 and selling it to third parties located in Country B that are not related persons with respect to CFC1 or CFC2. To determine whether CFC1's distributive share of Partnership's sales income is foreign base company sales income under section 954(d), CFC1 is treated as if it purchased Product A from CFC2 and sold it to third parties in Country B. Under section 954(d)(3), CFC2 is a related person with respect to CFC1. Thus, with respect to CFC1, the sales income is deemed to be derived from the purchase of personal property from a related person. Because the property purchased is both manufactured and sold for use outside of Country A, CFC1's country of organization, CFC1's distributive share of the sales income is foreign base company sales income.

(ii) Because Product A is both manufactured and sold for use within CFC2's country of organization, CFC2's distributive share of Partnership's sales income is not foreign base company sales income.

Example 3. CFC, a controlled foreign corporation organized in Country A, is an 80 percent partner in MJK Partnership, a Country B partnership. CFC purchased goods from J Corp, a Country C corporation that is a related person with respect to CFC. CFC sold the goods to MJK Partnership. In turn, MJK Partnership sold the goods to P Corp, a Country D corporation that is unrelated to CFC. P Corp sold the goods to unrelated customers in Country D. The goods were manufactured in Country C by persons unrelated to J Corp. CFC's distributive share of the income of MJK Partnership from the sale of goods to P Corp will be treated as income from the sale of goods purchased from a related person for purposes of section 954(d)(1) because CFC purchased the goods from J Corp, a related person. Because the goods were both manufactured and sold for use outside of Country A, CFC's distributive share of the income attributable to the sale of the goods is foreign base company sales income. Further, CFC's income from the sale of the goods to MJK Partnership will also be foreign base company sales income.

Example 4. The facts of are the same as *Example 3*, except that MJK Partnership purchased the goods from P Corp and sold those goods to CFC. CFC sold the goods to J Corp. J Corp sold the goods to unrelated customers in Country C. CFC's distributive share of the income of MJK Partnership from the sale of the goods by the partnership to itself will be treated as income from the sale of goods to a related person, for purposes of section 954(d)(1). Because the goods were both manufactured and sold for use outside of Country A, CFC's distributive share of income attributable to the sale of the goods is foreign base company sales income. Further, CFC's income from the sale of the goods to J Corp is also foreign base company sales income.

(h) *Applicability dates.*—(1) *Paragraph (d)(3) of this section.*—Paragraph (d)(3) of this section applies to taxable years of a controlled foreign corporation ending on or after December 16, 2019. For taxable years of a controlled foreign corporation ending on or after December 4, 2018, but ending before December 16, 2019, see § 1.954-1(d)(3) as contained in 26 CFR part 1 revised as of April 1, 2019.

(2) *Paragraph (g) of this section.*—Paragraph (g) of this section applies to taxable years of a controlled foreign corporation beginning on or after July 23, 2002.

(3) *Paragraphs (c)(1)(iii)(A)(3), (c)(1)(iv), and (d)(3)(i) of this section for taxable years beginning on or after* July 23, 2020. Paragraphs (c)(1)(iii)(A)(3), (c)(1)(iv), and (d)(3)(i) of this section apply to taxable years of a controlled foreign corporation beginning on or after July 23, 2020, and to taxable years of United States shareholders in which or with which such taxable years of foreign corporations end. In addition, taxpayers may choose to apply the rules in paragraphs (c)(1)(iii)(A)(3), (c)(1)(iv), and (d)(3)(i) of this section to taxable years of controlled foreign corporations that begin after December 31, 2017, and before July 23, 2020, and to taxable years of United States shareholders in which or with which such taxable years of the controlled foreign corporations end, provided that they consistently apply those rules and the rules in § 1.951A-2(c)(1)(iii), (c)(3)(ii), and (c)(7)and (8)to such taxable years. [Reg. § 1.954-1.]

☐ [*T.D.* 8618, 9-6-95. *Amended by T.D.* 8704, 12-31-96, *T.D.* 8767, 3-23-98, *T.D.* 8827, 7-12-99, *T.D.* 9008, 7-22-2002, *T.D.* 9883, 11-18-2019, *T.D.* 9882, 12-16-2019, *T.D.* 9902, 7-20-2020 *and T.D.* 9922, 11-2-2020.]

Proposed Amendment to Regulation

§ 1.954-1. Foreign base company income.

* * *

(c) * * *

(1) * * *

(i) *Deductions.*—(A) *Deductions against gross foreign base company income.*—

* * *

(B) *Special rule for deductible payments to certain non-fiscally transparent entities.*—Notwithstanding any other provision of this section, except as provided in paragraph (c)(1)(i)(C) of this section, an expense (including a distributive share of any expense) that would otherwise be allocable under section 954(b)(5) against the subpart F income of a controlled foreign corporation shall not be allocated against subpart F income of the controlled foreign corporation resulting from the payment giving rise to the expense if—

(*1*) Such expense arises from a payment between the controlled foreign corporation and a partnership in which the controlled foreign corporation is a partner and the partnership is not regarded as fiscally transparent, as defined in § 1.954-9(a)(7), by any country in which the controlled foreign corporation does business or has substantial assets; and

(*2*) The payment from which the expense arises would have reduced foreign tax, under § 1.954-9(a)(3), and would have fallen within the tax disparity rule of § 1.954-9(a)(5)(iv), if those provisions had been applicable to the payment.

(C) *Limitations.*—Paragraph (c)(1)(i)(B) of this section shall not apply to the extent that the controlled foreign corporation partner has no income against which to allocate the expense, other than its distributive share of a payment described in paragraph (c)(1)(i)(B) of this section. Similarly, to the extent an expense described in paragraph (c)(1)(i)(B) of this section exceeds the controlled foreign corporation partner's distributive share of the payment from which the expense arises, such excess amount of the expense may reduce subpart F income (other than such payment) to which it is properly allocable or apportionable under section 954(b)(5).

(D) *Example.*—The following example illustrates the application of paragraphs (c)(1)(i)(B) and (C) of this section:

Example. CFC, a controlled foreign corporation in Country A, is a 70 percent partner in partnership P, located in Country B. Country A's tax laws do not classify P as a fiscally transparent entity. The rate of tax in country B is 15 percent of the tax rate in country A. P loans $100 to CFC at a market rate of interest. In year 1, CFC pays P $10 of interest on the loan. The interest payment would have caused the recharacterization rules of § 1.954-9 to apply if the payment were made between the entities described in § 1.954-9(a)(2). CFC's distributive share of P's interest income is $7, which is foreign personal holding company income to CFC under section 954(c). Under paragraph (c)(1)(i)(B) of this section, $7 of the $10 interest expense may not be allocated against any of CFC's subpart F income. However, to the extent the remaining $3 of interest expense is properly allocable to subpart F income of CFC other than its distributive share of P's interest income, this expense may offset such other subpart F income.

(E) *Effective date.*—Paragraph (c)(1)(i)(B), (C) and (D) of this section shall be applicable for all payments made or accrued in taxable years commencing after [date that is 5 years after publication of the final regulations in the federal register], under hybrid arrangements, unless such payments are made pursuant to an arrangement that would qualify for permanent relief under § 1.954-9(c)(2) if made between a controlled foreign corporation and its hybrid branch, in which case the relief afforded under that section shall also be afforded under this section.

* * *

[Prop. Reg. § 1.954-1.]
[Proposed 7-13-99.]

Proposed Amendments to Regulation

§ 1.954-1. Foreign base company income.—(a) * * *

(2) *Gross foreign base company income.*—(i) *In general.*—The *gross foreign base company income* of a controlled foreign corporation, determined after the application of section 952(b) and § 1.952-1(b)(2), and after the application of the high-tax exception under section 954(b)(4) and paragraph (d) of this section, consists of the categories of gross income of the controlled foreign corporation described in paragraphs (a)(2)(i)(A) through (C) of this section.

(A) Foreign personal holding company income, as defined in section 954(c).

(B) Foreign base company sales income, as defined in section 954(d).

(C) Foreign base company services income, as defined in section 954(e).

(ii) *Foreign base company income for purposes of section 954(b).*—The term foreign base company income as used in section 954(b) refers to gross foreign base company income.

(3) *Adjusted gross foreign base company income.*—The *adjusted gross foreign base company income* of a controlled foreign corporation is the

gross foreign base company income of the controlled foreign corporation as adjusted by the de minimis rule in section 954(b)(3)(A) and paragraph (b)(1)(i) of this section, and the full inclusion rule in section 954(b)(3)(B) and paragraph (b)(1)(ii) of this section.

* * *

(5) *Adjusted net foreign base company income.*—The *adjusted net foreign base company income* of a controlled foreign corporation is the net foreign base company income of the controlled foreign corporation, reduced by the earnings and profits limitation of section 952(c)(1) and § 1.952-1(c), and increased by earnings and profits that are recharacterized as foreign base company income under section 952(c)(2) and § 1.952-1(f)(2)(ii). Unless otherwise provided (for example, in paragraph (a)(2)(ii) of this section), the term foreign base company income as used in the Internal Revenue Code and elsewhere in the Income Tax Regulations means adjusted net foreign base company income.

(6) *Insurance income.*—The *gross insurance income* of a controlled foreign corporation is all the gross income of the controlled foreign corporation, determined after the application of section 952(b) and § 1.952-1(b)(2), and after the application of the high-tax exception under section 954(b)(4) and paragraph (d) of this section, that is taken into account to determine the insurance income of the controlled foreign corporation under section 953. The *adjusted gross insurance income* of a controlled foreign corporation is the gross insurance income of the controlled foreign corporation as adjusted by the de minimis rule in section 954(b)(3)(A) and paragraph (b)(1)(i) of this section, and the full inclusion rule in section 954(b)(3)(B) and paragraph (b)(1)(ii) of this section. The *net insurance income* of a controlled foreign corporation is the adjusted gross insurance income of the controlled foreign corporation reduced under section 953 so as to take into account deductions (including taxes) properly allocable or apportionable to such income. The *adjusted net insurance income* of a controlled foreign corporation is the net insurance income of the controlled foreign corporation reduced by the earnings and profits limitation of section 952(c)(1) and § 1.952-1(c), and increased by earnings and profits that are recharacterized as insurance income under section 952(c)(2) and § 1.952-1(f)(2)(ii). The term insurance income as used in subpart F of the Internal Revenue Code and in the regulations under that subpart means adjusted net insurance income, unless otherwise provided.

(7) *Additional items of adjusted net foreign base company income or adjusted net insurance income by reason of section 952(c).*—The earnings and profits described in this paragraph (a)(7) are not subject to the de minimis rule in section 954(b)(3)(A) and paragraph (b)(1)(i) of this section, the full inclusion rule in section 954(b)(3)(B) and paragraph (b)(1)(ii) of this section, or the high-tax exception of section 954(b)(4) and paragraph (d) of this section.

* * *

(d) *High-tax exception.*—(1) *Application.*—(i) *In general.*—An item of gross income of a controlled foreign corporation for a CFC inclusion year qualifies for the high-tax exception under section 954(b)(4) and this paragraph (d)(1) only if—

(A) An election made under section 954(b)(4) and paragraph (d)(6) of this section is effective with respect to the controlled foreign corporation for the CFC inclusion year; and

(B) The tentative net item with respect to the item of gross income was subject to an effective rate of foreign tax, as determined under paragraph (d)(4) of this section, that is greater than 90 percent of the maximum rate of tax specified in section 11 for the CFC inclusion year. See paragraphs (d)(9)(iii)(A)(2)(*vi*) (Example 1) and (d)(9)(iii)(B)(2)(*vi*) (Example 2) of this section for illustrations of the application of the rules set forth in this paragraph (d)(1)(i)(B).

(ii) *Item of gross income.*—For purposes of this paragraph (d), an item of gross income means an item described in paragraph (d)(1)(ii)(A), (B), or (C) of this section. See paragraphs (d)(9)(iii)(A)(2)(*i*) (Example 1) and (d)(9)(iii)(B)(2)(*i*) (Example 2) of this section for illustrations of the application of the rule set forth in this paragraph (d)(1)(ii).

(A) *General gross item.*—A general gross item is the aggregate amount of all gross income, determined under federal income tax principles but without regard to items described in section 952(c)(2) and § 1.952-1(f)(2)(ii), that is attributable to a single tested unit (as provided in paragraph (d)(1)(iii) of this section) of the controlled foreign corporation in the CFC inclusion year and that is—

(*1*) In a single separate category (as defined in § 1.904-5(a)(4)(v);

(*2*) Not described in paragraph (d)(1)(ii)(B) of this section;

(*3*) Not passive foreign personal holding company income; and

(*4*) Of a type that would be treated as gross tested income, gross foreign base company income (as defined in paragraph (a)(2) of this section), or gross insurance income (as defined in paragraph (a)(6) of this section) (in all cases, determined without regard to the high-tax exception described in section 954(b)(4) and paragraph (d)(1) of this section).

(B) *Equity gross item.*—An equity gross item is the sum of gross income described in paragraph (d)(1)(ii)(A) of this section, determined without regard to paragraph (d)(1)(ii)(A)(2) of this section, that is also described in either paragraph (d)(1)(ii)(B)(*1*) or (2) of this section.

(*1*) *Income or gain arising from stock.*—Gross income described in this paragraph (d)(1)(ii)(B)(*1*) consists of dividends, income or gain recognized from dispositions of stock, and any similar items arising from stock that are taken into account by the tested unit, the entity an interest in which is the tested unit, or the branch the portion of the activities of which is the tested unit, as applicable, and subject to an exclusion, exemption, or other similar relief (such as a preferential tax rate) under the tax law of the country of tax residence of the tested unit or the entity, or the country in which the branch is located. For purposes of the preceding sentence, other similar relief does not include a deduction or credit against the tax imposed under such tax law for tax paid to another foreign country with respect to income attributable to the branch. Gross income described in this paragraph (d)(1)(ii)(B)(*1*) does not include gain recognized from dispositions of stock if the stock would be dealer property (as defined in § 1.954-2(a)(4)(v).

(*2*) *Income or gain arising from interests in pass-through entities.*—Gross income described in this paragraph (d)(1)(ii)(B)(2) is income or gain recognized on the disposition of, or a distribution with respect to, an interest in a pass-through entity (including an interest in a disregarded entity) that is attributable to the tested unit, the entity an interest in which is the tested unit, or the branch the portion of the activities of which is the tested unit, as applicable, and subject to an exclusion, exemption, or other similar relief (such as a preferential tax rate) under the tax law of the country of tax residence of the tested unit or the entity, or the country in which the branch is located. For purposes of the preceding sentence, other similar relief does not include a deduction or credit against the tax imposed under such tax law for tax paid to another foreign country with respect to income attributable to the branch.

(C) *Passive gross item.*—A passive gross item is the sum of the gross income described in paragraph (d)(1)(ii)(A) of this section (without regard to the exclusion of passive foreign personal holding company income under paragraph (d)(1)(ii)(A)(3) of this section) that constitutes a single item of passive foreign personal holding company income described in paragraph (c)(1)(iii)(B) of this section.

(iii) *Gross income attributable to a tested unit.*—(A) *Items properly reflected on an applicable financial statement.*—Gross income of a controlled foreign corporation is attributable to a tested unit of the controlled foreign corporation to the extent it is properly reflected, as modified under paragraph (d)(1)(iii)(B) of this section, on the applicable financial statement of the tested unit. All gross income of a controlled foreign corporation is attributable to a tested unit (but no portion of the gross income is attributable to more than one tested unit) of the controlled foreign corporation. See paragraphs (d)(9)(iii)(C)(2)(*ii*) and (d)(9)(iii)(C)(5) (Example 3) of this section for illustrations of the application of the rule set forth in this paragraph (d)(1)(iii)(A).

(B) *Adjustments to reflect disregarded payments.*—The principles of § 1.904-4(f)(2)(vi) apply to adjust gross income of the tested unit, to the extent thereof, to reflect disregarded payments. For purposes of this paragraph (d)(1)(iii)(B), the principles of § 1.904-4(f)(2)(vi) are applied taking into account the rules in paragraphs (d)(1)(iii)(B)(*1*) through (*5*) of this section. See paragraphs (d)(9)(iii)(A) (Example 1) and (d)(9)(iii)(B) (Example 2) of this section for examples that illustrate the application of the adjustments set forth in this paragraph (d)(1)(iii)(B).

(1) The controlled foreign corporation is treated as the foreign branch owner and any other tested units of the controlled foreign corporation are treated as foreign branches.

(2) The principles of § 1.904-4(f)(2)(vi)(A) apply in the case of disregarded payments between a foreign branch and another foreign branch without regard to whether either foreign branch makes a disregarded payment to, or receives a disregarded payment from, the foreign branch owner.

(3) The exclusion for payments described in § 1.904-4(f)(2)(vi)(C)(1) ("disregarded interest") does not apply to the extent of the amount of a disregarded payment that is deductible in the country of tax residence (or location, in the case of a branch) of the tested unit that is the payor.

(4) In the case of an amount of disregarded interest described in paragraph (d)(1)(iii)(B)(*3*) of this section, the rules in § 1.904-4(f)(2)(vi)(B) for determining how a disregarded payment is allocated to gross income of a foreign branch or foreign branch owner are applied by treating the disregarded payment as allocated and apportioned ratably to all of the gross income attributable to the tested unit that is making the disregarded payment. However, if a tested unit is both a payor and payee of an amount of disregarded interest described in paragraph (d)(1)(iii)(B)(*3*) of this section, the payments made are first allocable to the gross income allocated to it as a result of the receipt of amounts of disregarded interest described in paragraph (d)(1)(iii)(B)(*3*) of this section, to the extent thereof. If a tested unit makes and receives payments described in paragraph (d)(1)(iii)(B)(*3*) of this section to and from the same tested unit, the payments are netted so that paragraph (d)(1)(iii)(B)(*3*) of this section and the principles of § 1.904-4(f)(2)(vi) apply only to the net amount of such payments between the two tested units. If the payment described in paragraph (d)(1)(iii)(B)(*3*) of this section would (if regarded) be directly allocated under the principles of § 1.861-10T(b) or (c) if such payment were regarded for federal income tax purposes, then notwithstanding any other rule in this paragraph (d)(1)(iii)(B)(*4*), a disregarded payment is allocated to gross income of a tested unit under the principles of § 1.904-4(f)(2)(vi)(B) by applying the principles of § 1.861-10T.

(5) In the case of multiple disregarded payments, in lieu of the rules in § 1.904-4(f)(2)(vi)(F), disregarded payments are taken into account under paragraph (d)(1)(iii)(B) of this section under the rules provided in paragraphs (d)(1)(iii)(B)(*5*)(*i*) through (*iii*) of this section.

(i) Adjustments are first made with respect to disregarded payments received by a payee tested unit that are not themselves attributable to disregarded payments received by the payor tested unit. Second, adjustments are made with respect to disregarded payments made by the payee tested unit that are attributable to the income of that tested unit, adjusted as described in the preceding sentence. Third, adjustments are made with respect to amounts of disregarded interest received and paid, as described in paragraph (d)(1)(iii)(B)(*4*) of this section. Fourth, adjustments are made with respect to any other disregarded payments made or received.

(ii) Adjustments with respect to disregarded payments made are first made with respect to disregarded payments that would be definitely related to a single class of gross income under the principles of § 1.861-8; second, adjustments are made with respect to disregarded payments that would be definitely related to multiple classes of gross income under the principles of § 1.861-8, but that are not definitely related to all gross income of the tested unit; third, adjustments are made with respect to disregarded payments that would be definitely related to all gross income under the principles of § 1.861-8, other than payments described in paragraph (d)(1)(iii)(B)(*3*) of this section; and fourth, adjustments are made with respect to payments described in paragraph (d)(1)(iii)(B)(*3*) of this section and disregarded payments that would not be definitely related to any gross income under the principles of § 1.861-8.

(iii) Adjustments can be made only to the extent there is sufficient gross income (in the relevant income group) of the tested unit making the payment, taking into account the adjustments that increase gross income as provided in this paragraph (d)(1)(iii)(B)(*5*).

(iv) *Tentative net item.*—(A) *In general.*—Except as provided in paragraphs (d)(1)(iv)(B) and (C) of this section, a tentative net item with respect to an item of gross income described in paragraph (d)(1)(ii) of this section is determined by allocating and apportioning deductions for the CFC inclusion year (not including any items described in § 1.951A-2(c)(5) or (c)(6)) to the item of gross income under the principles of § 1.960-1(d)(3) by treating each single item of gross income described in paragraph (d)(1)(ii) of this section as gross income in a separate income group described in § 1.960-1(d)(2)(ii) and by treating all other income as assigned to a residual income group. A deduction for current year taxes (as defined in § 1.960-1(b)(4) imposed solely by reason of a disregarded payment that gives rise to an adjustment under paragraph (d)(1)(iii)(B) of this section, however, is allocated and apportioned under the principles of § 1.904-6(b)(2) in lieu of the rules under § 1.861-20(d)(3)(ii). See paragraph (d)(9)(iii)(A)(*2*)(*ii*) (Example 1) and (d)(9)(iii)(B)(*2*)(*iii*) (Example 2) of this section for illustrations of the application of the rule set forth in this paragraph (d)(1)(iv)(A).

(B) *Booking rule for deductions other than current year tax expense.*—Deductions (other than deductions for current year taxes) are attributable to a tested unit to the extent they are properly reflected on the applicable financial statement of the tested unit under the principles of paragraph (d)(1)(iii)(A) of this section. In applying the principles of § 1.960-1(d)(3) under paragraph (d)(1)(iv)(A) of this section, deductions (other than deductions for current year taxes) attributable to a tested unit are allocated and apportioned on the basis of the income and activities to which the expense relates, but are applied only to reduce the items of gross income described in paragraph (d)(1)(ii) of this section attributable to the same tested unit (including gross income that is attributed to the tested unit by reason of disregarded payments, and regardless of whether the tested unit has gross income in the relevant income group during the CFC inclusion year). In applying §§ 1.861-9 and 1.861-9T pursuant to § 1.960-1(d)(3), solely for purposes of paragraph (d)(1)(iv)(A) of this section interest deductions attributable to a tested unit are allocated and apportioned only on the basis of the assets (or gross income, in the case of a taxpayer that has elected the modified gross income method) of that tested unit. No interest deductions attributable to the tested unit are allocated and apportioned to the assets or gross income of another tested unit, or of a corporation, owned by the controlled foreign corporation indirectly through the tested unit. See paragraph (d)(9)(iii)(B)(*2*)(*ii*) (Example 2) of this section for illustrations of the application of the rule set forth in this paragraph (d)(1)(iv)(B).

(C) *Deduction or loss with respect to equity.*—Notwithstanding paragraph (d)(1)(iv)(A) of this section, if a tested unit takes into account a loss or deduction (including a deduction for foreign income taxes) with respect to a transaction involving stock or an interest in a pass-through entity, and income or gain with respect to the stock or interest is or would have been described in paragraph (d)(1)(ii)(B)(*1*) or (2) of this section, then for purposes of allocating and apportioning deductions under paragraph (d)(1)(iv)(A) of this section, the deduction or loss is allocated and apportioned solely to the item of gross income described in paragraph (d)(1)(ii)(B)(*1*) or (2) of this section, as applicable, with respect to such tested unit, regardless of whether there is any gross income included in such item during the CFC inclusion year.

(D) *Effect of potential and actual changes in taxes paid or accrued.*—Except as otherwise provided in this paragraph (d)(1)(iv)(D), the amount of current year taxes paid or accrued with respect to an item of gross income (as described in paragraph (d)(1)(ii) of this section) does not take into account any potential reduction in foreign income taxes that may occur by reason of a future distribution to shareholders of all or part of such income. However, to the extent the foreign income taxes paid or accrued by the controlled foreign corporation are reasonably certain to be returned to a shareholder by the foreign country imposing such taxes, directly or indirectly, through any means (including, but not limited to, a refund, credit, payment, discharge of an obligation, or any other method) on a subsequent distribution to such shareholder, the foreign income taxes are not treated as paid or accrued for purposes of paragraphs (d)(1)(iv) or (d)(5) of this section. In addition, foreign income taxes that have not been paid or accrued because they are contingent on a future distribution of earnings (or other similar transaction, such as a loan to a shareholder) are not taken into account for purposes of paragraph (d)(1)(iv) or (d)(5) of this section. If, pursuant to section 905(c) and § 1.905-3, a redetermination of U.S. tax liability is required to account for the effect of a foreign tax redetermination (as defined in § 1.905-3(a), paragraph (d)(1)(iv) and (d)(5) of this section are applied in the adjusted year taking into account the adjusted amount of the redetermined foreign tax.

(v) *Portfolio interest and treatment of certain income under foreign tax credit rules.*—Portfolio interest, as described in section 881(c), does not qualify for the high-tax exception under section 954(b)(4) and this paragraph (d). For rules concerning the treatment for foreign tax credit purposes of distributions of passive income excluded from foreign base company income, insurance income or tested income under section 954(b)(4) and this paragraph (d), see section 904(d)(3)(E) and § 1.904-4(c)(7)(iii).

(2) *Tested unit rules.*—(i) *In general.*—Subject to the combination rule in paragraph (d)(2)(iii) of this section, the term *tested unit* means any corporation, interest, or branch described in paragraphs (d)(2)(i)(A) through (C) of this section. See paragraph (d)(9)(iii)(C) of this section for an example that illustrates the application of the tested unit rules set forth in this paragraph (d)(2).

(A) A controlled foreign corporation (as defined in section 957(a)).

(B) An interest held directly or indirectly by a controlled foreign corporation in a pass-through entity that is—

(1) A tax resident (as described in § 1.267A-5(a)(23)(i) of any foreign country; or

(2) Not treated as fiscally transparent (as determined under the principles of § 1.267A-5(a)(8) for purposes of the tax law of the foreign country of which the controlled foreign corporation is a tax resident or, in the case of an interest in a pass-through entity held by a controlled foreign corporation indirectly through one or more other tested units, for purposes of the tax law of the foreign country of which the tested unit that directly (or indirectly through the fewest number of transparent interests) owns the interest is a tax resident.

(C) A branch (as described in § 1.267A-5(a)(2) the activities of which are carried on directly or indirectly (through one or more pass-through entities) by a controlled foreign corporation. However, in the case of a branch that does not give rise to a taxable presence under the tax law of the foreign country where the branch is located, the branch is a tested unit only if, under the tax law of the foreign country of which the controlled foreign corporation is a tax resident (or, if applicable, under the tax law of a foreign country of which the tested unit that directly (or indirectly, through the fewest number of transparent interests) carries on the activities of the branch is a tax resident), an exclusion, exemption, or other similar relief (such as a preferential rate) applies with respect to income attributable to the branch. For purposes of this paragraph (d)(2)(i)(C), similar relief does not include a deduction or credit against the tax imposed under such tax law for tax paid to another foreign country with respect to income attributable to the branch. If a controlled foreign corporation carries on directly or indirectly less than all of the activities of a branch (for example, if the activities are carried on indirectly through an interest in a partnership), then the rules in this paragraph (d)(2)(i)(C) apply separately with respect to the portion (or portions, if carried on indirectly through more than one chain of pass-through entities) of the activities carried on by the controlled foreign corporation. See paragraphs (d)(9)(iii)(C)*(3)* and (d)(9)(iii)(C)*(4)* (Example 3) of this section for illustrations of the application of the rules set forth in this paragraph (d)(2)(i)(C).

(ii) *Items attributable to only one tested unit.*—For purposes of paragraph (d) of this section, if an item is attributable to more than one tested unit in a tier of tested units, the item is considered attributable only to the lowest-tier tested unit. Thus, for example, if a controlled foreign corporation directly owns a branch tested unit described in paragraph (d)(2)(i)(C) of this section, and an item of gross income is (under the rules of paragraph (d)(1)(iii) of this section) attributable to both the branch tested unit and the controlled foreign corporation tested unit, then the item is considered attributable only to the branch tested unit.

(iii) *Combination rule.*—(A) *In general.*—Except as provided in paragraph (d)(2)(iii)(B) of this section, tested units of a controlled foreign corporation (including the controlled foreign corporation tested unit) that meet the requirements in paragraph (d)(2)(iii)(A)*(1)* of this section are treated as a single tested unit, and tested units that meet the requirements of paragraph (d)(2)(iii)(A)*(2)* of this section (after taking into account the application of paragraph (d)(2)(iii)(A)*(1)* of this section) are also treated as a single tested unit.

(1) Subject to tax in same foreign country.—The tested units are tax residents of, or located in (in the case of a tested unit that is branch, or a portion of the activities of a branch, that gives rise to a taxable presence under the tax law of a foreign country), the same foreign country. For purposes of this paragraph (d)(2)(iii)(A)*(1)*, in the case of a tested unit that is an interest in a pass-through entity or a portion of the activities of a branch, a reference to the tax residency or location of the tested unit means the tax residency of the entity the interest in which is the tested unit or the location of the branch, as applicable. See paragraphs (d)(9)(iii)(C)*(2)*(*i*) and (d)(9)(iii)(C)*(5)* (Example 3) for illustrations of the application of the rule set forth in this paragraph (d)(2)(iii)(A)*(1)*.

(2) De minimis gross income.—The gross income attributable to the tested unit (determined under paragraph (d)(1)(iii) of this section and translated into U.S. dollars, if necessary, at the appropriate exchange rate under section 989(b)(3)) is less than the lesser of one percent of gross income of the controlled foreign corporation, or $250,000. Appropriate adjustments are made for purposes of applying this paragraph (d)(2)(iii)(A)(2) if assets, including assets of or interests in a tested unit or a transparent entity, are transferred, including by issuance, contribution or distribution, if a significant purpose of the transfer is to qualify for the rule in this paragraph (d)(2)(iii), or if the rule is otherwise availed of with a significant purpose of avoiding the purposes of section 951, 951A, or 954(b)(4). A purpose may be a significant purpose even though it is outweighed by other purposes (taken together or separately). See paragraph (d)(9)(iii)(D) (Example 4) of this section for an example that illustrates the application of the rule set forth in this paragraph (d)(2)(iii)(A)(2).

(B) *Exception for nontaxed branches.*—The rule in paragraph (d)(2)(iii)(A) of this section does not apply to a tested unit that is described in paragraph (d)(2)(i)(C) of this section if the branch described in paragraph (d)(2)(i)(C) of this section does not give rise to a taxable presence under the tax law of the foreign country where the branch is located. See paragraph (d)(9)(iii)(C)*(4)* (Example 4) of this section for an illustration of the application of the rule set forth in this paragraph (d)(2)(iii)(B).

(C) *Effect of combination rule.*—If, pursuant to paragraph (d)(2)(iii)(A) of this section, tested units are treated as a single tested unit, then, solely for purposes of paragraph (d) of this section, items of gross income attributable to such tested units, and items of deduction and foreign taxes allocated and apportioned to such gross income, are aggregated for purposes of determining the combined tested unit's tentative net items, and foreign income taxes paid or accrued with respect to such tentative net items.

(3) *Applicable financial statement rules.*—(i) *In general.*—For purposes of this paragraph (d), the term *applicable financial statement* means a statement or information described in paragraphs (d)(3)(i)(A) through (H) of this section. A statement or information described in one of these paragraphs qualifies as an applicable financial statement only if the statement or information described in all preceding paragraphs is not readily available. For example, the statement or information described in paragraph (d)(3)(i)(C) of this section qualifies as an applicable financial statement only if the statement or information described in paragraphs (d)(3)(i)(A) and (B) of this section is not readily available. For purposes of paragraphs (d)(3)(i)(A) through (H) of this section, the term "separate-entity" includes the term "separate-branch," as applicable. For purposes of paragraph (d) of this section, in the case of a tested unit or a transparent interest that is an interest in a pass-through entity or a portion of the activities of a branch, a reference to the applicable financial statement of the tested unit or the transparent interest means the applicable financial statement of the entity or the branch, as applicable.

(A) An audited separate-entity financial statement that is prepared in accordance with U.S. generally accepted accounting principles ("U.S. GAAP").

(B) An audited separate-entity financial statement that is prepared on the basis of international financial reporting standards ("IFRS").

(C) An audited separate-entity financial statement that is prepared on the basis of the generally accepted accounting principles of the jurisdiction in which the entity is organized or the activities are located ("local-country GAAP").

(D) An unaudited separate-entity financial statement that is prepared in accordance with U.S. GAAP.

(E) An unaudited separate-entity financial statement that is prepared on the basis of IFRS.

(F) An unaudited separate-entity financial statement that is prepared on the basis of local-country GAAP.

(G) Separate-entity records used for tax reporting.

(H) Separate-entity records used for internal management controls or regulatory or other similar purposes.

(ii) *Failure to prepare an applicable financial statement.*—If an applicable financial statement is not prepared for a tested unit or a transparent interest, the items of gross income, deduction, disregarded payments, and any other items required to apply paragraph (d) of this section that would be properly reflected on an applicable financial statement of the tested unit or transparent interest must be determined. Such items are treated as properly reflected on the applicable financial statement of the tested unit or transparent interest for purposes of applying paragraph (d) of this section.

(iii) *Transparent interests.*—If a tested unit of a controlled foreign corporation or an entity an interest in which is a tested unit of a controlled foreign corporation holds a transparent interest, either directly or indirectly through one or more other transparent interests, then, for purposes of paragraph (d) of this section (and subject to the rule of paragraph (d)(2)(iii) of this section), items of the controlled foreign corporation properly reflected on the applicable financial statement of the transparent interest are treated as being properly reflected on the applicable financial statement of the tested unit, as modified under paragraph (d)(1)(iii)(B) of this section. See paragraph (d)(9)(iii)(C)(6) (Example 3) of this section for an illustration of the application of the rule set forth in this paragraph (d)(3)(iii).

(iv) *Items not taken into account for financial accounting purposes.*—For purposes of this paragraph (d), an item in a CFC inclusion year that is not taken into account in such year for financial accounting purposes, and therefore not property reflected on an applicable financial statement of a tested unit or a transparent interest, is treated as properly reflected on such applicable financial statement to the extent it would have been so reflected if the item were taken into account for financial accounting purposes in such CFC inclusion year.

(v) *Adjustments to items reflected on the applicable financial statement.*—(A) *In general.*—Appropriate adjustments are made if an item is included or not included on an applicable financial statement, or if a disregarded payment described in paragraph (d)(1)(iii)(B) of this section is made or not made, with a significant purpose of avoiding the purposes of section 951, 951A, 954(b)(4), or paragraph (d) of this section. Adjustments pursuant to this paragraph (d)(3)(v) include attributing all or a portion of the item to one or more tested units or transparent interests in a manner that reflects the substance of the transaction, or segregating all or a portion of the item and treating it as attributable to a separate item of gross income described in paragraph (d)(1)(ii) of this section. The combination rule of paragraph (d)(2)(iii)(A)(1) of this section does not apply to an item that is segregated and treated as a separate item of gross income under this paragraph (d)(3)(v). See also § 1.904-4(f)(2)(vi)(E) for rules relating to the determination of the amount of disregarded payments taken into account under paragraph (d)(1)(iii)(B) of this section.

(B) *Factually unrelated items.*—*(1) Gross income.*—Without limiting the scope of a significant avoidance purpose as described in paragraph (d)(3)(v)(A) of this section, gross income generally is treated as included on an applicable financial statement with a significant purpose of avoiding the purposes of section 951, 951A, 954(b)(4), or paragraph (d) of this section if it is factually unrelated to the other activities of the relevant entity or branch and is subject to tax at a materially different effective rate of foreign tax than the other activities of the tested unit (or entity, an interest in which is a tested unit) to which the item would otherwise be attributable, or is subject to a withholding tax imposed by a foreign country other than the country of residence of the tested unit. For purposes of this paragraph (d)(3)(v)(B)(*1*), an effective rate of foreign tax is materially different than the effective rate of foreign tax on other activities if it differs by at least 10 percentage points.

(2) Deductions.—Without limiting the scope of a significant avoidance purpose as described in paragraph (d)(3)(v)(A) of this section, a deduction generally is treated as included on an applicable financial statement with a significant purpose of avoiding the purposes of section 951, 951A, 954(b)(4), or paragraph (d) of this section if it is not incurred in connection with funding, or in the ordinary course of, the preexisting activities of the relevant entity or branch and is not deductible, in whole or in part, in the country of residence or location of the tested unit (or entity, an interest in which is a tested unit) to which the item would otherwise be attributable.

(4) *Effective rate at which foreign taxes are imposed.*—(i) *In general.*—For a CFC inclusion year of a controlled foreign corporation, the effective rate of foreign tax with respect to the tentative net items of the controlled foreign corporation is determined separately for each such item. The effective foreign tax rate at which taxes are imposed on a tentative net item is—

(A) The U.S. dollar amount of foreign income taxes paid or accrued with respect to the tentative net item under paragraph (d)(5) of this section; divided by

(B) The U.S. dollar amount of the tentative net item, increased by the amount of foreign income taxes described in paragraph (d)(4)(i)(A) of this section.

(ii) *Undefined value or negative effective foreign tax rate.*—If the amount described in paragraph (d)(4)(i)(A) of this section is positive and the amount described in paragraph (d)(4)(i)(B) of this section is zero or negative, the effective rate of foreign tax with respect to the tentative net item is deemed to be greater than 90 percent of the rate that would apply if the income were subject to the maximum rate of tax specified in section 11.

(5) *Foreign income taxes paid or accrued with respect to a tentative net item.*—For a CFC inclusion year, the amount of foreign income taxes paid or accrued by a controlled foreign corporation with respect to a tentative net item (as described in paragraph (d)(1)(iv) of this section) for purposes of section 954(b)(4) and this paragraph (d) is the amount of the controlled foreign corporation's current year taxes (as defined in § 1.960-1(b)(4) that are allocated and apportioned to the related item of gross income under the rules of paragraph (d)(1)(iv) of this section. See paragraphs (d)(9)(iii)(A)(*2*)(*iv*) (Example 1) and (d)(9)(iii)(B)(*2*)(*v*) (Example 2) of this section for illustrations of the application of this paragraph (d)(5).

(6) *Rules regarding the high-tax election.*—(i) *Manner.*—(A) *In general.*—An election is made under this paragraph (d)(6) by the controlling domestic shareholders (as defined in paragraph (d)(8)(iii) of this section) with respect to a controlled foreign corporation for a CFC inclusion year (a *high-tax election*) in accordance with the rules provided in forms or instructions and by—

(1) Filing the statement required under paragraph (d)(6)(vi)(A) of this section with a timely filed original federal income tax return, or with an amended federal income tax return for the U.S. shareholder inclusion year of each controlling domestic shareholder in which or with which such CFC inclusion year ends;

(2) Providing any notices required under paragraph (d)(6)(vi)(B) of this section;

(3) Substantiating, as described in paragraph (d)(6)(vii) of this section, its determination as to whether, with respect to each item of gross income, the requirement set forth in paragraph (d)(1)(i)(B) of this section is satisfied; and

(4) Providing any additional information required by applicable administrative pronouncements.

(B) *Election (or revocation) made with an amended income tax return.*—In the case of an election (or revocation) made with an amended federal income tax return—

(1) The election (or revocation) must be made on an amended federal income tax return duly filed within 24 months of the unextended due date of the original federal income tax return for the U.S. shareholder inclusion year with or within which the CFC inclusion year ends;

(2) Each United States shareholder of the controlled foreign corporation as of the end of the controlled foreign corporation's taxable year to which the election relates must file amended federal income tax returns (or timely original income tax returns if a return has not yet been filed) reflecting the effect of such election (or revocation) for the U.S. shareholder's inclusion year with or within which the CFC inclusion year ends as well as for any other taxable year in which the U.S. tax liability of the United States shareholder would be increased by reason of the election (or revocation) (or in the case of a partnership if any item reported by the partnership or any partnership-related item would change as a result of the election (or revocation)) within a single period no greater than six months within the 24-month period described in paragraph (d)(6)(i)(B)(*1*) of this section; and

(3) Each United States shareholder of the controlled foreign corporation as of the end of the controlled foreign corporation's taxable year to which the election relates must pay any tax due as a result of such adjustments within a single period no longer than six months within the 24-month period described in paragraph (d)(6)(i)(B)(*1*) of this section;

(C) *Special rules for United States shareholders that are domestic partnerships.*—In the case of a United States shareholder that is a domestic partnership, paragraphs (d)(6)(i)(A) and (B) and (d)(6)(iii) of this section are applied by substituting "Form 1065 (or successor form)" for "federal income tax return" and by substituting "amended Form 1065 (or successor form) or administrative adjustment request (as described in § 301.6227-1, as applicable," for "amended federal income tax return", each place that it appears.

(D) *Special rules for United States shareholders that hold an interest in the controlled foreign corporation through a partnership.*—A United States shareholder that is a partner in a partnership that is also a United States shareholder in the controlled foreign corporation must generally file an amended return, as required under paragraph (d)(6)(i)(B)(2) of this section, and must generally pay any additional tax owed as required under paragraph (d)(6)(i)(B)(*3*) of this section. However, in the case of a United States shareholder that is a partner in a partnership that duly files an administrative adjustment request under paragraph (d)(6)(i)(B)(*1*) or (2) of this section, the partner is treated as having satisfied the requirements of paragraphs (d)(6)(i)(B)(2) and (3) of this section with respect to the interest held through that partnership if:

(*1*) The partnership files an administrative adjustment request within the time described in paragraph (d)(6)(i)(B); and,

(*2*) The partnership and the partners comply with the requirements of section 6227. See § § 301.6227-1 through 301.6227-3 for rules relating to administrative adjustment requests.

(ii) *Scope.*—A high-tax election applies with respect to each item of gross income described in paragraph (d)(1)(ii) of this section of the controlled foreign corporation for the CFC inclusion year and is binding on all United States shareholders of the controlled foreign corporation.

(iii) *Revocation.*—A high-tax election may be revoked by the controlling domestic shareholders of the controlled foreign corporation in the same manner as prescribed for an election made on an amended federal income tax return as described in paragraph (d)(6)(i) of this section.

(iv) *Failure to satisfy election requirements.*—A high-tax election (or revocation) is valid only if all of the requirements in paragraph (d)(6)(i)(A) of this section, including the requirement to provide notice under paragraph (d)(6)(i)(A)(2) of this section, are satisfied.

(v) *Rules applicable to CFC groups.*—(A) *In general.*—In the case of a controlled foreign corporation that is a member of a CFC group, a high-tax election is made under paragraph (d)(6)(i) of this section, or revoked under paragraph (d)(6)(iii) of this section, with respect to all controlled foreign corporations that are members of the CFC group, and the rules in paragraphs (d)(6)(i) through (iv) of this section apply by reference to the CFC group.

(B) *Determination of the CFC group.*—(*1*) *Definition.*—Subject to the rules in paragraphs (d)(6)(v)(B)(2) and (*3*) of this section, the term *CFC group* means an affiliated group as defined in section 1504(a) without regard to section 1504(b)(1) through (6), except that section 1504(a) is applied by substituting "more than 50 percent" for "at least 80 percent" each place it appears, and section 1504(a)(2)(A) is applied by substituting "or" for "and." For purposes of this paragraph (d)(6)(v)(B), stock ownership is determined by applying the constructive ownership rules of section 318(a), other than section 318(a)(3)(A) and (B), by applying section 318(a)(4) only to options (as defined in § 1.1504-4(d) that are reasonably certain to be exercised as described in § 1.1504-4(g), and by substituting in section 318(a)(2)(C) "5 percent" for "50 percent."

(*2*) *Member of a CFC group.*—The determination of whether a controlled foreign corporation is included in a CFC group is made as of the close of the CFC inclusion year of the controlled foreign corporation that ends with or within the taxable years of the controlling domestic shareholders. One or more controlled foreign corporations are members of a CFC group if the requirements of paragraph (d)(6)(v)(B)(*1*) of this section are satisfied as of the end of the CFC inclusion year of at least one of the controlled foreign corporations, even if the requirements are not satisfied as of the end of the CFC inclusion year of all controlled foreign corporations. If the controlling domestic shareholders do not have the same taxable year, the determination of whether a controlled foreign corporation is a member of a CFC group is made with respect to the CFC inclusion year that ends with or within the taxable year of the majority of the controlling domestic shareholders (determined by voting power) or, if no such majority taxable year exists, the calendar year. See paragraph (d)(9)(iii)(E) (Example 5) of this section for an example that illustrates the application of the rule set forth in this paragraph (d)(6)(v)(B)(2).

(*3*) *Controlled foreign corporations included in only one CFC group.*—A controlled foreign corporation cannot be a member of more than one CFC group. If a controlled foreign corporation would be a member of more than one CFC group under paragraph (d)(6)(v)(E)(2) of this section, then ownership of stock of the controlled foreign corporation is determined by applying paragraph (d)(6)(v)(B) of this section without regard to section 1504(a)(2)(B) or, if applicable, by reference to the ownership existing as of the end of the first CFC inclusion year of a controlled foreign corporation that would cause a CFC group to exist.

(vi) *Rules regarding the statement and the notice requirements.*—The following rules apply for purposes of the statement and notice requirements in this paragraph (d)(6).

(A) *Statement required to be filed with a tax return.*—The statement required by paragraph (d)(6)(i)(A)(*1*) of this section must set forth the name, country of organization, and U.S. employer identification number (if applicable) of the foreign corporation, the name, address, stock interests, and U.S. employer identification number of each controlling domestic shareholder (or, if applicable, the agent described in § 1.1502-77(a) with respect to the consolidated group of which the controlling domestic shareholder is a member) approving the action, and the names, addresses, U.S. employer identification numbers, and stock interests of all other domestic shareholders notified of the action taken. Such statement must describe the nature of the action taken on behalf of the foreign corporation and the taxable year for which made, and identify a designated shareholder who retains a jointly executed consent confirming that such action has been approved by all of the controlling domestic shareholders and containing the signature of a principal officer of each such shareholder (or the agent described in § 1.1502-77(a), if applicable).

(B) *Notice.*—On or before the filing date described in paragraph (d)(6)(i)(A)(*1*) of this section (or paragraph (d)(6)(i)(B)(*1*) of this section if filing an amended income tax return), the controlling domestic shareholders must provide written notice of the election made to all other persons known by them to be domestic shareholders who own (within the meaning of section 958(a)) stock of the foreign corporation. Such notice must set forth the name, country of organization and U.S. employer identification number (if applicable) of the foreign corporation, and the names, addresses, and stock interests of the controlling domestic shareholders. Such notice must describe the nature of the action taken on behalf of the foreign corporation and the taxable year for which made, and identify a designated shareholder who retains a jointly executed consent confirming that such action has been approved by all of the controlling domestic shareholders and containing the signature of a principal officer of each such shareholder (or the agent described in § 1.1502-77(a), if applicable).

(vii) *Substantiation requirements.*—(A) *In general.*—If an election under section 954(b)(4) and paragraph (d)(6) of this section is in effect for a controlled foreign corporation for a CFC inclusion year, then each United States shareholder of that controlled foreign corporation with respect to the CFC inclusion year is required to maintain sufficient documentation (as described in paragraph (d)(6)(vii)(B) of this section) to establish that the taxpayer reasonably concluded that each item of gross income of the controlled foreign corporation satisfied (or did not satisfy) the requirement set forth in paragraph (d)(1)(i)(B) of this section. The substantiating documents must be in existence as of the filing date of the income tax return described in paragraph (d)(6)(i)(A) of this section (or paragraph (d)(6)(i)(B)(*1*) of this section if filing an amended income tax return) and must be provided to the Commissioner within 30 days of being requested by the Commissioner (unless otherwise agreed between the Commissioner and the taxpayer).

(B) *Sufficient documentation.*—For purposes of paragraph (d)(6)(vii)(A) of this section, the term sufficient documentation means documentation that accurately and completely describes the computations related to the high-tax exception under section 954(b)(4) and this paragraph (d)(6) with respect to each item of gross income of the controlled foreign corporation. Sufficient documentation must include the information described in paragraphs (d)(6)(vii)(B)(*1*) through (*5*) of this section.

(*1*) A description of each of the tested units and transparent interests of the controlled foreign corporation, including a detailed explanation of any tested units that are combined either under the same-country combination rule, or the de minimis combination rule.

(*2*) A detailed list of the items of gross income and deductions attributable to each tested unit and the applicable financial statement of each tested unit and transparent interest.

(3) A list of disregarded payments taken into account under paragraph (d)(1)(iii)(B) of this section for purposes of determining the gross income attributable to a tested unit.

(4) A list of current year foreign taxes paid or accrued with respect to each item of gross income, as described in paragraph (d)(5) of this section.

(5) The effective tax rate calculation for each item of gross income attributable to a tested unit, as described in paragraph (d)(4)(i) of this section.

(7) *Anti-abuse rule.*—Appropriate adjustments are made if an applicable instrument is issued or acquired, or a reverse hybrid is formed or availed of, with a significant purpose of avoiding the purposes of section 951, 951A, 954(b)(4), or paragraph (d) of this section. Adjustments pursuant to this paragraph (d)(7) include adjustments to foreign income taxes paid or accrued with respect to a tentative net item as determined under paragraph (d)(5) of this section, and adjustments to the tentative net item as determined under paragraph (d)(1)(iv) of this section. See paragraph (d)(9)(iii)(F) (Example 6) of this section for an example that illustrates the application of the anti-abuse rule set forth in this paragraph (d)(7).

(8) *Definitions.*—The following definitions apply for purposes of this paragraph (d).

(i) *Applicable instrument.*—The term *applicable instrument* means an instrument or arrangement described in paragraph (d)(8)(i)(A) or (B) of this section. For purposes of this paragraph (d)(8)(i), an instrument or arrangement includes a sale-repurchase transaction (including as described in § 1.861-2(a)(7), or other similar transaction or series of related transactions in which legal title to property is transferred and the property (or similar property, such as securities of the same class and issue) is reacquired or expected to be reacquired.

(A) *Deductions to issuer.*—An instrument or arrangement is described in this paragraph (d)(8)(i)(A) if, for federal income tax purposes, the instrument or arrangement gives rise to deductions to the issuer but, under the tax law of a foreign country, does not give rise to deductions (or gives rise to deductions that are disallowed), in whole or in part, to the issuer.

(B) *Income to holder.*—An instrument or arrangement is described in this paragraph (d)(8)(i)(B) if, under the tax law of a foreign country, the instrument or arrangement gives rise to income included in the holder's income but, for federal income tax purposes, does not give rise to income to the holder.

(ii) *CFC inclusion year.*—The term *CFC inclusion year* has the meaning provided in § 1.951A-1(f)(1).

(iii) *Controlling domestic shareholders.*—The term *controlling domestic shareholders* of a controlled foreign corporation means the United States shareholders (as defined in section 951(b) or 953(c)) who, in the aggregate, own (within the meaning of section 958(a)) more than 50 percent of the total combined voting power of all classes of the stock of such foreign corporation entitled to vote and who undertake to act on its behalf. If United States shareholders of the controlled foreign corporation do not, in the aggregate, own (within the meaning of section 958(a)) more than 50 percent of the total combined voting power of all classes of the stock of such foreign corporation entitled to vote, the controlling United States shareholders of the controlled foreign corporation are all those United States shareholders who own (within the meaning of section 958(a)) stock of such corporation.

(iv) *Disregarded entity.*—The term *disregarded entity* means an entity that is disregarded as an entity separate from its owner, as described in § 301.7701-2(c)(2)(i) of this chapter.

(v) *Disregarded payment.*—The term *disregarded payment* means any amount described in paragraph (d)(8)(v)(A) or (B) of this section.

(A) *Transfers to or from a disregarded entity.*—An amount described in this paragraph (d)(8)(iv)(A) is any amount that is transferred to or from a disregarded entity in connection with a transaction that is disregarded for federal income tax purposes and that is properly reflected on the applicable financial statement of a tested unit or a transparent interest.

(B) *Other disregarded amounts.*—An amount described in this paragraph (d)(8)(iv)(B) is any amount properly reflected on the applicable financial statement of a tested unit or transparent interest that would constitute an item of income, gain, deduction, or loss (other than an amount described in paragraph (d)(8)(iv)(A) of this section), a distribution to or contribution from the owner of the tested unit, transparent interest or entity, or a payment in exchange for property if the transaction to which the amount is attributable were regarded for federal income tax purposes.

(vi) *Indirectly.*—The term *indirectly,* when used in reference to ownership, means ownership through one or more pass-through entities.

(vii) *Pass-through entity.*—The term *pass-through entity* means a partnership, a disregarded entity, or any other person (whether domestic or foreign) other than a corporation to the extent that income, gain, deduction, or loss of the person is taken into account in determining the income or loss of a controlled foreign corporation that owns, directly or indirectly, interests in the person.

(viii) *Reverse hybrid.*—The term *reverse hybrid* has the meaning provided in § 1.909-2(b)(1)(iv).

(ix) *Transparent interest.*—The term *transparent interest* means an interest in a pass-through entity (or the activities of a branch) that is not a tested unit.

(x) *U.S. shareholder inclusion year.*—The term *U.S. shareholder inclusion year* has the meaning provided in § 1.951A-1(f)(7).

(9) *Examples.*—(i) *Scope.*—This paragraph (d)(9) provides presumed facts and examples illustrating the application of the rules in paragraph (d) of this section.

(ii) *Presumed facts.*—For purposes of the examples in paragraph (d)(9)(iii) of this section, except as otherwise stated, the following facts are presumed:

(A) USP is a domestic corporation.

(B) CFC1X and CFC2X are controlled foreign corporations organized in, and tax residents of, Country X.

(C) FDEX is a disregarded entity that is a tax resident of Country X.

(D) FDE1Y and FDE2Y are disregarded entities that are tax residents of Country Y.

(E) FPSY is an entity that is organized in, and a tax resident of, Country Y but is classified as a partnership for federal income tax purposes.

(F) CFC1X, CFC2X, and the interests in FDEX, FDE1Y, FDE2Y, and FPSY are tested units (the CFC1X tested unit, CFC2X tested unit, FDEX tested unit, FDE1Y tested unit, FDE2Y tested unit, and FPSY tested unit, respectively).

(G) CFC1X, CFC2X, FDEX, FDE1Y and FDE2Y conduct activities in the foreign country in which they are tax resident, and properly reflect items of income, gain, deduction, and loss on separate applicable financial statements.

(H) All entities have calendar taxable years (for both federal income tax purposes and for purposes of the relevant foreign country) and use the Euro (€) as their functional currency. At all relevant times € 1 = $1.

(I) The maximum rate of tax specified in section 11 for the CFC inclusion year is 21 percent.

(J) Neither CFC1X nor CFC2X directly or indirectly earns income described in section 952(b), or has any items of income, gain, deduction, or loss. In addition, no tested unit of CFC1X or CFC2X makes or receives disregarded payments.

(K) No tested unit is eligible for the de minimis combination rule of paragraph (d)(2)(iii)(A)(2) of this section.

(L) An election made under section 954(b)(4) and paragraph (d)(6) of this section is effective with respect to CFC1X and CFC2X, as applicable, for the CFC inclusion year.

(iii) *Examples.*—(A) *Example 1: Effect of disregarded interest.*—(1) *Facts—(i) Ownership.* USP owns all of the stock of CFC1X, and CFC1X owns all of the interests of FDE1Y.

(ii)Gross income and deductions (other than foreign income taxes). In Year 1, CFC1X generates € 100x of gross income from services performed for unrelated parties and properly reflects that gross income on the applicable financial statement of FDE1Y. The € 100x of services income is general category income under

§ 1.904-4(d). In Year 1, FDE1Y accrues and pays € 20x of interest to CFC1X that is deductible for Country Y tax purposes but is disregarded for federal income tax purposes. The € 20x of disregarded interest income received by CFC1X from FDE1Y is properly reflected on CFC1X's applicable financial statement, and the € 20x of disregarded interest expense paid from FDE1Y to CFC1X is properly reflected on FDE1Y's applicable financial statement.

(*iii*) *Foreign income taxes*. Country X imposes no tax on net income, and Country Y imposes a 25% tax on net income. For Country Y tax purposes, FDE1Y (which is not disregarded under Country Y tax law) has € 80x of taxable income (€ 100x of services income from the unrelated parties, less a € 20x deduction for the interest paid to CFC1X). Accordingly, FDE1Y incurs a Country Y income tax liability of € 20x ((€ 100x - € 20x) x 25%) with respect to Year 1, the U.S. dollar amount of which is $20x.

(2) *Analysis*—(*i*) *Items of gross income*. Under paragraph (d)(1)(ii) of this section, CFC1X has € 100x of general category gross income that is divided into two general gross items, one item that is attributable to the CFC1X tested unit and one item that is attributable to the FDE1Y tested unit under paragraph (d)(1)(iii) of this section. Without regard to the € 20x interest payment from FDE1Y to CFC1X, the gross income attributable to the CFC1X tested unit would be € 0 (that is, the € 20x of interest income properly reflected on the applicable financial statement of CFC1X would be reduced by € 20x, the amount attributable to the payment that is disregarded for federal income tax purposes). Similarly, without regard to the € 20x interest payment from FDE1Y to CFC1X, the gross income attributable to the FDE1Y tested unit would be € 100x (that is, the € 100x of services income properly reflected on the applicable financial statement of FDE1Y, unreduced by the € 20x disregarded payment made from FDE1Y to CFC1X). However, under paragraph (d)(1)(iii)(B) of this section, the gross income attributable to each of the CFC1X tested unit and the FDE1Y tested unit is adjusted by € 20x, the amount of the disregarded interest payment from FDE1Y to CFC1X that is deductible for Country Y tax purposes. Accordingly, the item of gross income attributable to the CFC1X tested unit (the "CFC1X general gross item") is € 20x (€ 0 + € 20x) and the item of gross income attributable to the FDE1Y tested unit (the "FDE1Y general gross item") is € 80x (€ 100x - € 20x), both of which are general gross items under paragraph (d)(1)(ii)(A) of this section.

(*ii*) *Foreign income tax deduction*. Under paragraph (d)(1)(iv) of this section, CFC1X's tentative net items are computed by treating the CFC1X general gross item and the FDE1Y general gross item each as in a separate income group (the "CFC1X income group" and the "FDE1Y income group") and by allocating and apportioning CFC1X's deductions for current year taxes between the income groups under the principles of § 1.960-1(d)(3) (CFC1X has no other deductions to allocate and apportion). Under paragraph (d)(1)(iv)(A) of this section, the € 20x deduction for Country Y income taxes is allocated and apportioned solely to the FDE1Y income group (the "FDE1Y group tax"). None of the Country Y taxes are allocated and apportioned to the CFC1X income group under paragraph (d)(1)(iv) of this section and the principles of § 1.904-6(b)(2), because none of the Country Y tax is imposed solely by reason of the disregarded interest payment.

(*iii*) *Tentative net items*. Under paragraph (d)(1)(iv)(A) of this section, the tentative net item with respect to the FDE1Y income group (the "FDE1Y tentative net item") is € 60x (the FDE1Y general gross item of € 80x, less the € 20x deduction for the FDE1Y group tax). The tentative net item with respect to the CFC1X income group (the "CFC1X tentative net item") is € 20x.

(*iv*) *Foreign income taxes paid or accrued with respect to a tentative net item*. Under paragraph (d)(5) of this section, the foreign income taxes paid or accrued with respect to a tentative net item is the U.S. dollar amount of the current year taxes that are allocated and apportioned to the item of gross income under the rules of paragraph (d)(1)(iv) of this section. Therefore, the foreign income taxes paid or accrued with respect to the FDE1Y tentative net item is $20x, the U.S. dollar amount of the FDE1Y group tax. The foreign income taxes paid or accrued with respect to the CFC1X tentative net item is $0, the U.S. dollar amount of the foreign tax allocated and apportioned to the CFC1X general gross item under paragraph (d)(1)(iv) of this section.

(*v*) *Effective foreign tax rate*. The effective foreign tax rate is determined under paragraph (d)(4) of this section by dividing the U.S. dollar amount of foreign income taxes paid or accrued with respect to each respective tentative net item by the U.S. dollar amount of the tentative net item increased by the U.S. dollar amount of the relevant foreign income taxes. Therefore, the effective foreign tax rate with respect to the FDEY1 tentative net item is 25%, calculated by dividing $20x (the U.S. dollar amount of the foreign income taxes paid or accrued with respect to the FDE1Y tentative net item under paragraph (d)(5) of this section) by $80x (the sum of $60x, the U.S. dollar amount of the FDE1Y tentative net item, and $20x, the U.S. dollar amount of the foreign income taxes paid or accrued with respect to the FDE1Y tentative net item). The CFC1X tentative net item is not subject to any foreign income tax, so is subject to an effective foreign tax rate of 0%, calculated as $0 (the U.S. dollar amount of the foreign income taxes paid or accrued with respect to the CFC1X tentative net item), divided by $20x (the U.S. dollar amount of the FDE1Y tentative net item).

(*vi*) *Qualification for the high-tax exception*. The FDE1Y tentative net item is subject to an effective foreign tax rate (25%) that is greater than 18.9% (90% of the 21% maximum rate of tax specified in section 11). Therefore, the requirement of paragraph (d)(1)(i)(B) of this section is satisfied, and the FDEY1 general gross item qualifies under paragraph (d)(1)(i) of this section for the high-tax exception of section 954(b)(4) and, under paragraphs (a)(2) and (a)(6) of this section, is excluded from the gross foreign base company income and gross insurance income, respectively, of CFC1X; in addition, the FDE1Y general gross item is excluded from gross tested income under section 951A(c)(2)(A)(i)(III) and § 1.951A-2(c)(1)(iii). The CFC1X tentative net item is subject to an effective foreign tax rate of 0%. Therefore, the CFC1X tentative net item does not satisfy the requirement of paragraph (d)(1)(i)(B) of this section, and the CFC1X general gross item does not qualify under paragraph (d)(1)(i) of this section for the high-tax exception of section 954(b)(4) and, under paragraphs (a)(2) and (a)(6) of this section, is not excluded from the gross foreign base company income and gross insurance income of CFC1X; in addition, the CFC1X general gross item is not excluded from gross tested income under section 951A(c)(2)(A)(i)(III) and § 1.951A-2(c)(1)(iii).

(B) *Example 2: Effect of disregarded payment for services*.—(1) *Facts*— (*i*) *Ownership*. USP owns all of the stock of CFC1X. CFC1X owns all of the interests of FDE1Y. FDE1Y is a tax resident of Country Y, but is treated as fiscally transparent for Country X tax purposes, so that FDE1Y is subject to tax in Country Y and that CFC1X is subject to tax in Country X with respect to FDE1Y's activities.

(*ii*) *Gross income, deductions (other than for foreign income taxes), and disregarded payments*. In Year 1, CFC1X generates € 1,000x of gross income from services to unrelated parties that would be gross tested income or gross foreign base company income without regard to paragraph (d)(1) of this section and that is properly reflected on the applicable financial statement of CFC1X. The € 1,000x of gross income for services is general category income under § 1.904-4(d). In Year 1, CFC1X accrues and pays € 480x of deductible expenses to unrelated parties, € 280x of which is properly reflected on CFC1X's applicable financial statement and is definitely related solely to CFC1X's gross income reflected on its applicable financial statement, and € 200x of which is properly reflected on FDE1Y's applicable financial statement and is definitely related solely to FDE1Y's gross income reflected on its applicable financial statement. Country X law does not provide rules for the allocation or apportionment of these deductions to particular items of gross income. In Year 1, CFC1X also accrues and pays € 325x to FDE1Y for support services performed by FDE1Y in Country Y; the payment is disregarded for federal income tax purposes. The € 325x of disregarded support services income received by FDE1Y from CFC1X is properly reflected on FDE1Y's applicable financial statement, and the € 325x of disregarded support services expense paid from CFC1X to FDE1Y is properly reflected on CFC1X's applicable financial statement.

(*iii*) *Foreign income taxes*. Country X imposes a 10% tax on net income, and Country Y imposes a 16% tax on net income. Country X allows a deduction, but not a credit, for foreign income taxes paid or accrued to another country (such as Country Y). For Country Y tax purposes, FDE1Y (which is not disregarded under Country Y tax law) has € 125x of taxable income (€ 325x of support services income received from CFC1X, less a € 200x deduction for expenses paid to unrelated parties). Accordingly, FDE1Y incurs a Country Y income tax liability with respect to Year 1 of € 20x (€ 125x x 16%), the U.S. dollar amount of which is $20x. For Country X tax purposes, CFC1X has € 500x of taxable income (€ 1,000x of gross income for services, less a € 480x deduction for expenses paid to unrelated parties by CFC1X and FDE1Y and a € 20x deduction for Country Y taxes; Country X does not allow CFC1X a deduction for the € 325x paid to FDE1Y for support services because the € 325x payment is disregarded for Country X tax purposes). Accordingly, CFC1X incurs a Country X income tax liability with respect to Year 1 of € 50x (€ 500x x 10%), the U.S. dollar amount of which is $50x.

(2) *Analysis*—(*i*) *Items of gross income*. Under paragraph (d)(1)(ii) of this section, CFC1X has € 1,000x of general category gross

income that is divided into two general gross items, one item that is attributable to the CFC1X tested unit and one item that is attributable to the FDE1Y tested unit under paragraph (d)(1)(iii) of this section. Without regard to the €325x payment for support services from CFC1X to FDE1Y, the gross income attributable to the CFC1X tested unit would be €1,000x (that is, the €1,000x of gross income from services properly reflected on the applicable financial statement of CFC1X, unreduced by the €325x payment from CFC1X to FDE1Y that is disregarded for federal income tax purposes). Similarly, without regard to the €325x payment for support services from CFC1X to FDE1Y, the gross income attributable to the FDE1Y tested unit would be €0 (that is, the €325x of services income properly reflected on the applicable financial statement of FDE1Y, reduced by the €325x disregarded payment). However, under paragraph (d)(1)(iii)(B) of this section, the gross income attributable to each of the CFCX1 tested unit and the FDE1Y tested unit is adjusted by €325x, the amount of the disregarded services payment from CFC1X to FDE1Y. Accordingly, the item of gross income attributable to the CFC1X tested unit (the "CFC1X general gross item") is €675x (€1,000x - €325x), and the item of gross income attributable to the FDE1Y tested unit (the "FDE1Y general gross item") is €325x (€0 + €325x), both of which are general gross items under paragraph (d)(1)(ii)(A) of this section.

(ii) *Deductions (other than for foreign income taxes).* Under paragraph (d)(1)(iv) of this section, CFC1X's tentative net items are computed by applying the principles of §1.960-1(d)(3), treating the CFC1X general gross item and the FDE1Y general gross item each as in a separate income group (the "CFC1X income group" and the "FDE1Y income group") and by allocating and apportioning CFC1X's deductions among the income groups. Under paragraph (d)(1)(iv)(B) of this section, the €280x of deductible expenses properly reflected on the applicable financial statement of the CFC1X tested unit are allocated and apportioned to the CFC1X income group, and the €200x of deductible expenses properly reflected on the applicable financial statement of the FDE1Y tested unit are allocated and apportioned to the FDE1Y income group.

(iii) *Foreign income tax deduction.* CFC1X accrues foreign income tax in Year 1 of €70x (€50x imposed by Country X and €20x imposed by Country Y). Under paragraph (d)(1)(iv)(A) of this section, the €70x of foreign income tax is allocated and apportioned under the principles of §1.960-1(d)(3)(ii) (or under the principles of §1.904-6(b)(2) in the case of tax imposed solely by reason of a disregarded payment that gives rise to an adjustment under paragraph (d)(1)(iii)(B) of this section) to the FDE1Y income group and the CFC1X income group. The Country Y tax of €20x is imposed solely by reason of FDE1Y's receipt of a €325x disregarded payment. As a result, the €20x of Country Y tax is allocated and apportioned to the FDE1Y income group under the principles of §1.904-6(b)(2). If Country X had allowed a deduction for the disregarded payment from CFC1X to FDE1Y and not otherwise imposed tax on CFC1X with respect to income of FDE1Y, the foreign tax imposed by Country X would relate only to the CFC1X income group, and no portion of it would be allocated and apportioned to the FDE1Y income group because the FDE1Y income would not be included in the Country X tax base. However, because gross income subject to tax in Country X corresponds to gross income that for federal income tax purposes is attributable to both the FDE1Y income group and the CFC1X income group, the €50x of foreign income tax imposed by Country X is allocated to both the FDE1Y income group and the CFC1X income group and must be apportioned between the two income groups under §1.861-20(e). Because Country X does not provide specific rules for the allocation or apportionment of the €500x of deductible expenses, §1.861-20(e) applies the principles of the section 861 regulations to determine the foreign law net income subject to Country X tax for purposes of apportioning the €50x of Country X tax between the income groups. CFC1X has €1,000x of gross income and €500x of deductible expenses under the tax laws of Country X, resulting in €500x of net foreign law income. Of the €1,000x of foreign law gross income, €325x corresponds to the gross income in the FDE1Y income group, and €675x corresponds to the gross income in the CFC1X income group. Applying federal income tax principles to allocate and apportion the foreign law deductions to foreign law gross income, €220x of the €500x foreign law deductions is allocated and apportioned to the FDE1Y income group and €280x is allocated and apportioned to the CFC1X income group. Of the total €500x of net foreign law income, €105x (€325x Country X gross income corresponding to the FDE1Y income group, less €220x allocable Country X expenses) corresponds to the FDE1Y income group and €395x (€675x Country X gross income corresponding to the CFC1X income group, less €280x allocable Country X expenses) corresponds to the CFC1X income group. Therefore, €10.5x (€50x x €105x/€500x) of Country X tax is allocated and apportioned to the FDE1Y income group, and €39.5x (€50x x €395x/€500x) is allocated and apportioned to the CFC1X income group. In total, €30.5x of foreign income tax (€10.5x of Country X tax and €20x of Country Y tax) is allocated and apportioned to the FDE1Y income group (the "FDE1Y group tax") and €39.5x of foreign income tax (all of which is Country X tax) is allocated and apportioned to the CFC1X income group (the "CFC1X group tax").

(iv) *Tentative net items.* Under paragraphs (d)(1)(iv)(A) and (B) of this section, the tentative net item in the FDE1Y income group (the "FDE1Y tentative net item") is €94.5x (the general gross item of €325x, less the allocated and apportioned deductions of €230.5x (the sum of deductions (other than for foreign income tax) of €200x and the FDE1Y group taxes of €30.5x)). The tentative net item in the CFC1X income group (the "CFC1X tentative net item") is €355.5x (the general gross item of €675x, less the allocated and apportioned deductions of €319.5x (the sum of deductions (other than for foreign income tax) of €280x and the CFC1X group tax of €39.5x)).

(v) *Foreign income taxes paid or accrued with respect to a tentative net item.* Under paragraph (d)(5) of this section, the foreign income taxes paid or accrued with respect to a tentative net item is the U.S. dollar amount of the current year taxes that are allocated and apportioned to the item of gross income under the rules of paragraph (d)(1)(iv) of this section. Therefore, the foreign income taxes paid or accrued with respect to the FDE1Y tentative net item is $30.5x, the U.S. dollar amount of the FDE1Y group tax. The foreign income tax paid or accrued with respect to the CFC1X tentative net item is $39.5x, the U.S. dollar amount of the CFC1X group tax.

(vi) *Effective foreign tax rate.* The effective foreign tax rate is determined under paragraph (d)(4) of this section by dividing the U.S. dollar amount of foreign income taxes with respect to each respective tentative net item by the U.S. dollar amount of the tentative net item increased by the U.S. dollar amount of the relevant foreign income taxes. Therefore, the effective foreign tax rate with respect to the FDE1Y tentative net item is 24.4%, calculated by dividing $30.5x (the U.S. dollar amount of the foreign income taxes paid or accrued with respect to the FDE1Y tentative net item under paragraph (d)(5)) by $125x (the sum of $94.5x, the U.S. dollar amount of the FDE1Y tentative net item, and $30.5x, the U.S. dollar amount of the foreign income taxes paid or accrued with respect to the FDE1Y tentative net item). The effective foreign tax rate with respect to the CFC1X tentative net item is 10%, calculated by dividing $39.5x (the U.S. dollar amount of the CFC1X group tax) by $395x (the sum of $355.5x, the U.S. dollar amount of the CFC1X tentative net item and $39.5x, the U.S. dollar amount of the foreign income tax paid or accrued with respect to the CFC1X tentative net item).

(vii) *Qualification for the high-tax exception.* The FDE1Y tentative net item is subject to an effective foreign tax rate (24.4%) that is greater than 18.9% (90% of the maximum rate of tax specified in section 11). Therefore, the requirement of paragraph (d)(1)(i)(B) of this section is satisfied, and the FDE1Y general gross item qualifies for the high-tax exception of section 954(b)(4) and, under paragraphs (a)(2) and (a)(6) of this section, is excluded from the gross foreign base company income and the gross insurance income, respectively, of CFC1X; in addition, the FDE1Y general gross item is excluded from gross tested income under section 951A(c)(2)(A)(i)(III) and §1.951A-2(c)(1)(iii). The CFC1X tentative net item is subject to an effective foreign tax rate (10%) that is not greater than 18.9%. Therefore, the CFC1X general gross item does not satisfy the requirement of paragraph (d)(1)(i)(B) of this section, does not qualify for the high-tax exception of section 954(b)(4) and, under paragraphs (a)(2) and (a)(6) of this section, is not excluded from the gross foreign base company income and gross insurance income of CFC1X; in addition, the CFC1X general gross item is not excluded from gross tested income under section 951A(c)(2)(A)(i)(III) and §1.951A-2(c)(1)(iii).

(C) *Example 3: Application of tested unit rules.*—(1) *Facts*—(i) *Ownership.* USP owns all of the stock of CFC1X. CFC1X directly owns all of the interests of FDEX and FDE1Y. In addition, CFC1X directly carries on activities in Country Y that constitute a branch (as described in §1.267A-5(a)(2) and that give rise to a taxable presence under Country Y tax law and Country X tax law (such branch, "FBY").

(ii) *Items reflected on applicable financial statement.* For the CFC inclusion year, CFC1X has a €20x item of gross income (Item A), which is properly reflected on the applicable financial statement of FBY, and a €30x item of gross income (Item B), which is properly reflected on the applicable financial statement of FDEX.

(2) *Analysis*—(i) *Identifying the tested units of CFC1X.* Without regard to the combination rule of paragraph (d)(2)(iii) of this section, CFC1X, CFC1X's interest in FDEX, CFC1X's interest in FDE1Y, and FBY would each be a tested unit of CFC1X. *See* paragraph (d)(2)(i) of this section. Pursuant to the combination rule, however, the FDE1Y

tested unit is combined with the FBY tested unit and treated as a single tested unit because FDE1Y is a tax resident of Country Y, the same country in which FBY is located (the "Country Y tested unit"). *See* paragraph (d)(2)(iii)(A)(*1*) of this section. The CFC1X tested unit (without regard to any items attributable to the FDEX, FDE1Y, or FBY tested units) is also combined with the FDEX tested unit and treated as a single tested unit because CFC1X and FDEX are both tax residents of County X (the "Country X tested unit"). *See* paragraph (d)(2)(iii)(A)(*1*) of this section.

(*ii*) *Computing the items of CFC1X.* Under paragraph (d)(1)(ii) of this section, an item of gross income is determined with respect to each of the Country Y tested unit and the Country X tested unit. To determine the item of gross income of each tested unit, the gross income that is attributable to the tested unit is determined under paragraph (d)(1)(iii) of this section. Under paragraph (d)(1)(iii)(A) of this section, only Item A is attributable to the Country Y tested unit, and only Item B is attributable to the Country X tested unit. Item A is not attributable to the Country X tested unit because it is not reflected on the applicable financial statement of the CFC1X tested unit or the FDEX tested unit, and an item of gross income is only attributable to one tested unit. *See* paragraph (d)(1)(iii)(A) of this section.

(*3*) *Alternative facts – branch does not give rise to a taxable presence in country where located*—(*i*) *Facts.* The facts are the same as in paragraph (d)(9)(iii)(C)(*1*) of this section (the original facts in this *Example 3*), except that FBY does not give rise to a taxable presence under Country Y tax law; moreover, Country X tax law does not provide an exclusion, exemption, or other similar relief with respect to income attributable to FBY.

(*ii*) *Analysis.* FBY is not a tested unit but is a transparent interest. *See* paragraphs (d)(2)(i)(C) and (d)(8)(ix) of this section. CFC1X has a tested unit in Country X that includes the CFC1X tested unit (without regard to any items related to the interest in FDEX or FDE1Y, but that includes FBY since it is a transparent interest and not a tested unit) and the interest in FDEX. *See* paragraph (d)(2)(iii) of this section. CFC1X has another tested unit in Country Y, the interest in FDE1Y.

(*4*) *Alternative facts — branch is a tested unit but is not combined*—(*i*) *Facts.* The facts are the same as in paragraph (d)(9)(iii)(C)(*1*) of this section (the original facts in this *Example 3*), except that FBY does not give rise to a taxable presence under Country Y tax law but Country X tax law provides an exclusion, exemption, or other similar relief (such as a preferential rate) with respect to income attributable to FBY.

(*ii*) *Analysis.* FBY is a tested unit. *See* paragraph (d)(2)(i)(C) of this section. CFC1X has two tested units in Country Y, the interest in FDE1Y and FBY. The interest in FDE1Y and FBY tested units are not combined because FBY does not give rise to a taxable presence under the tax law of Country Y. *See* paragraph (d)(2)(iii)(B) of this section. CFC1X also has a tested unit in Country X that includes the activities of CFC1X (without regard to any items related to the interest in FDEX, the interest in FDE1Y, or FBY) and the interest in FDEX.

(*5*) *Alternative facts – split ownership of tested unit*—(*i*) *Facts.* The facts are the same as in paragraph (d)(9)(iii)(C)(*1*) of this section (the original facts in this *Example 3*), except that USP also owns CFC2X, CFC1X does not own FDE1Y, and CFC1X and CFC2X own 60% and 40%, respectively, of the interests of FPSY.

(*ii*) *Analysis for CFC1X.* Under paragraph (d)(2)(iii)(A)(1) of this section, FBY and CFC1X's 60% interest in FPSY are combined and treated as a single tested unit of CFC1X ("CFC1X's Country Y tested unit"), and CFC1X's interest in FDEX and its other activities are combined and treated as a single tested unit of CFC1X ("CFC1X's Country X tested unit"). CFC1X's Country Y tested unit is attributed any item of CFC1X that is derived through its interest in FPSY to the extent the item is properly reflected on the applicable financial statement of FPSY. *See* paragraph (d)(1)(iii)(A) of this section.

(*iii*) *Analysis for CFC2X.* Under paragraphs (d)(2)(i)(A) and (d)(2)(i)(B)(*1*) of this section, CFC2X and CFC2X's 40% interest in FPSY are tested units of CFC2X. CFC2X's interest in FPSY is attributed any item of CFC2X that is derived through FPSY to the extent that it is properly reflected on the applicable financial statement of FPSY. *See* paragraph (d)(1)(iii)(A) of this section.

(*iv*) *Analysis for not combining CFC1X and CFC2X tested units.* None of the tested units of CFC1X are combined with the tested units of CFC2X under paragraph (d)(2)(iii)(A)(*1*) of this section because they are tested units of different controlled foreign corporations, and the combination rule only combines tested units of the same controlled foreign corporation.

(*6*) *Alternative facts – split ownership of transparent interest*—(*i*) *Facts.* The facts are the same as in paragraph (d)(9)(iii)(C)(*1*) of this section (the original facts in this *Example 3*), except that USP also owns CFC2X, CFC1X does not own FDE1Y, and CFC1X and CFC2X own 60% and 40%, respectively, of the interests in FPSY, but FPSY is not a tax resident of any foreign country and is fiscally transparent for Country X tax law purposes.

(*ii*) *Analysis for CFC1X.* CFC1X's interest in FPSY is not a tested unit but is a transparent interest. *See* paragraphs (d)(2)(i)(B) and (d)(8)(ix) of this section. Under paragraph (d)(3)(iii) of this section, any item of CFC1X that is derived through its interest in FPSY and is properly reflected on the applicable financial statement of FPSY is treated as properly reflected on the applicable financial statement of CFC1X.

(*iii*) *Analysis for CFC2X.* CFC2X's interest in FPSY is not a tested unit but is a transparent interest. *See* paragraphs (d)(2)(i)(B) and (d)(8)(ix) of this section. Under paragraph (d)(3)(iii) of this section, any item of CFC2X that is derived through its interest in FPSY and is properly reflected on the applicable financial statement of FPSY is treated as properly reflected on the applicable financial statement of CFC2X.

(D) *Example 4: Application of de minimis combination rule.*—(*1*) *Facts*—(*i*) *Ownership.* USP owns all of the stock of CFC1X, and CFC1X directly owns all of the interests of FDEW, FDEX, FDE1Y, FDE2Y, and FDEZ. FDEW and FDEZ are disregarded entities that are tax residents of Country W and Country Z, respectively.

(*ii*) *Gross income attributable to tested units.* Without regard to the combination rule of paragraph (d)(2)(iii) of this section, CFC1X, and CFC1X's interests in each of FDEW, FDEX, FDE1Y, FDE2Y, and FDEZ, would each be a tested unit of CFC1X. For the CFC inclusion year, and without regard to the combination rule of paragraph (d)(2)(iii) of this section, the U.S. dollar amount of the gross income attributable to the tested units of CFC1X (determined under paragraph (d)(1)(iii) of this section, and without regard to the combination rule in paragraph (d)(2)(iii) of this section) is as follows:

Table 1 to paragraph (d)(9)(iii)(D)(1)(ii).

Tested Unit	Gross Income
CFC1X	$19,500,000
FDEW	$100,000
FDEX	$100,000
FDE1Y	$175,000
FDE2Y	$50,000
FDEZ	$75,000
Total:	$20,000,000

(*2*) *Analysis*—(*i*) *Same country combination rule.* Pursuant to the same country combination rule in paragraph (d)(2)(iii)(A)(*1*) of this section, which applies before the de minimis combination rule in paragraph (d)(2)(iii)(A)(*2*) this section, the CFC1X tested unit (without regard to any items attributed to other tested units) is combined with CFC1X's interest in FDEX and treated as a single tested unit because CFC1X and FDEX are both tax residents of Country X (the "Country X tested unit"). CFC1X's interests in FDE1Y and FDE2Y are also combined under the same country combination rule and treated as a single tested unit because FDE1Y and FDE2Y are both tax residents of Country Y (the "Country Y tested unit").

(*ii*) *De minimis combination rule.* Pursuant to the de minimis combination rule in paragraph (d)(2)(iii)(A)(*2*) of this section, CFC1X's interests in FDEW and FDEZ are combined and treated as a single tested unit because the gross income attributable to each of these tested units ($100,000 attributable to CFC1X's interest in FDEW, and $75,000 attributable to CFC1X's interest in FDEZ) is less than $200,000, which is the lesser of 1% of CFCX's total gross income ($200,000) or $250,000. The Country X tested unit and the Country Y tested unit are not combined under the de minimis combination rule because the gross income attributable to these tested units ($19,600,000 attributable to the Country X tested unit, and $225,000 attributable to the Country Y tested unit) is not less than $200,000.

(E) *Example 5: CFC group - Controlled foreign corporations with different taxable years.*—(*1*) *Facts.* USP owns all of the stock of CFC1X and CFC2X. CFC2X has a taxable year ending November 30. On December 15, Year 1, USP sells all the stock of CFC2X to an unrelated party for cash.

(*2*) *Analysis.* The determination of whether CFC1X and CFC2X are in a CFC group is made as of the close of their CFC inclusion years that end with or within the taxable year ending December 31, Year 1, the taxable year of USP, the controlling domestic shareholder under paragraph (d)(8)(iii) of this section. *See* paragraph (d)(6)(v)(B)(2) of this section. Under paragraph (d)(6)(v)(B)(1) of this section, USP directly owns more than 50% of the stock of CFC1X as of December 31, Year 1, the end of CFC1X's CFC inclusion year. USP also directly owns more than 50% of the stock of CFC2X as of November 30, Year 1, the end of CFC2X's CFC inclusion year. Therefore, CFC1X and CFC2X are members of a CFC group and USP must consistently make high-tax elections, or revocations, under paragraph (d)(6) of this section with respect to CFC1X's taxable year ending December 31, Year 1, and CFC2X's taxable year ending November 30, Year 1. This is the case notwithstanding that USP does not directly own more than 50% of the stock of CFC2X as of December 31, Year 1, the end of CFC1X's CFC inclusion year. *See* paragraph (d)(6)(v)(B)(2) of this section.

(F) *Example 6: Application of anti-abuse rule to applicable instrument.*—(1) *Facts*—(i) *Ownership.* USP owns all the stock of CFC1X. CFC1X owns all the stock of CFCY, a controlled foreign corporation organized in Country Y. Under paragraph (d)(2)(i)(A) of this section, CFCY is a tested unit.

(ii) *Applicable instrument.* With a significant purpose of causing an item of gross income of CFCY to qualify for the high-tax exception described in section 954(b)(4) and paragraph (d)(1) of this section, CFCY issues an instrument to CFC1X. The instrument is treated as indebtedness that gives rise to deductible interest for federal income tax purposes and under the tax law of Country X, but payments or accruals with respect to the instrument are not deductible under the tax law of Country Y. During Year 1, CFCY accrues and pays € 20x with respect to the instrument held by CFC1X. For federal income tax purposes, the € 20x accrual is deductible interest expense. For Country Y tax purposes, neither the payment nor accrual is deductible. For Country X tax purposes, the € 20x payment is interest and included in income. CFCY has a general gross item that after taking into account the € 20x interest deduction on the instrument, but before taking into account the anti-abuse rule under paragraph (d)(7) of this section, would qualify for the high-tax exception in section 954(b)(4) and paragraph (d)(1) of this section; but for the € 20x interest deduction (for federal income tax purposes), the general gross item of CFCY would not qualify for the high-tax exception.

(2) *Analysis.* Under paragraph (d)(8)(i)(A) of this section, the instrument CFCY issues to CFC1X is an applicable instrument because it gives rise to deductions for federal income tax purposes but not, in whole or in part, under the tax law of Country Y. In addition, CFCY issues the instrument with a significant purpose of avoiding the purposes of section 951, 951A, 954(b)(4) or paragraph (d)(1) of this section. As a result, appropriate adjustments are made pursuant to the anti-abuse rule in paragraph (d)(7) of this section. The adjustments in this case would be an increase in the amount of the tentative net item described in paragraph (d)(1)(iv) of this section by € 20x, the amount of the payment on the applicable instrument that is deductible for federal income tax purposes, but not for Country Y tax purposes, such that CFCY's item of gross income does not qualify for the high-tax exception described in section 954(b)(4) and paragraph (d)(1) of this section.

* * *

(h) * * *

(3) *Paragraphs (a)(2) through (a)(7), (b)(1)(ii), (c)(1)(iii)(A)(3), (c)(1)(iv), and (d) of this section.*—Paragraphs (c)(1)(iii)(A)(3) and (c)(1)(iv) of this section apply to taxable years of a controlled foreign corporation beginning on or after July 23, 2020, and to taxable years of United States shareholders in which or with which such taxable years of foreign corporations end. Paragraphs (a)(2) through (7), (b)(1)(ii), and (d) of this section apply to taxable years of controlled foreign corporations beginning on or after [the date that final regulations are filed for public inspection], and to taxable years of United States shareholders in which or with which such taxable years of foreign corporations end. For the application of paragraphs (a)(2) through (7), (b)(1)(ii), and (d) (excluding paragraphs (d)(3)(i) and (d)(3)(ii)) of this section to taxable years of controlled foreign corporations beginning before [the date that final regulations are filed for public inspection], and to taxable years of United States shareholders in which or with which such taxable years of foreign corporations end, see § 1.954-1, as contained in 26 CFR part 1 revised as of April 1, 2020. For the application of paragraphs (d)(3)(i) and (ii) of this section to taxable years of controlled foreign corporations beginning on or after July 23, 2020, and before [the date final regulations are filed on public inspection], and to taxable years of United States shareholders in which or with which such taxable years of foreign corporations end, see § 1.954-1(d)(3)(i) and (ii), as in effect on September 21, 2020. [Prop. Reg. § 1.954-1.]

[Proposed 7-23-2020.]

Proposed Amendments to Regulation

☐ Section 1.954-1, as proposed to be amended in 85 FR 44650 (July 23, 2020), is further amended by removing the second sentence in paragraph (d)(1)(iv)(A).

§ 1.954-1. Foreign base company income.

[Proposed 11-12-2020.]

§ 1.954-2. Foreign personal holding company income.—(a) *Computation of foreign personal holding company income.*—(1) *Categories of foreign personal holding company income.*—For purposes of subpart F and the regulations under that subpart, foreign personal holding company income consists of the following categories of income—

(i) Dividends, interest, rents, royalties, and annuities as described in paragraph (b) of this section;

(ii) Gain from certain property transactions as described in paragraph (e) of this section;

(iii) Gain from commodities transactions as described in paragraph (f) of this section;

(iv) Foreign currency gain as described in paragraph (g) of this section; and

(v) Income equivalent to interest as described in paragraph (h) of this section.

(2) *Coordination of overlapping categories under foreign personal holding company provisions.*—(i) *In general.*—If any portion of income, gain or loss from a transaction is described in more than one category of foreign personal holding company income (as described in paragraph (a)(2)(ii) of this section), that portion of income, gain or loss is treated solely as income, gain or loss from the category of foreign personal holding company income with the highest priority.

(ii) *Priority of categories.*—The categories of foreign personal holding company income, listed from highest priority (paragraph (a)(2)(ii)(A) of this section) to lowest priority (paragraph (a)(2)(ii)(E) of this section), are—

(A) Dividends, interest, rents, royalties, and annuities, as described in paragraph (b) of this section;

(B) Income equivalent to interest, as described in paragraph (h) of this section without regard to the exceptions in paragraph (h)(1)(ii)(A) of this section;

(C) Foreign currency gain or loss, as described in paragraph (g) of this section without regard to the exclusion in paragraph (g)(2)(ii) of this section;

(D) Gain or loss from commodities transactions, as described in paragraph (f) of this section without regard to the exclusion in paragraph (f)(1)(ii) of this section; and

(E) Gain or loss from certain property transactions, as described in paragraph (e) of this section without regard to the exceptions in paragraph (e)(1)(ii) of this section.

(3) *Changes in the use or purpose for which property is held.*—(i) *In general.*—Under paragraphs (e), (f), (g) and (h) of this section, transactions in certain property give rise to gain or loss included in the computation of foreign personal holding company income if the controlled foreign corporation holds that property for a particular use or purpose. The use or purpose for which property is held is that use or purpose for which it was held for more than one-half of the period during which the controlled foreign corporation held the property prior to the disposition.

(ii) *Special rules.*—(A) *Anti-abuse rule.*—If a principal purpose of a change in use or purpose of property was to avoid including gain or loss in the computation of foreign personal holding company income, all the gain or loss from the disposition of the property is treated as foreign personal holding company income. A purpose may be a principal purpose even though it is outweighed by other purposes (taken together or separately).

(B) *Hedging transactions.*—The provisions of paragraph (a)(3)(i) of this section shall not apply to bona fide hedging transactions, as defined in paragraph (a)(4)(ii) of this section. A transaction will be treated as a bona fide hedging transaction only so long as it satisfies the requirements of paragraph (a)(4)(ii) of this section.

(iii) *Example.*—The following example illustrates the application of this paragraph (a)(3).

Example. At the beginning of taxable year 1, *CFC*, a controlled foreign corporation, purchases a building for investment. During taxable years 1 and 2, *CFC* derives rents from the building that are included in the computation of foreign personal holding company income under paragraph (b)(1)(iii) of this section. At the beginning of taxable year 3, *CFC* changes the use of the building by terminating all leases and using it in an active trade or business. At the beginning of taxable year 4, *CFC* sells the building at a gain. The building was not used in an active trade or business of *CFC* for more than one-half of the period during which it was held by *CFC*. Therefore, the building is considered to be property that gives rise to rents, as described in paragraph (e)(2) of this section, and gain from the sale is included in the computation of *CFC*'s foreign personal holding company income under paragraph (e) of this section.

(4) *Definitions and special rules.*—The following definitions and special rules apply for purposes of computing foreign personal holding company income under this section.

(i) *Interest.*—The term *interest* includes all amounts that are treated as interest income (including interest on a tax-exempt obligation) by reason of the Internal Revenue Code or Income Tax Regulations or any other provision of law. For example, interest includes stated interest, acquisition discount, original issue discount, de minimis original issue discount, market discount, de minimis market discount, and unstated interest, as adjusted by any amortizable bond premium or acquisition premium.

(ii) *Bona fide hedging transaction.*—(A) *Definition.*—The term *bona fide hedging transaction* means a transaction that meets the requirements of § 1.1221-2(a) through (d) and that is identified in accordance with the requirements of paragraph (a)(4)(ii)(B) of this section, except that in applying § 1.1221-2(b)(1), the risk being hedged may be with respect to ordinary property, section 1231 property, or a section 988 transaction. A transaction that hedges the liabilities, inventory or other assets of a related person (as defined in section 954(d)(3)), that is entered into to assume or reduce risks of a related person, or that is entered into by a person other than a person acting in its capacity as a regular dealer (as defined in paragraph (a)(4)(iv) of this section) to reduce risks assumed from a related person, will not be treated as a bona fide hedging transaction. For an illustration of how this rule applies with respect to foreign currency transactions, see paragraph (g)(2)(ii)(D) of this section.

(B) *Identification.*—The identification requirements of this section shall be satisfied if the taxpayer meets the identification and recordkeeping requirements of § 1.1221-2(f). However, for bona fide hedging transactions entered into prior to March 7, 1996, the identification and recordkeeping requirements of § 1.1221-2 shall not apply. Rather, for bona fide hedging transactions entered into on or after July 22, 1988 and prior to March 7, 1996, the identification and recordkeeping requirements shall be satisfied if such transactions are identified by the close of the fifth day after the day on which they are entered into. For bona fide hedging transactions entered into prior to July 22, 1988, the identification and recordkeeping requirements shall be satisfied if such transactions are identified reasonably contemporaneously with the date they are entered into, but no later than within the normal period prescribed under the method of accounting of the controlled foreign corporation used for financial reporting purposes.

(C) *Effect of identification and non-identification.*—*(1) Transactions identified.*—If a taxpayer identifies a transaction as a bona fide hedging transaction for purposes of this section, the identification is binding with respect to any loss arising from such transaction whether or not all of the requirements of paragraph (a)(4)(ii)(A) of this section are satisfied. Accordingly, such loss will be allocated against income that is not subpart F income (or, in the case of an election under paragraph (g)(3) of this section, against the category of subpart F income to which it relates) and apportioned among the categories of income described in section 904(d)(1). If the transaction is not in fact a bona fide hedging transaction described in paragraph (a)(4)(ii)(A) of this section, however, then any gain realized with respect to such transaction shall not be considered as gain from a bona fide hedging transaction. Accordingly, such gain shall be treated as gain from the appropriate category of foreign personal holding company income. Thus, the taxpayer's identification of the transaction as a hedging transaction does not itself operate to exclude gain from the appropriate category of foreign personal holding company income.

(2) Inadvertent identification.—Notwithstanding paragraph (a)(4)(ii)(C)*(1)* of this section, if the taxpayer identifies a transaction as a bona fide hedging transaction for purposes of this section, the characterization of the loss is determined as if the transaction had not been identified as a bona fide hedging transaction if—

(i) The transaction is not a bona fide hedging transaction (as defined in paragraph (a)(4)(ii)(A) of this section);

(ii) The identification of the transaction as a bona fide hedging transaction was due to inadvertent error; and

(iii) All of the taxpayer's transactions in all open years are being treated on either original or, if necessary, amended returns in a manner consistent with the principles of this section.

(3) Transactions not identified.—Except as provided in paragraphs (a)(4)(ii)(C)*(4)* and *(5)* of this section, the absence of an identification that satisfies the requirements of paragraph (a)(4)(ii)(B) of this section is binding and establishes that a transaction is not a bona fide hedging transaction. Thus, subject to the exceptions, the characterization of gain or loss is determined without reference to whether the transaction is a bona fide hedging transaction.

(4) Inadvertent error.—If a taxpayer does not make an identification that satisfies the requirements of paragraph (a)(4)(ii)(B) of this section, the taxpayer may treat gain or loss from the transaction as gain or loss from a bona fide hedging transaction if—

(i) The transaction is a bona fide hedging transaction (as defined in paragraph (a)(4)(ii)(A) of this section);

(ii) The failure to identify the transaction was due to inadvertent error; and

(iii) All of the taxpayer's bona fide hedging transactions in all open years are being treated on either original or, if necessary, amended returns as bona fide hedging transactions in accordance with the rules of this section.

(5) Anti-abuse rule.—If a taxpayer does not make an identification that satisfies all the requirements of paragraph (a)(4)(ii)(B) of this section but the taxpayer has no reasonable grounds for treating the transaction as other than a bona fide hedging transaction, then loss from the transaction shall be treated as realized with respect to a bona fide hedging transaction. Thus, a taxpayer may not elect to exclude loss from its proper characterization as a bona fide hedging transaction. The reasonableness of the taxpayer's failure to identify a transaction is determined by taking into consideration not only the requirements of paragraph (a)(4)(ii)(A) of this section but also the taxpayer's treatment of the transaction for financial accounting or other purposes and the taxpayer's identification of similar transactions as hedging transactions.

(iii) *Inventory and similar property.*—(A) *Definition.*—The term *inventory and similar property* (or *inventory or similar property*) means property that is stock in trade of the controlled foreign corporation or other property of a kind that would properly be included in the inventory of the controlled foreign corporation if on hand at the close of the taxable year (if the controlled foreign corporation were a domestic corporation), or property held by the controlled foreign corporation primarily for sale to customers in the ordinary course of its trade or business.

(B) *Hedging transactions.*—A bona fide hedging transaction with respect to inventory or similar property (other than a transaction described in section 988(c)(1) without regard to section 988(c)(1)(D)(i)) shall be treated as a transaction in inventory or similar property.

(iv) *Regular dealer.*—The term *regular dealer* means a controlled foreign corporation that—

(A) Regularly and actively offers to, and in fact does, purchase property from and sell property to customers who are not related persons (as defined in section 954(d)(3)) with respect to the controlled foreign corporation in the ordinary course of a trade or business; or

(B) Regularly and actively offers to, and in fact does, enter into, assume, offset, assign or otherwise terminate positions in property with customers who are not related persons (as defined in section 954(d)(3)) with respect to the controlled foreign corporation in the ordinary course of a trade or business.

(v) *Dealer property.*—(A) *Definition.*—Property held by a controlled foreign corporation is *dealer property* if—

(1) The controlled foreign corporation is a regular dealer in property of such kind (determined under paragraph (a)(4)(iv) of this section); and

(2) The property is held by the controlled foreign corporation in its capacity as a dealer in property of such kind without

regard to whether the property arises from a transaction with a related person (as defined in section 954(d)(3)) with respect to the controlled foreign corporation. The property is not held by the controlled foreign corporation in its capacity as a dealer if the property is held for investment or speculation on its own behalf or on behalf of a related person (as defined in section 954(d)(3)).

(B) *Securities dealers.*—If a controlled foreign corporation is a licensed securities dealer, only the securities that it has identified as held for investment in accordance with the provisions of section 475(b) or section 1236 will be considered to be property held for investment or speculation under this section. A licensed securities dealer is a controlled foreign corporation that is both a securities dealer, as defined in section 475, and a regular dealer, as defined in paragraph (a)(4)(iv) of this section, and that is either—

(1) registered as a securities dealer under section 15(a) of the Securities Exchange Act of 1934 or as a Government securities dealer under section 15C(a) of such Act; or

(2) licensed or authorized in the country in which it is chartered, incorporated, or organized to purchase and sell securities from or to customers who are residents of that country. The conduct of such securities activities must be subject to bona fide regulation, including appropriate reporting, monitoring, and prudential (including capital adequacy) requirements, by a securities regulatory authority in that country that regularly enforces compliance with such requirements and prudential standards.

(C) *Hedging transactions.*—A bona fide hedging transaction with respect to dealer property shall be treated as a transaction in dealer property.

(vi) *Examples.*—The following examples illustrate the application of paragraphs (a)(4)(ii), (iv) and (v) of this section.

Example 1. (i) CFC1 and CFC2 are related controlled foreign corporations (within the meaning of section 954(d)(3)) located in Countries F and G, respectively. *CFC1* and *CFC2* regularly purchase securities from and sell securities to customers who are not related persons with respect to *CFC1* or *CFC2* (within the meaning of section 954(d)(3)) in the ordinary course of their businesses and regularly and actively hold themselves out as being willing to, and in fact do, enter into either side of options, forward contracts, or other financial instruments. *CFC1* uses securities that are traded in securities markets in Country G to hedge positions that it enters into with customers located in Country F. *CFC1* is not a member of a securities exchange in Country G, so it purchases such securities from *CFC2* and unrelated persons that are registered as securities dealers in Country G and that are members of Country G securities exchanges. Such hedging transactions qualify as bona fide hedging transactions under paragraph (a)(4)(ii) of this section.

(ii) Transactions that *CFC1* and *CFC2* enter into with each other do not affect the determination of whether they are regular dealers. Because *CFC1* and *CFC2* regularly purchase securities from and sell securities to customers who are not related persons within the meaning of section 954(d)(3) in the ordinary course of their businesses and regularly and actively hold themselves out as being willing to, and in fact do, enter into either side of options, forward contracts, or other financial instruments, however, they qualify as regular dealers in such property within the meaning of paragraph (a)(4)(iv) of this section. Moreover, because *CFC1* purchases securities from *CFC2* as bona fide hedging transactions with respect to dealer property, the securities are dealer property under paragraph (a)(4)(v)(C) of this section. Similarly, because *CFC2* sells securities to *CFC1* in the ordinary course of its business as a dealer, the securities are dealer property under paragraph (a)(4)(v)(A) of this section.

Example 2. (i) *CFC* is a controlled foreign corporation located in Country B. *CFC* serves as the currency coordination center for the controlled group, aggregating currency risks incurred by the group and entering into hedging transactions that transfer those risks outside of the group. *CFC* regularly and actively holds itself out as being willing to, and in fact does, enter into either side of options, forward contracts, or other financial instruments with other members of the same controlled group. *CFC* hedges risks arising from such transactions by entering into transactions with persons who are not related persons (within the meaning of section 954(d)(3)) with respect to *CFC*. However, *CFC* does not regularly and actively hold itself out as being willing to, and does not, enter into either side of transactions with unrelated persons.

(ii) *CFC* is not a regular dealer in property under paragraph (a)(4)(iv) of this section and its options, forwards, and other financial instruments are not dealer property within the meaning of paragraph (a)(4)(v) of this section.

(vii) *Debt instrument.*—The term *debt instrument* includes bonds, debentures, notes, certificates, accounts receivable, and other evidences of indebtedness.

(5) *Special rules applicable to distributive share of partnership income.*—(i) [Reserved].

(ii) *Certain other exceptions applicable to foreign personal holding company income.*—To determine the extent to which a controlled foreign corporation's distributive share of an item of income of a partnership is foreign personal holding company income—

(A) The exceptions contained in section 954(c) that are based on whether the controlled foreign corporation is engaged in the active conduct of a trade or business, including section 954(c)(2) and paragraphs (b)(2) and (6), (e)(1)(ii) and (3)(ii), (iii) and (iv), (f)(1)(ii), (g)(2)(ii), and (h)(3)(ii) of this section, shall apply only if any such exception would have applied to exclude the income from foreign personal holding company income if the controlled foreign corporation had earned the income directly, determined by taking into account only the activities of, and property owned by, the partnership and not the separate activities or property of the controlled foreign corporation or any other person;

(B) A controlled foreign corporation's distributive share of partnership income will not be excluded from foreign personal holding company income under the exception contained in section 954(h) unless the controlled foreign corporation is an eligible controlled foreign corporation within the meaning of section 954(h)(2) (taking into account the income of the controlled foreign corporation and any partnerships or other qualified business units, within the meaning of section 989(a), of the controlled foreign corporation, including the controlled foreign corporation's distributive share of partnership income) and the partnership, of which the controlled foreign corporation is a partner, generates qualified banking or financing income within the meaning of section 954(h)(3) (taking into account only the income of the partnership);

(C) A controlled foreign corporation's distributive share of partnership income will not be excluded from foreign personal holding company income under the exception contained in section 954(i) unless the controlled foreign corporation is a qualifying insurance company, as defined in section 953(e)(3), and the income of the partnership would have been qualified insurance income, as defined in section 954(i)(2), if received by the controlled foreign corporation directly. See § 1.952-1(g)(1).

(iii) *Examples.*—The application of paragraph (a)(5)(ii) is demonstrated by the following examples:

Example 1. B Corp, a Country C corporation, is a controlled foreign corporation within the meaning of section 957(a). B Corp is an 80 percent partner of RKS Partnership, a Country D partnership whose principal office is located in Country D. RKS Partnership is a qualified business unit of B Corp, within the meaning of section 989(a). B Corp, including income earned through RKS Partnership, derives more than 70 percent of its gross income directly from the active and regular conduct of a lending or finance business, within the meaning of section 954(h)(4), from transactions in various countries with customers which are not related persons. Thus, B Corp is predominantly engaged in the active conduct of a banking, financing, or similar business within the meaning of section 954(h)(2)(A)(i). B Corp conducts substantial activity with respect to such business within the meaning of section 954(h)(2)(A)(ii). RKS Partnership derives more than 30 percent of its income from the active and regular conduct of a lending or finance business, within the meaning of section 954(h)(4), from transactions with customers which are not related persons and which are located solely within the home country of RKS Partnership, Country D. B Corp's distributive share of RKS Partnership's income from its lending or finance business will satisfy the special rule for income derived in the active conduct of banking, financing, or similar business of section 954(h). B Corp is an eligible controlled foreign corporation within the meaning of section 954(h)(2) and RKS Partnership generates qualified banking or financing income within the meaning of section 954(h)(3). B Corp does not have any foreign personal holding company income with respect to its distributive share of RKS Partnership income attributable to its lending or finance business income earned in Country D.

Example 2. D Corp, a Country F corporation, is a controlled foreign corporation within the meaning of section 957(a). D Corp is a qualifying insurance company, within the meaning of section 953(e)(3), that is engaged in the business of issuing life insurance contracts. D Corp has reserves of $100x, all of which are allocable to exempt contracts, and $10x of surplus, which is equal to 10 percent of the reserves allocable to exempt contracts. D Corp contributed the

$100x of reserves and $10x of surplus to DJ Partnership in exchange for a 40-percent partnership interest. DJ Partnership is an entity organized under the laws of Country G and is treated as a partnership under the laws of Country G and Country F. DJ Partnership earns $30x of investment income during the taxable year that is received from persons who are not related persons with respect to D Corp, within the meaning of section 954(d)(3). D Corp's distributive share of this investment income is $12x. This income is treated as earned by D Corp in Country F under the tax laws of Country F and meets the definition of exempt insurance income in section 953(e)(1). This $12x of investment income would be qualified insurance income, under section 954(i)(2), if D Corp had received the income directly, because the $110x invested by D Corp in DJ Partnership is equal to D Corp's reserves allocable to exempt contracts under section 954(i)(2)(A) and allowable surplus under section 954(i)(2)(B)(ii). Thus, D Corp's distributive share of DJ Partnership's income will be excluded from foreign personal holding company income under section 954(i).

(iv) [Reserved].

(v) *Effective date.*—This paragraph (a)(5) applies to taxable years of a controlled foreign corporation beginning on or after July 23, 2002.

(b) *Dividends, interest, rents, royalties, and annuities.*—(1) *In general.*—Foreign personal holding company income includes—

(i) Dividends, except certain dividends from related persons as described in paragraph (b)(4) of this section and distributions of previously taxed income under section 959(b);

(ii) Interest, except export financing interest as defined in paragraph (b)(2) of this section and certain interest received from related persons as described in paragraph (b)(4) of this section;

(iii) Rents and royalties, except certain rents and royalties received from related persons as described in paragraph (b)(5) of this section and rents and royalties derived in the active conduct of a trade or business as defined in paragraph (b)(6) of this section; and

(iv) Annuities.

(2) *Exclusion of certain export financing interest.*—(i) *In general.*—Foreign personal holding company income does not include interest that is export financing interest. The term *export financing interest* means interest that is derived in the conduct of a banking business and is export financing interest as defined in section 904(d)(2)(G). Solely for purposes of determining whether interest is export financing interest, property is treated as manufactured, produced, grown, or extracted in the United States if it is so treated under § 1.927(a)-1T(c).

(ii) *Exceptions.*—Export financing interest does not include income from related party factoring that is treated as interest under section 864(d)(1) or (6) after the application of section 864(d)(7).

(iii) *Conduct of a banking business.*—For purposes of this section, export financing interest is considered derived in the conduct of a banking business if, in connection with the financing from which the interest is derived, the corporation, through its own officers or staff of employees, engages in all the activities in which banks customarily engage in issuing and servicing a loan.

(iv) *Examples.*—The following examples illustrate the application of this paragraph (b)(2).

Example 1. (i) *DS*, a domestic corporation, manufactures property in the United States. In addition to selling inventory (property described in section 1221(1)), *DS* occasionally sells depreciable equipment it manufactures for use in its trade or business, which is property described in section 1221(2). Less than 50 percent of the fair market value, determined in accordance with section 904(d)(2)(G), of each item of inventory or equipment sold by *DS* is attributable to products imported into the United States. *CFC*, a controlled foreign corporation with respect to which *DS* is a related person (within the meaning of section 954(d)(3)), provides loans described in section 864(d)(6) to unrelated persons for the purchase of property from *DS*. This property is purchased exclusively for use or consumption outside the United States and outside *CFC's* country of incorporation.

(ii) If, in issuing and servicing loans made with respect to purchases from *DS* of depreciable equipment used in its trade or business, which is property described in section 1221(2) in the hands of *DS*, *CFC* engages in all the activities in which banks customarily engage in issuing and servicing loans, the interest accrued from these loans would be export financing interest meeting the requirements of this paragraph (b)(2) and, thus, not included in foreign personal holding company income. However, interest from the loans made with respect to purchases from *DS* of property that is inventory in the hands of *DS* cannot be export financing interest because it is treated as income from a trade or service receivable under section 864(d)(6) and the exception under section 864(d)(7) does not apply. Thus the interest from loans made with respect to this inventory is included in foreign personal holding company income under paragraph (b)(1)(ii) of this section.

Example 2. (i) DS, a domestic corporation, wholly owns two controlled foreign corporations organized in Country A, CFC1 and CFC2. CFC1 purchases from DS property that DS manufactures in the United States. CFC1 uses the purchased property as a component part of property that CFC1 manufactures in Country A within the meaning of § 1.954-3(a)(4). CFC2 provides loans described in section 864(d)(6) to unrelated persons in Country A for the purchase of the property that CFC1 manufactures in Country A.

(ii) The interest accrued from the loans by CFC2 is not export financing interest as defined in section 904(d)(2)(G) because the property sold by CFC1 is not manufactured in the United States under § 1.927(a)-1T(c). No portion of the interest is export financing interest as defined in this paragraph (b)(2). The full amount of the interest is, therefore, included in foreign personal holding company income under paragraph (b)(1)ii) of this section.

(3) *Treatment of tax exempt interest.*—For taxable years of a controlled foreign corporation beginning after March 3, 1997, foreign personal holding company income includes all interest income, including interest that is described in section 103 (see § 1.952-2(c)(1)).

(4) *Exclusion of dividends or interest from related persons.*—(i) *In general.*—(A) *Corporate payor.*—Foreign personal holding company income received by a controlled foreign corporation does not include dividends or interest if the payor—

(1) Is a corporation that is a related person with respect to the controlled foreign corporation, as defined in section 954(d)(3);

(2) Is created or organized under the laws of the same foreign country (the *country of incorporation*) as is the controlled foreign corporation; and

(3) Uses a substantial part of its assets in a trade or business in its country of incorporation, as determined under this paragraph (b)(4).

(B) *Payment by a partnership.*—For purposes of this paragraph (b)(4), if a partnership with one or more corporate partners makes a payment of interest, a corporate partner will be treated as the payor of the interest—

(1) If the interest payment gives rise to a partnership item of deduction under the Internal Revenue Code or Income Tax Regulations, to the extent that the item of deduction is allocable to the corporate partner under section 704(b); or

(2) If the interest payment does not give rise to a partnership item of deduction under the Internal Revenue Code or Income Tax Regulations, to the extent that a partnership item reasonably related to the payment would be allocated to that partner under an existing allocation under the partnership agreement (made pursuant to section 704(b)).

(ii) *Exceptions.*—(A) *Dividends.*—Dividends are excluded from foreign personal holding company income under this paragraph (b)(4) only to the extent that they are paid out of earnings and profits that are earned or accumulated during a period in which—

(1) The stock on which dividends are paid with respect to which the exclusion is claimed was owned by the recipient controlled foreign corporation directly, or indirectly through a chain of one or more subsidiaries each of which meets the requirements of paragraph (b)(4)(i)(A) of this section; and

(2) Each of the requirements of paragraph (b)(4)(i)(A) of this section is satisfied or, to the extent earned or accumulated during a taxable year of the related foreign corporation ending on or before December 31, 1962, during a period in which the payor was a related corporation as to the controlled foreign corporation and the other requirements of paragraph (b)(4)(i)(A) of this section were substantially satisfied.

(3) This paragraph (b)(4)(ii)(A) is illustrated by the following example:

Example. A, a domestic corporation, owns all of the stock of *B*, a corporation created and organized under the laws of Country Y, and *C*, a corporation created and organized under the laws of Country X. The taxable year of each of the corporations is the calendar year. In Year 1, *B* earns $100 of income from the sale of products in Country Y that it manufactured in Country Y. C had no earnings and profits in Year 1. On January 1 of Year 2, A contributes all of the stock of B and C to Newco, a Country Y corporation, in exchange for all of the stock of Newco. Neither *B* nor *C* earns any income in Year 2, but at the end of Year 2 *B* distributes the $100 accumulated earnings and profits to Newco. Newco's income from the distribution, $100, is foreign personal holding company income because the earnings and profits distributed by *B* were not earned or accumulated during a period in which the stock of *B* was owned by Newco and in which each of the requirements of paragraph (b)(4)(i)(A) of this section was satisfied.

(B) *Interest paid out of adjusted foreign base company income or insurance income.—(1) In general.*—Interest may not be excluded from the foreign personal holding company income of the recipient under this paragraph (b)(4) to the extent that the deduction for the interest is allocated under § 1.954-1(a)(4) and (c) to the payor's adjusted gross foreign base company income (as defined in § 1.954-1(a)(3)), adjusted gross insurance income (as defined in § 1.954-1(a)(6)), or any other category of income included in the computation of subpart F income under section 952(a).

(2) Rule for corporations that are both recipients and payors of interest.—If a controlled foreign corporation is both a recipient and payor of interest, the interest that is received will be characterized before the interest that is paid. In addition, the amount of interest paid or accrued, directly or indirectly, by the controlled foreign corporation to a related person (as defined in section 954(d)(3)) shall be offset against and eliminate any interest received or accrued, directly or indirectly, by the controlled foreign corporation from that related person. In a case in which the controlled foreign corporation pays or accrues interest to a related person, as defined in section 954(d)(3), and also receives or accrues interest indirectly from the related person, the smallest interest payment is eliminated and the amounts of all other interest payments are reduced by the amount of the smallest interest payment.

(C) *Coordination with sections 864(d) and 881(c).*—Income of a controlled foreign corporation that is treated as interest under section 864(d)(1) or (6), or that is portfolio interest, as defined by section 881(c), is not excluded from foreign personal holding company income under section 954(c)(3)(A)(i) and this paragraph (b)(4).

(iii) *Trade or business requirement.*—Except as otherwise provided under this paragraph (b)(4), the principles of section 367(a) apply for purposes of determining whether the payor has a trade or business in its country of incorporation and whether its assets are used in that trade or business. Property purchased or produced for use in a trade or business is not considered used in a trade or business before it is placed in service or after it is retired from service as determined in accordance with the principles of sections 167 and 168.

(iv) *Substantial assets test.*—A substantial part of the assets of the payor will be considered to be used in a trade or business located in the payor's country of incorporation for a taxable year only if the average value of the payor's assets for such year that are used in the trade or business and are located in such country equals more than 50 percent of the average value of all the assets of the payor (including assets not used in a trade or business). The average value of assets for the taxable year is determined by averaging the values of assets at the close of each quarter of the taxable year. The value of assets is determined under paragraph (b)(4)(v) of this section, and the location of assets used in a trade or business of the payor is determined under paragraphs (b)(4)(vi) through (xi) of this section.

(v) *Valuation of assets.*—For purposes of determining whether a substantial part of the assets of the payor are used in a trade or business in its country of incorporation, the value of assets shall be their fair market value (not reduced by liabilities), which, in the absence of affirmative evidence to the contrary, shall be deemed to be their adjusted basis.

(vi) *Location of tangible property.*—(A) *In general.*—Tangible property (other than inventory and similar property as defined in paragraph (a)(4)(iii) of this section, and dealer property as defined in paragraph (a)(4)(v) of this section) used in a trade or business is considered located in the country in which it is physically located.

(B) *Exception.*—An item of tangible personal property that is used in the trade or business of a payor in the payor's country of incorporation is considered located within the payor's country of incorporation while it is temporarily located elsewhere for inspection or repair if the property is not placed in service in a country other than the payor's country of incorporation and is not to be so placed in service following the inspection or repair.

(vii) *Location of intangible property.*—(A) *In general.*—Intangible property (other than inventory and similar property as defined in paragraph (a)(4)(iii) of this section, dealer property as defined in paragraph (a)(4)(v) of this section, and debt instruments) is considered located entirely in the payor's country of incorporation for a quarter of the taxable year only if the payor conducts all of its activities in connection with the use or exploitation of the property in that country during that entire quarter. For this purpose, the country in which the activities connected to the use or exploitation of the property are conducted is the country in which the expenses associated with these activities are incurred. Expenses incurred in connection with the use or exploitation of an item of intangible property are included in the computation provided by this paragraph (b)(4) if they would be deductible under section 162 or includible in inventory costs or the cost of goods sold if the payor were a domestic corporation. If the payor conducts such activities through an agent or independent contractor, then the expenses incurred by the payor with respect to the agent or independent contractor shall be deemed to be incurred by the payor in the country in which the expenses of the agent or independent contractor were incurred by the agent or independent contractor.

(B) *Exception for property located in part in the payor's country of incorporation.*—If the payor conducts its activities in connection with the use or exploitation of an item of intangible property, including goodwill (other than inventory and similar property, dealer property and debt instruments) during a quarter of the taxable year both in its country of incorporation and elsewhere, then the value of the intangible considered located in the payor's country of incorporation during that quarter is a percentage of the value of the item as of the close of the quarter. That percentage equals the ratio that the expenses incurred by the payor (described in paragraph (b)(4)(vii)(A) of this section) during the entire quarter by reason of activities that are connected with the use or exploitation of the item of intangible property and are conducted in the payor's country of incorporation bear to all expenses incurred by the payor during the entire quarter by reason of all such activities worldwide.

(viii) *Location of inventory and dealer property.*—(A) *In general.*—Inventory and similar property, as defined in paragraph (a)(4)(iii) of this section, and dealer property, as defined in paragraph (a)(4)(v) of this section, are considered located entirely in the payor's country of incorporation for a quarter of the taxable year only if the payor conducts all of its activities in connection with the production and sale, or purchase and resale, of such property in its country of incorporation during that entire quarter. If the payor conducts such activities through an agent or independent contractor, then the location of such activities is the place in which they are conducted by the agent or independent contractor.

(B) *Inventory and dealer property located in part in the payor's country of incorporation.*—If the payor conducts its activities in connection with the production and sale, or purchase and resale, of inventory or similar property or dealer property during a quarter of the taxable year both in its country of incorporation and elsewhere, then the value of the inventory or similar property or dealer property considered located in the payor's country of incorporation during each quarter is a percentage of the value of the inventory or similar property or dealer property as of the close of the quarter. That percentage equals the ratio that the costs and expenses incurred by the payor during the entire quarter by reason of activities connected with the production and sale, or purchase and resale, of inventory or similar property or dealer property that are conducted in the payor's country of incorporation bear to all costs or expenses incurred by the payor during the entire quarter by reason of all such activities worldwide. A cost incurred in connection with the production and sale or purchase and resale of inventory or similar property or dealer property is included in this computation if it—

(1) Would be included in inventory costs or otherwise capitalized with respect to inventory or similar property or dealer property under section 61, 263A, 471, or 472 if the payor were a domestic corporation; or

(2) Would be deductible under section 162 if the payor were a domestic corporation and is definitely related to gross income derived from such property (but not to all classes of gross income derived by the payor) under the principles of § 1.861-8.

(ix) *Location of debt instruments.*—For purposes of this paragraph (b)(4), debt instruments, other than debt instruments that are inventory or similar property (as defined in paragraph (a)(4)(iii) of this section) or dealer property (as defined in paragraph (a)(4)(v) of this section) are considered to be used in a trade or business only if they arise from the sale of inventory or similar property or dealer property by the payor or from the rendition of services by the payor in the ordinary course of a trade or business of the payor, and only until such time as interest is required to be charged under section 482. Debt instruments that arise from the sale of inventory or similar property or dealer property during a quarter are treated as having the same location, proportionately, as the inventory or similar property or dealer property held during that quarter. Debt instruments arising from the rendition of services in the ordinary course of a trade or business are considered located on a proportionate basis in the countries in which the services to which they relate are performed.

(x) *Treatment of certain stock interests.*—Stock in a controlled foreign corporation (lower-tier corporation) that is incorporated in the same country as the payor and that is more than 50-percent owned, directly or indirectly, by the payor within the meaning of section 958(a) shall be considered located in the payor's country of incorporation and, solely for purposes of section 954(c)(3), used in a trade or business of the payor in proportion to the value of the assets of the lower-tier corporation that are used in a trade or business in the country of incorporation. The location of assets used in a trade or business of the lower-tier corporation shall be determined under the rules of this paragraph (b)(4).

(xi) *Treatment of banks and insurance companies.*—[Reserved]

(5) *Exclusion of rents and royalties derived from related persons.*—(i) *In general.*—(A) *Corporate payor.*—Foreign personal holding company income received by a controlled foreign corporation does not include rents or royalties if—

(1) The payor is a corporation that is a related person with respect to the controlled foreign corporation, as defined in section 954(d)(3); and

(2) The rents or royalties are for the use of, or the privilege of using, property within the country under the laws of which the controlled foreign corporation receiving the payments is created or organized (the country of incorporation).

(B) *Payment by a partnership.*—For purposes of this paragraph (b)(5), if a partnership with one or more corporate partners makes a payment of rents or royalties, a corporate partner will be treated as the payor of the rents or royalties—

(1) If the rent or royalty payment gives rise to a partnership item of deduction under the Internal Revenue Code or Income Tax Regulations, to the extent the item of deduction is allocable to the corporate partner under section 704(b); or

(2) If the rent or royalty payment does not give rise to a partnership item of deduction under the Internal Revenue Code or Income Tax Regulations, to the extent that a partnership item reasonably related to the payment would be allocated to that partner under an existing allocation under the partnership agreement (made pursuant to section 704(b)).

(ii) *Exceptions.*—(A) *Rents or royalties paid out of adjusted foreign base company income or insurance income.*—Rents or royalties may not be excluded from the foreign personal holding company income of the recipient under this paragraph (b)(5) to the extent that deductions for the payments are allocated under section 954(b)(5) and §1.954-1(a)(4) and (c) to the payor's adjusted gross foreign base company income (as defined in §1.954-1(a)(3)), adjusted gross insurance income (as defined in §1.954-1(a)(6)), or any other category of income included in the computation of subpart F income under section 952(a).

(B) *Property used in part in the controlled foreign corporation's country of incorporation.*—If the payor uses the property both in the controlled foreign corporation's country of incorporation and elsewhere, the part of the rent or royalty attributable (determined under the principles of section 482) to the use of, or the privilege of using, the property outside such country of incorporation is included in the computation of foreign personal holding company income under this paragraph (b).

(6) *Exclusion of rents and royalties derived in the active conduct of a trade or business.*—Foreign personal holding company income shall not include rents or royalties that are derived in the active conduct of a trade or business and received from a person that is not a related person (as defined in section 954(d)(3)) with respect to the controlled foreign corporation. For purposes of this section, rents or royalties are derived in the active conduct of a trade or business only if the provisions of paragraph (c) or (d) of this section are satisfied.

(c) *Excluded rents.*—(1) *Active conduct of a trade or business.*—Rents will be considered for purposes of paragraph (b)(6) of this section to be derived in the active conduct of a trade or business if such rents are derived by the controlled foreign corporation (the lessor) from leasing any of the following—

(i) Property that the lessor, through its own officers or staff of employees, has manufactured or produced, or property that the lessor has acquired and, through its own officers or staff of employees, added substantial value to, but only if the lessor, through its officers or staff of employees, is regularly engaged in the manufacture or production of, or in the acquisition and addition of substantial value to, property of such kind;

(ii) Real property with respect to which the lessor, through its own officers or staff of employees, regularly performs active and substantial management and operational functions while the property is leased;

(iii) Personal property ordinarily used by the lessor in the active conduct of a trade or business, leased temporarily during a period when the property would, but for such leasing, be idle; or

(iv) Property that is leased as a result of the performance of marketing functions by such lessor through its own officers or staff of employees located in a foreign country or countries, if the lessor, through its officers or staff of employees, maintains and operates an organization either in such country or in such countries (collectively), as applicable, that is regularly engaged in the business of marketing, or of marketing and servicing, the leased property and that is substantial in relation to the amount of rents derived from the leasing of such property.

(2) *Special rules.*—(i) *Adding substantial value.*—For purposes of paragraph (c)(1)(i) of this section, the performance of marketing functions will not be considered to add substantial value to property.

(ii) *Substantiality of foreign organization.*—For purposes of paragraph (c)(1)(iv) of this section, whether an organization either in a foreign country or in foreign countries (collectively) is substantial in relation to the amount of rents is determined based on all the facts and circumstances. However, such an organization will be considered substantial in relation to the amount of rents if active leasing expenses, as defined in paragraph (c)(2)(iii) of this section, equal or exceed 25 percent of the adjusted leasing profit, as defined in paragraph (c)(2)(iv) of this section. In addition, for purposes of aircraft or vessels leased in foreign commerce, an organization will be considered substantial if active leasing expenses, as defined in paragraph (c)(2)(iii) of this section, equal or exceed 10 percent of the adjusted leasing profit, as defined in paragraph (c)(2)(iv) of this section. For purposes of paragraphs (c)(1)(iv) and (c)(2) of this section and §1.956-2(b)(1)(vi), the term *aircraft or vessels* includes component parts, such as engines that are leased separately from an aircraft or vessel.

(iii) *Active leasing expenses.*—The term *active leasing expenses* means the deductions incurred by an organization of the lessor in a foreign country that are properly allocable to rental income and that would be allowable under section 162 to the lessor if it were a domestic corporation, other than—

(A) Deductions for compensation for personal services rendered by shareholders of, or related persons (as defined in section 954(d)(3)) with respect to, the lessor;

(B) Deductions for amounts (including rents and royalties) paid or incurred by the lessor for the right to use the property (or a component thereof) that generated the rental income;

(C) Deductions that, although generally allowable under section 162, would be specifically allowable to the lessor (if the lessor were a domestic corporation) under any section of the Internal Revenue Code other than section 162;

(D) Deductions for payments made to agents or independent contractors with respect to the leased property other than payments for insurance, utilities and other expenses for like services, or for capitalized repairs; and

(E) Deductions for CST Payments or PCT Payments (as defined in §1.482-7(b)).

(iv) *Adjusted leasing profit.*—The term *adjusted leasing profit* means the gross income of the lessor from rents, reduced by the sum of—

(A) Amounts (including rents and royalties) paid or incurred by the lessor for the right to use the property (or a component thereof) that generated the rental income;

(B) The amounts that would be allowable to such lessor (if the lessor were a domestic corporation) as deductions under sections 167 or 168 with respect to such rental income; and

(C) The amounts paid by the lessor to agents or independent contractors with respect to such rental income other than payments for insurance, utilities and other expenses for like services, or for capitalized repairs.

(v) *Leased in foreign commerce.*—For purposes of paragraphs (c)(1)(iv) and (c)(2)(ii) of this section, an aircraft or vessel is considered to be leased in foreign commerce if the aircraft or vessel is used in foreign commerce and is used predominantly outside the United States. An aircraft or vessel is considered to be used in foreign commerce if it is used for the transportation of property or passengers between a port (or airport) in the United States and a port (or airport) in a foreign country or between foreign ports (or airports). An aircraft or vessel will be considered to be used predominantly outside the United States if more than 50 percent of the miles traversed during the taxable year in the use of the aircraft or vessel are traversed outside the United States or if the aircraft or vessel is located outside the United States more than 50 percent of the time during the taxable year.

(vi) *Leases acquired by the CFC lessor.*—Except as provided in this paragraph (c)(2)(vi), the exception in paragraph (c)(1)(iv) of this section will also apply to rents from leases acquired from any person, if following the acquisition the lessor performs active and substantial management, operational, and remarketing (including remarketing for purposes of re-leasing or selling the property) functions with respect to the leased property. However, if any person is claiming a benefit with respect to an acquired lease pursuant to section 921 or 114 of the Internal Revenue Code or section 101(d) of the American Jobs Creation Act of 2004, (Public Law 108-357 (118 Stat. 1418) (2004)), the rents from such lease, notwithstanding paragraphs (b)(6) and (c) of this section, are ineligible for the exception in section 954(c)(2)(A).

(vii) *Marketing of leases.*—Paragraph (c)(1)(iv) of this section can apply whether a lessor is engaged in the marketing of leases as a form of financing or is engaged in marketing the property as such, and regardless of whether the lease is classified as a finance lease or an operating lease for financial accounting purposes, so long as such lease is treated as a lease for Federal income tax purposes.

(viii) *Cost sharing arrangements (CSAs).*—For purposes of paragraphs (c)(1)(i) and (iv) of this section, CST Payments or PCT Payments (as defined in § 1.482-7(b)(1)) made by the lessor to another controlled participant (as defined in § 1.482-7(j)(1)(i)) pursuant to a CSA (as defined in § 1.482-7(a)) do not cause the activities undertaken by that other controlled participant to be considered to be undertaken by the lessor's own officers or staff of employees.

(3) *Examples.*—The application of this paragraph (c) is illustrated by the following examples:

Example 1. Controlled foreign corporation *A* is regularly engaged in the production of office machines which it sells or leases to others and services. Under paragraph (c)(1)(i) of this section, the rental income of Corporation *A* from these leases is derived in the active conduct of a trade or business for purposes of section 954(c)(2)(A).

Example 2. Controlled foreign corporation *D* purchases motor vehicles which it leases to others. In the conduct of its short-term leasing of such vehicles in foreign country X, Corporation *D* owns a large number of motor vehicles in country X which it services and repairs, leases motor vehicles to customers on an hourly, daily, or weekly basis, maintains offices and service facilities in country X from which to lease and service such vehicles, and maintains therein a sizable staff of its own administrative, sales, and service personnel. Corporation *D* also leases in country X on a long-term basis, generally for a term of one year, motor vehicles that it owns. Under the terms of the long-term leases, Corporation *D* is required to repair and service, during the term of the lease, the leased motor vehicles without cost to the lessee. By the maintenance in country X of office, sales, and service facilities and its complete staff of administrative, sales, and service personnel, Corporation *D* maintains and operates an organization therein that is regularly engaged in the business of marketing and servicing the motor vehicles that are leased. The deductions incurred by such organization satisfy the 25-percent test of paragraph (c)(2)(ii) of this section; thus, such organization is substantial in relation to the rents Corporation *D* receives from leasing the motor vehicles. Therefore, under paragraph (c)(1)(iv) of this section, such rents are derived in the active conduct of a trade or business for purposes of section 954(c)(2)(A).

Example 3. Controlled foreign corporation *E* owns a complex of apartment buildings that it has acquired by purchase. Corporation *E* engages a real estate management firm to lease the apartments, manage the buildings and pay over the net rents to Corporation *E*. The rental income of Corporation *E* from such leases is not derived in the active conduct of a trade or business for purposes of section 954(c)(2)(A).

Example 4. Controlled foreign corporation *F* acquired by purchase a twenty-story office building in a foreign country, three floors of which it occupies and the rest of which it leases. Corporation *F* acts as rental agent for the leasing of offices in the building and employs a substantial staff to perform other management and maintenance functions. Under paragraph (c)(1)(ii) of this section, the rents received by Corporation *F* from such leasing operations are derived in the active conduct of a trade or business for purposes of section 954(c)(2)(A).

Example 5. Controlled foreign corporation *G* owns equipment that it ordinarily uses to perform contracts in foreign countries to drill oil wells. For occasional brief and irregular periods it is unable to obtain contracts requiring immediate performance sufficient to employ all such equipment. During such a period it sometimes leases such idle equipment temporarily. After the expiration of such temporary leasing of the property, Corporation *G* continues the use of such equipment in the performance of its own drilling contracts. Under paragraph (c)(1)(iii) of this section, rents Corporation *G* receives from such leasing of idle equipment are derived in the active conduct of a trade or business for purposes of section 954(c)(2)(A).

Example 6. The facts are the same as in *Example 2*, except that controlled foreign corporation D purchases aircraft which it leases to others. If Corporation D incurs active leasing expenses, as defined in paragraph (c)(2)(iii) of this section, equal to or in excess of 10 percent of its adjusted leasing profit, as defined in paragraph (c)(2)(iv) of this section, the organization maintained and operated by Corporation D in country X is substantial in relation to the amount of rents Corporation D receives from leasing the aircraft. Therefore, under paragraph (c)(1)(iv) of this section, such rents are derived in the active conduct of a trade or business for purposes of section 954(c)(2)(A). If a particular aircraft subject to lease was not leased by the lessee corporation in foreign commerce, for example, because 50 percent or less of the miles during the taxable year were traversed outside the United States and the aircraft was located in the United States for 50 percent or more of the taxable year, Corporation D is not prevented from otherwise showing that it actively carries on a trade or business with regard to the rents derived from that aircraft under paragraph (c)(2)(ii) of this section, based on its facts and circumstances or a showing that active leasing expenses equal or exceed 25 percent of the adjusted leasing profit.

(d) *Excluded royalties.*—(1) *Active conduct of a trade or business.*—Royalties will be considered for purposes of paragraph (b)(6) of this section to be derived in the active conduct of a trade or business if such royalties are derived by the controlled foreign corporation (the licensor) from licensing—

(i) Property that the licensor, through its own officers or staff of employees, has developed, created, or produced, or property that the licensor has acquired and, through its own officers or staff of employees, added substantial value to, but only so long as the licensor, through its officers or staff of employees, is regularly engaged in the development, creation, or production of, or in the acquisition and addition of substantial value to, property of such kind; or

(ii) Property that is licensed as a result of the performance of marketing functions by such licensor through its own officers or staff of employees located in a foreign country or countries, if the licensor, through its officers or staff of employees, maintains and operates an organization either in such foreign country or in such foreign countries (collectively), as applicable, that is regularly engaged in the business of marketing, or of marketing and servicing, the licensed property and that is substantial in relation to the amount of royalties derived from the licensing of such property.

(2) *Special rules.*—(i) *Adding substantial value.*—For purposes of paragraph (d)(1)(i) of this section, the performance of marketing functions will not be considered to add substantial value to property.

(ii) *Substantiality of foreign organization.*—For purposes of paragraph (d)(1)(ii) of this section, whether an organization either in a foreign country or in foreign countries (collectively) is substantial in relation to the amount of royalties is determined based on all of the facts and circumstances. However, such an organization will be considered substantial in relation to the amount of royalties if active licensing expenses, as defined in paragraph (d)(2)(iii) of this section, equal or exceed 25 percent of the adjusted licensing profit, as defined in paragraph (d)(2)(iv) of this section.

(iii) *Active licensing expenses.*—The term *active licensing expenses* means the deductions incurred by an organization of the licensor in a foreign country that are properly allocable to royalty income and that would be allowable under section 162 to the licensor if it were a domestic corporation, other than—

(A) Deductions for compensation for personal services rendered by shareholders of, or related persons (as defined in section 954(d)(3)) with respect to, the licensor;

(B) Deductions for royalties paid or incurred;

(C) Deductions that, although generally allowable under section 162, would be specifically allowable to the licensor (if the controlled foeign corporation were a domestic corporation) under any section of the Internal Revenue Code other than section 162;

(D) Deductions for payments made to agents or independent contractors with respect to the licensed property; and

(E) Deductions for CST Payments or PCT Payments (as defined in § 1.482-7(b)).

(iv) *Adjusted licensing profit.*—The term *adjusted licensing profit* means the gross income of the licensor from royalties, reduced by the sum of—

(A) The royalties paid or incurred by the licensor with respect to such royalty income;

(B) The amounts that would be allowable to such licensor as deductions under section 167 or 197 (if the licensor were a domestic corporation) with respect to such royalty income; and

(C) The amounts paid by the licensor to agents or independent contractors with respect to such royalty income.

(v) *Cost sharing arrangements (CSAs).*—For purposes of paragraphs (d)(1)(i) and (ii) of this section, CST Payments or PCT Payments (as defined in § 1.482-7(b)(1)) made by the licensor to another controlled participant (as defined in § 1.482-7(j)(1)(i)) pursuant to a CSA (as defined in § 1.482-7(a)) do not cause the activities undertaken by that other controlled participant to be considered to be undertaken by the licensor's own officers or staff of employees.

(3) *Examples.*—The application of this paragraph (d) is illustrated by the following examples.

Example 1. Controlled foreign corporation *A*, through its own staff of employees, owns and operates a research facility in foreign country X. At the research facility, employees of Corporation *A* who are scientists, engineers, and technicians regularly perform experiments, tests, and other technical activities, that ultimately result in the issuance of patents that it sells or licenses. Under paragraph (d)(1)(i) of this section, royalties received by Corporation *A* for the privilege of using patented rights that it develops as a result of such research activity are derived in the active conduct of a trade or business for purposes of section 954(c)(2)(A), but only so long as the licensor is regularly engaged in the development, creation or production of, or in the acquisition of and addition of substantial value to, property of such kind.

Example 2. Assume that Corporation *A* in *Example 1*, in addition to receiving royalties for the use of patents that it develops, receives royalties for the use of patents that it acquires by purchase and licenses to others without adding any value thereto. Corporation *A* generally consummates royalty agreements on such purchased patents as the result of inquiries received by it from prospective licensees when the fact becomes known in the business community, as a result of the filing of a patent, advertisements in trade journals, announcements, and contacts by employees of Corporation *A*, that Corporation *A* has acquired rights under a patent and is interested in licensing its rights. Corporation *A* does not, however, maintain and operate an organization in a foreign country that is regularly engaged in the business of marketing the purchased patents. The royalties received by Corporation *A* for the use of the purchased patents are not derived in the active conduct of a trade or business for purposes of section 954(c)(2)(A).

Example 3. Controlled foreign corporation *B* receives royalties for the use of patents that it acquires by purchase. The primary business of Corporation *B*, operated on a regular basis, consists of licensing patents that it has purchased raw from inventors and, through the efforts of a substantial staff of employees consisting of scientists, engineers, and technicians, made susceptible to commercial application. For example, Corporation *B*, after purchasing patent rights covering a chemical process, designs specialized production equipment required for the commercial adaptation of the process and, by so doing, substantially increases the value of the patent. Under paragraph (d)(1)(i) of this section, royalties received by Corporation *B* from the use of such patent are derived in the active conduct of a trade or business for purposes of section 954(c)(2)(A).

Example 4. Controlled foreign corporation *C* receives royalties for the use of a patent that it developed through its own staff of employees at its facility in country X. Corporation *C* has developed no other patents. It does not regularly employ a staff of scientists, engineers or technicians to create new products to be patented. Further, it does not purchase and license patents developed by others to which it has added substantial value. The royalties received by Corporation *C* are not derived from the active conduct of a trade or business for purposes of section 954(c)(2)(A).

Example 5. Controlled foreign corporation *D* finances independent persons in the development of patented items in return for an ownership interest in such items from which it derives a percentage of royalty income, if any, subsequently derived from the use by others of the protected right. Corporation *D* also attempts to increase its royalty income from such patents by contacting prospective licensees and rendering to licensees advice that is intended to promote the use of the patented property. Corporation *D* does not, however, maintain and operate an organization in a foreign country that is regularly engaged in the business of marketing the patents. Royalties received by Corporation *D* for the use of such patents are not derived in the active conduct of a trade or business for purposes of section 954(c)(2)(A).

(e) *Certain property transactions.*—(1) *In general.*—(i) *Inclusions.*—Gain from certain property transactions described in section 954(c)(1)(B) includes the excess of gains over losses from the sale or exchange of—

(A) Property that gives rise to dividends, interest, rents, royalties or annuities, as described in paragraph (e)(2) of this section;

(B) Property that is an interest in a partnership, trust or REMIC; and

(C) Property that does not give rise to income, as described in paragraph (e)(3) of this section.

(ii) *Exceptions.*—Gain or loss from certain property transactions described in section 954(c)(1)(B) and paragraph (e)(1)(i) of this section does not include gain or loss from the sale or exchange of—

(A) Inventory or similar property, as defined in paragraph (a)(4)(iii) of this section;

(B) Dealer property, as defined in paragraph (a)(4)(v) of this section; or

(C) Property that gives rise to rents or royalties described in paragraph (b)(6) of this section that are derived in the active conduct of a trade or business from persons that are not related persons (as defined in section 954(d)(3)) with respect to the controlled foreign corporation.

(iii) *Treatment of losses.*—Section 1.954-1(c)(1)(ii) provides for the treatment of losses in excess of gains from the sale or exchange of property described in paragraph (e)(1)(i) of this section.

(iv) *Dual character property.*—Property may, in part, constitute property that gives rise to certain income as described in paragraph (e)(2) of this section or, in part, constitute property that does not give rise to any income as described in paragraph (e)(3) of this section. However, property that is described in paragraph (e)(1)(i)(B) of this section cannot be dual character property. Dual character property must be treated as two separate properties for purposes of paragraph (e)(2) or (3) of this section. Accordingly, the sale or exchange of such dual character property will give rise to gain or loss that in part must be included in the computation of foreign personal holding company income under paragraph (e)(2) or (3) of this section, and in part is excluded from such computation. Gain or loss from the disposition of dual character property must be bifurcated under this paragraph (e)(1)(iv) pursuant to the method that most reasonably reflects the relative uses of the property. Reasonable methods may include comparisons in terms of gross income generated or the physical division of the property. In the case of real property, the physical division of the property will in most cases be the most reasonable method available. For example, if a controlled foreign corporation owns an office building, uses 60 percent of the building in its trade or business, and rents out the other 40 percent, then 40 percent of the gain recognized on the disposition of the property would reasonably be treated as gain that is included in the computation of foreign personal holding company income under this paragraph (e)(1). This paragraph (e)(1)(iv) addresses the contemporaneous use of property for dual purposes. For rules concerning changes in the use of property affecting its classification for purposes of this paragraph (e), see paragraph (a)(3) of this section.

(2) *Property that gives rise to certain income.*—(i) *In general.*—Property the sale or exchange of which gives rise to foreign personal holding company income under this paragraph (e)(2) includes property that gives rise to dividends, interest, rents, royalties or annuities described in paragraph (b) of this section, including—

(A) Property that gives rise to export financing interest described in paragraph (b)(2) of this section; and

(B) Property that gives rise to income from related persons described in paragraph (b)(4) or (5) of this section.

(ii) *Gain or loss from the disposition of a debt instrument.*—Gain or loss from the sale, exchange or retirement of a debt instrument is included in the computation of foreign personal holding company income under this paragraph (e) unless—

(A) In the case of gain—

(1) It is interest (as defined in paragraph (a)(4)(i) of this section); or

(2) It is income equivalent to interest(as described in paragraph (h) of this section); and

(B) In the case of loss—

(1) It is directly allocated to, or treated as an adjustment to, interest income (as described in paragraph (a)(4)(i) of this section) or income equivalent to interest (as defined in paragraph (h) of this section) under any provision of the Internal Revenue Code or Income Tax Regulations; or

(2) It is required to be apportioned in the same manner as interest expense under section 864(e) or any other provision of the Internal Revenue Code or Income Tax Regulations.

(3) *Property that does not give rise to income.*—Except as otherwise provided in this paragraph (e)(3), for purposes of this section, the term *property that does not give rise to income* includes all rights and interests in property (whether or not a capital asset) including, for example, forwards, futures and options. Property that does not give rise to income shall not include—

(i) Property that gives rise to dividends, interest, rents, royalties or annuities described in paragraph (e)(2) of this section;

(ii) Tangible property (other than real property) used or held for use in the controlled foreign corporation's trade or business that is of a character that would be subject to the allowance for depreciation under section 167 or 168 and the regulations under those sections (including tangible property described in § 1.167(a)-2);

(iii) Real property that does not give rise to rental or similar income, to the extent used or held for use in the controlled foreign corporation's trade or business;

(iv) Intangible property (as defined in section 936(h)(3)(B)), goodwill or going concern value, to the extent used or held for use in the controlled foreign corporation's trade or business;

(v) Notional principal contracts (but see paragraphs (f)(2), (g)(2) and (h)(3) of this section for rules that include income from certain notional principal contracts in gains from commodities transactions, foreign currency gains and income equivalent to interest, respectively); or

(vi) Other property that is excepted from the general rule of this paragraph (e)(3) by the Commissioner in published guidance. See § 601.601(d)(2) of this chapter.

(f) *Commodities transactions.*—(1) *In general.*—(i) *Inclusion in foreign personal holding company income.*—Foreign personal holding company income includes the excess of gains over losses from commodities transactions.

(ii) *Exception.*—Gains and losses from qualified active sales and qualified hedging transactions are excluded from the computation of foreign personal holding company income under this paragraph (f).

(iii) *Treatment of losses.*—Section 1.954-1(c)(1)(ii) provides for the treatment of losses in excess of gains from commodities transactions.

(2) *Definitions.*—(i) *Commodity.*—For purposes of this section, the term *commodity* includes tangible personal property of a kind that is actively traded or with respect to which contractual interests are actively traded.

(ii) *Commodities transaction.*—The term *commodities transaction* means the purchase or sale of a commodity for immediate (spot) delivery or deferred (forward) delivery, or the right to purchase, sell, receive, or transfer a commodity, or any other right or obligation with respect to a commodity accomplished through a cash or off-exchange market, an interbank market, an organized exchange or board of trade, or an over-the-counter market, or in a transaction effected between private parties outside of any market. Commodities transactions include, but are not limited to—

(A) A futures or forward contract in a commodity;

(B) A leverage contract in a commodity purchased from a leverage transaction merchant;

(C) An exchange of futures for physical transaction;

(D) A transaction, including a notional principal contract, in which the income or loss to the parties is measured by reference to the price of a commodity, a pool of commodities, or an index of commodities;

(E) The purchase or sale of an option or other right to acquire or transfer a commodity, a futures contract in a commodity, or an index of commodities; and

(F) The delivery of one commodity in exchange for the delivery of another commodity, the same commodity at another time, cash, or nonfunctional currency.

(iii) *Qualified active sale.*—(A) *In general.*—The term *qualified active sale* means the sale of commodities in the active conduct of a commodities business as a producer, processor, merchant or handler of commodities if substantially all of the controlled foreign corporation's business is as an active producer, processor, merchant or handler of commodities. The sale of commodities held by a controlled foreign corporation other than in its capacity as an active producer, processor, merchant or handler of commodities is not a qualified active sale. For example, the sale by a controlled foreign corporation of commodities that were held for investment or speculation would not be a qualified active sale.

(B) *Active conduct of a commodities business.*—For purposes of this paragraph, a controlled foreign corporation is engaged in the active conduct of a commodities business as a producer, processor, merchant or handler of commodities only with respect to commodities for which each of the following conditions is satisfied—

(1) It holds the commodities directly, and not through an agent or independent contractor, as inventory or similar property (as defined in paragraph (a)(4)(iii) of this section) or as dealer property (as defined in paragraph (a)(4)(v) of this section); and

(2) With respect to such commodities, it incurs substantial expenses in the ordinary course of a commodities business from engaging in one or more of the following activities directly, and not through an independent contractor—

(i) Substantial activities in the production of the commodities, including planting, tending or harvesting crops, raising or slaughtering livestock, or extracting minerals;

(ii) Substantial processing activities prior to the sale of the commodities, including the blending and drying of agricultural commodities, or the concentrating, refining, mixing, crushing, aerating or milling of commodities; or

(iii) Significant activities as described in paragraph (f)(2)(iii)(B)(3) of this section.

(3) For purposes of paragraph (f)(2)(iii)(B)(2)(*iii*) of this section, the significant activities must relate to—

(i) The physical movement, handling and storage of the commodities, including preparation of contracts and invoices, arranging freight, insurance and credit, arranging for receipt, transfer or negotiation of shipping documents, arranging storage or warehousing, and dealing with quality claims;

(ii) Owning and operating facilities for storage or warehousing; or

(iii) Owning or chartering vessels or vehicles for the transportation of the commodities.

(C) *Substantially all.*—Substantially all of the controlled foreign corporation's business is as an active producer, processor, merchant or handler of commodities if the sum of its gross receipts from all of its qualified active sales (as defined in this paragraph (f)(2)(iii) without regard to the substantially all requirement) of commodities and its gross receipts from all of its qualified hedging transactions (as defined in paragraph (f)(2)(iv) of this section, applied without regard to the substantially all requirement of this paragraph (f)(2)(iii)(C)) equals or exceeds 85 percent of its total gross receipts for the taxable year (computed as though the corporation were a domestic corporation). In computing gross receipts, the District Director may disregard any sale or hedging transaction that has as a principal purpose manipulation of the 85 percent gross receipts test. A purpose may be a principal purpose even though it is outweighed by other purposes (taken together or separately).

(D) *Activities of employees of a related entity.*—For purposes of this paragraph (f), activities of employees of an entity related to the controlled foreign corporation, who are made available to and supervised on a day-to-day basis by, and whose salaries are paid by (or reimbursed to the related entity by), the controlled foreign corporation, are treated as activities engaged in directly by the controlled foreign corporation.

(iv) *Qualified hedging transaction entered into prior to January 31, 2003.*—(A) *In general.*—The term *qualified hedging transaction* means a bona fide hedging transaction, as defined in paragraph (a)(4)(ii) of this section, with respect to qualified active sales (other than transactions described in section 988(c)(1) without regard to section 988(c)(1)(D)(i)).

(B) *Exception.*—The term *qualified hedging transaction* does not include transactions that are not reasonably necessary to the conduct of business of the controlled foreign corporation as a producer, processor, merchant or handler of a commodity in the manner in which such business is customarily and usually conducted by others.

(C) *Effective date.*—This paragraph (f)(2)(iv) applies to gain or loss realized by a controlled foreign corporation with respect to a qualified hedging transaction entered into prior to January 31, 2003.

(v) *Qualified hedging transaction entered into on or after January 31, 2003.*—(A) *In general.*—The term *qualified hedging transaction* means a bona fide hedging transaction, as defined in paragraph (a)(4)(ii) of this section, with respect to one or more commodities transactions reasonably necessary to the conduct of any business by a producer, processor, merchant or handler of commodities in a manner in which such business is customarily and usually conducted by others. For purposes of this paragraph (f)(2)(v), a producer, processor, merchant or handler of commodities includes a controlled foreign corporation that regularly uses commodities in a manufacturing, construction, utilities, or transportation business.

(B) *Exception.*—The term *qualified hedging transaction* does not include a transaction described in section 988(c)(1) (without regard to section 988(c)(1)(D)(i)).

(C) *Examples.*—The following examples illustrate the provisions of this paragraph (f)(2)(v):

Example 1. CFC1 is a controlled foreign corporation located in country A. CFC1 manufactures and sells machinery in country B using aluminum and component parts purchased from third parties that contain significant amounts of aluminum. CFC1 conducts its manufacturing business in a manner in which such business is customarily and usually conducted by others. To protect itself against increases in the price of aluminum used in the machinery it manufactures, CFC1 enters into futures purchase contracts for the delivery of aluminum. These futures purchase contracts are bona fide hedging transactions. As CFC1 purchases aluminum and component parts containing significant amounts of aluminum in the spot market for use in its business, it closes out an equivalent amount of aluminum futures purchase contracts by entering into offsetting aluminum futures sales contracts. The aluminum futures purchase contracts are qualified hedging transactions as defined in paragraph (f)(2)(v)(A) of this section. Accordingly, any gain or loss on such aluminum futures purchase contracts is excluded from the computation of foreign personal holding company income.

Example 2. CFC2 is a controlled foreign corporation located in country B. CFC2 operates an airline business within country B in a manner in which such business is customarily and usually conducted by others. To protect itself against increases in the price of aviation fuel, CFC2 enters into forward contracts for the purchase of aviation fuel. These forward purchase contracts are bona fide hedging transactions. As CFC2 purchases aviation fuel in the spot market for use in its business, it closes out an equivalent amount of its forward purchase contracts for cash pursuant to a contractual provision that permits CFC2 to terminate the contract and make or receive a one-time payment representing the contract's fair market value. The aviation fuel forward purchase contracts are qualified hedging transactions as defined in paragraph (f)(2)(v)(A) of this section. Accordingly, any gain or loss on such aviation fuel forward purchase contracts is excluded from the computation of foreign personal holding company income.

(D) *Effective date.*—This paragraph (f)(2)(v) applies to gain or loss realized by a controlled foreign corporation with respect to a qualified hedging transaction entered into on or after January 31, 2003.

(vi) *Financial institutions not a producer, etc..*—For purposes of this paragraph (f), a corporation is not a producer, processor, merchant or handler of commodities if its business is primarily financial. For example, the business of a controlled foreign corporation is primarily financial if its principal business is making a market in notional principal contracts based on a commodities index.

(g) *Foreign currency gain or loss.*—(1) *Scope and purpose.*—This paragraph (g) provides rules for the treatment of foreign currency gains and losses. Paragraph (g)(2) of this section provides the general rule. Paragraph (g)(3) of this section provides an election to include foreign currency gains or losses that would otherwise be treated as foreign personal holding company income under this paragraph (g) in the computation of another category of subpart F income. Paragraph (g)(4) of this section provides an alternative election to treat any net foreign currency gain or loss as foreign personal holding company income. Paragraph (g)(5) of this section provides rules for certain gains and losses not subject to this paragraph (g).

(2) *In general.*—(i) *Inclusion.*—Except as otherwise provided in this paragraph (g), foreign personal holding company income includes the excess of foreign currency gains over foreign currency losses attributable to any section 988 transactions (foreign currency gain or loss). Section 1.954-1(c)(1)(ii) provides rules for the treatment of foreign currency losses in excess of foreign currency gains. However, if an election is made under paragraph (g)(4) of this section, the excess of foreign currency losses over foreign currency gains to which the election would apply may be apportioned to, and offset, other categories of foreign personal holding company income.

(ii) *Exclusion for business needs.*—(A) *General rule.*—Foreign currency gain or loss directly related to the business needs of the controlled foreign corporation is excluded from foreign personal holding company income.

(B) *Business needs.*—Foreign currency gain or loss is directly related to the business needs of a controlled foreign corporation if—

(1) The foreign currency gain or loss—

(i) Arises from a transaction (other than a hedging transaction) entered into, or property used or held for use, in the normal course of the controlled foreign corporation's trade or business, other than the trade or business of trading foreign currency;

(ii) Arises from a transaction or property that does not itself (and could not reasonably be expected to) give rise to subpart F income other than foreign currency gain or loss;

(iii) Does not arise from a transaction described in section 988(c)(1)(B)(iii); and

(iv) Is clearly determinable from the records of the controlled foreign corporation as being derived from such transaction or property; or

(2) The foreign currency gain or loss arises from a bona fide hedging transaction, as defined in paragraph (a)(4)(ii) of this section, with respect to a transaction or property that satisfies the requirements of paragraphs (g)(2)(ii)(B)(*1*)(*i*) through (*iii*) of this section, provided that any gain or loss arising from such transaction or property that is attributable to changes in exchange rates is clearly determinable from the records of the CFC as being derived from such transaction or property. For purposes of this paragraph (g)(2)(ii)(B)(*2*), a hedging transaction will satisfy the aggregate hedging rules of § 1.1221-2(c)(3) only if all (or all but a de minimis amount) of the aggregate risk being hedged arises in connection with transactions or property that satisfy the requirements of paragraphs (g)(2)(ii)(B)(*1*)(*i*) through (*iii*) of this section, provided that any gain or loss arising from such transactions or property that is attributable to changes in exchange rates is clearly determinable from the records of the CFC as being derived from such transactions or property.

(C) *Regular dealers.—(1) General rule.*—Transactions in dealer property (as defined in paragraph (a)(4)(v) of this section) described in section 988(c)(1)(B) or (C) that are entered into by a controlled foreign corporation that is a regular dealer (as defined in paragraph (a)(4)(iv) of this section) in such property in its capacity as a dealer will be treated as directly related to the business needs of the controlled foreign corporation under paragraph (g)(2)(ii)(A) of this section.

(2) Certain interest-bearing liabilities treated as dealer property.—(i) In general.—For purposes of this paragraph (g)(2)(ii)(C), an interest-bearing liability incurred by a controlled foreign corporation that is denominated in (or determined by reference to) a non-functional currency shall be treated as dealer property of the type described in paragraph (g)(2)(ii)(C)(*1*) of this section if the liability, by being denominated in such currency, reduces the controlled foreign corporation's currency risk with respect to dealer property, and the liability is identified on the controlled foreign corporation's records as a liability treated as dealer property before the close of the day on which the liability is incurred.

(ii) Failure to identify certain liabilities.—If a controlled foreign corporation identifies certain interest-bearing liabilities as liabilities treated as dealer property under paragraph (g)(2)(ii)(C)(*2*)(*i*) of this section but fails to so identify other interest-bearing liabilities that manage its currency risk with respect to assets held that constitute dealer property, the Commissioner may treat such other liabilities as properly identified as dealer property under paragraph (g)(2)(ii)(C)(*2*)(*i*) of this section if the Commissioner determines that the failure to identify such other liabilities had as one of its principal purposes the avoidance of Federal income tax.

(iii) Effective date.—This paragraph (g)(2)(ii)(C)(2) applies only to gain or loss from an interest-bearing liability entered into by a controlled foreign corporation on or after January 31, 2003.

(D) *Example.*—The following example illustrates the provisions of this paragraph (g)(2).

Example. (i) *CFC1* and *CFC2* are controlled foreign corporations located in Country B, and are members of the same controlled group. *CFC1* is engaged in the active conduct of a trade or business that does not produce any subpart F income. *CFC2* serves as the currency coordination center for the controlled group, aggregating currency risks incurred by the group and entering into hedging transactions that transfer those risks outside of the group. Pursuant to this arrangement, and to hedge the currency risk on a non-interest bearing receivable incurred by *CFC1* in the normal course of its business, on Day 1 *CFC1* enters into a forward contract to sell Japanese Yen to *CFC2* in 30 days. Also on Day 1, *CFC2* enters into a forward contract to sell Yen to unrelated Bank X on Day 30. *CFC2* is not a regular dealer in Yen spot and forward contracts, and the Yen is not the functional currency for either *CFC1* or *CFC2*.

(ii) Because the forward contract entered into by *CFC1* to sell Yen hedges a transaction entered into in the normal course of *CFC1*'s business that does not give rise to subpart F income, it qualifies as a bona fide hedging transaction as defined in paragraph (a)(4)(ii) of this section. Therefore, *CFC1*'s foreign exchange gain or loss from that forward contract will not be treated as foreign personal holding company income or loss under this paragraph (g).

(iii) Because the forward contract to purchase Yen was entered into by *CFC2* in order to assume currency risks incurred by *CFC1* it does not qualify as a bona fide hedging transaction, as defined in paragraph (a)(4)(ii) of this section. Thus, foreign exchange gain or loss recognized by *CFC2* from that forward contract will be foreign personal holding company income. Because *CFC2* entered into the forward contract to sell Yen in order to hedge currency risks of *CFC1*, that forward contract also does not qualify as a bona fide hedging transaction. Thus, *CFC2*'s foreign currency gain or loss arising from that forward contract will be foreign personal holding company income.

(iii) *Special rule for foreign currency gain or loss from an interest-bearing liability.*—Except as provided in paragraph (g)(2)(ii)(C)(2) or (g)(5)(iv) of this section, foreign currency gain or loss arising from an interest-bearing liability is characterized as subpart F income and non-subpart F income in the same manner that interest expense associated with the liability would be allocated and apportioned between subpart F income and non-subpart F income under §§1.861-9T and 1.861-12T.

(3) *Election to characterize foreign currency gain or loss that arises from a specific category of subpart F income as gain or loss in that category.—(i) In general.*—For taxable years of a controlled foreign corporation beginning on or after November 6, 1995, the controlling United States shareholders of the controlled foreign corporation may elect, under this paragraph (g)(3), to exclude foreign currency gain or loss otherwise includible in the computation of foreign personal holding company income under this paragraph (g) from the computation of foreign personal holding company income under this paragraph (g) and include such foreign currency gain or loss in the category (or categories) of subpart F income (described in section 952(a), or, in the case of foreign base company income, described in §1.954-1(c)(1)(iii)(A)(*1*) or (2)) to which such gain or loss relates. If an election is made under this paragraph (g)(3) with respect to a category (or categories) of subpart F income described in section 952(a), or, in the case of foreign base company income, described in §1.954-1(c)(1)(iii)(A)(*1*) or (2), the election shall apply to all foreign currency gain or loss that arises from—

(A) A transaction (other than a hedging transaction) entered into, or property used or held for use, in the normal course of the controlled foreign corporation's trade or business that gives rise to income in that category (or categories) and that is clearly determinable from the records of the controlled foreign corporation as being derived from such transaction or property; and

(B) A bona fide hedging transaction, as defined in paragraph (a)(4)(ii) of this section, with respect to a transaction or property described in paragraph (g)(3)(i)(A) of this section. For purposes of this paragraph (g)(3)(i)(B), a hedging transaction will satisfy the aggregate hedging rules of §1.1221-2(c)(3) only if all (or all but a de minimis amount) of the aggregate risk being hedged arises in connection with transactions or property that generate the same category of subpart F income described in section 952(a), or, in the case of foreign base company income, described in §1.954-1(c)(1)(iii)(A)(*1*) or (2).

(ii) *Time and manner of election.*—The controlling United States shareholders, as defined in §1.964-1(c)(5), make the election on behalf of the controlled foreign corporation by filing a statement with their original income tax returns for the taxable year of such United States shareholders ending with or within the taxable year of the controlled foreign corporation for which the election is made, clearly indicating that such election has been made. If the controlling United States shareholders elect to apply these regulations retroactively, under §1.954-0(a)(1)(ii), the election under this paragraph (g)(3) may be made by the amended return filed pursuant to the election under §1.954-0(a)(1)(ii). The controlling United States shareholders filing the election statement described in this paragraph (g)(3)(ii) must provide copies of the election statement to all other United States shareholders of the electing controlled foreign corporation. Failure to provide copies of such statement will not cause an election under this paragraph (g)(3) to be voidable by the controlled foreign corporation or the controlling United States shareholders. However, the District Director has discretion to void the election if it is determined that there was no reasonable cause for the failure to provide copies of such statement. The statement shall include the following information—

(A) The name, address, taxpayer identification number, and taxable year of each United States shareholder;

(B) The name, address, and taxable year of the controlled foreign corporation for which the election is effective; and

(C) Any additional information required by the Commissioner by administrative pronouncement.

(iii) *Revocation of election.*—This election is effective for the taxable year of the controlled foreign corporation for which it is made and all subsequent taxable years of such corporation unless revoked by or with the consent of the Commissioner.

(iv) *Example.*—The following example illustrates the provisions of this paragraph (g)(3).

Example. (i) *CFC*, a controlled foreign corporation, is a sales company that earns foreign base company sales income under section 954(d). *CFC* makes an election under this paragraph (g)(3) to treat foreign currency gains or losses that arise from a specific category (or categories) of subpart F income (as described in section 952(a), or, in the case of foreign base company income, as described in §1.954-1(c)(1)(iii)(A)(*1*) or (2)) as that type of income. *CFC* aggregates the currency risk on all of its transactions that generate foreign base company sales income and hedges this net currency exposure.

(ii) Assuming no more than a de minimis amount of risk in the pool of risks being hedged arises from transactions or property that generate income other than foreign base company sales income, pursuant to its election under (g)(3), CFC's net foreign currency gain from the pool and the hedging transactions will be treated as foreign base company sales income under section 954(d), rather than as foreign personal holding company income under section 954(c)(1)(D). If the pool of risks and the hedging transactions generate a net foreign base company sales loss, however, CFC must apply the rules of § 1.954-1(c)(1)(ii).

(4) *Election to treat all foreign currency gains or losses as foreign personal holding company income.*—(i) *In general.*—If the controlling United States shareholders make an election under this paragraph (g)(4), the controlled foreign corporation shall include in its computation of foreign personal holding company income the excess of foreign currency gains over losses or the excess of foreign currency losses over gains attributable to any section 988 transaction (except those described in paragraph (g)(5) of this section) and any section 1256 contract that would be a section 988 transaction but for section 988(c)(1)(D). Separate elections for section 1256 contracts and section 988 transactions are not permitted. An election under this paragraph (g)(4) supersedes an election under paragraph (g)(3) of this section.

(ii) *Time and manner of election.*—The controlling United States shareholders, as defined in § 1.964-1(c)(5), make the election on behalf of the controlled foreign corporation in the same time and manner as provided in paragraph (g)(3)(ii) of this section.

(iii) *Revocation of election.*—This election is effective for the taxable year of the controlled foreign corporation for which it is made and all subsequent taxable years of such corporation unless revoked by or with the consent of the Commissioner.

(5) *Gains and losses not subject to this paragraph.*—(i) *Capital gains and losses.*—Gain or loss that is treated as capital gain or loss under section 988(a)(1)(B) is not foreign currency gain or loss for purposes of this paragraph (g). Such gain or loss is treated as gain or loss from the sale or exchange of property that is included in the computation of foreign personal holding company income under paragraph (e)(1) of this section. Paragraph (a)(2) of this section provides other rules concerning income described in more than one category of foreign personal holding company income.

(ii) *Income not subject to section 988.*—Gain or loss that is not treated as foreign currency gain or loss by reason of section 988(a)(2) or (d) is not foreign currency gain or loss for purposes of this paragraph (g). However, such gain or loss may be included in the computation of other categories of foreign personal holding company income in accordance with its characterization under section 988(a)(2) or (d) (for example, foreign currency gain that is treated as interest income under section 988(a)(2) will be included in the computation of foreign personal holding company income under paragraph (b)(ii) of this section).

(iii) *Qualified business units using the dollar approximate separate transactions method.*—This paragraph (g) does not apply to any DASTM gain or loss computed under § 1.985-3(d). Such gain or loss is allocated under the rules of § 1.985-3(e)(2)(iv) or (e)(3). However, the provisions of this paragraph (g) do apply to section 988 transactions denominated in a currency other than the United States dollar or the currency that would be the qualified business unit's functional currency were it not hyperinflationary.

(iv) *Gain or loss allocated under § 1.861-9.*—[Reserved]

(h) *Income equivalent to interest.*—(1) *In general.*—(i) *Inclusion in foreign personal holding company income.*—Except as provided in this paragraph (h), foreign personal holding company income includes income equivalent to interest as defined in paragraph (h)(2) of this section.

(ii) *Exceptions.*—(A) *Liability hedging transactions.*—Income, gain, deduction or loss that is allocated and apportioned in the same manner as interest expense under the provisions of § 1.861-9T is not income equivalent to interest for purposes of this paragraph (h).

(B) *Interest.*—Amounts treated as interest under section 954(c)(1)(A) and paragraph (b) of this section are not income equivalent to interest for purposes of this paragraph (h).

(2) *Definition of income equivalent to interest.*—(i) *In general.*—The term *income equivalent to interest* includes income that is derived from—

(A) A transaction or series of related transactions in which the payments, net payments, cash flows or return predominantly reflect the time value of money;

(B) Transactions in which the payments (or a predominant portion thereof) are, in substance, for the use or forbearance of money;

(C) Notional principal contracts, to the extent provided in paragraph (h)(3) of this section;

(D) Factoring, to the extent provided in paragraph (h)(4) of this section;

(E) Conversion transactions, but only to the extent that gain realized with respect to such a transaction is treated as ordinary income under section 1258;

(F) The performance of services, to the extent provided in paragraph (h)(5) of this section;

(G) The commitment by a lender to provide financing, if any portion of such financing is actually provided;

(H) Transfers of debt securities subject to section 1058;

(I) Any guaranteed payments for the use of capital under section 707(c); and

(J) Other transactions, as provided by the Commissioner in published guidance. See § 601.601(d)(2) of this chapter.

(ii) *Income from the sale of property.*—Income from the sale of property will not be treated as income equivalent to interest by reason of paragraph (h)(2)(i)(A) or (B) of this section. Income derived by a controlled foreign corporation will be treated as arising from the sale of property only if the corporation in substance carries out sales activities. Accordingly, an arrangement that is designed to lend the form of a sales transaction to a transaction that in substance constitutes an advance of funds will be disregarded. For example, if a controlled foreign corporation acquires property on 30-day payment terms from one person and sells that property to another person on 90-day payment terms and at prearranged prices and terms such that the foreign corporation bears no substantial economic risk with respect to the purchase and sale other than the risk of non-payment, the foreign corporation has not in substance derived income from the sale of property.

(3) *Notional principal contracts.*—(i) *In general.*—Income equivalent to interest includes income from notional principal contracts denominated in the functional currency of the taxpayer (or a qualified business unit of the taxpayer, as defined in section 989(a)), the value of which is determined solely by reference to interest rates or interest rate indices, to the extent that the income from such transactions accrues on or after August 14, 1989.

(ii) *Regular dealers.*—Income equivalent to interest does not include income earned by a regular dealer (as defined in paragraph (a)(4)(iv) of this section) from notional principal contracts that are dealer property (as defined in paragraph (a)(4)(v) of this section).

(4) *Income equivalent to interest from factoring.*—(i) *General rule.*—Income equivalent to interest includes factoring income. Except as provided in paragraph (h)(4)(ii) of this section, the term *factoring income* includes any income (including any discount income or service fee, but excluding any stated interest) derived from the acquisition and collection or disposition of a factored receivable. The amount of income equivalent to interest realized with respect to a factored receivable is the difference (if a positive number) between the amount paid for the receivable by the foreign corporation and the amount that it collects on the receivable (or realizes upon its sale of the receivable). The rules of this paragraph (h)(4) apply only with respect to the tax treatment of factoring income derived from the acquisition and collection or disposition of a factored receivable and shall not affect the characterization of an expense or loss of either the person whose goods or services gave rise to a factored receivable or the obligor under a receivable.

(ii) *Exceptions.*—Factoring income shall not include—

(A) Income treated as interest under section 864(d)(1) or (6) (relating to income derived from trade or service receivables of related persons), even if such income is treated as not described in section 864(d)(1) by reason of the same-country exception of section 864(d)(7);

(B) Income derived from a factored receivable if payment for the acquisition of the receivable is made on or after the date on which stated interest begins to accrue, but only if the rate of stated interest equals or exceeds 120 percent of the Federal short-term rate (as defined under section 1274) (or the analogous rate for a currency other than the dollar) as of the date on which the receivable is acquired by the foreign corporation; or

(C) Income derived from a factored receivable if payment for the acquisition of the receivable by the foreign corporation is made only on or after the anticipated date of payment of all principal by the obligor (or the anticipated weighted average date of payment of a pool of purchased receivables).

(iii) *Factored receivable.*—For purposes of this paragraph (h)(4), the term *factored receivable* includes any account receivable or other evidence of indebtedness, whether or not issued at a discount and whether or not bearing stated interest, arising out of the disposition of property or the performance of services by any person, if such account receivable or evidence of indebtedness is acquired by a person other than the person who disposed of the property or provided the services that gave rise to the account receivable or evidence of indebtedness. For purposes of this paragraph (h)(4), it is immaterial whether the person providing the property or services agrees to transfer the receivable at the time of sale (as by accepting a third-party charge or credit card) or at a later time.

(iv) *Examples.*—The following examples illustrate the application of this paragraph (h)(4).

Example 1. DP, a domestic corporation, owns all of the outstanding stock of *FS*, a controlled foreign corporation. *FS* acquires accounts receivable arising from the sale of property by unrelated corporation X. The receivables have a face amount of $100, and after 30 days bear stated interest equal to at least 120 percent of the applicable Federal short-term rate (determined as of the date the receivables are acquired by *FS*). *FS* purchases the receivables from *X* for $95 on Day 1 and collects $100 plus stated interest from the obligor under the receivables on Day 40. Income (other than stated interest) derived by *FS* from the factored receivables is factoring income within the meaning of paragraph (h)(4)(i) of this section and, therefore, is income equivalent to interest.

Example 2. The facts are the same as in *Example 1*, except that, rather than collecting $100 plus stated interest from the obligor under the factored receivables on Day 40, *FS* sells the receivables to controlled foreign corporation *Y* on Day 15 for $97. Both the income derived by *FS* on the factored receivables and the income derived by *Y* (other than stated interest) on the receivables are factoring income within the meaning of paragraph (h)(4)(i) of this section, and therefore, constitute income equivalent to interest.

Example 3. The facts are the same as in *Example 1*, except that *FS* purchases the receivables from *X* for $98 on Day 30. Income derived by *FS* from the factored receivables is excluded from factoring income under paragraph (h)(4)(ii)(B) of this section and, therefore, does not give rise to income equivalent to interest.

Example 4. The facts are the same as in *Example 3*, except that it is anticipated that all principal will be paid by the obligor of the receivables by Day 30. Income derived by *FS* from this maturity factoring of the receivables is excluded from factoring income under paragraph (h)(4)(ii)(C) of this section and, therefore, does not give rise to income equivalent to interest.

Example 5. The facts are the same as in *Example 4*, except that *FS* sells the factored receivables to *Y* for $99 on day 45, at which time stated interest is accruing on the unpaid balance of $100. Because interest was accruing at the time *Y* acquired the receivables at a rate equal to at least 120 percent of the applicable Federal short-term rate, income derived by *Y* from the factored receivables is excluded from factoring income under paragraph (h)(4)(ii)(B) of this section and, therefore, does not give rise to income equivalent to interest.

Example 6. DP, a domestic corporation engaged in an integrated credit card business, owns all of the outstanding stock of *FS*, a controlled foreign corporation. On Day 1, individual *A* uses a credit card issued by *DP* to purchase shoes priced at $100 from *X*, a foreign corporation unrelated to *DP*, *FS*, or *A*. On Day 7, *X* transfers the receivable (which does not bear stated interest) arising from *A*'s purchase to *FS* in exchange for $95. *FS* collects $100 from *A* on Day 45. Income derived by *FS* on the factored receivable is factoring income within the meaning of paragraph (h)(4)(i) of this section and, therefore, is income equivalent to interest.

(5) *Receivables arising from performance of services.*—If payment for services performed by a controlled foreign corporation is not made until more than 120 days after the date on which such services are performed, then the income derived by the controlled foreign corporation constitutes income equivalent to interest to the extent that interest income would be imputed under the principles of section 483 or the original issue discount provisions (sections 1271 through 1275), if—

(i) Such provisions applied to contracts for the performance of services;

(ii) The time period referred to in sections 483(c)(1) and 1274(c)(1)(B) were 120 days rather than six months; and (iii) The time period referred to in section 483(c)(1)(A) were 120 days rather than one year.

(6) *Examples.*—The following examples illustrate the application of this paragraph (h).

Example 1. CFC, a controlled foreign corporation, promises that Corporation *A* may borrow up to $500 in principal for one year beginning at any time during the next three months at an interest rate of 10 percent. In exchange, Corporation *A* pays *CFC* a commitment fee of $2. Pursuant to this agreement, *CFC* lends $80 to Corporation *A*. As a result, the entire $2 fee is included in the computation of *CFC'S* foreign personal holding company income under paragraph (h)(2)(i)(G) of this section.

Example 2. (i) At the beginning of its current taxable year, *CFC*, a controlled foreign corporation, purchases at face value a one-year debt instrument issued by Corporation *A* having a $100 principal amount and bearing a floating rate of interest set at the LIBOR plus one percentage point. Contemporaneously, *CFC* borrows $100 from Corporation *B* for one year at a fixed interest rate of 10 percent, using the debt instrument as security.

(ii) During its current taxable year, *CFC* accrues $11 of interest from Corporation *A* on the bond. Because interest is excluded from the definition of income equivalent to interest under paragraph (h)(1)(ii)(B) of this section, the $11 is not income equivalent to interest.

(iii) During its current taxable year, *CFC* incurs $10 of interest expense with respect to the borrowing from Corporation *B*. That expense is allocated and apportioned to, and reduces, subpart F income to the extent provided in section 954(b)(5) and §§1.861-9T through 1.861-12T and 1.954-1(c).

Example 3. (i) On January 1, 1994, *CFC*, a controlled foreign corporation with the United States dollar as its functional currency, purchases at face value a 10-year debt instrument issued by Corporation *A* having a $100 principal amount and bearing a floating rate of interest set at the (LIBOR) plus one percentage point payable on December 31st of each year. *CFC* subsequently determines that it would prefer receiving a fixed rate of return. Accordingly, on January 1, 1995, *CFC* enters into a 9-year interest rate swap agreement with Corporation *B* whereby Corporation *B* promises to pay *CFC* on December 31st of each year an amount equal to 10 percent on a notional principal amount of $100. In exchange, *CFC* promises to pay Corporation *B* an amount equal to LIBOR plus one percentage point on the notional principal amount.

(ii) On December 31, 1995, *CFC* receives $9 of interest income from Corporation *A* with respect to the debt instrument. On the same day, *CFC* receives a total of $10 from Corporation *B* and pays $9 to Corporation *B* with respect to the interest rate swap.

(iii) The $9 of interest income is foreign personal holding income under section 954(c)(1). Pursuant to §1.446-3(d), *CFC* recognizes $1 of swap income for its 1995 taxable year that is also foreign personal holding company income because it is income equivalent to interest under paragraph (h)(2)(i)(C) of this section.

Example 4. (i) *CFC*, a controlled foreign corporation, purchases commodity X on the spot market for $100 and, contemporaneously, enter into a 3 month forward contract to sell commodity X for $104, a price set by the forward market.

(ii) Assuming that substantially all of *CFC*'s expected return is attributable to the time value of the net investment, as described in section 1258(c)(1), the transaction is a conversion transaction under section 1258(c). Accordingly, any gain treated as ordinary income under section 1258(a) will be foreign personal holding company income because it is income equivalent to interest under paragraph (h)(2)(i)(E) of this section.

(i) *Applicability dates.*—(1) *Paragraphs (c)(2)(v), through (vii).*—Paragraphs (c)(2)(v) through (vii) of this section and *Example 6* of paragraph (c)(3) of this section apply to taxable years of controlled foreign corporations beginning on or after May 2, 2006, and for taxable years of United States shareholders with or within which such taxable years of the controlled foreign corporations end. Taxpayers may elect to apply paragraphs (c)(2)(v) through (vii) to taxable years of controlled foreign corporations beginning after December 31, 2004, and for taxable years of United States shareholders with or within which such taxable years of the controlled foreign corporations end. If an election is made to apply §1.956–2(b)(1)(vi) to taxable years beginning after December 31, 2004, then the election must also be made for paragraphs (c)(2)(v) through (vii) of this section.

(2) *Paragraphs (c)(2)(iii)(B) and (c)(2)(iv)(A) of this section.*—Paragraphs (c)(2)(iii)(B) and (c)(2)(iv)(A) of this section apply for taxable years of controlled foreign corporations ending on or after November 19, 2019, and for the taxable years of United States shareholders in which or with which such taxable years end.

(3) *Other paragraphs.*—Paragraphs (c)(1)(i) and (d)(1)(i) of this section apply to rents or royalties, as applicable, received or accrued during taxable years of controlled foreign corporations ending on or after September 1, 2015, and to taxable years of United States shareholders in which or with which such taxable years end, but only with respect to property manufactured, produced, developed, or created, or in the case of acquired property, property to which substantial value has been added, on or after September 1, 2015. Paragraphs (c)(1)(iv), (c)(2)(ii), (c)(2)(iii)(E), (c)(2)(viii), (d)(1)(ii), (d)(2)(ii), (d)(2)(iii)(E), and (d)(2)(v) of this section apply to rents or royalties, as applicable, received or accrued during taxable years of controlled foreign corporations ending on or after September 1, 2015, and to taxable years of United States shareholders in which or with which such taxable years end, to the extent that such rents or royalties are received or accrued on or after September 1, 2015. See § 1.954-2(c)(1)(i), (c)(1)(iv), (c)(2)(ii), (c)(2)(iii), (d)(1)(i), (d)(1)(ii), (d)(2)(ii), and (d)(2)(iii), as contained in 26 CFR part 1 revised as of April 1, 2015, for rules applicable to rents or royalties, as applicable, received or accrued before September 1, 2015. Paragraph (h)(2)(i)(I) of this section applies to taxable years of controlled foreign corporations ending on or after December 16, 2019, and to taxable years of United States shareholders in which or with which such taxable years end. [Reg. § 1.954-2.]

☐ [*T.D.* 8618, 9-6-95. *Amended by T.D.* 8704, 12-31-96; *T.D.* 8985, 3-15-2002; *T.D.* 9008, 7-22-2002; *T.D.* 9039, 1-30-2003, *T.D.* 9141, 7-19-2004; *T.D.* 9240, 1-13-2006; *T.D.* 9326, 7-12-2007; *T.D.* 9406, 7-2-2008 (*corrected* 7-28-2008), *T.D.* 9525, 5-5-2011, *T.D.* 9733, 9-1-2015, *T.D.* 9792, 11-2-2016 (*corrected* 12-27-2016), *T.D.* 9883, 11-18-2019 *and T.D.* 9922, 11-2-2020.]

Proposed Amendments to Regulation

§ 1.954-2. Foreign personal holding company income.—(a) * * *

(5) *Special rules applicable to distributive share of partnership income.*—(i) *Application of related person exceptions where payment reduces foreign tax of payor.*—If a partnership receives an item of income that reduced the foreign income tax of the payor (determined under the principles of § 1.954-9(a)(3)), to determine the extent to which a controlled foreign corporation's distributive share of such item of income is foreign personal holding company income, the exceptions contained in section 954(c)(3) shall apply only if—

(A)*(1)* Any such exception would have applied to exclude the income from foreign personal holding company income if the controlled foreign corporation had earned the income directly (determined by testing, with reference to such controlled foreign corporation, whether an entity is a related person, within the meaning of section 954(d)(3), or is organized under the laws of, or uses property in, the foreign country in which the controlled foreign corporation is created or organized); and

(2) The distributive share of such income is not in respect of a payment made by the controlled foreign corporation to the partnership; and

(B)*(1)* The partnership is created or organized, and uses a substantial part of its assets in a trade or business in the country under the laws of which the controlled foreign corporation is created or organized (determined under the principles of paragraph (b)(4) of this section);

(2) The partnership is regarded as fiscally transparent, as defined in § 1.954-9(a)(7), by all countries under the laws of which the controlled foreign corporation is created or organized or has substantial assets; or

(3) The income is taxed in the year when earned at an effective rate of tax (determined under the principles of § 1.954-1(d)(2)) that is not less than 90 percent of, and not more than five percentage points less than, the effective rate of tax that would have applied to such income under the laws of the country in which the controlled foreign corporation is created or organized if such income were earned directly by the controlled foreign corporation partner from local sources.

(ii) *Certain other exceptions applicable to foreign personal holding company income.*—[Reserved].

(iii) *Effective date.*—Paragraph (a)(5)(i) of this section shall apply to all amounts paid or accrued in taxable years commencing after [date that is 5 years after publication of the final regulations in the federal register], under hybrid arrangements, unless such payments are made pursuant to an arrangement which would qualify for permanent relief under § 1.954-9(c)(2) if made between a controlled foreign corporation and its hybrid branch, in which case the relief afforded under that section shall also be afforded under this section.

(6) *Special rules applicable to exceptions from foreign personal holding company income treatment in circumstances involving hybrid branches.*—(i) *In general.*—In the case of a payment between a controlled foreign corporation (or its hybrid branch, as defined in § 1.954-9(a)(6)) and the hybrid branch of a related controlled foreign corporation, the exceptions contained in section 954(c)(3) shall apply only if the payment would have qualified for the exception if the payor were a separate controlled foreign corporation created or organized in the jurisdiction where foreign tax is reduced and the payee were a separate controlled foreign corporation created or organized under the laws of the jurisdiction in which the payment is subject to tax (other than a withholding tax).

(ii) *Exception where no tax reduction or tax disparity.*—Paragraph (a)(6)(i) of this section shall not apply unless the payment would have reduced foreign tax, under § 1.954-9(a)(3), and fallen within the tax disparity rule of § 1.954-9(a)(5)(iv) if those provisions had been applicable to the payment.

(iii) *Effective date.*—The rules of this section shall apply to all amounts paid or accrued in taxable years commencing after [date that is 5 years after publication of the final regulations in the federal register], under hybrid arrangements, unless such payments are made pursuant to an arrangement which would qualify for permanent relief under § 1.954-9(c)(2) if made between a controlled foreign corporation and its hybrid branch, in which case the relief afforded under that section shall also be afforded under this section.
[Prop. Reg. § 1.954-2.]
[Proposed 7-13-99.]

Proposed Amendments to Regulation

§ 1.954-2. Foreign personal holding company income.

* * *

(h) * * *

(3) *Notional principal contracts.*—(i) In general.—Income equivalent to interest includes income from notional principal contracts (as defined in § 1.446-3(c)) denominated in the functional currency of the taxpayer (or a qualified business unit of the taxpayer, as defined in section 989(a)), the value of which is determined solely by reference to interest rates or interest rate indices, to the extent that the income from such transactions accrues on or after August 14, 1989.

* * *

(iii) *Effective/applicability date.*—The rules of paragraph (h)(3) of this section apply to notional principal contracts as defined in § 1.446-3(c) that are entered into on or after the date of publication of a Treasury decision adopting these rules as final regulations in the **Federal Register**. Section 1.954-2(h)(3) as contained in 26 CFR part 1 revised April 1, 2011, continues to apply to notional principal contracts entered into before the date of publication of a Treasury decision adopting these rules as final regulations in the **Federal Register**.

* * *

[Prop. Reg. § 1.954-2.]
[Proposed 9-16-2011.]

Proposed Amendments to Regulation

§ 1.954-2. Foreign personal holding company income.—(a) * * *

(4) * * *

(ii) * * *

(A) * * * Additionally, the acquisition of a debt instrument by a controlled foreign corporation may be treated as a bona fide hedging transaction with respect to an interest-bearing liability of the controlled foreign corporation, provided that the acquisition of the debt instrument has the effect of managing the controlled foreign corporation's exchange rate risk with respect to the liability within the meaning of § 1.1221-2(c)(4) and (d), determined without regard to § 1.1221-2(d)(5), and otherwise meets the requirements of paragraph (a)(4)(ii) of this section. * * *

* * *

(g) * * *

(2) * * *

(ii) * * *

(C) *Foreign currency gains and losses arising from a transaction or property that gives rise to both non-subpart F income and subpart F income or from a bona fide hedging transaction with respect to such a transaction or property.—(1) In general.*—If a foreign currency gain or loss would be directly related to the business needs of the controlled foreign corporation pursuant to paragraph (g)(2)(ii)(B)(*1*) or (*2*) of this section except that it arises from a transaction or property that gives rise, or is reasonably expected to give rise, to both non-subpart F income and subpart F income (other than foreign currency gain or loss), or from a bona fide hedging transaction with respect to such a transaction or property, the amount of foreign currency gain or loss that is allocable to non-subpart F income under this paragraph (g)(2)(ii)(C)(*1*) is directly related to the business needs of the controlled foreign corporation. The amount of foreign currency gain or loss arising from a transaction or property described in this paragraph (g)(2)(ii)(C)(*1*), or from a bona fide hedging transaction with respect to such a transaction or property, that is allocable to non-subpart F income equals the product of the total amount of foreign currency gain or loss arising from the transaction or property and the ratio of non-subpart F income (other than foreign currency gain or loss) that the transaction or property gives rise to, or is reasonably expected to give rise to, to the total income that the transaction or property gives rise to, or is reasonably expected to give rise to. However, none of the foreign currency gain or loss arising from property that does not give rise to income (as defined in paragraph (e)(3) of this section), or from a bona fide hedging transaction with respect to such property, is allocable to non-subpart F income.

(*2*) *Financial statement hedging transaction with respect to a qualified business unit.*—If foreign currency gain or loss arises from a financial statement hedging transaction (as defined in this paragraph (g)(2)(ii)(C)(*2*)) with respect to a qualified business unit (as defined in § 1.989(a)-1) (QBU) of a controlled foreign corporation that is not treated as an entity separate from the controlled foreign corporation for federal income tax purposes, either because it is a branch or division of the controlled foreign corporation or because it is a business entity that is disregarded as separate from its owner under § 301.7701-3 of this chapter, the amount of the qualifying portion (as determined under this paragraph (g)(2)(ii)(C)(*2*)) of foreign currency gain or loss that is allocable to non-subpart F income under this paragraph (g)(2)(ii)(C)(*2*) is directly related to the business needs of the controlled foreign corporation. Generally, the controlled foreign corporation must allocate the qualifying portion of foreign currency gain or loss arising from the financial statement hedging transaction between subpart F income and non-subpart F income in the same proportion as it would characterize gain or loss determined under section 987 as subpart F income and non-subpart F income under the principles of § 1.987-6(b). A *financial statement hedging transaction* is a transaction that is entered into by a CFC for the purpose of managing exchange rate risk with respect to part or all of that CFC's net investment in a QBU that is included in the consolidated financial statements of a United States shareholder of the CFC (or a corporation that directly or indirectly owns such United States shareholder). The qualifying portion of foreign currency gain or loss is the amount of foreign currency gain or loss arising from a financial statement hedging transaction that is properly accounted for under U.S. generally accepted accounting principles as a cumulative foreign currency translation adjustment to shareholders' equity.

* * *

(iii) *Special rule for foreign currency gain or loss from an interest-bearing liability and bona fide hedges of an interest-bearing liability.*—Except as provided in paragraph (g)(2)(ii)(D)(*2*) or (g)(5)(iv) of this section, foreign currency gain or loss arising from an interest-bearing liability is characterized as subpart F income and non-subpart F income in the same manner that interest expense associated with the liability would be allocated and apportioned between subpart F income and non-subpart F income under §§ 1.861-9T and 1.861-12T. Likewise, foreign currency gain or loss arising from a bona fide hedging transaction entered into by the controlled foreign corporation that has the effect of managing exchange rate risk with respect to an interest-bearing liability that is not subject to paragraph (g)(2)(ii)(D)(*2*) (certain interest-bearing liabilities treated as dealer property) or (g)(5)(iv) (gain or loss allocated under § 1.861-9) of this section is characterized as subpart F income and non-subpart F income in the same manner that interest expense associated with the interest-bearing liability would be allocated and apportioned between subpart F income and non-subpart F income under §§ 1.861-9T and 1.861-12T. Paragraph (g)(2)(ii) of this section does not apply to any foreign currency gain or loss described in this paragraph (g)(2)(iii).

(3) * * *

(iii) *Revocation of election.*—This election is effective for the taxable year of the controlled foreign corporation for which it is made and all subsequent taxable years of such corporation unless revoked by the Commissioner or the controlling United States shareholders (as defined in § 1.964-1(c)(5)) of the controlled foreign corporation. The controlling United States shareholders of a controlled foreign corporation may revoke such corporation's election at any time. If an election has been revoked under this paragraph (g)(3)(iii), a new election under paragraph (g)(3) of this section cannot be made until the sixth taxable year following the year in which the previous election was revoked, and such subsequent election cannot be revoked until the sixth taxable year following the year in which the subsequent election was made. The controlling United States shareholders revoke an election on behalf of a controlled foreign corporation by filing a statement that clearly indicates such election has been revoked with their original or amended income tax returns for the taxable year of such United States shareholders ending with or within the taxable year of the controlled foreign corporation for which the election is revoked.

* * *

(4) * * *

(iii) *Revocation of election.*—This election is effective for the taxable year of the controlled foreign corporation for which it is made and all subsequent taxable years of such corporation unless revoked by the Commissioner or the controlling United States shareholders (as defined in § 1.964-1(c)(5)) of the controlled foreign corporation. The controlling United States shareholders of a controlled foreign corporation may revoke such corporation's election at any time. If an election has been revoked under this paragraph (g)(4)(iii), a new election under paragraph (g)(4) of this section cannot be made until the sixth taxable year following the year in which the previous election was revoked, and such subsequent election cannot be revoked until the sixth taxable year following the year in which the subsequent election was made. The controlling United States shareholders revoke an election on behalf of a controlled foreign corporation by filing a statement that clearly indicates such election has been revoked with their original or amended income tax returns for the taxable year of such United States shareholders ending with or within the taxable year of the controlled foreign corporation for which the election is revoked.

* * *

(i) * * *

(2) *Other paragraphs.*—* * * The second sentence of paragraph (a)(4)(ii)(A), paragraph (g)(2)(ii)(C)(*1*), and the second sentence of paragraph (g)(2)(iii) apply to a bona fide hedging transaction entered into on or after the date the proposed regulations are published as final regulations in the *Federal Register*. Paragraphs (g)(2)(ii)(C) (other paragraph (g)(2)(ii)(C)(*1*), insofar as it applies to a bona fide hedging transaction), (g)(3)(iii), and (g)(4)(iii) of this section apply to taxable years of controlled foreign corporations ending on or after the date that these regulations are published as final regulations in the *Federal Register*.

[Prop. Reg. § 1.954-2.]

[Proposed 12-19-2017.]

§ 4.954-2. Foreign personal holding company income; taxable years beginning after December 31, 1986.—

* * *

(b) *Dividends, etc.*—

* * *

(6) *Treatment of tax exempt interest.*—Foreign personal holding company income includes all interest income, including interest that is exempt from U.S. tax pursuant to section 103 ("tax-exempt interest"). However, the net foreign base company income of a controlled foreign corporation that is attributable to such tax-exempt interest shall be treated as tax-exempt interest in the hands of the U.S.

shareholders of the foreign corporation. Accordingly, any net foreign base company income that is included in the subpart F income of a U.S. shareholder and that is attributable to such tax-exempt interest shall remain exempt from the regular income tax, but potentially subject to the alternative minimum tax, in the hands of the U.S. shareholder.

* * *

[Reg. §4.954-2.]

□ [*T.D. 8216, 7-20-88. Amended by T.D. 8556, 7-22-94. Redesignated by T.D. 8618, 9-6-95.*]

§1.954-3. Foreign base company sales income.—(a) *Income included.*—(1) *In general.*—(i) *General rules.*—Foreign base company sales income of a controlled foreign corporation shall, except as provided in paragraphs (a)(2), (a)(3) and (a)(4) of this section, consist of gross income (whether in the form of profits, commissions, fees or otherwise) derived in connection with the purchase of personal property from a related person and its sale to any person, the sale of personal property to any person on behalf of a related person, the purchase of personal property from any person and its sale to a related person, or the purchase of personal property from any person on behalf of a related person. See section 954(d)(1). For purposes of the preceding sentence, except as provided in paragraphs (a)(2) and (a)(4) of this section, personal property sold by a controlled foreign corporation will be considered to be the same property that was purchased by the controlled foreign corporation regardless of whether the personal property is sold in the same form in which it was purchased, in a different form than the form in which it was purchased, or as a component part of a manufactured product. This section shall apply to the purchase and / or sale of personal property, whether or not such property was purchased and / or sold in the ordinary course of trade or business, except that income derived in connection with the sale of tangible personal property will not be considered to be foreign base company sales income if such property is sold to a person that is not a related person, as defined in §1.954-1(f), after substantial use has been made of the property by the controlled foreign corporation in its trade or business. This section shall not apply to the excess of gains over losses from sales or exchanges of securities or from futures transactions, to the extent such excess gains are includible in foreign personal holding company income of the controlled foreign corporation under §1.954-2; nor shall it apply to the sale of the controlled foreign corporation's property (other than its stock in trade or other property of a kind which would properly be included in its inventory if on hand at the close of the taxable year, or property held primarily for sale to customers in the ordinary course of its business) if substantially all the property of such corporation is sold pursuant to the discontinuation of the trade or business previously carried on by such corporation. The term "any person" as used in this paragraph (a)(1)(i) includes a related person as defined in §1.954-1(f).

(ii) *Special rule.*—*(a) In general.*—The term "personal property" as used in section 954(d) and this section shall not include agricultural commodities which are not grown in the United States (within the meaning of section 7701(a)(9)) in commercially marketable quantities. All of the agricultural commodities listed in Table I shall be considered grown in the United States in commercially marketable quantities. Bananas, black pepper, cocoa, coconut, coffee, crude rubber, and tea shall not be considered grown in the United States in commercially marketable quantities. All other agricultural commodities shall not be considered grown in the United States in commercially marketable quantities when, in consideration of all of the facts and circumstances of the individual case, such commodities are shown to be produced in the United States in insufficient quantity and quality to be marketed commercially. The term "agricultural commodities" includes, but is not limited to, livestock, poultry, fish produced in fish farms, fruit, furbearing animals as well as the products of truck farms, ranches, nurseries, ranges, and orchards. A fish farm is an area where fish are grown or raised (artificially protected and cared for), as opposed to merely caught or harvested. However, the term "agricultural commodities" shall not include timber (either standing or felled), or any commodity at least 50 percent of the fair market value of which is attributable to manufacturing or processing, determined in a manner consistent with the regulations under section 993(c) (relating to the definition of export property). For purposes of applying such regulations, the term "processing" shall be deemed not to include handling, packing, packaging, grading, storing, transporting, slaughtering, and harvesting. Subdivision (ii) shall apply in the computation of foreign base company sales income for taxable years of controlled foreign corporations beginning after December 31, 1975, and to taxable years of United States shareholders (within the meaning of section 951 (b)) within which or with which such taxable years of such foreign corporations end.

(b) Table.

Table I—Agricultural Commodities Grown in the United States in Commercially Marketable Quantities

Livestock and Products

Beeswax	Horses
Cattle and calves	Milk
Chickens	Mink
Chicken eggs	Mohair
Ducks	Rabbits
Geese	Sheep and lambs
Goats	Turkeys
Hogs	Wool
Honey	

Crops

Alfalfa	Eggplant	Peanuts
Almonds	Escarole	Pears
Apples	Figs	Peas
Apricots	Filberts	Peppers
Artichokes	Flaxseed	Plums and prunes
Asparagus	Garlic	Potatoes
Avocadoes	Grapes	Potted plants
Barley	Grapefruit	Raspberries
Beans	Grass seed	Rice
Beets	Hay	Rhubarb
Blackberries	Honeydew melons	Rye
Blueberries	Hops	Sorghum grain
Brussel sprouts	Lemons	Soybeans
Broccoli	Lettuce	Spinach
Bulbs	Limes	Strawberries
Cabbage	Macadamia nuts	Sugar beets
Cantaloupes	Maple syrup and sugar	Sugarcane
Carrots	Mint	Sweet potatoes
Cauliflower	Mushrooms	Tangelos
Celery	Nectarines	Tangerines
Cherries	Oats	Tobacco
Corn	Olives	Tomatoes
Cotton	Onions	Walnuts
Cranberries	Oranges	Watermelons
Cucumbers	Papayas	Wheat
Cut flowers	Pecans	
Dates	Peaches	

(iii) *Examples.*—The application of this subparagraph may be illustrated by the following examples:

Example 1. Controlled foreign corporation A, incorporated under the laws of foreign country X, is a wholly owned subsidiary of domestic corporation M. Corporation A purchases from M Corporation, a related person, articles manufactured in the United States and sells the articles to P, an unrelated person, for delivery and use in foreign country Y. Gross income of A Corporation derived from the purchase and sale of the personal property is foreign base company sales income.

Example 2. Corporation A in *Example 1* also purchases from P, an unrelated person, articles manufactured in country Y and sells the articles to foreign corporation B, a related person, for use in foreign country Z. Gross income of A Corporation derived from the purchase and sale of the personal property is foreign base company sales income.

Example (3). Controlled foreign corporation C, incorporated under the laws of foreign country X, is a wholly owned subsidiary of domestic corporation N. By contract, N Corporation agrees to pay C Corporation, a related person, a commission equal to 6 percent of the gross selling price of all personal property shipped by N Corporation as the result of orders solicited by C Corporation in foreign countries Y and Z. In fulfillment of such orders, N Corporation ships products manufactured by it in the United States. Corporation C does not assume title to the property sold. Gross commissions received by C Corporation from N Corporation in connection with the sale of such property for use in countries Y and Z constitute foreign base company sales income.

Example (4). Controlled foreign corporation D, incorporated under the laws of foreign country Y, is a wholly owned subsidiary of domestic corporation R. In 1964, D Corporation acquires a United States manufactured lathe from R Corporation. In 1972, after having made a substantial use of the lathe in its manufacturing business, D

Corporation sells the lathe to an unrelated person for use in foreign country Z. Gross income from the sale of the lathe is not foreign base company sales income since it is sold to an unrelated person after substantial use has been made of it by D Corporation in its business.

Example (5). Controlled foreign corporation E, incorporated under the laws of foreign country Y, is a wholly owned subsidiary of domestic corporation P. Corporation E purchases from P Corporation articles manufactured by P Corporation outside of country Y and sells the articles to F Corporation, an unrelated person, for use in foreign country Z. Corporation E finances the purchase of the articles by F Corporation by agreeing to accept payment over an extended period of time and receives not only the purchase price but also interest and service fees. All gross income of E Corporation derived in connection with the purchase and sale of the personal property, including interest and service fees derived from financing the sale to F Corporation, constitutes foreign base company sales income.

(2) *Property manufactured, produced, constructed, grown, or extracted within the country in which the controlled foreign corporation is created or organized.*—Foreign base company sales income does not include income derived in connection with the purchase and sale of personal property (or purchase or sale of personal property on behalf of a related person) in a transaction described in paragraph (a)(1) of this section if the property is manufactured, produced, constructed, grown, or extracted in the country under the laws of which the controlled foreign corporation which purchases and sells the property (or acts on behalf of a related person) is created or organized. See section 954(d)(1)(A). The principles set forth in paragraphs (a)(4)(ii) and (a)(4)(iii) of this section apply under this paragraph (a)(2) in determining what constitutes the manufacture, production, or construction of personal property, excluding the requirement set forth in paragraph (a)(4)(i) of this section that the provisions of paragraphs (a)(4)(ii) and (a)(4)(iii) of this section may only be satisfied through the activities of employees of the corporation manufacturing, producing, or constructing the personal property. The principles of paragraph (a)(4)(iv) of this section apply under this paragraph (a)(2) in determining what constitutes the manufacture, production, or construction of personal property but only when the personal property is manufactured, produced, or constructed by a person related to the controlled foreign corporation within the meaning of § 1.954-1(f). The application of this paragraph (a)(2) may be illustrated by the following examples:

Example (1). Controlled foreign corporation A, incorporated under the laws of foreign country X, is a wholly owned subsidiary of domestic corporation M. Corporation A purchases coffee beans grown in country X from foreign corporation P, a related person, and sells the beans to M Corporation, a related person, for use in the United States. Income from the purchase and sale of the coffee beans by A Corporation is not foreign base company sales income since the beans were grown in country X.

Example (2). Controlled foreign corporation B, incorporated under the laws of foreign country X, is a wholly owned subsidiary of controlled foreign corporation C, also incorporated under the laws of country X. Corporation B purchases and imports into country X rough diamonds mined in foreign country Y; in country X it cuts, polishes, and shapes the diamonds in a process which constitutes manufacturing within the meaning of subparagraph (4) of this paragraph. Corporation B sells the finished diamonds to C Corporation, a related person, which in turn sells them for use in foreign country Z. Since for purposes of this subparagraph the finished diamonds are manufactured in country X, gross income derived by C Corporation from their sale is not foreign base company sales income.

(3) *Property sold for use, consumption, or disposition within the country in which the controlled foreign corporation is created or organized.*—(i) *In general.*—Foreign base company sales income does not include income derived in connection with the purchase and sale of personal property (or purchase or sale of personal property on behalf of a related person) in a transaction described in subparagraph (1) of this paragraph, (*a*) if the property is sold for use, consumption, or disposition in the country under the laws of which the controlled foreign corporation which purchases and sells the property (or sells on behalf of a related person) is created or organized or (*b*), where the property is purchased by the controlled foreign corporation on behalf of a related person, if such property is purchased for use, consumption, or disposition in the country under the laws of which such controlled foreign corporation is created or organized. See section 954(d)(1)(B).

(ii) *Rules for determining country of use, consumption, or disposition.*—As a general rule, personal property which is sold to an unrelated person will be presumed for purposes of this subparagraph to have been sold for use, consumption, or disposition in the country of destination of the property sold; for such purpose, the occurrence in a country of a temporary interruption in shipment of goods shall not constitute such country the country of destination. However, if at the time of a sale or personal property to an unrelated person the controlled foreign corporation knew, or should have known from the facts and circumstances surrounding the transaction, that the property probably would not be used, consumed, or disposed of in the country of destination, the controlled foreign corporation must determine the country of ultimate use, consumption, or disposition of the property or the property will be presumed to have been used, consumed, or disposed of outside the country under the laws of which the controlled foreign corporation is created or organized. A controlled foreign corporation which sells personal property to a related person is presumed to sell such property for use, consumption, or disposition outside the country under the laws of which the controlled foreign corporation is created or organized unless such corporation establishes the use made of the property by the related person; once it has established that the related person has disposed of the property, the rules in the two preceding sentences relating to sales by a controlled foreign corporation to an unrelated person will apply at the first stage in the chain of distribution at which a sale is made by a related person to an unrelated person. Notwithstanding the preceding provisions of this subdivision, a controlled foreign corporation which sells personal property to any person all of whose business except for an insubstantial part consists of selling from inventory to retail customers at retail outlets all within one country may assume at the time of such sale to such person that such property will be used, consumed, or disposed of within such country.

(iii) *Fungible goods.*—For purposes of this subparagraph, a controlled foreign corporation which sells to a purchaser personal property which because of its fungible nature cannot reasonably be specifically traced to other purchasers and to the countries of ultimate use, consumption, or disposition shall, unless such corporation establishes a different disposition as being proper, treat such property as being sold, for ultimate use, consumption, or disposition in those countries, and to those other purchasers, in the same proportions in which property from the fungible mass of the first purchaser is sold in the regular course of business by such first purchaser. No apportionment need be made, however, on the basis of sporadic sales by the first purchaser. This subdivision shall apply only in a case where the controlled foreign corporation knew, or should have known from the facts and circumstances surrounding the transaction, the manner in which the first purchaser disposes of goods from the fungible mass.

(iv) *Illustrations.*—The application of this subparagraph may be illustrated by the following examples:

Example (1). Controlled foreign corporation A, incorporated under the laws of foreign country X, and controlled foreign corporation B, incorporated under the laws of foreign country Y, are related persons. Corporation A purchases from B Corporation electric transformers produced by B Corporation in country Y and sells the transformers to D Corporation, an unrelated person, for installation in a factory building being constructed in country X. Since the personal property purchased and sold by A Corporation is to be used within the country in which A Corporation is incorporated, income of A Corporation derived from the purchase and sale of the electric transformers is not foreign base company sales income.

Example (2). Controlled foreign corporation C, incorporated under the laws of foreign country X, is a wholly owned subsidiary of domestic corporation N. Corporation C purchases from N Corporation sewing machines manufactured in the United States by N Corporation and sells the sewing machines to retail department stores, unrelated persons, located in foreign country X. The entire activities of the department stores to which C Corporation sells the machines consist of selling goods from inventory to retail customers at retail outlets in country X. Under these circumstances, at the time of sale C Corporation may assume the sewing machines will be used, consumed, or disposed of in country X, and no attempt need be made by C Corporation to determine where the sewing machines will ultimately be used by the customers of the retail department stores. Gross income of C Corporation derived from the sales to the department stores located in country X is not foreign base company sales income.

Example (3). Controlled foreign corporation D, incorporated under the laws of foreign country Y, and controlled foreign corporation E, incorporated under the laws of foreign country X, are related persons. Corporation D purchases from E Corporation sulphur extracted by E Corporation from deposits located in country X. Corporation D sells the sulphur to F Corporation, an unrelated person, for delivery to F Corporation's storage facilities located in country Y. At the time of the sale of the sulphur from D Corporation to F Corporation, D Corporation knows that F Corporation is actively engaged in the business of selling a large amount of sulphur in country Y but also that F Corporation sells, in the normal course of its business, 25 percent of its sulphur for ultimate consumption in foreign country Z. However, D Corporation has no knowledge at the time of sale whether any portion of the particular shipment it sells to F Corporation will be resold by F Corporation for ultimate use, consumption, or disposition outside country Y. Moreover, delivery of the sulphur to F Corporation's storage facilities constitutes more than a temporary interruption in the shipment of the sulphur. Under such circumstances, D Corporation may, but is not required to, trace the ultimate disposition by F Corporation of the personal property sold to F Corporation; however, if D Corporation does not trace the ultimate disposition and if it does not establish a different disposition as being proper, 25 percent of the sulphur sold by D Corporation to F Corporation will be treated as being sold for consumption in country Z and 25 percent of the gross income from the sale of sulphur by D Corporation to F Corporation will be treated as foreign base company sales income.

Example (4). Controlled foreign corporation G, incorporated under the laws of foreign country X, is a wholly owned subsidiary of domestic corporation P. Corporation G purchases from P Corporation toys manufactured in the United States by P Corporation and sells the toys to R, an unrelated person, for delivery to a duty-free port in country X. Instructions for the assembly and operation of the toys are printed in a language which is not commonly used in country X. From the facts and circumstances surrounding the sales to R, G Corporation knows, or should know, that the toys will probably not be used, consumed, or disposed of within country X. Therefore, unless G Corporation determines the use to be made of the toys by R, such property will be presumed to have been sold by R for use, consumption, or disposition outside of country X, and the entire gross income of G Corporation derived from the sales will be considered foreign base company sales income.

(4) *Property manufactured or produced by the controlled foreign corporation.*—(i) *In general.*—Foreign base company sales income does not include income of a controlled foreign corporation derived in connection with the sale of personal property manufactured, produced, or constructed by such corporation. A controlled foreign corporation will have manufactured, produced, or constructed personal property which the corporation sells only if such corporation satisfies the provisions of paragraph (a)(4)(ii), (a)(4)(iii), or (a)(4)(iv) of this section through the activities of its employees (as defined in §31.3121(d)-1(c) of this chapter) with respect to such property. A controlled foreign corporation will not be treated as having manufactured, produced, or constructed personal property which the corporation sells merely because the property is sold in a different form than the form in which it was purchased. For rules of apportionment in determining foreign base company sales income derived from the sale of personal property purchased and used as a component part of property which is not manufactured, produced, or constructed, see paragraph (a)(5) of this section.

(ii) *Substantial transformation of property.*—If personal property purchased by a foreign corporation is substantially transformed by such foreign corporation prior to sale, the property sold by the selling corporation is manufactured, produced, or constructed by such selling corporation. The application of this paragraph (a)(4)(ii) may be illustrated by the following examples:

Example (1). Controlled foreign corporation A, incorporated under the laws of foreign country X, operates a paper factory in foreign country Y. Corporation A purchases from a related person wood pulp grown in country Y. Corporation A, by a series of processes, converts the wood pulp to paper which it sells for use in foreign country Z. The transformation of wood pulp to paper constitutes the manufacture or production of property for purposes of this subparagraph.

Example (2). Controlled foreign corporation B, incorporated under the laws of foreign country X, purchases steel rods from a related person which produces the steel in foreign country Y. Corporation B operates a machining plant in country X in which it utilizes the purchased steel rods to make screws and bolts. The transformation of steel rods to screws and bolts constitutes the manufacture or production of property for purposes of this subparagraph.

Example (3). Controlled foreign corporation C, incorporated under the laws of foreign country X, purchases tuna fish from unrelated persons who own fishing boats which catch such fish on the high seas. Corporation C receives such fish in country X in the condition in which taken from the fishing boats and in such country processes, cans, and sells the fish to related person D, incorporated under the laws of foreign country Y, for consumption in foreign country Z. The transformation of such fish into canned fish constitutes the manufacture or production of property for purposes of this subparagraph.

(iii) *Manufacture of a product when purchased components constitute part of the property sold.*—If purchased property is used as a component part of personal property which is sold, the sale of the property will be treated as the sale of a manufactured product, rather than the sale of component parts, if the assembly or conversion of the component parts into the final product by the selling corporation involves activities that are substantial in nature and generally considered to constitute the manufacture, production, or construction of property. Without limiting this substantive test, which is dependent on the facts and circumstances of each case, the operations of the selling corporation in connection with the use of the purchased property as a component part of the personal property which is sold will be considered to constitute the manufacture of a product if in connection with such property conversion costs (direct labor and factory burden) of such corporation account for 20 percent or more of the total cost of goods sold. In no event, however, will packaging, repackaging, labeling, or minor assembly operations constitute the manufacture, production, or construction of property for purposes of section 954(d)(1). The application of this paragraph (a)(4)(iii) may be illustrated by the following examples:

Example (1). Controlled foreign corporation A, incorporated under the laws of foreign country X, sells industrial engines for use, consumption, and disposition outside country X. Corporation A, in connection with the assembly of such engines, performs machining and assembly operations. In addition, A Corporation purchases, from related and unrelated persons, components manufactured in foreign country Y. On a per unit basis, A Corporation's selling price and costs of such engines are as follows:

Selling price			$400
Cost of goods sold:			
Material—			
Acquired from related persons	$100		
Acquired from others	40		
Total material		$140	
Conversion costs (direct labor and factory burden)		70	
Total cost of goods sold			$210
Gross profit			$190
Administrative and selling expenses			50
Taxable income			$140

The conversion costs incurred by A Corporation are more than 20 percent of total costs of goods sold ($70/$210 or 33 percent). Although the product sold, an engine, is not sufficiently distinguishable from the components to constitute a substantial transformation of the purchased parts within the meaning of subdivision (ii) of this subparagraph, A Corporation will be considered under this subdivision to have manufactured the product it sells.

Example (2). Controlled foreign corporation B, incorporated under the laws of foreign country X, operates an automobile assembly plant. In connection with such activity, B Corporation purchases from related persons assembled engines, transmissions, and certain other components, all of which are manufactured outside of country X; purchases additional components from unrelated persons; conducts stamping, machining, and subassembly operations; and has a substantial investment in tools, jigs, welding equipment, and other machinery and equipment used in the assembly of an automobile. On a per unit basis, B Corporation's selling price and costs of such automobiles are as follows:

Selling price			$2,500
Cost of goods sold:			
Material—			
Acquired from related persons	$1,200		
Acquired from others	275		
Total material		$1,475	
Conversion costs (direct labor and factory burden)		325	
Total cost of goods sold			$1,800
Gross profit			700
Administrative and selling expenses			300
Taxable income			$ 400

The product sold, an automobile, is not sufficiently distinguishable from the components purchased (the engine, transmission, etc.) to constitute a substantial transformation of purchased parts within the meaning of subdivision (ii) of this subparagraph. Although conversion costs of B Corporation are less than 20 percent of total cost of goods sold ($325/$1,800 or 18 percent), the operations conducted by B Corporation in connection with the property purchased and sold are substantial in nature and are generally considered to constitute the manufacture of a product. Corporation B will be considered under this subdivision to have manufactured the product it sells.

Example (3). Controlled foreign corporation C, incorporated under the laws of foreign country X, purchases from related persons radio parts manufactured in foreign country Y. Corporation C designs radio kits, packages component parts required for assembly of such kits, and sells the parts in a knocked-down condition to unrelated persons for use outside country X. These packaging operations of C Corporation do not constitute the manufacture, production, or construction of personal property for purposes of section 954(d)(1).

(iv) *Substantial contribution to manufacturing of personal property.—(a) In general.*—If an item of personal property would be considered manufactured, produced, or constructed (under the principles of paragraph (a)(4)(ii) or (a)(4)(iii) of this section) prior to sale by the controlled foreign corporation had all of the manufacturing, producing, and constructing activities undertaken with respect to that property prior to sale been undertaken by the controlled foreign corporation through the activities of its employees, then this paragraph (a)(4)(iv) applies. If this paragraph (a)(4)(iv) applies and if the facts and circumstances evince that the controlled foreign corporation makes a substantial contribution through the activities of its employees to the manufacture, production, or construction of the personal property sold, then the personal property sold by the controlled foreign corporation is manufactured, produced, or constructed by such controlled foreign corporation.

(b) Activities.—The determination of whether a controlled foreign corporation makes a substantial contribution through the activities of its employees to the manufacture, production, or construction of the personal property sold involves, but will not necessarily be limited to, consideration of the following activities:

(1) Oversight and direction of the activities or process pursuant to which the property is manufactured, produced, or constructed (under the principles of paragraph (a)(4)(ii) or (a)(4)(iii) of this section).

(2) Activities that are considered in, but that are insufficient to satisfy, the tests provided in paragraphs (a)(4)(ii) and (a)(4)(iii) of this section.

(3) Material selection, vendor selection, or control of the raw materials, work-in-process or finished goods.

(4) Management of manufacturing costs or capacities (for example, managing the risk of loss, cost reduction or efficiency initiatives associated with the manufacturing process, demand planning, production scheduling, or hedging raw material costs).

(5) Control of manufacturing related logistics.

(6) Quality control (for example, sample testing or establishment of quality control standards).

(7) Developing, or directing the use or development of, product design and design specifications, as well as trade secrets, technology, or other intellectual property for the purpose of manufacturing, producing, or constructing the personal property.

(c) Application of substantial contribution test.—When considering whether a controlled foreign corporation makes a substantial contribution to the manufacture, production, or construction of the personal property, the performance of any activity in paragraph (a)(4)(iv)(*b*) of this section will be taken into account. The performance or lack of performance of any particular activity in paragraph (a)(4)(iv)(*b*) of this section, or of a particular number of activities in (a)(4)(iv)(*b*) of this section, is not determinative. The weight accorded to the performance of any quantum of any activity (whether or not specified in paragraph (a)(4)(iv)(*b*) of this section) will vary with the facts and circumstances of the particular business. See paragraph (a)(4)(iv)(*d*) *Examples 8, 10* and *11* of this section. In determining whether the activities of the controlled foreign corporation constitute a substantial contribution, there is no minimum performance threshold before an activity can be considered. The fact that other persons make a substantial contribution to the manufacture, production, or construction of the personal property prior to sale does not preclude the controlled foreign corporation from making a substantial contribution to the manufacture, construction, or production of that property through the activities of its employees. See paragraph (a)(4)(iv)(*d*) *Example 9* of this section.

(d) Examples.—The rules of this paragraph (a)(4)(iv) are illustrated by the following examples:

Example 1. No substantial contribution to manufacturing. (i) *Facts.* FS, a controlled foreign corporation, purchases raw materials from a related person. The raw materials are manufactured (under the principles of paragraph (a)(4)(ii) or (a)(4)(iii) of this section) into Product X by CM, an unrelated corporation, pursuant to a contract manufacturing arrangement. CM physically performs the substantial transformation, assembly, or conversion outside of FS's country of organization. Product X is sold by FS for use outside of FS's country of organization. Under the terms of the contract, FS retains the right to control the raw materials, work-in-process, and finished goods, and the right to oversee and direct the activities or process pursuant to which Product X is manufactured by CM. FS owns the intellectual property used in the manufacturing process. However, FS does not exercise, through its employees, its powers to control the raw materials, work-in-process, or finished goods, and FS does not exercise its powers of oversight and direction. Likewise, FS does not, through its employees, develop or direct the use or development of the intellectual property for the purpose of manufacturing Product X.

(ii) *Result.* If the manufacturing activities undertaken with respect to Product X prior to sale had been undertaken by FS through the activities of its employees, FS would have satisfied the manufacturing exception contained in paragraph (a)(4)(ii) or (a)(4)(iii) of this section with respect to Product X. Therefore, this paragraph (a)(4)(iv) applies. FS does not satisfy the test under this paragraph (a)(4)(iv) because it does not make a substantial contribution through the activities of its employees to the manufacture of Product X. Mere contractual rights to control materials, contractual rights to oversee and direct the manufacturing activities or process pursuant to which the property is manufactured, and ownership of intellectual property are not sufficient to satisfy this paragraph (a)(4)(iv). Therefore, under the facts and circumstances of the business, FS is not considered to have manufactured Product X under paragraph (a)(4)(i) of this section.

Example 2. Substantial contribution to manufacturing. (i) *Facts.* Assume the same facts as in *Example 1*, except for the following. FS, through its employees, engages in product design and quality control and controls manufacturing related logistics. Employees of FS exercise the right to oversee and direct the activities of CM in the manufacture of Product X.

(ii) *Result.* If the manufacturing activities undertaken with respect to Product X prior to sale had been undertaken by FS through the activities of its employees, FS would have satisfied the manufacturing exception contained in paragraph (a)(4)(ii) or (a)(4)(iii) of this section with respect to Product X. Therefore, this paragraph (a)(4)(iv) applies. Under the facts and circumstances of the business, FS satisfies the test under this paragraph (a)(4)(iv) because it makes a substantial contribution through the activities of its employees to the manufacture of Product X. Therefore, FS is considered to have manufactured Product X under paragraph (a)(4)(i) of this section. The analysis and conclusion would be the same if CM were related to FS because the relationship between CM and FS is irrelevant for purposes of applying paragraph (a)(4) of this section.

Example 3. Raw materials procured by contract manufacturer. (i) *Facts.* FS, a controlled foreign corporation, enters into a contract with CM to manufacture (under the principles of paragraph (a)(4)(ii) or (a)(4)(iii) of this section) Product X. CM physically performs the substantial transformation, assembly, or conversion required to manufacture Product X outside of FS's country of organization. Product X is sold by FS to a related person for use outside of FS's country of organization. Employees of FS select the materials that will be used to manufacture Product X. FS does not own the materials or work-in-process during the manufacturing process. FS, through its employees, exercises oversight and direction of the manufacturing process and provides quality control. FS manages the manufacturing costs and capacities with respect to Product X by managing the risk of loss and engaging in demand planning and production scheduling.

(ii) *Result.* If the manufacturing activities undertaken with respect to Product X prior to sale had been undertaken by FS through the activities of its employees, FS would have satisfied the manufacturing exception contained in paragraph (a)(4)(ii) or (a)(4)(iii) of this section with respect to Product X. Therefore, this paragraph (a)(4)(iv) applies. Under the facts and circumstances of the business, FS satisfies the test under this paragraph (a)(4)(iv) because it makes a substantial contribution through the activities of its employees to the manufacture of Product X. Therefore, FS is considered to have manufactured Product X under paragraph (a)(4)(i) of this section.

Example 4. Physical conversion by employees of a person other than the contract manufacturer. (i) *Facts.* FS, a controlled foreign corporation organized in Country M, purchases raw materials from a related person. The raw materials are manufactured (under the principles of paragraph (a)(4)(ii) or (a)(4)(iii) of this section) into Product X by CM, an unrelated corporation, pursuant to a contract manufacturing arrangement. CM physically performs the substantial transformation, assembly, or conversion required to manufacture Product X outside of FS's country of organization. Product X is sold by FS for use outside of FS's country of organization. CM contracts with another corporation for its employees in order to operate CM's manufacturing plant and transform, assemble, or convert the raw materials into Product X. Apart from the physical performance of the substantial transformation, assembly, or conversion of the raw materials into Product X, employees of FS perform all of the other manufacturing activities required in connection with the manufacture of Product X (for example, oversight and direction of the manufacturing process; vendor selection; control of raw materials, work-in-process, and finished goods; control of manufacturing related logistics; and quality control).

(ii) *Result.* If the manufacturing activities undertaken with respect to Product X prior to sale had been undertaken by FS through the activities of its employees, FS would have satisfied the manufacturing exception contained in paragraph (a)(4)(ii) or (a)(4)(iii) of this section with respect to Product X. Therefore, this paragraph (a)(4)(iv) applies. Under the facts and circumstances of the business, FS satisfies the test under this paragraph (a)(4)(iv) because it makes a substantial contribution through the activities of its employees to the manufacture of Product X. Therefore, FS is considered to have manufactured Product X under paragraph (a)(4)(i) of this section.

Example 5. Automated manufacturing supervised by another person. (i) *Facts.* FS, a controlled foreign corporation, purchases raw materials from a related person. The raw materials are manufactured (under the principles of paragraph (a)(4)(ii) or (a)(4)(iii) of this section) into Product X by CM, an unrelated corporation selected by FS, pursuant to a contract manufacturing arrangement. CM physically performs the substantial transformation, assembly, or conversion outside of FS's country of organization. Product X is sold by FS to related and unrelated persons for use outside of FS's country of organization. At all times, FS retains ownership of the raw materials, work-in-process, and finished goods. FS retains the right to oversee and direct the activities or process pursuant to which Product X is manufactured by CM, but does not exercise, through its employees, its powers of oversight and direction. FS is the owner of sophisticated software and network systems that remotely and automatically (without human involvement) take orders, route them to CM, order raw materials, and perform quality control. FS has a small number of computer technicians who monitor the software and network systems to ensure that they are running smoothly and apply any necessary patches or fixes. The software and network systems were developed by employees of DP, the U.S. corporate parent of FS. DP's employees supervise the computer technicians, evaluate the results of the automated manufacturing business, and make ongoing operational decisions, including decisions related to acceptable performance of the manufacturing process, stoppages of that process, and decisions related to product and manufacturing process design. DP's employees develop and provide to FS all of the upgrades to the software and network systems. DP also has employees who direct and control other aspects of the manufacturing process such as vendor and material selection, management of the manufacturing costs and capacities, and the selection of CM. The need for DP's employees to direct the activities of the FS employees and otherwise contribute to the manufacturing process evinces that substantial operational responsibilities and decision making are required to be exercised by parties other than CM in order to manufacture Product X.

(ii) *Result.* If the manufacturing activities undertaken with respect to Product X prior to sale had been undertaken by FS through the activities of its employees, FS would have satisfied the manufacturing exception contained in paragraph (a)(4)(ii) or (a)(4)(iii) of this section with respect to Product X. Therefore, this paragraph (a)(4)(iv) applies. Under the facts and circumstance of the business, FS does not satisfy the test under this paragraph (a)(4)(iv) because it does not make a substantial contribution through the activities of its employees to the manufacture of Product X. Mere ownership of materials and intellectual property along with contractual rights to exercise powers of direction and control are not sufficient to satisfy this paragraph (a)(4)(iv). The employees of FS do not perform the amount of activity necessary to constitute a substantial contribution. FS is not considered to have manufactured Product X under paragraph (a)(4)(i) of this section.

Example 6. Automated manufacturing supervised by FS. (i) *Facts.* Assume the same facts as in *Example 5*, except for the following. FS, through its employees, engages in the activities undertaken by DP's employees in *Example 5*. DP's employees also contribute to product and manufacturing process design, and provide support and oversight to FS in connection with functions performed by FS through its employees.

(ii) *Result.* If the manufacturing activities undertaken with respect to Product X prior to sale had been undertaken by FS through the activities of its employees, FS would have satisfied the manufacturing exception contained in paragraph (a)(4)(ii) or (a)(4)(iii) of this section with respect to Product X. Therefore, this paragraph (a)(4)(iv) applies. Under the facts and circumstances of the business, FS satisfies the test under this paragraph (a)(4)(iv) because it makes a substantial contribution through the activities of its employees to the manufacture of Product X. This determination does not require a comparison between the activities of FS and the activities of DP. Selection of the contract manufacturer, even though not specifically identified in paragraph (a)(4)(iv)(*b*) of this section, is considered under paragraph (a)(4)(iv)(*c*) of this section in determining whether FS makes a substantial contribution to the manufacture of Product X through its employees. FS is considered to have manufactured Product X under paragraph (a)(4)(i) of this section.

Example 7. Automated manufacturing supervised by FS with purchased intellectual property. (i) *Facts.* Assume the same facts as in *Example 6*, except for the following. The software and network systems, and the upgrades to those systems, were purchased by FS rather than developed by employees of FS.

(ii) *Result.* If the manufacturing activities undertaken with respect to Product X prior to sale had been undertaken by FS through the activities of its employees, FS would have satisfied the manufacturing exception contained in paragraph (a)(4)(ii) or (a)(4)(iii) of this section with respect to Product X. Therefore, this paragraph (a)(4)(iv) applies. The lack of performance of software and network system development activities is not determinative under the facts and circumstances of the business. Therefore, FS satisfies the test under this paragraph (a)(4)(iv) because it makes a substantial contribution through the activities of its employees to the manufacture of Product X. This determination does not require a comparison between the activities of FS and the activities of DP. FS is considered to have manufactured Product X under paragraph (a)(4)(i) of this section.

Example 8. Manufacture without intellectual property. (i) *Facts.* FS, a controlled foreign corporation, purchases raw materials from a related person. The raw materials are manufactured (under the principles of paragraph (a)(4)(ii) or (a)(4)(iii) of this section) into Product X by CM, an unrelated corporation, pursuant to a contract manufacturing arrangement. CM physically performs the substantial transformation, assembly, or conversion outside of FS's country of organization. Product X is sold by FS for use outside of FS's country of organization. At all times, FS controls the raw materials, work-in-process, and finished goods. FS controls the manufacturing related logistics, manages the manufacturing costs and capacities, and provides quality control with respect to CM's manufacturing process and product. No intellectual property of significant value is required to manufacture Product X. FS does not own any intellectual property underlying Product X, or hold an exclusive or non-exclusive right to manufacture Product X.

(ii) *Result.* If the manufacturing activities undertaken with respect to Product X prior to sale had been undertaken by FS through the activities of its employees, FS would have satisfied the manufacturing exception contained in paragraph (a)(4)(ii) or (a)(4)(iii) of this section with respect to Product X. Therefore, this paragraph (a)(4)(iv) applies. Because use of intellectual property plays little or no role in the manufacture of Product X, it is not important to the substantial contribution analysis under paragraph (a)(4)(iv) of this section. Under the facts and circumstances of the business, FS satisfies the test under this paragraph (a)(4)(iv) because it makes a substantial contribution through the activities of its employees to the manufacture of Product X. Therefore, FS is considered to have manufactured Product X under paragraph (a)(4)(i) of this section.

Example 9. Substantial contribution by more than one CFC. (i) *Facts.* FS1 and FS2, unrelated controlled foreign corporations, contract with CM, an unrelated corporation, to manufacture (under the principles of paragraph (a)(4)(ii) or (a)(4)(iii) of this section) Product X. CM physically performs the substantial transformation, assembly, or conversion required to manufacture Product X outside of FS1's and FS2's respective countries of organization. Neither FS1 nor FS2 owns the materials or work-in-process during the manufacturing process. Product X is sold by FS1 and FS2 to persons related to FS1 and FS2, respectively, for disposition outside of FS1's and FS2's respective countries of organization. FS1, through its employees, designs Product X. FS1 directs the use of the product design and design specifications, and other intellectual property, for the purpose of manufacturing Product X. Employees of FS1 also select the materials that will be used to manufacture Product X, and the vendors that provide those materials. FS2, through its employees, designs the process for manufacturing Product X. FS2, through its employees, manages the manufacturing costs and capacities with respect to Product X. FS1 and FS2 each provide quality control and oversight and direction of CM's manufacturing activities with respect to different aspects of the manufacture of Product X.

(ii) *Result*. If the manufacturing activities undertaken with respect to Product X prior to sale had been undertaken by FS1 or FS2 through the activities of their employees, FS1 or FS2 would have satisfied the manufacturing exception contained in paragraph (a)(4)(ii) or (a)(4)(iii) of this section with respect to Product X. Therefore, this paragraph (a)(4)(iv) applies. The fact that other persons make a substantial contribution to the manufacture of personal property does not preclude a controlled foreign corporation from making a substantial contribution to the manufacture of personal property through the activities of its employees. In the analysis of whether FS1 or FS2 make a substantial contribution to the manufacture of Product X, each company takes into account its individual activities, including those of providing quality control and oversight and direction of the manufacture of Product X. In addition, no threshold level of activity is required, including with respect to providing quality control or oversight and direction of the activities or process pursuant to which Product X is manufactured, before FS1 and FS2 can take into account their respective activities. Under the facts and circumstances of the business, both FS1 and FS2 satisfy the test under this paragraph (a)(4)(iv) because each independently makes a substantial contribution through the activities of its employees to the manufacture of Product X. Therefore, FS1 and FS2 are each considered to have manufactured Product X under paragraph (a)(4)(i) of this section.

Example 10. Manufacture of products designed by CFC. (i) *Facts*. FS, a controlled foreign corporation, purchases raw materials from a related person. The raw materials are manufactured (under the principles of paragraph (a)(4)(ii) or (a)(4)(iii) of this section) into Product X by CM, an unrelated corporation, pursuant to a contract manufacturing arrangement. CM physically performs the substantial transformation, assembly, or conversion outside of FS's country of organization. Product X is sold by FS for use outside of FS's country of organization. Products in the X industry are distinguished (and vary widely in value) based on the raw materials used to make the product and the product design. FS designs the product and selects the materials that CM will use to manufacture Product X. FS also manages the manufacturing costs and capacities. Product X can be manufactured from the raw materials to FS's design specifications without significant oversight and direction, quality control, or control of manufacturing related logistics. The activities most relevant to the substantial contribution analysis under these facts are material selection, product design and management of the manufacturing costs and capacities.

(ii) *Result*. If the manufacturing activities undertaken with respect to Product X prior to sale had been undertaken by FS through the activities of its employees, FS would have satisfied the manufacturing exception contained in paragraph (a)(4)(ii) or (a)(4)(iii) of this section with respect to Product X. Therefore, this paragraph (a)(4)(iv) applies. Under the facts and circumstances of the business, FS makes a substantial contribution through the activities of its employees to the manufacture of Product X. FS satisfies the test under this paragraph (a)(4)(iv) because it makes a substantial contribution through the activities of its employees to the manufacture of Product X. Therefore, FS is considered to have manufactured Product X under paragraph (a)(4)(i) of this section.

Example 11. Direction and oversight of manufacturing and quality control through periodic visits. (i) *Facts*. FS, a controlled foreign corporation, purchases raw materials from a related person. The raw materials are manufactured (under the principles of paragraph (a)(4)(ii) or (a)(4)(iii) of this section) into Product X by CM, an unrelated corporation, pursuant to a contract manufacturing arrangement. CM physically performs the substantial transformation, assembly, or conversion outside of FS's country of organization. Product X is sold by FS for use outside of FS's country of organization. FS controls the raw material, work-in-process, and finished goods, manages the manufacturing costs and capacities, and provides oversight and direction of the manufacture of Product X. Employees of FS visit CM's manufacturing facility for one week each quarter and perform quality control tests on a random sample of the units of Product X produced during the week. In the X industry, quarterly visits to a manufacturing facility by qualified persons are sufficient to control the quality of manufacturing.

(ii) *Result*. If the manufacturing activities undertaken with respect to Product X prior to sale had been undertaken by FS through the activities of its employees, FS would have satisfied the manufacturing exception contained in paragraph (a)(4)(ii) or (a)(4)(iii) of this section with respect to Product X. Therefore, this paragraph (a)(4)(iv) applies. Under the facts and circumstances of the business, FS satisfies the test under this paragraph (a)(4)(iv) with respect to Product X because it makes a substantial contribution through the activities of its employees to the manufacture of Product X. Therefore, FS is considered to have manufactured Product X under paragraph (a)(4)(i) of this section.

(5) *Rules for apportionment of income derived from the sale of purchased components used in property not manufactured, produced, or constructed*.—The foreign base company sales income derived by a controlled foreign corporation for the taxable year from sales of personal property purchased and used as a component part of property which is not manufactured, produced, or constructed by such corporation within the meaning of subparagraph (4) of this paragraph shall, unless the records of the controlled foreign corporation show that a different apportionment of income is proper or unless all the income from such sales is treated as foreign base company sales income, be determined by first making for such year the following separate classifications and subclassifications with respect to the property which is sold and then by apportioning the income for such year from such sales in accordance with the rules of this subparagraph:

(i) A classification of the cost of components used in the property which is sold into two classes consisting of the cost of components manufactured, produced, constructed, grown, or extracted—

(*a*) Within the country under the laws of which the controlled foreign corporation is created or organized, and

(*b*) Outside such country;

(ii) A subclassification of the class described in subdivision (i)(*b*) of this subparagraph into—

(*a*) The cost of such components purchased from unrelated persons, and

(*b*) The cost of such components purchased from related persons;

(iii) A classification of the income derived from such sales into two classes consisting of income derived from sales for use, consumption, or disposition—

(*a*) Within the country under the laws of which the controlled foreign corporation is created or organized, and

(*b*) Outside such country; and

(iv) A subclassification of the class described in subdivision (iii)(*b*) of this subparagraph into income from—

(*a*) Sales to unrelated persons, and

(*b*) Sales to related persons. The foreign base company sales income for the taxable year from purchases of the property from related persons and sales to unrelated persons shall be the amount which bears to the amount described in subdivision (iv) (*a*) of this subparagraph the same ratio that the amount described in subdivision (ii)(*b*) of this subparagraph bears to the total cost of components used in the product which is sold. The foreign base company sales income for the taxable year from purchases of the property from related persons and sales to related persons is the amount which bears to the amount described in subdivision (iv) (*b*) of this subparagraph the same ratio that the amount described in subdivision (ii)(*b*) of this subparagraph bears to the total cost of components used in the product which is sold. The foreign base company sales income for the taxble year from purchases of the property from unrelated persons and sales to related persons is the amount which bears to the amount described in subdivision (iv)(*b*) of this subparagraph the same ratio that the amount described in subdivision (ii)(*a*) of this subparagraph bears to the total cost of components used in the product which is sold. The application of this subparagraph may be illustrated by the following examples:

Example (1). Controlled foreign corporation C, which is incorporated under the laws of foreign country X, uses the calendar year as the taxable year. For 1964, C Corporation purchases radio parts of which some are manufactured in foreign country Y; and others, in country X. Some of the parts manufactured in country Y are purchased from related persons. Corporation C uses the purchased parts in radio kits which it designs and sells for assembly by its customers, unrelated persons, some of whom use the kits outside country X. Unless the records of C Corporation show that a different apportionment of income is proper, the foreign base company sales income for 1964 is determined in the following manner upon the basis of the following factual classifications for such year:

Cost of components purchased from all persons:		
Manufactured within country X		$20
Manufactured outside country X		40
Total cost		60
Cost of components manufactured outside country X:		
Purchased from unrelated persons		10
Purchased from related persons		30
Total cost		40
Gross income from sales:		
Gross receipts from sales		$120
Cost of goods sold:		
Components	$60	
Direct labor and factory burden	10	70
Gross income		50
Gross income from sales:		
For use within country X		$26
For use outside country X		24
Gross income		50
Foreign base company sales income from purchases from related persons and sales to unrelated persons ($24× $30/$60)		12

Example (2). The facts are the same as in example (1) except that none of the purchases are from related persons and some of the sales for use outside country X are to related persons. Unless the records of C Corporation show that a different apportionment of income is proper, the foreign base company sales income for 1964 is determined in the following manner upon the basis of the following additional factual classification for such year:

Gross income from sales for use outside country X—	
To unrelated persons	$8
To related persons	16
Total gross income	24
Foreign base company sales income from purchases from unrelated persons and sales to related persons ($16 × $40/$60)	$10.67

Example (3). The facts are the same as in example (1) except that some of the sales for use outside country X are to related persons as in example (2). Unless the records of C Corporation show that a different apportionment of income is proper, the foreign base company sales income for 1964 is determined in the following manner:

Foreign base company sales income from purchases from related persons and sales to unrelated persons ($8 × $30/$60)	$4.00
Foreign base company sales income from purchases from related persons and sales to related persons ($16 × $30/$60)	8.00
Foreign base company sales income from purchases from unrelated persons and sales to related persons ($16 × $10/$60)	2.67
Total foreign base company sales income	$14.67

(6) *Special rule applicable to distributive share of partnership income.*—(i) *In general.*—To determine the extent to which a controlled foreign corporation's distributive share of any item of gross income of a partnership would have been foreign base company sales income if received by it directly, under § 1.952-1(g), the property sold will be considered to be manufactured, produced, or constructed by the controlled foreign corporation, within the meaning of paragraph (a)(4)(i) of this section, only if the manufacturing exception of paragraph (a)(4)(i) of this section would have applied to exclude the income from foreign base company sales income if the controlled foreign corporation had earned the income directly, determined by taking into account only the activities of the employees of, and property owned by, the partnership.

(ii) *Example.*—The application of paragraph (a)(6)(i) of this section is illustrated by the following example:

Example. CFC, a controlled foreign corporation organized under the laws of Country A, is an 80 percent partner in Partnership X, a partnership organized under the laws of Country B. Partnership X performs activities in Country B that would constitute the manufacture of Product O, within the meaning of paragraph (a)(4) of this section, if performed directly by CFC. Partnership X, through its sales offices in Country B, then sells Product O to Corp D, a corporation that is a related person with respect to CFC, within the meaning of section 954(d)(3), for use within Country B. CFC's distributive share of Partnership X's sales income is not foreign base company sales income because the manufacturing exception of paragraph (a)(4) of this section would have applied to exclude the income from foreign base company sales income if CFC had earned the income directly.

(iii) *Effective date.*—This paragraph (a)(6) applies to taxable years of a controlled foreign corporation beginning on or after July 23, 2002.

(b) *Branches of controlled foreign corporation treated as separate corporations.*—(1) *General rules for determining when to apply separate treatment.*—(i) *Sales or purchase branch.*—*(a) In general.*—If a controlled foreign corporation carries on purchasing or selling activities by or through a branch or similar establishment located outside the country under the laws of which such corporation is created or organized and the use of the branch or similar establishment for such activities has substantially the same tax effect as if the branch or similar establishment were a wholly owned subsidiary corporation of such controlled foreign corporation, the branch or similar establishment and the remainder of the controlled foreign corporation will be treated as separate corporations for purposes of determining foreign base company sales income of such corporation. See section 954(d)(2).

(b) Allocation of income and comparison of effective rates of tax.—The determination as to whether such use of the branch or similar establishment has the same tax effect as if it were a wholly owned subsidiary corporation of the controlled foreign corporation shall be made by allocating to such branch or similar establishment only that income derived by the branch or establishment which, when the special rules of subparagraph (2)(i) of this paragraph are applied, is described in paragraph (a) of this section (but determined without applying subparagraphs (2), (3), and (4) of such paragraph). The use of the branch or similar establishment for such activities will be considered to have substantially the same tax effect as if it were a wholly owned subsidiary corporation of the controlled foreign corporation if the income allocated to the branch or similar establishment under the immediately preceding sentence is, by statute, treaty obligation, or otherwise, taxed in the year when earned at an effective rate of tax that is less than 90 percent of, and at least 5 percentage points less than, the effective rate of tax which would apply to such income under the laws of the country in which the controlled foreign corporation is created or organized, if, under the laws of such country, the entire income of the controlled foreign corporation were considered derived by the corporation from sources within such country from doing business through a permanent establishment therein, received in such country, and allocable to such permanent establishment, and the corporation were managed and controlled in such country.

(c) Use of more than one branch.—If a controlled foreign corporation carries on purchasing or selling activities by or through more than one branch or similar establishment located outside the country under the laws of which such corporation is created or organized, then paragraph (b)(1)(i)(*b*) of this section shall be applied separately to the income derived by each such branch or similar establishment (by treating such purchasing or selling branch or similar establishment as if it were the only branch or similar establishment of the controlled foreign corporation and as if any such other branches or similar establishments were separate corporations) in determining whether the use of such branch or similar establishment has substantially the same tax effect as if such branch or similar establishment were a wholly owned subsidiary corporation of the controlled foreign corporation. See paragraph (b)(1)(ii)(*c*)(*1*) of this section for rules applicable to a controlled foreign corporation that carries on purchase or sales activities by or through one or more branches or similar establishments in addition to carrying on manufacturing activities by or through one or more branches or similar establishments.

(ii) *Manufacturing branch.*—*(a) In general.*—If a controlled foreign corporation carries on manufacturing, producing, constructing, growing, or extracting activities by or through a branch or similar establishment located outside the country under the laws of which such corporation is created or organized and the use of the branch or similar establishment for such activities with respect to personal property purchased or sold by or through the remainder of the controlled foreign corporation has substantially the same tax effect as if the branch or similar establishment were a wholly owned subsidiary corporation of such controlled foreign corporation, the branch or similar establishment and the remainder of the controlled foreign corporation will be treated as separate corporations for purposes of determining the foreign base company sales income of such corporation. See section 954(d)(2). The provisions of this paragraph (b)(1)(ii) will apply only if the controlled foreign corporation (including any branches or similar establishments of such controlled foreign corporation) manufactures, produces, or constructs such personal property within the meaning of paragraph (a)(4)(i) of this section, or carries on growing or extracting activities with respect to such personal property.

(b) Allocation of income and comparison of effective rates of tax.—The determination as to whether such use of the branch or similar establishment has substantially the same tax effect as if the branch or similar establishment were a wholly owned subsidiary corporation of the controlled foreign corporation shall be made by allocating to the remainder of such controlled foreign corporation only that income derived by the remainder of such corporation, which, when the special rules of subparagraph (2)(i) of this paragraph are applied, is described in paragraph (a) of this section (but determined without applying subparagraphs (2), (3), and (4) of such paragraph). The use of the branch or similar establishment for such activities will be considered to have substantially the same tax effect as if it were a wholly owned subsidiary corporation of the controlled foreign corporation if income allocated to the remainder of the controlled foreign corporation under the immediately preceding sentence is, by statute, treaty obligation, or otherwise, taxed in the year when earned at an effective rate of tax that is less than 90 percent of, and at least 5 percentage points less than, the effective rate of tax which would apply to such income under the laws of the country in which the branch or similar establishment is located, if, under the laws of such country, the entire income of the controlled foreign corporation were considered derived by such corporation from sources within such country from doing business through a permanent establishment therein, received in such country, and allocable to such permanent establishment, and the corporation were created or organized under the laws of, and managed and controlled in, such country.

(c) Use of more than one branch.—(1) Use of one or more sales or purchase branches in addition to a manufacturing branch.—If, with respect to personal property manufactured, produced, constructed, grown, or extracted by or through a branch or similar establishment located outside the country under the laws of which the controlled foreign corporation is created or organized, purchasing or selling activities are carried on by or through more than one branch or similar establishment, or by or through one or more branches or similar establishments located outside such country, of such corporation, then paragraph (b)(1)(ii)(*b*) of this section shall be applied separately to the income derived by each such purchasing or selling branch or similar establishment (by treating such purchasing or selling branch or similar establishment as though it alone were the remainder of the controlled foreign corporation) for purposes of determining whether the use of such manufacturing, producing, constructing, growing, or extracting branch or similar establishment has substantially the same tax effect as if such branch or similar establishment were a wholly owned subsidiary corporation of the controlled foreign corporation. If this rule applies, the sales or purchase branch rules contained in paragraph (b)(1)(i) of this section do not apply. The application of this paragraph (b)(1)(ii)(*c*)(*1*) is illustrated by the following example:

Example. All activities of controlled foreign corporation conducted through sales branches and manufacturing branch. (i) *Facts.* FS, a controlled foreign corporation organized under the laws of country M, operates three branches. Branch A, located in country A, manufactures Product X under the principles of paragraph (a)(4)(i) of this section. Branch B, located in Country B, sells Product X manufactured by Branch A to customers for use outside of Country B. Branch C, located in Country C sells Product X manufactured by Branch A to customers for use outside of Country C. FS does not conduct any manufacturing or selling activities apart from the activities of Branches A, B and C. Country M imposes an effective rate of tax on sales income of 0%. Country A imposes an effective rate of tax on sales income of 20%. Country B imposes an effective rate of tax on sales income of 20%. Country C imposes an effective rate of tax on sales income of 18%.

(ii) *Result.* Pursuant to this paragraph (b)(1)(ii)(*c*)(*1*), paragraph (b)(1)(ii)(*b*) of this section is applied to the sales income derived by Branch B by treating Branch B as though it alone were the remainder of the controlled foreign corporation. The use of Branch B does not have the same tax effect as if Branch B were a wholly owned subsidiary of FS because the tax rate applicable to the income allocated to Branch B under paragraph (b)(1)(ii)(*b*) of this section (20%) is not less than 90% of, and at least 5 percentage points less than, the effective rate of tax which would apply to such income under the laws of Country A (20%), the country in which Branch A is located. In addition, paragraph (b)(1)(ii)(*b*) of this section is applied separately to the sales income derived by Branch C by treating Branch C as though it alone were the remainder of the controlled foreign corporation. The use of Branch C does not have the same tax effect as if Branch C were a wholly owned subsidiary of FS because the tax rate applicable to the income allocated to Branch C under paragraph (b)(1)(ii)(*b*) of this section (18%) is not less than 90% of, and at least 5 percentage points less than, the effective rate of tax which would apply to such income under the laws of Country A (20%), the country in which Branch A is located. Pursuant to this paragraph (b)(1)(ii)(*c*)(*1*), the rules under paragraph (b)(1)(i) of this section for determining whether a sales or purchase branch is treated as a separate corporation from the remainder of the controlled foreign corporation do not apply.

(2) Use of more than one branch to manufacture, produce, construct, grow, or extract separate items of personal property.—If a controlled foreign corporation carries on manufacturing, producing, constructing, growing, or extracting activities with respect to separate items of personal property by or through more than one branch or similar establishment located outside the country under the laws of which such corporation is created or organized, then paragraphs (b)(1)(ii)(*b*) and (*c*) of this section will be applied separately to each such branch or similar establishment (by treating such manufacturing branch or similar establishment as if it were the only such branch or similar establishment of the controlled foreign corporation and as if any other such branches or similar establishments were separate corporations) for purposes of determining whether the use of such branch or similar establishment has substantially the same tax effect as if such branch or similar establishment were a wholly owned subsidiary corporation of the controlled foreign corporation. The application of this paragraph (b)(1)(ii)(*c*)(*2*) is illustrated by the following example:

Example. Multiple branches that satisfy paragraph (a)(4)(i). (i) *Facts.* FS is a controlled foreign corporation organized in Country M. FS operates two branches, Branch A and Branch B located in Country A and Country B, respectively. Branch A and Branch B each manufacture separate items of personal property (Product X and Product Y, respectively) within the meaning of paragraph (a)(4)(ii) or (iii) of this section. Raw materials used in the manufacture of Product X and Product Y are purchased by FS from an unrelated person. FS engages in activities in Country M to sell Product X and Product Y to a related person for use, disposition or consumption outside of Country M. Employees of FS located in Country M perform only sales functions. The effective rate of tax imposed in Country M on the income from the sales of Product X and Product Y is 10%. Country A imposes an effective rate of tax on sales income of 20%. Country B imposes an effective rate of tax on sales income of 12%.

(ii) *Result.* Pursuant to this paragraph (b)(1)(ii)(*c*)(*2*), paragraph (b)(1)(ii)(*b*) of this section is applied separately to Branch A and Branch B with respect to the sales income of FS attributable to Product X (manufactured by Branch A) and Product Y (manufactured by Branch B). Because the effective rate of tax on FS's sales income from the sale of Product X in Country M (10%) is less than 90% of, and at least 5 percentage points less than, the effective rate of tax that would apply to such income in the country in which Branch A is located (20%), the use of Branch A to manufacture Product X has substantially the same tax effect as if Branch A were a wholly owned subsidiary corporation of FS. Because the effective rate of tax on FS's sales income from the sale of Product Y in Country M (10%) is not less than 90% of, and at least 5 percentage points less than, the effective rate of tax that would apply to such income in the country in which Branch B is located (12%), the use of Branch B to manufacture Product Y does not have substantially the same tax effect as if Branch B were a wholly owned subsidiary corporation of FS. Consequently, only Branch A is treated as a separate corporation apart from the remainder of FS for purposes of determining foreign base company sales income from the sales of Product X.

(3) Use of more than one manufacturing branch, or one or more manufacturing branches and the remainder of the controlled foreign corporation, to manufacture, produce, or construct the same item of personal property.—(i) In general.—This paragraph (b)(1)(ii)(*c*)(3) applies to determine the location of manufacture, production, or construction of personal property for purposes of applying paragraph (b)(1)(i)(*b*) or (b)(1)(ii)(*b*) of this section where more than one branch or similar establishment of a controlled foreign corporation, or one or more branches or similar establishments of a controlled foreign corporation and the remainder of the controlled foreign corporation, each engage in manufacturing, producing, or constructing activities with respect to the same item of personal property which is then sold by the controlled foreign corporation. This paragraph (b)(1)(ii)(*c*)(3) is applied separately with respect to the income derived by each purchasing or selling branch or similar establishment or purchasing or selling remainder of the controlled foreign corporation as provided under paragraphs (b)(1)(i) and (b)(1)(ii) of this section. The location of manufacture, production, or construction is determined under paragraph (b)(1)(ii)(*c*)*(3)(ii)* of this section if one or more branches or similar establishments or the remainder of the controlled foreign corporation independently satisfies paragraph (a)(4)(i) of this section with respect to an item of personal property. The location of manufacture, production, or construction is determined under paragraph (b)(1)(ii)(*c*)*(3)(iii)* of this section if none of the branches or similar establishments or the remainder of the controlled foreign corporation independently satisfies paragraph (a)(4)(i) of this section with respect to an item of personal property, but the controlled foreign corporation as a whole makes a substantial contribution to the manufacture, production or construction of that property within the meaning of paragraph (a)(4)(iv) of this section. For purposes of this paragraph (b)(1)(ii)(*c*)(3), the location of any activity with respect to the manufacture, production, or construction of an item of personal property is determined under paragraph (b)(1)(ii)(*c*)*(3)(iv)* of this section. For purposes of this paragraph (b)(1)(ii)(*c*)(3), if multiple branches or similar establishments are located in a single jurisdiction, then the activities of those branches will be aggregated for purposes of determining whether a branch or remainder of the controlled foreign corporation satisfies paragraph (a)(4)(i) of this section.

(ii) Manufacture, production, or construction in one or more locations.—If only one branch or similar establishment or only the remainder of a controlled foreign corporation independently satisfies paragraph (a)(4)(i) of this section with respect to an item of personal property, then that branch or similar establishment or the remainder of the controlled foreign corporation will be the location of manufacture, production, or construction of that property for purposes of applying paragraph (b)(1)(i)(*b*) or (b)(1)(ii)(*b*) of this section to the income from the sale of that property. See paragraph (b)(1)(ii)(*c*)*(3)(v) Example 1* of this section. If more than one branch or similar establishment or one or more branches or similar establishments and the remainder of the controlled foreign corporation, each independently satisfy paragraph (a)(4)(i) of this section with respect to an item of personal property, then the location of manufacture, production, or construction of that property for purposes of applying paragraph (b)(1)(i)(*b*) or (b)(1)(ii)(*b*) of this section will be the location of that branch or similar establishment or the jurisdiction under the laws of which the remainder of the controlled foreign corporation is organized that satisfies paragraph (a)(4)(i) of this section and that would, after applying paragraph (b)(1)(ii)(*b*) of this section to such branch or similar establishment or paragraph (b)(1)(i)(*b*) of this section to the remainder of the controlled foreign corporation, impose the lowest effective rate of tax on the income allocated to such branch or the remainder of the controlled foreign corporation under such section (that is, either paragraph (b)(1)(i)(*b*) or (b)(1)(ii)(*b*) of this section). See paragraph (b)(1)(ii)(*c*)*(3)(v) Example 2* of this section.

(iii) No location independently satisfies manufacturing test.—If no branch or similar establishment or the remainder of the controlled foreign corporation independently satisfies paragraph (a)(4)(i) of this section with respect to an item of personal property but the controlled foreign corporation as a whole makes a substantial contribution to the manufacture, production, or construction of that property within the meaning of paragraph (a)(4)(iv) of this section, then for purposes of applying paragraph (b)(1)(i)(*b*) or (b)(1)(ii)(*b*) of this section, the location of manufacture, production, or construction with respect to the income derived by a purchasing or selling branch or similar establishment or the purchasing or selling remainder of the controlled foreign corporation in connection with the purchase or sale of that property will be the "tested manufacturing location" unless the "tested sales location" provides a greater contribution to the manufacture, production, or construction of the property. The tested manufacturing location is the location of any branch or similar establishment or remainder of the controlled foreign corporation that contributes to the manufacture, production, or construction of the personal property, if any, that would, after applying paragraph (b)(1)(ii)(*b*) of this section to such branch or similar establishment or paragraph (b)(1)(i)(*b*) of this section to the remainder of the controlled foreign corporation, be treated as a separate corporation and would impose the lowest effective rate of tax on the income allocated to such branch or similar establishment or to the remainder of the controlled foreign corporation under such section (that is, either paragraph (b)(1)(i)(*b*) or (b)(1)(ii)(*b*) of this section). The tested sales location is the location of the purchasing or selling branch or similar establishment or the remainder of the controlled foreign corporation by or through which the purchasing or selling activities are carried on with respect to the personal property. For purposes of this paragraph (b)(1)(ii)(*c*)*(3)(iii)*, the contribution to the manufacture, production, or construction of the personal property by the tested sales location will be deemed to include the activities of any branch or similar establishment or remainder of the controlled foreign corporation that would not be treated as a corporation separate from the tested sales location after the application of paragraph (b)(1)(i)(*b*) or (b)(1)(ii)(*b*) of this section. For purposes of this paragraph (b)(1)(ii)(*c*)*(3)(iii)*, the contribution of the tested manufacturing location to the manufacture, production, or construction of the personal property will be deemed to include any activities of any branch or similar establishment or remainder of the controlled foreign corporation that would be treated as a corporation separate from the tested sales location after the application of paragraph (b)(1)(i)(*b*) or (b)(1)(ii)(*b*) of this section. Whether the tested sales location provides a greater contribution to the manufacture, production, or construction of the personal property is determined by weighing the relative contributions to the manufacture, production, or construction of that property by the tested sales location and the tested manufacturing location under the facts and circumstances test provided in paragraph (a)(4)(iv) of this section. See paragraph (b)(1)(ii)(*c*)*(3)(v) Examples 3, 4, 5,* and *6* of this section. If the tested sales location provides a greater contribution to the manufacture, production, or construction of the personal property than the tested manufacturing location or if there is no tested manufacturing location, then the tested sales location is the location of manufacture, production, or construction of that property and the rules of paragraphs (b)(1)(i)(*a*) and (b)(1)(ii)(*a*) of this section will not apply with respect to the income derived by the tested sales location in connection with the purchase or sale of that property and the use of that purchasing or selling branch or similar establishment or the purchasing or selling remainder will not result in a branch being treated as a separate corporation for purposes of paragraph (b)(2)(ii) of this section.

(iv) Location of activity.—For purposes of paragraph (b)(1)(ii)(*c*)(3) of this section, the location of any activity with respect to the manufacture, production, or construction of an item of personal property is the location where the employees of the controlled foreign corporation perform such activity. For example, the location of any activity concerning intellectual property is determined based on where employees of the controlled foreign corporation develop or direct the use or development of the intellectual property, not on the formal assignment of that intellectual property.

(v) Examples.—The following examples illustrate the application of this paragraph (b)(1)(ii)(*c*)(3):

Example 1. Multiple branches contribute to the manufacture of a single product, only one branch satisfies paragraph (a)(4)(i). (i) *Facts.* FS is a controlled foreign corporation organized in Country M. FS operates three branches, Branch A, Branch B, and Branch C, located respectively in Country A, Country B, and Country C. Branch A, Branch B, and Branch C each performs different manufacturing activities with respect to the manufacture of Product X. Branch A, through the activities of employees of FS located in Country A, designs Product X. Branch B, through the activities of employees of FS located in Country B, provides quality control and oversight and direction. Branch C, through the activities of employees of FS located in Country C, manufactures Product X (within the meaning of paragraph (a)(4)(ii) or (a)(4)(iii of this section) using the designs developed by Branch A and under the oversight of the quality control personnel of Branch B. The activities of Branch A and Branch B do not independently satisfy paragraph (a)(4)(i) of this section. Employees of FS located in Country M purchase the raw materials used in the manufacture of Product X from a related person and control the work-in-process and finished goods throughout the manufacturing process. Employees of FS located in Country M also manage the manufacturing costs and capacities related to Product X. Further, employees of FS located in Country M oversee the coordination between the branches. The activities of the remainder of FS in Country M do not independently satisfy paragraph (a)(4)(i) of this section. Employees of FS located in Country M sell Product X to unrelated persons for use outside of Country M. The sales income from the sale of Product X is taxed in Country M at an effective rate of tax of 10%. Country C imposes an effective rate of tax of 20% on sales income.

(ii) *Result.* Country C is the location of manufacture for purposes of applying paragraph (b)(1)(ii)(*b*) of this section because only the activities of Branch C independently satisfy paragraph (a)(4)(i) of this section. The use of Branch C has substantially the same tax effect as if Branch C were a wholly owned subsidiary corporation of FS because the effective rate of tax on the sales income (10%) is less than 90% of, and at least 5 percentage points less than, the effective rate of tax that would apply to such income in the country in which Branch C is located (20%). Therefore, sales of Product X by the remainder of FS are treated as sales on behalf of Branch C. In determining whether the remainder of FS will qualify for the manufacturing exception under paragraph (a)(4)(iv) of this section, the activities of FS will include the activities of Branch A or Branch B, respectively, if each of those branches would not be treated as a separate corporation under paragraph (b)(1)(ii)(*b*) of this section, if that paragraph were applied independently to each of Branch A and Branch B. See paragraph (b)(2)(ii)(*a*) of this section.

Example 2. Multiple branches satisfy paragraph (a)(4)(i) with respect to the same product sold by the controlled foreign corporation. (i) *Facts.* Assume the same facts as in *Example 1,* except for the following. In addition to the design of Product X, Branch A also performs in Country A other manufacturing activities, including those ascribed to FS in *Example 1,* that are sufficient to qualify as manufacturing under paragraph (a)(4)(iv) of this section with respect to Product X. Country A imposes an effective rate of tax of 12% on sales income.

(ii) *Result.* Branch A and Branch C through their activities each independently satisfy the requirements of paragraph (a)(4)(i) of this section. Therefore, paragraph (b)(1)(ii)(*b*) of this section is applied by comparing the effective rate of tax imposed on the income from the sales of Product X against the lowest effective rate of tax that would apply to the sales income in either Country A or Country C if paragraph (b)(1)(ii)(*b*) of this section were applied separately to Branch A and Branch C. Country A imposes the lower effective rate of tax, and therefore, Branch A is treated as the location of manufacture for purposes of applying paragraph (b)(1)(ii)(*b*) of this section. The effective rate of tax in Country B is not considered because Branch B does not satisfy paragraph (a)(4)(i) of this section. Neither Branch A nor Branch C is treated as a separate corporation because the effective rate of tax on the sales income of FS from the sale of Product X (10%) is not less than 90% of, and at least 5 percentage points less than, the effective rate of tax that would apply to such income in the country in which Branch A is located (12%). Sales of Product X by the remainder of the controlled foreign corporation are not treated as made on behalf of any branch.

Example 3. Determining the location of manufacture when manufacturing activities performed by multiple branches and no branch independently satisfies paragraph (a)(4)(i). (i) *Facts.* FS, a controlled foreign corporation organized in Country M, purchases raw materials from a related person. The raw materials are manufactured (under the principles of paragraph (a)(4)(ii) or (a)(4)(iii) of this section) into Product X by CM, an unrelated corporation, pursuant to a contract manufacturing arrangement. CM physically performs the substantial transformation, assembly, or conversion of the raw materials in Country C. FS has two branches, Branch A and Branch B, located in Country A and Country B respectively. Branch A, through the activities of employees of FS located in Country A, designs Product X. Branch B, through the activities of employees of FS located in Country B, controls manufacturing related logistics, provides oversight and direction during the manufacturing process, and controls the raw materials and work-in-process. FS manages the manufacturing costs and capacities related to the manufacture of Product X through employees located in Country M. Further, employees of FS located in Country M oversee the coordination between the branches. Employees of FS located in Country M also sell Product X to unrelated persons for use outside of Country M. Country M imposes an effective rate of tax on sales income of 10%. Country A imposes an effective rate of tax on sales income of 20%, and Country B imposes an effective rate of tax on sales income of 24%. Neither the remainder of FS, nor any branch of FS independently satisfies paragraph (a)(4)(i) of this section. However, under the facts and circumstances of the business, FS as a whole provides a substantial contribution to the manufacture of Product X within the meaning of paragraph (a)(4)(iv) of this section.

(ii) *Result.* Based on the facts, neither the remainder of FS (through the activities of its employees in Country M) nor any branch of FS independently satisfies paragraph (a)(4)(i) of this section with respect to Product X, but FS, as a whole, provides a substantial contribution through the activities of its employees to the manufacture of Product X. The remainder of FS, Branch A, and Branch B each provides a contribution through the activities of employees to the manufacture of Product X. Therefore, FS must determine the location of manufacture under paragraph (b)(1)(ii)(*c*)(*3*)(*iii*) of this section. The tested sales location is Country M because the selling activities with respect to Product X are carried on by the remainder of FS. The location of Branch A is the tested manufacturing location because the effective rate of tax imposed on FS's sales income by Country M (10%) is less than 90% of, and at least 5 percentage points less than, the effective rate of tax that would apply to such income in Country A (20%), and Country A has the lowest effective rate of tax among the manufacturing branches that would, after applying paragraph (b)(1)(ii)(*b*) of this section, be treated as a separate corporation. The activities of Branch B will be included in the contribution of Branch A for purposes of determining the location of manufacture of Product X because the effective rate of tax imposed on the sales income by Country M (10%) is less than 90% of, and at least 5 percentage points less than, the effective rate of tax that would apply to such income in Country B (24%). Under the facts and circumstances of the business, the activities of the remainder of FS would not provide a greater contribution to the manufacture of Product X than the activities of Branch A and Branch B, considered together. Therefore, the location of manufacture is Country A, the location of Branch A.

Example 4. Manufacturing activities performed by multiple branches, no branch independently satisfies paragraph (a)(4)(i), selling activities carried on by remainder of the controlled foreign corporation, remainder contribution includes branch manufacturing activities. (i) *Facts.* The facts are the same as *Example 3,* except that the effective rate of tax on sales income in Country B is 12%. In addition, under the facts of the particular business, the activities of employees of FS located in Country B and Country M, if considered together, would provide a greater contribution to the manufacture of Product X than the activities of employees of FS located in Country A.

(ii) *Result.* Based on the facts, neither the remainder of FS (through activities of its employees in Country M) nor any branch of FS independently satisfies paragraph (a)(4)(i) of this section with respect to Product X, but FS, as a whole, provides a substantial contribution through the activities of its employees to the manufacture of Product X. The remainder of FS, Branch A, and Branch B each provide a contribution through the activities of their employees to the manufacture of Product X. Therefore, FS must determine the location of manufacture under paragraph (b)(1)(ii)(*c*)(*3*)(*iii*) of this section. The tested sales location is Country M because the selling activities with respect to Product X are carried on by the remainder of FS. The location of Branch A is the tested manufacturing location because the effective rate of tax imposed on FS's sales income by Country M (10%) is less than 90% of, and at least 5 percentage points less than, the effective rate of tax that would apply to such income in Country A (20%), and Branch A is the only branch that would, after applying paragraph (b)(1)(ii)(*b*) of this section, be treated as a separate corporation. The activities of Branch B will be included in the contribution of the remainder of FS for purposes of determining the location of manufacture of Product X because the effective rate of tax imposed on the sales income by Country M (10%) is not less than 90% of, and at least 5 percentage points less than, the effective rate of tax that would apply to such income in Country B (12%). Under a facts and circumstances analysis, considered together, the activities of Branch B and the remainder of FS would provide a greater contribution to the manufacture of Product X than the activities of Branch A. Therefore, the rules of paragraph (b)(1)(ii)(a) of this section will not apply with respect to the income derived by the remainder of FS in connection with the sale of Product X, and neither Branch A nor Branch B will be treated as a separate corporation for purposes of paragraph (b)(2)(ii) of this section.

Example 5. Manufacturing activities performed by multiple branches, no branch independently satisfies paragraph (a)(4)(i), sales carried on by remainder of the controlled foreign corporation and a sales branch. (i) *Facts.* The facts are the same as *Example 3,* except that sales of Product X are also carried on through Branch D in Country D, and Country D imposes a 16% effective rate of tax on sales income. In addition, under the facts and circumstances of the business, the activities of employees of FS located in Country A and Country M, considered together, would provide a greater contribution to the manufacture of Product X than the activities of employees of FS located in Country B.

(ii) *Result.* Based on the facts, neither the remainder of FS nor any branch of FS independently satisfies paragraph (a)(4)(i) of this section with respect to Product X, but FS, as a whole, provides a substantial contribution through the activities of its employees to the manufacture of Product X. The remainder of FS, Branch A, and Branch B each provide a contribution through the activities of their employees to the manufacture of Product X. Therefore, FS must determine the location of manufacture under paragraph (b)(1)(ii)(*c*)*(3)(iii)* of this section. Further, pursuant to paragraph (b)(1)(ii)(*c*)*(1)* of this section, paragraph (b)(1)(ii)(*c*)*(3)(iii)* of this section must be applied separately to the sales income derived by the remainder of FS and Branch D respectively. The results with respect to the income derived by the remainder of FS in connection with the sale of Product X in this *Example 5* are the same as in *Example 3*. However, paragraph (b)(1)(ii)(*c*)*(3)(iii)* of this section must also be applied with respect to Branch D because the sale of Product X is also carried on through Branch D. Thus, for purposes of that sales income, the location of Branch D is the tested sales location. The location of Branch B is the tested manufacturing location because the effective rate of tax imposed on Branch D's sales income by Country D (16%) is less than 90% of, and at least 5 percentage points less than, the effective rate of tax that would apply to such income in Country B (24%), and Branch B is the only branch that would, after applying paragraph (b)(1)(ii)(*b*) of this section, be treated as a separate corporation. The manufacturing activities performed in Country M by the remainder of FS and the manufacturing activities performed in Country A by Branch A will be included in Branch D's contribution to the manufacture of Product X for purposes of determining the location of manufacture of Product X with respect to Branch D's sales income because the effective rate of tax imposed on the sales income by Country D (16%) is not less than 90% of, and at least 5 percentage points less than, the effective rate of tax that would apply to such income in Country M (10%) and Country A (20%). Under the facts and circumstances of the business, the activities of Branch D, Branch A, and the remainder of FS, considered together, would provide a greater contribution to the manufacture of Product X than the activities of Branch B. Therefore, the rules of paragraph (b)(1)(ii)(*a*) of this section will not apply with respect to the income derived by Branch D in connection with the sale of Product X and the use of Branch D to sell Product X will not result in a branch being treated as a separate corporation for purposes of paragraph (b)(2)(ii) of this section.

Example 6. Determining the location of manufacture when employees of remainder of controlled foreign corporation travel to location of unrelated contract manufacturer to perform manufacturing activities. (i) *Facts.* FS, a controlled foreign corporation organized in Country M, purchases raw materials from a related person. The raw materials are manufactured (under the principles of paragraph (a)(4)(ii) or (a)(4)(iii) of this section) into Product X by CM, an unrelated corporation, pursuant to a contract manufacturing arrangement. CM physically performs the substantial transformation, assembly, or conversion of the raw materials in Country C. Employees of FS located in Country M sell Product X to unrelated persons for use outside of Country M. Employees of FS located in Country M engage in product design, manage the manufacturing costs and capacities with respect to Product X, and direct the use of intellectual property for the purpose of manufacturing Product X. Quality control and oversight and direction of the manufacturing process are conducted in Country C by employees of FS who are employed in Country M but who regularly travel to Country C. Branch A, located in Country A, is the only branch of FS. Product design with respect to Product X conducted by employees of FS located in Country A is supplemental to the bulk of the design work, which is done by employees of FS located in Country M. At all times, employees of Branch A control the raw materials, work-in-process and finished goods. Employees of FS located in Country A also control manufacturing related logistics with respect to Product X. Country M imposes an effective rate of tax on sales income of 10%. Country A imposes an effective rate of tax on sales income of 20%. Neither the remainder of FS nor Branch A independently satisfies paragraph (a)(4)(i) of this section. However, under the facts and circumstance of the business, FS as a whole (including Branch A) provides a substantial contribution to the manufacture of Product X within the meaning of paragraph (a)(4)(iv) of this section.

(ii) *Result.* Based on the facts, neither the remainder of FS nor Branch A independently satisfies paragraph (a)(4)(i) of this section with respect to Product X, but FS, as a whole, provides a substantial contribution through the activities of its employees to the manufacture of Product X. The remainder of FS and Branch A each provide a contribution through the activities of employees to the manufacture of Product X. Therefore, FS must determine the location of manufacture under paragraph (b)(1)(ii)(*c*)*(3)(iii)* of this section. The tested sales location is Country M because the selling activities with respect to Product X are carried on by the remainder of FS. The tested manufacturing location is the location of Branch A because the effective rate of tax imposed on the remainder of FS's sales income by Country M (10%) is less than 90% of, and at least 5 percentage points less than, the effective rate of tax that would apply to such income in Country A (20%), and Branch A is the only branch that would, after applying paragraph (b)(1)(ii)(*b*) of this section, be treated as a separate corporation. Although the activities of traveling employees are considered in determining whether FS, as a whole, makes a substantial contribution to the manufacture of Product X under paragraph (a)(4)(iv) of this section, the activities of the employees of FS that are performed in Country C are not taken into consideration in determining whether Country M, the jurisdiction under the laws of which FS is organized, is the location of manufacture under paragraph (b)(1)(ii)(*c*)*(3)(iii)* of this section. Activities of employees performed outside the jurisdiction in which the controlled foreign corporation is organized and outside a location in which the controlled foreign corporation maintains a branch or similar establishment, are not considered in determining the location of manufacture. Under the facts and circumstances of the business, the activities of employees of FS performed in Country M do not provide a greater contribution to the manufacture of Product X than the activities of employees of FS performed in Country A. Therefore, the location of manufacture is Country A, the location of Branch A.

(4) Use of more than one branch to manufacture, produce, construct, grow, or extract separate items of personal property.—For purposes of paragraphs (b)(1)(ii)(*c*)(2) and (b)(1)(ii)(*c*)*(3)* of this section, an *item* of personal property refers to an individual unit of personal property rather than a type or class of personal property.

(2) *Special rules.*—(i) *Determination of treatment as a wholly owned subsidiary corporation.*—For purposes of determining under this paragraph whether the use of a branch or similar establishment which is treated as a separate corporation has substantially the same tax effect as if the branch or similar establishment were a wholly owned subsidiary corporation of a controlled foreign corporation—

(a) Treatment as separate corporations.—The branch or similar establishment will be treated as a wholly owned subsidiary corporation of the controlled foreign corporation, and such branch or similar establishment will be deemed to be incorporated in the country in which it is located.

(b) Activities treated as performed on behalf of the remainder of corporation.—*(1)* With respect to purchasing or selling activities performed by or through the branch or similar establishment, such purchasing or selling activities will, with respect to personal property manufactured, produced, constructed, grown, or extracted by the remainder of the controlled foreign corporation, be treated as performed on behalf of the remainder of the controlled foreign corporation.

(2) With respect to purchasing or selling activities performed by or through the branch or similar establishment, such purchasing or selling activities will, with respect to personal property (other than property described in paragraph (b)(2)(i)(*b*)*(1)* of this section) purchased or sold, or purchased and sold, by the remainder of the controlled foreign corporation (or any branch treated as the remainder of the controlled foreign corporation), be treated as performed on behalf of the remainder of the controlled foreign corporation.

(c) Activities treated as performed on behalf of branch.—With respect to manufacturing, producing, constructing, growing, or extracting activities performed by or through the branch or similar establishment, purchasing or selling activities performed by or through the remainder of the controlled foreign corporation with respect to the personal property manufactured, produced, constructed, grown, or extracted by or through the branch or similar establishment shall be treated as performed on behalf of the branch or similar establishment.

(d) [Reserved].

(e) Tax laws to be taken into account.—Tax determinations shall be made by taking into account only the income, war profits, excess profits, or similar tax laws (or the absence of such laws) of the countries involved.

(ii) *Determination of foreign base company sales income.*—Once it has been determined under subparagraph (1) of this paragraph that a branch or similar establishment and the remainder of the controlled foreign corporation are to be treated as separate corporations, the determination of whether such branch or similar establishment, or the remainder of the controlled foreign corporation, as the case may be, has foreign base company sales income shall be made by applying the following rules:

(a) *Treatment as separate corporations.*—The branch or similar establishment will be treated as a wholly owned subsidiary corporation of the controlled foreign corporation, and such branch or similar establishment will be deemed to be incorporated in the country in which it is located. For purposes of applying the rules of this paragraph (b)(2)(ii), a branch or similar establishment of a controlled foreign corporation treated as a separate corporation purchasing or selling on behalf of the remainder of the controlled foreign corporation under paragraph (b)(2)(ii)(*b*) of this section, or the remainder of the controlled foreign corporation treated as a separate corporation purchasing or selling on behalf of a branch or similar establishment of the controlled foreign corporation under paragraph (b)(2)(ii)(*c*) of this section, will include the activities of any other branch or similar establishment or remainder of the controlled foreign corporation that would not be treated as a separate corporation (apart from the branch or similar establishment of a controlled foreign corporation that is treated as performing purchasing or selling activities on behalf of the remainder of the controlled foreign corporation under paragraph (b)(2)(ii)(*b*) of this section or the remainder of the controlled foreign corporation that is treated as performing purchasing or selling activities on behalf of the branch or similar establishment under paragraph (b)(2)(ii)(*c*) of this section) if the effective rate of tax imposed on the income of the purchasing or selling branch or similar establishment, or purchasing or selling remainder of the controlled foreign corporation, were tested under the principles of paragraph (b)(1)(i)(*b*) or (b)(1)(ii)(*b*) of this section against the effective rate of tax that would apply to such income if it were considered derived by such other branch or similar establishment or the remainder of the controlled foreign corporation.

(*b*) *Activities treated as performed on behalf of the remainder of corporation.*—*(1)* With respect to purchasing or selling activities performed by or through the branch or similar establishment, such purchasing or selling activities will, with respect to personal property manufactured, produced, constructed, grown, or extracted by the remainder of the controlled foreign corporation, be treated as performed on behalf of the remainder of the controlled foreign corporation.

(2) With respect to purchasing or selling activities performed by or through the branch or similar establishment, such purchasing or selling activities will, with respect to personal property (other than property described in paragraph (b)(2)(ii)(*b*)*(1)* of this section) purchased or sold, or purchased and sold, by the remainder of the controlled foreign corporation (or any branch treated as the remainder of the controlled foreign corporation), be treated as performed on behalf of the remainder of the controlled foreign corporation.

(*c*) *Activities treated as performed on behalf of branch.*—With respect to manufacturing, producing, constructing, growing, or extracting activities performed by or through the branch or similar establishment, purchasing or selling activities performed by or through the remainder of the controlled foreign corporation with respect to the personal property manufactured, produced, constructed, grown, or extracted by or through the branch or similar establishment shall be treated as performed on behalf of the branch or similar establishment.

(*d*) [Reserved].

(*e*) *Comparison with ordinary treatment.*—Income derived by a branch or similar establishment, or by the remainder of the controlled foreign corporation, will not be foreign base company sales income under paragraph (b) of this section if the income would not be foreign base company sales income if it were derived by a separate controlled foreign corporation under like circumstances.

(*f*) *Priority of application.*—If income derived by the branch or similar establishment, or by the remainder of the controlled foreign corporation, from a transaction would be classified as foreign base company sales income of such controlled foreign corporation under section 954(d)(1) and paragraph (a) of this section, the income shall, notwithstanding this paragraph, be treated as foreign base company sales income under paragraph (a) of this section and the branch or similar establishment shall not be treated as a separate corporation with respect to such income.

(3) *Inclusion of amounts in gross income of United States shareholders.*—A branch or similar establishment of a controlled foreign corporation and the remainder of such corporation shall be treated as separate corporations under this paragraph solely for purposes of determining the foreign base company sales income of each such corporation and for purposes of including an amount in subpart F income of the controlled foreign corporation under section 952(a). See section 954(b)(3) and paragraph (d)(4) of § 1.954-1 for rules relating to the treatment of a branch or similar establishment of a controlled foreign corporation and the remainder of such corporation as separate corporations for purposes of independently determining if the foreign base company income of each such corporation is less than 10 percent, or more than 70 percent, of its gross income. For all other purposes, however, a branch or similar establishment of a controlled foreign corporation and the remainder of such corporation shall not be treated as separate corporations. For example, if the controlled foreign corporation has a deficit in earnings and profits to which section 952(c) applies, the limitation of such section on the amount includible in the subpart F income of such corporation will apply. Moreover, income, war profits, or excess profits taxes paid by a branch or similar establishment to a foreign country will be treated as having been paid by the controlled foreign corporation for purposes of section 960 (relating to special rules for foreign tax credit) and the regulations thereunder. Also, income of a branch or similar establishment, treated as a separate corporation under this paragraph, will not be treated as dividend income of the controlled foreign corporation of which it is a branch or similar establishment.

(4) *Illustrations.*—The application of this paragraph (b) may be illustrated by the following examples:

Example (1). Controlled foreign corporation A, incorporated under the laws of foreign country X, is engaged in the manufacturing business in such country. Corporation A negotiates sales of its products for use outside of country X through a sales office, branch B, maintained in foreign country Y. These activities constitute the only activities of A Corporation. Country X levies an income tax at an effective rate of 50 percent on the income of A Corporation derived by the manufacturing plant in country X but does not tax the sales of income of A Corporation derived by branch B in country Y. Country Y levies an income tax at an effective rate of 10 percent on the sales income derived by branch B but does not tax the income of A Corporation derived by the manufacturing plant in country X. If the sales income derived by branch B were, under the laws of country X, derived from sources within country X by A Corporation, such income would be taxed by such country at an effective rate of 50 percent. In determining foreign base company sales income of A Corporation, branch B is treated as a separate wholly owned subsidiary corporation of A Corporation, the 10 percent rate of tax on branch B's income being less than 90 percent of, and at least 5 percentage points less than, the 50 percent rate. Income derived by branch B, treated as a separate corporation, from the sale by or through it for use, consumption, or disposition outside country Y of the personal property produced in country X is treated as income from the sale of personal property on behalf of A Corporation, a related person, and constitutes foreign base company sales income. The remainder of A Corporation, treated as a separate corporation, derives no foreign base company sales income since it produces the product which is sold.

Example (2). Controlled foreign corporation C is incorporated under the laws of foreign country X. Corporation C maintains branch B in foreign country Y. Branch B manufactures articles in country Y which are sold through the sales offices of C Corporation located in country X. These activities constitute the only activities of C Corporation. Country Y levies an income tax at an effective rate of 30 percent on the manufacturing profit of C Corporation derived by branch B but does not tax the sales income of C Corporation derived by the sales offices in country X. Country X does not impose an income, war profits, excess profits, or similar tax, and no tax is paid to any foreign country with respect to income of C Corporation which is not derived by branch B. If C Corporation were incorporated under the laws of country Y, the sales income of the sales offices in country X would be taxed by country Y at an effective rate of 30 percent. In determining foreign base company sales income of C Corporation, branch B is treated as a separate wholly owned subsidiary corporation of C Corporation, the zero rate of tax on the income derived by the remainder of C Corporation being less than 90 percent of, and at least 5 percentage points less than, the 30 percent rate. Branch B, treated as a separate corporation, derives no foreign base company sales income since it produces the product which is sold. Income derived by the remainder of C Corporation, treated as a separate corporation, from the sale by or through it for use, consumption, or disposition outside country X of the personal property produced in country Y is treated as income from the sale of personal property on behalf of branch B, a related person, and constitutes foreign base company sales income.

Example 3. (i) *Facts.* Corporation E, a controlled foreign corporation incorporated under the laws of foreign Country X, is a wholly owned subsidiary of Corporation D, also a controlled foreign corporation incorporated under the laws of Country X. Corporation E maintains Branch B in foreign Country Y. Both corporations use the calendar year as the taxable year. In 1964, Corporation E's sole activity, carried on through Branch B, consists of the purchase of articles manufactured in Country X by Corporation D, a related person, and the sale of the articles through Branch B to unrelated persons. One hundred percent of the articles sold through Branch B are sold for use outside Country X and 90% are also sold for use outside of Country Y. The income of Corporation E derived by Branch B from such transactions is taxed to Corporation E by Country X only at the time Corporation E distributes such income to Corporation D and is taxed on the basis of what the tax (a 40% effective rate) would have been if the income had been derived in 1964 by Corporation E from sources within Country X from doing business through a permanent establishment therein. Country Y levies an income tax at an effective rate of 50% on income derived from sources within such country, but the income of Branch B for 1964 is effectively taxed by Country Y at a 5% rate since under the laws of such country, only 10% of Branch B's income is derived from sources within such country. Corporation E makes no distributions to Corporation D in 1964.

(ii) *Result.* In determining foreign base company sales income of Corporation E for 1964, Branch B is treated as a separate wholly owned subsidiary corporation of Corporation E, the 5% rate of tax being less than 90% of, and at least 5 percentage points less than the 40% rate. Income derived by Branch B, treated as a separate corporation, from the purchase from a related person (Corporation D), of personal property manufactured outside of Country Y and sold for use, disposition, or consumption outside of Country Y constitutes foreign base company sales income. If, instead, Corporation D were unrelated to Corporation E, none of the income would be foreign base company sales income because Corporation E would be purchasing from and selling to unrelated persons and if Branch B were treated as a separate corporation it would likewise be purchasing from and selling to unrelated persons. Alternatively, if Corporation D were related to Corporation E, but Branch B manufactured the articles prior to sale under the principles of paragraph (a)(4)(iv) of this section, the income would not be foreign base company sales income because Branch B, treated as a separate corporation, would qualify for the manufacturing exception under paragraph (a)(4) of this section.

Example (4). Controlled foreign corporation F, incorporated under the laws of foreign country X, is a wholly owned subsidiary of domestic corporation M. Corporation F, through its branch B in foreign country Y, purchases from controlled foreign corporation G, a wholly owned subsidiary of M Corporation incorporated under the laws of foreign country Z, personal property which G Corporation manufactures in country Z. Corporation F sells such property for use in foreign country W. Since the income of F Corporation from such purchases and sales is classified as foreign base company sales income under section 954(d)(1) and paragraph (a) of this section, branch B will not be treated as a separate corporation with respect to such income even if the tax differential between countries X and Y would otherwise justify such treatment.

Example (5). Controlled foreign corporation A, incorporated under the laws of foreign country X, is engaged in manufacturing articles through its home office, located in country X, and selling such articles through branch B, located in foreign country Y, and through branch C, located in foreign country Z, for use outside country X. These activities constitute the only activities of A Corporation for its taxable year 1963. Each such country levies an income tax on only the income derived from sources within such country, and all income derived in 1963 by the home office, branch B, and branch C, respectively, is derived from sources within countries X, Y, and Z, respectively. The income and income taxes of A Corporation for 1963 are as follows:

	X Country	*Y Country*	*Z Country*
Income of:			
Home office	$200,000	. . .	. . .
Branch B	. . .	$100,000	. . .
Branch C	. . .	. . .	$100,000
Income tax	100,000	20,000	20,000
Effective rate of tax	50%	20%	20%

By applying subparagraph (1)(i) of this paragraph and by treating branch B as though it were the only branch of A Corporation, branch B is treated as a separate wholly owned subsidiary corporation of A Corporation in determining foreign base company sales income of A Corporation for 1963, the 20 percent rate of tax on the income of such branch being less than 90 percent of, and at least 5 percentage points less than, the 50 percent rate of tax which would apply to the income of branch B under the laws of country X if, under the laws of such country, all the income of A Corporation for 1963 derived through the home office and branch B were derived from sources within country X. Moreover, by applying subparagraph (1)(i) of this paragraph and by treating branch C as though it were the only branch of A Corporation, branch C is treated as a separate wholly owned subsidiary corporation of A Corporation, the 20 percent rate of tax on the income of such branch being less than 90 percent of, and at least 5 percentage points less than, the 50 percent rate of tax which would apply to the income of branch C under the laws of country X if, under the laws of such country, all the income of A Corporation for 1963 derived through the home office and branch C were derived from sources within country X. The income derived by branch B and branch C, respectively, each treated as a separate corporation, from the sale by or through each of them for use, consumption, or disposition outside country Y and country Z, respectively, is treated as income from the sale of personal property on behalf of A Corporation, a related person, and constitutes foreign base company sales income for 1963. The home office of A Corporation, treated as a separate corporation, derives no foreign base company sales income for 1963 since it produces the articles which are sold.

Example (6). [Reserved].

Example (7). [Reserved].

Example 8. Uniformly applicable incentive tax rate in one country. (i) *Facts.* FS is a controlled foreign corporation organized in Country M. FS operates one branch, Branch A, located in Country A. Branch A manufactures Product X within the meaning of paragraph (a)(4)(ii) or (a)(4)(iii) of this section. Raw materials used in the manufacture of Product X are purchased by FS from an unrelated person. FS engages in activities in Country M to sell Product X to a related person for use outside of Country M. Employees of FS located in Country M carry on only sales functions. The effective rate imposed in Country M on the income from the sale of Product X is 10%. Country A generally imposes an effective rate of tax on income of 20%, but imposes a uniformly applicable incentive rate of tax of 10% on manufacturing income and related sales income.

(ii) *Result.* The use of Branch A to manufacture Product X does not have substantially the same tax effect as if Branch A were a wholly owned subsidiary corporation of FS because the effective rate of tax on FS's sales income from the sale of Product X in Country M (10%) is not less than 90% of, and at least 5 percentage points less than, the effective rate of tax that would apply to such income in the country in which Branch A is located (10%). Consequently, pursuant to paragraph (b)(1)(ii)(b) of this section, Branch A is not treated as a separate corporation apart from the remainder of FS for purposes of determining foreign base company sales income.

Example 9. Manufacturing activities performed by multiple branches, no branch independently satisfies paragraph (a)(4)(i), selling activities carried on by remainder of the controlled foreign corporation, some branch manufacturing activities included in remainder contribution. (i) *Facts.* FS, a controlled foreign corporation organized in Country M, has three branches, Branch A, Branch B, and Branch C, located in Country A, Country B, and Country C respectively. FS purchases raw materials from a related person. The raw materials are manufactured (under the principles of paragraph (a)(4)(ii) or (a)(4)(iii) of this section) into Product X by CM, an unrelated corporation, pursuant to a contract manufacturing arrangement. CM physically performs the substantial transformation, assembly, or conversion required to manufacture Product X outside of FS's country of organization. FS manages the manufacturing costs and capacities with respect to the manufacture of Product X through employees located in Country M. Further, employees of FS located in Country M oversee the coordination between the branches. Branch A, through the activities of employees of FS located in Country A, designs Product X, controls manufacturing related logistics, and controls the raw materials and work-in-process during the manufacturing process. Branch B, through the activities of employees of FS located in Country B, provides quality control. Branch C, through the activities of employees of FS located in Country C, provides oversight and direction during the manufacturing process. Employees of FS located in Country M sell Product X to unrelated persons for use outside of Country M. Country M imposes an effective rate of tax on sales income of 10%. Country A imposes an effective rate of tax on sales income of 12%, Country B imposes an effective rate of tax on sales income of 24%, and Country C imposes an effective rate of tax on sales income of 25%. None of the remainder of FS, Branch A, Branch B, or Branch C independently satisfies paragraph (a)(4)(i) of this section. However, under the facts and circumstances of the business, FS, as a whole, provides a substantial contribution to the manufacture of Product X within the meaning of paragraph (a)(4)(iv) of this section. Under the facts and circumstances of the business, the activities of the remainder of FS and Branch A, if considered together, would not provide a greater contribution to the manufacture of Product X than the activities of Branch B and Branch C, if considered together. Under the facts and circumstances of the business, however, the activities of the employees of the remainder of FS and Branch A, if considered together, would constitute a substantial contribution to the manufacture of Product X.

(ii) *Result.* Based on the facts, neither the remainder of FS (through activities of its employees in Country M) nor any branch of FS independently satisfies paragraph (a)(4)(i) of this section with respect to Product X, but FS, as a whole, provides a substantial contribution through the activities of its employees to the manufacture of Product X. The remainder of FS, Branch A, Branch B, and Branch C each provide a contribution through the activities of employees to the manufacture of Product X. Therefore, FS must determine the location of manufacture under paragraph (b)(1)(ii)(*c*)(*3*)(*iii*) of this section. The tested sales location is Country M because the selling activities with respect to Product X are carried on by the remainder of FS. The location of Branch B is the tested manufacturing location because the effective rate of tax imposed on FS's sales income by Country M (10%) is less than 90% of, and at least 5 percentage points less than, the effective rate of tax that would apply to such income in Country B (24%), and Country B has the lowest effective rate of tax among the manufacturing branches that would, after applying paragraph (b)(1)(ii)(*b*) of this section, be treated as a separate corporation. The manufacturing activities performed in Country A by Branch A will be included in the contribution of the remainder of FS for purposes of determining the location of manufacture of Product X because the effective rate of tax imposed on the sales income by Country M (10%) is not less than 90% of, and at least 5 percentage points less than, the effective rate of tax that would apply to such income in Country A (12%). The manufacturing activities performed in Country C by Branch C will be included in the contribution of Branch B for purposes of determining the location of manufacture of Product X because the effective rate of tax imposed on the sales income by Country M (10%) is less than 90% of, and at least 5 percentage points less than, the effective rate of tax that would apply to such income in Country C (25%). Under the facts and circumstances of the business, the manufacturing activities of the remainder of FS and Branch A, considered together, would not provide a greater contribution to the manufacture of Product X than the activities of Branch B and Branch C, considered together. Therefore, the location of manufacture is Country B, the location of Branch B. In determining that Country B is the location of manufacture, it was determined that after applying paragraph (b)(1)(ii)(*b*) of this section Branch B would be treated as a separate corporation under paragraph (b)(1)(ii)(*a*) of this section for purposes of determining foreign base company sales income. To determine whether income from the sale of Product X is foreign base company sales income, the remainder of FS takes into account the activities of Branch A because, under paragraph (b)(2)(ii)(*a*) of this section, Branch A would not be treated as a separate corporation apart from FS. The remainder of FS is considered to have manufactured Product X under paragraph (a)(4)(i) of this section because the manufacturing activities of the remainder of FS and Branch A, considered together, would make a substantial contribution to the manufacture of Product X within the meaning of paragraph (a)(4)(iv) of this section. Therefore, income derived from the sale of Product X by the remainder of FS does not constitute foreign base company sales income.

(c) *Effective/applicability date.*—Paragraphs (a)(1)(i), (a)(1)(iii) *Example 1,* (a)(1)(iii) *Example 2,* (a)(2), (a)(4)(i), (a)(4)(ii), (a)(4)(iii), (a)(4)(iv), (a)(6)(i), (b)(1)(i)(*c*), (b)(1)(ii)(*a*), (b)(1)(ii)(*c*), (b)(2)(i)(*b*), (b)(2)(ii)(*a*), (b)(2)(ii)(*b*), (b)(2)(ii)(*e*), and (b)(4) *Example 3,* (b)(4) *Example 8,* and (b)(4) *Example 9* of this section shall apply to taxable years of controlled foreign corporations beginning after June 30, 2009, and for taxable years of United States shareholders in which or with which such taxable years of the controlled foreign corporations end.

(d) *Application of regulations to earlier taxable years.*—A taxpayer may choose to apply these regulations retroactively with respect to its open taxable years that began prior to July 1, 2009. The taxpayer may so choose if and only if the taxpayer and all members of the taxpayer's affiliated group (within the meaning of section 1504(a)) apply these regulations, in their entirety, to the earliest taxable year of each controlled foreign corporation that ends with or within an open taxable year of the taxpayer and to all subsequent taxable years. [Reg. § 1.954-3.]

☐ [*T.D. 6734, 5-14-64. Amended by T.D. 7497, 7-6-77, T.D. 7555, 7-25-78, T.D. 7893, 5-11-83; T.D. 7894, 5-11-83; T.D. 9008, 7-22-2002; T.D. 9438, 12-24-2008* (*corrected* 3-19-2009) *and T.D.* 9563, 12-15-2011.]

§ 1.954-4. Foreign base company services income.—(a) *Items included.*—Except as provided in paragraph (d) of this section, foreign base company services income means income of a controlled foreign corporation, whether in the form of compensation, commissions, fees, or otherwise, derived in connection with the performance of technical, managerial, engineering, architectural, scientific, skilled, industrial, commercial, or like services which—

(1) Are performed for, or on behalf of, a related person, as defined in paragraph (e)(1) of § 1.954-1, and

(2) Are performed outside the country under the laws of which the controlled foreign corporation is created or organized.

(b) *Services performed for, or on behalf of, a related person.*—(1) *Specific cases.*—For purposes of paragraph (a)(1) of this section, "services which are performed for, or on behalf of, a related person" include (but are not limited to) services performed by a controlled foreign corporation in a case where—

(i) The controlled foreign corporation is paid or reimbursed by, is released from an obligation to, or otherwise receives substantial financial benefit from, a related person for performing such services;

(ii) The controlled foreign corporation performs services (whether or not with respect to property sold by a related person) which a related person is, or has been, obligated to perform;

(iii) The controlled foreign corporation performs services with respect to property sold by a related person and the performance of such services constitutes a condition or a material term of such sale; or

(iv) Substantial assistance contributing to the performance of such services has been furnished by a related person or persons.

(2) *Special rules.*—(i) *Guaranty of performance.*—Subparagraph (1)(ii) of this paragraph shall not apply with respect to services performed by a controlled foreign corporation pursuant to a contract the performance of which is guaranteed by a related person, if (*a*) the related person's sole obligation with respect to the contract is to guarantee performance of such services, (*b*) the controlled foreign corporation is fully obligated to perform the services under the contract, and (*c*) the related person (or any other person related to the controlled foreign corporation) does not in fact (*1*) pay for performance of, or perform, any of such services the performance of which is so guaranteed or (*2*) pay for performance of, or perform, any significant services related to such services. If the related person (or any other person related to the controlled foreign corporation) does in fact pay for performance of, or perform, any of such services or any significant services related to such services, subparagraph (1)(ii) of this paragraph shall apply with respect to the services performed by the controlled foreign corporation pursuant to the contract the performance of which is guaranteed by the related person, even though such payment or performance is not considered to be substantial assistance for purposes of subparagraph (1)(iv) of this paragraph. For purposes of this subdivision, a related person shall be considered to guarantee performance of the services by the controlled foreign corporation whether it guarantees performance of such services by a separate contract of guaranty or enters into a service contract solely for purposes of guaranteeing performance of such services and immediately thereafter assigns the entire contract to the controlled foreign corporation for execution.

(ii) *Application of substantial assistance test.*—For purposes of subparagraph (1)(iv) of this paragraph—

(*a*) Assistance furnished by a related person or persons to the controlled foreign corporation shall include, but shall not be limited to, direction, supervision, services, know-how, financial assistance (other than contributions to capital), and equipment, material, or supplies.

(*b*) Assistance furnished by a related person or persons to a controlled foreign corporation in the form of direction, supervision, services, or know-how shall not be considered substantial unless either (*1*) the assistance so furnished provides the controlled foreign corporation with skills which are a principal element in producing the income from the performance of such services by such corporation or (*2*) the cost to the controlled foreign corporation of the assistance so furnished equals 50 percent or more of the total cost to the controlled foreign corporation of performing the services performed by such corporation. The term "cost," as used in this subdivision (*b*), shall be determined after taking into account adjustments, if any, made under section 482.

(*c*) Financial assistance (other than contributions to capital), equipment, material, or supplies furnished by a related person to a controlled foreign corporation shall be considered assistance only in that amount by which the consideration actually paid by the controlled foreign corporation for the purchase or use of such item is less than the arm's length charge for such purchase or use. The total of such amounts so considered to be assistance in the case of financial assistance, equipment, material, and supplies furnished by all related persons shall be compared with the profits derived by the controlled foreign corporation from the performance of the services to determine whether the financial assistance, equipment, material, and supplies furnished by a related person or persons are by themselves substantial assistance contributing to the performance of such services. For purposes of this subdivision (*c*), determinations shall be made after taking into account adjustments, if any, made under section 482 and the term "consideration actually paid" shall include any amount which is deemed paid by the controlled foreign corporation pursuant to such an adjustment.

(*d*) Even though assistance furnished by a related person or persons to a controlled foreign corporation in the form of direction, supervision, services, or know-how is not considered to be substantial under (*b*) of this subdivision and assistance furnished by a related person or persons in the form of financial assistance (other than contributions to capital), equipment, material, or supplies is not considered to be substantial under (*c*) of this subdivision, such assistance may nevertheless constitute substantial assistance when taken together or in combination with other assistance furnished by a related person or persons which in itself is not considered to be substantial.

(*e*) Assistance furnished by a related person or persons to a controlled foreign corporation in the form of direction, supervision, services, or know-how shall not be taken into account under (*b*) or (*d*) of this subdivision unless the assistance so furnished assists the controlled foreign corporation directly in the performance of the services performed by such corporation.

(iii) *Special rule applicable to distributive share of partnership income.*—A controlled foreign corporation's distributive share of a partnership's services income will be deemed to be derived from services performed for or on behalf of a related person, within the meaning of section 954(e)(1)(A), if the partnership is a related person with respect to the controlled foreign corporation, under section 954(d)(3), and, in connection with the services performed by the partnership, the controlled foreign corporation, or a person that is a related person with respect to the controlled foreign corporation, provided assistance that would have constituted substantial assistance contributing to the performance of such services, under paragraph (b)(2)(ii) of this section, if furnished to the controlled foreign corporation by a related person. This paragraph (b)(2)(iii) applies to taxable years of a controlled foreign corporation beginning on or after July 23, 2002.

(3) *Illustrations.*—The application of this paragraph may be illustrated by the following examples:

Example (1). Controlled foreign corporation A is paid by related corporation M for the installation and maintenance of industrial machines which M Corporation manufactures and sells to B Corporation. Such installation and maintenance services by A Corporation are performed for, or on behalf of, M Corporation for purposes of section 954(e).

Example (2). Controlled foreign corporation B enters into a contract with an unrelated person to drill an oil well in a foreign country. Domestic corporation M owns all the outstanding stock of B Corporation. Corporation B employs a relatively small clerical and administrative staff and owns the necessary well-drilling equipment. Most of the technical and supervisory personnel who oversee the drilling of the oil well by B Corporation are regular employees of M Corporation who are temporarily employed by B Corporation. In addition, B Corporation hires on the open market unskilled and semiskilled laborers to work on the drilling project. The services performed by B Corporation under the well-drilling contract are performed for, or on behalf of, a related person for purposes of section 954(e) because the services of the technical and supervisory personnel which are provided by M Corporation are of substantial assistance in the performance of such contract in that they assist B Corporation directly in the execution of the contract and provide B Corporation with skills which are a principal element in producing the income from the performance of such contract.

Example (3). Controlled foreign corporation F enters into a contract with an unrelated person to construct a dam in a foreign country. Domestic corporation M owns all the outstanding stock of F Corporation. Corporation F leases or buys from M Corporation, on an arm's length basis, the equipment and material necessary for the construction of the dam. The technical and supervisory personnel who design and oversee the construction of the dam are regular full-time employees of F Corporation who are not on loan from any related person. The principal clerical work, and the financial accounting, required in connection with the construction of the dam by F Corporation are performed, on a remunerated basis, by full-time employees of M Corporation. All other assistance F Corporation requires in completing the construction of the dam is paid for by that corporation and furnished by unrelated persons. The services performed by F Corporation under the contract for the construction of the dam are not performed for, or on behalf of, a related person for purposes of section 954(e) because the clerical and accounting services furnished by M Corporation do not assist F Corporation directly in the performance of the contract.

Example (4). Controlled foreign corporation D, a wholly owned subsidiary of domestic corporation M, procures and enters a contract with an unrelated person to construct a superhighway in a foreign country, but such person enters the contract only on the condition that M Corporation agrees to perform, or to pay for the performance by some person other than D Corporation of, the services called for by the contract if D Corporation should fail to complete their performance. Corporation D is capable of performing such contract. No related person as to D Corporation pays for, or performs, any services called for by the contract, or pays for, or performs, any significant services related to such services. The construction of the superhighway by D Corporation is not considered for purposes of section 954(e) to be the performance of services for, or on behalf of, M Corporation.

Example (5). Domestic corporation M is obligated under a contract with an unrelated person to construct a superhighway in a foreign country. At a later date M Corporation assigns the entire contract to its wholly owned subsidiary, controlled foreign corporation C, and the unrelated person releases M Corporation from any obligation under the contract. The construction of such highway by C Corporation is considered for purposes of section 954(e) to be the performance of services for, or on behalf of, M Corporation.

Example (6). Domestic corporation M enters a contract with an unrelated person to construct a superhighway in a foreign country. Corporation M immediately assigns the entire contract to its wholly owned subsidiary, controlled foreign corporation C. The unrelated person does not release M Corporation of its obligation under the contract, the sole purpose of these arrangements being to have M Corporation guarantee performance of the contract by C Corporation. Corporation C is capable of performing the construction contract. Neither M Corporation nor any other person related to C Corporation pays for, or performs, any services called for by the construction contract or at any time pays for, or performs, any significant services related to the services performed under such contract. The construction of the superhighway by C Corporation is not considered for purposes of section 954(e) to be the performance of services for, or on behalf of, M Corporation.

Example (7). The facts are the same as in example (6) except that M Corporation, preparatory to entering the construction contract, prepares plans and specifications which enable the submission of bids for the contract. Since M Corporation has performed significant services related to the services the performance of which it has guaranteed, the construction of such highway by C Corporation is considered for purposes of section 954(e) to be the performance of services for, or on behalf of, M Corporation.

Example (8). Domestic corporation M manufactures an industrial machine which requires specialized installation. Corporation M sells the machines for a basic price if the contract of sale contains no provision for installation. If, however, the customer agrees to employ controlled foreign corporation E, a wholly owned subsidiary of M Corporation, to install the machine and to pay E Corporation a specified installation charge, M Corporation sells the machine at a price which is less than the basic price. The installation services performed by E Corporation for customers of M Corporation purchasing the machine at the reduced price are considered for purposes of section 954(e) to be performed for, or on behalf of, M Corporation.

Example (9). Domestic corporation M manufactures and sells industrial machines with a warranty as to their performance conditional upon their installation and maintenance by a factory-authorized service agency. Controlled foreign corporation F, a wholly owned subsidiary of M Corporation, is the only authorized service agency. Any installation or maintenance services performed by F Corporation on such machines are considered for purposes of section 954(e) to be performed for, or on behalf of, M Corporation.

Example (10). Domestic corporation M manufactures electric office machines which it sells at a basic price without any provision for, or understanding as to, adjustment or maintenance of the machines. The machines require constant adjustment and maintenance services which M Corporation, certain wholly owned subsidiaries of

M Corporation, and certain unrelated persons throughout the world are qualified to perform. From among the numerous persons qualified and available to perform adjustment and maintenance services with respect to such office machines, foreign corporation B, a customer of M Corporation, employs controlled foreign corporation G, a wholly owned subsidiary of M Corporation, to adjust and maintain the office machines which B Corporation purchases from M Corporation. The adjustment and maintenance services performed by G Corporation for B Corporation are not considered for purposes of section 954(e) to be performed for, or on behalf of, M Corporation.

(c) *Place where services are performed.*—The place where services will be considered to have been performed for purposes of paragraph (a)(2) of this section will depend on the facts and circumstances of each case. As a general rule, services will be considered performed where the persons performing services for the controlled foreign corporation which derives income in connection with the performance of technical, managerial, architectural, engineering, scientific, skilled, industrial, commercial, or like services are physically located when they perform their duties in the execution of the service activity resulting in such income. Therefore, in many cases, total gross income of a controlled foreign corporation derived in connection with each service contract or arrangement performed for or on behalf of a related person must be apportioned, between income which is not foreign base company services income and that which is foreign base company services income, on a basis of employee-time spent within the foreign country under the laws of which the controlled foreign corporation is created or organized and employee-time spent without the foreign country under the laws of which such corporation is created or organized. In allocating time spent within and without the foreign country under the laws of which the controlled foreign corporation is created or organized, relative weight must also be given to the value of the various functions performed by persons in fulfillment of the service contract or arrangement. For example, clerical work will ordinarily be assigned little value, while services performed by technical, highly skilled, and managerial personnel will be assigned greater values in relation to the type of function performed by each individual.

(d) *Items excluded.*—Foreign base company services income does not include—

(1) Income derived in connection with the performance of services by a controlled foreign corporation if—

(i) The services directly relate to the sale or exchange of personal property by the controlled foreign corporation,

(ii) The property sold or exchanged was manufactured, produced, grown, or extracted by such controlled foreign corporation, and

(iii) The services were performed before the sale or exchange of such property by the controlled foreign corporation;

(2) Income derived in connection with the performance of services by a controlled foreign corporation if the services directly relate to an offer or effort to sell or exchange personal property which was, or would have been, manufactured, produced, grown, or extracted by such controlled foreign corporation whether or not a sale or exchange of such property was in fact consummated; or

(3) For taxable years beginning after December 31, 1975, foreign base company shipping income (as determined under § 1.954-6). [Reg. § 1.954-4.]

☐ [*T.D. 6734, 5-14-64. Amended by T.D. 6981, 11-12-68; T.D. 7894, 5-11-83 and T.D. 9008, 7-22-2002.*]

Proposed Regulation

§ 1.954-9. Hybrid branches.—(a) *Subpart F income arising from certain payments involving hybrid branches.*—(1) *Payment causing foreign tax reduction gives rise to additional subpart F income.*—The non-subpart F income of a controlled foreign corporation will be recharacterized as subpart F income, to the extent provided in paragraph (a)(5) of this section, if—

(i) A hybrid branch payment, as defined in paragraph (a)(6) of this section, is made between the entities described in paragraph (a)(2) of this section;

(ii) The hybrid branch payment reduces foreign tax, as determined under paragraph (a)(3) of this section; and

(iii) The hybrid branch payment is treated as falling within a category of foreign personal holding company income under the rules of paragraph (a)(4) of this section.

(2) *Hybrid branch payment between certain entities.*—(i) *In general.*—Paragraph (a)(1) of this section shall apply to hybrid branch payments between—

(A) A controlled foreign corporation and its hybrid branch;

(B) Hybrid branches of a controlled foreign corporation;

(C) A partnership in which a controlled foreign corporation is a partner (either directly or through one or more branches or other partnerships) and a hybrid branch of the partnership; or

(D) Hybrid branches of a partnership in which a controlled foreign corporation is a partner (either directly or through one or more branches or other partnerships).

(ii) *Hybrid branch payment involving partnership.*—(A) *Fiscally transparent partnership.*—To the extent of the controlled foreign corporation's proportionate share of a hybrid branch payment, the rules of paragraphs (a)(3), (4) and (5) of this section shall be applied by treating the hybrid branch payment between the partnership and the hybrid branch as if it were made directly between the controlled foreign corporation and the hybrid branch, or as if the hybrid branches of the partnership were hybrid branches of the controlled foreign corporation, if the hybrid branch payment is made between—

(1) A fiscally transparent partnership in which a controlled foreign corporation is a partner (either directly or through one or more branches or other fiscally transparent partnerships) and the partnership's hybrid branch; or

(2) Hybrid branches of a fiscally transparent partnership in which a controlled foreign corporation is a partner (either directly or through one or more branches or other fiscally transparent partnerships).

(B) *Non-fiscally transparent partnership.*—To the extent of the controlled foreign corporation's proportionate share of a hybrid branch payment, the rules of paragraphs (a)(3) and (4) and (a)(5)(iv) of this section shall be applied to the non-fiscally transparent partnership as if it were the controlled foreign corporation, if the hybrid branch payment is made between—

(1) A non-fiscally transparent partnership in which a controlled foreign corporation is a partner (either directly or through one or more branches or other partnerships) and the partnership's hybrid branch; or

(2) Hybrid branches of a non-fiscally transparent partnership in which a controlled foreign corporation is a partner (either directly or through one or more branches or other partnerships).

(C) *Examples.*—The following examples illustrate the application of this paragraph (a)(2)(ii):

Example 1. CFC, a controlled foreign corporation in Country A, is a 90 percent partner in partnership P, which is treated as fiscally transparent under the laws of Country A. P has a hybrid branch, BR, in Country B. P makes an interest payment of $100 to BR. Under Country A law, CFC's 90 percent share of the payment reduces CFC's Country A income tax. Under paragraph (a)(2)(ii)(A) of this section, the recharacterization rules of this section are applied by treating the payment as if made by CFC to BR. Ninety dollars of CFC's non-subpart F income, to the extent available, and subject to the earnings and profits and tax rate limitations of paragraph (a)(5) of this section, is recharacterized as subpart F income.

Example 2. CFC, a controlled foreign corporation in country A, is a 90 percent partner in partnership P, which is treated as fiscally transparent under the laws of Country A. P has two branches in Country B, BR1 and BR2. BR1 is treated as fiscally transparent under the laws of Country A. BR2 is a hybrid branch. BR1 makes an interest payment of $100 to BR2. Under paragraph (a)(2)(ii)(A) of this section, the payment by BR1, the fiscally transparent branch, is treated as a payment by P, and the deemed payment by P, a fiscally transparent partnership, is treated as made by CFC. Under Country A law, CFC's 90 percent share of BR1's payment reduces CFC's Country A income tax. Ninety dollars of CFC's non-subpart F income, to the extent available, and subject to the earnings and profits and tax rate limitations of paragraph (a)(5) of this section, is recharacterized as subpart F income.

(3) *Application when payment reduces foreign tax.*—For purposes of paragraph (a)(1) of this section, a hybrid branch payment reduces foreign tax when the foreign tax imposed on the income of the payor, or any person that is a related person with respect to the payor (as determined under the principles of section 954(d)(3)), is less than the foreign tax that would have been imposed on such income had the hybrid branch payment not been made, or the hybrid branch payment creates or increases a loss or deficit or other tax attribute which may be carried back or forward to reduce the foreign income tax of

the payor or any owner in another year (determined by taking into account any refund of such tax made to the payor, payee or any other person).

(4) *Hybrid branch payment that is included within a category of foreign personal holding company income.* (i) *In general.*—For purposes of paragraph (a)(1) of this section, whether the hybrid branch payment is treated as income included within a category of foreign personal holding company income is determined by treating a hybrid branch that is either the payor or recipient of the hybrid branch payment as a separate wholly-owned subsidiary corporation of the controlled foreign corporation that is incorporated in the jurisdiction under the laws of which such hybrid branch is created, organized for foreign law purposes, or has substantial assets. Thus, the hybrid branch payment will be treated as included within a category of foreign personal holding company income if, taking into account any specific exceptions for that category, the payment would be included within a category of foreign personal holding company income if the branch or branches were treated as separately incorporated for U.S. tax purposes.

(ii) *Extent to which controlled foreign corporation and hybrid branches treated as separate entities.*—For purposes of this section, other than the determination under paragraph (a)(4)(i) of this section, a controlled foreign corporation and its hybrid branch, a partnership and its hybrid branch, or hybrid branches shall not be treated as separate entities. Thus, for example, if a controlled foreign corporation, including all of its hybrid branches, has an overall deficit in earnings and profits to which section 952(c) applies, the limitation of such section on the amount includible in the subpart F income of such corporation will apply. Similarly, for purposes of applying the de minimis and full inclusion rules of section 954(b)(3), a controlled foreign corporation and its hybrid branch, or hybrid branches shall not be treated as separate corporations. Further, a hybrid branch payment that would reduce foreign personal holding company income under section 954(b)(5) if made between two separate entities will not create an expense if made between a controlled foreign corporation and its hybrid branch, a partnership and its hybrid branch, or hybrid branches.

(5) *Recharacterization of income attributable to current earnings and profits as subpart F income.*—(i) *General rule.*—Non-subpart F income of a controlled foreign corporation in an amount equal to the excess of earnings and profits of the controlled foreign corporation for the taxable year over subpart F income, as defined in section 952(a), will be recharacterized as subpart F income under paragraph (a)(1) of this section only to the extent provided under paragraphs (a)(5)(ii) through (vi) of this section.

(ii) *Subpart F income.*—For purposes of determining the excess of current earnings and profits over subpart F income under paragraph (a)(1) of this section, the amount of subpart F income is determined before the application of the rules of this section but after the application of the rules of sections 952(c) and 954(b). Further, such amount is determined by treating the controlled foreign corporation and all of its hybrid branches as a single corporation.

(iii) *Recharacterization limited to gross amount of hybrid branch payment.*—(A) *In general.*—The amount recharacterized as subpart F income under paragraph (a)(1) of this section is limited to the amount of the hybrid branch payment.

(B) *Exception for duplicative payments.*—[Reserved].

(iv) *Tax disparity rule.*—(A) *In general.*—Paragraph (a)(1) of this section will apply only if the hybrid branch payment falls within the tax disparity rule. The hybrid branch payment falls within the tax disparity rule if it is taxed in the year when earned at an effective rate of tax that is less than 90 percent of, and at least 5 percentage points less than, the hypothetical effective rate of tax imposed on the hybrid branch payment, as determined under paragraph (a)(5)(iv)(B) of this section.

(B) *Hypothetical effective rate of tax.*—*(1) In general.*—The hypothetical effective rate of tax imposed on the hybrid branch payment is—

(i) For the taxable year of the payor in which the hybrid branch payment is made, the amount of income taxes that would have been paid or accrued by the payor if the hybrid branch payment had not been made, less the amount of income taxes paid or accrued by the payor; divided by

(ii) The amount of the hybrid branch payment.

(2) Hypothetical effective rate of tax when hybrid branch payment causes or increases loss or deficit.—If the hybrid branch payment causes or increases a loss or deficit of the payor for foreign tax purposes, and such loss or deficit can be carried forward or back, the hypothetical effective rate of tax imposed on the hybrid branch payment is the effective rate of tax that would be imposed on the taxable income of the payor for the year in which the payment is made if the payor's taxable income were equal to the amount of the hybrid branch payment.

(C) *Examples.*—The application of this paragraph (a)(5)(iv) is illustrated by the following examples:

Example 1. In 2006, CFC organized in Country A had net income of $60 from manufacturing for Country A tax purposes. It also had a branch (BR) in Country B. BR is a hybrid entity under paragraph (a)(1) of this section. CFC made a payment of $40 to BR, which was a hybrid branch payment under paragraph (a)(6) of this section, and was treated by CFC as a deductible payment for Country A tax purposes. CFC paid $30 of Country A taxes in 2006. It would have paid $50 of Country A taxes without the deductible payment. Country A did not impose any withholding tax on the $40 payment to BR. Country B also did not impose a tax on the $40 received by BR. Therefore, the effective rate of tax on that payment is 0%. Furthermore, the hypothetical effective rate of tax on the $40 hybrid branch payment is 50% ($50 – $30/$40). The effective rate of tax (0%) is less than 90% of, and more than 5 percentage points less than, this hypothetical rate of tax of 50%. As a result, the $40 hybrid branch payment falls within the tax disparity rule of this paragraph (a)(5)(iv).

Example 2. Assume the same facts as in *Example 1,* except that CFC has a loss of $100 for the year for Country A tax purposes. Under Country A law, CFC can carry the loss forward for use in subsequent years. CFC paid no Country A taxes in 2006. The rate of tax in Country A is graduated from 20% to 50%. If the $40 hybrid branch payment were the only item of taxable income of CFC, Country A would have imposed tax at an effective rate of 30%. The effective rate of tax (0%) is less than 90% of, and more than 5 percentage points less than, the hypothetical effective rate of tax (30%) imposed on the hybrid branch payment. As a result, the $40 hybrid branch payment falls within the tax disparity rule of this paragraph (a)(5)(iv).

Example 3. Assume the same facts as in *Example 1,* except that Country B imposes tax on the $40 hybrid payment to BR at an effective rate of 50%. The effective rate of 50% is equal to the hypothetical effective rate of tax. As a result, the hybrid branch payment does not fall within the tax disparity rule of this paragraph (a)(5)(iv) and, thus, the recharacterization rules of paragraph (a)(1) of this section do not apply. See also the special high tax exception of paragraph (a)(5)(v) of this section.

(v) *Special high tax exception.*—(A) *In general.*—Paragraph (a)(1) of this section shall not apply if the non-subpart F income that would be recharacterized as subpart F income under this section was subject to foreign income taxes imposed by a foreign country or countries at an effective rate that is greater than 90 percent of the maximum rate of tax specified in section 11 for the taxable year of the controlled foreign corporation.

(B) *Effective rate of tax.*—The effective rate of tax imposed on the non-subpart F income that would be recharacterized as subpart F income under this section is determined under the principles of § 1.954-1(d)(2) and (3). See paragraph (b) of this section for the application of section 960 to amounts recharacterized as subpart F income under this section.

(vi) *No carryback or carryforward of amounts in excess of current year earnings and profits limitation.*—To the extent that some or all of the amount required to be recharacterized under this section is not recharacterized as subpart F income because the hybrid branch payment exceeds the amount that can be recharacterized, as determined under paragraph (a)(5)(i) of this section, this excess shall not be carried back or forward to another year.

(6) *Definitions for this section.*—For purposes of this section:

(i) *Arrangement* shall mean any agreement to pay interest, rents, royalties or similar amounts. It shall also include the declaration and payment of a dividend (but not an agreement or undertaking to pay future, unspecified dividends). An arrangement shall not, however, include the mere formation or acquisition (or similar event) of a hybrid branch that is intended to become a party to an arrangement.

(ii) *Entity* means any person that is treated by the United States or any jurisdiction as other than an individual.

(iii) *Hybrid branch* means an entity that—

(A) Is disregarded as an entity separate from its owner for federal tax purposes and is owned (including ownership through branches) by either a controlled foreign corporation or a partnership in which a controlled foreign corporation is a partner (either directly or indirectly through one or more branches or partnerships);

(B) Is treated as fiscally transparent by the United States; and

(C) Is treated as non-fiscally transparent by the country in which the payor entity, any owner of a fiscally-transparent payor entity, the controlled foreign corporation, or any intermediary partnership is created, organized or has substantial assets.

(iv) *Hybrid branch payment* means the gross amount of any payment (including any accrual) which, under the tax laws of any foreign jurisdiction to which the payor is subject, is regarded as a payment between two separate entities but which, under U.S. income tax principles, is not income to the recipient because it is between two parts of a single entity.

(7) *Fiscally transparent and non-fiscally transparent*.—For purposes of this section an entity shall be treated as fiscally transparent with respect to an interest holder of the entity, if such interest holder is required, under the laws of any jurisdiction to which it is subject, to take into account separately, on a current basis, such interest holder's share of all items which, if separately taken into account by such interest holder, would result in an income tax liability for the interest holder in such jurisdiction different from that which would result if the interest holder did not take the share of such items into account separately. A non-fiscally transparent entity is an entity that is not fiscally transparent under this paragraph (a)(7).

(b) *Application of section 960*.—For purposes of determining the amount of taxes deemed paid under section 960, the amount of non-subpart F income recharacterized as subpart F income under this section shall be treated as attributable to income in separate categories, as defined in § 1.904-5(a)(1), in proportion to the ratio of non-subpart F income in each such category to the total amount of non-subpart F income of the controlled foreign corporation for the taxable year.

(c) *Effective dates*.—(1) *In general*.—This section shall be applicable for all amounts paid or accrued in taxable years commencing after [date that is 5 years after publication of the final regulations in the federal register], under hybrid arrangements, except as otherwise provided.

(2) *Permanent relief*.—(i) *In general*.—This section shall not apply to any payments made under hybrid arrangements entered into before June 19, 1998. This exception shall be permanent so long as the arrangement is not substantially modified, within the meaning of paragraph (c)(2)(ii) of this section, on or after June 19, 1998.

(ii) *Substantial modification*.—(A) *In general*.—Substantial modification of a hybrid arrangement includes—

(1) The expansion of the hybrid arrangement (other than de minimis expansion);

(2) A more than 50% change in the U.S. ownership (direct or indirect) of any entity that is a party to the hybrid arrangement, other than—

(i) A transfer of ownership of such party within a controlled group determined under section 1563(a), without regard to section 1563(a)(4); or

(ii) A change in ownership of the entire controlled group (determined under section 1563(a), without regard to section 1563(a)(4)) of which such party is a member;

(3) Any measure taken by a party to the arrangement (or any related party) that materially increases the tax benefit of the hybrid arrangement, regardless of whether such measure alters the legal relationship between the parties to the arrangement. For example, in the case of a hybrid branch payment determined with reference to a percentage of sales, a growth in the amount of the hybrid branch payment (and, thus, the tax benefit) caused by a growth of sales will not, in general, be a substantial modification. However, in the case of a significant sales growth resulting from a transfer of assets by a related party, that transfer would be a measure which materially increased the benefit of the arrangement, and that arrangement would be deemed to have been substantially modified.

(B) *Transactions not treated as substantial modification*.—Substantial modification of a hybrid arrangement does not include—

(1) The daily reissuance of a demand loan by operation of law;

(2) The renewal of a loan, license or rental agreement on the same terms and conditions if—

(i) The renewal occurs pursuant to the terms of the agreement and without more than a de minimis amount of action of any party thereto;

(ii) As contemplated by the original agreement, the same parties agree to renew the agreement without modification; or

(iii) The renewal occurs solely by reason of a subsequent drawdown under a grandfathered master credit facility agreement;

(3) The renewal of a loan, license, or rental agreement by the same parties on terms which do not increase the tax benefit of the arrangement (other than a de minimis increase);

(4) The making of payments under a license agreement in respect of copyrights or patents (or know-how associated with such copyrights or patents), not in existence at the time the agreement was entered into, but only where the development of such property was anticipated by the agreement, and such property is substantially derived from (or otherwise incorporates substantial features of) copyrights and patents (or know-how associated with such copyrights or patents) in existence at the time of, and covered under, the original agreement;

(5) A final transfer pricing adjustment made by the taxation authorities of the jurisdiction in which the tax reduction occurs, so long as such adjustment would not have been a substantial valuation misstatement (as defined in section 6662(e)(1)(B)) if the adjustment had been made by the Internal Revenue Service; or

(6) A de minimis periodic adjustment by the parties to the arrangement made annually (or more frequently) to conform the payments to the requirements of section 482. [Prop. Reg. § 1.954-9.]

[Proposed 7-13-99.]

§ 1.954(c)(6)-1. Certain cases in which section 954(c)(6) exception not available.—(a) *Cross-references to other rules*.—For a non-exclusive list of rules that in certain cases limit the applicability of the exception to foreign personal holding company income under section 954(c)(6), see—

(1) Section 1.245A-5(d) (rules regarding the application of section 954(c)(6) to extraordinary disposition amounts);

(2) Section 1.245A-5(f) (rules regarding the application of section 954(c)(6) to tiered extraordinary reduction amounts);

(3) Section 1.245A(e)-1(c) (rules regarding tiered hybrid dividends);

(4) Section 1.367(b)-4(e)(4) (rules regarding income inclusion and gain recognition in certain exchanges following an inversion transaction);

(5) Section 964(e)(4)(A) (rules regarding certain gain from the sale or exchange of stock that is recharacterized as a dividend); and

(6) Section 1.7701(l)-4(e) (rules regarding recharacterization of certain transactions following an inversion transaction).

(b) *Applicability date*.—This section applies as of August 27, 2020. [Reg. 1.954(c)(6)-1.]

☐ [*T.D. 9909, 8-21-2020.*]

§ 1.956-1. Shareholder's pro rata share of the average of the amounts of United States property held by a controlled foreign corporation.—(a) *Overview and scope*.—(1) *In general*.—Subject to the provisions of section 951(a) and the regulations in this part, a United States shareholder of a controlled foreign corporation is required to include in gross income the amount determined under section 956 with respect to the shareholder for the taxable year but only to the extent not excluded from gross income under section 959(a)(2) and the regulations in this part. See § 1.958-1(d) for rules regarding the ownership of stock of a foreign corporation through a domestic partnership for purposes of section 956(a) and for purposes of any provision that specifically applies by reference to section 956(a) or the regulations in this part under section 956 that relate to section 956(a)

(2) *Reduction for certain United States shareholders*.—(i) *In general*.—For a taxable year of a controlled foreign corporation, the amount determined under section 956 with respect to each share of stock of the controlled foreign corporation owned (within the meaning of section 958(a)) by a United States shareholder is the amount that would be determined under section 956 with respect to such

share for the taxable year, absent the application of this paragraph (a)(2) for the taxable year (such amount, the *tentative section 956 amount*, and in the aggregate with respect to all shares owned (within the meaning of section 958(a)) by the United States shareholder, the *aggregate tentative section 956 amount*), reduced by the amount of the deduction under section 245A, if any, that the shareholder would be allowed if the shareholder received as a distribution from the controlled foreign corporation an amount equal to the tentative section 956 amount with respect to such share on the last day during the taxable year on which the foreign corporation is a controlled foreign corporation (*hypothetical distribution*).

(ii) *Determination of the amount of the deduction that would be allowed under section 245A with respect to a hypothetical distribution.*—For purposes of determining the amount of the deduction under section 245A that a United States shareholder would be allowed with respect to a share of stock of a controlled foreign corporation by reason of a hypothetical distribution, the rules in paragraphs (a)(2)(ii)(A) through (C) of this section apply—

(A) If a United States shareholder owns a share of stock of a controlled foreign corporation indirectly (within the meaning of section 958(a)(2)), then—

(1) Sections 245A(a) through (d), 246(a), and 959 apply to the hypothetical distribution as if the United States shareholder directly owned (within the meaning of section 958(a)(1)(A)) the share;

(2) Section 245A(e) applies to the hypothetical distribution as if the distribution were made to the United States shareholder through each entity by reason of which the United States shareholder indirectly owns such share and pro rata with respect to the equity that gives rise to such indirect ownership;

(3) To the extent that a distribution treated as made to a controlled foreign corporation pursuant to the hypothetical distribution by reason of paragraph (a)(2)(ii)(A)(2) of this section would be subject to section 245A(e)(2), the United States shareholder is treated as not being allowed a deduction under section 245A by reason of the hypothetical distribution; and

(4) Section 246(c) applies to the hypothetical distribution by substituting the phrase "owned (within the meaning of section 958(a))" for the term "held" each place it appears in section 246(c);

(B) Section 246(c) applies to the hypothetical distribution by substituting "the last day during the taxable year on which the foreign corporation is a controlled foreign corporation" for the phrase "the date on which such share becomes ex-dividend with respect to such dividend" in section 246(c)(1)(A); and

(C) The hypothetical distribution is treated as attributable first to earnings and profits of the controlled foreign corporation described in section 959(c)(2), then to earnings and profits of the controlled foreign corporation described in section 959(c)(3).

(3) *Examples.*—The examples in this paragraph (a)(3) illustrate the application of paragraph (a)(2) of this section.

(i) *Example 1*—(A) *Facts.* *(1)* USP, a domestic corporation, owns all of the single class of stock of FC, a foreign corporation. The stock of FC consists of 100 shares, and USP satisfies the holding period requirement of section 246(c) (as modified by paragraph (a)(2)(ii)(B) of this section) with respect to each share of FC stock. Any dividend from FC to USP would not constitute a hybrid dividend for purposes of section 245A(e). FC owns all of the stock of USS, a domestic corporation. FC's adjusted basis in the stock of USS is $0.

(2) The functional currency of FC is the U.S. dollar. FC has $100x of undistributed earnings as defined in section 245A(c)(2) at the end of the taxable year, $90x of which constitute undistributed foreign earnings as defined in section 245A(c)(3), and $10x of which are described in section 245(a)(5)(B) (that is, earnings attributable to a dividend that FC received from USS). None of the earnings and profits of FC are described in section 959(c)(1) or (2) or are earnings and profits attributable to income excluded from subpart F income under section 952(b). FC's applicable earnings (as defined in section 956(b)(1)) are $100x. FC also has held an obligation of USP with an adjusted basis of $120x on every day during the taxable year of FC, and such obligation was acquired while all of its stock was owned by USP.

(B) *Analysis.* Because USP directly owns all of the stock of FC at the end of FC's taxable year, USP's aggregate tentative section 956 amount with respect to FC is $100x, the lesser of USP's pro rata share of the average amounts of United States property held by FC ($120x) and its pro rata share of FC's applicable earnings ($100x). Under paragraph (a)(2)(i) of this section, USP's section 956 amount with respect to FC is its aggregate tentative section 956 amount with respect to FC reduced by the deduction under section 245A that USP would be allowed if USP received an amount equal to its aggregate tentative section 956 amount as a distribution with respect to the FC stock. USP would be allowed a $90x deduction under section 245A with respect to the foreign-source portion of the $100x hypothetical distribution (that is, an amount of the dividend that bears the same ratio to the dividend as the $90x of undistributed foreign earnings bears to the $100x of undistributed earnings). Accordingly, USP's section 956 amount with respect to FC is $10x, its aggregate tentative section 956 amount ($100x) with respect to FC reduced by the amount of the deduction that USP would have been allowed under section 245A with respect to the hypothetical distribution ($90x).

(ii) *Example 2*—(A) *Facts.* The facts are the same as in paragraph (a)(3)(i)(A) of this section (the facts in *Example 1*), except that all $100x of FC's undistributed earnings are described in section 959(c)(2).

(B) *Analysis.* As in paragraph (a)(3)(i)(B) of this section (the analysis in *Example 1*), USP's aggregate tentative section 956 amount with respect to FC is $100x, the lesser of USP's pro rata share of the average amounts of United States property held by FC ($120x) and its pro rata share of FC's applicable earnings ($100x). However, paragraph (a)(2) of this section does not reduce USP's section 956 amount because USP would not be allowed any deduction under section 245A with respect to the $100x hypothetical distribution by reason of section 959(a) and (d). Accordingly, USP's section 956 amount is $100x. However, under sections 959(a)(2) and 959(f)(1), USP's inclusion under section 951(a)(1)(B) with respect to FC is $0, because USP's section 956 amount with respect to FC does not exceed the earnings and profits of FC described in section 959(c)(2) with respect to USP. The $100x of earnings and profits of FC described in section 959(c)(2) are reclassified as earnings and profits described in section 959(c)(1).

(iii) *Example 3*—(A) *Facts.* The facts are the same as in paragraph (a)(3)(i)(A) of this section (the facts in *Example 1*), except that FC has $200x of undistributed earnings, which constitute undistributed foreign earnings as defined in section 245A(c)(3), of which $100x are described in section 959(c)(1)(A) and $100x are described in section 959(c)(3).

(B) *Analysis.* USP's aggregate tentative section 956 amount with respect to FC is $20x, the lesser of $20x, the excess of USP's pro rata share of the average amounts of United States property held by FC ($120x) over the earnings and profits described in section 959(c)(1)(A) with respect to USP ($100x), and its pro rata share of FC's applicable earnings ($100x). Under paragraph (a)(2)(i) of this section, USP's section 956 amount with respect to FC is its aggregate tentative section 956 amount with respect to FC reduced by the deduction under section 245A that USP would be allowed if USP received an amount equal to its aggregate tentative section 956 amount as a distribution with respect to the FC stock. USP would be allowed a $20x deduction under section 245A with respect to the foreign-source portion of the $20x hypothetical distribution, which, under paragraph (a)(2)(ii)(C) of this section, is treated as attributable to the earnings and profits of FC described in section 959(c)(3) despite the fact that FC has $100x of earnings and profits described in section 959(c)(1)(A) that would otherwise be distributed before earnings and profits described in section 959(c)(3). Accordingly, USP's section 956 amount with respect to FC is $0, its aggregate tentative section 956 amount ($20x) with respect to FC reduced by the amount of the deduction that USP would have been allowed under section 245A with respect to the hypothetical distribution after applying the rule in paragraph (a)(2)(ii)(C) of this section ($20x).

(iv) *Example 4*—(A) *Facts.* *(1)* USP, a domestic corporation, owns all of the single class of stock of FC1, a foreign corporation, and has held such stock for five years. FC1 has held 70% of the single class of stock of FC2, a foreign corporation, for three years. The other 30% of the FC2 stock has been held since FC2's formation by a foreign individual unrelated to USP or FC1. Any dividend from FC2 or FC1 to FC1 or USP, respectively, would not constitute a hybrid dividend for purposes of section 245A(e). FC2 has a calendar taxable year. On December 1, Year 1, FC1 acquires the remaining 30% of the stock of FC2 for cash. On June 30, Year 2, FC1 sells to a third party the 30% of FC2 stock acquired in Year 1 at no gain. FC2 made no distributions during Year 1.

(2) The functional currency of FC1 and FC2 is the U.S. dollar. For Year 1, FC2 has $120x of undistributed earnings as defined in section 245A(c)(2), all of which constitute undistributed foreign earnings. None of the earnings and profits of FC2 are described in section 959(c)(1) or (2) or are earnings and profits attributable to income excluded from subpart F income under section 952(b). FC2's applicable earnings (as defined in section 956(b)(1)) for Year 1 are $120x. FC2 has held an obligation of USP with an adjusted basis of $100x on every day of Year 1 that was acquired while USP owned all of the stock of FC1 and FC1 held 70% of the single class of stock of FC2.

(B) *Analysis.* Because USP indirectly owns (within the meaning of section 958(a)) all of the stock of FC2 at the end of Year 1, USP's aggregate tentative section 956 amount with respect to FC2 for Year 1 is $100x, the lesser of USP's pro rata share of the average amounts of United States property held by FC2 ($100x) and its pro rata share of FC2's applicable earnings ($120x). Under paragraph (a)(2)(i) of this section, USP's section 956 amount with respect to FC2 for Year 1 is its aggregate tentative section 956 amount with respect to FC2 reduced by the deduction under section 245A that USP would be allowed if USP received an amount equal to its aggregate tentative section 956 amount as a distribution with respect to the FC2 stock that USP owns indirectly within the meaning of section 958(a)(2). For purposes of determining the consequences of this hypothetical distribution, under paragraph (a)(2)(ii)(A)(1) of this section, USP is treated as owning the FC2 stock directly. In addition, under paragraph (a)(2)(ii)(A)(4) of this section, the holding period requirement of section 246(c) is applied by reference to the period during which USP owned (within the meaning of section 958(a)) the stock of FC2. Therefore, with respect to the hypothetical distribution from FC2 to USP, USP would satisfy the holding period requirement under section 246(c) with respect to the 70% of the FC2 stock that USP indirectly owned for three years through FC1, but not with respect to the 30% of the FC2 stock that USP indirectly owned through FC1 for a period of less than 365 days. Accordingly, USP's section 956 amount with respect to FC2 for Year 1 is $30x, its aggregate tentative section 956 amount ($100x) reduced by the amount of the deduction that USP would have been allowed under section 245A with respect to the hypothetical distribution ($70x).

(b) *Amount of United States property held indirectly by a controlled foreign corporation.*—(1) *General rule.*—For purposes of section 956, United States property held indirectly by a controlled foreign corporation includes—

(i) United States property held on behalf of the controlled foreign corporation by a trustee or a nominee;

(ii) United States property acquired by any other foreign corporation that is controlled by the controlled foreign corporation if a principal purpose of creating, organizing, or funding by any means (including through capital contributions or debt) the other foreign corporation is to avoid the application of section 956 with respect to the controlled foreign corporation; and

(iii) Property acquired by a partnership that is controlled by the controlled foreign corporation if the property would be United States property if held directly by the controlled foreign corporation, and a principal purpose of creating, organizing, or funding by any means (including through capital contributions or debt) the partnership is to avoid the application of section 956 with respect to the controlled foreign corporation.

(2) *Control.*—For purposes of paragraphs (b)(1)(ii) and (iii) of this section, a controlled foreign corporation controls a foreign corporation or partnership if the controlled foreign corporation and the other foreign corporation or partnership are related within the meaning of section 267(b) or section 707(b). For this purpose, in determining whether two corporations are members of the same controlled group under section 267(b)(3), a person is considered to own stock owned directly by such person, stock owned for the purposes of section 1563(e)(1), and stock owned with the application of section 267(c).

(3) *Coordination rule.*—Paragraph (b)(1)(iii) of this section applies only to the extent that the amount of United States property that is treated under that paragraph as held indirectly by a controlled foreign corporation through the partnership exceeds the sum of—

(i) The amount of United States property described in paragraph (b)(1)(iii) of this section that is treated as held by the controlled foreign corporation as a result of the application of § 1.956-4(b) with respect to the partnership; and

(ii) The amount of United States property that is treated as held by the controlled foreign corporation as a result of the application of § 1.956-4(c) with respect to any portion of an obligation attributable to the funding described in paragraph (b)(1)(iii) of this section of the partnership by the controlled foreign corporation.

(4) *Examples.*—The examples in this paragraph (b)(4) illustrate the rules of this paragraph (b). In each example, P is a United States citizen that wholly owns two controlled foreign corporations, FS1 and FS2.

(i) *Example 1.* (A) *Facts.* FS1 sells inventory to FS2 in exchange for trade receivables due in 60 days. Avoiding the application of section 956 with respect to FS1 was not a principal purpose of establishing the trade receivables. FS2 has no earnings and profits, and FS1 has substantial accumulated earnings and profits. FS2 makes a loan to P equal to the amount it owes FS1 under the trade receivables. FS2 pays the trade receivables according to their terms.

(B) *Result.* FS1 will not be considered to indirectly hold United States property under this paragraph (b) because the funding of FS2 through the sale of inventory in exchange for the establishment of trade receivables was not undertaken with a principal purpose of avoiding the application of section 956 with respect to FS1.

(ii) *Example 2.* (A) *Facts.* The facts are the same as in paragraph (b)(4)(i)(A) of this section (the facts in *Example 1*), except that, with a principal purpose of avoiding the application of section 956 with respect to FS1, FS1 and FS2 agree to defer FS2's payment obligation, and FS2 does not timely pay the receivables.

(B) *Result.* FS1 is considered to hold indirectly United States property under this paragraph (b) and § 1.956-2(a) because there was a funding of FS2, a principal purpose of which was to avoid the application of section 956 with respect to FS1.

(iii) *Example 3.* (A) *Facts.* FS1 has $100x of post-1986 undistributed earnings and profits and $100x post-1986 foreign income taxes, but does not have any cash. FS2 has earnings and profits of at least $100x, no post-1986 foreign income taxes, and substantial cash. Neither FS1 nor FS2 has earnings and profits described in section 959(c)(1) or section 959(c)(2). FS2 loans $100x to FS1. FS1 then loans $100x to P. An income inclusion by P of $100x under sections 951(a)(1)(B) and 956 with respect to FS1 would result in foreign income taxes deemed paid by P under section 960. A principal purpose of funding FS1 through the loan from FS2 is to avoid the application of section 956 with respect to FS2.

(B) *Result.* Under paragraph (b)(1)(ii) of this section, FS2 is considered to indirectly hold the $100x obligation of P that is held by FS1. As a result, P has an income inclusion of $100x under sections 951(a)(1)(B) and 956 with respect to FS2, and the foreign income taxes deemed paid by P under section 960 is $0. P does not have an income inclusion under sections 951(a)(1)(B) and 956 with respect to FS1 related to the $100x loan from FS1 to P.

(iv) *Example 4.* (A) *Facts.* FS1 deposits $100x with BK, an unrelated foreign financial institution. FS2 subsequently borrows $100x from BK. BK would not have loaned the $100x to FS2 on the same terms absent FS1's deposit. FS2 loans the $100x borrowed from BK to P. FS2 has no earnings and profits, and FS1 has substantial accumulated earnings and profits. A principal purpose for the transactions is to avoid the application of section 956 with respect to FS1.

(B) *Result.* FS1 is considered to hold indirectly United States property under this paragraph (b) and § 1.956-2(a) because FS1's deposit with BK, which facilitates BK's loan to FS2, is considered a funding by FS1 of FS2, a principal purpose of which was to avoid the application of section 956 with respect to FS1.

(v) *Example 5.* (A) *Facts.* FS1 sells inventory to FS2 in exchange for $100x. The sale occurred in the ordinary course of FS1's trade or business and FS2's trade or business, and the terms of the sale are consistent with terms that would be observed among parties dealing at arm's length. FS1 makes a $100x loan to P. FS2 has no earnings and profits, and FS1 has substantial accumulated earnings and profits.

(B) *Result.* FS2 will not be considered to indirectly hold United States property under this paragraph (b) because a sale in the ordinary course of business for cash on terms that are consistent with those that would be observed among parties dealing at arm's length does not constitute a funding.

(vi) *Example 6.* (A) *Facts.* In Year 1, FS2 loans $100x to FS1 to finance FS1's trade or business. The terms of the loan are consistent with those that would be observed among parties dealing at arm's length. In Year 2, FS1 repays the loan in accordance with the terms of the loan. Immediately after the repayment by FS1, FS2 loans $100x to P. FS2 has no earnings and profits, and FS1 has substantial accumulated earnings and profits.

(B) *Result.* FS1 will not be considered to indirectly hold United States property under this paragraph (b) because a repayment of a loan that has terms that are consistent with those that would be observed among parties dealing at arm's length and that is repaid consistent with those terms does not constitute a funding.

(vii) *Example 7.* (A) *Facts.* FS1 has substantial earnings and profits. P and FS1 are the only partners in FPRS, a foreign partnership. FS1 contributes $600x cash to FPRS in exchange for a 60% interest in the partnership, and P contributes real estate located outside the United States ($400x value) to FPRS in exchange for a 40% interest in the partnership. There are no special allocations in the FPRS partnership agreement. FPRS lends $100x to P. Under § 1.956-4(b) and § 1.956-2(a), FS1 is treated as holding United States property of $60x (60% x $100x) as a result of the FPRS loan to P. A principal purpose of creating, organizing, or funding FPRS is to avoid the application of section 956 with respect to FS1.

(B) *Result*. Before taking into account paragraph (b)(3) of this section, because FS1 controls FPRS and a principal purpose of creating, organizing, or funding FPRS was to avoid the application of section 956 with respect to FS1, FS1 is considered under paragraph (b)(1)(iii) of this section to indirectly hold the $100x obligation of P that would be United States property if held directly by FS1. However, under paragraph (b)(3) of this section, FS1 is treated as holding United States property under paragraph (b)(1)(iii) only to the extent the amount held indirectly under paragraph (b)(1)(iii) of this section exceeds the sum of the amount of the United States property that FS1 is treated as holding as a result of the application of § 1.956-4(b) with respect to FPRS. The amount of United States property that FS1 is treated as indirectly holding under paragraph (b)(1)(iii) of this section and § 1.956-2(a) ($100x) exceeds the amount determined under § 1.956-4(b) ($60x) by $40x. Thus, FS1 is considered to hold United States property within the meaning of section 956(c) in the amount of $100x ($60x under § 1.956-4(b) and $40x under paragraphs (b)(1)(iii) and (b)(3) of this section).

(viii) *Example 8*. (A) *Facts*. FS1 and FS2 have substantial earnings and profits. P and FS1 are the only partners in FPRS, a foreign partnership. There are no special allocations in the FPRS partnership agreement. P's liquidation value percentage with respect to FPRS is 40%, and FS1's liquidation value percentage with respect to FPRS is 60%. FS2 lends $100x to FPRS, and FPRS lends $100x to P. Under § 1.956-4(c) and § 1.956-2(a), FS2 is treated as holding United States property of $40x (40% x $100x) as a result of its loan to FPRS. A principal purpose of funding FPRS is to avoid the application of section 956 with respect to FS2.

(B) *Result*. Before taking into account paragraph (b)(3) of this section, because FS2 controls FPRS and a principal purpose of funding FPRS was to avoid the application of section 956 with respect to FS2, FS2 is considered under paragraph (b)(1)(iii) of this section to indirectly hold the $100x obligation of P that would be United States property if held directly by FS2. However, under paragraph (b)(3) of this section, FS2 is treated as holding United States property under paragraph (b)(1)(iii) only to the extent the amount held indirectly under paragraph (b)(1)(iii) of this section exceeds the amount of United States property that FS2 is treated as holding as a result of the application of § 1.956-4(c) with respect to the obligation with which FS2 funds FPRS. The amount of United States property that FS2 is treated as indirectly holding under paragraph (b)(1)(iii) of this section and § 1.956-2(a) ($100x) exceeds the amount determined under § 1.956-4(c) ($40x) by $60x. Thus, FS2 is considered to hold United States property within the meaning of section 956(c) in the amount of $100x ($40x under § 1.956-4(c) and $60x under paragraphs (b)(1)(iii) and (b)(3) of this section). P does not have an income inclusion under sections 951(a)(1)(B) and 956 with respect to FS1 related to the P obligation held by FPRS.

(c) - (d) [Reserved]

(e) *Amount attributable to property*.—(1) *General rule*.—Except as provided in subparagraph (2) of this paragraph, for purposes of paragraph (b)(1) of this section, the amount taken into account with respect to any United States property shall be its adjusted basis, as of the applicable determination date, reduced by any liability (other than a liability described in subparagraph (3) of this paragraph) to which such property is subject on such date. To be taken into account under this subparagraph, a liability must constitute a specific charge against the property involved. Thus, a liability evidenced by an open account or a liability secured only by the general credit of the controlled foreign corporation will not be taken into account. On the other hand, if a liability constitutes a specific charge against several items of property and cannot definitely be allocated to any single item of property, the liability shall be apportioned against each of such items of property in that ratio which the adjusted basis of such item on the applicable determination date bears to the adjusted basis of all such items at such time. A liability in excess of the adjusted basis of the property which is subject to such liability shall not be taken into account for the purpose of reducing the adjusted basis of other property which is not subject to such liability. See § 1.956-1(e)(6) for a special rule for determining amounts attributable to United States property acquired as the result of certain nonrecognition transactions.

(2) *Rule for pledges and guarantees*.—For purposes of this section, the amount of an obligation treated as held (before application of § 1.956-4(b)) as a result of a pledge or guarantee described in § 1.956-2(c) is the unpaid principal amount of the obligation on the applicable determination date.

(3) *Excluded charges*.—For purposes of subparagraph (1) of this paragraph, a specific charge created with respect to any item of property principally for the purpose of artificially increasing or decreasing the amount of a controlled foreign corporation's investment of earnings in United States property will not be recognized; whether a specific charge is created principally for such purpose will depend upon all the facts and circumstances of each case. One of the factors that will be considered in making such a determination with respect to a loan is whether the loan is from a related person, as defined in section 954(d)(3) and paragraph (e) of § 1.954-1.

(4) *Statement required*.—If for purposes of this section a United States shareholder of a controlled foreign corporation reduces the adjusted basis of property which constitutes United States property on the ground that such property is subject to a liability, he shall attach to his return a statement setting forth the adjusted basis of the property before the reduction and the amount and nature of the reduction.

(5) [Reserved]. For further guidance, see § 1.956-1T(e)(5).

(6) *Adjusted basis of property acquired in certain nonrecognition transactions*.—(i) *Scope*.—This paragraph (e)(6) provides rules for determining, solely for purposes of applying section 956, the adjusted basis of specified United States property acquired by a controlled foreign corporation pursuant to an exchange in which the controlled foreign corporation's basis in such specified United States property is determined under section 362(a). This paragraph (e)(6) also applies if specified United States property, the adjusted basis in which has been determined under these regulations, is transferred (in one or more subsequent exchanges) to a related person (within the meaning of section 954(d)(3)), pursuant to one or more exchanges in which the related person's adjusted basis in such property is determined, in whole or in part, by reference to the transferor controlled foreign corporation's adjusted basis in such property.

(ii) *Definition of specified United States property*.—For purposes of this paragraph (e)(6), *specified United States property* is stock of a domestic corporation described in section 956(c)(1)(B) or an obligation of a domestic corporation described in section 956(c)(1)(C) that is acquired by a controlled foreign corporation from the domestic issuing corporation. Specified United States property does not include property described in section 956(c)(2).

(iii) *Adjusted basis of specified United States property*.—Solely for purposes of applying section 956, the adjusted basis of specified United States property acquired by a controlled foreign corporation in connection with an exchange to which this paragraph (e)(6) applies shall be no less than the fair market value of any property transferred by the controlled foreign corporation in exchange for such specified United States property. For purposes of this paragraph (e)(6), the term *property* has the meaning set forth in section 317(a), but also includes any liability that is assumed by the controlled foreign corporation in connection with the exchange notwithstanding the application of section 357(a). The assumption of a liability by the controlled foreign corporation in connection with the exchange will be considered the transfer of property. The fair market value of such property will be the amount of the liability assumed. The fair market value of any property transferred by the controlled foreign corporation in exchange for the specified United States property shall be determined at the time of the exchange.

(iv) *Timing*.—For purposes of § 1.956-2(d)(1)(i)(*a*), a controlled foreign corporation that acquires specified United States property in an exchange to which this paragraph (e)(6) applies acquires an adjusted basis in such property at the time of the controlled foreign corporation's exchange of property for such specified United States property.

(v) *Transfers to related persons*.—If a controlled foreign corporation transfers specified United States property, the adjusted basis in which has been determined under this paragraph (e)(6), to a related person (within the meaning of section 954(d)(3)) (related person transferee) in one or more exchanges pursuant to which the related person transferee's adjusted basis in such specified United States property is determined, in whole or in part, by reference to the controlled foreign corporation's adjusted basis in such specified United States property, then, solely for purposes of applying section 956 following such exchange, the controlled foreign corporation's adjusted basis in any United States property received in the exchange (or exchanges) shall be no less than the aggregate adjusted basis of the specified United States property as determined under paragraph (e)(6)(iii) of this section, and the related person transferee's adjusted basis in such specified United States property shall be no less than the adjusted basis of such specified United States property in the hands of the controlled foreign corporation as determined under paragraph (e)(6)(iii) of this section. This paragraph (e)(6)(v) shall also apply in the case of one or more successive transfers of the specified United States property by a related person transferee to one or more persons related to the controlled foreign corporation (within the meaning of section 954(d)(3)). This paragraph (e)(6)(v) shall apply regardless of whether a subsequent transfer was part of a plan (or series of related transactions) that includes the controlled foreign corporation's acquisition of the specified United States property.

(vi) *Examples.*—The rules of this paragraph (e)(6) are illustrated by the following examples:

Example 1. (i) *Facts.* USP, a domestic corporation, is the common parent of an affiliated group that joins in the filing of a consolidated return. USP owns 100 percent of the stock of US1 and US2, both domestic corporations and members of the USP consolidated group. US1 owns 100 percent of the stock of CFC, a controlled foreign corporation. US2 issues $100x of its stock to CFC in exchange for $10x of CFC stock and $90x cash. US2's transfer of its stock to CFC is described in section 351, US2 recognizes no gain in the exchange under section 1032(a), and CFC's basis in the US2 stock acquired in the exchange is determined under section 362(a).

(ii) *Analysis.* The US2 stock acquired by CFC in the exchange constitutes specified United States property under paragraph (e)(6)(ii) of this section because CFC acquires the US2 stock from US2, the issuing corporation. Therefore, because CFC's adjusted basis in the US2 stock is determined under section 362(a), then for purposes of applying section 956, CFC's adjusted basis in the US2 stock shall, under paragraph (e)(6)(iii) of this section, be no less than $90x, the fair market value of the property exchanged by CFC for the US2 stock (the $10x of CFC stock issued in the exchange does not constitute property for purposes of paragraph (e)(6)(iii) of this section). Pursuant to paragraph (e)(6)(iv) of this section, for purposes of § 1.956-2(d)(1)(i)(*a*) CFC shall be treated as acquiring its adjusted basis of no less than $90x in the US2 stock at the time of its transfer of property to US2 in exchange for the US2 stock. The result would be the same if, instead of CFC transferring $90x of cash to US2 in the exchange, CFC assumes a $90x liability of US2.

Example 2. (i) *Facts.* USP, a domestic corporation, owns 100 percent of the stock of USS, a domestic corporation. USP also owns 100 percent of the stock of CFC, a controlled foreign corporation. USP's adjusted basis in its USS stock equals the fair market value of the USS stock, or $100x. USP transfers its USS stock to CFC in exchange for $100x of CFC stock. USP's transfer of its USS stock to CFC is described in section 351, USP recognizes no gain in the exchange under section 351(a), and CFC's adjusted basis in the USS stock acquired in the exchange, determined under section 362(a), equals $100x.

(ii) *Analysis.* The USS stock acquired by CFC in the exchange does not constitute specified United States property under paragraph (e)(6)(ii) of this section because CFC acquires the USS stock from USP. Therefore, CFC's adjusted basis in the USS stock, for purposes of section 956, is not determined under this paragraph (e)(6). Instead, CFC's adjusted basis in the USS stock is determined under the general rule of section 956(a) and under paragraphs (e)(1) through (4) of this section. As determined under section 362(a), CFC's adjusted basis in the USS stock is $100x.

Example 3. (i) *Facts.* USP, a domestic corporation, owns 100 percent of the stock of CFC1, a controlled foreign corporation. CFC1 holds specified United States property (within the meaning of paragraph (e)(6)(ii) of this section) with an adjusted basis of $30x for purposes of applying section 956 that was determined under paragraph (e)(6)(iii) of this section. CFC1 owns 100 percent of the stock of CFC2, a controlled foreign corporation. CFC1 transfers the specified United States property to CFC2 in an exchange described in section 351. CFC2's adjusted basis in the specified United States property is determined under section 362(a).

(ii) *Analysis.* In the section 351 exchange, CFC1 transferred specified United States property to CFC2 with an adjusted basis that was determined under paragraph (e)(6)(iii) of this section. Further, CFC2's adjusted basis in the specified United States property is determined under section 362(a) by reference, in whole or in part, to CFC1's adjusted basis in such property. Therefore, for purposes of applying section 956, pursuant to paragraph (e)(6)(v) of this section CFC2's adjusted basis in the specified United States property shall be no less than $30x. Paragraph (e)(6)(v) of this section would also apply if CFC2 subsequently transfers the specified United States property to another person related to CFC1 (within the meaning of section 954(d)(3)) if such related person's adjusted basis in the specified United States property is determined by reference, in whole or in part, to CFC2's adjusted basis in such property. See also § 1.956-1T(b)(4) if one of the principal purposes of CFC1's transfer of property to CFC2 was the avoidance of the application of section 956 with respect to CFC1.

(f) [Reserved]. For further guidance, see § 1.956-1T(f).

(g) *Applicability dates.*—(1) Paragraph (a)(1) of this section applies to taxable years of controlled foreign corporations ending on or after November 3, 2016, and to taxable years of United States shareholders in which or with which such taxable years end.

(2) Paragraph (b) of this section applies to taxable years of controlled foreign corporations ending on or after September 1, 2015, and to taxable years of United States shareholders in which or with which such taxable years end, with respect to property acquired on or after September 1, 2015. See paragraph (b)(4) of § 1.956-1T, as contained in 26 CFR part 1 revised as of April 1, 2015, for the rules applicable to taxable years of controlled foreign corporations ending before September 1, 2015, and property acquired before September 1, 2015. For purposes of this paragraph (g)(2), a deemed exchange of property pursuant to section 1001 on or after September 1, 2015 constitutes an acquisition of the property on or after that date.

(3) Paragraph (e)(2) of this section applies to taxable years of controlled foreign corporations ending on or after November 3, 2016, and taxable years of United States shareholders in which or with which such taxable years end, with respect to pledges or guarantees entered into on or after September 1, 2015. For purposes of this paragraph (g)(3), a pledgor or guarantor is treated as entering into a pledge or guarantee when there is a significant modification, within the meaning of § 1.1001-3(e), of an obligation with respect to which it is a pledgor or guarantor on or after September 1, 2015.

(4) Paragraphs (a)(2) and (3) of this section apply to taxable years of controlled foreign corporations beginning on or after July 22, 2019, and to taxable years of a United States shareholder in which or with which such taxable years of the controlled foreign corporations end. Notwithstanding the preceding sentence, a United States shareholder may apply paragraphs (a)(2) and (3) of this section to taxable years of controlled foreign corporations beginning after December 31, 2017, and to taxable years of the United States shareholder in which or with which such taxable years of the controlled foreign corporations end, provided that the United States shareholder and United States persons that are related (within the meaning of section 267 or 707) to the United States shareholder consistently apply those paragraphs with respect to all controlled foreign corporations in which they are United States shareholders for taxable years of the controlled foreign corporations beginning after December 31, 2017. For taxable years of controlled foreign corporations beginning before January 25, 2022, and taxable years of United States shareholders in which or with which such taxable years of foreign corporations end, see § 1.956-1(a)(2)(i) and (iii) and (a)(3)(iv) as in effect and contained in 26 CFR part 1, as revised April 1, 2021.

(5) Paragraph (e)(6) of this section applies to property acquired in exchanges occurring on or after June 24, 2011. [Reg. § 1.956-1.]

□ [*T.D. 6704, 2-19-64. Amended by T.D. 6795, 1-28-65, T.D. 7712, 8-6-80; T.D. 8209, 6-13-88; T.D. 9402, 6-23-2008, T.D. 9530, 6-23-2011, T.D. 9733, 9-1-2015 (corrected 10-28-2015), T.D. 9792, 11-2-2016, T.D. 9859, 5-22-2019 (corrected 6-24-2019) and T.D. 9960, 1-24-2022.*]

§ 1.956-1T. Shareholder's pro rata share of a controlled foreign corporation's increase in earnings invested in United States property (temporary).—(a) through (e)(4) [Reserved]

(5) *Exclusion for certain recourse obligations.*—For purposes of § 1.956-1(e)(1) of the regulations, in the case of an investment in United States property consisting of an obligation of a related person, as defined in section 954(d)(3) and paragraph (e) of § 1.954-1, a liability will not be recognized as a specific charge if the liability representing the charge is with recourse with respect to the general credit or other assets of the investing controlled foreign corporation.

(6) [Reserved]. For further guidance, see § 1.956-1(e)(6).

(f) *Effective/applicability date.*—Paragraph (e)(5) of this section applies to investments made on or after June 14, 1988.

(g) - (h) [Reserved]. [Temporary Reg. § 1.956-1T.]

□ [*T.D. 8209, 6-13-88. Amended by T.D. 9402, 6-23-2008, T.D. 9530, 6-23-2011, T.D. 9733 9-1-2015 (corrected 10-28-2015) and T.D. 9792, 11-2-2016 (corrected 12-27-2016).*]

§ 1.956-2. Definition of United States property.—(a) *Included property.*—(1) *In general.*—For purposes of section 956(a) and

§ 1.956-1, United States property is (except as provided in paragraph (b) of this section) any property acquired (within the meaning of paragraph (d)(1) of this section) by a foreign corporation (whether or not a controlled foreign corporation at the time) during any taxable year of such foreign corporation beginning after December 31, 1962, which is—

(i) Tangible property (real or personal) located in the United States;

(ii) Stock of a domestic corporation;

(iii) An obligation (as defined in paragraph (d)(2) of this section) of a United States person (as defined in section 957(d)), or

(iv) Any right to the use in the United States of—

(a) A patent or copyright,

(b) An invention, model, or design (whether or not patented),

(c) A secret formula or process, or

(d) Any other similar property right,

which is acquired or developed by the foreign corporation for use in the United States by any person. Whether a right described in this subdivision has been acquired or developed for use in the United States by any person is to be determined from all the facts and circumstances of each case. As a general rule, a right actually used principally in the United States will be considered to have been acquired or developed for use in the United States in the absence of affirmative evidence showing that the right was not so acquired or developed for such use.

(2) *Illustrations.*—The application of the provisions of this paragraph may be illustrated by the following examples:

Example (1). Foreign corporation R uses as a taxable year a fiscal year ending on June 30. Corporation R acquires on June 1, 1963, and holds on June 30, 1963, $100,000 of tangible property (not described in section 956(b)(2)) located in the United States. Corporation R's aggregate investment in United States property at the close of its taxable year ending June 30, 1963, is zero since the property which is acquired on June 1, 1963, is not acquired during a taxable year of R Corporation beginning after December 31, 1962. Assuming no change in R Corporation's aggregate investment in United States property during its taxable year ending June 30, 1964, R Corporation's increase in earnings invested in United States property for such taxable year is zero.

Example (2). Foreign corporation S uses the calendar year as a taxable year and is a controlled foreign corporation for its entire taxable year 1965. Corporation S is not a controlled foreign corporation at any time during its taxable years 1963 and 1964. Corporation S owns on December 31, 1964, $100,000 of tangible property (not described in section 956(b)(2)) located in the United States which it acquires during taxable years beginning after December 31, 1962. Corporation S's aggregate investment in United States property on December 31, 1964, is $100,000. Corporation S's current and accumulated earnings and profits (determined as provided in paragraph (b) of § 1.956-1) as of December 31, 1964, are in excess of $100,000. Assuming no change in S Corporation's aggregate investment in United States property during its taxable year 1965, S Corporation's increase in earnings invested in United States property for such taxable year is zero.

Example (3). Foreign corporation T uses the calendar year as a taxable year and is a controlled foreign corporation for its entire taxable years 1963, 1964, and 1966. At December 31, 1964, T Corporation's investment in United States property is $100,000. Corporation T is not a controlled foreign corporation at any time during its taxable year 1965 in which it acquires $25,000 of tangible property (not described in section 956 (b)(2)) located in the United States. On December 31, 1965, T Corporation holds the United States property of $100,000 which it held on December 31, 1964, and, in addition, the United States property acquired in 1965. Corporation T's aggregate investment in United States property at December 31, 1965, is $125,000. Corporation T's current and accumulated earnings and profits (determined as provided in paragraph (b) of § 1.956-1) as of December 31, 1965, are in excess of $125,000, and T Corporation pays no amount during 1965 to which section 959(c)(1) applies. Assuming no change in T Corporation's aggregate investment in United States property during its taxable year 1966, T Corporation's increase in earnings invested in United States property for such taxable year is zero.

(3) *Treatment of disregarded entities.*—For purposes of section 956, an obligation of a business entity (as defined in § 301.7701-2(a) of this chapter) that is disregarded as an entity separate from its owner for federal tax purposes under §§ 301.7701-1 through 301.7701-3 of this chapter is treated as an obligation of its owner.

(4) *Certain foreign stock and obligations held by expatriated foreign subsidiaries following an inversion transaction.*—(i) *General rule.*—Except as provided in paragraph (a)(4)(ii) of this section, for purposes of section 956 and paragraph (a) of this section, United States property includes an obligation of a foreign person and stock of a foreign corporation when the following conditions are satisfied—

(A) The obligation or stock is held by a controlled foreign corporation that is an expatriated foreign subsidiary, regardless of whether, when the obligation or stock was acquired, the acquirer was a controlled foreign corporation or an expatriated foreign subsidiary;

(B) The foreign person or foreign corporation is a non-EFS foreign related person, regardless of whether, when the obligation or stock was acquired, the foreign person or foreign corporation was a non-EFS foreign related person; and

(C) The obligation or stock was acquired—

(1) During the applicable period; or

(2) In a transaction related to the inversion transaction.

(ii) *Exceptions.*—For purposes of section 956 and paragraph (a) of this section, United States property does not include—

(A) Any obligation of a non-EFS foreign related person arising in connection with the sale or processing of property if the amount of the obligation at no time during the taxable year exceeds the amount that would be ordinary and necessary to carry on the trade or business of both the other party to the sale or processing transaction and the non-EFS foreign related person had the sale or processing transaction been made between unrelated persons; and

(B) Any obligation of a non-EFS foreign related person to the extent the principal amount of the obligation does not exceed the fair market value of readily marketable securities sold or purchased pursuant to a sale and repurchase agreement or otherwise posted or received as collateral for the obligation in the ordinary course of its business by a United States or foreign person which is a dealer in securities or commodities.

(iii) *Definitions.*—The definitions in § 1.7874-12 apply for the purposes of the application of paragraphs (a)(4), (c)(5), and (d)(2) of this section.

(iv) *Examples.*—The following examples illustrate the rules of this paragraph (a)(4). For purposes of the examples, FA, a foreign corporation, wholly owns DT, a domestic corporation, which, in turn, wholly owns FT, a foreign corporation that is a controlled foreign corporation. FA also wholly owns FS, a foreign corporation that is a controlled foreign corporation for its taxable year beginning January 1, 2017, but not for prior taxable years except as a result of a transaction described in the facts of an example. All entities have a calendar year tax year for U.S. tax purposes. FA acquired DT in an inversion transaction that was completed on January 1, 2015.

Example 1. (A) *Facts.* FT acquired an obligation of FS on January 31, 2015.

(B) *Analysis.* Pursuant to § 1.7874-12, DT is a domestic entity, FT is an expatriated foreign subsidiary, and FS is a non-EFS foreign related person. In addition, FT acquired the FS obligation during the applicable period. Thus, as of January 31, 2015, the obligation of FS is United States property with respect to FT for purposes of section 956(a) and this paragraph (a).

Example 2. (A) *Facts.* The facts are the same as in *Example 1* of this paragraph (a)(4)(iv), except that on February 15, 2015, FT contributed assets to FS in exchange for 60% of the stock of FS, by vote and value.

(B) *Analysis.* As a result of the transaction on February 15, 2015, FS became a controlled foreign corporation with respect to which an expatriated entity, DT, is a United States shareholder. Accordingly, under § 1.7874-12(a)(9), FS is an expatriated foreign subsidiary, and is therefore not a non-EFS foreign related person. Thus, as of February 15, 2015, the stock and obligation of FS are not United States property with respect to FT for purposes of section 956(a) and this paragraph (a). FS is not excluded from the definition of expatriated foreign subsidiary pursuant to § 1.7874-12(a)(9)(ii) because FS was not a CFC on the completion date.

Example 3. (A) *Facts.* Before the inversion transaction, FA also wholly owns USP, a domestic corporation, which, in turn, wholly owns, LFS, a foreign corporation that is a controlled foreign corporation. DT was not a United States shareholder of LFS on or before the completion date. On January 31, 2015, FT contributed assets to LFS in exchange for 60% of the stock of LFS, by vote and value. FT acquired an obligation of LFS on February 15, 2015.

(B) *Analysis.* LFS is a foreign related person. Because LFS was a controlled foreign corporation and a member of the EAG with respect to the inversion transaction on the completion date, and DT was not a United States shareholder with respect to LFS on or before the completion date, LFS is excluded from the definition of expatriated foreign subsidiary pursuant to § 1.7874-12(a)(9)(ii). Thus, pursuant to § 1.7874-12(a)(16), LFS is a non-EFS foreign related person, and the stock and obligation of LFS are United States property with respect to FT for purposes of section 956(a) and this paragraph (a). The fact that FT contributed assets to LFS in exchange for 60% of the stock of LFS does not change this result.

Example 4. (A) *Facts*. The facts are the same as in *Example 3* of this paragraph (a)(4)(iv), except that on February 10, 2015, LFS organized a new foreign corporation (LFSS), transferred all of its assets to LFSS, and liquidated, in a transaction treated as a reorganization described in section 368(a)(1)(F), and FT acquired an obligation of LFSS, instead of LFS, on February 15, 2015. On March 1, 2015, LFSS acquired an obligation of FS.

(B) *Analysis*. LFS is a controlled foreign corporation with respect to which USP, an expatriated entity, is a United States shareholder. USP is an expatriated entity because on the completion date, USP and DT became related to each other within the meaning of section 267(b). Because LFSS was not a member of the EAG with respect to the inversion transaction on the completion date, LFSS is not excluded from the definition of expatriated foreign subsidiary pursuant to § 1.7874-12(a)(9)(ii). Accordingly, under § 1.7874-12(a)(9)(i), LFFS is an expatriated foreign subsidiary and is therefore not a non-EFS foreign related person. Thus, the stock and obligation of LFSS are not United States property with respect to FT for purposes of section 956(a) and paragraph (a) of this section. However, because LFSS is an expatriated foreign subsidiary, pursuant to § 1.7874-12(a)(9), the obligation of FS, a non-EFS foreign related person, is United States property with respect to LFSS for purposes of section 956(a) and this paragraph (a).

(b) *Exceptions*.—(1) *Excluded property*.—For purposes of section 956(a) and paragraph (a) of this section, United States property does not include the following types of property held by a foreign corporation:

(i) Obligations of the United States.

(ii) Money.

(iii) Deposits with persons carrying on the banking business, unless the deposits serve directly or indirectly as a pledge or guarantee within the meaning of paragraph (c) of this section. See paragraph (e)(2) of § 1.956-1.

(iv) Property located in the United States which is purchased in the United States for export to, or use in, foreign countries. For purposes of this subdivision, property to be used outside the United States will be considered property to be used in a foreign country. Whether property is of a type described in this subdivision is to be determined from all the facts and circumstances in each case. Property which constitutes export trade assets within the meaning of section 971(c)(2) and paragraph (c)(3) if § 1.971-1, will be considered property of a type described in this subdivision.

(v) Any obligation (as defined in paragraph (d)(2) of this section) of a United States person (as defined in section 957(d)) arising in connection with the sale or processing of property if the amount of such obligation outstanding at any time during the taxable year of the foreign corporation does not exceed an amount which is ordinary and necessary to carry on trade or business of both the other party to the sale or processing transaction and the United States person, or, if the sale or processing transaction occurs between related persons, would be ordinary and necessary to carry on the trade or business of both the other party to the sale or processing transaction and the United States person if such persons were unrelated persons. Whether the amount of an obligation described in this subdivision is ordinary and necessary is to be determined from all the facts and circumstances in each case.

(vi) Any aircraft, railroad rolling stock, vessel, motor vehicle, or container used in the transportation of persons or property in foreign commerce and used predominantly outside the United States. Whether transportation property described in this paragraph (b)(1)(vi) is used in foreign commerce and predominantly outside the United States is to be determined from all the facts and circumstances of each case. As a general rule, such transportation property will be considered to be used predominantly outside the United States if 70 percent or more of the miles traversed (during the taxable year at the close of which a determination is made under section 956(a)(2)) in the use of such property are traversed outside the United States or if such property is located outside the United States 70 percent of the time during such taxable year. Notwithstanding the above, an aircraft or vessel, including component parts, is excluded from United States property if the aircraft or vessel is leased in foreign commerce (as the term is defined in § 1.954-2(c)(2)(v) and rents derived from leasing such aircraft or vessel are excluded from foreign personal holding company income under section 954(c)(2)(A).

(vii) An amount of assets described in paragraph (a) of this section of an insurance company equivalent to the unearned premiums or reserves which are ordinary and necessary for the proper conduct of that part of its insurance business which is attributable to contracts other than those described in section 953(a)(1) and the regulations thereunder. For purposes of this subdivision, a reserve will be considered ordinary and necessary for the proper conduct of an insurance business if, under the principles of paragraph (c) of § 1.953-4, such reserve would qualify as a reserve required by law. See paragraph (d)(3) of § 1.954-2 for determining, for purposes of this subdivision, the meaning of insurance company and of unearned premiums.

(viii) For taxable years beginning after December 31, 1975, the voting or nonvoting stock or obligations of an unrelated domestic corporation. For purposes of this subdivision, an unrelated domestic corporation is a domestic corporation which is neither a United States shareholder (as defined in section 951(b)) of the controlled foreign corporation making the investment, nor a corporation 25 percent or more of whose total combined voting power of all classes of stock entitled to vote is owned or considered as owned (within the meaning of section 958(b)) by United States shareholders of the controlled foreign corporation making the investment. The determination of whether a domestic corporation is an unrelated corporation is made immediately after each acquisition of stock or obligations by the controlled foreign corporations.

(ix) For taxable years beginning after December 31, 1975, movable drilling rigs or barges and other movable exploration and exploitation equipment (other than a vessel or an aircraft) when used on the Continental Shelf (as defined in section 638) of the United States in the exploration for, development, removal, or transportation of natural resources from or under ocean waters. Property used on the Continental Shelf includes property located in the United States which is being constructed or is in storage or in transit within the United States for use on the Continental Shelf. In general, the type of property which qualifies for the exception under this subdivision includes any movable property which would be entitled to the investment credit if used outside the United States in certain geographical areas of the Western Hemisphere pursuant to section 48(a)(2)(B)(x) (without reference to sections 49 and 50).

(x) An amount of—

(a) A controlled foreign corporation's assets described in paragraph (a) of this section equivalent to its earnings and profits which are accumulated after December 31, 1962, and are attributable to items of income described in section 952(b) and the regulations thereunder, reduced by the amount of

(b) The earnings and profits of such corporation which are applied in a taxable year of such corporation beginning after December 31, 1962, to discharge a liability on property, but only if the liability was in existence at the close of such corporation's taxable year immediately preceding its first taxable year beginning after December 31, 1962, and the property would have been United States property if it had been acquired by such corporation immediately before such discharge.

For purposes of this subdivision, distributions made by such corporation for any taxable year shall be considered first made out of earnings and profits for such year other than earnings and profits referred to in *(a)* of this subdivision.

(xi) [Reserved]. For further guidance, see § 1.956-2T(b)(1)(xi).

(2) *Statement required*.—If a United States shareholder of a controlled foreign corporation excludes any property from the United States property of such controlled foreign corporation on the ground that section 956(b)(2) applies to such excluded property, he shall attach to his return a statement setting forth, by categories described in paragraph (a)(1) of this section, the amount of United States property of the controlled foreign corporation and, by categories described in subparagraph (1) of this paragraph, the amount of such property which is excluded.

(c) *Treatment of pledges and guarantees*.—(1) *General rule*.—Except as provided in paragraph (c)(4) of this section, for purposes of section 956, any obligation of a United States person with respect to which a controlled foreign corporation or a partnership is a pledgor or guarantor will be considered to be held by the controlled foreign corporation or the partnership, as the case may be. See § 1.956-1(e)(2) for rules that determine the amount of the obligation treated as held by a pledgor or guarantor under this paragraph (c). For rules that treat an obligation of a foreign partnership as an obligation of the partners in the foreign partnership for purposes of section 956, see § 1.956-4(c).

(2) *Indirect pledge or guarantee.*—If the assets of a controlled foreign corporation or a partnership serve at any time, even though indirectly, as security for the performance of an obligation of a United States person, then, for purposes of paragraph (c)(1) of this section, the controlled foreign corporation or partnership will be considered a pledgor or guarantor of that obligation. If a partnership is considered a pledgor or guarantor of an obligation, a controlled foreign corporation that is a partner in the partnership will not also be treated as a pledgor or guarantor of the obligation solely as a result of its ownership of an interest in the partnership. For purposes of this paragraph, a pledge of stock of a controlled foreign corporation representing at least 66 2/3 percent of the total combined voting power of all classes of voting stock of such corporation will be considered an indirect pledge of the assets of the controlled foreign corporation if the pledge is accompanied by one or more negative covenants or similar restrictions on the shareholder effectively limiting the corporation's discretion to dispose of assets and/or incur liabilities other than in the ordinary course of business. See § 1.956-4(d) for guidance on the treatment of indirect pledges or guarantees of an obligation of a partnership attributed to its partners under § 1.956-4(c).

(3) *Illustrations.*—The following examples illustrate the application of this paragraph (c):

Example (1). A, a United States person, borrows $100,000 from a bank in foreign country X on December 31, 1964. On the same date controlled foreign corporation R pledges its assets as security for A's performance of A's obligation to repay such loan. The place at which or manner in which A uses the money is not material. For purposes of paragraph (b) of § 1.956-1, R Corporation will be considered to hold A's obligation to repay the bank $100,000, and, under the provisions of paragraph (e)(2) of § 1.956-1, the amount taken into account in computing R Corporation's aggregate investment in United States property on December 31, 1964, is the unpaid principal amount of the obligation on that date ($100,000).

Example (2). The facts are the same as in example (1), except that R Corporation participates in the transaction, not by pledging its assets as security for A's performance of A's obligation to repay the loan, but by agreeing to buy for $100,000 at maturity the note representing A's obligation if A does not repay the loan. Separate arrangements are made with respect to the payment of the interest on the loan. The agreement of R Corporation to buy the note constitutes a guarantee of A's obligation. For purposes of paragraph (b) of § 1.956-1, R Corporation will be considered to hold A's obligation to repay the bank $100,000, and, under the provisions of paragraph (e)(2) of § 1.956-1, the amount taken into account in computing R Corporation's aggregate investment in United States property on December 31, 1964, is the unpaid principal amount of the obligation on that date ($100,000).

Example (3). A, a United States person, borrows $100,000 from a bank on December 10, 1981, pledging 70 percent of the stock of X, a controlled foreign corporation, as collateral for the loan. A and X use the calendar year as their taxable year. In the loan agreement, among other things, A agrees not to cause or permit X Corporation to do any of the following without the consent of the bank:

(a) Borrow money or pledge assets, except as to borrowings in the ordinary course of business of X Corporation;

(b) Guarantee, assume, or become liable on the obligation of another, or invest in or lend funds to another;

(c) Merge or consolidate with any other corporation or transfer shares of any controlled subsidiary;

(d) Sell or lease (other than in the ordinary course of business) or otherwise dispose of any substantial part of its assets;

(e) Pay or secure any debt owing by X Corporation to A; and

(f) Pay any dividends, except in such amounts as may be required to make interest or principal payments on A's loan from the bank.

A retains the right to vote the stock unless a default occurs by A. Under paragraph (c)(2) of this section, the assets of X Corporation serve indirectly as security for A's performance of A's obligation to repay the loan and X Corporation will be considered a pledgor or guarantor with respect to that obligation. For purposes of paragraph (b) of § 1.956-1, X Corporation will be considered to hold A's obligation to repay the bank $100,000 and under paragraph (e)(2) of § 1.956-1, the amount taken into account in computing X Corporation's aggregate investment in United States property on December 31, 1981, is the unpaid principal amount of the obligation on that date.

Example 4. (i) *Facts.* USP, a domestic corporation, owns 70% of the stock of FS, a controlled foreign corporation, and a 90% interest in FPRS, a foreign partnership. X, an unrelated foreign person, owns 30% of the stock of FS. Y, an unrelated foreign person, owns a 10% interest in FPRS. There are no special allocations in the FPRS partnership agreement. FPRS borrows $100x from Z, an unrelated person. FS pledges its assets as security for FPRS's performance of its obligation to repay the $100x loan. USP's share of the $100x FPRS obligation, determined in accordance with its liquidation value percentage, is $90x. Under § 1.956-4(c), $90x of the FPRS obligation is treated as an obligation of USP for purposes of section 956.

(ii) *Result.* For purposes of section 956, under paragraph (c)(1) of this section, FS is considered to hold an obligation of USP in the amount of $90x, and thus is treated as holding United States property in the amount of $90x.

(4) *Special rule for certain conduit financing arrangements.*—The rule contained in subparagraph (1) of this paragraph shall not apply to a pledge or a guarantee by a controlled foreign corporation to secure the obligation of a United States person if such United States person is a mere conduit in a financing arrangement. Whether the United States person is a mere conduit in a financing arrangement will depend upon all the facts and circumstances in each case. A United States person will be considered a mere conduit in a financing arrangement in a case in which a controlled foreign corporation pledges stock of its subsidiary corporation, which is also a controlled foreign corporation, to secure the obligation of such United States person, where the following conditions are satisfied:

(i) Such United States person is a domestic corporation which is not engaged in the active conduct of a trade or business and has no substantial assets other than those arising out of its relending of the funds borrowed by it on such obligation to the controlled foreign corporation whose stock is pledged; and

(ii) The assets of such United States person are at all times substantially offset by its obligation to the lender.

(5) *Special guarantee and pledge rule for expatriated foreign subsidiaries.*—(i) *General rule.*—In applying paragraphs (c)(1) and (2) of this section to a controlled foreign corporation that is an expatriated foreign subsidiary, the phrase "of a United States person or a non-EFS foreign related person" is substituted for the phrase "of a United States person" each place it appears.

(ii) *Additional rules.*—The rule in paragraph (c)(5)(i) of this section—

(A) Applies regardless of whether, when the pledge or guarantee was entered into or treated as entered into, the controlled foreign corporation was a controlled foreign corporation or an expatriated foreign subsidiary, or a foreign person whose obligation is subject to the pledge or guarantee, or deemed pledge or guarantee, was a non-EFS foreign related person; and

(B) Applies to pledges or guarantees entered into, or treated pursuant to paragraph (c)(2) of this section as entered into—

(1) During the applicable period; or

(2) In a transaction related to the inversion transaction.

(d) *Definitions.*—(1) *Meaning of "acquired".*—(i) *Applicable rules.*—For purposes of this section—

(a) Property shall be considered acquired by a foreign corporation when such corporation acquires an adjusted basis in the property;

(b) Property which is an obligation of a United States person with respect to which a controlled foreign corporation is a pledgor or guarantor (within the meaning of paragraph (c) of this section) shall be considered acquired when the corporation becomes liable as a pledgor or guarantor or is otherwise considered a pledgor or guarantor (within the meaning of paragraph (c)(2) of this section); and

(c) Property shall not be considered acquired by a foreign corporation if—

(1) Such property is acquired in a transaction in which gain or loss would not be recognized under this chapter to such corporation if such corporation were a domestic corporation;

(2) The basis of the property acquired by the foreign corporation is the same as the basis of the property exchanged by such corporation; and

(3) The property exchanged by the foreign corporation was not United States property (as defined in paragraph (a)(1) of this section) but would have been such property if it had been acquired by such corporation immediately before such exchange.

(ii) *Illustrations.*—The application of the provisions of this subparagraph may be illustrated by the following examples:

Example (1). Foreign corporation R uses the calendar year as a taxable year and acquires before January 1, 1963, stock of domestic corporation M having as to R Corporation an adjusted basis of $10,000. The stock of M Corporation is not United States property of R Corporation on December 31, 1962, since it is not acquired in a taxable year of R Corporation beginning on or after January 1, 1963. On June 30, 1963, R Corporation sells the M Corporation stock for $15,000 in cash and expends such amount in acquiring stock of domestic corporation N which has as to R Corporation an adjusted basis of $15,000. For purposes of determining R Corporation's aggregate investment in United States property on December 31, 1963, R Corporation has, by virtue of acquiring the stock of N Corporation, acquired $15,000 of United States property.

Example (2). Foreign corporation S, a controlled foreign corporation for the entire period here involved, uses the calendar year as a taxable year and purchases for $100,000 on December 31, 1963, tangible property (not described in section 956(b)(2)) located in the United States and having a remaining estimated useful life of 10 years, subject to a mortgage of $80,000 payable in 5 annual installments. The property constitutes United States property as of December 31, 1963, and the amount taken into account for purposes of determining the aggregate amount of S Corporation's investment in United States property under paragraph (b) of § 1.956-1 is $20,000. No depreciation is sustained with respect to the property during the taxable year 1963. During the taxable year 1964, S Corporation pays $16,000 on the mortgage and sustains $10,000 of depreciation with respect to the property. As of December 31, 1964, the amount taken into account with respect to the property for purposes of determining the aggregate amount of S Corporation's investment in United States property under paragraph (b) of § 1.956-1 is $26,000, computed as follows:

Cost of property		$100,000
Less: Reserve for depreciation		10,000
Adjusted basis of property		90,000
Less: Liability to which property is subject:		
Gross amount of mortgage	$80,000	
Payment during 1964	16,000	$64,000
Amount taken into account (12/31/64)		$26,000

Example (3). Controlled foreign corporation T uses the calendar year as a taxable year and acquires on December 31, 1963, $10,000 of United States property not described in section 956(b)(2); no depreciation is sustained with respect to the property during 1963. Corporation T's current and accumulated earnings and profits (determined as provided in paragraph (b) of § 1.956-1) as of December 31, 1963, are in excess of $10,000, and T Corporation's United States shareholders include in their gross income under section 951(a)(1)(B) their pro rata share of T Corporation's increase ($10,000) for 1963 in earnings invested in United States property. On January 1, 1964, T Corporation acquires an additional $10,000 of United States property not described in section 956(b)(2). Each of the two items of property has an estimated useful life of 5 years, and T Corporation sustains $4,000 of depreciation with respect to such properties during its taxable year 1964. Corporation T's current and accumulated earnings and profits as of December 31, 1964, exceed $16,000, determined as provided in paragraph (b) of § 1.956-1. Corporation T pays no amounts during 1963 to which section 959(c)(1) applies. Corporation T's investment of earnings in United States property at December 31, 1964, is $16,000, and its increase for 1964 in earnings invested in United States property is $6,000.

Example (4). Foreign corporation U uses the calendar year as a taxable year and acquires before January 1, 1963, stock in domestic corporation M having as to U Corporation an adjusted basis of $10,000. On December 1, 1964, pursuant to a statutory merger described in section 368(a)(1), M Corporation merges into domestic corporation N, and U Corporation receives on such date one share of stock in N Corporation, the surviving corporation, for each share of stock it held in M Corporation. Pursuant to section 354 no gain or loss is recognized to U Corporation, and pursuant to section 358 the basis of the property received (stock of N Corporation) is the same as that of the property exchanged (stock of M Corporation). Corporation U is not considered for purposes of section 956 to have acquired United States property by reason of its receipt of the stock in N Corporation.

Example (5). The facts are the same as in example (4), except that U Corporation acquires the stock of M Corporation on February 1, 1963, rather than before January 1, 1963. For purposes of determining U Corporation's aggregate investment in United States property on December 31, 1963, U Corporation has, by virtue of acquiring the stock of M Corporation, acquired $10,000 of United States property. Corporation U pays no amount during 1963 to which section 959(c)(1) applies. The reorganization and resulting acquisition on December 1, 1964, by U Corporation of N Corporation's stock also represents an acquisition of United States property; however, assuming no other change in U Corporation's aggregate investment in United States property during 1964, U Corporation's increase for such year in earnings invested in United States property is zero.

(2) *Obligation defined.*—For purposes of section 956 and this section, the term "obligation" includes any bond, note, debenture, certificate, bill receivable, account receivable, note receivable, open account, or other indebtedness, whether or not issued at a discount and whether or not bearing interest, except that the term does not include—

(i) Any indebtedness arising out of the involuntary conversion of property which is not United States property within the meaning of paragraph (a) of this section;

(ii) Any obligation of a United States person (as defined in section 957(c)) arising in connection with the provision of services by a controlled foreign corporation to the United States person if the amount of the obligation outstanding at any time during the taxable year of the controlled foreign corporation does not exceed an amount which would be ordinary and necessary to carry on the trade or business of the controlled foreign corporation and the United States person if they were unrelated. The amount of the obligations shall be considered to be ordinary and necessary to the extent of such receivables that are paid within 60 days;

(iii) Any obligation of a non-EFS foreign related person arising in connection with the provision of services by an expatriated foreign subsidiary to the non-EFS foreign related person if the amount of the obligation outstanding at any time during the taxable year of the expatriated foreign subsidiary does not exceed an amount which would be ordinary and necessary to carry on the trade or business of the expatriated foreign subsidiary and the non-EFS foreign related person if they were unrelated. The amount of the obligations shall be considered to be ordinary and necessary to the extent of such receivables that are paid within 60 days; or

(iv) Any obligation of a United States person (as defined in section 957(c)) that is collected within 30 days from the time it is incurred (a *30-day obligation*), unless the controlled foreign corporation that holds the 30-day obligation holds for 60 or more calendar days during the taxable year in which it holds the 30-day obligation any obligations which, without regard to the exclusion described in this paragraph (d)(2)(iv), would constitute United States property within the meaning of section 956 and paragraph (a) of this section.

(e) *Effective/applicability date.*—The last sentence of paragraph (b)(1)(vi) of this section applies to taxable years of controlled foreign corporations beginning on or after May 2, 2006, and for taxable years of United States shareholders with or within which such taxable years of the controlled foreign corporations end. Taxpayers may elect to apply the rule of the last sentence of paragraph (b)(1)(vi) of this section to taxable years of controlled foreign corporations beginning after December 31, 2004, and for taxable years of United States shareholders with or within which such taxable years of the controlled foreign corporations end. If an election is made to apply the last two sentences of § 1.954-2(c)(2)(ii) and § 1.954-2(c)(2)(v) through (vii) to taxable years of a controlled foreign corporation beginning after December 31, 2004, then the election must also be made for the last sentence of paragraph (b)(1)(vi) of this section.

(f) [Reserved]. For further guidance, see § 1.956-2T(f).

(g) [Reserved]

(h) *Effective/applicability date.*—(1) Paragraph (a)(3) of this section applies to taxable years of controlled foreign corporations ending on or after November 3, 2016, and taxable years of United States shareholders in which or with which such taxable years end, with respect to obligations held on or after November 3, 2016.

(2) Paragraphs (c)(1), (c)(2), and *Example 4* of paragraph (c)(3) of this section apply to taxable years of controlled foreign corporations ending on or after November 3, 2016, and taxable years of United States shareholders in which or with which such taxable years end, with respect to pledges and guarantees entered into on or after September 1, 2015. For purposes of this paragraph (h)(2), a pledgor or guarantor is treated as entering into a pledge or guarantee when there is a significant modification, within the meaning of § 1.1001-3(e), of an obligation with respect to which it is a pledgor or guarantor on or after September 1, 2015.

(3) Except as otherwise provided in this paragraph (h)(3), paragraphs (a)(4) and (c)(5) of this section apply to obligations or stock acquired or to pledges or guarantees entered into, or treated as entered into, on or after September 22, 2014, but only if the inversion transaction was completed on or after September 22, 2014. The phrase ", regardless of whether, when the obligation or stock was acquired, the acquirer was a controlled foreign corporation or an expatriated foreign subsidiary" in paragraph (a)(4)(i)(A) of this section, the phrase "regardless of whether, when the obligation or stock was acquired, the foreign person or foreign corporation was a non-EFS foreign related person" in paragraph (a)(4)(i)(B) of this section, and paragraphs (a)(4)(i)(C)(2), (c)(5)(ii)(A), and (c)(5)(ii)(B)(2) of this section apply to obligations or stock acquired or pledges or guarantees entered into or treated as entered into on or after April 4, 2016, but only if the inversion transaction was completed on or after September 22, 2014. Paragraph (a)(4)(ii) of this section applies to obligations acquired on or after April 4, 2016. For inversion transactions completed on or after September 22, 2014, however, taxpayers may elect to apply paragraph (a)(4)(ii) of this section to an obligation acquired before April 4, 2016. For purposes of paragraph (a)(4)(i) of this section and this paragraph (h)(3), a deemed exchange of an obligation or stock pursuant to section 1001 constitutes an acquisition of the obligation or stock. For purposes of paragraph (c)(5) of this section and this paragraph (h)(3), a pledgor or guarantor or deemed pledgor or guarantor is treated as entering into a pledge or guarantee when there is a significant modification, within the meaning of § 1.1001-3(e), of an obligation with respect to which it is a pledgor or guarantor or is treated as a pledgor or guarantor.

(4) Paragraphs (d)(2)(i) and (ii) of this section are effective June 14, 1988, with respect to investments made on or after June 14, 1988.

(5) Paragraph (d)(2)(iii) of this section applies to obligations acquired on or after April 4, 2016, but only if the inversion transaction was completed on or after September 22, 2014. For inversion transactions completed on or after September 22, 2014, however, taxpayers may elect to apply paragraph (d)(2)(iii) of this section to an obligation acquired on or after September 22, 2014, and before April 4, 2016. For purposes of paragraph (d)(2)(iii) of this section and this paragraph (h)(5), a significant modification, within the meaning of § 1.1001-3(e), of an obligation on or after April 4, 2016, constitutes an acquisition of an obligation on or after April 4, 2016.

(6) Paragraph (d)(2)(iv) of this section applies to obligations held on or after September 16, 1988. See § 1.956-2T(d)(2)(v), as contained in 26 CFR part 1 revised as of April 1, 2017, for additional rules applicable to certain taxable years of a foreign corporation beginning before January 1, 2011. [Reg. § 1.956-2.]

☐ [*T.D. 6704, 2-19-64. Amended by T.D. 7712, 8-6-80, T.D. 7797, 11-24-81; T.D. 8209, 6-13-88; T.D. 9008, 7-22-2002; T.D. 9406, 7-2-2008; T.D. 9525, 5-5-2011; T.D. 9589, 5-10-2012; T.D. 9761, 4-4-2016; T.D. 9792, 11-2-2016 and T.D. 9834, 7-11-2018.*]

§ 1.956-2T. Definition of United States property (temporary).—(a)(1) through (3) [Reserved]. For further guidance, see § 1.956-2(a)(1) through (3).

(4) [Reserved.]

(b)(1) through (b)(1)(x) [Reserved]. For further guidance, see § 1.956-2(b)(1) through (b)(1)(x).

(xi) An obligation of a United States person arising from a nonperiodic payment by a controlled foreign corporation (within the meaning of section 957(a)) with respect to a notional principal contract described in § 1.446-3T(g)(4)(ii)(B)(1) or (2) if the following conditions are satisfied—

(A) The controlled foreign corporation that makes the nonperiodic payment is either a dealer in securities (within the meaning of section 475(c)(1)) or a dealer in commodities; and

(B) The conditions set forth in § 1.446-3T(g)(4)(ii)(C)(1) (relating to full margin or collateral in cash) are satisfied.

(C) *Examples*.—The following examples illustrate the application of this paragraph (b)(1)(xi):

Example 1. Full margin – cleared contract. (i) A domestic corporation (USC) wholly owns a controlled foreign corporation (CFC) that is a dealer in securities under section 475(c)(1). CFC enters into an interest rate swap contract with unrelated counterparty B. The contract is required to be cleared and is accepted for clearing by a U.S.-registered derivatives clearing organization (DCO). CFC is not a member of the DCO. CFC uses a U.S. affiliate (CM), which is a member of the DCO, as its clearing member to submit the contract to be cleared. CM is a domestic corporation that is wholly owned by USC. The standardized terms of the contract provide that, for a term of X years, CFC will pay B a fixed coupon of 1% per year and receive a floating coupon on a notional principal amount of $Y. When CFC and B enter into the contract, the market coupon for similar interest rate swaps is 2% per year. The DCO requires CFC to make an upfront payment to compensate B for the below-market annual coupon payments that B will receive, and CFC makes the upfront payment in cash. CFC makes the upfront payment through CM to the DCO, which then makes the payment to B. The DCO also requires B to post initial variation margin in an amount equal to the upfront payment and requires each party to post and collect daily variation margin in an amount equal to the change in the fair market value of the contract on a daily basis for the entire term of the contract. B posts the initial variation margin in U.S. dollars, which is received by CFC (through DCO and CM), and the parties post and collect daily variation margin in U.S. dollars.

(ii) Because the contract is subject to initial variation margin in an amount equal to the upfront payment and daily variation margin in an amount equal to the change in the fair market value of the contract on a daily basis for the entire term of the contract, the contract is described in § 1.446-3T(g)(4)(ii)(B)(*1*). Furthermore, because the additional conditions set forth in this paragraph (b)(1)(xi) are satisfied, the obligation of CM arising from the upfront payment by CFC does not constitute United States property for purposes of section 956.

Example 2. Full margin – uncleared contract. (i) Assume the same facts as in *Example 1*, except for the following. CFC's counterparty to the contract is USC, CM is not involved, and the contract is not required to be cleared and is not accepted for clearing by a U.S.-registered derivatives clearing organization. The contract requires CFC to make an upfront payment to compensate USC for the below-market annual coupon payments that USC will receive, and CFC makes the upfront payment in U.S. dollars. Pursuant to the requirements of a federal regulator, USC is obligated to post initial variation margin with CFC in an amount equal to CFC's upfront payment, and USC and CFC are obligated to post and collect daily variation margin in an amount equal to the change in the fair market value of the contract on a daily basis for the entire term of the contract. USC posts the initial variation margin in U.S. dollars, which is received by CFC, and the parties post and collect daily variation margin in U.S. dollars.

(ii) Because the contract is subject to initial variation margin in an amount equal to the upfront payment and daily variation margin in an amount equal to the change in the fair market value of the contract on a daily basis for the entire term of the contract, the contract is described in § 1.446-3T(g)(4)(ii)(B)(2). Furthermore, because the additional conditions set forth in this paragraph (b)(1)(xi) are satisfied, the obligation of USC arising from the upfront payment by CFC does not constitute United States property for purposes of section 956.

(b)(2) through (c)(4) [Reserved]. For further guidance, see § 1.956-2(b)(2) through (c)(4).

(5) [Reserved.]

(d)(1) [Reserved]. For further guidance, see § 1.956-2(d)(1).

(2) [Reserved.]

(e) [Reserved]. For further guidance see § 1.956-2(e).

(f) *Effective/applicability date*.—Paragraph (b)(1)(xi) of this section applies to payments described in § 1.956-2T(b)(1)(xi) made on or after May 8, 2015. Taxpayers may apply the rules of paragraph (b)(1)(xi) to payments made before May 8, 2015.

(g) *Expiration date*.—The applicability of paragraph (b)(1)(xi) of this section expires on May 7, 2018.

(h) [Reserved]

[Temporary Reg. § 1.956-2T.]

☐ [*T.D. 8209, 6-13-88. Amended by T.D. 9406, 7-2-2008; T.D. 9525, 5-5-2011, T.D. 9589, 5-10-2012; T.D. 9719, 5-7-2015; T.D. 9761, 4-4-2016 (corrected 6-22-2016 and 7-18-2016) and T.D. 9834, 7-11-2018.*]

§ 1.956-3. Certain trade or service receivables acquired from United States persons.—(a) *In general*.—For purposes of section 956(a) and § 1.956-1, the term "United States property" also includes any trade or service receivable if the trade or service receivable is acquired (directly or indirectly) from a related person who is a United States person (as defined in section 7701(a)(30)) (a *related United States person*) and the obligor under the receivable is a United States person. A trade or service receivable described in this paragraph is considered to be United States property notwithstanding the exceptions (other than subparagraph (H)) contained in section 956(c)(2). The terms "trade or service receivable" and "related person" have the respective meanings given to the terms by section 864(d) and the regulations thereunder, including § 1.864-8T(b). For purposes of this section, the exception in § 1.956-2T(d)(2)(ii) does not apply to trade or service receivables described in this paragraph.

(b) *Acquisition of a trade or service receivable.*—(1) *General rule.*—The rules of § 1.864-8T(c)(1) apply to determine whether a controlled foreign corporation has acquired a trade or service receivable.

(2) *Indirect acquisitions.*—(i) *Acquisition through unrelated person.*—A trade or service receivable is considered acquired from a related person when it is acquired from an unrelated person who acquired (directly or indirectly) the receivable from a person who is a related person to the acquiring person.

(ii) *Acquisition by nominee, pass-through entity, or related foreign corporation.*—A controlled foreign corporation is treated as holding a trade or service receivable that is held by a nominee on its behalf, or by a simple trust or other pass-through entity (other than a partnership) to the extent of its direct or indirect ownership or beneficial interest in such simple trust or other pass-through entity. See §§ 1.956-1(b) and 1.956-4(b) for rules that may treat a controlled foreign corporation as indirectly holding a trade or service receivable held by a foreign corporation or partnership. A controlled foreign corporation that is treated as holding a trade or service receivable held by another person (the *direct holder*) (or that would be treated as holding the receivable if the receivable were United States property or would be United States property if held directly by the controlled foreign corporation) is considered to have acquired the receivable from the person from whom the direct holder acquired the receivable. This paragraph (b)(2)(ii) does not limit the application of paragraph (b)(2)(iii) of this section. The following examples illustrate the application of this paragraph (b)(2)(ii):

Example 1. (i) *Facts.* A domestic corporation, P, wholly owns a controlled foreign corporation, FS, with substantial earnings and profits. FS contributes $200x of cash to a partnership, PRS, in exchange for an 80% partnership interest. An unrelated foreign person contributes real estate located in a foreign country with a fair market value of $50x to PRS for the remaining 20% partnership interest. There are no special allocations in the PRS partnership agreement. PRS uses the $200x of cash received from FS to purchase trade receivables from P. The obligors with respect to the trade receivables are United States persons that are not related to any partner in PRS. The liquidation value percentage, as determined under § 1.956-4(b), for FS with respect to PRS is 80%. A principal purpose of funding PRS (through FS's cash contribution) is to avoid the application of section 956 with respect to FS.

(ii) *Result.* Under § 1.956-4(b)(1), FS is treated as holding 80% of the trade receivables acquired by PRS from P, with a basis equal to $160x (80% x $200x, PRS's basis in the trade receivables). However, because FS controls PRS and a principal purpose of FS funding PRS was to avoid the application of section 956 with respect to FS, under § 1.956-1(b), if the trade receivables would be United States property if held directly by FS, FS additionally would be treated as holding the trade receivables to the extent that they exceed the amount of the receivables it holds under § 1.956-4(b), which is $40x ($200x - $160x). Accordingly, under this paragraph (b)(2)(ii), FS is treated as having acquired from P, a related United States person, the trade receivables that it is treated as holding with a basis equal to $200x ($160x + $40x). Thus, FS is treated as holding United States property with a basis of $200x under paragraph (a) of this section.

Example 2. (i) *Facts.* A domestic corporation, P, wholly owns a controlled foreign corporation, FS1, that has earnings and profits of at least $300x. FS1 organizes a foreign corporation, FS2, with a $200x cash contribution. FS2 uses the cash contribution to purchase trade receivables from P. The obligors with respect to the trade receivables are unrelated United States persons. A principal purpose of funding FS2 (through FS1's cash contribution) is to avoid the application of section 956 with respect to FS1.

(ii) *Result.* Under § 1.956-1(b), if the trade receivables held by FS2 were United States property, FS1 would be treated as holding the trade receivables held by FS2 because FS1 controls FS2 and a principal purpose of FS1 funding FS2 was to avoid the application of section 956 with respect to FS1. Accordingly, under this paragraph (b)(2)(ii), FS1 is treated as having acquired from P, a related United States person, the trade receivables that it would be treated as holding with a basis equal to $200x. Thus, FS1 is treated as holding United States property with a basis of $200x under paragraph (a) of this section.

(iii) *Swap or pooling arrangements.*—A trade or service receivable of a United States person is considered to be a trade or service receivable acquired from a related United States person and subject to the rules of this section when it is acquired in accordance with an arrangement that involves two or more groups of related persons, if the groups are unrelated to each other and the effect of the arrangement is that one or more persons in each group acquire (directly or indirectly) trade or service receivables from one or more unrelated United States persons who are also parties to the arrangement in exchange for reciprocal purchases of receivables from related United States persons. The following example illustrates the application of this paragraph (b)(2)(iii):

Example. (i) *Facts.* Controlled foreign corporations A, B, C, and D are wholly-owned subsidiaries of domestic corporations M, N, O, and P, respectively. M, N, O, and P are not related persons. According to a prearranged plan, A, B, C, and D each acquire trade or service receivables from M, N, O, and/or P. The obligors under some or all of the receivables acquired by each of A, B, C, and D are United States persons.

(ii) *Result.* The effect of the prearranged plan is that each of A, B, C, and D acquires trade or service receivables of United States persons from one or more unrelated United States persons who are also parties to the arrangement, in exchange for reciprocal purchases of receivables from a related United States person. Accordingly, each of A, B, C, and D is treated as holding a trade or service receivable acquired from a related United States person and is subject to the rules of this section. As a result, each of A, B, C, and D is treated as holding an amount of United States property equal to its adjusted basis in the receivables acquired pursuant to the arrangement with respect to which the obligors are United States persons.

(iv) *Financing arrangements.*—If a controlled foreign corporation participates (directly or indirectly) in a lending transaction that results in a loan to a United States person who purchases property described in section 1221(a)(1) *(inventory property)* or services from a related United States person, or to any person who purchases from a related United States person trade or service receivables under which the obligor is a United States person, or to a person who is a related person with respect to the purchaser, and if the loan would not have been made or maintained on the same terms but for the corresponding purchase, then the controlled foreign corporation is considered to have indirectly acquired a trade or service receivable described in paragraph (a) of this section. For purposes of this paragraph (b)(2)(iv), it is immaterial that the sums lent are not, in fact, the sums used to finance the purchase of the inventory property or services or trade or service receivables from a related United States person. The amount to be taken into account with respect to the United States property treated as held by a controlled foreign corporation as a result of the application of this paragraph (b)(2)(iv) is the lesser of the amount lent pursuant to a lending transaction described in this paragraph (b)(2)(iv) and the purchase price of the inventory property, services, or trade or service receivables. The following examples illustrate the application of this paragraph (b)(2)(iv):

Example 1. (i) *Facts.* P, a domestic corporation, owns all of the outstanding stock of FS1, a controlled foreign corporation. P sells inventory property for $200x to X, an unrelated United States person. FS1 makes a $100x short-term loan to X, which loan would not have been made or maintained on the same terms but for X's purchase of P's inventory property.

(ii) *Result.* FS1 directly participates in a lending transaction described in this paragraph (b)(2)(iv). Thus, FS1 is considered to have acquired a trade or service receivable described in paragraph (a) of this section. That is, FS1 is considered to have acquired a trade or service receivable of a United States person from a related United States person. As a result, FS1 is treated as holding United States property in the amount of $100x.

Example 2. (i) *Facts.* The facts are the same as in *Example 1* of this paragraph (b)(2)(iv), except that instead of loaning money to X directly, FS1 deposits $300x with an unrelated financial institution that loans $200x to X in order for X to purchase P's inventory property. The loan would not have been made or maintained on the same terms but for the corresponding deposit.

(ii) *Result.* FS1 is considered to have acquired a trade or service receivable described in paragraph (a) of this section because FS1 indirectly participates in a lending transaction described in this paragraph (b)(2)(iv). See Rev. Rul. 87-89, 1987-2 CB 195. That is, FS1 is considered to have acquired a trade or service receivable of a United States person from a related United States person. Thus, FS1 is treated as holding United States property in the amount of $200x.

Example 3. (i) *Facts.* P, a domestic corporation, owns all of the outstanding stock of FS1, a controlled foreign corporation. FS1 makes a $300x loan to U, an unrelated foreign corporation, in connection with U's purchase from P of receivables from the sale of inventory property by P to United States obligors for $200x.

(iii) *Result.* FS1 is considered to have acquired a trade or service receivable described in paragraph (a) of this section because FS1 directly participates in a lending transaction described in this paragraph (b)(2)(iv). That is, FS1 is considered to have acquired a trade or service receivable of a United States person from a related United States person. Thus, FS1 is treated as holding United States property in the amount of $200x.

(c) *Substitution of obligor.*—For purposes of this section, the substitution of another person for a United States obligor is disregarded, unless it can be demonstrated by the parties to the transaction that the primary purpose for the arrangement was not the avoidance of section 956. The following example illustrates the application of this paragraph (c):

Example. (i) *Facts.* P, a domestic corporation, owns all of the outstanding stock of FS1, a controlled foreign corporation with substantial accumulated earnings and profits. P sells inventory property to X, a domestic corporation unrelated to P. To pay for the inventory property, X arranges for a foreign financing entity to issue a note to P. P then sells the note to FS1. P and X cannot demonstrate that the primary purpose for X's assignment of the payment obligation to the foreign financing entity was not the avoidance of section 956.

(ii) *Result.* The substitution of the foreign financing entity for X is disregarded, and FS1 is treated as holding an obligation of a United States person acquired from a related United States person. Thus, FS1 is treated as holding United States property in the amount of the purchase price of the note.

(d) *Effective/applicability date.*—(1) Except as provided in paragraph (d)(2) of this section, this section applies to trade or service receivables acquired (directly or indirectly) after March 1, 1984.

(2) Paragraph (b)(2)(ii) of this section applies to taxable years of controlled foreign corporations ending on or after November 3, 2016, and taxable years of United States shareholders in which or with which such taxable years end, with respect to trade or service receivables acquired on or after September 1, 2015. For purposes of this paragraph (d), a significant modification, within the meaning of § 1.1001-3(e), of a trade or service receivable on or after September 1, 2015, constitutes an acquisition of the trade or service receivable on or after that date. [Reg. § 1.956-3.]

☐ [*T.D.* 9792, 11-2-2016.]

§ 1.956-4. Certain rules applicable to partnerships.—(a) *Overview.*—This section provides rules concerning the application of section 956 to certain obligations of and property held by a partnership. Paragraph (b) of this section provides rules concerning United States property held indirectly by a controlled foreign corporation through a partnership. Paragraph (c) of this section provides rules that generally treat obligations of a foreign partnership as obligations of the partners in the foreign partnership, as well as a special rule that treats a partner that is a United States person as owing additional amounts of a partnership obligation in certain circumstances. Paragraph (d) of this section sets forth a rule concerning the application of the indirect pledge or guarantee rule to obligations of partnerships. Paragraph (e) of this section provides that obligations of a domestic partnership are obligations of a United States person. Paragraph (f) of this section provides effective and applicability dates. See §§ 1.956-1(b) and 1.956-2(c) for additional rules applicable to partnerships.

(b) *Property held indirectly through a partnership.*—(1) *General rule.*—For purposes of section 956, a partner in a partnership is treated as holding its attributable share of any property held by the partnership (including an obligation that the partnership is treated as holding as a result of the application of § 1.956-2(c)). A partner's attributable share of partnership property is determined under the rules set forth in paragraph (b)(2) of this section. An upper-tier partnership's attributable share of the property of a lower-tier partnership is treated as property of the upper-tier partnership for purposes of applying this paragraph (b)(1) to the partners of the upper-tier partnership. For purposes of section 956, a partner's adjusted basis in the property of the partnership equals the partner's attributable share of the partnership's adjusted basis in the property, as determined under the rules set forth in paragraph (b)(2) of this section, taking into account any adjustments to basis under section 743(b) (with respect to the partner) or section 734(b) or any similar adjustments to basis. The rules in § 1.956-1(e)(2) apply to determine the amount of an obligation treated as held by a partnership as a result of the application of § 1.956-2(c). See § 1.956-1(b) for special rules that may treat a controlled foreign corporation as holding a greater amount of United States property held by a partnership than the amount determined under this section.

(2) *Methodology.*—(i) *Liquidation value percentage.*—(A) *Calculation.*—Except as otherwise provided in paragraph (b)(2)(ii) of this section, for purposes of paragraph (b)(1) of this section, a partner's attributable share of partnership property is determined in accordance with the partner's liquidation value percentage. For purposes of this paragraph (b)(2)(i) and paragraph (c)(1) of this section, the liquidation value of a partner's interest in a partnership is the amount of cash the partner would receive with respect to the interest if, on the applicable determination date, as provided in paragraph (b)(2)(i)(B) of this section, the partnership sold all of its assets for cash equal to the fair market value of such assets (taking into account section 7701(g)), satisfied all of its liabilities (other than those described in § 1.752-7), paid an unrelated third party to assume all of its § 1.752-7 liabilities in a fully taxable transaction, and then liquidated. A partner's liquidation value percentage is the ratio (expressed as a percentage) of the liquidation value of the partner's interest in the partnership divided by the aggregate liquidation value of all of the partners' interests in the partnership.

(B) *Determination date.*—The *determination date* with respect to a partnership is the most recent of—

(1) The formation of the partnership;

(2) An event described in § 1.704-1(b)(2)(iv)(*f*)*(5)* or § 1.704-1(b)(2)(iv)(*s*)*(1)* (a *revaluation event*), irrespective of whether the capital accounts of the partners are adjusted in accordance with § 1.704-1(b)(2)(iv)(*f*); or

(3) The first day of the partnership's taxable year, as determined under section 706, provided the liquidation value percentage determined for any partner on that day would differ from the most recently determined liquidation value percentage of that partner by more than 10 percentage points.

(ii) *Special allocations.*—For purposes of paragraph (b)(1) of this section, if a partnership agreement provides for the allocation of book income (or, where appropriate, book gain) from a subset of the property of the partnership to a partner other than in accordance with the partner's liquidation value percentage in a particular taxable year (a *special allocation*), then the partner's attributable share of that property is determined solely by reference to the partner's special allocation with respect to the property, provided the special allocation will be respected for federal income tax purposes under section 704(b) and the regulations thereunder and does not have a principal purpose of avoiding the purposes of section 956.

(3) *Examples.*—The following examples illustrate the rules of this paragraph (b):

Example 1. (i) *Facts.* USP, a domestic corporation, wholly owns FS, a controlled foreign corporation, which, in turn, owns an interest in FPRS, a foreign partnership. The remaining interest in FPRS is owned by an unrelated foreign person. FPRS holds non-depreciable property with an adjusted basis of $100x (the "FPRS property") that would be United States property if held by FS directly. At the close of quarter 1 of year 1, the liquidation value percentage, as determined under paragraph (b)(2) of this section, for FS with respect to FPRS is 25%. There are no special allocations in the FPRS partnership agreement.

(ii) *Result.* Under paragraph (b)(1) of this section, for purposes of section 956, FS is treated as holding its attributable share of the property held by FPRS with an adjusted basis equal to its attributable share of FPRS's adjusted basis in such property. Under paragraph (b)(2) of this section, FS's attributable share of property held by FPRS is determined in accordance with FS's liquidation value percentage, which is 25%. Thus, FS's attributable share of the FPRS property is 25%, and its attributable share of FPRS's basis in the FPRS property is $25x. Accordingly, for purposes of determining the amount of United States property held by FS as of the close of quarter 1 of year 1, FS is treated as holding United States property with an adjusted basis of $25x.

Example 2. (i) *Facts.* The facts are the same as in *Example 1* of this paragraph (b)(3), except that the FPRS partnership agreement, which satisfies the requirements of section 704(b), specially allocates 80% of the income with respect to the FPRS property to FS. The special allocation does not have a principal purpose of avoiding the purposes of section 956.

(ii) *Result.* Under paragraph (b)(1) of this section, for purposes of section 956, FS is treated as holding its attributable share of property held by FPRS with an adjusted basis equal to its attributable share of FPRS's adjusted basis in such property. In general, FS's attributable share of property held by FPRS is determined in accordance with FS's liquidation value percentage. However, because the special allocation does not have a principal purpose of avoiding the purposes of section 956, under paragraph (b)(2)(ii) of this section, FS's attributable share of the FPRS property is determined by reference to its special allocation. FS's special allocation percentage for the FPRS property is 80%, and thus FS's attributable share of the FPRS property is 80% and its attributable share of FPRS's basis in the FPRS property is $80x. Accordingly, for purposes of determining the amount of United States property held by FS as of the close of quarter 1 of year 1, FS is treated as holding United States property with an adjusted basis of $80x.

Example 3. (i) *Facts.* USP, a domestic corporation, wholly owns FS, a controlled foreign corporation, which, in turn, owns an interest in FPRS, a foreign partnership. USP owns the remaining interest in FPRS. FPRS holds property (the "FPRS property") that would be United States property if held by FS directly. The FPRS property has an adjusted basis of $100x and is anticipated to appreciate in value but generate relatively little income. The FPRS partnership agreement, which satisfies the requirements of section 704(b), specially allocates 80% of the income with respect to the FPRS property to USP and 80% of the gain with respect to the disposition of FPRS property to FS. The special allocation does not have a principal purpose of avoiding the purposes of section 956.

(ii) *Result.* Because the special allocation does not have a principal purpose of avoiding the purposes of section 956, under paragraph (b)(2)(ii) of this section, FS's attributable share of the FPRS property is determined by reference to a special allocation with respect to the FPRS property. Given the income and gain anticipated with respect to the FPRS property, it is appropriate to determine FS's attributable share of the property in accordance with the special allocation of gain. Accordingly, for purposes of determining the amount of United States property held by FS in each year that FPRS holds the FPRS property, FS's attributable share of the FPRS property is 80% and its attributable share of FPRS's basis in the FPRS property is $80x. Thus, FS is treated as holding United States property with an adjusted basis of $80x.

(c) *Obligations of a foreign partnership.*—(1) *In general.*—Except as provided in paragraphs (c)(2) and (c)(3) of this section, for purposes of section 956, an obligation of a foreign partnership is treated as a separate obligation of each of the partners in the partnership to the extent of each partner's share of the obligation. A partner's share of the partnership's obligation is determined in accordance with the partner's liquidation value percentage, as determined under the rules set forth in paragraph (b)(2)(i) of this section, without regard to the rules set forth in paragraph (b)(2)(ii) of this section. An upper-tier partnership's share of an obligation of a lower-tier partnership is treated as an obligation of the upper-tier partnership for purposes of applying this paragraph (c)(1) to the partners of the upper-tier partnership.

(2) *Exception for obligations of partnerships in which neither the lending controlled foreign corporation nor any person related to the lending controlled foreign corporation is a partner.*—For purposes of applying section 956 with respect to a controlled foreign corporation, an obligation of a foreign partnership is treated as an obligation of a foreign partnership, and not as an obligation of its partners, if neither the controlled foreign corporation nor any person related to the controlled foreign corporation within the meaning of section 954(d)(3) is a partner in the partnership. For purposes of section 956, an obligation treated as an obligation of a foreign partnership pursuant to this paragraph (c)(2) is not an obligation of a United States person.

(3) *Special obligor rule in the case of certain partnership distributions.*—(i) *General rule.*—For purposes of determining a partner's share of a foreign partnership's obligation under section 956, if the foreign partnership distributes an amount of money or property to a partner that is related to a controlled foreign corporation within the meaning of section 954(d)(3) and whose obligation would be United States property if held (or if treated as held) by the controlled foreign corporation, and the foreign partnership would not have made the distribution but for a funding of the partnership through an obligation held (or treated as held) by the controlled foreign corporation, notwithstanding § 1.956-1(e), the partner's share of the partnership obligation is the greater of—

(A) The partner's share of the partnership obligation as determined under paragraph (c)(1) of this section; and

(B) The lesser of the amount of the distribution to the partner that would not have been made but for the funding of the partnership and the amount of the obligation (as determined under § 1.956-1(e)).

(ii) *Deemed treatment.*—(A) For purposes of applying paragraph (c)(3)(i) of this section, in the case of a distribution of liquid assets by a foreign partnership to a partner, the foreign partnership is treated as if it would not have made the distribution of liquid assets to the partner but for the funding of the partnership through an obligation or obligations held (or treated as held) by the controlled foreign corporation to the extent the foreign partnership does not have sufficient liquid assets to make the distribution immediately prior to the distribution, without taking into account the obligation or obligations.

(B) If the controlled foreign corporation holds (or is treated as holding) multiple obligations of the foreign partnership, paragraph (c)(3)(ii)(A) of this section applies to the obligations in reverse chronological order starting with the obligation that was acquired (or the obligation with respect to which a pledge or guarantee was entered into) closest in time to the distribution. Paragraph (c)(3)(ii)(A) of this section applies to an obligation only to the extent that the full amount of the distribution is not otherwise treated, pursuant to paragraph (c)(3)(ii)(A) of this section, as if it would not have been made but for the funding of the partnership through one or more other obligations.

(C) For purposes of paragraph (c)(3)(ii) of this section, a significant modification, within the meaning of § 1.1001-3(e), of an obligation constitutes an acquisition of the obligation on or after that date, and a pledgor or guarantor is treated as entering into a pledge or guarantee when there is a significant modification, within the meaning of § 1.1001-3(e), of an obligation with respect to which it is a pledgor or guarantor.

(D) For purposes of paragraph (c)(3)(ii) of this section, liquid assets means cash or cash equivalents, marketable securities within the meaning of section 453(f)(2), or an obligation owed by a related person (within the meaning of section 954(d)(3)).

(4) *Examples.*—The following examples illustrate the rules of this paragraph (c):

Example 1. (i) *Facts.* USP, a domestic corporation, wholly owns FS, a controlled foreign corporation, and owns an interest in FPRS, a foreign partnership. At the close of quarter 1 of year 1, the liquidation value percentage, as determined under paragraph (b)(2)(i) of this section, for USP with respect to FPRS is 90%. X, a foreign person that is unrelated to USP or FS, owns the remaining interest in FPRS. FPRS borrows $100x from FS. FS's basis in the FPRS obligation is $100x.

(ii) *Result.* Under paragraph (c)(1) of this section, for purposes of section 956, the obligation of FPRS is treated as obligations of its partners (USP and X) in proportion to each partner's liquidation value percentage with respect to FPRS. Because USP, a partner in FPRS, is related to FS within the meaning of section 954(d)(3), the exception in paragraph (c)(2) of this section does not apply. Based on its liquidation value percentage, USP's share of the FPRS obligation is $90x. Accordingly, for purposes of section 956, $90x of the FPRS obligation held by FS is treated as an obligation of USP and is United States property within the meaning of section 956(c). Therefore, on the date the loan is made, FS is treated as holding United States property of $90x.

Example 2. (i) *Facts.* The facts are the same as in *Example 1* of this paragraph (c)(4), except that USP owns 40% of the stock of FS and is not a related person (as defined in section 954(d)(3)) with respect to FS. Y, a United States person that is unrelated to USP or X, owns the remaining 60% of the stock of FS.

(ii) *Result.* Because neither FS nor any person related to FS within the meaning of section 954(d)(3) is a partner in FPRS, the exception in paragraph (c)(2) of this section applies to treat the FPRS obligation as an obligation of a foreign partnership and not an obligation of a United States person. Therefore, paragraph (c)(1) of this section does not apply, and FS is not treated as holding United States property.

Example 3. (i) *Facts.* USP, a domestic corporation, wholly owns FS, a controlled foreign corporation. USP and FS own interests in FPRS, a foreign partnership. USP's liquidation value percentage with respect to FPRS is 60%, and FS's liquidation value percentage with respect to FPRS is 30%. USP2, a domestic corporation that is unrelated to USP and FS, also owns an interest in FPRS; its liquidation value percentage is 10%. FPRS borrows $100x from an unrelated person. FS guarantees the FPRS obligation.

(ii) *Result.* Under paragraph (c)(1) of this section, for purposes of section 956, the obligation of FPRS is treated as obligations of its partners (USP, FS, and USP2) in proportion to each partner's liquidation value percentage. Because USP, a partner in FPRS, is related to FS within the meaning of section 954(d)(3), and because FS is a partner in FPRS, the exception in paragraph (c)(2) of this section does not apply. Based on their liquidation value percentages, USP's share of the FPRS obligation is $60x, and USP2's share of the FPRS obligation is $10x. For purposes of section 956, $60x of the FPRS obligation is treated as an obligation of USP, and $10x of the FPRS obligation is treated as an obligation of USP2. Under §1.956-2(c)(1), FS is treated as holding the obligations of USP and USP2 that FS guaranteed. All of the exceptions to the definition of United States property contained in section 956 and §1.956-2 must be considered to determine whether the obligations of USP and USP2 that are treated as held by FS constitute United States property. Accordingly, the obligation of USP2 is not United States property under section 956(c)(2)(F) and §1.956-2(b)(1)(viii). The obligation of USP, however, is United States property within the meaning of section 956(c). Therefore, on the date the guarantee is made, FS is treated as holding United States property of $60x.

Example 4. (i) *Facts*. USP, a domestic corporation, wholly owns FS, a controlled foreign corporation. USP owns an interest in FPRS, a foreign partnership; its liquidation value percentage with respect to FPRS is 70%. A domestic corporation that is unrelated to USP and FS owns the remaining interest in FPRS; its liquidation value percentage is 30%. FPRS borrows $100x from FS and makes a distribution of $80x to USP. FPRS would not have made the distribution to USP but for the funding of FPRS by FS.

(ii) *Result*. Because USP, a partner in FPRS, is related to FS within the meaning of section 954(d)(3), the exception in paragraph (c)(2) of this section does not apply. Moreover, an obligation of USP held by FS would be United States property. USP's share of the FPRS obligation as determined under paragraph (c)(1) of this section in accordance with USP's liquidation value percentage is $70x. Under paragraph (c)(3) of this section, USP's share of the FPRS obligation is the greater of (i) USP's attributable share of the obligation, $70x, or (ii) the lesser of the amount of the distribution, $80x, or the amount of the obligation, $100x. For purposes of section 956, therefore, $80x of the FPRS obligation is treated as an obligation of USP and is United States property within the meaning of section 956(c). Thus, on the date the loan is made, FS is treated as holding United States property of $80x.

(d) *Limitation on a partner's indirect pledge or guarantee*.—For purposes of section 956 and §1.956-2(c), a controlled foreign corporation that is a partner in a partnership is not considered a pledgor or guarantor of the portion of an obligation of the partnership attributed to its partners that are United States persons under paragraph (c) of this section solely as a result of the attribution of a portion of the partnership's assets to the controlled foreign corporation under paragraph (b) of this section.

(e) *Obligations of a domestic partnership*.—For purposes of section 956, an obligation of a domestic partnership is an obligation of a United States person. See section 956(c)(2)(L) for an exception from the treatment of such an obligation as United States property.

(f) *Effective/applicability dates*.—(1) Paragraph (b) of this section applies to taxable years of controlled foreign corporations ending on or after November 3, 2016, and taxable years of United States shareholders in which or with which such taxable years end, with respect to property acquired on or after November 3, 2016. For purposes of this paragraph (f)(1), a deemed exchange of property pursuant to section 1001 on or after November 3, 2016, constitutes an acquisition of the property on or after that date. See §1.956-2(a)(3), as contained in 26 CFR part 1 revised as of April 1, 2016, for the rules applicable to taxable years of a controlled foreign corporation beginning on or after July 23, 2002, and ending before November 3, 2016, and with respect to property acquired before November 3, 2016, to taxable years of a controlled foreign corporation beginning on or after July 23, 2002.

(2) Except as otherwise provided in this paragraph (f)(2), paragraph (c) of this section applies to taxable years of controlled foreign corporations ending on or after November 3, 2016, and taxable years of United States shareholders in which or with which such taxable years end, with respect to obligations acquired, or pledges or guarantees entered into, on or after September 1, 2015, and, for purposes of paragraph (c)(3) of this section, in the case of distributions made on or after September 1, 2015. Paragraph (c)(3)(ii) of this section applies to taxable years of controlled foreign corporations ending on or after November 3, 2016, and taxable years of United States shareholders in which or with which such taxable years end, with respect to obligations acquired, or pledges or guarantees entered into, on or after September 1, 2015, and distributions made on or after November 3, 2016 For purposes of this paragraph (f)(2), a significant modification, within the meaning of §1.1001-3(e), of an obligation on or after September 1, 2015 constitutes an acquisition of the obligation on or after that date. Furthermore, for purposes of this paragraph (f)(2), a pledgor or guarantor is treated as entering into a pledge or guarantee when there is a significant modification, within the meaning of §1.1001-3(e), of an obligation with respect to which it is a pledgor or guarantor on or after September 1, 2015. See §1.956-1T(b)(5), as contained in 26 CFR part 1 revised as of April 1, 2016, for rules applicable to taxable years of controlled foreign corporations ending on or after September 1, 2015, and before November 3, 2016, and to taxable years of United States shareholders in which or with which such taxable years end, in the case of distributions made on or after September 1, 2015.

(3) Paragraph (d) of this section applies to taxable years of controlled foreign corporations ending on or after November 3, 2016, and taxable years of United States shareholders in which or with which such taxable years end, with respect to pledges or guarantees entered into on or after September 1, 2015. For purposes of this paragraph (f)(3), a pledgor or guarantor is treated as entering into a pledge or guarantee when there is a significant modification, within the meaning of §1.1001-3(e), of an obligation with respect to which it is a pledgor or guarantor on or after September 1, 2015.

(4) Paragraph (e) of this section applies to taxable years of controlled foreign corporations ending on or after November 3, 2016, and to taxable years of United States shareholders in which or with which such taxable years end, with respect to obligations held on or after November 3, 2016. [Reg. §1.956-4.]

□ [*T.D.* 9792, 11-2-2016 (*corrected* 12-27-2016).]

Proposed Amendments to Regulation

§1.956-4. Certain rules applicable to partnerships.

* * *

(b) * * *

(2) * * *

(ii) *Special allocations*.—Except as otherwise provided in paragraph (b)(2)(iii) of this section, for purposes of paragraph (b)(1) of this section, if a partnership agreement provides for the allocation of book income (or, where appropriate, book gain) from a subset of the property of the partnership to a partner other than in accordance with the partner's liquidation value percentage in a particular taxable year (a *special allocation*), then the partner's attributable share of that property is determined solely by reference to the partner's special allocation with respect to the property, provided the special allocation will be respected for Federal income tax purposes under section 704(b) and the regulations thereunder and does not have a principal purpose of avoiding the purposes of section 956.

(iii) *Limitation on special allocations in the case of a controlled partnership*.—Paragraph (b)(2)(ii) of this section does not apply to determine a partner's attributable share of partnership property in the case of a partnership controlled by the partner. For purposes of this paragraph (b)(2)(iii), a partner controls a partnership when the partner and the partnership are related within the meaning of section 267(b) or section 707(b), determined by substituting "at least 80 percent" for "more than 50 percent" wherever it appears.

(3) * * *

Example 2. (i) *Facts*. * * * FS does not control FPRS within the meaning of paragraph (b)(2)(iii) of this section.

(ii) *Result*. Under paragraph (b)(1) of this section, for purposes of section 956, FS is treated as holding its attributable share of the property held by FPRS with an adjusted basis equal to its attributable share of FPRS's adjusted basis in such property. In general, FS's attributable share of property held by FPRS is determined in accordance with FS's liquidation value percentage. However, because FS does not control FPRS within the meaning of paragraph (b)(2)(iii) of this section and because the special allocation does not have a principal purpose of avoiding the purposes of section 956, under paragraph (b)(2)(ii) of this section, FS's attributable share of the FPRS property is determined by reference to its special allocation. FS's special allocation percentage for the FPRS property is 80%, and thus FS's attributable share of the FPRS property is 80% and its attributable share of FPRS's basis in the FPRS property is $80x. Accordingly, for purposes of determining the amount of United States property held by FS as of the close of quarter 1 of year 1, FS is treated as holding United States property with an adjusted basis of $80x.

Example 3. (i) *Facts*. USP, a domestic corporation, wholly owns FS, a controlled foreign corporation, which, in turn, owns a 25% capital and profits interest in FPRS, a foreign partnership. The remaining 75% capital and profits interest in FPRS is owned by an unrelated foreign person. Thus, FS does not control FPRS within the meaning of paragraph (b)(2)(iii) of this section. FPRS holds property (the "FPRS property") that would be United States property if held by FS directly. The FPRS property has an adjusted basis of $100x and is anticipated to appreciate in value but generate relatively little income. The FPRS partnership agreement, which satisfies the requirements of section 704(b), specially allocates 80% of the income with respect to the FPRS property to the unrelated foreign person and 80% of the gain with respect to the disposition of FPRS property to FS. The special allocation does not have a principal purpose of avoiding the purposes of section 956.

(ii) *Result.* Because FPRS is not controlled by FS within the meaning of paragraph (b)(2)(iii) of this section, and the special allocation does not have a principal purpose of avoiding the purposes of section 956, under paragraph (b)(2)(ii) of this section, FS's attributable share of the FPRS property is determined by reference to a special allocation with respect to the FPRS property. Given the income and gain anticipated with respect to the FPRS property, it is appropriate to determine FS's attributable share of the property in accordance with the special allocation of gain. Accordingly, for purposes of determining the amount of United States property held by FS in each year that FPRS holds the FPRS property, FS's attributable share of the FPRS property is 80% and its attributable share of FPRS's basis in the FPRS property is $80x. Thus, FS is treated as holding United States property with an adjusted basis of $80x.

Example 4. (i) *Facts.* The facts are the same as in *Example 3* of this paragraph (b)(3), except that USP owns the 75% capital and profits interest in FPRS rather than an unrelated foreign person. Thus, FS controls FPRS within the meaning of paragraph (b)(2)(iii) of this section. At the close of quarter 1 of year 1, the liquidation value percentage, as determined under paragraph (b)(2) of this section, for FS with respect to FPRS is 25%.

(ii) *Result.* Because FPRS is controlled by FS within the meaning of paragraph (b)(2)(iii) of this section, under paragraph (b)(2)(iii) of this section, FS's attributable share of the FPRS property is not determined by reference to the special allocation of gain with respect to the FPRS property. Accordingly, for purposes of determining the amount of United States property held by FS in each year that FPRS holds the FPRS property, FS's attributable share of the FPRS property is determined under paragraph (b)(2)(i) in accordance with FS's liquidation value percentage, which is 25%, and its attributable share of FPRS's basis in the FPRS property is $25x. Thus, FS is treated as holding United States property with an adjusted basis of $25x.

* * *

(f) * * *

(1) Except as otherwise provided in this paragraph (f)(1), paragraph (b) of this section applies to taxable years of controlled foreign corporations ending on or after November 3, 2016, and taxable years of United States shareholders in which or with which such taxable years end, with respect to property acquired on or after November 3, 2016. Paragraphs (b)(2)(ii) and (iii) of this section, as well as *Example 2*, *Example 3*, and *Example 4* of paragraph (b)(3) of this section, apply to taxable years of controlled foreign corporations ending on or after the date of publication in the **Federal Register** of the Treasury decision adopting this rule as a final regulation, and taxable years of United States shareholders in which or with which such taxable years end, with respect to property acquired on or after the date of publication in the **Federal Register** of the Treasury decision adopting this rule as a final regulation. For purposes of this paragraph (f)(1), a deemed exchange of property pursuant to section 1001 on or after November 3, 2016 constitutes an acquisition of the property on or after that date, and a deemed exchange of property pursuant to section 1001 on or after the date of publication in the **Federal Register** of the Treasury decision adopting this rule as a final regulation constitutes an acquisition of the property on or after that date. See § 1.956-2(a)(3), as contained in 26 CFR part 1 revised as of April 1, 2016, for the rules applicable to taxable years of a controlled foreign corporation beginning on or after July 23, 2002, and ending before November 3, 2016, and with respect to property acquired before November 3, 2016, to taxable years of a controlled foreign corporation beginning on or after July 23, 2002. [Prop. Reg. § 1.956-4.]

[Proposed 11-3-2016 (corrected 12-28-2016).]

§1.957-1. Definition of controlled foreign corporation.—(a) *In general.*—The term *controlled foreign corporation* means any foreign corporation of which more than 50 percent (or such lesser amount as is provided in section 957(b) or section 953(c)) of either—

(1) The total combined voting power of all classes of stock of the corporation entitled to vote; or

(2) The total value of the stock of the corporation, is owned within the meaning of section 958(a), or (except for purposes of section 953(c)) is considered as owned by applying the rules of section 958(b) and § 1.958-2, by United States shareholders on any day during the taxable year of such foreign corporation. For the definition of the term *United States shareholder*, see sections 951(b) and 953(c)(1)(A). For the definition of the term *foreign corporation*, see § 301.7701-5 of this chapter (Procedure and Administration Regulations). For the treatment of associations as corporations, see section 7701(a)(3) and § § 301.7701-1 and 301.7701-2 of this chapter. For the definition of the term *stock*, see sections 958(a)(3) and 7701(a)(7). For the classification of a member in an association, joint stock company or insurance company as a shareholder, see section 7701(a)(8).

(b) *Percentage of total combined voting power owned by United States shareholders.*—(1) *Meaning of combined voting power.*—In determining for purposes of paragraph (a) of this section whether United States shareholders own the requisite percentage of total combined voting power of all classes of stock entitled to vote, consideration will be given to all the facts and circumstances of each case. In all cases, however, United States shareholders of a foreign corporation will be deemed to own the requisite percentage of total combined voting power with respect to such corporation—

(i) If they have the power to elect, appoint, or replace a majority of that body of persons exercising, with respect to such corporation, the powers ordinarily exercised by the board of directors of a domestic corporation;

(ii) If any person or persons elected or designated by such shareholders have the power, where such shareholders have the power to elect exactly one-half of the members of such governing body of such foreign corporation, either to cast a vote deciding an evenly divided vote of such body or, for the duration of any deadlock which may arise, to exercise the powers ordinarily exercised by such governing body; or

(iii) If the powers which would ordinarily be exercised by the board of directors of a domestic corporation are exercised with respect to such foreign corporation by a person whom such shareholders have the power to elect, appoint, or replace.

(2) *Shifting of formal voting power.*—Any arrangement to shift formal voting power away from United States shareholders of a foreign corporation will not be given effect if in reality voting power is retained. The mere ownership of stock entitled to vote does not by itself mean that the shareholder owning such stock has the voting power of such stock for purposes of section 957. For example, if there is any agreement, whether express or implied, that any shareholder will not vote his stock or will vote it only in a specified manner, or that sharehlders owning stock having not more than 50 percent of the total combined voting power will exercise voting power normally possessed by a majority of stockholders, then the nominal ownership of the voting power will be disregarded in determining which shareholders actually hold such voting power, and this determination will be made on the basis of such agreement. Moreover, where United States shareholders own shares of one or more classes of stock of a foreign corporation which has another class of stock outstanding, the voting power ostensibly provided such other class of stock will be deemed owned by any person or persons on whose behalf it is exercised or, if not exercised, will be disregarded if the percentage of voting power of such other class of stock is substantially greater than its proportionate share of the corporate earnings, if the facts indicate that the shareholders of such other class of stock do not exercise their voting rights independently or fail to exercise such voting rights, and if a principal purpose of the arrangement is to avoid the classification of such foreign corporation as a controlled foreign corporation under section 957.

(c) *Illustrations.*—The application of this section may be illustrated by the following examples:

Example (1). Foreign corporation R has two classes of capital stock outstanding, 60 shares of class A stock, and 40 shares of class B stock. Each share of each class of stock has one vote for all purposes. E, a United States person, owns 51 shares of class A stock. Corporation R is a controlled foreign corporation.

Example (2). Foreign corporation S has three classes of capital stock outstanding, consisting of 60 shares of class A stock, 40 shares of class B stock, and 200 shares of class C stock. The owners of a majority of class A stock are entitled to elect 6 of the 10 corporate directors, and the owners of a majority of the class B stock are entitled to elect the other 4 of the 10 directors. Class C stock has no voting rights. D, a United States person, owns all of the shares of the class C stock. He also owns 31 shares of class A stock and as such an owner can elect 6 members of the board of directors. None of the remaining shares of class A stock, or the 40 shares of class B stock, is owned, or considered as owned, within the meaning of section 958, by a United States person. Since, as owner of 31 shares of the class A stock, D has sufficient voting power to elect 6 directors, D has more than 50 percent of the total combined voting power of all classes of stock entitled to vote, and S Corporation is a controlled foreign corporation.

Example (3). M, a United States person, owns a 51-percent interest in R Company, a foreign company of which he is a member. The company, if it were domestic, would be taxable as a corporation. The remaining interest of 49 percent in the company is owned by seven other members none of whom is a United States person. The memorandum of association of R Company provides for only one manager, who with respect to the company exercises the powers ordinarily exercised by a board of directors of a domestic corporation. The manager is to be elected by unanimous agreement of all the members. Since M owns 51 percent of the company, he will be deemed to own more than 50 percent of the total combined voting power of all classes of stock of R Company entitled to vote, notwithstanding that he has power to elect a manager only with the agreement of the other members. Company R is a controlled foreign corporation.

Example (4). Domestic corporation M owns a 49-percent interest in S Company, a foreign company of which it is a member. The company, if it were domestic, would be taxable as a corporation. Company S is formed under the laws of foreign country Y. The remaining interest of 51 percent in S Company is owned by persons who are not United States persons. The organization contract of S Company provides for one manager, B, a citizen and resident of country Y who is an officer of M Corporation in charge of its foreign operations in such country, or any person M Corporation may at any time appoint to succeed B in such capacity. The manager has the sole authority with respect to S Company to exercise powers ordinarily exercised by a board of directors of a domestic corporation. Since M Corporation has the discretionary power to replace B and to appoint his successor as manager of S Company, the company is a controlled foreign corporation.

Example (5). N, a United States person, owns 50 percent of the outstanding shares of the only class of capital stock of foreign corporation R. An additional 48 percent of the outstanding shares is owned by foreign corporation S. The remaining 2 percent of shares is owned by P, a citizen and resident of foreign country T, who regularly acts as attorney for N in the conduct of N's business affairs in country T. All of the shares of the outstanding capital stock of R Corporation are bearer shares. At the time of the issuance of the shares to him, P places the certificates for such shares in a depository to which N has access. On several occasions N, with P's acquiescence, has taken such shares from the depository and, on one such occasion, used the shares as collateral in borrowing funds on a loan. Although dividends, when paid, are paid to P on his shares, his charges to N for legal fees are reduced by the amount of the dividends paid on such shares. Although P votes his shares at meetings of shareholders, the facts set forth above indicate an implied agreement between P and N that N is really to retain dominion over the stock. N is deemed to own the voting rights ostensibly attached to the stock owned by P, and R Corporation is a controlled foreign corporation.

Example (6). M, a domestic corporation which manufactures in the United States and distributes all of its production for foreign consumption through N, a person other than a related person or a United States person, forms foreign corporation S to purchase products from M Corporation and sell them to N. Corporations S and M have common directors. The outstanding capital stock of S Corporation consists of 10,000 shares of $100 par value class A stock, which has no voting rights except to vote for dissolution of the corporation on a share for share basis, and 500 shares of no par class B stock which has full voting rights. Each class of the outstanding stock is to participate on a share for share basis in any dividend. The class A stock has a preference as to assets on dissolution of the corporation to the extent of its par value as well as the right to participate with the class B stock in all other assets on a share for share basis. All of the shares of class A stock are issued to M Corporation in return for property having a value of $1 million. Of the class B stock, 300 of the shares are issued to N in return for $3,000 in cash and 200 shares are issued to M Corporation for $2,000 in cash. At stockholder meetings N never votes in opposition to M Corporation on important issues. Corporation S has average annual earnings of $200,000, all of which will be subpart F income if S Corporation is held to be a controlled foreign corporation. All such earnings are accumulated. Although N ostensibly has 60 percent of the voting power of S Corporation by virtue of his ownership of 300 shares of class B stock, he has the right to only approximately 3 percent of any dividends which may be paid by S Corporation; in addition, upon liquidation of S Corporation, N is entitled to share in the assets only after M Corporation has received the par value of its 10,000 shares of class A stock, or $1 million. Thus, the voting power owned by N is substantially greater than its proportionate share of the earnings of S Corporation. In addition, the facts set forth above indicate that N is not exercising his voting rights independently and that a principal purpose of the capitalization arrangement is to avoid classification of S Corporation as a controlled foreign corporation. For these reasons, the voting power ostensibly provided the class B stock will be deemed owned by M Corporation, and S Corporation is a controlled foreign corporation.

Example (7). Foreign corporation A, authorized to issue 100 shares of one class of capital stock, issues, for $1,000 per share, 45 shares to domestic corporation M, 45 shares to foreign corporation B, and 10 shares to foreign corporation C. Corporation C, a bank, lends $3 million to finance the operations of A Corporation. In the course of negotiating these financial arrangements, D, an officer of C Corporation, and E, an officer of M Corporation, orally agree that C Corporation will vote its stock as M Corporation directs. By virtue of such oral agreement M Corporation possesses the voting power ostensibly owned by C Corporation, and A Corporation is a controlled foreign corporation.

Example 8. For its prior taxable year, *JV*, a foreign corporation, had outstanding 1000 shares of class A stock, which is voting common, and 1000 shares of class B stock, which is nonvoting preferred. *DP*, a domestic corporation, and *FP*, a foreign corporation, each owned precisely 500 shares of both class A and class B stock, and each elected 5 of the 10 members of *JV*'s board of directors. The other facts and circumstances were such that *JV* was not a controlled foreign corporation on any day of the prior taxable year. On the first day of the current taxable year, *DP* purchased one share of class B stock from *FP*. *JV* was a controlled foreign corporation on the following day because over 50 percent of the total value in the corporation was held by a person that was a United States shareholder under section 951(b). See §1.951-1(f).

Example 9. The facts are the same as in *Example 8* except that the stock of *FP* was publicly traded, *FP* had one class of stock, and on the first day of the current taxable year *DP* purchased one share of *FP* stock on the foreign stock exchange instead of purchasing one share of *JV* stock from *FP*. *JV* became a controlled foreign corporation on the following day because over 50 percent of the total value in the corporation was held by a person that was a United States shareholder under section 951(b).

Example 10. *X*, a foreign corporation, is incorporated under the laws of country *Y*. Under the laws of country *Y*, *X* is considered a mutual insurance company. *X* issues insurance policies that provide the policyholder with the right to vote for directors of the corporation, the right to a share of the assets upon liquidation in proportion to premiums paid, and the right to receive policyholder dividends in proportion to premiums paid. Only policyholders are provided with the right to vote for directors, share in assets upon liquidation, and receive distributions. United States policyholders contribute 25 percent of the premiums and have 25 percent of the outstanding rights to vote for the board of directors. Based on these facts, the United States policyholders are United States shareholders owning the requisite combined voting power and value. Thus, *X* is a controlled foreign corporation for purposes of taking into account related person insurance income under section 953(c).

(d) *Effective date.*—Paragraphs (a) and (c) *Examples 8* through *10* of this section are effective for taxable years of a controlled foreign corporation beginning after March 7, 1996. [Reg. §1.957-1.]

☐ [*T.D. 6688, 10-30-63. Amended by T.D. 8216, 7-20-88; T.D. 8618, 9-6-95 and T.D. 8704, 12-31-96.*]

§1.957-3. United States person defined.—(a) *Basic rule.*—(1) *In general.*—The term *United States person* has the same meaning for purposes of sections 951 through 965 that it has under section 7701(a)(30) and the regulations under that section, except as provided in paragraphs (b) and (c) of this section, which provide, with respect to corporations organized in possessions of the United States, that certain residents of such possessions are not United States persons. The effect of determining that an individual is not a United States person for such purposes is to exclude such individual in determining whether a foreign corporation created or organized in, or under the laws of, a possession of the United States is a controlled foreign corporation. See §1.957-1 for the definition of the term "controlled foreign corporation."

(2) *Special provisions applicable to possessions of the United States.*—For purposes of this section—

(i) The term *possession of the United States* means the Puerto Rico or any section 931 possession;

(ii) The term *section 931 possession* has the same meaning that it has under § 1.931-1(c)(1);

(iii) The rules of § 1.937-1 will apply for determining whether an individual is a bona fide resident of a possession of the United States;

(iv) Except as provided in paragraph (b)(2) of this section, the rules of § 1.937-2 will apply for determining whether income is from sources within a possession of the United States; and

(v) The rules of § 1.937-3 will apply for determining whether income is effectively connected with the conduct of a trade or business in a possession of the United States.

(b) *Puerto Rico corporation and resident.*—An individual (who, without regard to this paragraph (b), is a United States person) will not be considered a United States person with respect to a foreign corporation created or organized in, or under the laws of, Puerto Rico for the taxable year of such corporation that ends with or within the taxable year of such individual if—

(1) Such individual is a bona fide resident of Puerto Rico during his entire taxable year in which or with which the taxable year of such foreign corporation ends; and

(2) A dividend received by such individual from such corporation during the taxable year of such corporation would, for purposes of section 933(1), be treated as income derived from sources within Puerto Rico. For purposes of this paragraph (b)(2), the rules of § 1.937-2(g)(1) will not apply.

(c) *Section 931 possession corporation and resident.*—An individual (who, without regard to this paragraph (c), is a United States person) will not be considered a United States person with respect to a foreign corporation created or organized in, or under the laws of, a section 931 possession for the taxable year of such corporation that ends with or within the taxable year of such individual if—

(1) Such individual is a bona fide resident of such section 931 possession during his entire taxable year in which or with which the taxable year of such foreign corporation ends; and

(2) Such corporation satisfies the following conditions—

(i) 80 percent or more of its gross income for the 3-year period ending at the close of the taxable year (or for such part of such period as such corporation or any predecessor has been in existence) was derived from sources within section 931 possessions or was effectively connected with the conduct of a trade or business in section 931 possessions; and

(ii) 50 percent or more of its gross income for such period (or part) was derived from the active conduct of a trade or business within section 931 possessions.

(d) *Effective/applicability date.*—This section applies to taxable years ending after April 9, 2008. [Reg. § 1.957-3.]

☐ [*T.D. 6683, 10-17-63. Amended by T.D. 9194, 4-6-2005 and T.D.* 9391, 4-4-2008.]

§ 1.958-1. Direct and indirect ownership of stock.—(a) *In general.*—Section 958(a) provides that, for purposes of sections 951 to 964 (other than sections 955(b)(1)(A) and (B) and 955(c)(2)(A)(ii) (as in effect before the enactment of the Tax Reduction Act of 1975), and 960(a)(1)), stock owned means—

(1) Stock owned directly; and

(2) Stock owned with the application of paragraph (b) of this section.

The rules of section 958(a) and this section provide a limited form of stock attribution primarily for use in determining the amount taxable to a United States shareholder under section 951(a). These rules also apply for purposes of other provisions of the Code and regulations which make express reference to section 958(a).

(b) *Stock ownership through foreign entities.*—For purposes of paragraph (a)(2) of this section, stock owned, directly or indirectly, by or for a foreign corporation, foreign partnership, foreign trust (within the meaning of section 7701(a)(31)) described in sections 671 through 679, or other foreign trust or foreign estate (within the meaning of section 7701(a)(31)) shall be considered as being owned proportionately by its shareholders, partners, grantors or other persons treated as owners under sections 671 through 679 of any portion of the trust that includes the stock, or beneficiaries, respectively. Stock considered to be owned by reason of the application of this paragraph shall, for purposes of reapplying this paragraph, be treated as actually owned by such person. Thus, this rule creates a chain of ownership; however, since the rule applies only to stock owned by a foreign entity, attribution under the rule stops with the first United States person in the chain of ownership running from the foreign entity. The application of this paragraph may be illustrated by the following example:

Example. Domestic corporation M owns 75 percent of the one class of stock in foreign corporation R, which in turn owns 80 percent of the one class of stock in foreign corporation S, which in turn owns 90 percent of the one class of stock in foreign corporation T. Under this paragraph, R Corporation is considered as owning 80 percent of the 90 percent of the stock which S Corporation owns in T Corporation, or 72 percent. Corporation M is considered as owning 75 percent of such 72 percent of the stock in T Corporation, or 54 percent. Since M Corporation is a domestic corporation, the attribution under this paragraph stops with M Corporation, even though, illustratively, such corporation is wholly owned by domestic corporation N.

(c) *Rules of application.*—(1) *Special rule for mutual insurance companies.*—For purposes of applying paragraph (a) of this section in the case of a foreign mutual insurance company, the term "stock" shall include any certificate entitling the holder to voting power in the corporation.

(2) *Amount of interest in foreign corporation, foreign partnership, foreign trust, or foreign estate.*—The determination of a person's proportionate interest in a foreign corporation, foreign partnership, foreign trust, or foreign estate will be made on the basis of all the facts and circumstances in each case. Generally, in determining a person's proportionate interest in a foreign corporation, the purpose for which the rules of section 958(a) and this section are being applied will be taken into account. Thus, if the rules of section 958 (a) are being applied to determine the amount of stock owned for purposes of section 951(a), a person's proportionate interest in a foreign corporation will generally be determined with reference to such person's interest in the income of such corporation. If the rules of section 958(a) are being applied to determine the amount of voting power owned for purposes of section 951(b) or 957, a person's proportionate interest in a foreign corporation will generally be determined with reference to the amount of voting power in such corporation owned by such person. However, any arrangement which artificially decreases a United States person's proportionate interest will not be recognized. See §§ 1.951-1 and 1.957-1.

(d) *Stock of foreign corporations owned through domestic partnerships.*—(1) *In general.*—Except as otherwise provided in paragraph (d)(2) of this section, for purposes of sections 951, 951A, and 956(a), and for purposes of any provision that specifically applies by reference to any of such sections or the regulations in this part under section 951, 951A, or sections 956 (but only as the regulations in this part under section 956 relate to section 956(a)), a domestic partnership is not treated as owning stock of a foreign corporation within the meaning of section 958(a). For purposes of determining the persons that own stock of the foreign corporation within the meaning of section 958(a) when the preceding sentence applies, stock of a foreign corporation owned by a domestic partnership is treated in the same manner as stock of a foreign corporation owned by a foreign partnership under section 958(a)(2) and paragraph (b) of this section.

(2) *Non-application for certain purposes.*—Paragraph (d)(1) of this section does not apply for purposes of—

(i) Determining whether any United States person is a United States shareholder (as defined in section 951(b));

(ii) Determining whether any foreign corporation is a controlled foreign corporation (CFC) (as defined in section 957(a));

(iii) Applying section 956(c) and (d);

(iv) Applying section 1248; or

(v) Determining whether any United States shareholder is a controlling domestic shareholder (as defined in § 1.964-1(c)(5)).

(3) *Examples.*—The following examples illustrate the application of this paragraph (d).

(i) *Example 1.*—(A) *Facts.* USP, a domestic corporation, and Individual A, a United States citizen unrelated to USP, own 95% and 5%, respectively, of PRS, a domestic partnership. PRS owns 100% of the single class of stock of FC, a foreign corporation.

(B) *Analysis.*—(*1*) *United States shareholder and CFC determinations.* Under paragraphs (d)(2)(i) and (ii) of this section, respectively, the determination of whether PRS, USP, and Individual A (each a United States person) are United States shareholders of FC, and whether FC is a controlled foreign corporation, is made without regard to paragraph (d)(1) of this section. PRS, a United States person, owns 100% of the total combined voting power or value of the FC stock within the meaning of section 958(a). Accordingly, PRS is a United States shareholder under section 951(b), and FC is a controlled foreign corporation under section 957(a). USP is also a United States shareholder of FC because it owns 95% of the total combined voting power or value of the FC stock under sections 958(b) and 318(a)(2)(A). Individual A, however, is not a United States shareholder of FC because Individual A owns only 5% of the total combined voting power or value of the FC stock under sections 958(b) and 318(a)(2)(A).

(2) *Application of sections 951 and 951A.* Under paragraph (d)(1) of this section, for purposes of sections 951 and 951A, PRS is not treated as owning (within the meaning of section 958(a)) the FC stock; instead, for purposes of determining the persons that own the FC stock within the meaning of section 958(a), the FC stock is treated as if it were owned by a foreign partnership under paragraph (b) of this section. Therefore, for purposes of sections 951 and 951A, USP is treated as owning 95% of the FC stock under section 958(a), and Individual A is treated as owning 5% of the FC stock under section 958(a). USP is a United States shareholder of FC, and therefore USP determines its income inclusions under sections 951 and 951A directly with respect to FC based on its ownership of FC stock under section 958(a). However, because Individual A is not a United States shareholder of FC, Individual A does not have an income inclusion under section 951 with respect to FC or a pro rata share of any amount of FC for purposes of section 951A. This is the case even though PRS is a United States shareholder of FC.

(ii) *Example 2.*—(A) *Facts.* USP, a domestic corporation, and Individual A, a United States citizen, own 90% and 10%, respectively, of PRS1, a domestic partnership. PRS1 and Individual B, a nonresident alien individual, own 90% and 10%, respectively, of PRS2, a domestic partnership. PRS2 owns 100% of the single class of stock of FC, a foreign corporation. USP, Individual A, and Individual B are unrelated to each other.

(B) *Analysis.*—(1) *United States shareholder and CFC determinations.* Under paragraphs (d)(2)(i) and (ii) of this section, the determination of whether PRS1, PRS2, USP, and Individual A (each a United States person) are United States shareholders of FC, and whether FC is a controlled foreign corporation, is made without regard to paragraph (d)(1) of this section. PRS2 owns 100% of the total combined voting power or value of the FC stock within the meaning of section 958(a). Accordingly, PRS2 is a United States shareholder under section 951(b), and FC is a controlled foreign corporation under section 957(a). Under sections 958(b) and 318(a)(2)(A), PRS1 is treated as owning 90% of the FC stock owned by PRS2. Accordingly, PRS1 is also a United States shareholder under section 951(b). Further, under section 958(b)(2), PRS1 is treated as owning 100% of the FC stock for purposes of determining the FC stock treated as owned by USP and Individual A under section 318(a)(2)(A). Therefore, USP is treated as owning 90% of the FC stock under section 958(b) (100% x 100% x 90%), and Individual A is treated as owning 10% of the FC stock under section 958(b) (100% x 100% x 10%). Accordingly, both USP and Individual A are also United States shareholders of FC under section 951(b).

(2) *Application of sections 951 and 951A.* Under paragraph (d)(1) of this section, for purposes of sections 951 and 951A, PRS1 and PRS2 are not treated as owning (within the meaning of section 958(a)) the FC stock; instead, for purposes of determining the persons that own the FC stock within the meaning of section 958(a), as the FC stock is treated as if it were owned by foreign partnerships under paragraph (b) of this section. Therefore, for purposes of determining the amount included in gross income under sections 951 and 951A, under section 958(a) USP is treated as owning 81% (100% x 90% x 90%) of the FC stock, and Individual A is treated as owning 9% (100% x 90% x 10%) of the FC stock. Because USP and Individual A are both United States shareholders of FC, USP and Individual A determine their respective inclusions under sections 951 and 951A directly with respect to FC based on their ownership of FC stock under section 958(a). This is the case even though PRS2 is a United States shareholder of FC.

(iii) *Example 3.*—(A) *Facts.* Individual A, a United States citizen, Individual B, a United States citizen unrelated to Individual A, and Individual C, a foreign person unrelated to both Individuals A and B, own 10%, 5%, and 85%, respectively, of PRS, a domestic partnership. PRS owns 100% of the single class of stock of FC, a foreign corporation. FC holds an account receivable from PRS that constitutes an obligation of a United States person within the meaning of section 956(c)(1)(C) and § 1.956-2(a)(1)(iii).

(B) *Analysis.*—(1) *United States shareholder and CFC determinations.* Under paragraphs (d)(2)(i) and (ii) of this section, respectively, the determination of whether PRS, Individual A, and Individual B (each a United States person) are United States shareholders of FC, and whether FC is a controlled foreign corporation, is made without regard to paragraph (d)(1) of this section. PRS, a United States person, owns 100% of the total combined voting power or value of the FC stock within the meaning of section 958(a). Accordingly, PRS is a United States shareholder under section 951(b), and FC is a controlled foreign corporation under section 957(a). Individual A is also a United States shareholder of FC because it owns 10% of the total combined voting power or value of the FC stock under sections 958(b) and 318(a)(2)(A). Individual B, however, is not a United States shareholder of FC because Individual B owns only 5% of the total combined voting power or value of the FC stock under sections 958(b) and 318(a)(2)(A).

(2) *Application of section 956(a).* Under paragraph (d)(1) of this section, for purposes of section 956(a), PRS is not treated as owning (within the meaning of section 958(a)) the FC stock; instead, for purposes of determining the persons that own the FC stock within the meaning of section 958(a), as the FC stock is treated as if it were owned by a foreign partnership under paragraph (b) of this section. Therefore, for purposes of section 956(a), under section 958(a) Individual A is treated as owning 10% of the FC stock, and Individual B is treated as owning 5% of the FC stock. Individual A is a United States shareholder of FC, and therefore Individual A determines the amount it must include in gross income under section 951(a)(1)(B) by reason of the PRS obligation held by FC based on its ownership of FC stock under section 958(a) as determined under paragraph (d)(1) of this section. However, because Individual B is not a United States shareholder of FC, Individual B does not have an amount to include in income under sections 956(a) and 951(a)(1)(B).

(3) *Application of section 956(c) and (d).* Under paragraph (d)(2)(iii) of this section, for purposes of section 956(c) and (d), the determination of whether FC holds United States property is made without regard to paragraph (d)(1) of this section. Therefore, PRS is treated as owning stock of FC within the meaning of section 958(a) for purposes of determining the amount of United States property held by FC arising from its account receivable from PRS.

(4) *Applicability dates.*—(i) *Paragraphs (d)(1) through (3) of this section.*—Paragraphs (d)(1) through (3) of this section apply to taxable years of foreign corporations beginning on or after January 25, 2022, and to taxable years of United States persons in which or with which such taxable years of foreign corporations end. For taxable years of a foreign corporation that precede the taxable years described in the preceding sentence, a domestic partnership may apply paragraphs (d)(1) through (3) of this section in their entirety to taxable years of a foreign corporation beginning after December 31, 2017, and to taxable years of the domestic partnership in which or with which such taxable years of the foreign corporation end, provided that the partnership, its partners that are United States shareholders of the foreign corporation, and other domestic partnerships that bear relationships described in section 267(b) or 707(b) to the partnership (and their United States shareholder partners) consistently apply paragraphs (d)(1) through (3) of this section with respect to all foreign corporations whose stock the domestic partnerships own within the meaning of section 958(a) (determined without regard to paragraph (d)(1) of this section).

(ii) *Rules applicable before January 25, 2022.*—For taxable years of foreign corporations beginning before January 25, 2022, and to taxable years of United States persons in which or with which such taxable years of foreign corporations end, see §§ 1.951-1(h) and 1.951A-1(e) as in effect and contained in 26 CFR part 1, as revised April 1, 2021.

(e) [Reserved]

(f) *Illustration.*—The application of this section may be illustrated by the following examples:

Example (1). United States persons A and B own 25 percent and 50 percent, respectively, of the one class of stock in foreign corporation M. Corporation M owns 80 percent of the one class of stock in foreign corporation N, and N Corporation owns 60 percent of the one class of stock in foreign corporation P. Under paragraph (b) of this section, M Corporation is considered to own 48 percent (80% of 60%) of the stock in P Corporation; such 48 percent is treated as actually owned by M Corporation for the purpose of again applying paragraph (b) of this section. Thus, A and B are considered to own 12 percent (25% of 48%) and 24 percent (50% of 48%), respectively, of the stock in P Corporation.

Example (2). United States person C is a 60-percent partner in foreign partnership X. Partnership X owns 40 percent of the one class of stock in foreign corporation Q. Corporation Q is a 50-percent partner in foreign partnership Y, and partnership Y owns 100 percent of the one class of stock in foreign corporation R. By the application of paragraph (b) of this section, C is considered to own 12 percent (60% of 40% of 50% of 100%) of the stock in R Corporation.

Example (3). Foreign trust Z was created for the benefit of United States persons D, E, and F. Under the terms of the trust instrument, the trust income is required to be divided into three equal shares. Each beneficiary's share of the income may either be accumulated for him or distributed to him in the discretion of the trustee. In 1970, the trust is to terminate and there is to be paid over to each beneficiary the accumulated income applicable to his share and one-third of the corpus. The corpus of trust Z is composed of 90 percent of the one class of stock in foreign corporation S. By the application of this section, each of D, E, and F is considered to own 30 percent (1/3 of 90 percent) of the stock in S Corporation.

Example (4). Among the assets of foreign estate W are Blackacre and a block of stock, consisting of 75 percent of the one class of stock of foreign corporation T. Under the terms of the will governing estate W, Blackacre is left to G, a nonresident alien, for life, remainder to H, a nonresident alien, and the block of stock is left to United States person K. By the application of this section, K is considered to own the 75 percent of the stock of T Corporation, and G and H are not considered to own any of such stock.

[Reg. § 1.958-1.]

□ [*T.D. 6889, 7-11-66. Amended by T.D. 7893, 5-11-83, T.D. 8955, 7-19-2001 and T.D. 9960, 1-24-2022 (corrected 2-18-2022).*]

Proposed Amendments to Regulation

§ 1.958-1. Direct and indirect ownership of stock.—

* * *

(d) * * *

(1) * * * Except as otherwise provided in paragraph (d)(2) of this section, for purposes of sections 951, 951A, 953(c), and 956(a) and § 1.964-1(c), and for purposes of any provision that specifically applies by reference to any of such sections or the regulations in this part under section 951, 951A, 953, or 956 (but only as the regulations in this part under section 953 or section 956 relate to section 953(c) or section 956(a), respectively), a domestic partnership is not treated as owning stock of a foreign corporation within the meaning of section 958(a). * * *

(2) * * *

(v) Applying section 953(c)(1)(A) for purposes of determining whether any foreign corporation is a controlled foreign corporation as defined in sections 953(c)(1)(B), 953(c)(3)(E), or 953(d)(1)(A).

* * *

(4) * * *

(i) * * * Notwithstanding the prior sentences, paragraph (d)(2)(v) of this section and the inclusion of the references to section 953(c) and § 1.964-1(c) in paragraph (d)(1) of this section apply to taxable years of foreign corporations beginning on or after [date of publication of the Treasury decision adopting these rules as final regulations in the **Federal Register**], and to taxable years of United States persons in which or with which such taxable years of foreign corporations end.

* * *

(e) *Elective entity treatment for certain S corporations.*—(1) *In general.*—Except as otherwise provided in this paragraph (e), with respect to an S corporation (as defined in section 1361(a)(1)), paragraph (d)(1) of this section shall not apply, and such S corporation shall be treated as owning stock of a foreign corporation within the meaning of section 958(a), if—

(i) The S corporation and its shareholders (where applicable) make the election described in paragraph (e)(2) of this section;

(ii) The S corporation made its election under section 1362(a) before June 22, 2019;

(iii) The S corporation would have been treated as owning stock of a controlled foreign corporation within the meaning of section 958(a) on June 22, 2019, if § 1.951A-1(e) (as in effect and contained in 26 CFR part 1, as revised April 1, 2021) did not apply to it;

(iv) The S corporation had transition accumulated earnings and profits (as defined in paragraph (e)(3) of this section) on September 1, 2020, or on the first day of any subsequent taxable year; and

(v) The S corporation maintains sufficient records to support the determination of the transition accumulated earnings and profits amount.

(2) *Election.*—(i) *Time and manner of making election.*—With respect to the first taxable year ending on or after September 1, 2020, an S corporation may irrevocably elect to apply the provisions of paragraph (e)(1) of this section on a timely-filed (including extensions) original Form 1120-S, "U.S. Income Tax Return for an S Corporation," by attaching a statement to such return including the contents of paragraph (e)(2)(ii) of this section. For taxable years of an S corporation ending before September 1, 2020, and after June 21, 2019, the S corporation and all of its shareholders may irrevocably elect to apply the provisions of paragraph (e)(1) of this section on timely-filed (including extensions) original returns or on amended returns filed by March 15, 2021, by attaching a statement including the contents of paragraph (e)(2)(ii) of this section thereto. An election described in Section 3.02 of Notice 2020-69, 2020-39 I.R.B. 604 that is filed (in the time and manner specified in Section 3.02 of Notice 2020-69) on or before [date of publication of the Treasury decision adopting these rules as final regulations in the **Federal Register**] is deemed to satisfy the election requirement of this paragraph (e)(2).

(ii) *Contents of election statement.*—The statement described in paragraph (e)(2)(i) of this section must:

(A) Identify that the S corporation and its shareholders (where applicable) are electing for the S corporation to be treated as owning stock of a foreign corporation within the meaning of section 958(a) under paragraph (e)(2) of this section;

(B) Include the amount of transition accumulated earnings and profits (as defined in paragraph (e)(3) of this section); and

(C) Where applicable, be signed by a person authorized to sign the S corporation's return that is required to be filed under section 6037.

(3) *Transition accumulated earnings and profits.*—(i) *In general.*—For purposes of this section, the term *transition accumulated earnings and profits* means, with respect to an S corporation and its shareholders, the amount of accumulated earnings and profits of the S corporation calculated as of September 1, 2020, reduced as described in paragraph (e)(3)(ii) of this section. Transition accumulated earnings and profits are not increased as a result of transactions occurring (or entity classification elections described in § 301.7701-3 of this chapter filed) after September 1, 2020. For purposes of this section, transition accumulated earnings and profits are not transferable to another person under any provision of the Code.

(ii) *Reduction solely by distributions.*—An S corporation with transition accumulated earnings and profits is treated as having no transition accumulated earnings and profits if, beginning after September 1, 2020, the S corporation distributes in one or more distributions a cumulative amount of accumulated earnings and profits equal to or greater than the amount of the S corporation's transition accumulated earnings and profits as of September 1, 2020.

(4) *Required aggregate treatment.*—In the case of an S corporation that has made an election under paragraph (e)(2) of this section and which satisfies the additional requirements of paragraph (e)(1) of this section, paragraph (d) of this section shall apply beginning with the S corporation's first taxable year for which the S corporation has no transition accumulated earnings and profits on the first day of that year, and to each subsequent taxable year of the S corporation.

(5) *Examples.*—The following examples illustrate the application of paragraph (e).

(i) *Example 1.*—(A) *Facts.* Individual A and Individual B, each a United States citizen, respectively own 5% and 95% of the single class of stock of SCX, an S corporation. SCX's sole asset is 100% of the single class of stock of FC, a controlled foreign corporation, which SCX has held since June 1, 2019. None of SCX, Individual A, or Individual B own shares, directly or indirectly, in any other controlled foreign corporation. Individual A, Individual B, SCX, and FC all use the calendar year as their taxable year. On January 1, 2021, SCX has transition accumulated earnings and profits of $100x and AAA of $0. SCX elects to apply the transition rules under paragraph (e)(1) of this section. During the 2021 taxable year, FC has $200x of tested income (within the meaning of § 1.951A-2(b)(1)) and $0 of qualified business asset investment (QBAI) (within the meaning of § 1.951A-3(b)).

(B) *Analysis.*—(1) *S corporation level.* As an electing S corporation with transition accumulated earnings and profits on the first day of the taxable year (January 1, 2021), SCX is treated as owning (within the meaning of section 958(a)) all the stock of FC for purposes of applying sections 951 and 951A and any provision that applies specifically by reference thereto. Accordingly, SCX, a United States shareholder of FC, determines its GILTI inclusion amount under § 1.951A-1(c)(1) for its 2021 taxable year. SCX's pro rata share of FC's tested income is $200x, and its pro rata share of FC's QBAI is $0. SCX's net CFC tested income (within the meaning of § 1.951A-1(c)(2)) is $200x, and its net deemed tangible income return (within the meaning of § 1.951A-1(c)(3)) is $0. As a result, SCX's GILTI inclusion amount for 2021 is $200x. At the end of 2021, SCX increases its AAA by $200x to reflect the GILTI inclusion amount. Because SCX computes its income as an individual under section 1363(b), it cannot take a section 250 deduction for any GILTI inclusion amount. See § 1.250(a)-1(c)(1).

(2) *S corporation shareholder level.* Neither Individual A nor Individual B is treated as owning the stock in FC within the meaning of section 958(a). Accordingly, Individual A and Individual B include in gross income their pro rata shares of SCX's GILTI inclusion amount as described in section 1366(a), which is $10x ($200x x 5%) for Individual A and $190x ($200x x 95%) for Individual B.

(ii) *Example 2.*—(A) *Facts.* The facts are the same as in paragraph (e)(5)(i) of this section, except that, on December 31, 2021, SCX distributes $300x to its shareholders. In addition, FC has an additional $200x of tested income (within the meaning of § 1.951A-2(b)(1)) and $0 of QBAI (within the meaning of § 1.951A-3(b)) during the 2022 taxable year.

(B) *Analysis.*—(1) *Determination of transition accumulated earnings and profits.* Before taking into account the distribution on December 31, 2021, the results for taxable year 2021 are the same as in paragraph (e)(5)(i)(B) of this section. For 2021, $200x, the portion of SCX's $300x distribution that does not exceed AAA, is subject to section 1368(c)(1). The remaining distribution of $100x is treated as a dividend under section 316 to the extent of SCX's accumulated earnings and profits. As of January 1, 2022, SCX has $0 of transition accumulated earnings and profits under paragraph (e)(3) of this section because the cumulative amount of SCX's distributions out of accumulated earnings and profits after September 1, 2020, equals or exceeds the amount of SCX's transition accumulated earnings and profits as of September 1, 2020.

(2) *S corporation level.* Because SCX has no transition accumulated earnings and profits as of January 1, 2022, paragraph (d) of this section applies to SCX for its taxable year 2022 and for each subsequent taxable year. As a result, for purposes of determining a GILTI inclusion amount in its taxable year 2022, SCX is not treated as owning (within the meaning of section 958(a)) the FC stock; instead, SCX is treated in the same manner as a foreign partnership for purposes of determining the FC stock owned by Individual A and Individual B under section 958(a)(2). Accordingly, SCX does not have a GILTI inclusion amount for its 2022 taxable year (or for any subsequent taxable year) and therefore will not increase its AAA as a result of GILTI inclusion amounts attributable to FC stock for its taxable year 2022 (or for any subsequent taxable year).

(3) *S corporation shareholder level.* With respect to Individual A, for purposes of determining the GILTI inclusion amount for taxable year 2022, Individual A is treated as owning 5% of the FC stock under section 958(a). Individual A is not a United States shareholder of FC because Individual A owns (within the meaning of section 958(a) and (b)) less than 10% of the FC stock. Accordingly, Individual A does not have a GILTI inclusion amount for taxable year 2022. With respect to Individual B, for purposes of determining the GILTI inclusion amount for taxable year 2022, Individual B is treated as owning 95% of the FC stock under section 958(a). In addition, Individual B is a United States shareholder of FC because Individual B owns (within the meaning of section 958(a) and (b)) at least 10% of the FC stock. Accordingly, Individual B's pro rata share of FC's tested income is $190x ($200x x 95%), and Individual B's pro rata share of FC's QBAI is $0. Individual B's net CFC tested income is $190x, and Individual B's net deemed tangible income return is $0. As a result, Individual B's GILTI inclusion amount for taxable year 2022 is $190x.

(6) *Applicability date.*—This paragraph (e) applies to taxable years of S corporations ending on or after September 1, 2020. Taxpayers may choose to apply this paragraph (e) to taxable years of S corporations ending on or after June 22, 2019, provided that the S corporation and its shareholders that are United States shareholders consistently apply the rules set forth in this paragraph (e) with respect to all controlled foreign corporations whose stock the S corporation owns within the meaning of section 958(a).

* * *

[Prop. Reg. § 1.958-1.]

[Proposed 1-25-2022.]

§ 1.958-2. Constructive ownership of stock.—(a) *In general.*—Section 958(b) provides that, for purposes of sections 951(b), 954(d)(3), 956(b)(2), and 957, the rules of section 318(a) as modified by section 958(b) and this section shall apply to the extent that the effect is to treat a United States person as a United States shareholder within the meaning of section 951(b), to treat a person as a related person within the meaning of section 954(d)(3), to treat the stock of a domestic corporation as owned by a United States shareholder of a controlled foreign corporation under section 956(b)(2), or to treat a foreign corporation as a controlled foreign corporation under section 957. The rules contained in this section also apply for purposes of other provisions of the Code and regulations which make express reference to section 958(b).

(b) *Members of family.*—(1) *In general.*—Except as provided in subparagraph (3) of this paragraph, an individual shall be considered as owning the stock owned, directly or indirectly, by or for—

(i) His spouse (other than a spouse who is legally separated from the individual under a decree of divorce or separate maintenance); and

(ii) His children, grandchildren, and parents.

(2) *Effect of adoption.*—For purposes of subparagraph (1)(ii) of this paragraph, a legally adopted child of an individual shall be treated as a child of such individual by blood.

(3) *Stock owned by nonresident alien individual.*—For purposes of this paragraph, stock owned by a nonresident alien individual (other than a foreign trust or foreign estate) shall not be considered as owned by a United States citizen or a resident alien individual. However, this limitation does not apply for purposes of determining whether the stock of a domestic corporation is owned or considered as owned by a United States shareholder under section 956(b)(2) and § 1.956-2(b)(1)(viii). See section 958(b)(1).

(c) *Attribution from partnerships, estates, trusts, and corporations.*—(1) *In general.*—Except as provided in subparagraph (2) of this paragraph—

(i) *From partnerships and estates.*—Stock owned, directly or indirectly, by or for a partnership or estate shall be considered as owned proportionately by its partners or beneficiaries.

(ii) *From trusts.*—(*a*) *To beneficiaries.*—Stock owned, directly or indirectly, by or for a trust (other than employees' trust described in section 401(a) which is exempt from tax under section 501(a)) shall be considered as owned by its beneficiaries in proportion to the actuarial interest of such beneficiaries in such trust.

(*b*) *To owner.*—Stock owned, directly or indirectly, by or for any portion of a trust of which a person is considered the owner under sections 671 to 679 (relating to grantors and others treated as substantial owners) shall be considered as owned by such person.

(iii) *From corporations.*—If 10 percent or more in value of the stock in a corporation is owned, directly or indirectly, by or for any person, such person shall be considered as owning the stock owned, directly or indirectly, by or for such corporation, in that proportion which the value of the stock which such person so owns bears to the value of all the stock in such corporation. See section 958(b)(3).

(2) *Rules of application.*—For purposes of subparagraph (1) of this paragraph, if a partnership, estate, trust, or corporation owns, directly or indirectly, more than 50 percent of the total combined voting power of all classes of stock entitled to vote in a corporation, it shall be considered as owning all the stock entitled to vote. See section 958(b)(2).

(d) *Attribution to partnerships, estates, trusts, and corporations.*—(1) *In general.*—Except as otherwise provided in paragraph (d)(2) of this section and § 1.954-1(f)—

(i) *To partnerships and estates.*—Stock owned, directly or indirectly, by or for a partner or a beneficiary of an estate shall be considered as owned by the partnership or estate.

(ii) *To trusts.—(a) From beneficiaries.*—Stock owned, directly or indirectly, by or for a beneficiary of a trust (other than an employees' trust described in section 401(a) which is exempt from tax under section 501(a)) shall be considered as owned by the trust, unless such beneficiary's interest in the trust is a remote contingent interest. For purposes of the preceding sentence, a contingent interest of a beneficiary in a trust shall be considered remote if, under the maximum exercise of discretion by the trustee in favor of such beneficiary, the value of such interest, computed actuarially, is 5 percent or less of the value of the trust property.

(b) From owner.—Stock owned, directly or indirectly, by or for a person who is considered the owner of any portion of a trust under sections 671 to 678 (relating to grantors and others treated as substantial owners) shall be considered as owned by the trust.

(iii) *To corporations.*—If 50 percent or more in value of the stock in a corporation is owned, directly or indirectly, by or for any person, such corporation shall be considered as owning the stock owned, directly or indirectly, by or for such person. This subdivision shall not be applied so as to consider a corporation as owning its own stock.

(2) [Reserved]

(e) *Options.*—Except as otherwise provided in § 1.954-1(f), if any person has an option to acquire stock, such stock shall be considered as owned by such person. For purposes of the preceding sentence, an option to acquire such an option, and each one of a series of such options, shall be considered as an option to acquire such stock.

(f) *Rules of application.*—For purposes of this section—

(1) *Stock treated as actually owned.*—(i) *In general.*—Except as provided in subdivisions (ii) and (iii) of this subparagraph, stock constructively owned by a person by reason of the application of paragraphs (b), (c), (d), and (e) of this section shall, for purposes of applying such paragraphs, be considered as actually owned by such person.

(ii) *Members of family.*—Stock constructively owned by an individual by reason of the application of paragraph (b) of this section shall not be considered as owned by him for purposes of again applying such paragraph in order to make another the constructive owner of such stock.

(iii) *Partnerships, estates, trusts, and corporations.*—Stock constructively owned by a partnership, estate, trust, or corporation by reason of the application of paragraph (d) of this section shall not be considered as owned by it for purposes of applying paragraph (c) of this section in order to make another the constructive owner of such stock.

(iv) *Option rule in lieu of family rule.*—For purposes of this subparagraph, if stock may be considered as owned by an individual under paragraph (b) or (e) of this section, it shall be considered as owned by him under paragraph (e).

(2) *Coordination of different attribution rules.*—For purposes of any one determination, stock which may be owned under more than one of the rules of § 1.958-1 and this section, or by more than one person, shall be owned under that attribution rule which imputes to the person, or persons, concerned the largest total percentage of such stock. The application of this subparagraph may be illustrated by the following examples:

Example (1). (a) United States persons A and B, and domestic corporation M, own 9 percent, 32 percent, and 10 percent, respectively, of the one class of stock in foreign corporation R. A also owns 10 percent of the one class of stock in M Corporation. For purposes of determining whether A is a United States shareholder with respect to R Corporation, 10 percent of the 10-percent interest of M Corporation in R Corporation is considered as owned by A. See paragraph (c)(1)(iii) of this section. Thus, A owns 10 percent (9% plus 10% of 10%) of the stock in R Corporation and is a United States shareholder with respect to such corporation. Corporations M and B, by reason of owning 10 percent and 32 percent, respectively, of the stock in R Corporation are United States shareholders with respect to such corporation.

(b) For purposes of determining whether R Corporation is a controlled foreign corporation, the 1 percent of the stock in R Corporation directly owned by M Corporation and considered as owned by A cannot be counted twice. Therefore, the total amount of stock in R Corporation owned by United States shareholders is 51 percent, determined as follows:

Stock ownership in R Corporation	(percent)
A	9
B	32
M Corporation	10
Total	51

Example (2). United States person C owns 10 percent of the one class of stock in foreign corporation N, which owns 60 percent of the one class of stock in foreign corporation S. Under paragraph (a)(2) of § 1.958-1, C is considered as owning 6 percent (10% of 60%) of the stock in S Corporation. Under paragraph (c)(1)(iii) and (2) of this section, N Corporation is considered as owning 100 percent of the stock in S Corporation and C is considered as owning 10 percent of such 100 percent, or 10 percent of the stock in S Corporation. Thus, for purposes of determining whether C is a United States shareholder with respect to S Corporation, the attribution rules of paragraph (c)(1)(iii) and (2) of this section are used inasmuch as C owns a larger total percentage of the stock of S Corporation under such rules.

(g) *Illustration.*—The application of this section may be illustrated by the following examples:

(1) *Example 1.*— United States persons A and B own 5 percent and 25 percent, respectively, of the one class of stock in foreign corporation M. Corporation M owns 60 percent of the one class of stock in foreign corporation N. Under paragraph (a)(2) of § 1.958-1, A and B are considered as owning 3 percent (5% of 60%) and 15 percent (25% of 60%), respectively, of the stock in N Corporation. Under paragraph (c)(2) of this section, M Corporation is treated as owning all the stock in N Corporation, and, under paragraph (c)(1)(iii) of this section, B is considered as owning 25 percent of such 100 percent, or 25 percent of the stock in N Corporation. Inasmuch as A owns less than 10 percent of the stock in M Corporation, he is not considered as owning, under paragraph (c)(1)(iii) of this section, any of the stock in N Corporation owned by M Corporation. Thus, the attribution rules of paragraph (a)(2) of § 1.958-1 are used with respect to A inasmuch as he owns a larger total percentage of the stock of N Corporation under such rules; and the attribution rules of paragraphs (c)(1)(iii) and (2) of this section are used with respect to B inasmuch as he owns a larger total percentage of the stock of N Corporation under such rules.

(2) *Example 2.*—United States person C owns 60 percent of the one class of stock in domestic corporation P; corporation P owns 60 percent of the one class of stock in foreign corporation Q; and corporation Q owns 60 percent of the one class of stock in foreign corporation R. Under paragraph (a)(2) of § 1.958-1, P Corporation is considered as owning 36 percent (60% of 60%) of the stock in R Corporation, and C is considered as owning none of the stock in R Corporation inasmuch as the chain of ownership stops at the first United States person and P Corporation is such a person. Under paragraph (c)(2) of this section, Q Corporation is treated as owning 100 percent of the stock in R Corporation, and under paragraph (c)(1)(iii) of this section, P Corporation is considered as owning 60 percent of such 100 percent, or 60 percent of the stock in R Corporation. For purposes of determining the amount of stock in R Corporation which C is considered as owning, P Corporation is treated under paragraph (c)(2) of this section as owning 100 percent of the stock in R Corporation; therefore, C is considered as owning 60 percent of the stock in R Corporation. Thus, the attribution rules of paragraphs (c)(1)(iii) and (2) of this section are used with respect to C and P Corporation inasmuch as they each own a larger total percentage of the stock of R Corporation under such rules.

(3) *Example 3.*—United States person D owns 25 percent of the one class of stock in foreign corporation S. D is also a 40-percent partner in domestic partnership X, which owns 50 percent of the one class of stock in domestic corporation T. Under paragraph (d)(1)(i) of this section, the 25 percent of the stock in S Corporation owned by D is considered as being owned by partnership X; since such stock is treated as actually owned by partnership X under paragraph (f)(1)(i) of this section, such stock is in turn considered as being owned by T Corporation under paragraph (d)(1)(iii) of this section. Thus, under paragraphs (d)(1) and (f)(1)(i) of this section, T Corporation is considered as owning 25 percent of the stock in S Corporation.

(4) *Example 4.*—Foreign corporation U owns 100 percent of the one class of stock in domestic corporation V and also 100 percent of the one class of stock in foreign corporation W. Because more than 50

percent in value of the stock of V Corporation is owned by its sole shareholder, U Corporation, V Corporation is considered under paragraph (d)(1)(iii) of this section as owning the stock owned by U Corporation in W Corporation, and accordingly is a United States shareholder of W Corporation.

(5) *Example 5.*—United States citizen E owns 15 percent of the one class of stock in foreign corporation Y, and United States citizen F, E's spouse, owns 5 percent of such stock. E and F's four nonresident alien grandchildren each own 20 percent of the stock in Y Corporation. Under paragraph (b)(1) of this section, E is considered as owning the stock owned by F in Y Corporation; however, by virtue of paragraph (b)(3) of this section, E may not be considered under paragraph (b)(1) of this section as owning any of the stock in Y Corporation owned by such grandchildren.

(6) *Example 6.*—United States person F owns 10 percent of the one class of stock in foreign corporation Z; corporation Z owns 10 percent of the one class of stock in foreign corporation K; and corporation K owns 100 percent of the one class of stock in foreign corporation L. United States person G, F's spouse, owns 9 percent of the stock in K Corporation. Under paragraph (c)(1)(iii) of this section or paragraph (a)(2) of § 1.958-1, F is considered as owning 1 percent (10% of 10% of 100%) of the stock in L Corporation by reason of his ownership of stock in Z Corporation, and, under paragraph (b)(1) of this section, G is considered as owning such 1 percent of the stock in L Corporation. Under paragraph (a)(2) of § 1.958-1, G is considered as owning 9 percent (9% of 100%) of the stock in L Corporation by reason of her ownership of stock in K Corporation, and, under paragraph (b)(1) of this section, F is considered as owning such 9 percent of the stock in L Corporation. Thus, for the purpose of determining whether F or G is a United States shareholder with respect to L Corporation, each of F and G is considered as owning a total of 10 percent of the stock in L Corporation by applying the rules of paragraph (a)(2) of § 1.958-1 and paragraphs (b)(1) and (c)(1)(iii) of this section.

(h) *Applicability date.*—Paragraphs (d)(1) and (e) of this section apply for taxable years of controlled foreign corporations ending on or after November 19, 2019, and for the taxable years of United States shareholders in which or with which such taxable years end. Paragraphs (d)(2) and (g)(4) of this section apply to taxable years of foreign corporations ending on or after October 1, 2019, and taxable years of United States shareholders in which or with which such taxable years of foreign corporations end. For taxable years of foreign corporations ending before October 1, 2019, and taxable years of United States shareholders in which or with which such taxable years of foreign corporations end, a taxpayer may apply such provisions to the last taxable year of a foreign corporation beginning before January 1, 2018, and each subsequent taxable year of the foreign corporation, and to taxable years of United States shareholders in which or with which such taxable years of the foreign corporation end, provided that the taxpayer and United States persons that are related (within the meaning of section 267 or 707) to the taxpayer consistently apply such provisions with respect to all foreign corporations. For taxable years of foreign corporations ending before October 1, 2019, and taxable years of United States shareholders in which or with which such taxable years of foreign corporations end, where the taxpayer does not apply the provisions of paragraphs (d)(2) and (g)(4) of this section, see paragraph (d)(2) and (g)(4) of this section as in effect and contained in 26 CFR part 1, as revised April 1, 2020. [Reg. § 1.958-2.]

☐ [*T.D.* 6889, 7-11-66. *Amended by T.D.* 7712, 8-6-80, *T.D.* 8955, 7-19-2001, *T.D.* 9883, 11-18-2019 *and T.D.* 9908, 9-21-2020.]

§ 1.959-1. Exclusion from gross income of United States persons of previously taxed earnings and profits.—(a) *In general.*—Sections 951 through 964 provide that certain types of income of controlled foreign corporations will be subject to United States income tax even though such amounts are not currently distributed to the United States shareholders of such corporations. The amounts so taxed to certain United States shareholders are described as subpart F income, previously excluded subpart F income withdrawn from investment in less developed countries, previously excluded subpart F income withdrawn from investment in foreign base company shipping operations, and increases in earnings invested in United States property. Section 959 provides that amounts taxed as subpart F income, as previously excluded subpart F income withdrawn from investment in less developed countries, or as previously excluded subpart F income withdrawn from investment in foreign base company shipping operations are not taxed again as increases in earnings invested in United States property. Section 959 also provides an exclusion whereby none of the amounts so taxed are taxed again when actually distributed directly, or indirectly through a chain of ownership described in section 958(a), to United States shareholders or to such shareholders' successors in interest. The exclusion also applies to amounts taxed to United States shareholders as income of one controlled foreign corporation and later distributed to another controlled foreign corporation in such a chain of ownership where such amounts would otherwise be again included in the income of such shareholders or their successors in interest as subpart F income of the controlled foreign corporation to which they are distributed. Section 959 also provides rules for the allocation of distributions to earnings and profits and for the non-dividend treatment of actual distributions which are excluded from gross income.

(b) *Actual distributions to United States persons.*—The earnings and profits for a taxable year of a foreign corporation attributable to amounts which are, or have been, included in the gross income of a United States shareholder of such corporation under section 951(a) shall not, when such amounts are distributed to such shareholder directly, or indirectly through a chain of ownership described in section 958(a), be again included in the gross income of such United States shareholder. See section 959(a)(1). Thus, earnings and profits attributable to amounts which are, or have been, included in the gross income of a United States shareholder of a foreign corporation under section 951(a)(1)(A)(i) as subpart F income, under section 951(a)(1)(A)(ii) as previously excluded subpart F income withdrawn from investment in less developed countries, under section 951(a)(1)(A)(iii) as previously excluded subpart F income withdrawn from investment in foreign base company shipping operations, or under section 951(a)(1)(B) as earnings invested in United States property, shall not be again included in the gross income of such shareholder when such amounts are actually distributed, directly or indirectly, to such shareholder. See paragraph (d) of this section for exclusion applicable to such shareholder's successor in interest. The application of this paragraph may be illustrated by the following example:

Example. (a) A, a United States shareholder, owns 100 percent of the only class of stock of R Corporation, a corporation organized on January 1, 1963, which is a controlled foreign corporation throughout the period here involved. Both A and R Corporation use the calendar year as a taxable year.

(b) During 1964, R Corporation derives $100 of subpart F income, and A includes such amount in his gross income under section 951(a)(1)(A)(i). Corporation R's current and accumulated earnings and profits (before taking into account distributions made during 1964) are $150. Also, during 1964, R Corporation distributes $50 to A. The $50 distribution is excludable from A's gross income for 1964 under this paragraph and § 1.959-3 because such distribution represents earnings and profits attributable to amounts which are included in A's gross income for such year under section 951(a).

(c) If instead of deriving the $100 of subpart F income in 1964, R Corporation derives such amount during 1963 and has earnings and profits for 1963 in excess of $100, A must include $100 in his gross income for 1963 under section 951(a)(1)(A)(i). However, the $50 distribution made by R Corporation to A during 1964 is excludable from A's gross income for such year under this paragraph and § 1.959-3 because such distribution represents earnings and profits attributable to amounts which have been included in A's gross income for 1963 under section 951(a).

(d) If, with respect to 1964—

(1) Instead of owning the stock of R Corporation directly, A owns such stock through a chain of ownership described in section 958(a), that is, A owns 100 percent of M Corporation which owns 100 percent of N Corporation which owns 100 percent of R Corporation,

(2) Both M and N Corporations use the calendar year as a taxable year and are controlled foreign corporations throughout the period here involved,

(3) Corporation R derives $100 of subpart F income and has earnings and profits in excess of $100,

(4) Neither M Corporation nor N Corporation has earnings and profits or a deficit in earnings and profits, and

(5) The $50 distribution is from R Corporation to N Corporation to M Corporation to A,

A must include $100 in his gross income for 1964 under section 951(a)(1)(A)(i) by reason of his indirect ownership of R Corporation. However, the $50 distribution is excludable from A's gross income for 1964 under this paragraph and § 1.959-3 because such distribution represents earnings and profits attributable to amounts which are included in A's gross income for such year under section 951(a) and are distributed indirectly to A through a chain of ownership described in section 958(a).

(c) *Excludable investment of earnings in United States property.*—The earnings and profits for a taxable year of a foreign corporation attributable to amounts which are, or have been, included in the gross income of a United States shareholder of such corporation under section 951(a)(1)(A) shall not, when such amounts would, but for section 959(a)(2) and this paragraph, be included under section 951(a)(1)(B) in the gross income of such shareholder directly, or indirectly through a chain of ownership described in section 958(a), be again included in the gross income of such United States shareholder. Thus, earnings and profits attributable to amounts which are, or have been, included in the gross income of a United States shareholder of a foreign corporation under section 951(a)(1)(A)(i) as subpart F income, under section 951(a)(1)(A)(ii) as previously excluded subpart F income withdrawn from investment in less developed countries, or under section 951(a)(1)(A)(iii) as previously excluded subpart F income withdrawn from investment in foreign base company shipping operations may be invested in United States property without being again included in such shareholder's income under section 951(a). Moreover, the first amounts deemed invested in United States property are amounts previously included in the gross income of a United States shareholder under section 951(a)(1)(A). See paragraph (d) of this section for exclusion applicable to such shareholder's successor in interest. The application of this paragraph may be illustrated by the following example:

Example. (a) A, a United States shareholder, owns 100 percent of the only class of stock of R Corporation, a corporation organized on January 1, 1963, which is a controlled foreign corporation throughout the period here involved. Both A and R Corporation use the calendar year as a taxable year.

(b) During 1964, R Corporation derives $35 of subpart F income, and A includes such amount in his gross income under section 951(a)(1)(A)(i). During 1964, R Corporation also invests $50 in tangible property (other than property described in section 956(b)(2)) located in the United States. Corporation R makes no distributions during the year, and its current earnings and profits are in excess of $50. Of the $50 investment of earnings in United States property, $35 is excludable from A's gross income for 1964 under section 959(a)(2) because such amount represents earnings and profits which are attributable to amounts which are included in A's gross income for such year under section 951(a)(1)(A)(i) and therefore may be invested in United States property without again being included in A's gross income. The remaining $15 is includible in A's gross income for 1964 under section 951(a)(1)(B).

(c) If, instead of deriving $35 of subpart F income in 1964, R Corporation has no subpart F income for 1964 but derives the $35 of subpart F income during 1963 and has earnings and profits for such year in excess of $35, A must include $35 in his gross income for 1963 under section 951(a)(1)(A)(i). However, of the $50 investment of earnings in United States property made by R Corporation during 1964, $35 is excludable from A's gross income for 1964 under section 959(a)(2) because such amount represents earnings and profits attributable to amounts which have been included in A's gross income for 1963 under section 951(a)(1)(A)(i). The remaining $15 is includible in A's gross income for 1964 under section 951(a)(1)(B).

(d) *Application of exclusions to shareholder's successor in interest.*—If a United States person (as defined in § 1.957-4) acquires from any person any portion of the interest in the foreign corporation of a United States shareholder referred to in paragraph (b) or (c) of this section, the rules of such paragraph shall apply to such acquiring person but only to the extent that the acquiring person establishes to the satisfaction of the district director the right to the exclusion provided by such paragraph. The information to be furnished by the acquiring person to the district director with his return for the taxable year to support such exclusion shall include:

(1) The name, address, and taxable year of the foreign corporation from which the distribution is received and of all other corporations, partnerships, trusts, or estates in any applicable chain of ownership described in section 958(a);

(2) The name, address, and (in the case of information required to be furnished after June 20, 1983) taxpayer identification number of the person from whom the stock interest was acquired;

(3) A description of the stock interest acquired and its relation, if any, to a chain of ownership described in section 958(a);

(4) The amount for which an exclusion under section 959(a) is claimed; and

(5) Evidence showing that the earnings and profits for which an exclusion is claimed are attributable to amounts which were included in the gross income of a United States shareholder under section 951(a), that such amounts were not previously excluded from the gross income of a United States person, and the identity of the United States shareholder including such amounts.

The acquiring person shall also furnish to the district director such other information as may be required by the district director in support of the exclusion.

Example. (a) A, a United States shareholder, owns 100 percent of the only class of stock of R Corporation, a corporation organized on January 1, 1964, and a controlled foreign corporation throughout the period here involved. Both A and R Corporation use the calendar year as a taxable year.

(b) During 1964, R Corporation has $100 of subpart F income and earnings and profits in excess of $100. A includes $100 in his gross income for 1964 under section 951(a)(1)(A)(i). During 1965, A sells 40 percent of his stock in R Corporation to B, a United States person who uses the calendar year as a taxable year. In 1965, R Corporation has no earnings and profits and experiences no increase in earnings invested in United States property. Corporation R distributes $40 to B on December 1, 1965. If B establishes his right to the exclusion to the satisfaction of the district director, he may exclude $40 from his gross income for 1965 under section 959(a)(1).

(c) If, instead of selling his 40-percent interest directly to B, A sells on February 1, 1965, 40 percent of his stock in R Corporation to C, a nonresident alien, and on October 1, 1965, B acquires the 40-percent interest in R Corporation from C, the result is the same as in paragraph (b) of this example, if B establishes his right to the exclusion to the satisfaction of the district director.

(d) If, instead of acquiring 40 percent, B acquires only 5 percent of A's stock in R Corporation and R Corporation distributes $5 to B during 1965, B is not a United States shareholder (within the meaning of section 951(b)) with respect to R Corporation since he owns only 5 percent of the stock of R Corporation. Notwithstanding, B may exclude the $5 distribution from his gross income for 1965 under section 959(a)(1) if he establishes his right to the exclusion to the satisfaction of the district director.

(e) If the facts are assumed to be the same as in paragraphs (a) and (b) of this example except that—

(1) A owns the stock of R Corporation indirectly through a chain of ownership described in section 958(a), that is, A owns 100 percent of M corporation which owns 100 percent of N Corporation which owns 100 percent of R Corporation,

(2) B acquires from N Corporation 40 percent of the stock in R Corporation,

(3) Both M Corporation and N Corporation are controlled foreign corporations which use the calendar year as a taxable year,

(4) Neither M Corporation nor N Corporation has any amount in 1964 or 1965 which is includible in gross income of United States shareholders under section 951(a), and

(5) Neither M Corporation nor N Corporation has a deficit in earnings and profits for 1964,

the result is the same as in paragraph (b) of this example if B establishes his right to the exclusion to the satisfaction of the district director. [Reg. § 1.959-1.]

□ *[T.D. 6795, 1-28-65. Amended by T.D. 7893, 5-11-83.]*

§ 1.959-2. Exclusion from gross income of controlled foreign corporations of previously taxed earnings and profits.—(a) *Applicable rule.*—The earnings and profits for a taxable year of a controlled foreign corporation attributable to amounts which are, or have been, included in the gross income of a United States shareholder under section 951(a) shall not, when distributed through a chain of ownership described in section 958(a), be also included in the gross income of another controlled foreign corporation in such chain for purposes of the application of section 951(a) to such other controlled foreign corporation with respect to such United States shareholder. See section 959(b). The exclusion from the income of such other foreign corporation also applies with respect to any other United States shareholder who acquires from such United States shareholder or any other person any portion of the interest of such United States shareholder in the controlled foreign corporation, but only to the extent the acquiring shareholder establishes to the satisfaction of the district director the right to such exclusion. An acquiring shareholder claiming the exclusion under section 959(b) shall furnish to the district director with his return for the taxable year the information required under paragraph (d) of § 1.959-1 to support the exclusion under this paragraph.

(b) *Illustration.*—The application of this section may be illustrated by the following example:

Example. (a) A, a United States shareholder, owns 100 percent of the only class of stock of M Corporation which in turn owns 100 percent of the only class of stock of N Corporation. A and corporations M and N use the calendar year as a taxable year and corporations M and N are controlled foreign corporations throughout the period here involved.

(b) During 1963, N Corporation invests $100 in tangible property (other than property described in section 956(b)(2)) located in the United States and has earnings and profits in excess of $100. A is required to include $100 in his gross income for 1963 under section 951(a)(1)(B) by reason of his indirect ownership of the stock of N Corporation. During 1963, M Corporation has no income or investments other than the income derived from a distribution of $100 from N Corporation. Corporation M has earnings and profits of $100 for 1963. Under paragraph (a) of § 1.954-2, the $100 distribution received by M Corporation from N Corporation would otherwise constitute subpart F income of M Corporation; however, by reason of section 959(b) and this section, this amount does not constitute gross income of M Corporation for purposes of determining amounts includible in A's gross income under section 951(a)(1)(A)(i).

(c) During 1964, N Corporation derives $100 of subpart F income and distributes $100 to M Corporation which has no subpart F income for 1964 but which invests the $100 distribution in tangible property (other than property described in section 956(b)(2)) located in the United States. Corporation N's earnings and profits for 1964 are in excess of $100, and M Corporation's current and accumulated earnings and profits (before taking into account distributions made during 1964) are in excess of $100. A is required with respect to N Corporation to include $100 in his gross income for 1964 under section 951(a)(1)(A)(i) by reason of his indirect ownership of the stock of N Corporation. The investment by M Corporation in United States property would otherwise constitute an investment of earnings in United States property to which section 956 applies; however, by reason of section 959(b) and this section, such amount does not constitute gross income of M Corporation for purposes of determining amounts includible in A's gross income under section 951(a)(1)(B).

(d) If during 1965, N Corporation invests $100 in tangible property (other than property described in section 956(b)(2)) located in the United States and has earnings and profits in excess of $100, A will be required with respect to N Corporation to include $100 in his gross income for 1965 under section 951(a)(1)(B), because the $100 of earnings and profits for 1964 attributable to N Corporation's subpart F income which was taxed to A in 1964 was distributed to M Corporation in such year.

(e) If, with respect to 1966—

(1) Corporation N owns 100 percent of the only class of stock of R Corporation,

(2) Corporation R derives $100 of subpart F income, has earnings and profits in excess of $100, and makes no distributions to N Corporation,

(3) Corporation N invests $25 in tangible property (other than property described in section 956(b)(2)) located in the United States and has current and accumulated earnings and profits in excess of $25, and

(4) Corporation M has no income or investments and does not have a deficit in earnings and profits,

the $100 of subpart F income derived by R Corporation is includible in A's gross income for 1966 under section 951(a)(1)(A)(i) and the $25 investment of earnings in United States property by N Corporation is includible in A's gross income for 1966 under section 951(a)(1)(B).

(f) If, however, the facts are the same as in paragraph (e) of this example except that—

(1) During 1966, R Corporation distributes $20 to N Corporation, and

(2) Corporation N makes no distributions during such year to M Corporation,

of the $25 investment in United States property by N Corporation, $20 is not includible in A's gross income for 1966 because such amount represents earnings and profits which are attributable to amounts included in A's gross income for such year under section 951(a)(1)(A)(i) with respect to R Corporation and which have been distributed to N Corporation by R Corporation. By reason of section 959(b) and this section, such $20 distribution to N Corporation does not constitute gross income of N Corporation for purposes of determining amounts includible in A's gross income under section 951(a)(1)(B); however, the remaining $5 of investment of earnings in United States property by N Corporation in 1966 is includible in A's gross income for such year under section 951(a)(1)(B). [Reg. § 1.959-2.]

□ [*T.D.* 6795, 1-28-65.]

§ 1.959-3. Allocation of distributions to earnings and profits of foreign corporations.—(a) *In general.*—For purposes of §§ 1.959-1 and 1.959-2, the source of the earnings and profits from which distributions are made by a foreign corporation as between earnings and profits attributable to increases in earnings invested in United States property, previously taxed subpart F income, previously excluded subpart F income withdrawn from investment in less developed countries, previously excluded subpart F income withdrawn from investment in foreign base company shipping operations, and other amounts shall be determined in accordance with section 959(c) and paragraphs (b) through (e) of this section.

(b) *Applicability of section 316(a).*—For purposes of this section, section 316(a) shall be applied, in determining the source of distributions from the earnings and profits of a foreign corporation, by first applying section 316(a)(2) and then by applying section 316(a)(1)—

(1) First, as provided by section 959(c)(1), to earnings and profits attributable to amounts included in gross income of a United States shareholder under section 951(a)(1)(B) (or which would have been so included but for section 959(a)(2) and paragraph (c) of § 1.959-1),

(2) Secondly, as provided by section 959(c)(2), to earnings and profits attributable to amounts included in gross income of a United States shareholder under section 951(a)(1)(A) (but reduced by amounts not included in such gross income under section 951(a)(1)(B) because of the exclusion provided by section 959(a)(2) and paragraph (c) of § 1.959-1), and

(3) Finally, as provided by section 959(c)(3), to other earnings and profits.

Thus, distributions shall be considered first attributable to amounts, if any, described in subparagraph (1) of this paragraph (first for the current taxable year and then for prior taxable years beginning with the most recent prior taxable year), secondly to amounts, if any, described in subparagraph (2) of this paragraph (first for the current taxable year and then for prior taxable years beginning with the most recent prior taxable year), and finally to the amounts, if any, described in subparagraph (3) of this paragraph (first for the current taxable year and then for prior taxable years beginning with the most recent prior taxable year). See, however, paragraph (e) of § 1.963-3 (applied as if section 963 had not been repealed by the Tax Reduction Act of 1975) for a special rule for determination of the source of distributions counting as minimum distributions. Earnings and profits are classified as to year and as to section 959(c) amount in the year in which such amounts are included in gross income of a United States shareholder under section 951(a) and are reclassified as to section 959(c) amount in the year in which such amounts would be so included but for the provisions of section 959(a)(2); any subsequent distribution of such amounts to a higher tier in a chain of ownership described in section 958(a) does not of itself change such classifications. For example, earnings and profits of a foreign corporation attributable to amounts of previously excluded subpart F income withdrawn from investment in less developed countries (or from investments in export trade assets or foreign base company shipping operations) shall be reclassified as amounts to which subparagraph (2), rather than subparagraph (3), of this paragraph applies for purposes of determining priority of distribution, and such earnings and profits shall be considered attributable to the taxable year in which the withdrawal occurs. This paragraph shall apply to distributions by one foreign corporation to another foreign corporation and by a foreign corporation to a United States person. The application of this paragraph may be illustrated by the following example:

Example. (a) M, a controlled foreign corporation is organized on January 1, 1963, and is 100-percent owned by A, a United States shareholder. Both A and M Corporation use the calendar year as a taxable year, and M Corporation is a controlled foreign corporation throughout the period here involved. As of December 31, 1966, M Corporation's accumulated earnings and profits of $450 (before taking into account distributions made in 1966) applicable to A's interest in such corporation are classified for purposes of section 959(c) as follows:

Year	Classification of earnings and profits for purposes of sec. 959 (c)(1)	(c)(2)	(c)(3)
1963	$100		
1964	100	$75	
1965		75	$50
1966			50

(b) During 1966, M Corporation makes three separate distributions to A of $150 each, and the source of such distributions under section 959(c) is as follows:

	Amount	Year	Allocation of distributions under sec. 959
Distribution # 1:	$100	1964	(c)(1)
	50	1963	(c)(1)
	150		
Distribution # 2:	$50	1963	(c)(1)
	75	1965	(c)(2)
	25	1964	(c)(2)
	150		
Distribution # 3:	$50	1964	(c)(2)
	50	1966	(c)(3)
	50	1965	(c)(3)
	150		

(c) If, in addition to the above facts—

(1) M Corporation owns throughout the period here involved 100 percent of the only class of stock of N Corporation, a controlled foreign corporation which uses the calendar year as a taxable year,

(2) Corporation N derives $60 of subpart F income for 1963 which A includes in his gross income for such year under section 951(a)(1)(A)(i),

(3) Corporation N has earnings and profits for 1963 of $60 but has neither earnings or profits nor a deficit in earnings and profits for 1964, 1965, or 1966, and

(4) During 1966, N Corporation invests $20 in tangible property (not described in section 956(b)(2)) located in the United States and distributes $45 to M Corporation,

the $20 investment of earnings in United States property is excludable from A's gross income for 1966, under section 959(a)(2) and paragraph (c) of § 1.959-1, with respect to N Corporation and the $45 dividend received by M Corporation does not, under section 959(b) and § 1.959-2, constitute gross income of M Corporation for 1966 for purposes of determining amounts includible in A's gross income under section 951(a)(1)(A)(i) with respect to M Corporation. However, the $45 dividend paid by N Corporation to M Corporation is allocated under section 959(c) and this paragraph to the earnings and profits of N Corporation as follows: $20 to 1963 earnings described in section 959(c)(1) and $25 to 1963 earnings described in section 959(c)(2). In such case, M Corporation's earnings and profits of $495 (before taking into account distributions made in 1966) would be classified as follows for purposes of section 959(c):

Year	Classification of earnings and profits for purposes of sec. 959 (c)(1)	(c)(2)	(c)(3)
1963	$120	$25	
1964	100	$75	
1965		75	$50
1966			50

(d) The three distributions to A in 1966 of $150 each would then have the following source under section 959(c):

	Amount	Year	Allocation of distributions under sec. 959
Distribution # 1:	$100	1964	(c)(1)
	50	1963	(c)(1)
	150		
Distribution # 2:	$70	1963	(c)(1)
	75	1965	(c)(2)
	5	1964	(c)(2)
	150		
Distribution # 3:	$70	1964	(c)(2)
	25	1963	(c)(2)
	50	1966	(c)(3)
	5	1965	(c)(3)
	150		

(c) *Treatment of deficits in earnings and profits.*—For purposes of this section, a United States shareholder's pro rata share (determined in accordance with the principles of paragraph (e) of § 1.951-1) of a foreign corporation's deficit in earnings and profits, determined under section 964(a) and § 1.964-1, for any taxable year shall be applied only to earnings and profits described in paragraph (b)(3) of this section.

(d) *Treatment of certain foreign taxes.*—For purposes of this section, any amount described in subparagraph (1), (2), or (3) of paragraph (b) of this section which is distributed by a foreign corporation through a chain of ownership described in section 958(a)(2) shall be reduced by any income, war profits, or excess profits taxes imposed on or with respect to such distribution by any foreign country or possession of the United States.

Example. (a) Domestic corporation M owns 100 percent of the only class of stock of foreign corporation A, which is incorporated under the laws of foreign country X and which, in turn, owns 100 percent of the only class of stock of foreign corporation B, which is incorporated under the laws of foreign country Y. All corporations use the calendar year as a taxable year and corporations A and B are controlled foreign corporations throughout the period here involved.

(b) During 1963, B Corporation (a less developed country corporation for 1963 within the meaning of § 1.955-5) derives $90 of subpart F income, after incurring $10 of foreign income tax allocable to such income under paragraph (c) of § 1.954-1, has earnings and profits in excess of $90, and makes no distributions. Corporation M must include $90 in its gross income for 1963 under section 951(a)(1)(A)(i) As of December 31, 1963, with respect to M Corporation, B Corporation has earnings and profits for 1963 described in section 959(c)(2) of $90.

(c) During 1964, B Corporation has neither earnings and profits nor a deficit in earnings and profits but distributes $90 to A Corporation, and, by reason of section 959(b) and § 1.959-2, such amount is not includible in the gross income of M Corporation for 1964 under section 951(a) with respect to A Corporation. Corporation A incurs a withholding tax of $13.50 on the $90 dividend distributed from B Corporation (15 percent of $90) and an additional foreign income tax of 10 percent or $7.65 by reason of the inclusion of the net distribution of $76.50 ($90 minus $13.50) in its taxable income for 1964. As of December 31, 1964, with respect to M Corporation, B Corporation's earnings and profits for 1963 described in section 959(c)(2) amount to zero ($90 minus $90); and A Corporation's earnings and profits for 1963 described in section 959(c)(2) amount to $68.85 ($90 minus $13.50 minus $7.65).

(e) *Determination of foreign tax credit.*—For purposes of applying section 902 and section 960 in determining the foreign tax credit allowable under section 901 in a case in which distributions are made by a second-tier corporation or a first-tier corporation, as the case may be, from its earnings and profits for a taxable year which are attributable to an amount included in the gross income of a United States shareholder under section 951(a) or which are attributable to amounts excluded from the gross income of such foreign corporation under section 959(b) and § 1.959-2 with respect to a United States shareholder, the rules of paragraph (b) of this section shall apply except that in applying subparagraph (1) or (2) of such paragraph—

(1) Distributions from the earnings and profits for such taxable year of the second-tier corporation shall be considered first attributable to its earnings and profits attributable to distributions from the earnings and profits of the foreign corporation, if any, next lower in the chain of ownership described in section 958(a), to the extent of such earnings and profits of the second-tier corporation, and then to the other earnings and profits of such second-tier corporation, and

(2) Distributions from the earnings and profits for such taxable year of the first-tier corporation shall be considered first attributable to its earnings and profits attributable to distributions from the earnings and profits of the second-tier corporation, to the extent of such earnings and profits of the first-tier corporation, and then to the other earnings and profits of such first-tier corporation.

For purposes of this paragraph, a second-tier corporation is a foreign corporation referred to in section 960(a)(1)(B), and a first-tier corporation is a foreign corporation referred to in section 960(a)(1)(A). The application of this paragraph may be illustrated by the following examples:

Example (1). (a) Domestic corporation A, a United States shareholder, owns 100 percent of the only class of stock of foreign corporation R which, in turn, owns 100 percent of the only class of stock of foreign corporation S. All corporations use the calendar year as a taxable year, and corporations R and S are controlled foreign corporations throughout the period here involved.

(b) Neither R Corporation nor S Corporation has subpart F income for 1963. During 1963, S Corporation increases by $100 its investment in tangible property (not described in section 956(b)(2)) located in the United States, makes no distributions, and has earnings and profits of $100. Corporation A must include $100 in its gross income for 1963 under section 951(a)(1)(B) with respect to S Corporation. During 1963, R Corporation also increases by $100 its investment in tangible property (not described in section 956(b)(2)) located in the United States, makes no distributions, and has earnings and profits of $100. Corporation A must include $100 in its gross income for 1963 under section 951(a)(1)(B) with respect to R Corporation.

(c) During 1964, S Corporation distributes $100 to R Corporation, and R Corporation distributes $100 to A Corporation. Neither corporation has any earnings or profits or deficit in earnings and profits for such year. At December 31, 1964, R Corporation has earnings and profits (computed before distributions to A Corporation made for the year) of $200, consisting of $100 of section 959(c)(1) amounts of R Corporation for 1963 and of $100 of section 959(c)(1) amounts of S Corporation for 1963. For purposes of determining the foreign tax credit under section 960 and the regulations thereunder, the $100 distribution by R Corporation shall be considered attributable to S Corporation's earnings and profits for 1963 described in section 959(c)(1).

Example (2). (a) Domestic corporation A, a United States shareholder, owns 100 percent of the only class of stock of foreign corporation T which, in turn, owns 100 percent of the only class of stock of foreign corporation U. All corporations use the calendar year as a taxable year, and corporations T and U are controlled foreign corporations throughout the period here involved.

(b) During 1964, T Corporation invests $100 in tangible property (not described in section 956(b)(2)) located in the United States. For 1964, T Corporation has no subpart F income and makes no distributions; A must include $100 in its gross income for 1964 under section 951(a)(1)(B) with respect to T Corporation. For 1964, U Corporation has no subpart F income or investment of earnings in United States property but U Corporation has $100 of earnings and profits which it distributes to T Corporation. At December 31, 1964, T Corporation has earnings and profits of $300, consisting of operating income of $100 for each of the years 1963 and 1964 and $100 in dividends received from the earnings and profits of U Corporation for 1964. These earnings and profits are classified as follows under section 959(c): $100 of section 959(c)(1) amounts of T Corporation for 1964, $100 of section 959(c)(3) amounts of U Corporation for 1964, and $100 of section 959(c)(3) amounts of T Corporation for 1963.

(c) During 1965 neither T Corporation nor U Corporation has any earnings and profits or deficit in earnings and profits or investment of earnings in United States property, but T Corporation distributes $100 to A Corporation. For purposes of determining the foreign tax credit under section 960 and the regulations thereunder, the $100 distribution of T Corporation shall be considered attributable to T Corporation's earnings and profits for 1964 described in section 959(c)(1).

(f) *Illustration.*—The application of this section may be illustrated by the following example:

Example. (a) M, a controlled foreign corporation is organized on January 1, 1963, and is wholly owned by A, a United States shareholder. Both A and Corporation M use the calendar year as a taxable year.

(b) Corporation M's earnings and profits (before distributions) for 1963 are $200, $100 of which is attributable to subpart F income. Corporation M's earnings and profits for such year also include $25 attributable to subpart F income which is excluded from M Corporation's foreign base company income under section 954(b)(1) as dividends, interest, and gains invested in qualified investments in less developed countries. Corporation M's increase in earnings invested in tangible property (not described in section 956(b)(2)) located in the United States for 1963, is $50, and M Corporation makes a distribution of such property during such year of $20. For purposes of section 959, A's interest in M Corporation's earnings and profits as of December 31, 1963, determined after the distribution of $20, is classified as follows:

Sec. 959(c)(1) amounts:		
Earnings for 1963 attributable to increased investment in United States property which would have been included in A's gross income but for application of sec. 959(a)(2) and § 1.959-1(c)	$50	
Less: Distribution for 1963 allocated under sec. 959(c)(1) and paragraph (b)(1) of this section to such amounts	20	$30
Sec. 959(c)(2) amounts:		
Earnings for 1963 attributable to subpart F income included in A's gross income under sec. 951(a)(1)(A)(i)	$100	
Less: Earnings for 1963 attributable to increased investment in United States property which would have been included in A's gross income but for application of sec. 959(a)(2) and § 1.959-1(c)	50	$50

Sec. 959(c)(3) amounts:			
Predistribution earnings for 1963		$200	
Less: Earnings for 1963 classified as:			
Sec. 959(c)(1) amounts	$50		
Sec. 959(c)(2) amounts	50	100	$100
A's total interest in M Corporation's earnings and profits			$180

For 1963, A is required to include $100 of subpart F income in his gross income under section 951(a)(1)(A)(i). He would have been required to include $50 in his gross income under section 951(a)(1)(B) as M Corporation's increase in earnings invested in United States property, except that section 959(a)(2) and paragraph (c) of § 1.959-1 provide in effect that earnings and profits taxed to A under section 951(a)(1)(A) with respect to M Corporation (whether in the current taxable year or in prior years) may be invested in United States property without again being included in gross income under section 951(a). The $20 dividend from M Corporation is excluded from A's gross income under section 959(a)(1) and paragraph (b) of § 1.959-1, since such distribution is allocated under section 959(c)(1) and paragraph (b)(1) of this section to amounts described in section 959(c)(1).

(c) During 1964, M Corporation's earnings and profits (before distributions) are $300, $75 of which is attributable to subpart F income. Corporation M has no change in investments in United States property during such year and withdraws $15 of previously excluded subpart F income from investment in less developed countries. Corporation M makes a cash distribution of $250 to A during 1964. For purposes of section 959, A's interest in M Corporation's earnings and profits as of December 31, 1964, determined after the distribution of $250, is classified as follows:

Sec. 959(c)(1) amounts:				
Sec. 959(c)(1) net amount for 1963 (as determined under paragraph (b) of this example)			$30	
Less: Distribution for 1964 allocated under sec. 959(c)(1) and paragraph (b)(1) of this section to such amount			30	$0
Sec. 959(c)(2) amounts:				
Sec. 959(c)(2) net amount for 1963 (as determined under paragraph (b) of this example)			$50	
Plus: Earnings for 1964 attributable to:				
Subpart F income for 1964 included in A's gross income under sec. 951(a)(1)(A)(i)			75	
Previously excluded subpart F income withdrawn in 1964 from investment in less developed countries and included in A's gross income under sec. 951(a)(1)(A)(ii)			15	
			$140	
Less: Distribution for 1964 allocated under sec. 959(c)(2) and paragraph (b)(2) of this section to such amounts			$140	0
Sec. 959(c)(3) amounts:				
Sec. 959(c)(3) net amount for 1963 (as determined under paragraph (b) of this example)			$100	
Plus: Sec. 959(c)(3) net amount for 1964:				
Predistribution earnings for 1964		$300		
Less:				
Earnings for 1964 classified as sec. 959(c)(1) amounts ($0) and as sec. 959(c)(2) amounts ($75 + $15)	$90			
Distributions for 1964 allocated under sec. 959(c)(3) and paragraph (b)(3) of this section	$80	$170	$130	$230
A's total interest in M Corporation's earnings and profits				$230

For 1964, A is required to include in his gross income under section 951(a)(1)(A)(i) $75 of subpart F income, and under section 951(a)(1)(A)(ii) $15 of previously excluded subpart F income withdrawn from investment in less developed countries. Of the $250 cash distribution, A may exclude $170 from his gross income under section 959(a)(1) and paragraph (b) of § 1.959-1 and $80 is includible in his gross income as a dividend.

(d) The source under section 959(c) of the 1964 distribution of $250 to A is as follows:

	Year	*Amount*
1963	$30	(c)(1)
1964	90	(c)(2)
1963	50	(c)(2)
1964	80	(c)(3)
Total	$250	

[Reg. § 1.959-3.]

☐ [*T.D. 6795, 1-28-65. Amended by T.D.* 7334, 12-20-74; *T.D.* 7545, 5-5-78 *and T.D.* 7893, 5-11-83.]

§ 1.959-4. Distributions to United States persons not counting as dividends.—Except as provided in section 960(a)(3) and § 1.960-1 any distribution to a United States person which is excluded from the gross income of such person under section 959(a)(1) and § 1.959-1 shall be treated for purposes of chapter 1 (relating to normal taxes and surtaxes) of subtitle A (relating to income taxes) of the Code as a distribution which is not a dividend. However, see paragraph (b)(1) of § 1.956-1, relating to the dividend limitation on the amount of a controlled foreign corporation's investment of earnings in United States property. [Reg. § 1.959-4.]

☐ [*T.D.* 6795, 1-28-65. *Amended by T.D.* 7120, 6-3-71.]

§ 1.960-1. Overview, definitions, and computational rules for determining foreign income taxes deemed paid under section 960(a), (b), and (d).—(a) *Overview.*—(1) *Scope of § § 1.960-1 through 1.960-3.*—This section and § § 1.960-2 and 1.960-3 provide rules to associate foreign income taxes of a controlled foreign corporation with the income that a domestic corporation that is a United States shareholder of the controlled foreign corporation takes into account in determining a subpart F inclusion or GILTI inclusion amount of the domestic corporation, as well as to associate foreign income taxes of a controlled foreign corporation with distributions of previously taxed earnings and profits. This section and § § 1.960-2 and 1.960-3 provide the exclusive rules for determining the foreign income taxes deemed paid by a domestic corporation under section 960. Therefore, only foreign income taxes of a controlled foreign corporation that are associated under these rules with a subpart F inclusion or GILTI inclusion amount of a domestic corporation that is a United States shareholder of the controlled foreign corporation, or with previously taxed earnings and profits, are eligible to be deemed paid. This section provides definitions and computational rules for determining foreign income taxes deemed paid under section 960(a), (b), and (d).

Section 1.960-2 provides rules for computing the amount of foreign income taxes deemed paid by a domestic corporation that is a United States shareholder of a controlled foreign corporation under section 960(a) and (d). Section 1.960-3 provides rules for computing the amount of foreign income taxes deemed paid by a domestic corporation that is a United States shareholder of a controlled foreign corporation, or by a controlled foreign corporation, under section 960(b). This section and § § 1.960-2 and 1.960-3 also apply for purposes of any provision that treats a taxpayer as a domestic corporation that is deemed to pay foreign income taxes or treats a foreign corporation as a controlled foreign corporation for purposes of section 960. See, for example, sections 962(a)(2) and 1293(f).

(2) *Scope of this section.*—Paragraph (b) of this section provides definitions for purposes of this section and § § 1.960-2 and 1.960-3. Paragraph (c) of this section provides computational rules to coordinate the various calculations under this section and § § 1.960-2 and 1.960-3. Paragraph (d) of this section provides rules for computing the income in an income group within a section 904 category, and for associating foreign income taxes with an income group. Paragraph (e) of this section provides a rule for the treatment of taxes associated with the residual income group. Paragraph (f) of this section provides an example illustrating the application of this section.

(b) *Definitions.*—The following definitions apply for purposes of this section and § § 1.960-2 and 1.960-3.

(1) *Annual PTEP account.*—The term *annual PTEP account* has the meaning set forth in § 1.960-3(c)(1).

(2) *Controlled foreign corporation.*—The term *controlled foreign corporation* means a foreign corporation described in section 957(a).

(3) *Current taxable year.*—The term *current taxable year* means the U.S. taxable year of a controlled foreign corporation that is an inclusion year, or during which the controlled foreign corporation receives a section 959(b) distribution or makes a section 959(a) distribution or a section 959(b) distribution.

(4) *Current year tax.*—The term *current year tax* means a foreign income tax that is paid or accrued by a controlled foreign corporation in a current taxable year (taking into account any adjustments resulting from a foreign tax redetermination (as defined in § 1.905-3(a)). See § 1.905-1 for rules on when foreign income taxes are considered paid or accrued for foreign tax credit purposes; see also § 1.367(b)-7(g) for rules relating to foreign income taxes associated with foreign section 381 transactions and hovering deficits.

(5) *Eligible current year tax.*—The term *eligible current year tax* means a current year tax, other than a current year tax for which a credit is disallowed or suspended at the level of the controlled foreign corporation. See, for example, section 245A(e)(3) and § 1.245A(d)-1(a)(2) and sections 901(k)(1), (l), and (m), 909, and 6038(c)(1)(B). An eligible current year tax, however, includes a current year tax that may be deemed paid but for which a credit is reduced or disallowed at the level of the United States shareholder. See, for example, sections 901(e), 901(j),901(k)(2), 908, 965(g), and 6038(c)(1)(A).

(6) *Foreign income tax.*—The term *foreign income tax* has the meaning provided in § 1.901-2(a).

(7) *Foreign taxable year.*—The term *foreign taxable year* has the meaning set forth in section 7701(a)(23), applied by substituting "under foreign law" for the phrase "under subtitle A."

(8) *Foreign taxable income.*—The term *foreign taxable income* means the base upon which a current year tax is imposed that comprises the items included in gross income under foreign law and the deductions allowed under foreign law. In the case of a current year tax that is imposed with respect to a taxable period, foreign taxable income includes all of the items taken into account under foreign law with respect to that period. See paragraph (d)(3)(ii)(A) of this section for rules for apportioning current year tax to section 904 categories or income groups on the basis of foreign taxable income.

(9) *GILTI inclusion amount.*—The term *GILTI inclusion amount* has the meaning set forth in § 1.951A-1(c)(1) (or, in the case of a member of a consolidated group, § 1.1502-51(b)).

(10) *Gross tested income.*—The term *gross tested income* has the meaning set forth in § 1.951A-2(c)(1).

(11) *Inclusion percentage.*—The term *inclusion percentage* has the meaning set forth in § 1.960-2(c)(2).

(12) *Inclusion year.*—The term *inclusion year* means the U.S. taxable year of a controlled foreign corporation which ends during or with the taxable year of a United States shareholder of the controlled foreign corporation in which the United States shareholder includes an amount in income under section 951(a)(1) or 951A(a) with respect to the controlled foreign corporation.

(13) *Income group.*—The term *income group* means a group of income described in paragraph (d)(2)(ii) of this section.

(14) *Partnership CFC.*—The term *partnership CFC* means, with respect to a U.S. shareholder partnership, a controlled foreign corporation stock of which is owned (within the meaning of section 958(a)) by the U.S. shareholder partnership.

(15) *Passive category.*—The term *passive category* means the separate category of income described in section 904(d)(1)(C) and § 1.904-4(b).

(16) *Previously taxed earnings and profits.*—The term *previously taxed earnings and profits* means earnings and profits described in section 959(c)(1) or (2), including earnings and profits described in section 959(c)(2) by reason of section 951A(f)(1) and § 1.951A-5(b)(1).

(17) *PTEP group.*—The term *PTEP group* has the meaning set forth in § 1.960-3(c)(2).

(18) *PTEP group taxes.*—The term *PTEP group taxes* has the meaning set forth in § 1.960-3(d)(1).

(19) *Recipient controlled foreign corporation.*—The term *recipient controlled foreign corporation* has the meaning set forth in § 1.960-3(b)(2).

(20) *Reclassified previously taxed earnings and profits.*—The term *reclassified previously taxed earnings and profits* has the meaning set forth in § 1.960-3(c)(4).

(21) *Reclassified PTEP group.*—The term *reclassified PTEP group* has the meaning set forth in § 1.960-3(c)(4).

(22) *Residual income group.*—The term *residual income group* has the meaning set forth in paragraph (d)(2)(ii)(D) of this section.

(23) *Section 904 category.*—The term *section 904 category* means a separate category of income described in § 1.904-5(a)(4)(v).

(24) *Section 951A category.*—The term *section 951A category* means the separate category of income described in section 904(d)(1)(A) and § 1.904-4(g).

(25) *Section 959 distribution.*—The term *section 959 distribution* means a section 959(a) distribution or a section 959(b) distribution.

(26) *Section 959(a) distribution.*—The term *section 959(a) distribution* means a distribution excluded from the gross income of a United States shareholder under section 959(a).

(27) *Section 959(b) distribution.*—The term *section 959(b) distribution* means a distribution excluded from the gross income of a controlled foreign corporation for purposes of section 951(a) under section 959(b).

(28) *Section 959(c)(2) PTEP group.*—The term *section 959(c)(2) PTEP group* has the meaning set forth in § 1.960-3(c)(4).

(29) *Subpart F inclusion.*—The term *subpart F inclusion* has the meaning set forth in § 1.960-2(b)(1).

(30) *Subpart F income.*—The term *subpart F income* has the meaning set forth in section 952 and § 1.952-1(a).

(31) *Subpart F income group.*—The term *subpart F income group* has the meaning set forth in paragraph (d)(2)(ii)(B)(*1*) of this section.

(32) *Tested foreign income taxes.*—The term *tested foreign income taxes* has the meaning set forth in § 1.960-2(c)(3).

(33) *Tested income.*—The term *tested income* means the amount with respect to a controlled foreign corporation that is described in section 951A(c)(2)(A) and § 1.951A-2(b)(1).

(34) *Tested income group*.—The term *tested income group* has the meaning set forth in paragraph (d)(2)(ii)(C) of this section.

(35) *United States shareholder*.—The term *United States shareholder* has the meaning set forth in section 951(b).

(36) *U.S. shareholder partner*.—The term *U.S. shareholder partner* means, with respect to a U.S. shareholder partnership and a partnership CFC of the U.S. shareholder partnership, a United States person that is a partner in the U.S. shareholder partnership and that is also a United States shareholder (as defined in section 951(b)) of the partnership CFC.

(37) *U.S. shareholder partnership*.—The term *U.S. shareholder partnership* means a domestic partnership (within the meaning of section 7701(a)(4)) that is a United States shareholder of one or more controlled foreign corporations.

(38) *U.S. taxable year*.—The term *U.S. taxable year* has the same meaning as that of the term *taxable year* set forth in section 7701(a)(23).

(c) *Computational rules*.—(1) *In general*.—For purposes of computing foreign income taxes deemed paid by either a domestic corporation that is a United States shareholder with respect to a controlled foreign corporation under § 1.960-2 or § 1.960-3 or by a controlled foreign corporation under § 1.960-3 for the current taxable year, the following rules apply in the following order, beginning with the lowest-tier controlled foreign corporation in a chain with respect to which the domestic corporation is a United States shareholder:

(i) First, items of gross income of the controlled foreign corporation for the current taxable year other than a section 959(b) distribution are assigned to section 904 categories and included in income groups within those section 904 categories under the rules in paragraph (d)(2) of this section. The receipt of a section 959(b) distribution by the controlled foreign corporation is accounted for under § 1.960-3(c)(3).

(ii) Second, deductions (other than for current year taxes) of the controlled foreign corporation for the current taxable year are allocated and apportioned to reduce gross income in the section 904 categories and the income groups within a section 904 category. See paragraph (d)(3)(i) of this section. Deductions for current year taxes (other than eligible current year taxes) of the controlled foreign corporation for the current taxable year are allocated and apportioned to reduce gross income in the section 904 categories and the income groups within a section 904 category. Additionally, the functional currency amounts of eligible current year taxes are allocated and apportioned to reduce gross income in the section 904 categories and the income groups within a section 904 category, and to reduce earnings and profits in the PTEP groups that were increased as provided in paragraph (c)(1)(i) of this section. No deductions other than eligible current year taxes are allocated and apportioned to PTEP groups. See paragraph (d)(3)(ii) of this section.

(iii) Third, for purposes of computing foreign taxes deemed paid, eligible current year taxes that were allocated and apportioned to income groups and PTEP groups in the section 904 categories are translated into U.S. dollars in accordance with section 986(a).

(iv) Fourth, eligible current year taxes deemed paid under section 960(a) and (d) by the domestic corporation with respect to income of the controlled foreign corporation are computed under the rules of § 1.960-2. In addition, foreign income taxes deemed paid under section 960(b)(2) with respect to the receipt of a section 959(b) distribution by the controlled foreign corporation are computed under the rules of § 1.960-3(b).

(v) Fifth, any previously taxed earnings and profits of the controlled foreign corporation resulting from subpart F inclusions and GILTI inclusion amounts with respect to the controlled foreign corporation's current taxable year are separated from other earnings and profits of the controlled foreign corporation and added to an annual PTEP account, and a PTEP group within the PTEP account, under the rules of § 1.960-3(c).

(vi) Sixth, paragraphs (c)(1)(i) through (iv) of this section are repeated for each next higher-tier controlled foreign corporation in the chain.

(vii) Seventh, with respect to the highest-tier controlled foreign corporation in a chain that is owned directly (or indirectly through a partnership) by the domestic corporation, foreign income taxes that are deemed paid under section 960(b)(1) in connection with the receipt of a section 959(a) distribution by the domestic corporation are computed under the rules of § 1.960-3(b).

(2) *Inclusion of current year items*.—For a current taxable year, the items of income and deductions (including for taxes), and the U.S. dollar amounts of current year taxes, that are included in the computations described in this section and assigned to income groups and PTEP groups for the taxable year are the items that the controlled foreign corporation accrues and takes into account during the current taxable year. An item of income with respect to a current taxable year does not include an amount included as subpart F income of a controlled foreign corporation by reason of the recharacterization of a recapture account established in a prior U.S. taxable year (and the corresponding earnings and profits) of the controlled foreign corporation under section 952(c)(2) and § 1.952-1(f).

(3) *Functional currency and translation*.—The computations described in this paragraph (c) that relate to income and earnings and profits are made in the functional currency of the controlled foreign corporation (as determined under section 985), and references to taxes deemed paid are to U.S. dollar amounts (translated in accordance with section 986(a)).

(d) *Computing income in a section 904 category and an income group within a section 904 category*.—(1) *Scope*.—This paragraph (d) provides rules for assigning gross income (including gains) of a controlled foreign corporation for the current taxable year to a section 904 category and income group within a section 904 category, and for allocating and apportioning deductions (including losses and current year taxes) and the U.S. dollar amount of eligible current year taxes of the controlled foreign corporation for the current taxable year among the section 904 categories, income groups within a section 904 category, and PTEP groups. For rules regarding maintenance of previously taxed earnings and profits in an annual PTEP account, and assignment of those previously taxed earnings and profits to PTEP groups, see § 1.960-3.

(2) *Assignment of gross income to section 904 categories and income groups within a category*.—(i) *Assigning items of gross income to section 904 categories*.—Items of gross income of the controlled foreign corporation for the current taxable year are first assigned to a section 904 category of the controlled foreign corporation under §§ 1.904-4 and 1.904-5, and under § 1.960-3(c)(1) in the case of gross income relating to a section 959(b) distribution received by the controlled foreign corporation. Income of a controlled foreign corporation, other than gross income relating to a section 959(b) distribution, cannot be assigned to the section 951A category. *See* § 1.904-4(g).

(ii) *Grouping gross income within a section 904 category*.—(A) *In general*.—Gross income within a section 904 category is assigned to an income group under the rules of this paragraph (d)(2)(ii), or to a PTEP group under the rules of § 1.960-3(c)(3). Gross income other than a section 959(b) distribution is assigned to a subpart F income group, tested income group, or residual income group.

(B) *Subpart F income groups*.—(*1*) *In general*.—The term *subpart F income group* means an income group within a section 904 category that consists of income that is described in paragraph (d)(2)(ii)(B)(*2*) of this section. Gross income that is treated as a single item of income under § 1.954-1(c)(1)(iii) is in a separate subpart F income group under paragraph (d)(2)(ii)(B)(*2*)(*i*) of this section. Items of gross income that give rise to income described in paragraph (d)(2)(ii)(B)(*2*)(*ii*) of this section are aggregated and treated as gross income in a separate subpart F income group. Similarly, items of gross income that give rise to income described in each one of paragraphs (d)(2)(ii)(B)(*2*)(*iii*) through (*v*) of this section are aggregated and treated as gross income in a separate subpart F income group.

(*2*) *Income in subpart F income groups*.—The income included in subpart F income groups is:

(*i*) Items of foreign base company income treated as a single item of income under § 1.954-1(c)(1)(iii);

(*ii*) Insurance income described in section 952(a)(1);

(*iii*) Income subject to the international boycott factor described in section 952(a)(3);

(*iv*) Income from certain bribes, kickbacks and other payments described in section 952(a)(4); and

(*v*) Income subject to section 901(j) described in section 952(a)(5).

(C) *Tested income groups.*—The term *tested income group* means an income group that consists of tested income within a section 904 category. Items of gross tested income in each section 904 category are aggregated and treated as gross income in a separate tested income group.

(D) *Residual income group.*—The term *residual income group* means the income group within a section 904 category that consists of income that is not in a subpart F income group, tested income group, or PTEP group.

(E) *Examples.*—The following examples illustrate the application of this paragraph (d)(2)(ii).

(*1*) *Example 1: Subpart F income groups*—(*i*) *Facts.* CFC, a controlled foreign corporation, is incorporated in Country X. CFC uses the "u" as its functional currency. At all relevant times, 1u=$1x. CFC earns from sources outside of Country X portfolio dividend income of 100,000u, portfolio interest income of 1,500,000u, and 70,000u of royalty income that is not derived from the active conduct of a trade or business. CFC also earns 50,000u from the sale of personal property to a related person for use outside of Country X that gives rise to foreign base company sales income under section 954(d). Finally, CFC earns 45,000u for performing consulting services outside of Country X for related persons that gives rise to foreign base company services income under section 954(e). None of the income is taxed by Country X. The dividend income is subject to a 15 percent third-country withholding tax after application of the applicable income tax treaty. The interest income and the royalty income are subject to no third-country withholding tax. CFC incurs no expenses.

(*ii*) *Analysis.* Under paragraph (d)(2)(i) of this section and § 1.904-4, the interest income, dividend income, and royalty income are passive category income and the sales and consulting income are general category income. Under paragraph (d)(2)(ii)(B) of this section, CFC has a separate subpart F income group within the passive category with respect to the 100,000u of dividend income, which is foreign personal holding company income described in § 1.954-1(c)(1)(iii)(A)(*1*)(*i*) (dividends, interest, rents, royalties and annuities) that falls within a single group of income under § 1.904-4(c)(3)(i) for passive income that is subject to withholding tax of fifteen percent or greater. CFC also has a separate subpart F income group within the passive category with respect to the 1,500,000u of interest income and the 70,000u of royalty income (in total 1,570,000u) which together are foreign personal holding company income described in § 1.954-1(c)(1)(iii)(A)(*1*)(*i*) (dividends, interest, rents, royalties and annuities) that falls within a single group of income under § 1.904-4(c)(3)(iii) for passive income that is subject to no withholding tax or other foreign tax. With respect to its 50,000u of sales income, CFC has a separate subpart F income group with respect to foreign base company sales income described in § 1.954-1(c)(1)(iii)(A)(*2*)(*i*) within the general category. With respect to its 45,000u of services income, CFC has a separate subpart F income group with respect to foreign base company services income described in § 1.954-1(c)(1)(iii)(A)(2)(*ii*) within the general category.

(*2*) *Example 2: Tested income groups*—(i) *Facts.* CFC, a controlled foreign corporation, is incorporated in Country X. CFC uses the "u" as its functional currency. At all relevant times, 1u=$1x. CFC earns 500u from the sale of goods to unrelated parties. CFC also earns 75u for performing consulting services for unrelated parties. All of its income is gross tested income. CFC incurs no deductions.

(*ii*) *Analysis.* Under paragraph (d)(2)(i) of this section and section 904 and § 1.904-4, the sales income and services income are both general category income. Under paragraph (d)(2)(ii)(C) of this section, with respect to the 500u of sales income and 75u services income (in total 575u), CFC has one tested income group within the general category.

(3) *Allocation and apportionment of deductions among section 904 categories, income groups within a section 904 category, and certain PTEP groups.*—(i) *In general.*—Gross income of the controlled foreign corporation in each income group within each section 904 category is reduced by deductions (including losses) of the controlled foreign corporation for the current taxable year under the rules in this paragraph (d)(3)(i). No deductions of the controlled foreign corporation for the current taxable year other than a deduction for eligible current year taxes imposed solely by reason of the receipt of a section 959(b) distribution are allocated or apportioned to reduce earnings and profits in a PTEP group.

(A) First, the rules of sections 861 through 865 and 904(d) (taking into account the rules of section 954(b)(5) and § 1.954-1(c), and section 951A(c)(2)(A)(ii) and § 1.951A-2(c)(3), as appropriate) apply to allocate and apportion to reduce gross income (or create a loss) in each section 904 category and income group within a section 904 category any deductions of the controlled foreign corporation that are definitely related to less than all of the controlled foreign corporation's gross income as a class. See paragraph (d)(3)(ii) of this section for special rules for allocating and apportioning current year taxes to section 904 categories, income groups, and PTEP groups.

(B) Second, related person interest expense is allocated to and apportioned among the subpart F income groups within the passive category under the principles of §§ 1.904-5(c)(2) and 1.954-1(c)(1)(i).

(C) Third, any remaining deductions are allocated and apportioned to reduce gross income (or create a loss) in the section 904 categories and income groups within each section 904 category under the rules referenced in paragraph (d)(3)(i)(A) of this section.

(ii) *Allocation and apportionment of a current year tax.*—(A) *In general.*—A current year tax is allocated and apportioned among the section 904 categories under the rules of § 1.904-6. An amount of the current year tax that is allocated and apportioned to a section 904 category is then allocated and apportioned among the income groups within the section 904 category under § 1.861-20 (as modified by § 1.904-6(c)) by treating each income group as a statutory grouping and treating the residual income group as the residual grouping. Therefore, foreign gross income attributable to a base difference is assigned to the residual income grouping under § 1.861-20(d)(2)(ii)(B). See, however, paragraph (d)(3)(ii)(B) of this section for special rules for applying § 1.861-20 in the case of PTEP groups. For purposes of determining foreign income taxes deemed paid under the rules in §§ 1.960-2 and 1.960-3, the U.S. dollar amount of eligible current year taxes is assigned to the section 904 categories, income groups, and PTEP groups (to the extent provided in paragraph (d)(3)(ii)(B) of this section) to which the eligible current year taxes are allocated and apportioned.

(B) *Foreign taxable income that includes previously taxed earnings and profits.*—For purposes of allocating and apportioning an eligible current year tax under this paragraph (d)(3)(ii), a PTEP group that is increased under § 1.960-3(c)(3) as a result of the receipt of a section 959(b) distribution in the current taxable year of the controlled foreign corporation is treated as an income group within the section 904 category. In such case, under § 1.861-20, the portion of the foreign gross income (as defined in § 1.861-20(b)(5)) that is characterized under Federal income tax principles as a distribution of previously taxed earnings and profits that results in the increase in the PTEP group in the current taxable year is assigned to that PTEP group. If a PTEP group is not treated as an income group under the first sentence of this paragraph (d)(3)(ii)(B), and the rules of § 1.861-20 would otherwise apply to assign foreign gross income to a PTEP group, that foreign gross income is instead assigned to the subpart F income group or tested income group to which the income that gave rise to the previously taxed earnings and profits would be assigned if the income were recognized by the recipient controlled foreign corporation under Federal income tax principles in the current taxable year. For example, a net basis or withholding tax imposed on a controlled foreign corporation's receipt of a section 959(b) distribution is allocated or apportioned to a PTEP group. In contrast, a withholding tax imposed on a disregarded payment from a disregarded entity to its controlled foreign corporation owner is never treated as related to a PTEP group, even if all of the controlled foreign corporation's earnings are previously taxed earnings and profits, because the payment that gives rise to the foreign gross income from which the tax was withheld does not constitute a section 959(b) distribution in the current taxable year. That foreign gross income, however, may be assigned to a subpart F income group or tested income group.

(e) *No deemed paid credit for current year taxes related to residual income group.*—Current year taxes paid or accrued by a controlled foreign corporation that are allocated and apportioned under paragraph (d)(3)(ii) of this section to a residual income group cannot be deemed paid under section 960 for any taxable year.

(f) *Example.*—The following example illustrates the application of this section and § 1.960-3.

(1) *Facts*—(i) *Income of CFC1 and CFC2.* CFC1, a controlled foreign corporation, conducts business in Country X. CFC1 uses the "u" as its functional currency. At all relevant times, 1u=$1x. CFC1 owns all of the stock of CFC2, a controlled foreign corporation. CFC1 and CFC2 both use the calendar year as their U.S. and foreign taxable years. In 2019, CFC1 earns 2,000,000u of gross income that is foreign oil and gas extraction income, within the meaning of section

907(c)(1), and 2,000,000u of interest income from unrelated persons, for both U.S. and Country X tax law purposes. Country X exempts interest income from tax. In 2019, CFC1 also receives a section 959(b) distribution from CFC2 of 4,000,000u of previously taxed earnings and profits attributable to an inclusion under section 965(a) for CFC2's 2017 U.S. taxable year. The inclusion under section 965(a) was income in the general category. There are no PTEP group taxes associated with the previously taxed earnings and profits distributed by CFC2 at the level of CFC2. The section 959(b) distribution is treated as a dividend taxable to CFC1 under Country X law. In 2019, CFC2 earns no gross income and receives no distributions.

(ii) *Pre-tax deductions of CFC1 and CFC2.* For both U.S. and Country X tax purposes, in 2019, CFC1 incurs 1,500,000u of deductible expenses other than current year taxes that are allocable to all gross income. For U.S. tax purposes, under § § 1.861-8 through 1.861-14T, 750,000u of such deductions are apportioned to each of CFC1's foreign oil and gas extraction income and interest income. Under Country X law, 1,000,000u of deductions are allocated and apportioned to the 4,000,000u treated as a dividend, and 500,000u of deductions are allocated and apportioned to the 2,000,000u of foreign oil and gas extraction income. Under Country X law, no deductions are allocable to the interest income. Country X imposes eligible current year tax of 900,000u on a base of 4,500,000u (6,000,000u gross income – 1,500,000u deductions) consisting of 3,000,000u (4,000,000u – 1,000,000u) attributable to CFC1's section 959(b) distribution and 1,500,000u (2,000,000u – 500,000u) attributable to CFC1's foreign oil and gas extraction income. In 2019, CFC2 has no expenses (including current year taxes).

(iii) *United States shareholders of CFC1.* All of the stock of CFC1 is owned (within the meaning of section 958(a)) by corporate United States shareholders that use the calendar year as their U.S. taxable year. In 2019, the United States shareholders of CFC1 include in gross income subpart F inclusions in the passive category totaling $1,250,000x with respect to 1,250,000u of subpart F income of CFC1.

(2) *Analysis*—(i) *CFC2.* Under paragraph (c)(1) of this section, the computational rules of paragraph (c)(1) of this section are applied beginning with CFC2. However, CFC2 has no gross income or expenses in 2019 (the "current taxable year"). Accordingly, the computational rules described in paragraphs (c)(1)(i) through (v) of this section are not relevant with respect to CFC2. Under paragraph (c)(1)(vi) of this section, the rules in paragraph (c)(1)(i) through (v) of this section are then applied to CFC1.

(ii) *CFC1*—(A) *Step 1.* Under paragraph (c)(1)(i) of this section, CFC1's items of gross income for the current taxable year are assigned to section 904 categories and included in income groups within those section 904 categories. In addition, CFC1's receipt of a section 959(b) distribution is assigned to a PTEP group. Under paragraph (d)(2)(i) of this section and § 1.904-4, the interest income is passive category income and the foreign oil and gas extraction income is general category income. Under paragraph (d)(2)(ii) of this section, the 2,000,000u of interest income is assigned to a subpart F income group (the "subpart F income group") within the passive category because it is foreign personal holding company income described in § 1.954-1(c)(1)(iii)(A)(*1*)(*i*) that falls within a single group of income under § 1.904-4(c)(3)(iii) for passive income that is subject to no withholding tax or other foreign tax. The 2,000,000u of foreign oil and gas extraction income is assigned to the residual income group within the general category. Under § 1.960-3(c), the 4,000,000u section 959(b) distribution is assigned to the PTEP group described in § 1.960-3(c)(2)(vii) within the 2017 annual PTEP account (the "PTEP group") within the general category.

(B) *Step 2*—(*1*) *Allocation and apportionment of deductions for expenses other than taxes.* Under paragraph (c)(1)(ii) of this section, CFC1's deductions for the current taxable year are allocated and apportioned among the section 904 categories, income groups within a section 904 category, and any PTEP groups that were increased as provided in paragraph (c)(1)(i) of this section. Under paragraph (d)(3)(i) of this section and § § 1.861-8 through 1.861-14T, 750,000u of deductions are allocated and apportioned to the residual income group within the general category, and 750,000u of deductions are allocated and apportioned to the subpart F income group within the passive category. Therefore, CFC1 has 1,250,000u (2,000,000u – 750,000u) of pre-tax income attributable to the residual income group within the general category and 1,250,000u (2,000,000u – 750,000u) of pre-tax income attributable to the subpart F income group within the passive category. For U.S. tax purposes, no deductions other than eligible current year taxes are allocated and apportioned to the 4,000,000u in CFC1's PTEP group.

(*2*) *Allocation and apportionment of current year taxes.* Under paragraph (c)(1)(ii) of this section, CFC1's current year taxes are allocated and apportioned among the section 904 categories, income groups within a section 904 category, and any PTEP groups that were increased as provided in paragraph (c)(1)(i) of this section. Under paragraphs (d)(3)(i) and (ii) of this section, for purposes of allocating and apportioning taxes to reduce the income in a section 904 category, an income group, or PTEP group, § 1.904-6(a)(1) and (ii) are applied to determine the amount of foreign taxable income, computed under Country X law but characterized under Federal income tax law, in each section 904 category, income group, and PTEP group that is included in the Country X tax base. For Country X purposes, 1,000,000u of deductions are apportioned to CFC1's PTEP group within the general category, 500,000u of deductions are apportioned to the residual income group within the general category, and no deductions are apportioned to the subpart F income group in the passive category. Therefore, for Country X purposes, CFC1 has 3,000,000u of foreign taxable income attributable to the PTEP group within the general category, 1,500,000u of foreign taxable income attributable to the residual income group within the general category, and no income attributable to the subpart F income group within the passive category. Under paragraph (d)(3)(ii) of this section, 600,000u (3,000,000u/4,500,000u x 900,000u) of the 900,000u eligible current year taxes paid by CFC1 are related to the PTEP group within the general category, and 300,000u (1,500,000u/4,500,000u x 900,000u) are related to the residual income group within the general category. No eligible current year taxes are allocated or apportioned to the subpart F income group within the passive category because the interest expense is exempt from Country X tax. Thus, for U.S. tax purposes, CFC1 has 3,400,000u of previously taxed earnings and profits (4,000,000u – 600,000u) in the PTEP group within the general category, 1,250,000u of income in the subpart F income group within the passive category, and 950,000u of income (1,250,000u – 300,000u) in the residual income group within the general category.

(C) *Step 3.* Under paragraph (c)(1)(iii) of this section, for purposes of computing foreign taxes deemed paid under section 960, CFC1 has $600,000x of foreign income taxes in the PTEP group within the general category and $300,000x of current year taxes in the residual income group within the general category. Under paragraph (e) of this section, the United States shareholders of CFC1 cannot claim a credit with respect to the $300,000x of taxes on CFC1's income in the residual income group.

(D) *Step 4.* Under paragraph (c)(1)(iv) of this section, the United States shareholders of CFC1 compute current year taxes deemed paid under section 960(a) and (d) and the rules of § 1.960-2. None of the Country X tax is allocated to CFC1's subpart F income group. Therefore, there are no current year taxes deemed paid by CFC1's United States shareholders with respect to their passive category subpart F inclusions. See § 1.960-2(b)(5) and (c)(7) for examples of the application of section 960(a) and (d) and the rules in § 1.960-2. Additionally, under paragraph (c)(1)(iv) of this section, foreign income taxes deemed paid under section 960(b)(2) by CFC1 are determined with respect to the section 959(b) distribution from CFC2 under the rules of § 1.960-3. There are no PTEP group taxes associated with the previously taxed earnings and profits distributed by CFC2 in the hands of CFC2. Therefore, there are no foreign income taxes deemed paid by CFC1 under section 960(b)(2) with respect to the section 959(b) distribution from CFC2. See § 1.960-3(e) for examples of the application of section 960(b) and the rules in § 1.960-3.

(E) *Step 5.* Under paragraph (c)(1)(v) of this section, previously taxed earnings and profits resulting from subpart F inclusions and GILTI inclusion amounts with respect to CFC1's current taxable year are separated from CFC1's other earnings and profits and added to an annual PTEP account and PTEP group within the PTEP account, under the rules of § 1.960-3(c). The United States shareholders of CFC1 include in gross income subpart F inclusions totaling $1,250,000x with respect to 1,250,000u of subpart F income of CFC1, and the subpart F inclusions are passive category income. Therefore, under § 1.960-3(c)(2), 1,250,000u of previously taxed earnings and profits resulting from the subpart F inclusions is added to CFC1's section 951(a)(1)(A) PTEP within the 2019 annual PTEP account within the passive category.

(F) *Step 6.* Paragraph (c)(1)(vi) of this section does not apply because CFC1 is the highest-tier controlled foreign corporation in the chain.

(G) *Step 7.* Paragraph (c)(1)(vii) of this section does not apply because CFC1 did not make a section 959(a) distribution. [Reg. § 1.960-1.]

☐ [*T.D.* 7120, 6-3-71. *Amended by T.D.* 7334, 12-20-74, *T.D.* 7481, 4-15-77, *T.D.* 7545, 5-5-78, *T.D.* 7649, 10-17-79, *T.D.* 7843, 11-5-82; *T.D.* 7961, 6-27-84, *T.D.* 8704, 12-31-96, *T.D.* 9882, 12-16-2019, *T.D.* 9922, 11-2-2020 *and T.D.* 9959, 12-28-2021.]

§1.960-2. Foreign income taxes deemed paid under sections 960(a) and (d).—(a) *Scope*.—Paragraph (b) of this section provides rules for computing the amount of foreign income taxes deemed paid by a domestic corporation that is a United States shareholder of a controlled foreign corporation under section 960(a). Paragraph (c) of this section provides rules for computing the amount of foreign income taxes deemed paid by a domestic corporation that is a United States shareholder of a controlled foreign corporation under section 960(d).

(b) *Foreign income taxes deemed paid under section 960(a)*.—(1) *In general*.—If a domestic corporation that is a United States shareholder of a controlled foreign corporation includes in gross income under section 951(a)(1)(A) its pro rata share of the subpart F income of the controlled foreign corporation (a *subpart F inclusion*), the domestic corporation is deemed to have paid the amount of the controlled foreign corporation's foreign income taxes that are properly attributable to the items of income in a subpart F income group of the controlled foreign corporation that give rise to the subpart F inclusion of the domestic corporation that is attributable to the subpart F income group. For each section 904 category, the domestic corporation is deemed to have paid foreign income taxes equal to the sum of the controlled foreign corporation's foreign income taxes that are properly attributable to the items of income in the subpart F income groups to which the subpart F inclusion is attributable. See §1.904-6(b)(1) for rules on assigning the foreign income tax to a section 904 category. No foreign income taxes are deemed paid under section 960(a) with respect to an inclusion under section 951(a)(1)(B).

(2) *Properly attributable*.—The amount of the controlled foreign corporation's foreign income taxes that are properly attributable to the items of income in the subpart F income group of the controlled foreign corporation to which a subpart F inclusion is attributable equals the domestic corporation's proportionate share of the eligible current year taxes of the controlled foreign corporation that are allocated and apportioned under §1.960-1(d)(3)(ii) to the subpart F income group. No other foreign income taxes are considered properly attributable to an item of income of the controlled foreign corporation.

(3) *Proportionate share*.—(i) *In general*.—A domestic corporation's proportionate share of the eligible current year taxes of a controlled foreign corporation that are allocated and apportioned under §1.960-1(d)(3)(ii) to a subpart F income group within a section 904 category of the controlled foreign corporation is equal to the total U.S. dollar amount of eligible current year taxes that are allocated and apportioned under §1.960-1(d)(3)(ii) to the subpart F income group multiplied by a fraction (not to exceed one), the numerator of which is the portion of the domestic corporation's subpart F inclusion that is attributable to the subpart F income group and the denominator of which is the total net income in the subpart F income group, both determined in the functional currency of the controlled foreign corporation. If the numerator or denominator of the fraction is zero or less than zero, then the proportionate share of the eligible current year taxes that are allocated and apportioned under §1.960-1(d)(3)(ii) to the subpart F income group is zero.

(ii) *Effect of qualified deficits*.—Neither an accumulated deficit nor any prior year deficit in the earnings and profits of a controlled foreign corporation reduces its net income in a subpart F income group. Accordingly, any such deficit does not affect the denominator of the fraction described in paragraph (b)(3)(i) of this section. However, the first sentence of this paragraph (b)(3)(ii) does not affect the application of section 952(c)(1)(B) for purposes of determining the domestic corporation's subpart F inclusion. Any reduction to the domestic corporation's subpart F inclusion under section 952(c)(1)(B) is reflected in the numerator of the fraction described in paragraph (b)(3)(i) of this section.

(iii) *Effect of current year E&P limitation or chain deficit*.—To the extent that an amount of income in a subpart F income group is excluded from the subpart F income of the controlled foreign corporation under section 952(c)(1)(A) or (C), the net income in the subpart F income group that is the denominator of the fraction described in paragraph (b)(3)(i) of this section is reduced (but not below zero) by the amount excluded. The domestic corporation's subpart F inclusion that is the numerator of the fraction described in paragraph (b)(3)(i) of this section is based on the controlled foreign corporation's subpart F income computed with the application of section 952(c)(1)(A) and (C). See §1.960-1(c)(2) for a rule regarding the treatment of an increase in the subpart F income of a controlled foreign corporation by reason of the recharacterization of a recapture account and the corresponding accumulated earnings and profits under section 952(c) and §1.952-1(f).

(4) *Domestic partnerships*.—For purposes of applying this paragraph (b), in the case of a domestic partnership that is a U.S. shareholder partnership with respect to a partnership CFC, the distributive share of a U.S. shareholder partner of the U.S. shareholder partnership's subpart F inclusion with respect to the partnership CFC is treated as a subpart F inclusion of the U.S. shareholder partner with respect to the partnership CFC.

(5) *Example*.—The following example illustrates the application of this paragraph (b).

(i) *Facts*. USP, a domestic corporation, owns 80% of the stock of CFC, a controlled foreign corporation. The remaining portion of the stock of CFC is owned by an unrelated person. USP and CFC both use the calendar year as their U.S. taxable year, and CFC also uses the calendar year as its foreign taxable year. CFC uses the "u" as its functional currency. At all relevant times, 1u=$1x. For its U.S. taxable year ending December 31, 2018, after the application of the rules in §1.960-1(d) the income of CFC after foreign taxes is assigned to the following income groups: 1,000,000u of dividend income in a subpart F income group within the passive category ("subpart F income group 1"); 2,400,000u of gain from commodities transactions in a subpart F income group within the passive category ("subpart F income group 2"); and 1,800,000u of foreign base company services income in a subpart F income group within the general category ("subpart F income group 3"). CFC has current year taxes, all of which are eligible current year taxes, translated into U.S. dollars, of $740,000x that are allocated and apportioned as follows: $50,000x to subpart F income group 1; $240,000x to subpart F income group 2; and $450,000x to subpart F income group 3. USP has a subpart F inclusion with respect to CFC of 4,160,000u = $4,160,000x, of which 800,000u is attributable to subpart F income group 1, 1,920,000u to subpart F income group 2, and 1,440,000u to subpart F income group 3.

(ii) *Analysis*—(A) *Passive category*. Under paragraphs (b)(2) and (3) of this section, the amount of CFC's foreign income taxes that are properly attributable to items of income in subpart F income group 1 to which a subpart F inclusion is attributable equals USP's proportionate share of the eligible current year taxes that are allocated and apportioned under §1.960-1(d)(3)(ii) to subpart F income group 1, which is $40,000x ($50,000x × 800,000u/1,000,000u). Under paragraphs (b)(2) and (3) of this section, the amount of CFC's foreign income taxes that are properly attributable to items of income in subpart F income group 2 to which a subpart F inclusion is attributable equals USP's proportionate share of the eligible current year taxes that are allocated and apportioned under §1.960-1(d)(3)(ii) to subpart F income group 2, which is $192,000x ($240,000x × 1,920,000u/2,400,000u). Accordingly, under paragraph (b)(1) of this section, USP is deemed to have paid $232,000x ($40,000x + $192,000x) of passive category foreign income taxes of CFC with respect to its $2,720,000x subpart F inclusion in the passive category.

(B) *General category*. Under paragraphs (b)(2) and (3) of this section, the amount of CFC's foreign income taxes that are properly attributable to items of income in subpart F income group 3 to which a subpart F inclusion is attributable equals USP's proportionate share of the eligible current year taxes that are allocated and apportioned under §1.960-1(d)(3)(ii) to subpart F income group 3, which is $360,000x ($450,000x × 1,440,000u/1,800,000u). CFC has no other subpart F income groups within the general category. Accordingly, under paragraph (b)(1) of this section, USP is deemed to have paid $360,000x of general category foreign income taxes of CFC with respect to its $1,440,000x subpart F inclusion in the general category.

(c) *Foreign income taxes deemed paid under section 960(d)*.—(1) *In general*.—If a domestic corporation that is a United States shareholder of one or more controlled foreign corporations includes an amount in gross income under section 951A(a) and §1.951A-1(b), the domestic corporation is deemed to have paid an amount of foreign income taxes equal to 80 percent of the product of its inclusion percentage multiplied by the sum of all tested foreign income taxes in the tested income group within each section 904 category of the controlled foreign corporation or corporations.

(2) *Inclusion percentage*.—The term *inclusion percentage* means, with respect to a domestic corporation that is a United States shareholder of one or more controlled foreign corporations, the domestic corporation's GILTI inclusion amount divided by the aggregate amount described in section 951A(c)(1)(A) and §1.951A-1(c)(2)(i) with respect to the United States shareholder.

(3) *Tested foreign income taxes.*—The term *tested foreign income taxes* means, with respect to a domestic corporation that is a United States shareholder of a controlled foreign corporation, the amount of the controlled foreign corporation's foreign income taxes that are properly attributable to tested income taken into account by the domestic corporation under section 951A and § 1.951A-1.

(4) *Properly attributable.*—The amount of the controlled foreign corporation's foreign income taxes that are properly attributable to tested income taken into account by the domestic corporation under section 951A(a) and § 1.951A-1(b) equals the domestic corporation's proportionate share of the eligible current year taxes of the controlled foreign corporation that are allocated and apportioned under § 1.960-1(d)(3)(ii) to the tested income group within each section 904 category of the controlled foreign corporation. No other foreign income taxes are considered properly attributable to tested income.

(5) *Proportionate share.*—A domestic corporation's proportionate share of eligible current year taxes of a controlled foreign corporation that are allocated and apportioned under § 1.960-1(d)(3)(ii) to a tested income group within a section 904 category of the controlled foreign corporation is the U.S. dollar amount of eligible current year taxes that are allocated and apportioned under § 1.960-1(d)(3)(ii) to a tested income group within a section 904 category of the controlled foreign corporation multiplied by a fraction (not to exceed one), the numerator of which is the portion of the tested income of the controlled foreign corporation in the tested income group within the section 904 category that is included in computing the domestic corporation's aggregate amount described in section 951A(c)(1)(A) and § 1.951A-1(c)(2)(i), and the denominator of which is the income in the tested income group within the section 904 category, both determined in the functional currency of the controlled foreign corporation. If the numerator or denominator of the fraction is zero or less than zero, the domestic corporation's proportionate share of the eligible current year taxes allocated and apportioned under § 1.960-1(d)(3)(ii) to the tested income group is zero.

(6) *Domestic partnerships.*—See § 1.951A-1(e) for rules regarding the determination of the GILTI inclusion amount of a U.S. shareholder partner.

(7) *Examples.*—The following examples illustrate the application of this paragraph (c).

(i) *Example 1: Directly owned controlled foreign corporation*—(A) *Facts.* USP, a domestic corporation, owns 100% of the stock of a number of controlled foreign corporations, including CFC1. USP and CFC1 each use the calendar year as their U.S. taxable year. CFC1 uses the "u" as its functional currency. At all relevant times, 1u=$1x. For its U.S. taxable year ending December 31, 2018, after application of the rules in § 1.960-1(d), the income of CFC1 is assigned to a single income group: 2,000u of income from the sale of goods in a tested income group within the general category ("tested income group"). CFC1 has current year taxes, all of which are eligible current year taxes, translated into U.S. dollars, of $400x that are all allocated and apportioned to the tested income group. For its U.S. taxable year ending December 31, 2018, USP has a GILTI inclusion amount determined by reference to all of its controlled foreign corporations, including CFC1, of $6,000x, and an aggregate amount described in section 951A(c)(1)(A) and § 1.951A-1(c)(2)(i) of $10,000x. All of the income in CFC1's tested income group is included in computing USP's aggregate amount described in section 951A(c)(1)(A) and § 1.951A-1(c)(2)(i).

(B) *Analysis.* Under paragraph (c)(5) of this section, USP's proportionate share of the eligible current year taxes that are allocated and apportioned under § 1.960-1(d)(3)(ii) to CFC1's tested income group is $400x ($400x × 2,000u/2,000u). Therefore, under paragraph (c)(4) of this section, the amount of foreign income taxes that are properly attributable to tested income taken into account by USP under section 951A(a) and § 1.951A-1(b) is $400x. Under paragraph (c)(3) of this section, USP's tested foreign income taxes with respect to CFC1 are $400x. Under paragraph (c)(2) of this section, USP's inclusion percentage is 60% ($6,000x/$10,000x). Accordingly, under paragraph (c)(1) of this section, USP is deemed to have paid $192 of the foreign income taxes of CFC1 (80% x 60% x $400x).

(ii) *Example 2: Controlled foreign corporation owned through domestic partnership*—(A) *Facts*—(*1*) US1, a domestic corporation, owns 95% of PRS, a domestic partnership. The remaining 5% of PRS is owned by US2, a domestic corporation that is unrelated to US1. PRS owns all of the stock of CFC1, a controlled foreign corporation. In addition, US1 owns all of the stock of CFC2, a controlled foreign corporation. US1, US2, PRS, CFC1, and CFC2 all use the calendar year as their taxable year. CFC1 and CFC2 both use the "u" as their functional currency. At all relevant times, 1u=$1x. For its U.S. taxable year ending December 31, 2018, after application of the rules in § 1.960-1(d), the income of CFC1 is assigned to a single income group: 300u of income from the sale of goods in a tested income group within the general category ("CFC1's tested income group"). CFC1 has current year taxes, all of which are eligible current year taxes, translated into U.S. dollars, of $100x that are all allocated and apportioned to CFC1's tested income group. The income of CFC2 is also assigned to a single income group: 200u of income from the sale of goods in a tested income group within the general category ("CFC2's tested income group"). CFC2 has current year taxes, all of which are eligible current year taxes, translated into U.S. dollars, of $20x that are allocated and apportioned to CFC2's tested income group.

(*2*) Under § 1.951A-1(e)(1), for purposes of determining the GILTI inclusion amount of US1 and US2, PRS is not treated as owning (within the meaning of section 958(a)) the stock of CFC1; instead, PRS is treated in the same manner as a foreign partnership for purposes of determining the stock of CFC1 owned by US1 and US2 under section 958(a)(2). Therefore, only US1 is a United States shareholder of CFC1. Taking into account both CFC1 and CFC2, US1 has a GILTI inclusion amount in the general category of $485x, and an aggregate amount described in section 951A(c)(1)(A) and § 1.951A-1(c)(2)(i) within the general category of $485x. 285u (95% x 300u) of the income in CFC1's tested income group and 200u of the income in CFC2's tested income group is included in computing US1's aggregate amount described in section 951A(c)(1)(A) and § 1.951A-1(c)(2)(i) within the general category. Because US2 is not a U.S. shareholder with respect to CFC1, US2 does not take into account CFC1's tested income in determining its GILTI inclusion amount.

(B) *Analysis*—(*1*) *US1*—(*i*) *CFC1.* Under paragraphs (c)(5) and (6) of this section, US1's proportionate share of the eligible current year taxes that are allocated and apportioned under § 1.960-1(d)(3)(ii) to CFC1's tested income group is $95x ($100x × 285u/300u). Therefore, under paragraph (c)(4) of this section, the amount of the foreign income taxes that are properly attributable to tested income taken into account by US1 under section 951A(a) and § 1.951A-1(b) is $95x. Under paragraph (c)(3) of this section, US1's tested foreign income taxes with respect to CFC1 are $95x. Under paragraph (c)(2) of this section, US1's inclusion percentage is 100% ($485x/$485x). Accordingly, under paragraph (c)(1) of this section, US1 is deemed to have paid $76x of the foreign income taxes of CFC1 (80% x 100% x $95x).

(*ii*) *CFC2.* Under paragraph (c)(5) of this section, US1's proportionate share of the eligible current year taxes that are allocated and apportioned under § 1.960-1(d)(3)(ii) to CFC2's tested income group is $20x ($20x x 200u/200u). Therefore, under paragraph (c)(4) of this section, the amount of foreign income taxes properly attributable to tested income taken into account by US1 under section 951A(a) and § 1.951A-1(b) is $20x. Under paragraph (c)(3) of this section, US1's tested foreign income taxes with respect to CFC2 are $20. Under paragraph (c)(2) of this section, US1's inclusion percentage is 100% ($485x/$485x). Accordingly, under paragraph (c)(1) of this section, US1 is deemed to have paid $16 of the foreign income taxes of CFC2 (80% x 100% x $20x).

(*2*) *US2.* US2 is not a United States shareholder of CFC1 or CFC2. Accordingly, under paragraph (c)(1) of this section, US2 is not deemed to have paid any of the foreign income taxes of CFC1 or CFC2. [Reg. § 1.960-2.]

☐ [*T.D. 7120, 6-3-71. Amended by T.D.* 7334, 12-20-74, *T.D.* 7649, 10-17-79, *T.D.* 7843, 11-3-82 *T.D.* 9882, 12-16-2019, *T.D.* 9922, 11-2-2020 *and T.D.* 9959, 12-28-2021 (*corrected* 7-26-2022).]

§ 1.960-3. Foreign income taxes deemed paid under section 960(b).—(a) *Scope.*—Paragraph (b) of this section provides rules for computing the amount of foreign income taxes deemed paid by a domestic corporation that is a United States shareholder of a controlled foreign corporation, or by a controlled foreign corporation, under section 960(b). Paragraph (c) of this section provides rules for the establishment and maintenance of PTEP groups within an annual PTEP account. Paragraph (d) of this section defines the term PTEP group taxes. Paragraph (e) of this section provides examples illustrating the application of this section.

(b) *Foreign income taxes deemed paid under section 960(b).*—(1) *Foreign income taxes deemed paid by a domestic corporation with respect to a section 959(a) distribution.*—If a controlled foreign corporation makes a distribution to a domestic corporation that is a United States shareholder with respect to the controlled foreign corporation and that distribution is, in whole or in part, a section 959(a) distribution with respect to a PTEP group within a section 904 category, the domestic corporation is deemed to have paid the amount of the foreign corporation's foreign income taxes that are properly attributable to the section 959(a) distribution with respect to the PTEP group and that have not been deemed to have been paid by a domestic corporation under section 960 for the current taxable year or any prior taxable year. See § 1.965-5(c)(1)(iii) for rules disallowing credits in relation to a distribution of certain previously taxed earnings and profits resulting from the application of section 965. For each section 904 category, the domestic corporation is deemed to have paid foreign income taxes equal to the sum of the controlled foreign corporation's foreign income taxes that are properly attributable to section 959(a) distributions with respect to all PTEP groups within the section 904 category. See § 1.904-6(b)(2) for rules on assigning the foreign income tax to a section 904 category.

(2) *Foreign income taxes deemed paid by a controlled foreign corporation with respect to a section 959(b) distribution.*—If a controlled foreign corporation (*distributing controlled foreign corporation*) makes a distribution to another controlled foreign corporation (recipient controlled foreign corporation) and the distribution is, in whole or in part, a section 959(b) distribution from a PTEP group within a section 904 category, the recipient controlled foreign corporation is deemed to have paid the amount of the distributing controlled foreign corporation's foreign income taxes that are properly attributable to the section 959(b) distribution from the PTEP group and that have not been deemed to have been paid by a domestic corporation under section 960 for the current taxable year or any prior taxable year. See § 1.904-6(b)(3) for rules on assigning the foreign income tax to a section 904 category.

(3) *Properly attributable.*—The amount of foreign income taxes that are properly attributable to a section 959 distribution from a PTEP group within a section 904 category equals the domestic corporation's or recipient controlled foreign corporation's proportionate share of the PTEP group taxes with respect to the PTEP group within the section 904 category. No other foreign income taxes are considered properly attributable to a section 959 distribution.

(4) *Proportionate share.*—A domestic corporation's or recipient controlled foreign corporation's proportionate share of the PTEP group taxes with respect to a PTEP group within a section 904 category is equal to the total amount of the PTEP group taxes with respect to the PTEP group multiplied by a fraction (not to exceed one), the numerator of which is the amount of the section 959 distribution from the PTEP group, and the denominator of which is the total amount of previously taxed earnings and profits in the PTEP group, both determined in the functional currency of the controlled foreign corporation. If the numerator or denominator of the fraction is zero or less than zero, then the proportionate share of the PTEP group taxes with respect to the PTEP group is zero.

(5) *Domestic partnerships.*—For purposes of applying this paragraph (b), in the case of a domestic partnership that is a U.S. shareholder partnership with respect to a partnership CFC, the distributive share of a U.S. shareholder partner of a U.S. shareholder partnership's section 959(a) distribution from the partnership CFC is treated as a section 959(a) distribution received by the U.S. shareholder partner from the partnership CFC.

(c) *Accounting for previously taxed earnings and profits.*—(1) *Establishment of annual PTEP account.*—A separate, annual account (*annual PTEP account*) must be established for the previously taxed earnings and profits of the controlled foreign corporation to which inclusions under section 951(a) and GILTI inclusion amounts of United States shareholders of the CFC are attributable. Each account must correspond to the inclusion year of the previously taxed earnings and profits and to the section 904 category to which the inclusions under section 951(a) or GILTI inclusion amounts were assigned at the level of the United States shareholders. Accordingly, a controlled foreign corporation may have an annual PTEP account in the section 951A category or a treaty category (as defined in § 1.861-13(b)(6)), even though income of the controlled foreign corporation that gave rise to the previously taxed earnings and profits cannot initially be assigned to the section 951A category or a treaty category.

(2) *PTEP groups within an annual PTEP account.*—The amount in an annual PTEP account is further assigned to one or more of the following groups of previously taxed earnings and profits (each, a *PTEP group*) within the account:

(i) Earnings and profits described in section 959(c)(1)(A) that were initially described in section 959(c)(2) by reason of section 965(a) ("reclassified section 965(a) PTEP");

(ii) Earnings and profits described in section 959(c)(1)(A) that were initially described in section 959(c)(2) by reason of section 965(b)(4)(A) ("reclassified section 965(b) PTEP");

(iii) Earnings and profits described in paragraphs (c)(2)(iii)(A) through (C) of this section (which are aggregated into a single PTEP group, "general section 959(c)(1) PTEP"):

(A) Earnings and profits described in section 959(c)(1)(A) by reason of section 951(a)(1)(B) and not by reason of section 959(a)(2);

(B) Earnings and profits described in section 959(c)(1)(A) that were initially described in section 959(c)(2) by reason of section 951(a)(1)(A) (other than earnings that were initially described in paragraphs (c)(2)(vi) through (ix) of this section); and

(C) Earnings and profits described in section 959(c)(1)(B), including by reason of section 959(a)(3) (before its repeal);

(iv) Earnings and profits described in section 959(c)(1)(A) that were initially described in section 959(c)(2) by reason of section 951A(f)(2) ("reclassified section 951A PTEP");

(v) Earnings and profits described in paragraphs (c)(2)(v)(A) through (C) of this section (which are aggregated into a single PTEP group, "reclassified section 245A(d) PTEP"):

(A) Earnings and profits described in section 959(c)(1)(A) that were initially described in section 959(c)(2) by reason of section 245A(e)(2);

(B) Earnings and profits described in section 959(c)(1)(A) that were initially described in section 959(c)(2) by reason of section 959(e); and

(C) Earnings and profits described in section 959(c)(1)(A) that were initially described in section 959(c)(2) by reason of section 964(e)(4);

(vi) Earnings and profits described in section 959(c)(2) by reason of section 965(a) ("section 965(a) PTEP");

(vii) Earnings and profits described in section 959(c)(2) by reason of section 965(b)(4)(A) ("section 965(b) PTEP");

(viii) Earnings and profits described in section 959(c)(2) by reason of section 951A(f)(2) ("section 951A PTEP");

(ix) Earnings and profits described in paragraphs (c)(2)(ix)(A) through (C) of this section (which are aggregated into a single PTEP group, "section 245A(d) PTEP"):

(A) Earnings and profits described in section 959(c)(2) by reason of section 245A(e)(2);

(B) Earnings and profits described in section 959(c)(2) by reason of section 959(e); and

(C) Earnings and profits described in section 959(c)(2) by reason of section 964(e)(4); and

(x) Earnings and profits described in section 959(c)(2) by reason of section 951(a)(1)(A) not otherwise described in paragraph (c)(2)(vi) through (ix) of this section ("section 951(a)(1)(A) PTEP").

(3) *Accounting for distributions of previously taxed earnings and profits.*—With respect to a recipient controlled foreign corporation that receives a section 959(b) distribution, such distribution amount is added to the annual PTEP account, and PTEP group within the annual PTEP account, that corresponds to the inclusion year and section 904 category of the annual PTEP account, and PTEP group within the annual PTEP account, from which the distributing controlled foreign corporation is treated as making the distribution under section 959. Similarly, with respect to a controlled foreign corporation that makes a section 959 distribution, such distribution amount reduces the annual PTEP account, and PTEP group within the annual PTEP account, that corresponds to the inclusion year and section 904 category of the annual PTEP account, and PTEP group within the annual PTEP account, from which the controlled foreign corporation is treated as making the distribution under section 959. Earnings and profits in a PTEP group are reduced by the amount of current year taxes that are allocated and apportioned to the PTEP group under § 1.960-1(d)(3)(ii), and the U.S. dollar amount of the taxes are added to an account of PTEP group taxes under the rules in paragraph (d)(1) of this section.

(4) *Accounting for reclassifications of earnings and profits described in section 959(c)(2) to earnings and profits described in section 959(c)(1).*—If an amount of previously taxed earnings and profits that is in a PTEP group described in paragraphs (c)(2)(vi) through (x) of this section (each, a section 959(c)(2) PTEP group) is reclassified as previously taxed earnings and profits described in section 959(c)(1) (reclassified previously taxed earnings and profits), the section 959(c)(2) PTEP group is reduced by the functional currency amount of the reclassified previously taxed earnings and profits. This amount is added to the corresponding PTEP group described in paragraph (c)(2)(i), (ii),

(iii) (by reason of paragraph (c)(2)(iii)(B) of this section), (iv) or (v) of this section (each, a reclassified PTEP group) in the same section 904 category and same annual PTEP account as the reduced section 959(c)(2) PTEP group.

(d) *PTEP group taxes.*—(1) *In general.*—The term *PTEP group taxes* means the U.S. dollar amount of foreign income taxes (translated in accordance with section 986(a)) that are paid, accrued, or deemed paid with respect to an amount in each PTEP group within an annual PTEP account. The foreign income taxes that are paid, accrued, or deemed paid with respect to a PTEP group within an annual PTEP account of a controlled foreign corporation are—

(i) The sum of—

(A) The current year taxes paid or accrued by the controlled foreign corporation that are allocated and apportioned to the PTEP group under § 1.960-1(d)(3)(ii);

(B) Foreign income taxes that are deemed paid under section 960(b)(2) and paragraph (b)(2) of this section by the controlled foreign corporation with respect to a section 959(b) distribution received by the controlled foreign corporation, the amount of which is added to the PTEP group under paragraph (c)(3) of this section; and

(C) In the case of a reclassified PTEP group of the controlled foreign corporation, reclassified PTEP group taxes that are attributable to the section 959(c)(2) PTEP group that corresponds to the reclassified PTEP group.

(ii) Reduced by—

(A) Foreign income taxes that were deemed paid under section 960(b)(2) and paragraph (b)(2) of this section by another controlled foreign corporation that received a section 959(b) distribution from the controlled foreign corporation, the amount of which is subtracted from the controlled foreign corporation's PTEP group under paragraph (c)(3) of this section;

(B) Foreign income taxes that were deemed paid under section 960(b)(1) and paragraph (b)(1) of this section by a domestic corporation that is a United States shareholder of the controlled foreign corporation that received a section 959(a) distribution from the controlled foreign corporation, the amount of which is subtracted from the controlled foreign corporation's PTEP group under paragraph (c)(3) of this section; and

(C) In the case of a section 959(c)(2) PTEP group of the controlled foreign corporation, reclassified PTEP group taxes.

(2) *Reclassified PTEP group taxes.*—Reclassified PTEP group taxes are foreign income taxes that are initially included in PTEP group taxes with respect to a section 959(c)(2) PTEP group under paragraph (d)(1)(i)(A) or (B) of this section multiplied by a fraction, the numerator of which is the portion of the previously taxed earnings and profits in the section 959(c)(2) PTEP group that become reclassified previously taxed earnings and profits, and the denominator of which is the total previously taxed earnings and profits in the section 959(c)(2) PTEP group.

(3) *Foreign income taxes deemed paid with respect to PTEP groups established for pre-2018 inclusion years.*—In the case of foreign income taxes paid or accrued in a taxable year of the controlled foreign corporation that began before January 1, 2018, with respect to an annual PTEP account, and a PTEP group within such account, that was established for an inclusion year that begins before January 1, 2018, the foreign income taxes are treated as PTEP group taxes of a controlled foreign corporation for purposes of this section only if those foreign income taxes were—

(i) Not included in a controlled foreign corporation's post-1986 foreign income taxes (as defined in section 902(c)(2) as in effect on December 21, 2017) used to compute foreign taxes deemed paid under section 902 (as in effect on December 21, 2017) in any taxable year that began before January 1, 2018; and

(ii) Not treated as deemed paid under section 960(a)(3) (as in effect on December 21, 2017) by a domestic corporation that was a United States shareholder of the controlled foreign corporation.

(e) *Examples.*—The following examples illustrate the application of this section.

(1) *Example 1: Establishment of PTEP groups and PTEP accounts*—(i) *Facts.* USP, a domestic corporation, owns all of the stock of CFC1, a controlled foreign corporation. CFC1 owns all of the stock of CFC2, a controlled foreign corporation. USP, CFC1, and CFC2 each use the calendar year as their U.S. taxable year. CFC1 and CFC2 use the "u" as their functional currency. At all relevant times, 1u = $1x. With respect to CFC2, USP includes in gross income a subpart F inclusion of 1,000,000u = $1,000,000x for the taxable year ending December 31, 2018. The inclusion is with respect to passive category income. In its U.S. taxable year ending December 31, 2019, CFC2 distributes 1,000,000u to CFC1. CFC2 has no earnings and profits except for the 1,000,000u of previously taxed earnings and profits resulting from USP's 2018 taxable year subpart F inclusion. CFC2's country of organization, Country X, imposes a withholding tax on CFC1 of 300,000u on CFC2's distribution to CFC1. Under § 1.960-1(d)(3)(ii), CFC1's 300,000u of current year taxes are allocated and apportioned to the PTEP group within the annual PTEP account within the section 904 category to which the 1,000,000u of previously taxed earnings and profits are assigned.

(ii) *Analysis*—(A) Under paragraph (c)(1) of this section, a separate annual PTEP account in the passive category for the 2018 taxable year is established for CFC2 as a result of USP's subpart F inclusion. Under paragraph (c)(2) of this section, this account contains one PTEP group, section 951(a)(1)(A) PTEP.

(B) Under paragraph (c)(3) of this section, in the 2019 taxable year, the 1,000,000u related to the section 959(b) distribution from CFC2 is added to CFC1's annual PTEP account for the 2018 taxable year in the passive category and to the section 951(a)(1)(A) PTEP within such account. Similarly, CFC2's 2018 taxable year annual PTEP account within the passive category, and the section 951(a)(1)(A) PTEP within such account, is reduced by the amount of the 1,000,000u section 959(b) distribution to CFC1. Additionally, CFC1's annual PTEP account for the 2018 taxable year in the passive category, and the section 951(a)(1)(A) PTEP within such account, is reduced by the 300,000u of withholding tax imposed on CFC1 by Country X. Therefore, CFC1's annual PTEP account for the 2018 taxable year within the passive category and the section 951(a)(1)(A) PTEP within such account is 700,000u.

(C) Under paragraph (d)(1) of this section, the 300,000u of withholding tax is translated into U.S. dollars and $300,000x is added to the PTEP group taxes with respect to CFC1's section 951(a)(1)(A) PTEP within the annual PTEP account for the 2018 taxable year within the passive category.

(2) *Example 2: Foreign income taxes deemed paid under section 960(b)*—(i) *Facts.* USP, a domestic corporation, owns 100% of the stock of CFC1, which in turn owns 60% of the stock of CFC2, which in turn owns 100% of the stock of CFC3. USP, CFC1, CFC2, and CFC3 all use the calendar year as their U.S. taxable year. CFC1, CFC2, and CFC3 all use the "u" as their functional currency. At all relevant times, 1u=$1x. On July 1, 2020, CFC2 distributes 600u to CFC1 and the entire distribution is a section 959(b) distribution ("distribution 1"). On October 1, 2020, CFC1 distributes 800u to USP and the entire distribution is a section 959(a) distribution ("distribution 2"). CFC1 and CFC2 make no other distributions in the year ending December 31, 2020, earn no other income, and incur no taxes on distribution 1 or distribution 2. Before taking into account distribution 1, CFC2 has 1,000u of section 951(a)(1)(A) PTEP within an annual PTEP account for the 2016 taxable year within the general category. The previously taxed earnings and profits in CFC2's PTEP group relate to subpart F income of CFC3 that was included by USP in 2016. CFC3 distributed the earnings and profits to CFC2 before the 2020 taxable year and, solely as a result of the distribution of the previously taxed earnings and profits, CFC2 incurred withholding and net basis tax, resulting in $150 of PTEP group taxes with respect to section 951(a)(1)(A) PTEP. Before taking into account distribution 1 and distribution 2, CFC1 has 200u in section 951A PTEP within an annual PTEP account for the 2018 taxable year within the section 951A category. The previously taxed earnings and profits in CFC1's PTEP group relate to the portion of a GILTI inclusion amount that was included by USP in 2018 and allocated to CFC2 under section 951A(f)(2) and § 1.951A-5(b)(2). CFC2 distributed the earnings and profits to CFC1 before the 2020 taxable year and, solely as a result of the distribution of the previously taxed earnings and profits, CFC1 incurred withholding and net basis tax, resulting in $25x of PTEP group taxes with respect to section 951A PTEP.

(ii) *Analysis*—(A) *Foreign income taxes deemed paid by CFC1.* With respect to distribution 1 from CFC2 to CFC1, under paragraph (b)(4) of this section CFC1's proportionate share of PTEP group taxes with respect to CFC2's section 951(a)(1)(A) PTEP within an annual PTEP account for the 2016 taxable year within the general category is $90x ($150x x 600u/1,000u). Under paragraph (b)(3) of this section, the amount of foreign income taxes that are properly attributable to distribution 1 is $90x. Accordingly, under paragraph (b)(2) of this section, CFC1 is deemed to have paid $90x of general category foreign income taxes of CFC2 with respect to its 600u section 959(b) distribution in the general category.

(B) *Adjustments to PTEP accounts of CFC1 and CFC2.* Under paragraph (c)(3) of this section, the 600u related to distribution 1 is added to CFC1's section 951(a)(1)(A) PTEP within an annual PTEP account for the 2016 taxable year within the general category. Similarly,

CFC2's section 951(a)(1)(A) PTEP within an annual PTEP account for the 2016 taxable year within the general category is reduced by 600u, the amount of the section 959(b) distribution to CFC1. Additionally, under paragraph (d) of this section, CFC1's PTEP group taxes with respect to its section 951(a)(1)(A) PTEP within an annual PTEP account for the 2016 taxable year within the general category are increased by $90 and CFC2's PTEP group taxes with respect to section 951(a)(1)(A) PTEP within an annual PTEP account for the 2016 taxable year within the general category are reduced by $90x.

(C) *Foreign income taxes deemed paid by USP.* With respect to distribution 2 from CFC1 to USP, because CFC1 has PTEP groups in more than one section 904 category, this section is applied separately to each section 904 category (that is, distribution 2 of 800u is applied separately to the 200u of CFC1's section 951A PTEP and 600u of CFC1's section 951(a)(1)(A) PTEP).

(*1*) *Section 951A category.* Under paragraph (b)(4) of this section, USP's proportionate share of PTEP group taxes with respect to CFC1's section 951A PTEP within an annual PTEP account for the 2018 taxable year within the section 951A category is $25x ($25x x 200u/200u). Under paragraph (b)(3) of this section, the amount of foreign income taxes within the section 951A category that are properly attributable to distribution 2 is $25x. Accordingly, under paragraph (b)(1) of this section USP is deemed to have paid $25x of section 951A category foreign income taxes of CFC1 with respect to its 200u section 959(a) distribution in the section 951A category.

(*2*) *General category.* Under paragraph (b)(4) of this section, USP's proportionate share of PTEP group taxes with respect to CFC1's section 951(a)(1)(A) PTEP within an annual PTEP account for the 2016 taxable year within the general category is $90x ($90x x 600u/600u). Under paragraph (b)(3) of this section, the amount of foreign income taxes that are properly attributable to distribution 2 is $90x. Accordingly, under paragraph (b)(1), USP is deemed to have paid $90x of general category foreign income taxes of CFC1 with respect to its 600u section 959(a) distribution in the general category. [Reg. § 1.960-3.]

☐ [*T.D. 7120, 6-3-71. Amended by T.D. 7481, 4-15-77, T.D. 7649, 10-17-79, T.D. 7843, 11-3-82, T.D. 9882, 12-16-2019 and T.D. 9922, 11-2-2020.*]

§ 1.960-4. Additional foreign tax credit in year of receipt of previously taxed earnings and profits.—(a) *Increase in section 904(a) limitation for the taxable year of exclusion.*—(1) *In general.*—The applicable limitation under section 904(a) for a taxpayer's taxable year (hereinafter in this section referred to as the "taxable year of exclusion") in which the taxpayer receives an amount which is excluded from gross income under section 959(a)(1) and which is attributable to a controlled foreign corporation's earnings and profits in respect of which an amount was required to be included in the gross income of such taxpayer under section 951(a) for a taxable year (hereinafter in this section referred to as the "taxable year of inclusion") previous to the taxable year of exclusion shall be increased under section 960(c)(1) by the amount described in paragraph (b) of this section if the conditions described in paragraph (a)(2) of this section are satisfied. For purposes of this section, an amount included in gross income under section 951A(a) is treated as an amount included in gross income under section 951(a). The amount of the increase in the foreign tax credit limitation allowed by this section is determined with regard to each separate category of income described in § 1.904-5(a)(4)(v).

(2) *Conditions under which increase in limitation is allowed for the taxable year of exclusion.*—The increase in limitation described in subparagraph (1) of this paragraph for the taxable year of exclusion shall be made only if the taxpayer—

(i) For the taxable year of inclusion either chose to claim a foreign tax credit as provided in section 901 or did not pay or accrue any foreign income taxes,

(ii) Chooses to claim a foreign tax credit as provided in section 901 for the taxable year of exclusion, and

(iii) For the taxable year of exclusion pays, accrues, or is deemed to have paid foreign income taxes with respect to the amount, described in subparagraph (1) of this paragraph, which is excluded from his gross income for such year under section 959(a)(1).

For purposes of determining the source of distributions in determining the foreign tax credit under section 960(b) and this section, see also paragraph (e) of § 1.959-3.

(b) *Amount of increase in limitation for the taxable year of exclusion.*—The amount of increase under section 960(c)(1) in the applicable limitation under section 904(a) for the taxable year of exclusion shall be—

(1) The amount by which the applicable section 904(a) limitation for the taxable year of inclusion was increased, determined as provided in paragraph (c) of this section, by reason of the inclusion of the amount in the taxpayer's income for such year under section 951(a), reduced by

(2) The amount of foreign income taxes allowed as a credit under section 901 for such taxable year of inclusion and which were allowable to such taxpayer solely by reason of the inclusion of such amount in his gross income under section 951(a), as determined under paragraph (d) of this section, and then by

(3) The additional reduction for such taxable year of inclusion arising by reason of increases in limitation under section 960(c)(1) for taxable years intervening between such taxable year of inclusion and such taxable year of exclusion, as determined under paragraph (e) of this section in respect of such inclusion under section 951(a),

except that the amount of increase determined under this paragraph for the taxable year of exclusion shall in no case exceed the amount of foreign income taxes paid, accrued, or deemed to be paid by such taxpayer for such taxable year of exclusion with respect to the amount, described in paragraph (a)(1) of this section, which is excluded from gross income for such year under section 959(a)(1).

(c) *Determination of increase in limitation for the taxable year of inclusion.*—The amount of the increase in the applicable limitation under section 904(a) for the taxable year of inclusion which arises by reason of the inclusion of the amount in gross income under section 951(a) shall be the amount of the applicable limitation under section 904(a) for such year reduced by the amount which would have been the applicable limitation under section 904(a) for such year if the amount had not been included in gross income for such year under section 951(a).

(d) *Determination of foreign income taxes allowed for taxable year of inclusion by reason of section 951(a) amount.*—The amount of foreign income taxes allowed as a credit under section 901 for the taxable year of inclusion which were allowable solely by reason of the inclusion of the amount in gross income for such year under section 951(a) shall be the amount of foreign income taxes allowed as a credit under section 901 for such year reduced by the amount of foreign income taxes which would have been allowed as a credit under section 901 for such year if the amount had not been included in gross income for such year under section 951(a). For purposes of this paragraph (d), the term "foreign income taxes" includes foreign income taxes paid or accrued, foreign income taxes deemed paid or accrued under section 904(c), and foreign income taxes deemed paid under section 960 (or section 902 with respect to taxable years of foreign corporations beginning before January 1, 2018), for the taxable year of inclusion.

(e) *Additional reduction for the taxable year of inclusion arising by reason of increases in limitation for intervening years.*—The amount of increase in the applicable limitation under section 904(a) for the taxable year of inclusion shall also be reduced, after first deducting the foreign income taxes described in paragraph (b)(2) of this section, by any increases in limitation which arise under section 960(c)(1)—by reason of any earlier exclusions under section 959(a)(1) in respect of the same inclusion under section 951(a) for such taxable year of inclusion—for the first, second, third, fourth, etc., succeeding taxable years of exclusion, in that order, which follow such taxable year of inclusion and precede the taxable year of exclusion in respect of which the increase in limitation under section 960(c)(1) and paragraph (b) of this section is being determined. The amount of any increase in limitation which arises under section 960(c)(1) for any such succeeding taxable year of exclusion shall be the amount of foreign income taxes allowed as a credit under section 901 for each such taxable year reduced by the amount of foreign income taxes which would have been allowed as a credit under section 901 for each such year if the limitation for each such year were not increased under section 960(c)(1). For any such succeeding taxable year of exclusion for which the taxpayer does not choose to claim a foreign tax credit as provided in section 901, the same increase in limitation under section 960(c)(1) shall be treated as having been made, for purposes of this paragraph, which would have been made for such taxable year if the taxpayer had chosen to claim the foreign tax credit for such year.

(f) *Examples.*—The application of this section may be illustrated by the following examples:

(1) *Example 1.* USP, a domestic corporation, owns all of the one class of stock of CFC, a controlled foreign corporation that uses the U.S. dollar as its functional currency. CFC, after paying foreign

income taxes of $10x, has earnings and profits for Year 1 of $90x, all of which are attributable to an amount required under section 951(a) to be included in USP's gross income for Year 1 because the income is general category foreign base company services income of CFC. Both corporations use the calendar year as the taxable year. For Year 2 and Year 3, CFC has no earnings and profits attributable to an amount required to be included in USP's gross income under section 951(a); for each such year it makes a distribution of $45x (from its section 951(a)(1)(A) PTEP within the annual PTEP account for Year 1) from which a foreign income tax of $6x is withheld. For each of Year 1, Year 2, and Year 3, USP derives taxable income of $50x from sources within the United States and claims a foreign tax credit under section 901, subject to the limitation under section 904. The U.S. tax payable by USP is determined as follows, assuming a corporate tax rate of 21%:

Table 1 to paragraph (f)(1)

Year 1		
Taxable income of USP:		
U.S. sources		$50.00x
Sources without the U.S.:		
Amount required to be included in USP's gross income under section 951(a)	$90.00x	
Foreign income taxes deemed paid by USP under section 960(a) and included in USP's gross income under section 78 ($10x x $90x/$90x)	$10.00x	$100.00x
Total taxable income		$150.00x
U.S. tax payable for Year 1:		
U.S. tax before credit ($150x x 21 %)		$31.50x
Credit: Foreign income taxes of $10x, but not to exceed the limitation of $21x for Year 1 ($100x/$150x x $31.50x) . . .		$10.00x
U.S. tax payable		$21.50x

Table 2 to paragraph (f)(1)

Year 2		
Taxable income of USP, consisting of income from U.S. sources		$50.00x
U.S. tax before credit ($50x x 21%)		$10.50x
Section 904 limitation for Year 2:		
Limitation for Year 2 before increase under section 960(c)(1) ($10.50x x $0/$50x)		0
Plus: Increase in limitation for Year 2 under sec. 960(c)(1):		
Amount by which Year 1 limitation was increased by reason of inclusion in USP's gross income under section 951(a) for Year 1 ($21x–[($50x x 21%) x $0/$50x])	$21.00x	
Less: Foreign income taxes allowed as a credit for Year 1 which were allowable solely by reason of such section 951(a) inclusion ($10x–$0)	$10.00x	
Balance	$11.00x	
But: Such balance not to exceed foreign income taxes paid by USP for Year 2 with respect to $45x distribution excluded under section 959(a)(1) ($6x tax withheld)	$6.00x	$6.00x
Limitation for Year 2		$6.00x
U.S. tax payable for Year 2:		
U.S. tax before credit ($50x x 21%)		$10.50x
Credit: Foreign income taxes of $6x, but not to exceed limitation of $6x for Year 2		$6.00x
U.S. tax payable		$4.50x

Table 3 to paragraph (f)(1)

Year 3		
Taxable income of USP, consisting of income from U.S. sources		$50.00x
U.S. tax before credit ($50x x 21%)		$10.50x
Section 904 limitation for Year 3:		
Limitation for Year 3 before increase under section 960(c)(1) ($10.50x x $0/$50x)		$0
Plus: Increase in limitation for Year 3 under section 960(c)(1):		
Amount by which Year 1 limitation was increased by reason of inclusion in USP's gross income under section 951(a) for Year 1 ($21x–[($50 x 21%) x $0/$50x])	$21.00x	
Less: Foreign income taxes allowed as a credit for Year 1 which were allowable solely by reason of such section 951(a) inclusion ($10x–$0)	$10.00x	
Tentative balance	$11.00x	
Less: Increase in limitation under section 960(c)(1) for Year 2 by reason of such sec. 951(a) inclusion	$6.00x	
Balance	$5.00x	
But: Such balance not to exceed foreign income taxes paid by USP for Year 3 with respect to $45x distribution excluded under section 959(a)(1) ($6x tax withheld)	$6.00x	$5.00x
Limitation for Year 3		$5.00x
U.S. tax payable for Year 3:		
U.S. tax before credit ($50x x 21%)		$10.50x
Credit: Foreign income taxes of $6, but not to exceed section 904(a) limitation of $5x		$5.00x
U.S. tax payable		$5.50x

(2) *Example 2.* The facts for Year 1 and Year 2 are the same as in paragraph (f)(1) of this section (the facts in *Example 1*), except that in Year 0, in which USP also claimed a foreign tax credit under section 901, USP pays $11x of foreign income taxes in excess of the general category limitation and such excess is not absorbed as a carryback to the prior year under section 904(c). Therefore, there is no increase under section 960(c)(1) in the limitation for Year 2 since the amount ($21x) by which the Year 1 limitation was increased by reason of the inclusion in USP's gross income for Year 1 under section 951(a), less the foreign income taxes ($21x) allowed as a credit which were allowable solely by reason of such inclusion is zero. The foreign income taxes so allowed as a credit for Year 1 which were allowable solely by reason of such section 951(a) inclusion consist of the $10 of foreign income taxes deemed paid for Year 1 under section 960(a) and the $11x of foreign income taxes for Year 0 carried over and deemed paid for Year 1 under section 904(c). [Reg. § 1.960-4.]

☐ [*T.D. 7120, 6-3-71. Amended by T.D. 7649, 10-17-79 T.D. 9882, 12-16-2019 and T.D. 9922, 11-2-2020.*]

§ 1.960-5. Credit for taxable year of inclusion binding for taxable year of exclusion.—(a) *Taxes not allowed as a deduction for taxable year of exclusion.*—In the case of any taxpayer who—

(1) Chooses to claim a foreign tax credit as provided in section 901 for the taxable year for which he is required to include in gross income under section 951(a) or 951A(a) an amount attributable to the earnings and profits of a controlled foreign corporation; and

(2) Does not choose to claim a foreign tax credit as provided in section 901 for a taxable year in which he receives an amount which is excluded from gross income under section 959(a)(1) and which is attributable to such earnings and profits of such controlled foreign corporation,

no deduction shall be allowed under section 164 for the taxable year of such exclusion for any foreign income taxes paid or accrued on or with respect to such excluded amount.

(b) *Example.*—The application of this section may be illustrated by the following example:

(1) *Facts.* USP, a domestic corporation, owns all the one class of stock of CFC, a controlled foreign corporation. Both corporations use the calendar year as the taxable year and the functional currency of CFC is the U.S. dollar. All of CFC's earnings and profits of $80x for Year 1 (after payment of foreign income taxes of $20x on its total income of $100x for such year) are attributable to amounts required under section 951(a) to be included in USP's gross income for Year 1 because such income is general category foreign base company services income of CFC. For Year 1, USP chooses to claim a foreign tax credit for the $20x of foreign income taxes which for such year are paid by CFC and deemed paid by USP under section 960(a) and § 1.960-2(b). In Year 2, CFC distributes the entire $80x of Year 1 previously taxed earnings and profits, from which a foreign income tax of $8x is withheld. Also in Year 2, CFC pays $40x of interest to USP, from which a foreign income tax of $4x is withheld. For Year 2, USP chooses to claim deductions for its creditable foreign income taxes under section 164 rather than a foreign tax credit under section 901.

(2) *Analysis.* Although USP does not choose to claim a foreign tax credit for Year 2, under section 960(c)(4) and paragraph (a) of this section it may not deduct the $8x of foreign income taxes under section 164. USP may, however, deduct under such section the foreign income tax of $4x which is withheld from the interest paid by CFC in Year 2. [Reg. § 1.960-5.]

☐ [*T.D. 7120, 6-3-71. Amended by T.D. 7649, 10-17-79 and T.D. 9882, 12-16-2019.*]

§ 1.960-6. Overpayments resulting from increase in limitation for taxable year of exclusion.—(a) *Amount of overpayment.*—If an increase in the limitation under section 960(c)(1) and § 1.960-4 for a taxable year of exclusion exceeds the tax (determined before allowance of any credits against tax) imposed by chapter 1 of the Code for such year, the amount of such excess shall be deemed an overpayment of tax for such year and shall be refunded or credited to the taxpayer in accordance with chapter 65 (section 6401 and following) of the Code.

(b) *Example.*—The application of this section may be illustrated by the following example:

(1) *Facts.* USP, a domestic corporation, owns all of the one class of stock of CFC, a controlled foreign corporation. Both corporations use the calendar year as the taxable year, and the functional currency of CFC is the U.S. dollar. For Year 1, CFC has total income of $100,000x on which it pays foreign income taxes of $20,000x. All of CFC's earnings and profits for Year 1 of $80,000x are attributable to an amount which is required under section 951(a) to be included in USP's gross income for Year 1 because such income is general category foreign base company services income of CFC. By reason of such income inclusion USP is deemed for Year 1 to have paid under section 960(a), and is required under section 78 to include in gross income for such year, the $20,000x ($20,000x x $80,000x/$80,000x) of foreign income taxes paid by CFC for such year. USP also derives $100,000x of taxable income from sources within the United States for Year 1. For Year 2, USP has $4,000x of taxable income, all of which is derived from sources within the United States. No part of CFC's earnings and profits for Year 2 is attributable to an amount required under section 951(a) or section 951A(a) to be included in USP's gross income. During Year 2, CFC makes one distribution consisting of its $80,000x earnings and profits for Year 1, all of which is excluded under section 959(a)(1) from USP's gross income for Year 2, and from which distribution foreign income taxes of $1,000x are withheld. For Year 1 and Year 2, USP claims the foreign tax credit under section 901, subject to the limitation of section 904.

(2) *Analysis.* The U.S. tax liability of USP is determined as follows for such years, assuming a corporate tax rate of 21%:

Table 1 to paragraph (b)(2)

Year 1

Taxable income of USP:		
U.S. sources		$100,000.00x
Sources without the U.S.:		
Amount required to be included in USP's gross income under section 951(a)	$80,000.00x	
Foreign income taxes deemed paid by USP under section 960(a) and included in USP's gross income under section 78 ($20,000x x $80,000x/$80,000x)	$20,000.00x	$100,000.00x
Total taxable income . . .		$200,000.00x
U.S. tax payable for Year 1:		
U.S. tax before credit ([$200,000x x 21%])		$42,000.00x
Credit: Foreign income taxes of $20,000x, but not to exceed limitation of $21,000x ($42,000x x $100,000x/$200,000x)		$20,000.00x
U.S. tax payable		$22,000.00x

Table 2 to paragraph (b)(2)

Year 2

Taxable income of USP, consisting of income from U.S. sources	$4,000x
U.S. tax before credit ($4,000x x 21%)	$840x
Section 904 limitation for Year 2:	
Limitation for Year 2 before increase under section 960(c)(1) ($840x x $0/$4,000x) . . .	$0

Plus: Increase in section 904 limitation for Year 2 under section 960(c)(1):		
Amount by which Year 1 limitation was increased by reason of inclusion in USP's gross income under section 951(a) for Year 1 ($21,000x– [$21,000x x $0/$100,000x])	$21,000x	
Less: Foreign income taxes allowed as a credit for Year 1 which were allowable solely by reason of such section 951(a) inclusion ($20,000x–$0)	$20,000x	
Balance	$1,000x	
But: Such balance not to exceed foreign income taxes paid by USP for Year 2 with respect to $80,000x distribution excluded under section 959(a)(1) ($1,000x tax withheld)	1,000x	1,000x
Limitation for Year 2		$1,000x
U.S. tax payable for Year 2:		
U.S. tax before credit ($4,000x x 21%)		$840x
Credit: Foreign income taxes of $1,000x, but not to exceed limitation of $1,000x for Year 2		$1,000x
U.S. tax payable		None
Overpayment of tax for Year 2:		
Increase in limitation under section 960(c)(1) for Year 2		$1,000x
Less: Tax imposed for Year 2 under chapter 1 of the Code		$840x
Excess treated as overpayment		$160x

[Reg. § 1.960-6.]

☐ *[T.D. 7120, 6-3-71. Amended by T.D. 7649, 10-17-79 and T.D. 9882, 12-16-2019.]*

§ 1.960-7. Applicability dates.—(a) Except as provided in paragraph (b) of this section, §§ 1.960-1 through 1.960-6 apply to each taxable year of a foreign corporation ending on or after December 4, 2018, and to each taxable year of a domestic corporation that is a United States shareholder of the foreign corporation in which or with which such taxable year of such foreign corporation ends.

(b) Section 1.960-1(c)(2) and (d)(3)(ii) apply to taxable years of a foreign corporation beginning after December 31, 2019, and to each taxable year of a domestic corporation that is a United States shareholder of the foreign corporation in which or with which such taxable year of such foreign corporation ends. For taxable years of a foreign corporation that end on or after December 4, 2018, and also begin before January 1, 2020, see § 1.960-1(c)(2) and (d)(3)(ii) as in effect on December 17, 2019. Paragraphs (b)(4), (5), and (6), (c)(1)(ii), (iii), and (iv), and (d)(3)(ii)(A) and (B) of § 1.960-1, and paragraphs (b)(2), (b)(3)(i), (b)(5)(i), (b)(5)(iv)(A), and (c)(4), (5), and (7) of § 1.960-2, apply to taxable years of foreign corporations beginning on or after December 28, 2021, and to each taxable year of a domestic corporation that is a United States shareholder of the foreign corporation in which or with which such taxable year of such foreign corporation ends. For taxable years of foreign corporations beginning before December 28, 2021, with respect to the paragraphs described in the preceding sentence, see §§ 1.960-1 and 1.960-2 as in effect on November 12, 2020. [Reg. § 1.960-7.]

☐ *[T.D. 7649, 10-17-79. Amended by T.D. 7843, 11-5-82, T.D. 9882, 12-16-2019, T.D. 9922, 11-2-2020 and T.D. 9959, 12-28-2021.]*

§ 1.961-1. Increase in basis of stock in controlled foreign corporations and of other property.—(a) *Increase in basis.*—(1) *In general.*—Except as provided in subparagraph (2) of this paragraph, the basis of a United States shareholder's—

(i) Stock in a controlled foreign corporation; or

(ii) Property (as defined in paragraph (b)(1) of this section) by reason of the ownership of which he is considered under section 958(a)(2) as owning stock in a controlled foreign corporation shall be increased under section 961(a), as of the last day in the taxable year of such corporation on which it is a controlled foreign corporation, by the amount required to be included with respect to such stock or such property in such shareholder's gross income under section 951(a) for his taxable year in which or with which such taxable year of such corporation ends. The increase in basis provided by the preceding sentence shall be made only to the extent to which such amount required to be included in gross income under section 951(a) was so included in gross income.

(2) *Limitation on amount of increase in case of election under section 962.*—In the case of a United States shareholder who makes the election under section 962 for the taxable year, the amount of the increase in basis provided by subparagraph (1) of this paragraph shall not exceed the amount of United States tax paid in accordance with such election with respect to the amounts included in such shareholder's gross income under section 951(a) for such year (as determined under § 1.962-1).

(b) *Rules of application.*—(1) *Property defined.*—The property of a United States shareholder referred to in paragraph (a)(1)(ii) of this section shall consist of—

(i) Stock in a foreign corporation;

(ii) An interest in a foreign partnership; or

(iii) A beneficial interest in a foreign estate or trust (as defined in section 7701(a)(31)).

(2) *Increase with respect to each share of stock.*—Any increase under paragraph (a) of this section in the basis of a United States shareholder's stock in a foreign corporation shall be made in the amount included in gross income under section 951(a) or in the amount of United States tax paid in accordance with an election under section 962, as the case may be, with respect to each share of such stock.

(c) *Illustration.*—The application of this section may be illustrated by the following examples:

Example (1). Domestic corporation M owns 800 of the 1,000 shares of the one class of stock in controlled foreign corporation R which owns all of the one class of stock in controlled foreign corporation S. Corporations M, R, and S use the calendar year as a taxable year. In 1964, S Corporation has $100,000 of earnings and profits after the payment of $11,250 of foreign income taxes, and $100,000 of subpart F income. Corporation R has no earnings and profits. With respect to S Corporation, M Corporation is required to include in gross income $80,000 (800/1,000 × $100,000) under section 951(a), and $9,000 ($80,000/$100,000 × $11,250) under section 78. On December 31, 1964, M Corporation must increase the basis of each share of its stock in R Corporation by $100 ($80,000/800).

Example (2). A, an individual United States shareholder, owns all of the 1,000 shares of the one class of stock in controlled foreign corporation T. Corporation T and A use the calendar year as a taxable year. In 1964, T Corporation has $80,000 of earnings and profits after the payment of $20,000 of foreign income taxes, and $80,000 of subpart F income. A makes the election under section 962 for 1964 and in accordance with such election pays a United States tax of $23,000 with respect to the $80,000 included in his gross income under section 951(a). On December 31, 1964, A must increase the basis of each share of his stock in T Corporation by $23 ($23,000/1,000). [Reg. § 1.961-1.]

☐ *[T.D. 6850, 9-15-65.]*

§ 1.961-2. Reduction in basis of stock in foreign corporations and of other property.—(a) *Reduction in basis.*—(1) *In general.*—Except as provided in subparagraph (2) of this paragraph, the adjusted basis of a United States person's—

(i) Stock in a foreign corporation;

(ii) Interest in a foreign partnership; or

(iii) Beneficial interest in a foreign estate or trust (as defined in section 7701(a)(31)),

with respect to which such United States person receives an amount which is excluded from gross income under section 959(a), shall be reduced under section 961(b), as of the time such person receives such excluded amount, by the sum of the amount so excluded and any income, war profits, or excess profits taxes imposed by any foreign country or possession of the United States on or with respect to the earnings and profits attributable to such excluded amount when such earnings and profits were actually distributed directly or indirectly through a chain or ownership described in section 958(a)(2).

(2) *Limitation on amount of reduction in case of election under section 962.*—In the case of a distribution of earnings and profits attributable to amounts with respect to which an election under section 962 has been made, the amount of the reduction in basis provided by subparagraph (1) of this paragraph shall not exceed the sum of—

(i) The amount of such distribution which is excluded from gross income under section 959(a) after the application of section 962(d) and § 1.962-3; and

(ii) Any income, war profits, or excess profits taxes imposed by any foreign country or possession of the United States on or with respect to the earnings and profits attributable to such excluded amount when such earnings and profits were actually distributed directly or indirectly through a chain of ownership described in section 958(a)(2).

(b) *Reduction with respect to each share of stock.*—Any reduction under paragraph (a) of this section in the adjusted basis of a United States person's stock in a foreign corporation shall be made with respect to each share of such stock in the sum of—

(1)(i) The amount excluded from gross income under section 959(a); or

(ii) The amount excluded from gross income under section 959(a) after the application of section 962(d) and § 1.962-3; and

(2) The amount of any income, war profits, or excess profits taxes imposed by any foreign country or possession of the United States on or with respect to the earnings and profits attributable to such excluded amount when such earnings and profits were actually distributed directly or indirectly through a chain of ownership described in section 958(a)(2).

(c) *Amount in excess of basis.*—To the extent that the amount of the reduction in the adjusted basis of property provided by paragraph (a) of this section exceeds such adjusted basis, the amount shall be treated as gain from the sale or exchange of property.

(d) *Illustration.*—The application of this section may be illustrated by the following examples:

Example (1). (a) Domestic corporation M owns all of the 1,000 shares of the one class of stock in controlled foreign corporation R, which owns all of the 500 shares of the one class of stock in controlled foreign corporation S. Each share of M Corporation's stock in R Corporation has a basis of $200. Corporations M, R, and S use the calendar year as a taxable year. In 1963, S Corporation has $100,000 of earnings and profits after the payment of $50,000 of foreign income taxes and $100,000 of subpart F income. For 1963, M Corporation includes $100,000 in gross income under section 951(a) with respect to S Corporation. In accordance with the provisions of § 1.961-1, M Corporation increases the basis of each of its 1,000 shares of stock in R Corporation to $300 ($200 + $100,000/1,000) as of December 31, 1963.

(b) On July 31, 1964, M Corporation sells 250 of its shares of stock in R Corporation to domestic corporation N at a price of $350 per share. Corporation N satisfies the requirements of paragraph (d) of § 1.959-1 so as to qualify as M Corporation's successor in interest. On September 30, 1964, the earnings and profits attributable to the $100,000 included in M Corporation's gross income under section 951(a) for 1963 are distributed to R Corporation which incurs a withholding tax of $10,000 on such distribution (10 percent of $100,000) and an additional foreign income tax of $33\frac{1}{3}$ percent or $30,000 by reason of the inclusion of the net distribution of $90,000 ($100,000 minus $10,000) in its taxable income for 1964. On June 30, 1965, R Corporation distributes the remaining $60,000 of such earnings and profits to corporations M and N: Corporation M receives $45,000 (750/1000 × $60,000) and excludes such amount from gross income under section 959(a); Corporation N receives $15,000 (250/1,000 × $60,000) and, as M Corporation's successor in interest, excludes such amount from gross income under section 959(a). As of June 30, 1965, M Corporation must reduce the adjusted basis of each of its 750 shares of stock in R Corporation to $200 ($300 minus ($45,000/750 + $10,000/1,000 + $30,000/1,000)); and N Corporation must reduce the basis of each of its 250 shares of stock in R Corporation to $250 ($350 minus ($15,000/250 + $10,000/1,000 + $30,000/1,000)).

Example (2). The facts are the same as in paragraph (a) of example (1), except that in addition, on July 31, 1964, R Corporation sells its 500 shares of stock in S Corporation to domestic corporation P at a price of $600 per share. Corporation P satisfies the requirements of paragraph (d) of § 1.959-1 so as to qualify as M Corporation's successor in interest. On September 30, 1964, S Corporation distributes $100,000 of earnings and profits to P Corporation, which earnings and profits are attributable to the $100,000 included in M Corporation's gross income under section 951(a) for 1963. Corporation P incurs a withholding tax of $10,000 on the distribution from S Corporation (10 percent of $100,000). As M Corporation's successor in interest, P Corporation excludes the $90,000 it receives from gross income under section 959(a). As of September 30, 1964, P Corporation must reduce the basis of each of its 500 shares of stock in S Corporation to $400 ($600 minus ($90,000/500 + $10,000/500)). [Reg. § 1.961-2.]

☐ [*T.D.* 6850, 9-15-65.]

§ 1.962-1. Limitation of tax for individuals on amounts included in gross income under section 951(a).—(a) *In general.*—An individual United States shareholder may, in accordance with § 1.962-2, elect to have the provisions of section 962 apply for his taxable year. In such case—

(1) The tax imposed under chapter 1 of the Internal Revenue Code on all amounts which are included in his gross income for such taxable year under section 951(a) shall (in lieu of the tax determined under section 1) be an amount equal to the tax which would be imposed under section 11 if such amounts were received by a domestic corporation (determined in accordance with paragraph (b)(1) of this section), and

(2) For purposes of applying sections 960(a) and 960(d) (relating to foreign tax credit) such amounts shall be treated as if received by a domestic corporation (as provided in paragraph (b)(2) of this section).

(3) Thus, an individual United States shareholder may elect to be subject to tax at corporate rates on amounts included in his gross income under section 951(a) and to have the benefit of a credit for certain foreign tax paid with respect to the earnings and profits attributable to such amounts. Section 962 also provides rules for the treatment of an actual distribution of earnings and profits previously taxed in accordance with an election of the benefits of this section. See § 1.962-3.

(b) *Rules of application.*—For purposes of this section—

(1) *Application of section 11.*—For purposes of applying section 11 for a taxable year as provided in paragraph (a)(1) of this section in the case of an electing United States shareholder—

(i) *Determination of taxable income.*—The term *taxable income* means the excess of—

(A) The sum of—

(*1*) All amounts required to be included in his gross income under section 951(a) for the taxable year with respect to a foreign corporation of which he is a United States shareholder, including—

(*i*) His section 965(a) inclusion amounts (as defined in § 1.965-1(f)(38)); and

(*ii*) His domestic pass-through owner shares (as defined in § 1.965-1(f)(21)) of section 965(a) inclusion amounts with respect to deferred foreign income corporations (as defined in § 1.965-1(f)(17)) of which he is a United States shareholder; plus

(*2*) His GILTI inclusion amount (as defined in § 1.951A-1(c)(1)) for the taxable year; plus

(*3*) All amounts which would be required to be included in his gross income under section 78 for the taxable year with respect to the amounts referred to in paragraph (b)(1)(i)(A)(*1*) and (2) of this section if the shareholder were a domestic corporation; over

(B) The sum of the following deductions, but no other deductions or amounts—

(*1*) His section 965(c) deduction amount (as defined in § 1.965-1(f)(42)) for the taxable year;

(*2*) His domestic pass-through owner shares of section 965(c) deduction amounts corresponding to the amounts referred to in paragraph (b)(1)(i)(A)(*1*)(*ii*) of this section; and

(*3*) The portion of the deduction under section 250 and § 1.250(a)-1 that would be allowed to a domestic corporation equal to the percentage applicable to global intangible low-taxed income for the taxable year under section 250(a)(1)(B) (including as modified by section 250(a)(3)(B)) multiplied by the sum of the amount described in paragraph (b)(1)(i)(A)(*2*) of this section and the amount described in paragraph (b)(1)(i)(A)(*3*) of this section that is attributable to the amount described in paragraph (b)(1)(i)(A)(2) of this section.

(ii) [Reserved]

(2) *Allowance of foreign tax credit.*—(i) *In general.*—Subject to the applicable limitation of section 904 and to the provisions of this paragraph (b)(2), there shall be allowed as a credit against the United States tax on the amounts described in paragraph (b)(1)(i) of this section the foreign income, war profits, and excess profits taxes deemed paid under section 960(a) or section 960(d) by the electing United States shareholder with respect to such amounts.

(ii) *Application of sections 960(a) and 960(d).*—In applying sections 960(a) and section 960(d) for purposes of this paragraph (b)(2) in the case of an electing United States shareholder, the term "domestic corporation" as used in sections 960(a), 960(d), and 78, and the term "corporation" as used in sections 901 and 960(d)(2)(A) and (B), are treated as referring to such shareholder with respect to the amounts described in paragraph (b)(1)(i) of this section.

(iii) *Carryback and carryover of excess tax deemed paid.*—For purposes of this paragraph (b)(2), other than with respect to section 951A category income (as defined in § 1.904-4(g)) (including section 951A category income that is reassigned to a separate category for income resourced under a treaty), any amount by which the foreign income, war profits, and excess profits taxes deemed paid by the electing United States shareholder for any taxable year under section 960 exceed the limitation determined under paragraph (b)(2)(iv)(A) of this section is treated as a carryback and carryover of excess tax paid under section 904(c), except that in no case will excess tax paid be deemed paid in another taxable year under section 904(c) if an election under section 962 by the shareholder does not apply for such taxable year. Such carrybacks and carryovers are applied only against the United States tax on amounts described in paragraph (b)(1)(i) of this section.

(iv) *Limitation on credit.*—For purposes of determining the limitation under section 904 on the amount of the credit for foreign income, war profits, and excess profit taxes—

(A) Deemed paid with respect to amounts described in subparagraph (1)(i) of this paragraph, the electing United States shareholder's taxable income shall be considered to consist only of the amounts described in such subparagraph (1)(i), and

(B) Paid with respect to amounts other than amounts described in subparagraph (1)(i) of this paragraph, the electing United States shareholder's taxable income shall be considered to consist only of amounts other than the amounts described in such subparagraph (1)(i).

(v) *Effect of choosing benefits of sections 901 to 905.*—The provisions of this subparagraph shall apply for a taxable year whether or not the electing United States shareholder chooses the benefits of subpart A of part III of subchapter N of chapter 1 (sections 901 to 905) of the Internal Revenue Code for such year.

(c) *Example.*—The application of this section may be illustrated by the following example.

(1) *Facts*—(i) Individual A is a U.S. resident who owns all of the shares of the one class of stock in CFC, a controlled foreign corporation. A and CFC each use the calendar year as their U.S. and foreign taxable years and the U.S. dollar as their functional currency. A owns no direct or indirect interest in any other controlled foreign corporation.

(ii) For the 2019 taxable year, CFC has $6,000,000 of pre-foreign tax earnings with respect to which it accrues and pays $1,000,000 of foreign income tax, leaving $5,000,000 of after-tax net income. Of this amount, $3,000,000 is general category tested income as defined in section 951A(c)(2), and $2,000,000 is passive category subpart F income described in sections 952 and 904(d)(1)(C) that is all in a single subpart F income group under §§ 1.954-1(c)(1)(iii) and 1.960-1(d)(2)(ii)(B)(2)(*i*). Of the $1,000,000 of foreign income taxes paid or accrued by CFC, $600,000 is allocated and apportioned to its general category tested income group and $400,000 is allocated and apportioned to its passive category subpart F income group under § 1.960-1(d)(3)(ii).

(iii) For the 2019 taxable year, A includes under section 951A(a) all $3,000,000 of the tested income of CFC as A's GILTI inclusion amount, as defined in § 1.951A-1(c)(1). In addition, A includes under section 951(a)(1) the $2,000,000 of passive category subpart F income of CFC.

(iv) For the 2019 taxable year, A earns $1,000,000 of foreign source passive category gross income and $3,000,000 of U.S. source gross income. A pays $100,000 of foreign withholding taxes with respect to the $1,000,000 of foreign source passive category gross income. A incurs $1,000,000 of deductible expenses for the 2019 taxable year that are definitely related to all of A's gross income and are properly allocated and apportioned under §§ 1.861-8(b)(5) and 1.861-8T(c)(1) among the section 904 statutory and residual groupings on the basis of the relative amounts of gross income in each grouping.

(v) A elects to apply section 962 and chooses to claim credits under section 901 for the 2019 taxable year.

(2) *Analysis with respect to section 962 taxable income*—(i) Section 962(a)(1) and § 1.962-1(a)(1) provide that when an individual United States shareholder elects to apply section 962 for a taxable year, the U.S. tax imposed with respect to amounts that the individual includes under section 951(a) (the "section 951(a) inclusions") equals the tax that would be imposed under section 11 if the amounts were included by a domestic corporation under section 951(a). For purposes of section 962, an amount included under section 951A is treated as an inclusion under section 951(a). See section 951A(f)(1)(A). Therefore, A has total section 951(a) inclusions of $5,000,000: a $2,000,000 passive category subpart F inclusion and a $3,000,000 GILTI inclusion amount. A is taxed at the corporate rates under section 11 with respect to these inclusions.

(ii) Section 962(a)(2), § 1.962-1(a)(2), and § 1.962-1(b)(2) provide that sections 960(a) and 960(d) apply to the section 951(a) inclusions of an electing individual United States shareholder as though the inclusions were received by a domestic corporation, and the electing individual United States shareholder is allowed a credit against the U.S. tax imposed with respect to the section 951(a) inclusions.

(iii) Section 960(a) deems a domestic corporation that is a United States shareholder of a controlled foreign corporation to pay the foreign income taxes paid or accrued by the foreign corporation that are properly attributable to the foreign corporation's items of income included in the domestic corporation's income under section 951(a). The foreign income taxes of a CFC that are properly attributable to such items are the domestic corporation's proportionate share of the taxes that are allocated and apportioned to the relevant subpart F income group. See § 1.960-1(c) and § 1.960-2(b). A owns 100 percent of CFC, and includes all of its subpart F income, which is in a single subpart F income group. Therefore, all of the $400,000 of foreign income taxes that are allocable to CFC's subpart F income are properly attributable to the section 951(a) inclusion of A, and A is deemed to pay these taxes.

(iv) Section 960(d) provides that a domestic corporation that has an inclusion in income under section 951A is deemed to pay an amount of foreign income taxes equal to 80 percent of the product of the domestic corporation's inclusion percentage multiplied by the sum of all tested foreign income taxes. Tested foreign income taxes are the foreign income taxes of a controlled foreign corporation that are properly attributable to its tested income that the domestic corporation takes into account under section 951A. The foreign income taxes that are properly attributable to the tested income taken into account by a domestic corporation are the domestic corporation's proportionate share of the controlled foreign corporation's foreign income taxes that are allocated and apportioned to the relevant tested income. See § 1.960-1(c) and § 1.960-2(c). Because A owns 100% of CFC and takes all $3,000,000 of CFC's tested income into account in computing A's GILTI inclusion amount, all $600,000 of the foreign income taxes that are allocated and apportioned to the general category tested income group of CFC are tested foreign income taxes. A has an inclusion percentage of 100 percent because A's GILTI inclusion amount equals all of A's share of the tested income of CFC. A is therefore deemed to pay under section 960(d) 80 percent of the $600,000 of tested foreign income taxes of CFC, or $480,000 of the tested foreign income taxes.

(v) Section 1.962-1(b)(1)(i)(A) provides that, for purposes of computing taxable income under section 962, gross income includes amounts that would be included under section 78 if the shareholder with the section 951(a) inclusions were a domestic corporation. Section 78 requires a domestic corporation to include in its gross income the foreign income taxes that it is deemed to pay under section 960, computed without regard to the 80 percent limitation under section 960(d), and to which the benefits of section 901 apply. See section 78. A therefore includes in gross income the $600,000 of foreign income taxes that A is deemed to pay under section 960(d), computed without regard to the 80 percent limitation, and the $400,000 of taxes that A is deemed to pay under section 960(a).

(vi) Section 1.962-1(b)(1)(i)(B)(*3*) provides that, for purposes of computing taxable income under section 962, gross income is reduced only by specified deductions, which include the deduction allowed to a domestic corporation under section 250 and § 1.250(a)-1 equal to 50 percent of the sum of the GILTI inclusion amount and the inclusion under section 78 with respect to the GILTI inclusion amount. See section 250(a). A is therefore allowed a deduction under section 250 equal to 50 percent of $3,600,000 (the $3,000,000 GILTI inclusion amount plus the $600,000 inclusion under section 78), or $1,800,000.

(vii) A's taxable income and pre-credit U.S. tax liability with respect to the section 951(a) inclusions are computed as follows:

Table 1 to Paragraph (c)(2)(vii)

Section 951(a) inclusions with respect to CFC	$5,000,000
Section 78 inclusions	$1,000,000
Deduction under section 250	($1,800,000)
Taxable income under section 962	$4,200,000
Pre-credit U.S. tax (0.21 x $4,200,000)	$882,000

(viii) Section 962 and §1.962-1(b)(2) provide that, in computing the section 904 limitation on the credit for foreign income taxes that an electing individual United States shareholder is deemed to pay under sections 960(a) and (d), the individual's taxable income for a taxable year is considered to consist only of section 951(a) inclusions and the deductions allowed under section 962. Section 904 limits the credit that a taxpayer may claim for the taxes that it pays or accrues, or is deemed to pay, to the amount of its U.S. tax that is attributable to the taxpayer's foreign source income, and applies this limitation separately with respect to each separate category of income. The limitation amount is computed by multiplying the taxpayer's total pre-credit U.S. tax by the ratio of the taxpayer's foreign source taxable income in a separate category for the taxable year to the taxpayer's total taxable income for the taxable year. See section 904(a) and §1.904-1(a).

(ix) A must compute the limitation on the credit for the foreign income taxes deemed paid under section 960(d) separately with respect to A's taxable income in the separate category described in section 904(d)(1)(A) (the "GILTI category"), namely, taxable income attributable to the GILTI inclusion amount. The limitation is computed using only A's 2019 taxable income under section 962 and the pre-credit U.S. tax of $882,000 on this income. A therefore computes the limitation by multiplying $882,000 by the ratio of A's foreign source GILTI category taxable income under section 962 to A's total taxable income under section 962, as follows:

Table 2 to Paragraph (c)(2)(ix)

GILTI inclusion amount	$3,000,000
Section 78 inclusion	$600,000
Section 250 deduction	($1,800,000)
Total GILTI category taxable income under section 962	$1,800,000
Ratio of GILTI category taxable income to total taxable income under section 962 ($1,800,000 / $4,200,000)	42.86%
Limitation amount (pre-credit U.S. tax of $882,000 x ($1,800,000 / $4,200,000))	$378,000

(x) A also must compute the limitation on the credit for the foreign income taxes deemed paid under section 960(a) separately with respect to the foreign source passive category taxable income under section 962, namely, A's taxable income attributable to the subpart F inclusion. A computes the limitation by multiplying A's pre-credit U.S. tax of $882,000 by the ratio of A's foreign source passive category taxable income under section 962 to A's total taxable income under section 962, as follows:

Table 3 to Paragraph (c)(2)(x)

Subpart F inclusion	$2,000,000
Section 78 inclusion	$400,000
Total foreign source passive category taxable income	$2,400,000
Ratio of foreign source passive category taxable income to total taxable income under section 962 ($2,400,000 / $4,200,000)	57.14%
Limitation amount (pre-credit U.S. tax of $882,000 x ($2,400,000 / $4,200,000))	$504,000

(xi) A may claim a foreign tax credit for $378,000 of the $480,000 of foreign income taxes deemed paid under section 960(d), and a foreign tax credit for all $400,000 of the foreign income taxes deemed paid under section 960(a), for a total foreign tax credit of $778,000. The U.S. tax on A's 2019 taxable income with respect to CFC under section 962 is reduced from $882,000 to $104,000 ($882,000 minus $778,000).

(3) *Analysis with respect to other income*—(i)A's taxable income and pre-credit U.S. tax liability with respect to A's other income is computed as follows:

Table 4 to Paragraph (c)(3)(i)

Gross income	$4,000,000
Deductions	$1,000,000
Taxable Income	$3,000,000
Pre-credit U.S. tax computed under section 1(j)	$1,074,988

(ii) A must compute a separate limitation on the credit for the foreign withholding taxes paid with respect to A's other foreign source passive category taxable income. Under §1.962-1(b)(2)(iv)(B), A's section 904 limitation on this income is computed on the basis of A's taxable income other than the amounts taken into account under §1.962-1(b)(1)(i). Accordingly, $250,000 of A's deductions ($1,000,000 x $1,000,000/$4,000,000) are apportioned to A's $1,000,000 of other foreign source passive category gross income, and $750,000 of deductions ($1,000,000 x $3,000,000/$4,000,000) are apportioned to A's $3,000,000 of U.S. source gross income, resulting in $750,000 of other foreign source passive category taxable income and $2,250,000 of U.S. source taxable income A computes the limitation by multiplying A's pre-credit U.S. tax on A's other income of $1,074,988 by the ratio of A's other foreign source passive category taxable income to A's other total taxable income, as follows:

Table 5 to Paragraph (c)(3)(ii)

Total other foreign source passive category taxable income	$750,000
Ratio of other foreign source passive category taxable income to total other taxable income ($750,000 / $3,000,000)	25%
Limitation amount (pre-credit U.S. tax of $1,074,988 x ($750,000 / $3,000,000))	$268,747

(iii) A may claim a foreign tax credit under section 901 for all $100,000 of the foreign withholding taxes on the other passive income. The U.S. tax on A's $3,000,000 of other taxable income is reduced from $1,074,988 to $974,988 ($1,074,88 minus $100,000).

(d) *Applicability dates.*—Except as otherwise provided in this paragraph (d), paragraph (b)(1)(i) of this section applies beginning the last taxable year of a foreign corporation that begins before January 1, 2018, and with respect to a United States person, for the taxable year in which or with which such taxable year of the foreign corporation ends. Paragraphs (b)(1)(i)(A)(2) and (b)(1)(i)(B)(3) of this section apply to taxable years of a foreign corporation that end on or after March 4, 2019, and with respect to a United States person, for the taxable year in which or with which such taxable year of the foreign corporation ends. Paragraphs (a)(2), (b)(1)(ii), (b)(2)(i) through (iii), and (c) of this section apply to taxable years of a foreign corporation that end on or after July 15, 2020, and with respect to a United States person, for the taxable year in which or with which such taxable year of the foreign corporation ends. For taxable years that precede the applicability dates described in the preceding two sentences, taxpayers may choose to apply the provisions of paragraphs (a)(2), (b)(1)(i)(A)(2), (b)(1)(i)(B)(3), (b)(1)(ii), (b)(2)(i) through (iii), and (c) of this section for taxable years of a foreign corporation beginning on or after January 1, 2018, and with respect to a United States person, for the taxable year in which or with which such taxable year of the foreign corporation ends. [Reg. § 1.962-1.]

☐ [*T.D.* 6858, 10-27-65. *Amended by T.D.* 7413, 3-25-76, *T.D.* 9846, 2-4-2019; *T.D.* 9849, 3-11-2019 *and T.D.* 9901, 7-9-2020.]

§ 1.962-2. Election of limitation of tax for individuals.—(a) *Who may elect.*—The election under section 962 may be made only by an individual (including a trust or estate) who is a United States shareholder (including an individual who is a United States shareholder because, by reason of section 958(b), he is considered to own stock of a foreign corporation owned (within the meaning of section 958(a)) by a domestic pass-through entity (as defined in § 1.965-1(f)(19))).

(b) *Time and manner of making election.*—A United States shareholder shall make an election under this section by filing a statement to such effect with his return for the taxable year with respect to which the election is made. The statement shall include the following information:

(1) The name, address, and taxable year of each controlled foreign corporation with respect to which the electing shareholder is a United States shareholder and of all other corporations, partnerships, trusts, or estates in any applicable chain of ownership described in section 958(a);

(2) The amounts, on a corporation-by-corporation basis, which are included in such shareholder's gross income for his taxable year under section 951(a);

(3) Such shareholder's pro rata share of the earnings and profits (determined under § 1.964-1) of each such controlled foreign corporation with respect to which such shareholder includes any amount in gross income for his taxable year under section 951(a) and the foreign income, war profits, excess profits, and similar taxes paid on or with respect to such earnings and profits;

(4) The amount of distributions received by such shareholder during his taxable year from each controlled foreign corporation referred to in subparagraph (1) of this paragraph from excludable section 962 earnings and profits (as defined in paragraph (b)(1)(i) of § 1.962-3), from taxable section 962 earnings and profits (as defined in paragraph (b)(1)(ii) of § 1.962-3), and from earnings and profits other than section 962 earnings and profits, showing the source of such amounts by taxable year; and

(5) Such further information as the Commissioner may prescribe by forms and accompanying instructions relating to such election.

(c) *Effect of election.*—(1) *In general.*—Except as provided in subparagraph (2) of this paragraph, an election under this section by a United States shareholder for a taxable year shall be applicable to all controlled foreign corporations with respect to which such shareholder includes any amount in gross income for his taxable year under section 951(a) and shall be binding for the taxable year for which such election is made.

(2) *Revocation.*—Upon application by the United States shareholder, an election made under this election may, subject to the approval of the Commissioner, be revoked. Approval will not be granted unless a material and substantial change in circumstances occurs which could not have been anticipated when the election was made. The application for consent to revocation shall be made by the United States shareholder's mailing a letter for such purpose to Commissioner of Internal Revenue, Attention: T.R., Washington, D.C. 20224 containing a statement of the facts upon which such shareholder relies in requesting such consent.

(d) *Applicability dates.*—Paragraph (a) of this section applies beginning the last taxable year of a foreign corporation that begins before January 1, 2018, and with respect to a United States person, for the taxable year in which or with which such taxable year of the foreign corporation ends. [Reg. § 1.962-2.]

☐ [*T.D.* 6858, 10-27-65. *Amended by T.D.* 9846, 2-4-2019 *and T.D.* 9849, 3-11-2019.]

§ 1.962-3. Treatment of actual distributions.—(a) *In general.*—Section 962(d) provides that the earnings and profits of a foreign corporation attributable to amounts which are, or have been, included in the gross income of an individual United States shareholder under section 951(a) by reason of such shareholder's ownership (within the meaning of section 958(a)) of stock in such corporation and with respect to which amounts an election under § 1.962-2 applies or applied shall, when such earnings and profits are distributed to such shareholder with respect to such stock, notwithstanding the provisions of section 959(a)(1), be included in his gross income to the extent that such earnings and profits exceed the amount of income tax paid by such shareholder under this chapter on the amounts to which such election applies or applied. Thus, when such shareholder receives an actual distribution of section 962 earnings and profits (as defined in paragraph (b)(1) of this section) from a foreign corporation, only the excludable section 962 earnings and profits (as defined in paragraph (b)(1)(i) of this section) may be excluded from his gross income.

(b) *Rules of application.*—For purposes of this section—

(1) *Section 962 earnings and profits defined.*—With respect to an individual United States shareholder, the term "section 962 earnings and profits" means the earnings and profits of a foreign corporation referred to in paragraph (a) of this section. Such earnings and profits include—

(i) *Excludable section 962 earnings and profits.*—Excludable section 962 earnings and profits which are the amount of the section 962 earnings and profits equal to the amount of income tax paid under this chapter by such shareholder on the amounts included in his gross income under section 951(a); and

(ii) *Taxable section 962 earnings and profits.*—Taxable section 962 earnings and profits which are the excess of section 962 earnings and profits over the amount described in subdivision (i) of this subparagraph.

(2) *Determinations made separately for each taxable year.*—If section 962 earnings and profits attributable to more than one taxable year are distributed by a foreign corporation, the determinations under this section shall be made separately with respect to each such taxable year.

(3) *Source of distributions.*—(i) *In general.*—Except as otherwise provided in this subparagraph, the provisions of paragraphs (a) through (d) of § 1.959-3 shall apply in determining the source of distributions of earnings and profits by a foreign corporation.

(ii) *Treatment of section 962 earnings and profits under § 1.959-3.*—For purposes of a section 959(c) amount and year classification under paragraph (b) of § 1.959-3, a distribution of earnings and profits by a foreign corporation shall be first allocated to earnings and profits other than section 962 earnings and profits (as defined in subparagraph (1) of this paragraph) and then to section 962 earnings and profits. Thus, distributions shall be considered first attributable to amounts described in paragraph (b)(1) of § 1.959-3 which are not section 962 earnings and profits and then to amounts described in such paragraph (b)(1) which are section 962 earnings and profits (first for the current taxable year and then for prior taxable years beginning with the most recent prior taxable year), secondly to amounts described in paragraph (b)(2) of § 1.959-3 which are not section 962 earnings and profits and then to amounts described in such paragraph (b)(2) which are section 962 earnings and profits (first for the current taxable year and then for prior taxable years beginning with the most recent prior taxable year), and finally to the amounts described in paragraph (b)(3) of § 1.959-3 (first for the current taxable year and then for prior taxable years beginning with the most recent prior taxable year).

(iii) *Allocation to excludable section 962 earnings and profits.*—A distribution of section 962 earnings and profits by a foreign corporation for any taxable year shall be considered first attributable to the excludable section 962 earnings and profits (as defined in subparagraph (1)(i) of this paragraph) and then to taxable section 962 earnings and profits.

(iv) *Allocation of deficits in earnings and profits.*—A United States shareholder's pro rata share (determined in accordance with the principles of paragraph (e) of § 1.951-1) of a foreign corporation's deficit in earnings and profits (determined under § 1.964-1) for any taxable year shall be applied in accordance with the provisions of paragraph (c) of § 1.959-3 except that such deficit shall also be applied to taxable section 962 earnings and profits (as defined in subparagraph (1)(ii) of this paragraph).

(4) *Distribution in exchange for stock.*—The provisions of this section shall not apply to a distribution of section 962 earnings and profits which is treated as in part or full payment in exchange for stock under subchapter C of chapter 1 of the Internal Revenue Code. The application of this subparagraph may be illustrated by the following example:

Example. Individual United States shareholder A owns 60 percent of the only class of stock in foreign corporation M, the basis of which is $10,000. Both A and M Corporation use the calendar year as a taxable year. In each of the taxable years 1964, 1965, and 1966, M Corporation has $1,000 of earnings and profits and $1,000 of subpart F income. With respect to each such amount, A includes $600 in gross income under section 951(a), makes the election under section 962, and pays a United States tax of $132 (22 percent of $600). Accordingly, A increases the basis of his stock in M Corporation under section 961(a) by $132 in each of the years 1964, 1965, and 1966, and thus on December 31, 1966, the adjusted basis for A's stock in M Corporation is $10,396. In 1967, M Corporation is completely liquidated (in a transaction described in section 331) and A receives $13,800, consisting of $1,800 of earnings and profits attributable to the amounts which A included in gross income under section 951(a) in 1964, 1965, and 1966, and $12,000 attributable to the other assets of M Corporation. No amount of the $3,404 gain realized by A on such distribution ($13,800 minus $10,396) may be excluded from gross income under section 959(a)(1). However, section 962(d) will not prevent any part of such $3,404 from being treated as a capital gain under section 331.

(5) *Illustration.*—The application of this paragraph may be illustrated by the following example:

Example. (a) M, a controlled foreign corporation is organized on January 1, 1963; A and B, individual United States shareholders, own 50 percent and 25 percent, respectively, of the only class of stock in M Corporation. Corporation M, A, and B use the calendar year as a taxable year, and M Corporation is a controlled foreign corporation throughout the period here involved. For the taxable years 1963, 1964, 1965, and 1966, A and B must include amounts in gross income under section 951(a) with respect to M Corporation. For the years 1963, 1965, and 1966, A makes the election under section 962. On January 1, 1967, B sells his 25-percent interest in M Corporation to A; A satisfies the requirements of paragraph (d) of § 1.959-1 so as to qualify as B's successor in interest. As of December 31, 1967, M Corporation's accumulated earnings and profits of $675 (before taking into account distributions made in 1967) applicable to A's interest (including his interest as B's successor in interest) in such corporation are classified under § 1.959-3 and this section for purposes of section 962(d) as follows:

Classification of earnings and profits for purposes of §1.962-3.

	Sec. 959(c) (1)			*Sec. 959(c) (2)*			*Sec. 959(c) (3)*
Year	*Non-sec. 962 earnings and profits*	*Excludable sec. 962 earnings and profits*	*Taxable sec. 962 earnings and profits*	*Non-sec. 962 earnings and profits*	*Excludable sec. 962 earnings and profits*	*Taxable sec. 962 earnings and profits*	
1963	$25	$11	$39	...	...	...	...
1964	75	...	...	$60	...	...	$15
1965	...	...	...	75	$33	$117	...
1966	...	...	...	50	22	78	...
1967	...	...	...	...	...	...	75

(b) During 1967, M Corporation makes three separate distributions to A of $200, $208, and $267. The source of such distributions under § 1.959-3 and this section is as follows:

	Amount	*Year*	*Classification of distributions under secs. 959 and 962(d)*
Distribution No. 1	$75	1964	(c)(1) non-sec. 962
	25	1963	(c)(1) non-sec. 962
	11	1963	(c)(1) excludable sec. 962
	39	1963	(c)(1) taxable sec. 962
	50	1966	(c)(2) non-sec. 962
	200		
Distribution No. 2	$22	1966	(c)(2) excludable sec. 962
	78	1966	(c)(2) taxable sec. 962
	75	1965	(c)(2) non-sec. 962
	33	1965	(c)(2) excludable sec. 962
	208		
Distribution No. 3	$117	1965	(c)(2) taxable sec. 962
	60	1964	(c)(2) non-sec. 962
	75	1967	(c)(3)
	15	1964	(c)(3)
	267		

(c) A must include $324 in his gross income for 1967. The source of these amounts is as follows:

Distribution	*Amount*	*Year*	*Classification*
No. 1	$39	1963	(c)(1) taxable sec. 962
No. 2	78	1966	(c)(2) taxable sec. 962
No. 3	117	1965	(c)(2) taxable sec. 962
	75	1967	(c)(3)
	15	1964	(c)(3)
Total	$324		

(c) *Treatment of shareholder's successor in interest.*—(1) *In general.*—If a United States person (as defined in § 1.957-4) acquires from any person any portion of the interest in the foreign corporation of a United States shareholder referred to in this section, the rules of paragraphs (a) and (b) of this section shall apply to such acquiring person. However, no exclusion of section 962 earnings and profits under paragraph (a) of this section shall be allowed unless such acquiring person establishes to the satisfaction of the district director his right to such exclusion. The information to be furnished by the acquiring person to the district director with his return for the taxable year to support such exclusion shall include:

(i) The name, address, and taxable year of the foreign corporation from which a distribution of section 962 earnings and profits is received and of all other corporations, partnerships, trusts, or estates in any applicable chain of ownership described in section 958(a);

(ii) The name and address of the person from whom the stock interest was acquired;

(iii) A description of the stock interest acquired and its relation, if any, to a chain of ownership described in section 958(a);

(iv) The amount for which an exclusion under paragraph (a) of this section is claimed; and

(v) Evidence showing that the section 962 earnings and profits for which an exclusion is claimed are attributable to amounts which were included in the gross income of a United States shareholder under section 951(a) subject to an election under § 1.962-2, that such amounts were not previously excluded from the gross income of a United States person, and the identity of the United States shareholder including such amount.

The acquiring person shall also furnish to the district director such other information as may be required by the district director in support of the exclusion.

(2) *Taxes previously deemed paid by an individual United States shareholder*.—If a corporate successor in interest of an individual United States shareholder receives a distribution of section 962 earnings and profits, the income, war profits, and excess profits taxes paid to any foreign country or to any possession of the United States in connection with such earnings and profits shall not be taken into account for purposes of section 902, to the extent such taxes were deemed paid by such individual United States shareholder under paragraph (b)(2) of § 1.962-1 and section 960(a)(1) for any prior taxable year. [Reg. § 1.962-3.]

□ [*T.D.* 6858, 10-27-65.]

Earnings and Profits of Foreign Corporations

§ 1.964-1. Determination of the earnings and profits of a foreign corporation.—(a)(1) *In general*.—For rules for determining the earnings and profits (or deficit in earnings and profits) of a foreign corporation for taxable years beginning before January 1, 1987, for purposes of sections 951 through 964, see 26 CFR § 1.964-1(a) (revised as of April 1, 2006). For taxable years beginning after December 31, 1986, except as otherwise provided in the Code and regulations, the earnings and profits (or deficit in earnings and profits) of a foreign corporation for its taxable year shall be computed for all federal income tax purposes substantially as if such corporation were a domestic corporation by—

(i) Preparing a profit and loss statement with respect to such year from the books of account regularly maintained by the corporation for the purpose of accounting to its shareholders;

(ii) Making the adjustments necessary to conform such statement to the accounting principles described in paragraph (b) of this section; and

(iii) Making the further adjustments necessary to conform such statement to the tax accounting standards described in paragraph (c) of this section.

(2) *Required adjustments*.—The computation described in paragraph (a)(1) of this section shall be made in the foreign corporation's functional currency (determined under section 985 and the regulations under that section) and may be made by following the procedures described in paragraphs (a)(1)(i) through (a)(1)(iii) of this section in an order other than the one listed, as long as the result so obtained would be the same. In determining earnings and profits, or the deficit in earnings and profits, of a foreign corporation under section 964, the amount of an illegal bribe, kickback, or other payment (within the meaning of section 162(c), as amended by section 288 of the Tax Equity and Fiscal Responsibility Act of 1982 in the case of payments made after September 3, 1982, and the regulations issued pursuant to section 964) paid after November 3, 1976, by or on behalf of the corporation during the taxable year of the corporation directly or indirectly to an official, employee, or agent in fact of a government shall not be taken into account to decrease such earnings and profits or to increase such deficit. No adjustment shall be required under paragraph (a)(1)(ii) or (iii) of this section unless it is material. Whether an adjustment is material depends on the facts and circumstances of the particular case, including the amount of the adjustment, its size relative to the general level of the corporation's total assets and annual profit or loss, the consistency with which the practice has been applied, and whether the item to which the adjustment relates is of a recurring or merely a nonrecurring nature. For the treatment of earnings and profits whose distribution is prevented by restrictions and limitations imposed by a foreign government, see section 964(b) and the regulations issued pursuant to section 964.

(3) *Translation into dollars*.—In the case of a foreign corporation with a functional currency other than the United States dollar (dollar), see sections 986(b) and 989(b) for rules regarding the time and manner of translating distributions or inclusions of the foreign corporation's earnings and profits into dollars.

(b) *Accounting adjustments*.—(1) *In general*.—The accounting principles to be applied in making the adjustments required by paragraph (a)(1)(ii) of this section shall be those accounting principles generally accepted in the United States for purposes of reflecting in the financial statements of a domestic corporation the operations of its foreign affiliates, including the following:

(i) *Clear reflection income*.—Any accounting practice designed for purposes other than the clear reflection on a current basis of income and expense for the taxable year shall not be given effect. For example, an adjustment will be required where an allocation is made to an arbitrary reserve out of current income.

(ii) *Physical assets, depreciation, etc*.—All physical assets (as defined in paragraph (e)(5)(ii) of this section), including inventory when reflected at cost, shall be taken into account at historical cost computed either for individual assets or groups of similar assets. The historical cost of such an asset shall not reflect any appreciation or depreciation in its value or in the relative value of the currency in which its cost was incurred. Depreciation, depletion, and amortization allowances shall be based on the historical cost of the underlying asset and no effect shall be given to any such allowance determined on the basis of a factor other than historical cost. For special rules for determining historical cost where assets are acquired during a taxable year beginning before January 1, 1950, or a majority interest in the foreign corporation is acquired after December 31, 1949, but before October 27, 1964, see subparagraph (2) of this paragraph.

(iii) *Valuation of assets and liabilities*.—Any accounting practice which results in the systematic undervaluation of assets or overvaluation of liabilities shall not be given effect, even though expressly permitted or required under foreign law, except to the extent allowable under paragraph (c) of this section. For example, an adjustment will be required where inventory is written down below market value. For the definition of market value, see paragraph (a) of § 1.471-4.

(iv) *Income equalization*.—Income and expense shall be taken into account without regard to equalization over more than one accounting period; and any equalization reserve or similar provision affecting income or expense shall not be given effect, even though expressly permitted or required under foreign law, except to the extent allowable under paragraph (c) of this section.

(v) *Foreign currency*.—If transactions effected in a foreign currency other than that in which the books of the corporation are kept are translated into the foreign currency reflected in the books, such translation shall be made in a manner substantially similar to that as prescribed in section 988 and the regulations under that section for the translation of foreign currency amounts into United States dollars.

(2) *Historical cost*.—For purposes of this section, the historical cost of an asset acquired by the foreign corporation during a taxable year beginning before January 1, 1963, shall be determined, if it is so elected by or on behalf of such corporation—

(i) In the event that the foreign corporation became a majority owned subsidiary of a United States person (within the meaning of section 7701(a)(30)) after December 31, 1949, but before October 27, 1964, and the asset was held by such foreign corporation at that time, as though the asset was purchased on the date during such period the foreign corporation first became a majority owned subsidiary at a price equal to its then fair market value, or

(ii) In the event that subdivision (i) of this subparagraph is inapplicable but the asset was acquired by the foreign corporation during a taxable year beginning before January 1, 1950, as though the asset were purchased on the first day of the first taxable year of the foreign corporation beginning after December 31, 1949, at a price equal to the undepreciated cost (cost or other basis minus book depreciation) of that asset as of that date as shown on the books of account of such corporation regularly maintained for the purpose of accounting to its shareholders.

For purposes of this subparagraph, a foreign corporation shall be considered a majority owned subsidiary of a United States person if, taking into account only stock acquired by purchase (as defined in section 334(b)(3)), the United States person owns (within the meaning of section 958(a)) more than 50 percent of the total combined voting power of all classes of stock of the foreign corporation entitled to vote. The election under this subparagraph shall be made for the first taxable year beginning after December 31, 1962, in which the foreign corporation is a controlled foreign corporation (within the meaning of section 957), or for which it is included in a chain or group under section 963(c)(2)(B) of 1975, (applied as if section 963 had not been repealed by the Tax Reduction Act of 1975) or has a deficit in earnings and profits sought to be taken into account under section 952(d), or pays a dividend that is included in the foreign base company shipping income of a controlled foreign corporation under § 1.954-6(f). Once made, such an election shall be irrevocable. For the time and manner in which an election may be made on behalf of a foreign corporation, see paragraph (c)(3) of this section.

(3) *Illustrations.*—The application of this paragraph may be illustrated by the following examples:

Example (1). Corporation M is a controlled foreign corporation which regularly maintains books of account for the purpose of accounting to its shareholders in accordance with the accounting practices prevalent in country X, the country in which it operates. As a consequence of those practices, the profit and loss statement prepared from these books of account reflects an allocation to an arbitrary reserve out of current income and depreciation allowances based on replacement values which are greater than historical cost. Adjustments are necessary to conform such statement to accounting principles generally accepted in the United States. Assuming these adjustments to be material, the unacceptable practices will have to be eliminated from the statement, an increase in the amount of profit (or a decrease in the amount of loss) thereby resulting.

Example (2). In 1973, Corporation N is a foreign corporation which is not a controlled foreign corporation but which is included in a chain, for minimum distribution purposes, under section 963(c)(2)(B). Corporation N regularly maintains books of account for the purpose of accounting to its shareholders in accordance with the accounting practices of country Y, the country in which it operates. As a consequence of those practices, the profit and loss statement prepared from these books of account reflects the inclusion in income of stock dividends and of corporate distributions representing a return of capital. Adjustments are necessary to conform such statement to accounting principles generally accepted in the United States. Assuming these adjustments to be material, the unacceptable practices will have to be eliminated from the statement, a decrease in the amount of profit (or increase in the amount of loss) thereby resulting.

(c) *Tax adjustments.*—(1) *In general.*—The tax accounting standards to be applied in making the adjustments required by paragraph (a)(1)(iii) of this section shall be the following:

(i) *Accounting methods.*—The method of accounting shall reflect the provisions of section 446 and the regulations thereunder.

(ii) *Inventories.*—Inventories shall be taken into account in accordance with the provisions of sections 471 and 472 and the regulations thereunder.

(iii) *Depreciation.*—Depreciation shall be computed as follows:

(a) For any taxable year beginning before July 1, 1972, depreciation shall be computed in accordance with section 167 and the regulations thereunder.

(b) If, for any taxable year beginning after June 30, 1972, 20 percent or more of the gross income from all sources of the corporation is derived from sources within the United States, then depreciation shall be computed in accordance with the provisions of § 1.312-15.

(c) If, for any taxable year beginning after June 30, 1972, less than 20 percent of the gross income from all sources of the corporation is derived from sources within the United States, then depreciation shall be computed in accordance with section 167 and the regulations thereunder.

(iv) *Elections.*—Effect shall be given to any election made in accordance with an applicable provision of the Code and the regulations thereunder and these regulations.

(v) *Taxable years.*—The period for computation of taxable income and earnings and profits known as the taxable year shall reflect the provisions of section 441 and the regulations under that section.

(vi) *Applicable requirements.*—Except as provided in paragraphs (c)(2) and (c) (3) of this section, any requirements imposed by the Code or applicable regulations with respect to making an election or adopting or changing a method of accounting or taxable year must be satisfied by or on behalf of the foreign corporation just as though it were a domestic corporation if such election or such adoption or change of method or taxable year is to be taken into account in the computation of its earnings and profits.

(2) *Adoption or change of method or taxable year.*—For the first taxable year of a foreign corporation beginning after April 25, 2006, in which such foreign corporation first qualifies as a controlled foreign corporation (as defined in section 957 or 953) or a noncontrolled section 902 corporation (as defined in section 904(d)(2)(E)), any method of accounting or taxable year allowable under this section may be adopted, and any election allowable under this section may be made, by such foreign corporation or on its behalf notwithstanding that, in previous years, its books or financial statements were prepared on a different basis, and notwithstanding that such election is required by the Code or regulations to be made in a prior taxable year. Any allowable methods adopted or elections made shall be reflected in the computation of the foreign corporation's earnings and profits for such taxable year, prior taxable years, and (unless the Commissioner consents to a change) subsequent taxable years. However, see section 898 for the rules regarding the taxable year of a specified foreign corporation as defined in section 898(b). Any allowable method of accounting or election that relates to events that first arise in a subsequent taxable year may be adopted or made by or on behalf of the foreign corporation for such year. Adjustments to the appropriate separate category (as defined in § 1.904-5(a)(1)) of earnings and profits and income of the foreign corporation shall be required under section 481 to prevent any duplication or omission of amounts attributable to previous years that would otherwise result from any change in a method of accounting. See paragraph (c)(3) of this section for the manner in which a method of accounting or a taxable year may be adopted or changed on behalf of the foreign corporation. See paragraph (c)(4) of this section for applicable rules if the amount of the foreign corporation's earnings and profits became significant for United States tax purposes before a method of accounting or taxable year was adopted by the foreign corporation or on its behalf in accordance with the rules of paragraph (c)(3) of this section. See paragraph (c)(6) of this section for special rules postponing the time for taking action by or on behalf of a foreign corporation until the amount of its earnings and profits becomes significant for U.S. tax purposes. See also §§ 1.985-5, 1.985-6, and 1.985-7 relating to adjustments to earnings and profits of a QBU required when the QBU changes its functional currency or begins to use the dollar approximate separate transactions method of accounting.

(3) *Action on behalf of corporation.*—(i) *In general.*—An election shall be deemed made, or an adoption or change in method of accounting or taxable year deemed effectuated, on behalf of the foreign corporation only if its controlling domestic shareholders (as defined in paragraph (c)(5) of this section)—

(A) Satisfy for such corporation any requirements imposed by the Internal Revenue Code or applicable regulations with respect to such election or such adoption or change in method or taxable year (including the provisions of sections 442 and 446 and the regulations under those sections, as well as any operative provisions), such as the filing of forms, the execution of consents, securing the permission of the Commissioner, or maintaining books and records in a particular manner. For purposes of this paragraph (c)(3)(i)(A), the books of the foreign corporation shall be considered to be maintained in a particular manner if the controlling domestic shareholders or the foreign corporation regularly keep the records and accounts required by section 964(c) and the regulations under that section in that manner;

(B) File the statement described in paragraph (c)(3)(ii) of this section, at the time and in the manner prescribed therein; and

(C) Provide the written notice required by paragraph (c)(3)(iii) of this section at the time and in the manner prescribed therein.

(ii) *Statement required to be filed with a tax return.*—The statement required by this paragraph (c)(3)(ii) shall set forth the name, country of organization, and U.S. employer identification number (if applicable) of the foreign corporation, the name, address, stock interests, and U.S. employer identification number of each controlling domestic shareholder (or, if applicable, the shareholder's common parent) approving the action, and the names, addresses, U.S. employer identification numbers, and stock interests of all other domestic shareholders notified of the action taken. Such statement shall describe the nature of the action taken on behalf of the foreign corporation and the taxable year for which made, and identify a designated shareholder who retains a jointly executed consent confirming that such action has been approved by all of the controlling domestic shareholders and containing the signature of a principal officer of each such shareholder (or its common parent). Each controlling domestic shareholder (or its common parent) shall file the statement with, and on or before the due date (including extensions) of, its own tax return (or information return, if applicable) for its taxable year with or within which ends the taxable year of the foreign corporation for which the election is made or for which the method of accounting or taxable year is adopted or changed. In the case of a controlling domestic shareholder that is the sole shareholder of a controlled foreign corporation, no separate statement need be filed if the information described in this paragraph (c)(3)(ii) is included on Form 5471 and Form 3115 or 1128, as applicable, filed with respect to the controlled foreign corporation with the shareholder's return for such taxable year.

(iii) *Notice.*—On or before the filing date described in paragraph (c)(3)(ii) of this section, the controlling domestic shareholders shall provide written notice of the election made or the adoption or change of method or taxable year effected to all other persons known by them to be domestic shareholders who own (within the meaning of section 958(a)) stock of the foreign corporation. Such notice shall set forth the name, country of organization and U.S. employer identification number (if applicable) of the foreign corporation, and the names, addresses, and stock interests of the controlling domestic shareholders. Such notice shall describe the nature of the action taken on behalf of the foreign corporation and the taxable year for which made, and identify a designated shareholder who retains a jointly executed consent confirming that such action has been approved by all of the controlling domestic shareholders and containing the signature of a principal officer of each such shareholder (or its common parent). However, the failure of the controlling domestic shareholders to provide such notice to a person required to be notified shall not invalidate the election made or the adoption or change of method or taxable year effected.

(4) *Effect of action or inaction by controlling domestic shareholders.*—(i) *In general.*—Any election, or adoption or change of method of accounting or taxable year made by the controlling domestic shareholders on behalf of the foreign corporation pursuant to paragraph (c)(3) of this section or any other provision of the regulations (for example, § 1.985-2(c)(2) or (3)) shall be reflected in the computation of the earnings and profits of such corporation under this section to the extent that it bears upon the federal income tax liability of the domestic shareholders of the foreign corporation. Any such action shall bind both the foreign corporation and its domestic shareholders as to the computation of the foreign corporation's earnings and profits for the taxable year of the foreign corporation for which the election is made or for which the method of accounting or taxable year is adopted or changed and in subsequent taxable years unless the Commissioner consents to a change. The preceding sentence shall apply regardless of—

(A) When the action was taken;

(B) Whether the foreign corporation was a controlled foreign corporation or a noncontrolled section 902 corporation at the time the action was taken;

(C) When ownership was acquired; or

(D) Whether the domestic shareholder received the written notice required by paragraph (c)(3)(iii) of this section.

(ii) *Inaction or untimely action.*—In the event that action by or on behalf of the foreign corporation is not undertaken by the time specified in paragraph (c)(6) of this section and such failure is shown to the satisfaction of the Commissioner to be due to reasonable cause, such action may be undertaken during any period of at least 30 days occurring after such showing is made which the Commissioner may specify as appropriate for this purpose. In the event that action by or on behalf of the foreign corporation is not undertaken by the time specified in paragraph (c)(6) of this section and such failure is not shown to the satisfaction of the Commissioner to be due to reasonable cause, earnings and profits shall be computed as if no elections had been made and any permissible accounting methods not requiring an election and reflected in the books of account regularly maintained by the foreign corporation for the purpose of accounting to its shareholders had been adopted. Accordingly, if the earnings and profits of a noncontrolled section 902 corporation became significant for United States income tax purposes in a taxable year beginning on or before April 25, 2006, the corporation's earnings and profits shall be computed as if no elections had been made and any permissible accounting methods not requiring an election and reflected in the books of account regularly maintained by the foreign corporation for purposes of accounting to its shareholders had been adopted. Thereafter, any change in a particular accounting method or methods or taxable year may be made by, or on behalf of, the foreign corporation only with the Commissioner's consent.

(iii) *Computation of earnings and profits by a minority shareholder prior to majority election or significant event.*—A shareholder of a foreign corporation may be required to compute the foreign corporation's earnings and profits before the foreign corporation or its controlling domestic shareholders make, or are required under this section to make, an election or adopt a method of accounting for federal income tax purposes. In such a case, the shareholder must compute earnings and profits in accordance with this section. Such computation shall be made as if no elections had been made and any permissible accounting methods not requiring an election and reflected in the books of account regularly maintained by the foreign corporation for the purpose of accounting to its shareholders had been adopted. However, a later, properly filed, and timely election or adoption of method by, or on behalf of, the foreign corporation shall not be treated as a change in accounting method.

(5) *Controlling domestic shareholders.*—(i) *Controlled foreign corporations.*—For purposes of this paragraph (c), the controlling domestic shareholders of a controlled foreign corporation shall be its controlling United States shareholders. The controlling United States shareholders of a controlled foreign corporation shall be those United States shareholders (as defined in section 951(b) or 953(c)) who, in the aggregate, own (within the meaning of section 958(a)) more than 50 percent of the total combined voting power of all classes of the stock of such foreign corporation entitled to vote and who undertake to act on its behalf. In the event that the United States shareholders of the controlled foreign corporation do not, in the aggregate, own (within the meaning of section 958(a)) more than 50 percent of the total combined voting power of all classes of the stock of such foreign corporation entitled to vote, the controlling United States shareholders of the controlled foreign corporation shall be all those United States shareholders who own (within the meaning of section 958(a)) stock of such corporation.

(ii) *Noncontrolled section 902 corporations.*—For purposes of this paragraph (c), the controlling domestic shareholders of a noncontrolled section 902 corporation that is not a controlled foreign corporation shall be its majority domestic corporate shareholders. The majority domestic corporate shareholders of a noncontrolled section 902 corporation shall be those domestic corporations that meet the ownership requirements of section 902(a) with respect to the noncontrolled section 902 corporation (or to a first-tier foreign corporation that is a member of the same qualified group (as defined in section 902(b)(2)) as the noncontrolled section 902 corporation) that, in the aggregate, own directly or indirectly more than 50 percent of the combined voting power of all of the voting stock of the noncontrolled section 902 corporation that is owned directly or indirectly by all domestic corporations that meet the ownership requirements of section 902(a) with respect to the noncontrolled section 902 corporation (or a relevant first-tier foreign corporation).

(6) *Action not required until significant.*—Notwithstanding any other provision of this paragraph, action by or on behalf of a foreign corporation (other than a foreign corporation subject to tax under section 882) to make an election or to adopt a taxable year or method of accounting shall not be required until the due date (including extensions) of the return for a controlling domestic shareholder's first taxable year with or within which ends the foreign corporation's first taxable year in which the computation of its earnings and profits is significant for United States tax purposes with respect to its controlling domestic shareholders (as defined in § 1.964-1(c)(5)). The filing of

the information return required by section 6038 shall not itself constitute a significant event. For taxable years beginning after April 25, 2006, events that cause a foreign corporation's earnings and profits to have United States tax significance include, without limitation:

(A) A distribution from the foreign corporation to its shareholders with respect to their stock.

(B) An amount is includible in gross income with respect to such corporation under section 951(a).

(C) An amount is excluded from subpart F income of the foreign corporation or another foreign corporation by reason of section 952(c).

(D) Any event making the foreign corporation subject to tax under section 882.

(E) The use by the foreign corporation's controlling domestic shareholders of the tax book value (or alternative tax book value) method of allocating interest expense under section 864(e)(4).

(F) A sale or exchange of the foreign corporation's stock of the controlling domestic shareholders that results in the recharacterization of gain under section 1248.

(7) *Revocation of election.*—Notwithstanding any other provision of this section, any election made by or on behalf of a foreign corporation (other than a foreign corporation subject to tax under section 882) may be modified or revoked by or on behalf of such corporation for the taxable year for which made whenever the consent of the Commissioner is secured for such modification or revocation, even though such election would be irrevocable but for this subparagraph.

(8) [Reserved].

(d) *Effective/applicability dates.*—Paragraphs (c)(1)(v) through (c)(6) of this section apply to taxable years ending on or after April 20, 2009. See 26 CFR §1.964-1T(c)(1)(v) through (c)(6) (revised as of April 1, 2009) for rules applicable to taxable years beginning after April 25, 2006, and ending before April 20, 2009. However, taxpayers may choose to apply paragraphs (c)(1)(v) through (c)(6) of this section in their entirety in lieu of 26 CFR §1.964-1T(c)(1)(v) through (c)(6) for periods covered by the temporary regulations, provided that appropriate adjustments are made to eliminate duplicate benefits arising from the application of paragraphs (c)(1)(v) through (c)(6) of this section to taxable years that are not open for assessment. [Reg. §1.964-1.]

☐ [*T.D.* 6764, 10-26-64. *Amended by T.D.* 6787, 12-28-64, *T.D.* 6829, 6-22-65, *T.D.* 6995, 1-17-69, *T.D.* 7221, 11-20-72, *T.D.* 7322, 8-23-74, *T.D.* 7545, 5-5-78, *T.D.* 7862, 12-16-82; *T.D.* 7893, 5-11-83; *T.D.* 9260, 4-20-2006 (*corrected* 12-22-2006) *and T.D.* 9452, 6-10-2009 (*corrected* 9-21-2009).]

Proposed Amendments to Regulation

§1.964-1. Determination of the earnings and profits of a foreign corporation.

* * *

(a)(4) *Example.*—The rules of this paragraph (a) are illustrated by the following example.

Example. (i) *Facts.* P, a domestic corporation, owns all of the outstanding stock of FX, a controlled foreign corporation. In preparing its books for purposes of accounting to its shareholders, FX uses an accounting method (Local Books Method) to determine the amount of its depreciation expense that does not conform to accounting principles generally accepted in the United States (U.S. GAAP) or to U.S. income tax accounting standards as described in paragraph (c). The amount of the adjustment necessary to conform the depreciation expense determined under the Local Books Method with the amount that would be determined under U.S. GAAP for purposes of paragraph (a)(1)(ii) of this section if FX were a domestic corporation is not material. However, the adjustment necessary to conform the amount of the depreciation expense under the Local Books Method to U.S. income tax accounting standards for purposes of paragraph (a)(1)(iii) of this section is material.

(ii) *Result.* Although FX is not required to make the adjustment necessary to conform the amount of its tax expense reserve deduction determined under the Local Books Method to the amount that would be determined under U.S. GAAP, FX is required to make the adjustment necessary to conform the amount of the depreciation expense determined under the Local Books Method to the amount of depreciation expense for the current year that would be allowed under U.S. income tax accounting standards as described in paragraph (c).

(b) * * *

(3) *Example.*—The rules of this paragraph (b) are illustrated by the following example.

* * *

(c) * * *

(1) *In general.*—Except as otherwise provided in the Code and regulations (for example, section 952(c)(3) (earnings and profits determined without regard to section 312(n)(4)-(6) for purposes of section 952(c)), the tax accounting standards to be applied in making the adjustments required by paragraph (a)(1)(iii) of this section shall be those applied to domestic corporations, including but not limited to the following:

* * *

(iii) *Depreciation and amortization.*—Depreciation and amortization shall be computed in accordance with the provisions of section 312(k) and the regulations under that section. In the case of a foreign corporation described in section 312(k)(4) (one with less than 20 percent U.S.-source gross income), depreciation and amortization of items that are not described in section 312(k)(2) or (k)(3) shall be determined under the rules for determining taxable income. For example, amortization for amortizable section 197 intangibles (as defined in section 197(c)) is calculated in accordance with section 197, and depreciation for real property is calculated in accordance with section 168(g)(2)(C)(iii). For any taxable year beginning before July 1, 1972, depreciation shall be computed in accordance with section 167 and the regulations under that section.

* * *

(v) *Taxable years.*—The period for computation of taxable income and earnings and profits known as the taxable year shall reflect the provisions of sections 441 and 898 and the regulations under those sections.

* * *

(2) *Adoption or change of method or taxable year.*—* * * Once adopted, a method of accounting or taxable year may be changed by or on behalf of the foreign corporation only in accordance with the applicable provisions of the Code and regulations. Adjustments to the appropriate separate category (as defined in §1.904-5(a)(1)) of earnings and profits and income of the foreign corporation (including a category of subpart F income described in section 952(a) or, in the case of foreign base company income, described in §1.954-1(c)(1)(iii)) shall be required under section 481 to prevent any duplication or omission of amounts attributable to previous years that would otherwise result from any change in a method of accounting. * * * See paragraph (c)(9) of this section for rules if the change in method of accounting is required in connection with an audit of the foreign corporation's controlling domestic shareholders (as defined in paragraph (c)(5) of this section).

* * *

(8) *Examples.*—The following examples illustrate the application of paragraph (c) of this section:

Example 1. P, a domestic corporation, owns all of the outstanding stock of FX, a controlled foreign corporation organized in 2012. In maintaining its books for the purpose of accounting to its shareholders, FX deducts additions to a reserve for bad debts. Assume that if FX were a domestic corporation, it would be required to use the specific charge-off method under section 166 with respect to allowable bad debt losses. In accordance with paragraph (c)(1)(i) of this section, FX's reserve deductions must be adjusted (if the adjustments are material) in order to compute its earnings and profits in accordance with U.S. income tax accounting standards as described in paragraph (c). Accordingly, P must compute FX's earnings and profits using the specific charge-off method of accounting for bad debts in accordance with section 166.

Example 2. FX, a controlled foreign corporation, maintains its books for the purpose of accounting to its shareholders by capitalizing research and experimental expenses. A, B, and C, the United States shareholders (as defined in section 951(b)) of FX, own 45 percent, 30 percent, and 25 percent, respectively, of its only class of outstanding stock. For the first taxable year of FX, pursuant to paragraph (c)(3) of this section, B and C adopt on its behalf the section 174 method of currently deducting research and experimental expenses. Regardless of whether A objects to this action or receives the notice required by paragraph (c)(3)(iii) of this section, adjustments must be made to reflect the use of the section 174 method in computing the earnings and profits of FX with respect to A as well as with respect to B and C.

Example 3. (i) P, a calendar year domestic corporation that uses the fair market value method of apportioning interest expense, owns all of the outstanding stock of FX, a controlled foreign corporation organized in 2002 that uses the calendar year as its taxable year for foreign tax purposes. On June 1, 2012, FX makes a distribution to P. Prior to that distribution, none of the significant events specified in paragraph (c)(6) of this section had occurred. In addition, neither P nor FX had ever made or adopted, or been required to make or adopt, an election or method of accounting or taxable year for United States tax purposes with respect to FX. FX does not act to make any election or adopt any method of accounting or a taxable year for United States tax purposes.

(ii) P must compute FX's earnings and profits for FX's 2002 through 2012 taxable years in order to determine if any portion of the 2012 distribution is taxable as a dividend and to determine P's deemed paid foreign tax credit on such portion under section 902. Under paragraph (c)(2) of this section, P may make an election or adopt a method or methods of accounting and a taxable year on behalf of FX by satisfying the requirements of paragraph (c)(3) of this section by the due date (with extensions) of P's Federal income tax return for 2012, its taxable year with which ends FX's 2012 taxable year. Under paragraph (c)(4) of this section, any such election or adoption will govern the computation of FX's earnings and profits for its taxable years beginning in 2002 and subsequent taxable years for purposes of determining the Federal income tax liability of P and any subsequent shareholders of FX in 2012 and subsequent taxable years, unless the Commissioner consents to a change.

(iii) If P fails to satisfy the requirements under paragraph (c)(3) of this section and such failure is not shown to the satisfaction of the Commissioner to be due to reasonable cause, the earnings and profits of FX will be computed on the basis of a calendar taxable year as if no elections were made and any permissible methods of accounting not requiring an election and reflected in FX's books were adopted. Any subsequent attempt by FX or P to change an accounting method or taxable year of FX shall be effective only if the Commissioner consents to the change.

Example 4. (i) The facts are the same as in *Example 3*, except that P owns 80 percent, rather than all, of the outstanding stock of FX. M, a calendar year domestic corporation, owns the remaining 20 percent of the stock of FX beginning in 2002. M uses the tax book value method to allocate its interest expense under section 864(e)(4).

(ii) M, but not P, must compute FX's earnings and profits beginning in 2002 in order to determine the adjustment under § 1.861-12(c) and § 1.861-12T(c) to M's basis in the stock of FX for M's 2002 through 2011 taxable years. Because P, the controlling domestic shareholder of FX, has not made or adopted, or been required to make or adopt, an election or a method of accounting or taxable year with respect to FX, the earnings and profits of FX for 2002 through 2011 will be computed on the basis of a calendar taxable year as if no elections were made and any permissible methods of accounting not requiring an election and reflected in FX's books were adopted. However, a properly filed, timely election or adoption of a method of accounting or taxable year by, or on behalf of, FX with respect to FX's taxable year ending in 2012, when FX's earnings and profits are first significant for United States tax purposes for P, FX's controlling domestic shareholder, shall not be treated as a change in accounting method or a change in taxable year for any pre-2012 taxable year of FX. M will not be required to recompute its basis adjustments for 2002 through 2011 by reason of P's adoption of a method or methods of accounting or taxable year with respect to FX for 2012. See paragraph (c)(4)(iii) of this section. However, any method of accounting or taxable year adopted on behalf of FX by P pursuant to this paragraph (c) with respect to FX is binding on P, FX, and M for purposes of computing FX's earnings and profits in 2002 and subsequent taxable years for purposes of determining the Federal income tax liability of P, M, and any subsequent shareholders of FX in 2012 and subsequent taxable years, unless the Commissioner consents to a change.

Example 5. (i) In 1987, P, a calendar year domestic corporation that uses the tax book value method to allocate its interest expense under section 864(e)(4), acquired 50 percent of the outstanding stock of 10/50 Corp, a noncontrolled section 902 corporation organized in 1980. For taxable years beginning on or before April 25, 2006, the provisions of this paragraph (c) did not provide a mechanism for shareholders of noncontrolled section 902 corporations to make elections or adopt methods of accounting or a taxable year on behalf of noncontrolled section 902 corporations. However, P had to compute 10/50 Corp's earnings and profits in order to determine the adjustment under § 1.861-12(c) and § 1.861-12T(c) to P's basis in the stock of 10/50 Corp beginning with P's 1987 taxable year.

(ii) For taxable years beginning on or before April 25, 2006, P was required to compute 10/50 Corp's earnings and profits as if any permissible method of accounting not requiring an election and reflected in 10/50 Corp's books had been adopted. See paragraph (c)(4)(ii) of this section. In taxable years beginning after April 25, 2006, in accordance with paragraph (c)(3) of this section P may request the consent of the Commissioner to change any method of accounting or the taxable year on behalf of 10/50 Corp.

(9) *Change of method on audit.*—If, in connection with an audit (or audits) of one or more shareholders of the foreign corporation who collectively would constitute the foreign corporation's controlling domestic shareholder(s) if they undertook to act on the corporation's behalf, the Commissioner determines that a method of accounting of the foreign corporation does not clearly reflect income, the computation of earnings and profits shall be made in a manner which, in the opinion of the Commissioner, does clearly reflect income. See section 446 and the related regulations. The Commissioner shall provide written notice of the change in method of accounting to each such shareholder and to all other persons known by the Commissioner to be domestic shareholders who own (within the meaning of section 958(a)) stock of the foreign corporation. However, the failure of the Commissioner to provide such notice to any such other person shall not invalidate the change of method, which shall bind both the foreign corporation and all of its domestic shareholders as to the computation of the foreign corporation's earnings and profits for the taxable year of the foreign corporation for which the method of accounting is changed and in subsequent taxable years unless the Commissioner consents to a change.

(d) *Effective/applicability date.*—This section applies in computing earnings and profits of foreign corporations in taxable years of foreign corporations beginning on or after the date of publication of these regulations as final regulations in the **Federal Register**, and taxable years of shareholders with or within which such taxable years of the foreign corporations end. See 26 CFR § 1.964-1 (revised as of April 1, 2011) for rules applicable to taxable years beginning before such date.

[Prop. Reg. § 1.964-1.]

[Proposed 11-4-2011.]

Proposed Amendments to Regulation

§ 1.964-1. Determination of the earnings and profits of a foreign corporation.—

* * *

(c) * * *

(2) * * * For the first taxable year of a foreign corporation in which such foreign corporation first qualifies as a controlled foreign corporation (as defined in section 957 or 953) or a foreign corporation (other than a controlled foreign corporation as defined in section 957 or 953) as to which a United States person that is a United States shareholder (within the meaning of section 951(b)) owns stock (within the meaning of section 958(a)) (such corporation, a "noncontrolled foreign corporation"), any method of accounting or taxable year allowable under this section may be adopted, and any election allowable under this section may be made, by such foreign corporation or on its behalf notwithstanding that, in previous years, its books or financial statements were prepared on a different basis, and notwithstanding that such election is required by the Code or regulations in this chapter to be made in a prior taxable year. * * *

(3) * * *

(iii) *Notice.*—(A) *In general.*—Except as otherwise provided in paragraph (c)(3)(iii)(B) of this section, on or before the filing date described in paragraph (c)(3)(ii) of this section, the controlling domestic shareholders must provide written notice of the election made or the adoption or change of method or taxable year effected to all other persons known by them to be United States persons that own (within the meaning of section 958(a)) stock of the foreign corporation *(domestic shareholders)* and to any other United States person that is a "Category 4 filer" of Form 5471, "Information Return of U.S. Persons With Respect to Certain Foreign Corporations," with respect to the foreign corporation (that is, certain United States persons that control, within the meaning of section 6038(e), the foreign corporation). Thus, for example, this notice is required to be provided to domestic shareholders that own (within the meaning of section 958(a)) stock in the foreign corporation through one or more domestic partnerships. The notice required in this paragraph (c)(3)(iii)(A) must set forth the name, country of organization, and U.S. employer identification number (if applicable) of the foreign corporation, and the names, addresses, and stock interests of the controlling domestic shareholders. Such notice must also describe the nature of the action taken on behalf of the foreign corporation and the taxable year for which made, and identify a designated shareholder that retains a jointly executed consent confirming that such action has been approved by all of the controlling domestic shareholders and containing the signature of a principal officer of each such shareholder (or its common parent). However, the failure of the controlling domestic shareholders to provide such notice to a person required to be notified does not invalidate the election made or the adoption or change of method or taxable year effected.

(B) *Special rule for domestic partnerships.*—A controlling domestic shareholder will be deemed to satisfy the notice requirement of paragraph (c)(3)(iii)(A) of this section with respect to any domestic shareholder that is a partner in a domestic partnership by providing notice to a domestic partnership (known to the controlling domestic shareholder) through which the domestic shareholder owns stock of the foreign corporation, instead of to the domestic shareholder.

* * *

(5) * * *

(ii) *Noncontrolled foreign corporations.*—For purposes of this paragraph (c), the controlling domestic shareholders of a noncontrolled foreign corporation are its majority domestic shareholders. The majority domestic shareholders of a noncontrolled foreign corporation are those United States shareholders (within the meaning of section 951(b)) that own (within the meaning of section 958(a)) stock in the noncontrolled foreign corporation and that, in the aggregate, own (within the meaning of section 958(a)), or are considered as owning by applying the rules of section 958(b), more than 50 percent of the combined voting power of all of the voting stock of the noncontrolled foreign corporation that is owned by all United States shareholders that own (within the meaning of section 958(a)), or are considered as owning by applying the rules of section 958(b), stock of the noncontrolled foreign corporation.

* * *

(8) *Stock owned through domestic partnerships.*—See § 1.958-1(d) for rules regarding the ownership of stock of a foreign corporation through a domestic partnership for purposes of paragraph (c) of this section and for purposes of any provision that specifically applies by reference to paragraph (c) of this section.

* * *

(d) *Applicability dates.*—* * * Notwithstanding the preceding sentences in this paragraph (d), paragraphs (c)(2), (c)(3)(ii) and (iii), (c)(4)(i)(B), (c)(4)(ii), (c)(5)(ii), and (c)(8) of this section apply to taxable years of foreign corporations beginning on or after [date of publication of the Treasury decision adopting these rules as final regulations in the **Federal Register**], and to taxable years of United States persons in which or with which such taxable years end. For taxable years of foreign corporations beginning before [date of publication of the Treasury decision adopting these rules as final regulations in the **Federal Register**], and to taxable years of foreign United States persons in which or with which such taxable years end, see § 1.964-1(c)(2), (c)(3)(ii) and (iii), (c)(4)(i)(B), (c)(4)(ii), and (c)(5)(ii) as in effect and contained in 26 CFR part 1, as revised April 1, 2021. [Prop. Reg. § 1.964-1.]

[Proposed 1-25-2022.]

§ 1.964-2. Treatment of blocked earnings and profits.—(a) *General rule.*—If, in accordance with paragraph (d) of this section, it is established to the satisfaction of the district director that any amount of the earnings and profits of a controlled foreign corporation for the taxable year (determined under § 1.964-1) was subject to a currency or other restriction or limitation imposed under the laws of any foreign country (within the meaning of paragraph (b) of this section) on its distribution to United States shareholders who own (within the meaning of section 958(a)) stock of such corporation, such amount shall not be included in earnings and profits for purposes of sections 952, 955 (as in effect both before and after the enactment of the Tax Reduction Act of 1975), and 956 for such taxable year. For rules governing the treatment of amounts with respect to which such restriction or limitation is removed, see paragraph (c) of this section.

(b) *Rules of application.*—For purposes of paragraph (a) of this section—

(1) *Period of restriction or limitation.*—An amount of earnings and profits of a controlled foreign corporation for any taxable year shall not be included in earnings and profits for purposes of sections 952, 955 (as in effect both before and after the enactment of the Tax Reduction Act of 1975), and 956 only if such amount of earnings and profits is subject to a currency or other restriction or limitation (within the meaning of subparagraph (2) of this paragraph) throughout the 150-day period beginning 90 days before the close of the taxable year and ending 60 days after the close of such taxable year.

(2) *Restriction or limitation defined.*—Whether earnings and profits of a controlled foreign corporation are subject to a currency or other restriction or limitation imposed under the laws of a foreign country must be determined on the basis of all the facts and circumstances in each case. Generally, such a restriction or limitation must prevent—

(i) The ready conversion (directly or indirectly) of such currency into United States dollars or into property of a type normally owned by such corporation in the operation of its business or other money which is readily convertible into United States dollars; or

(ii) The distribution of dividends by such corporation to its United States shareholders.

For purposes of this subparagraph, if a United States shareholder owns (within the meaning of section 958(a)), or is considered as owning by applying the rules of ownership of section 958(b), 80 percent or more of the total combined voting power of all classes of stock of a foreign corporation in a chain of ownership described in section 958(a), the distribution of dividends by such corporation to such shareholder will not be considered prevented solely by reason of the existence of a currency or other restriction or limitation at an intermediate tier in such chain if dividends may be distributed directly to such shareholders.

(3) *Foreign laws.*—A currency or other restriction or limitation on the distribution of earnings and profits may be imposed in a foreign country by express statutory provisions, executive orders or decrees, rules or regulations of a governmental agency, court decisions, the actions of appropriate officials who are acting within the scope of their authority, or by any similar official action. A currency restriction will not be considered to exist unless export restrictions are also imposed which prevent the exportation of property of a type normally owned by the controlled foreign corporation in the operation of its business which could be readily converted into United States dollars.

(4) *Voluntary restriction or limitation.*—A currency or other restriction or limitation arising from the voluntary act of the controlled foreign corporation or its United States shareholders during a taxable year beginning after December 31, 1962, will not be taken into account. For example, if a controlled foreign corporation—

(i) Issues a stock dividend which has the effect of capitalizing earnings and profits;

(ii) Elects to restrict its earnings and profits or to make certain investments as a means of avoiding current tax or securing a reduced rate of tax; or

(iii) Allocates earnings and profits to an optional or arbitrary reserve;

such restriction is voluntary and will not be taken into account.

(5) *Treatment of earnings and profits in cases of certain mandatory reserves.*—(i) *In general.*—If a controlled foreign corporation is required under the laws of a foreign country to establish a reserve out of earnings and profits for the taxable year, such earnings and profits shall be considered subject to a restriction or limitation by reason of such requirement only to the extent that the amount required to be included in such reserve at the close of the taxable year exceeds the accumulated earnings and profits (determined in accordance with subdivision (ii) of this subparagraph) of such corporation at the close of the preceding taxable year,

(ii) *Determination of earnings and profits.*—For purposes of determining the accumulated earnings and profits of a controlled foreign corporation under subdivision (i) of this subparagraph, such earnings and profits shall not include any amounts which are attributable to—

(a) Amounts which, for any prior taxable year, have been included in the gross income of a United States shareholder under section 951(a) and have not been distributed;

(b) Amounts which, for any prior taxable year, have been included in the gross income of a United States shareholder of such foreign corporation under section 551(b) and have not been distributed; or

(*c*) Amounts which become subject to a voluntary restriction or limitation (within the meaning of subparagraph (4) of this paragraph) during a taxable year beginning before January 1, 1963.

The rules of this subdivision apply only in determining the accumulated earnings and profits of a controlled foreign corporation for purposes of this subparagraph. See section 959 and the regulations thereunder for limitations on the exclusion from gross income of previously taxed earnings and profits.

(6) *Exhaustion of procedures for distributing earnings and profits.*—Earnings and profits of a controlled foreign corporation for a taxable year will not be considered subject to a currency or other restriction or limitation on their distribution unless the United States shareholders of such corporation demonstrate either that the available procedures for distributing such earnings and profits have been exhausted or that the use of such procedures will be futile. As a general rule, such procedures will be considered to have been exhausted if the foreign corporation applies for dollars (or foreign currency readily convertible into dollars) at the appropriate rate of exchange and complies with the applicable laws and regulations governing the acquisition and transfer of such currency including submission of the necessary documentation to the exchange authority. The fact that available procedures for distributing earnings and profits were exhausted without success with respect to a prior year is not, of itself, sufficient evidence that such procedures would not be successful with respect to the current taxable year.

(c) *Removal of restriction or limitation.*—(1) *In general.*—If, during any taxable year, a currency or other restriction or limitation (within the meaning of paragraph (b) of this section) imposed under the laws of a foreign country on the distribution of earnings and profits of a controlled foreign corporation to its United States shareholders is removed—

(i) *Treatment of deferred income.*—Each United States shareholder of such corporation on the last day in such year that such corporation is a controlled foreign corporation shall include in his gross income for such taxable year the amounts attributable to such earnings and profits which would have been includible in his gross income under section 951(a) for prior taxable years but for the existence of the currency or other restriction or limitation except that the amounts included under this subdivision (i) shall not exceed his pro rata share of—

(*a*) The earnings and profits upon which the restriction was removed determined on the basis of his stock ownership on the last day of the immediately preceding taxable year, and

(*b*) The applicable limitations under paragraph (c) of § 1.952-1, paragraph (b)(2) of § 1.955-1, paragraph (b)(2) of § 1.955A-1, or paragraph (b) of § 1.956-1, determined as of the last day of the immediately preceding taxable year, taking into account the provisions of subdivision (ii) of this subparagraph.

(ii) *Treatment of earnings and profits.*—For purposes of sections 952, 955 (as in effect both before and after the enactment of the Tax Reduction Act of 1975), and 956, the earnings and profits which are no longer subject to a currency or other restriction or limitation shall be treated as included in the corporation's earnings and profits for the year in which such earnings and profits were derived. Amounts with respect to which a currency or other restriction or limitation is removed shall be translated into United States dollars at the appropriate exchange rate for the translation period during which such currency or other restriction or limitation is removed. See paragraph (d) of § 1.964-1. Amounts with respect to which a currency or other restriction or limitation is removed shall not be taken into account in determining whether a deficiency distribution (within the meaning of § 1.963-6 (applied as if section 963 had not been repealed by the Tax Reduction Act of 1975)) is required to be made for the year in which such earnings and profits were derived.

(2) *Removal of restriction or limitation defined.*—An amount of earnings and profits shall be considered no longer subject to a limitation or restriction if and to the extent that—

(i) Money or property in such foreign country is readily convertible into United States dollars, or into other money or property of a type normally owned by such corporation in the operation of its business which is readily convertible into United States dollars;

(ii) Notwithstanding the existence of any laws or regulations forbidding the exchange of money or property into United States dollars, conversion is actually made into United States dollars, or other money or property of a type normally owned by such corporation in the operation of its business which is readily convertible into United States dollars; or

(iii) A mandatory reserve requirement (described in paragraph (b)(5) of this section) is removed either by a change in law of the foreign country imposing such requirement or by an accumulation of earnings and profits not subject to such requirement.

(3) *Distribution in foreign country.*—If, during any taxable year, earnings and profits previously subject to a currency or other restriction or limitation are distributed in a foreign country to one or more United States shareholders of a controlled foreign corporation directly, or indirectly through a chain of ownership described in section 958(a), such earnings and profits shall be considered no longer subject to a restriction or limitation. However, distributed amounts may be excluded from such shareholder's gross income for the taxable year of receipt if such shareholder elects a method of accounting under which the reporting of blocked foreign income is deferred until the income ceases to be blocked.

(4) *Source of distribution.*—If, during any taxable year, earnings and profits previously subject to a currency or other restriction or limitation are distributed to one or more United States shareholders of a controlled foreign corporation directly, or indirectly through a chain of ownership described in section 958(a), the source of such distribution shall be determined in accordance with the rules of § 1.959-3.

(5) *Illustration.*—The provisions of this paragraph may be illustrated by the following example:

Example. (a) M, a United States person, owns all of the only class of stock of A Corporation, a foreign corporation incorporated under the laws of foreign country X on January 1, 1963. Both M and A Corporations use the calendar year as a taxable year and A Corporation is a controlled foreign corporation throughout the period here involved.

(b) During 1963, A Corporation derives income of $100,000 all of which is subpart F income and has earnings and profits of $100,000. Under the laws of X Country, currency cannot be exported without a license. During the last 90 days of 1963 and the first 60 days of 1964, A Corporation can obtain a license to distribute only an amount equivalent to $10,000. M must include $10,000 in his gross income for 1963 under section 951(a)(1)(A)(i) and $90,000 of A Corporation's earnings and profits for 1963 are not taken into account for purposes of sections 952, 955, and 956.

(c) During 1964, A Corporation has no income and no earnings and profits. On June 1, 1964, A Corporation converts an amount equivalent to $20,000 into property of a type normally owned by such corporation in the operation of its business which is readily convertible into United States dollars but does not distribute such amount. Corporation A must include $20,000 in its earnings and profits for 1963 for purposes of sections 952, 955, and 956. M must include $20,000 in his gross income for 1964.

(d) During 1965, A Corporation has no income and no earnings and profits. On December 15, 1965, A Corporation distributes an amount equivalent to $15,000 to M in X Country. Neither M nor A Corporation can obtain a license to export currency from X Country. In his return for the taxable year 1965, M elects a method of accounting under which the reporting of blocked foreign income is deferred until the income ceases to be blocked. Accordingly, M does not include the $15,000 in his gross income for 1965.

(e) During 1966, A Corporation has no income and no earnings and profits. On February 1, 1966, notwithstanding the laws and regulations of X Country which forbid the exchange of X Country's currency into United States dollars, M converts an amount equivalent to $15,000 into a currency which is readily convertible into United States dollars. Since the income has ceased to be blocked, M must include $15,000 in his gross income for 1966.

(d) *Manner of claiming existence of restriction or limitation on distribution of earnings and profits.*—A United States shareholder claiming that an amount of the earnings and profits of a controlled foreign corporation for the taxable year was subject to a currency or other restriction or limitation imposed under the laws of a foreign country on its distribution shall file a statement with his return for the taxable year with or within which the taxable year of the foreign corporation ends which shall include—

(1) The name and address of the foreign corporation,

(2) A description of the classes of stock of the foreign corporation and a statement of the number of shares of each class owned (within the meaning of section 958(a)) or considered as owned (by

applying the rules of ownership of section 958(b)) by the United States shareholder,

(3) A description of the currency or other restriction or limitation on the distribution of earnings and profits,

(4) The total earnings and profits of the foreign corporation for the taxable year (before any amount is excluded from earnings and profits under this section) and the United States shareholder's pro rata share of such total earnings and profits,

(5) The United States shareholder's pro rata share of the amount of earnings and profits subject to a restriction or limitation on distribution,

(6) The amounts which would be includible in the United States shareholder's gross income under section 951(a) but for the existence of the currency or other restriction or limitation,

(7) A description of the available procedures for distributing earnings and profits and a statement setting forth the steps taken to exhaust such procedures or a statement setting forth the reasons that the use of such procedures would be futile, and

(8) The amount of distributions made in a foreign country and a statement as to whether a method of accounting has been elected under which the reporting of blocked income is deferred until such income ceases to be blocked, including an identification of the taxable year and place of filing of such election.

In addition, such United States shareholder shall furnish to the district director such other information as he may require to verify the status of a currency or other restriction or limitation. [Reg. § 1.964-2.]

☐ [*T.D. 6892, 8-22-66. Amended by T.D. 7545, 5-5-78 and T.D. 7893, 5-11-83.*]

§ 1.964-3. Records to be provided by United States shareholders.—(a) *Shareholder's responsibility for providing records.*—For purposes of verifying his income tax liability in respect of amounts includible in income under section 951 for the taxable year of a controlled foreign corporation each United States shareholder (as defined in section 951(b)) who owns (within the meaning of section 958(a)) stock of such corporation shall, within a reasonable time after demand by the district director, provide the district director—

(1) Such permanent books of account or records as are sufficient to satisfy the requirements of section 6001 and section 964(c), or true copies thereof, as are reasonably demanded, and

(2) If such books or records are not maintained in the English language, either (i) an accurate English translation of such books or records or (ii) the services of a qualified interpreter satisfactory to the district director. If such books or records are being used by another district director, the United States shareholder upon whom the district director has made a demand to provide such books or records shall file a statement of such fact with his district director, indicating the location of such books or records. For the length of time the United States shareholder of a controlled foreign corporation must cause such books or records as are under his control to be retained, see paragraph (e) of § 1.6001-1.

(b) *Records to be provided.*—Except as otherwise provided in paragraph (c) of this section, the requirements of section 6001 and section 964(c) for record keeping shall be considered satisfied if the books or records produced are sufficient to verify for the taxable year—

(1) The subpart F income of the controlled foreign corporation and, if any part of such income is excluded from the income of the United States shareholder under section 963 or section 970(a), the application of such exclusion,

(2) The previously excluded subpart F income of such corporation withdrawn from investment in less developed countries,

(3) The previously excluded subpart F income of such corporation withdrawn from investment in foreign base company shipping operations,

(4) The previously excluded export trade income of such corporation withdrawn from investment, and

(5) The increase in earnings invested by such corporation in United States property.

(c) *Special rules.*—Verification of the subpart F income of the controlled foreign corporation for the taxable year shall not be required if—

(1) It can be demonstrated to the satisfaction of the district director that—

(i) The locus and nature of such corporation's activities were such as to make it unlikely that the foreign base company income of such corporation (determined in accordance with paragraph (c)(3) of § 1.952-3) exceeded 5 percent of its gross income (determined in accordance with paragraph (b)(1) of § 1.952-3) for the taxable year (For taxable years to which § 1.952-3 does not apply, such amounts shall be determined under 26 CFR §§ 1.954-1(d)(3)(i) and (ii) (Rev. as of April 1, 1975)), and

(ii) If such corporation reinsures or issues insurance or annuity contracts in connection with United States risks, the 5-percent minimum premium requirement prescribed in paragraph (b) of § 1.953-1 has not been exceeded for the taxable year, or

(2) The United States shareholder's pro rata share of such subpart F income is excluded in full from his income under section 963 and the books or records verify the application of such exclusion. [Reg. § 1.964-3.]

☐ [*T.D. 6824, 5-10-65. Amended by T.D. 7893, 5-11-83.*]

Transition Tax

§ 1.965-1. Overview, general rules, and definitions.—(a) *Overview.*—(1) *In general.*—This section provides general rules and definitions under section 965. Section 1.965-2 provides rules relating to adjustments to earnings and profits and basis to determine and account for the application of section 965 and a rule that limits the amount of gain recognized under section 961(b)(2) by reason of distributions attributable to section 965 previously taxed earnings and profits (as defined in § 1.965-2(g)(1)(ii)) in the inclusion year. Section 1.965-3 provides rules regarding the determination of section 965(c) deductions. Section 1.965-4 sets forth rules that disregard certain transactions for purposes of section 965. Sections 1.965-5 and 1.965-6 provide rules with respect to foreign tax credits. Section 1.965-7 provides rules regarding elections and payments. Section 1.965-8 provides rules regarding affiliated groups, including consolidated groups. Section 1.965-9 provides dates of applicability. *See also* §§ 1.962-1 and 1.962-2 (providing rules regarding the application of section 962) and 1.986(c)-1 (providing rules regarding the application of section 986(c)).

(2) *Scope.*—Paragraph (b) of this section provides the general rules concerning section 965(a) inclusion amounts. Paragraph (c) of this section provides the general rule concerning section 965(c) deduction amounts. Paragraph (d) of this section provides a rule for specified foreign corporations that are not controlled foreign corporations. Paragraph (e) of this section treats certain controlled domestic partnerships as foreign partnerships for purposes of section 965. Paragraph (f) of this section provides definitions applicable for the section 965 regulations and §§ 1.962-1, 1.962-2, and 1.986(c)-1. Paragraph (g) of this section contains examples illustrating the general rules and definitions set forth in this section.

(b) *Section 965(a) inclusion amounts.*—(1) *Inclusion of the pro rata share of the section 965(a) earnings amount.*—For an inclusion year of a deferred foreign income corporation, the subpart F income of the deferred foreign income corporation (as otherwise determined for the inclusion year under section 952 and § 1.952-1) is increased by the section 965(a) earnings amount of the deferred foreign income corporation. *See* section 965(a). Accordingly, a section 958(a) U.S. shareholder with respect to a deferred foreign income corporation generally includes in gross income under section 951(a)(1) for the section 958(a) U.S. shareholder inclusion year its pro rata share of the section 965(a) earnings amount of the deferred foreign income corporation, translated (if necessary) into U.S. dollars using the spot rate on December 31, 2017, and subject to reduction under section 965(b), paragraph (b)(2) of this section, and § 1.965-8(b). The amount of the section 958(a) U.S. shareholder's inclusion with respect to a deferred foreign income corporation as a result of section 965(a) and this paragraph (b)(1), as reduced under section 965(b), paragraph (b)(2) of this section, and § 1.965-8(b), as applicable, is referred to as the *section 965(a) inclusion amount*. Neither the section 965(a) earnings amount nor the section 965(a) inclusion amount is subject to the rules or limitations in section 952 or limited by the accumulated earnings and profits of the deferred foreign income corporation on the date of the inclusion.

(2) *Reduction by the allocable share of the aggregate foreign E&P deficit.*—For purposes of determining a section 958(a) U.S. shareholder's section 965(a) inclusion amount with respect to a deferred foreign income corporation, the U.S. dollar amount of the section 958(a) U.S. shareholder's pro rata share of the section 965(a) earnings amount of the deferred foreign income corporation, translated (if

necessary) into U.S. dollars using the spot rate on December 31, 2017, is reduced by the deferred foreign income corporation's allocable share of the section 958(a) U.S. shareholder's aggregate foreign E&P deficit. *See* section 965(b). If the section 958(a) U.S. shareholder is a member of a consolidated group, under § 1.965-8(e), all section 958(a) U.S. shareholders that are members of the consolidated group are treated as a single section 958(a) U.S. shareholder for purposes of this paragraph (b)(2).

(c) *Section 965(c) deduction amounts.*—For a section 958(a) U.S. shareholder inclusion year, a section 958(a) U.S. shareholder is generally allowed a deduction in an amount equal to the section 965(c) deduction amount.

(d) *Treatment of specified foreign corporation as a controlled foreign corporation.*—A specified foreign corporation described in section 965(e)(1)(B) and paragraph (f)(45)(i)(B) of this section that is not otherwise a controlled foreign corporation is treated as a controlled foreign corporation solely for purposes of paragraph (b) of this section and sections 951, 961, and § 1.1411-10. *See* 965(e)(2).

(e) *Special rule for certain controlled domestic partnerships.*—(1) *In general.*—For purposes of the section 965 regulations, a controlled domestic partnership is treated as a foreign partnership for purposes of determining the section 958(a) U.S. shareholder of a specified foreign corporation and the section 958(a) stock of the specified foreign corporation owned by the section 958(a) U.S. shareholder if the following conditions are satisfied—

(i) Without regard to this paragraph (e), the controlled domestic partnership is a section 958(a) U.S. shareholder of the specified foreign corporation and thus owns section 958(a) stock of the specified foreign corporation (*tested section 958(a) stock*);

(ii) If the controlled domestic partnership (and all other controlled domestic partnerships in the chain of ownership of the specified foreign corporation) were treated as foreign—

(A) The specified foreign corporation would continue to be a specified foreign corporation; and

(B) At least one United States shareholder of the specified foreign corporation—

(1) Would be treated as a section 958(a) U.S. shareholder of the specified foreign corporation; and

(2) Would be treated as owning (within the meaning of section 958(a)) tested section 958(a) stock of the specified foreign corporation through another foreign corporation that is a direct or indirect partner in the controlled domestic partnership.

(2) *Definition of a controlled domestic partnership.*—For purposes of paragraph (e)(1) of this section, the term *controlled domestic partnership* means a domestic partnership that is controlled by a United States shareholder described in paragraph (e)(1)(ii)(B) of this section and persons related to the United States shareholder. For purposes of this paragraph (e)(2), control is determined based on all the facts and circumstances, except that a partnership will be deemed to be controlled by a United States shareholder and related persons if those persons, in the aggregate, own (directly or indirectly through one or more partnerships) more than 50 percent of the interests in the partnership capital or profits. For purposes of this paragraph (e)(2), a related person is, with respect to a United States shareholder, a person that is related (within the meaning of section 267(b) or 707(b)(1)) to the United States shareholder.

(f) *Definitions.*—This paragraph (f) provides definitions that apply for purposes of the section 965 regulations and §§ 1.962-1, 1.962-2, and 1.986(c)-1. Unless otherwise indicated, all amounts are expressed as positive numbers.

(1) *8 percent rate amount.*—The term *8 percent rate amount* means, with respect to a section 958(a) U.S. shareholder and a section 958(a) U.S. shareholder inclusion year, the excess, if any, of the section 958(a) U.S. shareholder's aggregate section 965(a) inclusion amount for the section 958(a) U.S. shareholder inclusion year over the amount of the section 958(a) U.S. shareholder's aggregate foreign cash position for the section 958(a) U.S. shareholder inclusion year as determined under § 1.965-3(c).

(2) *8 percent rate equivalent percentage.*—The term *8 percent rate equivalent percentage* means, with respect to a section 958(a) U.S. shareholder and a section 958(a) U.S. shareholder inclusion year, the percentage that would result in the 8 percent rate amount being subject to an 8 percent rate of tax determined by only taking into account a deduction equal to such percentage of such amount and the highest rate of tax specified in section 11 for the section 958(a) U.S. shareholder inclusion year. In the case of a section 958(a) U.S. shareholder inclusion year of a section 958(a) U.S. shareholder to which section 15 applies, the highest rate of tax under section 11 before the effective date of the change in rates and the highest rate of tax under section 11 after the effective date of such change will each be taken into account under the preceding sentence in the same proportions as the portion of the section 958(a) U.S. shareholder inclusion year that is before and after such effective date, respectively.

(3) *15.5 percent rate amount.*—The term *15.5 percent rate amount* means, with respect to a section 958(a) U.S. shareholder and a section 958(a) U.S. shareholder inclusion year, the amount of the section 958(a) U.S. shareholder's aggregate foreign cash position for the section 958(a) U.S. shareholder inclusion year as determined under § 1.965-3(c) to the extent it does not exceed the section 958(a) U.S. shareholder's aggregate section 965(a) inclusion amount for the section 958(a) U.S. shareholder inclusion year.

(4) *15.5 percent rate equivalent percentage.*—The term *15.5 percent rate equivalent percentage*, with respect to a section 958(a) U.S. shareholder and a section 958(a) U.S. shareholder inclusion year, has the meaning provided for the term "8 percent rate equivalent percentage" applied by substituting "15.5 percent rate amount" for "8 percent rate amount" and "15.5 percent rate of tax" for "8 percent rate of tax."

(5) *Accounts payable.*—The term *accounts payable* means payables arising from the purchase of property described in section 1221(a)(1) or section 1221(a)(8) or the receipt of services from vendors or suppliers, provided the payables have a term upon issuance of less than one year.

(6) *Accounts receivable.*—The term *accounts receivable* means receivables described in section 1221(a)(4) that have a term upon issuance of less than one year.

(7) *Accumulated post-1986 deferred foreign income.*—(i) *In general.*—The term *accumulated post-1986 deferred foreign income* means, with respect to a specified foreign corporation, the post-1986 earnings and profits of the specified foreign corporation except to the extent such earnings and profits—

(A) Are attributable to income of the specified foreign corporation that is effectively connected with the conduct of a trade or business within the United States and subject to tax under chapter 1;

(B) If distributed, would, in the case of a controlled foreign corporation, be excluded from the gross income of a United States shareholder under section 959; or

(C) If distributed, would, in the case of a controlled foreign corporation that has shareholders that are not United States shareholders on an E&P measurement date, be excluded from the gross income of such shareholders under section 959 if such shareholders were United States shareholders, determined by applying the principles of Revenue Ruling 82-16, 1982-1 C.B. 106.

(ii) *Earnings and profits attributable to subpart F income in the same taxable year as an E&P measurement date.*—For purposes of determining the accumulated post-1986 deferred foreign income of a specified foreign corporation as of an E&P measurement date, earnings and profits of the specified foreign corporation that are or would be, applying the principles of Revenue Ruling 82-16, 1982-1 C.B. 106, described in section 959(c)(2) by reason of subpart F income (as defined in section 952 without regard to section 965(a)) are described in section 965(d)(2)(B) and paragraph (f)(7)(i)(B) or (f)(7)(i)(C) of this section only to the extent that such income has been accrued by the specified foreign corporation as of the E&P measurement date. For rules regarding the interaction of sections 951, 956, 959, and 965 generally, see § 1.965-2(b).

(8) *Aggregate foreign cash position.*—(i) *In general.*—The term *aggregate foreign cash position* means, with respect to a section 958(a) U.S. shareholder that is not a member of a consolidated group, the greater of—

(A) The aggregate of the section 958(a) U.S. shareholder's pro rata share of the cash position of each specified foreign corporation determined as of the final cash measurement date of the specified foreign corporation; or

(B) One half of the sum of—

(1) The aggregate described in paragraph (f)(8)(i)(A) of this section determined as of the second cash measurement date of each specified foreign corporation, plus

(2) The aggregate described in paragraph (f)(8)(i)(A) of this section determined as of the first cash measurement date of each specified foreign corporation.

(ii) *Other rules.*—For rules for determining the aggregate foreign cash position for a section 958(a) U.S. shareholder inclusion year of the section 958(a) U.S. shareholder, see § 1.965-3(c). For the rule for determining the aggregate foreign cash position of a section 958(a) U.S. shareholder that is a member of a consolidated group, see § 1.965-8(e)(3). For rules disregarding certain assets for purposes of determining the aggregate foreign cash position of a section 958(a) U.S. shareholder, see § 1.965-3(b).

(9) *Aggregate foreign E&P deficit.*—The term *aggregate foreign E&P deficit* means, with respect to a section 958(a) U.S. shareholder, the lesser of—

(i) The aggregate of the section 958(a) U.S. shareholder's pro rata share of the specified E&P deficit of each E&P deficit foreign corporation, translated (if necessary) into U.S. dollars using the spot rate on December 31, 2017, or

(ii) The aggregate of the section 958(a) U.S. shareholder's pro rata share of the section 965(a) earnings amount of each deferred foreign income corporation, translated (if necessary) into U.S. dollars using the spot rate on December 31, 2017.

(10) *Aggregate section 965(a) inclusion amount.*—The term *aggregate section 965(a) inclusion amount* means, with respect to a section 958(a) U.S. shareholder, the sum of all of the section 958(a) U.S. shareholder's section 965(a) inclusion amounts.

(11) *Allocable share.*—The term *allocable share* means, with respect to a deferred foreign income corporation and an aggregate foreign E&P deficit of a section 958(a) U.S. shareholder, the product of the aggregate foreign E&P deficit and the ratio determined by dividing—

(i) The section 958(a) U.S. shareholder's pro rata share of the section 965(a) earnings amount of the deferred foreign income corporation, translated (if necessary) into U.S. dollars using the spot rate on December 31, 2017, by

(ii) The amount described in paragraph (f)(9)(ii) of this section with respect to the section 958(a) U.S. shareholder.

(12) *Bona fide hedging transaction.*—The term *bona fide hedging transaction* means a hedging transaction that meets (or that would meet if the specified foreign corporation were a controlled foreign corporation) the requirements of a bona fide hedging transaction described in § 1.954-2(a)(4)(ii), except that in the case of a specified foreign corporation that is not a controlled foreign corporation, the identification requirements of § 1.954-2(a)(4)(ii)(B) do not apply.

(13) *Cash-equivalent asset.*—(i) *In general.*—The term *cash-equivalent asset* means any of the following assets—

(A) Personal property which is of a type that is actively traded and for which there is an established financial market, other than a specified commodity;

(B) Commercial paper, certificates of deposit, the securities of the Federal government and of any State or foreign government;

(C) Any foreign currency;

(D) A short-term obligation; or

(E) Derivative financial instruments, other than bona fide hedging transactions.

(ii) *Specified commodity.*—The term *specified commodity* means a commodity held, or, for purposes of paragraph (f)(18) of this section, to be held, by a specified foreign corporation that, in the hands of the specified foreign corporation, is property described in section 1221(a)(1) or 1221(a)(8). This paragraph (f)(13)(ii) does not apply with respect to commodities held by a specified foreign corporation in its capacity as a dealer or trader in commodities.

(14) *Cash-equivalent asset hedging transaction.*—(i) *In general.*—The term *cash-equivalent asset hedging transaction* means a bona fide hedging transaction identified on a specified foreign corporation's books and records as hedging a cash-equivalent asset.

(ii) *Aggregate hedging transactions.*—For purposes of paragraph (f)(14)(i) of this section, the amount of a bona fide hedging transaction described in § 1.1221-2(c)(3) (an *aggregate hedging transaction*) that is treated as a cash-equivalent asset hedging transaction is the amount that bears the same proportion to the fair market value of the aggregate hedging transaction as the value of the cash-equivalent assets being hedged by the aggregate hedging transaction bears to the value of all assets being hedged by the aggregate hedging transaction.

(15) *Cash measurement dates.*—The term *cash measurement dates* means, with respect to a specified foreign corporation, the first cash measurement date, the second cash measurement date, and the final cash measurement date, collectively, and each a *cash measurement date*.

(16) *Cash position.*—(i) *General rule.*—The term *cash position* means, with respect to a specified foreign corporation, the sum of—

(A) Cash held by the corporation;

(B) The net accounts receivable of the corporation; and

(C) The fair market value of the cash-equivalent assets held by the corporation.

(ii) *Fair market value of cash-equivalent assets.*—For purposes of determining the fair market value of a cash-equivalent asset of a specified foreign corporation, the value of the cash-equivalent asset must be adjusted by the fair market value of any cash-equivalent asset hedging transaction with respect to the cash-equivalent asset, but only to the extent that the cash-equivalent asset hedging transaction does not reduce the fair market value of the cash-equivalent asset below zero.

(iii) *Measurement of derivative financial instruments.*—The amount of derivative financial instruments taken into account in determining the cash position of a specified foreign corporation is the aggregate fair market value of its derivative financial instruments that constitute cash-equivalent assets, provided such amount is not less than zero.

(iv) *Translation of cash position amounts.*—The cash position of a specified foreign corporation with respect to a cash measurement date must be expressed in U.S. dollars. For this purpose, the amounts described in paragraph (f)(16)(i) of this section must be translated (if necessary) into U.S. dollars using the spot rate on the relevant cash measurement date.

(17) *Deferred foreign income corporation.*—(i) *In general.*—The term *deferred foreign income corporation* means a specified foreign corporation that has accumulated post-1986 deferred foreign income greater than zero as of an E&P measurement date.

(ii) *Priority rule.*—If a specified foreign corporation satisfies the definition of a deferred foreign income corporation under section 965(d)(1) and paragraph (f)(17)(i) of this section, it is classified solely as a deferred foreign income corporation and not also as an E&P deficit foreign corporation even if it otherwise satisfies the requirements of section 965(b)(3)(B) and paragraph (f)(22) of this section.

(18) *Derivative financial instrument.*—The term *derivative financial instrument* includes a financial instrument that is one of the following—

(i) A notional principal contract,

(ii) An option contract,

(iii) A forward contract, other than a forward contract with respect to a specified commodity (as defined in paragraph (f)(13)(ii) of this section), but solely to the extent that the specified foreign corporation identified, or could have identified, the forward contract as a hedging transaction (within the meaning of § 1.1221-2(b)) with respect to one or more specified commodities held by the specified foreign corporation,

(iv) A futures contract,

(v) A short position in securities or commodities, other than a forward contract with respect to a specified commodity, but solely to the extent that the specified foreign corporation identified, or could have identified, the forward contract as a hedging transaction (within the meaning of § 1.1221-2(b)) with respect to one or more specified commodities held by the specified foreign corporation, or

(vi) Any financial instrument similar to one described in paragraphs (f)(18)(i) through (v) of this section.

(19) *Domestic pass-through entity.*—The term *domestic pass-through entity* means a pass-through entity that is a United States person (as defined in section 7701(a)(30)).

(20) *Domestic pass-through owner*.—The term *domestic pass-through owner* means, with respect to a domestic pass-through entity, a United States person (as defined in section 7701(a)(30)) that is a partner, shareholder, beneficiary, grantor, or owner, as the case may be, in the domestic pass-through entity. Notwithstanding the preceding sentence, the term does not include a partner, shareholder, beneficiary, grantor, or owner of the domestic pass-through entity that is itself a domestic pass-through entity but does include any other United States person that is an indirect partner, shareholder, beneficiary, grantor, or owner of the domestic pass-through entity through one or more other pass-through entities.

(21) *Domestic pass-through owner share*.—The term *domestic pass-through owner share* means, with respect to a domestic pass-through owner and a domestic pass-through entity, the domestic pass-through owner's share of the aggregate section 965(a) inclusion amount and the section 965(c) deduction amount, as applicable, of the domestic pass-through entity, including the domestic pass-through owner's share of the aggregate section 965(a) inclusion amount and section 965(c) deduction amount, as applicable, of a domestic pass-through entity owned indirectly by the domestic pass-through owner through one or more other pass-through entities.

(22) *E&P deficit foreign corporation*.—(i) *In general*.—The term *E&P deficit foreign corporation* means, with respect to a section 958(a) U.S. shareholder, a specified foreign corporation, other than a deferred foreign income corporation, if, as of November 2, 2017—

(A) The specified foreign corporation had a deficit in post-1986 earnings and profits,

(B) The corporation was a specified foreign corporation, and

(C) The shareholder was a United States shareholder of the corporation.

(ii) *Determination of deficit in post-1986 earnings and profits*.—In the case of a specified foreign corporation that has post-1986 earnings and profits that include earnings and profits described in section 959(c)(1) or 959(c)(2) (or both) and a deficit in earnings and profits (including hovering deficits, as defined in § 1.367(b)-7(d)(2)(i)), the specified foreign corporation has a deficit in post-1986 earnings and profits described in paragraph (f)(22)(i)(A) of this section only to the extent the deficit in post-1986 earnings and profits exceeds the aggregate of its post-1986 earnings and profits described in section 959(c)(1) and 959(c)(2).

(23) *E&P measurement dates*.—The term *E&P measurement dates* means November 2, 2017, and December 31, 2017, collectively, and each an *E&P measurement date*.

(24) *Final cash measurement date*.—The term *final cash measurement date* means, with respect to a specified foreign corporation, the close of the last taxable year of the specified foreign corporation that begins before January 1, 2018, and ends on or after November 2, 2017, if any.

(25) *First cash measurement date*.—The term *first cash measurement date* means, with respect to a specified foreign corporation, the close of the last taxable year of the specified foreign corporation that ends after November 1, 2015, and before November 2, 2016, if any.

(26) *Inclusion year*.—The term *inclusion year* means, with respect to a deferred foreign income corporation, the last taxable year of the deferred foreign income corporation that begins before January 1, 2018.

(27) *Net accounts receivable*.—The term *net accounts receivable* means, with respect to a specified foreign corporation, the excess (if any) of—

(i) The corporation's accounts receivable, over

(ii) The corporation's accounts payable (determined consistent with the rules of section 461).

(28) *Pass-through entity*.—The term *pass-through entity* means a partnership, S corporation, or any other person (whether domestic or foreign) other than a corporation to the extent that the income or deductions of the person are included in the income of one or more direct or indirect owners or beneficiaries of the person. For example, if a domestic trust is subject to federal income tax on a portion of its section 965(a) inclusion amount and its domestic pass-through owners are subject to tax on the remaining portion, the domestic trust is treated as a domestic pass-through entity with respect to such remaining portion.

(29) *Post-1986 earnings and profits*.—(i) *General rule*.—The term *post-1986 earnings and profits* means, with respect to a specified foreign corporation and an E&P measurement date, the earnings and profits (including earnings and profits described in section 959(c)(1) and 959(c)(2)) of the specified foreign corporation (computed in accordance with sections 964(a) and 986, subject to § 1.965-4(f), and by taking into account only periods when the foreign corporation was a specified foreign corporation) accumulated in taxable years beginning after December 31, 1986, and determined—

(A) As of the E&P measurement date, except as provided in paragraph (f)(29)(ii) of this section, and

(B) Without diminution by reason of dividends distributed during the last taxable year of the foreign corporation that begins before January 1, 2018, other than dividends distributed to another specified foreign corporation to the extent the dividends increase the post-1986 earnings and profits of the distributee specified foreign corporation.

(ii) *Foreign income taxes*.—For purposes of determining a specified foreign corporation's post-1986 earnings and profits as of the E&P measurement date on November 2, 2017, in the case in which foreign income taxes (as defined in section 901(m)(5)) of the specified foreign corporation accrue after November 2, 2017, but on or before December 31, 2017, and during the specified foreign corporation's U.S. taxable year that includes November 2, 2017, the specified foreign corporation's post-1986 earnings and profits as of November 2, 2017, are reduced by the applicable portion of such foreign income taxes. For purposes of the preceding sentence, the applicable portion of the foreign income taxes is the amount of the taxes that are attributable to the portion of the taxable income (as determined under foreign law) that accrues on or before November 2, 2017.

(iii) *Deficits in earnings and profits*.—Any deficit related to post-1986 earnings and profits, including a hovering deficit (as defined in § 1.367(b)-7(d)(2)(i)), of a specified foreign corporation is taken into account for purposes of determining the post-1986 earnings and profits (including a deficit) of the specified foreign corporation.

(30) *Pro rata share*.—The term *pro rata share* means, with respect to a section 958(a) U.S. shareholder of a specified foreign corporation, a deferred foreign income corporation, or an E&P deficit foreign corporation, as applicable—

(i) With respect to the section 965(a) earnings amount of a deferred foreign income corporation, the portion of the section 965(a) earnings amount that would be treated as distributed to the section 958(a) U.S. shareholder under § 1.951-1(e), determined as of the last day of the inclusion year of the deferred foreign income corporation on which it is a specified foreign corporation;

(ii) With respect to the specified E&P deficit of an E&P deficit foreign corporation, the portion of the specified E&P deficit allocated to the section 958(a) U.S. shareholder, determined by allocating the specified E&P deficit among the shareholders of the corporation's common stock in proportion to the liquidation value of the common stock held by the shareholders, determined as of the last day of the last taxable year of the E&P deficit foreign corporation that begins before January 1, 2018, provided that—

(A) If the corporation's common stock has a liquidation value of zero and there is at least one other class of equity with a liquidation preference relative to the common stock, then the specified E&P deficit is allocated as if it were distributed in a hypothetical distribution described in § 1.951-1(e)(1)(i) with respect to the most junior class of equity with a positive liquidation value to the extent of such liquidation value, and then to the next most junior class of equity to the extent of its liquidation value, and so on, applying § 1.951-1(e) by substituting "specified E&P deficit" for "subpart F income" each place it appears and treating the amount of current earnings and profits of the corporation for the year as being equal to the specified E&P deficit of the corporation for the year; and

(B) If the corporation's common stock has a liquidation value of zero and there is no other class of equity with a liquidation preference relative to the common stock, the specified E&P deficit is allocated among the common stock using any reasonable method consistently applied; and

(iii) With respect to the cash position of a specified foreign corporation on a cash measurement date, the portion of the cash position that would be treated as distributed to the section 958(a) U.S. shareholder under § 1.951-1(e) if the cash position were subpart

F income, determined as of the close of the cash measurement date and without regard to whether the section 958(a) U.S. shareholder is a section 958(a) U.S. shareholder of the specified foreign corporation as of any other cash measurement date of the specified foreign corporation, including the final cash measurement date of the specified foreign corporation.

(31) *Second cash measurement date.*—The term *second cash measurement date* means, with respect to a specified foreign corporation, the close of the last taxable year of the specified foreign corporation that ends after November 1, 2016, and before November 2, 2017, if any.

(32) *Section 958(a) stock.*—The term *section 958(a) stock* means, with respect to a specified foreign corporation, a deferred foreign income corporation, or an E&P deficit foreign corporation, as applicable, stock of the corporation owned (directly or indirectly) by a United States shareholder within the meaning of section 958(a).

(33) *Section 958(a) U.S. shareholder.*—The term *section 958(a) U.S. shareholder* means, with respect to a specified foreign corporation, a deferred foreign income corporation, or an E&P deficit foreign corporation, as applicable, a United States shareholder of such corporation that owns section 958(a) stock of the corporation.

(34) *Section 958(a) U.S. shareholder inclusion year.*—The term *section 958(a) U.S. shareholder inclusion year* means the taxable year of a section 958(a) U.S. shareholder in which or with which the last day of the inclusion year of a deferred foreign income corporation on which it is a specified foreign corporation occurs.

(35) *Section 965 regulations.*—The term *section 965 regulations* means the regulations under §§1.965-1 through 1.965-9, collectively.

(36) *Section 965(a) earnings amount.*—The term *section 965(a) earnings amount* means, with respect to a deferred foreign income corporation, the greater of the accumulated post-1986 deferred foreign income of the deferred foreign income corporation as of the E&P measurement date on November 2, 2017, or the accumulated post-1986 deferred foreign income of the deferred foreign income corporation as of the E&P measurement date on December 31, 2017, determined in each case in the functional currency of the specified foreign corporation. If the functional currency of a specified foreign corporation changes between the two E&P measurement dates, the comparison must be made in the functional currency of the specified foreign corporation as of December 31, 2017, by translating the specified foreign corporation's accumulated post-1986 deferred foreign income as of November 2, 2017, into the new functional currency using the spot rate on November 2, 2017.

(37) *Section 965(a) inclusion.*—The term *section 965(a) inclusion* means, with respect to a person and a deferred foreign income corporation, an amount included in income by the person by reason of section 965 with respect to the deferred foreign income corporation, whether because the person is a section 958(a) U.S. shareholder of the deferred foreign income corporation with a section 965(a) inclusion amount with respect to the deferred foreign income corporation or because the person is a domestic pass-through owner with respect to a domestic pass-through entity that is a section 958(a) U.S. shareholder of the deferred foreign income corporation and the person includes in income its domestic pass-through owner share of the section 965(a) inclusion amount of the domestic pass-through entity with respect to the deferred foreign income corporation.

(38) *Section 965(a) inclusion amount.*—The term *section 965(a) inclusion amount* has the meaning provided in paragraph (b)(1) of this section.

(39) *Section 965(a) previously taxed earnings and profits.*—The term *section 965(a) previously taxed earnings and profits* has the meaning provided in §1.965-2(c).

(40) *Section 965(b) previously taxed earnings and profits.*—The term *section 965(b) previously taxed earnings and profits* has the meaning provided in §1.965-2(d).

(41) *Section 965(c) deduction.*—The term *section 965(c) deduction* means, with respect to a person, an amount allowed as a deduction to the person by reason of section 965(c), whether because the person is a section 958(a) U.S. shareholder with a section 965(c) deduction amount or because the person is a domestic pass-through owner with respect to a domestic pass-through entity that is a section 958(a) U.S. shareholder and the person takes into account its domestic pass-through owner share of the section 965(c) deduction amount of the domestic pass-through entity.

(42) *Section 965(c) deduction amount.*—The term *section 965(c) deduction amount* means an amount equal to the sum of—

(i) A section 958(a) U.S. shareholder's 8 percent rate equivalent percentage of the section 958(a) U.S. shareholder's 8 percent rate amount for the section 958(a) U.S. shareholder inclusion year, plus

(ii) The section 958(a) U.S. shareholder's 15.5 percent rate equivalent percentage of the section 958(a) U.S. shareholder's 15.5 percent rate amount for the section 958(a) U.S. shareholder inclusion year.

(43) *Short-term obligation.*—The term *short-term obligation* means any obligation with a term upon issuance that is less than one year and any loan that must be repaid at the demand of the lender (or that must be repaid within one year of such demand), but does not include any accounts receivable.

(44) *Specified E&P deficit.*—The term *specified E&P deficit* means, with respect to an E&P deficit foreign corporation, the amount of the deficit described in paragraph (f)(22)(i)(A) of this section.

(45) *Specified foreign corporation.*—(i) *General rule.*—Except as provided in paragraph (f)(45)(iii) of this section, the term *specified foreign corporation* means—

(A) A controlled foreign corporation, or

(B) A foreign corporation of which one or more domestic corporations is a United States shareholder.

(ii) *Special attribution rule.*—(A) *In general.*—Solely for purposes of determining whether a foreign corporation is a specified foreign corporation within the meaning of section 965(e)(1)(B) and paragraph (f)(45)(i)(B) of this section, stock owned, directly or indirectly, by or for—

(1) A partner (*tested partner*) will not be considered as being owned by a partnership under sections 958(b) and 318(a)(3)(A) and §1.958-2(d)(1)(i) if the tested partner owns less than ten percent of the interests in the partnership's capital and profits; and

(2) A beneficiary (*tested beneficiary*) will not be considered as being owned by a trust under sections 958(b) and 318(a)(3)(B) and §1.958-2(d)(1)(ii) if the value of the interest of the tested beneficiary, computed actuarially, whether vested or contingent, current or remainder, is less than ten percent of the value of the trust property, assuming the maximum exercise of discretion in favor of the beneficiary.

(B) *Attribution for purposes of the ten percent standard.*—For purposes of paragraph (f)(45)(ii)(A) of this section, an interest in a partnership or trust owned by a partner or beneficiary other than the tested partner or tested beneficiary will be considered as being owned by the tested partner or tested beneficiary under the principles of sections 958(b) and 318, as modified by this paragraph (f)(45)(ii), as if interests in a partnership or trust were stock.

(iii) *Passive foreign investment companies.*—A foreign corporation that is a passive foreign investment company (as defined in section 1297) with respect to a United States shareholder and that is not a controlled foreign corporation is not a specified foreign corporation of the United States shareholder.

(46) *Spot rate.*—The term *spot rate* has the meaning provided in §1.988-1(d).

(47) *United States shareholder.*—The term *United States shareholder* has the meaning provided in section 951(b).

(g) *Examples.*—The following examples illustrate the definitions and general rules set forth in this section.

(1) *Example 1. Definition of specified foreign corporation.* (i) *Facts.* A, an individual, owns 1% of the interests in a partnership, PS, and 10% by vote and value of the stock of a foreign corporation, FC. PS owns 100% of the stock of a domestic corporation, DC. A United States citizen, USI, owns an additional 10% by vote and value of the stock of FC. The remaining 80% by vote and value of the stock of FC is owned by non-United States persons that are unrelated to A, USI, DC, and PS.

(ii) *Analysis.* (A) Absent the application of sections 958(b), 318(a)(3)(A), and 318(a)(3)(C), and §1.958-2(d)(1)(i) and (iii), FC would not be a specified foreign corporation because FC is not a controlled foreign corporation and there would be no domestic corporation that is a United States shareholder of FC. However, under sections 958(b) and 318(a)(3)(A) and § 1.958-2(d)(1)(i), absent the special attribution rule in paragraph (f)(45)(ii) of this section, PS would be treated as owning 10% of the stock of FC. As a result, under sections 958(b), 318(a)(5)(A), and 318(a)(3)(C), and § 1.958-2(f)(1)(i) and (d)(1)(iii), DC would be treated as owning the stock of FC treated as owned by PS, and thus DC would be a United States shareholder with respect to FC, causing FC to be a specified foreign corporation within the meaning of section 965(e)(1)(B) and paragraph (f)(45)(i)(B) of this section. The results would be the same whether A or PS or both are domestic or foreign persons.

(B) Under the special attribution rule in paragraph (f)(45)(ii) of this section, solely for purposes of determining whether a foreign corporation is a specified foreign corporation within the meaning of section 965(e)(1)(B) and paragraph (f)(45)(i)(B) of this section, the stock of FC owned by A is not considered as being owned by PS under sections 958(b) and 318(a)(3)(A) and § 1.958-2(d)(1)(i) because A owns less than 10% of the interests in PS's capital and profits. Accordingly, FC is not a specified foreign corporation within the meaning of section 965(e)(1)(B) and paragraph (f)(45)(i)(B) of this section.

(2) *Example 2. Definition of specified foreign corporation.* (i) *Facts.* The facts are the same as in paragraph(g)(1)(i) of this section (the facts in *Example 1*), except that A is a foreign corporation wholly owned by B, a foreign corporation, and B directly owns 9% of the interests in PS.

(ii) *Analysis.* Applying the principles of sections 958(b) and 318, as modified by paragraph (f)(45)(ii) of this section, as if the interest in PS were stock, A is treated as owning the interests in PS owned by B (in addition to the 1% interest in PS that A owns directly), and thus A is not treated as owning less than 10% of the interests in PS's capital and profits. Accordingly, the special attribution rule in paragraph (f)(45)(ii) of this section does not apply, and PS is treated as owning A's stock of FC for purposes of determining whether FC is a specified foreign corporation within the meaning of section 965(e)(1)(B) and paragraph (f)(45)(i)(B) of this section. Accordingly, under the analysis described in paragraph (ii)(A) of *Example 1* of paragraph (g)(1) of this section, FC is a specified foreign corporation within the meaning of section 965(e)(1)(B) and paragraph (f)(45)(i)(B) of this section.

(3) *Example 3. Determination of accumulated post-1986 deferred foreign income.* (i) *Facts.* USP, a domestic corporation, and FP, a foreign corporation unrelated to USP, have owned 70% and 30% respectively, by vote and value, of the only class of stock of FS, a foreign corporation, from January 1, 2016, until December 31, 2017. USP and FS both have a calendar year taxable year. FS had no income until its taxable year ending December 31, 2016, in which it had 100u of income, all of which constituted subpart F income, and USP included 70u in income with respect to FS under section 951(a)(1) for such year. FS earned no income in 2017. Therefore, FS's post-1986 earnings and profits are 100u as of both E&P measurement dates.

(ii) *Analysis.* Because USP included 70u in income with respect to FS under section 951(a)(1), 70u of such post-1986 earnings and profits would, if distributed, be excluded from the gross income of USP under section 959. Thus, FS's accumulated post-1986 deferred foreign income would be reduced by 70u pursuant to section 965(d)(2)(B) and paragraph (f)(7)(i)(B) of this section. Furthermore, under paragraph (f)(7)(i)(C) of this section, the accumulated post-1986 deferred foreign income of FS is reduced by amounts that would be excluded from the gross income of FP if FP were a United States shareholder, consistent with the principles of Revenue Ruling 82-16. Accordingly, FS's accumulated post-1986 deferred foreign income is reduced by the remaining 30u of the 100u of post-1986 earnings and profits to which USP's 70u of section 951(a)(1) income inclusions were attributable. As a result, FS's accumulated post-1986 deferred foreign income is 0u (100u minus 70u minus 30u).

(4) *Example 4. Determination of status as a deferred foreign income corporation or an E&P deficit foreign corporation; specified foreign corporation is solely a deferred foreign income corporation.* (i) *Facts.* USP, a domestic corporation, owns all of the stock of FS, a foreign corporation. As of November 2, 2017, FS has a deficit in post-1986 earnings and profits of 150u. As of December 31, 2017, FS has 200u of post-1986 earnings and profits. FS does not have earnings and profits that are attributable to income of the specified foreign corporation that is effectively connected with the conduct of a trade or business within the United States and subject to tax under chapter 1, or that, if distributed, would be excluded from the gross income of a United States shareholder under section 959 or from the gross income of another shareholder if such shareholder were a United States shareholder.

(ii) *Analysis.* FS's accumulated post-1986 deferred foreign income is equal to its post-1986 earnings and profits because no adjustment to post-1986 earnings and profits is made under section 965(d)(2) or § 1.965-1(f)(7). Under paragraph (f)(17)(i) of this section, FS is a deferred foreign income corporation because FS has accumulated post-1986 deferred foreign income greater than zero as of the E&P measurement date on December 31, 2017. In addition, under paragraph (f)(17)(ii) of this section, because FS is a deferred foreign income corporation, FS is not also an E&P deficit foreign corporation, notwithstanding that FS has a deficit in post-1986 earnings and profits as of the E&P measurement date on November 2, 2017.

(5) *Example 5. Determination of status as a deferred foreign income corporation or an E&P deficit foreign corporation; specified foreign corporation is neither a deferred foreign income corporation nor an E&P deficit foreign corporation.* (i) *Facts.* USP, a domestic corporation, owns all of the stock of FS, a foreign corporation. As of both November 2, 2017, and December 31, 2017, FS has 100u of earnings and profits described in section 959(c)(2) and a deficit of 90u in earnings and profits described in section 959(c)(3), all of which were accumulated in taxable years beginning after December 31, 1986, while FS was a specified foreign corporation. Accordingly, as of both November 2, 2017, and December 31, 2017, FS has 10u of post-1986 earnings and profits.

(ii) *Analysis.* (A) *Determination of status as a deferred foreign income corporation.* Under paragraph (f)(17) of this section, for purposes of determining whether FS is a deferred foreign income corporation, a determination must be made whether FS has accumulated post-1986 deferred foreign income greater than zero as of either the E&P measurement date on November 2, 2017, or the E&P measurement date on December 31, 2017. Under section 965(d)(2) and paragraph (f)(7) of this section, FS's accumulated post-1986 deferred foreign income is its post-1986 earnings and profits, except to the extent such earnings and profits are attributable to income of the specified foreign corporation that is effectively connected with the conduct of a trade or business within the United States and subject to tax under chapter 1, or that, if distributed, would be excluded from the gross income of a United States shareholder under section 959 or from the gross income of another shareholder if such shareholder were a United States shareholder. Disregarding FS's 100u of post-1986 earnings and profits described in paragraph (f)(7)(i)(B) of this section, FS has a 90u deficit in accumulated post-1986 deferred foreign income as of both E&P measurement dates. Accordingly, FS does not have accumulated post-1986 deferred foreign income greater than zero as of either E&P measurement date, and, therefore, FS is not a deferred foreign income corporation.

(B) *Determination of status as an E&P deficit foreign corporation.* Under paragraph (f)(22)(i) of this section, for purposes of determining whether FS is an E&P deficit foreign corporation, a determination must be made whether FS has a deficit in post-1986 earnings and profits as of the E&P measurement date on November 2, 2017. Under paragraph (f)(22)(ii) of this section, because the deficit in the earnings and profits of FS described in section 959(c)(3) of 90u does not exceed the earnings and profits of FS described in section 959(c)(2) of 100u, FS does not have a deficit in post-1986 earnings and profits as of the E&P measurement date on November 2, 2017, and, therefore, FS is not an E&P deficit foreign corporation. Accordingly, FS is neither a deferred foreign income corporation nor an E&P deficit foreign corporation.

(6) *Example 6. Application of currency translation rules.* (i) *Facts.* As of November 2, 2017, and December 31, 2017, USP, a domestic corporation, owns all of the stock of CFC1, an E&P deficit foreign corporation with the "u" as its functional currency; CFC2, an E&P deficit foreign corporation with the "v" as its functional currency; CFC3, a deferred foreign income corporation with the "y" as its functional currency; and CFC4, a deferred foreign income corporation with the "z" as its functional currency. USP, CFC1, CFC2, CFC3, and CFC4 each have a calendar year taxable year. As of December 31, 2017, 1u=$1, .75v=$1, .50y=$1, and .25z=$1. CFC1 has a specified E&P deficit of 100u, CFC2 has a specified E&P deficit of 120v, CFC3 has a section 965(a) earnings amount of 50y, and CFC4 has a section 965(a) earnings amount of 75z.

(ii) *Analysis.* (A) Under paragraph (f)(38) of this section, for purposes of determining USP's section 965(a) inclusion amounts with respect to CFC3 and CFC4, the section 965(a) earnings amount of each of CFC3 and CFC4 is translated into U.S. dollars at the spot rate on December 31, 2017, which equals $100 (50y at .50y=$1) and $300 (75z at .25z=$1), respectively. Furthermore, USP's pro rata share of the section 965(a) earnings amounts, as translated, is $100 and $300, respectively, or 100% of each section 965(a) earnings amount.

(B) Under paragraph (f)(9) of this section, for purposes of determining USP's aggregate foreign E&P deficit, the specified E&P deficit of each of CFC1 and CFC2 is translated into U.S. dollars at the spot rate on December 31, 2017, which equals $100 (100u at 1u=$1) and

$160 (120v at .75v=$1), respectively. Furthermore USP's pro rata share of each specified E&P deficit, as translated, is $100 and $160, respectively, or 100% of each specified E&P deficit. Therefore, USP's aggregate foreign E&P deficit is $260.

(C) Under section 965(b)(1) and paragraph (b)(2) of this section, for purposes of determining USP's section 965(a) inclusion amount with respect to each of CFC3 and CFC4, the U.S. dollar amount of USP's pro rata share of the section 965(a) earnings amount of each of CFC3 and CFC4 is reduced by each of CFC3 and CFC4's allocable share of USP's aggregate foreign E&P deficit. Under section 965(b)(2) and paragraph (f)(11) of this section, CFC3's allocable share of USP's aggregate foreign E&P deficit of $260 is $65 ($260 x ($100/$400)) and CFC4's allocable share of USP's aggregate foreign E&P deficit is $195 ($260 x ($300/400)). After reduction under section 965(b)(1) and paragraph (b)(2) of this section, the section 965(a) inclusion amount of USP with respect to CFC3 is $35 ($100-$65) and the section 965(a) inclusion amount of USP with respect to CFC4 is $105 ($300-$195). Under §1.965-2(c), the section 965(a) previously taxed earnings and profits of each of CFC3 and CFC4, translated into the respective functional currencies of CFC3 and CFC4 at the spot rate on December 31, 2017, are 17.5y ($35 at .50y=$1) and 26.25z ($105 at .25z=$1), respectively. Under §1.965-6(b)(1), for purposes of applying section 960(a)(1), the amounts treated as a dividend paid by each of CFC3 and CFC4, translated into the respective functional currencies of CFC3 and CFC4 at the spot rate on December 31, 2017, are 17.5y ($35 at .50y=$1) and 26.25z ($105 at .25z=$1).

(D) For purposes of determining the section 965(b) previously taxed earnings and profits of each of CFC3 and CFC4 under section 965(b)(4)(A) and §1.965-2(d)(1) as a result of the reduction to USP's section 965(a) inclusion amounts with respect to CFC3 and CFC4, the amount of the aggregate foreign E&P deficit of USP allocated to each of CFC3 and CFC4 under section 965(b)(2) and paragraph (f)(11) of this section, translated into the respective functional currencies of CFC3 and CFC4 at the spot rate on December 31, 2017, is 32.5y ($65 at .50y=$1) and 48.75z ($195 at .25z=$1), respectively.

(7) *Example 7. Determination of cash measurement dates and pro rata shares of cash positions.* (i) *Facts.* Except as otherwise provided, for all relevant periods, USP, a domestic corporation, has owned directly at least 10% of the stock of CFC1, CFC2, CFC3, and CFC4, each a foreign corporation. CFC1 and CFC2 have calendar year taxable years. CFC3 and CFC4 have taxable years that end on November 30. No entity has a short taxable year, except as a result of the transactions described below.

(A) USP transferred all of its stock of CFC2 to an unrelated person on June 30, 2016, at which point USP ceased to be a United States shareholder with respect to CFC2.

(B) CFC4 dissolved on December 30, 2010, and, as a result, its final taxable year ended on December 30, 2010.

(ii) *Analysis.* Each of CFC1, CFC2, CFC3, and CFC4 is a specified foreign corporation of USP, subject to the sale of CFC2 on June 30, 2016, and the dissolution of CFC4 on December 30, 2010. Under the definition of aggregate foreign cash position in paragraph (f)(8)(i) of this section, the definition of pro rata share of a cash position in paragraph (f)(30)(iii) of this section, and the definitions of the final cash measurement date, second cash measurement date, and first cash measurement date in paragraphs (f)(24), (25), and (31) of this section, the cash measurement dates of the specified foreign corporations to be taken into account by USP in determining its aggregate foreign cash position are summarized in the following table:

	Cash Measurement Dates		
	Final	Second	First
CFC1	December 31, 2017	December 31, 2016	December 31, 2015
CFC2	N/A	N/A	December 31, 2015
CFC3	November 30, 2018	November 30, 2016	November 30, 2015
CFC4	N/A	N/A	N/A

(8) *Example 8. Determination of section 958(a) U.S. shareholder in case of a controlled domestic partnership.* (i) *Facts.* USP, a domestic corporation, owns all of the stock of CFC1 and CFC2. CFC1 and CFC2 own 60% and 40%, respectively, of the interests in the capital and profits of DPS, a domestic partnership. DPS owns all of the stock of CFC3 and CFC4. This ownership structure has existed since the date of formation of CFC1, CFC2, CFC3, and CFC4. CFC1, CFC2, CFC3, and CFC4 are each a foreign corporation. USP, DPS, CFC1, CFC2, CFC3, and CFC4 have calendar year taxable years. On both E&P measurement dates, CFC3 has 50u of accumulated post-1986 deferred foreign income. On both E&P measurement dates, CFC4 has a deficit in post-1986 earnings and profits of 30u. On all cash measurement dates, CFC1, CFC2, and CFC3 each have a cash position of 0u, and CFC4 has a cash position of 200u.

(ii) *Analysis.* DPS is a controlled domestic partnership with respect to USP within the meaning of paragraph (e)(2) of this section because more than 50% of the interests in its capital and profits are owned by persons related to USP within the meaning of section 267(b), CFC1 and CFC2, and thus DPS is controlled by USP and related persons. Without regard to paragraph (e) of this section, DPS is a section 958(a) U.S. shareholder of CFC3 and CFC4, each of which is a controlled foreign corporation. If DPS were treated as foreign, CFC3 and CFC4 would each continue to be a controlled foreign corporation, and USP would be treated as a section 958(a) U.S. shareholder of each of CFC3 and CFC4, and would be treated as owning (within the meaning of section 958(a)) tested section 958(a) stock of each of CFC3 and CFC4 through CFC1 and CFC2, which are both partners in DPS. Thus, under paragraph (e)(1) of this section, DPS is treated as a foreign partnership for purposes of determining the section 958(a) U.S. shareholder of both CFC3 and CFC4 and the section 958(a) stock of both CFC3 and CFC4 owned by the section 958(a) U.S. shareholder. Thus, USP's pro rata share of CFC3's section 965(a) earnings amount is 50u, and its pro rata share of CFC4's specified E&P deficit is 30u. USP's aggregate foreign cash position is 200u. DPS is not a section 958(a) U.S. shareholder with respect to either CFC3 or CFC4. [Reg. §1.965-1.]

☐ [*T.D.* 9846, 2-4-2019 (*corrected* 4-9-2019).]

§1.965-2. Adjustments to earnings and profits and basis.—(a) *Scope.*—This section provides rules relating to adjustments to earnings and profits and basis to determine and account for the application of section 965(a) and (b) and §1.965-1(b) and a rule that limits the amount of gain recognized under section 961(b)(2) by reason of distributions attributable to section 965 previously taxed earnings and profits (as defined in paragraph (g)(1)(ii) of this section) in the inclusion year. Paragraph (b) of this section provides rules relating to adjustments to earnings and profits of a specified foreign corporation for purposes of applying sections 902, 959, 960, and 965. Paragraph (c) of this section provides rules regarding adjustments to earnings and profits by reason of section 965(a). Paragraph (d) of this section provides rules regarding adjustments to earnings and profits by reason of section 965(b). Paragraph (e) provides rules regarding adjustments to basis by reason of section 965(a). Paragraph (f) of this section provides an election to make certain adjustments to basis corresponding to adjustments to earnings and profits by reason of section 965(b). Paragraph (g) of this section provides rules that limit the amount of gain recognized in connection with the application of section 961(b)(2) and that require related reductions in basis. Paragraph (h) of this section provides rules regarding basis adjustments. Paragraph (i) of this section provides definitions that apply for purposes of this section. Paragraph (j) of this section provides examples illustrating the application of this section.

(b) *Determination of and adjustments to earnings and profits of a specified foreign corporation for purposes of applying sections 902, 959, 960, and 965.*—For the taxable year of a specified foreign corporation in which an E&P measurement date occurs, and the last taxable year of a specified foreign corporation that begins before January 1, 2018, and the taxable year of a section 958(a) U.S. shareholder in which or with which any such year ends, the adjustments to earnings and profits described in paragraphs (b)(1) through (b)(5) of this section apply in sequence. For purposes of determining the consequences under sections 902 and 960 of a distribution or an inclusion under section 951(a)(1), after the application of those paragraphs, the ordering rule in §1.960-1(i)(2) applies except that section 902 is applied with respect to any distributions from the specified foreign corporation described in paragraph (b)(2) of this section that are not disregarded under §1.965-4 before section 960 is applied with respect to an inclusion or distribution described in paragraph (b)(3), (b)(4), or (b)(5) of this section.

(1) Each of the subpart F income of the specified foreign corporation and the amount required to be included in income under section 1248, if any, are determined without regard to section 965(a),

but taking into account any relevant distributions, and earnings and profits of the specified foreign corporation that are described in section 959(c)(2) with respect to the section 958(a) U.S. shareholder are increased to the extent of the section 958(a) U.S. shareholder's inclusion under section 951(a)(1)(A) without regard to section 965(a) (including to the extent provided in section 959(e)).

(2) The treatment of a distribution by the specified foreign corporation to another specified foreign corporation that is made before January 1, 2018, and, in the case of a taxable year of a specified foreign corporation before its last taxable year that begins before January 1, 2018, any other distribution from the specified foreign corporation made before the relevant E&P measurement date, is determined under section 959.

(3) Each of the post-1986 earnings and profits (including a deficit) of the specified foreign corporation, the accumulated post-1986 deferred foreign income of the specified foreign corporation, the section 965(a) earnings amount of the specified foreign corporation, and the section 965(a) inclusion amount with respect to the specified foreign corporation, if any, is determined, taking into account the rules of § 1.965-4, and the earnings and profits (including a deficit) of the specified foreign corporation are adjusted as provided in paragraphs (c) and (d) of this section. For a rule disregarding subpart F income earned after an E&P measurement date for purposes of calculating accumulated post-1986 deferred foreign income as of the E&P measurement date, see § 1.965-1(f)(7)(ii).

(4) The treatment of distributions described in paragraph (b)(2) of this section that are disregarded under § 1.965-4 is redetermined (if necessary) and the treatment of all distributions from the specified foreign corporation other than those described in paragraph (b)(2) of this section is determined under section 959.

(5) An amount is determined under section 956 with respect to the specified foreign corporation and the section 958(a) U.S. shareholder; earnings and profits of the specified foreign corporation described in section 959(c)(2) with respect to the section 958(a) U.S. shareholder are reclassified as earnings and profits described in section 959(c)(1) with respect to the section 958(a) U.S. shareholder to the extent the amount determined under section 956 would, but for section 959(a)(2), be included by the section 958(a) U.S. shareholder under section 951(a)(1)(B); and earnings and profits described in section 959(c)(1) with respect to the section 958(a) U.S. shareholder are further increased to the extent of the section 958(a) U.S. shareholder's inclusion under section 951(a)(1)(B).

(c) *Adjustments to earnings and profits by reason of section 965(a).*—The earnings and profits of a deferred foreign income corporation described in section 959(c)(2) with respect to a section 958(a) U.S. shareholder are increased by an amount equal to the section 965(a) inclusion amount of the section 958(a) U.S. shareholder with respect to the deferred foreign income corporation, if any, translated (if necessary) into the functional currency of the deferred foreign income corporation using the spot rate on December 31, 2017, provided the section 965(a) inclusion amount is included in income by the section 958(a) U.S. shareholder. For purposes of the section 965 regulations, the earnings and profits described in section 959(c)(2) by reason of this paragraph (c) and the earnings and profits initially described in section 959(c)(2) by reason of this paragraph (c) but subsequently reclassified as earnings and profits described in section 959(c)(1), if any, are referred to as *section 965(a) previously taxed earnings and profits*. Furthermore, the earnings and profits (including a deficit) of the deferred foreign income corporation that are described in section 959(c)(3) (or that would be described in section 959(c)(3) but for the application of section 965(a) and the section 965 regulations) are reduced (or, in the case of a deficit, increased) by an amount equal to the section 965(a) previously taxed earnings and profits.

(d) *Adjustments to earnings and profits by reason of section 965(b).*—(1) *Adjustments to earnings and profits described in section 959(c)(2) and (c)(3) of deferred foreign income corporations.*—The earnings and profits of a deferred foreign income corporation described in section 959(c)(2) with respect to a section 958(a) U.S. shareholder are increased by an amount equal to the reduction to the section 958(a) U.S. shareholder's pro rata share of the section 965(a) earnings amount of the deferred foreign income corporation under section 965(b), § 1.965-1(b)(2), and § 1.965-8(b), as applicable, translated (if necessary) into the functional currency of the deferred foreign income corporation using the spot rate on December 31, 2017, provided the section 958(a) U.S. shareholder includes the section 965(a) inclusion amount (if any) with respect to the deferred foreign income corporation in income. For purposes of the section 965 regulations, the earnings and profits described in section 959(c)(2) by reason of this paragraph (d) and the earnings and profits initially described in section 959(c)(2) by reason of this paragraph (d) but subsequently reclassified as earnings and profits described in section 959(c)(1) are referred to as *section 965(b) previously taxed earnings and profits*, and are treated as having been previously included in the gross income of the section 958(a) U.S. shareholder under section 951 for purposes of section 1248(d)(1). Furthermore, the earnings and profits (including a deficit) described in section 959(c)(3) of the deferred foreign income corporation (or that would be described in section 959(c)(3) but for the application of section 965(b) and the section 965 regulations) are reduced (or, in the case of a deficit, increased) by an amount equal to the section 965(b) previously taxed earnings and profits.

(2) *Adjustments to earnings and profits described in section 959(c)(3) of E&P deficit foreign corporations.*—(i) *Increase in earnings and profits by an amount equal to the portion of the section 958(a) U.S. shareholder's pro rata share of the specified E&P deficit taken into account.*—(A) *In general.*—For an E&P deficit foreign corporation's last taxable year that begins before January 1, 2018, the earnings and profits of the E&P deficit foreign corporation described in section 959(c)(3) are increased by an amount equal to the portion of a section 958(a) U.S. shareholder's pro rata share of the specified E&P deficit of the E&P deficit foreign corporation taken into account under section 965(b), § 1.965-1(b)(2), and § 1.965-8(b), as determined under paragraph (d)(2)(ii) of this section, translated (if necessary) into the functional currency of the E&P deficit foreign corporation using the spot rate on December 31, 2017. For purposes of section 316, the earnings and profits of the E&P deficit foreign corporation attributable to the increase described in the preceding sentence are not treated as earnings and profits of the taxable year described in section 316(a)(2). See also § 1.965-6(b)(3) for the timing of this adjustment for purposes of determining foreign taxes deemed paid under sections 902 and 960.

(B) *Reduction of a qualified deficit.*—For purposes of section 952, a section 958(a) U.S. shareholder's pro rata share of the earnings and profits of an E&P deficit foreign corporation is increased by an amount equal to the portion of the section 958(a) U.S. shareholder's pro rata share of the specified E&P deficit of the E&P deficit foreign corporation taken into account under section 965(b), § 1.965-1(b)(2), or § 1.965-8(b), as applicable, as determined under paragraph (d)(2)(ii) of this section, translated (if necessary) into the functional currency of the E&P deficit foreign corporation using the spot rate on December 31, 2017, and such increase is attributable to the same activity to which the deficit so taken into account was attributable.

(ii) *Determination of portion of a section 958(a) U.S. shareholder's pro rata share of a specified E&P deficit taken into account.*—(A) *In general.*—The portion of a section 958(a) U.S. shareholder's pro rata share of a specified E&P deficit of an E&P deficit foreign corporation taken into account under section 965(b), § 1.965-1(b)(2), or § 1.965-8(b), as applicable, is 100 percent of the section 958(a) U.S. shareholder's pro rata share of the specified E&P deficit if either of the following conditions is satisfied:

(*1*) The section 958(a) U.S. shareholder (including a consolidated group of which the section 958(a) U.S. shareholder is a member) does not have an excess aggregate foreign E&P deficit (as defined in § 1.965-8(f)(7)(i)), or

(*2*) If the section 958(a) U.S. shareholder is a member of an affiliated group in which not all members are members of the same consolidated group, the amount described in § 1.965-8(f)(1)(i)(B) with respect to the affiliated group is equal to or greater than the amount described § 1.965-8(f)(1)(i)(A).

(B) *Designation of portion of a section 958(a) U.S. shareholder's pro rata share of a specified E&P deficit taken into account.*—If neither the condition in paragraph (d)(2)(ii)(A)(*1*) nor the condition in paragraph (d)(2)(ii)(A)(*2*) is satisfied with respect to a section 958(a) U.S. shareholder, then the section 958(a) U.S. shareholder must designate the portion taken into account by reporting to each E&P deficit foreign corporation of the section 958(a) U.S. shareholder, and maintaining, in its books and records, a statement setting forth the following information—

(*1*) The portion of the section 958(a) U.S. shareholder's pro rata share of the specified E&P deficit of the E&P deficit foreign corporation taken into account under section 965(b), § 1.965-1(b)(2), or § 1.965-8(b), as designated under § 1.965-8(c), as applicable, and

(*2*) In the case of an E&P deficit foreign corporation that has a qualified deficit (as determined under section 952 and § 1.952-1), the portion (if any) of the section 958(a) shareholder's pro rata share of the specified E&P deficit of the E&P deficit foreign corporation taken into account under paragraph (d)(2)(ii)(B)(*1*) of this section that is attributable to a qualified deficit, including the qualified activities to which such portion is attributable.

(e) *Adjustments to basis by reason of section 965(a).*—(1) *General rule.*—Except as provided in paragraph (e)(2) of this section, a section 958(a) U.S. shareholder's basis in section 958(a) stock of a deferred foreign income corporation, or a section 958(a) U.S. shareholder's basis in applicable property with respect to a deferred foreign income corporation, is increased by the section 958(a) U.S. shareholder's section 965(a) inclusion amount with respect to the deferred foreign income corporation included in income by the section 958(a) U.S. shareholder. *See* section 961(a).

(2) *Section 962 election.*—In the case of a section 958(a) U.S. shareholder who has made an election under section 962 for a section 958(a) U.S. shareholder's inclusion year, the increase in basis in the section 958(a) U.S. shareholder's section 958(a) stock of, or applicable property with respect to, a deferred foreign income corporation cannot exceed an amount equal to the amount of tax paid under chapter 1 of the Code with respect to the section 958(a) U.S. shareholder's section 965(a) inclusion amount with respect to the deferred foreign income corporation, taking into account any section 965(h) election made by the section 958(a) U.S. shareholder.

(f) *Adjustments to basis by reason of section 965(b).*—(1) *In general.*—Except as provided in paragraph (f)(2) of this section, no adjustments to basis of stock or property are made under section 961 (or any other provision of the Code) to take into account the reduction to a section 958(a) U.S. shareholder's pro rata share of the section 965(a) earnings amount of a deferred foreign income corporation under section 965(b), § 1.965-1(b)(2), or § 1.965-8(b), as applicable.

(2) *Election to make adjustments to basis to account for the application of section 965(b).*—(i) *In general.*—If a section 958(a) U.S. shareholder makes the election as provided in this paragraph (f)(2), the adjustments to basis described in paragraph (f)(2)(ii) of this section are made with respect to each deferred foreign income corporation and each E&P deficit foreign corporation in which the section 958(a) U.S. shareholder owns section 958(a) stock.

(ii) *Basis adjustments.*—(A) *Increase in basis with respect to a deferred foreign income corporation.*—(*1*) *In general.*—Except as provided in paragraphs (f)(2)(ii)(A)(*2*) and (C) of this section, a section 958(a) U.S. shareholder's basis in section 958(a) stock of a deferred foreign income corporation, or a section 958(a) U.S. shareholder's basis in applicable property with respect to a deferred foreign income corporation, is increased by an amount equal to the section 965(b) previously taxed earnings and profits of the deferred foreign income corporation with respect to the section 958(a) U.S. shareholder, translated (if necessary) into U.S. dollars using the spot rate on December 31, 2017.

(*2*) *Limited basis adjustment.*—A section 958(a) U.S. shareholder may, in lieu of applying paragraph (f)(2)(ii)(A)(*1*) of this section, designate the amount by which it increases its basis in section 958(a) stock of, or applicable property with respect to, a deferred foreign income corporation, provided that—

(*i*) The increase does not exceed the section 965(b) previously taxed earnings and profits of the deferred foreign income corporation with respect to the section 958(a) U.S. shareholder, translated (if necessary) into U.S. dollars using the spot rate on December 31, 2017; and

(*ii*) The aggregate amount of a section 958(a) U.S. shareholder's increases in basis with respect to stock or applicable property pursuant to paragraph (f)(2)(ii)(A)(*2*) of this section does not exceed the aggregate amount of the section 958(a) U.S. shareholder's reductions in basis pursuant to paragraph (f)(2)(ii)(B) of this section subject to the limitation under paragraph (f)(2)(ii)(B)(*2*) of this section.

(B) *Reduction in basis with respect to an E&P deficit foreign corporation.*—(*1*) In *general.* Except as provided in paragraphs (f)(2)(ii)(B)(*2*) and (f)(2)(ii)(C) of this section, a section 958(a) U.S. shareholder's basis in section 958(a) stock of an E&P deficit foreign corporation, or a section 958(a) U.S. shareholder's basis in applicable property with respect to an E&P deficit foreign corporation, is reduced by an amount equal to the portion of the section 958(a) U.S. shareholder's pro rata share of the specified E&P deficit of the E&P deficit foreign corporation taken into account under section 965(b), § 1.965-1(b)(2), and § 1.965-8(b), as applicable, as determined under paragraph (d)(2)(ii) of this section, translated (if necessary) into U.S. dollars using the spot rate on December 31, 2017. For rules requiring gain recognition, see paragraph (h)(3) of this section.

(*2*) *Limited basis adjustment.*—If a section 958(a) U.S. shareholder adjusts its basis in section 958(a) stock of, or applicable property with respect to, one or more deferred foreign income corporations under paragraph (f)(2)(ii)(A)(*2*) of this section, the section 958(a) U.S. shareholder's aggregate reductions in basis in section 958(a) stock of, or applicable property with respect to, an E&P deficit foreign corporation pursuant to paragraph (f)(2)(ii)(B)(*1*) of this section on a day may not exceed the amount of the section 958(a) U.S. shareholder's basis in the section 958(a) stock of, or applicable property with respect to, such E&P deficit foreign corporation, determined without taking into account specified basis adjustments to the section 958(a) stock of, or applicable property with respect to, such E&P deficit foreign corporation.

(C) *Section 962 election.*—In the case of a section 958(a) U.S. shareholder who has made an election under section 962 for a section 958(a) U.S. shareholder's inclusion year, the adjustments provided in paragraphs (f)(2)(ii)(A) and (B) of this section do not apply.

(iii) *Rules regarding the election.*—(A) *Consistency requirement.*—In order for the election described in this paragraph (f)(2) to be effective, a section 958(a) U.S. shareholder and each section 958(a) U.S. shareholder of an E&P deficit foreign corporation or of a deferred foreign income corporation with respect to which the second section 958(a) U.S. shareholder's pro rata share of the section 965(a) earnings amount is reduced under section 965(b), § 1.965-1(b)(2), or § 1.965-8(b) that is related to the first section 958(a) U.S. shareholder must make the election described in this paragraph (f)(2). For purposes of this paragraph (f)(2)(iii)(A), a person is treated as related to a section 958(a) U.S. shareholder if the person bears a relationship to the section 958(a) U.S. shareholder described in section 267(b) or 707(b).

(B) *Manner of making election.*—(*1*) *Timing.*—(*i*) *In general.*—Except as provided in paragraph (f)(2)(iii)(B)(*1*)(*ii*) of this section, the election provided in this paragraph (f)(2) must be made no later than the due date (taking into account extensions, if any) for the section 958(a) U.S. shareholder's return for the first taxable year that includes the last day of the last taxable year of a deferred foreign income corporation or E&P deficit foreign corporation of the shareholder that begins before January 1, 2018. Relief is not available under § 301.9100-2 or 301.9100-3 to file a late election. Except as provided in paragraph (f)(2)(iii)(B)(*1*)(*ii*) of this section, the election provided in this paragraph (f)(2) is irrevocable.

(*ii*) *Transition rule.*—If the due date referred to in paragraph (f)(2)(iii)(B)(*1*)(*i*) of this section occurs before May 6, 2019, the election must be made by May 6, 2019. In the case of an election made before February 5, 2019, the election may be revoked by attaching a statement, signed under penalties of perjury, to an amended return filed by May 6, 2019. The statement must contain the section 958(a) U.S. shareholder's name and taxpayer identification number and a statement that the section 958(a) U.S. shareholder and all related persons, as defined in paragraph (f)(2)(iii)(A) of this section, that are section 958(a) U.S. shareholders of E&P deficit foreign corporations or of deferred foreign income corporations with respect to which the section 958(a) U.S. shareholder's pro rata share of the section 965(a) earnings amount is reduced under section 965(b), § 1.965-1(b)(2), or § 1.965-8(b) revoke the election provided in this paragraph (f)(2).

(*2*) *Election statement.*—Except as otherwise provided in publications, forms, instructions, or other guidance, to make the election provided in this paragraph (f)(2), a section 958(a) U.S. shareholder must attach a statement, signed under penalties of perjury consistent with the rules for signatures applicable to the section 958(a) U.S. shareholders return, to its return for the first taxable year that includes the last day of the last taxable year of a deferred foreign income corporation or E&P deficit foreign corporation of the shareholder that begins before January 1, 2018. The statement must include the section 958(a) U.S. shareholder's name, taxpayer identification number, and a statement that the section 958(a) U.S. shareholder and all related persons, as defined in paragraph (f)(2)(iii)(A) of this section, that are section 958(a) U.S. shareholders of E&P deficit foreign corporations or of deferred foreign income corporations with respect to which the section 958(a) U.S. shareholder's pro rata share of the section 965(a) earnings amount is reduced under section 965(b), § 1.965-1(b)(2), or § 1.965-8(b) make the election provided in this paragraph (f)(2). If the section 958(a) U.S. shareholder increases its basis in stock or applicable property under paragraph (f)(2)(ii)(A)(2) of this section and decreases its basis in stock or applicable property pursuant to paragraph (f)(2)(ii)(B) of this section subject to the limitation under paragraph (f)(2)(ii)(B)(2) of this section, the election statement must so indicate. The attachment of an unsigned copy of the election statement to the timely-filed return for the relevant taxable year satisfies the signature requirement of this paragraph (f)(2)(iii)(B)(2) if the section 958(a) U.S. shareholder retains the original signed election statement in the manner specified by § 1.6001-1(e).

(g) *Gain reduction rule.*—(1) *Reduction in gain recognized under section 961(b)(2) by reason of distributions attributable to section 965 previously taxed earnings and profits in the inclusion year.*—(i) *In general.*—If a section 958(a) U.S. shareholder receives a distribution from a deferred foreign income corporation (including through a chain of ownership described under section 958(a)) during the inclusion year of the deferred foreign income corporation that is attributable to section 965 previously taxed earnings and profits of the deferred foreign income corporation, then the amount of gain that otherwise would be recognized under section 961(b)(2) by the section 958(a) U.S. shareholder with respect to the section 958(a) U.S. shareholder's section 958(a) stock of the deferred foreign income corporation or interest in applicable property with respect to the deferred foreign income corporation is reduced (but not below zero) by an amount equal to the section 965 previously taxed earnings and profits of the deferred foreign income corporation with respect to the section 958(a) U.S. shareholder, translated (if necessary) into U.S. dollars at the spot rate on December 31, 2017.

(ii) *Definition of section 965 previously taxed earnings and profits.*—For purposes of paragraph (g)(1)(i) of this section, the term *section 965 previously taxed earnings and profits* means, with respect to a deferred foreign income corporation and a section 958(a) U.S. shareholder, the sum of the section 965(a) previously taxed earnings and profits of the deferred foreign income corporation with respect to the section 958(a) U.S. shareholder, and, if the section 958(a) U.S. shareholder has made the election described in paragraph (f)(2) of this section, the section 965(b) previously taxed earnings and profits of the deferred foreign income corporation with respect to the section 958(a) U.S. shareholder.

(2) *Reduction in basis by an amount equal to the gain reduction amount.*—If a section 958(a) U.S. shareholder does not recognize gain under section 961(b)(2) by reason of paragraph (g)(1) of this section with respect to a distribution from a deferred foreign income corporation (including through a chain of ownership described under section 958(a)), the section 958(a) U.S. shareholder's basis in the section 958(a) stock of the deferred foreign income corporation, or the section 958(a) U.S. shareholder's basis in the applicable property with respect to the deferred foreign income corporation, is reduced by the amount of gain that would otherwise be recognized by the section 958(a) U.S. shareholder without regard to paragraph (g)(1) of this section.

(h) *Rules of application for specified basis adjustments.*—This paragraph (h) applies for purposes of making any adjustment to the basis of section 958(a) stock or applicable property with respect to a specified foreign corporation described in paragraph (e), (f)(2), or (g)(2) of this section (collectively, *specified basis adjustments*, and each a *specified basis adjustment*).

(1) *Timing of basis adjustments.*—Except as provided in paragraph (e)(2) of this section, a specified basis adjustment to section 958(a) stock or applicable property with respect to a specified foreign corporation is made as of the last day of the last taxable year of the specified foreign corporation that begins before January 1, 2018, on which it is a specified foreign corporation.

(2) *Netting of basis adjustments.*—If one or more specified basis adjustments occur on the same day with respect to the same section 958(a) stock or applicable property, a single basis adjustment is made as of the close of such day with respect to such stock or applicable property in an amount equal to the net amount, if any, of the increase or reduction, as applicable.

(3) *Gain recognition for reduction in excess of basis.*—The excess (if any) of a net reduction in basis with respect to section 958(a) stock or applicable property of a section 958(a) U.S. shareholder by reason of one or more specified basis adjustments over the section 958(a) U.S. shareholder's basis in such stock or applicable property without regard to the specified basis adjustments is treated as gain from the sale or exchange of property.

(4) *Adjustments with respect to each share.*—(i) *Section 958(a) stock.*—If a specified basis adjustment is made with respect to section 958(a) stock, the specified basis adjustment is made with respect to each share of the section 958(a) stock in a manner consistent with the section 958(a) U.S. shareholder's pro rata share of the section 965(a) earnings amount or specified E&P deficit, as applicable, by reason of such share.

(ii) *Applicable property.*—If a specified basis adjustment is made with respect to applicable property, the adjustment is made with respect to the applicable property in a manner consistent with the application of paragraph (h)(4)(i) of this section.

(5) *Stock or property for which adjustments are made.*—(i) *In general.*—Except as provided in paragraph (h)(5)(ii) of this section, a specified basis adjustment is made solely with respect to section 958(a) stock owned by the section 958(a) U.S. shareholder within the meaning of section 958(a)(1)(A) or applicable property owned directly by the section 958(a) U.S. shareholder.

(ii) *Special rule for an interest in a foreign pass-through entity.*—If the applicable property of the section 958(a) U.S. shareholder described in paragraph (h)(5)(i) of this section is an interest in a foreign pass-through entity, then, for purposes of determining the foreign pass-through entity's basis in section 958(a) stock or applicable property, as applicable, with respect to the section 958(a) U.S. shareholder, a specified basis adjustment is made with respect to section 958(a) stock or applicable property of the section 958(a) U.S. shareholder owned through the foreign pass-through entity in the same manner as if the section 958(a) stock or applicable property were owned directly by the section 958(a) U.S. shareholder. In the case of tiered foreign pass-through entities, this paragraph (h)(5)(ii) applies with respect to each foreign pass-through entity.

(i) *Definitions.*—This paragraph (i) provides definitions that apply for purposes of this section.

(1) *Applicable property.*—The term *applicable property* means, with respect to a section 958(a) U.S. shareholder and a specified foreign corporation, property owned by the section 958(a) U.S. shareholder (including through one or more foreign pass-through entities) by reason of which the section 958(a) U.S. shareholder is considered under section 958(a)(2) as owning section 958(a) stock of the specified foreign corporation.

(2) *Foreign pass-through entity.*—The term *foreign pass-through entity* means a foreign partnership or a foreign estate or trust (as defined in section 7701(a)(31)) (including a controlled domestic partnership treated as a foreign partnership pursuant to § 1.965-1(e)).

(3) *Property.*—The term *property* has the meaning provided in § 1.961-1(b)(1).

(j) *Examples.*—The following examples illustrate the application of this section.

(1) *Example 1. Determination of accumulated post-1986 deferred foreign income with subpart F income earned before E&P measurement date on November 2, 2017.* (i) *Facts.* USP, a domestic corporation, owns all of the stock of CFC1, a foreign corporation, which owns all of the stock of CFC2, also a foreign corporation. USP, CFC1, and CFC2 all have taxable years ending December 31, 2017. As of January 1, 2017, CFC1 has no earnings and profits, and CFC2 has 100u of earnings and profits described in section 959(c)(3) that were accumulated in taxable years beginning after December 31, 1986, while CFC2 was a specified foreign corporation, and $21x of post-1986 foreign income taxes. None of CFC2's earnings and profits are attributable to income treated as effectively connected with the conduct of a trade or business within the United States. On March 1, 2017, CFC1 earns 30u of subpart F income (as defined in section 952), and CFC2 earns 20u of subpart F income. No foreign income tax is imposed on CFC1's or CFC2's subpart F income. For purposes of section 904, the post-1986 undistributed earnings, subpart F income, and post-1986 foreign income taxes are in the general category. On July 1, 2017, CFC2 distributes 40u to CFC1. On November 1, 2017, CFC1 distributes 60u to USP. USP does not have an aggregate foreign E&P deficit. USP includes in gross income all amounts that it is required to include under section 951. No foreign income tax is imposed or withheld on the distribution by CFC2 to CFC1 or the distribution by CFC1 to USP.

(ii) *Analysis.* (A) *Adjustments to section 959(c) classification of earnings and profits for inclusion under section 951(a)(1)(A) without regard to section 965.* The distribution from CFC2 to CFC1 does not give rise to subpart F income to CFC1 due to the application of section 954(c)(6). Accordingly, USP's inclusion under section 951(a)(1)(A) without regard to section 965(a) is 30u with respect to CFC1 and 20u with respect to CFC2 for their taxable years ending December 31, 2017. As a result of the inclusions under section 951(a)(1)(A), CFC1 and CFC2 increase their earnings and profits described in section 959(c)(2) by 30u and 20u, respectively.

(B) *Distributions between specified foreign corporations before January 1, 2018.* The distribution of 40u from CFC2 to CFC1 is treated as a distribution of 20u out of earnings and profits described in section 959(c)(2) (attributable to inclusions under section 951(a)(1)(A) without regard to section 965(a)) and 20u out of earnings and profits described in section 959(c)(3).

(C) *Section 965(a) inclusion amount.* USP determines whether CFC1 and CFC2 are deferred foreign income corporations and, if so, determines its section 965(a) inclusion amounts with respect to CFC1 and CFC2. CFC1 and CFC2 are specified foreign corporations, and CFC1 and CFC2 each have accumulated post-1986 deferred foreign income greater than zero as of an E&P measurement date. Accordingly, CFC1 and CFC2 are deferred foreign income corporations. USP's section 965(a) inclusion amount with respect to each of CFC1 and CFC2, respectively, equals the section 965(a) earnings amount of CFC1 and CFC2, respectively.

(*1*) *CFC1 section 965(a) earnings amount.* The section 965(a) earnings amount with respect to CFC1 is 20u, the amount of its accumulated post-1986 deferred foreign income as of both November 2, 2017, and December 31, 2017, which is equal to 70u of post-1986 earnings and profits (30u earned and 40u attributable to the CFC2 distribution) reduced by 50u of such post-1986 earnings and profits described in section 959(c)(2) (30u earned and 20u attributable to the CFC2 distribution) under section 965(d)(2)(B) and § 1.965-1(f)(7)(i)(B). Under section 965(d)(3)(B) and § 1.965-1(f)(29)(i)(B), the post-1986 earnings and profits of CFC1 are not reduced by the 60u distribution to USP.

(*2*) *CFC2 section 965(a) earnings amount.* The section 965(a) earnings amount with respect to CFC2 is 80u, the amount of its accumulated post-1986 deferred foreign income as of both November 2, 2017, and December 31, 2017, which is equal to the amount of CFC2's post-1986 earnings and profits of 80u. CFC2's accumulated post-1986 deferred foreign income is equal to its post-1986 earnings and profits because CFC2 does not have earnings and profits that are attributable to income of the specified foreign corporation that is effectively connected with the conduct of a trade or business within the United States and subject to tax under chapter 1, or that, if distributed, would be excluded from the gross income of a United States shareholder under section 959 or from the gross income of another shareholder if such shareholder were a United States shareholder, and, therefore, no adjustment is made under section 965(d)(2) or § 1.965-1(f)(7). CFC2's 80u of post-1986 earnings and profits consists of 120u of earnings and profits that it earned, reduced by the 40u distribution to CFC1 under section 965(d)(3)(B) and § 1.965-1(f)(29)(i)(B). The amount of the reduction to the post-1986 earnings and profits of CFC2 for the 40u distribution is not limited by § 1.965-1(f)(29)(i)(B) because CFC1's post-1986 earnings and profits are increased by 40u as a result of the distribution. Furthermore, because the 40u distribution was made on July 1, 2017, which is before the E&P measurement date on November 2, 2017, § 1.965-4(f) is not relevant.

(*3*) *Effect on earnings and profits described in section 959(c)(2) and (3).* CFC1 and CFC2 increase their earnings and profits described in section 959(c)(2) by USP's section 965(a) inclusion amounts with respect to CFC1 and CFC2, 20u and 80u, respectively, and reduce their earnings and profits described in section 959(c)(3) by an equivalent amount.

(D) *Distribution to United States shareholder.* The distribution from CFC1 to USP is treated as a distribution of 60u out of the earnings and profits of CFC1 described in section 959(c)(2), which include earnings and profits attributable to the section 965(a) inclusion amount taken into account by USP.

(E) *Section 902 and section 960 consequences.* (*1*) *Distribution by and inclusions with respect to CFC2.* Under section 960, USP is deemed to pay $3.50x ($21x x (20u/120u)) of CFC2's post-1986 foreign income taxes as a result of its inclusion under section 951(a)(1)(A) without regard to section 965(a) with respect to CFC2. As a result of the distribution from CFC2 to CFC1, CFC2's post-1986 foreign income taxes are reduced, and CFC1's post-1986 foreign income taxes are increased, by the foreign income taxes deemed paid by CFC1 under section 902 of $3.50x (($21x-$3.50x) x (20u/120u-20u)). Under section 960, USP is deemed to pay $14x (($21x-$3.50x-$3.50x) x 80u/(120u-40u)) of CFC2's post-1986 foreign income taxes as a result of its section 965(a) inclusion with respect to CFC2. The taxes deemed paid by USP as a result of its section 965(a) inclusion with respect to CFC2 are subject to the applicable percentage disallowance under section 965(g).

(*2*) *Inclusions with respect to CFC1.* As determined in paragraph (j)(1)(ii)(E)(*1*) of this *section (paragraph (E)(1) in the analysis in this Example 1),* as a result of the distribution from CFC2 to CFC1, CFC1 is deemed under section 902 to pay $3.50x of CFC2's post-1986 foreign income taxes. Under section 960, USP is deemed to pay $2.10x ($3.50x x (30u/(30u+20u))) of CFC1's post-1986 foreign income taxes as a result of its inclusion under section 951(a)(1)(A) without regard to section 965(a) with respect to CFC1. Under section 960, USP is deemed to pay $1.40x (($3.50x-$2.10x) x 20u/(30u+20u-30u)) of CFC1's post-1986 foreign income taxes as a result of its section 965(a) inclusion with respect to CFC1. The taxes deemed paid by USP as a result of its section 965(a) inclusion with respect to CFC1 are subject to the applicable percentage disallowance under section 965(g).

(2) *Example 2. Determination of accumulated post-1986 deferred foreign income with subpart F income earned after E&P measurement date on November 2, 2017.* (i) *Facts.* The facts are the same as in paragraph (j)(1)(i) of this section (the facts in *Example 1*), except that on December 1, 2017, CFC1 earns an additional 50u of subpart F income (as defined in section 952), and neither CFC1 nor CFC2 has any post-1986 foreign income taxes.

(ii) *Analysis.* (A) *Adjustments to section 959(c) classification of earnings and profits for inclusion under section 951(a)(1)(A) without regard to section 965.* USP determines its inclusion under section 951(a)(1)(A) without regard to section 965(a), which is 80u with respect to CFC1 and 20u with respect to CFC2 for their taxable years ending December 31, 2017. As a result of the inclusions under section 951(a)(1)(A), CFC1 and CFC2 increase their earnings and profits described in section 959(c)(2) by 80u and 20u, respectively.

(B) *Distributions between specified foreign corporations before January 1, 2018.* The analysis is the same as in paragraph (j)(1)(ii)(B) of this section (paragraph (B) in the analysis in *Example 1*).

(C) *Section 965(a) inclusion amount.* USP determines whether CFC1 and CFC2 are deferred foreign income corporations and, if so, determines its section 965(a) inclusion amounts with respect to CFC1 and CFC2. CFC1 and CFC2 are specified foreign corporations, and CFC1 and CFC2 each have accumulated post-1986 deferred foreign income greater than zero as of an E&P measurement date. Accordingly, CFC1 and CFC2 are deferred foreign income corporations. USP's section 965(a) inclusion amount with respect to each of CFC1 and CFC2, respectively, equals the section 965(a) earnings amount of CFC1 and CFC2, respectively.

(*1*) *CFC1 section 965(a) earnings amount.* The section 965(a) earnings amount with respect to CFC1 is 20u, the greater of—

(*i*) The amount of its accumulated post-1986 deferred foreign income as of November 2, 2017, 20u, which is equal to 70u of post-1986 earnings and profits (30u earned and 40u attributable to the CFC2 distribution) reduced by 50u of such post-1986 earnings and profits described in section 959(c)(2) without regard to the subpart F income earned after November 2, 2017 (30u earned and 20u attributable to the CFC2 distribution) under section 965(d)(2)(B) and § 1.965-1(f)(7)(i)(B) and (ii), and

(*ii*) The amount of its accumulated post-1986 deferred foreign income as of December 31, 2017, 20u, which is equal to 120u of post-1986 earnings and profits (80u earned and 40u attributable to the CFC2 distribution) reduced by 100u of such post-1986 earnings and profits described in section 959(c)(2) with regard to the subpart F income earned on or before December 31, 2017 (80u earned and 20u attributable to the CFC2 distribution) under section 965(d)(2)(B) and § 1.965-1(f)(7)(i)(B) and (ii).

(*2*) *CFC2 section 965(a) earnings amount.* The analysis is the same as in paragraph (j)(1)(ii)(C)(*2*) of this section (paragraph (C)(2) in the analysis in *Example 1*)).

(*3*) *Effect on earnings and profits described in section 959(c)(2) and (3).* The analysis is the same as in paragraph (j)(1)(ii)(C)(*3*) of this section (paragraph (C)(3) in the analysis in *Example 1*).

(D) *Distribution to United States shareholder.* The analysis is the same as in paragraph (j)(1)(ii)(D) of this section (paragraph (D) in the analysis in *Example 1*).

(3) *Example 3. Determination of accumulated post-1986 deferred foreign income with subpart F income earned after E&P measurement date on November 2, 2017, but previously taxed earnings and profits attributable to the subpart F income distributed before E&P measurement date on November 2, 2017.* (i) *Facts.* The facts are the same as in paragraph (j)(1)(i) of this section (the facts in *Example 1*), except that on December 1, 2017, CFC2 earns an additional 50u of subpart F income (as defined in

section 952), and neither CFC1 nor CFC2 has any post-1986 foreign income taxes.

(ii) *Analysis.* (A) *Adjustments to section 959(c) classification of earnings and profits for inclusion under section 951(a)(1)(A) without regard to section 965.* USP determines its inclusion under section 951(a)(1)(A) without regard to section 965(a), which is 30u with respect to CFC1 and 70u with respect to CFC2 for their taxable years ending December 31, 2017. As a result of the inclusions under section 951(a)(1)(A), CFC1 and CFC2 increase their earnings and profits described in section 959(c)(2) by 30u and 70u, respectively.

(B) *Distributions between specified foreign corporations before January 1, 2018.* The distribution of 40u from CFC2 to CFC1 is treated as a distribution of 40u out of earnings and profits described in section 959(c)(2) (attributable to inclusions under section 951(a)(1)(A) without regard to section 965(a)).

(C) *Section 965(a) inclusion amount.* USP determines whether CFC1 and CFC2 are deferred foreign income corporations, and, if so, determines its section 965(a) inclusion amounts with respect to CFC1 and CFC2. Because USP wholly owns CFC1 and CFC2 under section 958(a) and USP does not have an aggregate foreign E&P deficit, USP's section 965(a) inclusion amount with respect to each of CFC1 and CFC2, respectively, equals the section 965(a) earnings amount, if any, of CFC1 and CFC2, respectively.

(*1*) *CFC1 section 965(a) earnings amount.* CFC1 is not a deferred foreign income corporation and does not have a section 965(a) earnings amount because the amount of its accumulated post-1986 deferred foreign income as of both November 2, 2017, and December 31, 2017, is 0u, which is equal to 70u of post-1986 earnings and profits (30u earned and 40u attributable to the CFC2 distribution) reduced by 70u of such post-1986 earnings and profits described in section 959(c)(2) (30u earned and 40u attributable to the CFC2 distribution) under section 965(d)(2)(B) and § 1.965-1(f)(7)(i)(B).

(*2*) *CFC2 section 965(a) earnings amount.* The section 965(a) earnings amount with respect to CFC2 is 100u, the greater of the amounts in paragraph (j)(3)(ii)(C)(*2*)(*i*) and (*ii*) of this section (paragraph (C)(2)(i) and (ii) in the analysis in this *Example 3*)—

(*i*) The amount of its accumulated post-1986 deferred foreign income as of November 2, 2017, 80u. CFC2's 80u of accumulated post-1986 deferred foreign income as of November 2, 2017, is equal to its 80u of post-1986 earnings and profits because no adjustment is made under section 965(d)(2) or § 1.965-1(f)(7), as CFC2 does not have earnings and profits that are attributable to income of the specified foreign corporation that is effectively connected with the conduct of a trade or business within the United States and subject to tax under chapter 1, or that, if distributed, would be excluded from the gross income of a United States shareholder under section 959 or from the gross income of another shareholder if such shareholder were a United States shareholder, without regard to the subpart F income earned after November 2, 2017. CFC2's 80u of post-1986 earnings and profits consists of 120u of earnings and profits that it earned, reduced by the 40u distribution to CFC1 under section 965(d)(3)(B) and § 1.965-1(f)(29)(i)(B). The amount of the reduction to the post-1986 earnings and profits of CFC2 for the 40u distribution is not limited by § 1.965-1(f)(29)(i)(B) because CFC1's post-1986 earnings and profits are increased by 40u as a result of the distribution. Furthermore, because the 40u distribution was made on July 1, 2017, which is before any E&P measurement date, § 1.965-4(f) is not relevant.

(*ii*) The amount of its accumulated post-1986 deferred foreign income as of December 31, 2017, 100u, which is equal to 130u of post-1986 earnings and profits reduced by 30u of such post-1986 earnings and profits described in section 959(c)(2) with regard to the subpart F income earned before December 31, 2017, under section 965(d)(2)(B) and § 1.965-1(f)(7)(i)(B) and (ii). CFC2's 130u of post-1986 earnings and profits consists of 170u of earnings and profits that it earned, reduced by the 40u distribution to CFC1 under section 965(d)(3)(B) and § 1.965-1(f)(29)(i)(B).

(*3*) *Effect on earnings and profits described in section 959(c)(2) and (3).* CFC2 increases its earnings and profits described in section 959(c)(2) by USP's section 965(a) inclusion amount with respect to CFC2, 100u, and reduces its earnings and profits described in section 959(c)(3) by an equivalent amount.

(D) *Distribution to United States shareholder.* The analysis is the same as in paragraph (j)(1)(ii)(D) of this section (paragraph (D) in the analysis in *Example 1*).

(4) *Example 4. Determination of accumulated post-1986 deferred foreign income with distribution made after E&P measurement date on November 2, 2017.* (i) *Facts.* USP, a domestic corporation, owns all of the stock of CFC1, a foreign corporation, which owns all of the stock of CFC2, also a foreign corporation. USP, CFC1, and CFC2 all have taxable years ending December 31, 2017. As of January 1, 2017, CFC1 has 10u of earnings and profits described in section 959(c)(3) that were accumulated in taxable years beginning after December 31, 1986, while CFC1 was a specified foreign corporation, and $2x of post-1986 foreign income taxes; and CFC2 has 100u of earnings and profits described in section 959(c)(3) that were accumulated in taxable years beginning after December 31, 1986, while CFC2 was a specified foreign corporation and $10x of post-1986 foreign income taxes. For purposes of section 904, the post-1986 undistributed earnings and post-1986 foreign income taxes are in the general category. None of CFC1's or CFC2's earnings and profits are attributable to income treated as effectively connected with the conduct of a trade or business within the United States. On December 1, 2017, CFC2 distributes 100u to CFC1, and CFC1 distributes 10u to USP. USP does not have an aggregate foreign E&P deficit. USP includes in gross income all amounts that it is required to include under section 951. No foreign income tax is imposed or withheld on the distribution by CFC2 to CFC1 or the distribution by CFC1 to USP. USP does not apply § 1.965-4(f)(3) to determine the post-1986 earnings and profits of CFC1 and CFC2.

(ii) *Analysis.* (A) *Adjustments to section 959(c) classification of earnings and profits for inclusion under section 951(a)(1)(A) without regard to section 965.* The distribution from CFC2 to CFC1 does not give rise to subpart F income to CFC1 due to the application of section 954(c)(6). Accordingly, USP does not have an inclusion under section 951(a)(1)(A) without regard to section 965(a) with respect to CFC1 or CFC2 for their taxable years ending December 31, 2017. As a result, neither CFC1 nor CFC2 has earnings and profits described in section 959(c)(2).

(B) *Distributions between specified foreign corporations before January 1, 2018.* The distribution of 100u from CFC2 to CFC1 is initially treated as a distribution out of earnings and profits described in section 959(c)(3).

(C) *Section 965(a) inclusion amount.* USP determines whether CFC1 and CFC2 are deferred foreign income corporations, and, if so, determines its section 965(a) inclusion amounts with respect to CFC1 and CFC2. CFC1 and CFC2 are specified foreign corporations, and CFC1 and CFC2 each have accumulated post-1986 deferred foreign income greater than zero as of an E&P measurement date. Accordingly, CFC1 and CFC2 are deferred foreign income corporations. USP's section 965(a) inclusion amount with respect to each of CFC1 and CFC2, respectively, equals the section 965(a) earnings amount of CFC1 and CFC2, respectively.

(*1*) *CFC1 section 965(a) earnings amount.* The section 965(a) earnings amount with respect to CFC1 is 10u, the amount of its accumulated post-1986 deferred foreign income as of both November 2, 2017, and December 31, 2017, which is equal to the amount of CFC1's post-1986 earnings and profits of 10u. CFC1's accumulated post-1986 deferred foreign income is equal to its post-1986 earnings and profits because CFC1 does not have earnings and profits that are attributable to income of the specified foreign corporation that is effectively connected with the conduct of a trade or business within the United States and subject to tax under chapter 1, or that, if distributed, would be excluded from the gross income of a United States shareholder under section 959 or from the gross income of another shareholder if such shareholder were a United States shareholder, and therefore no adjustment is made under section 965(d)(2) or § 1.965-1(f)(7). But for § 1.965-4(f), CFC1's post-1986 earnings and profits as of December 31, 2017, would be 110u, but because the distribution from CFC2 is a specified payment, it is disregarded in determining CFC1's post-1986 earnings and profits as of December 31, 2017, under § 1.965-4(f). Under section 965(d)(3)(B) and § 1.965-1(f)(29)(i)(B), the post-1986 earnings and profits of CFC1 are not reduced by the 10u distribution to USP.

(*2*) *CFC2 section 965(a) earnings amount.* The section 965(a) earnings amount with respect to CFC2 is 100u, the amount of its accumulated post-1986 deferred foreign income as of both November 2, 2017, and December 31, 2017, which is equal to the amount of CFC2's post-1986 earnings and profits of 100u. CFC2's accumulated post-1986 deferred foreign income is equal to its post-1986 earnings and profits because CFC2 does not have earnings and profits that are attributable to income of the specified foreign corporation that is effectively connected with the conduct of a trade or business within the United States and subject to tax under chapter 1, or that, if distributed, would be excluded from the gross income of a United States shareholder under section 959 or from the gross income of another shareholder if such shareholder were a United States shareholder, and therefore no adjustment is made under section 965(d)(2) or § 1.965-1(f)(7). But for § 1.965-4(f), CFC2's post-1986 earnings and profits as of December 31, 2017, would be 0u, but because the distribution to CFC1 is a specified payment, it is disregarded in determining CFC2's post-1986 earnings and profits as of December 31, 2017, under § 1.965-4(f).

(3) *Effect on earnings and profits described in section 959(c)(2) and (3).* CFC1 and CFC2 increase their earnings and profits described in section 959(c)(2) by USP's section 965(a) inclusion amounts with respect to CFC1 and CFC2, 10u and 100u, respectively, and reduce their earnings and profits described in section 959(c)(3) by an equivalent amount.

(D) *Distributions*—(1) *Distribution that is a specified payment.* The distribution from CFC2 to CFC1 is recharacterized as a distribution of 100u out of the earnings and profits of CFC2 described in section 959(c)(2), which include earnings and profits attributable to the section 965(a) inclusion amount taken into account by USP.

(2) *Distribution to United States shareholder.* The distribution from CFC1 to USP is treated as a distribution of 10u out of the earnings and profits of CFC1 described in section 959(c)(2), which include earnings and profits attributable to the section 965(a) inclusion amount taken into account by USP.

(E) *Section 902 and section 960 consequences.* Under section 960, USP is deemed to pay $10x ($10x x (100u/100u)) of CFC2's post-1986 foreign income taxes as a result of its section 965(a) inclusion with respect to CFC2 and $2x ($2x x (10u/10u) of CFC1's post-1986 foreign income taxes as a result of its section 965(a) inclusion with respect to CFC1. Such taxes are subject to the applicable percentage disallowance under section 965(g).

(5) *Example 5. Determination of accumulated post-1986 deferred foreign income with section 951(a)(1)(B) inclusion after E&P measurement date on November 2, 2017.* (i) *Facts.* USP, a domestic corporation, owns all of the stock of CFC, a foreign corporation. USP has a taxable year ending December 31, 2017, and CFC has a taxable year ending November 30, 2017. As of December 1, 2016, CFC has 110u of earnings and profits described in section 959(c)(3) that were accumulated in taxable years beginning after December 31, 1986, while CFC was a specified foreign corporation. CFC holds 150u of United States property throughout its taxable year ending November 30, 2017, but disposes of it on December 1, 2017, recognizing no gain or loss on the property. Between December 1, 2017, and December 31, 2017, CFC earns an additional 10u of income that does not constitute subpart F income or income treated as effectively connected with the conduct of a trade or business within the United States that gives rise to 10u of earnings and profits. USP includes in income all amounts that it is required to include under section 951.

(ii) *Analysis.* (A) *Section 965(a) inclusion amount.* USP determines whether CFC is a deferred foreign income corporation, and, if so, determines its section 965(a) inclusion amount with respect to CFC. CFC is a specified foreign corporation, and CFC has accumulated post-1986 deferred foreign income greater than zero as of an E&P measurement date. Accordingly, CFC is a deferred foreign income corporation. USP's section 965(a) inclusion amount with respect to CFC equals the section 965(a) earnings amount of CFC.

(1) *CFC section 965(a) earnings amount.* The section 965(a) earnings amount with respect to CFC is 110u, the greater of the amount of its accumulated post-1986 deferred foreign income as of November 2, 2017, which is 110u, and the amount of its accumulated post-1986 deferred foreign income as of December 31, 2017, which is 10u. CFC's accumulated post-1986 deferred foreign income as of November 2, 2017, is equal to its 110u of post-1986 earnings and profits, which are not reduced by the 110u of earnings and profits described in section 959(c)(1) as a result of USP's section 951(a)(1)(B) inclusion with respect to CFC as of December 31, 2017, because such amounts would not be excluded from the gross income of a United States shareholder under section 959 under section 965(d)(2) or §1.965-1(f)(7) if distributed on November 2, 2017. CFC's accumulated post-1986 deferred foreign income as of December 31, 2017, is equal to its 120u of post-1986 earnings and profits reduced by the 110u of earnings and profits described in section 959(c)(1) as a result of USP's section 951(a)(1)(B) inclusion with respect to CFC as of December 31, 2017, which would be excluded from the gross income of a United States shareholder under section 959 under section 965(d)(2) or §1.965-1(f)(7) if distributed on December 31, 2017.

(2) *Effect on earnings and profits described in section 959(c)(2) and (3).* In USP's taxable year ending December 31, 2018, CFC increases its earnings and profits described in section 959(c)(2) by USP's section 965(a) inclusion amount with respect to CFC, 110u, and reduces its earnings and profits described in section 959(c)(3) by an equivalent amount.

(B) *Section 956 inclusion.* In USP's taxable year ending December 31, 2017, USP increases its earnings and profits described in section 959(c)(1) by USP's amount included under sections 951(a)(1)(B) and 956 with respect to CFC, 110u, and reduces its earnings and profits described in section 959(c)(3) by an equivalent amount.

(6) *Example 6. Section 1248 inclusion.* (i) *Facts.* USP1, a domestic corporation, owns all of the stock of CFC, a foreign corporation, until it sells all of such stock to USP2, a domestic corporation, on December 1, 2017, in a sale on which USP1 recognizes $100x of gain. Throughout 2017, 1u=$1x. USP1, USP2, and CFC all have taxable years ending December 31, 2017. As of January 1, 2017, CFC has 100u of earnings and profits described in section 959(c)(3) that were accumulated in taxable years beginning after December 31, 1986, while CFC was wholly owned by USP1. On March 1, 2017, CFC distributes 20u to USP1. None of CFC's earnings and profits are attributable to income treated as effectively connected with the conduct of a trade or business within the United States. USP2 does not have an aggregate foreign E&P deficit. USP1 and USP2 include in income all amounts that they are required to include under sections 951 and 1248.

(ii) *Analysis.* (A) *Adjustments to section 959(c) classification of earnings and profits for section 1248 inclusion.* USP1's inclusion under section 1248 with respect to CFC is $80x ($100x-$20x). As a result of the inclusion under section 1248, under section 959(e), CFC increases its earnings and profits described in section 959(c)(2) by 80u.

(B) *Section 965(a) inclusion amount.* USP2 determines whether CFC is a deferred foreign income corporation and, if so, determines its section 965(a) inclusion amount with respect to CFC. CFC is a specified foreign corporation, and CFC has accumulated post-1986 deferred foreign income greater than zero as of an E&P measurement date. Accordingly, CFC is a deferred foreign income corporation. USP2's section 965(a) inclusion amount with respect to CFC equals the section 965(a) earnings amount of CFC. The section 965(a) earnings amount with respect to CFC is 20u, the amount of its accumulated post-1986 deferred foreign income as of both November 2, 2017, and December 31, 2017, which is equal to 100u of post-1986 earnings and profits reduced by 80u of such post-1986 earnings and profits described in section 959(c)(2) under section 965(d)(2)(B) and §1.965-1(f)(7)(i)(B). CFC increases its earnings and profits described in section 959(c)(2) by USP2's section 965(a) inclusion amount with respect to CFC, 20u, and reduces its earnings and profits that would be described in section 959(c)(3) but for the application of section 965(a) by an equivalent amount.

(C) *Distributions to United States shareholders.* The distributions from CFC to USP1 (including the deemed dividend under section 1248) are treated as distributions out of the earnings and profits of CFC described in section 959(c)(3).

(7) *Example 7. Distribution attributable to section 965(a) previously taxed earnings and profits.* (i) *Facts.* USP, a domestic corporation, owns all of the stock of CFC1, a specified foreign corporation that has no post-1986 earnings and profits (or deficit in post-1986 earnings and profits), and CFC1 owns all the stock of CFC2, a deferred foreign income corporation. USP is a calendar year taxpayer. CFC1's last taxable year beginning before January 1, 2018, ends on November 30, 2018; CFC2 has an inclusion year that ends on November 30, 2018. The functional currency of CFC1 and CFC2 is the U.S. dollar. USP's adjusted basis in the stock of CFC1 is zero. On January 1, 2018, CFC2 distributes $100x to CFC1, and CFC1 distributes $100x to USP. USP has a section 965(a) inclusion amount of $100x with respect to CFC2 that is taken into account for USP's taxable year ending December 31, 2018. CFC2 has no earnings and profits described in section 959(c)(1) or (2) other than section 965(a) previously taxed earnings and profits.

(ii) *Analysis.* Under paragraph (c) of this section, CFC2 has $100x of section 965(a) previously taxed earnings and profits with respect to USP. USP receives a distribution from CFC2 through a chain of ownership described in section 958(a) during the inclusion year of CFC2 that is attributable to the $100x of section 965(a) previously taxed earnings and profits of CFC2. Under paragraph (g)(1) of this section, the amount of gain that USP otherwise would recognize with respect to the stock of CFC1 under section 961(b)(2) is reduced (but not below zero) by $100x, the amount of CFC2's section 965(a) previously taxed earnings and profits with respect to USP. As of the close of November 30, 2018, USP's basis in CFC1 is increased under paragraph (e) of this section by USP's section 965(a) inclusion amount with respect to CFC2 ($100x), and is reduced under paragraph (g)(2) of this section by the amount of gain that would have been recognized by USP under section 961(b)(2) but for the application of paragraph (g)(1) of this section ($100x).

(8) *Example 8. Distribution attributable to section 965(b) previously taxed earnings and profits; parent-subsidiary.* (i) *Facts.* The facts are the same as in paragraph (j)(7)(i) of this section (the facts in *Example 7*), except that CFC1 has a specified E&P deficit of $100x. Because of the specified E&P deficit of CFC1, USP's section 965(a) inclusion amount with respect to CFC2 is reduced to zero pursuant to section 965(b)(1) and §1.965-1(b)(2). USP makes the election described in paragraph (f)(2) of this section.

(ii) *Analysis.* (A) *Application of the gain reduction rule.* Under paragraph (d)(1) of this section, CFC2 has $100x of section 965(b) previously taxed earnings and profits with respect to USP, and, under paragraph (d)(2) of this section, CFC1's earnings and profits described in section 959(c)(3) are increased by $100x to $0. USP receives a distribution from CFC2 through a chain of ownership described in section 958(a) during the inclusion year of CFC2 that is attributable to the $100x of section 965(b) previously taxed earnings and profits of CFC2. Under paragraph (g)(1) of this section, the amount of gain that USP otherwise would recognize with respect to the stock of CFC1 under section 961(b)(2) is reduced (but not below zero) by $100x, the amount of CFC2's section 965(b) previously taxed earnings and profits with respect to USP under paragraph (d)(1) of this section.

(B) *Adjustments to the basis of CFC1.* Because USP makes the election described in paragraph (f)(2) of this section, as of the close of November 30, 2018, USP's basis in CFC1 is increased under paragraph (f)(2)(ii)(A) of this section by an amount equal to CFC2's section 965(b) previously taxed earnings and profits with respect to USP under paragraph (d)(1) of this section ($100x), reduced under paragraph (f)(2)(ii)(B) of this section by an amount equal to the portion of the specified E&P deficit of CFC1 taken into account in determining USP's section 965(a) inclusion amount with respect to CFC2 ($100x), and reduced under paragraph (g)(2) of this section by the amount of gain that would have been recognized by USP with respect to the stock of CFC1 under section 961(b)(2) but for the application of paragraph (g)(1) of this section ($100x). Under paragraph (h)(2) and (3) of this section, the excess of the net reduction from the adjustments under paragraphs (f) and (g) of this section over USP's basis in the stock of CFC1 (in this case, $100x) is treated as gain recognized by USP from the sale or exchange of property.

(9) *Example 9. Distribution attributable to section 965(b) previously taxed earnings and profits; brother-sister.* (i) *Facts.* The facts are the same as in paragraph (j)(8)(i) of this section (the facts in *Example 8*), except that USP owns all the stock of CFC2, USP's adjusted basis in the stock of CFC2 is zero, CFC1 made no distributions, and on January 1, 2018, CFC2 distributes $100x to USP.

(ii) *Analysis.* (A) *Application of the gain reduction rule.* Under paragraph (d)(1) of this section, CFC2 has $100x of section 965(b) previously taxed earnings and profits with respect to USP, and, under paragraph (d)(2) of this section, CFC1's earnings and profits described in section 959(c)(3) (deficit of $100x) are increased by $100x to $0. USP receives a distribution from CFC2 during the inclusion year of CFC2 that is attributable to the $100x of section 965(b) previously taxed earnings and profits of CFC2. Under paragraph (g)(1) of this section, the amount of gain that USP otherwise would recognize with respect to the stock of CFC2 under section 961(b)(2) is reduced (but not below zero) by $100x, the amount of CFC2's section 965(b) previously taxed earnings and profits with respect to USP under paragraph (d)(1) of this section.

(B) *Adjustments to the basis of CFC1 and CFC2.* Because USP makes the election described in paragraph (f)(2) of this section, as of the close of November 30, 2018, USP's basis in the stock of CFC2 is increased under paragraph (f)(2)(ii)(A) of this section by the amount of CFC2's section 965(b) previously taxed earnings and profits with respect to USP under paragraph (d)(1) of this section ($100x) and reduced under paragraph (g)(2) of this section by the amount of gain that would have been recognized by USP with respect to the stock of CFC2 under section 961(b)(2) but for the application of paragraph (g)(1) of this section ($100x). As of the close of November 30, 2018, USP's basis in CFC1 is reduced under paragraph (f)(2)(ii)(B) of this section by an amount equal to the portion of USP's pro rata share of the specified E&P deficit of CFC1 taken into account in determining USP's section 965(a) inclusion amount with respect to CFC2 ($100x). Under paragraph (h)(3) of this section, the excess of the reduction under paragraph (f) of this section over USP's basis in the stock of CFC1 (in this case, $100x) is treated as gain recognized by USP from the sale or exchange of property. [Reg. § 1.965-2.]

□ [*T.D. 9846, 2-4-2019 (corrected 4-9-2019).*]

§ 1.965-3. Section 965(c) deductions.—(a) *Scope.*—This section provides rules regarding section 965(c) deductions and section 965(c) deduction amounts. Paragraph (b) of this section provides rules for disregarding certain assets for purposes of determining the aggregate foreign cash position of a section 958(a) U.S. shareholder. Paragraph (c) of this section provides rules for determining the aggregate foreign cash position for a section 958(a) U.S. shareholder inclusion year. Paragraph (d) of this section provides a rule regarding certain expatriated entities. Paragraph (e) of this section provides a rule for the treatment of section 965(c) deductions in connection with an election under section 962. Paragraph (f) of this section provides rules regarding the treatment of a section 965(c) deduction under certain provisions of the Internal Revenue Code. Paragraph (g) of this section provides a rule for domestic pass-through entities.

(b) *Rules for disregarding certain assets for determining aggregate foreign cash position.*—(1) *Disregard of certain obligations between related specified foreign corporations.*—In determining the aggregate foreign cash position of a section 958(a) U.S. shareholder, any account receivable, account payable, short-term obligation, or derivative financial instrument between a specified foreign corporation with respect to which the section 958(a) U.S. shareholder owns section 958(a) stock and a related specified foreign corporation on corresponding cash measurement dates is disregarded to the extent of the smallest of the product of the amount of the item on such corresponding cash measurement dates of each specified foreign corporation and the section 958(a) U.S. shareholder's ownership percentage of section 958(a) stock of the specified foreign corporation owned by the section 958(a) U.S. shareholder on such dates. For purposes of this paragraph (b)(1)(i), a specified foreign corporation is treated as a related specified foreign corporation with respect to another specified foreign corporation if, as of the cash measurement date referred to in the preceding sentence of each specified foreign corporation, the specified foreign corporations are related persons within the meaning of section 954(d)(3), substituting the term "specified foreign corporation" for "controlled foreign corporation" in each place that it appears.

(2) *Disregard of other assets upon demonstration of double-counting.*—For purposes of determining the aggregate foreign cash position of a section 958(a) U.S. shareholder, the section 958(a) U.S. shareholder's pro rata share of the cash position of a specified foreign corporation on a cash measurement date is reduced by amounts of net accounts receivable, actively traded property, and short-term obligations to the extent such amounts are attributable to amounts taken into account in determining the section 958(a) U.S. shareholder's pro rata share of the cash position of another specified foreign corporation on the corresponding cash measurement date of such other specified corporation and to the extent not disregarded pursuant to paragraph (b)(1) of this section. However, the preceding sentence applies only if the section 958(a) U.S. shareholder attaches a statement containing the information outlined in paragraphs (b)(2)(i) through (v) of this section to its timely filed return (taking into account extensions, if any) for the section 958(a) U.S. shareholder inclusion year, or, if the section 958(a) U.S. shareholder has multiple section 958(a) U.S. shareholder inclusion years, the later of such years. Relief is not available under § 301.9100-2 or 301.9100-3 to allow late filing of the statement. The statement must contain the following information with respect to each specified foreign corporation for which the cash position is reduced under this paragraph (b)(2)—

(i) A description of the asset that would be taken into account with respect to both specified foreign corporations,

(ii) A statement of the amount by which its pro rata share of the cash position of one specified foreign corporation is reduced,

(iii) A detailed explanation of why there would otherwise be double-counting, including the computation of the amount taken into account with respect to the other specified foreign corporation, and

(iv) An explanation of why paragraph (b)(1) of this section does not apply to disregard such amount.

(3) *Disregard of portion of cash position of noncorporate entities treated as specified foreign corporations.*—If an entity is treated as a specified foreign corporation of a section 958(a) U.S. shareholder pursuant to section 965(c)(3)(E), for purposes of determining the aggregate foreign cash position of the section 958(a) U.S. shareholder, the section 958(a) U.S. shareholder's pro rata share of the cash position of the entity (determined taking into account paragraphs (b)(1) and (b)(2) of this section) is reduced by the amount of the pro rata share attributable to deemed stock of the entity not owned (within the meaning of section 958(a), applied by treating domestic pass-through entities as foreign) by a specified foreign corporation of the section 958(a) U.S. shareholder (determined without taking into account section 965(c)(3)(E)).

(4) *Examples.*—The following examples illustrate the application of this paragraph (b).

(i) *Example 1.* (A) *Facts.* USP, a domestic corporation, owns all of the stock of CFC1, a foreign corporation. CFC1 owns 95% of the only class of stock of CFC2, also a foreign corporation, and 40% of the only class of stock of CFC3, also a foreign corporation. The remaining 5% of the only class of stock of CFC2 is owned by a person unrelated to USP, CFC1, and CFC2; and the remaining 60% of the only class of stock of CFC3 is owned by a person unrelated to USP and CFC1. USP, CFC1, and CFC3 have calendar year taxable years. CFC2 has a taxable year ending on November 30. On November 15, 2015, CFC1 makes a loan of $100x to CFC2, which is required to be and is, in fact, repaid on January 1, 2016. On November 15, 2016, CFC2 sells inventory to CFC1 in exchange for an account receivable of $200x, which is required to be and is, in fact, repaid on December 15, 2016. On August 1, 2017, CFC1 makes a loan of $300x to CFC3, which is required to be and is, in fact, repaid on January 31, 2018.

(B) *Analysis—(1) Loan from CFC1 to CFC2.* For purposes of determining the aggregate foreign cash position of USP, a section 958(a) U.S. shareholder of CFC1, under paragraph (b)(1) of this section, because CFC1 and CFC2 are related within the meaning of paragraph (b)(1) of this section, the short-term obligation of CFC2 held by CFC1 outstanding on the first cash measurement date of each specified foreign corporation, November 30, 2015, and December 31, 2015, respectively, is disregarded to the extent of 95%, the smallest ownership percentage of section 958(a) stock of CFC1 and CFC2 owned by USP on such first cash measurement dates. Accordingly, USP only takes into account $5 ($100 - 95% of $100) of the short-term obligation in determining CFC1's cash position for purposes of determining its aggregate foreign cash position.

(2) *Account receivable of CFC1 held by CFC2.* Because the account receivable of CFC1 held by CFC2 on its second cash measurement date, November 30, 2016, is not outstanding on CFC1's second cash measurement date, December 31, 2016, paragraph (b)(1) of this section does not apply to disregard any portion of such account receivable.

(3) *Loan from CFC1 to CFC3.* Because CFC3 is not related to CFC1 within the meaning of paragraph (b)(1) of this section, paragraph (b)(1) of this section does not apply to disregard any portion of such short-term obligation.

(ii) *Example 2.* (A) *Facts.* The facts are the same as in paragraph (b)(4)(i)(A) of this section (the facts in *Example 1*), except that on December 1, 2015, CFC1 sells 5% of the stock of CFC2 to an unrelated person.

(B) *Analysis.* The analysis is the same as in paragraph (b)(4)(i)(B) of this section (the analysis in *Example 1*), except that the short-term obligation of CFC2 held by CFC1 outstanding on both of their first cash measurement dates, November 30, 2015, and December 31, 2015, respectively, is disregarded under paragraph (b)(1) of this section to the extent of 90%, the smallest ownership percentage of section 958(a) stock of CFC1 and CFC2 by USP on such first cash measurement dates. Accordingly, USP takes into account $10 ($100 - 90% of $100) of the short-term obligation in determining CFC1's cash position for purposes of determining its aggregate foreign cash position.

(iii) *Example 3.* (A) *Facts.* USP, a domestic corporation, owns all of the stock of CFC1, a foreign corporation, which owns 45% of the only class of stock of CFC2, also a foreign corporation. The remainder of the CFC2 stock is actively traded on an established financial market but is not owned by any person related to USP or CFC1. USP, CFC1, and CFC2 have calendar year taxable years. The value of the CFC2 stock owned by CFC1 is $500x on each of the cash measurement dates. Also on each of the cash measurement dates, CFC2 has $300x of assets described in section 965(c)(3)(B) and § 1.965-1(f)(16) that are taken into account in determining its cash position.

(B) *Analysis.* For purposes of determining USP's aggregate foreign cash position, USP's pro rata share of the cash position of CFC1 on each cash measurement date may be reduced by the amount of the stock of CFC2 to the extent attributable to amounts taken into account in determining USP's pro rata share of the cash position of CFC2 on such cash measurement date (that is, to the extent of the $135x taken into account with respect to CFC2), provided USP attaches a statement to its timely filed return (taking into account extensions, if any) containing the following: a description of the CFC2 stock and the assets of CFC2 taken into account in determining its cash position; a statement that USP's pro rata share of the cash position of CFC1 is being reduced by $135x; the computation of the $135x taken into account with respect to CFC2; and an explanation of why paragraph (b)(1) of this section does not apply to disregard such amount.

(iv) *Example 4.* (A) *Facts.* USP, a domestic corporation, owns all of the stock of CFC1 and CFC2, each a foreign corporation. USP, CFC1, and CFC2 have calendar year taxable years. CFC1 buys goods on credit from a third party for $100x and thus has an account payable of $100x. CFC1 modifies the goods and sells to CFC2 for $105x in exchange for an account receivable of $105x. CFC2 modifies the goods and sells to another third party for $110x in exchange for an account receivable of $110x. All of the accounts payable and accounts receivable are outstanding on the final cash measurement date.

(B) *Analysis.* For purposes of determining USP's aggregate foreign cash position, on the final cash measurement date, CFC1 has net accounts receivable of $0 because, pursuant to paragraph (b)(1) of this section, CFC1's account receivable from CFC2 is disregarded, and CFC2 has net accounts receivable of $110x because, pursuant to paragraph (b)(1) of this section, CFC2's account payable to CFC1 is disregarded. USP cannot rely on the rule in paragraph (b)(2) of this section because no amounts attributable to CFC2's net accounts receivable are taken into account with respect to another specified foreign corporation.

(v) *Example 5.* (A) *Facts.* USP, a domestic corporation, owns all of the stock of CFC1 and CFC2, each a foreign corporation. USP and CFC1 own 60% and 40%, respectively, of the interests in the capital and profits of PS1, a partnership. PS1 and CFC2 own 70% and 30%, respectively, of the interests in the capital and profits of PS2, a partnership. On each cash measurement date, PS1's cash position of $100x consists entirely of cash, and PS2's cash position of $200x includes a $50x short-term obligation of CFC2.

(B) *Analysis.* (1) *Treatment of PS1.* Because an interest in PS1 is held by CFC1, a specified foreign corporation of USP, and PS1 would be a specified foreign corporation of USP if it were a foreign corporation, PS1 is treated as a specified foreign corporation of USP for purposes of determining USP's aggregate foreign cash position. Without regard to paragraph (b)(3) of this section, USP must take into account $100x, its pro rata share of PS1's cash position, for purposes of determining its aggregate foreign cash position. However, 60% of that amount is attributable to deemed stock of PS1 that is not owned (within the meaning of section 958(a)) by a specified foreign corporation of USP. Accordingly, pursuant to paragraph (b)(3) of this section, the amount of PS1's cash position that USP must take into account for purposes of determining its aggregate foreign cash position is reduced by $60x (60% of $100x) to $40x ($100x - $60x).

(2) *Treatment of PS2.* Because an interest in PS2 is held by CFC2, a specified foreign corporation of USP, and PS2 would be a specified foreign corporation of USP if it were a foreign corporation, PS2 is treated as a specified foreign corporation of USP for purposes of determining USP's aggregate foreign cash position. USP, CFC1, CFC2, PS1, and PS2 all have calendar year taxable years. For purposes of determining the aggregate foreign cash position of USP, a section 958(a) U.S. shareholder of PS2, under paragraph (b)(1) of this section, the short-term obligation of CFC2 held by PS2 outstanding on each cash measurement date of each specified foreign corporation is disregarded on such cash measurement dates. Accordingly, without regard to paragraph (b)(3) of this section, USP must take into account $150x ($200x - $50x) of PS2's cash position for purposes of determining its aggregate foreign cash position. However, 42% (60% x 70%) of that amount is attributable to deemed stock of PS2 that is not owned (within the meaning of section 958(a), applied by treating PS1 as foreign if it is a domestic pass-through entity) by a specified foreign corporation of USP (determined without taking into account section 965(c)(3)(E)). Accordingly, pursuant to paragraph (b)(3) of this section, the amount of PS2's cash position that USP must take into account for purposes of determining its aggregate foreign cash position is reduced by $63x (42% of $150x) to $87x ($150x - $63x).

(c) *Determination of aggregate foreign cash position for a section 958(a) U.S. shareholder inclusion year.—(1) Single section 958(a) U.S. shareholder inclusion year.*—If a section 958(a) U.S. shareholder has a single section 958(a) U.S. shareholder inclusion year, then the section 958(a) U.S. shareholder's aggregate foreign cash position for the section 958(a) U.S. shareholder inclusion year is equal to the aggregate foreign cash position of the section 958(a) U.S. shareholder.

(2) *Multiple section 958(a) U.S. shareholder inclusion years.*—If a section 958(a) U.S. shareholder has multiple section 958(a) U.S. shareholder inclusion years, then the section 958(a) U.S. shareholder's aggregate foreign cash position for each section 958(a) U.S. shareholder inclusion year is determined by allocating the aggregate foreign cash position to a section 958(a) U.S. shareholder inclusion year under paragraphs (c)(2)(i) and (c)(2)(ii) of this section.

(i) *Allocation to first section 958(a) U.S. shareholder inclusion year.*—A portion of the aggregate foreign cash position of the section 958(a) U.S. shareholder is allocated to the first section 958(a) U.S. shareholder inclusion year in an amount equal to the lesser of the section 958(a) U.S. shareholder's aggregate foreign cash position or the section 958(a) U.S. shareholder's aggregate section 965(a) inclusion amount for the section 958(a) U.S. shareholder inclusion year.

(ii) *Allocation to succeeding section 958(a) U.S. shareholder inclusion years.*—The amount of the section 958(a) U.S. shareholder's aggregate foreign cash position allocated to any succeeding section 958(a) U.S. shareholder inclusion year equals the lesser of the excess, if any, of the section 958(a) U.S. shareholder's aggregate foreign cash position over the aggregate amount of its aggregate foreign cash position allocated to preceding section 958(a) U.S. shareholder inclusion years under paragraph (c)(2)(i) of this section and this paragraph (c)(2)(ii) or the section 958(a) U.S. shareholder's aggregate section 965(a) inclusion amount for such succeeding section 958(a) U.S. shareholder inclusion year.

(3) *Estimation of aggregate foreign cash position.*—For purposes of determining the aggregate foreign cash position of a section 958(a) U.S. shareholder, the section 958(a) U.S. shareholder may assume that its pro rata share of the cash position of any specified foreign corporation whose last taxable year beginning before January 1, 2018, ends after the date the return for such section 958(a) U.S. shareholder inclusion year (the *estimated section 958(a) U.S. shareholder inclusion year*) is timely filed (taking into account extensions, if any) is zero as of the cash measurement date with which the taxable year of such specified foreign corporation ends. If a section 958(a) U.S. shareholder's pro rata share of the cash position of a specified foreign corporation is treated as zero pursuant to the preceding sentence, the amount described in § 1.965-1(f)(8)(i)(A) with respect to such section 958(a) U.S. shareholder in fact exceeds the amount described in § 1.965-1(f)(8)(i)(B) with respect to such section 958(a) U.S. shareholder, and the aggregate section 965(a) inclusion amount for the estimated section 958(a) U.S. shareholder inclusion year exceeds the amount described in § 1.965-1(f)(8)(i)(B) with respect to such section 958(a) U.S. shareholder, interest and penalties will not be imposed if such section 958(a) U.S. shareholder amends the return for the estimated section 958(a) U.S. shareholder inclusion year to account for the correct aggregate foreign cash position for the year. The amended return must be filed by the due date (taking into account extensions, if any) for the return for the year after the estimated section 958(a) U.S. shareholder inclusion year.

(4) *Examples.*—The following examples illustrate the application of this paragraph (c).

(i) *Example 1. Estimation of aggregate foreign cash position for a section 958(a) U.S. shareholder inclusion year*—(A) *Facts.* USP, a domestic corporation, owns all of the stock of CFC1, a foreign corporation, which owns all of the stock of CFC2, also a foreign corporation. USP is a calendar year taxpayer. CFC1 has a taxable year ending on December 31, and CFC2 has a taxable year ending on November 30. The cash position of CFC1 on each of December 31, 2015, December 31, 2016, and December 31, 2017, is $100x. The cash position of CFC2 on each of November 30, 2015, and November 30, 2016, is $200x. USP has a section 965(a) inclusion amount of $300x with respect to CFC1.

(B) *Analysis.* In determining its aggregate foreign cash position for its 2017 taxable year, USP may assume that its pro rata share of the cash position of CFC2 will be zero as of November 30, 2018, for purposes of filing its return due on April 18, 2018 (or due on October 15, 2018, with extension). Therefore, USP's aggregate foreign cash position is treated as $300x, which is the greater of (a) $300x, 50% of the sum of USP's pro rata shares of the cash position of CFC1 as of December 31, 2015, and December 31, 2016, and of the cash position of CFC2 as of November 30, 2015, and November 30, 2016, and (b) $100x, USP's pro rata share of the cash position of CFC1 as of December 31, 2017. If USP's pro rata share of the cash position of CFC2 as of November 30, 2018, in fact exceeds $200x, USP must amend its return for its 2017 taxable year to reflect the correct aggregate foreign cash position by the due date for its return for its 2018 taxable year, April 15, 2019 (or October 15, 2019, with extension).

(ii) *Example 2. Allocation of aggregate foreign cash position among section 958(a) U.S. shareholder inclusion years*—(A) *Facts.* The facts are the same as in paragraph (c)(4)(i)(A) of this section (the facts in *Example 1*), except that the cash position of each of CFC1 and CFC2 on all relevant cash measurement dates is $200x, with the result that USP has an aggregate foreign cash position determined under § 1.965-1(f)(8)(i) of $400x. For its 2017 taxable year, USP has a section 965(a) inclusion amount with respect to CFC1 of $300x, and for its 2018 taxable year, USP has a section 965(a) inclusion amount with respect to CFC2 of $300x.

(B) *Analysis.* Under paragraph (c)(2)(i) of this section, USP's aggregate foreign cash position for 2017 is $300x, which is the lesser of USP's aggregate foreign cash position determined under § 1.965-1(f)(8)(i) ($400x) or the section 965(a) inclusion amount ($300x) that USP takes into account in 2017. Under paragraph (c)(2)(ii) of this section, the amount of USP's aggregate foreign cash position for 2018 is $100x, USP's aggregate foreign cash position determined under § 1.965-1(f)(8)(i) ($400x) reduced by the amount of its aggregate foreign cash position for 2017 ($300x) under paragraph (c)(2)(i) of this section.

(d) *Increase of income by section 965(c) deduction of an expatriated entity.*—(1) *In general.*—If a person is allowed a section 965(c) deduction and the person (or a successor) first becomes an expatriated entity, with respect to a surrogate foreign corporation, at any time during the 10-year period beginning on December 22, 2017, then the tax imposed by chapter 1 of the Internal Revenue Code is increased for the first taxable year in which such person becomes an expatriated entity by an amount equal to 35 percent of the person's section 965(c) deductions, and no credits are allowed against such increase in tax. The preceding sentence applies only if the surrogate foreign corporation first becomes a surrogate foreign corporation on or after December 22, 2017.

(2) *Definition of expatriated entity.*—For purposes of paragraph (d)(1) of this section, the term *expatriated entity* has the same meaning given such term under section 7874(a)(2), except that such term does not include an expatriated entity if the surrogate foreign corporation with respect to the expatriated entity is treated as a domestic corporation under section 7874(b).

(3) *Definition of surrogate foreign corporation.*—For purposes of paragraph (d)(1) of this section, the term *surrogate foreign corporation* has the meaning given such term in section 7874(a)(2)(B).

(e) *Section 962 election.*—(1) *In general.*—In the case of an individual (including a trust or estate) that makes an election under section 962, any section 965(c) deduction taken into account under § 1.962-1(b)(1)(i)(B) in determining taxable income as used in section 11 is not taken into account for purposes of determining the individual's taxable income under section 1.

(2) *Example.*—The following example illustrates the application of the rule in this paragraph (e).

(i) *Facts.* USI, a United States citizen, owns 10% of the capital and profits of USPRS, a domestic partnership that has a calendar year taxable year, the remainder of which is owned by foreign persons unrelated to USI or USPRS. USPRS owns all of the stock of FS, a foreign corporation that is a controlled foreign corporation with a calendar year taxable year. USPRS has a section 965(a) inclusion amount with respect to FS of $1,000x and has a section 965(c) deduction amount of $700x. FS has no post-1986 foreign income taxes. USI makes a valid election under section 962 for 2017.

(ii) *Analysis.* USI's "taxable income" described in § 1.962-1(b)(1)(i) equals $100x (USI's domestic pass-through owner share of USPRS's section 965(a) inclusion amount) minus $70x (USI's domestic pass-through owner share of USPRS's section 965(c) deduction amount), or $30x. No other deductions are allowed in determining this amount. USI's tax on the $30x section 965(a) inclusion will be equal to the tax that would be imposed on such amount under section 11 if USI were a domestic corporation. Under paragraph (e)(1) of this section, USI cannot deduct $70x for purposes of determining USI's taxable income that is subject to tax under section 1.

(f) *Treatment of section 965(c) deduction under certain provisions of the Internal Revenue Code.*—(1) *Sections 62(a) and 63(d).*—A section 965(c) deduction is treated as a deduction described in section 62(a) and is not treated as an itemized deduction for any purpose of the Internal Revenue Code.

(2) *Sections 705, 1367, and 1368.*—(i) *Adjustments to basis.*—In the case of a domestic partnership or S corporation—

(A) The aggregate amount of its section 965(a) inclusions net of the aggregate amount of its section 965(c) deductions is treated as a separately stated item of net income solely for purposes of calculating basis under section 705(a) and § 1.705-1(a) and section 1367(a)(1) and § 1.1367-1(f), and

(B) The aggregate amount of its section 965(a) inclusions equal to the aggregate amount of its section 965(c) deductions is treated as income exempt from tax solely for purposes of calculating basis under sections 705(a)(1)(B), 1367(a)(1)(A), and § 1.1367-1(f).

(ii) *S corporation accumulated adjustments account.*—In the case of an S corporation, the aggregate amount of its section 965(a) inclusions equal to the aggregate amount of its section 965(c) deductions is treated as income not exempt from tax solely for purposes of determining whether an adjustment is made to an accumulated adjustments account under section 1368(e)(1)(A) and § 1.1368-2(a)(2).

(iii) *Example.*—The following example illustrates the application of this paragraph (f)(2).

(A) *Facts.* USI, a United States citizen, owns all of the stock of S Corp, an S corporation, which owns all of the stock of FS, a foreign corporation. S Corp has a section 965(a) inclusion of $1,000x with respect to FS and has a $700x section 965(c) deduction.

(B) *Analysis.* As a result of the application of paragraph (f)(2)(i)(A) of this section, solely for purposes of calculating basis under section 1367(a)(1) and § 1.1367-1(f), USI treats as a separately stated item of net income $300x (its pro rata share of the net of S Corp's $1,000x aggregate section 965(a) inclusion and S Corp's $700x aggregate section 965(c) deduction). Accordingly, USI's basis in S Corp is increased under section 1367(a)(1) by $300x. As a result of the application of paragraph (f)(2)(i)(B) of this section, an amount of S Corp's aggregate section 965(a) inclusion equal to its aggregate section 965(c) deduction, $700x, is treated as tax exempt income solely for purposes of calculating basis under section 1367(a)(1)(A) and § 1.1367-1(f), and accordingly, USI's basis in S Corp is further increased by its pro rata share of such amount, $700x. S Corp's accumulated adjustments account ("AAA") is increased under section 1368(e)(1)(A) by the $1,000x section 965(a) inclusion taken into account and reduced by the $700x section 965(c) deduction taken into account. In addition, as a result of the application of paragraph (f)(2)(ii) of this section, S Corp's AAA is further increased by an amount of S Corp's aggregate section 965(a) inclusion equal to its aggregate section 965(c) deduction, $700x, which is not treated as tax-exempt income for purposes of § 1.1368-2(a)(2).

(3) *Section 1411.*—For purposes of section 1411 and § 1.1411-4(f)(6), a section 965(c) deduction is not treated as being properly allocable to any section 965(a) inclusion.

(4) *Section 4940.*—For purposes of section 4940(c)(3)(A), a section 965(c) deduction is not treated as an ordinary and necessary expense paid or incurred for the production or collection of gross investment income.

(g) *Domestic pass-through entities.*—For purposes of determining a domestic pass-through owner share, a section 965(c) deduction amount of a domestic pass-through entity must be allocated to a domestic pass-through owner in the same proportion as an aggregate section 965(a) inclusion amount of the domestic pass-through entity for a section 958(a) U.S. shareholder inclusion year is allocated to the domestic pass-through owner. [Reg. § 1.965-3.]

☐ [*T.D.* 9846, 2-4-2019.]

§ 1.965-4. Disregard of certain transactions.—(a) *Scope.*—This section provides rules that disregard certain transactions for purposes of applying section 965 to a United States shareholder. Paragraph (b) of this section provides rules that disregard transactions undertaken with a principal purpose of changing the amount of a section 965 element of a United States shareholder. Paragraph (c) of this section provides rules that disregard certain changes in method of accounting and entity classification elections that would otherwise change the amount of a section 965 element. Paragraph (d) of this section defines the term section 965 element. Paragraph (e) of this section provides rules of application concerning paragraphs (b) and (c) of this section. Paragraph (f) of this section provides rules that disregard certain transactions occurring between E&P measurement dates. Paragraph (g) of this section provides examples illustrating the application of this section.

(b) *Transactions undertaken with a principal purpose of changing the amount of a section 965 element.*—(1) *General rule.*—Except as otherwise provided in paragraph (e)(3) of this section, a transaction is disregarded for purposes of determining the amounts of all section 965 elements of a United States shareholder if each of the following conditions is satisfied with respect to any section 965 element of the United States shareholder—

(i) The transaction occurs, in whole or in part, on or after November 2, 2017 (the *specified date*);

(ii) The transaction is undertaken with a principal purpose of changing the amount of a section 965 element of the United States shareholder; and

(iii) The transaction would, without regard to this paragraph (b)(1), change the amount of the section 965 element of the United States shareholder.

(2) *Presumptions and exceptions for the application of the general rule.*—(i) *Overview.*—Under paragraphs (b)(2)(iii) through (v) of this section, certain transactions are presumed to be undertaken with a principal purpose of changing the amount of a section 965 element of a United States shareholder for purposes of paragraph (b)(1) of this section. The presumptions described in paragraphs (b)(2)(iii) through (v) of this section may be rebutted only if facts and circumstances clearly establish that the transaction was not undertaken with a principal purpose of changing the amount of a section 965 element of a United States shareholder. A taxpayer that takes the position that the presumption is rebutted must attach a statement to its return for its taxable year in which or with which the relevant taxable year of the relevant specified foreign corporation ends disclosing that it has rebutted the presumption. In the case of a transaction described in paragraph (b)(2)(iii) or (iv) of this section, if the presumption does not apply because the transaction occurs in the ordinary course of business, whether the transaction was undertaken with a principal purpose of changing the amount of a section 965 element of a United States shareholder must be determined under all the facts and circumstances. Under paragraphs (b)(2)(iii) through (v) of this section, certain transactions are treated per se as being undertaken with a principal purpose of changing the amount of a section 965 element of a United States shareholder, and, therefore, such transactions are disregarded under paragraph (b)(1) of this section if the conditions of paragraphs (b)(1)(i) and (iii) of this section are satisfied. Further, under paragraph (b)(2)(iii) of this section, certain distributions are treated per se as not being undertaken with a principal purpose of changing the amount of a section 965 element of a United States shareholder and therefore are not disregarded under paragraph (b)(1) of this section.

(ii) *Definitions.*—(A) *Relatedness.*—For purposes of paragraphs (b)(2)(iii) through (v) of this section, a person is treated as related to a United States shareholder if, either immediately before or immediately after the transaction (or series of related transactions), the person bears a relationship to the United States shareholder described in section 267(b) or section 707(b).

(B) *Transfer.*—*(1) In general.*—For purposes of paragraphs (b)(2)(iii) and (v) of this section, the term *transfer* includes any disposition of stock or property, including a sale or exchange, contribution, distribution, issuance, redemption, recapitalization, or loan of stock or property, and includes an indirect transfer of stock or property.

(2) Indirect transfer.—For purposes of paragraph (b)(2)(ii)(B)(*1*) of this section, the term *indirect transfer* includes a transfer of property or stock owned by an entity through a transfer of an interest in such entity (or an interest in an entity that has a direct or indirect interest in such entity), and a transfer of property or stock to a person through a transfer of property or stock to a pass-through entity of which such person is a direct or indirect owner.

(iii) *Cash reduction transactions.*—(A) *General rule.*—For purposes of paragraph (b)(1) of this section, a cash reduction transaction is presumed to be undertaken with a principal purpose of changing the amount of a section 965 element of a United States shareholder. For this purpose, the term *cash reduction transaction* means a transfer of cash, accounts receivable, or cash-equivalent assets by a specified foreign corporation to a United States shareholder of the specified foreign corporation or a person related to a United States shareholder of the specified foreign corporation, or an assumption by a specified foreign corporation of an account payable of a United States shareholder of the specified foreign corporation or a person related to a United States shareholder of the specified foreign corporation, if such transfer or assumption would, without regard to paragraph (b)(1) of this section, reduce the aggregate foreign cash position of the United States shareholder. The presumption described in this paragraph (b)(2)(iii) does not apply to a cash reduction transaction that occurs in the ordinary course of business.

(B) *Per se rules for certain distributions.*—Notwithstanding the presumption described in paragraph (b)(2)(iii)(A) of this section, except in the case of a specified distribution, a cash reduction transaction that is a distribution by a specified foreign corporation to a United States shareholder of the specified foreign corporation is treated per se as not being undertaken with a principal purpose of changing the amount of a section 965 element of the United States shareholder for purposes of paragraph (b)(1) of this section. A specified distribution is treated per se as being undertaken with a principal purpose of changing the amount of a section 965 element of a United States shareholder for purposes of paragraph (b)(1) of this section. For purposes of this paragraph (b)(2)(iii)(B), the term *specified distribution* means a cash reduction transaction that is a distribution by a specified foreign corporation of a United States shareholder if and to the extent that, at the time of the distribution, there was a plan or intention for the distributee to transfer cash, accounts receivable, or cash-equivalent assets to any specified foreign corporation of the

United States shareholder or a distribution that is a non pro rata distribution to a foreign person that is related to the United States shareholder. For purposes of the preceding sentence, there is no plan or intention for the distributee to transfer cash, accounts receivable, or cash-equivalent assets to any specified foreign corporation of the United States shareholder if the transfer is pursuant to a legal obligation entered into before November 2, 2017. A taxpayer that takes the position that a cash reduction transaction is not a specified distribution because a transfer of cash, accounts receivable, or cash-equivalent asset is pursuant to a legal obligation entered into before November 2, 2017, must attach a statement to its return for its taxable year in which or with which the relevant taxable year of the relevant specified foreign corporation ends disclosing the position.

(iv) *E&P reduction transactions.*—(A) *General rule.*—For purposes of paragraph (b)(1) of this section, an E&P reduction transaction is presumed to be undertaken with a principal purpose of changing the amount of a section 965 element of a United States shareholder. For purposes of this paragraph (b)(2)(iv), the term *E&P reduction transaction* means a transaction between a specified foreign corporation and any of a United States shareholder of the specified foreign corporation, another specified foreign corporation of a United States shareholder of the specified foreign corporation, or any person related to a United States shareholder of the specified foreign corporation, if the transaction would, without regard to paragraph (b)(1) of this section, reduce either the accumulated post-1986 deferred foreign income or the post-1986 undistributed earnings (as defined in section 902(c)(1)) of the specified foreign corporation or another specified foreign corporation of any United States shareholder of such specified foreign corporation. The presumption described in this paragraph (b)(2)(iv)(A) does not apply to an E&P reduction transaction that occurs in the ordinary course of business.

(B) *Per se rule for specified transactions.*—A specified transaction is treated per se as being undertaken with a principal purpose of changing the amount of a section 965 element of a United States shareholder for purposes of paragraph (b)(1) of this section. For purposes of the preceding sentence, the term *specified transaction* means an E&P reduction transaction that involves one or more of the following: a complete liquidation of a specified foreign corporation to which section 331 applies; a sale or other disposition of stock by a specified foreign corporation; or a distribution by a specified foreign corporation that reduces the earnings and profits of the specified foreign corporation pursuant to section 312(a)(3).

(v) *Pro rata share transactions.*—(A) *General rule.*—For purposes of paragraph (b)(1) of this section, a pro rata share transaction is presumed to be undertaken with a principal purpose of changing the amount of a section 965 element of a United States shareholder. For this purpose, the term *pro rata share transaction* means either a pro rata share reduction transaction or an E&P deficit transaction.

(1) Definition of pro rata share reduction transaction.—For purposes of this paragraph (b)(2)(v)(A), the term *pro rata share reduction transaction* means a transfer of the stock of a specified foreign corporation by either a United States shareholder of the specified foreign corporation or a person related to a United States shareholder of the specified foreign corporation (including by the specified foreign corporation itself) to a person related to the United States shareholder if the transfer would, without regard to paragraph (b)(1) of this section, reduce the United States shareholder's pro rata share of the section 965(a) earnings amount of the specified foreign corporation, reduce the United States shareholder's pro rata share of the cash position of the specified foreign corporation, or both.

(2) Definition of E&P deficit transaction.—For purposes of this paragraph (b)(2)(v)(A), the term *E&P deficit transaction* means a transfer to either a United States shareholder or a person related to the United States shareholder of the stock of an E&P deficit foreign corporation by a person related to the United States shareholder (including by the E&P deficit foreign corporation itself) if the transfer would, without regard to paragraph (b)(1) of this section, increase the United States shareholder's pro rata share of the specified E&P deficit of the E&P deficit foreign corporation.

(B) *Per se rule for internal group transactions.*—An internal group transaction is treated per se as being undertaken with a principal purpose of changing the amount of a section 965 element of a United States shareholder for purposes of paragraph (b)(1) of this section. For purposes of the preceding sentence, the term *internal group transaction* means a pro rata share transaction if, immediately before or after the transfer, the transferor of the stock of the specified foreign corporation and the transferee of such stock are members of an affiliated group in which the United States shareholder is a member. For this purpose, the term *affiliated group* has the meaning set forth in section 1504(a), determined without regard to paragraphs (1) through (8) of section 1504(b), and the term *members of an affiliated group* means entities included in the same affiliated group. For purposes of identifying an affiliated group and the members of such group, each partner in a partnership, as determined without regard to this sentence, is treated as holding its proportionate share of the stock held by the partnership, as determined under the rules and principles of sections 701 through 777, and if one or more members of an affiliated group own, in the aggregate, at least 80 percent of the interests in a partnership's capital or profits, the partnership will be treated as a corporation that is a member of the affiliated group.

(C) *Example.*—The following example illustrates the application of the rules in this paragraph (b)(2)(v).

(1) Facts. FP, a foreign corporation, owns all of the stock of USP, a domestic corporation. USP owns all of the stock of FS, a foreign corporation. USP has a calendar year taxable year; FS's taxable year ends November 30. On January 2, 2018, USP transfers all of the stock of FS to FP in exchange for cash. On January 3, 2018, FS makes a distribution with respect to the stock transferred to FP. USP treats the transaction as a taxable sale of the FS stock and claims a dividends received deduction under section 245A with respect to its deemed dividend under section 1248(j) as a result of the sale. FS has post-1986 earnings and profits as of December 31, 2017, and no post-1986 earnings and profits that are attributable to income effectively connected with the conduct of a trade or business within the United States and subject to tax under chapter 1 or that, if distributed, would be excluded from the gross income of a United States shareholder under section 959.

(2) Analysis. The transfer of the stock of FS is a pro rata share reduction transaction and thus a pro rata share transaction because such transfer is by USP, a United States shareholder, to FP, a person related to USP, and the transfer would, without regard to the rule in paragraph (b)(1) of this section, reduce USP's pro rata share of the section 965(a) earnings amount of FS. Because USP and FP are also members of an affiliated group within the meaning of paragraph (b)(2)(v)(B) of this section, the transfer of the stock of FS is also an internal group transaction and is treated per se as being undertaken with a principal purpose of changing the amount of a section 965 element of USP. Accordingly, because the transfer occurs after the specified date and reduces USP's section 965(a) inclusion amount with respect to FS, the transfer is disregarded for purposes of determining any section 965 element of USP with the result that, among other things, USP's pro rata share of FS's section 965(a) earnings amount is determined as if USP owned (within the meaning of section 958(a)) 100% of the stock of FS on the last day of FS's inclusion year and no other person received a distribution with respect to such stock during such year. *See* section 951(a)(2)(A) and (B).

(c) *Disregard of certain changes in method of accounting and entity classification elections.*—(1) *Changes in method of accounting.*—Any change in method of accounting made for a taxable year of a specified foreign corporation that ends in 2017 or 2018 is disregarded for purposes of determining the amounts of all section 965 elements with respect to a United States shareholder if the change in method of accounting would, without regard to this paragraph (c)(1), change the amount of any section 965 element described in paragraph (d)(1) or (2) of this section with respect to the United States shareholder, or change the amount of the section 965 element described in paragraph (d)(3) of this section other than by reason of an increase in a section 965(a) inclusion amount with respect to the specified foreign corporation, regardless of whether the change in method of accounting is made with a principal purpose of changing the amount of a section 965 element with respect to the United States shareholder. The rule described in the preceding sentence applies regardless of whether the change in method of accounting was made in accordance with the procedures described in Rev. Proc. 2015-13, 2015-5 I.R.B. 419 (or successor), and regardless of whether the change in method of accounting was properly made, but it does not apply to a change in method of accounting for which the original and/or duplicate copy of any Form 3115, "Application for Change in Accounting Method," requesting the change was filed before the specified date (as defined in paragraph (b)(1) of this section).

(2) *Entity classification elections.*—Except as otherwise provided in paragraph (e)(3) of this section, an election under § 301.7701-3 to change the classification of an entity that is filed on or after the specified date (as defined in paragraph (b)(1) of this section) is

disregarded for purposes of determining the amounts of all section 965 elements of a United States shareholder if the election would, without regard to this paragraph (c)(2), change the amount of any section 965 element of the United States shareholder, regardless of whether the election is made with a principal purpose of changing the amount of a section 965 element of the United States shareholder. An election filed on or after the specified date is subject to the preceding sentence even if the election was filed with an effective date that is before the specified date.

(d) *Definition of a section 965 element.*—For purposes of paragraphs (b) and (c) of this section, the term *section 965 element* means, with respect to a United States shareholder, any of the following amounts (collectively, *section 965 elements*)—

(1) The United States shareholder's section 965(a) inclusion amount with respect to a specified foreign corporation;

(2) The aggregate foreign cash position of the United States shareholder; or

(3) The amount of foreign income taxes of a specified foreign corporation deemed paid by the United States shareholder under section 960 as a result of a section 965(a) inclusion.

(e) *Rules for applying paragraphs (b) and (c) of this section.*—(1) *Determination of whether there is a change in the amount of a section 965 element.*—For purposes of paragraphs (b) and (c) of this section, there is a change in the amount of a section 965 element of a United States shareholder as a result of a transaction, change in accounting method, or election to change an entity's classification, if, without regard to paragraph (b)(1), (c)(1), or (c)(2) of this section, the transaction, change in accounting method, or change in entity classification would—

(i) Reduce the amount described in paragraph (d)(1) of this section,

(ii) Reduce the amount described in paragraph (d)(2) of this section, but only if such amount is less than the United States shareholder's aggregate section 965(a) inclusion amount, or

(iii) Increase the amount described in paragraph (d)(3) of this section.

(2) *Treatment of domestic pass-through owners as United States shareholders.*—For purposes of paragraphs (b) and (c) of this section, if a domestic pass-through entity is a United States shareholder, then a domestic pass-through owner with respect to the domestic pass-through entity that is not otherwise a United States shareholder is treated as a United States shareholder.

(3) *Exception for certain incorporation transactions.*—(i) *In general.*—Paragraphs (b) and (c)(2) of this section do not apply to disregard a transfer of stock of a specified foreign corporation by a United States shareholder to a domestic corporation (for this purpose, including an S corporation), provided that—

(A) The transferee's section 965(a) inclusion amount with respect to the transferred stock of the specified foreign corporation is no lower than the transferor's section 965(a) inclusion amount with respect to the transferred stock of the specified foreign corporation, determined without regard to the transfer; and

(B) The transferee and the transferor determine their aggregate foreign cash position under paragraph (e)(3)(ii) of this section.

(ii) *Aggregate foreign cash position.*—In the case of a transfer described in paragraph (e)(3)(i) of this section, in order to rely on the exception in paragraph (e)(3)(i) of this section—

(A) The transferee must treat its pro rata share of the cash position of a specified foreign corporation as of a cash measurement date as of which it did not own the transferred stock of the specified foreign corporation as including the transferor's pro rata share of the cash position of the specified foreign corporation with respect to the transferred stock of the specified foreign corporation as of such cash measurement date for purposes of determining its aggregate foreign cash position; and

(B) The transferor must treat its pro rata share of the cash position of a specified foreign corporation as of a cash measurement date as of which it did not own the transferred stock of the specified foreign corporation as including the transferee's pro rata share of the cash position of the specified foreign corporation with respect to the transferred stock of the specified foreign corporation as of such cash measurement date for purposes of determining its aggregate foreign cash position.

(4) *Consequences of liquidation.*—(i) *In general.*—In the case of a liquidation of a specified foreign corporation that is disregarded for purposes of determining the section 965 elements of a United States shareholder pursuant to paragraph (b) or (c)(2) of this section, for purposes of determining the amounts of the section 965 elements of the United States shareholder, the date that is treated as the last day of the taxable year of the specified foreign corporation is the later of—

(A) The date of the liquidation; and

(B) The specified liquidation date, if any.

(ii) *Specified liquidation date.*—The term *specified liquidation date* means, in the case of a liquidation of a specified foreign corporation pursuant to an entity classification election that is disregarded for purposes of determining the section 965 elements of a United States shareholder—

(A) November 30, 2017, with respect to a United States shareholder that must include in income under § 1.367(b)-3 as a deemed dividend the all earnings and profits amount with respect to the United States shareholder's stock of the liquidating specified foreign corporation; or

(B) The date of filing of the entity classification election, with respect to all other United States shareholders.

(f) *Disregard of certain transactions occurring between E&P measurement dates.*—(1) *Disregard of specified payments.*—Except as provided in paragraph (f)(3) of this section, a specified payment made by a specified foreign corporation (*payor specified foreign corporation*) to another specified foreign corporation (*payee specified foreign corporation*) is disregarded for purposes of determining the post-1986 earnings and profits of each of the payor specified foreign corporation and the payee specified foreign corporation as of the E&P measurement date on December 31, 2017.

(2) *Definition of specified payment.*—For purposes of paragraph (f)(1) of this section, the term *specified payment* means any amount paid or accrued by the payor specified foreign corporation, including a distribution by the payor specified foreign corporation with respect to its stock, if each of the following conditions are satisfied:

(i) Immediately before or immediately after the payment or accrual of the amount, the payor specified foreign corporation and the payee specified foreign corporation are related within the meaning of section 954(d)(3), substituting the term "specified foreign corporation" for "controlled foreign corporation" in each place that it appears;

(ii) The payment or accrual of the amount occurs after November 2, 2017, and on or before December 31, 2017; and

(iii) The payment or accrual of the amount would, without regard to the application of paragraph (f)(1) of this section, reduce the post-1986 earnings and profits of the payor specified foreign corporation as of the E&P measurement date on December 31, 2017.

(3) *Non-application of disregard rule.*—A section 958(a) U.S. shareholder may determine the post-1986 earnings and profits of a specified foreign corporation without regard to paragraph (f)(1) of this section, provided that it and every section 958(a) U.S. shareholder related to the first section 958(a) U.S. shareholder determines the post-1986 earnings and profits of each of its specified foreign corporations without regard to paragraph (f)(1) of this section. For purposes of this paragraph (f)(3), a person is treated as related to a section 958(a) U.S. shareholder if the person bears a relationship to the section 958(a) U.S. shareholder described in section 267(b) or 707(b).

(4) *Examples.*—The following examples illustrate the application of the rules in this paragraph (f).

(i) *Example 1. Deductible payment between wholly owned specified foreign corporations is a specified payment.* (A) *Facts.* USP, a domestic corporation, owns all of the stock of CFC1, a foreign corporation, which owns all of the stock of CFC2, also a foreign corporation. USP, CFC1, and CFC2 have calendar year taxable years. On November 2, 2017, each of CFC1 and CFC2 has post-1986 earnings and profits of 100u. Neither CFC1 nor CFC2 has post-1986 earnings and profits that are attributable to income of the specified foreign corporation that is effectively connected with the conduct of a trade or business within the United States and subject to tax under chapter 1 or that, if distributed, would be excluded from the gross income of a United States shareholder under section 959 or from the gross income of another shareholder if such shareholder were a United States shareholder; therefore, no adjustment is made under section 965(d)(2) or § 1.965-1(f)(7), and each of CFC1's and CFC2's accumulated post-1986 deferred foreign income is equal to such corporation's post-1986 earnings and profits. On November 3, 2017, CFC2 makes a deductible payment of 10u to CFC1. The payment does not constitute subpart F income. CFC1 and CFC2 have no other items of income or deduction.

(B) *Analysis.* The payment from CFC2 to CFC1 is a specified payment because *(1)* CFC1 and CFC2 are related specified foreign corporations; *(2)* the payment occurs after November 2, 2017, and on or before December 31, 2017; and *(3)* the payment would, without regard to the application of the rule in paragraph (f)(1) of this section, reduce the post-1986 earnings and profits of CFC2 as of the E&P measurement date on December 31, 2017. Under paragraph (f)(1) of this section, the payment is disregarded, and CFC1 and CFC2 each have post-1986 earnings and profits of 100u as of December 31, 2017. Accordingly, the section 965(a) earnings amount of each of CFC1 and CFC2 is 100u.

(ii) *Example 2. Distribution is a specified payment.* (A) *Facts.* The facts are the same as in paragraph (f)(4)(i)(A) of this section (the facts in *Example 1*), except instead of a deductible payment to CFC1, CFC2 makes a 10u distribution on November 3, 2017, that, without regard to paragraph (f)(1) of this section would reduce the post-1986 earnings and profits of CFC2 as of the E&P measurement date on December 31, 2017, and increase the post-1986 earnings and profits of CFC1 as of the E&P measurement date on December 31, 2017, by 10u.

(B) *Analysis.* The distribution is a specified payment because *(1)* CFC1 and CFC2 are related specified foreign corporations; *(2)* the distribution occurs after November 2, 2017, and on or before December 31, 2017; and *(3)* the distribution would, without regard to the application of the rule in paragraph (f)(1) of this section, reduce the post-1986 earnings and profits of CFC2 as of the E&P measurement date on December 31, 2017. Under paragraph (f)(1) of this section, the distribution is disregarded with the result that CFC1 and CFC2 each have post-1986 earnings and profits of 100u as of the E&P measurement date on December 31, 2017, and a section 965(a) earnings amount of 100u.

(iii) *Example 3. Deductible payment between related (but not wholly owned) specified foreign corporations is a specified payment.* (A) *Facts.* The facts are the same as in paragraph (f)(4)(i)(A) of this section (the facts in *Example 1*), except that CFC1 owns only 51% of the only class of stock of CFC2, the remainder of which is owned by USI, a United States citizen unrelated to USP, CFC1, and CFC2.

(B) *Analysis.* The analysis is the same as in paragraph (f)(4)(i)(B) of this section (the analysis in *Example 1*); thus, the payment is disregarded with the result that CFC1 and CFC2 each have post-1986 earnings and profits of 100u as of the E&P measurement date on December 31, 2017, and a section 965(a) earnings amount of 100u.

(iv) *Example 4. Deductible payment between unrelated specified foreign corporations is not a specified payment.* (A) *Facts.* The facts are the same as in paragraph (f)(4)(i)(A) of this section (the facts in *Example 1*), except that CFC1 owns only 50% of the only class of stock of CFC2, the remainder of which is owned by USI, a United States citizen unrelated to USP, CFC1, and CFC2.

(B) *Analysis.* Paragraph (f)(1) of this section does not apply because CFC1 and CFC2 are not related. Thus, the payment is taken into account with the result that CFC1 has post-1986 earnings and profits of 110u as of the E&P measurement date on December 31, 2017, and a section 965(a) earnings amount of 110u.

(v) *Example 5. Deductible payment and income accrued from unrelated persons are not specified payments.* (A) *Facts.* The facts are the same as in paragraph (f)(4)(i)(A) of this section (the facts in *Example 1*), except that CFC2 does not make a deductible payment to CFC1, and, between E&P measurement dates, CFC2 accrues gross income of 20u from a person that is not related to CFC2, and CFC1 incurs a deductible expense of 20u to a person that is not related to CFC1.

(B) *Analysis.* Paragraph (f)(1) of this section does not apply because neither the deductible expense of CFC1 nor the income accrual by CFC2 are attributable to a specified payment.

(vi) *Example 6. Deductible payment and income accrued with respect to unrelated persons are not specified payments; deductible payment between wholly specified foreign corporations is a specified payment.* (A) *Facts.* The facts are the same as in paragraph (f)(4)(v)(A) of this section (the facts in *Example 5*), except that CFC2 also makes a deductible payment of 10u to CFC1 on November 3, 2017.

(B) *Analysis.* The deductible payment is a specified payment because *(1)* CFC1 and CFC2 are related specified foreign corporations; *(2)* the payment occurs after November 2, 2017, and on or before December 31, 2017; and *(3)* the deductible payment would, without regard to the application of the rule in paragraph (f)(1) of this section, reduce the post-1986 earnings and profits of CFC2 as of the E&P measurement date on December 31, 2017. Accordingly, under paragraph (f)(1) of this section, the deductible payment is disregarded with the result that CFC1 and CFC2 have 80u and 120u of post-1986 earnings and profits as of the E&P measurement date on December 31, 2017, respectively. Accordingly, CFC1 and CFC2 have section 965(a) earnings amounts of 100u and 120u, respectively. [Reg. § 1.965-4.]

☐ [*T.D. 9846, 2-4-2019.*]

§ 1.965-5. Allowance of a credit or deduction for foreign income taxes.—(a) *Scope.*—This section provides rules for the allowance of a credit or deduction for foreign income taxes in connection with the application of section 965. Paragraph (b) of this section provides rules under section 965(g) for the allowance of a credit or deduction for foreign income taxes paid or accrued. Paragraph (c) of this section provides rules for the allowance of a credit or deduction for foreign income taxes treated as paid or accrued in connection with the application of section 965. Paragraph (d) of this section defines the term applicable percentage.

(b) *Rules for foreign income taxes paid or accrued.*—(1) *In general.*—Neither a deduction (including under section 164) nor a credit under section 901 is allowed for the applicable percentage of any foreign income taxes paid or accrued with respect to any amount for which a section 965(c) deduction is allowed for a section 958(a) U.S. shareholder inclusion year. Neither a deduction (including under section 164) nor a credit under section 901 is allowed for the applicable percentage of any foreign income taxes attributable to a distribution of section 965(a) previously taxed earnings and profits or section 965(b) previously taxed earnings and profits. Accordingly, for example, no deduction or credit is allowed for the applicable percentage of any withholding taxes imposed on a United States shareholder by the jurisdiction of residence of the distributing foreign corporation with respect to a distribution of section 965(a) previously taxed earnings and profits or section 965(b) previously taxed earnings and profits. Similarly, for example, no deduction or credit is allowed for the applicable percentage of foreign income taxes imposed on a United States citizen by the citizen's jurisdiction of residence upon receipt of a distribution of section 965(a) previously taxed earnings and profits or section 965(b) previously taxed earnings and profits.

(2) *Attributing taxes to section 959(a) distributions of section 965 previously taxed earnings and profits.*—For purposes of paragraph (b)(1) of this section, foreign income taxes are attributable to a distribution of section 965(a) previously taxed earnings and profits or section 965(b) previously taxed earnings and profits if such taxes would be allocated and apportioned to a distribution of such previously taxed earnings and profits under the principles of § 1.904-6(a)(1)(iv), regardless of whether an actual distribution is made or recognized for Federal income tax purposes. Therefore, for example, a credit or deduction for the applicable percentage of foreign income taxes imposed on a United States shareholder that pays foreign tax on a distribution that is not recognized for Federal income tax purposes (for example, in the case of a consent dividend or stock dividend upon which a withholding tax is imposed) is not allowed under paragraph (b)(1) of this section to the extent it is attributable to a distribution of section 965(a) previously taxed earnings and profits or section 965(b) previously taxed earnings and profits under the principles of § 1.904-6(a)(1)(iv). For taxable years of foreign corporations beginning after December 31, 2019, in lieu of applying the principles of § 1.904-6 under this paragraph (b)(2), the rules in § 1.861-20 apply by treating the portion of a distribution attributable to section 965(a) previously taxed earnings and profits and the portion of a distribution attributable to section 965(b) previously taxed earnings and profits each as a statutory grouping, and the portion of the distribution that is attributable to other earnings and profits as the residual grouping. See § 1.861-20(g)(7) (*Example 6*).

(c) *Rules for foreign income taxes treated as paid or accrued.*—(1) *Disallowed credit.*—(i) *In general.*—A credit under section 901 is not allowed for the applicable percentage of any foreign income taxes treated as paid or accrued with respect to any amount for which a section 965(c) deduction is allowed for a section 958(a) U.S. shareholder inclusion year. For purposes of the preceding sentence, taxes treated as paid or accrued include foreign income taxes deemed paid under section 960(a)(1) with respect to a section 965(a) inclusion, foreign income taxes deemed paid under section 960(a)(3) (as in effect on December 21, 2017) or section 960(b) (as applicable to taxable years of controlled foreign corporations beginning after December 31, 2017) with respect to distributions of section 965(a) previously taxed earnings and profits or section 965(b) previously taxed earnings and profits, foreign income taxes allocated to an entity under § 1.901-2(f)(4), and a distributive share of foreign income taxes paid or accrued by a partnership.

(ii) *Foreign income taxes deemed paid under section 960(a)(3) (as in effect on December 21, 2017)*.—Foreign income taxes deemed paid by a domestic corporation under section 960(a)(3) with respect to a distribution of section 965(a) previously taxed earnings and profits or section 965(b) previously taxed earnings and profits include only the foreign income taxes paid or accrued by an upper tier foreign corporation with respect to a distribution of section 965(a) previously taxed earnings and profits or section 965(b) previously taxed earnings and profits from a lower-tier foreign corporation. No credit is allowed under section 960(a)(3) or any other section for foreign income taxes that would have been deemed paid under section 960(a)(1) with respect to the portion of a section 965(a) earnings amount that is reduced under § 1.965-1(b)(2) or § 1.965-8(b).

(iii) *Foreign income taxes deemed paid under section 960(b) (as applicable to taxable years of controlled foreign corporations beginning after December 31, 2017, and to taxable years of United States persons in which or with which such taxable years of foreign corporations end)*.—Paragraph (c)(1)(i) of this section applies to foreign income taxes deemed paid under section 960(b) (as in effect for a taxable year of a controlled foreign corporation beginning after December 31, 2017, and a taxable year of a United States person in which or with which such controlled foreign corporation's taxable year ends) only if such taxes are deemed paid under § 1.960-3(b)(1) with respect to distributions to a domestic corporation of section 965(a) previously taxed earnings and profits or section 965(b) previously taxed earnings and profits. *See also* § 1.960-3(c)(2)(i), (ii), (vi), or (vii). Foreign income taxes that would have been deemed paid under section 960(a)(1) (as in effect on December 21, 2017) with respect to the portion of a section 965(a) earnings amount that was reduced under § 1.965-1(b)(2) or § 1.965-8(b) are not eligible to be deemed paid under section 960(b) and § 1.960-3(b) or any other section of the Code.

(2) *Disallowed deduction*.—No deduction (including under section 164) is allowed for the applicable percentage of any foreign income taxes treated as paid or accrued with respect to any amount for which a section 965(c) deduction is allowed. Such taxes include foreign income taxes allocated to an entity under § 1.901-2(f)(4) and a distributive share of foreign income taxes paid or accrued by a partnership.

(3) *Coordination with section 78*.—(i) *In general*.—With respect to foreign income taxes deemed paid by a domestic corporation with respect to its section 965(a) inclusion amount for a section 958(a) U.S. shareholder inclusion year, section 78 applies only to so much of such taxes as bears the same proportion to the amount of such taxes as—

(A) The excess of—

(*1*) The section 965(a) inclusion amount for a section 958(a) U.S. shareholder inclusion year, over

(*2*) The section 965(c) deduction amount allowable with respect to such section 965(a) inclusion amount, bears to

(B) Such section 965(a) inclusion amount.

(ii) *Domestic corporation that is a domestic pass-through owner*.—With respect to foreign income taxes deemed paid by a domestic corporation attributable to such corporation's domestic pass-through owner share of a section 965(a) inclusion amount of a domestic pass-through entity, section 78 applies only to so much of such taxes as bears the same proportion to the amount of such taxes as the proportion determined under paragraph (c)(3)(i) of this section as applied to the domestic pass-through entity's section 965(a) inclusion amount for a section 958(a) U.S. shareholder inclusion year.

(d) *Applicable percentage*.—(1) *In general*.—For purposes of this section, except as provided in paragraph (d)(2) and (d)(3) of this section, the term *applicable percentage* means, with respect to a section 958(a) U.S. shareholder and a section 958(a) U.S. shareholder inclusion year, the amount (expressed as a percentage) equal to the sum of—

(i) 0.771 multiplied by the ratio of—

(A) The section 958(a) U.S. shareholder's 8 percent rate amount for the section 958(a) U.S. shareholder inclusion year, divided by

(B) The sum of the section 958(a) U.S. shareholder's 8 percent rate amount for the section 958(a) U.S. shareholder inclusion year plus the section 958(a) U.S. shareholder's 15.5 percent rate amount for the section 958(a) U.S. shareholder inclusion year; plus

(ii) 0.557 multiplied by the ratio of—

(A) The section 958(a) U.S. shareholder's 15.5 percent rate amount for the section 958(a) U.S. shareholder inclusion year, divided by

(B) The amount described in paragraph (d)(1)(i)(B) of this section.

(2) *No section 965(a) inclusion amount*.—If a section 958(a) U.S. shareholder does not have an aggregate section 965(a) inclusion amount, the section 958(a) U.S. shareholder's applicable percentage is 55.7 percent.

(3) *Applicable percentage for domestic pass-through owners*.—In the case of a domestic pass-through owner with respect to a domestic pass-through entity, the domestic pass-through owner's applicable percentage that is applied to foreign income taxes attributable to the domestic pass-through owner share of the section 965(a) inclusion amount or of distributions of section 965(a) previously taxed earnings and profits or section 965(b) previously taxed earnings and profits is equal to the applicable percentage determined under paragraph (d)(1) or (2) of this section, as applicable, with respect to the domestic pass-through entity.

(4) *Applicable percentage with respect to certain distributions of previously taxed earnings and profits*.—In the case of a distribution of section 965(a) previously taxed earnings and profits or section 965(b) previously taxed earnings and profits (other than with respect to a section 958(a) U.S. shareholder described in paragraph (d)(2) of this section), the applicable percentage that is applied to foreign income taxes attributable to the distribution is the applicable percentage that applied with respect to the section 958(a) U.S. shareholder and the section 958(a) U.S. inclusion year in which, or with which, the inclusion year of the relevant deferred foreign income corporation ends. For this purpose, the relevant deferred foreign income corporation is the deferred foreign income corporation with respect to which the section 958(a) U.S. shareholder had the section 965(a) inclusion as a result of which the section 965(a) previously taxed earnings and profits first arose (as described in § 1.965-2(c)) or the section 965(b) previously taxed earnings and profits first arose (as described in § 1.965-2(d)). [Reg. § 1.965-5.]

☐ [*T.D. 9846, 2-4-2019. Amended by T.D. 9882, 12-16-2019 and T.D.* 9922, 11-2-2020.]

§ 1.965-6. Computation of foreign income taxes deemed paid and allocation and apportionment of deductions.—(a) *Scope*.—This section provides rules for the computation of foreign income taxes deemed paid and the allocation and apportionment of deductions. Paragraph (b) of this section provides the general rules for the computation of foreign income taxes deemed paid under sections 902 and 960. Paragraph (c) of this section provides rules for allocation and apportionment of expenses. Paragraph (d) of this section provides rules for foreign income taxes associated with hovering deficits.

(b) *Computation of foreign incomes taxes deemed paid*.—(1) *In general*.—For purposes of determining foreign income taxes deemed paid under section 960(a)(1) with respect to a section 965(a) inclusion attributable to a deferred foreign income corporation that is a member of a qualified group (as defined in section 902(b)(2)), section 902 applies as if the section 965(a) inclusion, translated (if necessary) into the functional currency of the deferred foreign income corporation using the spot rate on December 31, 2017, were a dividend paid by the deferred foreign income corporation. For purposes of computing the amount of foreign income taxes deemed paid under section 960(a)(1), §§ 1.965-2(b), 1.965-5, sections 902 and 960, the regulations under those sections, and this section apply.

(2) *Dividend or inclusion in excess of post-1986 undistributed earnings*.—When the denominator of the section 902 fraction is positive but less than the numerator of such fraction, the section 902 fraction is one. When the denominator of the section 902 fraction is zero or less than zero, the section 902 fraction is zero, and no foreign taxes are deemed paid.

(3) *Treatment of adjustment under section 965(b)(4)(B)*.—For purposes of section 902(c)(1), the post-1986 undistributed earnings of an E&P deficit foreign corporation are increased under section 965(b)(4)(B) and § 1.965-2(d)(2)(i)(A) as of the first day of the foreign corporation's first taxable year following the E&P deficit foreign corporation's last taxable year that begins before January 1, 2018.

(4) *Section 902 fraction*.—The term *section 902 fraction* means, with respect to either a deferred foreign income corporation or an E&P deficit foreign corporation, the fraction that is—

(i) The dividends paid by, or the inclusion under section 951(a)(1) (including a section 965(a) inclusion) with respect to, the foreign corporation, as applicable (the *numerator*), divided by

(ii) The foreign corporation's post-1986 undistributed earnings or pre-1987 accumulated profits, as applicable (the *denominator*).

(c) *Allocation and apportionment of deductions.*—For purposes of allocating and apportioning expenses, a section 965(c) deduction does not result in any gross income, including a section 965(a) inclusion, being treated as exempt, excluded, or eliminated income within the meaning of section 864(e)(3) or § 1.861-8T(d). Similarly, a section 965(c) deduction does not result in the treatment of stock as an exempt asset within the meaning of section 864(e)(3) or § 1.861-8T(d). In addition, consistent with the general inapplicability of § 1.861-8T(d)(2) to earnings and profits described in section 959(c)(1) or 959(c)(2), neither section 965(a) previously taxed earnings and profits nor section 965(b) previously taxed earnings and profits are treated as giving rise to gross income that is exempt, excluded, or eliminated income. Similarly, the asset that gives rise to a section 965(a) inclusion, section 965(a) previously taxed earnings and profits, or section 965(b) previously taxed earnings and profits is not treated as a tax-exempt asset.

(d) *Hovering deficits.*—In the last taxable year that begins before January 1, 2018, of a deferred foreign income corporation that is also a foreign surviving corporation, as defined in § 1.367(b)-7(a), solely for purposes of determining the amount of related taxes that are included in post-1986 foreign income taxes under § 1.367(b)-7(d)(2)(iii)—

(1) The post-transaction earnings described in § 1.367(b)-7(d)(2)(ii) that can be offset by a hovering deficit include any post-transaction earnings earned in that year that were not considered accumulated because they were included in income under section 965 and § 1.965-1(b)(1) by a section 958(a) U.S. shareholder; and

(2) Any offset for purposes of § 1.367(b)-7(d)(2)(ii) is treated as occurring on the last day of the foreign surviving corporation's inclusion year. [Reg. § 1.965-6.]

□ [*T.D. 9846, 2-4-2019.*]

§ 1.965-7. Elections, payment, and other special rules.—(a) *Scope.*—This section provides rules regarding certain elections and payments. Paragraph (b) of this section provides rules regarding the section 965(h) election. Paragraph (c) of this section provides rules regarding the section 965(i) election. Paragraph (d) of this section provides rules regarding the section 965(m) election and a special rule for real estate investment trusts. Paragraph (e) of this section provides rules regarding the section 965(n) election. Paragraph (f) of this section provides rules regarding the election to use the alternative method for calculating post-1986 earnings and profits. Paragraph (g) of this section provides definitions that apply for purposes of this section.

(b) *Section 965(h) election.*—(1) *In general.*—Any person with a section 965(h) net tax liability (that is, a section 958(a) U.S. shareholder or a domestic pass-through owner with respect to a domestic pass-through entity that is a section 958(a) U.S. shareholder, but not a domestic pass-through entity itself) may elect under section 965(h) and this paragraph (b) to pay its section 965(h) net tax liability in eight installments. This election may be revoked only by paying the full amount of the remaining unpaid section 965(h) net tax liability.

(i) *Amount of installments.*—Except as provided in paragraph (b)(3) of this section, if a person makes a section 965(h) election, the amounts of the installments are—

(A) Eight percent of the section 965(h) net tax liability in the case of each of the first five installments;

(B) Fifteen percent of the section 965(h) net tax liability in the case of the sixth installment;

(C) Twenty percent of the section 965(h) net tax liability in the case of the seventh installment; and

(D) Twenty-five percent of the section 965(h) net tax liability in the case of the eighth installment.

(ii) *Increased installments due to a deficiency or a timely filed or amended return.*—(A) *In general.*—If a person makes a section 965(h) election, except as provided in paragraph (b)(1)(ii)(C) of this section, any deficiency or additional liability will be prorated to the installments described under paragraph (b)(1)(i) of this section if any of the following occur:

(1) A deficiency is assessed with respect to the person's section 965(h) net tax liability;

(2) The person files a return by the due date of the return (taking into account extensions, if any) increasing the amount of its section 965(h) net tax liability beyond that taken into account in paying the first installment described under paragraph (b)(1)(i) of this section; or

(3) The person files an amended return that reflects an increase in the amount of its section 965(h) net tax liability.

(B) *Timing.*—If the due date for the payment of an installment to which the deficiency is prorated has passed, the amount prorated to such installment must be paid on notice and demand by the Secretary, or, in the case of an additional liability reported on a return increasing the amount of the section 965(h) net tax liability after payment of the first installment or on an amended return, with the filing of the return. If the due date for the payment of an installment to which the deficiency or additional liability is prorated has not passed, then such amount will be due at the same time as, and as part of, the relevant installment.

(C) *Exception for negligence, intentional disregard, or fraud.*—If a deficiency or additional liability is due to negligence, intentional disregard of rules and regulations, or fraud with intent to evade tax, the proration rule of this paragraph (b)(1)(ii) will not apply, and the deficiency or additional liability (as well as any applicable interest and penalties) must be paid on notice and demand by the Secretary or, in the case of an additional liability reported on a return increasing the amount of the section 965(h) net tax liability after payment of the first installment or on an amended return, with the filing of the return.

(iii) *Due date of installments.*—(A) *In general.*—If a person makes a section 965(h) election, the first installment payment is due on the due date (without regard to extensions) for the return for the relevant taxable year. For purposes of this paragraph (b), the term *relevant taxable year* means, in the case in which the person is a section 958(a) U.S. shareholder, the section 958(a) U.S. shareholder inclusion year, or, in the case in which the person is a domestic pass-through owner, the taxable year in which the person has the section 965(a) inclusion to which the section 965(h) net tax liability is attributable. Each succeeding installment payment is due on the due date (without regard to extensions) for the return for the taxable year following the taxable year with respect to which the previous installment payment was made.

(B) *Extension for specified individuals.*—If a person is a specified individual with respect to a taxable year within which an installment payment is due pursuant to paragraph (b)(1)(iii)(A) of this section, then, for purposes of determining the due date of an installment payment under paragraph (b)(1)(iii)(A) of this section, the due date of the return (without regard to extensions) due within the taxable year will be treated as the fifteenth day of the sixth month following the close of the prior taxable year. This paragraph (b)(1)(iii)(B) is applicable regardless of whether the person is a specified individual with respect to the relevant taxable year.

(2) *Manner of making election.*—(i) *Eligibility.*—Any person with a section 965(h) net tax liability may make the section 965(h) election, provided that, with respect to the person, none of the acceleration events described in paragraph (b)(3)(ii) of this section has occurred before the election is made. Notwithstanding the preceding sentence, a person that would be eligible to make the section 965(h) election but for the occurrence of an event described in paragraph (b)(3)(ii) of this section may make the section 965(h) election if the exception described in paragraph (b)(3)(iii)(A) of this section applies.

(ii) *Timing.*—A section 965(h) election must be made no later than the due date (taking into account extensions, if any, or any additional time that would have been granted if the person had made an extension request) for the return for the relevant taxable year. Relief is not available under § 301.9100-2 or § 301.9100-3 to file a late election.

(iii) *Election statement.*—Except as otherwise provided in publications, forms, instructions, or other guidance, to make a section 965(h) election, a person must attach a statement, signed under penalties of perjury consistent with the rules for signatures applicable to the person's return, to its return for the relevant taxable year. The statement must include the person's name, taxpayer identification number, total net tax liability under section 965, section 965(h) net tax liability, section 965(i) net tax liability with respect to which a section 965(i) election is effective (if applicable), and the anticipated amounts of each installment described under paragraph (b)(1)(i) of this section. The statement must be filed in the manner prescribed in publications, forms, instructions, or other guidance. The attachment of an unsigned copy of the election statement to the timely filed return for the relevant taxable year satisfies the signature requirement of this paragraph (b)(2)(iii) if the person making the election retains the original signed election statement in the manner specified by § 1.6001-1(e).

(3) *Acceleration of payment.*—(i) *Acceleration.*—Notwithstanding paragraph (b)(1)(i) of this section, if a person makes a section 965(h) election and an acceleration event described in paragraph (b)(3)(ii) of this section subsequently occurs, then, except as provided in paragraph (b)(3)(iii) of this section, the unpaid portion of the remaining installments will be due on the date of the acceleration event (or in the case of a title 11 or similar case, the day before the petition is filed).

(ii) *Acceleration events.*—The following events are acceleration events for purposes of paragraph (b)(3)(i) of this section with respect to a person that has made a section 965(h) election—

(A) An addition to tax is assessed for the failure to timely pay an installment described in paragraph (b)(1)(i) of this section;

(B) A liquidation, sale, exchange, or other disposition of substantially all of the assets of the person (including in a title 11 or similar case, or, in the case of an individual, by reason of death);

(C) In the case of a person that is not an individual, a cessation of business by the person;

(D) Any event that results in the person no longer being a United States person, including a resident alien (as defined in section 7701(b)(1)(A)) becoming a nonresident alien (as defined in section 7701(b)(1)(B));

(E) In the case of a person that was not a member of any consolidated group, the person becoming a member of a consolidated group;

(F) In the case of a consolidated group, the group ceasing to exist (including by reason of the acquisition of a consolidated group within the meaning of § 1.1502-13(j)(5)) or the group otherwise discontinuing in the filing of a consolidated return; or

(G) A determination by the Commissioner described in the second sentence of paragraph (b)(3)(iii)(C)(*2*) of this section.

(iii) *Eligible section 965(h) transferee exception.*—(A) *In general.*—Paragraph (b)(3)(i) of this section does not apply (such that the unpaid portion of all remaining installments will not be due as of the date of the acceleration event) to a person with respect to which an acceleration event occurs if the requirements described in paragraphs (b)(3)(iii)(A)(*1*) and (*2*) of this section are satisfied. A person with respect to which an acceleration event described in this paragraph (b)(3)(iii)(A) occurs is referred to as an *eligible section 965(h) transferor.*

(*1*) *Requirement to have a covered acceleration event.*—The acceleration event satisfies the requirements of this paragraph (b)(3)(iii)(A)(*1*) if it is described in—

(*i*) Paragraph (b)(3)(ii)(B) of this section, and the acceleration event is a qualifying consolidated group member transaction within the meaning of paragraph (b)(3)(iii)(E) of this section;

(*ii*) Paragraph (b)(3)(ii)(B) of this section (other than, in the case of an individual, an acceleration event caused by reason of death) in a transaction that is not a qualifying consolidated group member transaction;

(*iii*) Paragraph (b)(3)(ii)(E) of this section;

(*iv*) Paragraph (b)(3)(ii)(F) of this section, and the acceleration event results from the acquisition of a consolidated group within the meaning of § 1.1502-13(j)(5), and the acquired consolidated group members join a different consolidated group as of the day following the acquisition;

(*v*) Paragraph (b)(3)(ii)(F) of this section, and the group ceases to exist as a result of the transfer of all of the assets of one or more members of the consolidated group to other members with only one entity remaining (the *successor entity*); or

(*vi*) Paragraph (b)(3)(ii)(F) of this section, and the group ceases to exist as a result of the termination of the subchapter S election pursuant to section 1362(d) of a shareholder of the common parent of the consolidated group and, for the shareholder's taxable year immediately following the termination, the shareholder joins in the filing of a consolidated return as a consolidated group that includes all of the former members of the former consolidated group.

(*2*) *Requirement to enter into a transfer agreement.*—An eligible section 965(h) transferor and an eligible section 965(h) transferee (as defined in paragraph (b)(3)(iii)(B)(*1*) of this section) must enter into an agreement with the Commissioner that satisfies the requirements of paragraph (b)(3)(iii)(B) of this section.

(B) *Transfer agreement.*—(*1*) *Eligibility.*—A transfer agreement that satisfies the requirements of this paragraph (b)(3)(iii)(B) must be entered into by an eligible section 965(h) transferor and an eligible section 965(h) transferee. For this purpose, the term *eligible section 965(h) transferee* refers to a single United States person that is not a domestic pass-through entity and that—

(*i*) With respect to an acceleration event described in paragraph (b)(3)(iii)(A)(*1*)(*i*) of this section, is a departing member (as defined in paragraph (b)(3)(iii)(E)(*1*)(*i*) of this section) or its qualified successor (as defined in paragraph (b)(3)(iii)(E)(*2*) of this section);

(*ii*) With respect to an acceleration event described in paragraph (b)(3)(iii)(A)(*1*)(*ii*) of this section, acquires substantially all of the assets of an eligible section 965(h) transferor;

(*iii*) With respect to an acceleration event described in paragraph (b)(3)(iii)(A)(*1*)(*iii*) of this section, is the agent (within the meaning of § 1.1502-77) of the consolidated group that the eligible section 965(h) transferor joins;

(*iv*) With respect to an acceleration event described in paragraph (b)(3)(iii)(A)(*1*)(*iv*) of this section, is the agent (within the meaning of § 1.1502-77) of the surviving consolidated group;

(*v*) With respect to an acceleration event described in paragraph (b)(3)(iii)(A)(*1*)(*v*) of this section, is the successor entity (within the meaning of paragraph (b)(3)(iii)(A)(*1*)(*v*) of this section); or

(*vi*) With respect an acceleration event described in paragraph (b)(3)(iii)(A)(*1*)(*vi*) of this section, is the agent (within the meaning of § 1.1502-77) of the consolidated group that includes the shareholder whose subchapter S election was terminated and all of the former members of the former consolidated group.

(*2*) *Filing requirements.*—(*i*) *In general.*—A transfer agreement must be timely filed. Except as provided in paragraph (b)(3)(iii)(B)(*2*)(*ii*) of this section, a transfer agreement is considered timely filed only if the transfer agreement is filed within 30 days of the date that the acceleration event occurs. The transfer agreement must be filed in accordance with the rules provided in publications forms, instructions, or other guidance. In addition, a duplicate copy of the transfer agreement must be attached to the returns of both the eligible section 965(h) transferee and the eligible section 965(h) transferor for the taxable year during which the acceleration event occurs filed by the due date for such returns (taking into account extensions, if any). Relief is not available under § 301.9100-2 or 301.9100-3 to file a transfer agreement late.

(*ii*) *Transition rule.*—If an acceleration event occurs on or before February 5, 2019, the transfer agreement must be filed by March 5, 2019, to be considered timely filed.

(*3*) *Signature requirement.*—The transfer agreement that is filed within 30 days of the acceleration event or by the due date specified in paragraph (b)(3)(iii)(B)(*2*)(*ii*) of this section must be signed under penalties of perjury by a person who is authorized to sign a return on behalf of the eligible section 965(h) transferor and a person who is authorized to sign a return on behalf of the eligible section 965(h) transferee.

(*4*) *Terms of agreement.*—A transfer agreement under this paragraph (b)(3)(iii)(B) must be entitled "Transfer Agreement Under Section 965(h)(3)" and must contain the following information and representations—

(*i*) A statement that the document constitutes an agreement by the eligible section 965(h) transferee to assume the liability of the eligible section 965(h) transferor for any unpaid installment payments of the eligible section 965(h) transferor under section 965(h);

(*ii*) A statement that the eligible section 965(h) transferee (and, if the eligible section 965(h) transferor continues in existence immediately after the acceleration event, the eligible section 965(h) transferor) agrees to comply with all of the conditions and requirements of section 965(h) and paragraph (b) of this section, as well as any other applicable requirements in the section 965 regulations;

(*iii*) The name, address, and taxpayer identification number of the eligible section 965(h) transferor and the eligible section 965(h) transferee;

(iv) The amount of the eligible section 965(h) transferor's section 965(h) net tax liability remaining unpaid, as determined by the eligible section 965(h) transferor, which amount is subject to adjustment by the Commissioner;

(v) A copy of the eligible section 965(h) transferor's most recent Form 965-A or Form 965-B, as applicable, if the eligible section 965(h) transferor has been required to file a Form 965-A or Form 965-B;

(vi) A detailed description of the acceleration event that led to the transfer agreement;

(vii) A representation that the eligible section 965(h) transferee is able to make the remaining payments required under section 965(h) and paragraph (b) of this section with respect to the section 965(h) net tax liability being assumed;

(viii) If the eligible section 965(h) transferor continues to exist immediately after the acceleration event, an acknowledgement that the eligible section 965(h) transferor and any successor to the eligible section 965(h) transferor will remain jointly and severally liable for any unpaid installment payments of the eligible section 965(h) transferor under section 965(h), including, if applicable, under § 1.1502-6;

(ix) A statement as to whether the leverage ratio of the eligible section 965(h) transferee and all subsidiary members of its affiliated group immediately after the acceleration event exceeds three to one, which ratio may be modified as provided in publications, forms, instructions, or other guidance;

(x) A certification by the eligible section 965(h) transferee stating that the eligible section 965(h) transferee waives the right to a notice of liability and consents to the immediate assessment of the portion of the section 965(h) net tax liability remaining unpaid; and

(xi) Any additional information, representation, or certification required by the Commissioner in publications, forms, instructions, or other guidance.

(5) Consolidated groups.—For purposes of this paragraph (b)(3)(iii)(B), in the case of a consolidated group, the terms "eligible section 965(h) transferor" and "eligible section 965(h) transferee" each refer to a consolidated group that is a party to a covered acceleration event described in paragraph (b)(3)(iii)(A)(*1*) of this section. In such a case, any transfer agreement under this paragraph (b)(3)(iii)(B) must be entered into by the agent (as defined in § 1.1502-77) of the relevant consolidated group.

(6) Leverage ratio.—For purposes of paragraph (b)(3)(iii)(B)(*4*)(*ix*) of this section, and except as otherwise provided in publications, forms, instructions, or other guidance, the term *leverage ratio* means the ratio that the total indebtedness of the eligible section 965(h) transferee bears to the sum of its money and all other assets reduced (but not below zero) by such total indebtedness. For this purpose, the amount taken into account with respect to any asset is the adjusted basis thereof for purposes of determining gain, and the amount taken into account with respect to any indebtedness with original issue discount is its issue price plus the portion of the original issue discount previously accrued as determined under the rules of section 1272 (determined without regard to subsection (a)(7) or (b)(4) thereof).

(C) *Consent of Commissioner.*—*(1) In general.*—Except as otherwise provided in publications, forms, instructions, or other guidance, if an eligible section 965(h) transferor and an eligible section 965(h) transferee file a transfer agreement in accordance with the provisions of paragraph (b)(3)(iii)(B) of this section, the eligible section 965(h) transferor and the eligible section 965(h) transferee will be considered to have entered into an agreement described in paragraph (b)(3)(iii)(A)(*2*) of this section with the Commissioner for purposes of section 965(h)(3) and paragraph (b)(3)(iii) of this section. If the Commissioner determines that additional information is necessary (for example, additional information regarding the ability of the eligible section 965(h) transferee to fully pay the remaining section 965(h) net tax liability), the eligible section 965(h) transferee must provide such information upon request.

(2) Material misrepresentations and omissions.—If the Commissioner determines that an agreement filed by an eligible section 965(h) transferor and an eligible section 965(h) transferee contains a material misrepresentation or material omission, or if the eligible section 965(h) transferee does not provide the additional information requested under paragraph (b)(3)(iii)(C)(*1*) of this section within a reasonable timeframe communicated by the Commissioner to the eligible section 965(h) transferee, then the Commissioner may reject the transfer agreement (effective as of the date of the related acceleration event). In the alternative, on the date that the Commissioner determines that the transfer agreement includes a material misrepresentation or material omission, the Commissioner may determine that an acceleration event has occurred with respect to the eligible section 965(h) transferee as of the date of the determination, such that any unpaid installment payments of the eligible section 965(h) transferor that were assumed by the eligible section 965(h) transferee become due on the date of the determination.

(D) *Effect of assumption.*—*(1) In general.*—If the exception in this paragraph (b)(3)(iii) applies with respect to an eligible section 965(h) transferor and an eligible section 965(h) transferee, the eligible section 965(h) transferee assumes all of the outstanding obligations and responsibilities of the eligible section 965(h) transferor with respect to the section 965(h) net tax liability as though the eligible section 965(h) transferee had included the section 965(a) inclusion in income. Accordingly, the eligible section 965(h) transferee is responsible for making payments and reporting with respect to any unpaid installment payments. In addition, for example, if an acceleration event described in paragraph (b)(3)(ii) of this section occurs with respect to an eligible section 965(h) transferee, any unpaid installment payments of the eligible section 965(h) transferor that were assumed by the eligible section 965(h) transferee will become due on the date of such event, subject to any applicable exception in paragraph (b)(3)(iii) of this section.

(2) Eligible section 965(h) transferor liability.—An eligible section 965(h) transferor (or a successor) remains jointly and severally liable for any unpaid installment payments of the eligible section 965(h) transferor that were assumed by the eligible section 965(h) transferee, as well as any penalties, additions to tax, or other additional amounts attributable to such net tax liability.

(E) *Qualifying consolidated group member transaction.*—*(1) Definition of qualifying consolidated group member transaction.*—For purposes of this paragraph (b)(3), the term *qualifying consolidated group member transaction* means a transaction in which—

(i) A member of a consolidated group (the *departing member*) ceases to be a member of the consolidated group (including by reason of the distribution, sale, or exchange of the departing member's stock);

(ii) The transaction results in the consolidated group (which is treated as a single person for this purpose under § 1.965-8(e)(1)) being treated as transferring substantially all of its assets for purposes of paragraph (b)(3)(ii)(B) of this section; and

(iii) The departing member either continues to exist immediately after the transaction or has a qualified successor.

(2) Definition of qualified successor.—For purposes of this paragraph (b)(3), the term *qualified successor* means, with respect to a departing member described in this paragraph (b)(3)(iii)(E), another domestic corporation (or consolidated group) that acquires substantially all of the assets of the departing member (including in a transaction described in section 381(a)(2)).

(3) Departure of multiple members of a consolidated group.—Multiple members that deconsolidate from the same consolidated group as a result of a single transaction are treated as a single departing member to the extent that, immediately after the transaction, they become members of the same (second) consolidated group, which would be treated as a single person under § 1.965-8(e)(1).

(c) *Section 965(i) election.*—(1) *In general.*—Each shareholder of an S corporation (including a person listed in § 1.1362-6(b)(2) with respect to a trust or estate, but not a domestic pass-through entity itself) that is a United States shareholder of a deferred foreign income corporation may elect under section 965(i) and this paragraph (c) to defer the payment of the shareholder's section 965(i) net tax liability with respect to the S corporation until the shareholder's taxable year that includes a triggering event described in paragraph (c)(3) of this section. This election may be revoked only by paying the full amount of the unpaid section 965(i) net tax liability.

(2) *Manner of making election.*—(i) *Eligibility.*—Each shareholder with a section 965(i) net tax liability with respect to an S corporation may make the section 965(i) election with respect to such S corporation, provided that, with respect to the shareholder, none of the triggering events described in paragraph (c)(3)(ii) of this section have occurred before the election is made. Notwithstanding the preceding sentence, a shareholder that would be eligible to make the section

965(i) election but for the occurrence of an event described in paragraph (c)(3)(ii) of this section may make the section 965(i) election if an exception described in paragraph (c)(3)(iv) of this section applies.

(ii) *Timing.*—A section 965(i) election must be made no later than the due date (taking into account extensions, if any) for the shareholder's return for each taxable year that includes the last day of the taxable year of the S corporation in which the S corporation has a section 965(a) inclusion to which the shareholder's section 965(i) net tax liability is attributable. Relief is not available under § 301.9100-2 or 301.9100-3 to make a late election.

(iii) *Election statement.*—Except as otherwise provided in publications, forms, instructions, or other guidance, to make a section 965(i) election, a shareholder must attach a statement, signed under penalties of perjury consistent with the rules for signatures applicable to the person's return, to its return for the taxable year that includes the last day of a taxable year of the S corporation in which the S corporation has a section 965(a) inclusion to which the shareholder's section 965(i) net tax liability is attributable. The statement must include the shareholder's name, taxpayer identification number, the name and taxpayer identification number of the S corporation with respect to which the election is made, the amount described in paragraph (g)(10)(i)(A) of this section as modified by paragraph (g)(6) of this section for purposes of determining the section 965(i) net tax liability with respect to the S corporation, the amount described in paragraph (g)(10)(i)(B) of this section, and the section 965(i) net tax liability with respect to the S corporation. The statement must be filed in the manner prescribed in publications, forms, instructions, or other guidance. The attachment of an unsigned copy of the election statement to the timely-filed return for the relevant taxable year satisfies the signature requirement of this paragraph (c)(2)(iii) if the shareholder retains the original signed election statement in the manner specified by § 1.6001-1(e).

(3) *Triggering events.*—(i) *In general.*—If a shareholder makes a section 965(i) election with respect to an S corporation, the shareholder defers payment of its section 965(i) net tax liability with respect to the S corporation until the shareholder's taxable year that includes the occurrence of a triggering event described in paragraph (c)(3)(ii) of this section with respect to the section 965(i) net tax liability with respect to the S corporation. If a triggering event described in paragraph (c)(3)(ii) of this section with respect to an S corporation occurs, except as provided in paragraph (c)(3)(iv) of this section, the shareholder's section 965(i) net tax liability with respect to the S corporation will be assessed as an addition to tax for the shareholder's taxable year that includes the triggering event.

(ii) *Triggering events.*—The following events are considered triggering events for purposes of paragraph (c)(3)(i) of this section with respect to a shareholder's section 965(i) net tax liability with respect to an S corporation—

(A) The corporation ceases to be an S corporation (determined as of the first day of the first taxable year that the corporation is not an S corporation);

(B) A liquidation, sale, exchange, or other disposition of substantially all of the assets of the S corporation (including in a title 11 or similar case), a cessation of business by the S corporation, or the S corporation ceasing to exist;

(C) The transfer of any share of stock of the S corporation by the shareholder (including by reason of death or otherwise) that results in a change of ownership for federal income tax purposes; or

(D) A determination by the Commissioner described in the second sentence of paragraph (c)(3)(iv)(C)(2) of this section.

(iii) *Partial transfers.*—If an S corporation shareholder transfers less than all of its shares of stock of the S corporation, the transfer will be a triggering event only with respect to the portion of a shareholder's section 965(i) net tax liability that is properly allocable to the transferred shares.

(iv) *Eligible section 965(i) transferee exception.*—(A) *In general.*—Paragraph (c)(3)(i) of this section will not apply (such that a shareholder's section 965(i) net tax liability with respect to an S corporation will not be assessed as an addition to tax for the shareholder's taxable year that includes the triggering event) if the requirements described in paragraphs (c)(3)(iv)(A)(*1*) and (*2*) of this section are satisfied. A shareholder with respect to which a triggering event described in this paragraph (c)(3)(iv)(A) occurs is referred to as an *eligible section 965(i) transferor*.

(*1*) *Requirement to have a covered triggering event.*—The triggering event satisfies the requirements of this paragraph (c)(3)(iv)(A)(*1*) if it is described in paragraph (c)(3)(ii)(C) of this section.

(*2*) *Requirement to enter into a transfer agreement.*—The shareholder with respect to which a triggering event occurs and an eligible section 965(i) transferee (as defined in paragraph (c)(3)(iv)(B)(*1*) of this section) must enter into an agreement with the Commissioner that satisfies the requirements of paragraph (c)(3)(iv)(B) of this section.

(B) *Transfer agreement.*—(*1*) *Eligibility.*—A transfer agreement that satisfies the requirements of this paragraph (c)(3)(iv)(B) may be entered into by an eligible section 965(i) transferor and an eligible section 965(i) transferee. For this purpose, the term *eligible section 965(i) transferee* refers to a single United States person that becomes a shareholder of the S corporation (including a person listed in § 1.1362-6(b)(2) with respect to a trust or estate, but not a domestic pass-through entity itself). In the case of a transfer that consists of multiple partial transfers (as described in paragraph (c)(3)(iii) of this section), a transfer agreement that satisfies the requirements of this paragraph (c)(3)(iv)(B) may be entered into by an eligible section 965(i) transferor and an eligible section 965(i) transferee for each partial transfer.

(*2*) *Filing requirements.*—(*i*) *In general.*—A transfer agreement must be timely filed. Except as provided in paragraphs (c)(3)(iv)(B)(*2*)(*ii*) and (*iii*) of this section, a transfer agreement is considered timely filed only if the transfer agreement is filed within 30 days of the date that the triggering event occurs. The transfer agreement must be filed in accordance with the rules provided in publications, forms, instructions, or other guidance. In addition, a duplicate copy of the transfer agreement must be attached to the returns of both the eligible section 965(i) transferee and the eligible section 965(i) transferor for the taxable year during which the triggering event occurs filed by the due date (taking into account extensions, if any) for such returns. Relief is not available under § 301.9100-2 or 301.9100-3 to file a transfer agreement late.

(*ii*) *Transition rule.*—If a triggering event occurs on or before February 5, 2019, the transfer agreement must be filed by March 5, 2019, to be considered timely filed.

(*iii*) *Death of eligible section 965(i) transferor.*—If the triggering event is the death of the eligible section 965(i) transferor, the transfer agreement must be filed by the later of the unextended due date for the eligible section 965(i) transferor's final income tax return or March 5, 2019.

(*3*) *Signature requirement.*—The transfer agreement that is filed within 30 days of the triggering event or by the due date specified in paragraph (c)(3)(iv)(B)(*2*)(*ii*) or (*iii*) of this section must be signed under penalties of perjury by a person who is authorized to sign a return on behalf of the eligible section 965(i) transferor and a person who is authorized to sign a return on behalf of the eligible section 965(i) transferee.

(*4*) *Terms of agreement.*—A transfer agreement under this paragraph (c)(3)(iv)(B) must be entitled "Transfer Agreement Under Section 965(i)(2)" and must contain the following information and representations:

(*i*) A statement that the document constitutes an agreement by the eligible section 965(i) transferee to assume the liability of the eligible section 965(i) transferor for the unpaid portion of the section 965(i) net tax liability, or, in the case of a partial transfer, for the unpaid portion of the section 965(i) net tax liability attributable to the transferred stock;

(*ii*) A statement that the eligible section 965(i) transferee agrees to comply with all of the conditions and requirements of section 965(i) and paragraph (c) of this section, including the annual reporting requirement, as well as any other applicable requirements in the section 965 regulations;

(*iii*) The name, address, and taxpayer identification number of the eligible section 965(i) transferor and the eligible section 965(i) transferee;

(*iv*) The amount of the eligible section 965(i) transferor's unpaid section 965(i) net tax liability or, in the case of a partial transfer, the unpaid portion of the section 965(i) net tax liability attributable to the transferred stock, each as determined by the eligible section 965(i) transferor, which amount is subject to adjustment by the Commissioner;

(v) A copy of the eligible section 965(i) transferor's most recent Form 965-A, if the eligible section 965(i) transferor has been required to file a Form 965-A;

(vi) A detailed description of the triggering event that led to the transfer agreement, including the name and taxpayer identification number of the S corporation with respect to which the section 965(i) election was effective;

(vii) A representation that the eligible section 965(i) transferee is able to pay the section 965(i) net tax liability being assumed;

(viii) An acknowledgement that the eligible section 965(i) transferor and any successor to the eligible section 965(i) transferor will remain jointly and severally liable for the section 965(i) net tax liability being assumed by the eligible section 965(i) transferee;

(ix) A statement as to whether the leverage ratio of the eligible section 965(i) transferee immediately after the triggering event exceeds three to one, which ratio may be modified as provided in publications, forms, instructions, or other guidance;

(x) Any additional information, representation, or certification required by the Commissioner in publications, forms, instructions, or other guidance.

(5) Special rule in the case of death of eligible section 965(i) transferor.—Except in the case of transfers to trusts, if the triggering event is the death of the eligible section 965(i) transferor, and the identity of the beneficiary or beneficiaries (in the case of multiple partial transfers) is determined as of the due date for the transfer agreement described in paragraph (c)(3)(iv)(B)(*2*)(*iii*) of this section, then the transfer may be treated as a transfer directly between the eligible 965(i) transferor and the beneficiary or beneficiaries. If, however, the identity of the beneficiary or beneficiaries is not determined as of the due date for the transfer agreement described in paragraph (c)(3)(iv)(B)(*2*)(*iii*) of this section, then the transfer must be treated first as a transfer between the eligible section 965(i) transferor and his or her estate at the time of death and second as a transfer between the estate and the beneficiary or beneficiaries when the shares are actually transferred to the beneficiary or beneficiaries. Separate transfer agreements must be filed for each transfer. The transfer from the eligible section 965(i) transferor to his or her estate is a transfer resulting from a triggering event that is the death of the eligible section 965(i) transferor, and the transfer agreement is subject to the timing rules in paragraph (c)(3)(iv)(B)(*2*)(*iii*) of this section. The transfer from the estate to the beneficiary or beneficiaries is not a transfer resulting from a triggering event that is the death of the eligible section 965(i) transferor, and the transfer agreement is subject to the timing rules in paragraph (c)(3)(iv)(B)(*2*)(*i*) and (*ii*) of this section.

(6) Leverage ratio.—For purposes of paragraph (c)(3)(iv)(B)(*4*)(*ix*) of this section, and except as otherwise provided in publications, forms, instructions, or other guidance, the term *leverage ratio* means the ratio that the total indebtedness of the eligible section 965(i) transferee bears to the sum of its money and all other assets reduced (but not below zero) by such total indebtedness. For this purpose, the amount taken into account with respect to any asset is the adjusted basis thereof for purposes of determining gain, and the amount taken into account with respect to any indebtedness with original issue discount is its issue price plus the portion of the original issue discount previously accrued as determined under the rules of section 1272 (determined without regard to subsection (a)(7) or (b)(4) thereof).

(C) *Consent of Commissioner.*—*(1) In general.*—Except as otherwise provided in publications, forms, instructions, or other guidance, if an eligible section 965(i) transferor and an eligible section 965(i) transferee file a transfer agreement in accordance with the provisions of paragraph (c)(3)(iv)(B) of this section, the eligible section 965(i) transferor and the eligible section 965(i) transferee will be considered to have entered into an agreement with the Commissioner for purposes of section 965(i)(2) and paragraph (c)(3)(iv) of this section. If the Commissioner determines that additional information is necessary (for example, additional information regarding the ability of the eligible section 965(i) transferee to pay the eligible section 965(i) transferor's unpaid section 965(i) net tax liability), the eligible section 965(i) transferee must provide such information upon request.

(2) Material misrepresentations and omissions.—If the Commissioner determines that an agreement filed by an eligible section 965(i) transferor and an eligible section 965(i) transferee contains a material misrepresentation or material omission, or if the eligible section 965(i) transferee does not provide the additional information requested under paragraph (c)(3)(iv)(C)(*1*) of this section within a reasonable timeframe communicated by the Commissioner to the eligible section 965(i) transferee, then the Commissioner may reject the transfer agreement (effective as of the date of the related triggering event). In the alternative, on the date that the Commissioner determines that the transfer agreement includes a material misrepresentation or material omission, the Commissioner may determine that a triggering event has occurred with respect to the eligible section 965(i) transferee as of the date of the determination, such that the unpaid section 965(i) net tax liability of the eligible section 965(i) transferor that was assumed by the eligible section 965(i) transferee becomes due on the date of the determination.

(D) *Effect of assumption.*—*(1) In general.*—When the exception in this paragraph (c)(3)(iv) applies with respect to an eligible section 965(i) transferor and an eligible section 965(i) transferee, the eligible section 965(i) transferee assumes all of the outstanding obligations and responsibilities of the eligible section 965(i) transferor with respect to the section 965(i) net tax liability with respect to the S corporation as though the eligible section 965(i) transferee had included the section 965(a) inclusion in income. Accordingly, the eligible section 965(i) transferee is responsible for making payments and reporting with respect to any unpaid section 965(i) net tax liability with respect to the S corporation. In addition, for example, if a triggering event described in paragraph (c)(3)(ii) of this section occurs with respect to an eligible section 965(i) transferee, any unpaid portion of the section 965(i) net tax liability of the eligible section 965(i) transferor that was assumed by the eligible section 965(i) transferee becomes due on the date of such event, subject to any applicable exception in paragraph (c)(3)(iv) or (v) of this section.

(2) Eligible section 965(i) transferor liability.—An eligible section 965(i) transferor remains jointly and severally liable for any unpaid installment payments of the eligible section 965(i) transferor that were assumed by the eligible section 965(i) transferee, as well as any penalties, additions to tax, or other additional amounts attributable to such net tax liability.

(v) *Coordination with section 965(h) election.*—(A) *In general.*—Subject to the limitation described in paragraph (c)(3)(v)(D) of this section, a shareholder that has made a section 965(i) election with respect to an S corporation, upon the occurrence of a triggering event with respect to such S corporation, may make a section 965(h) election with respect to the portion of the shareholder's section 965(i) net tax liability with respect to such S corporation that is assessed as an addition to tax for the shareholder's taxable year that includes the triggering event pursuant to paragraph (c)(3)(i) of this section as if such portion were a section 965(h) net tax liability.

(B) *Timing for election.*—A section 965(h) election made pursuant to section 965(i)(4) and paragraph (c)(3)(v)(A) of this section must be made no later than the due date (taking into account extensions, if any) for the shareholder's return for the taxable year in which the triggering event with respect to the S corporation occurs. Relief is not available under § 301.9100-2 or § 301.9100-3 to make a late election.

(C) *Due date for installment.*—If a shareholder makes a section 965(h) election pursuant to section 965(i)(4) and paragraph (c)(3)(v)(A) of this section, the payment of the first installment (as described in paragraph (b)(1)(i) of this section) must be made no later than the due date (without regard to extensions) for the shareholder's return of tax for the taxable year in which the triggering event with respect to the S corporation occurs.

(D) *Limitation.*—*(1) In general.*—Notwithstanding paragraph (c)(3)(v)(A) of this section, if the triggering event with respect to an S corporation is a triggering event described in paragraph (c)(3)(ii)(B) of this section, then the section 965(h) election may only be made with the consent of the Commissioner.

(2) Manner of obtaining consent.—*(i) In general.*—In order to obtain the consent of the Commissioner as required by paragraph (c)(3)(v)(D)(*1*) of this section, the shareholder intending to make the section 965(h) election must file the agreement described in paragraph (c)(3)(v)(D)(*4*) of this section within 30 days of the occurrence of the triggering event, except as described in paragraph (c)(3)(v)(D)(*2*)(*ii*) of this section. The agreement must be filed in accordance with the rules provided in publications, forms, instruc-

tions, or other guidance. In addition, a duplicate copy of the agreement must be filed, with the shareholder's timely-filed return for the taxable year during which the triggering event occurs (taking into account extensions, if any), along with the election statement described in paragraph (b)(2)(iii) of this section. Relief is not available under § 301.9100-2 or § 301.9100-3 to file an agreement late.

(*ii*) *Transition rule*.—If a triggering event occurs on or before February 5, 2019, the agreement must be filed by March 5, 2019, in order to be considered timely filed.

(*3*) *Signature requirement*.—The agreement that is filed within 30 days of the triggering event or by the due date specified in paragraph (c)(3)(v)(D)(*2*)(*ii*) of this section must be signed under penalties of perjury by the shareholder.

(*4*) *Terms of agreement*.—The agreement under this paragraph (c)(3)(v)(D) must be entitled "Consent Agreement Under Section 965(i)(4)(D)" and must contain the following information and representations—

(*i*) A statement that the shareholder agrees to comply with all of the conditions and requirements of section 965(h) and paragraph (b) of this section, as well as any other applicable requirements in the section 965 regulations;

(*ii*) The name, address, and taxpayer identification number of the shareholder;

(*iii*) The amount of the section 965(i) net tax liability under section 965 remaining unpaid with respect to which the section 965(h) election is made pursuant to section 965(i)(4)(D) and paragraph (c)(3)(v)(A) of this section, as determined by the shareholder, which amount is subject to adjustment by the Commissioner; and

(*iv*) A representation that the shareholder is able to make the payments required under section 965(h) and paragraph (b) of this section with respect to the portion of the total net tax liability under section 965 remaining unpaid described in paragraph (c)(3)(v)(D)(*4*)(*iii*) of this section.

(*v*) A statement as to whether the leverage ratio of the shareholder and all subsidiary members of its affiliated group immediately following the triggering event exceeds three to one; and

(*vi*) Any additional information, representation, or certification required by the Commissioner in publications, forms, instructions, or other guidance.

(*5*) *Consent of Commissioner*.—(*i*) *In general*.—If a shareholder files an agreement in accordance with the provisions of paragraph (c)(3)(v)(D) of this section, the shareholder will be considered to have obtained the consent of the Commissioner for purposes of section 965(i)(4)(D) and paragraph (c)(3)(v)(D)(*1*) of this section. However, if the Commissioner reviews the agreement and determines that additional information is necessary, the shareholder must provide such information upon request.

(*ii*) *Material misrepresentations and omissions*.—If the Commissioner determines that an agreement filed by a shareholder in accordance with the provisions of this paragraph (c)(3)(v)(D) contains a material misrepresentation or material omission, or if the shareholder does not provide the additional information requested under paragraph (c)(3)(v)(D)(*5*)(*i*) of this section within a reasonable timeframe communicated by the Commissioner to the shareholder, then the Commissioner may reject the agreement (effective as of the date of the related triggering event).

(*6*) *Leverage ratio*.—For purposes of paragraph (c)(3)(v)(D)(*4*)(*v*) of this section, and except as otherwise provided in publications, forms, instructions, or other guidance, the term *leverage ratio* means the ratio that the total indebtedness of the shareholder bears to the sum of its money and all other assets reduced (but not below zero) by such total indebtedness. For this purpose, the amount taken into account with respect to any asset is the adjusted basis thereof for purposes of determining gain, and the amount taken into account with respect to any indebtedness with original issue discount is its issue price plus the portion of the original issue discount previously accrued as determined under the rules of section 1272 (determined without regard to subsection (a)(7) or (b)(4) thereof).

(4) *Joint and several liability*.—If any shareholder of an S corporation makes a section 965(i) election, the S corporation is jointly and severally liable for the payment of the shareholder's section 965(i) net tax liability with respect to the S corporation, as well as any penalties, additions to tax, or other additional amounts attributable to such net tax liability.

(5) *Extension of limitation on collection*.—If an S corporation shareholder makes a section 965(i) election with respect to its section 965(i) net tax liability with respect to an S corporation, any limitation on the time period for the collection of the net tax liability shall not begin before the date of the triggering event with respect to the section 965(i) net tax liability.

(6) *Annual reporting requirement*.—(i) *In general*.—A shareholder that makes a section 965(i) election with respect to its section 965(i) net tax liability with respect to an S corporation is required to report the amount of its deferred net tax liability on its return of tax for the taxable year in which the election is made and on the return of tax for each subsequent taxable year until such net tax liability has been fully assessed.

(ii) *Failure to report*.—If a shareholder fails to report the amount of its deferred net tax liability as required with respect to any taxable year by the due date (taking into account extensions, if any) for the return of tax for that taxable year, five percent of such deferred net tax liability will be assessed as an addition to tax for such taxable year.

(d) *Section 965(m) election and special rule for real estate investment trusts*.—(1) *In general*.—A real estate investment trust may elect under section 965(m) and this paragraph (d) to defer the inclusion in gross income (for purposes of the computation of real estate investment trust taxable income under section 857(b)) of its REIT section 965 amounts and include them in income according to the schedule described in paragraph (d)(2) of this section. This election is revocable only by including in gross income (for purposes of the computation of real estate investment trust taxable income under section 857(b)) the full amount of the REIT section 965 amounts.

(2) *Inclusion schedule for section 965(m) election*.—If a real estate investment trust makes the section 965(m) election, the REIT section 965 amounts will be included in the real estate investment trust's gross income as follows—

(i) Eight percent of the REIT section 965 amounts in each taxable year in the five-taxable year period beginning with the taxable year the amount would otherwise be included;

(ii) Fifteen percent of the REIT section 965 amounts in the first year following the five year period described in paragraph (d)(2)(i) of this section;

(iii) Twenty percent of the REIT section 965 amounts in the second year following the five year period described in paragraph (d)(2)(i) of this section; and

(iv) Twenty-five percent of the REIT section 965 amounts in the third year following the five year period described in paragraph (d)(2)(i) of this section.

(3) *Manner of making election*.—(i) *Eligibility*.—A real estate investment trust with section 965(a) inclusions may make the section 965(m) election.

(ii) *Timing*.—A section 965(m) election must be made no later than the due date (taking into account extensions, if any) for the return for the first year of the five year period described in paragraph (d)(2)(i) of this section. Relief is not available under § 301.9100-2 or § 301.9100-3 to make a late election.

(iii) *Election statement*.—Except as otherwise provided in publications, forms, instructions, or other guidance, to make a section 965(m) election, a real estate investment trust must attach a statement, signed under penalties of perjury consistent with the rules for signatures applicable to the person's return, to its return for the taxable year in which it would otherwise be required to include the REIT section 965 amounts in gross income. The statement must include the real estate investment trust's name, taxpayer identification number, REIT section 965 amounts, and the anticipated amounts of each portion of the REIT section 965 amounts described under paragraph (d)(2) of this section, and the statement must be filed in the manner prescribed in publications, forms, instructions, or other guidance. The attachment of an unsigned copy of the election statement to the timely-filed return for the relevant taxable year satisfies the signature requirement of this paragraph (d)(3)(iii) if the real estate investment trust retains the original signed election statement in the manner specified by § 1.6001-1(e).

(4) *Coordination with section 965(h)*.—A real estate investment trust that makes the section 965(m) election may not also make a

section 965(h) election for any year with respect to which a section 965(m) election is in effect.

(5) *Acceleration of inclusion.*—If a real estate investment trust makes a section 965(m) election and subsequently there is a liquidation, sale, exchange, or other disposition of substantially all of the assets of the real estate investment trust (including in a title 11 or similar case), or a cessation of business by the real estate investment trust, any amount not yet included in gross income (for purposes of the computation of real estate investment trust taxable income under section 857(b)) as a result of the section 965(m) election will be so included as of the day before the date of the event. The unpaid portion of any tax liability with respect to such inclusion will be due on the date of the event (or in the case of a title 11 or similar case, the day before the petition is filed).

(6) *Treatment of section 965(a) inclusions of a real estate investment trust.*—Regardless of whether a real estate investment trust has made a section 965(m) election, and regardless of whether it is a United States shareholder of a deferred foreign income corporation, any section 965(a) inclusions of the real estate investment trust are not taken into account as gross income of the real estate investment trust for purposes of applying paragraphs (2) and (3) of section 856(c) for any taxable year for which the real estate investment trust takes into account a section 965(a) inclusion, including pursuant to paragraph (d)(2) of this section.

(e) *Section 965(n) election.*—(1) *In general.*—(i) *General rule.*—A person may elect to not take into account the amount described in paragraph (e)(1)(ii) of this section in determining its net operating loss under section 172 for the taxable year or in determining the amount of taxable income for such taxable year (computed without regard to the deduction allowable under section 172) that may be reduced by net operating loss carryovers or carrybacks to such taxable year under section 172. Except as provided in paragraph (e)(2)(ii)(B) of this section, the election for each taxable year is irrevocable. If the section 965(n) election creates or increases a net operating loss under section 172 for the taxable year, then the taxable income of the person for the taxable year cannot be less than the amount described in paragraph (e)(1)(ii) of this section. The amount of deductions equal to the amount by which a net operating loss is created or increased for the taxable year by reason of the section 965(n) election (the *deferred amount*) is not taken into account in computing taxable income or the separate foreign tax credit limitations under section 904 for that year. The source and separate category (as defined in § 1.904-5(a)(4)(v)) components of the deferred amount are determined in accordance with paragraph (e)(1)(iv) of this section.

(ii) *Applicable amount for section 965(n) election.*—If a person makes a section 965(n) election, the amount referred to in paragraph (e)(1)(i) of this section is the sum of—

(A) The person's section 965(a) inclusions for the taxable year reduced by the person's section 965(c) deductions for the taxable year, and

(B) In the case of a domestic corporation, the taxes deemed paid under section 960(a)(1) for the taxable year with respect to the person's section 965(a) inclusions that are treated as dividends under section 78.

(iii) *Scope of section 965(n) election.*—If a person makes a section 965(n) election, the election applies to both net operating losses for the taxable year for which the election is made and the net operating loss carryovers or carrybacks to such taxable year, each in their entirety. Any section 965(n) election made by the agent (within the meaning of § 1.1502-77) of a consolidated group applies to all net operating losses available to the consolidated group, including all components of the consolidated net operating loss deduction (as defined in § 1.1502-21(a)).

(iv) *Effect of section 965(n) election.*—(A) *In general.*—The section 965(n) election for a taxable year applies solely for purposes of determining the amount of net operating loss under section 172 for the taxable year and determining the amount of taxable income for the taxable year (computed without regard to the deduction allowable under section 172) that may be reduced by net operating loss carryovers or carrybacks to such taxable year under section 172. Paragraph (e)(1)(iv)(B) of this section provides a rule for coordinating the section 965(n) election's effect on section 172 with the computation of the separate foreign tax credit limitations under section 904.

(B) *Ordering rule for allocation and apportionment of deductions for purposes of the section 904 limitation.*—The effect of a section 965(n) election with respect to a taxable year on the computation of the separate foreign tax credit limitations under section 904 is computed as follows and in the following order.

(1) Deductions, including those that create or increase a net operating loss for the taxable year by reason of the section 965(n) election, are allocated and apportioned under §§ 1.861-8 through 1.861-17 to the relevant statutory and residual groupings, taking into account the amount described in paragraph (e)(1)(ii) of this section. The source and separate category of the net operating loss carryover or carryback to the taxable year, if any, is determined under the rules of § 1.904(g)-3(b), taking into account the amount described in paragraph (e)(1)(ii) of this section. Therefore, if the amount of the net operating loss carryover or carryback to the taxable year (as reduced by reason of the section 965(n) election) exceeds the U.S. source loss component of the net operating loss that is carried over under § 1.904(g)-3(b)(3)(i), but such excess is less than the potential carryovers (or carrybacks) of the separate limitation losses that are part of the net operating loss, the potential carryovers (or carrybacks) are proportionately reduced as provided in § 1.904(g)-3(b)(3)(ii) or (iii), as applicable.

(2) If a net operating loss is created or increased for the taxable year by reason of the section 965(n) election, the deferred amount (as defined in paragraph (e)(1)(i) of this section) is not allowed as a deduction for the taxable year. See paragraph (e)(1)(i) of this section. The deferred amount (which is the corresponding addition to the net operating loss for the taxable year) comprises a ratable portion of the deductions (including the deduction allowed under section 965(c)) allocated and apportioned to each statutory and residual grouping under paragraph (e)(1)(iv)(B)*(1)* of this section. Such ratable portion equals the deferred amount multiplied by a fraction, the numerator of which is the deductions allocated and apportioned to the statutory or residual grouping under paragraph (e)(1)(iv)(B)*(1)* of this section and the denominator of which is the total deductions described in paragraph (e)(1)(iv)(B)*(1)* of this section. Accordingly, the fraction described in the previous sentence takes into account the deferred amount.

(3) Taxable income and the separate foreign tax credit limitations under section 904 for the taxable year are computed without taking into account any deferred amount. Deductions allocated and apportioned to the statutory and residual groupings under paragraph (e)(1)(iv)(B)*(1)* of this section, to the extent deducted in the taxable year rather than deferred to create or increase a net operating loss, are combined with income in the statutory and residual groupings to which those deductions are assigned in order to compute the amount of separate limitation income or loss in each separate category and U.S. source income or loss for the taxable year. Section 904(b), (f), and (g) are then applied to determine the applicable foreign tax credit limitations for the taxable year.

(2) *Manner of making election.*—(i) *Eligibility.*—A person with a section 965(a) inclusion may make the section 965(n) election.

(ii) *Timing.*—(A) *In general.*—A section 965(n) election must be made no later than the due date (taking into account extensions, if any) for the person's return for the taxable year to which the election applies. Relief is not available under § 301.9100-2 or § 301.9100-3 of this chapter to make a late election.

(B) *Transition rule.*—In the case of a section 965(n) election made before June 21, 2019, the election may be revoked by attaching a statement, signed under penalties of perjury, to an amended return for the taxable year to which the election applies (the *election year*). The statement must include the person's name, taxpayer identification number, and a statement that the person revokes the section 965(n) election. The amended return to which the statement is attached must be filed by—

(1) In the case of a revocation with respect to an election due before February 5, 2019, the due date (taking into account extensions, if any, or any additional time that would have been granted if the person had made an extension request) for the return for the taxable year following the election year; or

(2) In the case of a revocation with respect to an election due on or after February 5, 2019, the due date (taking into account extensions, if any, or any additional time that would have been granted if the person had made an extension request) for the return for the election year.

(iii) *Election statement.*—Except as otherwise provided in publications, forms, instructions, or other guidance, to make a section

965(n) election, a person must attach a statement, signed under penalties of perjury consistent with the rules for signatures applicable to the person's return, to its return for the taxable year to which the election applies. The statement must include the person's name, taxpayer identification number, the amounts described in section 965(n)(2)(A) and paragraph (e)(1)(ii)(A) of this section and section 965(n)(2)(B) and paragraph (e)(1)(ii)(B) of this section, and the sum thereof, and the statement must be filed in the manner prescribed in publications, forms, instructions, or other guidance. The attachment of an unsigned copy of the election statement to the timely-filed return for the relevant taxable year satisfies the signature requirement of this paragraph (e)(2)(iii) if the person making the election retains the original signed election statement in the manner specified by § 1.6001-1(e).

(3) *Examples.*—The following examples illustrate the application of paragraph (e)(1)(iv) of this section.

(i) *Example 1: Net operating loss in inclusion year*—(A) *Facts.* USP, a domestic corporation, has a section 965(a) inclusion of $100x and has a section 965(c) deduction of $70x for its taxable year ending December 31, 2017. USP also includes in gross income the amount treated as dividends under section 78 of $50x (the foreign taxes deemed paid under section 960(a) for the taxable year with respect to USP's section 965(a) inclusion). The section 965(a) inclusion and the section 78 dividends are foreign source general category income. During the 2017 taxable year, USP also has U.S. source gross income of $150x and other deductions of $210x, comprising $60x of interest expense and $150x of other deductible expenses that are not definitely related to any gross income. USP's total tax book value of its assets, as determined under §§ 1.861-9(g)(2) and 1.861-9T(g)(3), is divided equally between assets that generate foreign source general category income and assets that generate U.S. source income. USP elects under paragraph (e)(1)(i) of this section to not take into account the amount described in paragraph (e)(1)(ii) of this section in determining its net operating loss under section 172 for the taxable year. Before taking into account the section 965(n) election, USP's total deductions are $280x ($210x + $70x) and USP's taxable income is $20x ($100x + $50x + $150x – $70x – $210x).

(B) *Analysis*—(1) The amount described in paragraph (e)(1)(ii) of this section is $80x ($100x section 965(a) inclusion – $70x section 965(c) deduction + $50x section 78 dividends). Not taking into account the $80x creates a net operating loss under section 172 of $60x ($20x taxable income without regard to the section 965(n) election – $80x) for the taxable year (the "deferred amount"). Under paragraph (e)(1)(i) of this section, the deferred amount of $60x constitutes a net operating loss and is not allowed as a deduction for the taxable year. USP's taxable income for the year is $80x ($100x + $50x + $150x – ($280x –$60x)).

(2) Under paragraph (e)(1)(iv)(B)(*1*) of this section, deductions are allocated and apportioned under §§ 1.861-8 through 1.861-17 to the relevant statutory and residual groupings, taking into account the amount described in paragraph (e)(1)(ii) of this section. Under § 1.861-8(b), USP's section 965(c) deduction is definitely related to the section 965(a) inclusion, and, therefore, is allocated solely to foreign source general category income. Under § 1.861-9T, based on USP's asset values, the interest expense of $60x is ratably apportioned $30x to foreign source general category income and $30x to U.S. source income. Under § 1.861-8(c)(3), based on $150x of gross U.S. source income and $150x of gross foreign source general category income, the other expenses of $150x are ratably apportioned $75x to foreign source general category income and $75x to U.S. source income. Therefore, USP's deductions allocated and apportioned to foreign source general category income are $175x ($70x + $30x + $75x) and its deductions allocated and apportioned to U.S. source income are $105x ($30x + $75x).

(3) Under paragraph (e)(1)(iv)(B)(*2*) of this section, the deferred amount of $60x comprises a ratable portion of the allocated and apportioned deductions. Therefore, $37.5x ($60x x $175x/$280x) of the deferred amount comprises deductions allocated and apportioned to foreign source general category income, and $22.5x ($60x x $105x/$280x) comprises deductions allocated and apportioned to U.S. source income.

(4) Under paragraph (e)(1)(iv)(B)(*3*) of this section, for purposes of the separate foreign tax credit limitation under section 904, foreign source general category income for the taxable year is computed without taking into account the $37.5x of the deferred amount that is attributable to the deductions allocated and apportioned to the foreign source general category. Therefore, for the 2017 taxable year, foreign source general category income is $12.5x ($100x section 965(a) inclusion + $50x section 78 dividends – ($175x deductions – $37.5x deferred amount). The remaining taxable income of $67.5x is U.S. source income.

(ii) *Example 2: Net operating loss carryover to the inclusion year*—(A) *Facts.* USP, a domestic corporation, has a section 965(a) inclusion of $100x and has a section 965(c) deduction of $60x for its taxable year ending December 31, 2017. USP also includes in gross income the amount treated as dividends under section 78 of $40x (the foreign taxes deemed paid under section 960(a) for the taxable year with respect to USP's section 965(a) inclusion). The section 965(a) inclusion and the section 78 dividends are foreign source general category income. USP also has U.S. source gross income of $200x, foreign source passive category gross income of $100x, and other deductions of $140x. Under § 1.861-8(b), USP's $60x section 965(c) deduction is definitely related to the section 965(a) inclusion, and, therefore, is allocated solely to foreign source general category income. Under §§ 1.861-8 through 1.861-17, USP allocates and apportions the other $140x of deductions as follows: $40x to foreign source general category income, $40x to foreign source passive category income, and $60x to U.S. source income. USP has a net operating loss of $260x for the 2016 taxable year consisting of a $120x U.S. source loss, a $75x general category separate limitation loss, and a $65x passive category separate limitation loss. Under paragraph (e)(1)(i) of this section, USP elects to not take into account the amount described in paragraph (e)(1)(ii) of this section in determining the amount of taxable income that may be reduced by net operating loss carryovers and carrybacks to the taxable year under section 172. USP's taxable income before taking into account the section 965(n) election and any net operating loss carryover deduction is $240x:

Table 1 to paragraph (e)(3)(ii)(A):

	General	Passive	US	Total
Section 965(a) inclusion	$100x			$100x
Section 78 dividend	$40x			$40x
Other gross income		$100x	$200x	$300x
Section 965(c) deduction	($60x)			($60x)
Other deductions	($40x)	($40x)	($60x)	($140x)
Net Income	$40x	$60x	$140x	$240x

(B) *Analysis*—(1) The amount described in paragraph (e)(1)(ii) of this section is $80x ($100x section 965(a) inclusion – $60x section 965(c) deduction + $40x section 78 dividends). As a result of the section 965(n) election, the net operating loss deduction allowed in the 2017 taxable year is reduced from $240x to $160x (the amount of USP's taxable income reduced by the amount described in paragraph (e)(1)(ii) of this section).

(2) Under paragraph (e)(1)(iv)(B)(*1*) of this section, the source and separate category of the net operating loss deduction allowed in the 2017 taxable year is determined under the rules of § 1.904(g)-3(b), taking into account the amount described in paragraph (e)(1)(ii) of this section. Under § 1.904(g)-3(b)(3)(i), first the $120x U.S. source component of the net operating loss is allocated to U.S. source income for the 2017 taxable year. Because the total tentative carryover under § 1.904(g)-3(b)(3)(ii) of $100x ($40x in the general category and $60x in the passive category) exceeds the remaining net operating loss deduction of $40x ($160x – $120x), the tentative carryover amount from each separate category is reduced proportionately, to $16x ($40x x $40x/$100x) for the general category and $24x ($40x x $60x/$100x) for the passive category. Accordingly, $16x of the general category component of the net operating loss is carried forward, and $24x of the passive category component of the net operating loss is carried forward and combined with income in the same respective categories for the 2017 taxable year. After allocation of the net operating loss carryover from 2016, USP's taxable income for the 2017 taxable year is as follows:

Table 1 to paragraph (e)(3)(ii)(B)(2):

	General	Passive	US	Total
Net income before NOL deduction	$40x	$60x	$140x	$240x
NOL deduction	($16x)	($24x)	($120x)	($160x)
Net income after NOL deduction	$24x	$36x	$20x	$80x

(f) *Election to use alternative method for calculating post-1986 earnings and profits.*—(1) *Effect of election for specified foreign corporations that do not have a 52-53-week taxable year.*—If an election is made under this paragraph (f) with respect to a specified foreign corporation that does not have a 52-53-week taxable year, the amount of the post-1986 earnings and profits (including a deficit) as of the E&P measurement date on November 2, 2017, is determined under paragraph (f)(3) of this section. The election described in this paragraph (f) is irrevocable. A specified foreign corporation that does not have a 52-53-week taxable year may not use the alternative method of determination in paragraph (f)(3) of this section for purposes of determining its post-1986 earnings and profits on the E&P measurement date on December 31, 2017.

(2) *Effect of election for specified foreign corporations that have a 52-53-week taxable year.*—If an election is made under this paragraph (f) with respect to a specified foreign corporation that has a 52-53-week taxable year, the amount of the post-1986 earnings and profits (including a deficit) as of both E&P measurement dates is determined under paragraph (f)(3) of this section. The election described in this paragraph (f) is irrevocable.

(3) *Computation of post-1986 earnings and profits using alternative method.*—With respect to an E&P measurement date, the post-1986 earnings and profits of a specified foreign corporation for which an election is properly made equals the sum of—

(i) The specified foreign corporation's post-1986 earnings and profits (including a deficit) determined as of the notional measurement date, as if it were an E&P measurement date, plus

(ii) The specified foreign corporation's annualized earnings and profits amount with respect to the notional measurement date.

(4) *Definitions.*—(i) *52-53-week taxable year.*—The term *52-53-week taxable year* means a taxable year described in § 1.441-2(a)(1).

(ii) *Annualized earnings and profits amount.*—The term *annualized earnings and profits amount* means, with respect to a specified foreign corporation, an E&P measurement date, and a notional measurement date, the amount equal to the product of the number of days between the notional measurement date and the E&P measurement date (not including the former, but including the latter) multiplied by the daily earnings amount of the specified foreign corporation. The annualized earnings and profits amount is expressed as a negative number if the E&P measurement date precedes the notional measurement date.

(iii) *Daily earnings amount.*—The term *daily earnings amount* means, with respect to a specified foreign corporation and a notional measurement date, the post-1986 earnings and profits (including a deficit) of the specified foreign corporation determined as of the close of the notional measurement date that were earned (or incurred) during the specified foreign corporation's taxable year that includes the notional measurement date, divided by the number of days that have elapsed in such taxable year as of the close of the notional measurement date.

(iv) *Notional measurement date.*—The term *notional measurement date* means—

(A) With respect to an E&P measurement date of a specified foreign corporation with a 52-53-week taxable year, the closest end of a fiscal month to such E&P measurement date, and

(B) With respect to the E&P measurement date on November 2, 2017, of all specified foreign corporations not described in paragraph (f)(4)(iv)(A) of this section, October 31, 2017.

(5) *Manner of making election.*—(i) *Eligibility.*—An election with respect to a specified foreign corporation to use the alternative method of calculating post-1986 earnings and profits as of an E&P measurement date pursuant to this paragraph (f) must be made on behalf of the specified foreign corporation by a controlling domestic shareholder (as defined in § 1.964-1(c)(5)) pursuant to the rules of § 1.964-1(c)(3), except that the controlling domestic shareholder is not required to file the statement described in § 1.964-1(c)(3)(ii).

(ii) *Timing.*—An election under this paragraph (f) must be made no later than the due date (taking into account extensions, if any) for the person's return for the first taxable year in which the person has a section 965(a) inclusion amount with respect to the specified foreign corporation or in which the person takes into account a specified E&P deficit with respect to the specified corporation for purposes of computing a section 965(a) inclusion amount with respect to another specified foreign corporation. Relief is not available under § 301.9100-2 or § 301.9100-3 to make a late election.

(iii) *Election statement.*—Except as otherwise provided in publications, forms, instructions, or other guidance, to make an election under this paragraph (f), a person must attach a statement, signed under penalties of perjury consistent with the rules for signatures applicable to the person's return, to the person's return for the taxable year described in paragraph (f)(5)(ii) of this section. The statement must include the person's name, taxpayer identification number, and the name and taxpayer identification number, if any, of each of the specified foreign corporations with respect to which the election is made, and the statement must be filed in the manner prescribed in instructions or other guidance. The attachment of an unsigned copy of the election statement to the timely-filed return for the relevant taxable year satisfies the signature requirement of this paragraph (f)(5)(iii) if the person making the election retains the original signed election statement in the manner specified by § 1.6001-1(e).

(6) *Examples.*—The following examples illustrate the application of this paragraph (f).

(i) *Example 1.* (A) *Facts.* FS, a foreign corporation, has a calendar year taxable year, and as of October 31, 2017, FS has post-1986 earnings and profits of 10,000u, 3,040u of which were earned during the taxable year that includes October 31, 2017. An election is properly made under paragraph (f)(5) of this section with respect to FS, allowing FS to determine its post-1986 earnings and profits under the alternative method with respect to its E&P measurement date on November 2, 2017.

(B) *Analysis.* As of the close of October 31, 2017, the notional measurement date with respect to the E&P measurement date on November 2, 2017, 304 days have elapsed in the taxable year of FS that includes October 31, 2017. Therefore, FS's daily earnings amount is 10u (3,040u divided by 304), and FS's annualized earnings and profits amount is 20u (10u multiplied by 2 (the number of days between the notional measurement date on October 31, 2017, and the E&P measurement date on November 2, 2017)). Accordingly, FS's post-1986 earnings and profits as of November 2, 2017, are 10,020u (its post-1986 earnings and profits as of October 31, 2017 (10,000u), plus its annualized earnings and profits amount (20u)).

(ii) *Example 2.* (A) *Facts.* The facts are the same as in paragraph (f)(6)(i)(A) of this section (the facts in *Example 1*), except that a deficit of 3,040u was incurred during the taxable year that includes October 31, 2017.

(B) *Analysis.* The analysis is the same as in paragraph (f)(6)(i)(B) of this section (the analysis in *Example 1*), except that FS's daily earnings amount is (10u) ((3,040u) divided by 304), and FS's annualized earnings and profits amount is (20u) ((10u) multiplied by 2 (the number of days between the notional measurement date on October 31, 2017, and the E&P measurement date on November 2, 2017)). Accordingly, FS's post-1986 earnings and profits as of November 2, 2017, are 9,980u (its post-1986 earnings and profits as of October 31, 2017 (10,000u), plus its annualized earnings and profits amount ((20u))).

(g) *Definitions.*—This paragraph (g) provides definitions that apply for purposes of this section.

(1) *Deferred net tax liability.*—The term *deferred net tax liability* means, with respect to any taxable year of a person, the amount of

the section 965(i) net tax liability the payment of which has been deferred under section 965(i) and paragraph (c) of this section.

(2) *REIT section 965 amounts.*—The term *REIT section 965 amounts* means, with respect to a real estate investment trust and a taxable year of the real estate investment trust, the aggregate amount of section 965(a) inclusions and section 965(c) deductions that would (but for section 965(m)(1)(B) and paragraph (d) of this section) be taken into account in determining the real estate investment trust's income for the taxable year.

(3) *Section 965(h) election.*—The term *section 965(h) election* means the election described in section 965(h)(1) and paragraph (b)(1) of this section.

(4) *Section 965(h) net tax liability.*—The term *section 965(h) net tax liability* means, with respect to a person that has made a section 965(h) election, the total net tax liability under section 965 reduced by the aggregate amount of the person's section 965(i) net tax liabilities, if any, with respect to which section 965(i) elections are effective.

(5) *Section 965(i) election.*—The term *section 965(i) election* means the election described in section 965(i)(1) and paragraph (c)(1) of this section.

(6) *Section 965(i) net tax liability.*—The term *section 965(i) net tax liability* means, with respect to an S corporation and a shareholder of the S corporation, in the case in which a section 965(i) election is made, the amount determined pursuant to paragraph (g)(10)(i) of this section by adding before the word "over" in (g)(10)(i)(A) of this section "determined as if the only section 965(a) inclusions included in income by the person are domestic pass-through entity shares of section 965(a) inclusions by the S corporation with respect to deferred foreign income corporations of which the S corporation is a United States shareholder."

(7) *Section 965(m) election.*—The term *section 965(m) election* means the election described in section 965(m)(1)(B) and paragraph (d)(1) of this section.

(8) *Section 965(n) election.*—The term *section 965(n) election* means the election described in section 965(n)(1) and paragraph (e)(1)(i) of this section.

(9) *Specified individual.*—The term *specified individual* means, with respect to a taxable year, a person described in § 1.6081-5(a)(5) or (6) who receives an extension of time to file and pay under § 1.6081-5(a) for the taxable year.

(10) *Total net tax liability under section 965.*—(i) *General rule.*—The term *total net tax liability under section 965* means, with respect to a person, the excess (if any) of—

(A) The person's net income tax for the taxable year in which the person includes a section 965(a) inclusion in income, over—

(B) The person's net income tax for the taxable year determined—

(1) Without regard to section 965, and

(2) Without regard to any income, deduction, or credit properly attributable to a dividend received (directly or through a chain of ownership described in section 958(a)) by the person (or, in the case of a domestic pass-through owner, by the person's domestic pass-through entity) from, or an inclusion under sections 951(a)(1)(B) and 956 with respect to, a deferred foreign income corporation and paid during, or included with respect to, the deferred foreign income corporation's inclusion year.

(ii) *Net income tax.*—For purposes of this paragraph (g)(10), the term *net income tax* means the regular tax liability (as defined in section 26(b)) reduced by the credits allowed under subparts A, B, and D of part IV of subchapter A of chapter 1 of subtitle A of the Internal Revenue Code.

(iii) *Foreign tax credits.*—The foreign tax credit disregarded in determining net income tax determined under paragraph (g)(10)(i)(B) of this section includes the credit for foreign income taxes deemed paid with respect to section 965(a) inclusions or foreign income taxes deemed paid with respect to a dividend, including a distribution that would have been treated as a dividend in the absence of section 965. The foreign tax credit disregarded under paragraph (g)(10)(i)(B) of this section also includes the credit for foreign income taxes imposed on distributions of section 965(a) previously taxed earnings and profits or 965(b) previously taxed earnings and profits made in the taxable year in which the person includes a section 965(a) inclusion in income. [Reg. § 1.965-7.]

❑ [*T.D. 9846, 2-4-2019 (corrected 4-9-2019). Amended by T.D. 9866, 6-14-2019 and T.D. 9882, 12-16-2019.*]

§ 1.965-8. Affiliated groups (including consolidated groups).—(a) *Scope.*—This section provides rules for applying section 965 and the section 965 regulations to members of an affiliated group (as defined in section 1504(a)), including members of a consolidated group (as defined in § 1.1502-1(h)). Paragraph (b) of this section provides guidance regarding the application of section 965(b)(5) to determine the section 965(a) inclusion amounts of a member of an affiliated group. Paragraph (c) of this section provides guidance for designating the source of aggregate unused E&P deficits. Paragraph (d) provides rules regarding earning and profits and stock basis adjustments. Paragraph (e) of this section provides rules that treat members of a consolidated group as a single person for certain purposes. Paragraph (f) of this section provides definitions that apply for purposes of this section. Paragraph (g) of this section provides examples illustrating the application of this section.

(b) *Reduction of E&P net surplus shareholder's pro rata share of the section 965(a) earnings amount of a deferred foreign income corporation by the allocable share of the applicable share of the aggregate unused E&P deficit.*—(1) *In general.*—This paragraph (b) applies after the application of § 1.965-1(b)(2) for purposes of determining the section 965(a) inclusion amount with respect to a deferred foreign income corporation of a section 958(a) U.S. shareholder that is both an E&P net surplus shareholder and a member of an affiliated group in which not all members are members of the same consolidated group. If this paragraph (b) applies, the U.S. dollar amount of the section 958(a) U.S. shareholder's pro rata share of the section 965(a) earnings amount of the deferred foreign income corporation is further reduced (but not below zero) by the deferred foreign income corporation's allocable share of the section 958(a) U.S. shareholder's applicable share of the affiliated group's aggregate unused E&P deficit.

(2) *Consolidated group as part of an affiliated group.*—If some, but not all, members of an affiliated group are members of a consolidated group, then the consolidated group is treated as a single member of the affiliated group for purposes of § 1.965-1(b)(2) and paragraph (b)(1) of this section.

(c) *Designation of portion of excess aggregate foreign E&P deficit taken into account.*—(1) *In general.*—This paragraph (c) provides rules for designating the source of an aggregate unused E&P deficit of an affiliated group that is not also a consolidated group taken into account under section 965(b)(5) and paragraph (b) of this section if the amount described in paragraph (f)(1)(i)(A) of this section with respect to the affiliated group exceeds the amount described in paragraph (f)(1)(i)(B) of this section with respect to the affiliated group. If this paragraph (c)(1) applies, each member of the affiliated group that is an E&P net deficit shareholder must designate by maintaining in its books and records a statement (identical to the statement maintained by all other such members) setting forth the portion of the excess aggregate foreign E&P deficit of the E&P net deficit shareholder taken into account under section 965(b)(5) and paragraph (b) of this section. See § 1.965-2(d)(2)(ii)(B) for a rule for designating the portion of a section 958(a) U.S. shareholder's pro rata share of a specified E&P deficit of an E&P deficit foreign corporation taken into account under section 965(b), § 1.965-1(b)(2), and paragraph (b) of this section, as applicable.

(2) *Consolidated group as part of an affiliated group.*—If some, but not all, members of an affiliated group are properly treated as members of a consolidated group, then the consolidated group is treated as a single member of the affiliated group for purposes of applying paragraph (c)(1) of this section.

(d) *Adjustments to earning and profits and stock basis.*—(1) [Reserved]

(2) *Consolidated groups.*—See § 1.1502-33(d)(1) for adjustments to members' earnings and profits and § 1.1502-32(b)(3) for adjustments to members' basis.

(e) *Treatment of a consolidated group or other affiliated group as a single section 958(a) U.S. shareholder or a single person.*—(1) *In general.*—All members of a consolidated group that are section 958(a) U.S. shareholders of a specified foreign corporation are treated as a single section 958(a) U.S. shareholder for purposes of section965(b), § 1.965-1(b)(2), and § 1.965-3. Furthermore, all members of a consolidated group are treated as a single person for purposes of paragraphs (h), (k), and (n) of section 965 and § 1.965-7. In addition, all members of an affiliated group that are section 958(a) U.S. shareholders of a specified foreign corporation are treated as a single section 958(a) U.S. shareholder for purposes of § 1.965-2(f). Thus, for example, any election governed by section 965(h) and § 1.965-7(b) must be made by the agent (within the meaning of § 1.1502-77) of the group as a single election on behalf of all members of the consolidated group. Similarly, the determination of whether the transfer of assets by one member to a non-member of the consolidated group would constitute an acceleration event under § 1.965-7(b)(3)(ii)(B) takes into account all of the assets of the consolidated group, which for purposes of this determination, includes all of the assets of each consolidated group member. In analyzing issues relating to the transfer of assets of a consolidated group, appropriate adjustments are made to prevent the duplication of assets or asset value.

(2) *Limitation.*—Paragraph (e)(1) of this section does not apply to treat all members of a consolidated group as a single section 958(a) U.S. shareholder or a single person, as applicable, for purposes of determining the amount of any member's inclusion under section 951 (including a section 965(a) inclusion), the foreign income taxes deemed paid with respect to a section 965(a) inclusion (see sections 960 and 902), or any purpose other than those specifically listed in paragraph (e)(1) of this section or another provision of the section 965 regulations.

(3) *Determination of section 965(c) deduction amount.*—For purposes of determining the section 965(c) deduction amount of any section 958(a) U.S. shareholder that is a member of a consolidated group, the aggregate foreign cash position of the section 958(a) U.S. shareholder is equal to the aggregate section 965(a) inclusion amount of the section 958(a) U.S. shareholder multiplied by the group cash ratio of the consolidated group.

(f) *Definitions.*—This paragraph (f) provides definitions that apply for purposes of applying the section 965 regulations to members of an affiliated group, including members of a consolidated group.

(1) *Aggregate unused E&P deficit.*—(i) *General rule.*—The term *aggregate unused E&P deficit* means, with respect to an affiliated group, the lesser of—

(A) The sum of the excess aggregate foreign E&P deficit with respect to each E&P net deficit shareholder that is a member of the affiliated group, or

(B) The amount determined under paragraph (f)(3)(ii) of this section.

(ii) *Reduction with respect to E&P net deficit shareholders that are not wholly owned by the affiliated group.*—If the group ownership percentage of an E&P net deficit shareholder is less than 100 percent, the amount of the excess aggregate foreign E&P deficit with respect to the E&P net deficit shareholder that is taken into account under paragraph (f)(1)(i) of this section is the product of the group ownership percentage multiplied by the excess aggregate foreign E&P deficit.

(2) *Allocable share.*—The term *allocable share* means, with respect to a deferred foreign income corporation and an E&P net surplus shareholder's applicable share of an aggregate unused E&P deficit of an affiliated group, the product of the E&P net surplus shareholder's applicable share of the affiliated group's aggregate unused E&P deficit and the ratio described in § 1.965-1(f)(11) with respect to the deferred foreign income corporation.

(3) *Applicable share.*—The term *applicable share* means, with respect to an E&P net surplus shareholder and an aggregate unused E&P deficit of an affiliated group, the amount that bears the same proportion to the affiliated group's aggregate unused E&P deficit as—

(i) The product of—

(A) The E&P net surplus shareholder's group ownership percentage, multiplied by

(B) The amount that would (but for section 965(b)(5) and paragraph (b) of this section) constitute the E&P net surplus shareholder's aggregate section 965(a) inclusion amount, bears to

(ii) The aggregate amount determined under paragraph (f)(3)(i) of this section with respect to all E&P net surplus shareholders that are members of the group.

(4) *Consolidated group aggregate foreign cash position.*—The term *consolidated group aggregate foreign cash position* means, with respect to a consolidated group, the aggregate foreign cash position (as defined in § 1.965-1(f)(8)(i)) determined by treating each member of the consolidated group that is a section 958(a) U.S. shareholder as a single section 958(a) U.S. shareholder pursuant to paragraph (e)(1) of this section.

(5) *E&P net deficit shareholder.*—The term *E&P net deficit shareholder* means a section 958(a) U.S. shareholder that has an excess aggregate foreign E&P deficit.

(6) *E&P net surplus shareholder.*—The term *E&P net surplus shareholder* means a section 958(a) U.S. shareholder that would (but for section 965(b)(5) and paragraph (b) of this section) have an aggregate section 965(a) inclusion amount greater than zero.

(7) *Excess aggregate foreign E&P deficit.*—The term *excess aggregate foreign E&P deficit* means, with respect to a section 958(a) U.S. shareholder, the amount, if any, by which the amount described in § 1.965-1(f)(9)(i) with respect to the section 958(a) U.S. shareholder exceeds the amount described in § 1.965-1(f)(9)(ii) with respect to the section 958(a) U.S. shareholder.

(8) *Group cash ratio.*—The term *group cash ratio* means, with respect to a consolidated group, the ratio of—

(i) The consolidated group aggregate foreign cash position, to

(ii) The sum of the aggregate section 965(a) inclusion amounts of all members of the consolidated group.

(9) *Group ownership percentage.*—The term *group ownership percentage* means, with respect to a section 958(a) U.S. shareholder that is a member of an affiliated group, the percentage of the value of the stock of the United States shareholder which is held by other includible corporations in the affiliated group. Notwithstanding the preceding sentence, the group ownership percentage of the common parent of the affiliated group is 100 percent. Any term used in this paragraph (f)(9) that is also used in section 1504 has the same meaning as when used in such section. Additionally, if the term is used in the context of a rule for which all members of a consolidated group are treated as a single section 958(a) U.S. shareholder under paragraph (e)(1) of this section, then the group ownership percentage is determined solely with respect to the value of the stock of the common parent of the consolidated group held by other includible corporations that are not members of the consolidated group.

(g) *Examples.*—The following examples illustrate the application of this section.

(1) *Example 1. Application of affiliated group rule.* (i) *Facts.* (A) *In general.* USP owns all of the stock of USS1, USS2, and USS3. Each of USP, USS1, USS2, and USS3 is a domestic corporation and is a member of an affiliated group of which USP is the common parent (the "USP Group"). The USP Group has not elected to file a consolidated federal income tax return. USS1 owns all of the stock of CFC1 and CFC2, USS2 owns all of the stock of CFC3, and USS3 owns all of the stock of CFC4. Each of CFC1, CFC2, CFC3, and CFC4 is a controlled foreign corporation within the meaning of section 957(a), and, therefore, each is a specified foreign corporation under section 965(e) and § 1.965-1(f)(45). Each of USP, USS1, USS2, USS3, CFC1, CFC2, CFC3, and CFC4 has the calendar year as its taxable year.

(B) *Facts relating to section 965.* CFC1 and CFC3 are deferred foreign income corporations with section 965(a) earnings amounts of $600x and $300x, respectively. CFC1 and CFC3 have cash positions of $0x and $50x, respectively, on each of their cash measurement dates. CFC2 and CFC4 are E&P deficit foreign corporations with specified E&P deficits of $400x and $100x, respectively. CFC2 and CFC4 have cash positions of $100x and $50x, respectively, on each of their cash measurement dates. The cash positions all consist solely of cash. CFC1, CFC2, CFC3, and CFC4 all use the U.S. dollar as their functional currency.

(ii) *Analysis.* (A) *Section 965(a) inclusion amounts before application of section 965(b)(5).* USS1 is a section 958(a) U.S. shareholder with respect to CFC1 and CFC2; USS2 is a section 958(a) U.S. shareholder with respect to CFC3; and USS3 is a section 958(a) U.S. shareholder with respect to CFC4. USS1's pro rata share of CFC1's section 965(a) earnings amount is $600x. Under section 965(b)(3)(A) and § 1.965-1(f)(9), USS1's aggregate foreign E&P deficit is $400x, the lesser of the aggregate of USS1's pro rata share of the specified E&P deficit of each E&P deficit foreign corporation ($400x) and the amount described in §1.965-1(f)(9)(ii) with respect to USS1 ($600x). Under section 965(b) and §1.965-1(b)(2), in determining its section 965(a) inclusion amount with respect to CFC1, USS1 reduces its pro rata share of the U.S. dollar amount of section 965(a) earnings amount of CFC1 by CFC1's allocable share of USS1's aggregate foreign E&P deficit. CFC1's allocable share of USS1's aggregate foreign E&P deficit is $400x, which is the product of USS1's aggregate foreign E&P deficit ($400x) and 1, which is the ratio determined by dividing USS1's pro rata share of the section 965(a) earnings amount of CFC1 ($600x), by the amount described in §1.965-1(f)(9)(ii) with respect to USS1 ($600x). Accordingly, under section 965(b) and §1.965-1(b)(2) (before applying section 965(b)(5) and paragraph (b) of this section), USS1's section 965(a) inclusion amount with respect to CFC1 would be $200x (USS1's pro rata share of the section 965(a) earnings amount of CFC1 of $600x reduced by CFC1's allocable share of USS1's aggregate foreign E&P deficit of $400x). Under section 965(b) and §1.965-1(b)(2) (before applying section 965(b)(5) and paragraph (b) of this section), USS2's section 965(a) inclusion amount with respect to CFC3 would be $300x (USS2's pro rata share of the section 965(a) earnings amount of CFC3).

(B) *Application of section 965(b)(5)—(1) Determination of E&P net surplus shareholders and E&P net deficit shareholders*. USS1 is an E&P net surplus shareholder because it would have an aggregate section 965(a) inclusion amount of $200x but for the application of section 965(b)(5) and paragraph (b) of this section. USS2 is also an E&P net surplus shareholder because it would have an aggregate section 965(a) inclusion amount of $300x but for the application of section 965(b)(5) and paragraph (b) of this section. USS3 is an E&P net deficit shareholder because it has an excess aggregate foreign E&P deficit of $100x.

(2) *Determining section 965(a) inclusion amounts under section 965(b)(5)*. Under section 965(b) and paragraph (b) of this section, for purposes of determining the section 965(a) inclusion amount of a section 958(a) U.S. shareholder with respect to a deferred foreign income corporation, if, after applying §1.965-1(b)(2), the section 958(a) U.S. shareholder is an E&P net surplus shareholder, then the U.S. dollar amount of the section 958(a) U.S. shareholder's pro rata share of the section 965(a) earnings amount of the deferred foreign income corporation is further reduced (but not below zero) by the deferred foreign income corporation's allocable share of the section 958(a) U.S. shareholder's applicable share of the affiliated group's aggregate unused E&P deficit. USS3 is the only E&P net deficit shareholder in the USP Group, and, therefore, the aggregate unused E&P deficit of the USP Group is equal to USS3's excess aggregate foreign E&P deficit ($100x). The applicable share of the USP Group's aggregate unused E&P deficit of each of USS1 and USS2, respectively, is an amount that bears the same proportion to the USP Group's aggregate unused E&P deficit as the product of the group ownership percentage of USS1 and USS2, respectively, multiplied by the amount that would (but for section 965(b)(5) and paragraph (b) of this section) constitute the aggregate section 965(a) inclusion amount of USS1 and USS2, respectively, bears to the aggregate of such amounts with respect to both USS1 and USS2. Therefore, USS1's applicable share of the USP Group's aggregate unused E&P deficit is $40 ($100x x ($200x/($200x + $300x))) and USS2's applicable share of the USP Group's aggregate unused E&P deficit is $60x ($100x x ($300x/($200x + $300x))). Because USS1 is a section 958(a) U.S. shareholder with respect to only one deferred foreign income corporation, the entire $40x of USS1's applicable share of the USP Group's aggregate unused E&P deficit is treated as CFC1's allocable share of USS1's applicable share of the USP Group's aggregate unused E&P deficit, and thus USS1's section 965(a) inclusion amount with respect to CFC1 is reduced to $160x ($200x - $40x). Because USS2 is a section 958(a) U.S. shareholder with respect to only one deferred foreign income corporation, the entire $60x of USS2's applicable share of the USP Group's aggregate unused E&P deficit is treated as CFC3's allocable share of USS2's applicable share of the USP Group's aggregate unused E&P deficit, and thus USS2's section 965(a) inclusion amount with respect to CFC3 is reduced to $240x ($300x - $60x).

(C) *Aggregate foreign cash position*. Under section 965(c) and §1.965-1(c), a section 958(a) U.S. shareholder that includes a section 965(a) inclusion amount in income is allowed a deduction equal to the section 965(c) deduction amount. The section 965(c) deduction amount is computed by taking into account the aggregate foreign cash position of the section 958(a) U.S. shareholder. Under §1.965-1(f)(8)(i), the aggregate foreign cash position of USS1 is $100x, and the aggregate foreign cash position of USS2 is $50x.

(D) *Section 965(c) deduction amount*. The section 965(c) deduction amount of USS1 is $102x, which is equal to (i) USS1's 8 percent rate equivalent percentage (77.1428571%) of its 8 percent rate amount for USS1's 2017 year ($60x ($160x - $100x)), plus USS1's 15.5 percent rate equivalent percentage (55.7142857%) of its 15.5 percent rate amount for USS1's 2017 year ($100x). The section 965(c) deduction amount of USS2 is $174.43x, which is equal to (i) USS2's 8 percent rate equivalent percentage (77.1428571%) of its 8 percent rate amount for USS2's 2017 year ($190x ($240x - $50x)), plus USS2's 15.5 percent rate equivalent percentage (55.7142857%) of its 15.5 percent rate amount for USS2's 2017 year ($50x). Because USS3 has no section 965(a) inclusion amount, it has no section 965(c) deduction amount and therefore is not allowed a section 965(c) deduction.

(2) *Example 2. Application to members of a consolidated group*. (i) *Facts*. The facts are the same as in paragraph (g)(1)(i) of this section (the facts in *Example 1*), except that the USP Group has elected to file a consolidated return.

(ii) *Analysis—(A) Section 965(a) inclusion amount—(1) Single section 958(a) U.S. shareholder treatment*. Because each of USS1, USS2, and USS3 is a section 958(a) U.S. shareholder of a specified foreign corporation and is a member of a consolidated group, paragraph (e)(1) of this section applies to treat USS1, USS2, and USS3 as a single section 958(a) U.S. shareholder for purposes of section 965(b) and §1.965-1(b)(2).

(2) *Determination of inclusion amount*. The single section 958(a) U.S. shareholder composed of USS1, USS2, and USS3 is a section 958(a) U.S. shareholder with respect to CFC1, CFC2, CFC3, and CFC4. Under §1.965-1(b)(2), in determining USS1's section 965(a) inclusion amount, the single section 958(a) U.S. shareholder decreases its pro rata share of the U.S. dollar amount of the section 965(a) earnings amount of CFC1 by CFC1's allocable share of the aggregate foreign E&P deficit of the single section 958(a) U.S. shareholder. CFC1's allocable share of the aggregate foreign E&P deficit is $333.33x, which is the product of the aggregate foreign E&P deficit of the single section 958(a) U.S. shareholder ($500x ($400x + $100x)) and .67, which is the ratio determined by dividing its pro rata share of the section 965(a) earnings amount of CFC1 ($600x) by the amount described in §1.965-1(f)(9)(ii) with respect to the single section 958(a) U.S. shareholder ($900x ($600x + $300x)). Therefore, USS1's section 965(a) inclusion amount with respect to CFC1 is $266.67 (its pro rata share of the section 965(a) earnings amount of CFC1 ($600) less CFC1's allocable share of the aggregate foreign E&P deficit of the single section 958(a) U.S. shareholder ($333.33x)). Similarly, under §1.965-1(b)(2), in determining the section 965(a) inclusion amount of USS2, the single section 958(a) U.S. shareholder decreases its pro rata share of the U.S. dollar amount of the section 965(a) earnings amount of CFC3 by CFC3's allocable share of the aggregate foreign E&P deficit of the single section 958(a) U.S. shareholder. CFC3's allocable share of the aggregate foreign E&P deficit is $166.67x, which is the product of the aggregate foreign E&P deficit of the single section 958(a) U.S. shareholder ($500x) and .33, which is the ratio determined by dividing its pro rata share of the section 965(a) earnings amount of CFC3 ($300x) by the amount described in §1.965-1(f)(9)(ii) with respect to the single section 958(a) U.S. shareholder ($900x ($600x + $300x)). Therefore, USS2's section 965(a) inclusion amount with respect to CFC3 is $133.33x (its pro rata share of the section 965(a) earnings amount of CFC3 ($300x) less CFC3's allocable share of the aggregate foreign E&P deficit of the single section 958(a) U.S. shareholder ($166.67x)).

(B) *Consolidated group aggregate foreign cash position*. Because USS1 and USS2 are members of a consolidated group, the aggregate foreign cash position of each of USS1 and USS2 is determined under paragraph (e)(3) of this section. Under paragraph (e)(3) of this section, the aggregate foreign cash position of each of USS1 and USS2 is equal to the aggregate section 965(a) inclusion amount of USS1 and USS2, respectively, multiplied by the group cash ratio of the USP Group, as determined pursuant to paragraph (f)(8) of this section. The group cash ratio of the USP Group is .50, which is the ratio of the USP Group's consolidated group aggregate foreign cash position ($200x ($50x + $100x + $50x)) and the sum of the aggregate section 965(a) inclusion amounts of all members of the USP Group ($400x ($266.67x + $133.33x)). Therefore, under paragraph (e)(3) of this section, the aggregate foreign cash positions of USS1 and USS2 are, respectively, $133.34x ($266.67x x ($200x/$400x)) and $66.67 ($133.33x x ($200x/400x)).

(C) *Section 965(c) deduction amount*. The section 965(c) deduction amount of USS1 is $177.14x, which is equal to (i) USS1's 8 percent rate equivalent percentage (77.1428571%) of its 8 percent rate amount for USS1's 2017 year ($133.33x ($266.67x - $133.34x)), plus USS1's 15.5 percent rate equivalent percentage (55.7142857%) of its 15.5 percent rate amount for USS1's 2017 year ($133.34x). The section 965(c) deduction amount of USS2 is $88.56x, which is equal to (i) USS2's 8 percent rate equivalent percentage (77.1428571%) of its 8 percent rate amount for USS2's 2017 year ($66.66x ($133.33x - $66.67x)), plus USS2's 15.5 percent rate equivalent percentage (55.7142857%) of its 15.5 percent rate amount for USS2's 2017 year ($66.67x). Because

USS3 has no section 965(a) inclusion amount, it has no section 965(c) deduction amount and therefore is not allowed a section 965(c) deduction. [Reg. § 1.965-8.]

☐ [*T.D. 9846, 2-4-2019 (corrected 4-9-2019).*]

§ 1.965-9. Applicability dates.—(a) *In general.*—Except as otherwise provided in this section, § § 1.965-1 through 1.965-8 apply beginning the last taxable year of a foreign corporation that begins before January 1, 2018, and with respect to a United States person, beginning the taxable year in which or with which such taxable year of the foreign corporation ends.

(b) *Applicability dates for rules disregarding certain transactions.*—Section 1.965-4 applies regardless of whether, with respect to a foreign corporation, the transaction, effective date of a change in method of accounting, effective date of an entity classification election, or specified payment described in § 1.965-4 occurred before the first day of the foreign corporation's last taxable year that begins before January 1, 2018, or, with respect to a United States person, the transaction, effective date of a change in method of accounting, effective date of an entity classification election, or specified payment described in § 1.965-4 occurred before the first day of the taxable year of the United States person in which or with which the taxable year of the foreign corporation ends.

(c) *Applicability date for certain portions of § 1.965-5.*—Paragraph (c)(1)(iii) of § 1.965-5 applies to taxable years of foreign corporations that both begin after December 31, 2017, and end on or after December 4, 2018, and with respect to a United States person, to the taxable years in which or with which such taxable years of the foreign corporations end. Section 1.965-5(b)(2) applies to taxable years of foreign corporations that end on or after December 16, 2019, and with respect to a United States person, to the taxable years in which or with which such taxable years of the foreign corporations end. [Reg. § 1.965-9.]

☐ [*T.D. 9846, 2-4-2019. Amended by T.D. 9882, 12-16-2019 and T.D. 9922, 11-2-2020.*]

Foreign Currency

§ 1.985-1. Functional currency.—(a) *Applicability and effective date.*—(1) *Purpose and scope.*—These regulations provide guidance with respect to defining the functional currency of a taxpayer and each qualified business unit (QBU), as defined in section 989 (a). Generally, a taxpayer and each QBU must make all determinations under subtitle A of the Code (relating to income taxes) in its respective functional currency. This section sets forth rules for determining when the functional currency is the United States dollar (dollar) or a currency other than the dollar. Section 1.985-2 provides an election to use the dollar as the functional currency for certain QBUs that absent the election would have a functional currency that is a hyperinflationary currency, and explains the effect of making the election. Section 1.985-3 sets forth the dollar approximate separate transactions method that certain QBUs must use to compute their income or loss or earnings and profits. Section 1.985-4 provides that the adoption of a functional currency is a method of accounting and sets forth conditions for a change in functional currency. Section 1.985-5 provides adjustments that are required to be made upon a change in functional currency. Finally, § 1.985-6 provides transition rules for a QBU that uses the dollar approximate separate transactions method for its first taxable year beginning after December 31, 1986.

(2) *Effective date.*—These regulations apply to taxable years beginning after December 31, 1986. However, any taxpayer desiring to apply temporary Income Tax Regulations § 1.985-0T through § 1.985-4T in lieu of these regulations to all taxable years beginning after December 31, 1986, and on or before OCT 20, 1989 may (on a consistent basis) so choose. For the text of the temporary regulations, see 53 Fed. Reg. 20308 (1988).

(b) *Dollar functional currency.*—(1) *In general.*—The dollar shall be the functional currency of a taxpayer or QBU described in paragraph (b)(1)(i) through (v) of this section regardless of the currency used in keeping its books and records (as defined in § 1.989(a)-1(d)). The dollar shall be the functional currency of—

(i) A taxpayer that is not a QBU (e.g., an individual);

(ii) A QBU that conducts its activities primarily in dollars. A QBU conducts its activities primarily in dollars if the currency of the economic environment in which the QBU conducts its activities is primarily the dollar. The facts and circumstances test set forth in paragraph (c)(2) of this section shall apply in making this determination;

(iii) Except as otherwise provided by ruling or administrative pronouncement, a QBU that has the United States, or any possession or territory of the United States where the dollar is the standard currency, as its residence (as defined in section 988(a)(3)(B));

(iv) A QBU that does not keep books and records in the currency of any economic environment in which a significant part of its activities is conducted. Whether a QBU keeps such books and records is determined in accordance with paragraph (c)(3) of this section; or

(v) A QBU that produces income or loss that is, or is treated as, effectively connected with the conduct of a trade or business within the United States.

(2) *QBUs operating in a hyperinflationary environment.*—(i) *Taxable years beginning on or before August 24, 1994.*—For taxable years beginning on or before August 24, 1994, see § 1.985-2 with respect to a QBU that elects to use, or is otherwise required to use, the dollar as its functional currency.

(ii) *Taxable years beginning after August 24, 1994.*—(A) *In general.*—For taxable years beginning after August 24, 1994, except as otherwise provided in paragraph (b)(2)(ii)(B) of this section, any QBU that otherwise would be required to use a hyperinflationary currency as its functional currency must use the dollar as its functional currency and compute income or loss or earnings and profits under the rules of § 1.985-3.

(B) *Exceptions.*—*(1) Certain QBU branches.*—The functional currency of a QBU that otherwise would be required to use a hyperinflationary currency as its functional currency and that is a branch of a foreign corporation having a non-dollar functional currency that is not hyperinflationary shall be the functional currency of the foreign corporation. Such QBU's income or loss or earnings and profits shall be determined under § 1.985-3 by substituting the functional currency of the foreign corporation for the dollar.

(2) Corporation that is not a controlled foreign corporation.—A foreign corporation (or its QBU branch) operating in a hyperinflationary environment is not required to use the dollar as its functional currency pursuant to paragraph (b)(2)(ii)(A) of this section if that foreign corporation is not a controlled foreign corporation as defined in section 957 or 953(c)(1)(B). However, a noncontrolled section 902 corporation, as defined in section 904(d)(2)(E), may elect to use the dollar (or, if appropriate, the currency specified in paragraph (b)(2)(ii)(B)(*1*) of this section) as its (or its QBU branch's) functional currency under the procedures set forth in § 1.985-2(c)(3).

(C) *Change in functional currency.*—*(1) In general.*—If a QBU is required to change its functional currency to the dollar under paragraph (b)(2)(ii)(A) of this section, or chooses or is required to change its functional currency to the dollar for any open taxable year (and all subsequent taxable years) under § 1.985-3(a)(2)(ii), the change is considered to be made with the consent of the Commissioner for purposes of § 1.985-4. A QBU changing functional currency must make adjustments described in § 1.985-7 if the year of change (as defined in § 1.481-1(a)(1)) begins after 1987, or the adjustments described in § 1.985-6 if the year of change begins in 1987. No adjustments under section 481 are required solely because of a change in functional currency described in this paragraph (b)(2)(ii)(C).

(2) Effective date.—This paragraph (b)(2)(ii)(C) applies to taxable years beginning after April 6, 1998. However, a taxpayer may choose to apply this paragraph (b)(2)(ii)(C) to all open years after December 31, 1986, provided each person, and each QBU branch of a person, that is related (within the meaning of § 1.985-2(d)(3)) also applies to this paragraph (b)(2)(ii)(C).

(D) *Hyperinflationary currency.*—For purposes of sections 985 through 989, the term hyperinflationary currency means the currency of a country in which there is cumulative inflation during the base period of at least 100 percent as determined by reference to the consumer price index of the country listed in the monthly issues of the "International Financial Statistics" or a successor publication of the International Monetary Fund. If a country's currency is not listed in the monthly issues of "International Financial Statistics," a QBU may use any other reasonable method consistently applied for determining the country's consumer price index. Base period means, with respect to any taxable year, the thirty-six calendar months immediately preceding the first day of the current calendar year. For this purpose, the cumulative inflation rate for the base period is based on compounded inflation rates. Thus, if for 1991, 1992, and 1993, a country's annual inflation rates are 29 percent, 25 percent, and 30 percent, respectively, the cumulative inflation rate for the three-year base period is 110 percent [((1.29 × 1.25 × 1.3) − 1.0 = 1.10) × 100 = 110%] and the currency of the country for the QBU's 1994 year is considered hyperinflationary. In making the determination whether a currency is hyperinflationary, the determination for purposes of United States generally accepted accounting principles may be used for income tax purposes provided the determination is based on criteria that is substantially similar to the rules previously set forth in this paragraph (b)(2)(ii)(D), the method of determination is applied consistently from year to year, and the same method is applied to all related persons as defined in § 1.985-3(e)(2)(vi).

(E) *Change in functional currency when currency ceases to be hyperinflationary.*—(1) *In general.*—A QBU that has been required to use the dollar as its functional currency under paragraph (b)(2) of this section, or has elected to use the dollar as its functional currency under paragraph (b)(2)(ii)(B)(2) of this section or § 1.985-2, must change its functional currency as of the first day of the first taxable year that follows three consecutive taxable years in which the currency of its economic environment, determined under paragraph (c)(2) of this section, is not a hyperinflationary currency. The functional currency of the QBU for such year shall be determined in accordance with paragraph (c) of this section. For purposes of § 1.985-4, the change is considered to be made with the consent of the Commissioner. See § 1.985-5 for adjustments that are required upon a change in functional currency.

(2) *Effective date.*—This paragraph (b)(2)(ii)(E) of this section applies to taxable years beginning after April 6, 1998.

(c) *Functional currency of a QBU that is not required to use the dollar.*—(1) *General rule.*—The functional currency of a QBU that is not required to use the dollar under paragraph (b) of this section shall be the currency of the economic environment in which a significant part of the QBU's activities is conducted, if the QBU keeps, or is presumed under paragraph (c) (3) of this section to keep, its books and records in such currency.

(2) *Economic environment.*—For purposes of section 985 and the regulations thereunder, the economic environment in which a significant part of a QBU's activities is conducted shall be determined by taking into account all the facts and circumstances.

(i) *Facts and circumstances.*—The facts and circumstances that are considered in determining the economic environment in which a significant part of a QBU's activities is conducted include, but are not limited to, the following:

(A) The currency of the country in which the QBU is a resident as determined under section 988 (a)(3)(B);

(B) The currencies of the QBU's cash flows;

(C) The currencies in which the QBU generates revenues and incurs expenses;

(D) The currencies in which the QBU borrows and lends;

(E) The currencies of the QBU's sales markets;

(F) The currencies in which pricing and other financial decisions are made;

(G) The duration of the QBU's business operations; and

(H) The significance and/or volume of the QBU's independent activities.

(ii) *Rate of inflation.*—The rate of inflation (regardless of how it is determined) shall not be a factor used to determine a QBU's economic environment.

(iii) *Consistency.*—A taxpayer must consistently apply the facts and circumstances test set forth in this paragraph (c) (2) in evaluating the economic environment of its QBUs, *e.g.,* its branches, that engage in the same or similar trades or businesses.

(3) *Books and records presumption.*—A QBU shall be presumed to keep books and records in the currency of the economic environment in which a significant part of its activities are conducted. The presumption may be overcome only if the QBU can demonstrate to the satisfaction of the district director that a substantial nontax purpose exists for not keeping any books and records in such currency. A taxpayer may not use this presumption affirmatively in determining a QBU's functional currency.

(4) *Multiple currencies.*—If a QBU has more than one currency that satisfies the requirements of paragraph (c) (1) of this section, the QBU may choose any such currency as its functional currency.

(5) *Relationship of United States accounting principles.*—In making the functional currency determination under this paragraph (c), the currency of the QBU for purposes of United States generally accepted accounting principles (GAAP) will ordinarily be accepted as the functional currency of the QBU for income tax purposes, provided that the GAAP determination is based on facts and circumstances substantially similar to those set forth in paragraph (c) (2) of this section.

(6) *Effect of changed circumstances.*—Regardless of any change in circumstances, a QBU may change its functional currency determined under this paragraph (c) only if the QBU complies with § 1.985-4 or the Commissioner's consent is considered to have been granted under § 1.985-2(d)(4) or § 1.985-3(a)(2)(ii). For special rules relating to the conversion to the euro, see § 1.985-8.

(d) *Single functional currency for a foreign corporation.*—(1) *General rule.*—This paragraph (d) applies to a foreign corporation that has two or more QBUs that do not have the same functional currency. The foreign corporation shall be treated as having a single functional currency for the corporation as a whole that is different from the functional currency of one or more of its QBUs. The determination of a foreign corporation's functional currency shall be made by first applying paragraph (d) (1) (i) and then paragraph (d) (1) (ii) of this section.

(i) *Step 1.*—Each QBU of the foreign corporation determines its functional currency in accordance with the rules set forth in paragraphs (b) and (c) of this section and § 1.985-2.

(ii) *Step 2.*—The foreign corporation determines its functional currency applying the principles of paragraphs (b) and (c) of this section to the corporation's activities as a whole. Thus, if a foreign corporation has two branches, the corporation shall determine its functional currency by applying the principles of paragraphs (b) and (c) of this section to the combined activities of the corporation and the branches.

For purposes of this paragraph (d)(1), if a QBU of a foreign corporation has the dollar as its functional currency under paragraph (b)(2) of this section, the QBU's activities shall be considered dollar activities of the corporation.

(2) *Translation of income or loss of QBUs having different functional currencies than the foreign corporation as a whole.*—Where the functional currency of a foreign corporation as a whole differs from the functional currency of one or more of its QBUs, each such QBU shall determine the amount of its income or loss or earnings and profits (or deficit in earnings and profits) in its functional currency under the principles of section 987 (relating to branch transactions). The amount of income or loss or earnings and profits (or deficit in earnings and profits) of each QBU in its functional currency shall then be translated into the foreign corporation's functional currency using the appropriate exchange rate as defined in section 989 (b) (4) for purposes of determining the corporation's income or loss or earnings and profits (or deficit in earnings and profits).

(e) *Translation of nonfunctional currency transactions.*—Except for a QBU using the dollar approximate separate transactions method described in § 1.985-3, *see* section 988 and the regulations thereunder for the treatment of nonfunctional currency transactions.

(f) *Examples.*—The provisions of this section are illustrated by the following examples:

Example (1). P, a domestic corporation, operates exclusively through foreign branch X in Country A. X is a QBU within the meaning of section 989 (a) and its residence is Country A as determined under section 988 (a) (3) (B). The currency of Country A is the LC. All of X's purchases, sales, and expenses are in the LC. The laws of A require X to keep books and records in the LC. It is determined that the LC is the currency of X under United States generally accepted accounting principles. This determination is based on facts and circumstances substantially similar to those set forth in paragraph (c) (2) of this section. Under these facts, while the functional currency of P is the dollar since its residence is the United States, the functional currency of X is the LC.

Example (2). P, a publicly-held domestic regulated investment company (as defined under section 851), operates exclusively through foreign branch B in Country R. B is a QBU within the meaning of section 989 (a) and its residence is Country R as determined under section 988 (a) (3) (B). The currency of Country R is the LC. B's principal activities consist of purchasing and selling stock and securities of Country R companies and securities issued by Country R. It is determined that the dollar is the currency of B under United States generally accepted accounting principles. This determination is not based on facts and circumstances substantially similar to those set forth in paragraph (c) (2) of this section. Under these facts, while the functional currency of P is the dollar since its residence is the United States, B may choose the LC as its functional currency because it has significant activities in the LC provided it keeps books and records in the LC. The fact that the dollar is the currency of B under generally accepted accounting principles is irrelevant for purposes of determining B's functional currency because the GAAP determination was not based on factors similar to those set forth in paragraph (c) (2) of this section.

Example (3). P, a domestic bank, operates through foreign branch X in Country R. X is a QBU within the meaning of section 989 (a) and its residence is Country R as determined under section 988 (a) (3) (B). The currency of Country R is the LC. The laws of R require X to keep books and records in the LC. The branch customarily loans dollars and LCs. In the case of its LC loans, X ordinarily fixes the terms of the loans by reference to a contemporary London Inter-Bank Offered Rate (LIBOR) on dollar deposits. For instance, the interest on the amount of the outstanding LC loan principal might equal LIBOR plus 2 percent and the amount of the outstanding LC loan principal would be adjusted to reflect changes in the dollar value of the LC. X is primarily funded with dollar-denominated funds borrowed from related and unrelated parties. X's only LC activities are paying local taxes, employee wages, and local expenses such as rent and electricity. Under these facts, X's activities are primarily conducted in dollars. Thus, although X keeps its books and records in LCs, X's functional currency is the dollar.

Example (4). S, a foreign corporation organized in Country U, is wholly-owned by P, a domestic corporation. The currency of Country U is the LC. S's sole function is acting as a financing vehicle for P and domestic corporations that are affiliated with P. All borrowing and lending transactions between S and P and its domestic affiliates are in dollars. Furthermore, primarily all of S's other borrowings are dollar-denominated or based on a dollar index. S's only LC activities are paying local taxes, employee wages, and local expenses such as rent and electricity. S keeps its books and records in the LC. Under these facts, S's activities are primarily conducted in dollars. Thus, although S keeps its books and records in LCs, S's functional currency is the dollar.

Example (5). D is a domestic corporation whose primary activity is the extraction of natural gas and oil through foreign branch X in Country Y. X is a QBU within the meaning of section 989 (a) and its residence is Country Y as determined under section 988 (a) (3) (B). The currency of Country Y is the LC. X bills a significant amount of its natural gas and oil sales in dollars and a significant amount in LCs. X also incurs significant LC and dollar expenses and liabilities. The laws of Country Y require X to keep its books and records in the LC. It is determined that the LC is the currency of X under United States generally accepted accounting principles. This determination is based on facts and circumstances substantially similar to those set forth in paragraph (c) (2) of this section. Absent other factors indicating that K primarily conducts its activities in the dollar, D could choose either the dollar or the LC as X's functional currency because X has significant activities in both the dollar and the LC, provided the books and records requirement is satisfied. If, instead, X's activities were determined to be primarily in the dollar, then X would have to use the dollar as its functional currency.

Example (6). S, a foreign corporation organized in Country U, is wholly-owned by P, a domestic corporation. The currency of U is the LC. S purchases the products it sells from related and unrelated parties, including P. These purchases are made in the LC. In addition, most of S's gross receipts are generated by transactions denominated in the LC. S attempts to determine its LC price for goods sold in such a manner as to obtain an LC equivalent of a certain dollar amount after reduction for all LC costs. However, local market conditions sometimes result in pricing adjustments. Thus, changes in the LC-dollar exchange rate from period to period generally result in corresponding changes in the LC price of S's products. S pays local taxes, employee wages, and other local expenses in the LC. It is determined that the dollar is the currency of S under United States generally accepted accounting principles. This determination is not based on facts and circumstances substantially similar to those set forth in paragraph (c) (2) of this section. Under these facts, S could choose either the dollar or the LC as its functional currency because S has significant activities in both the dollar and the LC, provided that the books and records requirement is satisfied.

Example (7). S, a foreign corporation organized in Country X, is wholly-owned by P, a domestic corporation. S conducts all of its operations through two branches. Branch A is located in Country F and branch B is located in Country G. S, A, and B are QBUs within the meaning of section 989 (a). Branch A's and branch B's residences are Country F and Country G respectively as determined under section 988 (a) (3) (B). The currency of Country F is the FC and the currency of Country G is the LC. The functional currencies of S, A, and B are determined in a two step procedure.

Step 1: The functional currency of branches A and B. Branch A and branch B both conduct all activities in their respective local currencies. The FC is the currency of branch A and the LC is the currency of branch B under United States generally accepted accounting principles. This determination is based on facts and circumstances substantially similar to those set forth in paragraph (c) (2) of this section. Under these facts, the functional currency of branch A is the FC and the functional currency of branch B is the LC.

Step 2: The functional currency of S. S's functional currency is determined by disregarding the fact that A and B are branches. When A's activities and B's activities are viewed as a whole, S determines that it only conducts significant activities in the LC. Therefore, S's functional currency is the LC. See Examples (9), (10), and (11) for how the earnings and profits of a foreign corporation, which has branches with different functional currencies, are determined.

Example (8). Assume the same facts as in Example (7), except that S does not exist and P conducts all of its operations through branch A and branch B. In this instance P's functional currency in Step 2 is the dollar, regardless of the fact that its branches' activities viewed as a whole are in the LC, because P is a taxpayer whose residence is the United States under section 988 (a) (3) (B) (i). Therefore, while the functional currency of branch A is the FC and the functional currency of branch B is the LC, the functional currency of P is the dollar because its residence is the United States.

Example (9). The facts are the same as in Example (7). In addition, assume that in 1987 branch A has earnings of 100 FC and branch B has earnings of 100 LC as determined under section 987. The weighted average exchange rate for the year is 1 FC/2 LC. Branch A's earnings are translated into 200 LC for purposes of computing S's earnings and profits in 1987. Thus, the total earnings and profits of S from branch A and branch B for 1987 is 300 LC.

Example (10). (i) X, a foreign corporation organized in Country W, is wholly-owned by P, a domestic corporation. Both X and P are calendar year taxpayers that began business during 1987. X operates exclusively through two branches, A and B both of which are located outside of Country W. The functional currency of X and A is the LC, while the functional currency of B is the DC as determined under section 985 and § 1.985-1. The earnings of B must be computed under section 987, relating to branch transactions. In 1987, A earns 900 LCs of nonsubpart F income and B earns 200 DCs of nonsubpart F income. Under section 904 (d) (2), A's income is financial service income and B's income is general limitation income. In order to determine X's earnings and profits, B's income must be translated into LCs (the functional currency of X). The weighted average exchange rate for 1987 is 1 LC/2 DC. Thus, in 1987 X's current earnings and profits (and its post-1986 undistributed earnings) are 1000 LCs consisting of 900 LCs of financial services income earned by A and 100 LCs (200 DC/2) of general limitation income earned by B. Neither A nor B makes any remittances during 1987.

(ii) In 1988, neither A nor B earns any income or generates any loss. On December 31, 1988, A remits 50 LCs directly to P. The remittance to P is considered to be remitted by A to X and then immediately distributed by X as a dividend. The 50 LC remittance does not result in an exchange gain or loss under section 987 to X because the functional currency of X and A is the LC. See section 987 (3). Under section 904 (d) (3) (D), the 50 LC dividend is treated as income in a separate category to the extent of the dividend's pro rata share of X's earnings and profits in each separate limitation category. Thus, 90 percent, or 45 LCs, is treated as financial services income, and 10 percent, or 5 LCs, is treated as general limitation income. After the dividend distribution, X has 950 LCs of accumulated earnings and profits (and post-1986 undistributed earnings) consisting of 855 LCs of financial service limitation income and 95 LCs of general limitation income.

Example (11). The facts are the same as in Example (10), except that A makes no remittance during 1988 but B remits 120 DCs to X on December 31, 1988, which X immediately converts into LCs, and X makes no dividend distribution during 1988. Assume that the appropriate exchange rate for the remittance is 1 LC/3 DCs. B's remittance triggers exchange loss to X. See section 987 (3). Under section 987, the exchange loss on the remittance is 20 LCs calculated as follows: 40 LCs, which is the LC value of the 120 DC remittance (120 DCs/3), less 60 LCs, their LC basis (120 DCs/2). This loss is sourced and characterized under section 987 and regulations thereunder.

Example (12). F, a foreign corporation, has gain from the disposition of a United States real property interest (as defined in section 897 (c)). The gain is taken into account as if F were engaged in a trade or business within the United States during the taxable year and as if such gain were effectively connected with such trade or business. F's disposition activity shall be treated as a separate QBU with a dollar functional currency because such activity produced income that is treated as effectively connected with a trade or business within the United States. Therefore, F must compute its gain from the disposition by giving the United States real property interest an historic dollar basis. [Reg. § 1.985-1.]

☐ [*T.D. 8263, 9-19-89. Amended by T.D. 8556, 7-22-94; T.D. 8765, 3-4-98 (corrected 3-31-98); T.D. 8776, 7-28-98 and T.D. 8927, 1-10-2001.*]

§ 1.985-2. Election to use the United States dollar as the functional currency of a QBU.—(a) *Background and scope.*—(1) *In general.*—This section permits an eligible QBU to elect to use the dollar as its functional currency for taxable years beginning on or before August 24, 1994. An election to use a dollar functional currency is not permitted for a QBU other than an eligible QBU. Paragraph (b) of this section defines an eligible QBU. Paragraph (c) of this section describes the time and manner for making the dollar election and paragraph (d) of this section describes the effect of making the election. For the definition of a QBU, see section 989(a). See § 1.985-1(b)(2)(ii) for rules requiring a QBU to use the dollar as its functional currency in taxable years beginning after August 24, 1994.

(2) *Exception.*—Pursuant to § 1.985-1(b)(2)(ii)(B)(2), the rules of paragraph (c)(3) of this section shall apply with respect to the procedure required to be followed by a noncontrolled section 902 corporation as defined in section 904(d)(2)(E) to elect the dollar as its (or its QBU branch's) functional currency and the application of § 1.985-3.

(b) *Eligible QBU.*—(1) *In general.*—The term "eligible QBU" means a QBU that could have used a hyperinflationary currency as its functional currency absent the dollar election. *See* § 1.985-1 for how a QBU determines its functional currency absent the dollar election.

(2) *Hyperinflationary currency.*—See § 1.985-1(b)(2)(ii)(D) for the definition of hyperinflationary currency.

(c) *Time and manner for dollar election.*—(1) *QBUs that are branches of United States persons.*—(i) *Rule.*—If an eligible QBU is a branch of a United States person, the dollar election shall be made by attaching a completed Form 8819 to the United States person's timely filed (taking extensions into account) tax return for the first taxable year for which the election is to be effective.

(ii) *Procedure prior to the issuance of Form 8819.*—In the absence of Form 8819, the election shall be made in accordance with § 1.985-2T(c)(1). Failure to file an amended return within the time period prescribed in § 1.985-2T(c)(1) shall not invalidate the dollar election if it is established to the satisfaction of the district director that reasonable cause existed for such failure. A subsequent election for 1988 will not prejudice the taxpayer with respect to such reasonable cause determination. Nevertheless, each United States person making an election under the § 1.985-2T(c)(1) must file a Form 8819 in the time and manner provided in the Form's instructions.

(2) *Eligible QBUs that are controlled foreign corporations or branches of controlled foreign corporations.*—(i) *Rule.*—If an eligible QBU is a controlled foreign corporation (as described in section 957), or a branch of a controlled foreign corporation, the election may be made either by the foreign corporation or by the controlling United States shareholders on behalf of the foreign corporation by—

(A) Filing a completed Form 8819 in the time and manner provided in the Form's instructions, and

(B) Providing the written notice required by paragraph (c)(2)(ii) of this section at the time and in the manner prescribed therein.

The term "controlling United States shareholders" means those United States shareholders (as defined in section 951(b)) who, in the aggregate, own (within the meaning of section 958(a)) greater than 50 percent of the total combined voting power of all classes of stock of the foreign corporation entitled to vote. If the foreign corporation is a controlled foreign corporation (as described in section 957) but the United States shareholders do not, in the aggregate, own the requisite voting power, the term "controlling United States shareholders" means all the United States shareholders (as defined in section 951(b)) who own (within the meaning of section 958(a)) stock of the controlled foreign corporation.

(ii) *Notice.*—Prior to filing Form 8819, the controlling United States shareholders (or the foreign corporation, if the dollar election is made by the corporation) shall provide written notice that the dollar election will be made to all United States persons known to be shareholders who own (within the meaning of section 958(a)) stock of the foreign corporation. Such notice shall also include all information required in Form 8819.

(iii) *Reasonable cause exception.*—Failure of the controlling United States shareholders (or the foreign corporation, if the dollar election is made by the corporation) to timely file Form 8819 or provide written notice to a United States person required to be notified by paragraph (c)(2)(ii) of this section shall not invalidate the dollar election, if it is established to the satisfaction of the district director that reasonable cause existed for such failure.

(iv) *Procedure prior to the issuance of Form 8819.*—In the absence of Form 8819, an eligible QBU described in paragraph (c)(2)(i) of this section shall make the dollar election in accordance with § 1.985-2T(c)(2). Nevertheless, the person or persons that made such election must file a Form 8819 in the time and manner provided in the Form's instructions.

(3) *Eligible QBUs that are noncontrolled foreign corporations or branches of noncontrolled foreign corporations.*—(i) *Rule.*—If an eligible QBU is a noncontrolled foreign corporation (a foreign corporation not described in section 957), or a branch of a noncontrolled foreign corporation, the dollar election must be made by the corporation or the majority domestic corporate shareholders on behalf of the corporation by applying the rules provided in paragraph (c)(2)(i)(A) and (B), (ii), (iii), and (iv) of this section substituting "majority domestic corporate shareholders" for "controlling United States shareholders" wherever it appears therein. The term "majority domestic corporate shareholders" means those domestic corporate shareholders (as described in section 902(a)) who, in the aggregate, own (within the meaning of section 958(a) greater than 50 percent of the total combined voting stock of all classes of stock of the noncontrolled foreign corporation entitled to vote that is owned (within the meaning of section 958(a)) by all the domestic corporate shareholders.

(ii) Procedure prior to the issuance of Form 8819. In the absence of Form 8819, an eligible QBU described in paragraph (c)(3)(i) of this section shall make the dollar election in accordance with § 1.985-2T(c)(3). Nevertheless, the person or persons that made such election must file a Form 8819 in the time and manner provided in the Form's instructions.

(4) *Others.*—Any other person making a dollar election under this section shall elect by filing Form 8819 and fulfilling any other notice requirements that may be required by the Commissioner.

(d) *Effect of dollar election.*—(1) *General rule.*—If a dollar election is made (or considered made under paragraph (d)(3) of this section) by or on behalf of an eligible QBU, the QBU shall be deemed to have the dollar as its functional currency. Each United States person that owns (within the meaning of section 958(a)) stock of a foreign corporation which has the dollar as its functional currency under § 1.985-2 must make all of its federal income tax calculations with respect to the foreign corporation using the dollar as the corporation's functional currency (regardless of when ownership was acquired or whether the United States person received the written notice required by paragraph (c)(2)(i)(B) of this section).

(2) *Computation.*—(i) *In general.*—Except as provided in paragraph (d)(2)(ii) of this section, any eligible QBU that pursuant to this § 1.985-2 has a dollar functional currency must compute income or loss or earnings and profits (or deficit in earnings and profits) in dollars using the dollar approximate separate transactions method described in § 1.985-3.

(ii) *Alternative method.*—An eligible QBU that has a dollar functional currency pursuant to this § 1.985-2 may use a method other than the dollar approximate separate transactions method described in § 1.985-3 only if the QBU demonstrates to the satisfaction of the Commissioner that it can properly employ such method. Generally, the QBU must show that it could compute foreign currency gain or loss under the principles of section 988 with respect to each of its section 988 transactions. If subsequently the QBU can no longer demonstrate to the satisfaction of the district director that it can properly employ such an alternative method, then the QBU will be deemed to have changed its method of accounting to the dollar approximate separate transactions method described in § 1.985-3. This change in accounting will be treated as having been made with the consent of the Commissioner. No adjustments under either § 1.985-5T (or any succeeding final regulation) or section 481(a) shall be required solely because of the change. Rather the QBU shall begin accounting for its operations under § 1.985-3 based on its books and records as of the time of the change.

(3) *Conformity.*—(i) *General rule.*—If a dollar election is made under this § 1.985-2 for an eligible QBU ("electing QBU"), then the dollar shall be the functional currency of any related person (regardless of when such person became related to the electing QBU) that is an eligible QBU, or any branch of any such related person that is an eligible QBU. For purposes of the preceding sentence, the term "related person" means any person with a relationship defined in section 267(b) to the electing QBU (or to the United States or foreign person of which the electing QBU is a part). In determining whether two or more corporations are members of the same controlled group under section 267(b)(3), a person is considered to own stock owned directly by such person, stock owned with the application of section 1563(e)(1), and stock owned with the application of section 267(c).

(ii) *Branches of United States and foreign persons.*—If a dollar election is made for a QBU branch of any person, each eligible QBU branch of such person shall have the dollar as its functional currency.

(4) *Required adjustments.*—If an eligible QBU's functional currency changes due to a dollar election, or due to the conformity requirements of paragraph (d)(3) of this section, such change shall be deemed for purposes of § 1.985-4 to be consented to by the Commissioner. No adjustments under section 481(a) shall be required solely because of the change. However, the QBU must make those adjustments required by § 1.985-5T (or any succeeding final regulation).

(5) *Taxable year conformity required.*—Generally, the adjustments required by paragraph (d)(4) of this section shall be made for a related person's taxable year—

(i) that includes the date in which the electing QBU made the dollar election if the person was related to such electing QBU at any time during the QBU's taxable year that includes such date, or

(ii) during which the person first becomes related to any electing QBU, in all other cases.

For purposes of this paragraph (d)(5), the date in which the electing QBU makes the dollar election shall be the last day of the electing QBU's taxable year. The district director may permit the related party to make such adjustments beginning one taxable year later if, in the district director's sole judgment, reasonable cause exists for the related party not being able to make the required adjustments for the earlier year.

(6) *Availability of election.*—A dollar election may be made by or on behalf of a QBU, or considered made under the conformity rule of paragraph (d)(3), in any year in which the QBU is an eligible QBU. If a dollar election is not made by or on behalf of a QBU for its first taxable year beginning after December 31, 1986 in which it is an eligible QBU, then any dollar election made by or on behalf of the QBU, or considered made under the conformity rules of paragraph (d)(3) of this section, that results in a change in the QBU's functional currency shall be treated as having been made with the consent of the Commissioner. In such a case, however, the taxpayer must make those adjustments required by § 1.985-5T (or any succeeding final regulation).

(7) *Effect of changed circumstances.*—Regardless of any change in circumstances (e.g., a currency ceases to qualify as hyperinflationary), a QBU whose functional currency is the dollar under this section may change its functional currency only if the QBU complies with § 1.985-4.

(8) *Examples.*—The provisions of this section are illustrated by the following examples.

Example (1). X is a calendar year domestic corporation that in 1987 establishes a branch, A, in Country Z. A's functional currency under section 985(b)(1) and (2) and § 1.985-1 is the "h", the currency of Country Z. The cumulative inflation in Country Z exceeds 100 percent for the thirty-six months prior to January 1987, as measured by the consumer price index of Country Z listed in the monthly issues of the "International Financial Statistics". Accordingly, A is an eligible QBU in 1987 because the h is a hyperinflationary currency. Thus, X may elect the dollar as the functional currency of A for 1987.

Example (2). The facts are the same as in Example (1). X does not elect the dollar as the functional currency of A for 1987. Rather, X elects the dollar as the functional currency of A for 1991, a year A is an eligible QBU. The election constitutes a change in A's functional currency that is made with the consent of the Commissioner. However, A must make the adjustments required under § 1.985-5T (or any succeeding final regulation).

Example (3). X is a domestic corporation that establishes A, an eligible QBU branch. X is wholly owned by domestic corporation Y. Y has an eligible QBU branch, B. Both X and Y are calendar year taxpayers. X makes a dollar election for A in 1987. Thus, A is an electing QBU. X and Y are related persons as defined in section 267(b) (*i.e.,* Y has a relationship under section 267(b)(3) to X, the corporation of which A is a part). Therefore, the dollar election by X for A in 1987 results in B, the eligible QBU branch of Y, also having the dollar as its functional currency for 1987.

Example (4). The facts are the same as in Example (3), except that Y does not have an eligible QBU branch but owns all the stock of C, a calendar year controlled foreign corporation, which is not itself an eligible QBU but which has an eligible QBU branch, D. X and C are related persons as defined in section 267(b) (*i.e.,* C has a relationship under section 267(b)(3) to X, the corporation of which A is a part). Therefore, the dollar election by X for A in 1987 results in D, the eligible QBU branch of C, also having the dollar as its functional currency for 1987.

Example (5). X, whose taxable year ends September 30, is an eligible QBU that does not use the dollar as its functional currency. X is wholly-owned by domestic corporation W. On January 1, 1989, X acquires all the stock of Y, an unrelated eligible QBU that made the dollar election under § 1.985-2. Y is a calendar year taxpayer. After the stock purchase, X and Y are related persons as defined in section 267(b). Under § 1.985-2(d)(3) and (5), the dollar shall be the functional currency of X, any person related to X, and any branch of such related person that is an eligible QBU beginning with the taxable year that includes December 31, 1989. Thus, X must change to the dollar for its taxable year beginning October 1, 1988. However, the district director may allow X to change to the dollar for its taxable year beginning October 1, 1989, provided reasonable cause exists. Those QBUs changing to the dollar as their functional currency as the result of the conformity requirements must make the adjustments required under § 1.985-5T (or any succeeding final regulation).

Example (6). The facts are the same as in Example (5), except that before X purchased the Y stock, X made the dollar election under § 1.985-2 but Y did not use the dollar as its functional currency. Under § 1.985-2(d)(3) and (5) the dollar shall be the functional currency of Y, any person related to Y, and any branch of such related person that is an eligible QBU beginning with the taxable year that includes September 30, 1989. Thus, Y must change to the dollar for its taxable year beginning January 1, 1989. However the district director may allow Y to change to the dollar for its taxable year beginning January 1, 1990, provided reasonable cause exists. Those QBUs changing to the dollar as their functional currency as the result of the conformity requirements must make the adjustments required under § 1.985-5T (or any succeeding final regulation). [Reg. § 1.985-2.]

☐ [*T.D. 8263, 9-19-89. Amended by T.D.* 8556, 7-22-94.]

§ 1.985-3. United States dollar approximate separate transactions method.—(a) *Scope and effective date.*—(1) *Scope.*—This section describes the United States dollar (dollar) approximate separate transactions method of accounting (DASTM). For all purposes of subtitle A, this method of accounting must be used to compute the gross income, taxable income or loss, or earnings and profits (or deficit in earnings and profits) of a QBU (as defined in section 989(a)) that has the dollar as its functional currency pursuant to § 1.985-1(b)(2).

(2) *Effective date.*—(i) *In general.*—This section is effective for taxable years beginning after August 24, 1994.

(ii) *DASTM prior-year election.*—A taxpayer may elect to apply this section to any open taxable year beginning after December 31,

1986 (whether or not DASTM has been previously elected for some or all of those years). In order to make this election, the taxpayer must apply § 1.985-3 to that year and all subsequent years. In addition, each person that is related (within the meaning of § 1.985-3(e)(2)(vi)) to the taxpayer on the last day of any taxable year for which the election is effective and that would have been eligible to elect DASTM must also apply these rules to that year and all subsequent years. A taxpayer that has not previously elected to apply DASTM to its prior taxable years may make the DASTM election for the pertinent years by filing amended returns and complying with the applicable election procedures of § 1.985-2. Form 8819 shall be attached to the return for the first year for which the election is to be effective. A taxpayer that has elected DASTM for prior taxable years and applied the rules under § 1.985-3 (as contained in the April 1, 1994 edition of 26 CFR part 1 (1.908 to 1.1000)) may amend its returns to apply the rules of this § 1.985-3. In either case, the DASTM election for prior taxable years shall be deemed to be made with the consent of the Commissioner.

(b) *Statement of method.*—Under DASTM, income or loss or earnings and profits (or a deficit in earnings and profits) of a QBU for its taxable year shall be determined in dollars by—

(1) Preparing an income or loss statement from the QBU's books and records (within the meaning of § 1.989(a)-1(d)) as recorded in the QBU's hyperinflationary currency (as defined in § 1.985-1(b)(2)(ii)(D));

(2) Making the adjustments necessary to conform such statement to United States generally accepted accounting principles and tax accounting principles (including reversing monetary correction adjustments required by local accounting principles);

(3) Translating the amounts of hyperinflationary currency as shown on such adjusted statement into dollars in accordance with paragraph (c) of this section; and

(4) Adjusting the resulting dollar income or loss or earnings and profits (or deficit in earnings and profits) and, where necessary, particular items of gross income, deductible expense or other amounts, in accordance with paragraph (e) of this section to reflect the amount of DASTM gain or loss as determined under paragraph (d) of this section.

(c) *Translation into United States dollars.*—(1) *In general.*—Except as otherwise provided in this paragraph (c), the amounts shown on the income or loss statement, as adjusted under paragraph (b)(2) of this section, shall be translated into dollars at the exchange rate (as defined in paragraph (c)(6) of this section) for the translation period (as defined in paragraph (c)(7) of this section) to which they relate. However, if the QBU previously changed its functional currency to the dollar, and the rules of § 1.985-5 (or, if applicable, § 1.985-5T, as contained in the April 1, 1993 edition of 26 CFR part 1 (1.908 to 1.1000)) applied in translating its balance sheet amounts into dollars, then the spot exchange rate applied under those rules shall be used to translate any amount that would otherwise be translated at a rate determined by reference to a translation period prior to the change in functional currency. For example, depreciation with respect to an asset acquired while the QBU had a nondollar functional currency shall be translated into dollars at the spot rate on the last day of the taxable year before the year of change to a dollar functional currency, rather than at the rate for the period in which the asset was acquired.

(2) *Cost of goods sold.*—The dollar value of cost of goods sold shall equal the sum of the dollar values of beginning inventory and purchases less the dollar value of closing inventory as these amounts are determined under paragraph (c)(3) of this section.

(3) *Beginning inventory, purchases, and closing inventory.*—(i) *Beginning inventory.*—Amounts representing beginning inventory shall be translated so as to obtain the same amount of dollars which represented such items in the closing inventory balance for the preceding taxable year.

(ii) *Purchases.*—Amounts representing items purchased or otherwise first included in inventory during the taxable year shall be translated at the exchange rate for the translation period in which the cost of such items was incurred.

(iii) *Closing inventory.*—(A) *In general.*—Amounts representing items included in the closing inventory balance shall be translated at the exchange rate for the translation period in which the cost of such items was incurred. However, if amounts representing items included in the closing inventory balance are either valued at market or written down to market value, they shall be translated at the exchange rate existing on the last day of the taxable year. For purposes of determining lower of cost or market, items of inventory included in the closing inventory balance shall be translated into dollars at the exchange rate for the translation period in which the cost of such items was incurred and compared with market as determined in the QBU's hyperinflationary currency translated into dollars at the exchange rate existing on the last day of the taxable year.

(B) *Determination of translation period.*—The method used to determine the translation period of amounts representing items of closing inventory for purposes of paragraph (c)(3)(iii)(A) of this section may be based upon reasonable approximations and averages, including rates of turnover, provided that the method is used consistently from year to year.

(4) *Depreciation, depletion, and amortization.*—Amounts representing allowances for depreciation, depletion, or amortization shall be translated at the exchange rate for the translation period in which the cost of the underlying asset was incurred, except as provided in paragraph (c)(1) of this section.

(5) *Prepaid expenses or income.*—Amounts representing expense or income paid or received in a prior taxable year shall be translated at the exchange rate for the translation period during which they were paid or received.

(6) *Exchange rate.*—The exchange rate for a translation period may be determined under any reasonable method, provided that the method is consistently applied to all translation periods and conforms to the taxpayer's method of financial accounting. Reasonable methods include the average of beginning and ending exchange rates for the translation period and the spot rate on the last day of the translation period. Once chosen, a method for determining an exchange rate can be changed only with the consent of the district director.

(7) *Translation period.*—(i) *In general.*—Except as provided in paragraphs (c)(3)(iii)(B) and (c)(7)(ii) of this section, a translation period shall be each month within a QBU's taxable year.

(ii) *Exception.*—A taxpayer may divide its taxable year into translation periods of equal length (with not more than one short period annually) that are less than one month. Once such a translation period is established, it may not be changed without the consent of the district director.

(8) *Dollar transactions.*—(i) *In general.*—Except as provided in paragraph (c)(8)(ii) of this section, no DASTM gain or loss is realized with respect to dollar transactions since the dollar is the functional currency of the QBU. Thus, the amount of any payment or receipt of dollars shall be reflected in the income or loss statement by the amount of such dollars. Also, the income or loss attributable to any transaction in which the amount that a QBU is entitled to receive (or is required to pay) by reason of such transaction is denominated in terms of the dollar, or is determined by reference to the value of the dollar, must be computed transaction by transaction. For example, if a foreign corporation lends 20 LC when 20 LC = $20 and is entitled to receive the LC equivalent of $20 at maturity plus a market rate of interest in dollars (or its LC equivalent), the loan is a dollar transaction. Similarly, this paragraph applies to any transaction that is determined to be a dollar transaction under section 988.

(ii) *Non-dollar functional currency.*—If pursuant to § 1.985-1(b)(2)(ii)(B)(*1*), a QBU is required to use a functional currency other than the dollar, then that currency shall be substituted for the dollar in applying paragraph (c)(8)(i) of this section.

(9) *Third currency transactions.*—A taxpayer may use any reasonable method of accounting for transactions described in section 988(c)(1)(B) and (C) that are denominated in, or determined by reference to, a currency other than the QBU's hyperinflationary currency or the dollar (third currency transactions) so long as such method is consistent with its method of financial accounting.

(10) *Examples.*—The provisions of this paragraph (c) are illustrated by the following examples:

Example 1. S is an accrual basis QBU that is required to use the dollar as its functional currency for its first taxable year beginning in 1994. S's hyperinflationary currency is the "h." During 1994, S accrues 100 dollars attributable to dollar-denominated sales. Because this is a dollar transaction under paragraph (c)(8) of this section, S's income or loss for 1994 shall reflect the 100 dollars (not the hyperinflationary value of such dollars when accrued).

Example 2. (i) S is an accrual basis QBU that is required to use the dollar as its functional currency for its first taxable year beginning in 1994. S's hyperinflationary currency is the "h." During 1994, S's sales amounted to 240,000,000h, its currently deductible expenses were 26,000,000h, and its total inventory purchases amounted to 100,000,000h. During January and February of 1994, S purchased depreciable assets for 80,000,000h and was allowed depreciation of 4,000,000h. At the end of 1994, S's closing inventory was 23,000,000h. No election to use a translation period other than the month is made, S had no transactions described in paragraph (c)(8) or (c)(9) of this section, and S's closing inventory was computed on the first-in, first-out inventory method. S's adjusted income or loss statement for 1994 is translated into dollars as follows:

	Hyperinflationary Currency	*Exchange Rate*	*United States Dollars*
Sales			
(Jan-Feb)	10,000,000 h	20:1 [1]	$ 500,000
(Mar-Apr)	20,000,000	21:1	952,381
(May-June)	50,000,000	22:1	2,272,727
(July)	50,000,000	23:1	2,173,913
(August)	20,000,000	26:1	769,231
(Sept.)	20,000,000	28:1	714,286
(Oct.)	20,000,000	29:1	689,655
(Nov.)	20,000,000	30:1	666,667
(Dec.)	30,000,000	31:1	967,742
Total	240,000,000 h		$9,706,602
Cost of Goods Sold:			
Opening Inventory	-0-		-0-
Purchases:			
(Jan-Feb)	15,000,000h	20:1	$ 750,000
(Mar-Apr)	10,000,000	21:1	476,190
(May-June)	30,000,000	22:1	1,363,636
(July)	20,000,000	23:1	869,565
(August)	10,000,000	26:1	384,615
(Sept.)	5,000,000	28:1	178,571
(Oct.)	5,000,000	29:1	172,414
(Nov.)	2,500,000	30:1	83,333
(Dec.)	2,500,000	31:1	80,645
Less Closing Inventory	(23,000,000)	[2]	(822,655)
	77,000,000 h		$3,536,314

[1] Where multiple months are indicated, the exchange rate applies for all months.
[2] See paragraph (ii) for this *Example.*

(ii) Since S uses the first-in, first-out inventory method, the closing inventory is assumed to consist of purchases made during the most recent translation period as follows:

	Hyperinflationary Currency	*Exchange Rate*	*United States Dollars*
December	2,500,000 h	31:1	$80,645
November	2,500,000	30:1	83,333
October	5,000,000	29:1	172,414
September	5,000,000	28:1	178,571
August	8,000,000	26:1	307,692
Total	23,000,000 h		$822,655
Non-Capitalized Expenses:			
(Jan-Feb)	4,000,000 h	20:1	$200,000
(Mar-Apr)	2,500,000	21:1	119,048
(May-June)	2,500,000	22:1	113,636
(July)	2,000,000	23:1	86,957
(August)	3,000,000	26:1	115,385
(Sept.)	3,000,000	28:1	107,143
(Oct.)	2,000,000	29:1	68,966
(Nov.)	3,000,000	30:1	100,000
(Dec.)	4,000,000	31:1	129,032
Total	26,000,000 h		$1,040,167
Depreciation	4,000,000 h	20:1	$200,000
Total Cost & Expenses	107,000,000 h		$4,776,481
Operating Profit	133,000,000 h		$4,930,121

(d) *Computation of DASTM gain or loss.*—(1) *Rule.*—DASTM gain or loss of a QBU equals—

(i) The net worth of the QBU (as determined under paragraph (d)(2) of this section) at the end of the taxable year minus the net worth of the QBU at the end of the preceding taxable year; plus

(ii) The dollar amount of the items described in paragraph (d)(3) of this section and minus the dollar amount of the items described in paragraph (d)(4) of this section; minus

(iii) The amount of dollar income or earnings and profits (or plus the amount of any dollar loss or deficit in earnings and profits) as determined for the taxable year pursuant to paragraphs (b)(1) through (b)(3) of this section.

(2) *Net worth.*—Net worth of a QBU at the end of any taxable year equals the aggregate dollar amount representing assets on the QBU's balance sheet at the end of the taxable year less the aggregate dollar amount representing liabilities on the balance sheet. Notwithstanding any other provision in this paragraph (d)(2), the district director may adjust the amount of any asset or liability if a purpose for acquiring (or disposing of) the asset or incurring (or discharging) the liability is to manipulate the composition of the balance sheet for any period during the taxable year in order to avoid tax. The taxpayer shall determine net worth by—

(i) Preparing a balance sheet as of the end of the taxable year from the QBU's books and records (within the meaning of § 1.989(a)-1(d)) as recorded in the QBU's hyperinflationary currency;

(ii) Making adjustments necessary to conform such balance sheet to United States generally accepted accounting principles and tax accounting principles (including reversing monetary correction adjustments required by local accounting principles); and

(iii) Translating the asset and liability amounts shown on the balance sheet into United States dollars in accordance with paragraph (d)(5) of this section.

(3) *Positive adjustments*.—(i) *In general*.—The items described in this paragraph (d)(3) are dividend distributions for the taxable year and any items that decrease net worth for the taxable year but that generally do not affect income or earnings and profits (or a deficit in earnings and profits). Such items include a transfer to the home office of a QBU branch and a return of capital.

(ii) *Translation*.—Except as provided by ruling or administrative pronouncement, items described in paragraph (d)(3)(i) of this section shall be translated into dollars as follows:

(A) If the item giving rise to the adjustment would be translated under paragraph (d)(5) of this section at the exchange rate for the last translation period of the taxable year if it were shown on the QBU's year-end balance sheet, such item shall be translated at the exchange rate on the date the item is transferred.

(B) If the item giving rise to the adjustment would be translated under paragraph (d)(5) of this section at the exchange rate for the translation period in which the cost of the item was incurred if it were shown on the QBU's year-end balance sheet, such item shall be translated at the same historical rate.

(iii) *Effective date*.—Paragraph (d)(3)(ii) of this section is applicable for any transfer, dividend, or distribution that is a return of capital that is made after March 8, 2005, and that gives rise to an adjustment under this paragraph (d)(3).

(4) *Negative adjustments*.—The items described in this paragraph (d)(4) are items that increase net worth for the taxable year but that generally do not affect income or loss or earnings and profits (or a deficit in earnings and profits). Such items include a capital contribution or a transfer from a home office to a QBU branch. Except as otherwise provided by ruling or administrative pronouncement, if the contribution or transfer is not in dollars, the amount of a capital contribution or transfer shall be translated into dollars at the exchange rate on the date made.

(5) *Translation of balance sheet*.—Asset and liability amounts shown on the balance sheet in hyperinflationary currency (adjusted pursuant to paragraph (d)(2)(ii) of this section) shall be translated into dollars as provided in this paragraph (d)(5). However, if the QBU previously changed its functional currency to the dollar and the rules of § 1.985-5 (or, if applicable, § 1.985-5T, as contained in the April 1, 1993 edition of 26 CFR part 1 (1.908 to 1.1000)) applied in translating its balance sheet amounts into dollars, then the spot exchange rate applied under those rules shall be used to translate any amount that would otherwise be translated at a rate determined by reference to a translation period prior to the change in functional currency. For example, the basis of real property acquired while the QBU had a nondollar functional currency shall be translated into dollars at the spot rate on the last day of the taxable year before the year of change to a dollar functional currency, rather than at the rate for the period in which the cost was incurred.

(i) *Closing inventory*.—Amounts representing items of inventory included in the closing inventory balance shall be translated in accordance with paragraph (c)(3)(iii) of this section.

(ii) *Bad debt reserves*.—Amounts representing bad debt reserves shall be translated at the exchange rate for the last translation period for the taxable year.

(iii) *Prepaid income or expense*.—Amounts representing expenses or income paid or received in a prior taxable year shall be translated in accordance with paragraph (c)(5) of this section.

(iv) *Hyperinflationary currency*.—Amounts of the hyperinflationary currency and hyperinflationary demand deposit balances shall be translated at the exchange rate for the last translation period of the taxable year.

(v) *Certain assets*.—(A) *In general*.—Amounts representing plant, real property, equipment, goodwill, and patents and other intangibles shall be translated at the exchange rate for the translation period in which the cost of the asset was incurred.

(B) *Adjustment to certain assets*.—Amounts representing depreciation, depletion, and amortization reserves shall be translated in accordance with paragraph (c)(4) of this section.

(vi) *Hyperinflationary debt obligations*.—Except as provided in paragraph (d)(5)(vii) of this section, amounts representing a hyperinflationary debt obligation (including accounts receivable and payable) shall be translated at the exchange rate for the last translation period for the taxable year.

(vii) *Accrued foreign income taxes*.—Amounts representing an accrued but unpaid foreign income tax shall be translated at the exchange rate on the last day of the last translation period of the taxable year of accrual.

(viii) *Certain hyperinflationary financial instruments*.—Amounts representing any item described in section 988(c)(1)(B)(iii) (relating to forward contracts, futures contracts, options, or similar financial instruments) denominated in or determined by reference to the hyperinflationary currency shall be translated at the exchange rate for the last translation period for the taxable year.

(ix) *Other assets and liabilities*.—Amounts representing assets and liabilities, other than those described in paragraphs (d)(5)(i) through (viii) of this section, shall be translated at the exchange rate for the translation period in which the cost of the asset or the amount of the liability was incurred.

(6) *Dollar transactions*.—Notwithstanding any other provisions of this paragraph (d), where the amount representing an item shown on the balance sheet reflects a dollar transaction (described in paragraph (c)(8) of this section), the transaction shall be taken into account in accordance with that paragraph.

(7) *Third currency transactions*.—A taxpayer may use any reasonable method of accounting for transactions described in section 988(c)(1)(B) and (C) that are denominated in, or determined by reference to, a currency other than the QBU's hyperinflationary currency or the dollar (third currency transactions), so long as such method is consistent with its method of financial accounting.

(8) *Character*.—The amount of DASTM gain or loss determined under paragraph (d)(1) of this section shall be ordinary income or loss.

(9) *Example*.—The provisions of this paragraph (d) are illustrated by the following example:

Example. (i) S, an accrual method calendar year foreign corporation, uses DASTM. S's hyperinflationary currency is the "h." S's net worth at December 31, 1993 was $3,246,495. For 1994, S's operating profit is 81,340,000h, or $2,038,200. S made a 5,000,000h distribution in April and again in December of 1994. S's translation period is the month. None of S's assets or liabilities reflect a dollar or third currency transaction described in paragraph (c)(8) or (c)(9) of this section, respectively. The exchange rate for each month in 1994 is as follows:

January	32h:$1
Feb.-Mar.	33:1
April-May	34:1
June	35:1
July	36:1
Aug.-Sept.	37:1
Oct.	38:1
Nov.	39:1
Dec.	40:1

interest expense generated by such liabilities (*e.g.*, prior to the application of § 1.861-9T or its successor regulation). To the extent DASTM gain on such liabilities exceeds interest expense, it shall be sourced or otherwise classified in the same manner that interest expense is allocated and apportioned under § 1.861-9T or its successor regulation. The amount of DASTM loss on interest-bearing liabilities computed under paragraph (e)(3)(vi) of this section (Step 6) shall be allocated and apportioned in the same manner that interest expense is allocated and apportioned under § 1.861-9T or its successor regulation (without regard to the exceptions to fungibility in § 1.861-10T or its successor regulation). For purposes of this section, an interest-bearing liability is a liability that requires payment of periodic interest (whether fixed or variable), has original issue discount, or would have interest imputed under subtitle A.

(B) *Allocation of DASTM gain or loss from interest-bearing liabilities that generate related person interest expense.*—DASTM gain or loss from interest-bearing liabilities that generate related person interest expense (as provided in section 954(b)(5)) shall be allocated for purposes of subtitle A (including sections 904 and 952) in the same manner that the related person interest expense of that debt is required to be allocated under the rules of section 954(b)(5) and § 1.904-5(c)(2).

(C) *Modified gross income method.*—In applying the modified gross income method described in § 1.861-9T(j) or its successor regulation, gross income shall be adjusted for any DASTM gain or loss from assets as provided in paragraph (e)(3)(v) of this section (Step 5) and any DASTM gain or loss with respect to short-term, non-interest-bearing trade payables as provided in paragraph (e)(3)(viii)(A) of this section.

(viii) *Step 8—adjust dollar income and expense by DASTM gain or loss from non-interest bearing liabilities.*—(A) *Short-term, non-interest-bearing trade payables.*—The taxpayer shall allocate DASTM gain or loss on short-term non-interest-bearing trade payables for purposes of subtitle A (including sections 904 and 952) to the same category or type of gross income as the cost or expense to which the trade payable relates. For this purpose, a short-term, non-interest-bearing trade payable is a non-interest-bearing liability with a term of 183 days or less that is incurred to purchase property or services to be used by the obligor in an active trade or business.

(B) *Excise tax payables.*—The taxpayer shall allocate DASTM gain or loss on excise tax payables for purposes of subtitle A (including sections 904 and 952) to the same category or type of gross income as would be derived from the activity to which the excise tax relates.

(C) *Other non-interest-bearing liabilities.*—*(1) In general.*—Except as provided in paragraphs (e)(3)(viii)(A), (e)(3)(viii)(B), and (e)(3)(viii)(C)*(2)* of this section, DASTM gain or loss on non-interest-bearing liabilities shall be allocated under paragraph (e)(3)(ix) of this section (Step 9).

(2) Tracing if substantial distortion of income.—DASTM gains and losses on liabilities described in paragraph (e)(3)(viii)(C)*(1)* of this section may be attributed to the same section 904(d) separate category or subpart F category as the transaction to which the liability relates if the taxpayer demonstrates to the satisfaction of the district director, or it is determined by the district director, that application of paragraph (e)(3)(viii)(C)*(1)* of this section results in a substantial distortion of income.

(ix) *Step 9—allocate residual DASTM gain or loss.*—If there is a difference between the net DASTM gain or loss determined under paragraphs (e)(3)(i) through (viii) of this section (Steps 1 through 8) and the DASTM gain or loss determined under paragraph (d) of this section, the amount of the difference must be allocated for purposes of subtitle A (including sections 904 and 952) to the QBU's gross income (computed under paragraphs (b)(1) through (3) of this section, as adjusted under paragraphs (e)(3)(i) through (viii) of this section (Steps 1 through 8)) on the basis of the relative amounts of each category or type of gross income. [Reg. § 1.985-3.]

☐ [T.D. 8263, 9-19-89. *Amended by T.D.* 8556, 7-22-94, *T.D.* 9320, 3-29-2007 *and T.D.* 9882, 12-16-2019.]

§ 1.985-4. Method of accounting.—(a) *Adoption or election.*—The adoption of, or the election to use, a functional currency shall be treated as a method of accounting. The functional currency shall be used for the year of adoption (or election) and for all subsequent taxable years unless permission to change is granted, or considered to be granted under § 1.985-2 or 1.985-8, by the Commissioner.

(b) *Condition for changing functional currencies.*—Generally, permission to change functional currencies shall not be granted unless significant changes in the facts and circumstances of the QBU's economic environment occur. If the determination of the functional currency of the QBU for purposes of United States generally accepted accounting principles (GAAP) is based on facts and circumstances substantially similar to those set forth in § 1.985-1(c)(2), then ordinarily the Commissioner will grant a taxpayer's request to change its functional currency (or the functional currency of its branch that is a QBU) to a new functional currency only if the taxpayer (or its QBU) also changes to the new functional currency for purposes of GAAP. However, permission to change will not necessarily be granted merely because the new functional currency will conform to the taxpayer's GAAP functional currency.

(c) *Relationship to certain other sections of the Code.*—Nothing in this section shall be construed to override the provisions of any other sections of the Code or regulations that require the use of consistent accounting methods. Such provisions must be independently satisfied separate and apart from the identification of a functional currency. For instance, while separate geographical divisions of a taxpayer's trade or business may have different functional currencies, such geographical divisions may nevertheless be required to consistently use other methods of accounting. [Reg. § 1.985-4.]

☐ [*T.D.* 8263, 9-19-89. *Amended by T.D.* 8776, 7-28-98 *and T.D.* 8927, 1-10-2001.]

Caution: The Treasury Department has identified Reg. §1.985-5, as amended by T.D. 9794, as a significant tax regulation that imposes an undue financial burden on U.S. taxpayers and/or adds undue complexity to the federal tax laws, pursuant to Executive Order 13789 (issued April 21, 2017) (Notice 2017-38, I.R.B. 2017-30, 147). In a subsequent report, published October 16, 2017, Treasury recommended planned actions that would reduce the burden of these regulations, including an extension of the application date of T.D. 9794 (see Notice 2022-34, I.R.B. 2022-34, 150).

§ 1.985-5. Adjustments required upon change in functional currency.—(a) *In general.*—This section applies in the case of a taxpayer or qualified business unit (QBU) (including a section 987 QBU (as defined in § 1.987-1(b)(2)) changing from one functional currency (old functional currency) to another functional currency (new functional currency). A taxpayer or QBU subject to the rules of this section shall make the adjustments set forth in the 3-step procedure described in paragraphs (b) through (e) of this section. Except as otherwise provided in this section, the adjustments shall be made on the last day of the last taxable year ending before the year of change (as defined in § 1.481-1(a)(1)). Gain or loss required to be recognized under paragraphs (b), (d)(2), (e)(2), and (e)(4)(iii) of this section is not subject to section 481 and, therefore, the full amount of the gain or loss must be included in income on the last day of the last taxable year ending before the year of change.

(b) *Step 1—Taking into account exchange gain or loss on certain section 988 transactions.*—The taxpayer or QBU shall recognize or otherwise take into account for all purposes of the Internal Revenue Code the amount of any unrealized exchange gain or loss attributable to a section 988 transaction (as defined in section 988(c)(1)(A) through (C)) that, after applying section 988(d), is denominated in terms of or determined by reference to the new functional currency. The amount of such gain or loss shall be determined without regard to the limitations of section 988(b) (that is, whether any gain or loss would be realized on the transaction as a whole). The character and source of such gain or loss shall be determined under section 988.

(c) *Step 2—Determining the new functional currency basis of property and the new functional currency amount of liabilities and any other relevant items.*—Except as otherwise provided in this section, the new functional currency adjusted basis of property and the new functional currency amount of liabilities and any other relevant items (for example, items described in section 988(c)(1)(B)(iii)) shall equal the product of the old functional currency adjusted basis or liability and the new functional currency/old functional currency spot rate on the last day of the last taxable year ending before the year of change.

(d) *Step 3A—Additional adjustments that are necessary when a QBU changes functional currency.*—(1) *QBU changing to a functional currency other than the owner's functional currency.*—(i) *Rule.*—If a QBU changes its functional currency, and after the change the QBU is a section 987

QBU that is subject to §§1.987-1 through 1.987-11 pursuant to §1.987-1(b)(1), then the adjustments described in either paragraph (d)(1)(ii) or (d)(1)(iii) of this section shall be taken into account for purposes of section 987.

(ii) *QBU and the owner had different functional currencies prior to the change.*—If the QBU and the owner of the QBU had different functional currencies prior to the change and as a result the QBU was a section 987 QBU prior to the change, then the adjustments described in paragraphs (d)(1)(ii)(A) and (d)(1)(ii)(B) of this section shall be taken into account.

(A) *Determining new historic rates.*—The historic rate (as defined in §1.987-1(c)(3)) for the year of change and subsequent taxable years with respect to a historic item (as defined in §1.987-1(e)) reflected on the balance sheet of the section 987 QBU immediately prior to the year of change shall be equal to the historic rate prior to the year of change (that is, a rate that translates the section 987 QBU's old functional currency into the owner's functional currency) divided by the spot rate (as defined in §1.987-1(c)(1)) for translating an amount denominated in the section 987 QBU's old functional currency into the section 987 QBU's new functional currency on the last day of the last taxable year ending before the year of change. For example, if a taxpayer with a U.S. dollar (USD) functional currency owns a section 987 QBU that changes from a British pound (GBP) functional currency to a euro (EUR) functional currency, the historic rate for translating a specific historic item of this section 987 QBU from GBP to USD is 1.50, and the spot rate for translating GBP to EUR on the last day of the last taxable year before the change is 1.30, then the new historic rate for translating this historic item from EUR to USD is 1.15 (1.50/1.30).

(B) *Determining the owner functional currency net value of the QBU on the last day of the last taxable year ending before the year of change under §1.987-4(d)(1)(i)(B).*—For purposes of determining the owner functional currency net value of the section 987 QBU on the last day of the last taxable year ending before the year of change under §1.987-4(d)(1)(i)(B) and §1.987-4(e), the section 987 QBU's marked items (as defined in §1.987-1(d)) shall be translated from the section 987 QBU's old functional currency into the owner's functional currency using the spot rate on the last day of the last taxable year ending before the year of change.

(iii) *QBU and the taxpayer had the same functional currency prior to the change.*—If a QBU that has the same functional currency as a taxpayer changes its functional currency to a new functional currency that is different than the functional currency of the taxpayer, and as a result the taxpayer becomes an owner of a section 987 QBU (see §1.987-1), the taxpayer and section 987 QBU will become subject to section 987 for the year of change and subsequent years.

(2) *QBU changing to the owner's functional currency.*—If a section 987 QBU changes its functional currency to the functional currency of its owner, the section 987 QBU shall be treated as if it terminated on the last day of the last taxable year ending before the year of change. See §§1.987-5 and 1.987-8 for the effect of a termination of a section 987 QBU that is subject to §§1.987-1 through 1.987-11.

(e) *Step 3B—Additional adjustments that are necessary when a taxpayer/owner changes functional currency.*—(1) *Corporations.*—The amount of a corporation's new functional currency earnings and profits and the amount of its new functional currency paid-in capital shall equal the old functional currency amounts of such items multiplied by the spot rate for translating an amount denominated in the corporation's old functional currency into the corporation's new functional currency on the last day of the last taxable year ending before the year of change. The foreign income taxes and accumulated profits or deficits in accumulated profits of a foreign corporation that were maintained in foreign currency for purposes of section 902 and that are attributable to taxable years of the foreign corporation beginning before January 1, 1987, also shall be translated into the new functional currency at the spot rate.

(2) *Collateral consequences to a United States shareholder of a corporation changing to the United States dollar as its functional currency.*—A United States shareholder (within the meaning of section 951(b) or section 953(c)(1)(A)) of a controlled foreign corporation (within the meaning of section 957 or section 953(c)(1)(B)) changing its functional currency to the dollar shall recognize foreign currency gain or loss computed under section 986(c) as if all previously taxed earnings and profits, if any, (including amounts attributable to pre-1987 taxable years that were translated from dollars into functional currency in the foreign corporation's first post-1986 taxable year) were distributed immediately prior to the change.

(3) *Taxpayers that are not corporations.*—[Reserved].

(4) *Adjustments to a section 987 QBU's balance sheet and net accumulated unrecognized section 987 gain or loss when an owner changes functional currency.*—(i) *Owner changing to a functional currency other than the section 987 QBU's functional currency.*—If an owner of a section 987 QBU, subject to §§1.987-1 through 1.987-11 pursuant to §1.987-1(b)(1), changes to a functional currency other than the functional currency of the section 987 QBU, the adjustments described in paragraphs (e)(4)(i)(A) through (C) of this section shall be taken into account for purposes of section 987.

(A) *Determining new historic rates.*—The historic rate (as defined in §1.987-1(c)(3)) for the year of change and subsequent taxable years with respect to a historic item (as defined in §1.987-1(e)) reflected on the balance sheet of the section 987 QBU immediately prior to the year of change shall be equal to the historic rate prior to the year of change (that is, a rate that translates the section 987 QBU's functional currency into the owner's old functional currency) divided by the spot rate for translating an amount denominated in the owner's new functional currency into the owner's old functional currency on the last day of the last taxable year ending before the year of change. For example, if a taxpayer that owns a section 987 QBU with a British pound functional currency changes from a U.S. dollar functional currency to a euro functional currency, and the historic rate for translating a specific item of the section 987 QBU from GBP to USD is 1.50 and the spot rate for translating EUR to USD on the last day of the last taxable year before the change is 1.10, then the new historic rate for translating this historic item from GBP to EUR is 1.36 (1.50/1.10).

(B) *Determining the owner functional currency net value of the section 987 QBU on the last day of the last taxable year ending before the year of change under §1.987-4(d)(1)(i)(B).*—For purposes of determining the change in the owner functional currency net value of the section 987 QBU on the last day of the last taxable year preceding the year of change under §§1.987-4(d)(1)(i)(B) and 1.987-4(e), the section 987 QBU's marked items shall be translated into the owner's new functional currency at the spot rate on the last day of the last taxable year ending before the year of change.

(C) *Translation of net accumulated unrecognized section 987 gain or loss.*—Any net accumulated unrecognized section 987 gain or loss determined under §1.987-4 shall be translated from the owner's old functional currency into the owner's new functional currency using the spot rate for translating an amount denominated in the owner's old functional currency into the owner's new functional currency on the last day of the last taxable year ending before the year of change.

(ii) *Taxpayer with the same functional currency as its QBU changing to a different functional currency.*—If a taxpayer with the same functional currency as its QBU changes to a new functional currency and as a result the taxpayer becomes an owner of a section 987 QBU (see §1.987-1), the taxpayer and the section 987 QBU shall become subject to section 987 for the year of change and subsequent years.

(iii) *Owner changing to the same functional currency as the section 987 QBU.*—If an owner changes its functional currency to the functional currency of its section 987 QBU, the section 987 QBU shall be treated as if it terminated on the last day of the last taxable year ending before the year of change. See §§1.987-5 and 1.987-8 for the consequences of a termination of a section 987 QBU that is subject to §§1.987-1 through 1.987-11.

(f) *Example.*—The provisions of this section are illustrated by the following example:

Example. (i) *Facts.* FC, a foreign corporation, owns all of the stock of DC, a domestic corporation. The Commissioner granted permission to change FC's functional currency from the British pound to the euro beginning January 1, 2020. The EUR/GBP exchange rate on December 31, 2019, is €1:£0.50.

(ii) *Determining new functional currency basis of property and liabilities.* The following table shows how FC must convert the items on its balance sheet from the British pound to the euro on December 31, 2019.

Assets:	GBP	EUR
Cash on hand	£40,000	€ 80,000
Accounts Receivable	£10,000	€ 20,000
Inventory	£100,000	€ 200,000
€ 100,000 Euro Bond (£100,000 historical basis)	£50,000	€ 100,000
Fixed assets:		
Property	£200,000	€ 400,000
Plant	£500,000	€ 1,000,000
Accumulated Depreciation	(£200,000)	(€ 400,000)
Equipment	£1,000,000	€ 2,000,000
Accumulated Depreciation	(£400,000)	(€ 800,000)
Total Assets	£1,300,000	€ 2,600,000
Liabilities:		
Accounts Payable	£50,000	€ 100,000
Long-term Liabilities	£400,000	€ 800,000
Paid-in-Capital	£800,000	€ 1,600,000
Retained Earnings	£50,000	€ 100,000
Total Liabilities and Equity	£1,300,000	€ 2,600,000

(iii) *Exchange gain or loss on section 988 transactions.* Under paragraph (b) of this section, FC will recognize a £50,000 loss (£50,000 current value minus £100,000 historical basis) on the Euro Bond resulting from the change in functional currency because, after the change, the Euro Bond will no longer be an asset denominated in a non-functional currency. The amount of FC's retained earnings on its December 31, 2019, balance sheet reflects the £50,000 loss on the Euro Bond.

(g) *Effective/applicability date.*—Generally, this regulation shall apply to taxable years beginning on or after one year after the first day of the first taxable year following December 7, 2016. If pursuant to § 1.987-11(b) a taxpayer applies §§ 1.987-1 through 1.987-11 beginning in a taxable year prior to the earliest taxable year described in § 1.987-11(a), then this section shall apply to taxable years of the taxpayer beginning on or after the first day of such prior taxable year. [Reg. § 1.985-5.]

☐ [*T.D. 8464, 12-31-92. Amended by T.D. 8765, 3-4-98 and T.D. 9794, 12-7-2016.*]

§ 1.985-6. Transition rules for a QBU that uses the dollar approximate separate transactions method for its first taxable year beginning in 1987.—(a) *In general.*—This section sets forth transition rules for a QBU that used the dollar approximate separate transactions method of accounting set forth in § 1.985-3 or § 1.985-3T (as contained in the April 1, 1989 edition of 26 CFR part 1 (1.908 to 1.1000)) for its first taxable year beginning in 1987 (DASTM QBU). A DASTM QBU must determine the dollar and hyperinflationary currency basis of its assets and the dollar and hyperinflationary currency amount of its liabilities that were acquired or incurred in taxable years beginning before January 1, 1987. In addition, a DASTM QBU must determine its net worth, including its retained earnings, at the end of the QBU's last taxable year beginning before January 1, 1987. This section provides rules for controlled foreign corporations (as defined in section 957 or section 953(c)(1)(B)), other foreign corporations, and branches of United States persons that must make these determinations.

(b) *Certain controlled foreign corporations.*—If a DASTM QBU was a controlled foreign corporation for its last taxable year beginning before January 1, 1987, and it had a significant event as described in § 1.964-1(c)(6) in a taxable year beginning before January 1, 1987, then the rules of this paragraph (b) shall apply.

(1) *Basis in assets and amount of liabilities.*—The hyperinflationary currency adjusted basis of the QBU's assets and the hyperinflationary currency amount of the QBU's liabilities acquired or incurred by the QBU in a taxable year beginning before January 1, 1987, shall be the basis or the amount as determined under § 1.964-1(e) prior to translation under § 1.964-1(e)(4). The dollar adjusted basis of such assets and the dollar amount of such liabilities shall be the adjusted basis or the amount as determined under the rules of § 1.964-1(e) after translation under § 1.964-1(e)(4).

(2) *Retained earnings.*—The dollar amount of the QBU's retained earnings at the end of its last taxable year beginning before January 1, 1987, shall be the dollar amount determined under § 1.964-1(e)(3).

(c) *All other foreign corporations.*—If a foreign corporation is a DASTM QBU that is not described in paragraph (b) of this section, then the hyperinflationary currency and dollar adjusted basis in the QBU's assets acquired in taxable years beginning before January 1, 1987, the hyperinflationary currency and dollar amount of the QBU's liabilities acquired or incurred in taxable years beginning before January 1, 1987, and the dollar amount of the QBU's net worth, including its retained earnings, at the end of its last taxable year beginning before January 1, 1987, shall be determined by applying the principles of § 1.985-3T or § 1.985-3. Thus, for example, the dollar basis of plant and equipment shall be determined using the appropriate historical exchange rate.

(d) *Pre-1987 section 902 amounts.*—(1) *Translation of pre-1987 section 902 accumulated profits and taxes into United States dollars.*—The foreign income taxes and accumulated profits or deficits in accumulated profits of a foreign corporation that were maintained in foreign currency for purposes of section 902 and that are attributable to taxable years of the foreign corporation beginning before January 1, 1987, shall be translated into dollars at the spot exchange rate on the first day of its first taxable year beginning after December 31, 1986. Once translated into dollars, these accumulated profits and taxes shall (absent a change in functional currency) remain in dollars for all federal income tax purposes.

(2) *Carryforward of accumulated deficits in accumulated profits from pre-1987 taxable years to post-1986 taxable years.*—For purposes of sections 902 and 960, the post-1986 undistributed earnings of a foreign corporation that is subject to the rules of this section shall be reduced by the dollar amount of the corporation's deficit in accumulated profits, if any, determined under section 902 and the regulations thereunder, that was accumulated at the end of the corporation's last taxable year beginning before January 1, 1987. The dollar amount of the accumulated deficit shall be determined by multiplying the foreign currency amount of such deficit by the spot exchange rate on the last day of the corporation's last taxable year beginning before January 1, 1987, and shall be taken into account on the first day of the corporation's first taxable year beginning after December 31, 1986. Post-1986 undistributed earnings may not be reduced by the dollar amount of a pre-1987 deficit in retained earnings determined under § 1.964-1(e).

(e) *Net worth branch.*—If a DASTM QBU is a branch of a United States person and the QBU used a net worth method of accounting for its last taxable year beginning before January 1, 1987, then the rules of this paragraph (e) shall apply. A net worth method of accounting is any method of accounting under which the taxpayer calculates the taxable income of a QBU based on the net change in the dollar value of the QBU's equity (assets minus liabilities) during the course of a taxable year, taking into account any contributions or remittances made during the year. *See, e.g.*, Rev. Rul. 75-106, 1975-1 C.B. 31. (See § 601.601(d)(2)(ii)(*b*) of this chapter).

(1) *Basis in assets and amount of liabilities.*—(i) *Hyperinflationary amounts.*—For the first taxable year beginning in 1987, the hyperinflationary currency adjusted basis of a QBU's assets or the hyperinflationary currency amounts of its liabilities acquired or incurred in a taxable year beginning before January 1, 1987 is the hyperinflationary currency basis or amount at the date when acquired or incurred, as adjusted according to United States generally accepted accounting and tax accounting principles. If a hyperinflationary currency basis or amount was not determined at such date, the dollar basis or amount, as adjusted according to United States generally accepted accounting and tax accounting principles, shall be translated into hyperinflationary currency at the spot exchange rate on the date when the asset or liability was acquired or incurred.

(ii) *Dollar amounts.*—For the first taxable year beginning in 1987, the dollar adjusted basis of the QBU's assets and the amounts of its liabilities shall be those amounts reflected on the QBU's dollar books and records at the end of the taxpayer's last taxable year beginning before January 1, 1987, after adjusting the books and records according to United States generally accepted accounting and tax accounting principles.

(2) *Ending net worth.*—The dollar amount of the QBU's net worth at the end of its last taxable year beginning before January 1, 1987 shall equal the QBU's net worth at that date as determined under paragraph (e)(1)(ii) of this section.

(f) *Profit and loss branch.*—If a DASTM QBU is a branch of a United States person and the QBU used a profit and loss method of accounting for its last taxable year beginning before January 1, 1987, then the United States person shall first apply the transition rules of § 1.987-5 in order to determine the beginning amount and dollar basis of the branch's EQ pool, the hyperinflationary currency basis of the branch's assets, and the hyperinflationary currency amounts of its liabilities. A profit and loss method of accounting is any method of accounting under which the taxpayer calculates the profits of a QBU by computing the QBU's profits in its functional currency and translating the net result into dollars. *See, e.g.*, Rev. Rul. 75-107, 1975-1 C.B. 32. (See § 601.601(d)(2)(ii)(*b*) of this chapter). The QBU and the taxpayer must then make the adjustments required by § 1.985-5, *e.g.*, the QBU must take into account unrealized exchange gain or loss on dollar-denominated section 988 transactions, the taxpayer must account for the deemed termination of the branch, and the taxpayer must translate the QBU's balance sheet items from hyperinflationary currency into dollars at the spot rate. [Reg. § 1.985-6.]

□ [*T.D.* 8464, 12-31-92.]

§ 1.985-7. Adjustments required in connection with a change to DASTM.—(a) *In general.*—If a QBU begins to use the dollar approximate separate transactions method of accounting set forth in § 1.985-3 (DASTM) in a taxable year beginning after April 6, 1998, adjustments shall be made as provided by this section. For the rules with respect to foreign corporations, see paragraph (b) of this section. For the rules with respect to adjustments to the income of United States shareholders of controlled foreign corporations, see paragraph (c) of this section. For the rules with respect to adjustments relating to QBU branches, see paragraph (d) of this section. For the effective date of this section, see paragraph (e). For purposes of applying this section, the look-back period shall be the period beginning with the first taxable year after the transition date and ending on the last day prior to the taxable year of change. The term transition date means the later of the last day of the last taxable year ending before the base period as defined in § 1.985-1(b)(2)(ii)(D) or the last day of the taxable year in which the QBU last applied DASTM. The taxable year of change shall mean the taxable year of change as defined in § 1.481-1(a)(1). The application of this paragraph may be illustrated by the following examples:

Example 1. A calendar year QBU that has not previously used DASTM operates in a country in which the functional currency of the country is hyperinflationary as defined under § 1.985-1(b)(2)(ii)(D) for the QBU's 1999 tax year. The look-back period is the period from January 1, 1996 through December 31, 1998, the transition date is December 31, 1995, and the taxable year of change is the taxable year beginning January 1, 1999.

Example 2. A QBU that has not previously used DASTM with a taxable year ending June 30, operates in a country in which the functional currency of the country is hyperinflationary for the QBU's tax year beginning July 1, 1999 as defined under § 1.985-1(b)(2)(ii)(D) (where the base period is the thirty-six calendar months immediately preceding the first day of the current calendar year 1999). The look-back period is the period from July 1, 1995 through June 30, 1999, the transition date is June 30, 1995, and the taxable year of change is the taxable year beginning July 1, 1999.

(b) *Adjustments to foreign corporations.*—(1) *In general.*—In the case of a foreign corporation, the corporation shall make the adjustments set forth in paragraphs (b)(2) through (4) of this section. The adjustments shall be made on the first day of the taxable year of change.

(2) *Treatment of certain section 988 transactions.*—(i) *Exchange gain or loss from section 988 transactions unrealized as of the transition date.*—A foreign corporation shall adjust earnings and profits by the amount of any unrealized exchange gain or loss that was attributable to a section 988 transaction (as defined in sections 988(c)(1)(A), (B), and (C)) that was denominated in terms of (or determined by reference to) the dollar and was held by the corporation on the transition date. Such gain or loss shall be computed as if recognized on the transition date and shall be reduced by any gain and increased by any loss recognized by the corporation with respect to such transaction during the look-back period. The amount of such gain or loss shall be determined without regard to the limitations of section 988(b) (i.e., whether any gain or loss would be realized on the transaction as a whole). The character and source of such gain or loss shall be determined under section 988. Proper adjustments shall be made to account for gain or loss taken into account by reason of this paragraph (b)(2). See § 1.985-5(f) *Example 1, footnote 1.*

(ii) *Treatment of a section 988 transaction entered into and terminated during the look-back period.*—A foreign corporation shall reduce earnings and profits by the amount of any gain, and increase earnings and profits by the amount of any loss, that was recognized with respect to any dollar denominated section 988 transactions entered into and terminated during the look-back period.

(3) *Opening balance sheet.*—The opening balance sheet of a foreign corporation for the taxable year of change shall be determined as if the corporation had changed its functional currency to the dollar by applying § 1.985-5(c) on the transition date and had translated its assets and liabilities acquired and incurred during the look-back period under § 1.985-3.

(4) *Earnings and profits adjustments.*—(i) *Pre-1987 accumulated profits.*—The foreign income taxes and accumulated profits or deficits in accumulated profits of a foreign corporation that are attributable to taxable years beginning before January 1, 1987, as stated on the transition date, and that were maintained for purposes of section 902 in the old functional currency, shall be translated into dollars at the spot rate in effect on the transition date. The applicable accumulated profits shall be reduced on a last-in, first-out basis by the aggregate dollar amount (translated from functional currency in accordance with the rules of section 989(b)) attributable to earnings and profits that were distributed (or treated as distributed) during the look-back period to the extent such amounts distributed exceed the earnings and profits calculated under (b)(4)(ii) or (b)(4)(iii), as applicable. See § 1.902-1(b)(2)(ii). Once translated into dollars, these pre-1987 taxes and accumulated profits or deficits in accumulated profits shall (absent a change in functional currency) remain in dollars for all federal income tax purposes.

(ii) *Post-1986 undistributed earnings of a CFC.*—In the case of a controlled foreign corporation (within the meaning of section 957 or section 953(c)(1)(B)) (CFC) or a foreign corporation subject to the rules of § 1.904-6(a)(2), the corporation's post-1986 undistributed earnings in each separate category as defined in § 1.904-5(a)(1) as of the first day of the taxable year of change (and prior to adjustment under paragraph (c)(1) of this section) shall equal the sum of—

(A) The corporation's post-1986 undistributed earnings and profits (or deficit in earnings and profits) in each separate category as defined in § 1.904-5(a)(1) as stated on the transition date translated into dollars at the spot rate in effect on the transition date; and

(B) The sum of the earnings and profits (or deficit in earnings and profits) in each separate category determined under § 1.985-3 for each post-transition date taxable year prior to the taxable year of change.

Such amount shall be reduced by the aggregate dollar amount (translated from functional currency in accordance with the rules of section 989(b)) attributable to earnings and profits that were distributed (or treated as distributed) during the look-back period out of post-1986 earnings and profits in such separate category. For purposes of applying this paragraph (b)(4)(ii)(B), the opening balance sheet for calculating earnings and profits under § 1.985-3 for the first post-transition year shall be translated into dollars pursuant to § 1.985-5(c).

(iii) *Post-1986 undistributed earnings of other foreign corporations.*—In the case of a foreign corporation that is not a CFC or subject to the rules of § 1.904-6(a)(2), the corporation's post-1986 undistributed earnings shall equal the sum of—

(A) The corporation's post-1986 undistributed earnings (or deficit) on the transition date translated into dollars at the spot rate in effect on the transition date; and

(B) The sum of the earnings and profits (or deficit in earnings and profits) determined under § 1.985-3 for each post-transition date taxable year (or such later year determined under section 902(c)(3)(A)) prior to the taxable year of change.

Such amount shall be reduced by the aggregate dollar amount (translated from functional currency in accordance with the rules of section 989(b)) that was distributed (or treated as distributed) during the look-back period out of post-1986 earnings and profits. For purposes of applying this paragraph (b)(4)(iii)(B), the opening balance sheet for calculating earnings and profits under § 1.985-3 for the first post-transition year shall be translated into dollars pursuant to § 1.985-5(c).

(c) *United States shareholders of controlled foreign corporations.*—(1) *In general.*—A United States shareholder (within the meaning of section 951(b) or section 953(c)(1)(B)) of a CFC that changes to DASTM shall make the adjustments set forth in paragraphs (c)(2) through (5) of this section on the first day of the taxable year of change. Adjustments under this section shall be taken into account by the shareholder (or such shareholder's successor in interest) ratably over four taxable years beginning with the taxable year of change. Similar rules shall apply in determining adjustments to income of United States persons who have made an election under section 1295 to treat a passive foreign investment company as a qualified electing fund.

(2) *Treatment under subpart F of income recognized on section 988 transactions.*—The character of amounts taken into account under paragraph (b)(2) of this section for purposes of sections 951 through 964, shall be determined on the transition date and to the extent characterized as subpart F income shall be taken into account in accordance with the rules of paragraph (c)(1) of this section. Such amounts shall retain their character for all federal income tax purposes (including sections 902, 959, 960, 961, 1248, and 6038).

(3) *Recognition of foreign currency gain or loss on previously taxed earnings and profits on the transition date.*—Gain or loss is recognized under section 986(c) as if all previously taxed earnings and profits as determined on the transition date, if any, were distributed on such date. Such gain or loss shall be reduced by any foreign currency gain and increased by any foreign currency loss that was recognized under section 986(c) with respect to distributions of previously taxed earnings and profits during the look-back period. Such amount shall be characterized in accordance with section 986(c) and taken into account in accordance with the rules of paragraph (c)(1) of this section.

(4) *Subpart F income adjustment.*—Subpart F income in a separate category shall be determined under § 1.985-3 for each look-back year. For this purpose, the opening DASTM balance sheet shall be determined under § 1.985-5. The sum of the difference (positive or negative) between the amount computed pursuant to § 1.985-3 and amount that was included in income for each year shall be taken into account in the taxable year of change pursuant to paragraph (c)(1) of this section. Such amounts shall retain their character for all federal income tax purposes (including sections 902, 959, 960, 961, 1248, and 6038). For rules applicable if an adjustment under this section results in a loss for the taxable year in a separate category, see section 904(f) and the regulations thereunder. The amount of previously taxed earnings and profits as determined under section 959(c)(2) shall be adjusted (positively or negatively) by the amount taken into account under this paragraph (c)(4) as of the first day of the taxable year of change.

(5) *Foreign tax credit.*—A United States shareholder of a CFC shall compute an amount of foreign taxes deemed paid under section 960 with respect to any positive adjustments determined under paragraph (c) of this section. The amount of foreign tax deemed paid shall be computed with reference to the full amount of the adjustment and to the post-1986 undistributed earnings determined under paragraph (b)(4)(i) and (ii) of this section and the post-1986 foreign income taxes of the CFC on the first day of the taxable year of change (i.e., without taking into account earnings and taxes for the taxable year of change). For purposes of section 960, the associated taxes in each separate category shall be allocated pro rata among, and deemed paid in, the shareholder's taxable years in which the income is taken into account. (No adjustment to foreign taxes deemed paid in prior years is required solely by reason of a negative adjustment to income under paragraph (c)(1) of this section).

(d) *QBU branches.*—(1) *In general.*—In the case of a QBU branch, the taxpayer shall make the adjustments set forth in paragraphs (d)(2) through (d)(4) of this section. Adjustments under this section shall be taken into account by the taxpayer ratably over four taxable years beginning with the taxable year of change.

(2) *Treatment of certain section 988 transactions.*—(i) *Exchange gain or loss from section 988 transactions unrealized as of the transition date.*—A QBU branch shall adjust income by the amount of any unrealized exchange gain or loss that was attributable to a section 988 transaction (as defined in sections 988(c)(1)(A), (B), and (C)) that was denominated in terms of (or determined by reference to) the dollar and was held by the QBU branch on the transition date. Such gain or loss shall be computed as if recognized on the transition date and shall be reduced by any gain and increased by any loss recognized by the QBU branch with respect to such transaction during the look-back period. The amount of such gain or loss shall be determined without regard to the limitations of section 988(b) (i.e., whether any gain or loss would be realized on the transaction as a whole). The character and source of such gain or loss shall be determined under section 988. Proper adjustments shall be made to account for gain or loss taken into account by reason of this paragraph (d)(2). See § 1.985-5(f) *Example 1, footnote 1.*

(ii) *Treatment of a section 988 transaction entered into and terminated during the look-back period.*—A QBU branch shall reduce income by the amount of any gain, and increase income by the amount of any loss, that was recognized with respect to any dollar denominated section 988 transactions entered into and terminated during the look-back period.

(3) *Deemed termination income adjustment.*—The taxpayer shall realize gain or loss attributable to the QBU branch's equity pool (as stated on the transition date) under the principles of section 987, computed as if the branch terminated on the transition date. Such amount shall be reduced by section 987 gain and increased by section 987 loss that was recognized by such taxpayer with respect to remittances during the look-back period.

(4) *Branch income adjustment.*—Branch income in a separate category shall be determined under § 1.985-3 for each look-back year. For this purpose, the opening DASTM balance sheet shall be determined under § 1.985-5. The sum of the difference (positive or negative) between the amount computed pursuant to § 1.985-3 and amount taken into account for each year shall be taken into account in the taxable year of change pursuant to paragraph (d)(1) of this section. Such amounts shall retain their character for all federal income tax purposes.

(5) *Opening balance sheet.*—The opening balance sheet of a QBU branch for the taxable year of change shall be determined as if the branch had changed its functional currency to the dollar by applying § 1.985-5(c) on the transition date and had translated its assets and liabilities acquired and incurred during the look-back period under § 1.985-3.

(e) *Effective date.*—This section is effective for taxable years beginning after April 6, 1998. However, a taxpayer may choose to apply this section to all open taxable years beginning after December 31, 1986, provided each person, and each QBU branch of a person, that is related (within the meaning of § 1.985-2(d)(3)) to the taxpayer also applies this section. [Reg. § 1.985-7.]

□ [*T.D. 8765, 3-4-98 (corrected 3-31-98).*]

§ 1.985-8. Special rules applicable to the European Monetary Union (conversion to euro).—(a) *Definitions.*—(1) *Legacy currency.*—A legacy currency is the former currency of a Member State of the European Community which is substituted for the euro in accordance with the Treaty establishing the European Community signed February 7, 1992. The term legacy currency shall also include the European Currency Unit.

(2) *Conversion rate.*—The conversion rate is the rate at which the euro is substituted for a legacy currency.

(b) *Operative rules.*—(1) *Initial adoption.*—A QBU (as defined in § 1.989(a)-1(b)) whose first taxable year begins after the euro has been substituted for a legacy currency may not adopt a legacy currency as its functional currency.

(2) *QBU with a legacy currency as its functional currency.*—(i) *Required change.*—A QBU with a legacy currency as its functional currency is required to change its functional currency to the euro beginning the first day of the first taxable year—

(A) That begins on or after the day that the euro is substituted for that legacy currency (in accordance with the Treaty on European Union); and

(B) In which the QBU begins to maintain its books and records (as described in § 1.989(a)-1(d)) in the euro.

(ii) Notwithstanding paragraph (b)(2)(i) of this section, a QBU with a legacy currency as its functional currency is required to change its functional currency to the euro no later than the last taxable year beginning on or before the first day such legacy currency is no longer valid legal tender.

(3) *QBU with a non-legacy currency as its functional currency.*—(i) *In general.*—A QBU with a non-legacy currency as its functional currency may change its functional currency to the euro pursuant to this § 1.985-8 if—

(A) Under the rules set forth in § 1.985-1(c), the euro is the currency of the economic environment in which a significant part of the QBU's activities are conducted;

(B) After conversion, the QBU maintains its books and records (as described in § 1.989(a)-1(d)) in the euro; and

(C) The QBU is not required to use the dollar as its functional currency under § 1.985-1(b).

(ii) *Time period for change.*—A QBU with a non-legacy currency as its functional currency may change its functional currency to the euro under this section only if it does so within the period set forth in paragraph (b)(2) of this section as if the functional currency of the QBU was a legacy currency.

(4) *Consent of Commissioner.*—A change made pursuant to paragraph (b) of this section shall be deemed to be made with the consent of the Commissioner for purposes of § 1.985-4. A QBU changing its functional currency to the euro pursuant to paragraph (b)(2) of this section must make adjustments as provided in paragraph (c) of this section. A QBU changing its functional currency to the euro pursuant to paragraph (b)(3) must make adjustments as provided in § 1.985-5.

(5) *Statement to file upon change.*—With respect to a QBU that changes its functional currency to the euro under paragraph (b) of this section, an affected taxpayer shall attach to its return for the taxable year of change a statement that includes the following: "TAXPAYER CERTIFIES THAT A QBU OF THE TAXPAYER HAS CHANGED ITS FUNCTIONAL CURRENCY TO THE EURO PURSUANT TO TREAS. REG. § 1.985-8." For purposes of this paragraph (b)(5), an affected taxpayer shall be in the case where the QBU is: a QBU of an individual U.S. resident (as a result of the activities of such individual), the individual; a QBU branch of a U.S. corporation, the corporation; a controlled foreign corporation (as described in section 957) (or QBU branch thereof), each United States shareholder (as described in section 951(b)); a partnership, each partner separately; a noncontrolled section 902 corporation (as described in section 904(d)(2)(E)) (or branch thereof), each domestic shareholder as described in § 1.902-1(a)(1); or a trust or estate, the fiduciary of such trust or estate.

(c) *Adjustments required when a QBU changes its functional currency from a legacy currency to the euro pursuant to paragraph (b)(2) of this section.*—(1) *In general.*—A QBU that changes its functional currency from a legacy currency to the euro pursuant to paragraph (b)(2) of this section must make the adjustments described in paragraphs (c)(2) through (5) of this section. Section 1.985-5 shall not apply.

(2) *Determining the euro basis of property and the euro amount of liabilities and other relevant items.*—The euro basis in property and the euro amount of liabilities and other relevant items shall equal the product of the legacy functional currency adjusted basis or amount of liabilities multiplied by the applicable conversion rate.

(3) *Taking into account exchange gain or loss on legacy currency section 988 transactions.*—(i) *In general.*—Except as provided in paragraphs (c)(3)(iii) and (iv) of this section, a legacy currency denominated section 988 transaction (determined after applying section 988(d)) outstanding on the last day of the taxable year immediately prior to the year of change shall continue to be treated as a section 988 transaction after the change and the principles of section 988 shall apply.

(ii) *Examples.*—The application of this paragraph (c)(3) may be illustrated by the following examples:

Example 1. X, a calendar year QBU on the cash method of accounting, uses the deutschmark as its functional currency. X is not described in section 1281(b). On July 1, 1998, X converts 10,000 deutschmarks (DM) into Dutch guilders (fl) at the spot rate of fl1 = DM1 and loans the 10,000 guilders to Y (an unrelated party) for one year at a rate of 10% with principal and interest to be paid on June 30, 1999. On January 1, 1999, X changes its functional currency to the euro pursuant to this section. Assume that the euro/deutschmark conversion rate is set by the European Council at €1 = DM2. Assume further that the euro/guilder conversion rate is set at €1 = fl2.25. Accordingly, under the terms of the note, on June 30, 1999, X will receive €4444.44 (fl10,000/2.25) of principal and €4444.44 (fl1,000/2.25) of interest. Pursuant to this paragraph (c)(3), X will realize an exchange loss on the principal computed under the principles of § 1.988-2(b)(5). For this purpose, the exchange rate used under § 1.988-2(b)(5)(i) shall be the guilder/euro conversion rate. The amount under § 1.988-2(b)(5)(ii) is determined by translating the fl10,000 at the guilder/deutschmark spot rate on July 1, 1998, and translating that deutschmark amount into euros at the deutschmark/euro conversion rate. Thus, X will compute an exchange loss for 1999 of €555.56 determined as follows: [€4444.44 (fl10,000/2.25) – €5000 ((fl10,000/1) /2) = -€555.56]. Pursuant to this paragraph (c)(3), the character and source of the loss are determined pursuant to section 988 and regulations thereunder. Because X uses the cash method of accounting for the interest on this debt instrument, X does not realize exchange gain or loss on the receipt of that interest.

Example 2. (i) X, a calendar year QBU on the accrual method of accounting, uses the deutschmark as its functional currency. On February 1, 1998, X converts 12,000 deutschmarks into Dutch guilders at the spot rate of fl1 = DM1 and loans the 12,000 guilders to Y (an unrelated party) for one year at a rate of 10% with principal and interest to be paid on January 31, 1999. In addition, assume the average rate (deutschmark/guilder) for the period from February 1, 1998, through December 31, 1998 is fl1.07 = DM1. Pursuant to § 1.988-2(b)(2)(ii)(C), X will accrue eleven months of interest on the note and recognize interest income of DM1028.04 (fl1100/1.07) in the 1998 taxable year.

(ii) On January 1, 1999, the euro will replace the deutschmark as the national currency of Germany pursuant to the Treaty on European Union signed February 7, 1992. Assume that on January 1, 1999, X changes its functional currency to the euro pursuant to this section. Assume that the euro/deutschmark conversion rate is set by the European Council at €1 = DM2. Assume further that the euro/guilder conversion rate is set at €1 = fl2.25. In 1999, X will accrue one month of interest equal to €44.44 (fl100/2.25). On January 31, 1999, pursuant to the note, X will receive interest denominated in euros of €533.33 (fl1200/2.25). Pursuant to this paragraph (c)(3), X will realize an exchange loss in the 1999 taxable year with respect to accrued interest computed under the principles of § 1.988-2(b)(3). For this purpose, the exchange rate used under § 1.988-2(b)(3)(i) is the guilder/euro conversion rate and the exchange rate used under § 1.988-2(b)(3)(ii) is the deutschmark/euro conversion rate. Thus, with respect to the interest accrued in 1998, X will realize exchange loss of €25.13 under § 1.988-2(b), (3) as follows: [€488.89 (fl1100/2.25) – €514.02 (DM1028.04/2) = -€25.13]. With respect to the one month of interest accrued in 1999, X will realize no exchange gain or loss since the exchange rate when the interest accrued and the spot rate on the payment date are the same.

(iii) X will realize exchange loss of €666.67 on repayment of the loan principal computed in the same manner as in Example 1 [€5333.33 (fl12,000/2.25) – €6000 fl12,000/1)/2)]. The losses with respect to accrued interest and principal are characterized and sourced under the rules of section 988.

(iii) *Special rule for legacy nonfunctional currency.*—The QBU shall realize or otherwise take into account for all purposes of the Internal Revenue Code the amount of any unrealized exchange gain or loss attributable to nonfunctional currency (as described in section 988(c)(1)(C)(ii)) that is denominated in a legacy currency as if the currency were disposed of on the last day of the taxable year immediately prior to the year of change. The character and source of the gain or loss are determined under section 988.

(iv) *Legacy currency denominated accounts receivable and payable.*—(A) *In general.*—A QBU may elect to realize or otherwise take into account for all purposes of the Internal Revenue Code the amount of any unrealized exchange gain or loss attributable to a legacy currency denominated item described in section 988(c)(1)(B)(ii) as if the item were terminated on the last day of the taxable year ending prior to the year of change.

(B) *Time and manner of election.*—With respect to a QBU that makes an election described in paragraph (c)(3)(iv)(A) of this section, an affected taxpayer (as described in paragraph (b)(5) of this section) shall attach a statement to its tax return for the taxable year ending immediately prior to the year of change which includes the following: "TAXPAYER CERTIFIES THAT A QBU OF THE TAXPAYER

HAS ELECTED TO REALIZE CURRENCY GAIN OR LOSS ON LEGACY CURRENCY DENOMINATED ACCOUNTS RECEIVABLE AND PAYABLE UPON CHANGE OF FUNCTIONAL CURRENCY TO THE EURO." A QBU making the election must do so for all legacy currency denominated items described in section 988(c)(1)(B)(ii).

(4) *Adjustments when a branch changes its functional currency to the euro.*—(i) *Branch changing from a legacy currency to the euro in a taxable year during which taxpayer's functional currency is other than the euro.*—If a branch changes its functional currency from a legacy currency to the euro for a taxable year during which the taxpayer's functional currency is other than the euro, the branch's euro equity pool shall equal the product of the legacy currency amount of the equity pool multiplied by the applicable conversion rate. No adjustment to the basis pool is required.

(ii) *Branch changing from a legacy currency to the euro in a taxable year during which taxpayer's functional currency is the euro.*—If a branch changes its functional currency from a legacy currency to the euro for a taxable year during which the taxpayer's functional currency is the euro, the taxpayer shall realize gain or loss attributable to the branch's equity pool under the principles of section 987, computed as if the branch terminated on the last day prior to the year of change. Adjustments under this paragraph (c)(4)(ii) shall be taken into account by the taxpayer ratably over four taxable years beginning with the taxable year of change.

(5) *Adjustments to a branch's accounts when a taxpayer changes to the euro.*—(i) *Taxpayer changing from a legacy currency to the euro in a taxable year during which a branch's functional currency is other than the euro.*—If a taxpayer changes its functional currency to the euro for a taxable year during which the functional currency of a branch of the taxpayer is other than the euro, the basis pool shall equal the product of the legacy currency amount of the basis pool multiplied by the applicable conversion rate. No adjustment to the equity pool is required.

(ii) *Taxpayer changing from a legacy currency to the euro in a taxable year during which a branch's functional currency is the euro.*—If a taxpayer changes its functional currency from a legacy currency to the euro for a taxable year during which the functional currency of a branch of the taxpayer is the euro, the taxpayer shall take into account gain or loss as determined under paragraph (c)(4)(ii) of this section.

(6) *Additional adjustments that are necessary when a corporation changes its functional currency to the euro.*—The amount of a corporation's euro currency earnings and profits and the amount of its euro paid-in capital shall equal the product of the legacy currency amounts of these items multiplied by the applicable conversion rate. The foreign income taxes and accumulated profits or deficits in accumulated profits of a foreign corporation that were maintained in foreign currency for purposes of section 902 and that are attributable to taxable years of the foreign corporation beginning before January 1, 1987, also shall be translated into the euro at the conversion rate.

(d) *Treatment of legacy currency section 988 transactions with respect to a QBU that has the euro as its functional currency.*—(1) *In general.*—This § 1.985-8(d) applies to a QBU that has the euro as its functional currency and that holds a section 988 transaction denominated in, or determined by reference to, a currency that is substituted by the euro. For example, this paragraph (d) will apply to a German QBU with the euro as its functional currency if the QBU is holding Country X currency or other section 988 transactions denominated in such currency on the day in the year 2005 when the euro is substituted for the Country X currency.

(2) *Principles of paragraph (c)(3) of this section shall apply.*—With respect to a QBU described in paragraph (d) of this section, the principles of paragraph (c)(3) of this section shall apply. For example, if a German QBU with the euro as its functional currency is holding a Country X currency denominated debt instrument on the day in the year 2005 when the euro is substituted for the Country X currency, the instrument shall continue to be treated as a section 988 transaction pursuant to the principles of paragraph (c)(3)(i) of this section. However, if such QBU holds Country X currency, the QBU shall take into account any unrealized exchange gain or loss pursuant to the principles of paragraph (c)(3)(iii) of this section as if the currency was disposed of on the day prior to the day the euro is substituted for the Country X currency. Similarly, if the QBU makes an election under the principles of paragraph (c)(3)(iv) of this section, the QBU shall take into account for all purposes of the Internal Revenue Code the amount of any unrealized exchange gain or loss attributable to a legacy currency denominated item described in section 988(c)(1)(B)(ii) as if the item were terminated on the day prior to the day the euro is substituted for the Country X currency.

(e) *Effective date.*—This section applies to tax years ending after July 29, 1998. [Reg. § 1.985-8.]

☐ [*T.D. 8927, 1-10-2001.*]

§ 1.986(a)-1. Translation of foreign income taxes for purposes of the foreign tax credit.—(a) *Translation of foreign income taxes taken into account when accrued.*—(1) *In general.*—For purposes of this section, the term *section 901 taxpayer* means the "taxpayer" described in § 1.901-2(f)(1) and so includes a partnership or a specified 10-percent owned foreign corporation (as defined in section 245A(b)) that has legal liability under foreign law for foreign income tax. Except as provided in paragraph (a)(2) of this section, in the case of a section 901 taxpayer that takes foreign income taxes (as defined in section 986(a)(4) (including taxes described in section 903)) into account when accrued, the amount of any foreign income taxes denominated in foreign currency that has been paid or accrued, including additional tax liability denominated in foreign currency, foreign income taxes withheld in foreign currency, or estimated foreign income taxes paid in foreign currency, are translated into dollars using the weighted average exchange rate (as defined in § 1.989(b)-1) (the "average exchange rate") for the section 901 taxpayer's U.S. taxable year (as defined in § 1.960-1(b)(37)) to which such foreign income taxes relate. *See* section 986(a)(1)(A). See section 988 and §§ 1.988-1(a)(2)(ii) and § 1.988-2(c) for rules for determining whether and the extent to which there is a foreign currency gain or loss when an accrued functional currency amount of foreign income tax denominated in nonfunctional currency differs from the functional currency amount paid.

(2) *Exceptions.*—(i) *Foreign income taxes not paid within 24 months.*—Any foreign income taxes denominated in foreign currency that are paid more than 24 months after the close of the section 901 taxpayer's U.S. taxable year to which they relate are translated into dollars using the spot rate on the date of payment of the foreign income taxes. *See* section 986(a)(1)(B)(i) and (a)(2)(A). For purposes of this section and § 1.905-3, the term *spot rate* has the meaning provided in § 1.988-1(d). To the extent any accrued foreign income taxes denominated in foreign currency remain unpaid more than 24 months after the close of the taxable year to which they relate, see § 1.905-3 and paragraph (c) of this section for the required adjustments.

(ii) *Foreign income taxes paid before taxable year begins.*—Any foreign income taxes denominated in foreign currency that are paid before the beginning of the section 901 taxpayer's U.S. taxable year to which such taxes relate are translated into dollars using the spot rate on the date of payment of the foreign income taxes. See section 986(a)(1)(B)(ii) and (a)(2)(A).

(iii) *Inflationary currency.*—Any foreign income taxes denominated in a foreign currency that is an inflationary currency in the section 901 taxpayer's U.S. taxable year to which the foreign income taxes relate, or in any subsequent taxable year up to and including the taxable year in which the taxes are paid, are translated into dollars using the spot rate on the date of payment of such taxes. For purposes of section 986(a)(1)(C) and this paragraph (a)(2)(iii), the term *inflationary currency* means the currency of a country in which there is cumulative inflation during the base period of at least 30 percent, as determined under the principles of § 1.985-1(b)(2)(ii)(D), where the base period, with respect to any taxable year, is the 36 months ending on the last day of such taxable year (in lieu of the base period described in § 1.985-1(b)(2)(ii)(D), which ends on the last day of the preceding calendar year). Accrued but unpaid foreign income taxes denominated in a foreign currency that is an inflationary currency in the taxable year accrued are translated into dollars at the spot rate on the last day of the section 901 taxpayer's U.S. taxable year to which such taxes relate (provisional year-end rate). However, a U.S. taxpayer that claims a foreign tax credit under section 901 may choose to translate accrued but unpaid foreign income taxes (including foreign income taxes deemed paid under section 960) denominated in a foreign currency that is an inflationary currency into dollars at the spot rate on the date of payment, in lieu of the provisional year-end rate, if such taxes are paid prior to the due date (with extensions) of the original Federal income tax return for the taxable year for which the credit is claimed and such return is timely filed. In all other cases, see § 1.905-3 and paragraph (c) of this section for required adjustments upon payment of accrued foreign income taxes denominated in an inflationary currency.

(iv) *Election to translate foreign income taxes using the spot rate as of date of payment.*—(A) *Eligibility to make election.*—An individual or corporate taxpayer (including a specified 10-percent owned foreign corporation) that is otherwise required to translate foreign income taxes that are denominated in foreign currency using the average exchange rate may elect to translate foreign income taxes described in this paragraph (a)(2)(iv) into dollars using the spot rate on the date of payment of the foreign income taxes, provided that the liability for such taxes is denominated in nonfunctional currency. For purposes of section 986(a)(1)(D) and this paragraph (a)(2)(iv), whether the currency in which a tax liability attributable to a qualified business unit (within the meaning of section 989(a)) (QBU) is denominated is a nonfunctional currency is determined by reference to the functional currency of the individual or corporate taxpayer and not that of the QBU of the taxpayer. Accrued but unpaid foreign income taxes subject to the election under this paragraph (a)(2)(iv) are translated at the provisional year-end rate. However, a taxpayer that claims a foreign tax credit under section 901 may choose to translate accrued but unpaid foreign income taxes (including foreign taxes deemed paid under section 960 with respect to a specified 10-percent owned foreign corporation that has made an election under this paragraph (a)(2)(iv)) into dollars at the spot rate on the date of payment, in lieu of the provisional year-end rate, if such taxes are paid prior to the due date (with extensions) of the original return for the taxable year for which the credit is claimed and such return is timely filed. In all other cases, see § 1.905-3 and paragraph (c) of this section for required adjustments upon payment of accrued foreign income taxes that are translated into dollars at the spot rate on the date of payment.

(B) *Scope of election.*—In general, an individual taxpayer may make an election under this paragraph (a)(2)(iv) for all foreign income taxes denominated in nonfunctional currency, or only for those foreign income taxes that are denominated in nonfunctional currency and that are attributable to the individual's non-QBU activities and all QBUs with dollar functional currencies. A corporate taxpayer may make an election under this paragraph (a)(2)(iv) for all foreign income taxes that are denominated in nonfunctional currency, or only for those foreign income taxes that are denominated in nonfunctional currency and that are attributable to all QBUs (including the corporate taxpayer) with dollar functional currencies. Therefore, an election under this paragraph (a)(2)(iv) may not be made for foreign income taxes that are denominated in a nonfunctional currency of the taxpayer and attributable to QBUs with non-dollar functional currencies, except as part of an election to translate all taxes denominated in nonfunctional currency at the spot rate on the date of payment. For purposes of this paragraph (a)(2)(iv)(B), foreign income tax is attributable to a QBU if the tax is properly recorded on the books and records of the QBU in accordance with sections 985 through 989. An election under this paragraph (a)(2)(iv) by a domestic corporation (or an individual that has made an election under section 962) does not apply to any taxes paid or accrued by foreign corporations with respect to which the individual or corporation is a United States shareholder. However, an election may be made on behalf of a foreign corporation to translate either all of the foreign corporation's foreign income taxes denominated in nonfunctional currency, or only the foreign income taxes denominated in nonfunctional currency that are attributable to the foreign corporation's QBUs with dollar functional currencies, using the spot rate on the date of payment. Such an election is made using the procedures under § 1.964-1(c)(3) that apply to permit controlling domestic shareholders to make or change a tax accounting election on behalf of a foreign corporation.

(C) *Time and manner of election.*—The election under this paragraph (a)(2)(iv) must be made by attaching a statement to the taxpayer's timely filed Federal income tax or information return (including extensions) for the first taxable year to which the election applies. The statement must identify whether the election under this paragraph (a)(2)(iv) is made for all foreign income taxes denominated in nonfunctional currency or only for those foreign income taxes that are denominated in nonfunctional currency and that are either attributable to the taxpayer's QBUs with dollar functional currencies or, in the case of an individual, attributable to non-QBU activities. Once made, the election under this paragraph (a)(2)(iv) applies for the taxable year for which made and all subsequent taxable years unless revoked with the consent of the Commissioner.

(D) *Example.*—*(1) Facts.*—USP, a domestic corporation that uses the calendar year as its taxable year, owns a partnership interest in PS, a non-hybrid partnership organized in Country X. USP also owns an equity interest in HPS, a Country X corporation that has filed an entity classification election under § 301.7701-3 of this chapter to be treated as a partnership for Federal income tax purposes. USP also owns 100% of CFC, a Country Y controlled foreign corporation that uses the U.S. dollar as its functional currency. PS and HPS each use a fiscal year ending November 30 as its taxable year both for Federal income tax purposes and for Country X tax purposes, and their functional currency is the Euro. HPS is the section 901 taxpayer of foreign income taxes denominated in Euros that it pays to Country X and properly records on its books and records. USP takes its distributive share of the HPS taxes into account under sections 702(a)(6) and 901(b)(5) and § § 1.702-1(a)(6) and 1.704-1(b)(4)(viii) in computing its foreign tax credit. USP is the section 901 taxpayer of Euro-denominated foreign income taxes it pays to Country X with respect to its distributive share of the income of PS, and also pays Country X taxes withheld in Euros from distributions from HPS to USP and properly records these taxes on its books and records. Pursuant to § 1.985-1(b)(1)(iii), USP's functional currency is the dollar. USP timely elects under § 1.986(a)-1(a)(2)(iv) to use the spot rate on the date of payment to translate into dollars its foreign income taxes denominated in nonfunctional currency that are attributable to all QBUs with dollar functional currencies.

(2) Result.—The Euro taxes paid by USP with respect to its distributive share of income from PS and the Euro taxes withheld from distributions from HPS are nonfunctional currency taxes attributable to USP, a QBU with a dollar functional currency. Accordingly, these taxes are translated into dollars at the spot rate on the date the taxes are paid. USP's distributive share of the Euro taxes paid by HPS are attributable to HPS, a Euro functional currency QBU of USP. Because these taxes are not attributable to a dollar QBU of USP, they are not covered by USP's election and so are translated into dollars at the average exchange rate for HPS's U.S. taxable year ending on November 30. See § 1.986(a)-1(a)(1). Foreign income taxes paid by CFC are not covered by USP's election; however, if USP so chooses it may make a separate election on behalf of CFC to use the spot rate on the date of payment to translate either all of CFC's nonfunctional currency taxes, or only those taxes that are attributable to CFC's dollar QBUs (which includes CFC). If instead USP had elected to use the spot rate on the date of payment to translate all of its foreign income taxes denominated in nonfunctional currency, rather than only those taxes attributable to QBUs with dollar functional currencies, then the spot rate on the date of payment would apply to translate all of the Euro taxes paid or accrued by USP, including its distributive share of taxes paid by HPS. However, this election would still not apply to taxes paid or accrued by CFC. See § 1.986(a)-1(a)(2)(iv)(B).

(v) *Regulated investment companies.*—In the case of a regulated investment company (as defined in section 851) which takes into account income on an accrual basis, foreign income taxes paid or accrued with respect to such income are translated into dollars using the spot rate on the date the income accrues. See section 986(a)(1)(E).

(b) *Translation of foreign income taxes taken into account when paid.*—In the case of a section 901 taxpayer that takes foreign income taxes into account when paid, the amount of any foreign income tax liability denominated in foreign currency, including additional income tax liability denominated in foreign currency or estimated foreign income taxes paid in foreign currency, are translated into dollars using the spot rate on the date of payment of such taxes. See section 986(a)(2)(A). Foreign income taxes withheld in foreign currency are translated into dollars using the spot rate on the date on which such taxes were withheld.

(c) *Refunds or other reductions of foreign income tax liability.*—In the case of a section 901 taxpayer that takes foreign income taxes into account when accrued, a reduction in the amount of previously-accrued foreign income taxes that is attributable to a refund of foreign income taxes, a credit allowed in lieu of a refund, or a reduction in or other downward adjustment to an accrued amount, including an adjustment on account of accrued foreign income taxes that were not paid by the date 24 months after the close of the U.S. taxable year to which such taxes relate, is translated into dollars using the exchange rate that was used to translate such amount when claimed as a credit or added to PTEP group taxes (as defined in § 1.960-3(d)(1)). In the case of foreign income taxes taken into account when accrued but translated into dollars on the date of payment, see § 1.905-3(b) for required adjustments to reflect a foreign tax redetermination (as defined in § 1.905-3(a)) attributable to a reduction in the amount of previously-accrued foreign income taxes that is attributable to a difference in exchange rates between the date or taxable year of accrual and the date of payment. In the case of a section 901 taxpayer that takes foreign income taxes into account when paid, a refund or other reduction in or downward adjustment to the amount of foreign income taxes is translated into dollars using the exchange rate that was used to translate such amount when claimed as a credit. If a refund or other reduction of foreign income taxes relates to foreign income taxes paid or accrued on more than one date, then the refund or other reduction is deemed to be derived from, and reduces, the payments of foreign income taxes in order, starting with the most recent payment of foreign income taxes first, to the extent thereof.

(d) *Allocation of refunds of foreign income taxes.*—Refunds of foreign income taxes are allocated to the same separate category as the foreign income taxes to which the refunded taxes relate. Refunds are related to foreign income taxes in a separate category if the foreign income tax that was refunded was imposed with respect to that separate category. See § 1.904-6 concerning the allocation of foreign income taxes to separate categories of income.

(e) *Basis of foreign currency refunded.*—(1) *Nonfunctional currency tax liability and dollar functional currency.*—If the functional currency of the QBU that paid the tax and received the refund is the dollar or the person receiving the refund is not a QBU, then the recipient's basis in the foreign currency refunded is the dollar value of the refund determined under paragraph (c) of this section by using the exchange rate that was used to translate such amount into dollars when claimed as a credit or added to PTEP group taxes.

(2) *Nonfunctional currency tax liability and non-dollar functional currency.*—If the functional currency of the QBU receiving the refund is not the dollar and is different from the currency in which the foreign income taxes were paid, then the recipient's basis in the refunded foreign currency is equal to the functional currency value of the nonfunctional currency refund, translated into functional currency at the appropriate exchange rate between the functional currency and the nonfunctional currency. Such exchange rate is determined under the principles of paragraph (c) of this section, substituting the words "functional currency" for the word "dollar" and using the exchange rate that was used to translate such amount into the QBU's functional currency when claimed as a credit or added to PTEP group taxes (as defined in § 1.960-3(d)(1)). If a QBU receives a refund of nonfunctional currency tax that is denominated in a currency that was the functional currency of the QBU when the refunded tax was claimed as a credit or added to PTEP group taxes, the QBU's basis in the nonfunctional currency received in the refund is determined by using the exchange rate used under § 1.985-5(c) when the QBU's functional currency changed. See § 1.905-3(b)(1)(ii)(C) (*Example* 3).

(3) *Functional currency tax liabilities.*—If the functional currency of the QBU receiving the refund is the currency in which the refund was made, then the recipient's basis in the currency received is the amount of the functional currency received. If the QBU receives a refund of functional currency tax that was denominated in a nonfunctional currency of the QBU when the tax was claimed as a credit or added to PTEP group taxes, the QBU will recognize the section 988 gain or loss that would have been recognized under § 1.985-5(b) if the refund had been received immediately before the QBU's functional currency changed.

(4) *Foreign currency gain or loss.*—For rules for determining subsequent foreign currency gain or loss on the disposition of nonfunctional currency, the basis of which is determined under this paragraph (e), see section 988(c)(1)(C).

(f) *Applicability dates.*—This section applies to taxable years ending on or after December 16, 2019, and to taxable years of foreign corporations which end with or within a taxable year of a United States shareholder ending on or after December 16, 2019. [Reg. § 1.986(a)-1.]

□ [*T.D.* 9882, 12-16-2019.]

»»→ Caution: The Treasury Department has identified Reg. § 1.987-1, as amended by T.D. 9794, as a significant tax regulation that imposes an undue financial burden on U.S. taxpayers and/or adds undue complexity to the federal tax laws, pursuant to Executive Order 13789 (issued April 21, 2017) (Notice 2017-38, I.R.B. 2017-30, 147). In a subsequent report, published October 16, 2017, Treasury recommended planned actions that would reduce the burden of these regulations, including an extension of the application date of T.D. 9794 (see Notice 2022-34, I.R.B. 2022-34, 150).

§ 1.987-1. Scope, definitions, and special rules.—(a) *In general.*—These regulations under section 987 (§§ 1.987-1 through 1.987-11) provide rules for determining the taxable income or loss of a taxpayer with respect to a section 987 QBU (as defined in paragraph (b)(2) of this section). Further, these regulations provide rules for determining the timing, amount, character, and source of section 987 gain or loss recognized with respect to a section 987 QBU. This section addresses the scope of these regulations and provides certain definitions, special rules, and the procedures for making the elections provided for in the regulations. Section 1.987-2 provides rules for attributing assets and liabilities and items of income, gain, deduction, and loss to an eligible QBU. It also provides rules regarding the translation of items transferred to a section 987 QBU. Section 1.987-3 provides rules for determining and translating the taxable income or loss of a taxpayer with respect to a section 987 QBU. Section 1.987-4 provides rules for determining net unrecognized section 987 gain or loss. Section 1.987-5 provides rules regarding the recognition of section 987 gain or loss. It also provides rules for determining an owner's basis in assets transferred from a section 987 QBU. Section 1.987-6 provides rules regarding the character and source of section 987 gain or loss. Section 1.987-7 provides rules with respect to section 987 aggregate partnerships. Section 1.987-8 provides rules regarding the termination of a section 987 QBU. Section 1.987-9 provides rules regarding the recordkeeping required under section 987. Section 1.987-10 provides transition rules. Section 1.987-11 provides the effective/applicability date of these regulations.

(b) *Scope of section 987 and definitions.*—(1) *Taxpayers subject to section 987.*—(i) *In general.*—Except as provided in paragraphs (b)(1)(ii) and (b)(6) of this section, an individual or corporation is subject to these regulations under section 987 if such person is an owner (as defined in paragraph (b)(4) of this section) of an eligible QBU (as defined in paragraph (b)(3) of this section) that is a section 987 QBU (as defined in paragraph (b)(2) of this section).

(ii) *Inapplicability to certain entities.*—Except as otherwise provided in paragraph (b)(1)(iii) of this section, these regulations under section 987 do not apply to specified entities described in this paragraph (b)(1)(ii), other than specified entities that engage in transactions primarily with related persons within the meaning of section 267(b) or section 707(b) that are not themselves specified entities. For this purpose, specified entities means banks, insurance companies, leasing companies, finance coordination centers, regulated investment companies, or real estate investment trusts. Further, except as otherwise provided in paragraph (b)(1)(iii) of this section, these regulations do not apply to trusts, estates, S corporations, and partnerships other than section 987 aggregate partnerships (as defined in paragraph (b)(5) of this section).

(iii) [Reserved]. For further guidance, see § 1.987-1T(b)(1)(iii).

(2) *Definition of a section 987 QBU.*—(i) *In general.*—A section 987 QBU is an eligible QBU (as defined in paragraph (b)(3) of this section) that has a functional currency different from its direct owner. A section 987 QBU also includes the assets and liabilities of an eligible QBU that are considered under paragraph (b)(5)(ii) of this section to be a section 987 QBU of a partner in a section 987 aggregate partnership (as defined in paragraph (b)(5) of this section). A section 987 QBU will continue to be treated as a section 987 QBU of the owner until a sale or other termination of the section 987 QBU as described in § 1.987-8(b). Except as provided in paragraph (b)(2)(ii) of this section, the functional currency of an eligible QBU shall be determined under § 1.985-1.

(ii) *Section 987 QBU grouping election.*—(A) *In general.*—Except as provided in paragraph (b)(2)(ii)(B) of this section, an owner may elect to treat, solely for purposes of section 987, all section 987 QBUs with the same functional currency that it directly owns as a single section 987 QBU.

(B) *Special grouping rules for section 987 QBUs owned indirectly through a section 987 aggregate partnership.*—An owner may elect to treat all section 987 QBUs with the same functional currency owned indirectly through a single section 987 aggregate partnership (as defined in paragraph (b)(5) of this section) as a single section 987 QBU. An owner may not treat section 987 QBUs as a single section 987 QBU if such QBUs are owned indirectly through different section 987 aggregate partnerships. Additionally, an owner may not treat section 987 QBUs that are owned both directly and indirectly through a section 987 aggregate partnership as a single section 987 QBU.

(3) *Definition of an eligible QBU.*—(i) *In general.*—Eligible QBU means a qualified business unit, as defined in § 1.989(a)-1, that is not subject to the Dollar Approximate Separate Transactions Method rules of § 1.985-3.

(ii) *Exclusion of certain entities.*—A corporation, partnership, trust, estate, or entity disregarded as an entity separate from its owner for Federal income tax purposes as described in § 301.7701-2(c)(2) (hereafter referred to as a "DE") is not an eligible QBU (even though such an entity may have activities that qualify as an eligible QBU).

(4) *Definition of owner.*—For purposes of these regulations under section 987, an owner is any person having direct or indirect ownership in an eligible QBU. Only an individual or corporation may be an owner of an eligible QBU. The term *owner* for section 987 purposes does not include an eligible QBU. For example, a section 987 QBU (QBU1) is not an owner of another section 987 QBU (QBU2) even if QBU1 owns the stock of QBU2.

(i) *Direct ownership.*—An individual or a corporation is a direct owner of an eligible QBU if the individual or corporation is the owner for Federal income tax purposes of the assets and liabilities of the eligible QBU.

(ii) *Indirect ownership.*—An individual or corporation that is a partner in a section 987 aggregate partnership (as defined in paragraph (b)(5) of this section) and is allocated, under § 1.987-7, all or a portion of the assets and liabilities of an eligible QBU of such partnership is an indirect owner of the eligible QBU.

(5) *Section 987 aggregate partnership.*—(i) *In general.*—A partnership is a section 987 aggregate partnership if:

(A) All of the interests in partnership capital and profits are owned, directly or indirectly, by persons related to each other within the meaning of sections 267(b) or 707(b). For purposes of this paragraph (b)(5), ownership of an interest in partnership capital or profits is determined in accordance with the rules for constructive ownership provided in section 267(c), other than section 267(c)(3); and

(B) The partnership has one or more eligible QBUs, at least one of which would be a section 987 QBU with respect to a partner if the partner owned the eligible QBU directly.

(ii) *Section 987 QBU of a partner.*—The assets and liabilities of an eligible QBU owned through a section 987 aggregate partnership and allocated to a partner under the principles of § 1.987-7(b) are considered to be a section 987 QBU of such partner if the partner has a functional currency different from that of the eligible QBU.

(iii) *Certain unrelated partners disregarded.*—In determining whether a partnership is a section 987 aggregate partnership, the interest of an unrelated partner shall be disregarded if the acquisition of such interest has as a principal purpose the avoidance of this paragraph (b)(5).

(6) [Reserved]. For further guidance, see § 1.987-1T(b)(6).

(7) *Examples illustrating paragraph (b) of this section.*—The following examples illustrate the principles of paragraph (b) of this section. U.S. Corp is a domestic corporation, has the U.S. dollar as its functional currency, and uses the calendar year as its taxable year. Except as otherwise provided, (i) Business A and Business B are eligible QBUs and have the euro and the Japanese yen, respectively, as their functional currencies and (ii) DE1 and DE2 are DEs, have no assets or liabilities, and conduct no activities.

Example 1. (i) *Facts.* U.S. Corp owns Business A and all of the interests in DE1. DE1 maintains a separate set of books and records that are kept in British pounds. DE1 owns pounds and all of the stock of a foreign corporation, FC. DE1 is liable to a lender on a pound-denominated obligation that was incurred to acquire the stock of FC. The FC stock, the pounds, and the liability incurred to acquire the FC stock are recorded on DE1's separate books and records. DE1 has no other assets or liabilities and conducts no activities (other than holding the FC stock and servicing its liability).

(ii) *Analysis.* (A) Pursuant to paragraph (b)(4)(i) of this section, U.S. Corp is the direct owner of Business A because it is the owner of the assets and liabilities of Business A. Because Business A is an eligible QBU with a functional currency that is different from the functional currency of its owner, U.S. Corp, Business A is a section 987 QBU (as defined in paragraph (b)(2) of this section). As a result, U.S. Corp and its section 987 QBU, Business A, are subject to section 987.

(B) Holding the stock of FC and pounds and servicing a liability does not constitute a trade or business within the meaning of § 1.989(a)-1(c). Because the activities of DE1 do not constitute a trade or business within the meaning of § 1.989(a)-1(c), such activities are not an eligible QBU. In addition, pursuant to paragraph (b)(3)(ii) of this section, DE1 itself is not an eligible QBU. As a result, neither DE1 nor its activities qualify as a section 987 QBU of U.S. Corp. Therefore, neither the activities of DE1 nor DE1 itself is subject to section 987. For the foreign currency treatment of payments on DE1's pound-denominated liability, see § 1.988-2(b).

Example 2. (i) *Facts.* U.S. Corp owns all of the interests in DE1. DE1 owns Business A and all of the interests in DE2. The only activities of DE1 are Business A activities and holding the interests in DE2. DE2 owns Business B and Business C. For purposes of this example, Business B does not maintain books and records that are separate from its owner, DE2. Instead, the activities of Business B are reflected on the books and records of DE2, which are maintained in Japanese yen. In addition, Business C has the U.S. dollar as its functional currency, maintains books and records that are separate from the books and records of DE2, and is an eligible QBU.

(ii) *Analysis.* (A) Pursuant to paragraph (b)(3)(ii) of this section, DE1 and DE2 are not eligible QBUs. Pursuant to paragraph (b)(3)(i) of this section, the Business B and Business C activities of DE2, and the Business A activities of DE1, are eligible QBUs. Moreover, pursuant to paragraph (b)(4) of this section, DE1 is not the owner of the Business A, Business B, or Business C eligible QBUs, and DE2 is not the owner of the Business B or Business C eligible QBUs. Instead, pursuant to paragraph (b)(4)(i) of this section, U.S. Corp is the direct owner of the Business A, Business B, and Business C eligible QBUs.

(B) Because Business A and Business B are eligible QBUs with functional currencies that are different than the functional currency of U.S. Corp, Business A and Business B are section 987 QBUs (as defined in paragraph (b)(2) of this section).

(C) The Business C eligible QBU has the same functional currency as U.S. Corp. Therefore, the Business C eligible QBU is not a section 987 QBU.

Example 3. (i) *Facts.* U.S. Corp owns all of the interests in DE1. DE1 owns Business A and Business B. For purposes of this example, assume Business B has the euro as its functional currency.

(ii) *Analysis.* (A) Pursuant to paragraph (b)(3)(ii) of this section, DE1 is not an eligible QBU. Moreover, pursuant to paragraph (b)(4) of this section, DE1 is not the owner of the Business A or Business B eligible QBUs. Instead, pursuant to paragraph (b)(4)(i) of this section, U.S. Corp is the direct owner of the Business A and Business B eligible QBUs.

(B) Business A and Business B constitute two separate eligible QBUs, each with the euro as its functional currency. Accordingly, Business A and Business B are section 987 QBUs of U.S. Corp. U.S. Corp may elect to treat Business A and Business B as a single section 987 QBU pursuant to paragraph (b)(2)(ii)(A) of this section. If such election is made, pursuant to paragraph (b)(4)(i) of this section, U.S. Corp would be the direct owner of the Business AB section 987 QBU that would include the activities of both the Business A section 987 QBU and the Business B section 987 QBU. In addition, pursuant to paragraph (b)(4) of this section, DE1 would not be treated as the owner of the Business AB section 987 QBU.

Example 4. (i) *Facts.* U.S. Corp owns all the stock of Y, a U.S. corporation that is a member of U.S. Corp's consolidated group. U.S. Corp also owns all the stock of CFC, a controlled foreign corporation (as defined in section 957(a)) of U.S. Corp with the Japanese yen as its functional currency. Y and CFC are the only partners in P, a foreign partnership. P owns DE1 and Business A. DE1 owns Business B.

(ii) *Analysis.* (A) Under paragraph (b)(5)(i) of this section, P is a section 987 aggregate partnership because Y and CFC own all the interests in partnership capital and profits, Y and CFC are related within the meaning of section 267(b), and the requirements of § 1.987-1(b)(5)(i)(B) are satisfied. Pursuant to paragraph (b)(3)(ii) of this section, P and DE1 are not eligible QBUs. Moreover, pursuant to paragraph (b)(4) of this section, for purposes of section 987, neither P nor DE1 is the owner of the Business B eligible QBU, and P is not the owner of the Business A eligible QBU. Instead, pursuant to paragraph (b)(4)(ii) of this section, Y and CFC are indirect owners of the Business A eligible QBU and the Business B eligible QBU to the extent they are allocated the assets and liabilities of such businesses under § 1.987-7.

(B) Because Business A and Business B are eligible QBUs with different functional currencies than Y, the portions of Business A and Business B allocated to Y under § 1.987-7 are section 987 QBUs of Y.

(C) Because the Business A eligible QBU has a different functional currency than CFC, the portion of Business A that is allocated to CFC under § 1.987-7 is a section 987 71 QBU, and CFC and its section 987 QBU are subject to section 987. Because the Business B eligible QBU has the same functional currency as CFC, the portion of Business B that is allocated to CFC under § 1.987-7 is not a section 987 QBU of CFC.

Example 5. (i) *Facts.* U.S. Corp owns all of the interests in DE1. DE1 owns Business A and all of the interests in DE2. DE2 owns Business B and all of the interests in DE3, an entity disregarded as an entity separate from its owner. DE3 owns Business C, which is an eligible QBU with the Russian ruble as its functional currency.

(ii) *Analysis.* Pursuant to paragraph (b)(3)(ii) of this section, DE1, DE2, and DE3 are not eligible QBUs, and the Business A, Business B, and Business C activities are eligible QBUs. Pursuant to paragraph (b)(4) of this section, an eligible QBU is not an owner of another eligible QBU. Accordingly, the Business A eligible QBU is not the owner of the Business B eligible QBU, and the Business B eligible QBU is not the owner of the Business C eligible QBU. Instead, pursuant to paragraph (b)(4) of this section, U.S. Corp is the direct owner of the Business A, Business B, and Business C eligible QBUs. Because each of the Business A, Business B, and Business C eligible QBUs has a different functional currency than U.S. Corp, such eligible QBUs are section 987 QBUs of U.S. Corp.

(c) *Exchange rates.*—Solely for purposes of section 987, the following definitions shall apply.

(1) *Spot rate.*—(i) *In general.*—Except as otherwise provided in this section, the spot rate means the rate determined under the principles of § 1.988-1(d)(1), (2), and (4) on the relevant date.

(ii) *Election to use a spot rate convention.*—(A) *In general—spot rate convention.*—An owner may elect to use a spot rate convention that reasonably approximates the spot rate determined in paragraph (c)(1)(i) of this section in lieu of such spot rate. A spot rate convention may be determined with respect to a spot rate at the beginning of a reasonable period, the end of a reasonable period, as an average of spot rates for a reasonable period, or by reference to spot and forward rates for a reasonable period. For this purpose, a reasonable period shall not exceed three months. For example, in lieu of the spot rate determined in paragraph (c)(1)(i) of this section, the spot rate for all transactions during a monthly period can be determined pursuant to one of the following conventions: the spot rate at the beginning of the current month or at the end of the preceding month; the monthly average of daily spot rates for the current or preceding month; or an average of the beginning and ending spot rates for the current or preceding month. Similarly, in lieu of the spot rate determined in paragraph (c)(1)(i) of this section, the spot rate can be determined pursuant to an average of the spot rate and the 30-day forward rate on a day of the preceding month. Use of a spot rate convention that is consistent with the convention used for financial accounting purposes is presumed to reasonably approximate the rate in paragraph (c)(1)(i) of this section. The Commissioner can rebut this presumption if the Commissioner determines that the use of the convention would not clearly reflect income based on the facts and circumstances available at the time of the election.

(B) [Reserved]. For further guidance, see § 1.987-1T(c)(1)(ii)(B).

(iii) *Election to use spot rates in lieu of yearly average exchange rates.*—A taxpayer may elect under this paragraph (c)(1)(iii) to use spot rates in lieu of yearly average exchange rates (as defined in paragraph (c)(2) of this section) for certain purposes. In particular, a taxpayer that makes this election must use the spot rate for purposes of determining the historic rate, as provided in paragraph (c)(3)(ii) of this section, and for purposes of translating items of income, gain, deduction, or loss of a section 987 QBU into the owner's functional currency, as described in § 1.987-3(c)(1). Additionally, a taxpayer that makes this election will be deemed also to elect to use the historic inventory method described in § 1.987-3(c)(2)(iv)(B).

(2) *Yearly average exchange rate.*—For purposes of section 987, the yearly average exchange rate is a rate that represents an average exchange rate for the taxable year (or, if the relevant period is less than a full taxable year, such portion of the taxable year) computed under any reasonable method. For example, an owner may determine the yearly average exchange rate based on a daily, monthly or quarterly averaging convention, whether weighted or unweighted, and may take into account forward rates for a period not to exceed three months. Use of an averaging convention that is consistent with the convention used for financial accounting purposes is presumed to be a reasonable method. The Commissioner can rebut this presumption if the Commissioner determines that the use of the convention would not have been expected to clearly reflect income based on the facts and circumstances available at the time of the election.

(3) *Historic rate.*—(i) *In general.*—Except as otherwise provided in these regulations, the historic rate is determined as described in paragraphs (c)(3)(i)(A) through (E) of this section.

(A) *Assets generally.*—In the case of an asset other than inventory that is acquired by a section 987 QBU (including through a transfer), the historic rate is the yearly average exchange rate applicable to the year of acquisition.

(B) *Inventory under the simplified inventory method.*—In the case of inventory with respect to which a taxpayer uses the simplified inventory method described in § 1.987-3(c)(2)(iv)(A), the historic rate for inventory accounted for under the last-in, first-out (LIFO) method of accounting is the yearly average exchange rate applicable to the year in which the inventory's LIFO layer arose. The historic rate for all other inventory of such a taxpayer is the yearly average exchange rate for the taxable year for which the determination of the historic rate for such inventory is relevant.

(C) *Inventory under the historic inventory method.*—In the case of inventory with respect to which a taxpayer has elected under § 1.987-3(c)(2)(iv)(B) to use the historic inventory method, each inventoriable cost with respect to such inventory may have a different historic rate. The historic rate for each inventoriable cost is the exchange rate at which such item would be translated under § 1.987-3 if it were not an inventoriable cost.

(D) *Liabilities generally.*—In the case of a liability that is incurred or assumed by a section 987 QBU, the historic rate is the yearly average exchange rate applicable to the year the liability is incurred or assumed.

(E) [Reserved]. For further guidance, see § 1.987-1T(c)(3)(i)(E).

(ii) *Historic rate when an election to use spot rates in lieu of yearly average exchange rates is in effect.*—A taxpayer that has elected under paragraph (c)(1)(iii) of this section to use spot rates in lieu of yearly average exchange rates must determine historic rates under paragraphs (c)(3)(i)(A) and (c)(3)(i)(D) of this section using the spot rate (as defined in paragraph (c)(1) of this section) for the date an asset is acquired by a section 987 QBU or a liability is assumed or incurred by a section 987 QBU in lieu of using the yearly average exchange rate.

(iii) *Date placed in service for depreciable or amortizable property.*—In the case of depreciable or amortizable property, an owner may determine the historic rate (whether a yearly average exchange rate or a spot rate, as applicable) by reference to the date such property is placed in service by the section 987 QBU rather than the date the property was acquired, provided that this convention is consistently applied for all such property attributable to that section 987 QBU.

(iv) *Changed functional currency.*—In the case of a section 987 QBU or an owner of a section 987 QBU that previously changed its functional currency, § 1.985-5(d)(1)(ii)(A) and § 1.985-5(e)(4)(i)(A), respectively, shall be taken into account in determining the historic rate for an item reflected on the balance sheet of the section 987 QBU immediately prior to the year of change.

(d) *Marked item.*—A marked item is an asset (marked asset) or liability (marked liability) that is properly reflected on the books and records of a section 987 QBU under § 1.987-2(b) and that—

(1) Is denominated in, or determined by reference to, the functional currency of the section 987 QBU, is not a section 988 transaction of the section 987 QBU, and would be a section 988 transaction if such item were held or entered into directly by the owner of the section 987 QBU;

(2) Is a prepaid expense or a liability for an advance payment of unearned income, in either case having an original term of one year or less on the date the prepaid expense or liability for an advance payment of unearned income arises; or

(3) [Reserved]. For further guidance, see § 1.987-1T(d)(3).

(e) *Historic item.*—A historic item is an asset (historic asset) or liability (historic liability) that is properly reflected on the books and records of a section 987 QBU under § 1.987-2(b) and that is not a marked item (as defined in paragraph (d) of this section).

(f) [Reserved]. For further guidance, see §1.987-1T(f).

(g) *Elections.*—(1) *In general.*—This paragraph (g) provides rules for making elections under section 987. Except as otherwise provided in paragraph (g)(2) of this section, such elections—

(i) May be made separately for each section 987 QBU;

(ii) Are made by the owner of the section 987 QBU (as defined in paragraph (b)(4) of this section); and

(iii) Must be made for the first taxable year in which the election is relevant in determining the section 987 taxable income or loss, or section 987 gain or loss, of the section 987 QBU and in which the regulations implementing the election are applicable with respect to the section 987 QBU.

(2) *Exceptions to the general rules.*—(i) *Consistency and timeliness requirements for certain elections.*—Notwithstanding paragraph (g)(1)(i) of this section, the following consistency and timeliness requirements apply:

(A) *Section 987 grouping election.*—Elections made pursuant to paragraph (b)(2)(ii) of this section (regarding the grouping of section 987 QBUs) are binding on all section 987 QBUs that are eligible to be grouped under the particular election (for example, election to group all euro QBUs owned by the same aggregate partnership), regardless of whether the section 987 QBU is established or acquired after the election is made and regardless of whether the section 987 QBU is identified on the election as required in paragraph (g)(3)(i)(A) of this section.

(B) through (C) [Reserved]. For further guidance, see §1.987-1T(g)(2)(i)(B) through (C).

(ii) *Persons making elections for QBUs owned by foreign corporations.*—Notwithstanding paragraph (g)(1)(ii) of this section, if a section 987 QBU is owned by a foreign corporation, elections shall be made in accordance with §1.964-1(c) by the foreign corporation's controlling domestic shareholders, as defined under §1.964-1(c)(5)(i) (dealing with controlled foreign corporations) and §1.964-1(c)(5)(ii) (dealing with noncontrolled section 902 corporations).

(3) *Manner of making elections.*—(i) *Election made by attaching statement to a return.*—Except as provided in paragraph (g)(3)(ii) of this section, elections shall be made under section 987 for each section 987 QBU by attaching a statement with the information required in this paragraph (g)(3)(i) to the timely filed tax return of the owner or, in the case of a foreign corporation, other applicable person for the first taxable year in which the election is required to be made under paragraph (g)(1)(iii) of this section.

(A) *Section 987 grouping election.*—The election provided in paragraph (b)(2)(ii) of this section must be titled "Section 987 Grouping Election Under §1.987-1(b)(2)(ii)" and provide the following information:

(1) The name, address, and functional currency of each section 987 QBU that the taxpayer is grouping together; and

(2) The owner's name and address.

(B) *Election to use a spot rate convention.*—An election under paragraph (c)(1)(ii) of this section to use a spot rate convention must be titled "Section 987 Election to Use a Spot Rate Convention Under §1.987-1(c)(1)(ii)" and provide the following information:

(1) A description of the convention; and

(2) The name and address of each section 987 QBU for which the election is being made.

(C) *Election to use spot rates in lieu of yearly average exchange rates.*—An election under paragraph (c)(1)(iii) of this section to use spot rates in lieu of yearly average exchange rates must be titled "Section 987 Election to Use Spot Rates in Lieu of Yearly Average Exchange Rates Under §1.987-1(c)(1)(iii)" and provide the following information:

(1) A description of the convention; and

(2) The name and address of each section 987 QBU for which the election is being made.

(D) *Election to use the historic inventory method.*—An election under §1.987-3(c)(2)(iv)(B) to use the historic inventory method shall be titled "Section 987 Election to Use the Historic Inventory Method Under §1.987-3(c)(2)(iv)(B)" and must provide the name and address of each section 987 QBU for which the election is being made.

(E) through (H) [Reserved]. For further guidance, see §1.987-1T(g)(3)(i)(E) through (H).

(ii) *Election made by filing a dedicated section 987 form.*—If the Commissioner publishes a form that provides the manner in which elections are made under section 987, the form shall govern the manner in which elections are made under section 987.

(4) *No change in method of accounting.*—An election under section 987 is not governed by the general rules concerning changes in methods of accounting. See also paragraph (g)(5) of this section.

(5) *Revocation of an election.*—Elections under section 987 may not be revoked without the consent of the Commissioner or his delegate. The Commissioner or his delegate will consider allowing a revocation of an election if the taxpayer can demonstrate significantly changed circumstances or such other circumstances that clearly demonstrate a substantial non-tax business reason for revoking the election. [Reg. §1.987-1.]

☐ *[T.D. 9794, 12-7-2016. Amended by T.D. 9795, 12-7-2016.]*

»»→ Caution: Temporary Reg. §1.987-1T, below, expired on December 6, 2019. The related proposed regulation, published in REG-128276-12 by cross-reference to the temporary regulation, may be relied upon for periods following the expiration date (see Notice 2022-34, I.R.B. 2022-34, 150).

§1.987-1T. Scope, definitions, and special rules (temporary).—(a) through (b)(1)(ii) [Reserved]. For further guidance, see §1.987-1(a) through (b)(1)(ii).

(iii) *Certain provisions applicable to all taxpayers.*—Notwithstanding §1.987-1(b)(1)(ii), paragraphs (b)(6) and (g)(3)(i)(E) of this section and §1.987-6T(b)(4) apply to any taxpayer that is an owner of a dollar QBU (as defined in paragraph (b)(6) of this section), and paragraphs (g)(2)(i)(B) and (g)(3)(i)(H) of this section and §§1.987-8T(d) and 1.987-12T apply to any taxpayer that is an owner of an eligible QBU (determined without regard to §1.987-1(b)(3)(ii)) that is subject to section 987.

(b)(2) through (b)(5) [Reserved]. For further guidance, see §1.987-1(b)(2) through (b)(5).

(6) *Dollar QBUs.*—(i) *In general.*—Except as provided in paragraphs (b)(1)(iii) and (b)(6)(iii) of this section, section 987 and the regulations thereunder do not apply with respect to an eligible QBU (determined without regard to §1.987-1(b)(3)(ii)) that has the U.S. dollar as its functional currency and that would be subject to section 987 if it had a functional currency other than the dollar (dollar QBU). This paragraph (b)(6) applies to all taxpayers, including entities described in §1.987-1(b)(1)(ii).

(ii) *Application of section 988 to a dollar QBU.*—(A) *In general.*—Except as provided in paragraphs (b)(6)(ii)(B) and (b)(6)(iii) of this section, a controlled foreign corporation (as defined in section 957(a)) (CFC) that is the owner of a dollar QBU applies section 988 with respect to any item that is properly reflected on the books and records of the dollar QBU and that would give rise to a section 988 transaction if such item were acquired, accrued, or entered into directly by the owner of the dollar QBU. Except as provided in paragraph (b)(6)(ii)(B) of this section, for purposes of determining the amount of section 988 gain or loss of the CFC, any item that is properly reflected on the books and records of the dollar QBU and that would give rise to a section 988 transaction if such item were acquired, accrued, or entered into directly by the owner of the dollar QBU is treated as properly reflected on the books and records of the owner of the dollar QBU, such that the amount of section 988 gain or loss with respect to such item is determined by reference to the owner's functional currency.

(B) *Section 988 gain or loss characterized as effectively connected income.*—Solely for the purpose of determining the amount of section 988 gain or loss of a CFC described in paragraph (b)(6)(ii)(A) of this section that is effectively connected with the conduct of a trade or business within the United States (ECI), any section 988 gain or loss that would be determined under section 988 as a result of the acquisition or accrual of any item and treated as ECI under §1.988-4(c) if the item were treated as properly reflected on the books and records of the dollar QBU is determined by treating such item as properly reflected on the books and records of the dollar QBU. Consequently, solely for that purpose, such section 988 gain or loss is determined by reference to the U.S. dollar.

(iii) *Election for a CFC to apply section 987 to a dollar QBU.*—(A) *In general.*—A CFC that is the owner of a dollar QBU may elect to apply section 987 and the regulations thereunder with respect to the dollar QBU in lieu of applying section 988 pursuant to paragraph (b)(6)(ii) of this section. If the dollar QBU or CFC is described in § 1.987-1(b)(1)(ii), however, the CFC must apply section 987 to the dollar QBU using the method it applied to the dollar QBU immediately prior to the effective date of this paragraph (b)(6) as provided in paragraph (h) of this section, provided such method was a reasonable interpretation of section 987, or, if no such method exists, a reasonable method.

(B) *Section 988 gain or loss characterized as effectively connected income.*—Solely for the purpose of determining the amount of section 988 gain or loss of a dollar QBU that is the subject of an election described in paragraph (b)(6)(iii)(A) of this section that is ECI, § 1.987-3T(b)(4)(i) and (ii) do not apply, and any section 988 gain or loss that would be determined under section 988 as a result of the acquisition or accrual of any item and treated as ECI under § 1.988-4(c) if the item were treated as properly reflected on the books and records of the dollar QBU is determined by treating such item as properly reflected on the books and records of the dollar QBU. Consequently, solely for that purpose, such section 988 gain or loss is determined by reference to the U.S. dollar. See § 1.987-6T(b)(4) for rules regarding the source of section 987 gain or loss with respect to a dollar QBU for which the CFC owner has made the election described in this paragraph.

(b)(7) through (c)(1)(ii)(A) [Reserved]. For further guidance, see § 1.987-1(b)(7) through (c)(1)(ii)(A).

(B) *Election inapplicable with respect to certain amounts.*—Except as provided in this paragraph (c)(1)(ii)(B), the election provided in § 1.987-1(c)(1)(ii)(A) does not apply for purposes of determining section 987 taxable income or loss (as defined in § 1.987-3(a)) with respect to a historic item (as defined in § 1.987-1(e)) if acquiring, accruing, or entering into such item gives rise to a section 988 transaction or specified owner functional currency transaction. However, the election provided in § 1.987-1(c)(1)(ii)(A) does apply for purposes of determining section 987 taxable income or loss with respect to a payable or receivable described in § 1.988-1(d)(3) under the circumstances described in § 1.988-1(d)(3).

(c)(2) through (c)(3)(i)(D) [Reserved]. For further guidance, see § 1.987-1(c)(2) through (c)(3)(i)(D).

(E) *Section 988 transactions and specified owner functional currency transactions.*—If acquiring, accruing, or entering into a historic item gives rise to a section 988 transaction of a section 987 QBU or a specified owner functional currency transaction described in § 1.987-3T(b)(4)(ii), the historic rate is the spot rate (as defined in paragraph (c)(1) of this section) on the date such item is acquired, accrued, or entered into. For this purpose, use of a spot rate convention under § 1.987-1(c)(1)(ii) is permitted only with respect to a payable or receivable described in § 1.988-1(d)(3) and only to the extent provided therein.

(c)(3)(ii) through (d)(2) [Reserved]. For further guidance, see § 1.987-1(c)(3)(ii) through (d)(2).

(3) Gives rise to a qualified short-term section 988 transaction (as defined in § 1.987-3T(b)(4)(iii)(B)) of the section 987 QBU, whether denominated in the functional currency of the owner or other nonfunctional currency with respect to the section 987 QBU, for which section 988 gain or loss is determined under § 1.987-3T(b)(4)(iii)(A) in, and by reference to, the functional currency of the section 987 QBU.

(e) [Reserved]. For further guidance, see § 1.987-1(e).

(f) *Examples.*—The following examples illustrate the application of § 1.987-1(d) and (e).

Example 1. U.S. Corp is a domestic corporation with the U.S. dollar as its functional currency and is the owner of Business A, a section 987 QBU that has the pound as its functional currency. Assume all transactions of Business A are entered into in the ordinary course of its business. U.S. Corp has not made an election under § 1.987-3T(b)(4)(iii)(C) to adopt a foreign currency mark-to-market method of accounting for qualified short-term section 988 transactions. Items reflected on Business A's balance sheet include £10,000, $1,000, a building with a basis of £100,000, a light general purpose truck with a basis of £30,000, a computer with a basis of £1,000, a 60-day receivable for ¥15,000, an account payable of £5,000, and a foreign currency contract within the meaning of section 1256(g)(2) that requires Business A to exchange £100 for $125 in 90 days. Under paragraph (d) of this section, the £10,000, the £5,000 account payable and the £/$ section 1256 foreign currency contract are marked items. The other items are historic items under this paragraph (e) of this section.

Example 2. The facts are the same as *Example 1* except that U.S. Corp has elected under § 1.987-3T(b)(4)(iii)(C) to adopt the foreign currency mark-to-market method of accounting for qualified short-term section 988 transactions of Business A. Under paragraphs (d) and (e) of this section, the £10,000, the $1,000, the ¥15,000 receivable, the £5,000 account payable, and the £/$ section 1256 foreign currency contract are marked items.

(g)(1) through (g)(2)(i)(A) [Reserved]. For further guidance, see § 1.987-1(g)(1) through (g)(2)(i)(A).

(B) *Annual deemed termination election.*—(*1*) *In general.*—Except as provided in paragraph (g)(2)(i)(B)(*2*) of this section, an election under § 1.987-8T(d) (annual deemed termination election) applies to all section 987 QBUs owned by the taxpayer, as well as to all section 987 QBUs owned by any person that has a relationship to the taxpayer described in section 267(b) or section 707(b) (substituting "and the profits interest" for "or the profits interest" in section 707(b)(1)(A) and substituting "and profits interests" for "or profits interests" in section 707(b)(1)(B)) on the last day of the first taxable year for which the election applies (a related person). If a taxpayer makes the election under § 1.987-8T(d), the first taxable year of a related person for which the election applies is the first taxable year that ends with or within a taxable year of the taxpayer for which the taxpayer's election applies. An election under § 1.987-8T(d) may not be revoked.

(*i*) *Fresh start taxpayers.*—A taxpayer to which § 1.987-10 applies that is required under § 1.987-10(a) to apply the fresh start transition method described in § 1.987-10(b) (fresh start taxpayer) may make the election under § 1.987-8T(d) only if the first taxable year for which the election would apply to the taxpayer is either the first taxable year beginning on or after the transition date (as defined in § 1.987-11(c)) in which the election is relevant or a subsequent taxable year in which the taxpayer's controlled group aggregate section 987 loss, if any, does not exceed $5 million. For purposes of this paragraph (g)(2)(i)(B), a taxpayer's controlled group aggregate section 987 loss means the aggregate net amount of section 987 loss that would be recognized pursuant to the election by the taxpayer and all other persons to whom the taxpayer's election would apply in the first taxable year of each person for which the election would apply.

(*ii*) *Other taxpayers.*—Other taxpayers, including taxpayers described in § 1.987-1(b)(1)(ii) and taxpayers described in § 1.987-10(c), must follow the election rules provided in paragraph (g)(2)(i)(B)(*1*)(*i*) of this section if any related party is a fresh start taxpayer. If no related party is a fresh start taxpayer, the election under § 1.987-8T(d) may be made only if the first taxable year for which the election would apply to the taxpayer is either the first taxable year beginning on or after December 7, 2016, in which the election is relevant or a subsequent taxable year in which the taxpayer's controlled group aggregate section 987 loss, if any, does not exceed $5 million.

(*2*) *QBU-by-QBU elections in certain circumstances.*—Notwithstanding paragraph (g)(2)(i)(B)(*1*) of this section, a taxpayer may make a separate election under § 1.987-8T(d) with respect to any section 987 QBU owned by the taxpayer if the first taxable year for which the election would apply to the taxpayer with respect to the section 987 QBU is a taxable year in which there is a section 987 gain recognized with respect to the section 987 QBU pursuant to the election, or is a taxable year in which there is a section 987 loss of $1 million or less that would be recognized with respect to the section 987 QBU pursuant to the election

(C) *Election to translate all items at the yearly average exchange rate.*—An election under § 1.987-3T(d) (election to translate all items at the yearly average exchange rate) may be made with respect to a section 987 QBU only if the first taxable year for which the election would apply is the first taxable year for which an election under § 1.987-8T(d) (annual deemed termination election) applies with respect to the section 987 QBU.

(g)(2)(ii) through (g)(3)(i)(D) [Reserved]. For further guidance, see § 1.987-1(g)(2)(ii) through (g)(3)(i)(D).

(E) *Election for a CFC to apply section 987 to a dollar QBU.*—An election under § 1.987-1T(b)(6)(iii) for a CFC to apply section 987 to a dollar QBU must be titled "Section 987 Election for a CFC to Apply

Section 987 to a Dollar QBU Under §1.987-1T(b)(6)(iii)" and must provide the name and address of each QBU for which the election is being made.

(F) *Election to apply the foreign currency mark-to-market method of accounting for qualified short term section 988 transactions.*—An election under §1.987-3T(b)(4)(iii)(C) to apply the foreign currency mark-to-market method of accounting for qualified short-term section 988 transactions must be titled "Section 987 Election to Use Foreign Currency Mark-to-Market Method of Accounting for Qualified Short-Term Section 988 Transactions Under §1.987-3(b)T(4)(iii)(C)" and must provide the name and address of each section 987 QBU for which the election is being made.

(G) *Election to translate all items at the yearly average exchange rate.*—An election under §1.987-3T(d) to translate all items at the yearly average exchange rate must be titled "Section 987 Election to Translate All Items at the Yearly Average Exchange Rate Under §1.987-3T(d)" and must provide the name and address of each section 987 QBU for which the election is being made.

(H) *Annual deemed termination election.*—An election under §1.987-8T(d) for an owner to deem all of its section 987 QBUs to terminate on the last day of each taxable year must be titled "Section 987 Annual Deemed Termination Election Under §1.987-8T(d)" and must provide the name and address of each section 987 QBU to which the election applies, including a section 987 QBU owned by a related person (within the meaning of paragraph (g)(2)(i)(B)(*1*) of this section).

(g)(4) through (6) [Reserved]. For further guidance, see §1.987-1(g)(4) through (6).

(h) *Effective/applicability date.*—Paragraphs (g)(2)(i)(B) and (g)(3)(i)(H) of this section apply to the first taxable year beginning on or after December 7, 2016. Paragraphs (b)(1)(iii), (b)(6), (c)(1)(ii)(B), (c)(3)(i)(E), (d)(3), (f), (g)(2)(i)(C), and (g)(3)(i)(E) through (G) of this section apply to taxable years beginning one year after the first day of the first taxable year following December 7, 2016. Notwithstanding the preceding sentence, if a taxpayer makes an election under §1.987-11(b), then paragraphs (b)(1)(iii), (b)(6), (c)(1)(ii)(B), (c)(3)(i)(E), (d)(3), (f), (g)(2)(i)(C), and (g)(3)(i)(E) through (G) of this section apply to taxable years to which §§1.987-1 through 1.987-10 apply as a result of such election.

(i) *Expiration date.*—The applicability of this section expires on December 6, 2019. [Temporary Reg. §1.987-1T.]

□ [*T.D. 9795, 12-7-2016.*]

»»→ Caution: The Treasury Department has identified Reg. §1.987-2, as amended by T.D. 9794, as a significant tax regulation that imposes an undue financial burden on U.S. taxpayers and/or adds undue complexity to the federal tax laws, pursuant to Executive Order 13789 (issued April 21, 2017) (Notice 2017-38, I.R.B. 2017-30, 147). In a subsequent report, published October 16, 2017, Treasury recommended planned actions that would reduce the burden of these regulations, including an extension of the application date of T.D. 9794 (see Notice 2022-34, I.R.B. 2022-34, 150).

§1.987-2. Attribution of items to eligible QBUs; definition of a transfer and related rules.—Attribution of items to eligible QBUs; definition of a transfer and related rules.—(a) *Scope and general principles.*—Paragraph (b) of this section provides rules for attributing assets and liabilities, and items of income, gain, deduction, and loss, to an eligible QBU. Assets and liabilities are attributed to a section 987 QBU for purposes of section 987. Items of income, gain, deduction, and loss are attributed to a section 987 QBU for purposes of computing the section 987 taxable income of the section 987 QBU and of its owner. Paragraph (c) of this section defines a transfer to or from a section 987 QBU. Paragraph (d) of this section provides translation rules for transfers to a section 987 QBU.

(b) *Attribution of items to an eligible QBU.*—(1) *General rules.*—Except as provided in paragraphs (b)(2) and (3) of this section, items are attributable to an eligible QBU to the extent they are reflected on the separate set of books and records, as defined in §1.989(a)-1(d), of the eligible QBU. In the case of a section 987 aggregate partnership, items reflected on the books and records of the partnership and deemed allocated to an eligible QBU of such partnership are considered to be reflected on the books and records of such eligible QBU. For purposes of this section, the term "item" refers to any asset or liability, and any item of income, gain, deduction, or loss. Items that are attributed to an eligible QBU pursuant to this section must be adjusted to conform to Federal income tax principles. Except as provided in §1.989(a)-1(d)(3), these attribution rules apply solely for purposes of section 987. For example, the allocation and apportionment of interest expense under section 864(e) is independent of the rules under section 987.

(2) *Exceptions for non-portfolio stock, interests in partnerships, and certain acquisition indebtedness.*—The following items shall not be considered to be on the books and records of an eligible QBU:

(i) Stock of a corporation (whether domestic or foreign), other than stock of a corporation reflected on the books and records (within the meaning of paragraph (b)(1) of this section) of an eligible QBU if the owner of the eligible QBU owns less than 10 percent of the total value of all classes of stock of such corporation. For this purpose, section 318(a) applies in determining ownership, except that in applying section 318(a)(2)(C), the phrase "10 percent" is used instead of the phrase "50 percent."

(ii) An interest in a partnership (whether domestic or foreign).

(iii) A liability that was incurred to acquire stock described in paragraph (b)(2)(i) of this section or that was incurred to acquire a partnership interest described in paragraph (b)(2)(ii) of this section.

(iv) Income, gain, deduction, or loss arising from the items described in paragraphs (b)(2)(i) through (iii) of this section. For example, a section 951 inclusion with respect to stock of a foreign corporation described in paragraph (b)(2)(i) of this section shall not be considered to be on the books and records of an eligible QBU.

(3) *Adjustments to items reflected on the books and records.*—(i) *General rule.*—If a principal purpose of recording (or failing to record) an item on the books and records of an eligible QBU is the avoidance of Federal income tax under, or through the use of, section 987, the item must be allocated between or among the eligible QBU, the owner of such eligible QBU, and any other persons, entities (including DEs), or other QBUs within the meaning of §1.989(a)-1(b) (including eligible QBUs) in a manner that reflects the substance of the transaction. For purposes of this paragraph (b)(3)(i), relevant factors for determining whether such Federal income tax avoidance is a principal purpose of recording (or failing to record) an item on the books and records of an eligible QBU shall include, but are not limited to, the factors set forth in paragraphs (b)(3)(ii) and (iii) of this section. The presence or absence of any factor or factors is not determinative. Moreover, the weight given to any factor (whether or not set forth in paragraphs (b)(3)(ii) and (iii) of this section) depends on the particular case.

(ii) *Factors indicating no tax avoidance.*—For purposes of paragraph (b)(3)(i) of this section, factors that may indicate that recording (or failing to record) an item on the books and records of an eligible QBU did not have as a principal purpose the avoidance of Federal income tax under, or through the use of, section 987 include the recording (or not recording) of an item:

(A) For a significant and bona fide business purpose;

(B) In a manner that is consistent with the economics of the underlying transaction;

(C) In accordance with generally accepted accounting principles (or similar comprehensive accounting standard);

(D) In a manner that is consistent with the treatment of similar items from year to year;

(E) In accordance with accepted conditions or practices in the particular trade or business of the eligible QBU;

(F) In a manner that is consistent with an explanation of existing internal accounting policies that is evidenced by documentation contemporaneous with the timely filing of a Federal income tax return for the taxable year; and

(G) As a result of a transaction between legal entities (for example, the transfer of an asset or the assumption of a liability), even if such transaction is not regarded for Federal income tax purposes (for example, a transaction between a DE and its owner).

(iii) *Factors indicating tax avoidance.*—For purposes of paragraph (b)(3)(i) of this section, factors that may indicate that a principal purpose of recording (or failing to record) an item on the books and records of an eligible QBU is the avoidance of Federal income tax under, or through the use of, section 987 include:

(A) The presence or absence of an item on the books and records that is the result of one or more transactions that are transitory, for example, due to a circular flow of cash or other property;

(B) The presence or absence of an item on the books and records that is the result of one or more transactions that do not have substance;

(C) The presence or absence of an item on the books and records that results in the taxpayer (or a person related to the taxpayer within the meaning of section 267(b) or section 707(b)) having offsetting positions with respect to the functional currency of a section 987 QBU; and

(D) The absence of any or all of the factors listed in paragraph (b)(3)(ii) of this section.

(4) *Assets and liabilities of a section 987 aggregate partnership or DE that are not attributed to an eligible QBU.*—Neither a section 987 aggregate partnership nor a DE is an eligible QBU and, thus, neither entity can be a section 987 QBU. See § 1.987-1(b)(2) and (3). As a result, a section 987 aggregate partnership or DE may own assets and liabilities that are not attributed to an eligible QBU as provided under this paragraph (b) and, therefore, are not subject to section 987. For the foreign currency treatment of such assets or liabilities, see § 1.988-1(a)(4).

(c) *Transfers to and from section 987 QBUs.*—(1) *In general.*—The following rules apply for purposes of determining whether there is a transfer of an asset or a liability from an owner to a section 987 QBU, or from a section 987 QBU to an owner. These rules apply solely for purposes of section 987.

(2) *Disregarded transactions.*—(i) *General rule.*—An asset or liability shall be treated as transferred to a section 987 QBU from its owner (whether direct owner or indirect owner, as defined in § 1.987-1(b)(4)) if, as a result of a disregarded transaction (as defined in paragraph (c)(2)(ii) of this section), such asset or liability is reflected on the books and records of the section 987 QBU within the meaning of paragraph (b) of this section. Similarly, an asset or liability shall be treated as transferred from a section 987 QBU to its owner if, as a result of a disregarded transaction, such asset or liability is no longer reflected on the books and records of the section 987 QBU within the meaning of paragraph (b) of this section.

(ii) *Definition of a disregarded transaction.*—For purposes of this section, a disregarded transaction means a transaction that is not regarded for Federal income tax purposes (for example, any transaction between separate section 987 QBUs of the same owner). For purposes of this paragraph (c), a disregarded transaction shall be treated as including the recording of an asset or liability on the books and records of an eligible QBU (as defined in § 1.987-1(b)(3)) of an owner, if the recording is the result of such asset or liability being removed from the books and records of a separate eligible QBU of the same owner, whether such separate eligible QBU is owned directly or is owned indirectly through the same entity (including through a DE or a section 987 aggregate partnership). Additionally, if an asset or liability that is attributable to a section 987 QBU within the meaning of paragraph (b) of this section is sold or exchanged (including in a nonrecognition transaction, such as an exchange under section 351) for an asset or liability that is not attributable to the section 987 QBU immediately after the sale or exchange, the sold or exchanged asset or liability that was attributable to the section 987 QBU immediately before the transaction shall be treated as transferred from the section 987 QBU to its direct or indirect owner in a disregarded transaction immediately before the sale or exchange for purposes of section 987 (including for purposes of recognizing section 987 gain or loss under § 1.987-5) and subsequently sold or exchanged by the owner. The preceding sentence shall not apply with respect to an acquisition or disposition of an interest in a section 987 aggregate partnership or in a DE, as described in paragraph (c)(5) of this section.

(iii) *Items derived from disregarded transactions ignored.*—For purposes of section 987, disregarded transactions shall not give rise to items of income, gain, deduction, or loss that are taken into account in determining section 987 taxable income or loss under § 1.987-3.

(3) *Transfers of assets to and from section 987 QBUs owned through section 987 aggregate partnerships.*—(i) *Contributions to section 987 aggregate partnerships.*—Solely for purposes of section 987, an asset shall be treated as transferred by an indirect owner (as defined in § 1.987-1(b)(4)(ii)) to a section 987 QBU of a partner (as defined in § 1.987-1(b)(5)(ii)) to the extent the indirect owner contributes the asset to the section 987 aggregate partnership that carries on the activities of the section 987 QBU, provided that, immediately prior to the contribution, the asset is not reflected on the books and records of the section 987 QBU within the meaning of paragraph (b) of this section and the asset is reflected on the books and records of the section 987 QBU immediately following such contribution. For purposes of this paragraph (c)(3)(i), deemed contributions of money described under section 752 shall be disregarded. See paragraph (c)(4)(ii) of this section for rules governing the assumption by a partner of liabilities of a section 987 aggregate partnership.

(ii) *Distributions from section 987 aggregate partnerships.*—Solely for purposes of section 987, an asset shall be treated as transferred from a section 987 QBU of a partner to its indirect owner to the extent the section 987 aggregate partnership that carries on the activities of the section 987 QBU distributes the asset to the indirect owner, provided that, immediately prior to such distribution, the asset is reflected on the books and records of the section 987 QBU within the meaning of paragraph (b) of this section, and the asset is not reflected on the books and records of the section 987 QBU immediately after such distribution. For purposes of this paragraph (c)(3)(ii), deemed distributions of money described under section 752 shall be disregarded. See paragraph (c)(4)(i) of this section for rules governing the assumption by a section 987 aggregate partnership of liabilities of a partner.

(4) *Transfers of liabilities to and from section 987 QBUs owned through section 987 aggregate partnerships.*—(i) *Assumptions of partner liabilities.*—Solely for purposes of section 987, a liability of the owner of a section 987 aggregate partnership shall be treated as transferred to a section 987 QBU of a partner if, and to the extent, the section 987 aggregate partnership assumes such liability, provided that, immediately prior to the transfer, the liability is not reflected on the books and records of the section 987 QBU within the meaning of paragraph (b) of this section, and the liability is reflected on the books and records of the section 987 QBU immediately following the transfer.

(ii) *Assumptions of section 987 aggregate partnership liabilities.*—Solely for purposes of section 987, a liability of a section 987 aggregate partnership shall be treated as transferred from a section 987 QBU of a partner to its indirect owner if, and to the extent, the indirect owner assumes such liability of the section 987 aggregate partnership, provided that, immediately prior to such assumption, the liability is reflected on the books and records of the section 987 QBU within the meaning of paragraph (b) of this section, and the liability is not reflected on the books and records of the section 987 QBU immediately following the transfer.

(5) *Acquisitions and dispositions of interests in DEs and section 987 aggregate partnerships.*—Solely for purposes of section 987, an asset or liability shall be treated as transferred to a section 987 QBU from its owner if, as a result of an acquisition (including by contribution) or disposition of an interest in a section 987 aggregate partnership or DE, such asset or liability is reflected on the books and records of the section 987 QBU. Similarly, an asset or liability shall be treated as transferred from a section 987 QBU to its owner if, as a result of an acquisition or disposition of an interest in a section 987 aggregate partnership or DE, the asset or liability is not reflected on the books and records of the section 987 QBU.

(6) *Changes in form of ownership.*—For purposes of this paragraph (c), mere changes in the form of ownership of an eligible QBU shall not result in a transfer to or from a section 987 QBU. Instead, the determination of whether a transfer has occurred in such case shall be made under paragraph (c)(5) of this section. For example, a transaction that causes a direct owner of an eligible QBU to become an indirect owner of the eligible QBU shall not, except to the extent provided in paragraph (c)(5) of this section, result in a transfer to or from a section 987 QBU. See, for example, Rev. Rul. 99-5 (1999-1 CB 434), Rev. Rul. 99-6 (1999-1 CB 432), § 601.601(d)(2) of this chapter, and section 708 and the applicable regulations.

(7) *Application of general tax law principles.*—General tax law principles, including the circular cash flow, step-transaction, economic substance, and substance-over-form doctrines, apply for purposes of determining whether there is a transfer of an asset or liability under this paragraph (c), including a transfer of an asset or liability pursuant to a disregarded transaction (as defined in paragraph (c)(2)(ii) of this section).

(8) *Interaction with § 1.988-1(a)(10).*—See § 1.988-1(a)(10) for rules regarding the treatment of an intra-taxpayer transfer of a section 988 transaction.

(9) *Certain disregarded transactions not treated as transfers.*—(i) *Combinations of section 987 QBUs.*—The combination of two or more separate section 987 QBUs (combining QBUs) that are directly owned by the same owner, or that are indirectly owned by the same

partner through a single section 987 aggregate partnership, into one section 987 QBU (combined QBU) does not give rise to a transfer of any combining QBU's assets or liabilities to the owner under § 1.987-2(c). In addition, transactions between the combining QBUs occurring in the taxable year of the combination do not result in a transfer of the combining QBUs' assets or liabilities to the owner under § 1.987-2(c). For this purpose, a combination occurs when the assets and liabilities that are properly reflected on the books and records of two or more combining QBUs begin to be properly reflected on the books and records of a combined QBU and the separate existence of the combining QBUs ceases. A combination may result from any transaction or series of transactions in which the combining QBUs become a combined QBU. For rules regarding the determination of net unrecognized section 987 gain or loss of a combined QBU, see § 1.987-4(f)(1).

(ii) *Change in functional currency from a combination.*—If, following a combination of section 987 QBUs described in paragraph (c)(9)(i) of this section, the combined section 987 QBU has a different functional currency than one or more of the combining section 987 QBUs, any such combining section 987 QBU is treated as changing its functional currency and the owner of the combined section 987 QBU must comply with the regulations under section 985 regarding the change in functional currency. See §§ 1.985-1(c)(6) and 1.985-5.

(iii) *Separation of section 987 QBUs.*—The separation of a section 987 QBU (separating QBU) into two or more section 987 QBUs (separated QBUs) that, after the separation, are directly owned by the same owner, or that are indirectly owned by the same partner through a single section 987 aggregate partnership, does not result in a transfer of the separating QBU's assets or liabilities to the owner under § 1.987-2(c). Additionally, transactions that occurred between the separating QBUs in the taxable year of the separation prior to the completion of the separation do not result in transfers for purposes of section 987. For this purpose, a separation occurs when the assets and liabilities that are properly reflected on the books and records of a separating QBU begin to be properly reflected on the books and records of two or more separated QBUs. A separation may result from any transaction or series of transactions in which a separating QBU becomes two or more separated QBUs. A separation may also result when a section 987 QBU that is subject to a grouping election under § 1.987-1(b)(2)(ii) changes its functional currency. For rules regarding the determination of net unrecognized section 987 gain or loss of a separated QBU, see § 1.987-4(f)(2).

(10) *Examples.*—The following examples illustrate the principles of this paragraph (c). For purposes of the examples, X and Y are domestic corporations, have the U.S. dollar as their functional currency, and use the calendar year as their taxable years. Furthermore, except as otherwise provided, Business A and Business B are eligible QBUs that have the euro and the Japanese yen, respectively, as their functional currencies, and DE1 and DE2 are DEs. For purposes of determining whether any of the transfers in these examples result in remittances, see § 1.987-5.

Example 1. Transfer to a directly owned section 987 QBU. (i) *Facts.* X owns all of the interests in DE1. DE1 owns Business A, which is a section 987 QBU of X. X owns €100 that are not reflected on the books and records of Business A. Business A is in need of additional capital and, as a result, X lends the €100 to DE1 for use in Business A in exchange for a note.

(ii) *Analysis.* (A) The loan from X to DE1 is not regarded for Federal income tax purposes (because it is an interbranch transaction) and therefore is a disregarded transaction (as defined in paragraph (c)(2)(ii) of this section). As a result, the DE1 note held by X and the liability of DE1 under the note are not taken into account under this section.

(B) As a result of the disregarded transaction, the €100 is reflected on the books and records of Business A. Therefore, X is treated as transferring €100 to its Business A section 987 QBU for purposes of section 987. This transfer is taken into account in determining the amount of any remittance for the taxable year under § 1.987-5(c). See § 1.988-1(a)(10)(ii) for the application of section 988 to X as a result of the transfer of non-functional currency to its section 987 QBU.

Example 2. Transfer to a directly owned section 987 QBU. (i) *Facts.* X owns Business A and Business B, both of which are section 987 QBUs of X. X owns equipment that is used in Business A and is reflected on the books and records of Business A. Because Business A has excess manufacturing capacity and X intends to expand the manufacturing capacity of Business B, the equipment formerly used in Business A is transferred to Business B for use by Business B. As a result of the transfer, the equipment is removed from the books and records of Business A and is recorded on the books and records of Business B.

(ii) *Analysis.* The transfer of the equipment from the books and records of Business A to the books and records of Business B is not regarded for Federal income tax purposes (because it is an interbranch transaction), and therefore it is a disregarded transaction for purposes of this paragraph (c). Therefore, for purposes of section 987, the Business A section 987 QBU is treated as transferring the equipment to X, and X is subsequently treated as transferring the equipment to the Business B section 987 QBU. These transfers are taken into account in determining the amount of any remittance for the taxable year under § 1.987-5(c).

Example 3. Intracompany sale of property between two section 987 QBUs. (i) *Facts.* X owns all of the interests in DE1 and DE2. DE1 and DE2 own Business A and Business B, respectively, both of which are section 987 QBUs of X. DE1 owns equipment that is used in Business A and is reflected on the books and records of Business A. For business reasons, DE1 sells a portion of the equipment used in Business A to DE2 in exchange for a fair market value amount of Japanese yen. The yen used by DE2 to acquire the equipment was generated by Business B and was reflected on Business B's books and records. Following the sale, the yen and the equipment will be used in Business A and Business B, respectively. As a result of such sale, the equipment is removed from the books and records of Business A and is recorded on the books and records of Business B. Similarly, as a result of the sale, the yen is removed from the books and records of Business B and is recorded on the books and records of Business A.

(ii) *Analysis.* (A) The sale of equipment between DE1 and DE2 is a transaction that is not regarded for Federal income tax purposes (because it is an interbranch transaction). Therefore the transaction is a disregarded transaction for purposes of paragraph (c) of this section. As a result, the sale is not taken into account under this section and, pursuant to paragraph (c)(2)(iii) of this section, the sale does not give rise to an item of income, gain, deduction, or loss for purposes of determining section 987 taxable income or loss under § 1.987-3. However, the yen and equipment exchanged by DE1 and DE2 in connection with the sale must be taken into account as a disregarded transaction under this paragraph (c).

(B) As a result of the disregarded transaction, the equipment ceases to be reflected on the books and records of Business A and becomes reflected on the books and records of Business B. Therefore, the Business A section 987 QBU is treated as transferring the equipment to X, and X is subsequently treated as transferring such equipment to the Business B section 987 QBU.

(C) Additionally, as a result of the disregarded transaction, the yen currency ceases to be reflected on the books and records of Business B and becomes reflected on the books and records of Business A. Therefore, the Business B section 987 QBU is treated as transferring the yen to X, and X is subsequently treated as transferring such yen from X to the Business A section 987 QBU. The transfers among Business A, Business B and X are taken into account in determining the amount of any remittance for the taxable year under § 1.987-5(c).

Example 4. Sale of property by a section 987 QBU to a corporation that is a member of the consolidated group. (i) *Facts.* X owns all of the stock of Y and all of the interests in DE1. DE1 owns Business A. X and Y file a consolidated return. Business A sells property to Y for €100.

(ii) *Analysis.* The sale of property by Business A to Y is not considered a transfer of property to X (and a corresponding transfer from X to Y) under paragraph (c) of this section because the transaction is regarded for Federal income tax purposes. Rather, for purposes of section 987, the transaction is considered to occur between Business A and Y.

Example 5. Transactions of a section 987 QBU owned through an aggregate partnership. (i) *Facts.* (A) X owns all of the stock of Y and a 50 percent interest in the capital and profits of P, a partnership. Y owns the other 50 percent interest in P. P owns 100 percent of the interests in DE1 and DE2. DE1 owns Business A and DE2 owns Business B.

(B) In connection with Business A, DE1 licenses intangible property to both DE2 and X. X enters into the license agreement in a transaction other than in its capacity as a partner of P and, therefore, the license is considered as occurring between P and one who is not a partner within the meaning of section 707(a). X uses the intangible property in its own trade or business in the U.S. DE2 uses the intangible property in Business B. Pursuant to the license agreement, X and DE2 pay a €30 and a €50 royalty, respectively, to DE1.

(ii) *Analysis.* (A) Under § 1.987-1(b)(5)(i), P is a section 987 aggregate partnership because X and Y own all the interests in partnership capital and profits, X and Y are related within the meaning of section 267(b), and the requirements of § 1.987-1(b)(5)(i)(B) are satisfied. X and Y each have a 50 percent allocable share of the assets and liabilities of Business A and Business B, as determined under § 1.987-7. Under § 1.987-1(b)(5)(ii), the assets and liabilities of Business A allocated to X are a section 987 QBU of X, and the assets and liabilities of Business A allocated to Y are a section 987 QBU of Y. Likewise, the assets and liabilities of Business B allocated to X are a section 987 QBU of X, and the assets and liabilities of Business B allocated to Y are a section 987 QBU of Y.

(B) The license from DE1 to DE2 is not regarded for Federal income tax purposes (because it is an interbranch agreement) and, as a result, royalty payments under the license are disregarded transactions. Thus, pursuant to paragraph (c)(2)(iii) of this section, DE1's receipt of the royalty pursuant to the license agreement does not give rise to an item of income, gain, deduction, or loss for purposes of determining section 987 taxable income or loss under § 1.987-3. However, the €50 that is paid from DE2 to DE1 pursuant to the license agreement must be taken into account under paragraph (c) of this section. Accordingly, €50 ceases to be reflected on the books and records of Business B and becomes reflected on the books and records of Business A. As a result, a 50 percent allocable share of the €50 royalty payment (€25) is treated as transferred from each of the Business B section 987 QBUs of X and Y, to X and Y, respectively. And subsequently, X and Y are treated as transferring their respective receipts of €25 to their respective Business A section 987 QBUs. These transfers are taken into account in determining the amount of any remittance to either of X or Y for the taxable year under § 1.987-5(c).

(C) The €30 royalty payment from X to DE1 is regarded for Federal income tax purposes (because it is a payment from a partnership to a separate entity). Accordingly, the royalty payment is not a disregarded transaction for purposes of this paragraph (c) and is therefore not treated as a transfer of an asset from an owner to a section 987 QBU. As a result, the payment is not taken into account in determining the amount of any remittance for the taxable year under § 1.987-5(c). Instead, the payment gives rise to an item of income and deduction that must be taken into account in computing section 987 taxable income or loss of Business A pursuant to § 1.987-3.

Example 6. Acquisition of an interest in a partnership. (i) *Facts.* (A) X owns all of the stock of Z, a domestic corporation with the dollar as its functional currency. X also owns all of the stock of Y and a 50 percent interest in the capital and profits of P, a partnership. Y owns the other 50 percent interest in P. P owns Business A, and P owns no other assets or liabilities other than those of Business A.

(B) Z contributes cash to P in exchange for a 20 percent interest in the capital and profits of P. The cash Z contributes to P is used in Business A and is reflected on Business A's books and records.

(ii) *Analysis.* (A) Under § 1.987-1(b)(5)(i), P is a section 987 aggregate partnership because X and Y own all the interests in partnership capital and profits, X and Y are related within the meaning of section 267(b), and the requirements of § 1.987-1(b)(5)(i)(B) are satisfied. Prior to the contribution to P by Z, X and Y each have a 50 percent allocable share of the assets and liabilities of Business A, as determined under § 1.987-7. Under § 1.987-1(b)(5)(ii), the assets and liabilities of Business A allocated to X are a section 987 QBU of X, and the assets and liabilities of Business A allocated to Y are a section 987 QBU of Y.

(B) Following Z's acquisition of a 20 percent interest in P, P remains a section 987 aggregate partnership because X, Y and Z own all the interests in partnership capital and profits; X, Y, and Z are related within the meaning of section 267(b); and the requirements of § 1.987-1(b)(5)(i)(B) are satisfied. Z acquires a 20 percent allocable share of the assets and liabilities of Business A, as determined under § 1.987-7. Under § 1.987-1(b)(5)(ii), the assets and liabilities of Business A allocated to Z are a section 987 QBU of Z (because Z becomes an indirect owner of Business A and Z and Business A have different functional currencies).

(C) As a result of Z's contribution of cash to Business A, through its contribution to P, each of X, Y, and Z are allocated a share of that Business A asset. Accordingly, under § 1.987-2(c)(5), Z is treated as contributing its allocable share of the cash to its Business A section 987 QBU. In addition, Z is treated as transferring X's and Y's respective allocable shares of the cash to X and Y, and X and Y are subsequently treated as transferring that cash to their respective Business A section 987 QBUs.

(D) In addition, as a result of Z's acquisition of its interest in P and Z's consequent acquisition of a Business A section 987 QBU, Z's allocable portion of the assets and liabilities of Business A (other than the cash) cease being reflected on the books and records of the respective Business A section 987 QBUs of each of X and Y. Those allocable portions of assets and liabilities from the Business A section 987 QBUs of X and Y are treated as if they are transferred from such section 987 QBUs to their respective owners, X and Y. These assets and liabilities are consequently recorded on the books and records of Z's Business A section 987 QBU. Accordingly, X and Y are treated as transferring those assets and liabilities to Z, and Z is treated as contributing those assets and liabilities to its new Business A section 987 QBU.

Example 7. Acquisition of an interest in a partnership. (i) *Facts.* The facts are the same as in *Example 6*, except that the cash that Z contributes to P in exchange for a 20 percent interest in P is not used in Business A and is not reflected on Business A's books and records. Instead, the cash is reflected on P's books and records.

(ii) *Analysis.* (A) Following Z's acquisition of a 20 percent interest in P, P remains a section 987 aggregate partnership because X, Y and Z own all the interests in partnership capital and profits; X, Y, and Z are related within the meaning of section 267(b); and the requirements of § 1.987-1(b)(5)(i)(B) are satisfied. Z acquires a 20 percent allocable share of the assets and liabilities of Business A, as determined under § 1.987-7. Under § 1.987-1(b)(5)(ii), the assets and liabilities of Business A allocated to Z are a section 987 QBU of Z (because Z becomes an indirect owner of Business A and Z and Business A have different functional currencies).

(B) As a result of Z's acquisition of its interest in P and Z's consequent acquisition of a Business A section 987 QBU, Z's allocable portion of the assets and liabilities of Business A cease being reflected on the books and records of the respective Business A section 987 QBUs of each of X and Y. Those allocable portions of assets and liabilities from the Business A section 987 QBUs of X and Y are treated as if they are transferred from such section 987 QBUs to their respective owners, X and Y. These assets and liabilities are consequently recorded on the books and records of Z's Business A section 987 QBU. Accordingly, X and Y are treated as transferring those assets and liabilities to Z, and Z is treated as contributing those assets and liabilities to its new Business A section 987 QBU.

Example 8. Conversion of a DE to a partnership through a sale of an interest. (i) *Facts.* X owns all of the stock of Y and all of the interests in DE1. DE1 owns Business A. Y acquires 50 percent of the DE1 interests from X for cash.

(ii) *Analysis.* (A) DE1 is converted to a partnership when Y purchases the 50 percent interest in DE1. For Federal income tax purposes, Y's purchase of 50 percent of X's interest in DE1 is treated as the direct purchase of 50 percent of the assets of Business A because DE1 is disregarded and Business A is treated as held directly by X. Immediately after the sale of 50 percent of Business A to Y, X and Y are treated as contributing their respective interests in the assets of Business A to a partnership. See Rev. Rul. 99-5 (1999-1 CB 434) (situation 1) and § 601.601(d)(2) of this chapter.

(B) For purposes of this paragraph (c), these deemed transactions are disregarded transactions. Under § 1.987-1(b)(5)(i), the newly formed partnership is a section 987 aggregate partnership because X and Y own all the interests in partnership capital and profits, X and Y are related within the meaning of section 267(b), and the requirements of § 1.987-1(b)(5)(i)(B) are satisfied. Because Y is a partner in a section 987 aggregate partnership that owns Business A and because Y and Business A have different functional currencies, Y's portion of the Business A assets and liabilities constitutes a section 987 QBU of Y.

(C) As a result of the conversion of DE1 to a partnership, Y acquires an allocable share of 50 percent of the assets and liabilities of Business A, as determined under § 1.987-7. Accordingly, 50 percent of the assets and liabilities of Business A cease being reflected on the books and records of X's section 987 QBU. Under § 1.987-2(b)(5), these amounts are treated as if they are transferred from X's section 987 QBU to X, and X is treated as transferring these assets and liabilities to Y. Accordingly, the assets and liabilities of Business A allocated to Y are treated as transferred by Y to Y's newly formed Business A section 987 QBU.

Example 9. Conversion of a DE to a partnership through a contribution. (i) *Facts.* X owns all of the stock of Y and all of the interests in DE1. DE1 owns Business A. Y contributes property (that is not then attributed to a section 987 QBU of Y) to DE1 in exchange for an interest in DE1. The property transferred by Y to DE1 is used in Business A and is reflected on the books and records of Business A.

(ii) *Analysis.* (A) DE1 is converted to a partnership when Y contributes property to DE1 in exchange for a 50 percent interest in DE1. For Federal income tax purposes, Y's contribution is treated as a contribution to a partnership in exchange for an ownership interest in the partnership. X is treated as contributing all of Business A to the partnership in exchange for a partnership interest. See Rev. Rul. 99-5 (situation 2), (1999-1 CB 434) and § 601.601(d)(2) of this chapter.

(B) For purposes of this paragraph (c), these deemed transactions are disregarded transactions. Under § 1.987-1(b)(5)(i), the newly formed partnership is a section 987 aggregate partnership because X and Y own all the interests in partnership capital and profits, X and Y are related within the meaning of section 267(b), and the requirements of § 1.987-1(b)(5)(i)(B) are satisfied. Because Y is a partner in a section 987 aggregate partnership that owns Business A and because Y and Business A have different functional currencies, Y's portion of the Business A assets and liabilities constitutes a section 987 QBU of Y.

(C) As a result of the conversion of DE1 to a partnership, Y acquires an allocable share of 50 percent of the assets and liabilities of Business A, as determined under § 1.987-7. Accordingly, under § 1.987-2(c)(5), Y is treated as contributing its allocable share of its contributed property to its Business A section 987 QBU. In addition, Y is treated as transferring X's allocable share of the contributed property to X, and X is subsequently treated as transferring that property to its Business A section 987 QBUs. In addition, Y's allocable share of the original (pre-conversion) assets and liabilities of Business A cease being reflected on the books and records of X's section 987 QBU. Under § 1.987-2(b)(5), these amounts are treated as if they are transferred from X's section 987 QBU to X, and X is treated as transferring these assets and liabilities to Y. Y is subsequently treated as transferring these assets and liabilities to Y's Business A section 987 QBU.

Example 10. Contribution of assets to a corporation. (i) *Facts.* X owns Business A. X forms Z, a domestic corporation, contributing 50 percent of its Business A assets and liabilities to Z in exchange for all of the stock of Z. X and Z do not file a consolidated tax return.

(ii) *Analysis.* Pursuant to paragraph (b)(2) of this section, the Z stock received in exchange for 50 percent of Business A's assets and liabilities is not reflected on the books and records of, and therefore is not attributable to, Business A for purposes of section 987 immediately after the exchange. As a result, pursuant to paragraph (c)(2)(i) and (ii) of this section, 50 percent of the assets and liabilities of Business A are treated as transferred from Business A to X in a disregarded transaction immediately before the exchange. The result would be the same even if X and Z filed a consolidated return.

Example 11. Circular transfers. (i) *Facts.* X owns Business A. On December 30, 2021, Business A purports to transfer € 100 to X. On January 2, 2022, X purports to transfer € 50 to Business A. On January 4, 2022, X purports to transfer another € 50 to Business A. As of the end of 2021, X has an unrecognized section 987 loss with respect to Business A, such that a remittance, if respected, would result in recognition of a foreign currency loss under section 987.

(ii) *Analysis.* Because the transfer by Business A to X is offset by the transfers from X to Business A that occurred in close temporal proximity, the Internal Revenue Service (IRS) may disregard the purported transfers to and from Business A for purposes of section 987 pursuant to general tax principles under paragraph (c)(7) of this section.

Example 12. Transfers without substance. (i) *Facts.* X owns Business A and Business B. On January 1, 2021, Business A purports to transfer € 100 to X. On January 4, 2021, X purports to transfer € 100 to Business B. The account in which Business B deposited the € 100 is used to pay the operating expenses and other costs of Business A. As of the end of 2021, X has an unrecognized section 987 loss with respect to Business A, such that a remittance, if respected, would result in recognition of a foreign currency loss under section 987.

(ii) *Analysis.* Because Business A continues to have use of the transferred property, the IRS may disregard the € 100 purported transfer from Business A to X for purposes of section 987 pursuant to general tax principles under paragraph (c)(7) of this section.

Example 13. Offsetting positions in section 987 QBUs. (i) *Facts.* X owns Business A and Business B. Each of Business A and Business B has the euro as its functional currency. X has not made a grouping election under § 1.987-1(b)(2)(ii). On January 1, 2021, X borrows € 1,000 from a third party lender, records the liability with respect to the borrowing on the books and records of Business A, and records the borrowed € 1,000 on the books and records of Business B. On December 31, 2022, when Business A has $100 of net unrecognized section 987 loss and Business B has $100 of net unrecognized section 987 gain resulting from the change in exchange rates with respect to the liability and the € 1,000, X terminates the Business A section 987 QBU.

(ii) *Analysis.* Because Business A and Business B have offsetting positions in the euro, the IRS will scrutinize the transaction under paragraph (b)(3) of this section to determine if a principal purpose of recording the euro-denominated liability on the books and records of Business A and the borrowed euros on the books and records of Business B was the avoidance of tax under section 987. If such a principal purpose is present, the IRS may reallocate the items (that is, the euros and the euro-denominated liability) between Business A, Business B, and X, under paragraph (c)(7) of this section to reflect the substance of the transaction.

Example 14. Offsetting positions with respect to a section 987 QBU and a section 988 transaction. (i) *Facts.* X owns all of the interests in DE1, and DE1 owns Business A. On January 1, 2021, X borrows € 1,000 from a third party lender and records the liability with respect to the borrowing on its books and records. X contributes the € 1,000 loan proceeds to DE1 and the € 1,000 are reflected on the books and records of Business A. On December 31, 2022, when Business A has $100 of net unrecognized section 987 loss resulting from the change in exchange rates with respect to the € 1,000 received from the borrowing, and when the euro-denominated borrowing, if repaid, would result in $100 of gain under section 988, X terminates the Business A section 987 QBU.

(ii) *Analysis.* Because X and Business A have offsetting positions in the euro, the IRS will scrutinize the transaction under paragraph (b)(3) of this section to determine whether a principal purpose of recording the borrowed euros on the books and records of Business A, or not recording the corresponding euro-denominated liability on the books and records of Business A, was the avoidance of tax under section 987. If such a principal purpose is present, the Commissioner may reallocate the items (that is, the euros and the euro-denominated liability) between Business A and X under paragraph (c)(7) of this section to reflect the substance of the transaction.

Example 15. Offsetting positions with respect to a section 987 QBU and a section 988 transaction. (i) *Facts.* X owns all of the stock of Y and all of the interests in DE1. DE1 owns Business A. X and Y file a consolidated return. On January 1, 2021, DE1 lends € 1,000 to Y. X records the receivable with respect to the loan on Business A's books and records. On December 31, 2022, when Business A has $100 of net unrecognized section 987 gain resulting from the loan, Y repays the € 1,000 liability. The repayment of the euro-denominated borrowing results in $100 of loss to Y under section 988. X claims a $100 loss on its consolidated return under section 988. Business A does not make any remittances to X in 2022, so the offsetting gain with respect to the loan receivable has not been recognized by X.

(ii) *Analysis.* Y, a related party to X, and Business A have offsetting positions in the euro. The IRS will scrutinize the transaction under paragraph (b)(3) of this section to determine whether a principal purpose of recording the euro-denominated receivable on the books and records of Business A, rather than on the books and records of X, was to avoid tax through the use of section 987. If such a principal purpose is present, the IRS may reallocate the euro-denominated receivable between Business A and X under paragraph (c)(7) of this section to reflect the substance of the transaction. Other provisions may also apply to defer or disallow the loss.

Example 16. Loan by section 987 QBU followed by immediate distribution to owner. (i) *Facts.* X owns all of the interests in DE1. DE1 owns Business A. On January 1, 2021, Business A borrows € 1,000 from a bank. On January 2, 2021, Business A distributes the € 1,000 it received from the bank to X. There are no other transfers between X and Business A during the year. At the end of the year, X has net unrecognized section 987 loss with respect to Business A such that a remittance would result in the recognition of foreign currency loss under section 987.

(ii) *Analysis.* Because the proceeds from the loan to Business A are immediately transferred to X and the distribution from Business A to X could result in the recognition of section 987 loss, the IRS may scrutinize the recording of the loan on the books of Business A and move the loan onto the books of X, resulting in the transfer not being taken into account for purposes of section 987 under paragraph (b)(3) of this section.

Example 17. Payment of interest by section 987 QBU on obligation of owner. (i) *Facts.* X owns all of the interests in DE1. DE1 owns business A. On January 1, X borrows € 1,000 from a bank. On July 1, Business A pays € 20 in interest on X's € 1,000 obligation to the bank.

(ii) *Analysis.* Under general tax law principles as provided in paragraph (c)(7) of this section, on July 1, 2021, Business A is treated for purposes of section 987 as making a transfer of € 20 to X, and X is treated as making a € 20 interest payment to the bank.

(d) *Translation of items transferred to a section 987 QBU.—*(1) *Marked items.—*The adjusted basis of a marked asset, or the amount of a marked liability, transferred to a section 987 QBU shall be translated into the section 987 QBU's functional currency at the spot rate (as defined in § 1.987-1(c)(1)) applicable to the date of transfer. If the asset or liability transferred is denominated in (or determined by reference to) the functional currency of the section 987 QBU (for example, cash or a note denominated in the functional currency of the section 987 QBU), no translation is required. See § 1.988-1(a)(10)(ii) for special rules regarding intra-taxpayer transfers.

(2) *Historic items.*—The adjusted basis of a historic asset, or the amount of a historic liability, transferred to a section 987 QBU shall be translated into the section 987 QBU's functional currency at the rate provided in § 1.987-1(c)(3).

(e) *Effective/applicability date.*—(1) *In general.*—Except as set forth in paragraph (e)(2) of this section, this section is applicable as specified in § 1.987-11.

(2) *Certain disregarded transactions not treated as transfers.*—Paragraph (c)(9) of this section applies to taxable years beginning on or after the day that is three years after the first day of the first taxable year following December 7, 2016. Notwithstanding the preceding sentence, if a taxpayer makes an election under § 1.987-11(b), then paragraph (c)(9) of this section applies to taxable years to which §§ 1.987-1 through 1.987-10 apply as a result of such election. [Reg. § 1.987-2.]

☐ [*T.D. 9794, 12-7-2016. Amended by T.D. 9795, 12-7-2016 and T.D.* 9857, 5-10-2019 (corrected 6-28-2019).]

»»→ Caution: The Treasury Department has identified Reg. §1.987-3, as amended by T.D. 9794, as a significant tax regulation that imposes an undue financial burden on U.S. taxpayers and/or adds undue complexity to the federal tax laws, pursuant to Executive Order 13789 (issued April 21, 2017) (Notice 2017-38, I.R.B. 2017-30, 147). In a subsequent report, published October 16, 2017, Treasury recommended planned actions that would reduce the burden of these regulations, including an extension of the application date of T.D. 9794 (see Notice 2022-34, I.R.B. 2022-34, 150).

§ 1.987-3. Determination of section 987 taxable income or loss of an owner of a section 987 QBU.—(a) *In general.*—This section provides rules for determining the taxable income or loss, or the earnings and profits, of an owner of a section 987 QBU (hereafter, section 987 taxable income or loss). Paragraph (b) of this section provides rules for determining items of income, gain, deduction, and loss, which generally must be determined in the section 987 QBU's functional currency. Paragraph (c) of this section provides rules for translating each item determined under paragraph (b) of this section into the functional currency of the owner of the section 987 QBU, if necessary. Paragraph (e) of this section provides examples illustrating the application of the rules of this section.

(b) *Determination of each item of income, gain, deduction, or loss in the section 987 QBU's functional currency.*—(1) *In general.*—Except as otherwise provided in this section, a section 987 QBU shall determine each item of income, gain, deduction, or loss of such section 987 QBU in its functional currency under Federal income tax principles.

(2) *Translation of items of income, gain, deduction, or loss that are denominated in a nonfunctional currency.*—(i) *In general.*—Except as otherwise provided in paragraphs (b)(2)(ii) and (b)(4) of this section, an item of income, gain, deduction, or loss that is denominated in (or determined by reference to) a nonfunctional currency (including the functional currency of the owner) shall be translated into the section 987 QBU's functional currency at the spot rate (as defined in § 1.987-1(c)(1)) on the date such item is properly taken into account, subject to the limitation under § 1.987-1(c)(1)(ii)(B) regarding the use of a spot rate convention. Examples 1, 2 and 6 of paragraph (e) of this section illustrate the application of this paragraph (b)(2)(i).

(ii) [Reserved]. For further guidance, see § 1.987-3T(b)(2)(ii).

(3) *Determination in the case of a section 987 QBU owned through a section 987 aggregate partnership.*—(i) *In general.*—Except as otherwise provided in this paragraph (b)(3), the taxable income or loss of a section 987 aggregate partnership, and the distributive share of any owner that is a partner in such partnership, shall be determined in accordance with the provisions of subchapter K of the Internal Revenue Code.

(ii) *Determination of each item of income, gain, deduction, or loss in the eligible QBU's functional currency.*—A section 987 aggregate partnership generally shall determine each item of income, gain, deduction, or loss reflected on the books and records of each of its eligible QBUs under § 1.987-2(b) in the functional currency of each such QBU.

(iii) *Allocation of items of income, gain, deduction, or loss of an eligible QBU.*—A section 987 aggregate partnership shall allocate the items of income, gain, deduction, or loss of each eligible QBU among its partners in accordance with each partner's distributive share of such income, gain, deduction, or loss as determined under subchapter K of the Internal Revenue Code.

(iv) *Translation of items into the owner's functional currency.*—To the extent the items referred to in paragraph (b)(3)(iii) of this section are allocated to a partner, the partner shall adjust the items to conform to Federal income tax principles and translate the items into the partner's functional currency as provided in paragraph (c) of this section.

(4) [Reserved]. For further guidance, see § 1.987-3T(b)(4).

(c) *Translation of items of income, gain, deduction, or loss of a section 987 QBU into the owner's functional currency.*—(1) *In general.*—Except as otherwise provided in this section, the exchange rate to be used by an owner in translating an item of income, gain, deduction, or loss attributable to a section 987 QBU into the owner's functional currency, if necessary, shall be the yearly average exchange rate (as defined in § 1.987-1(c)(2)) for the taxable year. However, an owner of a section 987 QBU that has elected under § 1.987-1(c)(1)(iii) to use spot rates in lieu of yearly average exchange rates must use the spot rate (as defined in § 1.987-1(c)(1)) for the date each item is properly taken into account.

(2) *Exceptions.*—(i) *Recovery of basis with respect to historic assets.*—Except as otherwise provided in this section, the exchange rate to be used by the owner in translating any recovery of basis (whether through a sale or exchange; deemed sale or exchange; cost recovery deduction such as depreciation, depletion or amortization; or otherwise) with respect to a historic asset (as defined in § 1.987-1(e)) shall be the historic rate as determined under § 1.987-1(c)(3) for the property to which such recovery of basis is attributable.

(ii) [Reserved]. For further guidance, see § 1.987-3T(c)(2)(ii).

(iii) *Gain or loss on the sale, exchange or other disposition of an interest in a section 987 aggregate partnership.*—[Reserved].

(iv) *Cost of goods sold computation.*—(A) *General rule—simplified inventory method.*—Cost of goods sold (COGS) for a taxable year shall be translated into the functional currency of the owner at the yearly average exchange rate (as defined in § 1.987-1(c)(2)) for the taxable year and adjusted as provided in paragraph (c)(3) of this section.

(B) *Election to use the historic inventory method.*—In lieu of using the simplified inventory method described in paragraph (c)(2)(iv)(A) of this section, the owner of a section 987 QBU may elect under this paragraph (c)(2)(iv)(B) to translate inventoriable costs (including current-year inventoriable costs and costs that were capitalized into inventory in prior years) that are included in COGS at the historic rate as determined under § 1.987-1(c)(3) for each such cost. As described in § 1.987-1(c)(1)(iii), a taxpayer that elects to use spot rates in lieu of yearly average exchange rates as provided in that section will be deemed to have made the election described in this paragraph (c)(2)(iv)(B).

(v) through (d) [Reserved]. For further guidance, see § 1.987-3T(c)(2)(v) through (d).

(e) *Examples.*—The following examples illustrate the application of this section. For purposes of the examples, U.S. Corp is a domestic corporation that uses the calendar year as its taxable year and has the U.S. dollar as its functional currency. Except as otherwise indicated, U.S. Corp is the owner of Business A, a section 987 QBU with the euro as its functional currency, and elects under paragraph (c)(2)(iv)(B) of this section to use the historic inventory method with respect to Business A but does not make any other elections under section 987. However, where it is specified that U.S. Corp elects to use spot rates in lieu of yearly average exchange rates under § 1.987-1(c)(1)(iii), U.S. Corp also elects under § 1.987-1(c)(1)(ii) to use a spot rate convention. Under this convention, sales booked during a particular month are translated at the average of the spot rates on the first and last day of the preceding month (the "convention rate"). Exchange rates used in these examples are selected for the purpose of illustrating the principles of this section. No inference (for example, whether a currency is hyperinflationary or not) is intended by their use. See § 1.987-4(g) for an illustration of the simplified inventory method described in paragraphs (c)(2)(iv)(A) and (c)(3) of this section.

Example 1. Business A properly accrues £100 of income from the provision of services. Under paragraph (b)(2)(i) of this section, the £100 is translated into €90 at the spot rate (as defined in § 1.987-1(c)(1)) on the date of accrual, without the use of a spot rate convention. In determining U.S. Corp's taxable income, the €90 of income is translated into dollars at the rate provided in paragraph (c)(1) of this section.

Example 2. Business A sells a historic asset consisting of non-inventory property for £100. Under paragraph (b)(2)(i) of this section, the £100 amount realized is translated into €85 at the spot rate (as defined in § 1.987-1(c)(1)) on the sale date without the use of a spot rate convention. In determining U.S. Corp's taxable income, the €85 is translated into dollars at the rate provided in paragraph (c)(1) of this section. The euro basis of the property is translated into dollars at the rate provided in paragraph (c)(2)(i) of this section (that is, the historic rate as determined under § 1.987-1(c)(3)).

Example 3. (i) Business A uses a first-in, first-out (FIFO) method of accounting for inventory. Business A sells 1,200 units of inventory in 2021 for €3 per unit. Business A's gross sales are translated under paragraph (c)(1) of this section at the yearly average exchange rate for the year of the sale. The yearly average exchange rate is €1 = $1.02 for 2020 and €1 = $1.05 for 2021. Thus, Business A's dollar gross sales will be computed as follows:

Gross Sales (2021)

Month	# of units	Amount in €	€/$ yearly average rate	Amount in $
Jan	100	€300	€1 = $1.05	$315.00
Feb	200	600	€1 = $1.05	630.00
March	0	0	€1 = $1.05	0
April	200	600	€1 = $1.05	630.00
May	100	300	€1 = $1.05	315.00
June	0	0	€1 = $1.05	0
July	100	300	€1 = $1.05	315.00
Aug	100	300	€1 = $1.05	315.00
Sept	0	0	€1 = $1.05	0
Oct	0	0	€1 = $1.05	0
Nov	100	300	€1 = $1.05	315.00
Dec	300	900	€1 = $1.05	945.00
	1,200			$3,780.00

(ii) The purchase price for each inventory unit was €1.50. Under § 1.987-1(c)(3)(i) and paragraph (c)(2)(iv)(B) of this section, the basis of each item of inventory is translated into dollars at the yearly average exchange rate for the year the inventory was acquired.

Opening Inventory and Purchases (2021)

Month	# of units	Amount in €	€/$ yearly average rate	Amount in $
Opening inventory (purchased in Dec. 2020)				
	100	€150	€1 = $1.02	$153.00
Purchases in 2021				
Jan	300	€450	€1 = $1.05	$472.50
Feb	0	0	€1 = $1.05	0
March	0	0	€1 = $1.05	0
April	300	450	€1 = $1.05	472.50
May	0	0	€1 = $1.05	0
June	0	0	€1 = $1.05	0
July	300	450	€1 = $1.05	472.50
Aug	0	0	€1 = $1.05	0
Sept	0	0	€1 = $1.05	0
Oct	0	0	€1 = $1.05	0
Nov	300	450	€1 = $1.05	472.50
Dec	0	0	€1 = $1.05	0
	1,200			$1,890.00

(iii) Because Business A uses a FIFO method for inventory, Business A is considered to have sold in 2021 the 100 units of opening inventory purchased in 2020 ($153.00), the 300 units purchased in January 2021 ($472.50), the 300 units purchased in April 2021 ($472.50), the 300 units purchased in July 2021 ($472.50), and 200 of the 300 units purchased in November 2021 ($315.00). Accordingly, Business A's translated dollar COGS for 2021 is $1,885.50. Business A's opening inventory for 2022 is 100 units of inventory with a translated dollar basis of $157.50.

(iv) Accordingly, for purposes of section 987 Business A has gross income in dollars of $1,894.50 ($3,780.00 - $1,885.50).

Example 4. (i) The facts are the same as in *Example 3* except that U.S. Corp properly elects under paragraph § 1.987-1(c)(1)(iii) to use spot rates in lieu of yearly average exchange rates. As a result, under paragraph (c)(3) of this section, U.S. Corp uses the convention rate to translate items of income, gain, deduction, or loss where such rate is appropriate. Thus, Business A's dollar gross sales will be computed as follows:

Gross Sales (2021)

Sales	# of units	Amount in €	€/$ convention rate	Amount in $
Jan	100	€300	€1 = $1.00	$300
Feb	200	600	€1 = $1.05	630
March	0	0	€1 = $1.03	0
April	200	600	€1 = $1.02	612
May	100	300	€1 = $1.04	312
June	0	0	€1 = $1.05	0
July	100	300	€1 = $1.06	318
Aug	100	300	€1 = $1.05	315
Sept	0	0	€1 = $1.06	0
Oct	0	0	€1 = $1.07	0
Nov	100	300	€1 = $1.08	324
Dec	300	900	€1 = $1.08	972
	1,200			$3,783

(ii) As in *Example 3*, the purchase price for each inventory unit was €1.50. Under § 1.987-3(c)(2)(iv)(B), U.S. Corp uses the convention rate as the historic rate in determining COGS.

Opening Inventory and Purchases (2021)

Month	# of units	Amount in €	€ /$ convention rate	Amount in $
Opening inventory (purchased in December 2020)				
	100	€ 150	€ 1 = $1.00	$150
Purchases in 2021				
Jan	300	€ 450	€ 1 = $1.00	$450
Feb	0	0	€ 1 = $1.05	0
March	0	0	€ 1 = $1.03	0
April	300	450	€ 1 = $1.02	459
May	0	0	€ 1 = $1.04	0
June	0	0	€ 1 = $1.05	0
July	300	450	€ 1 = $1.06	477
Aug	0	0	€ 1 = $1.05	0
Sept	0	0	€ 1 = $1.06	0
Oct	0	0	€ 1 = $1.07	0
Nov	300	450	€ 1 = $1.08	486
Dec	0	0	€ 1 = $1.08	0
	1,200			$1,872

(iii) As set forth in (i), Business A's gross sales are $3783.

(iv) Because Business A uses a FIFO method for inventory, Business A is considered to have sold in 2021 the 100 units of opening inventory purchased in December 2020 ($150), the 300 units purchased in January 2021 ($450), the 300 units purchased in April 2021 ($459), the 300 units purchased in July 2021 ($477), and 200 of the 300 units purchased in November 2021 ($324). Thus, Business A's COGS is $1,860.

(v) Accordingly, Business A has gross income in dollars of $1,923 ($3,783 - $1,860).

Example 5. The facts are the same as in *Example 3* except that during 2021, Business A incurred € 100 of depreciation expense with respect to a truck. No portion of the depreciation expense is an inventoriable cost. The truck was purchased on January 15, 2020. The yearly average exchange rate for 2020 was € 1 = $1.02. Under paragraph (c)(2)(i) of this section, the € 100 of depreciation is translated into dollars at the historic rate. Under § 1.987-1(c)(3)(i), the historic rate is the yearly average rate for 2020. Accordingly, U.S. Corp takes into account depreciation of $102 with respect to Business A in 2021.

Example 6. The facts are the same as in *Example 5* except that the € 100 of depreciation expense incurred during 2021 with respect to the truck is an inventoriable cost. As a result, the depreciation expense is capitalized into the 1,200 units of inventory purchased by Business A in 2021. Of those 1,200 units, 1,100 units are sold during the year, and 100 units become ending inventory. The portion of depreciation expense capitalized into inventory that is sold during 2021 is reflected in Business A's euro COGS and is translated at the € 1 = $1.02 yearly average exchange rate for 2020, the year in which the truck was purchased. The portion of the depreciation expense capitalized into the 100 units of ending inventory is not taken into account in 2021 but, rather, will be taken into account in the year the ending inventory is sold, translated at the € 1 = $1.02 yearly average exchange rate for 2020.

Example 7. Business A purchased raw land on October 16, 2020, for € 8,000 and sold the land on November 1, 2021, for € 10,000. The yearly average exchange rate was € 1 = $1.02 for 2020 and € 1 = $1.05 for 2021. Under paragraph (c)(1) of this section, the amount realized is translated into dollars at the yearly average exchange rate for 2021 (€ 10,000 x $1.05 = $10,500). Under paragraph (c)(2)(i) of this section, the basis is determined at the historic rate for 2020, which is the yearly average rate under section § 1.987-1(c)(3)(i) for such year (€ 8,000 x $1.02 = $8,160). Accordingly, the amount of gain reported by U.S. Corp on the sale of the land is $2,340 ($10,500 - $8,160).

Example 8. The facts are the same as in *Example 7* except that Business A properly elects under paragraph § 1.987-1(c)(1)(iii) to use spot rates in lieu of yearly average rates. Accordingly, the amount realized will be translated at the convention rate for the date of sale, and the basis will be translated at the convention rate for the date of purchase. The convention rate is € 1 = $1.01 for October 2020 and is € 1 = $1.08 for November 2021. Under these facts, the amount realized, translated into dollars at the convention rate for November 2021, is $10,800 (€ 10,000 x $1.08), and the basis, translated at the convention rate for October 2020, is $8,080 (€ 8,000 x $1.01). The amount of gain reported by U.S. Corp on the sale of the land is $2,720 ($10,800 - $8,080).

Example 9 through *Example 14* [Reserved]. For further guidance, see § 1.987-3T(e), *Example 9* through *Example 14*. [Reg. § 1.987-3.]

☐ [*T.D. 9794, 12-7-2016. Amended by T.D. 9795, 12-7-2016.*]

»»→ Caution: Temporary Reg. §1.987-3T, below, expired on December 6, 2019. The related proposed regulation, published in REG-128276-12 by cross-reference to the temporary regulation, may be relied upon for periods following the expiration date (see Notice 2022-34, I.R.B. 2022-34, 150).

§ 1.987-3T. Determination of section 987 taxable income or loss of an owner of a section 987 QBU (temporary).—(a) through (b)(2)(i) [Reserved]. For further guidance, see § 1.987-3(a) through (b)(2)(i).

(ii) *No translation of basis or amount realized with respect to a specified owner functional currency transaction treated as a historic asset.*—If the acquisition of a historic asset gives rise to a specified owner functional currency transaction described in paragraph (b)(4)(ii) of this section, the basis of the historic asset, and any amount realized on a disposition of the historic asset, is not translated if the amount is denominated in the owner's functional currency.

(3) [Reserved]. For further guidance, see § 1.987-3(b)(3).

(4) *Special rule for section 988 transactions.*—(i) *In general.*—Section 988 and the regulations thereunder apply to section 988 transactions of a section 987 QBU. For this purpose, whether a transaction is a section 988 transaction is determined by reference to the functional currency of the section 987 QBU. (But see paragraph (b)(4)(ii) of this section, providing that specified owner functional currency transactions are not treated as section 988 transactions.) However, except as provided in paragraph (b)(4)(iii)(A) of this section, section 988 gain or loss is determined in, and by reference to, the functional currency of the owner of the section 987 QBU rather than the functional currency of the section 987 QBU. Accordingly, in determining section 988 gain or loss of a section 987 QBU with respect to a section 988 transaction of the section 987 QBU, the amounts required under section 988 and the regulations thereunder to be translated on the applicable booking date or payment date with respect to the section 988 transaction are translated into the owner's functional currency at the rate required under section 988 and the regulations thereunder.

(ii) *Specified owner functional currency transactions not treated as section 988 transactions.*—Transactions of a section 987 QBU described in sections 988(c)(1)(B)(i), 988(c)(1)(B)(ii), and 988(c)(1)(C) (including the acquisition of nonfunctional currency as described in § 1.988-1(a)(1)), other than transactions described in paragraph (b)(4)(iii)(A) of this section, that are denominated in (or determined by reference to) the owner's functional currency (specified owner functional currency transactions) are not treated as section 988 transactions. Thus, no currency gain or loss is recognized by a section 987 QBU under section 988 with respect to such transactions.

(iii) *Determination of section 988 gain or loss for qualified short-term section 988 transactions.*—(A) *Determination by reference to the section 987 QBU's functional currency for certain transactions subject to a mark-to-market method of accounting.*—Section 988 gain or loss with respect to section 988 transactions described in paragraph (b)(4)(iii)(B) of this section that are accounted for under a mark-to-market method of accounting for Federal income tax purposes or under the foreign currency mark-to-market method of accounting described in paragraph (b)(4)(iii)(C) of this section, and any hedges entered into to manage risk with respect to such transactions within the meaning of § 1.1221-2(c)(4) (related hedges), must be determined in, and by reference to, the functional currency of the section 987 QBU (rather than the functional currency of its owner).

(B) *Qualified short-term section 988 transaction.*—A qualified short-term section 988 transaction is a section 988 transaction that occurs in the ordinary course of a section 987 QBU's business and has an original term of one year or less on the date the transaction is entered into by the section 987 QBU. The holding of currency that is nonfunctional currency (within the meaning of section 988(c)(1)(C)(ii)) to the section 987 QBU in the ordinary course of a section 987 QBU's trade or business also is treated as a qualified short-term section 988 transaction. Any transaction that is denominated in, or determined by reference to, a hyperinflationary currency, including the holding of hyperinflationary currency, is not considered a qualified short-term section 988 transaction. See §§1.988-2(b)(15), 1.988-2(d)(5), and 1.988-2(e)(7) for rules relating to transactions denominated in, or determined by reference to, a hyperinflationary currency.

(C) *Election to use a foreign currency mark-to-market method of accounting.*—A taxpayer may elect under this paragraph (b)(4)(iii)(C) to apply the foreign currency mark-to-market method of accounting described in this paragraph for all qualified short-term section 988 transactions described in paragraph (b)(4)(iii)(B) of this section, and any related hedges, that are properly attributable to a section 987 QBU on or after the effective date of the election and that are not otherwise accounted for under a mark-to-market method of accounting under section 475 or section 1256. Under the foreign currency mark-to-market method of accounting, the timing of section 988 gain or loss on section 988 transactions is determined under the principles of section 1256(a)(1). Thus, only section 988 gain or loss is taken into account under the foreign currency mark-to-market method of accounting. Appropriate adjustments must be made to prevent the section 988 gain or loss from being taken into account again under section 988 or another provision of the Code or regulations. A section 988 transaction subject to this election is not subject to the "netting rule" of section 988(b) and §1.988-2(b)(8), under which exchange gain or loss is limited to overall gain or loss realized in a transaction, in taxable years prior to the taxable year in which section 988 gain or loss would be recognized with respect to such section 988 transaction but for this election.

(iv) *Examples.*—Examples 10 through 13 of paragraph (e) of this section illustrate the application of this paragraph (b)(4).

(c)(1) through (c)(2)(i) [Reserved]. For further guidance, see §1.987-3(c)(1) through (c)(2)(i).

(ii) *Amount realized with respect to historic assets that are section 988 transactions.*—If the acquisition of a historic asset gave rise to a section 988 transaction described in paragraph (b)(4)(i) of this section, then in computing the total gain or loss on a disposition of the historic asset (some or all of which total gain or loss may be section 988 gain or loss described in section 988(b) and paragraph (b)(4)(i) of this section), the amount realized (determined, if necessary, under §1.987-3(b)(2)(i)) is translated into the owner's functional currency using the spot rate on the date such item is properly taken into account, subject to the limitation under §1.987-1T(c)(1)(ii)(B) regarding the use of a spot rate convention.

(iii) through (iv) [Reserved]. For further guidance, see §1.987-3(c)(2)(iii) through (iv).

(v) *Translation of income to account for certain foreign income tax claimed as a credit.*—The owner of a section 987 QBU claiming a credit under section 901 for foreign income taxes, other than foreign income taxes deemed paid under section 902 or section 960, that are properly reflected on the books and records of the section 987 QBU (the creditable tax amount) must determine section 987 taxable income or loss attributable to the section 987 QBU by reducing the amount of section 987 taxable income or loss that otherwise would be determined under this section by an amount equal to the creditable tax amount, translated into U.S. dollars using the yearly average exchange rate for the taxable year in which the creditable tax is accrued, and by increasing the resulting amount by an amount equal to the creditable tax amount, translated using the same exchange rate that is used to translate the creditable taxes into U.S. dollars under section 986(a). See *Example 14* of paragraph (e) of this section, for an illustration of this rule.

(d) *Election to translate all items at the yearly average exchange rate.*—Notwithstanding §1.987-3(c), a taxpayer that has made the annual deemed termination election described in §1.987-8T(d) may elect under this paragraph (d) to translate all items of income, gain, deduction, and loss with respect to a section 987 QBU determined under §1.987-3(b) in the functional currency of the section 987 QBU into the owner's functional currency, if necessary, at the yearly average exchange rate for the taxable year. *Example 9* of paragraph (e) of this section illustrates the application of this election.

(e) *Example 1* through *Example 8* [Reserved]. For further guidance, see §1.987-3(e), *Example 1* through *Example 8*.

Example 9. The facts are the same as in *Example 7*, except that U.S. Corp properly elects under paragraph (d) of this section to translate all items of income, gain, deduction, and loss with respect to Business A at the yearly average exchange rate. Accordingly, Business A's €2,000 gain on the sale of the land is translated at the yearly average exchange rate for 2021 of €1 = $1.05, and the amount of gain reported by U.S. Corp on the sale of the land is $2,100.

Example 10. Business A acquires £100 on August 27, 2021, for €120 and sells the pounds on November 17, 2021, for €125. The dollar-pound spot rate (without the use of a spot rate convention) is £1 = $1 on August 27, 2021, and £1 = $1.10 on November 17, 2021. The disposition of the pounds is a section 988 transaction of Business A under paragraph (b)(4)(i) of this section, and the pounds are a historic asset under §1.987-1(e). Section 988 gain or loss with respect to the disposition of the pounds is determined under paragraph (b)(4)(i) of this section and §1.988-2(a)(2) by reference to the dollar functional currency of Business A's owner. The dollar amount realized for the pounds is determined under paragraph (c)(2)(ii) of this section by translating £100 into $110 using the dollar-pound spot rate on November 17, 2021, without the use of a spot rate convention. The dollar basis in the pounds is determined under §1.987-3(c)(2)(i) by translating £100 into $100 using the historic rate described in §1.987-1T(c)(3)(i)(E), which is the dollar-pound spot rate on August 27, 2021, without the use of a spot rate convention. Thus, U.S. Corp takes into account $10 of section 988 gain with respect to Business A's disposition of £100.

Example 11. (i) Business A purchases a £100 2-year note for €75 on October 1, 2021, and receives a £100 repayment of principal with respect to the note on December 31, 2021. At the spot rates on October 1, 2021 (as defined in §1.987-1(c)(1)), without the use of a spot rate convention, Business A's €75 purchase price translates into £80 and $95. At the spot rates on December 31, 2021, without the use of a spot rate convention, the £100 principal amount on the note translates into €90 and $130, and £80 translates into $104.

(ii) The acquisition of the note is a section 988 transaction of Business A under paragraph (b)(4)(i) of this section, and the note is a historic asset under §1.987-1(e). To determine its section 987 taxable income or loss with respect to Business A, U.S. Corp must determine Business A's total gain or loss on the disposition of the note in U.S. Corp's dollar functional currency. Consistent with §1.988-2(b)(8), U.S. Corp also must determine whether some or all of that gain or loss constitutes section 987 gain or loss described in section 988(b).

(iii) To determine Business A's total gain or loss on the disposition of the note, Business A's basis and amount realized on the note must be determined in euros under §1.987-3(b), if necessary, and translated into dollars under §1.987-3(c). Business A has a €75 basis in the note that is translated into $95 under §1.987-3(c)(2)(i) at the historic rate described in §1.987-1T(c)(3)(i)(E), which is the spot rate on the date the note was acquired without the use of a spot rate convention. Business A's £100 amount realized on the note is translated into €90 under §1.987-3(b)(2)(i) using the spot rate on December 31, 2021, without the use of a spot rate convention. That €90 amount realized is then translated into $130 under paragraph (c)(2)(ii) of this section using the spot rate on December 31, 2021, without the use of a spot rate convention. Accordingly, the total gain with respect to the disposition of the note that is included in section 987 taxable income is $35 ($130 less $95).

(iv) U.S. Corp must determine whether some or all of the $35 total gain with respect to the note constitutes section 988 gain. The amount of section 988 gain realized with respect to the note is determined under §1.988-2(b)(5), which requires a comparison of the functional currency value of the principal amount of the note on the booking date and payment date spot rates, respectively, and defines the principal amount of the note as Business A's purchase price in units of nonfunctional currency, which is £80. Under paragraph (b)(4)(i) of this section, section 988 gain or loss with respect to the note is determined by reference to U.S. Corp's dollar functional currency, such that the amounts required under section 988 to be translated on the booking date and payment date are translated into the dollars at the booking date and payment date spot rates. Accordingly, Business A's £80 principal amount with respect to the note is translated at the booking date and payment date spots rates into $95 and $104, respectively. Thus, $9 ($104 less $95) of the $35 total gain taken into account by U.S. Corp as section 987 taxable income with respect to the note is section 988 gain. The remaining $26 of gain, which may be attributable to credit risk or another factor unrelated to currency fluctuations, is sourced and characterized without regard to section 988.

Example 12. The facts are the same as in *Example 11*, except that Business A is owned by a foreign corporation with a pound functional currency. Under paragraph (b)(4)(ii) of this section, the acquisition of the £100 2-year note is a specified owner functional currency transaction that is not treated as a section 988 transaction of Business A. Because the note is a historic asset under § 1.987-1(e), Business A's €75 basis in the note translates into £80 at the historic rate described in § 1.987-1T(c)(3)(i)(E), which provides that the historic rate is the spot rate for the date the note was acquired without the use of a spot rate convention. (If, instead, Business A had purchased the 5-year note for £80 rather than €75, then pursuant to paragraph (b)(2)(ii) of this section, Business A's basis in the note would have been determined without translating the £80 purchase price because it is denominated in the owner's functional currency.) Under paragraph (b)(2)(ii) of this section, the £100 amount realized with respect to the note is not translated because it is denominated in the owner's functional currency. Thus, the owner takes into account £20 (£100 less £80) of section 987 taxable income in 2021 with respect to the note.

Example 13. (i) Business A receives and accrues $100 of income from the provision of services on January 1, 2021. Business A continues to hold the $100 as a U.S. dollar-denominated demand deposit at a bank on December 31, 2021. U.S. Corp has elected under paragraph (b)(4)(iii)(C) of this section to use the foreign currency mark-to-market method of accounting for qualified short-term section 988 transactions entered into by Business A. The euro-dollar spot rate without the use of a spot rate convention is €1 = $1 on January 1, 2021, and €1 = $2 on December 31, 2021, and the yearly average exchange rate for 2021 is €1 = $1.50.

(ii) Under § 1.987-3(b)(2)(i), the $100 earned by Business A is translated into €100 at the spot rate on January 1, 2021, as defined in § 1.987-1(c)(1) without the use of a spot rate convention. In determining U.S. Corp's taxable income, the €100 of service income is translated into $150 at the yearly average exchange rate for 2021, as provided in § 1.987-3(c)(1).

(iii) The $100 demand deposit constitutes a qualified short-term section 988 transaction under paragraph (b)(4)(iii)(B) of this section because the demand deposit is treated as nonfunctional currency within the meaning of section 988(c)(1)(C)(ii). Because Business A uses the foreign currency mark-to-market method of accounting for qualified short-term section 988 transactions, under paragraph (b)(4)(iii)(A) of this section, section 988 gain or loss for such transactions is determined in, and by reference to, euros, the functional currency of Business A. Accordingly, section 988 gain or loss must be determined on Business A's holding of the $100 demand deposit in, and by reference to, the euro. Under § 1.988-2(a)(2), Business A is treated as having an amount realized of €50 when the $100 is marked to market at the end of 2021 under paragraph (b)(4)(iii)(C) of this section. Marking the dollars to market gives rise to a section 988 loss of €50 (€50 amount realized, less Business A's €100 basis in the $100). In determining U.S. Corp's taxable income, that €50 loss is translated into a $75 loss at the yearly average exchange rate for 2021, as provided in § 1.987-3(c)(1).

Example 14. (i) *Facts.* Business A earns €100 of revenue from the provision of services and incurs €30 of general expenses and €10 of depreciation expense during 2021. Except as otherwise provided, U.S. Corp uses the yearly average exchange rate described in § 1.987-1(c)(2) to translate items of income, gain, deduction, and loss of Business A. Business A is subject to income tax in Country X at a 25 percent rate. U.S. Corp claims a credit with respect to Business A's foreign income taxes and elects under section 986(a)(1)(D) to translate the foreign income taxes at the spot rate on the date the taxes were paid. The yearly average exchange rate for 2021 is €1 = $1.50. The historic rate used to translate the depreciation expense is €1 = $1.00. The spot rate on the date that Business A paid its foreign income taxes was €1 = $1.60.

(ii) *Analysis.* Because U.S. Corp has elected to translate foreign income taxes at the spot rate on the date such taxes were paid rather than at the yearly average exchange rate, U.S. Corp must make the adjustments described in paragraph (c)(2)(v) of this section. Accordingly, U.S. Corp determines its section 987 taxable income by reducing the section 987 taxable income or loss that otherwise would be determined under this section by €15, translated into U.S. dollars at the yearly average exchange rate (€1 = $1.50), and increasing the resulting amount by €15, translated using the same exchange rate that is used to translate the creditable taxes into U.S. dollars under section 986(a) (€1 = $1.60). Following these adjustments, Business A's section 987 taxable income for 2021 is $96.50, computed as follows:

	Amount in €	Translation Rate	Amount in $
Revenue	€100	€1 = $1.50	$150.00
General Expenses	(30)	€1 = $1.50	(45.00)
Depreciation	(10)	€1 = $1.50	(10.00)
Tentative section 987 taxable income	€60		$95.00
Adjustments under paragraph (c)(2)(v) of this section:			
Decrease by €15 tax translated at yearly average exchange rate (€1 = $1.50)			($22.50)
Increase by €15 tax translated at spot rate on payment date (€1 = $1.60)			24.00
Section 987 taxable income			$96.50

(f) *Effective/applicability date.*—This section applies to taxable years beginning on or after one year after the first day of the first taxable year following December 7, 2016. Notwithstanding the preceding sentence, if a taxpayer makes an election under § 1.987-11(b), then this section applies to taxable years to which §§ 1.987-1 through 1.987-10 apply as a result of such election.

(g) *Expiration date.*—The applicability of this section expires on December 6, 2019. [Temporary Reg. § 1.987-3T.]

☐ [*T.D. 9795, 12-7-2016.*]

»»→ Caution: The Treasury Department has identified Reg. §1.987-4, as amended by T.D. 9794, as a significant tax regulation that imposes an undue financial burden on U.S. taxpayers and/or adds undue complexity to the federal tax laws, pursuant to Executive Order 13789 (issued April 21, 2017) (Notice 2017-38, I.R.B. 2017-30, 147). In a subsequent report, published October 16, 2017, Treasury recommended planned actions that would reduce the burden of these regulations, including an extension of the application date of T.D. 9794 (see Notice 2022-34, I.R.B. 2022-34, 150).

§ 1.987-4. Determination of net unrecognized section 987 gain or loss of a section 987 QBU.—(a) *In general.*—The net unrecognized section 987 gain or loss of a section 987 QBU shall be determined by the owner annually as provided in paragraph (b) of this section in the owner's functional currency. Only assets and liabilities reflected on the books and records of the section 987 QBU under § 1.987-2(b) shall be taken into account.

(b) *Calculation of net unrecognized section 987 gain or loss.*—Net unrecognized section 987 gain or loss of a section 987 QBU for a taxable year shall equal the sum of:

(1) The section 987 QBU's net accumulated unrecognized section 987 gain or loss for all prior taxable years to which these regulations apply as determined in paragraph (c) of this section, and

(2) The section 987 QBU's unrecognized section 987 gain or loss for the current taxable year as determined in paragraph (d) of this section.

(c) *Net accumulated unrecognized section 987 gain or loss for all prior taxable years.*—(1) *In general.*—A section 987 QBU's net accumulated unrecognized section 987 gain or loss for all prior taxable years is the aggregate of the amounts determined under § 1.987-4(d) for all prior taxable years to which these regulations apply, reduced by the amounts taken into account under § 1.987-5 upon remittances for all such prior taxable years.

(2) *Coordination with § 1.987-12.*—For purposes of paragraph (c)(1) of this section, amounts taken into account under § 1.987-5 are determined without regard to § 1.987-12.

(d) *Calculation of unrecognized section 987 gain or loss for a taxable year.*—The unrecognized section 987 gain or loss of a section 987 QBU for a taxable year shall be determined under paragraphs (d)(1) through (8) of this section.

(1) *Step 1: Determine the change in the owner functional currency net value of the section 987 QBU for the taxable year.*—(i) *In general.*—The

change in the owner functional currency net value of the section 987 QBU for the taxable year shall equal—

(A) The owner functional currency net value of the section 987 QBU, determined in the functional currency of the owner under paragraph (e) of this section, on the last day of the taxable year; less

(B) The owner functional currency net value of the section 987 QBU, determined in the functional currency of the owner under paragraph (e) of this section, on the last day of the preceding taxable year. This amount shall be zero in the case of the section 987 QBU's first taxable year.

(ii) *Year section 987 QBU is terminated.*—If a section 987 QBU is terminated within the meaning of § 1.987-8 during an owner's taxable year, the owner functional currency net value of the section 987 QBU as provided in paragraph (d)(1)(i)(A) of this section shall be determined on the date the section 987 QBU is terminated.

(2) *Step 2: Increase the amount determined in step 1 by the amount of assets transferred from the section 987 QBU to the owner.*—(i) *In general.*—The amount determined in paragraph (d)(1) of this section shall be increased by the total amount of assets described in paragraph (d)(2)(ii) of this section transferred from the section 987 QBU to the owner during the taxable year translated into the owner's functional currency as provided in paragraph (d)(2)(ii) of this section.

(ii) *Assets transferred from the section 987 QBU to the owner during the taxable year.*—The assets transferred from the section 987 QBU to the owner for the taxable year shall equal the sum of:

(A) The amount of the section 987 QBU's functional currency and the aggregate adjusted basis of all marked assets (as defined in § 1.987-1(d)), after taking into account § 1.988-1(a)(10), transferred to the owner during the taxable year determined in the functional currency of the section 987 QBU and translated into the owner's functional currency at the spot rate (as defined in § 1.987-1(c)(1)) applicable to the date of transfer; and

(B) The aggregate adjusted basis of all historic assets (as defined in § 1.987-1(e)), after taking into account § 1.988-1(a)(10), transferred to the owner during the taxable year determined in the functional currency of the section 987 QBU and translated into the owner's functional currency at the historic rate for each such asset (as defined in § 1.987-1(c)(3)).

(3) *Step 3: Decrease the amount determined in steps 1 and 2 by the amount of assets transferred from the owner to the section 987 QBU.*—(i) *In general.*—The aggregate amount determined in paragraphs (d)(1) and (d)(2) of this section shall be decreased by the total amount of assets transferred from the owner to the section 987 QBU during the taxable year determined in the functional currency of the owner as provided in paragraph (d)(3)(ii) of this section.

(ii) *Total of all amounts transferred from the owner to the section 987 QBU during the taxable year.*—The total amount of assets transferred from the owner to the section 987 QBU for the taxable year shall equal the aggregate of:

(A) The total amount of functional currency of the owner transferred to the section 987 QBU during the taxable year; and

(B) The adjusted basis, determined in the functional currency of the owner, of any asset transferred to the section 987 QBU during the taxable year (after taking into account § 1.988-1(a)(10)).

(4) *Step 4: Decrease the amount determined in steps 1 through 3 by the amount of liabilities transferred from the section 987 QBU to the owner.*—The aggregate amount determined in paragraphs (d)(1) through (3) of this section shall be decreased by the aggregate amount of liabilities transferred from the section 987 QBU to the owner during the taxable year. The amount of such liabilities shall be translated into the functional currency of the owner at the spot rate (as defined in § 1.987-1(c)(1)) applicable on the date of transfer.

(5) *Step 5: Increase the amount determined in steps 1 through 4 by the amount of liabilities transferred from the owner to the section 987 QBU.*—The aggregate amount determined in paragraphs (d)(1) through (4) of this section shall be increased by the aggregate amount of liabilities transferred by the owner to the section 987 QBU during the taxable year. The amount of such liabilities shall be translated into the functional currency of the owner at the spot rate (as defined in § 1.987-1(c)(1)) applicable on the date of transfer.

(6) *Step 6: Decrease or increase the amount determined in steps 1 through 5 by the section 987 taxable income or loss, respectively, of the section 987 QBU for the taxable year.*—The aggregate amount determined in paragraphs (d)(1) through (5) of this section shall be decreased or increased by the section 987 taxable income or loss, respectively, computed under § 1.987-3 for the taxable year.

(7) *Step 7: Increase the amount determined in steps 1 through 6 by any expenses that are not deductible in computing the section 987 taxable income or loss of the section 987 QBU for the taxable year.*—The aggregate amount determined under paragraphs (d)(1) through (6) shall be increased by the amount of any expense or loss attributable to a section 987 QBU for the taxable year that is not deductible in computing the section 987 QBU's taxable income or loss for the year, including any foreign income taxes incurred by the section 987 QBU with respect to which the owner claims a credit (translated at the same rate at which such taxes were translated under section 986(a)).

(8) *Step 8: Decrease the amount determined in steps 1 through 7 by the amount of any tax-exempt income.*—The aggregate amount determined under paragraphs (d)(1) through (7) shall be decreased by the amount of any income or gain attributable to a section 987 QBU for the taxable year that is not included in computing the section 987 QBU's taxable income or loss for the year.

(e) *Determination of the owner functional currency net value of a section 987 QBU.*—(1) *In general.*—The owner functional currency net value of a section 987 QBU on the last day of a taxable year shall equal the aggregate amount of functional currency and the adjusted basis of each asset on the section 987 QBU's balance sheet on that day, less the aggregate amount of each liability on the section 987 QBU's balance sheet on that day, in each case translated into the owner's functional currency as provided in paragraph (e)(2) of this section. Such amount shall be determined by:

(i) Preparing a balance sheet for the relevant date from the section 987 QBU's books and records (within the meaning of § 1.989(a)-1(d)), as recorded in the section 987 QBU's functional currency and showing all assets and liabilities reflected on such books and records as provided in § 1.987-2(b);

(ii) Making adjustments necessary to conform the items reflected on the balance sheet described in paragraph (e)(1)(i) of this section to United States tax accounting principles; and

(iii) Translating the asset and liability amounts on the adjusted balance sheet described in paragraph (e)(1)(ii) of this section into the functional currency of the owner in accordance with paragraph (e)(2) of this section.

(2) *Translation of balance sheet items into the owner's functional currency.*—The amount of the section 987 QBU's functional currency, the basis of an asset, or the amount of a liability shall be translated as follows:

(i) *Marked item.*—A marked item (as defined in § 1.987-1(d)) shall be translated into the owner's functional currency at the spot rate (as defined in § 1.987-1(c)(1)) applicable to the last day of the relevant taxable year.

(ii) *Historic item.*—A historic item (as defined in § 1.987-1(e)) shall be translated into the owner's functional currency at the historic rate (as defined in § 1.987-1(c)(3)).

(f) *Combinations and separations.*—(1) *Combinations.*—The net unrecognized section 987 gain or loss of a combined QBU (as defined in § 1.987-2(c)(9)(i)) for a taxable year is determined under paragraph (b) of this section by taking into account the net accumulated unrecognized section 987 gain or loss of each combining QBU (as defined in § 1.987-2(c)(9)(i)) for all prior taxable years to which the regulations under section 987 apply, as determined under paragraph (c) of this section, and by treating the combining QBUs as having combined immediately prior to the beginning of the taxable year of combination. See paragraph (f)(3) of this section, *Example 1*, for an illustration of this rule.

(2) *Separations.*—The net unrecognized section 987 gain or loss of a separated QBU (as defined in § 1.987-2(c)(9)(iii)) for a taxable year is determined under paragraph (b) of this section by taking into account the separated QBU's share of the net accumulated unrecognized section 987 gain or loss of the separating QBU (as defined in § 1.987-2(c)(9)(iii)) for all prior taxable years to which the regulations under section 987 apply, as determined under paragraph (c) of this section, and by treating the separating QBU as having separated immediately prior to the beginning of the taxable year of separation. A separated QBU's share of the separating QBU's net accumulated unrecognized section 987 gain or loss for all such prior taxable years

is determined by apportioning the separating QBU's net accumulated unrecognized section 987 gain or loss for all such prior taxable years to each separated QBU in proportion to the aggregate adjusted basis of the gross assets properly reflected on the books and records of each separated QBU immediately after the separation. For purposes of determining the owner functional currency net value of the separated QBUs on the last day of the taxable year preceding the taxable year of separation under paragraphs (d)(1)(B) and (e) of this section, the balance sheets of the separated QBUs on that day will be deemed to reflect the assets and liabilities reflected on the balance sheet of the separating QBU on that day, apportioned between the separated QBUs in a reasonable manner that takes into account the assets and liabilities reflected on the balance sheets of the separated QBUs immediately after the separation. See paragraph (f)(3) of this section, *Example 2*, for an illustration of this rule.

(3) *Examples*.—The following examples illustrate the rules of paragraphs (f)(1) and (2) of this section.

(i) *Example 1. Combination of two section 987 QBUs that have the same owner*.—(A) *Facts*.—DC1, a domestic corporation, owns Entity A, a DE. Entity A conducts a business in France that constitutes a section 987 QBU (French QBU) that has the euro as its functional currency. French QBU has a net accumulated unrecognized section 987 loss from all prior taxable years to which the regulations under section 987 apply of $100. DC1 also owns Entity B, a DE. Entity B conducts a business in Germany that constitutes a section 987 QBU (German QBU) that has the euro as its functional currency. German QBU has a net accumulated unrecognized section 987 gain from all prior taxable years to which the regulations under section 987 apply of $110. During the taxable year, Entity A and Entity B merge under local law. As a result, the books and records of French QBU and German QBU are combined into a new single set of books and records. The combined entity has the euro as its functional currency.

(B) *Analysis*.—Pursuant to § 1.987-2(c)(9)(i), French QBU and German QBU are combining QBUs, and their combination does not give rise to a transfer that is taken into account in determining the amount of a remittance (as defined in § 1.987-5(c)). For purposes of computing net unrecognized section 987 gain or loss under this section for the year of the combination, the combination is deemed to have occurred on the last day of the owner's prior taxable year, such that the owner functional currency net value of the combined section 987 QBU at the end of that taxable year described under paragraph (d)(1)(B) of this section takes into account items reflected on the balance sheets of both French QBU and German QBU at that time. Additionally, any transactions between French QBU and German QBU occurring during the year of the merger will not result in transfers to or from a section 987 QBU. Pursuant to paragraph (f)(1) of this section, the combined QBU will have a net accumulated unrecognized section 987 gain from all prior taxable years of $10 (the $100 loss from French QBU plus the $110 gain from German QBU).

(ii) *Example 2. Separation of two section 987 QBUs that have the same owner*.—(A) *Facts*.—DC1, a domestic corporation, owns Entity A, a DE. Entity A conducts a business in the Netherlands that constitutes a section 987 QBU (Dutch QBU) that has the euro as its functional currency. The business of Dutch QBU consists of manufacturing and selling bicycles and scooters and is recorded on a single set of books and records. On the last day of Year 1, the adjusted basis of the gross assets of Dutch QBU is € 1,000. In Year 2, the net accumulated unrecognized section 987 loss of Dutch QBU from all prior taxable years is $200. During Year 2, Entity A separates the bicycle and scooter business such that each business begins to have its own books and records and to meet the definition of a section 987 QBU under § 1.987-1(b)(2) (hereafter, "bicycle QBU" and "scooter QBU"). There are no transfers between DC1 and Dutch QBU before the separation. After the separation, the aggregate adjusted basis of bicycle QBU's assets is € 600 and the aggregate adjusted basis of scooter QBU's assets is € 400. Each section 987 QBU continues to have the euro as its functional currency.

(B) *Analysis*.—Pursuant to § 1.987-2(c)(9)(iii), bicycle QBU and scooter QBU are separated QBUs, and the separation of Dutch QBU, a separating QBU, does not give rise to a transfer taken into account in determining the amount of a remittance (as defined in § 1.987-5(c)). For purposes of computing net unrecognized section 987 gain or loss under this section for Year 2, the separation will be deemed to have occurred on the last day of the owner's prior taxable year, Year 1. Pursuant to paragraph (f)(2) of this section, bicycle QBU will have a net accumulated unrecognized section 987 loss of $120 (€ 600/ € 1,000 x $200), and scooter QBU will have a net accumulated unrecognized section 987 loss of $80 (€ 400/ € 1,000 x $200).

(g) *Examples*.—The following examples illustrate the provisions of this section. For purposes of the examples, U.S. Corp is a domestic corporation that uses the calendar year as its taxable year and has the dollar as its functional currency. Except as otherwise indicated, U.S. Corp elects under § 1.987-3(c)(2)(iv)(B) to use the historic inventory method with respect to all of its section 987 QBUs but does not make other elections under section 987. Exchange rate and tax accounting (for example, depreciation rate) assumptions used in these examples are selected for the purpose of illustrating the principles of this section, and no inference is intended by their use. Additionally, the examples are not intended to demonstrate when activities constitute a trade or business within the meaning of § 1.989(a)-1(b)(2)(ii)(A) and § 1.989(a)-1(c) and therefore whether a section 987 QBU is considered to exist.

Example 1. (i) On July 1, 2021, U.S. Corp establishes Japan Branch, a section 987 QBU of U.S. Corp that has the yen as its functional currency, and transfers to Japan Branch $1,000 and raw land with a basis of $500. Japan Branch immediately exchanges the $1,000 for ¥100,000. On the same day, Japan Branch borrows ¥10,000. For the taxable year 2021, Japan Branch earns ¥2,000 per month (total of ¥12,000 for the six-month period from July 1, 2021, through December 31, 2021) for providing services and incurs ¥333.33 per month (total of ¥2,000 when rounded for the six-month period from July 1, 2021, through December 31, 2021) of related expenses. Assume that the spot rate on July 1, 2021, is $1 = ¥100; the spot rate on December 31, 2021, is $1 = ¥120; and the average rate for the period of July 1, 2021, to December 31, 2021, is $1 = ¥110. Thus, the ¥12,000 of services revenue when properly translated under § 1.987-3(c)(1) at the yearly average exchange rate equals $109.09 (¥12,000 x ($1 / ¥110)) = $109.09). The ¥2,000 of expenses translated at the same yearly average exchange rate equals $18.18 (¥2,000 x ($1 / ¥110) = $18.18). Thus, Japan Branch's net income translated into dollars equals $90.91 ($109.09 - $18.18 = $90.91).

(ii) Under paragraph (a) of this section, U.S. Corp must compute the net unrecognized section 987 gain or loss of Japan Branch for 2021. Because this is Japan Branch's first taxable year, the net unrecognized section 987 gain or loss (as defined under paragraph (b) of this section) is the branch's unrecognized section 987 gain or loss for 2021 as determined in paragraph (d) of this section. The calculation under paragraph (d) of this section is made as follows:

(iii) *Step 1*. Under paragraph (d)(1) of this section, U.S. Corp must determine the change in the owner functional currency net value (OFCNV) of Japan Branch for 2021 in dollars. The change in the OFCNV of Japan Branch for 2021 is equal to the OFCNV of Japan Branch determined in dollars on the last day of 2021, less the OFCNV of Japan Branch determined in dollars on the last day of the preceding taxable year.

(A) The OFCNV of Japan Branch determined in dollars on the last day of the current taxable year is determined under paragraph (e) of this section as the sum of the basis of each asset on Japan Branch's balance sheet on December 31, 2021, less the sum of each liability on Japan Branch's balance sheet on that date, translated into dollars as provided in paragraph (e)(2) of this section.

(B) For this purpose, Japan Branch will show the following assets and liabilities on its balance sheet for December 31, 2021:

(1) ¥120,000;

(2) Raw land with a basis of ¥55,000 ($500 translated under § 1.987-2(d)(2) at the historic rate of $1 = ¥110); and

(3) Liabilities of ¥10,000.

(C) Under paragraph (e)(2) of this section, U.S. Corp will translate these items as follows. The ¥120,000 is a marked asset and the ¥10,000 liability is a marked liability (as each is defined in § 1.987-1(d)). These items are translated into dollars on December 31, 2021, using the spot rate on December 31, 2021, of $1 = ¥120. The raw land is a historic asset (as defined in § 1.987-1(e)) and is translated into dollars under paragraph (e)(2)(ii) of this section at the historic rate, which under § 1.987-1(c)(3)(1)(A) is the yearly average exchange rate of $1 = ¥110 applicable to the year the land was transferred to the QBU. Thus, the OFCNV of Japan Branch on December 31, 2021, in dollars is $1,416.67 determined as follows:

Assets	Amount in ¥	Translation Rate	Amount in $
Yen	¥120,000	$1 = ¥120 (spot rate-12/31/21)	$1,000.00
Land	55,000	$1 = ¥110 (yearly average rate-2021)	500.00
Total assets			$1,500.00

Liabilities			
Bank Loan	¥10,000	$1 = ¥120 (spot rate-12/31/21)	$83.33
Total liabilities			$83.33
2021 ending OFCNV			$1,416.67

(D) Under paragraph (d)(1) of this section, the change in OFCNV of Japan Branch for 2021 is equal to the OFCNV of the branch determined in dollars on December 31, 2021, ($1,416.67) less the OFCNV of the branch determined in dollars on the last day of the preceding taxable year. Because this is the first taxable year of Japan Branch, the OFCNV of Japan Branch determined in dollars on the last day of the preceding taxable year is zero under paragraph (d)(1)(i)(B) of this section. Accordingly, the change in OFCNV of Japan Branch for 2021 is $1,416.67.

(iv) *Step 2.* Under paragraph (d)(2) of this section, the aggregate amount determined in paragraph (d)(1) of this section (step 1) is increased by the total amount of assets described in paragraph (d)(2)(ii) of this section transferred from the section 987 QBU to the owner during the taxable year translated into the owner's functional currency as provided in paragraph (d)(2)(ii) of this section. Because no such amounts were transferred, there is no change in the $1,416.67 determined in step 1.

(v) *Step 3.* Under paragraph (d)(3) of this section, the aggregate amount determined in paragraphs (d)(1) and (d)(2) of this section (steps 1 and 2) is decreased by the total amount of assets transferred from the owner to the section 987 QBU during the taxable year as determined in paragraph (d)(3)(ii) of this section in dollars. On July 1, 2021, U.S. Corp transferred to Japan Branch $1,000.00 (which Japan Branch immediately converted into ¥100,000) and raw land with a basis of $500.00 (equal to ¥55,000, translated under § 1.987-2(d)(2) at the historic rate of $1 = ¥110). Thus, the $1,416.67 determined under steps 1 and 2 is reduced by $1,500.00, resulting in ($83.33).

(vi) *Steps 4 and 5.* Because no liabilities were transferred by U.S. Corp to Japan Branch or by Japan Branch to U.S. Corp during the taxable year, the aggregate amount determined in paragraph (d)(3) of this section (Step 3) is not increased or decreased.

(vii) *Step 6.* Under paragraph (d)(6) of this section, the aggregate amount determined after applying paragraphs (d)(1) through (5) of this section (steps 1 through 5) is decreased by the section 987 taxable income of Japan Branch of $90.91 from ($83.33) to ($174.24).

(viii) *Steps 7 and 8.* Paragraphs (d)(7) and (d)(8) do not apply because Japan Branch does not have any tax-exempt or nondeductible items. Accordingly, the unrecognized section 987 loss of Japan Branch for 2021 is ($174.24), the amount determined after applying step 6.

Example 2. (i) U.S. Corp operates in the United Kingdom through U.K. Branch, a section 987 QBU of U.S. Corp that has the pound as its functional currency. U.S. Corp properly elects under § 1.987-1(c)(1)(ii) for U.K. Branch to use a spot rate convention (when permitted). Under the chosen convention, the spot rate (the "convention rate") for any transaction occurring during a month is the average of the pound spot rate and the 30-day forward rate for pounds on the next-to-last Thursday of the preceding month. The yearly average exchange rate was £1 = $0.90 for 2020, £1 = $1.00 for 2021, and £1 = $1.10 for 2022. The closing balance sheet of U.K. Branch in 2021 reflected the following assets:

(A) £100;

(B) A sales office purchased in 2020 with an adjusted basis of £1,000;

(C) A delivery truck purchased in 2020 with an adjusted basis of £200;

(D) Inventory of 100 units purchased in 2021 with a basis of £100; and

(E) Stock in ABC Corporation purchased in 2021 with a basis of £150, representing less than 10 percent of the total voting power and value of all classes of stock of ABC Corporation.

The closing balance sheet of U.K. Branch for 2021 reflected one liability, £50 of longterm debt entered into in 2020 with F Bank, an unrelated bank.

The office, truck, stock, and inventory are historic assets (as defined in § 1.987-1(e)). The £100 and long-term debt are marked items (as defined in § 1.987-1(d)). Assume that U.S. Corp translated U.K. Branch's 2021 closing balance sheet as follows:

Assets	Amount in £	Translation Rate	Amount in $
Pounds	£100.00	£1 = $1.05 (convention rate-Dec. 2021)	$105.00
Office	1,000.00	£1 = $0.90 (historic rate-2020)	900.00
Truck	200.00	£1 = $0.90 (historic rate-2020)	180.00
Stock	50.00	£1 = $1.00 (historic rate-2021)	150.00
Inventory	100.00	£1 = $1.00 (historic rate-2021)	100.00
Total assets			$1435.00
Liabilities			
Bank Loan	£50.00	£1 = $1.05 (convention rate-Dec. 2021)	$52.50
Total liabilities			$52.50
2021 ending OFCNV			$1,382.50

(ii) U.K. Branch uses the first-in, first-out (FIFO) method of accounting for inventory. In 2022, U.K. Branch sold 100 units of inventory for a total of £300 and purchased another 100 units of inventory for £100. There is depreciation of £33 with respect to the office and £40 with respect to the truck, and U.K. Branch incurred £30 of business expenses during 2022. Neither the depreciation nor the business expenses are inventoriable costs. All items of income earned and expenses incurred during 2022 are received and paid, respectively, in pounds. Under § 1.987-3, U.K. Branch's section 987 taxable income or loss is determined as follows:

Item	Amount in £	Translation Rate	Amount in $
Gross receipts	£300.00	£1 = $1.10 (yearly average rate-2022)	$330.00
Less: COGS	(100.00)	£1 = $1.00 (historic rate-2021)	(100.00)
Gross income			$230.00
Dep: Office	(33.00)	£1 = $0.90 (historic rate-2020)	($29.70)
Truck	(40.00)	£1 = $0.90 (historic rate-2020)	(36.00)
Other expenses	(30.00)	£1 = $1.10 (yearly average rate-2022)	(33.00)
Total expenses			($98.70)
Section 987 taxable income			$131.30

Accordingly, U.K. Branch has $131.30 of section 987 taxable income in 2022.

(iii) In December 2022, U.K. Branch transferred £30 to U.S. Corp, and U.S. Corp transferred a computer with a basis of $10 to U.K. Branch. U.S. Corp's net accumulated unrecognized section 987 gain or loss for all prior taxable years as determined in paragraph (c) of this section is $30.

(iv) The unrecognized section 987 gain or loss of U.K. Branch for 2022 is determined as follows:

(A) *Step 1.* Under paragraph (d)(1) of this section, the change in OFCNV for the taxable year must be determined. This amount is equal to the OFCNV of U.K. Branch determined under paragraph (e) of this section on the last day of 2022, less the OFCNV of U.K. Branch determined on the last day of 2021. The OFCNV of U.K. Branch on December 31, 2022, and the change in OFCNV for 2022, are determined as follows:

Assets	Amount in £	Translation Rate	Amount in $
Pounds	£240.00	£1 = $1.15 (convention rate-Dec. 2022)	$276.00
Office	967.00	£1 = $0.90 (historic rate-2020)	870.30
Truck	160.00	£1 = $0.90 (historic rate-2020)	144.00
Inventory	100.00	£1 = $1.10 (historic rate-2022)	110.00
Computer	9.09	£1 = $1.10 (historic rate-2022)	10.00
Stock	150.00	£1 = $1.00 (historic rate-2021)	150.00
Total assets			$1,560.30
Liabilities			
Bank Loan	£50.00	£1 = $1.15 (convention rate-Dec. 2022)	$57.50
Total liabilities			$57.50
2022 ending OFCNV			$1,502.80
Less: 2021 ending OFCNV			(1,382.50)
Change in OFCNV			$120.30

(B) *Step 2.* Under paragraph (d)(2) of this section, the aggregate amount determined in step 1 must be increased by the total amount of assets described in paragraph (d)(2)(ii) of this section transferred from U.K. Branch to U.S. Corp during the taxable year, translated into U.S. Corp's functional currency as provided in paragraph (d)(2)(ii) of this section. The amount of assets transferred from U.K. Branch to U.S. Corp during 2022 is determined as follows:

Asset	Amount in £	Translation Rate	Amount in $
£30	£30.00	£1 = $1.15 (convention rate-Dec. 2022)	$34.50

(C) *Step 3: Decrease the aggregate amount described in steps 1 and 2 by the owner's transfers to the section 987 QBU.* Under paragraph (d)(3) of this section, the aggregate amount determined in steps 1 and 2 must be decreased by the total amount of all assets transferred from U.S. Corp to U.K. Branch during the taxable year as determined in paragraph (d)(3)(ii) of this section. The amount of assets transferred from U.S. Corp to U.K. Branch during 2022 is determined as follows:

Asset	Amount in $
Computer	$10.00

(D) *Step 4.* Under paragraph (d)(4) of this section, the aggregate amount determined in steps 1 through 3 must be decreased by the aggregate amount of liabilities transferred by U.K. Branch to U.S. Corp. Under these facts, such amount is $0.

(E) *Step 5.* Under paragraph (d)(5) of this section, the aggregate amount determined in steps 1 through 4 must be increased by the aggregate amount of liabilities transferred by U.S. Corp to U.K. Branch. Under these facts, such amount is $0.

(F) *Step 6.* Under paragraph (d)(6) of this section, the aggregate amount determined in steps 1 through 5 is decreased or increased, respectively, by any section 987 taxable income or loss of U.K. Branch computed under § 1.987-3 for the taxable year. The amount of U.K. Branch's taxable income, as determined above, is $131.30.

(H) *Steps 7 and 8:* Paragraphs (d)(7) and (d)(8) do not apply because U.K. Branch does not have any tax-exempt income or nondeductible expense.

(v) *Summary.* Taking steps 1 through 8 into account, the amount of U.S. Corp's unrecognized section 987 gain or loss with respect to U.K. Branch in 2022 is computed as follows:

Step	Amount in $	Balance
1	+ $120.30	$120.30
2	+ 34.50	154.80
3	- 10.00	144.80
4	- 0	144.80
5	+ 0	144.80
6	- 131.30	13.50
7	+ 0	13.50
8	- 0	13.50

Thus, U.S. Corp's unrecognized section 987 gain for 2022 with respect to U.K. Branch is $13.50. As of the end of 2022, before taking into account the recognition of any section 987 gain or loss under § 1.987-5, U.S. Corp's net unrecognized section 987 gain is $43.50 (that is, $30.00 accumulated from prior years, plus $13.50 in 2022).

Example 3. (i) *Background.* U.S. Corp is the owner of Business A, a section 987 QBU that has the euro as its functional currency. Business A uses the FIFO method to account for inventory and uses the simplified inventory method described in § 1.987-3(c)(2)(iv)(A). On the last day of 2020, U.S. Corp begins Business A by contributing to Business A a building with a basis of $780, a machine with a basis of $300, and $100. On January 1, 2021, Business A converts the $100 into €100. The tax basis of the building and machine is translated into euros using the historic rate, which is the yearly average exchange rate for 2020, the year of the transfer. Accordingly, the building and the machine have a tax basis of €780 and €300, respectively, on December 31, 2020. The building and machine have annual depreciation of €20 and €30, respectively. Business A determines that 50 percent of the building depreciation should be allocated to the cost of goods manufactured (that is, treated as an inventoriable cost) and 50 percent should be allocated to selling, general and administrative (SG&A) expenses. The machine is used exclusively to manufacture inventory. Relevant exchange rates for purposes of this example are as follows:

Year	Yearly Average Exchange Rate	December 31 Spot Rate
2020	€1= $1.00	€1=$1.00
2021	€1=$1.50	€1=$2.00
2022	€1= $2.50	€1= $3.00

(ii) *Operations in 2021.* During 2021, Business A recognizes €140 of revenue from sales of finished goods. The related COGS is €70. Business A pays €10 in salaries allocable to SG&A. Inventoriable costs in 2021 include €10 of depreciation on the building and €30 of depreciation on the machine. Business A's balance sheet on December 31, 2021, shows no liabilities and the following assets: currency of €160, the building with an adjusted basis of €760, the machine with an adjusted basis of €270, and ending inventory with a FIFO cost basis of €40, comprising raw materials and finished goods.

(A) *Determination of income.* Under the simplified inventory method, Business A's income for 2021 is computed as follows:

Item	Amount in €	Translation Rate	Amount in $
Sales revenue	€ 140	€ 1 = $1.50 (yearly avg. rate-2021)	$210
COGS before adjustments	70	€ 1 = $1.50 (yearly avg. rate-2021)	$105
Adjustment for cost recovery deductions (see calculation below)			(20)
Adjustment for beginning inventory (none)			0
Adjusted COGS			$85
SG&A			
Depreciation on building (50%)	10	€ 1 = $1.00 (historic rate-2020)	$10
Salaries	10	€ 1 = $1.50 (yearly avg. rate-2021)	15
Total SG&A			$25
Section 987 net income (revenue less COGS and SG&A)			$100

COGS Adjustments

Adjustment for cost recovery deductions included in inventoriable costs

Depreciation Amount	Historic Rate	2021 Yearly Avg. Rate	Difference in Translation Rates	Adjustment (Depreciation x Change in Rates)
€ 10 (building)	1.00	1.50	(0.50)	($5)
€ 30 (machine)	1.00	1.50	(0.50)	($15)
Total adjustment for cost recovery deductions				($20)

(B) *Determination of OFCNV for 2020 and 2021.* Under the simplified inventory method, the OFCNV of Business A for 2020 and 2021 is determined under paragraph (e) of this section as follows:

OFCNV—End of 2021

Assets	Amount in €	Translation Rate	Amount in $
Euros	€ 160	€ 1 = $2.00 (year-end spot rate-2021)	$320
Building	760	€ 1 = $1.00 (historic rate-2020)	760
Machine	270	€ 1 = $1.00 (historic rate-2020)	270
Inventory	40	€ 1 = $1.50 (yearly average rate-2021)	60
Total assets			$1,410
Liabilities			
Total liabilities			$0
2021 ending OFCNV			$1,410

OFCNV—End of 2020

Assets	Amount in €	Translation Rate	Amount in $
Euros	€ 100	€ 1 = $1.00 (year-end spot rate-2020)	$100
Building	780	€ 1 = $1.00 (historic rate-2020)	780
Machine	300	€ 1 = $1.00 (historic rate-2020)	300
Total assets			$1,180
Liabilities			
Total liabilities			$0
2020 ending OFCNV			$1,180

(C) *Determination of net unrecognized section 987 gain or loss.* The net unrecognized section 987 gain or loss of Business A is determined under paragraph (d) of this section as follows (relevant steps only):

(1) *Step 1.* Under paragraph (d)(1) of this section, the change in OFCNV for the taxable year must be determined. This amount is equal to the OFCNV of Business A determined under paragraph (e) of this section on the last day of 2021, less the OFCNV of Business A determined on the last day of 2020.

2021 ending OFCNV	$1,410
Less: 2020 ending OFCNV	(1,180)
Change in OFCNV	$230

(2) *Step 6.* Under paragraph (d)(6) of this section, the aggregate amount determined in steps 1 through 5 must be decreased by the section 987 taxable income of Business A. The amount of Business A's taxable income for 2021, as determined above, is $100.

Change in OFCNV	$230
Less: section 987 taxable income	(100)
Unrecognized section 987 gain	$130
Plus: net accumulated unrecognized section 987 gain or loss from prior years	0
Net unrecognized section 987 gain	$130

(iii) *Operations in 2022.* During 2022, Business A recognizes € 180 of revenue from sales of finished goods. The related COGS is € 96. Business A pays € 10 in salaries allocable to SG&A. Inventoriable costs in 2022 include € 30 of depreciation on the machine and € 10 of depreciation on the building. Business A's balance sheet on December 31, 2022, shows no liabilities and the following assets: currency of € 260, the building with an adjusted basis of € 740, the machine with an adjusted basis of € 240, and ending inventory with a FIFO cost basis of € 54, comprising raw materials and finished goods.

(A) *Determination of income.* Under the simplified inventory method, Business A's income for 2022 is computed as follows:

Item	Amount in €	Translation Rate	Amount in $
Sales revenue	€ 180	€ 1 = $2.50 (yearly avg. rate-2022)	$450
COGS before adjustments	96	€ 1 = $2.50 (yearly avg. rate-2022)	$240
Adjustment for cost recovery deductions (see calculation below)			(60)
Adjustment for beginning inventory (see calculation below)			(40)
Adjusted COGS			$140
SG&A			
Depreciation on building (50%)	10	€ 1 = $1.00 (historic rate-2020)	$10
Salaries	10	€ 1 = $2.50 (yearly avg. rate-2022)	25
Total SG&A			$35
Section 987 net income (revenue less COGS and SG&A)			$275

COGS Adjustments

Adjustment for cost recovery deductions

Depreciation Amount	Historic Rate	2021 Yearly Avg. Rate	Difference in Translation Rates	Adjustment (Depreciation x Change in Rates)
€ 10 (building)	1.00	2.50	(1.50)	($15)
€ 30 (machine)	1.00	2.50	(1.50)	($45)
Total adjustment for cost recovery deductions				($60)

Adjustment for beginning inventory

Prior Year Ending Inventory	2021 Yearly Avg Rate.	2022 Yearly Avg Rate	Difference in Translation Rates	Adjustment (Inventory x Change in Rates)
€ 40	1.50	2.50	(1.00)	($40)
Total adjustment for beginning inventory				($40)

(B) *Determination of OFCNV*. Under the simplified inventory method, the OFCNV of Business A for 2022 is determined under paragraph (e) of this section as follows:

OFCNV—End of 2022

Assets	Amount in €	Translation Rate	Amount in $
Euros	€ 260	€ 1 = $3.00 (year-end spot rate-2022)	$780
Building	740	€ 1 = $1.00 (historic rate-2020)	740
Machine	240	€ 1 = $1.00 (historic rate-2020)	240
Inventory	54	€ 1 = $2.50 (yearly average rate-2022)	135
Total assets			$1,895
Liabilities			
Total liabilities			$0
2022 ending OFCNV			$1,895

(C) *Determination of net unrecognized section 987 gain or loss*. The net unrecognized section 987 gain of Business A is determined under paragraph (d) of this section as follows (relevant steps only):

(1) *Step 1*. Under paragraph (d)(1) of this section, the change in OFCNV for the taxable year must be determined. This amount is equal to the OFCNV of Business A determined under paragraph (e) of this section on the last day of 2022, less the OFCNV of Business A determined on the last day of 2021.

2022 ending OFCNV	$1,895
Less: 2021 ending OFCNV	(1,410)
Change in OFCNV	$485

(2) *Step 6*. Under paragraph (d)(6) of this section, the aggregate amount determined in steps 1 through 5 must be decreased by the section 987 taxable income of Business A. The amount of Business A's taxable income for 2022, as determined above, is $275.

Change in OFCNV	$485
Less: section 987 taxable income	(275)
Unrecognized section 987 gain 2022	$210
Plus: net accumulated unrecognized section 987 gain from prior year	130
Net unrecognized section 987 gain	$340

Example 4. (i) *Background*. The background facts about Business A are the same as in *Example 3*, except that Business A uses the dollar-value LIFO method to account for inventory.

(ii) *Operations in 2021*. The facts about Business A's operations in 2021 are the same as in *Example 3*.

(A) *Determination of income*. Under the simplified inventory method, Business A's income for 2021 is computed as follows:

Item	Amount in €	Translation Rate	Amount in $
Sales revenue	€ 140	€ 1 = $1.50 (yearly avg. rate-2021)	$210
COGS before adjustments	70	€ 1 = $1.50 (yearly avg. rate-2021)	$105
Adjustment for cost recovery deductions (same as *Example 1*)			(20)
Adjustment for LIFO liquidation (none)			0
Adjusted COGS			$85

Item	Amount in €	Translation Rate	Amount in $
SG&A			
Depreciation on building (50%)	10	€1 = $1.00 (historic rate-2020)	$10
Salaries	10	€1 = $1.50 (yearly avg. rate-2021)	15
Total SG&A			$25
Section 987 net income (revenue less COGS and SG&A)			$100

(B) *Determination of OFCNV for 2020 and 2021.* Under the simplified inventory method, the OFCNV of Business A for 2020 and 2021 is determined under paragraph (e) of this section as follows:

OFCNV—End of 2021

Assets	Amount in €	Translation Rate	Amount in $
Euros	€160	€1 = $2.00 (year-end spot rate-2021)	$320
Building	760	€1 = $1.00 (historic rate-2020)	760
Machine	270	€1 = $1.00 (historic rate-2020)	270
Inventory	40	€1 = $1.50 (historic rate-2021)	60
Total assets			$1,410
Liabilities			
Total liabilities			$0
2021 ending OFCNV			$1,410

OFCNV—End of 2020

Assets	Amount in €	Translation Rate	Amount in $
Euros	€100	€1 = $1.00 (year-end spot rate-2020)	$100
Building	780	€1 = $1.00 (historic rate-2020)	780
Machine	300	€1 = $1.00 (historic rate-2020)	300
Total assets			$1,180
Liabilities			
Total liabilities			$0
2020 ending OFCNV			$1,180

(C) *Determination of net unrecognized section 987 gain or loss.* The net unrecognized section 987 gain or loss of Business A for 2021 is determined under paragraph (d) of this section as follows (relevant steps only):

(1) *Step 1.* Under paragraph (d)(1) of this section, the change in OFCNV for the taxable year must be determined. This amount is equal to the OFCNV of Business A determined under paragraph (e) of this section on the last day of 2021, less the OFCNV of Business A determined on the last day of 2020.

2021 ending OFCNV	$1,410
Less: 2020 ending OFCNV	(1,180)
Change in OFCNV	$230

(2) *Step 6.* Under paragraph (d)(6) of this section, the aggregate amount determined in steps 1 through 5 must be decreased by the section 987 taxable income of Business A. The amount of Business A's taxable income for 2021, as determined above, is $100.

Change in OFCNV	$230
Less: section 987 taxable income	(100)
Unrecognized section 987 gain	$130
Plus: Net accumulated unrecognized section 987 gain or loss from prior years	0
Net unrecognized section 987 gain	$130

(iii) *Operations in 2022.* The facts about Business A's operations in 2022 are the same as in *Example 3*, except that due to Business A's dollar-value LIFO method of inventory accounting, Business A's balance sheet on December 31, 2022, reflects a 2021 layer of inventory with a LIFO cost basis of €40 and a 2022 layer of inventory with a LIFO cost basis of €10.80, and Business A's COGS is €99.20.

(A) *Determination of income.* Business A's income for 2022 is computed as follows:

Item	Amount in €	Translation Rate	Amount in $
Sales revenue	€180	€1 = $2.50 (yearly avg. rate-2022)	$450
COGS before adjustments	99.20	€1 = $2.50 (yearly avg. rate-2022)	$248
Adjustment for cost recovery deductions (same as *Example 3*)			(60)
Adjustment for LIFO liquidation (none)			0
Adjusted COGS			$188
SG&A			
Depreciation on building (50%)	10	€1 = $1.00 (historic rate-2020)	$10
Salaries	10	€1 = $2.50 (yearly avg. rate-2022)	25
Total SG&A			$35
Section 987 net income (revenue less COGS and SG&A)			$227

OFCNV—End of 2022

Assets	Amount in €	Translation Rate	Amount in $
Euros	€ 260.00	€ 1 = $3.00 (year-end spot rate-2022)	$780
Building	740.00	€ 1 = $1.00 (historic rate-2020)	740
Machine	240.00	€ 1 = $1.00 (historic rate-2020)	240
Inventory	10.80	€ 1 = $2.50 (historic rate-2022)	27
	40.00	€ 1 = $1.50 (historic rate-2021)	60
Total assets			$1,847
Liabilities			
Total liabilities			$0
2022 ending OFCNV			$1,847

(B) *Determination of net unrecognized section 987 gain or loss.* The net unrecognized section 987 gain of Business A for 2022 is determined under paragraph (d) of this section as follows (relevant steps only):

(1) *Step 1.* Under paragraph (d)(1) of this section, the change in OFCNV for the taxable year must be determined. This amount is equal to the OFCNV of Business A determined under paragraph (e) of this section on the last day of 2022, less the OFCNV of Business A determined on the last day of 2021.

2022 ending OFCNV	$1,847
Less: 2021 ending OFCNV	($1,410)
Change in OFCNV	$437

(2) *Step 6—Decrease the aggregate amount determined in steps 1 through 5 by the section 987 taxable income of the section 987 QBU for the taxable year.* Under paragraph (d)(6) of this section, the aggregate amount determined in steps 1 through 5 must be decreased by the section 987 taxable income of Business A. The amount of Business A's taxable income for 2022, as determined above, is $227.

Change in OFCNV	$437
Less: section 987 taxable income	(227)
Unrecognized section 987 gain 2022	$210
Plus: net accumulated unrecognized section 987 gain from prior years	130
Net unrecognized section 987 gain	$340

(iv) *Operations in 2023.* During 2023, Business A recognizes revenue of € 252 from sales of finished goods. The related COGS is € 140.80, reflecting a full liquidation of the 2022 inventory layer with a LIFO cost basis of $10.80 and a partial liquidation of inventory from the 2021 layer with a LIFO cost basis of $10.00. Business A pays € 10 in salaries allocable to SG&A. Inventoriable costs in 2023 include € 10 of depreciation on the building and € 30 of depreciation on the machine. Business A's balance sheet on December 31, 2023, shows no liabilities and the following assets: currency of € 422, the building with an adjusted basis of € 720, the machine with an adjusted basis of € 210, and a 2021 layer of ending inventory with a LIFO cost basis of € 30, comprising raw materials and finished goods. The yearly average exchange rate for 2023 is € 1 = $3.50, and the spot rate on December 31, 2023 is € 1 = $4.00.

(A) *Determination of income.* Business A's income for 2023 is computed as follows:

Item	Amount in €	Translation Rate	Amount in $
Sales revenue	€ 252	€ 1 = $3.50 (yearly avg. rate-2023)	$882
COGS before adjustments	140.80	€ 1 = $3.50 (yearly avg. rate-2023)	$492.80
Adjustment for cost recovery deductions (see calculation below)			(100.00)
Adjustment for LIFO liquidation (see calculation below)			(30.80)
Adjusted COGS			$362.00
SG&A			
Depreciation on building (50%)	10	€ 1 = $1.00 (historic rate-2020)	$10
Salaries	10	€ 1 = $3.50 (yearly avg. rate-2023)	35
Total SG&A			$45
Section 987 net income			$475

COGS Adjustments

Adjustment for cost recovery deductions

Depreciation Amount	Historic Rate	2023 Yearly Avg. Rate	Difference in Translation Rates	Adjustment (Depreciation x Change in Rates)
€ 10 (building)	1.00	3.50	(2.50)	($25)
€ 30 (machine)	1.00	3.50	(2.50)	($75)
Total adjustment for cost recovery deductions				($100)

Adjustment for LIFO liquidation

LIFO Liquidation Layer	Historic Rate	2023 Yearly Avg Rate	Difference in Translation Rates	Adjustment (Liquidated Layer x Change in Rates)
€ 10.80 (2022)	2.50	3.50	(1.00)	($10.80)
€ 10 (2021)	1.50	3.50	(2.00)	($20.00)
Total adjustment for liquidation of LIFO layers				($30.80)

(B) *Determination of OFCNV.* The OFCNV of Business A for 2023 is determined under paragraph (e) of this section as follows:

OFCNV—End of 2023

Assets	Amount in €	Translation Rate	Amount in $
Euros	€ 422	€ 1 = $4.00 (year-end spot rate-2023)	$1,688
Building	720	€ 1 = $1.00 (historic rate-2020)	720
Machine	210	€ 1 = $1.00 (historic rate-2020)	210
Inventory	30	€ 1 = $1.50 (historic rate-2021)	45
Total assets			$2,663
Liabilities			
Total liabilities			$0
2023 ending OFCNV			$2,663

(C) *Determination of net unrecognized section 987 gain or loss.* The net unrecognized section 987 gain of Business A is determined under paragraph (d) of this section as follows (relevant steps only):

(1) *Step 1.* Under paragraph (d)(1) of this section, the change in OFCNV for the taxable year must be determined. This amount is equal to the OFCNV of Business A determined under paragraph (e) of this section on the last day of 2023, less the OFCNV of Business A determined on the last day of 2022.

2023 ending OFCNV	$2,663
Less: 2022 ending OFCNV	(1,847)
Change in OFCNV	$816

(2) *Step 6—Decrease the aggregate amount determined in steps 1 through 5 by the section 987 taxable income of the section 987 QBU for the taxable year.* Under paragraph (d)(6) of this section, the aggregate amount determined in steps 1 through 5 must be decreased by the section 987 taxable income of Business A. The amount of Business A's taxable income for 2023, as determined above, is $475.

Change in OFCNV	$816
Less: section 987 taxable income	(475)
Unrecognized section 987 gain 2023	$341
Plus: net accumulated unrecognized section 987 gain from prior years	340
Net unrecognized section 987 gain	$681

(h) *Effective/applicability date.*—(1) *In general.*—Except as set forth in paragraph (h)(2) of this section, this section is applicable as specified in § 1.987-11.

(2) *Combinations and separations.*—Paragraphs (c)(2) and (f) of this section apply to taxable years beginning on or after the day that is three years after the first day of the first taxable year following December 7, 2016. Notwithstanding the preceding sentence, if a taxpayer makes an election under § 1.987-11(b), then paragraphs (c)(2) and (f) of this section applies to taxable years to which §§ 1.987-1 through 1.987-10 apply as a result of such election. [Reg. § 1.987-4.]

☐ *[T.D. 9794, 12-7-2016. Amended by T.D. 9795, 12-7-2016 and T.D. 9857, 5-10-2019 (corrected 6-28-2019).]*

»»→ Caution: The Treasury Department has identified Reg. §1.987-5, as amended by T.D. 9794, as a significant tax regulation that imposes an undue financial burden on U.S. taxpayers and/or adds undue complexity to the federal tax laws, pursuant to Executive Order 13789 (issued April 21, 2017) (Notice 2017-38, I.R.B. 2017-30, 147). In a subsequent report, published October 16, 2017, Treasury recommended planned actions that would reduce the burden of these regulations, including an extension of the application date of T.D. 9794 (see Notice 2022-34, I.R.B. 2022-34, 150).

§ 1.987-5. Recognition of section 987 gain or loss.—(a) *Recognition of section 987 gain or loss by the owner of a section 987 QBU.*—The taxable income of an owner of a section 987 QBU shall include the owner's section 987 gain or loss recognized with respect to the section 987 QBU for the taxable year. Except as otherwise provided, for any taxable year the owner's section 987 gain or loss recognized with respect to a section 987 QBU shall equal:

(1) The owner's net unrecognized section 987 gain or loss with respect to the section 987 QBU determined under § 1.987-4 on the last day of such taxable year (or, if earlier, on the day the section 987 QBU is terminated under § 1.987-8); multiplied by

(2) The owner's remittance proportion for the taxable year, as determined under paragraph (b) of this section.

(b) *Remittance proportion.*—The owner's remittance proportion with respect to a section 987 QBU for a taxable year shall equal:

(1) The remittance, as determined under paragraph (c) of this section, to the owner from the section 987 QBU for such taxable year; divided by

(2) The sum of

(A) The aggregate adjusted basis of the gross assets of the section 987 QBU as of the end of the taxable year that are reflected on its year-end balance sheet translated into the owner's functional currency as provided in § 1.987-4(e)(2) and

(B) The amount of the remittance as determined under paragraph (c) of this section.

(c) *Remittance.*—(1) *Definition.*—A remittance shall be determined in the owner's functional currency and shall equal the excess, if any, of:

(i) The aggregate of all amounts transferred from the section 987 QBU to the owner during the taxable year, as determined in paragraph (d) of this section; over

(ii) The aggregate of all amounts transferred from the owner to the section 987 QBU during the taxable year, as determined in paragraph (e) of this section.

(2) *Day when a remittance is determined.*—An owner's remittance from a section 987 QBU shall be determined on the last day of the owner's taxable year (or, if earlier, on the day the section 987 QBU is terminated under § 1.987-8).

(3) *Termination.*—A termination of a section 987 QBU as determined under § 1.987-8 is treated as a remittance of all the gross assets of the section 987 QBU to the owner on the date of such termination. See § 1.987-8(e). Accordingly, the remittance proportion in the case of a termination is 1.

(d) *Aggregate of all amounts transferred from the section 987 QBU to the owner for the taxable year.*—For purposes of paragraph (c)(1)(i) of this section, the aggregate amount transferred from the section 987 QBU to the owner for the taxable year shall be the aggregate amount of functional currency and the aggregate adjusted basis of the assets transferred, as determined in the owner's functional currency under § 1.987-4(d)(2). Solely for this purpose, the amount of liabilities transferred from the owner to the section 987 QBU, as determined in the owner's functional currency under § 1.987-4(d)(5), shall be treated as a transfer of assets from the section 987 QBU to the owner in an amount equal to the amount of such liabilities.

(e) *Aggregate of all amounts transferred from the owner to the section 987 QBU for the taxable year.*—For purposes of paragraph (c)(1)(ii) of this section, the aggregate of all amounts transferred from the owner to the section 987 QBU for the taxable year shall be the aggregate amount of functional currency and the aggregate adjusted basis of the assets transferred, as determined in the owner's functional currency under § 1.987-4(d)(3). Solely for this purpose, the amount of liabilities transferred from the section 987 QBU to the owner determined under § 1.987-4(d)(4) shall be treated as a transfer of assets from the owner to the section 987 QBU in an amount equal to the amount of such liabilities.

(f) *Determination of owner's adjusted basis in transferred assets.*—(1) *In general.*—The owner's adjusted basis in an asset received in a transfer from a section 987 QBU (whether or not such transfer is made in connection with a remittance, as defined in paragraph (c) of this section) shall be determined in the owner's functional currency under the rules prescribed in paragraphs (f)(2) and (f)(3) of this section.

(2) *Marked asset.*—The basis of a marked asset shall be the amount determined by translating the section 987 QBU's functional currency basis of the asset, after taking into account § 1.988-1(a)(10), into the owner's functional currency at the spot rate (as defined in § 1.987-1(c)(1)) applicable to the date of transfer.

(3) *Historic asset.*—The basis of a historic asset shall be the amount determined by translating the section 987 QBU's functional currency basis of the asset, after taking into account § 1.988-1(a)(10), into the owner's functional currency at the historic rate for the asset (as defined in § 1.987-1(c)(3)).

(g) *Example.*—The following example illustrates the calculation of section 987 gain or loss under this section:

Example. (i) U.S. Corp, a domestic corporation with the dollar as its functional currency, operates in the United Kingdom through Business A, a section 987 QBU with the pound as its functional currency. During 2021, the following transfers took place between U.S. Corp and Business A. On January 5, 2021, U.S. Corp transferred to Business A $300, which Business A used during the year to purchase services. On March 5, 2021, Business A transferred a machine to U.S. Corp. The pound adjusted basis of the machine when properly translated into dollars as described under § 1.987-4(d)(2)(ii)(B) and paragraph (d) of this section is $500. On November 1, 2021, Business A transferred pounds to U.S. Corp. The dollar amount of the pounds when properly translated as described under § 1.987-4(d)(2)(ii)(A) and paragraph (d) of this section is $2,300. On December 7, 2021, U.S Corp transferred a truck to Business A with an adjusted basis of $2,000.

(ii) At the end of 2021, Business A holds assets, properly translated into the owner's functional currency pursuant to § 1.987-4(e)(2), consisting of a computer with a pound adjusted basis equivalent to $500, a truck with a pound adjusted basis equivalent to $2,000, and pounds equivalent to $2,850. In addition, Business A has a pound liability entered into in 2020 with Bank A. All such assets and liabilities are reflected on the books and records of Business A. Assume that the net unrecognized section 987 gain for Business A as determined under § 1.987-4 as of the last day of 2021 is $80.

(iii) U.S. Corp's section 987 gain with respect to Business A is determined as follows:

(A) *Computation of amount of remittance.* Under paragraphs (c)(1) and (c)(2) of this section, U.S. Corp must determine the amount of the remittance for 2021 in the owner's functional currency (dollars) on the last day of 2021. The amount of the remittance for 2021 is $500, determined as follows:

Transfers from Business A to U.S. Corp in dollars:	
Machine	$500
Pounds	2,300
Aggregate transfers from Business A to U.S. Corp	$2,800
Transfers from U.S. Corp to Business A in dollars:	
U.S. dollars	$300
Truck	2,000
Aggregate transfers from U.S. Corp to Business A	$2,300
Computation of amount of remittance:	
Aggregate transfers from Business A to U.S. Corp	$2,800
Less: aggregate transfers from U.S. Corp to Business A	(2,300)
Total remittance	$500

(B) *Computation of section 987 QBU gross assets plus remittance.* Under paragraph (b)(2) of this section, Business A must determine the aggregate basis of its gross assets that are reflected on its year-end balance sheet translated into the owner's functional currency and must increase this amount by the amount of the remittance.

Computer	$500
Pounds	2,850
Truck	2,000
Aggregate gross assets	$5,350
Remittance	$500
Aggregate basis of Business A's gross assets at end of 2021, increased by amount of remittance	$5,850

(C) *Computation of remittance proportion.* Under paragraph (b) of this section, Business A must compute the remittance proportion by dividing the $500 remittance amount by the $5,850 sum of the aggregate basis of Business A's gross assets and the amount of the remittance. The resulting remittance proportion is 0.085.

(D) *Computation of section 987 gain or loss.* The amount of U.S. Corp's section 987 gain or loss that must be recognized with respect to Business A is determined under paragraph (a) of this section by multiplying the 0.085 remittance proportion by the $80 of net unrecognized section 987 gain. U.S. Corp's resulting recognized section 987 gain for 2021 is $6.80. [Reg. § 1.987-5.]

☐ *[T.D. 8367, 9-24-91. Amended by T.D. 9794, 12-7-2016.]*

»»→ Caution: The Treasury Department has identified Reg. § 1.987-6, as amended by T.D. 9794, as a significant tax regulation that imposes an undue financial burden on U.S. taxpayers and/or adds undue complexity to the federal tax laws, pursuant to Executive Order 13789 (issued April 21, 2017) (Notice 2017-38, I.R.B. 2017-30, 147). In a subsequent report, published October 16, 2017, Treasury recommended planned actions that would reduce the burden of these regulations, including an extension of the application date of T.D. 9794 (see Notice 2022-34, I.R.B. 2022-34, 150).

§ 1.987-6. Character and source of section 987 gain or loss.—(a) *Ordinary income or loss.*—Section 987 gain or loss is ordinary income or loss for Federal income tax purposes.

(b) *Character and source of section 987 gain or loss.*—(1) *In general.*—With respect to each section 987 QBU, the owner must determine the character and source of section 987 gain or loss in the year of a remittance under the rules of this paragraph (b) for all purposes of the Internal Revenue Code, including sections 904(d), 907, and 954.

(2) *Method required to characterize and source section 987 gain or loss.*—The owner must use the asset method set forth in § 1.861-9T(g) to characterize and source section 987 gain or loss. In applying the asset method, the owner must take into account only the assets of the section 987 QBU and must consistently determine the value of the assets on the basis of either the tax book value or the fair market value of the assets. The modified gross income method described in § 1.861-9T(j) cannot be used.

(3) *Coordination with section 954.*—Solely for purposes of determining the excess of foreign currency gains over foreign currency

losses characterized as foreign personal holding company income under section 954(c)(1)(D), section 987 gain or loss that is characterized pursuant to paragraph (b)(2) of this section by reference to assets that give rise to subpart F income shall be treated as foreign currency gain or foreign currency loss attributable to section 988 transactions not directly related to the business needs of the controlled foreign corporation.

(4) [Reserved]. For further guidance, see § 1.987-6T(b)(4).

(c) *Examples.*—The following examples illustrate the application of this section.

Example 1. CFC is a controlled foreign corporation as defined in section 957 with the Swiss franc (Sf) as its functional currency. CFC is the owner of Business A, a section 987 QBU that has the euro as its functional currency. For the year 2021, CFC recognizes section 987 gain of Sf10,000 under § 1.987-5. Applying the rules of this section, Business A has average total assets of Sf1,000,000, which generate income as follows: Sf750,000 of assets that generate foreign source general limitation income under section 904(d)(1)(A), none of which is subpart F income under section 952; and Sf250,000 of assets that generate foreign source passive income under section 904(d)(1)(B), all of which is subpart F income. Under paragraph (b) of this section, Sf7,500 (Sf750,000/Sf1,000,000 x Sf10,000) of the section 987 gain will be characterized as foreign source general limitation income that is not subpart F income under section 952, and Sf2,500 (Sf250,000/Sf1,000,000 x Sf10,000) will be characterized as foreign source passive income that is characterized as foreign personal holding company income under section 954(c)(1)(D). All of the section 987 gain is treated as ordinary income.

Example 2. The facts are the same as in *Example 1* except that: (a) CFC recognizes section 987 loss of Sf40,000, Sf10,000 of which is characterized under paragraph (b) of this section by reference to assets that give rise to subpart F income; and (b) CFC otherwise has Sf12,000 of net foreign currency gain determined under § 1.954-2(g) that is taken into account in determining the excess of foreign currency gain over foreign currency losses characterized as foreign personal holding company income under section 954(c)(1)(D). Under paragraph (b)(3) of this section, the Sf10,000 section 987 loss characterized by reference to assets that give rise to subpart F income is treated as foreign currency loss attributable to section 988 transactions not directly related to the business needs of the controlled foreign corporation for purposes of determining the excess of foreign currency gains over foreign currency losses characterized as foreign personal holding company income under section 954(c)(1)(D). Accordingly, CFC will aggregate the Sf10,000 section 987 loss with the Sf12,000 net foreign currency gain and will have Sf2,000 of net foreign currency gain characterized as foreign personal holding company income under section 954(c)(1)(D). [Reg. § 1.987-6.]

☐ [*T.D. 9794, 12-7-2016. Amended by T.D. 9795, 12-7-2016.*]

»»→ Caution: Temporary Reg. §1.987-6T, below, expired on December 6, 2019. The related proposed regulation, published in REG-128276-12 by cross-reference to the temporary regulation, may be relied upon for periods following the expiration date (see Notice 2022-34, I.R.B. 2022-34, 150).

§ 1.987-6T. Character and source of section 987 gain or loss (temporary).—(a) through (b)(3) [Reserved]. For further guidance, see § 1.987-6(a) through (b)(3).

(4) *Source of section 987 gain or loss with respect to a dollar QBU.*—The source of section 987 gain or loss with respect to a dollar QBU (as defined in § 1.987-1T(b)(6)(i)) for which the CFC owner has elected under § 1.987-1T(b)(6)(iii) to apply section 987 is determined by reference to the residence of the CFC owner. This paragraph (b)(4) applies to any CFC that has made the election under § 1.987-1T(b)(6)(iii), including a CFC described in § 1.987-1(b)(1)(ii).

(c) [Reserved]. For further guidance, see § 1.987-6(c).

(d) *Effective/applicability date.*—This section applies to taxable years beginning on or after one year after the first day of the first taxable year following December 7, 2016. Notwithstanding the preceding sentence, if a taxpayer makes an election under § 1.987-11(b), then this section applies to taxable years to which §§ 1.987-1 through 1.987-10 apply as a result of such election.

(e) *Expiration date.*—The applicability of this section expires on December 6, 2019. [Temporary Reg. § 1.987-6T.]

☐ [*T.D.* 9795, 12-7-2016.]

»»→ Caution: The Treasury Department has identified Reg. §1.987-7, as amended by T.D. 9794, as a significant tax regulation that imposes an undue financial burden on U.S. taxpayers and/or adds undue complexity to the federal tax laws, pursuant to Executive Order 13789 (issued April 21, 2017) (Notice 2017-38, I.R.B. 2017-30, 147). In a subsequent report, published October 16, 2017, Treasury recommended planned actions that would reduce the burden of these regulations, including an extension of the application date of T.D. 9794 (see Notice 2022-34, I.R.B. 2022-34, 150).

§ 1.987-7. Section 987 aggregate partnerships.—(a) *In general.*—This section provides rules for determining an owner's share of the assets and liabilities of an eligible QBU that is owned indirectly, as described in § 1.987-1(b)(4)(ii), through a section 987 aggregate partnership.

(b) [Reserved].

(c) *Coordination with subchapter K.*—[Reserved]. [Reg. § 1.987-7.]

☐ [*T.D. 9794, 12-7-2016. Amended by T.D. 9795, 12-7-2016 and T.D.* 9857, 5-10-2019.]

»»→ Caution: The Treasury Department has identified Reg. §1.987-8, as amended by T.D. 9794, as a significant tax regulation that imposes an undue financial burden on U.S. taxpayers and/or adds undue complexity to the federal tax laws, pursuant to Executive Order 13789 (issued April 21, 2017) (Notice 2017-38, I.R.B. 2017-30, 147). In a subsequent report, published October 16, 2017, Treasury recommended planned actions that would reduce the burden of these regulations, including an extension of the application date of T.D. 9794 (see Notice 2022-34, I.R.B. 2022-34, 150).

§ 1.987-8. Termination of a section 987 QBU.—(a) *Scope.*—This section provides rules regarding the termination of a section 987 QBU. Paragraph (b) of this section provides general rules for determining when a termination occurs. Paragraph (c) of this section provides exceptions to the general termination rules for certain transactions described in section 381(a). Paragraph (e) of this section describes certain effects of terminations. Paragraph (f) of this section contains examples that illustrate the principles of this section.

(b) *In general.*—Except as provided in paragraph (c) of this section, a section 987 QBU terminates if the conditions described in one of paragraphs (b)(1) through (4) is satisfied.

(1) *Trade or business ceases.*—A section 987 QBU ceases its trade or business. When a section 987 QBU ceases its trade or business is determined based on all the facts and circumstances, provided that an owner may continue to treat a section 987 QBU as a section 987 QBU for a reasonable period during the winding up of such trade or business, which period may in no event exceed two years from the date on which such QBU ceases its activities carried on for profit.

(2) *Substantially all assets transferred.*—The section 987 QBU transfers substantially all (within the meaning of section 368(a)(1)(C)) of its assets to its owner. For purposes of this paragraph (b)(2), the amount of assets transferred from the section 987 QBU to its owner as a result of a transaction shall be reduced by the amount of assets transferred from the owner to the section 987 QBU pursuant to the same transaction. See Examples 2, 5, and 6 in paragraph (f) of this section.

(3) *Owner no longer a CFC.*—A foreign corporation that is a controlled foreign corporation (as defined in section 957) that is the owner of a section 987 QBU ceases to be a controlled foreign corporation as a result of a transaction or series of transactions after which persons that were related to the corporation within the meaning of section 267(b) immediately before the transaction or series of transactions collectively own sufficient interests in the corporation such that the corporation would continue to be considered a controlled foreign corporation if such persons were United States shareholders within the meaning of section 951(b).

(4) *Owner ceases to exist.*—The owner of the section 987 QBU ceases to exist (including in connection with a transaction described in section 381(a)).

(c) *Transactions described in section 381(a).*—(1) *Liquidations.*—Notwithstanding paragraph (b) of this section, a termination does not occur when the owner of a section 987 QBU ceases to exist in a liquidation described in section 332, except in the following cases:

(i) The distributor is a domestic corporation and the distributee is a foreign corporation.

(ii) The distributor is a foreign corporation and the distributee is a domestic corporation.

(iii) The distributor and the distributee are both foreign corporations and the functional currency of the distributee is the same as the functional currency of the distributor's section 987 QBU.

(2) *Reorganizations.*—Notwithstanding paragraph (b) of this section, a termination does not occur when the owner of the section 987 QBU ceases to exist in a reorganization described in section 381(a)(2), except in the following cases:

(i) The transferor is a domestic corporation and the acquiring corporation is a foreign corporation.

(ii) The transferor is a foreign corporation and the acquiring corporation is a domestic corporation.

(iii) The transferor is a controlled foreign corporation immediately before the transfer, the acquiring corporation is a foreign corporation that is not a controlled foreign corporation immediately after the transfer, and the acquiring corporation was related to the transferor within the meaning of section 267(b) immediately before the transfer.

(iv) The transferor and the acquiring corporation are foreign corporations and the functional currency of the acquiring corporation is the same as the functional currency of the transferor's section 987 QBU.

(d) [Reserved]. For further guidance, see § 1.987-8T(d).

(e) *Effect of terminations.*—A termination of a section 987 QBU as determined in this section is treated as a remittance of all the gross assets of the section 987 QBU to its owner immediately before the section 987 QBU terminates. Thus, except as otherwise provided in these regulations under section 987, a termination results in the recognition of any net unrecognized section 987 gain or loss of the section 987 QBU. See § 1.987-5(c)(3).

(f) *Examples.*—The following examples illustrate the principles of this section. Except as otherwise provided, U.S. Corp is a domestic corporation that has the U.S. dollar as its functional currency, and Business A is a section 987 QBU.

Example 1. Cessation of operations. (i) *Facts.* U.S. Corp is the owner of Business A, a sales office of U.S. Corp in Country X. Business A ceases sales activities on December 31, 2021. During 2022, Business A sells all of the assets used in its sales activities and winds up its business, settling outstanding accounts.

(ii) *Analysis.* Business A's trade or business ceases on December 31, 2021. The cessation of Business A's trade or business causes a termination of the Business A section 987 QBU under paragraph (b)(1) of this section on December 31, 2021, unless U.S. Corp chooses to continue to treat Business A as a section 987 QBU until completion of the wind-up activities in 2022. If U.S. Corp chooses to continue to treat Business A as a section 987 QBU during the wind-up of Business A, Business A section 987 QBU would terminate under paragraph (b)(1) of this section upon completion of the wind-up in 2022.

Example 2. Transfer of a section 987 QBU to a member of a consolidated group. (i) *Facts.* U.S. Corp, the owner of Business A, transfers all the assets and liabilities of Business A to DS, a domestic corporation all of the stock of which is owned by U.S. Corp, in a transaction qualifying under section 351. U.S. Corp and DS are members of the same consolidated group.

(ii) *Analysis.* Pursuant to § 1.987-2(c)(2)(i) and (ii), as a result of the deemed exchange of the assets and liabilities of Business A for DS stock in a section 351 transaction, Business A is treated as transferring its assets and liabilities to U.S. Corp immediately before the transfer by U.S. Corp of the assets and liabilities to DS. Because a section 351 transaction is not a transaction described in section 381(a), the transfer of all of the assets of Business A to U.S. Corp causes a termination of the Business A section 987 QBU under paragraph (b)(2) of this section.

Example 3. Cessation of controlled foreign corporation status. (i) *Facts.* Foreign parent (FP) is a foreign corporation that owns all the stock of U.S. Corp, a domestic corporation. U.S. Corp owns all of the stock of FC, a controlled foreign corporation as defined in section 957. FC is the owner of Business A. FP contributes cash to FC in exchange for FC stock representing 60 percent of the voting power and value of all FC stock. FC no longer constitutes a controlled foreign corporation after the capital contribution.

(ii) *Analysis.* Because FC ceases to qualify as a controlled foreign corporation as a result of a transaction after which persons that were related to FC within the meaning of section 267(b) immediately before the transaction collectively own sufficient interests in FC such that the FC would continue to be considered a controlled foreign corporation if such persons were United States shareholders within the meaning of section 951(b), the Business A section 987 QBU terminates pursuant to paragraph (b)(3) of this section.

Example 4. Section 332 liquidation. (i) *Facts.* U.S. Corp owns all of the stock of FC, a foreign corporation. FC is the owner of Business A. Pursuant to a liquidation described in section 332, FC transfers all of its assets and liabilities to U.S. Corp.

(ii) *Analysis.* FC's liquidation causes a termination of the Business A section 987 QBU as provided in paragraph (b)(4) of this section because FC ceases to exist as a result of the liquidation. The exception for certain section 332 liquidations provided under paragraph (c)(1) of this section does not apply because U.S. Corp is a domestic corporation and FC is a foreign corporation. See paragraph (c)(1)(ii) of this section.

Example 5. Transfers to and from a section 987 QBU pursuant to the same transaction. (i) *Facts.* U.S. Corp owns 100 percent of DC1 and DC2, each a domestic corporation. DC1 owns Entity A, a DE that conducts a business (Business A) in Country X that constitutes a section 987 QBU of DC1. DC2 subsequently contributes property to Entity A in exchange for a 95 percent interest in Entity A. The property DC2 contributes to Entity A is used in the business conducted by Business A and is reflected on its books and records as provided under § 1.987-2(b).

(ii) *Analysis.* (A) For general Federal income tax purposes, Entity A is converted to a partnership when DC2 contributes property to Entity A in exchange for a 95 percent interest in Entity A. DC2's contribution is treated as a contribution to a partnership in exchange for an ownership interest in the partnership. DC1 is treated as contributing all of Business A to the partnership in exchange for a partnership interest. See Rev. Rul. 99-5 (situation 2), (1999-1 CB 434) and § 601.601(d)(2) of this chapter. For purposes of this section, these deemed transactions are not taken into account. See § 1.987-2(c) and § 1.987-2(c)(10), Example 9.

(B) Under § 1.987-1(b)(5)(i), Entity A is converted to a section 987 aggregate partnership when DC2 contributes property to Entity A in exchange for a 95 percent interest in Entity A because DC1 and DC2 own all the interests in partnership capital and profits, DC1 and DC2 are related within the meaning of section 267(b), and the requirements of § 1.987-1(b)(5)(i)(B) are satisfied. Because DC2 is a partner in a section 987 aggregate partnership that owns Business A and because DC2 and Business A have different functional currencies, DC2's portion of the Business A assets constitutes a section 987 QBU of DC2.

(C) As a result of the conversion of Entity A to a partnership, DC2 acquires an allocable share of 95 percent of the assets of Business A, as determined under § 1.987-7. Accordingly, under § 1.987-2(c)(5), DC2 is treated as contributing 95 percent of its contributed property to its Business A section 987 QBU. In addition, DC2 is treated as transferring 5 percent of the contributed property to DC1, and DC1 is subsequently treated as transferring that property to DC1's Business A section 987 QBU. In addition, 95 percent of the original (pre-conversion) assets of Business A cease being reflected on the books and records of DC1's section 987 QBU. Under § 1.987-2(b)(5), these amounts are treated as if they are transferred from DC1's section 987 QBU to DC1, and DC1 is treated as transferring these assets to DC2. DC2 is subsequently treated as transferring these assets to DC2's Business A section 987 QBU. The other 5 percent of the original (pre-conversion) assets are treated as remaining on the books and records of DC1's section 987 QBU and are not deemed to be transferred.

(D) For purposes of determining whether substantially all the assets of Business A were transferred from DC1's section 987 QBU as provided under paragraph (b)(2) of this section, the amount of assets transferred from Business A to DC1 under § 1.987-2(c) (95 percent of the assets held by Business A before the contribution by DC2) must be reduced by the 5 percent of the assets contributed by DC2, which were treated as transferred from DC2 to DC1 and subsequently transferred from DC1 to its Business A section 987 QBU, as a result of the formation of the section 987 aggregate partnership. Accordingly, the amount of assets transferred from DC1's section 987 QBU for purposes of paragraph (b)(2) of this section is equal to 95 percent of the original (pre-conversion) assets minus 5 percent of DC2's contributed assets.

Example 6. Deemed transfers to a CFC upon a check-the-box election. (i) *Facts.* In 2021, U.S. Corp forms an entity in a foreign country, Entity A. Entity A owns Business A, which has the pound as its functional currency. Entity A forms Entity B in another foreign country. Entity B owns Business B, a section 987 QBU that has the euro as its functional currency. At the time of formation, Entity A and Entity B elect to be DEs. In 2026, Entity A files an election on Form 8832 to be classified as a corporation under § 301.7701-3(g)(1)(iv) and becomes a CFC (FC) owned directly by U.S. Corp. FC has the pound as its functional currency.

(ii) *Analysis.* (A) Under § 1.987-1(b)(4)(i), U.S. Corp is the owner of Business A and Business B. In 2026, when Entity A elects to be classified as a corporation, U.S. Corp is deemed to contribute the assets and liabilities of Business A and Business B to FC under section 351 in exchange for FC stock. Pursuant to § 1.987-2(c)(2)(i) and (ii), as a result of the deemed exchange of the assets and liabilities of Business A and Business B for FC stock in a section 351 transaction, Business A and Business B are each treated as transferring their assets and liabilities to U.S. Corp immediately before U.S. Corp's transfer of such assets and liabilities to FC. The transfer of assets from Business A and Business B to U.S. Corp causes terminations of those section 987 QBUs under paragraph (b)(2) of this section. The assets and liabilities of Business A and Business B are now owned by FC, but because FC and Business A have the same functional currency, only Business B qualifies as a section 987 QBU to which section 987 applies.

(B) Terminations also would have occurred in 2026 if U.S. Corp had contributed Entity A and Entity B to an existing foreign corporation owned by U.S. Corp or to a newly created foreign corporation owned by U.S. Corp pursuant to a section 351 exchange because the transfer of all of the assets of Business A and Business B would cause terminations of those section 987 QBUs under paragraph (b)(2) of this section.

Example 7. Sale of a section 987 QBU to a member of a consolidated group. (i) *Facts.* U.S. Corp, the owner of Business A, sells all of the assets and liabilities of Business A to DS, a domestic corporation, in exchange for cash. U.S. Corp and DS are members of the same consolidated group. The cash received on the sale is recorded on the books of U.S. Corp.

(ii) *Analysis.* Pursuant to § 1.987-2(c)(2)(i) and (ii), Business A is treated as transferring all of its assets and liabilities to U.S. Corp immediately before the sale by U.S. Corp to DS. As a result of this deemed transfer from Business A to U.S. Corp, the Business A section 987 QBU terminates under paragraph (b)(2) of this section. [Reg. § 1.987-8.]

☐ [*T.D. 9794, 12-7-2016. Amended by T.D. 9795, 12-7-2016.*]

§ 1.987-8T. Termination of a section 987 QBU (temporary).—(a) through (c) [Reserved]. For further guidance, see § 1.987-8(a) through (c).

(d) *Annual deemed termination election.*—A taxpayer, including a taxpayer described in § 1.987-1(b)(1)(ii) to which §§ 1.987-1 through 1.987-11 generally do not apply, may elect under this paragraph (d) to deem all of the section 987 QBUs of which it is an owner to terminate on the last day of each taxable year for which the election is in effect. See § 1.987-8(e) regarding the effect of such a deemed termination. The owner of a section 987 QBU that is deemed to terminate under this paragraph is treated as having transferred all of the assets and liabilities attributable to such section 987 QBU to a new section 987 QBU on the first day of the following taxable year.

(e) through (f) [Reserved]. For further guidance, see § 1.987-8(e) through (f).

(g) *Effective/applicability date.*—This section applies to taxable years beginning on or after December 7, 2016.

(h) *Expiration date.*—The applicability of this section expires on December 6, 2019. [Temporary Reg. § 1.987-8T.]

☐ [*T.D. 9795, 12-7-2016.*]

»»→ Caution: The Treasury Department has identified Reg. §1.987-9, as amended by T.D. 9794, as a significant tax regulation that imposes an undue financial burden on U.S. taxpayers and/or adds undue complexity to the federal tax laws, pursuant to Executive Order 13789 (issued April 21, 2017) (Notice 2017-38, I.R.B. 2017-30, 147). In a subsequent report, published October 16, 2017, Treasury recommended planned actions that would reduce the burden of these regulations, including an extension of the application date of T.D. 9794 (see Notice 2022-34, I.R.B. 2022-34, 150).

§ 1.987-9. Recordkeeping requirements.—(a) *In general.*—A taxpayer that is an owner of a section 987 QBU shall keep a copy of each election made by the taxpayer in accordance with the rules of § 1.987-1(g)(3) (if not required to be made on a form published by the Commissioner regarding section 987) and such reasonable records as are sufficient to establish the section 987 QBU's taxable income or loss and section 987 gain or loss.

(b) *Supplemental information.*—An owner's obligation to maintain records under section 6001 and paragraph (a) of this section is not satisfied unless the following information is maintained in such records with respect to each section 987 QBU:

(1) The amount of the items of income, gain, deduction, or loss attributed to the section 987 QBU in the functional currency of the section 987 QBU.

(2) The amount of assets and liabilities attributed to the section 987 QBU in the functional currency of the section 987 QBU.

(3) The exchange rates used to translate items of income, gain, deduction, or loss of the section 987 QBU into the owner's functional currency and, if a spot rate convention is used, the manner in which such convention is determined.

(4) The exchange rates used to translate the assets and liabilities of the section 987 QBU into the owner's functional currency and, if a spot rate convention is used, the manner in which such convention is determined.

(5) The amount of the items of income, gain, deduction, or loss attributed to the section 987 QBU translated into the functional currency of the owner.

(6) The amount of assets and liabilities attributed to the section 987 QBU translated into the functional currency of the owner.

(7) The amount of assets and liabilities transferred by the owner to the section 987 QBU determined in the functional currency of the owner.

(8) The amount of assets and liabilities transferred by the section 987 QBU to the owner determined in the functional currency of the owner.

(9) The amount of the unrecognized section 987 gain or loss for the taxable year.

(10) The amount of the net accumulated unrecognized section 987 gain or loss at the close of the taxable year.

(11) If a remittance is made, the computations determined under § 1.861-9T(g) for purposes of sourcing and characterizing the remittance under § 1.987-5.

(12) The transition information required to be determined under § 1.987-10(e).

(c) *Retention of records.*—The records required by this section, or records that support the information required on a form published by the Commissioner regarding section 987, must be maintained and kept at all times available for inspection by the Internal Revenue Service for so long as the contents thereof may become relevant in the administration of the Internal Revenue Code.

(d) *Information on a dedicated section 987 form.*—The requirements of paragraph (b) of this section shall be satisfied if the taxpayer provides the specific information required on a form published by the Commissioner for this purpose. [Reg. § 1.987-9.]

☐ [*T.D. 9794, 12-7-2016.*]

»»→ Caution: The Treasury Department has identified Reg. §1.987-10, as amended by T.D. 9794, as a significant tax regulation that imposes an undue financial burden on U.S. taxpayers and/or adds undue complexity to the federal tax laws, pursuant to Executive Order 13789 (issued April 21, 2017) (Notice 2017-38, I.R.B. 2017-30, 147). In a subsequent report, published October 16, 2017, Treasury recommended planned actions that would reduce the burden of these regulations, including an extension of the application date of T.D. 9794 (see Notice 2022-34, I.R.B. 2022-34, 150).

§ 1.987-10. Transition rules.—(a) *Scope.*—These transition rules shall apply to any taxpayer that is an owner of a section 987 QBU pursuant to § 1.987-1(b)(4) on the transition date (as defined in § 1.987-11(c)). Except as provided in paragraph (c) of this section, a taxpayer to which this section applies must transition from the method previously used to comply with section 987 (the "prior section 987 method") to the method prescribed by these regulations pursuant to the fresh start transition method set forth in paragraph (b) of this section.

(b) *Fresh start transition method.*—(1) *In general.*—Pursuant to the fresh start transition method, and solely for purposes of this section, all section 987 QBUs of a taxpayer, other than section 987 QBUs subject to paragraph (c) of this section, are deemed to terminate on the day before the transition date. No section 987 gain or loss is determined or recognized as a result of the deemed termination. The owner of a section 987 QBU that is deemed to terminate under this section is treated as having transferred all of the assets and liabilities attributable to such QBU to a new section 987 QBU on the transition date. This deemed transfer of assets and liabilities is taken into account only for purposes of transitioning to these regulations under section 987 and shall not be taken into account in determining the amounts transferred from the owner to the section 987 QBU during the taxable year for purposes of § 1.987-5(c)(1)(ii).

(2) *Application of § 1.987-4.*—For purposes of applying § 1.987-4 with respect to a section 987 QBU described in paragraph (b)(1) of this section for the taxable year beginning on the transition date, the amount of assets and liabilities deemed transferred from the owner to the section 987 QBU on the transition date pursuant to paragraph (b)(1) of this section shall be determined by translating such assets and liabilities (without regard to whether the asset or liability is a marked item or a historic item) at the historic rate as determined under paragraph (b)(3) of this section.

(3) *Determination of historic rate.*—For purposes of applying these regulations with respect to a section 987 QBU described in paragraph (b)(1) of this section for taxable years beginning on or after the transition date, the historic rate (as defined in § 1.987-1(c)(3)) for an asset or liability deemed transferred under paragraph (b)(1) of this section from an owner to the section 987 QBU on the transition date shall be the historic rate under § 1.987-1(c)(3) determined by reference to the date the assets were acquired or liabilities entered into or assumed by the section 987 QBU deemed terminated (that is, without regard to the deemed termination or transfer described in paragraph (b)(1) of this section). However, if the owner is not able to determine reliably the historic rate for a particular asset or liability, then the historic rate must be determined based on reasonable assumptions (for example, assumptions about turnover and aging of accounts receivable), consistently applied.

(4) *Example.*—The provisions of this paragraph (b) are illustrated by the following example. Exchange rate assumptions used in the example are selected for the purpose of illustrating the principles of this section, and no inference is intended by their use. Additionally, the effect of depreciation is not taken into account for purposes of this example.

Example. (i) U.S. Corp is a domestic corporation with the dollar as its functional currency. U.S. Corp owns Business A, a U.K. branch with the pound as its functional currency. Business A was formed on January 1, year 1. U.S. Corp uses the method prescribed in the 1991 proposed section 987 regulations to determine the section 987 gain or loss of Business A. U.S. Corp contributed £6,000 to Business A on January 1, year 1. On the same day, Business A bought a truck for £4,000 and a computer for £1,000. Business A had profits determined under § 1.987-1(b)(1)(i) through (iii) of the 1991 proposed section 987 regulations of £250 in each of year 1, year 2, and year 3, and the yearly average exchange rate was used in each of those years to translate Business A's profits under the 1991 proposed section 987 regulations. The yearly average exchange rate was £1 = $1.10 in year 1, £1 = $1.20 in year 2, and £1 = $1.30 in year 3. Business A incurred a £50 loss in each of year 4 and year 5. Business A made no remittances to U.S. Corp in any year.

(ii) On January 1, year 5, Business A transitions to the method provided in these regulations pursuant to the fresh start transition method described in paragraph (b) of this section. Pursuant to paragraph (b)(1) of this section, Business A is deemed to terminate on December 31, year 4. However, no section 987 gain or loss is determined or recognized as a result of the deemed termination. Pursuant to paragraph (b)(2) of this section, for purposes of applying § 1.987-4 with respect to Business A for year 5, the amount of assets and liabilities transferred from U.S. Corp to Business A on the transition date shall be determined by translating all of Business A's assets at the historic rates for those assets as determined under § 1.987-1(c)(3) and paragraph (b)(3) of this section. Because U.S. Corp is not able to determine reliably the historic rate for the pound currency it is deemed to transfer to Business A, U.S. Corp determines the historic rate for these pounds based on a last-in, first-out cash flow assumption. Thus, it is assumed that the £50 loss in each of year 4 and year 5 first reduces the £250 earned in year 3. Accordingly, for purposes of determining the amount of assets and liabilities deemed transferred from U.S. Corp to Business A on January 1, year 5, U.S. Corp translates Business A's assets and liabilities as follows:

Assets	Amount in £	Translation Rate	Amount in $
Pounds	£1,000	£1 = $1.10 (yearly average rate-year 1)	$1,100
Pounds	250	£1 = $1.10 (yearly average rate-year 1)	275
Pounds	250	£1 = $1.20 (yearly average rate-year 2)	300
Pounds	150	£1 = $1.30 (yearly average rate-year 3)	195
Truck	4,000	£1 = $1.10 (yearly average rate-year 1)	4,400
Computer	1,000	£1 = $1.10 (yearly average rate-year 1)	1,100
Total assets			$7,370
Liabilities			
Total liabilities			$0

(c) *Transition of section 987 QBUs that applied the method set forth in the 2006 proposed section 987 regulations.*—(1) *In general.*—If, with respect to a particular section 987 QBU, a taxpayer's prior section 987 method was based on a reasonable application of the method described in the 2006 proposed section 987 regulations (REG-208270-86, 71 FR 52876), then the taxpayer shall apply these regulations under section 987 with respect to such section 987 QBU without regard to paragraph (b) of this section.

(2) *Application of § 1.987-4.*—For purposes of applying § 1.987-4 with respect to a section 987 QBU described in paragraph (c)(1) for the taxable year beginning on the transition date, the owner functional currency net value of the section 987 QBU on the last day of the preceding taxable year under § 1.987-4(d)(1)(B) shall be the amount that was determined under § 1.987-4(d)(1)(A) of the 2006 proposed section 987 regulations for the preceding taxable year. Additionally, for purposes of applying § 1.987-4 with respect to a section 987 QBU described in paragraph (c)(1) for all taxable years that end after the transition date, the section 987 QBU's net unrecognized section 987 gain or loss for all prior taxable years under § 1.987-4(c) shall take into account the aggregate of the amounts determined under § 1.987-4(d) of the 2006 proposed section 987 regulations for taxable years for which the taxpayer applied the 2006 proposed section 987 regulations, reduced by the amounts taken into account under § 1.987-5 of the 2006 proposed section 987 regulations upon a remittance for all such prior taxable years.

(3) *Use of prior historic rate.*—For purposes of applying these regulations under section 987 with respect to historic items (as defined in § 1.987-1(e)), other than inventory, that are reflected on the balance sheet of the section 987 QBU on the transition date, a taxpayer may use the same historic exchange rates as were used under the taxpayer's application of the 2006 proposed section 987 regulations in place of the historic rates that otherwise would be determined under § 1.987-1(c)(3), provided that, for all taxable years that end after the transition date, the taxpayer does so with respect to all historic items (other than inventory) that are reflected on the balance sheet of the section 987 QBU on the transition date.

(4) *Example.*—The provisions of this paragraph (c) are illustrated by the following example. Exchange rate assumptions used in the example are selected for the purpose of illustrating the principles of this section, and no inference is intended by their use. Additionally, the effect of depreciation is not taken into account for purposes of this example.

Example. (i) U.S. Corp is a domestic corporation with the dollar as its functional currency. U.S. Corp owns Business A, a U.K. branch with the pound as its functional currency. Business A was formed on January 1, year 1. U.S. Corp uses a reasonable application of the method described in the 2006 proposed section 987 regulations to determine the section 987 gain or loss of Business A. On January 1, year 5, Business A transitions to the method provided in these regulations pursuant to the method described in this paragraph (c). Business A's opening balance sheet on January 1, year 5, includes pounds, a truck acquired in year 2, inventory accounted for under the FIFO method, and no liabilities. These assets remain on the balance sheet on December 31, year 5.

(ii) Pursuant to paragraph (c)(3) of this section, U.S. Corp chooses to use the same historic exchange rates as were used under its application of the 2006 proposed regulations in place of the historic rates prescribed under § 1.987-1(c)(3) for purposes of applying these regulations with respect to historic items (other than inventory) held on the transition date.

(iii) The pounds are marked items under § 1.987-1(d). Because the pounds are marked items, for purposes of determining the owner functional currency net value of Business A on the last day of year 5 pursuant to § 1.987-4(e), the pounds are translated into dollars using the spot rate (as defined in § 1.987-1(c)(1)) applicable to the last day of year 5.

(iv) The truck held on Business A's balance sheet on January 1, year 5, is a historic item under § 1.987-1(e). For purposes of determining the owner functional currency net value of Business A on the last day of year 5 pursuant to § 1.987-4(e), the basis of the truck is translated into dollars using the spot rate on the day the truck was acquired in year 2, as determined under § 1.987-1(c)(3) of the 2006 proposed section 987 regulations. If U.S. Corp had not chosen pursuant to paragraph (c)(3) of this section to use the same historic exchange rates as were used under its application of the 2006 proposed regulations, the basis of the truck would have been translated into dollars using the historic rate described in § 1.987-1(c)(3), which is the yearly average exchange rate for year 5.

(v) The inventory held on Business A's balance sheet on January 1, year 5, is a historic item under § 1.987-1(e). For purposes of determining the owner functional currency net value of Business A on the last day of year 5 pursuant to § 1.987-4(e), the FIFO cost basis of the inventory is translated into dollars using the historic rate, which pursuant to § 1.987-1(c)(3)(i)(B) is the yearly average exchange rate for year 5.

(vi) Pursuant to paragraph (c)(3) of this section, for purposes of applying § 1.987-4 with respect to Business A for year 5, the owner functional currency net value of Business A on the last day of year 4 under § 1.987-4(d)(1)(B) is the amount that was determined under § 1.987-4(d)(1)(A) of the 2006 proposed section 987 regulations for year 4. Additionally, Business A's net unrecognized section 987 gain or loss for all prior years under § 1.987-4(c) shall take into account the aggregate of the amounts determined under § 1.987-4(d) of the 2006 proposed section 987 regulations for year 1 through year 4, reduced by the amounts taken into account under § 1.987-5 of the 2006 proposed section 987 regulations upon a remittance for all such prior taxable years.

(d) *Adjustments to avoid double counting.*—If a difference between the treatment of any item under these regulations and the treatment of the item under the taxpayer's prior section 987 method would result in income, gain, deduction or loss being taken into account more than once, then the net unrecognized section 987 gain or loss of the section 987 QBU, as determined under § 1.987-4(b) for the first taxable year for which these regulations apply, shall be adjusted to account for the difference.

(e) *Reporting.*—(1) *In general.*—Except as otherwise provided in this paragraph (e), the taxpayer must attach a statement titled "Section 987 Transition Information" to its timely filed return for the first taxable year to which these regulations under section 987 apply providing the following information:

(i) A description of each section 987 QBU to which these rules apply, the section 987 QBU's owner, the section 987 QBU's principal place of business, and a description of the prior section 987 method used by the taxpayer to determine section 987 gain or loss with respect to the section 987 QBU.

(ii) Any assumptions used by the taxpayer for determining the exchange rates used to translate the amount of assets and liabilities transferred to the section 987 QBU on the transition date, as provided in paragraph (b)(3) of this section.

(iii) With respect to each section 987 QBU subject to paragraph (c) of this section, a statement regarding whether historic items (as defined in § 1.987-1(c)(3)) are translated pursuant to paragraph (c)(2) of this section at the same historic rates as were used under the taxpayer's application of the 2006 proposed regulations or at the historic rates determined under § 1.987-1(c)(3).

(iv) With respect to each section 987 QBU with respect to which an adjustment is made pursuant to paragraph (d) of this section, a description of the adjustment and the basis for the computation of such adjustments.

(2) *Attachments not required where information is reported on a form.*—Paragraph (e) of this section shall not apply to the extent the information described in such paragraph is required to be reported on a form published by the Commissioner. [Reg. § 1.987-10.]

□ [*T.D.* 9794, 12-7-2016.]

Caution: The Treasury Department has identified Reg. §1.987-11, as amended by T.D. 9794, as a significant tax regulation that imposes an undue financial burden on U.S. taxpayers and/or adds undue complexity to the federal tax laws, pursuant to Executive Order 13789 (issued April 21, 2017) (Notice 2017-38, I.R.B. 2017-30, 147). In a subsequent report, published October 16, 2017, Treasury recommended planned actions that would reduce the burden of these regulations, including an extension of the application date of T.D. 9794 (see Notice 2022-34, I.R.B. 2022-34, 150).

§ 1.987-11. Effective/applicability date.—(a) *In general.*—Except as otherwise provided in this section, §§ 1.987-1 through 1.987-10 shall apply to taxable years beginning on or after one year after the first day of the first taxable year following December 7, 2016.

(b) *Application of these regulations to taxable years beginning after December 7, 2016.*—A taxpayer may apply these regulations under section 987 to taxable years beginning after December 7, 2016, provided the taxpayer consistently applies these regulations to such taxable years with respect to all section 987 QBUs directly or indirectly owned by the taxpayer on the transition date (as defined in paragraph (b)(2) of this section) as well as all section 987 QBUs directly or indirectly owned on the transition date by members that file a consolidated return with the taxpayer or by any controlled foreign corporation, as defined in section 957, in which a member owns more than 50 percent of the voting power or stock value, as determined under section 958(a).

(c) *Transition date.*—The transition date is the first day of the first taxable year to which these regulations under section 987 are applicable with respect to a taxpayer under this section. [Reg. § 1.987-11.]

□ [*T.D.* 9794, 12-7-2016.]

§ 1.987-12. Deferral of section 987 gain or loss.—(a) *In general.*—(1) *Overview.*—This section provides rules that defer the recognition of section 987 gain or loss that, but for this section, would be recognized in connection with certain QBU terminations and certain other transactions involving partnerships. This paragraph (a) provides an overview of this section and describes the section's scope of application, including with respect to QBUs subject to section 987 but to which §§ 1.987-1 through 1.987-11 generally do not apply. Paragraph (b) of this section describes the extent to which section 987 gain or loss is recognized under § 1.987-5 or similar principles in the taxable year of a deferral event (as defined in paragraph (b)(2) of this section) with respect to a QBU. Paragraph (c) of this section describes the extent to which section 987 gain or loss that, as a result of paragraph (b), is not recognized under § 1.987-5 or similar principles is recognized upon the occurrence of subsequent events. Paragraph (d) of this section describes the extent to which section 987 loss is recognized under § 1.987-5 or similar principles in the taxable year of an outbound loss event (as defined in paragraph (d)(2) of this section) with respect to a QBU. Paragraph (e) of this section provides rules for determining the source and character of gains and losses that, as a result of this section, are not recognized under § 1.987-5 or similar principles in the taxable year of a deferral event or outbound loss event. Paragraph (f) of this section defines controlled group and qualified successor for purposes of this section. Paragraph (g) of this section provides an anti-abuse rule. Paragraph (h) of this section provides examples illustrating the rules described in this section. Paragraph (i) of this section provides rules coordinating the application of this section with the fresh start transition method. Paragraph (j) of this section provides dates of applicability.

(2) *Scope.*—This section applies to any foreign currency gain or loss realized under section 987(3), including foreign currency gain or loss of an entity described in § 1.987-1(b)(1)(ii) (certain entities not otherwise subject to the regulations under section 987). References in this section to section 987 gain or loss refer to any foreign currency gain or loss realized under section 987(3), references to a section 987 QBU refer to any eligible QBU (as defined in § 1.987-1(b)(3)(i), but without regard to § 1.987-1(b)(3)(ii)) that is subject to section 987, and references to a section 987 aggregate partnership refer to any partnership for which the acquisition or disposition of a partnership interest could give rise to foreign currency gain or loss realized under section 987(3). Additionally, references to recognition of section 987 gain or loss under § 1.987-5 encompass any determination and recognition of gain or loss under section 987(3) that would occur but for this section. Accordingly, the principles of this section apply to a QBU subject to section 987 regardless of whether the QBU otherwise is subject to §§ 1.987-1 through 1.987-11. An owner of a QBU that is not subject to § 1.987-5 must adapt the rules set forth in this section as necessary to recognize section 987 gains or losses that are subject to this section consistent with the principles of this section.

(3) *Exceptions.*—(i) *Annual deemed termination elections.*—This section does not apply to section 987 gain or loss of a section 987 QBU with respect to which the annual deemed termination election described in § 1.987-8(d) is in effect.

(ii) *De minimis exception.*—This section does not apply to a section 987 QBU for a taxable year if the net unrecognized section 987 gain or loss of the section 987 QBU that, as a result of this section, would not be recognized under § 1.987-5 in the taxable year does not exceed $5 million.

(b) *Gain and loss recognition in connection with a deferral event.*—(1) *In general.*—Notwithstanding § 1.987-5, the owner of a section 987 QBU with respect to which a deferral event occurs (a deferral QBU) includes in taxable income section 987 gain or loss in connection with the deferral event only to the extent provided in paragraphs (b)(3) and (c) of this section. However, if the deferral event also constitutes an outbound loss event described in paragraph (d) of this section, the amount of loss recognized by the owner may be further limited under that paragraph.

(2) *Deferral event.*—(i) *In general.*—A deferral event with respect to a section 987 QBU means any transaction or series of transactions that satisfy the conditions described in paragraphs (b)(2)(ii) and (iii) of this section.

(ii) *Transactions.*—The transaction or series of transactions include either:

(A) A termination of the section 987 QBU other than any of the following terminations: a termination described in § 1.987-8(b)(3), a termination described in § 1.987-8(c), or a termination described solely in § 1.987-8(b)(1); or

(B) A disposition of part of an interest in a section 987 aggregate partnership or DE through which the section 987 QBU is owned, a disposition of part of a directly held section 987 QBU, or any contribution by another person to a section 987 aggregate partnership, DE, or section 987 QBU of assets that, immediately after the contribution, are not considered to be included on the books and records of an eligible QBU, provided that the contribution gives rise to a deemed transfer from the section 987 QBU to the owner. See paragraph (h) of this section, *Examples 1*, *2*, and *4*, for illustrations of this rule.

(iii) *Assets on books of successor QBU.*—Immediately after the transaction or series of transactions, assets of the section 987 QBU are reflected on the books and records of a successor QBU (as defined in paragraph (b)(4) of this section).

(3) *Gain or loss recognized under § 1.987-5 in the taxable year of a deferral event.*—In the taxable year of a deferral event with respect to a deferral QBU, the owner of the deferral QBU recognizes section 987 gain or loss as determined under § 1.987-5, except that, solely for purposes of applying § 1.987-5, all assets and liabilities of the deferral QBU that, immediately after the deferral event, are reflected on the books and records of a successor QBU are treated as not having been transferred and therefore as remaining on the books and records of the deferral QBU notwithstanding the deferral event.

(4) *Successor QBU.*—For purposes of this section, a section 987 QBU (potential successor QBU) is a successor QBU with respect to a section 987 QBU referred to in paragraph (b)(2)(ii) of this section if, immediately after the transaction or series of transactions described in that paragraph, the potential successor QBU satisfies all of the conditions described in paragraphs (b)(4)(i) through (iii) of this section.

(i) The books and records of the potential successor QBU reflect assets that, immediately before the transaction or series of transactions described in paragraph (b)(2)(ii) of this section, were reflected on the books and records of the section 987 QBU referred to in that paragraph.

(ii) The owner of the potential successor QBU and the owner of the section 987 QBU referred to in paragraph (b)(2)(ii) of this section immediately before the transaction or series of transactions described in that paragraph are members of the same controlled group.

(iii) In the case of a section 987 QBU referred to in paragraph (b)(2)(ii)(A) of this section, if the owner of the section 987 QBU immediately before the transaction or series of transactions described in that paragraph was a U.S. person, the potential successor QBU is owned by a U.S. person.

(c) *Recognition of deferred section 987 gain or loss in the taxable year of a deferral event and in subsequent taxable years.*—(1) *In general.*—(i) *Deferred section 987 gain or loss.*—A deferral QBU owner (as defined in paragraph (c)(1)(ii) of this section) recognizes section 987 gain or loss attributable to the deferral QBU that, as a result of paragraph (b) of this section, is not recognized in the taxable year of the deferral event under § 1.987-5 (deferred section 987 gain or loss) in the taxable year of the deferral event and in subsequent taxable years as provided in paragraphs (c)(2) through (4) of this section.

(ii) *Deferral QBU owner.*—For purposes of this paragraph (c), a deferral QBU owner means, with respect to a deferral QBU, the owner of the deferral QBU immediately before the deferral event, or the owner's qualified successor.

(2) *Recognition upon a subsequent remittance.*—(i) *In general.*—Except as provided in paragraph (c)(3) of this section, a deferral QBU owner recognizes deferred section 987 gain or loss in the taxable year of the deferral event and in subsequent taxable years upon a remittance from a successor QBU to the owner of the successor QBU (successor QBU owner) in the amount described in paragraph (c)(2)(ii) of this section.

(ii) *Amount.*—The amount of deferred section 987 gain or loss that is recognized pursuant to this paragraph (c)(2) in a taxable year of the deferral QBU owner is the outstanding deferred section 987 gain or loss (that is, the amount of deferred section 987 gain or loss not previously recognized) multiplied by the remittance proportion of the successor QBU owner with respect to the successor QBU for the taxable year ending with or within the taxable year of the deferral QBU owner, as determined under § 1.987-5(b) (and, to the extent relevant, paragraphs (b) and (c)(2)(iii) of this section) without regard to any election under § 1.987-8(d). For purposes of computing this remittance proportion, multiple successor QBUs of the same deferral QBU are treated as a single successor QBU. See paragraph (h) of this section, *Example 5*, for an illustration of this rule.

(iii) *Deemed remittance when a successor QBU ceases to be owned by a member of the deferral QBU owner's controlled group.*—For purposes of this paragraph (c)(2), in a taxable year of the deferral QBU owner in which a successor QBU ceases to be owned by a member of a controlled group that includes the deferral QBU owner, the successor QBU owner is treated as having a remittance proportion of 1. Accordingly, if there is only one successor QBU with respect to a deferral QBU and that successor QBU ceases to be owned by a member of the controlled group that includes the deferral QBU owner, all outstanding deferred section 987 gain or loss with respect to that deferral QBU will be recognized. This paragraph (c)(2)(iii) does not affect the application of §§ 1.987-1 through 1.987-11 to the successor QBU owner with respect to its ownership of the successor QBU.

(3) *Recognition of deferred section 987 loss in certain outbound successor QBU terminations.*—Notwithstanding paragraph (c)(2) of this section, if assets of the successor QBU (transferred assets) are transferred (or deemed transferred) in a transaction that would constitute an outbound loss event if the successor QBU had a net accumulated section 987 loss at the time of the exchange, then the deferral QBU owner recognizes outstanding deferred section 987 loss, if any, to the extent it would recognize loss under paragraph (d)(1) of this section if (i) the deferral QBU owner owned the successor QBU, (ii) the deferral QBU owner had net unrecognized section 987 loss with respect to the successor QBU equal to its outstanding deferred section 987 loss with respect to the deferral QBU, and (iii) the transferred assets were transferred (or deemed transferred) in an outbound loss event. Any outstanding deferred section 987 loss with respect to the deferral QBU that is not recognized as a result of the preceding sentence is recognized by the deferral QBU owner in the first taxable year in which the deferral QBU owner (including any qualified successor) ceases to be a member of a controlled group that includes the acquirer of the transferred assets or any qualified successor of such acquirer.

(4) *Special rules regarding successor QBUs.*—(i) *Successor QBU with respect to a deferral QBU that is a successor QBU.*—If a section 987 QBU is a successor QBU with respect to a deferral QBU that is a successor QBU with respect to another deferral QBU, the first-mentioned section 987 QBU is considered a successor QBU with respect to the second-mentioned deferral QBU. For example, if QBU A is a successor QBU with respect to QBU B, and QBU B is a successor QBU with respect to QBU C, then QBU A is a successor QBU with respect to QBU C.

(ii) *Separation of a successor QBU.*—If a successor QBU with respect to a deferral QBU separates into two or more separated QBUs (as defined in § 1.987-2(c)(9)(iii)), each separated QBU is considered a successor QBU with respect to the deferral QBU.

(iii) *Combination of a successor QBU.*—If a successor QBU with respect to a deferral QBU combines with another section 987 QBU of the same owner, resulting in a combined QBU (as defined in §1.987-2(c)(9)(i)), the combined QBU is considered a successor QBU with respect to the deferral QBU.

(d) *Loss recognition upon an outbound loss event.*—(1) *In general.*—Notwithstanding §1.987-5, the owner of a section 987 QBU with respect to which an outbound loss event occurs (an outbound loss QBU) includes in taxable income in the taxable year of an outbound loss event section 987 loss with respect to that section 987 QBU only to the extent provided in paragraph (d)(3) of this section.

(2) *Outbound loss event.*—An outbound loss event means, with respect to a section 987 QBU:

(i) Any termination of the section 987 QBU in connection with a transfer by a U.S. person of assets of the section 987 QBU to a foreign person that is a member of the same controlled group as the U.S. transferor immediately before the transaction or, if the transferee did not exist immediately before the transaction, immediately after the transaction (related foreign person), provided that the termination would result in the recognition of section 987 loss with respect to the section 987 QBU under §1.987-5 and paragraph (b) of this section but for this paragraph (d); or

(ii) Any transfer by a U.S. person of part of an interest in a section 987 aggregate partnership or DE through which the U.S. person owns the section 987 QBU to a related foreign person that has the same functional currency as the section 987 QBU, or any contribution by such a related foreign person to such a partnership or DE of assets that, immediately after the contribution, are not considered to be included on the books and records of an eligible QBU, provided that the transfer would result in the recognition of section 987 loss with respect to the section 987 QBU under §1.987-5 and paragraph (b) of this section but for this paragraph (d). See paragraph (h) of this section, *Example 3*, for an illustration of this rule.

(3) *Loss recognized upon an outbound loss event.*—In the taxable year of an outbound loss event with respect to an outbound loss QBU, the owner of the outbound loss QBU recognizes section 987 loss as determined under §1.987-5 and paragraphs (b) and (c) of this section, except that, solely for purposes of applying §1.987-5, the following assets and liabilities of the outbound loss QBU are treated as not having been transferred and therefore as remaining on the books and records of the outbound loss QBU notwithstanding the outbound loss event:

(i) In the case of an outbound loss event described in paragraph (d)(2)(i) of this section, assets and liabilities that, immediately after the outbound loss event, are reflected on the books and records of the related foreign person described in that paragraph or of an eligible QBU owned by such related foreign person; and

(ii) In the case of an outbound loss event described in paragraph (d)(2)(ii) of this section, assets and liabilities that, immediately after the outbound loss event, are reflected on the books and records of the eligible QBU from which the assets and liabilities of the outbound loss QBU are allocated and not on the books and records of a section 987 QBU.

(4) *Adjustment of basis of stock received in certain nonrecognition transactions.*—If an outbound loss event results from the transfer of assets of the outbound loss QBU in a transaction described in section 351 or section 361, the basis of the stock that is received in the transaction is increased by an amount equal to the section 987 loss that, as a result of this paragraph (d), is not recognized with respect to the outbound loss QBU in the taxable year of the outbound loss event (outbound section 987 loss).

(5) *Recognition of outbound section 987 loss that is not converted into stock basis.*—Outbound section 987 loss attributable to an outbound loss event that is not described in paragraph (d)(4) of this section is recognized by the owner of the outbound loss QBU in the first taxable year in which the owner or any qualified successor of the owner ceases to be a member of a controlled group that includes the related foreign person referred to in paragraph (d)(2)(i) or (ii) of this section, or any qualified successor of such person.

(e) *Source and character.*—(1) *Deferred section 987 gain or loss and certain outbound section 987 loss.*—The source and character of deferred section 987 gain or loss recognized pursuant to paragraph (c) of this section, and of outbound section 987 loss recognized pursuant to paragraph (d)(5) of this section, is determined under §1.987-6 as if such deferred section 987 gain or loss were recognized pursuant to §1.987-5 without regard to this section on the date of the related deferral event or outbound loss event.

(2) *Outbound section 987 loss reflected in stock basis.*—If loss is recognized on the sale or exchange of stock described in paragraph (d)(4) of this section within two years of the outbound loss event described in that paragraph, then, to the extent of the outbound section 987 loss, the source and character of the loss recognized on the sale or exchange is determined under §1.987-6 as if such loss were section 987 loss recognized pursuant to §1.987-5 without regard to this section on the date of the outbound loss event.

(f) *Definitions.*—(1) *Controlled group.*—For purposes of this section, a controlled group means all persons with the relationships to each other specified in sections 267(b) or Reg. §707(b).

(2) *Qualified successor.*—For purposes of this section, a qualified successor with respect to a corporation (transferor corporation) means another corporation (acquiring corporation) that acquires the assets of the transferor corporation in a transaction described in section 381(a), but only if (A) the acquiring corporation is a domestic corporation and the transferor corporation was a domestic corporation, or (B) the acquiring corporation is a controlled foreign corporation (as defined in section 957(a)) (CFC) and the transferor corporation was a CFC. A qualified successor of a corporation includes the qualified successor of a qualified successor of the corporation.

(g) *Anti-abuse.*—No section 987 loss is recognized under §1.987-5 or this section in connection with a transaction or series of transactions that are undertaken with a principal purpose of avoiding the purposes of this section.

(h) *Examples.*—The following examples illustrate the application of this section. For purposes of the examples, DC1 is a domestic corporation that owns all of the stock of DC2, which is also a domestic corporation, and CFC1 and CFC2 are CFCs. In addition, DC1, DC2, CFC1, and CFC2 are members of a controlled group as defined in paragraph (f)(1) of this section, and the de minimis rule of paragraph (a)(3)(ii) of this section is not applicable. Finally, except as otherwise provided, Business A is a section 987 QBU with the euro as its functional currency, there are no transfers between Business A and its owner, and Business A's assets are not depreciable or amortizable.

(1) *Example 1. Contribution of a section 987 QBU to a member of the controlled group.*—(i) *Facts.*—DC1 owns all of the interests in Business A. The balance sheet of Business A reflects assets with an aggregate adjusted basis of €1,000x and no liabilities. DC1 contributes €900x of Business A's assets to DC2 in an exchange to which section 351 applies. Immediately after the contribution, the remaining €100x of Business A's assets are no longer reflected on the books and records of a section 987 QBU. DC2, which has the U.S. dollar as its functional currency, uses the former Business A assets in a business (Business B) that constitutes a section 987 QBU. At the time of the contribution, Business A has net accumulated unrecognized section 987 gain of $100x.

(ii) *Analysis.*—(A) Under §1.987-2(c)(2)(ii), DC1's contribution of €900x of Business A's assets to DC2 is treated as a transfer of all of the assets of Business A to DC1, immediately followed by DC1's contribution of €900x of Business A's assets to DC2. The contribution of Business A's assets is a deferral event within the meaning of paragraph (b)(2) of this section because:

(1) The transfer from Business A to DC1 is a transfer of substantially all of Business A's assets to DC1, resulting in a termination of Business A under §1.987-8(b)(2); and

(2) Immediately after the transaction, assets of Business A are reflected on the books and records of Business B, a section 987 QBU owned by a member of DC1's controlled group and a successor QBU within the meaning of paragraph (b)(4) of this section. Accordingly, Business A is a deferral QBU within the meaning of paragraph (b)(1) of this section, and DC1 is a deferral QBU owner of Business A within the meaning of paragraph (c)(1)(ii) of this section.

(B) Under paragraph (b)(3) of this section, DC1's taxable income in the taxable year of the deferral event includes DC1's section 987 gain or loss determined with respect to Business A under §1.987-5, except that, for purposes of applying §1.987-5, all assets and liabilities of Business A that are reflected on the books and records of Business B immediately after Business A's termination are treated as not having been transferred and therefore as though they remained on Business A's books and records (notwithstanding the deemed transfer of those assets under §1.987-8(e)). Accordingly, in the taxable year of the deferral event, DC1 is treated as making a remittance of €100x, corresponding to the assets of Business A that are no longer reflected on the books and records of a section 987 QBU, and is treated as having a remittance proportion with respect to Business A of 0.1, determined by dividing the €100x remittance by the sum of the remittance and the €900x aggregate adjusted basis of the gross assets deemed to remain on Business A's books at the end of the year. Thus, DC1 recognizes $10x of section 987 gain in the taxable year of the deferral event. DC1's deferred section 987 gain equals $90x, which is the amount of section 987 gain that, but for the application of paragraph (b) of this section, DC1 would have recognized under § 1.987-5 ($100x), less the amount of section 987 gain recognized by DC1 under § 1.987-5 and this section ($10x).

(2) *Example 2. Election to be classified as a corporation.*—(i) *Facts.*—DC1 owns all of the interests in Entity A, a DE. Entity A conducts Business A, which has net accumulated unrecognized section 987 gain of $500x. Entity A elects to be classified as a corporation under § 301.7701-3(a). As a result of the election and pursuant to § 301.7701-3(g)(1)(iv), DC1 is treated as contributing all of the assets and liabilities of Business A to newly-formed CFC1, which has the euro as its functional currency. Immediately after the contribution, the assets and liabilities of Business A are reflected on CFC1's balance sheet.

(ii) *Analysis.*—Under § 1.987-2(c)(2)(ii), DC1's contribution of all of the assets and liabilities of Business A to CFC1 is treated as a transfer of all of the assets and liabilities of Business A to DC1, followed immediately by DC1's contribution of those assets and liabilities to CFC1. Because the deemed transfer from Business A to DC1 is a transfer of substantially all of Business A's assets to DC1, the Business A QBU terminates under § 1.987-8(b)(2). The contribution of Business A's assets is not a deferral event within the meaning of paragraph (b)(2) of this section because, immediately after the transaction, no assets of Business A are reflected on the books and records of a successor QBU within the meaning of paragraph (b)(4) of this section due to the fact that the assets of Business A are not reflected on the books and records of a section 987 QBU immediately after the termination as well as the fact that the requirement of paragraph (b)(4)(iii) of this section is not met. Accordingly, DC1 recognizes section 987 gain with respect to Business A under § 1.987-5 without regard to this section. Because the requirement of paragraph (b)(4)(iii) of this section is not met, the result would be the same even if the assets of Business A were transferred in a section 351 exchange to an existing foreign corporation that had a different functional currency than Business A.

(3) *Example 3. Outbound loss event.*—(i) *Facts.*—The facts are the same as in *Example 2 in paragraph (h)(2) of this section*, except that Business A has net accumulated unrecognized section 987 loss of $500x rather than net accumulated unrecognized section 987 gain of $500x.

(ii) *Analysis.*—(A) The analysis of the transactions under §§ 1.987-2(c)(2)(ii), 1.987-8(b)(2), and paragraph (b) of this section is the same as in *Example 2 in paragraph (h)(2) of this section*. However, the termination of Business A as a result of the transfer of the assets of Business A by a U.S. person (DC1) to a foreign person (CFC1) that is a member of DC1's controlled group is an outbound loss event described in paragraph (d)(2) of this section.

(B) Under paragraphs (d)(1) and (3) of this section, in the taxable year of the outbound loss event, DC1 includes in taxable income section 987 loss recognized with respect to Business A as determined under § 1.987-5, except that, for purposes of applying § 1.987-5, all assets and liabilities of Business A that are reflected on the books and records of CFC1, a related foreign person described in paragraph (d)(2) of this section, are treated as not having been transferred. Accordingly, DC1's remittance proportion with respect to Business A is 0, and DC1 recognizes no section 987 loss with respect to Business A. DC1's outbound section 987 loss is $500x, which is the amount of section 987 loss that DC1 would have recognized under § 1.987-5 ($500x) without regard to paragraph (d) of this section, less the amount of section 987 loss recognized by DC1 under paragraph (d)(3) of this section ($0). Under paragraph (d)(4) of this section, DC1 must increase its basis in its CFC1 shares by the amount of the outbound section 987 loss ($500x).

(4) *Example 4. Conversion of a DE to a partnership.*—(i) *Facts.*—(A) DC1 owns all of the interests in Entity A, a DE that conducts Business A. On the last day of Year 1, DC1 sells 50 percent of its interest in Entity A to DC2 (the Entity A sale).

(B) For Federal income tax purposes, Entity A is converted to a partnership when DC2 purchases the 50 percent interest in Entity A. DC2's purchase is treated as the purchase of 50 percent of the assets of Entity A (that is, the assets of Business A), which, prior to the purchase, were treated as held directly by DC1 for Federal income tax purposes. Immediately after DC2's deemed purchase of 50 percent of Business A assets, DC1 and DC2 are treated as contributing their respective interests in Business A assets to a partnership. *See* Rev. Rul. 99-5, 1999-1 CB 434 (situation 1). In connection with the deemed contribution, DC1 and DC2 agree to share equally in all items of the partnership's profits and loss, and, for purposes of § 1.987-7, to determine their share of assets and liabilities of the resulting partnership in accordance with their respective shares of partnership profits.

(ii) *Analysis.*—(A) The transactions deemed to occur under Rev. Rul. 99-5 are not taken into account for purposes of this section. The Entity A sale and resulting existence of a partnership, however, have consequences under section 987 and this section, as described in this Example 4 in paragraphs (h)(4)(ii)(B) through (D) of this section.

(B) Immediately after the Entity A sale, Entity A is a section 987 aggregate partnership within the meaning of § 1.987-1(b)(5) because DC1 and DC2 own all the interests in partnership capital and profits, DC1 and DC2 are related within the meaning of section 267(b), and the partnership has an eligible QBU (Business A) that would be a section 987 QBU with respect to a partner if owned by the partner directly. As a result of the Entity A sale, 50 percent of the assets and liabilities of Business A ceased to be reflected on the books and records of DC1's Business A section 987 QBU. As a result, such assets and liabilities are treated as if they were transferred from DC1's Business A section 987 QBU to DC1. Additionally, following DC2's acquisition of 50 percent of the interest in Entity A, DC2 is allocated 50 percent of the assets and liabilities of Business A under §§ 1.987-2(b). Because DC2 and Business A have different functional currencies, DC2's portion of the Business A assets and liabilities constitutes a section 987 QBU. Accordingly, 50 percent of the assets and liabilities of Business A are treated as transferred by DC2 to DC2's Business A section 987 QBU.

(C) The Entity A sale is a deferral event described in paragraph (b)(2) of this section because:

(*1*) The sale constitutes the disposition of part of an interest in a DE; and

(*2*) Immediately after the transaction, assets of DC1's Business A section 987 QBU are reflected on the books and records of DC1's Business A section 987 QBU and DC2's Business A section 987 QBU, each of which is a successor QBU with respect to DC1's Business A section 987 QBU within the meaning of paragraph (b)(4) of this section. Accordingly, DC1's Business A section 987 QBU is a deferral QBU within the meaning of paragraph (b)(1) of this section, and DC1 is a deferral QBU owner within the meaning of paragraph (c)(1)(ii) of this section. Under paragraph (b)(1) of this section, DC1 includes in taxable income section 987 gain or loss with respect to Business A in connection with the deferral event to the extent provided in paragraphs (b)(3) and (c) of this section.

(D) Under paragraph (b) of this section, in the taxable year of the Entity A sale, DC1 includes in taxable income section 987 gain or loss with respect to Business A as determined under § 1.987-5, except that, for purposes of applying § 1.987-5, all assets and liabilities of Business A that, immediately after the Entity A sale, are reflected on the books and records of successor QBUs are treated as though they were not transferred and therefore as remaining on the books and records of DC1's Business A section 987 QBU notwithstanding the Entity A sale. Accordingly, DC1's remittance amount under § 1.987-5 is $0, and DC1 recognizes no section 987 gain or loss with respect to Business A.

(5) *Example 5. Partial recognition of deferred gain or loss.*—(i) *Facts.*—DC1 owns all of the interests in Entity A, a DE that conducts Business A in Country X. During Year 1, DC1 contributes all of its interests in Entity A to DC2 in an exchange to which section 351 applies. At the time of the contribution, Business A has net accumulated unrecognized section 987 gain of $100x. After the contribution, Entity A continues to conduct business in Country X (Business B). In Year 3, as a result of a net transfer of property from Business B to DC2, DC2's remittance proportion with respect to Business B, as determined under § 1.987-5, is 0.25.

(ii) *Analysis.*—(A) For the reasons described in *Example 1 in paragraph (h)(1) of this section*, the contribution of Entity A by DC1 to DC2 results in a termination of Business A and a deferral event with respect to Business A, a deferral QBU; DC1 is a deferral QBU owner within the meaning of paragraph (c)(1)(ii) of this section; Business B is a successor QBU with respect to Business A; DC2 is a successor QBU owner; and the $100x of net accumulated unrecognized section

987 gain with respect to Business A becomes deferred section 987 gain as a result of the deferral event.

(B) Under paragraph (c)(1) of this section, DC1 recognizes deferred section 987 gain with respect to Business A in accordance with paragraphs (c)(2) through (4) of this section. Under paragraph (c)(2)(i) of this section, DC1 recognizes deferred section 987 gain in Year 3 as a result of the remittance from Business B to DC2. Under paragraph (c)(2)(ii) of this section, the amount of deferred section 987 gain that DC1 recognizes is $25x, which is DC1's outstanding deferred section 987 gain or loss ($100x) with respect to Business A multiplied by the remittance proportion (0.25) of DC2 with respect to Business B for the taxable year as determined under § 1.987-5(b).

(i) *Coordination with fresh start transition method.*—(1) *In general.*—If a taxpayer is a deferral QBU owner, or is or was the owner of an outbound loss QBU, and the taxpayer is required under § 1.987-10(a) to apply the fresh start transition method described in § 1.987-10(b) to the deferral QBU or outbound loss QBU, or would have been so required if the taxpayer had owned the deferral QBU or outbound loss QBU on the transition date (as defined in § 1.987-11(c)), the adjustments described in paragraphs (i)(2) and (3) of this section, as applicable, must be made on the transition date.

(2) *Adjustment to deferred section 987 gain or loss.*—The amount of any outstanding deferred section 987 gain or loss of a deferral QBU owner with respect to a deferral QBU described in paragraph (i)(1) of this section must be adjusted to equal the amount of outstanding deferred section 987 gain or loss that the deferral QBU owner would have had with respect to the deferral QBU on the transition date if, immediately before the deferral event, the deferral QBU had transitioned to the method prescribed by §§ 1.987-1 through 1.987-10 pursuant to the fresh start transition method.

(3) *Adjustments in the case of an outbound loss event.*—The basis of any stock described in paragraph (d)(4) of this section that was received in connection with the transfer (or deemed transfer) of assets of an outbound loss QBU described in paragraph (i)(1) of this section and that is held on the transition date must be adjusted to equal the basis that such stock would have had on the transition date if, immediately prior to the outbound loss event, the outbound loss QBU had transitioned to the method prescribed by §§ 1.987-1 through 1.987-10 pursuant to the fresh start transition method. If no such stock was received, the amount of any outbound section 987 loss with respect to the outbound loss QBU that may be recognized on or after the transition date pursuant to paragraph (d)(5) of this section must be adjusted to equal the amount of such loss that would be outstanding and that may be recognized pursuant to that paragraph if, immediately before the outbound loss event, the outbound loss QBU had transitioned to the method prescribed by §§ 1.987-1 through 1.987-10 pursuant to the fresh start transition method.

(j) *Applicability date.*—(1) *In general.*—Except as described in paragraph (j)(2) of this section, this section applies to any deferral event or outbound loss event that occurs on or after January 6, 2017. This section also applies to any deferral event or outbound loss event that occurs as a result of an entity classification election made under § 301.7701-3 that is filed on or after January 6, 2017, and that is effective before January 6, 2017.

(2) *Exceptions.*—(i) *Principal purpose.*—This section applies to any deferral event or outbound loss event occurring on or after December 7, 2016, if such deferral event or outbound loss event was undertaken with a principal purpose of recognizing section 987 loss.

(ii) *Entity classification.*—This section also applies to any deferral event or outbound loss event that occurs as a result of an entity classification election made under § 301.7701-3 that was filed on or after December 22, 2016, that was effective before December 7, 2016, and that was undertaken with a principal purpose of recognizing section 987 loss. [Reg. § 1.987-12.]

☐ [*T.D. 9795, 12-7-2016. Amended by T.D. 9857, 5-10-2019.*]

Caution: The Treasury Department has identified Reg. §1.988-1, as amended by T.D. 9794, as a significant tax regulation that imposes an undue financial burden on U.S. taxpayers and/or adds undue complexity to the federal tax laws, pursuant to Executive Order 13789 (issued April 21, 2017) (Notice 2017-38, I.R.B. 2017-30, 147). In a subsequent report, published October 16, 2017, Treasury recommended planned actions that would reduce the burden of these regulations, including an extension of the application date of T.D. 9794 (see Notice 2022-34, I.R.B. 2022-34, 150).

§ 1.988-1. Certain definitions and special rules.—(a) *Section 988 transaction.*—(1) *In general.*—The term "section 988 transaction" means any of the following transactions—

(i) A disposition of nonfunctional currency as defined in paragraph (c) of this section;

(ii) Any transaction described in paragraph (a)(2) of this section if any amount which the taxpayer is entitled to receive or is required to pay by reason of such transaction is denominated in terms of a nonfunctional currency or is determined by reference to the value of one or more nonfunctional currencies.

A transaction described in this paragraph (a) need not require or permit payment with a nonfunctional currency as long as any amount paid or received is determined by reference to the value of one or more nonfunctional currencies. The acquisition of nonfunctional currency is treated as a section 988 transaction for purposes of establishing the taxpayer's basis in such currency and determining exchange gain or loss thereon.

(2) *Description of transactions.*—The following transactions are described in this paragraph (a)(2).

(i) *Debt instruments.*—Acquiring a debt instrument or becoming an obligor under a debt instrument. The term "debt instrument" means a bond, debenture, note, certificate or other evidence of indebtedness.

(ii) *Payables, receivables, etc.*—Accruing, or otherwise taking into account, for purposes of subtitle A of the Internal Revenue Code, any item of expense or gross income or receipts which is to be paid or received after the date on which so accrued or taken into account. A payable relating to cost of goods sold, or a payable or receivable relating to a capital expenditure or receipt, is within the meaning of this paragraph (a)(2)(ii). Generally, a payable relating to foreign taxes (whether or not claimed as a credit under section 901) is within the meaning of this paragraph (a)(2)(ii). However, a payable of a domestic person relating to accrued foreign taxes of its qualified business unit (QBU branch) is not within the meaning of this paragraph (a)(2)(ii) if the QBU branch's functional currency is the U.S. dollar and the foreign taxes are claimed as a credit under section 901.

(iii) *Forward contract, futures contract, option contract, or similar financial instrument.*—Except as otherwise provided in this paragraph (a)(2)(iii) and paragraph (a)(4)(i) of this section, entering into or acquiring any forward contract, futures contract, option, warrant, or similar financial instrument.

(A) *Limitation for certain derivative instruments.*—A forward contract, futures contract, option, warrant, or similar financial instrument is within this paragraph (a)(2)(iii) only if the underlying property to which the instrument ultimately relates is a nonfunctional currency or is otherwise described in paragraph (a)(1)(ii) of this section. Thus, if the underlying property of an instrument is another financial instrument (*e.g.*, an option on a futures contract), then the underlying property to which such other instrument (*e.g.*, the futures contract) ultimately relates must be a nonfunctional currency. For example, a forward contract to purchase wheat denominated in a nonfunctional currency, an option to enter into a forward contract to purchase wheat denominated in a nonfunctional currency, or a warrant to purchase stock denominated in a nonfunctional currency is not described in this paragraph (a)(2)(iii). On the other hand, a forward contract to purchase a nonfunctional currency, an option to enter into a forward contract to purchase a nonfunctional currency, an option to purchase a bond denominated in or the payments of which are determined by reference to the value of a nonfunctional currency, or a warrant to purchase nonfunctional currency is described in this paragraph (a)(2)(iii).

(B) *Nonfunctional currency notional principal contracts.*—(*1*) *In general.*—The term "similar financial instrument" includes a notional principal contract only if the payments required to be made or received under the contract are determined with reference to a nonfunctional currency.

(*2*) *Definition of notional principal contract.*—The term "notional principal contract" means a contract (*e.g.*, a swap, cap, floor or collar) that provides for the payment of amounts by one party to another at specified intervals calculated by reference to a specified index upon a notional principal amount in exchange for specified consideration or a promise to pay similar amounts. For this purpose, a "notional principal contract" shall only include an instrument where the underlying property to which the instrument ultimately relates is money (*e.g.*, functional currency), nonfunctional currency, or property the value of which is determined by reference to an interest rate. Thus, the term "notional principal contract" includes a currency swap as defined in § 1.988-2(e)(2)(ii), but does not include a swap referenced to a commodity or equity index.

(C) *Effective date with respect to certain contracts.*—This paragraph (a)(2)(iii) does not apply to any forward contract, futures contract, option, warrant, or similar financial instrument entered into or acquired on or before October 21, 1988, if such instrument would have been marked to market under section 1256 if held on the last day of the taxable year.

(3) [Reserved]. For further guidance, see § 1.988-1T(a)(3).

(4) *Treatment of assets and liabilities of a section 987 aggregate partnership or DE that are not attributed to an eligible QBU.*—(i) *Scope.*—This paragraph (a)(4) applies to assets and liabilities of a section 987 aggregate partnership as defined in § 1.987-1(b)(5), or of an entity disregarded as an entity separate from its owner for Federal income tax purposes (DE), that are not attributable to an eligible QBU as defined in § 1.987-1(b)(3).

(ii) *Section 987 Aggregate Partnerships.*—For purposes of applying section 988 and the applicable regulations to transactions involving assets and liabilities described in paragraph (a)(4)(i) of this section that are held by a section 987 aggregate partnership, the owners of the section 987 aggregate partnership (within the meaning of § 1.987-1(b)(4)) shall be treated as owning their share of such assets and liabilities. Section 1.987-7(b) shall apply for purposes of determining an owner's share of such assets or liabilities.

(iii) *Disregarded entities.*—For purposes of applying section 988 and the applicable regulations to transactions involving assets and liabilities described in paragraph (a)(4)(i) of this section that are held by a DE, the owner of the DE (within the meaning of § 1.987-1(b)(4)) shall be treated as owning all such assets and liabilities.

(iv) *Example.*—The following example illustrates the application of paragraph (a)(4) of this section:

Example. Liability held through a section 987 aggregate partnership. (i) *Facts.* P, a foreign partnership, has two equal partners, X and Y. X is a domestic corporation with the dollar as its functional currency. Y is a foreign corporation wholly owned by X that has the yen as its functional currency. P is a section 987 aggregate partnership. On January 1, 2021, P borrowed yen and issued a note to the lender that obligated P to pay interest and repay principal to the lender in yen. Also on January 1, 2021, P used the yen it borrowed from the lender to acquire all of the stock of F, a foreign corporation, from an unrelated person. P also holds an eligible QBU (within the meaning of § 1.987-1(b)(3)) that has the yen as its functional currency. P maintains one set of books and records. The assets and liabilities of the eligible QBU are reflected on the books and records of P as provided under § 1.987-2(b). The F stock held by P, and the yen liability incurred to acquire the F stock, are also recorded on the books and records of P but, pursuant to § 1.987-2(b)(2)(i), are not considered to be reflected on the books and records of the eligible QBU for purposes of section 987.

(ii) *Analysis.* X's portion of the assets and liabilities of the eligible QBU owned by P is a section 987 QBU. Y's portion of the assets and liabilities of the eligible QBU owned by P is not a section 987 QBU because Y and the eligible QBU have the same functional currency. Because the F stock and yen-denominated liability incurred to acquire such stock are not considered reflected on the books and records of the eligible QBU, they are not subject to section 987. In addition, because the F stock and the yen-denominated liability incurred to acquire such stock are held by P (but not attributable to P's eligible QBU), X and Y are treated as owning their respective shares of such stock and liability pursuant to § 1.988-1(a)(4)(ii) for purposes of applying section 988. As a result, P's becoming the obligor on the portion of the yen-denominated note that is treated as an obligation of X is a section 988 transaction pursuant to paragraphs (a)(1)(ii), (a)(2)(ii) and (a)(3) of this section. Similarly, the dispositions of yen to make payments of interest and principal on the liability, to the extent such yen are treated as owned by X under paragraph (a)(4)(ii) of this section, are section 988 transactions under paragraphs (a)(1)(i) and (a)(3) of this section. To the extent the yen are treated as owned by the eligible QBU, see § 1.987-2(c) for the treatment of the payment of yen as a transfer from the eligible QBU to X. P's becoming the obligor on Y's portion of the yen-denominated note, and Y's portion of the yen disposed of in connection with payments on such note, are not section 988 transactions because Y has the yen as its functional currency.

(5) [Reserved]

(6) *Examples.*—The following examples illustrate the application of paragraph (a) of this section. The examples assume that X is a U.S. corporation on an accrual method with the calendar year as its taxable year. Because X is a U.S. corporation the U.S. dollar is its functional currency under section 985. The examples also assume that section 988(d) does not apply.

Example 1. On January 1, 1989, X acquires 10,000 Canadian dollars. On January 15, 1989, X uses the 10,000 Canadian dollars to purchase inventory. The acquisition of the 10,000 Canadian dollars is a section 988 transaction for purposes of establishing X's basis in such Canadian dollars. The disposition of the 10,000 Canadian dollars is a section 988 transaction pursuant to paragraph (a)(1) of this section.

Example 2. On January 1, 1989, X acquires 10,000 Canadian dollars. On January 15, 1989, X converts the 10,000 Canadian dollars to U.S. dollars. The acquisition of the 10,000 Canadian dollars is a section 988 transaction for purposes of establishing X's basis in such Canadian dollars. The conversion of the 10,000 Canadian dollars to U.S. dollars is a section 988 transaction pursuant to paragraph (a)(1) of this section.

Example 3. On January 1, 1989, X borrows 100,000 British pounds (£) for a period of 10 years and issues a note to the lender with a face amount of £100,000. The note provides for payments of interest at an annual rate of 10% paid quarterly in pounds and has a stated redemption price at maturity of £100,000. X's becoming the obligor under the note is a section 988 transaction pursuant to paragraphs (a)(1)(ii) and (2)(i) of this section. Because X is an accrual basis taxpayer, the accrual of interest expense under X's note is a section 988 transaction pursuant to paragraphs (a)(1)(ii) and (2)(ii) of this section. In addition, the acquisition of the British pounds to make payments under the note is a section 988 transaction for purposes of establishing X's basis in such pounds, and the disposition of such pounds is a section 988 transaction under paragraph (a)(1)(i) of this section. See § 1.988-2(b) with respect to the translation of accrued interest expense and the determination of exchange gain or loss upon payment of accrued interest expense.

Example 4. On January 1, 1989, X purchases at original issue for 74,621.54 British pounds (£) a 3-year bond maturing on December 31, 1991, at a stated redemption price of £100,000. The bond provides for no stated interest. The bond has a yield to maturity of 10% compounded semiannually and has £25,378.46 of original issue discount. The acquisition of the bond is a section 988 transaction as provided in paragraphs (a)(1)(ii) and (2)(i) of this section. The accrual of original issue discount with respect to the bond is a section 988 transaction under paragraphs (a)(1)(ii) and (2)(ii) of this section. See § 1.988-2(b) with respect to the translation of original issue discount and the determination of exchange gain or loss upon receipt of such amounts.

Example 5. On January 1, 1989, X sells and delivers inventory to Y for 10,000,000 Italian lira for payment on April 1, 1989. Under X's method of accounting, January 1, 1989 is the accrual date. Because X is an accrual basis taxpayer, the accrual of a nonfunctional currency denominated item of gross receipts on January 1, 1989, for payment after the date of accrual is a section 988 transaction under paragraphs (a)(1)(ii) and (2)(ii) of this section.

Example 6. On January 1, 1989, X agrees to purchase a machine from Y for delivery on March 1, 1990 for 1,000,000 yen. The agreement calls for X to pay Y for the machine on June 1, 1990. Under X's method of accounting, the expenditure for the machine does not accrue until delivery on March 1, 1990. The agreement to purchase the machine is not a section 988 transaction. In particular, the agreement to purchase the machine is not described in paragraph (a)(2)(ii) of this section because the agreement is not an item of expense taken into account under subtitle A (but rather is an agreement to purchase a capital asset in the future). However, the payable that will arise on the delivery date is a section 988 transaction under paragraphs (a)(1)(ii) and (2)(ii) of this section even though the payable relates to a capital expenditure. In addition, the disposition of yen to satisfy the payable on June 1, 1990, is a section 988 transaction under paragraph (a)(1)(i) of this section.

Example 7. On January 1, 1989, X purchases and takes delivery of inventory for 10,000 French francs with payment to be made on April 1, 1989. Under X's method of accounting, the expense accrues on January 1, 1989. On January 1, 1989, X also enters into a forward contract with a bank to purchase 10,000 French francs for $2,000 on April 1, 1989. Because X is an accrual basis taxpayer, the accrual of a nonfunctional currency denominated item of expense on January 1, 1989, for payment after the date of accrual is a section 988 transaction under paragraphs (a)(1)(ii) and (2)(ii) of this section. Entering into the forward contract to purchase the 10,000 French francs is a section 988 transaction under paragraphs (a)(1)(ii) and (2)(iii) of this section.

Example 8. On January 1, 1989, X acquires 100,000 Norwegian krone. On January 15, 1989, X purchases and takes delivery of 1,000 shares of common stock with the 100,000 krone acquired on January 1, 1989. On August 1, 1989, X sells the 1,000 shares of common stock and receives 120,000 krone in payment. On August 30, 1989, X converts the 120,000 krone to U.S. dollars. The acquisition of the 100,000 krone on January 1, 1989, and the acquisition of the 120,000 krone on August 1, 1989, are section 988 transactions for purposes of establishing the basis of such krone. The disposition of the 100,000 krone on January 15, 1989, and the 120,000 krone on August 30, 1989, are section 988 transactions as provided in paragraph (a)(1)(i) of this section. Neither the acquisition on January 15, 1989, nor the disposition on August 1, 1989, of the stock is a section 988 transaction.

Example 9. On May 11, 1989, X purchases a one year note at original issue for its issue price of $1,000. The note pays interest in dollars at the rate of 4 percent compounded semiannually. The amount of principal received by X upon maturity is equal to $1,000 plus the equivalent of the excess, if any, of (a) the Financial Times One Hundred Stock Index (an index of stocks traded on the London Stock Exchange hereafter referred to as the FT100) determined and translated into dollars on the last business day prior to the maturity date, over (b) £2,150, the "stated value" of the FT100, which is equal to 110% of the average value of the index for the six months prior to the issue date, translated at the exchange rate of £1 = $1.50. The purchase by X of the instrument described above is not a section 988 transaction because the index used to compute the principal amount received upon maturity is determined with reference to the value of stock and not nonfunctional currency.

Example 10. On April 9, 1989, X enters into an interest rate swap that provides for the payment of amounts by X to its counterparty based on 4% of a 10,000 yen principal amount in exchange for amounts based on yen LIBOR rates. Pursuant to paragraphs (a)(1)(ii) and (2)(iii) of this section, this yen for yen interest rate swap is a section 988 transaction.

Example 11. On August 11, 1989, X enters into an option contract for sale of a group of stocks traded on the Japanese Nikkei exchange. The contract is not a section 988 transaction within the meaning of §1.988-1(a)(2)(iii) because the underlying property to which the option relates is a group of stocks and not nonfunctional currency.

(7) *Special rules for regulated futures contracts and non-equity options.*—(i) *In general.*—Except as provided in paragraph (a)(7)(ii) of this section, paragraph (a)(2)(iii) of this section shall not apply to any regulated futures contract or non-equity option which would be marked to market under section 1256 if held on the last day of the taxable year.

(ii) *Election to have paragraph (a)(2)(iii) of this section apply.*—Notwithstanding paragraph (a)(7)(i) of this section, a taxpayer may elect to have paragraph (a)(2)(iii) of this section apply to regulated futures contracts and non-equity options as provided in paragraph (a)(7)(iii) and (iv) of this section.

(iii) *Procedure for making the election.*—A taxpayer shall make the election provided in paragraph (a)(7)(ii) of this section by sending to the Internal Revenue Service Center, Examination Branch, Stop Number 92, Kansas City, MO 64999 a statement titled "ELECTION TO TREAT REGULATED FUTURES CONTRACTS AND NON-EQUITY OPTIONS AS SECTION 988 TRANSACTIONS UNDER SECTION 988(c)(1)(D)(ii)" that contains the following:

(A) The taxpayer's name, address, and taxpayer identification number;

(B) The date the notice is mailed or otherwise delivered to the Internal Revenue Service Center;

(C) A statement that the taxpayer (including all members of such person's affiliated group as defined in section 1504 or in the case of an individual all persons filing a joint return with such individual) elects to have section 988(c)(1)(D)(i) and §1.988-1(a)(7)(i) not apply;

(D) The date of the beginning of the taxable year for which the election is being made;

(E) If the election is filed after the first day of the taxable year, a statement regarding whether the taxpayer has previously held a contract described in section 988(c)(1)(D)(i) or §1.988-1(a)(7)(i) during such taxable year, and if so, the first date during the taxable year on which such contract was held; and

(F) The signature of the person making the election (in the case of individuals filing a joint return, the signature of all persons filing such return).

The election shall be made by the following persons: in the case of an individual, by such individual; in the case of a partnership, by each partner separately; effective for taxable years beginning after March 17, 1992, in the case of tiered partnerships, each ultimate partner; in the case of an S corporation, by each shareholder separately; in the case of a trust (other than a grantor trust) or estate, by the fiduciary of such trust or estate; in the case of any corporation other than an S corporation, by such corporation (in the case of a corporation that is a member of an affiliated group that files a consolidated return, such election shall be valid and binding only if made by the common parent, as that term is used in §1.1502-77(a)); in the case of a controlled foreign corporation, by its controlling United States shareholders under §1.964-1(c)(3). With respect to a corporation (other than an S corporation), the election, when made by the common parent, shall be binding on all members of such corporation's affiliated group as defined in section 1504 that file a consolidated return. The election shall be binding on any income or loss derived from the partner's share (determined under the principles of section 702(a)) of all contracts described in section 988(c)(1)(D)(i) or paragraph (a)(7)(i) of this section in which the taxpayer holds a direct interest or indirect interest through a partnership or S corporation; however, the election shall not apply to any income or loss of a partnership for any taxable year if such partnership made an election under section 988(c)(1)(E)(iii)(V) for such year or any preceding year. Generally, a copy of the election must be attached to the taxpayer's income tax return for the first year it is effective. It is not required to be attached to subsequent returns. However, in the case of a partner, a copy of the election must be attached to the taxpayer's income tax return for every year during which the taxpayer is a partner in a partnership that engages in a transaction that is subject to the election.

(iv) *Time for making the election.*—(A) *In general.*—Unless the requirements for making a late election described in paragraph (a)(7)(iv)(B) of this section are satisfied, an election under section 988(c)(1)(D)(ii) and paragraph (a)(7)(ii) of this section for any taxable year shall be made on or before the first day of the taxable year or, if later, on or before the first day during such taxable year on which the taxpayer holds a contract described in section 988(c)(1)(D)(ii) and paragraph (a)(7)(ii) of this section. The election under section 988(c)(1)(D)(ii) and paragraph (a)(7)(ii) of this section shall apply to contracts entered into or acquired after October 21, 1988, and held on or after the effective date of the election. The election shall be effective as of the beginning of the taxable year and shall be binding with respect to all succeeding taxable years unless revoked with the prior consent of the Commissioner. In determining whether to grant revocation of the election, recapture of the tax benefit derived from the election in previous taxable years will be considered.

(B) *Late elections.*—A taxpayer may make an election under section 988(c)(1)(D)(ii) and paragraph (a)(7)(ii) of this section within 30 days after the time prescribed in the first sentence of paragraph (a)(7)(iv)(A) of this section. Such a late election shall be effective as of the beginning of the taxable year; however, any losses recognized during the taxable year with respect to contracts described in section 988(c)(1)(D)(ii) or paragraph (a)(7)(ii) of this section which were entered into or acquired after October 21, 1988, and held on or before the date on which the late election is mailed or otherwise delivered to the Internal Revenue Service Center shall not be treated as derived from a section 988 transaction. A late election must comply with the procedures set forth in paragraph (a)(7)(iii) of this section.

(v) *Transition rule.*—An election made prior to September 21, 1989 which satisfied the requirements of Notice 88-124, 1988-51 I.R.B. 6, shall be deemed to satisfy the requirements of paragraphs (a)(7)(iii) and (iv) of this section.

(vi) *General effective date provision.*—This paragraph (a)(7) shall apply with respect to futures contracts and options entered into or acquired after October 21, 1988.

(8) *Special rules for qualified funds.*—(i) *Definition of qualified fund.*—The term "qualified fund" means any partnership if—

(A) At all times during the taxable year (and during each preceding taxable year to which an election under section 988(c)(1)(E)(iii)(V) applied) such partnership has at least 20 partners and no single partner owns more than 20 percent of the interests in the capital or profits of the partnership;

(B) The principal activity of such partnership for such taxable year (and each such preceding taxable year) consists of buying and selling options, futures, or forwards with respect to commodities;

(C) At least 90 percent of the gross income of the partnership for the taxable year (and each such preceding year) consists of income or gains described in subparagraph (A), (B), or (G) of section 7704(d)(1) or gain from the sale or disposition of capital assets held for the production of interest or dividends;

(D) No more than a de minimis amount of the gross income of the partnership for the taxable year (and each such preceding taxable year) was derived from buying and selling commodities; and

(E) An election under section 988(c)(1)(E)(iii)(V) as provided in paragraph (a)(8)(iv) of this section applies to the taxable year.

(ii) *Special rules relating to paragraph (a)(8)(i)(A) of this section.*—(A) *Certain general partners.*—The interest of a general partner in the partnership shall not be treated as failing to meet the 20 percent ownership requirement of paragraph (a)(8)(i)(A) of this section for any taxable year of the partnership if, for the taxable year of the partner in which such partnership's taxable year ends, such partner (and each corporation filing a consolidated return with such partner) had no ordinary income or loss from a section 988 transaction (other than income from the partnership) which is exchange gain or loss (as the case may be).

(B) *Treatment of incentive compensation.*—For purposes of paragraph (a)(8)(i)(A) of this section, any income allocable to a general partner as incentive compensation based on profits rather than capital shall not be taken into account in determining such partner's interest in the profits of the partnership.

(C) *Treatment of tax exempt partners.*—The interest of a partner in the partnership shall not be treated as failing to meet the 20 percent ownership requirements of paragraph (a)(5)(8)(A) of this section if none of the income of such partner from such partnership is subject to tax under chapter 1 of subtitle A of the Internal Revenue Code (whether directly or through one or more pass-through entities).

(D) *Look-through rule.*—In determining whether the 20% ownership requirement of paragraph (a)(8)(i)(A) of this section is met with respect to any partnership, any interest in such partnership held by another partnership shall be treated as held proportionately by the partners in such other partnership.

(iii) *Other special rules.*—(A) *Related persons.*—Interests in the partnership held by persons related to each other (within the meaning of section 267(b) or 707(b)) shall be treated as held by one person.

(B) *Predecessors.*—Reference to any partnership shall include a reference to any predecessor thereof.

(C) *Treatment of certain debt instruments.*—Solely for purposes of paragraph (a)(8)(i)(D) of this section, any debt instrument which is described in both paragraph (a)(1)(ii) and (2)(i) of this section shall be treated as a commodity.

(iv) *Procedure for making the election provided in section 988(c)(1)(E)(iii)(V).*—A partnership shall make the election provided in section 988(c)(1)(E)(iii)(V) by sending to the Internal Revenue Service Center, Examination Branch, Stop Number 92, Kansas City, MO 64999 a statement titled "QUALIFIED FUND ELECTION UNDER SECTION 988(c)(1)(E)(iii)(V)" that contains the following:

(A) The partnership's name, address, and taxpayer identification number;

(B) The name, address and taxpayer identification number of the general partner making the election on behalf of the partnership;

(C) The date the notice is mailed or otherwise delivered to the Internal Revenue Service Center;

(D) A brief description of the activity of the partnership;

(E) A statement that the partnership is making the election provided in section 988(c)(1)(E)(iii)(V);

(F) The date of the beginning of the taxable year for which the election is being made;

(G) If the election is filed after the first day of the taxable year, then a statement regarding whether the partnership previously held an instrument referred to in section 988(c)(1)(E)(i) during such taxable year and, if so, the first date during the taxable year on which such contract was held; and

(H) The signature of the general partner making the election.

The election shall be made by a general partner with management responsibility of the partnership's activities and a copy of such election shall be attached to the partnership's income tax return (Form 1065) for the first taxable year it is effective. It is not required to be attached to subsequent returns.

(v) *Time for making the election.*—The election under section 988(c)(1)(E)(iii)(V) for any taxable year shall be made on or before the first day of the taxable year or, if later, on or before the first day during such year on which the partnership holds an instrument described in section 988(c)(1)(E)(i). The election under section 988(c)(1)(E)(iii)(V) shall apply to the taxable year for which made and all succeeding taxable years. Such election may only be revoked with the consent of the Commissioner. In determining whether to grant revocation of the election, recapture by the partners of the tax benefit derived from the election in previous taxable years will be considered.

(vi) *Operative rules applicable to qualified funds.*—(A) *In general.*—In the case of a qualified fund, any bank forward contract or any foreign currency futures contract traded on a foreign exchange which is not otherwise a section 1256 contract shall be treated as a section 1256 contract for purposes of section 1256.

(B) *Gains and losses treated as short-term.*—In the case of any instrument treated as a section 1256 contract under paragraph (a)(8)(vi)(A) of this section, subparagraph (A) of section 1256(a)(3) shall be applied by substituting "100 percent" for "40 percent" (and subparagraph (B) of such section shall not apply).

(vii) *Transition rule.*—An election made prior to September 21, 1989, which satisfied the requirements of Notice 88-124, 1988-51 I.R.B. 6, shall be deemed to satisfy the requirements of § 1.988-1(a)(8)(iv) and (v).

(viii) *General effective date rules.*—(A) The requirements of subclause (IV) of section 988(c)(1)(E)(iii) shall not apply to contracts entered into or acquired on or before October 21, 1988.

(B) In the case of any partner in an existing partnership, the 20 percent ownership requirements of subclause (I) of section 988(c)(1)(E)(iii) shall be treated as met during any period during which such partner does not own a percentage interest in the capital or profits of such partnership greater than 33 1/3 percent (or, if lower, the lowest such percentage interest of such partner during any period after October 21, 1988, during which such partnership is in existence). For purposes of the preceding sentence, the term "existing partnership" means any partnership if—

(*1*) such partnership was in existence on October 21, 1988, and principally engaged on such date in buying and selling options, futures, or forwards with respect to commodities; or

(*2*) a registration statement was filed with respect to such partnership with the Securities and Exchange Commission on or before such date and such registration statement indicated that the principal activity of such partnership will consist of buying and selling instruments referred to in paragraph (a)(8)(viii)(B)(*1*) of this section.

(9) *Exception for certain transactions entered into by an individual.*—(i) *In general.*—A transaction entered into by an individual which otherwise qualifies as a section 988 transaction shall be considered a section 988 transaction only to the extent expenses properly allocable to such transaction meet the requirements of section 162 or 212 (other than the part of section 212 dealing with expenses incurred in connection with taxes).

(ii) *Examples.*—The following examples illustrate the application of paragraph (a)(9) of this section.

Example 1. X is a U.S. citizen who therefore has the U.S. dollar as his functional currency. On January 1, 1990, X enters into a spot contract to purchase 10,000 British pounds (£) for $15,000 for delivery on January 3, 1990. Immediately upon delivery, X acquires at original issue a pound denominated bond with an issue price of £ 10,000. The bond matures on January 3, 1993, pays interest in pounds at a rate of 10% compounded semiannually, and has no original issue discount. Assume that all expenses properly allocable to these transactions would meet the requirements of section 212. Under § 1.988-2(d)(1)(ii), entering into the spot contract on January 1, 1990, is not a section 988 transaction. The acquisition of the pounds on January 3, 1990, under the spot contract is a section 988 transaction for purposes of establishing X's basis in the pounds. The disposition of the pounds and the acquisition of the bond by X are section 988 transactions. These transactions are not excluded from the definition of a section 988 transaction under paragraph (a)(9) of this section because expenses properly allocable to such transactions meet the requirements of section 212.

Example 2. X is a U.S. citizen who therefore has the dollar as his functional currency. In preparation for X's vacation, X purchases 1,000 British pounds (£) from a bank on June 1, 1989. During the period of X's vacation in the United Kingdom beginning June 10, 1989, and ending June 20, 1989, X spends £500 for hotel rooms, £ 300 for food and £200 for miscellaneous vacation expenses. The expenses properly allocable to such dispositions do not meet the requirements of section 162 or 212. Thus, the disposition of the pounds by X on his vacation are not section 988 transactions.

(10) *Intra-taxpayer transactions.*—(i) *In general.*—Except as provided in paragraph (a)(10)(ii) of this section, transactions between or among the taxpayer and/or qualified business units of that taxpayer ("intra-taxpayer transactions") are not section 988 transactions. See section 987 and the regulations thereunder.

(ii) *Certain intra-taxpayer transfers of section 988 transactions that result in the recognition of section 988 gain or loss.*—(A) *In general.*—Exchange gain or loss with respect to nonfunctional currency or any item described in paragraph (a)(2) of this section entered into with another taxpayer shall be realized upon a transfer (as defined under § 1.987-2(c)) of such currency or item from an owner to a section 987 QBU or from a section 987 QBU to an owner if as a result of such transfer —

(1) The currency or item loses its character as nonfunctional currency or as an item described in paragraph (a)(2) of this section; or

(2) The source of the exchange gain or loss could be altered absent the application of paragraph (a)(10)(ii)(B) of this section.

(B) *Computation of exchange gain or loss.*—Exchange gain or loss described in section (a)(10)(ii)(A) of this section shall be computed in accordance with § 1.988-2 (without regard to § 1.988-2(b)(8)) as if the nonfunctional currency or item described in paragraph (a)(2) of this section had been sold or otherwise transferred at fair market value between unrelated taxpayers. For purposes of the preceding sentence, a taxpayer must use a translation rate that is consistent with the translation conventions of the section 987 QBU to or from which, as the case may be, the item is being transferred. In the case of a gain or loss incurred in a transaction described in this paragraph (a)(10)(ii) that does not have a significant business purpose, the Commissioner may defer such gain or loss.

(iii) *Example.*—The following example illustrates the provisions of this paragraph (a)(10).

Example. (A) X, a corporation with the U.S. dollar as its functional currency, operates through foreign branches Y and Z. Y and Z are qualified business units as defined in section 989(a) with the LC as their functional currency. X computes Y's and Z's income under section 987 (relating to branch transactions). On November 12, 1988, Y transfers $25 to the home office of X when the fair market value of such amount equals LC120. Y has a basis of LC100 in the $25. Under paragraph (a)(10)(ii) of this section, Y realizes foreign source exchange gain of LC20 (LC120 – LC100) as the result of the $25 transfer. For purposes of determining whether the transfer is a remittance resulting in additional gain or loss, see section 987 and the regulations thereunder.

(B) If instead Y transfers the $25 to Z, exchange gain is not realized because the $25 is nonfunctional currency with respect to Z and if Z were to immediately convert the $25 into LCs, the gain would be foreign source. For purposes of determining whether the transfer is a remittance resulting in additional gain or loss, see section 987 and the regulations thereunder.

(11) *Authority to include or exclude transactions from section 988.*—(i) *In general.*—The Commissioner may recharacterize a transaction (or series of transactions) in whole or in part as a section 988 transaction if the effect of such transaction (or series of transactions) is to avoid section 988. In addition, the Commissioner may exclude a transaction (or series of transactions) which in form is a section 988 transaction from the provisions of section 988 if the substance of the transaction (or series of transactions) indicates that it is not properly considered a section 988 transaction.

(ii) *Example.*—The following example illustrates the provisions of this paragraph (a)(11).

Example. B is an individual with the U.S. dollar as its functional currency. B holds 500,000 Swiss francs which have a basis of $100,000 and a fair market value of $400,000 as of October 15, 1989. On October 16, 1989, B transfers the 500,000 Swiss francs to a newly formed U.S. corporation, X, with the dollar as its functional currency. On October 16, 1989, B sells the stock of X for $400,000. Assume the transfer to X qualified for nonrecognition under section 351. Because the sale of the stock of X is a substitute for the disposition of an asset subject to section 988, the Commissioner may recharacterize the sale of the stock as a section 988 transaction. The same result would obtain if B transferred the Swiss francs to a partnership and then sold the partnership interest.

(b) *Spot contract.*—A spot contract is a contract to buy or sell nonfunctional currency on or before two business days following the date of the execution of the contract. See § 1.988-2(d)(1)(ii) for operative rules regarding spot contracts.

(c) *Nonfunctional currency.*—The term "nonfunctional currency" means with respect to a taxpayer or a qualified business unit (as defined in section 989(a)) a currency (including the European Currency Unit) other than the taxpayer's or the qualified business unit's functional currency as defined in section 985 and the regulations thereunder. For rules relating to nonrecognition of exchange gain or loss with respect to certain dispositions of nonfunctional currency, see § 1.988-2(a)(1)(iii).

(d) *Spot rate.*—(1) *In general.*—Except as otherwise provided in this paragraph, the term "spot rate" means a rate demonstrated to the satisfaction of the District Director or the Assistant Commissioner (International) to reflect a fair market rate of exchange available to the public for currency under a spot contract in a free market and involving representative amounts. In the absence of such a demonstration, the District Director or the Assistant Commissioner (International), in his or her sole discretion, shall determine the spot rate from a source of exchange rate information reflecting actual transactions conducted in a free market. For example, the taxpayer or the District Director or the Assistant Commissioner (International) may determine the spot rate by reference to exchange rates published in the pertinent monthly issue of "International Financial Statistics" or a successor publication of the International Monetary Fund; exchange rates published by the Board of Governors of the Federal Reserve System pursuant to 31 U.S.C. section 5151; exchange rates published in newspapers, financial journals or other daily financial news sources; or exchange rates quoted by electronic financial news services.

(2) *Consistency required in valuing transactions subject to section 988.*—If the use of inconsistent sources of spot rate quotations results in the distortion of income, the District Director or the Assistant Commissioner (International) may determine the appropriate spot rate.

(3) *Use of certain spot rate conventions for payables and receivables denominated in nonfunctional currency.*—If consistent with the taxpayer's financial accounting, a taxpayer may utilize a spot rate convention determined at intervals of one quarter year or less for purposes of computing exchange gain or loss with respect to payables and receivables denominated in a nonfunctional currency that are incurred in the ordinary course of business with respect to the acquisition or sale of goods or the obtaining or performance of services. For example, if consistent with the taxpayer's financial accounting, a taxpayer may accrue all payables and receivables incurred during the month of January at the spot rate on December 31 or January 31 (or at an average of any spot rates occurring between these two dates) and record the payment or receipt of amounts in satisfaction of such payables and receivables consistent with such convention. The use of a spot rate convention cannot be changed without the consent of the Commissioner.

(4) *Currency where an official government established rate differs from a free market rate.*—(i) *In general.*—If a currency has an official government established rate that differs from a free market rate, the spot rate shall be the rate which most clearly reflects the taxpayer's income. Generally, this shall be the free market rate.

(ii) *Examples.*—The following examples illustrate the application of this paragraph (d)(4).

Example 1. X is an accrual method U.S. corporation with the dollar as its functional currency. X owns all the stock of a Country L subsidiary, CFC. CFC has the currency of Country L, the LC, as its functional currency. Country L imposes restrictions on the remittance of dividends. On April 1, 1990, CFC pays a dividend to X in the amount of LC100. Assume that the official government established rate is $1 = LC1 and the free market rate, which takes into account the remittance restrictions and which is the rate that most clearly reflects income, is $1 = LC4. On April 1, 1990, X donates the LC100 in a transaction that otherwise qualifies as a charitable contribution under section 170(c). Both the amount of the dividend income and the deduction under section 170 is $25 (LC100 × the free market rate, $.25).

Example 2. X, a corporation with the U.S. dollar as its functional currency, operates in foreign country L through branch Y. Y is a qualified business unit as defined in section 989(a). X computes Y's income under the dollar approximate separate transactions method as described in § 1.985-3. The currency of L is the LC. X can purchase legally United States dollars ($) in L only from the L government. In order to take advantage of an arbitrage between the official and secondary dollar to LC exchange rates in L:

(i) X purchases LC100 for $60 in L on the secondary market when the official exchange rate is $1 = LC1;

(ii) X transfers the LC100 to Y;

(iii) Y purchases $100 for LC100; and

(iv) Y transfers $65 ($100 less an L tax withheld of $35 on the transfer) to the home office of X.

Under paragraph (a)(7) of this section, the transfer of the LC100 by X to Y is a realization event. X has a basis of $60 in the LC100. Under these facts, the appropriate dollar to LC exchange rate for computing the amount realized by X is the official exchange rate. Therefore, X realizes $40 ($100 – $60) of U.S. source gain from the transfer to Y. The same result would obtain if Y rather than X purchased the LC100 on the secondary market in L with $60 supplied by X, because the substance of this transaction is that X is performing the arbitrage.

(e) *Exchange gain or loss*.—The term "exchange gain or loss" means the amount of gain or loss realized as determined in § 1.988-2 with respect to a section 988 transaction. Except as otherwise provided in these regulations (*e.g.*, § 1.988-5), the amount of exchange gain or loss from a section 988 transaction shall be separately computed for each section 988 transaction, and such amount shall not be integrated with gain or loss recognized on another transaction (whether or not such transaction is economically related to the section 988 transaction). See § 1.988-2(b)(8) for a special rule with respect to debt instruments.

(f) *Hyperinflationary currency*.—(1) *Definition*.—(i) *General rule*.—For purposes of section 988, a hyperinflationary currency means a currency described in § 1.985-1(b)(2)(ii)(D). Unless otherwise provided, the currency in any example used in §§ 1.988-1 through 1.988-5 is not a hyperinflationary currency.

(ii) *Special rules for determining base period*.—In determining whether a currency is hyperinflationary under § 1.985-1(b)(2)(ii)(D) for purposes of this paragraph (f), the following rules will apply:

(A) The base period means the thirty-six calendar month period ending on the last day of the taxpayer's (or qualified business unit's) current taxable year. Thus, for example, if for 1996, 1997, and 1998, a country's annual inflation rates are 6 percent, 11 percent, and 90 percent, respectively, the cumulative inflation rate for the three-year base period is 124% [((1.06 × 1.11 × 1.90) – 1.0 = 1.24) × 100 = 124%]. Accordingly, assuming the QBU has a calendar year as its taxable year, the currency of the country is hyperinflationary for the 1998 taxable year. This change in the § 1.985-1(b)(2)(ii)(D) base period shall not apply to any section 988 transaction of an entity described in section 851 (regulated investment company (RIC)) or section 856 (real estate investment trust (REIT)). The Service may, by notice, provide that the foregoing change in the § 1.985-1(b)(2)(ii)(D) base period does not apply to any section 988 transaction of an entity with distribution requirements similar to a RIC or REIT.

(B) The last sentence of § 1.985-1(b)(2)(ii)(D) shall not apply to alter the base period for purposes of this paragraph (f) in determining whether a currency is hyperinflationary for purposes of section 988. Accordingly, generally accepted accounting principles may not apply to alter the base period for purposes of this paragraph (f).

(2) *Effective date*.—Paragraph (f)(1) of this section shall apply to transactions entered into after February 14, 2000.

(g) *Fair market value*.—The fair market value of an item shall, where relevant, reflect an appropriate premium or discount for the time value of money (*e.g.*, the fair market value of a forward contract to buy or sell nonfunctional currency shall reflect the present value of the difference between the units of nonfunctional currency times the market forward rate at the time of valuation and the units of nonfunctional currency times the forward rate set forth in the contract). However, if consistent with the taxpayer's method of financial accounting (and consistently applied from year to year), the preceding sentence shall not apply to a financial instrument that matures within one year from the date of issuance or acquisition. Unless otherwise provided, the fair market value given in any example used in §§ 1.988-1 through 1.988-5 is deemed to reflect appropriately the time value of money. If the use of inconsistent sources of forward or other market rate quotations results in the distortion of income, the District Director or the Assistant Commissioner (International) may determine the appropriate rate.

(h) *Interaction with sections 1092 and 1256*.—Unless otherwise provided, it is assumed for purposes of §§ 1.988-1 through 1.988-5 that any contract used in any example is not a section 1256 contract and is not part of a straddle as defined in section 1092. No inference is intended regarding the application of section 1092 or 1256 unless expressly stated.

(i) *Effective date*.—Except as otherwise provided in this section, this section shall be effective for taxable years beginning after December 31, 1986. Thus, except as otherwise provided in this section, any payments made or received with respect to a section 988 transaction in taxable years beginning after December 31, 1986, are subject to this section. Generally, the revisions to paragraphs (a)(3), (a)(4), and (a)(10)(ii) of this section shall apply to taxable years beginning one year after the first day of the first taxable year following December 7, 2016. If pursuant to § 1.987-11(b) a taxpayer applies §§ 1.987-1 through 1.987-11 beginning in a taxable year prior to the earliest taxable year described in § 1.987-11(a), then the revisions to paragraphs (a)(3), (a)(4), and (a)(10)(ii) of this section shall apply to taxable years of the taxpayer beginning on or after the first day of such prior taxable year. [Reg. § 1.988-1.]

☐ [*T.D. 8400, 3-16-92. Amended by T.D. 8914, 12-29-2000 T.D. 9794, 12-7-2016 and T.D. 9795, 12-7-2016.*]

Caution: Temporary Reg. §1.988-1T, below, expired on December 6, 2019. The related proposed regulation, published in REG-128276-12 by cross-reference to the temporary regulation, may be relied upon for periods following the expiration date (see Notice 2022-34, I.R.B. 2022-34, 150).

§ 1.988-1T. Certain definitions and special rules (temporary).—(a)(1) through (a)(2) [Reserved]. For further guidance, see § 1.988-1(a)(1) through (2).

(3) *Specified owner functional currency transactions of a section 987 QBU not treated as section 988 transactions*.—Specified owner functional currency transactions, as defined in § 1.987-3T(b)(4)(ii), held by a section 987 QBU are not treated as section 988 transactions. Thus, no currency gain or loss shall be recognized by a section 987 QBU under section 988 with respect to such transactions.

(4) through (i) [Reserved]. For further guidance, see § 1.988-1(a)(4) through (i).

(j) *Effective/applicability date*.—This section applies to taxable years beginning on or after one year after the first day of the first taxable year following December 7, 2016. Notwithstanding the preceding sentence, if a taxpayer makes an election under § 1.987-11(b), then this section applies to taxable years to which §§ 1.987-1 through 1.987-10 apply as a result of such election.

(k) *Expiration date*.—The applicability of this section expires on December 6, 2019. [Temporary Reg. § 1.988-1T.]

☐ [*T.D. 9795, 12-7-2016.*]

Proposed Amendments to Regulation

§ 1.988-1. Certain definitions and special rules.—(a) * * *

(2) * * *

(iii) * * *

(B) * * *

(2) Definition of notional principal contract. Generally, the term "notional principal contract" means a contract defined in § 1.446-3(c). However, a "notional principal contract" shall only be considered as described in paragraph (a)(2)(iii)(B)(*1*) of this section if the underlying property to which the instrument ultimately relates is money (for example, functional currency), nonfunctional currency, or property the value of which is determined by reference to an interest rate. Thus, the term "notional principal contract" includes a currency

swap as defined in § 1.988-2(e)(2)(ii), but does not include a swap referenced to a commodity or equity index.

(C) * * * The rules of this paragraph (a)(2)(iii) apply to notional principal contracts as defined in § 1.446-3(c) that are entered into on or after the date of publication of a Treasury decision adopting these rules as final regulations in the **Federal Register.** Section 1.988-1(a)(2)(iii) as contained in 26 CFR part 1 revised April 1, 2011, continues to apply to notional principal contracts entered into before the date of publication of a Treasury decision adopting these rules as final regulations in the **Federal Register.**

[Prop. Reg. § 1.988-1.]
[Proposed 9-16-2011.]

§ 1.988-2. Recognition and computation of exchange gain or loss.—(a) *Disposition of nonfunctional currency.*—(1) *Recognition of exchange gain or loss.*—(i) *In general.*—Except as otherwise provided in this section, § 1.988-1(a)(7)(ii), and § 1.988-5, the recognition of exchange gain or loss upon the sale or other disposition of nonfunctional currency shall be governed by the recognition provisions of the Internal Revenue Code which apply to the sale or disposition of property (*e.g.*, section 1001 or, to the extent provided in regulations, section 1092). The disposition of nonfunctional currency in settlement of a forward contract, futures contract, option contract, or similar financial instrument is considered to be a sale or disposition of the nonfunctional currency for purposes of the preceding sentence.

(ii) *Clarification of section 1031.*—An amount of one nonfunctional currency is not "property of like kind" with respect to an amount of a different nonfunctional currency.

(iii) *Coordination with section 988(c)(1)(C)(ii).*—No exchange gain or loss is recognized with respect to the following transactions—

(A) An exchange of units of nonfunctional currency for different units of the same nonfunctional currency;

(B) The deposit of nonfunctional currency in a demand or time deposit or similar instrument (including a certificate of deposit) issued by a bank or other financial institution if such instrument is denominated in such currency;

(C) The withdrawal of nonfunctional currency from a demand or time deposit or similar instrument issued by a bank or other financial institution if such instrument is denominated in such currency;

(D) The receipt of nonfunctional currency from a bank or other financial institution from which the taxpayer purchased a certificate of deposit or similar instrument denominated in such currency by reason of the maturing or other termination of such instrument; and

(E) The transfer of nonfunctional currency from a demand or time deposit or similar instrument issued by a bank or other financial institution to another demand or time deposit or similar instrument denominated in the same nonfunctional currency issued by a bank or other financial institution.

The taxpayer's basis in the units of nonfunctional currency or other property received in the transaction shall be the adjusted basis of the units of nonfunctional currency or other property transferred. See paragraph (b) of this section with respect to the timing of interest income or expense and the determination of exchange gain or loss thereon.

(iv) *Example.*—The following example illustrates the provisions of paragraph (a)(1)(iii) of this section.

Example. X is a corporation on the accrual method of accounting with the U.S. dollar as its functional currency. On January 1, 1989, X acquires 1,500 British pounds (£) for $2,250 (£1 = $1.50). On January 3, 1989, when the spot rate is £ 1 = $1.49, X deposits the £1,500 with a British financial institution in a non-interest bearing demand account. On February 1, 1989, when the spot rate is £1 = $1.45, X withdraws the £1,500. On February 5, 1989, when the spot rate is £1 = $1.42, X purchases inventory in the amount of £ 1,500. Pursuant to paragraph (a)(1)(iii) of this section, no exchange loss is realized until February 5, 1989, when X disposes of the £1,500 for inventory. At that time, X realizes exchange loss in the amount of $120 computed under paragraph (a)(2) of this section. The loss is not an adjustment to the cost of the inventory.

(2) *Computation of gain or loss.*—(i) *In general.*—Exchange gain realized from the sale or other disposition of nonfunctional currency shall be the excess of the amount realized over the adjusted basis of such currency, and exchange loss realized shall be the excess of the adjusted basis of such currency over the amount realized.

(ii) *Amount realized.*—(A) *In general.*—The amount realized from the disposition of nonfunctional currency shall be determined under section 1001(b). A taxpayer that uses a spot rate convention under § 1.988-1(d)(3) to determine exchange gain or loss with respect to a payable shall determine the amount realized upon the disposition of nonfunctional currency paid in satisfaction of the payable in a manner consistent with such convention.

(B) *Exchange of nonfunctional currency for property.*—For purpose of paragraph (a)(2) of this section, the exchange of nonfunctional currency for property (other than nonfunctional currency) shall be treated as—

(*1*) An exchange of the units of nonfunctional currency for units of functional currency at the spot rate on the date of the exchange, and

(*2*) The purchase or sale of the property for such units of functional currency.

(C) *Example.*—The following example illustrates the provisions of paragraph (a)(2)(ii)(B) of this section.

Example. G is a U.S. corporation with the U.S. dollar as its functional currency. On January 1, 1989, G enters into a contract to purchase a paper manufacturing machine for 10,000,000 British pounds (£) for delivery on January 1, 1991. On January 1, 1991, when G exchanges £10,000,000 (which G purchased for $12,000,000) for the machine, the fair market value of the machine is $17,000,000. On January 1, 1991, the spot exchange rate is £1 = $1.50. Under paragraph (a)(2)(ii)(B) of this section, the transaction is treated as an exchange of £ 10,000,000 for $15,000,000 and the purchase of the machine for $15,000,000. Accordingly, in computing G's exchange gain of $3,000,000 on the disposition of the £10,000,000, the amount realized is $15,000,000. G's basis in the machine is $15,000,000. No gain is recognized on the bargain purchase of the machine.

(iii) *Adjusted basis.*—(A) *In general.*—Except as provided in paragraphs (a)(2)(iii)(B) and (C) of this section, the adjusted basis of nonfunctional currency is determined under the applicable provisions of the Internal Revenue Code (*e.g.*, sections 1011 through 1023). A taxpayer that uses a spot rate convention under § 1.988-1(d)(3) to determine exchange gain or loss with respect to a receivable shall determine the basis of nonfunctional currency received in satisfaction of such receivable in a manner consistent with such convention.

(B) *Determination of the basis of nonfunctional currency withdrawn from an account with a bank or other financial institution.*—(*1*) *In general.*—The basis of nonfunctional currency withdrawn from an account with a bank or other financial institution shall be determined under any reasonable method that is consistently applied from year to year by the taxpayer to all accounts denominated in a nonfunctional currency. For example, a taxpayer may use a first in first out method, a last in first out method, a prorata method (as illustrated in the example below), or any other reasonable method that is consistently applied. However, a method that consistently results in units of nonfunctional currency with the highest basis being withdrawn first shall not be considered reasonable.

(*2*) *Example.*—The following example illustrates the provisions of this paragraph (a)(2)(iii)(B).

Example. (i) X, a cash basis individual with the dollar as his functional currency, opens a demand account with a Swiss bank. Assume expenses associated with the demand account are deductible under section 212. The following chart indicates Swiss franc deposits to the account, Swiss franc interest credited to the account, the dollar basis of each deposit, and the determination of the aggregate dollar basis of all Swiss francs in the account. Assume that the taxpayer has properly translated all the amounts specified in the chart and that all transactions are subject to section 988.

Date	*Swiss francs Deposited*	*Interest Received*	*U.S. dollar Basis*	*Aggregate U.S. dollar Basis*
1/01/89	1000 Sf		$500	$500
3/31/89		50 Sf	$25	$525
6/30/89		50 Sf	$24	$549
9/30/89		50 Sf	$25	$574
12/31/89		50 Sf	$26	$600

(ii) On January 1, 1990, X withdraws 500 Swiss francs from the account. X may determine his basis in the Swiss francs by multiplying the aggregate U.S. dollar basis of Swiss francs in the account by a fraction the numerator of which is the number of Swiss francs withdrawn from the account and the denominator is the total number of Swiss francs in the account. Under this method, X's basis in the 500 Swiss francs is $250 computed as follows:

$$\frac{500 \text{ Sf}}{1200 \text{ Sf}} \times \$600 = \$250$$

(iii) X's basis in the Swiss francs remaining in the account is $350 ($600 – $250). X must use this method consistently from year to year with respect to withdrawals of nonfunctional currency from all of X's accounts.

(C) *Basis in refunded foreign income tax.*—See § 1.986(a)-1(e) for rules relating to the determination of basis in refunded foreign income tax denominated in nonfunctional currency.

(iv) *Purchase and sale of stock or securities traded on an established securities market by cash basis taxpayer.*—(A) *Amount realized.*—If stock or securities traded on an established securities market are sold by a cash basis taxpayer for nonfunctional currency, the amount realized with respect to the stock or securities (as determined on the trade date) shall be computed by translating the units of nonfunctional currency received into functional currency at the spot rate on the settlement date of the sale. This rule applies notwithstanding that the stock or securities are treated as disposed of on a date other than the settlement date under another section of the Code. See section 453(k).

(B) *Basis.*—If stock or securities traded on an established securities market are purchased by a cash basis taxpayer for nonfunctional currency, the basis of the stock or securities shall be determined by translating the units of nonfunctional currency paid into functional currency at the spot rate on the settlement date of the purchase.

(C) *Example.*—The following example illustrates the provisions of this paragraph (a)(2)(iv).

Example. On November 1, 1989 (the trade date), X, a calendar year cash basis U.S. individual, purchases stock for £100 for settlement on November 5, 1989. On November 1, 1989, the spot value of the £100 is $140. On November 5, 1989, X purchases £100 for $141 which X uses to pay for the stock. X's basis in the stock is $141. On December 30, 1990 (the trade date), X sells the stock for £110 for settlement on January 5, 1991. On December 30, 1990, the spot value of £110 is $165. On January 5, 1991, X transfers the stock and receives £110 which, translated at the spot rate, equal $166. Under section 453(k), the stock is considered disposed of on December 30, 1990. The amount realized with respect to such disposition is the value of the £110 on January 5, 1991 ($166). Accordingly, X's gain realized on December 30, 1990, from the disposition of the stock is $25 ($166 amount realized less $141 basis). X's basis in the £110 received from the sale of the stock is $166.

(v) *Purchase and sale of stock or securities traded on an established securities market by accrual basis taxpayer.*—For taxable years beginning after March 17, 1992, an accrual basis taxpayer may elect to apply the rules of paragraph (a)(2)(iv) of this section. The election shall be made by filing a statement with the taxpayer's first return in which the election is effective clearly indicating that the election has been made. A method so elected must be applied consistently from year to year and cannot be changed without the consent of the Commissioner.

(b) *Translation of interest income or expense and determination of exchange gain or loss with respect to debt instruments.*—(1) *Translation of interest income received with respect to a nonfunctional currency demand account.*—Interest income received with respect to a demand account with a bank or other financial institution which is denominated in (or the payments of which are determined by reference to) a nonfunctional currency shall be translated into functional currency at the spot rate on the date received or accrued or pursuant to any reasonable spot rate convention consistently applied by the taxpayer to all taxable years and to all accounts denominated in nonfunctional currency in the same financial institution. For example, a taxpayer may translate interest income received with respect to a demand account on the last day of each month of the taxable year, on the last day of each quarter of the taxable year, on the last day of each half of the taxable year, or on the last day of the taxable year. No exchange gain or loss is realized upon the receipt or accrual of interest income with respect to a demand account subject to this paragraph (b)(1).

(2) *Translation of nonfunctional currency interest income or expense received or paid with respect to a debt instrument described in § 1.988-1(a)(1)(ii) and (2)(i).*—(i) *Scope.*—(A) *In general.*—Paragraph (b) of this section only applies to debt instruments described in § 1.988-1(a) (1)(ii) and (2)(i) where all payments are denominated in, or determined with reference to, a single nonfunctional currency. Except as provided in paragraph (b)(2)(i)(B) of this section, this paragraph (b) shall not apply to contingent payment debt instruments.

(B) *Nonfunctional currency contingent payment debt instruments.*—(1) *Operative rules.*—See § 1.988-6 for rules applicable to contingent payment debt instruments for which one or more payments are denominated in, or determined by reference to, a nonfunctional currency.

(2) *Certain instruments are not contingent payment debt instruments.*—For purposes of sections 163(e) and 1271 through 1275 and the regulations thereunder, a debt instrument does not provide for contingent payments merely because the instrument is denominated in, or all payments of which are determined with reference to, a single nonfunctional currency. See § 1.988-6 for the treatment of nonfunctional currency contingent payment debt instruments.

(ii) *Determination and translation of interest income or expense.*—(A) *In general.*—Interest income or expense on a debt instrument described in paragraph (b)(2)(i) of this section (including original issue discount determined in accordance with sections 1271 through 1275 and 163(e) as adjusted for acquisition premium under section 1272(a)(7), and acquisition discount determined in accordance with sections 1281 through 1283) shall be determined in units of nonfunctional currency and translated into functional currency as provided in paragraphs (b)(2)(ii)(B) and (C) of this section. For purposes of sections 483, 1273(b)(5) and 1274, the nonfunctional currency in which an instrument is denominated (or by reference to which payments are determined) shall be considered money.

(B) *Translation of interest income or expense that is not required to be accrued prior to receipt or payment.*—With respect to an instrument described in paragraph (b)(2)(i) of this section, interest income or expense received or paid that is not required to be accrued by the taxpayer prior to receipt or payment shall be translated at the spot rate on the date of receipt or payment. No exchange gain or loss is realized with respect to the receipt or payment of such interest income or expense (other than the exchange gain or loss that might be realized under paragraph (a) of this section upon the disposition of the nonfunctional currency so received or paid).

(C) *Translation of interest income or expense that is required to be accrued prior to receipt or payment.*—With respect to an instrument described in paragraph (b)(2)(i) of this section, interest income or expense that is required to be accrued prior to receipt or payment (*e.g.*, under section 1272, 1281 or 163(e) or because the taxpayer uses an accrual method of accounting) shall be translated at the average rate (or other rate specified in paragraph (b)(2) (iii)(B) of this section) for the interest accrual period or, with respect to an interest accrual period that spans two taxable years, at the average rate (or other rate specified in paragraph (b)(2)(iii)(B) of this section) for the partial period within the taxable year. See paragraphs (b)(3) and (4) of this section for the determination of exchange gain or loss on the receipt or payment of accrued interest income or expense.

(iii) *Determination of average rate or other accrual convention.*—(A) *In general.*—For purposes of this paragraph (b), the average rate for an accrual period (or partial period) shall be a simple average of the spot exchange rates for each business day of such period or other average exchange rate for the period reasonably derived and consistently applied by the taxpayer.

(B) *Election to use spot accrual convention.*—For taxable years beginning after March 17, 1992, a taxpayer may elect to translate interest income and expense at the spot rate on the last day of the interest accrual period (and in the case of a partial accrual period, the spot rate on the last day of the taxable year). If the last day of the interest accrual period is within five business days of the date of receipt or payment, the taxpayer may translate interest income or expense at the spot rate on the date of receipt or payment. The election shall be made by filing a statement with the taxpayer's first return in which the election is effective clearly indicating that the election has been made. A method so elected must be applied consistently to all debt instruments from year to year and cannot be changed without the consent of the Commissioner.

(3) *Exchange gain or loss recognized by the holder with respect to accrued interest income.*—The holder of a debt instrument described in paragraph (b)(2)(i) of this section shall realize exchange gain or loss with respect to accrued interest income on the date such accrued interest income is received or the instrument is disposed of (including a deemed disposition under section 1001 that results from a material change in terms of the instrument). Except as otherwise provided in this paragraph (b) (*e.g.*, paragraph (b)(8) of this section), exchange gain or loss realized with respect to accrued interest income shall be recognized in accordance with the applicable recognition provisions of the Internal Revenue Code. The amount of exchange gain or loss so realized with respect to accrued interest income is determined for each accrual period by—

(i) Translating the units of nonfunctional currency interest income received with respect to such accrual period (as determined under the ordering rules of paragraph (b)(7) of this section) into functional currency at the spot rate on the date the interest income is received or the instrument is disposed of (or deemed disposed of), and

(ii) Subtracting from such amount the amount computed by translating the units of nonfunctional currency interest income accrued with respect to such income received at the average rate (or other rate specified in paragraph (b)(2) (iii)(B) of this section) for the accrual period.

(4) *Exchange gain or loss recognized by the obligor with respect to accrued interest expense.*—The obligor under a debt instrument described in paragraph (b)(2)(i) of this section shall realize exchange gain or loss with respect to accrued interest expense on the date such accrued interest expense is paid or the obligation to make payments is transferred or extinguished (including a deemed disposition under section 1001 that results from a material change in terms of the instrument). Except as otherwise provided in this paragraph (b) (*e.g.*, paragraph (b)(8) of this section), exchange gain or loss realized with respect to accrued interest expense shall be recognized in accordance with the applicable recognition provisions of the Internal Revenue Code. The amount of exchange gain or loss so realized with respect to accrued interest expense is determined for each accrual period by—

(i) Translating the units of nonfunctional currency interest expense accrued with respect to the amount of interest paid into functional currency at the average rate (or other rate specified in paragraph (b)(2)(iii)(B) of this section) for such accrual period; and

(ii) Subtracting from such amount the amount computed by translating the units of nonfunctional currency interest paid (or, if the obligation to make payments is extinguished or transferred, the units accrued) with respect to such accrual period (as determined under the ordering rules in paragraph (b)(7) of this section) into functional currency at the spot rate on the date payment is made or the obligation is transferred or extinguished (or deemed extinguished).

(5) *Exchange gain or loss recognized by the holder of a debt instrument with respect to principal.*—The holder of a debt instrument described in paragraph (b)(2)(i) of this section shall realize exchange gain or loss with respect to the principal amount of such instrument on the date principal (determined under the ordering rules of paragraph (b)(7) of this section) is received from the obligor or the instrument is disposed of (including a deemed disposition under section 1001 that results from a material change in terms of the instrument). For purposes of computing exchange gain or loss, the principal amount of a debt instrument is the holder's purchase price in units of nonfunctional currency. See paragraph (b)(10) of this section for rules regarding the amortization of that part of the principal amount that represents bond premium and the computation of exchange gain or loss thereon. If, however, the holder acquired the instrument in a transaction in which exchange gain or loss was realized but not recognized by the transferor, the nonfunctional currency principal amount of the instrument with respect to the holder shall be the same as that of the transferor. Except as otherwise provided in this paragraph (b) (*e.g.*, paragraph (b)(8) of this section), exchange gain or loss realized with respect to such principal amount shall be recognized in accordance with the applicable recognition provisions of the Internal Revenue Code. The amount of exchange gain or loss so realized by the holder with respect to principal is determined by—

(i) Translating the units of nonfunctional currency principal at the spot rate on the date payment is received or the instrument is disposed of (or deemed disposed of); and

(ii) Subtracting from such amount the amount computed by translating the units of nonfunctional currency principal at the spot rate on the date the holder (or a transferor from whom the nonfunctional principal amount is carried over) acquired the instrument (is deemed to acquire the instrument).

(6) *Exchange gain or loss recognized by the obligor of a debt instrument with respect to principal.*—The obligor under a debt instrument described in paragraph (b)(2)(i) of this section shall realize exchange gain or loss with respect to the principal amount of such instrument on the date principal (determined under the ordering rules of paragraph (b)(7) of this section) is paid or the obligation to make payments is transferred or extinguished (including a deemed disposition under section 1001 that results from a material change in terms of the instrument). For purposes of computing exchange gain or loss, the principal amount of a debt instrument is the amount received by the obligor for the debt instrument in units of nonfunctional currency. See paragraph (b)(10) of this section for rules regarding the amortization of that part of the principal amount that represents bond premium and the computation of exchange gain or loss thereon. If, however, the obligor became the obligor in a transaction in which exchange gain or loss was realized but not recognized by the transferor, the nonfunctional currency principal amount of the instrument with respect to such obligor shall be the same as that of the transferor. Except as otherwise provided in this paragraph (b) (*e.g.*, paragraph (b)(8) of this section), exchange gain or loss realized with respect to such principal shall be recognized in accordance with the applicable recognition provisions of the Internal Revenue Code. The amount of exchange gain or loss so realized by the obligor is determined by—

(i) Translating the units of nonfunctional currency principal at the spot rate on the date the obligor (or a transferor from whom the principal amount is carried over) became the obligor (or is deemed to have become the obligor); and

(ii) Subtracting from such amount the amount computed by translating the units of nonfunctional currency principal at the spot rate on the date payment is made or the obligation is transferred or extinguished (or deemed extinguished).

(7) *Payment ordering rules.*—(i) *Debt instruments subject to the rules of sections 163(e), or 1271 through 1288.*—In the case of a debt instrument described in paragraph (b)(2)(i) of this section that is subject to the rules of sections 163(e), or 1272 through 1288, units of nonfunctional currency (or an amount determined with reference to nonfunctional currency) received or paid with respect to such debt instrument shall be treated first as a receipt or payment of periodic interest under the principles of section 1273 and the regulations thereunder, second as a receipt or payment of original issue discount to the extent accrued as of the date of the receipt or payment, and finally as a receipt or payment of principal. Units of nonfunctional currency (or an amount determined with reference to nonfunctional currency) treated as a receipt or payment of original issue discount under the preceding sentence are attributed to the earliest accrual period in which original issue discount has accrued and to which prior receipts or payments have not been attributed. No portion thereof shall be treated as prepaid interest. These rules are illustrated by *Example 10* of paragraph (b)(9) of this section.

(ii) *Other debt instruments.*—In the case of a debt instrument described in paragraph (b)(2)(i) of this section that is not subject to the rules of section 163(e) or 1272 through 1288, whether units of nonfunctional currency (or an amount determined with reference to nonfunctional currency) received or paid with respect to such debt instrument are treated as interest or principal shall be determined under section 163 or other applicable section of the Code.

(8) *Limitation of exchange gain or loss on payment or disposition of a debt instrument.*—When a debt instrument described in paragraph (b)(2)(i) of this section is paid or disposed of, or when the obligation to make payments thereunder is satisfied by another person, or extinguished or assumed by another person, exchange gain or loss is computed with respect to both principal and any accrued interest (including original issue discount), as provided in paragraph (b)(3) through (7) of this section. However, pursuant to section 988(b)(1) and (2), the sum of any exchange gain or loss with respect to the principal and interest of any such debt instrument shall be realized only to the extent of the total gain or loss realized on the transaction. The gain or loss realized shall be recognized in accordance with the general principles of the Code. See *Examples 3, 4* and *6* of paragraph (b)(9) of this section.

(9) *Examples.*—The preceding provisions are illustrated in the following examples. The examples assume that any transaction involving an individual is a section 988 transaction.

Example 1. (i) X is an individual on the cash method of accounting with the dollar as his functional currency. On January 1, 1992, X converts $13,000 to 10,000 British pounds (£) at the spot rate of £1 = $1.30 and loans the £10,000 to Y for 3 years. The terms of the loan provide that Y will make interest payments of £1,000 on December 31 of 1992, 1993, and 1994, and will repay X's £10,000 principal on December 31, 1994. Assume the spot rates for the pertinent dates are as follows:

Date	*Spot rate (pounds to dollars)*
January 1, 1992	£1 = $1.30
December 31, 1992	£1 = $1.35
December 31, 1993	£1 = $1.40
December 31, 1994	£1 = $1.45

(ii) Under paragraph (b)(2)(ii)(B) of this section, X will translate the £1,000 interest payments at the spot rate on the date received. Accordingly, X will have interest income of $1,350 in 1992, $1,400 in 1993, and $1,450 in 1994. Because X is a cash basis taxpayer, X does not realize exchange gain or loss on the receipt of interest income.

(iii) Under paragraph (b)(5) of this section, X will realize exchange gain upon repayment of the £10,000 principal amount determined by translating the £10,000 at the spot rate on the date it is received (£10,000 × $1.45 = $14,500) and subtracting from such amount, the amount determined by translating the £10,000 at the spot rate on the date the loan was made (£10,000 × $1.30 = $13,000). Accordingly, X will realize an exchange gain of $1,500 on the repayment of the loan on December 31, 1994.

Example 2. (i) Assume the same facts as in *Example 1* except that X is an accrual method taxpayer and that average rates are as follows:

Accrual Period	*Average rate (pounds to dollars)*
1992	£1 = $1.32
1993	£1 = $1.37
1994	£1 = $1.42

(ii) Under paragraph (b)(2)(ii)(C) of this section, X will accrue the £1,000 interest payments at the average rate for the accrual period. Accordingly, X will have interest income of $1,320 in 1992, $1,370 in 1993, and $1,420 in 1994. Because X is an accrual basis taxpayer, X determines exchange gain or loss for each interest accrual period by translating the units of nonfunctional currency interest income received with respect to such accrual period at the spot rate on the date received and subtracting the amounts of interest income accrued for such period. Thus, X will realize $90 of exchange gain with respect to interest received under the loan, computed as follows:

Year	*Spot Value Interest Received*	*Accrued Interest @ Avg. Rate*	*Exch. Gain*
1992	$1,350	$1,320	$30
1993	$1,400	$1,370	$30
1994	$1,450	$1,420	$30
TOTAL			$90

(iii) Under paragraph (b)(5) of this section, X will realize exchange gain upon repayment of the £10,000 loan principal determined in the same manner as in *Example 1*. Accordingly, X will realize an exchange gain of $1,500 on the repayment of the loan principal on December 31, 1994.

Example 3. Assume the same facts as in *Example 1* except that X is a calendar year taxpayer on the accrual method of accounting that elects to use a spot rate convention to translate interest income as provided in § 1.988-2(b)(2)(iii)(B). Interest income is received by X on the last day of each accrual period. Under paragraph (b)(2)(ii)(C), X will translate the interest income at the spot rate on the last day of each interest accrual period. Accordingly, X will have interest income of $1,350 in 1992, and $1,400 in 1993, $1,450 in 1994. Because the rate at which the interest income is translated is the same as the rate on the day of receipt, X will not realize any exchange gain or loss with respect to the interest income. Under paragraph (b)(5) of this section, X will realize exchange gain upon repayment of the £10,000 loan principal determined in the same manner as in *Example 1*. Accordingly, X will realize an exchange gain of $1,500 on the repayment of the loan principal on December 31, 1994.

Example 4. Assume the same facts as in *Example 1* except that on December 31, 1993, X sells Y's note for 9,821.13 British pounds (£) after the interest payment. Under paragraph (b)(8) of this section, X will compute exchange gain on the £10,000 principal. The exchange gain is $1,000 [(£10,000 × $1.40) – (£10,000 × $1.30)]. This exchange gain, however, is only realized to the extent of the total gain on the disposition. X's total gain is $749.58 [(£9,821.13 × $1.40) – (£10,000 × $1.30)]. Thus, X will realize $749.58 of exchange gain (and will realize no market loss).

Example 5. (i) The facts are the same as in *Example 1* except that Y becomes insolvent and fails to repay the full £10,000 principal when due. Instead, X and Y agree to compromise the debt for a payment of £8,000 on December 31, 1994. Under paragraph (b)(8) of this section, X will compute exchange gain on the £10,000 originally booked. The exchange gain is $1,500 [(£10,000 × $1.45) – (£10,000 × $1.30) = $1,500]. This exchange gain, however, is only realized to the extent of the total gain on the disposition. X realizes an overall loss on the disposition of $1,400 [(£8,000 × $1.45) – (£10,000 × $1.30) = ($1,400)]. Thus, X will realize no exchange gain (and a $1400 market loss).

(ii) If the exchange rate on December 31, 1994, were £1 = $1.25, rather than £1 = $1.45, X would compute exchange loss under paragraph (b)(8) of this section, on the £10,000 originally booked. The exchange loss would be $500 [(£10,000 × $1.25) – (£10,000 × $1.30) = ($500)]. X's total loss on the disposition would be $3,000 [(£8,000 × $1.25) – (£10,000 × $1.30) = ($3,000)]. Thus, X would realize $500 of exchange loss and a $2,500 market loss on the disposition.

Example 6. (i) X is an individual with the dollar as his functional currency. X is on the cash method of accounting. On January 1, 1989, X borrows 10,000 British pounds (£) from Y, an unrelated person. The terms of the loan provide that X will make interest payments of £1,200 on December 31 of 1989 and 1990 and will repay Y's £10,000 principal on December 31, 1990. The spot rates for the pertinent dates are as follows:

DATE	*SPOT RATE (pounds to dollars)*
January 1, 1989	1 = $1.50
December 31, 1989	1 = $1.60
December 31, 1990	1 = $1.70

Assume that the basis of the £1,200 paid as interest by X on December 31, 1989 is $2,000, the basis of the £1,200 paid as interest by X on December 31, 1990, is $2,020 and the basis of the £10,000 principal paid by X on December 31, 1990 is $16,000.

(ii) Under paragraph (b)(2)(ii)(B) of this section, X translates the £1,200 interest payments at the spot rate on the day paid. Thus, X paid $1,920 (£1,200 × $1.60) of interest on December 31, 1989 and $2,040 (£1,200 × $1.70) of interest on December 31, 1990. In addition, X will realize exchange gain or loss on the disposition of the £1,200 on December 31, 1989 and 1990, under paragraph (a) of this section. Pursuant to paragraph (a)(2) of this section, X will realize an exchange loss of $80 [(£1,200 × $1.60) – $2,000] on December 31, 1989 and exchange gain of $20 [(£1,200 × $1.70) – $2,020] on December 31, 1990.

(iii) Under paragraph (b)(6) of this section, X will realize exchange loss on December 31, 1990 upon repayment of the £10,000 principal amount determined by translating the £10,000 received at the spot rate on January 1, 1989 (£10,000 × $1.50 = $15,000) and subtracting from such amount, the amount determined by translating the £ 10,000 paid at the spot rate on December 31, 1990 (£10,000 × $1.70 = $17,000). Thus, under paragraph (b)(6) of this section, X has an exchange loss with respect to the £10,000 principal of $2,000. Further, under paragraph (a)(2) of this section, X will realize an exchange gain upon disposition of the £10,000 on December 31, 1990. Under paragraph (a)(2) of this section, X will subtract his adjusted basis in the £10,000 ($16,000) from the amount realized upon the disposition of the £10,000 (£10,000 × $1.70 = $17,000) resulting in a gain of $1,000. Accordingly, X's combined exchange gain and loss realized on December 31, 1990 with respect to the repayment of the £10,000 is a $1,000 exchange loss.

Example 7. (i) X is a calendar year corporation on the accrual method of accounting and with the dollar as its functional currency. On January 1, 1989, X purchases at original issue for 82.64 Canadian dollars (C$) M corporation's 2 year note maturing on December 31, 1990, at a stated redemption price of C$ 100. The yield to maturity in Canadian dollars is 10 percent and the accrual period is the one year period beginning January 1 and ending December 31. The note has C$17.36 of original issue discount. Assume that the spot rates are as follows: C$1 = U.S.$.72 on January 1, 1989; C$1 = U.S.$.80 on January 1, 1990; C$1 = U.S.$.82 on December 31, 1990. Assume further that the average rate for 1989 is C$1 = U.S.$.76 and for 1990 is C$1 = U.S.$.81.

(ii) Under paragraph (b)(2)(ii)(A) of this section, X will determine its interest income in Canadian dollars. Accordingly, under section 1272, X must take into account original issue discount in the amount of C$8.26 on December 31, 1989 and C$9.10 on December 31, 1990. Pursuant to paragraph (b)(2)(ii)(C) of this section, X will translate these amounts into U.S. dollars at the average exchange rate for the relevant accrual period. Thus, the amount of interest income taken into account in 1989 is U.S.$6.28 (C$8.26 × U.S.$.76) and in 1990 is U.S.$7.37 (C$9.10 × U.S.$.81). Pursuant to paragraph (b)(3)(ii) of this section, X will realize exchange gain or loss with respect to the accrued interest determined for each accrual period by translating the Canadian dollars received with respect to such accrual period into U.S. dollars at the spot rate on the date the interest is received and subtracting from that amount the amount accrued in U.S. dollars. Thus, the amount of exchange gain realized on December 31, 1990, is U.S.$.58 (U.S.$.49 from 1989 + U.S.$.09 from 1990). Pursuant to paragraph (b)(5) of this section, X shall realize exchange gain or loss with respect to the principal (C$82.64) on December 31, 1990, computed by translating the C$82.64 at the spot rate on December 31, 1990 (U.S.$67.76) and subtracting the C$82.64 translated at the spot rate on January 1, 1989 (U.S.$59.50) for an exchange gain of U.S.$8.26. Thus, X's combined exchange gain is U.S.$8.84 (U.S.$.49 + U.S.$.09 + U.S.$8.26).

(iii) Assume instead that on January 1, 1990, X sells the note for C$86.95, which it immediately converts to U.S. dollars. X's exchange gain is computed under paragraph (b)(8) of this section with reference to the nonfunctional currency denominated principal amount (C$82.64) and the nonfunctional currency denominated accrued original issue discount (C$8.26). X will compute an exchange gain of U.S.$6.61 with respect to the issue price [(C$82.64 × U.S.$.80) – (C$82.64 × U.S.$.72)] and an exchange gain of U.S.$.33 with respect to the accrued original issue discount [(C$8.26 × U.S.$.80) – (C$8.26 × U.S.$.76)]. Accordingly, prior to the application of paragraph (b)(8) of this section, X's total exchange gain is U.S.$6.94 (U.S.$6.61 + U.S.$.33), and X's market loss is U.S.$3.16 [(C$90.90 – C$86.95) × U.S.$.80]. Pursuant to paragraph (b)(8) of this section, however, X's market loss on the note of U.S.$3.16 is netted against X's exchange gain of U.S.$6.94, resulting in a realized exchange gain of U.S.$3.78 and no market loss.

Example 8. (i) The facts are the same as in *Example 7* (i) except that on January 1, 1990, X contributes the M corporation note to Y, a wholly-owned U.S. subsidiary of X with the dollar as its functional currency, and Y collects C$100 from M corporation at maturity on December 31, 1990, when the spot rate is C$1= U.S.$.82. The transfer of the note from X to Y qualifies for nonrecognition of gain under section 351(a). On December 31, 1990, Y includes C$9.10 of accrued interest in income which translated at the average exchange rate of C$1 = U.S.$.81 for the year results in U.S.$7.37 of interest income.

(ii) Y's exchange gain is computed under paragraph (b)(3) of this section with respect to accrued interest income and paragraph (b)(5) of this section with respect to the nonfunctional currency principal amount. Under paragraph (b)(3) of this section, Y will realize exchange gain or loss for each accrual period computed by translating the units of nonfunctional currency interest income received with respect to such accrual period at the spot rate on the day received and subtracting the amounts of interest income accrued for such period. Thus, Y will realize $.49 of exchange gain with respect to original issue discount accrued in 1989 [(C$8.26 × U.S.$.82) – (C$8.26 × U.S.$.76) = U.S.$.49] and $.09 of exchange gain with respect to original issue discount accrued in 1990 [(C$9.10 × U.S.$.82) – (C$9.10 × U.S.$.81) = $.09].

(iii) Pursuant to paragraph (b)(5) of this section, the nonfunctional currency principal amount of the M bond in the hands of Y is C$82.64, the amount carried over from X, the transferor. Y's exchange gain with respect to the nonfunctional currency principal amount is $8.26 [(C$82.64 × U.S.$.82) – (C$82.64 × U.S.$.72) = U.S.$8.26]. Accordingly, Y's combined exchange gain is U.S.$8.84 ($.49 + $.09 + $8.26). Because the amount realized in Canadian dollars equals the adjusted issue price (C$100) on retirement of the M note, there is no market loss, and the netting rule of paragraph (b)(8) of this section does not limit realization of the exchange gain.

Example 9. (i) X is a calendar year corporation on the accrual method of accounting and with the dollar as its functional currency. X elects to use the spot rate convention to translate interest income as provided in paragraph (b)(2)(iii)(B) of this section. On January 31, 1992, X loans £1000 to Y, an unrelated person. Under the terms of the loan, Y will pay X interest of £50 on July 31, 1992, and January 31, 1993, and will repay the £ 1000 principal on January 31, 1993. Assume the following spot exchange rates.

DATE	*SPOT RATE (pounds to dollars)*
January 31, 1992	£1 = $1.50
July 31, 1992	£1 = $1.55
December 31, 1992	£1 = $1.60
January 31, 1993	£1 = $1.61

(ii) Under paragraph (b)(2)(ii)(C) of this section, X will translate the interest income at the spot rate on the last day of each interest accrual period (and in the case of a partial accrual period, at the spot rate on the last day of the taxable year). Accordingly, X will have interest income of $77.50 (£50 × $1.55) on July 31, 1992. Assuming under X's method of accounting that interest is accrued daily, X will accrue $66.50 (153/184 × £ 50) × $1.60) of interest income on December 31, 1992. On January 31, 1993, X will have interest income of $13.60 ((31/184 × £50) × $1.61). Because the rate at which the interest income is translated is the same as the rate on the day of receipt, X will not realize any exchange gain or loss with respect to the interest income received on July 31, 1992. However, X will realize exchange gain on the £41.50 (153/184 × £50) of accrued interest income of $.41 [(£41.50 × $1.61) – (£41.50 × $1.60) = $.41].

(iii) Under paragraph (b)(5) of this section, X will realize exchange gain upon repayment of the £ 100 principal amount determined by translating the £100 at the spot rate on the date it is received (£100 × $1.61 = $161.00) and subtracting from such amount, the amount determined by translating the £100 at the spot rate on the date the loan was made (£100 × $1.50 = $150.00). Accordingly, X will realize an exchange gain of $11 on the repayment of the loan on January 31, 1993.

Example 10. (i) X, a cash basis taxpayer with the dollar as its functional currency, has the calendar year as its taxable year. On January 1, 1992, X purchases at original issue for 65.88 British pounds (£) M corporation's 5-year bond maturing on December 31, 1996, having a stated redemption price at maturity of £100. The bond provides for annual payments of interest in pounds of 1 pound per year on December 31 of each year. The bond has 34.12 British pounds of original issue discount. The yield to maturity is 10 percent in British pounds and the accrual period is the one year period beginning January 1 and ending December 31 of each calendar year. The amount of original issue discount is determined in pounds for each accrual period by multiplying the adjusted issue price expressed in pounds by the yield and subtracting from such amount the periodic interest payments expressed in pounds for such period. The periodic interest payments are translated at the spot rate on the payment date (December 31 of each year). The original issue discount is translated at the average rate for the accrual period (January 1 through December 31). The following chart describes the determination of interest income with respect to the facts presented and provides other pertinent information.

Table 1

1 *Year (Dec. 31)*	2 *Periodic interest payments in pounds for the accrual period*	3 *Original issue discount in pounds for the accrual period*	4 *Issue price or adjusted issue price in pounds*	5 *Assumed spot rate on Dec. 31 (pounds to dollars)*	6 *Assumed average rate for accrual period (pounds to dollars)*	7 *Periodic interest payments in pounds multiplied by spot rate on the date of payment (column 2 times column 5)*	8 *Original issue discount in pounds multiplied by the average rate for the accrual period (column 3 times column 6)*	9 *Total interest income in dollars (column 7 plus column 8)*	10 *Adjusted issue price in dollars*
Issue Date			65.88	1 = $1.20					$79.06
1992	1	5.59	71.47	1 = $1.30	1 = $1.25	$1.30	$6.99	$8.29	$86.05
1993	1	6.15	77.62	1 = $1.40	1 = $1.35	$1.40	$8.30	$9.70	$94.35
1994	1	6.76	84.38	1 = $1.50	1 = $1.45	$1.50	$9.80	$11.30	$104.15
1995	1	7.44	91.82	1 = $1.60	1 = $1.55	$1.60	$11.53	$13.13	$115.68
1996	1	8.18	100.00	1 = $1.70	1 = $1.65	$1.70	$13.50	$15.20	$129.18

(ii) Because X is a cash basis taxpayer, X does not realize exchange gain or loss on the receipt of the £1 periodic interest payments. However, X will realize exchange gain on December 31, 1996 totaling $7.88 with respect to the original issue discount. Exchange gain is determined for each interest accrual period by translating the units of nonfunctional currency interest income received with respect to such accrual period at the spot rate on the date received and subtracting from such amount, the amount computed by translating the units of nonfunctional currency interest income accrued for such period at the average rate for the period. The following chart illustrates this computation:

Table 2

1 Year	2 OID accrued in pounds for each accrual period	3 Assumed spot rate on date payment received (pounds to dollars)	4 Interest received times spot rate on the date received (col. 2 times col. 3)	Assumed average rate for accrual period (pounds to dollars)	5	6 OID in pounds times the average rate for the accrual period (col. 2 times col. 5)	7 Exchange gain or loss (col. 4 less col. 6)
1992	5.59	1 = $1.70	$9.50	1 = $1.25		$6.99	$2.51
1993	6.15	1 = $1.70	$10.46	1 = $1.35		$8.30	$2.16
1994	6.76	1 = $1.70	$11.49	1 = $1.45		$9.80	$1.69
1995	7.44	1 = $1.70	$12.65	1 = $1.55		$11.53	$1.12
1996	8.18	1 = $1.70	$13.90	1 = $1.65		$13.50	$.40
						TOTAL	$7.88

(iii) X will also realize exchange gain with respect to the principal of the loan (*i.e.*, the issue price of 65.88 British pounds) on December 31, 1996 computed by translating the units of nonfunctional currency principal received at the spot rate on the date principal is received (65.88 British pounds × $1.70 = $112.00) and subtracting from such amount, the units of nonfunctional currency principal received translated at the spot rate on the date the instrument was acquired (65.88 British pounds × $1.20 = $79.06). Accordingly, X's exchange gain on the principal is $32.94 and X's total exchange gain with respect to the accrued interest and principal is $40.82. It should be noted that, under this fact pattern, the total exchange gain may be determined in an alternative fashion. Exchange gain may be computed by subtracting the adjusted issue price in dollars at maturity ($129.18—see column 10 of Table 1) from the amount computed by multiplying the stated redemption price at maturity in pounds times the spot rate on the maturity date (£100 × $1.70 = $170), which equals $40.82.

Example 11. (i) The facts are the same as in *Example 10* except that X makes an election under paragraph (b)(2)(iii) of this section to translate accrued interest on the last day of the accrual period. Accordingly, columns 8, 9 and 10 in Table 1 would change as follows:

1 Year (Dec. 31)	8 Original issue discount in pounds multiplied by the spot rate on last day of accrual period (Dec. 31)	9 Total interest income in dollars (column 7 plus column 8)	10 Adjusted issue price in dollars
			$ 79.06
1992	$ 7.27	$ 8.57	$ 87.63
1993	$ 8.61	$10.01	$ 97.64
1994	$10.14	$11.64	$109.28
1995	$11.90	$13.50	$122.78
1996	$13.91	$15.61	$138.39

(ii) Because X is a cash basis taxpayer, X does not realize exchange gain or loss on the receipt of the £1 periodic interest payments. However, X will realize exchange gain on December 31, 1993 totaling $6.18 with respect to the original issue discount. Exchange gain is determined for each interest accrual period by translating the units of nonfunctional currency interest income received with respect to such accrual period at the spot rate on the date received and subtracting from such amount, the amount computed by translating the units of nonfunctional currency interest income accrued for such period at the spot rate on the last day of the accrual period. Accordingly, columns 5, 6 and 7 of Table 2 would change as follows:

1 Year	5 Spot rate on last day of accrual period	6 OID in pounds times the spot rate on the last day of the accrual period (col. 2 times col. 3)	7 Exchange gain or loss (col. 4 less col. 6)
1992	$1.30	$ 7.27	$2.23
1993	$1.40	$ 8.61	$1.85
1994	$1.50	$10.14	$1.35
1995	$1.60	$11.90	$0.75
1996	$1.70	$13.90	$0.00
			$6.18

(iii) X will realize exchange gain with respect to the principal amount of the loan as provided in the preceding example.

Example 12. (i) C is a corporation that is a calendar year accrual method taxpayer with the dollar as its functional currency. On January 1, 1989, C lends 100 British pounds (£) in exchange for a note under the terms of which C will receive two equal payments of £ 57.62 on December 31, 1989, and December 31, 1990. Each payment of £57.62 represents the annual payment necessary to amortize the £100 principal amount at a rate of 10% compounded annually over a two year period. The following tables reflect the amounts of principal and interest that compose each payment and assumptions as to the relevant exchange rates:

Date	Principal	Interest
12/31/89	£47.62	£10.00
12/31/90	£52.38	£ 5.24

Date	Spot Rate £ 1 =	Average Rate for Year Ending
1/01/89	$1.30	
12/31/89	$1.40	$1.35
12/31/90	$1.50	$1.45

(ii) Because each interest payment is equal to the product of the outstanding principal balance of the obligation and a single fixed rate of interest, each stated interest payment constitutes periodic interest under the principles of section 1273. Accordingly, there is no original issue discount.

(iii) Because C is an accrual basis taxpayer, C will translate the interest income at the average rate for the annual accrual period pursuant to paragraph (b)(2)(ii)(C) of this section. Thus, C's interest income is $13.50 (£10.00 × $1.35) in 1989, and $7.60 (£5.24 × $1.45) in 1990. C will realize exchange gain or loss upon receipt of accrued interest computed in accordance with paragraph (b)(3) of this section. Thus, C will realize exchange gain in the amount of $ .50 [(£10.00 × $1.40) – $13.50] in 1989, and $ .26 [(£5.24 × $1.50) – $7.60] in 1990.

(iv) In addition, C will realize exchange gain or loss upon the receipt of principal each year computed under paragraph (b)(5) of this section. Thus, C will realize exchange gain in the amount of $4.76 [(£47.62 × $1.40) – (£47.62 × $1.30)] in 1989, and $10.48 [(£52.38 × $1.50) – (£52.38 × $1.30)] in 1990.

(10) *Treatment of bond premium.*—(i) *In general.*—Amortizable bond premium on a bond described in paragraph (b)(2)(i) of this section shall be computed in the units of nonfunctional currency in which the bond is denominated (or in which the payments are determined). Amortizable bond premium properly taken into account under section 171 or § 1.61-12 (or the successor provision thereof) shall reduce interest income or expense in units of nonfunctional currency. Exchange gain or loss is realized with respect to bond premium described in the preceding sentence by treating the portion of premium amortized with respect to any period as a return of principal. With respect to a holder that does not elect to amortize bond premium under section 171, the amount of bond premium will constitute a market loss when the bond matures. See paragraph (b)(8) of this section. The principles set forth in this paragraph (b)(10) shall apply to determine the treatment of acquisition premium described in section 1272(a)(7).

(ii) *Example.*—The following example illustrates the provisions of this paragraph (b)(10).

Example. (A) X is an individual on the cash method of accounting with the dollar as his functional currency. On January 1, 1989, X purchases Y corporation's note for 107.99 British pounds (£) from Z, an unrelated party. The note has an issue price of £100, a stated redemption price at maturity of £100, pays interest in pounds at the rate of 10% compounded annually, and matures on December 31, 1993. X elects to amortize the bond premium of £7.99 under the rules of section 171. Pursuant to paragraph (b)(10)(i) of this section, bond premium is determined and amortized in British pounds. Assume the amortization schedule is as follows:

Year Ending 12/31	Bond Premium Amortized	Unamortized Premium Plus Principal	Interest
		£107.99	
1989	£1.36	£106.63	£8.64
1990	£1.47	£105.16	£8.53
1991	£1.59	£103.57	£8.41
1992	£1.71	£101.86	£8.29
1993	£1.85	£100.00	£8.25

(B) The bond premium reduces X's pound interest income under the note. For example, the £ 10 stated interest payment made in 1989 is reduced by £1.36 of bond premium, and the resulting £8.64 interest income is translated into dollars at the spot rate on December 31, 1989. Exchange gain or loss is realized on the £1.36 bond premium based on the difference between the spot rates on January 1, 1989, the date the premium is paid to acquire the bond, and December 31, 1989, the date the bond premium is returned as part of the stated interest. The £1.36 bond premium reduces the unamortized premium plus principal to £106.63 (£107.99 – £1.36). On December 31, 1993, when the bond matures and the £7.99 of bond premium has been fully amortized, X will realize exchange gain or loss with respect to the remaining purchase price of £100.

(11) *Market discount.*—(i) *In general.*—Market discount as defined in section 1278(a)(2) shall be determined in units of nonfunctional currency in which the market discount bond is denominated (or in which the payments are determined). Accrued market discount (other than market discount currently included in income pursuant to section 1278(b)) shall be translated into functional currency at the spot rate on the date the market discount bond is disposed of. No part of such accrued market discount is treated as exchange gain or loss. Accrued market discount currently includible in income pursuant to section 1278(b) shall be translated into functional currency at the average exchange rate for the accrual period. Exchange gain or loss with respect to accrued market discount currently includible in income under section 1278(b) shall be determined in accordance with paragraph (b)(3) of this section relating to accrued interest income.

(ii) *Example.*—The following example illustrates the provisions of this paragraph (b)(11).

Example—(A) X is a calendar year corporation with the U.S. dollar as its functional currency. On January 1, 1990, X purchases a bond of M corporation for 96,530 British pounds (£). The bond, which was issued on January 1, 1989, has an issue price of £100,000, a stated redemption price at maturity of £100,000, and provides for annual pound payments of interest at 8 percent. The bond matures on December 31, 1991. X purchased the bond at a market discount of 3,470 pounds and did not elect to include the market discount currently in income under section 1278(b). X holds the bond to maturity and on December 31, 1991, receives payment of £100,000 (plus £8,000 interest) when the exchange rate is £1 = $1.50.

(B) Pursuant to paragraph (b)(11) of this section, X computes market discount in units of nonfunctional currency. Thus, the market discount as defined under section 1278(a)(2) is £ 3,470. Accrued market discount (other than market discount currently included in income pursuant to section 1278(b)) is translated at the spot rate on the date the market discount bond is disposed of. Accordingly, X will translate the accrued market discount of £3,470 at the spot rate on December 31, 1991 (£3,470 × $1.50 = $5,205). No exchange gain or loss is realized with respect to the £3,470 of accrued market discount. See paragraphs (b)(3) and (5) of this section for the realization and recognition of exchange gain or loss with respect to accrued interest and principal.

(12) *Tax exempt bonds.*—See § 1.988-3(c)(2), which characterizes exchange loss realized with respect to a nonfunctional currency tax exempt bond as a reduction of interest income.

(13) *Nonfunctional currency debt exchanged for stock of obligor.*—(i) *In general.*—Notwithstanding any other section of the Code other than section 267, 1091 or 1092, exchange gain or loss shall be realized and recognized by the holder and the obligor in accordance with the rules of paragraphs (b)(3) through (7) of this section with respect to the principal and accrued interest of a debt instrument described in paragraph (b)(2)(i) of this section that is acquired by the obligor in exchange for its stock, provided however, that such gain or loss shall be recognized only to the extent of the total gain or loss on the exchange (regardless of whether such gain or loss would otherwise be recognized). This rule shall apply whether the debt instrument is converted into stock according to its terms or exchanged pursuant to a separate agreement between the obligor and the holder. A debt instrument that is acquired by the obligor from a shareholder as a contribution to capital shall be treated for purposes of this section as exchanged for stock, whether or not additional stock is issued.

(ii) *Coordination with section 108.*—Section 988 and this section shall apply before section 108. Exchange gain realized by the obligor on an exchange described in paragraph (b)(13)(i) of this section shall not be treated as discharge of indebtedness income, but shall be considered to reduce the amount of the liability for purposes of computing the obligor's income on the exchange under section 108(e)(4), section 108(e)(6) or section 108(e)(10).

(iii) *Effective date.*—This paragraph (b)(13) shall be effective for exchanges of debt for stock effected after September 21, 1989.

(iv) *Examples.*—The following examples illustrate the operation of this paragraph (b)(13). In each such example, assume that sections 267, 1091 and 1092 do not apply.

Example 1. (i) X is a calendar year U.S. corporation with the U.S. dollar as its functional currency. On January 1, 1990 (the issue date), X acquired a convertible bond maturing on December 31, 1998, issued by Y corporation, a U.K. corporation with the British pound (£) as its functional currency. The issue price of the bond is £ 100,000, the stated redemption price at maturity is £100,000, and the bond provides for annual pound interest payments at the rate of 10%. The terms of the bond also provide that at any time prior to December 31, 1998, the holder may surrender all of his interest in the bond in exchange for 20 shares of Y common stock. On January 1, 1994, X surrenders his interest in the bond for 20 shares of Y common stock. Assume the following: (a) The spot rate on January 1, 1990, is £1 = $1.30, (b) The spot rate on January 1, 1994, is £1 = $1.50, and (c) The 20 shares of Y common stock have a market value of £200,000 on January 1, 1994.

(ii) Pursuant to paragraph (b)(13) of this section, X will realize and recognize exchange gain with respect to the issue price (£100,000) of the bond on January 1, 1994, when the bond is converted to stock. X will compute exchange gain pursuant to paragraph (b)(5) of this section by translating the issue price at the spot rate on the conversion date (£100,000 × $1.50 = $150,000) and subtracting from such amount the issue price translated at the spot rate on the date X acquired the bond (£100,000 × $1.30 = $130,000). Thus, X will realize and recognize $20,000 of exchange gain. X's basis in the 20 shares of Y common stock is $150,000 ($130,000 substituted basis + $20,000 recognized gain).

Example 2. (i) X, a foreign corporation with the British pound (£) as its functional currency, lends £100 at a market rate of interest to Y, its wholly-owned U.S. subsidiary, on January 1, 1990, on which date the spot exchange rate is £1 = $1. Y's functional currency is the U.S. dollar. On January 1, 1992, when the spot exchange rate is £1 = $.50, X cancels the debt as a contribution to capital. Pursuant to paragraph (b)(13) of this section, Y will realize and recognize exchange gain with respect to the £100 issue price of the debt instrument on January 1, 1992. Y will compute exchange gain pursuant to paragraph (b)(6) of this section by translating the issue price at the spot rate on the date Y became the obligor (£100 × $1 = $100) and subtracting from such amount the issue price translated at the spot rate on the date of extinguishment (£100 × $.50 = $50). Thus, Y will realize and recognize $50 of exchange gain.

(ii) Under section 108(e)(6), on the acquisition of its indebtedness from X as a contribution to capital Y is treated as having satisfied the debt with an amount of money equal to X's adjusted basis in the debt (£100). For purposes of section 108(e)(6), X's adjusted basis is translated into United States dollars at the spot rate on the date Y acquires the debt (£1 = $.50). Therefore, Y is treated as having satisfied the debt for $50. Pursuant to paragraph (b)(13) of this section, for purposes of section 108 the amount of the indebtedness is considered to be reduced by the exchange gain from $100 to $50. Accordingly, Y recognizes $50 of exchange gain and no discharge of indebtedness income on the extinguishment of its debt to X.

(iii) If X were a United States taxpayer with a dollar functional currency and a $100 basis in Y's obligation, X would realize and recognize an exchange loss of $50 under paragraph (b)(5) of this section on the contribution of the debt to Y. The recognized loss would reduce X's adjusted basis in the debt from $100 to $50, so that for purposes of applying section 108(e)(6) Y is treated as having satisfied the debt for $50. Accordingly, under these facts as well Y would recognize $50 of exchange gain and no discharge of indebtedness income.

Example 3. (i) X and Y are unrelated calendar year U.S. corporations with the U.S. dollar as their functional currency. On January 1, 1990 (the issue date), X acquires Y's bond maturing on December 31, 1999. The issue price of the bond is £100,000, the stated redemption price at maturity is £100,000, and the bond provides for annual pound interest payments at the rate of 10%. On January 1, 1994, X and Y agree that Y will redeem its bond from X in exchange for 20 shares of Y common stock. Assume the following:

(a) The spot rate on January 1, 1990, is £1 = $1.00,

(b) The spot rate on January 1, 1994, is £1 = $.50,

(c) Interest rates on equivalent bonds have increased so that as of January 1, 1994, the value of Y's bond has declined to £90,000, and

(d) The 20 shares of Y common stock have a market value of £90,000 as of January 1, 1994.

(ii) Pursuant to paragraph (b)(13) of this section, X will realize and recognize exchange loss with respect to the issue price (£100,000) of the bond on January 1, 1994, when the bond is exchanged for stock. X will compute exchange loss pursuant to paragraph (b)(5) of this section by translating the issue price at the spot rate on the exchange date (£100,000 × $.50 = $50,000) and subtracting from such amount the issue price translated at the spot rate on the date X acquired the bond (£100,000 × $1.00 = $100,000). Thus, X will compute $50,000 of exchange loss, all of which will be realized and recognized because it does not exceed the total $55,000 realized loss on the exchange ($45,000 worth of stock received less $100,000 basis in the exchanged bond).

(iii) Pursuant to paragraph (b)(13) of this section, Y will realize and recognize exchange gain with respect to the issue price, computed under paragraph (b)(6) of this section by translating the issue price at the spot rate on the date Y became the obligor (£100,000 × $1.00 = $100,000) and subtracting from such amount the issue price translated at the spot rate on the exchange date (£100,000 × $.50 = $50,000). Thus, Y will realize and recognize $50,000 of exchange gain. Under section 108(e)(10), on the transfer of stock to X in satisfaction of its indebtedness Y is treated as having satisfied the indebtedness with an amount of money equal to the fair market value of the stock (£90,000 × $.50 = $45,000). Pursuant to paragraph (b)(13) of this section, for purposes of section 108 the amount of the indebtedness is considered to be reduced by the recognized exchange gain from $100,000 to $50,000. Accordingly, Y recognizes an additional $5,000 of discharge of indebtedness income on the exchange.

Example 4. (i) The facts are the same as in *Example 3* except that interest rates on equivalent bonds have declined, rather than increased, so that the value of Y's bond on January 1, 1994, has risen to £112,500; and X and Y agree that Y will redeem its bond from X on that date in exchange for 25 shares of Y common stock worth £112,500. Pursuant to paragraphs (b)(13) and (b)(5) of this section, X will compute $50,000 of exchange loss on the exchange with respect to the £100,000 issue price of the bond. See Example 3. However, because X's total loss on the exchange is only $43,750 ($56,250 worth of stock received less $100,000 basis in the exchanged bond), under the netting rule of paragraph (b)(13) of this section the realized exchange loss is limited to $43,750.

(ii) Pursuant to paragraphs (b)(13) and (b)(6) of this section, Y will compute $50,000 of exchange gain with respect to the issue price. See *Example 3.* Under section 108(e)(10), Y is treated as having satisfied the $100,000 indebtedness with an amount of money equal to the fair market value of the stock (£112,500 × $.50 = $56,250), resulting in a total gain on the exchange of $43,750. Accordingly, under paragraph (b)(13) of this section Y's realized (and recognized) exchange gain on the exchange is limited to $43,750. Also pursuant to paragraph (b)(13) of this section, for purposes of section 108 the amount of the indebtedness is considered to be reduced by the recognized exchange gain from $100,000 to $56,250. Accordingly, Y recognizes no discharge of indebtedness income on the exchange.

(14) [Reserved]

(15) *Debt instruments and deposits denominated in hyperinflationary currencies.*—(i) *In general.*—If a taxpayer issues, acquires, or otherwise enters into or holds a hyperinflationary debt instrument (as defined in paragraph (b)(15)(vi)(A) of this section) or a hyperinflationary deposit (as defined in paragraph (b)(15)(vi)(B) of this section) on which interest is paid or accrued that is denominated in (or determined by reference to) a nonfunctional currency of the taxpayer, then the taxpayer shall realize exchange gain or loss with respect to such instrument or deposit for its taxable year determined by reference to the change in exchange rates between—

(A) The later of the first day of the taxable year, or the date the instrument was entered into (or an amount deposited); and

(B) The earlier of the last day of the taxable year, or the date the instrument (or deposit) is disposed of or otherwise terminated.

(ii) *Only exchange gain or loss is realized.*—No gain or loss is realized under paragraph (b)(15)(i) by reason of factors other than movement in exchange rates, such as the creditworthiness of the debtor.

(iii) *Special rule for synthetic, non-hyperinflationary currency debt instruments.*—(A) *General rule.*—Paragraph (b)(15)(i) does not apply to a debt instrument that has interest and principal payments that are to be made by reference to a currency or item that does not reflect hyperinflationary conditions in a country (within the meaning of § 1.988-1(f)).

(B) *Example.*—Paragraph (b)(15)(iii)(A) is illustrated by the following example:

Example. When the Turkish lira (TL) is a hyperinflationary currency, A, a U.S. corporation with the U.S. dollar as its functional currency, makes a 5 year, 100,000 TL-denominated loan to B, an unrelated corporation, at a 10% interest rate when 1,000 TL equals $1. Under the terms of the debt instrument, B must pay interest annually to A in amount of Turkish lira that is equal to $100. Also under the terms of the debt instrument, B must pay A upon maturity of the debt instrument an amount of Turkish lira that is equal to $1,000. Although the principal and interest are payable in a hyperinflationary currency, the debt instrument is a synthetic dollar debt instrument and is not subject to paragraph (b)(15)(i) of this section.

(iv) *Source and character of gain or loss.*—(A) *General rule for hyperinflationary conditions.* The rules of this paragraph (b)(15)(iv)(A) shall apply to any taxpayer that is either an issuer of (or obligor under) a hyperinflationary debt instrument or deposit and has currency gain on such debt instrument or deposit, or a holder of a hyperinflationary debt instrument or deposit and has currency loss on such debt instrument or deposit. For purposes of subtitle A of the Internal Revenue Code, any exchange gain or loss realized under paragraph (b)(15)(i) of this section is directly allocable to the interest expense or interest income, respectively, from the debt instrument or deposit (computed under this paragraph (b)), and therefore reduces or increases the amount of interest income or interest expense paid or accrued during that year with respect to that instrument or deposit. With respect to a debt instrument or deposit during a taxable year, to the extent exchange gain realized under paragraph (b)(15)(i) of this section exceeds interest expense of an issuer, or exchange loss realized under paragraph (b)(15)(i) of this section exceeds interest income of a holder or depositor, the character and source of such excess amount shall be determined under §§1.988-3 and 1.988-4.

(B) *Special rule for subsiding hyperinflationary conditions.*—If the taxpayer is an issuer of (or obligor under) a hyperinflationary debt instrument or deposit and has currency loss, or if the taxpayer is a holder of a hyperinflationary debt instrument or deposit and has currency gain, then for purposes of subtitle A of the Internal Revenue Code, the character and source of the currency gain or loss is determined under §§1.988-3 and 1.988-4. Thus, if an issuer has both interest expense and currency loss, the currency loss is sourced and characterized under section 988, and does not affect the determination of interest expense.

(v) *Adjustment to principal or basis.*—Any exchange gain or loss realized under paragraph (b)(15)(i) of this section is an adjustment to the functional currency principal amount of the issuer, functional currency basis of the holder, or the functional currency amount of the deposit. This adjusted amount or basis is used in making subsequent computations of exchange gain or loss, computing the basis of assets for purposes of allocating interest under §§1.861-9T through 1.861-12T and 1.882-5, or making other determinations that may be relevant for computing taxable income or loss.

(vi) *Definitions.*—(A) *Hyperinflationary debt instrument.*—A hyperinflationary debt instrument is a debt instrument that provides for—

(1) Payments denominated in or determined by reference to a currency that is hyperinflationary (as defined in §1.988-1(f)) at the time the taxpayer enters into or otherwise acquires the debt instrument; or

(2) Payments denominated in or determined by reference to a currency that is hyperinflationary (as defined in §1.988-1(f)) during the taxable year, and the terms of the instrument provide for the adjustment of principal or interest payments in a manner that reflects hyperinflation. For example, a debt instrument providing for a variable interest rate based on local conditions and generally responding to changes in the local consumer price index will reflect hyperinflation.

(B) *Hyperinflationary deposit.*—A hyperinflationary deposit is a demand or time deposit or similar instrument issued by a bank or other financial institution that provides for—

(1) Payments denominated in or determined by reference to a currency that is hyperinflationary (as defined in §1.988-1(f)) at the time the taxpayer enters into or otherwise acquires the deposit; or

(2) Payments denominated in or determined by reference to a currency that is hyperinflationary (as defined in §1.988-1(f)) during the taxable year, and the terms of the deposit provide for the adjustment of the deposit amount or interest payments in a manner that reflects hyperinflation.

(vii) *Interaction with other provisions.*—(A) *Interest allocation rules.*—In determining the amount of interest expense, this paragraph (b)(15) applies before §§1.861-9T through 1.861-12T, and 1.882-5.

(B) *DASTM.*—With respect to a qualified business unit that uses the United States dollar approximate separate transactions method of accounting described in §1.985-3, paragraph (b)(15)(i) of this section does not apply.

(C) *Interaction with section 988(a)(3)(C).*—Section 988(a)(3)(C) does not apply to a debt instrument subject to the rules of paragraph (b)(15)(i) of this section.

(D) *Hedging rules.*—To the extent §1.446-4 or 1.988-5 apply, the rules of paragraph (b)(15)(i) of this section will not apply. This paragraph (b)(15)(vii)(D) does not apply if the application of §1.988-5 results in hyperinflationary debt instrument or deposit described in paragraph (b)(15)(vi)(A) or (B) of this section.

(viii) *Effective date.*—This paragraph (b)(15) applies to transactions entered into after February 14, 2000.

(16) [Reserved]. For further guidance, see §1.988-2T(b)(16).

(17) *Coordination with installment method under section 453.*—[Reserved]

(18) *Interaction of section 988 and §1.1275-2(g).*—(i) *In general.*—If a principal purpose of structuring a debt instrument subject to section 988 and any related hedges is to achieve a result that is unreasonable in light of the purposes of section 163(e), section 988, sections 1271 through 1275, or any related section of the Internal Revenue Code, the Commissioner can apply or depart from the regulations under the applicable sections as necessary or appropriate to achieve a reasonable result. For example, if this paragraph (b)(18) applies to a multicurrency debt instrument and a hedge or hedges, the Commissioner can wholly or partially integrate transactions or treat portions of the debt instrument as separate instruments where appropriate. See also §1.1275-2(g).

(ii) *Unreasonable result.*—Whether a result is unreasonable is determined based on all the facts and circumstances. In making this determination, a significant fact is whether the treatment of the debt instrument is expected to have a substantial effect on the issuer's or a holder's U.S. tax liability. Another significant fact is whether the result is obtainable without the application of §1.988-6 and any related provisions (e.g., if the debt instrument and the contingency were entered into separately). A result will not be considered unreasonable, however, in the absence of an expected substantial effect on the present value of a taxpayer's tax liability.

(iii) *Effective date.*—This paragraph (b)(18) shall apply to debt instruments issued on or after October 29, 2004.

(c) *Item of expense or gross income or receipts which is to be paid or received after the date accrued.*—(1) *In general.*—Except as provided in §1.988-5, exchange gain or loss with respect to an item described in §1.988-1(a)(1)(ii) and (2)(ii) (other than accrued interest income or expense subject to paragraph (b) of this section) shall be realized on the date payment is made or received. Except as provided in the succeeding sentence, such exchange gain or loss shall be recognized in accordance with the applicable recognition provisions of the Internal Revenue Code. If the taxpayer's right to receive income, or obligation to pay an expense, is transferred or modified in a transaction in which gain or loss would otherwise be recognized, exchange gain or loss shall be realized and recognized only to the extent of the total gain or loss on the transaction.

(2) *Determination of exchange gain or loss with respect to an item of gross income or receipts.*—Exchange gain or loss realized on an item of gross income or receipts described in paragraph (c)(1) of this section shall be determined by multiplying the units of nonfunctional currency received by the spot rate on the payment date, and subtracting from such amount the amount determined by multiplying the units of nonfunctional currency received by the spot rate on the booking date. The term "spot rate on the payment date" means the spot rate determined under §1.988-1(d) on the date payment is received or otherwise taken into account. Pursuant to §1.988-1(d)(3), a taxpayer may use a spot rate convention for purposes of determining the spot rate on the payment date. The term "spot rate on the booking date" means the spot rate determined under §1.988-1(d) on the date the item of gross income or receipts is accrued or otherwise taken into account. Pursuant to §1.988-1(d)(3), a taxpayer may use a spot rate convention for purposes of determining the spot rate on the booking date.

(3) *Determination of exchange gain or loss with respect to an item of expense.*—Exchange gain or loss realized on an item of expense described in paragraph (c)(1) of this section shall be determined by multiplying the units of nonfunctional currency paid by the spot rate on the booking date and subtracting from such amount the amount determined by multiplying the units of nonfunctional currency paid by the spot rate on the payment date. The term "spot rate on the booking date" means the spot rate determined under § 1.988-1(d) on the date the item of expense is accrued or otherwise taken into account. Pursuant to § 1.988-1(d)(3), a taxpayer may use a spot rate convention for purposes of determining the spot rate on the booking date. The term "spot rate on the payment date" means the spot rate determined under § 1.988-1(d) on the date payment is made or otherwise taken into account. Pursuant to § 1.988-1(d)(3), a taxpayer may use a spot rate convention for purposes of determining the spot rate on the payment date.

(4) *Examples.*—The following examples illustrate the application of paragraph (c) of this section.

Example 1. X is a calendar year corporation with the dollar as its functional currency. X is on the accrual method of accounting. On January 15, 1989, X sells inventory for 10,000 Canadian dollars (C$). The spot rate on January 15, 1989, is C$1 = U.S. $.55. On February 23, 1989, when X receives payment of the C$10,000, the spot rate is C$1 = U.S. $.50. On February 23, 1989, X will realize exchange loss. X's loss is computed by multiplying the C$10,000 by the spot rate on the date the C$10,000 are received (C$10,000 × .50 = U.S. $5,000) and subtracting from such amount, the amount computed by multiplying the C$10,000 by the spot rate on the booking date (C$10,000 × .55 = U.S. $5,500). Thus, X's exchange loss on the transaction is U.S. $500 (U.S. $5,000 – U.S. $5,500).

Example 2. The facts are the same as in *Example 1* except that X uses a spot rate convention to determine the spot rate as provided in § 1.988-1(d)(3). Pursuant to X's spot rate convention, the spot rate at which a payable or receivable is booked is determined monthly for each nonfunctional currency payable or receivable by adding the spot rate at the beginning of the month and the spot rate at the end of the month and dividing by two. All payables and receivables in a nonfunctional currency booked during the month are translated into functional currency at the rate described in the preceding sentence. Further, the translation of nonfunctional currency paid with respect to a payable, and nonfunctional currency received with respect to a receivable, is also performed pursuant to the spot rate convention. Assume the spot rate determined under the spot rate convention for the month of January is C$1 = U.S. $.54 and for the month of February is C$1 = U.S. $.51. On the last date in February, X will realize exchange loss. X's loss is computed by multiplying the C$10,000 by the spot rate convention for the month of February (C$10,000 × U.S. $.51 = U.S. $5,100) and subtracting from such amount, the amount computed by multiplying the C$10,000 by the spot rate convention for the month of January (C$10,000 × U.S. $.54 = $5,400). Thus, X's exchange loss on the transaction is U.S. $300 (U.S. $5,100 – U.S. $5,400). X's basis in the C$10,000 is U.S. $5,400.

Example 3. The facts are the same as in *Example 2* except that X has a standing order with X's bank for the bank to convert any nonfunctional currency received in satisfaction of a receivable into U.S. dollars on the day received and to deposit those U.S. dollars in X's U.S. dollar bank account. X may use its convention to translate the amount booked into U.S. dollars, but must use the U.S. dollar amounts received from the bank with respect to such receivables to determine X's exchange gain or loss. Thus, if X receives payment of the C$10,000 on February 23, 1989, when the spot rate is C$1 = U.S.$ .50, X determines exchange gain or loss by subtracting the amount booked under X's convention (U.S.$5,400) from the amount of U.S. dollars received from the bank under the standing conversion order (assume $5,000). X's exchange loss is U.S.$400.

(d) *Exchange gain or loss with respect to forward contracts, futures contracts and option contracts.*—(1) *Scope.*—(i) *In general.*—This paragraph (d) applies to forward contracts, futures contracts and option contracts described in § 1.988-1(a)(1)(ii) and (2)(iii). For rules applicable to currency swaps and notional principal contracts described in § 1.988-1(a)(1)(ii) and (2)(iii), see paragraph (e) of this section.

(ii) *Treatment of spot contracts.*—Solely for purposes of this paragraph (d), a spot contract as defined in § 1.988-1(b) to buy or sell nonfunctional currency is not considered a forward contract or similar transaction described in § 1.988-1(a)(2)(iii) unless such spot contract is disposed of (or otherwise terminated) prior to making or taking delivery of the currency. For example, if a taxpayer with the dollar as its functional currency enters into a spot contract to purchase British pounds, and takes delivery of such pounds under the contract, the delivery of the pounds is not a realization event under section 988(c)(5) and paragraph (e)(4)(ii) of this section because the contract is not considered a forward contract or similar transaction described in § 1.988-1(a)(2)(iii). However, if the taxpayer sells or otherwise terminates the contract before taking delivery of the pounds, exchange gain or loss shall be realized and recognized in accordance with paragraphs (d)(2) and (3) of this section.

(2) *Realization of exchange gain or loss.*—(i) *In general.*—Except as provided in § 1.988-5, exchange gain or loss on a contract described in § 1.988-2(d)(1) shall be realized in accordance with the applicable realization section of the Internal Revenue Code (*e.g.*, sections 1001, 1092, and 1256). See also section 988(c)(5). For purposes of determining the timing of the realization of exchange gain or loss, sections 1092 and 1256 shall take precedence over section 988(c)(5).

(ii) *Realization by offset.*—(A) *In general.*—Except as provided in paragraphs (d)(2)(ii)(B) and (C) of this section, exchange gain or loss with respect to a transaction described in § 1.988-1(a)(1)(ii) and (2)(iii) shall not be realized solely because such transaction is offset by another transaction (or transactions).

(B) *Exception where economic benefit is derived.*—If a transaction described in § 1.988-1(a)(1)(ii) and (2)(iii) is offset by another transaction or transactions, exchange gain shall be realized to the extent the taxpayer derives, by pledge or otherwise, an economic benefit (*e.g.*, cash, property or the proceeds from a borrowing) from any gain inherent in such offsetting positions. Proper adjustment shall be made in the amount of any gain or loss subsequently realized for gain taken into account by reason of the preceding sentence. This paragraph (d)(2)(ii)(B) shall apply to transactions creating an offset after September 21, 1989.

(C) *Certain contracts traded on an exchange.*—If a transaction described in § 1.988-1(a)(1)(ii) and (2)(iii) is traded on an exchange and it is the general practice of the exchange to terminate offsetting contracts, entering into an offsetting contract shall be considered a termination of the contract being offset.

(iii) *Clarification of section 988(c)(5).*—If the delivery date of a contract subject to section 988(c)(5) and paragraph (d)(4)(ii) of this section is different than the date the contract expires, then for purposes of determining the date exchange gain or loss is realized, the term delivery date shall mean expiration date.

(iv) *Examples.*—The following examples illustrate the rules of this paragraph (d)(1) and (2).

Example 1. On August 1, 1989, X, a calendar year corporation with the dollar as its functional currency, enters into a forward contract with Bank A to buy 100 New Zealand dollars for $80 for delivery on January 31, 1990. (The forward purchase contract is not a section 1256 contract.) On November 1, 1989, the market price for the purchase of 100 New Zealand dollars for delivery on January 31, 1990, is $76. On November 1, 1989, X cancels its obligation under the forward purchase contract and pays Bank A $3.95 (the present value of $4 discounted at 12% for the period) in cancellation of such contract. Under section 1001(a), X realizes an exchange loss of $3.95 on November 1, 1989, because cancellation of the forward purchase contract for cash results in the termination of X's contract.

Example 2. X is a corporation with the dollar as its functional currency. On January 1, 1989, X enters into a currency swap contract with Bank A under which X is obligated to make a series of Japanese yen payments in exchange for a series of dollar payments. On February 21, 1992, X has a gain of $100,000 inherent in such contract as a result of interest rate and exchange rate movements. Also on February 21, 1992, X enters into an offsetting swap with Bank A to lock in such gain. If on February 21, 1992, X pledges the gain inherent in such offsetting positions as collateral for a loan, X's initial swap contract is treated as being terminated on February 21, 1992, under paragraph (d)(2)(ii)(B) of this section. Proper adjustment is made in the amount of any gain or loss subsequently realized for the gain taken into account by reason of paragraph (d)(2)(ii)(B) of this section.

Example 3. X is a calendar year corporation with the dollar as its functional currency. On October 1, 1989, X enters into a forward contract to buy 100,000 Swiss francs (Sf) for delivery on March 1, 1990, for $51,220. Assume that the contract is a section 1256 contract under section 1256(g)(2) and that section 1256(e) does not apply. Pursuant to section 1256(a)(1), the forward contract is treated as sold for its fair market value on December 31, 1989. Assume that the fair market value of the contract is $1,000 determined under § 1.988-1(g). Thus X will realize an exchange gain of $1,000 on December 31, 1989.

Such gain is subject to the character rules of § 1.988-3 and the source rules of § 1.988-4.

(v) *Extension of the maturity date of certain contracts.*—An extension of time for making or taking delivery under a contract described in paragraph (d)(1) of this section (*e.g.*, a historical rate rollover as defined in § 1.988-5(b)(2)(iii)(C)) shall be considered a sale or exchange of the contract for its fair market value on the date of the extension and the establishment of a new contract on such date. If, under the terms of the extension, the time value of any gain or loss recognized pursuant to the preceding sentence adjusts the price of the currency to be bought or sold under the new contract, the amount attributable to such time value shall be treated as interest income or expense for all purposes of the Code. However, the preceding sentence shall not apply and the amount attributable to the time value of any gain or loss recognized shall be treated as exchange gain or loss if the period beginning on the first date the contract is rolled over and ending on the date payment is ultimately made or received with respect to such contract does not exceed 183 days.

(3) *Recognition of exchange gain or loss.*—Except as provided in § 1.988-5 (relating to section 988 hedging transactions), exchange gain or loss realized with respect to a contract described in paragraph (d)(1) of this section shall be recognized in accordance with the applicable recognition provisions of the Internal Revenue Code. For example, a loss realized with respect to a contract described in paragraph (d)(1) of this section which is part of a straddle shall be recognized in accordance with the provisions of section 1092 to the extent such section is applicable.

(4) *Determination of exchange gain or loss.*—(i) *In general.*—Exchange gain or loss with respect to a contract described in § 1.988-2(d)(1) shall be determined by subtracting the amount paid (or deemed paid), if any, for or with respect to the contract (including any amount paid upon termination of the contract) from the amount received (or deemed received), if any, for or with respect to the contract (including any amount received upon termination of the contract). Any gain or loss determined according to the preceding sentence shall be treated as exchange gain or loss.

(ii) *Special rules where taxpayer makes or takes delivery.*—If the taxpayer makes or takes delivery in connection with a contract described in paragraph (d)(1) of this section, any gain or loss shall be realized and recognized in the same manner as if the taxpayer sold the contract (or paid another person to assume the contract) on the date on which he took or made delivery for its fair market value on such date. See paragraph (d)(2)(iii) of this section regarding the definition of the term "delivery date." This paragraph (d)(4)(ii) shall not apply in any case in which the taxpayer makes or takes delivery before June 11, 1987.

(iii) *Examples.*—The following examples illustrate the application of paragraph (d)(4) of this section.

Example 1. X is a calendar year corporation with the dollar as its functional currency. On October 1, 1989, when the six month forward rate is $.4907, X enters into a forward contract to buy 100,000 New Zealand dollars (NZD) for delivery on March 1, 1990. On March 1, 1990, when X takes delivery of the 100,000 NZD, the spot rate is 1NZD equals $.48. Pursuant to section 988(c)(5) and paragraph (d)(4)(ii) of this section, a taxpayer that takes delivery of nonfunctional currency under a forward contract that is subject to section 988 is treated as if the taxpayer sold the contract for its fair market value on the date delivery is taken. If X sold the contract on March 1, 1990, the transferee would require a payment of $1,070 [($.48 × 100,000NZD) − ($.4907 × 100,000NZD)] to compensate him for the loss in value of the 100,000NZD. Therefore, X realizes an exchange loss of $1,070. X has a basis in the 100,000NZD of $48,000.

Example 2. Assume the same facts as in *Example 1* except that the contract is for Swiss francs and is a section 1256 contract. Assume further that on December 31, 1989, the value to X of the contract as marked to market is $1,000. Pursuant to section 1256(a), X realizes an exchange gain of $1,000. Such gain, however, is characterized as ordinary income under § 1.988-3 and will be sourced under § 1.988-4.

Example 3. X is a calendar year corporation with the dollar as its functional currency. On May 2, 1989, X enters into an option contract with Bank A to purchase 50,000 Canadian dollars (C$) for U.S. $42,500 (C$1 = U.S. $.85) for delivery on or before September 18, 1989. X pays a $285 premium to Bank A to obtain the option contract. On September 18, 1989, when X exercises the option and takes delivery of the C$50,000, the spot rate is C$1 equals U.S. $.90. Pursuant to section 988(c)(5) and paragraph (d)(4)(ii) of this section, a taxpayer that takes delivery under an option contract that is subject to section 988 is treated as if the taxpayer sold the contract for its fair market value on the date delivery is taken. If X sold the contract for its fair market value on September 18, 1989, X would receive U.S. $2,500 [(C$50,000 × U.S. $.90) − (C$50,000 × U.S. $.85)]. Accordingly, X is deemed to have received U.S. $2,500 on the sale of the contract at its fair market value. X will realize U.S. $2,215 ($2,500 deemed received less $285 paid) of exchange gain with respect to the delivery of Canadian dollars under the option contract. X's basis in the 50,000 Canadian dollars is U.S. $45,000.

(5) *Hyperinflationary contracts.*—(i) *In general.*—If a taxpayer acquires or otherwise enters into a hyperinflationary contract (as defined in paragraph (d)(5)(ii) of this section) that has payments to be made or received that are denominated in (or determined by reference to) a nonfunctional currency of the taxpayer, then the taxpayer shall realize exchange gain or loss with respect to such contract for its taxable year determined by reference to the change in exchange rates between—

(A) The later of the first day of the taxable year, or the date the contract was acquired or entered into; and

(B) The earlier of the last day of the taxable year, or the date the contract is disposed of or otherwise terminated.

(ii) *Definition of hyperinflationary contract.*—A hyperinflationary contract is a contract described in paragraph (d)(1) of this section that provides for payments denominated in or determined by reference to a currency that is hyperinflationary (as defined in § 1.988-1(f)) at the time the taxpayer acquires or otherwise enters into the contract.

(iii) *Interaction with other provisions.*—(A) *DASTM.*—With respect to a qualified business unit that uses the United States dollar approximate separate transactions method of accounting described in § 1.985-3, this paragraph (d)(5) does not apply.

(B) *Hedging rules.*—To the extent § 1.446-4 or 1.988-5 apply, this paragraph (d)(5) does not apply.

(C) *Adjustment for subsequent transactions.*—Proper adjustments must be made in the amount of any gain or loss subsequently realized for gain or loss taken into account by reason of this paragraph (d)(5).

(iv) *Effective date.*—This paragraph (d)(5) is applicable to transactions acquired or otherwise entered into after February 14, 2000.

(e) *Currency swaps and other notional principal contracts.*—(1) *In general.*—Except as provided in paragraph (e)(2) of this section or in § 1.988-5, the timing of income, deduction and loss with respect to a notional principal contract that is a section 988 transaction shall be governed by section 446 and the regulations thereunder. Such income, deduction and loss is characterized as exchange gain or loss (except as provided in another section of the Internal Revenue Code (or regulations thereunder), § 1.988-5, or in paragraph (f) of this section).

(2) *Special rules for currency swaps.*—(i) *In general.*—Except as provided in paragraph (e)(2)(iii)(B) of this section, the provisions of this paragraph (e)(2) shall apply solely for purposes of determining the realization, recognition and amount of exchange gain or loss with respect to a currency swap contract, and not for purposes of determining the source of such gain or loss, or characterizing such gain or loss as interest. Except as provided in § 1.988-3(c), any income or loss realized with respect to a currency swap contract shall be characterized as exchange gain or loss (and not as interest income or expense). Any exchange gain or loss realized in accordance with this paragraph (e)(2) shall be recognized unless otherwise provided in an applicable section of the Code. For purposes of this paragraph (e)(2), a currency swap contract is a contract defined in paragraph (e)(2)(ii) of this section. With respect to a contract which requires the payment of swap principal prior to maturity of such contract, see paragraph (f) of this section. For purposes of this paragraph (e), the rules of paragraph (d)(2)(ii) of this section (regarding realization by offset) apply. See Example 2 of paragraph (d)(2)(iv) of this section.

(ii) *Definition of currency swap contract.*—(A) *In general.*—A currency swap contract is a contract involving different currencies between two or more parties to—

(1) Exchange periodic interim payments, as defined in paragraph (e)(2)(ii)(C) of this section, on or prior to maturity of the contract; and

(2) Exchange the swap principal amount upon maturity of the contract.

A currency swap contract may also require an exchange of the swap principal amount upon commencement of the agreement.

(B) *Swap principal amount.*—The swap principal amount is an amount of two different currencies which, under the terms of the currency swap contract, is used to determine the periodic interim payments in each currency and which is exchanged upon maturity of the contract. If such amount is not clearly set forth in the contract, the Commissioner may determine the swap principal amount.

(C) *Exchange of periodic interim payments.*—An exchange of periodic interim payments is an exchange of one or more payments in one currency specified by the contract for one or more payments in a different currency specified by the contract where the payments in each currency are computed by reference to an interest index applied to the swap principal amount. A currency swap contract must clearly indicate the periodic interim payments, or the interest index used to compute the periodic interim payments, in each currency.

(iii) *Timing and computation of periodic interim payments.*—(A) *In general.*—Except as provided in paragraph (e)(2)(iii)(B) of this section and § 1.988-5, the timing and computation of the periodic interim payments provided in a currency swap agreement shall be determined by treating—

(1) Payments made under the swap as payments made pursuant to a hypothetical borrowing that is denominated in the currency in which payments are required to be made (or are determined with reference to) under the swap, and

(2) Payments received under the swap as payments received pursuant to a hypothetical loan that is denominated in the currency in which payments are received (or are determined with reference to) under the swap.

Except as provided in paragraph (e)(2)(v) of this section, the hypothetical issue price of such hypothetical borrowing and loan shall be the swap principal amount. The hypothetical stated redemption price at maturity is the total of all payments (excluding any exchange of the swap principal amount at the inception of the contract) provided under the hypothetical borrowing or loan other than periodic interest payments under the principles of section 1273. For purposes of determining economic accrual under the currency swap, the number of hypothetical interest compounding periods of such hypothetical borrowing and loan shall be determined pursuant to a semiannual compounding convention unless the currency swap contract indicates otherwise. For purposes of determining the timing and amount of the periodic interim payments, the principles regarding the amortization of interest (see generally, sections 1272 through 1275 and 163(e)) shall apply to the hypothetical interest expense and income of such hypothetical borrowing and loan. However, such principles shall not apply to determine the time when principal is deemed to be paid on the hypothetical borrowing and loan. See paragraph (d)(2)(iii) of this section and *Example* 2 of paragraph (d)(5) of this section with respect to the time when principal is deemed to be paid. With respect to the translation and computation of exchange gain or loss on any hypothetical interest income or expense, see § 1.988-2(b). The amount treated as exchange gain or loss by the taxpayer with respect to the periodic interim payments for the taxable year shall be the amount of hypothetical interest income and exchange gain or loss attributable to such interest income from the hypothetical borrowing and loan for such year less the amount of hypothetical interest expense and exchange gain or loss attributable to the interest expense from such hypothetical borrowing and loan for such year.

(B) *Effect of prepayment for purposes of section 956.*—For purposes of section 956, the Commissioner may treat any prepayment of a currency swap as a loan.

(iv) *Timing and determination of exchange gain or loss with respect to the swap principal amount.*—Exchange gain or loss with respect to the swap principal amount shall be realized on the day the units of swap principal in each currency are exchanged. (See paragraph (e)(2)(ii)(A)(2) of this section which requires that the entire swap principal amount be exchanged upon maturity of the contract.) Such gain or loss shall be determined on the date of the exchange by subtracting the value (on such date) of the units of swap principal paid from the value of the units of swap principal received. This paragraph (e)(2)(iv) does not apply to an equal exchange of the swap principal amount at the commencement of the agreement at a market exchange rate.

(v) *Anti-abuse rules.*—(A) *Method of accounting does not clearly reflect income.*—If the taxpayer's method of accounting for income, expense, gain or loss attributable to a currency swap does not clearly reflect income, or if the present value of the payments to be made is not equivalent to that of the payments to be received (including the swap premium or discount, as defined in paragraph (e)(3)(ii) of this section) on the day the taxpayer enters into or acquires the contract, the Commissioner may apply principles analogous to those of section 1274 or such other rules as the Commissioner deems appropriate to clearly reflect income. For example, in order to clearly reflect income the Commissioner may determine the hypothetical issue price, the hypothetical stated redemption price at maturity, and the amounts required to be taken into account within a taxable year. Further, if the present value of the payments to be made is not equivalent to that of the payments to be received (including the swap premium or discount, as defined in paragraph (e)(3)(ii) of this section) on the day the taxpayer enters into or acquires the contract, the Commissioner may integrate the swap with another transaction (or transactions) in order to clearly reflect income.

(B) *Terms must be clearly stated.*—If the currency swap contract does not clearly set forth the swap principal amount in each currency, and the periodic interim payments in each currency (or the interest index used to compute the periodic interim payments in each currency), the Commissioner may defer any income, deduction, gain or loss with respect to such contract until termination of the contract.

(3) *Amortization of swap premium or discount in the case of off-market currency swaps.*—(i) *In general.*—An "off-market currency swap" is a currency swap contract under which the present value of the payments to be made is not equal to that of the payments to be received on the day the taxpayer enters into or acquires the contract (absent the swap premium or discount, as defined in paragraph (e)(3)(ii) of this section). Generally, such present values may not be equal if the swap exchange rate (as defined in paragraph (e)(3)(iii) of this section) is not the spot rate, or the interest indices used to compute the periodic interim payments do not reflect current values, on the day the taxpayer enters into or acquires the currency swap.

(ii) *Treatment of taxpayer entering into or acquiring an off-market currency swap.*—If a taxpayer that enters into or acquires a currency swap makes a payment (that is, the taxpayer pays a premium, "swap premium," to enter into or acquire the currency swap) or receives a payment (that is, the taxpayer enters into or acquires the currency swap at a discount, "swap discount") in order to make the present value of the amounts to be paid equal the amounts to be received, such payment shall be amortized in a manner which places the taxpayer in the same position it would have been in had the taxpayer entered into a currency swap contract under which the present value of the amounts to be paid equal the amounts to be received (absent any swap premium or discount). Thus, swap premium or discount shall be amortized as follows—

(A) The amount of swap premium or discount that is attributable to the difference between the swap exchange rate (as defined in paragraph (e)(3)(iii) of this section) and the spot rate on the date the contract is entered into or acquired shall be taken into account as income or expense on the date the swap principal amounts are taken into account; and

(B) The amount of swap premium or discount attributable to the difference in values of the periodic interim payments shall be amortized in a manner consistent with the principles of economic accrual. *Cf.*, section 171.

Any amount taken into account pursuant to this paragraph (e)(3)(ii) shall be treated as exchange gain or loss.

(iii) *Definition of swap exchange rate.*—The swap exchange rate is the single exchange rate set forth in the contract at which the swap principal amounts are determined. If the swap exchange rate is not clearly set forth in the contract, the Commissioner may determine such rate.

(iv) *Coordination with § 1.446-3(g)(4) regarding swaps with significant nonperiodic payments.*—The rules of § 1.446-3(g)(4) apply to any currency swap with a significant nonperiodic payment. Section 1.446-3(g)(4) applies before this paragraph (e)(3). Thus, if § 1.446-3(g)(4) applies, currency gain or loss may be realized on the loan. This paragraph (e)(3)(iv) applies to transactions entered into after February 14, 2000.

(4) *Treatment of taxpayer disposing of a currency swap.*—Any gain or loss realized on the disposition or the termination of a currency swap is exchange gain or loss.

(5) *Examples.*—The following examples illustrate the application of this paragraph (e).

Example 1. (i) C is an accrual method calendar year corporation with the dollar as its functional currency. On January 1, 1989, C enters into a currency swap with J with the following terms:

(1) the principal amount is $150 and 100 British pounds (£) (the equivalent of $150 on the effective date of the contract assuming a spot rate of £1 = $1.50 on January 1, 1989);

(2) C will make payments equal to 10% of the dollar principal amount on December 31, 1989, and December 31, 1990;

(3) J will make payments equal to 12% of the pound principal amount on December 31, 1989, and December 31, 1990; and

(4) on December 31, 1990, C will pay to J the $150 principal amount and J will pay to C the £ 100 principal amount.

Assume that the spot rate is £1 = $1.50 on January 1, 1989, £1 = $1.40 on December 31, 1989, and £1 = $1.30 on December 31, 1990. Assume further that the average rate for 1989 is £1 = $1.45 and for 1990 is £1 = $1.35.

(ii) Solely for determining the realization of gain or loss in accordance with paragraph (e)(2) of this section (and not for purposes of determining whether any payments are treated as interest), C will treat the dollar payments made by C as payments made pursuant to a dollar borrowing with an issue price of $150, a stated redemption price at maturity of $150, and yield to maturity of 10%. C will treat the pound payments received as payments received pursuant to a pound loan with an issue price of £100, a stated redemption price at maturity of £100, and a yield of 12% to maturity. Pursuant to § 1.988-2(b), C is required to compute hypothetical accrued pound interest income at the average rate for the accrual period and then determine exchange gain or loss on the day payment is received with respect to such accrued amount. Accordingly, C will accrue $17.40 (£12 × $1.45) in 1989 and $16.20 (£12 × $1.35) in 1990. C also will compute hypothetical exchange loss of $.60 on December 31, 1989 [(£12 × $1.40) − (£12 × $1.45)] and hypothetical exchange loss of $.60 on December 31, 1990 [£12 × $1.30) − (£12 × $1.35)]. All such hypothetical interest income and exchange loss are characterized and sourced as exchange gain and loss. Further, C is treated as having paid $15 ($150 × 10%) of hypothetical interest on December 31, 1989, and again on December 31, 1990. Such hypothetical interest expense is characterized and sourced as exchange loss. Thus, C will have a net exchange gain of $1.80 ($17.40 − $.60 − $15.00) with respect to the periodic interim payments in 1989 and a net exchange gain of $.60 ($16.20 − $.60 − $15.00) with respect to the periodic interim payments in 1990. Finally, C will realize an exchange loss on December 31, 1990 with respect to the exchange of the swap principal amount. This loss is determined by subtracting the value of the units of swap principal paid ($150) from the value of the units of swap principal received (£100 × $1.30 = $130) resulting in a $20 exchange loss.

Example 2. (i) C is an accrual method calendar year corporation with the dollar as its functional currency. On January 1, 1989, when the spot rate is £1 = $1.50, C enters into a currency swap contract with J under which C agrees to make and receive the following payments:

Date	*C Pays*	*J Pays*
December 31, 1989	$15.00	£12.00
December 31, 1990	$41.04	£12.00
December 31, 1991	$0.00	£12.00
December 31, 1992	$150.00	£112.00

(ii) Under paragraph (e)(2)(iii) of this section, C must treat the dollar periodic interim payments under the swap as made pursuant to a hypothetical dollar borrowing. The hypothetical issue price is $150 and the stated redemption price at maturity is $206.04. The amount of hypothetical interest expense must be amortized in accordance with economic accrual. Thus J must include and C must deduct periodic interim payment amounts as follows:

	Amount Taken into Account	*Adjusted Issue Price*
December 31, 1989	$15.00	150.00
December 31, 1990	$15.00	123.96
December 31, 1991	$12.40	136.36
December 31, 1992	$13.64	

(iii) Gain or loss with respect to the periodic interim payments of the currency swap is determined under paragraph (e)(2)(iii)(A) of this section with respect to the dollar cash flow amortized as set forth above and the corresponding pound cash flow as stated in the currency swap contract. Gain or loss with respect to the principal payments (*i.e.,* $150 and £100) exchanged on December 31, 1992, is determined under paragraph (e)(2)(iv) of this section on December 31, 1992, notwithstanding that under the principles regarding amortization of interest $26.04 would have been regarded as a payment of principal on December 31, 1990.

Example 3. (i) X is a corporation on the accrual method of accounting with the dollar as its functional currency and the calendar year as its taxable year. On January 1, 1989, X enters into a three year currency swap contract with Y with the following terms. The swap principal amount is $100 and the Swiss franc (Sf) equivalent of such amount which equals Sf200 translated at the swap exchange rate of $1 = Sf2. There is no initial exchange of the swap principal amount. The interest rates used to compute the periodic interim payments are 10% compounded annually for U.S. dollar payments and 5% compounded annually for Swiss franc payments. Thus, under the currency swap, X agrees to pay Y $10 (10% × $100) on December 31st of 1989, 1990 and 1991 and to pay Y the swap principal amount of $100 on December 31, 1991. Y agrees to pay X Sf10 (5% × Sf200) on December 31st of 1989, 1990 and 1991 and to pay X the swap principal amount of Sf200 on December 31, 1991. Assume that the average rate for 1989 and the spot rate on December 31, 1989, is $1 = Sf2.5.

(ii) Under paragraph (e)(2)(iii) of this section, on December 31, 1989, X will realize an exchange loss of $6 (the sum of $10 of loss by reason of the $10 periodic interim payment paid to Y and $4.00 of gain, the value of Sf10 on December 31, 1989, from the receipt of Sf10 on such date).

(iii) On January 1, 1990, X transfers its rights and obligations under the swap contract to Z, an unrelated corporation. Z has the dollar as its functional currency, is on the accrual method of accounting, and has the calendar year as its taxable year. On January 1, 1990, the exchange rate is $1 = Sf2.50. The relevant dollar interest rate is 8% compounded annually and the relevant Swiss franc interest rate is 5% compounded annually. Because of the movement in exchange and interest rates, the agreement between X and Z to transfer the currency swap requires X to pay Z $23.56 (the swap discount as determined under paragraph (e)(3) of this section).

(iv) Pursuant to paragraph (e)(4) of this section, X may deduct the loss of $23.56 in 1990. The loss is characterized under § 1.988-3 and sourced under § 1.988-4.

(v) Pursuant to paragraph (e)(3)(ii) of this section, Z is required to amortize the $23.56 received as follows. The amount of the $23.56 payment that is attributable to movements in exchange rates ($20) is taken into account on December 31, 1991, the date the swap principal amounts are exchanged, under paragraph (e)(3)(ii)(A) of this section. This amount is the present value (discounted at 10%, the rate under the currency swap contract used to compute the dollar periodic interim payments) of the financial asset required to compensate Z for the loss in value of the hypothetical Swiss franc loan resulting from movements in exchange rates between January 1, 1989 and January 1, 1990. This amount is determined by assuming that interest rates did not change from the date the swap originally was entered into (January 1, 1989), but that the exchange rate is $1 = Sf2.50. Under this assumption, a taxpayer undertaking the obligation to pay dollars under the currency swap on January 1, 1990, would only agree to pay $8 for Sf10 on December 31, 1990 and $88 for Sf210 on December 31, 1991, because the exchange rates have moved from $1 = Sf2 to $1 = Sf2.50. Thus, Z requires $2 on December 31, 1990 and $22 on December 31, 1991 to compensate for the amount of dollar payments Z is required to make in exchange for the Swiss francs received on December 31, 1990 and 1991. The present value of $2 on December 31, 1990 and $22 on December 31, 1991 discounted at the rate for U.S. dollar payments of 10% is $20 ($1.82 + $18.18). This amount is discounted at the rate for U.S. dollar payments (i.e., at the historic rate) because the amount of the $23.56 payment received by Z that is attributable to movements in interest rates is computed and amortized separately as provided in the following paragraph.

(vi) Pursuant to paragraph (e)(3)(ii)(B) of this section, Z is required to amortize the portion of the $23.56 payment attributable to movements in interest rates under principles of economic accrual over the term of the currency swap agreement. The amount of the $23.56 payment that is attributable to movements in interest rates (assuming that exchange rates have not changed) is the present value ($3.56) of the excess ($2.00 in 1990 and $2.00 in 1991) of the periodic interim payments Z is required to pay under the currency swap agreement ($10 in 1990 and $10 in 1991) over the amount Z would be required to pay if the currency swap agreement reflected current interest rates on the day Z acquired the swap contract ($8 in 1990 and $8 in 1991) discounted at the appropriate dollar interest rate on January 1, 1990. Thus, under principles of economic accrual (e.g., see section 171 of the Code), Z will include in income $1.72 on December 31, 1990, the amount that, when added to the interest ($.28) on the $3.56 computed at the 8% rate on the date Z acquired the currency swap contract, will equal the $2.00 needed to compensate Z for the movement in interest rates between January 1, 1989 and January 1, 1990. Z also will include in income $1.85 on December 31, 1991, the amount that, when added to the interest ($.15) on the $1.85 (the remaining balance of the $3.56 payment) computed at the 8% rate on the date Z acquired the currency swap contract, will equal the $2.00 needed to compensate Z for the movement in interest rates between January 1, 1990 and January 1, 1991. This amount is computed assuming exchange rates have not changed because the amount attributable to movements in exchange rates is computed and amortized separately under the preceding paragraph.

(6) *Special effective date for rules regarding currency swaps.*—Paragraph (e)(3) of this section regarding amortization of swap premium or discount in the case of off-market currency swaps shall be effective for transactions entered into after September 21, 1989, unless such swap premium or discount was paid or received pursuant to a binding contract with an unrelated party that was entered into prior to such date. For transactions entered into prior to this date, see Notice 89-21, 1989-8 I.R.B. 23.

(7) *Special rules for currency swap contracts in hyperinflationary currencies.*—(i) *In general.*—If a taxpayer enters into a hyperinflationary currency swap (as defined in paragraph (e)(7)(iv) of this section), then the taxpayer realizes exchange gain or loss for its taxable year with respect to such instrument determined by reference to the change in exchange rates between—

(A) The later of the first day of the taxable year, or the date the instrument was entered into (by the taxpayer); and

(B) The earlier of the last day of the taxable year, or the date the instrument is disposed of or otherwise terminated.

(ii) *Adjustment to principal or basis.*—Proper adjustments are made in the amount of any gain or loss subsequently realized for gain or loss taken into account by reason of this paragraph (e)(7).

(iii) *Interaction with DASTM.*—With respect to a qualified business unit that uses the United States dollar approximate separate transactions method of accounting described in §1.985-3, this paragraph (e)(7) does not apply.

(iv) *Definition of hyperinflationary currency swap contract.*—A hyperinflationary currency swap contract is a currency swap contract that provides for—

(A) Payments denominated in or determined by reference to a currency that is hyperinflationary (as defined in §1.988-1(f)) at the time the taxpayer enters into or otherwise acquires the currency swap; or

(B) Payments that are adjusted to take into account the fact that the currency is hyperinflationary (as defined in §1.988-1(f)) during the current taxable year. A currency swap contract that provides for periodic payments determined by reference to a variable interest rate based on local conditions and generally responding to changes in the local consumer price index is an example of this latter type of currency swap contract.

(v) *Special effective date for nonfunctional hyperinflationary currency swap contracts.*—This paragraph (e)(7) applies to transactions entered into after February 14, 2000.

(f) *Substance over form.*—(1) *In general.*—If the substance of a transaction described in §1.988-1(a)(1) differs from its form, the timing, source, and character of gains or losses with respect to such transaction may be recharacterized by the Commissioner in accordance with its substance. For example, if a taxpayer enters into a transaction that it designates a "currency swap contract" that requires the prepayment of all payments to be made or to be received (but not both), the Commissioner may recharacterize the contract as a loan. In applying the substance over form principle, separate transactions may be integrated where appropriate. See also §1.861-9T(b)(1).

(2) *Example.*—The following example illustrates the provisions of this paragraph (f).

Example. (i) On January 1, 1990, X, a U.S. corporation with the dollar as its functional currency, enters into a contract with Y under which X will pay Y $100 and Y will pay X LC100 on January 1, 1990, and X will pay Y LC109.3 and Y will pay X $133 on December 31, 1992. On January 1, 1990, the spot exchange rate is LC1 = $1 and the 3 year forward rate is LC1 = $.8218. X's cash flows are summarized below:

Date	Dollar	LC
1/1/90	(100)	100
12/31/90	0	0
12/31/91	0	0
12/31/92	133	(109.3)

(ii) X and Y designate this contract as a "currency swap." Notwithstanding this designation, for purposes of determining the timing, source, and character with respect to the transaction, the transaction is characterized by the Commissioner in accordance with its substance. Thus, the January 1, 1990, exchange by X of $100 for LC 100 is treated as a spot purchase of LCs by X and the December 31, 1992, exchange by X at 109.3 LC for $133 is treated as a forward sale of LCs by X. Under such treatment there would be no tax consequences to X under paragraph (e)(2) of this section in 1990, 1991, and 1992 with respect to this transaction other than the realization of exchange gain or loss on the sale of the LC109.3 on December 31, 1992. Calculation of such gain or loss would be governed by the rules of paragraph (d) of this section.

(g) *Effective date.*—Except as otherwise provided in this section, this section shall be effective for taxable years beginning after December 31, 1986. Thus, except as otherwise provided in this section, any payments made or received with respect to a section 988 transaction in taxable years beginning after December 31, 1986, are subject to this section.

(h) *Timing of income and deductions from notional principal contracts.*—Except as otherwise provided (e.g., in §1.988-5 or 1.446-3(g)), income or loss from a notional principal contract described in §1.988-1(a)(2)(iii)(B) (other than a currency swap) is exchange gain or loss. For the rules governing the timing of income and deductions with respect to notional principal contracts, see §1.446-3. See paragraph (e)(2) of this section with respect to currency swaps.

(i) [Reserved]. For further guidance, see §1.988-2T(i). [Reg. §1.988-2.]

☐ [*T.D.* 8400, 3-16-92. *Amended by T.D.* 8491, 10-8-93; *T.D.* 8860, 1-12-2000, *T.D.* 9157, 8-27-2004, *T.D.* 9795, 12-7-2016 *and T.D.* 9882, 12-16-2019.]

»»→ Caution: Temporary Reg. §1.988-2T, below, expired on December 6, 2019. The related proposed regulation, published in REG-128276-12 by cross-reference to the temporary regulation, may be relied upon for periods following the expiration date (see Notice 2022-34, I.R.B. 2022-34, 150).

§1.988-2T. Recognition and computation of exchange gain or loss (temporary).—(a) through (b)(15) [Reserved]. For further guidance, see §1.988-2(a) through (b)(15).

(16) *Deferral of loss on certain related-party debt instruments.*—(i) *Treatment of creditor.*—For rules applicable to a corporation included in a controlled group that is a creditor under a debt instrument see §1.267(f)-1(e).

(ii) *Treatment of debtor.*—(A) *In general.*—Exchange loss realized under § 1.988-2(b)(4) or (b)(6) is deferred if—

(*1*) The loss is realized by a debtor with respect to a loan from a person that has a relationship to the debtor described in section 267(b) or section 707(b); and

(*2*) The transaction resulting in the realization of exchange loss has as a principal purpose the avoidance of Federal income tax.

(B) *Recognition of deferred loss.*—Any exchange loss that is deferred under paragraph (b)(16)(ii)(A) of this section is deferred until the end of the term of the loan, determined immediately prior to the transaction.

(17) through (h) [Reserved]. For further guidance, see § 1.988-2(b)(17) through (h).

(i) *Special rules for section 988 transactions of a section 987 QBU.*—For rules regarding section 988 transactions of a section 987 QBU, see § 1.987-3T(b)(4) for section 987 QBUs in general and § 1.987-1T(b)(6) for dollar QBUs.

(j) *Effective/applicability date.*—Paragraph (b)(16) of this section applies to any exchange loss realized on or after December 7, 2016. Paragraph (i) of this section applies to taxable years beginning on or after one year after the first day of the first taxable year following December 7, 2016. Notwithstanding the preceding sentence, if a taxpayer makes an election under § 1.987-11(b), then paragraph (i) of this section applies to taxable years to which §§ 1.987-1 through 1.987-10 apply as a result of such election.

(k) *Expiration date.*—The applicability of this section expires on December 6, 2019. [Temporary Reg. § 1.988-2T.]

□ [*T.D. 9795, 12-7-2016.*]

§ 1.988-3. Character of exchange gain or loss.—(a) *In general.*—The character of exchange gain or loss recognized on a section 988 transaction is governed by section 988 and this section. Except as otherwise provided in section 988(c)(1)(E), section 1092, § 1.988-5 and this section, exchange gain or loss realized with respect to a section 988 transaction (including a section 1256 contract that is also a section 988 transaction) shall be characterized as ordinary gain or loss. Accordingly, unless a valid election is made under paragraph (b) of this section, any section providing special rules for capital gain or loss treatment, such as sections 1233, 1234, 1234A, 1236 and 1256(f)(3), shall not apply.

(b) *Election to characterize exchange gain or loss on certain identified forward contracts, futures contracts and option contracts as capital gain or loss.*—(1) *In general.*—Except as provided in paragraph (b)(2) of this section, a taxpayer may elect, subject to the requirements of paragraph (b)(3) of this section, to treat any gain or loss recognized on a contract described in § 1.988-2(d)(1) as capital gain or loss, but only if the contract—

(i) Is a capital asset in the hands of the taxpayer;

(ii) Is not part of a straddle within the meaning of section 1092(c) (without regard to subsections (c) (4) or (e)); and

(iii) Is not a regulated futures contract or nonequity option with respect to which an election under section 988(c)(1)(D)(ii) is in effect.

If a valid election under this paragraph (b) is made with respect to a section 1256 contract, section 1256 shall govern the character of any gain or loss recognized on such contract.

(2) *Special rule for contracts that become part of a straddle after an election is made.*—If a contract which is the subject of an election under paragraph (b)(1) of this section becomes part of a straddle within the meaning of section 1092(c) (without regard to subsections (c)(4) or (e)) after the date of the election, the election shall be invalid with respect to gains from such contract and the Commissioner, in his sole discretion, may invalidate the election with respect to losses.

(3) *Requirements for making the election.*—A taxpayer elects to treat gain or loss on a transaction described in paragraph (b)(1) of this section as capital gain or loss by clearly identifying such transaction on its books and records on the date the transaction is entered into. No specific language or account is necessary for identifying a transaction referred to in the preceding sentence. However, the method of identification must be consistently applied and must clearly identify the pertinent transaction as subject to the section 988(a)(1)(B) election. The Commissioner, in his sole discretion, may invalidate any purported election that does not comply with the preceding sentence.

(4) *Verification.*—A taxpayer that has made an election under § 1.988-3(b)(3) must attach to his income tax return a statement which sets forth the following:

(i) A description and the date of each election made by the taxpayer during the taxpayer's taxable year;

(ii) A statement that each election made during the taxable year was made before the close of the date the transaction was entered into;

(iii) A description of any contract for which an election was in effect and the date such contract expired or was otherwise sold or exchanged during the taxable year;

(iv) A statement that the contract was never part of a straddle as defined in section 1092; and

(v) A statement that all transactions subject to the election are included on the statement attached to the taxpayer's income tax return.

In addition to any penalty that may otherwise apply, the Commissioner, in his sole discretion, may invalidate any or all elections made during the taxable year under § 1.988-3(b)(1) if the taxpayer fails to verify each election as provided in this § 1.988-3(b)(4). The preceding sentence shall not apply if the taxpayer's failure to verify each election was due to reasonable cause or bona fide mistake. The burden of proof to show reasonable cause or bona fide mistake made in good faith is on the taxpayer.

(5) *Independent verification.*—(i) *Effect of independent verification.*—If the taxpayer receives independent verification of the election in paragraph (b)(3) of this section, the taxpayer shall be presumed to have satisfied the requirements of paragraphs (b)(3) and (4) of this section. A contract that is a part of a straddle as defined in section 1092 may not be independently verified and shall be subject to the rules of paragraph (b)(2) of this section.

(ii) *Requirements for independent verification.*—A taxpayer receives independent verification of the election in paragraph (b)(3) of this section if—

(A) The taxpayer establishes a separate account(s) with an unrelated broker(s) or dealer(s) through which all transactions to be independently verified pursuant to this paragraph (b)(5) are conducted and reported.

(B) Only transactions entered into on or after the date the taxpayer establishes such account may be recorded in the account.

(C) Transactions subject to the election of paragraph (b)(3) of this section are entered into such account on the date such transactions are entered into.

(D) The broker or dealer provides the taxpayer a statement detailing the transactions conducted through such account and includes on such statement the following: "Each transaction identified in this account is subject to the election set forth in section 988(a)(1)(B)."

(iii) *Special effective date for independent verification.*—The rules of this paragraph (b)(5) shall be effective for transactions entered into after March 17, 1992.

(6) *Effective date.*—Except as otherwise provided, this paragraph (b) is effective for taxable years beginning on or after September 21, 1989. For prior taxable years, any reasonable contemporaneous election meeting the requirements of section 988(a)(1)(B) shall satisfy this paragraph (b).

(c) *Exchange gain or loss treated as interest.*—(1) *In general.*—Except as provided in this paragraph (c)(1), exchange gain or loss realized on a section 988 transaction shall not be treated as interest income or expense. Exchange gain or loss realized on a section 988 transaction shall be treated as interest income or expense as provided in paragraph (c)(2) of this section with regard to tax exempt bonds, § 1.988-2(e)(2)(ii)(B), § 1.988-5, and in administrative pronouncements. See § 1.861-9T(b), providing rules for the allocation of certain items of exchange gain or loss in the same manner as interest expense.

(2) *Exchange loss realized by the holder on nonfunctional currency tax exempt bonds.*—Exchange loss realized by the holder of a debt instrument the interest on which is excluded from gross income under section 103(a) or any similar provision of law shall be treated as an offset to and reduce total interest income received or accrued with respect to such instrument. Therefore, to the extent of total interest

income, no exchange loss shall be recognized. This paragraph (c)(2) shall be effective with respect to debt instruments acquired on or after June 24, 1987.

(d) *Effective date.*—Except as otherwise provided in this section, this section shall be effective for taxable years beginning after December 31, 1986. Thus, except as otherwise provided in this section, any payments made or received with respect to a section 988 transaction in taxable years beginning after December 31, 1986, are subject to this section. Thus, for example, a payment made prior to January 1, 1987, under a forward contract that results in the deferral of a loss under section 1092 to a taxable year beginning after December 31, 1986, is not characterized as an ordinary loss by virtue of paragraph (a) of this section because payment was made prior to January 1, 1987. [Reg. § 1.988-3.]

☐ *[T.D. 8400, 3-16-92.]*

»»→ Caution: The Treasury Department has identified Reg. § 1.988-4, as amended by T.D. 9794, as a significant tax regulation that imposes an undue financial burden on U.S. taxpayers and/or adds undue complexity to the federal tax laws, pursuant to Executive Order 13789 (issued April 21, 2017) (Notice 2017-38, I.R.B. 2017-30, 147). In a subsequent report, published October 16, 2017, Treasury recommended planned actions that would reduce the burden of these regulations, including an extension of the application date of T.D. 9794 (see Notice 2022-34, I.R.B. 2022-34, 150).

§ 1.988-4. Source of gain or loss realized on a section 988 transfer.—(a) *In general.*—Except as otherwise provided in § 1.988-5 and this section, the source of exchange gain or loss shall be determined by reference to the residence of the taxpayer. This rule applies even if the taxpayer has made an election under § 1.988-3(b) to characterize exchange gain or loss as capital gain or loss. This section takes precedence over section 865.

(b) *Qualified business unit.*—(1) *In general.*—The source of exchange gain or loss shall be determined by reference to the residence of the qualified business unit of the taxpayer on whose books the asset, liability, or item of income or expense giving rise to such gain or loss is properly reflected.

(2) *Proper reflection on the books of the taxpayer or qualified business unit.*—(i) *In general.*—For purposes of paragraph (b)(1) of this section, the principles of § 1.987-2(b) shall apply in determining whether an asset, liability, or item of income or expense is reflected on the books and records of a qualified business unit.

(ii) *Effective/applicability date.*—Generally, paragraph (b)(2)(i) of this section shall apply to taxable years beginning on or after one year after the first day of the first taxable year following December 7, 2016. If pursuant to § 1.987-11(b) a taxpayer applies §§ 1.987-1 through 1.987-11 beginning in a taxable year prior to the earliest taxable year described in § 1.987-11(a), then paragraph (b)(2)(i) of this section shall apply to taxable years of the taxpayer beginning on or after the first day of such prior taxable year.

(c) *Effectively connected exchange gain or loss.*—Notwithstanding paragraphs (a) and (b) of this section, exchange gain or loss that under principles similar to those set forth in § 1.864-4(c) arises from the conduct of a United States trade or business shall be sourced in the United States and such gain or loss shall be treated as effectively connected to the conduct of a United States trade or business for purposes of sections 871(b) and 882(a)(1).

(d) *Residence.*—(1) *In general.*—Except as otherwise provided in this paragraph (d), for purposes of sections 985 through 989, the residence of any person shall be—

(i) In the case of an individual, the country in which such individual's tax home (as defined in section 911(d)(3)) is located;

(ii) In the case of a corporation, partnership, trust or estate which is a United States person (as defined in section 7701(a)(30)), the United States; and

(iii) In the case of a corporation, partnership, trust or estate which is not a United States person, a country other than the United States.

If an individual does not have a tax home (as defined in section 911(d)(3)), the residence of such individual shall be the United States if such individual is a United States citizen or a resident alien and shall be a country other than the United States if such individual is not a United States citizen or resident alien. If the taxpayer is a U.S. person and has no principal place of business outside the United States, the residence of the taxpayer is the United States. Notwithstanding paragraph (d)(1)(ii) of this section, if a partnership is formed or availed of to avoid tax by altering the source of exchange gain or loss, the source of such gain or loss shall be determined by reference to the residence of the partners rather than the partnership.

(2) *Exception.*—In the case of a qualified business unit of any taxpayer (including an individual), the residence of such unit shall be the country in which the principal place of business of such qualified business unit is located.

(3) *Partner in a partnership not engaged in a U.S. trade or business under section 864(b)(2).*—The determination of residence shall be made at the partner level (without regard to whether the partnership is a qualified business unit of the partners) in the case of partners in a partnership that are not engaged in a U.S. trade or business by reason of section 864(b)(2).

(e) *Special rule for certain related party loans.*—(1) *In general.*—In the case of a loan by a United States person or a related person to a 10 percent owned foreign corporation, or a corporation that meets the 80 percent foreign business requirements test of section 861(c)(1), other than a corporation subject to § 1.861-11T(e)(2)(i), which is denominated in, or determined by reference to, a currency other than the U.S. dollar and bears interest at a rate at least 10 percentage points higher than the Federal mid-term rate (as determined under section 1274(d)) at the time such loan is entered into, the following rules shall apply—

(i) For purposes of section 904 only, such loan shall be marked to market annually on the earlier of the last business day of the United States person's (or related person's) taxable year or the date the loan matures; and

(ii) Any interest income earned with respect to such loan for the taxable year shall be treated as income from sources within the United States to the extent of any notional loss attributable to such loan under paragraph (d)(1)(i) of this section.

(2) *United States person.*—For purposes of this paragraph (e), the term "United States person" means a person described in section 7701(a)(30).

(3) *Loans by related foreign persons.*—(i) *In general.*—[Reserved]

(ii) *Definition of related person.*—For purposes of this paragraph (e), the term "related person" has the meaning given such term by section 954(d)(3) except that such section shall be applied by substituting "United States person" for "controlled foreign corporation" each place such term appears.

(4) *10 percent owned foreign corporation.*—For purposes of this paragraph (e), the term "10 percent owned foreign corporation" means any foreign corporation in which the United States person owns directly or indirectly (within the meaning of section 318(a)) at least 10 percent of the voting stock.

(f) *Exchange gain or loss treated as interest under § 1.988-3.*—Notwithstanding the provisions of this section, any gain or loss realized on a section 988 transaction that is treated as interest income or expense under § 1.988-3(c)(1) shall be sourced or allocated and apportioned pursuant to section 861(a)(1), 862(a)(1), or 864(e) as the case may be.

(g) *Exchange gain or loss allocated in the same manner as interest under § 1.861-9T.*—The allocation and apportionment of exchange gain or loss under § 1.861-9T shall not affect the source of exchange gain or loss for purposes of sections 871(a), 881, 1441, 1442 and 6049.

(h) *Effective date.*—This section shall be effective for taxable years beginning after December 31, 1986. Thus, any payments made or received with respect to a section 988 transaction in taxable years beginning after December 31, 1986, are subject to this section. [Reg. § 1.988-4.]

☐ *[T.D. 8400, 3-16-92. Amended by T.D. 9794, 12-7-2016.]*

§ 1.988-5. Section 988(d) hedging transactions.—(a) *Integration of a nonfunctional currency debt instrument and a § 1.988-5(a) hedge.*—(1) *In general.*—This paragraph (a) applies to a qualified hedging transaction as defined in this paragraph (a)(1). A qualified hedging transaction is an integrated economic transaction, as provided in paragraph (a)(5) of this section, consisting of a qualifying debt instrument as defined in paragraph (a)(3) of this section and a § 1.988-5(a) hedge as defined in paragraph (a)(4) of this section. If a taxpayer enters into a transaction that is a qualified hedging transaction, no exchange gain or loss is recognized by the taxpayer on the qualifying debt instrument or on the § 1.988-5(a) hedge for the period that either is part of a qualified hedging transaction, and the transactions shall be integrated as provided in paragraph (a)(9) of this section. However, if the qualified hedging transaction results in a synthetic nonfunctional currency denominated debt instrument, such instrument shall be subject to the rules of § 1.988-2(b).

(2) *Exception.*—This paragraph (a) does not apply with respect to a qualified hedging transaction that creates a synthetic asset or liability denominated in, or determined by reference to, a currency other than the U.S. dollar if the rate that approximates the Federal short-term rate in such currency is at least 20 percentage points higher than the Federal short term rate (determined under section 1274(d)) on the date the taxpayer identifies the transaction as a qualified hedging transaction.

(3) *Qualifying debt instrument.*—(i) *In general.*—A qualifying debt instrument is a debt instrument described in § 1.988-1(a)(2)(i), regardless of whether denominated in, or determined by reference to, nonfunctional currency (including dual currency debt instruments, multi-currency debt instruments and contingent payment debt instruments). A qualifying debt instrument does not include accounts payable, accounts receivable or similar items of expense or income.

(ii) *Special rule for debt instrument of which all payments are proportionately hedged.*—If a debt instrument satisfies the requirements of paragraph (a)(3)(i) of this section, and all principal and interest payments under the instrument are hedged in the same proportion, then for purposes of this paragraph (a), that portion of the instrument that is hedged is eligible to be treated as a qualifying debt instrument, and the rules of this paragraph (a) shall apply separately to such qualifying debt instrument. See Example 8 in paragraph (a)(9)(iv) of this section.

(4) *Section 1.988-5(a) hedge.*—(i) *In general.*—A § 1.988-5(a) hedge (hereinafter referred to in this paragraph (a) as a "hedge") is a spot contract, futures contract, forward contract, option contract, notional principal contract, currency swap contract, similar financial instrument, or series or combination thereof, that when integrated with a qualifying debt instrument permits the calculation of a yield to maturity (under principles of section 1272) in the currency in which the synthetic debt instrument is denominated (as determined under paragraph (a) (9)(ii)(A) of this section).

(ii) *Retroactive application of definition of currency swap contract.*—A taxpayer may apply the definition of currency swap contract set forth in § 1.988-2(e)(2)(ii) in lieu of the definition of swap agreement in section 2(e)(5) of Notice 87-11, 1987-1 C.B. 423 to transactions entered into after December 31, 1986 and before September 21, 1989.

(5) *Definition of integrated economic transaction.*—A qualifying debt instrument and a hedge are an integrated economic transaction if all of the following requirements are satisfied—

(i) All payments to be made or received under the qualifying debt instrument (or amounts determined by reference to a nonfunctional currency) are fully hedged on the date the taxpayer identifies the transaction under paragraph (a) of this section as a qualified hedging transaction such that a yield to maturity (under principles of section 1272) in the currency in which the synthetic debt instrument is denominated (as determined under paragraph (a)(9)(ii)(A) of this section) can be calculated. Any contingent payment features of the qualifying debt instrument must be fully offset by the hedge such that the synthetic debt instrument is not classified as a contingent payment debt instrument. See *Examples 6* and *7* of paragraph (a)(9)(iv) of this section.

(ii) The hedge is identified in accordance with paragraph (a)(8) of this section on or before the date the acquisition of the financial instrument (or instruments) constituting the hedge is settled or closed.

(iii) None of the parties to the hedge are related. The term "related" means the relationships defined in section 267(b) or section 707(b).

(iv) In the case of a qualified business unit with a residence, as defined in section 988(a)(3)(B), outside of the United States, both the qualifying debt instrument and the hedge are properly reflected on the books of such qualified business unit throughout the term of the qualified hedging transaction.

(v) Subject to the limitations of paragraph (a)(5) of this section, both the qualifying debt instrument and the hedge are entered into by the same individual, partnership, trust, estate, or corporation. With respect to a corporation, the same corporation must enter into both the qualifying debt instrument and the hedge whether or not such corporation is a member of an affiliated group of corporations that files a consolidated return.

(vi) With respect to a foreign person engaged in a U.S. trade or business that enters into a qualifying debt instrument or hedge through such trade or business, all items of income and expense associated with the qualifying debt instrument and the hedge (other than interest expense that is subject to § 1.882-5), would have been effectively connected with such U.S. trade or business throughout the term of the qualified hedging transaction had this paragraph (a) not applied.

(6) *Special rules for legging in and legging out of integrated treatment.*—(i) *Legging in.*—"Legging in" to integrated treatment under this paragraph (a) means that a hedge is entered into after the date the qualifying debt instrument is entered into or acquired, and the requirements of this paragraph (a) are satisfied on the date the hedge is entered into ("leg in date"). If a taxpayer legs into integrated treatment, the following rules shall apply—

(A) Exchange gain or loss shall be realized with respect to the qualifying debt instrument determined solely by reference to changes in exchange rates between—

(1) The date the instrument was acquired by the holder, or the date the obligor assumed the obligation to make payments under the instrument; and

(2) The leg in date.

(B) The recognition of such gain or loss will be deferred until the date the qualifying debt instrument matures or is otherwise disposed of.

(C) The source and character of such gain or loss shall be determined on the leg in date as if the qualifying debt instrument was actually sold or otherwise terminated by the taxpayer.

(ii) *Legging out.*—With respect to a qualifying debt instrument and hedge that are properly identified as a qualified hedging transaction, "legging out" of integrated treatment under this paragraph (a) means that the taxpayer disposes of or otherwise terminates all or any portion of the qualifying debt instrument or the hedge before maturity of the qualified hedging transaction. For purposes of the preceding sentence, if the taxpayer changes a material term of the qualifying debt instrument (for example, exercises an option to change the interest rate or index, or the maturity date) or the hedge (for example, changes the interest or exchange rates underlying the hedge, or the expiration date) before maturity of the qualified hedging transaction, the taxpayer will be deemed to have disposed of or otherwise terminated all or any portion of the qualifying debt instrument or the hedge, as applicable. A taxpayer that disposes of or terminates a qualified hedging transaction (that is, disposes of or terminates both the qualifying debt instrument and the hedge in their entirety on the same day) is considered to have disposed of or otherwise terminated the synthetic debt instrument rather than legging out. See paragraph (a)(9)(iv) of this section, *Example 10* for an illustration of this rule. If a taxpayer legs out of integrated treatment, the following rules apply:

(A) The transaction will be treated as a qualified hedging transaction during the time the requirements of this paragraph (a) were satisfied.

(B) If all of the instruments comprising the hedge (each such instrument, a component) are disposed of or otherwise terminated, the qualifying debt instrument is treated as sold or otherwise terminated by the taxpayer for its fair market value on the date the hedge is disposed of or otherwise terminated (the leg-out date), and any gain or loss (including gain or loss resulting from factors other than movements in exchange rates) from the identification date to the leg-out date is realized and recognized on the leg-out date. The spot rate on the leg-out date is used to determine exchange gain or loss on the debt instrument for the period beginning on the leg-out date and ending on the date such instrument matures or is disposed of or otherwise terminated. Proper adjustment must be made to reflect any gain or loss taken into account. The netting rule of § 1.988-2(b)(8) applies. See paragraph (a)(9)(iv) of this section, *Example 4* and *Example 5* for an illustration of this rule.

(C) If a hedge has more than one component (and such components have been properly identified as being part of the qualified hedging transaction) and at least one but not all of the components that comprise the hedge has been disposed of or otherwise terminated, or if part of any component of the hedge has been terminated (whether a hedge consists of a single or multiple components), the date such component (or part thereof) is disposed of or terminated is considered the leg-out date and the qualifying debt instrument is treated as sold or otherwise terminated by the taxpayer for its fair market value in accordance with the rules of paragraph (a)(6)(ii)(B) of this section on such leg-out date. In addition, all of the remaining components (or parts thereof) that have not been disposed of or otherwise terminated are treated as sold by the taxpayer for their fair market value on the leg-out date, and any gain or loss from the identification date to the leg-out date is realized and recognized on the leg-out date. To the extent relevant, the spot rate on the leg-out date is used to determine exchange gain or loss on the remaining components (or parts thereof) for the period beginning on the leg-out date and ending on the date such components (or parts thereof) are disposed of or otherwise terminated. See paragraph (a)(9)(iv) of this section, *Example 11* for an illustration of this rule.

(D) If the qualifying debt instrument is disposed of or otherwise terminated in whole or in part, the date of such disposition or termination is considered the leg-out date. Accordingly, the hedge (including all components making up the hedge in their entirety) that is part of the qualified hedging transaction is treated as sold by the taxpayer for its fair market value on the leg-out date, and any gain or loss from the identification date to the leg-out date is realized and recognized on the leg-out date. To the extent relevant, the spot rate on the leg-out date is used to determine exchange gain or loss on the hedge (including all components thereof) for the period beginning on the leg-out date and ending on the date such hedge is disposed of or otherwise terminated.

(E) Except as provided in paragraph (a)(8)(iii) of this section (regarding identification by the Commissioner), the part of the qualified hedging transaction that has not been disposed of or otherwise terminated (that is, the remaining debt instrument in its entirety even if partially hedged, or the remaining components of the hedge) cannot be part of a qualified hedging transaction for any period after the leg-out date.

(F) If a taxpayer legs out of a qualified hedging transaction and realizes a net gain with respect to the debt instrument that is disposed of or otherwise terminated, then paragraph (a)(6)(ii)(B), (C), and (D) of this section, as appropriate, will not apply if during the period beginning 30 days before the leg-out date and ending 30 days after that date the taxpayer enters into another transaction that, taken together with any remaining components of the hedge, hedges at least 50 percent of the remaining currency flow with respect to the qualifying debt instrument that was part of the qualified hedging transaction or, if appropriate, an equivalent amount under the hedge (or any remaining components thereof) that was part of the qualified hedging transaction. Similarly, in a case in which a hedge has multiple components that are part of a qualified hedging transaction, if the taxpayer legs out of a qualified hedging transaction by terminating one such component or a part of one or more such components and realizes a net gain with respect to the terminated component, components, or portions thereof, then paragraphs (a)(6)(ii)(B), (C), and (D) of this section, as appropriate, will not apply if the remaining components of the hedge (including parts thereof) by themselves hedge at least 50 percent of the remaining currency flow with respect to the qualifying debt instrument that was part of the qualified hedging transaction. See paragraph (a)(9)(iv) of this section, *Example 11* for an illustration of this rule.

(7) *Transactions part of a straddle.*—At the discretion of the Commissioner, a transaction shall not satisfy the requirements of paragraph (a)(5) of this section if the debt instrument making up the qualified hedging transaction is part of a straddle as defined in section 1092(c) prior to the time the qualified hedging transaction is identified.

(8) *Identification requirements.*—(i) *Identification by the taxpayer.*—A taxpayer must establish a record and before the close of the date the hedge is entered into, the taxpayer must enter into the record for each qualified hedging transaction the following information—

(A) The date the qualifying debt instrument and hedge were entered into;

(B) The date the qualifying debt instrument and the hedge are identified as constituting a qualified hedging transaction;

(C) The amount that must be deferred, if any, under paragraph (a)(6) of this section and the source and character of such deferred amount;

(D) A description of the qualifying debt instrument and the hedge; and

(E) A summary of the cash flow resulting from treating the qualifying debt instrument and the hedge as a qualified hedging transaction.

(ii) *Identification by trustee on behalf of beneficiary.*—A trustee of a trust that enters into a qualified hedging transaction may satisfy the identification requirements described in paragraph (a)(8)(i) of this section on behalf of a beneficiary of such trust.

(iii) *Identification by the Commissioner.*—If—

(A) A taxpayer enters into a qualifying debt instrument and a hedge but fails to comply with one or more of the requirements of this paragraph (a), and

(B) On the basis of all the facts and circumstances, the Commissioner concludes that the qualifying debt instrument and the hedge are, in substance, a qualified hedging transaction,

then the Commissioner may treat the qualifying debt instrument and the hedge as a qualified hedging transaction. The Commissioner may identify a qualifying debt instrument and a hedge as a qualified hedging transaction regardless of whether the qualifying debt instrument and the hedge are held by the same taxpayer.

(9) *Taxation of qualified hedging transactions.*—(i) *In general.*—(A) *General rule.*—If a transaction constitutes a qualified hedging transaction, the qualifying debt instrument and the hedge are integrated and treated as a single transaction with respect to the taxpayer that has entered into the qualified hedging transaction during the period that the transaction qualifies as a qualified hedging transaction. Neither the qualifying debt instrument nor the hedge that makes up the qualified hedging transaction shall be subject to section 263(g), 1092 or 1256 for the period such transactions are integrated. However, the qualified hedging transaction may be subject to section 263(g) or 1092 if such transaction is part of a straddle.

(B) *Special rule for income or expense of foreign persons effectively connected with a U.S. trade or business.*—Interest income of a foreign person resulting from a qualified hedging transaction entered into by such foreign person that satisfies the requirements of paragraph (a)(5)(vii) of this section shall be treated as effectively connected with a U.S. trade or business. Interest expense of a foreign person resulting from a qualified hedging transaction entered into by such foreign person that satisfies the requirements of paragraph (a)(5)(vii) of this section shall be allocated and apportioned under § 1.882-5 of the regulations.

(C) *Special rule for foreign persons that enter into qualified hedging transactions giving rise to U.S. source income not effectively connected with a U.S. trade or business.*—If a foreign person enters into a qualified hedging transaction that gives rise to U.S. source interest income (determined under the source rules for synthetic asset transactions as provided in this section) not effectively connected with a U.S. trade or business of such foreign person, for purposes of sections 871(a), 881, 1441, 1442 and 6049, the provisions of this paragraph (a) shall not apply and such sections of the Internal Revenue Code shall be applied separately to the qualifying debt instrument and the hedge. To the extent relevant to any foreign person, if the requirements of this paragraph (a) are otherwise met, the provisions of this paragraph (a) shall apply for all other purposes of the Internal Revenue Code (*e.g.*, for purposes of calculating the earnings and profits of a controlled foreign corporation that enters into a qualified hedging transaction through a qualified business unit resident outside the United States, income or expense with respect to such qualified hedging transaction shall be calculated under the provisions of this paragraph (a)).

(ii) *Income tax effects of integration.*—The effect of integrating and treating a transaction as a single transaction is to create a synthetic debt instrument for income tax purposes, which is subject to the original issue discount provisions of sections 1272 through 1288 and 163(e), the terms of which are determined as follows:

(A) *Denomination of synthetic debt instrument.*—In the case where the qualifying debt instrument is a borrowing, the denomination of the synthetic debt instrument is the same as the currency paid under the terms of the hedge to acquire the currency used to make payments under the qualifying debt instrument. In the case where the qualifying debt instrument is a lending, the denomination of the synthetic debt instrument is the same as the currency received under the terms of the hedge in exchange for amounts received under the qualifying debt instrument. For example, if the hedge is a forward contract to acquire British pounds for dollars, and the qualifying debt instrument is a borrowing denominated in British pounds, the synthetic debt instrument is considered a borrowing in dollars.

(B) *Term and accrual periods.*—The term of the synthetic debt instrument shall be the period beginning on the identification date and ending on the date the qualifying debt instrument matures or such earlier date that the qualifying debt instrument or hedge is disposed of or otherwise terminated. Unless otherwise clearly indicated by the payment interval under the hedge, the accrual period shall be a six month period which ends on the dates determined under section 1272(a)(5).

(C) *Issue price.*—The issue price of the synthetic debt instrument is the adjusted issue price of the qualifying debt instrument translated into the currency in which the synthetic debt instrument is denominated at the spot rate on the identification date.

(D) *Stated redemption price at maturity.*—In the case where the qualifying debt instrument is a borrowing, the stated redemption price at maturity shall be determined under section 1273(a)(2) on the identification date by reference to the amounts to be paid under the hedge to acquire the currency necessary to make interest and principal payments on the qualifying debt instrument. In the case where the qualifying debt instrument is a lending, the stated redemption price at maturity shall be determined under section 1273(a)(2) on the identification date by reference to the amounts to be received under the hedge in exchange for the interest and principal payments received pursuant to the terms of the qualifying debt instrument.

(iii) *Source of interest income and allocation of expense.*—Interest income from a synthetic debt instrument described in paragraph (a)(9)(ii) of this section shall be sourced by reference to the source of income under sections 861(a)(1) and 862(a)(1) of the qualifying debt instrument. The character for purposes of section 904 of interest income from a synthetic debt instrument shall be determined by reference to the character of the interest income from qualifying debt instrument. Interest expense from a synthetic debt instrument described in paragraph (a)(9)(ii) of this section shall be allocated and apportioned under §§1.861-8T through 1.861-12T or the successor sections thereof or under §1.882-5.

(iv) *Examples.*—The following examples illustrate the application of this paragraph (a)(9).

Example 1. (i) K is a U.S. corporation with the U.S. dollar as its functional currency. On December 24, 1989, K agrees to close the following transaction on December 31, 1989. K will borrow from an unrelated party on December 31, 1989, 100 British pounds (£) for 3 years at a 10 percent rate of interest, payable annually, with no principal payment due until the final installment. K will also enter into a currency swap contract with an unrelated counterparty under the terms of which—

(a) K will swap, on December 31, 1989, the £100 obtained from the borrowing for $100; and

(b) K will exchange dollars for pounds pursuant to the following table in order to obtain the pounds necessary to make payments on the pound borrowing:

DATE	*U.S. Dollars*	*Pounds*
December 31, 1990	8	10
December 31, 1991	8	10
December 31, 1992	108	110

(ii) The interest rate on the borrowing is set and the exchange rates on the swap are fixed on December 24, 1989. On December 31, 1989, K borrows the £100 and swaps such pounds for $100. Assume K has satisfied the identification requirements of paragraph (a)(8) of this section.

(iii) The pound borrowing (which constitutes a qualifying debt instrument under paragraph (a)(3) of this section) and the currency swap contract (which constitutes a hedge under paragraph (a)(4) of this section) are a qualified hedging transaction as defined in paragraph (a)(1) of this section. Accordingly, the pound borrowing and the swap are integrated and treated as one transaction with the following consequences:

(A) The integration of the pound borrowing and the swap results in a synthetic dollar borrowing with an issue price of $100 under section 1273(b)(2).

(B) The total amount of interest and principal of the synthetic dollar borrowing is equal to the dollar payments made by K under the currency swap contract (i.e., $8 in 1990, $8 in 1991, and $108 in 1992).

(C) The stated redemption price at maturity (defined in section 1273(a)(2)) is $100. Because the stated redemption price equals the issue price, there is no OID on the synthetic dollar borrowing.

(D) K may deduct the annual interest payments of $8 under section 163(a) (subject to any limitations on deductibility imposed by other provisions of the Code) according to its regular method of accounting. K has also paid $100 as a return of principal in 1992.

(E) K must allocate and apportion its interest expense with respect to the synthetic dollar borrowing under the rules of §§1.861-8T through 1.861-12T.

Example 2. (i) K, a U.S. corporation, has the U.S. dollar as its functional currency. On December 24, 1989, when the spot rate for Swiss francs (Sf) is Sf1 = $1, K enters into a forward contract to purchase Sf100 in exchange for $100.04 for delivery on December 31, 1989. The Sf100 are to be used for the purchase of a franc denominated debt instrument on December 31, 1989. The instrument will have a term of 3 years, an issue price of Sf100, and will bear interest at 6 percent, payable annually, with no repayment of principal until the final installment. On December 24, 1989, K also enters into a series of forward contracts to sell the franc interest and principal payments that will be received under the terms of the franc denominated debt instrument for dollars according to the following schedule:

Date	*U.S. Dollars*	*Francs*
December 31, 1990	6.12	6
December 31, 1991	6.23	6
December 31, 1992	112.16	106

(ii) On December 31, 1989, K takes delivery of the Sf100 and purchases the franc denominated debt instrument. Assume K satisfies the identification requirements of paragraph (a)(8) of this section. The purchase of the franc debt instrument (which constitutes a qualifying debt instrument under paragraph (a)(3) of this section) and the series of forward contracts (which constitute a hedge under paragraph (a)(4) of this section) are a qualified hedging transaction under paragraph (a)(1) of this section. Accordingly, the franc debt instrument and all the forward contracts are integrated and treated as one transaction with the following consequences:

(A) The integration of the franc debt instrument and the forward contracts results in a synthetic dollar debt instrument in an amount equal to the dollars exchanged under the forward contract to purchase the francs necessary to acquire the franc debt instrument. Accordingly, the issue price is $100.04 (section 1273(b)(2) of the Code).

(B) The total amount of interest and principal received by K with respect to the synthetic dollar debt instrument is equal to the dollars received under the forward sales contracts (i.e., $6.12 in 1990, $6.23 in 1991, and $112.16 in 1992).

(C) The synthetic dollar debt instrument is an installment obligation and its stated redemption price at maturity is $106.15 (i.e., $6.12 of the payments in 1990, 1991, and 1992 are treated as periodic interest payments under the principles of section 1273). Because the stated redemption price at maturity exceeds the issue price, under section 1273(a)(1) the synthetic dollar debt instrument has OID of $6.11.

(D) The yield to maturity of the synthetic dollar debt instrument is 8.00 percent, compounded annually. Assuming K is a calendar year taxpayer, it must include interest income of $8.00 in 1990 (of which $1.88 constitutes OID), $8.15 in 1991 (of which $2.03 constitutes OID), and $8.32 in 1992 (of which $2.20 constitutes OID). The amount of the final payment received by K in excess of the interest income includible is a return of principal and a payment of previously accrued OID.

(E) The source of the interest income shall be determined by applying sections 861(a)(1) and 862(a)(1) with reference to the franc interest income that would have been received had the transaction not been integrated.

Example 3. (i) K is an accrual method U.S. corporation with the U.S. dollar as its functional currency. On January 1, 1992, K borrows

100 British pounds (£) for 3 years at a 10% rate of interest payable on December 31 of each year with no principal payment due until the final installment. The spot rate on January 1, 1992, is £1 = $1.50. On January 1, 1993, when the spot rate is £1 = $1.60, K enters into a currency swap contract with an unrelated counterparty under the terms of which K will exchange dollars for pounds pursuant to the following table in order to obtain the pounds necessary to make the remaining payments on the pound borrowing:

DATE	*U.S. Dollars*	*Pounds*
December 31, 1993	12.80	10
December 31, 1994	12.80	10
December 31, 1994	160.00	100

(ii) Assume that British pound interest rates are still 10% and that K properly identifies the pound borrowing and the currency swap contract as a qualified hedging transaction as provided in paragraph (a)(8) of this section. Under paragraph (a)(6)(i) of this section, K must realize exchange gain or loss with respect to the pound borrowing determined solely by reference to changes in exchange rates between January 1, 1992 and January 1, 1993. (Thus, gain or loss from other factors such as movements in interest rates or changes in credit quality of K are not taken into account). Recognition of such gain or loss is deferred until K terminates its pound borrowing. Accordingly, K must defer exchange loss in the amount of $10 [(£100 × 1.50) – (£100 × 1.60)].

(iii) Additionally, the qualified hedging transaction is treated as a synthetic U.S. dollar debt instrument with an issue date of January 1, 1993, and a maturity date of December 31, 1994. The issue price of the synthetic debt instrument is $160 (£100 × 1.60, the spot rate on January 1, 1993) and the total amount of interest and principal is $185.60. The accrual period is the one year period beginning on January 1 and ending December 31 of each year. The stated redemption price at maturity is $160. Thus, K is treated as paying $12.80 of interest in 1993, $12.80 of interest in 1994, and $160 of principal in 1994. The interest expense from the synthetic instrument is allocated and apportioned in accordance with the rules of §§1.861-8T through 1.861-12T. Sections 263(g), 1092, and 1256 do not apply to the positions comprising the synthetic dollar borrowing.

Example 4. (i) K is an accrual method U.S. corporation with the U.S. dollar as its functional currency. On January 1, 2013, K borrows 100 British pounds (£) for 3 years at a 10% rate of interest payable on December 31 of each year with no principal payment due until the final installment. The spot rate on January 1, 2013, is £1 = $1.50. Also on January 1, 2013, K enters into a currency swap contract with an unrelated counterparty under the terms of which K will exchange dollars for pounds pursuant to the following table in order to obtain the pounds necessary to make the remaining payments on the pound borrowing:

DATE	*U.S. Dollars*	*Pounds*
December 31, 2013	12.00	10
December 31, 2014	12.00	10
December 31, 2015	162.00	110

(ii) Assume that K properly identifies the pound borrowing and the currency swap contract as a qualified hedging transaction as provided in paragraph (a)(1) of this section.

(iii) The pound borrowing (which constitutes a qualifying debt instrument under paragraph (a)(3) of this section) and the currency swap contract (which constitutes a hedge under paragraph (a)(4) of this section) are a qualified hedging transaction as defined in paragraph (a)(1) of this section. Accordingly, the pound borrowing and the swap are integrated and treated as one transaction with the following consequences:

(A) The integration of the pound borrowing and the swap results in a synthetic dollar borrowing with an issue price of $150 under section 1273(b)(2).

(B) The total amount of interest and principal of the synthetic dollar borrowing is equal to the dollar payments made by K under the currency swap contract (i.e., $12 in 2013, $12 in 2014, and $162 in 2015).

(C) The stated redemption price at maturity (defined in section 1273(a)(2)) is $150. Because the stated redemption price equals the issue price, there is no OID on the synthetic dollar borrowing.

(D) K may deduct the annual interest payments of $12 under section 163(a) (subject to any limitations on deductibility imposed by other provisions of the Code) according to its regular method of accounting. K has also paid $150 as a return of principal in 2015.

(E) K must allocate and apportion its interest expense from the synthetic instrument under the rules of §§1.861-8T through 1.861-12T.

(iv) Assume that on January 1, 2014, the spot exchange rate is £1 = $1.60, interest rates have not changed since January 1, 2013, (accordingly, assume that the market value of K's bond in pounds has not changed) and that K transfers its rights and obligations under the currency swap contract in exchange for $10. Under §1.988-2(e)(3)(iii), K will include in income as exchange gain $10 on January 1, 2014. Pursuant to paragraph (a)(6)(ii) of this section, the pound borrowing and the currency swap contract are treated as a qualified hedging transaction for 2013. The loss inherent in the pound borrowing from January 1, 2013, to January 1, 2014, is realized and recognized on January 1, 2014. Such loss is exchange loss in the amount of $10.00 [(£100 × $1.50, the spot rate on January 1, 2013) – (£100 × $1.60, the spot rate on January 1, 2014)]. For purposes of determining exchange gain or loss on the £100 principal amount of the debt instrument for the period January 1, 2014, to December 31, 2015, the spot rate on January 1, 2014 is used rather than the spot rate on the issue date. Thus, assuming that the spot rate on December 31, 2015, the maturity date, is £1 = $1.80, K realizes exchange loss in the amount of $20 [(£100 × $1.60) – (£100 × $1.80)]. Except as provided in paragraph (a)(8)(iii) (regarding identification by the Commissioner), the pound borrowing cannot be part of a qualified hedging transaction for any period subsequent to the leg out date.

Example 5. (i) K, a U.S. corporation, has the U.S. dollar as its functional currency. On January 1, 2013, when the spot rate for Swiss francs (Sf) is Sf1 = $.50, K converts $100 to Sf200 and purchases a franc denominated debt instrument. The instrument has a term of 3 years, an adjusted issue price of Sf200, and will bear interest at 5 percent, payable annually, with no repayment of principal until the final installment. The U.S. dollar interest rate on an equivalent instrument is 8% on January 1, 2013, compounded annually. On January 1, 2013, K also enters into a series of forward contracts to sell the franc interest and principal payments that will be received under the terms of the franc denominated debt instrument for dollars according to the following schedule:

DATE	*U.S. Dollars*	*Francs*
December 31, 2013	5.14	10
December 31, 2014	5.29	10
December 31, 2015	114.26	210

(ii) Assume K satisfies the identification requirements of paragraph (a)(8) of this section. Assume further that on January 1, 2014, the spot exchange rate is Sf1 = U.S.$ .5143, the U.S. dollar interest rate is 10%, compounded annually, and the Swiss franc interest rate is the same as on January 1, 2013 (5%, compounded annually). On January 1, 2014, K disposes of the forward contracts that were to mature on December 31, 2014, and December 31, 2015 and incurs a loss of $3.62 (the present value of $.10 with respect to the 2014 contract and $4.27 with respect to the 2015 contract).

(iii) The purchase of the franc debt instrument (which constitutes a qualifying debt instrument under paragraph (a)(3) of this section) and the series of forward contracts (which constitute a hedge under paragraph (a)(4) of this section) are a qualified hedging transaction under paragraph (a)(1) of this section. Accordingly, the franc debt instrument and all the forward contracts are integrated for the period beginning January 1, 2013, and ending January 1, 2014.

(A) The integration of the franc debt instrument and the forward contracts results in a synthetic dollar debt instrument with an issue price of $100.

(B) The total amount of interest and principal to be received by K with respect to the synthetic dollar debt instrument is equal to the dollars to be received under the forward sales contracts (i.e., $5.14 in 2013, $5.29 in 2014, and $114.26 in 2015).

(C) The synthetic dollar debt instrument is an installment obligation and its stated redemption price at maturity is $109.27 (i.e.,

$5.14 of the payments in 2013, 2014, and 2015 is treated as periodic interest payments under the principles of section 1273). Because the stated redemption price at maturity exceeds the issue price, under section 1273(a)(1) the synthetic dollar debt instrument has OID of $9.27.

(D) The yield to maturity of the synthetic dollar debt instrument is 8.00 percent, compounded annually. Assuming K is a calendar year taxpayer, it must include interest income of $8.00 in 2013 (of which $2.86 constitutes OID).

(E) The source of the interest income is determined by applying sections 861(a)(1) and 862(a)(1) with reference to the franc interest income that would have been received had the transaction not been integrated.

(iv) Because K disposed of the forward contracts on January 1, 2014, the rules of paragraph (a)(6)(ii) of this section shall apply. Accordingly, the $3.62 loss from the disposition of the forward contracts is realized and recognized on January 1, 2014. Additionally, K is deemed to have sold the franc debt instrument for $102.86, its fair market value in dollars on January 1, 2014. K will compute gain or loss with respect to the deemed sale of the franc debt instrument by subtracting its adjusted basis in the instrument ($102.86—the value of the Sf200 issue price at the spot rate on the identification date plus $2.86 of original issue discount accrued on the synthetic dollar debt instrument for 2013) from the amount realized on the deemed sale of $102.86. Thus K realizes and recognizes no gain or loss from the deemed sale of the debt instrument. The dollar amount used to determine exchange gain or loss with respect to the franc debt instrument is the Sf200 issue price on January 1, 2014, translated into dollars at the spot rate on January 1, 2014, of Sf1 = U.S.$ .5143. Except as provided in paragraph (a)(8)(iii) of this section (regarding identification by the Commissioner), the franc borrowing cannot be part of a qualified hedging transaction for any period subsequent to the leg out date.

Example 6. (i) K is a U.S. corporation with the dollar as its functional currency. On January 1, 1992, K issues a debt instrument with the following terms: the issue price is $1,000, the instrument pays interest annually at a rate of 8% on the $1,000 principal amount, the instrument matures on December 31, 1996, and the amount paid at maturity is the greater of zero or $2,000 less the U.S. dollar value (determined on December 31, 1996) of 150,000 Japanese yen.

(ii) Also on January 1, 1992, K enters into the following hedges with respect to the instrument described in the preceding paragraph: a forward contract under which K will sell 150,000 yen for $1,000 on December 31, 1996 (note that this forward rate assumes that interest rates in yen and dollars are equal); and an option contract that expires on December 31, 1996, under which K has the right (but not the obligation) to acquire 150,000 yen for $2,000. K will pay for the option by making payments to the writer of the option equal to $5 each December 31 from 1992 through 1996.

(iii) The net economic effect of these transactions is that K has created a liability with a principal amount and amount paid at maturity of $1,000, with an interest cost of 8.5% (8% on debt instrument, 0.5% option price) compounded annually. For example, if on December 31, 1996, the spot exchange rate is $1 = 100 yen, K pays $500 on the bond [$2,000 – (150,000 yen/$100)], and $500 in satisfaction of the forward contract [$1,000 – (150,000 yen/$100)]. If instead the spot exchange rate on December 31, 1996 is $1 = 200 yen, K pays $1,250 on the bond [$2,000 – (150,000 yen/$200)] and K receives $250 in satisfaction of the forward contract [$1,000 – (150,000 yen/$200)]. Finally, if the spot exchange rate on December 31, 1996 is $1 = 50 yen, K pays $0 on the bond [$2,000 – (150,000 yen/$50), but the bond holder is not required under the terms of the instrument to pay additional principal]; K exercises the option to buy 150,000 yen for $2,000; and K then delivers the 150,000 yen as required by the forward contract in exchange for $1,000.

(iv) Assume K satisfies the identification requirements of paragraph (a)(8) of this section. The debt instrument described in paragraph (i) of this *Example 6* (which constitutes a qualifying debt instrument under paragraph (a)(3) of this section) and the forward contract and option contract described in paragraph (ii) of this example (which constitute a hedge under paragraph (a)(4) of this section and are collectively referred to hereafter as "the contracts") together are a qualified hedging transaction under paragraph (a)(1) of this section. Accordingly, with respect to K, the debt instrument and the contracts are integrated, resulting in a synthetic dollar debt instrument with an issue price of $1000, a stated redemption price at maturity of $1000 and a yield to maturity of 8.5% compounded annually (with no original issue discount). K must allocate and apportion its annual interest expense of $85 under the rules of §§1.861-8T through 1.861-12T.

Example 7. (i) R is a U.S. corporation with the dollar as its functional currency. On January 1, 1995, R issues a debt instrument with the following terms: the issue price is 504 British pounds (£), the instrument pays interest at a rate of 3.7% (compounded semi-annually) on the £504 principal amount, the instrument matures on December 31, 1999, with a repayment at maturity of the £ 504 principal plus the proportional gain, if any, in the "Financial Times" 100 Stock Exchange (FTSE) index (determined by the excess of the value of the FTSE index on the maturity date over the value of the FTSE on the issue date, divided by the value of the FTSE index on the issue date, multiplied by the number of FTSE index contracts that could be purchased on the issue date for £504).

(ii) Also on January 1, 1995, R enters into a contract with a bank under which on January 1, 1995, R will swap the £504 for $1,000 (at the current spot rate). R will make U.S. dollar payments to the bank equal to 8.15% on the notional principal amount of $1,000 (compounded semiannually) for the period beginning January 1, 1995 and ending December 31, 1999. R will receive pound payments from the bank equal to 3.7% on the notional principal amount of £504 (compounded semi-annually) for the period beginning January 1, 1995 and ending December 31, 1999. On December 31, 1999, R will swap with the bank $1,000 for £504 plus the proportional gain, if any, in the FTSE index (computed as provided above).

(iii) Economically, both the indexed debt instrument and the hedging contract are hybrid instruments with the following components. The indexed debt instrument is composed of a par pound debt instrument that is assumed to have a 10.85% coupon (compounded semi-annually) plus an embedded FTSE equity index option for which the investor pays a premium of 7.15% (amortized semi-annually) on the pound principal amount. The combined effect is that the premium paid by the investor partially offsets the coupon payments resulting in a return of 3.7% (10.85% – 7.15%). Similarly, the dollar payments under the hedging contract to be made by R are computed by multiplying the dollar notional principal amount by an 8.00% rate (compounded semi-annually) which the facts assume would be the rate paid on a conventional currency swap plus a premium of 0.15% (amortized semi-annually) on the dollar notional principal amount for an embedded FTSE equity index option.

(iv) Assume R satisfies the identification requirements of paragraph (a)(8) of this section. The indexed debt instrument described in paragraph (i) of this *Example 7* constitutes a qualifying debt instrument under paragraph (a)(3) of this section. The hedging contract described in paragraph (ii) of this *Example 7* constitutes a hedge under paragraph (a)(4) of this section. Since both the pound exposure of the indexed debt instrument and the exposure to movements of the FTSE embedded in the indexed debt instrument are hedged such that a yield to maturity can be determined in dollars, the transaction satisfies the requirement of paragraph (a)(5)(i) of this section. Assuming the transactions satisfy the other requirements of paragraph (a)(5) of this section, the indexed debt instrument and hedge are a qualified hedging transaction under paragraph (a)(1) of this section. Accordingly, with respect to R, the debt instrument and the contracts are integrated, resulting in a synthetic dollar debt instrument with an issue price of $1000, a stated redemption price at maturity of $1000 and a yield to maturity of 8.15% compounded semi-annually (with no original issue discount). K must allocate and apportion its interest expense from the synthetic instrument under the rules §§1.861-8T through 1.861-12T.

Example 8. (i) K is a U.S. corporation with the U.S. dollar as its functional currency. On December 24, 1992, K agrees to close the following transaction on December 31, 1992. K will borrow from an unrelated party on December 31, 1992, 200 British pounds (£) for 3 years at a 10 percent rate of interest, payable annually, with no principal payment due until the final installment. K will also enter into a currency swap contract with an unrelated counterparty under the terms of which—

(A) K will swap, on December 31, 1992, £ 100 obtained from the borrowing for $100; and

(B) K will exchange dollars for pounds pursuant to the following table:

DATE	*U.S. Dollars*	*Pounds*
December 31, 1993	8	10
December 31, 1994	8	10
December 31, 1995	108	110

(ii) The interest rate on the borrowing is set and the exchange rates on the swap are fixed on December 24, 1992. On December 31, 1992, K borrows the £200 and swaps £100 for $100. Assume K has satisfied the identification requirements of paragraph (a)(8) of this section.

(iii) The £200 debt instrument satisfies the requirements of paragraph (a)(3)(i) of this section. Because all principal and interest payments under the instrument are hedged in the same proportion (50% of all interest and principal payments are hedged), 50% of the payments under the £200 instrument (principal amount of £100 and annual interest of £10) are treated as a qualifying debt instrument for purposes of paragraph (a) of this section. Thus, the distinct £100 borrowing and the currency swap contract (which constitutes a hedge under paragraph (a)(4) of this section) are a qualified hedging transaction as defined in paragraph (a)(1) of this section. Accordingly, £100 of the pound borrowing and the swap are integrated and treated as one synthetic dollar transaction with the following consequences:

(A) The integration of £100 of the pound borrowing and the swap results in a synthetic dollar borrowing with an issue price of $100 under section 1273(b)(2).

(B) The total amount of interest and principal of the synthetic dollar borrowing is equal to the dollar payments made by K under the currency swap contract (i.e., $8 in 1993, $8 in 1994, and $108 in 1995).

(C) The stated redemption price at maturity (defined in section 1273(a)(2)) is $100. Because the stated redemption price equals the issue price, there is no OID on the synthetic dollar borrowing.

(D) K may deduct the annual interest payments of $8 under section 163(a) (subject to any limitations on deductibility imposed by other provisions of the Code) according to its regular method of accounting. K has also paid $100 as a return of principal in 1995.

(E) K must allocate and apportion its interest expense from the synthetic instrument under the rules of §§1.861-8T through 1.861-12T.

That portion of the £200 pound debt instrument that is not hedged (*i.e.*, £100) is treated as a separate debt instrument subject to the rules of §1.988-2(b) and §§1.861-8T through 1.861-12T.

Example 9. (i) K is an accrual method U.S. corporation with the U.S. dollar as its functional currency. On January 1, 1992, K borrows 100 British pounds (£) for 3 years at a 10% rate of interest payable on December 31 of each year with no principal payment due until the final installment. On the same day, K enters into a currency swap agreement with an unrelated bank under which K agrees to the following:

(A) On January 1, 1992, K will exchange the £100 borrowed for $150.

(B) For the period beginning January 1, 1992 and ending December 31, 1994, K will pay at the end of each month an amount determined by multiplying $150 by one month LIBOR less 65 basis points and receive from the bank on December 31st of 1992, 1993, and 1994, £10.

(C) On December 31, 1994, K will exchange $150 for £100.

Assume K satisfies the identification requirements of paragraph (a)(8) of this section.

(ii) The pound borrowing (which constitutes a qualifying debt instrument under paragraph (a)(3) of this section) and the currency swap contract (which constitutes a hedge under paragraph (a)(4) of this section) are a qualified hedging transaction as defined in paragraph (a)(1) of this section. Accordingly, the pound borrowing and the swap are integrated and treated as one transaction with the following consequences:

(A) The integration of the pound borrowing and the swap results in a synthetic dollar borrowing with an issue price of $150 under section 1273(b)(2).

(B) The total amount of interest and principal of the synthetic dollar borrowing is equal to the dollar payments made by K under the currency swap contract.

(C) The stated redemption price at maturity (defined in section 1273(a)(2)) is $150. Because the stated redemption price equals the issue price, there is no OID on the synthetic dollar borrowing.

(D) K may deduct the monthly variable interest payments under section 163(a) (subject to any limitations on deductibility imposed by other provisions of the Code) according to its regular method of accounting. K has also paid $150 as a return of principal in 1994.

(E) K must allocate and apportion its interest expense from the synthetic instrument under the rules of §§1.861-8T through 1.861-12T.

Example 10. (i) K is an accrual method U.S. corporation with the U.S. dollar as its functional currency. On January 1, 1992, K loans 100 British pounds (£) for 3 years at a 10% rate of interest payable on December 31 of each year with no principal payment due until the final installment. The spot rate on January 1, 1992, is £1 = $1.50. Also on January 1, 1992, K enters into a currency swap contract with an unrelated counterparty under the terms of which K will exchange pounds for dollars pursuant to the following table:

DATE	*Pounds*	*Dollars*
December 31, 1992	10	12
December 31, 1993	10	12
December 31, 1994	110	162

(ii) Assume that K properly identifies the pound borrowing and the currency swap contract as a qualified hedging transaction as provided in paragraph (a)(1) of this section.

(iii) The pound loan (which constitutes a qualifying debt instrument under paragraph (a)(3) of this section) and the currency swap contract (which constitutes a hedge under paragraph (a)(4) of this section) are a qualified hedging transaction as defined in paragraph (a)(1) of this section. Accordingly, the pound loan and the swap are integrated and treated as one transaction with the following consequences:

(A) The integration of the pound loan and the swap results in a synthetic dollar loan with an issue price of $150 under section 1273(b)(2).

(B) The total amount of interest and principal of the synthetic dollar loan is equal to the dollar payments received by K under the currency swap contract (i.e., $12 in 1992, $12 in 1993, and $162 in 1994).

(C) The stated redemption price at maturity (defined in section 1273(a)(2)) is $150. Because the stated redemption price equals the issue price, there is no OID on the synthetic dollar loan.

(D) K must include in income as interest $12 in 1992, 1993, and 1994.

(E) The source of the interest income shall be determined by applying sections 861(a)(1) and 862(a)(1) with reference to the pound interest income that would have been received had the transaction not been integrated.

(iv) On January 1, 1993, K transfers both the pound loan and the currency swap to B, its wholly owned U.S. subsidiary, in exchange for B stock in a transfer that satisfies the requirements of section 351. Under paragraph (a)(6) of this section, the transfer of both instruments is not "legging out." Rather, K is considered to have transferred the synthetic dollar loan to B in a transaction in which gain or loss is not recognized. B's basis in the loan under section 362 is $100.

Example 11. (i) K is a domestic corporation with the U.S. dollar as its functional currency. On January 1, 2013, K borrows 100 British pounds (£) for two years at a 10% rate of interest payable on December 31 of each year with no principal payment due until maturity on December 31, 2014. Assume that the spot rate on January 1, 2013, is £1=$1. On the same date, K enters into two swap contracts with an unrelated counterparty that economically results in the transformation of the fixed rate £100 borrowing to a floating rate dollar borrowing. The terms of the swaps are as follows:

(A) *Swap #1, Currency swap.* On January 1, 2013, K will exchange £100 for $100.

(*1*) On December 31 of both 2013 and 2014, K will exchange $8 for £10;

(*2*) On December 31, 2014, K will exchange $100 for £100.

(B) *Swap #2, Interest rate swap.* On December 31 of both 2013 and 2014, K will pay LIBOR times a notional principal amount of $100 and will receive 8% times the same $100 notional principal amount.

(ii) Assume that K properly identifies the pound borrowing and the swap contracts as a qualified hedging transaction as provided in paragraph (a)(8)(i) of this section and that the other relevant requirements of paragraph (a) of this section are satisfied.

(iii) On January 1, 2014, the spot exchange rate is £1=$2; the U.S. dollar LIBOR rate of interest is 9%; the market value of K's note in pounds has not changed; and K terminates swap #2. Because interest rates have increased from 8% to 9%, K will incur a loss of ($.92) (the present value of the ($1) difference between the 8% and 9% interest payments discounted at the current interest rate of 9%) with respect to the termination of such swap on January 1, 2014. Pursuant to paragraph (a)(6)(ii)(C) of this section, K must treat swap #1 as having been sold for its fair market value on the leg-out date, which is the date swap #2 is terminated. K must realize and recognize gain of $100.92 (the present value of £110 discounted in pounds to equal £100 x $2 ($200) less the present value of $108 ($99.08)). The loss inherent in the pound borrowing from January 1, 2013 to January 1, 2014 is realized and recognized on January 1, 2014. Such loss is exchange loss in the amount of $100 (the present value of £110 that was to be paid at the end of the year discounted at pound interest rates to equal £100 times the change in exchange rates (£100 x $1, the spot rate on January 1, 2013) - (£100 x $2, the spot rate on January 1, 2014)). Pursuant to paragraph (a)(6)(ii)(E) of this section, except as provided in paragraph (a)(8)(iii) of this section (regarding identification by the Commissioner), the pound borrowing and currency swap cannot be part of a qualified hedging transaction for any period after the leg-out date.

(iv) Assume the facts are the same as in paragraph (iii) of this *Example* except that on January 1, 2014, the U.S. dollar LIBOR rate of interest is 7% rather than 9%. When K terminates swap #2, K will realize gain of $0.93 (the present value of the ($1) difference between the 8% and 7% interest payments discounted at the current interest rate of 7%) received with respect to the termination on January 1, 2014. Fifty percent or more of the remaining pound cash flow of the pound borrowing remains hedged after the termination of swap #2. Accordingly, under paragraph (a)(6)(ii)(F) of this section, paragraphs (a)(6)(ii)(B) and (C) of this section do not apply, and the gain on swap #1 and the loss on the qualifying debt instrument are not taken into account. Thus, K will include in income $0.93 realized from the termination of swap #2.

(10) *Transition rules and effective dates for certain provisions.*—(i) *Coordination with Notice 87-11.*—Any transaction entered into prior to September 21, 1989 which satisfied the requirements of Notice 87-11, 1987-1 C.B. 423, shall be deemed to satisfy the requirements of paragraph (a) of this section.

(ii) *Prospective application to contingent payment debt instruments.*—In the case of a contingent payment debt instrument, the definition of qualifying debt instrument set forth in paragraph (a)(3)(i) of this section applies to transactions entered into after March 17, 1992.

(iii) *Prospective application of partial hedging rule.*—Paragraph (a)(3)(ii) of this section is effective for transactions entered into after March 17, 1992.

(iv) *Effective/applicability dates for legging in and legging out rules.*—(A) The rules of paragraph (a)(6)(i) of this section are effective for qualified hedging transactions that are legged into after March 17, 1992.

(B) The rules of paragraph (a)(6)(ii) and *Example 11* of paragraph (a)(9)(iv) of this section apply to leg-outs that occur on or after September 6, 2012.

(b) *Hedged executory contracts.*—(1) *In general.*—If the taxpayer enters into a hedged executory contract as defined in paragraph (b)(2) of this section, the executory contract and the hedge shall be integrated as provided in paragraph (b)(4) of this section.

(2) *Definitions.*—(i) *Hedged executory contract.*—A hedged executory contract is an executory contract as defined in paragraph (b)(2)(ii) of this section that is the subject of a hedge as defined in paragraph (b)(2)(iii) of this section, provided that the following requirements are satisfied—

(A) The executory contract and the hedge are identified as a hedged executory contract as provided in paragraph (b)(3) of this section.

(B) The hedge is entered into (*i.e.*, settled or closed, or in the case of nonfunctional currency deposited in an account with a bank or other financial institution, such currency is acquired and deposited) on or after the date the executory contract is entered into and before the accrual date as defined in paragraph (b)(2)(iv) of this section.

(C) The executory contract is hedged in whole or in part throughout the period beginning with the date the hedge is identified in accordance with paragraph (b)(3) of this section and ending on or after the accrual date.

(D) None of the parties to the hedge are related. The term related means the relationships defined in section 267(b) and section 707(c)(1).

(E) In the case of a qualified business unit with a residence, as defined in section 988(a)(3)(B), outside of the United States, both the executory contract and the hedge are properly reflected on the books of the same qualified business unit.

(F) Subject to the limitations of paragraph (b)(2)(i)(E) of this section, both the executory contract and the hedge are entered into by the same individual, partnership, trust, estate, or corporation. With respect to a corporation, the same corporation must enter into both the executory contract and the hedge whether or not such corporation is a member of an affiliated group of corporations that files a consolidated return.

(G) With respect to a foreign person engaged in a U.S. trade or business that enters into an executory contract or hedge through such trade or business, all items of income and expense associated with the executory contract and the hedge would have been effectively connected with such U.S. trade or business throughout the term of the hedged executory contract had this paragraph (b) not applied.

(ii) *Executory contract.*—(A) *In general.*—Except as provided in paragraph (b)(2)(ii)(B) of this section, an executory contract is an agreement entered into before the accrual date to pay nonfunctional currency (or an amount determined with reference thereto) in the future with respect to the purchase of property used in the ordinary course of the taxpayer's business, or the acquisition of a service (or services), in the future, or to receive nonfunctional currency (or an amount determined with reference thereto) in the future with respect to the sale of property used or held for sale in the ordinary course of the taxpayer's business, or the performance of a service (or services), in the future. Notwithstanding the preceding sentence, a contract to buy or sell stock shall be considered an executory contract. (Thus, for example, a contract to sell stock of an affiliate is an executory contract for this purpose.) On the accrual date, such agreement ceases to be considered an executory contract and is treated as an account payable or receivable.

(B) *Exceptions.*—An executory contract does not include a section 988 transaction. For example, a forward contract to purchase nonfunctional currency is not an executory contract. An executory contract also does not include a transaction described in paragraph (c) of this section.

(C) *Effective date for contracts to buy or sell stock.*—That part of paragraph (b)(2)(ii)(A) of this section which provides that a contract to buy or sell stock shall be considered an executory contract applies to contracts to buy or sell stock entered into on or after March 17, 1992.

(iii) *Hedge.*—(A) *In general.*—For purposes of this paragraph (b), the term hedge means a deposit of nonfunctional currency in a hedging account (as defined in paragraph (b)(3)(iii)(D) of this section), a forward or futures contract described in § 1.988-1(a)(1)(ii) and (2)(iii), or combination thereof, which reduces the risk of exchange rate fluctuations by reference to the taxpayer's functional currency with respect to nonfunctional currency payments made or received under an executory contract. The term hedge also includes an option contract described in § 1.988-1(a)(1)(ii) and (2)(iii), but only if the option's expiration date is on or before the accrual date. The premium paid for an option that lapses shall be integrated with the executory contract.

(B) *Special rule for series of hedges.*—A series of hedges as defined in paragraph (b)(3)(iii)(A) of this section shall be considered a hedge if the executory contract is hedged in whole or in part throughout the period beginning with the date the hedge is identified in accordance with paragraph (b)(3)(i) of this section and ending on or after the accrual date. A taxpayer that enters into a series of hedges will be deemed to have satisfied the preceding sentence if the hedge that succeeds a hedge that has been terminated is entered into no later than the business day following such termination.

(C) *Special rules for historical rate rollovers.*—(*1*) *Definition.*—A historical rate rollover is an extension of the maturity date of a forward contract where the new forward rate is adjusted on the rollover date to reflect the taxpayer's gain or loss on the contract as of the rollover date plus the time value of such gain or loss through the new maturity date.

(*2*) *Certain historical rate rollovers considered a hedge.*—A historical rate rollover is considered a hedge if the rollover date is before the accrual date.

(3) *Treatment of time value component of certain historical rate rollovers that are hedges.*—Interest income or expense determined under § 1.988-2(d)(2)(v) with respect to a historical rate rollover shall be considered part of a hedge if the period beginning on the first date a hedging contract is rolled over and ending on the date payment is made or received under the executory contract does not exceed 183 days. Such interest income or expense shall not be recognized and shall be an adjustment to the income from, or expense of, the services performed or received under the executory contract, or to the amount realized or basis of the property sold or purchased under the executory contract. For the treatment of such interest income or expense that is not considered part of a hedge, see § 1.988-2(d)(2)(v).

(D) *Special rules regarding deposits of nonfunctional currency in a hedging account.*—A hedging account is an account with a bank or other financial institution used exclusively for deposits of nonfunctional currency used to hedge executory contracts. For purposes of determining the basis of units in such account that comprise the hedge, only those units in the account as of the accrual date shall be taken into consideration. A taxpayer may adopt any reasonable convention (consistently applied to all hedging accounts) to determine which units comprise the hedge as of the accrual date and the basis of the units as of such date.

(E) *Interest income on deposit of nonfunctional currency in a hedging account.*—Interest income on a deposit of nonfunctional currency in a hedging account may be taken into account for purposes of determining the amount of a hedge if such interest is accrued on or before the accrual date. However, such interest income shall be included in income as provided in section 61. For example, if a taxpayer with the dollar as its functional currency enters into an executory contract for the purchase and delivery of a machine in one year for 100 British pounds (£), and on such date deposits £90.91 in a properly identified bank account that bears interest at the rate of 10%, the interest that accrues prior to the accrual date shall be included in income and may be considered a hedge.

(iv) *Accrual date.*—The accrual date is the date when the item of income or expense (including a capital expenditure) that relates to an executory contract is required to be accrued under the taxpayer's method of accounting.

(v) *Payment date.*—The payment date is the date when payment is made or received with respect to an executory contract or the subsequent corresponding account payable or receivable.

(3) *Identification rules.*—(i) *Identification by the taxpayer.*—A taxpayer must establish a record and before the close of the date the hedge is entered into, the taxpayer must enter into the record a clear description of the executory contract and the hedge and indicate that the transaction is being identified in accordance with paragraph (b)(3) of this section.

(ii) *Identification by the Commissioner.*—If a taxpayer enters into an executory contract and a hedge but fails to satisfy one or more of the requirements of paragraph (b) of this section and, based on the facts and circumstances, the Commissioner concludes that the executory contract in substance is hedged, then the Commissioner may apply the provisions of paragraph (b) of this section as if the taxpayer had satisfied all of the requirements therein, and may make appropriate adjustments. The Commissioner may apply the provisions of paragraph (b) of this section regardless of whether the executory contract and the hedge are held by the same taxpayer.

(4) *Effect of hedged executory contract.*—(i) *In general.*—If a taxpayer enters into a hedged executory contract, amounts paid or received under the hedge by the taxpayer are treated as paid or received by the taxpayer under the executory contract, or any subsequent account payable or receivable, or that portion to which the hedge relates. Also, the taxpayer recognizes no exchange gain or loss on the hedge. If an executory contract, on the accrual date, becomes an account payable or receivable, the taxpayer recognizes no exchange gain or loss on such payable or receivable for the period covered by the hedge.

(ii) *Partially hedged executory contracts.*—The effect of integrating an executory contract and a hedge that partially hedges such contract is to treat the amounts paid or received under the hedge as paid or received under the portion of the executory contract being hedged, or any subsequent account payable or receivable. The income or expense of services performed or received under the executory contract, or the amount realized or basis of property sold or purchased under the executory contract, that is attributable to that portion of the executory contract that is not hedged shall be translated into functional currency on the accrual date. Exchange gain or loss shall be realized when payment is made or received with respect to any payable or receivable arising on the accrual date with respect to such unhedged amount.

(iii) *Disposition of a hedge or executory contract prior to the accrual date.*—(A) *In general.*—If a taxpayer identifies an executory contract as part of a hedged executory contract as defined in paragraph (b)(2) of this section, and disposes of (or otherwise terminates) the executory contract prior to the accrual date, the hedge shall be treated as sold for its fair market value on the date the executory contract is disposed of and any gain or loss shall be realized and recognized on such date. Such gain or loss shall be an adjustment to the amount received or expended with respect to the disposition or termination, if any. The spot rate on the date the hedge is treated as sold shall be used to determine subsequent exchange gain or loss on the hedge. If a taxpayer identifies a hedge as part of a hedged executory contract as defined in paragraph (b)(2) of this section, and disposes of the hedge prior to the accrual date, any gain or loss realized on such disposition shall not be recognized and shall be an adjustment to the income from, or expense of, the services performed or received under the executory contract, or to the amount realized or basis of the property sold or purchased under the executory contract.

(B) *Certain events in a series of hedges treated as a termination of the hedged executory contract.*—If the rules of paragraph (b)(2)(iii)(B) of this section are not satisfied, the hedged executory contract shall be terminated and the provisions of paragraph (b)(4)(iii)(A) of this section shall apply to any gain or loss previously realized with respect to such hedge. Any subsequent hedging contracts entered into to reduce the risk of exchange rate movements with respect to such executory contract shall not be considered a hedge as defined in paragraph (b)(2)(iii) of this section.

(C) *Executory contracts between related persons.*—If an executory contract is between related persons as defined in section 267(b) and 707(b), and the taxpayer disposes of the hedge or terminates the executory contract prior to the accrual date, the Commissioner may redetermine the timing, source, and character of gain or loss from the hedge or the executory contract if he determines that a significant purpose for disposing of the hedge or terminating the executory contract prior to the accrual date was to affect the timing, source, or character of income, gain, expense, or loss for Federal income tax purposes.

(iv) *Disposition of a hedge on or after the accrual date.*—If a taxpayer identifies a hedge as part of a hedged executory contract as defined in paragraph (b)(2) of this section, and disposes of the hedge on or after the accrual date, no gain or loss is recognized on the hedge and the booking date as defined in § 1.988-2(c)(2) of the payable or receivable for purposes of computing exchange gain or loss shall be the date such hedge is disposed of. See *Example 3* of paragraph (b)(4)(iv) of this section.

(v) *Sections 263(g), 1092, and 1256 do not apply.*—Sections 263(g), 1092, and 1256 do not apply with respect to an executory contract or hedge which comprise a hedged executory contract as defined in paragraph (b)(2) of this section. However, sections 263(g), 1092 and 1256 may apply to the hedged executory contract if such transaction is part of a straddle.

(vi) *Examples.*—The principles set forth in paragraph (b) of this section are illustrated in the following examples. The examples assume that K is an accrual method, calendar year U.S. corporation with the dollar as its functional currency.

Example 1. (i) On January 1, 1992, K enters into a contract with JPF, a Swiss machine manufacturer, to pay 500,000 Swiss francs for delivery of a machine on June 1, 1993. Also on January 1, 1992, K enters into a foreign currency forward agreement to purchase 500,000 Swiss francs for $250,000 for delivery on June 1, 1993. K properly identifies the executory contract and the hedge in accordance with paragraph (b)(3)(i) of this section. On June 1, 1993, K takes delivery of the 500,000 Swiss francs (in exchange for $250,000) under the forward contract and makes payment of 500,000 Swiss francs to JPF in exchange for the machine. Assume that the accrual date is June 1, 1993.

(ii) Under paragraph (b)(1) of this section, the hedge is integrated with the executory contract. Therefore, K is deemed to have paid $250,000 for the machine and there is no exchange gain or loss on the foreign currency forward contract. K's basis in the machine is $250,000. Section 1256 does not apply to the forward contract.

Example 2. (i) On January 1, 1992, K enters into a contract with S, a Swiss machine manufacturer, to pay 500,000 Swiss francs for delivery of a machine on June 1, 1993. Under the contract, K is not obligated to pay for the machine until September 1, 1993. On February 1, 1992, K enters into a foreign currency forward agreement to purchase 500,000 Swiss francs for $250,000 for delivery on September 1, 1993. K properly identifies the executory contract and the hedge in accordance with paragraph (b)(3) of this section. On June 1, 1993, K takes delivery of [the] machine. Assume that under K's method of accounting the delivery date is the accrual date. On September 1, 1993, K takes delivery of the 500,000 Swiss francs (in exchange for $250,000) under the forward contract and makes payment of 500,000 Swiss francs to S.

(ii) Under paragraph (b)(1) of this section, the hedge is integrated with the executory contract. Therefore K is deemed to have paid $250,000 for the machine and there is no exchange gain or loss on the foreign currency forward contract. Thus K's basis in the machine is $250,000. In addition, no exchange gain or loss is recognized on the payable in existence from June 1, 1993, to September 1, 1993. Section 1256 does not apply to the forward contract.

Example 3. The facts are the same as in *Example 2* except that K disposed of the forward contract on August 1, 1993 for $10,000. Pursuant to paragraph (b)(4)(iv) of this section, K does not recognize the $10,000 gain. K's basis in the machine is $250,000 (the amount fixed by the forward contract), regardless of the amount in dollars that K actually pays to acquire the Sf500,O00 when K pays for the machine. K has a payable with a booking date of August 1, 1993, payable on September 1, 1993 for 500,000 Swiss francs. Thus, K will realize exchange gain or loss on the difference between the amount booked on August 1, 1993 and the amount paid on September 1, 1993 under § 1.988-2(c).

Example 4. (i) On January 1, 1992, K enters into a contract with S, a Swiss machine repair firm, to pay 500,000 Swiss francs for repairs to be performed on June 1, 1992. Under the contract, K is not obligated to pay for the repairs until September 1, 1992. On February 1, 1992, K enters into a foreign currency forward agreement to purchase 500,000 Swiss francs for $250,000 for delivery on August 1, 1992. K properly identifies the executory contract and the hedge in accordance with paragraph (b)(3) of this section. On June 1, 1992, S performs the repair services. Assume that under K's method of accounting this date is the accrual date. On August 1, 1992, K takes delivery of the 500,000 Swiss francs (in exchange for $250,000) under the forward contract. On the same day, K deposits the Sf500,000 in a separate account with a bank and properly identifies the transaction as a continuation of the hedged executory contract. On September 1, 1992, K makes payment of the Sf500,000 in the account to S.

(ii) Under paragraph (b)(1) of this section, the hedge is integrated with the executory contract. Therefore K is deemed to have paid $250,000 for the services and there is no exchange gain or loss on the foreign currency forward contract or on the disposition of Sf500,000 in the account. Any interest on the Swiss francs in the account is included in income but is not considered part of the hedge (because the amount paid for the services must be set on or before the accrual date). In addition, no exchange gain or loss is recognized on the payable in existence from June 1, 1992, to September 1, 1992. Section 1256 does not apply to the forward contract.

Example 5. (i) On January 1, 1992, K enters into a contract with S, a Swiss machine manufacturer, to pay 500,000 Swiss francs for delivery of a machine on June 1, 1993. Under the contract, K is not obligated to pay for the machine until September 1, 1993. On February 1, 1992, K enters into a foreign currency forward agreement to purchase 250,000 Swiss francs for $125,000 for delivery on September 1, 1993. K properly identifies the executory contract and the hedge in accordance with paragraph (b)(3) of this section. On June 1, 1993, K takes delivery of the machine. Assume that under K's method of accounting the delivery date is the accrual date. Assume further that the exchange rate is Sf1 = $.50 on June 1, 1993. On August 30, 1993, K purchases Sf250,000 for $135,000. On September 1, 1993, K takes delivery of the 250,000 Swiss francs (in exchange for $125,000) under the forward contract and makes payment of 500,000 Swiss francs (the Sf250,000 received under the contract plus the Sf250,000 purchased on August 30, 1993) to S. Assume the spot rate on September 1, 1993, is 1 Sf1 = $.5420 (Sf250,000 equal $135,500).

(ii) Under paragraph (b)(1) of this section, the partial hedge is integrated with the executory contract. K is deemed to have paid $250,000 for the machine [$125,000 on the hedged portion of the Sf500,000 and $125,000 ($.50, the spot rate on June 1, 1993, times Sf250,000) on the unhedged portion of the Sf500,000]. K's basis in the machine therefore is $250,000. K recognizes no exchange gain or loss on the foreign currency forward contract but K will realize exchange gain of $500 on the disposition of the Sf250,000 purchased on August 30, 1993 under § 1.988-2(a). In addition, exchange loss is realized on the unhedged portion of the payable in existence from June 1, 1993, to September 1, 1993. Thus, K will realize exchange loss of $10,500 ($125,000 booked less $135,500 paid) under § 1.988-2 (c) on the payable. Section 1256 does not apply to the forward contract.

Example 6. (i) On January 1, 1990, K enters into a contract with S, a Swiss steel manufacturer, to buy steel for 1,000,000 Swiss francs (Sf) for delivery and payment on December 31, 1990. On January 1, 1990, the spot rate is Sf1 = $.50, the U.S. dollar interest rate is 10% compounded annually, and the Swiss franc rate is 5% compounded annually. Under K's method of accounting, the delivery date is the accrual date.

(ii) Assume that on January 1, 1990, K enters into a foreign currency forward contract to buy Sf1,000,000 for $523,800 for delivery on December 31, 1990. K properly identifies the executory contract and the hedge in accordance with paragraph (b)(3) of this section. Pursuant to paragraph (b)(2)(iii) of this section, the forward contract constitutes a hedge. Assuming that the requirements of paragraph (b)(2)(i) of this section are satisfied, the executory contract to buy steel and the forward contract are integrated under paragraph (b)(1) of this section. Thus, K is deemed to have paid $523,800 for the steel and will have a basis in the steel of $523,800. No gain or loss is realized with respect to the forward contract and section 1256 does not apply to such contract.

(iii) Assume instead that on January 1, 1990, K enters into a foreign currency forward contract to buy Sf1,000,OOO for $512,200 for delivery on July 1, 1990. K properly identifies the executory contract and the hedge in accordance with paragraph (b)(3) of this section. On July 1, 1990, when the spot rate is Sf1 = $.53, K cancels the forward contract in exchange for $17,800 ($530,000 – $512,200). On July 1, 1990, K enters into a second forward agreement to buy Sf1,000,000 for $542,900 for delivery on December 31, 1990. K properly identifies the second forward agreement as a hedge in accordance with paragraph (b)(3) of this section. Pursuant to paragraph (b)(2)(iii) of this section, the forward contract entered into on January 1, 1990, and the forward contract entered into on July 1, 1990, constitute a hedge. Assuming that the requirements of paragraph (b)(2)(i) of this section are satisfied, the executory contract to buy steel and the forward agreements are integrated under paragraph (b)(1) of this section. Thus, K is deemed to have paid $525,100 for the steel (the forward price in the second forward agreement of $542,900 less the gain on the first forward agreement of $17,800) and will have a basis in the steel of $525,100. No gain is realized with respect to the forward contracts and section 1256 does not apply to such contracts.

(iv) Assume instead that on January 1, 1990, K enters into a foreign currency forward contract to buy Sf1,000,000 for $512,200 for delivery on July 1, 1990. K properly identifies the executory contract and the hedge in accordance with paragraph (b)(3) of this section. On July 1, 1990, when the spot rate is Sf1 = $.53, K enters into a historical rate rollover of its $17,800 gain ($530,000 – $512,200) on the forward agreement. Thus, K enters into a second foreign currency forward agreement to buy Sf1,000,000 for $524,210 for delivery on December 31, 1990. (The forward price of $524,210 is the market forward price on July 1, 1990 for the purchase of Sf1,000,000 for delivery on December 31, 1990 of $542,900 less the $17,800 gain on January 1, 1990 contract and less the time value of such gain of $890.) K properly identifies the second forward agreement as a hedge in accordance with paragraph (b)(3) of this section. On December 31, 1990, when the spot rate is Sf1 = $.54, K takes delivery of the Sf1,000,000 (in exchange for $524,210) and purchases the steel for Sf1,000,000. Pursuant to paragraph (b)(2)(iii) of this section, the forward contract entered into on January 1, 1990, and the forward contract entered into on July 1, 1990, which incorporates the rollover of K's gain on the January 1, 1990 contract, constitute a hedge. Assuming that the requirements of paragraph (b)(2)(i) of this section are satisfied, the executory contract to buy steel and the forward agreements are integrated under paragraph (b)(1) of this section. Because the period from the rollover date to the date payment is made under the executory contract does not exceed 183 days, the $890 of interest income is considered part of the hedge and is not recognized. Thus, K is deemed to have paid $524,210 for the steel and will have a basis in the steel of $524,210. No gain is realized with respect to the forward contracts and section 1256 does not apply to such contracts.

(v) Assume instead that on January 1, 1990, K purchases Sf952,380.95 (the present value of Sf1,000,000 to be paid on December 31, 1990) for $476,190.48 and on the same day deposits the Swiss francs in a separate bank account that bears interest at a rate of 5%, compounded annually. K properly identifies the transaction as a hedged executory contract. Over the period beginning January 1, 1990, and ending December 31, 1990, K receives Sf47,619.05 in interest on the account that is included in income and that has a basis of $25,714.29. (Assume that under § 1.988-2(b)(1), K uses the spot rate of

Sf1 = $.54 to translate the interest income). On December 31, 1990, K makes payment of the Sf1,000,000 principal and accrued interest in the account to S. Pursuant to paragraph (b)(2)(iii) of this section, the principal in the bank account and the interest constitute a hedge. Under paragraph (b)(1) of this section, the hedge is integrated with the executory contract. Therefore K is deemed to have paid $501,904.77 (the basis of the principal deposited plus the basis of the interest) for the steel and there is no exchange gain or loss on the disposition of the Sf1,000,000. K's basis in the steel therefore is $501,904.77.

(5) *References to this paragraph (b).*—If the rules of this paragraph (b) are referred to in another paragraph of this section (*e.g.*, paragraph (c) of this section), then the rules of this paragraph (b) shall be applied for purposes of such other paragraph by substituting terms appropriate for such other paragraph. For example, paragraph (c)(2) of this section refers to the identification rules of paragraph (b)(3) of this section. Accordingly, for purposes of paragraph (c)(2), the rules of paragraph (b)(3) will be applied by substituting the term "stock or security" for "executory contract".

(c) *Hedges of period between trade date and settlement date on purchase or sale of publicly traded stock or security.*—If a taxpayer purchases or sells stocks or securities which are traded on an established securities market and—

(1) Hedges all or part of such purchase or sale for any part of the period beginning on the trade date and ending on the settlement date; and

(2) Identifies the hedge and the underlying stock or securities as an integrated transaction under the rules of paragraph (b)(3) of this section;

then any gain or loss on the hedge shall be an adjustment to the amount realized or the adjusted basis of the stock or securities sold or purchased (and shall not be taken into account as exchange gain or loss). The term hedge means a deposit of nonfunctional currency in a hedging account (within the meaning of paragraph (b)(2)(iii)(D) of this section), or a forward or futures contract described in § 1.988-1(a)(1)(ii) and (2)(iii), or combination thereof, which reduces the risk of exchange rate fluctuations for any portion of the period beginning on the trade date and ending on the settlement date. The provisions of paragraphs (b)(2)(i)(D) through (G), and (b)(2)(iii)(D) and (E) of this section shall apply. Sections 263(g), 1092, and 1256 do not apply with respect to stock or securities and a hedge which are subject to this paragraph (c).

(d) [Reserved]

(e) *Advance rulings regarding net hedging and anticipatory hedging systems.*—In his sole discretion, the Commissioner may issue an advance ruling addressing the income tax consequences of a taxpayer's system of hedging either its net nonfunctional currency exposure or anticipated nonfunctional currency exposure. The ruling may address the character, source, and timing of both the section 988 transaction(s) making up the hedge and the underlying transactions being hedged. The procedures for obtaining a ruling shall be governed by such pertinent revenue procedures and revenue rulings as the Commissioner may provide. The Commissioner will not issue a ruling regarding hedges of a taxpayer's investment in a foreign subsidiary.

(f) [Reserved]

(g) *General effective date.*—Except as otherwise provided in this section, the rules of this section shall apply to qualified hedging transactions, hedged executory contracts and transactions described in paragraph (c) of this section entered into on or after September 21, 1989. This section shall apply even if the transaction being hedged (*e.g.*, the debt instrument) was entered into or acquired prior to such date. The effective date regarding advance rulings for net and anticipatory hedging shall be governed by such revenue procedures that the Commissioner may publish. [Reg. § 1.988-5.]

☐ [*T.D.* 8400, 3-16-92. *Amended by T.D.* 9598, 9-5-2012 *and T.D.* 9736, 9-3-2015.]

§ 1.988-6. Nonfunctional currency contingent payment debt instruments.—(a) *In general.*—(1) *Scope.*—This section determines the accrual of interest and the amount, timing, source, and character of any gain or loss on nonfunctional currency contingent payment debt instruments described in this paragraph (a)(1) and to which § 1.1275-4(a) would otherwise apply if the debt instrument were denominated in the taxpayer's functional currency. Except as provided by the rules in this section, the rules in § 1.1275-4 (relating to contingent payment debt instruments) apply to the following instruments—

(i) A debt instrument described in § 1.1275-4(b)(1) for which all payments of principal and interest are denominated in, or determined by reference to, a single nonfunctional currency and which has one or more non-currency related contingencies;

(ii) A debt instrument described in § 1.1275-4(b)(1) for which payments of principal or interest are denominated in, or determined by reference to, more than one currency and which has no non-currency related contingencies;

(iii) A debt instrument described in § 1.1275-4(b)(1) for which payments of principal or interest are denominated in, or determined by reference to, more than one currency and which has one or more non-currency related contingencies; and

(iv) A debt instrument otherwise described in paragraph (a)(1)(i), (ii) or (iii) of this section, except that the debt instrument is described in § 1.1275-4(c)(1) rather than § 1.1275-4(b)(1) (e.g., the instrument is issued for non-publicly traded property).

(2) *Exception for hyperinflationary currencies.*—(i) *In general.*—Except as provided in paragraph (a)(2)(ii) of this section, this section shall not apply to an instrument described in paragraph (a)(1) of this section if any payment made under such instrument is determined by reference to a hyperinflationary currency, as defined in § 1.985-1(b)(2)(ii)(D). In such case, the amount, timing, source and character of interest, principal, foreign currency gain or loss, and gain or loss relating to a non-currency contingency shall be determined under the method that reflects the instrument's economic substance.

(ii) *Discretion as to method.*—If a taxpayer does not account for an instrument described in paragraph (a)(2)(i) of this section in a manner that reflects the instrument's economic substance, the Commissioner may apply the rules of this section to such an instrument or apply the principles of § 1.988-2(b)(15), reasonably taking into account the contingent feature or features of the instrument.

(b) *Instruments described in paragraph (a)(1)(i) of this section.*—(1) *In general.*—Paragraph (b)(2) of this section provides rules for applying the noncontingent bond method (as set forth in § 1.1275-4(b)) in the nonfunctional currency in which a debt instrument described in paragraph (a)(1)(i) of this section is denominated, or by reference to which its payments are determined (the denomination currency). Paragraph (b)(3) of this section describes how amounts determined in paragraph (b)(2) of this section shall be translated from the denomination currency of the instrument into the taxpayer's functional currency. Paragraph (b)(4) of this section describes how gain or loss (other than foreign currency gain or loss) shall be determined and characterized with respect to the instrument. Paragraph (b)(5) of this section describes how foreign currency gain or loss shall be determined with respect to accrued interest and principal on the instrument. Paragraph (b)(6) of this section provides rules for determining the source and character of any gain or loss with respect to the instrument. Paragraph (b)(7) of this section provides rules for subsequent holders of an instrument who purchase the instrument for an amount other than the adjusted issue price of the instrument. Paragraph (c) of this section provides examples of the application of paragraph (b) of this section. See paragraph (d) of this section for the determination of the denomination currency of an instrument described in paragraph (a)(1)(ii) or (iii) of this section. See paragraph (e) of this section for the treatment of an instrument described in paragraph (a)(1)(iv) of this section.

(2) *Application of noncontingent bond method.*—(i) *Accrued interest.*—Interest accruals on an instrument described in paragraph (a)(1)(i) of this section are initially determined in the denomination currency of the instrument by applying the noncontingent bond method, set forth in § 1.1275-4(b), to the instrument in its denomination currency. Accordingly, the comparable yield, projected payment schedule, and comparable fixed rate debt instrument, described in § 1.1275-4(b)(4), are determined in the denomination currency. For purposes of applying the noncontingent bond method to instruments described in this paragraph, the applicable Federal rate described in § 1.1275-4(b)(4)(i) shall be the rate described in § 1.1274-4(d) with respect to the denomination currency.

(ii) *Net positive and negative adjustments.*—Positive and negative adjustments, and net positive and net negative adjustments, with respect to an instrument described in paragraph (a)(1)(i) of this section are determined by applying the rules of § 1.1275-4(b)(6) (and § 1.1275-4(b)(9)(i) and (ii), if applicable) in the denomination currency. Accordingly, a net positive adjustment is treated as additional interest (in the denomination currency) on the instrument. A net negative adjustment first reduces interest that otherwise would be accrued by the taxpayer during the current tax year in the denomination currency. If a net negative adjustment exceeds the interest that would otherwise be accrued by the taxpayer during the current tax year in the denomination currency, the excess is treated as ordinary loss (if the taxpayer is a holder of the instrument) or ordinary income (if the taxpayer is the issuer of the instrument). The amount treated as ordinary loss by a holder with respect to a net negative adjustment is limited, however, to the amount by which the holder's total interest inclusions on the debt instrument (determined in the denomination currency) exceed the total amount of the holder's net negative adjustments treated as ordinary loss on the debt instrument in prior taxable years (determined in the denomination currency). Similarly, the amount treated as ordinary income by an issuer with respect to a net negative adjustment is limited to the amount by which the issuer's total interest deductions on the debt instrument (determined in the denomination currency) exceed the total amount of the issuer's net negative adjustments treated as ordinary income on the debt instrument in prior taxable years (determined in the denomination currency). To the extent a net negative adjustment exceeds the current year's interest accrual and the amount treated as ordinary loss to a holder (or ordinary income to the issuer), the excess is treated as a negative adjustment carryforward, within the meaning of § 1.1275-4(b)(6)(iii)(C), in the denomination currency.

(iii) *Adjusted issue price.*—The adjusted issue price of an instrument described in paragraph (a)(1)(i) of this section is determined by applying the rules of § 1.1275-4(b)(7) in the denomination currency. Accordingly, the adjusted issue price is equal to the debt instrument's issue price in the denomination currency, increased by the interest previously accrued on the debt instrument (determined without regard to any net positive or net negative adjustments on the instrument) and decreased by the amount of any noncontingent payment and the projected amount of any contingent payment previously made on the instrument. All adjustments to the adjusted issue price are calculated in the denomination currency.

(iv) *Adjusted basis.*—The adjusted basis of an instrument described in paragraph (a)(1)(i) of this section is determined by applying the rules of § 1.1275-4(b)(7) in the taxpayer's functional currency. In accordance with those rules, a holder's basis in the debt instrument is increased by the interest previously accrued on the debt instrument (translated into functional currency), without regard to any net positive or net negative adjustments on the instrument (except as provided in paragraph (b)(7) or (8) of this section, if applicable), and decreased by the amount of any noncontingent payment and the projected amount of any contingent payment previously made on the instrument to the holder (translated into functional currency). See paragraph (b)(3)(iii) of this section for translation rules.

(v) *Amount realized.*—The amount realized by a holder and the repurchase price paid by the issuer on the scheduled or unscheduled retirement of a debt instrument described in paragraph (a)(1)(i) of this section are determined by applying the rules of § 1.1275-4(b)(7) in the denomination currency. For example, with regard to a scheduled retirement at maturity, the holder is treated as receiving the projected amount of any contingent payment due at maturity, reduced by the amount of any negative adjustment carryforward. For purposes of translating the amount realized by the holder into functional currency, the rules of paragraph (b)(3)(iv) of this section shall apply.

(3) *Treatment and translation of amounts determined under noncontingent bond method.*—(i) *Accrued interest.*—The amount of accrued interest, determined under paragraph (b)(2)(i) of this section, is translated into the taxpayer's functional currency at the average exchange rate, as described in § 1.988-2(b)(2)(iii)(A), or, at the taxpayer's election, at the appropriate spot rate, as described in § 1.988-2(b)(2)(iii)(B).

(ii) *Net positive and negative adjustments.*—(A) *Net positive adjustments.*—A net positive adjustment, as referenced in paragraph (b)(2)(ii) of this section, is translated into the taxpayer's functional currency at the spot rate on the last day of the taxable year in which the adjustment is taken into account under § 1.1275-4(b)(6), or, if earlier, the date the instrument is disposed of or otherwise terminated.

(B) *Net negative adjustments.*—A net negative adjustment is treated and, where necessary, is translated from the denomination currency into the taxpayer's functional currency under the following rules:

(1) The amount of a net negative adjustment determined in the denomination currency that reduces the current year's interest in that currency shall first reduce the current year's accrued but unpaid interest, and then shall reduce the current year's interest which was accrued and paid. No translation is required.

(2) The amount of a net negative adjustment treated as ordinary income or loss under § 1.1275-4(b)(6)(iii)(B) first is attributable to accrued but unpaid interest accrued in prior taxable years. For this purpose, the net negative adjustment shall be treated as attributable to any unpaid interest accrued in the immediately preceding taxable year, and thereafter to unpaid interest accrued in each preceding taxable year. The amount of the net negative adjustment applied to accrued but unpaid interest is translated into functional currency at the same rate used, in each of the respective prior taxable years, to translate the accrued interest.

(3) Any amount of the net negative adjustment remaining after the application of paragraphs (b)(3)(ii)(B)*(1)* and *(2)* of this section is attributable to interest accrued and paid in prior taxable years. The amount of the net negative adjustment applied to such amounts is translated into functional currency at the spot rate on the date the debt instrument was issued or, if later, acquired.

(4) Any amount of the net negative adjustment remaining after application of paragraphs (b)(3)(ii)(B)*(1)*, *(2)* and *(3)* of this section is a negative adjustment carryforward, within the meaning of § 1.1275-4(b)(6)(iii)(C). A negative adjustment carryforward is carried forward in the denomination currency and is applied to reduce interest accruals in subsequent years. In the year in which the instrument is sold, exchanged or retired, any negative adjustment carryforward not applied to interest reduces the holder's amount realized on the instrument (in the denomination currency). An issuer of a debt instrument described in paragraph (a)(1)(i) of this section who takes into income a negative adjustment carryforward (that is not applied to interest) in the year the instrument is retired, as described in § 1.1275-4(b)(6)(iii)(C), translates such income into functional currency at the spot rate on the date the instrument was issued.

(iii) *Adjusted basis.*—(A) *In general.*—Except as otherwise provided in this paragraph and paragraph (b)(7) or (8) of this section, a holder determines and maintains adjusted basis by translating the denomination currency amounts determined under § 1.1275-4(b)(7)(iii) into functional currency as follows:

(1) The holder's initial basis in the instrument is determined by translating the amount paid by the holder to acquire the instrument (in the denomination currency) into functional currency at the spot rate on the date the instrument was issued or, if later, acquired.

(2) An increase in basis attributable to interest accrued on the instrument is translated at the rate applicable to such interest under paragraph (b)(3)(i) of this section.

(3) Any noncontingent payment and the projected amount of any contingent payments determined in the denomination currency that decrease the holder's basis in the instrument under § 1.1275-4(b)(7)(iii) are translated as follows:

(i) The payment first is attributable to the most recently accrued interest to which prior amounts have not already been attributed. The payment is translated into functional currency at the rate at which the interest was accrued.

(ii) Any amount remaining after the application of paragraph (b)(3)(iii)(A)*(3)(i)* of this section is attributable to principal. Such amounts are translated into functional currency at the spot rate on the date the instrument was issued or, if later, acquired.

(B) *Exception for interest reduced by a negative adjustment carryforward.*—Solely for purposes of this § 1.988-6, any amounts of accrued interest income that are reduced as a result of a negative adjustment carryforward shall be treated as principal and translated at the spot rate on the date the instrument was issued or, if later, acquired.

(iv) *Amount realized.*—(A) *Instrument held to maturity.*—*(1) In general.*—With respect to an instrument held to maturity, a holder translates the amount realized by separating such amount in the denomination currency into the component parts of interest and principal that make up adjusted basis prior to translation under paragraph (b)(3)(iii) of this section, and translating each of those component parts of the amount realized at the same rate used to translate the respective component parts of basis under paragraph (b)(3)(iii) of this section. The amount realized first shall be translated by reference to the component parts of basis consisting of accrued interest during the taxpayer's holding period as determined under paragraph (b)(3)(iii) of this section and ordering such amounts on a last in first out basis. Any remaining portion of the amount realized shall be translated by reference to the rate used to translate the component of basis consisting of principal as determined under paragraph (b)(3)(iii) of this section.

(2) Subsequent purchases at discount and fixed but deferred contingent payments.—For purposes of this paragraph (b)(3)(iv) of this section, any amount which is required to be added to adjusted basis under paragraph (b)(7) or (8) of this section shall be treated as additional interest which was accrued on the date the amount was added to adjusted basis. To the extent included in amount realized, such amounts shall be translated into functional currency at the same rates at which they were translated for purposes of determining adjusted basis. See paragraphs (b)(7)(iv) and (b)(8) of this section for rules governing the rates at which the amounts are translated for purposes of determining adjusted basis.

(B) *Sale, exchange, or unscheduled retirement.*—*(1) Holder.*—In the case of a sale, exchange, or unscheduled retirement, application of the rule stated in paragraph (b)(3)(iv)(A) of this section shall be as follows. The holder's amount realized first shall be translated by reference to the principal component of basis as determined under paragraph (b)(3)(iii) of this section, and then to the component of basis consisting of accrued interest as determined under paragraph (b)(3)(iii) of this section and ordering such amounts on a first in first out basis. Any gain recognized by the holder (i.e., any excess of the sale price over the holder's basis, both expressed in the denomination currency) is translated into functional currency at the spot rate on the payment date.

(2) Issuer.—In the case of an unscheduled retirement of the debt instrument, any excess of the adjusted issue price of the debt instrument over the amount paid by the issuer (expressed in denomination currency) shall first be attributable to accrued unpaid interest, to the extent the accrued unpaid interest had not been previously offset by a negative adjustment, on a last-in-first-out basis, and then to principal. The accrued unpaid interest shall be translated into functional currency at the rate at which the interest was accrued. The principal shall be translated at the spot rate on the date the debt instrument was issued.

(C) *Effect of negative adjustment carryforward with respect to the issuer.*—Any amount of negative adjustment carryforward treated as ordinary income under § 1.1275-4(b)(6)(iii)(C) shall be translated at the exchange rate on the day the debt instrument was issued.

(4) *Determination of gain or loss not attributable to foreign currency.*—A holder of a debt instrument described in paragraph (a)(1)(i) of this section shall recognize gain or loss upon sale, exchange, or retirement of the instrument equal to the difference between the amount realized with respect to the instrument, translated into functional currency as described in paragraph (b)(3)(iv) of this section, and the adjusted basis in the instrument, determined and maintained in functional currency as described in paragraph (b)(3)(iii) of this section. The amount of any gain or loss so determined is characterized as provided in § 1.1275-4(b)(8), and sourced as provided in paragraph (b)(6) of this section.

(5) *Determination of foreign currency gain or loss.*—(i) *In general.*—Other than in a taxable disposition of the debt instrument, foreign currency gain or loss is recognized with respect to a debt instrument described in paragraph (a)(1)(i) of this section only when payments are made or received. No foreign currency gain or loss is recognized with respect to a net positive or negative adjustment, as determined under paragraph (b)(2)(ii) of this section (except with respect to a positive adjustment described in paragraph (b)(8) of this section). As described in this paragraph (b)(5), foreign currency gain or loss is determined in accordance with the rules of § 1.988-2(b).

(ii) *Foreign currency gain or loss attributable to accrued interest.*—The amount of foreign currency gain or loss recognized with respect to payments of interest previously accrued on the instrument is determined by translating the amount of interest paid or received into functional currency at the spot rate on the date of payment and subtracting from such amount the amount determined by translating the interest paid or received into functional currency at the rate at which such interest was accrued under the rules of paragraph (b)(3)(i) of this section. For purposes of this paragraph, the amount of any payment that is treated as accrued interest shall be reduced by the amount of any net negative adjustment treated as ordinary loss (to the holder) or ordinary income (to the issuer), as provided in paragraph (b)(2)(ii) of this section. For purposes of determining whether the payment consists of interest or principal, see the payment ordering rules in paragraph (b)(5)(iv) of this section.

(iii) *Principal.*—The amount of foreign currency gain or loss recognized with respect to payment or receipt of principal is determined by translating the amount paid or received into functional currency at the spot rate on the date of payment or receipt and subtracting from such amount the amount determined by translating the principal into functional currency at the spot rate on the date the instrument was issued or, in case of the holder, if later, acquired. For purposes of determining whether the payment consists of interest or principal, see the payment ordering rules in paragraph (b)(5)(iv) of this section.

(iv) *Payment ordering rules.*—(A) *In general.*—Except as provided in paragraph (b)(5)(iv)(B) of this section, payments with respect to an instrument described in paragraph (a)(1)(i) of this section shall be treated as follows:

(1) A payment shall first be attributable to any net positive adjustment on the instrument that has not previously been taken into account.

(2) Any amount remaining after applying paragraph (b)(5)(iv)(A)*(1)* of this section shall be attributable to accrued but unpaid interest, remaining after reduction by any net negative adjustment, and shall be attributable to the most recent accrual period to the extent prior amounts have not already been attributed to such period.

(3) Any amount remaining after applying paragraphs (b)(5)(iv)(A)*(1)* and *(2)* of this section shall be attributable to principal. Any interest paid in the current year that is reduced by a net negative adjustment shall be considered a payment of principal for purposes of determining foreign currency gain or loss.

(B) *Special rule for sale or exchange or unscheduled retirement.*—Payments made or received upon a sale or exchange or unscheduled retirement shall first be applied against the principal of the debt instrument (or in the case of a subsequent purchaser, the purchase price of the instrument in denomination currency) and then against accrued unpaid interest (in the case of a holder, accrued while the holder held the instrument).

(C) *Subsequent purchaser that has a positive adjustment allocated to a daily portion of interest.*—A positive adjustment that is allocated to a daily portion of interest pursuant to paragraph (b)(7)(iv) of this section shall be treated as interest for purposes of applying the payment ordering rule of this paragraph (b)(5)(iv).

(6) *Source of gain or loss.*—The source of foreign currency gain or loss recognized with respect to an instrument described in paragraph (a)(1)(i) of this section shall be determined pursuant to § 1.988-4. Consistent with the rules of § 1.1275-4(b)(8), all gain (other than foreign currency gain) on an instrument described in paragraph (a)(1)(i) of this section is treated as interest income for all purposes. The source of an ordinary loss (other than foreign currency loss) with respect to an instrument described in paragraph (a)(1)(i) of this section shall be determined pursuant to § 1.1275-4(b)(9)(iv). The source of a capital loss with respect to an instrument described in paragraph (a)(1)(i) of this section shall be determined pursuant to § 1.865-1(b)(2).

(7) *Basis different from adjusted issue price.*—(i) *In general.*—The rules of § 1.1275-4(b)(9)(i), except as set forth in this paragraph (b)(7), shall apply to an instrument described in paragraph (a)(1)(i) of this section purchased by a subsequent holder for more or less than the instrument's adjusted issue price.

(ii) *Determination of basis.*—If an instrument described in paragraph (a)(1)(i) of this section is purchased by a subsequent holder, the subsequent holder's initial basis in the instrument shall equal the amount paid by the holder to acquire the instrument, translated into functional currency at the spot rate on the date of acquisition.

(iii) *Purchase price greater than adjusted issue price.*—If the purchase price of the instrument (determined in the denomination currency) exceeds the adjusted issue price of the instrument, the holder shall, consistent with the rules of § 1.1275-4(b)(9)(i)(B), reasonably allocate such excess to the daily portions of interest accrued on the instrument or to a projected payment on the instrument. To the extent attributable to interest, the excess shall be reasonably allocated over the remaining term of the instrument to the daily portions of interest accrued and shall be a negative adjustment on the dates the daily portions accrue. On the date of such adjustment, the holder's adjusted basis in the instrument is reduced by the amount treated as a negative adjustment under this paragraph (b)(7)(iii), translated into functional currency at the rate used to translate the interest which is offset by the negative adjustment. To the extent related to a projected payment, such excess shall be treated as a negative adjustment on the date the payment is made. On the date of such adjustment, the holder's adjusted basis in the instrument is reduced by the amount treated as a negative adjustment under this paragraph (b)(7)(iii), translated into functional currency at the spot rate on the date the instrument was acquired.

(iv) *Purchase price less than adjusted issue price.*—If the purchase price of the instrument (determined in the denomination currency) is less than the adjusted issue price of the instrument, the holder shall, consistent with the rules of § 1.1275-4(b)(9)(i)(C), reasonably allocate the difference to the daily portions of interest accrued on the instrument or to a projected payment on the instrument. To the extent attributable to interest, the difference shall be reasonably allocated over the remaining term of the instrument to the daily portions of interest accrued and shall be a positive adjustment on the dates the daily portions accrue. On the date of such adjustment, the holder's adjusted basis in the instrument is increased by the amount treated as a positive adjustment under this paragraph (b)(7)(iv), translated into functional currency at the rate used to translate the interest to which it relates. For purposes of determining adjusted basis under paragraph (b)(3)(iii) of this section, such increase in adjusted basis shall be treated as an additional accrual of interest during the period to which the positive adjustment relates. To the extent related to a projected payment, such difference shall be treated as a positive adjustment on the date the payment is made. On the date of such adjustment, the holder's adjusted basis in the instrument is increased by the amount treated as a positive adjustment under this paragraph (b)(7)(iv), translated into functional currency at the spot rate on the date the adjustment is taken into account. For purposes of determining the amount realized on the instrument in functional currency under paragraph (b)(3)(iv) of this section, amounts attributable to the excess of the adjusted issue price of the instrument over the purchase price of the instrument shall be translated into functional currency at the same rate at which the corresponding adjustments are taken into account under this paragraph (b)(7)(iv) for purposes of determining the adjusted basis of the instrument.

(8) *Fixed but deferred contingent payments.*—In the case of an instrument with a contingent payment that becomes fixed as to amount before the payment is due, the rules of § 1.1275-4(b)(9)(ii) shall be applied in the denomination currency of the instrument. For this purpose, foreign currency gain or loss shall be recognized on the date payment is made or received with respect to the instrument under the principles of paragraph (b)(5) of this section. Any increase or decrease in basis required under § 1.1275-4(b)(9)(ii)(D) shall be taken into account at the same exchange rate as the corresponding net positive or negative adjustment is taken into account.

(c) *Examples.*—The provisions of paragraph (b) of this section may be illustrated by the following examples. In each example, assume that the instrument described is a debt instrument for federal income tax purposes. No inference is intended, however, as to whether the instrument is a debt instrument for federal income tax purposes. The examples are as follows:

Example 1. Treatment of net positive adjustment—(i) *Facts.* On December 31, 2004, Z, a calendar year U.S. resident taxpayer whose functional currency is the U.S. dollar, purchases from a foreign corporation, at original issue, a zero-coupon debt instrument with a non-currency contingency for £1000. All payments of principal and interest with respect to the instrument are denominated in, or determined by reference to, a single nonfunctional currency (the British pound). The debt instrument would be subject to § 1.1275-4(b) if it were denominated in dollars. The debt instrument's comparable yield, determined in British pounds under paragraph (b)(2)(i) of this section and § 1.1275-4(b), is 10 percent, compounded annually, and the projected payment schedule, as constructed under the rules of § 1.1275-4(b), provides for a single payment of £1210 on December 31, 2006 (consisting of a noncontingent payment of £975 and a projected payment of £235). The debt instrument is a capital asset in the hands of Z. Z does not elect to use the spot-rate convention described in § 1.988-2(b)(2)(iii)(B). The payment actually made on December 31, 2006, is £1300. The relevant pound/dollar spot rates over the term of the instrument are as follows:

Date	Spot rate (pounds to dollars)
Dec. 31, 2004	£1.00 = $1.00
Dec. 31, 2005	£1.00 = $1.10
Dec. 31, 2006	£1.00 = $1.20

Accrual period	Average rate (pounds to dollars)
2005	£1.00 = $1.05
2006	£1.00 = $1.15

(ii) *Treatment in 2005*—(A) *Determination of accrued interest.* Under paragraph (b)(2)(i) of this section, and based on the comparable yield, Z accrues £100 of interest on the debt instrument for 2005 (issue price of £1000 × 10 percent). Under paragraph (b)(3)(i) of this section, Z translates the £100 at the average exchange rate for the accrual period ($1.05 × £100 = $105). Accordingly, Z has interest income in 2005 of $105.

(B) *Adjusted issue price and basis.* Under paragraphs (b)(2)(iii) and (iv) of this section, the adjusted issue price of the debt instrument determined in pounds and Z's adjusted basis in dollars in the debt instrument are increased by the interest accrued in 2005. Thus, on January 1, 2006, the adjusted issue price of the debt instrument is £1100. For purposes of determining Z's dollar basis in the debt instrument, the $1000 basis ($1.00 × £1000 original cost basis) is increased by the £100 of accrued interest, translated at the rate at which interest was accrued for 2005. See paragraph (b)(3)(iii) of this section. Accordingly, Z's adjusted basis in the debt instrument as of January 1, 2006, is $1105.

(iii) *Treatment in 2006*—(A) *Determination of accrued interest.* Under paragraph (b)(2)(i) of this section, and based on the comparable yield, Z accrues £110 of interest on the debt instrument for 2006 (adjusted issue price of £1100 × 10 percent). Under paragraph (b)(3)(i) of this section, Z translates the £110 at the average exchange rate for the accrual period ($1.15 × £110 = $126.50). Accordingly, Z has interest income in 2006 of $126.50.

(B) *Effect of net positive adjustment.* The payment actually made on December 31, 2006, is £1300, rather than the projected £1210. Under paragraph (b)(2)(ii) of this section, Z has a net positive adjustment of £90 on December 31, 2006, attributable to the difference between the amount of the actual payment and the amount of the projected payment. Under paragraph (b)(3)(ii)(A) of this section, the £90 net positive adjustment is treated as additional interest income and is translated into dollars at the spot rate on the last day of the year ($1.20 × £90 = $108). Accordingly, Z has a net positive adjustment of $108 resulting in a total interest inclusion for 2006 of $234.50 ($126.50 + $108 = $234.50).

(C) *Adjusted issue price and basis.* Based on the projected payment schedule, the adjusted issue price of the debt instrument immediately before the payment at maturity is £1210 (£1100 plus £110 of accrued interest for 2006). Z's adjusted basis in dollars, based only on the noncontingent payment and the projected amount of the contingent payment to be received, is $1231.50 ($1105 plus $126.50 of accrued interest for 2006).

(D) *Amount realized.* Even though Z receives £1300 at maturity, for purposes of determining the amount realized, Z is treated under paragraph (b)(2)(v) of this section as receiving the projected amount of the contingent payment on December 31, 2006. Therefore, Z is treated as receiving £1210 on December 31, 2006. Under paragraph (b)(3)(iv) of this section, Z translates its amount realized into dollars and computes its gain or loss on the instrument (other than foreign currency gain or loss) by breaking the amount realized into its component parts. Accordingly, £100 of the £1210 (representing the interest accrued in 2005) is translated at the rate at which it was accrued (£1 = $1.05), resulting in an amount realized of $105; £110 of the £1210 (representing the interest accrued in 2006) is translated into dollars at the rate at which it was accrued (£1 = $1.15), resulting in an amount realized of $126.50; and £1000 of the £1210 (representing a return of principal) is translated into dollars at the spot rate on the date the instrument was purchased (£1 = $1), resulting in an amount realized of $1000. Z's total amount realized is $1231.50, the same as its basis, and Z recognizes no gain or loss (before consideration of foreign currency gain or loss) on retirement of the instrument.

(E) *Foreign currency gain or loss.* Under paragraph (b)(5) of this section Z recognizes foreign currency gain under section 988 on the instrument with respect to the consideration actually received at maturity (except for the net positive adjustment), £1210. The amount of recognized foreign currency gain is determined based on the difference between the spot rate on the date the instrument matures and the rates at which the principal and interest were taken into account. With respect to the portion of the payment attributable to interest accrued in 2005, the foreign currency gain is $15 [£100 × ($1.20 – $1.05)]. With respect to interest accrued in 2006, the foreign currency gain equals $5.50 [£110 × ($1.20 – $1.15)]. With respect to principal, the foreign currency gain is $200 [£1000 × ($1.20 – $1.00)]. Thus, Z recognizes a total foreign currency gain on December 31, 2006, of $220.50.

(F) *Source.* Z has interest income of $105 in 2005, interest income of $234.50 in 2006 (attributable to £110 of accrued interest and the £90 net positive adjustment), and a foreign currency gain of $220.50 in 2006. Under paragraph (b)(6) of this section and section 862(a)(1), the interest income is sourced by reference to the residence of the payor and is therefore from sources without the United States. Under paragraph (b)(6) of this section and § 1.988-4, Z's foreign currency gain of $220.50 is sourced by reference to Z's residence and is therefore from sources within the United States.

Example 2. Treatment of net negative adjustment—(i) *Facts.* Assume the same facts as in *Example 1*, except that Z receives £975 at maturity instead of £1300.

(ii) *Treatment in 2005.* The treatment of the debt instrument in 2005 is the same as in Example 1. Thus, Z has interest income in 2005 of $105. On January 1, 2006, the adjusted issue price of the debt instrument is £1100, and Z's adjusted basis in the instrument is $1105.

(iii) *Treatment in 2006*—(A) *Determination of accrued interest.* Under paragraph (b)(2)(i) of this section and based on the comparable yield, Z's accrued interest for 2006 is £110 (adjusted issue price of £1100 × 10 percent). Under paragraph (b)(3)(i) of this section, the £110 of accrued interest is translated at the average exchange rate for the accrual period ($1.15 × £110 = $126.50).

(B) *Effect of net negative adjustment.* The payment actually made on December 31, 2006, is £975, rather than the projected £1210. Under paragraph (b)(2)(ii) of this section, Z has a net negative adjustment of £235 on December 31, 2006, attributable to the difference between the amount of the actual payment and the amount of the projected payment. Z's accrued interest income of £110 in 2006 is reduced to zero by the net negative adjustment. Under paragraph (b)(3)(ii)(B)(*1*) of this section the net negative adjustment which reduces the current year's interest is not translated into functional currency. Under paragraph (b)(2)(ii) of this section, Z treats the remaining £125 net negative adjustment as an ordinary loss to the extent of the £100 previously accrued interest in 2005. This £100 ordinary loss is attributable to interest accrued but not paid in the preceding year. Therefore, under paragraph (b)(3)(ii)(B)(*2*) of this section, Z translates the loss into dollars at the average rate for such year (£1 = $1.05). Accordingly, Z has an ordinary loss of $105 in 2006. The remaining £25 of net negative adjustment is a negative adjustment carryforward under paragraph (b)(2)(ii) of this section.

(C) *Adjusted issue price and basis.* Based on the projected payment schedule, the adjusted issue price of the debt instrument immediately before the payment at maturity is £1210 (£1100 plus £110 of accrued interest for 2006). Z's adjusted basis in dollars, based only on the noncontingent payments and the projected amount of the contingent payments to be received, is $1231.50 ($1105 plus $126.50 of accrued interest for 2006).

(D) *Amount realized.* Even though Z receives £975 at maturity, for purposes of determining the amount realized, Z is treated under paragraph (b)(2)(v) of this section as receiving the projected amount of the contingent payment on December 31, 2006, reduced by the amount of Z's negative adjustment carryforward of £25. Therefore, Z is treated as receiving £1185 (£1210 – £25) on December 31, 2006. Under paragraph (b)(3)(iv) of this section, Z translates its amount realized into dollars and computes its gain or loss on the instrument (other than foreign currency gain or loss) by breaking the amount realized into its component parts. Accordingly, £100 of the £1185 (representing the interest accrued in 2005) is translated at the rate at which it was accrued (£1 = $1.05), resulting in an amount realized of $105; £110 of the £1185 (representing the interest accrued in 2006) is translated into dollars at the rate at which it was accrued (£1 = $1.15), resulting in an amount realized of $126.50; and £975 of the £1185 (representing a return of principal) is translated into dollars at the spot rate on the date the instrument was purchased (£1 = $1), resulting in an amount realized of $975. Z's amount realized is $1206.50 ($105 + $126.50 + $975 = $1206.50), and Z recognizes a capital loss (before consideration of foreign currency gain or loss) of $25 on retirement of the instrument ($1206.50 – $1231.50 = –$25).

(E) *Foreign currency gain or loss.* Z recognizes foreign currency gain with respect to the consideration actually received at maturity, £975. Under paragraph (b)(5)(ii) of this section, no foreign currency gain or loss is recognized with respect to unpaid accrued interest reduced to zero by the net negative adjustment resulting in 2006. In addition, no foreign currency gain or loss is recognized with respect to unpaid accrued interest from 2005, also reduced to zero by the ordinary loss. Accordingly, Z recognizes foreign currency gain with respect to principal only. Thus, Z recognizes a total foreign currency gain on December 31, 2006, of $195 [£975 × ($1.20 – $1.00)].

(F) *Source.* In 2006, Z has an ordinary loss of $105, a capital loss of $25, and a foreign currency gain of $195. Under paragraph (b)(6) of this section and § 1.1275-4(b)(9)(iv), the $105 ordinary loss generally reduces Z's foreign source passive income under section 904(d) and the regulations thereunder. Under paragraph (b)(6) of this section and § 1.865-1(b)(2), the $25 capital loss is sourced by reference to how interest income on the instrument would have been sourced. Therefore, the $25 capital loss generally reduces Z's foreign source passive income under section 904(d) and the regulations thereunder. Under paragraph (b)(6) of this section and § 1.988-4, Z's foreign currency gain of $195 is sourced by reference to Z's residence and is therefore from sources within the United States.

Example 3. Negative adjustment and periodic interest payments—(i) *Facts.* On December 31, 2004, Z, a calendar year U.S. resident taxpayer whose functional currency is the U.S. dollar, purchases from a foreign corporation, at original issue, a two-year debt instrument with a non-currency contingency for £1000. All payments of principal and interest with respect to the instrument are denominated in, or determined by reference to, a single nonfunctional currency (the British pound). The debt instrument would be subject to § 1.1275-4(b) if it were denominated in dollars. The debt instrument's comparable yield, determined in British pounds under §§ 1.988-2(b)(2) and 1.1275-4(b), is 10 percent, compounded semiannually. The debt instrument provides for semiannual interest payments of £30 payable each June 30, and December 31, and a contingent payment at maturity on December 31, 2006, which is projected to equal £1086.20 (consisting of a noncontingent payment of £980 and a projected payment of £106.20) in addition to the interest payable at maturity. The debt instrument is a capital asset in the hands of Z. Z does not elect to use the spot-rate convention described in § 1.988-2(b)(2)(iii)(B). The payment actually made on December 31, 2006, is £981.00. The relevant pound/dollar spot rates over the term of the instrument are as follows:

Date	Spot rate (pounds to dollars)
Dec. 31, 2004	£1.00 = $1.00
June 30, 2005	£1.00 = $1.20
Dec. 31, 2005	£1.00 = $1.40
June 30, 2006	£1.00 = $1.60
Dec. 31, 2006	£1.00 = $1.80

Accrual period	Average rate (pounds to dollars)
Jan. – June 2005	£1.00 = $1.10
July – Dec. 2005	£1.00 = $1.30
Jan. – June 2006	£1.00 = $1.50
July – Dec. 2006	£1.00 = $1.70

(ii) *Treatment in 2005*—(A) *Determination of accrued interest.* Under paragraph (b)(2)(i) of this section, and based on the comparable yield, Z accrues £50 of interest on the debt instrument for the January-June accrual period (issue price of £1000 × 10 percent/2). Under paragraph (b)(3)(i) of this section, Z translates the £50 at the average exchange rate for the accrual period ($1.10 × £50 = $55.00). Similarly, Z accrues £51 of interest in the July-December accrual period [(£1000 + £50 – £30) × 10 percent/2], which is translated at the average exchange rate for the accrual period ($1.30 × £51 = $66.30). Accordingly, Z accrues $121.30 of interest income in 2005.

(B) *Adjusted issue price and basis*—(*1*) *January-June accrual period.* Under paragraphs (b)(2)(iii) and (iv) of this section, the adjusted issue price of the debt instrument determined in pounds and Z's adjusted basis in dollars in the debt instrument are increased by the interest accrued, and decreased by the interest payment made, in the January-June accrual period. Thus, on July 1, 2005, the adjusted issue price of the debt instrument is £1020 (£1000 + £50 – £30 = £1020). For purposes of determining Z's dollar basis in the debt instrument, the $1000 basis is increased by the £50 of accrued interest, translated, under paragraph (b)(3)(iii) of this section, at the rate at which interest was accrued for the January-June accrual period ($1.10 × £50 = $55). The resulting amount is reduced by the £30 payment of interest made during the accrual period, translated, under paragraph (b)(3)(iii) of this section and § 1.988-2(b)(7), at the rate applicable to accrued interest ($1.10 × £30 = $33). Accordingly, Z's adjusted basis as of July 1, 2005, is $1022 ($1000 + $55 – $33).

(2) *July-December accrual period.* Under paragraphs (b)(2)(iii) and (iv) of this section, the adjusted issue price of the debt instrument determined in pounds and Z's adjusted basis in dollars in the debt instrument are increased by the interest accrued, and decreased by the interest payment made, in the July-December accrual period. Thus, on January 1, 2006, the adjusted issue price of the instrument is £1041 (£1020 + £51 – £30 = £1041). For purposes of determining Z's dollar basis in the debt instrument, the $1022 basis is increased by the £51 of accrued interest, translated, under paragraph (b)(3)(iii) of this section, at the rate at which interest was accrued for the July-December accrual period ($1.30 × £51 = $66.30). The resulting amount is reduced by the £30 payment of interest made during the accrual period, translated, under paragraph (b)(3)(iii) of this section and § 1.988-2(b)(7), at the rate applicable to accrued interest ($1.30 × £30 = $39). Accordingly, Z's adjusted basis as of January 1, 2006, is $1049.30 ($1022 + $66.30 – $39).

(C) *Foreign currency gain or loss.* Z will recognize foreign currency gain on the receipt of each £30 payment of interest actually received during 2005. The amount of foreign currency gain in each case is determined, under paragraph (b)(5)(ii) of this section, by reference to the difference between the spot rate on the date the £30 payment was made and the average exchange rate for the accrual period during which the interest accrued. Accordingly, Z recognizes $3 of foreign currency gain on the January-June interest payment [£30 × ($1.20 – $1.10)], and $3 of foreign currency gain on the July-December interest payment [£30 × ($1.40 – $1.30)]. Z recognizes in 2005 a total of $6 of foreign currency gain.

(D) *Source.* Z has interest income of $121.30 and a foreign currency gain of $6. Under paragraph (b)(6) of this section and section 862(a)(1), the interest income is sourced by reference to the residence of the payor and is therefore from sources without the United States. Under paragraph (b)(6) of this section and § 1.988-4, Z's foreign currency gain of $6 is sourced by reference to Z's residence and is therefore from sources within the United States.

(iii) *Treatment in 2006—*(A) *Determination of accrued interest.* Under paragraph (b)(2)(i) of this section, and based on the comparable yield, Z's accrued interest for the January-June accrual period is £52.05 (adjusted issue price of £1041 × 10 percent/2). Under paragraph (b)(3)(i) of this section, Z translates the £52.05 at the average exchange rate for the accrual period ($1.50 × £52.05 = $78.08). Similarly, Z accrues £53.15 of interest in the July-December accrual period [(£1041 + £52.05 – £30) × 10 percent/2], which is translated at the average exchange rate for the accrual period ($1.70 × £53.15 = $90.35). Accordingly, Z accrues £105.20, or $168.43, of interest income in 2006.

(B) *Effect of net negative adjustment.* The payment actually made on December 31, 2006, is £981.00, rather than the projected £1086.20. Under paragraph (b)(2)(ii)(B) of this section, Z has a net negative adjustment of £105.20 on December 31, 2006, attributable to the difference between the amount of the actual payment and the amount of the projected payment. Z's accrued interest income of £105.20 in 2006 is reduced to zero by the net negative adjustment. Elimination of the 2006 accrued interest fully utilizes the net negative adjustment.

(C) *Adjusted issue price and basis—*(1) *January-June accrual period.* Under paragraphs (b)(2)(iii) and (iv) of this section, the adjusted issue price of the debt instrument determined in pounds and Z's adjusted basis in dollars in the debt instrument are increased by the interest accrued, and decreased by the interest payment made, in the January-June accrual period. Thus, on July 1, 2006, the adjusted issue price of the debt instrument is £1063.05 (£1041 + £52.05 – £30 = £1063.05). For purposes of determining Z's dollar basis in the debt instrument, the $1049.30 adjusted basis is increased by the £52.05 of accrued interest, translated, under paragraph (b)(3)(iii) of this section, at the rate at which interest was accrued for the January-June accrual period ($1.50 × £52.05 = $78.08). The resulting amount is reduced by the £30 payment of interest made during the accrual period, translated, under paragraph (b)(3)(iii) of this section and § 1.988-2(b)(7), at the rate applicable to accrued interest ($1.50 × £30 = $45). Accordingly, Z's adjusted basis as of July 1, 2006, is $1082.38 ($1049.30 + $78.08 – $45).

(2) *July-December accrual period.* Under paragraphs (b)(2)(iii) and (iv) of this section, the adjusted issue price of the debt instrument determined in pounds and Z's adjusted basis in dollars in the debt instrument are increased by the interest accrued, and decreased by the interest payment made, in the July-December accrual period. Thus, immediately before maturity on December 31, 2006, the adjusted issue price of the instrument is £1086.20 (£1063.05 + £53.15 – £30 = £1086.20). For purposes of determining Z's dollar basis in the debt instrument, the $1082.38 adjusted basis is increased by the £53.15 of accrued interest, translated, under paragraph (b)(3)(iii) of this section, at the rate at which interest was accrued for the July-December accrual period ($1.70 × £53.15 = $90.36). The resulting amount is reduced by the £30 payment of interest made during the accrual period, translated, under paragraph (b)(3)(iii) of this section and § 1.988-2(b)(7), at the rate applicable to accrued interest ($1.70 × £30 = $51). Accordingly, Z's adjusted basis on December 31, 2006, immediately prior to maturity is $1121.74 ($1082.38 + $90.36 – $51).

(D) *Amount realized.* Even though Z receives £981.00 at maturity, for purposes of determining the amount realized, Z is treated under paragraph (b)(2)(v) of this section as receiving the projected amount of the contingent payment on December 31, 2006. Therefore, Z is treated as receiving £1086.20 on December 31, 2006. Under paragraph (b)(3)(iv) of this section, Z translates its amount realized into dollars and computes its gain or loss on the instrument (other than foreign currency gain or loss) by breaking the amount realized into its component parts. Accordingly, £20 of the £1086.20 (representing the interest accrued in the January-June 2005 accrual period, less £30 interest paid) is translated into dollars at the rate at which it was accrued (£1 = $1.10), resulting in an amount realized of $22; £21 of the £1086.20 (representing the interest accrued in the July-December 2005 accrual period, less £30 interest paid) is translated into dollars at the rate at which it was accrued (£1 = $1.30), resulting in an amount realized of $27.30; £22.05 of the £1086.20 (representing the interest accrued in the January-June 2006 accrual period, less £30 interest paid) is translated into dollars at the rate at which it was accrued (£1 = $1.50), resulting in an amount realized of $33.08; £23.15 of the £1086.20 (representing the interest accrued in the July 1-December 31, 2006 accrual period, less the £30 interest payment) is translated into dollars at the rate at which it was accrued (£1 = $1.70), resulting in an amount realized of $39.36; and £1000 (representing principal) is translated into dollars at the spot rate on the date the instrument was purchased (£1 = $1), resulting in an amount realized of $1000. Accordingly, Z's total amount realized is $1121.74 ($22 + $27.30 + $33.08 + $39.36 + $1000), the same as its basis, and Z recognizes no gain or loss (before consideration of foreign currency gain or loss) on retirement of the instrument.

(E) *Foreign currency gain or loss.* Z recognizes foreign currency gain with respect to each £30 payment actually received during 2006. These payments, however, are treated as payments of principal for this purpose because all 2006 accrued interest is reduced to zero by the net negative adjustment. See paragraph (b)(5)(iv)(A)(*3*) of this section. The amount of foreign currency gain in each case is determined, under paragraph (b)(5)(iii) of this section, by reference to the difference between the spot rate on the date the £30 payment is made and the spot rate on the date the debt instrument was issued. Accordingly, Z recognizes $18 of foreign currency gain on the January-June 2006 interest payment [£30 × ($1.60 – $1.00)], and $24 of foreign currency gain on the July-December 2006 interest payment [£30 × ($1.80 – $1.00)]. Z separately recognizes foreign currency gain with respect to the consideration actually received at maturity, £981.00. The amount of such gain is determined based on the difference between the spot rate on the date the instrument matures and the rates at which the principal and interest were taken into account. With respect to the portion of the payment attributable to interest accrued in January-June 2005 (other than the £30 payments), the foreign currency gain is $14 [£20 × ($1.80 – $1.10)]. With respect to the portion of the payment attributable to interest accrued in July-December 2005 (other than the £30 payments), the foreign currency gain is $10.50 [£21 × ($1.80 – $1.30)]. With respect to the portion of the payment attributable to interest accrued in 2006 (other than the £30 payments), no foreign currency gain or loss is recognized under paragraph (b)(5)(ii) of this section because such interest was reduced to zero by the net negative adjustment. With respect to the portion of the payment attributable to principal, the foreign currency gain is $752 [£940 × ($1.80 – $1.00)]. Thus, Z recognizes a foreign currency gain of $42 on receipt of the two £30 payments in 2006, and $776.50 ($14 + $10.50 + $752) on receipt of the payment at maturity, for a total 2006 foreign currency gain of $818.50.

(F) *Source.* Under paragraph (b)(6) of this section and § 1.988-4, Z's foreign currency gain of $818.50 is sourced by reference to Z's residence and is therefore from sources within the United States.

Example 4. Purchase price greater than adjusted issue price—(i) *Facts.* On July 1, 2005, Z, a calendar year U.S. resident taxpayer whose functional currency is the U.S. dollar, purchases a debt instrument with a non-currency contingency for £1405. All payments of principal and interest with respect to the instrument are denominated in, or determined by reference to, a single nonfunctional currency (the British pound). The debt instrument would be subject to § 1.1275-4(b) if it were denominated in dollars. The debt instrument was originally issued by a foreign corporation on December 31, 2003, for an issue price of £1000, and matures on December 31, 2006. The debt instrument's comparable yield, determined in British pounds under

§§1.988-2(b)(2) and 1.1275-4(b), is 10.25 percent, compounded semiannually, and the projected payment schedule for the debt instrument (determined as of the issue date under the rules of §1.1275-4(b)) provides for a single payment at maturity of £1349.70 (consisting of a noncontingent payment of £1000 and a projected payment of £349.70). At the time of the purchase, the adjusted issue price of the debt instrument is £1161.76, assuming semiannual accrual periods ending on June 30 and December 31 of each year. The increase in the value of the debt instrument over its adjusted issue price is due to an increase in the expected amount of the contingent payment. The debt instrument is a capital asset in the hands of Z. Z does not elect to use the spot-rate convention described in §1.988-2(b)(2)(iii)(B). The payment actually made on December 31, 2006, is £1400. The relevant pound/dollar spot rates over the term of the instrument are as follows:

Date	Spot rate (pounds to dollars)
July 1, 2005	£1.00 = $1.00
Dec. 31, 2006	£1.00 = $2.00

Accrual period	Average rate (pounds to dollars)
July 1 – December 31, 2005	£1.00 = $1.50
January 1 – June 30, 2006	£1.00 = $1.50
July 1 – December 31, 2006	£1.00 = $1.50

(ii) *Initial basis.* Under paragraph (b)(7)(ii) of this section, Z's initial basis in the debt instrument is $1405, Z's purchase price of £1405, translated into functional currency at the spot rate on the date the debt instrument was purchased (£1 = $1).

(iii) *Allocation of purchase price differential.* Z purchased the debt instrument for £1405 when its adjusted issue price was £1161.76. Under paragraph (b)(7)(iii) of this section, Z allocates the £243.24 excess of purchase price over adjusted issue price to the contingent payment at maturity. This allocation is reasonable because the excess is due to an increase in the expected amount of the contingent payment and not, for example, to a decrease in prevailing interest rates.

(iv) *Treatment in 2005—(A) Determination of accrued interest.* Under paragraph (b)(2)(i) of this section, and based on the comparable yield, Z accrues £59.54 of interest on the debt instrument for the July-December 2005 accrual period (issue price of £1161.76 × 10.25 percent/2). Under paragraph (b)(3)(i) of this section, Z translates the £59.54 of interest at the average exchange rate for the accrual period ($1.50 × £59.54 = $89.31). Accordingly, Z has interest income in 2005 of $89.31.

(B) *Adjusted issue price and basis.* Under paragraphs (b)(2)(iii) and (iv) of this section, the adjusted issue price of the debt instrument determined in pounds and Z's adjusted basis in dollars in the debt instrument are increased by the interest accrued in July-December 2005. Thus, on January 1, 2006, the adjusted issue price of the debt instrument is £1221.30 (£1161.76 + £59.54). For purposes of determining Z's dollar basis in the debt instrument on January 1, 2006, the $1405 basis is increased by the £59.54 of accrued interest, translated at the rate at which interest was accrued for the July-December 2005 accrual period. Paragraph (b)(3)(iii) of this section. Accordingly, Z's adjusted basis in the instrument, as of January 1, 2006, is $1494.31 [$1405 + (£59.54 × $1.50)].

(v) *Treatment in 2006—(A) Determination of accrued interest.* Under paragraph (b)(2)(i) of this section, and based on the comparable yield, Z accrues £62.59 of interest on the debt instrument for the January-June 2006 accrual period (issue price of £1221.30 × 10.25 percent/2). Under paragraph (b)(3)(i) of this section, Z translates the £62.59 of accrued interest at the average exchange rate for the accrual period ($1.50 × £62.59 = $93.89). Similarly, Z accrues £65.80 of interest in the July-December 2006 accrual period [(£1221.30 + £62.59) × 10.25 percent/2], which is translated at the average exchange rate for the accrual period ($1.50 × £65.80 = $98.70). Accordingly, Z accrues £128.39, or $192.59, of interest income in 2006.

(B) *Effect of positive and negative adjustments—(1) Offset of positive adjustment.* The payment actually made on December 31, 2006, is £1400, rather than the projected £1349.70. Under paragraph (b)(2)(ii) of this section, Z has a positive adjustment of £50.30 on December 31, 2006, attributable to the difference between the amount of the actual payment and the amount of the projected payment. Under paragraph (b)(7)(iii) of this section, however, Z also has a negative adjustment of £243.24, attributable to the excess of Z's purchase price for the debt instrument over its adjusted issue price. Accordingly, Z will have a net negative adjustment of £192.94 (£50.30 – £243.24 = –£192.94) for 2006.

(2) *Offset of accrued interest.* Z's accrued interest income of £128.39 in 2006 is reduced to zero by the net negative adjustment. The net negative adjustment which reduces the current year's interest is not translated into functional currency. Under paragraph (b)(2)(ii) of this section, Z treats the remaining £64.55 net negative adjustment as an ordinary loss to the extent of the £59.54 previously accrued interest in 2005. This £59.54 ordinary loss is attributable to interest accrued but not paid in the preceding year. Therefore, under paragraph (b)(3)(ii)(B)(2) of this section, Z translates the loss into dollars at the average rate for such year (£1 = $1.50). Accordingly, Z has an ordinary loss of $89.31 in 2006. The remaining £5.01 of net negative adjustment is a negative adjustment carryforward under paragraph (b)(2)(ii) of this section.

(C) *Adjusted issue price and basis—(1) January-June accrual period.* Under paragraph (b)(2)(iii) of this section, the adjusted issue price of the debt instrument on July 1, 2006, is £1283.89 (£1221.30 + £62.59 = £1283.89). Under paragraphs (b)(2)(iv) and (b)(3)(iii) of this section, Z's adjusted basis as of July 1, 2006, is $1588.20 ($1494.31 + $93.89).

(2) *July-December accrual period.* Based on the projected payment schedule, the adjusted issue price of the debt instrument immediately before the payment at maturity is £1349.70 (£1283.89 + £65.80 accrued interest for July-December). Z's adjusted basis in dollars, based only on the noncontingent payments and the projected amount of the contingent payments to be received, is $1686.90 ($1588.20 plus $98.70 of accrued interest for July-December).

(3) *Adjustment to basis upon contingent payment.* Under paragraph (b)(7)(iii) of this section, Z's adjusted basis in the debt instrument is reduced at maturity by £243.24, the excess of Z's purchase price for the debt instrument over its adjusted issue price. For this purpose, the adjustment is translated into functional currency at the spot rate on the date the instrument was acquired (£1 = $1). Accordingly, Z's adjusted basis in the debt instrument at maturity is $1443.66 ($1686.90 – $243.24).

(D) *Amount realized.* Even though Z receives £1400 at maturity, for purposes of determining the amount realized, Z is treated under paragraph (b)(2)(v) of this section as receiving the projected amount of the contingent payment on December 31, 2006, reduced by the amount of Z's negative adjustment carryforward of £5.01. Therefore, Z is treated as receiving £1344.69 (£1349.70 – £5.01) on December 31, 2006. Under paragraph (b)(3)(iv) of this section, Z translates its amount realized into dollars and computes its gain or loss on the instrument (other than foreign currency gain or loss) by breaking the amount realized into its component parts. Accordingly, £59.54 of the £1344.69 (representing the interest accrued in 2005) is translated at the rate at which it was accrued (£1 = $1.50), resulting in an amount realized of $89.31; £62.59 of the £1344.69 (representing the interest accrued in January-June 2006) is translated into dollars at the rate at which it was accrued (£1 = $1.50), resulting in an amount realized of $93.89; £65.80 of the £1344.69 (representing the interest accrued in July-December 2006) is translated into dollars at the rate at which it was accrued (£1 = $1.50), resulting in an amount realized of $98.70; and £1156.76 of the £1344.69 (representing a return of principal) is translated into dollars at the spot rate on the date the instrument was purchased (£1 = $1), resulting in an amount realized of $1156.76. Z's amount realized is $1438.66 ($89.31 + $93.89 + $98.70 + $1156.76), and Z recognizes a capital loss (before consideration of foreign currency gain or loss) of $5 on retirement of the instrument ($1438.66 - $1443.66 = –$5).

(E) *Foreign currency gain or loss.* Z recognizes foreign currency gain under section 988 on the instrument with respect to the entire consideration actually received at maturity, £1400. While foreign currency gain or loss ordinarily would not have arisen with respect to £50.30 of the £1400, which was initially treated as a positive adjustment in 2006, the larger negative adjustment in 2006 reduced this positive adjustment to zero. Accordingly, foreign currency gain or loss is recognized with respect to the entire £1400. Under paragraph (b)(5)(ii) of this section, however, no foreign currency gain or loss is recognized with respect to unpaid accrued interest reduced to zero by the net negative adjustment resulting in 2006, and no foreign currency gain or loss is recognized with respect to unpaid accrued interest from 2005, also reduced to zero by the ordinary loss. Therefore, the entire £1400 is treated as a return of principal for the purpose of determining foreign currency gain or loss, and Z recognizes a total foreign currency gain on December 31, 2001, of $1400 [£1400 × ($2.00 – $1.00)].

(F) *Source.* Z has an ordinary loss of $89.31, a capital loss of $5, and a foreign currency gain of $1400. Under paragraph (b)(6) of this section and §1.1275-4(b)(9)(iv), the $89.31 ordinary loss generally reduces Z's foreign source passive income under section 904(d) and the regulations thereunder. Under paragraph (b)(6) of this section and §1.865-1(b)(2), the $5 capital loss is sourced by reference to how interest income on the instrument would have been sourced. Therefore, the $5 capital loss generally reduces Z's foreign source passive income under section 904(d) and the regulations thereunder. Under paragraph (b)(6) of this section and § 1.988-4, Z's foreign currency gain of $1400 is sourced by reference to Z's residence and is therefore from sources within the United States.

Example 5. Sale of an instrument with a negative adjustment carryforward—(i) *Facts.* On December 31, 2003, Z, a calendar year U.S. resident taxpayer whose functional currency is the U.S. dollar, purchases at original issue a debt instrument with non-currency contingencies for £1000. All payments of principal and interest with respect to the instrument are denominated in, or determined by reference to, a single nonfunctional currency (the British pound). The debt instrument would be subject to § 1.1275-4(b) if it were denominated in dollars. The debt instrument's comparable yield, determined in British pounds under §§ 1.988-2(b)(2) and 1.1275-4(b), is 10 percent, compounded annually, and the projected payment schedule for the debt instrument provides for payments of £310 on December 31, 2005 (consisting of a noncontingent payment of £50 and a projected amount of £260) and £990 on December 31, 2006 (consisting of a noncontingent payment of £940 and a projected amount of £50). The debt instrument is a capital asset in the hands of Z. Z does not elect to use the spot-rate convention described in § 1.988-2(b)(2)(iii)(B). The payment actually made on December 31, 2005, is £50. On December 30, 2006, Z sells the debt instrument for £940. The relevant pound/dollar spot rates over the term of the instrument are as follows:

Date	Spot rate (pounds to dollars)
Dec. 31, 2003	£1.00 = $1.00
Dec. 31, 2005	£1.00 = $2.00
Dec. 30, 2006	£1.00 = $2.00

Accrual period	Average rate (pounds to dollars)
January 1 –December 31, 2004	£1.00 = $2.00
January 1 –December 31, 2005	£1.00 = $2.00
January 1 –December 31, 2006	£1.00 = $2.00

(ii) *Treatment in 2004*—(A) *Determination of accrued interest.* Under paragraph (b)(2)(i) of this section, and based on the comparable yield, Z accrues £100 of interest on the debt instrument for 2004 (issue price of £1000 × 10 percent). Under paragraph (b)(3)(i) of this section, Z translates the £100 at the average exchange rate for the accrual period ($2.00 × £100 = $200). Accordingly, Z has interest income in 2004 of $200.

(B) *Adjusted issue price and basis.* Under paragraphs (b)(2)(iii) and (iv) of this section, the adjusted issue price of the debt instrument determined in pounds and Z's adjusted basis in dollars in the debt instrument are increased by the interest accrued in 2004. Thus, on January 1, 2005, the adjusted issue price of the debt instrument is £1100. For purposes of determining Z's dollar basis in the debt instrument, the $1000 basis ($1.00 × £1000 original cost basis) is increased by the £100 of accrued interest, translated at the rate at which interest was accrued for 2004. See paragraph (b)(3)(iii) of this section. Accordingly, Z's adjusted basis in the debt instrument as of January 1, 2005, is $1200 ($1000 + $200).

(iii) *Treatment in 2005*—(A) *Determination of accrued interest.* Under paragraph (b)(2)(i) of this section, and based on the comparable yield, Z's accrued interest for 2005 is £110 (adjusted issue price of £1100 × 10 percent). Under paragraph (b)(3)(i) of this section, the £110 of accrued interest is translated at the average exchange rate for the accrual period ($2.00 × £110 = $220).

(B) *Effect of net negative adjustment.* The payment actually made on December 31, 2005, is £50, rather than the projected £310. Under paragraph (b)(2)(ii) of this section, Z has a net negative adjustment of £260 on December 31, 2005, attributable to the difference between the amount of the actual payment and the amount of the projected payment. Z's accrued interest income of £110 in 2005 is reduced to zero by the net negative adjustment. Under paragraph (b)(3)(ii)(B)(*1*) of this section, the net negative adjustment which reduces the current year's interest is not translated into functional currency. Under paragraph (b)(2)(ii) of this section, Z treats the remaining £150 net negative adjustment as an ordinary loss to the extent of the £100 previously accrued interest in 2004. This £100 ordinary loss is attributable to interest accrued but not paid in the preceding year. Therefore, under paragraph (b)(3)(ii)(B)(*2*) of this section, Z translates the loss into dollars at the average rate for such year (£1 = $2.00). Accordingly, Z has an ordinary loss of $200 in 2005. The remaining £50 of net negative adjustment is a negative adjustment carryforward under paragraph (b)(2)(ii) of this section.

(C) *Adjusted issue price and basis.* Based on the projected payment schedule, the adjusted issue price of the debt instrument on January 1, 2006 is £900, i.e., the adjusted issue price of the debt instrument on January 1, 2005 (£1100), increased by the interest accrued in 2005 (£110), and decreased by the projected amount of the December 31, 2005, payment (£310). See paragraph (b)(2)(iii) of this section. Z's adjusted basis on January 1, 2006 is Z's adjusted basis on January 1, 2005 ($1200), increased by the functional currency amount of interest accrued in 2005 ($220), and decreased by the amount of the payments made in 2005, based solely on the projected payment schedule, (£310). The amount of the projected payment is first attributable to the interest accrued in 2005 (£110), and then to the interest accrued in 2004 (£100), and the remaining amount to principal (£100). The interest component of the projected payment is translated into functional currency at the rates at which it was accrued, and the principal component of the projected payment is translated into functional currency at the spot rate on the date the instrument was issued. See paragraph (b)(3)(iii) of this section. Accordingly, Z's adjusted basis in the debt instrument, following the increase of adjusted basis for interest accrued in 2005 ($1200 + $220 = $1420), is decreased by $520 ($220 + $200 + $100 = $520). Z's adjusted basis on January 1, 2006 is therefore, $900.

(D) *Foreign currency gain or loss.* Z will recognize foreign currency gain on the receipt of the £50 payment actually received on December 31, 2005. Based on paragraph (b)(5)(iv) of this section, the £50 payment is attributable to principal since the accrued unpaid interest was completely eliminated by the net negative adjustment. The amount of foreign currency gain is determined, under paragraph (b)(5)(iii) of this section, by reference to the difference between the spot rate on the date the £50 payment was made and the spot rate on the date the debt instrument was issued. Accordingly, Z recognizes $50 of foreign currency gain on the £50 payment. [($2.00 – $1.00) × £50 = $50]. Under paragraph (b)(6) of this section and § 1.988-4, Z's foreign currency gain of $50 is sourced by reference to Z's residence and is therefore from sources within the United States.

(iv) *Treatment in 2006*—(A) *Determination of accrued interest.* Under paragraph (b)(2)(i) of this section, and based on the comparable yield, Z accrues £90 of interest on the debt instrument for 2006 (adjusted issue price of £900 × 10 percent). Under paragraph (b)(3)(i) of this section, Z translates the £90 at the average exchange rate for the accrual period ($2.00 × £90 = $180). Accordingly, prior to taking into account the 2005 negative adjustment carryforward, Z has interest income in 2006 of $180.

(B) *Effect of net negative adjustment.* The £50 negative adjustment carryforward from 2005 is a negative adjustment for 2006. Since there are no other positive or negative adjustments, there is a £50 negative adjustment in 2006 which reduces Z's accrued interest income by £50. Accordingly, after giving effect to the £50 negative adjustment carryforward, Z will accrue $80 of interest income. [(£90 – £50) × $2.00 = $80].

(C) *Adjusted issue price.* Under paragraph (b)(2)(iii) of this section, the adjusted issue price of the debt instrument determined in pounds is increased by the interest accrued in 2006 (prior to taking into account the negative adjustment carryforward). Thus, on December 30, 2006, the adjusted issue price of the debt instrument is £990.

(D) *Adjusted basis.* For purposes of determining Z's dollar basis in the debt instrument, Z's $900 adjusted basis on January 1, 2006, is increased by the accrued interest, translated at the rate at which interest was accrued for 2006. See paragraph (b)(3)(iii)(A) of this section. Note, however, that under paragraph (b)(3)(iii)(B) of this section the amount of accrued interest which is reduced as a result of the negative adjustment carryforward, i.e., £50, is treated for purposes of this section as principal, and is translated at the spot rate on the date the instrument was issued, i.e., £1.00 = $1.00. Accordingly, Z's adjusted basis in the debt instrument as of December 30, 2006, is $1030 ($900 + $50 + $80).

(E) *Amount realized.* Z's amount realized in denomination currency is £940, i.e., the amount of pounds Z received on the sale of the debt instrument. Under paragraph (b)(3)(iv)(B)(*1*) of this section, Z's amount realized is first translated by reference to the principal component of basis (including the amount which is treated as principal under paragraph (b)(3)(iii)(B) of this section) and then the remaining amount realized, if any, is translated by reference to the accrued unpaid interest component of adjusted basis. Thus, £900 of Z's amount realized is translated by reference to the principal component of adjusted basis. The remaining £40 of Z's amount realized is treated as principal under paragraph (b)(3)(iii)(B) of this section, and is also is translated by reference to the principal component of adjusted basis. Accordingly, Z's amount realized in functional currency is $940. (No part of Z's amount realized is attributable to the interest accrued on the debt instrument.) Z realizes a loss of $90 on the sale of the debt instrument ($1030 basis – $940 amount realized). Under paragraph (b)(4) of this section and § 1.1275-4(b)(8), $80 of the loss is characterized as ordinary loss, and the remaining $10 of loss is characterized as capital loss. Under § § 1.988-6(b)(6) and 1.1275-4(b)(9)(iv) the $80 ordinary loss is treated as a deduction that is definitely related to the interest income accrued on the debt instrument. Similarly, under § § 1.988-6(b)(6) and 1.865-1(b)(2) the $10 capital loss is also allocated to the interest income from the debt instrument.

(F) *Foreign currency gain or loss.* Z recognizes foreign currency gain with respect to the £940 he received on the sale of the debt instrument. Under paragraph (b)(5)(iv) of this section, the £940 Z received is attributable to principal (and the amount which is treated as principal under paragraph (b)(3)(iii)(B) of this section). Thus, Z recognizes foreign currency gain on December 31, 2006, of $940. [($2.00 – $1.00) × £940]. Under paragraph (b)(6) of this section and § 1.988-4, Z's foreign currency gain of $940 is sourced by reference to Z's residence and is therefore from sources within the United States.

(d) *Multicurrency debt instruments.*—(1) *In general.*—Except as provided in this paragraph (d), a multicurrency debt instrument described in paragraph (a)(1)(ii) or (iii) of this section shall be treated as an instrument described in paragraph (a)(1)(i) of this section and shall be accounted for under the rules of paragraph (b) of this section. Because payments on an instrument described in paragraph (a)(1)(ii) or (iii) of this section are denominated in, or determined by reference to, more than one currency, the issuer and holder or holders of the instrument are required to determine the denomination currency of the instrument under paragraph (d)(2) of this section before applying the rules of paragraph (b) of this section.

(2) *Determination of denomination currency.*—(i) *In general.*—The denomination currency of an instrument described in paragraph (a)(1)(ii) or (iii) of this section shall be the predominant currency of the instrument. Except as otherwise provided in paragraph (d)(2)(ii) of this section, the predominant currency of the instrument shall be the currency with the greatest value determined by comparing the functional currency value of the noncontingent and projected payments denominated in, or determined by reference to, each currency on the issue date, discounted to present value (in each relevant currency), and translated (if necessary) into functional currency at the spot rate on the issue date. For this purpose, the applicable discount rate may be determined using any method, consistently applied, that reasonably reflects the instrument's economic substance. If a taxpayer does not determine a discount rate using such a method, the Commissioner may choose a method for determining the discount rate that does reflect the instrument's economic substance. The predominant currency is determined as of the issue date and does not change based on subsequent events (e.g., changes in value of one or more currencies).

(ii) *Difference in discount rate of greater than 10 percentage points.*—This § 1.988-6(d)(2)(ii) applies if no currency has a value determined under paragraph (d)(2)(i) of this section that is greater than 50% of the total value of all payments. In such a case, if the difference between the discount rate in the denomination currency otherwise determined under (d)(2)(i) of this section and the discount rate determined under paragraph (d)(2)(i) of this section with respect to any other currency in which payments are made (or determined by reference to) pursuant to the instrument is greater than 10 percentage points, then the Commissioner may determine the predominant currency under any reasonable method.

(3) *Issuer/holder consistency.*—The issuer determines the denomination currency under the rules of paragraph (d)(2) of this section and provides this information to the holders of the instrument in a manner consistent with the issuer disclosure rules of § 1.1275-2(e). If the issuer does not determine the denomination currency of the instrument, or if the issuer's determination is unreasonable, the holder of the instrument must determine the denomination currency under the rules of paragraph (d)(2) of this section. A holder that determines the denomination currency itself must explicitly disclose this fact on a statement attached to the holder's timely filed federal income tax return for the taxable year that includes the acquisition date of the instrument.

(4) *Treatment of payments in currencies other than the denomination currency.*—For purposes of applying the rules of paragraph (b) of this section to debt instruments described in paragraph (a)(1)(ii) or (iii) of this section, payments not denominated in (or determined by reference to) the denomination currency shall be treated as non-currency-related contingent payments. Accordingly, if the denomination currency of the instrument is determined to be the taxpayer's functional currency, the instrument shall be accounted for under § 1.1275-4(b) rather than under this section.

(e) *Instruments issued for nonpublicly traded property.*—(1) *Applicability.*—This paragraph (e) applies to debt instruments issued for nonpublicly traded property that would be described in paragraph (a)(1)(i), (ii), or (iii) of this section, but for the fact that such instruments are described in § 1.1275-4(c)(1) rather than § 1.1275-4(b)(1). For example, this paragraph (e) generally applies to a contingent payment debt instrument denominated in a nonfunctional currency that is issued for non-publicly traded property. Generally the rules of § 1.1275-4(c) apply except as set forth by the rules of this paragraph (e).

(2) *Separation into components.*—An instrument described in this paragraph (e) is not accounted for using the noncontingent bond method of § 1.1275-4(b) and paragraph (b) of this section. Rather, the instrument is separated into its component payments. Each noncontingent payment or group of noncontingent payments which is denominated in a single currency shall be considered a single component treated as a separate debt instrument denominated in the currency of the payment or group of payments. Each contingent payment shall be treated separately as provided in paragraph (e)(4) of this section.

(3) *Treatment of components consisting of one or more noncontingent payments in the same currency.*—The issue price of each component treated as a separate debt instrument which consists of one or more noncontingent payments is the sum of the present values of the noncontingent payments contained in the separate instrument. The present value of any noncontingent payment shall be determined under § 1.1274-2(c)(2), and the test rate shall be determined under § 1.1274-4 with respect to the currency in which each separate instrument is considered denominated. No interest payments on the separate debt instrument are qualified stated interest payments (within the meaning of § 1.1273-1(c)) and the de minimis rules of section 1273(a)(3) and § 1.1273-1(d) do not apply to the separate debt instrument. Interest income or expense is translated, and exchange gain or loss is recognized on the separate debt instrument as provided in § 1.988-2(b)(2), if the instrument is denominated in a nonfunctional currency.

(4) *Treatment of components consisting of contingent payments.*—(i) *General rule.*—A component consisting of a contingent payment shall generally be treated in the manner provided in § 1.1275-4(c)(4). However, except as provided in paragraph (e)(4)(ii) of this section, the test rate shall be determined by reference to the U.S. dollar unless the dollar does not reasonably reflect the economic substance of the contingent component. In such case, the test rate shall be determined by reference to the currency which most reasonably reflects the economic substance of the contingent component. Any amount received in nonfunctional currency from a component consisting of a contingent payment shall be translated into functional currency at the spot rate on the date of receipt. Except in the case when the payment becomes fixed more than six months before the payment is due, no foreign currency gain or loss shall be recognized on a contingent payment component.

(ii) *Certain delayed contingent payments.*—(A) *Separate debt instrument relating to the fixed component.*—The rules of § 1.1275-4(c)(4)(iii) shall apply to a contingent component the payment of which becomes fixed more than 6 months before the payment is due. For this purpose, the denomination currency of the separate debt instrument relating to the fixed payment shall be the currency in which payment is to be made and the test rate for such separate debt instrument shall be determined in the currency of that instrument. If the separate debt instrument relating to the fixed payment is denominated in nonfunctional currency, the rules of § 1.988-2(b)(2) shall apply to that instrument for the period beginning on the date the payment is fixed and ending on the payment date.

(B) *Contingent component.*—With respect to the contingent component, the issue price considered to have been paid by the issuer to the holder under § 1.1275-4(c)(4)(iii)(A) shall be translated, if necessary, into the functional currency of the issuer or holder at the spot rate on the date the payment becomes fixed.

(5) *Basis different from adjusted issue price.*—The rules of § 1.1275-4(c)(5) shall apply to an instrument subject to this paragraph (e).

(6) *Treatment of a holder on sale, exchange, or retirement.*—The rules of § 1.1275-4(c)(6) shall apply to an instrument subject to this paragraph (e).

(f) *Rules for nonfunctional currency tax exempt obligations described in § 1.1275-4(d).*—(1) *In general.*—Except as provided in paragraph (f)(2) of this section, section 1.988-6 shall not apply to a debt instrument the interest on which is excluded from gross income under section 103(a).

(2) *Operative rules.*—[RESERVED].

(g) *Effective date.*—This section shall apply to debt instruments issued on or after October 29, 2004. [Reg. § 1.988-6.]

☐ [*T.D.* 9157, 8-27-2004.]

Proposed Regulation

§ 1.988-7. Election to mark-to-market foreign currency gain or loss on section 988 transactions.—(a) *In general.*—Except as provided in paragraph (b) of this section, a taxpayer may elect under this section to apply the foreign currency mark-to-market method of accounting described in this section with respect to all section 988 transactions (including the acquisition and holding of nonfunctional currency described in section 988(c)(1)(C)(ii)). Under the foreign currency mark-to-market method of accounting, the timing of section 988 gain or loss on section 988 transactions is determined under the principles of section 1256. Only section 988 gain or loss is taken into account under the foreign currency mark-to-market method of accounting. Consistent with section 1256(a)(2), appropriate adjustments must be made to prevent the section 988 gain or loss from being taken into account again under section 988 or another provision of the Code or regulations. A section 988 transaction subject to this election is not subject to the "netting rule" of section 988(b) and § 1.988-2(b)(8), under which exchange gain or loss is limited to overall gain or loss realized in a transaction, in taxable years prior to the taxable year in which section 988 gain or loss would be recognized with respect to such section 988 transaction but for this election.

(b) *Exceptions.*—The election described in paragraph (a) of this section does not apply to:

(1) Any security, commodity, or section 1256 contract that is marked to market under any other provision, including section 475 or section 1256;

(2) Any security, commodity, or section 1256 contract that, pursuant to an election or an identification made by the taxpayer, is excepted from mark-to-market treatment under another provision, including section 475 or section 1256;

(3) Any transaction of a qualified business unit (as defined in section 1.989(a)-1(b)) that is subject to section 987; or

(4) Any section 988 transaction denominated in, or determined by reference to, a hyperinflationary currency. See § 1.988-2(b)(15), (d)(5), and (e)(7) for rules relating to such transactions.

(c) *Time and manner of election.*—A taxpayer makes the election under paragraph (a) of this section by filing a statement that clearly indicates that such election has been made with the taxpayer's timely-filed original federal income tax return for the taxable year for which the election is made. In the case of a controlled foreign corporation, the controlling United States shareholders (as defined in § 1.964-1(c)(5)) make the election under paragraph (a) of this section on behalf of the controlled foreign corporation by filing a statement that clearly indicates that such election has been made with their timely-filed, original federal income tax returns for the taxable year of such United States shareholders ending with or within the taxable year of the controlled foreign corporation for which the election is made.

(d) *Revocation and subsequent election.*—A taxpayer may revoke its election under paragraph (a) of this section at any time. If an election has been revoked under this paragraph (d), a new election under paragraph (a) of this section cannot be made until the sixth taxable year following the year in which the previous election was revoked, and such subsequent election cannot be revoked until the sixth taxable year following the year in which the subsequent election was made. A taxpayer revokes the election by filing a statement that clearly indicates that such election has been revoked with its original or amended federal income tax return for the taxable year for which the election is revoked. In the case of a controlled foreign corporation, the controlling United States shareholders revoke the election on behalf of the controlled foreign corporation by filing a statement that clearly indicates that such election has been revoked with their original or amended federal income tax returns for the taxable year of such United States shareholders ending with or within the taxable year of the controlled foreign corporation for which the election is revoked.

(e) *Applicability dates.*—This section applies to taxable years of taxpayers (including controlled foreign corporations) ending on or after the date these regulations are published as final regulations in the *Federal Register*.

[Prop. Reg. § 1.988-7.]

[Proposed 12-19-2017.]

»»→ Caution: The Treasury Department has identified Reg. §1.989(a)-1, as amended by T.D. 9794, as a significant tax regulation that imposes an undue financial burden on U.S. taxpayers and/or adds undue complexity to the federal tax laws, pursuant to Executive Order 13789 (issued April 21, 2017) (Notice 2017-38, I.R.B. 2017-30, 147). In a subsequent report, published October 16, 2017, Treasury recommended planned actions that would reduce the burden of these regulations, including an extension of the application date of T.D. 9794 (see Notice 2022-34, I.R.B. 2022-34, 150).

§ 1.989(a)-1. Definition of a Qualified Business Unit.—(a) *Applicability.*—(1) *In general.*—This section provides rules relating to the definition of the term "qualified business unit" (QBU) within the meaning of section 989.

(2) *Effective date.*—These rules shall apply to taxable years beginning after December 31, 1986. However, any person may apply on a consistent basis § 1.989(a)-1T(c) of the Temporary Income Tax Regulations in lieu of § 1.989(a)-1(c) to all taxable years beginning after December 31, 1986, and on or before February 3, 1990. For the text of the temporary regulation, see 53 FR 20612 (June 8, 1988).

(b) *Definition of a qualified business unit.*—(1) *In general.*—A QBU is any separate and clearly identified unit of a trade or business of a taxpayer provided that separate books and records are maintained.

(2) *Application of the QBU definition.*—(i) *Persons.*—(A) *Corporations.*—A corporation is a QBU.

(B) *Individuals.*—An individual is not a QBU.

(C) *Partnerships.*—A partnership, other than a section 987 aggregate partnership as defined in § 1.987-1(b)(5), is a QBU.

(D) *Trusts and estates.*—A trust or estate is a QBU of a beneficiary.

(ii) *Activities.*—Activities of a corporation, partnership, trust, estate, or individual qualify as a QBU if—

(A) The activities constitute a trade or business; and

(B) A separate set of books and records is maintained with respect to the activities.

(3) *Special rule.*—Any activity (wherever conducted and regardless of its frequency) that produces income or loss that is, or is treated as, effectively connected with the conduct of a trade or business within the United States shall be treated as a separate QBU, provided the books and records requirement of paragraph (d)(2) of this section is satisfied.

(4) *Effective/applicability date.*—Generally, the revisions to paragraph (b)(2)(i) of this section shall apply to taxable years beginning on or after one year after the first day of the first taxable year following December 7, 2016. If pursuant to § 1.987-11(b) a taxpayer applies §§ 1.987-1 through 1.987-11 beginning in a taxable year prior to the earliest taxable year described in § 1.987-11(a), then the effective date of the revisions to paragraph (b)(2)(i) of this section with respect to the taxpayer shall apply to taxable years of the taxpayer beginning on or after the first day of such prior taxable year.

(c) *Trade or business.*—The determination as to whether activities constitute a trade or business is ultimately dependent upon an examination of all the facts and circumstances. Generally, a trade or business for purposes of section 989(a) is a specific unified group of activities that constitutes (or could constitute) an independent economic enterprise carried on for profit, the expenses related to which are deductible under section 162 or 212 (other than that part of section 212 dealing with expenses incurred in connection with taxes).

To constitute a trade or business, a group of activities must ordinarily include every operation which forms a part of, or a step in, a process by which an enterprise may earn income or profit. Such group of activities must ordinarily include the collection of income and the payment of expenses. It is not necessary that the activities carried out by a QBU constitute a different trade or business from those carried out by other QBUs of the taxpayer. A vertical, functional, or geographic division of the same trade or business may be a trade or business for this purpose provided that the activities otherwise qualify as a trade or business under this paragraph (c). However, activities that are merely ancillary to a trade or business will not constitute a trade or business under this paragraph (c). Activities of an individual as an employee are not considered by themselves to constitute a trade or business under this paragraph (c).

(d) *Separate books and records.*—(1) *General rule.*—Except as provided in paragraph (d)(2) of this section, a separate set of books and records shall include books of original entry and ledger accounts, both general and subsidiary, or similar records. For example, in the case of a taxpayer using the cash receipts and disbursements method of accounting, the books of original entry include a cash receipts and disbursements journal where each receipt and each disbursement is recorded. Similarly, in the case of a taxpayer using an accrual method of accounting, the books of original entry include a journal to record sales (accounts receivable) and a journal to record expenses incurred (accounts payable). In general, a journal represents a chronological account of all transactions entered into by an entity for an accounting period. A ledger account, on the other hand, chronicles the impact during an accounting period of the specific transactions recorded in the journal for that period upon the various items shown on the entity's balance sheet (*i.e.*, assets, liabilities, and capital accounts) and income statement (*i.e.*, revenues and expenses).

(2) *Special rule.*—For purposes of paragraph (b)(3) of this section, books and records include books and records used to determine income or loss that is, or is treated as, effectively connected with the conduct of a trade or business within the United States.

(3) *Proper reflection on the books of the taxpayer or qualified business unit.*—The principles of § 1.987-2(b) shall apply in determining whether an asset, liability, or item of income or expense is reflected on the books of a qualified business unit (and therefore is attributable to such unit).

(4) *Effective/applicability date.*—Generally, the revisions to paragraph (d)(3) of this section shall apply to taxable years beginning on or after one year after the first day of the first taxable year following December 7, 2016. If pursuant to § 1.987-11(b) a taxpayer applies §§ 1.987-1 through 1.987-11 beginning in a taxable year prior to the earliest taxable year described in § 1.987-11(a), then the revisions to paragraph (b)(2)(i) of this section shall apply with respect to taxable years of the taxpayer beginning on or after the first day of such prior taxable year.

(e) *Examples.*—The provisions of this section may be illustrated by the following examples:

Example (1). Corporation X is a domestic corporation. Corporation X manufactures widgets in the U.S. for export. Corporation X sells widgets in the United Kingdom through a branch office in London. The London office has its own employees and solicits and processes orders. Corporation X maintains in the U.S. a separate set of books and records for all transactions conducted by the London office. Corporation X is a QBU under paragraph (b)(2)(i) of this section because of its corporate status. The London branch office is a QBU under paragraph (b)(2)(ii) of this section because (1) the sale of widgets is a trade or business as defined in paragraph (c) of this section; and (2) a complete and separate set of books and records (as described in paragraph (d) of this section) is maintained with respect to its sales operations.

Example (2). A domestic corporation incorporates a wholly-owned subsidiary in Switzerland. The domestic corporation is a manufacturer that markets its product abroad primarily through the Swiss subsidiary. To facilitate sales of the parent's product in Europe, the Swiss subsidiary has branch offices in France and West Germany that are responsible for all marketing operations in those countries. Each branch has its own employees, solicits and processes orders, and maintains a separate set of books and records. The domestic corporation and the Swiss subsidiary are both QBUs under paragraph (b)(2)(i) of this section because of their corporate status. The French and West German branches are QBUs of the Swiss subsidiary. They satisfy paragraph (b)(2)(ii) because each constitutes a trade or business (as defined in paragraph (c) of this section) and because separate sets of books and records (as described in paragraph (d) of this section) of their respective operations is maintained. Each branch is considered to have a trade or business although each is a geographical division of the same trade or business.

Example (3). W is a domestic corporation that manufactures product X in the United States for sale worldwide. All of W's sales functions are conducted exclusively in the United States. W employs individual Q to work in France. Q's sole function is to act as a courier to deliver sales documents to customers in France. With respect to Q's activities in France, a separate set of books and records as described in paragraph (d) is maintained. Under paragraph (c) of this section, Q's activities in France do not constitute a QBU since they are merely ancillary to W's manufacturing and selling business. Q is not considered to have a QBU because an individual's activities as an employee are not considered to constitute a trade or business of the individual under paragraph (c).

Example (4). The facts are the same as in example (3) except that the courier function is the sole activity of a wholly-owned French subsidiary of W. Under paragraph (b)(2)(i) of this section, the French subsidiary is considered to be a QBU.

Example (5). A corporation incorporated in the Netherlands is a subsidiary of a domestic corporation and a holding company for the stock of one or more subsidiaries incorporated in other countries. The Dutch corporation's activities are limited to paying its directors and its administrative expenses, receiving capital contributions from its United States parent corporation, contributing capital to its subsidiaries, receiving dividend distributions from its subsidiaries, and distributing dividends to its domestic parent corporation. Under paragraph (b)(2)(i) of this section, the Netherlands corporation is considered to be a QBU.

Example (6). Taxpayer A, an individual resident of the United States, is engaged in a trade or business wholly unrelated to any type of investment activity. A also maintains a portfolio of foreign currency-denominated investments through a foreign broker. The broker is responsible for all activities necessary to the management of A's investments and maintains books and records as described in paragraph (d) of this section, with respect to all investment activities of A. A's investment activities qualify as a QBU under paragraph (b)(2)(ii) of this section to the extent the activities engaged in by A generate expenses that are deductible under section 212 (other than that part of section 212 dealing with expenses incurred in connection with taxes).

Example (7). Taxpayer A, an individual resident of the United States, is the sole shareholder of foreign corporation (FC) whose activities are limited to trading in stocks and securities. FC is a QBU under paragraph (b)(2)(i) of this section.

Example (8). Taxpayer A, an individual resident of the United States, markets and sells in Spain and in the United States various products produced by other United States manufacturers. A has an office and employs a salesman to manage A's activities in Spain, maintains a separate set of books and records with respect to his activities in Spain, and is engaged in a trade or business as defined in paragraph (c) of this section. Therefore, under paragraph (b)(2)(ii) of this section, the activities of A in Spain are considered to be a QBU.

Example (9). Foreign corporation FX is incorporated in Mexico and is wholly owned by a domestic corporation. The domestic corporation elects to treat FX as a domestic corporation under section 1504(d). FX operates entirely in Mexico and maintains a separate set of books and records with respect to its activities in Mexico. FX is a QBU under paragraph (b)(2)(i) of this section. The activities of FX in Mexico also constitute a QBU under paragraph (b)(2)(ii) of this section.

Example (10). F, a foreign corporation, computes a gain of $100 from the disposition of a United States real property interest (as defined in section 897(c)). The gain is taken into account as if F were engaged in a trade or business in the United States and as if such gain were effectively connected with such trade or business. F is a QBU under paragraph (b)(2)(i) of this section because of its corporate status. F's disposition activity constitutes a separate QBU under paragraph (b)(3) of this section. [Reg. § 1.989(a)-1.]

☐ [*T.D. 8279, 1-3-90. Amended by T.D. 9794, 12-7-2016.*]

§ 1.989(b)-1. Definition of weighted average exchange rate.—For purposes of section 989(b)(3) and (4), the term "weighted average exchange rate" means the simple average of the daily exchange rates (determined by reference to a qualified source of exchange rates described in § 1.988-1(d)(1)), excluding weekends, holidays and any other nonbusiness days for the taxable year. [Reg. § 1.989(b)-1.]

☐ [*T.D. 8263, 9-19-89. Amended by T.D. 8367, 9-24-91 and T.D. 9452, 6-10-2009.*]

Domestic International Sales Corporations

§1.994-1. Inter-company pricing rules for DISC's.—

* * *

(e) *Methods of applying paragraphs (c) and (d) of this section.*—(1) *Limitation on DISC income ("no loss" rule).*—(i) *In general.*—Except as otherwise provided in this subparagraph, neither the gross receipts method nor the combined taxable income method may be applied to cause in any taxable year a loss to the related supplier, but either method may be applied to the extent it does not cause a loss. A loss to a related supplier would result if the taxable income of the DISC would exceed the combined taxable income of the related supplier and the DISC. If, however, there is no combined taxable income of the DISC and the related supplier (because, for example, a combined loss is incurred), a transfer price (or commission) will not be deemed to cause a loss to the related supplier if it allows the DISC to recover an amount not in excess of its costs (if any).

* * *

[Reg. § 1.994-1.]

☐ [*T.D. 7364, 7-15-75. Amended by T.D. 7435, 9-29-76; T.D. 7854, 11-6-82 and T.D. 7984, 10-11-84.*]

International Boycott Determinations

§7.999-1. Computation of the international boycott factor (Temporary).—(a) *In general.*—Sections 908(a), 952(a)(3), and 995(b)(1)(F) provide that certain benefits of the foreign tax credit, deferral of earnings of foreign corporations, and DISC are denied if a person or a member of a controlled group (within the meaning of section 993(a)(3)) that includes that person participates in or cooperates with an international boycott (within the meaning of section 999(b)(3)). The loss of tax benefits may be determined by multiplying the otherwise allowable tax benefits by the "international boycott factor." Section 999(c)(1) provides that the international boycott factor is to be determined under regulations prescribed by the Secretary. The method of computing the international boycott factor is set forth in paragraph (c) of this section. A special rule for computing the international boycott factor of a person that is a member of two or more controlled groups is set forth in paragraph (d). Transitional rules for making adjustments to the international boycott factor for years affected by the effective dates are set forth in paragraph (e). The definitions of the terms used in this section are set forth in paragraph (b).

(b) *Definitions.*—For purposes of this section:

(1) *Boycotting country.*—In respect of a particular international boycott, the term "boycotting country" means any country described in section 999(a)(1)(A) or (B) that requires participation in or cooperation with that particular international boycott.

(2) *Participation in or cooperation with an international boycott.*—For the definition of the term "participation in or cooperation with an international boycott", see section 999(b)(3) and Parts H through M of the Treasury Department's International Boycott Guidelines.

(3) *Operations in or related to a boycotting country.*—For the definitions of the terms "operations", "operations in a boycotting country", "operations related to a boycotting country", and "operations with the government, a company, or a national of a boycotting country", see Part B of the Treasury Department's International Boycott Guidelines.

(4) *Clearly demonstrating clearly separate and identifiable operations.*—For the rules for "clearly demonstrating clearly separate and identifiable operations", see Part D of the Treasury Department's International Boycott Guidelines.

(5) *Purchase made from a country.*—The terms "purchase made from a boycotting country" and "purchases made from any country other than the United States" mean, in respect of any particular country, the gross amount paid in connection with the purchase of, the use of, or the right to use:

(i) Tangible personal property (including money) from a stock of goods located in that country,

(ii) Intangible property (other than securities) in that country,

(iii) Securities by a dealer to a beneficial owner that is a resident of that country (but only if the dealer knows or has reason to know the country of residence of the beneficial owner),

(iv) Real property located in that country, or

(v) Services performed in, and the end product of services performed in, that country (other than payroll paid to a person that is an officer or employee of the payor).

(6) *Sales made to a country.*—The terms "sales made to a boycotting country" and "sales made to any country other than the United States" mean, in respect of any particular country, the gross receipts from the sale, exchange, other disposition, or use of:

(i) Tangible personal property (including money) for direct use, consumption, or disposition in that country,

(ii) Services performed in that country.

(iii) The end product of services (wherever performed) for direct use, consumption, or disposition in that country,

(iv) Intangible property (other than securities) in that country,

(v) Securities by a dealer to a beneficial owner that is a resident of the country (but only if the dealer knows or has reason to know the country of residence of the beneficial owner), or

(vi) Real property located in that country.

To determine the country of direct use, consumption, or disposition of tangible personal property and the end product of services, see paragraph (b)(10) of this section.

(7) *Sales made from a country.*—The terms "sales made from a boycotting country" and "sales made from any country other than the United States" mean, in respect of a particular country, the gross receipts from the sale, exchange, other disposition, or use of:

(i) Tangible personal property (including money) from a stock of goods located in that country,

(ii) Intangible property (other than securities) in that country, or

(iii) Services performed in, and the end product of services performed in, that country.

However, gross receipts from any such sale, exchange, other disposition, or use by a person that are included in the numerator of that person's international boycott factor by reason of paragraph (b)(6) of this section shall not again be included in the numerator by reason of this subparagraph.

(8) *Payroll paid or accrued for services performed in a country.*—The terms "payroll paid or accrued for services performed in a boycotting country" and "payroll paid or accrued for services performed in any country other than the United States" mean, in respect of a particular country, the total amount paid or accrued as compensation to officers and employees, including wages, salaries, commissions, and bonuses, for services performed in that country.

(9) *Services performed partly within and partly without a country.*—(i) *In general.*—Except as provided in paragraph (b)(9)(ii) of this section, for purposes of allocating to a particular country:

(A) The gross amount paid in connection with the purchase or use of,

(B) The gross receipts from the sale, exchange, other disposition or use of, and

(C) The payroll paid or accrued

for services performed, or the end product of services performed, partly within and partly without that country, the amount paid, received, or accrued to be allocated to that country, unless the facts and circumstances of a particular case warrant a different amount, will be that amount that bears the same relation to the total amount paid, received, or accrued as the number of days of performance of the services within that country bears to the total number of days of performance of services for which the total amount is paid, received, or accrued.

(ii) *Transportation, telegraph, and cable services.*—Transportation, telegraph, and cable services performed partly within one country and partly within another country are allocated between the two countries as follows:

(A) In the case of a purchase of such services performed from Country A to Country B, fifty percent of the gross amount paid is deemed to be a purchase made from Country A and the remaining fifty percent is deemed to be a purchase made from Country B.

(B) In the case of a sale of such services performed from Country A to Country B, fifty percent of the gross receipts is deemed to be a sale made from Country B and the remaining fifty percent is deemed to be a sale made to Country B.

(10) *Country of use, consumption, or disposition.*—As a general rule, the country of use, consumption, or disposition of tangible personal property (including money) and the end product of services (wherever performed) is deemed to be the country of destination of the tangible personal property or the end product of the services. (Thus, if legal services are performed in one country and an opinion is given for use by a client in a second country, the end product of the legal services is used, consumed, or disposed of in the second country.) The occurrence in a country of a temporary interruption in the shipment of the tangible personal property or the delivery of the end product of services shall not constitute such country the country of destination. However, if at the time of the transaction the person providing the tangible personal property or the end product of services knew, or should have known from the facts and circumstances surrounding the transaction, that the tangible personal property or the end product of services probably would not be used, consumed, or disposed of in the country of destination, that person must determine the country of ultimate use, consumption or disposition of the tangible personal property or the end product of services. Notwithstanding the preceding provisions of this subparagraph, a person that sells, exchanges, otherwise disposes of, or makes available for use, tangible personal property to any person all of whose business except for an insubstantial part consists of selling from inventory to retail customers at retail outlets all within one country may assume at the time of such sale to such person that the tangible personal property will be used, consumed, or disposed of within such country.

(11) *Controlled group taxable year.*—The term "controlled group taxable year" means the taxable year of the controlled group's common parent corporation. In the event that no common parent corporation exists, the members of the group shall elect the taxable year of one of the members of the controlled group to serve as the controlled group taxable year. The taxable year election is a binding election to be changed only with the approval of the Secretary or his delegate. The election is to be made in accordance with the procedures set forth in the instructions to Form 5713, the International Boycott Report.

(c) *Computation of international boycott factor.*—(1) *In general.*—The method of computing the international boycott factor of a person that is not a member of a controlled group is set forth in paragraph (c)(2) of this section. The method of computing the international boycott factor of a person that is a member of a controlled group is set forth in paragraph (c)(3) of this section. For purposes of paragraphs (c)(2) and (3), purchases and sales made by, and payroll paid or accrued by, a partnership are deemed to be made or paid or accrued by a partner in that proportion that the partner's distributive share bears to the purchases and sales made by, and the payroll paid or accrued by, the partnership. Also for purposes of paragraphs (c)(2) and (3), purchases and sales made by, and payroll paid or accrued by, a trust referred to in section 671 are deemed to be made both by the trust (for purposes of determining the trust's international boycott factor), and by a person treated under section 671 as the owner of the trust (but only in that proportion that the portion of the trust that such person is considered as owning under sections 671 through 679 bears to the purchases and sales made by, and the payroll paid and accrued by, the trust).

(2) *International boycott factor of a person that is not a member of a controlled group.*—The international boycott factor to be applied by a person that is not a member of a controlled group (within the meaning of section 993(a)(3)) is a fraction.

(i) The numerator of the fraction is the sum of the—

(A) Purchases made from all boycotting countries associated in carrying out a particular international boycott,

(B) Sales made to or from all boycotting countries associated in carrying out a particular international boycott, and

(C) Payroll paid or accrued for services performed in all boycotting countries associated in carrying out a particular international boycott by that person during that person's taxable year, minus the amount of such purchases, sales, and payroll that is clearly demonstrated to be attributable to clearly separate and identifiable operations in connection with which there was no participation in or cooperation with that international boycott.

(ii) The denominator of the fraction is the sum of the—

(A) Purchases made from any country other than the United States,

(B) Sales made to or from any country other than the United States, and

(C) Payroll paid or accrued for services performed in any country other than the United States

by that person during that person's taxable year.

(3) *International boycott factor of a person that is a member of a controlled group.*—The international boycott factor to be applied by a person that is a member of a controlled group (within the meaning of section 993(a)(3)) shall be computed in the manner described in paragraph (c)(2) of this section, except that there shall be taken into account the purchases and sales made by, and the payroll paid or accrued by, each member of the controlled group during each member's own taxable year that ends with or within the controlled group taxable year that ends with or within that person's taxable year.

(d) *Computation of the international boycott factor of a person that is a member of two or more controlled groups.*—The international boycott factor to be applied under sections 908(a), 953(a)(3), and 995(b)(1)(F) by a person that is a member of two or more controlled groups shall be determined in the manner described in paragraph (c)(3), except that the purchases, sales, and payroll included in the numerator and denominator shall include the purchases, sales, and payroll of that person and of all other members of the two or more controlled groups of which that person is a member.

(e) *Transitional rules.*—(1) *Pre-November 3, 1976 boycotting operations.*—The international boycott factor to be applied under sections 908(a), 952(a)(3), and 995(b)(1)(F) by a person that is not a member of a controlled group, for that person's taxable year that includes November 3, 1976, or a person that is a member of a controlled group, for the controlled group taxable year that includes November 3, 1976, shall be computed in the manner described in paragraphs (c)(2) and (c)(3), respectively, of this section. However, that the following adjustments shall be made:

(i) There shall be excluded from the numerators described in paragraphs (c)(2)(i) and (c)(3)(i) of this section purchases, sales, and payroll clearly demonstrated to be attributable to clearly separate and identifiable operations—

(A) That were completed on or before November 3, 1976, or

(B) In respect of which it is demonstrated that the agreements constituting participation in or cooperation with the international boycott were renounced, the renunciations were communicated on or before November 3, 1976, to the governments or persons with which the agreements were made, and the agreements have not been reaffirmed after November 3, 1976, and

(ii) The international boycott factor resulting after the numerator has been modified in accordance with paragraph (e)(1)(i) of this section shall be further modified by multiplying it by a fraction. The numerator of that fraction shall be the number of days in that person's taxable year (or, if applicable, in that person's controlled group taxable year) remaining after November 3, 1976, and the denominator shall be 366.

The principles of this subparagraph are illustrated in the following example:

Example. Corporation A, a calendar year taxpayer, is not a member of a controlled group. During the 1976 calendar year, Corporation A had three operations in a boycotting country under three separate contracts, each of which contained agreements constituting participation in or cooperation with an international boycott. Each contract was entered into on or after September 2, 1976. Operation (1) was completed on November 1, 1976. The sales made to a boycotting country in connection with Operation (1) amounted to $10. Operation (2) was not completed during the taxable year, but on November 1, 1976, Corporation A communicated a renunciation of the boycott agreement covering that operation to the government of the boycotting country. The sales made to a boycotting country in connection with Operation (2) amounted to $40. Operation (3) was not completed during the taxable year, nor was any renunciation of the boycott agreement made. The sales made to a boycotting country in connection with Operation (3) amounted to $25. Corporation A had no purchases made from, sales made from, or payroll paid or accrued for services performed in, a boycotting country. Corporation A had $500 of purchases made from, sales made from, sales made to, and payroll paid or accrued for services performed in, countries other than the United States. Company A's boycott factor for 1976, computed under paragraph (c)(2) of this section (before the application of this subparagraph) would be:

$$\frac{\$10 + \$40 + \$25}{\$500} = \frac{\$75}{\$500}$$

However, the $10 is eliminated from the numerator by reason of paragraph (e)(j)(1)(A) of this section, and the $40 is eliminated from the numerator by reason of paragraph (e)(j)(1)(B) of this section. Thus, before the application of paragraph (e)(1)(ii) of this section, Corporation A's international boycott factor is $25/$500. After the application of paragraph (e)(1)(ii), Corporation A's international boycott factor is:

$$\frac{\$25}{\$500} \times \frac{58}{366}$$

(2) *Pre-December 31, 1977 boycotting operations.*—The international boycott factor to be applied under sections 908(a), 952(a)(3), and 995(b)(1)(P) by a person that is not a member of a controlled group, for that person's taxable year that includes December 31, 1977, or by a person that is a member of a controlled group, for the controlled group taxable year that includes December 31, 1977, shall be computed in the manner described in paragraphs (c)(2) and (c)(3), respectively, of this section. However, the following adjustments shall be made:

(i) There shall be excluded from the numerators described in paragraphs (c)(2)(i) and (c)(3)(i) of this section purchases, sales, and payroll clearly demonstrated to be attributable to clearly separate and identifiable operations that were carried out in accordance with the terms of binding contracts entered into before September 3, 1976, and—

(A) That were completed on or before December 31, 1977, or

(B) In respect of which it is demonstrated that the agreements constituting participation in or cooperation with the international boycott were renounced, the renunciations were communicated on or before December 31, 1977, to the governments or persons with which the agreements were made, and the agreements were not reaffirmed after December 31, 1977, and

(ii) In the case of clearly separate and identifiable operations that are carried out in accordance with the terms of binding contracts entered into before September 2, 1976, but that do not meet the requirements of paragraph (e)(2)(i) of this section, the numerators described in paragraphs (e)(2)(i) and (e)(3)(i) of this section shall be adjusted by multiplying the purchases, sales, and payroll clearly demonstrated to be attributable to those operations by a fraction, the numerator of which is the number of days in such person's taxable year (or, if applicable, in such person's controlled group taxable year) remaining after December 31, 1977, and the denominator of which is 365.

The principles of this subparagraph are illustrated in the following example:

Example. Corporation A is not a member of a controlled group and reports on the basis of a July 1-June 30 fiscal year. During the 1977-1978 fiscal year, Corporation A had 2 operations carried out pursuant to the terms of separate contracts, each of which had a clause that constituted participation in or cooperation with an international boycott. Neither operation was completed during the fiscal year, nor were either of the boycotting clauses renounced. Operation (1) was carried out in accordance with the terms of a contract entered into on November 15, 1976. Operation (2) was carried out in accordance with the terms of a binding contract entered into before September 2, 1976. Corporation A had sales made to a boycotting country in connection with Operation (1) in the amount of $50, and in connection with Operation (2) in the amount of $100. Corporation A had sales made to countries other than the United States in the amount of $500. Corporation A had no purchases made from, sales made from, or payroll paid or accrued for services performed in, any country other than the United States. In the absence of this subparagraph, Corporation A's international boycott factor would be

$$\frac{\$50 + \$100}{\$500}$$

However, by reason of the application of this subparagraph, Corporation A's international boycott factor is reduced to

$$\frac{[(\$50 + \$100)\ (181/365)]}{\$500}$$

(3) *Incomplete controlled group taxable year.*—If, at the end of the taxable year of a person that is a member of a controlled group, the controlled group taxable year that includes November 3, 1976 has not ended, or the taxable year of one or more members of the controlled group that includes November 3, 1976 has not ended, then the international boycott factor to be applied under sections 908(a), 952(a)(3) and 955(b)(1)(P) by such person for the taxable year shall be computed in the manner described in paragraph (c)(3) of this section. However, the numerator and the denominator in that paragraph shall include only the purchases, sales, and payroll of those members of the controlled group whose taxable years ending after November 3, 1976 have ended as the end of the taxable year of such person.

(f) *Effective date.*—This section applies to participation in or cooperation with an international boycott after November 3, 1976. In the case of operations which constitute participation in or cooperation with an international boycott and which are carried out in accordance with the terms of a binding contract entered into before September 2, 1976, this section applies to such participation or cooperation after December 31, 1977. [Temporary Reg. §7.999-1.]

☐ [*T.D. 7467, 2-24-77.*]

Tax Consequences of Transition to Using Reference Rates Other Than Interbank Offered Rates

§1.1001-6. Transition from certain interbank offered rates.—(a) *In general.*—This section provides rules relating to the modification of the terms of a contract as part of the transition away from the London Interbank Offered Rate and certain other interbank offered rates. In general, paragraphs (b) through (g) of this section provide the operative rules for a covered modification. Paragraph (h) of this section defines certain terms that are used in these operative rules, such as *covered modification, qualified rate, discontinued IBOR, associated modification,* and *qualified one-time payment.* Paragraph (j) of this section describes certain modifications that are not covered modifications and provides examples that illustrate the operation of the rules in paragraph (j) of this section. For rules regarding original issue discount on certain debt instruments that provide for a rate referencing a discontinued IBOR, see §1.1275-2(m). For rules regarding certain interests in a REMIC that provide for a rate referencing a discontinued IBOR, see §1.860G-1(e).

(b) *Treatment under section 1001.*—(1) *Covered modifications.*—A covered modification of a contract is not treated as the exchange of property for other property differing materially in kind or in extent for purposes of §1.1001-1(a). For example, if the terms of a debt instrument that pays interest at a rate referencing the U.S.-dollar London Interbank Offered Rate (USD LIBOR) are modified to provide that the debt instrument pays interest at a qualified rate referencing the Secured Overnight Financing Rate published by the Federal Reserve Bank of New York (SOFR) and the modification is not described in paragraph (j) of this section, the modification is not treated as the exchange of property for other property differing materially in kind or in extent for purposes of §1.1001-1(a).

(2) *Contemporaneous noncovered modifications.*—If a covered modification is made at the same time as a noncovered modification, §1.1001-1(a) or §1.1001-3, as appropriate, applies to determine whether the noncovered modification results in the exchange of property for other property differing materially in kind or in extent. In applying §1.1001-1(a) or §1.1001-3 for this purpose, the covered modification is treated as part of the terms of the contract prior to the noncovered modification. For example, if the parties to a debt instrument modify the interest rate in a manner that is a covered modification and contemporaneously extend the final maturity date of the debt instrument, which is a noncovered modification, only the extension of the final maturity date is analyzed under §1.1001-3 and, for purposes of that analysis, the modified interest rate is treated as a term of the instrument prior to the extension of the final maturity date.

(c) *Effect of a covered modification on integrated transactions and hedging transactions.*—(1) *In general.*—Except as otherwise provided in paragraph (c)(2) of this section, the rules in paragraphs (c)(1)(i) through (iv) of this section determine the effect of a covered modification on an integrated transaction under § 1.1275-6, a qualified hedging transaction under § 1.988-5(a), a hedging transaction under § 1.446-4, or a qualified hedging transaction under § 1.148-4(h).

(i) A covered modification of one or more contracts that are part of an integrated transaction under § 1.1275-6 is treated as not legging out of the integrated transaction, provided that, no later than the end of the 90-day period beginning on the date of the first covered modification of any such contract, the financial instrument that results from any such covered modifications satisfies the requirements to be a § 1.1275-6 hedge (as defined in § 1.1275-6(b)(2)) with respect to the qualifying debt instrument that results from any such covered modification. If a taxpayer enters into a financial instrument intended to mitigate the economic effect of a temporary mismatch of the legs of the integrated transaction during that 90-day period (a *§ 1.1275-6 interim hedge*), the integration of the § 1.1275-6 interim hedge with the other components of the integrated transaction during the 90-day period is treated as not legging into a new integrated transaction and the termination of the § 1.1275-6 interim hedge before the end of the 90-day period is treated as not legging out of the existing integrated transaction.

(ii) A covered modification of one or more contracts that are part of a qualified hedging transaction under § 1.988-5(a) is treated as not legging out of the qualified hedging transaction, provided that, no later than the end of the 90-day period beginning on the date of the first covered modification of any such contract, the financial instrument or series or combination of financial instruments that results from any such covered modifications satisfies the requirements to be a § 1.988-5(a) hedge (as defined in § 1.988-5(a)(4)) with respect to the qualifying debt instrument that results from any such covered modification. If a taxpayer enters into a financial instrument intended to mitigate the economic effect of a temporary mismatch of the legs of the qualified hedging transaction during that 90-day period (a *§ 1.988-5(a) interim hedge*), the integration of the § 1.988-5(a) interim hedge with the other components of the qualified hedging transaction during the 90-day period is treated as not legging into a new qualified hedging transaction and the termination of the § 1.988-5(a) interim hedge before the end of the 90-day period is treated as not legging out of the existing qualified hedging transaction.

(iii) A covered modification of one leg of a transaction subject to the hedge accounting rules in § 1.446-4 is not treated as a disposition or termination (within the meaning of § 1.446-4(e)(6)) of either leg of the transaction.

(iv) A covered modification of a qualified hedge or of the tax-advantaged bonds with which the qualified hedge is integrated under § 1.148-4(h)(1) is treated as not terminating the qualified hedge under § 1.148-4(h)(3)(iv)(B), provided that, no later than the end of the 90-day period beginning on the date of the first covered modification of either the qualified hedge or the hedged bonds, the qualified hedge that results from any such covered modification satisfies the requirements to be a qualified hedge (determined by applying the special rules for certain modifications of qualified hedges under § 1.148-4(h)(3)(iv)(C)) with respect to the hedged bonds that result from any such covered modification. Solely for purposes of determining whether the qualified hedge that results from a covered modification satisfies the requirements to be a qualified hedge with respect to the hedged bonds that result from any such covered modification in the preceding sentence, a qualified one-time payment with respect to the hedge or the hedged bonds (or both) is allocated in a manner consistent with the allocation of a termination payment for a variable yield issue under § 1.148-4(h)(3)(iv)(H) and treated as a series of periodic payments. This paragraph (c)(1)(iv) does not apply if, prior to any covered modifications, the qualified hedge and the tax-advantaged bond are integrated under § 1.148-4(h)(4).

(2) *Fallback rates.*—If a covered modification of a contract that is part of an integrated transaction under § 1.1275-6 is described in paragraph (h)(1)(ii) or (iii) of this section, that covered modification is treated as not legging out of the integrated transaction. If a covered modification of a contract that is part of a qualified hedging transaction under § 1.988-5(a) is described in paragraph (h)(1)(ii) or (iii) of this section, that covered modification is treated as not legging out of the qualified hedging transaction. If a covered modification of a qualified hedge or of the tax-advantaged bonds with which the qualified hedge is integrated under § 1.148-4(h) is described in paragraph (h)(1)(ii) or (iii) of this section, that covered modification is treated as not terminating the qualified hedge under § 1.148-4(h)(3)(iv)(B).

(d) *Coordination with provision for existing obligations under chapter 4.*—A modification of a contract is not a material modification of that contract for purposes of § 1.1471-2(b)(2)(iv) to the extent the modification is a covered modification. See paragraph (b)(2) of this section for rules that apply for purposes of § 1.1471-2(b)(2)(iv) when a modification to a contract includes both a covered modification and a contemporaneous noncovered modification.

(e) *Coordination with fast-pay stock rules.*—A covered modification of stock is not a significant modification in the terms of the stock or the related agreements or a significant change in the relevant facts and circumstances for purposes of § 1.7701(l)-3(b)(2)(ii). If a covered modification is made at the same time as, or as part of a plan that includes, a noncovered modification and the noncovered modification is a significant modification in the terms of the stock or the related agreements or a significant change in the relevant facts and circumstances, then § 1.7701(l)-3(b)(2)(ii) applies to determine whether the stock is fast-pay stock, taking into account all the facts and circumstances (including both the covered and noncovered modification).

(f) *Coordination with rules for investment trusts.*—A covered modification of a contract held by an investment trust does not manifest a power to vary the investment of the certificate holders for purposes of § 301.7701-4(c)(1) of this chapter. Further, a covered modification of an ownership interest in an investment trust does not manifest a power to vary the investment of the certificate holder for purposes of § 301.7701-4(c)(1) of this chapter.

(g) [Reserved]

(h) *Definitions.*—(1) *Covered modification.*—A *covered modification* is a modification or portion of a modification of the terms of a contract that is described in one or more of paragraphs (h)(1)(i) through (iii) of this section and that is not described in any of paragraphs (j)(1) through (5) of this section. Any modification of the terms of a contract described in section 4.02 of Rev. Proc. 2020-44, 2020-45 I.R.B. 991, or described in other guidance published in the Internal Revenue Bulletin that supplements the list of modifications described in section 4.02 of Rev. Proc. 2020-44 or the definitions on which that section relies (see § 601.601(d)(2)(ii)(a) of this chapter) is treated as a covered modification. For purposes of this section, a modification of the terms of a contract includes any modification of the terms of the contract, regardless of the form of the modification (for example, a modification may be an exchange of one contract for another, an amendment to the existing contract, or a modification accomplished indirectly through one or more transactions with third parties) and regardless of whether the modification is evidenced by an express agreement (oral or written), conduct of the parties, or otherwise. For purposes of this section, a contract includes but is not limited to a debt instrument, a derivative contract, stock, an insurance contract, and a lease agreement.

(i) The terms of the contract are modified to replace an operative rate that references a discontinued IBOR with a qualified rate, to add an obligation for one party to make a qualified one-time payment (if any), and to make associated modifications (if any).

(ii) The terms of the contract are modified to include a qualified rate as a fallback to an operative rate that references a discontinued IBOR and to make associated modifications (if any).

(iii) The terms of the contract are modified to replace a fallback rate that references a discontinued IBOR with a qualified rate and to make associated modifications (if any).

(2) *Noncovered modification.*—A *noncovered modification* is any modification or portion of a modification of the terms of a contract that is not a covered modification.

(3) *Qualified rate.*—(i) *In general.*—A *qualified rate* is any of the rates described in paragraph (h)(3)(ii) of this section, provided that the interest rate benchmark to which the rate refers and the discontinued IBOR identified in paragraph (h)(1)(i), (ii), or (iii) of this section are based on transactions conducted in the same currency or are otherwise reasonably expected to measure contemporaneous variations in the cost of newly borrowed funds in the same currency. For purposes of paragraphs (h)(1)(ii) and (iii) of this section, a single qualified rate may be comprised of one or more fallback rates (for example, a waterfall of fallback rates). Paragraph (h)(3)(iii) of this section provides additional rules for determining whether one or more fallback rates constitute a qualified rate, and paragraph (h)(3)(iv) of this section provides examples illustrating the operation of those rules.

(ii) *Rates.*—The following rates are described in this paragraph (h)(3)(ii):

(A) A qualified floating rate, as defined in § 1.1275-5(b), but without regard to the limitations on multiples set forth in § 1.1275-5(b) (examples of qualified floating rates generally include SOFR, the Sterling Overnight Index Average, the Tokyo Overnight Average Rate, the Swiss Average Rate Overnight, and the euro short-term rate administered by the European Central Bank);

(B) An alternative, substitute, or successor rate selected, endorsed, or recommended by the central bank, reserve bank, monetary authority, or similar institution (including any committee or working group thereof) as a replacement for a discontinued IBOR or its local currency equivalent in that jurisdiction;

(C) A rate selected, endorsed, or recommended by the Alternative Reference Rates Committee as a replacement for USD LIBOR, provided that the Federal Reserve Bank of New York is an ex officio member of the Alternative Reference Rates Committee at the time of the selection, endorsement, or recommendation;

(D) A rate that is determined by reference to a rate described in paragraph (h)(3)(ii)(A), (B), or (C) of this section, including a rate determined by adding or subtracting a specified number of basis points to or from the rate or by multiplying the rate by a specified number; and

(E) A rate identified for purposes of this section as a qualified rate in guidance published in the Internal Revenue Bulletin (see § 601.601(d)(2)(ii)(a) of this chapter).

(iii) *Rules for fallback rates.*—(A) *Multiple fallback rates.*—If the rate being tested as a qualified rate is comprised of more than one fallback rate, the rate is a qualified rate only if each individual fallback rate separately satisfies the requirements to be a qualified rate.

(B) *Indeterminable fallback rate.*—Except as provided in paragraph (h)(3)(iii)(C) of this section, if it is not possible to determine at the time of the modification being tested as a covered modification whether a fallback rate satisfies the requirements set forth in the first sentence of paragraph (h)(3)(i) of this section (for example, the calculation agent will determine the fallback rate at the time that the fallback rate is triggered based on factors that are not guaranteed to produce a rate described in paragraph (h)(3)(ii) of this section), the fallback rate is treated as not satisfying the requirements to be a qualified rate.

(C) *Fallback rate is a remote contingency.*—If the likelihood that any value will ever be determined under the contract by reference to a fallback rate is remote (determined at the time of the modification being tested as a covered modification), that fallback rate is treated as satisfying the requirements to be a qualified rate.

(iv) *Examples.*—The following examples illustrate the application of the rules in paragraphs (h)(3)(i) through (iii) of this section to qualified rates comprised of one or more fallback rates.

(A) *Example 1: Addition of a single fallback rate.*—(*1*) *Facts.* B is the issuer and L is the holder of a debt instrument that pays interest semiannually in U.S. dollars at a rate of six-month USD LIBOR and that contains no fallback provisions to address the pending discontinuation of six-month USD LIBOR. On July 1, 2022, B and L modify the debt instrument to add such fallback provisions (the *new fallbacks*). The new fallbacks provide that, upon the discontinuation of six-month USD LIBOR, six-month USD LIBOR will be replaced by a fallback rate equal to CME Group's forward-looking SOFR term rate of a six-month tenor (*six-month CME Term SOFR*) plus a fixed spread that will be determined at the time of six-month USD LIBOR's discontinuation. Six-month USD LIBOR will be discontinued on June 30, 2023.

(*2*) *Analysis.* The fallback rate is a qualified floating rate and is, therefore, described in paragraph (h)(3)(ii)(A) of this section. Moreover, because both six-month USD LIBOR and six-month CME Term SOFR are based on transactions conducted in U.S. dollars, the fallback rate satisfies the currency requirement in paragraph (h)(3)(i) of this section. As further provided in paragraph (h)(3)(i) of this section, B and L must also apply the rules in paragraph (h)(3)(iii)(A), (B), and (C) of this section to determine if the fallback rate is a qualified rate. Because the rate being tested as a qualified rate (*i.e.*, the fallback rate) is comprised of only one fallback rate, paragraph (h)(3)(iii)(A) of this section has no effect. As discussed elsewhere in this paragraph (h)(3)(iv)(A)(*2*), it is evident at the time of the fallback rate's addition that the fallback rate satisfies the requirements set forth in the first sentence of paragraph (h)(3)(i) of this section, so paragraph (h)(3)(iii)(B) of this section has no effect. Because it appears likely at the time of the modification that the fallback rate will be used to determine interest on the debt instrument, paragraph (h)(3)(iii)(C) of this section has no effect. In summary, the fallback rate is described in paragraph (h)(3)(ii)(A) of this section and satisfies the currency requirement in paragraph (h)(3)(i) of this section, and none of the rules in paragraph (h)(3)(iii) of this section affect the analysis. Therefore, the fallback rate is a qualified rate.

(B) *Example 2: Addition of a single indeterminable fallback rate.*—(*1*) *Facts.* The facts are the same as in paragraph (h)(3)(iv)(A)(*1*) of this section (*Example 1*), except that the new fallbacks provide that, upon the discontinuation of six-month USD LIBOR, B will select a replacement for six-month USD LIBOR based on the industry standard at the time of selection.

(*2*) *Analysis.* As provided in paragraph (h)(3)(i) of this section, B and L must apply the rule in paragraph (h)(3)(iii)(B) of this section to determine whether the fallback rate is a qualified rate. Because it is not possible to determine at the time of the fallback rate's addition in 2022 whether the fallback rate (*i.e.*, the replacement rate that B will select in 2023) satisfies the requirements set forth in the first sentence of paragraph (h)(3)(i) of this section, the fallback rate is treated as not satisfying the requirements to be a qualified rate under paragraph (h)(3)(iii)(B) of this section. Therefore, the fallback rate is not a qualified rate.

(C) *Example 3: Addition of a fallback waterfall that is a qualified rate.*—(*1*) *Facts.* The facts are the same as in paragraph (h)(3)(iv)(A)(*1*) of this section (*Example 1*), except that the new fallbacks provide for a fallback waterfall. The first tier of the fallback waterfall provides that, upon the discontinuation of six-month USD LIBOR, six-month USD LIBOR will be replaced by a fallback rate equal to six-month CME Term SOFR plus a fixed spread that will be determined at the time of six-month USD LIBOR's discontinuation. The second tier of the fallback waterfall provides that, upon the discontinuation of six-month CME Term SOFR, B will select a replacement for the fallback rate in the first tier of the fallback waterfall based on the industry standard at the time of selection. At the time of the fallback waterfall's addition, the likelihood that six-month CME Term SOFR will be discontinued is remote.

(*2*) *Analysis of the fallback waterfall.* As provided in paragraph (h)(3)(i) of this section, B and L must apply the rules in paragraphs (h)(3)(iii)(A), (B) and (C) of this section to determine whether the fallback waterfall is a qualified rate. Under paragraph (h)(3)(iii)(A) of this section, because the rate being tested as a qualified rate (*i.e.*, the fallback waterfall) is comprised of more than one fallback rate, the fallback waterfall is a qualified rate only if each individual fallback rate (*i.e.*, fallback rates in the first and second tiers of the fallback waterfall) separately satisfies the requirements to be a qualified rate. As concluded in paragraphs (h)(3)(iv)(C)(*3*) and (*4*) of this section, the fallback rates in the first and second tiers of the fallback waterfall separately satisfy the requirements to be a qualified rate. Therefore, the fallback waterfall is a qualified rate.

(*3*) *Analysis of the first tier of the fallback waterfall.* Because the fallback rate in the first tier of the fallback waterfall is the same as the fallback rate in paragraph (h)(3)(iv)(A)(*1*) of this section (*Example 1*), the analysis of the fallback rate in the first tier of the fallback waterfall is the same as the analysis of the fallback rate in paragraph (h)(3)(iv)(A)(2) of this section (*Example 1*). Accordingly, the fallback rate in the first tier of the fallback waterfall separately satisfies the requirements to be a qualified rate.

(*4*) *Analysis of the second tier of the fallback waterfall.* The fallback rate in the second tier of the fallback waterfall is the same as the fallback rate in paragraph (h)(3)(iv)(B)(*1*) of this section (*Example 2*). However, unlike the fallback rate in paragraph (h)(3)(iv)(B)(*1*) of this section (*Example 2*), the likelihood that the amount of interest on the debt instrument will ever be determined by reference to the fallback rate in the second tier of the fallback waterfall is remote. Accordingly, under paragraph (h)(3)(iii)(C) of this section, the fallback rate in the second tier of the fallback waterfall is treated as satisfying the requirements to be a qualified rate.

(D) *Example 4: Addition of a fallback waterfall that is not a qualified rate.*—(*1*) *Facts.* The facts are the same as in paragraph (h)(3)(iv)(A)(*1*) of this section (*Example 1*), except that the new fallbacks provide for a fallback waterfall. The first tier of the fallback waterfall provides that, upon the discontinuation of six-month USD LIBOR, six-month USD LIBOR will be replaced by a stated fallback rate (*Fallback Rate X*). Fallback Rate X, which is equal to an interest rate benchmark (*Benchmark X*) plus a fixed spread, satisfies the requirements set forth in the first sentence of paragraph (h)(3)(i) of this section. The second tier of the fallback waterfall provides that, upon the discontinuation of Benchmark X, B will select a replacement for

Fallback Rate X based on the industry standard at the time of selection. At the time of the fallback waterfall's addition, the likelihood that Benchmark X will be discontinued is not remote.

(2) *Analysis of the fallback waterfall.* As provided in paragraph (h)(3)(i) of this section, B and L must apply the rules in paragraphs (h)(3)(iii)(A), (B) and (C) of this section to determine whether the fallback waterfall is a qualified rate. Under paragraph (h)(3)(iii)(A) of this section, because the rate being tested as a qualified rate (*i.e.*, the fallback waterfall) is comprised of more than one fallback rate, the fallback waterfall is a qualified rate only if each individual fallback rate (*i.e.*, the fallback rates in the first and second tiers of the fallback waterfall) separately satisfies the requirements to be a qualified rate. As concluded in paragraph (h)(3)(iv)(D)(*3*) of this section, the fallback rate in the second tier of the fallback waterfall is treated as not satisfying the requirements to be a qualified rate. Therefore, the fallback waterfall is not a qualified rate.

(3) *Analysis of the second tier of the fallback waterfall.* As provided in paragraphs (h)(3)(i) and (h)(3)(iii)(A) of this section, B and L must apply the rules in paragraphs (h)(3)(iii)(B) and (C) of this section to determine whether the fallback rate in the second tier of the fallback waterfall is a qualified rate. Because the likelihood that Benchmark X will be discontinued is not remote, paragraph (h)(3)(iii)(C) of this section has no effect on the analysis of the fallback rate in the second tier of the fallback waterfall. Under paragraph (h)(3)(iii)(B) of this section, because it is not possible to determine at the time of the fallback waterfall's addition in 2022 whether the fallback rate in the second tier of the fallback waterfall (*i.e.*, the replacement rate that B will select in 2023) satisfies the requirements set forth in the first sentence of paragraph (h)(3)(i) of this section, the fallback rate in the second tier of the fallback waterfall is treated as not satisfying the requirements to be a qualified rate.

(4) *Discontinued IBOR.*—A *discontinued IBOR* is any interbank offered rate described in paragraph (h)(4)(i) or (ii) of this section but only during the period beginning on the date of the announcement described in paragraph (h)(4)(i) or (ii) of this section and ending on the date that is one year after the date on which the administrator of the interbank offered rate ceases to provide the interbank offered rate.

(i) The administrator of the interbank offered rate announces that the administrator has ceased or will cease to provide the interbank offered rate permanently or indefinitely, and no successor administrator is expected as of the time of the announcement to continue to provide the interbank offered rate; or

(ii) The regulatory supervisor for the administrator of the interbank offered rate, the central bank for the currency of the interbank offered rate, an insolvency official with jurisdiction over the administrator for the interbank offered rate, a resolution authority with jurisdiction over the administrator for the interbank offered rate, a court, or an entity with similar insolvency or resolution authority over the administrator for the interbank offered rate announces that the administrator of the interbank offered rate has ceased or will cease to provide the interbank offered rate permanently or indefinitely, and no successor administrator is expected as of the time of the announcement to continue to provide the interbank offered rate.

(5) *Associated modification.*—An *associated modification* is a modification of the technical, administrative, or operational terms of a contract that is reasonably necessary to adopt or to implement the modifications described in paragraph (h)(1)(i), (ii), or (iii) of this section other than associated modifications. An associated modification also includes an incidental cash payment intended to compensate a counterparty for small valuation differences resulting from a modification of the administrative terms of a contract, such as the valuation differences resulting from a change in observation period. Examples of associated modifications include a change to the definition of interest period or a change to the timing and frequency of determining rates and making payments of interest (for example, delaying payment dates on a debt instrument by two days to allow sufficient time to compute and pay interest at a qualified rate computed in arrears).

(6) *Qualified one-time payment.*—A *qualified one-time payment* is a single cash payment that is intended to compensate the other party or parties for all or part of the basis difference between the discontinued IBOR identified in paragraph (h)(1)(i), (ii), or (iii) of this section and the interest rate benchmark to which the qualified rate refers.

(i) [Reserved]

(j) *Modifications excluded from the definition of covered modification.*—A modification or portion of a modification described in any of paragraphs (j)(1) through (5) of this section is excluded from the definition of covered modification in paragraph (h)(1) of this section and therefore is a noncovered modification.

(1) The terms of the contract are modified to change the amount or timing of contractual cash flows and that change is intended to induce one or more parties to perform any act necessary to consent to a modification to the contract described in paragraph (h)(1)(i), (ii), or (iii) of this section. See paragraph (j)(6)(iii) of this section (*Example 3*).

(2) The terms of the contract are modified to change the amount or timing of contractual cash flows and that change is intended to compensate one or more parties for a modification to the contract not described in paragraph (h)(1)(i), (ii), or (iii) of this section. See paragraph (j)(6)(v) of this section (*Example 5*).

(3) The terms of the contract are modified to change the amount or timing of contractual cash flows and that change is either a concession granted to a party to the contract because that party is experiencing financial difficulty or a concession secured by a party to the contract to account for the credit deterioration of another party to the contract. See paragraph (j)(6)(vi) of this section (*Example 6*).

(4) The terms of the contract are modified to change the amount or timing of contractual cash flows and that change is intended to compensate one or more parties for a change in rights or obligations that are not derived from the contract being modified. See paragraph (j)(6)(vii) of this section (*Example 7*). If each contract in a given portfolio of contracts has the same parties, those parties modify more than one contract in the portfolio (each such contract is a *modified portfolio contract*), and those modifications provide for a single, aggregate qualified one-time payment with respect to all modified portfolio contracts, then the portion of the qualified one-time payment allocable to any one modified portfolio contract is treated for purposes of this paragraph (j)(4) as not intended to compensate for a change in rights or obligations derived from any other modified portfolio contract.

(5) The terms of the contract are modified to change the amount or timing of contractual cash flows and the modification is identified for purposes of this paragraph (j)(5) in guidance published in the Internal Revenue Bulletin (see § 601.601(d)(2)(ii)(a) of this chapter) as having a principal purpose of achieving a result that is unreasonable in light of the purpose of this section.

(6) *Examples.*—The following examples illustrate the operation of the rules in paragraphs (j)(1) through (4) of this section.

(i) *Example 1: Covered modification.*—(A) *Facts.* B is the issuer and L is the holder of a debt instrument that pays interest semiannually at a rate of six-month USD LIBOR plus 100 basis points. On July 1, 2022, B and L modify the debt instrument to replace that original rate with CME Group's forward-looking SOFR term rate of a six-month tenor (*six-month CME Term SOFR*) plus an adjustment spread of 42.826 basis points plus 100 basis points (the whole modification is the *LIBOR replacement modification with basis adjustment spread*). B and L chose the adjustment spread of 42.826 basis points because that is the adjustment spread used or recommended by the International Swaps and Derivatives Association and the Alternative Reference Rates Committee for similar substitutions or replacements of six-month USD LIBOR with a tenor-adjusted variant of SOFR.

(B) *Analysis.* The parties have modified the terms of the debt instrument to replace a rate referencing a discontinued IBOR (*i.e.*, six-month USD LIBOR plus 100 basis points) with a qualified rate (*i.e.*, six-month CME Term SOFR plus 142.826 basis points). The LIBOR replacement modification with basis adjustment spread is described in paragraph (h)(1)(i) of this section and not described in any of paragraphs (j)(1) through (5) of this section. Therefore, the LIBOR replacement modification with basis adjustment spread is a covered modification of the debt instrument.

(ii) *Example 2: Covered modification with qualified one-time payment.*—(A) *Facts.* The facts are the same as in paragraph (j)(6)(i)(A) of this section (*Example 1*), except that, instead of the LIBOR replacement modification with basis adjustment spread, B and L modify the debt instrument by replacing the original rate of six-month USD LIBOR plus 100 basis points with six-month CME Term SOFR plus 100 basis points and by obligating B to make a cash payment to L equal to the present value of the adjustment spread of 42.826 basis points with respect to the debt instrument (this payment is the *basis adjustment payment*, and the whole modification is the *LIBOR replacement modification with basis adjustment payment*).

(B) *Analysis.* The parties have modified the terms of the debt instrument to replace a rate referencing a discontinued IBOR (*i.e.*, six-month USD LIBOR plus 100 basis points) with a qualified rate (*i.e.*, six-month CME Term SOFR plus 100 basis points) and have added an obligation for B to make the basis adjustment payment, which is a single cash payment that is intended to compensate L for the basis difference between the discontinued IBOR identified in paragraph (h)(1)(i) of this section (*i.e.*, six-month USD LIBOR) and the interest rate benchmark to which the qualified rate refers (*i.e.*, six-month CME Term SOFR). Accordingly, the basis adjustment payment is a qualified one-time payment as defined in paragraph (h)(6) of this section, and the LIBOR replacement modification with basis adjustment payment is described in paragraph (h)(1)(i) of this section. Because it is described in paragraph (h)(1)(i) of this section and not described in any of paragraphs (j)(1) through (5) of this section, the LIBOR replacement modification with basis adjustment payment is a covered modification of the debt instrument.

(iii) *Example 3: Inducement spread.*—(A) *Facts.* The facts are the same as in paragraph (j)(6)(i)(A) of this section (*Example 1*), except that the debt instrument is part of a widely held issue of debt with identical terms. Under the trust indenture applicable to the debt instrument, if B proposes a modification of the terms of the debt and all holders of the debt consent to that modification, the terms of the debt are modified as B proposed. In accordance with the trust indenture, B proposes the LIBOR replacement modification with basis adjustment spread on January 1, 2022. To induce holders such as L to perform the acts necessary to consent to the LIBOR replacement modification with basis adjustment spread, B also proposes to increase the interest rate paid to each consenting holder by an additional spread of 10 basis points (the *inducement spread*). All holders, including L, consent to B's proposed modifications by June 1, 2022. On July 1, 2022, the debt instrument is modified to implement the LIBOR replacement modification with basis adjustment spread and to increase the interest rate by the inducement spread. Once all modifications are effective, the debt instrument pays interest at a rate of six-month CME Term SOFR plus 152.826 basis points.

(B) *Analysis.* As concluded in paragraph (j)(6)(i)(B) of this section (*Example 1*), the portion of these modifications that implements the LIBOR replacement modification with basis adjustment spread is a covered modification of L's debt instrument. However, the portion of these modifications that increases the interest rate by the inducement spread changes the amount of cash flows on L's debt instrument, and that change is intended to induce L to perform the acts necessary to consent to a modification to the debt instrument described in paragraph (h)(1)(i) of this section (*i.e.*, the LIBOR replacement modification with basis adjustment spread). Therefore, the portion of the modification that increases the interest rate by the inducement spread is described in paragraph (j)(1) of this section and, consequently, is a noncovered modification of L's debt instrument. See paragraph (b)(2) of this section for the treatment of a contemporaneous noncovered modification.

(iv) *Example 4: Consent fee.*—(A) *Facts.* The facts are the same as in paragraph (j)(6)(iii)(A) of this section (*Example 3*), except that, instead of proposing to increase the interest rate paid to each consenting holder by the inducement spread, B proposes to make a cash payment to each consenting holder (the *consent fee*) at the time of the modification. Thus, when the proposed modification occurs on July 1, 2022, B pays all holders, including L, the consent fee. Once all modifications are effective, the debt instrument pays interest at a rate of six-month CME Term SOFR plus 142.826 basis points.

(B) *Analysis.* As concluded in paragraph (j)(6)(i)(B) of this section (*Example 1*), the LIBOR replacement modification with basis adjustment spread is a covered modification of L's debt instrument. However, B's obligation to pay the consent fee is also a modification of L's debt instrument but is not a covered modification because it is not described in paragraph (h)(1)(i) of this section. In particular, B's obligation to pay the consent fee is not an associated modification because it is not a modification of the technical, administrative, or operational terms of L's debt instrument and is not intended to compensate for valuation differences resulting from a modification of the administrative terms of L's contract. Nor is the consent fee a qualified one-time payment because it is not intended to compensate L for any part of the basis difference between the discontinued IBOR identified in paragraph (h)(1)(i) of this section (*i.e.*, six-month USD LIBOR) and the interest rate benchmark to which the qualified rate refers (*i.e.*, six-month CME Term SOFR). See paragraph (b)(2) of this section for the treatment of a contemporaneous noncovered modification.

(v) *Example 5: Compensation for a modification to a customary financial covenant.*—(A) *Facts.* The facts are the same as in paragraph (j)(6)(i)(A) of this section (*Example 1*), except that, at the same time as and for reasons unrelated to the LIBOR replacement modification with basis adjustment spread, B and L also modify customary financial covenants in the debt instrument in a manner that benefits B. In exchange for the modification of customary financial covenants, B agrees to add another 30 basis points to the rate such that, once all modifications are effective, the debt instrument pays interest at a rate of six-month CME Term SOFR plus 172.826 basis points.

(B) *Analysis.* As concluded in paragraph (j)(6)(i)(B) of this section (*Example 1*), the portion of these modifications that implements the LIBOR replacement modification with basis adjustment spread is a covered modification of the debt instrument. However, the portion of these modifications that modifies customary financial covenants is not related to the replacement of LIBOR and, therefore, is not described in any of paragraphs (h)(1)(i), (ii), or (iii) of this section and, therefore, is a noncovered modification of the debt instrument. Moreover, the portion of these modifications that adds 30 basis points to the rate changes the amount of cash flows on the debt instrument, and the parties intend that change to compensate L for a modification to the debt instrument not described in paragraph (h)(1)(i), (ii), or (iii) of this section (*i.e.*, the modification of customary financial covenants). Therefore, the portion of these modifications that adds those 30 basis points to the rate is described in paragraph (j)(2) of this section and, consequently, is a noncovered modification of the debt instrument. See paragraph (b)(2) of this section for the treatment of a contemporaneous noncovered modification.

(vi) *Example 6: Workout of distressed debt.*—(A) *Facts.* The facts are the same as in paragraph (j)(6)(i)(A) of this section (*Example 1*), except that B's financial condition has deteriorated since the issue date of the debt instrument and, to decrease the risk of B's default or bankruptcy, L agrees to subtract 50 basis points from the rate such that, once all modifications are effective, the debt instrument pays interest at a rate of six-month CME Term SOFR plus 92.826 basis points.

(B) *Analysis.* As concluded in paragraph (j)(6)(i)(B) of this section (*Example 1*), the portion of these modifications that implements the LIBOR replacement modification with basis adjustment spread is a covered modification of the debt instrument. However, the portion of these modifications that subtracts 50 basis points from the rate changes the amount of cash flows on the debt instrument, and that change is a concession granted to B because B is experiencing financial difficulty. Therefore, the portion of these modifications that subtracts those 50 basis points from the rate is described in paragraph (j)(3) of this section and, consequently, is a noncovered modification of the debt instrument. See paragraph (b)(2) of this section for the treatment of a contemporaneous noncovered modification.

(vii) *Example 7: Change in rights or obligations not derived from the modified contract.*—(A) *Facts.* B is the issuer and L is the holder of a debt instrument (*Debt X*) with respect to which the facts are the same as in paragraph (j)(6)(i)(A) of this section (*Example 1*). In addition, B and L are the issuer and holder, respectively, of a second debt instrument (*Debt Y*). At the same time that the LIBOR replacement modification with basis adjustment spread occurs with respect to Debt X, B and L also modify customary financial covenants in Debt Y in a manner that benefits B. In exchange for the modification of customary financial covenants in Debt Y, B agrees to add another 30 basis points to the rate on Debt X such that, once all modifications are effective, Debt X pays interest at a rate of six-month CME Term SOFR plus 172.826 basis points.

(B) *Analysis.* As concluded in paragraph (j)(6)(i)(B) of this section (*Example 1*), the portion of these modifications that implements the LIBOR replacement modification with basis adjustment spread is a covered modification of Debt X. However, the portion of these modifications that adds 30 basis points to the rate on Debt X changes the amount of cash flows on Debt X, and the parties intend that change to compensate L for a change in rights or obligations that are not derived from Debt X (*i.e.*, the modification of customary financial covenants in Debt Y). Therefore, the portion of these modifications that adds those 30 basis points to the rate on Debt X is described in paragraph (j)(4) of this section and, consequently, is a noncovered modification of Debt X. See paragraph (b)(2) of this section for the treatment of a contemporaneous noncovered modification.

(k) *Applicability date.*—This section applies to a modification of the terms of a contract that occurs on or after March 7, 2022. A taxpayer may choose to apply this section to modifications of the terms of contracts that occur before March 7, 2022, provided that the taxpayer and all related parties (within the meaning of section 267(b) or section 707(b)(1) or within the meaning of § 1.150-1(b) for a taxpayer that is a State or local governmental unit (as defined in § 1.103-1(a)) or a 501(c)(3) organization (as defined in section 150(a)(4))) apply this section to all modifications of the terms of contracts that occur before that date. See section 7805(b)(7). [Reg. § 1.001-6.]

☐ [*T.D. 9961, 12-30-2021.*]

Sales of Controlled Corporation Stock

§ 1.1248-1. Treatment of gain from certain sales or exchanges of stock in certain foreign corporations.—(a) *In general.*—(1) If a United States person (as defined in section 7701(a)(30)) recognizes gain on a sale or exchange after December 31, 1962, of stock in a foreign corporation, and if in respect of such person the conditions of subparagraph (2) of this paragraph are satisfied, then the gain shall be included in the gross income of such person as a dividend to the extent of the earnings and profits of such corporation attributable to such stock under § 1.1248-2 or 1.1248-3, whichever is applicable, which were accumulated in taxable years of such foreign corporation beginning after December 31, 1962, during the period or periods such stock was held (or was considered as held by reason of the application of section 1223, taking into account § 1.1248–8) by such person while such corporation was a controlled foreign corporation. See section 1248(a). See § 1.1248-8 for additional rules regarding the attribution of earnings and profits to the stock of a foreign corporation following certain nonrecognition transactions. For computation of earnings and profits attributable to such stock if there are any "lower tier" corporations, see paragraph (a)(3) and (4) of § 1.1248-2 or paragraph (a) of § 1.1248-3, whichever is applicable. In general, the amount of gain to be included in a person's gross income as a dividend under section 1248(a) shall be determined separately for each share of stock sold or exchanged. However, such determination may be made in respect of a block of stock if earnings and profits attributable to the block are computed under § 1.1248-2 or 1.1248-3. See paragraph (b) of § 1.1248-2 and paragraph (a)(5) of § 1.1248-3. For the limitation on the tax attributable to an amount included in an individual's gross income as a dividend under section 1248(a), see section 1248(b) and § 1.1248-4. For the treatment, under certain circumstances, of the sale or exchange of stock in a domestic corporation as the sale or exchange of stock held by the domestic corporation in a foreign corporation, see section 1248(e) and § 1.1248-6. For the nonapplication of section 1248 in certain circumstances, see section 1248(g) and paragraph (e) of this section. For the requirement that the person establish the amount of earnings and profits attributable to the stock sold or exchanged and, for purposes of section 1248(b), the amount of certain taxes, see section 1248(h) and § 1.1248-7.

(2) In respect of a United States person who sells or exchanges stock in a foreign corporation, the conditions referred to in subparagraph (1) of this paragraph are satisfied only if (i) such person owned, within the meaning of section 958(a), or was considered as owning by applying the rules of ownership of section 958(b), 10 percent or more of the total combined voting power of all classes of stock entitled to vote of such foreign corporation at any time during the 5-year period ending on the date of the sale or exchange, and (ii) at such time such foreign corporation was a controlled foreign corporation (as defined in section 957).

(3) For purposes of subparagraph (2) of this paragraph, (i) a foreign corporation shall not be considered to be a controlled foreign corporation at any time before the first day of its first taxable year beginning after December 31, 1962, and (ii) the percentage of the total combined voting power of stock of a foreign corporation owned (or considered as owned) by a United States person shall be determined in accordance with the principles of section 951(b) and the regulations thereunder.

(4) For purposes of paragraph (a)(1) of this section, if a foreign partnership sells or exchanges stock of a corporation, the partners in such foreign partnership shall be treated as selling or exchanging their proportionate share of the stock of such corporation. Stock which is considered to have been sold or exchanged by a partner by reason of the application of this paragraph (a)(4) shall for purposes of applying such sentence be treated as actually sold or exchanged by such partner.

(5) The application of this paragraph may be illustrated by the following examples:

Example (1). Corporation F is a foreign corporation which has outstanding 100 shares of one class of stock. F was a controlled foreign corporation for the period beginning on January 1, 1963, and ending on June 30, 1965, but was not a controlled foreign corporation at any time thereafter. On December 31, 1965, Brown, a United States person who has owned 15 shares of F stock since 1962, sells 7 of his 15 shares and recognizes gain with respect to each share sold. Since Brown owned stock representing at least 10 percent of the total combined voting power of F at a time during the 5-year period ending on December 31, 1965, while F was a controlled foreign corporation, the conditions of subparagraph (2) of this paragraph are satisfied. Therefore, section 1248(a) applies to the gain recognized by Brown to the extent of the earnings and profits attributable under § 1.1248-3 to such shares.

Example (2). Assume the same facts as in example (1). Assume further that on February 1, 1970, Brown sells the remainder of his shares in F Corporation and recognizes gain with respect to each share sold. Even though Brown did not own stock representing at least 10 percent of the total combined voting power of F on February 1, 1970, nevertheless, in respect of each of the 8 shares of F stock which he sold on such date, the conditions of subparagraph (2) of this paragraph are satisfied since Brown owned stock representing at least 10 percent of such voting power at a time during the 5-year period ending on February 1, 1970, while F was a controlled foreign corporation. Therefore, section 1248(a) applies to the gain recognized by Brown to the extent of the earnings and profits attributable under § 1.1248-3 to such shares. If, however, Brown had sold the remainder of his shares in F on July 1, 1970, since the last date on which Brown owned stock representing at least 10 percent of the total combined voting power of F while F was a controlled foreign corporation was June 30, 1965, a date which is not within the 5-year period ending July 1, 1970, the conditions of subparagraph (2) of this paragraph would not be satisfied and section 1248(a) would not apply.

Example (3). Corporation G, a foreign corporation created in 1950, has outstanding 100 shares of one class of stock and uses the calendar year as its taxable year. Corporation X, a United States person, owns 60 shares of G stock and has owned such stock since G was created. Corporation Y, a United States person, owned 15 shares of the G stock from 1950 until December 1, 1962, on which date it sold 10 of such shares. On December 31, 1963, Y sells its remaining 5 shares of the G stock and recognizes gain on the sale. Since G is not considered to be a controlled foreign corporation at any time before January 1, 1963, and since Y did not own stock representing at least 10 percent of the total combined voting power of G at any time on or after such date, the conditions of subparagraph (2) of this paragraph are not satisfied and section 1248(a) does not apply.

Example (4). (i) *Facts.* X, a domestic corporation, and Y, a foreign corporation that is not a controlled foreign corporation, are partners in foreign partnership Z. X has a 60% interest in Z, and Y has a 40% interest in Z. All parties are calendar year taxpayers. On January 1, year 1, Z forms foreign corporation H, a controlled foreign corporation that conducts a business in Country C. Z and H's functional currency is the United States dollar. In years 1 and 2, H did not earn subpart F income as defined in section 952(a). On December 31, year 2, Z sells all of the H stock for $600 when Z's adjusted basis in the stock is $100. Therefore, Z recognizes a gain of $500 on the sale, of which $300 is allocable to X as a 60% partner. At the time of the sale, H had $300 of earnings and profits, $180 of which (that is, 60% of $300) is attributable to X's 60% share of the H stock.

(ii) *Result.* Pursuant to section 1248(a) and paragraphs (a)(1) and (4) of this section, X and Y are treated as selling 60% and 40%, respectively, of the H stock. X includes in its gross income as a dividend $180 of the gain recognized on the sale. Because Y is a foreign corporation that is not a CFC, neither section 1248 nor section 964 applies to the sale of Y's 40% share of the H stock.

(iii) *Alternative facts.* If, instead, X owned its 60% interest in Z through another foreign partnership, the result would be the same.

(b) *Sale or exchange.*—For purposes of section 1248(a), the term sale or exchange includes the receipt of a distribution which is treated as in exchange for stock under section 302(a) (relating to distributions in redemption of stock) or section 331(a) (relating to distributions in complete liquidation of a corporation). For purposes of section 1248(a), gain recognized by a shareholder under section 301(c)(3) in connection with a distribution of property by a corporation with respect to its stock shall be treated as gain from the sale or exchange of stock of such corporation.

(c) *Gain recognized.*—Section 1248(a) applies to a sale or exchange of stock in a foreign corporation only if gain is recognized in whole or in part upon the sale or exchange. Thus, for example, if a United States person exchanges stock in a foreign corporation and no gain is recognized on the exchange under section 332, 351, 354, 355, 356, or

361, taking into account the application of section 367, then no amount is includible in the gross income of the person as a dividend under section 1248(a). But see §§1.1248(f)-1 and 1.1248(f)-2, providing that a domestic distributing corporation must include in gross income amounts under section 1248(f) as a result of certain foreign stock distributed pursuant to section 337, 355(c)(1), or 361(c)(1) (in certain cases without regard to the amount of gain realized by the domestic distributing corporation in the distribution).

(d) *Credit for foreign taxes.*—(1) If a domestic corporation includes an amount in its gross income as a dividend under section 1248(a) upon a sale or exchange of stock in a foreign corporation (referred to as a "first tier" corporation), and if on the date of the sale or exchange the domestic corporation owns directly at least 10 percent of the voting stock of the first tier corporation—

(i) The foreign tax credit provisions of sections 901 through 908 shall apply in the same manner and subject to the same conditions and limitations as if the first tier corporation on such date distributed to the domestic corporation as a dividend that portion of the amount included in gross income under section 1248(a) which does not exceed the earnings and profits of the first tier corporation attributable to the stock under §1.1248-2 or §1.1248-3, as the case may be, and

(ii) If on such date such first tier corporation owns directly 50 percent or more of the voting stock of a "lower tier" corporation described in paragraph (a)(3) of §1.1248-2 or paragraph (a)(3) of §1.1248-3, as the case may be (referred to as a "second tier" corporation), then the foreign tax credit provisions of sections 901 through 905 shall apply in the same manner and subject to the same conditions and limitations as if on such date (*a*) the domestic corporation owned directly that percentage of the stock in the second tier corporation which such domestic corporation is considered to own by reason of the application of section 958(a)(2), and (*b*) the second tier corporation had distributed to the domestic corporation as a dividend that portion of the amount included in gross income under section 1248(a) which does not exceed the earnings and profits of the second tier corporation attributable to such stock under §1.1248-2 or §1.1248-3, as the case may be.

(2) A credit shall not be allowed under subparagraph (1) of this paragraph in respect of taxes which are not actually paid or accrued. For the inclusion as a dividend in the gross income of a domestic corporation of an amount equal to the taxes deemed paid by such corporation under section 902(a)(1), see section 78.

(3) If subparagraph (1)(ii) of this paragraph applies, and if the amount included in gross income under section 1248(a) upon the sale or exchange of the stock in a first tier corporation described in subparagraph (1)(ii) of this paragraph is less than the sum of the earnings and profits of the first tier corporation attributable to such stock under §1.1248-2 or §1.1248-3, as the case may be, plus the earnings and profits of the second tier corporation attributable to such stock under §1.1248-2 or 1.1248-3, as the case may be, then the amount considered distributed to the domestic corporation as a dividend shall be determined by multiplying the amount included in gross income under section 1248(a) by—

(i) For purposes of applying subparagraph (1)(i) of this paragraph, the percentage that (*a*) the earnings and profits of the first tier corporation attributable to such stock under §1.1248-2 or §1.1248-3, as the case may be, bears to (*b*) the sum of the earnings and profits of the first tier corporation attributable to such stock under §1.1248-2 or §1.1248-3, as the case may be, plus the earnings and profits of the second tier corporation attributable to such stock under §1.1248-2 or §1.1248-3, as the case may be, and

(ii) For purposes of applying subparagraph (1)(ii) of this paragraph, the percentage that (*a*) the earnings and profits of the second tier corporation attributable to such stock under §1.1248-2 or 1.1248-3, as the case may be, bears to (*b*) the sum referred to in subdivision (i)(*b*) of this subparagraph.

(4) The provisions of this paragraph may be illustrated by the following examples:

Example (1). On June 30, 1964, domestic corporation D owns 10 percent of the voting stock of controlled foreign corporation X. On such date, D sells a share of X stock and includes $200 of the gain on the sale in its gross income as a dividend under section 1248(a). X does not own any stock of a lower tier corporation referred to in paragraph (a)(3) of §1.1248-3. D uses the calendar year as its taxable year and instead of deducting foreign taxes under section 164, D chooses the benefits of the foreign tax credit provisions for 1964. If D had included $200 in its gross income as a dividend with respect to a distribution from X on June 30, 1964, the amount of the foreign income taxes paid by X which D would be deemed to have paid under section 902(a) in respect of such distribution would be $60. Thus, in respect of the $200 included in D's gross income as a dividend under section 1248(a), and subject to the applicable limitations and conditions of sections 901 through 905, D is entitled under this paragraph to a foreign tax credit of $60 for 1964.

Example (2). On June 30, 1965, domestic corporation D owns all of the voting stock of foreign corporation Y, and Y (the first tier corporation) owns all of the voting stock of foreign corporation Z (a second tier corporation). On such date, D sells a block of Y stock and includes $400 of the gain on the sale in its gross income as a dividend under section 1248(a). The earnings and profits attributable under §1.1248-3 to the block are $600 from Y and $1,800 from Z. D uses the calendar year as its taxable year and instead of deducting foreign taxes under section 164, D chooses the benefits of the foreign tax credit provisions for 1965. For purposes of applying the foreign tax credit provisions, Y is considered under subparagraph (3) of this paragraph to have distributed to D a dividend of $100 ($400 × 600/2400) and Z is considered to have so distributed to D a dividend of $300 ($400 × 1800/2400). If D had included $100 in its gross income as a dividend with respect to a distribution from Y on June 30, 1965, the amount of foreign income taxes paid by Y which D would be deemed to have paid under section 902(a) in respect of such distribution is $80. If D had owned the stock in Z directly, and if D had included $300 in its gross income as a dividend with respect to a distribution from Z, the amount of foreign income taxes paid by Z which D would be deemed to have paid under section 902(a) in respect of such distribution is $120. Thus, in respect of the $400 included in D's gross income as a dividend under section 1248(a), and subject to the applicable limitations and conditions of sections 901 through 905, D is entitled under this paragraph to a foreign tax credit of $200 ($80 plus $120) for 1965.

(e) *Exceptions.*—Under section 1248(g), this section and §§1.1248-2 through 1.1248-8 do not apply to:

(1) Distributions to which section 303 (relating to distributions in redemption of stock to pay death taxes) applies; or

(2) Any amount to the extent that the amount is, under any other provision of the Internal Revenue Code (Code), treated as- -

(i) A dividend;

(ii) Gain from the sale of an asset which is not a capital asset; or

(iii) Gain from the sale of an asset held for not more than 1 year.

(f) *Installment method.*—(1) Gain from a sale or exchange to which section 1248 applies may be reported under the installment method if such method is otherwise available under section 453 of the Code. In such case, the income (other than interest) in each installment payment shall be deemed to consist of gain which is included in gross income under section 1248 as a dividend until all such gain has been reported, and the remaining portion (if any) of such income shall be deemed to consist of gain to which section 1248 does not apply. For treatment of amounts as interest on certain deferred payments, see section 483.

(2) The application of this paragraph may be illustrated by the following example:

Example. Jones contracts to sell stock in a controlled foreign corporation for $5,000 to be paid in 10 equal payments of $500 each, plus a sufficient amount of interest so that section 483 does not apply. He properly elects under section 453 to report under the installment method gain of $1,000 which is includible in gross income under section 1248 as a dividend and gain of $500 which is a long-term capital gain. Accordingly, $150 of each of the first 6 installment payments and $100 of the seventh installment payment are included in gross income under section 1248 as a dividend, and $50 of the seventh installment payment and $150 of each of the last 3 installment payments are long-term capital gain.

(g) *Effective/applicability date.*—(1) The third sentence in paragraph (a)(1), paragraph (a)(4), and paragraph (a)(5), *Example 4*, of this section apply to income inclusions that occur on or after July 30, 2007. A taxpayer may elect to apply paragraph (a)(4) of this section to income inclusions in open taxable years provided that it consistently applies paragraph (a)(4) of this section for income inclusions in the first year for which the election is applicable and in all subsequent years.

(2) Paragraph (b) of this section applies to distributions that occur on or after February 10, 2009.

(3) Paragraphs (c) and (e) of this section apply to transactions occurring on or after April 18, 2013. [Reg. §1.1248-1.]

☐ [*T.D. 6779, 12-21-64. Amended by T.D. 7728, 10-31-80; T.D. 7961, 6-20-84; T.D. 9345, 7-27-2007 T.D. 9444, 2-10-2009; T.D. 9585, 4-23-2012 and T.D.* 9614, 3-18-2013.]

§ 1.1248-2. Earnings and profits attributable to a block of stock in simple cases.—(a) *General.*—(1) *Manner of computation.*—For purposes of paragraph (a)(1) of § 1.1248-1, if a United States person sells or exchanges a block of stock (as defined in paragraph (b) of this section) in a foreign corporation, and if the conditions of paragraph (c) of this section are satisfied in respect of the block, then the earnings and profits attributable to the block which were accumulated in taxable years of the corporation beginning after December 31, 1962, during the period such block was held (or was considered to be held by reason of the application of section 1223, taking into account § 1.1248-8) by such person while such corporation was a controlled foreign corporation, shall be computed in accordance with the steps set forth in subparagraphs (2), (3), and (4) of this paragraph.

(2) *Step 1.*—(i) For each taxable year of the corporation beginning after December 31, 1962, the earnings and profits accumulated for each such taxable year by the corporation shall be computed in the manner prescribed in paragraph (d) of this section, and

(ii) for the period the person held (or is considered to have held by reason of the application of section 1223, taking into account § 1.1248-8) the block, the amount of earnings and profits attributable to the block shall be computed in the manner prescribed in paragraph (e) of this section.

(3) *Step 2.*—If the conditions of paragraph (c)(5)(ii) of this section must be satisfied in respect of stock in a "lower tier" foreign corporation which such person owns within the meaning of section 958(a)(2), then (i) the earnings and profits accumulated for each such taxable year by such lower tier corporation shall be computed in the manner prescribed in paragraph (d) of this section, and (ii) for the period the person held (or is considered to have held by reason of the application of section 1223, taking into account § 1.1248-8) the block, the amount of earnings and profits of the lower tier corporation attributable to the block shall be computed in the manner prescribed in paragraph (e) of this section applied as if such person owned directly the percentage of such stock in such lower tier corporation which such person owns within the meaning of section 958(a)(2).

(4) *Step 3.*—The amount of earnings and profits attributable to the block shall be the sum of the amounts computed under steps 1 and 2.

(b) *Block of stock.*—For purposes of this section, the term "block of stock" means a group of shares sold or exchanged in one transaction, but only if—

(1) The amount realized, basis, and holding period are identical for each such share, and

(2) In case, during the period the person held (or is considered to have held by reason of the application of section 1223) such shares, any amount was included under section 951 in the gross income of the person (or another person) in respect of the shares, the excess under paragraph (e)(3)(ii) of this section (computed as if each share were a block) is identical for each such share.

(c) *Conditions to application.*—This section shall apply only if the following conditions are satisfied:

(1)(i) On each day of the period during which the block of stock was held (or is considered as held by reason of the application of section 1223) by the person during taxable years of the corporation beginning after December 31, 1962, the corporation is a controlled foreign corporation, and

(ii) on no such day is the corporation a foreign personal holding company (as defined in section 552) or a foreign investment company (as defined in section 1246(b)).

(2) The corporation had only one class of stock, and the same number of shares of such stock were outstanding, on each day of each taxable year of the corporation beginning after December 31, 1962, any day of which falls within the period referred to in subparagraph (1) of this paragraph.

(3) For each taxable year referred to in subparagraph (2) of this paragraph, the corporation is not a less developed country corporation (as defined in section 902(d)).

(4) For each taxable year referred to in subparagraph (2) of this paragraph, the corporation does not make any distributions out of its earnings and profits other than distributions which, under section 316 (as modified by section 959), are considered to be out of earnings and profits accumulated in taxable years beginning after December 31, 1962, during the period such person held (or is considered to have held by reason of the application of section 1223, taking into account § 1.1248-8) the block while such corporation was a controlled foreign corporation.

(5)(i) If (*a*) on the date of the sale or exchange such person, by reason of his ownership of such block, owns within the meaning of section 958(a)(2) stock in another foreign corporation (referred to as a "lower tier" corporation), and (*b*) the conditions of paragraph (a)(2) of § 1.1248-1 would be satisfied by such person in respect of such stock in the lower tier corporation if such person were deemed to have sold or exchanged such stock in the lower tier corporation on the date he actually sold or exchanged such block in the first tier corporation, then the conditions of subdivision (ii) of this subparagraph must be satisfied.

(ii) In respect of stock in such lower tier corporation, (*a*) the conditions set forth in subparagraphs (1) through (4) of this paragraph (applied as if such person owned directly such stock in such lower tier corporation) must be met and (*b*) such person must own within the meaning of section 958(a)(2) the same percentage of the shares of such stock on each day which falls within the period referred to in subparagraph (1) of this paragraph.

(d) *Earnings and profits accumulated for a taxable year.*—(1) *General.*—For purposes of this section, the earnings and profits accumulated for a taxable year of a foreign corporation shall be the earnings and profits for such year computed in accordance with the rules prescribed in § 1.964-1 (relating to determination of earnings and profits for a taxable year of a controlled foreign corporation) and reduced by any distributions therefrom. If the stock in the corporation is sold or exchanged before any action is taken by or on behalf of the corporation under paragraph (c) of § 1.964-1, the computation of earnings and profits under § 1.964-1 for purposes of this section shall be made as if no elections had been made and no accounting method had been adopted.

(2) *Special rules.*—(i) The earnings and profits of the corporation accumulated—

(*a*) For any taxable year beginning before January 1, 1967 (computed without any reduction for distributions), shall not include the excess of any item includible in gross income of the foreign corporation under section 882(b) as gross income derived from sources within the United States, and

(*b*) For any taxable year beginning after December 31, 1966 (computed without any reduction for distributions), shall not include the excess of any item includible in gross income of the foreign corporation under section 882(b)(2) as income effectively connected for that year with the conduct by such corporation of a trade or business in the United States, whether derived from sources within or from sources without the United States,

over any deductions allocable to such item under section 882(c). However, if the sale or exchange of stock in the foreign corporation by the United States person occurs before January 1, 1967, the provisions of (*a*) of this subdivision apply with respect to such sale or exchange even though the taxable year begins after December 31, 1966. See section 1248(d)(4). Any item which is required to be excluded from gross income, or which is taxed at a reduced rate, under an applicable treaty obligation of the United States shall not be excluded under this subdivision from earnings and profits accumulated for a taxable year (computed without any reduction for distributions).

(ii) If a foreign corporation adopts a plan of complete liquidation in a taxable year of the corporation beginning after December 31, 1962, and if because of the application of section 337(a) gain or loss would not be recognized by the corporation from the sale or exchange of property if the corporation were a domestic corporation, then the earnings and profits of the corporation accumulated for the taxable year (computed without any reduction for distributions) shall be determined without regard to the amount of such gain or loss. See section 1248(d)(2). For the nonapplication of section 337(a) to a liquidation by a collapsible corporation (as defined in section 341) and to certain other liquidations, see section 337(c).

(e) *Earnings and profits attributable to block.*—(1) *General.*—Except as provided in subparagraph (3) of this paragraph, the earnings and profits attributable to a block of stock of a controlled foreign corporation for the period a United States person held (or is considered to have held by reason of the application of section 1223, taking into account § 1.1248-8) the block are an amount equal to—

(i) The sum of the earnings and profits accumulated for each taxable year of the corporation beginning after December 31, 1962 (computed under paragraph (d) of this section) during such period, multiplied by

(ii) The percentage that (*a*) the number of shares in the block, bears to (*b*) the total number of shares of the corporation outstanding during such period.

(2) *Special rule.*—For purposes of computing the sum referred to in subparagraph (1)(i) of this paragraph, in case the block was held (or is considered as held by reason of the application of section 1223, taking into account § 1.1248-8) during a taxable year beginning after December 31, 1962, but not on each day of such taxable year, there shall be included in such sum only that portion which bears the same ratio to (i) the total earnings and profits for such taxable year computed under paragraph (d) of this section), as (ii) the number of days during such taxable year the block was held (or is considered as so held), bears to (iii) the total number of days in such taxable year.

(3) *Amounts included in gross income under section 951.*—(i) If, during the period the person held (or is considered to have held by reason of the application of section 1223, taking into account § 1.1248-8) the block, any amount was included under section 951 in the gross income of such person (or of another person whose holding of the stock sold or exchanged is, by reason of the application of section 1223, attributed to such person) in respect of the block, then the earnings and profits attributable to the block for such period shall be an amount equal to (*a*) the earnings and profits attributable to the block which would have been computed under subparagraph (1) of this paragraph if this subparagraph did not apply, reduced by (*b*) the excess computed under subdivision (ii) of this subparagraph. See section 1248(d)(1).

(ii) The excess computed under this subdivision is the excess (if any) of (*a*) amounts included under section 951 in the gross income of such person (or such other person) in respect of the block during such period, over (*b*) the portion of such amounts which, in any taxable year of such person (or such other person), resulted in an exclusion from the gross income of such person (or such other person) under section 959(a)(1) (relating to exclusion from gross income of distributions of previously taxed earnings and profits).

(iii) This subparagraph shall apply notwithstanding an election under section 962 by such person to be subject to tax at corporate rates.

(4) *Example.*—The application of this paragraph may be illustrated by the following examples:

Example (1). On May 26, 1965, Green, a United States person, purchases at its fair market value a block of 25 of the 100 outstanding shares of the only class of stock of controlled foreign corporation F. He sells the block on January 1, 1968. In respect of the block, Green did not include any amount in his gross income under section 951. F uses the calendar year as its taxable year and does not own stock in any lower tier corporation referred to in paragraph (c)(5)(i) of this section. All of the conditions of paragraph (c) of this section are satisfied in respect of the block. The earnings and profits accumulated by F (computed under paragraph (d) of this section) are $10,000 for 1965, $13,000 for 1966, and $11,000 for 1967. The earnings and profits of F attributable to the block are $7,500, determined as follows:

Sum of earnings and profits accumulated by F during period block was held:

For 1965 (219/365 × $10,000)	$6,000
For 1966	13,000
For 1967	11,000
Sum	$30,000
Multiplied by:	
Number of shares in block (25), divided by total number of shares outstanding (100)	25%
Earnings and profits attributable to block	$7,500

Example (2). Assume the same facts as in example (1) except that in respect of the block Green includes in his gross income under section 951 the total amount of $2,800 for 1965 and 1966, and because of such inclusion the amount of $2,300 which was distributed to Green by F on January 15, 1967, is excluded from his gross income under section 959(a)(1). Accordingly, the earnings and profits of F attributable to the block are $7,000, determined as follows:

Earnings and profits attributable to the block, as computed in example (1)	$7,500
Minus:	
Excess of amount included in Green's gross income under section 951 ($2,800), over portion thereof which resulted in an exclusion under section 959(a)(1) ($2,300)	$500
Earnings and profits attributable to block	$7,000

Example (3). Assume the same facts as in example (1) except that on each day beginning on January 1, 1966 (the date controlled foreign corporation G was organized) through January 1, 1968, F owns 80 of the 100 outstanding shares of the only class of G stock. Since, by reason of his ownership of 25 shares of F stock, Green owns within the meaning of section 958(a)(2) the equivalent of 20 shares of G stock (25/100 of 80 shares), G is a lower tier corporation referred to in paragraph (c)(5)(i)(*a*) of this section. If Green had sold the 20 shares of G stock on January 1, 1968, the date he actually sold the block of F stock, the conditions of paragraph (a)(2) of § 1.1248-1 would be satisfied in respect of the G stock, and, accordingly, the conditions of paragraph (c)(5)(ii) of this section must be satisfied. Assume further that such conditions are satisfied, that G uses the calendar year as its taxable year, and that the earnings and profits accumulated by G (computed under paragraph (d) of this section) are $19,000 for 1966 and $21,000 for 1967. The earnings and profits of F and of G attributable to the block are $15,500, determined as follows:

Sum of earnings and profits accumulated by G for period Green owned G stock within the meaning of section 958(a)(2) ($19,000 plus $21,000)	$40,000
Multiplied by:	
Number of G shares deemed owned within the meaning of section 958(a)(2) by Green (20), divided by total number of G shares outstanding (100)	20%
Earnings and profits of G attributable to block	$8,000
Earnings and profits of F attributable to block, as determined in example (1)	7,500
Total earnings and profits attributable to block	$15,500

[Reg. § 1.1248-2.]

☐ [*T.D. 6779, 12-21-64. Amended by T.D. 7293, 11-27-73 and T.D.* 9345, 7-27-2007.]

§ 1.1248-3. Earnings and profits attributable to stock in complex cases.—(a) *General.*—(1) *Manner of computation.*—For purposes of paragraph (a)(1) of § 1.1248-1, if a United States person sells or exchanges stock in a foreign corporation, and if the provisions of § 1.1248-2 do not apply, then the earnings and profits attributable to the stock which were accumulated in taxable years of the corporation beginning after December 31, 1962, during the period or periods such stock was held (or was considered to be held by reason of the application of section 1223, taking into account § 1.1248-8) by such person while such corporation was a controlled foreign corporation, shall be computed in accordance with the steps set forth in subparagraphs (2), (3), and (4) of this paragraph.

(2) *Step 1.*—For each taxable year of the corporation beginning after December 31, 1962, (i) the earnings and profits accumulated for such taxable year by the corporation shall be computed in the manner prescribed in paragraph (b) of this section, (ii) the person's "tentative ratable share" of such earnings and profits shall be computed in the manner prescribed in paragraph (c) or (d) (whichever is applicable) of this section, and (iii) the person's "ratable share" of such earnings and profits shall be computed by adjusting the tentative ratable share in the manner prescribed in paragraph (e) of this section.

(3) *Step 2.*—If the provisions of paragraph (f) of this section (relating to earnings and profits of "lower tier" foreign corporations) apply, the amount of the person's ratable share of the earnings and profits accumulated by each "lower tier" corporation attributable to any such taxable year (i) shall be computed in the manner prescribed by paragraph (f) of this section,, and (ii) shall be added to such person's ratable share for such taxable year determined in step 1.

(4) *Step 3.*—The amount of earnings and profits attributable to the share shall be the sum of the ratable shares computed for each such taxable year in the manner prescribed in steps 1 and 2.

(5) *Share or block.*—In general, the computation under this paragraph shall be made separately for each share of stock sold or exchanged, except that if a group of shares constitute a block of stock the computation may be made in respect of the block. For purposes of this section, the term "block of stock" means a group of shares sold or exchanged in one transaction, but only if (i) the amount realized, basis, and holding period are identical for each such share, and (ii) the adjustments (if any) under paragraphs (e) and (f)(5) of this section of the tentative ratable shares would be identical for each such share if such adjustments were computed separately for each such share.

(6) *Deficit in earnings and profits.*—For purposes of this section and §§1.1248-2 through 1.1248-8, in respect of a taxable year, the term "earnings and profits accumulated" for a taxable year (but only if computed under paragraph (b) of this section) includes a deficit in earnings and profits accumulated for such taxable year. Similarly, a tentative ratable share, or a ratable share, may be a deficit.

(7) *Examples.*—The application of the provisions of this paragraph may be illustrated by the following examples:

Example (1). On December 31, 1967, Brown sells 10 shares of stock in foreign corporation X, which uses the calendar year as its taxable year. The 10 shares constitute a block of stock under subparagraph (5) of this paragraph. Under step 1, Brown's ratable shares of the earnings and profits of X attributable to the block are as follows:

Taxable year of X	*Ratable shares*
1963	$100
1964	150
1965	−50 (deficit)
1966	50
1967	100
Sum	$350

The amount of the earnings and profits attributable to such block under step 3 is $350.

Example (2). Assume the same facts as in example (1), except that in respect of X there are "lower tier" corporations Y and Z to which the provisions of paragraph (f) of this section apply. Brown's ratable shares of the earnings and profits of X, Y, and Z attributable to the block under steps 1 and 2 for each taxable year of X are as follows:

Taxable year of X	X	Y	Z	*Total*
		Ratable shares		
1963	$100	$40	$20	$160
1964	150	40	−60	130
1965	−50	30	50	30
1966	50	50	30	130
1967	100	−40	40	100
Sum	$350	$120	$80	$550

The amount of the earnings and profits attributable to such block under step 3 is $550.

(b) *Earnings and profits accumulated for a taxable year.*—(1) *General.*—For purposes of this section, the earnings and profits accumulated for a taxable year of a foreign corporation shall be the earnings and profits for such year, computed in accordance with the rules prescribed in §1.964-1 (relating to determination of earnings and profits for a taxable year of a controlled foreign corporation), except that (i) the special rules of subparagraph (2) of this paragraph shall apply, and (ii) adjustments shall be made under subparagraph (3) of this paragraph for distributions made by the corporation during such taxable year. If the stock in the corporation is sold or exchanged before any action is taken by or on behalf of the corporation under paragraph (c) of §1.964-1, the computation of earnings and profits under §1.964-1 for purposes of this section shall be made as if no elections had been made and no accounting method had been adopted. The amount of earnings and profits accumulated for a taxable year of a foreign corporation, as computed under this paragraph, is not necessarily the same amount as the earnings and profits of the taxable year computed under section 316(a)(2) or paragraph (d) of §1.1248-2. Thus, for example, if a distribution with respect to stock is in excess of the amount of earnings and profits of the taxable year computed under section 316(a)(2), such excess is treated under section 316(a)(1) or paragraph (d) of §1.1248-2 as made out of any earnings and profits accumulated in prior taxable years, whereas the amount of such excess may create, or increase, a deficit in the earnings and profits accumulated for the taxable year as computed under this paragraph. See subparagraph (3) of this paragraph.

(2) *Special rules.*—(i) The earnings and profits of the corporation accumulated—

(a) For any taxable year beginning before January 1, 1967, shall not include the excess of any item includible in gross income of the foreign corporation under section 882(b) as gross income derived from sources within the United States, and

(b) For any taxable year beginning after December 31, 1966, shall not include the excess of any item includible in gross income of the foreign corporation under section 882(b)(2) as income effectively connected for that year with the conduct by such corporation of a trade or business in the United States, whether derived from sources within or from sources without the United States,

over any deductions allocable to such item under section 882(c). However, if the sale or exchange of stock in the foreign corporation by the U.S. person occurs before January 1, 1967, the provisions of *(a)* of this subdivision apply with respect to such sale or exchange even though the taxable year begins after December 31, 1966. See section 1248(d)(4). Any item which is required to be excluded from gross income, or which is taxed at a reduced rate, under an applicable treaty obligation of the United States shall not be excluded under this subdivision from earnings and profits accumulated for a taxable year.

(ii) If a foreign corporation adopts a plan of complete liquidation in a taxable year of the corporation beginning after December 31, 1962, and if because of the application of section 337(a) gain or loss would not be recognized by the corporation from the sale or exchange of property if the corporation were a domestic corporation, then the earnings and profits of the corporation accumulated for the taxable year shall be determined without regard to the amount of such gain or loss. See section 1248(d)(2). For the nonapplication of section 337(a) to a liquidation by a collapsible corporation (as defined in section 341) and to certain other liquidations, see section 337(c).

(3) *Adjustment for distributions.*—(i) The earnings and profits of a foreign corporation accumulated for a taxable year (computed without regard to this subparagraph) shall be reduced (if necessary below zero so as to create a deficit), or a deficit in such earnings and profits shall be increased, by the amount of the distributions (other than in redemption of stock under section 302(a) or 303) made by the corporation in respect of its stock during such taxable year *(a)* out of such earnings and profits, or *(b)* out of earnings and profits accumulated for prior taxable years beginning after December 31, 1962 (computed under this paragraph). Except for purposes of applying this subparagraph, the application of the preceding sentence shall not affect the amount of earnings and profits accumulated for any such prior taxable year.

(ii) The application of this subparagraph may be illustrated by the following examples:

Example (1). X Corporation, which uses the calendar year as its taxable year, was organized on January 1, 1965, and was a controlled foreign corporation on each day of 1965. The amount of X's earnings and profits accumulated for 1965 (computed under this paragraph without regard to the adjustment for distributions under this subparagraph) is $400,000, of which $100,000 is distributed by X as dividends during 1965. The amount of X's earnings and profits accumulated for 1965 (computed under this paragraph) is $300,000 (that is, $400,000 minus $100,000). The result would be the same even if X was not a controlled foreign corporation on each day of 1965.

Example (2). Assume the same facts as in example (1). Assume further that the amount of X's earnings and profits accumulated for 1966 (computed under this paragraph without regard to the adjustment for distributions under this subparagraph) is $150,000, and that X distributes the amount of $260,000 as dividends during 1966. Since $150,000 of the distribution is from earnings and profits accumulated for 1966 (computed without regard to the adjustment for distributions under this subparagraph), and since $110,000 is from earnings and profits accumulated for 1965, the earnings and profits of X accumulated for 1966 are a deficit of $110,000 (that is, $150,000 minus $260,000). However, the earnings and profits accumulated for 1965 are still $300,000 for purposes of computing in the manner prescribed in paragraph (c) of this section a person's tentative ratable share.

(c) *Tentative ratable share if earnings and profits accumulated for a taxable year not less than zero.*—(1) *General rule.*—For purposes of paragraph (a)(2)(ii) of this section, in respect of a share (or block) of stock in a foreign corporation, if the amount of the earnings and profits accumulated for a taxable year of the corporation (computed under paragraph (b) of this section), beginning after December 31, 1962, is not less than zero, then the person's tentative ratable share for such taxable year shall be equal to—

(i) *(a)* Such amount (if the computation is made in respect of a block, multiplied by the number of shares in the block), divided by *(b)* the number of shares in the corporation outstanding, or deemed under subparagraph (2) of this paragraph to be outstanding, on each day of such taxable year, multiplied by

(ii) The percentage that *(a)* the number of days in such taxable year of the corporation during the period the person held (or was considered to have held by reason of the application of section 1223, taking into account § 1.1248-8) the share (or block) while the corporation was a controlled foreign corporation, bears to *(b)* the total number of days in such taxable year.

(2) *Shares deemed outstanding for a taxable year.*—For purposes of this section and § § 1.1248-4 through 1.1248-7, if the number of shares of stock in a foreign corporation outstanding on each day of a taxable year of the corporation is not constant, then the number of such shares deemed outstanding on each such day shall be the sum of the fractional amounts in respect of each share outstanding on any day of the taxable year. The fractional amount in respect of a share shall be determined by dividing (i) the number of days in the taxable year during which such share was outstanding (excluding the day the share became outstanding, but including the day the share ceased to be outstanding), by (ii) the total number of days in such taxable year.

(3) *Examples.*—The application of subparagraphs (1) and (2) of this paragraph may be illustrated by the following examples:

Example (1). On each day of 1964, S owns a block consisting of 30 of the 100 shares of the only class of stock outstanding in F Corporation, and on each such day F is a controlled foreign corporation. F uses the calendar year as its taxable year and F's earnings and profits accumulated for 1964 (computed under paragraph (b) of this section) are $10,000. S's tentative ratable share with respect to the block is $3,000, computed as follows:

Earnings and profits accumulated for taxable year	$10,000
Multiplied by:	
Number of shares in block (30), divided by number of shares outstanding (100)	30%
Multiplied by:	
Number of days in 1964 S held block while F was a controlled foreign corporation (365), divided by number of days in 1964 (365)	100%
Tentative ratable share for block	$3,000

Example (2). On December 31, 1964, X Corporation, a controlled foreign corporation which uses the calendar year as its taxable year, had 100 shares of one class of stock outstanding, 15 of which were owned by T. T's 15 shares were redeemed by X on March 14, 1965. On December 31, 1965, in addition to the remaining 85 shares, 10 new shares of stock (which were issued on May 26, 1965) were outstanding. Thus, during 1965, 15 shares were outstanding for 73 days, 10 for 219 days, and 85 for 365 days. The earnings and profits (computed under paragraph (b) of this section) accumulated for X's taxable year ending on December 31, 1965, are $18,800. T's tentative ratable share with respect to one share of stock is $40, computed as follows:

Earnings and profits accumulated for taxable year		$18,800
Divided by:		
Number of shares deemed outstanding on each day of 1965:		
15 for 73 days (15 × 73/365)	3	
10 for 219 days (10 × 219/365)	6	
85 for 365 days (85 × 365/365)	85	
Total number of shares deemed outstanding each day of 1965		94
Earnings and profits accumulated per share		$200
Multiplied by:		
Number of days in 1965 T held his share while X was a controlled foreign corporation (73), divided by number of days in 1965 (365)		20%
T's tentative ratable share per share of stock		$40

Example (3). Assume the same facts as in example (2) except that X was not a controlled foreign corporation after January 31, 1965. T's tentative ratable share with respect to one share of stock for 1965 is $17, computed as follows:

Earnings and profits accumulated per share, determined in example (2)	$200
Multiplied by:	
Number of days in 1965 T held X stock while X was a controlled foreign corporation (31), divided by number of days in 1965 (365)	8.5%
Tentative ratable share	$17

(4) *More than one class of stock.*—If a foreign corporation for a taxable year has more than one class of stock outstanding, then before applying subparagraphs (1) and (2) of this paragraph the earnings and profits accumulated for the taxable year of the corporation (computed under paragraph (b) of this section) shall be allocated to each class of stock in accordance with the principles of paragraph (e)(2) and (3) of § 1.951-1, applied as if the corporation were a controlled foreign corporation on each day of such taxable year.

(d) *Tentative ratable share if deficit in earnings and profits accumulated for taxable year.*—(1) *General rule.*—For purposes of paragraph (a)(2)(ii) of this section, in respect of a share (or block) of stock in a foreign corporation, if there is a deficit in the earnings and profits accumulated for a taxable year of the corporation (computed under paragraph (b) of this section) beginning after December 31, 1962, the person's tentative ratable share for such taxable year shall be an amount equal to the sum of the partial tentative ratable shares computed under subparagraphs (2) and (3) of this paragraph.

(2) *Operating deficit.*—The partial tentative ratable share under this subparagraph is computed in 2 steps. First, compute (under paragraph (b) of this section without regard to the adjustment for distributions under subparagraph (3) thereof) the deficit (if any) in earnings and profits accumulated for such taxable year. Second, compute the partial tentative ratable share in the same manner as the tentative ratable share for such taxable year would be computed under paragraph (c) of this section if such deficit were the amount referred to in paragraph (c)(1)(i)*(a)* of this section.

(3) *Deficit from distributions.*—The partial tentative ratable share under this subparagraph is computed in 2 steps. First, compute and treat as a deficit only that portion of the adjustment for distributions under paragraph (b)(3) of this section for such taxable year which is attributable under subparagraph (4) of this paragraph to distributions out of earnings and profits accumulated during prior taxable years of the corporation beginning after December 31, 1962, during the period or periods the corporation was a controlled foreign corporation and the share (or block) of stock was owned by a United States shareholder (as defined in section 951(b) and the regulations thereunder). Second, compute the partial tentative ratable share for such taxable year in the same manner as the tentative ratable share for such taxable year would be computed under paragraph (c) of this section if (i) such deficit were the amount referred to in paragraph (c)(1)(i)*(a)* of this section, and (ii) the corporation were a controlled foreign corporation on each day of such taxable year.

(4) *Order of distributions.*—For purposes of applying subparagraph (3) of this paragraph only, the adjustment for distributions under paragraph (b)(3) of this section for a taxable year of a foreign corporation shall be treated as attributable first to distributions of earnings and profits for the taxable year (computed under paragraph (b) of this section without regard to such adjustment) to the extent thereof, and then to distributions out of the most recent of earnings and profits accumulated during prior taxable years beginning after December 31, 1962 (computed under paragraph (b) of this section). If the foreign corporation was a controlled foreign corporation during a prior taxable year for a period or periods which was only part of such prior taxable year, then for purposes of the preceding sentence (i) such taxable year shall be divided into periods the corporation was or was not a controlled foreign corporation, (ii) distributions of the earnings and profits accumulated during such prior taxable year shall be considered made from the most recent period first, and (iii) the earnings and profits accumulated during such prior taxable year shall be allocated to a period during such year in the same proportion as the number of days in the period bears to the number of days in such year. Except for purposes of applying subparagraph (3) of this paragraph, the application of this subparagraph shall not affect the amount of earnings and profits accumulated for any such prior taxable year (computed under paragraph (b) of this section).

(5) *Examples.*—The application of this paragraph may be illustrated by the following examples:

Example (1). On each day of 1965 X Corporation, which uses the calendar year as its taxable year, was a controlled foreign corporation having 100 shares of one class of stock outstanding, a block of 25 of which were owned by T, who acquired them in 1962 and sold them in 1967. The deficit in X's earnings and profits accumulated for 1965 (computed under paragraph (b) of this section without regard to the adjustment for distributions under subparagraph (3) thereof) is $100,000, and thus in respect of the block T's partial tentative ratable share computed under subparagraph (2) of this paragraph is a deficit of $25,000 (that is, $100,000 × 25/100). During 1965 X does not make any distributions in respect of its stock, and thus in respect of the block T's partial tentative ratable share computed under subparagraph (3) of this paragraph is zero. Accordingly, T's tentative ratable share in respect of the block of X stock for 1965 is a deficit of $25,000. If, however, X was a controlled foreign corporation for only 292 days during 1965, T's tentative ratable share in respect of the block for 1965 would be a deficit of $20,000 (that is, $25,000 × 292/365).

Example (2). (i) Assume the same facts as in example (1) except that at no time during 1965 is X a controlled foreign corporation and that during 1965 X distributes $80,000 with respect to its stock. Assume further that X was a controlled foreign corporation on each day of 1964, but only for the first 146 days of 1963, and that X's earnings and profits accumulated for prior taxable years computed under paragraph (b) of this section are $70,000 for 1964 and $20,000 for 1963.

(ii) Since X was not a controlled foreign corporation on any day of 1965, in respect of the block T's partial tentative ratable share computed under subparagraph (2) of this paragraph is zero.

(iii) The partial tentative ratable share under subparagraph (3) of this paragraph is computed in the following manner: For 1965 the adjustment for distributions under paragraph (b)(3) of this section is $80,000. Under subparagraph (4) of this paragraph $70,000 of such adjustment is attributable to the distribution of all of the earnings and profits accumulated during 1964, on every day of which X was a controlled foreign corporation, and $10,000 of the adjustment is attributable to the distribution of $10,000 of the earnings and profits accumulated for 1963. The portion of the earnings and profits accumulated by X in 1963 attributable to the first 146 days in 1963 during which X was a controlled foreign corporation is $8,000 (that is, $20,000 × 146/365), and the portion attributable to the period in 1963 during which X was not a controlled foreign corporation is $12,000 (that is, $20,000 × 219/365). Under subparagraph (4)(ii) of this paragraph, the distribution in 1965 of $10,000 of earnings and profits accumulated during 1963 is attributable to the more recent period in 1963, that is, the period X was not a controlled foreign corporation. Accordingly, the portion of the adjustment for distributions under paragraph (b)(3) of this section attributable to earnings and profits accumulated during periods X was a controlled foreign corporation is $70,000, and in respect of the block T's partial tentative ratable share under subparagraph (3) of this paragraph is a deficit of $17,500 (that is, $70,000 × 25/100).

(iv) T's tentative ratable share in respect of the block of X stock for 1965 is a deficit of $17,500 (that is, the sum of the partial tentative ratable share for the block computed under subparagraph (2) of this paragraph, zero, plus the partial tentative ratable share for the block computed under subparagraph (3) of this paragraph, a deficit of $17,500).

(v) Assume that X had 100 shares of one class of stock outstanding on each day of 1964 and 1963. Notwithstanding the distributions in 1965 of earnings and profits accumulated during 1964 and 1963 (computed under paragraph (b) of this section), nevertheless, in respect of the block T's tentative ratable share for 1964 is $17,500 (that is, earnings and profits accumulated during 1964 so computed of $70,000, multiplied by 25 shares/100 shares) and in respect of the block T's tentative ratable share for 1963 is $2,000 (that is, earnings and profits accumulated during 1963 so computed of $20,000, multiplied by 25 shares/100 shares, and multiplied by the percentage that the number of days in 1963 on which X was a controlled foreign corporation bears to the total number of days in 1963, 146/365).

Example (3). Assume the same facts as in example (2) except that X was a controlled foreign corporation on each day of 1965. The tentative ratable share with respect to the block of stock for 1965 is a deficit of $42,500, that is, the sum of the partial tentative ratable share under subparagraph (2) of this paragraph (as determined in example (1)), a deficit of $25,000, plus the partial tentative ratable share under subparagraph (3) of this paragraph (as determined in example (2)), a deficit of $17,500.

(6) *More than one class of stock.*—If a foreign corporation for a taxable year has more than one class of stock outstanding, then before applying subparagraph (1) of this paragraph the earnings and profits accumulated for the taxable year of the corporation (computed under paragraph (b) of this section) shall be allocated to each class of stock in accordance with the principles of paragraph (e)(2) and (3) of § 1.951-1, applied as if the corporation were a controlled foreign corporation on each day of such taxable year.

(e) *Ratable share of earnings and profits accumulated for a taxable year.*—(1) *In general.*—For purposes of paragraph (a)(2)(iii) of this section, in respect of a share (or block) of stock in a foreign corporation, the person's ratable share of the earnings and profits accumulated for a taxable year beginning after December 31, 1962, shall be an amount equal to the tentative ratable share computed under paragraph (c) or (d) (as the case may be) of this section, adjusted in the manner prescribed in subparagraphs (2) through (6) of this paragraph.

(2) *Amounts included in gross income under section 951.*—(i) In respect of a share (or block) of stock in a foreign corporation, a person's tentative ratable share for a taxable year of the corporation (computed under paragraph (c) of this section) shall be reduced (but not below zero) by the excess of *(a)* the amount, if any, included (in respect of such corporation for such taxable year) under section 951 in the gross income of such person or (during the period such share, or block, was considered to be held by such person by reason of the application of section 1223, taking into account § 1.1248-8) in the gross income of any other person who held such share (or block), over *(b)* the portion of such amount which, in any taxable year of such person or such other person, resulted in an exclusion from the gross income of such person or such other person of an amount under section 959(a)(1) (relating to exclusion from gross income of distributions of previously taxed earnings and profits). See section 1248(d)(1). This subdivision shall apply notwithstanding an election under section 962 by such person to be subject to tax at corporate rates.

(ii) The application of this subparagraph may be illustrated by the following example:

Example. On December 31, 1975, Brown sells one share of stock in X Corporation, a controlled foreign corporation which has never been a less developed country corporation (as defined in section 902(d)). Both Brown and X use the calendar year as the taxable year. In respect of his share, Brown's tentative ratable share for 1971 (computed under paragraph (c) of this section) is $35. In respect of his share, Brown included $4 in his gross income for 1971 under section 951, and the amount of $3, which was distributed to him by X on January 15, 1972, is excluded from Brown's gross income under section 959(a)(1). In respect of the stock, Brown's ratable share for 1971 is $34, determined as follows:

Tentative ratable share	$35
Minus:	
Excess of amount of tentative ratable share included in Brown's gross income under section 951 ($4), over portion thereof which resulted in exclusion under section 959(a)(1)($3)	1
Ratable share	$34

(3) *Amounts included in gross income under section 551.*—In respect of a share (or block) of stock in a foreign corporation, a person's tentative ratable share for a taxable year of the corporation (computed under paragraph (c) of this section) shall be reduced (but not below zero) by the amount, if any, included (in respect of such corporation for such taxable year) under section 551 in the gross income of such person or (during the period such share, or block, was considered to be held by such person by reason of the application of section 1223, taking into account § 1.1248-8) in the gross income of any other person who held such share (or block).

(4) *Less developed country corporations.*—(i) If the foreign corporation was a less developed country corporation as defined in section 902(d) for a taxable year of the corporation, and if the person who sold or exchanged a share (or block) of stock in such corporation satisfies the requirements of paragraph (a) of § 1.1248-5 in respect of such stock, then his ratable share for such taxable year shall be zero. See section 1248(d)(3).

(ii) The application of this subparagraph may be illustrated by the following example:

Example. Assume the same facts as in the example in subparagraph (2)(ii) of this paragraph except that X was a less developed country corporation for 1971. Assume further that Brown satisfies the requirements of paragraph (a) of § 1.1248-5. Brown's ratable share in respect of the stock for 1971 is zero.

(5) *Qualified shareholder of foreign investment company.*—In respect of a share (or block) of stock in a foreign corporation which was a foreign investment company described in section 1246(b)(1), if the election under section 1247(a) to distribute income currently was in effect for a taxable year of the company, and if the person who sold or exchanged the stock (or another person who actually owned the stock during such taxable year and whose holding of the stock is attributed by reason of the application of section 1223, taking into account § 1.1248-8, to the person who sold or exchanged the stock) was a qualified shareholder (as defined in section 1247(c)) for his taxable year in which or with which such taxable year of the company ends, then the ratable share in respect of the share (or block) for such taxable year of the company shall be zero. See section 1248(d)(5). In case gain is recognized under section 1246 in respect of a share (or block), see section 1248(f)(3)(B).

(6) *Adjustment for certain distributions.*—If (i) the person who sold or exchanged the share or block (or another person who actually owned the share or block and whose holding of the share or block is attributed by reason of the application of section 1223 to such person, taking into account § 1.1248-8) received a distribution during a taxable year of the corporation, and (ii) such distribution was not included in the gross income of such person (or such other person) by reason of the application of section 959(a)(1) to amounts which were included under section 951(a)(1) in the gross income of a United States shareholder whose holding of the share or block is not attributed by reason of the application of section 1223 to such person, taking into account § 1.1248-8 (or such other person), then the amount of such distribution shall be added to such person's tentative ratable share for such taxable year. Thus, for example, such tentative ratable share may be increased, or a deficit reduced, by the amount of such distribution.

(f) *Earnings and profits of subsidiaries of foreign corporations.*—(1) *Application of paragraph.*—(i) In respect of a person who sells or exchanges stock in a foreign corporation (referred to as a "first tier" corporation), the provisions of this paragraph shall apply if the following 3 conditions exist:

(a) The conditions of paragraph (a)(2) of § 1.1248-1 are satisfied by the person in respect of such stock;

(b) By reason of his ownership of such stock, on the date of such sale or exchange such person owned, within the meaning of section 958(a)(2), stock in another foreign corporation (referred to as a "lower tier" corporation); and

(c) The conditions of paragraph (a)(2) of § 1.1248-1 would be satisfied by such person in respect of such stock in the lower tier corporation if such person were deemed to have sold or exchanged such stock in the lower tier corporation on the date he actually sold or exchanged such stock in the first tier corporation.

(ii) If the provisions of this paragraph apply, *(a)* the person's tentative ratable share (or shares) of the earnings and profits accumulated by the lower tier corporation attributable to a taxable year of the first tier corporation shall be computed under subparagraph (2) or (4) of this paragraph, whichever is applicable, and *(b)* such person's ratable share (or shares) for the lower tier corporation attributable to a taxable year of the first tier corporation shall be computed under subparagraph (5) of this paragraph. For the manner of taking into account the ratable share for a lower tier corporation, see paragraph (a)(3) of this section.

(iii) The application of this subparagraph may be illustrated by the following example:

Example. On each day of 1964 and 1965 corporations X and Y are controlled foreign corporations, and each has outstanding 100 shares of one class of stock. On January 15, 1965, T, a United States person, owns one share of stock in X and X directly owns 20 shares of stock in Y. Thus, T owns, within the meaning of section 958(a)(2), stock in Y. On that date, T sells his share in X and satisfies the conditions of paragraph (a)(2) of § 1.1248-1 in respect of his stock in X. Assuming that the conditions of paragraph (a)(2) of § 1.1248-1 would be satisfied by T in respect of the stock he indirectly owns in Y if, on January 15, 1965, he were deemed to have sold such stock in Y, the provisions of this paragraph apply.

(2) *Tentative ratable share (of lower tier corporation attributable to a taxable year of first tier corporation) not less than zero.*—If the provisions of this paragraph apply to a sale or exchange by a United States person of a share (or block) of stock in a first tier corporation, and if the amount of earnings and profits accumulated (computed under paragraph (b) of this section) for a taxable year (beginning after December 31, 1962) of the lower tier corporation is not less than zero, then in respect of the share (or block) such person's tentative ratable share of the earnings and profits accumulated for such taxable year of the lower tier corporation attributable to any taxable year (beginning after December 31, 1962) of such first tier corporation shall be an amount equal to—

(i) *(a)* Such amount of earnings and profits accumulated for such taxable year of the lower tier corporation (if the computation is made in respect of a block in the first tier corporation, multiplied by the number of shares in the block), divided by *(b)* the number of shares in the first tier corporation outstanding, or deemed under paragraph (c)(2) of this section to be outstanding, on each day of such taxable year of the first tier corporation, multiplied by

(ii) The percentage that *(a)* the number of days during the period or periods in such taxable year of the first tier corporation on which such person held (or was considered to have held by reason of the application of section 1223, taking into account § 1.1248-8) the share (or block) in the first tier corporation while the first tier corporation owned (within the meaning of section 958(a)) stock of such lower tier corporation at times while such lower tier corporation was a controlled foreign corporation, bears to *(b)* the total number of days in such taxable year of the first tier corporation, multiplied by

(iii) The percentage that *(a)* the average number of shares in the lower tier corporation which were owned within the meaning of section 958(a) by the first tier corporation during such period or periods (referred to in subdivision (ii)*(a)* of this subparagraph), bears to *(b)* the total number of such shares outstanding, or deemed under the principles of paragraph (c)(2) of this section to be outstanding, during such period or periods, multiplied by

(iv) The percentage that *(a)* the number of days in such taxable year of the lower tier corporation which fall within the taxable year of the first tier corporation, bears to *(b)* the total number of days in such taxable year of the lower tier corporation.

(3) *Examples.*—The application of subparagraph (2) of this paragraph may be illustrated by the following examples:

Example (1). In a year subsequent to 1969, Brown, a United States person, sells 5 of his shares of stock in X Corporation in a transaction as to which the provisions of this paragraph apply. Brown had purchased the 5 shares prior to 1969. On each day of 1969 X Corporation actually had 100 shares of one class of stock outstanding. On each such day X Corporation directly owned all of the shares of stock in Y Corporation, and Y Corporation directly owned all of the shares of stock in Z Corporation. Z Corporation on each such day was a controlled foreign corporation. Both X and Z use the calendar year as the taxable year. Z's earnings and profits accumulated for 1969 (computed under paragraph (b) of this section) are $2,000. Brown's tentative ratable share of the earnings and profits accumulated by Z attributable to the 1969 calendar year of X is $20 per share, computed as follows:

(i) Z's earnings and profits for 1969 ($2,000), divided by the number of shares in X deemed outstanding each day of 1969 (100) $20

Multiplied by:

(ii) Since on each day of 1969 Brown (by reason of owning directly his shares in X) owned, within the meaning of section 958(a)(2), stock in Z while Z was a controlled foreign corporation, the percentage determined under subparagraph (2)(ii) of this paragraph equals 100%

Multiplied by:

(iii) Since on each day of 1969 X owned 100 percent of the stock of Y while Y owned 100 percent of the stock in Z, the percentage determined under subparagraph (2)(iii) equals 100%

Multiplied by:

(iv) Since X and Z each use the same taxable year, the percentage determined under subparagraph (2)(iv) of this paragraph equals 100%

Total $20

Example (2). Assume the same facts as in example (1), except that Brown sold his stock in X on October 19, 1969. Brown's tentative ratable share of the earnings and profits accumulated by Z attributable to the 1969 calendar year of X is $16 per share, computed as follows:

(i) The amount determined in subdivision (i) of example (1)	$20
Multiplied by:	
(ii) The number of days in the period during 1969 Brown (by reason of owning directly his stock in X) owned, within the meaning of section 958(a)(2), his stock in Z while Z was a controlled foreign corporation (292), divided by the number of days in 1969 (365), equals	80%
Multiplied by:	
(iii) The percentage determined in subdivision (iii) of example (1)	100%
Multiplied by:	
(iv) The percentage determined in subdivision (iv) of example (1)	100%
Total	$16

Example (3). Assume the same facts as in examples (1) and (2), except that on each day during 1969 Y owned (within the meaning of section 958(a)(2)) 81 of the 100 shares of Z's outstanding stock. Brown's tentative ratable share of the earnings and profits accumulated by Z attributable to the 1969 calendar year of X is $12.96 per share, computed as follows:

(i) The amount determined in subdivision (i) of example (1)	$20
Multiplied by:	
(ii) The percentage determined in subdivision (ii) of example (2)	80%
Multiplied by:	
(iii) The average number of shares in Z which were owned (within the meaning of section 958(a)) by X during the applicable period (81), divided by the total number of shares in Z during such period (100)	81%
Multiplied by:	
(iv) The percentage determined in subdivision (iv) of example (1)	100%
Total	$12.96

The result would be the same if X owned (within the meaning of section 958(a)(2)) 81 percent of the stock in Y while Y so owned 100 percent of the stock in X, or if X so owned 90 percent of the stock in Y while Y so owned 90 percent of the stock in Z.

Example (4). Assume the same facts as in example (3), except that Z Corporation uses a fiscal year ending June 30 as its taxable year. Assume further that Z's earnings and profits accumulated for its fiscal year ending June 30, 1969, and for its fiscal year ending June 30, 1970, are $3,000 and $2,000, respectively. Brown's tentative ratable share of the earnings and profits accumulated by Z attributable to the 1969 calendar year of X is $16.17 per share, computed as follows:

	In respect of Z's taxable year ending June 30, 1969	June 30, 1970
(i) Z's earnings and profits, divided by the number of shares in X deemed outstanding on each day of 1969:		
$3,000/100	$30	
$2,000/100		$20
Multiplied by:		
(ii) The percentage determined in subdivision (ii) of example (2)	80%	80%
Multiplied by:		
(iii) The percentage determined in subdivision (iii) of example (3)	81%	81%
Multiplied by:		
(iv) Number of days in Z's taxable year which fall within 1969, divided by total number of days in Z's taxable year:		
181/365	49.6%	
184/365		50.4%
Totals	$9.64	$6.53

(v) Sum of tentative ratable shares of Z attributable to X's 1969 calendar year:

For Z's taxable year ending	
June 30, 1969	$ 9.64
June 30, 1970	6.53
Sum	$16.17

(4) *Deficit in tentative ratable share of lower tier corporation attributable to a taxable year of first tier corporation.*—(i) If there is a deficit in the earnings and profits accumulated for a taxable year of a lower tier corporation beginning after December 31, 1962 (computed under paragraph (b) of this section), the person's tentative ratable share for such taxable year of such lower tier corporation attributable to a taxable year of a first tier corporation shall not be computed under subparagraph (2) of this paragraph but shall be an amount equal to the sum of the partial tentative ratable shares computed under subdivisions (ii) and (iii) of this subparagraph.

(ii) The partial tentative ratable share under this subdivision is computed in 2 steps. First, compute (under paragraph (b) of this section without regard to the adjustments for distributions under subparagraph (3) thereof) the deficit (if any) in earnings and profits accumulated for such taxable year of such lower tier corporation. Second, compute the partial tentative ratable share in the same manner as such tentative ratable share would be computed under subparagraph (2) of this paragraph if such deficit were the amount referred to in subparagraph (2)(i)*(a)* of this paragraph.

(iii) The partial tentative ratable share under this subdivision is computed in 2 steps. First, compute and treat as a deficit the portion of the adjustment for distributions under paragraph (b)(3) of this section for such taxable year which is attributable under paragraph (d)(4) of this section to distributions of earnings and profits accumulated during prior taxable years of the lower tier corporation beginning after December 31, 1962, during the period or periods such lower tier corporation was a controlled foreign corporation and the percentage of the stock of such lower tier corporation (which the person owns within the meaning of section 958(a)(2)) was owned within the meaning of section 958(a) by a United States shareholder (as defined in section 951(b) and the regulations thereunder). Second, compute the partial tentative ratable share in the same manner as such tentative ratable share would be computed under subparagraph (2) of this paragraph if *(a)* such deficit were the amount referred to in subparagraph (2)(i)*(a)* of this paragraph, and *(b)* such lower tier corporation were a controlled foreign corporation on each day of such taxable year.

(5) *Ratable share of lower tier corporation attributable to a first tier corporation.*—(i) If the provisions of this paragraph apply in respect of a share of stock in a first tier corporation, a person's ratable share of the earnings and profits accumulated by the lower tier corporation attributable to a taxable year of the first tier corporation shall be an amount equal to the tentative ratable share computed under subparagraph (2) or (4) of this paragraph, adjusted in the manner prescribed in this subparagraph.

(ii) If the first tier corporation and the lower tier corporation use the same taxable year, then in respect of a share (or block) of stock in the first tier corporation the person's tentative ratable share of the accumulated earnings and profits of the lower tier corporation attributable to the taxable year of the first tier corporation (computed under subparagraph (2) of this paragraph) shall be reduced (but not below zero) by the excess of *(a)* the amount, if any, included (in respect of such lower tier corporation for its taxable year) under section 951 in the gross income of such person or (during the period such stock was considered to be held by such person by reason of the application of section 1223, taking into account § 1.1248-8) in the gross income of any other person who held such stock, over *(b)* the portion of such amount which, in any taxable year of such person or such other person, resulted in an exclusion from the gross income of such person or such other person of an amount under section 959(a)(1). For an illustration of the principles in the preceding sentence, see the example in paragraph (e)(2)(ii) of this section.

(iii) If the first tier corporation and the lower tier corporation do not use the same taxable year, and if there would be an excess computed under subdivision (ii) of this subparagraph in respect of a taxable year of the lower tier corporation (were the taxable years of such corporations the same), then such person's tentative ratable share of the accumulated earnings and profits for a taxable year of the lower tier corporation attributable to such taxable year of the first tier corporation shall be reduced (but not below zero) by an amount which bears the same ratio to *(a)* such excess, as *(b)* the number of days in the taxable year of the lower tier corporation which fall within the taxable year of the first tier corporation, bears to *(c)* the total number of days in the taxable year of the first tier corporation.

(iv) If the first tier corporation and the lower tier corporation use the same taxable year, then in respect of a share (or block) of stock in the first tier corporation the person's tentative ratable share of the accumulated earnings and profits of the lower tier corporation attributable to the taxable year of the first tier corporation (computed under subparagraph (2) of this paragraph) shall be reduced (but not below zero) by the amount, if any, included (in respect of such corporation for such taxable year) under section 551, by reason of the application of section 555(b), in the gross income of such person or (during the period such share (or block) was considered to be held by such person by reason of the application of section 1223, taking into account § 1.1248-8) in the gross income of any other person who held such share (or block).

(v) If the first tier corporation and the lower tier corporation do not use the same taxable year, and if there would be a reduction in the person's tentative ratable share of the accumulated earnings and profits of the lower tier corporation attributable to the taxable year of the first tier corporation by an amount computed under subdivision (iv) of this subparagraph in respect of a taxable year of the lower tier corporation (were the taxable years of such corporations the same), then such person's tentative ratable share of the accumulated earnings and profits for a taxable year of the lower tier corporation attributable to such taxable year of the first tier corporation shall be reduced by an amount which bears the same ratio to *(a)* such amount, as *(b)* the number of days in the taxable year of the lower tier corporation which fall within the taxable year of the first tier corporation, bears to *(c)* the total number of days in the taxable year of the first tier corporation.

(vi) If the lower tier corporation was a less developed country corporation as defined in section 902(d) for a taxable year of the corporation, see paragraph (g) of this section.

(g) *Lower tier corporation a less developed country corporation.*—(1) *General.*—If the lower tier corporation was a less developed country corporation as defined in section 902(d) for a taxable year of such corporation, and if the person who sold or exchanged a share (or block) of stock in the first tier corporation satisfies on the date of such sale or exchange—

(i) The requirements of paragraph (a)(1) of § 1.1248-5 with respect to such stock, and

(ii) The requirements of paragraph (d)(1) of § 1.1248-5 with respect to any stock of the lower tier corporation which such person, by reason of his direct ownership of such stock in the first tier corporation, owned within the meaning of section 958(a)(2),

then such person's ratable share (or a deficit in such ratable share) for such taxable year of the lower tier corporation attributable to a taxable year of the first tier corporation (determined without regard to this paragraph) shall be reduced by an amount computed by multiplying such ratable share (so determined without regard to this paragraph) by the percentage computed under either subparagraph (2) or (4) of this paragraph, whichever is applicable.

(2) *Percentage for second tier corporation.*—For purposes of subparagraph (1) of this paragraph, if stock of a lower tier corporation (hereinafter referred to as a "second tier" corporation) is owned directly by the first tier corporation on the date of the sale or exchange referred to in such subparagraph (1), the percentage under this subparagraph shall be computed by dividing (i) the number of shares of stock of the second tier corporation which the first tier corporation has owned directly for an uninterrupted 10-year period ending on such date, by (ii) the total number of shares of the stock of such second tier corporation owned directly by such first tier corporation on such date.

(3) *Examples.*—The provisions of subparagraph (2) of this paragraph may be illustrated by the following examples:

Example (1). On January 1, 1966, Smith, a United States person, recognizes gain upon the sale of one share of the only class of stock of F Corporation, which he has owned continuously since 1955. He includes a portion of the gain in his gross income as a dividend under section 1248(a). On January 1, 1966, F owns directly 60 shares of the 100 outstanding shares of the only class of stock of G Corporation, which F acquired in 1955 and owned continuously until such sale. F uses a taxable year ending June 30, and G uses the calendar year as the taxable year. For 1964, G was a less developed country corporation, and on each day of 1964 G was a controlled foreign corporation. Smith's ratable share for G's taxable year ending December 31, 1964, attributable to F's taxable year ending June 30, 1965 (determined without regard to this paragraph) is $6.00. Since the percentage computed under subparagraph (2) of this paragraph is 100 percent (60 shares divided by 60 shares), Smith's ratable share for G's taxable year ending December 31, 1964, attributable to F's taxable year ending June 30, 1965 (after the application of subparagraph (2) of this paragraph) is zero (that is, $6.00 reduced by 100 percent of $6.00).

Example (2). Assume the same facts as in example (1) except that of the 60 shares of G Corporation which F Corporation owned on January 1, 1966, 20 shares were acquired in 1961. The percentage computed under subparagraph (2) of this paragraph is 66²/₃ percent (40 shares divided by 60 shares). Accordingly, Smith's ratable share for G's taxable year ending December 31, 1964, attributable to F's taxable year ending June 30, 1965 (after the application of subparagraph (2) of this paragraph) is $2.00 (that is, $6.00 reduced by 66²/₃ percent of $6.00).

(4) *Percentage for lower tier corporations other than second tier corporation.*—For purposes of subparagraph (1) of this paragraph, if stock of a lower tier corporation (other than a second tier corporation) is owned within the meaning of section 958(a)(2) by the first tier corporation on the date of the sale or exchange referred to in such subparagraph (1), the percentage under this subparagraph shall be computed in the following manner:

(i) First, determine the percentage for the second tier corporation in accordance with subparagraph (2) of this paragraph.

(ii) Second, determine a partial percentage for each other lower tier corporation in the same manner as the percentage for the second tier corporation is determined. Thus, for example, the partial percentage for a third tier corporation is determined by dividing *(a)* the number of shares of stock of the third tier corporation which the second tier corporation has owned directly for an uninterrupted 10-year period ending on the date of the sale or exchange referred to in subparagraph (1) of this paragraph, by *(b)* the total number of shares of stock of such third tier corporation owned directly by such second tier corporation on such date.

(iii) Third, the percentage for a third tier corporation is the percentage for the second tier corporation multiplied by the partial percentage for the third tier corporation. The percentage for a fourth tier corporation is the percentage for the third tier corporation (as determined in the preceding sentence) multiplied by the partial percentage for the fourth tier corporation. In a similar manner, the percentage for any other lower tier corporation may be determined.

(5) *Example.*—The application of subparagraph (4) of this paragraph may be illustrated by the following example:

Example. On January 1, 1967, Brown, a United States person recognizes gain upon the sale of one share of the only class of stock of W Corporation, which he has owned continuously since 1955. He includes a portion of the gain in his gross income as a dividend under section 1248(a). W is the first tier corporation of a chain of foreign corporations W, X, Y, and Z. W and Z each use the calendar year as the taxable year. For 1964, Z was a less developed country corporation and on each day of 1964 Z was a controlled foreign corporation. Additional facts are set forth in the table below:

(1) Corporation	(2) Shares directly owned by preceding tier — For uninterrupted 10-year period ending 1/1/67	(3) on 1/1/67	(4) Col. (2) divided by Col. (3) (percent)
X	40	60	66²/3
Y	30	40	75
Z	20	30	66²/3

For 1964, the percentage referred to in subparagraph (4) of this paragraph for Z is 33¹/3 percent (66²/3% × 75% × 66²/3%).

(6) *Special rule.*—For purposes of applying the provisions of this paragraph, a lower tier corporation may be treated as a second tier corporation with respect to any of its stock which is owned directly by a first tier corporation whereas such lower tier corporation may be treated as a lower tier corporation other than a second tier corporation with respect to other stock in such lower tier corporation which is owned (within the meaning of section 958(a)(2)) by such first tier corporation. Thus, for example, if corporations X, Y, and Z are foreign corporations, X is a first tier corporation owning directly 100 percent of the stock of Y and 40 percent of the stock of Z, and in addition Y owns directly 60 percent of the stock of Z, then the 40 percent of the Z stock (which X owns directly) is considered to be stock in a second tier corporation and the 60 percent of the Z stock (which Y owns directly and which X is considered to own within the meaning of section 958(a)(2)) is considered to be stock in a third tier corporation. [Reg. § 1.1248-3.]

☐ [*T.D. 6779, 12-21-64. Amended by T.D.* 7293, 11-27-73; *T.D.* 7545, 5-5-78; *T.D.* 9345, 7-27-2007 *and T.D.* 9614, 3-18-2013.]

§ 1.1248-4. Limitation on tax applicable to individuals.—(a) *General rule.*—(1) *Limitation on tax.*—Under section 1248(b), if during a taxable year an individual sells or exchanges stock in a foreign corporation, then in respect of the stock the increase in the individual's income tax liability for such taxable year which is attributable (under paragraph (b) of this section) to the amount included in his gross income as a dividend under section 1248(a) shall not be greater than an amount equal to the sum of—

(i) The excess, computed under paragraph (c) of this section in respect of the stock, of the United States taxes which would have been paid by the corporation over the taxes (including United States taxes) actually paid by the corporation, plus

(ii) An amount equal to the increase in the individual's income tax liability which would be attributable to the inclusion in his gross income for such taxable year, as long-term capital gain, of an amount equal to the excess of *(a)* the amount included in the individual's gross income as a dividend under section 1248(a) in respect of such stock, over *(b)* the excess referred to in subdivision (i) of this subparagraph.

(2) *Share or block.*—In general, the limitation on tax attributable (under paragraph (b) of this section) to the amount included in an individual's gross income as a dividend under section 1248(a) shall be determined separately for each share of stock sold or exchanged. However, such determination may be made in respect of a block of stock if earnings and profits attributable to the block are computed under § 1.1248-2 or 1.1248-3. See paragraph (b) of § 1.1248-2 and paragraph (a)(5) of § 1.1248-3.

(3) *Application of limitation.*—The provisions of subparagraph (1) of this paragraph shall not apply unless the individual establishes—

(i) In the manner prescribed in § 1.1248-7, the amount of the earnings and profits of the corporation attributable under paragraph (a)(1) of § 1.1248-2 or under paragraph (a)(1) of § 1.1248-3, whichever is applicable, to the stock, and

(ii) The amount equal to the sum described in subparagraph (1) of this paragraph, computed in accordance with the provisions of this section.

(4) *Example.*—The provisions of this paragraph may be illustrated by the following example:

Example. On December 31, 1966, Smith, a United States person, sells a share of stock of X Corporation which he has owned continuously since December 31, 1965, and includes $100 of the gain on the sale in his gross income as a dividend under section 1248(a). Both X and Smith use the calendar year as the taxable year. The increase in Smith's income tax liability for 1966 which is attributable (under paragraph (b) of this section) to the inclusion of the $100 in his gross income as a dividend is $70. X was a controlled foreign corporation on each day of 1966. The excess, computed under paragraph (c) of this section in respect of the share, of the United States taxes which X would have paid over the taxes (including United States taxes) actually paid by X is $49. Under section 1248(b), the limitation on the tax attributable to the $100 included by Smith in his gross income as a dividend under section 1248(a) is $61.75, computed as follows:

(i)	Excess, computed under paragraph (c) of this section, of United States taxes which X Corporation would have paid in 1966 over the taxes actually paid by X in 1966		$49.00
(ii)	The amount determined under subparagraph (1)(ii) of this paragraph:		
	The amount Smith included in his gross income as a dividend under section 1248(a)	$100.00	
	Less the excess referred to in subdivision (i) of this example	$49.00	
	Difference	$51.00	
	Increase in Smith's tax liability attributable to including $51 in his gross income as long-term capital gain (25 percent of $51)		$12.75
(iii)	Limitation on tax		$61.75

(b) *Tax attributable to amount treated as dividend.*—(1) *General.*—For purposes of paragraph (a)(1) of this section, in respect of a share (or block) of stock in a foreign corporation sold or exchanged by an individual during a taxable year, the tax attributable to the amount included in his gross income as a dividend under section 1248(a) shall be the amount which bears the same ratio to (i) the excess of *(a)* his income tax liability for the taxable year determined without regard to section 1248(b) over *(b)* such tax liability determined as if the portion of the total gain recognized during the taxable year which is treated as a dividend under section 1248(a) had not been recognized, as (ii) the amount included as a dividend under section 1248(a) in respect of the share (or block), bears to (iii) the total amount included as a dividend under section 1248(a) in the individual's gross income for such taxable year.

(2) *Examples.*—The application of this paragraph may be illustrated by the following examples:

Example (1). (i) During 1963, Brown, an unmarried United States person, sells a block of stock in a controlled foreign corporation. On the sale, he recognizes $22,000 gain, of which $18,000 is treated as a dividend under section 1248(a) and $4,000 as long-term capital gain. Brown computes his income tax liability for his taxable year ending December 31, 1963, under section 1201 (relating to alternative tax) in accordance with the additional facts assumed in the following table:

	Computation of income tax liability without regard to section 1248(b)	*Computation of income tax liability as if the gain treated as a dividend under section 1248(a) had not been recognized*
Income from salary	$300,000	$300,000
Long-term capital gain resulting from sale of stock, less deduction for capital gains under section 1202 ($4,000 less $2,000)	2,000	2,000
Amount treated as a dividend under section 1248(a)	$18,000	0
Adjusted gross income	$320,000	$302,000
Charitable contribution of $100,000 to church (limited under section 170(b) to 30 percent of adjusted gross income)	(96,000)	(90,600)
Other itemized deductions and personal exemption	(7,700)	(7,700)
Taxable income	$216,300	$203,700
Less 50 percent of $4,000	2,000	2,000
Amount subject to partial tax under section 1201(b)(1)	$214,300	$201,700
Partial tax	$169,833	$158,367
25 percent of $4,000	1,000	1,000
Tax liability	$170,833	$159,367

(ii) The tax attributable to the $18,000 treated as a dividend under section 1248(a) is $11,466 ($170,833 minus $159,367).

Example (2). Assume the same facts as in example (1) except that the $18,000 treated as a dividend under section 1248(a) is attributable to the sale of a block of stock in X Corporation and a block of stock in Y Corporation. Assume further that $10,000 of the gain on the block of X stock was treated as a dividend and that $8,000 of the gain on the block of Y stock was treated as a dividend. Thus, the tax attributable to the amount treated as a dividend in respect of the block of X stock is $6,370 ($10,000/$18,000 of $11,466) and the amount in respect of the block of Y stock is $5,096 ($8,000/$18,000 of $11,466). The result would be the same if both blocks of stock were blocks of stock in the same corporation.

(c) *Excess (of United States taxes which would have been paid over taxes actually paid) attributable to a share.*—(1) *General.*—For purposes of paragraph (a)(1)(i) of this section—

(i) The term "taxes" means income, war profits, or excess profits taxes, and

(ii) The excess (and the portion of such excess attributable to an individual's share or block of stock in a foreign corporation) of the United States taxes which would have been paid by the corporation over the taxes (including United States taxes) actually paid by the corporation, for the period or periods the stock was held (or was considered to be held by reason of the application of section 1223) by the individual in taxable years of the corporation beginning after December 31, 1962, while the corporation was a controlled foreign corporation, shall be computed in accordance with the steps set forth in subparagraphs (2), (3), and (4) of this paragraph.

(2) *Step 1.*—For each taxable year of the corporation beginning after December 31, 1962, in respect of the individual's share (or block) of such stock (i) the taxable income of the corporation shall be computed in the manner prescribed in paragraph (d) of this section, and (ii) the excess (and the portion of such excess attributable to the stock) of the United States taxes which would have been paid by the corporation on such taxable income over the taxes (including United States taxes) actually paid by the corporation shall be computed in the manner prescribed in paragraph (e) of this section.

(3) *Step 2.*—If during such taxable year the corporation is a first tier corporation to which paragraph (f) of this section applies, (i) the excess (and the portion of such excess attributable to the individual's share, or block, of stock in the first tier corporation) of the United States taxes which would have been paid by any lower tier corporation over the taxes (including United States taxes) actually paid by such lower tier corporation shall be computed under paragraph (f) of this section, and (ii) such portion shall be added to the portion of the excess attributable to the individual's share (or block) of such stock as determined in step 1 for such taxable year.

(4) *Step 3.*—The excess, in respect of the individual's share (or block), of the United States taxes which would have been paid by the corporation over the taxes actually paid by the corporation shall be the sum of the portions computed for each such taxable year in the manner prescribed in steps 1 and 2.

(d) *Taxable income.*—For purposes of paragraph (c)(2)(i) of this section, taxable income shall be computed in respect of an individual's share (or block) in accordance with the following rules:

(1) *Application of principles of § 1.952-2.*—Except as otherwise provided in this paragraph, the principles of paragraphs (a)(1), (b)(1), and (c) of § 1.952-2 (other than subparagraphs (2)(iii)*(b)*, (2)(v), (5)(i), and (6) of such paragraph (c)) shall apply.

(2) *Effect of elections.*—In respect of a taxable year of a foreign corporation, no effect shall be given to an election or an adoption of accounting method unless for such taxable year effect is given to such election or adoption of accounting method under paragraph (d)(1) of § 1.1248-2 or paragraph (b)(1) of § 1.1248-3, whichever is applicable.

(3) The deductions for certain dividends received provided in sections 243, 244, and 245 shall not be allowed.

(4) *Deduction for taxes.*—In computing the amount of the deduction allowed under section 164, there shall be excluded income, war profits, or excess profits taxes paid or accrued which are imposed by the authority of any foreign country or possession of the United States.

(5) *Capital loss carryover.*—In determining the amount of a net capital loss to be carried forward under section 1212 to the taxable year—

(i) No net capital loss shall be carried forward from a taxable year beginning before January 1, 1963.

(ii) The portion of a net capital loss or a capital gain net income (net capital gain for taxable years beginning before January 1, 1977) for a taxable year beginning after December 31, 1962, which shall be taken into account shall be the amount of such loss or gain (as the case may be), multiplied by the percentage which *(a)* the number of days in such taxable year during which the individual held (or was considered to have held by reason of the application of section 1223) the share (or block) of stock sold or exchanged while the corporation was a controlled foreign corporation, bears to *(b)* the total number of days in such taxable year.

(iii) The application of this subparagraph may be illustrated by the following examples:

Example (1). Corporation X is a foreign corporation which was created on January 1, 1963, and which uses the calendar year as its taxable year. X was a controlled foreign corporation on each day of the period March 15, 1963, through December 31, 1965, but was not a controlled foreign corporation on any day during the period January 1, 1963, through March 14, 1963. On December 31, 1965, Smith, a United States person, sells a share of X stock which he has owned continuously since January 1, 1963. A portion of the gain recognized on the sale is includible in Smith's gross income as a dividend under section 1248(a). X had a net capital loss (determined without regard to subchapter N, chapter 1 of the Code) of $200 for 1963. Since, however, X was a controlled foreign corporation for only 292 days in 1963, for purposes of determining the net capital loss carryover to 1964 the portion of the net capital loss of $200 for 1963 which Smith takes into account under subdivision (ii) of this subparagraph is $160

(292/365 of $200), and, accordingly, the amount of the net capital loss carryover to 1964 is $160.

Example (2). Assume the same facts as in example (1), except that X was not a controlled foreign corporation on any day of the period May 26, 1964, through June 30, 1965. Assume further that X had a net capital gain (capital gain net income for taxable years beginning after December 31, 1976) (determined without regard to subchapter N, chapter 1, of the Code) of $160 for 1964. In computing X's taxable income for 1964 under this paragraph, Smith applies the net capital loss carryover of $160 from 1963 to reduce the net capital gain (capital gain net income for taxable years beginning after December 31, 1976) of $160 for 1964 to zero. Since, however, X was a controlled foreign corporation for only 146 days in 1964, for purposes of computing the portion of the 1963 capital loss of $160 which is a net capital loss carryover to 1965, the portion of the 1964 capital gain which Smith takes into account under subdivision (ii) of this subparagraph is $63.83 (146/366 of $160). Thus, the net capital loss carryover to 1965 is $96.17 ($160 minus $63.83).

(6) *Net operating loss deduction.*—(i) The individual shall reduce the taxable income (computed under subparagraphs (1) through (5) of this paragraph) of the corporation for the taxable year by the amount of the net operating loss deduction of the corporation computed under section 172, as modified in the manner prescribed in this subparagraph.

(ii) The rules of subparagraphs (1) through (5) of this paragraph shall apply for purposes of determining the excess referred to in section 172(c) and the taxable income referred to in section 172(b)(2).

(iii) A net operating loss shall not be carried forward from, or carried back to, a taxable year beginning before January 1, 1963.

(iv) The portion of a net operating loss incurred, or of taxable income earned, in a taxable year beginning after December 31, 1962, which shall be taken into account under section 172(b)(2) shall be the amount of such loss or income (as the case may be), multiplied by the percentage which *(a)* the number of days in such taxable year during which the individual held (or was considered to have held by reason of the application of section 1223) the share (or block) of stock sold or exchanged while the corporation was a controlled foreign corporation, bears to *(b)* the total number of days in such taxable year.

(v) For illustrations of the principles of this subparagraph, see the examples relating to net capital loss carryovers in subparagraph (5)(iii) of this paragraph.

(7) *Adjustment for amount previously included in gross income of United States shareholders.*—In respect of the individual's share (or block) of stock sold or exchanged, the taxable income of the corporation for the taxable year (determined without regard to this subparagraph and subparagraph (8) of this paragraph) shall be reduced (but not below zero) by an amount equal to the sum of the amounts included under section 951 in the gross income of United States shareholders (as defined in section 951(b)) of the corporation for the taxable year.

(8) *Adjustment for distributions.*—In respect of the individual's share (or block) of stock sold or exchanged, the taxable income of the corporation for the taxable year (determined without regard to this subparagraph) shall be reduced (but not below zero) by the amount of the distributions (other than in redemption of stock under section 302(a) or 303) made by the corporation out of earnings and profits of such taxable year (within the meaning of section 316(a)(2)). For purposes of the preceding sentence, distributions shall be taken into account only to the extent not excluded from the gross income of the United States shareholders of the corporation under section 959.

(e) *Excess attributable to a share (or block) of stock.*—(1) *Excess of United States taxes which would have been paid over taxes actually paid.*—For purposes of paragraph (c)(2)(ii) of this section, in respect of a taxable year of a foreign corporation, the portion of the excess under this subparagraph which is attributable to an individual's share (or block) of such stock shall be an amount equal to—

(i) The excess (if any) of *(a)* the United States taxes which would have been paid by the corporation on its taxable income (computed under paragraph (d) of this section) for the taxable year had it been taxed as a domestic corporation under chapter 1 of the Code (but without regard to subchapters F, G, H, L, M, N, S, and T thereof) for such taxable year, over *(b)* the income, war profits, or excess profits taxes actually paid by the corporation during such taxable year (including such taxes paid to the United States),

(ii) Multiplied by the percentage that *(a)* the number of days in such taxable year of the corporation during the period or periods the share (or block) was held (or was considered as held by reason of the application of section 1223) by the individual while the corporation was a controlled foreign corporation, bears to *(b)* the total number of days in such taxable year,

(iii) If the computation is made in respect of a block, multiplied by the number of shares in the block, and

(iv) Divided by the number of shares in the corporation outstanding, or deemed under paragraph (c)(2) of § 1.1248-3 to be outstanding, on each day of such taxable year.

(2) *Example.*—The provisions of this paragraph may be illustrated by the following example:

Example. (i) Jones, a United States person, owns on each day of 1963 10 shares of the 100 shares of the only class of outstanding stock of X Corporation. He sells one of such shares on December 31, 1963. X Corporation is a controlled foreign corporation on each day of 1963 and Jones and X each use the calendar year as the taxable year. For 1963, the excess of the United States taxes which would have been paid by X had it been taxable as a domestic corporation over the taxes (including United States taxes) actually paid by X is $23,500, computed as follows:

Amount subject to partial tax under section 1201 (a)(1), as computed by Jones:		
Taxable income		$300,000
Less excess of net long-term capital gain over net short-term capital loss		100,000
Amount subject to partial tax		$200,000
Excess determined under subparagraph (1)(i) of this paragraph:		
30 percent × $25,000	$7,500	
52 percent × $175,000	91,000	
Partial tax		$98,500
25 percent × $100,000		25,000
United States taxes X would have paid (alternative tax computed under section 1201(a))		$123,500
Less income taxes X actually paid to: United States	$10,000	
foreign countries	90,000	
Total		$100,000
Excess		$23,500
Multiplied by:		
Percentage determined under subparagraph (1)(ii) of this paragraph:		
Since on each day of 1963, Jones held the share of X stock while X was a controlled foreign corporation, the percentage equals		100 %
Total		$23,500

(ii) The portion of the excess determined in subdivision (i) of this example which is attributable to the share held by Jones is $235, that is, the amount of such excess ($23,500), divided by the number of shares of X deemed to be outstanding on each day of 1963 (100).

(3) *More than one class of stock.*—If a foreign corporation for a taxable year has more than one class of stock outstanding, then before applying subparagraph (1) of this paragraph the excess (if any) which would be determined under subparagraph (1)(i) of this paragraph shall be allocated to each class of stock in accordance with the principles of paragraph (e)(2) and (3) and § 1.951-1, applied as if the corporation were a controlled foreign corporation on each day of such taxable year.

(f) *Subsidiaries of foreign corporations.*—(1) *Excess for lower tier corporation attributable to taxable year of first tier corporation.*—For purposes of paragraph (c)(3) of this section, if the provisions of paragraph (a)(3) of § 1.1248-2 or paragraph (f) of § 1.1248-3 apply in the case of the sale or exchange by an individual of a share (or block) of stock in a first tier corporation, then in respect of a taxable year of a lower tier corporation (beginning after December 31, 1962) which includes at least one day which falls within a taxable year of the first tier corporation (beginning after December 31, 1962), the portion of the excess under this subparagraph attributable to the share shall be an amount equal to—

(i) The excess (if any) of *(a)* the United States taxes which would have been paid by the lower tier corporation on its taxable income (computed under paragraph (g) of this section) for such taxable year of the lower tier corporation had it been taxed as a domestic corporation under chapter 1 of the Code (but without regard to subchapters F, G, H, L, M, N, and T thereof) for such taxable year of the lower tier corporation, over *(b)* the income, war profits, or excess profits taxes actually paid by the lower tier corporation during such taxable year (including such taxes paid to the United States),

(ii) Multiplied by each of the percentages described under paragraph (f)(2)(ii), (iii), and (iv) of § 1.1248-3 in respect of such taxable year of the first tier corporation,

(iii) If the computation is made in respect of a block of stock, multiplied by the number of shares in the block, and

(iv) Divided by the number of shares in the first tier corporation outstanding, or deemed under paragraph (c)(2) of § 1.1248-3 to be outstanding, on each day of such taxable year of the first tier corporation.

(2) *More than one class of stock.*—If a foreign corporation for a taxable year has more than one class of stock outstanding, then before applying subparagraph (1) of this paragraph the principles of paragraph (e)(3) of this section shall apply.

(g) *Taxable income of lower tier corporations.*—(1) *General.*—For purposes of paragraph (f)(1)(i) of this section, in respect of the individual's share (or block) the taxable income of a lower tier corporation shall be computed in the manner provided in paragraph (d) of this section, except as provided in this paragraph.

(2) *Capital loss carryover.*—For purposes of subparagraph (1) of this paragraph, the provisions of paragraph (d)(5)(ii) of this section shall not apply. In determining the amount of a net capital loss to be carried forward under section 1212 to the taxable year of a lower tier corporation, the portion of a net capital loss or a capital gain net income (net capital gain for taxable years beginning before January 1, 1977) for a taxable year of the lower tier corporation beginning after December 31, 1962, which shall be taken into account shall be the amount of such loss or gain (as the case may be), multiplied by the percentage which (i) the number of days in such taxable year during the period or periods the individual held (or was considered to have held by reason of the application of section 1223) the share (or block) of stock in the first tier corporation sold or exchanged while the first tier corporation owned (within the meaning of section 958(a)) stock in the lower tier corporation while the lower tier corporation was a controlled foreign corporation, bears to (ii) the total number of days in such taxable year.

(3) *Net operating loss deduction.*—For purposes of subparagraph (1) of this paragraph, the provisions of paragraph (d)(6)(iv) of this section shall not apply. In determining the amount of the net operating loss deduction for a taxable year of a lower tier corporation, the portion of a net operating loss incurred, or of taxable income earned, in a taxable year of the lower tier corporation beginning after December 31, 1962, which shall be taken into account under section 172(b)(2) shall be the amount of such loss or income (as the case may be) multiplied by the percentage described in subparagraph (2) of this paragraph for such taxable year. [Reg. § 1.1248-4.]

☐ [*T.D.* 6779, 12-21-64. *Amended by T.D.* 7545, 5-5-78 *and T.D.* 7728, 10-31-80.]

§ 1.1248-5. Stock ownership requirements for less developed country corporations.—(a) *General rule.*—(1) *Requirements.*—For purposes of paragraph (e)(4) of § 1.1248-3, a United States person shall be considered as satisfying the requirements of this paragraph with respect to a share (or block) of stock of a foreign corporation if on the date he sells or exchanges such share (or block)—

(i) The 10-year stock ownership requirement of paragraph (b) of this section is met with respect to such share (or block), and

(ii) In the case of a United States person which is a domestic corporation, the requirement of paragraph (c) of this section, if applicable, is met.

(2) *Ownership of stock.*—For purposes of this section—

(i) The rules for determining ownership of stock prescribed by section 958(a) and (b) shall apply.

(ii) Stock owned by a United States person who is an individual, estate, or trust which was acquired by reason of the death of the predecessor in interest of such United States person shall be considered as owned by such United States person during the period such stock was owned by such predecessor in interest, and during the period such stock was owned by any other predecessor in interest if between such United States person and such other predecessor in interest there was no transfer other than by reason of the death of an individual.

(b) *10-year stock ownership requirement.*—(1) *General.*—A United States person meets the 10-year stock ownership requirement with respect to a share (or block) of stock in a foreign corporation which he sells or exchanges only if the share (or block) was owned (under the rules of paragraph (a)(2) of this section) by such person for a continuous period of at least 10 years ending on the date of the sale or exchange. See the first sentence of section 1248(d)(3). Thus, for example, if Jones, a United States person, sells a share of stock in a foreign corporation on January 1, 1965, the 10-year stock ownership requirement is met with respect to the share only if the share was owned (under the rules of paragraph (a)(2) of this section) by Jones continuously from January 1, 1955, to January 1, 1965. If a foreign corporation has not been in existence for at least 10 years on the date of the sale or exchange of the share, the 10-year stock ownership requirement cannot be met.

(2) *Special rule.*—For purposes of this paragraph, a United States person shall be considered to have owned stock during the period he was considered to have held the stock by reason of the application of section 1223.

(c) *Disqualification of domestic corporation as a result of changes in ownership of its stock.*—(1) *General.*—(i) For purposes of paragraph (a)(1)(ii) of this section, the requirement of this paragraph must be met only if, on at least one day during the 10-year period ending on the date of the sale or exchange by a domestic corporation of a share of stock in a foreign corporation, one or more noncorporate United States shareholders (as defined in subdivision (iii) of this subparagraph) own more than 50 percent of the total combined voting power of all classes of stock entitled to vote of the domestic corporation.

(ii) The requirement of this paragraph is that if one or more persons are noncorporate United States shareholders on the first such day (referred to in subdivision (i) of this subparagraph), such person or persons continue after such first day, at all times during the remainder of such 10-year period, to own in the aggregate more than 50 percent of the total combined voting power of all classes of stock entitled to vote of the domestic corporation. For purposes of determining whether a domestic corporation meets the requirement of this paragraph, the stock owned by a United States person who is a noncorporate United States shareholder of a domestic corporation on such first day shall not be counted at any time after he ceases during such ten-year period to be a noncorporate United States shareholder of such corporation.

(iii) For purposes of this paragraph, the term "noncorporate United States shareholder" means, with respect to a domestic corporation, a United States person who is an individual, estate, or trust and who owns 10 percent or more of the total combined voting power of all classes of stock of such domestic corporation.

(iv) For purposes of this paragraph, the percentage of the total combined voting power of stock of a foreign corporation owned by a United States person shall be determined in accordance with the principles of section 951(b) and the regulations thereunder.

(2) *Examples.*—The application of this paragraph may be illustrated by the following examples:

Example (1). During the entire period beginning December 31, 1954, and ending December 31, 1964, domestic corporation N owns all the stock of controlled foreign corporation X, a less developed country corporation. On December 31, 1964, N recognizes gain upon the sale of all its X stock. A, B, and C, who are unrelated individuals, were the only United States persons owning, or considered as owning, 10 percent or more of the total combined voting power of all classes of stock entitled to vote of N at any time during the 10-year period December 31, 1954, through December 31, 1964. The percentages of the total combined voting power in N, which A, B, and C owned during such 10-year period, are as follows:

Owner	*Dec. 31, 1954- Apr. 1, 1957 Percent*	*Apr. 2, 1957-Oct. 1, 1959 Percent*	*Oct. 2, 1959-Dec. 31, 1964 Percent*
A	20	20	20
B	9	30	30
C	30	15	9

Domestic corporation N does not meet the requirement of this paragraph with respect to the stock of controlled foreign corporation X for the following reasons:

(i) April 2, 1957, is the first day (during the 10-year period ending on December 31, 1964, the date N sells the X stock) on which noncorporate United States shareholders of N own more than 50 percent of the total combined voting power in N, and thus the requirement of this paragraph must be met. See subparagraph (1)(i) of this paragraph. Although A, B, and C did own, in the aggregate, more than 50 percent of such voting power before April 2, 1957, the voting power owned by B is not counted because B was not a noncorporate United States shareholder of N before such date.

(ii) Although C is a noncorporate United States shareholder on April 2, 1957, C ceases to own 10 percent or more of the total combined voting power in N on October 2, 1959. Thus, after October 1, 1959, the N stock which C owns is not counted for purposes of determining whether the more-than-50-percent stock ownership test is met. See subparagraph (1)(ii) of this paragraph. Accordingly, after October 1, 1959, the requirement of this paragraph is not met.

Example (2). Assume the same facts as in example (1), except that B's wife owns directly 5 percent of the total combined voting power in N from December 31, 1954, to December 31, 1964. On the basis of the assumed facts, N meets the requirement of this paragraph with respect to the stock of controlled foreign corporation X for the following reasons:

(i) December 31, 1954, is the first day (of the 10-year period ending on the date N sells the X stock) on which noncorporate United States shareholders of N own more than 50 percent of the total combined voting power in N. B is a noncorporate United States shareholder on such date because he owns, and is considered as owning, 14 percent of the total combined voting power in N (9 percent directly, and, under section 958(b), 5 percent constructively). Thus, on December 31, 1954, noncorporate United States shareholders A, B, and C own, in the aggregate, more than 50 percent of the total combined voting power in N.

(ii) A, B, and C, the noncorporate United States shareholders of N on December 31, 1954, own, and are considered as owning, more than 50 percent of the total voting power of N from December 31, 1954, to October 1, 1959. Since beginning on October 2, 1959, A owns 20 percent and B owns, and is considered as owning, 35 percent of the total combined voting power in N, A and B own, and are considered as owning, more than 50 percent of the total combined voting power in N from October 2, 1959, to December 31, 1964. Therefore, the requirement of this paragraph is met.

(d) *Application of section to lower tier corporation.*—(1) *General.*—For purposes of paragraph (g)(1)(ii) of §1.1248-3, a United States person satisfies the requirements of this subparagraph in respect of stock of a lower tier corporation which such person, by reason of his direct ownership of the share (or block) of the first tier corporation sold or exchanged, owned within the meaning of section 958(a)(2) on the date he sold or exchanged such share (or block), if on such date—

(i) The 10-year stock ownership requirement of paragraph (b) of this section is met by such person with respect to any stock in the lower tier corporation which such person so owned, and

(ii) In the case of a United States person which is a domestic corporation, the requirement of paragraph (c) of this section, if applicable, is met.

(2) *Special rule.*—For purposes of this paragraph, in applying paragraphs (b) and (c) of this section, the sale or exchange of a share (or block) of stock in a first tier corporation by a United States person shall be deemed to be the sale or exchange of any stock in a lower tier corporation which the person, by reason of his direct ownership of such share (or block) of the first tier corporation, owned within the meaning of section 958(a)(2) on the date he actually sold or exchanged such share (or block) in the first tier corporation. [Reg. §1.1248-5.]

☐ [*T.D. 6779, 12-21-64.*]

§1.1248-6. Sale or exchange of stock in certain domestic corporations.—(a) *General rule.*—If a United States person recognizes gain upon the sale or exchange of a share (or block) of stock of a domestic corporation which was formed or availed of principally for the holding, directly or indirectly, of stock of one or more foreign corporations, and if the conditions of paragraph (a)(2) of §1.1248-1 would be met by such person in respect of the share (or block) if the domestic corporation were a foreign corporation, then section 1248 shall apply in respect of such gain in accordance with the rules provided in paragraph (b) of this section. See paragraph (d) of this section for a rule suspending the application of this section in certain circumstances.

(b) *Application.*—(1) The gain referred to in paragraph (a) of this section shall be included in the gross income of the United States person as a dividend under section 1248(a) to the extent of the earnings and profits attributable under §1.1248-2 or §1.1248-3, whichever is applicable, to the share (or block), computed, however, in accordance with the following rules:

(i) The domestic corporation shall be treated as if it were a first tier foreign corporation;

(ii) If, after the application of subdivision (i) of this subparagraph, the provisions of paragraph (a)(3) of §1.1248-2 or paragraph (f) of §1.1248-3 (as the case may be) would apply in respect of a foreign corporation the stock of which is owned (within the meaning of section 958(a)) by the domestic corporation treated as the first tier corporation, such foreign corporation shall be considered a lower tier corporation;

(iii) Except to the extent provided in subdivision (iv) of this subparagraph, the earnings and profits of the domestic corporation treated as the first tier corporation accumulated for a taxable year, as computed under paragraph (d) of §1.1248-2 or paragraph (b) of §1.1248-3 (as the case may be), shall be considered to be zero; and

(iv) If, during a taxable year, a domestic corporation treated as the first tier corporation realizes gain upon the sale or exchange of stock in a foreign corporation, and solely by reason of the application of section 337 (relating to certain liquidations) the gain was not recognized, then the earnings and profits of such domestic corporation accumulated for the taxable year as computed under paragraph (d) of §1.1248-2 or paragraph (b) of §1.1248-3 (as the case may be), shall be considered to be an amount equal to the portion of such gain realized during the taxable year which, if section 337 had not applied, would have been treated as a dividend under section 1248(a).

(2) If the person selling or exchanging the stock in the domestic corporation is an individual, the limitation on tax attributable to the amount included in his gross income as a dividend under subparagraph (1) of this paragraph shall be determined, in accordance with the principles of paragraph (f) of §1.1248-4, by treating the domestic corporation as a first tier corporation.

(3)(i) If the earnings and profits of the foreign corporation or corporations (or of the domestic corporation treated as a first tier corporation) to be taken into account under subparagraph (1) of this paragraph are not established in the manner provided in paragraph (a)(1) of §1.1248-7, all of the gain from the sale or exchange of the share (or block) of the domestic corporation shall be treated as a dividend.

(ii) To the extent that the person does not establish, in the manner provided in paragraph (c) of §1.1248-7, the foreign taxes paid by such foreign corporation or corporations to be taken into account for purposes of computing the limitation on tax attributable to a share, such foreign taxes shall not be taken into account for purposes of such computation.

(c) *Corporation formed or availed of principally for holding stock of foreign corporations.*—Whether or not a domestic corporation is formed or availed of principally for the holding, directly or indirectly, of stock of one or more foreign corporations shall be determined on the basis of all the facts and circumstances of each particular case.

(d) *Temporary suspension of section 1248(e).*—Section 1248(e) and the rules of this section do not apply to a sale, exchange, or other disposition of the stock of a domestic corporation during a period when capital gains are taxed at a rate that equals or exceeds the rate at which ordinary income is taxed.

(e) *Effective/applicability date.*—Paragraph (d) of this section applies to a sale, exchange, or other disposition of the stock of a domestic corporation on or after September 21, 1987. [Reg. § 1.1248-6.]

☐ [*T.D. 6779, 12-21-64. Amended by T.D. 9614, 3-18-2013.*]

§ 1.1248-7. Taxpayer to establish earnings and profits and foreign taxes.—(a) *In general.*—(1) *Earnings and profits.*—If a taxpayer sells or exchanges stock in a foreign corporation which was a controlled foreign corporation and the Commissioner determines that the taxpayer has not established the amount of the earnings and profits of the corporation attributable to the stock under § 1.1248-2 or § 1.1248-3, whichever is applicable, all the gain from such sale or exchange shall be treated as a dividend under section 1248(a). See section 1248(h). A taxpayer shall be considered to have established such amount if—

(i) He attaches to his income tax return, filed on or before the last day prescribed by law (including extensions thereof) for his taxable year in which he sold or exchanged the stock, the schedule prescribed by paragraph (b) of this section or, if such last day is before April 1, 1965, he files such schedule before such date with the district director with whom such return was filed, and

(ii) He establishes in the manner prescribed by paragraph (d) of this section the correctness of each amount shown on such schedule.

(2) Notwithstanding an omission of information from, or an error with respect to an amount shown on, the schedule referred to in subparagraph (1)(i) of this paragraph, a taxpayer shall be considered to have complied with such subparagraph (1)(i) if—

(i) He establishes that such omission or error was inadvertent, or due to reasonable cause and not due to willful neglect, and that he has substantially complied with the requirements of this section, and

(ii) The taxpayer corrects such omission or error at the time when he complies with paragraph (d) of this section.

(3) For the requirement to establish the amount of foreign taxes to be taken into account for purposes of section 1248(b), see paragraph (c) of this section.

(b) *Schedule attached to return.*—(1) The taxpayer shall attach to his income tax return for his taxable year in which he sold or exchanged the stock, a schedule showing his name, address, and identifying number. Except to the extent provided in paragraph (e) of this section, the schedule shall also show the amount of the earnings and profits attributable under paragraph (a) of § 1.1248-2 or paragraph (a) of § 1.1248-3 (as the case may be) to the stock, and, in order to support the computation of such amount, any additional information required by subparagraphs (2), (3), (4), and (5) of this paragraph.

(2) The schedule shall also show for the first tier corporation, and for each lower tier corporation as to which information is required under subparagraph (4) of this paragraph, (i) the name of the corporation, (ii) the country under whose laws the corporation is created or organized, and (iii) the last day of the taxable year which the corporation regularly uses in computing its income.

(3) If the amount of earnings and profits attributable to a block of stock sold or exchanged are computed under § 1.1248-2, the schedule shall also show—

(i) For each taxable year of the corporation, beginning after December 31, 1962, during the period the taxpayer held (or was considered to have held by reason of the application of section 1223, taking into account § 1.1248-8) the block, (*a*) the earnings and profits accumulated for each such taxable year computed under paragraph (d) of § 1.1248-2, and (*b*) the sum thereof computed under paragraph (e)(1)(i) and (2) of § 1.1248-2,

(ii) The number of shares in the block and the total number of shares of the corporation outstanding during such period,

(iii) If during the period the person held (or is considered to have held by reason of the application of section 1223, taking into account § 1.1248-8) the block any amount was included under section 951 in the gross income of such person (or another person) in respect of the block, the computation of the excess referred to in paragraph (e)(3)(ii) of § 1.1248-2, and

(iv) If the amount of earnings and profits of a lower tier corporation attributable to the block are computed under paragraph (a)(3) of § 1.1248-2, (*a*) the number of shares in the lower tier corporation which the taxpayer owns within the meaning of section 958(a)(2), (*b*) the total number of shares of such lower tier corporation outstanding during such period, and (*c*) in respect of such lower tier corporation, the information prescribed in subdivisions (i) and (iii) of this subparagraph.

(4) If the amount of earnings and profits attributable to a share (or block) sold or exchanged are computed under § 1.1248-3, the schedule shall also show for each taxable year of the corporation beginning after December 31, 1962, any day of which falls in a period or periods the taxpayer held (or was considered to have held by reason of the application of section 1223, taking into account § 1.1248-8) the stock while the corporation was a controlled foreign corporation—

(i) The number of days in such period or periods, but only if such number is less than the total number of days in such taxable year,

(ii) The earnings and profits accumulated for the taxable year computed under paragraph (b) of § 1.1248-3,

(iii) The number of shares in the corporation outstanding, or deemed under paragraph (c)(2) of § 1.1248-3 to be outstanding, on each day of the taxable year,

(iv) The taxpayer's tentative ratable share computed under paragraph (c) or (d) (as the case may be) of § 1.1248-3,

(v) The amount of, and a short description of each adjustment to, the tentative ratable share under paragraph (e) of § 1.1248-3, and

(vi) The amount of the ratable share referred to in paragraph (e)(1) of § 1.1248-3.

(5) In respect of a taxable year referred to in subparagraph (4) of this paragraph of a first tier corporation, if the taxpayer is required to compute under paragraph (f)(5) of § 1.1248-3 his ratable share of the earnings and profits for a taxable year of the lower tier corporation attributable to such taxable year of such first tier corporation, then for such taxable year of the lower tier corporation the schedule shall show—

(i) The earnings and profits accumulated for the taxable year of the lower tier corporation, computed under paragraph (b) of § 1.1248-3,

(ii) Each percentage described in paragraph (f)(2)(ii), (iii), and (iv) of § 1.1248-3,

(iii) The amount of the taxpayer's tentative ratable share computed under paragraph (f)(2) or (4) (as the case may be) of § 1.1248-3,

(iv) The amount of, and a short description of each adjustment to, the tentative ratable share under paragraph (f)(5) of § 1.1248-3, and

(v) The amount of the ratable share referred to in paragraph (f)(5)(i) of § 1.1248-3.

(c) *Foreign taxes.*—(1) If the taxpayer fails to establish any portion of the amount of any foreign taxes which he is required to establish by subparagraph (2) of this paragraph, then such portion shall not be taken into account under section 1248(b)(1)(B).

(2) The taxpayer shall establish in respect of the stock he sells or exchanges the amount of the foreign taxes described in section 1248(b)(1)(B) paid by the first tier corporation for each taxable year of such corporation for which the information is required under paragraph (b)(3) or (4) of this section, and the amount of such taxes paid by each lower tier corporation for each taxable year (as to which information is required under paragraph (b)(3)(iv) or (5) of this section) of each such lower tier corporation. A taxpayer shall be considered to have established the amount of such foreign taxes if—

(i) He attaches to the schedule described in paragraph (b) of this section a supplementary schedule which, except to the extent provided in paragraph (e) of this section, sets forth the amount of such foreign taxes for each taxable year (of the first tier corporation and of each such lower tier corporation) as to which such amount must be established under this subparagraph, and

(ii) He establishes in the manner prescribed by paragraph (d)(2) of this section the correctness of each amount shown on such supplementary schedule.

(d) *Establishing amounts on schedules.*—(1) A taxpayer shall be considered to have established, in respect of the stock he sold or exchanged, the correctness of an amount shown on a schedule described in paragraph (b) of this section only if he produces or provides within 180 days after demand by the district director (or within such longer period to which such director consents)—

(i) The books of original entry, or similar systematic accounting records maintained by any person or persons on a current basis as supplements to such books, which establish to the satisfaction of the district director the correctness of each such amount, and

(ii) In respect of any such books or records which are not in the English language, either an accurate English translation of any such records as are demanded, or the services of a qualified interpreter satisfactory to such director.

(2) A shareholder shall be considered to have established in respect of such stock the correctness of an amount shown on a supplementary schedule described in paragraph (c) of this section

only if he produces or provides within 180 days after demand by the district director (or within such longer period to which such director consents)—

(i) Evidence described in paragraph (a)(2) of § 1.905-2 of such amount, or

(ii) Secondary evidence of such amount, in the same manner and to the same extent as would be permissible under paragraph (b) of § 1.905-2 in the case of a taxpayer who claimed the benefits of the foreign tax credit in respect of such amount.

(e) *Insufficient information at time return is filed.*—If stock in a foreign corporation, which was a controlled foreign corporation, is sold or exchanged by a taxpayer during a taxable year of the corporation (or of a lower tier corporation) which ends after the last day of the taxpayer's taxable year in which the sale or exchange occurs, and if—

(1) For the taxpayer's taxable year, the last day referred to in paragraph (a)(1) of this section for filing his income tax return with a schedule prescribed in paragraph (b) of this section, and, if applicable, with a supplemental schedule prescribed in paragraph (c) of this section, or

(2) The last day referred to in paragraph (a)(1) of this section (that is, April 1, 1965) for filing any such schedule or schedules with the district director with whom such return was filed,

is not later than 90 days after the close of such taxable year of any such corporation, then such return with such schedule or schedules may be filed, or any such schedule or schedules may be filed, on the basis of estimates of amounts or percentages (for any such taxable year of any such corporation) required to be shown on any such schedule or schedules. If any such estimate differs from the actual amount or percentage, the taxpayer shall, within 90 days after the close of any such taxable year of any such corporation, file (or attach to a claim for refund or amended return filed) at the office of the district director with whom he filed the return a new schedule or schedules showing the actual amounts or percentages. [Reg. § 1.1248-7.]

☐ [*T.D. 6779, 12-21-64. Amended by T.D. 9345, 7-27-2007 and T.D. 9614, 3-18-2013.*]

§ 1.1248-8. Earnings and profits attributable to stock following certain non-recognition transactions.—(a) *Scope.*—This section sets forth rules for the attribution of earnings and profits for purposes of section 1248 and § 1.1248-1(a)(1) and to supplement the rules in §§ 1.1248-2 and 1.1248-3 with respect to—

(1) *Stock that an exchanging shareholder receives, or an acquiring corporation receives, in restructuring transactions.*—Except as otherwise provided in this paragraph (a), stock of a foreign corporation that an exchanging shareholder receives, or an acquiring corporation receives, pursuant to a restructuring transaction (as defined in paragraph (b)(1)(vii) of this section) in which the holding period of such stock is determined by application of section 1223(1) or 1223(2), whichever is appropriate. This section shall not apply to an exchange otherwise described in this paragraph (a)(1) if, as a result of the exchange, the exchanging shareholder is required to include in income as a deemed dividend the section 1248 amount pursuant to § 1.367(b)-4(b). See paragraphs (b)(2) and (3) of this section;

(2) *Nonexchanging shareholders.*—Stock of a foreign corporation that participates in a restructuring transaction that is held by a nonexchanging shareholder (as defined in paragraph (b)(1)(vi) of this section) in the restructuring transaction. See paragraph (b)(4) of this section;

(3) *Section 381 transactions..*—Stock of a foreign corporation that receives assets in a transfer to which section 361(a) or (b) applies in connection with a reorganization described in section 368(a)(1)(A), (C), (D), (F), or (G), or in a distribution to which section 332 applies, and to which section 381(c)(2)(A) and § 1.381(c)(2)-1(a) apply. See paragraph (b)(6) of this section; or

(4) *Section 332 liquidations.*—Stock of a foreign corporation that receives the assets and liabilities of a foreign corporation in a complete liquidation described in section 332 if the foreign distributee is a foreign corporate shareholder (as defined in paragraph (b)(1)(v) of this section) of the liquidating corporation. See paragraph (c) of this section.

(b) *Earnings and profits attributable to stock following a restructuring transaction.*—(1) *Definitions.*—The following definitions apply for purposes of this section:

(i) *Acquired corporation* is a corporation whose stock or assets are acquired in exchange for stock in (or stock in and other property of) either the acquiring corporation or a foreign corporation that controls, within the meaning of section 368(c), the acquiring corporation in a restructuring transaction.

(ii) *Acquiring corporation* is a corporation that acquires the stock or assets of an acquired corporation in a restructuring transaction.

(iii) *Controlled foreign corporation* is a corporation described in either section 953(c)(1)(B) or section 957.

(iv) *Exchanging shareholder* is a person that exchanges—

(A) In a restructuring transaction qualifying as a nonrecognition transaction within the meaning of section 7701(a)(45) and described in section 354, 356, or 361(a) or (b), stock in an acquired corporation for stock in either a foreign acquiring corporation or a foreign corporation that is in control, within the meaning of section 368(c), of an acquiring corporation (whether domestic or foreign); or

(B) In a restructuring transaction qualifying as a nonrecognition transaction within the meaning of section 7701(a)(45) and described in section 351, property (including stock) for stock in a foreign acquiring corporation.

(v) *Foreign corporate shareholder* is a foreign corporation that—

(A) Owns stock of another foreign corporation; and

(B) Has a section 1248 shareholder that is also a section 1248 shareholder of the other foreign corporation.

(vi) *Non-exchanging shareholder* is, at the time the acquiring corporation participates in a restructuring transaction, either a section 1248 shareholder or a foreign corporate shareholder of the acquiring corporation that is not an exchanging shareholder with respect to that corporation.

(vii) *Restructuring transaction* is a transaction qualifying as a nonrecognition transaction within the meaning of section 7701(a)(45) and described in section 351, 354, 356, or 361.

(viii) *Section 1248 shareholder* is any United States person that satisfies the ownership requirements of section 1248(a)(2) and § 1.1248-1(a)(2) with respect to a foreign corporation.

(2) *Earnings and profits attributable to stock that an exchanging shareholder receives in a restructuring transaction.*—Where, in a restructuring transaction, an exchanging shareholder receives stock in a foreign corporation, the holding period of which is determined under section 1223(1), and the exchanging shareholder is either a section 1248 shareholder or a foreign corporate shareholder with respect to that foreign corporation immediately after the restructuring transaction, the earnings and profits attributable to the stock the exchanging shareholder receives shall be determined pursuant to the rules in paragraphs (b)(2)(i), (ii), and (iii) of this section.

(i) *Exchanging shareholder exchanges property that is not stock of a foreign acquired corporation with respect to which the exchanging shareholder is a section 1248 shareholder or a foreign corporate shareholder.*—Except as provided in paragraph (b)(2)(iv) of this section, where the exchanging shareholder exchanges in a restructuring transaction property that is not stock of a foreign acquired corporation with respect to which the exchanging shareholder is a section 1248 shareholder or a foreign corporate shareholder immediately before the transaction, the earnings and profits attributable to the stock that the exchanging shareholder receives in the restructuring transaction will be determined in accordance with § 1.1248-2 or § 1.1248-3, whichever is applicable, without regard to any portion of the section 1223(1) holding period in that stock that is before the restructuring transaction. See paragraph (b)(7), *Example 1* of this section.

(ii) *Exchanging shareholder exchanges stock of a foreign corporation with respect to which the exchanging shareholder is either a section 1248 shareholder or a foreign corporate shareholder.*—Except as provided in paragraph (b)(2)(iii) of this section, where the exchanging shareholder exchanges in a restructuring transaction stock of a foreign acquired corporation with respect to which the exchanging shareholder is either a section 1248 shareholder or a foreign corporate shareholder immediately before such restructuring transaction, the earnings and profits attributable to the stock that the exchanging shareholder receives in the restructuring transaction shall be the sum of the earnings and profits attributable to—

(A) The stock of the foreign acquired corporation exchanged (determined in accordance with § 1.1248-2 or § 1.1248-3, whichever is applicable, and this section, if applicable) that was accumulated before the restructuring transaction; and

(B) The stock of the foreign corporation that the exchanging shareholder receives in the restructuring transaction (determined in accordance with §1.1248-2 or §1.1248-3, whichever is applicable, and this section, if applicable), without regard to any portion of the section 1223(1) holding period in that stock that is prior to the restructuring transaction. See paragraph (b)(7) *Example 2*, *Example 4*, and *Example 6* of this section.

(iii) *Exchanging shareholder receives stock in a foreign corporation that controls a domestic acquiring corporation.*—Where the acquiring corporation is a domestic corporation and the exchanging shareholder receives in a restructuring transaction stock in a foreign corporation that controls (within the meaning of section 368(c)) the domestic acquiring corporation, the earnings and profits attributable to the stock that the exchanging shareholder receives in the restructuring transaction shall consist solely of the amount of earnings and profits attributable to such stock (determined in accordance with §1.1248-2 or §1.1248-3, whichever is applicable, and this section, if applicable) without regard to any portion of the section 1223(1) holding period in that stock that is prior to the restructuring transaction. See paragraph (b)(7) *Example 5* of this section.

(iv) *Exchanging shareholder exchanges stock of a domestic acquired corporation for stock of a foreign corporation with respect to which the exchanging shareholder is a section 1248 shareholder after the exchange.*—If there is a restructuring transaction described in §1.1248(f)-1(b)(3) to which the exception provided by §1.1248(f)-2(c) applies with respect to a distribution by a domestic acquired corporation of stock of a foreign corporation to one or more exchanging shareholders, the earnings and profits attributable to a portion of a share of stock as provided under §1.1248(f)-2(c)(2) (or a whole share, if no division is required) will be determined pursuant to paragraphs (b)(2)(iv)(A) and (b)(2)(iv)(B) of this section.

(A) The earnings and profits attributable to a portion of a share of stock as provided under §1.1248(f)-2(c)(2)(i) (or a whole share, if no division is required) will be determined in accordance with §1.1248-2 or §1.1248-3 (and this section, as applicable), without regard to any portion of the section 1223(1) holding period in that portion of a share (or whole share) that is before the restructuring transaction.

(B) The earnings and profits attributable to a portion of a share of stock as provided under §1.1248(f)-2(c)(2)(ii) (or whole share, if no division is required) is the amount in paragraph (b)(2)(iv)(B)(*1*) of this section, increased by the amounts described in paragraph (b)(2)(iv)(B)(*2*) of this section.

(*1*) The amount equal to the product of the ratio of the value of the share of stock to the value of all shares of stock received by the exchanging shareholder multiplied by the amount in paragraph (b)(2)(iv)(B)(*1*)(*i*) of this section, reduced by the amount in paragraph (b)(2)(iv)(B)(*1*)(*ii*) of this section.

(*i*) The amount equal to the product of the exchanging shareholder's ownership interest percentage (within the meaning of §1.367(a)-7(f)(7)) in the domestic acquired corporation multiplied by the earnings and profits attributable to the block of stock of the foreign corporation transferred in the section 361 exchange that relates to the portion (or whole share), determined in accordance with §1.1248-2 or §1.1248-3 (and this section, as applicable) immediately before the restructuring transaction (and without taking into account the application of sections 367 and 1248 to the transfer of the stock of the foreign corporation in the section 361 exchange).

(*ii*) The amount of any dividend included in the domestic acquiring corporation's gross income under section 1248(a) on the transfer of the block of stock of the foreign corporation, which relates to the portion or whole share, in the section 361 exchange by reason of gain recognized under §§1.367(a)-6 or 1.367(a)-7(c)(2) attributable to the exchanging shareholder.

(*2*) The earnings and profits determined in accordance with §1.1248-2 or §1.1248-3 (and this section, as applicable), without regard to any portion of the section 1223(1) holding period in that stock that is before the restructuring transaction. See §1.1248(f)-2(e), *Example 2* and *Example 3*.

(3) *Earnings and profits attributable to stock in a foreign corporation certain acquiring corporations receive in a restructuring transaction.*—Where an acquiring corporation receives, in a restructuring transaction, stock in a foreign acquired corporation, the holding period of which is determined under section 1223(2), and the acquiring corporation is either a section 1248 shareholder or a foreign corporate shareholder with respect to that foreign acquired corporation immediately after the restructuring transaction, the earnings and profits attributable to the foreign acquired corporation stock that the acquiring corporation receives shall be determined pursuant to the rules in paragraphs (b)(3)(i) and (ii) of this section.

(i) *Stock of a foreign corporation with respect to which the exchanging shareholder is neither a section 1248 shareholder nor a foreign corporate shareholder.*—The earnings and profits attributable to the stock of the foreign acquired corporation that the acquiring corporation receives in a restructuring transaction where the exchanging shareholder is neither a section 1248 shareholder nor a foreign corporate shareholder with respect to that foreign acquired corporation immediately before the restructuring transaction shall be determined in accordance with §1.1248-2 or §1.1248-3, whichever is applicable, without regard to any portion of the section 1223(2) holding period in that stock that is prior to the restructuring transaction.

(ii) *Stock of a foreign corporation with respect to which the exchanging shareholder is either a section 1248 shareholder or a foreign corporate shareholder.*—The earnings and profits attributable to the stock of a foreign acquired corporation that the acquiring corporation receives in the restructuring transaction where the exchanging shareholder is either a section 1248 shareholder or a foreign corporate shareholder with respect to that foreign corporation immediately before the restructuring transaction shall be determined in accordance with §1.1248-2 or §1.1248-3, whichever is applicable, with regard to the portion of the section 1223(2) holding period of the stock that the exchanging shareholder took into account for purposes of attributing earnings and profits to that stock (determined in accordance with this section). See paragraph (b)(7) *Example 3*, *Example 5*, and *Example 7* of this section.

(4) *Earnings and profits attributable to stock held by a non-exchanging shareholder in a foreign acquiring corporation.*—(i) Except to the extent paragraph (b)(4)(ii) of this section applies, the earnings and profits attributable to stock of a foreign acquiring corporation held by a non-exchanging shareholder immediately prior to a restructuring transaction continue to be attributed to such stock, and the earnings and profits of the acquired corporation accumulated prior to the restructuring transaction attributable to the stock of an acquired corporation are not attributed to the non-exchanging shareholder's stock in the foreign acquiring corporation. See §1.1248-2 or §1.1248-3 (whichever is applicable) and, as applicable, paragraph (b)(6) of this section; see also paragraph (b)(7) *Example 2* and *Example 4* of this section.

(ii) Where a non-exchanging shareholder holds stock in a foreign corporation that is also an exchanging shareholder and a foreign acquiring corporation in the same restructuring transaction—

(A) The earnings and profits attributable to such stock shall be the sum of the earnings and profits attributable to the stock of such foreign corporation immediately before the restructuring transaction (including amounts attributed under section 1248(c)(2)) and the earnings and profits attributable to the stock of the foreign acquiring corporation accumulated after the restructuring transaction (including amounts attributed under section 1248(c)(2)); and

(B) Paragraph (b)(6) of this section applies. See paragraph (b)(7) *Example 8* of this section.

(iii) Where the acquiring corporation is a foreign corporate shareholder with respect to stock of a foreign acquired corporation, paragraph (b)(3) of this section shall not apply for purposes of determining the earnings and profits attributable to stock in the foreign acquiring corporation owned by a non-exchanging shareholder thereof (see section 1248(c)(2)). See paragraph (b)(7) *Example 6* of this section.

(5) *Reduction in earnings and profits attributable to stock to prevent multiple inclusions with respect to the same earnings and profits.*—To the extent consistent with the principles of section 1248, adjustments to earnings and profits attributable to stock shall be made such that section 1223(1) and (2) and this section are applied in a manner that results in earnings and profits being taken into account only once. Thus, for example, when a controlled foreign corporation sells or exchanges all or part of the stock of another foreign corporation to which earnings and profits are attributable pursuant to this paragraph (b) or paragraph (c) of this section, proportionate reductions shall be made to the earnings and profits attributed to the stock of the selling foreign corporate shareholder owned by a section 1248 shareholder. See paragraph (b)(7) *Example 7* of this section.

(6) *Special rule regarding section 381.*—Solely for purposes of determining the earnings and profits (or deficit in earnings and profits) attributable to stock pursuant to this paragraph (b), the earnings and profits of a corporation shall not include earnings and profits that are treated as received or incurred under section 381(c)(2)(A) and §1.381(c)(2)-1(a). See paragraph (b)(7) *Example 4* of this section.

(7) *Examples.*—The application of this paragraph (b) is illustrated by the following examples. Unless otherwise indicated, in the following examples assume that—

(i) There is no immediate gain recognition pursuant to section 367(a)(1) and the regulations under that section (either through operation of the rules or because the appropriate parties have entered into a gain recognition agreement under § § 1.367(a)-3(b) and 1.367(a)-8);

(ii) There is no income inclusion required pursuant to section 367(b) and the regulations under that section, and all reporting requirements in those regulations are complied with;

(iii) References to earnings and profits are to earnings and profits that would be includible in income as a dividend under section 1248 and the regulations under that section if stock to which the earnings and profits are attributable were sold or exchanged by its shareholder;

(iv) Each corporation has only a single class of stock outstanding and uses the calendar year as its taxable year; and

(v) Each transaction is unrelated to all other transactions.

Example 1. A section 351 exchange of property other than stock in a foreign corporation with respect to which the exchanging shareholder is either a section 1248 shareholder or a foreign corporate shareholder. (i) *Facts.* DC1, a domestic corporation, has owned all the stock of CFC, a foreign corporation, since CFC's formation on January 1, year 3. On December 31, year 5, DC2, a domestic corporation unrelated to DC1, contributes property it has held since January 1, year 1, to CFC in exchange for voting stock of CFC in a restructuring transaction that is an exchange under section 351. The property that DC2 contributes is not stock in a foreign corporation with respect to which DC2 was either a section 1248 shareholder or a foreign corporate shareholder. DC2 receives 80% of the voting stock of CFC in the restructuring transaction and its holding period in that CFC stock, determined pursuant to section 1223(1), began on January 1, year 1. CFC has $100 of accumulated earnings and profits on December 31, year 5. On December 31, year 7, when the accumulated earnings and profits of CFC are $200, DC2, a section 1248 shareholder with respect to CFC, sells its CFC stock.

(ii) *Result.* Under paragraph (b)(2)(i) of this section, the earnings and profits attributable to the CFC stock sold by DC2 are $80. This amount consists of none of the $100 of earnings and profits accumulated by CFC before the restructuring transaction, and 80% of the $100 of earnings and profits of CFC accumulated after the restructuring transaction.

Example 2. A section 351 exchange of controlled foreign corporation stock by a United States person for stock in a controlled foreign corporation in a restructuring transaction. (i) *Facts.* The facts are the same as in *Example 1* except as follows. The property that DC2 contributes is 100% of the stock in CFC2, a foreign corporation. DC2 has owned all the stock of CFC2 since CFC2's formation on January 1, year 2, and CFC2 has $200 of earnings and profits as of December 31, year 5. CFC2 does not accumulate any additional earnings and profits from December 31, year 5, to December 31, year 7. On December 31, year 7, when the accumulated earnings and profits of CFC are $200, DC2, a section 1248 shareholder with respect to CFC, sells its CFC stock. Also on that date, DC1 sells its CFC stock.

(ii) *Result.* (A) *DC2 sale.* Pursuant to paragraph (b)(2)(ii) of this section, the earnings and profits attributable to the CFC stock sold by DC2 are $280. This amount consists of all of the $200 of earnings and profits of CFC2 accumulated before the restructuring transaction (see also section 1248(c)(2)), none of the $100 of earnings and profits accumulated by CFC before the restructuring transaction, and 80% of the $100 of earnings and profits of CFC accumulated after the restructuring transaction.

(B) *DC1 sale.* Pursuant to paragraph (b)(4) of this section, the earnings and profits attributable to the CFC stock sold by DC1, a non-exchanging shareholder in the restructuring transaction, are $120. This amount consists of all of the $100 of earnings and profits of CFC accumulated before the restructuring transaction, none of the $200 of earnings and profits of CFC2 accumulated before the restructuring transaction, and 20% of the $100 of earnings and profits of CFC accumulated after the restructuring transaction.

Example 3. A section 351 exchange of controlled foreign corporation stock by a United States person for stock in a domestic corporation in a restructuring transaction. (i) *Facts.* DC1, a domestic corporation, has owned all of the stock of CFC, a foreign corporation, since CFC's formation on January 1, year 1. DC1 has also owned all the stock of DC2, a domestic corporation, since DC2's formation on January 1, year 1. On December 31, year 2, DC1 contributes the stock of CFC to DC2 in exchange for stock in DC2 in a restructuring transaction that is an exchange described in section 351. On December 31, year 2, CFC has $100 of accumulated earnings and profits. DC2 has a basis in the CFC stock determined under section 362, and is considered to have held the CFC stock since January 1, year 1, pursuant to section 1223(2). On December 31, year 4, when the accumulated earnings and profits of CFC are still $100, DC2 sells its CFC stock.

(ii) *Result.* Under paragraph (b)(3)(ii) of this section, $100 of accumulated earnings and profits of CFC is attributable to the stock of CFC sold by DC2, even though DC2 did not hold the stock of CFC during the time CFC accumulated the earnings and profits.

Example 4. Acquisition of a controlled foreign corporation by a controlled foreign corporation in a reorganization described in section 368(a)(1)(C) (or section 368(a)(1)(B)). (i) *Facts.* DC1, a domestic corporation, has owned all the stock of CFC1, a foreign corporation, since its formation on January 1, year 1. DC2, a domestic corporation unrelated to DC1, has owned all of the stock of CFC2, a foreign corporation, since its formation on January 1, year 2. On December 31, year 3, pursuant to a restructuring transaction that is a reorganization described in section 368(a)(1)(C), CFC1 transfers all of its assets to CFC2 in exchange for 25% of the voting stock of CFC2. CFC1 distributes the CFC2 stock to DC1 and the CFC1 stock is cancelled. DC1's holding period in the CFC2 stock, determined under section 1223(1), begins on January 1, year 1. On December 31, year 3, CFC1 has $100 of accumulated earnings and profits and CFC2 has $200 of accumulated earnings and profits. CFC2 succeeds to the $100 of CFC1 accumulated earnings and profits in the reorganization under section 381. From January 1, year 4 to December 31, year 5, CFC2 incurred a deficit in earnings and profits in the amount of ($200). On December 31, year 5, both DC1 and DC2 sell their stock in CFC2.

(ii) *Result.* (A) *DC1.* Pursuant to paragraph (b)(2)(ii) of this section, $50 of earnings and profits is attributable to the CFC2 stock sold by DC1. This amount consists of $100 of CFC1's earnings and profits accumulated before the restructuring transaction, reduced by 25% of CFC2's ($200) post-restructuring transaction deficit in earnings and profits. None of the $200 of CFC2's earnings and profits accumulated by CFC2 prior to the reorganization is attributed to the CFC2 stock sold by DC1. Also, none of the earnings and profits CFC2 succeeded to under section 381 is attributed to the CFC2 stock sold by DC1, pursuant to paragraph (b)(6) of this section.

(B) *DC2.* Pursuant to paragraph (b)(4) of this section, there is $50 of accumulated earnings and profits attributable to the CFC2 stock sold by DC2. This amount consists of all of the $200 of CFC2's earnings and profits accumulated by CFC2 prior to the reorganization, reduced by 75% of CFC2's deficit in earnings and profits in the amount of ($200) incurred after the restructuring transaction. None of the $100 of CFC1 accumulated earnings and profits succeeded to under section 381 is attributable to the CFC2 stock sold by DC2, pursuant to paragraph (b)(6) of this section.

(C) *Section 368(a)(1)(B) reorganization.* If, instead of DC1 acquiring its 25% interest in CFC2 pursuant to a reorganization described in section 368(a)(1)(C), DC1 had transferred the stock of CFC1 to CFC2 in exchange for 25% of the voting stock of CFC2 in a reorganization described in section 368(a)(1)(B), the results would be the same as described in paragraphs (ii) (A) and (B) of this *Example 4.*

Example 5. Acquisition of the stock of a foreign corporation that controls a domestic acquiring corporation in a triangular reorganization described in section 368(a)(1)(C). (i) *Facts.* DC1, a domestic corporation, has owned all the stock of CFC1, a foreign corporation, since its formation on January 1, year 1. CFC1 has owned all the stock of CFC2, a foreign corporation, since its formation on January 1, year 1. FC, a foreign corporation that is not a controlled foreign corporation, has owned all of the stock of DC2, a domestic corporation, since its formation on January 1, year 2. On December 31, year 3, pursuant to a restructuring transaction that was a triangular reorganization described in section 368(a)(1)(C), CFC1 transfers all of its assets, including the CFC2 stock, to DC2 in exchange for 60% of the voting stock of FC. CFC1 transfers the voting stock of FC to DC1 and the CFC1 stock is cancelled. Pursuant to section 1223(1), DC1 is considered to have held the stock of FC since January 1, year 1. Under section 1223(2), DC2 is considered to have held the stock of CFC2 since January 1, year 1. On December 31, year 3, CFC1 has $100 of earnings and profits, CFC2 has $300 of earnings and profits, and FC has $200 of earnings and profits. DC1 includes the $100 all earnings and profits amount attributable to its CFC1 stock in income as a deemed dividend under § 1.367(b)-3 upon the exchange of CFC1 stock for FC stock. Pursuant to the lower-tier earnings exclusion of § 1.367(b)-2(d)(3)(ii), that amount does not include the $300 of earnings and profits of CFC2. From January 1, year 4, until December 31, year 5, FC (now a controlled foreign corporation) accumulates an additional $50 of earnings and profits. From January 1, year 4 until December 31, year 5, CFC2 accumulates an additional $100 of earnings and profits. On December 31, year 5, DC1 sells its stock in FC and DC2 sells its stock in CFC2.

(ii) *Result.* (A) *DC1.* Pursuant to paragraph (b)(2)(iii) of this section, there is $30 of earnings and profits attributable to the stock of FC sold by DC1. This amount consists of 60% of the $50 of earnings and profits accumulated by FC after the restructuring transaction, and none of the earnings and profits accumulated by CFC1, CFC2, or FC before the restructuring transaction.

(B) *DC2.* Pursuant to paragraph (b)(3)(ii) of this section, there is $400 of earnings and profits attributable to the stock of CFC2 sold by DC2. This amount consists of all of the earnings and profits accumulated by CFC2 during DC2's section 1223(2) holding period.

Example 6. Acquisition of the stock of a foreign corporation that controls a foreign acquiring corporation in a reorganization described in section 368(a)(1)(C). (i) *Facts.* DC1, a domestic corporation, has owned all the stock of CFC1, a foreign corporation, since its formation on January 1, year 1. CFC1 has owned all the stock of CFC2, a foreign corporation, since its formation on January 1, year 1. FC, a foreign corporation that is not a controlled foreign corporation, has owned all of the stock of FC2, a foreign corporation, since its formation on January 1, year 2. On December 31, year 3, pursuant to a restructuring transaction that was a triangular reorganization described in section 368(a)(1)(C), CFC1 transfers all of its assets, including the CFC2 stock, to FC2 in exchange for 60% of the voting stock of FC. CFC1 transfers the voting stock of FC to DC1 and the CFC1 stock is cancelled. Pursuant to section 1223(1), DC1 is considered to have held the stock of FC since January 1, year 1. Under section 1223(2), FC2 is considered to have held the stock of CFC2 since January 1, year 1. On December 31, year 3, CFC1 has $100 of earnings and profits, CFC2 has $300 of earnings and profits, FC has $200 of earnings and profits, and FC2 has no earnings and profits. From January 1, year 4, until December 31, year 5, FC (now a controlled foreign corporation) accumulates an additional $50 of earnings and profits. From January 1, year 4 until December 31, year 5, CFC2 accumulates an additional $100 of earnings and profits. FC2, a controlled foreign corporation after the restructuring transaction, accumulates $100 of earnings and profits from January 1, year 4, until December 31, year 5. On December 31, year 5, DC1 sells its stock in FC.

(ii) *Result.* Pursuant to paragraphs (b)(2)(ii) and (b)(4)(iii) of this section, there is $550 of earnings and profits attributable to the stock of FC sold by DC1. This amount consists of all $400 of the CFC1 and CFC2 earnings and profits accumulated before the restructuring transaction (see also section 1248(c)(2)), and 60% of the $250 of the earnings and profits accumulated by FC, FC2, and CFC2 after the restructuring transaction.

Example 7. Acquisition of controlled foreign corporation stock by a controlled foreign corporation in a reorganization described in section 368(a)(1)(B), followed by a sale of the acquired stock by the acquiring controlled foreign corporation. (i) *Facts.* DC1, a domestic corporation, has owned all of the outstanding stock of CFC1, a foreign corporation, since its formation on January 1, year 1. CFC1 has owned all of the outstanding stock of CFC3, a foreign corporation, since its formation on January 1, year 1. DC2, a domestic corporation unrelated to DC1, has owned all of the outstanding stock of CFC2, a foreign corporation, since its formation on January 1, year 2. On December 31, year 3, pursuant to a restructuring transaction that is a reorganization described in section 368(a)(1)(B), CFC1 transfers all of the stock of CFC3 to CFC2 in exchange for 40% of CFC2's stock. On December 31, year 3, CFC2 and CFC3 have, respectively, $40 and $20 of earnings and profits. On December 31, year 5, when the accumulated earnings and profits of CFC3 are $50 ($20 of earnings and profits as of December 31, year 3, plus $30 of earnings and profits generated from January 1, year 4, through December 31, year 5), CFC2 sells the stock of CFC3 in a transaction to which section 964(e) applies.

(ii) *Result.* (A) *CFC2.* Pursuant to paragraph (b)(3)(ii) of this section, there is $50 of earnings and profits attributable to the CFC3 stock sold by CFC2. This amount consists of the accumulated earnings and profits attributable to CFC2's entire section 1223(2) holding period in the CFC3 stock.

(B) *CFC1, DC2, and DC1.* Under paragraph (b)(5) of this section, the earnings and profits attributable to the CFC2 stock held by CFC1 and DC2, and the earnings and profits attributable to the CFC1 stock held by DC1, will be reduced (regardless of whether CFC2 recognizes gain on its sale of CFC3 stock).

(*1*) *CFC1.* The earnings and profits attributable to the CFC2 stock held by CFC1 will be reduced by $32, or the amount of earnings and profits as of December 31, year 5, that would have been attributable to the CFC2 stock held by CFC1 pursuant to paragraph (b)(2)(ii) of this section. This amount consists of all of the $20 of earnings and profits accumulated by CFC3 before the restructuring transaction and 40% of the $30 of earnings and profits accumulated by CFC3 after the restructuring transaction (.40 × $30 = $12).

(*2*) *DC1.* The earnings and profits attributable to the CFC1 stock held by DC1 will also be reduced by $32, or the amount of earnings and profits that would have been attributable to the CFC1 stock held by DC1 as of December 31, year 5.

(*3*) *DC2.* The earnings and profits attributable to the CFC2 stock held by DC2 will be reduced by $18, or the amount of earnings and profits that would have been attributable to the CFC2 stock held by DC2 as of December 31, year 5, under paragraph (b)(4) of this section. This amount consists of 60% of the $30 (.60 × $30 = $18) of earnings and profits accumulated by CFC3 after the restructuring transaction.

(C) *Partial sale by CFC2.* If, instead of selling 100% of the CFC3 stock, on December 31, year 5, CFC2 sells only 50% of its CFC3 stock, paragraph (b)(5) of this section requires CFC1 to reduce the earnings and profits of CFC3 attributable to its CFC2 stock to $16. Similarly, DC1 would be required to reduce the earnings and profits of CFC3 attributable to its CFC1 stock by $16. Paragraph (b)(5) of this section also requires DC2 to reduce the CFC3 earnings and profits attributable to its CFC2 stock by $9. These reductions occur without regard to whether CFC2 recognizes gain on its sale of CFC3 stock.

Example 8. Acquisition of the assets of a lower-tier controlled foreign corporation by an upper-tier controlled foreign corporation in a restructuring transaction described in section 368(a)(1)(C). (i) *Facts.* DC, a domestic corporation, has owned all the stock of CFC1, a controlled foreign corporation, since its formation on January 1, year 1. CFC1 is a holding company that has owned 79% of the stock of CFC2, a controlled foreign corporation, since its formation on January 1, year 1. The other 21% of CFC2 stock is owned by X, an unrelated party. On December 31, year 1, CFC2 has $200 of earnings and profits. On December 31, year 1, CFC1 has no accumulated earnings and profits. On December 31, year 1, pursuant to a restructuring transaction described in section 368(a)(1)(C), CFC2 transfers all its properties to CFC1. In exchange, CFC1 assumes the liabilities of CFC2 and transfers to CFC2 voting stock representing 21% of the stock of CFC1. CFC2 distributes the voting stock to X and liquidates. The liabilities assumed do not exceed 20% of the value of the properties of CFC2. From January 1, year 2, to December 31, year 3, CFC1 accumulates $100 of earnings and profits. On December 31, year 3, DC sells its CFC1 stock.

(ii) *Result.* Pursuant to paragraph (b)(4)(ii) of this section, there is $237 of earnings and profits attributable to DC's CFC1 stock. This amount consists of 79% of CFC2's $200 of earnings and profits accumulated before the restructuring transaction (see section 1248(c)(2)), and 79% of CFC1's $100 of earnings and profits accumulated after the restructuring transaction. Pursuant to paragraph (b)(6) of this section, none of CFC2's $200 of earnings and profits to which CFC1 succeeded under section 381 would be attributable to DC's CFC1 stock.

(c) *Earnings and profits attributable to stock of a foreign distributee corporation that is a foreign corporate shareholder with respect to a foreign liquidating corporation.*—(1) *General rule.*—If a foreign corporation (liquidating corporation) makes a distribution of property in complete liquidation under section 332 to a foreign corporation (distributee), and immediately before the liquidation the distributee was a foreign corporate shareholder with respect to the liquidating foreign corporation, the amount of earnings and profits attributable to the distributee stock upon its subsequent sale or exchange will be determined under this paragraph (c)(1). The earnings and profits attributable will be the sum of the earnings and profits attributable to the stock of the distributee immediately before the liquidation (including amounts attributed under section 1248(c)(2)) and the earnings and profits attributable to the stock of the distributee accumulated after the liquidation (including amounts attributed under section 1248(c)(2)).

(2) *Special rule regarding section 381.*—Solely for purposes of determining the earnings and profits (or deficit in earnings and profits) attributable to stock under this paragraph (c), the attributed earnings and profits of a corporation shall not include earnings and profits that are treated as received or incurred pursuant to section 381(c)(2)(A) and § 1.381(c)(2)-1(a).

(3) *Example.*—(i) *Facts.*—DC, a domestic corporation, has owned all of the stock of CFC1, a foreign corporation, since its formation on January 1, year 1. CFC1 is an operating company that has owned all of the stock of CFC2, a foreign corporation, since its formation on January 1, year 1. On December 31, year 2, CFC1 has $200 of accumulated earnings and profits and CFC2 has a ($200) deficit in earnings

and profits. On December 31, year 2, CFC2 distributes all of its assets and liabilities to CFC1 in a liquidation to which section 332 applies. From January 1, year 3, until December 31, year 4, CFC1 accumulates no additional earnings and profits. On December 31, year 4, DC sells its stock in CFC1.

(ii) *Result.*—Pursuant to paragraph (c)(1) of this section, there are no earnings and profits attributable to DC's CFC1 stock. This amount consists of the sum of the earnings and profits attributable to the CFC1 stock immediately before the liquidation (100% of the $200 accumulated earnings and profits of CFC1 and 100% of CFC2's ($200) deficit in earnings and profits) and the amount of earnings and profits accumulated after the section 332 liquidation (see also section 1248(c)(2)).

(d) *Effective/applicability dates.*—(1) *General rule.*—Except as provided in paragraph (d)(2) of this section, this section applies to income inclusions that occur on or after July 30, 2007.

(2) *Exception.*—Paragraph (b)(2)(iv) of this section applies to restructuring transactions occurring on or after April 18, 2013. [Reg. § 1.1248-8.]

☐ *[T.D. 9345, 7-27-2007. Amended by T.D. 9614, 3-18-2013 and T.D.* 9803, 12-15-2016.]

§ 1.1248(f)-1. Certain nonrecognition distributions.—(a) *Scope and purpose.*—This section and §§ 1.1248(f)-2 and 1.1248(f)-3 provide rules under section 1248(f) that apply when a domestic corporation (domestic distributing corporation) distributes stock of a foreign corporation (foreign distributed corporation) in a distribution to which section 337, 355(c)(1), or 361(c)(1) applies. Paragraph (b) of this section provides the general rule that requires the domestic distributing corporation, depending on the type of distribution, to include in gross income either the section 1248 amount or the total section 1248(f) amount. Paragraph (c) of this section provides definitions that apply for purposes of this section and §§ 1.1248(f)-2 and 1.1248(f)-3. Section 1.1248(f)-2 provides exceptions to the general rule contained in paragraph (b) of this section that apply, depending on the type of distribution. Section 1.1248(f)-3 provides reasonable cause relief procedures for failures to timely comply with certain filing requirements and effective/applicability dates.

(b) *General rule.*—(1) *Section 337 distribution.*—This paragraph (b)(1) applies if a domestic distributing corporation that is a section 1248 shareholder of a foreign distributed corporation distributes stock of the foreign distributed corporation in a distribution to which section 337 applies (section 337 distribution). Except as provided in § 1.1248(f)-2(a), the domestic distributing corporation must, notwithstanding any other provision of subtitle A of the Internal Revenue Code (Code), include in gross income as a dividend the section 1248 amount with respect to the stock of the foreign distributed corporation. This paragraph (b)(1) applies only to the extent the domestic distributing corporation does not recognize gain with respect to the stock of the foreign distributed corporation as a result of the section 337 distribution under another provision of subtitle A of the Code.

(2) *Existing stock distribution under section 355 or 361.*—This paragraph (b)(2) applies to the extent a domestic distributing corporation distributes stock of the foreign distributed corporation that is not received in a section 361 exchange that is part of the plan of distribution, provided the distribution is described in section 355(c)(1) or section 361(c)(1) (existing stock distribution). Except as provided in § 1.1248(f)-2(b), the domestic distributing corporation must, notwithstanding any other provision of subtitle A of the Code, include in gross income as a dividend the section 1248 amount with respect to the stock of the foreign distributed corporation. This paragraph (b)(2) only applies to the extent the domestic distributing corporation does not recognize gain with respect to the stock of the foreign distributed corporation as a result of the existing stock distribution under another provision of subtitle A of the Code.

(3) *New stock distribution under section 361.*—This paragraph (b)(3) applies to the extent a domestic distributing corporation distributes stock of the foreign distributed corporation that is received in a section 361 exchange that is part of the plan of distribution (and, to the extent applicable, also distributes any cash or other property), provided the distribution is described in section 361(c)(1) (new stock distribution). Except as provided in § 1.1248(f)-2(c), the domestic distributing corporation must, notwithstanding any other provision of subtitle A of the Code, include in gross income as a dividend the total section 1248(f) amount with respect to the stock of each foreign corporation transferred in the section 361 exchange. This paragraph (b)(3) applies without regard to the amount of gain realized by the domestic distributing corporation in the new stock distribution.

(c) *Definitions.*—Except as otherwise provided, the following definitions apply for purposes of this section and §§ 1.1248(f)-2 and 1.1248(f)-3:

(1) *80-percent distributee* is a corporation described in section 337(c).

(2) *Block of stock* has the meaning provided in § 1.1248-2(b).

(3) *Distributee* is a shareholder of the domestic distributing corporation that receives one or more shares of stock of a foreign distributed corporation in an existing stock distribution (as defined in paragraph (b)(2) of this section) or a new stock distribution (as defined in paragraph (b)(3) of this section).

(4) *Hypothetical section 1248 amount* is, with respect to each distributee or non-stock distributee, the amount in paragraph (c)(4)(i) of this section, reduced by the amount in paragraph (c)(4)(ii) of this section computed with respect to the stock of each foreign corporation transferred in the section 361 exchange by the domestic distributing corporation for which there is not an income inclusion under § 1.367(b)-4(b)(1)(i).

(i) The amount that the domestic distributing corporation would have included in income as a deemed dividend under § 1.367(b)-4(b)(1)(i) if the requirements of § 1.367(b)-4(b)(1)(ii)(A) (involving the receipt of foreign stock in an exchange to which § 1.367(a)-7(c) applies) had not been satisfied and that would have been attributable to such distributee or non-stock distributee under § 1.367(a)-7(e)(4) (providing rules to attribute deemed income inclusions under § 1.367(b)-4 to persons described in § 1.367(a)-3(e)(3)(iii)(A)).

(ii) The amount of gain recognized by the domestic distributing corporation under § 1.367(a)-7(c)(2) attributable to such distributee or non-stock distributee and allocable to the stock of such foreign corporation under § 1.367(a)-7(e)(1), but only to the extent such gain is treated as a dividend under section 1248(a).

(5) *Non-stock distributee* is a shareholder of the domestic distributing corporation that receives cash or other property but no shares of stock of the foreign distributed corporation in a new stock distribution (as defined in paragraph (b)(3) of this section).

(6) *Postdistribution amount* is the section 1248 amount with respect to the stock (or a portion of a share of stock) of the foreign distributed corporation received by a distributee, computed immediately after the distribution, but without taking into account any adjustments to the basis of the stock under § 1.1248(f)-2(b)(3) (in the case of an existing stock distribution) or adjustments to the basis of stock or income inclusions under § 1.1248(f)-2(c)(3) (in the case of a new stock distribution). The postdistribution amount in the stock of a foreign distributed corporation received in an existing stock distribution is determined based on the distributee's holding period in the stock as adjusted under § 1.1248(f)-2(b)(2). The postdistribution amount in the stock (or a portion of a share of stock, as applicable) of a foreign distributed corporation received in a new stock distribution is determined after applying the rules in §§ 1.1248-8(b)(2)(iv) and 1.1248(f)-2(c)(2).

(7) *Section 358 basis* is the basis in stock as determined under section 358.

(8) *Section 361 exchange* is an exchange described in section 361(a) or (b).

(9) *Section 1248 amount* is the net positive earnings and profits (if any) attributable to the stock of the foreign distributed corporation, determined in accordance with § 1.1248-2 or § 1.1248-3 (taking into account § 1.1248-8, if applicable), and that would be included in gross income as a dividend under section 1248(a) if the stock were sold by the domestic distributing corporation in a transaction in which all realized gain is recognized.

(10) *Section 1248(f) amount* is the amount in paragraph (c)(10)(i) of this section, reduced by the amount in paragraph (c)(10)(ii) of this section computed with respect to the stock of each foreign corporation transferred in the section 361 exchange by the domestic distributing corporation for which the domestic distributing corporation does not have an income inclusion under § 1.367(b)-4(b)(1)(i).

(i) The amount that the domestic distributing corporation would have included in income as a dividend under § 1.367(b)-4(b)(1)(i) if the requirements of § 1.367(b)-4(b)(1)(ii)(A) (involving the receipt of foreign stock in an exchange to which § 1.367(a)-7(c) applies) had not been satisfied.

(ii) The amount of gain recognized by the domestic distributing corporation under § 1.367(a)-7(c)(2) and allocable to the stock of such foreign corporation under § 1.367(a)-7(e)(1), but only to the extent such gain is treated as a dividend under section 1248(a).

(11) *Section 1248(f) block amount* is the portion of the section 1248(f) amount, as defined in paragraph (c)(10) of this section, that relates to a block of stock of the foreign corporation if more than a single block of stock of the foreign corporation is transferred in the section 361 exchange.

(12) *Section 1248 shareholder* is a domestic corporation that satisfies the ownership requirements of section 1248(a)(2) with respect to a foreign corporation, except that a domestic corporation, other than a domestic distributing corporation, that is a regulated investment company (as defined in section 851(a)), a real estate investment trust (as defined in section 856(a)), or an S corporation (as defined in section 1361(a)) cannot be a section 1248 shareholder.

(13) *Timely filed return* is a U.S. income tax return filed on or before the due date set forth in section 6072(b), including any extensions of time to file the return granted under section 6081.

(14) *Total section 1248(f) amount* is the sum of each section 1248(f) amount (as defined in paragraph (c)(10) of this section). [Reg. § 1.248(f)-1.]

☐ [*T.D. 9614, 3-18-2013. Amended by T.D. 9760, 3-18-2016.*]

§ 1.1248(f)-2. Exceptions for certain distributions and attribution rules.—(a) *Section 337 stock distribution.*—(1) *General exception.*—In the case of a section 337 distribution (as defined in § 1.1248-1(b)(1)), § 1.1248(f)-1(b)(1) shall not apply to the distribution of stock of the foreign distributed corporation to the 80-percent distributee if the conditions of paragraphs (a)(1)(i), (a)(1)(ii) and (a)(1)(iii) of this section are satisfied.

(i) *80-percent distributee is a section 1248 shareholder.*—Immediately after the section 337 distribution, the 80-percent distributee is a section 1248 shareholder with respect to the foreign distributed corporation.

(ii) *Holding period.*—The 80-percent distributee is treated as holding the stock of the foreign distributed corporation received in the section 337 distribution for the period during which the stock was held by the domestic distributing corporation.

(iii) *Basis.*—The 80-percent distributee's basis in the stock of the foreign distributed corporation received in the section 337 distribution does not exceed the domestic distributing corporation's basis in such stock at the time of the section 337 distribution.

(2) *Elective exception.*—If the conditions of paragraph (a)(1)(ii) or (a)(1)(iii) of this section are not otherwise satisfied, the domestic distributing corporation and the 80-percent distributee may elect to make adjustments to the 80-percent distributee's holding period or basis in the stock of the foreign distributed corporation, as appropriate, such that the conditions described in paragraphs (a)(1)(ii) and (iii) of this section are satisfied. The conditions and procedures for making the election are described in paragraph (a)(3) of this section. See paragraphs (a)(4) and (5) of this section for adjustments that are required as a result of making the election.

(3) *Election and reporting.*—(i) *Statement required by domestic distributing corporation and 80-percent distributee.*—(A) *In general.*—The domestic distributing corporation and the 80-percent distributee make the election described in paragraph (a)(2) of this section by each including a statement, described in paragraph (a)(3)(i)(B) of this section, with a timely filed return for the taxable year during which the section 337 distribution occurs, and by entering into a written agreement described in paragraph (a)(3)(ii) of this section. If the domestic distributing corporation or the 80-percent distributee are members of a consolidated group at the time of the section 337 distribution but not the common parent, the common parent of the consolidated group makes the election on behalf of the domestic distributing corporation or the 80-percent distributee. The election described in paragraph (a)(2) of this section and made pursuant to this paragraph (a)(3) is irrevocable.

(B) *Form and content.*—The statement of election must be entitled, "STATEMENT TO ELECT TO APPLY EXCEPTION UNDER § 1.1248(f)-2(a)(2)," state that the domestic distributing corporation and the 80-percent distributee have entered into a written agreement described in paragraph (a)(3)(ii) of this section, set forth the date of the agreement and the names of the parties to the agreement, and the adjustments to the 80-percent distributee's holding period and/or basis determined under section 334 in the stock of the foreign distributed corporation received in the section 337 distribution required under paragraphs (a)(4) and (a)(5) of this section.

(ii) *Written agreement.*—The domestic distributing corporation and the 80-percent distributee must enter into a written agreement described in this paragraph (a)(3)(ii) on or before the due date (including extensions) of the domestic distributing corporation's U.S. income tax return for the taxable year during which the section 337 distribution occurs. Both the domestic distributing corporation and the 80-percent distributee must retain the original or a copy of the agreement as part of its records in the manner specified by § 1.6001-1(e). Both the domestic distributing corporation and the 80-percent distributee must provide a copy of the agreement to the Internal Revenue Service within 30 days of the receipt of a request for the agreement in connection with an examination of the taxable year during which the section 337 distribution occurs. The written agreement must—

(A) State the document is an agreement under paragraph (a)(3)(ii) of this section;

(B) Provide the name and taxpayer identification number (if any) of the domestic distributing corporation, the 80-percent distribute, and the foreign distributed corporation;

(C) With respect to the 80-percent distributee, state the holding period in the stock of the foreign distributed corporation received in the section 337 distribution as adjusted under paragraph (a)(4) of this section; and

(D) With respect to the 80-percent distributee, identify the basis as determined under section 334 of the stock of the foreign distributed corporation received in the section 337 distribution and the adjustment (if any) to such basis under paragraph (a)(5) of this section.

(4) *Holding period adjustment.*—For purposes of section 1248, immediately after the section 337 distribution, the 80-percent distributee's holding period in the stock of the foreign distributed corporation received in the section 337 distribution shall equal the domestic distributing corporation's holding period in such stock at the time of the section 337 distribution.

(5) *Basis adjustments.*—If the domestic distributing corporation's section 1248 amount with respect to the stock of the foreign distributed corporation received by the 80-percent distributee in the section 337 distribution exceeds the 80-percent distributee's postdistribution amount with respect to such stock (excess amount), the 80-percent distributee's basis as determined under section 334 in such stock shall be reduced by the excess amount.

(b) *Existing stock distribution under sections 355 or 361.*—In the case of an existing stock distribution (as defined in § 1.1248(f)-1(b)(2)), § 1.1248(f)-1(b)(2) shall not apply to the distribution of stock of the foreign distributed corporation to a distributee that is a section 1248 shareholder with respect to the foreign distributed corporation immediately after the distribution if the domestic distributing corporation and all distributees that are section 1248 shareholders elect to apply the provisions of this paragraph (b) in accordance with paragraph (b)(1) of this section. See paragraphs (b)(2) and (3) of this section for adjustments that may be required if an election is made to apply the provisions of this paragraph (b).

(1) *Election and reporting.*—(i) *Statement required by domestic distributing corporation and section 1248 shareholders.*—(A) *In general.*—The domestic distributing corporation and all distributees that are section 1248 shareholders elect to apply the provisions of paragraph (b) of this section by each including a statement, described in paragraph (b)(1)(i)(B) of this section, with a timely filed return for the taxable year during which the existing stock distribution occurs and by entering into a written agreement described in paragraph (b)(1)(ii) of this section. If the domestic distributing corporation or a section 1248 shareholder is a member of a consolidated group but not the common parent, the common parent of the consolidated group makes the election on behalf of the domestic distributing corporation or section 1248 shareholder. The election made under this paragraph (b)(1) is irrevocable.

(B) *Form and content.*—The statement of election must be entitled, "ELECTION TO APPLY EXCEPTION UNDER § 1.1248(f)-2(b)," state that the domestic distributing corporation and all distributees that are section 1248 shareholders have entered into a written agreement described in paragraph (b)(1)(ii) of this section, the date of the agreement and the names of the parties to the agreement, and set forth any required adjustment to each section

1248 shareholder's holding period or section 358 basis (if any) in the stock of the foreign distributed corporation received in the existing stock distribution under paragraph (b)(2) or (b)(3) of this section, respectively.

(ii) *Written agreement*.—The domestic distributing corporation and the section 1248 shareholders must enter into a written agreement described in this paragraph (b)(1)(ii) on or before the due date (including extensions) of the domestic distributing corporation's U.S. income tax return for the taxable year during which the existing stock distribution occurs. Each party to the agreement must retain the original or a copy of the agreement as part of its records in the manner specified by § 1.6001-1(e). Each party to the agreement must provide a copy of the agreement to the Internal Revenue Service within 30 days of the receipt of a request for the agreement in connection with an examination of the taxable year during which the existing stock distribution occurs. The written agreement must—

(A) State the document is an agreement under paragraph (b)(1)(ii) of this section;

(B) Provide the name and taxpayer identification number (if any) of the domestic distributing corporation, the foreign distributed corporation, and each section 1248 shareholder;

(C) With respect to each section 1248 shareholder, state the holding period in the stock of the foreign distributed corporation received in the existing stock distribution as adjusted under paragraph (b)(2) of this section; and

(D) With respect to each section 1248 shareholder, identify the basis under section 358 of the stock of the foreign distributed corporation received in the existing stock distribution and the adjustment (if any) to the basis under paragraph (b)(3) of this section.

(2) *Holding period adjustments*.—For purposes of section 1248, immediately after the existing stock distribution, each section 1248 shareholder's holding period in each share of stock of the foreign distributed corporation received in the existing stock distribution will be equal to the domestic distributing corporation's holding period in the share of stock at the time of the existing stock distribution.

(3) *Basis adjustments*.—If the domestic distributing corporation's section 1248 amount with respect to a share of stock of the foreign distributed corporation received by a section 1248 shareholder in the existing stock distribution exceeds the section 1248 shareholder's postdistribution amount with respect to the share of stock (excess amount), the section 1248 shareholder's section 358 basis in the share of stock is reduced by the excess amount. For an illustration of the rule in this paragraph (b)(3), see paragraph (e) of this section, *Example 1* and *Example 3*.

(c) *New stock distribution under section 361*.—In the case of a new stock distribution (as defined in § 1.1248(f)-1(b)(3)), the amount that the domestic distributing corporation is required to include in gross income as a dividend under § 1.1248(f)-1(b)(3) (total section 1248(f) amount) is reduced by the sum of the portions of any section 1248(f) amount attributable under paragraph (d) of this section to stock of the foreign distributed corporation distributed to distributees that are section 1248 shareholders, but only if the domestic distributing corporation and all the distributees that are section 1248 shareholders elect to apply the provisions of this paragraph (c) in accordance with paragraph (c)(1) of this section. See paragraphs (c)(2), (c)(3), and (c)(4) of this section for adjustments or income inclusions that are required if an election is made to apply the provisions of this paragraph (c). The adjustments or income inclusions provided in paragraphs (c)(2), (c)(3), and (c)(4) of this section apply after any adjustments required under section 367(a)(5) and § 1.367(a)-7(c). For illustrations of this exception, see paragraph (e) of this section, *Example 2* and *Example 3* and § 1.367(a)-3(e)(8), *Example 3*.

(1) *Election and reporting*.—(i) *Statement required by domestic distributing corporation and section 1248 shareholders*.—(A) *In general*.—The domestic distributing corporation and all distributees that are section 1248 shareholders elect to apply the provisions of paragraph (c) of this section by each including a statement, in the form and containing the information listed in paragraph (c)(1)(i)(B) of this section, with a timely filed return for the taxable year during which the new stock distribution occurs and by entering into a written agreement described in paragraph (c)(1)(ii) of this section. If the domestic distributing corporation or a section 1248 shareholder is a member of a consolidated group at the time of the new stock distribution but is not the common parent, the common parent of the consolidated group makes the election on behalf of the domestic distributing corporation or section 1248 shareholder. The election made under this paragraph (c)(1) is irrevocable.

(B) *Form and content*.—The statement of election must be entitled, "ELECTION TO APPLY EXCEPTION UNDER § 1.1248(f)-2(c)," state that the domestic distributing corporation and each distributee that is a section 1248 shareholder have entered into a written agreement described in paragraph (c)(1)(ii) of this section, the date of the agreement and the names of the parties to the agreement, and describe, with respect to each section 1248 shareholder, the extent to which the shares of stock of the foreign distributed corporation received in the new stock distribution are divided into portions under paragraph (c)(2) of this section, any adjustments to the section 358 basis of the stock under paragraph (c)(3) of this section, and the amount the domestic distributing corporation must include in gross income as a dividend under paragraph (c)(3) of this section.

(ii) *Written agreement*.—The domestic distributing corporation and all distributees that are section 1248 shareholders must enter into a written agreement described in this paragraph (c)(1)(ii) on or before the due date (including extensions) of the domestic distributing corporation's U.S. income tax return for the taxable year during which the new stock distribution occurs. Each party to the agreement must retain the original or a copy of the agreement as part of its records in the manner specified by § 1.6001-1(e). Each party to the agreement must provide a copy of the agreement to the Internal Revenue Service within 30 days of the receipt of a request for the agreement in connection with an examination of the taxable year during which the new stock distribution occurs. The written agreement must—

(A) State the document is an agreement under paragraph (c)(1)(ii) of this section;

(B) Provide the name and taxpayer identification number (if any) of the domestic distributing corporation, the foreign distributed corporation, and each section 1248 shareholder;

(C) With respect to each section 1248 shareholder, describe the extent to which the shares of stock of the foreign distributed corporation are divided into portions under paragraph (c)(2) of this section;

(D) With respect to each section 1248 shareholder, state the amount of earnings and profits attributable to the stock (or each block of stock, as applicable) of each foreign corporation transferred in the section 361 exchange that is attributable under § 1.1248-8(b)(2)(iv) to the stock of the foreign distributed corporation received in the new stock distribution;

(E) With respect to each section 1248 shareholder, state the amount of the section 1248(f) amount with respect to the stock (or each block of stock, as applicable) of each foreign corporation transferred in the section 361 exchange that is attributable under § 1.1248(f)-2(d) to the stock of the foreign distributed corporation received in the new stock distribution;

(F) With respect to each section 1248 shareholder, state the amount of the adjustment to the section 358 basis of the stock of the foreign distributed corporation under paragraph (c)(3) of this section; and

(G) With respect to each section 1248 shareholder, state the amount the domestic distributing corporation must include in gross income as a dividend under paragraph (c)(3) of this section.

(2) *Portions*.—If the domestic distributing corporation transfers property, other than a single block of stock of a foreign corporation with respect to which the domestic distributing corporation is a section 1248 shareholder immediately before the section 361 exchange, to the foreign distributed corporation in the section 361 exchange that precedes the new stock distribution, then each share of stock of the foreign distributed corporation received by a distributee that is a section 1248 shareholder must be divided into portions as follows:

(i) One portion attributable to all property transferred in the section 361 exchange, other than property that is stock of a foreign corporation with respect to which the domestic distributing corporation is a section 1248 shareholder immediately before the section 361 exchange; and

(ii) One portion attributable to each block of stock of each foreign corporation transferred in the section 361 exchange with respect to which the domestic distributing corporation is a section 1248 shareholder immediately before the section 361 exchange. For the determination of the earnings and profits attributable to the stock (or block of stock, as applicable) of each foreign corporation transferred in the section 361 exchange that are attributable to a portion of a share of stock of the foreign distributed corporation, see

§ 1.1248-8(b)(2)(iv). For the determination of the section 1248(f) amount with respect to the stock (or block of stock, as applicable) of each foreign corporation transferred in the section 361 exchange that is attributable to a portion of a share of stock of the foreign distributed corporation, see paragraph (d)(2) of this section.

(3) *Basis adjustments and income inclusions.*—If the section 1248(f) amount attributable to a portion of a share of stock (or whole share, if no division is required) (as determined under paragraph (d) of this section) of the foreign distributed corporation received by a distributee that is a section 1248 shareholder in the new stock distribution exceeds the section 1248 shareholder's postdistribution amount in the portion (or whole share, if no division is required) (excess amount), then the section 1248 shareholder's section 358 basis in the portion as determined under paragraph (c)(4) of this section (or whole share, if no division is required), as adjusted under § 1.367(a)-7(c)(3), is reduced by the excess amount, but not below zero. To the extent the excess amount exceeds the section 358 basis in the portion (or whole share, if no division is required), the domestic distributing corporation must include that portion of the section 1248(f) amount attributable to the portion of the share (or whole share, if no division is required) in gross income as a dividend. For an illustration of this rule, see paragraph (e) of this section, *Example 2*, and § 1.367(a)-3(e)(8), *Example 3*.

(4) *Divided shares of stock.*—(i) *Basis.*—The basis of a portion of a share of stock of the foreign distributed corporation created under paragraph (c)(2) of this section is the product of the section 1248 shareholder's section 358 basis, as adjusted under § 1.367(a)-7(c)(3), in the share of stock multiplied by the ratio of the basis determined under section 362 (taking into account any gain or deemed dividends recognized under section 367) of the property (section 362 basis) to which the portion relates, to the aggregate section 362 basis of all property received by the foreign distributed corporation in the section 361 exchange. For illustrations of this rule, see paragraph (e) of this section, *Example 2*, and § 1.367(a)-3(e)(8), *Example 3*.

(ii) *Fair market value.*—The fair market value of a portion of a share of stock of the foreign distributed corporation created under paragraph (c)(2) of this section is the product of the fair market value of the share of stock multiplied by the ratio of the fair market value of the property to which the portion relates to the aggregate fair market value of all property received by the foreign distributed corporation in the section 361 exchange. For illustrations of this rule, see paragraph (e) of this section, *Example 2*, and § 1.367(a)-3(e)(8), *Example 3*.

(iii) *Subsequent exchanges.*—For purposes of determining the gain realized on the sale or exchange of a share of stock of the foreign distributed corporation that has divided portions under paragraph (c)(2) of this section, the amount realized on the sale or exchange of the share will be allocated to each divided portion based on the relative fair market value of the property to which the portion relates as determined at the time of the reorganization.

(iv) *Duration of divided shares.*—Shares of stock of the foreign distributed corporation that are divided into portions under paragraph (c)(2) of this section must be divided so long as section 1248(a) would apply to a sale or exchange of the shares.

(d) *Attribution of all or a portion of section 1248(f) amount to certain stock of the foreign distributed corporation.*—This paragraph (d) applies if there is a new stock distribution for which an election under § 1.1248(f)-2(c)(1) is made. This paragraph (d) provides rules for attributing all or a portion, as applicable, of the section 1248(f) amount with respect to the stock of each foreign corporation transferred in the section 361 exchange by the domestic distributing corporation to shares of stock, or to portions of shares of stock, as applicable, received in the foreign distributed corporation and distributed to one or more distributees that are section 1248 shareholders with respect to the foreign distributed corporation. Paragraph (d)(1) of this section provides rules to attribute the applicable section 1248(f) amount among shares of stock of the foreign distributed corporation received by one or more distributees that are section 1248 shareholders. If shares of stock are divided into portions under paragraph (c)(2) of this section, paragraph (d)(2) of this section provides additional rules to attribute the applicable section 1248 amount to portions of shares of stock received by one or more distributees that are section 1248 shareholders.

(1) *Attribution of all or a portion of section 1248(f) amount among shares of stock.*—With respect to one or more shares of stock of the foreign distributed corporation distributed to a distributee that is a section 1248 shareholder, the portion of the section 1248(f) amount with respect to the stock of the foreign corporation transferred in the section 361 exchange that is equal to the distributee's hypothetical section 1248 amount is attributed among those shares of stock of the foreign distributed corporation based on the ratio of the value of a share distributed to the distributee to the value of all shares of stock distributed to the distributee (attributable share amount).

(2) *Attribution of all or a portion of section 1248(f) amount to portions of a share of stock.*—(i) *Single block of stock.*—If a single block of stock of the foreign corporation is transferred in the section 361 exchange, the attributable share amount (as determined under paragraph (d)(1) of this section) is attributed to the portion of the share that relates to the single block of stock of the foreign corporation.

(ii) *Multiple blocks of stock.*—If multiple blocks of stock of the foreign corporation are transferred in the section 361 exchange, the attributable share amount (as determined under paragraph (d)(1) of the section) is attributed among the portions of the share that relate to such multiple blocks of stock of the foreign corporation. The portion of the attributable share amount that is attributable to a portion to which a block of stock relates is that amount that bears the same ratio that the section 1248(f) block amount with respect to that block of stock bears to the section 1248(f) amount with respect to the stock of the foreign corporation.

(e) *Examples.*—The rules of this section are illustrated by the following examples. See also § 1.367(a)-3(e)(8), *Example 3*. For purposes of the examples, unless otherwise indicated: DP and DC are domestic corporations; X is a United States citizen; FP is a foreign corporation; CFC1, CFC2, and FA are controlled foreign corporations; each corporation has a single class of stock outstanding and uses the calendar year as its taxable year; each shareholder of a corporation owns a single block of stock in the corporation; DC owns Business A, which consists solely of property whose fair market value exceeds its basis and could satisfy the requirements of the active foreign trade or business exception under section 367(a)(3) and § 1.367(a)-2; DC owns no other assets and has no liabilities; the requirements in § 1.367(a)-7(c)(5) are satisfied; no earnings and profits of a foreign corporation are described in section 1248(d); and none of the foreign corporations in the examples is a surrogate foreign corporation (within the meaning of section 7874) as a result of the transactions described in the examples because one or more of the conditions of section 7874(a)(2)(B) is not satisfied.

Example 1. Existing stock distribution under section 355(c)(1); gain recognition and adjustment to stock basis. (i) *Facts.* DP, FP, and X own 80%, 10%, and 10%, respectively, of the outstanding stock of DC. DP's DC stock has a $140x basis, $160x fair market value, and a 2-year holding period. DC wholly owns CFC1. DC's CFC1 stock has a $50x basis, $100x fair market value (therefore a gain of $50x), $25x of earnings and profits attributable to it for purposes of section 1248, and a $25x section 1248 amount (computed as the lesser of $50x gain in the CFC1 stock and $25x of section 1248 earnings and profits), and a 3-year holding period. On December 31, year 3, DC distributes all of the CFC1 stock to DP, FP, and X on a pro-rata basis in a distribution to which section 355 applies. The fair market value of the CFC1 stock received by DP, FP, and X is $80x, $10x, and $10x, respectively. After the distribution, DP's stock in DC has a fair market value of $80x and DP's section 358 basis in the CFC1 stock is $70x (a pro rata portion, or 50%, of DP's $140x basis in the DC stock immediately before the distribution). See § 1.358-2(a)(iv).

(ii) *Result.* (A) Under § 1.367(e)-1(b)(1), DC must recognize $5x gain on the distribution of CFC1 stock to FP (10% of the $50x gain in the CFC1 stock). Under § 1.367(b)-5(b)(1)(ii), DC must also recognize $5x gain on the distribution of CFC1 stock to X (10% of the $50x gain in the CFC1 stock). Of the aggregate $10x gain recognized by DC, $5x is recharacterized as a dividend under section 1248(a), computed as 20% of the $25x section 1248 amount with respect to the CFC1 stock. See § 1.1248-1 for additional consequences.

(B) DC's distribution of CFC1 stock to DP is described in section 1248(f)(1) and § 1.1248(f)-1(b)(2) because the distribution is pursuant to section 355(c)(1) (an existing stock distribution). As a result, the general rule is that DC must include in gross income as a dividend the section 1248 amount with respect to the CFC1 stock distributed to DP, or $20x (computed as 80% of the $25x section 1248 amount). However, if DP and DC make the election under paragraph (b)(1) of this section, § 1.1248(f)-1(b)(2) will not apply to DC's distribution of CFC1 stock to DP. If DP and DC make the election, then:

(*1*) Under paragraph (b)(2) of this section, for purposes of section 1248, immediately after the distribution DP will have a 3-year holding period in the CFC1 stock, the same holding period DC had in the CFC1 stock at the time of the distribution.

(2) Under paragraph (b)(3) of this section, DP's section 358 basis in the CFC1 stock ($70x) is reduced by $10x, the amount by which DC's section 1248 amount with respect to the CFC1 stock ($20x) distributed to DP exceeds DP's postdistribution amount with respect to the CFC1 stock ($10x). Under § 1.1248(f)-1(c)(6), DP's postdistribution amount equals the amount that DP would include in gross income as a dividend under section 1248(a) if DP sold the CFC1 stock immediately after the distribution, or $10x, which is computed as the lesser of the $10x gain in the CFC1 stock ($80x fair market value, less $70x basis) and $20x of section 1248 earnings and profits attributable to the CFC1 stock, taking into account DP's 3-year holding period in the stock as required by paragraph (b)(2) of this section. As adjusted under paragraph (b)(3) of this section, DP's basis in the CFC1 stock is $60x ($70x basis, less $10x required basis reduction).

Example 2. New stock distribution under section 361(c)(1); adjustment to stock basis. (i) *Facts.* DP wholly owns DC. DP's DC stock has a $180x basis and $200x fair market value. DC wholly owns CFC1 and CFC2. DC's CFC1 stock has a $70x basis, $100x fair market value (therefore a gain of $30x), $40x of earnings and profits attributable to it for purposes of section 1248, and a section 1248 amount of $30x (computed as the lesser of the $30x gain in CFC1 stock and $40x section 1248 earnings and profits). DC's CFC2 stock has a $130x basis, $100x fair market value (therefore a loss of $30x), $80x of earnings and profits attributable to it for purposes of section 1248, and a section 1248 amount of $0x (computed as the lesser of the $0x gain and $80x section 1248 earnings and profits). On December 31, Year 1, in a reorganization described in section 368(a)(1)(F), DC transfers the CFC1 stock and the CFC2 stock to FA, a newly formed corporation, in exchange for 100 shares of FA stock. DC distributes the 100 shares of FA stock to DP. DC's transfer of the CFC1 stock and CFC2 stock to FA in exchange for FA stock qualifies as a section 361 exchange, and DC's distribution of the 100 shares of FA stock to DP is pursuant to section 361(c)(1). DP exchanges its DC stock for the 100 shares of FA stock pursuant to section 354. Immediately after the transaction, DP wholly owns FA. DP and DC elect to apply the provisions of § 1.367(a)-7(c) in accordance with § 1.367(a)-7(c)(5). Pursuant to § 1.367(a)-3(e)(3)(iii)(A), DP properly files a gain recognition agreement with respect to the CFC1 stock that satisfies the conditions of §§ 1.367(a)-3(e)(6) and 1.367(a)-8.

(ii) *Result.* (A) DC does not recognize gain under § 1.367(a)-3(e)(2) with respect to the transfer of the CFC1 stock to FA because the three conditions in § 1.367(a)-3(e)(3)(i), (e)(3)(ii), and (e)(3)(iii) are satisfied. First, § 1.367(a)-3(e)(3)(i) is satisfied because the requirements of § 1.367(a)-7(c) are satisfied, including that an election is made to apply § 1.367(a)-7(c). Second, the requirements under § 1.367(a)-3(e)(3)(ii) related to transfers of domestic stock are not applicable because CFC1 is a foreign corporation. Third, because DC owns all the stock of FA immediately after DC's receipt of the FA stock in the section 361 exchange but prior to, and without taking into account, DC's distribution of the FA stock to DP, for purposes of satisfying the requirements of § 1.367(a)-3(e)(3)(iii), DP properly files a gain recognition agreement with respect to the CFC1 stock that satisfies the conditions of §§ 1.367(a)-3(e)(6) and 1.367(a)-8. Furthermore, DC is not required to recognize gain under § 1.367(a)-7(c)(2)(ii), and DP is not required to reduce its $180x section 358 basis in the FA stock under § 1.367(a)-7(c)(3), because the inside gain (within the meaning of § 1.367(a)-7(f)(5)) is $0x ($200x aggregate fair market value of CFC1 stock and CFC2 stock, less $200x aggregate basis of CFC1 stock and CFC2 stock). In addition, DC is not required to include in income as a deemed dividend the $30x section 1248 amount with respect to the CFC1 stock under § 1.367(b)-4(b)(1)(i) because immediately after DC's receipt of the FA stock in the section 361 exchange but prior to, and without taking into account, DC's distribution of the FA stock to DP, CFC1 and FA are controlled foreign corporations as to which DC is a section 1248 shareholder. See § 1.367(b)-4(b)(1)(ii)(A). With respect to the transfer of the CFC2 stock to FA, DC's section 1248 amount with respect to the CFC2 stock is $0x; therefore, § 1.367(b)-4(b)(1)(i) has no application.

(B) Under § 1.1248(f)-1(b)(3), as a result of the section 361(c)(1) distribution of the FA stock to DP (a new stock distribution), the general rule is that DC must include in gross income as a dividend the total section 1248(f) amount (defined in § 1.1248(f)-1(c)(14)). The total section 1248(f) amount is $30x, the sum of the section 1248(f) amount (defined in § 1.1248(f)-1(c)(10)) with respect to the CFC1 stock ($30x) and CFC2 stock ($0x). The section 1248(f) amount with respect to the CFC1 stock is the amount that DC would have included in income as a deemed dividend under § 1.367(b)-4(b)(1)(i) with respect to the CFC1 stock if the requirements under § 1.367(b)-4(b)(1)(ii)(A) had not been satisfied ($30x), less the amount of gain recognized by DC under § 1.367(a)-7(c)(2) that is allocable to the CFC1 stock under § 1.367(a)-7(e)(1) and treated as a dividend under section 1248(a) ($0x). Similarly, the section 1248(f) amount with respect to the CFC2 stock is the amount that DC would have included in income as a deemed dividend under § 1.367(b)-4(b)(1)(i) with respect to the CFC2 stock if the requirements under § 1.367(b)-4(b)(1)(ii)(A) had not been satisfied ($0x), less the amount of gain recognized by DC under § 1.367(a)-7(c)(2) that is allocable to the CFC2 stock under § 1.367(a)-7(e)(1) and treated as a dividend under section 1248(a) ($0x).

(C) If, however, DP and DC make the election provided in paragraph (c)(1) of this section, the amount that DC is required to include in gross income as a dividend under § 1.1248(f)-1(b)(3) (the total section 1248(f) amount of $30x) is reduced to the extent the section 1248(f) amount with respect to the CFC1 stock ($30x) and CFC2 stock ($0x) is attributable under paragraph (d) of this section to the shares of FA stock distributed to one or more distributees that are section 1248 shareholders of FA. The only distributee is DP, and DP is a section 1248 shareholder with respect to FA. If DP and DC elect to apply paragraph (c) of this section, then:

(*1*) Under paragraph (d)(1) of this section, the portion of the section 1248(f) amount with respect to the CFC1 stock that is attributed to the shares of FA stock distributed to DP is equal to DP's hypothetical section 1248 amount (as defined in § 1.1248(f)-1(c)(4)) with respect to the CFC1 stock. Because DP is the only shareholder of DC, DP's hypothetical section 1248 amount equals the section 1248(f) amount with respect to the CFC1 stock ($30x). The $30x hypothetical section 1248 amount is attributed pro rata (based on relative values) among the 100 shares of FA stock distributed to DP, and the attributable share amount (as defined in paragraph (d)(1) of this section) is $.30x. Paragraph (d)(1) of this section has no application with respect to the CFC2 stock because there is no section 1248(f) amount with respect to the CFC2 stock.

(*2*) If the shares of FA stock are divided into portions, the rules of paragraph (d)(2) of this section apply to attribute the attributable share amount ($.30x) to portions of shares of FA stock distributed to DP. Under paragraph (c)(2)(ii) of this section, the 100 shares of FA stock are divided into two portions, one portion related to the single block of CFC1 stock and one portion related to the single block of CFC2 stock. Under paragraph (d)(2)(i) of this section, the attributable share amount of $.30x is attributed to the portion of the 100 shares of FA stock that relates to the single block of CFC1 stock. Thus, all of the $30x section 1248(f) amount with respect to the CFC1 stock is attributable to the 100 shares of FA stock.

(*3*) Because the election under paragraph (c)(1) of this section is made, the total section 1248(f) amount ($30x) that DC is otherwise required to include in gross income as a dividend under § 1.1248(f)-1(b)(3) is reduced by $30x, the portion of the section 1248(f) amount with respect to the CFC1 stock that is attributable under paragraph (d) of this section to the shares of FA stock distributed to DP. Thus, the amount DC is required to include in gross income as a dividend under § 1.1248(f)-1(b)(3) is $0x ($30x less $30x).

(*4*) Under paragraph (c)(4)(i) of this section, the basis of each portion is the product of DP's section 358 basis in the share of FA stock multiplied by the ratio of the section 362 basis of the property (CFC1 stock or CFC2 stock, as applicable) to which the portion relates, to the aggregate section 362 basis of all property (CFC1 stock and CFC2 stock) received by FA in the section 361 exchange. Under paragraph (c)(4)(ii) of this section, the fair market value of each portion is the product of the fair market value of the share of FA stock multiplied by the ratio of the fair market value of the property (CFC1 stock or CFC2 stock, as applicable) to which the portion relates, to the aggregate fair market value of all property (CFC1 stock and CFC2 stock) received by FA in the section 361 exchange. The section 362 basis of the CFC1 stock and CFC2 stock is $70x and $130x, respectively, for a total section 362 basis of $200x. The CFC1 stock and CFC2 stock each has a fair market value of $100x, for a total fair market value of $200x. Therefore, the portions attributable to the CFC1 stock have an aggregate basis of $63x ($180x multiplied by $70x/$200x) and fair market value of $100x ($200x multiplied by $100x/$200x), resulting in aggregate gain in such portions of $37x (or $.37x per portion in each of the 100 shares). The portions attributable to the CFC2 stock have an aggregate basis of $117x ($180x multiplied by $130x/$200x) and fair market value of $100x ($200x multiplied by $100x/$200x), resulting in aggregate losses in such portions of $17x (or $.17x per portion in each of the 100 shares).

(*5*) Under § 1.1248-8(b)(2)(iv), the $40x earnings and profits attributable to the single block of CFC1 stock are attributed to the portions of the 100 shares of FA stock that relate to the CFC1 stock. Similarly, the $80x of earnings and profits attributable to the single block of CFC2 stock are attributed to the portions of the 100 shares of the FA stock that relate to the CFC2 stock. Thus, DP's postdistribution amount (defined in § 1.1248(f)-1(c)(6)) with respect to the portions of the shares of FA attributable to the CFC1 stock is $37x, the lesser of the aggregate gain in the portions attributable to the CFC1 stock of $37x (computed in paragraph (ii)(C)(*4*) of this *Example 2*) and the $40x earnings and profits attributable to such portions. Furthermore, DP's postdistribution amount with respect to the portions of the shares of FA attributable to the CFC2 stock is $0x, the lesser of the aggregate gain in the portions attributable to the CFC2 stock of $0x (computed in paragraph (ii)(C)(*4*) of this *Example 2* to be an aggregate loss of $17x) and the $80x earnings and profits attributable to such portions.

(*6*) Under paragraph (c)(3) of this section, DP's section 358 basis in the portions of the 100 shares of FA stock attributable to the CFC1 stock ($63x, computed in paragraph (ii)(C)(*4*) of this *Example 2*) is reduced by the amount (if any) by which the section 1248(f) amount attributable to such portions under paragraph (d) of this section ($30x, as computed in paragraph (ii)(C)(2) of this *Example 2*) exceeds DP's postdistribution amount with respect to such portions ($37x, computed in paragraph (ii)(C)(*5*) of this *Example 2*). Thus, there is no basis reduction in the portions of the 100 shares of FA stock attributable to the CFC1 stock. DP's section 358 basis in the portions of the 100 shares of FA stock attributable to the CFC2 stock is not reduced because the section 1248(f) amount attributable to such portions under paragraph (d) of this section is $0x (computed in paragraph (ii)(C)(2) of this *Example 2*), which equals DP's postdistribution amount with respect to such portions of $0x (as computed in paragraph (ii)(C)(*5*) of this *Example 2*).

Example 3. Combined existing stock distribution and new stock distribution under sections 355(c)(1) and 361(c)(1). (i) *Facts.* DP owns all 100 outstanding shares of stock of DC. DP's DC stock has a $180x basis (each of the 100 shares having a basis of $18), $200x fair market value, and 2-year holding period. DC owns all 60 shares of the outstanding stock of CFC1; all such shares constitute a single block of stock. DC's CFC1 stock has a $50x basis, $60x fair market value, $30x of earnings and profits attributable to it for purposes of section 1248, a $10x section 1248 amount (computed as the lesser of $10x gain and $30x of section 1248 earnings and profits), and a 3-year holding period. DC also owns all 40 shares of the outstanding stock of CFC2; all such shares constitute a single block of stock. DC's CFC2 stock has a $30x basis, $40x fair market value, $20x of earnings and profits attributable to it for purposes of section 1248, and a $10x section 1248 amount (computed as the lesser of $10x gain and $20x of section 1248 earnings and profits). DC also owns Business A, which has a fair market value of $100x. On December 31, year 4, in a divisive reorganization described in section 368(a)(1)(D), DC transfers the CFC2 stock to CFC1 in exchange for 40 shares of newly issued CFC1 stock. DC's transfer of the CFC2 stock to CFC1 qualifies as a section 361 exchange. DC then distributes the 100 shares of CFC1 stock (60 shares held prior to the transaction and 40 shares received in the section 361 exchange) to DP in a transaction that qualifies under section 355. DP properly files a gain recognition agreement with respect to the CFC2 stock that satisfies the conditions of §§ 1.367(a)-3(e)(6) and 1.367(a)-8. DP and DC properly make the elections provided in § 1.367(a)-7(c)(5) and paragraphs (b) and (c) of this section.

(ii) *Result.* (A) DC does not recognize gain under § 1.367(a)-3(e)(2) with respect to the transfer of the CFC2 stock to CFC1 because the three conditions in § 1.367(a)-3(e)(3)(i), (e)(3)(ii), and (e)(3)(iii) are satisfied. First, § 1.367(a)-3(e)(3)(i) is satisfied because the requirements of § 1.367(a)-7(c) are satisfied, including that an election is made to apply § 1.367(a)-7(c). Second, the requirements under § 1.367(a)-3(e)(3)(ii) related to transfers of domestic stock are not applicable because CFC2 is a foreign corporation. Third, because DC and DP own all the stock of CFC1 for purposes of satisfying the requirements of § 1.367(a)-3(e)(3)(iii), DP properly files a gain recognition agreement with respect to the CFC2 stock that satisfies the conditions of §§ 1.367(a)-3(e)(6) and 1.367(a)-8. See paragraph (ii)(G) of this example for the computation of the amount of gain subject to the gain recognition agreement. In addition, DC is not required to include in income as a dividend the $10x section 1248 amount with respect to the CFC2 stock under § 1.367(b)-4(b)(1)(i) because immediately after DC's receipt of the CFC1 stock in the section 361 exchange but prior to, and without taking into account, DC's distribution of the CFC1 stock to DP, CFC1 and CFC2 are controlled foreign corporations as to which DC is a section 1248 shareholder. See § 1.367(b)-4(b)(1)(ii)(A).

(B) DC is not required to recognize gain under § 1.367(a)-7(c)(2)(i) because DP, a control group member (as defined in § 1.367(a)-7(f)(1)), owns 100% of DC. DC is not required to recognize gain under § 1.367(a)-7(c)(2)(ii) because the amount described in § 1.367(a)-7(c)(2)(ii)(A) ($10x) does not exceed the amount described in § 1.367(a)-7(c)(2)(ii)(B) ($40x). The $10x described in § 1.367(a)-7(c)(2)(ii)(A) equals the product of the inside gain (as defined in § 1.367(a)-7(f)) ($10x) multiplied by DP's ownership interest percentage (as defined in § 1.367(a)-7(f)) (100%), reduced by the sum of the amounts in § 1.367(a)-7(c)(2)(ii)(A)(*1*), (c)(2)(ii)(A)(*2*), and (c)(2)(ii)(A)(*3*) ($0x). Under § 1.367(a)-7(f)(5), the $10x of inside gain is the amount by which the aggregate fair market value of the section 367(a) property (CFC2 stock with a fair market value of $40x) exceeds the sum of the inside basis ($30x) of such property, and $0x (the product of the section 367(a) percentage (100%) multiplied by DC's deductible liabilities assumed by CFC1 ($0x)). Under § 1.367(a)-7(f)(4), the $30x inside basis equals the aggregate basis of the section 367(a) property transferred in the section 361 exchange ($30x), increased by any gain or deemed dividends recognized by DC with respect to the section 367(a) property under section 367 ($0x). The $40x described in § 1.367(a)-7(c)(2)(ii)(B) is the product of the section 367(a) percentage (100%) multiplied by the fair market value of the 40 shares of CFC1 stock received by DC in the section 361 exchange and distributed to DP ($40x).

(C) Under section 358, DP must allocate the $180x basis in its 100 shares of DC stock between the 100 shares of DC stock (fair market value of $100x) and the 100 shares of CFC1 stock (fair market value of $100x) held after the distribution based on the relative fair market values of the shares. Accordingly, after the allocation of the basis under section 358, but prior to the application of § 1.367(a)-7(c)(3), the basis of DP's DC stock is $90x and the basis of DP's CFC1 stock is $90x. With respect to the $90x basis in the 100 shares of CFC1 stock, $36x is attributable to the 40 shares of CFC1 stock received by DC in the section 361 exchange ($90x multiplied by 40/100), and $54x is attributable to the 60 shares of CFC1 stock owned by DC prior to the section 361 exchange ($90x multiplied by 60/100). See § 1.358-2(a)(2)(iv).

(D) Pursuant to § 1.367(a)-7(c)(3)(ii), any adjustment to DP's basis in the CFC1 stock required under § 1.367(a)-7(c)(3)(i) can only be made with respect to the 40 shares of CFC1 stock received by DC in the section 361 exchange. Under § 1.367(a)-7(c)(3)(i)(A), DP must reduce its section 358 basis ($36x) in the 40 shares of CFC1 stock by $6x, the amount by which DP's attributable inside gain ($10x), reduced by the sum of the amounts in § 1.367(a)-7(c)(2)(ii)(A)(*1*), (c)(2)(ii)(A)(*2*), and (c)(2)(ii)(A)(*3*) ($0x) (as computed in paragraph (ii)(B) of this *Example 3*) exceeds DP's outside gain (as defined in § 1.367(a)-7(f)) ($4x). DP's $4x outside gain equals the product of the section 367(a) percentage (as defined in § 1.367(a)-7(f)) (100%) multiplied by the amount by which the fair market value ($40x) of the 40 shares of CFC1 stock is greater than DP's section 358 basis in the stock ($36x). After the $6x reduction to stock basis required under § 1.367(a)-7(c)(3), but before the application of § 1.1248(f)-2(c)(3), DP's basis in the 40 shares of CFC1 stock is $30x.

(E) DC's distribution of the 40 shares of newly issued CFC1 stock is subject to § 1.1248(f)-1(b)(3) (a new stock distribution). Except as provided in § 1.1248(f)-2(c), under § 1.1248(f)-1(b)(3) DC must include in gross income as a dividend the total section 1248(f) amount (as defined in § 1.1248(f)-1(c)(14)). The total section 1248(f) amount is $10x, the sum of the section 1248(f) amount (as defined in § 1.1248(f)-1(c)(10)) with respect to the stock of each foreign corporation transferred in the section 361 exchange. Only the CFC2 stock is transferred in the section 361 exchange; therefore, the total section 1248(f) amount is equal to the section 1248(f) amount with respect to the CFC2 stock ($10x). The $10x section 1248(f) amount with respect to the CFC2 stock is the amount that DC would have included in income as a deemed dividend under § 1.367(b)-4(b)(1)(i) with respect to the CFC2 stock if the requirements of § 1.367(b)-4(b)(1)(ii)(A) had not been satisfied ($10x), reduced by the amount of gain recognized by DC under § 1.367(a)-7(c)(2) allocable to the CFC2 stock and treated as a dividend under section 1248(a) (in this case, $0x, as described in paragraph (ii)(B) of this *Example 3*).

(F) However, because DC and DP (a section 1248 shareholder of CFC1 immediately after the distribution) elect to apply the provisions of § 1.1248(f)-2(c) (as provided in § 1.1248(f)-2(c)(*1*)), the amount that DC is required to include in income as a dividend under § 1.1248(f)-1(b)(3) ($10x total section 1248(f) amount as computed in paragraph (ii)(E) of this *Example 3*) is reduced by the sum of the portions of the section 1248(f) amount with respect to the CFC2 stock that is attributable (under the rules of § 1.1248(f)-2(d)) to the 40 shares of CFC1 stock distributed to DP. As stated in the facts, the election is made to apply § 1.1248(f)-2(c).

(*1*) Under paragraph (d)(1) of this section, the portion of the section 1248(f) amount with respect to the CFC2 stock that is attributed to the 40 shares of CFC1 stock distributed to DP is equal to DP's hypothetical section 1248 amount (as defined in § 1.1248(f)-1(c)(4)) with respect to the CFC2 stock. Because DP is the only shareholder of DC, DP's hypothetical section 1248 amount equals the section 1248(f) amount with respect to the CFC2 stock ($10x). The $10x hypothetical section 1248 amount is attributed pro rata (based on relative values) among the 40 shares of CFC1 stock distributed to DP, and the attributable share amount (as defined in paragraph (d)(1) of this section) is $.25x.

(2) The 40 shares of CFC1 stock are not divided into portions under paragraph (c)(2) of this section because the only property transferred by DC to CFC1 is a single block of stock of CFC2. If the 40 shares of CFC1 stock were required to be divided into portions, however, the rules of paragraph (d)(2) of this section apply to attribute the attributable share amount ($.25x) to portions of shares of CFC1 stock distributed to DP.

(3) Because the election under paragraph (c)(1) of this section is made, the total section 1248(f) amount ($10x) that DC is otherwise required to include in gross income as a dividend under § 1.1248(f)-1(b)(3) is reduced by $10x, the portion of the section 1248(f) amount with respect to the CFC2 stock that is attributable under paragraph (d) of this section to the 40 shares of CFC1 stock distributed to DP. Thus, the amount DC is required to include in gross income as a dividend under § 1.1248(f)-1(b)(3) is $0x ($30x less $30x).

(4) Under § 1.1248-8(b)(2)(iv), the $20x earnings and profits attributable to the single block of CFC2 stock are attributed pro rata to the 40 shares of CFC1 stock. Thus, DP's postdistribution amount (defined in § 1.1248(f)-1(c)(6)) with respect to the 40 shares of CFC1 stock attributable to the CFC2 stock is $10x, the lesser of the aggregate gain in the 40 shares of CFC1 stock of $10x ($40x fair market value, less $30x section 358 basis, as described in paragraph (ii)(D) of this *Example 3*) and the $20x earnings and profits attributable to such shares.

(5) Under paragraph (c)(3) of this section, DP's section 358 basis in the 40 shares of CFC1 stock ($30x) is reduced by the amount (if any) by which the section 1248(f) amount attributable to such shares under paragraph (d) of this section ($10x, as computed in paragraph (ii)(E) of this *Example 3*) exceeds DP's postdistribution amount with respect to such shares ($10x). Thus, there is no basis reduction in the 40 shares of CFC1 stock.

(G) Pursuant § 1.367(a)-3(e)(6), the amount of gain subject to the gain recognition agreement entered into by DP with respect to the CFC2 stock is $10x, which is the product of DP's ownership interest percentage (100%) multiplied by the gain realized by DC in the 361 exchange prior to taking into account the application of any other provision of section 367 ($10x), reduced by the sum of the amounts described in § 1.367(a)-3(e)(6)(i)(A), (e)(6)(i)(B), (e)(6)(i)(C), and (e)(6)(i)(D) ($0x).

(H) DC's distribution of the 60 shares of CFC1 stock it held before the section 361 exchange is subject to § 1.1248(f)-1(b)(2) (an existing stock distribution); however, because DC and DP make the election provided in paragraph (b)(1) of this section, § 1.1248(f)-1(b)(2) does not apply to the distribution.

(1) Under paragraph (b)(2) of this section, for purposes of section 1248, DP will have a 3-year holding period in the 60 shares of CFC1 stock received, the same holding period that DC had in the 60 shares of CFC1 stock.

(2) Under paragraph (b)(3) of this section, DP's section 358 basis in the 60 shares of CFC1 stock received ($54x, as computed in paragraph (ii)(C) of this *Example 3*) is reduced by $4x, the amount by which DC's section 1248 amount ($10x) with respect to the 60 shares of CFC1 stock exceeds DP's postdistribution amount ($6x) with respect to the 60 shares of CFC1 stock. Under § 1.1248(f)-1(c)(6), DP's postdistribution amount with respect to the 60 shares of CFC1 stock equals the amount that DP would include in gross income as a dividend under section 1248(a) if DP sold the 60 shares of CFC1 stock immediately after the distribution, or $6x, which is computed as the lesser of the $6x gain in the such shares of CFC1 stock ($60x fair market value, less $54x basis) and $30x of section 1248 earnings and profits attributable to the CFC1 stock, taking into account DP's 3-year holding period in the stock as required by paragraph (b)(2) of this section. As adjusted under paragraph (b)(3) of this section, DP's basis in the 60 shares of CFC1 stock is $50x ($54x basis, less $4x basis reduction).

(f) *Applicable cross-references.*—For rules relating to the attribution of earnings and profits to the stock of a foreign corporation following certain nonrecognition transactions, see § 1.1248-8. For rules relating to a transfer of property by a domestic corporation to a foreign corporation in a section 361 exchange that precedes a new stock distribution, see § 1.367(a)-7. If the property transferred includes stock of a corporation, see also §§ 1.367(a)-3(e) and 1.367(b)-4. For other rules that may apply if a domestic corporation distributes the stock of a foreign corporation in a new stock distribution or an existing stock distribution satisfying the requirements of section 355, see §§ 1.367(b)-5(b)(1) and 1.367(e)-1. [Reg. § 1.1248(f)-2.]

☐ [*T.D. 9614, 3-18-2013. Amended by T.D. 9760, 3-18-2016 and T.D. 9803, 12-15-2016.*]

§ 1.1248(f)-3. Reasonable cause and effective/applicability dates.—(a) *Reasonable cause for failure to comply.*—(1) *Request for relief.*—If an 80-percent distributee, a distributee that is a section 1248 shareholder, or the domestic distributing corporation (reporting person) fails to timely comply with any requirement under § 1.1248(f)-2, the failure shall be deemed not to have occurred if the reporting person is able to demonstrate that the failure was due to reasonable cause and not willful neglect using the procedure set forth in paragraph (a)(2) of this section. Whether the failure to timely comply was due to reasonable cause and not willful neglect will be determined by the Director of Field Operations, Cross Border Activities Practice Area of Large Business & International (Director) based on all the facts and circumstances.

(2) *Procedures for establishing that a failure to timely comply was due to reasonable cause and not willful neglect.*—(i) *Time of submission.*—A reporting person's statement that the failure to timely comply was due to reasonable cause and not willful neglect will be considered only if, promptly after the reporting person becomes aware of the failure, an amended return is filed for the taxable year to which the failure relates that includes the information that should have been included with the original return for such taxable year or that otherwise complies with the rules of this section, and that includes a written statement explaining the reasons for the failure to timely comply.

(ii) *Notice requirement.*—In addition to the requirements of paragraph (a)(2)(i) of this section, the reporting person must comply with the notice requirements of this paragraph (a)(2)(ii). If any taxable year of the reporting person is under examination when the amended return is filed, a copy of the amended return and any information required to be included with such return must be delivered to the Internal Revenue Service personnel conducting the examination. If no taxable year of the reporting person is under examination when the amended return is filed, a copy of the amended return and any information required to be included with such return must be delivered to the Director.

(b) *Effective/applicability date.*—(1) *General rule.*—Except as provided in paragraph (b)(2)(ii) of this section, §§ 1.1248(f)-1 and 1.1248(f)-2 apply to distributions occurring on or after April 18, 2013. The provisions of § 1.1248(f)-3(a) apply to distributions occurring on or after April 17, 2013.

(2) *Transactions described in Notice 87-64.*—(i) *Gain not otherwise recognized.*—For distributions occurring on or after September 21, 1987, and before April18, 2013, section 1248(f)(1) shall not apply to the extent the domestic distributing corporation recognizes gain with respect to the stock of the foreign distributed corporation as a result of the distribution under another provision of subtitle A of the Internal Revenue Code.

(ii) *Section 355 distributions.*—Taxpayers may apply the provisions of § 1.1248(f)-2(b) to distributions occurring on or after September 21, 1987. [Reg. § 1.1248(f)-3.]

☐ [*T.D. 9614, 3-18-2013. Amended by T.D. 9760, 3-18-2016.*]

§ 1.1249-1. Gain from certain sales or exchanges of patents, etc., to foreign corporations.—(a) *General rule.*—Section 1249 provides that if gain is recognized from the sale or exchange after December 31, 1962, of a patent, an invention, model, or design (whether or not patented), a copyright, a secret formula or process, or any other similar property right (not including property such as goodwill, a trademark, or a trade brand) to any foreign corporation by any United States person (as defined in section 7701(a)(30)) which controls such foreign corporation, and if such gain would (but for the provisions of section 1249) be gain from the sale or exchange of a capital asset or of property described in section 1231, then such gain shall be considered as gain from the sale or exchange of property which is neither a capital asset nor property described in section 1231. Section 1249 applies only to gain recognized in taxable years beginning after December 31, 1962.

(b) *Control.*—For purposes of paragraph (a) of this section, the term "control" means, with respect to any foreign corporation, the ownership, directly or indirectly, of stock possessing more than 50 percent of the total combined voting power of all classes of stock entitled to vote. For purposes of the preceding sentence, the rules for determining ownership of stock provided by section 958(a) and (b), and the principles for determining percentage of total combined voting power owned by United States shareholders provided by paragraphs (b) and (c) of § 1.957-1, shall apply. [Reg. § 1.1249-1.]

☐ [*T.D. 6765, 11-2-64.*]

Proposed Regulation

§ 1.1256(g)-2. Foreign currency contract defined.—(a) *Foreign currency contract.*—For purposes of section 1256, the term *foreign currency contract* means a forward contract that—

(1) Requires delivery of, or the settlement of which depends on the value of, a foreign currency that is a currency in which positions are also traded through regulated futures contracts;

(2) Is traded in the interbank market; and

(3) Is entered into at arm's length at a price determined by reference to the price in the interbank market.

(b) *Applicability date.*—This section applies to contracts entered into on or after [date 30 days after date of publication of the final rule in the **Federal Register**]. [Prop. Reg. § 1.1256(g)-2.]

[Proposed 7-6-2022.]

Passive Foreign Investment Companies

§ 1.1291-1. Taxation of U.S. persons that are shareholders of section 1291 funds.—(a) through (b)(2)(i) [Reserved].

(b)(2)(ii) *Pedigreed QEF.*—A PFIC is a *pedigreed QEF* with respect to a shareholder if the PFIC has been a QEF with respect to the shareholder for all taxable years during which the corporation was a PFIC that are included wholly or partly in the shareholder's holding period of the PFIC stock.

(iii) through (iv) [Reserved].

(v) *Section 1291 fund.*—A PFIC is a *section 1291 fund* with respect to a shareholder unless the PFIC is a pedigreed QEF with respect to the shareholder or a section 1296 election is in effect with respect to the shareholder.

(b)(3) through (6) [Reserved].

(7) *Shareholder.*—A *shareholder* is a United States person that directly owns stock of a PFIC (a direct shareholder), or that is an indirect shareholder (as defined in section 1298(a) and paragraph (b)(8) of this section), except as provided in paragraph (e) of this section. For purposes of sections 1291 and 1298, a domestic partnership or S corporation (as defined in section 1361(a)(1)) is not treated as a shareholder of a PFIC except for purposes of any information reporting requirements, including the requirement to file an annual report under section 1298(f). In addition, to the extent that a person is treated under sections 671 through 678 as the owner of a portion of a domestic trust, the trust is not treated as a shareholder of a PFIC with respect to PFIC stock held by that portion of the trust, except for purposes of the information reporting requirements of § 1.1298-1(b)(3)(i) (imposing an information reporting requirement on domestic liquidating trusts and fixed investment trusts).

(8) *Indirect shareholder.*—(i) *In general.*—An *indirect shareholder* of a PFIC is a United States person that indirectly owns stock of a PFIC. A person indirectly owns stock when it is treated as owning stock of a corporation owned by another person, including another United States person, under this paragraph (b)(8). In applying this paragraph (b)(8), the determination of a person's indirect ownership is made on the basis of all the facts and circumstances in each case; the substance rather than the form of ownership is controlling, taking into account the purposes of sections 1291 through 1298.

(ii) *Ownership through a corporation.*—(A) *Ownership through a non-PFIC foreign corporation.*—A person that directly or indirectly owns 50 percent or more in value of the stock of a foreign corporation that is not a PFIC is considered to own a proportionate amount (by value) of any stock owned directly or indirectly by the foreign corporation.

(B) *Ownership through a PFIC.*—A person that directly or indirectly owns stock of a PFIC is considered to own a proportionate amount (by value) of any stock owned directly or indirectly by the PFIC. Section 1297(d) does not apply in determining whether a corporation is a PFIC for purposes of this paragraph (b)(8)(ii)(B).

(C) *Ownership through a domestic corporation.*—*(1) In general.*—Solely for purposes of determining whether a person satisfies the ownership threshold described in paragraph (b)(8)(ii)(A) of this section, a person that directly or indirectly owns 50 percent or more in value of the stock of a domestic corporation is considered to own a proportionate amount (by value) of any stock owned directly or indirectly by the domestic corporation.

(2) Non-duplication.—Paragraph (b)(8)(ii)(C)*(1)* of this section does not apply to treat a United States person as owning (other than for purposes of applying the ownership threshold in paragraph (b)(8)(ii)(A) of this section) stock of a PFIC that is directly owned or considered owned indirectly within the meaning of this paragraph (b)(8) by another United States person (determined without regard to paragraph (b)(8)(ii)(C)*(1)*). See *Example 1* of paragraph (b)(8)(iv) of this section.

(3) S corporations.—The 50 percent limitation in paragraph (b)(8)(ii)(C)*(1)* of this section does not apply with respect to stock owned directly or indirectly by an S corporation. See paragraph (b)(8)(iii)(B) of this section for rules regarding stock owned directly or indirectly by an S corporation.

(iii) *Ownership through pass-through entities.*—(A) *Partnerships.*—If a foreign or domestic partnership directly or indirectly owns stock, the partners of the partnership are considered to own such stock proportionately in accordance with their ownership interests in the partnership.

(B) *S Corporations.*—If an S corporation directly or indirectly owns stock, each S corporation shareholder is considered to own such stock proportionately in accordance with the shareholder's ownership interest in the S corporation.

(C) *Estates and nongrantor trusts.*—If a foreign or domestic estate or nongrantor trust (other than an employees' trust described in section 401(a) that is exempt from tax under section 501(a)) directly or indirectly owns stock, each beneficiary of the estate or trust is considered to own a proportionate amount of such stock. For purposes of this paragraph (b)(8)(iii)(C), a nongrantor trust is any trust or portion of a trust that is not treated as owned by one or more persons under sections 671 through 679.

(D) *Grantor trusts.*—If a foreign or domestic trust directly or indirectly owns stock, a person that is treated under sections 671 through 679 as the owner of any portion of the trust that holds an interest in the stock is considered to own the interest in the stock held by that portion of the trust.

(iv) *Successive application.*—Stock considered to be owned by a person by reason of paragraphs (b)(8)(ii) or (iii) is of this section, for purposes of applying such paragraphs, considered to be actually owned by such person. Subject to the limitations provided in section 1298(a) and paragraphs (b)(8)(ii) and (b)(8)(iii) of this section, this paragraph applies by successively considering a person as actually owning its proportionate share of stock or other equity interest directly held by an entity directly owned by the person. Paragraph (b)(8)(ii)(C)*(2)* of this section applies after the other subparagraphs of paragraph (b)(8) of this section.

(v) *Examples.*—The rules of this paragraph (b)(8) are illustrated by the following examples:

(A) *Example 1.*—*(1) Facts.* A is a United States person who owns 49% of the stock of FC1, a foreign corporation that is not a PFIC, and separately all of the stock of DC, a domestic corporation that is not an S corporation. DC, in turn, owns the remaining 51% of the stock of FC1, and FC1 owns 100 shares of stock in a PFIC that is not a controlled foreign corporation (CFC) within the meaning of section 957(a). The remainder of the PFIC's shares are owned by unrelated foreign persons.

(2) Results—*(i) Treatment of DC.* Under paragraph (b)(8)(ii)(A) of this section, DC is considered to actually own 51 shares of the PFIC stock directly held by FC1 because DC directly owns 50% or more of the stock of FC1.

(ii) Treatment of A. In determining whether A is considered to own 50% or more of the value of FC1 for purposes of applying

paragraphs (b)(8)(ii)(A) and (b)(8)(iv) of this section to the PFIC stock held through FC1, A is considered under paragraphs (b)(8)(ii)(C)(*1*) and (b)(8)(iv) of this section as indirectly owning all the stock of FC1 that DC directly owns, before the application of paragraph (b)(8)(ii)(C)(*2*) of this section. Because A also directly owns 49% of the stock of FC1, before the application of paragraph (b)(8)(ii)(C)(2) of this section A would be treated as owning all 100 shares of PFIC stock held by FC1. However, because 51 shares of the PFIC stock held by FC1 are indirectly owned by DC under paragraph (b)(8)(ii)(A) of this section, pursuant to the limitation imposed by paragraph (b)(8)(ii)(C)(2) of this section, only the remaining 49 shares of the PFIC stock are considered as indirectly owned by A under paragraph (b)(8) of this section.

(B) *Example 2.*—(*1*) *Facts.* B, a United States citizen, owns 50% of the interests in Foreign Partnership, a foreign partnership treated as a partnership for U.S. federal income tax purposes, the remaining interests in which are owned by an unrelated foreign person. Foreign Partnership owns 100% of the stock of FC1 and 50% of the stock of FC2, the remainder of which is owned by an unrelated foreign person. Both FC1 and FC2 are foreign corporations that are not PFICs. FC1 and FC2 each own 50% of the stock of FC3, a foreign corporation that is a PFIC.

(2) *Results.* Under paragraphs (b)(8)(iii)(A) and (b)(8)(iv) of this section, for purposes of determining whether B is a shareholder of FC3, B is considered to actually own 50% (50% x 100%) of the stock of FC1 and 25% (50% x 50%) of the stock of FC2. Under paragraphs (b)(8)(ii)(A) and (b)(8)(iv) of this section, B is then considered to own 25% (50% x 100% x 50%) of the stock of FC3 indirectly through FC1, and thus is a shareholder of FC3 for purposes of the PFIC provisions. Because B is considered to own less than 50% of FC2, B is not considered to own any stock of FC3 indirectly through FC2.

(C) *Example 3.*—(*1*) *Facts.* The facts are the same as in paragraph (b)(8)(v)(B)(*1*) of this section (the facts in *Example 2*), except that B owns 40% of the interests in Foreign Partnership.

(2) *Results.* Under paragraph (b)(8)(iii)(A) and (b)(8)(iv) of this section, for purposes of determining whether B is a shareholder of FC3, B is considered to actually own 40% (40% x 100%) of the stock of FC1 and 20% (40% x 50%) of the stock of FC2, and thus is not considered to own 50% or more of the stock of FC1 or FC2. Under paragraphs (b)(8)(ii)(A) and (b)(8)(iv) of this section, B is not considered to own any stock of FC3 indirectly through FC1 or FC2.

(D) *Example 4.*—(*1*) *Facts.* The facts are the same as in paragraph (b)(8)(v)(C)(*1*) of this section (the facts in *Example 3*), except that FP owns only 80% of FC1 and B also directly owns 20% of FC1.

(2) *Results.* Under paragraph (b)(8)(iii)(A) and (b)(8)(iv) of this section, for purposes of determining whether B is a shareholder of FC3, B is considered to own 32% (40% x 80%) of the stock of FC1 and 20% (40% x 50%) of the stock of FC2. Because B directly owns 20% of FC1, B is considered to actually own 52% (32% + 20%) of the stock of FC1 in total. Under paragraphs (b)(8)(ii)(A) and (b)(8)(iv) of this section, B is considered to own 26% (52% x 50%) of the stock of FC3 indirectly through FC1, and thus is a shareholder of FC3 for purposes of the PFIC provisions. B is not considered to own any stock of FC3 indirectly through FC2.

(c) *Coordination with other PFIC rules.*

(1) and (2) [Reserved].

(3) *Coordination with section 1296: distributions and dispositions.*—If PFIC stock is marked to market under section 1296 for any taxable year, then, except as provided in §1.1296-1(i), section 1291 and the regulations thereunder shall not apply to any distribution with respect to section 1296 stock (as defined in §1.1296-1(a)(2)), or to any disposition of such stock, for such taxable year.

(4) *Coordination with mark to market rules under chapter 1 of the Internal Revenue Code other than section 1296.*—(i) *In general.*—If PFIC stock is marked to market for any taxable year under section 475 or any other provision of chapter 1 of the Internal Revenue Code, other than section 1296, regardless of whether the application of such provision is mandatory or results from an election by the taxpayer or another person, then, except as provided in paragraph (c)(4)(ii) of this section, section 1291 and the regulations thereunder shall not apply to any distribution with respect to such PFIC stock or to any disposition of such PFIC stock for such taxable year. See §§1.1295-1(i)(3) and 1.1296-1(h)(3)(i) for rules regarding the automatic termination of an existing election under section 1295 or section 1296 when a taxpayer marks to market PFIC stock under section 475 or any other provision of chapter 1 of the Internal Revenue Code.

(ii) *Coordination rule.*—(A) Notwith-standing any provision in this section to the contrary, the rule of paragraph (c)(4)(ii)(B) of this section shall apply to the first taxable year in which a United States person marks to market its PFIC stock under a provision of chapter 1 of the Internal Revenue Code, other than section 1296, if such foreign corporation was a PFIC for any taxable year, prior to such first taxable year, during the United States person's holding period (as defined in section 1291(a)(3)(A) and §1.1296-1(f)) in such stock, and for which such corporation was not treated as a QEF with respect to such United States person.

(B) For the first taxable year of a United States person that marks to market its PFIC stock under any provision of chapter 1 of the Internal Revenue Code, other than section 1296, such United States person shall, in lieu of the rules under which the United States person marks to market, apply the rules of §1.1296-1(i)(2) and (3) as if the United States person had made an election under section 1296 for such first taxable year.

(d) [Reserved].

(e) *Exempt organization as shareholder.*—(1) *In general.*—If the shareholder of a PFIC is an organization exempt from tax under this chapter, section 1291 and these regulations apply to such shareholder only if a dividend from the PFIC would be taxable to the organization under subchapter F.

(2) *Ownership through certain tax-exempt organizations and accounts.*—To the extent a United States person owns stock of a PFIC through an organization or account described in §1.1298-1(c)(1), that person is not treated as a shareholder with respect to the PFIC stock.

(f) through (i) [Reserved].

(j) *Applicability dates.*—(1) Paragraphs (c)(3) and (4) of this section apply for taxable years beginning on or after May 3, 2004.

(2) Paragraph (e)(1) of this section is applicable on and after April 1, 1992.

(3) Except as otherwise provided in paragraph (j)(4) of this section, paragraphs (b)(2)(ii) and (v), (b)(7) and (8), and (e)(2) of this section apply to taxable years of shareholders ending on or after December 31, 2013.

(4) Paragraphs (b)(8)(iv) and (b)(8)(v)(A), (B), (C), and (D) of this section apply for taxable years of shareholders beginning on or after January 14, 2021. A shareholder may choose to apply such paragraphs for any open taxable year beginning before January 14, 2021, provided that, with respect to a tested foreign corporation, the shareholder consistently applies such paragraphs and the provisions of §§1.1297-1 (except that consistent treatment is not required with respect to §1.1297-1(c)(1)(i)(A)), 1.1297-2, 1.1297-4, 1.1297-6, 1.1298-2, and 1.1298-4 for such year and all subsequent years. [Reg. §1.1291-1.]

☐ [*T.D. 8750, 12-31-97. Redesignated by T.D. 8870, 2-4-2000. Amended by T.D. 9123, 4-30-2004, T.D. 9806, 12-27-2016 and T.D. 9936, 1-14-2021.*]

Proposed Regulation

§1.1291-1. Taxation of U.S. persons that are shareholders of section 1291 funds.—(a) *In general.*—A U.S. person that is a shareholder (within the meaning of paragraph (b)(7) of this section) of a section 1291 fund (as defined in paragraph (b)(2)(v) of this section) is subject to the special rules under section 1291 and these regulations with respect to gain recognized on direct and indirect dispositions of stock of the section 1291 fund and upon certain direct and indirect distributions by the section 1291 fund. This section provides definitions and rules applicable to all PFICs and their shareholders. For rules governing the taxation of distributions and dispositions, *see* §§1.1291-2 and 1.1291-3, respectively. For rules governing the determination of the deferred tax amount, *see* §1.1291-4. For rules governing the determination of the foreign tax credit that a shareholder of a section 1291 fund may claim on distributions and certain dispositions, *see* §1.1291-5. For rules governing the recognition of gain on a direct or indirect disposition of stock of a section 1291 fund notwithstanding an otherwise applicable nonrecognition provision, *see* §1.1291-6. For guidance for regulated investment companies making a mark-to-market election, *see* §1.1291-8. For the time and manner of making the deemed sale and dividend elections under section 1291(d)(2), *see* §§1.1291-9 and 1.1291-10, respectively.

(b) *Definitions.*—(1) *PFIC.*—(i) *In general.*—A passive foreign investment company (PFIC) is a foreign corporation that satisfies either the income test of section 1296(a)(1) or the asset test of section 1296(a)(2). A corporation will not be treated as a PFIC with respect to a shareholder for those days included in the shareholder's holding period before the shareholder became a United States person within the meaning of section 7701(a)(30).

(ii) *PFIC characterization continued.*—A corporation will be treated as a PFIC with respect to a shareholder even if the corporation satisfies neither the income test nor the asset test of section 1296(a), if the corporation (or its predecessor in a reorganization described in section 368(a)(1)(F)) was a section 1291 fund with respect to the shareholder at any time during the shareholder's holding period of the corporation's stock.

(2) *Types of PFICs.*—(i) *QEF.*—A PFIC is a qualified electing fund (QEF) with respect to a shareholder that has elected under section 1295 to be taxed currently on its share of the PFIC's earnings and profits pursuant to section 1293.

(ii) [Withdrawn by REG-113350-13 on December 31, 2013.]

(iii) *Unpedigreed QEF.*—A PFIC is an unpedigreed QEF for a taxable year if—

(A) An election under section 1295 is in effect for that year;

(B) The PFIC has been a QEF with respect to the shareholder for at least one, but not all, of the taxable years that are included wholly or partly in the shareholder's holding period of the PFIC stock and during which the corporation was a PFIC; and

(C) The shareholder has not made an election under section 1291(d)(2) and § 1.1291-9 or 1.1291-10 with respect to the PFIC to purge the prior PFIC years from the shareholder's holding period.

For the effect on a shareholder's holding period of an election under section 1291(d)(2), *see* §§ 1.1291-9(f) and 1.1291-10(f).

(iv) *Nonqualified fund.*—A PFIC is a nonqualified fund with respect to a shareholder if the shareholder has not elected under section 1295 to treat the PFIC as a QEF.

(v) [Withdrawn by REG-113350-13 on December 31, 2013.]

(3) *PrePFIC year and day.*—A prePFIC year is a taxable year (or portion thereof) of the shareholder, included in its holding period of the stock of a corporation, during which the corporation was not a PFIC within the meaning of paragraph (b)(1) of this section. A prePFIC day is a day in a prePFIC year of the shareholder. Thus, the days in a taxable year of a shareholder beginning after 1986 that are included in a taxable year of the corporation that began before 1987 are prePFIC days.

(4) *Prior PFIC year and day.*—A prior PFIC year is a taxable year (or portion thereof) of a shareholder, other than the current shareholder year, included in its holding period of stock of a corporation during which the corporation was a section 1291 fund. A prior PFIC day is a day in a prior PFIC year of a shareholder.

(5) *Current shareholder year.*—The current shareholder year is the taxable year of the shareholder in which occurs a distribution by, or disposition of stock of, a section 1291 fund.

(6) *Stock.*—The term stock includes any equity interest in a corporation, without regard to whether there is a certificate or other representation of the equity interest in the corporation. For a rule that treats an option holder as a shareholder of a section 1291 fund, *see* § 1.1291-1(d).

(7) [Withdrawn by REG-113350-13 on December 31, 2013.]

(8) [Withdrawn by REG-113350-13 on December 31, 2013.]

(c) *Coordination with QEF rules.*—(1) *Pedigreed QEFs.*—Section 1291 and these regulations do not apply to direct and indirect distributions by, and direct and indirect dispositions of stock of, a PFIC that, with respect to the shareholder, is a pedigreed QEF as defined in paragraph (b)(2)(ii) of this section.

(2) *Unpedigreed QEFs.*—Section 1291 and these regulations apply to direct and indirect distributions by, and direct and indirect dispositions of stock of, a PFIC that, with respect to the shareholder, is an unpedigreed QEF, as defined in paragraph (b)(2)(iii) of this section. For the treatment under section 1291 and these regulations of inclusions in income under section 1293(a) and distributions of amounts not includible in income by reason of section 1293(c), *see* § 1.1291-2(b)(2).

(d) *Option holder as shareholder.*—If a U.S. person has an option to acquire stock of a PFIC (other than stock with respect to which the PFIC is a pedigreed QEF), such option is considered to be stock of a section 1291 fund for purposes of applying section 1291 and these regulations to a disposition of the option. For purposes of this paragraph (d), the exercise of an option is not a disposition to which section 1291 applies. For purposes of this paragraph (d), an option to acquire an option, and each one of a series of such options, are considered an option to acquire stock. For the holding period of stock acquired upon the exercise of an option, *see* § 1.1291-1(h)(3).

(e) *Exempt organization as shareholder.*—If the shareholder of a section 1291 fund is an organization exempt from tax under this chapter, section 1291 and these regulations apply to such shareholder only if a dividend from the section 1291 fund would be taxable to the organization under subchapter F.

(f) *Excess distribution from sources within Puerto Rico.*—A deferred tax amount, as defined in § 1.1291-4, will be determined under section 1291 and these regulations on amounts derived from sources within Puerto Rico (within the meaning of section 933(1)) by an individual shareholder who is a bona fide resident of Puerto Rico, but only to the extent such amounts are allocated under § 1.1291-2(e)(2) to a taxable year in the shareholder's holding period during which the shareholder was not entitled to the benefits of section 933.

(g) *Regulated investment companies and real estate investment trusts.*—A regulated investment company, as defined in section 851, and a real estate investment trust, as defined in section 856, that are shareholders of a section 1291 fund are taxable under section 1291 and these regulations on direct or indirect distributions from a section 1291 fund and on direct or indirect dispositions of the stock of a section 1291 fund, and are therefore liable for the deferred tax amount, as defined in section 1291(c) and § 1.1291-4. For a mark-to-market election that may be made by a regulated investment company that is a shareholder of a section 1291 fund, *see* § 1.1291-8.

(h) *Holding period.*—(1) *In general.*—Except as otherwise provided in this paragraph (h), § 1.1291-6(b)(5), 1.1291-9(f), or 1.1291-10(f), a shareholder's holding period of stock of a PFIC is determined under the general rules of the Code and regulations concerning the holding period of stock. The following example illustrates the rule of this paragraph (h)(1).

Example. T purchased the stock of FC, a foreign corporation, on December 31, 1985. FC has qualified as a PFIC since its taxable year beginning January 1, 1987. For purposes of sections 1291 through 1297 and the regulations under those sections, as well as other provisions of the Code and regulations, T's holding period of the FC stock began on January 1, 1986.

(2) *Stock acquired from U.S. decedent or domestic estate.*—For purposes of section 1291 and these regulations, a shareholder's holding period of a share of stock of a PFIC includes the period the share was held by another U.S. person if the shareholder acquired the share by reason of the death of that other U.S. person (the decedent), the PFIC was a section 1291 fund with respect to the decedent, and the decedent did not recognize gain pursuant to § 1.1291-6(c)(2)(iii) (or would not have recognized gain had there been any) on the transfer to the shareholder.

(3) *Stock acquired upon exercise of option.*—The holding period of a share of stock of a PFIC acquired upon the exercise of an option includes the period the option was held. The following example illustrates the rule of this paragraph (h)(3).

Example. X is a domestic corporation that owns all of the stock of Y, a PFIC. On January 1, 1993, X issues a debt instrument to G, a U.S. person. Under the terms of the instrument, G may convert the debt instrument into 20 shares of the stock of Y on any date prior to the maturity date of December 31, 2002. On August 14, 1997, G exercises the conversion right and receives 20 shares of Y stock. Pursuant to § 1.1291-1(h)(3), G's holding period of the Y stock begins at the time of the acquisition of the debt instrument, not at the time of acquisition of the Y stock.

(4) *Stock owned directly and indirectly.*—(i) *In general.*—Except as provided in paragraph (h)(2), (3), (4)(ii), (5), or (6) of this section, 1.1291-6(b)(5), 1.1291-9(f), or 1.1291-10(f), a shareholder's holding period of stock of a PFIC owned indirectly begins on the first day that a shareholder is considered to own stock of the PFIC (or of another PFIC that was a predecessor of that PFIC) under

§ 1.1291-1(b)(8). If a shareholder has owned a share of stock of a PFIC both directly and indirectly, the shareholder's holding period of that share begins on the earlier of—

(A) The first day that the shareholder owned the stock of the PFIC directly; or

(B) The first day that the shareholder was an indirect shareholder with respect to the share of stock of the PFIC (or of another PFIC that was a predecessor of that PFIC).

(ii) *Examples.*—The following examples illustrate the operation of the rule of paragraph (h)(4)(i) of this section.

Example 1. A's holding period of stock of X began on August 14, 1990. X is a corporation that always has been an S corporation. At the time A acquired the X stock, X held stock of FC, a PFIC. For purposes of sections 1291 through 1297, A's holding period of the FC stock began on August 14, 1990, even though X's holding period of that stock began on an earlier day.

Example 2. B, a U.S. person, owns all the stock of FP, a foreign corporation that is not a PFIC; under section 1223, B's holding period of the FP stock began on August 1, 1987. FP owns 50 percent of the stock of FS, a foreign corporation that is not a PFIC; FP's holding period of the FS stock began on December 13, 1987. FS owns 10 percent of FC, a PFIC; under section 1223, FS's holding period of the FC stock began on November 20, 1986. For purposes of section 1291, B's holding period of the FC stock began on December 13, 1987, the first day that ownership of the FC stock is attributed to B under § 1.1291-1(b)(8).

(iii) *Section 1291 fund stock held by former C corporation.*—For purposes of § 1.1291-2(e)(2)(i), if an S corporation's holding period of stock of a section 1291 fund includes any period during which the S corporation was a C corporation, the S corporation shareholder's holding period is the S corporation's holding period of such stock.

(5) *New holding period.*—If a shareholder recognizes all of the gain realized on a direct or indirect disposition of stock of a section 1291 fund, within the meaning of § 1.1291-3(c), (d), or (e), but continues to be a shareholder with respect to such stock immediately after such disposition, the shareholder's holding period for such stock will be treated as beginning on the day after the disposition. For an illustration of this rule as applied to a disposition pursuant to § 1.1291-3(d) (regarding pledged stock), *see* § 1.1291-3(d)(7), *Example 1.*

(6) *Stock transferred to a member of a consolidated return group.*—For the holding period of stock of a section 1291 fund transferred from one member of a consolidated return group to another member of the group for purposes of § 1.1291-2(e)(2)(i), *see* § 1.1291-3(f).

(7) *PFIC character of holding period.*—(i) *In general.*—If a shareholder's holding period of stock of a PFIC includes a period described in section 1223(1), the character of the days in such latter period as prePFIC or prior PFIC days is determined by reference to the character of those days in the shareholder's holding period immediately prior to the exchange. If a shareholder's holding period of stock of a PFIC includes a period described in section 1223(2), the character of the days in such latter period as prePFIC or prior PFIC days is determined by reference to the character, immediately prior to the transfer, of those days in the holding period of the person from whom the stock was acquired.

(ii) *Anti-avoidance rule.*—If a shareholder's holding period of stock of a PFIC includes a period described in section 1223(1), the character of the days in such latter period will be deemed to be prior PFIC days if a purpose for the exchange described in section 1223(1) was avoidance of the interest charge rules under section 1291.

(i) [Withdrawn by REG-113350-13 on December 31, 2013.]

(j) *Effective date.*—(1) *In general.*—Except as otherwise provided in this paragraph (j), §§ 1.1291-1 through 1.1291-9 and the new parts of § 1.1291-10 are effective on April 11, 1992. However, sections 1291 through 1297, inclusive, are effective for taxable years of foreign corporations beginning after December 31, 1986. Accordingly, shareholders of PFICs are subject to sections 1291 through 1297 with respect to transactions occurring within those taxable years. Shareholders of section 1291 funds, in determining their liability under sections 1291 through 1297 during those years, must apply reasonable interpretations of the statute and legislative history and employ reasonable methods to preserve the interest charge.

(2) *Section 1.1291-3(d)(6).*—For purposes of applying section 1297(b)(6), concerning a disposition resulting from the use of PFIC stock as security for a loan, the transition rule provided in § 1.1291-3(d)(6) is effective for taxable years of foreign corporations beginning after 1986.

(3) *Section 1.1291-8.*—Section 1.1291-8 is effective for taxable years of RICs ending after [*INSERT DATE OF PUBLICATION OF THIS DOCUMENT AS A FINAL REGULATION*]. [Prop. Reg. § 1.1291-1.]

[Proposed 4-1-92 (partial withdrawals 12-31-2013).]

Proposed Amendments to Regulation

§ 1.1291-1. Taxation of U.S. persons that are shareholders of section 1291 funds.—

***

(b) ***

(7) *Shareholder.*—Except as otherwise provided in this paragraph (b)(7) or paragraph (e) of this section, a shareholder of a PFIC is a United States person that directly owns stock of a PFIC (a direct shareholder), or that is an indirect shareholder (as defined in paragraph (b)(8) of this section). Notwithstanding the previous sentence, neither a domestic partnership nor an S corporation (as defined in section 1361(a)(1)) is treated as a shareholder of a PFIC. In addition, to the extent that a person is treated under sections 671 through sections 678 as the owner of a portion of a domestic trust, the trust is not treated as a shareholder of a PFIC with respect to PFIC stock held by that portion of the trust, except for purposes of the information reporting requirements of § 1.1298-1(b)(3)(i) (imposing an information reporting requirement on domestic liquidating trusts and fixed investment trusts).

***

(c) ***

(4) ***

(i) *In general.*—If PFIC stock is marked to market for any taxable year under section 475 or any other provision of chapter 1 of the Internal Revenue Code, other than section 1296, regardless of whether the application of such provision is mandatory or results from an election by the shareholder (as defined in paragraph (b)(7) of this section) or another person, then, except as provided in paragraph (c)(4)(ii) of this section, section 1291 and the regulations in this part thereunder do not apply to any distribution with respect to such PFIC stock or to any disposition of such PFIC stock for such taxable year. See §§ 1.1295-1(i)(3) and 1.1296-1(h)(3)(i) for rules regarding the automatic termination of an existing election under section 1295 or section 1296 when a shareholder marks to market PFIC stock under section 475 or any other provision of chapter 1 of the Internal Revenue Code.

(ii) ***

(A) Notwithstanding any provision in this section to the contrary, with respect to a shareholder (as defined in paragraph (b)(7) of this section), the rule of paragraph (c)(4)(ii)(B) of this section applies to the first taxable year in which the shareholder's PFIC stock is marked to market under a provision of chapter 1 of the Internal Revenue Code, other than section 1296, if such foreign corporation was a PFIC for any taxable year before the taxable year in which the PFIC stock is marked to market, which is during the shareholder's holding period (as defined in section 1291(a)(3)(A) and § 1.1296-1(f)) in such stock, and for which such corporation was not treated as a QEF with respect to such shareholder.

(B) For the first taxable year of a shareholder in which the shareholder's PFIC stock is marked to market under any provision of chapter 1 of the Internal Revenue Code, other than section 1296, such shareholder, in lieu of the rules under which the stock is marked to market, applies the rules of § 1.1296-1(i)(2) and (3) as if an election had been made under section 1296 for such first taxable year.

(5) *Coordination with section 1297(d).*—(i) *In general.*—For purposes of section 1297(d), with respect to a partner or S corporation shareholder that would be considered an indirect shareholder, through its ownership in a domestic partnership or S corporation, with respect to a foreign corporation that is a PFIC and a controlled foreign corporation (as defined in section 957), the term "qualified portion" does not include any portion of such indirect shareholder's holding period during which it was not a United States shareholder (as defined in section 951(b)) with respect to the foreign corporation.

(ii) *Transition rule.*—For taxable years of shareholders beginning before [date of publication of the Treasury decision adopting these rules as final regulations in the **Federal Register**], or for taxable years of shareholders of an S corporation in which the S corporation elects to apply § 1.958-1(e), for purposes of section 1297(d), a partner's or S corporation shareholder's qualified portion with respect to the foreign corporation includes the portion of its holding period during which it—

(A) Is an indirect shareholder under paragraph (b)(8)(iii)(A) or (B) of this section with respect to the foreign corporation; and

(B) Included in gross income its distributive or pro rata share of any amount that the domestic partnership or S corporation, respectively, included under sections 951(a)(1) and 951A(a) with respect to stock in the foreign corporation (treating the requirement in this paragraph (c)(5)(ii)(B) as not satisfied to the extent § 1.958-1(d)(1) through (3) is applied with respect to the domestic partnership or S corporation before their general applicability date under § 1.958-1(d)(4) or the domestic partnership or S corporation relied on the earlier proposed version of such provisions). See, for example, § 1.951A-1(e)(2).

* * *

(j) * * *

(5) Paragraphs (b)(7), (c)(4)(i), (c)(4)(ii)(A) and (B), and (c)(5) of this section apply to taxable years of shareholders beginning on or after [date of publication of the Treasury decision adopting these rules as final regulations in the **Federal Register**].

For taxable years of shareholders beginning before [date of publication of the Treasury decision adopting these rules as final regulations in the **Federal Register**], see § 1.1291-1(b)(7), (c)(4)(i), and (c)(4)(ii)(A) and (B) as in effect and contained in 26 CFR part 1, as revised April 1, 2021. [Prop. Reg. § 1.1291-1.]

[Proposed 1-25-2022.]

Proposed Regulation

§ 1.1291-2. Taxation of distributions by section 1291 funds.—(a) *In general.*—Notwithstanding section 301 and the regulations under that section, a shareholder is subject to the rules of section 1291, this section, and § 1.1291-4 with respect to a distribution (including an indirect distribution as defined in paragraph (f) of this section) by a section 1291 fund, if any portion of such distribution is an excess distribution. An excess distribution is defined in paragraph (c)(1) of this section. Under paragraph (e)(2)(i) of this section, the excess distribution is allocated ratably over the shareholder's holding period of the stock of the section 1291 fund. The portions of the excess distribution allocated to the current shareholder year and to prePFIC years are included in the shareholder's gross income as ordinary income in the current shareholder year under paragraph (e)(2)(ii) of this section. The portions of the excess distribution allocated to prior PFIC years are not included in the shareholder's gross income pursuant to paragraph (e)(2)(iii) of this section. Instead, the shareholder incurs tax plus interest (the deferred tax amount) on those portions of the excess distribution, as provided in § 1.1291-4.

(b) *Distribution.*—(1) *In general.*—For purposes of section 1291 and these regulations, unless otherwise provided in this paragraph (b), a distribution is any actual or constructive transfer of money or property by a section 1291 fund with respect to its stock. For example, a distribution includes a transfer of stock taxable pursuant to section 305(b) and (c), a transfer in redemption of stock taxable under section 301 pursuant to section 302(d), and an amount treated as a dividend under section 78. A distribution, however, does not include a transfer that qualifies under section 305(a) or 355(a). Transfers with respect to stock that are treated as dispositions of the stock under § 1.1291-3 are not treated as distributions under this section. For transfers with respect to stock (including transfers that qualify under section 355(a)) that are treated as dispositions, *see* § 1.1291-3.

(2) *Coordination with current inclusion rules.*—(i) *Deemed dividend or income inclusions; distributions of previously taxed amounts.*—Amounts included in gross income under section 551(a), 951(a), or 1293(a), and transfers of amounts not included in gross income by reason of section 551(d), 959, or 1293(c), are not treated as distributions for purposes of this section. The following example illustrates the rule of this paragraph (b)(2)(i).

Example. USP, a domestic corporation, purchased in 1989 10 percent of the stock of FC, a section 1291 fund that also is a CFC. Both USP and FC use the calendar year as their taxable year. In 1989, USP, pursuant to section 951(a)(1), included in income $100 of subpart F income of FC, none of which was distributed in 1989. The $100 of subpart F income is not treated as a distribution taxable under section 1291. In 1990, FC did not have any subpart F income. In that year, FC distributed $200 to USP. Of the $200 distribution, $100 had been previously taxed to USP. Because $100 of the $200 distribution is not included in gross income by reason of section 959, pursuant to § 1.1291-2(b)(2) that amount is not treated as a distribution for purposes of § 1.1291-2(c)(2)(i). Therefore, the total distribution, for purposes of calculating the excess distribution for 1990, is $100.

(ii) *Other rules.*—For treatment of amounts that would be taxable in the same taxable year under section 951(a) or 1293(a) and section 1291, *see* § § 1.1291-2(f)(3) and 1.1291-3(e)(4)(ii).

(3) *Section 304 transactions.*—(i) *In general.*—If, in a transaction described in section 304(a), the issuing corporation is a section 1291 fund, any amount treated as paid out of the earnings and profits of such section 1291 fund by virtue of section 304(b)(2) is treated as an excess distribution by such fund for purposes of section 1291 and this section. In addition, the transfer of the stock of such fund will be treated as a disposition to which § § 1.1291-3 and 1.1291-6 apply. If, in a transaction described in section 304(a), the acquiring corporation is a section 1291 fund, any amount paid by such corporation to the transferor is treated as a distribution by such fund (notwithstanding the provisions of section 304(b)(2)), and the transferor is treated for purposes of section 1291 and this section as the owner of any stock of the fund that it owns directly or constructively under section 304(c). The following example illustrates the rule of this paragraph (b)(3)(i).

Example. USP, a domestic corporation, owns all the stock of FS1 and FS2. FS1 and FS2 each have accumulated earnings and profits of $100 that were not previously taxed under any other section of the Code. FS1, but not FS2, is a PFIC. USP has not elected under section 1295 to treat FS1 as a QEF. However, USP plans to make a section 1295 election to treat FS1 as a QEF, as well as the deemed dividend election under section 1291(d)(2)(B) to purge USP's holding period of the FS1 stock of its prior PFIC years. Before it makes those elections, USP plans to sell the stock of FS1 to FS2 for its fair market value of $200. The transfer of the FS1 stock to FS2 is a transaction to which section 304 applies. Section 304(b)(2) provides that $100 of the $200 payment to USP is treated as paid directly by FS1 out of its earnings and profits. Pursuant to § 1.1291-2(b)(3)(i), the $100 distribution to USP is taxable as an excess distribution. The transfer will not be a taxable disposition under § 1.1291-3 because USP's interest in FS1 is not reduced as a result of the transfer. *See* section 304(a)(1) and § 1.1291-6(c)(1)(i).

(ii) *Limitation.*—[Reserved]

(c) *Excess distribution and nonexcess distribution.*—(1) *Excess distribution.*—An excess distribution is that portion of any direct or indirect distribution with respect to a share of stock of a section 1291 fund during the current shareholder year that is the ratable portion (as defined in paragraph (c)(4) of this section) of the total excess distribution (as defined in paragraph (c)(3) of this section), if any. Except as provided in § 1.1291-5, an excess distribution and the taxation thereof are determined without regard to the amount or character of the earnings and profits of the section 1291 fund. Except as provided in paragraph (d)(2) of this section (concerning shares of stock having the same holding period), the excess distribution is calculated separately for each share of stock held.

(2) *Nonexcess distribution.*—(i) *In general.*—A nonexcess distribution with respect to a share of section 1291 stock is the portion of the total amount of all distributions during the current shareholder year with respect to the share that does not exceed 125 percent of the average amount of the distributions with respect to the share during the three taxable years of the shareholder's holding period (or during the lesser number of taxable years in the shareholder's holding period) that immediately precede the current shareholder year. Distributions in any of the preceding three (or fewer) taxable years of the shareholder included in the shareholder's holding period that began before 1987 are included in determining the nonexcess distribution.

(ii) *Amount not included in income.*—The portion of an excess distribution in a prior taxable year that was not included in income pursuant to § 1.1291-2 (e)(2)(iii) is not treated as a distribution in that prior year for purposes of paragraph (c)(2)(i) or (iii) of this section. For an illustration of the rule of this paragraph (c)(2)(ii), *see* paragraph (e)(4), *Example 1*, of this section.

(iii) *Distributions received by predecessors.*—If a shareholder's holding period of the stock of a section 1291 fund includes the period the stock was held by another person, distributions made during the holding period of such other person with respect to the stock will be treated as if they had been received by the shareholder for purposes of paragraph (c)(2)(i) of this section.

(3) *Total excess distribution.*—(i) *In general.*—The total excess distribution with respect to a share of stock of a section 1291 fund is the excess, if any, of—

(A) The total amount of all distributions during the current shareholder year with respect to the share, over

(B) The nonexcess distribution with respect to that stock.

(ii) *Exception.*—Notwithstanding paragraph (c)(3)(i) of this section, the total excess distribution is zero for the taxable year of the shareholder in which the shareholder's holding period of the stock begins. The following example illustrates the rule of this paragraph (c)(3)(ii).

Example. On January 1, 1989, X, a U.S. person, gave his son Y, also a U.S. person, one share of stock of FC, a section 1291 fund, that X had purchased in 1986. Y purchased another share of FC stock on January 3, 1989. Y did not make the section 1295 election with respect to FC. In 1989, FC distributed $100 for each outstanding share of its stock. Pursuant to § 1.1291-2(c)(3)(ii), no portion of the distribution in respect of the share Y purchased in 1989 is treated as an excess distribution. However, the distribution paid to Y with respect to the stock given to him by his father may be wholly or partly an excess distribution. Although Y first held that share of FC stock in 1989, Y's holding period includes the period X held that share of stock, as provided in section 1223(2), and therefore does not begin in 1989.

(4) *Ratable portion.*—The total excess distribution is allocated ratably to each distribution received with respect to a share of stock during the current shareholder year. A distribution's ratable portion of the total excess distribution is the product of the total excess distribution and the ratio of the distribution to the total distribution with respect to the share of stock during the current shareholder year. Each ratable portion of the total excess distribution is an excess distribution.

(d) *Special rules.*—The following rules apply for purposes of calculating the nonexcess distribution and the total excess distribution—

(1) *Stock acquired during the year.*—In general, a distribution in a prior taxable year with respect to a share of stock may only be taken into account in determining a nonexcess distribution under paragraph (c)(2)(i) of this section if the shareholder was a shareholder at the time of such distribution, or the distribution was received by a person whose holding period of the stock is included in the shareholder's holding period. However, with respect to a prior taxable year during which a person became a shareholder, the shareholder may instead take into account the total amount (or portion thereof) that the shareholder determines was actually paid by the section 1291 fund with respect to that share of stock during that taxable year. No other annualization rule will apply under section 1291(b)(3)(C). The following example illustrates the rule of this paragraph (d)(1).

Example. R, a U.S. person, became an indirect shareholder of one share of FC stock on August 1, 1991. R did not elect under section 1295 to treat FC, a PFIC, as a QEF. R and FC both use the calendar year as their taxable years. R determines, based on dividend information provided in FC's 1991 annual report, that FC distributed $100 with respect to each outstanding share of its stock at the end of each quarter during that year. For purposes of calculating nonexcess distributions in 1992, 1993, and 1994, R may treat $400 as the amount received in 1991. If R had been unable to determine the amount distributed in 1991 before August 1, the 1991 distribution would have been limited to the $200 actually distributed after August 1 with respect to the one share of FC stock attributed to R.

(2) *Calculations for shares with same holding period.*—The calculation of the nonexcess distribution and the total excess distribution may be made on an aggregate basis for shares of stock having the same holding period (block of stock). The following example illustrates the rule of this paragraph (d)(2).

Example. (i) *Facts.* X, a U.S. person that is a calendar year taxpayer, owns 12 shares of stock of FC, a PFIC. X has not elected under section 1295 to treat FC as a QEF. X acquired two of the 12 shares on December 31, 1986 (Block #1), four shares on December 31, 1987 (Block #2), and six shares on December 31, 1988 (Block #3). On June 30 of 1987 and 1988, FC distributed $10 in respect of each outstanding share of its stock; no portion of either distribution was an excess distribution. On June 30, 1989, FC distributed $30 in respect of each outstanding share of its stock. For purposes of determining the taxation of the 1989 distribution, the excess distribution may be calculated for each of the three blocks of stock held by X instead of on a share-by-share basis.

(ii) *Block #1 excess distribution.* The nonexcess distribution for Block #1 is $25 (125% times $20 [($20 + $20)/2]). The total excess distribution for Block #1 is $35 ($60 – $25).

(iii) *Block #2 excess distribution.* The nonexcess distribution for Block #2 is $50 (125% × $40, the distribution made in the only preceding taxable year in the holding period of the Block #2 shares). The total excess distribution for Block #2 is $70 ($120 – $50).

(iv) *Block #3.* There is no excess distribution with respect to the Block #3 stock because the first taxable year of the holding period of that block of stock is 1989, the taxable year of the distribution.

(3) *Effect of nontaxable distribution or exchange.*—(i) *Tax-free distributions of stock.*—A distribution with respect to a share of stock, made during the shareholder's holding period for the share but before a distribution of stock under section 305(a) with respect to that share, will be treated ratably as a distribution with respect to the shares in the block of stock composed of the original share and the shares distributed with respect to that share pursuant to the stock distribution.

(ii) *Nontaxable exchange of stock.*—Distributions with respect to stock include distributions with respect to stock exchanged therefor in a nonrecognition transfer in which gain was not recognized pursuant to § 1.1291-6(c).

(iii) *Example.*—The following example illustrates the rule of paragraph (d)(3) of this section.

Example. On December 31, 1985, X, a U.S. person, purchased one share of stock of FC, a corporation. FC has been a section 1291 fund with respect to X since FC's taxable year that began January 1, 1987. In both 1986 and 1987, FC distributed $6 with respect to each share of its stock. FC transferred all its assets and liabilities to F, a PFIC, in a transaction that qualified as a reorganization defined in section 368(a)(1)(C) and that was effective on January 1, 1988. X exchanged his share of FC stock for one share of stock of F in an exchange to which section 354 applied and no gain was recognized pursuant to § 1.1291-6(c)(1). On December 31, 1988, F distributed $3 with respect to each share of its stock. No part of the 1986, 1987, and 1988 distributions was an excess distribution. On December 31, 1989, F distributed $10 with respect to each share of its stock. In calculating the total excess distribution for 1989, the $6 distributions paid in 1986 and 1987 by FC with respect to the FC stock held by X, as well as the $3 distribution paid by F in 1988 on the F stock received in exchange for the FC stock, are taken into account. Accordingly, the total excess distribution for 1989 is $3.75 ($10 – [125% × $5 (the average distribution for the three preceding taxable years)]).

(4) *Distributions in a foreign currency.*—(i) *In general.*—Except as provided in paragraph (d)(4)(ii) of this section, the nonexcess distribution and the total excess distribution are determined in U.S. dollars. Each distribution that must be taken into account for purposes of the calculation is translated into the U.S. dollar at the spot rate (within the meaning of § 1.988-1T (d)) on the date on which such distribution was made. The following example illustrates the rule of this paragraph (d)(4)(i).

Example. USP, a domestic corporation, purchased on December 31, 1986, five percent of the stock of FC, a country X corporation that is a section 1291 fund with respect to USP. The functional currency of FC is the "LC", the currency of country X. FC made no distributions during 1987. FC distributed $100 to USP on August 1, 1988; LC20 on November 20, 1989; and 100 units of country Y currency on December 13, 1990. In order to calculate the 1989 and 1990 excess distributions, USP must convert the 1989 distribution of LC20 into U.S. dollars at the spot rate on November 20, 1989, and the 1990 distribution of 100 units of country Y currency into U.S. dollars at the spot rate on December 13, 1990.

(ii) *Exception.*—If all distributions that must be taken into account for purposes of calculating the nonexcess distribution and the total excess distribution for the current shareholder year were made in a single currency (other than the U.S. dollar), the nonexcess distribution and total excess distribution will be determined in the currency in which the distributions were made. Each ratable portion of a total excess distribution determined in a foreign currency is translated into U.S. dollars at the spot rate on the date of the distribution to which the ratable portion is allocated.

(5) *Adjustments for section 642(c) charitable deduction.*—(i) *In general.*—A trust that is permitted to deduct the amount of its fixed

annual charitable obligation from gross income pursuant to section 642(c)(1) (the section 642(c) deduction) generally may adjust an excess distribution from a section 1291 fund as provided in this paragraph (d)(5) by the amount of the section 642(c) deduction. Except as otherwise provided in this paragraph (d)(5), the trust may adjust an excess distribution if, in satisfaction of its fixed annual obligation, it distributes—

(A) amounts received from the section 1291 fund;

(B) the stock of a section 1291 fund; or

(C) the proceeds from the sale thereof, to an organization described in section 170(c), as required under the terms of the governing instrument of the trust.

The adjustment provided in this paragraph (d)(5) is limited to the amount of the trust's fixed annual charitable obligation.

(ii) *Exception.*—This paragraph (d)(5) does not apply to a grantor of a trust if the grantor deducted from income, as provided in section 170(f)(2)(B), the value of an interest in any share of stock of the section 1291 fund upon its transfer to the trust.

(iii) *Adjustments.*—(A) *Corpus consisting only of section 1291 fund stock.*—Where the assets of the trust consist only of stock of one or more section 1291 funds, the section 642(c) deduction first reduces the nonexcess distributions, if any, determined under paragraph (c)(2)(i) of this section. The amount of the section 642(c) deduction remaining after reduction of the nonexcess distributions reduces the portions of the excess distributions allocated to the prePFIC and current shareholder years. Finally, the amount of the section 642(c) deduction remaining after the prior two reductions reduces pro rata the portions of the excess distributions allocated to the prior PFIC years. The deferred tax amount, as defined in § 1.1291-4, is determined with respect to the adjusted allocations of the excess distributions.

(B) *Corpus consisting of section 1291 fund stock and other property.*—*(1) Income from both section 1291 fund stock and other property.*—A distribution of income in satisfaction of a fixed annual charitable obligation is treated as distributed out of income, if any, derived from the trust property other than the stock of a section 1291 fund to the extent thereof, before being treated as distributed out of amounts received from a section 1291 fund. An adjustment will be permitted in the manner provided in paragraph (d)(5)(iii)(A) of this section only after the deduction permitted under section 642(c) has reduced income from other property to zero.

(2) Use of corpus to satisfy obligation.—The trust will not be entitled to the adjustment permitted under this paragraph (d)(5) if the trust uses stock of a section 1291 fund instead of its other property to satisfy its fixed annual charitable obligation.

(6) *PFIC for part of current shareholder year.*—This paragraph (d)(6) applies if the section 1291 fund first qualified as a PFIC for its taxable year beginning after the first day of the current shareholder year and therefore is a section 1291 fund for only a portion of the current shareholder year. Distributions during the portion of the current shareholder year before the corporation qualified as a PFIC are taken into account for purposes of calculating the nonexcess distribution and the total excess distribution. However, those distributions are taxable under the general rules applicable to distributions by a corporation to its shareholder with respect to its stock, notwithstanding that a ratable portion thereof may be an excess distribution within the meaning of paragraph (c)(1) of this section. The following example illustrates the rule of this paragraph (d)(6).

Example. X, a U.S. person, purchased one share of stock of FC, a corporation, on December 31, 1986. X uses the calendar year as its taxable year; FC's taxable year ends November 30. FC first qualified as a PFIC for its taxable year that began December 1, 1990. X did not elect under section 1295 to treat FC as a QEF. X received a distribution of $100 in 1987, but did not receive another distribution from FC until August 1, 1990, when FC distributed $100 per share. On December 13, 1990, FC made another $100 per share distribution. The August distribution is taken into account for purposes of calculating the nonexcess distribution and total excess distribution for 1990 and the ratable portion of the December 13 distribution that is an excess distribution. However, pursuant to § 1.1291-2(d)(6), the August distribution is not subject to section 1291 notwithstanding that a ratable portion of that distribution is an excess distribution within the meaning of § 1.1291-2(c)(1). The August distribution is included in X's 1990 gross income to the extent provided in section 301(c).

(e) *Taxation of a distribution and effect on earnings and profits.*—(1) *Nonexcess distribution.*—A nonexcess distribution, as defined in paragraph (c)(2)(i) of this section, is taxable to a shareholder according to the general rules of taxation applicable to distributions made by a corporation to a shareholder with respect to its stock. *See, e.g.*, section 301 and the regulations under that section.

(2) *Excess distribution.*—(i) *In general.*—To determine the taxation of an excess distribution, the excess distribution is first allocated pro rata to each day in the shareholder's holding period (as determined under § 1.1291-1(h)) of the share of stock with respect to which the distribution was made. The holding period of a share of stock of a section 1291 fund is treated as ending on (and including) the date of each excess distribution solely for purposes of allocating the excess distribution.

(ii) *Allocations included in income.*—The portions of an excess distribution allocated to prePFIC years and the current shareholder year are included in the shareholder's gross income for the current shareholder year as ordinary income.

(iii) *Allocations not included in income.*—The portions of an excess distribution allocated to prior PFIC years are not included in the shareholder's gross income for purposes of this title. These amounts are subject to the deferred tax amount. The deferred tax amount is an additional liability of the shareholder for tax and interest for the current shareholder year. For the calculation of the deferred tax amount and the foreign tax credit that may be taken to reduce the deferred tax amount, *see* §§ 1.1291-4 and 1.1291-5.

(3) *Allocation of earnings and profits.*—For purposes of determining the taxation of a nonexcess distribution and calculating the foreign tax credit under § 1.1291-5, the earnings and profits of a section 1291 fund are allocated proportionately between the nonexcess distribution (as defined in paragraph (c)(2)(i) of this section) and the total excess distribution (as defined in paragraph (c)(3) of this section) and reduced (but not below zero) by the amounts thereof.

(4) *Examples.*—The following examples illustrate the operation of paragraphs (c), (d), and (e) of this section.

Example 1. (i) *Facts.* X, a U.S. person, purchased a share of stock of FC, a corporation, on December 31, 1985. FC has been a section 1291 fund since its taxable year that began January 1, 1987. X received distributions from FC of $50 on December 31, 1987, $80 on December 31, 1988, and $150 on December 31, 1989. FC made no distributions in 1986.

(ii) *1987 excess distribution.* Because X did not receive a distribution from FC during 1986, the only preceding taxable year in its holding period, the total distribution of $50 is the total excess distribution for 1987. That amount is allocated pro rata over X's two-year holding period, as provided in § 1.1291-2(e)(2)(i): $25 is allocated to 1986, a prePFIC year, and $25 to 1987, the current shareholder year. The entire $50 therefore is included in X's gross income for 1987 as ordinary income.

(iii) *1988 excess distribution.* In 1988, of the $80 total distribution, $31.25 (125% × $25 [(0 + $50) / 2]) is the nonexcess distribution, and is taxable as a corporate distribution as provided in section 301(c). The total excess distribution for 1988, $48.75 ($80 – $31.25), is allocated over X's three-year holding period; $16.25 is allocated to each year. The portions of the excess distribution allocated to the prePFIC year (1986) and the current shareholder year (1988) total $32.50; that amount is included in X's gross income as ordinary income. The $16.25 portion of the excess distribution allocated to 1987, the prior PFIC year, is not included in X's gross income, but is subject to the deferred tax amount. Of the $80 distribution, $63.75 ($31.25 + $32.50) is included in X's gross income in 1988.

(iv) *1989 excess distribution.* In 1989, of the $150 total distribution, $47.40 (125% × $37.90 [(0 + $50 + $63.75) / 3]) is the nonexcess distribution, and is taxable as a corporate distribution as provided in section 301(c). The total excess distribution for 1989, $102.60 ($150 –$47.40), is allocated over X's four-year holding period; $25.65 is allocated to each year. The portions of the excess distribution allocated to the prePFIC year (1986) and the current shareholder year (1989) total $51.30; that amount is included in X's gross income as ordinary income. The portions of the excess distribution allocated to the prior PFIC years (1987 and 1988) total $51.30; that amount is not included in X's gross income but is subject to the deferred tax amount. Of the total $150 distribution, $98.70 ($47.40 + $51.30) is included in X's gross income in 1989.

Example 2. (i) *Facts.* X, a U.S. person with a calendar taxable year, purchased 1,000 shares of stock of FC, a corporation, on December 31, 1985. FC has been a section 1291 fund since its taxable year that began January 1, 1987. FC distributed $100,000 to X on January 31, 1989, and $200,000 to X on July 31, 1989. X determined the total excess distribution for 1989 to be $150,000.

(ii) *January 31 distribution.* The excess distribution allocated to the January 31 distribution, which is the ratable portion of the total excess distribution allocated to the $100,000 distribution made on that date, is $50,000 [$150,000 × ($100,000 / $300,000)]. For purposes of allocating the $50,000 excess distribution over X's holding period, X's holding period is treated as ending on (and including) January 31, 1989. X thus held the stock for 1,127 days (365 days in both 1986 and 1987, 366 days in 1988, and 31 days in 1989) at the time of the January 31 distribution. The $50,000 excess distribution allocated to the January 31 distribution is allocated pro rata to the 1,127 days; approximately $44.37 is allocated to each day in the holding period. The total allocations to each of the taxable years in X's holding period are as follows:

TAXABLE YEAR	*TOTAL ALLOCATION PER YEAR*
1986	$16,193.70
1987	$16,193.70
1988	$16,237.70
1989	$ 1,374.90
Excess distribution:	$50,000.00

The allocation to 1986, the prePFIC year, and the allocation to 1989, the current shareholder year, are included in X's gross income for 1989 as ordinary income. The allocations to 1987 and 1988, the prior PFIC years, are not included in X's gross income in 1989, but are subject to the deferred tax amount.

(iii) *July 31 distribution.* The excess distribution allocated to the July 31 distribution, which is the ratable portion of the total excess distribution allocated to the distribution made on that date, is $100,000 [$150,000 × ($200,000 / $300,000)]. For purposes of the allocation of this excess distribution, X's holding period is treated as ending on July 31, 1989. X thus held the stock for 1,308 days (365 days in both 1986 and 1987, 366 days in 1988, and 212 days in 1989) at the time of the July 31 distribution. The $100,000 excess distribution allocated to the July 31 excess distribution is allocated pro rata to the 1,308 days; approximately $76.45 is allocated to each day in the holding period. The total allocations of the July 31 excess distribution to each of the taxable years in X's holding period are as follows:

TAXABLE YEAR	*TOTAL ALLOCATION PER YEAR*
1986	$27,905.20
1987	$ 27,905.20
1988	$ 27,981.65
1989	$ 16,207.95
Excess distribution:	$100,000.00

The portions of the excess distribution allocated to 1986, the prePFIC year, and to 1989, the current shareholder year, are included as ordinary income in X's gross income for 1989. The portions of the excess distribution allocated to 1987 and 1988, the prior PFIC years, are not included in X's gross income in 1989, but are subject to the deferred tax amount.

Example 3. (i) *Facts.* X, a U.S. person, holds six shares of the stock of FC, a section 1291 fund. Two shares were purchased on December 31, 1986 (Block #1), and four shares were purchased on December 31, 1987 (Block #2). On June 30 of 1987 and 1988, FC distributed $10,000 in respect of each outstanding share of its stock. No portion of the distributions in either year was an excess distribution. On June 30, 1989, FC distributed $30,000 in respect of each outstanding share of its stock.

(ii) *Calculation of the 1989 excess distributions.* The excess distribution is determined separately for each block of stock.

(A) *Block #1 excess distribution.* The nonexcess distribution for Block #1 is $25,000 [125% times ($20,000 + $20,000) / 2]. The total excess distribution for Block #1 is $35,000 ($60,000 – $25,000).

(B) *Block #2 excess distribution.* The nonexcess distribution for Block #2 is $50,000 [125% times $40,000 (the distribution received in the only preceding taxable year included in X's holding period]. The total excess distribution for Block #2 is $70,000 ($120,000 – $50,000).

(iii) *Block #1 allocation.* The holding period of the Block #1 stock began on January 1, 1987, and ended, for purposes of section 1291, on June 30, 1989, for a total of 912 days (365 days in 1987, 366 days in 1988 and 181 days in 1989). The $35,000 excess distribution for Block #1 is allocated pro rata to each of the 912 days. Accordingly, approximately $38.38 is allocated to each day. The total allocations to each of the taxable years in X's holding period are as follows:

TAXABLE YEAR	*TOTAL ALLOCATION PER YEAR*
1987	$14,007.70
1988	$14,046.10
1989	$ 6,946.20
Excess distribution:	$35,000.00

The portion of the excess distribution allocated to 1989, the current shareholder year, of $6,946.20, is included as ordinary income in X's gross income for 1989. The portions of the excess distribution allocated to the prior PFIC years, 1987 and 1988, an aggregate of $28,053.80, are not included in X's gross income in 1989, but are subject to the deferred tax amount.

(iv) *Block #2 allocation.* The holding period of the Block #2 stock began on January 1, 1988, and ended, for purposes of section 1291, on June 30, 1989, for a total of 547 days (366 days in 1988 and 181 days in 1989). The excess distribution of $70,000 in respect of the Block #2 stock is allocated pro rata to each of the 547 days. Accordingly, approximately $127.97 is allocated to each day. The total allocations to each of the taxable years in X's holding period are as follows:

TAXABLE YEAR	*TOTAL ALLOCATION PER YEAR*
1988	$46,837.40
1989	$23,162.60
Excess distribution:	$70,000.00

The portion of the excess distribution allocated to 1989, the current shareholder year, of $23,162.60, is included as ordinary income in X's gross income for 1989. The portion of the excess distribution allocated to 1988, $46,837.40, is not included in X's gross income in 1989, but is subject to the deferred tax amount.

Example 4. X is a U.S. person that owns all the stock of FC, a section 1291 fund. At the end of its 1991 taxable year, FC has accumulated earnings and profits, before reduction for distributions made during the year, of $100, none of which was previously taxed to X under section 951 or 1293. FC distributes $200 to X on the last day of FC's taxable year. X determines that, of the $200 distribution, $50 is a nonexcess distribution, and $150 is the total excess distribution. FC's earnings and profits of $100 are allocated proportionately between the nonexcess distribution of $50 and the excess distribution of $150, and reduced to zero. Accordingly, $25 of FC's earnings and profits are allocated to the nonexcess distribution and $75 of FC's earnings and profits are allocated to the excess distribution. Therefore, $25 of the $50 nonexcess distribution is taxable as a dividend under section 301(c)(1), and the remaining $25 is taxable to the extent provided in section 301(c)(2) and (3). The excess distribution of $150 is taxable as provided in § 1.1291-2(e)(2).

(f) *Indirect distributions.*—(1) *In general.*—A distribution (as defined in § 1.1291-2(b)) by a section 1291 fund to the actual owner of stock of the section 1291 fund is an indirect distribution if such stock is considered owned by a U.S. person pursuant to § 1.1291-1(b)(8). Except as otherwise provided in this paragraph (f), an indirect shareholder is taxable on the total distribution paid by the section 1291 fund with respect to the stock attributed to the indirect shareholder, as if the indirect shareholder had actually received that amount. The following example illustrates the rule of this paragraph (f)(1).

Example. (i) X, an S corporation under section 1361, purchased 100 shares of stock of FC, a corporation, on December 31, 1985. FC has been a section 1291 fund since its taxable year that began January 1, 1987. A purchased 10 percent of the stock of X on December 31, 1986, and thus became an indirect shareholder of 10 shares of FC stock. Pursuant to § 1.1291-1(h)(4)(i), A's holding period of the FC stock began on January 1, 1987.

(ii) FC distributed $5 per share of stock to its shareholders in 1986, and $8 per share in 1987. In 1987 A is treated as receiving a distribution of $80 from FC. A did not have a total excess distribution in 1987, the taxable year in which A's holding period of the FC stock began.

(iii) FC distributed $12 per share in 1988, all of which was paid on June 30, 1988. A therefore is treated as receiving a distribution of $120 from FC. The nonexcess distribution is $100 [125% times $80]. Accordingly, the excess distribution is $20 ($120 – $100). That amount is allocated under § 1.1291-2(e)(2)(i) to each day in A's holding period of the FC stock, which began on January 1, 1987, and ended, for purposes of the allocation of the excess distribution, on June 30, 1988.

(2) *Pass-through entities.*—(i) *Taxation of trusts, estates, and their beneficiaries.*—[Reserved]

(ii) *Information reporting.*—(A) *In general.*—A domestic partnership that is a direct or indirect shareholder of a section 1291 fund must separately state the total distribution as a distribution from a section 1291 fund on its federal income tax return (if any) and on any Schedule K-1 filed by the partnership or provided to a partner to which a distributive share of the distribution from the section 1291 fund is allocated pursuant to section 704. In addition, the partnership must state on the Schedule K-1 the information needed by the partner to compute its excess distribution with respect to such total distribution, and provide the name, address and stock basis, where appropriate, of the actual owner of the section 1291 fund that paid the distribution (or whose stock was transferred in an indirect disposition). Any partner receiving such a Schedule K-1 that is itself a domestic partnership is in turn obligated to separately state such information according to the same rules. Similar rules apply to S corporations.

(B) *Trusts and estates.*—[Reserved]

(3) *Coordination with subpart F.*—If, but for this paragraph (f)(3), an indirect distribution would be taxable to an indirect shareholder under this section and also included in the gross income of the indirect shareholder under section 551(a), 951(a)(1), or 1293(a), the indirect distribution is taxable only under this section.

(4) *Exceptions.*—(i) *Distribution to sole shareholder.*—A distribution by a section 1291 fund (distributing fund) to another section 1291 fund (distributee fund) will not be taxable to the direct shareholder of the distributee fund if—

(A) The distributee fund owns all the stock of the distributing fund; and

(B) The distributing fund distributed all its earnings and profits in the current shareholder year and annually distributed all its earnings and profits for each year that is included in the shareholder's holding period of the distributing fund.

(ii) *Other exceptions.*—[Reserved]

(5) *Adjustment to basis.*—The shareholder's adjusted basis of the stock or other property that is owned directly by the shareholder and through which ownership of the section 1291 fund is attributed to the shareholder is increased by the amount of the indirect distribution taxed to the shareholder pursuant to paragraph (f)(1) of this section.

(6) *Treatment of previously taxed amounts.*—The principles of sections 959 and 961 apply with respect to amounts previously taxed under this paragraph (f). The following example illustrates the rule of this paragraph (f)(6).

Example. USP owns 50% of CFC1. CFC1 and its wholly owned subsidiary, CFC2, are both controlled foreign corporations within the meaning of section 957(a), but are not PFICs. CFC2 owns 10% of the stock of NQF, a PFIC. USP is an indirect shareholder of NQF pursuant to § 1.1291-1(b)(8)(ii). USP has not elected to treated NQF as a QEF. In 1992, NQF distributes $100 to CFC2, and CFC1 distributes $100 to USP, but CFC2 makes no distributions to CFC1. At the end of 1992, CFC1 has accumulated earnings and profits of $200, none of which was previously taxed to USP under section 951(a)(1). USP is taxable pursuant to § 1.1291-2(f) on its pro rata share of the indirect distribution paid to CFC2, and also is taxable on CFC1's distribution pursuant to section 301(c). No part of the distribution by CFC1 to USP is attributable to the amount taxed to USP under § 1.1291-2(f) because no part of the distribution can be attributed to NQF's distribution to CFC2. [Prop. Reg. § 1.1291-2.]

[Proposed 4-1-92.]

Proposed Regulation

§ 1.1291-3. Dispositions.—(a) *Purpose and scope.*—Any direct or indirect disposition of stock of a section 1291 fund within the meaning of paragraphs (b), (c), (d), and (e) of this section is taxable to the extent provided in section 1291, this section, and § 1.1291-6. For dispositions of stock of a section 1291 fund that qualify for nonrecognition treatment, *see* § 1.1291-6. Gain is determined on a share-by-share basis and is taxed as an excess distribution as provided in § 1.1291-2(e)(2). Unless otherwise provided under another provision of the Code, a loss realized on a disposition of stock of a section 1291 fund is not recognized.

(b) *Disposition.*—(1) *In general.*—For purposes of this section, a disposition is any transaction or event that constitutes an actual or deemed transfer of property for any purpose of the Code and the regulations thereunder, including (but not limited to) a sale, exchange, gift, or transfer at death, an exchange pursuant to a liquidation or section 302(a) redemption, or a distribution described in section 311, 336, 337, 355(c) or 361(c). For purposes of this paragraph (b), any person receiving a distribution that qualifies under section 355 will be treated as disposing of all of its stock in the distributing corporation (whether or not there is an actual disposition of such stock) in exchange for stock of the distributing corporation, the controlled corporation, or both, as the case may be.

(2) *Change of U.S. residence or citizenship.*—If a shareholder of a section 1291 fund becomes a nonresident alien for U.S. tax purposes, the shareholder will be treated as having disposed of the shareholder's stock in the section 1291 fund for purposes of section 1291 on the last day that the shareholder is a U.S. person. Termination of an election under section 6013(g) is treated as a change of residence (within the meaning of this paragraph (b)(2)) of the spouse who was a resident solely by reason of the section 6013(g) election.

(c) *Direct disposition of stock of a section 1291 fund.*—Except to the extent provided in § 1.1291-6, a direct shareholder of a section 1291 fund recognizes all gain that it realizes on a disposition of the stock of such fund.

(d) *Stock of a section 1291 fund used as security for an obligation.*—(1) *In general.*—Except to the extent provided in paragraphs (d)(3) and (6) of this section, the use of stock of a section 1291 fund as security for the performance of an obligation of a direct or indirect shareholder (or of a person related within the meaning of section 267(b) to that shareholder), in connection with a loan, guarantee, margin account, or otherwise (a pledge of stock), is a transaction that results in a disposition of the stock of the section 1291 fund within the meaning of paragraph (b) of this section. Such pledged stock will be treated as having been disposed of on the later of the date when such stock is first used as security with respect to such obligation, or the first day of the first taxable year of the foreign corporation as a PFIC. Such pledged stock will be treated as having been disposed of for consideration equal to the lesser of—

(i) The unpaid principal of the obligation secured by the stock on the date of disposition; or

(ii) The fair market value of the stock immediately before such disposition.

(2) *Indirect pledge.*—A pledge of stock of a section 1291 fund, as described in paragraph (d)(1) of this section, will be deemed to occur if such stock serves indirectly as security for the performance of an obligation described in that paragraph, and a principal purpose for the structure of the security arrangement was to avoid the rule of that paragraph.

(3) *Requirement of gain realized.*—This paragraph (d) does not apply if the shareholder would realize a loss on an actual disposition of the stock of the section 1291 fund at the time the obligation was secured by the stock.

(4) *Increase in value of pledged stock.*—An increase in the value of stock being used to secure the performance of an obligation will not be treated as a disposition of the stock unless the pledged stock is used to secure additional principal or new indebtedness.

(5) *Adjustment to basis; holding period.*—If stock of a section 1291 fund is treated as disposed of under this paragraph (d), adjustments to basis will be made in accordance with rules similar to those in § 1.1291-6(b)(4). For the holding period of pledged stock, *see* § 1.1291-1(h)(5).

(6) *Transition rule.*—Stock of a section 1291 fund that secured an obligation within the meaning of paragraph (d)(1) of this section as of the effective date of section 1297(b)(6) is not treated as disposed of as of the first day of the first taxable year of the foreign corporation as a PFIC, unless such stock continued to secure such obligation 180 days after the effective date. For a special effective date pertaining to this rule, *see* § 1.1291-1(j)(2).

(7) *Examples.*—The following examples illustrate the operation of this paragraph (d).

Example 1. On November 20, 1995, X, a U.S. person that was a shareholder of FC, a section 1291 fund, used its stock in FC, valued immediately before the loan at $120,000, as security for a $100,000 loan. X's basis in the stock is $70,000. The pledge is treated as a disposition of the stock for $100,000, which is the lesser of the loan principal secured by the stock and the fair market value of the stock. S recognizes $30,000 on the disposition, which gain is taxed as an excess distribution under section 1291 and § 1.1291-2(e)(2). X's basis in the FC stock is increased by $30,000, the amount of gain recognized on the deemed disposition. The holding period of the pledged stock is not adjusted to reflect the disposition because the full amount of the gain inherent in the stock was not recognized (*see* § 1.1291-1(h)(5)).

Example 2. The facts are the same as in *Example 1.* In addition, on August 12, 1996, X borrows an additional $30,000 (for a total outstanding loan balance on that day of $130,000). The value of the FC stock immediately before the additional loan is $130,000. Pursuant to § 1.1291-3(d)(4), there is a disposition within the meaning of § 1.1291-3(d)(1) to the extent the value of the FC stock secures additional indebtedness. The FC stock first secured a loan of $100,000, which was less than its full value. The second loan results in a disposition to the extent that the previously unrecognized appreciation and any additional appreciation secure additional indebtedness. Accordingly, there is an excess distribution of $30,000. X's basis in its FC stock is increased by $30,000, the amount of gain recognized. X's holding period in the FC stock for section 1291 purposes is treated as beginning on the day after the effective date of the second borrowing (*see* § 1.1291-1(h)(5)).

(e) *Indirect dispositions.*—(1) *In general.*—Except as otherwise provided in this paragraph (e) and § 1.1291-6, an indirect shareholder of a section 1291 fund is taxable under section 1291 and this section on an indirect disposition of stock of the section 1291 fund.

(2) *Indirect disposition defined.*—An indirect disposition is—

(i) Any disposition of stock of a section 1291 fund by its actual owner if such stock is attributed to an indirect shareholder under § 1.1291-1(b)(8);

(ii) Any disposition, by an indirect shareholder or any other person, of any interest in a person, if by virtue of such interest the indirect shareholder was treated as owning stock of a section 1291 fund under § 1.1291-1(b)(8); or

(iii) Any other transaction as a result of which an indirect shareholder's ownership of a section 1291 fund is reduced or terminated.

Paragraph (e)(2)(i) of this section applies without regard to whether the indirect shareholder's ownership of a section 1291 fund is changed by the disposition. However, paragraph (e)(2)(ii) of this section does not apply if the disposition does not result in a reduction in the indirect shareholder's ownership of the fund or an increase in the basis of the stock of the fund in the hands of the actual owner.

(3) *Examples.*—The following examples illustrate paragraph (e)(2) of this section.

Example 1. T, a U.S. person, and M, a foreign person, are equal partners of FP, a foreign partnership that owns 10 shares of stock of FC, a PFIC. Pursuant to § 1.1291-1(b)(8)(iii), T is an indirect shareholder of one-half of the shares of FC stock held by FP. T did not elect under section 1295 to treat FC as a QEF. On August 14, 1994, H, a U.S. person, joins the partnership as an equal partner. As a result of H's acquisition of one-third of FP, H is an indirect shareholder of one-third of the FC stock held by FP. H's acquisition of the FP interest is a disposition pursuant to § 1.1291-3(e)(2)(iii), taxable to T, of one-third of T's interest in the FC stock.

Example 2. E, a U.S. person, and R, a foreign person, each own 50% of the outstanding stock of Distributing, a foreign corporation that is not a PFIC or a controlled foreign corporation within the meaning of section 957(a). Distributing owns all the stock of Controlled, a PFIC. Pursuant to § 1.1291-1(b)(8)(ii)(A), E is an indirect shareholder of Controlled. E did not elect under section 1295 to treat Controlled as a QEF. In a transaction that qualifies under section 355(a), Distributing distributes all the Controlled stock to R. As a result of the distribution, E's interest in Controlled is terminated. The distribution is an indirect disposition of E's ownership of Controlled, within the meaning of § 1.1291-3(e)(2)(i), taxable to E under § 1.1291-3(e).

Example 3. C, a U.S. person, owns 51% of the stock of CFC, a foreign corporation that is not a PFIC. Several foreign persons own the remaining 49% of CFC. CFC owns 100 shares of FYZ, a PFIC. Pursuant to § 1.1291-1(b)(8)(ii)(A), C is an indirect shareholder of 51 shares of the FYZ stock held by CFC. C did not elect under section 1295 to treat FYZ as a QEF. To raise capital, CFC makes a public offering of its stock. After the offering, C owns only 35% of the CFC stock. The reduction of C's ownership of CFC terminated C's indirect ownership of the FYZ stock, and therefore is an indirect disposition of the FYZ stock, pursuant to § 1.1291-3(e)(2)(iii), taxable to C under § 1.1291-3(e).

(4) *General rules.*—(i) *Amount and treatment of gain.*—If a shareholder with respect to a share of stock of a section 1291 fund is taxable on an indirect disposition of that share, the shareholder is treated as recognizing an amount of gain with respect to that share equal to the shareholder's pro rata share of the gain realized by the actual owner of that share (in the case of a disposition described in paragraph (e)(2)(i) of this section), or the gain the actual owner would have realized on an actual disposition of such stock (in the case of other dispositions). The gain taxable to the shareholder is an excess distribution, taxable in the manner provided in § 1.1291-2(e)(2). The gain is allocated over the shareholder's holding period of the stock of the section 1291 fund as determined in § 1.1291-1(h)(4).

(ii) *Coordination with current inclusion rules.*—If gain from an indirect disposition would be taxable to a shareholder under this section, and would, but for this paragraph (e)(4)(ii), also be included in the gross income of the shareholder under section 551(a), 951(a)(1), or 1293(a), the indirect disposition is taxable only under this section.

(iii) *Adjustment to basis; holding period.*—The shareholder's adjusted basis of the stock or other property that is owned directly by the shareholder and through which ownership of the section 1291 fund is attributed to the shareholder is increased by the amount of gain recognized by the shareholder pursuant to paragraph (e)(4)(i) of this section. In addition, solely for purposes of determining the subsequent treatment under the Code of a direct or indirect shareholder of the stock of the section 1291 fund treated as transferred in an indirect disposition, the adjusted basis of the actual owner of the stock of the section 1291 fund is increased by the amount of gain recognized by the shareholder. For the holding period rule for stock that is treated as disposed of under paragraph (e)(2) of this section, *see* § 1.1291-1(h)(5).

(iv) *Treatment of previously taxed amounts.*—The principles of sections 959 and 961 apply with respect to distributions by a foreign corporation through which a shareholder was considered to own stock of a section 1291 fund, to the extent that such distributions are attributable to amounts previously taxed under this paragraph (e) on a disposition of the stock of such fund.

(5) *Pass-through entities.*—(i) *Section 1291 fund stock held by former C corporation.*—Solely for purposes of calculating the aggregate amount of interest under § 1.1291-4(d)(1), the S corporation shareholder's gain is determined without regard to section 1366(f)(2). Accordingly, the excess distribution for this purpose includes the amount of the S corporation's liability for tax attributable to the built-in gain in the stock of the section 1291 fund pursuant to section 1374. For an illustration of the rule of this paragraph (e)(5)(i), *see* § 1.1291-4(e), *Example 2*. For the taxation of the S corporation on the disposition of the stock of a section 1291 fund, *see* section 1374.

(ii) *Taxation of trusts, estates, and their beneficiaries.*—[Reserved]

(iii) *Information reporting.*—The information reporting obligations to which pass-through entities are subject with respect to indirect distributions also apply with respect to indirect dispositions. *See* § 1.1291-2(f)(2)(ii).

(6) *Exceptions.*—(i) *Disposition of PFIC's wholly-owned PFIC.*—A direct shareholder of a section 1291 fund (first-tier fund) will not be taxable on an indirect disposition of a section 1291 fund (second-tier fund) that is a wholly owned subsidiary of the first-tier fund if the second-tier fund annually distributed all its earnings and profits for each year that is included in the shareholder's holding period of the second-tier fund.

(ii) *Other exceptions.*—[Reserved]

(f) *Transfers within a consolidated group.*—For purposes of applying sections 1291 through 1297 to the stock of a PFIC, transfers by one member of a consolidated group to another member are ignored. Thus, the basis of the transferred stock in the hands of the transferee is the adjusted basis of such stock in the hands of the transferor, and the holding period of such stock held by a member of the consolidated group includes the holding period of all members of the group that have transferred the stock.

(g) *Installment sales.*—If the gain from a disposition of a share of stock of a section 1291 fund is reported on the installment basis, there is an excess distribution on the receipt of each installment or portion thereof in the amount of the gain to be reported in accordance with section 453 with respect to such share. For purposes of allocating each excess distribution under § 1.1291-2(e)(2)(i), the holding period of the transferred stock, which begins on the date determined under § 1.1291-1(h), is treated as ending on the date of each installment.

(h) *Series of liquidation distributions.*—For purposes of allocating the gain recognized on a distribution of property that is one of a series of distributions in liquidation of a section 1291 fund, the holding period of the stock of the liquidating corporation, which begins on the date determined under § 1.1291-1(h), is treated as ending on the date of each liquidation distribution with respect to which gain is recognized.

(i) *Sections 1246 and 1248 inapplicable.*—Sections 1246 and 1248 do not apply to the disposition of stock of a section 1291 fund that is taxable under section 1291. *See* sections 1246(g) and 1248(g)(2).

(j) *Estate tax deduction.*—If a shareholder acquired the stock of a section 1291 fund from a decedent (other than a decedent who was a nonresident alien at all times during the holding period of the stock), and the decedent did not recognize any gain on the transfer of his or her stock at death pursuant to § 1.1291-6(c)(2)(iii)(A), the shareholder may deduct from gross income, for the taxable year of the disposition of the stock of the section 1291 fund that is taxable to the shareholder, an amount equal to that portion of the decedent's estate tax deemed paid which is attributable to the excess of (A) the value at which such stock was taken into account for purposes of determining the value of the decedent's gross estate, over (B) the value at which it would have been so taken into account if such value had been the basis of the stock in the hands of the shareholder determined under § 1.1291-6(b)(4)(iii). [Prop. Reg. § 1.1291-3.]

[Proposed 4-1-92.]

Proposed Regulation

§ 1.1291-4. The deferred tax amount.—(a) *In general.*—The deferred tax amount is the sum of the aggregate increases in taxes (defined in paragraph (c)(5) of this section) and the aggregate amount of interest (defined in paragraph (d) of this section) determined with respect to the aggregate increases in taxes. The deferred tax amount is computed for the portions of each excess distribution allocated to different prior PFIC years, as defined in § 1.1291-1(b)(4).

(b) *Character of deferred tax amount.*—The aggregate increases in taxes are an additional amount of tax imposed on the shareholder for the current shareholder year. The aggregate increases in taxes are treated as an income tax for purposes of subtitle F (Procedure and Administration), and therefore will be assessed, collected, paid, and subject to penalties and interest in the same manner as other taxes on income. The aggregate amount of interest is treated as interest under section 6601. To determine the extent to which such interest may be deducted for federal income tax purposes, *see* section 163 and the regulations under that section.

(c) *Increase in tax.*—(1) *In general.*—An increase in tax is determined for each portion of an excess distribution allocated to a prior PFIC year. Each increase in tax is determined by multiplying the amount of the excess distribution allocated to the prior PFIC year by the highest statutory rate of tax in effect under either section 1 or section 11, as applicable, for that prior PFIC year.

(2) *Rate of tax in effect.*—The highest statutory rate of tax is determined without regard to the actual rate of tax to which the shareholder was subject in that prior PFIC year. The rate of tax in effect in the case of a distribution or disposition taxable to an indirect shareholder is the rate in effect for the indirect shareholder. For taxable years of the shareholder beginning after 1987 and before January 1, 1991, the highest statutory rate of tax in effect under section 1 is 28 percent. If there was a change of tax rates during a taxable year, the highest rate of tax is determined in the manner described in section 15(e) using the highest statutory rates of tax in effect before and after the change of rates.

(3) *Reduction for foreign taxes.*—To the extent provided in section 1291(g) and § 1.1291-5, each increase in tax is reduced by the foreign tax credit calculated with respect to the increase in tax.

(4) *Net increase in tax.*—The net increase in tax is the amount of the increase in tax after reduction for creditable foreign taxes. *See* paragraph (d) of this section.

(5) *Aggregate increases in taxes.*—The term aggregate increases in taxes means the sum of all net increases in tax calculated for an excess distribution.

(d) *Aggregate amount of interest.*—(1) *In general.*—The aggregate amount of interest is the sum of the interest charges computed on all net increases in tax calculated for an excess distribution. An interest charge is computed separately for the interest period of each net increase in tax by using the applicable rates and method under section 6621. The interest period for a net increase in tax is the period beginning on the due date of the income tax return for the prior PFIC year for which the net increase in tax was computed and ending on the due date for the income tax return for the current shareholder year. For purposes of this paragraph, the term due date means the date prescribed by law, determined without regard to extensions, for filing the income tax return for the taxable year of the shareholder.

(2) *Reduction for interest paid under section 453A(c).*—A disposition may be subject to both sections 1291 and 453A(c). The aggregate amount of interest determined in paragraph (d)(1) of this section is reduced by the amount of interest paid under section 453A(c) that is attributable to an excess distribution arising from the disposition. The shareholder may use any reasonable method of determining the amount of the reduction.

(e) *Examples.*—The following examples illustrate the rules of this section.

Example 1. (i) *Facts.* X is a domestic corporation that is a calendar year taxpayer. The due date (without regard to extensions) for its federal income tax return is March 15. X acquired a share of stock of FC, a corporation, on December 31, 1986, for $500. FC has been a section 1291 fund with respect to X since FC's taxable year that began January 1, 1987. On December 31, 1990, X sold the FC stock for $1000. X did not incur any foreign tax on the disposition of the FC stock. X's gain on the sale, $500, is taxed as an excess distribution. The excess distribution is allocated pro rata over X's four-year holding period. Accordingly, $125 is allocated to each year in X's holding period. The $125 allocated to 1990, the current shareholder year, is included in X's ordinary income for that year. The allocations to 1987, 1988 and 1989, the prior PFIC years, are subject to the deferred tax amount under § 1.1291-4.

(ii) *Calculation of the 1987 increase in tax.* The increase in tax for the $125 allocated to 1987 is determined in the manner described in section 15(e) by using a weighted average rate. The weighted average rate is 40 percent:

46% rate: 181/365 × 46%	=	22.81%
34% rate: 184/365 × 34%	=	17.14%
		39.95%

The increase in tax for 1987 is $49.94 ($125 × 39.95%).

(iii) *Calculation of the other increases in tax.* The highest statutory rate of tax applicable to X that was in effect for both 1988 and 1989 was 34 percent. The increase in tax for each of 1988 and 1989 is $42.50 ($125 × 34%).

Year of Allocation	Increase in Tax
1987	$49.94
1988	42.50
1989	42.50

Example 2. (i) *Facts.* The facts are the same as in *Example 1* except that X was a C corporation until it elected to be treated as an S corporation effective for its taxable year beginning January 1, 1988. A is a U.S. person who has been a shareholder of X since January 1, 1988. A's holding period of the FC stock began on January 1, 1988, pursuant to § 1.1291-1(h)(4)(i). As of January 1, 1988, the FC stock had appreciated in value to $800; X therefore had $300 of built-in gain within the meaning of section 1374. Assume X pays a built-in gain tax of $102 because of the sale of the FC stock in 1990.

(ii) *Calculation of the aggregate increases in taxes owed by A.* The $500 gain recognized, reduced as provided in section 1366(f)(2) by the amount of built-in gain tax of $102 paid by X pursuant to section 1374 to $398, is taxable to A as an excess distribution as provided in § 1.1291-2(e)(2). The $398 excess distribution is allocated pro rata over X's four-year holding period (not A's three-year holding period) as provided in § 1.1291-3(e)(5). The allocation of $99.50 to 1990, the current shareholder year, is included in A's ordinary income. The allocations of $99.50 to 1987, 1988, and 1989 are not included in income, but are subject to the deferred tax amount. The aggregate increases in taxes are determined based on those $99.50 allocations.

(A) *Calculation of the 1987 increase in tax.* The highest statutory rate of tax applicable to A that was in effect in 1987 was 38.5 percent. The increase in tax for the portion of the excess distribution allocated to 1987 is $38.31 ($99.50 × 38.5%).

(B) *Calculation of the other increases in tax.* The highest statutory rate of tax applicable to A that was in effect for both 1988 and 1989 is 28 percent. The increase in tax for each of 1988 and 1989 is $27.86 ($99.50 × 28%).

(C) *Calculation of the aggregate increases in taxes.* The aggregate increases in taxes are $94.03 ($38.31 + 27.86 + 27.86).

(iii) *Calculation of the aggregate amount of interest.* For purposes of calculating the aggregate amount of interest, the reduction provided under section 1366(f)(2) is disregarded and the excess distribution is $500. Accordingly, for purposes of calculating the aggregate amount of interest, $125 is allocated to 1987, 1988, and 1989.

(A) *Calculation of the 1987 hypothetical increase in tax.* The highest statutory rate of tax applicable to A that was in effect in 1987 was 38.5 percent. The hypothetical increase in tax for the portion of the excess distribution allocated to 1987 is $48.12 ($125 × 38.5%).

(B) *Calculation of the other hypothetical increases in tax.* The highest statutory rate of tax applicable to A that was in effect for both 1988 and 1989 is 28 percent. The hypothetical increase in tax for each of 1988 and 1989 is $35.00 ($125 × 28%).

Year of Allocation	Increase in Tax
1987	$48.12
1988	35.00
1989	35.00

(C) *Interest charge.* Interest on each of the three hypothetical increases in tax ($48.12, $35, and $35) is computed using the rates and method provided in section 6621 for the respective interest period. The following are the interest periods:

Interest Period	
Beginning on	*Ending on*
April 15, 1988	April 15, 1991
April 15, 1989	April 15, 1991
April 15, 1990	April 15, 1991

(iv) *The deferred tax amount.* The deferred tax amount is the sum of the aggregate increases in taxes determined in (ii) and the aggregate amount of interest determined in (iii). [Prop. Reg. § 1.1291-4.]

(iv) *Aggregate increases in taxes.* The aggregate increases in taxes are $134.94 ($49.94 + $42.50 + $42.50).

(v) *Interest charge.* Interest on each of the three increases in tax ($49.94, $42.50, and $42.50) is computed using the rates and method provided in section 6621 for the respective interest period. The following are the interest periods:

Interest Period	
Beginning on	*Ending on*
March 15, 1988	March 15, 1991
March 15, 1989	March 15, 1991
March 15, 1990	March 15, 1991

[Proposed 4-1-92.]

Proposed Regulation

§ 1.1291-5. Coordination with the foreign tax credit rules.—(a) *Scope.*—This section provides rules for determining the amount of foreign tax credit that a shareholder may claim on a distribution from a section 1291 fund, and in certain cases, on a disposition of stock of a section 1291 fund. This section applies to a shareholder that has chosen under section 901 for the current shareholder year to claim a credit for foreign taxes paid. The rules of this section apply separately with respect to each section 1291 fund in which the shareholder directly or indirectly owns stock. For purposes of this section, an S corporation is treated as a partnership, and its shareholders as partners of the partnership. *See* section 1373.

(b) *Distributions from section 1291 funds to shareholders that are not entitled to a foreign tax credit for foreign taxes deemed paid.*—(1) *Rule.*—If a section 1291 fund makes a distribution with respect to which a shareholder (other than a shareholder described in paragraph (c) of this section) is subject to tax under § 1.1291-2, and the shareholder would be entitled to a foreign tax credit for foreign taxes paid (including withholding taxes) with respect to such distribution, but not for foreign taxes deemed paid with respect to such distribution (determined in both cases without regard to section 1291 and this section), the foreign tax credit with respect to that distribution is determined under the steps provided in this paragraph (b). The excess distribution is treated as foreign source income described in section 904(d)(1)(A).

(i) *Step 1.*—The shareholder determines the total excess distribution under § 1.1291-2 (c)(3), and the excess distribution taxes. The excess distribution taxes are the creditable foreign taxes (within the meaning of section 1291(g)(2)(A)), paid or accrued with respect to the total distribution for the current shareholder year, allocated to the total excess distribution as follows:

$$\frac{\text{Foreign taxes paid with respect to the total distribution}}{} \times \frac{\text{Total excess distribution}}{\text{Total distribution}}$$

The remainder of the creditable foreign taxes are allocated to the nonexcess distribution.

(ii) *Step 2.*—The shareholder allocates the total excess distribution and the excess distribution taxes ratably to each distribution received during the shareholder's taxable year in the manner provided in § 1.1291-2 (c)(4). The shareholder then allocates each excess distribution and the excess distribution taxes allocated to that distribution to each taxable year included in the shareholder's holding period based on the number of days in each such taxable year.

(iii) *Step 3.*—The shareholder determines the tentative increase in tax for each prior PFIC year. The term tentative increase in tax means the increase in tax determined in the manner provided in § 1.1291-4(c) for each prior PFIC year. The tentative increase in tax for a prior PFIC year is the foreign tax credit limitation for the excess distribution taxes allocated to that prior PFIC year.

(iv) *Step 4.*—The shareholder claims as a foreign tax credit with respect to an increase in tax for a prior PFIC year the lesser of the tentative increase in tax for that year determined in *Step 3* or the excess distribution taxes allocated to that prior PFIC year in *Step 2*.

(v) *Step 5.*—The shareholder determines the net increase in tax for each prior PFIC year by reducing the tentative increase in tax for a prior PFIC year determined in *Step 3* by the foreign tax credit determined for that year in *Step 4*. For the calculation of the interest charge for each net increase in tax, *see* § 1.1291-4(d).

(vi) *Step 6.*—The portions of the excess distribution and excess distribution taxes allocated to the current shareholder year and pre-PFIC years, if any, as well as the creditable foreign taxes allocated to the nonexcess distribution, are taken into account in the current shareholder year under the general foreign tax credit rules.

(2) *Carryovers disallowed.*—The amount by which the excess distribution taxes allocated to a prior PFIC year exceed the tentative increase in tax for that year may not be claimed as a foreign tax credit against any federal income tax.

(c) *Distributions from section 1291 funds that are CFCs.*—(1) *Rule.*—If a controlled foreign corporation (CFC) (as defined in section 904(d)(4)) that is a section 1291 fund makes a distribution with respect to which a United States shareholder (also as defined in section 904(d)(4)) is subject to tax under § 1.1291-2, the foreign tax credit with respect to that excess distribution is determined by applying the rules of section 1291(g) on a separate category basis within the meaning of section 904. *See* section 904(d)(3)(A) and the regulations under that section. A distribution described in this paragraph (c) from a section 1291 fund is foreign source income except to the extent the distribution is determined to be derived from U.S. sources pursuant to section 904(g). The foreign tax credit of a United States shareholder with respect to a distribution by a CFC that is taxable as an excess distribution to the shareholder under § 1.1291-2(e)(2) is determined according to the following steps.

(i) *Step 1.*—The shareholder determines—

(A) The separate category or categories (as defined in § 1.904-5(a)(1)) to which the total distribution (including the amount of the gross-up determined under section 78) for the taxable year is allocable under the rules of section 904(d)(3) and the regulations under that section (*see* § 1.904-5(c)(4));

(B) The creditable foreign taxes, which are the foreign taxes paid or deemed paid on the distribution (determined without regard to section 1291 and this section) with respect to each separate category under the rules of sections 901, 902, 904, and 960 and the regulations under those sections (*see* § 1.904-6(b)(3)); and

(C) The portion of the total distribution (including the gross-up) in each separate category that is from U.S. sources pursuant to section 904(g) (*see* § 1.904-5(m)(4) and (6)).

Solely for purposes of section 1291, any portion of the total excess distribution that would not be allocated to a separate category under normally applicable rules because it exceeds the fund's earnings and profits is deemed to be foreign source income allocated to the separate category defined in section 904(d)(1)(A).

(ii) *Step 2.*—The shareholder determines—

(A) The total excess distribution under § 1.1291-2(c)(3) with respect to the total distribution (including the gross-up); and

(B) The portion of the total excess distribution allocable to each separate category (the separate category excess distribution). Each separate category excess distribution is calculated as follows:

$$\frac{\text{Distribution allocable to a separate category (including gross-up) (\textit{Step 1} (A))}}{\text{Total distribution (including gross-up)}} \times \begin{array}{c}\text{Total excess}\\ \text{distribution}\\ \text{(\textit{Step 2} (A))}\end{array}$$

(iii) *Step 3.*—The shareholder determines the U.S. source portion of each separate category excess distribution as follows:

$$\frac{\begin{array}{c}\text{U.S. source portion of distribution allocable to a separate category}\\ \text{(\textit{Step 1} (C))}\end{array}}{\begin{array}{c}\text{Total distribution allocable to that category}\\ \text{(\textit{Step 1} (A))}\end{array}} \times \begin{array}{c}\text{Separate category excess distribution}\\ \text{(\textit{Step 2} (B))}\end{array}$$

(iv) *Step 4.*—The shareholder determines the excess distribution taxes with respect to each separate category (separate category excess distribution taxes) as follows:

$$\begin{array}{c}\text{Creditable foreign taxes with respect to the}\\ \text{distribution and allocable to the separate}\\ \text{category (\textit{Step 1} (B))}\end{array} \times \frac{\begin{array}{c}\text{Separate category excess}\\ \text{distribution (\textit{Step 2} (B))}\end{array}}{\begin{array}{c}\text{Total distribution allocable to}\\ \text{that category (\textit{Step 1} (A))}\end{array}}$$

(v) *Step 5.*—(A) The shareholder allocates—

(1) The separate category excess distribution;

(2) The separate category excess distribution taxes; and

(3) The U.S. source portion of the separate category excess distribution ratably to each distribution received during the shareholder's taxable year in the manner provided in § 1.1291-2(c)(4).

(B) The shareholder then allocates—

(1) The amount determined in *Step* 5 (A)*(1)* for each distribution to each taxable year included in the shareholder's holding period based on the number of days in each such taxable year;

(2) The amount determined in *Step* 5 (A)*(2)* for each distribution to each taxable year included in the shareholder's holding period based on the number of days in each such taxable year; and

(3) The amount determined in *Step* 5 (A)*(3)* for each distribution to each taxable year included in the shareholder's holding period based on the number of days in each such taxable year.

Solely for purposes of determining the foreign tax credit limitation for the current shareholder year, the portion of an excess distribution that is allocated to the current shareholder year and prePFIC years, and included in income, is treated as a dividend from a CFC that is not a PFIC. The excess distribution taxes allocated to that portion of the excess distribution are treated as foreign taxes paid with respect to a dividend from a CFC that is not a PFIC and taken into account in the current shareholder year under general foreign tax credit rules.

(vi) *Step 6.*—The shareholder determines a tentative increase in tax for each prior PFIC year for each allocation of a separate category excess distribution determined under *Step 5* (B)*(1)* (separate category tentative increase in tax).

(vii) *Step 7.*—The shareholder determines a foreign tax credit limitation for each prior PFIC year to which the separate category excess distribution is allocated. The limitation is determined as follows:

$$\begin{array}{c}\text{Separate category tentative increase in tax}\\ \text{for prior PFIC year (\textit{Step 6})}\end{array} \times \frac{\begin{array}{c}\text{Foreign source separate category excess}\\ \text{distribution allocated to that prior PFIC year}\\ \text{(\textit{Step 5}(B)(1) – \textit{Step 5}(B)(3))}\end{array}}{\begin{array}{c}\text{Separate category excess distribution allocated}\\ \text{to that prior PFIC year (\textit{Step 5}(B)(1))}\end{array}}$$

(viii) *Step 8.*—The shareholder may claim a foreign tax credit for each separate category tentative increase in tax. The foreign tax credit for a prior PFIC year is the lesser of the foreign tax credit limitation determined in *Step 7* for the prior PFIC year or the amount of the separate category excess distribution taxes allocated to that prior PFIC year under *Step 5* (B)(2).

(ix) *Step 9.*—The shareholder determines the separate category net increase in tax for each prior PFIC year by reducing the separate category tentative increase in tax determined for that year in *Step 6* by the amount of the foreign tax credit determined for that year in *Step 8*. For the calculation of the interest charge on each net increase in tax, *see* § 1.1291-4(d).

(2) *Carryovers disallowed.*—The amount by which the excess distribution taxes allocated to a prior PFIC year exceed the separate category tentative increase in tax for that year may not be claimed as a foreign tax credit against any federal income tax.

(3) *Example.*—The following example illustrates the rules of paragraph (c) of this section.

Example. (i) *Facts.* USP, a domestic corporation, has been a United States shareholder of FC, a CFC that is a section 1291 fund, since December 31, 1986. USP and FC both use the calendar year as their taxable year. USP has not included any amount in income under section 951 with respect to FC. On March 31, 1989, FC distributed $1000 to USP. As of that date, USP had held the FC stock for 821 days (365 days in 1987, 366 days in 1988, and 90 days in 1989). USP elects to credit foreign taxes for 1989, and determines the total creditable taxes with respect to the distribution from FC to be $485, $425 of which are deemed paid taxes and $60 of which are withholding taxes. The total distribution for 1989, including the section 78 gross-up, is $1425.

(ii) *Step 1: Determination of separate category income, U.S. source portions, and foreign taxes.* Applying the look through rules of section 904(d)(3), USP determines that $1125 of the total distribution of $1425 is allocable to distributions from a noncontrolled section 902 corporation, and that the remaining $300 is allocable to general limitation income. USP determines that $390 of creditable foreign taxes were paid and deemed paid with respect to the distributions from the noncontrolled section 902 corporation, and $95 were paid and deemed paid with respect to the general limitation income. USP determines that the distributions from the noncontrolled section 902 corporation and the general limitation income are from foreign sources. Accordingly, *Steps 3* and *5* (A)(3) will not be performed.

(iii) *Step 2: Calculation of total excess distribution and separate category excess distributions.* USP determines, based on FC distributions during the preceding three taxable years, that the total excess distribution for the current taxable year is $800. Of that amount, $631.58 [[$1125 (distribution allocable to distributions from a noncontrolled section 902 corporation)/$1425 (total distribution)] × $800 (total excess distribution)] is allocable to distributions from a noncontrolled section 902 corporation, and $168.42 [[$300 (distribution allocable to general limitation income)/$1425 (total distribution)]× $800 (total excess distribution)] is allocable to general limitation income.

(iv) *Step 4: Calculation of separate category excess distribution taxes.* USP calculates the excess distribution taxes (EDT) allocable to the separate category excess distributions. The noncontrolled section 902 corporation excess distribution taxes are $218.95 [$390 (creditable foreign taxes paid and deemed paid with respect to distributions from a noncontrolled section 902 corporation) × [$631.58 (noncontrolled section 902 corporation excess distribution)/$1125 (distribution from noncontrolled section 902 corporation)]], and the general limitation excess distribution taxes are $53.33 [$95 (creditable foreign taxes paid and deemed paid with respect to general limitation income) × [$168.42 (general limitation income excess distribution)/$300 (distribution allocable to general limitation income)]].

(v) *Step 5: Allocations of separate category excess distributions and excess distribution taxes over holding period.* The separate category excess distributions and the separate category EDT are allocated to each taxable year in USP's holding period based on the number of days in each such taxable year. (Discrepancies may be observed in the following presentation. These discrepancies reflect rounding to the nearest penny of the different calculations performed.)

(A) *Noncontrolled section 902 corporation excess distribution:* $.77 of the noncontrolled section 902 corporation excess distribution ($631.58/821 days) and $.27 of EDT ($218.95/821 days) are allocated to each day. The allocations to each taxable year are as follows:

	Allocations to taxable year	
Taxable year in holding period	*Excess distribution*	*EDT*
1987 (365 days)	$281.05	$98.55
1988 (366 days)	281.82	98.82
1989 (90 days)	69.30	24.30 .

(B) *General limitation excess distribution:* $.21 of the general limitation excess distribution ($168.42/821 days) and $.065 of EDT ($53.33/821 days) are allocated to each day. The allocations to each taxable year are as follows:

	Allocations to taxable year	
Taxable year in holding period	*Excess distribution*	*EDT*
1987 (365 days)	$76.65	$23.73
1988 (366 days)	76.86	23.79
1989 (90 days)	18.90	5.85

(vi) *Step 6: Calculation of separate category tentative increases in taxes.* USP determines the tentative increases in tax (TIIT) for the allocations of each separate category excess distribution to 1987 and 1988, the prior PFIC years in USP's holding period. The noncontrolled section 902 corporation excess distribution TIIT for 1987 is $112.28 [$281.05 (allocation of noncontrolled section 902 corporation excess distribution to 1987) × 39.95% (the highest corporate tax rate in effect in 1987)], and for 1988, $95.82 [$281.82 (allocation of noncontrolled section 902 corporation excess distribution to 1988) × 34% (highest corporate tax rate in effect in 1988)]. The general limitation excess distribution TIIT for 1987 is $30.62 [$76.65 (allocation of general limitation income excess distribution to 1987) × 39.95% (highest corporate tax rate in effect in 1987)], and for 1988, $26.13 [$76.86 (allocation of general limitation income excess distribution to 1988) × 34% (highest corporate tax rate in effect in 1988)].

(vii) *Step 7: Calculation of the foreign tax credit limitations.* USP determines the foreign tax credit (FTC) limitations for each prior PFIC year on a separate category basis. The FTC limitations are the same as the tentative increases in tax because none of the separate category distributions are from U.S. sources. Therefore, the FTC limitation for the noncontrolled section 902 corporation excess distribution for 1987 is $112.28, and for 1988, $95.82. The FTC limitation for the general limitation excess distribution for 1987 is $30.62, and for 1988, $26.13.

(viii) *Step 8: Calculation of the foreign tax credit.* The FTC for the noncontrolled section 902 corporation excess distribution for 1987 is $98.55 [lower of $112.28 (1987 noncontrolled section 902 corporation FTC limitation) and $98.55 (1987 noncontrolled section 902 corporation EDT)], and for 1988, $95.82 [lower of $95.82 (1988 noncontrolled section 902 corporation FTC limitation) and $98.82 (1988 noncontrolled section 902 corporation EDT)]. The FTC for the general limitation excess distribution for 1987 is $23.73 [lower of $30.62 (1987 general limitation FTC limitation) and $23.73 (1987 general limitation income EDT)], and for 1988 is $23.79 [lower of $26.13 (1988 general limitation income FTC limitation) and $23.79 (1988 general limitation EDT)].

(ix) *Step 9: Calculation of the separate category net increases in taxes.* As provided in § 1.1291-4(c)(3), USP determines the net increase in tax (NIIT) for each separate category excess distribution allocated to a prior PFIC year. The noncontrolled section 902 corporation NIIT for 1987 is $13.73 [$112.28 (1987 noncontrolled section 902 corporation TIIT) less $98.55 (1987 noncontrolled section 902 corporation FTC)], and the noncontrolled section 902 corporation NIIT for 1988 is 0 [$95.82 (1988 noncontrolled section 902 corporation TIIT) less $95.82 (1988 noncontrolled section 902 corporation FTC)]. The general limitation income NIIT for 1987 is $6.89 [$30.62 (1987 general limitation income TIIT) less $23.73 (1987 general limitation income FTC)], and the general limitation NIIT for 1988 is $2.34 [$26.13 (1988 general limitation income TIIT) less $23.79 (1988 general limitation income FTC)]. An interest charge is calculated for each NIIT as provided in § 1.1291-4(d). The $3 excess of noncontrolled section 902 EDT allocated to 1988 ($98.82) over the FTC limitation calculated for the 1988 allocation of the noncontrolled section 902 excess distribution ($95.82) may not be used to reduce any federal income tax. The calculations of *Steps 5* through *9* are summarized as follows:

(A) *Noncontrolled section 902 corporation excess distribution:*

Taxable year (days) in holding period	*Allocations to taxable year—Step 5* Excess distribution	*EDT*	*Step 6* *TIIT*	*Step 8* *FTC*	*Step 9* *NIIT*
1987 (365)	$281.05	$98.55	$112.28	$98.55	$13.73
1988 (366)	281.82	98.82	95.82	95.82	0
1989 (90)	69.30	24.30			

(B) *General limitation income excess distribution:*

Taxable year (days) in holding period	*Allocations to taxable year—Step 5* Excess distribution	*EDT*	*Step 6* *TIIT*	*Step 8* *FTC*	*Step 9* *NIIT*
1987 (365)	$76.65	$23.73	$30.62	$23.73	$6.89
1988 (366)	76.86	23.79	26.13	23.79	2.34
1989 (90)	69.30	24.30			

(x) *Current shareholder year foreign tax credit.* The allocations of the separate category excess distributions to 1989, the current shareholder year, are included in USP's ordinary income. Such income is treated as a dividend from a CFC that is not a PFIC, and the EDT allocated to that income are treated as foreign taxes paid with respect to a dividend from a CFC that is not a PFIC.

(d) *Distributions from section 1291 funds that are noncontrolled section 902 corporations.*—If a noncontrolled section 902 corporation (as defined in section 904(d)(2)(E) and the regulations under that section) that is a section 1291 fund makes a distribution with respect to which a domestic shareholder (as defined in section 902 and the regulations under that section) is subject to tax under § 1.1291-2, the rules of paragraph (c) of this section apply for purposes of determining the amount of the foreign tax credit with respect to that distribution; however, the only separate category is described in section 904(d)(1)(E). This paragraph (d) does not apply to a United States shareholder of a CFC to whom paragraph (c) of this section applies.

(e) *Section 1248 gain.*—For purposes of determining the foreign tax credit under this section, a shareholder treats gain from a disposition of stock of a section 1291 fund as a distribution only to the extent that the gain would be, but for section 1291, includible in gross income as a dividend under section 1248. [Prop. Reg. § 1.1291-5.]

[Proposed 4-1-92.]

Proposed Regulation

§ 1.1291-6. Nonrecognition transfers of stock of section 1291 funds.—(a) *In general.*—(1) *Scope.*—This section provides rules concerning the recognition of gain by a shareholder on a direct or indirect disposition of stock of a section 1291 fund that results from a transaction in which, but for section 1291 and these regulations, there would not be full recognition of gain under the Code and regulations (the transaction hereinafter referred to as a nonrecognition transfer). This section also provides coordination between section 1291 and other provisions of the Code and regulations under which gain must be recognized in transactions that would otherwise be entitled to nonrecognition.

(2) *Nonrecognition transfers.*—A nonrecognition transfer includes, but is not limited to, a gift, a transfer by reason of death, a distribution to a beneficiary by a trust or estate (other than a distribution to which section 643(e)(3) applies), and a transfer in which gain or loss is not fully recognized pursuant to any of the following provisions: Sections 311(a), 332, 336(e), 337, 351, 354, 355, 361, 721, 731, 852(b)(6), 1036, and 1041.

(3) *Application of section to transfer of stock of a pedigreed QEF.*—This section does not apply to a nonrecognition transfer of stock of a pedigreed QEF. The following example illustrates the rule of this paragraph (a)(3).

Example. X is a U.S. person that is a shareholder of FC, a corporation. FC owns all the stock of FS. Both FC and FS are pedigreed QEFs with respect to X. Pursuant to a plan of complete liquidation, satisfying the requirements of section 332, FS distributes all its assets and liabilities to FC. No gain or loss will be recognized to FC, FS, or X under section 1291(f) or 1297(b)(5).

(b) *Recognition of gain or loss.*—(1) *In general.*—Unless otherwise provided in paragraph (c) of this section, a shareholder recognizes gain on any direct or indirect disposition of stock of a section 1291 fund in accordance with the rules of § 1.1291-3, without regard to whether the disposition is a result of a nonrecognition transfer as defined in paragraph (a)(2) of this section.

(2) *Coordination with other recognition provisions.*—A direct or indirect disposition of stock to which an exception to the gain recognition rule of paragraph (b)(1) of this section applies will nevertheless be a disposition taxable under § 1.1291-3 if the gain must be recognized pursuant to another provision of the Code or regulations. For coordination with section 367, *see* paragraph (d)(1) of this section.

(3) *No recognition of loss.*—This section does not permit or require the recognition of loss on a direct or indirect disposition of stock of a section 1291 fund if such loss would not otherwise be recognized under another section of the Code or regulations. For the effect on the holding period of a disposition resulting from a nonrecognition transfer that would be subject to the gain recognition rule but for the fact that a loss is realized, *see* paragraph (b)(5) of this section.

(4) *Special basis rules.*—(i) *Direct shareholders.*—If the gain recognition rule of paragraph (b)(1) of this section applies to a nonrecognition transfer in which a direct shareholder transfers stock of a section 1291 fund, proper adjustment is made to the basis of such stock in the hands of the transferee, as well as to the basis of the property, if any, received by the shareholder in the transaction.

(ii) *Indirect shareholders.*—If the gain recognition rule of paragraph (b)(1) of this section applies to a disposition by an indirect shareholder that results from a nonrecognition transfer, the shareholder's adjusted basis of the stock or other property owned directly by the shareholder through which ownership of the section 1291 fund is attributed to the shareholder is increased by the amount of gain recognized by the shareholder. In addition, solely for purposes of determining the subsequent treatment under the Code and regulations of a direct or indirect shareholder of the stock of the section 1291 fund treated as disposed of, the adjusted basis of the actual owner of the stock of the section 1291 fund is increased by the amount of gain recognized by the shareholder.

(iii) *Stock acquired by reason of death.*—Unless all of the gain is recognized to a shareholder (the decedent) pursuant to paragraph (c)(2)(iii)(B) of this section, the basis of stock received on the death of the decedent by the decedent's estate (other than a foreign estate within the meaning of section 7701(a)(31)), or directly by another U.S. person, is the lower of the fair market value or adjusted basis of the transferred stock in the hands of the shareholder immediately before death. If gain is recognized by the decedent, the decedent's adjusted basis of the stock of the section 1291 fund is increased by the gain recognized with respect thereto.

(iv) *Assets distributed in certain subsidiary liquidations.*—The bases of the assets of a section 1291 fund distributed to an 80 percent corporate distributee (within the meaning of section 337(c)), in complete liquidation of the section 1291 fund pursuant to section 332, is increased by the amount by which the gain recognized by the shareholder exceeds the amount that would have been taxed as a dividend under section 367(b). Except as otherwise provided in this paragraph (b)(4)(iv), the adjusted basis of each distributed asset is increased (but not in excess of its fair market value) by a pro rata portion of the excess described in the preceding sentence, based on the realized but unrecognized gain with respect to such asset relative to the realized but unrecognized gain with respect to all distributed assets. For purposes of the preceding sentence, money is not treated as an asset. The adjusted basis of a receivable may not be increased pursuant to this paragraph (b)(4)(iv) to an amount that exceeds the receivable's face amount.

(5) *Special holding period rule for transfers subject to gain recognition rule.*—If a loss is realized on a direct or indirect disposition of stock of a section 1291 fund in a transaction in which any gain, if realized, would have been recognized under this section, the shareholder's holding period for stock received in the transaction, if any, as well as the transferee's holding period of the transferred stock, begins on the day after the disposition, but only for purposes of applying sections 1291 through 1297 to the shareholder or the transferee with respect to such stock, as appropriate.

(c) *Exceptions to general rule.*—(1) *Transfer of section 1291 fund stock for PFIC stock.*—Gain is not recognized on a direct or indirect disposition of stock of a section 1291 fund that results from a nonrecognition transfer if in the transfer, stock of the section 1291 fund, or an interest in another person that causes the shareholder to be an indirect shareholder, is exchanged solely for either—

(i) Stock of the same or another corporation that either qualifies under section 1296(a) as a PFIC for its taxable year that includes the day after the nonrecognition transfer or is the acquiring foreign corporation in a section 368(a)(1)(F) reorganization; or

(ii) An interest in another person that owns directly or indirectly stock of the transferred section 1291 fund or of another PFIC, but only to the extent (by value) that the shareholder is treated under § 1.1291-1(b)(8) as owning after the transfer at least as great an interest in the section 1291 fund or other PFIC that the indirect shareholder owned before the transfer. Stock in another PFIC owned before the transfer is not taken into account for purposes of the preceding sentence. For the definition of an indirect disposition, *see* generally § 1.1291-3(e)(2).

(2) *Transfer to U.S. person.*—(i) *In general.*—Unless otherwise provided, a shareholder does not recognize gain on a direct or indirect disposition of stock of a section 1291 fund that results from a nonrecognition transfer if immediately after the transfer such stock is owned or considered owned by a U.S. person (U.S. transferee), provided that—

(A) The basis of the stock that is the subject of the disposition, in the hands of its actual owner immediately after the transfer, is no greater than the basis of such stock in the hands of its actual owner immediately before the transfer;

(B) The U.S. transferee's holding period for the transferred stock is at least as long as the holding period of the shareholder immediately before the transfer; and

(C) The aggregate ownership (determined under § 1.1291-1(b)(8)) of the shareholder and the U.S. transferee immediately after the transfer (determined without regard to stock held by the U.S. transferee prior to the transfer) is the same as or greater than the shareholder's proportionate ownership immediately before the transfer.

This paragraph (c)(2)(i) does not apply to a transfer to a partnership, S corporation, trust or estate. For those rules, *see* paragraph (c)(3) of this section.

(ii) *Transitory ownership.*—Gain is not recognized to a domestic corporation that is a party to a reorganization within the meaning of section 368(b) if, pursuant to a plan of reorganization, the corporation acquires stock of a PFIC that is a party to the reorganization in exchange for the domestic corporation's assets, and transfers the PFIC stock under section 361(c) to a shareholder that is a U.S. person in exchange for the shareholder's stock of the domestic corporation.

(iii) *Transfer by reason of death.*—(A) *In general.*—Except as provided in paragraph (c)(2)(iii)(B) of this section, gain is not recognized to a shareholder upon a disposition of stock of a section 1291 fund that results from a nonrecognition transfer to the shareholder's domestic estate or directly to another U.S. person upon the death of the shareholder.

(B) *Exception.*—Gain is recognized to a shareholder on the transfer of stock of a section 1291 fund to the shareholder's domestic estate if, pursuant to the terms of the will, the section 1291 fund stock may be transferred to either a foreign beneficiary or a trust established in the will.

(iv) *Section 355 distribution of stock of section 1291 fund.*—Gain is not recognized to a shareholder that is the distributing corporation upon a direct or indirect disposition of stock of a section 1291 fund that results from the distribution of stock of a controlled corporation to another U.S. person (the distributee) in a transaction qualifying under section 355(a) if the distributee is a shareholder with respect to such stock immediately after the distribution. The distributee in such a transaction takes a holding period in the stock of the controlled corporation equal to the longer of the holding period determined under section 1223(1) or the distributing corporation's holding period of the stock of the controlled corporation. If the controlled corporation is itself the section 1291 fund, the distributee in such a transaction takes a basis in the stock of the controlled corporation equal to the lesser of the adjusted basis determined under section 358 or the distributing corporation's adjusted basis of the stock of the controlled corporation immediately prior to the distribution.

(v) *Gifts incurring gift tax.*—If a shareholder makes a gift of stock of a section 1291 fund to a U.S. person and thereby incurs gift tax, the shareholder will not recognize gain, but will be liable for the deferred tax amount as if the shareholder recognized gain in the amount of the gift tax that is added to the basis of the transferred stock under section 1015(d). The adjusted basis of the transferred stock may only be increased, to the extent provided in section 1015(d), by the amount of gift tax paid. The following example illustrates the rule of this paragraph (c)(2)(v).

Example. M, a U.S. person, purchased 1,000 shares of NQF, a PFIC, on December 31, 1989. M did not elect to treat NQF as a QEF. M gave the NQF stock to her daughter, H, also a U.S. person, on December 31, 1993. M paid $100x of gift tax. As provided in section 1015(a) and (d)(6), H's adjusted basis in the NQF stock is M's adjusted basis, increased by $60x of gift tax paid. As a result, pursuant to § 1.1291-6(c)(2)(v), M is liable for the deferred tax amount that M would have owed if M recognized $60x of gain on a taxable transfer of the NQF stock. For purposes of calculating the deferred tax amount, the $60x is allocated over M's four-year holding period, with the deferred tax amount calculated with respect to the $45x allocated to 1991, 1992, and 1993. Other than for the $60x of gift tax paid, there are no further adjustments to H's basis in the NQF.

(vi) *Exception inapplicable.*—Paragraph (c)(2) of this section does not apply to a disposition of stock of a section 1291 fund that results from a nonrecognition transfer of stock of a section 1291 fund if the U.S. transferee is—

(A) An organization that will not be subject to section 1291 and these regulations pursuant to § 1.1291-1(e) with respect to that section 1291 fund; or

(B) A trust, including a testamentary trust or other irrevocable trust, that is not a grantor trust or beneficiary-owned section 678 trust to which paragraph (c)(3)(iv) of this section applies.

(3) *Transfers involving pass-through entities.*—(i) *Section 721 transfer to partnership.*—Gain is not recognized to a shareholder on a disposition of stock of a section 1291 fund that results from a transfer to a partnership under section 721, but only to the extent that the shareholder is treated as owning such stock immediately after the transfer pursuant to § 1.1291-1(b)(8)(iii)(A).

(ii) *Section 731 distribution by partnership.*—Gain is not recognized to a partner on a disposition of stock of a section 1291 fund that results from a distribution under section 731, but only to the extent that the partner is treated as owning such stock immediately after the distribution pursuant to § 1.1291-1(b)(8).

(iii) *Transfer to S corporation.*—Gain is not recognized to a shareholder on a disposition of stock of a section 1291 fund that results from a transfer to an S corporation under section 351, but only to the extent that the shareholder is treated as owning such stock immediately after the transfer pursuant to § 1.1291-1(b)(8)(iii)(B).

(iv) *Transfer to grantor trust.*—Gain is not recognized on a disposition of stock of a section 1291 fund that results from a nonrecognition transfer to a trust by the grantor of the trust if the grantor is treated as owning the portion of the trust that includes both the income and corpus portions of the stock that is disposed of. If a person other than the grantor is treated as the owner of the portion of a beneficiary-owned section 678 trust that includes the income and corpus portions of the stock transferred to the trust, that person is treated as acquiring the stock by gift from the grantor, which is a transfer subject to the general rules of this section. Stock owned directly or indirectly by a grantor of a grantor trust or by a beneficiary of a beneficiary-owned section 678 trust will be treated as transferred by the grantor or other person considered the owner thereof for purposes of this section at the time the grantor or beneficiary is no longer considered the owner of both the income and corpus portions of the stock of the section 1291 fund. For special rules applicable to a grantor or beneficiary-owned section 678 trust, *see* sections 671 through 679 and the regulations under those sections.

(4) *Transfer to nonresident alien spouse who files joint return.*—Gain is not recognized on a disposition of stock of a section 1291 fund that results from a nonrecognition transfer to the shareholder's nonresident alien spouse who has made the election under section 6013(g) and is treated as a resident for purposes of chapter 1 of the Code. A termination of the election pursuant to section 6013(g)(4) will be treated as a disposition of the stock by the transferee spouse as provided in § 1.1291-3(b)(2).

(d) *Special rules.*—(1) *Section 367 or 1492 transfer.*—(i) *Gain recognition transfer.*—If the gain recognition rule of paragraph (b)(1) of this section applies to a disposition of stock of a section 1291 fund that results from a transfer with respect to which section 367 or 1492 requires the shareholder to recognize gain or include an amount in income as a distribution under section 301, the gain realized on the transfer is taxable as an excess distribution as provided in § 1.1291-2(e)(2). The excess, if any, of the amount to be included in income pursuant to section 367(b) over the gain realized is taxable as provided in the regulations under section 367(b).

(ii) *Disposition to which exception applies.*—If an exception to the gain recognition rule of paragraph (b)(1) of this section applies to a disposition to which section 367(b) applies, and section 367(b) requires the shareholder to include an amount in income as a distribution taxable under section 301, that amount is an excess distribution taxable as provided in § 1.1291-2(e)(2).

(2) *Taxable year of disposition by reason of death.*—A disposition of stock of a section 1291 fund by reason of a shareholder's death, to which the gain recognition rule of paragraph (b)(1) or (c)(2)(iii)(B) of this section applies, will be treated as a disposition by the shareholder effected immediately before death and taxable to the shareholder in the shareholder's last taxable year.

(3) *Section 643(e)(3) election.*—An election by a foreign estate or trust under section 643(e)(3) will not apply to stock of a section 1291 fund distributed to a U.S. person if the gain recognized by reason of the election is not taxable in the United States.

(e) *Receipt of nonqualifying property.*—If a nonrecognition transfer results in a disposition of stock of a section 1291 fund to which an exception to the gain recognition rule of paragraph (b)(1) of this section would apply but for the fact that the property received in the transfer includes money or property (nonqualifying property) in addition to property permitted to be received pursuant to paragraph (c) of this section, gain is recognized only to the extent of the nonqualifying property. If such nonqualifying property is treated as a distribution by the section 1291 fund under otherwise applicable provisions of the Code, the distribution will be taxable on an excess distribution as provided in § 1.1291-2(e)(2).

(f) *Examples.*—The following examples illustrate the operation of this section.

Example 1. A is a shareholder of PFIC, a corporation organized under the laws of Country X. PFIC is a section 1291 fund with respect to A. To avoid expropriation of the assets of PFIC by the government of Country X, PFIC's management has decided to relocate to Country Y. To effect the relocation, PFIC adopted a plan of reorganization pursuant to which PFIC will transfer all of its assets to Newco, a newly organized Country Y corporation, in exchange for Newco stock and the assumption of PFIC's liabilities in a transaction that will qualify as a reorganization described in section 368(a)(1)(F). PFIC will distribute the Newco stock to its shareholders in exchange for its stock. A will transfer all of its PFIC stock in exchange for Newco stock of equal value. A will not recognize gain on the transfer of PFIC stock in exchange for Newco stock pursuant to section 354 and § 1.1291-6(c)(1)(i), and the days in A's holding period of the Newco stock will retain the prePFIC and prior PFIC character of the days in A's holding period of the PFIC stock pursuant to § 1.1291-1(h)(7). *See* § 1.1291-1(b)(1)(ii).

Example 2. X is a domestic corporation that owns 75 percent of F, a foreign corporation that is not a PFIC. F owns 100 percent of the stock of FS, a PFIC. X is treated under § 1.1291-1(b)(8)(ii)(A) as owning 75 percent of the stock of FS. X has not elected under section 1295 to treat FS as a QEF. FC, a foreign corporation, will acquire substantially all the assets of F in exchange for FC stock and the assumption of the liabilities of F in a transaction that will qualify as a reorganization described in section 368(a)(1)(C). FC never qualified as a PFIC and will not qualify as a PFIC at the beginning of the day after the transaction. F will distribute the FC stock to its shareholders in exchange for their F stock. X will transfer all its F stock to F in exchange for FC stock of equal value. After the reorganization, X will hold 49 percent of the outstanding FC stock, and therefore will no longer be treated under § 1.1291-1(b)(8)(ii)(A) as owning stock of FS. Pursuant to §§ 1.1291-6(b)(1) and 1.1291-3(e)(1), X will be taxed on the indirect disposition of the FS stock.

Example 3. X, a domestic corporation, owns stock of PFIC, a corporation that is a section 1291 fund with respect to X. Pursuant to a plan of reorganization, X will transfer to FC, a foreign corporation, substantially all of its assets in exchange for FC voting stock and FC's assumption of the liabilities of X in a transaction that will qualify as a reorganization described in section 368(a)(1)(C). It is assumed that the transaction is not taxable under section 367(a) (including section 367(a)(5)). X will distribute the FC stock to its shareholders in exchange for their X stock. FC is not a PFIC and will not qualify as a PFIC for the taxable year that includes the day after the transfer. In addition, after the reorganization, no U.S. person will own 50 percent or more of FC. Pursuant to § 1.1291-6(b)(1), section 361(a) will not apply to X's transfer of the PFIC stock to FC. X therefore will recognize the gain realized on the transfer of the stock of PFIC. The gain will be taxed to X as an excess distribution pursuant to § 1.1291-3.

Example 4. X, a domestic corporation, satisfies the stock ownership requirements specified in section 332(b) with respect to PFIC, a corporation that is a section 1291 fund with respect to X. Pursuant to a plan of complete liquidation, PFIC will distribute all its assets and liabilities to X in exchange for its stock and liquidate. Pursuant to § 1.1291-6(b)(1) and (d)(1)(i), section 332(a) will not apply to the complete liquidation of PFIC. X therefore will recognize gain on the disposition of the stock of PFIC, which gain will be taxed as an excess distribution pursuant to § 1.1291-3. The adjusted basis of the assets of X will be increased as provided in § 1.1291-6(b)(4)(iv).

Example 5. USP, a domestic corporation, owns all the stock of USS, also a domestic corporation. USS owns stock of FS, a corporation that is a section 1291 fund with respect to USS. Pursuant to a plan of reorganization that will qualify under section 368(a)(1)(C), USS will transfer substantially all its assets to FC, a PFIC, in exchange for FC stock and the assumption by FC of the liabilities of USS. USS will transfer the FC stock to USP in exchange for its stock. Pursuant to § 1.1291-6(c)(1), section 361 applies to USS's transfer to FC of the FS stock. As provided in § 1.1291-6(c)(2)(ii), USS will not recognize any gain on the transfer of the FC stock to USP in exchange for its stock.

Example 6. A, a U.S. person, owns all the stock of FC, a corporation that is both a controlled foreign corporation and a section 1291 fund with respect to A. Pursuant to a reorganization plan, FC will transfer all its assets to F, a foreign corporation that is a PFIC but not a controlled foreign corporation after the transfer, in exchange for F stock and the assumption of FC's liabilities in a transaction that will qualify as a reorganization described in section 368(a)(1)(C). FC will distribute the F stock to A in exchange for A's FC stock. A will not recognize gain on the transfer of FC stock in exchange for F stock pursuant to section 354 and § 1.1291-6(c)(1). However, the regulations under section 367(b) require A to include a certain amount in gross income as a distribution taxable under section 301. As provided in § 1.1291-6(d)(1)(ii), A will treat that amount as an excess distribution taxable as provided in § 1.1291-2(e)(2).

Example 7. M, a U.S. person, purchased 100 shares of the stock of NQF on December 31, 1989, for $100. NQF is a corporation that is a section 1291 fund with respect to M. On January 1, 1992, when the 100 shares of NQF stock had a fair market value of $200, M transferred its NQF stock to P, a domestic partnership, of which M and N, also a U.S. person, are equal partners. After the transfer to P, M will be considered to own only 50 shares of the NQF stock pursuant to § 1.1291-1(b)(8)(iii)(A), notwithstanding that gain recognized with respect to all 100 shares would be allocated to M pursuant to section 704(c). M therefore is taxable on the disposition of 50 shares of NQF stock in accordance with § 1.1291-6(c)(3)(i).

(g) *Reporting requirements for transfers entitled to nonrecognition treatment under this section.*—If an exception to the gain recognition rule of paragraph (b)(1) of this section applies wholly or partly to a disposition of stock of a section 1291 fund that results from a nonrecognition transfer, the shareholder must provide the following information in an attachment to Form 8621, which must be filed with the shareholder's federal income tax return for the taxable year in which the transfer occurs:

(1) A complete description of the transfer, including a complete description of the stock, securities or other property received directly or indirectly in the transfer.

(2) The name, address, and taxpayer identification number (if available) of the transferor and transferee of the transferred property.

(3) A statement citing the applicable exception to the gain recognition rule and stating why the exception is applicable.

(h) *Transfers involving QEF stock.*—For rules concerning the effect of a transfer of stock of a QEF on the section 1295 election, *see* § 1.1295-1. [Prop. Reg. § 1.1291-6.]

[Proposed 4-1-92.]

Proposed Regulation

§ 1.1291-7. Section 1291(e) rules similar to section 1246.—[Reserved]

[Proposed 4-1-92.]

§ 1.1291-9. Deemed dividend election.—(a) *Deemed dividend election.*—(1) *In general.*—This section provides rules for making the election under section 1291(d)(2)(B) (deemed dividend election). Under that section, a shareholder (as defined in paragraph (j)(3) of this section) of a PFIC that is an unpedigreed QEF may elect to include in income as a dividend the shareholder's pro rata share of the post-1986 earnings and profits of the PFIC attributable to the stock held on the qualification date (as defined in paragraph (e) of this section), provided the PFIC is a controlled foreign corporation (CFC) within the meaning of section 957(a) for the taxable year for which the shareholder elects under section 1295 to treat the PFIC as a QEF (section 1295 election). If the shareholder makes the deemed dividend election, the PFIC will become a pedigreed QEF with respect to the shareholder. The deemed dividend is taxed under section 1291 as an excess distribution received on the qualification date. The excess distribution determined under this paragraph (a) is allocated under section 1291(a)(1)(A) only to those days in the shareholder's holding period during which the foreign corporation qualified as a PFIC. For purposes of the preceding sentence, the holding period of the PFIC stock with respect to which the election is made ends on the day before the qualification date. For the definitions of PFIC, QEF, unpedigreed QEF, and pedigreed QEF, see paragraph (j)(1) and (2) of this section.

(2) *Post-1986 earnings and profits defined.*—(i) *In general.*—For purposes of this section, the term post-1986 earnings and profits means the undistributed earnings and profits, within the meaning of section 902(c)(1), as of the day before the qualification date, that were accumulated and not distributed in taxable years of the PFIC beginning after 1986 and during which it was a PFIC, but without regard to whether the earnings relate to a period during which the PFIC was a CFC.

(ii) *Pro rata share of post-1986 earnings and profits attributable to shareholder's stock.*—(A) *In general.*—A shareholder's pro rata share of the post-1986 earnings and profits of the PFIC attributable to the stock held by the shareholder on the qualification date is the amount of post-1986 earnings and profits of the PFIC accumulated during any portion of the shareholder's holding period ending at the close of the day before the qualification date and attributable, under the principles of section 1248 and the regulations under that section, to the PFIC stock held on the qualification date.

(B) *Reduction for previously taxed amounts.*—A shareholder's pro rata share of the post-1986 earnings and profits of the PFIC does not include any amount that the shareholder demonstrates to the satisfaction of the Commissioner (in the manner provided in paragraph (d)(2) of this section) was, pursuant to another provision of the law, previously included in the income of the shareholder, or of another U.S. person if the shareholder's holding period of the PFIC stock includes the period during which the stock was held by that other U.S. person.

(b) *Who may make the election.*—A shareholder of an unpedigreed QEF that is a CFC for the taxable year of the PFIC for which the shareholder makes the section 1295 election may make the deemed dividend election provided the shareholder held stock of that PFIC on the qualification date. A shareholder is treated as holding stock of the PFIC on the qualification date if its holding period with respect to that stock under section 1223 includes the qualification date. A shareholder may make the deemed dividend election without regard to whether the shareholder is a United States shareholder within the meaning of section 951(b). A deemed dividend election may be made by a shareholder whose pro rata share of the post-1986 earnings and profits of the PFIC attributable to the PFIC stock held on the qualification date is zero.

(c) *Time for making the election.*—The shareholder makes the deemed dividend election in the shareholder's return for the taxable year that includes the qualification date. If the shareholder and the PFIC have the same taxable year, the shareholder makes the deemed dividend election in either the original return for the taxable year for which the shareholder makes the section 1295 election, or in an amended return for that year. If the shareholder and the PFIC have different taxable years, the deemed dividend election must be made in an amended return for the taxable year that includes the qualification date. If the deemed dividend election is made in an amended return, the amended return must be filed by a date that is within three years of the due date, as extended under section 6081, of the original return for the taxable year that includes the qualification date.

(d) *Manner of making the election.*—(1) *In general.*—A shareholder makes the deemed dividend election by filing Form 8621 and the attachment to Form 8621 described in paragraph (d)(2) of this section with the return for the taxable year of the shareholder that includes the qualification date, reporting the deemed dividend as an excess distribution pursuant to section 1291(a)(1), and paying the tax and interest due on the excess distribution. A shareholder that makes the deemed dividend election after the due date of the return (determined without regard to extensions) for the taxable year that includes the qualification date must pay additional interest, pursuant to section 6601, on the amount of the underpayment of tax for that year.

(2) *Attachment to Form 8621.*—The shareholder must attach a schedule to Form 8621 that demonstrates the calculation of the shareholder's pro rata share of the post-1986 earnings and profits of the PFIC that is treated as distributed to the shareholder on the qualification date pursuant to this section. If the shareholder is claiming an exclusion from its pro rata share of the post-1986 earnings and profits for an amount previously included in its income or the income of another U.S. person, the shareholder must include the following information:

(i) The name, address, and taxpayer identification number of each U.S. person that previously included an amount in income, the amount previously included in income by each such U.S. person, the provision of the law pursuant to which the amount was previously included in income, and the taxable year or years of inclusion of each amount; and

(ii) A description of the transaction pursuant to which the shareholder acquired, directly or indirectly, the stock of the PFIC from another U.S. person, and the provisions of law pursuant to which the shareholder's holding period includes the period the other U.S. person held the CFC stock.

(e) *Qualification date.*—(1) *In general.*—Except as otherwise provided in this paragraph (e), the qualification date is the first day of the PFIC's first taxable year as a QEF (first QEF year).

(2) *Elections made after March 31, 1995, and before January 27, 1997.*—(i) *In general.*—The qualification date for deemed dividend elections made after March 31, 1995, and before January 27, 1997, is the first day of the shareholder's election year. The shareholder's election year is the taxable year of the shareholder for which it made the section 1295 election.

(ii) *Exception.*—A shareholder who made the deemed dividend election after May 1, 1992, and before January 27, 1997, may elect to change its qualification date to the first day of the first QEF year, provided the periods of limitations on assessment for the taxable year that includes that date and for the shareholder's election year have not expired. A shareholder changes the qualification date by filing amended returns, with revised Forms 8621 and the attachments described in paragraph (d)(2) of this section, for the shareholder's election year and the shareholder's taxable year that includes the first day of the first QEF year, and making all appropriate adjustments and payments.

(3) *Examples.*—The rules of this paragraph (e) are illustrated by the following examples:

Example 1—(i) *Eligibility to make deemed dividend election.* A is a U.S. person who files its income tax return on a calendar year basis. On January 2, 1994, A purchased one percent of the stock of M, a PFIC with a taxable year ending November 30. M was both a CFC and a PFIC, but not a QEF, for all of its taxable years. On December 3, 1996, M made a distribution to its shareholders. A received $100, all of which A reported in its 1996 return as an excess distribution as provided in section 1291(a)(1). A decides to make the section 1295 election in A's 1997 taxable year to treat M as a QEF effective for M's taxable year beginning December 1, 1996. Because A did not make the section 1295 election in 1994, the first year in its holding period of M stock that M qualified as a PFIC, M would be an unpedigreed QEF and A would be subject to both sections 1291 and 1293. A, however, may elect under section 1291(d)(2) to purge the years M was not a QEF from A's holding period. If A makes the section 1291(d)(2) election, the December 3 distribution will not be taxable under section 1291(a). Because M is a CFC, even though A is not a U.S. shareholder within the meaning of section 951(b), A may make the deemed dividend election under section 1291(d)(2)(B).

(ii) *Making the election.* Under paragraph (e)(1) of this section, the qualification date, and therefore the date of the deemed dividend, is December 1, 1996. Accordingly, to make the deemed dividend election, A must file an amended return for 1996, and include the deemed dividend in income in that year. As a result, M will be a pedigreed QEF as of December 1, 1996, and the December 3, 1996, distribution will not be taxable as an excess distribution. Therefore, in its amended return, A may report the December 3, 1996, distribution consistent with section 1293 and the general rules applicable to corporate distributions.

Example 2. X, a U.S. person, owned a five percent interest in the stock of FC, a PFIC with a taxable year ending June 30. X never made the section 1295 election with respect to FC. X transferred her interest in FC to her granddaughter, Y, a U.S. person, on February 14, 1996. The transfer qualified as a gift for federal income tax purposes, and no gain was recognized on the transfer (see Regulation Project INTL-656-87, published in 1992-1 C.B. 1124; see § 601.601(d)(2)(ii)(*b*) of this chapter). As provided in section 1223(2), Y's holding period includes the period that X held the FC stock. Y decides to make the section 1295 election in her 1996 return to treat FC as a QEF for its taxable year beginning July 1, 1995. However, because Y's holding period includes the period that X held the FC stock, and FC was a PFIC but not a QEF during that period, FC will be an unpedigreed QEF with respect to Y unless Y makes a section 1291(d)(2) election. Although Y did not actually own the stock of FC on the qualification date (July 1, 1995), Y's holding period includes that date. Therefore, provided FC is a CFC for its taxable year beginning July 1, 1995, Y may make a section 1291(d)(2)(B) election to treat FC as a pedigreed QEF.

(f) *Adjustment to basis.*—A shareholder that makes the deemed dividend election increases its adjusted basis of the stock of the PFIC owned directly by the shareholder by the amount of the deemed dividend. If the shareholder makes the deemed dividend election with respect to a PFIC of which it is an indirect shareholder, the shareholder's adjusted basis of the stock or other property owned directly by the shareholder, through which ownership of the PFIC is attributed to the shareholder, is increased by the amount of the deemed dividend. In addition, solely for purposes of determining the subsequent treatment under the Code and regulations of a shareholder of the stock of the PFIC, the adjusted basis of the direct owner of the stock of the PFIC is increased by the amount of the deemed dividend.

(g) *Treatment of holding period.*—For purposes of applying sections 1291 through 1297 to the shareholder after the deemed dividend, the shareholder's holding period of the stock of the PFIC begins on the qualification date. For other purposes of the Code and regulations, this holding period rule does not apply.

(h) *Coordination with section 959(e).*—For purposes of section 959(e), the entire deemed dividend is treated as included in gross income under section 1248(a).

(i) *Election inapplicable to shareholder of a former PFIC or of a section 1297(e) PFIC.*—A shareholder may not make the section 1295 and deemed dividend elections if the foreign corporation is a former PFIC (as defined in paragraph (j)(2)(iv) of this section) or a section 1297(e) PFIC (as defined in paragraph (j)(2)(v) of this section) with respect to the shareholder. For the rules regarding the election by a shareholder of a former PFIC, see § 1.1298-3. For the rules regarding the election by a shareholder of a section 1297(e) PFIC, see § 1.1297-3.

(j) *Definitions.*—(1) *Passive foreign investment company (PFIC).*—A passive foreign investment company (PFIC) is a foreign corporation that satisfies either the income test of section 1296(a)(1) or the asset test of section 1296(a)(2). A corporation will not be treated as a PFIC with respect to a shareholder for those days included in the shareholder's holding period when the shareholder, or a person whose holding period of the stock is included in the shareholder's holding period, was not a United States person within the meaning of section 7701(a)(30).

(2) *Types of PFICs.*—(i) *Qualified electing fund (QEF).*—A PFIC is a qualified electing fund (QEF) with respect to a shareholder that has elected, under section 1295, to be taxed currently on its share of the PFIC's earnings and profits pursuant to section 1293.

(ii) *Pedigreed QEF.*—A PFIC is a pedigreed QEF with respect to a shareholder if the PFIC has been a QEF with respect to the shareholder for all taxable years during which the corporation was a PFIC that are included wholly or partly in the shareholder's holding period of the PFIC stock.

(iii) *Unpedigreed QEF.*—A PFIC is an unpedigreed QEF for a taxable year if—

(A) An election under section 1295 is in effect for that year;

(B) The PFIC has been a QEF with respect to the shareholder for at least one, but not all, of the taxable years during which the corporation was a PFIC that are included wholly or partly in the shareholder's holding period of the PFIC stock; and

(C) The shareholder has not made an election under section 1291(d)(2) and this section or § 1.1291-10 with respect to the PFIC to purge the nonQEF years from the shareholder's holding period.

(iv) *Former PFIC.*—A foreign corporation is a former PFIC with respect to a shareholder if the corporation satisfies neither the income test of section 1297(a)(1) nor the asset test of section 1297(a)(2), but its stock, held by that shareholder, is treated as stock of a PFIC, pursuant to section 1298(b)(1), because the corporation was a PFIC that was not a QEF at some time during the shareholder's holding period of the stock.

(v) *Section 1297(e) PFIC.*—A foreign corporation is a section 1297(e) PFIC with respect to a shareholder (as defined in paragraph (j)(3) of this section) if—

(A) The foreign corporation qualifies as a PFIC under section 1297(a) on the first day on which the qualified portion of the shareholder's holding period in the foreign corporation begins, as determined under section 1297(e)(2); and

(B) The stock of the foreign corporation held by the shareholder is treated as stock of a PFIC, pursuant to section 1298(b)(1), because, at any time during the shareholder's holding period of the stock, other than the qualified portion, the corporation was a PFIC that was not a QEF.

(3) A shareholder is a United States person that is a shareholder as defined in § 1.1291-1(b)(7) or an indirect shareholder as defined in § 1.1291-1(b)(8), except as provided in § 1.1291-1(e).

(k) *Effective/applicability date.*—(1) The rules of this section, except for paragraph (j)(2)(v) of this section, are applicable as of April 1, 1995.

(2) The rules of paragraph (j)(2)(v) of this section are applicable as of December 8, 2005.

(3) Paragraph (j)(3) of this section applies to taxable years of shareholders ending on or after December 31, 2013. [Reg. § 1.1291-9.]

☐ [*T.D.* 8701, 12-26-96. *Amended by T.D.* 8750, 12-31-97; *T.D.* 9231, 12-7-2005; *T.D.* 9360, 9-26-2007, *T.D.* 9650, 12-30-2013 *and T.D.* 9806, 12-27-2016.]

§ 1.1291-10. Deemed sale election.—(a) *Deemed sale election.*—This section provides rules for making the election under section 1291(d)(2)(A) (deemed sale election). Under that section, a shareholder (as defined in § 1.1291-9(j)(3)) of a PFIC that is an unpedigreed QEF may elect to recognize gain with respect to the stock of the unpedigreed QEF held on the qualification date (as defined in paragraph (e) of this section). If the shareholder makes the deemed sale election, the PFIC will become a pedigreed QEF with respect to the shareholder. A shareholder that makes the deemed sale election is treated as having sold, for its fair market value, the stock of the PFIC that the shareholder held on the qualification date. The gain recognized on the deemed sale is taxed under section 1291 as an excess distribution received on the qualification date. In the case of an election made by an indirect shareholder, the amount of gain to be recognized and taxed as an excess distribution is the amount of gain that the direct owner of the stock of the PFIC would have realized on an actual sale or other disposition of the stock of the PFIC indirectly owned by the shareholder. Any loss realized on the deemed sale is not recognized. For the definitions of PFIC, QEF, unpedigreed QEF, and pedigreed QEF, see § 1.1291-9(j)(1) and (2).

(b) *Who may make the election.*—A shareholder of an unpedigreed QEF may make the deemed sale election provided the shareholder held stock of that PFIC on the qualification date. A shareholder is treated as holding stock of the PFIC on the qualification date if its holding period with respect to that stock under section 1223 includes the qualification date. A deemed sale election may be made by a shareholder that would realize a loss on the deemed sale.

(c) *Time for making the election.*—The shareholder makes the deemed sale election in the shareholder's return for the taxable year that includes the qualification date. If the shareholder and the PFIC have the same taxable year, the shareholder makes the deemed sale election in either the original return for the taxable year for which the shareholder makes the section 1295 election, or in an amended return for that year. If the shareholder and the PFIC have different taxable years, the deemed sale election must be made in an amended return for the taxable year that includes the qualification date. If the deemed sale election is made in an amended return, the amended return must be filed by a date that is within three years of the due date, as extended under section 6081, of the original return for the taxable year that includes the qualification date.

(d) *Manner of making the election.*—A shareholder makes the deemed sale election by filing Form 8621 with the return for the taxable year of the shareholder that includes the qualification date, reporting the gain as an excess distribution pursuant to section 1291(a), and paying the tax and interest due on the excess distribution. A shareholder that makes the deemed sale election after the due date of the return (determined without regard to extensions) for the taxable year that includes the qualification date must pay additional interest, pursuant to section 6601, on the amount of the underpayment of tax for that year. A shareholder that realizes a loss on the deemed sale reports the loss on Form 8621, but does not recognize the loss.

(e) *Qualification date.*—(1) *In general.*—Except as otherwise provided in this paragraph (e), the qualification date is the first day of the PFIC's first taxable year as a QEF (first QEF year).

(2) *Elections made after March 31, 1995, and before January 27, 1997.*—(i) *In general.*—The qualification date for deemed sale elections made after March 31, 1995, and before January 27, 1997, is the first day of the shareholder's election year. The shareholder's election year is the taxable year of the shareholder for which it made the section 1295 election.

(ii) *Exception.*—A shareholder who made the deemed sale election after May 1, 1992, and before January 27, 1997, may elect to change its qualification date to the first day of the first QEF year, provided the periods of limitations on assessment for the taxable year that includes that date and for the shareholder's election year have not expired. A shareholder changes the qualification date by filing amended returns, with revised Forms 8621, for the shareholder's election year and the shareholder's taxable year that includes the first day of the first QEF year, and making all appropriate adjustments and payments.

(f) *Adjustments to basis.*—(1) *In general.*—A shareholder that makes the deemed sale election increases its adjusted basis of the PFIC stock owned directly by the amount of gain recognized on the deemed sale. If the shareholder makes the deemed sale election with respect to a PFIC of which it is an indirect shareholder, the shareholder's adjusted basis of the stock or other property owned directly by the shareholder, through which ownership of the PFIC is attributed to the shareholder, is increased by the amount of gain recognized by the shareholder. In addition, solely for purposes of determining the subsequent treatment under the Code and regulations of a shareholder of the stock of the PFIC, the adjusted basis of the direct owner of the stock of the PFIC is increased by the amount of gain recognized on the deemed sale. A shareholder shall not adjust the basis of any stock with respect to which the shareholder realized a loss on the deemed sale.

(2) *Adjustment of basis for section 1293 inclusion with respect to deemed sale election made after March 31, 1995, and before January 27, 1997.*—For purposes of determining the amount of gain recognized with respect to a deemed sale election made after March 31, 1995, and before January 27, 1997, by a shareholder that treats the first day of the shareholder's election year as the qualification date, the adjusted basis of the stock deemed sold includes the shareholder's section 1293(a) inclusion attributable to the period beginning with the first day of the PFIC's first QEF year and ending on the day before the qualification date.

(g) *Treatment of holding period.*—For purposes of applying sections 1291 through 1297 to the shareholder after the deemed sale, the shareholder's holding period of the stock of the PFIC begins on the qualification date, without regard to whether the shareholder recognized gain on the deemed sale. For other purposes of the Code and regulations, this holding period rule does not apply.

(h) *Election inapplicable to shareholder of former PFIC.*—A shareholder may not make the section 1295 and deemed sale elections if the foreign corporation is a former PFIC (as defined in § 1.1291-9(j)(2)(iv)) with respect to the shareholder. For the rules regarding the election by a shareholder of a former PFIC, see 1.1297-3T.

(i) *Effective date.*—The rules of this section are applicable as of April 1, 1995. [Reg. § 1.1291-10.]

☐ [*T.D.* 8701, 12-26-96.]

§ 1.1293-1. Current taxation of income from qualified electing funds.—(a) *In general.*—[Reserved].

(1) *Other rules.*—[Reserved].

(2) *Net capital gain defined.*—(i) *In general.*—This paragraph (a)(2) defines the term net capital gain for purposes of sections 1293 and 1295 and the regulations under those sections. The QEF, as defined in § 1.1291-9(j)(2)(i), in determining its net capital gain for a taxable year, may either—

(A) Calculate and report the amount of each category of long-term capital gain provided in section 1(h) that was recognized by the PFIC in the taxable year;

(B) Calculate and report the amount of net capital gain recognized by the PFIC in the taxable year, stating that that amount is subject to the highest capital gain rate of tax applicable to the shareholder; or

(C) Calculate its earnings and profits for the taxable year and report the entire amount as ordinary earnings.

(ii) *Effective date.*—Paragraph (a)(2)(i) of this section is applicable to sales by QEFs during their taxable years ending on or after May 7, 1997.

(b) *Other rules.*—[Reserved].

(c) *Application of rules of inclusion with respect to stock held by a pass through entity.*—(1) *In general.*—If a domestic pass through entity makes a section 1295 election, as provided in paragraph (d)(2) of this section, with respect to the PFIC shares that it owns, directly or indirectly, the domestic pass through entity takes into account its pro rata share of the ordinary earnings and net capital gain attributable to the QEF shares held by the pass through entity. A U.S. person that indirectly owns QEF shares through the domestic pass through entity accounts for its pro rata shares of ordinary earnings and net capital gain attributable to the QEF shares according to the general rules applicable to inclusions of income from the domestic pass through entity. For the definition of pass through entity, see § 1.1295-1(j).

(2) *QEF stock transferred to a pass through entity.*—(i) *Pass through entity makes a section 1295 election.*—If a shareholder transfers stock subject to a section 1295 election to a domestic pass through entity of which it is an interest holder and the pass through entity makes a section 1295 election with respect to that stock, as provided in § 1.1295-1(d)(2), the shareholder takes into account its pro rata shares of the ordinary earnings and net capital gain attributable to the QEF shares under the rules applicable to inclusions of income from the pass through entity.

(ii) *Pass through entity does not make a section 1295 election.*—If the pass through entity does not make a section 1295 election with respect to the PFIC, the shares of which were transferred to the pass through entity subject to the 1295 election of the shareholder, the shareholder continues to be subject, in its capacity as an indirect shareholder, to the income inclusion rules of section 1293 and reporting rules required of shareholders of QEFs. Proper adjustments to reflect an inclusion in income under section 1293 by the indirect shareholder must be made, under the principles of § 1.1291-9(f), to the basis of the indirect shareholder's interest in the pass through entity.

(3) *Effective date.*—Paragraph (c) of this section is applicable to taxable years of shareholders beginning after December 31, 1997. [Reg. § 1.1293-1.]

☐ [*T.D. 8750, 12-31-97. Redesignated and amended by T.D. 8870, 2-4-2000.*]

Proposed Regulations

§ 1.1293-1. Current taxation of income from qualified electing funds.—(a) *In general.*—Pursuant to section 1293(a)(1), every U.S. person that is a direct or indirect shareholder of a PFIC during a taxable year of the PFIC for which the shareholder has in effect a section 1295 election (within the meaning of § 1.1295-1(a)) includes in gross income the shareholder's pro rata share of the ordinary earnings and net capital gain of such fund for that taxable year. Such amounts are included in income in the taxable year of the shareholder in which or with which the taxable year of the PFIC ends. Section 1293 applies to a shareholder of a pedigreed QEF (as defined in § 1.1291-1(b)(2)(ii)) only for those taxable years during which the corporation qualifies as a PFIC under section 1296(a). Section 1293 applies to a shareholder of an unpedigreed QEF (as defined in § 1.1291-1(b)(2)(iii)) for those taxable years during which the corporation is a PFIC (as defined in § 1.1291-1(b)(1)).

(b) *Other rules.*—[Reserved][Prop. Reg. § 1.1293-1.]
[Proposed 4-1-92.]

Proposed Amendments to Regulation

§ 1.1293-1. Current taxation of income from qualified electing funds.—(a) * * *

(3) *Pass-through entity defined.*—For purposes of this section, the term *pass-through entity* has the meaning provided in § 1.1295-1(j)(2).

(4) *Applicability dates.*—Paragraph (a)(3) of this section applies to taxable years of shareholders beginning on or after [date of publication of the Treasury decision adopting these rules as final regulations in the **Federal Register**].

* * *

(c) * * *

(1) *In general.*—Except as otherwise provided in this paragraph (c), a shareholder that makes a section 1295 election as provided in § 1.1295-1(d)(2) with respect to stock in a PFIC that it is treated as owning by reason of an interest in a pass-through entity, or a shareholder that is treated as owning stock in a QEF by reason of an interest in a domestic partnership that has made a preexisting partnership section 1295 election (within the meaning of § 1.1295-1(d)(2)(i)(13)) or in an S corporation that has made a preexisting S corporation section 1295 election (within the meaning of § 1.1295-1(d)(2)(ii)(13)), includes in income its pro rata share of ordinary earnings and net capital gain attributable to the QEF stock as if the shareholder directly owned its share of the QEF stock held by the pass-through entity.

(2) *Section 1295 election made by domestic nongrantor trust or domestic estate.*—Notwithstanding paragraph (c)(1) of this section, if a domestic nongrantor trust or domestic estate makes a section 1295 election as provided in § 1.1295-1(d)(2)(iii)(A)(*1*) with respect to PFIC stock that it owns, the domestic nongrantor trust or domestic estate includes in income its pro rata share of ordinary earnings and net capital gain attributable to the QEF stock. A shareholder that is treated as owning such QEF stock by reason of an interest in the domestic nongrantor trust or domestic estate accounts for its pro rata share of ordinary earnings and net capital gain attributable to such stock according to the general rules applicable to inclusions of income from the domestic nongrantor trust or domestic estate.

(3) *QEF stock transferred to a pass-through entity.*—(i) *In general.*—Except as otherwise provided in this paragraph (c)(3), if a shareholder transfers stock in a PFIC subject to a section 1295 election to a pass-through entity in which it is an interest holder, such shareholder continues to include in income its pro rata share of ordinary earnings and net capital gain attributable to the QEF stock held by the transferee pass-through entity, under paragraph (c)(1) of this section. Proper adjustments to reflect an inclusion in income under section 1293 by the indirect shareholder must be made, under the principles of § 1.1291-9(f), to the basis of the indirect shareholder's interest in the pass-through entity.

(ii) *Shareholders other than the transferor.*—Except as otherwise provided in this paragraph (c)(3), if a shareholder transfers stock in a PFIC subject to a section 1295 election to a pass-through entity and such stock is not subject to a preexisting QEF election made by the pass-through entity, any other person that becomes a shareholder of such PFIC as a result of the transfer will be subject to the income inclusion rules of this section only if such person makes a section 1295 election with respect to the transferred PFIC stock under § 1.1295-1(d)(2).

(iii) *QEF stock transferred to domestic nongrantor trust.*—Notwithstanding paragraphs (c)(3)(i) and (ii) of this section, if a shareholder transfers stock in a PFIC subject to a section 1295 election to a domestic nongrantor trust in which it is a beneficiary, and the transferee domestic nongrantor trust makes a section 1295 election with respect to that stock pursuant to § 1.1295-1(d)(2)(iii)(A)(*1*), the domestic nongrantor trust, and the transferor and any person that becomes a shareholder of the QEF as a result of the transfer, take into account their share of ordinary earnings and net capital gain attributable to the QEF shares under paragraph (c)(2) of this section. If the transferee domestic nongrantor trust does not make a section 1295 election with respect to the transferred PFIC stock, the transferor continues to be subject, in its capacity as an indirect shareholder, to the income inclusion rules of paragraph (c)(1) of this section.

(4) *Applicability date.*—Paragraph (c) of this section applies to taxable years of shareholders beginning on or after [date of publication of the Treasury decision adopting these rules as final regulations in the **Federal Register**]. For taxable years of shareholders beginning before [date of publication of the Treasury decision adopting these rules as final regulations in the **Federal Register**], see § 1.1293-1(c), as in effect and contained in 26 CFR part 1, as revised April 1, 2021. [Prop. Reg. § 1.1293-1.]

[Proposed 1-25-2022.]

Proposed Regulation

§ 1.1293-2. Special inclusion rules for special preferred QEF election.—(a) *In general.*—A shareholder (including a shareholder that is a pass-through entity, as described in § 1.1295-2(c)(1)) that makes a special preferred QEF election under § 1.1295-2 must, regardless of the shareholder's method of accounting, include in income in respect of each share subject to the election, an annual amount (preferred QEF amount) determined according to the rules of paragraph (b) of this section. A shareholder that makes a special preferred QEF election must include the preferred QEF amount in income under this section for each year in which the taxpayer continues to hold a share that is subject to the election. The rules of this section apply in lieu of the general rules of section 1293 and § 1.1293-1.[1]

(b) *Preferred QEF amount.*—(1) *In general.*—The preferred QEF amount for any share subject to a special preferred QEF election is the sum of the ratable daily portion of each periodic dividend amount (as described in paragraph (b)(2) of this section) on the share for the taxable year of the shareholder to which that portion relates, plus the preferred discount amount (as defined below), if any, for the taxable year. For purposes of this section, the preferred discount amount for a taxable year is the amount that bears the same ratio to the total amount of preferred discount (as described in § 1.1295-2(b)(2)(i)) on the share as the number of days that the taxpayer held the share in the taxable year bears to the number of days after the date the taxpayer acquired the share and up to (and including) the share's redemption date as established under the principles of § 1.305-5(b). Notwithstanding the preceding sentence, the preferred discount amount for a taxable year is zero if the preferred discount on the share at the time of its acquisition by the shareholder was less than an amount equal to 1/4 of 1 percent of the redemption price of the stock, multiplied by the number of complete years from the date of acquisition of the stock to the redemption date of the stock.

(2) *Periodic dividend amount.*—A periodic dividend amount is the amount payable with respect to a share, whether on a cumulative or noncumulative basis, for a period (wholly or partly within the shareholder's taxable year) for which dividends on the share are calculated

[1] This proposed regulation was published on April 1, 1992, at 57 Fed. Reg. 11024.

based upon the redemption or liquidation price of the share multiplied by a fixed percentage rate.

(c) *Special rules of application.*—(1) *Earnings and profits disregarded.*—The amounts to be included in income pursuant to this section are determined without regard to the earnings and profits of the foreign corporation with respect to which the special preferred QEF election applies.

(2) *Year of inclusion.*—The shareholder includes the preferred QEF amount in its taxable year without regard to the taxable year of the foreign corporation with respect to which the special preferred QEF election applies.

(3) *Character of inclusions.*—The shareholder includes all preferred QEF amounts in income as ordinary earnings.

(4) *Treatment of distributions.*—Distributions received by a shareholder on shares subject to a special preferred QEF election that are paid out of earnings and profits of the foreign corporation are not included in gross income of the shareholder to the extent the distributions do not exceed the preferred QEF amounts (other than any portion of preferred QEF amounts consisting of preferred discount amounts) previously includible in income pursuant to this section. These distributions will, however, be treated as dividends for all other purposes of the Code and regulations. Amounts distributed to a shareholder with respect to shares subject to a special preferred QEF election that exceed amounts previously included in income under this section with respect to such shares are treated for all purposes of the Code and regulations as a distribution of property subject to the rules of section 301.

(5) *Basis adjustment rules.*—The adjusted basis of a shareholder in shares that are subject to a special preferred QEF election shall be—

(i) Increased by any amount that is included in the gross income of the shareholder under paragraph (a) of this section; and

(ii) Decreased by any dividends (not to exceed the amount included in gross income under paragraph (a) of this section) actually paid to the shareholder in respect of such shares.

(6) *Effect limited to electing shareholder.*—This section does not apply to the foreign corporation with respect to which a special preferred QEF election applies. Accordingly, the provisions of this section will not affect the foreign corporation's calculation of its earnings and profits for any purpose of the Code or regulations. In addition, the rules of this section apply only for purposes of determining the tax consequences for holders of shares subject to the election. Thus, the election shall have no effect on the application of the Code or regulations with respect to the tax consequences of the ownership of shares that are not subject to the election, including for purposes of determining whether any distributions from the foreign corporation with respect to such shares should be treated as having been included in the income of any United States person pursuant to section 1293(c) or section 959.

(d) *Examples.*—The following examples illustrate the rules of paragraphs (a), (b) and (c) of this section. Although these examples assume a 30-day month, 360-day year, any reasonable counting method may be used to compute the length of accrual periods. For purposes of simplicity, the relevant amounts as stated are rounded to two decimal places. However, the computations do not reflect any such rounding convention. The examples are as follows:

Example 1. Preferred QEF amount—(i) *Facts.* (A) On May 1, 1998, A, an individual who files his returns on a calendar year basis, purchased for $10,000 in a single secondary market transaction 100 shares of nonconvertible Class A $100 par value preferred stock (the Class A Stock) of FC, a foreign corporation with a taxable year ending on March 31.

(B) The terms of the Class A Stock provide for a mandatory redemption of the Class A Stock by the issuer at par on June 1, 2012. The Class A Stock is not redeemable pursuant to an issuer call or holder put on any other date. Each share of Class A Stock provides for a semi-annual cumulative distribution payable in dollars on June 1 and December 1 equal to one-half the product of the par value of the Class A Stock and the applicable annual dollar LIBOR in effect on the distribution date immediately prior to the relevant distribution date. The shares of the Class A stock are qualified preferred shares in the hands of A. A purchases no other qualified preferred shares of FC during its 1998 or 1999 taxable years.

(C) A made a special preferred QEF election for A's taxable year ended December 31, 1998, which applies to the Class A Stock acquired by A on May 1, 1998. FC is a PFIC under section 1296 for its taxable year ending March 31, 1999, but FC is not a PFIC for its taxable year ending March 31, 2000. FC paid no current dividends on June 1, 1998, and December 1, 1998, paid the June 1, 1999, dividend currently on June 1, 1999, together with accumulated distributions from June 1, 1998, and December 1, 1998, and paid the December 1, 1999, dividend currently on December 1, 1999. The applicable annual LIBOR is 8 percent on December 1, 1997, 7 percent on June 1, 1998, 9 percent on December 1, 1998, 10 percent on June 1, 1999, and 9 percent on December 1, 1999. FC had sufficient earnings and profits, within the meaning of section 312, for its taxable year ending on March 31, 2000, so that actual distributions to all shareholders of Class A Stock in that year were treated as paid out of earnings and profits of FC.

(ii) *Tax consequences to A for A's taxable year ending December 31, 1998.* As required under paragraph (a) of this section, A must include in gross income for its 1998 taxable year the 1998 preferred QEF amount. The preferred QEF amount, as determined under paragraph (b) of this section, for A's 1998 taxable year is the ratable portion of each periodic dividend amount for that year. For 1998, there are three periodic dividend amounts: The periodic dividend amount for the period from December 1, 1997, to June 1, 1998 (periodic dividend amount 1), the periodic dividend amount for the period from June 1, 1998, to December 1, 1998 (periodic dividend amount 2), and the periodic dividend amount for the period from December 1, 1998, to June 1, 1999 (periodic dividend amount 3). Periodic dividend amount 1 in respect of each share owned by A is $4 (1/2 multiplied by the applicable annual LIBOR of 8 percent set on December 1, 1997, multiplied by the $100 amount payable on redemption). Because A acquired the shares on May 1, 1998, A's ratable portion of periodic dividend amount 1 for 1998 is approximately $.67 (30/180 multiplied by $4) per share. Periodic dividend amount 2 in respect of each share owned by A is $3.50 (1/2 multiplied by the applicable annual LIBOR of 7 percent set on June 1, 1998, multiplied by $100). Because A owned the shares for the entire period associated with periodic dividend amount 2, A's ratable portion of periodic dividend amount 2 for 1998 is the full $3.50 per share. Periodic dividend amount 3 in respect of each share owned by A is $4.50 (1/2 multiplied by the applicable annual LIBOR of 9 percent set on December 1, 1998, multiplied by $100). Because the portion of 1998 associated with periodic dividend amount 3 is only the month of December, 1998, A's ratable portion of periodic dividend amount 3 for 1998 is approximately $.75 (30/180 multiplied by $4.50). Accordingly, A's preferred QEF amount for 1998 is approximately $4.92 ($.67 + $3.5 + $.75) per share. A must include approximately $492 (approximately $4.92 per share, multiplied by 100 shares) in income as ordinary earnings for its 1998 tax year even though FC paid no actual dividend to shareholders of Class A Stock for the period in 1998 during which A held the Class A Stock.

(iii) *Tax consequences to A for A's taxable year ending December 31, 1999.* As required under paragraph (a) of this section, A includes in gross income for its 1999 taxable year its preferred QEF amount for 1999. The preferred QEF amount, as determined under paragraph (b) of this section, for A's 1999 taxable year is the ratable portion of each periodic dividend amount for that year. For 1999, there are three periodic dividend amounts: The periodic dividend amount for the period from December 1, 1998, to June 1, 1999 (periodic dividend amount 1), the periodic dividend amount for the period from June 1, 1999, to December 1, 1999 (periodic dividend amount 2), and the periodic dividend amount for the period from December 1, 1999, to June 1, 2000 (periodic dividend amount 3). Periodic dividend amount 1 in respect of each share owned by A is $4.50 (1/2 multiplied by the applicable annual LIBOR of 9 percent set on December 1, 1998, multiplied by $100). Because A held each share of Class A Stock for five months in 1999 for the period associated with periodic dividend amount 1, A's ratable portion of periodic dividend amount 1 for 1999 is approximately $3.75 (150/180 multiplied by $4.50). Periodic dividend amount 2 in respect of each share owned by A is $5 (1/2 multiplied by the applicable annual LIBOR of 10 percent set on June 1, 1999, multiplied by $100). Because A owned the share for the entire period associated with periodic dividend amount 2, A's ratable portion of periodic dividend amount 2 for 1999 is the full $5. Periodic dividend amount 3 in respect of each share owned by A is $4.50 (1/2 multiplied by the applicable annual LIBOR of 9 percent set on December 1, 1999, multiplied by $100). Because A held each share of Class A Stock for one month in 1999 for the period associated with periodic dividend amount 3, A's ratable portion of periodic dividend amount 3 for 1999 is approximately $.75 (30/180 multiplied by $4.50). Accordingly, A's preferred QEF amount for 1998 is approximately $9.50 ($3.75 + $5 + $.75). A must include approximately $950 ($9.50

per share, multiplied by 100 shares) in income as ordinary income for its 1999 taxable year even though FC was not a PFIC for FC's taxable year ending in 2000. The current distributions and arrearages actually paid to A with respect to the Class A Stock are not includible in income by A under paragraph (c)(4) of this section because they constitute amounts previously included in income.

Example 2. Preferred Discount—(i) *Facts*. The facts are the same as in *Example 1* except that A acquired the 100 shares of Class A Stock for $9000.

(ii) *Tax Consequences to A for A's taxable year ending December 31, 1990*. (A) Because the Class A Stock is fixed term preferred stock (as described in § 1.1295-2(b)(1)(vii)) and A acquired each share of the Class A stock with $10 of preferred discount, as described in § 1.1295-2(b)(2), A's preferred QEF amount to be included by A for the taxable year consists of the sum of the ratable daily portion of each periodic dividend amount, as calculated in paragraph (d)(ii) of *Example 1* of this section, plus the preferred discount amount described in paragraph (b)(1) of this section.

(B) The preferred discount amount with respect to each share is approximately $.47 ($10 multiplied by 240 days/5070 days to maturity). A must include approximately $47 ($.47 per share, multiplied by 100 shares), together with the amount calculated in paragraph (d)(ii) of *Example 1* of this section, in income as ordinary earnings for its 1998 tax year even though FC paid no actual dividend to shareholders of Class A Shares for the period in 1998 during which A held the Class A Stock.

(iii) *Tax consequences to A for A's taxable year ending December 31, 1999*. The portion of the preferred discount on each share includible under paragraph (a) of this section is approximately $.71 ($10 multiplied by 360 days/5070 days to maturity). A must include this amount, together with the amount calculated in paragraph (d)(iii) of *Example 1* of this section, in income as ordinary earnings for its 1999 tax year even though FC was not a PFIC for FC's taxable year ending in 2000. The current distributions and arrearages actually paid to A in 1999 with respect to the Class A Stock are not includible in income by A under paragraph (c)(4) of this section, because they constitute amounts previously included in income.

(e) *Effective date*.—The rules under this section apply with respect to qualified preferred stock subject to a special preferred QEF election made after the date that is 30 days after the date of publication of this document as a final regulation. [Prop. Reg. § 1.1293-2.]

[Proposed 12-24-96.]

§ 1.1294-1T. Election to extend the time for payment of tax on undistributed earnings of a qualified electing fund (Temporary).—(a) *Purpose and scope*.—This section provides rules for making the annual election under section 1294. Under that section, a U.S. person that is a shareholder in a qualified electing fund (QEF) may elect to extend the time for payment of its tax liability which is attributable to its share of the undistributed earnings of the QEF. In general, a QEF is a passive foreign investment company (PFIC), as defined in section 1296, that makes the election under section 1295. Under section 1293, a U.S. person that owns, or is treated as owning, stock of a QEF at any time during the taxable year of the QEF shall include in gross income, as ordinary income, its pro rata share of the ordinary earnings of the QEF for the taxable year and, as long-term capital gain, its pro rata share of the net capital gain of the QEF for the taxable year. The shareholder's share of the earnings shall be included in the shareholder's taxable year in which or with which the taxable year of the QEF ends.

(b) *Election to extend time for payment*.—(1) *In general*.—A U.S. person that is a shareholder of a QEF on the last day of the QEF's taxable year may elect under section 1294 to extend the time for payment of that portion of its tax liability which is attributable to the inclusion in income pursuant to section 1293 of the shareholder's share of the QEF's undistributed earnings. The election under section 1294 may be made only with respect to undistributed earnings, and interest is imposed under section 6601 on the amount of the tax liability which is subject to the extension. This interest must be paid on the termination of the election.

(2) *Exception*.—An election under this § 1.1294-1T cannot be made for a taxable year of the shareholder if any portion of the QEF's earnings is includible in the gross income of the shareholder for such year under either section 551 (relating to foreign personal holding companies) or section 951 (relating to controlled foreign corporations).

(3) *Undistributed earnings*.—(i) *In general*.—For purposes of this § 1.1294-1T the term "undistributed earnings" means the excess, if any, of the amount includible in gross income by reason of section 1293(a) for the shareholder's taxable year (the includible amount) over the sum of (A) the amount of any distribution to the shareholder during the QEF's taxable year and (B) the portion of the includible amount that is attributable to stock in the QEF that the shareholder transferred or otherwise disposed of before the end of the QEF's year. For purposes of this paragraph, a distribution will be treated as made from the most recently accumulated earnings and profits.

(ii) *Effect of a loan, pledge or guarantee*.—A loan, pledge, or guarantee described in § 1.1294-1T(e)(2) or (4) will be treated as a distribution of earnings for purposes of paragraph (b)(3)(i)(A). If earnings are treated as distributed in a taxable year by reason of a loan, pledge or guarantee described in § 1.1294-1T(e)(2) or (4), but the amount of the deemed distribution resulting therefrom was less than the amount of the actual loan by the QEF (or the amount of the loan secured by the pledge or guarantee), earnings derived by the QEF in a subsequent taxable year will be treated as distributed in such subsequent year to the shareholder for purposes of paragraph (b)(3)(i)(A) by virture of such loan, but only to the extent of the difference between the outstanding principal balance on the loan in such subsequent year and the prior years' deemed distributions resulting from the loan. For this purpose, the outstanding principal balance on a loan in a taxable year shall be treated as equal to the greatest amount of the outstanding balance at any time during such year.

Example (1). (i) *Facts*. *FC* is a PFIC that made the election under section 1295 to be a QEF for its taxable year beginning January 1, 1987. *S* owned 500 shares, or 50 percent, of *FC* throughout the first six months of 1987, but on June 30, 1987 sold 10 percent, or 50 shares, of the *FC* stock that it held. *FC* had $100,000*x* of ordinary earnings but no net capital gain in 1987. No part of *FC*'s earnings is includible in *S*'s income under either section 551 or 951. *FC* made no distributions to its shareholders in 1987. *S*'s pro rata share of income is determined by attributing *FC*'s income ratably to each day in *FC*'s year. Accordingly, *FC*'s daily earnings are $274*x* ($100,000*x*/365). *S*'s share of the earnings of *FC* is $47,484*x*, determined as follows.

FC's daily earnings × number of days percentage held by *S* × percentage of ownership in *FC*.

Accordingly, *S*'s pro rata share of *FC*'s earnings for the first six months of *FC*'s year deemed earned while *S* held 50 percent of *FC*'s stock is $24,797*x* ($274*x* × 181 days × 50%). *S*'s pro rata share of *FC*'s earnings for the remainder of *FC*'s year deemed earned while S held 45 percent of *FC*'s stock is $22,687*x* ($274*x* × 184 days × 45%). Therefore, *S*'s total share of *FC*'s earnings to be included in income under section 1293 is $47,484*x* ($24,797*x* + $22,687*x*).

(ii) *Election*. *S* intends to make the election under section 1294 to defer the payment of its tax liability that is attributable to the undistributed earnings of *FC*. The amount of current year undistributed earnings as defined in § 1.1294-1T(b)(3) with respect to which *S* can make the election is the excess of *S*'s inclusion in gross income under section 1293(a) for the taxable year over the sum of (1) the cash and other property distributed to *S* during *FC*'s tax year out of earnings included in income pursuant to section 1293(a), and (2) the earnings attributable to stock disposed of during *FC*'s tax year. Because *S* sold 10 percent, or 50 shares, of the *FC* stock that it held during the first six months of the year, 10 percent of its share of the earnings for that part of the year, which is $2,480*x* ($24,797*x* × 10%), is attributable to the shares sold. *S* therefore cannot make the election under section 1294 to extend the time for payment of its tax liability on that amount. Accordingly, *S* can make the election under section 1294 with respect to its tax on $45,004*x* ($47,484*x* less $2,480*x*), which is its pro rata share of *FC*'s earnings, reduced by the earnings attributable to the stock disposed of during the year.

Example (2). (i) *Facts*. The facts are the same as in Example (1) with the following exceptions. *S* did not sell any *FC* stock during 1987. Therefore, because *S* held 50 percent of the *FC* stock throughout 1987, *S*'s pro rata share of *FC*'s ordinary earnings was $50,000*x*, no part of which was includible in *S*'s income under either section 551 or 951. There were no actual distributions of earnings to *S* in 1988. On December 31, 1987, *S* pledged the FC stock as security for a bank loan of $75,000*x*. The pledge is treated as a disposition of the *FC* stock and therefore a distribution of *S*'s share of the undistributed earnings of *FC* up to the amount of the loan principal. *S*'s entire share of the undistributed earnings of *FC* are deemed distributed as a result of the pledge of the *FC* stock. *S* therefore cannot make the election under section 1294 to extend the time for payment of its tax liability on its share of *FC*'s earnings for 1987.

(ii) *Deemed distribution.* In 1988, *FC* has ordinary earnings of $100,000*x* but no net capital gain. *S*'s pro rata share of *FC*'s 1988 ordinary earnings was $50,000*x*. *S*'s loan remained outstanding throughout 1988; the highest loan balance during 1988 was $74,000*x*. Of *S*'s share of the ordinary earnings of *FC* of $50,000*x*, $24,000*x* is deemed distributed to *S*. This is the amount by which the highest loan balance for the year ($74,000*x*) exceeds the portion of the undistributed earnings of *FC* deemed distributed to *S* in 1987 by reason of the pledge ($50,000*x*). *S* may make the election under section 1294 to extend the time for payment of its tax liability on $26,000*x*, which is the amount by which *S*'s includible amount for 1988 exceeds the amount deemed distributed to S during 1988.

(c) *Time for making the election.*—(1) *In general.*—An election under this § 1.1294-1T may be made for any taxable year in which a shareholder reports income pursuant to section 1293. Except as provided in paragraph (c)(2), the election shall be made by the due date, as extended, of the tax return for the shareholder's taxable year for which the election is made.

(2) *Exception.*—An election under this section may be made within 60 days of receipt of notification from the QEF of the shareholder's pro rata share of the ordinary earnings and net capital gain if notification is received after the time for filing the election provided in paragraph (c)(1) (and requires the filing of an amended return to report income pursuant to section 1293). If the notification reports an increase in the shareholder's pro rata share of the earnings previously reported to the shareholder by the QEF, the shareholder may make the election under this paragraph (c)(2) only with respect to the amount of such increase.

(d) *Manner of making the election.*—(1) *In general.*—A shareholder shall make the election by (i) attaching to its return for the year of the election Form 8621 or a statement containing the information and representations required by this section and (ii) filing a copy of Form 8621 or the statement with the Internal Revenue Service Center, P.O. Box 21086, Philadelphia, Pennsylvania 19114.

(2) *Information to be included in the election statement.*—If a statement is used in lieu of Form 8621, the statement should be identified, in a heading, as an election under section 1294 of the Code. The statement must include the following information and representations:

(i) The name, address, and taxpayer identification number of the electing shareholder and the taxable year of the shareholder for which the election is being made;

(ii) The name, address and taxpayer identification number of the QEF if provided to the shareholder;

(iii) A statement that the shareholder is making the election under section 1294 of the Code;

(iv) A schedule containing the following information:

(A) the ordinary earnings and net capital gain for the current year included in the shareholder's income under section 1293;

(B) the amount of cash and other property distributed by the QEF during its taxable year with respect to stock held directly or indirectly by the shareholder during that year, identifying the amount of such distributions that is paid out of current earnings and profits and the amount paid out of each prior year's earnings and profits; and

(C) the undistributed PFIC earnings tax liability (as defined in paragraph (f) of this section) for the taxable year, payment of which is being deferred by reason of the election under section 1294;

(v) The number of shares of stock held in the QEF during the QEF's taxable year which gave rise to the section 1293 inclusion and the number of such shares transferred, deemed transferred or otherwise disposed of by the electing shareholder before the end of the QEF's taxable year, and the date of transfer; and

(vi) The representations of the electing shareholder that—

(A) No part of the QEF's earnings for the taxable year is includible in the electing shareholder's gross income under either section 551 or 951 of the Code;

(B) The election is made only with respect to the shareholder's pro rata share of the undistributed earnings of the QEF; and

(C) The electing shareholder, upon termination of the election to extend the date for payment, shall pay the undistributed PFIC earnings tax liability attributable to those earnings to which the termination applies as well as interest on such tax liability pursuant to section 6601. Payment of this tax and interest must be made by the due date (determined without extensions) of the tax return for the taxable year in which the termination occurs.

(e) *Termination of the extension.*—The election to extend the date for payment of tax will be terminated in whole or in part upon the occurrence of any of the following events:

(1) The QEF's distribution of earnings to which the section 1294 extensic pay tax is attributable; the extension will terminate only with respect to the tax attributable to the earnings that were distributed.

(2) The electing shareholder's transfer of stock in the QEF (or use thereof as security for a loan) with respect to which an election under this § 1.1294-1T was made. The election will be terminated with respect to the undistributed earnings attributable to the shares of the stock transferred. In the case of a pledge of the stock, the election will be terminated with respect to undistributed earnings equal to the amount of the loan for which the stock is pledged.

(3) Revocation of the QEF's election as a QEF or cessation of the QEF's status as a PFIC. A revocation of the QEF election or cessation of PFIC status will result in the complete termination of the extension.

(4) A loan of property by the QEF directly or indirectly to the electing shareholder or related person, or a pledge or guarantee by the QEF with respect to a loan made by another party to the electing shareholder or related person. The election will be terminated with respect to undistributed earnings in an amount equal to the amount of the loan, pledge, or guarantee.

(5) A determination by the District Director pursuant to section 1294(c)(3) that collection of the tax is in jeopardy. The amount of undistributed earnings with respect to which the extension is terminated under this paragraph (d)(5) will be left to the discretion of the District Director.

(f) *Undistributed PFIC earnings tax liability.*—The electing shareholder's tax liability attributable to the ordinary earnings and net capital gain included in gross income under section 1293 shall be the excess of the tax imposed under chapter 1 of the Code for the taxable year over the tax that would be imposed for the taxable year without regard to the inclusion in income under section 1293 of the undistributed earnings as defined in paragraph (b)(3) of this section.

Example. The facts are the same as in § 1.1294-1T(b)(3), *Example (1),* with the following exceptions. *S*, a domestic corporation, did not dispose of any *FC* stock in 1987. Therefore, because *S* held 50 percent of the *FC* stock throughout 1987, *S*'s pro rata share of *FC*'s ordinary earnings was $50,000*x*. In addition to $50,000*x* of ordinary earnings from *FC*, *S* had $12,500*x* of domestic source income and $6,000*x* of expenses (other than interest expense) not definitely related to any gross income. These expenses are apportioned, pursuant to § 1.861-8(c)(2), on a pro rata basis between the domestic and foreign source income—$1,200*x* of expenses, or one-fifth, to domestic source income, and $4,800*x* of expenses, or four-fifths, to the section 1293 inclusion. *FC* paid foreign taxes of $25,000*x* in 1987. Accordingly, *S* is entitled to claim as an indirect foreign tax credit pursuant to section 1293(f) a proportionate amount of the foreign taxes paid by *FC*, which is $12,500*x* ($25,000*x* × $50,000*x* / $100,000*x*). *S* is taxed in the U.S. at the rate of 34 percent. The amount for payment is determined as follows:

1987 Tax Liability (with section 1293 inclusion)

Source	*U.S.*		*Foreign*
Income	12,500x		0
Section 1293	0		50,000x
Expenses	– 1,200x		– 4,800x
Taxable income	11,300x		45,200x
Total taxable income		56,500x	
U.S. income tax rate		×34%	
Pre-credit U.S. tax		19,210x	
Foreign tax credit		12,500x	
1987 Tax Liability		6,710x	

1987 Tax Liability (without section 1293 inclusion)

Source	U.S.	Foreign
Income	12,500x	0
Expenses	– 6,000x	
Taxable income	6,500x	
U.S. tax rate	×34%	
U.S. tax	2,210x	
Foreign tax credit	0	
Hypothetical 1987 Tax Liability	2,210x	

The amount of tax, payment of which *S* may defer pursuant to section 1294, is \$4,500*x* (\$6,710*x* less \$2,210*x*).

(g) *Authority to require a bond.*—Pursuant to the authority granted in section 6165 and in the manner provided therein, and subject to notification, the District Director may require the electing shareholder to furnish a bond to secure payment of the tax, the time for payment of which is extended under this section. If the electing shareholder does not furnish the bond within 60 days after receiving a request from the District Director, the election will be revoked.

(h) *Annual reporting requirement.*—The electing shareholder must attach Form 8621 or a statement to its income tax return for each year during which an election under this section is outstanding. The statement must contain the following information: (1) the total amount of undistributed earnings as of the end of the taxable year to which the outstanding elections apply; (2) the total amount of the undistributed PFIC earnings tax liability and accrued interest charge as of the end of the year; (3) the total amount of distributions received during the taxable year; and (4) a description of the occurrence of any other termination event described in paragraph (e) of this section that occurred during the taxable year. The electing shareholder also shall file by the due date, as extended, for its return a copy of Form 8621 or the statement with the Philadelphia Service Center, P.O. Box 21086, Philadelphia, Pennsylvania 19114. [Temporary Reg. § 1.1294-1T.]

☐ [*T.D.* 8178, 2-26-88.]

§ 1.1295-1. Qualified electing funds.—(a) *In general.*—[Reserved].

(b) *Application of section 1295 election.*—[Reserved].

(1) *Election personal to shareholder.*—[Reserved].

(2) *Election applicable to specific corporation only*—

(i) *In general.*—[Reserved].

(ii) *Stock of QEF received in a nonrecognition transfer.*—[Reserved].

(iii) *Exception for options.*—A shareholder's section 1295 election does not apply to any option to buy stock of the PFIC.

(3) *Application of general rules to stock held by a pass through entity.*—(i) *Stock subject to a section 1295 election transferred to a pass through entity.*—A shareholder's section 1295 election will not apply to a domestic pass through entity to which the shareholder transfers stock subject to a section 1295 election, or to any other U.S. person that is an interest holder or beneficiary of the domestic pass through entity. However, as provided in paragraph (c)(2)(iv) of this section (relating to a transfer to a domestic pass through entity of stock subject to a section 1295 election), a shareholder that transfers stock subject to a section 1295 election to a pass through entity will continue to be subject to the section 1295 election with respect to the stock indirectly owned through the pass through entity and any other stock of that PFIC owned by the shareholder.

(ii) *Limitation on application of pass through entity's section 1295 election.*—Except as provided in paragraph (c)(2)(iv) of this section, a section 1295 election made by a domestic pass through entity does not apply to other stock of the PFIC held directly or indirectly by the interest holder or beneficiary.

(iii) *Effect of partnership termination on section 1295 election.*—Termination of a section 1295 election made by a domestic partnership by reason of the termination of the partnership under section 708(b) will not terminate the section 1295 election with respect to partners of the terminated partnership that are partners of the new partnership. Except as otherwise provided, the stock of the PFIC of which the new partners are indirect shareholders will be treated as stock of a QEF only if the new domestic partnership makes a section 1295 election with respect to that stock.

(iv) *Characterization of stock held through a pass through entity.*—Stock of a PFIC held through a pass through entity will be treated as stock of a pedigreed QEF with respect to an interest holder or beneficiary only if—

(A) In the case of PFIC stock acquired (other than in a transaction in which gain is not recognized pursuant to regulations under section 1291(f) with respect to that stock) and held by a domestic pass through entity, the pass through entity makes the section 1295 election and the PFIC has been a QEF with respect to the pass through entity for all taxable years that are included wholly or partly in the pass through entity's holding period of the PFIC stock and during which the foreign corporation was a PFIC within the meaning of § 1.1291-9(j)(1); or

(B) In the case of PFIC stock transferred by an interest holder or beneficiary to a pass through entity in a transaction in which gain is not fully recognized (including pursuant to regulations under section 1291(f)), the pass through entity makes the section 1295 election with respect to the PFIC stock transferred for the taxable year in which the transfer was made. The PFIC stock transferred will be treated as stock of a pedigreed QEF by the pass through entity, however, only if that stock was treated as stock of a pedigreed QEF with respect to the interest holder or beneficiary at the time of the transfer, and the PFIC has been a QEF with respect to the pass through entity for all taxable years of the PFIC that are included wholly or partly in the pass through entity's holding period of the PFIC stock during which the foreign corporation was a PFIC within the meaning of § 1.1291-9(j).

(v) *Characterization of stock distributed by a partnership.*—In the case of PFIC stock distributed by a partnership to a partner in a transaction in which gain is not fully recognized, the PFIC stock will be treated as stock of a pedigreed QEF by the partners only if that stock was treated as stock of a pedigreed QEF with respect to the partnership for all taxable years of the PFIC that are included wholly or partly in the partnership's holding period of the PFIC stock during which the foreign corporation was a PFIC within the meaning of § 1.1291-9(j), and the partner has a section 1295 election in effect with respect to the distributed PFIC stock for the partner's taxable year in which the distribution was made. If the partner does not have a section 1295 election in effect, the stock shall be treated as stock in a section 1291 fund. See paragraph (k) of this section for special applicability date of paragraph (b)(3)(v) of this section.

(4) *Application of general rules to a taxpayer filing a joint return under section 6013.*—A section 1295 election made by a taxpayer in a joint return, within the meaning of section 6013, will be treated as also made by the spouse that joins in the filing of that return. See paragraph (k) of this section for special applicability date of paragraph (b)(4) of this section.

(c) *Effect of section 1295 election.*—(1) *In general.*—Except as otherwise provided in this paragraph (c), the effect of a shareholder's section 1295 election is to treat the foreign corporation as a QEF with respect to the shareholder for each taxable year of the foreign corporation ending with or within a taxable year of the shareholder for which the election is effective. A section 1295 election is effective for the shareholder's election year and all subsequent taxable years of the shareholder unless invalidated, terminated or revoked as provided in paragraph (i) of this section. The terms shareholder and shareholder's election year are defined in paragraph (j) of this section.

(2) *Years to which section 1295 election applies.*—(i) *In general.*—Except as otherwise provided in this paragraph (c), a foreign corporation with respect to which a section 1295 election is made will be treated as a QEF for its taxable year ending with or within the shareholder's election year and all subsequent taxable years of the foreign corporation that are included wholly or partly in the shareholder's holding period (or periods) of stock of the foreign corporation.

(ii) *Effect of PFIC status on election.*—A foreign corporation will not be treated as a QEF for any taxable year of the foreign corporation that the foreign corporation is not a PFIC under section 1297(a) and is not treated as a PFIC under section 1298(b)(1). Therefore, a shareholder shall not be required to include pursuant to section 1293 the shareholder's pro rata share of ordinary earnings and net capital gain for such year and shall not be required to satisfy the section 1295 annual reporting requirement of paragraph (f)(2) of this section for such year. Cessation of a foreign corporation's status as a PFIC will not, however, terminate a section 1295 election. Thus, if the foreign corporation is a PFIC in any taxable year after a year in which it is not treated as a PFIC, the shareholder's original election under section 1295 continues to apply and the shareholder must take into account its pro rata share of ordinary earnings and net capital gain for such year and comply with the section 1295 annual reporting requirement.

(iii) *Effect on election of complete termination of a shareholder's interest in the PFIC.*—Complete termination of a shareholder's direct and indirect interest in stock of a foreign corporation will not terminate a shareholder's section 1295 election with respect to the foreign corporation. Therefore, if a shareholder reacquires a direct or indirect interest in any stock of the foreign corporation, that stock is considered to be stock for which an election under section 1295 has been made and the shareholder is subject to the income inclusion and reporting rules required of a shareholder of a QEF.

(iv) *Effect on section 1295 election of transfer of stock to a domestic pass through entity.*—The transfer of a shareholder's direct or indirect interest in stock of a foreign corporation to a domestic pass through entity (as defined in paragraph (j) of this section) will not terminate the shareholder's section 1295 election with respect to the foreign corporation, whether or not the pass through entity makes a section 1295 election. For the rules concerning the application of section 1293 to stock transferred to a domestic pass through entity, see § 1.1293-1(c).

(v) *Examples.*—The following examples illustrate the rules of this paragraph (c)(2).

Example 1. In 1998, C, a U.S. person, purchased stock of FC, a foreign corporation that is a PFIC. Both FC and C are calendar year taxpayers. C made a timely section 1295 election to treat FC as a QEF in C's 1998 return, and FC was therefore a pedigreed QEF. C included its shares of FC's 1998 ordinary earnings and net capital gain in C's 1998 income and did not make a section 1294 election to defer the time for payment of tax on that income. In 1999, 2000, and 2001, FC did not satisfy either the income or asset test of section 1296(a), and therefore was neither a PFIC nor a QEF. C therefore did not have to include its pro rata shares of the ordinary earnings and net capital gain of FC pursuant to section 1293, or satisfy the section 1295 annual reporting requirements for any of those years. FC qualified as a PFIC again in 2002. Because C had made a section 1295 election in 1998, and the election had not been invalidated, terminated, or revoked, within the meaning of paragraph (i) of this section, C's section 1295 election remains in effect for 2002. C therefore is subject in 2002 to the income inclusion and reporting rules required of shareholders of QEFs.

Example 2. The facts are the same as in Example (1) except that FC did not lose PFIC status in any year and C sold all the FC stock in 1999 and repurchased stock of FC in 2002. Because C had made a section 1295 election in 1998 with respect to stock of FC, and the election had not been invalidated, terminated, or revoked, within the meaning of paragraph (i) of this section, C's section 1295 election remained in effect and therefore applies to the stock of FC purchased by C in 2002. C therefore is subject in 2002 to the income inclusion and reporting rules required of shareholders of QEFs.

Example 3. The facts are the same as in Example (2) except that C is a partner in domestic partnership P and C transferred its FC stock to P in 1999. Because C had made a section 1295 election in 1998 with respect to stock of FC, and the election had not been invalidated, terminated, or revoked, within the meaning of paragraph (i) of this section, C's section 1295 election remains in effect with respect to its indirect interest in the stock of FC. If P does not make the section 1295 election with respect to the FC stock, C will continue to be subject, in C's capacity as an indirect shareholder of FC, to the income inclusion and reporting rules required of shareholders of QEFs in 1999 and subsequent years for that portion of the FC stock C is treated as owning indirectly through the partnership. If P makes the section 1295 election, C will take into account its pro rata shares of the ordinary earnings and net capital gain of the FC under the rules applicable to inclusions of income from P.

(d) *Who may make a section 1295 election.*—(1) *General rule.*—Except as otherwise provided in this paragraph (d), any U.S. person that is a shareholder (as defined in paragraph (j) of this section) of a PFIC, including a shareholder that holds stock of a PFIC in bearer form, may make a section 1295 election with respect to that PFIC. The shareholder need not own directly or indirectly any stock of the PFIC at the time the shareholder makes the section 1295 election provided the shareholder is a shareholder of the PFIC during the taxable year of the PFIC that ends with or within the taxable year of the shareholder for which the section 1295 election is made. Except in the case of a shareholder that is an exempt organization that may not make a section 1295 election, as provided in paragraph (d)(6) of this section, in a chain of ownership only the first U.S. person that is a shareholder of the PFIC may make the section 1295 election.

(2) *Application of general rule to pass through entities.*—(i) *Partnerships.*—(A) *Domestic partnership.*—A domestic partnership that holds an interest in stock of a PFIC makes the section 1295 election with respect to that PFIC. The partnership election applies only to the stock of the PFIC held directly or indirectly by the partnership and not to any other stock held directly or indirectly by any partner. As provided in § 1.1293-1(c)(1), shareholders owning stock of a QEF by reason of an interest in the partnership take into account the section 1293 inclusions with respect to the QEF shares owned by the partnership under the rules applicable to inclusions of income from the partnership.

(B) *Foreign partnership.*—A U.S. person that holds an interest in a foreign partnership that, in turn, holds an interest in stock of a PFIC makes the section 1295 election with respect to that PFIC. A partner's election applies to the stock of the PFIC owned directly or indirectly by the foreign partnership and to any other stock of the PFIC owned by that partner. A section 1295 election by a partner applies only to that partner.

(ii) *S corporation.*—An S corporation that holds an interest in stock of a PFIC makes the section 1295 election with respect to that PFIC. The S corporation election applies only to the stock of the PFIC held directly or indirectly by the S corporation and not to any other stock held directly or indirectly by any S corporation shareholder. As provided in § 1.1293-1(c)(1), shareholders owning stock of a QEF by reason of an interest in the S corporation take into account the section 1293 inclusions with respect to the QEF shares under the rules applicable to inclusions of income from the S corporation.

(iii) *Trust or estate.*—(A) *Domestic trust or estate.*—*(1) Nongrantor trust or estate.*—A domestic nongrantor trust or a domestic estate that holds an interest in stock of a PFIC makes the section 1295 election with respect to that PFIC. The trust or estate's election applies only to the stock of the PFIC held directly or indirectly by the trust or estate and not to any other stock held directly or indirectly by any beneficiary. As provided in § 1.1293-1(c)(1), shareholders owning stock of a QEF by reason of an interest in a domestic trust or estate take into account the section 1293 inclusions with respect to the QEF shares under the rules applicable to inclusions of income from the trust or estate.

(2) Grantor trust.—A U.S. person that is treated under sections 671 through 678 as the owner of the portion of a domestic trust that owns an interest in stock of a PFIC makes the section 1295 election with respect to that PFIC. If that person ceases to be treated as the owner of the portion of the trust that owns an interest in the PFIC stock and is a beneficiary of the trust, that person's section 1295 election will continue to apply to the PFIC stock indirectly owned by that person under the rules of paragraph (c)(2)(iv) of this section as if the person had transferred its interest in the PFIC stock to the trust.

However, the stock will be treated as stock of a PFIC that is not a QEF with respect to other beneficiaries of the trust, unless the trust makes the section 1295 election as provided in paragraph (d)(2)(iii)(A)(*1*) of this section.

(B) *Foreign trust or estate.*—(*1*) *Nongrantor trust or estate.*—A U.S. person that is a beneficiary of a foreign nongrantor trust or estate that holds an interest in stock of a PFIC makes the section 1295 election with respect to that PFIC. A beneficiary's section 1295 election applies to all the PFIC stock owned directly and indirectly by the trust or estate and to the other PFIC stock owned directly or indirectly by the beneficiary. A section 1295 election by a beneficiary applies only to that beneficiary.

(*2*) *Grantor trust.*—A U.S. person that is treated under sections 671 through 679 as the owner of the portion of a foreign trust that owns an interest in stock of a PFIC stock makes the section 1295 election with respect to that PFIC. If that person ceases to be treated as the owner of the portion of the trust that owns an interest in the PFIC stock and is a beneficiary of the trust, that person's section 1295 election will continue to apply to the PFIC stock indirectly owned by that person under the rules of paragraph (c)(2)(iv) of this section. However, as provided in paragraph (d)(2)(iii)(B)(*1*) of this section, any other shareholder that is a beneficiary of the trust and that wishes to treat the PFIC as a QEF must make the section 1295 election.

(iv) *Indirect ownership of the pass through entity or the PFIC.*—The rules of this paragraph (d)(2) apply whether or not the shareholder holds its interest in the pass through entity directly or indirectly and whether or not the pass through entity holds its interest in the PFIC directly or indirectly.

(3) *Indirect ownership of a PFIC through other PFICs.*—(i) *In general.*—An election under section 1295 shall apply only to the foreign corporation for which an election is made. Therefore, if a shareholder makes an election under section 1295 to treat a PFIC as a QEF, that election applies only to stock in that foreign corporation and not to the stock in any other corporation which the shareholder is treated as owning by virtue of its ownership of stock in the QEF.

(ii) *Example.*—The following example illustrates the rules of paragraph (d)(3)(i) of this section:

Example. In 1988, T, a U.S. person, purchased stock of FC, a foreign corporation that is a PFIC. FC also owns the stock of SC, a foreign corporation that is a PFIC. T makes an election under section 1295 to treat FC as a QEF. T's section 1295 election applies only to the stock T owns in FC, and does not apply to the stock T indirectly owns in SC.

(4) *Member of consolidated return group as shareholder.*—Pursuant to § 1.1502-77(a), the common parent of an affiliated group of corporations that join in filing a consolidated income tax return makes a section 1295 election for all members of the affiliated group. An election by a common parent will be effective for all members of the affiliated group with respect to interests in PFIC stock held at the time the election is made or at any time thereafter. A separate election must be made by the common parent for each PFIC of which a member of the affiliated group is a shareholder.

(5) *Option holder.*—A holder of an option to acquire stock of a PFIC may not make a section 1295 election that will apply to the option or to the stock subject to the option.

(6) *Exempt organization.*—A tax-exempt organization that is not taxable under section 1291, pursuant to § 1.1291-1(e), with respect to a PFIC may not make a section 1295 election with respect to that PFIC. In addition, such an exempt organization will not be subject to any section 1295 election made by a domestic pass through entity.

(e) *Time for making a section 1295 election.*—(1) *In general.*—Except as provided in § 1.1295-3, a shareholder making the section 1295 election must make the election on or before the due date, as extended under section 6081 (election due date), for filing the shareholder's income tax return for the first taxable year to which the election will apply. The section 1295 election must be made in the original return for that year, or in an amended return, provided the amended return is filed on or before the election due date.

(2) *Examples.*—The following examples illustrate the rules of paragraph (e)(1) of this section:

Example 1. In 1998, C, a domestic corporation, purchased stock of FC, a foreign corporation that is a PFIC. Both C and FC are calendar year taxpayers. C wishes to make the section 1295 election for its taxable year ended December 31, 1998. The section 1295 election must be made on or before March 15, 1999, the due date of C's 1998 income tax return as provided by section 6072(b). On March 14, 1999, C files a request for a three-month extension of time to file its 1998 income tax return under section 6081(b). C's time to file its 1998 income tax return and to make the section 1295 election is thereby extended to June 15, 1999.

Example 2. The facts are the same as in *Example 1* except that on May 1, 1999, C filed its 1998 income tax return and failed to include the section 1295 election. C may file an amended income tax return for 1998 to make the section 1295 election provided the amended return is filed on or before the extended due date of June 15, 1999.

(f) *Manner of making a section 1295 election and the annual election requirements of the shareholder.*—(1) *Manner of making the election.*—A shareholder must make a section 1295 election by—

(i) Completing Form 8621 in the manner required by that form and this section for making the section 1295 election;

(ii) Attaching Form 8621 to its federal income tax return filed by the election due date for the shareholder's election year; and

(iii) Receiving and reflecting in Form 8621 the information provided in the PFIC Annual Information Statement described in paragraph (g)(1) of this section, the Annual Intermediary Statement described in paragraph (g)(3) of this section, or the applicable combined statement described in paragraph (g)(4) of this section, for the taxable year of the PFIC ending with or within the taxable year for which Form 8621 is being filed. If the PFIC Annual Information Statement contains a statement described in paragraph (g)(1)(ii)(C) of this section, the shareholder must attach a statement to Form 8621 that indicates that the shareholder rather than the PFIC calculated the PFIC's ordinary earnings and net capital gain.

(2) *Annual election requirements.*—(i) *In general.*—A shareholder that makes a section 1295 election with respect to a PFIC held directly or indirectly, for each taxable year to which the section 1295 election applies, must—

(A) Complete Form 8621 in the manner required by that form and this section;

(B) Attach Form 8621 to its federal income tax return filed by the due date of the return, as extended; and

(C) Receive and reflect in Form 8621 the PFIC Annual Information Statement described in paragraph (g)(1) of this section, the Annual Intermediary Statement described in paragraph (g)(3) of this section, or the applicable combined statement described in paragraph (g)(4) of this section, for the taxable year of the PFIC ending with or within the taxable year for which Form 8621 is being filed. If the PFIC Annual Information Statement contains a statement described in paragraph (g)(1)(ii)(C) of this section, the shareholder must attach a statement to its Form 8621 that the shareholder rather than the PFIC provided the calculations of the PFIC's ordinary earnings and net capital gain.

(ii) *Retention of documents.*—For all taxable years subject to the section 1295 election, the shareholder must retain copies of all Forms 8621, with their attachments, and PFIC Annual Information Statements or Annual Intermediary Statements. Failure to produce those documents at the request of the Commissioner in connection with an examination may result in invalidation or termination of the shareholder's section 1295 election.

(3) *Effective date.*—See paragraph (k) of this section for special applicability date of paragraph (f) of this section.

(g) *Annual election requirements of the PFIC or intermediary.*—(1) *PFIC Annual Information Statement.*—For each year of the PFIC ending in a taxable year of a shareholder to which the shareholder's section 1295 election applies, the PFIC must provide the shareholder with a PFIC Annual Information Statement. The PFIC Annual Information Statement is a statement of the PFIC, signed by the PFIC or an authorized representative of the PFIC, that contains the following information and representations—

(i) The first and last days of the taxable year of the PFIC to which the PFIC Annual Information Statement applies;

(ii) Either—

(A) The shareholder's pro rata shares of the ordinary earnings and net capital gain (as defined in § 1.1293-1(a)(2)) of the PFIC for the taxable year indicated in paragraph (g)(1)(i) of this section; or

(B) Sufficient information to enable the shareholder to calculate its pro rata shares of the PFIC's ordinary earnings and net capital gain, for that taxable year; or

(C) A statement that the foreign corporation has permitted the shareholder to examine the books of account, records, and other documents of the foreign corporation for the shareholder to calculate the amounts of the PFIC's ordinary earnings and the net capital gain according to federal income tax accounting principles and to calculate the shareholder's pro rata shares of the PFIC's ordinary earnings and net capital gain;

(iii) The amount of cash and the fair market value of other property distributed or deemed distributed to the shareholder during the taxable year of the PFIC to which the PFIC Annual Information Statement pertains; and

(iv) Either—

(A) A statement that the PFIC will permit the shareholder to inspect and copy the PFIC's permanent books of account, records, and such other documents as may be maintained by the PFIC to establish that the PFIC's ordinary earnings and net capital gain are computed in accordance with U.S. income tax principles, and to verify these amounts and the shareholder's pro rata shares thereof; or

(B) In lieu of the statement required in paragraph (g)(1)(iv)(A) of this section, a description of the alternative documentation requirements approved by the Commissioner, with a copy of the private letter ruling and the closing agreement entered into by the Commissioner and the PFIC pursuant to paragraph (g)(2) of this section.

(2) *Alternative documentation.*—In rare and unusual circumstances, the Commissioner will consider alternative documentation requirements necessary to verify the ordinary earnings and net capital gain of a PFIC other than the documentation requirements described in paragraph (g)(1)(iv)(A) of this section. Alternative documentation requirements will be allowed only pursuant to a private letter ruling and a closing agreement entered into by the Commissioner and the PFIC describing an alternative method of verifying the PFIC's ordinary earnings and net capital gain. If the PFIC has not obtained a private letter ruling from the Commissioner approving an alternative method of verifying the PFIC's ordinary earnings and net capital gain by the time a shareholder is required to make a section 1295 election, the shareholder may not use an alternative method for that taxable year.

(3) *Annual Intermediary Statement.*—In the case of a U.S. person that is an indirect shareholder of a PFIC that is owned through an intermediary, as defined in paragraph (j) of this section, an Annual Intermediary Statement issued by an intermediary containing the information described in paragraph (g)(1) of this section and reporting the indirect shareholder's pro rata share of the ordinary earnings and net capital gain of the QEF as described in paragraph (g)(1)(ii)(A) of this section, may be provided to the indirect shareholder in lieu of the PFIC Annual Information Statement if the following conditions are satisfied—

(i) The intermediary receives a copy of the PFIC Annual Information Statement or the intermediary receives an annual intermediary statement from another intermediary which contains a statement that the other intermediary has received a copy of the PFIC Annual Information Statement and represents that the conditions of paragraphs (g)(3)(ii) and (g)(3)(iii) of this section are met;

(ii) The representations and information contained in the Annual Intermediary Statement reflect the representations and information contained in the PFIC Annual Information Statement; and

(iii) The PFIC Annual Information Statement issued to the intermediary contains either the representation set forth in paragraph (g)(1)(iv)(A) of this section, or, if alternative documentation requirements were approved by the Commissioner pursuant to paragraph (g)(2) of this section, a copy of the private letter ruling and closing agreement between the Commissioner and the PFIC, agreeing to an alternative method of verifying PFIC ordinary earnings and net capital gain as described in paragraph (g)(2) of this section;

(4) *Combined statements.*—(i) *PFIC Annual Information Statement.*—A PFIC that owns directly or indirectly any stock of one or more PFICs with respect to which a shareholder may make the section 1295 election may prepare a PFIC Annual Information Statement that combines with its own information and representations the information and representations of all the PFICs. The PFIC may use any format for a combined PFIC Annual Information Statement provided the required information and representations are separately stated and identified with the respective corporations.

(ii) *Annual Intermediary Statement.*—An intermediary described in paragraph (g)(3) of this section that owns directly or indirectly stock of one or more PFICs with respect to which an indirect shareholder may make the section 1295 election may prepare an Annual Intermediary Statement that combines with its own information and representations the information and representations with respect to all the PFICs. The intermediary may use any format for a combined Annual Intermediary Statement provided the required information and representations are separately stated and identified with the intermediary and the respective corporations.

(5) *Effective date.*—See paragraph (k) of this section for special applicability date of paragraph (g) of this section.

(h) *Transition rules.*—Taxpayers may rely on Notice 88-125 (1988-2 C.B. 535) (see § 601.601(d)(2) of this chapter), for rules on making and maintaining elections for shareholder election years (as defined in paragraph (j) of this section) beginning after December 31, 1986, and before January 1, 1998. Elections made under Notice 88-125 must be maintained as provided in § 1.1295-1 for taxable years beginning after December 31, 1997. A section 1295 election made prior to February 2, 1998, that was intended to be effective for the taxable year of the PFIC that began during the shareholder's election year will be effective for that taxable year of the foreign corporation provided that it is clear from all the facts and circumstances that the shareholder intended the election to be effective for that taxable year of the foreign corporation.

(i) *Invalidation, termination, or revocation of section 1295 election.*—(1) *Invalidation or termination of election at the discretion of the Commissioner.*—(i) *In general.*—The Commissioner, in the Commissioner's discretion, may invalidate or terminate a section 1295 election applicable to a shareholder if the shareholder, the PFIC, or any intermediary fails to satisfy the requirements for making a section 1295 election or the annual election requirements of this section to which the shareholder, PFIC, or intermediary is subject, including the requirement to provide, on request, copies of the books and records of the PFIC or other documentation substantiating the ordinary earnings and net capital gain of the PFIC.

(ii) *Deferral of section 1293 inclusion.*—The Commissioner may invalidate any pass through entity section 1295 election with respect to an interest holder or beneficiary if the section 1293 inclusion with respect to that interest holder or beneficiary is not included in the gross income of either the pass through entity, an intermediate pass through entity, or the interest holder or beneficiary within two years of the end of the PFIC's taxable year due to nonconforming taxable years of the interest holder and the pass through entity or any intermediate pass through entity.

(iii) *When effective.*—Termination of a shareholder's section 1295 election will be effective for the taxable year of the PFIC determined by the Commissioner in the Commissioner's discretion. An invalidation of a shareholder's section 1295 election will be effective for the first taxable year to which the section 1295 election applied, and the shareholder whose election is invalidated will be treated as if the section 1295 election was never made.

(2) *Shareholder revocation.*—(i) *In general.*—In the Commissioner's discretion, upon a finding of a substantial change in circumstances, the Commissioner may consent to a shareholder's request to revoke a section 1295 election. Request for revocation must be made by the shareholder that made the election and at the time and in the manner provided in paragraph (i)(2)(ii) of this section.

(ii) *Time for and manner of requesting consent to revoke.*—(A) *Time.*—The shareholder must request consent to revoke the section 1295 election no later than 12 calendar months after the discovery of the substantial change of circumstances that forms the basis for the shareholder's request to revoke the section 1295 election.

(B) *Manner of making request.*—A shareholder requests consent to revoke a section 1295 election by filing a ruling request with the Office of the Associate Chief Counsel (International). The ruling request must satisfy the requirements, including payment of the user fee, for filing ruling requests with that office.

(iii) *When effective.*—Unless otherwise determined by the Commissioner, revocation of a section 1295 election will be effective for the first taxable year of the PFIC beginning after the date the Commissioner consents to the revocation.

(3) *Automatic termination.*—If a United States person, or the United States shareholder on behalf of a controlled foreign corporation, makes an election pursuant to section 1296 and the regulations thereunder with respect to PFIC stock for which a QEF election is in effect, or marks to market such stock under another provision of chapter 1 of the Internal Revenue Code, the QEF election is automatically terminated with respect to such stock that is marked to market under section 1296 or another provision of chapter 1 of the Internal Revenue Code. Such termination shall be effective on the last day of the shareholder's taxable year preceding the first taxable year for which the section 1296 election is in effect or such stock is marked to market under another provision of chapter 1 of the Internal Revenue Code.

Example. Corp Y, a domestic corporation, owns directly 100 shares of marketable stock in foreign corporation FX, a PFIC. Corp Y also owns a 50 percent interest in FP, a foreign partnership that owns 200 shares of FX stock. Accordingly, under section 1298(a)(3) and §1.1296-1(e)(1), Corp Y is treated as indirectly owning 100 shares of FX stock. Corp Y also owns 100 percent of the stock of FZ, a foreign corporation that is not a PFIC. FZ owns 100 shares of FX stock, and therefore under section 1298(a)(2)(A), Corp Y is treated as owning the 100 shares of FX stock owned by FZ. For taxable year 2005, Corp Y has a QEF election in effect with respect to all 300 shares of FX stock that it owns directly or indirectly. See generally §1.1295-1(c)(1). For taxable year 2006, Corp Y makes a timely election pursuant to section 1296 and the regulations thereunder. For purposes of section 1296, Corp Y is treated as owning stock held indirectly through a partnership, but not through a foreign corporation. Section 1296(g); §1.1296-1(e)(1). Accordingly, Corp Y's section 1296 election covers the 100 shares it owns directly and the 100 shares it owns indirectly through FP, but not the 100 shares owned by FZ. With respect to the first 200 shares, Corp Y's QEF election is automatically terminated effective December 31, 2005. With respect to the 100 shares Corp Y owns through foreign FZ, Corp Y's QEF election remains in effect unless invalidated, terminated, or revoked pursuant to this paragraph (i).

(4) *Effect of invalidation, termination, or revocation.*—An invalidation, termination, or revocation of a section 1295 election—

(i) Terminates all section 1294 elections, as provided in §1.1294-1T(e), and the undistributed PFIC earnings tax liability and interest thereon are due by the due date, without regard to extensions, for the return for the last taxable year of the shareholder to which the section 1295 election applies;

(ii) In the Commissioner's discretion, results in a deemed sale of the QEF stock on the last day of the PFIC's last taxable year as a QEF, in which gain, but not loss, will be recognized and with respect to which appropriate basis and holding period adjustments will be made; and

(iii) Subjects the shareholder to any other terms and conditions that the Commissioner determines are necessary to ensure the shareholder's compliance with sections 1291 through 1298 or any other provisions of the Code.

(5) *Effect after invalidation, termination, or revocation.*—(i) *In general.*—Without the Commissioner's consent, a shareholder whose section 1295 election was invalidated, terminated, or revoked under this paragraph (i) may not make the section 1295 election with respect to the PFIC before the sixth taxable year in which the invalidation, termination, or revocation became effective.

(ii) *Special rule.*—Notwithstanding paragraph (i)(5)(i) of this section, a shareholder whose section 1295 election was terminated pursuant to paragraph (i)(3) of this section, and either whose section 1296 election has subsequently been terminated because its PFIC stock ceased to be marketable or who no longer marks to market such stock under another provision of chapter 1 of the Internal Revenue Code, may make a section 1295 election with respect to its PFIC stock before the sixth taxable year in which its prior section 1295 election was terminated.

(j) *Definitions.*—For purposes of this section—

Intermediary is a nominee or shareholder of record that holds stock on behalf of the shareholder or on behalf of another person in a chain of ownership between the shareholder and the PFIC, and any direct or indirect beneficial owner of PFIC stock (including a beneficial owner that is a pass through entity) in the chain of ownership between the shareholder and the PFIC.

Pass through entity is a partnership, S corporation, trust, or estate.

Shareholder has the same meaning as the term shareholder in §1.1291-9(j)(3), except that for purposes of this section, a partnership and an S corporation also are treated as shareholders. Furthermore, unless otherwise provided, an interest holder of a pass through entity, which is treated as a shareholder of a PFIC, also will be treated as a shareholder of the PFIC.

Shareholder's election year is the taxable year of the shareholder for which it made the section 1295 election.

(k) *Effective dates.*—Except as otherwise provided, paragraphs (b)(2)(iii), (b)(3), (b)(4), and (c) through (j) of this section are applicable to taxable years of shareholders beginning after December 31, 1997. However, taxpayers may apply the rules under paragraphs (b)(4), (f) and (g) of this section to a taxable year beginning before January 1, 1998, provided the statute of limitations on the assessment of tax has not expired as of April 27, 1998, and, in the case of paragraph (b)(4) of this section, the taxpayers who filed the joint return have consistently applied the rules of that section to all taxable years following the year the election was made. Paragraph (b)(3)(v) of this section is applicable as of February 7, 2000, however, a taxpayer may apply the rules to a taxable year prior to the applicable date provided the statute of limitations on the assessment of tax for that taxable year has not expired. Paragraphs (i)(3) and (i)(5)(ii) of this section are applicable for taxable years beginning on or after May 3, 2004. [Reg. §1.1295-1.]

☐ *[T.D. 8750, 12-31-97. Redesignated and amended by T.D. 8870, 2-4-2000. Amended by T.D. 9123, 4-30-2004.]*

Proposed Regulation

§1.1295-1. Qualified electing funds.—(a) *In general.*—This section provides certain rules under section 1295 applicable to a U.S. person that has elected to treat a PFIC (as defined in §1.1291-1(b)(1)) as a QEF (as defined in §1.1291-1(b)(2)(i)). A U.S. person that has elected to treat a PFIC as a QEF is taxable annually, pursuant to section 1293, on its pro rata share of the ordinary earnings and net capital gain of the QEF.

(b) *Application of section 1295 election.*—(1) *Election personal to shareholder.*—An election under section 1295 and this section (section 1295 election) applies only to the shareholder that makes the election. Accordingly, a shareholder's section 1295 election will not apply to a U.S. transferee (as defined in §1.1291-6(c)(2)(i)) of stock of a PFIC with respect to which the shareholder made a section 1295 election. A section 1295 election made by a common parent of a consolidated group as agent for members of the group is considered made by each member of the group that owns stock of the PFIC at the time of the election and at any time thereafter.

(2) *Election applicable to specific corporation only.*—(i) *In general.*—Only a corporation with respect to which a shareholder makes a section 1295 election is a QEF. The shareholder's section 1295 election applies to all the stock of the QEF that the shareholder owns at the time of the election or acquires thereafter. Except as provided in paragraph (b)(2)(ii) of this section, if a shareholder transfers stock of a QEF in exchange for stock of another PFIC, the latter PFIC is not a QEF unless the shareholder makes a section 1295 election to treat it as a QEF. If a shareholder disposes of stock of a QEF in exchange for stock of another PFIC in a nonrecognition transfer (as defined in §1.1291-6(a)(2)) effected prior to April 1, 1992, and the shareholder has consistently treated the other PFIC as a QEF, the shareholder may make a section 1295 election with respect to the other PFIC whose stock was received for the taxable year of the PFIC that includes the day the transfer was effected. Such election must be made by the later of—

(A) The due date provided in section 1295(b); or

(B) The due date for the return for the taxable year of the shareholder that includes April 1, 1992.

For the deadline for making the section 1295 election in the case of nonrecognition transfers effected after April 1, 1992, *see* section 1295(b).

(ii) *Stock of QEF received in a nonrecognition transfer.*—If a U.S. person is a U.S. transferee (as defined in §1.1291-6(c)(2)(i)) of stock of a PFIC in a nonrecognition transfer in which the shareholder disposing of such stock does not fully recognize the gain with respect to such stock, and the U.S. transferee, at the time of the transaction, has in effect a section 1295 election with respect to that PFIC, the section 1295 election will apply to the newly acquired stock on the day after the transaction. The newly acquired stock will be treated as stock of an unpedigreed QEF for which an election under section 1291(d)(2) and §1.1291-9 or 1.1291-10 may be made. For purposes of making a section 1291(d)(2) election pursuant to this paragraph (b)(2)(ii), the qualification date is the day after the nonrecognition transaction. The following example illustrates the rule of this paragraph (b)(2)(ii).

Example. (i) X, a domestic corporation, owns stock of NQF, a section 1291 fund with respect to X, and stock of FC, a pedigreed QEF with respect to X. Pursuant to a plan of reorganization, X and the other shareholders of NQF exchange their NQF stock for voting stock of FC in a transaction that qualifies as a reorganization described in section 368(a)(1)(C). Pursuant to § 1.1291-6(c)(1), the gain recognition rule of § 1.1291-6(b)(1) does not apply to X's disposition of NQF stock. X therefore does not recognize gain on the exchange of NQF stock for FC stock. X's adjusted basis in the FC stock received in the reorganization is equal to X's adjusted basis in the NQF stock immediately prior to the transfer. The holding period of the FC stock received includes the period during which X held the NQF stock, and, as provided in § 1.1291-1(h)(7), the character of the days during that period as prePFIC and prior PFIC carry over to the FC stock.

(ii) As provided in § 1.1295-1(b)(2)(ii), the section 1295 election that X made with respect to FC applies to the FC stock received in the reorganization. However, because the holding period of the FC stock received in exchange for the NQF stock includes days that are treated as prior PFIC days, the FC stock received in the reorganization is treated as stock of an unpedigreed QEF. X may make an election under section 1291(d)(2) to purge the holding period of the FC stock received of the prior PFIC days carried over with the NQF holding period.

[Prop. Reg. § 1.1295-1.]

[Proposed 4-1-92.]

Proposed Amendments to Regulation

§ 1.1295-1. Qualified electing funds.—

* * *

(b) * * *

(3) *Application of general rules to stock held by a pass through entity.—*(i) *Stock subject to a section 1295 election transferred to a domestic nongrantor trust or domestic estate.—*A shareholder's section 1295 election will not apply to a domestic nongrantor trust or domestic estate to which the shareholder transfers stock subject to a section 1295 election, or to any other United States person that is a beneficiary of the domestic nongrantor trust or estate. However, as provided in paragraph (c)(2)(iv) of this section (relating to a transfer to a domestic pass through entity of stock subject to a section 1295 election), a shareholder that transfers stock subject to a section 1295 election to a domestic nongrantor trust or domestic estate will continue to be subject to the section 1295 election with respect to the stock indirectly owned through the domestic nongrantor trust or domestic estate and any other stock of that PFIC owned by the shareholder.

(ii) *Limitation on application of domestic nongrantor trust's or domestic estate's section 1295 election.—*Except as provided in paragraph (c)(2)(iv) of this section, a section 1295 election made by a domestic nongrantor trust or domestic estate does not apply to other stock of the PFIC held directly or indirectly by the beneficiary.

(iii) *Effect of partnership termination on preexisting partnership section 1295 election.—*The termination of a preexisting partnership section 1295 election (within the meaning of paragraph (d)(2)(i)(B) of this section) by reason of the termination of the partnership under section 708(b) will not terminate the section 1295 election with respect to partners of the terminated partnership that are partners of the new partnership (continuing partners). The stock of the PFIC of which a new partner (partners other than continuing partners) is an indirect shareholder will be treated as stock of a QEF with respect to such partner only if the new partner makes or has made a section 1295 election with respect to that stock under paragraph (d)(2)(i)(A) of this section.

(iv) *Characterization of stock held through a pass-through entity.—*Stock of a PFIC held through a pass-through entity will be treated as stock of a pedigreed QEF with respect to a shareholder (as defined in paragraph (j)(3) of this section) that is treated as owning such stock by reason of an interest in the pass-through entity only if—

(A) In the case of PFIC stock acquired (other than in a transaction in which gain is not fully recognized, including pursuant to regulations in this part under section 1291(f)) and held by a domestic pass-through entity, the domestic pass-through entity has made a preexisting section 1295 election under paragraph (d)(2)(i)(B) or (d)(2)(ii)(B) of this section, or makes an election under paragraph (d)(2)(iii)(A)(*1*) of this section, and the PFIC has been a QEF with respect to the pass-through entity for all taxable years that are included in the pass-through entity's holding period of the PFIC stock and during which the foreign corporation was a PFIC within the meaning of § 1.1291-9(j)(1);

(B) In the case of PFIC stock acquired (other than in a transaction in which gain is not fully recognized, including pursuant to regulations in this part under section 1291(f)) and held by a domestic pass-through entity, other than PFIC stock described in paragraph (b)(3)(iv)(A) of this section, through which the shareholder is treated as owning such PFIC stock, the shareholder makes the section 1295 election under paragraph (d)(2)(i)(A), (d)(2)(ii)(A), (d)(2)(iii)(A)(*2*), or (d)(2)(iii)(B) of this section, and the PFIC has been a QEF with respect to the shareholder for all taxable years that are included in the shareholder's holding period for the PFIC stock, and during which the foreign corporation was a PFIC within the meaning of § 1.1291-9(j)(1); or

(C) In the case of PFIC stock transferred by an interest holder or beneficiary to a pass-through entity in a transaction in which gain is not fully recognized (including pursuant to regulations in this part under section 1291(f)), if the pass-through entity made a preexisting section 1295 election under paragraph (d)(2)(i)(B) or (d)(2)(ii)(B) of this section with respect to the PFIC stock, or the shareholder or pass-through entity, as applicable, makes a section 1295 election under paragraph (d)(2)(i)(A), (d)(2)(ii)(A), (d)(2)(iii)(A)(*1*) or (*2*), or (d)(2)(iii)(B) of this section, in each case for the taxable year in which the transfer was made, or the shareholder's section 1295 election continues pursuant to paragraph (c)(2)(iv) of this section. If the foreign corporation was a PFIC within the meaning of § 1.1291-9(j) at the time of the transfer, the PFIC stock transferred will be treated as stock of a pedigreed QEF with respect to a transferor, however, only if that stock was treated as stock of a pedigreed QEF with respect to the transferor at the time of the transfer. In all cases subject to this paragraph (b)(3)(iv)(C), the PFIC stock will be treated as stock of a pedigreed QEF only if the PFIC has been a QEF for all taxable years of the PFIC that are included wholly or partly in the shareholder's holding period of the PFIC stock during which the foreign corporation was a PFIC within the meaning of § 1.1291-9(j).

(v) *Characterization of stock distributed by a partnership.—*In the case of PFIC stock distributed by a partnership to one or more partners in a transaction in which gain is not fully recognized (including pursuant to regulations in this part under section 1291(f)), the PFIC stock will be treated as stock of a pedigreed QEF by a shareholder only if that stock was treated as stock of a pedigreed QEF with respect to the shareholder immediately before the distribution, or, in the case of a distribution of PFIC stock by a partnership to one or more partners in the first year of the distributee partner or partners' holding period of the PFIC stock, the distributee partner or partners make an election as provided in paragraph (d)(2) of this section.

* * *

(d) * * *

(1) *General rule.—*Except as otherwise provided in this paragraph (d), any shareholder (as defined in paragraph (j)(3) of this section) of a PFIC, including a shareholder that holds stock of a PFIC in bearer form, may make a section 1295 election with respect to that PFIC. The shareholder need not own directly or indirectly any stock of the PFIC when the shareholder makes the section 1295 election provided the shareholder is a shareholder of the PFIC during the taxable year of the PFIC that ends with or within the taxable year of the shareholder for which the section 1295 election is made.

(2) * * *

(i) * * *

(A) *In general.—*If a partnership (domestic or foreign) holds stock of a PFIC, the section 1295 election with respect to such PFIC is made by a shareholder (as defined in paragraph (j)(3) of this section) indirectly owning the PFIC stock by reason of its interest in the partnership. A section 1295 election made by a shareholder under this paragraph (d)(2)(i)(A) applies to the stock of the PFIC indirectly owned by the shareholder by reason of its interest in the partnership and to any other stock of the PFIC owned by the shareholder. A shareholder making an election under this paragraph (d)(2)(i)(A) must do so in the form and manner provided in paragraph (f) of this section. The shareholder must also notify the partnership of the election no later than 30 days after filing the return in which the election is made; the shareholder may notify the partnership in any reasonable manner. However, the failure of the shareholder to notify the partnership of its election does not invalidate an otherwise valid election under this paragraph (d)(2)(i)(A). A shareholder making an election under this paragraph (d)(2)(i)(A) accounts for its pro rata share of ordinary earnings and net capital gain attributable to the QEF stock as provided in § 1.1293-1(c)(1).

(B) *Preexisting section 1295 election by domestic partnership.*—Any section 1295 election made by a domestic partnership with respect to a PFIC effective for taxable years of the PFIC ending on or before [date of publication of the Treasury decision adopting these rules as final regulations in the **Federal Register**] *(preexisting partnership section 1295 election)* will be treated as if it were made by each shareholder that is treated as owning stock in the PFIC by reason of its interest in the domestic partnership on or before such date, and the stock in the PFIC will continue to be treated as stock in a QEF to such shareholder; any partner that becomes a shareholder of the PFIC by acquiring an interest in the domestic partnership after [date of publication of the Treasury decision adopting these rules as final regulations in the **Federal Register**] and wishes to have a section 1295 election applicable with respect to the PFIC may make a section 1295 election under paragraph (d)(2)(i)(A) of this section with respect to stock treated as owned by reason of its interest in the domestic partnership. A shareholder that is treated as owning stock of a QEF by reason of an interest in a domestic partnership that has made a preexisting partnership section 1295 election accounts for its pro rata share of the ordinary earnings and net capital gain attributable to such QEF stock as provided in § 1.1293-1(c)(1).

(ii) *S corporation.*—(A) *In general.*—If an S corporation holds stock of a PFIC, the section 1295 election with respect to such PFIC is made by a shareholder (as defined in paragraph (j)(3) of this section) indirectly owning the PFIC stock by reason of its interest in the S corporation. A section 1295 election made by a shareholder under this paragraph (d)(2)(ii)(A) applies to the stock of the PFIC held by the shareholder by reason of its interest in the S corporation and to any other stock of the PFIC held by the shareholder. A shareholder making an election under this paragraph (d)(2)(ii)(A) must do so in the form and manner provided in paragraph (f) of this section. The shareholder must also notify the S corporation of the election no later than 30 days after filing the return in which the election is made; the shareholder may notify the S corporation in any reasonable manner. However, the failure of the shareholder to notify the S corporation of its election does not invalidate an otherwise valid election under this paragraph (d)(2)(ii)(A). A shareholder making an election under this paragraph (d)(2)(ii)(A) accounts for its pro rata share of ordinary earnings and net capital gain attributable to the QEF stock as provided in § 1.1293-1(c)(1).

(B) *Preexisting section 1295 election by S corporation.*—Any section 1295 election made by an S corporation with respect to a PFIC effective for taxable years of such PFIC ending on or before [date of publication of the Treasury decision adopting these rules as final regulations in the **Federal Register**] *(preexisting S corporation section 1295 election)* will be treated as if it were made by each shareholder that is treated as owning stock in the PFIC by reason of its interest in the S corporation on or before such date, and the stock in the PFIC will continue to be treated as stock in a QEF to such shareholder; any S corporation shareholder that becomes a shareholder of the PFIC by acquiring an interest in the S corporation after [date of publication of the Treasury decision adopting these rules as final regulations in the **Federal Register**] and wishes to have a section 1295 election applicable with respect to the PFIC may make a section 1295 election under paragraph (d)(2)(ii)(A) of this section with respect to stock treated as owned by reason of its interest in the S corporation. A shareholder that is treated as owning stock of a QEF by reason of an interest in an S corporation that has made a preexisting S corporation section 1295 election accounts for its pro rata share of the ordinary earnings and net capital gain attributable to the QEF stock as provided in § 1.1293-1(c)(1).

* * *

(f) * * *

(2) * * *

(i) *In general.*—A shareholder that makes a section 1295 election with respect to a PFIC, or a shareholder that is treated as owning stock in a QEF by reason of an interest in a domestic partnership that has made a preexisting partnership section 1295 election (within the meaning of paragraph (d)(2)(i)(B) of this section) or by reason of an interest in an S corporation that has made a preexisting S corporation section 1295 election (within the meaning of paragraph (d)(2)(ii)(B) of this section), for each taxable year to which the section 1295 election applies, must—

* * *

(3) *Preexisting partnership or S corporation section 1295 election.*—A shareholder that is treated as owning stock in a QEF by reason of an interest in a domestic partnership that has made a preexisting partnership section 1295 election or by reason of an interest in an S corporation that has made a preexisting S corporation section 1295 election does not need to make a section 1295 election with respect to such QEF under the rules of paragraph (f)(1) of this section. However, such shareholder must comply with the annual election requirements as provided in paragraph (f)(2) of this section.

(4) *Notice requirement for partners and S corporation shareholders.*—See paragraphs (d)(2)(i)(A) and (d)(2)(ii)(A) of this section for a notice requirement for partners and S corporation shareholders making a section 1295 election under this section. * * * * *

(j) *Definitions.*—For purposes of this section—

(1) *Intermediary.*—The term *intermediary* means a nominee or shareholder of record that holds stock on behalf of the shareholder or on behalf of another person in a chain of ownership between the shareholder and the PFIC, and any direct or indirect beneficial owner of PFIC stock (including a beneficial owner that is a pass-through entity) in the chain of ownership between the shareholder and the PFIC.

(2) *Pass-through entity.*—The term *pass-through entity* means a partnership, S corporation, trust, or estate.

(3) *Shareholder.*—The term *shareholder* has the meaning provided in § 1.1291-1(b)(7).

(4) *Shareholder's election year.*—The term *shareholder's election year* means the taxable year of the shareholder for which it makes the section 1295 election.

(k) *Applicability dates.*—* * * Paragraphs (b)(3), (d)(1), (d)(2)(i) and (ii), (f)(2)(i), (f)(3) and (4), and (j) of this section apply to taxable years of shareholders beginning on or after [date of publication of the Treasury decision adopting these rules as final regulations in the **Federal Register**]. For taxable years of shareholders beginning before [date of publication of the Treasury decision adopting these rules as final regulations in the **Federal Register**], see § 1.1295-1(b)(3), (d)(1), (d)(2)(i) and (ii), (f)(2)(i), (i)(1)(ii), and (j) as in effect and contained in 26 CFR part 1, as revised April 1, 2021. [Prop. Reg. § 1.1295-1.]

[Proposed 1-25-2022.]

Proposed Regulation

§ 1.1295-2. Special preferred QEF election.—(a) *In general.*—This section provides rules permitting certain shareholders to make a special election under section 1295 (special preferred QEF election) in lieu of the election described in § 1.1295-1[1] and Notice 88-125, 1988-2 C.B. 535 (see § 601.601(d)(2)(ii)(*b*) of this chapter), with respect to certain preferred shares (qualified preferred shares) of a foreign corporation that certifies either that it is a PFIC (as defined in § 1.1291-1(b)(1)(i))[1] or that it reasonably believes that it is a PFIC. In order to make a special preferred QEF election, a shareholder must satisfy the stock ownership requirement of paragraph (c)(2) of this section. A special preferred QEF election of a shareholder applies only to those qualified preferred shares acquired and held directly by the shareholder in the taxable year of the shareholder for which the election is made. A shareholder making a special preferred QEF election must account for dividend income on shares subject to the election under the special income inclusion rules described in § 1.1293-2, rather than under the general income inclusion rules of section 1293 and § 1.1293-1. In addition, for purposes of determining the tax consequences of owning shares subject to the special preferred QEF election, an electing shareholder must treat the foreign corporation as a PFIC for the entire period during which the shareholder continues to hold any of such shares. Paragraph (b) of this section defines qualified preferred share. Paragraph (c) of this section provides rules for determining who may make the special preferred QEF election. Paragraph (d) of this section provides rules concerning the effect of the election. Paragraph (e) of this section provides rules for the time and manner of making the election. Paragraph (f) of this

[1] This proposed regulation was published on April 1, 1992, at 57 Fed. Reg. 11024.

section sets forth the annual reporting requirement for the election. Paragraph (g) of this section provides rules concerning the possible termination or invalidation of the election. For the applicability date of this section, see paragraph (h) of this section.

(b) *Qualified preferred share defined.*—(1) *In general.*—For purposes of this section, a share of a foreign corporation is a qualified preferred share only if—

(i) The share was originally issued for cash or in exchange for qualified preferred shares of the foreign corporation in a transaction to which section 354(a)(1) applied;

(ii) If the share were to constitute a debt obligation, the share would be in registered form within the meaning of § 5f.103-1(c) of this chapter;

(iii) All amounts payable with respect to the share are denominated in U.S. dollars and are not determined by reference to the value of a currency other than the U.S. dollar;

(iv) The share is limited and preferred as to dividends and does not participate in corporate growth to any significant extent within the meaning of section 1504(a)(4)(B);

(v) The share has a fixed redemption or liquidation price;

(vi) The share provides for cumulative or noncumulative dividend rights that are limited to an annual (or shorter period) amount computed by multiplying either the redemption or liquidation price of the share by a specified index described in § 1.446-3(c)(2)(i), (iii), or (iv) (specified index), or by a specified index periodically re-established pursuant to an auction reset mechanism, set in advance of the period with respect to which the specified index applies;

(vii) If the share may be redeemed under circumstances described in § 1.305-5(b) such that redemption premium (as described in § 1.305-5(b)) could be treated under section 305(c) as a constructive distribution (fixed term preferred stock), the share was not issued with redemption premium exceeding the de minimis amount described in section 305(c)(1) and § 1.305-5(b)(1);

(viii) If the share may not be redeemed under circumstances described in § 1.305-5(b) such that redemption premium would not be treated under section 305 as a constructive distribution (perpetual preferred stock), the share does not provide shareholders with the right to receive an amount upon liquidation or redemption that exceeds the issue price of the share (as determined under the principles of section 1273(b)) by an amount in excess of 5 percent of such liquidation or redemption amount;

(ix) If redeemable, the share is redeemable only in whole and not in part and is not subject to mandatory redemption within five years of the issue date of the share. Further, the share is not subject to a holder put or issuer call that, based on all the facts and circumstances as of the issue date of the share, is more likely than not to be exercised at a time within five years of the issue date;

(x) If convertible, the share is not convertible into a share other than a share meeting all the conditions set forth in paragraphs (b)(1)(i) through (b)(1)(ix) of this section; and

(xi) The issuer of the share has indicated in an offering document relating to the original issuance of the share or in a written statement available to U.S. holders that the issuer has no current intention or belief that it will not pay dividends on the share on a current basis and that the share meets the conditions set forth in paragraphs (b)(1)(i) through (b)(1)(x) of this section and this paragraph (b)(1)(xi).

(2) *Special rules for shares acquired in secondary market transactions.*—(i) *Fixed term preferred stock.*—A share of fixed term preferred stock (as described in paragraph (b)(1)(vii) of this section) that satisfies the conditions set forth in paragraph (b)(1) of this section and that is acquired in a transaction other than in connection with the initial issuance of the share (a secondary market transaction), shall constitute a qualified preferred share with respect to a shareholder, but only if the shareholder acquires the share for cash and the share has preferred discount (as defined below) that is less than or equal to an amount equal to 1 percent of the redemption price, multiplied by the number of complete years from the date of acquisition of the share to the redemption date as established under the principles of § 1.305-5(b). Sales of shares to bond houses, brokers, or similar persons or organizations acting in the capacity as underwriters, placement agents, or wholesalers are ignored for purposes of determining whether a share is acquired in connection with the initial issuance of the share. For purposes of this section, the preferred discount for a share is the excess of the redemption price of the share payable on the redemption date over the shareholder's acquisition cost for the share.

(ii) *Perpetual preferred stock.*—A share of perpetual preferred stock, within the meaning of paragraph (b)(1)(viii) of this section, that satisfies the conditions set forth in paragraph (b)(1) of this section and that is acquired in a secondary market transaction, shall constitute a qualified preferred share with respect to the shareholder, but only if the shareholder acquires the share for cash and the amount payable upon liquidation of the share exceeds the shareholder's acquisition cost for the share by an amount less than or equal to 10 percent of such liquidation amount.

(iii) *Examples.*—The following examples illustrate the rules of this paragraph (b)(2).

Example 1—(i) *Facts.* On May 1, 1998, A, an individual who files her return on a calendar year basis, purchases for $9000 cash in a single secondary market transaction (as defined in paragraph (b)(2)(i) of this section) 100 shares of nonconvertible Class A $100 par value preferred stock (Class A Stock) of FC, a foreign corporation with a taxable year ending March 31. The terms of the Class A Stock satisfy all the conditions described in paragraph (b)(1) of this section and provide for a mandatory redemption of the Class A Stock by the issuer in U.S. dollars at par on June 1, 2012. The Class A Stock is not redeemable pursuant to an issuer call or holder put on any other date.

(ii) *Analysis.* In order for A to make a special preferred QEF election with respect to the Class A Stock acquired by A, the Class A Stock acquired must constitute qualified preferred shares. Although the Class A Stock meets the requirements for qualified preferred shares set forth in paragraph (b)(1) of this section, the stock also must satisfy the requirements described in paragraph (b)(2) because A acquired the stock in a secondary market transaction. Because the terms of the Class A Stock provide that the stock will be redeemed by the issuer on June 1, 2012, the stock constitutes fixed term preferred stock within the meaning of paragraph (b)(1)(vii) of this section. A purchased the Class A Stock for $90 per share, representing a $10 discount ($100 June 1, 2012, per share redemption price less $90 acquisition cost). Because this $10 discount, which constitutes preferred discount within the meaning of paragraph (b)(2)(i) of this section, is less than $14 (1 percent of the redemption price multiplied by 14 (the number of complete years until the mandatory redemption date)), the Class A Stock acquired by A satisfies the conditions of paragraph (b)(2)(i) of this section and therefore constitutes qualified preferred shares.

Example 2—(i) *Facts.* The facts are the same as in *Example 1*, except that A acquires the 100 shares of Class A Stock for $8000.

(ii) *Analysis.* In this case, A purchased the Class A Stock for $80 per share, representing a $20 discount ($100 June 1, 2012, redemption price less $80 acquisition cost). Because this $20 of preferred discount is greater than $14 (1 percent of the redemption price multiplied by 14 (the number of complete years until the mandatory redemption date)), the Class A Stock fails to satisfy the conditions of paragraph (b)(2)(i) of this section and therefore fails to qualify as qualified preferred shares.

(c) *Who may make the election.*—(1) *In general.*—A U.S. person that acquires qualified preferred shares for cash or in a nonrecognition transaction described in § 1.1291-6(a)[2] (nonrecognition transaction) and that holds such shares directly may make a special preferred QEF election, provided that, in the case of shares acquired in a nonrecognition transaction, either the qualified preferred shares are treated as stock of a pedigreed QEF, as defined in § 1.1291-1(b)(2)(ii), immediately prior to the nonrecognition transaction, or the gain, if any, realized on the transaction would be recognized under § 1.1291-6(b) with respect to the nonrecognition transaction. A special preferred QEF election will not apply to any shares with respect to which the electing shareholder is an indirect shareholder, within the meaning of § 1.1291-1(b)(8). Solely for purposes of this section, partnerships, S corporations, trusts and estates (pass-through entities) that directly own qualified preferred shares are treated as shareholders that may make a special preferred QEF election. A shareholder may not make a special preferred QEF election if at any time the shareholder made a section 1295 election (other than a special preferred QEF election) with respect to the foreign corporation. A shareholder may not make a special preferred QEF election unless the shareholder satisfies the stock ownership requirements set forth in paragraph (c)(2) of this section, and the shareholder receives from the foreign corporation the statement described in paragraph (c)(3) of this section.

[2] This proposed regulation was published on April 1, 1992, at 57 Fed. Reg. 11024.

(2) *Ownership requirement.*—A holder of qualified preferred shares of a foreign corporation may make a special preferred QEF election only if, at all times during the taxable year of the shareholder, the shareholder does not own, directly, indirectly, or constructively, within the meaning of section 958, five percent or more of the vote or value of any class of stock of the foreign corporation. The five percent vote or value limitation must be satisfied for each taxable year of the shareholder during which the shareholder continues to hold shares subject to the special preferred QEF election.

(3) *Statement from corporation.*—A shareholder may make the special preferred QEF election only if the foreign corporation has provided a written statement relating to the taxable year of the corporation that ends with or within the taxable year of the shareholder for which the election is made certifying either that the foreign corporation is, or that it reasonably believes that it is, a PFIC, and that it is not a controlled foreign corporation within the meaning of section 957(a) for such taxable year of the corporation. The statement must be provided directly to the electing shareholder or in a disclosure or other document generally available to all U.S. holders. Electing shareholders must retain a copy of the statement for their records.

(d) *Effect of election.*—(1) *In general.*—Unless terminated or invalidated pursuant to paragraph (g) of this section, shares subject to a special preferred QEF election will be treated as shares of a pedigreed QEF (as defined in § 1.1291-1(b)(2)(ii)) for all taxable years of the foreign corporation that are included wholly or partly in the shareholder's holding period of the shares. A special preferred QEF election applies to all qualified preferred shares owned directly by the shareholder that are acquired in the taxable year of the election. Separate special preferred QEF elections may be made for qualified preferred shares acquired in other taxable years of the taxpayer. A special preferred QEF election is personal to the shareholder that made the election and does not apply to a transferee of the shares. A shareholder that has made a special preferred QEF election may not make, with respect to the foreign corporation, any other election permitted under sections 1291 through 1297 and the regulations under those sections, including a section 1295 election as described in § 1.1295-1 and Notice 88-125, 1988-2 C.B. 535 (see § 601.601(d)(2)(ii)(*b*) of this chapter), for any period during which the special preferred QEF election remains in effect with respect to any shares of the shareholder.

(2) *Continued PFIC Characterization.*—By making the special preferred QEF election, the shareholder agrees to treat the foreign corporation as a PFIC with respect to qualified preferred shares subject to the election at all times during its holding period for such shares, without regard to whether the foreign corporation is a PFIC for any taxable year of the foreign corporation during which the preferred QEF election remains in effect.

(3) *Section 1293 inclusions.*—For each taxable year of the shareholder to which an election under this section applies, the shareholder must include in income the preferred QEF amount, as defined in § 1.1293-2, in the manner and under the rules provided in that section.

(e) *Time for and manner of making the special preferred QEF election.*—(1) *Time for making the election.*—A special preferred QEF election must be made on or before the due date, as extended, for filing the shareholder's return for the taxable year during which the shareholder acquired the qualified preferred shares for which the election is being made. A special preferred QEF election may not be made for those shares at any other time pursuant to any other provision of the Code or regulations.

(2) *Manner of making the election.*—(i) *In general.*—A shareholder makes the special preferred QEF election under this section for all qualified preferred shares of a foreign corporation acquired during the shareholder's taxable year by checking the appropriate box in Form 8621 (Return by a Shareholder of a Passive Foreign Investment Company or Qualified Electing Fund), Part I, for making the section 1295 election, and indicating in the margin of Part I that the shareholder is making a special preferred QEF election with respect to certain specified shares. The shareholder also must report the preferred QEF amount for the taxable year of the election on Line 6a of Part II of Form 8621. In addition, the shareholder must attach to Form 8621 the statement (preferred QEF statement) described in paragraph (e)(2)(ii) of this section, signed by the shareholder under penalties of perjury, stating that the information and representations provided in the preferred QEF statement are true, correct, and complete to the best of the shareholder's knowledge and belief.

(ii) *Preferred QEF statement contents.*—The preferred QEF statement must include the following information and representations:

(A) The first taxable year of the shareholder for which the special preferred QEF election is made;

(B) The number of shares subject to the election, their acquisition date(s) and acquisition price(s), and the class designation(s) of the shares;

(C) A representation by the shareholder that it did not at any time during its taxable year own directly, indirectly, or constructively, within the meaning of section 958, five percent or more of the vote or value of any class of stock of the foreign corporation with respect to which the election applies;

(D) A representation by the shareholder that it has obtained the written statement described in paragraph (c)(3) of this section; and

(E) A representation by the shareholder that it has never made a section 1295 election other than a special preferred QEF election with respect to the foreign corporation.

(f) *Annual reporting requirement.*—For each taxable year of a shareholder during which the shareholder holds shares of a foreign corporation subject to one or more special preferred QEF elections, the shareholder must file Form 8621 with respect to the foreign corporation regardless of whether the foreign corporation is or is not a PFIC under section 1296 during any portion of the taxable year. The shareholder must indicate in the margin of Part I of Form 8621 the number of special preferred QEF elections of the shareholder that remain in effect with respect to the foreign corporation. In addition, the shareholder must report, on Line 6a of Part II of Form 8621, the aggregate of the preferred QEF amounts for all relevant special preferred QEF elections in effect for the taxable year.

(g) *Termination or invalidation of election.*—(1) *In general.*—A sale, exchange or other disposition of a share that is subject to a special preferred QEF election will terminate the special preferred QEF election with respect to that share. In addition, the Commissioner may, in the Commissioner's discretion, terminate or invalidate a special preferred QEF election if a shareholder that made the election fails to satisfy the initial or ongoing requirements of the election. Once made, a special preferred QEF election may not be terminated or invalidated by the shareholder.

(2) *Effect of termination or invalidation.*—Termination of a special preferred QEF election by the Commissioner will be effective on the first day of the shareholder's first taxable year following the last taxable year of the shareholder for which the requirements of the election are satisfied. For purposes of sections 1291 through 1297 and the regulations thereunder, the holding period of qualified preferred shares subject to an election that has been terminated will be treated as beginning on the effective date of the termination. A shareholder that has made an election that is invalidated by the Commissioner will be treated for purposes of sections 1291 through 1297 and the regulations thereunder as if the shareholder never made the election.

(h) *Effective date.*—An election under this section may only be made with respect to qualified preferred shares that are issued after the date that is 30 days after the date of publication of this document as a final regulation. [Prop. Reg. § 1.1295-2.]

[Proposed 12-24-96.]

§ 1.1295-3. Retroactive elections.—(a) *In general.*—This section prescribes the exclusive rules under which a shareholder, as defined in § 1.1295-1(j), may make a section 1295 election for a taxable year after the election due date, as defined in § 1.1295-1(e) (retroactive election). Therefore, a shareholder may not seek such relief under any other provision of the law, including § 301.9100 of this chapter. Paragraph (b) of this section describes the general rules for a shareholder to preserve the ability to make a retroactive election. These rules require that the shareholder possess reasonable belief as of the election due date that the foreign corporation was not a PFIC for its taxable year that ended in the shareholder's taxable year to which the election due date pertains, and that the shareholder file a Protective Statement to preserve its ability to make a retroactive election. Paragraph (c) of this section establishes the terms, conditions and other requirements with respect to a Protective Statement required to be filed under the general rules. Paragraph (d) of this section sets forth factors that establish a shareholder's reasonable belief that a foreign corporation was not a PFIC. Paragraph (e) of this section prescribes special rules for certain shareholders that are deemed to satisfy the reasonable belief requirement and therefore are not required to file a Protective Statement. Paragraph (f) of this section describes the limited circumstances under which the Commissioner may permit a shareholder that lacked the requisite reasonable belief or failed to satisfy the requirements of paragraph (b) or (e) of this section to make a retroactive election. Paragraph (g) of this section provides the time for and manner of making a retroactive election. Paragraph (h) of this section provides the effective date of this section.

(b) *General rule.*—Except as provided in paragraphs (e) and (f) of this section, a shareholder may make a retroactive election for a taxable year of the shareholder (retroactive election year) only if the shareholder—

(1) Reasonably believed, within the meaning of paragraph (d) of this section, that as of the election due date, as defined in § 1.1295-1(e), the foreign corporation was not a PFIC for its taxable year that ended during the retroactive election year;

(2) Filed a Protective Statement with respect to the foreign corporation, applicable to the retroactive election year, in which the shareholder described the basis for its reasonable belief and extended, in the manner provided in paragraph (c)(4) of this section, the periods of limitations on the assessment of taxes determined under sections 1291 through 1298 with respect to the foreign corporation (PFIC related taxes) for all taxable years of the shareholder to which the Protective Statement applies; and

(3) Complied with the other terms and conditions of the Protective Statement.

(c) *Protective Statement.*—(1) *In general.*—A Protective Statement is a statement executed under penalties of perjury by the shareholder, or a person authorized to sign a federal income tax return on behalf of the shareholder, that preserves the shareholder's ability to make a retroactive election. To file a Protective Statement that applies to a taxable year of the shareholder, the shareholder must reasonably believe as of the election due date that the foreign corporation was not a PFIC for the foreign corporation's taxable year that ended during the retroactive election year. The Protective Statement must contain—

(i) The shareholder's reasonable belief statement, as described in paragraph (c)(2) of this section;

(ii) The shareholder's agreement extending the periods of limitations on the assessment of PFIC related taxes for all taxable years to which the Protective Statement applies, as provided in paragraph (c)(4) of this section; and

(iii) The following information and representations—

(A) The shareholder's name, address, taxpayer identification number, and the shareholder's first taxable year to which the Protective Statement applies;

(B) The foreign corporation's name, address, and taxpayer identification number, if any; and

(C) The highest percentage of shares of each class of stock of the foreign corporation held directly or indirectly by the shareholder during the shareholder's first taxable year to which the Protective Statement applies.

(2) *Reasonable belief statement.*—The Protective Statement must contain a reasonable belief statement, as described in paragraph (c)(1) of this section. The reasonable belief statement is a description of the shareholder's basis for its reasonable belief that the foreign corporation was not a PFIC for its taxable year that ended with or within the shareholder's first taxable year to which the Protective Statement applies. If the Protective Statement applies to a taxable year or years described in paragraph (c)(5)(ii) of this section, the reasonable belief statement must describe the shareholder's basis for its reasonable belief that the foreign corporation was not a PFIC for the foreign corporation's taxable year or years that ended in such taxable year or years of the shareholder. The reasonable belief statement must discuss the application of the income and asset tests to the foreign corporation and the factors, including those stated in paragraph (d) of this section, that affect the results of those tests.

(3) *Who executes and files the Protective Statement.*—The person that executes and files the Protective Statement is the person that makes the section 1295 election, as provided in § 1.1295-1(d).

(4) *Waiver of the periods of limitations.*—(i) *Time for and manner of extending periods of limitations.*—(A) *In general.*—A shareholder that files the Protective Statement with the Commissioner must extend the periods of limitations on the assessment of all PFIC related taxes for all of the shareholder's taxable years to which the Protective Statement applies, as provided in this paragraph (c)(4). The shareholder is required to execute the waiver on such form as the Commissioner may prescribe for purposes of this paragraph (c)(4). Until that form is published, the shareholder must execute a statement in which the shareholder agrees to extend the periods of limitations on the assessment of all PFIC related taxes for all the shareholder's taxable years to which the Protective Statement applies, as provided in this paragraph (c)(4), and agrees to the restrictions in paragraph (c)(4)(ii)(A) of this section. The shareholder or a person authorized to sign the shareholder's federal income tax return must sign the form or statement. A properly executed form or statement authorized by this paragraph (c)(4) will be deemed consented to and signed by a Service Center Director or the Assistant Commissioner (International) for purposes of § 301.6501(c)-1(d) of this chapter.

(B) *Application of general rule to domestic partnerships.—(1) In general.*—A domestic partnership that holds an interest in stock of a PFIC satisfies the waiver requirement of paragraph (c)(4) of this section pursuant to the rules of this paragraph (c)(4)(i)(B)(*1*). The partnership must file one or more waivers obtained or arranged under this paragraph (c)(4)(i)(B) as part of the Protective Statement, as provided in paragraph (c)(1) of this section. The partnership must either—

(*i*) Obtain from each partner the partner's waiver of the periods of limitations;

(*ii*) Obtain from each partner a duly executed power of attorney under § 601.501 of this chapter authorizing the partnership to extend that partner's periods of limitations, and execute a waiver on behalf of the partners; or

(*iii*) In the case of a domestic partnership governed by the unified audit and litigation procedures of sections 6221 through 6233 (TEFRA partnership), arrange for the tax matters partner (or any other person authorized to enter into an agreement to extend the periods of limitations), as provided in section 6229(b), to execute a waiver on behalf of all the partners.

(2) Special rules.—(i) Addition of partner to non-TEFRA partnership.—In the case of any individual who becomes a partner in a domestic partnership other than a TEFRA partnership (non-TEFRA partnership) in a taxable year subsequent to the year in which the partnership filed a Protective Statement, the partner and the partnership must comply with the rules applicable to non-TEFRA partnerships, as provided in paragraph (c)(4)(i)(B)(*1*) of this section, by the due date, as extended, for the federal income tax return of the partnership for the taxable year during which the individual became a partner. Failure to so comply will render the Protective Statement invalid with respect to the partnership and partners.

(ii) Change in status from non-TEFRA partnership to TEFRA partnership.—If a partnership is a non-TEFRA partnership in one taxable year but becomes a TEFRA partnership in a subsequent taxable year, the partnership must file one or more waivers obtained or arranged under this paragraph (c)(4)(i)(B)(*2*)(*ii*), as part of the Protective Statement, as provided in paragraph (c)(1) of this section. The partnership must either obtain from any new partner the partner's waiver described in this paragraph (c)(4); obtain from the new partner a duly executed power of attorney under § 601.501 of this chapter authorizing the partnership to extend the partner's periods of limitations, and execute a waiver on behalf of the new partner; or arrange for the tax matters partner (or any other person authorized to enter into an agreement to extend the periods of limitations) to execute a waiver on behalf of all the partners. In each case, the partnership must attach any new waiver of a partner's periods of limitations, and a copy of the Protective Statement to its federal income tax return for that taxable year.

(C) *Application of general rule to domestic nongrantor trusts and domestic estates.*—A domestic nongrantor trust or a domestic estate that holds an interest in stock of a PFIC satisfies the waiver requirement of this paragraph (c)(4) at the entity level. For this purpose, such entity must comply with rules similar to those applicable to non-TEFRA partnerships, as provided in paragraph (c)(4)(i)(B)(*1*) of this section.

(D) *Application of general rule to S corporations.*—An S corporation that holds an interest in stock of a PFIC satisfies the waiver requirement of this paragraph (c)(4) at the S corporation level. For this purpose, the S corporation must comply with rules similar to those applicable to non-TEFRA partnerships, as provided in paragraph (c)(4)(i)(B)(*1*) of this section. However, in the case of an S corporation that was governed by the unified audit corporate proceedings of sections 6241 through 6245 for any taxable year to which a Protective Statement applies (former TEFRA S corporation), the tax matters person (or any other person authorized to enter into such an agreement), as was provided in sections 6241 through 6245, may execute a waiver described in this paragraph (c)(4) that applies to such taxable year; for any other taxable year, the former TEFRA S corporation must comply with rules similar to those applicable to non-TEFRA partnerships.

(E) *Effect on waiver of complete termination of a pass through entity or pass through entity's business.*—The complete termination of a pass through entity described in paragraphs (c)(4)(i)(B) through (D) of this section, or a pass through entity's trade or business, will not terminate a waiver that applies to a partner, shareholder, or beneficiary.

(F) *Application of general rule to foreign partnerships, foreign trusts, domestic or foreign grantor trusts, and foreign estates.*—A U.S. person that is a partner or beneficiary of a foreign partnership, foreign trust, or foreign estate that holds an interest in stock of a PFIC satisfies the waiver requirement of this paragraph (c)(4) at the partner or beneficiary level. A U.S. person that is treated under sections 671 through 679 as the owner of the portion of a domestic or foreign trust that owns an interest in PFIC stock also satisfies the waiver requirement at the owner level. A waiver by a partner or beneficiary applies only to that partner or beneficiary, and is not affected by a complete termination of the entity or the entity's trade or business.

(ii) *Terms of waiver.*—(A) *Scope of waiver.*—The waiver of the periods of limitations is limited to the assessment of PFIC related taxes. If the period of limitations for a taxable year affected by a retroactive election has expired with respect to the assessment of other non-PFIC related taxes, no adjustments, other than consequential changes, may be made by the Internal Revenue Service or by the shareholder to any other items of income, deduction, or credit for that year. If the period of limitations for refunds or credits for a taxable year affected by a retroactive election is open only by virtue of the assessment period extension and section 6511(c), no refund or credit is allowable on grounds other than adjustments to PFIC related taxes and consequential changes.

(B) *Period of waiver.*—The extension of the periods of limitations on the assessment of PFIC related taxes will be effective for all of the shareholder's taxable years to which the Protective Statement applies. In addition, the waiver, to the extent it applies to the period of limitations for a particular year, will terminate with respect to that year no sooner than three years from the date on which the shareholder files an amended return, as provided in paragraph (g) of this section, for that year. For the suspension of the running of the period of limitations for the collection of taxes for which a shareholder has elected under section 1294 to extend the time for payment, as provided in paragraph (g)(3)(ii) of this section, see sections 6503(i) and 6229(h).

(5) *Time of and manner for filing a Protective Statement.*—(i) *In general.*—Except as provided in paragraph (c)(5)(ii) of this section, a Protective Statement must be attached to the shareholder's federal income tax return for the shareholder's first taxable year to which the Protective Statement will apply. The shareholder must file its return and the copy of the Protective Statement by the due date, as extended under section 6081, for the return.

(ii) *Special rule for taxable years ended before January 2, 1998.*—A shareholder may file a Protective Statement that applies to the shareholder's taxable year or years that ended before January 2, 1998, provided the period of limitations on the assessment of taxes for any such year has not expired (open year). The shareholder must file the Protective Statement applicable to such open year or years, as provided in paragraph (c)(5)(i) of this section, by the due date, as extended, for the shareholder's return for the first taxable year ending after January 2, 1998.

(6) *Applicability of the Protective Statement.*—(i) *In general.*—Except as otherwise provided in this paragraph (c)(6), a Protective Statement applies to the shareholder's first taxable year for which the Protective Statement was filed and to each subsequent taxable year. The Protective Statement will not apply to any taxable year of the shareholder during which the shareholder does not own any stock of the foreign corporation or to any taxable year thereafter. Accordingly, if the shareholder has not made a retroactive election with respect to the previously owned stock by the time the shareholder reacquires stock of the foreign corporation, the shareholder must file another Protective Statement to preserve its right to make a retroactive election with respect to the later acquired stock. For the rule that provides that a section 1295 election made with respect to a foreign corporation applies to stock of that corporation acquired after a lapse in ownership, see § 1.1295-1(c)(2)(iii).

(ii) *Invalidity of the Protective Statement.*—A shareholder will be treated as if it never filed a Protective Statement if—

(A) The shareholder failed to make a retroactive election by the date prescribed for making the retroactive election in paragraph (g)(1) of this section; or

(B) The waiver of the periods of limitations terminates (by reason of a court decision or other determination) with respect to any taxable year before the expiration of three years from the date of filing of an amended return for that year pursuant to paragraph (g) of this section.

(7) *Retention of Protective Statement and information demonstrating reasonable belief.*—A shareholder that files a Protective Statement must retain a copy of the Protective Statement and its attachments and must, for each taxable year of the shareholder to which the Protective Statement applies, retain information sufficient to demonstrate the shareholder's reasonable belief that the foreign corporation was not a PFIC for the taxable year of the foreign corporation ending during each such taxable year of the shareholder.

(d) *Reasonable belief.*—(1) *In general.*—A foreign corporation is a PFIC for a taxable year if the foreign corporation satisfies either the income or asset test of section 1297(a). To determine whether a shareholder had reasonable belief that the foreign corporation is not a PFIC under section 1297(a), the shareholder must consider all relevant facts and circumstances. Reasonable belief may be based on a variety of factors, including reasonable asset valuations as well as reasonable interpretations of the applicable provisions of the Code, regulations, and administrative guidance regarding the direct or indirect ownership of the income or assets of the foreign corporation, the proper character of that income or those assets, and similar issues. Reasonable belief may be based on reasonable predictions regarding income to be earned and assets to be owned in subsequent years where qualification of the foreign corporation as a PFIC for the current taxable year will depend on the qualification of the corporation as a PFIC in a subsequent year. Reasonable belief may be based on an analysis of generally available financial information of the foreign corporation. To determine whether a shareholder had reasonable belief that the foreign corporation was not a PFIC, the Commissioner may consider the size of the shareholder's interest in the foreign corporation.

(2) *Knowledge of law required.*—Reasonable belief must be based on a good faith effort to apply the Code, regulations, and related administrative guidance. Any person's failure to know or apply these provisions will not form the basis of reasonable belief.

(e) *Special rules for qualified shareholders.*—(1) *In general.*—A shareholder that is a qualified shareholder, as defined in paragraph (e)(2) of this section, for a taxable year of the shareholder is not required to satisfy the reasonable belief requirement of paragraph (b)(1) of this section or file a Protective Statement to preserve its ability to make a retroactive election with respect to such taxable year. Accordingly, a qualified shareholder may make a retroactive election for any open taxable year in the shareholder's holding period. The retroactive election will be treated as made in the earliest taxable year of the shareholder during which the foreign corporation qualified as a PFIC (including a taxable year ending prior January 2, 1998) and the shareholder will be treated as a shareholder of a pedigreed QEF, as defined in § 1.1291-9(j)(2)(ii), provided the shareholder—

(i) Has been a qualified shareholder with respect to the foreign corporation for all taxable years of the shareholder included in the shareholder's holding period during which the foreign corporation was a PFIC, or in the case of taxable years ending before January 2, 1998, the shareholder satisfies the criteria of a qualified shareholder, for all such years; or

(ii) Has been a qualified shareholder, or in the case of taxable years ending before January 2, 1998, satisfies the criteria of a qualified shareholder, for all taxable years in its holding period before it filed a Protective Statement, which Protective Statement is applicable to all subsequent years, beginning with the first taxable year in which the shareholder is not a qualified shareholder.

(2) *Qualified shareholder.*—A shareholder will be treated as a qualified shareholder for a taxable year if the shareholder did not file

a Protective Statement applicable to an earlier taxable year included in the shareholder's holding period of the stock of the foreign corporation currently held and—

(i) At all times during the taxable year the shareholder owned, within the meaning of section 958, directly, indirectly, or constructively, less than two percent of the vote and value of each class of stock of the foreign corporation; and

(ii) With respect to the taxable year of the foreign corporation ending within the shareholder's taxable year, the foreign corporation or U.S. counsel for the foreign corporation indicated in a public filing, disclosure statement or other notice provided to U.S. persons that are shareholders of the foreign corporation (corporate filing) that the foreign corporation—

(A) Reasonably believes that it is not or should not constitute a PFIC for the corporation's taxable year; or

(B) Is unable to conclude that it is not or should not be a PFIC (due to certain asset valuation or interpretation issues, or because PFIC status will depend on the income or assets of the foreign corporation in the corporation's subsequent taxable years) but reasonably believes that, more likely than not, it ultimately will not be a PFIC.

(3) *Exceptions.*—Notwithstanding paragraph (e)(2)(ii) of this section, a shareholder will not be treated as a qualified shareholder for a taxable year of the shareholder if the shareholder knew or had reason to know that a corporate filing regarding the foreign corporation's PFIC status was inaccurate, or knew that the foreign corporation was a PFIC for the taxable year of the foreign corporation ending with or within such taxable year of the shareholder. For purposes of this paragraph, a shareholder will be treated as knowing that a foreign corporation was a PFIC if the principal activity of the foreign corporation, directly or indirectly, is owning or trading a diversified portfolio of stock, securities, or other financial contracts.

(f) *Special consent.*—(1) *In general.*—A shareholder that has not satisfied the requirements of paragraph (b) or (e) of this section may request the consent of the Commissioner to make a retroactive election for a taxable year of the shareholder provided the shareholder satisfies the requirements set forth in this paragraph (f). The Commissioner will grant relief under this paragraph (f) only if—

(i) The shareholder reasonably relied on a qualified tax professional, within the meaning of paragraph (f)(2) of this section;

(ii) Granting consent will not prejudice the interests of the United States government, as provided in paragraph (f)(3) of this section;

(iii) The shareholder requests consent under paragraph (f) of this section before a representative of the Internal Revenue Service raises upon audit the PFIC status of the corporation for any taxable year of the shareholder; and

(iv) The shareholder satisfies the procedural requirements set forth in paragraph (f)(4) of this section.

(2) *Reasonable reliance on a qualified tax professional.*—(i) *In general.*—Except as provided in paragraph (f)(2)(ii) of this section, a shareholder is deemed to have reasonably relied on a qualified tax professional only if the shareholder reasonably relied on a qualified tax professional (including a tax professional employed by the shareholder) who failed to identify the foreign corporation as a PFIC or failed to advise the shareholder of the consequences of making, or failing to make, the section 1295 election. A shareholder will not be considered to have reasonably relied on a qualified tax professional if the shareholder knew, or reasonably should have known, that the foreign corporation was a PFIC and of the availability of a section 1295 election, or knew or reasonably should have known that the qualified tax professional—

(A) Was not competent to render tax advice with respect to the ownership of shares of a foreign corporation; or

(B) Did not have access to all relevant facts and circumstances.

(ii) *Shareholder deemed to have not reasonably relied on a qualified tax professional.*—For purposes of this paragraph (f)(2), a shareholder is deemed to have not reasonably relied on a qualified tax professional if the shareholder was informed by the qualified tax professional that the foreign corporation was a PFIC and of the availability of the section 1295 election and related tax consequences, but either chose not to make the section 1295 election or was unable to make a valid section 1295 election.

(3) *Prejudice to the interests of the United States government.*—(i) *General rule.*—Except as otherwise provided in paragraph (f)(3)(ii) of this section, the Commissioner will not grant consent under paragraph (f) of this section if doing so would prejudice the interests of the United States government. The interests of the United States government are prejudiced if granting relief would result in the shareholder having a lower tax liability, taking into account applicable interest charges, in the aggregate for all years affected by the retroactive election (other than by a de minimis amount) than the shareholder would have had if the shareholder had made the section 1295 election by the election due date. The time value of money is taken into account for purposes of this computation.

(ii) *Elimination of prejudice to the interests of the United States government.*—Notwithstanding the general rule of paragraph (f)(3)(i) of this section, if granting relief would prejudice the interests of the United States government, the Commissioner may, in the Commissioner's sole discretion, grant consent to make the election provided the shareholder enters into a closing agreement with the Commissioner that requires the shareholder to pay an amount sufficient to eliminate any prejudice to the United States government as a consequence of the shareholder's inability to file amended returns for closed taxable years.

(4) *Procedural requirements.*—(i) *Filing instructions.*—A shareholder requests consent under paragraph (f) of this section to make a retroactive election by filing with the Office of the Associate Chief Counsel (International) a ruling request that includes the affidavits required by this paragraph (f)(4). The ruling request must satisfy the requirements, including payment of the user fee, for ruling requests filed with that office.

(ii) *Affidavit from shareholder.*—The shareholder, or a person authorized to sign a federal income tax return on behalf of the shareholder, must submit a detailed affidavit describing the events that led to the failure to make a section 1295 election by the election due date, and to the discovery thereof. The shareholder's affidavit must describe the engagement and responsibilities of the qualified tax professional as well as the extent to which the shareholder relied on the tax professional. The shareholder must sign the affidavit under penalties of perjury. An individual who signs for an entity must have personal knowledge of the facts and circumstances at issue.

(iii) *Affidavits from other persons.*—The shareholder must submit detailed affidavits from individuals having knowledge or information about the events that led to the failure to make a section 1295 election by the election due date, and to the discovery thereof. These individuals must include the qualified tax professional upon whose advice the shareholder relied, as well as any individual (including an employee of the shareholder) who made a substantial contribution to the return's preparation, and any accountant or attorney, knowledgeable in tax matters, who advised the shareholder with regard to its ownership of the stock of the foreign corporation. Each affidavit must describe the individual's engagement and responsibilities as well as the advice concerning the tax treatment of the foreign corporation that the individual provided to the shareholder. Each affidavit also must include the individual's name, address, and taxpayer identification number, and must be signed by the individual under penalties of perjury.

(iv) *Other information.*—In connection with a request for consent under this paragraph (f), a shareholder must provide any additional information requested by the Commissioner.

(v) *Notification of Internal Revenue Service.*—The shareholder must notify the branch of the Associate Chief Counsel (International) considering the request for relief under this paragraph (f) if, while the shareholder's request for consent is pending, the Internal Revenue Service begins an examination of the shareholder's return for the retroactive election year or for any subsequent taxable year during which the shareholder holds stock of the foreign corporation.

(vi) *Who requests special consent under this paragraph (f) and who enters into a closing agreement.*—The person that requests consent under this paragraph (f) is the person that makes the section 1295 election, as provided in § 1.1295-1(d). If a shareholder is required to enter into a closing agreement with the Commissioner, as described in paragraph (f)(3)(ii) of this section, rules similar to those under paragraphs (c)(4)(i)(B) through (E) of this section apply for purposes of determining the person that enters into the closing agreement.

(g) *Time for and manner of making a retroactive election.*—(1) *Time for making a retroactive election.*—(i) *In general.*—Except as otherwise provided in paragraph (g)(1)(ii) of this section, a shareholder must make a retroactive election, in the manner provided in paragraph (g)(2) of this section, on or before the due date, as extended, for the shareholder's return—

(A) In the case of a shareholder that makes a retroactive election pursuant to paragraph (b) or (e) of this section, for the taxable year in which the shareholder determines or reasonably should have determined that the foreign corporation was a PFIC; or

(B) In the case of a shareholder that obtains the consent of the Commissioner pursuant to paragraph (f) of this section, for the taxable year in which such consent is granted.

(ii) *Transition rule.*—A shareholder that files a Protective Statement for a taxable year described in paragraph (c)(5)(ii) of this section may make a retroactive election by the due date, as extended, for the return for the first taxable year ended after January 2, 1998, even if the shareholder determined or should have determined that the foreign corporation was a PFIC for a year described in paragraph (c)(5)(ii) of this section at any time on or before January 2, 1998.

(iii) *Ownership not required at time retroactive election is made.*—The shareholder need not own shares of the foreign corporation at the time the shareholder makes a retroactive election with respect to the foreign corporation.

(2) *Manner of making a retroactive election.*—A shareholder that has satisfied the requirements of paragraph (b) or (e) of this section, or a shareholder that has been granted consent under paragraph (f) of this section, must make a retroactive election in the manner provided in Form 8621 for making a section 1295 election, and must attach Form 8621 to an amended return for the later of the retroactive election year or the earliest open taxable year of the shareholder. The shareholder also must file an amended return for each of its subsequent taxable years affected by the retroactive election. In each amended return the shareholder must redetermine its income tax liability for that year to take into account the assessment of PFIC related taxes. If the period of limitations for the assessment of taxes for a taxable year affected by the retroactive election has expired except to the extent the waiver of limitations, described in paragraph (c)(4) of this section, has extended such period, no adjustments, other than consequential changes, may be made to any other items of income, deduction, or credit in that year. In addition, the shareholder must pay all taxes and interest owing by reason of the PFIC and QEF status of the foreign corporation in those years (except to the extent a section 1294 election extends the time to pay the taxes and interest). A shareholder that filed a Protective Statement must attach to Form 8621 filed with each amended return a representation that the shareholder, until the taxable year in which it determined or reasonably should have determined that the foreign corporation was a PFIC, reasonably believed, within the meaning of paragraph (d) of this section, that the foreign corporation was not a PFIC in the taxable year for which the amended return is filed, and in all other taxable years to which the Protective Statement applies. A shareholder that entered into a closing agreement must comply with the terms of that agreement, as provided in paragraph (f)(3)(ii) of this section, to eliminate any prejudice to the United States government's interests, as described in paragraph (f)(3) of this section.

(3) *Who makes the retroactive election.*—The person that makes the retroactive election is the person that makes the section 1295 election, as provided in § 1.1295-1(d). A partner, shareholder, or beneficiary for which a pass through entity, as described in paragraphs (c)(4)(i)(B) through (D) of this section, filed a Protective Statement may make a retroactive election, if the pass through entity completely terminates its business or otherwise ceases to exist.

(4) *Other elections.*—(i) *Section 1291(d)(2) election.*—If the foreign corporation for which the shareholder makes a retroactive election will be treated as an unpedigreed QEF, as defined in § 1.1291-9(j)(2)(iii), with respect to the shareholder, the shareholder may make an election under section 1291(d)(2) to purge its holding period of the years or parts of years before the effective date of the retroactive election. If the qualification date, within the meaning of § 1.1291-9(e) or 1.1291-10(e), falls in a taxable year for which the period of limitations has expired, the shareholder may treat the first day of the retroactive election year as the qualification date. The shareholder may make a section 1291(d)(2) election at the time that it makes the retroactive election, but no later than two years after the date that the amended return in which the retroactive election is made is filed. For the requirements for making a section 1291(d)(2) election, see §§ 1.1291-9 and 1.1291-10.

(ii) *Section 1294 election.*—A shareholder may make an election under section 1294 to extend the time for payment of tax on the shareholder's pro rata shares of the ordinary earnings and net capital gain of the foreign corporation reported in the shareholder's amended return, and section 6621 interest attributable to such tax, but only to the extent the tax and interest are attributable to earnings that have not been distributed to the shareholder. The shareholder must make a section 1294 election for a taxable year at the time that it files its amended return for that year, as provided in paragraph (g)(1) of this section. For the requirements for making a section 1294 election, see § 1.1294-1T.

(h) *Effective date.*—The rules of this section are effective as of January 2, 1998. [Reg. § 1.1295-3.]

□ [*T.D. 8750, 12-31-97. Redesignated and amended by T.D. 8870, 2-4-2000.*]

§ 1.1296-1. Mark to market election for marketable stock.—(a) *Definitions.*—(1) *Eligible RIC.*—An *eligible RIC* is a regulated investment company that offers for sale, or has outstanding, any stock of which it is the issuer and which is redeemable at net asset value, or that publishes net asset valuations at least annually.

(2) *Section 1296 stock.*—The term *section 1296 stock* means marketable stock in a passive foreign investment company (PFIC), including any PFIC stock owned directly or indirectly by an eligible RIC, for which there is a valid section 1296 election. Section 1296 stock does not include stock of a foreign corporation that previously had been a PFIC, and for which a section 1296 election remains in effect.

(3) *Unreversed inclusions.*—(i) *General rule.*—The term *unreversed inclusions* means with respect to any section 1296 stock, the excess, if any, of—

(A) The amount of mark to market gain included in gross income of the United States person under paragraph (c)(1) of this section with respect to such stock for prior taxable years; over

(B) The amount allowed as a deduction to the United States person under paragraph (c)(3) of this section with respect to such stock for prior taxable years.

(ii) *Section 1291 adjustment.*—The amount referred to in paragraph (a)(3)(i)(A) of this section shall include any amount subject to section 1291 under the coordination rule of paragraph (i)(2)(ii) of this section.

(iii) *Example.*—An example of the computation of unreversed inclusions is as follows:

Example. A, a United States person, acquired stock in Corp X, a foreign corporation, on January 1, 2005 for $150. At such time and at all times thereafter, Corp X was a PFIC and A's stock in Corp X was marketable. For taxable years 2005 and 2006, Corp X was a nonqualified fund subject to taxation under section 1291. A made a timely section 1296 election with respect to the X stock, effective for taxable year 2007. The fair market value of the X stock was $200 as of December 31, 2006, and $240 as of December 31, 2007. Additionally, Corp X made no distribution with respect to its stock for the taxable years at issue. In 2007, pursuant to paragraph (i)(2)(ii) of this section, A must include the $90 gain in the X stock in accordance with the rules of section 1291 for purposes of determining the deferred tax amount and any applicable interest. Nonetheless, for purposes of determining the amount of the unreversed inclusions pursuant to paragraph (a)(3)(ii) of this section, A will include the $90 of gain that was taxed under section 1291 and not the interest thereon.

(iv) *Special rule for regulated investment companies.*—In the case of a regulated investment company which had elected to mark to market the PFIC stock held by such company as of the last day of the taxable year preceding such company's first taxable year for which such company makes a section 1296 election, the amount referred to in paragraph (a)(3)(i)(A) of this section shall include amounts previously included in gross income by the company pursuant to such mark to market election with respect to such stock for prior taxable years. For further guidance, see Notice 92-53 (1992-2 C.B. 384) (see also 601.601(d)(2) of this chapter).

(b) *Application of section 1296 election.*—(1) *In general.*—Any United States person and any controlled foreign corporation (CFC) that owns directly, or is treated as owning under this section, marketable stock, as defined in § 1.1296-2, in a PFIC may make an election to mark to market such stock in accordance with the provisions of section 1296 and this section.

(2) *Election applicable to specific United States person.*—A section 1296 election applies only to the United States person (or CFC that is treated as a U.S. person under paragraph (g)(2) of this section) that makes the election. Accordingly, a United States person's section 1296 election will not apply to a transferee of section 1296 stock.

(3) *Election applicable to specific corporation only.*—A section 1296 election is made with respect to a single foreign corporation, and thus a separate section 1296 election must be made for each foreign corporation that otherwise meets the requirements of this section. A United States persons section 1296 election with respect to stock in a foreign corporation applies to all marketable stock of the corporation that the person owns directly, or is treated as owning under paragraph (e) of this section, at the time of the election or that is subsequently acquired.

(c) *Effect of election.*—(1) *Recognition of gain.*—If the fair market value of section 1296 stock on the last day of the United States person's taxable year exceeds its adjusted basis, the United States person shall include in gross income for its taxable year the excess of the fair market value of such stock over its adjusted basis (mark to market gain).

(2) *Character of gain.*—Mark to market gain, and any gain on the sale or other disposition of section 1296 stock, shall be treated as ordinary income.

(3) *Recognition of loss.*—If the adjusted basis of section 1296 stock exceeds its fair market value on the last day of the United States persons taxable year, such person shall be allowed a deduction for such taxable year equal to the lesser of the amount of such excess or the unreversed inclusions with respect to such stock (mark to market loss).

(4) *Character of loss.*—(i) *Losses not in excess of unreversed inclusions.*—Any mark to market loss allowed as a deduction under paragraph (c)(3) of this section, and any loss on the sale or other disposition of section 1296 stock, to the extent that such loss does not exceed the unreversed inclusions attributable to such stock, shall be treated as an ordinary loss, deductible in computing adjusted gross income.

(ii) *Losses in excess of unreversed inclusions.*—Any loss recognized on the sale or other disposition of section 1296 stock in excess of any prior unreversed inclusions will be subject to the rules generally applicable to losses provided elsewhere in the Internal Revenue Code and the regulations thereunder.

(5) *Application of election to separate lots of stock.*—In the case in which a United States person purchased or acquired shares of stock in a PFIC at different prices, the rules of this section shall be applied in a manner consistent with the rules of § 1.1012-1.

(6) *Source rules.*—The source of any amount included in gross income under paragraph (c)(1) of this section, or the allocation and apportionment of any amount allowed as a deduction under paragraph (c)(3) of this section, shall be determined in the same manner as if such amounts were gain or loss (as the case may be) from the sale of stock in the PFIC.

(7) *Examples.*—The following examples illustrate this paragraph (c):

Example 1. Treatment of gain as ordinary income. A, a United States individual, purchases stock in FX, a foreign corporation that is not a PFIC, in 1990 for $1,000. On January 1, 2005, when the fair market value of the FX stock is $1,100, FX becomes a PFIC. A makes a timely section 1296 election for taxable year 2005. On December 31, 2005, the fair market value of the FX stock is $1,200. For taxable year 2005, A includes $200 of mark to market gain (the excess of the fair market value of FX stock ($1,200) over A's adjusted basis ($1,000)) in gross income as ordinary income and pursuant to paragraph (d)(1) of this section increases his basis in the FX stock by that amount.

Example 2. Treatment of gain as capital gain. The facts are the same as in *Example 1.* For taxable year 2006, FX does not satisfy either the asset test or the income test of section 1297(a). A does not revoke the section 1296 election it made with respect to the FX stock. On December 1, 2006, A sells the FX stock when the fair market value of the stock is $1,500. For taxable year 2006, A includes $300 of gain (the excess of the fair market value of FX stock ($1,500) over A's adjusted basis ($1,200)) in gross income as long-term capital gain because at the time of sale of the FX stock by A, FX did not qualify as a PFIC, and, therefore, the FX stock was not section 1296 stock at the time of the disposition. Further, A's holding period for non-PFIC purposes was more than one year.

Example 3. Treatment of losses as ordinary where they do not exceed unreversed inclusions. The facts are the same as in *Example 1.* On December 1, 2006, A sells the stock in FX for $1,100. At that time, A's unreversed inclusions (the amount A included in income as mark to market gain) with respect to the stock in FX are $200. Accordingly, for taxable year 2006, A recognizes a loss on the sale of the FX stock of $100, (the fair market value of the FX stock ($1,100) minus A's adjusted basis ($1,200) in the stock) that is treated as an ordinary loss because the loss does not exceed the unreversed inclusions attributable to the stock of FX.

Example 4. Treatment of losses as long-term capital losses. The facts are the same as in *Example 3*, except that FX does not satisfy either the asset test or the income test of section 1297(a) for taxable year 2006. For taxable year 2006, A's $100 loss from the sale of the FX stock is treated as long-term capital loss because at the time of the sale of the FX stock by A FX did not qualify as a PFIC, and, therefore, the FX stock was not section 1296 stock at the time of the disposition. Further, A's holding period in the FX stock for non-PFIC purposes was more than one year.

Example 5. Long-term capital loss treatment of losses in excess of unreversed inclusions. The facts are the same as in *Example 3*, except that A sells his FX stock for $900. At the time of A's sale of the FX stock on December 1, 2006, A's unreversed inclusions with respect to the FX stock are $200. Accordingly, the $300 loss recognized by A on the disposition is treated as an ordinary loss to the extent of his unreversed inclusions ($200). The amount of the loss in excess of A's unreversed inclusions ($100) will be treated as a long-term capital loss because A's holding period in the FC stock for non-PFIC purposes was more than one year.

Example 6. Application of section 1296 election to separate lots of stock. On January 1, 2005, Corp A, a domestic corporation, purchased 100 shares (first lot) of stock in FX, a PFIC, for $500 ($5 per share). On June 1, 2005, Corp A purchased 100 shares (second lot) of FX stock for $1,000 ($10 per share). Corp A made a timely section 1296 election with respect to its FX stock for taxable year 2005. On December 31, 2005, the fair market value of FX stock was $8 per share. For taxable year 2005, Corp A includes $300 of gain in gross income as ordinary income under paragraph (c)(1) of this section with respect to the first lot, and adjusts its basis in that lot to $800 pursuant to paragraph (d)(1) of this section. With respect to the second lot, Corp A is not permitted to recognize a loss under paragraph (c)(3) of this section for taxable year 2005. Although Corp A's adjusted basis in that stock exceeds its fair market value by $200, Corp A has no unreversed inclusions with respect to that particular lot of stock. On July 1, 2006, Corp A sells 100 shares of FX stock for $900. Assuming that Corp A adequately identifies (in accordance with the rules of § 1.1012-1(c)) the shares of FX stock sold as being from the second lot, Corp A recognizes $100 of long term capital loss pursuant to paragraph (c)(4)(ii) of this section.

(d) *Adjustment to basis.*—(1) *Stock held directly.*—The adjusted basis of the section 1296 stock shall be increased by the amount included in the gross income of the United States person under paragraph (c)(1) of this section with respect to such stock, and decreased by the amount allowed as a deduction to the United States person under paragraph (c)(3) of this section with respect to such stock.

(2) *Stock owned through certain foreign entities.*—(i) In the case of section 1296 stock that a United States person is treated as owning through certain foreign entities pursuant to paragraph (e) of this section, the basis adjustments under paragraph (d)(1) of this section shall apply to such stock in the hands of the foreign entity actually holding such stock, but only for purposes of determining the subsequent treatment under chapter 1 of the Internal Revenue Code of the United States person with respect to such stock. Such increase or decrease in the adjusted basis of the section 1296 stock shall constitute an adjustment to the basis of partnership property only with respect to the partner making the section 1296 election. Corresponding adjustments shall be made to the adjusted basis of the United States person's interest in the foreign entity and in any intermediary entity described in paragraph (e) of this section through which the United States person holds the PFIC stock.

(ii) *Example.*—The following example illustrates this paragraph (d)(2):

Example. FP is a foreign partnership. Corp A, a domestic corporation, owns a 20 percent interest in FP. Corp B, a domestic corporation, owns a 30 percent interest in FP. Corp C, a foreign corporation, with no direct or indirect shareholders that are U.S. persons, owns a 50% interest in FP. Corp A, Corp B, and FP all use a calendar year for their taxable year. In 2005, FP purchases stock in FX, a foreign corporation and a PFIC, for $1,000. Corp A makes a timely section 1296 election for taxable year 2005. On December 31, 2005, the fair market value of the PFIC stock is $1,100. Corp A includes $20 of ordinary income in taxable year 2005 under paragraphs (c)(1) and (2) of this section. Corp A increases its basis in its FP partnership interest by $20. FP increases its basis in the FX stock to $1,020 solely for purposes of determining the subsequent treatment of Corp A, under chapter 1 of the Internal Revenue Code, with respect to such stock. In 2006, FP sells the FX stock for $1,200. For purposes of determining the amount of gain of Corp A, FP will be treated as having $180 in gain of which $20 is allocated to Corp A. Corp A's $20 of gain will be treated as ordinary income under paragraph (c)(2) of this section. For purposes of determining the amount of gain attributable to Corp B, FP will be treated as having $200 gain, $60 of which will be allocated to Corp B.

(3) *Stock owned indirectly by an eligible RIC.*—Paragraph (d)(2) of this section shall also apply to an eligible RIC which is an indirect shareholder under § 1.1296-2(f) of stock in a PFIC and has a valid section 1296 election in effect with respect to the PFIC stock.

(4) *Stock acquired from a decedent.*—In the case of stock of a PFIC that is acquired by bequest, devise, or inheritance (or by the decedent's estate) and with respect to which a section 1296 election was in effect as of the date of the decedent's death, notwithstanding section 1014 or section 1022, the basis of such stock in the hands of the person so acquiring it shall be the adjusted basis of such stock in the hands of the decedent immediately before his death (or, if lesser, the basis that would have been determined under section 1014 or section 1022 without regard to this paragraph (d)).

(5) *Transition rule for individuals becoming subject to United States income taxation.*—(i) *In general.*—If any individual becomes a United States person in a taxable year beginning after December 31, 1997, solely for purposes of this section, the adjusted basis, before adjustments under this paragraph (d), of any section 1296 stock owned by such individual on the first day of such taxable year shall be treated as being the greater of its fair market value or its adjusted basis on such first day.

(ii) An example of the transition rule for individuals becoming subject to United States income taxation is as follows:

Example. A, a nonresident alien individual, purchases marketable stock in FX, a PFIC, for $50 in 1995. On January 1, 2005, A becomes a United States person and makes a timely section 1296 election with respect to the stock in accordance with paragraph (h) of this section. The fair market value of the FX stock on January 1, 2005, is $100. The fair market value of the FX stock on December 31, 2005, is $110. Under paragraph (d)(5)(i) of this section, A computes the amount of mark to market gain or loss for the FX stock in 2005 by reference to an adjusted basis of $100, and therefore A includes $10 in gross income as mark to market gain under paragraph (c)(1) of this section. Additionally, under paragraph (d)(1) of this section, A's adjusted basis in the FX stock for purposes of this section is increased to $110 (and to $60 for all other tax purposes). A sells the FX stock in 2006 for $120. For purposes of applying section 1001, A must use its original basis of $50, with any adjustments under paragraph (d)(1) of this section, $10 in this case, and therefore A recognizes $60 of gain. Under paragraph (c)(2) of this section (which is applied using an adjusted basis of $110), $10 of such gain is treated as ordinary income. The remaining $50 of gain from the sale of the FX stock is long term capital gain because A held such stock for more than one year.

(e) *Stock owned through certain foreign entities.*—(1) *In general.*—Except as provided in paragraph (e)(2) of this section, the following rules shall apply in determining stock ownership for purposes of this section. PFIC stock owned, directly or indirectly, by or for a foreign partnership, foreign trust (other than a foreign trust described in sections 671 through 679), or foreign estate shall be considered as being owned proportionately by its partners or beneficiaries. PFIC stock owned, directly or indirectly, by or for a foreign trust described in sections 671 through 679 shall be considered as being owned proportionately by its grantors or other persons treated as owners under sections 671 through 679 of any portion of the trust that includes the stock. The determination of a person's proportionate interest in a foreign partnership, foreign trust or foreign estate will be made on the basis of all the facts and circumstances. Stock considered owned by reason of this paragraph shall, for purposes of applying the rules of this section, be treated as actually owned by such person.

(2) *Stock owned indirectly by eligible RICs.*—The rules for attributing ownership of stock contained in § 1.1296-2(f) will apply to determine the indirect ownership of PFIC stock by an eligible RIC.

(f) *Holding period.*—Solely for purposes of sections 1291 through 1298, if section 1296 applied to stock with respect to the taxpayer for any prior taxable year, the taxpayer's holding period in such stock shall be treated as beginning on the first day of the first taxable year beginning after the last taxable year for which section 1296 so applied.

(g) *Special rules.*—(1) *Certain dispositions of stock.*—To the extent a United States person is treated as actually owning stock in a PFIC under paragraph (e) of this section, any disposition which results in the United States person being treated as no longer owning such stock, and any disposition by the person owning such stock, shall be treated as a disposition by the United States person of the stock in the PFIC.

(2) *Treatment of CFC as a United States person.*—In the case of a CFC that owns, or is treated as owning under paragraph (e) of this section, section 1296 stock:

(i) Other than with respect to the sourcing rules in paragraph (c)(6) of this section, this section shall apply to the CFC in the same manner as if such corporation were a United States person. The CFC will be treated as a foreign person for purposes of applying the source rules of paragraph (c)(6).

(ii) For purposes of subpart F of part III of subchapter N of the Internal Revenue Code—

(A) Amounts included in the CFC's gross income under paragraph (c)(1) or (i)(2)(ii) of this section shall be treated as foreign personal holding company income under section 954(c)(1)(A); and

(B) Amounts allowed as a deduction under paragraph (c)(3) of this section shall be treated as a deduction allocable to foreign personal holding company income for purposes of computing net foreign base company income under § 1.954-1(c).

(iii) A United States shareholder, as defined in section 951(b), of the CFC shall not be subject to section 1291 with respect to any stock of the PFIC for the period during which the section 1296 election is in effect for that stock, and the holding period rule of paragraph (f) of this section shall apply to such United States shareholder.

(iv) The rules of this paragraph (g)(2) shall not apply to a United States person that is a shareholder of the PFIC for purposes of section 1291, but is not a United States shareholder under section 951(b) with respect to the CFC making a section 1296 election.

(3) *Timing of inclusions for stock owned through certain foreign entities.*—In the case of section 1296 stock that a United States person is treated as owning through certain foreign entities pursuant to paragraph (e) of this section, the mark to market gain or mark to market loss is determined in accordance with paragraphs (c) and (i)(2)(ii) of this section as of the last day of the taxable year of the foreign partnership, foreign trust or foreign estate and then included in the taxable year of such United States person that includes the last day of the taxable year of the entity.

(h) *Elections.*—(1) *Timing and manner for making a section 1296 election.*—(i) *United States persons.*—A United States person that owns marketable stock in a PFIC, or is treated as owning marketable stock under paragraph (e) of this section, on the last day of the taxable year of such person, and that wants to make a section 1296 election, must make a section 1296 election for such taxable year on or before the due date (including extensions) of the United States person's income tax return for that year. The section 1296 election must be made on the Form 8621, "Return by a Shareholder of a Passive Foreign Investment Company or Qualified Electing Fund", included with the original tax return of the United States person for that year, or on an amended return, provided that the amended return is filed on or before the election due date.

(ii) *Controlled foreign corporations.*—A section 1296 election by a CFC shall be made by its controlling United States shareholders, as defined in § 1.964-1(c)(5), and shall be included with the Form 5471, "Information Return of U.S. Persons With Respect To Certain Foreign Corporations", for that CFC by the due date (including extensions) of the original income tax returns of the controlling United States shareholders for that year. A section 1296 election by a CFC shall be binding on all United States shareholders of the CFC.

(iii) *Retroactive elections for PFIC stock held in prior years.*—A late section 1296 election may be permitted only in accordance with § 301.9100 of this chapter.

(2) *Effect of section 1296 election.*—(i) A section 1296 election will apply to the taxable year for which such election is made and remain in effect for each succeeding taxable year unless such election is revoked or terminated pursuant to paragraph (h)(3) of this section.

(ii) *Cessation of a foreign corporation as a PFIC.*—A United States person will not include mark to market gain or loss pursuant to paragraph (c) of this section with respect to any stock of a foreign corporation for any taxable year that such foreign corporation is not a PFIC under section 1297 or treated as a PFIC under section 1298(b)(1) (taking into account the holding period rule of paragraph (f) of this section). Cessation of a foreign corporation's status as a PFIC will not, however, terminate a section 1296 election. Thus, if a foreign corporation is a PFIC in a taxable year after a year in which it is not treated as a PFIC, the United States person's original election (unless revoked or terminated in accordance with paragraph (h)(3) of this section) continues to apply and the shareholder must include any mark to market gain or loss in such year.

(3) *Revocation or termination of election.*—(i) *In general.*—A United States person's section 1296 election is terminated if the section 1296 stock ceases to be marketable; if the United States person elects, or is required, to mark to market the section 1296 stock under another provision of chapter 1 of the Internal Revenue Code; or if the Commissioner, in the Commissioner's discretion, consents to the United States person's request to revoke its section 1296 election upon a finding of a substantial change in circumstances. A substantial change in circumstances for this purpose may include a foreign corporation ceasing to be a PFIC.

(ii) *Timing of termination or revocation.*—Where a section 1296 election is terminated automatically (e.g., the stock ceases to be marketable), section 1296 will cease to apply beginning with the taxable year in which such termination occurs. Where a section 1296 election is revoked with the consent of the Commissioner, section 1296 will cease to apply beginning with the first taxable year of the United States person after the revocation is granted unless otherwise provided by the Commissioner.

(4) *Examples.*—The operation of the rules of this paragraph (h) is illustrated by the following examples:

Example 1. A, a United States person, owns stock in FX, a PFIC. A makes a QEF election in 1996 with respect to the FX stock. For taxable year 2005, A makes a timely section 1296 election with respect to its stock, and thus its QEF election is automatically terminated pursuant to § 1.1295-1(i)(3). In 2006, A's stock in FX ceases to be marketable, and therefore its section 1296 election is automatically terminated under paragraph (h)(3) of this section. Beginning with taxable year 2006, A is subject to the rules of section 1291 with respect to its FX stock unless it makes a new QEF election. See § 1.1295-1(i)(5).

Example 2. The facts are the same as in *Example 1*, except that A's stock in FX becomes marketable again in 2007. A may make a new section 1296 election with respect to the FX stock for its taxable year 2007, or thereafter. A will be subject to the coordination rules under paragraph (i) of this section unless it made a new QEF election in 2006.

(i) *Coordination rules for first year of election.*—(1) *In general.*—Notwithstanding any provision in this section to the contrary, the rules of this paragraph (i) shall apply to the first taxable year in which a section 1296 election is effective with respect to marketable stock of a PFIC if such foreign corporation was a PFIC for any taxable year, prior to such first taxable year, during the United States person's holding period (as defined in paragraph (f) of this section) in such stock, and for which such corporation was not treated as a QEF with respect to such United States person.

(2) *Shareholders other than regulated investment companies.*—For the first taxable year of a United States person (other than a regulated investment company) for which a section 1296 election is in effect with respect to the stock of a PFIC, such United States person shall, in lieu of the rules of paragraphs (c) and (d) of this section—

(i) Apply the rules of section 1291 to any distributions with respect to, or disposition of, section 1296 stock;

(ii) Apply section 1291 to the amount of the excess, if any, of the fair market value of such section 1296 stock on the last day of the United States person's taxable year over its adjusted basis, as if such amount were gain recognized from the disposition of stock on the last day of the taxpayer's taxable year; and

(iii) Increase its adjusted basis in the section 1296 stock by the amount of excess, if any, subject to section 1291 under paragraph (i)(2)(ii) of this section.

(3) *Shareholders that are regulated investment companies.*—For the first taxable year of a regulated investment company for which a section 1296 election is in effect with respect to the stock of a PFIC, such regulated investment company shall increase its tax under section 852 by the amount of interest that would have been imposed under section 1291(c)(3) for such taxable year if such regulated investment company were subject to the rules of paragraph (i)(2) of this section, and not this paragraph (i)(3). No deduction or increase in basis shall be allowed for the increase in tax imposed under this paragraph (i)(3).

(4) The operation of the rules of this paragraph (i) is illustrated by the following examples:

Example (1). A, a United States person and a calendar year taxpayer, owns marketable stock in FX, a PFIC that it acquired on January 1, 1992. At all times, A's FX stock was a nonqualified fund subject to taxation under section 1291. A made a timely section 1296 election effective for taxable year 2005. At the close of taxable year 2005, the fair market value of A's FX stock exceeded its adjusted basis by $10. Pursuant to paragraph (i)(2)(ii) of this section, A must treat the $10 gain under section 1291 as if the FX stock were disposed of on December 31, 2005. Further, A increases its adjusted basis in the FX stock by the $10 in accordance with paragraph (i)(2)(iii) of this section.

Example (2). Assume the same facts as in *Example (1)*, except that A is a RIC that had not made an election prior to 2005 to mark to market the PFIC stock. In taxable year 2005, A includes $10 of ordinary income under paragraph (c)(1) of this section, and such amount is not subject to section 1291. A also increases its tax imposed under section 852 by the amount of interest that would have been determined under section 1291(c)(3), and no deduction is permitted for such amount. Finally, under paragraph (d)(1) of this section, A increases its adjusted basis in the FX stock by $10.

(j) *Effective/applicability date.*—The provisions in this section are applicable for taxable years beginning on or after May 3, 2004. The provisions of paragraph (d)(4) of this section relating to section 1022 are effective on and after January 19, 2017. [Reg. § 1.1296-1.]

☐ [*T.D. 9123, 4-30-2004. Amended by T.D. 9811, 1-18-2017.*]

Proposed Amendments to Regulation

§ 1.1296-1. Mark to market election for marketable stock.—(a) * * *

(4) *Shareholder.*—The term *shareholder* has the meaning provided in § 1.1291-1(b)(7).

* * *

(e) * * *

(1) *In general.*—Except as provided in paragraph (e)(2) of this section, the following rules apply in determining stock ownership for purposes of this section. PFIC stock owned, directly or indirectly, by or for a partnership (domestic or foreign), S corporation, foreign trust (other than a foreign trust that is described in sections 671 through 679), or foreign estate is considered as being owned proportionately by its partners, shareholders, or beneficiaries, respectively. PFIC stock owned, directly or indirectly, by or for a trust (domestic or foreign) described in sections 671 through 679 is considered as being owned proportionately by its grantors or other persons treated as owners under sections 671 through 679 of any portion of the trust that includes the stock. The determination of a person's proportionate interest in a partnership, S corporation, trust, or estate will be made on the basis of all the facts and circumstances. Stock considered owned by a person by reason of this paragraph is treated as actually owned by such person for purposes of applying the rules of this section.

* * *

(h) * * *

(1) * * *

(i) *Shareholders.*—Except as otherwise provided in this paragraph (h), a shareholder (as defined in paragraph (a)(4) of this section) that owns marketable stock in a PFIC, or is treated as owning marketable stock under paragraph (e) of this section, on the last day of the shareholder's taxable year, must make a section 1296 election for such taxable year on or before the due date (including extensions) of its income tax return for that year. The section 1296 election must be made on the Form 8621, "Return by a Shareholder of a Passive Foreign Investment Company or Qualified Electing Fund" (or successor form), included with the original or superseding tax return of the shareholder for that year.

(A) *Preexisting section 1296 election.*—Notwithstanding paragraph (h)(1)(i) of this section, any section 1296 election with respect to a PFIC made by a domestic partnership or S corporation effective for taxable years of the PFIC ending on or before [date of publication of the Treasury decision adopting these rules as final regulations in the **Federal Register**] *(preexisting section 1296 election)* will continue to apply, and any stock in the PFIC that a shareholder is treated as owning by reason of its interest in the domestic partnership or S corporation on or before such date will continue to be treated as section 1296 stock to such shareholder; any person that becomes a shareholder of the PFIC by acquiring an interest in the domestic partnership or S corporation after such date that wishes for a section 1296 election to apply with respect to the PFIC may make a section 1296 election as provided in paragraphs (b)(1) and (h)(1)(i) of this section. A shareholder that is treated as owning section 1296 stock by reason of an interest in a domestic partnership or S corporation that has made a preexisting 1296 election under this paragraph (h)(1)(i)(A) accounts for its share, through its ownership in the domestic partnership or S corporation, of any mark to market gain recognized under paragraph (c)(1) of this section and any mark to market loss under paragraph (c)(3) of this section as if it owned the section 1296 stock directly.

(B) *Notice.*—A shareholder that makes a section 1296 election with respect to section 1296 stock owned through a partnership or S corporation must notify the partnership or S corporation of the election no later than 30 days after filing the return in which the election is made; the shareholder may provide such notification in any reasonable manner. However, the failure of the shareholder to notify the partnership or S corporation of its election will not invalidate an otherwise valid section 1296 election. * * * * *

(j) *Applicability date.*—Except as otherwise provided in this paragraph (j), the provisions in this section apply to taxable years beginning on or after May 3, 2004. The provisions of paragraph (d)(4) of this section relating to section 1022 apply on and after January 19, 2017. The provisions of paragraphs (a)(4); (b)(1) through (3); (c)(1), (3), and (5); (d)(1) and (d)(2)(i); (e)(1); (f); (g)(1), (g)(2)(i), and (g)(3); (h)(1)(i) and (ii), (h)(2)(ii), and (h)(3)(i) and (ii); and (i)(1), (i)(2) introductory text, and (i)(2)(ii) apply to taxable years of shareholders beginning on or after [date of publication of the Treasury decision adopting these rules as final regulations in the **Federal Register**]. For taxable years of shareholders beginning before [date of publication of the Treasury decision adopting these rules as final regulations in the **Federal Register**], see § 1.1296-1(b)(1) through (3); (c)(1), (3), and (5); (d)(1) and (d)(2)(i); (e)(1); (f); (g)(1), (g)(2)(i), and (g)(3); (h)(1)(i) and (ii), (h)(2)(ii), and (h)(3)(i) and (ii); and (i)(1), (i)(2) introductory text, and (i)(2)(ii) as in effect and contained in 26 CFR part 1, as revised April 1, 2021. [Prop. Reg. § 1.1296-1.]

[Proposed 1-25-2022.]

§ 1.1296-2. Definition of marketable stock.—(a) *General rule.*—For purposes of section 1296, the term *marketable stock* means—

(1) Passive foreign investment company (PFIC) stock that is regularly traded, as defined in paragraph (b) of this section, on a qualified exchange or other market, as defined in paragraph (c) of this section;

(2) Stock in certain PFICs, as described in paragraph (d) of this section; and

(3) Options on stock that is described in paragraph (a)(1) or (2) of this section, to the extent provided in paragraph (e) of this section.

(b) *Regularly traded.*—(1) *General rule.*—For purposes of paragraph (a)(1) of this section, a class of stock that is traded on one or more qualified exchanges or other markets, as defined in paragraph (c) of this section, is regularly traded on such exchanges or markets for any calendar year during which such class of stock is traded, other than in de minimis quantities, on at least 15 days during each calendar quarter.

(2) *Special rule for year of initial public offering.*—For the calendar year in which a corporation initiates a public offering of a class of stock for trading on one or more qualified exchanges or other markets, as defined in paragraph (c) of this section, such class of stock meets the requirements of paragraph (b)(1) of this section for such year if the stock is regularly traded on such exchanges or markets, other than in de minimis quantities, on 1/6 of the days remaining in the quarter in which the offering occurs, and on at least 15 days during each remaining quarter of the taxpayer's calendar year. In cases where a corporation initiates a public offering of a class of stock in the fourth quarter of the calendar year, such class of stock meets the requirements of paragraph (b)(1) of this section in the calendar year of the offering if the stock is regularly traded on such exchanges or markets, other than in de minimis quantities, on the greater of 1/6 of the days remaining in the quarter in which the offering occurs, or 5 days.

(3) *Anti-abuse rule.*—Trades that have as one of their principal purposes the meeting of the trading requirements of paragraph (b)(1) or (2) of this section shall be disregarded. Further, a class of stock shall not be treated as meeting the trading requirement of paragraph (b)(1) or (2) of this section if there is a pattern of trades conducted to meet the requirement of paragraph (b)(1) or (2) of this section. Similarly, paragraph (b)(2) of this section shall not apply to a public offering of stock that has as one of its principal purposes to avail itself of the reduced trading requirements under the special rule for the calendar year of an initial public offering. For purposes of applying the immediately preceding sentence, consideration will be given to whether the trading requirements of paragraph (b)(1) of this section are satisfied in the subsequent calendar year.

(c) *Qualified exchange or other market.*—(1) *General rule.*—For purposes of paragraph (a)(1) of this section, the term *qualified exchange or other market* means, for any calendar year—

(i) A national securities exchange that is registered with the Securities and Exchange Commission or the national market system established pursuant to section 11A of the Securities Exchange Act of 1934 (15 U.S.C. 78f); or

(ii) A foreign securities exchange that is regulated or supervised by a governmental authority of the country in which the market is located and which has the following characteristics—

(A) The exchange has trading volume, listing, financial disclosure, surveillance, and other requirements designed to prevent fraudulent and manipulative acts and practices, to remove impediments to and perfect the mechanism of a free and open, fair and orderly, market, and to protect investors; and the laws of the country in which the exchange is located and the rules of the exchange ensure that such requirements are actually enforced; and

(B) The rules of the exchange effectively promote active trading of listed stocks.

(2) *Exchange with multiple tiers.*—If an exchange in a foreign country has more than one tier or market level on which stock may be separately listed or traded, each such tier shall be treated as a separate exchange.

(d) *Stock in certain PFICs.*—(1) *General rule.*—Except as provided in paragraph (d)(2) of this section, a foreign corporation is a corporation described in section 1296(e)(1)(B), and paragraph (a)(2) of this section, if the foreign corporation offers for sale or has outstanding stock of which it is the issuer and which is redeemable at its net asset value and if the foreign corporation satisfies the following conditions with respect to the class of shares held by the electing taxpayer—

(i) At all times during the calendar year, the foreign corporation has more than one hundred shareholders with respect to the class, other than shareholders who are related under section 267(b);

(ii) At all times during the calendar year, the class of shares of the foreign corporation is readily available for purchase by the general public at its net asset value and the foreign corporation does not require a minimum initial investment of greater than $10,000 (U.S.);

(iii) At all times during the calendar year, quotations for the class of shares of the foreign corporation are determined and published no less frequently than on a weekly basis in a widely-available permanent medium not controlled by the issuer of the shares, such as a newspaper of general circulation or a trade publication;

(iv) No less frequently than annually, independent auditors prepare financial statements of the foreign corporation that include balance sheets (statements of assets, liabilities, and net assets) and statements of income and expenses, and those statements are made available to the public;

(v) The foreign corporation is supervised or regulated as an investment company by a foreign government or an agency or instrumentality thereof that has broad inspection and enforcement authority and effective oversight over investment companies;

(vi) At all times during the calendar year, the foreign corporation has no senior securities authorized or outstanding, including any debt other than in de minimis amounts;

(vii) Ninety percent or more of the gross income of the foreign corporation for its taxable year is passive income, as defined in section 1297(a)(1) and the regulations thereunder; and

(viii) The average percentage of assets held by the foreign corporation during its taxable year which produce passive income or which are held for the production of passive income, as defined in section 1297(a)(2) and the regulations thereunder, is at least 90 percent.

(2) *Anti-abuse rule.*—If a foreign corporation undertakes any actions that have as one of their principal purposes the manipulation of the net asset value of a class of its shares, for the calendar year in which the manipulation occurs, the shares are not marketable stock for purposes of paragraph (d)(1) of this section.

(e) [Reserved]

(f) *Special rules for regulated investment companies (RICs).*—(1) *General rule.*—In the case of any RIC that is offering for sale, or has outstanding, any stock of which it is the issuer and which is redeemable at net asset value, if the RIC owns directly or indirectly, as defined in section 1298(a), stock in any passive foreign investment company, that stock will be treated as marketable stock owned by that RIC for purposes of section 1296. Except as provided in paragraph (f)(2) of this section, in the case of any other RIC that publishes net asset valuations at least annually, if the RIC owns directly or indirectly, as defined in section 1298(a), stock in any passive foreign investment company, that stock will be treated as marketable stock owned by that RIC for purposes of section 1296.

(2) [Reserved]

(g) *Effective date.*—This section applies to shareholders whose taxable year ends on or after January 25, 2000 for stock in a foreign corporation whose taxable year ends with or within the shareholder's taxable year. In addition, shareholders may elect to apply these regulations to any taxable year beginning after December 31, 1997, for stock in a foreign corporation whose taxable year ends with or within the shareholder's taxable year. [Reg. § 1.1296-2.]

☐ [*T.D. 8867, 1-25-2000. Redesignated and amended by T.D. 9123, 4-30-2004.*]

§ 1.1297-1. Definition of passive foreign investment company.—(a) *Overview.*—This section provides rules concerning the income test set forth in section 1297(a)(1) and the asset test set forth in section 1297(a)(2). Paragraph (b) of this section provides a rule relating to the definition of gross income with respect to certain dividends that are excluded from gross income under section 1502 for purposes of section 1297. Paragraph (c) of this section provides rules relating to the definition of passive income for purposes of section 1297. Paragraph (d) of this section provides rules relating to the asset test of section 1297. See §§ 1.1297-2 and 1.1297-6 for additional rules concerning the treatment of the income and assets of a corporation subject to look-through treatment under section 1297(c). Paragraph (e) of this section provides rules relating to the determination of passive foreign investment company (PFIC) status for stapled entities. Paragraph (f) of this section provides definitions applicable for this section, and paragraph (g) of this section provides the applicability date of this section.

(b) *Dividends included in gross income.*—(1) *General rule.*—For purposes of section 1297, gross income includes dividends that are excluded from gross income under section 1502 and § 1.1502-13.

(2) *Example.*—(i) *Facts.* USP is a domestic corporation that owns 30% of TFC, a foreign corporation. The remaining 70% of TFC is owned by FP, a foreign corporation that is unrelated to USP. TFC owns 25% of the value of USS1, a domestic corporation. USS1 owns 80% of the value of USS2, a domestic corporation. USS1 and USS2 are members of an affiliated group (as defined in section 1504(a)) filing a consolidated return. USS2 distributes a dividend to USS1 that is excluded from USS1's income pursuant to § 1.1502-13 for purposes of determining the U.S. Federal income tax liability of the affiliated group of which USS1 and USS2 are members.

(ii) *Results.* Although the dividend received by USS1 from USS2 is excluded from USS1's income for purposes of determining the U.S. Federal income tax liability of the affiliated group of which USS1 and USS2 are members, pursuant to paragraph (b)(1) of this section, for purposes of section 1297, USS1's gross income includes the USS2 dividend. Accordingly, for purposes of section 1297, TFC's gross income includes 25% of the dividend received by USS1 from USS2 pursuant to section 1297(c) and § 1.1297-2(b)(2)(ii). See section 1298(b)(7) and § 1.1298-4 for rules concerning the characterization of the USS2 dividend.

(c) *Passive income.*—(1) *Foreign personal holding company income.*—(i) *General rule.*—For purposes of section 1297(b)(1), except as otherwise provided in section 1297(b)(2), this section, and § 1.1297-6, the term *passive income* means income of a kind that would be foreign personal holding company income as defined under section 954(c). For the purpose of this paragraph (c)(1)—

(A) The exceptions to foreign personal holding company income in section 954(c)(1), section 954(c)(2)(A) (relating to active rents and royalties), section 954(c)(2)(B) (relating to export financing income), and section 954(c)(2)(C) (relating to dealers) are taken into account;

(B) The exceptions in section 954(c)(3) (relating to certain income received from related persons), section 954(c)(6) (relating to certain amounts received from related controlled foreign corporations), and section 954(i) (relating to entities engaged in the active conduct of an insurance business) are not taken into account;

(C) The rules in section 954(c)(4) (relating to sales of certain partnership interests) and section 954(c)(5) (relating to certain commodity hedging transactions) are taken into account; and

(D) An entity is treated as a controlled foreign corporation within the meaning of section 957(a) for purposes of applying an exception to foreign personal holding company income in section 954(c)(1)(B)'s flush language, (1)(C)(ii), (1)(D), (4), and (5) and § 1.954-2 and for purposes of identifying whether a person is a related person with respect to such entity within the meaning of section 954(d)(3).

(ii) *Determination of gross income or gain on a net basis for certain items of foreign personal holding company income.*—For purposes of section 1297, the excess of gains over losses from property transactions described in section 954(c)(1)(B), the excess of gains over losses from transactions in commodities described in section 954(c)(1)(C), the excess of foreign currency gains over foreign currency losses described in section 954(c)(1)(D), and positive net income from notional principal contracts described in section 954(c)(1)(F) are taken into account as gross income. The excess of gains over losses (or, with respect to notional principal contracts, positive net income) for a category of transactions is calculated by a tested foreign corporation taking into account individual items of gain or loss (or, with respect to notional principal contracts, net income or net deduction) recognized by the tested foreign corporation and those items of gain or loss (or, with respect to notional principal contracts, net income or net deduction) treated as recognized by the tested foreign corporation with respect to its look-through subsidiaries and look-through partnerships pursuant to section 1297(c) and § 1.1297-2(b)(2) or (2).

(iii) *Amounts treated as dividends.*—For purposes of section 1297, the term dividend includes all amounts treated as dividends for purposes of this chapter, including amounts treated as dividends pursuant to sections 302, 304, 356(a)(2), 964(e), and 1248.

(2) [Reserved].

(3) *Passive treatment of dividends and distributive share of partnership income.*—For purposes of section 1297, a tested foreign corporation's share of dividends received from a corporation that is not a look-through subsidiary (as defined in § 1.1297-2(g)(3)) and distributive share of any item of income of a partnership that is not a look-through partnership (as defined in § 1.1297-2(g)(4)) with respect to a tested foreign corporation are treated as passive income, except to the extent that the item of income would not be treated as passive under section 1297(b)(2)(C) and paragraph (c)(4) of this section.

(4) *Exception for certain interest, dividends, rents, and royalties received from a related person.*—(i) *In general.*—For purposes of section 1297(b)(2)(C), interest, dividends, rents, or royalties actually received or accrued by a tested foreign corporation are considered received or accrued from a related person only if the payor of the interest, dividend, rent, or royalty is a related person (within the meaning of section 954(d)(3)) with respect to the tested foreign corporation, taking into account paragraph (c)(1)(i)(D) of this section. For rules determining when amounts received or accrued by a look-through subsidiary or look-through partnership (and treated as received di-

rectly by a tested foreign corporation pursuant to section 1297(c) and § 1.1297-2(b)(2) and (b)(3)) are treated as received from a related person, see § 1.1297-2(d).

(ii) *Ordering rule.*—Gross income that is interest, a dividend, or a rent or royalty that is, in each case, received or accrued from a related person is allocated to income that is not passive under the rules of this paragraph (c)(4). If the related person is also a look-through subsidiary or a look-through partnership with respect to the tested foreign corporation, this paragraph (c)(4) applies after the application of the intercompany income rules of § 1.1297-2(c).

(iii) *Allocation of interest.*—For purposes of section 1297(b)(2)(C), interest that is received or accrued, as applicable based on the recipient's method of accounting, from a related person is allocated to income of the related person that is not passive income in proportion to the ratio of the portion of the related person's non-passive gross income for its taxable year that ends with or within the taxable year of the recipient to the total amount of the related person's gross income for the taxable year. If the related person does not have gross income for the taxable year that ends with or within the taxable year of the recipient, the interest is either allocated to income of the related person that is not passive income to the extent the related person's deduction for the interest would be allocable to non-passive income of the related person under the principles of §§ 1.861-9 through 1.861-13T, applied in a reasonable and consistent manner taking into account the general operation of the PFIC rules and the purpose of section 1297(b)(2)(C) or, alternatively, at the election of the tested foreign corporation is treated as allocated entirely to passive income.

(iv) *Allocation of dividends.*—(A) *In general.*—For purposes of section 1297(b)(2)(C), the principles of § 1.316-2(a) apply in determining from what year's earnings and profits a dividend from a related person is treated as distributed. A dividend is considered to be distributed, first, out of the earnings and profits of the taxable year of the related person that includes the date the dividend is distributed (current earnings and profits) and that ends with or within the taxable year of the recipient; second, out of the earnings and profits accumulated for the immediately preceding taxable year of the related person; third, out of the earnings and profits accumulated for the second preceding taxable year of the related person; and so forth. For purposes of paragraph (c)(4)(iv) of this section, the principles of § 1.243-4(a)(6) apply with respect to a deficit in an earnings and profits account for a prior year.

(B) *Dividends paid out of current earnings and profits.*—To the extent that a dividend is paid out of current earnings and profits of the related person for its taxable year that ends with or within the taxable year of the recipient, the dividend is treated as paid ratably out of earnings and profits attributable to passive income and to non-passive income. The portion of the current earnings and profits that is treated as paid out of non-passive income of the related person may be determined by multiplying the current earnings and profits by the ratio of the related person's non-passive gross income as determined under this section (including paragraph (c)(1)(ii) of this section) for the taxable year to its total gross income as determined under this section (including paragraph (c)(1)(ii) of this section) for that year.

(C) *Dividends paid out of accumulated earnings and profits.*—To the extent that a dividend from a related person is treated as paid out of the related person's accumulated earnings and profits, the dividend is treated as paid ratably out of accumulated earnings and profits of the related person for prior taxable years (beginning with the most recently accumulated) that are attributable to passive income and to non-passive income, which may be determined in the same manner as in paragraph (c)(4)(iv)(B) of this section. Alternatively, the accumulated earnings and profits may be allocated based on the ratio of accumulated earnings and profits that are attributable to passive income and to non-passive income during either the related party period or the three-year period. The related party period is the entire period during which the related person was related to the recipient. The three-year period is the three taxable years immediately preceding the related person's taxable year that ends with or within the current taxable year of the recipient. The three-year period may be used only if the related person has been related to the recipient for a period longer than the three taxable years immediately preceding the recipient's taxable year.

(v) *Allocation of rents and royalties.*—For purposes of section 1297(b)(2)(C), rents and royalties that are received or accrued, as applicable based on the recipient's method of accounting, from a related person are allocable to income of the related person that is not passive income to the extent the related person's deduction for the rent or royalty is allocable to non-passive gross income of the related person under the principles of §§ 1.861-8 through 1.861-14T.

(vi) *Determination of whether amounts are received or accrued from a related person.*—For purposes of section 1297(b)(2)(C), the determination of whether interest, dividends, rents, and royalties were received or accrued from a related person is made on the date of the receipt or accrual, as applicable based on the recipient's method of accounting, of the interest, dividend, rent, or royalty.

(vii) *Allocation of distributive share of income from related partnership.*—For purposes of section 1297(a)(1), a tested foreign corporation includes its distributive share as provided in section 704 of the separate items of passive or non-passive income from a partnership that is a related person (and not a look-through partnership) with respect to the tested foreign corporation for the taxable year of the tested foreign corporation.

(d) *Asset test.*—(1) *Calculation of average annual value (or adjusted bases).*—(i) *General rule.*—For purposes of section 1297, the calculation of the average percentage of assets held by a tested foreign corporation during its taxable year that produce passive income or that are held for the production of passive income is determined based on the average of the fair market values, or the average of the adjusted bases, as appropriate, of the passive assets and total assets held (including assets treated as held pursuant to section 1297(c) and § 1.1297-2(b)(2)(i) and (b)(3)) by the foreign corporation on the last day of each measuring period *(measuring date)* of the foreign corporation's taxable year. The average of the fair market values (or the average of the adjusted bases) of the foreign corporation's passive assets or total assets for the taxable year is equal to the sum of the values (or adjusted bases) of the passive assets or total assets, as applicable, on each measuring date of the foreign corporation's taxable year, divided by the number of measuring dates in the taxable year.

(ii) *Measuring period.*—(A) *General rule.*—Except as otherwise provided in paragraph (d)(1)(ii)(B) of this section, the measuring periods for a tested foreign corporation are the four quarters that make up the foreign corporation's taxable year.

(B) *Election to use alternative measuring period.*—The average percentage of assets held by a tested foreign corporation during its taxable year that produce passive income or that are held for the production of passive income may be calculated using a period that is shorter than a quarter (such as a week or month). The same period must be used to measure the assets of the foreign corporation for the first year (including a short taxable year) that this alternative measuring period is used, and for any and all subsequent years, unless a revocation is made. An election to use an alternative measuring period or a revocation of such an election must be made in accordance with the rules of paragraph (d)(1)(iv) of this section.

(C) *Short taxable year.*—For purposes of applying section 1297 to a tested foreign corporation that has a taxable year of less than twelve months (short taxable year), the average values (or adjusted bases) are determined based on the measuring dates of the foreign corporation's taxable year that fall within the short taxable year, and by treating the last day of the short taxable year as a measuring date.

(iii) *Adjusted basis election.*—An election under section 1297(e)(2)(B) with respect to an eligible tested foreign corporation or a revocation of such an election may be made by the tested foreign corporation or alternatively by the owner (as defined in paragraph (d)(1)(iv) of this section). If made by the owner, the election must be made in accordance with the rules of paragraph (d)(1)(iv) of this section.

(iv) *Time and manner of elections and revocations.*—(A) *Elections.*—An owner (as defined in this paragraph (d)(1)(iv)) of a foreign corporation makes an election described in paragraph (d)(1)(ii)(B) or (d)(1)(iii) of this section for a taxable year in the manner provided in the Instructions to Form 8621 (or successor form), if the owner is required to file a Form 8621 (or successor form) with respect to the foreign corporation for the taxable year of the owner in which or with which the taxable year of the foreign corporation for which the election is made ends. If the owner is not required to file Form 8621 (or successor form) with respect to the foreign corporation for the taxable year, the owner makes such an election by filing a written statement providing for the election and attaching the statement to an original or amended Federal income tax return for the taxable year of the owner in which or with which the taxable year of the foreign corporation for which the election is made ends clearly indicating that such election has been made. An election can be made by an owner only if the owner's taxable year for which the election is made, and all taxable years that are affected by the election, are not closed by the period of limitations on assessments under section 6501. Elections described in paragraphs (d)(1)(ii)(B) and (d)(1)(iii) of this section are not eligible for relief under § 301.9100-3 of this chapter. For purposes of this paragraph (d)(1)(iv), an owner of a foreign corporation is a United States person that is eligible under § 1.1295-1(d) to make a section 1295 election with respect to the foreign corporation, or would be eligible under § 1.1295-1(d) to make a section 1295 election if the foreign corporation were a PFIC.

(B) *Revocations and subsequent elections.*—An election described in paragraph (d)(1)(ii)(B) or (d)(1)(iii) of this section made pursuant to paragraph (d)(1)(iv)(A) of this section is effective for the taxable year of the foreign corporation for which it is made and all subsequent taxable years of such corporation unless revoked by the Commissioner or the owner (as defined in paragraph (d)(1)(iv)(A) of this section) of the foreign corporation. The owner of a foreign corporation may revoke such an election at any time. If an election described in paragraph (d)(1)(ii)(B) or (d)(1)(iii) of this section has been revoked under this paragraph (d)(1)(iv)(B), a new election described in paragraph (d)(1)(ii)(B) or (d)(1)(iii) of this section, as applicable, cannot be made until the sixth taxable year following the year for which the previous election was revoked, and such subsequent election cannot be revoked until the sixth taxable year following the year for which the subsequent election was made. The owner revokes the election for a taxable year in the manner provided in the Instructions to Form 8621 (or successor form), if the owner is required to file a Form 8621 (or successor form) with respect to the foreign corporation for the taxable year of the owner in which or with which the taxable year of the foreign corporation for which the election is revoked ends, or by filing a written statement providing for the revocation and attaching the statement to an original or amended Federal income tax return for the taxable year of the owner in which or with which the taxable year of the foreign corporation for which the election is revoked ends clearly indicating that such election has been revoked, if the owner is not required to file Form 8621 (or successor form) with respect to the foreign corporation for the taxable year.

(v) *Method of measuring assets.*—(A) *Publicly traded foreign corporations.*—For purposes of section 1297, the assets of a publicly traded foreign corporation as defined in paragraph (f)(7) of this section (including assets treated as held pursuant to section 1297(c) and § 1.1297-2(b)(2)(i) and (b)(3)(i), other than assets of a look-through subsidiary described in paragraph (d)(1)(v)(B) of this section) must be measured for all measuring periods of the taxable year on the basis of value.

(B) *Non-publicly traded controlled foreign corporation.*—(*1*) *In general.*—For purposes of section 1297, the assets of a controlled foreign corporation that is not described in paragraph (d)(1)(v)(A) of this section (including assets treated as held pursuant to section 1297(c) and § 1.1297-2(b)(2)(i) and (b)(3)(i), other than assets held by a look-through subsidiary described in paragraph (d)(1)(v)(A) of this section) must be measured for all measuring periods of the taxable year during which the foreign corporation is a controlled foreign corporation on the basis of adjusted basis.

(*2*) *Controlled foreign corporation determination.*—For purposes of section 1297(e)(2)(A) and this paragraph (d)(1)(v), the term *controlled foreign corporation* has the meaning provided in section 957, determined without applying subparagraphs (A), (B), and (C) of section 318(a)(3) so as to consider a United States person as owning stock which is owned by a person who is not a United States person.

(C) *Other foreign corporations.*—(*1*) *In general.*—Except as provided in paragraph (d)(1)(v)(C)(*2*) of this section, the assets of a foreign corporation that is not described in paragraphs (d)(1)(v)(A) or (d)(1)(v)(B) of this section (including assets treated as held pursuant to section 1297(c) and § 1.1297-2(b)(2)(i) and (b)(3)(i), other than assets held by a look-through subsidiary described in paragraphs (d)(1)(v)(A) or (d)(1)(v)(B) of this section) are measured for all measuring periods of the taxable year on the basis of value, unless a tested foreign corporation or a shareholder makes an election under section 1297(e)(2)(B) in accordance with paragraph (d)(1)(iii) of this section. In the case of a foreign corporation that is described in paragraph (d)(1)(v)(B) of this section for some but not all measuring periods during a taxable year, this paragraph (d)(1)(v)(C)(*1*) applies to the remaining measuring period or periods during that taxable year.

(*2*) *Lower-tier subsidiaries.*—(*i*) *Lower-tier subsidiaries that are publicly traded foreign corporations.*—For purposes of applying section 1297(a)(2) to the assets of a foreign corporation that is a lower-tier subsidiary of a foreign corporation that directly or indirectly owns all or part of the lower-tier subsidiary (a parent foreign corporation), if the lower-tier subsidiary is described in paragraph (d)(1)(v)(A), the rules of paragraph (d)(1)(v)(A) apply. The previous sentence applies both for purposes of applying section 1297(a)(2) to the lower-tier subsidiary as a tested foreign corporation, and for purposes of applying section 1297(a)(2) to a parent foreign corporation with respect to the assets of the lower-tier subsidiary.

(*ii*) *Lower-tier subsidiaries that are non-publicly traded controlled foreign corporations.*—For purposes of applying section 1297(a)(2) to the assets of a foreign corporation that is a lower-tier subsidiary of a parent foreign corporation, if the lower-tier subsidiary is described in paragraph (d)(1)(v)(B), the rules of paragraph (d)(1)(v)(B) apply. The previous sentence applies both for purposes of applying section 1297(a)(2) to the lower-tier subsidiary as a tested foreign corporation, and for purposes of applying section 1297(a)(2) to a parent foreign corporation with respect to the assets of the lower-tier subsidiary.

(*iii*) *Other lower-tier subsidiaries.*—For purposes of applying section 1297(a)(2) to a foreign corporation that is a lower-tier subsidiary of a parent foreign corporation, if the lower-tier subsidiary is not described in paragraphs (d)(1)(v)(A) or (d)(1)(v)(B) of this section, the assets of the lower-tier subsidiary (including assets treated as held pursuant to section 1297(c) and § 1.1297-2(b)(2)(i) and (b)(3)(i)) must be measured under the rules of the same paragraph of this section (d)(1)(v) that applies to the parent foreign corporation. The previous sentence applies both for purposes of applying section 1297(a)(2) to the lower-tier subsidiary as a tested foreign corporation, and for purposes of applying section 1297(a)(2) to a parent foreign corporation. If a tested foreign corporation indirectly owns a lower-tier subsidiary that is not described in paragraphs (d)(1)(v)(A) or (d)(1)(v)(B) of this section through one or more other foreign corporations, the status of any parent foreign corporation in that chain of corporations that is described in paragraph (d)(1)(v)(A) of this section, or if there is no such parent foreign corporation then the status of any parent foreign corporation in that chain of corporations that is described in paragraph (d)(1)(v)(B) of this section, determines the basis on which the assets of the lower-tier subsidiary are measured. In the case of a foreign corporation that is a lower-tier subsidiary with respect to more than one parent foreign corporation, this rule applies separately to measure the assets of the lower-tier subsidiary with respect to each parent foreign corporation.

(D) [Reserved].

(E) *Examples.*—The following examples illustrate the application of this paragraph (d)(1)(v).

(*1*) *Example 1.*—(*i*) *Facts.* USP, a domestic corporation, owns 60% of TFC1, which is a foreign corporation. The remaining 40% of TFC1's stock is regularly traded on a national securities exchange that is registered with the Securities and Exchange Commission and continues to be until September 1 of the taxable year, when USP acquires all of TFC1's stock pursuant to a tender offer. TFC1 owns 30% of the stock of FS1, a foreign corporation that is neither a publicly traded foreign corporation nor a controlled foreign corporation.

(*ii*) *Results.* TFC1 is a controlled foreign corporation with respect to USP. TFC1 also is a publicly traded foreign corporation until September 1 of the taxable year. For purposes of section 1297, the assets of TFC1 (including the assets of FS1 treated as held by TFC1 pursuant to section 1297(c)) and must be measured on the basis of value for each measuring period ending before September 1, pursuant to paragraph (d)(1)(v)(A) of this section. For purposes of applying section 1297 to FS1 as a tested foreign corporation with respect to USP, the assets of FS1 must be measured using the same method as is used for TFC1's assets, pursuant to paragraph (d)(1)(v)(C)(*2*) of this section.

(2) *Example 2.*—(*i*) *Facts.* A, a United States person, owns 1% of the stock of TFC2, a foreign corporation that is neither a publicly traded foreign corporation nor a controlled foreign corporation. TFC2 owns 25% of the stock of FS2, a foreign corporation that is neither a publicly traded foreign corporation nor a controlled foreign corporation.

(ii) *Results.* For purposes of applying section 1297 to TFC2, the assets of TFC2 (including the assets of FS2 treated as held by TFC2 pursuant to section 1297(c) and § 1.1297-2(b)(2)(i)) are measured for all measuring periods of the taxable year on the basis of value, unless A or TFC2 makes an election under section 1297(e)(2)(B) in accordance with paragraph (d)(1)(iii) of this section, pursuant to paragraph (d)(1)(v)(C)(*1*) of this section. For purposes of applying section 1297 to FS2 as a tested foreign corporation with respect to A, the assets of FS2 must be measured using the same method as is used for TFC2's assets, pursuant to paragraph (d)(1)(v)(C)(*2*) of this section.

(3) *Example 3.*—(i) *Facts.* The facts are the same as in paragraph (d)(1)(v)(E)(*2*)(*i*) (the facts in Example 2), except that the 75% of FS2's stock not owned by TFC2 is owned by TFC3, a publicly traded foreign corporation that is neither related to TFC2 nor to A. B, a United States person that is neither related to A nor to TFC2, owns 1% of the stock of TFC3.

(*ii*) *Results.* For purposes of applying section 1297 to TFC2, the results are the same as in paragraph (d)(1)(v)(E)(*2*)(*ii*) (the results in Example 2). For purposes of applying section 1297 to FS2 as a tested foreign corporation with respect to A, the assets of FS2 must be measured using the same method as is used for TFC2's assets, pursuant to paragraph (d)(1)(v)(C)(*2*) of this section. For purposes of applying section 1297 to TFC3, the assets of TFC3 must be measured by reference to value pursuant to paragraph (d)(1)(v)(A) because it is a publicly traded corporation. For purposes of applying section 1297 to FS2 as a tested foreign corporation with respect to B, the assets of FS2 must be measured by reference to value because TFC3 is a publicly traded foreign corporation, pursuant to paragraphs (d)(1)(v)(C)(*2*) and (d)(1)(v)(A) of this section.

(2) [Reserved].

(3) *Dual-character assets.*—(i) *General rule.*—Except as otherwise provided in paragraph (d)(3)(ii) or (d)(3)(iii) of this section and in § 1.1297-2(c), for purposes of section 1297, an asset (or portion of an asset) that produces both passive income and non-passive income during a taxable year (dual-character asset), including stock and other assets that produce passive and non-passive income under section 1297(b)(2)(C) and paragraph (c)(4) of this section, is treated as two assets for each measuring period in the taxable year, one of which is a passive asset and one of which is a non-passive asset. The value (or adjusted basis) of the dual-character asset is allocated between the passive asset and the non-passive asset in proportion to the relative amounts of passive income and non-passive income produced by the asset (or portion of an asset) during the taxable year. See paragraph (d)(3)(iii) of this section for a special rule concerning stock that has previously produced dividends subject to the exception provided in section 1297(b)(2)(C). For purposes of section 1297(b)(2)(C), a partnership interest in a partnership that is a related person to the tested foreign corporation is treated as producing passive or non-passive income in proportion to the tested foreign corporation's distributive share of partnership passive or non-passive income for the taxable year under paragraph (c)(4)(vii) of this section.

(ii) *Special rule when only part of an asset produces income.*—For purposes of section 1297, when only a portion of an asset produces income during a taxable year or a portion of a taxable year, the asset is treated as two assets for that period, one of which is characterized as a passive asset or a non-passive asset based on the income that it produces, and one of which is characterized based on the income that it is held to produce. The value (or adjusted basis) of the asset is allocated between the two assets pursuant to the method that most reasonably reflects the uses of the property. In the case of real property, an allocation based on the physical use of the property generally is the most reasonable method.

(iii) *Special rule for stock that previously produced income that was excluded from passive income under section 1297(b)(2)(C).*—Stock with respect to which no dividends are received during a taxable year, but with respect to which dividends were received during one or both of the prior two taxable years, is characterized based on the relative portion of the dividends received that was passive or non-passive. If the dividends were in whole excluded from passive income under section 1297(b)(2)(C) and paragraph (c)(4)(iv) of this section, the stock is treated as a single non-passive asset. If the dividends were in part excluded from passive income under section 1297(b)(2)(C) and paragraph (c)(4)(iv) of this section, the stock is treated as two assets, one of which is a passive asset and one of which is a non-passive asset. The value (or adjusted basis) of the stock is allocated between the two assets in proportion to the average percentage of aggregate dividends received in the prior two taxable years that were characterized as passive income and the average percentage of aggregate dividends received in the prior two years that were characterized as non-passive income, for the previous two taxable years pursuant to section 1297(b)(2)(C) and paragraph (c)(4)(iv) of this section. If the tested foreign corporation did not receive any dividends from the stock for the current taxable year or within either of the prior two taxable years of the tested foreign corporation, then the stock is treated as a passive asset.

(iv) *Example.*—The following example illustrates the application of this paragraph (d)(3).

(A) *Facts.* (*1*) USP is a domestic corporation that owns 30% of TFC, a foreign corporation. The remaining 70% of TFC is owned by FP, a foreign corporation that is unrelated to USP. TFC owns 20% of the value of FS1, a foreign corporation, and FP owns the remaining 80% of the value of FS1. FP, TFC, and FS1 are not controlled foreign corporations within the meaning of section 957(a), and each has a calendar year taxable year.

(*2*) In Year 1, FS1 had current earnings and profits of $1000x, attributable to passive income of $500x and non-passive income of $500x, and paid $300x of dividends to TFC. In Year 2, FS1 had current earnings and profits of $1000x, attributable to passive income of $100x and non-passive income of $900x, and paid $100x of dividends to TFC. In Year 3, FS1 has passive income of $200x and non-passive income of $800x and does not pay a dividend.

(*3*) Throughout Year 3, TFC holds an obligation of FS1 with respect to which FS1 pays $100x of interest.

(*4*) In addition to the stock in FS1 and the FS1 obligation, TFC holds an office building, 40% of which is rented to FP throughout Year 3 for $100x per quarter. During Year 3, FP has only passive income. The remaining 60% of the office building is leased throughout Year 3 to an unrelated person for $300x per quarter, and TFC's own officers or staff of employees regularly perform active and substantial management and operational functions while the property is leased.

(B) *Results.* (*1*) For purposes of section 1297(b)(2)(C), FP is a "related person" with respect to TFC because FP owns more than 50% of the vote or value of TFC, and FS1 is a "related person" with respect to TFC because FP owns more than 50% of the vote or value of both TFC and of FS1.

(*2*) Under paragraph (c)(4)(iv) of this section, the dividends paid by FS1 in Year 1 were characterized as 50% passive income ($150x) and 50% non-passive income ($150x). Under paragraph (c)(4)(iv) of this section, the dividends paid by FS1 in Year 2 were characterized as 10% passive income ($10x) and 90% non-passive income ($90x). Accordingly, the average percentage of dividends for the previous two taxable years that were characterized as passive income is 40% (((10% x $100x) + (50% x $300x))/($100x + $300x)), and the average percentage of dividends characterized as non-passive income is 60% (((90% x $100x) + (50% x $300x))/($100x + $300x)). Thus, under paragraph (d)(3)(iii) of this section, 60% of each share of stock of FS1 is characterized as a non-passive asset and 40% is characterized as a passive asset for each quarter of Year 3 for purposes of applying section 1297(a)(2) to determine whether TFC is a PFIC.

(*3*) Under paragraph (c)(4)(iii) of this section, the interest received by TFC from FS1 is characterized as 20% ($200x/($200x + $800x)) passive income and thus 80% non-passive income for purposes of applying section 1297(a)(1) to determine whether TFC is a PFIC. Accordingly, under paragraph (d)(3)(i) of this section, 20% of the obligation of FS1 is characterized as a passive asset and 80% as a non-passive asset for each quarter of Year 3 for purposes of applying section 1297(a)(2) to determine whether TFC is a PFIC.

(*4*) Under paragraph (c)(4)(v) of this section, the rent received from FP throughout Year 3 is characterized as 100% passive income. Under paragraph (c)(1)(i)(A) of this section and section 954(c)(2)(A), the rent received from the unrelated person is characterized as 100% non-passive income. Accordingly, under paragraph (d)(3)(i) of this section, the 40% of the office building rented to FP has a value of 25% (($100x x 4)/ (($100x x 4) +($300x x 4))) of the value of the office building and that 25% is a passive asset, and the 60% of the office building rented to the unrelated person has a value of 75% (($300x x 4)/(($100x x 4) +($300x x 4))) of the value of the office building and is a non-passive asset for purposes of applying section 1297(a)(2) to determine whether TFC is a PFIC.

(4) *Passive treatment of stock and partnership interests.*—For purposes of section 1297(a)(2), shares of stock in a corporation that is not a look-through subsidiary (as defined in § 1.1297-2(g)(3)) and partnership interests in a partnership that is not a look-through partnership (as defined in § 1.1297-2(g)(4)) with respect to a tested foreign corporation for a taxable year or portion thereof are treated as passive assets for the taxable year or relevant portion thereof, except to the extent the stock or partnership interest is treated as a dual-character asset under section 1297(b)(2)(C) and paragraph (d)(3) of this section because it produces both passive and non-passive income, or the stock or partnership interest produces solely non-passive income for the taxable year under section 1297(b)(2)(C) and paragraph (c)(4) of this section or under paragraph (d)(5) of this section.

(5) *Dealer property.*—For purposes of section 1297(a)(2), an asset that produces, or would produce upon disposition, income or gain that is, or would be, excluded from passive income pursuant to section 954(c)(2)(C) is treated as a non-passive asset.

(e) *Stapled stock.*—If a United States person that would be a shareholder (within the meaning of § 1.1291-1(b)(7) and (b)(8)) of a stapled entity (as defined in section 269B(c)(2)) owns stock in all entities that are stapled entities with respect to each other and the shares are stapled interests (as defined in section 269B(c)(3)), the United States person's interests in the stapled entities are treated as an interest in a single entity that holds all of the assets of the stapled entities, conducts all of the activities of the stapled entities, and derives all of the income of the stapled entities for all purposes of the PFIC regime.

(f) *Definitions.*—The following definitions apply for purposes of this section and § 1.1297-2:

(1) *Measuring date.*—The term *measuring date* has the meaning provided in paragraph (d)(1)(i) of this section.

(2) *Measuring period.*—The term *measuring period* means a three-month period or an alternative measuring period, within the meaning provided in paragraph (d)(1)(ii) of this section.

(3) *Non-passive asset.*—The term *non-passive asset* means an asset other than a passive asset.

(4) *Non-passive income.*—The term *non-passive income* means income other than passive income.

(5) *Passive asset.*—The term *passive asset* means an asset that produces passive income, or which is held for the production of passive income, taking into account the rules in paragraphs (c) and (d) of this section.

(6) *Passive income.*—The term *passive income* has the meaning provided in paragraph (c)(1) of this section.

(7) *Publicly traded foreign corporation.*—The term *publicly traded foreign corporation* means a foreign corporation the stock of which is regularly traded on an exchange described in section 1297(e)(3), other than in de minimis quantities, for at least twenty trading days during a taxable year.

(8) *Related person.*—For purposes of applying the rules of this section and § 1.1297-2 with respect to section 1297(b)(2)(C), the term means a *related person* within the meaning of section 954(d)(3).

(9) *Tested foreign corporation.*—The term *tested foreign corporation* means a foreign corporation the PFIC status of which is being tested under section 1297(a).

(g) *Applicability date.*—(1) *In general.*—Except as otherwise provided in paragraph (g)(2) of this section, the rules of this section apply to taxable years of shareholders beginning on or after January 14, 2021. A shareholder may choose to apply such rules for any open taxable year beginning before January 14, 2021, provided that, with respect to a tested foreign corporation, the shareholder consistently applies the provisions of this section (except that consistent treatment is not required with respect to paragraph (c)(1)(i)(A) of this section) and § 1.1291-1(b)(8)(iv) and (b)(8)(v)(A), (B), (C) , and (D) and §§ 1.1297-2, 1.1298-2, and 1.1298-4 for such year and all subsequent years.

(2) *Paragraph (d)(1)(v)(B)(2) of this section.*—Paragraph (d)(1)(v)(B)(2) of this section applies to taxable years of shareholders ending on or after October 1, 2019. For taxable years of shareholders ending before October 1, 2019, a shareholder may apply paragraph (d)(1)(v)(B)(2) of this section to the last taxable year of a foreign corporation beginning before January 1, 2018, and each subsequent taxable year of the foreign corporation, provided that the shareholder and United States persons that are related (within the meaning of section 267 or section 707) to the taxpayer consistently apply such paragraph with respect to all foreign corporations. [Reg. § 1.1297-1.]

☐ [*T.D. 9936, 1-14-2021 (corrected 3-9-2021).*]

Proposed Amendments to Regulation

§ 1.1297-1. Definition of passive foreign investment company.—

* * *

(c) * * *

(1) * * *

(i) * * *

(B) The exceptions in sections 954(c)(3) (relating to certain income received from related persons), 954(c)(6) (relating to certain amounts received from related controlled foreign corporations), 954(h) (relating to entities engaged in the active conduct of a banking, financing, or similar business), and 954(i) (relating to entities engaged in the active conduct of an insurance business) are not taken into account.* * *

* * *

(2) *Exception for certain income derived in the active conduct of a banking business by a foreign bank.*—(i) *In general.*—For purposes of section 1297(b)(2)(A), income of a tested foreign corporation is treated as non-passive if—

(A) The income would not be treated as foreign personal holding company income under section 954(h) (relating to entities engaged in the active conduct of a banking, financing, or similar business) if the tested foreign corporation (and, to the extent relevant, any related person as defined by section 954(d)(3)) were a controlled foreign corporation within the meaning of section 957(a); and

(B) The tested foreign corporation is a foreign bank that is engaged in the active conduct of a banking business (within the meaning of section 954(h)(2)(B)(ii)) and the income is derived in the conduct of that banking business.

(ii) *Foreign bank determination.*—A tested foreign corporation will be treated as a foreign bank only if it—

(A) is licensed by federal or state bank regulatory authorities to do business as a bank in the United States, or is licensed or authorized by a bank regulatory authority in the country in which it is chartered or incorporated (or, in the case of a qualified business unit, in the country in which the unit maintains its principal office) to do business as a bank in that country, including to—

(*1*) Accept bank deposits from residents of that country; and

(*2*) Carry out one or more of the activities listed in section 954(h)(4), and

(B) regularly receives bank deposits from and carries out one or more of the activities listed in section 954(h)(4) with unrelated customers in the ordinary course of a banking business.

* * *

(d) * * *

(1) * * *

(v) * * *

(D) *Valuation.*—For purposes of determining the value of assets during a measuring period when the shares of a tested foreign corporation are not publicly traded, valuation may be determined on the basis of periodic financial accounting statements provided at least annually. If the tested foreign corporation or one or more shareholders has actual knowledge or reason to know based on readily accessible information that the financial accounting statements do not reflect a reasonable estimate of an asset's value and the information provides a more reasonable estimate of the asset's value, then the information must be used to determine the value of the assets to which it relates.

* * *

(2) *Working capital.*—For purposes of section 1297(a)(2), an amount of currency denominated in functional currency (as defined in section 985(b)) held in a non-interest bearing financial account that is held for the present needs of an active trade or business and is no greater than the amount necessary to cover operating expenses incurred in the ordinary course of the trade or business of the tested foreign corporation (for example, accounts payable for ordinary operating expenses) and reasonably expected to be paid within 90 days is not treated as a passive asset. For purposes of the preceding sentence, cash equivalents are not treated as currency, and amounts held for purposes other than to meet the ordinary course operating expenses of the trade or business, including for the purpose of providing for (i) future diversification into a new trade or business, (ii) expansion of trade or business activities, (iii) future plant replacement, or (iv) future business contingencies, are treated as passive assets.

* * *

(g) * * *

(1) *In general.*—Except as otherwise provided, the rules of this section apply to taxable years of shareholders beginning on or after January 14, 2021.

* * *

(3) *Paragraphs (c)(1)(i)(B), (c)(2), (d)(1)(v)(D), and (d)(2) of this section.*—Paragraphs (c)(1)(i)(B), (c)(2), (d)(1)(v)(D), and (d)(2) of this section apply to taxable years of shareholders beginning on or after [the date these regulations are filed as final regulations in the **Federal Register**]. A shareholder may choose to apply the paragraphs in the preceding sentence for any open taxable year beginning before [the date these regulations are filed as final regulations in the **Federal Register**] without regard to whether the rules of this section are applied consistently, provided that once applied, each rule must be applied for each subsequent taxable year beginning before [the date these regulations are filed as final regulations in the **Federal Register**]. [Prop. Reg. § 1.1297-1.]

[Proposed 1-15-2021 (corrected 3-5-2021).]

§ 1.1297-2. Special rules regarding look-through subsidiaries and look-through partnerships.—(a) *Overview.*—This section provides rules concerning the treatment of income and assets of a look-through subsidiary (as defined in § 1.1297-2(g)(3)) or look-through partnership (as defined in § 1.1297-2(g)(4)) for purposes of determining whether a tested foreign corporation (as defined in § 1.1297-1(f)(9)) is a passive foreign investment company (PFIC) under section 1297(a). Paragraph (b) of this section provides guidance for purposes of section 1297(c) on how to determine a tested foreign corporation's ownership in a corporation and how to determine a tested foreign corporation's proportionate share of a look-through subsidiary's or look-through partnership's assets and income. Paragraph (c) of this section provides rules that eliminate certain income and assets related to look-through subsidiaries and look-through partnerships for purposes of determining a tested foreign corporation's PFIC status. Paragraph (d) of this section provides a rule to determine whether certain income received or accrued by look-through subsidiaries and look-through partnerships is received or accrued from a related person for purposes of section 1297(b)(2)(C). Paragraph (e) of this section provides rules concerning the attribution of activities from qualified affiliates (as defined in § 1.1297-2(e)(2)) for purposes of characterizing the income and assets of a look-through subsidiary or look-through partnership. Paragraph (f) of this section provides rules for determining the amount of gain from the direct or indirect sale or exchange of stock of a look-through subsidiary or partnership interests in a partnership described in section 954(c)(4) that is taken into account under section 1297(a) and for determining the passive or non-passive character of gain from the sale of a look-through subsidiary. Paragraph (g) of this section provides definitions applicable for this section, and paragraph (h) of this section provides the applicability date of this section.

(b) *General rules.*—(1) *Tested foreign corporation's ownership of a corporation.*—For purposes of section 1297(c) and this section, the principles of section 958(a) and the regulations in this chapter under that section applicable to determining direct or indirect ownership by value apply to determine a tested foreign corporation's percentage ownership (by value) in the stock of another corporation. These principles apply whether an intermediate entity is domestic or foreign.

(2) *Tested foreign corporation's proportionate share of the assets and income of a look-through subsidiary.*—(i) *Proportionate share of subsidiary assets.*—For each measuring period (as defined in § 1.1297-1(f)(2)), a tested foreign corporation is treated as if it held its proportionate share of each asset of a look-through subsidiary, determined based on the tested foreign corporation's percentage ownership (by value) (as determined under paragraph (b)(1) of this section)) of the look-through subsidiary on the measuring date (as defined in § 1.1297-1(f)(1)). A tested foreign corporation's proportionate share of a look-through subsidiary's asset is treated as producing passive income, or being held to produce passive income, to the extent the asset produced, or was held to produce, passive income in the hands of such look-through subsidiary under the rules of paragraph (b)(2)(ii) of this section.

(ii) *Proportionate share of subsidiary income.*—(A) *General rule.*—A tested foreign corporation is treated as if it received directly its proportionate share of each item of gross income or loss of a corporation for a taxable year if the corporation is a look-through subsidiary with respect to the tested foreign corporation for the taxable year of the tested foreign corporation. In such case, a tested foreign corporation's proportionate share of a look-through subsidiary's gross income or loss is determined based on the corporation's average percentage ownership (by value) of the look-through subsidiary. The exceptions to passive income in section 1297(b)(2) and the relevant exceptions to foreign personal holding company income in section 954(c) that are based on whether income is derived in the active conduct of a business or whether a corporation is engaged in the active conduct of a business apply to such income only if the exception would have applied to exclude the income from passive income or foreign personal holding company income in the hands of the subsidiary, determined by taking into account only the activities of the subsidiary except as provided in paragraph (e) of this section. See paragraph (d) of this section for rules determining whether a person is a related person for purposes of applying section 1297(b)(2)(C) in the case of income received or accrued by a subsidiary that is treated as received directly by a tested foreign corporation pursuant to this paragraph (b)(2).

(B) *Partial year.*—When a corporation is not a look-through subsidiary with respect to a tested foreign corporation for an entire taxable year of the tested foreign corporation, the tested foreign corporation may be treated as if it received directly its proportionate share of the gross income or loss of the first corporation for each measuring period in the year for which the first corporation is a look-through subsidiary, if the conditions in paragraph (g)(3)(ii)(B) of this section are satisfied. In such case, a tested foreign corporation's proportionate share of a look-through subsidiary's gross income or loss is determined based on the tested foreign corporation's percentage ownership (by value) (as determined under paragraph (b)(1) of this section) of the look-through subsidiary on the relevant measuring date.

(iii) *Coordination of section 1297(c) with section 1298(b)(7).*—A tested foreign corporation is not treated under section 1297(c) and this paragraph (b) as holding its proportionate share of the assets of a domestic corporation, or receiving directly its proportionate share of the gross income or loss of the domestic corporation, if the stock of the domestic corporation is treated as an asset that is not a passive asset (as defined in § 1.1297-1(f)(5)) that produces income that is not passive income (as defined in § 1.1297-1(f)(6)) under section 1298(b)(7) (concerning the treatment of certain foreign corporations owning stock in certain 25-percent-owned domestic corporations). See § 1.1298-4 for rules governing the application of section 1298(b)(7).

(3) *Tested foreign corporation's proportionate share of the assets and income of a look-through partnership.*—(i) *Proportionate share of partnership assets.*—For each measuring period (as defined in § 1.1297-1(f)(2)), a tested foreign corporation is treated as if it held its proportionate share of each asset of a look-through partnership, determined based on the tested foreign corporation's percentage ownership (by value) (as determined under paragraph (b)(1) of this section) of the look-through partnership on the measuring date (as defined in § 1.1297-1(f)(1)). A tested foreign corporation's proportionate share of a look-through partnership's asset is treated as producing passive income, or being held to produce passive income, to the extent the asset produced, or was held to produce, passive income in the hands of the partnership under the rules in paragraph (b)(3)(ii) of this section.

(ii) *Proportionate share of partnership income.*—(A) *General rule.*—A tested foreign corporation is treated as if it received directly its proportionate share of any item of gross income or loss of a partnership that is a look-through partnership with respect to the tested foreign corporation for the taxable year of the tested foreign corporation. The exceptions to passive income in section 1297(b)(2) and the relevant exceptions to foreign personal holding company income in section 954(c) that are based on whether income is derived in the active conduct of a business or whether a corporation is engaged in the active conduct of a business apply to such income only if the exception would have applied to exclude the income from passive income or foreign personal holding company income in the hands of the partnership, determined by taking into account only the activities of the partnership except as provided in paragraph (e) of this section. See paragraph (d) of this section for rules determining whether a person is a related person for purposes of applying section 1297(b)(2)(C) in the case of income received or accrued by a partnership that is treated as received directly by a tested foreign corporation pursuant to this paragraph (b)(3).

(B) *Partial year.*—When a partnership is not a look-through partnership with respect to a tested foreign corporation for an entire taxable year of the tested foreign corporation, the tested foreign corporation may be treated as if it received directly its proportionate share of the gross income of the partnership for each measuring period in the year for which the partnership is a look-through partnership, provided that the conditions set forth in paragraph (g)(3)(ii)(B) of this section would be satisfied if the partnership were a corporation.

(4) *Examples.*—The following examples illustrate the rules of this paragraph (b). For purposes of these examples, USP is a domestic corporation; TFC, LTS, and FS are foreign corporations that are not controlled foreign corporations within the meaning of section 957(a); USP owns 30% of TFC; and LTS owns 25% of the only class of FS stock.

(i) *Example 1.*—(A) *Facts.* TFC directly owns 80% of the only class of LTS stock for TFC's and LTS's entire taxable year.

(B) *Results*—(1) *LTS.* Under paragraph (b)(1) of this section and pursuant to the principles of section 958(a), LTS owns 25% of the value of FS. Under paragraph (b)(2)(i) and (ii) of this section, in determining whether LTS is a PFIC under section 1297(a), LTS is treated as if it held 25% of each of FS's assets on each of the measuring dates in its taxable year and received directly 25% of the gross income of FS for the taxable year.

(2) *TFC.* Under paragraph (b)(1) of this section and pursuant to the principles of section 958(a), TFC owns 80% of the value of LTS and indirectly owns 20% of the value of FS. Under paragraph (b)(2) of this section, in determining whether TFC is a PFIC under section 1297(a), TFC is treated as if it held 80% of each of LTS's assets on each of the measuring dates in its taxable year and received directly 80% of the gross income of LTS for the taxable year. However, because TFC indirectly owns less than 25% of FS, FS is not a look-through subsidiary with respect to TFC and, therefore, TFC is treated as if it held a 20% interest in the stock of FS (and not the assets of FS), and received 80% of any dividends paid from FS to LTS (and not any income of FS).

(ii) *Example 2.*—(A) *Facts.* TFC directly owns 25% of the only class of LTS stock on the last day of each of the first three quarters of its taxable year but disposes of its entire interest in LTS during the fourth quarter of its taxable year.

(B) *Results.* Under paragraph (b)(1) and pursuant to the principles of section 958(a), on each of its first three measuring dates, TFC owns 25% of the value of LTS and indirectly owns 6.25% of the value of FS. Under paragraph (g)(3) of this section, if information about the gross income of LTS for each of the first three quarters of its taxable year is available to TFC, LTS is treated as a look-through subsidiary with respect to TFC for those quarters because TFC owned 25% of the value of LTS on the measuring dates with respect to those measuring periods. In that case, under paragraph (b)(2) of this section, in determining whether TFC is a PFIC under section 1297(a), TFC is treated as if it held 25% of each of LTS's assets and received directly 25% of the gross income of LTS on each of the first three measuring dates in its taxable year. For each of its first three quarters, if LTS is treated as a look-through subsidiary with respect to TFC under paragraph (g)(3) of this section, then TFC is treated as if it held a 6.25% interest in the stock of FS (and not the assets of FS) and received 25% of any dividends paid from FS to LTS (and not any income of FS). Under paragraph (g)(3) of this section, if information about the gross income of LTS for each of the first three quarters of its taxable year is not available to TFC, then LTS is not a look-through subsidiary with respect to TFC.

(iii) *Example 3.*—(A) *Facts.* TFC directly owns 100% of the only class of LTS stock for TFC's and LTS's entire taxable year. TFC sells one item of property described in section 954(c)(1)(B)(i) for a gain of $25x and another for a loss of $10x, and no exception from passive income applies to either amount. During the taxable year, FS sells one item of property described in section 954(c)(1)(B)(i) for a gain of $50x and another for a loss of $55x; no exception from passive income applies to either amount.

(B) *Results.* Under paragraph (b)(1) of this section and pursuant to the principles of section 958(a), TFC owns 100% of the value of LTS, and TFC indirectly owns 25% of the value of FS. Under paragraph (b) of this section, in determining whether TFC is a PFIC under section 1297(a), TFC is treated as if it held 100% of LTS's assets on each of the measuring dates in its taxable year and received directly 100% of the gross income of LTS for the taxable year. Furthermore, TFC is treated as if it held 25% of each of FS's assets and received directly 25% of the gross income of FS. Pursuant to § 1.1297-1(c)(1)(ii), the excess of gains over losses from property transactions described in section 954(c)(1)(B) is taken into account as gross income for purposes of section 1297, and items of gain or loss of look-through subsidiaries are treated as recognized by a tested foreign corporation. Accordingly, TFC takes into account the net $5x loss from the sales of property by FS. TFC's income from its own sales of property constitutes passive income pursuant to § 1.1297-1(c) and section 954(c)(1)(B), although, pursuant to § 1.1297-1(c)(1)(ii), only the excess of gains over losses, $15x ($25x - $10x), is taken into account as gross income for purposes of section 1297. As a result, TFC's income (including the $5x loss from FS), all of which is passive income, equals $10x ($15x - $5x) of gross income.

(c) *Elimination of certain intercompany assets and income.*—(1) *General rule for asset test.*—(i) *LTS stock.*—For purposes of section 1297(a)(2), a tested foreign corporation does not take into account the value (or adjusted basis) of stock of a look-through subsidiary *(LTS stock)*, including LTS stock that the tested foreign corporation is treated as owning on a measuring date pursuant to section 1297(c) and paragraph (b)(2) or (b)(3) of this section. Furthermore, for purposes of section 1297(a)(2), a tested foreign corporation does not take into account the value (or adjusted basis) of its own stock that it is treated as owning on a measuring date pursuant to section 1297(c) and paragraph (b)(2) or (b)(3) of this section.

(ii) *LTS obligation.*—For purposes of section 1297(a)(2), a tested foreign corporation does not take into account the value (or adjusted basis) of its proportionate share of a direct LTS obligation, an indirect LTS obligation or a TFC obligation that it is treated as owning on a measuring date. The term *direct LTS obligation* means a debt obligation of, lease to, or license to a look-through subsidiary *(LTS debt, LTS lease,* and *LTS license,* respectively, and *LTS obligation* collectively) from the tested foreign corporation that the tested foreign corporation owns on a measuring date, and the term *indirect LTS obligation* means a LTS obligation from a look-through subsidiary that the tested foreign corporation is treated as owning on a measuring date pursuant to section 1297(c) and paragraph (b)(2) or (b)(3) of this section. The term *TFC obligation* means a debt obligation of, lease to, or a license to the tested foreign corporation from a look-through subsidiary that the tested foreign corporation is treated as owning on a measuring date pursuant to section 1297(c) and paragraph (b)(2) or (b)(3) of this section. The tested foreign corporation's proportionate share of a LTS obligation or a TFC obligation is the value (or adjusted basis) of the item multiplied by the tested foreign corporation's percentage ownership (by value) in each relevant look-through subsidiary. For purposes of section 1297(a)(2) and § 1.1297-1(d) as applied to a tested foreign corporation, property subject to a LTS lease or LTS license or a lease or license to the tested foreign corporation is characterized as either producing passive income or non-passive income (or both) by taking into account the activities of the qualified affiliates (as defined in paragraph (e)(2) of this section) of the entity that owns the property. For this purpose, the activities of the entity that owns the property that is subject to the lease or license are not taken into account to the extent that they relate to the lease or license.

(2) *General rule for income test.*—(i) *LTS stock.*—For purposes of section 1297(a)(1), a tested foreign corporation does not take into account dividends derived with respect to LTS stock, including dividends that the tested foreign corporation is treated as receiving on a measuring date pursuant to section 1297(c) and paragraph (b)(2) or (b)(3) of this section; provided that, notwithstanding the foregoing, a tested foreign corporation takes into account dividends that are attributable to income that was not treated as received directly by the tested foreign corporation pursuant to paragraph (b)(2) of this section. For this purpose, the rules of § 1.1297-1(c)(4)(iv)(A) apply to

determine the earnings and profits from which a dividend is paid, substituting the term "look-through subsidiary" for "related person."

(ii) *LTS obligation.*—For purposes of section 1297(a)(1), a tested foreign corporation does not take into account its proportionate share of interest, rents, or royalties derived with respect to direct or indirect LTS obligations or TFC obligations. The tested foreign corporation's proportionate share of interest, rents, or royalties is the amount of the item multiplied by the tested foreign corporation's percentage ownership (by value) in each relevant look-through subsidiary.

(3) *Partnerships.*—For purposes of section 1297(a)(1) and (a)(2), the principles of paragraphs (c)(1) and (2) of this section apply with respect to ownership interests in, debt of, and leases or licenses to a look-through partnership (as defined in paragraph (g)(4) of this section), and with respect to distributions and the distributive shares of income from a look-through partnership and interest, rents, or royalties derived with respect to the debt, leases or licenses of a look-through partnership.

(4) *Examples.*—The following examples illustrate the rules of this paragraph (c). For purposes of these examples, USP is a domestic corporation; USP owns 30% of TFC; TFC, LTS, LTS1, LTS2, and FS are foreign corporations that are not controlled foreign corporations within the meaning of section 957(a); FPS is a foreign partnership; and TFC, LTS1, and LTS2 measure assets for purposes of section 1297(a)(2) based on value.

(i) *Example 1.*—(A) *Facts.* TFC directly owns 80% of the only class of LTS stock for TFC's and LTS's entire taxable year, and LTS is a look-through subsidiary (as defined in paragraph (g)(3) of this section) with respect to TFC. LTS owns 25% of the only class of FS stock, and FS is a look-through subsidiary with respect to LTS. Pursuant to the principles of section 958(a), TFC owns 80% of the value of LTS, LTS owns 25% of the value of FS, and TFC indirectly owns 20% of the value of FS. During the first quarter of the taxable year, LTS received a $20x dividend from FS.

(B) *Results*—*(1) LTS.* Under paragraph (c)(1)(i) of this section, for purposes of applying section 1297(a)(2) to LTS, LTS's assets do not include the stock of FS. Under paragraph (c)(2)(i) of this section, for purposes of applying section 1297(a)(1) to LTS, LTS's income does not include the $20x dividend from FS.

(2) TFC. Under paragraph (c)(1)(i) of this section, for purposes of applying section 1297(a)(2) to TFC, TFC's assets do not include the stock of LTS. Under paragraph (b)(2)(ii)(A) of this section, for purposes of applying section 1297(a)(1) to TFC, TFC is treated as receiving directly the income of LTS. Because TFC indirectly owns less than 25% of FS, FS is not a look-through subsidiary with respect to TFC and, therefore, TFC's assets include the value of TFC's 20% interest in the stock of FS and do not include 20% of FS's assets. Similarly, TFC is treated as if it received $16x (80% x $20x) of the $20x dividend paid from FS to LTS (and not any income of FS). Because the dividend constitutes gross income to LTS (although it is eliminated for purposes of applying section 1297(a)(1) to LTS), TFC is treated as receiving the dividend from FS directly under paragraph (b)(2)(ii)(A) of this section. Because the dividend is from a subsidiary that is not a look-through subsidiary with respect to TFC, paragraph (c)(2)(i) of this section does not apply to eliminate the $16x dividend for purposes of section 1297(a).

(ii) *Example 2.*—(A) *Facts.* TFC directly owns 40% of the value of LTS1 stock on each of the measuring dates, and thus is treated under paragraph (b)(1) of this section as owning 40% of LTS1's assets on each of the measuring dates. TFC's assets include a loan to LTS1 with a balance of $1,000x on each of the measuring dates. During the first quarter of the taxable year, TFC received $20x of dividends from LTS1, which were attributable to income of LTS1 treated as received directly by TFC pursuant to paragraph (b)(2) of this section, and $30x of interest on the loan, both of which were paid in cash.

(B) *Results.* Under paragraph (c)(1)(i) of this section, for purposes of applying section 1297(a), TFC's assets do not include the stock of LTS1, and TFC's income does not include the $20x of dividends received from LTS1 pursuant to paragraph (c)(2)(i) of this section. Similarly, under paragraph (c)(1)(ii) of this section TFC's assets include only $600x ($1,000x loan – (40% x $1,000x)) of the loan to LTS1, and under paragraph (c)(2)(ii) of this section, TFC's income includes only $18x ($30x interest – (40% x $30x)) of the interest from LTS1. However, TFC's assets include the entire $50x of cash ($20x of dividends and $30x of interest) received from LTS1.

(iii) *Example 3.*—(A) *Facts.* The facts are the same as in paragraph (c)(4)(ii)(A) of this section (the facts in *Example 2*), except that TFC also directly owns 30% of the value of LTS2 stock on each of the measuring dates, and thus is treated under paragraph (b)(1) of this section as owning 30% of LTS2's assets, and LTS1's assets also include a loan to LTS2 with a balance of $200x on each of the measuring dates. During the first quarter of the taxable year, LTS1 received $5x of interest on the loan, which was paid in cash.

(B) *Results.* The results are the same as in paragraph (c)(4)(ii)(B) of this section (the results in *Example 2*), except that TFC's assets also do not include the stock of LTS2. Similarly, although TFC would be treated under paragraph (b)(2) of this section as owning $80x (40% x $200x) of the LTS1 loan to LTS2, under paragraph (c)(1)(ii) of this section TFC does not take into account its proportionate share of an indirect LTS obligation and accordingly, TFC does not take into account $24x (30% x $80x) of the loan to LTS2. As a result, TFC's assets include only $56x ($80x-$24x) of the LTS1 loan to LTS2. Furthermore, although TFC would be treated under paragraph (b)(2) of this section as receiving $2x (40% x $5x) of the interest received by LTS1 from LTS2, under paragraph (c)(2)(ii) of this section TFC does not take into account its proportionate share of interest with respect to an indirect LTS obligation and thus, TFC does not take into account $0.60x (30% x $2x) of the interest received by LTS1. Accordingly, TFC's income includes only $1.40x ($2x-$0.60x) of the interest from LTS2. Furthermore, TFC's assets include $2x (40% x $5x) of LTS1's cash received from LTS2.

(iv) *Example 4.*—(A) *Facts.* TFC directly owns 80% of the value of LTS1 stock on each of the measuring dates, and thus is treated under paragraph (b)(1) of this section as owning 80% of LTS1's assets on each of the measuring dates. TFC also directly owns 50% of the value in FPS on each of the measuring dates. LTS1's assets include the remaining 50% of the value in FPS and a loan to FPS with a balance of $500x on each of the measuring dates. FPS's assets include a loan to TFC with a balance of $1000x on each of the measuring dates. During the first measuring period of the taxable year, FPS received $30x of interest from TFC, and LTS1 received $15x of interest from FPS, both of which were paid in cash. During the last measuring period of the taxable year, FPS received $80x of income from an unrelated person in cash and distributed $60x of such income in cash to TFC and LTS1 in proportion to their interests in FPS.

(B) *Results.* Under paragraph (c)(1)(i) and (ii) of this section, for purposes of applying section 1297(a), TFC's assets do not include the stock of LTS1, the interests in FPS owned by TFC directly and through LTS1, any of the loan by FPS to TFC, or any of the loan by LTS1 to FPS. Similarly, under paragraph (c)(2)(i) and (ii) of this section, TFC's income does not include any of the $30x of interest received by FPS from TFC, any of the $15x of interest received by LTS1 from FPS, or any of the $60x of distributions received by TFC and LTS1 from FPS. However, on each of the measuring dates, TFC's assets include $27x ((50% x $30x) + (80% x 50% x $30x)) of the $30 of cash received by FPS from TFC and $12x (80% x $15x) of the $15x of cash received by LTS1 from FPS. Moreover, on the last measuring date of the taxable year, TFC's assets include $18x ((50% x $20x) + (80% x 50% x $20x)) of the $20x ($80x - $60x) of cash received by FPS from the unrelated person and retained by FPS and $54x ((50% x $60x) + (80% x 50% x $60x)) of the $60x cash received by FPS from the unrelated person and distributed. Furthermore, TFC's income includes $72x ((50% x $80x) + (80% x 50% x $80x)) of the $80x of income received by FPS from an unrelated person.

(v) *Example 5.*—(A) *Facts.* TFC directly owns 80% of the value of the stock of LTS1 and 60% of the value of the stock of LTS2 on each of the measuring dates, and thus is treated under paragraph (b)(1) of this section as owning 80% of LTS1's assets and 60% of LTS2's assets on each of the measuring dates. TFC's assets include a license for the use of its intangible property by LTS1 with a value of $5,000x on each of the measuring dates, LTS1's assets include a sub-license of such license to LTS2 with a value of $2,000x on each of the measuring dates, and LTS2's assets include a lease of its building to LTS1 with a value of $4,000x on each of the measuring dates. LTS1 and LTS2 each use the intangible property that is the subject of the license and sublicense in its respective trade or business, and LTS1 uses the building in its trade or business. During the last quarter of the taxable year, TFC received a royalty of $500x from LTS1 with respect to the license, and LTS1 received a royalty of $200x from LTS2 with respect to the sub-license, both of which were paid in cash. LTS2 received $100x of rent paid in cash from LTS1 during each quarter of the taxable year with respect to the building lease.

(B) *Results*—*(1) Asset test.* Under paragraph (c) of this section, for purposes of applying section 1297(a)(2) to TFC's final measuring period, the following analysis applies. TFC's assets do not include the stock of LTS1 and LTS2. Similarly, TFC's assets include only $1,000x ($5,000x license – (80% x $5,000x)) of the license to LTS1. However, TFC's assets include the entire $500x of cash it received from LTS1 as a result of the royalty. Moreover, although TFC would be treated under paragraph (b)(2) of this section as owning $1,600x (80% x $2,000x) of the LTS1 sub-license to LTS2, under paragraph (c)(1)(ii) of this section TFC does not take into account its proportionate share of an indirect LTS obligation, and accordingly TFC does not take into account $960x (60% x $1,600x) of LTS1's sub-license to LTS2. As a result, TFC's assets include $640x ($1,600x - $960x) of the sub-license. In addition, TFC's assets include $160x (80% x $200x) of LTS1's cash received from LTS2 as a result of the royalty to LTS1. Similarly, although TFC would be treated under paragraph (b)(2) of this section as owning $2,400x (60% x $4,000x) of the LTS2 lease to LTS1, under paragraph (c)(1)(ii) of this section TFC does not take into account $1,920x (80% x $2,400x) of the LTS2 building lease, and accordingly, its assets include $480x ($2,400x - $1,920x) of the lease. TFC's assets also include $240x (60% x $100x x 4) of LTS2's cash received from LTS1 as a result of the rental payment to LTS2.

(2) *Income test.* Under paragraph (c)(2)(ii) of this section, because TFC does not take into account its proportionate share of a direct LTS obligation, TFC's income includes only $100x ($500x royalty – (80% x $500x)) of the royalties from LTS1. Furthermore, although TFC would be treated under paragraph (b)(2) of this section as receiving $160x (80% x $200x) of the royalty received by LTS1 from LTS2, under paragraph (c)(2)(ii) of this section TFC does not take into account its proportionate share of royalties derived with respect to an indirect LTS obligation, and accordingly TFC does not take into account $96x (60% x $160x) of the royalty received by LTS1. As a result, TFC's income includes only $64x ($160x - $96x) of the royalty from LTS2. Similarly, although TFC would be treated under paragraph (b)(2) of this section as receiving $240x (60% x $100x x 4) of the rent received by LTS2 from LTS1, under paragraph (c)(2)(ii) of this section TFC does not take into account its proportionate share of rent derived with respect to an indirect LTS obligation, and accordingly TFC does not take into account $192x (80% x $240) of the rent received by LTS2. Therefore, TFC's income includes only $48 ($240x - $192x) of the rent received from LTS1.

(3) *Treatment of intangible and rental property.* For purposes of determining whether the intangible property that TFC owns and the building that TFC is treated as owning under paragraph (b)(2) of this section is held in the production of passive income, the activities performed by TFC and its qualified affiliates with respect to the property are taken into account under paragraphs (c)(1)(ii) and (e) of this section. Because TFC is the common parent of the affiliated group (as determined under paragraph (e)(2) of this section) that includes LTS1 and LTS2, LTS1 and LTS2 are qualified affiliates of TFC and the activities of their officers and employees with respect to the intangible property and building are taken into account to determine whether the building and intangible property would be treated as passive assets.

(d) *Related person determination for purposes of section 1297(b)(2)(C).*—(1) *General rule.*—For purposes of section 1297(b)(2)(C), interest, dividends, rents or royalties received or accrued by a look-through subsidiary (and treated as received directly by a tested foreign corporation pursuant to section 1297(c) and paragraph (b)(2) of this section) are considered received or accrued from a related person only if the payor of the interest, dividend, rent or royalty is a related person (within the meaning of section 954(d)(3)) with respect to the look-through subsidiary, taking into account § 1.1297-1(c)(1)(i)(D). Similarly, for purposes of 1297(b)(2)(C), interest, dividends, rents or royalties received or accrued by a look-through partnership (and treated as received directly by a tested foreign corporation pursuant to paragraph (b)(3) of this section) are considered received or accrued from a related person only if the payor of the interest, dividend, rent or royalty is a related person (within the meaning of section 954(d)(3)) with respect to the look-through partnership, taking into account § 1.1297-1(c)(1)(i)(D).

(2) *Example.*—The following example illustrates the rule of this paragraph (d).

(i) *Facts.* USP is a domestic corporation that owns 30% of TFC. TFC directly owns 30% of the value of FS1 stock, and thus under paragraph (b) of this section is treated as owning 30% of FS1's assets and earning 30% of FS1's gross income. The remaining FS1 stock is owned by an unrelated foreign person. FS1 directly owns 60% of the vote of FS2 stock and 20% of the value of FS2 stock. The remaining vote and value of FS2 stock are owned by an unrelated foreign person. TFC, FS1, and FS2 are foreign corporations that are not controlled foreign corporations within the meaning of section 957(a). FS1 receives a $100x dividend from FS2.

(ii) *Results.* Pursuant to section 1297(c) and paragraph (b)(2) of this section, TFC is treated as receiving directly $30x of the dividend income received by FS1. FS2 is a related person (within the meaning of section 954(d)(3)) with respect to FS1 for purposes of section 1297(b)(2)(C) because FS1 owns more than 50% of the vote of FS2. FS2 is not a related person (within the meaning of section 954(d)(3)) with respect to TFC for purposes of section 1297(b)(2)(C) because TFC indirectly does not own more than 50% of the vote or value of the FS2 stock. Under paragraph (d)(1) of this section, for purposes of determining whether the dividend income received by FS1 is subject to the exception in section 1297(b)(2)(C) for purposes of testing the PFIC status of TFC, the dividend is treated as received from a related person because FS1 and FS2 are related persons within the meaning of section 1297(b)(2)(C). Therefore, to the extent the dividend income received by FS1 would be properly allocable to income of FS2 that is not passive income, the dividend income that TFC is treated as receiving under section 1297(c) and paragraph (b)(2)(ii) of this section is treated as non-passive income (as defined in § 1.1297-1(f)(4)).

(e) *Treatment of activities of certain look-through subsidiaries and look-through partnerships for purposes of certain exceptions.*—(1) *General rule.*—An item of income received by a tested foreign corporation (including an amount treated as received or accrued pursuant to section 1297(c) and paragraph (b)(2) or (b)(3) of this section) that would be passive income in the hands of the entity that actually received or accrued it is not passive if the item would be excluded from foreign personal holding company income under the following exceptions contained in section 954(c) that are based on whether the entity is engaged in the active conduct of a trade or business, determined by taking into account the activities performed by the officers and employees of the tested foreign corporation as well as activities performed by the officers and employees of any qualified affiliate of the tested foreign corporation—

(i) Section 954(c)(1)(B) and § 1.954-2(e)(1)(ii) and (3)(ii), (iii) and (iv);

(ii) Section 954(c)(1)(C) and § 1.954-2(f)(1)(ii) and (2)(iii)(D);

(iii) Section 954(c)(1)(D) and § 1.954-2(g)(2)(ii);

(iv) Section 954(c)(2)(A) and § 1.954-2(b)(6), (c), and (d);

(v) Section 954(c)(2)(B) and § 1.954-2(b)(2); and

(vi) Section 954(c)(2)(C) and § 1.954-2(h)(3)(ii).

(2) *Qualified affiliate.*—The term *qualified affiliate* means a corporation or a partnership that is included in an affiliated group that includes the tested foreign corporation. For purposes of this paragraph (e), the term *affiliated group* has the meaning provided in section 1504(a), except that—

(i) The affiliated group is determined without regard to sections 1504(a)(2)(A), (b)(2) and (b)(3) ;

(ii) Subject to paragraph (e)(2)(iii) of this section, a partnership is treated as an includible corporation;

(iii) The common parent of the affiliated group is not a domestic corporation or domestic partnership;

(iv) Section 1504(a)(2)(B) is applied by substituting "more than 50 percent" for "at least 80 percent";

(v) A foreign corporation or foreign partnership must be the common parent of the affiliated group;

(vi) Subject to paragraph (e)(2)(vii) of this section, a partnership is included as a member of the affiliated group if more than 50 percent of the value of its capital interests or profits interests is owned by one or more corporations or partnerships that are included in the affiliated group; and

(vii) A corporation or a partnership that is not the common parent of an affiliated group is included in the affiliated group only if it would be a look-through subsidiary or look-through partnership, as applicable, of the common parent if the common parent were a tested foreign corporation.

(3) *Examples.*—The following examples illustrate the rule of this paragraph (e).

(i) *Example 1.*—(A) *Facts.* USP is a domestic corporation that directly owns 20% of the outstanding stock of FS1. The remaining 80% of the outstanding stock of FS1 is directly owned by a foreign person that is not related to USP. FS1 directly owns 100% of the value of the outstanding stock of FS2 and directly owns 80% of the value of the outstanding stock of FS3. The remaining 20% of the value of the outstanding stock of FS3 is directly owned by a foreign person that is not related to USP. FS2 directly owns 80% of the value of the outstanding stock of FS4. The remaining 20% of the value of the outstanding stock of FS4 is directly owned by a foreign person that is not related to USP. FS1, FS2, FS3 and FS4 are all organized in Country A and are not controlled foreign corporations within the meaning of section 957(a). FS4 owns real property that is leased to a person that is not a related person, but does not perform any activities. FS1 and FS2 also do not perform any activities. Officers and employees of FS3 in Country A perform activities with respect to the real property of FS4 that, if performed by officers or employees of FS4, would allow the rental income in the hands of FS4 to qualify for the exception from foreign personal holding company income in section 954(c)(2)(A) and § 1.954-2(b)(6) and (c)(1)(ii).

(B) *Results*—(1) *Qualified affiliates.* FS1 is the common parent of the affiliated group (as determined under paragraph (e)(2) of this section) that includes FS2, FS3, and FS4 because (i) FS1 owns more than 50% by value of FS2 and FS3, (ii) FS2 owns more than 50% by value of FS4, and (iii) FS2, FS3, and FS4 would be look-through subsidiaries with respect to FS1 if FS1 were the tested foreign corporation. Accordingly, each of FS1, FS2, FS3 and FS4 are qualified affiliates (as determined under paragraph (e)(2) of this section) with respect to the other members of the group for purposes of determining whether FS1, FS2, FS3, or FS4 is a "PFIC."

(2) *FS1 and FS2.* Under this paragraph (e), for purposes of determining whether the rental income actually received by FS4 with respect to the real property owned and rented by FS4 and treated under section 1297(c) and paragraph (b)(2) of this section as received directly by FS1 or by FS2, respectively, is passive income for purposes of section 1297, the activities of FS3 are taken into account because FS3 is a qualified affiliate of FS1 and FS2, respectively. Thus, the exception in section 954(c)(2)(A) would apply, and the rental income treated as received by FS1 or by FS2, respectively, would be treated as non-passive income for purposes of determining whether FS1 or FS2 is a PFIC.

(3) *FS4.* Under this paragraph (e), for purposes of determining whether the rental income received by FS4 with respect to the real property owned and rented by FS4 is passive income for purposes of section 1297, the activities of FS3 are taken into account, because FS3 is a qualified affiliate of FS4. Thus, the exception in section 954(c)(2)(A) would apply, and the rental income received by FS4 would be treated as non-passive income for purposes of determining whether FS4 is a PFIC.

(ii) *Example 2.*—(A) *Facts.* The facts are the same as in paragraph (e)(3)(i)(A) of this section (the facts in *Example 1*), except that FS2 also owns real property that is leased to a person that is not a related person, and the officers and employees of FS2 in Country A engage in activities that would allow rental income received by FS2 with respect to its real property to qualify for the exception in section 954(c)(2)(A) and § 1.954-2(b)(6) and § 1.954-2(c)(1)(iv), relying on the rule in § 1.954-2(c)(2)(ii) that provides that an organization is substantial in relation to rents if active leasing expenses equal or exceed 25% of adjusted leasing profit. However, the active leasing expenses of FS1 are less than 25% of its adjusted leasing profit, which includes the rental income of FS4 treated as received directly by FS1 as well as the rental income of FS2 treated as received directly by FS1.

(B) *Results.* Because FS2's rental income constitutes non-passive income as a result of the application of § 1.1297-1(c)(1)(i)(A) and section 954(c)(2)(A), it is treated as non-passive income that FS1 is treated as receiving directly under section 1297(c) and paragraph (b)(2) of this section for purposes of determining whether FS1 is a PFIC, and accordingly, it is not necessary to rely on paragraph (e) of this section.

(iii) *Example 3.*—(A) *Facts.* The facts are the same as in paragraph (e)(3)(i)(A) of this section (the facts in *Example 1*), except that USP directly owns 60% of the outstanding stock of FS1.

(B) *Results.* Under paragraph (e)(2)(iii) of this section, USP cannot be the common parent of an affiliated group for purposes of paragraph (e)(2) of this section because it is a domestic corporation. Because FS1 is a foreign corporation, FS1 may be the common parent of an affiliated group for purposes of paragraph (e)(2) of this section. The results therefore are the same as in paragraph (e)(3)(i)(B) of this section (the results in Example 1).

(f) *Gain on disposition of a look-through subsidiary or look-through partnership.*—(1) [Reserved].

(2) *Amount of gain taken into account from disposition of look-through subsidiary.*—For purposes of section 1297(a)(1), section 1298(b)(3), and § 1.1298-2, the amount of gain that is taken into account by a tested foreign corporation from the tested foreign corporation's direct disposition of stock of a look-through subsidiary, or an indirect disposition resulting from the disposition of stock of a look-through subsidiary by other look-through subsidiaries or by look-through partnerships, is the residual gain. The residual gain equals the total gain recognized by the tested foreign corporation (including gain treated as recognized by the tested foreign corporation pursuant to section 1297(c) and paragraph (b)(2) or (b)(3) of this section) from the disposition of the stock of the look-through subsidiary reduced (but not below zero) by unremitted earnings. *Unremitted earnings* are the excess (if any) of the aggregate income (if any) taken into account by the tested foreign corporation pursuant to section 1297(c) and paragraph (b)(2) or (b)(3) of this section with respect to the stock of the disposed-of look-through subsidiary (including with respect to any other look-through subsidiary, to the extent it is owned by the tested foreign corporation indirectly through the disposed-of look-through subsidiary) over the aggregate dividends (if any) received by the tested foreign corporation from the disposed-of look-through subsidiary with respect to the stock, determined without regard to paragraph (c)(2)(i) of this section. For purposes of this paragraph (f)(2), the amount of gain derived from the disposition of stock of a look-through subsidiary and income of and dividends received from the look-through subsidiary is determined on a share-by-share basis under a reasonable method.

(3) *Characterization of residual gain as passive income.*—For purposes of section 1297(a)(1), section 1298(b)(3), and § 1.1298-2, the residual gain from the direct or indirect disposition of stock of a look-through subsidiary is characterized as passive income or non-passive income based on the relative amounts of passive assets and non-passive assets (as defined in § 1.1297-1(f)(5) and (3), respectively) of the disposed-of look-through subsidiary (and any other look-through subsidiary to the extent owned indirectly through the look-through subsidiary) treated as held by the tested foreign corporation on the date of the disposition of the look-through subsidiary. For the purpose of this paragraph (f)(3), the relative amounts of passive assets and non-passive assets held by the look-through subsidiary are measured under the same method (value or adjusted bases) used to measure the assets of the tested foreign corporation for purposes of section 1297(a)(2).

(4) *Gain taken into account from disposition of 25%-owned partnerships and look-through partnerships.*—(i) *Section 954(c)(4) partnerships.*—The amount of gain derived from a tested foreign corporation's direct or indirect (through a look-through subsidiary or look-through partnership) disposition of partnership interests in a partnership described in section 954(c)(4) (treating the tested foreign corporation as if it were a controlled foreign corporation) that is taken into account by the tested foreign corporation for purposes of section 1297(a)(1), section 1298(b)(3), and § 1.1298-2 is determined under section 954(c)(4).

(ii) *Look-through partnerships.*—In the case of a look-through partnership that is not described in paragraph (f)(4)(i) of this section, the principles of paragraphs (f)(2) and (f)(3) of this section apply to determine the amount and characterization of gain derived from a tested foreign corporation's direct or indirect (through a look-through subsidiary or look-through partnership) disposition of partnership interests of the look-through partnership that is taken into account by the tested foreign corporation for purposes of section 1297(a)(1), section 1298(b)(3), and § 1.1298-2.

(5) *Examples.*—The following examples illustrate the rules of this paragraph (f). For purposes of the examples in this paragraph (f)(5), USP is a domestic corporation, TFC and FS are foreign corporations that are not controlled foreign corporations within the meaning of section 957(a), and USP, TFC, and FS each has a single class of stock with 100 shares outstanding and a calendar taxable year.

(i) *Example 1.*—(A) *Facts.* USP owned 30% of the outstanding stock of TFC throughout Years 1, 2, 3, and 4. In Year 1, TFC purchased 5 shares of FS stock, representing 5% of the stock of FS, from an unrelated person. On the first day of Year 3, TFC purchased 20 shares of FS stock, representing 20% of the stock of FS, from an unrelated person. TFC owned 25% of the outstanding stock of FS throughout Years 3 and 4. Before Year 3, TFC did not include any amount in income with respect to FS under section 1297(c)(2). During Years 3 and 4, for purposes of section 1297(a)(1), TFC included in income, in the aggregate, $40x of income with respect to FS under section 1297(c) and paragraph (b)(2) of this section. TFC did not receive dividends from FS during Year 1, 2, 3, or 4. For purposes of section 1297(a)(2), TFC measures its assets based on their fair market value as provided under section 1297(e). On the last day of Year 4, TFC recognizes a loss with respect to the sale of 5 shares of FS stock, and a $110x gain with respect to the sale of 20 shares of FS stock. On the date of the sale, FS owns non-passive assets with an aggregate fair market value of $150x, and passive assets with an aggregate fair market value of $50x.

(B) *Results*. For purposes of applying section 1297(a)(1) to TFC for Year 4, TFC must take into account $78x of residual gain, as provided by paragraph (f)(2) of this section, which equals the amount by which the $110x gain recognized on the sale of 20 shares in FS exceeds the aggregate pro rata share of $32x income ($40x x 20/25) taken into account by TFC with respect to the 20 shares in FS under section 1297(c) and paragraph (b)(2) of this section during Years 3 and 4. There is zero residual gain on the sale of 5 shares of FS stock because they were sold at a loss. Under paragraph (f)(3) of this section, $58.50x of the residual gain is non-passive income ($78x x ($150x/$200x)) and $19.50x is passive income ($78x x ($50x/$200x)).

(ii) *Example 2*.—(A) *Facts*. The facts are the same as in paragraph (f)(5)(i)(A) of this section (the facts in *Example 1*), except that in Year 1, TFC purchased 15 shares of FS stock, representing 15% of the stock of FS, from an unrelated person, and on the first day of Year 3, TFC purchased an additional 15 shares of FS stock, representing 15% of the stock of FS, from an unrelated person, and on the last day of Year 4, TFC recognizes gain of $10x of the sale of 15 shares of FS stock purchased in Year 1, and gain of $60x on the sale of the other 15 shares of FS stock purchased in Year 3.

(B) *Results*. For purposes of applying section 1297(a)(1) to TFC for Year 4, TFC must take into account $40x of residual gain with respect to the 15 shares acquired in Year 3, as provided by paragraph (f)(2) of this section, which equals the amount by which the $60x gain recognized on the sale of those 15 shares exceeds the aggregate pro rata share of $20x income ($40x x 15/30) taken into account by TFC with respect to those 15 shares in FS under section 1297(c)(2) during Years 3 and 4. There is zero residual gain on the sale of the 15 shares of FS stock acquired in Year 1 because the $10x of gain does not exceed the aggregate pro rata share of $20x income taken into account by TFC with respect to those 15 shares of FS under section 1297(c) and paragraph (b)(2) of this section. Under paragraph (f)(3) of this section, $30x of the residual gain is non-passive income ($40x x ($150x/$200x)) and $10x is passive income ($40x x ($50x/$200x)).

(iii) *Example 3*.—(A) *Facts*. The facts are the same as in paragraph (f)(5)(ii)(A) of this section (the facts in *Example 2*), except that TFC received, in the aggregate, $20x of dividends from FS during Year 2.

(B) *Results*. The results are the same as in paragraph (f)(5)(ii)(B) of this section (the results in *Example 2*) with respect to the 15 shares acquired in Year 3 ($40x of residual gain attributable to the 15 shares acquired in Year 3). For purposes of applying section 1297(a)(1) to TFC for Year 4, TFC must also take into account $10x of residual gain with respect to the 15 shares acquired in Year 1. As provided by paragraph (f)(2) of this section, the residual gain equals the amount by which the $10x gain recognized on the sale of those 15 shares exceeds the unremitted earnings with respect to those shares. The unremitted earnings with respect to the 15 shares acquired in Year 1 are $0x, the amount by which the pro rata share of aggregate income ($20x) taken into account by TFC with respect to those 15 shares of FS stock under section 1297(c) and paragraph (b)(2) of this section in Years 3 and 4 exceeds the aggregate pro rata amount of dividends with respect to those 15 shares of FS stock ($20x) received by TFC from FS in Year 2. Total residual gain therefore is $50x ($40x + $10x). Under paragraph (f)(3) of this section, $37.50x of the residual gain is non-passive income ($50x x ($150x/$200x)) and $12.50x is passive income ($50x x ($50x/$200x)).

(g) *Definitions*.—The following definitions apply for purposes of § 1.1297-1 and this section:

(1) *Direct LTS obligation*.—The term *direct LTS obligation* has the meaning provided in paragraph (c)(1)(ii) of this section.

(2) *Indirect LTS obligation*.—The term *indirect LTS obligation* has the meaning provided in paragraph (c)(1)(ii) of this section.

(3) *Look-through subsidiary*.—The term *look-through subsidiary* means, with respect to a tested foreign corporation, a corporation as to which the asset test of paragraph (g)(3)(i) and the income test of paragraph (g)(3)(ii) of this section are satisfied on each measuring date during the taxable year of a tested foreign corporation. If a corporation satisfies both the asset test of paragraph (g)(3)(i) and the income test of paragraph (g)(3)(ii)(B) for some but not all measuring periods within the taxable year of a tested foreign corporation, the subsidiary is treated as a look-through subsidiary only for those measuring periods in which both tests are satisfied.

(i) For purposes of section 1297(a)(2) and paragraph (b)(2)(i) of this section, a corporation at least 25 percent of the value of the stock of which is owned (as determined under paragraph (b)(1) of this section) by the tested foreign corporation on the measuring date (as defined in § 1.1297-1(f)(1));

(ii) For purposes of section 1297(a)(1), either—

(A) For the taxable year, a corporation with respect to which the average percentage ownership (which is equal to the percentage ownership (by value) (as determined under paragraph (b)(1) of this section) on each measuring date during the taxable year, divided by the number of measuring dates in the year) by the tested foreign corporation during the tested foreign corporation's taxable year is at least 25 percent; or

(B) For a measuring period (as defined in § 1.1297-1(f)(2)), a corporation at least 25 percent of the value of the stock of which is owned (as determined under paragraph (b)(1) of this section) by the tested foreign corporation on the measuring date, provided all items of gross income of the corporation for each of the measuring periods in the taxable year for which the tested foreign corporation owns at least 25 percent of the value (as determined under paragraph (b)(1) of this section) on the relevant measuring dates can be established; and

(iii) For purposes of paragraph (f) of this section and § 1.1298-2, a corporation at least 25 percent of the value of the stock of which is owned (as determined under paragraph (b)(1) of this section) by the tested foreign corporation immediately before the disposition of stock of the corporation.

(4) *Look-through partnership*.—(i) *In general*.—The term *look-through partnership* means, with respect to a tested foreign corporation—

(A) A partnership that would be a look-through subsidiary (as defined in paragraph (g)(3) of this section) if such partnership were a corporation; or

(B) A partnership that is not described in paragraph (g)(4)(i)(A) of this section, if the tested foreign corporation satisfies both of the active partner tests set forth in paragraphs (g)(4)(ii)(A) and (B) of this section on the measurement date or for the taxable year, as applicable, unless an election is made under paragraph (g)(4)(iii) of this section.

(ii) *Active partner test*.—(A) *Partnership interest under asset test*.—For purposes of paragraph (b)(3)(i) of this section, paragraph (g)(4)(i)(B) of this section applies for the measuring period only if the tested foreign corporation would not be a PFIC if section 1297(a)(1) and (2) and the regulations thereunder were applied to the tested foreign corporation without regard to any partnership interest owned by the tested foreign corporation that is not a partnership described in paragraph (g)(4)(i)(A) of this section. For purposes of the preceding sentence, the active partner test is applied on the measurement date (as defined in § 1.1297-1(f)(1)).

(B) *Partnership income under income test*.—For purposes of paragraph (b)(3)(ii) of this section, paragraph (g)(4)(i)(B) of this section applies for the taxable year of the tested foreign corporation or for a measuring period (as defined in § 1.1297-1(f)(2)), as applicable, only if the tested foreign corporation would not be a PFIC if section 1297(a)(1) and (2) and the regulations thereunder were applied to the tested foreign corporation without regard to any partnership interest owned by the tested foreign corporation that is not a partnership described in paragraph (g)(4)(i)(A) of this section. For purposes of the preceding sentence, the active partner test is applied on the measuring date (as defined in § 1.1297-1(f)(1)) or for the taxable year, as applicable using the same period that was used under paragraph (g)(3)(ii) of this section.

(iii) *Election*.—For any taxable year, an election may be made with respect to a partnership described in paragraph (g)(4)(i)(B) of this section to not apply the provisions of this paragraph (g)(4) to such partnership.

(iv) *Examples*.—The following examples illustrate the rules of this paragraph (g)(4). For purposes of the examples in this paragraph (g)(4)(iv), TFC is a foreign corporation that is not a controlled foreign corporation; FC1 and FC2 are foreign corporations that are not controlled foreign corporations; FPS is a foreign partnership; TFC owns 100% of the single class of stock of FC1 and FC2; FC2 owns 10% of the value of FPS, and the remaining 90% of FPS is owned by an unrelated foreign person; and TFC, FC1, FC2, and FPS are all calendar year taxpayers.

(A) *Example 1.*—(1) *Facts.* During Year 1, FC1 generated $100x of non-passive income, FC2 generated $150x of non-passive income, and FPS generated $50x of income. On all of the measurement dates in Year 1, FC1 has assets with a value of $1000x that FC1 uses in its trade or business generating non-passive income, FC2 has assets with a value of $1500x that FC2 uses in its trade or business generating non-passive income, and FPS has assets with a value of $500x.

(2) *Results*—(i) *Active partner test with respect to partnership interest.* Pursuant to section 1297(c) and § 1.1297-2(b)(2), TFC is treated as holding directly the assets held by FC1 and FC2. For purposes of the active partner test under paragraph (g)(4)(ii)(B) of this section, TFC does not take into account its interest in FPS to determine whether it would be a PFIC. Because 100% ($2500x/$2500x) of the assets of FC1 and FC2 that TFC is treated as directly holding, without taking into account the interest in FPS, generates non-passive income, TFC satisfies the active partner test in paragraph (g)(4)(ii)(B) of this section.

(ii) *Active partner test with respect to partnership income.* Pursuant to section 1297(c) and paragraph (b)(2) of this section, TFC is treated as if it received directly its proportionate share of income of FC1 and FC2. For purposes of the active partner test under paragraph (g)(4)(ii)(A) of this section, TFC does not take into account its interest in FPS to determine whether it would be a PFIC. Because 100% ($250x/$250x) of the income of FC1 and FC2 that TFC is treated as directly receiving, without taking into account the interest in FPS, is non-passive income, TFC satisfies the active partner test in paragraph (g)(4)(ii)(A) of this section with respect to the income of FPS.

(iii) *Qualification of look-through partnership.* For purposes of paragraph (b)(3) of this section, FPS qualifies as a look-through partnership because TFC satisfies the active partner tests of both paragraphs (g)(4)(ii)(A) and (B) of this section. Unless an election is made not to treat FPS as a look-through partnership under paragraph (g)(4)(iii) of this section, TFC is treated as receiving directly $5x of income (10% x $50x), TFC's pro rata share of the income of FPS, the character of which is determined at the level of FPS for purposes of section 1297. In addition, TFC is treated as holding directly $50x of FPS's assets (10% x $500x), TFC's proportionate share of the assets held by FPS. The character of those assets as passive or non-passive is determined in the hands of FPS for purposes of section 1297.

(B) *Example 2.*—(1) *Facts.* During Year 1, FC1 generated $50x of passive income, FC2 earned $175x of non-passive income, and FPS generated $50x of income. On all of the measurement dates in Year 1, FC1 has assets with a value of $1100x that produce passive income, and FC2 has assets with a value of $900x that FC2 uses in its trade or business generating non-passive income. The value of FPS is $1000x taking into account its assets and liabilities.

(2) *Results*—(i) *Active partner test with respect to partnership interest.* Pursuant to section 1297(c) and § 1.1297-2(b)(2), TFC is treated as holding directly the assets held by FC1 and FC2. For purposes of the active partner test under paragraph (g)(4)(ii)(B) of this section, TFC does not take into account its interest in FPS to determine whether it would be a PFIC. Accordingly, 55% ($1100x/$2000x) of the assets that TFC is treated as directly holding, without taking into account the interest in FPS, generate passive income.

(ii) *Active partner test with respect to partnership income.* Pursuant to section 1297(c) and § 1.1297-2(b)(2), TFC is treated as if it received directly its proportionate share of income of FC1 and FC2. For purposes of the active partner test under paragraph (g)(4)(ii)(A) of this section, TFC does not take into account its interest in FPS to determine whether it would be a PFIC. Accordingly, 77.8% ($175x/$225x) of the income that TFC is treated as directly receiving, without taking into account the interest in FPS, is non-passive income.

(iii) *Failure to qualify as look-through partnership.* TFC satisfies the active partner test in paragraph (g)(4)(ii)(A) of this section but does not satisfy the active partner test in paragraph (g)(4)(ii) (B) of this section. Therefore, FPS does not qualify as a look-though partnership. Under paragraph (b)(3)(iii) of this section, TFC's share of income with respect to FPS is treated as passive income for purposes of section 1297 and TFC's $100x interest (10% x $1000x) in FPS is treated as a passive asset for purposes of section 1297.

(5) *LTS debt.*—The term *LTS debt* has the meaning provided in paragraph (c)(1)(ii) of this section.

(6) *LTS lease.*—The term *LTS lease* has the meaning provided in paragraph (c)(1)(ii) of this section.

(7) *LTS license.*—The term *LTS license* has the meaning provided in paragraph (c)(1)(ii) of this section.

(8) *LTS obligation.*—The term *LTS obligation* has the meaning provided in paragraph (c)(1)(ii) of this section.

(9) *LTS stock.*—The term *LTS stock* has the meaning provided in paragraph (c)(1)(i) of this section.

(10) *Qualified affiliate.*—The term *qualified affiliate* has the meaning provided in paragraph (e)(2) of this section.

(11) *Residual gain.*—The term *residual gain* has the meaning provided in paragraph (f)(2) of this section.

(12) *TFC obligation.*—The term *TFC obligation* has the meaning provided in paragraph (c)(1)(ii) of this section.

(13) *Unremitted earnings.*—The term *unremitted earnings* has the meaning provided in paragraph (f)(2) of this section.

(h) *Applicability date.*—The rules of this section apply to taxable years of shareholders beginning on or after January 14, 2021. A shareholder may choose to apply such rules for any open taxable year beginning before January 14, 2021, provided that, with respect to a tested foreign corporation, the shareholder consistently applies the provisions of § 1.1291-1(b)(8)(iv) and (b)(8)(v)(A), (B), (C), and (D) and §§ 1.1297-1 (except that consistent treatment is not required with respect to § 1.1297-1(c)(1)(i)(A)), 1.1298-2, and 1.1298-4 for such year and all subsequent years. [Reg. § 1.1297-2.]

☐ [*T.D. 9936, 1-14-2021 (corrected 3-9-2021).*]

Proposed Amendments to Regulation

§ 1.1297-2. Special rules regarding look-through subsidiaries and look-through partnerships.—

* * *

(b) * * *

(2) * * *

(ii) * * *

(A) * * * The exceptions to passive income in section 1297(b)(2) and the relevant exceptions to foreign personal holding company income in sections 954(c) and (h) that are based on whether income is derived in the active conduct of a business or whether a corporation is engaged in the active conduct of a business apply to such income only if the exception would have applied to exclude the income from passive income or foreign personal holding company income in the hands of the subsidiary, determined by taking into account only the activities of the subsidiary except as provided in paragraph (e) of this section. * * *

* * *

(3) * * *

(ii) * * *

(A) * * * The exceptions to passive income in section 1297(b)(2) and the relevant exceptions to foreign personal holding company income in sections 954(c) and (h) that are based on whether income is derived in the active conduct of a business or whether a corporation is engaged in the active conduct of a business apply to such income only if the exception would have applied to exclude the income from passive income or foreign personal holding company income in the hands of the partnership, determined by taking into account only the activities of the partnership except as provided in paragraph (e) of this section. * * *

* * *

(c) * * *

(2) * * *

(i) *LTS stock.*—For purposes of section 1297, a tested foreign corporation does not take into account dividends derived with respect to LTS stock, including dividends that the tested foreign corporation is treated as receiving on a measurement date pursuant to section 1297(c) and paragraphs (b)(2) or (b)(3) of this section. * * *

* * *

(4) * * *

(ii) * * *

(A) * * * During the first quarter of the taxable year, TFC received $20x of dividends from LTS1 and $30x of interest on the loan, both of which were paid in cash.

* * *

(e) * * *

(4) *Active banking business.*—For purposes of § 1.1297-1(c)(2), the activities of the employees of a person that is a related person with respect to a look-through subsidiary or partnership are taken into account to the extent provided in section 954(h)(3)(E).

* * *

(f) *Gain on disposition of a look-through subsidiary or look-through partnership.*—(1) *Stock basis adjustment.*—For purposes of determining gain in paragraph (2) of this paragraph (f), a tested foreign corporation's basis in the stock of a look-through subsidiary is decreased, but not below zero, by the aggregate amount of distributions made by the look-through subsidiary with respect to the look-through subsidiary's stock that are attributable to income of the look-through subsidiary not treated as received directly by the tested foreign corporation pursuant to paragraph (b)(2) of this section.

(2) *Amount of gain taken into account.*—The amount of gain derived from a tested foreign corporation's direct disposition of stock of a look-through subsidiary, or an indirect disposition resulting from the disposition of stock of a look-through subsidiary by other look-through subsidiaries or by look-through partnerships, that is taken into account by the tested foreign corporation for purposes of section 1297(a)(1), section 1298(b)(3), and § 1.1298-2 is the residual gain. The residual gain equals the total gain recognized by the tested foreign corporation (including gain treated as recognized by the tested foreign corporation pursuant to section 1297(c) and paragraph (b)(2) of this section or § 1.1297-1(c)(2)) from the disposition of the stock of the look-through subsidiary reduced (but not below zero) by unremitted earnings. *Unremitted earnings* are the excess (if any) of the aggregate income (if any) taken into account by the tested foreign corporation pursuant to section 1297(c) and paragraph (b)(2) of this section or § 1.1297-1(c)(2) with respect to the stock of the disposed-of look-through subsidiary (including with respect to any other look-through subsidiary, to the extent it is owned by the tested foreign corporation indirectly through the disposed-of look-through subsidiary) over the aggregate dividends (if any) received by the tested foreign corporation from the disposed-of look-through subsidiary with respect to the stock other than dividends described in paragraph (f)(1) of this section. For purposes of this paragraph (f)(2), the amount of gain derived from the disposition of stock of a look-through subsidiary and income of and dividends received from the look-through subsidiary is determined on a share-by-share basis, determined under a reasonable method.

* * *

(h) *Applicability date.*—Except as otherwise provided, the rules of this section apply to taxable years of shareholders beginning on or after January 14, 2021. * * * Paragraphs (b)(2)(ii)(A), (b)(3)(ii)(A), (c)(2)(i), (c)(4)(ii)(A), (e)(4), (f)(1), and (f)(2) of this section apply to taxable years of shareholders beginning on or after [the date these regulations are filed as final regulations in the **Federal Register**]. A shareholder may choose to apply the paragraphs in the preceding sentence for any open taxable year beginning before [the date these regulations are filed as final regulations in the **Federal Register**] without regard to whether the rules of this section are applied consistently, provided that once applied, each rule must be applied for each subsequent taxable year beginning before [the date these regulations are filed as final regulations in the **Federal Register**]. [Prop. Reg. § 1.1297-2.]

[Proposed 1-15-2021.]

§ 1.1297-3. Deemed sale or deemed dividend election by a U.S. person that is a shareholder of a section 1297(e) PFIC.—(a) *In general.*—A shareholder (as defined in § 1.1291-9(j)(3)) of a foreign corporation that is a section 1297(e) passive foreign investment company (PFIC) (as defined in § 1.1291-9(j)(2)(v)) with respect to such shareholder, shall be treated for tax purposes as holding stock in a PFIC and therefore continues to be subject to taxation under section 1291 unless the shareholder makes a purging election under section 1298(b)(1). A purging election under section 1298(b)(1) is made under rules similar to the rules of section 1291(d)(2). Section 1291(d)(2) allows a shareholder to purge the continuing PFIC taint by either making a deemed sale election or a deemed dividend election.

(b) *Application of deemed sale election rules.*—(1) *Eligibility to make the deemed sale election.*—A shareholder of a foreign corporation that is a section 1297(e) PFIC with respect to such shareholder may make a deemed sale election under section 1298(b)(1) by applying the rules of this paragraph (b).

(2) *Effect of the deemed sale election.*—A shareholder making the deemed sale election with respect to a section 1297(e) PFIC shall be treated as having sold all of its stock in the section 1297(e) PFIC for its fair market value on the controlled foreign corporation (CFC) qualification date, as defined in paragraph (d) of this section. A deemed sale under this section is treated as a disposition subject to taxation under section 1291. Thus, the gain from the deemed sale is taxed as an excess distribution received on the CFC qualification date. In the case of an election made by an indirect shareholder, the amount of gain to be recognized and taxed as an excess distribution is the amount of gain that the direct owner of the stock of the PFIC would have realized on an actual sale or disposition of the stock of the PFIC indirectly owned by the shareholder. Any loss realized on the deemed sale is not recognized. After the deemed sale election, the shareholder's stock with respect to which the election was made under this paragraph (b) shall not be treated as stock in a PFIC and the shareholder shall not be subject to taxation under section 1291 with respect to such stock unless the qualified portion of the shareholder's holding period ends, as determined under section 1297(e)(2), and the foreign corporation thereafter qualifies as a PFIC under section 1297(a).

(3) *Time for making the deemed sale election.*—Except as provided in paragraph (e) of this section, a shareholder shall make the deemed sale election under this paragraph (b) and section 1298(b)(1) in the shareholder's original or amended return for the taxable year that includes the CFC qualification date (election year). If the deemed sale election is made in an amended return, the return must be filed by a date that is within three years of the due date, as extended under section 6081, of the original return for the election year.

(4) *Manner of making the deemed sale election.*—A shareholder makes the deemed sale election under this paragraph (b) by filing Form 8621, "Return by a Shareholder of a Passive Foreign Investment Company or Qualified Electing Fund", with the return of the shareholder for the election year, reporting the gain as an excess distribution pursuant to section 1291(a) as if such sale occurred under section 1291(d)(2), and paying the tax and interest due on the excess distribution. A shareholder that makes the deemed sale election after the due date of the return (determined without regard to extensions) for the election year must pay additional interest, pursuant to section 6601, on the amount of underpayment of tax for that year. An electing shareholder that realizes a loss shall report the loss on Form 8621, but shall not recognize the loss.

(5) *Adjustments to basis.*—A shareholder that makes the deemed sale election increases its adjusted basis of the PFIC stock owned directly by the amount of gain recognized on the deemed sale. If the shareholder makes the deemed sale election with respect to a PFIC of which it is an indirect shareholder, the shareholder's adjusted basis of the stock or other property owned directly by the shareholder, through which ownership of the PFIC is attributed to the shareholder, is increased by the amount of gain recognized by the shareholder. In addition, solely for purposes of determining the subsequent treatment under the Internal Revenue Code (Code) and regulations of a shareholder of the stock of the PFIC, the adjusted basis of the direct owner of the stock of the PFIC is increased by the amount of gain recognized on the deemed sale. A shareholder shall not adjust the basis of any stock with respect to which the shareholder realized a loss on the deemed sale, which loss is not recognized under paragraph (b)(2) of this section.

(6) *Treatment of holding period.*—If a shareholder of a foreign corporation has made a deemed sale election, then, for purposes of applying sections 1291 through 1298 to such shareholder after the deemed sale, the shareholder's holding period in the stock of the foreign corporation begins on the CFC qualification date, without regard to whether the shareholder recognized gain on the deemed sale. For other purposes of the Code and regulations, this holding period rule does not apply.

(c) *Application of deemed dividend election rules.*—(1) *Eligibility to make the deemed dividend election.*—A shareholder of a foreign corporation that is a section 1297(e) PFIC with respect to such shareholder may make the deemed dividend election under the rules of this paragraph (c). A deemed dividend election may be made by a shareholder whose pro rata share of the post-1986 earnings and profits of the PFIC attributable to the PFIC stock held on the CFC qualification date is zero.

(2) *Effect of the deemed dividend election.*—A shareholder making the deemed dividend election with respect to a section 1297(e) PFIC

shall include in income as a dividend its pro rata share of the post-1986 earnings and profits of the PFIC attributable to all of the stock it held, directly or indirectly on the CFC qualification date, as defined in paragraph (d) of this section. The deemed dividend is taxed under section 1291 as an excess distribution received on the CFC qualification date. The excess distribution determined under this paragraph (c) is allocated under section 1291(a)(1)(A) only to each day of the shareholder's holding period of the stock during which the foreign corporation qualified as a PFIC. For purposes of the preceding sentence, the shareholder's holding period of the PFIC stock ends on the day before the CFC qualification date. After the deemed dividend election, the shareholder's stock with respect to which the election was made under this paragraph (c) shall not be treated as stock in a PFIC and the shareholder shall not be subject to taxation under section 1291 with respect to such stock unless the qualified portion of the shareholder's holding period ends, as determined under section 1297(e)(2), and the foreign corporation thereafter qualifies as a PFIC under section 1297(a).

(3) *Post-1986 earnings and profits defined.*—(i) *In general.*—(A) *General rule.*—For purposes of this section, the term post-1986 earnings and profits means the post-1986 undistributed earnings, within the meaning of section 902(c)(1) (determined without regard to section 902(c)(3)), as of the day before the CFC qualification date, that were accumulated and not distributed in taxable years of the PFIC beginning after 1986 and during which it was a PFIC, without regard to whether the earnings related to a period during which the PFIC was a CFC.

(B) *Special rule.*—If the CFC qualification date is a day that is after the first day of the taxable year, the term post-1986 earnings and profits means the post-1986 undistributed earnings, within the meaning of section 902(c)(1) (determined without regard to section 902(c)(3)), as of the close of the taxable year that includes the CFC qualification date. For purposes of this computation, only earnings and profits accumulated in taxable years during which the foreign corporation was a PFIC shall be taken into account, but without regard to whether the earnings related to a period during which the PFIC was a CFC.

(ii) *Pro rata share of post-1986 earnings and profits attributable to shareholder's stock.*—(A) *In general.*—A shareholder's pro rata share of the post-1986 earnings and profits of the PFIC attributable to the stock held by the shareholder on the CFC qualification date is the amount of post-1986 earnings and profits of the PFIC accumulated during any portion of the shareholder's holding period ending at the close of the day before the CFC qualification date and attributable, under the principles of section 1248 and the regulations under that section, to the PFIC stock held on the CFC qualification date.

(B) *Reduction for previously taxed amounts.*—A shareholder's pro rata share of the post-1986 earnings and profits of the PFIC does not include any amount that the shareholder demonstrates to the satisfaction of the Commissioner (in the manner provided in paragraph (c)(5)(ii) of this section) was, pursuant to another provision of the law, previously included in the income of the shareholder, or of another U.S. person if the shareholder's holding period of the PFIC stock includes the period during which the stock was held by that other U.S. person.

(4) *Time for making the deemed dividend election.*—Except as provided in paragraph (e) of this section, the shareholder shall make the deemed dividend election under this paragraph (c) and section 1298(b)(1) in the shareholder's original or amended return for the taxable year that includes the CFC qualification date (election year). If the deemed dividend election is made in an amended return, the return must be filed by a date that is within three years of the due date, as extended under section 6081, of the original return for the election year.

(5) *Manner of making the deemed dividend election.*—(i) *In general.*—A shareholder makes the deemed dividend election by filing Form 8621 and the attachment to Form 8621 described in paragraph (c)(5)(ii) of this section with the return of the shareholder for the election year, reporting the deemed dividend as an excess distribution pursuant to section 1291(a)(1), and paying the tax and interest due on the excess distribution. A shareholder that makes the deemed dividend election after the due date of the return (determined without regard to extensions) for the election year must pay additional interest, pursuant to section 6601, on the amount of underpayment of tax for that year.

(ii) *Attachment to Form 8621.*—The shareholder must attach a schedule to Form 8621 that demonstrates the calculation of the shareholder's pro rata share of the post-1986 earnings and profits of the PFIC that is treated as distributed to the shareholder on the CFC qualification date, pursuant to this paragraph (c). If the shareholder is claiming an exclusion from its pro rata share of the post-1986 earnings and profits for an amount previously included in its income or the income of another U.S. person, the shareholder must include the following information:

(A) The name, address and taxpayer identification number of each U.S. person that previously included an amount in income, the amount previously included in income by each such U.S. person, the provision of law, pursuant to which the amount was previously included in income, and the taxable year or years of inclusion of each amount.

(B) A description of the transaction pursuant to which the shareholder acquired, directly or indirectly, the stock of the PFIC from another U.S. person, and the provision of law pursuant to which the shareholder's holding period includes the period the other U.S. person held the CFC stock.

(6) *Adjustments to basis.*—A shareholder that makes the deemed dividend election increases its adjusted basis of the stock of the PFIC owned directly by the shareholder by the amount of the deemed dividend. If the shareholder makes the deemed dividend election with respect to a PFIC of which it is an indirect shareholder, the shareholder's adjusted basis of the stock or other property owned directly by the shareholder, through which ownership of the PFIC is attributed to the shareholder, is increased by the amount of the deemed dividend. In addition, solely for purposes of determining the subsequent treatment under the Code and regulations of a shareholder of the stock of the PFIC, the adjusted basis of the direct owner of the stock of the PFIC is increased by the amount of the deemed dividend.

(7) *Treatment of holding period.*—If the shareholder of a foreign corporation has made a deemed dividend election, then, for purposes of applying sections 1291 through 1298 to such shareholder after the deemed dividend, the shareholder's holding period of the stock of the foreign corporation begins on the CFC qualification date. For other purposes of the Code and regulations, this holding period rule does not apply.

(8) *Coordination with section 959(e).*—For purposes of section 959(e), the entire deemed dividend is treated as having been included in gross income under section 1248(a).

(d) *CFC qualification date.*—For purposes of this section, the CFC qualification date is the first day on which the qualified portion of the shareholder's holding period in the section 1297(e) PFIC begins, as determined under section 1297(e).

(e) *Late purging elections requiring special consent.*—(1) *In general.*—This section prescribes the exclusive rules under which a shareholder of a section 1297(e) PFIC may make a section 1298(b)(1) election after the time prescribed in paragraph (b)(3) or (c)(4) of this section for making a deemed sale or a deemed dividend election has elapsed (late purging election). Therefore, a shareholder may not seek such relief under any other provisions of the law, including § 301.9100-3 of this chapter. A shareholder may request the consent of the Commissioner to make a late deemed sale or deemed dividend election for the taxable year of the shareholder that includes the CFC qualification date provided the shareholder satisfies the requirements set forth in this paragraph (e). The Commissioner may, in his discretion, grant relief under this paragraph (e) only if—

(i) In a case where the shareholder is requesting consent under this paragraph (e) after December 31, 2005, the shareholder requests such consent before a representative of the Internal Revenue Service (IRS) raises upon audit the PFIC status of the foreign corporation for any taxable year of the shareholder;

(ii) The shareholder has agreed in a closing agreement with the Commissioner, described in paragraph (e)(3) of this section, to eliminate any prejudice to the interests of the U.S. government, as determined under paragraph (e)(2) of this section, as a consequence of the shareholder's inability to file amended returns for its taxable year in which the CFC qualification date falls or an earlier closed taxable year in which the shareholder has taken a position that is inconsistent with the treatment of the foreign corporation as a PFIC; and

(iii) The shareholder satisfies the procedural requirements set forth in paragraph (e)(3) of this section.

(2) *Prejudice to the interests of the U.S. government.*—The interests of the U.S. government are prejudiced if granting relief would result in the shareholder having a lower tax liability (other than by a de minimis amount), taking into account applicable interest charges, for the taxable year that includes the CFC qualification date (or a prior taxable year in which the taxpayer took a position on a return that was inconsistent with the treatment of the foreign corporation as a PFIC) than the shareholder would have had if the shareholder had properly made the section 1298(b)(1) election in the time prescribed in paragraph (b)(2) or (c)(3) of this section (or had not taken a position in a return for an earlier year that was inconsistent with the status of the foreign corporation as a PFIC). The time value of money is taken into account for purposes of this computation.

(3) *Procedural requirements.*—(i) *In general.*—The amount due with respect to a late purging election is determined in the same manner as if the purging election had been timely filed. However, the shareholder is also liable for interest on the amount due, pursuant to section 6601, determined for the period beginning on the due date (without extensions) for the taxpayer's income tax return for the year in which the CFC qualification date falls and ending on the date the late purging election is filed with the IRS.

(ii) *Filing instructions.*—A late purging election is made by filing a completed Form 8621-A, "Return by a Shareholder Making Certain Late Elections to End Treatment as a Passive Foreign Investment Company."

(4) *Time and manner of making late election.*—(i) *Time for making a late purging election.*—A shareholder may make a late purging election in the manner provided in paragraph (e)(4)(ii) of this section at any time. The date the election is filed with the IRS will determine the amount of interest due under paragraph (e)(3) of this section.

(ii) *Manner of making a late purging election.*—A shareholder makes a late purging election by completing Form 8621-A in the manner required by that form and this section and filing that form with the Internal Revenue Service, DP 8621-A, Ogden, UT 84201.

(5) *Multiple late elections.*—(i) *General rule.*—A shareholder of a foreign corporation may make multiple late purging elections under the rules of this paragraph (e) or § 1.1298-3(e) to the same extent such multiple purging elections could have been made if those purging elections had been filed within the time prescribed under paragraph (b)(3) or (c)(4) of this section or § 1.1298-3(b)(3) or (c)(4).

(ii) *Example.*—The rule of this paragraph (e)(5) is illustrated by the following example:

Example. (i) In 1991, X, a U.S person, acquired a five percent interest in the stock of FC, a controlled foreign corporation, as defined in section 957(a). In years 1991, 1992, 1995, 1996 and 1997, FC satisfied either the income test or the asset test of section 1297(a). X did not make a QEF election with regard to FC. In years 1993 and 1994, FC did not satisfy either the income or the asset test of section 1297(a). In 1998, X acquired additional stock in FC such that X was a U.S. shareholder (as defined in section 951(b)) of FC.

(ii) Because FC qualified as a PFIC in 1991, FC will be treated as a PFIC with respect to all of the stock held by X, under the "once a PFIC always a PFIC" rule of section 1298(b)(1), unless X makes an election to purge the PFIC taint. Because X ceased to satisfy either the income or asset test in 1993, X could have made an election under § 1.1298-3 to purge the PFIC taint of FC for that year if X had filed such an election within the time prescribed under § 1.1298-3(b)(3) or (c)(4). If X had done so, the stock X held in FC would not be treated as stock in a PFIC for the years 1993 and 1994. Because X became a U.S. shareholder of FC in 1998, X then could have made a deemed sale or deemed dividend election under this section to purge the PFIC taint of FC for the years 1995 through 1997 if X had filed within the time prescribed under paragraph (b)(3) or (c)(4) of this section. Accordingly, X may make a late purging election to purge the PFIC taint of FC for the years 1991 and 1992 under the rules of § 1.1298-3(e) and may also make a late purging election to purge the PFIC taint of FC for the years 1995 through 1997 under the rules of this paragraph (e).

(f) *Effective/applicability date.*—The rules of this section are applicable as of December 8, 2005. [Reg. § 1.1297-3.]

☐ [*T.D. 9360, 9-26-2007 (corrected 10-17-2007).*]

§ 1.1297-4. Qualifying insurance corporation.—(a) *Scope.*—This section provides rules for determining whether a foreign corporation is a qualifying insurance corporation for purposes of section 1297(f). Paragraph (b) of this section provides the general rule for determining whether a foreign corporation is a qualifying insurance corporation. Paragraph (c) of this section describes the 25 percent test in section 1297(f)(1)(B). Paragraph (d) of this section contains rules for applying the alternative facts and circumstances test in section 1297(f)(2). Paragraph (e) of this section contains rules limiting the amount of applicable insurance liabilities for purposes of the 25 percent test described in paragraph (c) of this section and the alternative facts and circumstances test described in paragraph (d) of this section. Paragraph (f) of this section provides definitions that apply for purposes of this section. Paragraph (g) of this section provides the applicability date of this section.

(b) *Qualifying insurance corporation.*—For purposes of section 1297(b)(2)(B), this section, and §§ 1.1297-5 and 1.1297-6, with respect to a U.S. person, a qualifying insurance corporation (QIC) is a foreign corporation that—

(1) Is an insurance company as defined in section 816(a) that would be subject to tax under subchapter L if the corporation were a domestic corporation; and

(2) Satisfies—

(i) The 25 percent test described in paragraph (c) of this section; or

(ii) The requirements for an election to apply the alternative facts and circumstances test as described in paragraph (d) of this section and a United States person has made an election as described in paragraph (d)(5) of this section.

(c) *25 percent test.*—A foreign corporation satisfies the 25 percent test if the amount of its applicable insurance liabilities exceeds 25 percent of its total assets. This determination is made on the basis of the applicable insurance liabilities and total assets reported on the corporation's applicable financial statement for the applicable reporting period.

(d) *Election to apply the alternative facts and circumstances test.*—(1) *In general.*—A United States person that owns stock in a foreign corporation that fails to qualify as a QIC solely because of the 25 percent test may elect to treat the stock of the corporation as stock of a QIC if the foreign corporation—

(i) Is predominantly engaged in an insurance business as described in paragraph (d)(2) of this section;

(ii) Failed to satisfy the 25 percent test solely due to runoff-related circumstances, as described in paragraph (d)(3) of this section, or rating-related circumstances, as described in paragraph (d)(4) of this section; and

(iii) Reports an amount of applicable insurance liabilities that is at least 10 percent of the amount of the total assets on the corporation's applicable financial statement for the applicable reporting period.

(2) *Predominantly engaged in an insurance business.*—(i) *In general.*—A foreign corporation is not considered predominantly engaged in an insurance business in any taxable year unless more than half of the business of the foreign corporation is the issuing of insurance or annuity contracts or the reinsuring of risks underwritten by insurance companies. This determination is made based on the character of the business actually conducted in the taxable year. The fact that a foreign corporation has been holding itself out as an insurer for a long period is not determinative of whether the foreign corporation is predominantly engaged in an insurance business.

(ii) *Facts and circumstances.*—Facts and circumstances to consider in determining whether a foreign corporation is predominantly engaged in an insurance business include (but are not limited to)—

(A) Claims payment patterns for the current year and prior years;

(B) The foreign corporation's loss exposure as calculated for a regulator or for a credit rating agency, or, if those are not calculated, for internal pricing purposes;

(C) The percentage of gross receipts constituting premiums for the current and prior years; and

(D) The number and size of insurance contracts issued or taken on through reinsurance by the foreign corporation.

(iii) *Examples of facts indicating a foreign corporation is not predominantly engaged in an insurance business.*—Examples of facts that may indicate a foreign corporation is not predominantly engaged in an insurance business include (but are not limited to)—

(A) A small overall number of insured risks with low likelihood but large potential costs;

(B) Employees and agents of the foreign corporation focused to a greater degree on investment activities than underwriting activities; and

(C) Low loss exposure.

(3) *Runoff-related circumstances.*—During the annual reporting period covered by the applicable financial statement, a foreign corporation fails to satisfy the 25 percent test solely due to runoff-related circumstances only if the corporation—

(i) Was engaged in the process of terminating its pre-existing, active conduct of an insurance business (within the meaning of section 1297(b)(2)(B)) under the supervision of its applicable insurance regulatory body or pursuant to any court-ordered receivership proceeding (liquidation, rehabilitation, or conservation) and fails to satisfy the 25 percent test because the corporation is required to hold additional assets due to its business being in runoff;

(ii) Has no plan or intention to enter into, and did not issue or enter into, any insurance, annuity, or reinsurance contract, other than a contractually obligated renewal of an existing insurance contract or a reinsurance contract pursuant to and consistent with the termination of its active conduct of an insurance business; and

(iii) Made payments during the annual reporting period covered by the applicable financial statement as required to satisfy claims under insurance, annuity, or reinsurance contracts.

(4) *Rating-related circumstances.*—A foreign corporation fails to satisfy the 25 percent test solely due to rating-related circumstances only if—

(i) The 25 percent test is not met due to capital and surplus amounts that a generally recognized credit rating agency considers necessary for the foreign corporation to obtain a public rating with respect to its financial strength, and the foreign corporation maintains such capital and surplus in order to obtain the minimum credit rating necessary for the annual reporting period by the foreign corporation to be able to write the business in its regulatory or board supervised business plan. This paragraph (c)(4)(i) applies only if the foreign corporation is a mortgage insurance company (as defined in paragraph (f)(10) of this section) or if more than half of the foreign corporation's net written premiums for the annual reporting period (or the average of the net written premiums for the foreign corporation's annual reporting period and the two immediately preceding annual reporting periods) are from insurance coverage against the risk of loss from a catastrophic loss event (that is, a low frequency but high severity loss event); or

(ii) The foreign corporation is a financial guaranty insurance company (as defined in paragraph (f)(5) of this section).

(5) *Election.*—(i) *In general.*—A United States person may make the election under section 1297(f)(2) for its taxable year if the foreign corporation directly provides the United States person a statement, signed by a responsible officer of the foreign corporation or an authorized representative of the foreign corporation, or the foreign corporation (or its foreign parent corporation on its behalf) makes a publicly available statement (such as in a public filing, disclosure statement, or other notice provided to United States persons that are shareholders of the foreign corporation) that it satisfied the requirements of section 1297(f)(2) and paragraph (d)(1) of this section during the foreign corporation's applicable reporting period. However, a United States person may not rely upon any statement by the foreign corporation (or its foreign parent corporation) to make the election under section 1297(f)(2) if the shareholder knows or has reason to know based on reasonably accessible information that the statement made by the foreign corporation (or its foreign parent corporation) was incorrect.

(ii) *Information provided by foreign corporation.*—In addition to a statement that the foreign corporation satisfied the requirements of section 1297(f)(2) and paragraph (d)(1) of this section, the statement described in paragraph (d)(5)(i) of this section also must include:

(A) The ratio of applicable insurance liabilities to total assets for the applicable reporting period; and

(B) A statement indicating whether the failure to satisfy the 25 percent test described in paragraph (c) of this section was the result of runoff-related or rating-related circumstances, along with a brief description of those circumstances.

(iii) *Time and manner for making the election.*—Except as provided in paragraph (d)(5)(iv), the election described in paragraph (d)(1) of this section may be made by a United States person who owns stock in the foreign corporation by completing the appropriate part of Form 8621 (or successor form) for each taxable year of the United States person in which the election applies. A United States person must attach the Form 8621 (or successor form) to its original or amended Federal income tax return for the taxable year of the United States person to which the election relates. A United States person can attach the Form 8621 (or successor form) to an amended return for the taxable year of the United States person to which the election relates if the United States person can demonstrate the reason for not filing the form with its original return was due to reasonable cause.

(iv) *Deemed election for small shareholders in publicly traded companies.*—(A) *In general.* A United States person who owns publicly traded stock in a foreign corporation will be deemed to make the election under section 1297(f)(2) with respect to the foreign corporation and its subsidiaries if the following requirements are satisfied:

(1) The stock of the foreign corporation that is owned by the United States person (including stock owned indirectly) has a value of $25,000 or less ($50,000 or less in the case of a joint return) on the last day of the United States person's taxable year and on any day during the taxable year on which the United States person disposes of stock of the foreign corporation; and

(2) If the United States person owns stock of the foreign corporation indirectly through a domestic partnership, domestic trust, domestic estate, or S corporation (a *domestic pass-through entity*), the stock of the foreign corporation that is owned by the domestic pass-through entity has a value of $25,000 or less on the last day of the taxable year of the domestic pass-through entity that ends with or within the United States person's taxable year and on any day during the taxable year of the domestic pass-through entity on which it disposes of stock of the foreign corporation.

(B) *Publicly traded stock.*—For the purpose of paragraph (d)(5)(iv)(A) of this section, stock is publicly traded if it would be treated as marketable stock within the meaning of section 1296(e) and § 1.1296-2 (without regard to § 1.1296-2(d)) if the election under section 1297(f)(2) is not made.

(v) *Options.*—If a United States person is considered to own stock in a foreign corporation by reason of holding an option, the United States person may make the election under section 1297(f)(2) (or may be deemed to make an election under paragraph (d)(5)(iv) of this section) with respect to the foreign corporation or its subsidiaries in the same manner as if the United States person owned stock in the foreign corporation.

(6) *Stock ownership.*—For purposes of this section, ownership of stock in a foreign corporation means either direct ownership of such stock or indirect ownership determined using the rules specified in § 1.1291-1(b)(8) (but without regard to the 50 percent ownership requirement of § 1.1291-1(b)(8)(ii)(A)).

(e) *Rules limiting the amount of applicable insurance liabilities.*—(1) *In general.*—For purposes of determining whether a foreign corporation satisfies the 25 percent test described in paragraph (c) of this section or the 10 percent test described in paragraph (d)(1)(iii) of this section, the rules of this paragraph (e) apply to limit the amount of applicable insurance liabilities of the foreign corporation.

(2) *General limitation on applicable insurance liabilities.*—The amount of applicable insurance liabilities may not exceed any of the amounts described in paragraphs (e)(2)(i) to (iii) of this section. This paragraph (e)(2) applies after applying paragraph (e)(3) of this section.

(i) The amount of applicable insurance liabilities of the foreign corporation shown on any financial statement that the foreign corporation filed or was required to file with its applicable insurance regulatory body for the financial statement's applicable reporting period;

(ii) If the foreign corporation's applicable financial statement is prepared on the basis of either GAAP or IFRS, the amount of the foreign corporation's applicable insurance liabilities determined on the basis of its applicable financial statement, whether or not the foreign corporation files the statement with its applicable insurance regulatory body; or

(iii) The amount of applicable insurance liabilities required for the foreign corporation by the applicable law or regulation of the jurisdiction of the applicable insurance regulatory body at the end of the applicable reporting period (or a lesser amount of applicable insurance liabilities, if the foreign corporation is holding a lesser amount as a permitted practice of the applicable regulatory body).

(3) *Discounting.*—If an applicable financial statement or a financial statement described in paragraph (e)(2) of this section is prepared on the basis of an accounting method other than GAAP or IFRS and does not discount applicable insurance liabilities on an economically reasonable basis, the amount of applicable insurance liabilities may not exceed the amount of applicable insurance liabilities on the financial statement reduced by applying the discounting methods that would apply under either GAAP or IFRS to the insurance or annuity contracts to which the applicable insurance liabilities at issue relate. The foreign corporation may choose whether to apply either GAAP or IFRS discounting methods for this purpose.

(4) [Reserved].

(5) [Reserved].

(f) *Definitions.*—The following definitions apply for purposes of this section.

(1) *Applicable financial statement.*—The term *applicable financial statement* means the foreign corporation's financial statement prepared for financial reporting purposes, listed in paragraphs (f)(1)(i) through (iii) of this section, and that has the highest priority. The financial statements are, in order of descending priority—

(i) *GAAP statements.*—A financial statement that is prepared in accordance with GAAP;

(ii) *IFRS statements.*—A financial statement that is prepared in accordance with IFRS; or

(iii) *Regulatory annual statement.*—A financial statement required to be filed with the applicable insurance regulatory body.

(iv) [Reserved].

(2) *Applicable insurance liabilities.*—(i) *In general.*—The term *applicable insurance liabilities* means, with respect to any life or property and casualty insurance business—

(A) Reported losses (which are expected payments to policyholders for sustained losses related to insured events under an insurance contract that have occurred and have been reported to, but not paid by, the insurer as of the financial statement end date), and incurred but not reported losses (which are expected payments to policyholders for sustained losses relating to insured events under an insurance contract that have occurred but have not been reported to the insurer as of the financial statement end date);

(B) Unpaid loss adjustment expenses (including reasonable estimates of anticipated loss adjustment expenses) associated with investigating, defending, settling, and adjusting paid losses, unpaid reported losses, and incurred but not reported losses (of the type described in paragraph (f)(2)(i)(A) of this section) as of the financial statement end date; and

(C) The aggregate amount of reserves (excluding deficiency, contingency, or unearned premium reserves) held as of the financial statement end date to mature or liquidate potential, future claims for death, annuity, or health benefits that may become payable under contracts providing, at the time the reserve is computed, coverage for mortality or morbidity risks;

(D) Provided, however, that—

(1) No item or amount shall be taken into account more than once in determining applicable insurance liabilities;

(2) The applicable insurance liabilities eligible to be taken into account in applying this paragraph (f)(2) include only the applicable insurance liabilities of the foreign corporation whose QIC status is being determined; and

(3) [Reserved].

(ii) *Amounts not specified in paragraph (f)(2)(i) of this section.*—Amounts not specified in paragraph (f)(2)(i) of this section are not applicable insurance liabilities. For example, the term applicable insurance liability does not include any amount held by an insurance company as a deposit liability that is not an insurance liability, such as a funding agreement, a guaranteed investment contract, premium or other deposit funds, structured settlements, or any other substantially similar contract issued by an insurance company. The term applicable insurance liabilities also does not include the amount of any reserve for a life insurance or annuity contract the payments of which do not depend on the life or life expectancy of one or more individuals.

(3) *Applicable insurance regulatory body.*—The term *applicable insurance regulatory body* means the entity that has been established by law to license or authorize a corporation to engage in an insurance business, to regulate insurance company solvency, and, in the case of an applicable financial statement described in paragraph (f)(1)(iii), is the entity to which the applicable financial statement is provided.

(4) *Applicable reporting period.*—The term *applicable reporting period* is the last annual reporting period for a financial statement ending with or within the taxable year of a U.S. person owning stock in a foreign corporation, within the meaning of paragraph (d)(6) of this section.

(5) *Financial guaranty insurance company.*—The term *financial guaranty insurance company* means any insurance company whose sole business is to insure or reinsure only the type of business written by, or that would be permitted to be written by, a company licensed under, and compliant with, a U.S. state law, modeled after the Financial Guaranty Insurance Guideline as established by National Association of Insurance Companies, that specifically governs the licensing and regulation of financial guaranty insurance companies.

(6) *Financial statements.*—(i) *In general.*—The term *financial statement* means a statement prepared for a legal entity for a reporting period in accordance with the rules of a financial accounting or statutory accounting standard that includes a complete balance sheet, statement of income, and a statement of cash flows (or equivalent statements under the applicable reporting standard).

(ii) [Reserved].

(iii) [Reserved].

(7) *Generally accepted accounting principles or GAAP.*—The term *generally accepted accounting principles* or *GAAP* means United States generally accepted accounting principles described in standards established and made effective by the Financial Accounting Standards Board.

(8) *Insurance business.*—For purposes of this section, § 1.1297-5, and § 1.1297-6, *insurance business* means the business of issuing insurance and annuity contracts and the reinsuring of risks underwritten by insurance companies, together with those investment activities and administrative services that are required to support (or are substantially related to) insurance, annuity, or reinsurance contracts issued or entered into by the foreign corporation.

(9) *International financial reporting standards* or *IFRS.*—The term *international financial reporting standards* or *IFRS* means accounting standards established and made effective by the International Accounting Standards Board.

(10) *Mortgage insurance company.*—For purposes of this section, *mortgage insurance company* means any insurance company whose sole business is to insure or reinsure against a lender's loss of all or a portion of the principal amount of a mortgage loan upon default of the mortgagor.

(11) *Total assets.*—For purposes of section 1297(f) and this section, a foreign corporation's *total assets* are the aggregate value of the real property and personal property that the foreign corporation reports on its applicable financial statement as of the financial statement end date.

(g) *Applicability date.*—The rules of this section apply to taxable years of shareholders beginning on or after January 14, 2021. A shareholder may choose to apply such rules for any open taxable year beginning after December 31, 2017 and before January 14, 2021, provided that, with respect to a tested foreign corporation, it consistently applies the provisions of this section and § 1.1297-6 for such year and all subsequent years. [Reg. § 1.1297-4.]

☐ *[T.D. 9936, 1-14-2021 (corrected 3-9-2021).]*

Proposed Amendments to Regulation

§ 1.1297-4. Qualifying insurance corporation.—

* * *

(e) * * *

(4) *Corresponding adjustment to total assets.*—For purposes of determining whether a foreign corporation satisfies the 25 percent test or the 10 percent test, the amount of total assets reported on the

foreign corporation's applicable financial statement may be reduced as described in paragraphs (e)(4)(i) through (iii) of this section.

(i) *Consolidated applicable financial statement.*—If a foreign corporation's applicable financial statement is prepared on a consolidated basis, the amount of total assets may be reduced by the amount of liabilities of another entity that are reported on the applicable financial statement and would be treated as applicable insurance liabilities but for the application of paragraphs (e)(2) or (f)(2)(i)(D)(2) of this section.

(ii) *Insurance risk transferred through reinsurance.*—If the applicable financial statement is prepared on the basis of an accounting method that measures insurance liabilities without a reduction for amounts that may be recovered from other parties through reinsurance and the amount that may be recovered through reinsurance is reported as an asset on the applicable financial statement (rather than as a reduction in the amount of an insurance liability), the foreign corporation's total assets may be reduced by the amount of the corporation's insurance liabilities that are reinsured to another party and are excluded from the definition of applicable insurance liabilities under paragraph (f)(2)(i)(D)(3) of this section.

(iii) No amount may be used more than once to reduce total assets under paragraphs (e)(4)(i) and (ii) of this section.

(5) *Example.*—The following example illustrates the application of paragraph (e)(4) of this section.

(i) *Facts.* P, a foreign corporation, issues property and casualty insurance contracts and has a consolidated applicable financial statement (AFS) constructed using IFRS accounting principles, including those of IFRS 17, for the applicable reporting period. The AFS reports insurance contract liabilities for incurred claims that meet the requirements of paragraphs (f)(2)(i)(A) and (f)(2)(i)(B) of this section in an amount equal to 1,100x, 200x of which are liabilities under contracts issued by S, a wholly owned insurance subsidiary, and 900x of which are liabilities under contracts issued by P. The AFS also reports 2,500x of total assets, including 250x of assets related to P's insurance contract liabilities for incurred claims that are recoverable from unrelated parties through reinsurance.

(ii) *Results*—(A) Reduction to applicable insurance liabilities (*AIL*). Under paragraph (f)(2)(i)(D)(2) of this section, only AIL of the foreign corporation whose QIC status is being determined may be included in AIL. Thus, P's AIL do not include the 200x of insurance contract liabilities on P's consolidated AFS that are liabilities under contracts issued by S. Under paragraph (f)(2)(i)(D)(3) of this section, the amount of insurance liabilities determined under paragraphs (f)(2)(i)(A) through (C) and (D)(*1*) and (2) of this section are reduced by an amount equal to the assets reported on P's AFS that represent amounts relating to those liabilities that may be recoverable from other parties through reinsurance. Thus, P's AIL are reduced by an amount equal to the 250x of assets for incurred claims related to the insurance liabilities of P that are recoverable from another party through reinsurance. Assuming no other limitation applies (such as those contained in paragraph (e) of this section), P's AIL equals 650x (1,100x-200x-250x).

(B) *Reduction to total assets.* Pursuant to paragraph (e)(4)(i) of this section, P may reduce its total assets by amounts of liabilities of another entity that are excluded from P's AIL because of paragraphs (e)(2) or (f)(2)(i)(D)(2) of this section. Under paragraph (f)(2)(i)(D)(2) of this section, P's AIL may include only the liabilities of P, the entity whose QIC status is being determined. Therefore, P may reduce its total assets by 200x, the amount of liabilities under contracts issued by S that are included on P's AFS but excluded from P's AIL. Pursuant to paragraph (e)(4)(ii) of this section, P may also reduce its total assets by 250x, the amount of P's liabilities that are reinsured by another party and excluded from the definition of AIL under paragraph (f)(2)(i)(D)(*3*) of this section. After these adjustments, P has total assets of 2,050x (2,500x-200x-250x).

(C) *AIL to total assets tests.* Accordingly, for purposes of the 25 percent and 10 percent tests, P has AIL of 650x and total assets of 2,050x, for a test ratio of 650x/2,050x, or 31.7%.

(f) *Definitions.*—* * *

(1) *Applicable financial statement.*—The term applicable financial statement means the foreign corporation's financial statement prepared for the financial reporting purposes listed in paragraphs (f)(1)(i) through (iii) of this section that has the highest priority, including priority within paragraphs (f)(1)(i)(B) and (f)(1)(ii) of this section. Subject to paragraph (f)(1)(iv) of this section, the financial statements are, in order of descending priority—

(i) *GAAP statements.*—A financial statement that is prepared in accordance with GAAP and is:

(A) A Form 10-K (or successor form), or annual statement to shareholders, filed with the United States Securities and Exchange Commission (SEC), or filed by the taxpayer with an agency of a foreign government that is equivalent to the SEC, and has reporting standards not less stringent than the standards required by the SEC;

(B) An audited financial statement of the taxpayer that is used for:

(*1*) Credit purposes;

(*2*) Reporting to shareholders, partners, or other proprietors, or to beneficiaries;

(*3*) Filing with the Federal government or any Federal agency, other than the SEC or the Internal Revenue Service or an applicable insurance regulatory body, or filing with a state or foreign government or an agency of a state or foreign government, other than an agency that is equivalent to the SEC or the Internal Revenue Service or is an applicable insurance regulatory body; or

(*4*) Any other substantial non-tax purpose, including filing with the applicable insurance regulatory body; or

(ii) *IFRS statements.*—A financial statement that is prepared in accordance with IFRS and is described in paragraphs (f)(1)(i)(A) or (B) of this section, in the order of priority set forth in those paragraphs; or

(iii) *Regulatory annual statement.*—An audited financial statement required to be filed with the applicable insurance regulatory body that is not prepared in accordance with GAAP or IFRS.

(iv) *Priority of financial statements.*—(A) A financial statement that takes into account assets and liabilities of affiliates of the foreign corporation that are not owned in whole or part by the foreign corporation is not treated as an applicable financial statement for purposes of paragraphs (f)(1)(i) and (ii) of this section, and is not treated as an applicable financial statement for purposes of paragraph (f)(1)(iii) of this section unless it is the only financial statement described in paragraph (f)(1)(iii) of this section.

(B) A financial statement that is described in more than one clause listed in paragraphs (f)(1)(i) through (iii) of this section is treated for purposes of this paragraph (f)(1) as described solely in the highest priority clause. If a foreign corporation has more than one financial statement with equal priority under paragraphs (f)(1)(i) through (iii) of this section, a non-consolidated financial statement has priority over other financial statements.

(2) *Applicable insurance liabilities.*—* * *

(i) * * *

(D) * * *

(3) Amounts of liabilities determined under paragraphs (f)(2)(i)(A) through (C) and (D)(*1*) and (2) are reduced by an amount equal to the assets reported on the corporation's financial statement as of the financial statement end date that represent amounts relating to those liabilities that may be recoverable from other parties through reinsurance. If a foreign corporation's financial statement is prepared on a consolidated basis, to the extent not reduced already under paragraphs (f)(2)(i)(A) through (C) and (D)(*1*) and (2), liabilities are reduced by an amount equal to the assets relating to those liabilities that may be recoverable through reinsurance from another entity included in the consolidated financial statement, regardless of whether the reinsurance transaction is eliminated in the preparation of the consolidated financial statement.

* * *

(6) *Financial statements.*—(i) *In general.*—The term *financial statement* means a statement prepared for a legal entity for a reporting period in accordance with the rules of a financial accounting or statutory accounting standard that includes a complete balance sheet, statement of income, a statement of cash flows (or equivalent statements under the applicable reporting standard), and related exhibits, schedules, forms, and footnotes that usually accompany the balance sheet, income statement, and cash flow statement.

(ii) *Consolidated and non-consolidated financial statement.*—The term *consolidated financial statement* means a financial statement of a consolidated group of entities that includes a parent and its subsidiaries presented as those of a single economic entity, prepared in accordance with GAAP, IFRS, or another financial or statutory accounting standard. A *non-consolidated financial statement* means a financial statement that is not prepared on a consolidated basis and that accounts for investments in subsidiaries on a cost or equity basis.

(iii) *Audited financial statement.*—The term *audited financial statement* means a financial statement that has been examined by an independent auditor that has provided an opinion that the financial statement presents fairly in all material respects the financial position of the audited company (and its subsidiaries and controlled entities, if relevant) and the results of their operations and cash flows in accordance with GAAP or IFRS, or an equivalent opinion under GAAP, IFRS, or another financial accounting or statutory accounting standard.

* * *

(g) *Applicability date.*—(1) *General applicability date.*—Except as provided in paragraph (g)(2) of this section, this section applies to taxable years of shareholders beginning on or after January 14, 2021.

(2) *Exception.*—Paragraphs (e)(4), (e)(5), (f)(1), (f)(2)(i)(D)(3), and (f)(6) of this section apply to taxable years of United States persons that are shareholders in foreign corporations beginning on or after [the date these regulations are filed as final regulations in the **Federal Register**].

(3) *Early application.*—(i) A shareholder may choose to apply the rules of this section (other than paragraphs (f)(1), (f)(2)(i)(D)(3), and (f)(6) of this section) for any open taxable year beginning after December 31, 2017 and before the applicability dates described in paragraphs (g)(1) and (2) of this section, provided that, with respect to a tested foreign corporation, it consistently applies those rules and the rules described in § 1.1297-6(f)(3) for such year and all subsequent years.

(ii) A shareholder may choose to apply paragraphs (f)(1), (f)(2)(i)(D)(3), and (f)(6) of this section for any open taxable year beginning after December 31, 2017 and before [the date these regulations are filed as final regulations in the **Federal Register**], provided that, with respect to a tested foreign corporation, it consistently applies the rules of this section, § 1.1297-5, and § 1.1297-6 for such year and all subsequent years. [Prop. Reg. § 1.1297-4.]

[Proposed 1-15-2021 (corrected 3-5-2021).]

§ 1.1297-5. [Reserved]

☐ [*T.D.* 9936, 1-14-2021.]

Proposed Amendments to Regulation

§ 1.1297-5. Active conduct of an insurance business.—(a) *Scope.*—This section provides rules pertaining to the exception from passive income under section 1297(b)(2)(B) for income derived in the active conduct of an insurance business. Paragraph (b) of this section sets forth the options for a qualifying insurance company (QIC) to qualify as engaged in the active conduct of an insurance business and describes circumstances under which a QIC will not be engaged in the active conduct of an insurance business. Paragraph (c) of this section describes the factual requirements that are sufficient to show that a QIC is engaged in the active conduct of an insurance business for purposes of section 1297(b)(2)(B). Paragraph (d) of this section describes an alternative active conduct percentage test, pursuant to which a QIC may be deemed to be engaged in the active conduct of an insurance business for purposes of section 1297(b)(2)(B). Paragraph (e) of this section describes the circumstances under which officers and employees of certain entities related to a QIC may be treated as if they were employees of the QIC. Paragraph (f) of this section provides definitions applicable to this section. Paragraph (g) of this section provides the applicability date of this section.

(b) *Active conduct of an insurance business.*—(1) *In general.*—A QIC is engaged in the active conduct of an insurance business only if it satisfies—

(i) the factual requirements test in paragraph (c) of this section; or

(ii) the active conduct percentage test in paragraph (d) of this section.

(2) *Exceptions.*—Notwithstanding paragraph (b)(1) of this section, a QIC is not engaged in the active conduct of an insurance business if either of the following circumstances apply—

(i) It has no employees or only a nominal number of employees and relies exclusively or almost exclusively upon independent contractors (disregarding for this purpose any related entity that has entered into a contract designating its status as an independent contractor with respect to the QIC) to perform its core functions;

(ii) It is a vehicle that has the effect of securitizing or collateralizing insurance risks underwritten by other insurance or reinsurance companies or is an insurance linked securities fund that invests in securitization vehicles, and its stock (or a financial instrument, note, or security that is treated as equity for U.S. tax purposes) is designed to provide an investment return that is tied to the occurrence of a fixed or predetermined portfolio of insured risks, events, or indices related to insured risks.

(c) *Factual Requirements Test.*—(1) *In general.*—A QIC satisfies the factual requirements test of paragraph (b)(1)(i) of this section if all the following are met—

(i) The officers and employees of the QIC carry out substantial managerial and operational activities on a regular and continuous basis with respect to its core functions as described in paragraph (c)(2) of this section; and

(ii) The officers and employees of the QIC perform virtually all of the active decision-making functions relevant to underwriting functions as described in paragraph (c)(3) of this section.

(2) *Substantial managerial and operational activities with respect to core functions.*—(i) *Substantial managerial and operational activities.*—Substantial managerial and operational activities with respect to a QIC's core functions requires all of the following—

(A) Establishing the strategic, overall parameters with respect to each core function;

(B) Establishing, or reviewing and approving, detailed plans to implement the strategic, overall parameters for each of the QIC's core functions;

(C) Managing, controlling and supervising the execution of the detailed plans to carry out each of the QIC's core functions;

(D) Establishing criteria for the hiring of employees or independent contractors to execute the detailed plans to carry out each of the QIC's core functions, and if independent contractors are hired, prescribing the goals and objectives of the engagement, the scope of work, evaluation criteria for contractor eligibility and for submissions by prospective contractors, and criteria and budget for the work to be performed;

(E) Reviewing the conduct of the work performed by employees or independent contractors to ensure that it meets the goals, standards, criteria, timeline, and budget specified by the QIC, and taking appropriate action if it does not; and

(F) Conducting each of the requirements above by officers or senior employees of the QIC, which officers or employees are experienced in the conduct of those activities and devote all or virtually all of their work to those activities and similar activities for related entities.

(ii) *Regular and continuous basis.*—Carrying out managerial and operational activities on a regular and continuous basis requires that the parameters and plans described in paragraphs (c)(2)(i)(A) and (B) of this section are regularly reviewed and updated and that the activities described in paragraphs (c)(2)(i)(C) and (E) of this section are carried out on a daily or other frequent basis as part of the ordinary course of the QIC's operations.

(3) *Performance of virtually all of the active decision-making functions relevant to a QIC's underwriting activities.*—(i) *Active decision-making functions.*—Active decision-making functions are the underwriting activities that are most important to decisions of the QIC relating to the assumption of specific insurance risks.

(ii) *Performance requirements.*—Performance of virtually all of the active decision-making functions relating to underwriting activities requires all of the following—

(A) Carrying out virtually all of the activities related to a QIC's decision to assume an insurance risk, as set forth in the definition of underwriting activities, by employees and not by independent contractors; and

(B) Evaluating, analyzing, and conducting virtually all of the decision-making with respect to executing an insurance contract on a contract-by-contract basis, including determining whether the contract meets the QIC's criteria with respect to the risks to be undertaken and pricing and is otherwise sound and appropriate.

(iii) *Exclusions.*—The following activities are not active decision-making functions relevant to a QIC's core functions—

(A) Development of underwriting policies or parameters that are changed infrequently without further ongoing, active involvement in the day-to-day decision-making related to these functions; and

(B) Clerical or ministerial functions with respect to underwriting that do not involve the exercise of discretion or business judgment.

(4) *Number of officers and employees.*—The number of officers and employees actively engaged in each core function is a relevant factor in determining whether the factual requirements in paragraph (c)(1) of this section have been satisfied.

(d) *Active conduct percentage test.*—A QIC satisfies the active conduct percentage test of paragraph (b)(1)(ii) and will be deemed to be engaged in an active insurance business for the applicable reporting period only if it satisfies the percentage requirement in paragraph (d)(1) of this section and, to the extent core functions are outsourced, the oversight requirement in paragraph (d)(2) of this section.

(1) *Percentage test.*—For the applicable reporting period covered by the applicable financial statement, total costs incurred by the QIC with respect to the QIC's officers and employees for services rendered with respect to its core functions (other than investment activities) equals or exceeds 50 percent of total costs incurred by the QIC with respect to the QIC's officers and employees and any other person or entities for services rendered with respect to its core functions (other than investment activities).

(2) *Outsourcing.*—To the extent the QIC outsources any part of its core functions to unrelated entities, officers and employees of the QIC with experience and relevant expertise must select and supervise the person that performs the outsourced functions, establish objectives for performance of the outsourced functions, and prescribe rigorous guidelines relating to the outsourced functions which are routinely evaluated and updated.

(e) *Related officers and employees.*—For purposes of this section, a QIC's officers and employees are considered to include the officers and employees of a related entity if the requirements of this paragraph (e) are satisfied. In determining whether an activity is carried out by employees, the activities of persons that are independent contractors and that are not related entities are disregarded. An entity may be a related entity regardless of whether it has entered into a contract designating its status as an independent contractor with respect to the QIC. An entity is treated as a related entity only if the requirements of this paragraph (e) are satisfied.

(1) *Modified qualified affiliate requirement.*—The entity is a qualified affiliate of the QIC within the meaning of § 1.1297-2(e)(2) (determined by treating the QIC as the tested foreign corporation) except that, for purposes of this section, section 1504(a)(2)(A) (with "more than 50 percent" substituted for "at least 80 percent") also applies for purposes of determining qualified affiliate status.

(2) *Oversight and supervision requirement.*—The QIC exercises regular oversight and supervision over the services performed by the related entity's officers and employees for the QIC.

(3) *Compensation requirement.*—The QIC either—

(i) Pays directly all the compensation costs of the related entity's officers and employees attributable to core functions performed by those officers and employees on behalf of the QIC;

(ii) Reimburses the related entity for the portion of its expenses, including compensation costs and related expenses (determined in accordance with section 482 and taking into account all expenses that would be included in the total services costs under § 1.482-9(j) and § 1.482-9(k)(2)) for the performance by its officers and employees of core functions on behalf of the QIC; or

(iii) Otherwise pays arm's length compensation in accordance with section 482 on a fee-related basis to the related entity for services related to core functions.

(f) *Definitions.*—The following definitions apply solely for purposes of this section.

(1) *Applicable reporting period.*—The term *applicable reporting period* has the meaning set forth in § 1.1297-4(f)(4).

(2) *Compensation costs.*—The term *compensation costs* means all amounts incurred by the QIC during the applicable reporting period with respect to an officer and employee (including, for example, wages, salaries, deferred compensation, employee benefits, and employer payroll taxes).

(3) *Contract and claims management activities.*—The term *contract and claims management activities* means performing the following activities with respect to an insurance or annuity contract: Monitoring a contract (or group of contracts) over its life cycle (that is, maintaining the information on contractual developments, insured risk and occurrences, and maintaining accounts on premiums, claims reserves, and commissions); performing loss and claim reporting (establishing and maintaining loss reporting systems, developing reliable claims statistics, defining and adjusting claims provisions and introducing measures to protect and reduce claims in future); and all the activities related to a policyholder's claim, including processing the claims report, examining coverage, handling the claim (working out the level of the claim, clarifying causes, claims reduction measures, legal analysis) and seeking recovery of funds due to the QIC.

(4) *Core functions.*—The term *core functions* means the QIC 's underwriting, investment, contract and claims management, and sales activities; however, contract and claims management activities will not be considered to be a core function of a reinsurance company with respect to indemnity reinsurance contracts to the extent that the ceding company has agreed to retain this core function under a reinsurance contract.

(5) *Investment activities.*—The term *investment activities* means investment in equity and debt instruments and related hedging transactions and other assets of a kind typically held for investment, for the purpose of producing income to meet obligations under the insurance, annuity, or reinsurance contracts.

(6) *Qualifying insurance corporation or QIC.*—The term *qualifying insurance corporation* or *QIC* has the meaning described in § 1.1297-4(b).

(7) *Sales activities.*—The term *sales activities* means sales, marketing, and customer relations with respect to insurance or reinsurance policies.

(8) *Total costs.*—With respect to the QIC's own officers and employees (and without regard to related officers and employees described in paragraph (e) of this section), the term *total costs* means the compensation costs of those officers and employees and related expenses (determined in accordance with section 482 and taking into account all expenses that would be included in the total services costs under § 1.482-9(j) and § 1.482-9(k)(2)) for services performed related to core functions. With respect to services performed by related officers and employees and unrelated persons or entities, the term *total costs* means the amount paid or accrued to the related or unrelated persons or entities for the services related to core functions. For purposes of this section, total costs, however, do not include any ceding commissions paid or accrued with respect to reinsurance contracts or commissions or fees paid or accrued to brokers or sales agents to procure reinsurance contracts.

(9) *Underwriting activities.*—The term *underwriting activities* means the performance of activities related to a QIC's decision to assume an insurance risk (for example, the decision to enter into an insurance or reinsurance contract, setting underwriting policy, risk classification and selection, designing or tailoring insurance or reinsurance products to meet market or customer requirements, performing actuarial analysis with respect to insurance products, and performing analysis for purposes of setting premium rates or calculating reserves, and risk retention).

(10) *Virtually all.*—The term *virtually all* means all, other than a *de minimis* portion, measured on any reasonable basis.

(g) *Applicability date.*—This section applies to taxable years of shareholders beginning on or after [the date these regulations are filed as final regulations in the **Federal Register**]. A shareholder may choose to apply the rules of this section for any open taxable year beginning after December 31, 2017 and before [the date these regulations are filed as final regulations in the **Federal Register**], provided that, with respect to a tested foreign corporation, it consistently applies the rules of this section, § 1.1297-4, and § 1.1297-6 for such year and all subsequent years. [Prop. Reg. § 1.1297-5.]

[Proposed 1-15-2021 (corrected 3-5-2021).]

§1.1297-6. Exception from the definition of passive income for active insurance income.—(a) *Scope*.—This section provides rules pertaining to the exception from passive income under section 1297(b)(2)(B) for income derived in the active conduct of an insurance business and rules related to certain income of a qualifying domestic insurance corporation. Paragraph (b) of this section provides a general rule that excludes from passive income certain income of a qualifying insurance corporation (QIC), as defined in §1.1297-4(b), and certain income of a qualifying domestic insurance corporation. Paragraph (c) of this section provides rules excluding certain assets for purposes of the passive asset test under section 1297(a)(2). Paragraph (d) of this section provides rules concerning the treatment of income and assets of certain look-through subsidiaries and look-through partnerships of a QIC. Paragraph (e) of this section provides rules relating to qualifying domestic insurance corporations. Paragraph (f) of this section provides the applicability date of this section.

(b) *Exclusion from passive income of active insurance income*.—For purposes of section 1297 and §1.1297-1, passive income does not include—

(1) Income that a QIC derives in the active conduct of an insurance business (within the meaning of section 1297(b)(2)(B)); and

(2) Income of a qualifying domestic insurance corporation.

(c) *Exclusion of assets for purposes of the passive asset test under section 1297(a)(2)*.—For purposes of section 1297 and §1.1297-1, passive assets (as defined in §1.1297-1(f)(5)), do not include—

(1) Assets of a QIC available to satisfy liabilities of the QIC related to its insurance business (as defined in §1.1297-4(f)(8)), if the QIC is engaged in the active conduct of an insurance business (within the meaning of section 1297(b)(2)(B)); and

(2) Assets of a qualifying domestic insurance corporation.

(d) *Treatment of income and assets of certain look-through subsidiaries and look-through partnerships for purposes of the section 1297(b)(2)(B) exception*.—(1) *General rule*.—For purposes of applying paragraphs (b)(1) and (c)(1) of this section, a QIC is treated as receiving the income or holding the assets of a look-through subsidiary or look-through partnership to the extent provided in section 1297(c) and §1.1297-2(b)(2) or §1.1297-2(b)(3). Subject to the limitation of paragraph (d)(2) of this section, a QIC's proportionate share of the income or assets of a look-through subsidiary or look-through partnership may be treated as earned or held directly by the QIC, and thus as non-passive under paragraphs (b)(1) and (c)(1) of this section, if the requirements of those paragraphs are satisfied.

(2) *Limitation*.—A QIC that is engaged in the active conduct of an insurance business (within the meaning of section 1297(b)(2)(B)) may not treat its proportionate share of the income or assets of a look-through subsidiary or look-through partnership as non-passive to the extent that it exceeds the greater of—

(i) The QIC's proportionate share of the income or assets, respectively, of the look-through subsidiary or look-through partnership multiplied by a fraction, the numerator of which is the net equity value of the interests held by the QIC in the look-through subsidiary or look-through partnership, and the denominator of which is the value of the QIC's proportionate share of the assets of the look-through subsidiary or look-through partnership; and

(ii) The QIC's proportionate share of the income or assets, respectively, of the look-through subsidiary or look-through partnership that are treated as non-passive in the hands of the look-through subsidiary or look-through partnership.

(3) *Examples*.—The following examples illustrate the rules of this section.

(i) *Example 1: QIC holds all the stock of an investment subsidiary*.—(A) *Facts*.

(*1*) F1 is a foreign corporation. In Year 1, F1 meets the definition of a QIC under section 1297(f) and §1.1297-4 and is engaged in the active conduct of an insurance business within the meaning of section 1297(b)(2)(B). Throughout Year 1, F1 owns all the stock of F2, a foreign corporation that is not a QIC and is engaged solely in the investment of passive assets. The stock of F2 is an asset that is available to satisfy liabilities of F1 related to its insurance business within the meaning of paragraph (c)(1) of this section. The assets of F1 are measured on the basis of value under §1.1297-1(d)(1)(v)(C).

(*2*) Throughout Year 1, F2 owns assets with a value of $1,000x and adjusted bases of $500x, all of which are treated as passive in the hands of F2. F2 has outstanding debt with a principal amount of $250x. On the financial statement end date of F1's applicable financial statement, the net equity value of the F2 stock held by F1 is $750x. In Year 1, F2 earned $100x of income that is treated as passive in the hands of F2.

(B) *Result*—(*1*) Because F1 owns all of the stock of F2, F2 is a look-through subsidiary of F1 within the meaning of §1.1297-2(g)(3). Under section 1297(c) and §1.1297-2(b)(2), F1 is treated as if it held 100% of the assets of F2 and received directly 100% of the income of F2. Under paragraph (d)(1) of this section, because F1 is engaged in the active conduct of an insurance business and the stock of F2 is an asset that is available to satisfy the insurance liabilities of F1, F1 treats its proportionate share of the income and assets of F2 as non-passive. The amount of income and assets that is treated as non-passive is subject to the limitation of paragraph (d)(2) of this section.

(*2*) Under paragraph (d)(2) of this section, the amount of F1's proportionate share of F2's income that is treated as non-passive cannot exceed the greater of two amounts: $75x, which is F1's proportionate share of F2's income ($100x) multiplied by 75% (the net equity value of the F2 stock held by F1, which is $750x, divided by the value of F1's proportionate share of F2's assets, which is $1,000x); and zero, which is F1's proportionate share of the income of F2 that is treated as non-passive in the hands of F2. Therefore, for the purpose of characterizing F1's proportionate share of F2's income, $75x is treated as non-passive, and $25x is treated as passive.

(*3*) Under paragraph (d)(2) of this section, the amount of F1's proportionate share of F2's assets that is treated as non-passive cannot exceed the greater of two amounts: $750x, which is F1's proportionate share of F2's assets ($1,000x) multiplied by 75% (the net equity value of the F2 stock held by F1, which is $750x, divided by the value of F1's proportionate share of F2's assets, which is $1,000x); and zero, which is F1's proportionate share of the assets of F2 that are treated as non-passive in the hands of F2. Therefore, for the purpose of characterizing F1's proportionate share of the assets of F2, $750x is treated as non-passive, and $250x is treated as passive.

(C) *Alternative facts*—(*1*) *Facts*. The facts are the same as in paragraph (d)(3)(i)(A) of this section (paragraph (A) of this Example 1), except that the assets of F1 are measured on the basis of adjusted basis under §1.1297-1(d)(1)(v)(C) pursuant to a valid election under §1.1297-1(d)(1)(iii).

(*2*) *Result*. The result with respect to F1's proportionate share of the income of F2 is the same as in paragraph (d)(3)(i)(B)(*2*) of this section (paragraph (B)(*2*) of this Example 1). Because the assets of F1 are measured on the basis of adjusted basis under §1.1297-1(d)(1)(v)(C), F1's proportionate share of the passive assets of F2 is equal to $500x (100% of $500x adjusted bases). Under paragraph (d)(2) of this section, the amount of F1's proportionate share of F2's assets that may be treated as non-passive cannot exceed the greater of two amounts: $375x, which is F1's proportionate share of F2's passive assets ($500x) multiplied by 75% (the net equity value of the F2 stock held by F1, which is $750x, divided by the value of F1's proportionate share of F2's assets, which is $1,000x); and zero, which is F1's proportionate share of the assets of F2 that are treated as non-passive in the hands of F2. Therefore, for the purpose of characterizing F1's proportionate share of the assets of F2, $375x is treated as non-passive, and $125x is treated as passive.

(ii) *Example 2: QIC holds all the stock of an operating subsidiary*.—(A) *Facts*.

(*1*) F1 is a foreign corporation. In Year 1, F1 meets the definition of a QIC under section 1297(f) and §1.1297-4 and is engaged in the active conduct of an insurance business within the meaning of section 1297(b)(2)(B). Throughout Year 1, F1 owns all the stock of F2, a foreign corporation engaged in a manufacturing business that is not a QIC. The stock of F2 is an asset that is available to satisfy liabilities of F1 related to its insurance business within the meaning of paragraph (c)(1) of this section. The assets of F1 are measured on the basis of value under §1.1297-1(d)(1)(v)(C).

(*2*) Throughout Year 1, F2 owns assets with a value of $1,200x, of which $1,000x is treated as non-passive and $200x is treated as passive in the hands of F2. F2 has outstanding debt of $600x. On the financial statement end date of F1's applicable financial statement, the net equity value of the F2 stock held by F1 is $600x. In Year 1, F2 earned $120x of income, of which, in the hands of F2, $100x is treated as non-passive and $20x is treated as passive.

(B) *Result*—(*1*) Because F1 owns all the stock of F2, F2 is a look-through subsidiary of F1 within the meaning of §1.1297-2(g)(3). Under section 1297(c) and §1.1297-2(b)(2), F1 is treated as if it held 100% of the assets of F2 and received directly 100% of the income of F2. Under paragraph (d)(1) of this section, because F1 is engaged in the active conduct of an insurance business and the stock of F2 is an asset that is available to satisfy the insurance liabilities of F1, F1 treats its proportionate share of the income and assets of F2 as non-passive. The amount of income and assets that is treated as non-passive is subject to the limitation of paragraph (d)(2) of this section.

(2) Under paragraph (d)(2) of this section, the amount of F1's proportionate share of F2's income that is treated as non-passive cannot exceed the greater of two amounts: $60x, which is F1's proportionate share of F2's income ($120x) multiplied by 50% (the net equity value of the F2 stock held by F1, which is $600x, divided by the value of F1's proportionate share of F2's assets, which is $1,200x); and $100x, which is F1's proportionate share of the income of F2 that is treated as non-passive in the hands of F2. Therefore, for the purpose of characterizing F1's proportionate share of F2's income, $100x is treated as non-passive, and $20x is treated as passive.

(3) Under paragraph (d)(2) of this section, the amount of F1's proportionate share of F2's assets that is treated as non-passive cannot exceed the greater of two amounts: $600x, which is F1's proportionate share of F2's income ($1,200x) multiplied by 50% (the net equity value of the F2 stock held by F1, which is $600x, divided by the value of F1's proportionate share of F2's assets, which is $1,200x); and $1,000x, which is F1's proportionate share of the assets of F2 that are treated as non-passive in the hands of F2. Therefore, for the purpose of characterizing F1's proportionate share of the assets of F2, $1,000x is treated as non-passive, and $200x is treated as passive.

(e) *Qualifying domestic insurance corporation*.—(1) *General rule*.—A domestic corporation (or a foreign corporation that is treated as a domestic corporation pursuant to a valid section 953(d) election and that computes its reserves as a domestic insurance company would under subchapter L) is a qualifying domestic insurance corporation if it is—

(i) Subject to tax as an insurance company under subchapter L of the Internal Revenue Code;

(ii) Subject to federal income tax on its net income; and

(iii) A look-through subsidiary of a tested foreign corporation.

(2) [Reserved].

(3) [Reserved].

(f) *Applicability date*.—The rules of this section apply to taxable years of shareholders beginning on or after January 14, 2021. A shareholder may choose to apply such rules for any open taxable year beginning after December 31, 2017 and before January 14, 2021, provided that, with respect to a tested foreign corporation, it consistently applies the provisions of this section and § 1.1297-4, for such year and all subsequent years. [Reg. § 1.1297-6.]

☐ [*T.D.* 9936, 1-14-2021.]

Proposed Amendments to Regulation

§ 1.1297-6. Exception from the definition of passive income for active insurance income.—

* * *

(b) *Exclusion from passive income of active insurance income*.—* * *

(2) * * * See paragraph (e)(2)(i) of this section for additional rules regarding the amount of income of a qualifying domestic insurance corporation that is treated as non-passive.

* * *

(c) *Exclusion of assets for purposes of the passive asset test under section 1297(a)(2)*.—* * *

(2) * * * See paragraph (e)(2)(ii) of this section for additional rules regarding the amount of assets of a qualifying domestic insurance corporation that are treated as non-passive.

* * *

(e) *Qualifying domestic insurance corporation*.—* * *

(2) *Qualifying domestic insurance corporation non-passive asset and income limitations*.—For purposes of section 1297 and § 1.1297-1—

(i) *Qualifying domestic insurance corporation's non-passive assets*.—The amount of passive assets of a qualifying domestic insurance corporation that may be treated as non-passive is equal to the lesser of the passive assets of the corporation (determined without application of paragraph (c)(2) of this section) or the corporation's non-passive asset limitation (as defined in paragraph (e)(2)(iii) of this section).

(ii) *Qualifying domestic insurance corporation's non-passive income*.—The amount of passive income of a qualifying domestic insurance corporation that may be treated as non-passive is equal to the lesser of the passive income of the corporation (determined without application of paragraph (b)(2) of this section) or the corporation's passive income multiplied by the proportion that its non-passive asset limitation (as defined in paragraph (e)(2)(iii) of this section) bears to its total passive assets (determined without application of paragraph (c)(2) of this section).

(iii) *Non-passive asset limitation*.—For purposes of paragraph (e) of this section, the non-passive asset limitation equals the corporation's total insurance liabilities multiplied by the applicable percentage. The applicable percentage is—

(A) 400 percent of total insurance liabilities, for a company taxable under Part II of Subchapter L; and

(B) 200 percent of total insurance liabilities, for a company taxable under Part I of Subchapter L.

(iv) *Total insurance liabilities*.—For purposes of paragraph (e) of this section—

(A) *Companies taxable under Part I of Subchapter L*.—In the case of a company taxable under part I of Subchapter L, the term *total insurance liabilities* means the sum of the total reserves (as defined in section 816(c)) plus (to the extent not included in total reserves) the items referred to in paragraphs (3), (4), (5), and (6) of section 807(c).

(B) *Companies taxable under Part II of Subchapter L*.—In the case of a company taxable under part II of Subchapter L, the term *total insurance liabilities* means the sum of unearned premiums (determined under § 1.832-4(a)(8)) and unpaid losses.

(3) *Example*.—The following example illustrates the application of this section.

(i) *Facts*. X, a qualifying domestic insurance corporation within the meaning of paragraph (e)(1) of this section, is a nonlife insurance company taxable under part II of Subchapter L. X has passive assets of $1000x, total insurance liabilities of $200x, and passive income of $100x.

(ii) *Result*—(A) *Non-passive asset limitation*. The applicable percentage for nonlife insurance companies is 400%. Pursuant to paragraph (e)(2)(iii) of this section, X has a non-passive asset limitation of $800x, which is equal to its total insurance liabilities of $200x multiplied by 400%. Under paragraph (e)(2)(i) of this section, $800x of X's passive assets (equal to the lesser of the non-passive asset limitation ($800x) or passive assets ($1000x)) are treated as non-passive, and $200x remains passive.

(B) *Non-passive income limitation*. X has a non-passive asset limitation of $800x. The proportion of its non-passive asset limitation ($800x) to its total passive assets ($1000x) is 80%. Pursuant to paragraph (e)(2)(ii) of this section, X has $80x of passive income treated as non-passive (equal to the lesser of passive income ($100x) or 80% times $100x) and $20x remains passive.

(f) *Applicability date*.—(1) *General applicability date*.—Except as provided in paragraph (f)(2) of this section, this section applies to taxable years of shareholders beginning on or after January 14, 2021.

(2) *Exception*.—Paragraphs (e)(2) and (e)(3) of this section apply to taxable years of shareholders beginning on or after [the date these regulations are filed as final regulations in the **Federal Register**].

(3) *Early application*.—A shareholder may choose to apply the rules of this section (other than paragraphs (e)(2), and (e)(3) of this section) for any open taxable year beginning after December 31, 2017 and before January 14, 2021, provided that, with respect to a tested foreign corporation, it consistently applies those rules and the rules described in § 1.1297-4(g)(3)(i) for such year and all subsequent years. [Prop. Reg. § 1.1297-6.]

[Proposed 1-15-2021.]

§ 1.1298-1. Section 1298(f) annual reporting requirements for United States persons that are shareholders of a passive foreign investment company.—(a) *Overview*.—This section provides rules regarding the reporting requirements under section 1298(f) applicable to a United States person that is a shareholder (as defined in § 1.1291-1(b)(7)) of a passive foreign investment company (PFIC). Paragraph (b) of this section provides the section 1298(f) annual reporting requirements generally applicable to United States persons. Paragraph (c) of this section sets forth exceptions to reporting for certain shareholders. Paragraph (d) of this section provides rules regarding the time and manner of filing the annual report. Paragraph

(e) of this section sets forth the requirement to file a separate annual report with respect to each PFIC. Paragraph (f) of this section coordinates the requirement to file an annual report under section 1298(f) with the requirement to file an annual report under other provisions of the Internal Revenue Code (Code). Paragraph (g) of this section sets forth examples illustrating the application of this section. Paragraph (h) of this section provides effective/applicability dates.

(b) *Requirement to file.*—(1) *General rule.*—Except as otherwise provided in this section, a United States person that is a shareholder of a PFIC must complete and file Form 8621, "Information Return by a Shareholder of a Passive Foreign Investment Company or Qualified Electing Fund" (or successor form), under section 1298(f) and these regulations for the PFIC if, during the shareholder's taxable year, the shareholder—

(i) Directly owns stock of the PFIC;

(ii) Is an indirect shareholder under § 1.1291-1(b)(8) that holds any interest in the PFIC through one or more entities, each of which is foreign; or

(iii) Is an indirect shareholder under § 1.1291-1(b)(8)(iii)(D) that is treated under sections 671 through 678 as the owner of any portion of a trust described in section 7701(a)(30)(E) that owns, directly or indirectly through one or more entities, each of which is foreign, any interest in the PFIC.

(2) *Additional requirement to file for certain indirect shareholders.*—(i) *General rule.*—Except as otherwise provided in this section, an indirect shareholder that owns an interest in a PFIC through one or more United States persons also must file Form 8621 (or successor form) with respect to the PFIC under section 1298(f) and these regulations if, during the indirect shareholder's taxable year, the indirect shareholder is—

(A) Treated as receiving an excess distribution (within the meaning of section 1291(b)) with respect to the PFIC;

(B) Treated as recognizing gain that is treated as an excess distribution (under section 1291(a)(2)) as a result of a disposition of the PFIC;

(C) Required to include an amount in income under section 1293(a) with respect to the PFIC (QEF inclusion);

(D) Required to include or deduct an amount under section 1296(a) with respect to the PFIC (MTM inclusion); or

(E) Required to report the status of a section 1294 election with respect to the PFIC (see § 1.1294-1T(h)).

(ii) *Exception to indirect shareholder reporting for certain QEF inclusions and MTM inclusions.*—Except as otherwise provided in this paragraph (b)(2)(ii), the filing requirements under paragraph (b) of this section do not apply with respect to an interest in a PFIC owned by an indirect shareholder described in paragraph (b)(2)(i)(C) or (D) of this section if another shareholder through which the indirect shareholder owns such interest in the PFIC timely files Form 8621 (or successor form) with respect to the PFIC under paragraph (b)(1) or (2) of this section. However, the exception in this paragraph (b)(2)(ii) does not apply with respect to a PFIC owned by an indirect shareholder described in paragraph (b)(2)(i)(C) of this section that owns the PFIC through a domestic partnership or S corporation if the domestic partnership or S corporation does not make a qualified electing fund election with respect to the PFIC (see § 1.1293-1(c)(2)(ii), addressing QEF stock transferred to a pass through entity that does not make a section 1295 election).

(3) *Special rules for estates and trusts.*—(i) *Domestic liquidating trusts and fixed investment trusts.*—A United States person that is treated under sections 671 through 678 as the owner of any portion of a trust described in section 7701(a)(30)(E) that owns, directly or indirectly, any interest in a PFIC is not required under section 1298(f) and these regulations to file Form 8621 (or successor form) with respect to the PFIC if the trust is either a domestic liquidating trust under § 301.7701-4(d) of this chapter created pursuant to a court order issued in a bankruptcy under Chapter 7 (11 U.S.C. 701 *et seq.*) of the Bankruptcy Code or a confirmed plan under Chapter 11 (11 U.S.C. 1101 *et seq.*) of the Bankruptcy Code, or a widely held fixed investment trust under § 1.671-5. Such a trust itself is treated as a shareholder for purposes of section 1298(f) and these regulations, and thus, except as otherwise provided in this section, the trust is required under section 1298(f) and these regulations to file Form 8621 (or successor form) with respect to the PFIC as provided in paragraphs (b)(1) and (2) of this section.

(ii) *Beneficiaries of foreign estates and trusts.*—A United States person that is considered to own an interest in a PFIC because it is a beneficiary of an estate described in section 7701(a)(31)(A) or a trust described in section 7701(a)(31)(B) that owns, directly or indirectly, stock of a PFIC, and that has not made an election under section 1295 or 1296 with respect to the PFIC, is not required under section 1298(f) and these regulations to file Form 8621 (or successor form) with respect to the stock of the PFIC that it is considered to own through the estate or trust if, during the beneficiary's taxable year, the beneficiary is not treated as receiving an excess distribution (within the meaning of section 1291(b)) or as recognizing gain that is treated as an excess distribution (under section 1291(a)(2)) with respect to the stock.

(c) *Exceptions.*—(1) *Exception if shareholder is a tax-exempt entity.*—A shareholder that is an organization exempt under section 501(a) to the extent that it is described in section 501(c), 501(d), or 401(a), a state college or university described in section 511(a)(2)(B), a plan described in section 403(b) or 457(b), an individual retirement plan or annuity as defined in section 7701(a)(37), or a qualified tuition program described in section 529, a qualified ABLE program described in 529A, or a Coverdell education savings account described in section 530 is not required under section 1298(f) and these regulations to file Form 8621 (or successor form) with respect to a PFIC unless the income derived with respect to the PFIC stock would be taxable to the organization under subchapter F of Subtitle A of the Code.

(2) *Exception if aggregate value of shareholder's PFIC stock is $25,000 or less, or value of shareholder's indirect PFIC stock is $5,000 or less.*—(i) *General rule.*—A shareholder is not required under section 1298(f) and these regulations to file Form 8621 (or successor form) with respect to a section 1291 fund (as defined in § 1.1291-1(b)(2)(v)) for a shareholder's taxable year if—

(A) On the last day of the shareholder's taxable year:

(1) The value of all PFIC stock owned directly or indirectly under section 1298(a) and § 1.1291-1(b)(8) by the shareholder is $25,000 or less; or

(2) The section 1291 fund stock is indirectly owned by the shareholder under section 1298(a)(2)(B) and § 1.1291-1(b)(8)(ii)(B), and the value of the section 1291 fund stock indirectly owned by the shareholder is $5,000 or less;

(B) The shareholder is not treated as receiving an excess distribution (within the meaning of section 1291(b)) with respect to the section 1291 fund during the taxable year or as recognizing gain treated as an excess distribution under section 1291(a)(2) as the result of a disposition of the section 1291 fund during the taxable year; and

(C) An election under section 1295 has not been made to treat the section 1291 fund as a qualified electing fund with respect to the shareholder.

(ii) *Determination of the $25,000 threshold in the case of indirect ownership.*—For purposes of determining the value of stock held by a shareholder for purposes of paragraph (c)(2)(i)(A)(*1*) of this section, the shareholder must take into account the value of all PFIC stock owned directly or indirectly under section 1298(a) and § 1.1291-1(b)(8), except for PFIC stock that is—

(A) Owned through another United States person that itself is a shareholder of the PFIC (including a domestic partnership or S corporation treated as a shareholder of a PFIC for purposes of information reporting requirements applicable to a shareholder);

(B) Owned through a PFIC under section 1298(a)(2)(B) and § 1.1291-1(b)(8)(ii)(B); or

(C) Marked to market for the shareholder's taxable year under any provision of chapter 1 of the Internal Revenue Code other than section 1296, provided the rules of § 1.1296-1(i)(2) and (3) do not apply to the shareholder with respect to the PFIC stock pursuant to § 1.1291-1(c)(4)(ii) for the shareholder's taxable year.

(iii) *Application of the $25,000 exception to shareholders who file a joint return.*—In the case of a joint return, the exception described in paragraph (c)(2)(i)(A)(*1*) of this section shall apply if the value of all PFIC stock owned directly or indirectly (as determined under section 1298(a), § 1.1291-1(b)(8), and paragraph (c)(2)(ii) of this section) by both spouses is $50,000 or less, and all of the other applicable requirements of paragraph (c)(2) of this section are met.

(iv) *Reliance on periodic account statements.*—A shareholder may rely upon periodic account statements provided at least annually to determine the value of a PFIC unless the shareholder has actual knowledge or reason to know based on readily accessible information that the statements do not reflect a reasonable estimate of the PFIC's value.

(3) *Exception for PFIC stock marked to market under a provision other than section 1296.*—A shareholder is not required under section 1298(f) and these regulations to file Form 8621 (or successor form) with respect to a PFIC for any taxable year in which the PFIC is marked to market under any provision of chapter 1 of the Internal Revenue Code other than section 1296, provided the rules of § 1.1296-1(i)(2) and (3) do not apply to the shareholder with respect to the PFIC pursuant to § 1.1291-1(c)(4)(ii) for the taxable year.

(4) *Exception for PFIC stock held through certain foreign pension funds.*—A shareholder who is a member or beneficiary of, or participant in, a plan, trust, scheme, or other arrangement that is treated as a foreign pension fund (or equivalent) under an income tax treaty to which the United States is a party and that owns, directly or indirectly, an interest in a PFIC is not required under section 1298(f) and these regulations to file Form 8621 (or successor form) with respect to the PFIC interest if, pursuant to the applicable income tax treaty, the income earned by the foreign pension fund may be taxed as the income of the shareholder only when and to the extent the income is paid to, or for the benefit of, the shareholder.

(5) *Exception for certain shareholders who are dual resident taxpayers.*—(i) *General rule.*—Subject to the provisions of paragraphs (c)(5)(ii) and (iii) of this section, a shareholder is not required under section 1298(f) and these regulations to file Form 8621 (or successor form) with respect to a PFIC for a taxable year, or the portion of a taxable year, in which the shareholder is a dual resident taxpayer (within the meaning of § 301.7701(b)-7(a)(1) of this chapter) who is treated as a nonresident alien of the United States for purposes of computing his or her United States income tax liability pursuant to § 301.7701(b)-7 of this chapter.

(ii) *Dual resident taxpayer filing as a nonresident alien at end of taxable year.*—If a shareholder to whom this paragraph (c)(5) applies computes his or her U.S. income tax liability as a nonresident alien on the last day of the taxable year and complies with the filing requirements of § 301.7701(b)-7(b) and (c) of this chapter and, in particular, such individual timely files with the Internal Revenue Service Form 1040NR, "U.S. Nonresident Alien Income Tax Return," or Form 1040NR-EZ, "U.S. Income Tax Return for Certain Nonresident Aliens With No Dependents," as applicable, and attaches thereto a properly completed Form 8833, "Treaty-Based Return Position Disclosure Under Section 6114 or 7701(b)," and the schedule required by § 1.6012-1(b)(2)(ii)(*b*) (if applicable), such shareholder will not be required under section 1298(f) and these regulations to file Form 8621 (or successor form) with respect to the taxable year, or the portion of the taxable year, covered by Form 1040NR (or Form 1040NR-EZ).

(iii) *Dual resident taxpayer filing as resident alien at end of taxable year.*—If a shareholder to whom this paragraph (c)(5) applies computes his or her U.S. income tax liability as a resident alien on the last day of the taxable year and complies with the filing requirements of § 1.6012-1(b)(2)(ii)(*a*) and, in particular such shareholder timely files with the Internal Revenue Service Form 1040, "U.S. Individual Income Tax Return," or Form 1040EZ, "Income Tax Return for Single and Joint Filers With No Dependents," as applicable, and attaches a properly completed Form 8833 to the schedule required by § 1.6012-1(b)(2)(ii)(*a*), such shareholder will not be required under section 1298(f) and these regulations to file Form 8621 (or successor form) with respect to the portion of the taxable year reflected on the schedule to such Form 1040 or Form 1040EZ required by § 1.6012-1(b)(2)(ii)(*a*).

(6) *Exception for certain domestic partnerships.*—A shareholder that is a domestic partnership is not required under section 1298(f) and these regulations to file Form 8621 (or successor form) with respect to a PFIC directly or indirectly held by the domestic partnership for a taxable year if each person that directly or indirectly owns an interest in the domestic partnership for its taxable year in which or with which the taxable year of the partnership ends is either—

(i) Not a shareholder of the PFIC as defined by § 1.1291-1(b)(7);

(ii) A tax-exempt entity or account not required to file Form 8621 with respect to the stock of the PFIC under paragraph (c)(1) of this section;

(iii) A dual resident taxpayer not required to file Form 8621 with respect to the stock of the PFIC under paragraph (c)(5) of this section; or

(iv) A domestic partnership not required to file Form 8621 with respect to the stock of the PFIC under this paragraph (c)(6).

(7) *Exception for certain short-term ownership of PFIC stock.*—A shareholder is not required under section 1298(f) and these regulations to file Form 8621 (or successor form) with respect to a section 1291 fund (as defined in § 1.1291-1(b)(2)(v)) for a taxable year when the shareholder—

(i) Acquires the section 1291 fund in the taxable year or the immediately preceding taxable year;

(ii) Is a shareholder of the section 1291 fund for a total of 30 days or less during the period beginning 29 days before the first day of the shareholder's taxable year and ending 29 days after the close of the shareholder's taxable year; and

(iii) Is not treated as receiving an excess distribution (within the meaning of section 1291(b)) with respect to the section 1291 fund, including any gain recognized that is treated as an excess distribution under section 1291(a)(2) as a result of the disposition of the section 1291 fund.

(8) *Exception for certain bona fide residents of certain U.S. territories.*—A shareholder is not required under section 1298(f) and these regulations to file Form 8621 (or successor form) with respect to a PFIC for a taxable year when the shareholder—

(i) Is a bona fide resident (as defined by section 937(a)) of Guam, the Northern Mariana Islands, or the United States Virgin Islands; and

(ii) Is not required to file an income tax return with the Internal Revenue Service with respect to such taxable year.

(9) *Exception for taxable years ending before December 31, 2013.*—A United States person is not required under section 1298(f) and these regulations to file an annual report with respect to a PFIC for a taxable year of the United States person ending before December 31, 2013.

(d) *Time and manner for filing.*—A United States person required under section 1298(f) and these regulations to file Form 8621 (or successor form) with respect to a PFIC must attach the form to its Federal income tax return (or information return, if applicable) for the taxable year to which the filing obligation relates on or before the due date (including extensions) for the filing of the return, or must separately file the form in accordance with the instructions for the form when the United States person is not required to file a Federal income tax return (or information return, if applicable) for the taxable year. In the case of any failure to report information that is required to be reported pursuant to section 1298(f) and these regulations, the time for assessment of tax will be extended pursuant to section 6501(c)(8).

(e) *Separate annual report for each PFIC.*—(1) *General rule.*—If a United States person is required under section 1298(f) and these regulations to file Form 8621 (or successor form) with respect to more than one PFIC, the United States person must file a separate Form 8621 (or successor form) for each PFIC.

(2) *Special rule for shareholders who file a joint return.*—United States persons that file a joint return may file a single Form 8621 (or successor form) with respect to a PFIC in which they jointly or individually own an interest.

(f) *Coordination rule.*—A United States person that is a shareholder of a PFIC may file a single Form 8621 (or successor form) with respect to the PFIC that contains all of the information required to be reported pursuant to section 1298(f) and these regulations and any other information reporting requirements or election rules under other provisions of the Code.

(g) *Examples.*—The following examples illustrate the rules of this section:

Example 1. General requirement to file. (i) *Facts.* In 2013, J, a United States citizen, directly owns an interest in Partnership X, a domestic partnership, which, in turn, owns an interest in A Corp, which is a PFIC. In addition, J directly owns an interest in Partnership Y, a foreign partnership, which, in turn, owns an interest in A Corp. Neither J nor Partnership X has made a qualified electing fund election under section 1295 or a mark to market election under section 1296 with respect to A Corp. As of the last day of 2013, the value of Partnership X's interest in A Corp is $200,000, and the value of J's proportionate share of Partnership Y's interest in A Corp is $100,000. During 2013, J is not treated as receiving an excess distribution or recognizing gain treated as an excess distribution with respect to A Corp. Partnership X timely files a Form 8621 under section

1298(f) and paragraph (b)(1) of this section with respect to A Corp for 2013.

(ii) *Results.* J is the first United States person in the chain of ownership with respect to J's interest in A Corp held through Partnership Y. Under paragraph (b)(1) of this section, J must file a Form 8621 under section 1298(f) with respect to J's interest in A Corp held through Partnership Y because J is an indirect shareholder of A Corp under § 1.1291-1(b)(8) that holds PFIC stock through a foreign entity (Partnership Y), and there are no other United States persons in the chain of ownership. The fact that Partnership X filed a Form 8621 with respect to A Corp does not relieve J of the obligation under paragraph (b)(1) of this section to file a Form 8621 with respect to J's interest in A Corp held through Partnership Y. J has no filing obligation under section 1298(f) and paragraph (b)(2) of this section with respect to J's proportionate share of Partnership X's interest in A Corp.

Example 2. Application of the $25,000 exception. (i) *Facts.* In 2013, J, a United States citizen, directly owns stock of A Corp, B Corp, and C Corp, all of which were PFICs during 2013. As of the last day of 2013, the value of J's interests was $5,000 in A Corp, $10,000 in B Corp, and $4,000 in C Corp. J timely filed an election under section 1295 to treat A Corp as a qualified electing fund for the first year in which A Corp qualified as a PFIC, and a mark-to-market election under section 1296 with respect to the stock of B Corp. J did not make a qualified electing fund election under section 1295 or a mark to market election under section 1296 with respect to C Corp. J did not receive an excess distribution or recognize gain treated as an excess distribution in respect of C Corp during 2013.

(ii) *Results.* Under paragraph (b)(1) of this section, J must file separate Forms 8621 with respect to A Corp and B Corp for 2013. However, J is not required to file a Form 8621 with respect to C Corp because J owns, in the aggregate, PFIC stock with a value of less than $25,000 on the last day of J's taxable year, C Corp is not subject to a qualified electing fund election or mark to market election with respect to J, and J did not receive an excess distribution in respect of C Corp or recognize gain treated as an excess distribution in respect of C Corp during 2013. Therefore, J qualifies for the $25,000 exception in paragraph (c)(2) of this section with respect to C Corp.

Example 3. Application of the $25,000 exception to indirect shareholder. (i) *Facts.* E, a United States citizen, directly owns an interest in Partnership X, a domestic partnership. Partnership X, in turn, directly owns an interest in A Corp and B Corp, both of which are PFICs. Partnership X timely filed an election under section 1295 to treat B Corp as a qualified electing fund for the first year in which B Corp qualified as a PFIC. In addition, E directly owns an interest in C Corp, which is a PFIC. C Corp, in turn, owns an interest in D Corp, which is a PFIC. E has not made a qualified electing fund election under section 1295 or a mark to market election under section 1296 with respect to A Corp, C Corp, or D Corp. As of the last day of 2013, the value of Partnership X's interest in A Corp is $30,000, the value of Partnership X's interest in B Corp is $30,000, the value of E's indirect interest in A Corp is $10,000, the value of E's indirect interest in B Corp is $10,000, the value of E's interest in C Corp is $20,000, and the value of C Corp's interest in D Corp is $10,000. During 2013, E did not receive an excess distribution, or recognize gain treated as an excess distribution, with respect to A Corp, C Corp, or D Corp. Partnership X timely files Forms 8621 under section 1298(f) and paragraph (b)(1) of this section with respect to A Corp and B Corp for 2013.

(ii) *Results.* Under paragraph (b) of this section, E does not have to file a Form 8621 under section 1298(f) and these regulations with respect to A Corp because E is not the United States person that is at the lowest tier in the chain of ownership with respect to A Corp and E did not receive an excess distribution or recognize gain treated as an excess distribution with respect to A Corp. Furthermore, under paragraph (b)(2)(ii) of this section, E does not have to file a Form 8621 under section 1298(f) and these regulations with respect to B Corp because Partnership X timely filed a Form 8621 with respect to B Corp. In addition, under paragraph (c)(2)(ii)(A) of this section, E does not take into account the value of A Corp and B Corp, which E owns through Partnership X, in determining whether E qualifies for the $25,000 exception. Further, under paragraph (c)(2)(ii)(B) of this section, E does not take into account the value of D Corp in determining whether E qualifies for the $25,000 exception. Therefore, even though E is the United States person that is at the lowest tier in the chain of ownership with respect to C Corp and D Corp, E does not have to file a Form 8621 with respect to C Corp or D Corp because E qualifies for the $25,000 exception set forth in paragraph (c)(2)(i)(A)(*1*) of this section.

Example 4. Indirect shareholder's requirement to file. (i) *Facts.* The facts are the same as in *Example 3* of this paragraph (g), except that the value of E's interest in C Corp is $30,000 and the value of E's proportionate share of C Corp's interest in D Corp is $3,000.

(ii) *Results.* The results are the same as in *Example 3* of this paragraph (g) with respect to E having no requirement to file a Form 8621 under section 1298(f) and these regulations with respect to A Corp and B Corp. However, under the facts in this *Example 4*, E does not qualify for the $25,000 exception under paragraph (c)(2)(i)(A)(*1*) of this section with respect to C Corp because the value of E's interest in C Corp is $30,000. Accordingly, E must file a Form 8621 under section 1298(f) and these regulations with respect to C Corp. However, E does qualify for the $5,000 exception under paragraph (c)(2)(i)(A)(*2*) of this section with respect to D Corp, and thus does not have to file a Form 8621 with respect to D Corp.

Example 5. Application of the domestic partnership exception. (i) *Facts.* Tax Exempt Entity A and Tax Exempt Entity B are both organizations exempt under section 501(a) because they are described in section 501(c). Tax Exempt Entity A and Tax Exempt Entity B own all the interests in Partnership X, a domestic partnership, which, in turn, owns, an interest in Partnership Y, also a domestic partnership. The remaining interests in Partnership Y are owned by F Corp, a foreign corporation owned solely by individuals that are not residents or citizens of the United States. Partnership Y owns an interest in A Corp, which is a PFIC. Any income derived with respect to A Corp would not be taxable to Tax Exempt Entity A or Tax Exempt Entity B under subchapter F of Subtitle A of the Code. Tax Exempt Entity A, Tax Exempt Entity B, Partnership X, and Partnership Y all are calendar year taxpayers.

(ii) *Results.* Under paragraph (c)(1) of this section, Tax Exempt Entity A and Tax Exempt Entity B do not have to file Form 8621 under section 1298(f) and these regulations with respect to A Corp because neither entity would be subject to tax under subchapter F of Subtitle A of the Code with respect to income derived from A Corp. In addition, under paragraph (c)(6) of this section, neither Partnership X nor Partnership Y is required to file Form 8621 under section 1298(f) and these regulations with respect to A Corp because all of the direct and indirect interests in Partnership X and Partnership Y are owned by persons described in paragraph (c)(1) of this section or persons that are not a shareholder of A Corp as defined by § 1.1291-1(b)(7).

(h) *Applicability dates.*—(1) Except as provided in paragraph (h)(2) of this section, this section applies to taxable years of shareholders ending on or after December 31, 2013.

(2) Paragraph (c)(9) of this section applies to taxable years of shareholders ending before December 31, 2013. [Reg. § 1.1298-1.]

☐ [*T.D. 9806, 12-27-2016.*]

Proposed Amendments to Regulation

§ 1.1298-1. Section 1298(f) annual reporting requirements for United States persons that are shareholders of a passive foreign investment company.—

* * *

(b) * * *

(1) *General rule.*—Except as otherwise provided in this section, a United States person that is a shareholder of a PFIC (as defined in § 1.1291-1(b)(7)) must complete and file Form 8621, "Information Return by a Shareholder of a Passive Foreign Investment Company or Qualified Electing Fund" (or successor form), under section 1298(f) and this section for the PFIC if, during the shareholder's taxable year, the shareholder—

(i) Directly owns stock of the PFIC; or

(ii) Is an indirect shareholder under § 1.1291-1(b)(8) that holds any interest in the PFIC through one or more entities, domestic or foreign, each of which is not a shareholder of such PFIC within the meaning of § 1.1291-1(b)(7).

(2) *Additional requirement to file for certain beneficiaries of domestic estates and domestic nongrantor trusts.*—(i) *General rule.*—Except as otherwise provided in this section, an indirect shareholder that owns an interest in a PFIC by reason of an interest in a domestic estate or domestic nongrantor trust (as described in § 1.1291-1(b)(8)(iii)(C)) also must file Form 8621 (or successor form) with respect to the PFIC under section 1298(f) and this section if, during the indirect shareholder's taxable year, the indirect shareholder is—

* * *

(ii) *Exception to indirect shareholder reporting for certain QEF inclusions and MTM inclusions.*—The filing requirements under paragraph (b)(2)(i) of this section do not apply with respect to an interest in a PFIC owned by an indirect shareholder described in paragraph (b)(2)(i)(C) or (D) of this section if the domestic nongrantor trust or domestic estate through which the indirect shareholder owns such interest in the PFIC timely files Form 8621 (or successor form) with respect to the PFIC under paragraph (b)(1) of this section.

* * *

(h) * * *

(3) Paragraphs (b)(1) and (b)(2)(i) and (ii) of this section apply to taxable years of shareholders beginning on or after [date of publication of the Treasury decision adopting these rules as final regulations in the **Federal Register**]. For taxable years of shareholders beginning before [date of publication of the Treasury decision adopting these rules as final regulations in the **Federal Register**], see § 1.1298-1(b)(1) and (b)(2)(i) and (ii) as in effect and contained in 26 CFR part 1, as revised April 1, 2021. [Prop. Reg. § 1.1298-1.]

[Proposed 1-25-2022.]

§ 1.1298-2. Rules for certain corporations changing businesses.—(a) *Overview*.—This section provides rules under section 1298(b)(3) and 1298(g) that apply to certain foreign corporations that dispose of one or more active trades or businesses for purposes of determining whether a foreign corporation is treated as a passive foreign investment company (PFIC). Paragraph (b) of this section provides a rule that applies to certain foreign corporations that dispose of one or more active trades or businesses. Paragraph (c) of this section provides special rules. Paragraph (d) of this section provides a rule for the treatment of the disposition of the stock of a look-through subsidiary (as defined in § 1.1297-2(g)(3)) or partnership interests in a look-through partnership (as defined in § 1.1297-2(g)(4)). Paragraph (e) of this section provides guidance on when a tested foreign corporation can apply the change of business exception. Paragraph (f) provides examples illustrating the application of the rules in this section. Paragraph (g) provides the applicability date for this section.

(b) *Change of business exception*.—A corporation is not treated as a PFIC for a taxable year if—

(1) Neither the corporation (nor any predecessor) was a PFIC for any prior taxable year;

(2) Either—

(i) Substantially all of the passive income of the corporation for the taxable year is attributable to proceeds from the disposition of one or more active trades or businesses; or

(ii) Following the disposition of one or more active trades or businesses, substantially all of the passive assets of the corporation on each of the measuring dates that occur during the taxable year and after the disposition are attributable to proceeds from the disposition; and

(3) The corporation reasonably does not expect to be and is not a PFIC for either of the first two taxable years following the taxable year.

(c) *Special rules*.—The rules in this paragraph (c) apply for purposes of section 1298(b)(3) and this section.

(1) Income is attributable to proceeds from the disposition of one or more active trades or businesses to the extent the income is derived from the investment of the proceeds from the disposition of assets used in the active trades or businesses.

(2) Assets are attributable to proceeds from the disposition of one or more active trades or businesses only to the extent the assets are the proceeds of the disposition of assets used in the active trades or businesses, or are derived from the investment of the proceeds.

(3) The determination of the existence of an active trade or business and whether assets are used in an active trade or business is made under § 1.367(a)-2(d)(2), (3), and (5), except that officers and employees do not include the officers and employees of related entities as provided in § 1.367(a)-2(d)(3). However, if activities performed by the officers and employees of a lookthrough subsidiary of a corporation or of a look-through partnership (including a look-through subsidiary or a look-through partnership with respect to which paragraph (d) of this section applies) would be taken into account by the corporation pursuant to § 1.1297-2(e) if it applied, such activities are taken into account for purposes of the determination of the existence of an active trade or business and the determination of whether assets are used in an active trade or business.

(4) In the case of a corporation that satisfies the condition in paragraph (b)(2)(ii) of this section, the condition in paragraph (b)(3) of this section is deemed to be satisfied if the corporation completely liquidates by the end of the taxable year following the year with respect to which the tested foreign corporation applies the exception in paragraph (b) of this section.

(d) *Disposition of stock of a look-through subsidiary or partnership interests in a look-through partnership*.—For purposes of paragraph (b) of this section, the proceeds from a tested foreign corporation's disposition of the stock of a look-through subsidiary or of partnership interests in a look-through partnership are treated as proceeds from the disposition of a proportionate share of the assets held by the look-through subsidiary or look-through partnership on the date of the disposition, based on the method (value or adjusted bases) used to measure the assets of the tested foreign corporation for purposes of section 1297(a)(2). The proceeds attributable to assets used by the look-through subsidiary or look-through partnership in an active trade or business are treated as proceeds attributable to the disposition of an active trade or business.

(e) *Application of change of business exception*.—A tested foreign corporation can apply the exception in paragraph (b) of this section with respect to a taxable year of a disposition of an active trade or business or an immediately succeeding taxable year, but cannot apply the exception with respect to more than one taxable year for a disposition.

(f) *Examples*.—The following examples illustrate the rules of this section. For purposes of these examples: USP is a domestic corporation; TFC and FS are foreign corporations that are not controlled foreign corporations (within the meaning of section 957(a)); each corporation has outstanding a single class of stock; USP has owned its interest in TFC since the formation of TFC; each of USP, TFC, and FS have a calendar taxable year; and for purposes of section 1297(a)(2), TFC measures the amount of its assets based on value.

(1) *Example 1*.—(i) *Facts*. (A) USP owns 15% of the outstanding stock of TFC. TFC owns 30% of the outstanding stock of FS. FS operates an active trade or business and 100% of its assets are used in the active trade or business. The value of FS's non-passive assets (as defined in § 1.1297-1(f)(3)) is $900x; the value of FS's passive assets (which include cash and cash equivalents) is $100x. TFC has not been treated as a PFIC for any taxable year before Year 1 and has no predecessor. In addition to holding the FS stock, TFC directly conducts its own active trade or business. The value of TFC's non-passive assets (other than FS stock) is $50x; the value of TFC's passive assets (other than FS stock and assets received during Year 1) is $30x. TFC earns $1x of non-passive income (as defined in § 1.1297-1(f)(4)) from its directly conducted active trade or business.

(B) On January 1, Year 1, TFC sells all of its FS stock for $300x. The residual gain computed under § 1.1297-2(f)(2) on the sale of the FS stock is $10x. Under § 1.1297-2(f)(3), $9x of residual gain is characterized as non-passive income and $1x of residual gain is characterized as passive income. TFC earned $5x of passive income from the investment of the proceeds from the disposition of the FS stock during each quarter of Year 1, and TFC maintained those earnings ($20x in total) as well as the disposition proceeds in cash for the remainder of the year. TFC reinvests the proceeds of the FS stock sale in an active trade or business during Year 2, and, thus, TFC is not a PFIC in Year 2 and Year 3. Less than 75% of TFC's gross income in Year 1 is passive income (($20x + $1x)/($10x + $20x + $1x) = 68%). However, subject to the application of section 1298(b)(3) and this section, TFC would be a PFIC in Year 1 under section 1297(a)(2) because the proceeds from the sale of the FS stock ($300x) together with TFC's other passive assets exceed 50% of TFC's total assets on each quarterly measuring date. For example, on the first quarterly measuring date TFC's ratio of passive assets to total assets is (($300x + $30x + $5x)/($300x + $30x + $5x + $50x)) and on the fourth quarterly measuring date TFC's ratio of passive assets to total assets is (($300x + $30x + $20x)/($300x + $30x + $20x + $50x)), each of which exceeds 87%. Therefore, TFC chooses to apply the change of business exception in paragraph (b) of this section to Year 1.

(ii) *Results*. (A) Under paragraph (d) of this section, for purposes of applying section 1298(b)(3)(B)(i) in Year 1, TFC's proceeds from the disposition of the stock of FS that are attributable to assets used by FS in an active trade or business are considered as from the disposition of an active trade or business. Because 100% of FS's assets are used in its active trade or business, all of TFC's proceeds are considered as from the disposition of an active trade or business. Therefore, under paragraph (c)(1) of this section, the passive income considered attributable to proceeds from a disposition of one or more active trades or businesses is $20x (from investment of disposition proceeds). Because TFC reasonably does not expect to be a PFIC in Year 2 and Year 3, and TFC is not, in fact, a PFIC for those years, TFC will not be treated as a PFIC in Year 1 by reason of section 1298(b)(3) and paragraph (b) of this section, based on the satisfaction of the condition in paragraph (b)(2)(i) of this section, because the 95% ($20x/($20x + $1x)) of TFC's passive income for Year 1 that is attributable to proceeds of the disposition of FS's active trade or business constitutes substantially all of its passive income.

(B) TFC would also not be treated as a PFIC in Year 1 by reason of section 1298(b)(3) and paragraph (b) of this section, based on the satisfaction of the condition in paragraph (b)(2)(ii) of this section, because the over 91% of TFC's passive assets on the quarterly measuring dates during Year 1 following the disposition of the stock of FS that is attributable to proceeds of the disposition of FS's active trade or business constitutes substantially all of its passive assets. For example, on the first quarterly measuring date TFC's ratio of passive assets attributable to the proceeds of the disposition of FS's active trade or business to its total passive assets is 91% ($305x/($305x + $30x)), and the same ratio for the fourth quarterly measuring date is 91.4% ($320x/($320x + $30x)).

(C) Under paragraph (e) of this section, TFC cannot claim the section 1298(b)(3) exception in relation to the income attributable to the proceeds of the FS stock sale in Year 2 because TFC already claimed the exception for Year 1.

(2) *Example 2.*—(i) *Facts.* The facts are the same as in paragraph (f)(1)(i) of this section (the facts in *Example 1*), except that during the first quarter of Year 1, TFC earned only $4x of passive income ($1x per quarter) from the investment of the proceeds from the disposition of the FS stock and earned $12x of passive income ($3x per quarter) from its other passive assets and maintained such earnings in cash for the remainder of the year.

(ii) *Results.* The results are the same as in paragraph (f)(1)(ii) of this section (the results in *Example 1*), except that under paragraph (c)(1) of this section, the passive income considered attributable to proceeds from a disposition of one or more active trades or businesses is $4x (from investment of disposition proceeds). Because 24% ($4x/($4x + $12x + $1x)) of TFC's passive income for Year 1 is attributable to proceeds of the disposition of FS's active trade or business, and 24% does not constitute substantially all of TFC's passive income for Year 1, TFC does not qualify for the exception from treatment as a PFIC in section 1298(b)(3) and paragraph (b)(2)(i) of this section for Year 1. However, under paragraphs (b)(2)(ii) and (d) of this section, more than $300x ($300x disposition proceeds + amounts earned from investment of disposition proceeds) of TFC's passive assets held on each quarterly measuring date after the disposition is considered attributable to the disposition of an active trade or business. Because TFC reasonably does not expect to be a PFIC in Year 2 and Year 3, and TFC is not, in fact, a PFIC for those years, TFC will not be treated as a PFIC in Year 1 by reason of paragraph (b) of this section, based on the satisfaction of the condition in paragraph (b)(2)(ii) of this section, assuming that the average 89% of TFC's passive assets on the quarterly measuring dates during Year 1 following the disposition of the stock of FS that is attributable to proceeds of the disposition of FS's active trade or business constitutes substantially all of its passive assets.

(g) *Applicability date.*—The rules of this section apply to taxable years of shareholders beginning on or after January 14, 2021. A shareholder may choose to apply such rules for any open taxable year beginning before January 14, 2021, provided that, with respect to the tested foreign corporation, the shareholder consistently applies the provisions of this section and § 1.1291-1(b)(8)(iv) and (b)(8)(v)(A), (B), (C) and (D) and §§ 1.1297-1 (except that consistent treatment is not required with respect to § 1.1297-1(c)(1)(i)(A)), 1.1297-2, and 1.1298-4 for such year and all subsequent years. [Reg. § 1.1298-2.]

☐ [*T.D. 9936*, 1-14-2021 (*corrected* 3-9-2021).]

§ 1.1298-3. Deemed sale or deemed dividend election by a U.S. person that is a shareholder of a former PFIC.—(a) *In general.*—A shareholder (as defined in § 1.1291-9(j)(3)) of a foreign corporation that is a former PFIC, (as defined in § 1.1291-9(j)(2)(iv)) with respect to such shareholder, shall be treated for tax purposes as holding stock in a PFIC and therefore continues to be subject to taxation under section 1291 unless the shareholder makes a purging election under section 1298(b)(1). A purging election under section 1298(b)(1) is made under rules similar to the rules of section 1291(d)(2). Section 1291(d)(2) allows a shareholder to purge the continuing PFIC taint by making either a deemed sale election or a deemed dividend election.

(b) *Application of deemed sale election rules.*—(1) *Eligibility to make the deemed sale election.*—A shareholder of a foreign corporation that is a former PFIC with respect to such shareholder may make a deemed sale election under section 1298(b)(1) by applying the rules of this paragraph (b).

(2) *Effect of deemed sale election.*—A shareholder making the deemed sale election with respect to a former PFIC shall be treated as having sold all its stock in the former PFIC for its fair market value on the termination date, as defined in paragraph (d) of this section. A deemed sale is treated as a disposition subject to taxation under section 1291. Thus, gain from the deemed sale is taxed under section 1291 as an excess distribution received on the termination date. In the case of an election made by an indirect shareholder, the amount of gain to be recognized and taxed as an excess distribution is the amount of gain that the direct owner of the stock of the PFIC would have realized on an actual sale or disposition of the stock of the PFIC indirectly owned by the shareholder. Any loss realized on the deemed sale is not recognized. After the deemed sale election, the shareholder's stock with respect to which the election was made under this paragraph (b) shall not be treated as stock in a PFIC and the shareholder shall not be subject to taxation under section 1291 with respect to such stock unless the foreign corporation thereafter qualifies as a PFIC under section 1297(a).

(3) *Time for making the deemed sale election.*—Except as provided in paragraph (e) of this section, the shareholder shall make the deemed sale election under this paragraph (b) and section 1298(b)(1) in the shareholder's original or amended return for the taxable year that includes the termination date (election year). If the deemed sale election is made in an amended return, the return must be filed by a date that is within three years of the due date, as extended under section 6081, of the original return for the election year.

(4) *Manner of making the deemed sale election.*—A shareholder makes the deemed sale election under this paragraph (b) by filing Form 8621 ("Return by a Shareholder of a Passive Foreign Investment Company or Qualified Electing Fund") with the return of the shareholder for the election year, reporting the gain as an excess distribution pursuant to section 1291(a) as if such deemed sale occurred under section 1291(d)(2), and paying the tax and interest due on the excess distribution. A shareholder that makes the deemed sale election after the due date of the return (determined without regard to extensions) for the election year must pay additional interest, pursuant to section 6601, on the amount of underpayment of tax for that year. An electing shareholder that realizes a loss shall report the loss on Form 8621, but shall not recognize the loss.

(5) *Adjustments to basis.*—A shareholder that makes the deemed sale election increases its adjusted basis of the PFIC stock owned directly by the amount of gain recognized on the deemed sale. If the shareholder makes the deemed sale election with respect to a PFIC of which it is an indirect shareholder, the shareholder's adjusted basis of the stock or other property owned directly by the shareholder, through which ownership of the PFIC is attributed to the shareholder, is increased by the amount of gain recognized by the shareholder. In addition, solely for purposes of determining the subsequent treatment under the Code and regulations of a shareholder of the stock of the PFIC, the adjusted basis of the direct owner of the stock of the PFIC is increased by the amount of gain recognized on the deemed sale. A shareholder shall not adjust the basis of any stock with respect to which the shareholder realized a loss on the deemed sale, but which loss is not recognized under paragraph (b)(2) of this section.

(6) *Treatment of holding period.*—If a shareholder of a foreign corporation has made a deemed sale election, then, for purposes of applying sections 1291 through 1298 to such shareholder after the deemed sale, the shareholder's holding period in the stock of the foreign corporation begins on the day following the termination, without regard to whether the shareholder recognized gain on the deemed sale. For other purposes of the Code and regulations, this holding period rule does not apply.

(c) *Application of deemed dividend election rules.*—(1) *Eligibility to make the deemed dividend election.*—A shareholder of a foreign corporation that is a former PFIC with respect to such shareholder may make the deemed dividend election under the rules of this paragraph (c) provided the foreign corporation was a controlled foreign corporation (as defined in section 957(a) (CFC)) during its last taxable year as a PFIC. A shareholder may make the deemed dividend election without regard to whether the shareholder is a United States shareholder within the meaning of section 951(b). A deemed dividend election may be made by a shareholder whose pro rata share of the post-1986 earnings and profits of the PFIC attributable to the PFIC stock held on the termination date is zero.

(2) *Effect of the deemed dividend election.*—A shareholder making the deemed dividend election with respect to a former PFIC shall include in income as a dividend its pro rata share of the post-1986 earnings and profits of the PFIC attributable to all of the stock it held, directly or indirectly on the termination date, as defined in paragraph (d) of this section. The deemed dividend is taxed under section 1291 as an excess distribution received on the termination date. The excess distribution determined under this paragraph (c) is allocated under section 1291(a)(1)(A) only to each day of the shareholder's holding period of the stock during which the foreign corporation qualified as a PFIC. For purposes of the preceding sentence, the shareholder's holding period of the PFIC stock ends on the termination date. After the deemed dividend election, the shareholder's stock with respect to which the election was made under this paragraph (c) shall not be treated as stock in a PFIC and the shareholder shall not be subject to taxation under section 1291 with respect to such stock unless the foreign corporation thereafter qualifies as a PFIC under section 1297(a).

(3) *Post-1986 earnings and profits defined.*—(i) *In general.*—For purposes of this section, the term *post-1986 earnings and profits* means the post-1986 undistributed earnings, within the meaning of section 902(c)(1) (determined without regard to section 902(c)(3)), as of the close of the taxable year that includes the termination date. For purposes of this computation, only earnings and profits accumulated in taxable years during which the foreign corporation was a PFIC shall be taken into account, without regard to whether the earnings relate to a period during which the PFIC was a CFC.

(ii) *Pro rata share of post-1986 earnings and profits attributable to shareholder's stock.*—(A) *In general.*—A shareholder's pro rata share of the post-1986 earnings and profits of the PFIC attributable to the stock held by the shareholder on the termination date is the amount of post-1986 earnings and profits of the PFIC accumulated during any portion of the shareholder's holding period ending at the close of the termination date and attributable, under the principles of section 1248 and the regulations under that section, to the PFIC stock held on the termination date.

(B) *Reduction for previously taxed amounts.*—A shareholder's pro rata share of the post-1986 earnings and profits of the PFIC does not include any amount that the shareholder demonstrates to the satisfaction of the Commissioner (in the manner provided in paragraph (c)(5)(ii) of this section) was, pursuant to another provision of the law, previously included in the income of the shareholder, or of another U.S. person if the shareholder's holding period of the PFIC stock includes the period during which the stock was held by that other U.S. person.

(4) *Time for making the deemed dividend election.*—Except as provided in paragraph (e) of this section, the shareholder shall make the deemed dividend election under this paragraph (c) and section 1298(b)(1) in the shareholder's original or amended return for the taxable year that includes the termination date (election year). If the deemed dividend election is made in an amended return, the return must be filed by a date that is within three years of the due date, as extended under section 6081, of the original return for the election year.

(5) *Manner of making the deemed dividend election.*—(i) *In general.*—A shareholder makes the deemed dividend election by filing Form 8621 and the attachment to Form 8621 described in paragraph (c)(5)(ii) of this section with the return of the shareholder for the election year, reporting the deemed dividend as an excess distribution pursuant to section 1291(a)(1), and paying the tax and interest due on the excess distribution. A shareholder that makes the deemed dividend election after the due date of the return (determined without regard to extensions) for the election year must pay additional interest, pursuant to section 6601, on the amount of underpayment of tax for that year.

(ii) *Attachment to Form 8621.*—The shareholder must attach a schedule to Form 8621 that demonstrates the calculation of the shareholder's pro rata share of the post-1986 earnings and profits of the PFIC that is treated as distributed to the shareholder on the termination date pursuant to this paragraph (c). If the shareholder is claiming an exclusion from its pro rata share of the post-1986 earnings and profits for an amount previously included in its income or the income of another U.S. person, the shareholder must include the following information:

(A) The name, address, and taxpayer identification number of each U.S. person that previously included an amount in income, the amount previously included in income by each such U.S. person, the provision of law pursuant to which the amount was previously included in income, and the taxable year or years of inclusion of each amount.

(B) A description of the transaction pursuant to which the shareholder acquired, directly or indirectly, the stock of the PFIC from another U.S. person, and the provision of law pursuant to which the shareholder's holding period includes the period the other U.S. person held the CFC stock.

(6) *Adjustments to basis.*—A shareholder that makes the deemed dividend election increases its adjusted basis of the stock of the PFIC owned directly by the shareholder by the amount of the deemed dividend. If the shareholder makes the deemed dividend election with respect to a PFIC of which it is an indirect shareholder, the shareholder's adjusted basis of the stock or other property owned directly by the shareholder, through which ownership of the PFIC is attributed to the shareholder, is increased by the amount of the deemed dividend. In addition, solely for purposes of determining the subsequent treatment under the Code and regulations of a shareholder of the stock of the PFIC, the adjusted basis of the direct owner of the stock of the PFIC is increased by the amount of the deemed dividend.

(7) *Treatment of holding period.*—If the shareholder of a foreign corporation has made a deemed dividend election, then, for purposes of applying sections 1291 through 1298 to such shareholder after the deemed dividend, the shareholder's holding period of the stock of the foreign corporation begins on the day following the termination date. For other purposes of the Code and regulations, this holding period rule does not apply.

(8) *Coordination with section 959(e).*—For purposes of section 959(e), the entire deemed dividend is treated as having been included in gross income under section 1248(a).

(d) *Termination date.*—For purposes of this section, the termination date is the last day of the last taxable year of the foreign corporation during which it qualified as a PFIC under section 1297(a).

(e) *Late purging elections requiring special consent.*—(1) *In general.*—This section prescribes the exclusive rules under which a shareholder of a former PFIC may make a section 1298(b)(1) election after the time prescribed in paragraph (b)(3) or (c)(4) of this section for making a deemed sale or a deemed dividend election has elapsed (late purging election). Therefore, a shareholder may not seek such relief under any other provisions of the law, including § 301.9100-3 of this chapter. A shareholder may request the consent of the Commissioner to make a late purging election for the taxable year of the shareholder that includes the termination date provided the shareholder satisfies the requirements set forth in this paragraph (e). The Commissioner may, in his discretion, grant relief under this paragraph (e) only if—

(i) In a case where the shareholder is requesting consent under this paragraph (e) after December 31, 2005, the shareholder requests such consent before a representative of the Internal Revenue Service raises upon audit the PFIC status of the foreign corporation for any taxable year of the shareholder;

(ii) The shareholder has agreed in a closing agreement with the Commissioner, described in paragraph (e)(3) of this section, to eliminate any prejudice to the interests of the U.S. government, as determined under paragraph (e)(2) of this section, as a consequence of the shareholder's inability to file amended returns for its taxable year in which the termination date falls or an earlier closed taxable year in which the shareholder has taken a position that is inconsistent with the treatment of the foreign corporation as a PFIC; and

(iii) The shareholder satisfies the procedural requirements set forth in paragraph (e)(3) of this section.

(2) *Prejudice to the interests of the U.S. government.*—The interests of the U.S. government are prejudiced if granting relief would result in the shareholder having a lower tax liability (other than by a de minimis amount), taking into account applicable interest charges, for the taxable year that includes the termination date (or a prior taxable year in which the taxpayer took a position on a return that was inconsistent with the treatment of the foreign corporation as a PFIC) than the shareholder would have had if the shareholder had properly made the section 1298(b)(1) election in the time prescribed in para-

graph (b)(2) or (c)(3) of this section (or had not taken a position in a return for an earlier year that was inconsistent with the status of the foreign corporation as a PFIC). The time value of money is taken into account for purposes of this computation.

(3) *Procedural requirements.*—(i) *In general.*—The amount due with respect to a late purging election is determined in the same manner as if the purging election had been timely filed. However, the shareholder is also liable for interest on the amount due, pursuant to section 6601, determined for the period beginning on the due date (without extensions) for the taxpayer's income tax return for the year in which the termination date falls and ending on the date the late purging election is filed with the IRS.

(ii) *Filing instructions.*—A late purging election is made by filing a completed Form 8621-A, "Return by a Shareholder Making Certain Late Elections to End Treatment as a Passive Foreign Investment Company."

(4) *Time and manner of making late election.*—(i) *Time for making a late purging election.*—A shareholder may make a late purging election in the manner provided in paragraph (e)(4)(ii) of this section at any time. The date the election is filed with the IRS will determine the amount of interest due under paragraph (e)(3) of this section.

(ii) *Manner of making a late purging election.*—A shareholder makes a late purging election by completing Form 8621-A in the manner required by that form and this section and filing that form with the Internal Revenue Service, DP 8621-A, Ogden, UT 84201.

(5) *Multiple late elections* .—For rules regarding the circumstances under which a shareholder of a foreign corporation may make multiple late purging elections under this paragraph (e) or § 1.1297-3(e), see § 1.1297-3(e)(5).

(f) *Effective/applicability date.*—The rules of this section are applicable as of December 8, 2005. [Reg. § 1.1298-3.]

☐ [*T.D.* 9231, 12-7-2005. *Amended by T.D.* 9360, 9-26-2007.]

§ 1.1298-4. Rules for certain foreign corporations owning stock in 25-percent-owned domestic corporations.—(a) *Overview.*—This section provides rules under section 1298(b)(7) that apply to certain foreign corporations that own stock in 25-percent-owned domestic corporations (as defined in paragraph (b) of this section) for purposes of determining whether a foreign corporation is a passive foreign investment company (PFIC). Paragraph (b) of this section provides the general rule. Paragraph (c) of this section provides rules concerning ownership of 25-percent-owned domestic corporations or qualified stock (as defined in paragraph (b)(2) of this section) through partnerships. Paragraph (d) of this section provides rules for determining whether a foreign corporation is subject to the tax imposed by section 531 (the section 531 tax) and for waiving treaty benefits that would prevent the imposition of such tax. Paragraph (e) of this section provides an anti-abuse rule for the application of section 1298(b)(7). Paragraph (f) provides the applicability date for this section.

(b) *Treatment of certain foreign corporations owning stock in a 25-percent-owned domestic corporation.*—(1) *General rule.*—Except as otherwise provided in paragraph (e) of this section, when a tested foreign corporation (as defined in § 1.1297-1(f)) is subject to the section 531 tax (or waives any benefit under any treaty that would otherwise prevent the imposition of the tax), and owns (directly or indirectly under the rules in paragraph (c) of this section) at least 25 percent (by value) of the stock of a domestic corporation (a *25-percent-owned domestic corporation*), for purposes of determining whether the foreign corporation is a PFIC, any qualified stock held directly or indirectly under the rules in paragraph (c) of this section by the 25-percent-owned domestic corporation is treated as an asset that does not produce passive income (and is not held for the production of passive income), and any amount included in gross income with respect to the qualified stock is not treated as passive income.

(2) *Qualified stock and second-tier domestic corporation.*—For purposes of this section, the term *qualified stock* means any stock in a C corporation that is a domestic corporation and that is not a regulated investment company or real estate investment trust and the term second-tier corporation means the corporation.

(c) *Indirect ownership of stock through a partnership.*—For purposes of paragraph (b)(1) of this section, a tested foreign corporation that is a partner in a partnership is considered to own its proportionate share of any stock of a domestic corporation held by the partnership, and a domestic corporation that is a partner in a partnership is considered to own its proportionate share of any qualified stock held by the partnership. An upper-tier partnership's attributable share of the stock of a domestic corporation or of qualified stock held by a lower-tier partnership is treated as held by the upper-tier partnership for purposes of applying the rule in this paragraph (c).

(d) *Section 531 tax.*—(1) *Subject to section 531 tax.*—For purposes of paragraph (b) of this section, a tested foreign corporation is considered subject to the section 531 tax regardless of whether the tax is imposed on the corporation and of whether the requirements of § 1.532-1(c) are met.

(2) *Waiver of treaty benefits.*—(i) *Tested foreign corporation that files, or is required to file, a Federal income tax return.*—For purposes of paragraph (b) of this section, a tested foreign corporation that files, or is required to file, a Federal income tax return waives the benefit under a treaty that would otherwise prevent the imposition of the section 531 tax by attaching to its original or amended return for the taxable year for which section 1298(b)(7) and paragraph (b)(1) of this section are applied or any prior taxable year a statement that it irrevocably waives treaty protection against the imposition of the section 531 tax, effective for all prior, current, and future taxable years, provided the taxable year for which the return is filed and all subsequent taxable years are not closed by the period of limitations on assessments under section 6501.

(ii) *Tested foreign corporation that is not required to file a Federal income tax return.*—For purposes of paragraph (b) of this section, a tested foreign corporation that is not required to file a Federal income tax return waives the benefit under a treaty that would otherwise prevent the imposition of the section 531 tax by a date no later than nine months following the close of the taxable year for which section 1298(b)(7) and paragraph (b)(1) of this section are applied by—

(A) Adopting a resolution or similar governance document that confirms that it has irrevocably waived any treaty protection against the imposition of the section 531 tax, effective for all prior, current, and future taxable years, and maintaining a copy of the resolution (or other governance document) in its records; or

(B) In the case of a tested foreign corporation described in section 1297(e)(3), including in its public filings a statement that it irrevocably waives treaty protection against the imposition of the section 531 tax, effective for all prior, current, and future taxable years.

(e) *Anti-abuse rule.*—(1) *General rule.*—Paragraph (b) of this section does not apply with respect to qualified stock in a second-tier domestic corporation owned by a 25-percent-owned domestic corporation if a principal purpose for the formation of, acquisition of, or holding of stock of the 25-percent-owned domestic corporation or the second-tier domestic corporation, or for the capitalization or other funding of the second-tier domestic corporation, is to hold passive assets (as defined in § 1.1297-1(f)(5)) through the second-tier domestic corporation to avoid classification of the tested foreign corporation as a PFIC.

(2) [Reserved].

(3) [Reserved].

(f) *Applicability date.*—The rules of this section apply to taxable years of shareholders beginning on or after January 14, 2021. A shareholder may choose to apply such rules for any open taxable year beginning before January 14, 2021, provided that, with respect to a tested foreign corporation, the shareholder consistently applies the provisions of this section and § 1.1291-1(b)(8)(iv) and (b)(8)(v)(A), (B), (C), and (D) and §§ 1.1297-1 *(except that consistent treatment is not required with respect to § 1.1297-1(c)(1)(i)(A))*, 1.1297-2, and 1.1298-2 for such year and all subsequent years. [Reg. § 1.1298-4.]

☐ [*T.D.* 9936, 1-14-2021 (*corrected* 3-9-2021).]

Proposed Amendments to Regulation

§ 1.1298-4. Rules for certain foreign corporations owning stock in 25-percent-owned domestic corporations.—

* * *

(e) * * *

(2) *Safe harbor.*—Paragraph (e)(1) of this section will not apply if paragraph (e)(2)(i) or (e)(2)(ii) of this section applies.

(i) *Active business within United States.*—The value of the assets of the second-tier domestic corporation used or held for use in an active trade or business within the U.S. is more than 80 percent of the fair market value of the gross assets of such corporation. For purposes of this paragraph (e)(2)—

(A) The value of the assets of the second-tier domestic corporation takes into account its pro-rata share of the value of the assets of its domestic subsidiary qualified affiliates and does not take into account the stock of such affiliates;

(B) The term *domestic subsidiary qualified affiliate* means each member of the affiliated group (as defined in section 1504(a) applied by substituting "more than 50 percent" for "at least 80 percent" each place it appears), treating the second-tier domestic corporation as the common parent of such affiliated group; and

(C) For purposes of this paragraph (e)(2), the determination of the existence of an active trade or business and whether assets are used in an active trade or business is made under § 1.367(a)-2(d)(2), (3), and (5) except that officers and employees of related entities as provided in § 1.367(a)-2(d)(3) include only the officers and employees of related domestic entities within the meaning of section 267(b) or 707(b)(1).

(ii) *Businesses undergoing change and new businesses.*—(A) *In general.*—The second-tier domestic corporation engages in an active U.S. trade or business that satisfies paragraph (e)(2)(i) of this section by the end of the transition period following the testing date.

(B) *Testing date.*—For purposes of this paragraph (e)(2)(ii), the term "testing date" means the last day of the month in which either—

(1) The second-tier domestic corporation is created or organized or is acquired, directly or indirectly, by the tested foreign corporation; or

(2) A second-tier domestic corporation that previously satisfied (e)(2)(i) of this paragraph (e) disposes of, to a person that is not related within the meaning of section 267(b) or 707(b)(1), substantially all of the assets used or held for use in its active U.S. trade or business.

(C) *Transition period.*—For purposes of this paragraph (e)(2)(ii), the term "transition period" means thirty-six months after the testing date as defined in paragraph (e)(2)(ii)(B)*(1)* or (2) of this section.

(D) *Inapplicability.*—This paragraph (e)(2)(ii) does not apply for any taxable year (including previous taxable years) of the tested foreign corporation if the second-tier domestic corporation does not engage in an active U.S. trade or business that satisfies paragraph (e)(2)(i) of this section by the end of the transition period following a testing date.

(3) *Examples.*—The following examples illustrate the rules of this paragraph (e). For purposes of these examples, TFC is a foreign corporation that is not a controlled foreign corporation (within the meaning of section 957(a)) and that is subject to the section 531 tax, USS1 and USS2 are domestic corporations for TFC's entire taxable year, TFC owns 100% of the single class of stock of USS1, and USS1 owns 100% of the single class of stock of USS2.

(i) *Example 1.*—(A) *Facts.* USS2 operates an active trade or business within the United States within the meaning of § 1.367(a)-2(d)(2), (3), and (5). Throughout TFC's Year 1, the value of USS2's assets is $100x, and the value of USS2's assets that are used or held for use in its active trade or business within the United States is $20x. USS2 was not created, organized, or acquired within the preceding thirty-six months and has not disposed of an active trade or business within the United States within the preceding thirty-six months.

(B) *Results.* Paragraph (e)(2)(i) of this section does not apply in Year 1 even though USS2 is engaged in an active trade or business within the United States because only 20% ($20x/$100x) of its assets are used or held for use in an active U.S. trade or business within the meaning of § 1.367(a)-2(d)(2), (3), and (5), an amount that is not more than 80% of the fair market value of the total gross assets of USS2. Accordingly, the general rule in paragraph (e)(1) of this section will apply if there is a principal purpose to hold passive assets through USS2, the second-tier domestic corporation, to avoid classification of TFC, the tested foreign corporation, as a PFIC.

(ii) *Example 2.*—(A) *Facts.* The facts are the same as in as in paragraph (e)(4)(i)(A) of this section (the facts in *Example 1*), except that USS2 also has an investment in USS3, a wholly owned domestic subsidiary of USS2. Throughout TFC's taxable Year 1, the value of USS3's assets is $400x and USS3 uses 100% of its assets in an active trade or business within the United States within the meaning of § 1.367(a)-2(d)(2), (3), and (5).

(B) *Results.* Because USS3 is a domestic subsidiary qualified affiliate of USS2, USS2's pro-rata share of the assets of USS3 is taken into account to determine whether USS2 satisfies paragraph (e)(2)(i) of this section. Accordingly, USS2 takes into account $400x (its pro-rata share) of USS3's assets in addition to the $100x of its own assets and, thus, is treated for purposes of paragraph (e)(2)(i) of this section as owning $500x of assets, with 84% ($420x/$500x) of such assets being used or held for use in an active trade or business within the United States within the meaning of § 1.367(a)-2(d)(2), (3), and (5). Therefore, paragraph (e)(2)(i) of this section applies in Year 1 and the general rule in paragraph (e)(1) of this section does not apply.

(iii) *Example 3.*—(A) *Facts.* Throughout Year 1, USS2 uses 100% of its assets in an active trade or business within the United States within the meaning of § 1.367(a)-2(d)(2), (3), and (5), and thus satisfied paragraph (e)(2)(i) of this section in Year 1. On the first day of Year 2, USS2 disposes of all of those assets for cash. On the seventh day of Year 5 (before the end of the first month in Year 5), USS2 invests the cash in assets that it immediately begins to use in an active trade or business in the United States.

(B) *Results.* Because USS2, the second-tier domestic corporation, engages in an active U.S. trade or business that satisfies paragraph (e)(2)(i) of this section by the end of thirty-six months after the last day of the month in which it disposed of its entire active U.S. trade or business that previously satisfied paragraph (e)(2)(i) of this section, paragraph (e)(2)(ii) of this section applies in Year 2, Year 3, and Year 4, and the general rule in paragraph (e)(1) of this section does not apply.

(iv) *Example 4.*—(A) *Facts.* The facts are the same as in paragraph (e)(4)(iii)(A) of this section (the facts in *Example 3*), except that at the end of the first month of Year 5, USS2 is still in negotiations to purchase assets to be used in an active trade or business in the United States within the meaning of § 1.367(a)-2(d)(2), (3), and (5), and USS2 does not complete the purchase of such assets until the third month of Year 5.

(B) *Results.* The safe harbor in paragraph (e)(2)(ii) of this section does not apply for Year 2, Year 3, or Year 4, because USS2, the second-tier domestic corporation, did not engage in an active U.S. trade or business that satisfied paragraph (e)(2)(i) of this section by the end of the thirty-six month transition period after the end of the month in which it sold its prior active trade or business. Accordingly, the general rule in paragraph (e)(1) of this section will apply if there is a principal purpose to hold passive assets through USS2, the second-tier domestic corporation, to avoid classification of TFC, the tested foreign corporation, as a PFIC.

(f) *Applicability date.*—Except as otherwise provided, the rules of this section apply to taxable years of shareholders beginning on or after January 14, 2021. * * * Paragraphs (e)(2) and (3) of this section apply to taxable years of shareholders beginning on or after **[DATE OF FILING OF FINAL RULE IN THE FEDERAL REGISTER]**. A shareholder may choose to apply the paragraphs in the preceding sentence for any open taxable year beginning before **[DATE OF FILING OF FINAL RULE IN THE FEDERAL REGISTER]** without regard to whether the rules of this section are applied consistently, provided that once applied, each rule must be applied for each subsequent taxable year beginning before **[DATE OF FILING OF FINAL RULE IN THE FEDERAL REGISTER]**. [Prop. Reg. § 1.1298-4.]

[Proposed 1-15-2021.]

Net Investment Income Tax

§ 1.1411-1. General rules.—(a) *General rule.*—Except as otherwise provided, all Internal Revenue Code (Code) provisions that apply for chapter 1 purposes in determining taxable income (as defined in section 63(a)) of a taxpayer also apply in determining the tax imposed by section 1411.

(b) *Adjusted gross income.*—All references to an individual's adjusted gross income are treated as references to adjusted gross income as defined in section 62, and all references to an estate's or trust's adjusted gross income are treated as references to adjusted gross income as defined in section 67(e). However, there may be additional adjustments to adjusted gross income because of investments in controlled foreign corporations (CFCs) or passive foreign investment companies (PFICs). See § 1.1411-10(e).

(c) *Effect of section 1411 and the regulations thereunder for other purposes.*—The inclusion or exclusion of items of income, gain, loss, or deduction in determining net investment income for purposes of section 1411, and the assignment of items of income, gain, loss, or deduction to a particular category of net investment income under section 1411(c)(1)(A), does not affect the treatment of any item of income, gain, loss, or deduction under any provision of the Code other than section 1411.

(d) *Definitions.*—The following definitions apply for purposes of calculating net investment income under section 1411 and the regulations thereunder—

(1) The term *gross income from annuities* under section 1411(c)(1)(A) includes the amount received as an annuity under an annuity, endowment, or life insurance contract that is includible in gross income as a result of the application of section 72(a) and section 72(b), and an amount not received as an annuity under an annuity contract that is includible in gross income under section 72(e). In the case of a sale of an annuity, to the extent the sales price of the annuity does not exceed its surrender value, the gain recognized would be treated as gross income from an annuity within the meaning of section 1411(c)(1)(A)(i) and § 1.1411-4(a)(1)(i). However, if the sales price of the annuity exceeds its surrender value, the seller would treat the gain equal to the difference between the basis in the annuity and the surrender value as gross income from an annuity described in section 1411(c)(1)(A)(i) and § 1.1411-4(a)(1)(i) and the excess of the sales price over the surrender value as gain from the disposition of property included in section 1411(c)(1)(A)(iii) and § 1.1411-4(a)(1)(iii). The term *gross income from annuities* does not include amounts paid in consideration for services rendered. For example, distributions from a foreign retirement plan that are paid in the form of an annuity and include investment income that was earned by the retirement plan does not constitute income from an annuity within the meaning of section 1411(c)(1)(A)(i).

(2) The term *controlled foreign corporation (CFC)* is as defined in section 953(c)(1)(B) or 957(a).

(3) The term *gross income from dividends* includes any item treated as a dividend for purposes of chapter 1. See also § 1.1411-10 for additional amounts that constitute gross income from dividends. The term *gross income from dividends* includes, but is not limited to, amounts treated as dividends—

(i) Pursuant to subchapter C that are included in gross income (including constructive dividends);

(ii) Pursuant to section 1248(a), other than as provided in § 1.1411-10;

(iii) Pursuant to § 1.367(b)-2(e)(2);

(iv) Pursuant to section 1368(c)(2); and

(v) Substitute dividends that represent payments made to the transferor of a security in a securities lending transaction or a sale-repurchase transaction.

(4) The term *excluded income* means:

(i) Items of income excluded from gross income in chapter 1. For example, interest on state and local bonds excluded from gross income under section 103 and gain from the sale of a principal residence excluded from gross income under section 121.

(ii) Items of income not included in net investment income, as determined under § § 1.1411-4 and 1.1411-10. For example, wages, unemployment compensation, Alaska Permanent Fund Dividends, alimony, and Social Security Benefits.

(iii) Items of gross income and net gain specifically excluded by section 1411, the regulations thereunder, or other guidance published in the Internal Revenue Bulletin. For example, gains from the disposition of property used in a trade of business not described in section 1411(c)(2) under § 1.1411-4(d)(4)(i), distributions from certain Qualified Plans described in section 1411(c)(5) and § 1.1411-8, income taken into account in determining self-employment income that is subject to tax under section 1401(b) described in section 1411(c)(6) and § 1.1411-9, and section 951(a) inclusions from a CFC for which a § 1.1411-10(g) election is not in effect.

(5) The term *individual* means any natural person.

(6) The term *gross income from interest* includes any item treated as interest income for purposes of chapter 1 and substitute interest that represents payments made to the transferor of a security in a securities lending transaction or a sale-repurchase transaction.

(7) The term *married* and *married taxpayer* has the same meaning as in section 7703.

(8) The term *net investment income (NII)* means net investment income as defined in section 1411(c) and § 1.1411-4, as adjusted pursuant to the rules described in § 1.1411-10(c).

(9) The term *passive foreign investment company (PFIC)* is as defined in section 1297(a).

(10) The term *gross income from rents* includes amounts paid or to be paid principally for the use of (or the right to use) tangible property.

(11) The term *gross income from royalties* includes amounts received from mineral, oil, and gas royalties, and amounts received for the privilege of using patents, copyrights, secret processes and formulas, goodwill, trademarks, tradebrands, franchises, and other like property.

(12) The term *trade or business* refers to a trade or business within the meaning of section 162.

(13) The term *United States person* is as defined in section 7701(a)(30).

(14) The term *United States shareholder* is as defined in section 951(b).

(e) *Disallowance of certain credits against the section 1411 tax.*—Amounts that may be credited against only the tax imposed by chapter 1 of the Code may not be credited against the section 1411 tax imposed by chapter 2A of the Code unless specifically provided in the Code. For example, the foreign income, war profits, and excess profits taxes that are allowed as a foreign tax credit by section 27(a), section 642(a), and section 901, respectively, are not allowed as a credit against the section 1411 tax. [Reg. § 1.1411-1.]

***

□ [*T.D. 9644, 11-26-2013.*]

§ 1.1411-2. Application to individuals.—(a) *Individual to whom tax applies.*—(1) *In general.*—Section 1411 applies to an individual who is a citizen or resident of the United States (within the meaning of section 7701(a)(30)(A)). Section 1411 does not apply to nonresident alien individuals (within the meaning of section 7701(b)(1)(B)). See paragraph (a)(2)(vi) of this section for special rules regarding bona fide residents of United States territories.

(2) *Special rules.*—(i) *Dual resident individuals treated as residents of a foreign country under an income tax treaty.*—A dual resident taxpayer (as defined in § 301.7701(b)-7(a)(1)) who determines that he or she is a resident of a foreign country for treaty purposes pursuant to an income tax treaty between the United States and the foreign country and who claims benefits of the treaty as a nonresident of the United States will be treated as a nonresident alien of the United States for purposes of paragraph (a)(1) of this section.

(ii) *Dual-status resident aliens.*—A dual-status individual who is a resident of the United States for a portion of a taxable year and a nonresident alien for the other portion of the taxable year will not be subject to section 1411 with respect to the portion of the year for which that individual is treated as a nonresident alien. The only income the individual must take into account for purposes of section 1411 is the income he or she receives during the portion of the year for which he or she is treated as a resident of the United States. The threshold amount under paragraph (d)(1) of this section applies.

(iii) *Joint returns in the case of a nonresident alien individual married to a United States citizen or resident.*—(A) *Default treatment.*—In the case of a United States citizen or resident who is married to a nonresident alien individual, the spouses will be treated as married filing separately for purposes of section 1411. For purposes of calculating the tax imposed under section 1411(a)(1), the United States citizen or resident spouse will be subject to the threshold amount for a married taxpayer filing a separate return in paragraph (d)(1)(ii) of this section, and the nonresident alien spouse will not be subject to tax under section 1411. In accordance with the rules for married individuals filing separate returns, the spouse that is a United States citizen or resident must determine his or her own net investment income and modified adjusted gross income.

(B) *Taxpayer election.*—Married taxpayers who file a joint Federal income tax return pursuant to a section 6013(g) election for purposes of chapter 1 and chapter 24 also may elect to be treated as making a section 6013(g) election for purposes of chapter 2A (relating to the tax imposed by section 1411).

(1) *Effect of election.*—For purposes of calculating the tax imposed under section 1411(a)(1), the effect of an election under section 6013(g) is to include the combined income of the United States citizen or resident spouse and the nonresident spouse in the section 1411(a)(1) calculation and to apply the threshold amount for a taxpayer making a joint return as set out in paragraph (d)(1)(i) of this section.

(2) *Procedural requirements for making election.*—Taxpayers with a section 6013(g) election in effect for chapter 1 and chapter 24 purposes for any taxable year beginning after December 31, 2012, or taxpayers making a section 6013(g) election for chapter 1 and chapter 24 purposes in any taxable year beginning after December 31, 2012, who want to apply their section 6013(g) election for purposes of chapter 2A must make the election for the first taxable year beginning after December 31, 2013, in which the United States taxpayer is subject to tax under section 1411. The determination of whether the United States taxpayer is subject to tax under section 1411 is made without regard to the effect of the section 6013(g) election described in paragraph (a)(2)(iii)(B) of this section. The election, if made, must be made in the manner prescribed by forms, instructions, or in other guidance on an original or amended return for the taxable year for which the election is made. An election can be made on an amended return only if the taxable year for which the election is made, and all taxable years that are affected by the election, are not closed by the period of limitations on assessments under section 6501. Further, once made, the duration and termination of the section 6013(g) election for chapter 2A is governed by the rules of section 6013(g)(2) through (g)(6) and the regulations thereunder.

(3) *Ineffective elections.*—In the event a taxpayer makes an election described in paragraph (a)(2)(iii)(B) of this section and subsequently determines that such taxpayer does not meet the criteria for making such election in such tax year described in paragraph (a)(2)(iii)(B)(2) of this section, then such original election will have no effect for that year and all future years. In such a case, the taxpayer should make appropriate adjustments to properly reflect the ineffective election. However, notwithstanding the previous sentence, if a taxpayer meets the criteria for the same election in a subsequent year, such taxpayer is deemed to treat such original election as being made in that subsequent year unless the taxpayer files (or amends) the return for such subsequent year to report the taxpayer's net investment income tax without the original election. Furthermore, this paragraph (a)(2)(iii)(B)(3) shall not apply if a taxpayer does not meet the criteria described in paragraph (a)(2)(iii)(B)(2) of this section for making such election in such tax year solely as a result of the carryback of a net operating loss pursuant to section 172.

(iv) *Joint returns for a year in which nonresident alien married to a United States citizen or resident becomes a United States resident.*—(A) *Default treatment.*—In the case of a United States citizen or resident who is married to an individual who is a nonresident alien individual at the beginning of any taxable year, but is a United States resident at the close of such taxable year, each spouse will be treated as married filing separately for the entire year for purposes of section 1411. For purposes of calculating the tax imposed under section 1411(a)(1), each spouse will be subject to the threshold amount for a married taxpayer filing a separate return in paragraph (d)(1)(ii) of this section. The spouse who becomes a United States resident during the tax year will be subject to section 1411 only with respect to income received for the portion of the year for which he or she is treated as a United States resident. Each spouse must determine his or her own net investment income and modified adjusted gross income.

(B) *Taxpayer election.*—Married taxpayers who file a joint Federal income tax return pursuant to a section 6013(h) election for purposes of chapter 1 and chapter 24 also may elect to be treated as making a section 6013(h) election for purposes of chapter 2A for such tax year.

(1) *Effect of election.*—For purposes of calculating the tax imposed under section 1411(a)(1), the effect of an election under section 6013(h) is to include the combined income of the United States citizen or resident spouse and the dual-status resident spouse in the section 1411(a)(1) calculation and to apply the threshold amount for a taxpayer making a joint return as set out in paragraph (d)(1)(i) of this section.

(2) *Procedural requirements for making election.*—Taxpayers who make a section 6013(h) election for purposes of chapter 1 and chapter 24 for any taxable year beginning after December 31, 2012, may elect to have their section 6013(h) election apply for purposes of chapter 2A. The election, if made, must be made in the manner prescribed by forms, instructions, or in other guidance on an original or amended return for the taxable year for which the election is made. An election can be made on an amended return only if the taxable year for which the election is made, and all taxable years that are affected by the election, are not closed by the period of limitations on assessments under section 6501. Further, in all cases, once made, the section 6013(h) election is governed by the rules of section 6013(h)(2) and the regulations thereunder.

(iv) *Grantor trusts.*—For rules regarding the treatment of owners of grantor trusts, see § 1.1411-3(b)(1)(v).

(v) *Bankruptcy estates.*—A bankruptcy estate administered under chapter 7 (relating to liquidations) or chapter 11 (relating to reorganizations) of the Bankruptcy Code (Title 11 of the United States Code) of a debtor who is an individual is treated as a married taxpayer filing a separate return for purposes of section 1411. See § 1.1411-2(d)(1)(ii).

(vi) *Bona fide residents of United States territories.*—(A) *Applicability.*—An individual who is a bona fide resident of a United States territory is subject to the tax imposed by section 1411(a)(1) only if the individual is required to file an income tax return with the United States upon application of section 931, 932, 933, or 935 and the regulations thereunder. With respect to an individual described in this paragraph (a)(2)(vi)(A), the amount excluded from gross income under section 931 or 933 and any deduction properly allocable or chargeable against amounts excluded from gross income under section 931 or 933, respectively, is not taken into account in computing modified adjusted gross income under paragraph (c) of this section or net investment income (within the meaning of § 1.1411-1(d)).

(B) *Coordination with exception for nonresident aliens.*—An individual who is both a bona fide resident of a United States territory and a nonresident alien individual with respect to the United States is not subject to taxation under section 1411(a)(1).

(C) *Definitions.*—For purposes of this section—

(1) *Bona fide resident.*—The term *bona fide resident* has the meaning provided under section 937(a).

(2) *United States territory.*—The term *United States territory* means American Samoa, Guam, the Northern Mariana Islands, Puerto Rico, or the United States Virgin Islands.

(b) *Calculation of tax.*—(1) *In general.*—In the case of an individual described in paragraph (a)(1) of this section, the tax imposed by section 1411(a)(1) for each taxable year is equal to 3.8 percent of the lesser of—

(i) Net investment income for such taxable year; or

(ii) The excess (if any) of—

(A) The modified adjusted gross income (as defined in paragraph (c) of this section) for such taxable year; over

(B) The threshold amount (as defined in paragraph (d) of this section).

(2) *Example.*—During Year 1 (a year in which section 1411 is in effect), A, an unmarried United States citizen, has modified adjusted gross income (as defined in paragraph (c) of this section) of $190,000, which includes $50,000 of net investment income. A has a zero tax imposed under section 1411 because the threshold amount for a single individual is $200,000 (as provided in paragraph (d)(1)(iii) of this section). If during Year 2, A has modified adjusted gross income of $220,000, which includes $50,000 of net investment income, then the individual has a section 1411 tax of $760 (3.8% multiplied by $20,000, the lesser of $50,000 net investment income or $20,000 excess of modified adjusted gross income over the threshold amount).

(c) *Modified adjusted gross income.*—(1) *General rule.*—For purposes of section 1411, the term *modified adjusted gross income* means adjusted gross income increased by the excess of—

(i) The amount excluded from gross income under section 911(a)(1); over

(ii) The amount of any deductions (taken into account in computing adjusted gross income) or exclusions disallowed under section 911(d)(6) with respect to the amounts described in paragraph (c)(1)(i) of this section.

(2) *Rules with respect to CFCs and PFICs.*—Additional rules in § 1.1411-10(e)(1) apply to an individual that is a United States shareholder of a controlled foreign corporation (CFC) or that is a United States person that directly or indirectly owns an interest in a passive foreign investment company (PFIC). [Reg. § 1.1411-2.]

* * *

□ [*T.D. 9644, 11-26-2013 (corrected 3-31-2014).*]

§ 1.1411-10. Controlled foreign corporations and passive foreign investment companies.—(a) *In general.*—This section provides rules that apply to an individual, estate, or trust that is a United States shareholder of a controlled foreign corporation (CFC), or that is a United States person that directly or indirectly owns an interest in a passive foreign investment company (PFIC). In addition, this section provides rules that apply to an individual, estate, or trust that owns an interest in a domestic partnership or an S corporation that is either a United States shareholder of a CFC or that has made an election under section 1295 to treat a PFIC as a qualified electing fund (QEF). References in this section to an election under paragraph (g) of this section being in effect relate to an election that is applicable to the person that is determining the section 1411 consequences with respect to holding a particular CFC or QEF.

(b) *Amounts derived from a trade or business described in § 1.1411-5.*—(1) *In general.*—Except as provided in paragraph (b)(2) of this section, an amount included in gross income under section 951(a) or section 1293(a) that is also income derived from a trade or business described in section 1411(c)(2) and § 1.1411-5 (applying the relevant rules in § 1.1411-4(b)) is taken into account as net investment income under section 1411(c)(1)(A)(ii) and § 1.1411-4(a)(1)(ii) for purposes of section 1411 and the regulations thereunder when it is taken into account for purposes of chapter 1, and the rules in paragraphs (c) through (g) of this section do not apply to that amount. For purposes of section 1411 and the regulations thereunder, an amount included in gross income under section 1296(a) that is also income derived from a trade or business described in section 1411(c)(2) and § 1.1411-5 (applying the relevant rules in § 1.1411-4(b)), is net investment income within the meaning of section 1411(c)(1)(A)(ii) and § 1.1411-4(a)(1)(ii), and the rules in paragraph (c)(2)(ii) of this section do not apply to that amount.

(2) *Coordination rule for changes in trade or business status.*—With respect to stock of a CFC or QEF for which an election under paragraph (g) of this section is not in effect, the rules in paragraphs (c) through (f) of this section apply to a distribution of earnings and profits described in paragraph (c)(1)(i)(A) of this section that was not taken into account as net investment income under paragraph (b) of this section.

(c) *Calculation of net investment income.*—(1) *Dividends.*—For purposes of section 1411(c)(1)(A)(i) and § 1.1411-4(a)(1)(i), net investment income is calculated by taking into account the amount of dividends described in this paragraph (c)(1).

(i) *Distributions of previously taxed earnings and profits.*—(A) *Rules when an election under paragraph (g) of this section is not in effect with respect to the shareholder.*—*(1) General rule.*—Except as otherwise provided in this paragraph (c)(1)(i), with respect to stock of a CFC or QEF for which an election under paragraph (g) of this section is not in effect, a distribution of earnings and profits that is not treated as a dividend for chapter 1 purposes under section 959(d) or section 1293(c) is a dividend for purposes of section 1411(c)(1)(A)(i) and § 1.1411-4(a)(1)(i) if the distribution is attributable to amounts that are or have been included in gross income for chapter 1 purposes under section 951(a) or section 1293(a) in a taxable year beginning after December 31, 2012. Solely, for this purpose, distributions of earnings and profits attributable to amounts that are or have been included in gross income for chapter 1 purposes under section 951(a) or section 1293(a) are considered first attributable to those earnings and profits, if any, derived from the current taxable year, and then from prior taxable years beginning with the most recent prior taxable year, and with respect to amounts included under section 951(a), without regard to whether the earnings and profits are described in section 959(c)(1) or section 959(c)(2).

(2) Exception for distributions attributable to earnings and profits previously taken into account for purposes of section 1411.—A distribution of earnings and profits that is not treated as a dividend for chapter 1 purposes under section 959(d) or section 1293(c) is not treated as a dividend for purposes of section 1411(c)(1)(A)(i) and § 1.1411-4(a)(1)(i), to the extent that an individual, estate, or trust establishes, by providing information that is similar to, and in the same manner as, the information described in § 1.959-1(d) (relating to previously taxed earnings and profits), that the distribution is attributable to—

(i) Amounts included in gross income by any person for chapter 1 purposes under section 951(a) or section 1293(a) that have been taken into account by any person as net investment income by reason of paragraph (b) of this section or an election under paragraph (g) of this section; or

(ii) Amounts included in gross income by any person as a dividend pursuant to section 1248(a) that, by reason of paragraph (c)(3)(ii) of this section, have been taken into account by any person as net investment income under section 1411(c)(1)(A)(i) and § 1.1411-4(a)(1)(i).

(B) *Rule when an election under paragraph (g) of this section is in effect with respect to the shareholder.*—Except as otherwise provided in this paragraph (c)(1)(i), if an election under paragraph (g) of this section is in effect, a distribution of earnings and profits that is not treated as a dividend for chapter 1 purposes under section 959(d) or section 1293(c) is not treated as a dividend for purposes of section 1411(c)(1)(A)(i) and § 1.1411-4(a)(1)(i).

(C) *Special rule for certain distributions related to 2013 taxable years.*—*(1) Scope.*—The rule in this paragraph (c)(1)(i)(C) applies to individuals, estates, and trusts that were subject to section 1411 during a taxable year that began after December 31, 2012, and before January 1, 2014, and that satisfy all of the conditions set forth in paragraph (c)(1)(i)(C)(2) of this section. This rule also applies to all domestic partnerships and S corporations that satisfy all of the conditions set forth in paragraph (c)(1)(i)(C)(2) of this section.

(2) Rule.—A distribution of earnings and profits from a CFC or QEF, with respect to which an election under paragraph (g) is in effect, that is not treated as a dividend for chapter 1 purposes under section 959(d) or section 1293(c) is a dividend for purposes of section 1411(c)(1)(A)(i) and § 1.1411-4(a)(1)(i) to the extent that—

(i) The distribution of earnings and profits is attributable to an amount included by an individual, estate, trust, domestic partnership, S corporation or common trust fund in gross income for chapter 1 purposes under section 951(a) or section 1293(a) with respect to the CFC or QEF for a taxable year that began after December 31, 2012, and before January 1, 2014;

(ii) The individual, estate, trust, domestic partnership, S corporation, or common trust fund made the election under paragraph (g) of this section with respect to the CFC or QEF in a taxable year that began after December 31, 2013; and

(iii) The individual, estate, trust, domestic partnership, S corporation, or common trust fund did not make the election described in paragraph (g)(4)(iii) of this section (concerning making an election under paragraph (g) of this section for a taxable year that begins before January 1, 2014).

(3) Ordering rule.—Solely, for purposes of this paragraph (c)(1)(i)(C)*(3)*, distributions of earnings and profits attributable to amounts that have been included in gross income for chapter 1 purposes under section 951(a) or section 1293(a) are considered first attributable to the earnings and profits derived from a taxable year that began after December 31, 2012, and before January 1, 2014.

(ii) *Excess distributions that constitute dividends.*—To the extent an excess distribution within the meaning of section 1291(b) constitutes a dividend within the meaning of section 316(a), the amount is included in net investment income for purposes of section 1411(c)(1)(A)(i) and § 1.1411-4(a)(1)(i).

(2) *Net gain.*—For purposes of section 1411(c)(1)(A)(iii) and § 1.1411-4(a)(1)(iii), the rules in this paragraph (c)(2) apply in determining net gain attributable to the disposition of property.

(i) *Gains treated as excess distributions.*—Gains treated as excess distributions under section 1291(a)(2) are included in determining net gain attributable to the disposition of property for purposes of section 1411(c)(1)(A)(iii) and § 1.1411-4(a)(1)(iii).

(ii) *Inclusions and deductions with respect to section 1296 mark to market elections.*—Amounts included in gross income under section 1296(a)(1) and amounts allowed as a deduction under section 1296(a)(2) are taken into account in determining net gain attributable to the disposition of property for purposes of section 1411(c)(1)(A)(iii) and § 1.1411-4(a)(1)(iii).

(iii) *Gain or loss attributable to the disposition of stock of CFCs and QEFs.*—With respect to stock of a CFC or QEF for which an election under paragraph (g) of this section is not in effect, for purposes of calculating the net gain under § § 1.1411-4(a)(1)(iii) and 1.1411-4(d) that is attributable to the direct or indirect disposition of that stock (including for purposes of determining gain or loss on the direct or indirect disposition of that stock by a domestic partnership, S corporation, or common trust fund), basis is determined in accordance with the provisions of paragraph (d) of this section.

(iv) *Gain or loss attributable to the disposition of interests in domestic partnerships or S corporations that own directly or indirectly stock of CFCs or QEFs.*—With respect to stock of a CFC or QEF for which an election under paragraph (g) of this section is not in effect, for purposes of calculating the net gain under § § 1.1411-4(a)(1)(iii) and 1.1411-4(d) that is attributable to the disposition of an interest in a domestic partnership or S corporation that directly or indirectly owns that stock, basis is determined in accordance with the provisions of paragraph (d) of this section.

(3) *Application of section 1248.*—With respect to stock of a CFC or QEF for which an election under paragraph (g) of this section is not in effect, for purposes of section 1411 and § 1.1411-4—

(i) In determining the gain recognized on the sale or exchange of stock of a foreign corporation for section 1248(a) purposes, basis is determined in accordance with the provisions of paragraph (d) of this section; and

(ii) Section 1248(a) applies without regard to the exclusion for certain earnings and profits under sections 1248(d)(1) and (d)(6), except that those exclusions will apply with respect to the earnings and profits of a foreign corporation that are attributable to:

(A) Amounts taken into account as net investment income under paragraph (b) of this section; and

(B) Amounts previously included in gross income for chapter 1 purposes under section 951(a) or section 1293(a) in a taxable year beginning before December 31, 2012, and that have not yet been distributed. For this purpose, the determination of whether earnings and profits that are attributable to amounts previously taxed in a taxable year beginning before December 31, 2012, have been distributed is determined based on the rules described in paragraph (c)(1)(i) of this section.

(4) *Amounts distributed by an estate or trust.*—Net investment income of a beneficiary of an estate or trust includes the beneficiary's share of distributable net income, as described in sections 652 and 662 and as modified by paragraph (f) of this section, to the extent that the beneficiary's share of distributable net income includes items that, if they had been received directly by the beneficiary, would have been described in this paragraph (c).

(5) *Properly allocable deductions.*—(i) *General rule.*—For purposes of section 1411(c)(1)(B) and § 1.1411-4(f), the section 163(d)(1) investment expense deduction may be calculated by—

(A) Increasing the amount of investment income determined for chapter 1 purposes under section 163(d)(4)(B) by the amount of dividends described in § 1.1411-10(c) that are derived from a CFC or QEF with respect to which an election under paragraph (g) of this section is not in effect;

(B) Decreasing the amount of investment income determined for chapter 1 purposes under section 163(d)(4)(B) by the amount included in gross income for chapter 1 purposes under section 951(a) or section 1293(a) that is attributable to a CFC or QEF with respect to which an election under paragraph (g) of this section is not in effect; and

(C) Increasing or decreasing, as applicable, the amount of investment income for chapter 1 purposes under section 163(d)(4)(B) by the difference between the amount calculated with respect to a disposition under paragraphs (c)(2)(iii) and (c)(2)(iv) of this section and the amount of the gain or loss attributable to the relevant disposition as calculated for chapter 1 purposes.

(ii) *Additional rules.*—For purposes of section 1411(c)(1)(B) and § 1.1411-4(f), if the method of calculation described in paragraph (c)(5)(i) of this section is applied:

(A) The amount of investment interest not allowed as a deduction under section 163(d)(2) must be calculated consistent with the method of calculation described in paragraph (c)(5)(i).

(B) The method of calculation must be adopted by an individual, estate, or trust no later than the first year in which the individual, estate, or trust is subject to section 1411.

(C) The method of calculation must be applied with respect to all CFCs and QEFs for all taxable years with respect to which an election under paragraph (g) of this section is not in effect.

(D) A method of calculation under this paragraph is a method of accounting, which must be applied consistently, and may only be changed by the taxpayer by securing the consent of the Commissioner in accordance with § 1.446-1(e) and following the administrative procedures issued under § 1.446-1(e)(3)(ii).

(d) *Conforming basis adjustments.*—(1) *Basis adjustments under sections 961 and 1293.*—(i) *Stock held by individuals, estates, or trusts.*—With respect to stock of a CFC or QEF which is held by an individual, estate, or trust, either directly or indirectly through one or more entities each of which is foreign, for which an election under paragraph (g) of this section is not in effect—

(A) The basis increases made pursuant to sections 961(a) and 1293(d) for amounts included in gross income for chapter 1 purposes under sections 951(a) and 1293(a) in taxable years beginning after December 31, 2012, are not taken into account for purposes of section 1411 and the regulations thereunder; and

(B) The basis decreases made pursuant to sections 961(b) and 1293(d) attributable to amounts treated as dividends for purposes of section 1411 under paragraph (c)(1)(i) of this section are not taken into account for purposes of section 1411 and the regulations thereunder.

(ii) *Stock held by domestic partnerships or S corporations.*—(A) *Rule when an election under paragraph (g) of this section is not in effect.*—The rules of this paragraph (d)(1)(ii)(A) apply with respect to stock of a CFC or QEF held directly by a domestic partnership or S corporation, or indirectly through one or more entities each of which is foreign, for which an election under paragraph (g) of this section is not in effect. If an individual, estate, or trust is a shareholder of an S corporation, or if an individual, estate, or trust directly, or through one or more tiers of passthrough entities (including an S corporation), owns an interest in a domestic partnership, the S corporation or domestic partnership, as the case may be, will not take into account for purposes of section 1411 and the regulations thereunder the basis increases made by the domestic partnership or S corporation pursuant to sections 961(a) and 1293(d) for amounts included in gross income for chapter 1 purposes under sections 951(a) and 1293(a) for taxable years beginning after December 31, 2012, and the basis decreases made by the domestic partnership or S corporation pursuant to sections 961(b) and 1293(d) attributable to amounts treated as dividends for purposes of section 1411 under paragraph (c)(1)(i) of this section (the section 1411 recalculated basis). If the domestic partnership or S corporation disposes of the stock of a CFC or QEF, the section 1411 recalculated basis will be used to determine the distributive share or pro rata share of the gain or loss for purposes of section 1411 for partners or shareholders.

(B) *Rules when an election under paragraph (g) of this section is in effect.*—If an election under paragraph (g) of this section is in effect with respect to stock of a CFC or QEF held directly or indirectly by a domestic partnership or S corporation, the partner's distributive share or the shareholder's pro rata share of the gain or loss for purposes of section 1411 is the same as the distributive share or pro rata share of the gain or loss for purposes of chapter 1. See *Example 6* of paragraph (h) of this section.

(2) *Special rules for partners that own interests in domestic partnerships that own directly or indirectly stock of CFCs or QEFs.*—The rules of this paragraph (d)(2) apply with respect to stock of a CFC or QEF for which an election under paragraph (g) of this section is not in effect, and that is held by a domestic partnership, either directly or indirectly through one or more entities each of which is foreign. In such a case, the basis increases provided under section 705(a)(1)(A) to the partners for purposes of chapter 1 that are attributable to amounts that the domestic partnership includes or included in gross income under section 951(a) or section 1293(a) for a taxable year beginning after December 31, 2012, are not taken into account for purposes of section 1411. Instead, each partner's adjusted basis in the partnership interest is increased by its share of any distributions to the partnership from the CFC or QEF that are treated as dividends for purposes of section 1411 under paragraph (c)(1)(i) of this section. Similar rules

apply when the stock of the CFC or QEF is held in a tiered partnership structure. For purposes of determining net investment income under section 1411 and the regulations thereunder, the partner's adjusted basis in the partnership interest as calculated under this paragraph (d)(2) is used to determine all tax consequences related to tax basis (for example, loss limitation rules and the characterization of partnership distributions).

(3) *Special rules for S corporation shareholders that own interests in S corporations that own directly or indirectly stock of CFCs or QEFs.*—The rules of this paragraph (d)(3) apply with respect to stock of a CFC or QEF for which an election under paragraph (g) of this section is not in effect, and that is held by an S corporation, directly or indirectly through one or more entities each of which is foreign. In such case, the basis increases provided in section 1367(a)(1)(A) to its shareholders for chapter 1 purposes that are attributable to amounts that the S corporation includes or included in gross income for chapter 1 purposes under section 951(a) or section 1293(a) for taxable years beginning after December 31, 2012, are not taken into account for purposes of section 1411. Instead, each shareholder's adjusted basis of stock in the S corporation is increased by its share of the distributions to the S corporation from the CFC or QEF that are treated as dividends for purposes of section 1411 under paragraph (c)(1)(i) of this section. Similar rules apply when the S corporation holds an interest in a CFC or QEF through a partnership. For purposes of determining net investment income under section 1411 and the regulations thereunder, the shareholder's adjusted basis in the stock of the S corporation as calculated under this paragraph (d)(3) is used to determine all tax consequences related to tax basis (for example, loss limitation rules and the characterization of S corporation distributions).

(4) *Special rules for participants in common trust funds.*—Rules similar to the rules in paragraphs (d)(2) and (3) of this section apply to ownership interests in common trust funds (as defined in section 584).

(e) *Conforming adjustments to modified adjusted gross income and adjusted gross income.*—(1) *Individuals.*—Solely for purposes of section 1411(a)(1)(B)(i) and the regulations thereunder, the term *modified adjusted gross income* means modified adjusted gross income as defined in § 1.1411-2(c)(1)—

(i) Increased by amounts included in net investment income under paragraphs (c)(1)(i), (c)(1)(ii), (c)(2)(i), and (c)(4) of this section that are not otherwise included in gross income for chapter 1 purposes;

(ii) Increased or decreased, as applicable, by the difference between the amount calculated with respect to a disposition under paragraphs (c)(2)(iii) and (iv) of this section and the amount of the gain or loss attributable to the relevant disposition as calculated for chapter 1 purposes;

(iii) Decreased by any amount included in gross income for chapter 1 purposes under section 951(a) or section 1293(a) attributable to a CFC or QEF with respect to which no election under paragraph (g) of this section is in effect; and

(iv) To the extent the section 163(d)(1) investment interest expense deduction is calculated using the method of calculation set forth in paragraph (c)(5) of this section and the deduction is taken into account under § 1.1411-4(f)(2), increased or decreased, as appropriate, by the difference between the amount of the section 163(d)(1) investment interest expense deduction calculated under paragraph (c)(5) of this section and the amount calculated for chapter 1 purposes.

(2) *Estates and trusts.*—Solely for purposes of section 1411(a)(2)(B)(i) and the regulations thereunder, the term *adjusted gross income* means adjusted gross income as defined in § 1.1411-3(a)(1)(ii)(B)(*1*) adjusted by the following amounts to the extent those amounts are not distributed by the estate or trust—

(i) Increased by amounts included in net investment income under paragraphs (c)(1)(i), (c)(1)(ii), (c)(2)(i), and (c)(4) of this section that are not otherwise included in gross income for chapter 1 purposes;

(ii) Increased or decreased, as applicable, by the difference between the amount calculated with respect to a disposition under paragraphs (c)(2)(iii) and (iv) of this section and the amount of the gain or loss attributable to the relevant disposition as calculated for chapter 1 purposes;

(iii) Decreased by any amount included in gross income for chapter 1 purposes under section 951(a) or section 1293(a) attributable to a CFC or QEF with respect to which no election under paragraph (g) of this section is in effect; and

(iv) To the extent the section 163(d)(1) investment interest expense deduction is calculated using the method of calculation set forth in paragraph (c)(5) of this section and taken into account under § 1.1411-4(f)(2), increased or decreased, as appropriate, by the difference between the amount of the section 163(d)(1) investment interest expense deduction calculated under paragraph (c)(5) of this section and the amount calculated for chapter 1 purposes.

(f) *Application to estates and trusts.*—All of the items described in paragraph (c) of this section are included in the net investment income of an estate or trust or its beneficiaries. The amounts described in paragraphs (e)(2)(i) through (iv) of this section, regardless of whether the estate or trust receives those amounts directly or indirectly through another estate or trust, increase or decrease, as applicable, the estate's or trust's distributable net income for purposes of section 1411. The estate or trust, or the beneficiaries thereof, must take those amounts into account in a manner reasonably consistent with the general operating rules for estates and trusts in § 1.1411-3 and subchapter J in computing the undistributed net investment income of the estate or trust and the net investment income of the beneficiaries.

(g) *Election with respect to CFCs and QEFs.*—(1) *Effect of election.*—If an election under paragraph (g) of this section is made with respect to a CFC or QEF, amounts included in gross income for chapter 1 purposes under section 951(a) or section 1293(a)(1)(A) with respect to the CFC or QEF in taxable years beginning with the taxable year for which the election is made are treated as net investment income for purposes of § 1.1411-4(a)(1)(i), and amounts included in gross income under section 1293(a)(1)(B) with respect to the QEF in taxable years beginning with the taxable year for which the election is made are taken into account in calculating net gain attributable to the disposition of property under § 1.1411-4(a)(1)(iii). See paragraphs (c)(1)(i)(B) and (c)(1)(i)(C) of this section for the effect of this election on certain distributions of previously taxed earnings and profits.

(2) *Years to which election applies.*—(i) *In general.*—An election under paragraph (g) of this section applies to the taxable year for which it is made and all subsequent taxable years, and applies to all subsequently acquired interests in the CFC or QEF. An election under paragraph (g) of this section is irrevocable.

(ii) *Termination of interest in CFC or QEF.*—Complete termination of a person's interest in the CFC or QEF does not terminate the person's election under paragraph (g) of this section with respect to the CFC or QEF. Thus, if the person reacquires stock of the CFC or QEF, that stock is considered to be stock for which an election under paragraph (g) of this section has been made and is in effect.

(iii) *Termination of partnership.*—If a domestic partnership that makes the election under paragraph (g) of this section is terminated pursuant to section 708(b)(1)(B), the election is binding on the new partnership.

(3) *Who may make the election.*—An individual, estate, trust, domestic partnership, S corporation, or common trust fund may make an election under paragraph (g) of this section with respect to each CFC or QEF that it holds directly or indirectly through one or more entities, each of which is foreign. In addition, an individual, estate, trust, domestic partnership, S corporation, or common trust fund may make an election under paragraph (g) of this section with respect to a CFC or QEF that it holds indirectly through a domestic partnership, S corporation, estate, trust, or common trust fund if the domestic partnership, S corporation, estate, trust, or common trust fund does not make the election. The election, if made, for an estate or trust must be made by the fiduciary of that estate or trust.

(4) *Time and manner for making the election.*—(i) *Individuals, estates, and trusts.*—(A) *General rule.*—Except as otherwise provided in this paragraph, in order for an election under paragraph (g) of this section by an individual, estate, or trust (other than a CRT) with respect to a CFC or QEF to be effective, the election must be made no later than the first taxable year beginning after December 31, 2013, during which the individual, estate, or trust—

(*1*) Includes an amount in gross income for chapter 1 purposes under section 951(a) or section 1293(a) with respect to the CFC or QEF; and

(*2*) Is subject to tax under section 1411 or would be subject to tax under section 1411 if the election were made with respect to the stock of the CFC or QEF.

(B) *Special rule for charitable remainder trusts (CRTs).*—Except as otherwise provided in this paragraph, in order for an election under paragraph (g) of this section by a CRT with respect to a CFC or QEF to be effective, the election must be made no later than the first taxable year beginning after December 31, 2013, during which the CRT includes an amount in gross income for chapter 1 purposes under section 951(a) or section 1293(a) with respect to the CFC or QEF.

(ii) *Certain domestic passthrough entities.*—Except as otherwise provided in this paragraph, in order for an election under paragraph (g) of this section by a domestic partnership, S corporation, or common trust fund with respect to a CFC or a QEF to be effective, the election must be made no later than the first taxable year beginning after December 31, 2013, during which the domestic partnership S corporation, or common trust fund—

(A) Includes an amount in gross income for chapter 1 purposes under section 951(a) or section 1293(a) with respect to the CFC or QEF; and

(B) Has a direct or indirect owner that is subject to tax under section 1411 or would be subject to tax under section 1411 if the election were made.

(iii) *Taxable years that begin before January 1, 2014.*—(A) *Individuals, estates, or trusts.*—An individual, estate, or trust may make an election under paragraph (g) of this section for a taxable year that begins before January 1, 2014.

(B) *Certain domestic passthrough entities.*—A domestic partnership, S corporation, or common trust fund may make an election under paragraph (g) of this section for a taxable year that begins before January 1, 2014, provided that all of its partners, shareholders, or participants, as the case may be, consent to the election. In the case of a partner, shareholder, or participant that is a partnership, S corporation, or common trust fund, all of the partners, shareholders, and participants also must consent to the election.

(iv) *Time for making election.*—In all cases, the election under paragraph (g) of this section must be made in the manner prescribed by forms, instructions, or in other guidance on the individual's, estate's, trust's, domestic partnership's, S corporation's, or common trust fund's original or amended return for the taxable year for which the election is made. An election can be made on an amended return only if the taxable year for which the election is made, and all taxable years that are affected by the election, are not closed by the period of limitations on assessments under section 6501. An individual, estate, trust, domestic partnership, S corporation, or common trust fund may not seek an extension of time to make the election under any other provision of the law, including § 301.9100 of this chapter.

(h) *Examples.*—The following examples illustrate the rules of this section. In each example, unless otherwise indicated, the individuals, the foreign corporation (FC), the QEF (QEF), and the partnership (PRS) use a calendar taxable year. Further, the gross income or gain with respect to an interest in FC is not derived in a trade or business described in § 1.1411-5.

Example 1. (i) *Facts.* A, a United States citizen, is the sole shareholder of FC, a controlled foreign corporation (within the meaning of section 957). A is a United States shareholder (within the meaning of section 951(b)) with respect to FC. In 2012, A includes $40,000 in gross income for chapter 1 purposes under section 951(a)(1)(A) with respect to FC. On December 31, 2012, A's basis in the stock of FC for chapter 1 purposes is $500,000, which includes an increase to basis under section 961(a) of $40,000. The amount of FC's earnings and profits that are described in section 959(c)(2) is $40,000, the amount of FC's earnings and profits that are described in section 959(c)(3) is $20,000, and FC does not have any earnings and profits that are described in section 959(c)(1). No election is made under paragraph (g) of this section. During 2013, A does not include any amounts in income under section 951(a) with respect to FC, A does not receive any distributions from FC, and there is no change in the amount of FC's earnings and profits. In 2014, A includes $10,000 in gross income for chapter 1 purposes under section 951(a)(1)(A) with respect to FC. As a result, A's basis in the stock of FC for chapter 1 purposes increases by $10,000 to $510,000 pursuant to section 961(a). During 2015, FC distributes $30,000 to A, which is not treated as a dividend for purposes of chapter 1 under section 959(d). As a result, A's basis in the stock of FC for chapter 1 purposes is decreased by $30,000 to $480,000 pursuant to section 961(b).

(ii) *Results for section 1411 purposes.* In 2014, A does not include the $10,000 section 951(a) income inclusion in A's net investment income under section 1411(c)(1)(A)(i) and § 1.1411-4(a)(1)(i). Pursuant to paragraph (e)(1)(iii) of this section, A decreases A's modified adjusted gross income for section 1411 purposes by $10,000 in 2014, and pursuant to paragraph (d)(1)(i) of this section, A's adjusted basis is not increased by $10,000 and remains at $500,000. In 2015, pursuant to paragraph (c)(2)(i) of this section, A includes $10,000 of the distribution of previously taxed earnings and profits as a dividend for purposes of determining A's net investment income because $10,000 of the $30,000 distribution is attributable to amounts that A included in gross income for chapter 1 purposes under section 951(a) in a tax year that began after December 31, 2012. Pursuant to paragraph (e)(1)(i) of this section, A increases A's modified adjusted gross income for section 1411 purposes by $10,000 in 2015. Under paragraph (d)(1)(i) of this section, A's adjusted basis is not decreased by the $10,000 that is treated as a dividend for section 1411 purposes, and thus, A's adjusted basis in FC for section 1411 purposes is decreased under section 961 only by $20,000 to $480,000.

Example 2. (i) *Facts.* Same facts as *Example 1.* In addition, during 2016, A includes $15,000 in gross income for chapter 1 purposes under section 951(a)(1)(A) with respect to FC. As a result, A's basis in the stock of FC for chapter 1 purposes increases by $15,000 to $495,000 pursuant to section 961(a). During 2017, A sells all of A's shares of FC for $550,000 and, prior to the application of section 1248, recognizes $55,000 ($550,000 minus $495,000) of long-term capital gain for chapter 1 purposes. For purposes of calculating the amount included in income as a dividend pursuant to section 1248(a) for chapter 1 purposes, the earnings and profits of FC attributable to A's shares in FC which were accumulated after December 31,1962 and during the period which A held the stock while FC was a controlled foreign corporation is $55,000, $35,000 of which is excluded pursuant to section 1248(d)(1). Therefore, after the application of section 1248, for chapter 1 purposes, upon the sale of the FC stock, A recognizes $35,000 of long-term capital gain and a $20,000 dividend.

(ii) *Results for section 1411 purposes.* (A) In 2016, A does not include the $15,000 section 951(a)(1)(A) income inclusion in A's net investment income under section 1411(c)(1)(A)(i) and § 1.1411-1(a)(1)(i). Pursuant to paragraph (e)(1)(ii) of this section, A decreases A's modified adjusted gross income for section 1411 purposes by $15,000, and, pursuant to paragraph (d)(1)(i) of this section, A's adjusted basis remains at $480,000.

(B) During 2017, prior to the application of section 1248, A recognizes $70,000 ($550,000 minus $480,000) of gain for section 1411 purposes. Pursuant to paragraph (c)(3) of this section, for section 1411 purposes, section 1248(a) applies to the gain on the sale of FC calculated for section 1411 purposes ($70,000) and section 1248(d)(1) does not apply, except with respect to the $20,000 of earnings and profits of FC that are attributable to amounts previously included in income for chapter 1 purposes under section 951 for a taxable year beginning before December 31, 2012. Accordingly, for purposes of calculating the amount of income includible as a dividend under section 1248(a), A has $55,000 of earnings and profits, $20,000 of which is excluded pursuant to section 1248(d)(1). Therefore, after the application of section 1248, for section 1411 purposes A has $35,000 of long-term capital gain and a $35,000 dividend. For purposes of calculating net investment income in 2017, A includes $35,000 as a dividend under section 1411(c)(1)(A)(i) and § 1.1411-4(a)(1)(i) and $35,000 as a gain under section 1411(c)(1)(A)(iii) and § 1.1411-4(a)(1)(iii).

Example 3. (i) *Facts.* Same facts as *Example 2,* except that A timely makes an election under paragraph (g)(4)(i) of this section for 2014 (and thus for all subsequent years).

(ii) *Results for section 1411 purposes.* A does not have any adjustments to A's modified adjusted gross income for section 1411 purposes for 2014, 2015, 2016 or 2017 because the election under paragraph (g)(4)(i) of this section was timely made. Pursuant to paragraph (g)(2) of this section, for purposes of calculating A's net investment income in 2014, the $10,000 that A included in income for chapter 1 purposes under section 951(a) is net investment income for purposes of section 1411(c)(1)(A)(i) and § 1.1411-4(a)(1)(i). A has no amount of net investment income with respect to FC in 2015. Pursuant to paragraph (g)(2) of this section, for purposes of calculating A's net investment income in 2016, the $15,000 that A included in income for chapter 1 purposes under section 951(a) is net investment income for purposes of section 1411(c)(1)(A)(i) and § 1.1411-4(a)(1)(i). For purposes of calculating A's net investment income in 2017, the amount of gain on the disposition of the FC shares is the same as the amount calculated for chapter 1 purposes. Applying section 1248, A includes $35,000 as a gain under section 1411(c)(1)(A)(iii) and § 1.1411-4(a)(1)(iii), and $20,000 as a dividend under section 1411(c)(1)(A)(i) and § 1.1411-4(a)(1)(i).

Example 4. Domestic partnership holding QEF stock. (i) *Facts.* (A) C, a United States citizen, owns a 50% interest in PRS, a domestic partnership. D, a United States citizen, and E, a United States citizen, each own a 25% interest in PRS. All allocations of partnership income and losses are pro rata based on ownership interests. PRS owns an interest in QEF, a foreign corporation that is a passive foreign investment company (within the meaning of section 1297(a)). PRS, a United States person, made an election under section 1295 with respect to QEF applicable to the first year of its holding period in QEF. As of December 31, 2012, for chapter 1 purposes, C's basis in his partnership interest is $100,000, D's basis in his partnership interest is $50,000, E's basis in his partnership interest is $50,000, and PRS's adjusted basis in its QEF stock is $80,000, which includes an increase in basis under section 1293(d) of $40,000. As of December 31, 2012, the amount of QEF's earnings that have been included in income by PRS under section 1293(a), but have not been distributed by QEF, is $40,000. PRS also has cash of $60,000 and domestic C corporation stock with an adjusted basis of $60,000. During 2013, PRS does not include any amounts in income under section 1293(a) with respect to QEF, PRS does not receive any distributions from QEF, and there are no adjustments to the basis of C, D, or E in their interests in PRS.

(B) During 2014, PRS has income of $40,000 under section 1293(a) with respect to QEF and has no other partnership income. PRS does not make an election under paragraph (g) of this section.

(C) During 2015, QEF distributes $60,000 to PRS. PRS has no income for the year.

(ii) *Results for 2014.* (A) For chapter 1 purposes, as a result of the $40,000 income inclusion under section 1293(a), PRS's basis in its QEF stock is increased by $40,000 under section 1293(d)(1) to $120,000. Under § 1.1293-1(c)(1) and section 702, C's, D's, and E's distributive shares of the section 1293(a) income inclusion are $20,000, $10,000, and $10,000, respectively. Under section 705(a)(1)(A), C increases his adjusted basis in his partnership interest by $20,000 to $120,000, and D and E each increase his adjusted basis in his partnership interest by $10,000 to $60,000.

(B) For section 1411 purposes, pursuant to paragraph (d)(1)(ii) of this section, PRS's basis in QEF is not increased by the $40,000 income inclusion (it remains at $80,000). Because PRS did not make an election under paragraph (g) of this section, C, D and E do not have net investment income with respect to the income inclusion, and pursuant to paragraph (d)(2) of this section, they do not increase their adjusted bases in their interests in PRS (each remains at $50,000). Pursuant to paragraph (e)(1)(ii) of this section, C reduces his modified adjusted gross income by $20,000, and D and E each reduce their modified adjusted gross income by $10,000.

(iii) *Results for 2015.* (A) For chapter 1 purposes, the distribution of $60,000 from QEF to PRS is not a dividend under section 1293(c), and PRS decreases its basis in QEF by $60,000 under section 1293(d)(2) to $60,000.

(B) Pursuant to paragraph (c)(1)(i) of this section, $40,000 of the distribution is a dividend for section 1411 purposes because PRS included $40,000 in gross income for chapter 1 purposes under section 1293(a) in a tax year that began after December 31, 2012. For section 1411 purposes, pursuant to paragraph (d)(1)(ii) of this section, section 1293(d) will not apply to reduce PRS's basis in QEF to the extent of the $40,000 of the distribution that is treated as a dividend under paragraph (c)(2)(i) of this section. Thus, PRS's basis in QEF is decreased only by $20,000 for purposes of section 1411 and is $60,000. The $40,000 distribution of previously taxed earnings and profits that is treated as a dividend for section 1411 purposes is allocated $20,000 to C, $10,000 to D, and $10,000 to E. Because PRS did not make an election under paragraph (g) of this section, pursuant to paragraph (c)(2)(i) of this section, C has $20,000 of net investment income, and D and E each has $10,000 of net investment income as a result of the distribution by QEF, and pursuant to paragraph (d)(2) of this section, C increases his adjusted basis in PRS by $20,000 to $120,000, and D and E each increases his adjusted basis in PRS by $10,000 to $60,000. Pursuant to paragraph (e)(1)(i) of this section, C increases his modified adjusted gross income by $20,000, and D and E each increases his modified adjusted gross income by $10,000.

Example 5. Sale of partnership interest. (i) *Facts.* Same facts as *Example 4.* In addition, in 2016, D sells his entire interest in PRS to F for $100,000.

(ii) *Results for 2016.* For chapter 1 purposes, D has a gain of $40,000 ($100,000 minus $60,000). For section 1411 purposes, D has a gain of $40,000 ($100,000 minus $60,000), and thus, has net investment income of $40,000. No adjustments to modified adjusted gross income are necessary under paragraph (e) of this section.

Example 6. Domestic partnership's sale of QEF stock. (i) *Facts.* Same facts as *Example 4.* In addition, in 2016 PRS has income of $60,000 under section 1293(a) with respect to QEF, and in 2017, PRS sells its entire interest in QEF for $170,000.

(ii) *Results for 2016.* (A) For chapter 1 purposes, as a result of the $60,000 income inclusion under section 1293(a), PRS's basis in its QEF stock is increased by $60,000 under section 1293(d)(1) to $120,000. Under § 1.1293-1(c)(1) and section 702, C's, D's, and E's distributive shares of the section 1293(a) income inclusion are $30,000, $15,000, and $15,000 respectively. Under section 705(a)(1)(A), C increases his adjusted basis in his partnership interest by $30,000 to $150,000, and D and E each increases his adjusted basis in his partnership interest by $15,000 to $75,000.

(B) For section 1411 purposes, pursuant to paragraph (d)(1)(ii) of this section, PRS's basis in QEF is not increased by the $60,000 income inclusion (it remains at $60,000). Because PRS did not make an election under paragraph (g) of this section, C, D and E do not have net investment income with respect to the income inclusion, and pursuant to paragraph (d)(2) of this section, they do not increase their adjusted bases in their interests in PRS (C remains at $120,000, and D and E each remain at $60,000). Pursuant to paragraph (e)(1)(ii) of this section, C reduces his modified adjusted gross income by $30,000, and D and E each reduce their modified adjusted gross income by $15,000.

(iii) *Results for 2017.* (A) For chapter 1 purposes, PRS has a gain of $50,000 ($170,000 minus $120,000), which is allocated 50% ($25,000) to C, 25% ($12,500) to D, and 25% ($12,500) to E.

(B) Based on PRS's basis in the stock of QEF for section 1411 purposes, PRS has a gain for section 1411 purposes of $110,000 ($170,000 minus $60,000), which in the absence of an election by PRS under paragraph (g) of this section, results in gain of $55,000 to C, $27,500 to D, and $27,500 to E. Therefore, C has net investment income of $55,000, and D and E each have net investment income of $27,500. Pursuant to paragraph (e)(1)(ii) of this section, C increases his modified adjusted gross income by $30,000, and D and E each increase their modified adjusted gross income by $15,000.

(i) *Effective/applicability date.*—This section applies to taxable years beginning after December 31, 2013. However, taxpayers may apply this section to taxable years beginning after December 31, 2012, in accordance with § 1.1411-1(f). [Reg. § 1.1411-10.]

□ [*T.D. 9644, 11-26-2013 (corrected 3-31-2014).*]

Proposed Amendments to Regulation

§ 1.1411-10. Controlled foreign corporations and passive foreign investment companies.—

* * *

(g) * * *

(3) *Who may make the election.*—(i) *In general.*—An individual, estate, or trust may make an election under paragraph (g) of this section with respect to each CFC or QEF that it holds directly or indirectly through one or more entities, each of which is a foreign entity or a domestic pass-through entity. The election, if made, for an estate or trust must be made by the fiduciary of the estate or trust.

(ii) *Special rule for certain S corporations.*—For taxable years in which an S corporation elects to apply § 1.958-1(e), the S corporation may make an election under this paragraph (g)(3)(ii) with respect to each CFC that it holds, directly or indirectly. If an S corporation does not make the election under this paragraph (g)(3)(ii), the election may be made by its shareholders that are individuals, estates, or trusts instead.

(4) * * *

(iii) *Time for making election.*—The election under paragraph (g) of this section must be made in the manner prescribed by forms, instructions, or in other guidance on the individual's, estate's, or trust's original or amended return for the taxable year for which the election is made. An election can be made on an amended return only if the taxable year for which the election is made, and all taxable years that are affected by the election, are not closed by the period of limitations on assessments under section 6501. Extensions of time to make the election are not available under any other provision of the law, including § 301.9100 of this chapter.

* * *

(i) *Applicability dates.*—Except as otherwise provided in this paragraph (i), this section applies to taxable years beginning after December 31, 2013. However, taxpayers may apply this section to taxable years beginning after December 31, 2012, in accordance with

§1.1411-1(f). Paragraphs (g)(3) and (g)(4)(iii) of this section apply to taxable years beginning on or after [date of publication of the Treasury decision adopting these rules as final regulations in the **Federal Register**]. For taxable years beginning before [date of publication of the Treasury decision adopting these rules as final regulations in the **Federal Register**], see paragraphs (g)(3) and (g)(4)(iii) of this section as in effect and contained in 26 CFR part 1, as revised April 1, 2021. [Prop. Reg. §1.1411-10.]

[Proposed 1-25-2022.]

Withholding Taxes

§1.1441-1. Requirement for the deduction and withholding of tax on payments to foreign persons.—(a) *Purpose and scope.*—This section, §§1.1441-2 through 1.1441-9, and 1.1443-1 provide rules for withholding under sections 1441, 1442, and 1443 when a payment is made to a foreign person. This section provides definitions of terms used in chapter 3 of the Internal Revenue Code (Code) and regulations thereunder. It prescribes procedures to determine whether an amount must be withheld under chapter 3 of the Code and documentation that a withholding agent may rely upon to determine the status of a payee or a beneficial owner as a U.S. person or as a foreign person and other relevant characteristics of the payee that may affect a withholding agent's obligation to withhold under chapter 3 of the Code and the regulations thereunder. Special procedures regarding payments to foreign persons that act as intermediaries are also provided. Section 1.1441-2 defines the income subject to withholding under sections 1441, 1442, and 1443 and the regulations under these sections. Section 1.1441-3 provides rules regarding the amount subject to withholding and rules for coordinating withholding under this section with withholding under section 1445 and under chapter 4 of the Code. Section 1.1441-4 provides exemptions from withholding for, among other things, certain income effectively connected with the conduct of a trade or business in the United States, including certain compensation for the personal services of an individual. Section 1.1441-5 provides rules for withholding on payments made to flow-through entities and other similar arrangements. Section 1.1441-6 provides rules for claiming a reduced rate of withholding under an income tax treaty. Section 1.1441-7 defines the term withholding agent and provides due diligence rules governing a withholding agent's obligation to withhold. Section 1.1441-8 provides rules for relying on claims of exemption from withholding for payments to a foreign government, an international organization, a foreign central bank of issue, or the Bank for International Settlements. Sections 1.1441-9 and 1.1443-1 provide rules for relying on claims of exemption from withholding for payments to foreign tax exempt organizations and foreign private foundations.

(b) *General rules of withholding.*—(1) *Requirement to withhold on payments to foreign persons.*—A withholding agent must withhold 30 percent of any payment of an amount subject to withholding made to a payee that is a foreign person unless it can reliably associate the payment with documentation upon which it can rely to treat the payment as made to a payee that is a U.S. person or as made to a beneficial owner that is a foreign person entitled to a reduced rate of withholding. However, a withholding agent making a payment to a foreign person need not withhold where the foreign person assumes responsibility for withholding on the payment under chapter 3 of the Code and the regulations thereunder as a qualified intermediary (see paragraphs (e)(5) and (e)(6) of this section), as a U.S. branch of a foreign person (see paragraph (b)(2)(iv) of this section), as a withholding foreign partnership (see §1.1441-5(c)(2)(i)), or as a withholding foreign trust (see §1.1441-5(e)(5)(v)). When withholding under chapter 4 was applied to a payment, the withholding obligation under this section is satisfied. See §1.1441-3(a)(2). This section (dealing with general rules of withholding and claims of foreign or U.S. status by a payee or a beneficial owner) and §§1.1441-4, 1.1441-5, 1.1441-6, 1.1441-8, 1.1441-9, and 1.1443-1 provide rules for determining whether documentation is required as a condition for reducing the rate of withholding on a payment to a foreign beneficial owner or to a U.S. payee and if so, the nature of the documentation upon which a withholding agent may rely in order to reduce such rate. Paragraph (b)(2) of this section prescribes the rules for the determination of who the payee is, the extent to which a payment is treated as made to a foreign payee, and reliable association of a payment with documentation. Paragraph (b)(3) of this section describes the applicable presumptions for determining the payee's status as U.S. or foreign and the payee's other characteristics (*e.g.*, as an owner or intermediary, as an individual, partnership, corporation, etc.). Paragraph (b)(4) of this section lists the types of payments for which the 30-percent withholding rate may be reduced. Because the treatment of a payee as a U.S. or a foreign person also has consequences for purposes of making an information return under the provisions of chapter 61 of the Code and for withholding under other provisions of the Code, such as sections 3402, 3405, or 3406, paragraph (b)(5) of this section lists applicable provisions outside chapter 3 of the Code that require certain payees to establish their foreign status (*e.g.*, in order to be exempt from information reporting). Paragraph (b)(6) of this section describes the withholding obligations of a foreign person making a payment that it has received in its capacity as an intermediary. Paragraph (b)(7) of this section describes the liability of a withholding agent that fails to withhold at the required 30-percent rate in the absence of documentation. Paragraph (b)(8) of this section deals with adjustments and refunds in the case of overwithholding. Paragraph (b)(9) of this section deals with determining the status of the payee when the payment is jointly owned. See paragraph (c)(6) of this section for a definition of beneficial owner. See §1.1441-7(a) for a definition of withholding agent. See §1.1441-2(a) for the determination of an amount subject to withholding. See §1.1441-2(e) for the definition of a payment and when it is considered made. Except as otherwise provided, the provisions of this section apply only for purposes of determining a withholding agent's obligation to withhold under chapter 3 of the Code and the regulations thereunder.

(2) *Determination of payee and payee's status.*—(i) *In general.*—Except as otherwise provided in this paragraph (b)(2) and §1.1441-5(c)(1) and (e)(3), a payee is the person to whom a payment is made, regardless of whether such person is the beneficial owner of the amount (as defined in paragraph (c)(6) of this section). A foreign payee is a payee who is a foreign person. A U.S. payee is a payee who is a U.S. person. Generally, the determination by a withholding agent of the U.S. or foreign status of a payee and of its other relevant characteristics (*e.g.*, as a beneficial owner or intermediary, or as an individual, corporation, or flow-through entity) is made on the basis of a withholding certificate that is a Form W-8 or a Form 8233 (indicating foreign status of the payee or beneficial owner) or a Form W-9 (indicating U.S. status of the payee). The provisions of this paragraph (b)(2), paragraph (b)(3) of this section, and §1.1441-5(c), (d), and (e) dealing with determinations of payee and applicable presumptions in the absence of documentation apply only to payments of amounts subject to withholding under chapter 3 of the Code (within the meaning of §1.1441-2(a)). However, for a payment that is both an amount subject to withholding under chapter 3 and a withholdable payment under chapter 4, first apply the rules of §1.1471-3 for determining the payee of a withholdable payment under chapter 4 and the applicable presumptions in the absence of documentation applicable to such payments. See also §1.6049-5(d) for payments of amounts that are not subject to withholding under chapter 3 of the Code (or the regulations thereunder) but that may be reportable under provisions of chapter 61 of the Code (and the regulations thereunder). See paragraph (d) of this section for documentation upon which the withholding agent may rely in order to treat the payee or beneficial owner as a U.S. person. See paragraph (e) of this section for documentation upon which the withholding agent may rely in order to treat the payee or beneficial owner as a foreign person. For applicable presumptions of status in the absence of documentation, see paragraph (b)(3) of this section and §1.1441-5(d). For definitions of a foreign person and U.S. person, see paragraph (c)(2) of this section.

(ii) *Payments to a U.S. agent of a foreign person.*—A withholding agent making a payment to a U.S. person (other than to a U.S. branch that is treated as a U.S. person pursuant to paragraph (b)(2)(iv) of this section) and who has actual knowledge that the U.S. person receives the payment as an agent of a foreign person must treat the payment as made to the foreign person. However, the withholding agent may treat the payment as made to the U.S. person if the U.S. person is a financial institution and the withholding agent has no reason to believe that the financial institution will not comply with its obligation to withhold. See paragraph (c)(5) of this section for the definition of a financial institution.

(iii) *Payments to wholly-owned entities.*—(A) *Foreign-owned domestic entity.*—A payment to a wholly-owned domestic entity that is disregarded for federal tax purposes under §301.7701-2(c)(2) of this chapter as an entity separate from its owner and whose single owner is a foreign person shall be treated as a payment to the owner of the entity, subject to the provisions of paragraph (b)(2)(iv) of this section.

For purposes of this paragraph (b)(2)(iii)(A), a domestic entity means a person that would be treated as a U.S. person if it had an election in effect under § 301.7701-3(c)(1)(i) of this chapter to be treated as a corporation. For example, a limited liability company, A, organized under the laws of the State of Delaware, opens an account at a U.S. bank. Upon opening of the account, the bank requests A to furnish a Form W-9 as required under section 6049(a) and the regulations under that section. A does not have an election in effect under § 301.7701-3(c)(1)(i) of this chapter and, therefore, is not treated as an organization taxable as a corporation, including for purposes of the exempt recipient provisions in § 1.6049-4(c)(1). If A has a single owner and the owner is a foreign person (as defined in paragraph (c)(2) of this section), then A may not furnish a Form W-9 because it may not represent that it is a U.S. person for purposes of the provisions of chapters 3, 4, and 61 of the Code, and section 3406. Therefore, A must furnish a Form W-8 with the name, address, and taxpayer identifying number (TIN) (if required) of the foreign person who is the single owner in the same manner as if the account were opened directly by the foreign single owner. See § § 1.894-1(d) and 1.1441-6(b)(2) for special rules where the entity's owner is claiming a reduced rate of withholding under an income tax treaty.

(B) *Foreign entity.*—A payment to a wholly-owned foreign entity that is disregarded under § 301.7701-2(c)(2) of this chapter as an entity separate from its owner shall be treated as a payment to the single owner of the entity, subject to the provisions of paragraph (b)(2)(iv) of this section if the foreign entity has a U.S. branch in the United States. For purposes of this paragraph (b)(2)(iii)(B), a foreign entity means a person that would be treated as a foreign person if it had an election in effect under § 301.7701-3(c)(1)(i) of this chapter to be treated as a corporation. See § § 1.894-1T(d) and 1.1441-6(b)(2) for special rules where the foreign entity or its owner is claiming a reduced rate of withholding under an income tax treaty. Thus, for example, if the foreign entity's single owner is a U.S. person, the payment shall be treated as a payment to a U.S. person. Therefore, based on the saving clause in U.S. income tax treaties, such an entity may not claim benefits under an income tax treaty even if the entity is organized in a country with which the United States has an income tax treaty in effect and treats the entity as a non-fiscally transparent entity. See § 1.894-1T(d)(6), *Example 10.* Unless it has actual knowledge or reason to know that the foreign entity to whom the payment is made is disregarded under § 301.7701-2(c)(2) of this chapter, a withholding agent may treat a foreign entity as an entity separate from its owner unless it can reliably associate the payment with a withholding certificate from the entity's owner.

(iv) *Payments to a U.S. branch of certain foreign banks or foreign insurance companies.*—(A) *U.S. branch treated as a U.S. person in certain cases.*—A payment to a U.S. branch of a foreign person is a payment to a foreign person. However, a U.S. branch of a foreign person that is described in this paragraph (b)(2)(iv)(A) may agree to be treated as a U.S. person for purposes of withholding on specified payments to the U.S. branch. If a U.S. branch agrees to be treated as a U.S. person with a withholding agent, it is required to act as a U.S. person with respect to all other withholding agents, including when acting as an intermediary with respect to withholdable payments for purposes of chapter 4. See § 1.1471-3(a)(3)(vi). In such cases, the U.S. branch is treated as a payee that is a U.S. person. See paragraph (C) of this section for additional requirements for the U.S. branch when treated as a payor that is a U.S. person. Notwithstanding the preceding sentence, a withholding agent making a payment to a U.S. branch treated as a U.S. person under this paragraph (b)(2)(iv)(A) shall not treat the branch as a U.S. person for purposes of reporting the payment made to the branch. Therefore, a payment to such U.S. branch shall be reported on Form 1042-S under § 1.1461-1(c) and § 1.1474-1(d)(1)(i) for a payment of U.S. source FDAP income that is a chapter 4 reportable amount as defined in § 1.1471-1(b)(18). Further, a U.S. branch that is treated as a U.S. person under this paragraph (b)(2)(iv)(A) shall not be treated as a U.S. person for purposes of the withholding certificate it provides to a withholding agent. Therefore, the U.S. branch must furnish a U.S. branch withholding certificate on a Form W-8IMY as provided in paragraph (e)(3)(v) of this section and not a Form W-9. An agreement to treat a U.S. branch as a U.S. person must be evidenced by a U.S. branch withholding certificate described in paragraph (e)(3)(v) of this section furnished by the U.S. branch to the withholding agent. A U.S. branch described in this paragraph (b)(2)(iv)(A) and eligible to be treated as a U.S. person is any U.S. branch of a foreign bank subject to regulatory supervision by the Federal Reserve Board or a U.S. branch of a foreign insurance company required to file an annual statement on a form approved by the National Association of Insurance Commissioners with the Insurance Department of a State, a Territory, or the District of Columbia. In addition, a territory financial institution (including a territory financial institution that is a flow-through entity) will be treated as a U.S. branch for purposes of this paragraph (b)(2)(iv)(A) and therefore is eligible to be treated as a U.S. person. The Internal Revenue Service (IRS) may approve a list of U.S. branches that may be eligible for treatment as U.S. persons under this paragraph (b)(2)(iv)(A) (see § 601.601(d)(2) of this chapter). See § 1.6049-5(c)(5)(vi) for the treatment of U.S. branches as U.S. payors if they make a payment that is subject to reporting under chapter 61 of the Code. Also see § 1.6049-5(d)(1)(ii) for the treatment of U.S. branches as foreign payees under chapter 61 of the Code.

(B) *Consequences to the withholding agent.*—Any person that is otherwise a withholding agent regarding a payment to a U.S. branch described in paragraph (b)(2)(iv)(A) of this section shall treat the payment in one of the following ways—

(1) As a payment to a U.S. person, in which case the withholding agent is not responsible for withholding on such payment to the extent it can reliably associate the payment with a withholding certificate described in paragraph (e)(3)(v) of this section that has been furnished by the U.S. branch under its agreement with the withholding agent to be treated as U.S. person;

(2) As a payment directly to the persons whose names are on withholding certificates or other appropriate documentation forwarded by the U.S. branch to the withholding agent when no agreement is in effect to treat the U.S. branch as a U.S. person for such payment, to the extent the withholding agent can reliably associate the payment with such certificates or documentation;

(3) As a payment to a foreign person of income that is effectively connected with the conduct of a trade or business in the United States if the withholding agent has obtained an EIN for the branch and cannot reliably associate the payment with a withholding certificate from a U.S. branch (or any other certificate or other appropriate documentation from another person). See § 1.1441-4(a)(2)(ii); or

(4) As a payment to a foreign person of income that is not effectively connected with the conduct of a trade or business in the United States if the withholding agent has not obtained an EIN for the branch and cannot reliably associate the payment with a withholding certificate from the U.S. branch.

(C) *Consequences to the U.S. branch.*—A U.S. branch that is treated as a U.S. person under paragraph (b)(2)(iv)(A) of this section shall be treated as a separate person for purposes of section 1441(a) and all other provisions of chapters 3 and 4 of the Code and the regulations thereunder (other than for purposes of reporting the payment to the U.S. branch under § 1.1461-1(c) and § 1.1474-1(d)(1)(i) for a chapter 4 reportable amount by a withholding agent) or for purposes of the documentation such a branch must furnish under paragraph (e)(3)(v) of this section) for any payment that it receives as such. Thus, the U.S. branch shall be responsible for withholding on a payment as a U.S. person in accordance with the provisions under chapters 3 and 4 of the Code and the regulations thereunder and other applicable withholding provisions of the Code. For this purpose, it shall obtain and retain documentation from payees or beneficial owners of the payments that it receives as an intermediary as a U.S. person in the same manner as if it were a separate entity. For example, if a U.S. branch receives a payment as an intermediary on behalf of customers of its home office and the home office is a qualified intermediary, the U.S. branch must obtain a qualified intermediary withholding certificate described in paragraph (e)(3)(ii) of this section from its home office. Similarly, if a U.S. branch of an FFI treated as a U.S. person receives a payment on behalf of another branch of the FFI that is treated as a nonparticipating FFI, the U.S. branch must withhold on the payment made to the other branch as if it were a separate person to the extent required under chapter 4. In addition, a U.S. branch that has not provided documentation to the withholding agent for a payment that is, in fact, not effectively connected income is a withholding agent with respect to that payment. See paragraph (b)(6) of this section and § 1.1441-4(a)(2)(ii).

(D) *Definition of payment to a U.S. branch.*—A payment is treated as a payment to a U.S. branch of a foreign bank or foreign insurance company if the payment is credited to an account maintained in the United States in the name of a U.S. branch of the foreign person, or the payment is made to an address in the United States where the U.S. branch is located and the name of the U.S. branch appears on documents (in written or electronic form) associated with the payment (e.g., the check mailed or a letter addressed to the branch).

(E) *Payments to other U.S. branches.*—Similar withholding procedures may apply to payments to U.S. branches that are not described in paragraph (b)(2)(iv)(A) of this section to the extent permitted by the IRS. Any such branch must establish that its situation is analogous to that of a U.S. branch described in paragraph (b)(2)(iv)(A) of this section. In the alternative, the branch must establish that the withholding and reporting requirements under chapter 3 of the Code and the regulations thereunder impose an undue administrative burden and that the collection of the tax imposed by section 871(a) or 881(a) on the foreign person (or its members in the case of a foreign partnership) will not be jeopardized by the exemption from withholding. Generally, an undue administrative burden will be found to exist in a case where the person entitled to the income, such as a foreign insurance company, receives from the withholding agent income on securities issued by a single corporation, some of which is, and some of which is not, effectively connected with conduct of a trade or business within the United States and the criteria for determining the effective connection are unduly difficult to apply because of the circumstances under which such securities are held. No exemption from withholding shall be granted under this paragraph (b)(2)(iv)(E) unless the person entitled to the income complies with such other requirements as may be imposed by the IRS and unless the IRS is satisfied that the collection of the tax on the income involved will not be jeopardized by the exemption from withholding. The IRS may prescribe such procedures as are necessary to make these determinations (see § 601.601(d)(2) of this chapter).

(v) *Payments to a foreign intermediary.*—(A) *Payments treated as made to persons for whom the intermediary collects the payment.*—Except as otherwise provided in paragraph (b)(2)(v)(B) of this section, the payee of a payment to a person that the withholding agent may treat as a foreign intermediary in accordance with the provisions of paragraph (b)(3)(ii)(C) or (b)(3)(v)(A) of this section is the person or persons for whom the intermediary collects the payment. Thus, for example, the payee of a payment that the withholding agent can reliably associate with a withholding certificate from a qualified intermediary (defined in paragraph (e)(5)(ii) of this section) that does not assume primary withholding responsibility or a payment to a nonqualified intermediary are the persons for whom the qualified intermediary or nonqualified intermediary acts and not to the intermediary itself. See paragraph (b)(3)(v) of this section for presumptions that apply if the payment cannot be reliably associated with valid documentation. For similar rules for payments to flow-through entities, see § 1.1441-5(c)(1) and (e)(3).

(B) *Payments treated as made to foreign intermediary.*—The payee of a payment to a person that the withholding agent may treat as a qualified intermediary is the qualified intermediary to the extent that the qualified intermediary assumes primary withholding responsibility under paragraph (e)(5)(iv) of this section for the payment. For example if a qualified intermediary assumes primary withholding responsibility under chapter 3 of the Internal Revenue Code but does not assume primary reporting or withholding responsibility under chapter 61 or section 3406 of the Internal Revenue Code and therefore provides Forms W-9 for U.S. non-exempt recipients, the qualified intermediary is the payee except to the extent the payment is reliably associated with a Form W-9 from a U.S. non-exempt recipient.

(vi) *Other payees.*—A payment to a person described in § 1.6049-4(c)(1)(ii) that the withholding agent would treat as a payment to a foreign person without obtaining documentation for purposes of information reporting under section 6049 (if the payment were interest) is treated as a payment to a foreign payee for purposes of chapter 3 of the Code and the regulations thereunder (or to a foreign beneficial owner to the extent provided in paragraph (e)(1)(ii)(A)(*6*) or (*7*) of this section). Further, a payment that the withholding agent can reliably associate with documentary evidence described in § 1.6049-5(c)(1) relating to the payee is treated as a payment to a foreign payee. See § 1.1441-5(b)(1) and (c)(1) for payee determinations for payments to partnerships. See § 1.1441-5(e) for payee determinations for payments to foreign trusts or foreign estates.

(vii) *Rules for reliably associating a payment with a withholding certificate or other appropriate documentation.*—(A) *Generally.*—The presumption rules of paragraph (b)(3) of this section and §§ 1.1441-5(d) and (e)(6) and 1.6049-5(d) apply to any payment, or portion of a payment, that a withholding agent cannot reliably associate with valid documentation. Generally, a withholding agent can reliably associate a payment with valid documentation if, prior to the payment, it holds valid documentation (either directly or through an agent), it can reliably determine how much of the payment relates to the valid documentation, and it has no actual knowledge or reason to know that any of the information, certifications, or statements in, or associated with, the documentation are incorrect. Special rules apply for payments made to intermediaries, flow-through entities, and certain U.S. branches. See paragraph (b)(2)(vii)(B) through (F) of this section. The documentation referred to in this paragraph (b)(2)(vii) is documentation described in paragraphs (c)(16) and (17) of this section upon which a withholding agent may rely to treat the payment as a payment made to a payee or beneficial owner, and to ascertain the characteristics of the payee or beneficial owner that are relevant to withholding or reporting under chapter 3 of the Internal Revenue Code and the regulations thereunder. A withholding agent that is not required to obtain documentation with respect to a payment is considered to lack documentation for purposes of this paragraph (b)(2)(vii). For example, a withholding agent paying U.S. source interest to a person that is an exempt recipient, as defined in § 1.6049-4(c)(1)(ii), is not required to obtain documentation from that person in order to determine whether an amount paid to that person is reportable under an applicable information reporting provision under chapter 61 of the Internal Revenue Code. The withholding agent must, however, treat the payment as made to an undocumented person for purposes of chapter 3 of the Internal Revenue Code. Therefore, the presumption rules of paragraph (b)(3)(iii) of this section apply to determine whether the person is presumed to be a U.S. person (in which case, no withholding is required under this section), or whether the person is presumed to be a foreign person (in which case 30-percent withholding is required under this section). See paragraph (b)(3)(v) of this section for special reliance rules in the case of a payment to a foreign intermediary and § 1.1441-5(d) and (e)(6) for special reliance rules in the case of a payment to a flow-through entity.

(B) *Special rules applicable to a withholding certificate from a nonqualified intermediary or flow-through entity.*—(*1*) In the case of a payment made to a nonqualified intermediary, a flow-through entity (as defined in paragraph (c)(23) of this section), or a U.S. branch described in paragraph (b)(2)(iv) of this section (other than a U.S. branch that is treated as a U.S. person), a withholding agent can reliably associate the payment with valid documentation only to the extent that, prior to the payment, the withholding agent can allocate the payment to a valid nonqualified intermediary, flow-through entity, or U.S. branch withholding certificate (and a withholding certificate provided by a nonparticipating FFI with respect to a portion of a payment that is a withholdable payment allocated to an exempt beneficial owner as described in § 1.1471-3(c)(3)(iii)(B)(*4*)); the withholding agent can reliably determine how much of the payment relates to valid documentation provided by a payee as determined under paragraph (c)(12) of this section (*i.e.*, a person that is not itself an intermediary, flow-through entity, or U.S. branch); and the withholding agent has sufficient information to report the payment on Form 1042-S or Form 1099, if reporting is required. See, however, paragraph (e)(3)(iv) of this section for when a nonqualified intermediary may report payees to the withholding agent in a chapter 4 withholding rate pool, in which case a withholding agent need not associate the portion of the payment attributable to such payees with documentation from each such payee. See also paragraph (e)(3)(iii) of this section for the requirements of a nonqualified intermediary withholding certificate, paragraph (e)(3)(v) of this section for the requirements of a U.S. branch withholding certificate, and §§ 1.1441-5(c)(3)(iii) and (e)(5)(iii) for the requirements of a flow-through withholding certificate (including the requirements for a withholding certificate associated with a withholdable payment). Thus, a payment cannot be reliably associated with valid documentation provided by a payee to the extent such documentation is lacking or unreliable, or to the extent that information required to allocate and report all or a portion of the payment to each payee is lacking or unreliable. If a withholding certificate attached to an intermediary, U.S. branch, or flow-through withholding certificate is another intermediary, U.S. branch, or flow-through withholding certificate, the rules of this paragraph (b)(2)(vii)(B) apply by treating the share of the payment allocable to the other intermediary, U.S. branch, or flow-through entity as if the payment were made directly to such other entity. See paragraph (e)(3)(iv)(D) of this section for rules permitting information allocating a payment to documentation to be received after the payment is made.

(*2*) The rules of paragraph (b)(2)(vii)(B)(*1*) of this section are illustrated by the following examples. Each example illustrates a payment that is not a withholdable payment and, as a result of which, neither the chapter 4 status of the NQI nor payee specific documentation with respect to the chapter 4 status is required to be provided to the withholding agent (and no withholding applies under chapter 4 on each payment). See paragraph (e)(3)(iv)(C) of this section for the requirements of a withholding statement provided by a nonqualified intermediary that receives a withholdable payment and for an example illustrating the requirements of an NQI providing a withholding statement to a withholding agent for a withholdable payment.

Example 1. WA, a withholding agent, makes a payment of U.S. source interest with respect to a grandfathered obligation as described in § 1.1471-2(b) (and thus the payment is not a withholdable payment) to NQI, an intermediary that is a nonqualified intermediary. NQI provides a valid intermediary withholding certificate under paragraph (e)(3)(iii) of this section. NQI does not, however, provide valid documentation from the persons on whose behalf it receives the interest payment, and, therefore, the interest payment cannot be reliably associated with valid documentation provided by a payee. WA must apply the presumption rules of paragraph (b)(3)(v) of this section to the payment.

Example 2. The facts are the same as in *Example 1*, except that NQI does attach valid beneficial owner withholding certificates (as defined in paragraph (e)(2)(i) of this section) from A, B, C, and D establishing their statuses as foreign persons. NQI does not, however, provide WA with any information allocating the payment among A, B, C, and D and, therefore, WA cannot determine the portion of the payment that relates to each beneficial owner withholding certificate. The interest payment cannot be reliably associated with valid documentation from a payee, and WA must apply the presumption rules of paragraph (b)(3)(v) of this section to the payment. See, however, paragraph (e)(3)(iv)(D) of this section providing for alternative procedures that allow a nonqualified intermediary to provide allocation information after a payment is made.

Example 3. The facts are the same as in *Example 2*, except that NQI provides allocation information associated with its intermediary withholding certificate indicating that 25% of the interest payment is allocable to A and 25% to B. NQI does not provide any allocation information regarding the remaining 50% of the payment. WA may treat 25% of the payment as made to A and 25% as made to B. The remaining 50% of the payment cannot be reliably associated with valid documentation from a payee, however, since NQI did not provide information allocating the payment. Thus, the remaining 50% of the payment is subject to the presumption rules of paragraph (b)(3)(v) of this section.

Example 4. WA makes a payment of U.S. source interest to NQI1, an intermediary that is not a qualified intermediary. NQI1 provides WA with a valid nonqualified intermediary withholding certificate as well valid beneficial owner withholding certificates from A and B and a valid nonqualified intermediary withholding certificate from NQI2. NQI2 has provided valid beneficial owner documentation from C sufficient to establish C's status as a foreign person. Based on information provided by NQI1, WA can allocate 20% of the interest payment to A, and 20% to B. Based on information that NQI2 provided NQI1 and that NQI1 provides to WA, WA can allocate 60% of the payment to NQI2, but can only allocate one half of that payment (30%) to C. Therefore, WA cannot reliably associate the remainder of the payment made to NQI2 (30% of the total payment) with valid documentation and must apply the presumption rules of paragraph (b)(3)(v) of this section to that portion of the payment.

(C) *Special rules applicable to a withholding certificate provided by a qualified intermediary that does not assume primary withholding responsibility.*—*(1)* If a payment is made to a qualified intermediary that does not assume primary withholding responsibility under chapters 3 and 4 of the Code or primary Form 1099 reporting and backup withholding responsibility under chapter 61 and section 3406 of the Code for the payment, a withholding agent can reliably associate the payment with valid documentation only to the extent that, prior to the payment, the withholding agent has received a valid qualified intermediary withholding certificate described in paragraph (e)(3)(ii) of this section and the withholding agent can reliably determine the portion of the payment that relates to a chapter 3 withholding rate pool, as defined in paragraph (c)(44) of this section; a chapter 4 withholding rate pool (including for a withholdable payment as described in paragraph (e)(5)(v)(C)*(2)* of this section), as defined in paragraph (c)(48) of this section; or a pool attributable to U.S. exempt recipients. In the case of a withholding rate pool attributable to a U.S. non-exempt recipient, a payment cannot be reliably associated with valid documentation unless, prior to the payment, the qualified intermediary has provided the U.S. person's Form W-9 (or, in the absence of the form, the name, address, and TIN, if available, of the U.S. person) and sufficient information for the withholding agent to report the payment on Form 1099. See, however, paragraph (e)(5)(v)(C)*(3)* of this section for alternative procedures for allocating payments among U.S. non-exempt recipients and paragraphs (e)(5)(v)(C)*(1)* and *(2)* of this section for when a chapter 4 withholding rate pool of U.S. payees may be provided by a qualified intermediary instead of documentation with respect to each U.S. non-exempt recipient.

(2) The rules of this paragraph (b)(2)(vii)(C) are illustrated by the following examples:

Example 1. WA, a withholding agent, makes a payment of U.S. source dividends that is a withholdable payment to QI. QI provides WA with a valid qualified intermediary withholding certificate on which it indicates that it does not assume primary withholding responsibility under chapters 3 and 4 or primary Form 1099 reporting and backup withholding responsibility under chapter 61 and section 3406. QI does not provide any information allocating the dividend to withholding rate pools. WA cannot reliably associate the payment with valid payee documentation and therefore must apply the presumption rules applicable to a withholdable payment under § 1.1471-3(f)(5) to determine the status of the payee for purposes of chapter 4. See *Example 2* for an application of the presumption rules under § 1.1471-3(f).

Example 2. WA makes a payment of U.S. source dividends that is a withholdable payment to QI, which is an NFFE. QI has 5 customers: A, B, C, D, and E, all of whom are individuals except for C. QI has obtained valid documentation from A and B establishing their entitlement to a 15% rate of tax on U.S. source dividends under an income tax treaty. C is a U.S. person that is an exempt recipient as defined in paragraph (c)(20) of this section. D and E are U.S. non-exempt recipients who have provided Forms W-9 to QI. A, B, C, D, and E are each entitled to 20% of the dividend payment. QI provides WA with a valid qualified intermediary withholding certificate as described in paragraph (e)(3)(ii) of this section with which it associates the Forms W-9 from D and E. QI associates the following allocation information with its qualified intermediary withholding certificate: 40% of the payment is allocable to the 15% chapter 3 withholding rate pool, and 20% is allocable to each of D and E. QI does not provide any allocation information regarding the remaining 20% of the payment. WA cannot reliably associate 20% of the payment with valid documentation and, therefore, must apply the presumption rules applicable to a withholdable payment. Because QI is receiving a withholdable payment as an intermediary, under paragraph (b)(3)(iii) of this section WA must apply the presumption rule of § 1.1471-3(f)(5) to treat the portion of the payment that cannot reliably be associated with valid documentation as made to a nonparticipating FFI account holder of QI. As a result, WA is required to withhold at a 30% rate of tax under chapter 4. See § 1.1441-3(a)(2) permitting WA to credit the amount withheld under chapter 4 against the liability for tax due on the payment under section 1441 or 1442. The 40% of the payment allocable to the 15% withholding rate pool and the portion of the payments allocable to D and E are payments that can be reliably associated with documentation.

(D) *Special rules applicable to a withholding certificate provided by a qualified intermediary that assumes primary withholding responsibility under chapter 3 and chapter 4 of the Internal Revenue Code.*—*(1)* In the case of a payment made to a qualified intermediary that assumes primary withholding responsibility under chapters 3 and 4 of the Code with respect to that payment (but does not assume primary Form 1099 reporting and backup withholding responsibility under chapter 61 of the Code and section 3406), a withholding agent can reliably associate the payment with valid documentation only to the extent that, prior to the payment, the withholding agent has received a valid qualified intermediary withholding certificate and the withholding agent can reliably determine the portion of the payment that relates to the withholding rate pool for which the qualified intermediary assumes primary withholding responsibility and the portion of the payment attributable to withholding rate pools for each U.S. non-exempt recipient for whom the qualified intermediary has provided a Form W-9 (or, in absence of the form, the name, address, and TIN, if available, of the U.S. non-exempt recipient). See paragraph (e)(5)(iv) of this section (requiring a qualified intermediary assuming primary withholding responsibility under chapter 3 to assume primary withholding responsibility under chapter 4). See also paragraph (e)(5)(v)(C)*(3)* of this section for alternative allocation procedures for payments made to U.S. persons that are not exempt recipients and paragraphs (e)(5)(v)(C)*(1)* and *(2)* of this section for when a qualified intermediary may provide a chapter 4 withholding rate pool of U.S. payees to a withholding agent instead of documentation with respect to each U.S. non-exempt recipient.

(2) Examples.—The following examples illustrate the rules of paragraph (b)(2)(vii)(D)*(1)* of this section. See also the example in paragraph (e)(5)(v)(D) for rules for reporting of U.S. non-exempt

recipients when a qualified intermediary that is an FFI reports a U.S. account under chapter 4.

Example 1. WA makes a payment of U.S. source interest that is a withholdable payment to QI, a qualified intermediary that is an NFFE. QI provides WA with a withholding certificate that indicates that QI will assume primary withholding responsibility under chapters 3 and 4 of the Code with respect to the payment. In addition, QI attaches a Form W-9 from A, a U.S. non-exempt recipient, as defined in paragraph (c)(21) of this section, and provides the name, address, and TIN of B, a U.S. person that is also a non-exempt recipient but who has not provided a Form W-9. QI associates a withholding statement with its qualified intermediary withholding certificate indicating that 10% of the payment is attributable to A and 10% to B, and that QI will assume primary withholding responsibility under chapters 3 and 4 with respect to the remaining 80% of the payment. WA can reliably associate the entire payment with valid documentation. Although under the presumption rule of paragraph (b)(3)(v) of this section, an undocumented person receiving U.S. source interest is generally presumed to be a foreign person, WA has actual knowledge that B is a U.S. non-exempt recipient and therefore must report the payment on Form 1099 and backup withhold on the interest payment under section 3406.

Example 2. The facts are the same as in *Example 1*, except that no information has been provided for the 20% of the payment that is allocable to A and B. Thus, QI has accepted withholding responsibility for 80% of the payment but has provided no information for the remaining 20%. In this case, 20% of the payment cannot be reliably associated with valid documentation, and, under paragraph (b)(3)(iii) of this section, WA must apply the presumption rule of § 1.1471-3(f)(5) to treat the payment as made to a nonparticipating FFI and withhold 30% of the gross amount of the payment (because the payment is a withholdable payment and is treated as made to a foreign payee under paragraph (b)(3)(v) of this section). See *Example 2* in paragraph (b)(2)(vii)(C)(*2*) and § 1.1471-3(f)(1).

(E) *Special rules applicable to a withholding certificate provided by a qualified intermediary that assumes primary Form 1099 reporting and backup withholding responsibility but not primary withholding under chapter 3 and chapter 4.*—(*1*) If a payment is made to a qualified intermediary that assumes primary Form 1099 reporting and backup withholding responsibility for the payment (but does not assume primary withholding responsibility under chapters 3 and 4 of the Code), a withholding agent can reliably associate the payment with valid documentation only to the extent that, prior to the payment, the withholding agent has received a valid qualified intermediary withholding certificate and the withholding agent can reliably determine the portion of the payment that relates to a withholding rate pool or pools provided as part of the qualified intermediary's withholding statement and the portion of the payment for which the qualified intermediary assumes primary Form 1099 reporting and backup withholding responsibility. See paragraph (e)(5)(v)(C)(*2*) of this section for when a qualified intermediary may include a chapter 4 withholding rate pool on a withholding statement provided to a withholding agent with respect to a withholdable payment.

(*2*) The following example illustrates the rules of paragraph (b)(2)(vii)(D)(*1*) of this section:

Example. WA, a withholding agent, makes a payment of U.S. source dividends that is a withholdable payment to QI, a qualified intermediary that is a participating FFI. QI has provided WA with a valid qualified intermediary withholding certificate. QI states on its withholding statement accompanying the certificate that it assumes primary Form 1099 reporting and backup withholding responsibility but does not assume primary withholding responsibility under chapters 3 and 4 of the Code. QI represents that 15% of the dividend is subject to a 30% rate of withholding, 75% of the dividend is subject to a 15% rate of withholding. QI represents that it assumes primary Form 1099 reporting and backup withholding for the remaining 10% of the payment and will not need to provide a chapter 4 withholding rate pool with respect to this portion of the payment or documentation with respect to U.S. non-exempt recipients. WA can reliably associate the entire payment with valid documentation.

(F) *Special rules applicable to a withholding certificate provided by a qualified intermediary that assumes primary withholding responsibility under chapter 3 and chapter 4 and primary Form 1099 reporting and backup withholding responsibility and a withholding certificate provided by a withholding foreign partnership or a withholding foreign trust.*—If a payment is made to a qualified intermediary that assumes both primary withholding responsibility under chapters 3 and 4 of the Code and primary Form 1099 reporting and backup withholding responsibility under chapter 61 and section 3406 of the Code for the payment, a withholding agent can reliably associate a payment with valid documentation provided that it receives a valid qualified intermediary withholding certificate as described in paragraph (e)(3)(ii) of this section. In the case of a payment made to a withholding foreign partnership or a withholding foreign trust, the withholding agent can reliably associate the payment with valid documentation to the extent it can associate the payment with a valid withholding certificate described in § 1.1441-5(c)(2)(iv) or in § 1.1441-5(e)(5)(v) (respectively). See paragraph (e)(5)(iv) of this section, providing that a qualified intermediary assuming primary withholding responsibility under chapter 3 must also assume primary withholding responsibility under chapter 4 with respect to a withholdable payment.

(3) *Presumptions regarding payee's status in the absence of documentation.*—(i) *General rules.*—A withholding agent that cannot, prior to the payment, reliably associate (within the meaning of paragraph (b)(2)(vii) of this section) a payment of an amount subject to withholding (as described in § 1.1441-2(a)) with valid documentation may rely on the presumptions of this paragraph (b)(3) to determine the status of the person receiving the payment as a U.S. or a foreign person and the person's other relevant characteristics (*e.g.*, as an owner or intermediary, as an individual, trust, partnership, or corporation). The determination of withholding and reporting requirements applicable to payments to a person presumed to be a foreign person is governed only by the provisions of chapters 3 and 4 of the Code and the regulations thereunder. For the determination of withholding and reporting requirements applicable to payments to a person presumed to be a U.S. person, see chapter 61 of the Code, section 3402, 3405, or 3406, and, with respect to the reporting requirements of a participating FFI or registered deemed-compliant FFI, see chapter 4 of the Code and the related regulations. A presumption that a payee is a foreign payee is not a presumption that the payee is a foreign beneficial owner. Therefore, the provisions of this paragraph (b)(3) have no effect for purposes of reducing the withholding rate if associating the payment with documentation of foreign beneficial ownership is required as a condition for such rate reduction. See paragraph (b)(3)(ix) of this section for consequences to a withholding agent that fails to withhold in accordance with the presumptions set forth in this paragraph (b)(3) or if the withholding agent has actual knowledge or reason to know of facts that are contrary to the presumptions set forth in this paragraph (b)(3). See paragraph (b)(2)(vii) of this section for rules regarding the extent to which a withholding agent can reliably associate a payment with documentation.

(ii) *Presumptions of classification as individual, corporation, partnership, etc.*—(A) *In general.*—A withholding agent that cannot reliably associate a payment with a valid withholding certificate or that has received valid documentary evidence under §§ 1.1441-1(e)(1)(ii)(A)(*2*) and 1.6049-5(c)(1) or (4) but cannot determine a payee's classification from the documentary evidence must apply the rules of this paragraph (b)(3)(ii) to determine the payee's classification as an individual, trust, estate, corporation, or partnership. The fact that a payee is presumed to have a certain status under the provisions of this paragraph (b)(3)(ii) does not mean that it is excused from furnishing documentation if documentation is otherwise required to obtain a reduced rate of withholding under this section. For example, if, for purposes of this paragraph (b)(3)(ii), a payee is presumed to be a tax-exempt organization based on § 1.6049-4(c)(1)(ii)(B), the withholding agent cannot rely on this presumption to reduce the rate of withholding on payments to such person (if such person is also presumed to be a foreign person under paragraph (b)(3)(iii)(A) of this section) because a reduction in the rate of withholding for payments to a foreign tax-exempt organization generally requires that a valid Form W-8 described in § 1.1441-9(b)(2) be furnished to the withholding agent.

(B) *No documentation provided.*—If the withholding agent cannot reliably associate a payment with a valid withholding certificate or valid documentary evidence, it must presume that the payee is an individual, a trust, or an estate, if the payee appears to be such person (*e.g.*, based on the payee's name or information in the customer file). In the absence of reliable indications that the payee is an individual, a trust, or an estate, the withholding agent must presume that the payee is a corporation or one of the persons enumerated under § 1.6049-4(c)(1)(ii)(B) through (Q) if it can be so treated under § 1.6049-4(c)(1)(ii)(A)(*1*) or any one of the paragraphs under § 1.6049-4(c)(1)(ii)(B) through (Q) without the need to furnish documentation. If the withholding agent cannot treat a payee as a person described in § 1.6049-4(c)(1)(ii)(A)(*1*) through (Q), then the payee shall be presumed to be a partnership. If such a partnership is presumed to be foreign, it is not the beneficial owner of the income paid to it. See paragraph (c)(6) of this section. If such a partnership is presumed to be domestic, it is a U.S. non-exempt recipient for purposes of chapter 61 of the Code.

(C) *Documentary evidence furnished for offshore obligation.*—If the withholding agent receives valid documentary evidence, as described in § 1.6049-5(c)(1) or (c)(4), with respect to an offshore obligation from an entity but the documentary evidence does not establish the entity's classification as a corporation, trust, estate, or partnership, the withholding agent may presume (in the absence of actual knowledge otherwise) that the entity is the type of person enumerated under § 1.6049-4(c)(1)(ii)(B) through (Q) if it can be so treated under any one of those paragraphs without the need to furnish documentation. If the withholding agent cannot treat a payee as a person described in § 1.6049-4(c)(1)(ii)(B) through (Q), then the payee shall be presumed to be a corporation unless the withholding agent knows, or has reason to know, that the entity is not classified as a corporation for U.S. tax purposes. If a payee is, or is presumed to be, a corporation under this paragraph (b)(3)(ii)(C) and a foreign person under paragraph (b)(3)(iii) of this section, a withholding agent shall not treat the payee as the beneficial owner of income if the withholding agent knows, or has reason to know, that the payee is not the beneficial owner of the income. For this purpose, a withholding agent will have reason to know that the payee is not a beneficial owner if the documentary evidence indicates that the payee is a bank, broker, intermediary, custodian, or other agent, or is treated under § 1.6049-4(c)(1)(ii)(B) through (Q) as such a person. A withholding agent may, however, treat such a person as a beneficial owner if the foreign person provides a statement, in writing and signed by a person with authority to sign the statement, that is attached to the documentary evidence and that states that the foreign person is the beneficial owner of the income.

(iii) *Presumption of U.S. or foreign status.*—A payment that the withholding agent cannot reliably associate with documentation is presumed to be made to a U.S. person, except as otherwise provided in this paragraph (b)(3)(iii), in paragraphs (b)(3)(iv) and (v) of this section, or in § 1.1441-5(d) or (e). A withholding agent must treat a payee that is presumed or known to be a trust but for which the withholding agent cannot determine the type of trust in accordance with the presumptions specified in § 1.1441-5(e)(6)(ii). In the case of a payment that is a withholdable payment, a withholding agent must apply the presumption rule under § 1.1471-3(f) for purposes of chapter 4.

(A) *Payments to exempt recipients.*—*(1) In general.*—If a withholding agent cannot reliably associate a payment with documentation from the payee and the payee is an exempt recipient (as determined under the provisions of § 1.6049-4(c)(1)(ii) in the case of interest, or under similar provisions under chapter 61 of the Code applicable to the type of payment involved, but not including a payee that the withholding agent may treat as a foreign intermediary in accordance with paragraph (b)(3)(v) of this section), the payee is presumed to be a foreign person and not a U.S. person—

(i) If the withholding agent has actual knowledge of the payee's employer identification number and that number begins with the two digits "98";

(ii) If the withholding agent's communications with the payee are mailed to an address in a foreign country;

(iii) If the name of the payee indicates that the entity is the type of entity that is on the per se list of foreign corporations contained in § 301.7701-2(b)(8)(i) of this chapter (and, in the case of a name which contains the designation "corporation" or "company," the withholding agent has a document that reasonably demonstrates the payee was incorporated in the relevant jurisdiction);

(iv) If the payment is made with respect to an offshore obligation (as defined in paragraph (c)(37) of this section); or

(v) With respect to an account opened after July 1, 2014, if the withholding agent has a telephone number for the person outside of the United States.

(2) Special rule for withholdable payments made to exempt recipients.—Notwithstanding the provisions of paragraph (b)(3)(iii)(A)*(1)* of this section, a payment that is also a withholdable payment made to an entity determined to be an exempt recipient under § 1.6049-4(c)(1)(ii)(A)*(1)*, (F), (G), (H), (M), (O), (P), or (Q) in the case of interest (or under similar provisions in chapter 61 applicable to the type of income) shall be presumed made to a foreign payee in the absence of documentation (including documentary evidence) establishing the entity as a U.S. person. Additionally, a withholding agent may apply the rule provided in this paragraph (b)(3)(iii)(A)*(2)* instead of the rule in provided in paragraph (b)(3)(iii)(A)*(1)* of this section for all payments with respect to an obligation. The provisions of this paragraph (b)(3)(iii)(A)*(2)* will not apply, however, to a withholdable payment made with respect to a preexisting obligation to a payee that the withholding agent determined prior to July 1, 2014, to be a U.S. exempt recipient.

(B) *Scholarships and grants.*—A payment representing taxable scholarship or fellowship grant income that does not represent compensation for services (but is not excluded from tax under section 117) and that a withholding agent cannot reliably associate with documentation is presumed to be made to a foreign person if the withholding agent has a record that the payee has a U.S. visa that is not an immigrant visa. See section 871(c) and § 1.1441-4(c) for applicable tax rate and withholding rules.

(C) *Pensions, annuities, etc.*—A payment from a trust described in section 401(a), an annuity plan described in section 403(a), a payment with respect to any annuity, custodial account, or retirement income account described in section 403(b), or a payment from an individual retirement account or individual retirement annuity described in section 408 that a withholding agent cannot reliably associate with documentation is presumed to be made to a U.S. person only if the withholding agent has a record of a Social Security number for the payee and relies on a mailing address described in the following sentence. A mailing address is an address used for purposes of information reporting or otherwise communicating with the payee that is an address in the United States or in a foreign country with which the United States has an income tax treaty in effect and the treaty provides that the payee, if an individual resident in that country, would be entitled to an exemption from U.S. tax on amounts described in this paragraph (b)(3)(iii)(C). Any payment described in this paragraph (b)(3)(iii)(C) that is not presumed to be made to a U.S. person is presumed to be made to a foreign person. A withholding agent making a payment to a person presumed to be a foreign person may not reduce the 30-percent amount of withholding required on such payment unless it receives a withholding certificate described in paragraph (e)(2)(i) of this section furnished by the beneficial owner. For reduction in the 30-percent rate, see §§ 1.1441-4(e) or 1.1441-6(b).

(D) *Payments with respect to offshore obligations.*—A payment is presumed made to a foreign payee if the payment is made outside the United States (as defined in § 1.6049-5(e)) with respect to an offshore obligation (as defined in paragraph (c)(37) of this section) and the withholding agent does not have actual knowledge that the payee is a U.S. person. See § 1.6049-5(d)(2) and (3) for exceptions to this rule.

(E) *Certain payments for services.*—A payment for services is presumed to be made to a foreign person if—

(1) The payee is an individual;

(2) The withholding agent does not know, or have reason to know, that the payee is a U.S. citizen or resident;

(3) The withholding agent does not know, or have reason to know, that the income is (or may be) effectively connected with the conduct of a trade or business within the United States; and

(4) All of the services for which the payment is made were performed by the payee outside of the United States.

(iv) *Grace period.*—A withholding agent may choose to apply the provisions of § 1.6049-5(d)(2)(ii) regarding a 90-day grace period for purposes of this paragraph (b)(3) (by applying the term withholding agent instead of the term payor) to amounts described in § 1.1441-6(c)(2) and to amounts covered by a Form 8233 described in § 1.1441-4(b)(2)(ii). Thus, for these amounts, a withholding agent may choose to treat the payee as a foreign person and withhold under chapter 3 of the Code (and the regulations thereunder) while awaiting documentation. For purposes of determining the rate of withholding under this section, the withholding agent must withhold at the unreduced 30-percent rate at the time that the amounts are credited to an account. For reporting of amounts credited both before and after the grace period, see § 1.1461-1(c)(4)(i)(A). The following adjustments shall be made at the expiration of the grace period:

(A) If, at the end of the grace period, the documentation is not furnished in the manner required under this section and the account holder is presumed to be a U.S. non-exempt recipient, then backup withholding only applies to amounts credited to the account after the expiration of the grace period. Amounts credited to the account during the grace period shall be treated as owned by a foreign payee and adjustments must be made to correct any underwithholding on such amounts in the manner described in § 1.1461-2.

(B) If, at the end of the grace period, the documentation is not furnished in the manner required under this section, or if documentation is furnished that does not support the claimed rate reduction, and the account holder is presumed to be a foreign person then adjustments must be made to correct any underwithholding on amounts credited to the account during the grace period, based on the adjustment procedures described in § 1.1461-2.

(v) *Special rules applicable to payments to foreign intermediaries.*—(A) *Reliance on claim of status as foreign intermediary.*—The presumption rules of paragraph (b)(3)(v)(B) of this section apply to a payment made to an intermediary (whether the intermediary is a qualified or nonqualified intermediary) that has provided a valid withholding certificate under paragraph (e)(3)(ii) or (iii) of this section (or has provided documentary evidence described in paragraph (b)(3)(ii)(C) of this section that indicates it is a bank, broker, custodian, intermediary, or other agent) to the extent the withholding agent cannot treat the payment as being reliably associated with valid documentation under the rules of paragraph (b)(2)(vii) of this section. For this purpose, a U.S. person's foreign branch that is a qualified intermediary defined in paragraph (e)(5)(ii) of this section shall be treated as a foreign intermediary. A payee that the withholding agent may not reliably treat as a foreign intermediary under this paragraph (b)(3)(v)(A) is presumed to be a payee other than an intermediary whose classification as an individual, corporation, partnership, etc., must be determined in accordance with paragraph (b)(3)(ii) of this section to the extent relevant. In addition, such payee is presumed to be a U.S. or a foreign payee based upon the presumptions described in paragraph (b)(3)(iii) of this section. The provisions of paragraph (b)(3)(v)(B) of this section are not relevant to a withholding agent that can reliably associate a payment with a withholding certificate from a person representing to be a qualified intermediary to the extent the qualified intermediary has assumed primary withholding responsibility in accordance with paragraph (e)(5)(iv) of this section.

(B) *Beneficial owner documentation or allocation information is lacking or unreliable.*—Except as otherwise provided in this paragraph (b)(3)(v)(B), any portion of a payment that the withholding agent may treat as made to a foreign intermediary (whether a nonqualified or a qualified intermediary) but that the withholding agent cannot treat as reliably associated with valid documentation under the rules of paragraph (b)(2)(vii) of this section is presumed made to an unknown, undocumented foreign payee. As a result, a withholding agent must deduct and withhold 30 percent from any payment of an amount subject to withholding. If a withholding certificate attached to an intermediary certificate is another intermediary withholding certificate or a flow-through withholding certificate, the rules of this paragraph (b)(3)(v)(B) (or § 1.1441-5(d)(3) or (e)(6)(iii)) apply by treating the portion of the payment allocable to the other intermediary or flow-through entity as if it were made directly to the other intermediary or flow-through entity. Any payment of an amount subject to withholding that is presumed made to an undocumented foreign person must be reported on Form 1042-S. See § 1.1461-1(c). See § 1.6049-5(d) for payments that are not subject to withholding under chapter 3. However, in the case of a payment that is a withholdable payment made to a foreign intermediary, the presumption rules under § 1.1471-3(f)(5) shall apply.

(vi) *U.S. branches and territory financial institutions not treated as U.S. persons.*—The rules of paragraph (b)(3)(v)(B) of this section shall apply to payments to a U.S. branch or a territory financial institution described in paragraph (b)(2)(iv)(A) of this section that has provided a withholding certificate as described in paragraph (e)(3)(v) of this section on which it has not agreed to be treated as a U.S. person.

(vii) *Joint payees.*—(A) *In general.*—Except as provided in paragraph (b)(3)(vii)(B) of this section and this paragraph (b)(3)(vii)(A), if a withholding agent makes a payment to joint payees and cannot reliably associate the payment with valid documentation from all payees, the payment is presumed made to an unidentified U.S. person. If, however, a withholding agent makes a payment that is a withholdable payment and any joint payee does not appear, by its name and other information contained in the account file, to be an individual, then the entire amount of the payment will be treated as made to an undocumented foreign person. See paragraph (b)(3)(iii) of this section for presumption rules that apply in the case of a payment that is a withholdable payment. However, if one of the joint payees provides a Form W-9 furnished in accordance with the procedures described in §§ 31.3406(d)-1 through 31.3406(d)-5 of this chapter, the payment shall be treated as made to that payee. See § 31.3406(h)-2 of this chapter for rules to determine the relevant payee if more than one Form W-9 is provided. For purposes of applying this paragraph (b)(3), the grace period rules in paragraph (b)(3)(iv) of this section shall apply only if each payee meets the conditions described in paragraph (b)(3)(iv) of this section.

(B) *Special rule for offshore obligations.*—If a withholding agent makes a payment to joint payees and cannot reliably associate a payment with valid documentation from all payees, the payment is presumed made to an unknown foreign payee if the payment is made outside the United States (as defined in § 1.6049-5(e)) with respect to an offshore obligation (as defined in § 1.6049-5(c)(1)).

(viii) *Rebuttal of presumptions.*—A payee or beneficial owner may rebut the presumptions described in this paragraph (b)(3) by providing reliable documentation to the withholding agent or, if applicable, to the IRS.

(ix) *Effect of reliance on presumptions and of actual knowledge or reason to know otherwise.*—(A) *General rule.*—Except as otherwise provided in paragraph (b)(3)(ix)(B) of this section, a withholding agent that withholds on a payment under section 3402, 3405, or 3406 in accordance with the presumptions set forth in this paragraph (b)(3) shall not be liable for withholding under this section even if it is later established that the beneficial owner of the payment is, in fact, a foreign person. Similarly, a withholding agent that withholds on a payment under this section in accordance with the presumptions set forth in this paragraph (b)(3) shall not be liable for withholding under section 3402 or 3405 or for backup withholding under section 3406 even if it is later established that the payee or beneficial owner is, in fact, a U.S. person. A withholding agent that, instead of relying on the presumptions described in this paragraph (b)(3), relies on its own actual knowledge to withhold a lesser amount, not withhold, or not report a payment, even though reporting of the payment or withholding a greater amount would be required if the withholding agent relied on the presumptions described in this paragraph (b)(3), shall be liable for tax, interest, and penalties to the extent provided under section 1461 and the regulations under that section. See paragraph (b)(7) of this section for provisions regarding such liability if the withholding agent fails to withhold in accordance with the presumptions described in this paragraph (b)(3).

(B) *Actual knowledge or reason to know that amount of withholding is greater than is required under the presumptions or that reporting of the payment is required.*—Notwithstanding the provisions of paragraph (b)(3)(ix)(A) of this section, a withholding agent may not rely on the presumptions described in this paragraph (b)(3) to the extent it has actual knowledge or reason to know that the status or characteristics of the payee or of the beneficial owner are other than what is presumed under this paragraph (b)(3) and, if based on such knowledge or reason to know, it should withhold (under this section or another withholding provision of the Code) an amount greater than would be the case if it relied on the presumptions described in this paragraph (b)(3) or it should report (under this section or under another provision of the Code) an amount that would not otherwise be reportable if it relied on the presumptions described in this paragraph (b)(3). In such a case, the withholding agent must rely on its actual knowledge or reason to know rather than on the presumptions set forth in this paragraph (b)(3). Failure to do so and, as a result, failure to withhold the higher amount or to report the payment, shall result in liability for tax, interest, and penalties to the extent provided under sections 1461 and 1463 and the regulations under those sections.

(x) *Examples.*—The provisions of this paragraph (b)(3) are illustrated by the following examples:

Example 1. A withholding agent, W, makes a payment of U.S. source interest with respect to a grandfathered obligation as described in § 1.1471-2(b) (and thus the payment is not a withholdable payment) to X, Inc. with respect to an account W maintains for X, Inc. outside the United States. W cannot reliably associate the payment to X, Inc. with documentation. Under § 1.6049-4(c)(1)(ii)(A)(*1*), W may treat X, Inc. as a corporation that is an exempt recipient under chapter 61. Thus, under the presumptions described in paragraph (b)(3)(iii) of this section as applicable to a payment to an exempt recipient that is not a withholdable payment, W must presume that X, Inc. is a foreign person (because the payment is made with respect to an offshore obligation). However, W knows that X, Inc. is a U.S. person who is an exempt recipient. W may not rely on its actual knowledge to not withhold under this section. If W's knowledge is, in fact, incorrect, W would be liable for tax, interest, and, if applicable, penalties, under section 1461. W would be permitted to reduce or eliminate its liability for the tax by establishing, in accordance with paragraph (b)(7) of this section, that the tax is not due or has been satisfied. If W's actual knowledge is, in fact, correct, W may nevertheless be liable for tax, interest, or penalties under section 1461 for the amount that W should have withheld based upon the presumptions. W would be permitted to reduce or eliminate its liability for the tax by establishing, in accordance with paragraph (b)(7) of this section, that its actual knowledge was, in fact, correct and that no tax or a lesser amount of tax was due.

Example 2. A withholding agent, W, makes a payment of U.S. source interest with respect to a grandfathered obligation as described in § 1.1471-2(b) (and thus the payment is not a withholdable payment) to Y who does not qualify as an exempt recipient under § 1.6049-4(c)(1)(ii). W cannot reliably associate the payment to Y with documentation. Under the presumptions described in paragraph (b)(3)(iii) of this section, W must presume that Y is a U.S. person who is not an exempt recipient for purposes of section 6049. However, W knows that Y is a foreign person. W may not rely on its actual knowledge to withhold under this section rather than backup withhold under section 3406. If W's knowledge is, in fact, incorrect, W would be liable for tax, interest, and, if applicable, penalties, under section 3403. If W's actual knowledge is, in fact, correct, W may nevertheless be liable for tax, interest, or penalties under section 3403 for the amount that W should have withheld based upon the presumptions. Paragraph (b)(7) of this section does not apply to provide relief from liability under section 3403.

Example 3. A withholding agent, W, makes a payment of U.S. source dividends to X, Inc. with respect to an account that X, Inc. opened with W after June 30, 2014. W cannot reliably associate the payment to X, Inc. with documentation but may treat X, Inc. as an exempt recipient for purposes of this section applying the rules of § 1.6042-3(b)(1)(vii). However, because the dividend payment is a withholdable payment and W did not determine the chapter 3 status of X, Inc. before July 1, 2014, W may treat X, Inc. as a U.S. person that is an exempt recipient only if W obtains documentary evidence supporting X, Inc.'s status as a U.S. person. See paragraph (b)(3)(iii)(A)(2) of this section.

Example 4. A withholding agent, W, is a plan administrator who makes pension payments to person X with a mailing address in a foreign country with which the United States has an income tax treaty in effect. Under that treaty, the type of pension income paid to X is taxable solely in the country of residence. The plan administrator has a record of X's U.S. social security number. W has no actual knowledge or reason to know that X is a foreign person. W may rely on the presumption of paragraph (b)(3)(iii)(C) of this section in order to treat X as a U.S. person. Therefore, any withholding and reporting requirements for the payment are governed by the provisions of section 3405 and the regulations under that section.

(4) *List of exemptions from, or reduced rates of, withholding under chapter 3 of the Code.*—A withholding agent that has determined that the payee is a foreign person for purposes of paragraph (b)(1) of this section must determine whether the payee is entitled to a reduced rate of withholding under section 1441, 1442, or 1443. This paragraph (b)(4) identifies items for which a reduction in the rate of withholding may apply and whether the rate reduction is conditioned upon documentation being furnished to the withholding agent. Documentation required under this paragraph (b)(4) is documentation that a withholding agent must be able to associate with a payment upon which it can rely to treat the payment as made to a foreign person that is the beneficial owner of the payment in accordance with paragraph (e)(1)(ii) of this section. This paragraph (b)(4) also cross-references other sections of the Code and applicable regulations in which some of these exceptions, exemptions, or reductions are further explained. See, for example, paragraph (b)(4)(viii) of this section, dealing with effectively connected income, that cross-references § 1.1441-4(a); see paragraph (b)(4)(xv) of this section, dealing with exemptions from, or reductions of, withholding under an income tax treaty, that cross-references § 1.1441-6. This paragraph (b)(4) is not an exclusive list of items to which a reduction of the rate of withholding may apply and, thus, does not preclude an exemption from, or reduction in, the rate of withholding that may otherwise be allowed under the regulations under the provisions of chapter 3 of the Code for a particular item of income identified in this paragraph (b)(4). The exclusions and limitations specified in this paragraph (b)(4) apply for purposes of chapter 3. Additional withholding and documentation requirements may apply to withholding agents under chapter 4 with respect to payments that are withholdable payments. See, for example, § 1.1471-2(a) requiring withholding on withholdable payments made to certain FFIs and § 1.1471-2(a)(4) for payments exempted from withholding under section 1471(a).

(i) Portfolio interest described in section 871(h) or 881(c) and substitute interest payments described in § 1.871-7(b)(2) or § 1.881-2(b)(2) are exempt from withholding under section 1441(a). See § 1.871-14 for regulations regarding portfolio interest and section 1441(c)(9) for the exemption from withholding for portfolio interest. Documentation establishing foreign status is required for interest on an obligation in registered form to qualify as portfolio interest. See section 871(h)(2)(B)(ii) and § 1.871-14(c)(1)(ii)(C). For special documentation rules regarding foreign-targeted registered obligations described in § 1.871-14(e)(2) (and issued before January 1, 2016), see § 1.871-14(e)(3) and (4) and, in particular, § 1.871-14(e)(4)(i)(A) and (ii)(A) regarding when the withholding agent must receive the documentation. The documentation furnished for purposes of qualifying interest as portfolio interest serves as the basis for the withholding exemption for purposes of this section and establishing foreign status for purposes of section 6049. See § 1.6049-5(b)(8). Documentation establishing foreign status is not required for qualifying interest on an obligation in bearer form described in § 1.871-14(b)(1) (and issued before March 19, 2012) as portfolio interest. However, in certain cases, documentation for portfolio interest on a bearer obligation may have to be furnished in order to establish foreign status for purposes of the information reporting provisions of section 6049 and backup withholding under section 3406. See § 1.6049-5(b)(7).

(ii) Bank deposit interest and similar types of deposit interest (including original issue discount) described in section 871(i)(2)(A) or 881(d) that are from sources within the United States are exempt from withholding under section 1441(a). See section 1441(c)(10). Documentation establishing foreign status is not required for purposes of this withholding exemption but may have to be furnished for purposes of the information reporting provisions of section 6049 and backup withholding under section 3406. See § 1.6049-5(d)(3)(iii) for exceptions to the foreign payee and exempt recipient rules regarding this type of income. See also § 1.6049-5(b)(11) for applicable documentation exemptions for certain bank deposit interest paid on obligations in bearer form.

(iii) Bank deposit interest (including original issue discount) described in section 861(a)(1)(B) is exempt from withholding under sections 1441(a) as income that is not from U.S. sources. Documentation establishing foreign status is not required for purposes of this withholding exemption but may have to be furnished for purposes of the information reporting provisions of section 6049 and backup withholding under section 3406. Reporting requirements for payments of such interest are governed by section 6049 and the regulations under that section. See § 1.6049-5(b)(12) and alternative documentation rules under § 1.6049-5(c)(1).

(iv) Interest or original issue discount from sources within the United States on certain short-term obligations described in section 871(g)(1)(B) or 881(a)(3) is exempt from withholding under sections 1441(a). Documentation establishing foreign status is not required for purposes of this withholding exemption but may have to be furnished for purposes of the information reporting provisions of section 6049 and backup withholding under section 3406. See § 1.6049-5(b)(12) for applicable documentation for establishing foreign status and § 1.6049-5(d)(3)(iii) for exceptions to the foreign payee and exempt recipient rules regarding this type of income. See also § 1.6049-5(b)(10) for applicable documentation exemptions for certain obligations in bearer form.

(v) Income from sources without the United States is exempt from withholding under sections 1441(a). Documentation establishing foreign status is not required for purposes of this withholding exemption but may have to be furnished for purposes of the information reporting provisions of section 6049 or other applicable provisions of chapter 61 of the Code and backup withholding under section 3406. See, for example, § 1.6049-5(b)(6) and (12) and alternative documentation rules under § 1.6049-5(c). See also paragraph (b)(5) of this section for cross references to other applicable provisions of the regulations under chapter 61 of the Code.

(vi) Distributions from certain domestic corporations described in section 871(i)(2)(B) or 881(d) are exempt from withholding under section 1441(a). See section 1441(c)(10). Documentation establishing foreign status is not required for purposes of this withholding exemption but may have to be furnished for purposes of the information reporting provisions of section 6042 and backup withholding under section 3406. See § 1.6042-3(b)(1)(iii) through (vi).

(vii) Dividends paid by certain foreign corporations that are treated as income from sources within the United States by reason of section 861(a)(2)(B) are exempt from withholding under section 884(e)(3) to the extent that the distributions are paid out of earnings and profits in any taxable year that the corporation was subject to branch profits tax for that year. Documentation establishing foreign status is not required for purposes of this withholding exemption but may have to be furnished for purposes of the information reporting provisions of section 6042 and backup withholding under section 3406. See § 1.6042-3(b)(1)(iii) through (vii).

(viii) Certain income that is effectively connected with the conduct of a U.S. trade or business is exempt from withholding under section 1441(a). See section 1441(c)(1). Documentation establishing foreign status and status of the income as effectively connected must be furnished for purposes of this withholding exemption to the extent required under the provisions of § 1.1441-4(a). Documentation furnished for this purpose also serves as documentation establishing foreign status for purposes of applicable information reporting provisions under chapter 61 of the Code and for backup withholding under section 3406. See, for example, § 1.6041-4(a)(1).

(ix) Certain income with respect to compensation for personal services of an individual that are performed in the United States is exempt from withholding under section 1441(a). See section 1441(c)(4) and § 1.1441-4(b). However, such income may be subject to withholding as wages under section 3402. Documentation establishing foreign status must be furnished for purposes of any withholding exemption or reduction to the extent required under § 1.1441-4(b) or 31.3401(a)(6)-1(e) and (f) of this chapter. Documentation furnished for this purpose also serves as documentation establishing foreign status for purposes of information reporting under section 6041. See § 1.6041-4(a)(1).

(x) Amounts described in section 871(f) that are received as annuities from certain qualified plans are exempt from withholding under section 1441(a). See section 1441(c)(7). Documentation establishing foreign status must be furnished for purposes of the withholding exemption as required under § 1.1441-4(d). Documentation furnished for this purpose also serves as documentation establishing foreign status for purposes of information reporting under section 6041. See § 1.6041-4(a)(1).

(xi) Payments to a foreign government (including a foreign central bank of issue) that are excludable from gross income under section 892(a) are exempt from withholding under section 1442. See § 1.1441-8(b). Documentation establishing status as a foreign government is required for purposes of this withholding exemption. Payments to a foreign government are exempt from information reporting under chapter 61 of the Code (see § 1.6049-4(c)(1)(ii)(F)).

(xii) Payments of certain interest income to a foreign central bank of issue or the Bank for International Settlements that are exempt from tax under section 895 are exempt from withholding under section 1442. Documentation establishing eligibility for such exemption is required to the extent provided in § 1.1441-8(c)(1). Payments to a foreign central bank of issue or to the Bank for International Settlements are exempt from information reporting under chapter 61 of the Code (see § 1.6049-4(c)(1)(ii)(H) and (M)).

(xiii) Amounts derived by a foreign central bank of issue from bankers' acceptances described in section 871(i)(2)(C) or 881(d) are exempt from tax and, therefore, from withholding. See section 1441(c)(10). Documentation establishing foreign status is not required for purposes of this withholding exemption if the name of the payee and other facts surrounding the payment reasonably indicate that the beneficial owner of the payment is a foreign central bank of issue as defined in § 1.861-2(b)(4). See § 1.1441-8(c)(2) for withholding procedures. See also §§ 1.6049-4(c)(1)(ii)(H) and 1.6041-3(q)(8) for a similar exemption from information reporting.

(xiv) Payments to an international organization from investments in the United States of stocks, bonds, or other domestic securities or from interest on deposits in banks in the United States of funds belonging to such international organization are exempt from tax under section 892(b) and, thus, from withholding. Documentation establishing status as an international organization is not required if the name of the payee and other facts surrounding the payment reasonably indicate that the beneficial owner of the payment is an international organization within the meaning of section 7701(a)(18). See § 1.1441-8(d). Payments to an international organization are exempt from information reporting under chapter 61 of the Code (see § 1.6049-4(c)(1)(ii)(G)).

(xv) Amounts may be exempt from, or subject to a reduced rate of, withholding under an income tax treaty. Documentation establishing eligibility for benefits under an income tax treaty is required for this purpose as provided under § 1.1441-6. Documentation furnished for this purpose also serves as documentation establishing foreign status for purposes of applicable information reporting provisions under chapter 61 of the Code and for backup withholding under section 3406. See, for example, § 1.6041-4(a)(1).

(xvi) Amounts of scholarships and grants paid to certain exchange or training program participants that do not represent compensation for services but are not excluded from tax under section 117 are subject to a reduced rate of withholding of 14-percent under section 1441(b). Documentation establishing foreign status is required for purposes of this reduction in rate as provided under § 1.1441-4(c). This income is not subject to information reporting under chapter 61 of the Code nor to backup withholding under section 3406. The compensatory portion of a scholarship or grant is reportable as wage income. See § 1.6041-3(o).

(xvii) Amounts paid to a foreign organization described in section 501(c) are exempt from withholding under section 1441 to the extent that the amounts are not income includible under section 512 in computing the organization's unrelated business taxable income and are not subject to the tax imposed by section 4948(a). Documentation establishing status as a tax-exempt organization is required for purposes of this exemption to the extent provided in § 1.1441-9. Amounts includible under section 512 in computing the organization's unrelated business taxable income are subject to withholding to the extent provided in section 1443(a) and § 1.1443-1(a). Gross investment income (as defined in section 4940(c)(2)) of a private foundation is subject to withholding at a 4-percent rate to the extent provided in section 1443(b) and § 1.1443-1(b). Payments to a tax-exempt organization are exempt from information reporting under chapter 61 of the Code and the regulations thereunder (see § 1.6049-4(c)(1)(ii)(B)(1)).

(xviii) Per diem amounts for subsistence paid by the U.S. government to a nonresident alien individual who is engaged in any program of training in the United States under the Mutual Security Act of 1954 are exempt from withholding under section 1441(a). See section 1441(c)(6). Documentation of foreign status is not required under § 1.1441-4(e) for purposes of establishing eligibility for this exemption. See § 1.6041-3(p).

(xix) Interest with respect to tax-free covenant bonds issued prior to 1934 is subject to special withholding procedures set forth in § 1.1461-1 in effect prior to January 1, 2001 (see § 1.1461-1 as contained in 26 CFR part 1, revised April 1, 1999).

(xx) Income from certain gambling winnings of a nonresident alien individual is exempt from tax under section 871(j) and from withholding under section 1441(a). See section 1441(c)(11). Documentation establishing foreign status is not required for purposes of this exemption but may have to be furnished for purposes of the information reporting provisions of section 6041 and backup withholding under section 3406. See §§ 1.6041-1 and 1.6041-4(a)(1).

(xxi) Amounts paid with respect to a notional principal contract described in § 1.871-15(a)(7), an equity-linked instrument described in § 1.871-15(a)(4), or a securities lending or sale-repurchase transaction described in § 1.871-15(a)(13) are exempt from withholding under section 1441(a) as dividend equivalents under section 871(m) if the transaction is not a section 871(m) transaction within the meaning of § 1.871-15(a)(12), if the transaction is subject to the exception described in § 1.871-15(k), or if the payment is not a dividend equivalent pursuant to § 1.871-15(c)(2). However, the amounts may be subject to withholding under section 1441(a) if they are subject to tax under any section other than section 871(m). For purposes of this withholding exemption, it is not necessary for the payee to provide documentation establishing that a notional principal contract or equity-linked instrument has a delta (as described in § 1.871-15(g)) that is less than 0.80 or does not have substantial equivalence (as defined in § 1.871-15(h)) with the underlying security. For purposes of the withholding exemption regarding corporate acquisitions described in § 1.871-15(k), the exemption only applies if the long party furnishes, under penalties of perjury, a written statement to the withholding agent certifying that it satisfies the requirements of § 1.871-15(k).

(xxii) Certain payments to qualified derivatives dealers (as described in paragraph (e)(6) of this section). For purposes of this withholding exemption, the qualified derivatives dealer must furnish to the withholding agent the documentation described in paragraph (e)(3)(ii) of this section. A withholding agent that makes a payment to a qualified intermediary that is acting as a qualified derivatives dealer is not required to withhold on the following payments if the withholding agent can reliably associate the payment with a valid qualified intermediary withholding certificate as described in paragraph (e)(3)(ii) of this section, including the certification described in paragraph (e)(3)(ii)(E):

(A) A payment with respect to a potential section 871(m) transaction that is not an underlying security;

(B) A payment of a dividend equivalent; or

(C) A payment of a dividend in 2017.

(xxiii) Amounts paid with respect to a potential section 871(m) transaction that is only a section 871(m) transaction as a result of applying § 1.871-15(n) to treat certain transactions as combined transactions, if the withholding agent is able to rely on one or more of the presumptions provided in § 1.871-15(n)(3)(i) or (ii) (applying those paragraphs whether or not the withholding agent is a short party by substituting "withholding agent" for "short party"), and the withholding agent does not otherwise have actual knowledge that the long party (or a related person within the meaning of section 267(b) or section 707(b)) entered into the potential section 871(m) transaction in connection with any other potential section 871(m) transactions. The ability of one or more withholding agents to rely on the presumptions provided in section 1.871-15(n)(3) does not affect the withholding tax obligations or liability of any party to the transaction that cannot rely on the presumptions. Notwithstanding the withholding exemption provided to the withholding agent in this paragraph (b)(4)(xxii), the long party may still be liable for tax on dividend equivalent amounts with respect to such combined transactions under section 871(m).

(xxiv) Any payments not otherwise mentioned in this paragraph (b)(4) shall be subject to withholding at the rate of 30-percent if it is an amount subject to withholding (as defined in § 1.1441-2(a)) unless and to the extent the IRS may otherwise prescribe in published guidance (see § 601.601(d)(2) of this chapter) or unless otherwise provided in regulations under chapter 3 of the Code.

(5) *Establishing foreign status under applicable provisions of chapter 61 of the Code.*—This paragraph (b)(5) identifies relevant provisions of the regulations under chapter 61 of the Code that exempt payments from information reporting, and therefore, from backup withholding under section 3406, based on the payee's status as a foreign person. Many of these exemptions require that the payee's foreign status be established in order for the exemption to apply. The regulations under applicable provisions of chapter 61 of the Code generally provide that the documentation described in this section may be relied upon for purposes of determining foreign status.

(i) Payments to a foreign person that are governed by section 6041 (dealing with certain trade or business income) are exempt from information reporting under § 1.6041-4(a).

(ii) Payments to a foreign person that are governed by section 6041A (dealing with remuneration for services and certain sales) are exempt from information reporting under § 1.6041A-1(d)(3).

(iii) Payments to a foreign person that are governed by section 6042 (dealing with dividends) are exempt from information reporting under § 1.6042-3(b)(1)(iii) through (vi).

(iv) Payments to a foreign person that are governed by section 6044 (dealing with patronage dividends) are exempt from information reporting under § 1.6044-3(c)(1).

(v) Payments to a foreign person that are governed by section 6045 (dealing with broker proceeds) are exempt from information reporting under § 1.6045-1(g).

(vi) Payments to a foreign person that are governed by section 6049 (dealing with interest) to a foreign person are exempt from information reporting under § 1.6049-5(b)(6) through (15).

(vii) Payments to a foreign person that are governed by section 6050N (dealing with royalties) are exempt from information reporting under § 1.6050N-1(c).

(viii) Payments to a foreign person that are governed by section 6050P (dealing with income from cancellation of debt) are exempt from information reporting under section 6050P or the regulations under that section except to the extent provided in Notice 96-61 (1996-2 CB 227); see also § 601.601(b)(2) of this chapter.

(ix) Payments to a foreign person that are governed by section 6050W (dealing with payment card and third party network transactions) are exempt from information reporting under § 1.6050W-1(a)(5)(ii).

(6) *Rules of withholding for payments by a foreign intermediary or certain U.S. branches.*—(i) *In general.*—A foreign intermediary described in paragraph (e)(3)(i) of this section or a U.S. branch or territory financial institution described in paragraph (b)(2)(iv) of this section that receives an amount subject to withholding (as defined in § 1.1441-2(a)) shall be required to withhold (if another withholding agent has not withheld the full amount required) and report such payment under chapter 3 of the Code and the regulations thereunder except as otherwise provided in this paragraph (b)(6). A nonqualified intermediary, U.S. branch, or territory financial institution described in paragraph (b)(2)(iv) of this section (other than a U.S. branch or territory financial institution that is treated as a U.S. person) shall not be required to withhold or report if it has provided a valid nonqualified intermediary withholding certificate or a U.S. branch withholding certificate, it has provided all of the information required by paragraph (e)(3)(iv) of this section (withholding statement), and it does not know, and has no reason to know, that another withholding agent failed to withhold the correct amount or failed to report the payment correctly under § 1.1461-1(c). The withholding requirement of a nonqualified intermediary under the previous sentence also excludes a case in which withholding under chapter 4 was applied by a withholding agent on the payment. See § 1.1441-3(a)(2) (coordinating withholding under chapter 3 with withholding applied under chapter 4 of the Code). A qualified intermediary's obligations to withhold and report shall be determined in accordance with its qualified intermediary withholding agreement.

(ii) *Examples.*—The following examples illustrate the rules of paragraph (b)(6)(i) of this section and coordinate rules for withholding that apply under chapter 4 with those that apply under chapter 3. See also paragraph (e)(3)(iv)(C) of this section for the requirements of withholding statements provided by nonqualified intermediaries.

Example 1. FB, a foreign bank, acts as intermediary for five different individuals, A, B, C, D, and E, each of whom owns U.S. securities that generate U.S. source dividends (that are withholdable payments). The dividends are paid by USWA, a U.S. withholding agent. FB furnished USWA with a nonqualified intermediary withholding certificate, described in paragraph (e)(3)(iii) of this section, on which FB certifies its status as a participating FFI (such that withholding under chapter 4 does not apply), to which it attached valid withholding certificates for A, B, C, D, and E. The withholding certificates from A and B claim a 15% reduced rate of withholding under an income tax treaty. C, D, and E claim no reduced rate of withholding. FB provides a withholding statement that meets all of the requirements of paragraph (e)(3)(iv) of this section, including information allocating 20% of each dividend payment to each of A, B, C, D, and E. FB does not have actual knowledge or reason to know that USWA did not withhold the correct amounts or report the dividends on Forms 1042-S to each of A, B, C, D, and E. FB is not required to withhold or to report the dividends to A, B, C, D, and E.

Example 2. The facts are the same as in *Example 1*, except that FB did not provide any information for USWA to determine how much of the dividend payments were made to A, B, C, D, and E. Because USWA could not reliably associate the dividend payments with documentation under paragraph (b)(2)(vii) of this section with respect to a payment that is a withholdable payment, USWA applied the presumption rule of § 1.1471-3(f)(5) and withheld 30% from all dividend payments under chapter 4 and filed a Form 1042-S reporting the payment to an account holder of FB that is a non-participating FFI. FB is deemed to know that USWA did not report the payment to A, B, C, D, and E because it did not provide all of the information required on a withholding statement under paragraph (e)(3)(iv) of this section (*i.e.*, allocation information). Although FB is not required to withhold on the payment under this section because the full 30% withholding was imposed by USWA, it is required to report the payments on Forms 1042-S to A, B, C, D, and E. FB's intentional failure to do so will subject it to intentional disregard penalties under sections 6721 and 6722.

(7) *Liability for failure to obtain documentation timely or to act in accordance with applicable presumptions.*—(i) *General rule.*—A withholding agent that cannot reliably associate a payment with valid documentation on the date of payment and that does not withhold under this section, or withholds at less than the 30-percent rate prescribed under section 1441(a) and paragraph (b)(1) of this section, is liable under section 1461 for the tax required to be withheld under chapter 3 of the Code and the regulations thereunder, without the benefit of a reduced rate unless—

(A) The withholding agent has appropriately relied on the presumptions described in paragraph (b)(3) of this section (including the grace period described in paragraph (b)(3)(iv) of this section) in order to treat the payee as a U.S. person or, if applicable, on the presumptions described in § 1.1441-4(a)(2)(ii) or (a)(3)(i) to treat the payment as effectively connected income;

(B) The withholding agent can demonstrate to the satisfaction of the district director or the Assistant Commissioner (International) that the proper amount of tax, if any, was in fact paid to the IRS;

(C) No documentation is required under section 1441 or this section in order for a reduced rate of withholding to apply; or

(D) The withholding agent has complied with the provisions of § 1.1441-6(c) or (g).

(ii) *Proof that tax liability has been satisfied.*—(A) *In general.*—Proof of payment of tax may be established for purposes of paragraph (b)(7)(i)(B) of this section on the basis of a Form 4669 (or such other form as the IRS may prescribe in published guidance (see § 601.601(d)(2) of this chapter)) establishing the amount of tax, if any, actually paid by or for the beneficial owner on the income. Proof that a reduced rate of withholding was, in fact, appropriate under the provisions of chapter 3 of the Code and the regulations thereunder may also be established after the date of payment by the withholding agent on the basis of a valid withholding certificate or other appropriate documentation received after that date that was effective as of the date of payment. A withholding certificate furnished after the date of payment will be considered effective as of the date of the payment if the certificate contains a signed affidavit (either at the bottom of the form or on an attached page) that states that the information and representations contained on the certificate were accurate as of the time of the payment. A withholding certificate received within 30 days after the date of the payment will not be considered to be unreliable solely because it does not contain the affidavit described in the preceding sentence. However, in the case of a withholding certificate of an individual received more than a year after the date of payment, the withholding agent will be required to obtain, in addition to the withholding certificate and affidavit, documentary evidence, as described in § 1.1471-3(c)(5)(i), that supports the individual's claim of foreign status or documentary evidence described in § 1.1441-6(c)(4)(i) to support any treaty claim made on the certificate. In the case of a withholding certificate of an entity received more than a year after the date of payment, the withholding agent will be required to obtain, in addition to the withholding certificate and affidavit, documentary evidence described in § 1.1471-3(c)(5)(i) that supports the entity's claim of foreign status or documentary evidence described in § 1.1441-6(c)(4)(ii) to support any treaty claim made on the certificate. If documentation other than a withholding certificate is submitted from a payee more than a year after the date of payment, the withholding agent will be required to obtain from the payee a withholding certificate and affidavit supporting the claim of chapter 3 status as of the time of the payment. See, however, paragraph (b)(7)(ii)(B) of this section for special rules that apply when a withholding certificate is received after the date of the payment to claim that income is effectively connected with the conduct of a U.S. trade or business. See § 1.1471-3(c)(7)(ii) for additional requirements that may apply under chapter 4 for documentation obtained after the date of payment of a withholdable payment.

(B) *Special rules for establishing that income is effectively connected with the conduct of a U.S. trade or business.*—A withholding certificate received after the date of payment to claim under § 1.1441-4(a)(1) that income is effectively connected with the conduct of a U.S. trade or business will be considered effective as of the date of the payment if the certificate contains a signed affidavit (either at the bottom of the form or on an attached page) that states that the information and representations contained on the certificate were accurate as of the time of the payment. The signed affidavit must also state that the beneficial owner has included the income on its U.S. income tax return for the taxable year in which it is required to report the income or, alternatively, that the beneficial owner intends to include the income on a U.S. income tax return for the taxable year in which it is required to report the income and the due date for filing such return (including any applicable extensions) is after the date on which the affidavit is signed. A certificate received within 30 days after the date of the payment will not be considered to be unreliable solely because it does not contain the affidavit described in the preceding sentences.

(iii) *Liability for interest and penalties.*—For payments made after December 31, 2000, if a withholding agent fails to deduct and withhold any tax imposed under sections 1441 or 1442, and the tax against which such tax may be credited under section 1462 is paid, then the amount of tax required to be deducted and withheld shall not be collected from the withholding agent. However, the withholding agent is not relieved from liability for interest or any penalties or additions to the tax otherwise applicable in respect of the failure to deduct and withhold. See section 1463. Further, in the event that a tax liability is assessed against the beneficial owner under section 871, 881, or 882 and interest under section 6601(a) is assessed against, and collected from, the beneficial owner, the interest charge imposed on the withholding agent shall be abated to that extent so as to avoid the imposition of a double interest charge.

(iv) *Special rule for determining validity of withholding certificate containing inconsequential errors.*—A withholding agent may treat a withholding certificate as valid when the certificate includes an error described as an inconsequential error in § 1.1471-3(c)(7)(i) for which the withholding agent obtains documentation sufficient for supporting a payee's claim of status as a foreign person or, for a payee that is an entity, its classification to the extent permitted under § 1.1471-3(c)(7)(i). For example, if the country of residence is abbreviated in an ambiguous way on a beneficial owner withholding certificate provided to establish the beneficial owner's foreign status, a withholding agent may treat the withholding certificate as valid if it has obtained documentary evidence supporting that the beneficial owner's residence is in a country other than the United States.

(v) *Special effective date.*—See paragraph (f)(2)(ii) of this section for the special effective date applicable to this paragraph (b)(7).

(8) *Adjustments, refunds, or credits of overwithheld amounts.*—If the amount withheld under section 1441, 1442, or 1443 is greater than the tax due by the withholding agent or the taxpayer, adjustments may be made in accordance with the procedures described in § 1.1461-2(a). Alternatively, refunds or credits may be claimed in accordance with the procedures described in § 1.1464-1, relating to refunds or credits claimed by the beneficial owner, or § 1.6414-1, relating to refunds or credits claimed by the withholding agent. If an amount was withheld under section 3406 or is subsequently determined to have been paid to a foreign person, see paragraph (b)(3)(vii) of this section and § 31.6413(a)-3(a)(1) of this chapter.

(9) *Payments to joint owners.*—A payment to joint owners that requires documentation in order to reduce the rate of withholding under chapter 3 of the Code and the regulations thereunder does not qualify for such reduced rate unless the withholding agent can reliably associate the payment with documentation from each owner. Notwithstanding the preceding sentence, a payment to joint owners qualifies as a payment exempt from withholding under this section if any one of the owners provides a certificate of U.S. status on a Form W-9 in accordance with paragraph (d)(2) or (3) of this section or the withholding agent can associate the payment with an intermediary or flow-through withholding certificate upon which it can rely to treat the payment as made to a U.S. payee under paragraph (d)(4) of this section. See § 31.3406(h)-2(a)(3)(i)(B) of this chapter.

(c) *Definitions.*—The following definitions apply for purposes of sections 1441 through 1443, 1461, and regulations under those sections. For definitions of terms used in these regulations that are defined under sections 1471 through 1474, see subparagraphs (43) through (56) of this paragraph.

(1) *Withholding.*—The term *withholding* means the deduction and withholding of tax at the applicable rate from the payment.

(2) *Foreign and U.S. person.*—(i) *In general.*—The term foreign person means any person that is not a U.S. person, including a QI branch of a U.S. financial institution (as defined in § 1.1471-1(b)(109). Such a branch continues to be a U.S. payor for purposes of chapter 61 of the Code. See § 1.6049-5(c)(4). A U.S. person is a person described in section 7701(a)(30), the U.S. government (including an agency or instrumentality thereof), a State (including an agency or instrumentality thereof), or the District of Columbia (including an agency or instrumentality thereof).

(ii) *Dual residents.*—Individuals will not be treated as U.S. persons for purposes of this section for a taxable year or any portion of a taxable year for which they are a dual resident taxpayer (within the meaning of § 301.7701(b)-7(a)(1) of this chapter) who is treated as a nonresident alien pursuant to § 301.7701(b)-7(a)(1) of this chapter for purposes of computing their U.S. tax liability.

(3) *Individual.*—(i) *Alien individual.*—The term *alien individual* means an individual who is not a citizen or a national of the United States. See § 1.1-1(c).

(ii) *Nonresident alien individual.*—The term *nonresident alien individual* means persons described in section 7701(b)(1)(B), alien individuals who are treated as nonresident aliens pursuant to § 301.7701(b)-7 of this chapter for purposes of computing their U.S. tax liability, or an alien individual who is a resident of Puerto Rico, Guam, the Commonwealth of Northern Mariana Islands, the U.S. Virgin Islands, or American Samoa as determined under § 301.7701(b)-1(d) of this chapter. An alien individual who has made an election under section 6013(g) or (h) to be treated as a resident of the United States is nevertheless treated as a nonresident alien individual for purposes of withholding under chapter 3 of the Code and the regulations thereunder.

(4) *Certain foreign corporations.*—For purposes of this section, a corporation created or organized in Guam, the Commonwealth of Northern Mariana Islands, the U.S. Virgin Islands, and American Samoa, is not treated as a foreign corporation if the requirements of sections 881(b)(1)(A), (B), and (C) are met for such corporation. Further, a payment made to a foreign government or an international

organization shall be treated as a payment made to a foreign corporation for purposes of withholding under chapter 3 of the Code and the regulations thereunder.

(5) *Financial institution and foreign financial institution (or FFI).*—The term financial institution means a person described in § 1.1471-1(b)(50). The term foreign financial institution or FFI has the meaning set forth in § 1.1471-1(b)(47).

(6) *Beneficial owner.*—(i) *General rule.*—This paragraph (c)(6) defines the term *beneficial owner* for payments of income other than a payment for which a reduced rate of withholding is claimed under an income tax treaty. The term *beneficial owner* means the person who is the owner of the income for tax purposes and who beneficially owns that income. A person shall be treated as the owner of the income to the extent that it is required under U.S. tax principles to include the amount paid in gross income under section 61 (determined without regard to an exclusion or exemption from gross income under the Internal Revenue Code). Beneficial ownership of income is determined under the provisions of section 7701(l) and the regulations under that section and any other applicable general U.S. tax principles, including principles governing the determination of whether a transaction is a conduit transaction. Thus, a person receiving income in a capacity as a nominee, agent, or custodian for another person is not the beneficial owner of the income. In the case of a scholarship, the student receiving the scholarship is the beneficial owner of that scholarship. In the case of a payment of an amount that is not income, the beneficial owner determination shall be made under this paragraph (c)(6) as if the amount were income.

(ii) *Special rules.*—(A) *General rule.*—The beneficial owners of income paid to an entity described in this paragraph (c)(6)(ii) are those persons described in paragraphs (c)(6)(ii)(B) through (D) of this section.

(B) *Foreign partnerships.*—The beneficial owners of income paid to a foreign partnership (whether a nonwithholding or a withholding foreign partnership) are the partners in the partnership, unless they themselves are not the beneficial owners of the income under this paragraph (c)(6). For example, a partnership (first tier) that is a partner in another partnership (second tier) is not the beneficial owner of income paid to the second tier partnership since the first tier partnership is not the owner of the income under U.S. tax principles. Rather, the partners of the first tier partnership are the beneficial owners (to the extent they are not themselves persons that are not beneficial owners under this paragraph (c)(6)). See § 1.1441-5(b) for applicable withholding procedures for payments to a domestic partnership. See also § 1.1441-5(c)(3)(ii) for applicable withholding procedures for payments to a foreign partnership where one of the partners (at any level in the chain of tiers) is a domestic partnership.

(C) *Foreign simple trusts and foreign grantor trusts.*—The beneficial owners of income paid to a foreign simple trust, as described in paragraph (c)(23) of this section, are the beneficiaries of the trust, unless they themselves are not the beneficial owners of the income under this paragraph (c)(6). The beneficial owners of income paid to a foreign grantor trust, as described in paragraph (c)(26) of this section, are the persons treated as the owners of the trust, unless they themselves are not the beneficial owners of the income under this paragraph (c)(6).

(D) *Other foreign trusts and foreign estates.*—The beneficial owner of income paid to a foreign complex trust as defined in paragraph (c)(25) of this section or to a foreign estate is the foreign complex trust or estate itself.

(7) *Withholding agent.*—For a definition of the term *withholding agent* and applicable rules, see § 1.1441-7.

(8) *Person.*—For purposes of the regulations under chapter 3 of the Code, the term *person* shall mean a person described in section 7701(a)(1) and the regulations under that section and a U.S. branch to the extent treated as a U.S. person under paragraph (b)(2)(iv) of this section. For purposes of the regulations under chapter 3 of the Code, the term *person* does not include a wholly-owned entity that is disregarded for federal tax purposes under § 301.7701-2(c)(2) of this chapter as an entity separate from its owner. See paragraph (b)(2)(iii) of this section for procedures applicable to payments to such entities.

(9) *Source of income.*—The source of income is determined under the provisions of part I (section 861 and following), subchapter N, chapter 1 of the Code and the regulations under those provisions.

(10) *Chapter 3 of the Code (or chapter 3).*—For purposes of the regulations under sections 1441, 1442, and 1443, any reference to chapter 3 of the Code (or chapter 3) shall not include references to sections 1445 and 1446, unless the context indicates otherwise.

(11) *Reduced rate.*—For purposes of regulations under chapter 3 of the Code, and other withholding provisions of the Code, the term *reduced rate,* when used in regulations under chapter 3 of the Code, shall include an exemption from tax.

(12) *Payee.*—For purposes of chapter 3 of the Code, the term payee of a payment is determined under paragraph (b)(2) of this section, § 1.1441-5(c)(1) (relating to partnerships), and § 1.1441-5(e)(2) and (3) (relating to trusts and estates) and includes foreign persons, U.S. exempt recipients, and U.S. non-exempt recipients. A nonqualified intermediary and a qualified intermediary (to the extent it does not assume primary withholding responsibility) are not payees if they are acting as intermediaries and not the beneficial owner of income. In addition, a flow-through entity (other than a withholding foreign partnership, withholding foreign trust, or qualified intermediary that assumes primary withholding responsibility) is not a payee unless the income is (or is deemed to be) effectively connected with the conduct of a trade or business in the United States. See § 1.6049-5(d)(1) for rules to determine the payee for purposes of chapter 61 of the Code. See §§ 1.1441-1(b)(3), 1.1441-5(d), and (e)(6) and § 1.6049-5(d)(3) for presumption rules that apply if a payee's identity cannot be determined on the basis of valid documentation. For purposes of chapter 4, the term payee has the meaning set forth in § 1.1471-3(a) with respect to a withholdable payment.

(13) *Intermediary.*—An *intermediary* means, with respect to a payment that it receives, a person that, for that payment, acts as a custodian, broker, nominee, or otherwise as an agent for another person, regardless of whether such other person is the beneficial owner of the amount paid, a flow-through entity, or another intermediary.

(14) *Nonqualified intermediary.*—A *nonqualified intermediary* means any intermediary that is not a U.S. person and not a qualified intermediary, as defined in paragraph (e)(5)(ii) of this section, or a qualified intermediary that is not acting in its capacity as a qualified intermediary with respect to a payment. For example, to the extent an entity that is a qualified intermediary provides another withholding agent with a foreign beneficial owner withholding certificate as defined in paragraph (e)(2)(i) of this section, the entity is not acting in its capacity as a qualified intermediary. Notwithstanding the preceding sentence, a qualified intermediary is acting as a qualified intermediary to the extent it provides another withholding agent with Forms W-9, or other information regarding U.S. non-exempt recipients pursuant to its qualified intermediary agreement with the IRS.

(15) *Qualified intermediary.*—The term *qualified intermediary* is defined in paragraph (e)(5)(ii) of this section.

(16) *Withholding certificate.*—The term withholding certificate means a Form W-8 described in paragraph (e)(2)(i) of this section (relating to foreign beneficial owners), paragraphs (e)(3)(i) or (e)(5)(i) of this section (relating to foreign intermediaries or qualified intermediaries), § 1.1441-5(c)(2)(iv), (c)(3)(iii), and (e)(5)(iii) (relating to flow through entities), a Form 8233 described in § 1.1441-4(b)(2), a Form W-9 as described in paragraph (d) of this section, a statement described in § 1.871-14(c)(2)(v) (relating to portfolio interest), or any other certificates that under the Code or regulations certifies or establishes the status of a payee or beneficial owner as a U.S. or a foreign person.

(17) *Documentary evidence; other appropriate documentation.*—The terms documentary evidence or other appropriate documentation refer to documentary evidence that may be provided for payments made outside the United States with respect to offshore obligations in accordance with § 1.6049-5(c)(1) or any other evidence that under the Code or regulations certifies or establishes the status of a payee or beneficial owner as a U.S. or foreign person. See §§ 1.1441-6(b)(2), (c)(3) and (4) (relating to treaty benefits), and 1.6049-5(c)(1) and (4) (relating to chapter 61 reporting). Also see § 1.1441-4(a)(3)(ii) regarding documentary evidence for notional principal contracts.

(18) *Documentation.*—The term *documentation* refers to both withholding certificates, as defined in paragraph (c)(16) of this section, and documentary evidence or other appropriate documentation, as defined in paragraph (c)(17) of this section.

(19) *Payor.*—The term *payor* is defined in § 31.3406(a)-2 of this chapter and § 1.6049-4(a)(2) and generally includes a withholding agent, as defined in § 1.1441-7(a). The term also includes any person that makes a payment to an intermediary, flow-through entity, or U.S. branch that is not treated as a U.S. person to the extent the intermediary, flow through, or U.S. branch provides a Form W-9 or other appropriate information relating to a payee so that the payment can be reported under chapter 61 of the Internal Revenue Code and, if required, subject to backup withholding under section 3406. This latter rule does not preclude the intermediary, flow-through entity, or U.S. branch from also being a payor.

(20) *Exempt recipient.*—The term *exempt recipient* means a person that is exempt from reporting under chapter 61 of the Internal Revenue Code and backup withholding under section 3406 and that is described in §§ 1.6041-3(q), 1.6045-2(b)(2)(i), and 1.6049-4(c)(1)(ii), and § 5f.6045-1(c)(3)(i)(B) of this chapter. Exempt recipients are not exempt from withholding under chapter 3 of the Internal Revenue Code unless they are U.S. persons or foreign persons entitled to an exemption from withholding under chapter 3.

(21) *Non-exempt recipient.*—A *non-exempt recipient* is any person that is not an exempt recipient under paragraph (c)(20) of this section.

(22) *Reportable amounts.*—*Reportable amounts* are defined in paragraph (e)(3)(vi) of this section.

(23) *Flow-through entity.*—A flow-through entity means any entity that is described in this paragraph (c)(23) and that may provide documentation on behalf of its partners, beneficiaries, or owners to a withholding agent. The entities described in this paragraph are a foreign partnership (other than a withholding foreign partnership), a foreign simple trust (other than a withholding foreign trust) that is described in paragraph (c)(24) of this section, a foreign grantor trust (other than a withholding foreign trust) that is described in paragraph (c)(26) of this section, or, for any payments for which a reduced rate of withholding under an income tax treaty is claimed, any entity to the extent the entity is considered to be fiscally transparent under section 894 with respect to the payment by an interest holder's jurisdiction.

(24) *Foreign simple trust.*—A *foreign simple trust* is a foreign trust that is described in section 651(a).

(25) *Foreign complex trust.*—A foreign complex trust is a foreign trust other than a foreign simple trust or foreign grantor trust.

(26) *Foreign grantor trust.*—A *foreign grantor trust* is a foreign trust but only to the extent all or a portion of the income of the trust is treated as owned by the grantor or another person under sections 671 through 679.

(27) *Partnership.*—The term *partnership* means any entity treated as a partnership under § 301.7701-2 or -3 of this chapter.

(28) *Nonwithholding foreign partnership (or NWP).*—A nonwithholding foreign partnership is a foreign partnership that is not a withholding foreign partnership, as defined in § 1.1441-5(c)(2)(i).

(29) *Withholding foreign partnership (or WP).*—A withholding foreign partnership is defined in § 1.1441-5(c)(2)(i).

(30) *Possessions of the United States or U.S. territory.*—For purposes of the regulations under chapters 3 and 61 of the Code, the term possessions of the United States or U.S. territory means Guam, American Samoa, the Northern Mariana Islands, Puerto Rico, or the Virgin Islands.

(31) *Amount subject to chapter 3 withholding.*—An amount subject to withholding under chapter 3 is an amount described in § 1.1441-2(a).

(32) *EIN.*—The term EIN means an employer identification number (also known as a federal tax identification number) described in § 301.6109-1(a)(1)(i).

(33) *Flow-through withholding certificate.*—The term flow-through withholding certificate means a Form W-8IMY submitted by a foreign partnership, foreign simple trust, or foreign grantor trust.

(34) *Foreign payee.*—The term foreign payee means any payee other than a U.S. payee.

(35) *Intermediary withholding certificate.*—The term intermediary withholding certificate means a Form W-8IMY submitted by an intermediary or qualified intermediary.

(36) *Nonwithholding foreign trust (or NWT).*—The term nonwithholding foreign trust or NWT means a foreign trust as defined in section 7701(a)(31)(B) that is a simple trust or grantor trust and is not a withholding foreign trust.

(37) *Payment with respect to an offshore obligation.*—The term payment with respect to an offshore obligation means a payment made outside of the United States, within the meaning of § 1.6049-5(e), with respect to an offshore obligation (as defined in § 1.6049-5(c)(1), § 1.6041-1(d), or § 1.6042-3(b) (depending on the type of payment)).

(38) *Permanent residence address.*—(i) *In general.*—The term *permanent residence address* is the address in the country of which the person claims to be a resident for purposes of that country's income tax. In the case of a withholding certificate furnished in order to claim a reduced rate of withholding under an income tax treaty, whether a person is a resident of a treaty country must be determined in the manner prescribed under the applicable treaty. See § 1.1441-6(b). The address of a financial institution with which the person maintains an account, a post office box, or an address used solely for mailing purposes is not a permanent residence address unless such address is the only address used by the person and appears as the person's registered address in the person's organizational documents. Further, an address that is provided subject to a hold mail instruction (as defined in paragraph (c)(38)(ii) of this section) is not a permanent residence address unless the person provides the documentary evidence described in paragraph (c)(38)(ii) of this section. If the person is an individual who does not have a tax residence in any country, the permanent residence address is the place at which the person normally resides. If the person is an entity and does not have a tax residence in any country, then the permanent residence address of the entity is the place at which the person maintains its principal office.

(ii) *Hold mail instruction.*—The term *hold mail instruction* means a current instruction by a person to keep the person's mail until such instruction is amended. An instruction to send all correspondence electronically is not a hold mail instruction. An address that is subject to a hold mail instruction may be used as a permanent residence address if the person has also provided the withholding agent with documentary evidence described in § 1.1471-3(c)(5)(i) (without regard to the requirement in § 1.1471-3(c)(5)(i) that the documentary evidence contain a permanent residence address). The documentary evidence described in § 1.1471-3(c)(5)(i) must support the person's claim of foreign status or, in the case of a person that is claiming treaty benefits, must support residence in the country where the person is claiming a reduced rate of withholding under an income tax treaty. If, after a withholding certificate is provided, a person's permanent residence address is subsequently subject to a hold mail instruction, the addition of the hold mail instruction is a change in circumstances requiring the person to provide the documentary evidence described in this paragraph (c)(38)(ii) in order for a withholding agent to use the address as a permanent residence address.

(39) *Standing instructions to pay amounts.*—The term standing instructions to pay amounts has the meaning set forth in § 1.1471-1(b)(126).

(40) *Territory financial institution.*—The term territory financial institution has the meaning set forth in § 1.1471-1(b)(130).

(41) *TIN.*—The term TIN means the tax identifying number assigned to a person under section 6109.

(42) *Withholding foreign trust (or WT).*—The term withholding foreign trust (or WT) means a foreign grantor trust or foreign simple trust that has executed the agreement described in § 1.1441-5(e)(5)(v).

(43) *Certified deemed-compliant FFI.*—The term certified deemed-compliant FFI means an FFI described in § 1.1471-5(f)(2).

(44) *Chapter 3 withholding rate pool.*—The term chapter 3 withholding rate pool has the meaning described in paragraph (e)(5)(v)(C)(*1*) of this section.

(45) *Chapter 3 status.*—The term chapter 3 status refers to the attributes of a payee relevant for determining the rate of withholding with respect to a payment made to the payee for purposes of chapter 3.

(46) *Chapter 4 of the Code (or chapter 4).*—The term chapter 4 of the Code (or chapter 4) means sections 1471 through 1474 and the regulations thereunder.

(47) *Chapter 4 status.*—The term chapter 4 status means a person's status as a U.S. person, a specified U.S. person, an individual that is a foreign person, a participating FFI, a deemed-compliant FFI, a restricted distributor, an exempt beneficial owner, a nonparticipating FFI, a territory financial institution, an excepted NFFE, or a passive NFFE.

(48) *Chapter 4 withholding rate pool.*—The term chapter 4 withholding rate pool has the meaning set forth § 1.1471-1(b)(20). For when a withholding statement may include a chapter 4 withholding rate pool of U.S. payees for purposes of this section and § 1.1441-5, however, see paragraph (e)(3)(iv)(A) of this section (for a withholding statement provided by a nonqualified intermediary) or paragraph (e)(5)(v)(C)(*2*) of this section (for a withholding statement provided by a qualified intermediary).

(49) *Deemed-compliant FFI.*—The term deemed-compliant FFI means an FFI that is treated, pursuant to section 1471(b)(2) and § 1.1471-5(f), as meeting the requirements of section 1471(b). The term deemed-compliant FFI also includes a QI branch of a U.S. financial institution that is a reporting Model 1 FFI.

(50) *GIIN (or Global Intermediary Identification Number).*—The term GIIN or Global Intermediary Identification Number means the identification number that is assigned to a participating FFI or registered deemed-compliant FFI. The term GIIN or Global Intermediary Identification Number also includes the identification number assigned to a reporting Model 1 FFI (as defined in § 1.1471-1(b)(114)) for purposes of identifying such entity to withholding agents. All GIINs will appear on the IRS FFI list.

(51) *NFFE.*—The term NFFE or non-financial foreign entity has the meaning set forth in § 1.1471-1(b)(80).

(52) *Nonparticipating FFI.*—The term nonparticipating FFI means an FFI other than a participating FFI, a deemed-compliant FFI, or an exempt beneficial owner.

(53) *Participating FFI.*—The term participating FFI has the meaning set forth in § 1.1471-1(b)(91).

(54) *Preexisting obligation.*—The term preexisting obligation has the meaning set forth in § 1.1471-1(b)(104).

(55) *Registered deemed-compliant FFI.*—The term registered deemed-compliant FFI has the meaning set forth in § 1.1471-5(f)(1).

(56) *Withholdable payment.*—The term withholdable payment has the meaning set forth in § 1.1473-1(a).

(d) *Beneficial owner's or payee's claim of U.S. status.*—(1) *In general.*—Under paragraph (b)(1) of this section, a withholding agent is not required to withhold under chapter 3 of the Code on payments to a U.S. payee, to a person presumed to be a U.S. payee in accordance with the provisions of paragraph (b)(3) of this section, or to a person that the withholding agent may treat as a U.S. beneficial owner of the payment. Absent actual knowledge or reason to know otherwise, a withholding agent may rely on the provisions of this paragraph (d) in order to determine whether to treat a payee or beneficial owner as a U.S. person.

(2) *Payments for which a Form W-9 is otherwise required.*—A withholding agent may treat as a U.S. payee any person who is required to furnish a Form W-9 and who furnishes it in accordance with the procedures described in §§ 31.3406(d)-1 through 31.3406(d)-5 of this chapter (including the requirement that the payee furnish its taxpayer identifying number (TIN)) if the withholding agent meets all the requirements described in § 31.3406(h)-3(e) of this chapter regarding reliance by a payor on a Form W-9. Providing a Form W-9 or valid substitute form shall serve as a statement that the person whose name is on the form is a U.S. person. Therefore, a foreign person, including a U.S. branch treated as a U.S. person under paragraph (b)(2)(iv) of this section, shall not provide a Form W-9. A U.S. branch of a foreign person may establish its status as a foreign person exempt from reporting under chapter 61 and backup withholding under section 3406 by providing a withholding certificate on Form W-8.

(3) *Payments for which a Form W-9 is not otherwise required.*—In the case of a payee who is not required to furnish a Form W-9 under section 3406 (e.g., a person exempt from reporting under chapter 61 of the Internal Revenue Code), the withholding agent may treat the payee as a U.S. payee if the payee provides the withholding agent with a Form W-9 or a substitute form described in § 31.3406(h)-3(c)(2) of this chapter (relating to forms for exempt recipients) that contains the payee's name, address, and TIN. The form must be signed under penalties of perjury by the payee if so required by the form or by § 31.3406(h)-3 of this chapter. Providing a Form W-9 or valid substitute form shall serve as a statement that the person whose name is on the certificate is a U.S. person. A Form W-9 or valid substitute form shall not be provided by a foreign person, including any U.S. branch of a foreign person whether or not the branch is treated as a U.S. person under paragraph (b)(2)(iv) of this section. See paragraph (e)(3)(v) of this section for withholding certificates provided by U.S. branches described in paragraph (b)(2)(iv) of this section. The procedures described in § 31.3406(h)-2(a) of this chapter shall apply to payments to joint payees. A withholding agent that receives a Form W-9 to satisfy this paragraph (d)(3) must retain the form in accordance with the provisions of § 31.3406(h)-3(g) of this chapter, if applicable, or of paragraph (e)(4)(iii) of this section (relating to the retention of withholding certificates) if § 31.3406(h)-3(g) of this chapter does not apply. The rules of this paragraph (d)(3) are only intended to provide a method by which a withholding agent may determine that a payee is a U.S. person and do not otherwise impose a requirement that documentation be furnished by a person who is otherwise treated as an exempt recipient for purposes of the applicable information reporting provisions under chapter 61 of the Internal Revenue Code (e.g., § 1.6049-4(c)(1)(ii) for payments of interest).

(4) *When a payment to an intermediary or flow-through entity may be treated as made to a U.S. payee.*—A withholding agent that makes a payment to an intermediary (whether a qualified intermediary or nonqualified intermediary), a flow-through entity, or a U.S. branch or territory financial institution described in paragraph (b)(2)(iv) of this section may treat the payment as made to a U.S. payee to the extent that, prior to the payment, the withholding agent can reliably associate the payment with a Form W-9 described in paragraph (d)(2) or (3) of this section attached to a valid intermediary, flow-through, or U.S. branch withholding certificate described in paragraph (e)(3)(i) of this section or to the extent the withholding agent can reliably associate the payment with a Form W-8 described in paragraph (e)(3)(v) of this section that evidences an agreement to treat a U.S. branch or territory financial institution described in paragraph (b)(2)(iv) of this section as a U.S. person. In addition, a withholding agent may treat the payment as made to a U.S. payee only if it complies with the electronic confirmation procedures described in paragraph (e)(4)(v) of this section, if required, and it has not been notified by the IRS that any of the information on the withholding certificate or other documentation is incorrect or unreliable. In the case of a Form W-9 that is required to be furnished for a reportable payment that may be subject to backup withholding, the withholding agent may be notified in accordance with section 3406(a)(1)(B) and the regulations under that section. See applicable procedures under section 3406(a)(1)(B) and the regulations under that section for payors who have been notified with regard to such a Form W-9. Withholding agents who have been notified in relation to other Forms W-9, including under section 6724(b) pursuant to section 6721, may rely on the withholding certificate or other documentation only to the extent provided under procedures as prescribed by the IRS (see § 601.601(d)(2) of this chapter).

(e) *Beneficial owner's claim of foreign status.*—(1) *Withholding agent's reliance.*—(i) *In general.*—Absent actual knowledge or reason to know otherwise, a withholding agent may treat a payment as made to a foreign beneficial owner in accordance with the provisions of paragraph (e)(1)(ii) of this section. See paragraph (e)(4)(viii) of this section for applicable reliance rules. See paragraph (b)(4) of this section for a description of payments for which a claim of foreign status is relevant for purposes of claiming a reduced rate of withholding for purposes of section 1441, 1442, or 1443. See paragraph (b)(5) of this section for a list of payments for which a claim of foreign status is relevant for other purposes, such as claiming an exemption from information reporting under chapter 61 of the Code.

(ii) *Payments that a withholding agent may treat as made to a foreign person that is a beneficial owner.*—(A) *General rule.*—The withholding agent may treat a payment as made to a foreign person that is a beneficial owner if it complies with the requirements described in paragraph (e)(1)(ii)(B) of this section and, then, only to the extent—

(1) That the withholding agent can reliably associate the payment with a beneficial owner withholding certificate described in paragraph (e)(2) of this section furnished by the person whose name is on the certificate or attached to a valid foreign intermediary, flow-through, or U.S. branch withholding certificate;

(2) That the payment is made outside the United States (within the meaning of §1.6049-5(e)) with respect to an offshore obligation (within the meaning of paragraph (c)(37) of this section) and the withholding agent can reliably associate the payment with documentary evidence described in §§1.1441-6(c)(3) or (4), or 1.6049-5(c)(1) relating to the beneficial owner;

(3) That the withholding agent can reliably associate the payment with a valid qualified intermediary withholding certificate, as described in paragraph (e)(3)(ii) of this section, and the qualified intermediary has provided sufficient information for the withholding agent to allocate the payment to a chapter 3 withholding rate pool;

(4) That the withholding agent can reliably associate the payment with a withholding certificate described in §1.1441-5(c)(3)(iii) or (e)(5)(iii) from a flow-through entity claiming the income is effectively connected income;

(5) That the withholding agent identifies the payee as a U.S. branch described in paragraph (b)(2)(iv) of this section, the payment to which it treats as effectively connected income in accordance with §1.1441-4(a)(2)(ii) or (3);

(6) That the withholding agent identifies the payee as an international organization (or any wholly-owned agency or instrumentality thereof) as defined in section 7701(a)(18) that has been designated as such by executive order (pursuant to 22 U.S.C. 288 through 288(f)); or

(7) That the withholding agent pays interest from bankers' acceptances and identifies the payee as a foreign central bank of issue (as defined in §1.861-2(b)(4)).

(B) *Additional requirements.*—In order for a payment described in paragraph (e)(1)(ii)(A) of this section to be treated as made to a foreign beneficial owner, the withholding agent must hold the documentation (if required) prior to the payment, comply with the electronic confirmation procedures described in paragraph (e)(4)(v) of this section (if required), and must not have been notified by the IRS that any of the information on the withholding certificate or other documentation is incorrect or unreliable. If the withholding agent has been so notified, it may rely on the withholding certificate or other documentation only to the extent provided under procedures prescribed by the IRS (see §601.601(d)(2) of this chapter). See paragraph (b)(2)(vii) of this section for rules regarding reliable association of a payment with a withholding certificate or other appropriate documentation.

(2) *Beneficial owner withholding certificate.*—(i) *In general.*—A beneficial owner withholding certificate is a statement by which the beneficial owner of the payment represents that it is a foreign person and, if applicable, claims a reduced rate of withholding under section 1441. A separate withholding certificate must be submitted to each withholding agent. If the beneficial owner receives more than one type of payment from a single withholding agent, the beneficial owner may have to submit more than one withholding certificate to the single withholding agent for the different types of payments as may be required by the applicable forms and instructions, or as the withholding agent may require (such as to facilitate the withholding agent's compliance with its obligations to determine withholding under this section or the reporting of the amounts under §1.1461-1(b) and (c)). For example, if a beneficial owner claims that some but not all of the income it receives is effectively connected with the conduct of a trade or business in the United States, it may be required to submit two separate withholding certificates, one for income that is not effectively connected and one for income that is so connected. See §1.1441-6(b)(2) for special rules for determining who must furnish a beneficial owner withholding certificate when a benefit is claimed under an income tax treaty. See paragraph (e)(4)(ix) of this section for reliance rules in the case of certificates held by another person or at a different branch location of the same person. For purposes of a qualified intermediary acting as a qualified derivatives dealer, a qualified intermediary withholding certificate, as described in paragraph (e)(3)(ii) of this section is a beneficial owner withholding certificate for purposes of treaty claims for dividends.

(ii) *Requirements for validity of certificate.*—(A) *In general.*—A beneficial owner withholding certificate is valid for purposes of a payment of an amount subject to chapter 3 withholding only if it is provided on a Form W-8 or a Form 8233 in the case of personal services income described in §1.1441-4(b) or certain scholarship or grant amounts described in §1.1441-4(c) (or a substitute form described in paragraph (e)(4)(vi) of this section or such other form as the IRS may prescribe). A Form W-8 is valid only if its validity period has not expired, it is signed under penalties of perjury by the beneficial owner, and it contains all of the information required on the form. The required information is the beneficial owner's name, permanent residence address (as defined in §1.1441-1(c)(38)), TIN (if required), a certification that the person is not a U.S. citizen (if the person is an individual) or a certification of the country under the laws of which the beneficial owner is created, incorporated, or governed (if a person other than an individual), the classification of the entity, and such other information as may be required by the regulations under section 1441 or by the form or accompanying instructions in addition to, or in lieu of, the information described in this paragraph (e)(2)(ii) (including when a foreign TIN and an individual's date of birth are required). A beneficial owner withholding certificate must also include the chapter 4 status of a beneficial owner when required for chapter 4 purposes in order to be valid. See paragraph (e)(4)(vii) of this section for circumstances in which a TIN is required on a beneficial owner withholding certificate.

(B) *Requirement to collect foreign TIN and date of birth.*—*(1) In general.*—In addition to the general requirements of paragraph (e)(2)(ii)(A) of this section, except as provided in paragraphs (e)(2)(ii)(B)(4), through (6) of this section, a beneficial owner withholding certificate provided by an account holder to document an account that is maintained at a U.S. branch or office of a withholding agent that is a financial institution is valid for purposes of a payment of U.S. source income reportable on Form 1042-S (before the application of this paragraph (e)(2)(ii)(B)) made on or after January 1, 2018, only if it contains the account holder's taxpayer identification number issued by the account holder's jurisdiction of tax residence (foreign TIN) or a reasonable explanation for the absence of a foreign TIN (as described in paragraph (e)(2)(ii)(B)(3) of this section) and, in the case of an individual account holder, the account holder's date of birth, unless the withholding agent has the account holder's date of birth in its files. A withholding agent is permitted to obtain a foreign TIN on a written statement signed by an account holder that includes an acknowledgment that such statement is part of the withholding certificate if the withholding agent associates such statement with the account holder's withholding certificate. A withholding agent will be treated as having the account holder's date of birth in its files if it obtains the date of birth on a written statement (including a written statement transmitted by email) from the account holder. A withholding agent may rely on the foreign TIN and date of birth contained in the withholding certificate unless it knows or has reason to know that the foreign TIN or date of birth is incorrect. Therefore, a withholding agent will not be required to validate the format or other specifications of the foreign TIN against the applicable jurisdiction's TIN system. For purposes of this paragraph (e)(2)(ii)(B), a change of address to another jurisdiction other than the United States is a change in circumstances for purposes of a withholding agent's reliance on a foreign TIN of the account holder (or reasonable explanation for its absence).

(2) Definitions.—For purposes of this paragraph (e)(2)(ii)(B), the term "account" means a financial account as defined in §1.1471-5(b) (substituting "U.S. office or branch of a financial institution" for "FFI"); the term "account holder" has the meaning described in §1.1471-5(a)(3); and the term "financial institution" means an entity that is a depository institution, custodial institution, investment entity, or a specified insurance company, each as defined in §1.1471-5(e).

(3) Requirements for reasonable explanation of the absence of a foreign TIN.—A withholding agent may rely on a reasonable explana-

tion for the absence of a foreign TIN on a beneficial owner withholding certificate only if the explanation addresses why the account holder was not issued a foreign TIN. An explanation provided in the instructions for, as applicable, Forms W-8BEN, W-8BEN-E, W-8ECI, W-8EXP, or Form W-8IMY is a reasonable explanation. If an account holder provides an explanation other than as described in the preceding sentence, the withholding agent must determine whether the explanation is reasonable. A reasonable explanation may be provided on the withholding certificate or on a separate attached statement associated with the form. A withholding agent may rely on a reasonable explanation described in this paragraph (e)(2)(ii)(B)(*3*) unless it has actual knowledge that the account holder has a foreign TIN.

(*4*) *Exceptions to the requirement to obtain a foreign TIN (or reasonable explanation for its absence).*—(*i*) *Jurisdictions with which the United States does not have an agreement relating to the exchange of tax information.*—A beneficial owner withholding certificate is not required to include a foreign TIN (or reasonable explanation for its absence) for an account holder resident of a jurisdiction that is not identified, in an applicable revenue procedure (see § 601.601(d)(2) of this chapter), as a jurisdiction that has in effect with the United States an income tax or other convention or bilateral agreement relating to the exchange of tax information within the meaning of section 6103(k)(4), under which the United States agrees to provide, as well as receive, tax information. A withholding agent that applies the exception described in the preceding sentence is, however, required to obtain the foreign TIN (or reasonable explanation for its absence) of each account holder resident in a jurisdiction that is added to the list on the applicable revenue procedure, before the time for filing Form 1042-S (with any applicable extension) for payments made during the calendar year following the calendar year in which the revenue procedure was published that added the jurisdiction to the list.

(*ii*) *Jurisdictions that do not issue foreign TINs.*—A beneficial owner withholding certificate is not required to include a foreign TIN (or reasonable explanation for its absence) for an account holder resident of a jurisdiction that has been identified by the IRS on a list of jurisdictions that either do not issue foreign TINs to their residents or have requested that their residents not be required to provide foreign TINs to withholding agents for purposes of this paragraph (e)(2)(ii)(B). A withholding agent that applies the exception described in the preceding sentence is, however, required to obtain the foreign TIN (or reasonable explanation for its absence) of each account holder resident in a jurisdiction that is removed from the list of jurisdictions referenced in the preceding sentence before the time for filing Form 1042-S (with any applicable extension) for payments made during the calendar year following the calendar year in which the jurisdiction is removed from the list. A list of jurisdictions that either do not issue taxpayer identification numbers to their residents or that have requested to be included on the list is available at https://www.irs.gov/businesses/corporations/list-of-jurisdictions-that-do-not-issue-foreign-tins (or any replacement page on the IRS website or as provided in published guidance).

(*iii*) *Account holder that is a government, international organization, foreign central bank of issue, or resident of a U.S. territory.*—A beneficial owner withholding certificate is not required to include a foreign TIN (or reasonable explanation for its absence) if the withholding agent has obtained a valid withholding certificate under paragraph (e)(2)(ii)(A) of this section or other documentation on which it may rely for purposes of the section 1441 regulations to treat the account holder as a government, an international organization, a foreign central bank of issue, or a resident of a U.S. territory. Thus, for example, a withholding agent may apply the exception provided in this paragraph (e)(2)(ii)(B)(*4*)(*iii*) with respect to an account holder claiming exemption under section 892 or otherwise identifying itself as a foreign government on a beneficial owner withholding certificate when the withholding agent may rely upon the claim of exemption under § 1.1441-8(b) or the claim of status as a foreign government under § 1.1441-7(b)(1) and (2).

(*5*) *Transition rules for the foreign TIN requirement for a beneficial owner withholding certificate signed before January 1, 2018.*—(*i*) *Payments made before January 1, 2020.*—For payments made before January 1, 2020, an otherwise valid beneficial owner withholding certificate signed before January 1, 2018, is not treated as invalid if it does not include a foreign TIN (or a reasonable explanation for its absence) as required under paragraph (e)(2)(ii)(B) of this section until the earlier of—

(*A*) the expiration date of the validity period of the withholding certificate (if applicable); or

(*B*) the date when a change in circumstances (including for chapter 4 purposes) requires a revised withholding certificate.

(*ii*) *Payments made after December 31, 2019.*—For payments made after December 31, 2019, an otherwise valid beneficial owner withholding certificate signed before January 1, 2018, is not treated as invalid if it does not include a foreign TIN (or a reasonable explanation for its absence) as required under paragraph (e)(2)(ii)(B) of this section until the earlier of the date described in paragraph (e)(2)(ii)(B)(*5*)(*i*)(*A*) or (*B*) of this section, provided the withholding agent either—

(*A*) obtains from the account holder its foreign TIN (or reasonable explanation for its absence) on a written statement (including a written statement transmitted by email) which the withholding agent associates with the account holder's withholding certificate, or

(*B*) already has the account holder's foreign TIN in the withholding agent's files, which the withholding agent associates with the account holder's withholding certificate.

(*iii*) *Limitation on standard of knowledge.*—If a withholding agent maintains an account on December 31, 2017, that is documented with a valid beneficial owner withholding certificate as of that date, the withholding agent's reason to know that the foreign TIN is incorrect, or actual knowledge that an account holder has a foreign TIN despite providing a reasonable explanation as described in paragraph (e)(2)(ii)(B)(*3*) of this section, is limited to electronically searchable information (as defined in § 1.1471-1(b)(38)) that is in the withholding agent's files.

(*6*) *Transition rule for the date of birth requirement for a beneficial owner withholding certificate signed before January 1, 2018.*—For an otherwise valid beneficial owner withholding certificate signed before January 1, 2018, a withholding agent is not required to treat the withholding certificate as invalid for payments made before January 1, 2019, to an account holder solely because the withholding certificate does not include the account holder's date of birth and the date of birth is not in the withholding agent's files.

(3) *Intermediary, flow-through, or U.S. branch withholding certificate.*—(i) *In general.*—An intermediary withholding certificate is a Form W-8 by which a payee represents that it is a foreign person and that it is an intermediary (whether a qualified or nonqualified intermediary) with respect to a payment and not the beneficial owner. See paragraphs (e)(3)(ii) and (iii) of this section. A flow-through withholding certificate is a Form W-8 used by a flow-through entity as defined in paragraph (c)(23) of this section. See § 1.1441-5(c)(3)(iii) (a nonwithholding foreign partnership), § 1.1441-5(e)(5)(iii) (a foreign simple trust or foreign grantor trust) or § 1.1441-6(b)(2) (foreign entity presenting claims on behalf of its interest holders for a reduced rate of withholding under an income tax treaty). A U.S. branch certificate is a Form W-8 furnished under paragraph (e)(3)(v) of this section by a U.S. branch described in paragraph (b)(2)(iv) of this section. See paragraph (e)(4)(viii) of this section for applicable reliance rules.

(ii) *Intermediary withholding certificate from a qualified intermediary.*—A qualified intermediary shall provide a qualified intermediary withholding certificate for withholdable payments or reportable amounts received by the qualified intermediary. See paragraph (e)(3)(vi) of this section for the definition of reportable amount. A qualified intermediary withholding certificate is valid only if it is furnished on a Form W-8, an acceptable substitute form, or such other form as the IRS may prescribe, it is signed under penalties of perjury by a person with authority to sign for the qualified intermediary, its validity has not expired, and it contains the following information, statement, and certifications—

(A) The name, permanent residence address, qualified intermediary employer identification number (QI-EIN), and the country under the laws of which the qualified intermediary is created, incorporated, or governed. If required for purposes of chapter 4 or if the qualified intermediary is a participating FFI or registered deemed-compliant FFI and certifies that it is providing (or will provide) a chapter 4 withholding rate pool of U.S. payees under § 1.6049-4(c)(4) with respect to accounts that the qualified intermediary maintains, the withholding certificate must also include the chapter 4 status of the qualified intermediary and its GIIN (if applicable). See paragraph (e)(5)(ii) for the chapter 4 status required of a qualified intermediary, including when a qualified intermediary withholding certificate may include a chapter 4 status of limited FFI (as defined in § 1.1471-1(b)(77)). A qualified intermediary that does not act in its capacity as a qualified intermediary must not use its QI-

EIN. Rather, it should provide a nonqualified intermediary withholding certificate, if it is acting as an intermediary, and should use the taxpayer identification number (if any) that it uses for all other purposes and GIIN (if applicable);

(B) A certification that, with respect to accounts it identifies on its withholding statement (as described in paragraph (e)(5)(v) of this section), the qualified intermediary is not acting for its own account but is acting as a qualified intermediary;

(C) A certification that the qualified intermediary has provided, or will provide, a withholding statement as required by paragraph (e)(5)(v) of this section;

(D) A certification that the qualified intermediary meets the requirements of § 1.6049-4(c)(4) when the qualified intermediary provides (or will provide) a withholding statement associated with its Form W-8 that allocates a payment to a chapter 4 withholding rate pool of U.S. payees that hold accounts with the qualified intermediary. Additionally, when the qualified intermediary provides a chapter 4 withholding rate pool of U.S. payees that do not hold accounts maintained by the qualified intermediary, the qualified intermediary provides a certification on the Form W-8 that the qualified intermediary has obtained (or will obtain) documentation from the intermediary or flow through entity allocating the payment to the pool to establish that the entity's status is as a participating FFI, registered deemed-compliant FFI, or qualified intermediary under § 1.1471-3(d)(4) (or, as applicable, § 1.1471-3(e)(4)(vi)(B) or § 1.1441-1(b)(2)(vii)); and

(E) In the case of any payment with respect to a potential section 871(m) transaction (including any dividend equivalent payment within the meaning of § 1.871-15(i)) or underlying security (as defined in § 1.871-15(a)(15)) received by a qualified intermediary acting as a qualified derivatives dealer, a certification that the home office or branch receiving the payment, as applicable, meets the requirements to act as a qualified derivatives dealer as further described in paragraph (e)(6) of this section and that the qualified derivatives dealer assumes primary withholding and reporting responsibilities under chapters 3, 4, and 61, and section 3406 with respect to any payments it makes with respect to potential section 871(m) transactions;

(F) Any other information, certifications, or statements as may be required by the form or accompanying instructions in addition to, or in lieu of, the information and certifications described in this paragraph (e)(3)(ii) or paragraph (e)(3)(v) of this section. See paragraph (e)(5)(v) of this section for the requirements of a withholding statement associated with the qualified intermediary withholding certificate.

(iii) *Intermediary withholding certificate from a nonqualified intermediary.*—A nonqualified intermediary shall provide a nonqualified intermediary withholding certificate for reportable amounts received by the nonqualified intermediary. See paragraph (e)(3)(vi) of this section for the definition of reportable amount. A nonqualified intermediary withholding certificate is valid only to the extent it is furnished on a Form W-8, an acceptable substitute form, or such other form as the IRS may prescribe, it is signed under penalties of perjury by a person authorized to sign for the nonqualified intermediary, it contains the information, statements, and certifications described in this paragraphs (e)(3)(iii) and (iv) of this section, its validity has not expired, and the withholding certificates and other appropriate documentation for all persons to whom the certificate relates are associated with the certificate. Withholding certificates and other appropriate documentation consist of beneficial owner withholding certificates described in paragraph (e)(2)(i) of this section, intermediary and flow-through withholding certificates described in paragraph (e)(3)(i) of this section, withholding foreign partnership and withholding foreign trust certificates described in § 1.1441-5(c)(2)(iv) and (e)(5)(iii), documentary evidence described in §§ 1.1441-6(c)(3) or (4) and 1.6049-5(c)(1), and any other documentation or certificates applicable under other provisions of the Code or regulations that certify or establish the status of the payee or beneficial owner as a U.S. or a foreign person. If a nonqualified intermediary is acting on behalf of another nonqualified intermediary or a flow-through entity, then the nonqualified intermediary must associate with its own withholding certificate the other nonqualified intermediary withholding certificate or the flow-through withholding certificate and separately identify all of the withholding certificates and other appropriate documentation that are associated with the withholding certificate of the other nonqualified intermediary or flow-through entity. Nothing in this paragraph (e)(3)(iii) shall require an intermediary to furnish original documentation. Copies of certificates or documentary evidence may be transmitted to the U.S. withholding agent, in which case the nonqualified intermediary must retain the original documentation for the same time period that the copy is required to be retained by the withholding agent under paragraph (e)(4)(iii) of this section and must provide it to the withholding agent upon request. For purposes of this paragraph (e)(3)(iii), a valid intermediary withholding certificate also includes a statement described in § 1.871-14(c)(2)(v) furnished for interest to qualify as portfolio interest for purposes of sections 871(h) and 881(c). The information and certifications required on a Form W-8 described in this paragraph (e)(3)(iii) are as follows—

(A) The name and permanent resident address of the nonqualified intermediary, chapter 4 status (if required for chapter 4 purposes or if the nonqualified intermediary provides the certification described in paragraph (e)(3)(iii)(D) of this section), GIIN (if applicable), and the country under the laws of which the nonqualified intermediary is created, incorporated, or governed;

(B) A certification that the nonqualified intermediary is not acting for its own account;

(C) If the nonqualified intermediary withholding certificate is used to transmit withholding certificates or other appropriate documentation for more than one person on whose behalf the nonqualified intermediary is acting, a withholding statement associated with the Form W-8 that provides all the information required by paragraph (e)(3)(iv) of this section;

(D) If the nonqualified intermediary provides a withholding statement associated with the Form W-8 allocating a payment to a chapter 4 withholding rate pool of U.S. payees, a certification that the nonqualified intermediary meets the requirements of § 1.6049-4(c)(4) with respect to any payees included in such pool that hold accounts maintained (as defined in § 1.1471-5(b)(5)) by the nonqualified intermediary; and

(E) Any other information, certifications, or statements as may be required by the form or accompanying instructions in addition to, or in lieu of, the information, certifications, and statements described in this paragraph (e)(3)(iii) or paragraph (e)(5)(iv) of this section.

(iv) *Withholding statement provided by nonqualified intermediary.*—(A) *In general.*—A nonqualified intermediary shall provide a withholding statement required by this paragraph (e)(3)(iv) to the extent the nonqualified intermediary is required to furnish, or does furnish, documentation for payees on whose behalf it receives reportable amounts (as defined in paragraph (e)(3)(vi) of this section) or to the extent it otherwise provides the documentation of such payees to a withholding agent. A nonqualified intermediary, however, that is subject to withholding under chapter 4 due to its chapter 4 status as a nonparticipating FFI need not provide a withholding statement unless it is providing documentation to allocate a portion of the payment as made to an exempt beneficial owner as described in § 1.1471-3(c)(3)(iii)(B)(4). A nonqualified intermediary that is subject to withholding under chapter 4 due to its chapter 4 status is not required to disclose to the withholding agent information regarding persons for whom it collects reportable amounts unless it has actual knowledge that any such person is a U.S. non-exempt recipient as defined in paragraph (c)(21) of this section. Information regarding U.S. non-exempt recipients required under this paragraph (e)(3)(iv) must be provided irrespective of any requirement under foreign law that prohibits the disclosure of the identity of an account holder of a nonqualified intermediary or financial information relating to such account holder. A nonqualified intermediary is not required to provide information on a withholding statement regarding U.S. non-exempt recipients, provided that the nonqualified intermediary is a participating FFI (including a reporting Model 2 FFI) or registered deemed-compliant FFI (including a reporting Model 1 FFI) that identifies on the withholding statement the portion of a payment allocable to a chapter 4 withholding rate pool of U.S. payees to the extent that the nonqualified intermediary is permitted to include such U.S. payees in a pool under § 1.6049-4(c)(4)(iii). See § 1.1471-3(d)(4) for the requirements of an entity to identify itself as a participating FFI or registered deemed-compliant FFI to a withholding agent for purposes of chapter 4. Although a nonqualified intermediary is not required to provide documentation and other information required by this paragraph (e)(3)(iv) for persons other than U.S. non-exempt recipients not included in a chapter 4 withholding rate pool of U.S. payees, a withholding agent that does not receive documentation and such information must apply the presumption rules of paragraph (b) of this section, §§ 1.1441-5(d) and (e)(6), 1.6049-5(d), and 1.1471-3(f)(5) (for a withholdable payment) or the withholding agent shall be liable for tax, interest, and penalties. A withholding agent must apply the presumption rules even if it is not required under chapter 61 of the Code to obtain documentation to treat a payee as an exempt recipient and even though it has actual knowledge that the payee is a U.S. person. For example, if a nonqualified intermediary receives a payment that is not a withholdable payment and fails to provide a withholding agent with a Form W-9 for an account holder that is a U.S. exempt recipient that is not included in a chapter 4 withholding rate pool of U.S. payees to the extent permitted in this paragraph (e)(3)(iv)(A), the withholding agent must presume (even if it has actual knowledge that the account holder is a U.S. exempt recipient) that the account holder is an undocumented foreign person with respect to amounts subject to chapter 3 withholding. See paragraph (b)(3)(v) of this section for applicable presumptions. Therefore, the withholding agent must withhold 30 percent from the payment even though if a Form W-9 had been provided, no withholding or reporting on the payment attributable to a U.S. exempt recipient would apply. Further, a nonqualified intermediary that fails to provide the documentation and the information under this paragraph (e)(3)(iv) for another withholding agent to report the payments on Forms 1042-S (including under the requirements of § 1.1474-1(d)(2) for a payment of a chapter 4 reportable amount) and Forms 1099 is not relieved of its responsibility to file information returns. See paragraph (b)(6) of this section. Therefore, unless the nonqualified intermediary itself files such returns and provides copies to the payees, it shall be liable for penalties under sections 6721 (failure to file information returns), and 6722 (failure to furnish payee statements), including the penalties under those sections for intentional failure to file information returns. In addition, failure to provide either the documentation or the information required by this paragraph (e)(3)(iv) results in a payment not being reliably associated with valid documentation. Therefore, the beneficial owners of the payment are not entitled to reduced rates of withholding and if the full amount required to be held under the presumption rules is not withheld by the withholding agent, the nonqualified intermediary must withhold the difference between the amount withheld by the withholding agent and the amount required to be withheld. Failure to withhold shall result in the nonqualified intermediary being liable for tax under section 1461, interest, and penalties, including penalties under section 6656 (failure to deposit) and section 6672 (failure to collect and pay over tax).

(B) *General requirements.*—A withholding statement must be provided prior to the payment of a reportable amount and must contain the information specified in paragraph (e)(3)(iv)(C) of this section. The statement must be updated as often as required to keep the information in the withholding statement correct prior to each subsequent payment. The withholding statement forms an integral part of the withholding certificate provided under paragraph (e)(3)(iii) of this section, and the penalties of perjury statement provided on the withholding certificate shall apply to the withholding statement. The withholding statement may be provided in any manner the nonqualified intermediary and the withholding agent mutually agree, including electronically. If the withholding statement is provided electronically as part of a system established by the withholding agent or nonqualified intermediary to provide the statement, however, there must be sufficient safeguards to ensure that the information received by the withholding agent is the information sent by the nonqualified intermediary and all occasions of user access that result in the submission or modification of the withholding statement information must be recorded. In addition, the electronic system must be capable of providing a hard copy of all withholding statements provided by the nonqualified intermediary. A withholding statement may otherwise be transmitted by a nonqualified intermediary via email or facsimile to a withholding agent under the requirements specified in paragraph (e)(4)(iv)(D) of this section (substituting the term withholding statement for the term Form W-8 or the term document, as applicable). A withholding agent will be liable for tax, interest, and penalties in accordance with paragraph (b)(7) of this section to the extent it does not follow the presumption rules of paragraph (b)(3) of this section or §§ 1.1441-5(d) and (e)(6), and 1.6049-5(d) for any payment of a reportable amount, or portion thereof, for which it does not have a valid withholding statement prior to making a payment. A withholding agent may not treat as valid an allocation of a payment to a chapter 4 withholding rate pool of U.S. payees described in paragraph (e)(3)(iv)(A) of this section or an allocation of a payment to a chapter 4 withholding rate pool of recalcitrant account holders described in paragraph (e)(3)(iv)(C)(2) of this section unless the withholding agent identifies the nonqualified intermediary maintaining the account (as described in § 1.1471-5(b)(5)) as a participating FFI (including a reporting Model 2 FFI) or registered deemed-compliant FFI (including a reporting Model 1 FFI) by applying the rules of § 1.1471-3(d)(4). Additionally, in the case of a withholdable payment that is an amount subject to withholding made on or after April 1, 2017, a withholding agent may not treat as valid an allocation of the payment to a chapter 4 withholding rate pool of U.S. payees unless the nonqualified intermediary identifies the pool of U.S. payees as one described in § 1.1471-3(c)(3)(iii)(B)(*2*)(*iii*) (or by describing such payees consistent with the description provided in § 1.1471-3(c)(3)(iii)(B)(*2*)(*iii*)).

(C) *Content of withholding statement.*—The withholding statement provided by a nonqualified intermediary must contain the information required by this paragraph (e)(3)(iv)(C).

(1) In general.—Except as otherwise provided by paragraph (e)(3)(iv)(C)(*2*) and (*3*) of this section), the withholding statement provided by a nonqualified intermediary must contain the information required by this paragraph (e)(3)(iv)(C)(*1*).

(i) Except as otherwise provided in (e)(3)(iv)(A) of this section (which excludes reporting of information with respect to certain U.S. persons on the withholding statement), the withholding statement must contain the name, address, TIN (if any), and the type of documentation (documentary evidence, Form W-9, or type of Form W-8) for every person from whom documentation has been received by the nonqualified intermediary and provided to the withholding agent and whether that person is a U.S. exempt recipient, a U.S. non-exempt recipient, or a foreign person. See paragraphs (c)(2), (20), and (21) of this section for the definitions of foreign person, U.S. exempt recipient, and U.S. non-exempt recipient. In the case of a foreign person, the statement must indicate whether the foreign person is a beneficial owner or an intermediary, flow-through entity, U.S. branch, or territory financial institution described in paragraph (b)(2)(iv) of this section and include the type of recipient, based on recipient codes applicable for chapter 3 purposes used for filing Forms 1042-S, if the foreign person is a recipient as defined in § 1.1461-1(c)(1)(ii).

(ii) The withholding statement must allocate each payment, by income type, to every payee required to be reported on the withholding statement for whom documentation has been provided (including U.S. exempt recipients except as provided in paragraph (e)(3)(iv)(A) of this section). Any payment that cannot be reliably associated with valid documentation from a payee shall be treated as made to an unknown payee in accordance with the presumption rules of paragraph (b) of this section and §§ 1.1441-5(d) and (e)(6) and 1.6049-5(d). For this purpose, a type of income is determined by the types of income required to be reported on Forms 1042-S or 1099, as appropriate. Notwithstanding the preceding sentence, deposit interest (including original issue discount) described in section 871(i)(2)(A) or 881(d) and interest or original issue discount on short-term obligations as described in section 871(g)(1)(B) or 881(e) is only required to be allocated to the extent it is required to be reported on Form 1099 or Form 1042-S. See § 1.6049-8 (regarding reporting of bank deposit interest to certain foreign persons). If a payee receives income through another nonqualified intermediary, flow-through entity, or U.S. branch or territory financial institution described in paragraph (e)(2)(iv) of this section (other than a U.S. branch or territory financial institution treated as a U.S. person), the withholding statement must also state, with respect to the payee, the name, address, and TIN, if known, of the other nonqualified intermediary or U.S. branch from which the payee directly receives the payment or the flow-through entity in which the payee has a direct ownership interest. If another nonqualified intermediary, flow-through entity, or U.S. branch fails to allocate a payment, the name of the nonqualified intermediary, flow-through entity, or U.S. branch that failed to allocate the payment shall be provided with respect to such payment.

(iii) If a payee is identified as a foreign person, the nonqualified intermediary must specify the rate of withholding to which the payee is subject, the payee's country of residence and, if a reduced rate of withholding is claimed, the basis for that reduced rate (*e.g.*, treaty benefit, portfolio interest, exempt under section 501(c)(3), 892, or 895). The allocation statement must also include the TINs of those foreign persons for whom such a number is required under paragraph (e)(4)(vii) of this section or § 1.1441-6(b)(1) (regarding claims for treaty benefits for which a TIN is provided unless a foreign tax identifying number described in § 1.1441-6(b)(1) is provided). In the case of a claim of treaty benefits, the nonqualified intermediary's withholding statement must also state whether the limitation on benefits and section 894 statements required by § 1.1441-6(c)(5) have been provided, if required, in the beneficial owner's Form W-8 or associated with such owner's documentary evidence.

(iv) The withholding statement must also contain any other information the withholding agent reasonably requests in order to fulfill its obligations under chapter 3 and chapter 61 of the Code, and section 3406.

(2) *Nonqualified intermediary withholding statement for withholdable payments.*—This paragraph (e)(3)(iv)(C)(*2*) modifies the requirements of a withholding statement described in paragraph (e)(3)(iv)(C)(*1*) of this section that is provided by a nonqualified intermediary with respect to a reportable amount that is a withholdable payment. For such a payment, the requirements applicable to a withholding statement described in paragraph (e)(3)(iv)(A) through (e)(3)(iv)(C)(*1*) of this section shall apply, except that—

(*i*) The withholding statement must include the chapter 4 status (using the applicable status code used for filing Form 1042-S) and GIIN (when required for chapter 4 purposes under §1.1471-3(d)) of each other intermediary or flow-through entity that is a foreign person and that receives the payment, excluding an intermediary or flow-through entity that is an account holder of or interest holder in a withholding foreign partnership, withholding foreign trust, or intermediary acting as a qualified intermediary for the payment;

(*ii*) If the nonqualified intermediary that is a participating FFI or registered deemed-compliant FFI provides a withholding statement described in §1.1471-3(c)(3)(iii)(B)(*2*) (describing an FFI withholding statement), the withholding statement may include chapter 4 withholding rate pools with respect to the portions of the payment allocated to nonparticipating FFIs and recalcitrant account holders (to the extent permitted on an FFI withholding statement described in that paragraph) in lieu of providing specific payee information with respect to such persons on the statement (including persons subject to chapter 4 withholding) as described in paragraph (e)(3)(iv)(C)(*1*) of this section;

(*iii*) If the nonqualified intermediary provides a withholding statement described in §1.1471-3(c)(3)(iii)(B)(*3*) (describing a chapter 4 withholding statement), the withholding statement may include chapter 4 withholding rate pools with respect to the portions of the payment allocated to nonparticipating FFIs; and

(*iv*) For a payment allocated to a payee that is a foreign person (other than a person included in a chapter 4 withholding rate pool described in paragraphs (e)(3)(iv)(C)(*2*)(*ii*) and (*iii*) of this section) that is reported on a withholding statement described in §1.1471-3(c)(3)(iii)(B)(2) or (3), the withholding statement must include the chapter 4 status of the payee (unless an exception applies for purposes of providing such status under chapter 4) and, for a payee other than an individual, the recipient code for chapter 4 purposes used for filing Form 1042-S; and

(*v*) To the extent that a withholdable payment is not reportable on a Form 1042-S, Form 1099 under the rules of chapter 61, or Form 8966 "FATCA Report," no allocation of the payment is required on the withholding statement.

(3) *Alternative withholding statement.*—(i) In lieu of a withholding statement containing all of the information described in paragraph (e)(3)(iv)(C)(*1*) and (2) of this section, a withholding agent may accept from a nonqualified intermediary a withholding statement that meets all of the requirements of this paragraph (e)(3)(iv)(C)(*3*)(*i*) with respect to a payment. The withholding statement described in this paragraph (e)(3)(iv)(C)(*3*)(*i*) may be provided only by a nonqualified intermediary that provides the withholding agent with the withholding certificates from the beneficial owners (that is, not documentary evidence) before the payment is made.

(*A*) The withholding statement is not required to contain all of the information specified in paragraphs (e)(3)(iv)(C)(*1*) and (2) of this section that is also included on a withholding certificate (for example, name, address, TIN (if any), chapter 4 status, GIIN (if any)). The withholding statement is also not required to specify the rate of withholding to which each foreign payee is subject, provided that all of the information necessary to make such determination is provided on the withholding certificate. A withholding agent that uses the withholding statement may not apply a different rate from that which the withholding agent may reasonably conclude from the information on the withholding certificate.

(*B*) The withholding statement must allocate the payment to every payee required to be reported as described in paragraph (e)(3)(iv)(C)(*1*)(*ii*) of this section.

(*C*) The withholding statement must also contain any other information the withholding agent reasonably requests in order to fulfill its obligations under chapters 3, 4, and 61, and section 3406.

(*D*) The withholding statement must contain a representation from the nonqualified intermediary that the information on the withholding certificates is not inconsistent with any other account information the nonqualified intermediary has for the beneficial owners for determining the rate of withholding with respect to each payee (applying the standards of knowledge applicable to a withholding agent's reliance on a withholding certificate in the regulations under section 1441 and, for a withholdable payment, the regulations under section 1471).

(*ii*) In lieu of a withholding statement that includes a recipient code for chapter 4 purposes used for filing Form 1042-S, a withholding agent may accept a nonqualified intermediary withholding statement that contains all of the information described in paragraph (e)(3)(iv)(C)(*1*) and (*2*) of this section (or an alternative withholding statement permitted under paragraph (e)(3)(iv)(C)(*3*)(i) of this section) but that does not provide a recipient code for chapter 4 purposes used for filing Form 1042-S for a payee as required in paragraph (e)(3)(iv)(C)(*2*)(*iv*) of this section if the withholding agent is able to determine such payee's recipient code based on other information included on or with the withholding statement or in the withholding agent's records with respect to the payee.

(4) *Example.*—This example illustrates the principles of paragraph (e)(3)(iv)(C) of this section. WA makes a withholdable payment of U.S. source dividends to NQI, a nonqualified intermediary. NQI provides WA with a valid intermediary withholding certificate under paragraph (e)(3)(iii) of this section that includes NQI's certification of its status for chapter 4 purposes as a participating FFI. NQI provides a withholding statement on which NQI allocates 20% of the payment to a chapter 4 withholding rate pool of recalcitrant account holders of NQI for purposes of chapter 4 and allocates 80% of the payment equally to A and B, individuals that are account holders of NQI. NQI also provides WA with valid beneficial owner withholding certificates from A and B establishing their status as foreign persons entitled to a 15% rate of withholding under an applicable income tax treaty. Because NQI has certified its status as a participating FFI, withholding under chapter 4 is not required with respect to NQI. See §1.1471-2(a)(4). Based on the documentation NQI provided to WA with respect to A and B, WA can reliably associate the payment with valid documentation on the portion of the payment allocated to them and, because the payment is a withholdable payment, may rely on the allocation of the payment for NQI's recalcitrant account holders in a chapter 4 withholding rate pool in lieu of payee information with respect to such account holders. See paragraph (e)(3)(iv)(C)(2) of this section for the special rules for a withholding statement provided by a nonqualified intermediary for a withholdable payment. Also see §1.1471-2(a) for WA's withholding requirements under chapter 4 with respect to the portion of the payment allocated to NQI's recalcitrant account holders and §1.1441-3(a)(2) for coordinating withholding under chapter 3 for payments to which withholding is applied under chapter 4.

(D) *Alternative procedures.*—(*1*) *In general.*—Under the alternative procedures of this paragraph (e)(3)(iv)(D), a nonqualified intermediary may provide information allocating a payment of a reportable amount to each payee (including U.S. exempt recipients) otherwise required under paragraph (e)(3)(iv)(B)(2) of this section after a payment is made. To use the alternative procedure of this paragraph (e)(3)(iv)(D), the nonqualified intermediary must inform the withholding agent on a statement associated with its nonqualified intermediary withholding certificate that it is using the procedure under this paragraph (e)(3)(iv)(D) and the withholding agent must agree to the procedure. If the requirements of the alternative procedure are met, a withholding agent, including the nonqualified intermediary using the procedures, can treat the payment as reliably associated with documentation and, therefore, the presumption rules of paragraph (b)(3) of this section and §§1.1441-5(d) and (e)(6) and 1.6049-5(d) do not apply even though information allocating the payment to each payee has not been received prior to the payment. See paragraph (e)(3)(iv)(D)(*7*) of this section, however, for a nonqualified intermediary's liability for tax and penalties if the requirements of this paragraph (e)(3)(iv)(D) are not met. These alternative procedures shall not be used for payments that are allocable to U.S. non-exempt recipients except as provided in paragraph (e)(3)(iv)(D)(*2*)(*ii*) of this section. Therefore, a nonqualified intermediary is required to provide a withholding agent with information allocating payments of reportable amounts to U.S. non-exempt recipients prior to the payment being made by the withholding agent.

(*2*) *Withholding rate pools.*—(*i*) *In general.*—In place of the information required in paragraph (e)(3)(iv)(C)(2) of this section allocating payments to each payee, the nonqualified intermediary must provide a withholding agent with withholding rate pool information prior to the payment of a reportable amount. The withholding statement must contain all other information required by paragraph (e)(3)(iv)(C) of this section. Further, each payee listed in the withholding statement must be assigned to an identified withholding rate pool. To the extent a nonqualified intermediary is required to provide, or does provide, documentation, the alternative procedures do not relieve the nonqualified intermediary from the requirement to provide documentation prior to the payment being made. Therefore, withholding certificates or other appropriate documentation and all information required by paragraph (e)(3)(iv)(C) of this section (other than allocation information) must be provided to a withholding agent before any new payee receives a reportable amount. In addition, the withholding statement must be updated by assigning a new payee to a withholding rate pool prior to the payment of a reportable amount. A withholding rate pool is a payment of a single type of income, determined in accordance with the categories of income used to file Form 1042-S, that is subject to a single rate of withholding. A withholding rate pool may be established by any reasonable method to which the nonqualified intermediary and a withholding agent agree (*e.g.*, by establishing a separate account for a single withholding rate pool, or by dividing a payment made to a single account into portions allocable to each withholding rate pool). The nonqualified intermediary shall determine withholding rate pools based on valid documentation or, to the extent a payment cannot be reliably associated with valid documentation, the presumption rules of paragraph (b)(3) of this section and §§1.1441-5(d) and (e)(6) and 1.6049-5(d).

(ii) Withholding rate pools for chapter 4 purposes.—This paragraph (e)(3)(iv)(D)(2)(*ii*) modifies the provisions of paragraph (e)(3)(iv)(D)(2)(*i*) of this section with respect to the withholding rate pools permitted for the alternative procedures described in paragraph (e)(3)(iv)(D)(*1*) of this section in the case of a payment that is allocable on a withholding statement to a chapter 4 withholding rate pool as described in this paragraph. In the case of a withholdable payment, a nonqualified intermediary may include reportable amounts allocable to a chapter 4 withholding rate pool (other than a chapter 4 withholding rate pool of U.S. payees) in a 30-percent rate pool together with a withholding rate pool for amounts subject to chapter 3 withholding at the 30-percent rate. For a payment of a reportable amount that is allocable to a chapter 4 withholding rate pool of U.S. payees on a withholding statement, a nonqualified intermediary may include such amount in a single withholding rate pool with the amount of the payment that is exempt from withholding under chapter 3 instead of providing documentation regarding U.S. non-exempt recipients included in the pool or separately allocating the amount to the chapter 4 withholding rate pool. To the extent that a nonqualified intermediary allocates an amount to any chapter 4 withholding rate pool, the nonqualified intermediary is required to notify the withholding agent of the allocation before receiving the payment and is not required to provide documentation with respect to the payees included in such pool. The nonqualified intermediary shall determine the chapter 4 withholding rate pools permitted to be used under this paragraph (e)(3)(iv)(D)(2)(*ii*) in accordance with the nonqualified intermediary's applicable chapter 4 status and under §1.1471-3(c)(3)(iii)(B)(2) (for an FFI withholding statement) or (c)(3)(iii)(B)(*3*) (for a chapter 4 withholding statement) or under §1.6049-4(c)(4) for a chapter 4 withholding rate pool of U.S. payees (or similar applicable coordination rule in chapter 61 for payments other than interest). Additionally, the nonqualified intermediary shall identify those payees to which withholding under chapter 4 applies that are not included in a chapter 4 reporting pool (including payees that could be included in a chapter 4 withholding rate pool for whom the nonqualified intermediary chooses to provide payee specific information).

(3) Allocation information.—The nonqualified intermediary must provide the withholding agent with sufficient information to allocate the income in each withholding rate pool to each payee (including U.S. exempt recipients or any chapter 4 withholding rate pool identified by the withholding agent under paragraph (e)(3)(iv)(D)(2)(*ii*) of this section) within the pool no later than January 31 of the year following the year of payment. Any payments that are not allocated to payees for whom documentation has been provided or a chapter 4 withholding rate pool referred to in the previous sentence shall be allocated to an undocumented payee in accordance with the presumption rules of paragraph (b)(3) of this section and §§1.1441-5(d) and (e)(6) and 1.6049-5(d), and 1.1471-3(f)(5) (for a withholdable payment for chapter 4 purposes). Notwithstanding the preceding sentence, deposit interest (including original issue discount) described in section 871(i)(2)(A) or 881(d) and interest or original issue discount on short-term obligations as described in section 871(g)(1)(B) or 881(e) is not required to be allocated to a U.S. exempt recipient or a foreign payee, except as required under §1.6049-8 (regarding reporting of deposit interest paid to certain foreign persons).

(4) Failure to provide allocation information.—Except as provided in paragraph (e)(3)(iv)(D)(*5*) of this section, if a nonqualified intermediary fails to provide allocation information, if required, by January 31 for any withholding rate pool to the extent required in paragraph (e)(3)(iv)(D)(*3*) of this section, a withholding agent shall not apply the alternative procedures of this paragraph (e)(3)(iv)(D) to any payments of reportable amounts paid after January 31 in the taxable year following the calendar year for which allocation information was not given and any subsequent taxable year. Further, the alternative procedures shall be unavailable for any other withholding rate pool (other than a chapter 4 withholding rate pool as otherwise permitted) even though allocation information was given for that other pool. Therefore, the withholding agent must withhold on a payment of a reportable amount in accordance with the presumption rules of paragraph (b)(3) of this section, and §§1.1441-5(d) and (e)(6) and 1.6049-5(d), and 1.1471-3(f)(5) (for a withholdable payment for chapter 4 purposes), unless the nonqualified intermediary provides all of the information, including information sufficient to allocate the payment to each specific payee or chapter 4 withholding rate pool (as permitted), required by paragraph (e)(3)(iv)(A) through (C) of this section prior to the payment. A nonqualified intermediary must allocate at least 90 percent of the income required to be allocated for each withholding rate pool as required under this paragraph (e)(3)(iv)(D)(*4*) or the nonqualified intermediary will be treated as having failed to provide allocation information for purposes of this paragraph (e)(3)(iv)(D). For purposes of the allocation, a nonqualified intermediary is required to identify by January 31 the portion of the payment that is allocated to each chapter 4 withholding rate pool (rather than the payees included in each such pool). See paragraph (e)(3)(iv)(D)(*7*) of this section for liability for tax and penalties if a nonqualified intermediary fails to provide allocation information in whole or in part.

(5) Cure provision.—A nonqualified intermediary may cure any failure to provide allocation information by providing the required allocation information to the withholding agent no later than February 14 following the calendar year of payment. If the withholding agent receives the allocation information by that date, it may apply the adjustment procedures of §1.1461-2 (or of §1.1474-2 for an amount withheld under chapter 4) to any excess withholding for payments made on or after February 1 and on or before February 14. Any nonqualified intermediary that fails to cure by February 14 may request the ability to use the alternative procedures of this paragraph (e)(3)(iv)(D) by submitting a request, in writing, to the IRS. The request must state the reason that the nonqualified intermediary did not comply with the alternative procedures of this paragraph (e)(3)(iv)(D) and steps that the nonqualified intermediary has taken, or will take, to ensure that no failures occur in the future. If the IRS determines that the alternative procedures of this paragraph (e)(3)(iv)(D) may apply, a determination to that effect will be issued by the IRS to the nonqualified intermediary.

(6) Form 1042-S reporting in case of allocation failure.—If a nonqualified intermediary fails to provide allocation information by February 14 following the year of payment for a withholding rate pool, the withholding agent must file Forms 1042-S for payments made to each payee in that pool (other than U.S. exempt recipients) in the prior calendar year by pro rating the payment to each payee (including U.S. exempt recipients) listed in the withholding statement for that withholding rate pool, treating as a payee for this purpose each chapter 4 withholding rate pool identified by the nonqualified intermediary under paragraph (e)(3)(iv)(D)(2)(*ii*) of this section. If the nonqualified intermediary fails to allocate 10 percent or less of an amount required to be allocated for a withholding rate pool, a withholding agent shall report the unallocated amount as paid to a single unknown payee in accordance with the presumption rules of paragraph (b) of this section and §§1.1441-5(d) and (e)(6) and 1.6049-5(d), and §1.1471-3(f)(5) (for a withholdable payment for chapter 4 purposes). The portion of the payment that can be allocated to specific recipients, as defined in §1.1461-1(c)(1)(ii), shall be reported to each recipient in accordance with the rules of §1.1461-1(c) and §1.1474-1(d)(2) (for a withholdable payment).

(7) Liability for tax, interest, and penalties.—If a nonqualified intermediary fails to provide allocation information by February 14 following the year of payment for all or a portion of the payments made to any withholding rate pool, the withholding agent from whom the nonqualified intermediary received payments of reportable amounts shall not be liable for any tax, interest, or penalties, due solely to the errors or omissions of the nonqualified intermediary. See §1.1441-7(b)(2) through (10) for the due diligence requirements of a withholding agent. Because failure by the nonqualified intermediary to provide allocation information results in a payment not being reliably associated with valid documentation, the beneficial owners

for whom the nonqualified intermediary acts are not entitled to a reduced rate of withholding. Therefore, the nonqualified intermediary, as a withholding agent, shall be liable for any tax not withheld by the withholding agent in accordance with the presumption rules, interest on the under withheld tax if the nonqualified intermediary fails to pay the tax timely, and any applicable penalties, including the penalties under sections 6656 (failure to deposit), 6721 (failure to file information returns) and 6722 (failure to file payee statements). Failure to provide allocation information for more than 10 percent of the payments made to a particular withholding rate pool will be presumed to be an intentional failure within the meaning of sections 6721(e) and 6722(c). The nonqualified intermediary may rebut the presumption.

(8) Applicability to flow-through entities and certain U.S. branches.—See paragraph (e)(3)(v) of this section and §1.1441-5(c)(3)(iv) and (e)(5)(iv) for the applicability of this paragraph (e)(3)(iv) to U.S. branches described in paragraph (b)(2)(iv) of this section (other than U.S. branches treated as U.S. persons) and flow-through entities.

(E) *Notice procedures.*—The IRS may notify a withholding agent that the alternative procedures of paragraph (e)(3)(iv)(D) of this section are not applicable to a specified nonqualified intermediary, a U.S. branch described in paragraph (b)(2)(iv) of this section, or a flow-through entity. If a withholding agent receives such a notice, it must commence withholding under this section or chapter 4 (if applicable) in accordance with the presumption rules of paragraph (b)(3) of this section and §§1.1441-5(d) and (e)(6), 1.6049-5(d), and 1.1471-3(f)(5) (for a withholdable payment for chapter 4 purposes) unless the nonqualified intermediary, U.S. branch, or flow-through entity complies with the procedures in paragraphs (e)(3)(iv)(A) through (C) of this section. In addition, the IRS may notify a withholding agent, in appropriate circumstances, that it must apply the presumption rules of paragraph (b)(3) of this section and §§1.1441-5(d) and (e)(6), 1.6049-5(d), and §1.1471-3(f)(5) (for a withholdable payment for chapter 4 purposes) to payments made to a nonqualified intermediary, a U.S. branch, or a flow-through entity even if the nonqualified intermediary, U.S. branch, or flow-through entity provides allocation information prior to the payment. A withholding agent that receives a notice under this paragraph (e)(3)(iv)(E) must commence withholding in accordance with the presumption rules within 30 days of the date of the notice. The IRS may withdraw its prohibition against using the alternative procedures of paragraph (e)(3)(iv)(D) of this section, or its requirement to follow the presumption rules, if the nonqualified intermediary, U.S. branch, or flow-through entity can demonstrate to the satisfaction of the IRS that it is capable of complying with the rules under chapter 3 of the Code and any other conditions required by the IRS.

(v) *Withholding certificate from certain U.S. branches (including territory financial institutions).*—A U.S. branch certificate is a withholding certificate provided by a U.S. branch (including a territory financial institution) described in paragraph (b)(2)(iv) of this section that is not the beneficial owner of the income. The withholding certificate is provided with respect to reportable amounts and must state that such amounts are not effectively connected with the conduct of a trade or business in the United States. The withholding certificate must either transmit the appropriate documentation for the persons for whom the branch receives the payment (*i.e.*, as an intermediary) or be provided as evidence of its agreement with the withholding agent to be treated as a U.S. person with respect to any payment associated with the certificate. A U.S. branch withholding certificate is valid only if it is furnished on a Form W-8, an acceptable substitute form, or such other form as the IRS may prescribe, it is signed under penalties of perjury by a person authorized to sign for the branch, its validity has not expired, and it contains the information, statements, and certifications described in this paragraph (e)(3)(v). If the certificate is furnished to transmit withholding certificates and other documentation, it must contain the information, certifications, and statements described in paragraphs (e)(3)(v)(A) through (C) of this section and in paragraphs (e)(3)(iii) and (iv) (alternative procedures) of this section, applying the term U.S. branch instead of the term nonqualified intermediary. If the certificate is furnished pursuant to an agreement to treat the U.S. branch or territory financial institution as a U.S. person (which agreement must be for purposes of chapter 4 in addition to this section in the case of a payment that is a withholdable payment), the information and certifications required on the withholding certificate are limited to the following—

(A) The name of the territory financial institution or person of which the U.S. branch is a part, the address of the territory financial institution or U.S. branch;

(B) A certification that the payments associated with the certificate are not effectively connected with the conduct of its trade or business in the United States;

(C) The EIN of the U.S. branch or territory financial institution;

(D) When required for chapter 4 purposes, the chapter 4 status and GIIN (if applicable) of the entity of which the U.S. branch is a part; and

(E) Any other information, certifications, or statements as may be required by the form or accompanying instructions in addition to, or in lieu of, the information and certification described in this paragraph (e)(3)(v).

(vi) *Reportable amounts.*—For purposes of chapter 3 of the Internal Revenue Code, a nonqualified intermediary, qualified intermediary, flow-through entity, and U.S. branch described in paragraph (b)(2)(iv) of this section (other than a U.S. branch that agrees to be treated as a U.S. person) must provide a withholding certificate and associated documentation and other information with respect to reportable amounts. For purposes of the regulations under chapter 3 of the Internal Revenue Code, the term reportable amount means an amount subject to withholding within the meaning of §1.1441-2(a), bank deposit interest (including original issue discount) and similar types of deposit interest described in section 871(i)(2)(A) or 881(d) that are from sources within the United States, and any amount of interest or original issue discount from sources within the United States on the redemption of certain short-term obligations described in section 871(g)(1)(B) or 881(e). Reportable amounts shall not include amounts received on the sale or exchange (other than a redemption) of an obligation described in section 871(g)(1)(B) or 881(e) that is effected at an office outside the United States. See §1.6045-1(g)(3) to determine whether a sale is effected at an office outside the United States. Reportable amounts also do not include payments with respect to deposits with banks and other financial institutions that remain on deposit for a period of two weeks or less, to amounts of original issue discount arising from a sale and repurchase transaction that is completed within a period of two weeks or less, or to amounts described in §1.6049-5(b)(7), (10) or (11) (relating to certain obligations issued in bearer form). While short-term OID and bank deposit interest are not subject to withholding under chapter 3 of the Internal Revenue Code, such amounts may be subject to information reporting under section 6049 if paid to a U.S. person who is not an exempt recipient described in §1.6049-4(c)(1)(ii) and to backup withholding under section 3406 in the absence of documentation. See §1.6049-5(d)(3)(iii) for applicable procedures when such amounts are paid to a foreign intermediary.

(4) *Applicable rules.*—The provisions in this paragraph (e)(4) describe procedures applicable to withholding certificates on Form W-8 or Form 8233 (or a substitute form) or documentary evidence furnished to establish foreign status. These provisions do not apply to Forms W-9 (or their substitutes). For corresponding provisions regarding Form W-9 (or a substitute form), see section 3406 and the regulations under that section.

(i) *Who may sign the certificate.*—(A) *In general.*—A withholding certificate (including an acceptable substitute) may be signed by any person authorized to sign a declaration under penalties of perjury on behalf of the person whose name is on the certificate as provided in section 6061 and the regulations under that section (relating to who may sign generally for an individual, estate, or trust, which includes certain agents who may sign returns and other documents), section 6062 and the regulations under that section (relating to who may sign corporate returns), and section 6063 and the regulations under that section (relating to who may sign partnership returns). A person authorized to sign a withholding certificate includes an officer or director of a corporation, a partner of a partnership, a trustee of a trust, an executor of an estate, any foreign equivalent of the former titles, and any other person that has been provided written authorization by the individual or entity named on the certificate to sign documentation on such person's behalf.

(B) *Electronic signatures.*—A withholding agent, regardless of whether the withholding agent has established an electronic system pursuant to paragraph (e)(4)(iv)(A) or (e)(4)(iv)(C) of this section, may accept a withholding certificate with an electronic signature, provided the electronic signature meets the requirements of paragraph (e)(4)(iv)(B)(3)(*ii*) of this section. In addition, the withholding certificate must reasonably demonstrate to the withholding agent that the form has been electronically signed by the recipient identified on the form (or a person authorized to sign for the recipient). For example, a withholding agent may treat as signed for purposes of the requirements for a valid withholding certificate, a withholding certificate that has in the signature block the name of the person authorized to sign, a time and date stamp, and a statement that the certificate has been electronically signed. However, a withholding agent may not treat a withholding certificate with a typed name in the signature line and no other information as signed for purposes of the requirements for a valid withholding certificate. A withholding agent may also rely upon, in addition to the contents of a withholding certificate, other documentation or information it has collected to support that a withholding certificate was electronically signed by the recipient identified on the form (or other person authorized to sign for the recipient), provided that the withholding agent does not have actual knowledge that the documentation or information is incorrect.

(ii) *Period of validity.*—(A) *General rule.*—*(1) Withholding certificates and documentary evidence.*—Except as provided otherwise in paragraphs (e)(4)(ii)(B) and (C) of this section and this paragraph (e)(4)(ii)(A), a withholding certificate described in paragraph (e)(2)(i) of this section, or a certificate described in § 1.871-14(c)(2)(v) (furnished to qualify interest as portfolio interest for purposes of sections 871(h) and 881(c)), will remain valid until the earlier of the last day of the third calendar year following the year in which the withholding certificate is signed or the day that a change in circumstances occurs that makes any information on the certificate incorrect. For example, a withholding certificate signed on September 30, 2015, remains valid through December 31, 2018, unless circumstances change that make the information on the form no longer correct. Documentary evidence described in § 1.6049-5(c)(1) provided to establish a payee's foreign status shall remain valid until the last day of the third calendar year following the year in which the documentary evidence is provided to the withholding agent except as provided in paragraph (e)(4)(ii)(B) of this section; however, if such documentary evidence contains an expiration date, it may be treated as valid until that expiration date if doing so would provide a longer period of validity than the three-year period. Additionally, a withholding certificate or documentary evidence with a period of validity that is valid on December 31, 2013, will not be treated as invalid based solely on the period described in this paragraph (e)(4)(ii) before January 1, 2015. Notwithstanding the validity periods prescribed by this paragraph (e)(4)(ii)(A) and paragraphs (e)(4)(ii)(B) and (C) of this section, a withholding certificate and documentary evidence will cease to be valid if a change in circumstances makes the information on the documentation incorrect.

(2) Documentary evidence for treaty claims and treaty statements.—Documentary evidence described in § 1.1441-6(c)(3) or (4) shall remain valid until the last day of the third calendar year following the year in which the documentary evidence is provided to the withholding agent, except as provided in paragraph (e)(4)(ii)(B) of this section. A statement regarding entitlement to treaty benefits described in § 1.1441-6(c)(5) (treaty statement) shall remain valid until the last day of the third calendar year following the year in which the treaty statement is provided to the withholding agent except as provided in this paragraph (e)(4)(ii)(A)(2). A treaty statement provided by an entity that identifies a limitation on benefits provision for a publicly traded corporation shall not expire at the time provided in the preceding sentence if a withholding agent determines, based on publicly available information at each time for which the treaty statement would otherwise be renewed, that the entity is publicly traded. Notwithstanding the second sentence of this paragraph (e)(4)(ii)(A)(2), a treaty statement provided by an entity that identifies a limitation on benefits provision for a government or tax-exempt organization (other than a tax-exempt pension trust or pension fund) shall remain valid indefinitely. Notwithstanding the validity periods (or exceptions thereto) prescribed in this paragraph (e)(4)(ii)(A)(2), a treaty statement will cease to be valid if a change in circumstances makes the information on the statement unreliable or incorrect. For accounts opened and treaty statements obtained prior to January 6, 2017 (including those from publicly traded corporations, governments, and tax-exempt organizations), the treaty statement will expire January 1, 2020.

(B) *Indefinite validity period.*—Notwithstanding paragraph (e)(4)(ii)(A) of this section, the certificates (or parts of certificates) and documentary evidence described in paragraphs (e)(4)(ii)(B)*(1)* through *(11)* of this section shall remain valid until a change in circumstances makes the information on the documentation incorrect under paragraph (e)(4)(ii)(D)*(3)*. See, however, § 1.1471-3(c)(6)(ii) for when a withholding certificate or documentary evidence remains valid (or is subject to renewal) when also provided with respect to a withholdable payment made to an entity (including an intermediary) for purposes of whether a withholding agent may continue to rely on the entity's claim of chapter 4 status. Additionally, the provisions of paragraphs (e)(4)(ii)(B)*(1)*, (2), and *(11)* of this section do not apply to documentary evidence or a withholding certificate furnished prior to July 1, 2014. (For documentary evidence or a withholding certificate furnished after December 31, 2000, and before July 1, 2014, see this section as in effect and contained in 26 CFR part 1, as revised April 1, 2013.)

(1) A beneficial owner withholding certificate (other than the portion of the certificate making a claim for treaty benefits) and documentary evidence supporting a claim of foreign status when both are provided together by an individual claiming foreign status, if the withholding agent does not have a current U.S. residence address or U.S. mailing address for the payee, does not have one or more current U.S. telephone numbers that are the only telephone numbers the withholding agent has for the payee, and, for a payment described in § 1.6049-5(c)(1), the withholding agent has not been provided standing instructions to make a payment to an account in the United States for the obligation. For purposes of the preceding sentence, a beneficial owner withholding certificate and documentary evidence supporting the individual's claim of foreign status will be treated as provided together if they are provided within 30 days of each other, regardless of which the withholding agent receives first.

(2) A beneficial owner withholding certificate (other than the portion of the certificate making a claim for treaty benefits) and documentary evidence provided by an entity supporting the entity's claim of foreign status, if both are received by the withholding agent before the validity period of either the withholding certificate or the documentary evidence would otherwise expire under paragraph (e)(4)(ii)(A) of this section. See, however, § 1.1471-3(c)(6)(ii) for rules regarding indefinite validity for chapter 4 purposes.

(3) A beneficial owner withholding certificate provided by an entity claiming status as a tax-exempt entity under section 501(c) that is not a foreign private foundation under section 509, provided that the withholding agent reports at least one payment annually to the entity under § 1.1461-1(c).

(4) A certificate described in paragraph (e)(3)(ii) of this section (a qualified intermediary withholding certificate) but not including the withholding certificates, documentary evidence, statements, or other information associated with the certificate.

(5) A certificate described in paragraph (e)(3)(iii) of this section (a nonqualified intermediary certificate), but not including the withholding certificates, documentary evidence, statements, or other information associated with the certificate.

(6) A certificate described in paragraph (e)(3)(v) of this section (a U.S. branch (including a territory financial institution) withholding certificate that is not provided by the beneficial owner), but not including the withholding certificates, documentary evidence, statements, or other information associated with the certificate.

(7) A certificate furnished by a person representing to be an integral part of a foreign government (within the meaning of § 1.892-2T(a)(2)) in accordance with § 1.1441-8(b), or by a person representing to be a foreign central bank of issue (within the meaning of § 1.861-2(b)(4)) or the Bank for International Settlements in accordance with § 1.1441-8(c)(1).

(8) A withholding certificate provided by a withholding foreign trust described in § 1.1441-5(e)(5)(v).

(9) A certificate described in § 1.1441-5(c)(2)(iv) (dealing with a certificate from a person representing to be a withholding foreign partnership).

(10) A certificate described in § 1.1441-5(c)(3)(iii) (a withholding certificate from a nonwithholding foreign partnership) or in § 1.1441-5(e)(5)(iii) (a withholding certificate of a foreign simple or foreign grantor trust) but not including the withholding certificates, documentary evidence, statements, or other information required to be associated with the certificate; and

(11) Documentary evidence that is not generally renewed or amended (such as a certificate of incorporation).

(C) *Withholding certificate for effectively connected income.*—Notwithstanding paragraph (e)(4)(ii)(B) of this section, the period of validity of a withholding certificate furnished to a withholding agent to claim a reduced rate of withholding for income that is effectively connected with the conduct of a trade or business within the United States shall be limited to the three-year period described in paragraph (e)(4)(ii)(A) of this section.

(D) *Change in circumstances.—(1) Defined.*—A certificate or documentation becomes invalid from the date of a change in circumstances affecting the correctness of the certificate or documentation to the extent provided in this paragraph (e)(4)(ii)(D). For purposes of this section, a person is considered to have a change in circumstances only if such change affects the person's claim of chapter 3 status. Thus, for example, a change of address is not a change in circumstances with respect to a claim of only foreign status under this paragraph (e)(4)(ii)(D) if the change is to another address outside the United States, but is a change in circumstances if the change is to an address in the United States. However, see paragraph (e)(2)(ii)(B)(*1*) of this section for a special rule for a change of address for purposes of reliance on a foreign TIN (or a reasonable explanation for the absence of a foreign TIN) included on a beneficial owner withholding certificate.

(2) Obligation to notify a withholding agent of a change in circumstances.—If a change in circumstances makes any information on a certificate or other documentary evidence incorrect, then the person whose name is on the certificate or other documentation must inform the withholding agent within 30 days of the change and furnish a new certificate or new documentary evidence. If an intermediary (including a U.S. branch or territory financial institution described in paragraph (b)(2)(iv)(A) of this section) or a flow-through entity becomes aware that a certificate or other appropriate documentation it has furnished to the person from whom it collects a payment is no longer valid because of a change in the circumstances of the person who issued the certificate or furnished the other appropriate documentation, then the intermediary or flow-through entity must notify the person from whom it collects the payment of the change of circumstances within 30 days of the date that it knows or has reason to know of the change in circumstances. It must also obtain a new withholding certificate or new appropriate documentation to replace the existing certificate or documentation the validity of which has expired due to the change in circumstances to continue to treat the person who provided the certificate or documentary evidence under its claimed chapter 3 status.

(3) Withholding agent's obligation with respect to a change in circumstances.—A withholding agent may rely on a certificate without having to inquire into possible changes of circumstances that may affect the validity of the statement, unless it knows or has reason to know that circumstances have changed, as permitted under paragraph (e)(4)(viii) of this section. A withholding agent is required to notify any person providing documentary evidence (in lieu of a withholding certificate) of the person's obligation to notify the withholding agent of a change in circumstances. However, a withholding agent may choose to apply the provisions of paragraph (b)(3)(iv) of this section regarding the 90-day grace period as of that date while awaiting a new certificate or documentation or while seeking information regarding changes, or suspected changes, in the person's circumstances. A withholding agent may also require a new certificate at any time prior to a payment, even though the withholding agent has no actual knowledge or reason to know that any information stated on the certificate has changed.

(iii) *Retention of documentation.*—A withholding agent must retain each withholding certificate and other documentation for purposes of this section for as long as it may be relevant to the determination of the withholding agent's tax liability under section 1461 and §1.1461-1. A withholding agent may retain a withholding certificate or documentary evidence that is an original, certified copy, or a scanned document (as described in paragraph (e)(4)(iv)(D) of this section). A withholding agent may also retain a withholding certificate by other means (such as microfiche) that allows a reproduction of the document provided that the withholding agent has recorded its receipt of a form described in the preceding sentence and is able to produce a hard copy of the form. See §1.6049-5(c)(1) for the requirements for maintaining documentary evidence that also apply for purposes of determining a payee's U.S. or foreign status for purposes of chapter 3.

(iv) *Electronic transmission of information.*—(A) *In general.*—A withholding agent may establish a system for a beneficial owner or payee to electronically furnish a Form W-8, an acceptable substitute Form W-8, or such other form as the IRS may prescribe. The system must meet the requirements described in paragraph (e)(4)(iv)(B) of this section. See paragraph (e)(4)(iv)(D) of this section for other cases in which a Form W-8 (or other documentation) may be furnished electronically.

(B) *Requirements.—(1) In general.*—The electronic system must ensure that the information received is the information sent, and must document all occasions of user access that result in the submission renewal, or modification of a Form W-8. In addition, the design and operation of the electronic system, including access procedures, must make it reasonably certain that the person accessing the system and furnishing Form W-8 is the person named in the Form.

(2) Same information as paper Form W-8.—The electronic transmission must provide the withholding agent or payor with exactly the same information as the paper Form W-8.

(3) Perjury statement and signature requirements.—The electronic transmission must contain an electronic signature by the person whose name is on the Form W-8 and the signature must be under penalties of perjury in the manner described in this paragraph (e)(4)(iv)(B)(*3*).

(i) Perjury statement.—The perjury statement must contain the language that appears on the paper Form W-8. The electronic system must inform the person whose name is on the Form W-8 that the person must make the declaration contained in the perjury statement and that the declaration is made by signing the Form W-8. The instructions and the language of the perjury statement must immediately follow the person's certifying statements and immediately precede the person's electronic signature.

(ii) Electronic signature.—The act of the electronic signature must be effected by the person whose name is on the electronic Form W-8. The signature must also authenticate and verify the submission. For this purpose, the terms *authenticate* and *verify* have the same meanings as they do when applied to a written signature on a paper Form W-8. An electronic signature can be in any form that satisfies the foregoing requirements. The electronic signature must be the final entry in the person's Form W-8 submission.

(4) Requests for electronic Form W-8 data.—Upon request by the Internal Revenue Service during an examination, the withholding agent must supply a hard copy of the electronic Form W-8 and a statement that, to the best of the withholding agent's knowledge, the electronic Form W-8 was filed by the person whose name is on the form. The hard copy of the electronic Form W-8 must provide exactly the same information as, but need not be identical to, the paper Form W-8.

(C) *Form 8233.*—A withholding agent may establish a system for a beneficial owner or payee to provide Form 8233 electronically, provided the system meets the requirements of paragraph (e)(4)(iv)(B)(*1*) through (*4*) of this section (replacing "Form W-8" with "Form 8233" each place it appears).

(D) *Forms and documentary evidence received by facsimile or email.*—A withholding agent may rely upon an otherwise valid Form W-8 (or documentary evidence) received by facsimile or a form or document scanned and received electronically, such as, for example, an image embedded in an email or as a Portable Document Format (.pdf) attached to an email. A withholding agent may not rely on a form or document received by such means, however, if the withholding agent knows that the form or document was transmitted to the withholding agent by a person not authorized to do so by the person required to execute the form. A withholding agent may establish other procedures to authenticate and verify a form or document sent by such means and may reject any form or document that fails to satisfy the requirements of such procedures. A taxpayer may apply this paragraph (e)(4)(iv)(D) to all of its open tax years, including tax years that are currently under examination by the IRS.

(E) *Third party repositories.*—A withholding certificate will be considered furnished for purposes of this section (including paragraph (e)(1)(ii)(A)(*1*) of this section) by the person providing the certificate, and a withholding agent may rely on an otherwise valid withholding certificate received electronically from a third party repository, if the withholding certificate was uploaded or provided to a third party repository and there are processes in place to ensure that the withholding certificate can be reliably associated with a specific request from the withholding agent and a specific authorization from the person providing the certificate (or an agent of the person providing the certificate) for the withholding agent making the request to receive the withholding certificate. For purposes of the preceding sentence, a withholding agent must be able to reliably associate each payment with a specific request and authorization except when the withholding agent is permitted to rely on the withholding certificate on an obligation-by-obligation basis or as otherwise permitted under paragraph (e)(4)(ix) of this section (treating the withholding certificate as obtained by the withholding agent and furnished by a customer for purposes of this paragraph (e)(4)(iv)(E)). A third party repository may also be used for withholding statements, and a withholding agent may also rely on an otherwise valid withholding statement, if the intermediary providing the withholding certificates and withholding statement through the repository provides an updated withholding statement in the event of any change in the information previously provided (for example, a change in the composition of a partnership or a change in the allocation of payments to the partners) and ensures there are processes in place to update withholding agents when there is a new withholding statement (and withholding certificates, as necessary) in the event of any change that would affect the validity of the prior withholding certificates or withholding statement. A third party repository, for purposes of this paragraph, is an entity that maintains withholding certificates (including certificates accompanied by withholding statements) but is not an agent of the applicable withholding agent or the person providing the certificate.

(F) *Examples.*—This paragraph contains examples to illustrate the rules of paragraph (e)(4)(iv)(E) of this section.

(*1*) *Example 1.* A, a foreign corporation, completes a Form W-8BEN-E and a Form W-8ECI and uploads the forms to X, a third party repository (X is an entity that maintains withholding certificates on an electronic data aggregation site). WA, a withholding agent, enters into a contract with A under which it will make payments to A of U.S. source FDAP that are not effectively connected with A's conduct of a trade or business in the United States. X is not an agent of WA or A. Before receiving a payment, A sends WA an email with a link that authorizes WA to access A's Form W-8BEN-E on X's system. The link does not authorize WA to access A's Form W-8ECI. X's system meets the requirements of a third party repository, and WA can treat the Form W-8BEN-E as furnished by A.

(*2*) *Example 2.* The facts are the same as Example 1 of this paragraph (e)(4)(iv)(F), and WA and A enter into a second contract under which WA will make payments to A that are effectively connected with A's conduct of a trade or business in the United States. A sends WA an email with a link that gives WA access to A's Form W-8ECI on X's system. The link in this second email does not give WA access to A's Form W-8BEN-E. A's email also clearly indicates that the link is associated with payments received under the second contract. X's system meets the requirements of a third party repository, and WA can treat the Form W-8ECI as furnished by A.

(*3*) *Example 3.* FP is a foreign partnership that is acting on behalf of its partners, A and B, who are both foreign individuals. FP completes a Form W-8IMY and uploads it to X, a third party repository. FP also uploads Forms W-8BEN from both A and B and a valid withholding statement allocating 50% of the payment to A and 50% to B. WA is a withholding agent that makes payments to FP as an intermediary for A and B. FP sends WA an email with a link to its Form W-8IMY on X's system. The link also provides WA access to FP's withholding statement and A's and B's Forms W-8BEN. FP also has processes in place that ensure it will provide a new withholding statement or withholding certificate to X's repository in the event of a change in the information previously provided that affects the validity of the withholding statement and that ensure it will update WA if there is a new withholding statement. X's system meets the requirements of a third party repository, and WA can treat the Form W-8IMY (and withholding statement) as furnished by FP. In addition, because FP is acting as an agent of A and B, the beneficial owners, WA can treat the Forms W-8BEN for A and B as furnished by A and B.

(v) *Additional procedures for certificates provided electronically.*—The IRS may prescribe procedures in a revenue procedure (see § 601.601(d)(2) of this chapter) or may issue other appropriate guidance (including a written directive for revenue agents) to further prescribe the conditions by which the IRS will determine that a system developed by a withholding agent to permit beneficial owners and payees to provide Forms W-8 electronically satisfies the requirements of paragraph (e)(4)(iv)(B) of this section.

(vi) *Acceptable substitute form.*—A withholding agent may substitute its own form instead of an official Form W-8 or 8233 (or such other official form as the IRS may prescribe). Such a substitute for an official form will be acceptable if it contains provisions that are substantially similar to those of the official form, it contains the same certifications relevant to the transactions as are contained on the official form and these certifications are clearly set forth, and the substitute form includes a signature-under penalties-of-perjury statement identical to the one stated on the official form. The substitute form is acceptable even if it does not contain all of the provisions contained on the official form, so long as it contains those provisions that are relevant to the transaction for which it is furnished (including those required for purposes of chapter 4). For example, a withholding agent that pays no income for which treaty benefits are claimed may develop a substitute form that is identical to the official form, except that it does not include information regarding claims of benefits under an income tax treaty. Similarly, a withholding agent that is not required to determine the chapter 4 status of a payee providing a form may develop a substitute form that does not contain chapter 4 statuses. A withholding agent who uses a substitute form must furnish instructions relevant to the substitute form only to the extent and in the manner specified in the instructions to the official form. A withholding agent may use a substitute form that is written in a language other than English and may accept a form that is filled out in a language other than English, but the withholding agent must make available an English translation of the form and its contents to the IRS upon request. A withholding agent may refuse to accept a certificate from a payee or beneficial owner (including the official Form W-8 or 8233) if the certificate provided is not an acceptable substitute form provided by the withholding agent, but only if the withholding agent furnishes the payee or beneficial owner with an acceptable substitute form within 5 business days of receipt of an unacceptable form from the payee or beneficial owner. In that case, the substitute form is acceptable only if it contains a notice that the withholding agent has refused to accept the form submitted by the payee or beneficial owner and that the payee or beneficial owner must submit the acceptable form provided by the withholding agent in order for the payee or beneficial owner to be treated as having furnished the required withholding certificate.

(vii) *Requirement of taxpayer identifying number.*—A TIN must be stated on a withholding certificate when required by this paragraph (e)(4)(vii) for the withholding certificate to be valid for purposes of this section. A TIN is required to be stated on—

(A) A withholding certificate on which a beneficial owner is claiming the benefit of a reduced rate under an income tax treaty (other than for amounts described in § 1.1441-6(c)(2) or amounts for which a foreign tax identifying number has been provided, as described in § 1.1441-6(c)(2));

(B) A withholding certificate on which a beneficial owner is claiming exemption from withholding because income is effectively connected with a U.S. trade or business;

(C) A withholding certificate on which a beneficial owner is claiming exemption from withholding under section 871(f) for certain annuities received under qualified plans;

(D) A withholding certificate on which a beneficial owner is claiming an exemption based solely on a foreign organization's claim of tax exempt status under section 501(c) or private foundation status (however, a TIN is not required from a foreign private foundation that is subject to the 4-percent tax under section 4948(a) on income if that income would be exempt from withholding but for section 4948(a) (e.g., portfolio interest));

(E) A withholding certificate from a person representing to be a qualified intermediary described in paragraph (e)(5)(ii) of this section;

(F) A withholding certificate from a person representing to be a withholding foreign partnership or a withholding foreign trust;

(G) A withholding certificate provided by a foreign organization that is described in section 501(c);

(H) A withholding certificate from a person representing to be a U.S. branch or territory financial institution described in paragraph (b)(2)(iv) of this section; and

(I) A withholding certificate provided by an entity acting as a qualified securities lender, as defined for purposes of chapter 3, with respect to a substitute dividend paid in a securities lending or similar transaction.

(viii) *Reliance rules.*—A withholding agent may rely on the information and certifications stated on withholding certificates or other documentation without having to inquire into the veracity of this information or certification, unless it has actual knowledge or reason to know that the information or certification is incorrect. In the case of amounts described in § 1.1441-6(c)(2), a withholding agent described in § 1.1441-7(b)(3) has reason to know that the information or certifications on a certificate are incorrect only to the extent provided in § 1.1441-7(b)(4) through (6). See § 1.1441-6(b)(1) for reliance on representations regarding eligibility for a reduced rate under an income tax treaty. Paragraphs (e)(4)(viii)(A) and (B) of this section provide examples of such reliance.

(A) *Classification.*—A withholding agent may rely on the claim of entity classification indicated on the withholding certificate that it receives from or for the beneficial owner, unless it has actual knowledge or reason to know that the classification claimed is incorrect. A withholding agent may not rely on a person's claim of classification other than as a corporation if the name of the corporation indicates that the person is a per se corporation described in § 301.7701-2(b)(8)(i) of this chapter unless the certificate contains a statement that the person is a grandfathered per se corporation described in § 301.7701-2(b)(8) of this chapter and that its grandfathered status has not been terminated. In the absence of reliable representation or information regarding the classification of the payee or beneficial owner, see § 1.1441-1(b)(3)(ii) for applicable presumptions.

(B) *Status of payee as an intermediary or as a person acting for its own account.*—A withholding agent may rely on the type of certificate furnished as indicative of the payee's status as an intermediary or as an owner, unless the withholding agent has actual knowledge or reason to know otherwise. For example, a withholding agent that receives a beneficial owner withholding certificate from a foreign financial institution may treat the institution as the beneficial owner, unless it has information in its records that would indicate otherwise or the certificate contains information that is not consistent with beneficial owner status (*e.g.*, sub-account numbers that do not correspond to accounts maintained by the withholding agent for such person or names of one or more persons other than the person submitting the withholding certificate). If the financial institution also acts as an intermediary, the withholding agent may request that the institution furnish two certificates, *i.e.*, a beneficial owner certificate described in paragraph (e)(2)(i) of this section for the amounts that it receives as a beneficial owner, and an intermediary withholding certificate described in paragraph (e)(3)(i) of this section for the amounts that it receives as an intermediary. In the absence of reliable representation or information regarding the status of the payee as an owner or as an intermediary, see paragraph (b)(3)(v)(A) for applicable presumptions.

(C) *Reliance on a prior version of a withholding certificate.*—Upon the issuance by the IRS of an updated version of a withholding certificate, a withholding agent may continue to accept the prior version of the withholding certificate until the later of six full months after the revision date shown on the updated withholding certificate or the end of the calendar year the updated withholding certificate is issued, unless the IRS has issued guidance that indicates that the period for accepting a prior version is shortened or extended (including in the instructions to the form), such as when there is a new payee status required to be established using the form. A withholding agent may continue to rely upon a previously signed prior version of the withholding certificate until its period of validity expires.

(ix) *Certificates to be furnished to withholding agent for each obligation unless exception applies.*—Unless otherwise provided in paragraphs (e)(4)(ix)(A) through (D) of this section, a withholding agent that is a financial institution with which a customer may open an account shall obtain a withholding certificate or documentary evidence on an obligation-by-obligation basis and may not rely upon such documentation collected by another person or another branch of the withholding agent.

(A) *Exception for certain branch or account systems or system maintained by agent.*—A withholding agent may rely on a withholding certificate or documentary evidence furnished by a customer as part of a single branch system, universal account system, or shared account system described in § 1.1471-3(c)(8) (substituting the term chapter 3 status for chapter 4 status each place it appears in that paragraph). Furthermore, a withholding agent may rely on a shared documentation system maintained by an agent as described in § 1.1471-3(c)(9)(i) (also substituting the term chapter 3 status for chapter 4 status each place it appears in that paragraph).

(B) *Reliance on certification provided by introducing brokers.*—*(1) In general.*—A withholding agent may rely on the certification of a broker indicating the broker's determination of a payee's chapter 3 status and that the broker holds a valid beneficial owner withholding certificate described in paragraph (e)(2)(i) of this section or other appropriate documentation for that beneficial owner with respect to any readily tradable instrument, as defined in § 31.3406(h)-1(d) of this chapter, if the broker is a United States person (including a U.S. branch treated as a U.S. person under paragraph (b)(2)(iv) of this section) that is acting as the agent of a beneficial owner. A withholding agent may also rely on a certification described in the preceding sentence that is provided by a qualified intermediary that makes payments to beneficial owners that it receives from the withholding agent. The certification must be in writing or in electronic form and contain all of the information required of a nonqualified intermediary under paragraphs (e)(3)(iv)(B) and (C) of this section. If a broker chooses to use this paragraph (e)(4)(ix)(B), that broker will be solely responsible for applying the rules of § 1.1441-7(b) to the withholding certificates or other appropriate documentation and shall be liable for any underwithholding as a result of the broker's failure to apply such rules. See § 1.1471-3(c)(9)(iii) for a similar allowance that applies to a broker's determination of a payee's chapter 4 status for purposes of chapter 4. For purposes of this paragraph (e)(4)(ix)(B), the term *broker* means a person treated as a broker under § 1.6045-1(a).

(2) Example.—The following example illustrates the rules of this paragraph (e)(4)(x)(B) with respect to a U.S. broker:

Example. SCO is a U.S. securities clearing organization that provides clearing services for correspondent broker, CB, a U.S. corporation. Pursuant to a fully disclosed clearing agreement, CB fully discloses the identity of each of its customers to SCO. Part of SCO's clearing duties include the crediting of income and gross proceeds of readily tradable instruments (as defined in § 31.3406(h)-1(d)) to each customer's account. For each disclosed customer that is a foreign beneficial owner, CB provides SCO with information required under paragraphs (e)(3)(iv)(B) and (C) of this section that is necessary to apply the correct rate of withholding and to file Forms 1042-S. SCO may use the representations and beneficial owner information provided by CB to determine the proper amount of withholding and to file Forms 1042-S. CB is responsible for determining the validity of the withholding certificates or other appropriate documentation under § 1.1441-1(b).

(C) *Reliance on documentation and certifications provided between principals and agents.*—*(1) Withholding agent as agent.*—A withholding agent that acts on behalf of a principal may rely upon documentation (or copies of documentation) obtained from the principal, and, with respect to a principal that is a U.S. withholding agent, a qualified intermediary (when acting as such for determining a payee's status), or a withholding foreign partnership or withholding foreign trust with respect to a partner, owner, or beneficiary in the partnership or trust, the withholding agent may rely upon certification provided by the principal for purposes of determining a payee's chapter 3 status. Thus an agent (such as a paying agent or transfer agent) may not rely upon a certification provided by a principal that is a participating FFI but is not also a qualified intermediary, withholding foreign partnership, or withholding foreign trust for purposes of this section, even though it may rely on the certification when provided solely for purposes of chapter 4 under § 1.1471-3(c)(9)(iv).

(2) Withholding agent as principal.—A withholding agent may also rely on documentation collected by an agent of the withholding agent in order to fulfill its chapter 3 obligations because such agent's actions are imputed to the principal (the withholding agent). For example, a withholding agent may contract an agent to collect Forms W-8 from account holders on its behalf, but the withholding agent remains liable for any tax liability resulting from a failure of the agent to comply with the requirements of chapter 3.

(D) *Reliance upon documentation for accounts acquired in merger or bulk acquisition for value.*—A withholding agent that acquires an account from a predecessor or transferor in a merger or bulk acquisition of accounts for value is permitted to rely upon valid documentation (or copies of valid documentation) collected by the predecessor or transferor for determining the chapter 3 status of an account holder of such an account. In addition, a withholding agent that acquires an account in a merger or bulk acquisition of accounts for value, other than a related party transaction, from a U.S. withholding agent (or a qualified intermediary when the withholding agent is also a qualified intermediary) may also rely upon the predecessor's or transferor's determination of the account holder's chapter 3 status for a transition period of the lesser of six months from the date of the merger or until the acquirer knows that the claim of entity classification and status is inaccurate or a change in circumstances occurs with respect to the account. At the end of the transition period, the acquirer will be permitted to rely upon the predecessor's determination as to the chapter 3 status of the account holder only if the documentation that the acquirer has for the account holder, including documentation obtained from the predecessor or transferor, supports the status claimed. An acquirer that discovers at the end of the transition period that the chapter 3 status assigned by the predecessor or transferor to the account holder was incorrect and has not withheld as it would have been required to but for its reliance upon the predecessor's determination, will be required to withhold on future payments, if any, made to the account holder the amount of tax that should have been withheld during the transition period but for the erroneous classification as to the account holder's status. For purposes of this paragraph (e)(4)(ix)(D), a related party transaction is a merger or sale of accounts in which the acquirer is in the same expanded affiliated group, within the meaning of § 1.1471-5(i)(2), as the predecessor or transferor either prior to or after the merger or acquisition or the predecessor or transferor (or shareholders of the predecessor or transferor) obtain a controlling interest in the acquirer or in a newly formed entity created for purposes of the merger or acquisition. See § 1.1471-3(c)(9)(v) for a similar reliance rule that applies for purposes of chapter 4.

(5) *Qualified intermediaries.*—(i) *In general.*—A qualified intermediary, as defined in paragraph (e)(5)(ii) of this section, may furnish a qualified intermediary withholding certificate to a withholding agent. The withholding certificate provides certifications on behalf of other persons for the purpose of claiming and verifying reduced rates of withholding under section 1441 or 1442 and for the purpose of reporting and withholding under other provisions of the Code, such as the provisions under chapter 61 and section 3406 (and the regulations under those provisions), or for the qualified derivative dealer (if applicable). Furnishing such a certificate is in lieu of transmitting to a withholding agent withholding certificates or other appropriate documentation for the persons for whom the qualified intermediary receives the payment, including interest holders in a qualified intermediary that is fiscally transparent under the regulations under section 894. Although the qualified intermediary is required to obtain withholding certificates or other appropriate documentation from beneficial owners, payees, or interest holders pursuant to its agreement with the IRS, it is generally not required to attach such documentation to the intermediary withholding certificate. Notwithstanding the preceding sentence, a qualified intermediary must provide a withholding agent with the Forms W-9, or disclose the names, addresses, and taxpayer identifying numbers, if known, of those U.S. non-exempt recipients for whom the qualified intermediary receives reportable amounts (within the meaning of paragraph (e)(3)(vi) of this section) to the extent required in the qualified intermediary's agreement with the IRS. When a qualified intermediary is acting as a qualified derivatives dealer, the withholding certificate entitles a withholding agent to make payments with respect to potential section 871(m) transactions that are not underlying securities and dividend equivalent payments on underlying securities to the qualified derivatives dealer free of withholding. A withholding agent is required to withhold on all other U.S. source FDAP payments made to a qualified derivatives dealer as required by applicable law. Paragraph (e)(6) of this section contains detailed rules prescribing the circumstances in which a qualified intermediary can act as a qualified derivatives dealer. A person may claim qualified intermediary status before an agreement is executed with the IRS if it has applied for such status and the IRS authorizes such status on an interim basis under such procedures as the IRS may prescribe.

(ii) *Definition of qualified intermediary.*—With respect to a payment to a foreign person, the term qualified intermediary means a person that is a party to a withholding agreement with the IRS where such person is—

(A) A foreign financial institution that is a participating FFI (including a reporting Model 2 FFI), a registered deemed-compliant FFI (including a reporting Model 1 FFI), an FFI treated as a deemed-compliant FFI under an applicable IGA that is subject to due diligence and reporting requirements with respect to its U.S. accounts similar to those applicable to a registered deemed-compliant FFI under § 1.1471-5(f)(1), excluding a U.S. branch of any of the foregoing entities, or any other category of FFI identified in a qualified intermediary withholding agreement as eligible to act as a qualified intermediary;

(B) A foreign branch or office of a U.S. financial institution or a foreign branch or office of a U.S. clearing organization that is either a reporting Model 1 FFI or agrees to the reporting requirements applicable to a participating FFI with respect to its U.S. accounts;

(C) A foreign person that is a home office or has a branch that is an eligible entity as described in paragraph (e)(6)(ii) of this section, without regard to the requirement that the person be a qualified intermediary; or

(D) Any other person acceptable to the IRS.

(iii) *Withholding agreement.*—(A) *In general.*—The IRS may, upon request, enter into a withholding agreement with a foreign person described in paragraph (e)(5)(ii) of this section pursuant to such procedures as the IRS may prescribe in published guidance (see § 601.601(d)(2) of this chapter). Under the withholding agreement, a qualified intermediary shall generally be subject to the applicable withholding and reporting provisions applicable to withholding agents and payors under chapters 3, 4, and 61 of the Code, section 3406, the regulations under those provisions, and other withholding provisions of the Code, except to the extent provided under the agreement.

(B) *Terms of the withholding agreement.*—The withholding agreement shall specify the obligations of the qualified intermediary under chapters 3 and 4 including, for a qualified intermediary that is an FFI, the documentation, withholding, and reporting obligations required of a participating FFI or registered deemed-compliant FFI (including a reporting Model 1 FFI as defined in § 1.1471-1(b)(114)) with respect to each branch of the qualified intermediary other than a U.S. branch that is treated as a U.S. person under paragraph (b)(2)(iv)(A) of this section. The withholding agreement will specify the type of certifications and documentation upon which the qualified intermediary may rely to ascertain the classification (*e.g.*, corporation or partnership), status (*i.e.*, U.S. or foreign and chapter 4 status) of beneficial owners and payees who receive reportable amounts, reportable payments, and withholdable payments collected by the qualified intermediary for purposes of chapters 3, 4, and 61, section 3406, and, if necessary, entitlement to the benefits of a reduced rate under an income tax treaty. The withholding agreement shall specify if, and to what extent, the qualified intermediary may assume primary withholding responsibility in accordance with paragraph (e)(5)(iv) of this section. It shall also specify the extent to which applicable return filing and information reporting requirements are modified so that, in appropriate cases, the qualified intermediary may report payments to the IRS on an aggregated basis, without having to disclose the identity of beneficial owners and payees. However, the qualified intermediary may be required to provide to the IRS the name and address of those foreign customers who benefit from a reduced rate under an income tax treaty pursuant to the withholding agreement for purposes of verifying entitlement to such benefits, particularly under an applicable limitation on benefits provision. Under the withholding agreement, a qualified intermediary may agree to act as an acceptance agent to perform the duties described in § 301.6109-1(d)(3)(iv)(A) of this chapter. The withholding agreement may specify the manner in which applicable procedures for adjustments for underwithholding and overwithholding, including refund procedures, apply to qualified intermediaries and the extent to which applicable procedures may be modified. In particular, a withholding agreement may allow a qualified intermediary to claim refunds of overwithheld amounts. In addition, the withholding agreement shall specify the manner in which the IRS will verify compliance with the agreement, including the time and manner for which a qualified intermediary will be required to certify to the IRS regarding its compliance with the withholding agreement (including its performance of a periodic review) and the types of information required to be disclosed as part of the certification. In appropriate cases, the IRS may require review procedures be performed by an approved reviewer (in addition to those performed as part of the periodic review) and may conduct a review of the reviewer's findings. The withholding agreement may include provisions for the assessment and collection of tax in the event that failure to comply with the terms of the withholding agreement results in the failure by the withholding agent or the qualified intermediary to withhold and deposit the required amount of tax. Further, the withholding agreement may specify the procedures by which amounts withheld are to be deposited, if different from the deposit procedures under the Code and applicable regulations. To determine whether to enter a withholding agreement and the terms of any particular withholding agreement, the IRS will consider the type of local know-your-customer laws and practices to which the entity is subject (if the entity is an FFI), as well as the extent and nature of supervisory and regulatory control exercised under the laws of the foreign country over the foreign entity.

(iv) *Assignment of primary withholding responsibility.*—Any person (whether a U.S. person or a foreign person) who meets the definition of a withholding agent under § 1.1441-7(a) (for payments subject to chapter 3 withholding) and § 1.1473-1(d) (for withholdable payments) is required to withhold and deposit any amount withheld under §§ 1.1461-1(a) and 1.1474-1(b) and to make the returns prescribed by §§1.1461-1(b) and (c), and by 1.1474-1(c), and (d). Under its qualified intermediary withholding agreement, a qualified intermediary may, however, inform a withholding agent from which it receives a payment that it will assume the primary obligation to withhold, deposit, and report amounts under chapters 3 and 4 of the Code and/or under chapter 61 and section 3406 of the Code. For assuming withholding obligations as described in the previous sentence, a qualified intermediary that assumes primary withholding responsibility for payments made to an account under chapter 3 is also required to assume primary withholding responsibility under chapter 4 for payments made to the account that are withholdable payments. Additionally, a qualified intermediary may represent that it assumes chapter 61 reporting and section 3406 obligations for a payment when the qualified intermediary meets the requirements of §1.6049-4(c)(4)(i) or (ii) for the payment. If a withholding agent makes a payment of an amount subject to withholding under chapter 3, a reportable payment (as defined in section 3406(b)), or a withholdable payment to a qualified intermediary that represents to the withholding agent that it has assumed primary withholding responsibility for the payment, the withholding agent is not required to withhold on the payment. The withholding agent is not required to determine that the qualified intermediary actually performs its primary withholding responsibilities. A qualified intermediary that assumes primary withholding responsibility under chapters 3 and 4 or primary reporting and backup withholding responsibility under chapter 61 and section 3406 is not required to assume primary withholding responsibility for all accounts it has with a withholding agent but must assume primary withholding responsibility for all payments made to any one account that it has with the withholding agent.

(v) *Withholding statement.*—(A) *In general.*—A qualified intermediary must provide each withholding agent from which it receives reportable amounts as a qualified intermediary with a written statement (the withholding statement) containing the information specified in paragraph (e)(5)(v)(B) of this section. A withholding statement is not required, however, if all of the information a withholding agent needs to fulfill its withholding and reporting requirements is contained in the withholding certificate. The qualified intermediary withholding agreement will require the qualified intermediary to include information in its withholding statement relating to withholdable payments for purposes of withholding under chapter 4 as described in paragraph (e)(5)(v)(C)(2) of this section. The withholding statement forms an integral part of the qualified intermediary's qualified intermediary withholding certificate, and the penalties of perjury statement provided on the withholding certificate shall apply to the withholding statement as well. The withholding statement may be provided in any manner, and in any form, to which qualified intermediary and the withholding agent mutually agree, including electronically. If the withholding statement is provided electronically, the statement must satisfy the requirements described in paragraph (e)(3)(iv) of this section (applicable to a withholding statement provided by a nonqualified intermediary). The withholding statement shall be updated as often as necessary for the withholding agent to meet its reporting and withholding obligations under chapters 3, 4, and 61 and section 3406. For purposes of this section, a withholding agent will be liable for tax, interest, and penalties in accordance with paragraph (b)(7) of this section to the extent it does not follow the presumption rules of paragraph (b)(3) of this section, §§1.1441-5(d) and (e)(6), and 1.6049-5(d) for a payment, or portion thereof, for which it does not have a valid withholding statement prior to making a payment.

(B) *Content of withholding statement.*—The withholding statement must contain sufficient information for a withholding agent to apply the correct rate of withholding on payments from the accounts identified on the statement and to properly report such payments on Forms 1042-S and Forms 1099, as applicable. The withholding statement must—

(1) Designate those accounts for which the qualified intermediary acts as a qualified intermediary;

(2) Designate those accounts for which qualified intermediary assumes primary withholding responsibility under chapter 3 and chapter 4 of the Code and/or primary reporting and backup withholding responsibility under chapter 61 and section 3406;

(3) If applicable, designate those accounts for which the qualified intermediary is acting as a qualified securities lender with respect to a substitute dividend paid in a securities lending or similar transaction;

(4) If a qualified intermediary is acting as a qualified derivatives dealer, designate the accounts:

(i) For which the qualified derivatives dealer is receiving payments with respect to potential section 871(m) transactions or underlying securities as a qualified derivatives dealer;

(ii) For which the qualified derivatives dealer is receiving payments with respect to potential section 871(m) transactions (and that are not underlying securities) for which withholding is not required;

(iii) For which qualified derivatives dealer is receiving payments with respect to underlying securities for which withholding is required; and

(iv) If applicable, identifying the home office or branch that is treated as the owner for U.S. federal income tax purposes; and

(5) Provide information regarding withholding rate pools, as described in paragraph (e)(5)(v)(C) of this section.

(C) *Withholding rate pools.*—*(1) In general.*—Except to the extent it has assumed both primary withholding responsibility under chapters 3 and 4 of the Code and primary Form 1099 reporting and backup withholding responsibility under chapter 61 and section 3406 with respect to a payment, a qualified intermediary shall provide as part of its withholding statement the chapter 3 withholding rate pool information that is required for the withholding agent to meet its withholding and reporting obligations under chapters 3 and 61 of the Code and section 3406. See, however, paragraph (e)(5)(v)(C)(2) of this section for when a qualified intermediary may provide a chapter 4 withholding rate pool (as described in paragraph (c)(48) of this section) with respect to a payment that is a withholdable payment. A chapter 3 withholding rate pool is a payment of a single type of income, determined in accordance with the categories of income reported on Form 1042-S, that is subject to a single rate of withholding paid to a payee that is a foreign person and for which withholding under chapter 4 does not apply. A chapter 3 withholding rate pool may be established by any reasonable method on which the qualified intermediary and a withholding agent agree (*e.g.*, by establishing a separate account for a single chapter 3 withholding rate pool, or by dividing a payment made to a single account into portions allocable to each chapter 3 withholding rate pool). A qualified intermediary may include a separate pool for account holders that are U.S. exempt recipients or may include such accounts in a chapter 3 withholding rate pool to which withholding does not apply. The withholding statement must identify the chapter 4 exemption code (as provided in the instructions to Form 1042-S) applicable to the chapter 3 withholding rate pools contained on the withholding statement. To the extent a qualified intermediary does not assume primary Form 1099 reporting and backup withholding responsibility under chapter 61 and section 3406, a qualified intermediary's withholding statement must establish a separate withholding rate pool for each U.S. non-exempt recipient account holder that the qualified intermediary has disclosed to the withholding agent unless the qualified intermediary uses the alternative procedures in paragraph (e)(5)(v)(C)(3) of this section or the account holder is a payee that the qualified intermediary is permitted to include in a chapter 4 withholding rate pool of U.S. payees. A qualified intermediary that is a participating FFI or registered deemed-compliant FFI may include a chapter 4 withholding rate pool of U.S. payees on a withholding statement by applying the rules under paragraph (e)(3)(iv)(A) of this section (by substituting "qualified intermediary" for "nonqualified intermediary") with respect to an account that it maintains (as described in §1.1471-5(b)(5)) for the payee of the payment. A qualified intermediary shall determine withholding rate pools based on valid documentation that it obtains under its withholding agreement with the IRS, or if a payment cannot be reliably associated with valid documentation, under the applicable presumption rules. If a qualified intermediary has an account holder that is another intermediary (whether a qualified intermediary or a nonqualified intermediary) or a flow-through entity, the qualified intermediary may combine the account holder information provided by the other intermediary or flow-through entity with the qualified intermediary's direct account holder information to determine the qualified intermediary's chapter 3 withholding rate pools and each of the qualified intermediary's chapter 4 withholding rate pools to the extent provided in its withholding agreement with the IRS.

(2) Withholding rate pool requirements for a withholdable payment.—This paragraph (e)(5)(v)(C)(2) modifies the requirements of a withholding statement described in paragraph (e)(5)(v)(C)(1) of this section provided by a qualified intermediary with respect to a withholdable payment (including a reportable amount that is a withholdable payment). For such a payment, the regulations applicable to a withholding statement described in paragraph (e)(5)(v)(C)(1) of this section shall apply, except that—

(*i*) If the qualified intermediary provides a withholding statement described in § 1.1471-3(c)(3)(iii)(B)(*2*) (describing an FFI withholding statement), the withholding statement may include a chapter 4 withholding rate pool with respect to the portion of the payment allocated to a single pool of recalcitrant account holders (without the need to subdivide into the pools described in § 1.1471-4(d)(6)), including both account holders of the qualified intermediary and of any participating FFI, registered deemed-compliant FFI, or other qualified intermediary for whom the first-mentioned qualified intermediary receives the payment, and nonparticipating FFIs (to the extent permitted) in lieu of reporting chapter 3 withholding rate pools with respect to such persons as described in paragraph (e)(5)(v)(C)(*1*) of this section); or

(*ii*) If the qualified intermediary provides a withholding statement described in § 1.1471-3(c)(3)(iii)(B)(*3*) (describing a chapter 4 withholding statement), the withholding statement may include a chapter 4 withholding rate pool with respect to the portion of the payment allocated to nonparticipating FFIs.

(*3*) *Alternative procedure for U.S. non-exempt recipients.*—If permitted under its withholding agreement with the IRS, a qualified intermediary may, by mutual agreement with a withholding agent, establish a single zero withholding rate pool that includes U.S. non-exempt recipient account holders for whom the qualified intermediary has provided Forms W-9 prior to the withholding agent paying any reportable payments, as defined in the qualified intermediary withholding agreement, and foreign persons for which no withholding is required under chapters 3 and 4, and may include payments allocated to a chapter 4 withholding rate pool of U.S. payees. In such a case, the qualified intermediary may also establish a separate withholding rate pool (subject to 28-percent withholding, or other applicable statutory back-up withholding tax rate) that includes only U.S. non-exempt recipient account holders for whom a qualified intermediary has not provided Forms W-9 prior to the withholding agent paying any reportable payments. If a qualified intermediary chooses the alternative procedure of this paragraph (e)(5)(v)(C)(*3*), the qualified intermediary must provide the information required by its withholding agreement to the withholding agent no later than January 15 of the year following the year in which the payments are paid. Failure to provide such information will result in the application of penalties to the qualified intermediary under sections 6721 and 6722, as well as any other applicable penalties, and may result in the termination of the qualified intermediary's withholding agreement with the IRS. A withholding agent shall not be liable for tax, interest, or penalties for failure to backup withhold or report information under chapter 61 of the Code due solely to the errors or omissions of the qualified intermediary. If a qualified intermediary fails to provide the allocation information required by this paragraph (e)(5)(v)(C)(*3*), with respect to U.S. non-exempt recipients, the withholding agent shall report the unallocated amount paid from the withholding rate pool to an unknown recipient, or otherwise in accordance with the appropriate Form 1099 and the instructions accompanying the form.

(D) *Example.*—The following example illustrates the application of paragraph (e)(5)(v)(C) of this section for a qualified intermediary providing chapter 4 withholding rate pools on an FFI withholding statement provided to a withholding agent. WA makes a payment of U.S. source interest that is a withholdable payment to QI, a qualified intermediary that is an FFI and a non-U.S. payor (as defined in § 1.6049-5(c)(5)), and A and B are account holders of QI (as defined under § 1.1471-5(a)) and are both U.S. nonexempt recipients (as defined paragraph (c)(21) of this section). Ten percent of the payment is attributable to both A and B. A has provided WA with a Form W-9, but B has not provided WA with a Form W-9. QI assumes primary withholding responsibility under chapters 3 and 4 with respect to the payment, 80 percent of which is allocable to foreign payees who are account holders other than A and B. As a participating FFI, QI is required to report with respect to its U.S. accounts under § 1.1471-4(d) (as incorporated into its qualified intermediary agreement). Provided that QI reports A's account as a U.S. account under the requirements referenced in the preceding sentence, QI is not required to provide WA with a Form W-9 from A and may instead include A in a chapter 4 withholding rate pool of U.S. payees, allocating 10% of the payment to this pool. See § 1.6049-4(c)(4)(iii) concerning when reporting under section 6049 for a payment of interest is not required when an FFI that is a non-U.S. payor reports an account holder receiving the payment under its chapter 4 requirements. With respect to B, the interest payment is subject to backup withholding under section 3406. Because B is a recalcitrant account holder of QI for withholdable payments and because QI assumes primary chapter 4 withholding responsibility, however, QI may include the portion of the payment allocated to B with the remaining 80% of the payment for which QI assumes primary withholding responsibility. WA can reliably associate the full amount of the payment based on the withholding statement and does so regardless of whether WA knows B is a U.S. non-exempt recipient that is receiving a portion of the payment. See § 31.3406(g)-1(e) (providing exemption to backup withholding when withholding was applied under chapter 4).

(6) *Qualified derivatives dealers.*—(i) *In general.*—To act as a qualified derivatives dealer under a qualified intermediary withholding agreement, the home office or branch that is a qualified intermediary must be an eligible entity as described in paragraph (e)(6)(ii) of this section and, in accordance with the qualified intermediary agreement, must—

(A) Furnish to a withholding agent a qualified intermediary withholding certificate (described in paragraph (e)(3)(ii) of this section) that indicates that the home office or branch receiving the payment is a qualified derivatives dealer with respect to the payments associated with the withholding certificate;

(B) Agree to assume the primary withholding and reporting responsibilities, including the documentation provisions under chapters 3, 4, and 61, and section 3406, the regulations under those provisions, and other provisions of the Internal Revenue Code, for payments made as a qualified derivatives dealer with respect to potential section 871(m) transactions. For this purpose, a qualified derivatives dealer is required to obtain a withholding certificate or other appropriate documentation from each counterparty to whom the qualified derivatives dealer makes a reportable payment (including a dividend equivalent payment within the meaning of § 1.871-15(i)). The qualified derivatives dealer is also required to determine whether any payment it makes with respect to a potential section 871(m) transaction is, in whole or in part, a dividend equivalent;

(C) Agree to remain liable for tax under section 881, if any, on any payment with respect to a potential section 871(m) transaction (including a dividend equivalent payment within the meaning of § 1.871-15(i)) and underlying securities as defined in § 1.871-15(a)(15) (including dividends) it receives as a qualified derivatives dealer, or in the case of dividend equivalents received in its equity derivatives dealer capacity, the taxes required pursuant to § 1.871-15(q);

(D) Comply with the compliance review procedures applicable to a qualified intermediary that acts as a qualified derivatives dealer under the qualified intermediary withholding agreement, which will specify the time and manner in which a qualified derivatives dealer must:

(*1*) Certify to the IRS that it has complied with the obligations to act as a qualified derivatives dealer (including its performance of a periodic review applicable to a qualified derivatives dealer);

(*2*) Report to the IRS any amounts subject to reporting on Forms 1042-S (including dividend equivalent payments that it made);

(*3*) Report to the IRS on the appropriate U.S. federal tax return, its tax liabilities, including its tax liability pursuant to § 1.871-15(q)(1) and any other taxes on payments with respect to potential section 871(m) transactions or underlying securities as defined in § 1.871-15(a)(15) it receives; and

(*4*) Respond to inquiries from the IRS about obligations it has assumed as a qualified derivatives dealer in a timely manner;

(E) Agree to act as a qualified derivatives dealer for all payments made as a principal with respect to potential section 871(m) transactions and all payments received as a principal with respect to potential section 871(m) transactions and underlying securities as defined in § 1.871-15(a)(15) (including dividend equivalent payments within the meaning of § 1.871-15(i)), excluding any payments made or received by the qualified derivatives dealer to the extent the payment is treated as effectively connected with the conduct of a trade or business within the United States within the meaning of section 864, and not act as a qualified derivatives dealer for any other payments. For purposes of this paragraph (E), any securities lending or sale-repurchase transaction that the qualified intermediary enters into that is a section 871(m) transaction is treated as entered into as a principal unless the qualified intermediary determines that it is acting as an intermediary with respect to that transaction; and

(F) Each home office or branch must qualify and be approved for qualified derivatives dealer status and must represent itself as a qualified derivatives dealer on its Form W-8IMY and separately identify the home office or branch as the recipient on a withholding statement (if necessary). The home office means a foreign person, excluding any branches of the foreign person, that applies for qualified derivatives dealer status. Each home office or branch that obtains qualified derivatives dealer status must be treated as a separate qualified derivatives dealer.

(ii) *Definition of eligible entity.*—An eligible entity is a home office or branch that is a qualified intermediary and that, treating the home office or branch as a separate entity, is—

(A) An equity derivatives dealer subject to regulatory supervision as a dealer by a governmental authority in the jurisdiction in which it was organized or operates;

(B) A bank or bank holding company subject to regulatory supervision as a bank or bank holding company (as applicable) by a governmental authority in the jurisdiction in which it was organized or operates or an entity that is wholly-owned (directly or indirectly) by a bank or bank holding company subject to regulatory supervision as a bank or bank holding company (as applicable) by a governmental authority in the jurisdiction in which the bank or bank holding company (as applicable) was organized or operates and that in its equity derivatives dealer capacity—

(1) Issues potential section 871(m) transactions to customers; and

(2) Receives dividends with respect to stock or dividend equivalent payments with respect to potential section 871(m) transactions that hedge potential section 871(m) transactions that it issued;

(C) A foreign branch of a U.S. financial institution, if the foreign branch would meet the requirements of paragraph (A) or (B) of this section if it were a separate entity; or

(D) Any person otherwise acceptable to the IRS.

(f) *Effective/applicability date.*—(1) *In general.*—Except as otherwise provided in paragraphs (e)(2)(ii)(B), (e)(4)(iv)(D), (f)(2), and (f)(3) of this section, this section applies to payments made on or after January 6, 2017. (For payments made after June 30, 2014 (except for payments to which paragraph (e)(4)(iv)(D) applies, in which case, substitute March 5, 2014, for June 30, 2014), and before January 6, 2017, see this section as in effect and contained in 26 CFR part 1, as revised April 1, 2016. For payments made after December 31, 2000, and before July 1, 2014, see this section as in effect and contained in 26 CFR part 1, as revised April 1, 2013.)

(2) *Lack of documentation for past years.*—A taxpayer may elect to apply the provisions of paragraphs (b)(7)(i)(B), (ii), and (iii) of this section, dealing with liability for failure to obtain documentation timely, to all of its open tax years, including tax years that are currently under examination by the IRS. The election is made by simply taking action under those provisions in the same manner as the taxpayer would take action for payments made after December 31, 2000.

(3) *Special rules related to section 871(m).*—Paragraphs (b)(4)(xxi), (b)(4)(xxiii), (e)(3)(ii)(E), and (e)(6) of this section apply to payments made on or after September 18, 2015. Paragraphs (e)(5)(ii)(C) and (e)(5)(v)(B)(4) of this section apply to payments made on or after on January 19, 2017. [Reg. § 1.1441-1.]

☐ [*T.D.* 6187, 7-5-56. *Amended by T.D.* 6592, 2-27-62; *T.D.* 6908, 12-30-66; *T.D.* 7157, 12-29-71; *T.D.* 7385, 10-28-75; *T.D.* 7670, 1-30-80; *T.D.* 8734, 10-6-97; *T.D.* 8804, 12-30-98; *T.D.* 8856, 12-29-99 (*corrected* 3-27-2000); *T.D.* 8881, 5-15-2000 (*corrected* 4-5-2001); *T.D.* 9023, 11-21-2002; *T.D.* 9253, 3-13-2006; *T.D.* 9323, 4-11-2007 *T.D.* 9658, 2-28-2014 (*corrected* 6-30-2014), *T.D.* 9734, 9-17-2015 (*corrected* 12-4-2015), *T.D.* 9808, 12-30-2016 (*corrected* 6-29-2017), *T.D.* 9815, 1-19-2017 (*corrected* 10-25-2017) *and T.D.* 9890, 12-27-2019.]

§ 1.1441-2. Amounts subject to withholding.—(a) *In general.*—For purposes of the regulations under chapter 3 of the Internal Revenue Code, the term *amounts subject to withholding* means amounts from sources within the United States that constitute either fixed or determinable annual or periodical income described in paragraph (b) of this section or other amounts subject to withholding described in paragraph (c) of this section. For purposes of this paragraph (a), an amount shall be treated as being from sources within the United States if the source of the amount cannot be determined at the time of payment. See § 1.1441-3(d)(1) for determining the amount to be withheld from a payment in the absence of information at the time of payment regarding the source of the amount. Amounts subject to withholding include amounts that are not fixed or determinable annual or periodical income and upon which withholding is specifically required under a provision of this section or another section of the regulations under chapter 3 of the Internal Revenue Code (such as corporate distributions upon which withholding is required under § 1.1441-3(c)(1) that do not constitute dividend income). Amounts subject to withholding do not include—

(1) Amounts described in § 1.1441-1(b)(4)(i) to the extent they involve interest on obligations in bearer form or on foreign-targeted registered obligations (but, in the case of a foreign-targeted registered obligation, only to the extent of those amounts paid to a registered owner that is a financial institution within the meaning of section 871(h)(5)(B) or a member of a clearing organization which member is the beneficial owner of the obligation);

(2) Amounts described in § 1.1441-1(b)(4)(ii) (dealing with bank deposit interest and similar types of interest (including original issue discount) described in section 871(i)(2)(A) or 881(d));

(3) Amounts described in § 1.1441-1(b)(4)(iv) (dealing with interest or original issue discount on certain short-term obligations described in section 871(g)(1)(B) or 881(e));

(4) Amounts described in § 1.1441-1(b)(4)(xx) (dealing with income from certain gambling winnings exempt from tax under section 871(j));

(5) Amounts paid as part of the purchase price of an obligation sold or exchanged between interest payment dates, unless the sale or exchange is part of a plan the principal purpose of which is to avoid tax and the withholding agent has actual knowledge or reason to know of such plan;

(6) Original issue discount paid as part of the purchase price of an obligation sold or exchanged in a transaction other than a redemption of such obligation, unless the purchase is part of a plan the principal purpose of which is to avoid tax and the withholding agent has actual knowledge or reason to know of such plan; and

(7) Insurance premiums paid with respect to a contract that is subject to the section 4371 excise tax.

(8) Amounts of United States source gross transportation income, as defined in section 887(b)(1), that is taxable under section 887(a).

(b) *Fixed or determinable annual or periodical income.*—(1) *In general.*—(i) *Definition.*—For purposes of chapter 3 of the Internal Revenue Code and the regulations thereunder, fixed or determinable annual or periodical income includes all income included in gross income under section 61 (including original issue discount) except for the items specified in paragraph (b)(2) of this section. Items of income that are excluded from gross income under a provision of law without regard to the U.S. or foreign status of the owner of the income, such as interest excluded from gross income under section 103(a) or qualified scholarship income under section 117, shall not be treated as fixed or determinable annual or periodical income under chapter 3 of the Internal Revenue Code. Income excluded from gross income under section 892 (income of foreign governments) or section 115 (income of a U.S. possession) is fixed or determinable annual or periodical income since the exclusion from gross income under those sections is dependent on the foreign status of the owner of the income. See § 1.306-3(h) for treating income from the disposition of section 306 stock as fixed or determinable annual or periodical income.

(ii) *Manner of payment.*—The term *fixed or determinable annual or periodical* is merely descriptive of the character of a class of income. If an item of income falls within the class of income contemplated in the statute and described in paragraph (a) of this section, it is immaterial whether payment of that item is made in a series of payments or in a single lump sum. Further, the income need not be paid annually if it is paid periodically; that is to say, from time to time, whether or not at regular intervals. The fact that a payment is not made annually or periodically does not, however, prevent it from being fixed or determinable annual or periodical income (e.g., a lump sum payment). In addition, the fact that the length of time during which the payments are to be made may be increased or diminished in accordance with someone's will or with the happening of an event does not disqualify the payment as determinable or periodical. For this purpose, the share of the fixed or determinable annual or periodical income of an estate or trust from sources within the United States which is required to be distributed currently, or which has been paid or credited during the taxable year, to a nonresident alien beneficiary of such estate or trust constitutes fixed or determinable annual or periodical income.

(iii) *Determinability of amount.*—An item of income is fixed when it is to be paid in amounts definitely pre-determined. An item of income is determinable if the amount to be paid is not known but there is a basis of calculation by which the amount may be ascertained at a later time. For example, interest is determinable even if it is contingent in that its amount cannot be determined at the time of payment of an amount with respect to a loan because the calculation of the interest portion of the payment is contingent upon factors that are not fixed at the time of the payment. For purposes of this section, an amount of income does not have to be determined at the time that the payment is made in order to be determinable. An amount of income described in paragraph (a) of this section which the withholding agent knows is part of a payment it makes but which it cannot calculate exactly at the time of payment, is nevertheless determinable if the determination of the exact amount depends upon events expected to occur at a future date. In contrast, a payment which may be income in the future based upon events that are not anticipated at the time the payment is made is not determinable. For example, loan proceeds may become income to the borrower when and to the extent the loan is canceled without repayment. While the cancellation of the debt is income to the borrower when it occurs, it is not determinable at the time the loan proceeds are disbursed to the borrower if the lack of repayment leading to the cancellation of part or all of the debt was not anticipated at the time of disbursement. The fact that the source of an item of income cannot be determined at the time that the payment is made does not render a payment not determinable. See § 1.1441-3(d)(1) for determining the amount to be withheld from a payment in the absence of information at the time of payment regarding the source of the amount.

(2) *Exceptions.*—For purposes of chapter 3 of the Code and the regulations thereunder, the items of income described in this paragraph (b)(2) are not fixed or determinable annual or periodical income—

(i) Gains derived from the sale of property (including market discount and option premiums), except for gains described in paragraph (b)(3) or (c) of this section; and

(ii) Any other income that the Internal Revenue Service (IRS) may determine, in published guidance (see § 601.601(d)(2) of this chapter), is not fixed or determinable annual or periodical income.

(3) *Original issue discount.*—(i) *Amount subject to tax.*—An amount representing original issue discount is fixed or determinable annual or periodical income that is subject to tax under sections 871(a)(1)(C) and 881(a)(3) to the extent provided in those sections and this paragraph (b)(3) if not otherwise excluded under paragraph (a) of this section. An amount of original issue discount is subject to tax with respect to a foreign beneficial owner of an obligation carrying original issue discount upon a sale or exchange of the obligation or when a payment is made on such obligation. The amount taxable is the amount of original issue discount that accrued while the foreign person held the obligation up to the time that the obligation is sold or exchanged or that a payment is made on the obligation, reduced by any amount of original issue discount that was taken into account prior to that time (due to a payment made on the obligation). In the case of a payment made on the obligation, the tax due on the amount of original issue discount may not exceed the amount of the payment reduced by the tax imposed on any portion of the payment that is qualified stated interest.

(ii) *Amounts subject to withholding.*—A withholding agent must withhold on the taxable amount of original issue discount paid on the redemption of an original issue discount obligation unless an exception to withholding applies (e.g., portfolio interest or treaty exception). In addition, withholding is required on the taxable amount of original issue discount upon the sale or exchange of an original issue discount obligation, other than in a redemption, to the extent the withholding agent has actual knowledge or reason to know that the sale or exchange is part of a plan the principal purpose of which is to avoid tax. If a withholding agent cannot determine the taxable amount of original issue discount on the redemption of an original issue discount obligation (or on the sale or exchange of such an obligation if the principal purpose of the sale is to avoid tax), then it must withhold on the entire amount of original issue discount accrued from the date of issue until the date of redemption (or the date the obligation is sold or exchanged) determined on the basis of the most recently published "List of Original Issue Discount Instruments" (IRS Publication 1212, available from the IRS Forms Distribution Center) or similar list published by the IRS as if the beneficial owner of the obligation had held the obligation since its original issue.

(iii) *Exceptions to withholding.*—To the extent that this paragraph (b)(3) applies to require withholding by a person other than an issuer of an original issue discount obligation, or the issuer's agent, it shall apply only to obligations issued after December 31, 2000.

(4) *Securities lending transactions and equivalent transactions.*—See §§ 1.871-7(b)(2) and 1.881-2(b)(2) regarding the character of substitute payments as fixed and determinable annual or periodical income. Such amounts constitute income subject to withholding to the extent they are from sources within the United States, as determined under section §§ 1.861-2(a)(7) and 1.861-3(a)(6). See §§ 1.6042-3(a)(2) and 1.6049-5(a)(5) for reporting requirements applicable to substitute dividend and interest payments, respectively.

(5) *REMIC residual interests.*—Amounts subject to withholding include an excess inclusion described in § 1.860G-3(b)(2) and the portion of an amount described in § 1.860G-3(b)(1) that is an excess inclusion.

(6) *Dividend equivalents.*—Amounts subject to withholding include a dividend equivalent described in section 871(m) and the regulations thereunder. For this purpose, the amount of a dividend equivalent includes any gross amount that is used in computing any net amount that is transferred to or from the taxpayer under the terms of the transaction or any other payment described in section 871(m) and the regulations thereunder.

(c) *Other income subject to withholding.*—Withholding is also required on the following items of income—

(1) Gains described in sections 631(b) or (c), relating to treatment of gain on disposal of timber, coal, or domestic iron ore with a retained economic interest; and

(2) Gains subject to the 30-percent tax under section 871(a)(1)(D) or 881(a)(4), relating to contingent payments received from the sale or exchange of patents, copyrights, and similar intangible property.

(d) *Exceptions to withholding where no money or property is paid or lack of knowledge.*—(1) *General rule.*—A withholding agent who is not related to the recipient or beneficial owner has an obligation to withhold under section 1441 only to the extent that, at any time between the date that the obligation to withhold would arise (but for the provisions of this paragraph (d)) and the due date for the filing of return on Form 1042 (including extensions) for the year in which the payment occurs, it has control over, or custody of money or property owned by the recipient or beneficial owner from which to withhold an amount and has knowledge of the facts that give rise to the payment. The exemption from the obligation to withhold under this paragraph (d) shall not apply, however, to distributions with respect to stock or if the lack of control or custody of money or property from which to withhold is part of a pre-arranged plan known to the withholding agent to avoid withholding under section 1441, 1442, or 1443. For purposes of this paragraph (d), a withholding agent is related to the recipient or beneficial owner if it is related within the meaning of section 482. Any exemption from withholding pursuant to this paragraph (d) applies without a requirement that documentation be furnished to the withholding agent. However, documentation may have to be furnished for purposes of the information reporting provisions under chapter 61 of the Code and backup withholding under section 3406. The exemption from withholding under this paragraph (d) is not a determination that the amounts are not fixed or determinable annual or periodical income, nor does it constitute an exemption from reporting the amount under § 1.1461-1(b) and (c).

(2) *Cancellation of debt.*—A lender of funds who forgives any portion of the loan is deemed to have made a payment of income to the borrower under § 1.61-12 at the time the event of forgiveness occurs. However, based on the rules of paragraph (d)(1) of this section, the lender shall have no obligation to withhold on such amount to the extent that it does not have custody or control over money or property of the borrower at any time between the time that the loan is forgiven and the due date (including extensions) of the Form 1042 for the year in which the payment is deemed to occur. A payment received by the lender from the borrower in partial settlement of the debt obligation does not, for this purpose, constitute an amount of money or property belonging to the borrower from which the withholding tax liability can be satisfied.

(3) *Satisfaction of liability following underwithholding by withholding agent.*—A withholding agent who, after failing to withhold the proper amount from a payment, satisfies the underwithheld amount out of its own funds may cause the beneficial owner to realize income to the extent of such satisfaction or may be considered to have advanced funds to the beneficial owner. Such determination depends upon the contractual arrangements governing the satisfaction of such tax liability (e.g., arrangements in which the withholding agent agrees to pay the amount due under section 1441 for the beneficial owner) or applicable laws governing the transaction. If the satisfaction of the tax liability is considered to constitute an advance of funds by the withholding agent to the beneficial owner and the withholding agent fails to collect the amount from the beneficial

owner, a cancellation of indebtedness may result, giving rise to income to the beneficial owner under § 1.61-12. While such income is annual or periodical fixed or determinable, the withholding agent shall have no liability to withhold on such income to the extent the conditions set forth in paragraphs (d)(1) and (2) of this section are satisfied with respect to this income. Contrast the rules of this paragraph (d)(3) with the rules in § 1.1441-3(f)(1) dealing with a situation in which the satisfaction of the beneficial owner's tax liability itself constitutes additional income to the beneficial owner. See, also, § 1.1441-3(c)(2)(ii)(B) for a special rule regarding underwithholding on corporate distributions due to underestimating an amount of earnings and profits.

(4) *Withholding exemption inapplicable.*—The exemption in § 1.1441-2(d) from the obligation to withhold shall not apply to amounts described in § 1.860G-3(b)(1) (regarding certain partnership allocations of REMIC net income with respect to a REMIC residual interest).

(e) *Payment.*—(1) *General rule.*—A payment is considered made to a person if that person realizes income whether or not such income results from an actual transfer of cash or other property. For example, realization of income from cancellation of debt results in a deemed payment. A payment is considered made when the amount would be includible in the income of the beneficial owner under the U.S. tax principles governing the cash basis method of accounting. A payment is considered made whether it is made directly to the beneficial owner or to another person for the benefit of the beneficial owner (e.g., to the agent of the beneficial owner). Thus, a payment of income is considered made to a beneficial owner if it is paid in complete or partial satisfaction of the beneficial owner's debt to a creditor. In the event of a conflict between the rules of this paragraph (e)(1) governing whether a payment has occurred and its timing and the rules of § 31.3406(a)-4 of this chapter, the rules in § 31.3406(a)-4 of this chapter shall apply to the extent that the application of section 3406 is relevant to the transaction at issue.

(2) *Income allocated under section 482.*—A payment is considered made to the extent income subject to withholding is allocated under section 482. Further, income arising as a result of a secondary adjustment made in conjunction with a reallocation of income under section 482 from a foreign person to a related U.S. person is considered paid to a foreign person unless the taxpayer to whom the income is reallocated has entered into a repatriation agreement with the IRS and the agreement eliminates the liability for withholding under this section. For purposes of determining the liability for withholding, the payment of income is deemed to have occurred on the last day of the taxable year in which the transactions that give rise to the allocation of income and the secondary adjustments, if any, took place.

(3) *Blocked income.*—Income is not considered paid if it is blocked under executive authority, such as the President's exercise of emergency power under the Trading with the Enemy Act (50 U.S.C. App. 5), or the International Emergency Economic Powers Act (50 U.S.C. 1701 et seq).. However, on the date that the blocking restrictions are removed, the income that was blocked is considered constructively received by the beneficial owner (and therefore paid for purposes of this section) and subject to withholding under § 1.1441-1. Any exemption from withholding pursuant to this paragraph (e)(3) applies without a requirement that documentation be furnished to the withholding agent. However, documentation may have to be furnished for purposes of the information reporting provisions under chapter 61 of the Code and backup withholding under section 3406. The exemption from withholding granted by this paragraph (e)(3) is not a determination that the amounts are not fixed or determinable annual or periodical income.

(4) *Special rules for dividends.*—For purposes of sections 1441 and 6042, in the case of stock for which the record date is earlier than the payment date, dividends are considered paid on the payment date. In the case of a corporate reorganization, if a beneficial owner is required to exchange stock held in a former corporation for stock in a new corporation before dividends that are to be paid with respect to the stock in the new corporation will be paid on such stock, the dividend is considered paid on the date that the payee or beneficial owner actually exchanges the stock and receives the dividend. See § 31.3406(a)-4(a)(2) of this chapter.

(5) *Certain interest accrued by a foreign corporation.*—For purposes of sections 1441 and 6049, a foreign corporation shall be treated as having made a payment of interest as of the last day of the taxable year if it has made an election under § 1.884-4(c)(1) to treat accrued interest as if it were paid in that taxable year.

(6) *Payments other than in U.S. dollars.*—For purposes of section 1441, a payment includes amounts paid in a medium other than U.S. dollars. See § 1.1441-3(e) for rules regarding the amount subject to withholding in the case of such payments.

(7) *Payments of dividend equivalents.*—(i) *In general.*—Subject to paragraphs (e)(7)(iv), (vi), and (vii) of this section, a payment of a dividend equivalent is not considered to be made until the later of when—

(A) The amount of a dividend equivalent is determined as provided in § 1.871-15(j)(2), and

(B) A payment occurs with respect to the section 871(m) transaction after the amount of a dividend equivalent is determined as provided in § 1.871-15(j)(2).

(ii) *Payment.*—For purposes of paragraph (e)(7) of this section, a payment occurs with respect to a section 871(m) transaction when—

(A) Money or other property is paid to or by the long party, unless the section 871(m) transaction is described in § 1.871-15(i)(3)(i), in which case a payment is treated as being made at the end of the applicable calendar quarter;

(B) The long party sells, exchanges, transfers, or otherwise disposes of the section 871(m) transaction (including by settlement, offset, termination, expiration, lapse, or maturity); or

(C) The section 871(m) transaction is transferred to an account that is not maintained by the withholding agent or the long party terminates the account relationship with the withholding agent.

(iii) *Premiums and other upfront payments.*—When a long party pays a premium or other upfront payment to the short party at the time a section 871(m) transaction is issued, the premium or other upfront payment is not treated as a payment for purposes of paragraph (e)(7)(ii)(A) of this section.

(iv) *Option to withhold on dividend payment date.*—A withholding agent may withhold on the payment date described in paragraph (e)(4) of this section for the applicable dividend on the underlying security (the dividend payment date) if it withholds on that date for all section 871(m) transactions of the same type (for example, securities lending or sale-repurchase transaction, NPC, or ELI) and satisfies the requirements to paragraph (e)(7)(v) of this section.

(v) *Changes to time of withholding.*—This paragraph describes how a withholding agent changes the time that it withholds on a dividend equivalent payment to a time described in paragraph (e)(7)(i) or (iv) of this section and these requirements must be satisfied for a withholding agent to change the time it withholds. A withholding agent must apply the change consistently to all transactions of the same type entered into on or after the change. For transactions of the same type entered into before the change, a withholding agent must withhold under the original approach throughout the term of the transaction. When a withholding agent changes the time that it will withhold, the withholding agent must notify each payee in writing that it will withhold using the approach described in paragraph (e)(7)(i) or (iv) of this section, as applicable, before the time for determining the payee's first dividend equivalent payment (as determined under § 1.871-15(j)(2)). With respect to transactions held by an intermediary or foreign flow-through entity, a withholding agent is treated as providing notice to each payee holding that transaction through the entity when it notifies the intermediary or foreign flow-through entity of the time it will withhold, as described in the preceding sentence, provided that the intermediary or foreign flow-through entity agrees to provide the same notice to each payee. The withholding agent must attach a statement to its relevant income tax return (filed by the due date, including extensions) for the year of the change notifying the IRS of the change and when it applies, identifying the type of section 871(m) transaction to which the change applies, and certifying that it has notified its payees. For purposes of this paragraph, a withholding agent will be considered to have entered into a transaction on the first date the withholding agent becomes responsible for withholding on the transaction (based on the rule in paragraph (e)(7)(ix) of this section).

(vi) *Withholding by qualified derivatives dealers.*—A withholding agent that is acting as a qualified derivatives dealer must withhold with respect to a dividend equivalent payment on the payment date described in paragraph (e)(4) of this section for the applicable dividend on the underlying security and must notify each payee in writing that it will withhold on the dividend payment date before the time for determining the payee's first dividend equivalent payment (as determined under § 1.871-15(j)(2)).

(vii) *Withholding with respect to derivatives that reference partnerships.*—To the extent that a withholding agent is required to withhold with respect to a partnership interest described in § 1.871-15(m), the liability for withholding arises on March 15 of the year following the year in which the payment of a dividend equivalent (determined under § 1.871-15(i)) occurs.

(viii) *Notification to holders of withholding timing.*—If a withholding agent is required to notify a payee of when it will withhold under paragraph (e)(7)(v) of this section, it may use the reporting methods prescribed in § 1.871-15(p)(3)(i).

(ix) *Withholding agent responsibility.*—A withholding agent is only responsible for dividend equivalent amounts determined (as provided in § 1.871-15(j)(2)) during the period the withholding agent is a withholding agent for the section 871(m) transaction.

(f) *Effective/applicability date.*—This section applies to payments made after December 31, 2000. Paragraph (a)(8) of this section applies to payments made on or after January 6, 2017; however, taxpayers may apply paragraph (a)(8) to any open tax year. Paragraphs (b)(5) and (d)(4) of this section apply to payments made after August 1, 2006. Paragraph (b)(6) of this section applies to payments made on or after January 23, 2012. Paragraph (e)(7) of this section applies to payments made on or after January 19, 2017. [Reg. § 1.1441-2.]

☐ *[T.D. 6187, 7-5-56. Amended by T.D. 6464, 5-11-60, T.D. 6592, 2-27-62, T.D. 6841, 7-26-65, T.D. 6873, 1-24-66, T.D. 6908, 12-30-66; T.D. 7977, 9-19-84; T.D. 8734, 10-6-97; T.D. 8804, 12-30-98; T.D. 8856, 12-29-99; T.D. 8881, 5-15-2000; T.D. 9272, 7-31-2006; T.D. 9415, 7-11-2008 (corrected 8-5-2008); T.D. 9572, 1-19-2012, T.D. 9648, 12-4-2013, T.D. 9734, 9-17-2015, T.D. 9808, 12-30-2016, T.D. 9815, 1-19-2017 (corrected 10-25-2017) and T.D. 9890, 12-27-2019.]*

§ 1.1441-3. Determination of amounts to be withheld.—(a) *General rule.*—(1) *Withholding on gross amount.*—Except as otherwise provided in regulations under section 1441, the amount subject to withholding under § 1.1441-1 is the gross amount of income subject to withholding that is paid to a foreign person. The gross amount of income subject to withholding may not be reduced by any deductions, except to the extent that one or more personal exemptions are allowed as provided under § 1.1441-4(b)(6).

(2) *Coordination with chapter 4.*—A withholding agent making a payment that is both a withholdable payment and an amount subject to withholding under § 1.1441-2(a) and that has withheld tax as required under chapter 4 from such payment is not required to withhold under this section notwithstanding paragraph (a)(1) of this section. See § 1.1474-6(b)(1) for the allowance for a withholding agent to credit withholding applied under chapter 4 against its liability for tax due under sections 1441, 1442, or 1443, and see § 1.1474-6(b)(1) for the rule allowing a withholding agent to credit withholding applied under chapter 4 against its liability for tax due under sections 1441, 1442, or 1443, and § 1.1474-6(b)(2) for when such withholding is considered applied by a withholding agent. If the withholdable payment is not required to be withheld upon under chapter 4, then the withholding agent must apply the provisions of § 1.1441-1 to determine whether withholding is required under sections 1441, 1442, or 1443.

(b) *Withholding on payments on certain obligations.*—(1) *Withholding at time of payment of interest.*—When making a payment on an interest-bearing obligation, a withholding agent must withhold under § 1.1441-1 upon the gross amount of stated interest payable on the interest payment date, regardless of whether the payment constitutes a return of capital or the payment of income within the meaning of section 61. To the extent an amount was withheld on an amount of capital rather than interest, see the rules for adjustments, refunds, or credits under § 1.1441-1(b)(8).

(2) *No withholding between interest payment dates.*—(i) *In general.*—A withholding agent is not required to withhold under § 1.1441-1 upon interest accrued on the date of a sale or exchange of a debt obligation when that sale occurs between two interest payment dates (even though the amount is treated as interest under § 1.61-7(c) or (d) and is subject to tax under section 871 or 881). See § 1.6045-1(c) for reporting requirements by brokers with respect to sale proceeds. See § 1.61-7(c) regarding the character of payments received by the acquirer of an obligation subsequent to such acquisition (that is, as a return of capital or interest accrued after the acquisition). Any exemption from withholding pursuant to this paragraph (b)(2)(i) applies without a requirement that documentation be furnished to the withholding agent. However, documentation may have to be furnished for purposes of the information reporting provisions under section 6045 or 6049 and backup withholding under section 3406. The exemption from withholding granted by this paragraph (b)(2) is not a determination that the accrued interest is not fixed or determinable annual or periodical income under section 871(a) or 881(a).

(ii) *Anti-abuse rule.*—The exemption in paragraph (b)(2)(i) of this section does not apply if the sale of securities is part of a plan the principal purpose of which is to avoid tax by selling and repurchasing securities and the withholding agent has actual knowledge or reason to know of such plan.

(c) *Corporate distributions.*—(1) *General rule.*—A corporation making a distribution with respect to its stock or any intermediary (described in § 1.1441-1(c)(13)) making a payment of such a distribution is required to withhold under section 1441, 1442, or 1443 on the entire amount of the distribution, unless it elects to reduce the amount of withholding under the provisions of this paragraph (c). Any exceptions from withholding provided by this paragraph (c) apply without any requirement to furnish documentation to the withholding agent. However, documentation may have to be furnished for purposes of the information reporting provisions under section 6042 or 6045 and backup withholding under section 3406. See § 1.1461-1(c) to determine whether amounts excepted from withholding under this section are considered amounts that are subject to reporting.

(2) *Exception to withholding on distributions.*—(i) *In general.*—An election described in paragraph (c)(1) of this section is made by actually reducing the amount of withholding at the time that the payment is made. An intermediary that makes a payment of a distribution is not required to reduce the withholding based on the distributing corporation's estimates under this paragraph (c)(2), even if the distributing corporation itself elects to reduce the withholding on payments of distributions that it itself makes to foreign persons. Conversely, an intermediary may elect to reduce the amount of withholding with respect to the payment of a distribution even if the distributing corporation does not so elect for the payments of distributions that it itself makes of distributions to foreign persons. The amounts with respect to which a distributing corporation or intermediary may elect to reduce the withholding are as follows:

(A) A distributing corporation or intermediary may elect to not withhold on a distribution to the extent it represents a nontaxable distribution payable in stock or stock rights.

(B) A distributing corporation or intermediary may elect to not withhold on a distribution to the extent it represents a distribution in part or full payment in exchange for stock.

(C) A distributing corporation or intermediary may elect to not withhold on a distribution (actual or deemed) to the extent it is not paid out of accumulated earnings and profits or current earnings and profits, based on a reasonable estimate determined under paragraph (c)(2)(ii) of this section.

(D) A regulated investment company or intermediary may elect to not withhold on a distribution representing a capital gain dividend (as defined in section 852(b)(3)(C)) or an exempt interest dividend (as defined in section 852(b)(5)(A)) based on the applicable procedures described under paragraph (c)(3) of this section.

(E) A U.S. Real Property Holding Corporation (defined in section 897(c)(2)) or a real estate investment trust (defined in section 856) or intermediary may elect to not withhold on a distribution to the extent it is subject to withholding under section 1445 and the regulations under that section. See paragraph (c)(4) of this section for applicable procedures.

(ii) *Reasonable estimate of accumulated and current earnings and profits on the date of payment.*—(A) *General rule.*—A reasonable estimate for purposes of paragraph (c)(2)(i)(C) of this section is a determination made by the distributing corporation at a time reasonably close to the date of payment of the extent to which the distribution will constitute a dividend, as defined in section 316. The determination is based upon the anticipated amount of accumulated earnings and profits and current earnings and profits for the taxable year in which the distribution is made, the distributions made prior to the distribution for which the estimate is made and all other relevant facts and circumstances. A reasonable estimate may be made based on the procedures described in § 31.3406(b)(2)-4(c)(2) of this chapter.

(B) *Procedures in case of underwithholding.*—A distributing corporation or intermediary that is a withholding agent with respect to a distribution and that determines at the end of the taxable year in which the distribution is made that it underwithheld under section 1441 on the distribution shall be liable for the amount underwithheld as a withholding agent under section 1461. However, for purposes of this section and § 1.1461-1, any amount underwithheld paid by a distributing corporation, its paying agent, or an intermediary shall not be treated as income subject to additional withholding even if that amount is treated as additional income to the shareholders unless the additional amount is income to the shareholder as a result of a contractual arrangement between the parties regarding the satisfaction of the shareholder's tax liabilities. In addition, no penalties shall be imposed for failure to withhold and deposit the tax if—

(1) The distributing corporation made a reasonable estimate as provided in paragraph (c)(2)(ii)(A) of this section; and

(2) Either—

(i) The corporation or intermediary pays over the underwithheld amount on or before the due date for filing a Form 1042 for the calendar year in which the distribution is made, pursuant to § 1.1461-2(b); or

(ii) The corporation or intermediary is not a calendar year taxpayer and it files an amended return on Form 1042X (or such other form as the Commissioner may prescribe) for the calendar year in which the distribution is made and pays the underwithheld amount and interest within 60 days after the close of the taxable year in which the distribution is made.

(C) *Reliance by intermediary on reasonable estimate.*—For purposes of determining whether the payment of a corporate distribution is a dividend, a withholding agent that is not the distributing corporation may, absent actual knowledge or reason to know otherwise, rely on representations made by the distributing corporation regarding the reasonable estimate of the anticipated accumulated and current earnings and profits made in accordance with paragraph (c)(2)(ii)(A) of this section. Failure by the withholding agent to withhold the required amount due to a failure by the distributing corporation to reasonably estimate the portion of the distribution treated as a dividend or to properly communicate the information to the withholding agent shall be imputed to the distributing corporation. In such a case, the Internal Revenue Service (IRS) may collect from the distributing corporation any underwithheld amount and subject the distributing corporation to applicable interest and penalties as a withholding agent.

(D) *Example.*—The rules of this paragraph (c)(2) are illustrated by the following example:

Example. (i) *Facts.* Corporation X, a publicly traded corporation with both U.S. and foreign shareholders and a calendar year taxpayer, has an accumulated deficit in earnings and profits at the close of 2000. In 2001, Corporation X generates $1 million of current earnings and profits each month and makes an $18 million distribution, resulting in a $12 million dividend. Corporation X plans to make an additional $18 million distribution on October 1, 2002. Approximately one month before that date, Corporation X's management receives an internal report from its legal and accounting department concerning Corporation X's estimated current earnings and profits. The report states that Corporation X should generate only $5.1 million of current earnings and profits by the close of the third quarter due to costs relating to substantial organizational and product changes, but these changes will enable Corporation X to generate $1.3 million of earnings and profits monthly for the last quarter of the 2002 fiscal year. Thus, the total amount of current and earnings and profits for 2002 is estimated to be $9 million.

(ii) *Analysis.* Based on the facts in paragraph (i) of this *Example*, including the fact that earnings and profits estimate was made within a reasonable time before the distribution, Corporation X can rely on the estimate under paragraph (c)(2)(ii)(A) of this section. Therefore, Corporation X may treat $9 million of the $18 million of the October 1, 2002, distribution to foreign shareholders as a nondividend distribution.

(3) *Special rules in the case of distributions from a regulated investment company.*—(i) *General rule.*—If the amount of any distributions designated as being subject to section 852(b)(3)(C) or (5)(A), or 871(k)(1)(C) or (2)(C), exceeds the amount that may be designated under those sections for the taxable year, then no penalties will be asserted for any resulting underwithholding if the designations were based on a reasonable estimate (made pursuant to the same procedures as are described in paragraph (c)(2)(ii)(A) of this section) and the adjustments to the amount withheld are made within the time period described in paragraph (c)(2)(ii)(B) of this section. Any adjustment to the amount of tax due and paid to the IRS by the withholding agent as a result of underwithholding shall not be treated as a distribution for purposes of section 562(c) and the regulations thereunder. Any amount of U.S. tax that a foreign shareholder is treated as having paid on the undistributed capital gain of a regulated investment company under section 852(b)(3)(D) may be claimed by the foreign shareholder as a credit or refund under § 1.1464-1.

(ii) *Reliance by intermediary on reasonable estimate.*—For purposes of determining whether a payment is a distribution designated as subject to section 852(b)(3)(C) or (5)(A), or 871(k)(1)(C) or (2)(C), a withholding agent that is not the distributing regulated investment company may, absent actual knowledge or reason to know otherwise, rely on the designations that the distributing company represents have been made in accordance with paragraph (c)(3)(i) of this section. Failure by the withholding agent to withhold the required amount due to a failure by the regulated investment company to reasonably estimate the required amounts or to properly communicate the relevant information to the withholding agent shall be imputed to the distributing company. In such a case, the IRS may collect from the distributing company any underwithheld amount and subject the company to applicable interest and penalties as a withholding agent.

(4) *Coordination with withholding under section 1445.*—(i) *In general.*—A distribution from a U.S. Real Property Holding Corporation (USRPHC) (or from a corporation that was a USRPHC at any time during the five-year period ending on the date of distribution) with respect to stock that is a U.S. real property interest under section 897(c) or from a Real Estate Investment Trust (REIT) or other entity that is a qualified investment entity (QIE) under section 897(h)(4) with respect to its stock is subject to the withholding provisions under section 1441 (or section 1442 or 1443) and section 1445. A USRPHC (other than a REIT or other entity that is a QIE) making a distribution shall be treated as satisfying its withholding obligations under both sections if it withholds in accordance with one of the procedures described in either paragraph (c)(4)(i)(A) or (B) of this section. A USRPHC must apply the same withholding procedure to all the distributions made during the taxable year. However, the USRPHC may change the applicable withholding procedure from year to year. For rules regarding distributions by REITs and other entities that are QIEs, see paragraph (c)(4)(i)(C) of this section. To the extent withholding under sections 1441, 1442, or 1443 applies under this paragraph (c)(4)(i) to any portion of a distribution that is a withholdable payment, see paragraph (a)(2) of this section for rules coordinating withholding under chapter 4.

(A) *Withholding under section 1441.*—The USRPHC may choose to withhold on a distribution only under section 1441 (or 1442 or 1443) and not under section 1445. In such a case, the USRPHC must withhold under section 1441 (or 1442 or 1443) on the full amount of the distribution, whether or not any portion of the distribution represents a return of basis or capital gain. If a reduced tax rate under an income tax treaty applies to the distribution by the USRPHC, then the applicable rate of withholding on the distribution shall be no less than 15 percent for distributions after February 16, 2016, and no less than 10 percent for distributions on or before February 16, 2016, unless the applicable treaty specifies an applicable lower rate for distributions from a USRPHC, in which case the lower rate may apply.

(B) *Withholding under both sections 1441 and 1445.*—As an alternative to the procedure described in paragraph (c)(4)(i)(A) of this section, a USRPHC may choose to withhold under both sections 1441 (or 1442 or 1443) and 1445 under the procedures set forth in this paragraph (c)(4)(i)(B). The USRPHC must make a reasonable estimate of the portion of the distribution that is a dividend under paragraph (c)(2)(ii)(A) of this section, and must—

(1) Withhold under section 1441 (or 1442 or 1443) on the portion of the distribution that is estimated to be a dividend under paragraph (c)(2)(ii)(A) of this section; and

(2) Withhold under section 1445(e)(3) and § 1.1445-5(e) on the remainder of the distribution (except for any portion paid to a withholding qualified holder (as defined in § 1.1445-1(g)(11)) or on such smaller portion based on a withholding certificate obtained in accordance with § 1.1445-5(e)(3)(iv).

(C) *Coordination with REIT/QIE withholding.*—In the case of a distribution from a REIT or other entity that is a QIE, withholding is required as described in paragraph (c)(4)(i)(C)(*1*) and (2) of this section.

(*1*) Withholding is required under section 1441 (or section 1442 or 1443) on—

(*i*) The portion of the distribution that is not designated (for REITs) or reported (for regulated investment companies that are QIEs) as a capital gain dividend, a return of basis, or a distribution in excess of a shareholder's adjusted basis in the stock of the REIT or QIE that is treated as a capital gain under section 301(c)(3); and

(*ii*) Any portion of a capital gain dividend from a REIT or other entity that is a QIE that is not treated as gain attributable to the sale or exchange of a U.S. real property interest pursuant to the second sentence of section 897(h)(1)).

(*2*) Withholding is required under section 1445 with respect to—

(*i*) A distribution in excess of a shareholder's adjusted basis in the stock of the REIT or QIE is, unless the interest in the REIT or QIE is not a U.S. real property interest (for example, an interest in a domestically controlled REIT or QIE under section 897(h)(2)) or the distribution is paid to a withholding qualified holder (as defined in § 1.1445-1(g)(11)); and

(*ii*) Any portion of a capital gain dividend that is attributable to the sale or exchange of a U.S. real property interest under section 897(h)(1), unless it is paid to a withholding qualified holder (as defined in § 1.1445-1(g)(11)). See § 1.1445-8.

(ii) *Intermediary reliance rule.*—A withholding agent that is not the distributing USRPHC must withhold under paragraph (c)(4)(i) of this section, but may, absent actual knowledge or reason to know otherwise, rely on representations made by the USRPHC regarding the determinations required under paragraph (c)(4)(i) of this section. Failure by the withholding agent to withhold the required amount due to a failure by the distributing USRPHC to make these determinations in a reasonable manner or to properly communicate the determinations to the withholding agent shall be imputed to the distributing USRPHC. In such a case, the IRS may collect from the distributing USRPHC any underwithheld amount and subject the distributing USRPHC to applicable interest and penalties as a withholding agent.

(iii) *Applicability date.*—Paragraphs (c)(4)(i), (c)(4)(i)(B)(2), and (c)(4)(i)(C) of this section apply to distributions made by a USRPHC or a QIE occurring on or after December 29, 2022. For distributions made by a USRPHC or a QIE occurring before December 29, 2022, see § 1.1441-3(c)(4)(i), § 1.1441-3(c)(4)(i)(B)(2), and § 1.1441-3(c)(4)(i)(c), as contained in 26 CFR part 1, revised as of April 1, 2021.

(d) *Withholding on payments that include an undetermined amount of income.*—(1) *In general.*—Where the withholding agent makes a payment and does not know at the time of payment the amount that is subject to withholding because the determination of the source of the income or the calculation of the amount of income subject to tax depends upon facts that are not known at the time of payment, then the withholding agent must withhold an amount under § 1.1441-1 based on the entire amount paid that is necessary to ensure that the tax withheld is not less than 30 percent (or other applicable percentage) of the amount that could be from sources within the United States or income subject to tax. See § 1.1471-2(a)(5) for similar rules under chapter 4 that apply to payments made to payees that are entities. The amount so withheld shall not exceed 30 percent of the amount paid. With respect to a payment described in paragraph (d)(1) or (2) of this section, the withholding agent may elect to retain 30 percent of the payment to hold in escrow until the earlier of the date that the amount of income from sources within the United States or the taxable amount can be determined or one year from the date the amount is placed in escrow, at which time the withholding becomes due under § 1.1441-1, or, to the extent that withholding is not required, the escrowed amount must be paid to the payee.

(2) *Withholding on certain gains.*—Absent actual knowledge or reason to know otherwise, a withholding agent may rely on a claim regarding the amount of gain described in § 1.1441-2(c) if the beneficial owner withholding certificate, or other appropriate withholding certificate, states the beneficial owner's basis in the property giving rise to the gain. In the absence of a reliable representation on a withholding certificate, the withholding agent must withhold an amount under § 1.1441-1 that is necessary to assure that the tax withheld is not less than 30 percent (or other applicable percentage) of the recognized gain. For this purpose, the recognized gain is determined without regard to any deduction allowed by the Code from the gains. The amount so withheld shall not exceed 30 percent of the amount payable by reason of the transaction giving rise to the recognized gain. See § 1.1441-1(b)(8) regarding adjustments in the case of overwithholding.

(e) *Payments other than in U.S. dollars.*—(1) *In general.*—The amount of a payment made in a medium other than U.S. dollars is measured by the fair market value of the property or services provided in lieu of U.S. dollars. The withholding agent may liquidate the property prior to payment in order to withhold the required amount of tax under section 1441 or obtain payment of the tax from an alternative source. However, the obligation to withhold under section 1441 is not deferred even if no alternative source can be located. Thus, for purposes of withholding under chapter 3 of the Code, the provisions of § 31.3406(h)-2(b)(2)(ii) of this chapter (relating to backup withholding from another source) shall not apply. If the withholding agent satisfies the tax liability related to such payments, the rules of paragraph (f) of this section apply.

(2) *Payments in foreign currency.*—If the amount subject to withholding tax is paid in a currency other than the U.S. dollar, the amount of withholding under section 1441 shall be determined by applying the applicable rate of withholding to the foreign currency amount and converting the amount withheld into U.S. dollars on the date of payment at the spot rate (as defined in § 1.988-1(d)(1)) in effect on that date. A withholding agent making regular or frequent payments in foreign currency may use a month-end spot rate or a monthly average spot rate. In addition, such as withholding agent may use the spot rate on the date the amount of tax is deposited (within the meaning of § 1.6302-2(a)), provided that such deposit is made within seven days of the date of the payment giving rise to the obligation to withhold. A spot rate convention must be used consistently for all non-dollar amounts withheld and from year to year. Such convention cannot be changed without the consent of the Commissioner. The U.S. dollar amount so determined shall be treated by the beneficial owner as the amount of tax paid on the income for purposes of determining the final U.S. tax liability and, if applicable, claiming a refund or credit of tax.

(f) *Tax liability of beneficial owner satisfied by withholding agent.*—(1) *General rule.*—In the event that the satisfaction of a tax liability of a beneficial owner by a withholding agent constitutes income to the beneficial owner and such income is of a type that is subject to withholding, the amount of the payment deemed made by the withholding agent for purposes of this paragraph (f) shall be determined under the gross-up formula provided in this paragraph (f)(1). Whether the payment of the tax by the withholding agent constitutes a satisfaction of the beneficial owner's tax liability and whether, as such, it constitutes additional income to the beneficial owner, must be determined under all the facts and circumstances surrounding the transaction, including any agreements between the parties and applicable law. The formula described in this paragraph (f)(1) is as follows:

$$\text{Payment} = \frac{\text{Gross payment without withholding}}{1 - (\text{tax rate})}$$

(2) *Example.*—The following example illustrates the provisions of this paragraph (f):

Example. College X awards a qualified scholarship within the meaning of section 117(b) to foreign student, FS, who is in the United States on an F visa. FS is a resident of a country that does not have an income tax treaty with the United States. The scholarship is $20,000 to be applied to tuition, mandatory fees and books, plus benefits in kind consisting of room and board and roundtrip air transportation. College X agrees to pay any U.S. income tax owed by FS with respect to the scholarship. The fair market value of the room and board measured by the amount College X charges non-scholarship students is $6,000. The cost of the roundtrip air transportation is $2,600. Therefore, the total fair market value of the scholarship received by FS is $28,600. However, the amount taxable is limited to the fair market value of the benefits in kind ($8,600) because the portion of the scholarship amount for tuition, fees, and books is not included in gross income under section 117. The applicable rate of withholding is 14 percent under section 1441(b). Therefore, under the gross-up formula, College X is deemed to make a payment of $10,000 ($8,600 divided by (1 – .14). The U.S. tax that must be deducted and withheld from the payment under section 1441(b) is $1,400 (.14 × $10,000).

College X reports scholarship income of $30,000 and $1,400 of U.S. tax withheld on Forms 1042 and 1042-S.

(g) *Conduit financing arrangements.*—(1) *Duty to withhold.*—A financed entity or other person required to withhold tax under section 1441 with respect to a financing arrangement that is a conduit financing arrangement within the meaning of § 1.881-3(a)(2)(iv) shall be required to withhold under section 1441 as if the district director had determined, pursuant to § 1.881-3(a)(3), that all conduit entities that are parties to the conduit financing arrangement should be disregarded. The amount of tax required to be withheld shall be determined under § 1.881-3(d). The withholding agent may withhold tax at a reduced rate if the financing entity establishes that it is entitled to the benefit of a treaty that provides a reduced rate of tax on a payment of the type deemed to have been paid to the financing entity. Section 1.881-3(a)(3)(ii)(E) shall not apply for purposes of determining whether any person is required to deduct and withhold tax pursuant to this paragraph (g), or whether any party to a financing arrangement is liable for failure to withhold or entitled to a refund of tax under sections 1441 or 1461 to 1464 (except to the extent the amount withheld exceeds the tax liability determined under § 1.881-3(d)). See § 1.1441-7(f) relating to withholding tax liability of the withholding agent in conduit financing arrangements subject to § 1.881-3.

(2) *Effective date.*—This paragraph (g) is effective for payments made by financed entities on or after September 11, 1995. This paragraph shall not apply to interest payments covered by section 127(g)(3) of the Tax Reform Act of 1984, and to interest payments with respect to other debt obligations issued prior to October 15, 1984 (whether or not such debt was issued by a Netherlands Antilles corporation).

(h) *Dividend equivalents.*—(1) *Withholding on gross amount.*—The gross amount of a dividend equivalent described in section 871(m) and the regulations thereunder is subject to withholding in an amount equal to the gross amount of the dividend equivalent used in computing any net amount that is transferred to or from the taxpayer. Withholding is required on the amount of the dividend equivalent calculated under § 1.871-15(j).

(2) *Reliance by withholding agent on reasonable determinations.*—For purposes of determining whether a payment is a dividend equivalent and the timing and amount of a dividend equivalent under section 871(m), a withholding agent may rely on the information received from the party to the transaction that is required (as provided in § 1.871-15(p)) to make those determinations, unless the withholding agent knows or has reason to know that the information is incorrect. When a withholding agent fails to withhold the required amount because the party described in § 1.871-15(p) fails to reasonably determine or timely provide information regarding whether a transaction is a section 871(m) transaction, the timing and amount of any dividend equivalent, or any other information required to be provided pursuant to § 1.871-15(p), and the withholding agent relied, absent actual knowledge to the contrary, on that party's determination or did not timely receive required information, then the failure to withhold is imputed to the party required to make the determinations described in § 1.871-15(p). In that case, the IRS may collect any underwithheld amount from the party to the transaction that was required to make the determinations described in § 1.871-15(p) or timely provide the information and subject that party to applicable interest and penalties as if the party were a withholding agent with respect to the payment of the dividend equivalent made pursuant to the section 871(m) transaction.

(3) *Effective/applicability date.*—Except for the first sentence of paragraph (h)(1), this paragraph (h) applies to payments made on or after September 18, 2015. The first sentence of paragraph (h)(1) of this section, applies to payments made on or after January 23, 2012.

(i) *Effective/applicability date.*—Except as otherwise provided in paragraphs (g)(2) and (h)(3) of this section, this section applies to payments made on or after January 6, 2017. (For payments made after June 30, 2014, and before January 6, 2017, see this section as in effect and contained in 26 CFR part 1, revised April 1, 2016. For payments made after December 31, 2000, see this section as in effect and contained in 26 CFR part 1 as revised April 1, 2013.) [Reg. § 1.1441-3.]

☐ [*T.D. 6187, 7-5-56. Amended by T.D. 6592, 2-27-62; T.D. 6636, 2-25-63; T.D. 6669, 8-26-63; T.D. 6777, 12-15-64; T.D. 6908, 12-30-66; T.D. 7378, 9-29-75; T.D. 7977, 9-19-84; T.D. 8611, 8-10-95; T.D. 8734, 10-6-97; T.D. 8804, 12-30-98; T.D. 8856, 12-29-99; T.D. 8881, 5-15-2000; T.D. 9253, 3-13-2006; T.D. 9572, 1-19-2012; T.D. 9648, 12-4-2013, T.D. 9658, 2-28-2014, T.D. 9734, 9-17-2015 and T.D. 9808, 12-30-2016 (corrected 6-29-2017) and T.D. 9971, 12-28-2022.*]

Proposed Amendments to Regulation

§ 1.1441-3. Determination of amounts to be withheld.—

* * *

(c) * * *

(5) *Special rules for certain distributions to which section 302 applies.*—(i) *Withholding responsibility.*—(A) *General rule.*—A corporation that makes a public section 302 distribution, or any intermediary (described in § 1.1441-1(c)(13)) making a payment of such a distribution, is required to withhold under section 1441, 1442 or 1443 on the entire amount of the distribution unless the provisions of paragraph (c)(5)(iii) of this section have been applied. The provisions of paragraph (c)(2)(i)(B) or (d)(1) of this section do not apply to a public section 302 distribution.

(B) *Effective/applicability date.*—The rules of this paragraph (c)(5) apply to public section 302 distributions made after December 31, 2008.

(ii) *Definitions.*—Solely for purposes of this paragraph (c)(5), the following definitions shall apply:

(A) Public section 302 distribution means a distribution by a corporation in redemption of its stock for which there is an established financial market within the meaning of § 1.1092(d)-1.

(B) Section 302 payment means payment of a public section 302 distribution.

(C) Distributing corporation means a corporation making or treated as making a public section 302 distribution.

(iii) *Escrow procedure.*—(A) *Application.*—*(1) In general.*—The escrow procedure in this paragraph (c)(5)(iii) may be applied only by an intermediary (described in § 1.1441-1(c)(13)) that is a U.S. financial institution. A U.S. financial institution making a section 302 payment to a foreign account holder, and applying this escrow procedure, is not required to withhold on the entire amount of a section 302 payment under the general rule of paragraph (c)(5)(i).

(B) *Escrow account.*—*(1) In general.*—A U.S. financial institution shall set aside in an escrow account on the date it receives a section 302 payment from a distributing corporation with respect to stock of a foreign account holder 30 percent (or the applicable dividend rate provided by a tax treaty for a qualifying foreign account holder) of the amount and shall credit the foreign account holder's account with the balance of the section 302 payment.

(2) Qualified intermediaries.—The amount set aside, under paragraph (c)(5)(iii)(B)(1) of this section shall include 30 percent (or the applicable dividend rate provided by a treaty) of the amount paid to any qualified intermediary (QI) (whether or not the QI has assumed primary withholding responsibility) and to any withholding foreign partnership or withholding foreign trust (WP/WT).

(C) *Request for section 302 payment certification.*—On or before the date it receives the section 302 payment, the U.S. financial institution shall provide the following information and instructions, in writing, to the foreign beneficial owner—

(1) The total number of distributing corporation's shares outstanding before and after the public section 302 distribution;

(2) An explanation of the conditions under which the section 302 payment will be treated as a dividend or a payment in exchange for stock for Federal income tax purposes (including an explanation of any applicable constructive ownership rules); and

(3) A request that the beneficial owner of the account provide a certification (section 302 payment certification), within 60 days of the section 302 payment, stating whether the section 302 payment is either a dividend or a payment in exchange for stock under the Internal Revenue Code.

(D) *Content of section 302 payment certification.*—The section 302 payment certification must include the following information:

(1) The beneficial owner's name and account number.

(2) The distributing corporation's name.

(3) The total shares of the distributing corporation outstanding immediately before and immediately after the public section 302 distribution.

(4) A certification from the beneficial owner that either—

(i) The section 302 payment is a payment in exchange for stock because the beneficial owner's proportionate interest has been reduced but not completely terminated;

(ii) The section 302 payment is a payment in exchange for stock because the beneficial owner's interest in the distributing corporation is completely terminated; or

(iii) The section 302 payment is a dividend.

(5) With respect to the certifications in paragraph (c)(5)(iii)(D)(4)(i) and (ii) of this section, the number of shares actually and constructively owned by the beneficial owner before and after the distribution and the beneficial owner's percentage ownership before and after the distribution.

(6) A penalties of perjury statement.

(7) The signature of the beneficial owner and date of signature.

(E) *Receipt of section 302 payment certification.—(1) Payment in exchange for stock.*—If, within the 60-day period described in paragraph (c)(5)(iii)(C)(3), the U.S. financial institution receives from the foreign beneficial owner a section 302 payment certification stating that the section 302 payment is a payment in exchange for stock, and if the U.S. financial institution does not know or have reason to know that the information in the section 302 payment certification is unreliable or incorrect, the U.S. financial institution shall credit the account with the amount set aside with respect to the beneficial owner who provides the certification. The entire amount paid (including the amount initially set aside) shall be reported as capital gains on Form 1042-S Foreign Person's U.S. Source Income Subject to Withholding.

(2) Unreliable or incorrect exchange certification.—If the U.S. financial institution knows or has reason to know that the information in the section 3 02 payment certification is unreliable or incorrect, the U.S. financial institution shall treat the payment as a payment for which no section 302 payment certification has been received and shall follow the withholding and reporting procedures in paragraph (c)(5)(iii)(E)(4) of this section.

(3) Dividend.—If, within the 60-day period, the U.S. financial institution receives a section 302 payment certification from the foreign beneficial owner stating that the section 302 payment is a dividend, the U.S. financial institution shall treat the amount set aside as tax withheld as of the time it receives the section 302 payment certification, and shall deposit that amount pursuant to the applicable regulations. The entire amount paid shall be reported on Form 1042-S as dividends.

(4) No timely certification received.—If, within the 60-day period, the U.S. financial institution does not receive a section 302 payment certification, or is treated under paragraph (c)(5)(iii)(E)(2) of this section as not receiving a section 302 payment certification, the U.S. financial institution shall treat the amount set aside as tax withheld as of the 61st day, and shall deposit that amount pursuant to the applicable regulations. The entire amount paid shall be reported on Form 1042-S as dividends.

(5) Late certification.—If, after the 60-day period has expired, the U.S. financial institution receives a section 3 02 payment certification from a foreign beneficial owner that the section 302 payment is a payment in exchange for stock and the conditions stated in § 1.1461-2(a) are satisfied, the U.S. financial institution may apply the refund or offset procedures of that paragraph.

(6) Determination of incorrect treatment.—If, after the 60-day period has expired, the U.S. financial institution determines that the section 302 payment was incorrectly treated as a distribution in exchange for stock, the procedures set forth regarding underwithholding in § 1.1461-2(b) are applicable.

(7) Undocumented beneficial owners.—The U.S. financial institution shall withhold at 30 percent on the entire amount paid to a beneficial owner that is not properly documented under §§ 1.1441-1, 1.1441-5, etc. and that is presumed to be a foreign person, whether or not the U.S. financial institution has received a section 302 payment certification from such beneficial owner. The U.S. financial institution shall report the entire amount paid on Form 1042-S as dividends.

(F) *Amounts in excess of section 302 payment.*—If the amount the U.S. financial institution credits to the account of the foreign beneficial owner from the escrow account includes an amount in excess of the section 302 payment, such as interest accrued on the escrowed funds, the U.S. financial institution shall report and withhold on such excess amount in accordance with the rules under Chapter 3 of the Internal Revenue Code.

(G) *U.S. non-exempt recipients.*—The U.S. financial institution shall treat beneficial owners that are U.S. non-exempt recipients, and that hold stock in the distributing corporation through QIs, WPs/WTs, NQIs and flow-throughs, in accordance with the section 302 payment certifications obtained from those U.S. non-exempt recipients and shall instruct foreign intermediaries and foreign flow-through entities to do the same.

(H) *Notice to distributing corporation.*—The U.S. financial institution shall notify the distributing corporation, in writing, by the filing date of Form 1042-S, of the aggregate amount of the section 302 payment that the U.S. financial institution has reported on Forms 1042-S as capital gains, and the aggregate amount of the section 302 payment that it has reported on Forms 1042-S as dividends.

(I) *Application of Escrow Procedure to Qualified Intermediaries.*—As provided in paragraph (c)(5)(iii)(A) of this section, only the U.S. financial institution may establish an escrow account and the amounts set aside in the escrow account shall include 30 percent (or the applicable treaty rate applicable to dividends) on payments made to a direct account holder that is a QI (including a QI that has assumed primary withholding responsibility). Under the procedure described in paragraph (c)(5)(iii)(I)(3), a QI shall provide the U.S. financial institution with a withholding statement as required in the QI Agreement. If there is a chain of QIs, each QI in the chain shall apply the procedure. The procedures described in this paragraph (I) shall be applied to withholding foreign partnerships and withholding foreign trusts within the meaning of §§ 1.1441-5(c)(2) and (e)(5)(v), respectively, in the same manner as the procedures apply to a QI.

(1) Request for section 302 payment certification.—The U.S. financial institution shall provide the information and instructions described in paragraph (c)(5)(iii)(C) of this section to the QI, and the QI shall provide the same information and instructions to its account holders including account holders that are U.S. non-exempt recipients.

(2) Content of section 302 payment certification.—The content of the section 302 payment certification shall include the information described in paragraph (c)(5)(iii)(D) of this section.

(3) Receipt of section 302 payment certification.—(i) Payment in exchange for stock.—If, within the 60-day period described in paragraph (c)(5)(iii)(C), the QI receives from the beneficial owner a section 302 payment certification stating that the section 302 payment is a payment in exchange for stock and if the QI does not know or have reason to know that the information in the section 302 payment certification is unreliable or incorrect, the QI shall reflect such treatment in its withholding statement provided to the U.S. financial institution, and, based upon the withholding statement, the U.S. financial institution shall release payment from its escrow and the QI shall credit the beneficial owner's account with the amount set aside by the U.S. financial institution with respect to the beneficial owner who provided the certification. The entire amount paid (including the amount initially set aside) shall be reported on the QI's pooled basis Form 1042-S as capital gains.

(ii) Unreliable or incorrect exchange certification.—If the QI knows or has reason to know that the information in the section 302 payment certification is unreliable or incorrect, the QI shall treat the payment as a payment for which no section 302 payment certification has been received and shall follow the withholding and reporting procedures in paragraph (c)(5)(iii)(I)(3)(iv) of this section.

(iii) Dividend.—If, within the 60-day period, QI receives a section 302 payment certification stating that the section 302 payment is a dividend, the QI shall reflect such treatment in its withholding statement and shall treat the payment as a dividend for purposes of its reporting and withholding responsibilities under the QI agreement. The entire amount paid shall be reported on its pooled basis Form 1042-S as dividends.

(iv) No timely certification received.—If, within the 60-day period, the QI does not receive a section 302 payment certification, or is treated under paragraph (c)(5)(iii)(I)(3)(ii) of this section as not receiving a section 302 payment certification, the QI shall reflect such treatment in its withholding statement provided to the U.S. financial institution and shall treat the payment as a dividend for purposes of its reporting and withholding responsibilities under the QI agreement. The entire amount paid shall be reported on its pooled basis Form 1042-S as dividends.

(v) Late certification.—If, after the 60-day period has expired, the QI receives a section 302 payment certification from a beneficial owner that the section 302 payment is a payment in exchange for stock and the conditions stated in the QI agreement regarding the refund and offset procedures are satisfied, the QI may apply such refund or offset procedures.

(vi) Determination of incorrect treatment.—If, after the 60-day period has expired, the QI determines that the section 302 payment was incorrectly treated as a distribution in exchange for stock, the procedures set forth regarding adjustments for underwithholding in the QI agreement are applicable.

(vii) Undocumented beneficial owners.—The QI shall withhold at 30 percent on the entire amount paid to a beneficial owner that is not properly documented and that is presumed to be a foreign person, whether or not the QI has received a section 302 payment certification from such beneficial owner. The QI shall report the entire amount paid on its pooled basis Form 1042-S as dividends.

(4) U.S. non-exempt recipients.—The QI shall treat direct account holders that are U.S. non-exempt recipients, and that hold stock in the distributing corporation, in accordance with the section 302 payment certifications obtained from those U.S. non-exempt recipients and shall instruct foreign intermediaries and foreign flow-through entities to do the same.

(J) *Intermediaries that are not qualified intermediaries.*—If the U.S. financial institution has an account holder that is an intermediary that is not a QI ("NQI"), the U.S. financial institution shall apply the rules of paragraph (c)(5)(iii)(J)(1) through (4) of this section. Where the provisions of this paragraph (J) refer only to the U.S. financial institution, they shall apply in the same manner to a QI or WP/WT and where they refer to an NQI, they shall apply in the same manner to a flow-through that is not a WP or WT.

(1) The U.S. financial institution shall provide the information and instructions described in paragraph (c)(5)(iii)(C) of this section to the NQI and the NQI shall provide the same information and instructions to its account holders.

(2) The content of the section 302 payment certification shall include the information described in paragraph (c)(5)(iii)(D) of this section.

(3) The NQI shall provide the section 302 payment certification to the U.S. financial institution together with the otherwise required documentation and a withholding statement made in accordance with the section 302 payment certification.

(4) The U.S. financial institution shall treat the section 3 02 payment as a dividend or a payment in exchange for stock based on the information and documentation provided to it under paragraph (c)(5)(iii)(J)(3) of this section. The U.S. financial institution shall withhold and report on a specific payee basis in accordance with this information.

* * *

[Prop. Reg. § 1.1441-3.]

[Proposed 10-17-2007.]

§ 1.1441-4. Exemptions from withholding for certain effectively connected income and other amounts.—(a) *Certain income connected with a U.S. trade or business.*—(1) *In general.*—No withholding is required under section 1441 on income otherwise subject to withholding if the income is (or is deemed to be) effectively connected with the conduct of a trade or business within the United States and is includible in the beneficial owner's gross income for the taxable year. For purposes of this paragraph (a), an amount is not deemed to be includible in gross income if the amount is (or is deemed to be) effectively connected with the conduct of a trade or business within the United States and the beneficial owner claims an exemption from tax under an income tax treaty because the income is not attributable to a permanent establishment in the United States. To claim a reduced rate of withholding because the income is not attributable to a permanent establishment, see § 1.1441-6(b)(1). This paragraph (a) does not apply to income of a foreign corporation to which section 543(a)(7) applies for the taxable year or to compensation for personal services performed by an individual. See paragraph (b) of this section for compensation for personal services performed by an individual.

(2) *Withholding agent's reliance on a claim of effectively connected income.*—(i) *In general.*—Absent actual knowledge or reason to know otherwise, a withholding agent may rely on a claim of exemption based upon paragraph (a)(1) of this section if, prior to the payment to the foreign person, the withholding agent can reliably associate the payment with a Form W-8 upon which it can rely to treat the payment as made to a foreign beneficial owner in accordance with § 1.1441-1(e)(1)(ii). For purposes of this paragraph (a), a withholding certificate is valid only if, in addition to other applicable requirements, it includes the taxpayer identifying number of the person whose name is on the Form W-8 and represents, under penalties of perjury, that the amounts for which the certificate is furnished are effectively connected with the conduct of a trade or business in the United States and is includable in the beneficial owner's gross income for the taxable year. In the absence of a reliable claim that the income is effectively connected with the conduct of a trade or business in the United States, the income is presumed not to be effectively connected, except as otherwise provided in paragraph (a)(2)(ii) or (3) of this section. See § 1.1441-1(e)(4)(ii)(C) for the period of validity applicable to a certificate provided under this section and § 1.1441-1(e)(4)(ii)(D) for changes in circumstances arising during the taxable year indicating that the income to which the certificate relates is not, or is no longer expected to be, effectively connected with the conduct of a trade or business within the United States. A withholding certificate shall be effective only for the item or items of income specified therein. The provisions of § 1.1441-1(b)(3)(iv) dealing with a 90-day grace period shall apply for purposes of this section.

(ii) *Special rules for U.S. branches of foreign persons.*—(A) *U.S. branches of certain foreign banks or foreign insurance companies.*—A payment to a U.S. branch described in § 1.1441-1(b)(2)(iv)(B)(*3*) is presumed to be effectively connected with the conduct of a trade or business in the United States without the need to furnish a certificate if the withholding agent obtains an EIN for the entity, unless the U.S. branch provides a U.S. branch withholding certificate described in § 1.1441-1(e)(3)(v) that represents otherwise. If no certificate is furnished but the income is not, in fact, effectively connected income, then the branch must withhold whether the payment is collected on behalf of other persons or on behalf of another branch of the same entity. See § 1.1441-1(b)(2)(iv) and (b)(6) for general rules applicable to payments to U.S. branches of foreign persons.

(B) *Other U.S. branches.*—See § 1.1441-1(b)(2)(iv)(E) for similar procedures for other U.S. branches to the extent provided in a determination letter from the IRS.

(3) *Income on notional principal contracts.*—(i) *General rule.*—Except as otherwise provided in paragraph (a)(3)(iii) of this section, a withholding agent that pays amounts attributable to a notional principal contract described in § 1.863-7(a) or § 1.988-2(e) shall have no obligation to withhold on the amounts paid under the terms of the notional principal contract regardless of whether a withholding certificate is provided. However, a withholding agent must file returns under § 1.1461-1(b) and (c) reporting the income that it must treat as effectively connected with the conduct of a trade or business in the United States under the provisions of this paragraph (a)(3). Except as otherwise provided in paragraph (a)(3)(ii) of this section, a withholding agent must treat the income as effectively connected with the conduct of a U.S. trade or business if the income is paid to, or to the account of, a qualified business unit of a foreign person located in the United States or, if the payment is paid to, or to the account of, a qualified business unit of a foreign person located outside the United States, the withholding agent knows, or has reason to know, the payment is effectively connected with the conduct of a trade or business within the United States. Income on a notional principal contract does not include the amount characterized as interest under the provisions of § 1.446-3(g)(4).

(ii) *Exception for certain payments.*—A payment shall not be treated as effectively connected with the conduct of a trade or business within the United States for purposes of paragraph (a)(3)(i) of this section even if no withholding certificate is furnished if the payee provides a representation in a master agreement that governs the transactions in notional principal contracts between the parties (for example an International Swaps and Derivatives Association (ISDA) Agreement, including the Schedule thereto) or in the confirmation on the particular notional principal contract transaction that the payee is a U.S. person or a non-U.S. branch of a foreign person.

(iii) *Exception for specified notional principal contracts.*—A withholding agent that makes a payment attributable to a specified notional principal contract described in section 871(m) and the regulations thereunder that is not treated as effectively connected with the conduct of a trade or business within the United States is obligated to withhold on the amount of the payment that is a dividend equivalent.

(b) *Compensation for personal services of an individual.*—(1) *Exemption from withholding.*—Withholding is not required under § 1.1441-1 from salaries, wages, remuneration, or any other compensation for personal services of a nonresident alien individual if such compensation is effectively connected with the conduct of a trade or business within the United States and—

(i) Such compensation is subject to withholding under section 3402 (relating to withholding on wages) and the regulations under that section;

(ii) Such compensation would be subject to withholding under section 3402 but for the provisions of section 3401(a) (not including section 3401(a)(6)) and the regulations under that section. This paragraph (b)(1)(ii) does not apply to payments to a nonresident alien individual from any trust described in section 401(a), any annuity plan described in section 403(a), any annuity, custodial account, or retirement income account described in section 403(b), or an individual retirement account or individual retirement annuity described in section 408. Instead, these payments are subject to withholding under this section to the extent they are exempted from the definition of wages under section 3401(a)(12) or to the extent they are from an annuity, custodial account, or retirement income account described in section 403(b), or an individual retirement account or individual retirement annuity described in section 408. Thus, for example, payments to a nonresident alien individual from a trust described in section 401 (a) are subject to withholding under section 1441 and not under section 3405 or section 3406;

(iii) Such compensation is for services performed by a nonresident alien individual who is a resident of Canada or Mexico and who enters and leaves the United States at frequent intervals;

(iv) Such compensation is, or will be, exempt from the income tax imposed by chapter 1 of the Code by reason of a provision of the Internal Revenue Code or a tax treaty to which the United States is a party;

(v) Such compensation is paid after January 3, 1979 as a commission or rebate paid by a ship supplier to a nonresident alien individual, who is employed by a nonresident alien individual, foreign partnership, or foreign corporation in the operation of a ship or ships of foreign registry, for placing orders for supplies to be used in the operation of such ship or ships with the supplier. See section 162(c) and the regulations thereunder for denial of deductions for illegal bribes, kickbacks, and other payments; or

(vi) Compensation that is exempt from withholding under section 3402 by reason of section 3402(e), provided that the employee and his employer enter into an agreement under section 3402(p) to provide for the withholding of income tax upon payments of amounts described in § 31.3401(a)-3(b)(1) of this chapter. An employee who desires to enter into such an agreement should furnish his employer with Form W-4 (withholding exemption certificate) (or such other form as the Internal Revenue Service (IRS) may prescribe). See section 3402(f) and the regulations thereunder and § 31.3402(p)-1 of this chapter.

(2) *Manner of obtaining withholding exemption under tax treaty.*—(i) *In general.*—In order to obtain the exemption from withholding by reason of a tax treaty provided by paragraph (b)(1)(iv) of this section, a nonresident alien individual must submit a withholding certificate (described in paragraph (b)(2)(ii) of this section) to each withholding agent from whom amounts are to be received. A separate withholding certificate must be filed for each taxable year of the alien individual. If the withholding agent is satisfied that an exemption from withholding is warranted (see paragraph (b)(2)(iii) of this section), the withholding certificate shall be accepted in the manner set forth in paragraph (b)(2)(iv) of this section. The exemption from withholding becomes effective for payments made at least ten days after a copy of the accepted withholding certificate is forwarded to the IRS. The withholding agent may rely on an accepted withholding certificate only if the IRS has not objected to the certificate. For purposes of this paragraph (b)(2)(i), the IRS will be considered to have not objected to the certificate if it has not notified the withholding agent within a 10-day period beginning from the date that the withholding certificate is forwarded to the IRS pursuant to paragraph (b)(2)(v) of this section. After expiration of the 10-day period, the withholding agent may rely on the withholding certificate retroactive to the date of the first payment covered by the certificate. The fact that the IRS does not object to the withholding certificate within the 10-day period provided in this paragraph (b)(2)(i) shall not preclude the IRS from examining the withholding agent at a later date with respect to facts that the withholding agent knew or had reason to know regarding the payment and eligibility for a reduced rate and that were not disclosed to the IRS as part of the 10-day review process.

(ii) *Withholding certificate claiming withholding exemption.*—The statement claiming an exemption from withholding shall be made on Form 8233 (or an acceptable substitute or such other form as the IRS may prescribe). Form 8233 shall be dated, signed by the beneficial owner under penalties of perjury, and contain the following information—

(A) The individual's name, permanent residence address, taxpayer identifying number (or a copy of a completed Form W-7 or SS-5 showing that a number has been applied for), and the U.S. visa number, if any;

(B) The individual's current immigration status and visa type;

(C) The individual's original date of entry into the United States;

(D) The country that issued the individual's passport and the number of such passport, or the individual's permanent address if a citizen of Canada or Mexico;

(E) The taxable year, for which the statement is to apply the compensation to which it relates, and the amount (or estimated amount if exact amount not known) of such compensation;

(F) A statement that the individual is not a citizen or resident of the United States;

(G) The number of personal exemptions claimed by the individual;

(H) A statement as to whether the compensation to be paid to him or her during the taxable year is or will be exempt from income tax and the reason why the compensation is exempt;

(I) If the compensation is exempt from withholding by reason of an income tax treaty to which the United States is a party, the tax treaty and provision under which the exemption from withholding is claimed and the country of which the individual is a resident;

(J) Sufficient facts to justify the claim in exemption from withholding; and

(K) Any other information as may be required by the form or accompanying instructions in addition to, or in lieu of, the information described in this paragraph (b)(2)(ii).

(iii) *Review by withholding agent.*—The exemption from withholding provided by paragraph (b)(1)(iv) of this section shall not apply unless the withholding agent accepts (in the manner provided in paragraph (b)(2)(iv) of this section) the statement on Form 8233, "Exemption From Withholding on Compensation for Independent (and Certain Dependent) Personal Services of a Nonresident Alien Individual," (or successor form) supplied by the nonresident alien individual. Before accepting the statement, the withholding agent must examine the statement. If the withholding agent knows or has reason to know that any of the facts or assertions on Form 8233 may be false or that the eligibility of the individual's compensation for the exemption cannot be readily determined, the withholding agent may not accept the statement on Form 8233 and is required to withhold under this section. If the withholding agent accepts the statement and subsequently finds that any of the facts or assertions contained on Form 8233 may be false or that the eligibility of the individual's compensation for the exemption can no longer be readily determined, then the withholding agent shall promptly so notify the IRS by letter, and the withholding agent is not relieved of liability to withhold on any amounts still to be paid. If the withholding agent is notified by the IRS that the eligibility of the individual's compensation for the exemption is in doubt or that such compensation is not eligible for the exemption, the withholding agent is required to withhold under this section. The rules of this paragraph (b)(2) are illustrated by the following examples.

Example 1. C, a nonresident alien individual, submits Form 8233 to W, a withholding agent. The statement on Form 8233 does not include all the information required by paragraph (b)(2)(ii) of this section. Therefore, W has reason to know that he or she cannot readily determine whether C's compensation for personal services is eligible for an exemption from withholding and, therefore, W must withhold.

Example 2. D, a nonresident alien individual, is performing services for W, a withholding agent. W has accepted a statement on Form 8233 submitted by D, according to the provisions of this section. W receives notice from the IRS that the eligibility of D's compensation for a withholding exemption is in doubt. Therefore, W has reason to know that the eligibility of the compensation for a withholding exemption cannot be readily determined, as of the date W receives the notification, and W must withhold tax under section 1441 on amounts paid after receipt of the notification.

Example 3. E, a nonresident alien individual, submits Form 8233 to W, a withholding agent for whom E is to perform personal services. The statement contains all the information requested on Form 8233. E claims an exemption from withholding based on a personal exemption amount computed on the number of days E will perform personal services for W in the United States. If W does not know or have reason to know that any statement on the Form 8233 is false or that the eligibility of E's compensation for the withholding exemption cannot be readily determined, W can accept the statement on Form 8233 and exempt from withholding the appropriate amount of E's income.

(iv) *Acceptance by withholding agent.*—If after the review described in paragraph (b)(2)(iii) of this section the withholding agent is satisfied that an exemption from withholding is warranted, the withholding agent may accept the statement by making a certification, verified by a declaration that it is made under the penalties of perjury, on Form 8233. The certification shall be—

(A) That the withholding agent has examined the statement,

(B) That the withholding agent is satisfied that an exemption from withholding is warranted, and

(C) That the withholding agent does not know or have reason to know that the individual's compensation is not entitled to the exemption or that the eligibility of the individual's compensation for the exemption cannot be readily determined.

(v) *Copies of Form 8233.*—The withholding agent shall forward one copy of each Form 8233 that is accepted under paragraph (b)(2)(iv) of this section to the IRS within five days of such acceptance. The withholding agent shall retain a copy of Form 8233.

(3) *Withholding agreements.*—Compensation for personal services of a nonresident alien individual who is engaged during the taxable year in the conduct of a trade or business within the United States may be wholly or partially exempted from the withholding required by § 1.1441-1 if an agreement is reached between the IRS and the alien individual with respect to the amount of withholding required. Such agreement shall be available in the circumstances and in the manner set forth by the Internal Revenue Service, and shall be effective for payments covered by the agreement that are made after the agreement is executed by all parties. The alien individual must agree to timely file an income tax return for the current taxable year.

(4) *Final payment exemption.*—(i) *General rule.*—Compensation for independent personal services of a nonresident alien individual who is engaged during the taxable year in the conduct of a trade or business within the United States may be wholly or partially exempted from the withholding required by § 1.1441-1 from the final payment of compensation for independent personal services. This exemption does not apply to wages. This exemption from withholding is available only once during an alien individual's taxable year and is obtained by the alien individual presenting to the withholding agent a letter in duplicate from a district director stating the amount of compensation subject to the exemption and the amount that would otherwise be withheld from such final payment under section 1441 that shall be paid to the alien individual due to the exemption. The alien individual shall attach a copy of the letter to his or her income tax return for the taxable year for which the exemption is effective.

(ii) *Final payment of compensation for personal services.*—For purposes of this paragraph, final payment of compensation for personal services means the last payment of compensation, other than wages, for personal services rendered within the United States that the individual expects to receive from any withholding agent during the taxable year.

(iii) *Manner of applying for final payment exemption.*—In order to obtain the final payment exemption provided by paragraph (b)(4)(i) of this section, the nonresident alien individual (or his or her agent) must file the forms and provide the information required by the district director. Ordinary and necessary business expenses may be taken into account if substantiated to the satisfaction of the district director. The alien individual must submit a statement, signed by him or her and verified by a declaration that it is made under the penalties of perjury, that all the information provided is true and that to his or her knowledge no relevant information has been omitted. The information required to be submitted includes, but is not limited to—

(A) A statement by each withholding agent from whom amounts of gross income effectively connected with the conduct of a trade or business within the United States have been received by the alien individual during the taxable year, of the amount of such income paid and the amount of tax withheld, signed and verified by a declaration that it is made under penalties of perjury;

(B) A statement by the withholding agent from whom the final payment of compensation for personal services will be received, of the amount of such final payment and the amount which would be withheld under § 1.1441-1 if a final payment exemption under paragraph (b)(4)(i) of this section is not granted, signed and verified by a declaration that it is made under penalties of perjury;

(C) A statement by the individual that he or she does not intend to receive any other amounts of gross income effectively connected with the conduct of a trade or business within the United States during the current taxable year;

(D) The amount of tax which has been withheld (or paid) under any other provision of the Code or regulations with respect to any income effectively connected with the conduct of a trade or business within the United States during the current taxable year;

(E) The amount of any outstanding tax liabilities (and interest and penalties relating thereto) from the current taxable year or prior taxable periods; and

(F) The provision of any income tax treaty under which a partial or complete exemption from withholding may be claimed, the country of the individual's residence, and a statement of sufficient facts to justify an exemption pursuant to such treaty.

(iv) *Letter to withholding agent.*—If the district director is satisfied that the information provided under paragraph (b)(4)(iii) of this section is sufficient, the district director will, after coordination with the Director of the Foreign Operations District, ascertain the amount of the alien individual's tentative income tax for the taxable year with respect to gross income that is effectively connected with the conduct of a trade or business within the United States. After the tentative tax has been ascertained, the district director will provide the alien individual with a letter to the withholding agent stating the amount of the final payment of compensation for personal services that is exempt from withholding, and the amount that would otherwise be withheld under section 1441 that shall be paid to the alien individual due to the exemption. The amount of compensation for personal services exempt from withholding under this paragraph (b)(4) shall not exceed $5,000.

Example 1. On July 15, 1983, B, a nonresident alien individual, appears before a district director with the information required by paragraph (b)(4)(iii) of this section. B has received personal service income in 1983 from which $3,000 has been withheld under section 1441. On August 1, 1983, B will receive $5,000 in personal service income from W. B does not intend to receive any other income subject to U.S. tax during 1983. Taking into account B's substantiated deductible business expenses, the district director computes the tentative tax liability on B's income effectively connected with the conduct of a trade or business in the United States during 1983 (including the $5,000 payment to be made on August 1, 1983) to be $3,300. B does not owe U.S. tax for any other taxable periods. The amount of B's final payment exemption is determined as follows:

(1) The amount of total withholding is $4,500 ($3,000 previously withheld plus $1,500, 30% of the $5,000 final payment);

(2) The amount of tentative excess withholding is $1,200 (total withholding of $4,500 minus B's tentative tax liability of $3,300); and

(3) To allow B to receive $1,200 of the amount which would otherwise have been withheld from the final payment, the district director allows a withholding exemption for $4,000 of B's final payment. W must withhold $300 from the final payment.

Example 2. The facts are the same as in Example 1 except B will receive a final payment of compensation on August 1, 1983, in the amount of $10,000 and B's tentative tax liability is $3,900. The amount of B's final payment exemption is determined as follows:

(1) The amount of total withholding is $6,000 ($3,000 previously withheld plus $3,000, 30% of the $10,000 final payment);

(2) The amount of tentative excess withholding is $2,100 (total withholding of $6,000 minus B's tentative tax liability of $3,900); and

(3) To allow B to receive $2,100 of the amount which would otherwise be withheld from the final payment, $7,000 of the final payment would have to be exempt from withholding; however, as no more than $5,000 of the final payment can be exempt from withholding under this paragraph (b)(4), the district director allows a withholding exemption for $5,000 of B's final payment. B must file a claim for refund at the end of the taxable year to obtain a refund of $600. W must withhold $1,500 from the final payment.

(5) *Requirement of return.*—The tentative tax determined by the district director under paragraph (b)(4)(iv) of this section or by the Director of the Foreign Operations District under the withholding agreement procedure of paragraph (b)(3) of this section shall not constitute a final determination of the income tax liability of the nonresident alien individual, nor shall such determination constitute a tax return of the nonresident alien individual for any taxable period. An alien individual who applies for or obtains an exemption from withholding under the procedures of paragraphs (b)(2), (3), or (4) of this section is not relieved of the obligation to file a return of income under section 6012.

(6) *Personal exemption.*—(i) *In general.*—To determine the tax to be withheld at source under § 1.1441-1 from remuneration paid for personal services performed within the United States by a nonresident alien individual and from scholarship and fellowship income described in paragraph (c) of this section, a withholding agent may take into account one personal exemption pursuant to sections 873(b)(3) and 151 regardless of whether the income is effectively connected. For purposes of withholding under section 1441 on remuneration for personal services, the exemption must be prorated upon a daily basis for the period during which the personal services are performed within the United States by the nonresident alien individual by dividing by 365 the number of days in the period during which the individual is present in the United States for the purpose of performing the services and multiplying the result by the amount of the personal exemption in effect for the taxable year. See § 31.3402(f)(6)-1 of this chapter.

(ii) *Multiple exemptions.*—More than one personal exemption may be claimed in the case of a resident of a contiguous country or a national of the United States under section 873(b)(3). In addition, residents of a country with which the United States has an income tax treaty in effect may be eligible to claim more than one personal exemption if the treaty so provides. Claims for more than one personal exemption shall be made on the withholding certificate furnished to the withholding agent. The exemption must be prorated on a daily basis in the same manner as described in paragraph (b)(6)(i) of this section.

(iii) *Special rule where both certain scholarship and compensation income are received.*—The fact that both non-compensatory scholarship income and compensation income (including compensatory scholarship income) are received during the taxable year does not entitle the taxpayer to claim more than one personal exemption amount (or more than the additional amounts permitted under paragraph (b)(6)(ii) of this section). Thus, if a nonresident alien student receives non-compensatory taxable scholarship income from one withholding agent and compensation income from another withholding agent, no more than the total personal exemption amount permitted under the Internal Revenue Code or under an income tax treaty may be taken into account by both withholding agents. For this purpose, the withholding agent may rely on a representation from the beneficial owner that the exemption amount claimed does not exceed the amount permissible under this section.

(c) *Special rules for scholarship and fellowship income.*—(1) *In general.*—Under section 871(c), certain amounts paid as a scholarship or fellowship for study, training, or research in the United States to a nonresident alien individual temporarily present in the United States as a nonimmigrant under section 101(a)(15)(F), (J), (M), or (Q) of the Immigration and Nationality Act are treated as income effectively connected with the conduct of a trade or business within the United States. The amounts described in the preceding sentence are those amounts that do not represent compensation for services. Such amounts (as described in the second sentence of section 1441(b)) are subject to withholding under section 1441, but at the lower rate of 14 percent. That rate may be reduced under the provisions of an income tax treaty. Claims of a reduced rate under an income tax treaty shall be made under the procedures described in § 1.1441-6(b)(1). Therefore, claims for reduction in withholding under an income tax treaty on amounts described in this paragraph (c)(1) may not be made on a Form 8233. However, if the payee is receiving both compensation for personal services (including compensatory scholarship income) and non-compensatory scholarship income described in this paragraph (c)(1) from the same withholding agent, claims for reduction of withholding on both types of income may be made on Form 8233.

(2) *Alternate withholding election.*—A withholding agent may elect to withhold on the amounts described in paragraph (c)(1) of this section at the rates applicable under section 3402, as if the income were wages. Such election shall be made by obtaining a Form W-4 (or an acceptable substitute or such other form as the IRS may prescribe) from the beneficial owner. The fact that the withholding agent asks the beneficial owner to furnish a Form W-4 for such fellowship or scholarship income or to take such income into account in preparing such Form W-4 shall serve as notice to the beneficial owner that the income is being treated as wages for purposes of withholding tax under section 1441.

(d) *Annuities received under qualified plans.*—Withholding is not required under section § 1.1441-1 in the case of any amount received as an annuity if the amount is exempt from tax under section 871(f) and the regulations under that section. The withholding agent may exempt the payment from withholding if, prior to payment, it can reliably associate the payment with documentation upon which it can rely to treat the payment as made to a beneficial owner in accordance with § 1.1441-1(e)(1)(ii). A beneficial owner withholding certificate furnished for purposes of claiming the benefits of the exemption under this paragraph (d) is valid only if, in addition to other applicable requirements, it contains a taxpayer identifying number.

(e) *Per diem of certain alien trainees.*—Withholding is not required under section 1441(a) and § 1.1441-1 on per diem amounts paid for subsistence by the United States Government (directly or by contract) to any nonresident alien individual who is engaged in any program of training in the United States under the Mutual Security Act of 1954, as amended (22 U.S.C. chapter 24). This rule shall apply even though such amounts are subject to tax under section 871. Any exemption from withholding pursuant to this paragraph (e) applies without a requirement that documentation be furnished to the withholding agent. However, documentation may have to be furnished for purposes of the information reporting provisions under section 6041 and backup withholding under section 3406. The exemption from withholding granted by this paragraph (e) is not a determination that the amounts are not fixed or determinable annual or periodical income.

(f) *Failure to receive withholding certificates timely or to act in accordance with applicable presumptions.*—See applicable procedures described in § 1.1441-1(b)(7) in the event the withholding agent does not hold an appropriate withholding certificate or other appropriate documentation at the time of payment or does not act in accordance with applicable presumptions described in paragraph (a)(2)(i), (2)(ii), or (3) of this section.

(g) *Effective/applicability date.*—This section applies to payments made on or after January 6, 2017. (For payments made after June 30, 2014, and before January 6, 2017, see this section as in effect and contained in 26 CFR part 1, revised April 1, 2016. For payments made after December 31, 2000, see this section as in effect and contained in 26 CFR part 1 revised April 1, 2013.) [Reg. § 1.1441-4.]

☐ [*T.D.* 6187, 7-5-56. *Amended by T.D.* 6229, 4-22-57; *T.D.* 6592, 2-27-62; *T.D.* 6908, 12-30-66; *T.D.* 6922, 6-16-67; *T.D.* 7378, 9-29-75; *T.D.* 7582, 1-2-79; *T.D.* 7777, 5-18-81; *T.D.* 7842, 11-2-82; *T.D.* 7977, 9-19-84; *T.D.* 8015, 3-25-85; *T.D.* 8288, 2-2-90; *T.D.* 8734, 10-6-97; *T.D.* 8804, 12-30-98; *T.D.* 8856, 12-29-99; *T.D.* 8881, 5-15-2000; *T.D.* 9572, 1-19-2012 (*corrected* 3-7-2012); *T.D.* 9648, 12-4-2013, *T.D.* 9658, 2-28-2014, *T.D.* 9808, 12-30-2016 (*corrected* 6-29-2017) *and T.D.* 9890, 12-27-2019.]

§ 1.1441-5. Withholding on payments to partnerships, trusts, and estates.—(a) *In general.*—This section describes the rules that apply to payments made to partnerships, trusts, and estates. Paragraph (b) of this section prescribes the rules that apply to a withholding agent making a payment to a U.S. partnership, trust, or estate. It also prescribes the obligations of a U.S. partnership, trust, or estate that makes a payment to a foreign partner, beneficiary, or owner. Paragraph (c) of this section prescribes rules that apply to a withholding agent that makes a payment to a foreign partnership. Paragraph (d) of this section provides presumption rules that apply to payments made to foreign partnerships. Paragraph (e) of this section prescribes rules, including presumption rules, that apply to a withholding agent that makes a payment to a foreign trust or foreign estate.

(b) *Rules applicable to U.S. partnerships, trusts, and estates.*—(1) *Payments to U.S. partnerships, trusts, and estates.*—No withholding is required under section 1.1441-1(b)(1) on a payment of an amount subject to withholding (as defined in § 1.1441-2(a)) that a withholding agent may treat as made to a U.S. payee. Therefore, if a withholding agent can reliably associate (within the meaning of § 1.1441-2(b)(vii)) a Form W-9 provided in accordance with § 1.1441-1(d)(2) or (4) by a U.S. partnership, U.S. trust, or a U.S. estate the withholding agent may treat the payment as made to a U.S. payee and the payment is not subject to withholding under section 1441 even though the partnership, trust, or estate may have foreign partners, beneficiaries, or owners. A withholding agent is also not required to withhold under section 1441 on a payment it makes to an entity presumed to be a U.S. payee under paragraphs (d)(2) and (e)(6)(ii) of this section.

(2) *Withholding by U.S. payees.*—(i) *U.S. partnerships.*—(A) *In general.*—A U.S. partnership is required to withhold under § 1.1441-1 as a withholding agent on an amount subject to withholding (as defined in § 1.1441-2(a)) that is includible in the gross income of a partner that is a foreign person. Subject to paragraph (b)(2)(v) of this section, a U.S. partnership shall withhold when any distributions that include amounts subject to withholding (including guaranteed payments made by a U.S. partnership) are made. To the extent a foreign partner's distributive share of income subject to withholding has not actually been distributed to the foreign partner, the U.S. partnership must withhold on the foreign partner's distributive share of the income on the earlier of the date that the statement required under section 6031(b) is mailed or otherwise provided to the partner or the due date for furnishing the statement.

(B) *Effectively connected income of partners.*—Withholding on items of income that are effectively connected income in the hands of the partners who are foreign persons is governed by section 1446 and not by this section. In such a case, partners in a domestic partnership are not required to furnish a withholding certificate in order to claim an exemption from withholding under section 1441(c)(1) and § 1.1441-4.

(ii) *U.S. simple trusts.*—A U.S. trust that is described in section 651(a) (a U.S. simple trust) is required to withhold under chapter 3 of the Internal Revenue Code as a withholding agent on the distributable net income includible in the gross income of a foreign beneficiary to the extent the distributable net income is an amount subject to withholding (as defined in § 1.1441-2(a)). A U.S. simple trust shall withhold when a distribution is made to a foreign beneficiary. The U.S. trust may make a reasonable estimate of the portion of the distribution that constitutes distributable net income consisting of an amount subject to withholding and apply the appropriate rate of withholding to the estimated amount. If, at the end of the taxable year in which the distribution is made, the U.S. simple trust determines that it underwithheld under section 1441 or 1442, the trust shall be liable as a withholding agent for the amount under withheld under section 1461. No penalties shall be imposed for failure to withhold and deposit the tax if the U.S. simple trust's estimate was reasonable and the trust pays the underwithheld amount on or before the due date of Form 1042 under section 1461. Any payment of underwithheld amounts by the U.S. simple trust shall not be treated as income subject to additional withholding even if that amount is treated as additional income to the foreign beneficiary, unless the additional amount is income to the foreign beneficiary as a result of a contractual arrangement between the parties regarding the satisfaction of the foreign beneficiary's tax liability. To the extent a U.S. simple trust is required to, but does not, distribute such income to a foreign beneficiary, the U.S. trust must withhold on the foreign beneficiary's allocable share at the time the income is required (without extension) to be reported on Form 1042-S under § 1.1461-1(c).

(iii) *U.S. complex trusts and U.S. estates.*—A U.S. trust that is not a trust described in section 651(a) (see paragraph (b)(2)(ii) of this section) or sections 671 through 679 (see paragraph (b)(2)(iv) of this section) (a U.S. complex trust) is required to withhold under chapter 3 of the Internal Revenue Code (Code) as a withholding agent on the distributable net income includible in the gross income of a foreign beneficiary to the extent the distributable net income consists of an amount subject to withholding (as defined in § 1.1441-2(a)) that is, or is required to be, distributed currently. The U.S. complex trust shall withhold when a distribution is made to a foreign beneficiary. The trust may use the same procedures regarding an estimate of the amount subject to withholding as a U.S. simple trust under paragraph (b)(2)(ii) of this section. To the extent an amount subject to withholding is required to be, but is not actually, distributed, the U.S. complex trust must withhold on the foreign beneficiary's allocable share at the time the income is required to be reported on Form 1042-S under § 1.1461-1(c), without extension. A U.S. estate is required to withhold under chapter 3 of the Code on the distributable net income includible in the gross income of a foreign beneficiary to the extent the distributable net income consists of an amount subject to withholding (as defined in § 1.1441-2(a)) that is actually distributed. A U.S. estate may also use the reasonable estimate procedures of paragraph (b)(2)(ii) of this section. However, those procedures apply to an estate that has a taxable year other than a calendar year only if the estate files an amended return on Form 1042 for the calendar year in which the distribution was made and pays the underwithheld tax and interest within 60 days after the close of the taxable year in which the distribution was made.

(iv) *U.S. grantor trusts.*—A U.S. trust that is described in section 671 through 679 (a U.S. grantor trust) must withhold on any income includible in the gross income of a foreign person that is treated as an owner of the grantor trust to the extent the amount includible consists of an amount that is subject to withholding (as described in § 1.1441-2(a)). The withholding must occur at the time the income is received by, or credited to, the trust.

(v) *Subsequent distribution.*—If a U.S. partnership or U.S. trust withholds on a foreign partner, beneficiary, or owner's share of an amount subject to withholding before the amount is actually distributed to the partner, beneficiary, or owner, withholding is not required when the amount is subsequently distributed.

(vi) *Coordination with chapter 4 requirements for U.S. partnerships, trusts, and estates.*—To the extent that a U.S. partnership is required to withhold on an amount under chapter 4 with respect to a partner, beneficiary, or owner, the partnership, trust, or estate must apply the rules described in § 1.1473-1(a)(5) to determine when it must withhold on the amount under chapter 4. In a case in which withholding applies under chapter 4 to such an amount, see § 1.1441-3(a)(2) to coordinate with withholding that otherwise applies to such an amount under this paragraph (b).

(c) *Foreign partnerships.*—(1) *Determination of payee.*—(i) *Payments treated as made to partners.*—Except as otherwise provided in paragraph (c)(1)(ii) or (iv) of this section, the payees of a payment to a person that the withholding agent may treat as a nonwithholding foreign partnership under paragraph (c)(3)(i) or (d)(2) of this section are the partners (looking through partners that are foreign intermediaries or flow-through entities) as follows—

(A) If the withholding agent can reliably associate a partner's distributive share of the payment with a valid Form W-9 provided under § 1.1441-1 (d), the partner is a U.S. payee;

(B) If the withholding agent can reliably associate a partner's distributive share of the payment with a valid Form W-8, or other appropriate documentation, provided under § 1.1441-1 (e)(1)(ii), the partner is a payee that is a foreign beneficial owner;

(C) If the withholding agent can reliably associate a partner's distributive share of the payment with a qualified intermediary withholding certificate under § 1.1441-1(e)(3)(ii), a nonqualified intermediary withholding certificate under § 1.1441-1(e)(3)(iii), or a U.S. branch certificate under § 1.1441-1(e)(3)(v) (including one provided by a territory financial institution), then the rules of § 1.1441-1(b)(2)(v) shall apply to determine who the payee is in the same manner as if the partner's distributive share of the payment had been paid directly to such intermediary or U.S. branch or territory financial institution;

(D) If the withholding agent can reliably associate the partner's distributive share with a withholding foreign partnership certificate under paragraph (c)(2)(iv) of this section or a nonwithholding foreign partnership certificate under paragraph (c)(3)(iii) of this section, then the rules of this paragraph (c)(1)(i) or paragraph (c)(1)(ii) of this section shall apply to determine whether the payment is treated as made to the partners of the higher-tier partnership under this paragraph (c)(1)(i) or to the higher-tier partnership itself (under the rules of paragraph (c)(1)(ii) of this section) in the same manner as if the partner's distributive share of the payment had been paid directly to the higher-tier foreign partnership;

(E) If the withholding agent can reliably associate the partner's distributive share with a withholding certificate described in paragraph (e) of this section regarding a foreign trust or estate, then the rules of paragraph (e) of this section shall apply to determine who the payees are; and

(F) If the withholding agent cannot reliably associate the partner's distributive share with a withholding certificate or other appropriate documentation, the partners are considered to be the payees and the presumptions described in paragraph (d)(3) of this section shall apply to determine their classification and status.

(ii) *Payments treated as made to the partnership.*—A payment to a person that the withholding agent may treat as a foreign partnership is treated as a payment to the foreign partnership and not to its partners only if—

(A) The withholding agent can reliably associate the payment with a withholding certificate described in paragraph (c)(2)(iv) of this section (withholding certificate of a withholding foreign partnership);

(B) The withholding agent can reliably associate the payment with a withholding certificate described in paragraph (c)(3)(iii) of this section (nonwithholding foreign partnership) certifying that the payment is income that is effectively connected with the conduct of a trade or business in the United States; or

(C) The withholding agent can treat the income as effectively connected income under the presumption rules of § 1.1441-4(a)(2)(ii) or (3)(i).

(iii) *Rules for reliably associating a payment with documentation.*—For rules regarding the reliable association of a payment with documentation, see § 1.1441-1(b)(2)(vii). In the absence of documentation, see §§ 1.1441-1(b)(3) and 1.6049-5(d) and paragraphs (d) and (e)(6) of this section for applicable presumptions.

(iv) *Coordination with chapter 4 for payments made to foreign partnerships.*—A withholding agent that makes a payment of U.S. source FDAP income to a foreign partnership that is a withholdable payment to which withholding under chapter 4 applies must apply the rules described in § 1.1473-1(a)(5)(vi) to determine when the payment is treated as made to a partner in the partnership for purposes of chapter 4. In a case in which withholding applies under chapter 4 to a withholdable payment made to a foreign partnership, see § 1.1441-3(a)(2) to coordinate with withholding otherwise required under this paragraph (c) with respect to the amount of the payment included in the gross income of a partner. For when a withholding agent may reliably associate a withholdable payment with a chapter 4 withholding rate pool in lieu of obtaining documentation for each payee include in the pool, see § 1.1441-1(e)(3)(iv)(C)(2) (substituting the term *nonwithholding foreign partnership* for the term *nonqualified intermediary*).

(v) *Examples.*—The rules of paragraphs (c)(1)(i) and (ii) of this section are illustrated by the following examples. Each example assumes that all payments are not withholdable payments and thus no withholding applies under chapter 4.

Example 1. FP is a nonwithholding foreign partnership organized in Country X. FP has two partners, FC, a foreign corporation, and USP, a U.S. partnership. USWH, a U.S. withholding agent, makes a payment of U.S. source interest to FP that is not a withholdable payment. FP has provided USWH with a valid nonwithholding foreign partnership certificate, as described in paragraph (c)(3)(iii) of this section, with which it associates a beneficial owner withholding certificate from FC and a Form W-9, "Request for Taxpayer Identification Number and Certification," from USP together with the withholding statement required by paragraph (c)(3)(iv) of this section. USWH can reliably associate the payment of interest with the withholding certificates from FC and USP. Under paragraph (c)(1)(i) of this section, the payees of the interest payment are FC and USP.

Example 2. The facts are the same as in *Example 1,* except that FP1, a nonwithholding foreign partnership, is a partner in FP rather than USP. FP1 has two partners, A and B, both foreign persons. FP provides USWH with a valid nonwithholding foreign partnership certificate, as described in paragraph (c)(3)(iii) of this section, with which it associates a beneficial owner withholding certificate from FC and a nonwithholding foreign partnership certificate from FP1. In addition, foreign beneficial owner withholding certificates from A and B are associated with the nonwithholding foreign partnership withholding certificate from FP1. FP also provides the withholding statement required by paragraph (c)(3)(iv) of this section. USWH can reliably associate the interest payment with the withholding certificates provided by FC, A, and B. Therefore, under paragraph (c)(1)(i) of this section, the payees of the interest payment are FC, A, and B.

Example 3. USWH makes a payment of U.S. source dividends to WFP, a withholding foreign partnership, that is not a withholdable payment. WFP has two partners, FC1 and FC2, both foreign corporations. USWH can reliably associate the payment with a valid withholding foreign partnership withholding certificate from WFP. Therefore, under paragraph (c)(1)(ii)(A) of this section, WFP is the payee of the interest.

Example 4. USWH makes a payment of U.S. source royalties that is not a withholdable payment to FP, a foreign partnership. USWH can reliably associate the royalties with a valid withholding certificate from FP on which FP certifies that the income is effectively connected with the conduct of a trade or business in the United States. Therefore, under paragraph (c)(1)(ii)(B) of this section, FP is the payee of the royalties.

(2) *Withholding foreign partnerships.*—(i) *Reliance on claim of withholding foreign partnership status.*—A withholding foreign partnership is a foreign partnership that has entered into an agreement with the IRS, as described in paragraph (c)(2)(ii) of this section, with respect to distributions and guaranteed payments it makes to its partners. A withholding agent that can reliably associate a payment with a certificate described in paragraph (c)(2)(iv) of this section may treat the person to whom it makes the payment as a withholding foreign partnership for purposes of withholding under chapters 3 and 4 of the Code, information reporting under chapter 61 of the Code, backup withholding under section 3406, and withholding under other provisions of the Code. Furnishing such a certificate is in lieu of transmitting to a withholding agent withholding certificates or other appropriate documentation for its partners. Although the withholding foreign partnership generally will be required to obtain withholding certificates or other appropriate documentation from its partners pursuant to its agreement with the IRS, it generally will not be required to attach such documentation to its withholding foreign partnership withholding certificate to the extent it is permitted to act as a withholding foreign partnership with respect to the payment under its agreement. In addition, the IRS may permit a foreign partnership to act as a qualified intermediary under § 1.1441-1(e)(5)(ii)(D) with respect to its partners in appropriate circumstances.

(ii) *Withholding agreement.*—The IRS may, upon request, enter into a withholding agreement with a foreign partnership pursuant to such procedures as the IRS may prescribe in published guidance (see § 601.601(d)(2) of this chapter). Under the withholding agreement, a foreign partnership shall generally be subject to the applicable withholding and reporting provisions applicable to withholding agents and payors as defined in § 1.6049-4(a) under chapters 3, 4, and 61 of the Code, section 3406, the regulations under those provisions, and other withholding provisions of the Code, except to the extent provided under the withholding agreement. Under the withholding agreement, a foreign partnership may agree to act as an acceptance agent to perform the duties described in § 301.6109-1(d)(3)(iv)(A) of this chapter. For a foreign partnership that is an FFI, the withholding agreement will require the partnership to assume the requirements of a participating FFI, a registered deemed-compliant FFI, or an FFI treated as a deemed-compliant FFI under an applicable IGA that is subject to due diligence and reporting requirements with respect to its U.S. accounts similar to those applicable to a registered deemed-compliant FFI under § 1.1471-5(f)(1). The withholding agreement may specify the manner in which applicable procedures for adjustments for underwithholding and overwithholding, including refund procedures, apply to the withholding foreign partnership and its partners and the extent to which applicable procedures may be modified. In particular, the withholding agreement may allow a withholding foreign partnership to claim refunds of overwithheld amounts on behalf of its customers. In addition, the withholding agreement must specify the manner in which the IRS will verify the partnership's compliance with its agreement, including the requirements for a periodic review of the partnership's compliance with the withholding agreement and the procedures for the partnership to certify to its compliance with the withholding agreement. A withholding foreign partnership must file a return on Form 1042, "Annual Withholding Tax Return for U.S. Source Income of Foreign Persons," and information returns on Form 1042-S, "Foreign Person's U.S. Source Income Subject to Withholding." The withholding agreement may also require a withholding foreign partnership to file a partnership return under section 6031(a) and partner statements under 6031(b), including for each U.S. partner to the extent required in the agreement. Additionally, a partnership that is an FFI will be required to file Form 8966, "FATCA Report" to the extent provided in the withholding agreement.

(iii) *Withholding responsibility.*—A withholding foreign partnership must assume primary withholding responsibility under both chapters 3 and 4 of the Code to the extent required in the withholding agreement. It is not required to provide information to the withholding agent regarding each partner's distributive share of the payment (including a withholdable payment). The withholding foreign partnership will be responsible for reporting the payments under §§1.1461-1(c), 1.1474-1(d), and chapter 61 of the Code and filing Form 1042 (to the extent required in the withholding agreement). A withholding agent making a payment to a withholding foreign partnership is not required to withhold any amount under chapters 3 and 4 of the Code on the payment unless it has actual knowledge or reason to know that the foreign partnership is not acting as a withholding foreign partnership with respect to the payment or has not withheld to the extent required. The withholding foreign partnership shall withhold the payments under the same procedures and at the same time as prescribed for withholding by a U.S. partnership under paragraph (b)(2) of this section, except that, for purposes of determining the partner's status, the provisions of paragraph (d)(4) of this section shall apply.

(iv) *Withholding certificate from a withholding foreign partnership.*—The rules of §1.1441-1(e)(4) shall apply to withholding certificates described in this paragraph (c)(2)(iv). A withholding certificate furnished by a withholding foreign partnership is valid with regard to any partner on whose behalf the certificate is furnished only if it is furnished on a Form W-8, an acceptable substitute form, or such other form as the IRS may prescribe, it is signed under penalties of perjury by a partner with authority to sign for the partnership, its validity has not expired, and it contains the information, statement, and certifications described in this paragraph (c)(2)(iv) as follows—

(A) The name, permanent residence address (as described in §1.1441-1(e)(2)(ii)), the employer identification number of the partnership, the country under the laws of which the partnership is created or governed, the chapter 4 status of the partnership if required for purposes of chapter 4 or if the partnership provides (or will provide) a withholding statement associated with the Form W-8 allocating a payment to a chapter 4 withholding rate pool of U.S. payees under §1.6049-4(c)(4) with respect to its partners, and the GIIN of the partnership (if applicable). If the partnership provides (or will provide) a chapter 4 withholding rate pool of U.S. payees as described in the preceding sentence, the partnership must certify to its chapter 4 status as a participating FFI (including a reporting Model 2 FFI) or registered deemed-compliant FFI (including a reporting Model 1 FFI);

(B) A certification that the partnership is a withholding foreign partnership within the meaning of paragraph (c)(2)(i) of this section, and, for a partnership that is an FFI receiving a withholdable payment, a certification that the partnership is acting as a participating FFI, a registered deemed-compliant FFI, or a nonreporting IGA FFI (as defined in §1.1471-1(b)(83)); and

(C) Any other information, certifications or statements as may be required by the withholding foreign partnership agreement with the IRS or the form or accompanying instructions in addition to, or in lieu of, the information, statements, and certifications described in this paragraph (c)(2)(iv).

(3) *Nonwithholding foreign partnerships.*—(i) *Reliance on claim of foreign partnership status.*—A withholding agent may treat a person as a nonwithholding foreign partnership if it receives from that person a nonwithholding foreign partnership withholding certificate as described in paragraph (c)(3)(iii) of this section. A withholding agent that does not receive a nonwithholding foreign partnership withholding certificate or does not receive a valid withholding certificate from an entity it knows, or has reason to know, is a foreign partnership must apply the presumption rules of §§1.1441-1(b)(3) and 1.6049-5(d) and paragraphs (d) and (e)(6) of this section. In addition, to the extent a withholding agent cannot, prior to a payment, reliably associate the payment with valid documentation from a payee that is associated with the nonwithholding foreign partnership withholding certificate or has insufficient information to report the payment on Form 1042-S or Form 1099, to the extent reporting is required, the withholding agent must apply the presumption rules. See §1.1441-1(b)(2)(vii)(A) and (B) for rules regarding reliable association. See, however, §1.1441-1(e)(3)(iv)(C)(2) for when a withholding agent may reliably associate a withholdable payment with a chapter 4 withholding rate pool in lieu of obtaining documentation for each payee included in the pool (substituting the term nonwithholding foreign partnership for the term nonqualified intermediary). See also §1.1441-1(e)(3)(iv)(A) for when a withholding agent may reliably associate a payment with a chapter 4 withholding rate pool of U.S. payees. See paragraph (c)(3)(iv) of this section and §1.1441-1(e)(3)(iv) for alternative procedures permitting allocation information to be received after a payment is made.

(ii) *Reliance on claim of reduced withholding by a partnership for its partners.*—This paragraph (c)(3)(ii) describes the manner in which a withholding agent may rely on a claim of reduced withholding when making a payment to a nonwithholding foreign partnership. To the extent that a withholding agent treats a payment to a nonwithholding foreign partnership as a payment to the nonwithholding foreign partnership's partners (whether direct or indirect) in accordance with paragraph (c)(1)(i) of this section, it may rely on a claim for reduced withholding by the partner if, prior to the payment, the withholding agent can reliably associate the payment (within the meaning of §1.1441-1(b)(2)(vii)) with a valid withholding certificate or other appropriate documentation from the partner that establishes entitlement to a reduced rate of withholding. A withholding certificate or other appropriate documentation that establishes entitlement to a reduced rate of withholding is a beneficial owner withholding certificate described in §1.1441-1(e)(2)(i), documentary evidence described in §1.1441-6(c)(3) or (4) or §1.6049-5(c)(1) (for a partner claiming to be a foreign person and a beneficial owner, determined under the provisions of §1.1441-1(c)(6)), a Form W-9 described in §1.1441-1(d) (for a partner claiming to be a U.S. payee), a withholding foreign partnership withholding certificate described in paragraph (c)(2)(iv) of this section, or a withholding statement allocating the payment to a chapter 4 withholding rate pool of U.S. payees. For when the withholding agent can reliably associate the payment with a chapter 4 withholding rate pool, see paragraph (c)(3)(i) of this section. See also §1.1441-3(a)(2) (coordinating withholding under chapter 3 when withholding under chapter 4 is applied to a payment). Unless a nonwithholding foreign partnership withholding certificate is provided for income claimed to be effectively connected with the conduct of a trade or business in the United States, a claim must be presented for each portion of the payment that represents an item of income includible in the distributive share of a partner as required under paragraph (c)(3)(iii)(C) of this section. When making a claim for several partners, the partnership may present a single nonwithholding foreign partnership withholding certificate to which the partners' certificates or other appropriate documentation are associated. Where the nonwithholding foreign partnership withholding certificate is provided for income claimed to be effectively connected with the conduct of a trade or business in the United States under paragraph (c)(3)(iii)(D) of this section, the claim may be presented without having to identify any partner's distributive share of the payment.

(iii) *Withholding certificate from a nonwithholding foreign partnership.*—A nonwithholding foreign partnership shall provide a nonwithholding foreign partnership withholding certificate with respect to reportable amounts received by the nonwithholding foreign partnership. A nonwithholding foreign partnership withholding certificate is valid only to the extent it is furnished on a Form W-8 (or an acceptable substitute form or such other form as the IRS may prescribe), it is signed under penalties of perjury by a partner with authority to sign for the partnership, its validity has not expired, and it contains the information, statements, and certifications described in this paragraph (c)(3)(iii) and paragraph (c)(3)(iv) of this section, and the withholding certificates and other appropriate documentation for all the persons to whom the certificate relates are associated with the certificate. The rules of §1.1441-1(e)(4) shall apply to withholding certificates described in this paragraph (c)(3)(iii). No withholding certificates or other appropriate documentation from persons who derive income through a partnership (whether or not U.S. exempt recipients) are required to be associated with the nonwithholding foreign partnership withholding certificate if the certificate is furnished solely for income claimed to be effectively connected with the conduct of a trade or business in the United States. Withholding certificates and other appropriate documentation that may be associated with the nonwithholding foreign partnership withholding certificate consist of beneficial owner withholding certificates under §1.1441-1(e)(2)(i), intermediary withholding certificates under §1.1441-1(e)(3)(i), withholding foreign partnership withholding certificates under paragraph (c)(2)(iv) of this section, nonwithholding foreign partnership withholding certificates under this paragraph (c)(3)(iii), withholding certificates from foreign trusts or estates under paragraph (e) of this section, documentary evidence described in §1.1441-6(c)(3) or (4) or documentary evidence described in §1.6049-5(c)(1), and any other documentation or certificates applicable under other provisions of the Internal Revenue Code or regulations that certify or establish the status of the payee or beneficial owner as a U.S. or a foreign person. Nothing in this paragraph (c)(3)(iii) shall require a nonwithholding foreign partnership to furnish original documentation. Copies of certificates or documentary evidence may be transmitted to the U.S. withholding agent, in which case the nonwithholding foreign partnership must retain the original documentation for the same time period that the copy is required to be retained by the withholding agent under § 1.1441-1(e)(4)(iii) and must provide it to the withholding agent upon request. The information, statement, and certifications required on the withholding certificate are as follows—

(A) The name, permanent residence address (as described in § 1.1441-1(e)(2)(ii)), the employer identification number of the partnership, if any, the country under the laws of which the partnership is created or governed, and the chapter 4 status of the partnership (for a nonwithholding foreign partnership receiving a withholdable payment or providing a withholding statement associated with the Form W-8 allocating a payment to a chapter 4 withholding rate pool of U.S. payees), and the GIIN of the partnership (if applicable);

(B) A certification that the person whose name is on the certificate is a foreign partnership;

(C) A withholding statement associated with the nonwithholding foreign partnership withholding certificate that provides all of the information required by paragraph (c)(3)(iv) of this section and § 1.1441-1(e)(3)(iv). No withholding statement is required, however, for a nonwithholding foreign partnership withholding certificate furnished for income claimed to be effectively connected with the conduct of a trade or business in the United States;

(D) A certification that the income is effectively connected with the conduct of a trade or business in the United States, if applicable; and

(E) Any other information, certifications, or statements required by the form or accompanying instructions in addition to, or in lieu of, the information and certifications described in this paragraph (c)(3)(iii).

(iv) *Withholding statement provided by nonwithholding foreign partnership and coordination with chapter 4.*—The provisions of § 1.1441-1(e)(3)(iv) (regarding a withholding statement) shall apply to a nonwithholding foreign partnership by substituting the term nonwithholding foreign partnership for the term nonqualified intermediary, including when a nonwithholding foreign partnership may provide to a withholding agent a withholding statement that includes a chapter 4 withholding rate pool in lieu of information with respect to each partner that is a payee of a payment.

(v) *Withholding and reporting by a foreign partnership.*—A nonwithholding foreign partnership described in this paragraph (c)(3) that receives an amount subject to withholding (as defined in § 1.1441-2(a)) shall be required to withhold and report such payment under chapter 3 of the Code and the regulations thereunder except as otherwise provided in this paragraph (c)(3)(v). A nonwithholding foreign partnership shall not be required to withhold and report if it has provided a valid nonwithholding foreign partnership withholding certificate, it has provided all of the information required by paragraph (c)(3)(iv) of this section (withholding statement), and it does not know, and has no reason to know, that another withholding agent failed to withhold the correct amount or failed to report the payment correctly under § 1.1461-1(c). A nonwithholding foreign partnership is also not required to withhold and report under this paragraph (c)(3) to the extent that withholding under chapter 4 was applied to a payment that is includible in the gross income of a partner in the partnership. See also § 1.1441-3(a)(2) for coordination rules when withholding under chapter 4 has been applied to a withholdable payment. A withholding foreign partnership's obligations to withhold and report shall be determined in accordance with its withholding foreign partnership agreement.

(d) *Presumption rules.*—(1) *In general.*—This paragraph (d) contains the applicable presumptions for a withholding agent (including a partnership) to determine the classification and status of a partnership and its partners in the absence of documentation. The provisions of § 1.1441-1(b)(3)(iv) (regarding the 90-day grace period) and § 1.1441-1(b)(3)(vii) through (ix) shall apply for purposes of this paragraph (d).

(2) *Determination of partnership status as U.S. or foreign in the absence of documentation.*—In the absence of a valid representation of U.S. partnership status in accordance with paragraph (b)(1) of this section or of foreign partnership status in accordance with paragraph (c)(2)(i) or (c)(3)(i) of this section, the withholding agent shall determine the classification of the payee under the presumptions set forth in § 1.1441-1(b)(3)(ii). If the withholding agent treats the payee as a partnership under § 1.1441-1(b)(3)(ii), the withholding agent shall apply the presumptions set forth in § 1.1441-1(b)(3)(iii)(A)(*1*) (applied by substituting the term *partnership* for the term *exempt recipient*) to determine whether to treat the partnership as a U.S. person or foreign person. For rules regarding reliable association with a withholding certificate from a domestic or a foreign partnership, see § 1.1441-1(b)(2)(vii).

(3) *Determination of partners' status in the absence of certain documentation.*—If a nonwithholding foreign partnership has provided a nonwithholding foreign partnership withholding certificate under paragraph (c)(3)(iii) of this section that would be valid except that the withholding agent cannot reliably associate all or a portion of the payment with valid documentation from a partner of the partnership, then the withholding agent may apply the presumption rule of this paragraph (d)(3) with respect to all or a portion of the payment for which documentation has not been received. See § 1.1441-1(b)(2)(vii)(A) and (B) for rules regarding reliable association. The presumption rule of this paragraph (d)(3) also applies to a person that is presumed to be a foreign partnership under the rule of paragraph (d)(2) of this section. Any portion of a payment that the withholding agent cannot treat as reliably associated with valid documentation from a partner may be presumed made to a foreign payee. As a result, any payment of an amount subject to withholding is subject to withholding at a rate of 30 percent. Any payment that is presumed to be made to an undocumented foreign payee must be reported on Form 1042-S. See § 1.1461-1(c). For a payment described in this paragraph (d)(3) that is a withholdable payment, see § 1.1471-3(f)(5) for the presumption rule for determining the payee's chapter 4 status to determine whether withholding under chapter 4 applies to the payment.

(4) *Determination by a withholding foreign partnership of the status of its partners.*—Except as otherwise provided in the agreement described in paragraph (c)(2) of this section, a withholding foreign partnership shall determine whether the partners or some other persons are the payees of the partners' distributive shares of any payment made by a withholding foreign partnership by applying the rules of § 1.1441-1(b)(2), paragraph (c)(1) of this section (in the case of a partner that is a foreign partnership), and paragraph (e)(3) of this section (in the case of a partner that is a foreign estate or a foreign trust). Further, the provisions of paragraph (d)(3) of this section shall apply to determine the status of partners and the applicable withholding rates to the extent that, at the time the foreign partnership is required to withhold on a payment, it cannot reliably associate the amount with documentation for any one or more of its partners.

(e) *Foreign trusts and estates.*—(1) *In general.*—This paragraph (e) provides rules applicable to payments of amounts subject to withholding (as defined in § 1.1441-2(a)) that a withholding agent may treat as made to any foreign trust or a foreign estate. For rules relating to payments to a U.S. trust or a U.S. estate, see paragraph (b) of this section. For the definitions of foreign simple trust, foreign complex trust, and foreign grantor trust, see § 1.1441-1(c)(24), (25), and (26).

(2) *Payments to foreign complex trusts and foreign estates.*—Under § 1.1441-1(c)(6)(ii)(D), a foreign complex trust or foreign estate is generally considered to be the beneficial owner of income paid to the foreign complex trust or foreign estate. See paragraph (e)(4) of this section for rules describing when a withholding agent may treat a payment as made to a foreign complex trust or a foreign estate.

(3) *Payees of payments to foreign simple trusts and foreign grantor trusts.*—(i) *Payments for which beneficiaries and owners are payees.*—For purposes of the regulations under chapters 3 and 61 of the Internal Revenue Code and section 3406, a foreign simple trust is not a beneficial owner or a payee of a payment. Also, a foreign grantor trust (or a portion of a trust that is a foreign grantor trust) is not considered a beneficial owner or a payee of a payment. Except as otherwise provided in paragraph (e)(3)(ii) of this section, the payees of a payment made to a person that the withholding agent may treat as a foreign simple trust or a foreign grantor trust (or a portion of a trust that is a foreign grantor trust) are determined under the rules of this paragraph (e)(3)(i). The payees shall be treated as the beneficial owners if they may be so treated under § 1.1441-1(c)(6)(ii)(C) and they provide documentation supporting their status as the beneficial owners. The payees of a payment to a foreign simple trust or foreign grantor trust are determined as follows—

(A) If the withholding agent can reliably associate a payment with a valid Form W-9 provided under § 1.1441-1(d) from a beneficiary or owner of the foreign trust, then the beneficiary or owner is a U.S. payee;

(B) If the withholding agent can reliably associate a payment with a valid Form W-8, or other appropriate documentation, provided under § 1.1441-1(e)(1)(ii) from a beneficiary or owner of the foreign trust, then the beneficiary or owner is a payee that is a foreign beneficial owner;

(C) If the withholding agent can reliably associate a payment with a qualified intermediary withholding certificate under § 1.1441-1(e)(3)(ii), a nonqualified intermediary withholding certificate under § 1.1441-1(e)(3)(ii), or a U.S. branch withholding certificate under § 1.1441-1(e)(3)(v), then the rules of § 1.1441-1(b)(2)(v) shall apply to determine the payee in the same manner as if the payment had been paid directly to such intermediary or U.S. branch;

(D) If the withholding agent can reliably associate a payment with a withholding foreign partnership withholding certificate under paragraph (c)(2)(iv) of this section or a nonwithholding foreign partnership withholding certificate under paragraph (c)(3)(iii) of this section, then the rules of paragraph (c)(1)(i) or (ii) of this section shall apply to determine the payee;

(E) If the withholding agent can reliably associate the payment with a foreign simple trust withholding certificate or a foreign grantor trust withholding certificate (both described in paragraph (e)(5)(iii) of this section) from a second or higher-tier foreign simple trust or foreign grantor trust, then the rules of this paragraph (e)(3)(i) or paragraph (e)(3)(ii) of this section shall apply to determine whether the payment is treated as made to a beneficiary or owner of the higher-tier trust or to the trust itself in the same manner as if the payment had been made directly to the higher-tier trust; and

(F) If the withholding agent cannot reliably associate a payment with a withholding certificate or other appropriate documentation, the payees shall be determined by applying the presumptions described in paragraph (e)(6) of this section.

(ii) *Payments for which trust is payee.*—A payment to a person that the withholding agent may treat as made to a foreign trust under paragraph (e)(5)(iii) of this section is treated as a payment to the trust, and not to a beneficiary of the trust, only if—

(A) The withholding agent can reliably associate the payment with a foreign complex trust withholding certificate under paragraph (e)(4) of this section;

(B) The withholding agent can reliably associate the payment with a foreign simple trust withholding certificate under paragraph (e)(5)(iii) of this section certifying that the payment is income that is treated as effectively connected with the conduct of a trade or business in the United States; or

(C) The withholding agent can treat the income as effectively connected income under the presumption rules of § 1.1441-4(a)(3)(i).

(iii) *Coordination with chapter 4 for payments made to foreign simple trusts and foreign grantor trusts.*—A withholding agent that makes a payment of U.S. source FDAP income to a foreign simple trust or foreign grantor trust that is a withholdable payment to which withholding under chapter 4 applies must apply the rules described in § 1.1473-1(a)(5)(vi) to determine when the payment is treated as made to a beneficiary or owner of the trust for purposes of chapter 4. In a case in which withholding applies under chapter 4 to a withholdable payment made to a foreign simple trust or foreign grantor trust, see § 1.1441-3(a)(2) to coordinate withholding otherwise required under this paragraph (e) with respect to the amount of the payment included in the gross income of the payee of the payment. For when a withholding agent may reliably associate a withholdable payment with a chapter 4 withholding rate pool in lieu of obtaining documentation for each payee included in the pool, see § 1.1441-1(e)(3)(iv)(C)(2) (substituting the term *nonwithholding foreign trust* for the term *nonqualified intermediary).*

(4) *Reliance on claim of foreign complex trust or foreign estate status.*—A withholding agent may treat a payment as made to a foreign complex trust or a foreign estate if the withholding agent can reliably associate the payment with a beneficial owner withholding certificate described in § 1.1441-1(e)(2)(i) or other documentary evidence under § 1.1441-6(c)(3) or (4) (regarding a claim for treaty benefits) or § 1.6049-5(c)(1) (regarding documentary evidence to establish foreign status for purposes of chapter 61 of the Internal Revenue Code) that establishes the foreign complex trust or foreign estate's status as a beneficial owner. See paragraph (e)(6) of this section for presumption rules if documentation is lacking.

(5) *Foreign simple trust and foreign grantor trust.*—(i) *Reliance on claim of foreign simple trust or foreign grantor trust status.*—A withholding agent may treat a person as a foreign simple trust or foreign grantor trust if it receives from that person a foreign simple trust or foreign grantor trust withholding certificate as described in paragraph (e)(5)(iii) of this section. A withholding agent must apply the presumption rules of §§ 1.1441-1(b)(3) and 1.6049-5(d) and paragraphs (d) and (e)(6) of this section to the extent it cannot, prior to the payment, reliably associate a payment (within the meaning of § 1.1441-1(b)(2)(vii)) with a valid foreign simple trust or foreign grantor trust withholding certificate, it cannot reliably determine how much of the payment relates to valid documentation provided by a payee (*e.g.*, a person that is not itself a nonqualified intermediary, flow-through entity, or U.S. branch) associated with the foreign simple trust or foreign grantor trust withholding certificate, or it does not have sufficient information to report the payment on Form 1042-S or Form 1099, if reporting is required. See § 1.1441-1(b)(2)(vii)(A) and (B). See, however, § 1.1441-1(e)(3)(iv)(C)(2) for when a withholding agent may reliably associate a withholdable payment with a chapter 4 withholding rate pool in lieu of obtaining documentation for each payee included in a pool (substituting the term *nonwithholding foreign trust* for the term *nonqualified intermediary).* See also § 1.1441-1(e)(3)(iv)(A) for when a withholding agent may reliably associate a payment with a chapter 4 withholding rate pool of U.S. payees.

(ii) *Reliance on claim of reduced withholding by a foreign simple trust or foreign grantor trust for its beneficiaries or owners.*—This paragraph (e)(5)(ii) describes the manner in which a withholding agent may rely on a claim of reduced withholding when making a payment to a foreign simple trust or foreign grantor trust. To the extent that a withholding agent treats a payment to a foreign simple trust or foreign grantor trust as a payment to payees other than the trust in accordance with paragraph (e)(3)(i) of this section, it may rely on a claim for reduced withholding by a beneficiary or owner if, prior to the payment, the withholding agent can reliably associate the payment (within the meaning of § 1.1441-1(b)(2)(vii)) with a valid withholding certificate or other appropriate documentation from a payee or beneficial owner that establishes entitlement to a reduced rate of withholding. A withholding certificate or other appropriate documentation that establishes entitlement to a reduced rate of withholding is a beneficial owner withholding certificate described in § 1.1441-1(e)(2)(i) or documentary evidence described in § 1.1441-6(c)(3) or (4) or in § 1.6049-5(c)(1) (for a beneficiary or owner claiming to be a foreign person and a beneficial owner, determined under the provisions of § 1.1441-1(c)(6)), a Form W-9 described in § 1.1441-1(d) (for a beneficiary or owner claiming to be a U.S. payee), a withholding foreign partnership withholding certificate described in paragraph (c)(2)(iv) of this section, or a withholding statement allocating the payment to a chapter 4 withholding rate pool of U.S. payees. For when the withholding agent can reliably associate the payment with a chapter 4 withholding rate pool, see paragraph (c)(3)(i) of this section. See also § 1.1441-3(a)(2) (coordinating withholding under chapter 3 when withholding under chapter 4 is applied to a withholdable payment). Unless a foreign simple trust or foreign grantor trust withholding certificate is provided for income treated as income effectively connected with the conduct of a trade or business in the United States, a claim must be presented for each payee's portion of the payment. When making a claim for several payees, the trust may present a single foreign simple trust or foreign grantor trust withholding certificate with which the payees' certificates or other appropriate documentation are associated. Where the foreign simple trust or foreign grantor trust withholding certificate is provided for income that is treated as effectively connected with the conduct of a trade or business in the United States under paragraph (e)(5)(iii)(D) of this section, the claim may be presented without having to identify any beneficiary's or grantor's distributive share of the payment.

(iii) *Withholding certificate from foreign simple trust or foreign grantor trust.*—A withholding certificate furnished by a foreign simple trust or a foreign grantor trust that is not a withholding foreign trust (within the meaning of paragraph (e)(5)(v) of this section) is valid only if it is furnished on a Form W-8, an acceptable substitute form, or such other form as the IRS may prescribe, it is signed under penalties of perjury by a trustee, its validity has not expired, it contains the information, statements, and certifications required by this paragraph (e)(5)(iii) and § 1.1441-1(e)(3)(iv), and the withholding certificates or other appropriate documentation for all of the payees (as determined under paragraph (e)(3)(i) of this section) to whom the certificate relates are associated with the foreign simple trust or foreign grantor trust withholding certificate. The rules of § 1.1441-1(e)(4) shall apply to withholding certificates described in this paragraph (e)(5)(iii). No withholding certificates or other appropriate documentation from persons who derive income through a foreign simple trust or a foreign grantor trust (whether or not U.S. exempt recipients) are required to be associated with the foreign simple trust or foreign grantor trust withholding certificate if the certificate is furnished solely for income that is treated as effectively connected with the conduct of a trade or business in the United States. Withholding certificates and other appropriate documentation (as determined under paragraph (e)(3)(i) of this section) that may be associated with a foreign simple trust or foreign grantor trust withholding certificate consist of beneficial owner withholding certificates under § 1.1441-1(e)(2)(i), intermediary withholding certificates under § 1.1441-1(e)(3)(i), withholding foreign partnership withholding certificates under paragraph (c)(2)(iv) of this section, nonwithholding foreign partnership withholding certificates under paragraph (c)(3)(iii) of this section, withholding certificates from foreign trusts or estates under paragraph (e)(4) or (5)(iii) of this section, documentary evidence described in § § 1.1441-6(c)(3) or (4), or 1.6049-5(c)(1), and any other documentation or certificates applicable under other provisions of the Internal Revenue Code or regulations that certify or establish the status of the payee or beneficial owner as a U.S. or a foreign person. Nothing in this paragraph (e)(5)(iii) shall require a foreign simple trust or foreign grantor trust to provide original documentation. Copies of certificates or documentary evidence may be passed up to the U.S. withholding agent, in which case the foreign simple trust or foreign grantor trust must retain the original documentation for the same time period that the copy is required to be retained by the withholding agent under § 1.1441-1(e)(4)(iii) and must provide it to the withholding agent upon request. The information, statement, and certifications required on a foreign simple trust or foreign grantor trust withholding certificate are as follows—

(A) The name, permanent residence address (as described in § 1.1441-1(e)(2)(ii)), the employer identification number, if required, of the trust, the country under the laws of which the trust is created, the chapter 4 status of the trust if required for purposes of chapter 4 or if the trust provides (or will provide) a withholding statement associated with the Form W-8 allocating a payment to a chapter 4 withholding rate pool of U.S. payees under § 1.6049-4(c)(4) with respect to the nonwithholding foreign trust's owners and beneficiaries, and the GIIN of the trust (if applicable). If a nonwithholding foreign trust provides (or will provide) a chapter 4 withholding rate pool of U.S. payees as described in the preceding sentence, the trust must certify to its chapter 4 status as a participating FFI (including a reporting Model 2 FFI) or registered deemed-compliant FFI (including a reporting Model 1 FFI);

(B) A certification that the person whose name is on the certificate is a foreign simple trust or a foreign grantor trust;

(C) A withholding statement associated with the foreign simple trust or foreign grantor trust withholding certificate that provides all of the information required by paragraph (e)(5)(iv) of this section. No withholding statement is required, however, for a foreign simple trust withholding certificate furnished for income that is treated as effectively connected with the conduct of a trade or business in the United States;

(D) A certification on a foreign simple trust withholding certificate that the income is treated as effectively connected with the conduct of a trade or business in the United States, if applicable; and

(E) Any other information, certifications, or statements required by the form or accompanying instructions in addition to, or in lieu of, the information, certifications, and statements described in this paragraph (e)(5)(iii);

(iv) *Withholding statement provided by a foreign simple trust or foreign grantor trust and coordination with chapter 4.*—The provisions of § 1.1441-1(e)(3)(iv) (regarding a withholding statement) shall apply to a foreign simple trust or foreign grantor trust by substituting the term *foreign simple trust* or *foreign grantor trust* for the term *nonqualified intermediary*, including when a withholding statement provided by a foreign simple trust or foreign grantor trust may include a chapter 4 withholding rate pool in lieu of information with respect to each owner or beneficiary that is a payee of a payment.

(v) *Withholding foreign trusts.*—The IRS may enter into a withholding agreement with a foreign trust to treat the trust or estate as a withholding foreign trust. Such a withholding agreement shall generally follow the same principles as a withholding agreement with a withholding foreign partnership under paragraph (c)(2)(ii) of this section. A withholding agent may treat a payment to a withholding foreign trust in the same manner the withholding agent would treat a payment (including a withholdable payment) to a withholding foreign partnership. See § 1.1441-1(e)(5)(ii)(D). For a withholding foreign trust that is an FFI, the withholding agreement will require the withholding foreign trust to assume the requirements of either a participating FFI, registered deemed-compliant FFI, or an FFI treated as a deemed-compliant FFI under an applicable IGA that is subject to due diligence and reporting requirements with respect to its U.S. accounts similar to those applicable to a registered deemed-compliant FFI under § 1.1471-5(f)(1).

(6) *Presumption rules.*—(i) *In general.*—This paragraph (e)(6) contains the applicable presumptions for a withholding agent (including a trust or estate) to determine the classification and status of a trust or estate and its beneficiaries or owners in the absence of valid documentation. The provisions of § 1.1441-1(b)(3)(iv) (regarding the 90-day grace period) and § 1.1441-1(b)(3)(vii) through (ix) shall apply for purposes of this paragraph (e)(6).

(ii) *Determination of status as U.S. or foreign trust or estate in the absence of documentation.*—In the absence of valid documentation that establishes the U.S. status of a trust or estate under paragraph (b)(1) of this section and of documentation that establishes the foreign status of a trust or estate under paragraph (e)(4) or (e)(5)(iii) of this section, the withholding agent shall determine the classification of the payee based upon the presumptions set forth in § 1.1441-1(b)(3)(ii). If, based upon those presumptions, the withholding agent classifies the payee as a trust or estate, the withholding agent shall apply the presumptions set forth in § 1.1441-1(b)(3)(iii)(A)(*1*) (applied by substituting the term *trust* for the term *exempt recipient*) to determine whether the trust or estate is a U.S. person or foreign person. An undocumented payee presumed to be a foreign trust shall be presumed to be a foreign complex trust. If a withholding agent has documentary evidence that establishes that an entity is a foreign trust, but the withholding agent cannot determine whether the foreign trust is a complex trust, a simple trust, or foreign grantor trust, the withholding agent shall presume that the trust is a foreign complex trust. Notwithstanding the preceding sentence, in the case of a foreign trust with a settlor that is a U.S. person for which a withholding agent has both a U.S. address and TIN, the withholding agent shall presume that the trust is a grantor trust when it cannot determine the status of the trust as a simple trust, complex trust, or grantor trust. See § 1.1471-3(f)(4) and (5) to determine the status of the payee for purposes of chapter 4.

(iii) *Determination of beneficiary or owner's status in the absence of certain documentation.*—If a foreign simple trust or foreign grantor trust has provided a foreign simple trust or foreign grantor trust withholding certificate under paragraph (e)(5)(iii) of this section but the payment to such trust cannot be reliably associated with valid documentation from a specific beneficiary or owner of the trust, then any portion of a payment that a withholding agent cannot treat as reliably associated with valid documentation from a beneficiary or owner may be presumed made to a foreign payee. As a result, any payment of an amount subject to withholding is subject to withholding at a rate of 30 percent. Any such payment that is presumed to be made to an undocumented foreign person must be reported on Form 1042-S. See § 1.1461-1(c).

(f) *Failure to receive withholding certificate timely or to act in accordance with applicable presumptions.*—See applicable procedures described in § 1.1441-1(b)(7) in the event the withholding agent does not hold an appropriate withholding certificate or other appropriate documentation at the time of payment or fails to rely on the presumptions set forth in § 1.1441-1(b)(3) or in paragraph (d) or (e) of this section. For a payment that is a withholdable payment, see § 1.1471-3(f) for the presumption rule for determining the payee's chapter 4 status.

(g) *Effective/applicability date.*—This section applies to payments made on or after January 6, 2017. (For payments made after June 30, 2014, and before January 6, 2017, see this section as in effect and contained in 26 CFR Part 1, as revised April 1, 2016. For payments made after December 31, 2000, and before July 1, 2014, see this section as in effect and contained in 26 CFR Part 1, as revised April 1, 2013.) [Reg. § 1.1441-5.]

☐ [*T.D.* 6187, 7-5-56. *Amended by T.D.* 6238, 6-10-57; *T.D.* 6908, 12-30-66; *T.D.* 7277, 5-14-73; *T.D.* 7842, 11-2-82; *T.D.* 7977, 9-19-84; *T.D.* 8160, 9-8-87; *T.D.* 8411, 4-24-92; *T.D.* 8734, 10-6-97; *T.D.* 8804, 12-30-98; *T.D.* 8856, 12-29-99; *T.D.* 8881, 5-15-2000 (*corrected* 4-5-2001), *T.D.* 9658. 2-28-2014 *and T.D.* 9808, 12-30-2016.]

§ 1.1441-6. Claim of reduced withholding under an income tax treaty.—(a) *In general.*—The rate of withholding on a payment of income subject to withholding may be reduced to the extent provided under an income tax treaty in effect between the United States and a foreign country. Most benefits under income tax treaties are to foreign persons who reside in the treaty country. In some cases, benefits are available under an income tax treaty to U.S. citizens or

U.S. residents or to residents of a third country. See paragraph (b)(5) of this section for claims of benefits by U.S. persons. If the requirements of this section are met, the amount withheld from the payment may be reduced at source to account for the treaty benefit. See, however, § 1.1471-2(a) and § 1.1472-1(b) for when withholding at source on a withholdable payment may not be reduced to account for a treaty benefit such that the beneficial owner of the payment may need to file a claim for refund to obtain a refund for the overwithheld amount of tax. See also § 1.1441-4(b)(2) for rules regarding claims of a reduced rate of withholding under an income tax treaty in the case of compensation from personal services and § 1.1441-4(c)(1) for rules regarding claims of a reduced rate of withholding under an income tax treaty in the case of scholarship and fellowship income.

(b) *Reliance on claim of reduced withholding under an income tax treaty.*—(1) *In general.*—The withholding imposed under section 1441, 1442, or 1443 on any payment to a foreign person is eligible for reduction under the terms of an income tax treaty only to the extent that such payment is treated as derived by a resident of an applicable treaty jurisdiction, such resident is a beneficial owner, and all other requirements for benefits under the treaty are satisfied. See section 894 and the regulations under section 894 to determine whether a resident of a treaty country derives the income. Absent actual knowledge or reason to know otherwise, a withholding agent may rely on a claim that a beneficial owner is entitled to a reduced rate of withholding based upon an income tax treaty if, prior to the payment, the withholding agent can reliably associate the payment with a beneficial owner withholding certificate, as described in § 1.1441-1(e)(2), that contains the information necessary to support the claim, or, in the case of a payment of income described in paragraph (c)(2) of this section made outside the United States with respect to an offshore obligation, documentary evidence described in paragraphs (c)(3), (c)(4), and (c)(5) of this section. See § 1.6049-5(e) for the definition of payments made outside the United States and § 1.6049-5(c)(1) for the definition of an offshore obligation. For purposes of this paragraph (b)(1), a beneficial owner withholding certificate described in § 1.1441-1(e)(2)(i) contains information necessary to support the claim for a treaty benefit only if it includes the beneficial owner's taxpayer identifying number (except as otherwise provided in paragraph (c)(1) and (g) of this section, or the beneficial owner provides its foreign tax identifying number issued by its country of residence and such country has with the United States an income tax treaty or information exchange agreement in effect), includes the representations that the beneficial owner derives the income under section 894 and the regulations under section 894, if required, and with regard to a beneficial owner that is an entity, includes a statement that the entity meets the limitation on benefits provisions of the treaty, if any. For claims for treaty benefits for scholarship and fellowship income, the beneficial owner withholding certificate must contain the beneficial owner's U.S. taxpayer identifying number (not a foreign taxpayer identifying number). The withholding certificate must also contain any other representations required by this section and any other information, certifications, or statements as may be required by the form or accompanying instructions in addition to, or in place of, the information and certifications described in this section. Absent actual knowledge or reason to know that the claims are unreliable or incorrect (applying the standards of knowledge in § 1.1441-7(b)), a withholding agent may rely on the claims made on a withholding certificate or on documentary evidence. A withholding agent may also rely on the information contained in a withholding statement provided under §§ 1.1441-1(e)(3)(iv) and 1.1441-5(c)(3)(iv) and (e)(5)(iv) to determine whether the appropriate statements regarding section 894 and limitation on benefits have been provided in connection with documentary evidence. The Internal Revenue Service (IRS) may apply the provisions of § 1.1441-1(e)(1)(ii)(B) to notify the withholding agent that the certificate cannot be relied upon to grant benefits under an income tax treaty. See § 1.1441-1(e)(4)(viii) regarding reliance on a withholding certificate by a withholding agent. The provisions of § 1.1441-1(b)(3)(iv) dealing with a 90-day grace period shall apply for purposes of this section.

(i) *Identification of limitation on benefits provisions.*—In conjunction with the representation that the beneficial owner meets the limitation on benefits provision of the applicable treaty, if any, required by paragraph (b)(1) of this section, a beneficial owner withholding certificate must also identify the specific limitation on benefits provision of the article (if any, or a similar provision) of the treaty upon which the beneficial owner relies to claim the treaty benefit. A withholding agent may rely on the beneficial owner's claim regarding its reliance on a specific limitation on benefits provision absent actual knowledge that such claim is unreliable or incorrect.

(ii) *Reason to know based on existence of treaty.*—For purposes of this paragraph (b)(1), a withholding agent's reason to know that a beneficial owner's claim to a reduced rate of withholding under an income tax treaty is unreliable or incorrect includes a circumstance where the beneficial owner is claiming benefits under an income tax treaty that does not exist or is not in force. A withholding agent may determine whether a tax treaty is in existence and is in force by checking the list maintained on the IRS Web site at https://www.irs.gov/businesses/international-businesses/united-states-income-tax-treaties-a-to-z (or any replacement page on the IRS Web site) or in the State Department's annual Treaties in Force publication.

(2) *Payment to fiscally transparent entity.*—(i) *In general.*—If the person claiming a reduced rate of withholding under an income tax treaty is an interest holder of an entity that is considered to be fiscally transparent (as defined in the regulations under section 894) by the interest holder's jurisdiction with respect to an item of income, then, with respect to such income derived by that person through the entity, the entity shall be treated as a flow-through entity and may provide a flow-through withholding certificate with which the withholding certificate or other documentary evidence of the interest holder that supports the claim for treaty benefits is associated. In the case of a payment that is a withholdable payment, see, however, § 1.1471-3(c) for determining the payee of the payment and §§ 1.1471-2(a) and 1472-1(b) for when withholding at source may apply to the payment based on the status of the payee notwithstanding a claim for treaty benefits made under this paragraph (b)(2) by an interest holder in the payee. In such a case, the interest holder may file a claim for refund of the overwithheld amount of tax. For purposes of this paragraph (b)(2)(i), interest holders do not include any direct or indirect interest holders that are themselves treated as fiscally transparent entities with respect to that income by the interest holder's jurisdiction. See § 1.1441-1(c)(23) and (e)(3)(i) for the definition of flow-through entity and flow-through withholding certificate. The entity may provide a beneficial owner withholding certificate, or beneficial owner documentation, with respect to any remaining portion of the income to the extent the entity is receiving income and is not treated as fiscally transparent by its own jurisdiction. Further, the entity may claim a reduced rate of withholding with respect to the portion of a payment for which it is not treated as fiscally transparent if it meets all the requirements to make such a claim and, in the case of treaty benefits, it provides the documentation required by paragraph (b)(1) of this section. If dual claims, as described in paragraph (b)(2)(iii) of this section, are made, multiple withholding certificates may have to be furnished. Multiple withholding certificates may also have to be furnished if the entity receives income for which a reduction of withholding is claimed under a provision of the Internal Revenue Code (*e.g.*, portfolio interest) and income for which a reduction of withholding is claimed under an income tax treaty.

(ii) *Certification by qualified intermediary.*—Notwithstanding paragraph (b)(2)(i) of this section, a foreign entity that is fiscally transparent, as defined in the regulations under section 894, that is also a qualified intermediary for purposes of claiming a reduced rate of withholding under an income tax treaty for its interest holders (who are deriving the income paid to the entity as residents of an applicable treaty jurisdiction) may furnish a single qualified intermediary withholding certificate, as described in § 1.1441-1(e)(3)(ii), for amounts for which it claims a reduced rate of withholding under an income tax treaty on behalf of its interest holders.

(iii) *Dual treatment.*—Under paragraph (b)(2)(i) of this section, a withholding agent may make a payment to a foreign entity that is simultaneously claiming to be the beneficial owner of a portion of the income (whether or not it is also claiming a reduced rate of tax on its own behalf) and a reduced rate on behalf of persons in their capacity as interest holders in the entity with respect to the same, or a different, portion of the income. If the same portion of a payment may be reliably associated with both the entity's claim and an interest holder's claim, the withholding agent may choose to reject both claims and request new documentation and information allocating the payment among the beneficial owners of the payment or the withholding agent may choose which claim to apply. If the entity and the interest holder's claims are reliably associated with separate portions of the payment, the withholding agent may, at its option, accept such dual claims based on withholding certificates or other appropriate documentation furnished by the entity and its interest holders with respect to their respective shares of the payment even though this will result in the withholding agent treating the entity differently with respect to different portions of the same payment. Alternatively, the withholding agent may choose to apply only the claim made by the entity, provided the entity may be treated as a beneficial owner of the income. If the withholding agent does not accept claims for a reduced rate of withholding presented by any one or more of the interest holders, or by the entity, any interest holder or the entity may subsequently claim a refund or credit of any amount so withheld to the extent the interest holder's or entity's share of such withholding exceeds the amount of tax due.

(iv) *Examples.*—The following examples illustrate the rules of paragraph (b)(2) of this section. Each of the following examples describes a payment of U.S. source royalties, which are not withholdable payments under chapter 4. See § 1.1473-1(a)(4)(iii) (describing nonfinancial payments that are not treated as withholdable payments). Thus, withholding under chapter 4 shall not apply with respect to the U.S. source royalties in any of the following examples:

(A) *Example 1.*—(i) *Facts.* Entity E is a business organization formed under the laws of country Y. Country Y has an income tax treaty with the United States. The treaty contains a limitation on benefits provision. E receives U.S. source royalties from withholding agent W and claims a reduced rate of withholding under the U.S.-Y tax treaty on its own behalf (rather than on behalf of its interest holders). E furnishes a beneficial owner withholding certificate described in paragraph (b)(1) of this section that represents that E is a resident of country Y (within the meaning of the U.S.-Y tax treaty), is the beneficial owner of the income, derives the income under section 894 and the regulations under section 894, and is not precluded from claiming benefits by the treaty's limitation on benefits provision.

(ii) *Analysis.* Absent actual knowledge or reason to know otherwise, as described in paragraph (b)(1) of this section, W may rely on the representations made by E to apply a reduced rate of withholding.

(B) *Example 2.*—(i) *Facts.* The facts are the same as under *Example 1*, except that one of E's interest holders, H, is an entity organized in country Z. The U.S.-Z tax treaty reduces the rate on royalties to zero whereas the rate on royalties under the U.S.-Y tax treaty applicable to E is 5%. H is not fiscally transparent under country Z's tax law with respect to such income. H furnishes a beneficial owner withholding certificate to E that represents that H derives, within the meaning of section 894 and the regulations under section 894, its share of the royalty income paid to E as a resident of country Z, is the beneficial owner of the royalty income, and is not precluded from claiming treaty benefits by virtue of the limitation on benefits provision in the U.S.-Z treaty. E furnishes to W a flow-through withholding certificate described in § 1.1441-1(e)(3)(i) to which it attaches H's beneficial owner withholding certificate and a withholding statement for the portion of the payment that H claims as its distributive share of the royalty income. E also furnishes to W a beneficial owner withholding certificate for itself for the portion of the payment that H does not claim as its distributive share.

(ii) *Analysis.* Absent actual knowledge or reason to know otherwise, as described in paragraph (b)(1) of this section, W may rely on the documentation furnished by E to treat the royalty payment to a single foreign entity (E) as derived by different residents of tax treaty countries as a result of the claims presented under different treaties. W may, at its option, grant dual treatment, that is, a reduced rate of zero percent under the U.S.-Z treaty on the portion of the royalty payment that H claims to derive as a resident of country Z and a reduced rate of 5% under the U.S.-Y treaty for the balance. However, under paragraph (b)(2)(iii) of this section, W may, at its option, treat E as the only relevant person deriving the royalty and grant benefits under the U.S.-Y treaty only.

(C) *Example 3.*—(i) *Facts.* E is a business organization formed under the laws of country X. Country X has an income tax treaty with the United States. E has two interest holders, H1, organized in country Y, and H2, organized in country Z. E receives from W, a U.S. withholding agent, a payment of U.S. source royalties and interest, with respect to an obligation issued before July 1, 2014, that is eligible for the portfolio interest exception under sections 871(h) and 881(c), provided W receives the appropriate beneficial owner statement required under section 871(h)(5). E is classified as a corporation under U.S. tax law principles. Country X, E's country of organization, treats E as an entity that is not fiscally transparent with respect to items of income under the regulations under section 894. Under the U.S.-X income tax treaty, royalties are subject to a 5% rate of withholding. Country Y, H1's country of organization, treats E as fiscally transparent with respect to items of income under section 894 and H1 as not fiscally transparent with respect to items of income. Under the country Y-U.S. income tax treaty, royalties are exempt from U.S. tax. Country Z, H2's country of organization, treats E as not fiscally transparent under section 894 with respect to items of income. E provides W with a flow-through beneficial owner withholding certificate with which it associates a beneficial owner withholding certificate from H1. H1's withholding certificate states that H1 is a resident of country Y, derives the royalty income under section 894, meets the applicable limitation on benefits provisions of the U.S.-Y treaty, and is the beneficial owner of the income. The withholding statement attached to E's flow-through withholding certificate allocates one-half of the royalty payment to H1. E also provides W with a beneficial owner withholding certificate for the interest income and the remaining one-half of the royalty income. The withholding certificate states that E is a resident of country X, derives the royalty income under section 894, meets the limitation on benefits provisions of the U.S.-X treaty, and is the beneficial owner of the income.

(ii) *Analysis.* Absent actual knowledge or reason to know that the claims are incorrect, as described in paragraph (b)(1), W may treat one-half of the royalty derived by E as subject to a 5% withholding rate and one-half of the royalty as derived by H1 and subject to no withholding. Further, it may treat all of the interest as being paid to E and as qualifying for the portfolio interest exception. W can, at its option, treat the entire royalty as paid to E and subject it to withholding at a 5% rate of withholding. In that case, H1 would be entitled to claim a refund with respect to its one-half of the royalty.

(D) *Example 4.*—*(1) Facts.* Entity E is a business organization formed under the laws of Country Y. Country Y has an income tax treaty with the United States that contains a limitation on benefits provision. E receives U.S. source royalties from withholding agent W. E furnishes a beneficial owner withholding certificate to W claiming a reduced rate of withholding under the U.S.-Country Y tax treaty. However, E's beneficial owner withholding certificate does not specifically identify the limitation on benefits provision that E satisfies.

(2) Analysis. Because E's withholding certificate does not specifically identify the limitation on benefits provision under the U.S.-Country Y tax treaty that E satisfies as required by paragraph (b)(1)(i) of this section, W cannot rely on E's withholding certificate to apply the reduced rate of withholding claimed by E.

(3) *Certified TIN.*—The IRS may issue guidance requiring a foreign person claiming treaty benefits and for whom a TIN is required to establish with the IRS, at the time the TIN is requested or after the TIN is issued, that the person is a resident in a treaty country and meets other conditions (such as limitation on benefits provisions) of the treaty. See § 601.601(d)(2) of this chapter.

(4) *Claim of benefits under an income tax treaty by a U.S. person.*—In certain cases, a U.S. person may claim the benefit of an income tax treaty. For example, under certain treaties, a U.S. citizen residing in the treaty country may claim a reduced rate of U.S. tax on certain amounts representing a pension or an annuity from U.S. sources. Claims of treaty benefits by a U.S. person may be made by furnishing a Form W-9 to the withholding agent or such other form as the IRS may prescribe in published guidance (see § 601.601(d)(2) of this chapter).

(c) *Exemption from requirement to furnish a taxpayer identifying number and special documentary evidence rules for certain income.*—(1) *General rule.*—In the case of income described in paragraph (c)(2) of this section, a withholding agent may rely on a beneficial owner withholding certificate described in paragraph (b)(1) of this section without regard to the requirement that the withholding certificate include the beneficial owner's taxpayer identifying number. In the case of a payment of income not described in paragraph (c)(2) of this section, a withholding agent may rely on a withholding certificate that includes the beneficial owner's foreign taxpayer identifying number described in paragraph (b)(1) of this section instead of the beneficial owner's taxpayer identifying number. In the case of payments of income described in paragraph (c)(2) of this section made outside the United States (as defined in § 1.6049-5(e)) with respect to an offshore obligation (as defined in § 1.6049-5(c)(1)), a withholding agent may, as an alternative to a withholding certificate described in paragraph (b)(1) of this section, rely on a certificate of residence described in paragraph (c)(3) of this section or documentary evidence described in paragraph (c)(4) of this section, relating to the beneficial owner, that the withholding agent has reviewed and maintains in its records in accordance with § 1.1441-1(e)(4)(iii). In the case of a payment to a person other than an individual, the certificate of residence or documentary evidence must be accompanied by the statements described in paragraphs (c)(5)(i) and (ii) of this section regarding limitation on benefits and whether the amount paid is derived by such person or by one of its interest holders. The withholding agent maintains the reviewed documents by retaining the original, certified copy, or photocopy (microfiche, electronic scan, or similar means of electronic storage) of such documents. With respect to documentary evidence, the withholding agent must also note in its records the date on which the documents were received and reviewed. This paragraph (c)(1) shall not apply to amounts that are exempt from withholding based on a claim that the income is effectively connected with the conduct of a trade or business in the United States.

(2) *Income to which special rules apply.*—The income to which paragraph (c)(1) of this section applies is dividends and interest from stocks and debt obligations that are actively traded, dividends from any redeemable security issued by an investment company registered under the Investment Company Act of 1940 (15 U.S.C. 80a-1), dividends, interest, or royalties from units of beneficial interest in a unit investment trust that are (or were upon issuance) publicly offered and are registered with the Securities and Exchange Commission under the Securities Act of 1933 (15 U.S.C. 77a), and amounts paid with respect to loans of securities described in this paragraph (c)(2). With respect to a dividend equivalent described in section 871(m) and the regulations thereunder, this paragraph (c)(2) applies to the extent that the underlying security described in section 871(m) and the regulations thereunder satisfies the requirements of this paragraph (c)(2). For purposes of this paragraph (c)(2), a stock or debt obligation is actively traded if it is actively traded within the meaning of section 1092(d) and §1.1092(d)-1 when documentation is provided.

(3) *Certificate of residence.*—A certificate of residence referred to in paragraph (c)(1) of this section is a certification issued by an appropriate tax official of the treaty country of which the taxpayer claims to be a resident that the taxpayer has filed its most recent income tax return as a resident of that country (within the meaning of the applicable tax treaty). The certificate of residence must have been issued by such official within three years prior to its being presented to the withholding agent, or such other period as the IRS may prescribe in published guidance (see §601.601(d)(2) of this chapter). See §1.1441-1(e)(4)(ii)(A) for the period during which a withholding agent may rely on a certificate of residence. The competent authorities may agree to a different procedure for certifying residence, in which case such procedure shall govern for payments made to a person claiming to be a resident of the country with which such an agreement is in effect.

(4) *Documentary evidence establishing residence in the treaty country.*—(i) *Individuals.*—For an individual, the documentary evidence referred to in paragraph (c)(1) of this section is any documentation that includes the individuals name, address, and photograph, is an official document issued by an authorized governmental body (i.e., a government or agency thereof, or a municipality), and has been issued no more than three years prior to presentation to the withholding agent. A document older than three years may be relied upon as proof of residence only if it is accompanied by additional evidence of the person's residence in the treaty country (e.g., a bank statement, utility bills, or medical bills). Documentary evidence must be in the form of original documents or certified copies thereof.

(ii) *Persons other than individuals.*—For a person other than an individual, the documentary evidence referred to in paragraph (c)(1) of this section is any documentation that includes the name of the entity and the address of its principal office in the treaty country, and is an official document issued by an authorized governmental body (e.g., a government or agency thereof, or a municipality).

(5) *Statements regarding entitlement to treaty benefits.*—(i) *Statement regarding conditions under a limitation on benefits provision.*—In addition to the documentary evidence described in paragraph (c)(4)(ii) of this section, a taxpayer that is not an individual must provide a statement that it meets one or more of the conditions set forth in the limitation on benefits article (if any, or in a similar provision) contained in the applicable tax treaty and must identify the specific limitation on benefits provision of the article (if any, or a similar provision) of the treaty upon which the taxpayer relies to claim the treaty benefit. A withholding agent may rely on the taxpayer's claim on a treaty statement regarding its reliance on a specific limitation on benefits provision absent actual knowledge that such claim is unreliable or incorrect.

(ii) *Statement regarding whether the taxpayer derives the income.*—A taxpayer that is not an individual must also provide, in addition to the documentary evidence and the statement described in paragraph (c)(5)(i) of this section, a statement that any income for which it intends to claim benefits under an applicable income tax treaty is income that will properly be treated as derived by itself as a resident of the applicable treaty jurisdiction within the meaning of section 894 and the regulations thereunder. This requirement does not apply if the taxpayer furnishes a certificate of residence that certifies that fact.

(d) *Joint owners.*—In the case of a payment to joint owners, each owner must furnish a withholding certificate or, if applicable, documentary evidence or a certificate of residence. The applicable rate of withholding on a payment of income to joint owners shall be the highest applicable rate.

(e) *Competent authority.*—The procedures described in this section may be modified to the extent the U.S. competent authority may agree with the competent authority of a country with which the United States has an income tax treaty in effect.

(f) *Failure to receive withholding certificate timely.*—See applicable procedures described in §1.1441-1(b)(7) in the event the withholding agent does not hold an appropriate withholding certificate or other appropriate documentation at the time of payment.

(g) *Special taxpayer identifying number rule for certain foreign individuals claiming treaty benefits.*—(1) *General rule.*—Except as provided in paragraph (c) or (g)(2) of this section, for purposes of paragraph (b)(1) of this section, a withholding agent may not rely on a beneficial owner withholding certificate, described in paragraph (b)(1) of this section, that does not include the beneficial owner's taxpayer identifying number (TIN).

(2) *Special rule.*—For purposes of satisfying the TIN requirement of paragraph (b)(1) of this section, a withholding agent may rely on a beneficial owner withholding certificate, described in such paragraph, without regard to the requirement that the withholding certificate include the beneficial owner's TIN, if—

(i) A withholding agent, who is also an acceptance agent, as defined in §301.6109-1(d)(3)(iv) of this chapter (the payor), has entered into an acceptance agreement that permits the acceptance agent to request an individual taxpayer identification number (ITIN) on an expedited basis because of the circumstances of payment or unexpected nature of payments required to be made by the payor;

(ii) The payor was required to make an unexpected payment to the beneficial owner who is a foreign individual;

(iii) An ITIN for the beneficial owner cannot be received by the payor from the Internal Revenue Service (IRS) because the IRS is not issuing ITINs at the time of payment or any time prior to the time of payment when the payor has knowledge of the unexpected payment;

(iv) The unexpected payment to the beneficial owner could not be reasonably delayed to permit the payor to obtain an ITIN for the beneficial owner on an expedited basis; and

(v) The payor satisfies the provisions of paragraph (g)(3) of this section.

(3) *Requirement that an ITIN be requested during the first business day following payment.*—The payor must submit a beneficial owner payee application for an ITIN (Form W-7 "Application for IRS Individual Taxpayer Identification Number") that complies with the requirements of §301.6109-1(d)(3)(ii) of this chapter, and also the certification described in §301.6109-1(d)(3)(iv)(A)(*4*) of this chapter, to the IRS during the first business day after payment is made.

(4) *Definition of unexpected payment.*—For purposes of this section, an *unexpected payment* is a payment that, because of the nature of the payment or the circumstances in which it is made, could not reasonably have been anticipated by the payor or beneficial owner during a time when the payor or beneficial owner could obtain an ITIN from the IRS. For purposes of this paragraph (g)(4), a payor or beneficial owner will not lack the requisite knowledge of the forthcoming payment solely because the amount of the payment is not fixed.

(5) *Examples.*—The rules of this paragraph (g) are illustrated by the following examples:

Example 1. G, a citizen and resident of Country Y, a country with which the United States has an income tax treaty that exempts U.S. source gambling winnings from U.S. tax, is visiting the United States for the first time. During his visit, G visits Casino B, a casino that has entered into a special acceptance agent agreement with the IRS that permits Casino B to request an ITIN on an expedited basis. During that visit, on a Sunday, G wins $5000 in slot machine play at Casino B and requests immediate payment from Casino B. ITINs are not available from the IRS on Sunday and would not again be available until Monday. G, who does not have an individual taxpayer identification number, furnishes a beneficial owner withholding certificate, described in § 1.1441-1(e)(2), to the Casino upon winning at the slot machine. The beneficial owner withholding certificate represents that G is a resident of Country Y (within the meaning of the U.S.—Y tax treaty) and meets all applicable requirements for claiming benefits under the U.S.—Y tax treaty. The beneficial owner withholding certificate does not, however, contain an ITIN for G. On the following Monday, Casino B faxes a completed Form W-7, including the required certification, for G, to the IRS for an expedited ITIN. Pursuant to paragraph (b) and (g)(2) of this section, absent actual knowledge or reason to know otherwise, Casino B, may rely on the documentation furnished by G at the time of payment and pay the $5000 to G without withholding U.S. tax based on the treaty exemption.

Example 2. The facts are the same as *Example 1*, except G visits Casino B on Monday. G requests payment Monday afternoon. In order to pay the winnings to G without withholding the 30 percent tax, Casino B must apply for and obtain an ITIN for G because an expedited ITIN is available from the IRS at the time of the $5000 payment to G.

Example 3. The facts are the same as *Example 1*, except G requests payment fifteen minutes before the time when the IRS begins issuing ITINs. Under these facts, it would be reasonable for Casino B to delay payment to G. Therefore, Casino B must apply for and obtain an ITIN for G if G wishes to claim an exemption from U.S. withholding tax under the U.S.—Y tax treaty at the time of payment.

Example 4. P, a citizen and resident of Country Z, is a lawyer and a well-known expert on real estate transactions. P is scheduled to attend a three-day seminar on complex real estate transactions, as a participant, at University U, a U.S. university, beginning on a Saturday and ending on the following Monday, which is a holiday. University U has entered into a special acceptance agent agreement with the IRS that permits University U to request an ITIN on an expedited basis. Country Z is a country with which the United States has an income tax treaty that exempts certain income earned from the performance of independent personal services from U.S. tax. It is P's first visit to the United States. On Saturday, prior to the start of the seminar, Professor Q, one of the lecturers at the seminar, cancels his lecture. That same day the Dean of University U offers P $5000, to replace Professor Q at the seminar, payable at the conclusion of the seminar on Monday. P agrees. P gives her lecture Sunday afternoon. ITINs are not available from the IRS on that Saturday, Sunday, or Monday. After the seminar ends on Monday, P, who does not have an ITIN, requests payment for her teaching. P furnishes a beneficial owner withholding certificate, described in § 1.1441-1(e)(2), to University U that represents that P is a resident of Country Z (within the meaning of the U.S.—Z tax treaty) and meets all applicable requirements for claiming benefits under the U.S.—Z tax treaty. The beneficial owner withholding certificate does not, however, contain an ITIN for P. On Tuesday, University U faxes a completed Form W-7, including the required certification, for P, to the IRS for an expedited ITIN. Pursuant to paragraph (b) and (g)(2) of this section, absent actual knowledge or reason to know otherwise, University U may rely on the documentation furnished by P and pay $5000 to P without withholding U.S. tax based on the treaty exemption.

(h) *Dividend equivalents.*—The rate of withholding on a dividend equivalent may be reduced to the extent provided under an income tax treaty in effect between the United States and a foreign country. For this purpose, a dividend equivalent as described in section 871(m) and the regulations thereunder is treated as a dividend from sources within the United States. To receive a reduced rate of withholding with respect to a dividend equivalent, a foreign person must satisfy the other requirements described in this section.

(i) *Effective/applicability dates.*—(1) *General rule.*—Except as otherwise provided in paragraphs (i)(2) and (3) of this section, this section applies to payments made on or after January 6, 2017. (For payments made after June 30, 2014 (except for payments to which paragraph (c)(1) applies, in which case substitute March 5, 2014, for June 30, 2014), and before January 6, 2017, see this section as in effect and contained in 26 CFR part 1, revised April 1, 2016. For payments made after December 31, 2001, and before July 1, 2014, see this section as in effect and contained in 26 CFR part 1 revised April 1, 2013.)

(2) *Dividend equivalents.*—Paragraph (h) of this section applies to payments made on or after December 5, 2013.

(3) *Effective/applicability date.*—Paragraphs (b)(1)(i) and (ii), (b)(2)(iv)(D), and (c)(5)(i) of this section apply to withholding certificates and treaty statements provided on or after January 6, 2017. [Reg. § 1.1441-6.]

☐ [*T.D.* 7157, 12-29-71. *Amended by T.D.* 7842, 11-2-82; *T.D.* 7977, 9-19-84; *T.D.* 8734, 10-6-97; *T.D.* 8804, 12-30-98; *T.D.* 8856, 12-29-99 (*corrected* 3-27-2000); *T.D.* 8881, 5-15-2000; *T.D.* 8977, 1-16-2002; *T.D.* 9023, 11-21-2002; *T.D.* 9253, 3-13-2006 (*corrected* 5-1-2006); *T.D.* 9648, 12-4-2013, *T.D.* 9658, 2-28-2014, *T.D.* 9808, 12-30-2016 *and T.D.* 9890, 12-27-2019 (*corrected* 3-5-2020).]

§ 1.1441-7. General provisions relating to withholding agents.—(a) *Withholding agent defined.*—(1) *In general.*—For purposes of chapter 3 of the Internal Revenue Code and the regulations under such chapter, the term *withholding agent* means any person, U.S. or foreign, that has the control, receipt, custody, disposal, or payment of an item of income of a foreign person subject to withholding, including (but not limited to) a foreign intermediary described in § 1.1441-1(e)(3)(i), a foreign partnership, or a U.S. branch described in § 1.1441-1(b)(2)(iv)(A) or (E). See §§ 1.1441-1(b)(2) and (3) and 1.1441-5(c), (d), and (e), for rules to determine whether a payment is considered made to a foreign person. Any person who meets the definition of a withholding agent is required to deposit any tax withheld under § 1.1461-1(a) and to make the returns prescribed by § 1.1461-1(b) and (c), except as otherwise may be required by a qualified intermediary withholding agreement, a withholding foreign partnership agreement, or a withholding foreign trust agreement. When several persons qualify as withholding agents with respect to a single payment, only one tax is required to be withheld and deposited. See § 1.1461-1. A person who, as a nominee described in § 1.6031(c)-1T, has furnished to a partnership all of the information required to be furnished under § 1.6031(c)-1T(a) shall not be treated as a withholding agent if it has notified the partnership that it is treating the provision of information to the partnership as a discharge of its obligations as a withholding agent.

(2) *Withholding agent with respect to dividend equivalents.*—Each person that is a party to any contract or arrangement that provides for the payment of a dividend equivalent, as described in section 871(m) and the regulations thereunder, is treated as having control and custody of the payment.

(3) *Examples.*—The following examples illustrate the rules of paragraphs (a)(1) and (a)(2) of this section:

Example 1. USB is a broker organized in the United States. USB pays U.S. source dividends and interest, which are amounts subject to withholding under § 1.1441-2(a), to FC, a foreign corporation that has an investment account with USB. USB is a withholding agent as defined in paragraph (a)(1) of this section.

Example 2. USB is a bank organized in the United States. FB is a bank organized in country X. FB has an omnibus account with USB through which FB invests in debt and equity instruments that pay amounts subject to withholding as defined in § 1.1441-2(a). FB is a nonqualified intermediary, as defined in § 1.1441-1(c)(14). Both USB and FB are withholding agents as defined in paragraph (a)(1) of this section.

Example 3. The facts are the same as in *Example 2*, except that FB is a qualified intermediary. Both USB and FB are withholding agents as defined in paragraph (a)(1) of this section.

Example 4. FB is a bank organized in country X. FB has a branch in the United States. FB's branch has customers that are foreign persons who receive amounts subject to withholding, as defined in § 1.1441-2(a). FB is a withholding agent under paragraph (a)(1) of this section and is required to withhold and report payments of amounts subject to withholding in accordance with chapter 3 of the Internal Revenue Code.

Example 5. X is a foreign corporation. X pays dividends to shareholders who are foreign persons. Under section 861(a)(2)(B), a portion of the dividends are from sources within the United States and constitute amounts subject to withholding within the meaning of § 1.1441-2(a). The dividends are not subject to tax under section 884(a). See section 884(e)(3). X is a withholding agent under paragraph (a)(1) of this section.

Example 6. FC, a foreign corporation, enters into a notional principal contract (NPC) with Bank X, a bank organized in the United States. The NPC is a specified NPC for purposes of section 871(m) and the regulations thereunder. FC is the long party to the contract and Bank X is the short party. The NPC references a specified number of shares of dividend-paying common stock issued by a domestic corporation. As the long party, FC receives payments from Bank X based on any appreciation in the value of the common stock and dividends paid with respect to the common stock. As the short party, Bank X receives payment from FC based on any depreciation in the value of the common stock and a payment based on LIBOR. Bank X is a withholding agent because Bank X is deemed to have control and custody of a dividend equivalent as a party to the NPC. If FC's tax liability under section 881 has not been satisfied in full by Bank X as withholding agent, FC is required to file a return on Form 1120-F (U.S. Income Tax Return of a Foreign Corporation).

Example 7. CO is a domestic clearing organization. CO serves as a central counterparty clearing and settlement service provider for derivatives exchanges in the United States. CB is a broker organized in Country X, a foreign country, and a clearing member of CO. CB is a nonqualified intermediary, as defined in § 1.1441-1(c)(14). FC is a foreign corporation that has an account with CB. FC instructs CB to purchase a call option that is a specified ELI (as described in § 1.871-15(e)). CB effects the trade for FC on the exchange. The exchange matches FC's order with an order for a written call option with the same terms. The exchange then sends the matched trade to CO, which clears the trade. CB and the clearing member representing the person who sold the call option settle the trade with CO. Upon receiving the matched trade, the option contracts are novated and CO becomes the counterparty to CB and the counterparty to the clearing member representing the person who sold the call option. To the extent that there is a dividend equivalent with respect to the call option, both CO and CB are withholding agents as described in paragraph (a)(1) of this section. As a withholding agent, CO and CB must each determine whether it is obligated to withhold under chapter 3 of the Internal Revenue Code and the regulations thereunder.

Example 8. FCO is a foreign clearing organization. FCO serves as a central counterparty clearing and settlement service provider for derivatives exchanges in Country A, a foreign country. CB is a broker organized in Country A, and a clearing member of FCO. CB is a nonqualified intermediary, as defined in § 1.1441-1(c)(14). FC is a foreign corporation that has an account with CB. FC instructs CB to purchase a call option that is a section 871(m) transaction. CB effects the trade for FC on the exchange. The exchange matches FC's order with an order for a written call option with the same terms. The exchange then sends the matched trade to FCO, which clears the trade. CB and the clearing member representing the call option seller settle the trade with FCO. Upon receiving the matched trade, the option contracts are novated and FCO becomes the counterparty to CB and the counterparty to the clearing member representing the call option seller. To the extent that there is a dividend equivalent with respect to the call option, both FCO and CB are withholding agents as described in paragraph (a)(1) of this section.

Example 9. The facts are the same as Example 8, except that CB is a qualified intermediary, as defined in § 1.1441-1(c)(15), that has assumed the primary obligation to withhold, deposit, and report amounts under chapters 3 and 4 of Internal Revenue Code. CB provides a written statement to FCO representing that it has assumed primary withholding responsibility for any dividend equivalent payment with respect to the call option. FCO, therefore, is not required to withhold on a dividend equivalent payment to CB.

(4) *Effective/applicability date.*—Paragraph (a)(2) of this section and *Example 6* apply on or after January 23, 2012. *Example 7, Example 8,* and *Example 9* of paragraph (a)(3) of this section apply beginning January 19, 2017.

(b) *Standards of knowledge.*—(1) *In general.*—A withholding agent must withhold at the full 30-percent rate under section 1441, 1442, or 1443(a) or at the full 4-percent rate under section 1443(b) if it has actual knowledge or reason to know that a claim of U.S. status or of a reduced rate of withholding under section 1441, 1442, or 1443 is unreliable or incorrect. A withholding agent shall be liable for tax, interest, and penalties to the extent provided under sections 1461 and 1463 and the regulations under those sections if it fails to withhold the correct amount despite its actual knowledge or reason to know the amount required to be withheld. For purposes of the regulations under sections 1441, 1442, and 1443, a withholding agent may rely on information or certifications contained in, or associated with, a withholding certificate or other documentation furnished by or for a beneficial owner or payee unless the withholding agent has actual knowledge or reason to know that the information or certifications are incorrect or unreliable and, if based on such knowledge or reason to know, it should withhold (under chapter 3 of the Code or another withholding provision of the Code) an amount greater than would be the case if it relied on the information or certifications, or it should report (under chapter 3 of the Code or under another provision of the Code) an amount that would not otherwise be reportable if it relied on the information or certifications. See § 1.1441-1(e)(4)(viii) for applicable reliance rules. A withholding agent that has received notification by the Internal Revenue Service (IRS) that a claim of U.S. status or of a reduced rate is incorrect has actual knowledge beginning on the date that is 30 calendar days after the date the notice is received. A withholding agent that fails to act in accordance with the presumptions set forth in § § 1.1441-1(b)(3), 1.1441-4(a), 1.1441-5(d) and (e), or 1.1441-9(b)(3) may also be liable for tax, interest, and penalties. See § 1.1441-1(b)(3)(ix) and (7). In the case of a withholding agent making a withholdable payment to a payee that the withholding agent is required to treat as a foreign entity, see § 1.1471-3(e) for standards of knowledge and § § 1.1471-2 and 1.1472-1(b) for withholding that may apply under chapter 4. A withholding agent is allowed to apply the rules under paragraphs (b)(5) and (b)(8) of this section as in effect and contained in 26 CFR part 1 revised April 1, 2013, to accounts opened, and obligations entered into, by an entity on or after July 1, 2014, and before January 1, 2015.

(2) *Reason to know.*—A withholding agent shall be considered to have reason to know if its knowledge of relevant facts or of statements contained in the withholding certificates or other documentation is such that a reasonably prudent person in the position of the withholding agent would question the chapter 3 claims made. For an obligation other than a preexisting obligation, a withholding agent will have reason to know that a chapter 3 claim made by the holder of the obligation (account holder) is unreliable or incorrect if any information contained in its account opening files or other files pertaining to the obligation (account information), including documentation collected for purposes of AML due diligence (as defined under § 1.1471-1(b)(4)), conflicts with the account holder's claim. A withholding agent will not, however, be considered to have reason to know that a person's chapter 3 claim is unreliable or incorrect based on documentation collected for AML due diligence until the date that is 30 days after the obligation is executed (or the account is opened for an obligation that is an account with a financial institution).

(3) *Financial institutions—limits on reason to know.*—(i) *In general.*—For purposes of this paragraph (b)(3) and paragraphs (b)(4) through (10) of this section, the terms withholding certificate, documentary evidence, and documentation are defined in § 1.1441-1(c)(16), (17), and (18). Except as otherwise provided in paragraphs (b)(4) through (9) of this section, a withholding agent that is a financial institution under § 1.1471-5(e), an insurance company (without regard to whether such company is a specified insurance company), or a broker or dealer in securities that maintains or opens an account for a beneficial owner (a direct account holder) has reason to know that documentation provided by the direct account holder is unreliable or incorrect only if one or more of the circumstances described in paragraphs (b)(4) through (9) of this section exist. If a direct account holder has provided documentation that is unreliable or incorrect under the rules of paragraph (b)(4) through (9) of this section, the withholding agent may require new documentation. Alternatively, the withholding agent may rely on the documentation originally provided if the rules of paragraphs (b)(4) through (9) of this section permit such reliance based on additional statements and documentation obtained by the withholding agent from the beneficial owner. Paragraph (b)(10) of this section provides rules regarding reason to know for withholding agents that receive beneficial owner documentation from persons (indirect account holders) that have an account relationship with, or an ownership interest in, a direct account holder of the withholding agent. Paragraph (b)(11) of this section provides limitations on a withholding agent's reason to know for multiple obligations held by the same person. Paragraph (b)(12) of this section defines a reasonable explanation provided by an individual with respect to the individual's claim of foreign status. For rules regarding reliance on Form W-9, see § 31.3406(h)-3(e)(2) of this chapter. For payments that are withholdable payments, see § 1.1471-3(e)(3) and (4) for additional rules regarding a withholding agent's reason to know with respect to a payee's claim of chapter 4 status and § 1.1471-3(f) for presumption rules that apply when the claim of chapter 4 status is unreliable or incorrect.

(ii) *Limits on reason to know for preexisting obligations.*—With respect to a preexisting obligation, a withholding agent that has documented the foreign status of the direct account holder for purposes of chapter 3 or chapter 61 before July 1, 2014, may continue to rely on such documentation without regard to a U.S. phone number or U.S. place of birth. If, however, the withholding agent reviews documentation for an individual account holder claiming foreign status that contains a U.S. place of birth (as described in paragraph (b)(5)(ii) of this section) or if the withholding agent is notified of a change in circumstances under the criteria of paragraphs (b)(5) and (8) of this section (as effective on July 1, 2014), the obligation will be treated as having experienced a change in circumstances under § 1.1441-1(e)(4)(ii)(D) as of the date that the withholding agent reviews the documentation or receives the notification, and the withholding agent will then have reason to know that the documentation is unreliable or incorrect. With respect to an obligation held by an entity, a withholding agent is not required to treat the additional U.S. indicia described in this paragraph (b) as a change in circumstances under § 1.1441-1(e)(4)(ii)(D) before January 1, 2015. See § 1.1441-1(b)(3)(iv) for the grace period following a change in circumstances. For purposes of this rule, a direct account holder will be considered documented prior to July 1, 2014, without regard to whether the withholding agent obtains renewal documentation for the account holder on or after July 1, 2014, pursuant to the requirements of § 1.1441-1(e)(4)(ii)(A).

(4) *Rules applicable to withholding certificates.*—(i) *In general.*—A withholding agent has reason to know that a beneficial owner withholding certificate provided by a direct account holder is unreliable or incorrect if the withholding certificate is incomplete with respect to any item on the certificate that is relevant to the claims made by the direct account holder, the withholding certificate contains any information that is inconsistent with the direct account holder's claim, the withholding agent has account information that is inconsistent with the direct account holder's claim, or the withholding certificate lacks information necessary to establish entitlement to a reduced rate of withholding. For purposes of establishing a direct account holder's status as a foreign person or resident of a treaty country a withholding certificate shall be considered unreliable or inconsistent with an account holder's claims only if it is not reliable under the rules of paragraphs (b)(5) and (6) of this section. See, however, § 1.1441-1(e)(2)(ii)(B) for additional reliance standards that apply to a withholding certificate that is required to include an account holder's foreign TIN. A withholding agent that relies on an agent to review and maintain a withholding certificate is considered to know or have reason to know the facts within the knowledge of the agent.

(ii) *Examples.*—The rules of paragraph (b)(4) of this section are illustrated by the following examples:

Example 1. F, a foreign person that has a direct account relationship with USB, a bank that is a U.S. person, provides USB with a beneficial owner withholding certificate for the purpose of claiming a reduced rate of withholding on U.S. source dividends (which is a withholdable payment). F resides in a treaty country that has a limitation on benefits provision in its income tax treaty with the United States. The withholding certificate includes a certification of F's status for chapter 4 purposes to except the payment from withholding under chapter 4, but does not contain a statement regarding limitation on benefits or deriving the income under section 894 as required by § 1.1441-6(b)(1). USB cannot rely on the withholding certificate to grant a reduced rate of withholding for chapter 3 purposes because it is incomplete with respect to the claim made by F.

Example 2. F, a foreign person and entity that has a direct account relationship with USB, a broker that is a U.S. person, provides USB with a withholding certificate for the purpose of claiming the portfolio interest exception under section 881(c) with respect to interest paid on an obligation issued before July 1, 2014. The payment of interest is not a withholdable payment under § 1.1471-2(b) (referring to payments made with respect to grandfathered obligations), and, therefore, withholding does not apply to the payment under chapter 4. See § 1.1441-3(c)(4)(i) for rules coordinating withholding under chapters 3 and 4. F indicates on its withholding certificate, however, that it is a partnership. USB may not treat F as a beneficial owner of the interest for purposes of the portfolio interest exception because F has indicated on its withholding certificate that it is a foreign partnership, and such entity classification is inconsistent with its claim as a beneficial owner.

(5) *Withholding certificate—establishment of foreign status.*—A withholding agent has reason to know that a beneficial owner withholding certificate (as defined in § 1.1441-1(e)(2), but excluding a Form W-8ECI) provided by a direct account holder is unreliable or incorrect for purposes of establishing the account holder's status as a foreign person as set forth in paragraphs (b)(5)(i) through (iii) of this section.

(i) *Classification of U.S. status, U.S. address, or U.S. telephone number.*—A withholding certificate is unreliable or incorrect if the withholding agent has classified the person as a U.S. person in its account information, the withholding certificate has a current permanent residence address (as defined in § 1.1441-1(e)(2)(ii)) in the United States, the withholding certificate has a current mailing address in the United States, the withholding agent has a current residence or mailing address as part of its account information that is an address in the United States, or the direct account holder notifies the withholding agent of a new residence or mailing address in the United States (whether or not provided on a withholding certificate). A withholding agent also has reason to know that a withholding certificate provided by a person is unreliable or incorrect if the withholding agent has a current telephone number for the account holder in the United States and has no telephone number for the account holder outside of the United States. When any of the foregoing U.S. indicia are present, a withholding agent may nevertheless rely on the beneficial owner withholding certificate to establish the account holder's foreign status if it may do so under the provisions of paragraph (b)(5)(i)(A) or (B) of this section.

(A) A withholding agent may treat a direct account holder as a foreign person if the beneficial owner withholding certificate has been provided by an individual and—

(1) The withholding agent has in its possession or obtains documentary evidence establishing foreign status (as described in § 1.1471-3(c)(5)(i)) that does not contain a U.S. address and the individual provides the withholding agent with a reasonable explanation, in writing, supporting the claim of foreign status (as defined in paragraph (b)(12) of this section);

(2) For a payment made outside the U.S. with respect to an offshore obligation (as described in § 1.6049-5(c)(1)), the withholding agent has in its possession or obtains documentary evidence establishing foreign status (as described in § 1.1471-3(c)(5)(i)), that does not contain a U.S. address;

(3) For a payment made with respect to an offshore obligation (with offshore obligation defined as in § 1.6049-5(c)(1)), the withholding agent classifies the individual as a resident of the country in which the obligation is maintained, the withholding agent is required to report a payment made to the individual annually on a tax information statement that is filed with the tax authority of the country in which the office is located as part of that country's resident reporting requirements, and that country has a tax information exchange agreement or income tax treaty in effect with the United States; or

(4) For a case in which the withholding agent classified the account holder as a U.S. person in its account information, the withholding agent has in its possession or obtains documentary evidence described in § 1.1471-3(c)(5)(i)(B) evidencing citizenship in a country other than the United States.

(B) A withholding agent may treat a direct account holder as a foreign person if the beneficial owner withholding certificate has been provided by an entity that the withholding agent does not know, or does not have reason to know, is a flow-through entity and—

(1) The withholding agent has in its possession or obtains documentation establishing foreign status that substantiates that the entity is actually organized or created under the laws of a foreign country; or

(2) For a payment made with respect to an offshore obligation (with offshore obligation defined as in § 1.6049-5(c)(1)), the withholding agent classifies the entity as a resident of the country in which the account is maintained, the withholding agent is required to report a payment made to the entity annually on a tax information statement that is filed with the tax authority of the country in which the office is located as part of that country's resident reporting requirements, and that country has a tax information exchange agreement or income tax treaty in effect with the United States.

(ii) *U.S. place of birth.*—A withholding agent has reason to know that a withholding certificate claiming foreign status provided by a direct account holder that is an individual is unreliable or incorrect if the withholding agent has, either on accompanying documentation or as part of its account information, an unambiguous indication of a place of birth for the individual in the United States. A withholding agent may treat the individual as a foreign person, notwithstanding the U.S. place of birth, if the withholding agent has in its possession or obtains documentary evidence described in § 1.1471-3(c)(5)(i)(B) evidencing citizenship in a country other than the United States and either a copy of the individual's Certificate of Loss of Nationality of the United States or a reasonable written explanation of the account holder's renunciation of U.S. citizenship or the reason the account holder did not obtain U.S. citizenship at birth.

(iii) *Standing instructions with respect to offshore obligations.*—A beneficial owner withholding certificate is unreliable or incorrect if it is provided with respect to an offshore obligation (as defined in § 1.6049-5(c)(1)) of a direct account holder that has provided standing instructions to pay amounts to an address or an account maintained in the United States. The withholding agent may treat the account holder as a foreign person, however, if the account holder provides either a reasonable explanation in writing that supports its foreign status or documentary evidence establishing foreign status described in §1.1471-3(c)(5)(i).

(6) *Withholding certificate—claim of reduced rate of withholding under treaty.*—A withholding agent has reason to know that a withholding certificate (other than Form W-9) provided by a direct account holder is unreliable or incorrect for purposes of establishing that the account holder is a resident of a country with which the United States has an income tax treaty if it is described in paragraphs (b)(6)(i) through (iii) of this section.

(i) *Permanent residence address.*—A beneficial owner withholding certificate is unreliable or incorrect if the permanent residence address on the beneficial owner withholding certificate is not in the country whose treaty is invoked, or the direct account holder notifies the withholding agent of a new permanent residence address that is not in the treaty country. A withholding agent may, however, treat a direct account holder as entitled to a reduced rate of withholding under an income tax treaty if the account holder provides a reasonable explanation for the permanent residence address outside the treaty country (*e.g.*, the address is the address of a branch of the beneficial owner located outside the treaty country in which the entity is a resident) or the withholding agent has in its possession or obtains documentary evidence described in §1.1471-3(c)(5)(i) that establishes residency in a treaty country.

(ii) *Mailing address.*—A beneficial owner withholding certificate is unreliable or incorrect if the permanent residence address on the withholding certificate is in the applicable treaty country but the withholding certificate contains a mailing address outside the treaty country or the withholding agent has a current mailing address as part of its account information for the direct account holder that is outside the treaty country. A mailing address that is a P.O. Box, in-care-of address, or address at a financial institution (if the financial institution is not a beneficial owner) shall not preclude a withholding agent from treating the account holder as a resident of a treaty country if such address is in the treaty country. If a withholding agent has a mailing address (whether or not contained on the withholding certificate) outside the applicable treaty country, the withholding agent may nevertheless treat a direct account holder as a resident of an applicable treaty country if—

(A) The withholding agent has in its possession or obtains documentary evidence described in §1.1471-3(c)(5)(i) supporting the account holder's claim of residence in the applicable treaty country (and the additional documentation does not contain an address outside the treaty country);

(B) The withholding agent has in its possession, or obtains, documentation that establishes that the direct account holder is an entity organized in a treaty country (or an entity managed and controlled in a treaty country, if the applicable treaty so requires);

(C) The withholding agent knows that the address outside the applicable treaty country (other than a P.O. box, or in-care-of address) is a branch of the account holder that is an entity that is a resident of the applicable treaty country; or

(D) The withholding agent obtains a written statement from the direct account holder that reasonably establishes entitlement to treaty benefits.

(iii) *Standing instructions.*—A beneficial owner withholding certificate is unreliable or incorrect to establish entitlement to a reduced rate of withholding under an income tax treaty if the direct account holder has standing instructions to pay amounts directing the withholding agent to pay amounts from its account to an address or an account outside the treaty country unless the account holder provides a reasonable explanation, in writing, or the withholding agent has in its possession or obtains documentary evidence described in §1.1471-3(c)(5)(i) establishing the account holder's residence in the applicable treaty country.

(7) *Documentary evidence.*—A withholding agent shall not treat documentary evidence provided by a direct account holder as valid if the documentary evidence does not reasonably establish the identity of the person presenting the documentary evidence. For example, documentary evidence is not valid if it is provided in person by a direct account holder that is a natural person and the photograph or signature on the documentary evidence, if any, does not match the appearance or signature of the person presenting the document. A withholding agent shall not rely on documentary evidence to reduce the rate of withholding that would otherwise apply under the presumption rules of §§1.1441-1(b)(3), 1.1441-5(d) and (e)(6), and 1.6049-5(d) if the documentary evidence contains information that is inconsistent with the direct account holder's claim of a reduced rate of withholding, the withholding agent has other account information that is inconsistent with the direct account holder's claim, or the documentary evidence lacks information necessary to establish entitlement to a reduced rate of withholding. For example, if a direct account holder provides documentary evidence to claim treaty benefits and the documentary evidence establishes the direct account holder's status as a foreign person and a resident of a treaty country, but the account holder fails to provide the treaty statements required by §1.1441-6(c)(5), the documentary evidence does not establish the direct account holder's entitlement to a reduced rate of withholding. For purposes of establishing a direct account holder's status as a foreign person or resident of a country with which the United States has an income tax treaty, documentary evidence shall be considered unreliable or incorrect only if it is not reliable under the rules of paragraph (b)(8) or (9) of this section.

(8) *Documentary evidence—establishment of foreign status.*—A withholding agent has reason to know that documentary evidence is unreliable or incorrect for purposes of establishing the direct account holder's status as a foreign person if the documentary evidence is described in paragraphs (b)(8)(i), (ii), (iii), or (iv) of this section.

(i) *Documentary evidence received prior to January 1, 2001.*—A withholding agent shall not treat documentary evidence provided by a direct account holder before January 1, 2001, as valid for purposes of establishing the account holder's status as a foreign person if it has actual knowledge that the account holder is a U.S. person or if it has a mailing or residence address for the account holder in the United States. If a withholding agent has an address for the direct account holder in the United States, the withholding agent may nevertheless treat the account holder as a foreign person if it can so treat the account holder under the rules of paragraph (b)(8)(ii) of this section. See, however, paragraph (b)(3)(ii) of this section regarding changes in circumstances with respect to preexisting obligations.

(ii) *Documentary evidence received after December 31, 2000.*—A withholding agent shall not treat documentary evidence provided by an account holder after December 31, 2000, as valid for purposes of establishing the direct account holder's foreign status if the withholding agent does not have a permanent residence address for the account holder. Documentary evidence is also unreliable or incorrect to establish a direct account holder's status as a foreign person if the withholding agent has classified the account holder as a U.S. person in its account information, if the withholding agent has a current mailing or permanent residence address (whether or not on the documentation) for the direct account holder in the United States, the direct account holder notifies the withholding agent of a new residence or mailing address in the United States, or if the withholding agent has a current telephone number for the account holder in the United States and has no telephone number for the account holder outside of the United States. Notwithstanding the foregoing, a withholding agent may rely on documentary evidence as establishing the direct account holder's foreign status if it may do so under the provisions of paragraph (b)(8)(ii)(A) or (B) of this section.

(A) *Treatment of individual's foreign status.*—A withholding agent may treat a direct account holder that is an individual as a foreign person even if it has any of the U.S. indicia described in this paragraph for the account holder if—

(1) The withholding agent has in its possession or obtains additional documentary evidence supporting the claim of foreign status (described in §1.1471-3(c)(5)(i)) that does not contain a U.S. address and a reasonable explanation in writing supporting the account holder's foreign status;

(2) The withholding agent obtains a valid beneficial owner withholding certificate on Form W-8 and the Form W-8 contains a permanent residence address outside the United States and a mailing address outside the United States (or if a mailing address is inside the United States the account holder provides a reasonable explanation in writing supporting the account holder's foreign status); or

(3) For a payment made with respect to an offshore obligation (with offshore obligation defined as in §1.6049-5(c)(1)), the withholding agent classifies the individual as a resident of the country in which the obligation is maintained, the withholding agent is required to report a payment made to the individual annually on a tax information statement that is filed with the tax authority of the

country in which the office is located as part of that country's resident reporting requirements, and that country has a tax information exchange agreement or income tax treaty in effect with the United States.

(B) *Presumption of entity's foreign status.*—A withholding agent may treat a direct account holder that is an entity (other than a flow-through entity) as a foreign person even if it has any of the U.S. indicia described in this paragraph for the account holder in the United States if—

(1) The withholding agent has in its possession or obtains documentary evidence establishing foreign status that substantiates that the entity is actually organized or created under the laws of a foreign country;

(2) The withholding agent obtains a valid beneficial owner withholding certificate on Form W-8 and the Form W-8 contains a permanent residence address outside the United States and a mailing address outside the United States (or if a mailing address is inside the United States the account holder provides additional documentary evidence sufficient to establish the account holder's foreign status); or

(3) For a payment made with respect to an offshore obligation (with offshore obligation defined as in § 1.6049-5(c)(1)), the withholding agent classifies the entity as a resident of the country in which the account is maintained, the withholding agent is required to report a payment made to the entity annually on a tax information statement that is filed with the tax authority of the country in which the office is located as part of that country's resident reporting requirements, and that country has a tax information exchange agreement or income tax treaty in effect with the United States.

(iii) *U.S. place of birth.*—A withholding agent has reason to know that documentary evidence provided by a direct account holder to support an individual's foreign status is unreliable or incorrect if the withholding agent has, either on the documentary evidence or as part of its account information, an unambiguous indication of a place of birth for the individual in the United States. A withholding agent may treat the individual as a foreign person, notwithstanding the U.S. birth place, if the withholding agent has in its possession or obtains documentary evidence described in § 1.1471-3(c)(5)(i)(B) evidencing citizenship in a country other than the United States and a copy of the individual's Certificate of Loss of Nationality of the United States. Alternatively, a withholding agent may treat the individual as a foreign person if the withholding agent obtains a valid beneficial owner withholding certificate on Form W-8 from the individual that establishes the account holder's foreign status, documentary evidence described in § 1.1471-3(c)(5)(i)(B) evidencing citizenship in a country other than the United States, and a reasonable written explanation of the individual's renunciation of U.S. citizenship or the reason the individual did not obtain U.S. citizenship at birth.

(iv) *Standing instructions with respect to offshore obligations.*—Documentary evidence is unreliable or incorrect if it is provided with respect to an offshore obligation (as defined in § 1.6049-5(c)(1)) of a direct account holder that has provided the withholding agent with standing instructions to pay amounts to an address or an account maintained in the United States. The withholding agent may treat the direct account holder as a foreign person, however, if the account holder provides either a reasonable explanation in writing that supports its foreign status or a valid beneficial owner withholding certificate claiming foreign status.

(9) *Documentary evidence—claim of reduced rate of withholding under treaty.*—A withholding agent has reason to know that documentary evidence is unreliable or incorrect for purposes of establishing that a direct account holder is a resident of a country with which the United States has an income tax treaty if it is described in paragraph (b)(9)(i) or (ii) of this section.

(i) *Permanent residence address and mailing address.*—Documentary evidence is unreliable or incorrect if the withholding agent has a current mailing or current permanent residence address for the direct account holder (whether or not on the documentary evidence) that is outside the applicable treaty country, or the withholding agent has no permanent residence address for the account holder. If a withholding agent has a current mailing or current permanent residence address for the direct account holder outside the applicable treaty country, the withholding agent may nevertheless treat a direct account holder as a resident of an applicable treaty country if the withholding agent—

(A) Has in its possession or obtains additional documentary evidence described in § 1.1471-3(c)(5)(i) supporting the direct account holder's claim of residence in the applicable treaty country (and the documentary evidence does not contain an address outside the applicable treaty country, a P.O. box, an in-care-of address, or the address of a financial institution);

(B) Has in its possession or obtains documentary evidence described in § 1.1471-3(c)(5)(i) that establishes the direct account holder is an entity organized in a treaty country (or an entity managed and controlled in a treaty country, if the applicable treaty so requires); or

(C) Obtains a valid beneficial owner withholding certificate on Form W-8 that contains a permanent residence address and a mailing address in the applicable treaty country.

(ii) *Standing instructions.*—Documentary evidence is unreliable or incorrect if the direct account holder has provided the withholding agent with standing instructions to pay amounts to an address or an account maintained outside the treaty country unless the direct account holder provides a reasonable explanation, in writing, establishing the direct account holder's residence in the applicable treaty country, or a valid beneficial owner withholding certificate that contains a permanent residence address and a mailing address in the applicable treaty country.

(10) *Indirect account holders.*—A withholding agent that receives documentation from a payee through a nonqualified intermediary, a flow-through entity, or a U.S. branch (including a territory financial institution) described in § 1.1441-1(b)(2)(iv) (other than a U.S. branch or territory financial institution that is treated as a U.S. person) has reason to know that the documentation is unreliable or incorrect if a reasonably prudent person in the position of a withholding agent would question the claims made. This standard requires, but is not limited to, a withholding agent's compliance with the rules of paragraphs (b)(10)(i) through (iv).

(i) The withholding agent must review the withholding statement described in § 1.1441-1(e)(3)(iv) and may not rely on information in the statement to the extent the information does not support the claims made for any payee. For this purpose, a withholding agent may not treat a payee as a foreign person if an address in the United States is provided for such payee and may not treat a person as a resident of a country with which the United States has an income tax treaty if the address for that person is outside the applicable treaty country. Notwithstanding a U.S. address or an address outside a treaty country, the withholding agent may treat a payee as a foreign person or a foreign person as a resident of a treaty country if the withholding statement is accompanied by a valid withholding certificate and documentary evidence (as described in § 1.1471-3(c)(5)(i)) or a reasonable explanation is provided, in writing, by the nonqualified intermediary, flow-through entity, or U.S. branch supporting the payee's foreign status or the foreign person's residency in a treaty country.

(ii) The withholding agent must review each withholding certificate in accordance with the requirements of paragraphs (b)(5) and (6) of this section and verify that the information on the withholding certificate is consistent with the information on the withholding statement required under § 1.1441-1(e)(3)(iv). If there is a discrepancy between the withholding certificate and the withholding statement, the withholding agent may choose to rely on the withholding certificate, if valid, and instruct the nonqualified intermediary, flow-through entity, or U.S. branch to correct the withholding statement or apply the presumption rules of §§ 1.1441-1(b), 1.1441-5(d) and (e)(6), 1.6049-5(d), and 1.1471-3(f) (for a withholdable payment for chapter 4 purposes) to the payment allocable to the payee who provided the withholding certificate. If the withholding agent chooses to rely upon the withholding certificate, the withholding agent is required to instruct the intermediary or flow-through entity to correct the withholding statement and confirm that the intermediary or flow-through entity does not know or have reason to know that the withholding certificate is unreliable or inaccurate.

(iii) The withholding agent must review the documentary evidence provided by the nonqualified intermediary, flow-through entity, or U.S. branch to determine that there is no obvious indication that the payee is a U.S. non-exempt recipient or that the documentary evidence does not establish the identity of the person who provided the documentation (*e.g.*, the documentary evidence does not appear to be an identification document).

(iv) If the beneficial owner is claiming a reduced rate of withholding under an income tax treaty, the rules of § 1.1441-6(b)(1)(ii) also apply to determine whether the withholding agent has reason to know that a claim for treaty benefits is unreliable or incorrect.

(11) *Limits on reason to know for multiple obligations belonging to a single person.*—A withholding agent that maintains multiple obligations for a single person will have reason to know that a claim of foreign status for the person is inaccurate based on account information for another obligation held by the person only to the extent that—

(i) The withholding agent's computerized systems link the obligations by reference to a data element such as client number, EIN, or foreign tax identifying number and consolidates the account information and payment information for the obligations; or

(ii) The withholding agent has treated the obligations as consolidated obligations for purposes of sharing documentation pursuant to § 1.1441-1(e)(4)(ix).

(12) *Reasonable explanation supporting claim of foreign status.*—A reasonable explanation supporting an individual's claim of foreign status for purposes of paragraphs (b)(5) and (8) of this section means a written statement prepared by the individual or the individual's completion of a checklist provided by the withholding agent, stating that the individual meets the requirements of one of paragraphs (b)(12)(i) through (iv) of this section.

(i) The individual certifies that he or she—

(A) Is a student at a U.S. educational institution and holds the appropriate visa;

(B) Is a teacher, trainee, or intern at a U.S. educational institution or a participant in an educational or cultural exchange visitor program, and holds the appropriate visa;

(C) Is a foreign individual assigned to a diplomatic post or a position in a consulate, embassy, or international organization in the United States; or

(D) Is a spouse or unmarried child under the age of 21 years of one of the persons described in paragraphs (b)(12)(i)(A) through (C) of this section;

(ii) The individual provides information demonstrating that he or she has not met the substantial presence test set forth in § 301.7701(b)-1(c) of this chapter (*e.g.*, a written statement indicating the number of days present in the United States during the three-year period that includes the current year);

(iii) The individual certifies that he or she meets the closer connection exception described in § 301.7701(b)-2, states the country to which the individual has a closer connection, and demonstrates how that closer connection has been established; or

(iv) With respect a payment entitled to a reduced rate of tax under a U.S. income tax treaty, the individual certifies that he or she is treated as a resident of a country other than the United States and is not treated as a U.S. resident or U.S. citizen for purposes of that income tax treaty.

(13) *Additional guidance.*—The IRS may prescribe other circumstances for which a withholding certificate or documentary evidence is unreliable or incorrect in addition to the circumstances described in paragraph (b) of this section to establish an account holder's status as a foreign person or a beneficial owner entitled to a reduced rate of withholding in published guidance (see § 601.601(d)(2) of this chapter).

(c) *Agent.*—(1) *In general.*—A withholding agent may authorize an agent to fulfill its obligations under chapter 3 if the requirements of paragraph (c)(2) of this section are satisfied. The acts of an agent of a withholding agent (including the receipt of withholding certificates, the payment of amounts of income subject to withholding, and the deposit of tax withheld) are imputed to the withholding agent on whose behalf it is acting.

(2) *Authorized agent.*—An agent is an authorized agent only if—

(i) There is a written agreement between the withholding agent and the person acting as agent that clearly provides which obligations under chapter 3 that the agent is authorized to fulfill;

(ii) A Form 8655, "Reporting Agent Authorization," is filed with the IRS by a withholding agent if its agent (including any sub-agent) acts as a reporting agent for filing Form 1042 on behalf of the withholding agent and the agent (or sub-agent) identifies itself (instead of the withholding agent) as the filer on the Form 1042;

(iii) Books and records and relevant personnel of the agent (including any sub-agent) are available to the withholding agent (on a continuous basis, including after termination of the relationship) in order to evaluate the withholding agent's compliance with the provisions of chapters 3, 4, and 61 of the Code, section 3406, and the regulations under those provisions; and

(iv) The U.S. withholding agent remains fully liable for the acts of its agent (or for any sub-agent) and does not assert any of the defenses that may otherwise be available, including under common law principles of agency in order to avoid tax liability under the Code.

(3) *Liability of withholding agent acting through an agent.*—An authorized agent is subject to the same withholding and reporting obligations that apply to any withholding agent under the provisions of chapter 3 of the Code and the regulations thereunder. See the instructions to Form 1042-S for the manner for filing the form when an authorized agent acts on behalf of a withholding agent. Except as otherwise provided in the QI, WP, and WT agreements, an authorized agent does not benefit from the special procedures or exceptions that may apply to a QI, WP, or WT. A withholding agent acting through an authorized agent is liable for any failure of the agent, such as failure to withhold an amount or make payment of tax, in the same manner and to the same extent as if the agent's failure had been the failure of the withholding agent. For this purpose, the agent's actual knowledge or reason to know shall be imputed to the withholding agent. The withholding agent's liability shall exist irrespective of the fact that the authorized agent is also a withholding agent and is itself separately liable for failure to comply with the provisions of the regulations under section 1441, 1442, or 1443. However, the same tax, interest, or penalties shall not be collected more than once.

(d) *United States obligations.*—If the United States is a withholding agent for an item of interest, including original issue discount, on obligations of the United States or of any agency or instrumentality thereof, the withholding obligation of the United States is assumed and discharged by—

(1) The Commissioner of the Public Debt, for interest paid by checks issued through the Bureau of the Public Debt;

(2) The Treasurer of the United States, for interest paid by him or her, whether by check or otherwise;

(3) Each Federal Reserve Bank, for interest paid by it, whether by check or otherwise; or

(4) Such other person as may be designated by the IRS.

(e) *Assumed obligations.*—If, in connection with the sale of a corporation's property, payment on the bonds or other obligations of the corporation is assumed by a person, then that person shall be a withholding agent to the extent amounts subject to withholding are paid to a foreign person. Thus, the person shall withhold such amounts under § 1.1441-1 as would be required to be withheld by the seller or corporation had no such sale or assumption been made.

(f) *Conduit financing arrangements.*—(1) *Liability of withholding agent.*—Subject to paragraph (f)(2) of this section, any person that is required to deduct and withhold tax under § 1.1441-3(g) is made liable for that tax by section 1461. A person that is required to deduct and withhold tax but fails to do so is liable for the payment of the tax and any applicable penalties and interest.

(2) *Exception for withholding agents that do not know of conduit financing arrangement.*—(i) *In general.*—A withholding agent will not be liable under paragraph (f)(1) of this section for failing to deduct and withhold with respect to a conduit financing arrangement unless the person knows or has reason to know that the financing arrangement is a conduit financing arrangement. This standard shall be satisfied if the withholding agent knows or has reason to know of facts sufficient to establish that the financing arrangement is a conduit financing arrangement, including facts sufficient to establish that the participation of the intermediate entity in the financing arrangement is pursuant to a tax avoidance plan. A withholding agent that knows only of the financing transactions that comprise the financing arrangement will not be considered to know or have reason to know of facts sufficient to establish that the financing arrangement is a conduit financing arrangement.

(ii) *Examples.*—The following examples illustrate the operation of paragraph (d)(2) of this section. Each example assumes that withholding under chapter 4 does not apply.

Example 1. (i) DS is a U.S. subsidiary of FP, a corporation organized in Country N, a country that does not have an income tax treaty with the United States. FS is a special purpose subsidiary of FP that is incorporated in Country T, a country that has an income tax treaty with the United States that prohibits the imposition of withholding tax on payments of interest. FS is capitalized with

$10,000,000 in debt from BK, a Country N bank, and $1,000,000 in capital from FS.

(ii) On May 1, 1995, C, a U.S. person, purchases an automobile from DS in return for an installment note. On July 1, 1995, DS sells a number of installment notes, including C's, to FS in exchange for $10,000,000. DS continues to service the installment notes for FS, and C is not notified of the sale of its obligation and continues to make payments to DS. But for the withholding tax on payments of interest by DS to BK, DS would have borrowed directly from BK, pledging the installment notes as collateral.

(iii) The C installment note is a financing transaction, whether held by DS or by FS, and the FS note held by BK also is a financing transaction. After FS purchases the installment note, and during the time the installment note is held by FS, the transactions constitute a financing arrangement, within the meaning of §1.881-3(a)(2)(i). BK is the financing entity, FS is the intermediate entity, and C is the financed entity. Because the participation of FS in the financing arrangement reduces the tax imposed by section 881 and because there was a tax avoidance plan, FS is a conduit entity.

(iv) Because C does not know or have reason to know of the tax avoidance plan (and by extension that the financing arrangement is a conduit financing arrangement), C is not required to withhold tax under section 1441. However, DS, who knows that FS's participation in the financing arrangement is pursuant to a tax avoidance plan and is a withholding agent for purposes of section 1441, is not relieved of its withholding responsibilities.

Example 2. Assume the same facts as in *Example 1* except that C receives a new payment booklet on which DS is described as "agent." Although C may deduce that its installment note has been sold, without more C has no reason to know of the existence of a financing arrangement. Accordingly, C is not liable for failure to withhold, although DS still is not relieved of its withholding responsibilities.

Example 3. (i) DC is a U.S. corporation that is in the process of negotiating a loan of $10,000,000 from BK1, a bank located in Country N, a country that does not have an income tax treaty with the United States. Before the loan agreement is signed, DC's tax lawyers point out that interest on the loan would not be subject to withholding tax if the loan were made by BK2, a subsidiary of BK1 that is incorporated in Country T, a country that has an income tax treaty with the United States that prohibits the imposition of withholding tax on payments of interest. BK1 makes a loan to BK2 to enable BK2 to make the loan to DC. Without the loan from BK1 to BK2, BK2 would not have been able to make the loan to DC.

(ii) The loan from BK1 to BK2 and the loan from BK2 to DC are both financing transactions and together constitute a financing arrangement within the meaning of §1.881-3(a)(2)(i). BK1 is the financing entity, BK2 is the intermediate entity, and DC is the financed entity. Because the participation of BK2 in the financing arrangement reduces the tax imposed by section 881 and because there is a tax avoidance plan, BK2 is a conduit entity.

(iii) Because DC is a party to the tax avoidance plan (and accordingly knows of its existence), DC must withhold tax under section 1441. If DC does not withhold tax on its payment of interest, BK2, a party to the plan and a withholding agent for purposes of section 1441, must withhold tax as required by section 1441.

Example 4. (i) DC is a U.S. corporation that has a long-standing banking relationship with BK2, a U.S. subsidiary of BK1, a bank incorporated in Country N, a country that does not have an income tax treaty with the United States. DC has borrowed amounts of as much as $75,000,000 from BK2 in the past. On January 1, 1995, DC asks to borrow $50,000,000 from BK2. BK2 does not have the funds available to make a loan of that size. BK2 considers asking BK1 to enter into a loan with DC but rejects this possibility because of the additional withholding tax that would be incurred. Accordingly, BK2 borrows the necessary amount from BK1 with the intention of on-lending to DC. BK1 does not make the loan directly to DC because of the withholding tax that would apply to payments of interest from DC to BK1. DC does not negotiate with BK1 and has no reason to know that BK1 was the source of the loan.

(ii) The loan from BK2 to DC and the loan from BK1 to BK2 are both financing transactions and together constitute a financing arrangement within the meaning of §1.881-3(a)(2)(i). BK1 is the financing entity, BK2 is the intermediate entity, and DC is the financed entity. The participation of BK2 in the financing arrangement reduces the tax imposed by section 881. Because the participation of BK2 in the financing arrangement reduces the tax imposed by section 881 and because there was a tax avoidance plan, BK2 is a conduit entity.

(iii) Because DC does not know or have reason to know of the tax avoidance plan (and by extension that the financing arrangement is a conduit financing arrangement), DC is not required to withhold tax under section 1441. However, BK2, who is also a withholding agent under section 1441 and who knows that the financing arrangement is a conduit financing arrangement, is not relieved of its withholding responsibilities.

(g) *Effective/applicability date.*—Except as otherwise provided in paragraph (a)(4) of this section, this section applies to payments made on or after January 6, 2017. (For payments made after June 30, 2014, and before January 6, 2017, see this section as in effect and contained in 26 CFR part 1, as revised April 1, 2016. For payments made after December 31, 2000, and before July 1, 2014, see this section as in effect and contained in 26 CFR part 1, as revised April 1, 2013.) [Reg. §1.1441-7.]

☐ [*T.D.* 7977, 9-19-84. *Amended by T.D.* 8611, 8-10-95; *T.D.* 8734, 10-6-97; *T.D.* 8804, 12-30-98; *T.D.* 8856, 12-29-99; *T.D.* 8881, 5-15-2000 (*corrected* 4-5-2001); *T.D.* 9572, 1-19-2012 (*corrected* 3-7-2012); *T.D.* 9648, 12-4-2013, *T.D.* 9658, 2-28-2014, *T.D.* 9734, 9-17-2015, *T.D.* 9808, 12-30-2016, *T.D.* 9815, 1-19-2017 (*corrected* 10-25-2017) *and T.D.* 9890, 12-27-2019.]

§1.1441-8. Exemption from withholding for payments to foreign governments, international organizations, foreign central banks of issue, and the Bank for International Settlements.—(a) *Foreign governments.*—Under section 892, certain specific types of income received by foreign governments are excluded from gross income and are exempt from taxation, unless derived from the conduct of a commercial activity or received from or by a controlled commercial entity. Accordingly, withholding is not required under §1.1441-1 with regard to any item of income which is exempt from taxation under section 892.

(b) *Reliance on claim of exemption by foreign government.*—Absent actual knowledge or reason to know otherwise, the withholding agent may rely upon a claim of exemption made by the foreign government if, prior to the payment, the withholding agent can reliably associate the payment with documentation upon which it can rely to treat the payment as made to a beneficial owner in accordance with §1.1441-1(e)(1)(ii). A Form W-8 furnished by a foreign government for purposes of claiming an exemption under this paragraph (b) is valid only if, in addition to other applicable requirements, it certifies that the income is, or will be, exempt from taxation under section 892 and the regulations under that section and whether the person whose name is on the certificate is an integral part of a foreign government (as defined in §1.892-2T(a)(2)) or a controlled entity (as defined in §1.892-2T(a)(3)).

(c) *Income of a foreign central bank of issue or the Bank for International Settlements.*—(1) *Certain interest income.*—Section 895 provides for the exclusion from gross income of certain income derived by a foreign central bank of issue, or by the Bank for International Settlements, from obligations of the United States or of any agency or instrumentality thereof or from interest on deposits with persons carrying on the banking business if the bank is the owner of the obligations or deposits and does not hold the obligations or deposits for, or use them in connection with, the conduct of a commercial banking function or other commercial activity by such bank. See §1.895-1. Absent actual knowledge or reason to know that a foreign central bank of issue, or the Bank for International Settlements, is operating outside the scope of the exclusion granted by section 895 and the regulations under that section, the withholding agent may rely on a claim of exemption if, prior to the payment, the withholding agent can reliably associate the payment with documentation upon which it can rely to treat the foreign central bank of issue or the Bank for International Settlements as the beneficial owner of the payment in accordance with §1.1441-1(e)(1)(ii). A Form W-8 furnished by a foreign central bank of issue or the Bank for International Settlements for purposes of claiming an exemption under this paragraph (c)(1) is valid only if, in addition to other applicable requirements, it certifies that the person whose name is on the certificate is a foreign central bank of issue, or the Bank for International Settlements, and that the bank does not, and will not, hold the obligations or the bank deposits covered by the Form W-8 for, or use them in connection with, the conduct of a commercial banking function or other commercial activity.

(2) *Bankers' acceptances.*—Interest derived by a foreign central bank of issue from bankers' acceptances is exempt from tax under sections 871(i)(2)(C) and 881(d) and §1.861-2(b)(4). With respect to bankers' acceptances, a withholding agent may treat a payee as a foreign central bank of issue without requiring a withholding certificate if the name of the payee and other facts surrounding the pay-

ment reasonably indicate that the payee or beneficial owner is a foreign central bank of issue, as defined in § 1.861-2(b)(4).

(d) *Exemption for payments to international organizations.*—A payment to an international organization (within the meaning of section 7701(a)(18)) is exempt from withholding on any payment. A withholding agent may treat a payee as an international organization without requiring a withholding certificate if the name of the payee is one that is designated as an international organization by executive order (pursuant to 22 U.S.C. 288 through 288(f)) and other facts surrounding the transaction reasonably indicate that the international organization is the beneficial owner of the payment.

(e) *Failure to receive withholding certificate timely and other applicable procedures.*—See applicable procedures described in § 1.1441-1(b)(7) in the event the withholding agent does not hold a valid withholding certificate described in paragraph (b) or (c)(1) of this section or other appropriate documentation at the time of payment. Further, the provisions of § 1.1441-1(e)(4) shall apply to withholding certificates and other documents related thereto furnished under the provisions of this section.

(f) *Effective date.*—(1) *In general.*—This section applies to payments made after December 31, 2000.

(2) *Transition rules.*—For purposes of this section, the validity of a Form 8709 that was valid on January 1, 1998, under the regulations in effect prior to January 1, 2001 (see 26 CFR part 1, revised April 1, 1999) and expired, or will expire, at any time during 1998, is extended until December 31, 1998. The validity of a Form 8709 that is valid on or after January 1, 1999, remains valid until its validity expires under the regulations in effect prior to January 1, 2001 (see 26 CFR part 1, revised April 1, 1999) but in no event shall such a form remain valid after December 31, 2000. The rule in this paragraph (f)(2), however, does not apply to extend the validity period of a Form 8709 that expires solely by reason of changes in the circumstances of the person whose name is on the certificate. Notwithstanding the first three sentences of this paragraph (f)(2), a withholding agent may choose to not take advantage of the transition rule in this paragraph (f)(2) with respect to one or more withholding certificates valid under the regulations in effect prior to January 1, 2001 (see 26 CFR part 1, revised April 1, 1999) and, therefore, to require withholding certificates conforming to the requirements described in this section (new withholding certificates). For purposes of this section, a new withholding certificate is deemed to satisfy the documentation requirement under the regulations in effect prior to January 1, 2001 (see 26 CFR part 1, revised April 1, 1999). Further, a new withholding certificate remains valid for the period specified in § 1.1441-1(e)(4)(ii), regardless of when the certificate is obtained. [Reg. § 1.1441-8.]

☐ [*T.D.* 8211, *6-24-88. Redesignated and amended by T.D.* 8734, 10-6-97 *and amended by T.D.* 8804, 12-30-98 *and T.D.* 8856, 12-29-99.]

§ 1.1441-9. Exemption from withholding on exempt income of a foreign tax-exempt organization, including foreign private foundations.—(a) *Exemption from withholding for exempt income.*—No withholding is required under section 1441(a) or 1442, and the regulations under those sections, on amounts paid to a foreign organization that is described in section 501(c) to the extent that the amounts are not income includible under section 512 in computing the organization's unrelated business taxable income. See, however, § 1.1443-1 for withholding on payments of unrelated business income to foreign tax-exempt organizations and on payments subject to tax under section 4948. For a foreign organization to claim an exemption from withholding under section 1441(a) or 1442 based on its status as an organization described in section 501(c), it must furnish the withholding agent with a withholding certificate described in paragraph (b)(2) of this section. A foreign organization described in section 501(c) may choose to claim a reduced rate of withholding under the procedures described in other sections of the regulations under section 1441 and not under this section. In particular, if an organization chooses to claim benefits under an income tax treaty, the withholding procedures applicable to claims of such a reduced rate are governed solely by the provisions of § 1.1441-6 and not of this section.

(b) *Reliance on foreign organization's claim of exemption from withholding.*—(1) *General rule.*—A withholding agent may rely on a claim of exemption under this section only if, prior to the payment, the withholding agent can reliably associate the payment with a valid withholding certificate described in paragraph (b)(2) of this section.

(2) *Withholding certificate.*—A withholding certificate under this paragraph (b)(2) is valid only if it is a Form W-8 and if, in addition to other applicable requirements, the Form W-8 includes the taxpayer identifying number of the organization whose name is on the certificate, and it certifies that the Internal Revenue Service (IRS) has issued a favorable determination letter (and the date thereof) that is currently in effect, what portion, if any, of the amounts paid constitute income includible under section 512 in computing the organization's unrelated business taxable income, and, if the organization is described in section 501(c)(3), whether it is a private foundation described in section 509. Notwithstanding the preceding sentence, if the organization cannot certify that it has been issued a favorable determination letter that is still in effect, its withholding certificate is nevertheless valid under this paragraph (b)(2) if the organization attaches to the withholding certificate an opinion that is acceptable to the withholding agent from a U.S. counsel (or any other person as the IRS may prescribe in published guidance (see § 601.601(d)(2) of this chapter)) concluding that the organization is described in section 501(c). If the determination letter or opinion of counsel to which the withholding certificate refers concludes that the organization is described in section 501(c)(3), and the certificate further certifies that the organization is not a private foundation described in section 509, an affidavit of the organization setting forth sufficient facts concerning the operations and support of the organization for the Internal Revenue Service (IRS) to determine that such organization would be likely to qualify as an organization described in section 509(a)(1), (2), (3), or (4) must be attached to the withholding certificate. An organization that provides an opinion of U.S. counsel or an affidavit may provide the same opinion or affidavit to more than one withholding agent provided that the opinion is acceptable to each withholding agent who receives it in conjunction with a withholding certificate. Any such opinion of counsel or affidavit must be renewed whenever there is a change in facts or circumstances that are relevant to determine the organization's status under section 501(c) or, if relevant, that the organization is or is not a private foundation described in section 509.

(3) *Presumptions in the absence of documentation.*—Notwithstanding paragraph (b)(1) of this section, if the organization's certification with respect to whether amounts paid constitute income includible under section 512 in computing the organization's unrelated business taxable income is not reliable or is lacking but all other certifications are reliable, the withholding agent may rely on the certificate but the amounts paid are presumed to be income includible under section 512 in computing the organization's unrelated business taxable income. If the certification regarding private foundation status is not reliable, the withholding agent may rely on the certificate but the amounts paid are presumed to be paid to a foreign beneficial owner that is a private foundation.

(4) *Reason to know.*—Reliance by a withholding agent on the information and certifications stated on a withholding certificate is subject to the agent's actual knowledge or reason to know that such information or certification is incorrect as provided in § 1.1441-7(b). For example, a withholding agent must cease to treat a foreign organization's claim for exemption from withholding based on the organization's tax-exempt status as valid beginning on the earlier of the date on which such agent knows that the IRS has given notice to such foreign organization that it is not an organization described in section 501(c) or the date on which the IRS gives notice to the public that such foreign organization is not an organization described in section 501(c). Similarly, a withholding agent may no longer rely on a certification that an amount is not subject to tax under section 4948 beginning on the earlier of the date on which such agent knows that the IRS has given notice to such foreign organization that it is subject to tax under section 4948 or the date on which the IRS gives notice that such foreign organization is a private foundation within the meaning of section 509(a).

(c) *Failure to receive withholding certificate timely and other applicable procedures.*—See applicable procedures described in § 1.1441-1(b)(7) in the event the withholding agent does not hold a valid withholding certificate or other appropriate documentation at the time of payment. Further, the provisions of § 1.1441-1(e)(4) shall apply to withholding certificates and other documents related thereto furnished under the provisions of this section.

* * *

[Reg. § 1.1441-9.]

☐ [*T.D.* 8734, 10-6-97. *Amended by T.D.* 8804, 12-30-98; *T.D.* 8856, 12-29-99 *and T.D.* 8881, 5-15-2000.]

§1.1442-3. Tax exempt income of a foreign tax-exempt corporation.—For regulations providing for a claim of exemption for income exempt from tax under section 501(a) of a foreign tax-exempt corporation, see §1.1441-9. See §1.1443-1 for withholding rules applicable to foreign private foundations and to the unrelated business income of foreign tax-exempt organizations. [Reg. §1.1442-3.]

☐ [*T.D.* 8734, 10-6-97 (T.D. 8804 delayed the effective date of T.D. 8734 from January 1, 1999, to January 1, 2000; T.D. 8856 further delayed the effective date of T.D. 8734 until January 1, 2001).]

§1.1445-1. Withholding on dispositions of U.S. real property interests by foreign persons: In general.—(a) *Purpose and scope of regulations.*—These regulations set forth rules relating to the withholding requirements of section 1445. In general, section 1445(a) provides that any person who acquires a U.S. real property interest from a foreign person must withhold a tax of 15 percent (10 percent in the case of dispositions described in paragraph (b)(2) of this section) from the amount realized by the transferor foreign person (or a lesser amount established by agreement with the Internal Revenue Service). Section 1445(e) provides special rules requiring withholding on distributions and certain other transactions by corporations, partnerships, trusts, and estates. This §1.1445-1 provides general rules concerning the withholding requirement of section 1445(a), as well as definitions applicable under both sections 1445(a) and 1445(e). Section 1.1445-2 provides for various situations in which withholding is not required under section 1445(a). Section 1.1445-3 provides for adjustments to the amount required to be withheld by transferees under section 1445(a). Section 1.1445-4 prescribes the duties of agents in transactions subject to withholding under either section 1445(a) or 1445(e). Section 1.1445-5 provides rules concerning the withholding required under section 1445(e), while §1.1445-6 provides for adjustments to the amount required to be withheld under section 1445(e). Finally, §1.1445-7 provides rules concerning the treatment of a foreign corporation that has made an election under section 897(i) to be treated as a domestic corporation.

(b) *Duty to withhold.*—(1) *In general.*—Except as provided in paragraph (b)(2) and §§1.1445-2 and 1.1445-3, transferees of U.S. real property interests are required to deduct and withhold a tax equal to 15 percent of the amount realized by the transferor if the transferor is a foreign person. Neither the transferee's duty to withhold nor the amount required to be withheld is affected by the amount of cash to be paid by the transferee. Amounts withheld must be reported and paid over in accordance with the requirements of paragraph (c) of this section. Failures to withhold and pay over are subject to the liabilities set forth in paragraph (e) of this section. If two or more persons are joint transferees of a U.S. real property interest, each such person is subject to the obligation to withhold. That obligation is fulfilled with respect to each such person if any one of them withholds and pays over the required amount in accordance with the rules of this section. If the amount realized (as defined in paragraph (g)(5) of this section) by the transferor is zero, then no withholding is required. For example, if a real property interest is transferred as a gift (i.e., the recipient does not assume any liabilities or furnish any other consideration to the transferor) then no withholding is required.

(2) *Reduced rate for certain residences.*—Transferees of U.S. real property interests are required to deduct and withhold a tax equal to 10 percent of the amount realized by the transferor if the transferor is a foreign person and the following requirements are satisfied:

(i) the property is acquired by the transferee for use by the transferee as a residence;

(ii) the amount realized for the property does not exceed $1,000,000; and

(iii) section 1445(b)(5) does not apply to the disposition. See §1.1445-2(d)(1).

(3) *U.S. real property interest owned jointly by foreign and non-foreign transferors.*—The amount subject to withholding under paragraph (b)(1) of this section with respect to the transfer of a U.S. real property interest owned by one or more foreign persons (as defined in §1.897-1(k)) and one or more non-foreign persons shall be determined by allocating the amount realized from the transfer between (or among) such transferors based upon the capital contribution of each transferor with respect to the property and by aggregating the amounts allocated to any foreign person (or persons). For this purpose, a husband and wife will each be deemed to have contributed 50 percent of the aggregate capital contributed by such husband and wife. See §1.1445-1(f)(3)(iv) with respect to the crediting of the amount withheld between or among joint foreign transferors.

(4) *Options to acquire a U.S. real property interest.*—(i) *No withholding on grant of option.*—No withholding is required under section 1445 with respect to any amount realized by the grantor on the grant of an option to acquire a U.S. real property interest.

(ii) *No withholding upon lapse of option.*—No withholding is required under section 1445 with respect to any amount realized by the grantor upon the lapse of an option to acquire a U.S. real property interest.

(iii) *Withholding required upon the sale or exchange of option.*—A transferee of an option to acquire a U.S. real property interest must deduct and withhold a tax equal to 15 percent of the amount realized by the transferor upon the disposition. This paragraph (b)(4)(iii) does not apply to require withholding upon the initial grant of an option.

(iv) *Withholding required on exercise of option.*—If the holder exercises an option to purchase a U.S. real property interest, the amount paid for the option shall be considered an amount realized by the grantor/transferor upon the transfer of the property with respect to which the option was granted, and shall thus be subject to withholding on the day that such underlying property is transferred. The preceding sentence applies regardless of whether or not the terms of the option specifically provide that the option price is applied to the purchase price.

(5) *Exceptions and modifications.*—The duty to withhold under section 1445(a) is subject to the exceptions and modifications contained in §§1.1445-2 and 1.1445-3. Generally, §1.1445-2 provides rules for determining that withholding is not required because either the transferor is not a foreign person or the interest transferred is not a U.S. real property interest. In addition, §1.1445-2 provides exceptions to the withholding requirement, including a rule that exempts from withholding any person who acquires a U.S. real property interest for use as a residence for a contract price of $300,000 or less. If withholding is required under section 1445(a), §1.1445-3 allows the amount withheld to be modified pursuant to a withholding certificate issued by the Internal Revenue Service. If a transferee cannot withhold the full amount required because the first payment of consideration for the transfer does not involve sufficient cash (or other liquid assets convertible into cash, such as foreign currency), then a withholding certificate must be obtained pursuant to §1.1445-3.

(c) *Reporting and paying over of withheld amounts.*—(1) *In general.*—A transferee must report and pay over any tax withheld by the 20th day after the date of the transfer. Forms 8288 and 8288-A are used for this purpose, and must be filed at the location as provided in the instructions to Forms 8288 and 8288-A. Pursuant to section 7502 and regulations thereunder, the timely mailing of Forms 8288 and 8288-A will be treated as their timely filing. Form 8288-A will be stamped by the IRS to show receipt, and a stamped copy will be mailed by the IRS to the transferor (at the address reported on the form) for the transferor's use. See §§1.1445-1(f) and 1.1445-3(f). Forms 8288 and 8288-A are required to include the identifying numbers of both the transferor and the transferee, as provided in paragraph (d) of this section. If any identifying number as required by such forms is not provided, the transferee must still report and pay over any tax withheld on Form 8288, although the transferor cannot obtain a credit or refund of tax on the basis of a Form 8288-A that does not include the transferor's identifying number (see paragraph (f)(2) of this section).

(2) *Pending application for withholding certificate.*—(i) *In general.*—(A) *Delayed reporting and payment with respect to application submitted by transferee.*—If an application for a withholding certificate with respect to a transfer of a U.S. real property interest is submitted to the Internal Revenue Service by the transferee on the day of or at any time prior to the transfer, the transferee must withhold 15 percent (10 percent in the case of dispositions described in paragraph (b)(2) of this section) of the amount realized as required by paragraph (b) of this section. However, the amount withheld, or a lesser amount as determined by the Service, need not be reported and paid over to the Service until the 20th day following the Service's final determination with respect to the application for a withholding certificate. For this purpose, the Service's final determination occurs on the day when the withholding certificate is mailed to the transferee by the Service or when a notification denying the request for a withholding certificate is mailed to the transferee by the Service. An application is submitted to the Service on the day it is actually received by the Service at the address provided in §1.1445-1(g)(10) or, under the

rules of section 7502, on the day it is mailed to the Service at the address provided in § 1.1445-1(g)(10).

(B) *Delayed reporting and payment with respect to application submitted by transferor.*—If an application for a withholding certificate with respect to a transfer of a U.S. real property interest is submitted to the Internal Revenue Service by the transferor on the day of or any time prior to the transfer, such transferor must provide notice to the transferee prior to the transfer. No particular form is required but the notice must set forth the name, address, and taxpayer identification number of the transferor, a brief description of the property which is the subject of the application, and the date the application was submitted to the Service. The transferee must withhold 15 percent (10 percent in the case of dispositions described in paragraph (b)(2) of this section) of the amount realized as required in paragraph (b) of this section but need not report or pay over to the Service such amount (or a lesser amount as determined by the Service) until the 20th day following the Service's final determination with respect to the application. The Service will send a copy of the withholding certificate or copy of the notification denying the request for a withholding certificate to the transferee. For this purpose, the Service's final determination will be deemed to occur on the day when the copy of the withholding certificate or the copy of the notification denying the request for a withholding certificate is mailed by the Service to the transferee (or transferees). An application is submitted to the Service on the day it is actually received by the Service at the address provided in § 1.1445-1(g)(10) or, under the rules of § 7502, on the day it is mailed to the Service at the address provided in § 1.1445-1(g)(10).

(ii) *Anti-abuse rule.*—(A) *In general.*—A transferee that in reliance upon the rules of this paragraph (c)(2) fails to report and pay over amounts withheld by the 20th day following the date of the transfer, shall be subject to the payment of interest and penalties if the relevant application for a withholding certificate (or an amendment to the application for a withholding certificate) was submitted for a principal purpose of delaying the transferee's payment to the IRS of the amount withheld. Interest and penalties shall be assessed on the amount that is ultimately paid over (or collected pursuant to the agreement) with respect to the period between the 20th day after the date of the transfer and the date on which payment is made (or collected).

(B) *Presumption.*—A principal purpose of delaying payment of the amount withheld shall be presumed if—

(1) The transferee applies for a withholding certificate pursuant to § 1.1445-3(c) based on a determination of the transferor's maximum tax liability, and

(2) Such liability is ultimately determined to be equal to 90 percent or more of the amount that was otherwise required to be withheld and paid over.

However, the presumption created by the previous sentence may be rebutted by evidence establishing that delaying payment of the amount withheld was not a principal purpose of the transaction.

(d) *Contents of Forms 8288 and 8288-A.*—(1) *Transactions subject to section 1445(a).*—Any person that is required to file Forms 8288 and 8288-A pursuant to section 1445(a) and the rules of this section must set forth thereon the following information:

(i) The name, identifying number, and home address (in the case of an individual) or office address (in the case of any entity) of the transferee(s) filing the return;

(ii) The name, identifying number, and home address (in the case of an individual) or office address (in the case of any entity) of the transferor(s);

(iii) A brief description of the U.S. real property interest transferred, including its location and the nature of any substantial improvements in the case of real property, and the class or type and amount of interests transferred in the case of interests in a corporation that constitute U.S. real property interests;

(iv) The date of the transfer;

(v) The amount realized by the transferor, as defined in paragraph (g)(5) of this section;

(vi) The amount withheld by the transferee and whether withholding is at the statutory or reduced rate; and

(vii) Such other information as the Commissioner may require.

For purposes of paragraph (d)(1)(i) and (ii), mailing addresses may be provided in addition to, but not in lieu of, home addresses or office addresses.

(2) *Transactions subject to section 1445(e).*—Any person that is required to file Forms 8288 and 8288-A pursuant to the rules of § 1.1445-5 must set forth thereon the following information:

(i) The name, identifying number, and office address of the entity or fiduciary filing the return;

(ii) The amount withheld by the entity or fiduciary;

(iii) The date of the transfer;

(iv) In the case of a transaction subject to withholding pursuant to section 1445(e)(1) and § 1.1445-5(c):

(A) A brief description of the U.S. real property interest transferred, as described in paragraph (d)(1)(iii) of this section;

(B) The name, identifying number, and home address (in the case of an individual) or office address (in the case of an entity) of each holder of an interest in the entity that is a foreign person; and

(C) Each such interest-holder's pro rata share of the amount withheld;

(v) In the case of a distribution subject to withholding pursuant to section 1445(e)(2) and § 1.1445-5(d):

(A) A brief description of the U.S. real property interest transferred, as described in paragraph (d)(1)(iii) of this section; and

(B) The amount of gain recognized upon the distribution by the corporation.

(vi) In the case of a distribution subject to withholding pursuant to section 1445(e)(3) and § 1.1445-5(e):

(A) A brief description of the property distributed by the corporation;

(B) The name, identifying number, and home address (in the case of an individual) or office address (in the case of an entity) of each holder of an interest in the entity that is a foreign person;

(C) The amount realized upon the distribution by each such foreign interest holder; and

(D) Each foreign interest-holder's pro rata share of the amount withheld; and

(vii) Such other information as the Commissioner may require.

(e) *Liability of transferee upon failure to withhold.*—(1) *In general.*—Every person required to deduct and withhold tax under section 1445 is made liable for that tax by section 1461. Therefore, a person that is required to deduct and withhold tax but fails to do so may be held liable for the payment of the tax and any applicable penalties and interest.

(2) *Transferor's liability not otherwise satisfied.*—(i) *Tax and penalties.*—Except as provided in paragraph (e)(3) of this section, if a transferee is required to deduct and withhold tax under section 1445 but fails to do so, then the tax shall be assessed against and collected from that transferee. Such person may also be subject to any of the civil and criminal penalties that apply. Corporate officers or other responsible persons may be subject to a civil penalty under section 6672 equal to the amount that should have been withheld and paid over.

(ii) *Interest.*—If a transferee is required to deduct and withhold tax under section 1445 but fails to do so, then such transferee shall be liable for the payment of interest pursuant to section 6601 and the regulations thereunder. Interest shall be payable with respect to the period between—

(A) The last date on which the tax imposed under section 1445 was required to be paid over by the transferee, and

(B) The date on which such tax is actually paid. Interest shall be payable with respect to the entire amount that is required to be deducted and withheld. However, if the Service issues a withholding certificate providing for withholding of a reduced amount, then, for the period after the issuance of the certificate, interest shall be payable with respect to that reduced amount.

(3) *Transferor's liability otherwise satisfied.*—(i) *Tax and penalties.*—If a transferee is required to deduct and withhold tax under section 1445 but fails to do so, and the transferor's tax liability with respect to the transfer was satisfied (or was established to be zero) by—

(A) The transferor's filing of an income tax return (and payment of any tax due) with respect to the transfer, or

(B) The issuance of a withholding certificate by the Internal Revenue Service establishing that the transferor's maximum tax liability is zero,

then the tax required to be withheld under section 1445 shall not be collected from the transferee. Such transferee's liability for tax, and the requirement that such person file Forms 8288 and 8288-A, shall be deemed to have been satisfied as of the date on which the transferor's income tax return was filed or the withholding certificate was issued. No penalty shall be imposed on or collected from such person for failure to return or pay the tax, unless such failure was fraudulent and for the purpose of evading payment. A transferee that seeks to avoid liability for tax and penalties pursuant to the rule of paragraph (e)(3)(i) must provide sufficient information for the Service to determine whether the transferor's tax liability was satisfied (or was established to be zero).

(ii) *Interest.*—If a transferee is required to deduct and withhold tax under section 1445 but fails to do so, then such person shall be liable for the payment of interest under section 6601 and regulations thereunder. Such transferee's liability for the payment of interest shall not be excused by reason of the deemed satisfaction, pursuant to subdivision (i) of this paragraph (e)(3), of the transferee's liability under section 1445, because the deemed satisfaction of that liability is the equivalent of the late payment of a liability, on which interest must be paid. Interest shall be payable with respect to the period between—

(A) The last date on which the tax imposed under section 1445 was required to be paid over, and

(B) The date (established from information supplied to the Service by the transferee) on which any tax due is paid with respect to the transferor's relevant income tax return, or the date the withholding certificate is issued establishing that the transferor's maximum tax liability is zero.

Interest shall be payable with respect to the entire amount that is required to be deducted and withheld. However, if the Service issues a withholding certificate providing for withholding of a reduced amount, then for the period after the issuance of the certificate interest shall be payable with respect to that reduced amount.

(4) *Coordination with entity withholding rules.*—For purposes of section 1445(e) and § § 1.1445-5, 1.1445-6, 1.1445-7, and 1.1445-8T, the rules of this paragraph (e) shall be applied by—

(i) Substituting the words "person required to withhold" for the word "transferee" each place it appears in this paragraph (e), and

(ii) Substituting the words "person subject to withholding" for the word "transferor" each place it appears in this paragraph (e).

(f) *Effect of withholding on transferor.*—(1) *In general.*—The withholding of tax under section 1445(a) does not excuse a foreign person that disposes of a U.S. real property interest from filing a U.S. tax return with respect to the income arising from the disposition. Form 1040NR, 1041, or 1120F, as appropriate, must be filed, and any tax due must be paid, by the filing deadline generally applicable to such person. (The return may be filed by such later date as is provided in an extension granted by the Internal Revenue Service.) Any tax withheld under section 1445(a) shall be credited against the amount of income tax as computed in such return.

(2) *Manner of obtaining credit or refund.*—A stamped copy of Form 8288-A will be provided to the transferor by the Service (under paragraph (c) of this section) if the Form 8288-A is complete, including the transferor's identifying number. Except as provided in paragraph (f)(3) of this section, a stamped copy of Form 8288-A must be attached to the transferor's return to establish the amount withheld that is available as a credit. If the amount withheld under section 1445(a) constitutes less than the full amount of the transferor's U.S. tax liability for that taxable year, then a payment of estimated tax may be required to be made pursuant to section 6154 or 6654 prior to the filing of the income tax return for that year. Alternatively, if the amount withheld under section 1445(a) exceeds the transferor's maximum tax liability with respect to the disposition (as determined by the IRS), then the transferor may seek an early refund of the excess pursuant to § 1.1445-3T(g), or a normal refund upon filing of a tax return.

(3) *Special rules.*—(i) *Failure to receive Form 8288-A.*—If a stamped copy of Form 8288-A has not been provided to the transferor by the Service, the transferor may establish the amount of tax withheld by the transferee by attaching to its return substantial evidence (*e.g.*, closing documents) of such amount. Such a transferor must attach to its return a statement which supplies all of the information required by § 1.1445-1(d), including the transferor's identifying number.

(ii) *U.S. persons subjected to withholding.*—If a transferee withholds tax under section 1445(a) with respect to a person who is not a foreign person, such person may credit the amount of any tax withheld against his income tax liability in accordance with the provisions of this § 1.1445-1(f) or apply for an early refund under § 1.1445-3(g).

(iii) *Refund in case of installment sale.*—A transferor that takes gain into account in accordance with the provisions of section 453 shall not be entitled to a refund of the amount withheld, unless a withholding certificate providing for such a refund is obtained from the Internal Revenue Service pursuant to the provisions of § 1.1445-3.

(iv) *Joint foreign transferors.*—If two or more foreign persons jointly transfer a U.S. real property interest, each transferor shall be credited with such portion of the amount withheld as such transferors mutually agree. Such transferors must request that the transferee reflect the agreed-upon crediting of the amount withheld on the Forms 8288-A filed by the transferee. If the foreign transferors fail to request that the transferee reflect the agreed-upon crediting of the amount withheld by the 10th day after the date of transfer, the transferee must credit the amount withheld equally between (or among) the foreign transferors. In such case, the transferee is indemnified pursuant to section 1461 against any claim by a transferor objecting to the resulting division of credits. For rules regarding the amount realized allocated to joint foreign and non-foreign transferors, see § 1.1445-1(b)(2).

(g) *Definitions.*—(1) *In general.*—Unless otherwise specified, the definitions of terms provided in § 1.897-1 shall apply for purposes of this section and § § 1.1445-2 through 1.1445-7. For purposes of section 1445 and the regulations thereunder, definitions of other relevant terms are provided in this paragraph (g). In addition, the term "residence" is defined in § 1.1445-2(d)(1), the terms "transferor's agent" and "transferee's agent" are defined in § 1.1445-4(f), and the term "relevant taxpayer" is defined in § 1.1445-6(a)(2).

(2) *Transfer.*—The term "transfer" means any transaction that would constitute a disposition for any purpose of the Internal Revenue Code and regulations thereunder. For purposes of § § 1.1445-5 and 1.1445-6, the term includes distributions to shareholders of a corporation, partners of a partnership, and beneficiaries of a trust or estate.

(3) *Transferor.*—The term "transferor" means any person, foreign or domestic, that disposes of a U.S. real property interest by sale, exchange, gift or any other transfer. The term "U.S. real property interest" is defined in § 1.897-1(c).

(4) *Transferee.*—The term "transferee" means any person, foreign or domestic, that acquires a U.S. real property interest by purchase, exchange, gift, or any other transfer.

(5) *Amount realized.*—The amount realized by the transferor for the transfer of a U.S. real property interest is the sum of:

(i) The cash paid, or to be paid,

(ii) The fair market value of other property transferred, or to be transferred, and

(iii) The outstanding amount of any liability assumed by the transferee or to which the U.S. real property interest is subject immediately before and after the transfer. The term "cash paid or to be paid" does not include stated or unstated interest or original issue discount (as determined under the rules of sections 1271 through 1275).

(6) *Contract price.*—The contract price of a U.S. real property interest is the sum that is agreed to by the transferee and transferor as the total amount of consideration to be paid for the property. That amount will generally be equal to the amount realized by the transferor, as defined in paragraph (b)(5) of this section.

(7) *Fair market value.*—The fair market value of property means the price at which the property would change hands between an unrelated willing buyer and willing seller, neither being under any compulsion to buy or to sell and both having reasonable knowledge of all relevant facts.

(8) *Date of transfer.*—The date of transfer of a U.S. real property interest is the first date on which consideration is paid (or a liability assumed) by the transferee. However, for purposes of section 1445(e)(2), (3), and (4) and § 1.1445-5(c)(1)(iii) and 1.1445-5(c)(3) only, the date of transfer is the date of the distribution that gives rise to the obligation to withhold. For purposes of this paragraph (g)(8), the payment of consideration does not include the payment, prior to the

passage of legal or equitable title (other than pursuant to an initial contract for purchase), of earnest money, a good-faith deposit, or any similar sum that is primarily intended to bind the transferee or transferor to the entering or performance of a contract. Such a payment will not constitute a payment of consideration solely because it may ultimately be applied against the amount owed to the transferor by the transferee. Such a payment is presumed to be earnest money, a good faith deposit, or a similar sum if it is subject to forfeiture in the event of a failure to enter into a contract or a breach of contract. However, a payment that is not forfeitable may nevertheless be found to constitute earnest money, a good faith deposit, or a similar sum.

(9) *Identifying number.*—Pursuant to § 1.897-1(p), an individual's identifying number is the social security number or the identification number assigned by the Internal Revenue Service (see § 301.6109-1 of this chapter). The identifying number of any other person is its United States employer identification number.

(10) *Address for correspondence.*—Any written communication to the Internal Revenue Service described in this section is to be mailed to the address specified in the Instructions for Form 8288 under the heading "Where To File."

(11) *Withholding qualified holder.*—A withholding qualified holder means a qualified holder (under § 1.897(l)-1(d)), and a foreign partnership all of the interests of which are held by qualified holders (under § 1.897(l)-1(d)), including through one or more partnerships.

(h) *Applicability dates.*—The requirement in paragraphs (c)(2)(i)(B), (d)(1)(i) and (ii), (d)(2)(i), (d)(2)(iv)(B), and (d)(2)(vi)(B) of this section that taxpayer identification numbers be provided (in all cases) is applicable for dispositions of U.S. real property interests occurring after November 3, 2003. The withholding rates set forth in paragraphs (a), (b)(1), (b)(2), (b)(4)(iii), (c)(2)(i)(A), and (c)(2)(i)(B) of this section apply to dispositions after February 16, 2016. For dispositions on or before February 16, 2016, see paragraphs (a), (b)(1), (b)(3)(iii), (c)(2)(i)(A), and (c)(2)(i)(B) of this section as contained in 26 CFR part 1 revised as of April 1, 2015. [Reg. § 1.1445-1.]

☐ [*T.D.* 8113, 12-18-86. *Amended by T.D.* 8647, 12-20-95 *T.D.* 9082, 8-4-2003, *T.D.* 9751, 2-17-2016 *and T.D.* 9971, 12-28-2022.]

§ 1.1445-2. Situations in which withholding is not required under section 1445(a).—(a) *Purpose and scope of section.*—This section provides rules concerning various situations in which withholding is not required under section 1445(a). In general, a transferee has a duty to withhold under section 1445(a) only if both of the following are true:

(1) The transferor is a foreign person; and

(2) The transferee is acquiring a U.S. real property interest.

Thus, paragraphs (b) and (c) of this section provide rules under which a transferee of property can ascertain that he has no duty to withhold because one or the other of the two key elements is missing. Under paragraph (b), a transferee may determine that no withholding is required because the transferor is not a foreign person. Under paragraph (c), a transferee may determine that no withholding is required because the property acquired is not a U.S. real property interest. Finally, paragraph (d) of this section provides rules concerning exceptions to the withholding requirement.

(b) *Transferor not a foreign person.*—(1) *In general.*—No withholding is required under section 1445 if the transferor of a U.S. real property interest is not a foreign person. Therefore, paragraph (b)(2) of this section provides rules pursuant to which the transferor can provide a certification of non-foreign status to inform the transferee that withholding is not required. A transferee that obtains such a certification must retain that document for five years, as provided in paragraph (b)(3) of this section. Except to the extent provided in paragraph (b)(4) of this section, the obtaining of this certification excuses the transferee from any liability otherwise imposed by section 1445 and § 1.1445-1(e). However, section 1445 and the rules of this section do not impose any obligation upon a transferee to obtain a certification from the transferor; thus, a transferee may instead rely upon other means to ascertain the non-foreign status of the transferor. If, however, the transferee relies upon other means and the transferor was, in fact, a foreign person, then the transferee is subject to the liability imposed by section 1445 and § 1.1445-1(e).

A transferee is in no event required to rely upon other means to ascertain the non-foreign status of the transferor and may demand a certification of non-foreign status. If the certification is not provided, the transferee may withhold tax under section 1445 and will be considered, for purposes of sections 1461 through 1463, to have been required to withhold such tax.

(2) *Transferor's certification of non-foreign status.*—(i) *In general.* The rules in this paragraph (b)(2)(i) apply for purposes of the transferor's certification of non-foreign status (including a certification of non-foreign status provided by a withholding qualified holder (as defined in § 1.1445-1(g)(11)).

(A) A transferee of a U.S. real property interest is not required to withhold under section 1445(a) if, before or at the time of the transfer, the transferor furnishes to the transferee a certification that is signed under penalties of perjury and

(*1*) States that the transferor is not a foreign person; and

(*2*) Sets forth the transferor's name, identifying number and home address (in the case of an individual) or office address (in the case of an entity).

(B) For purposes of paragraph (b)(2)(i)(A) of this section, a foreign person is a nonresident alien individual, foreign corporation, foreign partnership, foreign trust, or foreign estate, except that a withholding qualified holder (as defined in § 1.1445-1(g)(11)) is not a foreign person. Additionally, a foreign corporation that has made a valid election under section 897(i) is generally not treated as a foreign person for purposes of section 1445. In this regard, see § 1.1445-7. Pursuant to § 1.897-1(p), an individual's identifying number is the individual's Social Security number and any other person's identifying number is its U.S. employer identification number (EIN), or, if the transferor is a withholding qualified holder (as defined in § 1.1445-1(g)(11)) that does not have a U.S. taxpayer identification number, a foreign tax identification number issued by its jurisdiction of residence. A certification pursuant to this paragraph (b) must be verified as true and signed under penalties of perjury by a responsible officer in the case of a corporation, by a general partner in the case of a partnership, and by a trustee, executor, or equivalent fiduciary in the case of a trust or estate. No particular form is needed for a certification pursuant to this paragraph (b), nor is any particular language required, so long as the document meets the requirements of this paragraph (b)(2)(i), except that, with respect to a certification submitted by a withholding qualified holder (as defined in § 1.1445-1(g)(11)), the transferor must state on the certification that it is treated as a non-foreign person because it is a withholding qualified holder and must further specify whether it qualifies as a withholding qualified holder because it is a qualified holder under § 1.897(l)-1(d) or a foreign partnership that satisfies the requirements of § 1.1445-1(g)(11). Samples of acceptable certifications are provided in paragraph (b)(2)(iv) of this section.

(ii) *Foreign corporation that has made election under section 897(i).*—A foreign corporation that has made a valid election under section 897(i) to be treated as a domestic corporation for purposes of section 897 may provide a certification of non-foreign status pursuant to this paragraph (b)(2). However, an electing foreign corporation must attach to such certification a copy of the acknowledgment of the election provided to the corporation by the Internal Revenue Service pursuant to § 1.897-3(d)(4). An acknowledgement is valid for this purpose only if it states that the information required by § 1.897-3 has been determined to be complete.

(iii) *Disregarded entities.*—A disregarded entity may not certify that it is the transferor of a U.S. real property interest, as the disregarded entity is not the transferor for U.S. tax purposes, including sections 897 and 1445. Rather, the owner of the disregarded entity is treated as the transferor of property and must provide a certificate of non-foreign status to avoid withholding under section 1445. A disregarded entity for these purposes means an entity that is disregarded as an entity separate from its owner under § 301.7701-3 of this chapter, a qualified REIT subsidiary as defined in section 856(i), or a qualified subchapter S subsidiary under section 1361(b)(3)(B). Any domestic entity must include in its certification of non-foreign status with respect to the transfer a certification that it is not a disregarded entity. This paragraph (b)(2)(iii) and the sample certification provided in paragraph (b)(2)(iv)(B) of this section (to the extent it addresses disregarded entities) is applicable for dispositions occurring [after]September 4, 2003.

(iv) *Sample certifications.*—(A) *Individual transferor.*—"Section 1445 of the Internal Revenue Code provides that a transferee (buyer) of a U.S. real property interest must withhold tax if the transferor (seller) is a foreign person. To inform the transferee (buyer) that withholding of tax is not required upon my disposition of a U.S. real property interest, I, [*name of transferor*], hereby certify the following:

1. I am not a nonresident alien for purposes of U.S. income taxation;

2. My U.S. taxpayer identifying number (Social Security number) is ___; and

3. My home address is ___

I understand that this certification may be disclosed to the Internal Revenue Service by the transferee and that any false statement I have made here could be punished by fine, imprisonment, or both.

Under penalties of perjury I declare that I have examined this certification and to the best of my knowledge and belief it is true, correct, and complete.
[Signature and Date]"

(B) *Entity transferor.*—"Section 1445 of the Internal Revenue Code provides that a transferee of a U.S. real property interest must withhold tax if the transferor is a foreign person. For U.S. tax purposes (including section 1445), the owner of a disregarded entity (which has legal title to a U.S. real property interest under local law) will be the transferor of the property and not the disregarded entity. To inform the transferee that withholding of tax is not required upon the disposition of a U.S. real property interest by [name of transferor], the undersigned hereby certifies the following on behalf of [name of the transferor]:

1. [Name of transferor] is not a foreign corporation, foreign partnership, foreign trust, or foreign estate (as those terms are defined in the Internal Revenue Code and Income Tax Regulations);

2. [Name of transferor] is not a disregarded entity as defined in § 1.1445-2(b)(2)(iii);

3. [Name of transferor]'s U.S. employer identification number is ___; and

4. [Name of transferor]'s office address is ___.

[Name of transferor] understands that this certification may be disclosed to the Internal Revenue Service by transferee and that any false statement contained herein could be punished by fine, imprisonment, or both.

Under penalties of perjury I declare that I have examined this certification and to the best of my knowledge and belief it is true, correct, and complete, and I further declare that I have authority to sign this document on behalf of [name of transferor].
[Signature(s) and date]
[Title(s)]"

(v) *Form W-9.*—For purposes of paragraph (b)(2)(i) of this section, a certification of non-foreign status includes a valid Form W-9, *Request for Taxpayer Identification Number and Certification*, or its successor, submitted to the transferee by the transferor.

(vi) *Form W-8EXP.*—A certification of non-foreign status may be made by a withholding qualified holder (as defined under § 1.1445-1(g)(11)) as provided in paragraph (b)(2)(i) of this section to certify its qualified holder status. A certification of non-foreign status under paragraph (b)(2)(i) of this section also includes a certification made on a Form W-8EXP (or its successor) that states that the transferor is treated as a non-foreign person because it is a withholding qualified holder and must further specify whether it qualifies as a withholding qualified holder because it is a qualified holder under § 1.897(l)-1(d) or a foreign partnership that satisfies the requirements of § 1.1445-1(g)(11). The certification must also meet all of the other requirements for a valid Form W-8EXP (or its successor) as provided on the form and the instructions to the form. A qualified holder may not provide a certification of non-foreign status on a Form W-9 (or its successor) as permitted in paragraph (b)(2)(v) of this section.

(3) *Transferee must retain certification.*—If a transferee obtains a transferor's certification pursuant to the rules of this paragraph (b), then the transferee must retain that certification until the end of the fifth taxable year following the taxable year in which the transfer takes place. The transferee must retain the certification, and make it available to the Internal Revenue Service when requested in accordance with the requirements of section 6001 and regulations thereunder.

(4) *Reliance upon certification not permitted.*—(i) *In general.*—A transferee may not rely upon a transferor's certification pursuant to this paragraph (b) under the circumstances set forth in either subdivision (ii) or (iii) of this paragraph (b)(4). In either of those circumstances, a transferee's withholding obligation shall apply as if a certification had never been obtained, and the transferee is fully liable pursuant to section 1445 and § 1445-1(e) for any failure to withhold.

(ii) *Failure to attach IRS acknowledgment of election.*—A transferee that knows that the transferor is a foreign corporation may not rely upon a certification of non-foreign status provided by the corporation on the basis of election under section 897(i), unless there is attached to the certification a copy of the acknowledgment by the Internal Revenue Service of the corporation's election, as required by paragraph (b)(2)(ii) of this section.

(iii) *Knowledge of falsity.*—A transferee is not entitled to rely upon a transferor's certification if prior to or at the time of the transfer the transferee either—

(A) Has actual knowledge that the transferor's certification is false; or

(B) Receives a notice that the certification is false from a transferor's or transferee's agent, pursuant to § 1.1445-4.

(iv) *Belated notice of false certification.*—If after the date of the transfer a transferee receives a notice that a certification is false, then that transferee is entitled to rely upon the certification only with respect to consideration that was paid prior to receipt of the notice. Such a transferee is required to withhold a full 15 percent of the amount realized from the consideration that remains to be paid to the transferor if possible. Thus, if 15 percent or more of the amount realized remains to be paid to the transferor then the transferee is required to withhold and pay over the full 15 percent. The transferee must do so by withholding and paying over the entire amount of each successive payment of consideration to the transferor until the full 15 percent of the amount realized has been withheld and paid over. Amounts so withheld must be reported and paid over by the 20th day following the date on which each such payment of consideration is made. A transferee that is subject to the rules of this paragraph (b)(4)(iv) may not obtain a withholding certificate pursuant to § 1.1445-3, but must instead withhold and pay over the amounts required by this paragraph. For dispositions described in § 1.1445-1(b)(2), this paragraph shall be applied by replacing "15 percent" with "10 percent" each time it appears.

(c) *Transferred property not a U.S. real property interest.*—(1) *In general.*—No withholding is required under section 1445 if the transferee acquires only property that is not a U.S. real property interest. As defined in section 897(c) and § 1.897-1(c), a U.S. real property interest includes certain interests in U.S. corporations, as well as direct interests in real property and certain associated personal property. This paragraph (c) provides rules pursuant to which a person acquiring an interest in a U.S. corporation may determine that withholding is not required because that interest is not a U.S. real property interest. To determine whether an interest in tangible property constitutes a U.S. real property interest the acquisition of which would be subject to withholding, see § 1.897-1(b) and (c).

(2) *Interests in publicly traded entities.*—No withholding is required under section 1445(a) upon the acquisition of an interest in a domestic corporation if any class of stock of the corporation is regularly traded on an established securities market. This exemption shall apply if the disposition is incident to an initial public offering of stock pursuant to a registration statement filed with the Securities and Exchange Commission. Similarly, no withholding is required under section 1445(a) upon the acquisition of an interest in a publicly traded partnership or trust. However, the rule of this paragraph (c)(2) shall not apply to the acquisition, from a single transferor (or related transferors as defined in § 1.897-1(i)) in a single transaction (or related transactions), of an interest described in § 1.897-1(c)(2)(iii)(B) (relating to substantial amounts of non-publicly traded interests in publicly traded corporations) or to similar interests in publicly traded partnerships or trusts. The person making an acquisition described in the preceding sentence must otherwise determine whether withholding is required, pursuant to section 1445 and the regulations thereunder. Transactions shall be deemed to be related if they are undertaken within 90 days of one another or if it can otherwise be shown that they were undertaken in pursuance of a prearranged plan.

(3) *Transferee receives statement that interest in corporation is not a U.S. real property interest.*—(i) *In general.*—No withholding is required under section 1445(a) upon the acquisition of an interest in a domestic corporation, if the transferor provides the transferee with a copy of a statement, issued by the corporation pursuant to § 1.897-2(h), certifying that the interest is not a U.S. real property interest. In

general, a corporation may issue such a statement only if the corporation was not a U.S. real property holding corporation at any time during the previous five years (or the period in which the interest was held by its present holder, if shorter) or if interests in the corporation ceased to be United States real property interests under section 897(c)(1)(B). (A corporation may not provide such a statement based on its determination that the interest in question is an interest solely as a creditor.) See § 1.897-2(f) and (h). The corporation may provide such a statement directly to the transferee at the transferor's request. The transferor must request such a statement prior to the transfer, and shall, to the extent possible, specify the anticipated date of the transfer. A corporation's statement may be relied upon for purposes of this paragraph (c)(3) only if the statement is dated not more than 30 days prior to the date of the transfer. A transferee may also rely upon a corporation's statement that is voluntarily provided by the corporation in response to a request from the transferee, if that statement otherwise complies with the requirements of this paragraph (c)(3) and § 1.897-2(h).

(ii) *Reliance on statement not permitted.*—A transferee is not entitled to rely upon a statement that a corporation is not a U.S. real property holding corporation if, prior to or at the time of the transfer, the transferee either—

(A) Has actual knowledge that the statement is false, or

(B) Receives a notice that the statement is false from a transferor's or transferee's agent, pursuant to § 1.1445-4.

Such a transferee's withholding obligations shall apply as if a statement had never been given, and such a transferee may be held fully liable pursuant to § 1.1445-1(e) for any failure to withhold.

(iii) *Belated notice of false statement.*—If after the date of the transfer, a transferee receives notice that a statement provided under § 1.1445-2(c)(3)(i) (that an interest in a corporation is not a U.S. real property interest) is false, then such transferee may rely on the statement only with respect to consideration that was paid prior to the receipt of the notice. Such a transferee is required to withhold a full 15 percent of the amount realized from the consideration that remains to be paid to the transferor, if possible. Thus, if 15 percent or more of the amount realized remains to be paid to the transferor, then the transferee is required to withhold any pay over the full 15 percent. The transferee must do so by withholding and paying over the entire amount of each successive payment of consideration to the transferor, until the full 15 percent of the amount realized has been withheld and paid over. Amounts so withheld must be reported and paid over by the 20th day following the date on which each such payment of consideration is made. A transferee that is subject to the rules of this paragraph 1.1445-2(c)(3)(iii) may not obtain a withholding certificate pursuant to § 1.1445-3, but must instead withhold and pay over the amounts required by this paragraph.

(d) *Exceptions to requirement of withholding.*—(1) *Purchase of residence for $300,000 or less.*—No withholding is required under section 1445(a) if one or more individual transferees acquire a U.S. real property interest for use as a residence and the amount realized on the transaction is $300,000 or less. For purposes of this section, a U.S. real property interest is acquired for use as a residence if on the date of the transfer the transferee (or transferees) has definite plans to reside at the property for at least 50 percent of the number of days that the property is used by any person during each of the first two 12-month periods following the date of the transfer. The number of days that the property will be vacant is not taken into account in determining the number of days such property is used by any person. A transferee shall be considered to reside at a property on any day on which a member of the transferee's family, as defined in section 267(c)(4), resides at the property. No form or other document need be filed with the Internal Revenue Service to establish a transferee's entitlement to rely upon the exception provided by this paragraph (d)(1). A transferee who fails to withhold in reliance upon this exception, but who does not in fact reside at the property for the minimum number of days set forth above, shall be liable for the failure to withhold (if the transferor was a foreign person and did not pay the full U.S. tax due on any gain recognized upon the transfer). However, if the transferee establishes that the failure to reside the minimum number of days was caused by a change in circumstances that could not reasonably have been anticipated at the time of the transfer, then the transferee shall not be liable for the failure to withhold. The exception provided by paragraph (d)(1) does not apply in any case where the transferee is other than an individual even if the property is acquired for or on behalf of an individual who will use the property as a residence. However, this exception applies regardless of the organizational structure of the transferor (i.e., regardless of whether the transferor is an individual, partnership, trust, corporation, etc.).

(2) *Coordination with nonrecognition provisions.*—(i) *In general.*—A transferee shall not be required to withhold under section 1445(a) with respect to the transfer of a U.S. real property interest if—

(A) The transferor notifies the transferee, in the manner described in paragraph (d)(2)(iii) of this section, that by reason of the operation of a nonrecognition provision of the Internal Revenue Code or the provisions of any United States treaty the transferor is not required to recognize any gain or loss with respect to the transfer; and

(B) By the 20th day after the date of the transfer the transferee mails a copy of the transferor's notice to the Internal Revenue Service, at the address provided in § 1.1445-1(g)(10), together with a cover letter setting forth the name, identifying number, and home address (in the case of an individual) or office address (in the case of an entity) of the transferee providing the notice to the Service.

The rule of this paragraph (d)(2)(i) is subject to the exceptions set forth in paragraph (d)(2)(ii). For purposes of this paragraph (d)(2) a nonrecognition provision is any provision of the Internal Revenue Code for not recognizing gain or loss.

(ii) *Exceptions.*—A transferee may not rely upon the rule of paragraph (d)(2)(i) of this section, and must therefore withhold under section 1445(a) with respect to the transfer of a U.S. real property interest, if either:

(A) The transferor qualifies for nonrecognition treatment with respect to part, but not all, of the gain realized by the transferor upon the transfer; or

(B) The transferee knows or has reason to know that the transferor is not entitled to the nonrecognition treatment claimed by the transferor.

In either of the above circumstances the transferee or transferor may request a withholding certificate from the Internal Revenue Service pursuant to the rules of § 1.1445-3.

(iii) *Contents of the notice.*—No particular form is required for a transferor's notice to a transferee that the transferor is not required to recognize gain or loss with respect to a transfer. The notice must be verified as true and signed under penalties of perjury by the transferor, by a responsible officer in the case of a corporation, by a general partner in the case of a partnership, and by a trustee or equivalent fiduciary in the case of a trust or estate. The following information must be set forth in paragraphs labeled to correspond with the designation set forth as follows—

(A) A statement that the document submitted constitutes a notice of a nonrecognition transaction or a treaty provision pursuant to the requirements of § 1.1445-2(d)(2);

(B) The name, identifying number, and home address (in the case of an individual) or office address (in the case of an entity) of the transferor submitting the notice;

(C) A statement that the transferor is not required to recognize any gain or loss with respect to the transfer;

(D) A brief description of the transfer; and

(E) A brief summary of the law and facts supporting the claim that recognition of gain or loss is not required with respect to the transfer.

(iv) *No notice allowed.*—The provisions of this paragraph (d)(2) do not apply to exclusions from income under section 121, to simultaneous like-kind exchanges under section 1031 that do not qualify for nonrecognition treatment in their entirety (see paragraph (d)(2)(ii)(A) of this section), and to nonsimultaneous like-kind exchanges under section 1031 where the transferee cannot determine that the exchange has been completed and all the conditions for nonrecognition have been satisfied at the time it is otherwise required to pay the section 1445 withholding tax and file the withholding tax return (Form 8288, "U.S. Withholding Tax Return for Dispositions by Foreign Persons of U.S. Real Property Interests"). In these cases, the transferee is excused from withholding only upon the timely application for and receipt of a withholding certificate under § 1.1445-3 (see § 1.1445-3(b)(5) and (6) for specific rules applicable to transactions under sections 121 and 1031). This paragraph (d)(2)(iv) is applicable for dispositions and exchanges occurring [after] September 4, 2003.

(3) *Special procedural rules applicable to foreclosures.*—(i) *Amount to be withheld.*—(A) *Foreclosures.*—A transferee that acquires a U.S. real property interest pursuant to a repossession or foreclosure on such property under a mortgage, security agreement, deed of trust or

other instrument securing a debt must withhold tax under section 1445(a) equal to 15 percent (10 percent in the case of dispositions described in § 1.1445-1(b)(2)) of the amount realized on such sale. Such amount must be reported and paid over to the Service under the general rules of § 1.1445-1. However, if the transferee complies with the notice requirements of § 1.1445-2(d)(3)(ii) and (iii), such transferee may report and pay over to the Service on or before the 20th day following the final determination by a court or trustee with jurisdiction over the foreclosure action, the lesser of:

(1) the amount otherwise required to be withheld under section 1445(a), or

(2) the "alternative amount" as defined in the succeeding sentence.

The alternative amount is the entire amount, if any, determined by a court or trustee with jurisdiction over the matter, that accrues to the debtor/transferor out of the amount realized from the foreclosure sale. The amount of any mortgage, lien, or other security agreement secured by the property, that is terminated, assumed by another person, or otherwise extinguished (as to the debtor/transferor) shall not be treated as an amount that accrues to the debtor/transferor for purposes of this § 1.1445-2(d)(3)(i)(A). If the alternative amount is zero, no withholding is required. Any difference between the amount withheld at the time of the foreclosure sale and the amount to be reported and paid over to the Service must be transferred to the court or trustee with jurisdiction over the foreclosure action. Amounts withheld, if any, are to be reported and paid over to the Service by using Forms 8288 and 8288-A in conformity with § 1.1445-1(d).

(B) *Deeds in lieu of foreclosures.*—A transferee of a U.S. real property interest pursuant to a deed in lieu of foreclosure must withhold tax equal to 15 percent (10 percent in the case of dispositions described in § 1.1445-1(b)(2)) of the amount realized by the debtor/transferor on the transfer. However, no withholding is required if:

(1) The transferee is the only person with a security interest in the property,

(2) No cash or other property (other than incidental fees incurred with respect to the transfer) is paid, directly or indirectly, to any person with respect to the transfer, and

(3) The notice requirements of § 1.1445-2(d)(3) are satisfied.

The amount withheld, if any, must be reported and paid over to the Service not later than the 20th day following the date of transfer. In a case where withholding would otherwise be required, a withholding certificate may be requested in accordance with § 1.1445-3.

(ii) *Notice to the court or trustee in a foreclosure action.*—(A) *Notice on day of purchase.*—A transferee in a foreclosure sale that chooses to use the special rules applicable to foreclosures must provide notice to the court or trustee with jurisdiction over the foreclosure action on the day the property is transferred with respect to such transferee's withholding obligation. No particular form is necessary but the notice must set forth the transferee's name, home address in the case of an individual, office address in the case of an entity, a brief description of the property, the date of the transfer, the amount realized on the sale of the foreclosed property and the amount withheld under section 1445(a).

(B) *Notice whether amount withheld or alternative amount is reported and paid over the Service.*—A purchaser/transferee in a foreclosure that chooses to use the special rules applicable to foreclosures must provide notice to the court or trustee with jurisdiction over the foreclosure action regarding whether the amount withheld or the alternative amount will be (or has been) reported and paid over to the Service. The notice should set forth all the information required by the preceding paragraph (d)(3)(ii)(A), the amount withheld or alternative amount that will be (or has been) reported and paid over to the Service, and the amount that will be (or has been) paid over to the court or trustee.

(iii) *Notice to the Service.*—(A) *General rule.*—A transferee that in reliance upon the rules of this paragraph (d)(3) withholds an alternative amount (or does not withhold because the alternative amount is zero) must, on or before the 20th day following the final determination by a court or trustee in a foreclosure action or on or before the 20th day following the date of the transfer with respect to a transfer pursuant to a deed in lieu of foreclosure, provide notice thereof to the Assistant Commissioner (International) at the address provided in § 1.1445-1(g)(10). (The filing of such a notice shall not relieve a creditor of any obligation it may have to file a notice pursuant to section 6050J and the regulations thereunder.) No particular form is required but the following information must be set forth in paragraphs labelled to correspond with the numbers set forth below.

(1) A statement that the notice constitutes a notice of foreclosure action or transfer pursuant to a deed in lieu of foreclosure under § 1.1445-2(d)(3).

(2) The name, identifying number, and home address (in the case of an individual) or office address (in the case of an entity) of the purchaser/transferee.

(3) The name, identifying number, and home address (in the case of an individual) or office address (in the case of an entity) of the debtor/transferor.

(4) In a foreclosure action, the date of the final determination by a court or trustee regarding the distribution of the amount realized from the foreclosure sale. In a transfer pursuant to a deed in lieu of foreclosure, the date the property is transferred to the purchaser/transferee.

(5) A brief description of the property.

(6) The amount realized from the foreclosure sale or with respect to the transfer pursuant to a deed in lieu of foreclosure.

(7) The alternative amount.

(B) *Special rule for lenders required to file Form 1099-A where the alternative amount is zero.*—A person required under section 6050J to file Form 1099-A does not have to comply with the notice requirement of § 1.1445-2(d)(3)(iii)(A) if the alternative amount is zero. In such case, the filing of the Form 1099-A will be deemed to satisfy the notice requirement of § 1.1445-2(d)(3)(iii)(A).

(iv) *Requirements not applicable.*—A transferee is not required to withhold tax or provide notice pursuant to the rules of this paragraph (d)(3) if no substantive withholding liability applies to the transfer of the property by the debtor/transferor. For example, if the debtor/transferor provides the transferee with a certification of non-foreign status pursuant to paragraph (b) of this section, then no substantive withholding liability would exist with respect to the acquisition of the property from the debtor transferor. In such a case, no withholding of tax or notice to the Internal Revenue Service is required of the transferee with respect to the repossession or foreclosure.

(v) *Anti-abuse rule.*—If a U.S. real property interest is transferred in foreclosure or pursuant to a deed in lieu of foreclosure for a principal purpose of avoiding the requirements of section 1445(a), then the provisions of this paragraph (d)(3) shall not apply to the transfer and the transferee shall be fully liable for any failure to withhold with respect to the transfer. A principal purpose to avoid section 1445(a) will be presumed (subject to rebuttal on the basis of all relevant facts and circumstances) if:

(A) The transferee acquires property in which it, or a related party, has a security interest;

(B) The security interest did not arise in connection with the debtor/transferor's or a related party's or predecessor in interest's acquisition, improvement, or maintenance of the property; and

(C) The total amount of all debts secured by the property exceeds 90 percent of the fair market value of the property.

(4) *Installment payments.*—A transferee of a U.S. real property interest is not required to withhold under section 1445 when making installment payments on an obligation arising out of a disposition that took place before January 1, 1985. With respect to dispositions that take place after December 31, 1984, the transferee shall be required to satisfy its entire withholding obligation within the time specified in § 1.1445-1(c) regardless of the amount actually paid by the transferee. Thereafter, no withholding is required upon further installment payments on an obligation arising out of the transfer. A transferee that is unable to satisfy its entire withholding obligation within the time specified in § 1.1445-1(c) may request a withholding certificate pursuant to § 1.1445-3.

(5) *Acquisitions by governmental bodies.*—No withholding of tax is required under section 1445 with respect to any acquisition of property by the United States, a state or possession of the United States, a political subdivision thereof, or the District of Columbia.

(6) [Reserved.]

(7) *Withholding certificate obtained by transferee or transferor.*—No withholding is required under section 1445(a) if the transferee is provided with a withholding certificate that so specifies. Either the

transferor or the transferee may seek a withholding certificate from the Internal Revenue Service, pursuant to the provisions of § 1.1445-3.

(8) *Amount realized by transferor is zero.*—If the amount realized by the transferor on a transfer of a U.S. real property interest is zero, no withholding is required.

(e) *Applicability dates.*—The requirement in paragraphs (d)(2)(i)(B), (d)(2)(iii)(B), and (d)(3)(iii)(A)(2) and (3) of this section that taxpayer identification numbers be provided (in all cases) is applicable for dispositions of U.S. real property interests occurring after November 3, 2003. The exclusion of entities described in section 897(l) from the definition of foreign person in paragraph (b)(2)(i) of this section applies to dispositions and distributions after December 18, 2015, and the withholding rates set forth in paragraphs (b)(4)(iv), (c)(3)(iii), and (d)(3)(i) of this section apply to dispositions after February 16, 2016. For dispositions on or before February 16, 2016, see paragraphs (b)(4)(iv), (c)(3)(iii), and (d)(3)(i) of this section as contained in 26 CFR part 1 revised as of April 1, 2015. Paragraph (b)(2)(v) of this section applies to certifications provided on or after May 7, 2019, except that a taxpayer may choose to apply paragraph (b)(2)(v) of this section with respect to certifications provided before May 7, 2019. Paragraphs (b)(2)(i) and (b)(2)(vi) of this section, apply with respect to dispositions of U.S. real property interests and distributions described in section 897(h) occurring on or after December 29, 2022. For dispositions of U.S. real property interests and distributions described in section 897(h) occurring before December 29, 2022, see § 1.1445-2(b)(2)(i) and 1.1445-2(b)(2)(vi), as contained in 26 CFR part 1, revised as of April 1, 2021. [Reg. § 1.1445-2.]

□ [*T.D.* 8113, 12-18-86. *Amended by T.D.* 8198, 5-4-88, *T.D.* 9082, 8-4-2003, *T.D.* 9751, 2-17-2016, *T.D.* 9926, 11-27-2020 *and T.D.* 9971, 12-28-2022.]

§ 1.1445-3. Adjustments to amount required to be withheld pursuant to withholding certificate.—(a) *In general.*—Withholding under section 1445(a) may be reduced or eliminated pursuant to a withholding certificate issued by the Internal Revenue Service in accordance with the rules of this section. A withholding certificate may be issued by the Service in cases where reduced withholding is appropriate (see paragraph (c) of this section), where the transferor is exempt from U.S. tax (see paragraph (d) of this section), or where an agreement for the payment of tax is entered into with the Service (see paragraph (e) of this section). A withholding certificate that is obtained prior to a transfer notifies the transferee that no withholding is required. A withholding certificate that is obtained after a transfer has been made may authorize a normal refund or an early refund pursuant to paragraph (g) of this section. Either a transferee or transferor may apply for a withholding certificate. The Internal Revenue Service will act upon an application for a withholding certificate not later than the 90th day after it is received. Solely for this purpose (i.e., determining the day upon which the 90-day period commences), an application is received by the Service on the date that all information necessary for the Service to make a determination is provided by the applicant. In no event, however, will a withholding certificate be issued without the transferor's identifying number. (For rules regarding whether an application for a withholding certificate has been timely submitted, see § 1.1445-1(c)(2).) The Service may deny a request for a withholding certificate where, after due notice, an applicant fails to provide information necessary for the Service to make a determination. The Service will act upon an application for an early refund not later than the 90th day after it is received. An application for an early refund must either (1) include a copy of a withholding certificate issued by the Service with respect to the transaction, or (2) be combined with an application for a withholding certificate. Where an application for an early refund is combined with an application for a withholding certificate, the Service will act upon both applications not later than the 90th day after receipt. In the case of an application for a certificate based on nonconforming security under paragraph (e)(3)(v) of this section, and in unusually complicated cases, the Service may be unable to provide a final withholding certificate by the 90th day. In such a case the Service will notify the applicant, by the 45th day after receipt of the application, that additional processing time will be necessary. The Service's notice may request additional information or explanation concerning particular aspects of the application, and will provide a target date for final action (contingent upon the applicant's timely submission of any requested information). A withholding certificate issued pursuant to the provisions of this section serves to fulfill the requirements of section 1445(b)(4) concerning qualifying statements, section 1445(c)(1) concerning the transferor's maximum tax liability, or section 1445(c)(2) concerning the Secretary's authority to prescribe reduced withholding.

(b) *Applications for withholding certificates.*—(1) *In general.*—An application for a withholding certificate must be submitted to the address provided in § 1.1445-1(g)(10). An application for a withholding certificate must be signed by a responsible officer in the case of a corporation, by a general partner in the case of a partnership, by a trustee, executor, or equivalent fiduciary in the case of a trust or estate, and in the case of an individual by the individual himself. A duly authorized agent may sign the application but the application must contain a valid power of attorney authorizing the agent to sign the application on behalf of the applicant. The person signing the application must verify under penalties of perjury that all representations made in connection with the application are true, correct, and complete to his knowledge and belief. No particular form is required for an application, but the application must set forth the information described in paragraphs (b)(2), (3), and (4), and to the extent applicable, paragraph (b)(5) or (6) of this section.

(2) *Parties to the transaction.*—The application must set forth the name, address, and identifying number of the person submitting the application (specifying whether that person is the transferee or transferor), and the name, address, and identifying number of other parties to the transaction (specifying whether each such party is a transferee or transferor). The Service will deny the application if complete information, including the identifying numbers of all the parties, is not provided. Thus, for example, the applicant should determine if an identifying number exists for each party, and, if none exists for a particular party, the applicant should notify the particular party of the obligation to get an identifying number before the application can be submitted to the Service. The address provided in the case of an individual must be that individual's home address, and the address provided in the case of an entity must be that entity's office address. A mailing address may be provided in addition to, but not in lieu of, a home address or office address.

(3) *Real property interest to be transferred.*—The application must set forth information concerning the U.S. real property interest with respect to which the withholding certificate is sought, including the type of interest, the contract price, and, in the case of an interest in real property, its location and general description, or in the case of an interest in a U.S. real property holding corporation, the class or type and amount of the interest.

(4) *Basis for certificate.*—(i) *Reduced withholding.*—If a withholding certificate is sought on the basis of a claim that reduced withholding is appropriate, the application must include:

(A) A calculation of the maximum tax that may be imposed on the disposition in accordance with paragraph (c)(2) of this section. Such calculation must be accompanied by a copy of the relevant contract and depreciation schedules or other evidence that confirms the contract price and adjusted basis of the property. If no depreciation schedules are provided, the application must state the nature of the use of the property and why depreciation was not allowable. Evidence that supports any claimed adjustment to the maximum tax on the disposition must also be provided;

(B) A calculation of the transferor's unsatisfied withholding liability, or evidence supporting the claim that no such liability exists, in accordance with paragraph (c)(3) of this section; and

(C) In the case of a request for a special reduction of withholding pursuant to paragraph (c)(4) of this section, a statement of law and facts in support of the request.

(ii) *Exemption.*—If a withholding certificate is sought on the basis of the transferor's exemption from U.S. tax, the application must set forth a brief statement of the law and facts that support the claimed exemption. In this regard, see paragraph (d) of this section.

(iii) *Agreement.*—If a withholding certificate is sought on the basis of an agreement for the payment of tax, the application must include a signed copy of the agreement proposed by the applicant and a copy of the security instrument (if any) proposed by the applicant. In this regard, see paragraph (e) of this section.

(5) *Special rule for exclusions from income under section 121.*—A withholding certificate may be sought on the basis of a section 121 exclusion as a reduction in the amount of tax due under paragraph (c)(2)(v) of this section. The application must include information establishing that the transferor, who is a nonresident alien individual at the time of the sale (and is therefore subject to sections 897 and 1445) is entitled to claim the benefits of section 121. For example, a claim for reduced withholding as a result of section 121 must include

information that the transferor occupied the U.S. real property interest as his or her personal residence for the required period of time.

(6) *Special rule for like-kind exchanges under Section 1031.*—A withholding certificate may be requested with respect to a like-kind exchange under section 1031 as a transaction subject to a nonrecognition provision under paragraph (c)(2)(ii) of this section. The application must include information substantiating the requirements of section 1031. The IRS may require additional information during the course of the application process to determine that the requirements of section 1031 are satisfied. In the case of a deferred like-kind exchange, the withholding agent is excused from reporting and paying the withholding tax to the IRS within 20 days after the transfer only if an application for a withholding certificate is submitted prior to or on the date of transfer. See § 1.1445-1(c)(2) for rules concerning delayed reporting and payment where an application for a withholding certificate has been submitted to the IRS prior to or on the date of transfer.

(c) *Adjustment of amount required to be withheld.*—(1) *In general.*—The Internal Revenue Service may issue a withholding certificate that excuses withholding or that permits the transferee to withhold an adjusted amount reflecting the transferor's maximum tax liability. The transferor's maximum tax liability is the sum of—

(i) The maximum amount which could be imposed as tax under section 871 or 882 upon the transferor's disposition of the subject real property interest, as determined under paragraph (c)(2) of this section, and

(ii) The transferor's unsatisfied withholding liability with respect to the subject real property interest, as determined under paragraph (c)(3) of this section.

In addition, the Internal Revenue Service may issue a withholding certificate that permits the transferee to withhold a reduced amount if the Service determines pursuant to paragraph (c)(4) of this section that reduced withholding will not jeopardize the collection of tax.

(2) *Maximum tax imposed on disposition.*—The first element of the transferor's maximum tax liability is the maximum amount which the transferor could be required to pay as tax upon the disposition of the subject real property interest. In the case of an individual transferor that amount will generally be the contract price of the property minus its adjusted basis, multiplied by the maximum individual income tax rate applicable to long-term capital gain. In the case of a corporate transferor, that amount will generally be the contract price of the property minus its adjusted basis, multiplied by the maximum corporate income tax rate applicable to long-term capital gain. However, that amount must be adjusted to take into account the following:

(i) Any reduction of tax to which the transferor is entitled under the provisions of a U.S. income tax treaty;

(ii) The effect of any nonrecognition provision that is applicable to the transaction;

(iii) Any losses realized and recognized upon the previous disposition of U.S. real property interests during the taxable year;

(iv) Any amount that is required to be treated as ordinary income; and

(v) Any other factor that may increase or reduce the tax upon the disposition.

(3) *Transferor's unsatisfied withholding liability.*—(i) *In general.*—The second element of the transferor's maximum tax liability is the transferor's unsatisfied withholding liability. That liability is the amount of any tax that the transferor was required to but did not withhold and pay over under section 1445 upon the acquisition of the subject U.S. real property interest or a predecessor interest. The transferor's unsatisfied withholding liability is included in the calculation of maximum tax liability so that such prior withholding liability can be satisfied by the transferee's withholding upon the current transfer. Alternatively, the transferor's unsatisfied withholding liability may be disregarded for purposes of calculating the maximum tax liability, if either—

(A) Such prior withholding liability is fully satisfied by a payment that is made with the application submitted pursuant to this section; or

(B) An agreement is entered into for the payment of that liability pursuant to the rules of paragraph (e) of this section. Because section 1445 only requires withholding after December 31, 1984, no transferor's unsatisfied withholding liability can exist unless the transferor acquired the subject or predecessor real property interest after that date. For purposes of this paragraph (c), a predecessor interest is one that was exchanged for the subject U.S. real property interest in a transaction in which the transferor was not required to recognize the full amount of the gain or loss realized upon the transfer.

(ii) *Evidence that no unsatisfied withholding liability exists.*—For purposes of paragraph (b)(4)(i)(B) of this section (concerning information that must be submitted with an application for a withholding certificate), evidence that the transferor has no unsatisfied withholding liability includes any one of the following documents:

(A) Evidence that the transferor acquired the subject or predecessor real property interest prior to January 1, 1985;

(B) A copy of the Form 8288 that was filed by the transferor, and proof of payment of the amount shown due thereon, with respect to the transferor's acquisition of the subject or predecessor real property interest;

(C) A copy of a withholding certificate with respect to the transferor's acquisition of the subject or predecessor real property interest, plus a copy of Form 8288 and proof of payment with respect to any withholding required under that certificate;

(D) A copy of the non-foreign certification furnished by the person from whom the subject or predecessor U.S. real property interest was acquired, executed at the time of that acquisition;

(E) Evidence that the transferor purchased the subject or predecessor real property for $300,000 or less, and a statement, signed by the transferor under penalties of perjury, that the transferor purchased the property for use as a residence within the meaning of § 1.1445-2(d)(1);

(F) Evidence that the person from whom the transferor acquired the subject or predecessor U.S. real property interest fully paid any tax imposed on that transaction pursuant to section 897;

(G) A copy of a notice of nonrecognition treatment provided to the transferor pursuant to § 1.1445-2(d)(2) by the person from whom the transferor acquired the subject or predecessor U.S. real property interest; and

(H) A statement, signed by the transferor under penalties of perjury, setting forth the facts and circumstances that supported the transferor's conclusion that no withholding was required under section 1445(a) with respect to the transferor's acquisition of the subject or predecessor real property interest.

(4) *Special reduction of amount required to be withheld.*—The Internal Revenue Service may, in its discretion, issue a withholding certificate that permits the transferee to withhold a reduced amount based upon a determination that reduced withholding will not jeopardize the collection of tax. A transferor that requests a withholding certificate pursuant to this paragraph (c)(4) is required pursuant to paragraph (b)(4)(i)(C) of this section to submit a statement of law and facts in support of the request. That statement must explain why the transferor is unable to enter into an agreement for the payment of tax pursuant to paragraph (e) of this section.

(d) *Transferor's exemption from U.S. tax.*—(1) *In general.*—The Internal Revenue Service will issue a withholding certificate that excuses all withholding by a transferee if it is established that:

(i) The transferor's gain from the disposition of the subject U.S. real property interest will be exempt from U.S. tax, and

(ii) The transferor has no unsatisfied withholding liability.

For the available exemptions, see paragraph (d)(2) of this section. The transferor's unsatisfied withholding liability shall be determined in accordance with the provisions of paragraph (c)(3) of this section. A transferor that is entitled to a reduction of (rather than an exemption from) U.S. tax may obtain a withholding certificate to that effect pursuant to the provisions of paragraph (c) of this section.

(2) *Available exemptions.*—A transferor's gain from the disposition of a U.S. real property interest may be exempt from U.S. tax because either:

(i) The transferor is an integral part or controlled entity of a foreign government and the disposition of the subject property is not a commercial activity, as determined pursuant to section 892 and the regulations thereunder; or

(ii) The transferor is entitled to the benefits of an income tax treaty that provides for such an exemption (subject to the limitations imposed by section 1125(c) of Pub. L. 96-499, which, in general, overrides such benefits as of January 1, 1985).

(e) *Agreement for the payment of tax.*—(1) *In general.*—The Internal Revenue Service will issue a withholding certificate that excuses withholding or that permits a transferee to withhold a reduced amount, if either the transferee or the transferor enters into an agreement for the payment of tax pursuant to the provisions of this paragraph (e). An agreement for the payment of tax is a contract between the Service and any other person that consists of two necessary elements. Those elements are—

(i) A contract between the Service and the other person, setting forth in detail the rights and obligations of each; and

(ii) A security instrument or other form of security acceptable to the Director, Foreign Operations District.

(2) *Contents of agreement.*—(i) *In general.*—An agreement for the payment of tax must cover an amount described in subdivision (ii) or (iii) of this paragraph (e)(2). The agreement may either provide adequate security for the payment of the chosen amount in accordance with paragraph (e)(3) of this section, or provide for the payment of that amount through a combination of security and withholding of tax by the transferee.

(ii) *Tax that would otherwise be withheld.*—An agreement for the payment of tax may cover the amount of tax that would otherwise be required to be withheld pursuant to section 1445(a). In addition to the amount computed pursuant to section 1445(a), the applicant must agree to pay interest upon that amount, at the rate established under section 6621, with respect to the period between the date on which the tax imposed by section 1445(a) would otherwise be due (*i.e.*, the 20th day after the date of transfer) and the date on which the transferor's payment of tax with respect to the disposition will be due under the agreement. The amount of interest agreed upon must be paid by the applicant regardless of whether or not the Service is required to draw upon any security provided pursuant to the agreement. The interest may be paid either with the return or by the Service drawing upon the security.

(iii) *Maximum tax liability.*—An agreement for the payment of tax may cover the transferor's maximum tax liability, determined in accordance with paragraph (c) of this section. The agreement must also provide for the payment of an additional amount equal to 25 percent of the amount determined under paragraph (c) of this section. This additional amount secures the interest and penalties that would accrue between the date of a failure to file a return and pay tax with respect to the disposition, and the date on which the Service collects upon that liability pursuant to the agreement. Such additional amount will only be collected if the Service finds it necessary to draw upon any security provided due to the transferor's failure to file a return and pay tax with respect to the relevant disposition.

(3) *Major types of security.*—(i) *In general.*—The following are the major types of security acceptable to the Service. Further details with respect to the terms and conditions of each type may be specified by Revenue Procedure.

(ii) *Bond with surety or guarantor.*—The Service may accept as security with respect to a transferor's tax liability a bond that is executed with a satisfactory surety or guarantor. Only the following persons may act as surety or guarantor for this purpose:

(A) A surety company holding a certificate of authority from the Secretary as an acceptable surety on Federal bonds, as listed in Treasury Department Circular No. 570, published annually in the Federal Register on the first working day of July;

(B) A person that is engaged within or without the United States in the conduct of a banking, financing, or similar business under the principles of § 1.864-4(c)(5) and that is subject to U.S. or foreign local or national regulation of such business, if that person is otherwise acceptable to the Service; and

(C) A person that is engaged within or without the United States in the conduct of an insurance business that is subject to U.S. or foreign local or national regulation, if that person is otherwise acceptable to the Service.

(iii) *Bond with collateral.*—The Service may accept as security with respect to a transferor's tax liability a bond that is secured by acceptable collateral. All collateral must be deposited with a responsible financial institution acting as escrow agent or, in the Service's discretion, with the Service. Only the following types of collateral are acceptable:

(A) Bonds, notes, or other public debt obligations of the United States, in accordance with the rules of 31 CFR Part 225; and

(B) A certified cashier's, or treasurer's check, drawn on an entity acceptable to the Service that is engaged within or without the United States in the conduct of a banking, financing, or similar business under the principles of § 1.864-4(c)(5) and that is subject to U.S. or foreign local or national regulation of such business.

(iv) *Letter of credit.*—The Service may accept as security with respect to a transferor's tax liability an irrevocable letter of credit. The Service may accept a letter of credit issued by an entity acceptable to the Service that is engaged within or without the United States in the conduct of a banking, financing or similar business under the principles of § 1.884-4(c)(5) and that is subject to U.S. or foreign local or national regulation of such business. However, the Director will accept a letter of credit from an entity that is not engaged in trade or business in the United States only if such letter may be drawn on an advising bank within the United States.

(v) *Guarantees and other nonconforming security.*—(A) *Guarantee.*—The Service may in its discretion accept as security with respect to a transferor's tax liability the applicant's guarantee that it will pay such liability. The Service will in general accept such a guarantee only from a corporation, foreign or domestic, any class of stock of which is regularly traded on an established securities market on the date of the transfer.

(B) *Other forms of security.*—The Service may in unusual circumstances and at its discretion accept any form of security that it finds to be adequate. An application for a withholding certificate that proposes a form of security that does not conform with any of the preferred types set forth in paragraph (e)(3)(ii) through (iv) of this section or any relevant Revenue Procedure must include:

(1) A detailed statement of the facts and circumstances supporting the use of the proposed form of security, and

(2) A memorandum of law concerning the validity and enforceability of the proposed form of security.

(4) *Terms of security instrument.*—Any security instrument that is furnished pursuant to this section must provide that—

(i) The amount of each deposit of estimated tax that will be required with respect to the gain realized on the subject disposition may be collected by levy upon the security as of the date following the date on which each such deposit is due (unless such deposit is timely made);

(ii) The entire amount of the liability may be collected by levy upon the security at any time during the nine months following the date on which the payment of tax with respect to the subject disposition is due, subject to release of the security upon the full payment of the tax and any interest and penalties due. If the transferor requests an extension of time to file a return with respect to the disposition, then the Director may require that the term of the security instrument be extended until the date that is nine months after the filing deadline as extended.

(f) *Amendments to application for withholding certificate.*—(1) *In general.*—An applicant for a withholding certificate may amend an otherwise complete application by submitting an amending statement to the address provided in § 1.1445-1(g)(10). The amending statement shall provide the information required by § 1.1445-3(f)(3) and must be signed and accompanied by a penalties of perjury statement in accordance with § 1.1445-3(b)(1).

(2) *Extension of time for the Service to process requests for withholding certificates.*—(i) *In general.*—If an amending statement is submitted, the time in which the Internal Revenue Service must act upon the amended application shall be extended by 30 days.

(ii) *Substantial amendments.*—If an amending statement is submitted and the Service finds that the statement substantially amends the facts of the underlying application or substantially alters the terms of the withholding certificate as requested in the initial application, the time within which the Service must act upon the amended application shall be extended by 60 days. The applicant shall be so notified.

(iii) *Amending statement received after the requested withholding certificate has been signed on behalf of the Service.*—If an amending statement is received after the withholding certificate, drafted in response to the underlying application, has been signed on behalf of the Service and prior to the day such certificate is mailed to the applicant, the time in which the Service must act upon the amended application shall be extended by 90 days. The applicant will be so notified.

(3) *Information required to be submitted.*—No particular form is required for an amending statement but the statement must provide the following information:

(i) *Identification of applicant.*—The amending statement must set forth the name, address and identifying number of the person submitting the amending statement (specifying whether that person is the transferee or transferor).

(ii) *Date of underlying application.*—The amending statement must set forth the date of the underlying application for a withholding certificate.

(iii) *Real property interest to be (or that has been) transferred.*—The amending statement must set forth a brief description of the real property interest with respect to which the underlying application for a withholding certificate was submitted.

(iv) *Amending information.*—The amending statement must fully set forth the basis for the amendment including any modification of the facts supporting the application for a withholding certificate and any change sought in the terms of the withholding certificate.

(g) *Early refund of overwithheld amounts.*—If a transferor receives a withholding certificate pursuant to this section, and an amount greater than that specified in the certificate was withheld by the transferee, then pursuant to the rules of this paragraph (g) the transferor may apply for a refund (without interest) of the excess amount prior to the date on which the transferor's tax return is due (without extensions). (Any interest payable on refunds issued after the filing of a tax return shall be determined in accordance with the provisions of section 6611 and regulations thereunder.) An application for an early refund must be delivered to the address provided in § 1.1445-1(g)(10). No particular form is required for the application, but the following information must be set forth in separate paragraphs numbered to correspond with the number given below:

(1) Name, address, and identifying number of the transferor seeking the refund;

(2) Amount required to be withheld pursuant to the withholding certificate issued by Internal Revenue Service;

(3) Amount withheld by the transferee (attach a copy of Form 8288-A stamped by IRS pursuant to § 1.1445-1(c));

(4) Amount to be refunded to the transferor. An application for an early refund cannot be processed unless the required copy of Form 8288-A (or substantial evidence of the amount withheld in the case of a failure to receive Form 8288-A as provided in § 1.1445-1(f)(3)) is attached to the application. If an application for a withholding certificate based upon the transferor's maximum tax liability is submitted after the transfer takes place, then that application may be combined with an application for an early refund. The Service will act upon a claim for refund within the time limits set forth in paragraph (a) of this section.

(h) *Effective date for taxpayer identification numbers.*—The requirement in paragraphs (b)(2), (f)(3)(i), and (g)(1) of this section that taxpayer identification numbers be provided (in all cases) is applicable for dispositions of U.S. real property interests occurring after November 3, 2003. [Reg. § 1.1445-3.]

☐ [*T.D. 8113, 12-18-86. Amended by T.D. 9082, 8-4-2003 and T.D. 9751, 2-17-2016.*]

Proposed Amendments to Regulation

§ 1.1445-3. Adjustments to amount required to be withheld pursuant to withholding certificate.—

***

(e) ***

(5) *Special rule for gain deferred under section 1400Z-2(a).*—The Internal Revenue Service will issue a withholding certificate under this paragraph (e) that excuses withholding or that permits a transferee to withhold a reduced amount if the transferor has obtained an eligibility certificate under § 1.1400Z2(a)-2 from the IRS with respect to the transfer. The amount by which the transferee may reduce the withholding (including a reduction to zero) is the amount of security provided on the eligibility certificate. If this paragraph (e)(5) applies, the requirements in paragraphs (e)(1) through (e)(4) of this section are deemed to have been satisfied. This paragraph (e)(5) applies to any covered transfer defined in § 1.1400Z2(a)-2(c)(2) that occurs after [DATE OF PUBLICATION OF FINAL RULE]. [Prop. Reg. § 1.1445-3.]

[Proposed 4-14-2021.]

§ 1.1445-4. Liability of agents.—(a) *Duty to provide notice of false certification or statement to transferee.*—A transferee's or transferor's agent must provide notice to the transferee if either—

(1) The transferee is furnished with a non-U.S. real property interest statement pursuant to § 1.1445-2(c)(3) and the agent knows that the statement is false; or

(2) The transferee is furnished with a non-foreign certification pursuant to § 1.1445-2(b)(2) and either (i) the agent knows that the certification is false, or (ii) the agent represents a transferor that is a foreign corporation.

An agent that represents a transferor that is a foreign corporation is not required to provide notice to the transferee if the foreign corporation provided a nonforeign certification to the transferee prior to such agent's employment and the agent does not know that the corporation did so.

(b) *Duty to provide notice of false certification or statement to entity or fiduciary.*—A transferee's or transferor's agent must provide notice to an entity or fiduciary that plans to carry out a transaction described in section 1445(e)(1), (2), (3), or (4) if either—

(1) The entity or fiduciary is furnished with a non-U.S. real property interest statement pursuant to § 1.1445-5(b)(4)(iii) and the agent knows that such statement is false; or

(2) The entity or fiduciary is furnished with a non-foreign certification pursuant to § 1.1445-5(b)(3)(ii) and either (i) the agent knows that such certification is false, or (ii) the agent represents a foreign corporation that made such a certification.

(c) *Procedural requirements.*—(1) *Notice to transferee, entity, or fiduciary.*—An agent who is required by this section to provide notice must do so in writing as soon as possible after learning of the false certification or statement, but not later than the date of the transfer (prior to the transferee's payment of consideration). If an agent first learns of a false certification or statement after the date of the transfer, notice must be given by the third day following that discovery. The notice must state that the certification or statement is false and may not be relied upon. The notice must also explain the possible consequences to the recipient of a failure to withhold. The notice need not disclose the information on which the agent's statement is based. The following is an example of an acceptable notice: "This is to notify you that you may be required to withhold tax in connection with *(describe transaction)*. You have been provided with a certification of nonforeign status (or a non-U.S. real property interest statement) in connection with that transaction. I have learned that that document is false. Therefore, you may not rely upon it as a basis for failing to withhold under section 1445 of the Internal Revenue Code. Section 1445 provides that any person who acquires a U.S. real property interest from a foreign person after February 16, 2016, must withhold a tax equal to 15 percent (10 percent in the case of dispositions described in § 1.1445-1(b)(2)) of the total purchase price. (The term 'U.S. real property interest' includes real property, stock in U.S. corporations whose assets are primarily real property, and some personal property associated with realty.) Any person who is required to withhold but fails to do so can be held liable for the tax. Thus, if you do not withhold the 15 percent tax (10 percent tax in the case of dispositions described in § 1.1445-1(b)(2)) from the total that you pay on this transaction, you could be required to pay the tax yourself, if what you are acquiring is a U.S. real property interest and the transferor is a foreign person. Tax that is withheld must be promptly paid over to the IRS using Form 8288. For further information see sections 897 and 1445 of the Internal Revenue Code and the related regulations."

(2) *Notice to be filed with IRS.*—An agent who is required by paragraph (a) or (b) of this section to provide notice to a transferee, entity, or fiduciary must furnish a copy of that notice to the Internal Revenue Service by the date on which the notice is required to be given to the transferee, entity, or fiduciary. The copy of the notice must be delivered to the address provided in § 1.1445-1(g)(10), and must be accompanied by a cover letter stating that the copy is being filed pursuant to the requirements of this § 1.1445-4(c)(2).

(d) *Effect on recipient.*—A transferee, entity, or fiduciary that receives a notice pursuant to this section prior to the date of the transfer from any agent of the transferor or transferee may not rely upon the subject certification or statement for purposes of excusing withholding pursuant to § 1.1445-2 or § 1.1445-5. Therefore, the recipient of a notice may be held liable for any failure to deduct and withhold tax under section 1445 as if such certification or statement had never been given. For special rules concerning the effect of the receipt of a notice after the date of the transfer, see §§1.1445-2(b)(4)(iv) and 1.1445-5(c), (d) and (e).

(e) *Failure to provide notice.*—Any agent who is required to provide notice but who fails to do so in the manner required by paragraph (a) or (b) of this section shall be held liable for the tax that the recipient of the notice would have been required to withhold under section 1445 if such notice had been given. However, an agent's liability under this paragraph (e) is limited to the amount of compensation that that agent derives from the transaction. In addition, an agent who assists in the preparation of, or fails to disclose knowledge of, a false certification or statement may be liable for civil or criminal penalties.

(f) *Definition of transferor's or transferee's agent.*—(1) *In general.*—For purposes of this section, the terms "transferor's agent" and "transferee's agent" mean any person who represents the transferor or transferee (respectively)—

(i) In any negotiation with another person (or another person's agent) relating to the transaction; or

(ii) In settling the transaction.

(2) *Transactions subject to section 1445(e).*—In the case of transactions subject to section 1445(e), the following definitions apply.

(i) The term "transferor's agent" means any person that represents or advises an entity or fiduciary with respect to the planning, arrangement, or consummation by the entity of a transaction described in section 1445(e)(1), (2), (3), or (4).

(ii) The term "transferee's agent" means any person that represents or advises the holder of an interest in an entity with respect to the planning, arrangement or consummation by the entity of a transaction described in section 1445(e)(1), (2), (3), or (4).

(3) *Exclusion of settlement officers and clerical personnel.*—For purposes of this section, a person shall not be treated as a transferor's agent or transferee's agent with respect to any transaction solely because such person performs one or more of the following activities:

(i) The receipt and disbursement of any portion of the consideration for the transaction;

(ii) The recording of any document in connection with the transaction; or

(iii) Typing, copying, and other clerical tasks;

(iv) The obtaining of title insurance reports and reports concerning the condition of the real property that is the subject of the transaction; or

(v) The transmission or delivery of documents between the parties.

(4) *Exclusion for governing body of a condominium association and the board of directors of a cooperative housing corporation.*—The members of a board, committee or other governing body of a condominium association and the board of directors and officers of a cooperative housing corporation will not be deemed agents of the transferor or transferee if such individuals function exclusively in their capacity as representatives of such association or corporation with respect to the transaction. In addition, the managing agent of a cooperative housing corporation or condominium association will not be deemed to be an agent of the transferee or transferor if such person functions exclusively in its capacity as a managing agent. If a person's activities include advising the transferee or transferor with respect to the transfer, this exclusion shall not apply. [Reg. §1.1445-4.]

☐ [*T.D. 8113, 12-18-86. Amended by T.D. 9082, 8-4-2003 and T.D.* 9751, 2-17-2016.]

Proposed Amendments to Regulation

§1.1445-4. Liability of agents.—(a) ***

(2) The transferee is furnished with a non-foreign certification pursuant to §1.1445-2(b)(2) or a certification regarding qualified holder status provided on Form W-8EXP and either:

(i) The agent knows that the certification is false; or

(ii) The agent represents a transferor that is a foreign corporation that is not a qualified holder. An agent that represents a transferor that is a foreign corporation is not required to provide notice to the transferee if the foreign corporation provided a non-foreign certification or certification regarding qualified holder status provided on Form W-8EXP, as applicable, to the transferee prior to such agent's employment and the agent does not know that the corporation did so.

(b) ***

(2) The entity or fiduciary is furnished with a non-foreign certification pursuant to §1.1445-5(b)(3)(ii) or a certification regarding qualified holder status provided on Form W-8EXP and either:

(i) The agent knows that such certification is false; or

(ii) The agent represents a foreign corporation (other than a qualified holder) that made such a certification.

***

(g) *Certain applicability dates.*—Paragraphs (a)(2) and (b)(2) of this section, as revised by the Treasury decision adopting these rules as final regulations, apply with respect to dispositions of U.S. real property interests and distributions described in section 897(h) occurring on or after the date of publication of the Treasury decision adopting these rules as final regulations in the **Federal Register**. [Prop. Reg. §1.1445-4.]

[Proposed 6-7-2019.]

§1.1445-5. Special rules concerning distributions and other transactions by corporations, partnerships, trusts, and estates.—(a) *Purpose and scope.*—This section provides special rules concerning the withholding that is required under section 1445(e) upon distributions and other transactions involving domestic or foreign corporations, partnerships, trusts, and estates. Paragraph (b) of this section provides rules that apply generally to the various withholding requirements set forth in this section. Under section 1445(e)(1) and paragraph (c) of this section, a domestic partnership or the fiduciary of a domestic trust or estate is required to withhold tax upon the entity's disposition of a U.S. real property interest if any foreign persons are partners or beneficiaries of the entity. Paragraph (d) provides rules concerning the requirement of section 1445(e)(2) that a foreign corporation withhold tax upon its distribution of a U.S. real property interest to its interest-holders. Finally, under section 1445(e)(3) and paragraph (e) of this section a domestic U.S. real property holding corporation is required to withhold tax upon certain distributions to interest-holders that are foreign persons. Paragraphs (f) and (g) of this section are reserved to provide rules concerning transactions involving interests in partnerships, trusts, and estates that will be subject to withholding pursuant to section 1445(e)(4) and (5).

(b) *Rules of general application.*—(1) *Double withholding not required.*—If tax is required to be withheld with respect to a transfer of property in accordance with the rules of this section, then no additional tax is required to be withheld by the transferee of the property with respect to that transfer pursuant to the general rules of section 1445(a) and §1.1445-1. For rules coordinating the withholding under section 1441 (or section 1442 or 1443) and under section 1445 on distributions from a corporation, see §1.1441-3(b)(4). If a transfer of a U.S. real property interest described in section 1445(e) is exempt from withholding under the rules of this section, then no withholding is required under the general rules of section 1445(a) and §1.1445-1.

(2) *Coordination with nonrecognition provisions.*—(i) *In general.*—Withholding shall not be required under the rules of this section with respect to a transfer described in section 1445(e) of a U.S. real property interest if—

(A) By reason of the operation of a nonrecognition provision of the Internal Revenue Code or the provisions of any treaty of the United States no gain or loss is required to be recognized by the foreign person with respect to which withholding would otherwise be required; and

(B) The entity or fiduciary that is otherwise required to withhold complies with the notice requirements of paragraph (b)(2)(ii) of this section. The entity or fiduciary must determine whether gain or loss is required to be recognized pursuant to the rules of section 897 and the applicable nonrecognition provisions of the Internal Revenue Code. An entity or fiduciary may obtain a withholding certificate from the Internal Revenue Service that confirms the applicability of a nonrecognition provision, but is not required to do so. For purposes of this paragraph (b)(2), a nonrecognition provision is any provision of the Internal Revenue Code for not recognizing gain or loss. If nonrecognition treatment is available only with respect to part of the gain realized on a transfer, the exemption from withholding provided by this paragraph (b)(2) shall not apply. In such cases a withholding certificate may be sought pursuant to the provisions of §1.1445-6.

(ii) *Notice of nonrecognition transfer.*—An entity or fiduciary that fails to withhold tax with respect to a transfer in reliance upon the rules of this paragraph (b)(2) must by the 20th day after the date of the transfer deliver a notice thereof to the address provided in §1.1445-1(g)(10). No particular form is required for a notice of transfer, but the following information must be set forth in paragraphs labelled to correspond with the letter set forth below:

(A) A statement that the document submitted constitutes a notice of a nonrecognition transfer pursuant to the requirements of §1.1445-5(b)(2)(ii);

(B) The name, office address, and identifying number of the entity of fiduciary submitting the notice;

(C) The name, identifying number, and home address (in the case of an individual) or office address (in the case of an entity) of each foreign person with respect to which withholding would otherwise be required;

(D) A brief description of the transfer; and

(E) A brief statement of the law and facts supporting the claim that recognition of gain or loss is not required with respect to the transfer.

(3) *Interest-holder not a foreign person.*—(i) *In general.*—Pursuant to the provisions of paragraphs (c) and (e) of this section, an entity or fiduciary is required to withhold with respect to certain transfers of property if a holder of an interest in the entity is a foreign person. For purposes of determining whether a holder of an interest is a foreign person, an entity or fiduciary may rely upon a certification of non-foreign status provided by that person in accordance with paragraph (b)(3)(ii) of this section. Except to the extent provided in paragraph (b)(3)(iii) of this section, such a certification excuses the entity or fiduciary from any liability otherwise imposed pursuant to section 1445(e) and regulations thereunder. However, no obligation is imposed upon an entity or fiduciary to obtain certifications from interest-holders; an entity or fiduciary may instead rely upon other means to ascertain the non-foreign status of an interest-holder. If the entity or fiduciary does rely upon other means but the interest-holder proves, in fact, to be a foreign person, then the entity or fiduciary is subject to any liability imposed pursuant to section 1445 and regulations thereunder. An entity or fiduciary is not required to rely upon other means to ascertain the non-foreign status of an interest-holder and may demand a certification of non-foreign status. If the certification is not provided, the entity or fiduciary may withhold tax under section 1445 and will be considered, for purposes of sections 1461 through 1463, to have been required to withhold such tax.

(ii) *Interest-holder's certification of non-foreign status.*—(A) *In general.*—For purposes of this section, an entity or fiduciary may treat any holder of an interest in the entity as a U.S. person if that interest-holder furnishes to the entity or fiduciary a certification stating that the interest-holder is not a foreign person, in accordance with the provisions of paragraph (b)(3)(ii)(B) of this section. In general, a foreign person is a nonresident alien individual, foreign corporation, foreign partnership, foreign trust, or foreign estate, except that a withholding qualified holder (as defined in §1.1445-1(g)(11)) is not a foreign person for purposes of this section.

(B) *Procedural rules.*—The rules in this paragraph (b)(3)(ii)(B) apply for purposes of the interest-holder's certification of non-foreign status (including a certification of non-foreign status provided by a withholding qualified holder (as defined in §1.1445-1(g)(11)).

(1) An interest-holder's certification of non-foreign status must be signed under penalties of perjury and must state

(i) That the interest-holder is not a foreign person; and

(ii) The interest-holder's name, identifying number, home address (in the case of an individual), or office address (in the case of an entity), and place of incorporation (in the case of a corporation).

(2) For purposes of paragraph (b)(3)(ii)(B)*(1)* of this section, an individual's identifying number is the individual's Social Security number and any other person's identifying number is its U.S. employer identification number (see §1.897-1(p)), or, if the interest-holder is a withholding qualified holder (as defined in §1.1445-1(g)(11)) that does not have a U.S. taxpayer identification number, a foreign tax identification number issued by its jurisdiction of residence. The certification must be signed by a responsible officer in the case of a corporation, by a general partner in the case of a partnership, and by a trustee, executor, or equivalent fiduciary in the case of a trust or estate. No particular form is needed for a certification pursuant to this paragraph (b)(3)(ii), nor is any particular language required, so long as the document meets the requirements of this paragraph, except that, with respect to certification submitted by a withholding qualified holder (as defined in §1.1445-1(g)(11)), the transferor must state on the certification that it is treated as a non-foreign person because it is a withholding qualified holder and must further specify whether it qualifies as a withholding qualified holder because it is a qualified holder under §1.897(l)-1(d) or a foreign partnership that satisfies the requirements of §1.1445-1(g)(11). Samples of acceptable certifications are provided in paragraph (b)(3)(ii)(E) of this section.

(3) An entity may rely upon a certification pursuant to this paragraph (b)(3)(ii)(B) for a period of two calendar years following the close of the calendar year in which the certification was given. If an interest holder becomes a foreign person (or no longer is treated as a withholding qualified holder (as defined in §1.1445-1(g)(11)) and therefore is no longer treated as a non-foreign person for purposes of withholding under section 1445 within the period described in the preceding sentence, the interest-holder must notify the entity before any further dispositions or distributions and upon receipt of such notice (or any other notification of the foreign status of the interest-holder) the entity may no longer rely upon the prior certification. An entity that obtains and relies upon a certification must retain that certification with its books and records for a period of three calendar years following the close of the last calendar year in which the entity relied upon the certification.

(C) *Foreign corporation that has made an election under section 897(i).*—A foreign corporation that has made a valid election under section 897(i) to be treated as a domestic corporation for purposes of section 897 may provide a certifi-cation of non-foreign status pursuant to this paragraph (b)(3)(ii). However, an electing foreign corporation must attach to such certification a copy of the acknowledgment of the election provided to the corporation by the Internal Revenue Service pursuant to §1.897-3(d)(4).

An acknowledgment is valid for this purpose only if it states that the information required by §1.897-3 has been determined to be complete.

(D) *Form W-8EXP.*—A certification of non-foreign status can be made by a withholding qualified holder (as defined in §1.1445-1(g)(11) as provided in this paragraph (b)(3)(ii) to certify its qualified holder status. A certification of non-foreign status under this paragraph (b)(3)(ii) also includes a certification made on a Form W-8EXP that states that the interest-holder is treated as a non-foreign person because it is a withholding qualified holder and must further specify whether it qualifies as a withholding qualified holder because it is a qualified holder under §1.897(l)-1(d) or a foreign partnership that satisfies the requirements of §1.1445-1(g)(11). The certification must also meet all of the other requirements for a valid Form W-8EXP as provided on the form and the instructions to the form. A qualified holder may not provide a certification of non-foreign status on a Form W-9, as described in paragraph (b)(3)(iv) of this section.

(iii) *Reliance upon certification not permitted.*—An entity or fiduciary may not rely upon an interest-holder's certification of non-foreign status if, prior to or at the time of the transfer with respect to which withholding would be required, the entity or fiduciary either—

(A) Has actual knowledge that the certification is false;

(B) Has received a notice that the certification is false from a transferor's or transferee's agent, pursuant to §1.1445-4; or

(C) Has received from a corporation that it knows to be a foreign corporation a certification that does not have attached to it a copy of the IRS acknowledgment of the corporation's election under section 897(i), as required by paragraph (b)(3)(ii)(C) of this section.

Such an entity's or fiduciary's withholding obligations shall apply as if a statement had never been given, and such an entity or fiduciary may be held fully liable pursuant to §1.1445-1(e) for any failure to withhold. For special rules concerning an entity's belated receipt of a notice concerning a false certification, see paragraphs (c)(2)(ii) and (e)(2)(iii) of this section.

(iv) *Form W-9.*—For purposes of paragraph (b)(3)(i) of this section, a certification of non-foreign status includes a valid Form W-9, *Request for Taxpayer Identification Number and Certification*, or its successor, submitted to the transferee by the transferor.

(4) *Property transferred not a U.S. real property interest.*—(i) *In general.*—Pursuant to the provisions of paragraphs (c) and (d) of this section, an entity or fiduciary is required to withhold with respect to certain transfers of property, if the property transferred is a U.S. real property interest. (In addition, taxable distributions of U.S. real property interests by domestic or foreign partnerships, trusts, and estates will be subject to withholding pursuant to section 1445(e)(4) and paragraph (f) of this section after publication of a Treasury decision

under sections 897(e)(2) and (g).) As defined in section 897(c) and §1.897-1(c), a U.S. real property interest includes certain interests in U.S. corporations, as well as direct interests in real property and certain associated personal property. This paragraph (b)(4) provides rules pursuant to which an entity (or fiduciary thereof) that transfers an interest in a U.S. corporation may determine that withholding is not required because the interest transferred is not a U.S. real property interest. To determine whether an interest in tangible property constitutes a U.S. real property interest the transfer of which would be subject to withholding, see §1.897-1(b) and (c).

(ii) *Interests in publicly traded entities.*—Withholding is not required under paragraph (c) or (d) of this section upon an entity's transfer of an interest in a domestic corporation if any class of stock of the corporation is regularly traded on an established securities market. This exemption shall apply to a disposition incident to an initial public offering of stock pursuant to a registration statement filed with the Securities and Exchange Commission. Similarly, no withholding is required under paragraph (c) or (d) of this section upon an entity's transfer of an interest in a publicly traded partnership or trust. However, the rule of this paragraph (b)(4)(ii) shall not apply to the transfer, to a single transferee (or related transferees as defined in §1.897-1(i)) in a single transaction (or related transactions), of an interest described in §1.897-1(c)(2)(iii)(B) (relating to substantial amounts of non-publicly traded interests in publicly traded corporations) or of similar interests in publicly traded partnerships or trusts. The entity making a transfer described in the preceding sentence must otherwise determine whether withholding is required, pursuant to section 1445(e) and the regulations thereunder. Transactions shall be deemed to be related if they are undertaken within 90 days of one another or if if can otherwise be shown that they were undertaken in pursuance of a prearranged plan.

(iii) *Corporation's statement that interest is not a U.S. real property interest.*—(A) *In general.*—No withholding is required under paragraph (c) or (d) of this section upon an entity's transfer of an interest in a domestic corporation if, prior to the transfer, the entity or fiduciary obtains a statement, issued by the corporation pursuant to §1.897-2(h), certifying that the interest is not a U.S. real property interest. In general, a corporation may issue such a statement only if the corporation was not a U.S. real property holding corporation at any time during the previous five years (or the period in which the interest was held by its present holder, if shorter) or if interests in the corporation ceased to be United States real property interests under section 897(c)(1)(B). (A corporation may not provide such a statement based on its determination that the interest in question is an interest solely as a creditor.) See §1.897-2(f) and (h). A corporation's statement may be relied upon for purposes of this paragraph (b)(4)(iii) only if the statement is dated not more than 30 days prior to the date of the transfer.

(B) *Reliance on statement not permitted.*—An entity or fiduciary is not entitled to rely upon a statement that an interest in a corporation is not a U.S. real property interest if, prior to or at the time of the transfer, the entity or fiduciary either—

(*1*) Has actual knowledge that the statement is false, or

(*2*) Receives a notice that the statement is false from a transferor's or transferee's agent, pursuant to §1.1445-4.

Such an entity's or fiduciary's withholding obligations shall apply as if a statement had never been given, and such an entity or fiduciary may be held fully liable pursuant to §1.1445-1(e) for any failure to withhold. For special rules concerning an entity's belated receipt of a notice concerning a false statement, see paragraphs (c)(2)(iii) and (d)(2)(i) of this section.

(5) *Reporting and paying over of withheld amounts.*—(i) *In general.*—An entity or fiduciary must report and pay over to the Internal Revenue Service any tax withheld pursuant to section 1445(e) and this section by the 20th day after the date of the transfer (as defined in §1.1445-1(g)(8)). Forms 8288 and 8288-A are used for this purpose and must be filed at the location as provided in the instructions to Forms 8288 and 8288-A. The contents of Forms 8288 and 8288-A are described in §1.1445-1(d). Pursuant to section 7502 and regulations thereunder, the timely mailing of Forms 8288 and 8288-A by U.S. mail will be treated as their timely filing. Form 8288-A will be stamped by the Internal Revenue Service to show receipt, and a stamped copy will be mailed by the Service to the interest holder if the Form 8288 is complete, including the transferor's identifying number, at the address shown on the form, for the interest-holder's use. See paragraph (b)(7) of this section.

If an application for a withholding certificate with respect to a transfer of a U.S. real property interest was submitted to the Internal Revenue Service on the day of or at any time prior to the transfer, the entity or fiduciary must withhold the amount required under section 1445(e) and the rules of this section. However, the amount withheld, or a lesser amount as determined by the Service, need not be reported and paid over to the Service until the 20th day following the Service's final determination. For this purpose, the Service's final determination occurs on the day when the withholding certificate is mailed to the applicant by the Service or when notification denying the request for a withholding certificate is mailed to the applicant by the Service. An application is submitted to the Service on the day it is actualy received by the Service at the address provided in §1.1445-1(g)(10) or, under the rules of section 7502, on the day it is mailed to the Service at the address provided in §1.1445-1(g)(10), concerning the issuance of withholding certificates see §1.1445-6.

(ii) *Anti-abuse rule.*—An entity or fiduciary that in reliance upon the rules of this paragraph (b)(5)(ii) fails to report and pay over amounts withheld by the 20th day following the date of the transfer, shall be subject to the payment of interest and penalties if the relevant application for a withholding certificate (or an amendment of the application for a withholding certificate) was submitted for a principle purpose of delaying the payment to the IRS of the amount withheld. Interest and penalties shall be assessed on the amount that is ultimately paid over with respect to the period between the 20th day after the date of the transfer and the date on which payment is made.

(6) *Liability upon failure to withhold.*—For rules regarding liability upon failure to withhold under section 1445(e) and this §1.1445-5, see §1.1445-1(e).

(7) *Effect of withholding by entity or fiduciary upon interest holder.*—The withholding of tax under section 1445(e) does not excuse a foreign person that is subject to U.S. tax by reason of the operation of section 897 from filing a U.S. tax return. Thus, Form 1040NR, 1041, or 1120F as appropriate must be filed and any tax due must be paid by the filing date otherwise applicable to such person (or any extension therof). The tax withheld with respect to the foreign person under section 1445(e) (as shown on Form 8288-A) shall be credited against the amount of income tax as computed in such return, but only if the stamped copy of Form 8288-A provided to the entity or fiduciary (under paragraph (b)(5) of this section) is attached to the return or substantial evidence of the amount of tax withheld is attached to the return in accordance with the succeeding sentence. If a stamped copy of Form 8288-A has not been provided to the interest-holder by the Service, the interest-holder may establish the amount of tax withheld by the entity or fiduciary by attaching to its return substantial evidence of such amount. Such an interest-holder must attach to its return a statement which supplies all of the information required by §1.1445-1(d)(2). If the amount withheld under section 1445(e) constitutes less than the full amount of the foreign person's U.S. tax liability for that taxable year, then a payment of estimated tax may be required to be made pursuant to section 6154 or 6654 prior to the filing of the income tax return for that year. Alternatively, if the amount withheld under section 1445(e) exceeds the foreign person's maximum tax liability with respect to the transaction (as *reflected* in a withholding certificate issued by the Internal Revenue Service pursuant to §1.1445-6), then the foreign person may seek an early refund of the excess pursuant to §1.1445-6(g). A foreign person that takes gain into account in accordance with the provisions of section 453 shall not be entitled to a refund of the amount withheld unless a withholding certificate providing for such a refund is obtained pursuant to §1.1445-6.

If an entity or fiduciary withholds tax under section 1445(e) with respect to a beneficial owner of an interest who is not a foreign person, such beneficial owner may credit the amount of any tax withheld against his income tax liability in accordance with the provisions of this §1.1445-5(b)(7) or apply for an early refund under §1.1445-6(g).

(8) *Effective dates.*—(i) *Partnership, trust, and estate dispositions of U.S. real property interests.*—The provisions of section 1445(e)(1) and paragraph (c) of this section, requiring withholding upon certain dispositions of U.S. real property interests by domestic partnerships, trusts and estates, shall apply to any disposition on or after January 1, 1985.

(ii) *Certain distributions by foreign corporations.*—The provisions of section 1445(e)(2) and paragraph (d) of this section requiring withholding upon distributions of U.S. real property interest by foreign corporations, shall apply to distributions made on or after January 1, 1985.

(iii) *Distributions by certain domestic corporations to foreign shareholders.*—The provisions of section 1445(e)(3) and paragraph (e)(1) of this section, requiring withholding upon distributions in redemption of stock under section 302(a) or liquidating distributions under Part II of subchapter C of the Internal Revenue Code by U.S. real property holding corporations to foreign shareholders, shall apply to distributions made on or after January 1, 1985. The provisions of section 1445(e)(3) and paragraph (e)(1) of this section requiring withholding on distributions under section 301 by U.S. real property holding corporations to foreign shareholders shall apply to distributions made after August 20, 1996. The provisions of paragraph (e) of this section providing for the coordination of withholding between sections 1445 and 1441 (or 1442 or 1443) for distributions under section 301 by U.S. real property holding corporations to foreign shareholders apply to distributions after December 31, 2000 (see § 1.1441-3(c)(4) and (h)).

(iv) *Taxable distributions by domestic or foreign partnerships, trusts, and estates.*—The provisions of section 1445(e)(4), requiring withholding upon certain taxable distributions by domestic or foreign partnerships, trusts, and estates, shall apply to distributions made on or after the effective date of a Treasury decision under section 897(e)(2)(B)(ii) and (g).

(v) [Removed]

(vi) *Tiered partnerships.*—No withholding is required upon the disposition of a U.S. real property interest by a partnership which is directly owned, in whole or in part, by another domestic partnership (but only to the extent that the amount realized is attributable to the partnership interest of that other partnership) until the effective date of a Treasury Decision published under section 1445(e) providing rules governing this matter.

(c) *Dispositions of U.S. real property interests by domestic partnerships, trusts, and estates.*—(1) *Withholding required.*—(i) *In general.*—If a domestic partnership, trust, or estate disposes of a U.S. real property interest and any partner, beneficiary, or owner of the entity is a foreign person, then the partnership or the trustee, executor, or equivalent fiduciary of the trust or estate must withhold tax with respect to each such foreign person in accordance with the provisions of subdivision (ii), (iii), or (iv) of this paragraph (c)(1) (as applicable). The withholding obligation imposed by this paragraph (c) applies to the fiduciary of a trust even if the grantor of the trust or another person is treated as the owner of the trust or any portion thereof for purposes of the Internal Revenue Code. Thus, the withholding obligation imposed by this paragraph (c) applies to the trustee of a land trust or similar arrangement, even if such a trustee is not ordinarily treated under the applicable provisions of local law as a true fiduciary.

(ii) *Disposition by partnership.*—A partnership must withhold a tax equal to the rate specified in section 1445(e)(1) multiplied by the amount of each foreign partner's distributive share of the gain realized by the partnership upon the disposition of each U.S. real property interest. Such distributive share of the gain must be determined pursuant to the principles of section 704 and the regulations thereunder. For the rules applicable to partnerships, interests in which are regularly traded on an established securities market, see § 1.1445-8.

(iii) *Disposition by trust or estate.*—(A) *In general.*—A trustee, fiduciary, executor or equivalent fiduciary (hereafter collectively referred to as the fiduciary) of a trust or estate having one or more foreign beneficiaries must withhold tax in accordance with the rules of this § 1.1445-5(c)(1)(iii). Such a fiduciary must establish a U.S. real property interest account and must enter in such account all gains and losses realized during the taxable year of the trust or estate from dispositions of U.S. real property interests. The fiduciary must withhold a tax equal to the rate specified in section 1445(e)(1) multiplied by the amount of any distribution to a foreign beneficiary that is attributable to the balance in the U.S. real property interest account on the day of the distribution. A distribution from a trust or estate to a beneficiary (domestic or foreign) shall, solely for purposes of section 1445(e)(1), be deemed to be attributable first to any balance in the U.S. real property interest account and then to other amounts. However, a distribution that occurs prior to the transfer of a U.S. real property interest in a taxable year or at any other time when the amount contained in the U.S. real property interest account is zero, is not subject to withholding under this § 1.1445-5(c)(1)(iii). The U.S. real property interest account is reduced by the amount distributed to all beneficiaries (domestic and foreign) attributable to such account during the taxable year of the trust or estate. Any ending balance of the U.S. real property interest account not distributed by the close of the taxable year of the trust or estate is cancelled and is not carried over (or carried back) to any other year. Thus, the beginning balance of such account in any taxable year of the trust or estate is always zero. For rules applicable to grantor trusts see § 1.1445-5(c)(1)(iv). For rules applicable to trusts, interests in which are regularly traded on an established securities market and real estate investment trusts, see § 1.1445-8.

(B) *Example.*—The following example illustrates the rules of paragraph (c)(1)(iii)(A) of this section.

On January 1, 1994, A establishes a domestic trust (which has as its taxable year, the calendar year) for the benefit of B, a nonresident alien, and C, a U.S. citizen. The trust is not a trust subject to sections 671 through 679. Under the terms of the trust, the trustee, T, is given discretion to distribute income and corpus of the trust to provide for the reasonable needs of B and C. During the trust's 1994 tax year, T disposes of three parcels of vacant land located in the United States. The following chart illustrates the computation of the amount subject to withholding under section 1445 with respect to distributions made by T to B and C during 1994. In 1994, the relevant rate of withholding (that is, the rate specified in section 1445(e)(1)) was 35%.

Date	*Parcel sold*	*Gains or (loss) realized*	*Distributions to C*	*Distributions to B (before withholding)*	*Section 1445 withholding (35% rate)*	*U.S. real property interest account*
1/01/94						-0-
3/01/94	Parcel 1	140,000				140,000
3/05/94			5,000	10,000	3,500	125,000
3/15/94			10,000	5,000	1,750	110,000
5/01/94	Parcel 2	300,000				410,000
5/15/94	Parcel 3	(50,000)				360,000
12/01/94			170,000	170,000	59,500	20,000
1/01/95						-0-

(iv) *Disposition by grantor trust.*—The trustee or equivalent fiduciary of a trust that is subject to the provisions of subpart E of part 1 of subchapter J (sections 671 through 679) must withhold a tax equal to the rate specified in section 1445(e)(1) multiplied by the amount of the gain realized from each disposition of a U.S. real property interest to the extent such gain is allocable to a portion of the trust treated as owned by a foreign person under subpart E of part I of subchapter J.

(2) *Withholding not required under paragraph (c).*—(i) [Removed]

(ii) *Interest-holder not a foreign person.*—(A) *In general.*—A domestic partnership, trust, or estate that disposes of a U.S. real property interest shall not be required to withhold with respect to any partner or beneficiary that it determines, pursuant to the rules of paragraph (b)(3) of this section, not to be a foreign person.

(B) *Belated notice of false certification.*—If after the date of the transfer a partnership or fiduciary learns that a partner's or beneficiary's certification of non-foreign status is false, then that partnership or fiduciary shall be required to withhold, with respect to the foreign partner or beneficiary that gave the false certification, the lesser of—

(1) The amount otherwise required to be withheld under the rules of this paragraph (c), or

(2) An amount equal to that partner's or beneficiary's remaining interests in the income or assets of the partnership, trust, or estate.

Amounts so withheld must be reported and paid over by the 60th day following the date on which the partnership or fiduciary learns that the certification is false. For rules concerning the notifications of false certifications that may be required to be given to partnerships and fiduciaries, see § 1.1445-4(b).

(iii) *Property disposed of not a U.S. real property interest.*—(A) *In general.*—No withholding is required under this paragraph (c) if a domestic partnership, trust, or estate that disposes of property determines pursuant to the rules of paragraph (b)(4) of this section that the property disposed of is not a U.S. real property interest.

(B) *Belated notice of false statement.*—If after the date of the transfer a partnership or fiduciary learns that a corporation's statement (that an interest in the corporation is not a U.S. real property interest) is false, then that partnership or fiduciary shall be required to withhold, with respect to each foreign partner or beneficiary, the lesser of—

(1) The amount otherwise required to be withheld under the rules of this paragraph (c), or

(2) An amount equal to that partner's or beneficiary's remaining interests in the income or assets of the partnership, trust, or estate.

Amounts so withheld must be reported and paid over by the 60th day following the date on which the partnership or fiduciary learns that the statement is false. For rules concerning the notifications of false statements that may be required to be given to partnerships or fiduciaries, see § 1.1445-4(b).

(iv) *Withholding certificate.*—No withholding is required under this paragraph (c) with respect to the transfer of a U.S. real property interest if the Internal Revenue Service issues a withholding certificate that so provides. For rules concerning the issuance of withholding certificates, see § 1.1445-6.

(v) *Nonrecognition transactions.*—For special rules concerning transactions entitled to nonrecognition of gain or loss, see paragraph (b)(2) of this section.

(3) *Large partnerships or trusts.*—(i) *In general.*—If a partnership or trust has more than 100 partners or beneficiaries, then the partnership or fiduciary of the trust may elect to withhold in accordance with the provisions of this § 1.1445-5(c)(3) in lieu of withholding in the manner required by § 1.1445-5(c)(1). However, the rules of this § 1.1445-5(c)(3) shall not apply to any partnership or trust interests in which are regularly traded on an established securities market except as described in § 1.1445-8(c)(1). The rules of this § 1.1445-5(c)(3) shall not apply to any real estate investment trust. *See* § 1.1445-8.

(ii) *Amount to be withheld.*—A partnership or trust electing to withhold under this paragraph (c)(3) shall withhold from each distribution to a foreign person an amount equal to the rate specified in section 1445(e)(1) multiplied by of the amount attributable to section 1445(e)(1) transfers.

(iii) *Amounts attributable to section 1445(e)(1) transfers.*—A distribution is attributable to section 1445(e)(1) transfers to the extent of the partner's or beneficiary's proportionate share of the current balance of the entity's section 1445(e)(1) account. A distribution from a partnership or trust that has made an election under this § 1.1445-5(c)(3) shall be deemed first to be attributable to a section 1445(e)(1) transfer to the extent of the balance in the section 1445(e)(1) account. An entity's section 1445(e)(1) account shall be equal to—

(A) The total amount of net gain realized by the entity upon all transfers of U.S. real property interests carried out by the entity after the date of its election under this § 1.1445-5(c)(3); minus

(B) The total amount of all distributions by the entity to domestic and foreign distributees from such account.

(iv) *Special rules for entities that make recurring sales of growing crops and timber.*—An entity that makes an election under § 1.1445-5(c)(3) and that makes recurring sales of growing crops and timber may further elect to determine the amount subject to withholding under the rules of this § 1.1445-5(c)(3)(iv). Such an entity must withhold from each distribution to a foreign partner or beneficiary an amount equal to 15 percent of such partner's or beneficiary's proportionate share of the current balance of the entity's gross section 1445(e)(1) account. An entity's gross section 1445(e)(1) account equals—

(A) The total amount realized by the entity upon all transfers of U.S. real property interests carried out by the entity after the date of its election under this § 1.1445-5(c)(3)(iv); minus

(B) The total amount of all distributions to domestic and foreign distributees from such account.

An entity that elects to compute the amount subject to withholding under this § 1.1445-5(c)(3)(iv), shall make such election in accordance with § 1.1445-5(c)(3)(vi) and shall be subject to the provisions otherwise applicable under § 1.1445-5(c)(3).

(v) *Procedural rules.*—An election under paragraph (c)(3) may be made by filing a notice thereof at the address provided in § 1.1445-1(g)(10). The notice must be submitted by a general partner (in the case of a partnership) or the trustee or equivalent fiduciary (in the case of a trust). The notice must set forth the name, office address, and identifying number of the partnership or fiduciary making the election, and, in the case of a partnership, must include the name, office address, and identifying number of the general partner submitting the election. An election under this paragraph (c)(3) may be revoked only with the consent of the Internal Revenue Service. Consent of the Service may be requested by filing an application to revoke the election at the address stated above. This application must include all information provided to the Service with the election notice and must provide an explanation of the reasons for revoking the election. The application to revoke an election must also specify the amount remaining to be distributed in the section 1445(e)(1) account or the gross section 1445(e)(1) account. An entity that ceases to qualify under section 1.1445-5(c)(3) because such entity does not have more than 100 partners or beneficiaries may revoke its election only with the consent of the Internal Revenue Service.

(d) *Distributions of U.S. real property interests by foreign corporations.*—(1) *In general.*—A foreign corporation that distributes a U.S. real property interest must deduct and withhold a tax equal to the rate specified in section 1445(e)(2) multiplied by of the amount of gain recognized by the corporation on the distribution. The amount of gain required to be recognized by the corporation must be detemined pursuant to the rules of section 897 and any other applicable section. For special rules concerning the applicability of a nonrecognition provision to a distribution, see paragraph (b)(2) of this section. The withholding liability imposed by this paragraph (d) applies to the same taxpayer that owes the related substantive income tax liability pursuant to the operation of section 897. Only one such liability will be assessed and collected from a foreign corporation, but separate penalties for failures to comply with the two requirements will be asserted.

(2) *Withholding not required.*—(i) *Property distributed not a U.S. real property interest.*—(A) *In general.*—No withholding is required under this paragraph (d) if a foreign corporation that distributes property determines pursuant to the rules of paragraph (b)(3) of this section that the property distributed is not a U.S. real property interest.

(B) *Belated notice of false statement.*—If after the date of a distribution described in paragraph (d)(1) of this section a foreign corporation learns that another corporation's statement (that an interest in that other corporation is not a U.S. real property interest) is false, then the foreign corporation may not rely upon that statement for any purpose. Such a foreign corporation's withholding obligations under this paragaph (d) shall apply as if a statement had never been given, and such a corporation may be held fully liable pursuant to § 1.1445-5(b)(5) for any failure to withhold. Amounts withheld pursuant to the rule of this paragraph (d)(2)(i)(B) must be reported and paid over by the 60th day following the date on which the foreign corporation learns that the statement is false. No penalties or interest will be assessed for failures to withhold prior to that date. For rules concerning the notifications of false statements that may be required to be given to foreign corporations, see § 1.1445-4(b).

(ii) *Withholding certificate.*—No withholding is required under this paragraph (d) with respect to a foreign corporation's distribution of a U.S. real property interest if the distributing corporation obtains a withholding certificate from the Internal Revenue Service that so provides. For rules concerning the issuance of withholding certificates, see § 1.1445-6.

(e) *Distributions to foreign persons by U.S. real property holding corporations.*—(1) *In general.*—A domestic corporation that distributes any property to a foreign person that holds an interest in the corporation must deduct and withhold a tax equal to 15 percent of the fair market value of the property distributed to the foreign person, if—

(i) The foreign person's interest in the corporation constitutes a U.S. real property interest under the provisions of section 897 and regulations thereunder; and

(ii) There is a distribution of property in redemption of stock treated as an exchange under section 302(a), in liquidation of the corporation pursuant to the provisions of Part II of subchapter C of the Internal Revenue Code (sections 331 through section 346), or with respect to stock under section 301 that is not made out of earnings and profits of the corporation.

(2) *Coordination rules for Section 301 distributions.*—If a domestic corporation makes a distribution of property under section 301 to a foreign person whose interest in such corporation constitutes a U.S. real property interest under the provisions of section 897 and the regulations thereunder, then see § 1.1441-3(c)(4) for rules coordinating withholding obligations under sections 1445 and 1441 (or 1442 or 1443)).

(3) *Withholding not required.*—(i) *Foreign person's interest not a U.S. real property interest.*—Withholding is required under this paragraph (e) only with respect to distributions to foreign persons holding interests in the corporation that constitute U.S. real property interests. In general, a foreign person's interest in a domestic corporation constitutes a U.S. real property interest if the corporation was a U.S. real property holding corporation at any time during the shorter of (A) the period in which the foreign person held the interest or (B) the previous five years (but not earlier than June 19, 1980). See section 897(c) and §§ 1.897-1(c) and 1.897-2(b) and (h). However, an interest in such a corporation ceases to be a U.S. real property interest after all of the U.S. real property interests held by the corporation itself are disposed of in transactions on which gain or loss is recognized. See section 897(c)(1)(B) and § 1.897-2(f)(2). Thus, if a U.S. real property holding corporation in the process of liquidation does not elect section 337 nonrecognition treatment upon its sale of all U.S. real property interests held by the corporation, and recognizes gain or loss upon such sales, interests in that corporation cease to be U.S. real property interests. Therefore, no withholding would be required with respect to that corporation's subsequent liquidating distribution to a foreign shareholder of property other than a U.S. real property interest.

(ii) *Nonrecognition transactions.*—For special rules concerning the applicability of a nonrecognition provision to a distribution described in paragraph (e)(1) of this section, see paragraph (b)(2) of this section.

(iii) *Interest-holder not a foreign person.*—(A) *In general.*—A domestic corporation shall not be required to withhold under this paragraph (e) with respect to a distribution of property to any distributee that it determines, pursuant to the rules of paragraph (b)(3) of this section, not to be a foreign person.

(B) *Belated notice of false certification.*—If after the date of a distribution described in paragraph (e)(1) of this section a domestic corporation learns that an interest-holder's certification of non-foreign status is false, then the corporation may rely upon that certification only if the person providing the false certification holds (or held) less than 10 percent of the value of the outstanding stock of the corporation. With respect to less than 10 percent interest-holders, no withholding is required under this paragraph (e) upon receipt of a belated notice of false certification. With respect to 10 percent or greater interest-holders, the corporation's withholding obligations under this paragraph (e) shall apply as if a certification had never been given, and such a corporation may be held fully liable pursuant to § 1.1445-5(b)(6) for any failure to withhold as of the date specified in this § 1.1445-5(e)(3)(iii)(B). Amounts withheld pursuant to the rule of this paragraph (e)(3)(iii)(B) must be reported and paid over by the 60th day following the date on which the corporation learns that the certification is false. No penalties or interest for failures to withhold will be assessed prior to that date. For rules concerning the notifications of false certifications that may be required to be given to U.S. real property holding corporations, see § 1.1445-4(b).

(iv) *Withholding certificate.*—No withholding, or reduced withholding, is required under this paragraph (e) with respect to a domestic corporation's distribution of property if the distributing corporation obtains a withholding certificate from the Internal Revenue Service that so provides. For rules concerning the issuance of withholding certificates, see § 1.1445-6.

(f) *Taxable distributions by domestic or foreign partnerships, trusts, or estates.*—[Reserved]

(g) *Dispositions of interests in partnerships, trusts, and estates.*—[Reserved]

(h) *Applicability dates.*—The requirement in paragraphs (b)(2)(ii)(B) and (C) of this section that taxpayer identification numbers be provided (in all cases) is is applicable for dispositions of U.S. real property interests occurring after November 3, 2003. The withholding rates set forth in paragraphs (c)(3)(iv) and (e)(1) of this section apply to distributions after February 16, 2016. For distributions on or before February 16, 2016, see paragraphs (c)(3)(iv) and (e)(1) of this section as contained in 26 CFR part 1 revised as of April 1, 2015. Paragraph (b)(3)(iv) of this section applies to certifications provided on or after May 7, 2019, except that a taxpayer may choose to apply paragraph (b)(3)(iv) of this section with respect to certifications provided before May 7, 2019. Paragraphs (c) and (d) of this section apply to distributions on or after November 30, 2020. Paragraph (b)(3)(ii)(A) of this section applies with respect to dispositions of U.S. real property interests and distributions described in section 897(h) occurring on or after December 29, 2022. For dispositions of U.S. real property interests and distributions described in section 897(h) occurring before December 29, 2022, see § 1.1445-5(b)(3)(ii)(A), as contained in 26 CFR part 1, revised as of April 1, 2021. [Reg. § 1.1445-5.]

☐ [*T.D.* 8113, 12-18-86. *Amended by T.D.* 8198, 5-4-88; *T.D.* 8321, 12-6-90; *T.D.* 8647, 12-20-95; *T.D.* 8734, 10-6-97 (T.D. 8804 delayed the effective date of T.D. 8734 from January 1, 1999, to January 1, 2000; T.D. 8856 further delayed the effective date of T.D. 8734 until January 1, 2001), *T.D.* 9082, 8-4-2003, *T.D.* 9751, 2-17-2016 (*corrected* 4-25-2016), *T.D.* 9926, 11-27-2020 *and T.D.* 9971, 12-28-2022.]

§ 1.1445-6. Adjustments pursuant to withholding certificate of amount required to be withheld under section 1445(e).—(a) *Withholding certificate for purposes of section 1445(e).*—(1) *In general.*—Pursuant to the provisions of § 1.1445-5(c)(2)(iv), (d)(2)(ii), and (e)(2)(iv), withholding under section 1445(e) may be reduced or eliminated pursuant to a withholding certificate issued by the Internal Revenue Service in accordance with the rules of this § 1.1445-6. A withholding certificate may be issued in cases where adjusted withholding is appropriate (e.g., because of the applicability of a nonrecognition provision—see paragraph (c) of this section), where the relevant taxpayers are exempt from U.S. tax (see paragraph (d) of this section), or where an agreement for the payment of tax is entered into with the Service (see paragraph (e) of this section). A withholding certificate that is obtained prior to a transfer allows the entity or fiduciary to withhold a reduced amount or excuses withholding entirely. A withholding certificate that is obtained after a transfer has been made may authorize a normal refund or an early refund pursuant to paragraph (g) of this section. The Internal Revenue Service will act upon an application for a withholding certificate not later than the 90th day after it is received. (The Service may deny a request for a withholding certificate where, after due notice, an applicant fails to provide the information necessary to make a determination.) Solely for this purpose (i.e., determining the day upon which the 90 day period commences), an application is received by the Service on the date when all information necessary for the Service to make a determination is provided by the applicant. In no event, however, will a withholding certificate be issued without the transferor's identifying number. (For rules regarding whether an application has been timely submitted, see § 1.1445-5(b)(5).) The Internal Revenue Service will act upon an application for an early refund not later than the 90th day after it is received. An application for an early refund must either (i) include a copy of a withholding certificate issued by the Service with respect to the transaction, or (ii) be combined with an application for a withholding certificate. Where an application for an early refund is combined with an application for a withholding certificate, the Service will act upon both applications not later than the 90th day after receipt. Either an entity, a fiduciary, or a relevant taxpayer (as defined in paragraph (a)(2) of this section) may apply for a withholding certificate. An entity or fiduciary may apply for a withholding certificate with respect to all or less than all relevant taxpayers. For special rules concerning the issuance of a withholding certificate to a foreign corporation that has made an election under section 897(i), see § 1.1445-7(d).

(2) *Relevant taxpayer.*—For purposes of this section, the term "relevant taxpayer" means any foreign person that will bear substantive income tax liability by reason of the operation of section 897 with respect to a transaction upon which withholding is required under section 1445(e).

(b) *Applications for withholding certificates.*—(1) *In general.*—An application for a withholding certificate pursuant to this § 1.1445-6 must be submitted in the manner provided in § 1.1445-3(b). However, in lieu of the information required to be submitted pursuant to § 1.1445-3(b)(4), the applicant must provide the information required by paragraph (b)(2) of this section. In addition, the information required by paragraph (b)(3) of this section must be submitted with the application.

(2) *Basis for certificate.*—(i) *Adjusted withholding.*—If a withholding certificate is sought on the basis of a claim that adjusted withholding is appropriate, the application must include a calculation, in accordance with paragraph (c) of this section, of the maximum tax that may be imposed on each relevant taxpayer with respect to which adjusted withholding is sought. The application must also include all evidence necessary to substantiate the claimed calculation, such as records of adjustments to basis or appraisals of fair market value.

(ii) *Exemption.*—If a withholding certificate is sought on the basis of a relevant taxpayer's exemption from U.S. tax, the application must set forth a brief statement of the law and facts that support the claimed exemption. See paragraph (d) of this section.

(iii) *Agreement.*—If a withholding certificate is sought on the basis of an agreement for the payment of tax, the application must include a copy of the agreement proposed by the applicant and a copy of the security instrument (if any) proposed by the applicant. In this regard, see paragraph (e) of this section.

(3) *Relevant taxpayers.*—An application for withholding certificate pursuant to this section must include all of the following information: the name, identifying number, and home address (in the case of an individual) or office address (in the case of an entity) of each relevant taxpayer with respect to which adjusted withholding is sought.

(c) *Adjustment of amount required to be withheld.*—The Internal Revenue Service may issue a withholding certificate that excuses withholding, or that permits an entity or fiduciary to withhold an adjusted amount reflecting the relevant taxpayers' maximum tax liability. A relevant taxpayer's maximum tax liability is the maximum amount which that taxpayer could be required to pay as tax by reason of the transaction upon which withholding is required. In the case of an individual taxpayer that amount will generally be the gain realized by the individual, multiplied by the maximum individual income tax rate applicable to long term capital gain. In the case of a corporate taxpayer, that amount will generally be the gain realized by the corporation, multiplied by the maximum corporate income tax rate applicable to long term capital gain. However, that amount must be adjusted to take into account the following:

(1) Any reduction of tax to which the relevant taxpayer is entitled under the provisions of a U.S. income tax treaty;

(2) The effect of any nonrecognition provision that is applicable to the transaction;

(3) Any losses previously realized and recognized by the relevant taxpayer during the taxable year by reason of the operation of section 897;

(4) Any amount realized upon the subject transfer by the relevant taxpayer that is required to be treated as ordinary income under any provision of the Code; and

(5) Any other factor that may increase or reduce the tax upon the transaction.

(d) *Relevant taxpayer's exemption from U.S. tax.*—(1) *In general.*—The Internal Revenue Service will issue a withholding certificate that excuses withholding by an entity or fiduciary if it is established that a relevant taxpayer's income from the transaction will be exempt from U.S. tax. For the available exemptions, see paragraph (d)(2) of this section. If a relevant taxpayer is entitled to a reduction of (rather than an exemption from) U.S. tax, then the entity or fiduciary may obtain a withholding certificate to that effect pursuant to the provisions of paragraph (c) of this section.

(2) *Available exemptions.*—A relevant taxpayer's income from a transaction with respect to which withholding is required under section 1445(e) may be exempt from U.S. tax because either:

(i) The relevant taxpayer is an integral part or controlled entity of a foreign government and the subject income is exempt from U.S. tax pursuant to section 892 and the regulations thereunder; or

(ii) The relevant taxpayer is entitled to the benefits of an income tax treaty that provides for such an exemption (subject to the limitations imposed by section 1125(c) of Pub. L. 96-499, which, in general, overrides such benefits as of January 1, 1985).

(e) *Agreement for the payment of tax.*—(1) *In general.*—The Internal Revenue Service will issue a withholding certificate that excuses withholding or that permits an entity or fiduciary to withhold a reduced amount, if the entity, fiduciary, or a relevant taxpayer enters into an agreement for the payment of tax pursuant to the provisions of this paragraph (e). An agreement for the payment of tax is a contract between the Service and the entity, fiduciary, or relevant taxpayer that consists of two necessary elements. Those elements are—

(i) A contract between the Service and the other person, setting forth in detail the rights and obligations of each; and

(ii) A security instrument or other form of security acceptable to the Assistant Commissioner (International).

(2) *Contents of agreement.*—(i) *In general.*—An agreement for the payment of tax must cover an amount described in subdivision (ii) or (iii) of this paragraph (e)(2). The agreement may either provide adequate security for the payment of the chosen amount with respect to the relevant taxpayer in accordance with paragraph (e)(3) of this section, or provide for the payment of that amount through a combination of security and withholding of tax by the entity or fiduciary.

(ii) *Tax that would otherwise be withheld.*—An agreement for the payment of tax may cover the amount of tax that would otherwise be required to be withheld with respect to the relevant taxpayer pursuant to section 1445(e). In addition to the amount computed pursuant to section 1445(e), the applicant must agree to pay interest upon that amount, at the rate established under section 6621, with respect to the period between the date on which withholding tax under section 1445(e) would otherwise be due and the date on which the relevant taxpayer's payment of tax with respect to the disposition will be due. The amount of interest agreed upon must be paid by the applicant regardless of whether or not the Service is required to draw upon any security provided pursuant to the agreement. The interest may be paid either with the return or by the Service drawing upon the security.

(iii) *Maximum tax liability.*—An agreement for the payment of tax may cover the relevant taxpayer's maximum tax liability, determined in accordance with paragraph (c) of this section. The agreement must also provide for the payment of an additional amount equal to 25 percent of the amount determined under paragraph (c) of this section. This additional amount secures the interest and penalties that would accrue between the date of the relevant taxpayer's failure to file a return and pay tax with respect to the disposition, and the date on which the Service collects upon that liability pursuant to the agreement.

(iv) *Allocation of payment.*—An agreement for the payment of tax pursuant to this section must set forth an allocation of the payment provided for by the agreement among the relevant taxpayers with respect to which the withholding certificate is sought. In the case of an agreement that covers an amount described in subdivision (ii) of this paragraph (e)(2), such allocation must be based upon the amount that would otherwise be required to be withheld with respect to each relevant taxpayer. In the case of an agreement that covers an amount described in subdivision (iii) of this paragraph (e)(2), such allocation must be based upon each relevant taxpayer's maximum tax liability.

(3) *Major types of security.*—The major types of security that are acceptable to the Internal Revenue Service for purposes of this section are described in § 1.1445-3(e)(3).

(4) *Terms of security instrument.*—Any security instrument that is furnished pursuant to this section must contain the terms described in § 1.1445-3(e)(4).

(f) *Amendments to application for withholding certificates.*—(1) *In general.*—An applicant for a withholding certificate may amend an otherwise complete application by submitting an amending statement to the address provided in § 1.1445-1(g)(10). The amending statement shall provide the information required by § 1.1445-6(f)(3) and must be signed and accompanied by a penalties of perjury statement in accordance with § 1.1445-6(b).

(2) *Extension of time for the Service to process requests for withholding certificates.*—(i) *In general.*—If an amending statement is submitted, the time in which the Internal Revenue Service must act upon the amended application shall be extended by 30 days.

(ii) *Substantial amendments.*—If an amending statement is submitted and the Service finds that the statement substantially amends to the facts of the underlying application or substantially alters the terms of the withholding certificate as requested in the initial application, the time within which the Service must act upon the amended application shall be extended by 60 days. The applicant shall be so notified.

(iii) *Amending statement received after the requested withholding certificate has been signed on behalf of the Service.*—If an amending statement is received after the withholding certificate, drafted in response to the underlying application, has been signed on behalf of the Service and prior to the day such certificate is mailed to the applicant, the time in which the Service must act upon the amended application shall be extended by 90 days.

(3) *Information required to be submitted.*—No particular form is required for an amending statement but the statement must provide the following information:

(i) *Identification of applicant.*—The amending statement must set forth the name, address, and identifying number of the person submitting the amending statement.

(ii) *Date of application.*—The amending statement must set forth the date of the underlying application for a withholding certificate.

(iii) *Real property interest to be (or that has been) transferred.*—The amending statement must set forth a brief description of the real property interest with respect to which the underlying application for a withholding certificate was submitted.

(iv) *Amending information.*—The amending statement must fully set forth the basis for the amendment including any modification of the facts supporting the application for a withholding certificate and any change sought in the terms of the withholding certificate.

(g) *Early refund of overwithheld amounts.*—If the Internal Revenue Service issues a withholding certificate pursuant to this section, and an amount greater than that specified in the certificate was withheld by the entity or fiduciary, then pursuant to the rules of this paragraph (g) a relevant taxpayer may apply for an early refund of a proportionate share of the excess amount (without interest) prior to the date on which the relevant taxpayer's return is due (without extensions). An application for an early refund must be delivered to the address provided in § 1.1445-1(g)(10). No particular form is required for the application, but the following information must be set forth in separate paragraphs numbered to correspond with the numbers given below:

(1) Name, address, and identifying number of the relevant taxpayer seeking the refund;

(2) Amount required to be withheld pursuant to withholding certificate;

(3) Amount withheld by entity or fiduciary (attach a copy of Form 8388-A stamped by IRS pursuant to § 1.1445-5(b)(4) or provide substantial evidence of the amount withheld in the case of a failure to receive Form 8288-A, as provided in § 1.1445-5(b)(7));

(4) Amount to be refunded to the relevant taxpayer.

An application for an early refund cannot be processed unless the required copy of Form 8288-A or substantial evidence of the amount withheld in the case of a failure to receive Form 8288-A (as provided in § 1.1445-5(b)(7)) is attached to the application. If an application for a withholding certificate is submitted after the transfer takes place, then that application may be combined with an application for an early refund. The Service will act upon a claim for refund within the time limits set forth in § 1.1445-6(a)(1).

(h) *Effective date for taxpayer identification numbers.*—The requirement in paragraphs (b)(3), (f)(3)(i), and (g)(1) of this section that taxpayer identification numbers be provided (in all cases) is applicable for dispositions of U.S. real property interests occurring after November 3, 2003. [Reg. § 1.1445-6.]

□ [*T.D.* 8113, 12-18-86. *Amended by T.D.* 9082, 8-4-2003 *and T.D.* 9751, 2-17-2016.]

§ 1.1445-7. Treatment of foreign corporation that has made an election under section 897(i) to be treated as a domestic corporation.—(a) *In general.*—Pursuant to section 897(i) a foreign corporation may elect to be treated as a domestic corporation for purposes of sections 897 and 6039C. A foreign corporation that has made such an election shall also be treated as a domestic corporation for purposes of the withholding required under section 1445, in accordance with the provisions of this section.

(b) *Withholding under section 1445(a).*—(1) *Dispositions by corporation.*—A foreign corporation that has made an election under section 897(i) may provide a transferee with a certification of non-foreign status in connection with the corporation's disposition of a U.S. real property interest. However, in accordance with the provisions of §§ 1.1445-2(b)(2)(ii) and 1.1445-5(b)(3)(ii)(C), such an electing foreign corporation must attach to such certification a copy of the acknowledgment of the election provided to the corporation by the Internal Revenue Service pursuant to § 1.897-3(d)(4) which states that the information required by § 1.897-3 has been determined to be complete.

(2) *Dispositions of interests in corporation.*—Dispositions of interests in electing foreign corporations shall be subject to the withholding requirements of section 1445(a) and the rules of §§ 1.1445-1 through 1.1445-4. Therefore, if a foreign person disposes of an interest in such a corporation, and that interest is a U.S. real property interest under the provisions of section 897 and regulations thereunder, then the transferee is required to withhold under section 1445(a).

(c) *Withholding under section 1445(e).*—Because a foreign corporation that has made an election under section 897(i) is treated as a domestic corporation for purposes of determining withholding obligations under section 1445, such a corporation is not subject to the requirement of section 1445(e)(2) that a foreign corporation withhold at the corporate capital gain rate from the gain recognized upon the distribution of a U.S. real property interest. Such a corporation is subject to the provisions of section 1445(e)(3). Thus, if interests in an electing corporation constitute U.S. real property interests, then the corporation is required to withhold with respect to the non-dividend distribution of any property to an interest-holder that is a foreign person. See § 1.1445-5(e). Dividend distributions (distributions that are described in section 301) shall be treated as provided in sections 897(f), 1441 and 1442. In addition, if interests in an electing foreign corporation do not constitute U.S. real property interests, then distributions by such corporation shall be treated as provided in sections 897(f) (if applicable), 1441 and 1442. Approved by the Office of Management and Budget under control number 545-0902. [Reg. § 1.1445-7.]

□ [*T.D.* 8113, 12-18-86.]

§ 1.1445-8. Special rules regarding publicly traded partnerships, publicly traded trusts and real estate investment trusts (REITS).—(a) *Entities to which this section applies.*—The rules of this section apply to—

(1) Any partnership or trust, interests in which are regularly traded on an established securities market (regardless of the number of its partners or beneficiaries), and

(2) Any REIT (regardless of the form of its organization).

For purposes of paragraph (a)(1) of this section, the rules of section 1445(e)(1) and this section shall not apply to a publicly traded partnership (as defined in section 7704) which is treated as a corporation under section 7704(a), or to those entities that are classified as "associations" and taxed as corporations. See § 301.7701-2.

(b) *Obligation to withhold.*—(1) *In general.*—An entity described in paragraph (a) of this section is not required to withhold under the provisions of § 1.1445-5(c), which states the withholding requirements of domestic partnerships, trusts and estates upon the disposition of U.S. real property interests. Except as otherwise provided in this paragraph (b), an entity described in paragraph (a) of this section shall be liable to withhold tax upon the distribution of any amount attributable to the disposition of a U.S. real property interest, with respect to each holder of an interest in the entity that is a foreign person. The amount to be withheld is described in paragraph (c) of this section.

(2) *Publicly traded partnerships.*—Publicly traded partnerships which comply with the withholding procedures under section 1446 will be deemed to have satisfied their withholding obligations under this paragraph (b).

(3) *Special rule for certain distributions to nominees.*—In the case of a person that—

(i) Is a nominee (as defined in paragraph (d) of this section),

(ii) Receives a distribution attributable to the disposition of a U.S. real property interest directly from an entity described in paragraph (a) of this section or indirectly from such entity through a nominee,

(iii) Receives the distribution for payment to any foreign person, or the account of any foreign person, and

(iv) Receives a qualified notice pursuant to paragraph (f) of this section,

then the obligation to withhold in accordance with the general rules of section 1445(e)(1) and this paragraph (b) shall be imposed solely on that person to the extent of the amount specified by the qualified notice. A person obligated to withhold by reason of this paragraph (b)(3) is referred to as a withholding agent.

(4) *Person designated to act for withholding agent.*—The rules stated in § 1.1441-7(b)(1) and (2) regarding a person designated to act for a withholding agent shall apply for purposes of this section.

(5) *Effect of withholding exemption granted under § 1.1441-4(f).*—A letter issued by a district director under the provisions of § 1.1441-4(f), which exempts a person from withholding under section 1441 or section 1442, shall also exempt that person from withholding under this paragraph (b), if—

(i) The letter identifies another person as the withholding agent for purposes of section 1441 or 1442, and

(ii) Such other person enters into a written agreement, with the district director who issued the letter, to be the withholding agent for purposes of this paragraph (b).

The exemption granted, and the corresponding withholding obligation imposed, by this paragraph (b)(5) shall apply with respect to the first distribution made after execution of the agreement described in the preceding sentence and shall continue to apply to all distributions made during the period in which the exemption granted under § 1.1441-4(f) is in effect.

(6) *Payment other than in money.*—The rule stated in § 1.1441-7(c) regarding payment other than in money shall apply for purposes of this section.

(c) *Amount to be withheld.*—(1) *Distribution from a publicly traded partnership or publicly traded trust.*—The amount to be withheld under this section with respect to a distribution by a publicly traded partnership or publicly traded trust shall be computed in the manner described in § 1.1445-5(c)(3)(ii) and (iii), subject to the rules of this section.

(2) *REITs.*—(i) *In general.*—The amount to be withheld with respect to a distribution by a REIT, under this section shall be equal to the highest rate specified in section 1445(e)(1) multiplied by the amount described in paragraph (c)(2)(ii) of this section.

(ii) *Amount subject to withholding.*—(A) *In general.*—Except as otherwise provided in paragraph (c)(2)(ii)(C) of this section, the amount subject to withholding is the amount of any distribution, determined with respect to each share or certificate of beneficial interest, designated by a REIT as a capital gain dividend, multiplied by the number of shares or certificates of beneficial interest owned by the foreign person. Solely for purposes of this paragraph, the largest amount of any distribution occurring after March 7, 1991 that could be designated as a capital gain dividend under section 857(b)(3)(C) shall be deemed to have been designated by a REIT as a capital gain dividend regardless of the amount actually designated.

(B) *Distribution attributable to net short-term capital gain from the disposition of a U.S. real property interest.*—[Reserved]

(C) *Designation of prior distribution as capital gain dividend.*—If a REIT makes an actual designation of a prior distribution, in whole or in part, as a capital gain dividend, such prior distribution shall not be subject to withholding under this section. Rather, a REIT must characterize and treat as a capital gain dividend distribution (solely for purposes of section 1445(e)(1)) each distribution, determined with respect to each share or certificate of beneficial interest, made on the day of, or any time subsequent to, such designation as a capital gain dividend until such characterized amounts equal the amount of the prior distribution designated as a capital gain dividend. The provisions of this paragraph shall not be applicable in any taxable year in which the REIT adopts a formal or informal resolution or plan of complete liquidation.

(iii) *Example.*—The following example illustrates the rules of paragraph (c)(2)(ii)(C) of this section.

In the first quarter of 1988, XYZ REIT makes a dividend distribution of $2X. In the second quarter of 1988, XYZ sells real property, recognizing a long term capital gain of $15X, and makes a dividend distribution of $5X. In the third quarter of 1988, XYZ makes a distribution of $3X. In the fourth quarter of 1988, XYZ sells real property recognizing a long term capital loss of $2X. Within 30 days after the close of the taxable year, XYZ designates a capital gain dividend for the year of $13X. It subsequently makes a fourth quarter distribution of $7X. Since XYZ has made an actual designation of prior distributions during the taxable year as capital gain dividends, withholding on those prior distributions will not be required. However, the REIT must characterize, solely for purposes of § 1445(e)(1), a total amount of $13X of dividend distributions as capital gain dividends. Therefore, the fourth quarter dividend distribution of $7X must be characterized as a capital gain dividend subject to withholding under this section. In addition, XYZ will be required to characterize an additional $6X of subsequent dividend distributions as capital gain dividends.

(d) *Definition of nominee.*—For purposes of this section, the term "nominee" means a domestic person that holds an interest in an entity described in paragraph (a) of this section on behalf of another domestic or foreign person.

(e) *Determination of non-foreign status by withholding agent.*—A withholding agent may rely on a certification of non-foreign status pursuant to § 1.1445-5(b)(3)(ii) to determine whether an interest holder is not a foreign person. Reliance on these documents will excuse the withholding agent from liability imposed under section 1445(e)(1) in the absence of actual knowledge that the interest holder is a foreign person. A withholding agent may also employ other means to determine the status of an interest holder, but, if the agent relies on such other means and the interest holder proves, in fact, to be a foreign person (or, is not a withholding qualified holder (as defined in § 1.1445-1(g)(11)) and therefore is not treated as a non-foreign person for purposes of withholding under section 1445), then the withholding agent is subject to any liability imposed pursuant to section 1445 and the regulations thereunder for failure to withhold. See also § 1.1445-5(b)(3)(ii)(B)(3) for the period during which a withholding agent may rely on a certification of non-foreign status submitted by a withholding qualified holder (as defined in § 1.1445-1(g)(11)), which applies under this paragraph (e).

(f) *Qualified notice.*—A qualified notice for purposes of paragraph (b)(3)(iv) of this section is a notice provided in the manner described in § 1.1446-4(b)(4) by a partnership, trust, or REIT regarding a distribution that is attributable to the disposition of a United States real property interest. In the case of a REIT, a qualified notice is only a notice of a distribution, all or any portion of which the REIT actually designates, or characterizes in accordance with paragraph (c)(2)(ii)(C) of this section, as a capital gain dividend in the manner described in § 1.1446-4(b)(4), with respect to each share or certificate of beneficial interest. A deemed designation under paragraph (c)(2)(ii)(A) of this section may not be the subject of a qualified notice under this paragraph (f). A person described in paragraph (b)(3) of this section is treated as receiving a qualified notice when the notice is provided in accordance with § 1.1446-4(b)(4).

(g) *Reporting and paying over withheld amounts.*—With respect to an amount withheld under this section, a withholding agent is not required to conform to the requirements of § 1.1445-5(b)(5) but is required to report and pay over to the Internal Revenue Service any amount required to be withheld pursuant to the rules and procedures of section 1461, the regulations thereunder and § 1.6302-2. Forms 1042 and 1042S are to be used for this purpose.

(h) *Early refund procedure not available.*—The early refund procedure set forth in § 1.1445-6(g) shall not apply to amounts withheld under the rules of this section. For adjustment of over-withheld amounts, see § 1.1461-4.

(i) *Liability upon failure to withhold.*—For rules regarding liability upon failure to withhold under § 1445(e) and this section, see § 1.1445-1(e).

(j) *Applicability dates.*—Paragraph (c)(2)(i) of this section applies to distributions on or after November 30, 2020. Paragraph (e) of this section applies with respect to distributions made on or after December 29, 2022. For distributions made before December 29, 2022, see § 1.1445-8(e) as contained in 26 CFR part 1, as revised April 1, 2021.

Paragraph (f) of this section applies to distributions made on or after January 1, 2022. For distributions made before January 1, 2022, see § 1.1445-8(f) as contained in 26 CFR part 1, revised as of April 1, 2020. [Reg. § 1.1445-8.]

☐ [*T.D.* 8321, 12-6-90. *Amended by T.D.* 8647, 12-20-95, *T.D.* 9926, 11-27-2020 *and T.D.* 9971, 12-28-2022.]

§ 1.1445-10T. Special rule for foreign governments (Temporary).—(a) This section provides a temporary regulation that, if and when adopted as a final regulation, will add a new paragraph (d)(6) to § 1.1445-2. Paragraph (b) of this section would then appear as paragraph (d) (6) of § 1.1445-2.

(b) *Foreign government.*—(1) *As transferor.*—A foreign government is subject to U.S. taxation under section 897 on the disposition of a U.S. real property interest except to the extent specifically otherwise provided in the regulations issued under section 892. A foreign government that disposes of a U.S. real property interest that is not subject to taxation as specifically provided by the regulations under section 892 may present a notice of nonrecognition treatment pursuant to paragraph (d)(2) of this section that specifically cites the provision of such regulation, and thereby avoids withholding by the transferee of the property. A foreign government that disposes of a U.S. real property interest or the transferee of the property may obtain a withholding certificate from the Internal Revenue Service that confirms the applicability of section 892, but neither is required to do so. Rules concerning the issuance of withholding certificates are provided in § 1.1445-3.

(2) *As transferee.*—A foreign government or international organization that acquires a U.S. real property interest is fully subject to section 1445 and the regulations thereunder. Therefore, such an entity is required to withhold tax upon the acquisition of a U.S. real property interest from a foreign person.

(c) *Effective date.*—The rules of this section shall be effective for transfers, exchanges, distributions and other dispositions occurring on or after June 6, 1988. [Temporary Reg. § 1.1445-10T.]

☐ [*T.D.* 8198, 5-4-88.]

§ 1.1445-11T. Special rules requiring withholding under § 1.1445-5 (Temporary).—(a) *Purpose and scope.*—This section provides temporary regulations that, if and when adopted as a final regulation, will add certain new paragraphs within § 1.1445-5(b) and (c). The paragraphs of this section would then appear as set forth below. Paragraph (b) of this section would then appear as paragraph (b)(8)(v) of § 1.1445-5. Paragraph (c) of this section would then appear as paragraph (c)(2)(i) of § 1.1445-5. Paragraph (d) of this section would then appear as paragraph (g) of § 1.1445-5.

(b) *Disposition of interests in partnerships, trusts, and estates.*—The provisions of section 1445(e)(5), requiring withholding upon certain dispositions of interests in partnerships, trusts, and estates, that own directly or indirectly a U.S. real property interest shall apply to dispositions on or after the effective date of a later Treasury decision under section 897(g) of the Code except in the case of dispositions of interests in partnerships in which fifty percent of the value of the gross assets consist of U.S. real property interests and ninety percent or more of the value of the gross assets consist of U.S. real property interests plus any cash or cash equivalents. The provisions of section 1445(e)(5), shall apply, however, to dispositions after June 6, 1988, of interests in partnerships in which fifty percent or more of the value of the gross assets consist of U.S. real property interests, and ninety percent or more of the value of the gross assets consist of U.S. real property interests plus any cash or cash equivalents. See paragraph (d) of this section.

(c) *Transactions covered elsewhere.*—No withholding is required under this paragraph (c) with respect to the distribution of a U.S. real property interest by a partnership, trust, or estate. Such distributions shall be subject to withholding under section 1445(e)(4) and paragraph (f) of this § 1.1445-5 on the effective date of a later Treasury decision published under section 897(g) of the Code. No withholding is required at this time for distributions described in the preceding sentence. See paragraph (b)(8)(iv) of this § 1.1445-5. No withholding is required under this paragraph with respect to the disposition of an interest in a trust, estate, or partnership except in the case of a partnership in which fifty percent or more of the value of the gross assets consist of U.S. real property interests, and ninety percent or more of the value of the gross assets consist of U.S. real property interests plus any cash or cash equivalents. See paragraph (b)(8)(v) of § 1.1445-5. Withholding shall be required as provided in section 1445(e)(5) and paragraph (g) of this section with respect to the disposition after June 6, 1988, of an interest in a partnership in which fifty percent or more of the value of the gross assets consist of U.S. real property interests, and ninety percent or more of the value of the gross assets consist of U.S. real property interests plus any cash or cash equivalents.

(d) *Dispositions of interests in partnerships, trusts, and estates.*—(1) *Withholding required on disposition of certain partnership interests.*—Withholding is required under section 1445(e)(5) and this paragraph with respect to the disposition by a foreign partner of an interest in a domestic or foreign partnership in which fifty percent or more of the value of the gross assets consist of U.S. real property interests, and ninety percent or more of the value of the gross assets consist of U.S. real property interests plus any cash or cash equivalents. For purposes of this paragraph cash equivalents means any asset readily convertible into cash (whether or not denominated in U.S. dollars), including, but not limited to, bank accounts, certificates of deposit, money market accounts, commercial paper, U.S. and foreign treasury obligations and bonds, corporate obligations and bonds, precious metals or commodities, and publicly traded instruments. The taxpayer on filing an income tax return for the year of the disposition may demonstrate the extent to which the gain on the disposition of the interest is not attributable to U.S. real property interests. A taxpayer is also permitted by § 1.1445-3 to apply for a withholding certificate in instances where reduced withholding is appropriate.

(2) *Withholding not required.*—(i) *Transferee receives statement that interest in partnership is not described in paragraph (d)(1).*—No withholding is required under paragraph (d)(1) of this section upon the disposition of a partnership interest otherwise described in that paragraph if the transferee is provided a statement, issued by the partnership and signed by a general partner under penalties of perjury no earlier than 30 days before the transfer, certifying that fifty percent or more of the value of the gross assets does not consist of U.S. real property interests, or that ninety percent or more of the value of the gross assets of the partnership does not consist of U.S. real property interests plus cash or cash equivalents.

(ii) *Reliance on statement not permitted.*—A transferee is not entitled to rely upon a statement described in paragraph (d)(2)(i) of this section if, prior to or at the time of the transfer, the transferee either—

(A) Has actual knowledge that the statement is false, or

(B) Receives a notice, pursuant to § 1.1445-4.

Such a transferee's withholding obligations shall apply as if the statement had never been given, and such a transferee may be held fully liable pursuant to § 1.1445-1(e) for any failure to withhold.

(iii) *Belated notice of false statement.*—If, after the date of the transfer, a transferee receives notice that a statement provided under paragraph (d)(2)(i) of this section is false, then such transferee may rely on the statement only with respect to consideration that was paid prior to the receipt of the notice. Such a transferee is required to withhold a full 10 percent of the amount realized from the consideration that remains to be paid to the transferor. Thus, if 10 percent or more of the amount realized remains to be paid to the transferor, then the transferee is required to withhold and pay over the full 10 percent. The transferee must do so by withholding and paying over the entire amount of each successive payment of consideration to the transferor, until the full 10 percent of the amount realized has been withheld and paid over. Amounts so withheld must be reported and paid over by the 20th day following the date on which each such payment of consideration is made. A transferee that is subject to the rules of this § 1.1445-10T(d)(2)(iii) may not obtain a withholding certificate pursuant to § 1.1445-3, but must instead withhold and pay over the amounts required by this paragraph.[1]

(e) *Effective date.*—The rules of this section are effective for transactions after June 6, 1988. [Temporary Reg. § 1.1445-11T.]

☐ [*T.D.* 8198, 5-4-88. *Amended by T.D.* 9751, 2-17-2016.]

[1] Section 324(a) of the Protecting Americans from Tax Hikes Act of 2015 (Public Law 114-113) increased the withholding rate under section 1445(e)(5) to 15 percent, applicable to dispositions after February 16, 2016.

§1.1446-1. Witholding tax on foreign partners' share of effectively connected taxable income.—(a) *In general.*—If a domestic or foreign partnership has effectively connected taxable income (ECTI) as computed under §1.1446-2 for any partnership tax year, and any portion of such taxable income is allocable under section 704 to a foreign partner, then the partnership must pay a withholding tax under section 1446 (1446 tax) at the time and in the manner prescribed in this section, and §§1.1446-2 through 1.1446-6.

(b) *Steps in determining 1446 tax obligation.*—In general, a partnership determines its 1446 tax as follows. The partnership determines whether it has any foreign partners in accordance with paragraph (c) of this section. If the partnership does not have any foreign partners (including any person presumed to be foreign under paragraph (c) of this section and any domestic trust treated as foreign under §1.1446-3(d)) during its taxable year, it generally will not have a 1446 tax obligation. If the partnership has one or more foreign partners, it then determines under §1.1446-2 whether it has ECTI any portion of which is allocable under section 704 to one or more of the foreign partners. If the partnership has ECTI allocable under section 704 to one or more of its foreign partners, the partnership computes its 1446 tax, pays over 1446 tax, and reports the amount paid in accordance with the rules in §1.1446-3. For special rules applicable to publicly traded partnerships, see §1.1446-4. For special rules applicable to tiered partnership structures, see §1.1446-5. For special rules that may apply in determining the amount of 1446 tax due with respect to a partner, see §1.1446-6.

(c) *Determining whether a partnership has a foreign partner.*—(1) *In general.*—Except as otherwise provided in this section, §1.1446-3, and §1.1446-5, only a partnership that has at least one foreign partner during the partnership's taxable year can have a 1446 tax liability. Generally, the term foreign partner means any partner of the partnership that is not a U.S. person within the meaning of section 7701(a)(30). Thus, a partner of the partnership is generally a foreign partner if the partner is a nonresident alien, foreign partnership (see §1.1446-5 for rules that allow a lower-tier partnership to look through an upper-tier foreign partnership to the partners of such partnership for purposes of computing its 1446 tax), foreign corporation (which includes a foreign government pursuant to section 892(a)(3)), foreign estate or trust (see paragraph (c) (2) of this section for rules that instruct a partnership to consider the grantor or other owner of a trust under subpart E of subchapter J as the partner for purposes of computing the partnership's 1446 tax), as those terms are defined under section 7701 and the regulations thereunder, or a foreign organization described in section 501(c), or other foreign person. A person also is a foreign partner if the person is presumed to be a foreign person under paragraph (c)(3) of this section. For purposes of this section, a partner that is treated as a U.S. person for all income tax purposes (by election or otherwise, see e.g., sections 953(d) and 1504(d)) will not be a foreign partner, provided the partner has provided the partnership a valid Form W-9, "Request for Taxpayer Identification Number and Certification," or the partnership uses other means to determine that the partner is not a foreign partner (see paragraph (c)(3) of this section). A partner that is treated as a U.S. person only for certain specified purposes is considered a foreign partner for purposes of section 1446, and a partnership must pay 1446 tax on the portion of ECTI allocable to that partner. For example, a partnership must generally pay 1446 tax on ECTI allocable to a foreign corporate partner that has made an election under section 897(i).

(2) *Submission of Forms W-8BEN, W-8IMY, W-8ECI, W-8EXP, and W-9.*—(i) *In general.*—Except as otherwise provided in this paragraph (c)(2) or paragraph (c)(3) of this section, a partnership must generally determine whether a partner is a foreign partner, and the partner's tax classification (e.g., corporate or non-corporate), by obtaining a withholding certificate from the partner that is a Form W-8BEN, "Certificate of Foreign Status of Beneficial Owner for United States Tax Withholding," Form W-8IMY, "Certificate of Foreign Intermediary, Flow-Through Entity, or Certain U.S. Branches for United States Tax Withholding," Form W-8ECI, "Certificate of Foreign Person's Claim for Exemption from Withholding on Income Effectively Connected With the Conduct of a Trade or Business in the United States," Form W-8EXP, "Certificate of Foreign Government or other Foreign Organization for United States Tax Withholding," or a Form W-9, as applicable, or an acceptable substitute form permitted under paragraph (c)(5) of this section. Generally, a foreign partner that is a nonresident alien, a foreign estate or trust (other than a grantor trust described in this paragraph (c) (2)), a foreign corporation, or a foreign government should provide a valid Form W-8BEN.

(ii) *Withholding certificate applicable to each type of partner.*—A partner that submits a valid Form W-8 (e.g., Form W-8BEN) for purposes of section 1441 or 1442 will generally satisfy the documentation requirements of this section provided that the submission of such form is not inconsistent with the rules of this paragraph (c)(2) or paragraph (c)(3) of this section. The following rules shall apply for purposes of this section.

(A) *U.S. person.*—A partner that is a U.S. person (other than a grantor trust described in this paragraph (c)(2)), including a domestic partnership and domestic simple or complex trust (including an estate), shall provide a valid Form W-9.

(B) *Nonresident alien.*—A Form W-8 (e.g., Form W-8BEN) submitted by a nonresident alien for purposes of withholding under section 1441 will generally be accepted for purposes of section 1446. If no such form is submitted for purposes of section 1441, such nonresident alien shall submit Form W-8BEN for purposes of section 1446.

(C) *Foreign partnership.*—A partner that is a foreign partnership generally shall provide a valid Form W-8IMY for purposes of section 1446. See §1.1446-5 (permitting a lower-tier partnership to look through an upper-tier foreign partnership in certain circumstances when computing 1446 tax).

(D) *Disregarded entities.*—An entity that is disregarded as an entity separate from its owner under §301.7701-3 of this chapter (whether domestic or foreign) shall not submit a Form W-8 (e.g., Form W-8BEN) or Form W-9. Instead, the owner of such entity for Federal tax purposes shall submit appropriate documentation to comply with this section. See §§301.7701-1 through 301.7701-3 of this chapter for determining the U.S. Federal tax classification of a partner.

(E) *Domestic and foreign grantor trusts.*—To the extent that a grantor or other person is treated as the owner of any portion of a trust under subpart E of subchapter J of the Internal Revenue Code, such trust shall provide documentation under this paragraph (c)(2) to identify the trust as a grantor trust and provide documentation on behalf of the grantor or other person treated as the owner of all or a portion of such trust as required by this paragraph (c)(2). If such trust is a foreign trust, the trust shall submit Form W-8IMY to the partnership identifying itself as a foreign grantor trust and shall provide such documentation (e.g., Forms W-8BEN, W-8IMY, W-8ECI, W-8EXP, or W-9) and information pertaining to its grantor or other owner to the partnership that permits the partnership to reliably associate (within the meaning of §1.1441-1(b)(2)(vii)) such portion of the trust's allocable share of partnership ECTI with the grantor or other person that is the owner of such portion of the trust. If such trust is a domestic trust, the trust shall furnish the partnership a statement under penalty of perjury that the trust is, in whole or in part, a domestic grantor trust and such statement shall identify that portion of the trust that is treated as owned by a grantor or another person under subpart E of subchapter J of the Internal Revenue Code. The trust shall also provide such documentation and information (e.g., Forms W-8BEN, W-8IMY, W-8ECI, W-8EXP, or W-9) pertaining to its grantor or other owner(s) to the partnership that permits the partnership to reliably associate (within the meaning of §1.1441-1(b)(2)(vii)) such portion of the trust's allocable share of partnership ECTI with the grantor or other person that is the owner of such portion of the trust.

(F) *Nominees.*—Where a nominee holds an interest in a partnership on behalf of another person, the beneficial owner of the partnership interest, not the nominee, shall submit a Form W-8 (e.g., Form W-8BEN) or Form W-9 to the partnership or nominee that is the withholding agent.

(G) *Foreign governments, foreign tax-exempt organizations and other foreign persons.*—A Form W-8 (e.g., Form W-8EXP) submitted by a partner that is a foreign government, foreign tax-exempt organization, or other foreign person for purposes of withholding under §§1441 through 1443 will also operate to establish the foreign status of such partner under this section. However, except as set forth in §1.1446-2(b)(4)(iii) (regardingwithholding qualified holders (as defined in §1.1445-1(g)(11)) and §1.1446-3(c)(3) (regarding certain tax-exempt organizations described in section 501(c)), the submission of Form W-8EXP (or successor) will have no effect on whether there is a 1446 tax due with respect to such partner's allocable share of partnership ECTI. For example, a partnership must still pay 1446 tax with respect to a foreign government partner's allocable share of ECTI because such partner is treated as a foreign corporation under section 892(a)(3). If no Form W-8 is submitted for purposes of withholding under sections 1441 through 1443, then such government, tax-exempt organization, or person must generally submit Form W-8BEN.

(H) *Foreign corporations, certain foreign trusts, and foreign estates.*—Consistent with the rules of this paragraph (c)(2) and paragraph (c)(3) of this section, a foreign corporation, a foreign trust (other than a foreign grantor trust described in paragraph (c)(2)(ii)(E) of this section), or a foreign estate may generally submit any appropriate Form W-8 (for example, Form W-8BEN-E or Form W-8IMY) to the partnership to establish its foreign status for purposes of section 1446. In addition, a foreign entity may also submit a certification of non-foreign status (including a Form W-8EXP) described in § 1.1445-5(b)(3)(ii) for purposes of documenting itself as a withholding qualified holder (as defined in § 1.1445-1(g)(11)).

(iii) *Effect of Forms W-8BEN, W-8IMY, W-8ECI, W-8EXP, W-9, and statement.*—(A) *Partnership reliance on withholding certificate.*—In general, for purposes of this section, a partnership may rely on a valid Form W-8 (e.g., Form W-8BEN) or Form W-9, or statement described in this paragraph (c)(2) from a partner, beneficial owner, or grantor trust to determine whether that person, beneficial owner, or the owner of a grantor trust, is a non-foreign or foreign partner for purposes of computing 1446 tax, and if such person is a foreign partner, to determine whether or not such person is a corporation for U.S. tax purposes. The rules of paragraph (c)(3) of this section shall apply to a partnership that receives a Form W-8IMY from a foreign grantor trust or a statement described in this paragraph (c)(2) from a domestic grantor trust, but does not receive a Form W-8 (e.g., Form W-8BEN) or Form W-9 identifying such grantor or other person. Further, a partnership may not rely on a Form W-8 or Form W-9, or statement described in this paragraph (c)(2), and such form or statement is therefore not valid for any installment period or Form 8804 filing date during which the partnership has actual knowledge or has reason to know that any information on the withholding certificate or statement is incorrect or unreliable and, if based on such knowledge or reason to know, the partnership should pay 1446 tax in an amount greater than would be the case if it relied on the certificate or statement.

(B) *Reason to know.*—A partnership has reason to know that information on a withholding certificate or statement is incorrect or unreliable if its knowledge of relevant facts or statements contained on the form or other documentation is such that a reasonably prudent person in the position of the withholding agent would question the claims made. See §§ 1.1441-1(e)(4)(viii) and 1.1441-7(b)(1) and (2).

(C) *Subsequent knowledge and impact on penalties.*—If the partnership does not have actual knowledge or reason to know that a Form W-8BEN, Form W-8IMY, Form W-8ECI, Form W-8EXP, Form W-9, or statement received from a partner, beneficial owner, or grantor trust contains incorrect or unreliable information, but it subsequently determines that the certificate or statement contains incorrect or unreliable information, and, based on such knowledge the partnership should pay 1446 tax in an amount greater than would be the case if it relied on the certificate or statement, then the partnership will not be subject to penalties for its failure to pay the 1446 tax in reliance on such certificate or statement for any installment payment date prior to the date that the determination is made. See §§ 1.1446-1(c)(4) and 1.1446-3 concerning penalties for failure to pay the withholding tax when a partnership knows or has reason to know that a withholding certificate or statement is incorrect or unreliable.

(iv) *Requirements for certificates to be valid.*—Except as otherwise provided in this paragraph (c), for purposes of this section, the validity of a Form W-9 shall be determined under section 3406 and § 31.3406(h)-3(e) of this chapter which establish when such form may be reasonably relied upon. A Form W-8BEN, Form W-8IMY, Form W-8ECI, or Form W-8EXP is only valid for purposes of this section if its validity period has not expired, the partner submitting the form has signed it under penalties of perjury, and it contains all the required information.

(A) *When period of validity expires.*—For purposes of this section, a Form W-8BEN, Form W-8IMY, Form W-8ECI, or Form W-8EXP submitted by a partner shall be valid until the end of the period of validity determined for such form under § 1.1441-1(e). With respect to a foreign partnership submitting Form W-8IMY, the period of validity of such form shall be determined under § 1.1441-1(e) as if such foreign partnership submitted the form required of a nonwithholding foreign partnership. See § 1.1441-1(e)(4)(ii).

(B) *Required information for Forms W-8BEN, W-8IMY, W-8ECI, and W-8EXP.*—Forms W-8BEN, W-8IMY, W-8ECI, and W-8EXP submitted under this section must contain the partner's name, permanent address and Taxpayer Identification Number (TIN), the country under the laws of which the partner is formed, incorporated or governed (if the person is not an individual), the classification of the partner for U.S. Federal tax purposes (e.g., partnership, corporation), and any other information required to be submitted by the forms or instructions for such form, as applicable.

(v) *Partner must provide new withholding certificate when there is a change in circumstances.*—The principles of § 1.1441-1(e)(4)(ii)(D) shall apply when a change in circumstances has occurred (including situations where the status of a U.S. person changes) that requires a partner to provide a new withholding certificate.

(vi) *Partnership must retain withholding certificates.*—A partnership or nominee who has responsibility for paying 1446 tax under this section or § 1.1446-4 must retain each withholding certificate, statement, and other information received from its direct and indirect partners for as long as it may be relevant to the determination of the withholding agent's 1446 tax liability under section 1461 and the regulations thereunder.

(3) *Presumptions in the absence of valid Form W-8BEN, Form W-8IMY, Form W-8ECI, Form W-8EXP, Form W-9, or statement.*—Except as otherwise provided in this paragraph (c)(3), a partnership that does not receive a valid Form W-8BEN, Form W-8IMY, Form W-8ECI, Form W-8EXP, Form W-9, or statement required by paragraph (c)(2) of this section from a partner, beneficial owner, or grantor trust, or a partnership that receives a withholding certificate or statement but has actual knowledge or reason to know that the information on the certificate or statement is incorrect or unreliable, must presume that the partner is a foreign person. Except as provided in § 1.1446-3(a)(2) and § 1.1446-5(c)(2), a partnership that knows that a partner is an individual shall treat the partner as a nonresident alien. Except as provided in § 1.1446-3(a)(2) and § 1.1446-5(c)(2), a partnership that knows that a partner is an entity shall treat the partner as a corporation if the entity is a corporation as defined in § 301.7701-2(b)(8) of this chapter. See § 1.1446-3(a)(2) which prohibits a partnership in certain circumstances from considering preferential tax rates in computing its 1446 tax when the presumption and rules of this paragraph (c)(3) apply. In all other cases, the partnership shall treat the partner as either a nonresident alien or a foreign corporation, whichever classification results in a higher 1446 tax being due, and shall pay the 1446 tax in accordance with this presumption. Except as provided in § 1.1446-5(c)(2), the presumption set forth in this paragraph (c)(3) that a partner is a foreign person shall not apply to the extent that the partnership relies on other means to ascertain the non-foreign status of a partner and the partnership is correct in its determination that such partner is a U.S. person. A partnership is in no event required to rely upon other means to determine the non-foreign status of a partner and may demand that a partner furnish an acceptable certificate under this section. If a certificate is not provided in such circumstances, the partnership may presume that the partner is a foreign partner, and for purposes of sections 1461 through 1463, will be considered to have been required to pay 1446 tax on such partner's allocable share of partnership ECTI.

(4) *Consequences when partnership knows or has reason to know that Form W-8BEN, Form W-8IMY, Form W-8ECI, Form W-8EXP, or Form W-9 is incorrect or unreliable and does not withhold.*—If a partnership has actual knowledge or has reason to know that a Form W-8BEN, Form W-8IMY, Form W-8ECI, Form W-8EXP, Form W-9, or statement required by paragraph (c)(2) of this section submitted by a partner, beneficial owner, or grantor trust contains incorrect or unreliable information (either because the certificate or statement when given to the partnership contained incorrect information or because there has been a change in facts that makes information on the certificate or statement incorrect), and the partnership pays less than the full amount of 1446 tax due on ECTI allocable to that partner, the partnership shall be fully liable under section 1461 and § 1.1461-3 (§ 1.1461-1 for publicly traded partnerships subject to § 1.1446-4) and § 1.1446-3, and for all applicable penalties and interest, for any failure to pay the 1446 tax for the period during which the partnership has such knowledge or reason to know that the certificate contained incorrect or unreliable information and for all subsequent installment periods. If a partner, beneficial owner, or grantor trust submits a new

valid Form W-8BEN, Form W-8IMY, Form W-8ECI, Form W-8EXP, Form W-9, or statement, as applicable, the partnership may rely on that documentation when paying 1446 tax (or any installment of such tax) for any payment date that has not passed at the time such form is received.

(5) *Acceptable substitute form.*—A partnership or withholding agent responsible for paying 1446 tax (or any installment of such tax) may substitute its own form for the official version of Form W-8 (e.g., Form W-8BEN) that is recognized under this section to ascertain the identity of its partners, provided such form is consistent with § 1.1441-1(e)(4)(vi). All references under this section or §§ 1.1446-2 through 1.1446-6 to a Form W-8 (e.g., Form W-8BEN, Form W-8IMY, Form W-8ECI, Form W-8EXP) shall include the acceptable substitute form recognized under this paragraph (c)(5). [Reg. § 1.1446-1.]

□ [*T.D. 9200, 5-13-2005. Amended by T.D. 9394, 4-28-2008 and T.D.* 9971, 12-28-2022.]

§ 1.1446-2. Determining a partnership's effectively connected taxable income allocable to foreign partners under section 704.—(a) *In general.*—A partnership's effectively connected taxable income (ECTI) is generally the partnership's taxable income as computed under section 703, with adjustments as provided in section 1446(c) and this section, and computed with consideration of only those partnership items which are effectively connected (or treated as effectively connected) with the conduct of a trade or business in the United States. For purposes of determining the section 1446 withholding tax (1446 tax) or any installment of such tax under § 1.1446-3, partnership ECTI allocable under section 704 to foreign partners is the sum of the allocable shares of ECTI of each of the partnership's foreign partners as determined under paragraph (b) of this section. See § 1.1446-6 (special rules permitting the partnership to consider partner-level deductions and losses to reduce the partnership's 1446 tax). The calculation of partnership ECTI allocable to foreign partners as set forth in paragraph (b) of this section and the partnership's withholding tax obligation are partnership-level computations solely for purposes of determining the 1446 tax. Therefore, any deduction that is not taken into account in calculating a partner's allocable share of partnership ECTI (e.g., percentage depletion), but which is a deduction that under U.S. tax law the foreign partner is otherwise entitled to claim, can still be claimed by the foreign partner when computing its U.S. tax liability and filing its U.S. income tax return, subject to any restriction or limitation that otherwise may apply.

(b) *Computation.*—(1) *In general.*—A foreign partner's allocable share of partnership ECTI for the partnership's taxable year that is allocable under section 704 to a particular foreign partner is equal to that foreign partner's distributive share of partnership gross income and gain for the partnership's taxable year that is effectively connected and properly allocable to the partner under section 704 and the regulations thereunder, reduced by the foreign partner's distributive share of partnership deductions for the partnership taxable year that are connected with such income under section 873(a) or 882(c) and properly allocable to the partner under section 704 and the regulations thereunder, in each case, after application of the rules of this section. See § 1.1446-6 (special rules permitting the partnership to consider partner-level deductions and losses to reduce the partnership's 1446 tax). For these purposes, a foreign partner's distributive share of effectively connected gross income and gain and the deductions connected with such income shall be computed by considering allocations that are respected under the rules of section 704 and § 1.704-1(b)(1), including special allocations in the partnership agreement (as defined in § 1.704-1(b)(2)(ii) (*h*)), and adjustments to the basis of partnership property described in section 743 pursuant to an election by the partnership under section 754 (see § 1.743-1(j)). The character of effectively connected partnership items (capital versus ordinary) shall be separately considered only to the extent set forth in paragraph (b)(3)(v) of this section and, when applicable, sections 1.1446-3(a)(2) (consideration of preferential rates when computing 1446 tax) and section 1.1446-6 (special rules permitting the partnership to consider partner-level deductions and losses to reduce the partnership's 1446 tax).

(2) *Income and gain rules.*—For purposes of computing a foreign partner's allocable share of partnership ECTI under this paragraph (b), the following rules shall apply with respect to partnership income and gain.

(i) *Application of the principles of section 864.*—The determination of whether a partnership's items of gross income are effectively connected shall be made by applying the principles of section 864 and the regulations thereunder.

(ii) *Income treated as effectively connected.*—A partnership's items of gross income that are effectively connected include any income that is treated as effectively connected income, including partnership income subject to a partner's election under section 871(d) or section 882(d), any partnership income treated as effectively connected with the conduct of a U.S. trade or business pursuant to section 897, and any other items of partnership income treated as effectively connected under another provision of the Internal Revenue Code, without regard to whether those amounts are taxable to the partner. A partner that makes the election under section 871(d) or section 882(d) shall furnish to the partnership a statement that indicates that such election has been made. See § 1.871-10(d)(3). If a partnership receives a valid Form W-8ECI from a partner, the partner is deemed, for purposes of section 1446, to have effectively connected income subject to withholding under section 1446 to the extent of the items identified on the form.

(iii) *Exempt income.*—A foreign partner's allocable share of partnership ECTI does not include income or gain exempt from U.S. tax by reason of a provision of the Internal Revenue Code. A foreign partner's allocable share of partnership ECTI also does not include income or gain exempt from U.S. tax by operation of any U.S. income tax treaty or reciprocal agreement. In the case of income excluded by reason of a treaty provision, such income must be derived by a resident of an applicable treaty jurisdiction, the resident must be the beneficial owner of the item, and all other requirements for benefits under the treaty must be satisfied. The partnership must have received from the partner a valid withholding certificate, that is, Form W-8BEN (see § 1.1446-1(c)(2)(iii) regarding when a Form W-8BEN is valid for purposes of this section), containing the information necessary to support the claim for treaty benefits required in the forms and instructions. In addition, for purposes of this section, the withholding certificate must contain the beneficial owner's taxpayer identification number.

(3) *Deductions and losses.*—For purposes of computing a foreign partner's allocable share of partnership ECTI under this paragraph (b), the following rules shall apply with respect to deductions and losses.

(i) *Oil and gas interests.*—The deduction for depletion with respect to oil and gas wells shall be allowed, but the amount of such deduction shall be determined without regard to sections 613 and 613A.

(ii) *Charitable contributions.*—The deduction for charitable contributions provided in section 170 shall not be allowed.

(iii) *Net operating losses and other suspended or carried losses.*—Except as provided in § 1.1446-6, the net operating loss deduction of any foreign partner provided in section 172 shall not be taken into account. Further, except as provided in § 1.1446-6, the partnership shall not take into account any suspended losses (e.g., losses in excess of a partner's basis in the partnership, see section 704(d)) or any capital loss carrybacks or carryovers available to a foreign partner.

(iv) *Interest deductions.*—The rules of this paragraph (b)(3)(iv) shall apply for purposes of determining the amount of interest expense that is allocable to income which is (or is treated as) effectively connected with the conduct of a trade or business for purposes of calculating a foreign partner's allocable share of partnership ECTI. In the case of a non-corporate foreign partner, the rules of § 1.861-9T(e)(7) shall apply. In the case of a corporate foreign partner, the rules of § 1.882-5 shall apply by treating the partnership as a foreign corporation and using the partner's pro-rata share of the partnership's assets and liabilities for these purposes. For these purposes, the rules governing elections under § 1.882-5(a)(7) shall be made at the partnership level.

(v) *Limitation on capital losses.*—Losses from the sale or exchange of capital assets allocable under section 704 to a partner shall be allowed only to the extent of gains from the sale or exchange of capital assets allocable under section 704 to such partner.

(vi) *Other deductions.*—No deduction shall be allowed for personal exemptions provided in section 151 or the additional itemized deductions for individuals provided in part VII of subchapter B of the Internal Revenue Code (section 211 and following).

(vii) *Limitations on deductions.*—Except as provided in §1.1446-6 and this paragraph (b)(3), any limitations on losses or deductions that apply at the partner level when determining ECTI allocable to a foreign partner shall not be taken into account.

(4) *Other rules.*—(i) *Exclusion of items allocated to U.S. partners.*—Except as provided in §1.1446-5(e), in computing partnership ECTI, the partnership shall not take into account any item of income, gain, loss, or deduction to the extent allocable to any partner that is not a foreign partner, as that term is defined in §1.1446-1(c).

(ii) *Partnership credits.*—See §1.1446-3(a) providing that the 1446 tax is computed without regard to a partner's distributive share of the partnership's tax credits.

(iii) *Special rule for qualified holders.*—With respect to a foreign partner that is a withholding qualified holder (as defined in §1.1445-1(g)(11)), the foreign partner's allocable share of partnership ECTI does not include gain or loss that is not taken into account under §1.897(l)-1(b) and that is not otherwise treated as effectively connected with a trade or business in the United States. The partnership must have received from the partner a valid certificate of non-foreign status (including a Form W-8EXP) described in §1.1445-2(b)(2)(i) or §1.1445-5(b)(3)(ii). See §1.1446-1(c)(2)(ii)(G) and (H) regarding documentation of withholding qualified holders.

(5) *Examples.*—The following examples illustrate the application of this section. In considering the examples, disregard the potential application of §1.1446-3(b)(2)(v)(F) (relating to the de minimis exception to paying 1446 tax). The examples are as follows:

Example 1. Limitation on capital losses. PRS partnership has two equal partners, A and B. A is a nonresident alien and B is a U.S. citizen. A provides PRS with a valid Form W-8BEN, and B provides PRS with a valid Form W-9. PRS has the following annualized tax items for the relevant installment period, all of which are effectively connected with its U.S. trade or business and are allocated equally between A and B: $100 of long-term capital gain, $400 of long-term capital loss, $300 of ordinary income, and $100 of ordinary deductions. Assume that these allocations are respected under section 704(b) and the regulations thereunder. Accordingly, A's allocable share of PRS's effectively connected items includes $50 of long-term capital gain, $200 of long-term capital loss, $150 of ordinary income, and $50 of ordinary deductions. In determining A's allocable share of partnership ECTI, the amount of the long-term capital loss that may be taken into account pursuant to paragraph (b)(3)(v) of this section is limited to A's allocable share of gain from the sale or exchange of capital assets. Accordingly, A's share of partnership ECTI allocable under section 704 pursuant to §1.1446-2 is $100 ($150 of ordinary income less $50 of ordinary deductions, plus $50 of capital gain less $50 of capital loss).

Example 2. Limitation on capital losses—special allocations. PRS partnership has two equal partners, A and B. A and B are both nonresident aliens. A and B each provide PRS with a valid Form W-8BEN. PRS has the following annualized tax items for the relevant installment period, all of which are effectively connected with its U.S. trade or business: $200 of long-term capital gain, $200 of long-term capital loss, and $400 of ordinary income. A and B have equal shares in the ordinary income, however, pursuant to the partnership agreement, capital gains and losses are subject to special allocations. The long-term capital gain is allocable to A, and the long-term capital loss is allocable to B. Assume that these allocations are respected under section 704(b) and the regulations thereunder. Pursuant to paragraph (b)(3)(v) of this section, A's allocable share of partnership ECTI under §1.1446-2 is $400 (consisting of $200 of ordinary income and $200 of long-term capital gain), and B's allocable share of partnership ECTI is $200 (consisting of $200 of ordinary income).

Example 3. Withholding tax obligation where partner has net operating losses. PRS partnership has two equal partners, FC, a foreign corporation, and DC, a domestic corporation. FC and DC provide a valid Form W-8BEN and Form W-9, respectively, to PRS. Both FC and PRS are on a calendar taxable year. PRS is engaged in the conduct of a trade or business in the United States and for its first installment period during its taxable year has $100 of annualized ECTI that is allocable to FC. As of the beginning of the taxable year, FC had an unused effectively connected net operating loss carryover in the amount of $300. FC's net operating loss carryover is not taken into account in determining FC's allocable share of partnership ECTI under §1.1446-2 and, absent the application of §1.1446-6 (permitting a foreign partner to certify deductions and losses reasonably expected to be available to reduce the partner's U.S. income tax liability on the effectively connected income or gain allocable from the partnership), is not considered in computing the 1446 tax installment payment due on behalf of FC. Accordingly, PRS must pay 1446 tax with respect to the $100 of ECTI allocable to FC.

[Reg. §1.1446-2.]

☐ [*T.D. 9200, 5-13-2005. Amended by T.D. 9394, 4-28-2008 and T.D. 9971, 12-28-2022.*]

§1.1446-3. Time and manner of calculating and paying over the 1446 tax.—(a) *In general.*—(1) *Calculating 1446 tax.*—This section provides rules for calculating, reporting, and paying over the section 1446 withholding tax (1446 tax). A partnership's 1446 tax equals the amount determined under this section and shall be paid in installments during the partnership's taxable year (see paragraph (d)(1) of this section for installment payment due dates), with any remaining tax due paid with the partnership's annual return required to be filed pursuant to paragraph (d) of this section. For these purposes, a partnership shall not take into account either a partner's liability for any other tax imposed under any other provision of the Internal Revenue Code (e.g., section 55 or 884) or a partner's distributive share of the partnership's tax credits when determining the amount of the partnership's 1446 tax.

(2) *Applicable percentage.*—(i) *In general.*—Except as provided in this paragraph (a)(2), in the case of a foreign partner that is a corporation for U.S. tax purposes, the applicable percentage is the highest rate of tax specified in section 11(b) for such taxable year. Except as provided in this paragraph (a)(2) and §1.1446-5, in the case of a foreign partner that is not a corporation for U.S. tax purposes (e.g., a partnership, individual, trust or estate), the applicable percentage is the highest rate of tax specified in section 1.

(ii) *Special types of income or gain.*—Except as otherwise provided, a partnership is permitted to consider as the applicable percentage under this paragraph (a)(2) the highest rate of tax applicable to a particular type of income or gain allocable to a partner (e.g., long-term capital gain allocable to a non-corporate partner, unrecaptured section 1250 gain, collectibles gain under section 1(h)), to the extent of a partner's allocable share of such income or gain. Consideration of the highest rate of tax applicable to a particular type of income or gain under the previous sentence shall be made without regard to the amount of such partner's income. A partnership is not permitted to consider the highest rate of tax applicable to a particular type of income or gain under this paragraph (a)(2)(ii) if the application of the preferential rate depends upon the corporate or non-corporate status of the person reporting the income or gain and, either no documentation has been provided to the partnership under §1.1446-1 to establish the corporate or non-corporate status of the partner required to pay tax on the income or gain, or the partnership is otherwise required to compute and pay 1446 tax on such portion of the income or gain using the highest applicable percentage under section 1446(b). See e.g., §§1.1446-1(c)(3) (presumption of foreign status in the absence of documentation) and 1.1446-5(c)(2) (requirement to pay 1446 tax at higher of rates in section 1446(b) where a lower-tier partnership cannot reliably associate income with a partner of the upper-tier partnership).

(b) *Installment payments.*—(1) *In general.*—Except as provided in §1.1446-4 for certain publicly traded partnerships, a partnership must pay its 1446 tax by making installment payments of the 1446 tax based on the amount of partnership effectively connected taxable income (ECTI) allocable under section 704 to its foreign partners, without regard to whether the partnership makes any distributions to its partners during the partnership's taxable year. The amount of the installment payments is determined in accordance with this paragraph (b), and the tax must be paid at the times set forth in paragraph (d) of this section. Subject to paragraphs (b)(2)(v) and (b)(3)(ii) of this section, in computing its first installment of 1446 tax for a taxable year, a partnership must decide whether it will pay its 1446 tax for the entire taxable year by using the safe harbor set forth in paragraph (b)(3)(i) of this section, or by using one of several annualization methods available under paragraph (b)(2)(ii) of this section for computing partnership ECTI allocable to foreign partners. In the case of a partnership's underpayment of an installment of 1446 tax, the partnership shall be subject to an addition to the tax equal to the amount determined under section 6655, as modified by this section, as if such partnership were a corporation, as well as any other applicable interest and penalties. See §1.1446-3(f). Section 6425 (permitting an adjustment for an overpayment of estimated tax by a corporation) shall not apply to a partnership's payment of its 1446 tax.

(2) *Calculation.*—(i) *Application of the principles of section 6655.*—(A) *In general.*—Installment payments of 1446 tax required during the partnership's taxable year are based upon partnership ECTI for the portion of the partnership taxable year to which the payments relate, and, except as set forth in this paragraph (b)(2) or paragraph (b)(3) of this section, shall be calculated using the principles of section 6655. The principles of section 6655, except as otherwise provided in § 1.6655-2, are applied to annualize the partnership's items of effectively connected income, gain, loss, and deduction to determine each foreign partner's allocable share of partnership ECTI. Each foreign partner's allocable share of partnership ECTI is then multiplied by the relevant applicable percentage for the type of income allocable to the foreign partner under paragraph (a)(2) of this section. The respective 1446 tax amounts are then added for each foreign partner to yield an annualized 1446 tax with respect to such partner. The installment of 1446 tax due with respect to a foreign partner equals the excess of the section 6655(e)(2)(B)(ii) percentage of the annualized 1446 tax for that partner (or, if applicable, the adjusted seasonal amount) for the relevant installment period, over the aggregate amount of 1446 tax installment payments previously paid with respect to that partner during the partnership's taxable year. The partnership's total 1446 tax installment payment equals the sum of the installment payments due for such period on behalf of all the partnership's foreign partners.

(B) *Calculation rules when certificates are submitted under § 1.1446-6.*—*(1)* To the extent applicable, in computing the 1446 tax due with respect to a foreign partner, a partnership may consider a certificate received from such partner under § 1.1446-6(c)(1)(i) or (ii) and the amount of state and local taxes permitted to be considered under § 1.1446-6(c)(1)(iii). For the purposes of applying this paragraph (b)(2)(i)(B), a partnership shall first annualize the partner's allocable share of the partnership's items of effectively connected income, gain, deduction, and loss before—

(i) Considering under § 1.1446-6(c)(1)(i) the partner's certified deductions and losses;

(ii) Determining under § 1.1446-6(c)(1)(ii) whether the 1446 tax otherwise due with respect to that partner is less than $1,000 (determined with regard to any certified deductions or losses); or

(iii) Considering under § 1.1446-6(c)(1)(iii) the amount of state and local taxes withheld and remitted on behalf of the partner.

(2) The amount of the limitation provided in § 1.1446-6(c)(1)(i)(C) shall be based on the partner's allocable share of these annualized amounts. For any installment period in which the partnership considers a partner's certificate, the partnership must also consider the following events to the extent they occur prior to the due date for paying the 1446 tax for such installment period—

(i) The receipt of an updated certificate or status update from the partner under § 1.1446-6(c)(2)(ii)(B) certifying an amount of deductions or losses that is less than the amount reflected on the superseded certificate (see § 1.1446-6(e)(2) *Example 4*);

(ii) The failure to receive an updated certificate or status update from the partner that should have been provided under § 1.1446-6(c)(2)(ii)(B); and

(iii) The receipt of a notification from the IRS under § 1.1446-6(c)(3) or (5) (see § 1.1446-6(e)(2) *Example 5*).

(ii) *Annualization methods.*—A partnership that decides to annualize its income for the taxable year shall use one of the annualization methods set forth in section 6655(e) and the regulations thereunder, and as described in the forms and instructions for Form 8804, "Annual Return for Partnership Withholding Tax (Section 1446)," Form 8805, "Foreign Partner's Information Statement of Section 1446 Withholding Tax," and Form 8813, "Partnership Withholding Tax Payment Voucher."

(iii) *Partner's estimated tax payments.*—In computing its installment payments of 1446 tax, a partnership may not take into account a partner's estimated tax payments.

(iv) *Partner whose interest terminates during the partnership's taxable year.*—If a partner's interest in the partnership terminates prior to the end of the partnership's taxable year, the partnership shall take into account the income that is allocable to the partner for the portion of the partnership taxable year that the person was a partner.

(v) *Exceptions and modifications to the application of the principles under section 6655.*—To the extent not otherwise modified in §§ 1.1446-1 through 1.1446-7 or inconsistent with those rules, the principles of section 6655 apply to the calculation of the installment payments of 1446 tax made by a partnership as set forth in this paragraph (b)(2)(v).

(A) *Inapplicability of special rules for large corporations.*—The principles of section 6655(d)(2), concerning large corporations (as defined in section 6655(g)(2)), shall not apply.

(B) *Inapplicability of special rules regarding early refunds.*—The principles of section 6655(h), applicable to amounts excessively credited or refunded under section 6425, shall not apply. See paragraph (b)(1) of this section providing that section 6425 shall not apply for purposes of the 1446 tax. This paragraph (b)(2)(v)(B) shall apply to 1446 tax paid by a partnership or nominee, as well as to amounts that a partner is deemed to have paid for estimated tax purposes by reason of the partnership's or nominee's 1446 tax payments under § 1.1446-3(d)(1)(i).

(C) *Period of underpayment.*—The period of the underpayment set forth in section 6655(b)(2) shall end on the earlier of the date the partnership is required to file Form 8804 (as provided in paragraph (d)(1)(iii) of this section and without regard to extensions), or with respect to any portion of the underpayment, the date on which such portion is paid.

(D) *Other taxes.*—Section 6655 shall be applied without regard to any references to alternative minimum taxable income and modified alternative minimum taxable income.

(E) *1446 tax treated as tax under section 11.*—The principles of section 6655(g)(1) shall be applied to treat the 1446 tax as a tax imposed by section 11, and any partnership required to pay such tax shall be treated as a corporation.

(F) *Application of section 6655(f).*—A partnership subject to section 1446 shall apply section 6655(f) after aggregating the 1446 tax due (or any installment of such tax) for all its foreign partners. See § 1.1446-6(c)(1)(ii) for an exception to this rule when a nonresident alien partner certifies to the partnership that the partnership investment is the nonresident alien partner's only activity giving rise to effectively connected items.

(G) *Application of section 6655(i).*—If a partnership has a taxable year of less than 12 months, the partnership is required to pay 1446 tax (including installments of such tax) in accordance with this section § 1.1446-3, if the partnership has ECTI allocable under section 704 to foreign partners. In such a case, the partnership shall adjust its installment payments of 1446 tax in a reasonable manner (e.g., the annualized amounts of ECTI estimated to be allocable to a foreign partner, and the section 6655(e)(2)(B)(ii) percentage to be applied to each installment) to account for the short-taxable year. However, if the partnership's taxable year is a period of less than 4 months, the partnership shall not be required to make installment payments of 1446 tax, but will only be required to file Forms 8804 and 8805 in accordance with this section § 1.1446-3, and report and pay the appropriate 1446 tax for the short-taxable year.

(H) *Current year tax safe harbor.*—The safe harbor set forth in section 6655(d)(1)(B)(i) shall apply to a partnership subject to section 1446.

(I) *Prior year tax safe harbor.*—The safe harbor set forth in section 6655(d)(1)(B)(ii) shall not apply and instead the safe harbor set forth in paragraph (b)(3) of this section applies.

(3) *1446 tax safe harbor.*—(i) *In general.*—The addition to tax under section 6655 shall not apply to a partnership with respect to a current installment of 1446 tax if—

(A) The average of the amount of the current installment and prior installments during the taxable year is at least 25 percent of the total 1446 tax (without regard to § 1.1446-6) for the prior taxable year;

(B) The prior taxable year consisted of twelve months;

(C) The partnership timely files (including extensions) an information return under section 6031 for the prior year; and

(D) The amount of ECTI for the prior taxable year is not less than 50 percent of the ECTI shown on the annual return of section 1446 withholding tax that is (or will be) timely filed for the current year.

(ii) *Permission to change to standard annualization method.*—Except as otherwise provided in this paragraph (b)(3)(ii), if a partnership decides to pay its 1446 tax for the first installment period based upon the safe harbor method set forth in paragraph (b)(3)(i), the partnership must use the safe harbor method for each installment payment made during the partnership's taxable year. Notwithstanding the previous sentence, if a partnership paying over 1446 tax during the taxable year pursuant to this paragraph (b)(3) determines during an installment period (based upon the standard option annualization method set forth in section 6655(e) and the regulations thereunder, as modified by the forms and instructions to Forms 8804, 8805, and 8813) that it will not qualify for the safe harbor in this paragraph (b)(3) because the prior year's ECTI will not meet the 50-percent threshold in paragraph (b)(3)(i)(D) of this section, then the partnership is permitted, without being subject to the addition to the tax under section 6655 (as applied through this section), to pay over its 1446 tax for the period in which such determination is made, and all subsequent installment periods during the taxable year, using the standard option annualization method. A change pursuant to this paragraph shall be disclosed in a statement attached to the Form 8804 the partnership files for the taxable year and shall include information to allow the IRS to determine whether the change was appropriate.

(c) *Coordination with other withholding rules.*—(1) *Fixed or determinable, annual or periodical income.*—Fixed or determinable, annual or periodical income subject to tax under section 871(a) or section 881 is not subject to withholding under section 1446, and such income is subject to the withholding requirements of sections 1441 and 1442 and the regulations thereunder.

(2) *Real property gains.*—(i) *Domestic partnerships.*—Except as otherwise provided in this paragraph (c)(2), a domestic partnership that is otherwise subject to the withholding requirements of sections 1445 and 1446 will be subject to the payment and reporting requirements of section 1446 only and not section 1445(e)(1) and the regulations thereunder, with respect to partnership gain from the disposition of a U.S. real property interest (as defined in section 897(c)). A partnership that has complied with the requirements of section 1446 will be deemed to satisfy the withholding requirements of section 1445 and the regulations thereunder. However, a domestic partnership that would otherwise be exempt from section 1445 withholding by operation of a nonrecognition provision must continue to comply with the requirements of § 1.1445-5(b)(2). In the event that amounts are withheld under section 1445(e) at the time of the disposition of a U.S. real property interest, such amounts may be credited against the partnership's 1446 tax. A partnership that fails to comply fully with the requirements of section 1446 pursuant to this paragraph (c)(2) shall be liable for any unpaid 1446 tax and subject to any applicable addition to the tax, interest, and penalties under section 1446. See § 1.1446-4(f)(4) for rules coordinating the withholding liability of publicly traded partnerships under sections 1445 and 1446.

(ii) *Foreign partnerships.*—A foreign partnership that is subject to withholding under section 1445(a) during its taxable year may credit the amount withheld under section 1445(a) against its section 1446 tax liability for that taxable year only to the extent such amount is allocable to foreign partners.

(3) *Coordination with section 1443.*—A partnership that has ECTI allocable under section 704 to a foreign organization described in section 501(c) shall be required to pay 1446 tax on such ECTI only to the extent such ECTI is includible under section 512 and section 513 in computing the organization's unrelated business taxable income. The certificate procedure available under § 1.1441-9(b)(1) by which a partner may set forth the amounts it believes will and will not be includible in its computation of unrelated business taxable income under section 512 and section 513 shall also apply to a partner in a partnership subject to section 1446. Such certificate shall be made by a partner in the same manner as under § 1.1441-9(b)(2). A partnership that determines that the partner's certificate as to certain partnership items is unreliable or lacking must presume, consistent with § 1.1441-9(b)(3) (regarding amounts includible under section 512 in computing the organization's unrelated business taxable income), that such partnership items would be includible in computing the partner's UBTI.

(4) *Coordination with section 1446(f).*—A partnership that is directly or indirectly subject to withholding under section 1446(f)(1) during its taxable year may credit the amount withheld under section 1446(f)(1) against its section 1446 tax liability for that taxable year only to the extent the amount is allocable to foreign partners.

(d) *Reporting and crediting the 1446 tax.*—(1) *Reporting 1446 tax.*—This paragraph (d) sets forth the rules for reporting and crediting the 1446 tax paid by a partnership. To the extent that 1446 tax is paid on ECTI allocable to a domestic trust (including a grantor or other person treated as an owner of a portion of such trust) or a grantor or other person treated as the owner of a portion of a foreign trust, the rules of this paragraph (d) applicable to a foreign trust or its beneficiaries shall be applied to such domestic or foreign trust and its beneficiaries or owners, as applicable, so that appropriate credit for the 1446 tax may be claimed by the trust, beneficiary, grantor, or other person.

(i) *Reporting of installment tax payments and notification to partners of installment tax payments.*—Each partnership required to make an installment payment of 1446 tax must file Form 8813, "Partnership Withholding Tax Payment Voucher (Section 1446)," in accordance with the instructions to that form. Form 8813 is generally used to transmit an installment payment of 1446 tax to the IRS with respect to partnership ECTI estimated to be allocated to foreign partners. However, see § 1.1446-6(d)(3) (relating to circumstances where a partnership must file Form 8813 when no payment is required under section 1446). Except as provided in this section, a partnership must notify each foreign partner of the 1446 tax paid on the partner's behalf when the partnership makes an installment payment of 1446 tax. The notice required to be given to a foreign partner under the previous sentence must be provided within 10 days of the installment payment due date, or, if paid later, the date such installment payment is made. A foreign partner generally may credit an installment of 1446 tax paid by the partnership on the partner's behalf against the partner's estimated tax that the partner must pay during the partner's own taxable year. See § 1.1446-5(b) (relating to tiered partnership structures). However, a foreign partner may not obtain an early refund of such amounts under the estimated tax rules. See § 1.1446-3(b)(2)(v)(B). See paragraph (d)(2) of this section for the amount of 1446 tax a partner may credit against its U.S. income tax liability. No particular form is required for a partnership's notification to a foreign partner, but each notification must include the partnership's name, the partnership's Taxpayer Identification Number (TIN), the partnership's address, the partner's name, the partner's TIN, the partner's address, the annualized ECTI estimated to be allocated to the foreign partner (or prior year's safe harbor amount, if applicable), and the amount of tax paid on behalf of the partner for both the current and any prior installment periods during the partnership's taxable year. Notwithstanding any other provision of this paragraph (d), a withholding agent is not required to notify a partner of an installment of 1446 tax paid on the partner's behalf, unless requested by the partner, if—

(A) The partnership's agent responsible for providing notice pursuant to this paragraph is the same person that acts as an agent of the foreign partner for purposes of filing the partner's U.S. Federal income tax return for the partner's taxable year that includes the installment payment date; or

(B) The partnership has at least 500 foreign partners and the total 1446 tax that the partnership determines will be required to be paid for the partnership taxable year on behalf of such partner (based on paragraph (b)(2)(ii) or (3) of this section) with respect to the partner's allocable share of ECTI is less than $1,000.

(ii) *Payment due dates.*—The 1446 tax is calculated based on partnership ECTI allocable under section 704 to foreign partners during the partnership's taxable year, as determined under section 706. Installment payments of the 1446 tax generally must be made during the partnership's taxable year in which such income is derived. A partnership must pay to the Internal Revenue Service a portion of its estimated annual 1446 tax in installments on or before the 15th day of the fourth, sixth, ninth, and twelfth months of the partnership's taxable year as provided in section 6655. Any additional amount determined to be due is to be paid with the filing of the annual return of tax required under paragraph (d)(1)(iii) of this section and clearly designated as for the prior taxable year. Form 8813 should not be submitted for a payment made under the preceding sentence.

(iii) *Annual return and notification to partners.*—Every partnership (except a publicly traded partnership subject to § 1.1446-4) that has effectively connected gross income for the partnership's taxable year allocable under section 704 to one or more of its foreign partners (or is treated as having paid 1446 tax under § 1.1446-5(b)), must file Form 8804, "Annual Return for Partnership Withholding Tax (Section 1446)." Additionally, every partnership that is required to file Form 8804 also must file Form 8805, "Foreign Partner's Information Statement of Section 1446 Withholding Tax," for each of its foreign partners on whose behalf it paid 1446 tax, and furnish Form 8804 and the Forms 8805 to the Internal Revenue Service and the respective Form 8805 to each of its partners. Notwithstanding the previous sentence, a partnership that considers a foreign partner's certificate under § 1.1446-6 when computing its 1446 tax on Form 8804 is required to furnish such partner and the Internal Revenue Service a Form 8805, even if the form submitted to the partner shows no payment of 1446 tax on behalf of the partner. Forms 8804 and 8805 are separate from Form 1065, "U.S. Return of Partnership Income," and the attachments thereto, and are not to be filed as part of the partnership's Form 1065. A partnership must generally file Forms 8804 and 8805 on or before the due date for filing the partnership's Form 1065. See § 1.6031(a)-1(c) for rules concerning the due date of a partnership's Form 1065. However, with respect to partnerships described in § 1.6081-5(a)(1), Forms 8804 and 8805 are not due until the 15th day of the sixth month following the close of the partnership's taxable year.

(iv) *Information provided to beneficiaries of foreign trusts and estates.*—A foreign trust or estate that is a partner in a partnership subject to withholding under section 1446 shall be provided Form 8805 by the partnership. The foreign trust or estate must provide to each of its beneficiaries a copy of the Form 8805 furnished by the partnership. In addition, the foreign trust or estate must provide a statement for each of its beneficiaries to inform each beneficiary of the amount of the credit that may be claimed under section 33 (as determined under this section) for the 1446 tax paid by the partnership. Until an official Internal Revenue Service form is available, the statement from a foreign trust or estate that is described in this paragraph (d)(1)(iv) shall contain the following information—

(A) Name, address, and TIN of the foreign trust or estate;

(B) Name, address, and TIN of the partnership;

(C) The amount of the partnership's ECTI allocated to the foreign trust or estate for the partnership taxable year (as shown on the Form 8805 provided to the trust or estate);

(D) The amount of 1446 tax paid by the partnership on behalf of the foreign trust or estate (as shown on Form 8805 to the trust or estate);

(E) Name, address, and TIN of the beneficiary of the foreign trust or estate;

(F) The amount of the partnership's ECTI allocated to the trust or estate for purposes of section 1446 that is to be included in the beneficiary's gross income; and

(G) The amount of 1446 tax paid by the partnership on behalf of the foreign trust or estate that the beneficiary is entitled to claim on its return as a credit under section 33.

(v) *Attachments required of foreign trusts and estates.*—The statement furnished to each foreign beneficiary under this paragraph (d)(1) must also be attached to the foreign trust or estate's U.S. Federal income tax return filed for the taxable year that includes the installment periods to which the statement relates.

(vi) *Attachments required of beneficiaries of foreign trusts and estates.*—The beneficiary of the foreign trust or estate must attach the statement provided by the trust or estate pursuant to paragraph (d)(1)(iv) of this section, along with a copy of the Form 8805 furnished by the partnership to such trust or estate, to its U.S. income tax return for the year in which it claims a credit for the 1446 tax. See § 1.1446-3(d)(2)(ii) for additional rules regarding a partner or beneficial owner claiming a credit for the 1446 tax.

(vii) *Information provided to beneficiaries of foreign trusts and estates that are partners in certain publicly traded partnerships.*—A statement similar to the statement required by paragraph (d)(1)(iv) of this section shall be provided by trusts or estates that hold interests in publicly traded partnerships subject to § 1.1446-4.

(2) *Crediting 1446 tax against a partner's U.S. tax liability.*—(i) *In general.*—A partnership's payment of 1446 tax on the portion of ECTI allocable to a foreign partner generally relates to the partner's U.S. income tax liability for the partner's taxable year in which the partner is subject to U.S. tax on that income. Subject to paragraphs (d)(2)(ii) and (iii) of this section, a partner may claim as a credit under section 33 the 1446 tax paid by the partnership with respect to ECTI allocable to that partner. The partner may not claim an early refund of these amounts under the estimated tax rules. See paragraph (d)(1)(i) of this section regarding a partner's ability to credit an installment of 1446 tax paid on the partner's behalf against the partner's estimated tax payments due for the taxable year. See also § 1.1446-5(b) (relating to tiered partnership structures).

(ii) *Substantiation for purposes of claiming the credit under section 33.*—A partner may credit the amount paid under section 1446 with respect to such partner against its U.S. income tax liability only if it attaches proof of payment to its U.S. income tax return for the partner's taxable year in which the items comprising such partner's allocable share of partnership ECTI are included in the partner's income. Except as provided in the next sentence, proof of payment consists of a copy of the Form 8805 the partnership provides to the partner (or in the case of a beneficiary of a foreign trust or estate, the statement required under paragraph (d)(1)(iv) or (vii) of this section to be provided by such trust or estate and a copy of the related Form 8805 furnished to such trust or estate), but only if the name and TIN on the Form 8805 (or the statement provided by a foreign trust or estate) match the name and TIN on the partner's U.S. tax return, and such form (or statement) identifies the partner (or beneficiary) as the person entitled to the credit under section 33. In the case of a partner of a publicly traded partnership that is subject to withholding on distributions under § 1.1446-4, proof of payment consists of a copy of the Form 1042-S, "Foreign Person's U.S. Source Income Subject to Withholding," provided to the partner by the partnership.

(iii) *Special rules for apportioning the tax credit under section 33.*—(A) *Foreign trusts and estates.*—Section 1446 tax paid on the portion of ECTI allocable under section 704 to a foreign trust or estate that the foreign trust or estate may claim as a credit under section 33 shall bear the same ratio to the total 1446 tax paid on behalf of the trust or estate as the total ECTI allocable to such trust or estate and not distributed (or treated as distributed) to the beneficiaries of such trust or estate, and, accordingly not deducted under section 651 or section 661 in calculating the trust or estate's taxable income, bears to the total ECTI allocable to such trust or estate. The 1446 tax that a foreign trust or estate is not entitled to claim as a credit under this paragraph (d)(2) may be claimed as a credit by the beneficiary of such trust or estate that includes the partnership ECTI allocated to the trust or estate in gross income under section 652 or section 662 (whether distributed or deemed to be distributed and with the same character as effectively connected income as in the hands of the trust or estate). In the case of a foreign trust or estate with multiple beneficiaries, each beneficiary may claim a portion of the 1446 tax that may be claimed by all beneficiaries under the previous sentence as a credit in the same proportion as the amount of ECTI included in such beneficiary's gross income bears to the total amount of ECTI included by all beneficiaries. The trust or estate must provide each beneficiary with a copy of the Form 8805 provided to it by the partnership and prepare the statement required by paragraph (d)(1)(iv) of this section.

(B) *Use of domestic trusts to circumvent section 1446.*—This paragraph (d)(2)(iii)(B) shall apply if a partnership knows or has reason to know that a foreign person holds its interest in the partnership through a domestic trust, and such domestic trust was formed or availed of with a principal purpose of avoiding the 1446 tax. The use of a domestic trust may have a principal purpose of avoiding the 1446 tax even though the tax avoidance purpose is outweighed by other purposes when taken together. In such case, a partnership is required to pay 1446 tax under this paragraph as if the domestic trust was a foreign trust for purposes of section 1446 and the regulations thereunder. Accordingly, all applicable additions to the tax, interest, and penalties shall apply to the partnership for its failure to pay 1446 tax under this paragraph (d)(2)(iii)(B), commencing with the installment period during which the partnership knows or has reason to know that this paragraph (d)(2)(iii)(B) applies. A publicly traded partnership within the meaning of § 1.1446-4 (or a nominee required to pay 1446 tax under § 1.1446-4) will not be considered to know or have reason to know a domestic trust is being used to avoid the 1446 tax under this paragraph (d)(2)(iii)(B), provided the interest held in such entity by the domestic trust is publicly traded.

(iv) *Refunds to withholding agent.*—A withholding agent (i.e., the partnership) may obtain a refund of the 1446 tax paid (or deemed paid under § 1.1446-5(b)) to the extent of the excess of the amount paid to the Internal Revenue Service by the partnership, over the partnership's section 1446 tax liability as determined by the sum of the total tax creditable to each partner indicated on all Forms 8805 for the taxable year. If a partnership issues Form 8805 to a partner, then the partnership may not claim a refund for any amount of tax shown on that form as paid on behalf of the partner. If a partnership incorrectly withholds upon a United States person under section 1446 of the Internal Revenue Code and issues a Form 8805 to that person, the partnership may not file for a refund of the amount incorrectly withheld. Instead, the United States person may file for a refund of that amount on its annual return. For rules concerning refunds to withholding agents who pay 1446 tax on distributions of effectively connected income or gain under § 1.1446-4 (i.e., publicly traded partnerships or nominees), see § 1.1464-1.

(v) *1446 tax treated as cash distribution to partners.*—Except as otherwise provided in this paragraph (d)(2)(v), a partnership's payment of 1446 tax on behalf of a foreign partner is treated under section 1446(d) and this section as a deemed distribution of money to the partner on the earliest of the day on which the partnership paid the tax, the last day of the partnership's taxable year for which the amount was paid, or the last day on which the partner owned an interest in the partnership during the taxable year for which the tax was paid. However, a deemed distribution of money under section 1446(d) resulting from a partnership's installment payment of 1446 tax on behalf of a partner is treated as an advance or drawing of money under § 1.731-1(a)(1)(ii) to the extent of the partner's distributive share of income for the partnership taxable year. The rule treating a deemed distribution as an advance or drawing of money under this paragraph (d)(2)(v) applies only for purposes of determining the tax results of the deemed distribution to the partner under sections 705, 731, and 733, and does not affect the date that the partnership is considered to have paid any installment of 1446 tax for purposes of section 6655 (as applied through this section) or the date a foreign partner is deemed to have paid estimated tax by reason of such installment payment. See paragraph (d)(1)(i) of this section (permitting a partner to credit 1446 tax paid on the partner's behalf against the partner's estimated tax obligation). An amount treated as an advance or drawing of money is taken into account at the end of the partnership taxable year or the last day during the partnership's taxable year on which the partner owned an interest in the partnership. Any 1446 tax paid after the close of the partnership's taxable year, including amounts paid with the filing of Form 8804, that are on account of partnership ECTI allocated to partners for the prior taxable year shall be treated under section 1446(d) and this section as a distribution from the partnership on the earlier of the last day of the partnership's prior taxable year for which the tax is paid, or the last day in such prior taxable year on which such foreign partner held an interest in the partnership.

(vi) *Examples.*—The following examples illustrate the application of this section. In considering the examples, disregard the potential application of paragraph (b)(2)(v)(F) of this section (relating to the de minimis exception to paying 1446 tax). The examples are as follows:

(A) *Example 1. Simple trust that reports entire amount of ECTI.*—PRS is a partnership that has two partners, FT, a foreign trust, and A, a U.S. person. FT is a simple trust under section 651. FT and A each provide PRS with a valid Form W-8BEN and Form W-9, respectively. FT has one beneficiary, NRA, a nonresident alien. PRS and FT each maintain a calendar taxable year. PRS estimated for each installment period during the partnership's taxable year that FT would be allocated $100 of ECTI for the taxable year, and that all such ECTI would be ordinary in character. Assume that the allocation of the $100 would be respected under section 704(b) and the regulations thereunder. PRS pays installments of 1446 tax based upon its estimates and timely pays a total of $37 of 1446 tax over the course of the partnership's taxable year ($100 ECTI × .37). Assume that PRS' estimates of ECTI allocable to FT during the taxable year equal the actual amount of ECTI allocable to FT for the taxable year. Assume also that FT's only income for the taxable year is the $100 of income from PRS, and that, pursuant to the terms of the trust's governing instrument and local law, the $100 of ECTI is not included in FT's fiduciary accounting income and the deemed distribution of the $37 withholding tax paid under paragraph (d)(2)(v) of this section is not included in FT's fiduciary accounting income. Accordingly, the $100 of ECTI is not income required to be distributed by FT, and FT may not claim a deduction under section 651 for this amount. FT must report the $100 of ECTI in its gross income and may claim a credit under section 33 as determined under paragraph (d)(2)(iii) of this section of $37 for the 1446 tax paid by PRS. NRA is not required to include any of the ECTI in gross income and accordingly may not claim a credit for any amount of the $37 of 1446 tax PRS paid.

(B) *Example 2. Simple trust that distributes a portion of ECTI to the beneficiary.*.—Assume the same facts as in paragraph (d)(2)(vi)(A) of this section (*Example 1*), except that PRS distributes $60 to FT, which FT includes in its fiduciary accounting income under local law. FT will report the $100 of ECTI in its gross income and may claim a deduction for the $60 required to be distributed under section 651(a) to NRA. Pursuant to paragraph (d)(2)(iii) of this section, FT may claim a $14.8 credit under section 33 for the 1446 tax PRS paid ($40/$100 multiplied by $37). NRA is required to include the $60 of the ECTI in gross income under section 652 (as ECTI) and may claim a $22.2 credit under section 33 for the 1446 tax PRS paid ($37 less $14.8 or $60/$100 multiplied by $37).

(C) *Example 3. Complex trust that distributes entire ECTI to the beneficiary.*—Assume the same facts as in paragraph (d)(2)(vi)(A) of this section (*Example 1*), except that FT is a complex trust under section 661. PRS distributes $60 to FT, which FT includes in its fiduciary accounting income. FT distributes the $60 of fiduciary accounting income to NRA and also properly distributes an additional $40 to NRA from FT's principal. FT will report the $100 of ECTI in its gross income and may deduct the $60 required to be distributed to NRA under section 661(a)(1) and may deduct the $40 distributed to NRA under section 661(a)(2). Pursuant to paragraph (d)(2)(iii) of this section, FT may not claim a credit under section 33 for any of the $37 of 1446 tax paid by PRS. NRA is required to include $100 of the ECTI in gross income under section 662 (as ECTI) and may claim a $37 credit under section 33 for the 1446 tax paid by PRS ($37 less $0).

(e) *Liability of partnership for failure to withhold.*—(1) *In general.*—Every partnership required to pay 1446 tax is made liable for that tax by section 1461. Therefore, a partnership that is required to pay 1446 tax but fails to do so, or pays less than the amount required under this section, is liable under section 1461 for the payment of the tax required to be withheld under chapter 3 of the Internal Revenue Code and the regulations thereunder unless, and to the extent, the partnership can demonstrate pursuant to paragraph (e)(2) of this section, to the satisfaction of the Commissioner or his delegate, that a foreign partner has paid the full amount of tax required to be paid by such partner to the Internal Revenue Service. See paragraph (e)(3) of this section and section 1463 regarding a partnership's liability for penalties and interest even though a foreign partner has satisfied the underlying tax liability. See also § 1.1461-3 for applicable penalties when a partnership fails to pay 1446 tax. See paragraph (b) of this section for an addition to the tax under section 6655 when there is an underpayment of 1446 tax.

(2) *Proof that tax liability has been satisfied and deemed payment of 1446 tax.*—Proof of payment of tax may be established for purposes of paragraph (e)(1) of this section consistent with § 1.1445-1(e)(3). Under that standard, a partnership must provide sufficient information to the IRS to determine that the partner's tax liability was satisfied or established to be zero in accordance with the rules of this section. Under this section, a partnership's liability for 1446 tax shall be deemed to have been satisfied (deemed payment), to the extent of the 1446 tax due with respect to the ECTI allocable to a foreign partner, on the later of the date that such partner is considered to have paid all tax that is required to be shown on such partner's U.S. income tax return under section 6513(a) and (b)(2) (prescribing the date tax is considered paid for purposes of sections 6511(b)(2), (c), and 6512), or the last date for payment of the 1446 tax without extensions (the unextended due date for Form 8804). The deemed payment rule of this paragraph (e)(2) shall apply for purposes sections of 1446, 1461, and 1463, and any additions to the tax, interest, or penalties potentially applicable to such partnership under section 1446, including sections 6601, 6651, and 6655. Any deemed payment of 1446 tax under this paragraph (e)(2) shall not be treated as a deemed distribution under section 1446(d) and this section.

(3) *Liability for interest, penalties, and additions to the tax.*—(i) *Partnership.*—Notwithstanding paragraph (e)(2) of this section, a partnership that fails to pay 1446 tax is not relieved from liability under section 6655 (as applied through this section) or for interest under section 6601, when applicable. See § 1.1463-1. Such liability may exist even if there is no underlying tax liability due from a foreign partner on its allocable share of partnership ECTI. The addition to the tax under section 6655 or the interest charge under section 6601 that is required by those sections shall be imposed as set forth in those sections, as modified by this section. The section 6601 interest charge shall accrue beginning on the last date prescribed for payment of the 1446 tax due under section 1461 (which is the due date, without extensions, for filing Form 8804). The section 6601 interest charge shall stop accruing on the 1446 tax liability on the date, and to the extent, that the unpaid tax liability under section 1446 is satisfied (or is deemed satisfied under this paragraph (e)). Further, a partnership's liability under section 6655 (as applied through this section) for any underpaid installment payment shall accrue beginning on the relevant installment payment date, and shall stop accruing on the earlier of the date (and to the extent) that the 1446 tax liability is actually satisfied or the date prescribed in paragraph (b)(2)(v)(C) of this section. See paragraph (e)(4) of this section for examples illustrat-

ing that a partner's payment of estimated tax has no effect on the partnership's calculation of its addition to the tax under section 6655 and this section. See § 1.1461-3 for a list of the additions to tax, interest, and penalties that may apply to a partnership that fails to comply with section 1446. See § 1.1446-6(d)(2)(i) for exceptions to the application of the addition to the tax under section 6655 (as applied through this section) when a partnership reasonably relies on a foreign partner's certificate to reduce 1446 tax.

(ii) *Foreign partner.*—A foreign partner is permitted to reduce any addition to the tax under section 6654 or section 6655 by the amount of any section 6655 addition to the tax paid by the partnership with respect to the partnership's failure to pay adequate installment payments of the 1446 tax on ECTI allocable to the foreign partner.

(4) *Examples.*—The following examples illustrate the application of this section. In considering the examples, disregard the potential application of paragraph (b)(2)(v)(F) of this section (relating to the de minimis exception to paying 1446 tax). Further, in each of the examples where a partnership is deemed to have paid 1446 tax with respect to ECTI allocable to a partner, it is assumed that the partnership has presented to the IRS the appropriate information under paragraph (e)(2) of this section for the IRS to conclude that the deemed payment is appropriate. The examples are as follows:

(i) *Example 1. Foreign partnership fails to pay 1446 tax and sole foreign partner fails to pay all tax required to be shown on partner's U.S. income tax return.*—(A) PRS is a foreign partnership engaged in a trade or business in the United States and has two equal partners, A, a U.S. person, and B, a nonresident alien. PRS is described in § 1.6081-5(a) (PRS keeps its books and records outside the United States and Puerto Rico) and, therefore, is required to file Form 8804 by the 15th day of the 6th month following the close of its taxable year. Both partners and PRS are calendar year taxpayers. PRS has received a valid Form W-9 and W-8BEN from A and B, respectively, but has not received any other documents or certificates. B is engaged in multiple trades or businesses (including the PRS partnership) that give rise to effectively connected income. PRS will use an acceptable annualization method under this section for computing its 1446 tax.

(B) In PRS's first year of operations (Year 1), PRS estimates for each installment period described in § 1.1446-3 that B will be allocated $100 of ordinary ECTI for the taxable year. Therefore, for each installment period PRS is required to pay one fourth of the tax on the annualized ECTI allocable to B, or $9.25 (.25 X ($100 X .37)). PRS fails to make any installment payments. PRS's operations actually result in $100 of ECTI allocated to B. Therefore, PRS was required to have paid 1446 tax of $37 on or before the due date, without extensions, for filing its Form 8804 which is June 15, Year 2 (the last date prescribed for payment of the 1446 tax). PRS does not file Forms 8804 or 8805.

(C) B pays estimated taxes and makes the following payments on the following dates: June 15, Year 1 - $20, September 15, Year 1 - $15, and January 15, Year 2 - $10. B's total estimated tax payments equal $45. B files its U.S. Federal income tax return timely on June 15, Year 2, and reports all effectively connected income required to be shown on its return. Assume that B's total correct tax liability as shown on the return is $50. B does not make a payment with its return and so B still owes $5 to the Internal Revenue Service (excluding any interest, penalties, and additions to the tax that may apply). Assume that B is not subject to an addition to the tax under section 6654.

(D) Under the rules of paragraph (e)(2) of this section, for purposes of sections 1446, 1461, and 1463, PRS is not considered to have paid any 1446 tax because B has not paid all of B's U.S. income tax liability.

(E) Further, under the principles of section 6655 and the rules of § 1.1446-3(e), a partner's estimated tax payments will not affect the calculation of a partnership's addition to the tax. Accordingly, PRS will be liable under the principles of section 6655 and § 1.1446-3 for failing to withhold for each installment payment. The addition to the tax will accrue beginning with the due date of each installment payment on the $9.25 underpayment for each respective installment period and will continue to accrue until June 15, Year 2 (the date prescribed in paragraph (b)(2)(v)(C) of this section).

(F) Further, beginning on June 15, Year 2 (the last date prescribed for payment of 1446 tax without extensions), PRS will be liable for interest under section 6601 with respect to the unpaid 1446 tax, $37. This interest will stop accruing on the earlier of the date that the 1446 tax is paid by PRS or is deemed paid under paragraph (e)(2) of this section by reason of B's payment of its full tax liability.

(G) Further, beginning on June 15, Year 2 (the due date for filing Form 8804), PRS will be liable for the addition to the tax under section 6651(a)(1) for failing to file Form 8804. This addition to the tax accrues on the amount required to be shown as the 1446 tax liability on Form 8804, $37. This addition to the tax will accrue at the rate of 5 percent per month until the date that PRS files Form 8804 for Year 1, or the maximum accrual of the penalty (25 percent of the tax required to be shown on the return) under that section has been reached.

(H) PRS may be liable for other penalties and additions to the tax for its failure to withhold or to furnish statements to its foreign partner B. See § 1.1461-3 for a list of the penalties that may apply.

(ii) *Example 2. Foreign partnership fails to pay 1446 tax but sole foreign partner pays all tax required to be shown on the partner's U.S. income tax return.*—The facts are the same as paragraph (e)(4)(i)(A) of this section (*Example 1*), except that B pays $5 with the filing of B's return and has therefore paid all tax required to be shown on B's return within the meaning of paragraph (e)(2) of this section.

(A) For purposes of sections 1446, 1461, and 1463, PRS is deemed to have paid its 1446 tax liability under paragraph (e) (2) of this section as of the later of the date that B is considered to have paid its tax under section 6513(a) and (b)(2) (June 15, Year 2) and the last date for PRS to pay its 1446 tax without extensions (also June 15, Year 2). Therefore, PRS is deemed to have paid all of its 1446 tax liability as of June 15, Year 2. PRS has no continuing liability for 1446 tax under section 1461, however, additions to the tax, interest, and penalties may apply.

(B) For purposes of section 6655 and § 1.1446-3, under paragraph (e)(2) PRS is deemed to have paid its 1446 tax on June 15, Year 2. Even if B had fully paid its tax liability as of March 15, Year 2, the rule in paragraph (e) (2) of this section would not deem PRS to have paid its 1446 tax until June 15, Year 2. As a result, B's estimated tax payments will have no effect on PRS's calculation of its addition to the tax. The addition to the tax under 6655 and § 1.1446-3 shall begin to accrue on each installment date with respect to the underpaid installment ($8.75), and will stop accruing on June 15, Year 2, the date prescribed in paragraph (b)(2)(v)(C) of this section.

(C) Because PRS is deemed to have paid its full 1446 tax liability as of June 15, Year 2 (the last date prescribed for payment of 1446 tax without extensions), PRS is not subject to an interest charge under section 6601, or a failure to file penalty under section 6651 (see section 6651(b)(1)).

(D) PRS may be liable for other penalties and additions to the tax for its failure to withhold or to furnish statements to its foreign partner B. See § 1.1461-3 for a list of the penalties that may apply.

(E) If PRS had several foreign partners, PRS would conduct the same analysis as set forth above with respect to each partner. That is, under paragraph (e) of this section, PRS may be deemed to have paid 1446 tax with respect to the ECTI allocable to some but not all of its foreign partners.

(iii) *Example 3. Domestic partnership fails to pay 1446 tax but sole foreign partner fully pays all tax required to be shown on partner's U.S. income tax return.*—The facts are the same as paragraph (e)(4)(ii) introductory text of this section (*Example 2*), except that PRS is a domestic partnership whose last date prescribed for paying 1446 tax without extensions (i.e., generally the unextended due date for Form 8804) is March 15, Year 2.

(A) For purposes of sections 1446, 1461, and 1463, PRS is deemed to have paid its 1446 tax liability on the later of the date that B is considered to have paid tax under section 6513(a) and (b)(2) (June 15, Year 2) and the last date for paying 1446 tax without extensions (i.e., the unextended due date for Form 8804, March 15, Year 2). Accordingly, PRS is not considered to have fully paid its 1446 tax liability until June 15, Year 2. PRS has no continuing liability for 1446 tax under section 1461, however, additions to the tax, interest, and penalties may apply.

(B) For purposes of section 6655 and § 1.1446-3, PRS is subject to an underpayment addition to the tax that accrues on the same amount as in paragraphs (e)(4)(i) and (ii) of this section (*Examples 1* and 2), respectively, in paragraphs (e)(4)(i) and (e)(4)(ii) of this section, respectively because PRS is not deemed to have paid 1446 tax under paragraph (e)(2) of this section until June 15, Year 2. The addition to the tax will stop accruing on the date prescribed in paragraph (b)(2)(v)(C) of this section (i.e., March 15, Year 2, the due date, without extensions, for filing Form 8804).

(C) For purposes of section 6601, as of the last date prescribed for paying 1446 tax without extensions (March 15, Year 2), PRS has not paid or been deemed to have paid any 1446 tax. Accordingly, the interest charge under section 6601 shall begin to accrue on March 15, Year 2, and shall accrue until the 1446 liability is paid or deemed to have been paid. In this case, the interest charge will accrue until June 15, Year 2, the date that PRS is deemed to have paid its 1446 tax under paragraph (e)(2) of this section.

(D) For purposes of section 6651(a)(1), as of March 15, Year 2, PRS's amount required to be shown as tax on its Form 8804 is $37. This amount cannot be reduced under section 6651(b)(1) because PRS is not deemed to have paid 1446 tax under paragraph (e)(2) of this section until June 15, Year 2, a date falling after the last date for PRS to pay its 1446 tax, March 15, Year 2. Accordingly, the failure to file penalty will begin to accrue on March 15, Year 2 (filing due date for Form 8804), and shall stop accruing on the earlier of the date that PRS files Form 8804 or the maximum accrual of the penalty (25 percent of the amount required to be shown as tax on the return) is reached.

(E) PRS may be liable for other penalties and additions to the tax for its failure to withhold or to furnish statements to its foreign partner B. See § 1.1461-3 for a list of the penalties that may apply.

(f) *Effect of withholding on partner*.—The payment of the 1446 tax by a partnership does not excuse a foreign partner to which a portion of ECTI is allocable from filing a U.S. tax or informational return, as appropriate, with respect to that income. Information concerning installment payments of 1446 tax paid during the partnership's taxable year on behalf of a foreign partner shall be provided to such foreign partner in accordance with paragraph (d) of this section and such information may be taken into account by the foreign partner when computing the partner's estimated tax liability during the taxable year. Form 1040NR, "U.S. Nonresident Alien Income Tax Return," Form 1065, "U.S. Return of Partnership Income," Form 1120F, "U.S. Income Tax Return of a Foreign Corporation," or such other return as appropriate, must be filed by the partner, and any tax due must be paid, by the filing deadline (including extensions) generally applicable to such person. Pursuant to paragraph (d) of this section, a partner may generally claim a credit under section 33 for its share of any 1446 tax paid by the partnership against the amount of income tax (or 1446 tax in the case of tiers of partnerships) as computed in such partner's return. See § 1.1446-3(e)(3)(ii) for rules permitting a partner to reduce its addition to tax under section 6654 or section 6655. [Reg. § 1.1446-3.]

☐ [*T.D.* 9200, 5-13-2005. *Amended by T.D.* 9394, 4-28-2008 (*corrected* 6-10-2020), *T.D.* 9821, 7-18-2017, *T.D.* 9892, 1-29-2020 *and T.D.* 9926, 11-27-2020.]

Proposed Amendments to Regulation

§ 1.1446-3. Time and manner of calculating and paying over the 1446 tax.—

* * *

(b) * * *

(2) * * *

(i) * * *

(B) * * *

(1) To the extent applicable, in computing the 1446 tax due with respect to a foreign partner, a partnership may consider a certificate received from such partner under § 1.1446-6(c)(1)(i), (ii) or (iv) and the amount of state and local taxes permitted to be considered under § 1.1446-6(c)(1)(iii). For this purpose, a partnership shall first consider under § 1.1446-6(c)(1)(iv) the partner's permitted deferral amounts and then annualize the partner's allocable share of the partnership's items of effectively connected income, gain, deduction, and loss before—

* * *

[Prop. Reg. § 1.1446-3.]

[Proposed 4-14-2021.]

§ 1.1446-4. Publicly traded partnerships.—(a) *In general*.—This section sets forth rules for applying the section 1446 withholding tax (1446 tax) to publicly traded partnerships. A publicly traded partnership (as defined in paragraph (b) of this section) that has effectively connected gross income, gain or loss must pay 1446 tax by withholding from distributions to a foreign partner. Publicly traded partnerships that withhold on distributions must pay over and report any 1446 tax as provided in paragraph (c) of this section, and generally are not to pay over and report the 1446 tax under the rules in § 1.1446-3. The amount of the withholding tax on distributions, other than distributions excluded under paragraph (f) of this section, that are made during any partnership taxable years, equals the applicable percentage (defined in paragraph (b)(2) of this section) of such distributions. For penalties and additions to the tax for failure to comply with this section, see §§ 1.1461-1 and 1.1461-3.

(b) *Definitions*.—(1) *Publicly traded partnership*.—For purposes of this section, the term publicly traded partnership has the same meaning as in section 7704 (including the regulations thereunder), but does not include a publicly traded partnership treated as a corporation under that section.

(2) *Applicable percentage*.—For purposes of this section, applicable percentage shall have the meaning as set forth in § 1.1446-3(a)(2), except that the partnership or nominee required to pay 1446 tax may not consider a preferential rate in computing the 1446 tax due with respect to a partner.

(3) *Nominee*.—For purposes of this section, the term nominee means a person that holds an interest in a publicly traded partnership on behalf of a foreign person and that is either a U.S. person, a qualified intermediary (as defined in § 1.1441-1(e)(5)(ii)) that assumes primary withholding responsibility for the distribution, or a U.S. branch of a foreign person that agrees to be treated as a U.S. person (as described in § 1.1441-1(b)(2)(iv)) with respect to the distribution. For purposes of this paragraph (b)(3), a U.S. branch or a qualified intermediary is a nominee only if it assumes primary withholding responsibility for the distribution for all purposes of chapters 3 and 4 of subtitle A of the Code.

(4) *Qualified notice*.—For purposes of this section, a qualified notice is a notice from a publicly traded partnership that states the amount of a distribution that is attributable to each type of income described in paragraphs (f)(3)(i) through (v) of this section. A qualified notice may also include the information described in § 1.1446(f)-4(b)(3) (relating to the 10-percent exception to withholding under section 1446(f)(1)) and the information described in § 1.1446(f)-4(c)(2)(iii) (relating to an adjustment to the amount realized for withholding under section 1446(f)(1)). The notice must be posted in a readily accessible format in an area of the primary public website of the publicly traded partnership that is dedicated to this purpose, and a copy of the notice must be delivered to any registered holder that is a nominee. A qualified notice must be posted and delivered to the registered holder by the date required for providing notice with respect to distributions described in 17 CFR 240.10b-17(b)(1) or (3) issued pursuant to the Securities Exchange Act of 1934 (15 U.S.C. 78a) and contain the information described therein as it would relate to the distribution. The publicly traded partnership must keep the notice accessible to the public for ten years on its primary public website or the primary public website of any successor organization. No specific format is required unless otherwise prescribed by the Commissioner in forms or instructions or in publications or guidance published in the Internal Revenue Bulletin (see §§ 601.601(d)(2) and 601.602 of this chapter). See paragraph (d) of this section regarding when a nominee is considered to have received a qualified notice.

(c) *Paying and reporting 1446 tax*.—The withholding tax required under this section is to be paid pursuant to the rules and procedures of section 1461, §§ 1.1461-1, 1.1461-2, and 1.6302-2, as supplemented by the rules of this section. A withholding agent under this section must use Form 1042,"Annual Withholding Tax Return for U.S. Source Income of Foreign Persons," and Form 1042-S,"Foreign Person's U.S. Source Income Subject to Withholding," to report withholding from distributions under this section. See § 1.1461-1(b). Further, a withholding agent under this section may obtain a refund for 1446 tax paid in accordance with section 1464 and the regulations thereunder. See § 1.1446-3(d)(1)(iv) and (vii) (relating to a foreign trust or estate that holds an interest in a publicly traded partnership) and § 1.1446-5(d) (relating to a publicly traded partnership that is part of a tiered partnership structure) for additional guidance.

(d) *Rules for nominees required to withhold tax under section 1446*.—(1) *In general*.—A nominee that receives a distribution from a publicly traded partnership (or another nominee) that is to be paid to (or for the account of) any foreign person is treated as a withholding agent under this section. A nominee that fails to withhold pursuant to this section is subject to liability under section 1461, as well as applicable penalties and interest, as if the nominee were the partnership responsible for withholding. A nominee that receives a qualified notice that meets the requirements in paragraph (b)(4) of this section must withhold based on the amounts specified on the qualified notice. A nominee is treated as receiving a qualified notice on the date that the notice is posted to the publicly traded partnership's website or is received by the nominee in accordance with paragraph (b)(4) of this section. If a nominee properly withholds based on the amounts specified on a qualified notice, the nominee is not liable for any underwithholding on amounts that are effectively connected income, gain, or loss. Rather, the publicly traded partnership that issued the qualified notice is liable under section 1461 for underwithholding on such amounts. If a nominee does not receive a qualified notice that meets the requirements in paragraph (b)(4) of this section, or to the extent the qualified notice does not specify an amount, the nominee must withhold on the full amount of the distribution with respect to—

(i) A foreign partner that is a corporation, at the greater of the highest rate of tax specified in section 11(b) or 881 (without regard to any reduction in the rate of tax permitted under an applicable income tax treaty);

(ii) A foreign partner that is not a corporation, at the greater of the highest rate of tax specified in section 1 or 871 (without regard to any reduction in the rate of tax permitted under an applicable income tax treaty); or

(iii) A foreign partner whose classification cannot be determined, at the higher of the rate determined under paragraph (d)(1)(i) or (ii) of this section.

(2) *Exception to nominee's withholding.*—A nominee is not required to withhold under paragraph (d)(1) of this section to the extent that it makes a payment of a distribution to a qualified intermediary or U.S. branch that is also a nominee for the distribution under paragraph (b)(3) of this section. For purposes of the preceding sentence, a nominee may treat a qualified intermediary or U.S. branch as a nominee for a distribution based on, respectively, a valid qualified intermediary withholding certificate described in § 1.1441-1(e)(3)(ii) or a valid U.S. branch withholding certificate described in § 1.1446(f)-4(a)(2)(ii)(B) on which the qualified intermediary or U.S. branch represents that it assumes primary withholding responsibility with respect to the distribution.

(e) *Determining foreign status of partners.*—Except as provided in this paragraph (e), the rules of § 1.1446-1 shall apply in determining whether a partner of a publicly traded partnership is a foreign partner for purposes of the 1446 tax. A partnership or nominee obligated to withhold under this section shall be entitled to rely on any of the forms acceptable under § 1.1446-1 that it receives from persons on whose behalf it holds interests in the partnership to the same extent a partnership is entitled to rely on such forms under those rules. If a partnership or nominee pays a distribution to an entity that provides a valid qualified intermediary withholding certificate described in § 1.1441-1(e)(3)(ii) indicating that the entity does not assume primary withholding responsibility for the distribution, for withholding under this section the partnership or nominee may instead rely on a withholding statement that allocates the distribution to—

(1) A chapter 3 withholding rate pool (as described in § 1.1441-1(e)(5)(v)(C)) consisting of account holders that are foreign persons subject to withholding at the highest rate of tax specified in section 1;

(2) A chapter 3 withholding rate pool (as described in § 1.1441-1(e)(5)(v)(C)) consisting of account holders that are foreign persons subject to withholding at the highest rate of tax specified in section 11(b);

(3) A chapter 3 withholding rate pool (as described in § 1.1441-1(e)(5)(v)(C)) consisting of account holders that are foreign persons not subject to withholding; or

(4) Each account holder for which a form acceptable under § 1.1446-1 is provided.

(f) *Distributions subject to withholding.*—(1) *In general.*—Except as provided in this paragraph (f)(1), a publicly traded partnership must withhold at the applicable percentage with respect to any actual distribution made to a foreign partner. The amount of a distribution subject to 1446 tax includes the amount of any 1446 tax required to be withheld on the distribution. In the case of a partnership (upper-tier partnership) that receives a partnership distribution from another partnership in which it is a partner (lower-tier partnership) (i.e., a tiered structure described in § 1.1446-5), any 1446 tax that was paid by the lower-tier partnership may be credited by the upper-tier partnership and shall be treated as a distribution under section 1446. For example, a foreign publicly traded partnership, UTP, owns an interest in domestic publicly traded partnership, LTP. LTP makes a distribution subject to section 1446 of $100 to UTP during its taxable year beginning January 1, 2020, and withholds 37 percent (the highest rate in section 1) ($37) of that distribution under section 1446. UTP receives a net distribution of $63 which it immediately redistributes to its partners. UTP has a liability to pay 37 percent of the total actual and deemed distribution it makes to its foreign partners as a section 1446 withholding tax. UTP may credit the $37 withheld by LTP against this liability as if it were paid by UTP. See § § 1.1462-1(b) and 1.1446-5(b)(1). When UTP distributes the $63 it actually receives from LTP to its partners, UTP is treated for purposes of section 1446 as if it made a distribution of $100 to its partners ($63 actual distribution and $37 deemed distribution). UTP's partners (U.S. and foreign) may claim a credit against their U.S. income tax liability for their allocable share of the $37 of 1446 tax paid on their behalf.

(2) *In-kind distributions.*—If a publicly traded partnership distributes property other than money, the partnership shall not release the property until it has funds sufficient to enable the partnership to pay over in money the required 1446 tax.

(3) *Ordering rule relating to distributions.*—Distributions from publicly traded partnerships are deemed to be paid out of the following types of income in the order indicated—

(i) Amounts attributable to income described in section 1441 or 1442 that are not effectively connected with the conduct of a trade or business in the United States and are subject to withholding under § 1.1441-2(a);

(ii) Amounts attributable to income described in section 1441 or 1442 that are not effectively connected with the conduct of a trade or business in the United States and are not subject to withholding under § 1.1441-2(a);

(iii) Amounts attributable to income effectively connected with the conduct of a trade or business in the United States that are not subject to withholding under § § 1.1446-1 through 1.1446-6;

(iv) Amounts subject to withholding under § § 1.1446-1 through 1.1446-6; and

(v) Amounts not listed in paragraphs (f)(3)(i) through (iv) of this section.

(4) *Coordination with section 1445(e)(1).*—Except as otherwise provided in this section, a publicly traded partnership that complies with the requirements of withholding under section 1446 and this section will be deemed to have satisfied the requirements of section 1445(e)(1) and the regulations thereunder. Notwithstanding the excluded amounts set forth in paragraph (f)(3) of this section, distributions subject to withholding at the applicable percentage shall include the following—

(i) Amounts subject to withholding under section 1445(e)(1) upon distribution pursuant to an election under § 1.1445-5(c)(3) of the regulations; and

(ii) Amounts not subject to withholding under section 1445 because the distributee is a partnership or is a foreign corporation that has made an election under section 897(i). [Reg. § 1.1446-4.]

☐ [*T.D.* 9200, 5-13-2005 *Amended by T.D.* 9926, 11-27-2020 (*corrected* 3-5-2021).]

§ 1.1446-5. Tiered partnership structures.—(a) *In general.*—The rules of this section shall apply in cases where a partnership (lower-tier partnership) that has effectively connected taxable income (ECTI), has a partner that is a partnership (upper-tier partnership). Except as provided in paragraph (e) of this section, if an upper-tier domestic partnership directly owns an interest in a lower-tier partnership, the lower-tier partnership is not required to pay the section 1446 withholding tax (1446 tax) with respect to the upper-tier partnership's allocable share of net income, regardless of whether the upper-tier domestic partnership's partners are foreign. Paragraph (b) of this section prescribes the reporting requirements for upper-tier and lower-tier partnerships subject to section 1446. Paragraph (c) of this section prescribes rules requiring a lower-tier partnership to look through an upper-tier foreign partnership to a partner of such upper-tier partnership to the extent it has sufficient documentation to determine the status of such partner and determine such partner's indirect share of the lower-tier partnership's effectively connected taxable income (ECTI). Paragraph (d) of this section prescribes rules applicable to a publicly traded partnership in a tiered partnership structure. Paragraph (e) of this section prescribes rules permitting a domestic upper-tier partnership to elect to apply the look through rules of paragraph (c) of this section. Paragraph (f) of this section sets forth examples illustrating the rules of this section.

(b) *Reporting requirements.*—(1) *In general.*—Notwithstanding paragraph (c) of this section, to the extent that an upper-tier partnership that is a foreign partnership is a partner in a lower-tier partnership, and the lower-tier partnership has paid 1446 tax (including installment payments of such tax) with respect to ECTI allocable to the upper-tier partnership, the lower-tier partnership shall comply with § § 1.1446-1 through 1.1446-3 and provide the upper-tier partnership notice of such payments and a copy of the statements and forms filed with respect to the upper-tier partnership's interest in the lower-tier partnership (e.g., Form 8805, "Foreign Partner's Information Statement of Section 1446 Withholding Tax"). The upper-tier partnership may treat the 1446 tax (or any installment of such tax) paid by the lower-tier partnership on its behalf as a credit against its liability to pay 1446 tax (or any installment of such tax), as if the upper-tier partnership actually paid over the amounts at the time that the amounts were paid by the lower-tier partnership. See § 1.1462-1(b) and § 1.1446-3(d). To the extent required in § 1.1446-3(d)(1)(iii), the upper-tier partnership will file Form 8804, "Annual Return for Partnership Withholding Tax (Section 1446)," and Form 8805, "Foreign Partner's Information Statement of Section 1446 Withholding Tax," for each of its foreign partners with respect to its 1446 tax obligation. To the extent the upper-tier partnership does not claim a refund of the 1446 tax it paid (or is considered to have paid), the upper-tier partnership will pass the credit for the 1446 tax paid to its partners on the Forms 8805 it issues. See § 1.1446-3(d). The rules of this paragraph (b) shall apply to an upper-tier and lower-tier partnership to the extent that an election has been made and consented to under paragraph (e) of this section.

(2) *Publicly traded partnerships.*—In the case of an upper-tier foreign partnership that is a publicly traded partnership, the rules of § 1.1446-4(c) shall apply. See also paragraph (d) of this section.

(c) *Look through rules for foreign upper-tier partnerships.*—For purposes of computing the 1446 tax obligation of a lower-tier partnership, if an upper-tier foreign partnership owns an interest in the lower-tier partnership, the upper-tier partnership's allocable share of ECTI from the lower-tier partnership shall be treated as allocable to a partner of the upper-tier partnership, to the extent of such partner's indirect share of such ECTI (as if such partner were a direct partner in the lower-tier partnership), if—

(1) The upper-tier foreign partnership furnishes the lower-tier partnership a valid Form W-8IMY, "Certificate of Foreign Intermediary, Flow Through Entity, or Certain U.S. Branches for United States Tax Withholding," indicating that it is a look-through foreign partnership for purposes of section 1446; and

(2) The lower-tier partnership can reliably associate (within the meaning of § 1.1441-1(b)(2)(vii)) effectively connected partnership items allocable to the upper-tier partnership (and indirectly to such partner) with a Form W-8 (e.g., Form W-8BEN), Form W-9, "Request for Taxpayer Identification Number and Certification," or other form acceptable under § 1.1446-1, establishing the status of such partner provided by the upper-tier partnership. The lower-tier partnership required to pay 1446 tax must be able to provide the information necessary for the IRS to determine the chain of ownership, allocation of effectively connected items at each partnership level, as well as to the ultimate beneficial owner of the effectively connected items, and whether the amount of 1446 tax paid was appropriate. This information should permit each partnership in the tiered structure and the IRS to reliably associate any effectively connected items allocable to such upper-tier partnership, as well as to the ultimate beneficial owner of the effectively connected items. The principles of § 1.1441-1(b)(2)(vii) shall apply to determine whether a lower-tier partnership can reliably associate effectively connected partnership items allocable to the upper-tier partnership with a partner of the upper-tier partnership. To the extent the lower-tier partnership receives a valid Form W-8IMY from the upper-tier partnership but cannot reliably associate a portion of the upper-tier partnership's allocable share of effectively connected partnership items with a partner of such upper-tier partnership, then the lower-tier partnership shall pay 1446 tax on such portion at the higher of the applicable percentages in section 1446(b). See § 1.1446-3(a)(2) for the treatment of any income or gain potentially subject to a preferential rate. If a lower-tier partnership has not received a valid Form W-8IMY from the upper-tier partnership, the lower-tier partnership shall withhold on the upper-tier partnership's entire allocable share of ECTI at the higher of the applicable percentages in section 1446(b). The look through regime set forth in this paragraph (c) is for purposes of computing the lower-tier partnership's 1446 tax obligation only and does not alter the persons considered to be partners in the lower-tier partnership for partnership reporting purposes (e.g., issuing Form 8805, Schedule K-1).

(d) *Publicly traded partnerships.*—(1) *Upper-tier publicly traded partnership.*—The rules set forth in paragraph (c) shall not apply to look through an upper-tier partnership whose interests are publicly traded (as defined in § 1.1446-4(b)(1)).

(2) *Lower-tier publicly traded partnership.*—The look through rules of paragraph (c) of this section shall apply, if the requirements of that paragraph are met, to a lower-tier partnership that is a publicly traded partnership within the meaning of § 1.1446-4(b)(1) only if the upper-tier partnership is not described in paragraph (d)(1) of this section. For example, a lower-tier publicly traded partnership (or nominee) shall look through an upper-tier foreign partnership (or domestic partnership to the extent an election is made and consented to under paragraph (e) of this section) when computing its 1446 tax liability, provided the upper-tier partnership is not a publicly traded partnership and the appropriate documentation needed to satisfy the standards set forth in § 1.1441-1(b)(2)(vii) and paragraph (c) of this section have been furnished.

(e) *Election by a domestic upper-tier partnership to apply look through rules.*—(1) *In general.*—Subject to the rules of this paragraph (e), a domestic partnership that is a partner in a lower-tier partnership may elect to apply the rules of this section 1.1446-5 and have the lower-tier partnership look through such upper-tier partnership to the partners of such domestic partnership for purposes of computing the lower-tier partnership's 1446 tax liability. A domestic partnership shall make this election by attaching to the Form W-9 submitted to the lower-tier partnership, a written statement and information (described in paragraph (e)(2) of this section) that identifies the upper-tier partnership as a domestic partnership and that states that such partnership is making the election under this paragraph (e). This paragraph (e)(1) shall not apply to a publicly traded partnership described in § 1.1446-4(b)(1). See paragraph (d)(1) of this section.

(2) *Information required for valid election statement.*—In addition to the requirements of paragraphs (e)(1) and (3) of this section, the election statement submitted under this paragraph (e)(2) is not valid and cannot be accepted by the lower-tier partnership pursuant to paragraph (e)(3) of this section unless the upper-tier partnership attaches valid documentation pursuant to § 1.1446-1 (e.g., Form W-8BEN) with respect to one or more of its foreign partners. The information and documentation submitted with the election must comply with the rules of this section to permit the lower-tier partnership to reliably associate (within the meaning of § 1.1441-1(b)(2)(vii)) at least a portion of the upper-tier partnership's allocable share of ECTI with one or more foreign partners of the upper-tier partnership. The election statement must identify the upper-tier partnership by name, address, and TIN, and specify the percentage interest the domestic partnership holds in the lower-tier partnership. The statement may also include such information the upper-tier partnership deems necessary to enable the lower-tier partnership to apply the provisions of this section. If at any time the upper-tier partnership determines that the information or documentation previously provided to the lower- tier partnership is no longer correct, the upper-tier partnership shall update such information and documentation. Except as provided in paragraph (e)(3) of this section, an election that is effective under this paragraph (e) shall apply for subsequent taxable years until such upper-tier partnership revokes the election in writing. A revocation under this section shall be effective for any installment due date arising more than 15 days subsequent to the date that the lower-tier partnership receives such revocation.

(3) *Consent of lower-tier partnership.*—An election made under this paragraph (e) is not effective until the lower-tier partnership consents in writing to the upper-tier partnership that it agrees to apply the provisions of this section. A lower-tier partnership may not consent to an election submitted under this paragraph (e) for any installment date or Form 8804 filing date arising within 15 days of the lower-tier partnership's receipt of such election. The lower-tier partnership's written consent must specify the extent to which it will look through the upper-tier partnership in computing its 1446 tax (or any installment of such tax). To the extent that the lower-tier partnership does not consent to an election to apply the look through provisions of paragraph (c) of this section, the lower-tier partnership shall consider such portion of the upper-tier partnership's allocable share of ECTI as allocable to a domestic person for purposes of computing its 1446 tax obligation. A lower-tier partnership that has consented to an election under this paragraph (e) may revoke or modify its consent, in writing, at any time.

(f) *Examples.*—The following examples illustrate the provisions of this section. In considering the examples, disregard the potential application of § 1.1446-3(b)(2)(v)(F) (relating to the de minimis exception to paying 1446 tax). The examples are as follows:

Example 1. Sufficient documentation—tiered partnership structure. (i) Nonresident alien (NRA) and foreign corporation (FC) are partners in PRS, a foreign partnership, and share profits and losses in PRS 70 and 30 percent, respectively. All of PRS's partnership items are allocated based upon each partner's respective ownership interest and it is assumed that these allocations are respected under section 704(b) and the regulations thereunder. NRA and FC each furnish PRS with a valid Form W-8BEN establishing themselves as a foreign individual and foreign corporation, respectively. PRS holds a 40 percent interest in the profits, losses and capital of LTP, a lower-tier partnership. NRA holds the remaining 60 percent interest in profits, losses and capital of LTP. All of LTP's partnership items are allocated based upon each partner's respective ownership interest and it is assumed that these allocations are respected under section 704(b) and the regulations thereunder. LTP has $100 of annualized ECTI for the relevant installment period. All of this income is ordinary income and there is no potential application of a preferential rate applicable percentage under § 1.1446-3(a)(2). Further, § 1.1446-6 does not apply. PRS has no income other than the income allocated from LTP. PRS provides LTP with a valid Form W-8IMY indicating that it is a foreign partnership and attaches the valid Form W-8BENs executed by NRA and FC, as well as a statement describing the allocation of PRS's effectively connected items among its partners. The information that PRS submits to LTP is sufficient to permit LTP to reliably associate (within the meaning of § 1.1441-1(b)(2)(vii)) PRS's allocable share of effectively connected items with NRA and FC pursuant to this section. Further, NRA provides a valid Form W-8BEN to LTP.

(ii) LTP must pay 1446 tax on the $60 allocable to its direct partner NRA using the applicable percentage for non-corporate partners (the highest rate in section 1).

(iii) With respect to the effectively connected partnership items that LTP can reliably associate with NRA through PRS (70 percent of PRS's 40 percent allocable share ($40), or $28), LTP will pay 1446 tax on NRA's allocable share of LTP's ECTI (as determined by looking through PRS) using the applicable percentage for non-corporate partners (the highest rate in section 1).

(iv) With respect to the effectively connected partnership items that LTP can reliably associate with FC through PRS (30 percent of PRS's 40 percent allocable share ($40), or $12), LTP will pay 1446 tax on FC's allocable share of LTP's ECTI (as determined by looking through PRS) using the applicable percentage for corporate partners (the highest rate in section 11).

(v) LTP's payment of the 1446 tax is treated as a distribution to NRA and PRS, its direct partners, that those partners may credit against their respective tax obligations. PRS will report its 1446 tax obligation with respect to its direct foreign partners, NRA and FC, on the Form 8804 and Forms 8805 that it files with the Internal Revenue Service pursuant to paragraph (b) of this section and will credit the amount withheld by LTP on its Form 8804. This credit will satisfy PRS's 1446 tax liability as reported on the Form 8804 it files because PRS's only income is from LTP, and LTP paid 1446 tax with respect to all of PRS's allocable share in LTP by looking through to PRS's partners NRA and FC. Further, PRS will pass along the credit for the 1446 tax withheld by LTP to its partners, NRA and FC on the Form 8805 issued to each partner. The credit passed to each partner on Form 8805 will be treated as a distribution to the respective partners under section 1446(d).

Example 2. Insufficient documentation—tiered partnership structure. (i) LTP is a domestic partnership that has two equal partners A and PRS. A is a nonresident alien and PRS is a foreign partnership that has two equal foreign partners, C and D. Neither A nor PRS provides LTP with a valid Form W-8 or Form W-9. Neither C nor D provides PRS with a valid Form W-8 or Form W-9. Pursuant to § 1.1446-1(c)(3), LTP must presume that PRS is a foreign person subject to withholding under section 1446 at the higher of the highest rate under section 1 or section 11(b)(1). LTP has also not received any documentation with respect to A. LTP must presume that A is a foreign person, and, if LTP knows that A is an individual, compute and pay 1446 tax, subject to § 1.1446-3(a)(2), based on that knowledge.

(ii) Assume a change of facts where C provides a form W-8 (e.g., Form W-8BEN) to PRS, and PRS in turn, furnishes that form to LTP along with its Form W-8IMY, and information regarding how effectively connected items are allocated to C and D. Based upon the additional facts, LTP can reliably associate one-half of PRS's allocable share of ECTI with documentation related with C. Therefore, under paragraph (c)(2) of this section, LTP will look through PRS to C when computing its 1446 tax to the extent of C's indirect share and will not look through with respect to the remainder of PRS's allocable share (D's indirect share). [Reg. § 1.1446-5.]

□ [*T.D. 9200, 5-13-2005. Amended by T.D. 9394, 4-28-2008.*]

§ 1.1446-6. Special rules to reduce a partnership's 1446 tax with respect to a foreign partner's allocable share of effectively connected taxable income.—(a) *In general.*—(1) *Purpose and scope.*—This section provides rules regarding when a partnership required to pay withholding tax under section 1446 (1446 tax), or an installment of 1446 tax, may consider certain partner-level deductions and losses in computing its 1446 tax obligation under § 1.1446-3, or otherwise not pay a de minimis amount of 1446 tax due with respect to a nonresident alien individual partner. A partnership determines the applicability of the rules of this section on a partner-by-partner basis for each installment period and when completing its Form 8804, "Annual Return for Partnership Withholding Tax (Section 1446)," and paying 1446 tax for the partnership taxable year. Except with respect to certain state and local taxes paid by the partnership on behalf of the partner, to apply the rules of this section with respect to a foreign partner, the partnership must receive a certificate from such partner for each partnership taxable year. Paragraph (b) of this section identifies the foreign partners to which this section applies. Paragraph (c) of this section identifies the deductions and losses that a foreign partner may certify to the partnership as well as the state and local taxes paid by the partnership on behalf of the foreign partner that can be taken into account without a certification, and establishes an exception that permits a partnership to not pay a de minimis amount of 1446 tax with respect to a nonresident alien partner. Paragraph (c) of this section also sets forth the requirements for a valid certificate. Paragraphs (a)(2) and (d) of this section establish when a partnership may rely on and consider a foreign partner's certificate in computing its 1446 tax, and the effects of relying on such a certificate. Paragraph (d) of this section also describes the effects of a partnership relying on a certificate (including an updated certificate) and the reporting requirements of a partnership with respect to a certificate. Paragraph (e) of this section sets forth examples that illustrate the rules of this section. Paragraph (f) of this section provides the Effective/Applicability date. Paragraph (g) of this section provides a transition rule.

(2) *Reasonable reliance on a certificate.*—Subject to § 1.1446-2 and the rules of this section, a partnership receiving a certificate (including an updated certificate or status update under paragraph (c)(2)(ii)(B) of this section) of deductions and losses from a partner provided in accordance with the provisions of this section may reasonably rely on such certificate (to the extent of the certified deductions and losses or other representations set forth in the certificate) until such time that it has actual knowledge or reason to know that the certificate is defective or that the time for receiving an updated certificate or status update from the partner under paragraph (c)(2)(ii)(B) of this section has expired. For this purpose, a partnership shall be considered to have actual knowledge or reason to know that a certificate is defective upon receipt of written notification from the IRS under paragraph (c)(3) or (c)(5) of this section.

(b) *Foreign partner to whom this section applies.*—(1) *In general.*—Except as otherwise provided in paragraph (b)(3) of this section, a foreign partner to whom this section applies is a foreign partner that meets the requirements of this paragraph (b)(1).

(i) The partner has provided valid documentation to the partnership to which a certificate is submitted under this section in accordance with § 1.1446-1.

(ii) If the partner's current taxable year is the first taxable year in which the partner submits a certificate to any partnership, the partner has filed (or will file) a qualifying U.S. income tax return for each of its three taxable years ending before the end of the partnership's taxable year for which the partner is submitting a certificate (regardless of whether it was a partner in that partnership during each of these years). A qualifying U.S. income tax return for a taxable year that is prior to the first taxable year the partner submits a certificate to any partnership is a U.S. income tax return filed within the time specified in paragraph (b)(2)(iii) of this section.

(iii) If the current taxable year of the partner is not the first taxable year in which the partner submits a certificate to any partnership, the partner met the requirements in paragraph (b)(1)(ii) of this section for the first taxable year in which it submitted a certificate to any partnership and has filed (or will file) a qualifying U.S. income tax return for its first taxable year in which it submitted a certificate to any partnership and each subsequent taxable year ending before the beginning of the current taxable year (regardless of whether it was a partner in any partnership during each of those years). A qualifying U.S. income tax return for a taxable year that is prior to the taxable year the partner submits a certificate to any partnership is a U.S. income tax return filed within the time specified in paragraph (b)(2)(iii) of this section.

(iv) The partner files a qualifying U.S. income tax return (within the meaning of paragraph (b)(2)(iii) of this section) for its taxable year in which a certificate is provided to any partnership.

(2) *Definitions.*—(i) *U.S. income tax return.*—A U.S. income tax return means a Form 1040NR, "U.S. Nonresident Alien Income Tax

Return," in the case of a nonresident alien individual and a Form 1120F, "U.S. Income Tax Return of a Foreign Corporation," in the case of a foreign corporation.

(ii) *Timely-filed.*—Only for purposes of this section, a U.S. income tax return shall be considered timely-filed if the return is filed on or before the due date set forth in section 6072(c), plus any extension of time to file such return granted under section 6081.

(iii) *Qualifying U.S. income tax return.*—A U.S. income tax return shall constitute a qualifying U.S. income tax return if the return reports income or gain that is effectively connected with a U.S. trade or business or deductions or losses properly allocated and apportioned to such activities and if the return is described in paragraph (b)(2)(iii)(A), (B), or (C) of this section. A protective return described in § 1.874-1(b)(6) or § 1.882-4(a)(3)(vi) is not a qualifying U.S. income tax return for purposes of this section.

(A) A U.S. income tax return for a partner's preceding taxable year in which it did not submit a certificate to any partnership (but not including a taxable year following the first taxable year in which the partner submitted a certificate to any partnership), with a due date as set forth in section 6072(c), not including any extensions of time to file, which falls before the beginning of the current partnership taxable year for which the certificate is provided is described in this paragraph (b)(2)(iii)(A) if the return is filed and all amounts due with respect to such return (including interest, penalties, and additions to tax, if any) are paid on or before the earlier of—

(1) The date that is one year after the due date set forth in section 6072(c) for such return, not including any extensions of time to file; or

(2) The date on which the certificate for the current partnership taxable year is submitted to the partnership.

(B) A U.S. income tax return for a partner's preceding taxable year in which it did not submit a certificate to any partnership (but not including a taxable year following the first taxable year in which the partner submitted a certificate to any partnership), with a due date as set forth in section 6072(c), not including any extensions of time to file, which falls within the current partnership taxable year for which the certificate is provided is described in this paragraph (b)(2)(iii)(B) if the return is timely-filed and all amounts due with respect to such return are timely paid.

(C) A U.S. income tax return for a taxable year in which the partner submits a certificate to any partnership and for a taxable year following the first taxable year in which the partner submits a certificate to any partnership is described in this paragraph (b)(2)(iii)(C) if the return is timely-filed and all amounts due with such return are timely paid with respect to such return.

(3) *Special rules.*—(i) In the case of a partnership (upper-tier partnership) that is a partner in another partnership (lower-tier partnership)—

(A) The rules of this section may apply to reduce or eliminate the 1446 tax (or any installment of such tax) of the lower-tier partnership with respect to a foreign partner of the upper-tier partnership only to the extent the provisions of § 1.1446-5 apply to look through the upper-tier partnership to the foreign partner of such upper-tier partnership and the certificate described in paragraph (c) of this section is provided by such foreign partner to the upper-tier partnership and, in turn, provided to the lower-tier partnership with other appropriate documentation (see § 1.1446-5(c) and (e));

(B) An upper-tier partnership that submits a certificate of deductions and losses or a de minimis certificate to a lower-tier partnership may not submit that certificate to another lower-tier partnership;

(C) An upper-tier partnership that relies on a certificate submitted to it by a foreign partner under this section for computing its 1446 tax due on effectively connected taxable income (ECTI) allocable to that partner (other than ECTI allocable to it from a lower-tier partnership) may not submit that certificate to any lower-tier partnership; and

(D) In addition to any other information required by this section, a lower-tier partnership must submit with a Form 8813, "Partnership Withholding Tax Payment Voucher (Section 1446)," and Form 8805, "Foreign Partner's Information Statement of Section 1446 Withholding Tax," for which it relies on a certificate from an upper-tier partnership to reduce the 1446 tax due with respect to a foreign partner of the upper-tier partnership, sufficient information so that the IRS may reliably associate the ECTI and the certificate of deductions and losses with the partner in the upper-tier partnership submitting the certificate, including the name, taxpayer identification number (TIN) and allocation of effectively connected items at each partnership tier, as well as to the ultimate upper-tier partner submitting the certificate.

(ii) This section shall not apply to a partner that is a foreign estate or its beneficiaries.

(iii) This section shall not apply to a partner that is a trust or to its beneficiaries, except to the extent that such trust is owned by a grantor or other person under subpart E of subchapter J of the Internal Revenue Code, the documentation requirements of § 1.1446-1 have been met by the grantor or other owner of such trust, and the certificate described in paragraph (c) of this section is provided by the grantor or other owner of such trust to the partnership.

(iv) This section shall not apply to a partner in a publicly-traded partnership subject to § 1.1446-4.

(c) *Reduction of 1446 tax with respect to a foreign partner.*—(1) *General rules.*—Under paragraph (c)(1)(i) of this section a foreign partner to whom this section applies may certify to a partnership for a partnership taxable year that it has certain deductions (other than charitable deductions) and losses properly allocated and apportioned to gross income that is effectively connected (or treated as effectively connected) with the conduct of the partner's trade or business in the United States, and that the partner reasonably expects those deductions and losses to be available and claimed on the partner's U.S. income tax return to be filed for that taxable year. Under paragraph (c)(1)(ii) of this section, a nonresident alien individual partner to whom this section applies may also certify to a partnership for a partnership taxable year that its only investment or activity giving rise to effectively connected items for the partnership's taxable year that ends with or within the partner's taxable year is (and will be) the partner's investment in the partnership. A certificate submitted by a foreign partner to a partnership under this section must be in accordance with the form and requirements set forth in paragraph (c)(2)(ii) of this section. Under paragraph (c)(1)(iii) of this section, a partnership may take into account certain state and local taxes withheld by the partnership on behalf of the partner.

(i) *Certified deductions and losses.*—(A) *Deductions and losses from the partnership.*—Under this paragraph (c)(1)(i)(A), a partner may certify to a partnership for a partnership taxable year deductions (other than charitable deductions) and losses properly allocated and apportioned to gross income which is effectively connected (or treated as effectively connected) with the conduct of the partner's trade or business in the United States, that are reported on a Form 1065 (Schedule K-1), "Partner's Share of Income, Credits, Deductions, etc.," issued (or to be issued) to the partner by the partnership for a prior partnership taxable year, that are (or will be) reported on a qualifying U.S. income tax return for a partner's taxable year that ends before the installment due date or the close of the partnership taxable year for which the partner is certifying such deductions and losses, and that the partner reasonably expects to be available and claimed on a qualifying U.S. income tax return for the partner's taxable year ending with or after the close of the partnership taxable year. A partner that has a loss reported on a Form 1065 (Schedule K-1) issued (or to be issued) to the partner by the partnership for a prior partnership taxable year, but that is not (and will not be) reported on a qualifying U.S. income tax return for a prior taxable year of the partner because the loss is suspended under section 704(d) may also certify such suspended loss to the partnership under this paragraph (c)(1)(i)(A).

(B) *Deductions and losses from other sources.*—Under this paragraph (c)(1)(i)(B), a foreign partner may certify to a partnership for a partnership taxable year deductions (other than charitable deductions) and losses properly allocated and apportioned to gross income that is effectively connected (or treated as effectively connected) with the conduct of the partner's trade or business in the United States and that are from sources other than the partnership to whom the certificate is submitted if the deductions and losses are (or will be) reported on a qualifying U.S. income tax return of the partner for a taxable year that ends before the installment due date or the close of the partnership taxable year for which the partner is certifying the deductions and losses and the partner reasonably expects the deductions and losses to be available and claimed on the a qualifying U.S. income tax return filed for its taxable year ending with or after the close of the partnership taxable year. Any deductions and losses certified under this paragraph (c)(1)(i)(B) that are allocated to the partner from another partnership must be reported on a Form 1065 (Schedule K-1) issued (or to be issued) to the partner by such other partnership. However, the partner may not certify any deduction or loss allocated to it from another partnership that is suspended under section 704(d).

(C) *Limit on the consideration of a partner's net operating loss deduction.*—A partnership may not consider a net operating loss deduction (as determined under section 172) certified by the partner under this paragraph (c)(1)(i) in an amount greater than the percentage limitation, if any, provided in section 56(a)(4) and (d) multiplied by the partner's allocable share of ECTI from the partnership reduced by all other certified deductions and losses whether or not taken into account by the partnership, as well as deductions considered under paragraph (c)(1)(iii) of this section.

(D) *Limitation on losses subject to certain partner level limitations.*—Pursuant to paragraph (c)(2)(i) of this section, a partner must identify any certified losses or deductions that are subject to special limitations at the partner level (for example, sections 465 and 469) and provide information to the partnership that will allow the partnership to take the special limitations into account. For example, where a partner certifies a loss to the partnership that is a passive activity loss under section 469, the partner shall identify the activities the partnership conducts that the partner expects will be passive activities. The partnership shall then ensure that these limitations are taken into account when determining the 1446 tax due with respect to the partner.

(E) *Certification of deductions and losses to other partnerships.*—Deductions and losses certified to a partnership for a taxable year of the partnership may not be certified for the taxable year of another partnership that begins or ends with or within the taxable year of the partnership to which the deductions and losses were certified.

(F) *Partner level use of deductions and losses certified to a partnership.*—Any deductions and losses certified to a partnership for a taxable year of the partner and considered by the partnership in computing its section 1446 tax due may not be considered by that partner for the same taxable year in computing the amount of its required installments under section 6654(d) or 6655(d) on income unrelated to the partnership to which the partner has submitted the certificate.

(ii) *De minimis certificate for nonresident alien individual partners.*—(A) *In general.*—Under this paragraph (c)(1)(ii), a nonresident alien individual partner to whom this section applies and that satisfies the requirements of paragraph (c)(1)(ii)(B) of this section may certify to a partnership that its only activity giving rise to effectively connected income, gain, deduction, or loss for the partnership's taxable year that ends with or within the partner's taxable year is (and will be) the partner's investment in the partnership. A partnership that receives a certificate from a nonresident alien partner under this paragraph (c)(1)(ii) and that may reasonably rely on such certificate is not required to pay 1446 tax (or any installment of such tax) with respect to such partner if the partnership estimates that the annualized (or, in the case of a partnership completing its Form 8804, the actual) 1446 tax otherwise due with respect to such partner is less than $1,000, without taking into account any deductions or losses certified by the partner to the partnership under paragraph (c)(1)(i) of this section or any amounts under paragraph (c)(1)(iii) of this section.

(B) *Requirements for exception.*—The requirements of this paragraph (c)(1)(ii)(B) are met if the nonresident individual alien partner's only activity giving rise to effectively connected income, gain, deduction, or loss for the partnership taxable year that ends with or within the partner's taxable year is (and will be) the partner's investment in the partnership. For this purpose, if the partner has (or has reason to expect to have) income or gain described in section 864(c)(6), such income or gain shall be considered derived from a separate investment activity. A certificate submitted by a nonresident alien individual partner under this paragraph (c)(1)(ii) is valid even if such certificate does not certify deductions and losses to partnership under this section. A nonresident alien individual partner that submits a certificate to a partnership under this paragraph (c)(1)(ii) must notify the partnership in writing and revoke such certificate within 10 days of the date that the partner invests or otherwise engages in another activity that may give rise to effectively connected income, gain, deduction, or loss for the partner's taxable year. For example, while an investment in a U.S. real property interest (as defined in section 897(c)) would not give rise to an activity requiring a notification (unless an election is in effect under section 871(d)), the disposition of the U.S. real property interest would give rise to an activity requiring a notification.

(iii) *Consideration of certain current year state and local taxes.*—In addition to any deductions and losses certified by a foreign partner to a partnership under paragraph (c)(1)(i) of this section, the partnership may consider as a deduction of such partner 90-percent of any state and local income taxes withheld and remitted by the partnership on behalf of such partner with respect to the partner's allocable share of partnership ECTI. The partnership may consider the amount of state and local taxes of the foreign partner determined under this paragraph (c)(1)(iii) regardless of whether the foreign partner submits a certificate to the partnership under paragraph (c)(1)(i) or (ii) of this section.

(2) *Form and time of certification.*—(i) *Form of certification.*—A partner's certification to a partnership under paragraph (c)(1)(i) or (iii) of this section shall be made using Form 8804-C, "Certificate Of Partner-Level Items to Reduce Section 1446 Withholding" in accordance with the instructions of the form and the rules of this section.

(ii) *Time for certification provided to partnership.*—(A) *First certificate submitted for a partnership's taxable year.*—Provided the other requirements of this section are met, a partnership may only rely on the first certificate received from a foreign partner for any 1446 tax installment due or Form 8804 filing due (without regard to extensions) on or after the date on which the certificate is received. See §1.1446-3 for 1446 tax installment due dates. See also paragraph (e) of this section for examples illustrating the rules of this paragraph (c)(2).

(B) *Updated certificates and status updates.*—*(1) Preceding year tax returns not yet filed.*—If a foreign partner's U.S. income tax return for a preceding taxable year has not been filed as of the time the partner submits to the partnership its first certificate under this paragraph (c), the certificate shall specify this fact and set forth the filing due date for such return set forth in section 6072(c), plus any extension of time to file such return granted under section 6081 and the regulations under section 6081. The partner shall also submit an updated certificate to the partnership in accordance with this paragraph (c) within 10 days of the date the partner files its U.S. income tax return for any such taxable year. In addition, prior to the partnership's final 1446 tax installment due date the partner shall provide to the partnership, under penalties of perjury, a status update regarding any U.S. income tax return for the prior taxable year that has not (or will not) be filed as of the final installment due date. The status update must identify the due date, set forth in section 6072(c), plus any extension of time to file such return granted under section 6081 and the regulations under section 6081, for any un-filed return identified in the first certificate and state whether the first certificate submitted may continue to be considered by the partnership. If the partnership does not receive an updated certificate or a status update from the partner prior to the partnership's final installment due date, the partnership shall disregard the partner's certificate when computing the 1446 tax due with respect to that partner for the final installment period and when completing its Form 8804 for the taxable year. In addition, the foreign partner shall not be permitted to submit an additional or substitute certificate for the disregarded certificate. See §1.1446-3(b)(2)(i) for computation requirements for installment payments of 1446 tax when a partnership receives, or fails to receive, an updated certificate or status update. See also paragraph (e)(2) *Examples 4 and 8* of this section. Notwithstanding this paragraph (c)(2)(ii)(B)(1), a partner that can meet the requirements of this section for a subsequent partnership taxable year may submit a certificate to the partnership under this section for such taxable year.

(2) Other circumstances requiring an updated certificate.—If at any time during the partnership taxable year the partner determines that its most recent certificate furnished to the partnership for such taxable year is incorrect, then the partner shall submit to the partnership an updated certificate in accordance with this paragraph (c) within 10 days of such determination. For example, if the partner determines that the amount or character of the certified deductions or losses is incorrect, the partner shall submit an updated certificate to the partnership. See §1.1446-3(b)(2)(i) for computation requirements for installment payments of 1446 tax when a partnership receives an updated certificate.

(3) Form and content of updated certificate.—The updated certificate required by this paragraph (c)(2)(ii) must be provided using the form and instructions identified in paragraph (c)(2)(i) of this section. The updated certificate must indicate that it is an updated certificate filed in accordance with this paragraph (c)(2)(ii). The partner is not required to attach to the updated certificate a copy of the certificate that is being updated (superseded certificate).

(4) *Partnership consideration of an updated certificate.*—A partnership may consider an updated certificate, that meets the requirements of this paragraph (c), that is received prior to an installment due date in the same partnership taxable year for which the superseded certificate was provided, or prior to the due date of its Form 8804 (without regard to extensions) to be filed for the year the superseded certificate was provided. A partnership must consider an updated certificate that meets all the requirements of this paragraph (c) if it would increase the amount of 1446 tax the partnership would pay by the next installment due date, if any, or the due date of its Form 8804. An updated certificate considered by the partnership under this paragraph (c)(2)(ii)(B)(4) supersedes all prior certificates submitted by the foreign partner for the same partnership taxable year, beginning with the installment period or Form 8804 filing date for which the partnership considers the updated certificate. See paragraph (e)(2) *Example 4* of this section.

(3) *Notification to partnership when a partner's certificate cannot be relied upon.*—If the IRS determines, in its discretion based on all the facts and circumstances, that a foreign partner's certificate is defective (or that it lacks information sufficient to make this determination after providing written request for such information to the partnership), the IRS shall notify the partnership of such determination in writing. Upon receipt of such written notification, the partnership shall not rely on any certificate submitted by that foreign partner for the partnership taxable year to which the defective certificate relates (or any subsequent partnership taxable year), until the IRS provides written notification to the partnership revoking or modifying the original written notification. For purposes of this section, a foreign partner's certificate of deductions and losses shall be defective if—

(i) The partner is not described in paragraph (b) of this section;

(ii) Any deductions or losses set forth in such certificate are not described in paragraph (c)(1)(i) of this section;

(iii) The timing requirements under paragraph (c)(2) of this section for submitting an original certificate, an updated certificate or a status update to the partnership are not met;

(iv) The certificate does not include all of the information required by paragraph (c)(2)(i) of this section;

(v) Any representation made on the certificate is incorrect;

(vi) The actual amount of deductions and losses available to the partner is less than the amount of deductions and losses certified to the partnership for the partnership taxable year and considered by the partnership in determining its 1446 tax due; or

(vii) There is a failure to comply with any other provision of this section.

(4) *Partner to receive copy of notice.*—If the IRS notifies a partnership under paragraph (c)(3) of this section that a certificate of a foreign partner is defective, the IRS shall send a copy of such notice to the partner's address as shown on the certificate. The partnership shall also promptly furnish a copy of the IRS notice to such partner.

(5) *Notification to partnership when no foreign partner's certificate can be relied upon.*—If the IRS determines, in its discretion based on all the facts and circumstances, that there would be a substantial reduction in section 1446 tax as a result of the submission of one or more defective certificates or that a substantial portion of all certificates being submitted by partners to the partnership and by the partnership to the IRS are defective (or lack information sufficient to make this determination), then the IRS shall notify the partnership of such determination in writing. Upon receipt of such written notification, the partnership shall not rely on any certificate submitted by any partner for the partnership taxable year to which the notice relates or any subsequent partnership taxable year, until the IRS provides written notification to the partnership revoking or modifying the original notice.

(6) *Partnership notification to partner regarding use of deductions and losses.*—Unless § 1.1446-3(d)(1)(i)(A) or (B) applies (relating to waiver of notice of tax paid during the partnership taxable year), a partnership must notify each foreign partner of the amount of such partner's certified deductions and losses and state and local taxes, if any, taken into account under this paragraph (c) in determining the 1446 tax due with respect to such partner for each installment period or Form 8804 filing date, as applicable.

(7) *Partner's certificate valid only for partnership taxable year for which submitted.*—A partnership that receives a certificate from a partnership under this paragraph (c) shall consider such certificate only for the partnership taxable year for which the certificate is submitted, as set forth on the certificate.

(d) *Effect of certificate of deductions and losses on partners and partnership.*—(1) *Effect on partner.*—(i) *No effect on liability for income tax of foreign partner.*—A foreign partner that certifies deductions and losses to a partnership under this section is not relieved of liability for income tax on its allocable share of ECTI from the partnership. Further, the submission of a certificate under this section does not constitute an acceptance by the IRS of the amount or character of the deductions or losses certified therein.

(ii) *No effect on partner's estimated tax obligations.*—A foreign partner that certifies deductions and losses to a partnership under this section is not relieved of any estimated tax obligation otherwise applicable to such partner with respect to income or gain allocated to such partner from the partnership.

(iii) *No effect on partner's obligation to file U.S. income tax return.*—The submission of a certificate under paragraph (c) of this section does not relieve the foreign partner from its obligation to file a U.S. income tax return even if as a result of the partnership considering the certificate the partner would have no additional tax due with such return. See also § 1.1446-3(f).

(2) *Effect on partnership.*—(i) *Reasonable reliance to relieve partnership from addition to tax under section 6655.*—A partnership that has reasonably relied on a certificate received from a foreign partner and complied with the filing requirements of paragraph (d)(3)(i) of this section, shall not be liable for any addition to tax under section 6655 (as applied through § 1.1446-3) for any period during which the partnership reasonably relied on such certificate, even if such certificate is later determined to be defective or the partner submits an updated certificate under paragraph (c)(2) of this section that increases the 1446 tax due with respect to such partner.

(ii) *Continuing liability for withholding tax under section 1461 and for applicable interest and penalties.*—(A) *In general.*—Except as otherwise provided in this section, a partnership that has reasonably relied on a certificate received from a foreign partner and complied with the filing requirements of paragraph (d)(3)(i) of this section, is not relieved from liability for the 1446 tax (or any installment of such tax) under section 1461, any additions to the tax, interest or penalties. However, the partnership may be relieved of additions to the tax or penalties in certain circumstances. See §§ 301.6651-1(c) and 301.6724-1 of this chapter. Further, see § 1.1446-3(e) which deems a partnership to have paid 1446 tax with respect to ECTI allocable to a partner in certain circumstances. See also paragraph (e)(2) *Example 5* of this section.

(B) *Certificate defective because of amount or character of deductions and losses.*—If a certificate is determined to be defective because the actual amount of deductions and losses available to the partner is less than the amount reflected on the certificate (other than when it is determined that the partner certified the same deduction or loss to more than one partnership), or because the character of the certified deductions and losses is erroneous, the partnership shall be liable for 1446 tax under section 1461 (or any installment of such tax) with respect to such partner to the extent the partnership considered an amount of certified deductions and losses greater than the amount actually available to the partner and permitted to be used under §§ 1.1446-1 through 1.1446-5 and this section, or to the extent that the proper character of the certified deductions and losses results in a greater amount of 1446 tax due with respect to such partner. See paragraph (e)(2) *Example 6* of this section.

(3) *Partnership level rules and requirements.*—(i) *Filing requirement.*—A partnership that relies in whole or in part on a certificate received from a partner under this section in computing its 1446 tax due with respect to such partner must still file Form 8813 or Form 8804 and 8805, whichever is applicable, for the period for which the certificate is considered, even if as a result of relying on the certificate no 1446 tax (or an installment of such tax) is due with respect to such foreign partner. See generally § 1.1446-3(d)(1). Except as otherwise provided in this paragraph (d)(3)(i), the partnership must attach a copy of the foreign partner's certificate, and the computation of the 1446 tax due with respect to such partner, to both the Form 8813 and Form 8805 filed with the IRS for any installment period or year for which such certificate is considered in computing the partnership's 1446 tax. See § 1.1446-3(d)(1)(iii) requiring the partnership to furnish Form 8805 to the IRS and such foreign partner even if no 1446 tax is paid on behalf of the partner. The partnership must include in that

computation the amount of state and local taxes described in paragraph (c)(1)(iii) of this section taken into account in computing the 1446 tax due with respect to that partner. The partnership must also attach a computation of the 1446 tax due with respect to a partner for whom only state and local taxes described in paragraph (c)(1)(iii) are taken into account. For an installment period other than the first installment period for which the partnership considers a foreign partner's certificate or updated certificate, the partnership may, instead of attaching any partner's certificate, attach to Form 8813 a list containing the name, TIN, the amount of certified deductions and losses, and the amount of state and local taxes the partnership may consider under paragraph (c)(1)(iii) of this section for each foreign partner whose certificate was relied upon. For purposes of the preceding sentence, if the partnership is relying on a certificate received under paragraph (c)(1)(ii) of this section, instead of providing the amounts described in the prior sentence, it should attach a statement to Form 8813 which provides that, relying on that certificate, no 1446 tax is due with respect to that partner.

(ii) *Reasonable cause for failure to timely file a valid certificate and computation.*—This paragraph (d)(3)(ii) provides the sole source of relief for a partnership that fails to timely file a valid certificate or attach a computation of 1446 tax as required under paragraph (d)(3)(i) of this section. To permit the partnership to reasonably rely on such certificate, the partnership shall be considered to have satisfied the requirements of paragraph (d)(3)(i) of this section if the partnership demonstrates that such failure was due to reasonable cause and not willful neglect and if once the partnership becomes aware of the failure, the partnership attaches the certificate and computation, as well as a written statement setting forth the reasons for the failure to comply with the requirements of paragraph (d)(3)(i) of this section, to an amended Form 8813 or amended Forms 8804 and 8805 for the relevant period. All such submissions should be sent to the address provided in the instructions to Form 8804-C.

(A) *Determining reasonable cause.*—In determining whether the partnership has reasonable cause, the Director shall consider whether the partnership acted reasonably and in good faith considering all the facts and circumstances.

(B) *Notification.*—If the IRS has notified, as provided in paragraph (c)(3) of this section, the partnership that the certificate is defective or that no foreign partner's certificate may be relied upon, as provided in paragraph (c)(5) of this section, the partnership will be deemed not to have acted reasonably and in good faith. Otherwise, the Director shall notify the partnership in writing within 120 days of the amended filing if it is determined that the failure to comply was not due to reasonable cause, or if additional time will be needed to make such determination. If the Director fails to notify the partnership within 120 days of the amended filing, the partnership shall be considered to have demonstrated to the Director that such failure was due to reasonable cause and not willful neglect.

(e) *Examples.*—(1) The rules of this section are illustrated by the examples in paragraph (e)(2) of this section. In 2008, the relevant rate of withholding for foreign partners that were not corporations (that is, the highest rate in section 1 as specified in § 1.1446-3(a)(2)(i)) was 35%, and the due date for filing Form 8804 for domestic calendar year partnerships (that is, the date specified in § 1.1446-3(d)(1)(iii)) was April 15. Except as otherwise provided, in each example assume:

(i) Section 1.1446-3(b)(2)(v)(F) (relating to the de minimis exception to paying 1446 tax) does not apply;

(ii) Paragraph (c)(1)(ii) of this section (relating to a nonresident alien individual partner whose sole investment generating effectively connected income or gain is the partnership) does not apply;

(iii) All income and losses are ordinary;

(iv) For purposes of applying paragraph (c)(1)(i)(C) of this section, the percentage limitation under section 56(a)(4) and (d) is 90 percent;

(v) Any loss is not a passive activity loss within the meaning of section 469;

(vi) The partnership uses an acceptable annualization method under § 1.1446-3;

(vii) NRA is a nonresident alien individual who maintains a calendar taxable year for U.S. tax purpose;

(viii) B and C are U.S. individuals who maintain a calendar taxable year; and

(ix) Any partnership maintains a calendar taxable year.

(2) The examples are as follows:

Example 1. Qualifying U.S. income tax return. (i) NRA and B form a partnership (PRS) in year 4 to conduct a trade or business in the United States. NRA and B provide PRS appropriate documentation under § 1.1446-1 to establish their status for purposes of section 1446. NRA submits a certificate to PRS (using Form 8804-C) on March 20, year 4, to be considered by PRS in determining its 1446 tax due with respect to NRA for the first installment period in the year 4. The Form 8804-C states that NRA reasonably expects to have an effectively connected net operating loss of $5,000 available to offset its allocable share of ECTI from PRS in year 4. Prior to year 4, NRA had not submitted a certificate to a partnership under this section. NRA filed (or will file) its year 1 U.S. income tax return on March 11, year 3, its year 2 U.S. income tax return on February 12, year 4; its year 3 U.S. income tax return on April 13, year 4; and its year 4 U.S. income tax return on May 14, year 5. NRA paid or (will pay) all amounts due with respect to the returns (including interest, penalties, and additions to tax, if any) by the date they are filed. NRA's years 1 though 3 U.S. income tax returns report income or gain effectively connected with a U.S. trade or business or deductions or losses properly allocated and apportioned to such activities.

(ii) To be eligible to submit a certificate of deductions and losses to PRS under this section, NRA must satisfy the requirements of paragraph (b)(1) of this section. In accordance with § 1.1446-1, NRA provided valid documentation to PRS to establish its status for purposes of section 1446. NRA's year 1 U.S. income tax return is a qualifying U.S. income tax return because it reported income or gain effectively connected with a U.S. trade or business or deductions or losses properly allocated and apportioned to such activities and is described under paragraph (b)(2)(iii)(A) of this section. Although NRA filed its year 1 return after the due date of the return (determined under section 6072(c) without regard to any extension of time to file) the return was filed on March 11, year 3, which was on or before the earlier of June 15, year 3, the date one year after its section 6072(c) due date without regard to any extension of time to file, and March 20, year 4, the date on which NRA submitted the certificate to PRS. NRA's year 2 U.S. income tax return is a qualifying U.S. income tax return because it reported income or gain effectively connected with a U.S. trade or business or deductions or losses properly allocated and apportioned to such activities and is described under paragraph (b)(2)(iii)(A) of this section. Although NRA filed its year 2 return after the due date of the return (determined under section 6072(c) without regard to any extension of time to file) the return was filed on February 12, year 4, which was on or before the earlier of June 15, year 4, the date one year after its section 6072(c) due date without regard to any extension of time to file, and March 20, year 4, the date on which NRA submitted the certificate to PRS. NRA's year 3 U.S. income tax return is a qualifying U.S. income tax return because it reported income or gain effectively connected with a U.S. trade or business or deductions or losses properly allocated and apportioned to such activities and is described under paragraph (b)(2)(iii)(B) of this section. Because NRA filed its year 3 U.S. income tax return on April 13, year 4, the return will be considered timelyfiled under paragraph (b)(2)(ii) of this section, as the due date under section 6072(c) was June 15, year 4. NRA's year 4 U.S. income tax return is a qualifying U.S. income tax return because it reported income or gain effectively connected with a U.S. trade or business or deductions or losses properly allocated and apportioned to such activities and is described under paragraph (b)(2)(iii)(C) of this section. Because NRA filed its year 4 U.S. income tax return on May 14, year 5, the return will be considered timelyfiled under paragraph (b)(2)(ii) of this section. Accordingly, NRA meets the conditions of paragraph (b)(1) of this section and is eligible to provide a certificate of deductions and losses to PRS for year 4.

Example 2. Subsequent year qualifying U.S. income tax return. (i) Assume the same facts as in Example 1. Further, NRA and C form a second partnership (XYZ) in year 7 to conduct a trade or business in the United States. NRA and C provide XYZ appropriate documentation under § 1.1446-1 to establish their status for purposes of section 1446. NRA did not submit a certificate under this section to any partnership for years 5 and 6. NRA submits a certificate to XYZ (using Form 8804-C) on April 10, year 7, to be considered by XYZ in determining its 1446 tax due with respect to NRA for its first installment period in year 7. The certificate states that NRA reasonably expects to have an effectively connected net operating loss of $8,000 available to offset its allocable share of ECTI from XYZ in year 7. Further, the certificate contains all of the necessary representations required under this section. NRA will file its U.S. income tax return for year 5 on March 25, year 7, (after its section 6072(c) due date and any extension of time to file that could have been granted under section 6081), its U.S. income tax return for year 6 on April 26, year 7; and its U.S. income tax return for year 7 on May 27, year 8. NRA will pay all amounts due with the returns (including interest, penalties, and additions to tax, if any) by the dates they are filed. NRA's years 5, 6, and 7 U.S. income tax returns will report income or gain that is effectively connected with a U.S. trade or business or deductions or losses properly allocated and apportioned to such activities.

(ii) To be eligible to submit a certificate of deductions and losses to XYZ under this section, NRA must satisfy the requirements of paragraph (b)(1) of this section. NRA provided valid documentation to XYZ in accordance with § 1.1446-1. As described in Example 1, NRA's year 4 U.S. income tax return is a qualifying U.S. income tax return because it will report income or gain effectively connected with a U.S. trade or business and is described under paragraph (b)(2)(iii)(C) of this section. Although NRA's year 5 U.S. income tax return reports income or gain effectively connected with a U.S. trade or business or deductions or losses properly allocated and apportioned to such activities it is not qualifying U.S. tax return under paragraph (b)(2)(iii) of this section. Because NRA submitted a certificate to PRS in year 4, to constitute a qualifying U.S. tax income return the year 5 U.S. income tax return must be timely-filed and all amounts due with such return must be timely paid. See paragraph (b)(2)(iii)(C) of this section. However, NRA will not file its U.S. income tax return for year 5 until March 25, year 7, (after its section 6072(c) due date and any extension of time to file that could have been granted under section 6081). Because the year 5 tax return is not a qualifying U.S. income tax return under paragraph (b)(2)(iii) of this section, NRA does not satisfy the requirements of paragraph (b)(1)(ii) of this section and, therefore, may not submit a certificate of deductions and losses to XYZ under this section in year 7.

Example 3. General application of the rules of this section. NRA and B form a partnership (PRS) to conduct a trade or business in the United States. NRA and B are equal partners under the partnership agreement. NRA and B provide PRS appropriate documentation under § 1.1446-1 to establish their status for purposes of section 1446. Prior to the formation of PRS, NRA had not invested in or engaged in the conduct of a U.S. trade or business. PRS incurs a $1,500 effectively connected net operating loss in years 1 and 2. The loss incurred in each is allocated equally between NRA and B. NRA has filed a qualifying U.S. income tax return (within the meaning of paragraph (b)(2)(iii) of this section) for years 1 and 2 that report its allocable share of effective connected net operating loss allocated to it from PRS, as reported on the Form 1065 (Schedule K- 1) issued to NRA for each year.

(i) In year 3, NRA may not submit a certificate to PRS under paragraph (c) because it will not have filed qualifying U.S. income tax returns for the preceding three years. In year 3, PRS has ECTI of $1,000 that is allocated equally between NRA and B. PRS satisfies its 1446 tax obligation with respect to NRA for year 3.

(ii) In year 4, PRS estimates that it will have ECTI of $4,000, which will be allocated equally between NRA and B. On or before April 15th of year 4 (the first installment due date), NRA submits a certificate to PRS under this section (using Form 8804-C) certifying that it reasonably expects to have an effectively connected net operating loss of $1,000 ($750 loss in both years 1 and 2, less $500 of income in year 3) available to offset its allocable share of ECTI from PRS in year 4. As of the date the certificate is submitted, NRA has received the Form 1065 (Schedule K-1) from PRS for year 3 but has not yet filed its U.S. income tax return for year 3.

(iii) With respect to year 4, and based upon paragraph (b)(1) of this section, NRA can include year 3 (NRA's preceding taxable year) as one of the preceding three years that it has filed or will file qualifying U.S. income tax returns (within the meaning of paragraph (b)(2)(iii) of this section). Therefore, provided PRS has, in accordance with paragraph (a)(2) of this section, no actual knowledge or reason to know the certificate is defective, PRS may reasonably rely on NRA's certificate. Accordingly, PRS may consider NRA's certificate to reduce the 1446 tax that would otherwise be required to be paid on NRA's behalf. Specifically, subject to paragraph (c)(1)(i)(C) of this section, the $1,000 of net losses that have been reported on Forms 1065 (Schedule K-1) issued to NRA that are available to reduce NRA's U.S. income tax on NRA's allocable share of effectively connected income or gain allocable from PRS may be used to reduce the $2,000 of ECTI estimated to be allocable to NRA. As a result, PRS must pay 1446 tax on only $1,100 of NRA's allocable share of partnership ECTI for the first installment period in year 5 ($2,000 – ($1,000 × .90)). PRS must pay 1446 tax of $96.25 for its first installment period with respect to the ECTI allocable to NRA ($1,100 (net ECTI after considering certified losses) x .35 (withholding tax rate) x .25 (section 6655(e)(2)(B) percentage for the first installment period)). See § 1.1446-3(b)(2). Pursuant to paragraph (d)(3) of this section, PRS must attach NRA's certificate and PRS's computation of its 1446 tax obligation with respect to NRA to its Form 8813, "Partnership Withholding Tax Payment Voucher (Section 1446)," filed for the first installment period. Under paragraph (c)(2)(ii)(B) of this section, NRA is required to provide an updated certificate on or before the 10th day after NRA files its U.S. income tax return for year 3, even if the updated certificate results in no change to the amount of deductions and losses reported on the superseded certificate.

(iv) The results are the same if NRA had not yet received a Form 1065 (Schedule K-1) from PRS for year 3. See paragraph (c)(1)(i)(A) of this section.

Example 4. Updated certificate submitted for losses. On January 1, year 8, NRA and B form a partnership (PRS) to conduct a trade or business in the United States. NRA and B are equal partners in PRS. NRA and B provide PRS appropriate documentation under § 1.1446-1 to establish their status for purposes of section 1446. During years 1 through 7 NRA held an interest in another partnership (XYZ) that conducted a trade or business in the United States. NRA timely-filed (within the meaning of paragraph (b)(2) of this section) U.S. income tax returns for years 1 through 6 reporting its allocable year of ECTI (or loss) from XYZ (and timely paid all tax shown on such returns). NRA files its U.S. income tax return for year 7 on June 9, year 8 (and timely pays all tax due with such return). Therefore, NRA has filed qualifying U.S. income tax returns (within the meaning of paragraph (b)(2)(iii) of this section) for years 1 through 7. During years 1 through 7, NRA's only investment generating effectively connected items was its interest in XYZ. The XYZ partnership liquidated and ceased doing business on December 31, year 7.

(i) On or before April 15, year 8, PRS receives from NRA a valid certificate under this section using Form 8804-C in which NRA certifies that it reasonably expects to have available effectively connected net operating losses in the amount of $5,000. Among other statements made in accordance with paragraph (c) of this section, NRA represents that it has not yet filed its year 7 U.S. income tax return, but will timely file such return (and timely pay all tax due with such return). For its first installment period in year 8, PRS estimates that it will earn taxable income of $10,000 for the year which will be allocated equally to NRA and B (NRA's allocable share of PRS's ECTI is $5,000).

(ii) Provided PRS has, in accordance with paragraph (a)(2) of this section, no actual knowledge or reason to know the certificate is defective, PRS may reasonably rely on NRA's certificate when computing its 1446 tax obligation for the first installment period. PRS is limited under paragraph (c)(1)(i)(C) of this section and PRS may only consider $4,500 ($5,000 × .90) of the certified net operating loss. After consideration of the certified loss, PRS owes 1446 tax in the amount of $43.75 for the first installment period ($5,000 estimated allocable ECTI less $4,500 (certified loss as limited under paragraph (c)(1)(i)(C)) x .35 (1446 tax applicable percentage) x .25 (section 6655(e)(2)(B) percentage for the first installment period)). See § 1.1446-3(b)(2). Pursuant to paragraph (d)(3) of this section, PRS must attach a copy of NRA's certificate and the computation of 1446 tax due with respect to NRA to the Form 8813 filed with respect to NRA.

(iii) PRS's estimate of ECTI allocable to NRA for the second installment period remains unchanged from the first installment period. On June 10, year 8, NRA provides PRS an updated certificate reporting that NRA now reasonably expects to have an effectively connected net operating loss of $4,000 available to offset its allocable share of ECTI from PRS in year 4. NRA provided the updated certificate within 10 days of filing its U.S. income tax return for the year 7 taxable year, as required by paragraph (c)(2)(ii)(B) of this section. Provided the updated certificate is otherwise valid, PRS may rely on the updated certificate for the second installment period (due date June 15, year 8). Even if the updated certificate were not valid, PRS could no longer rely on the original certificate.

(iv) Under paragraph (d) of this section, PRS is not relieved from liability for the 1446 tax due with respect to NRA under section 1461 if it relies on a certificate determined to be defective, or if it receives an updated certificate reporting an amount of deductions and losses less than the amount reported on the superseded certificate. Under the principles of section 6655 (as applied through § 1.1446-3), PRS is required to have paid 50-percent of the annualized 1446 tax due with respect to NRA on or before the due date of the second installment period (section 6655(e)(2)(B) percentage for the second installment period). Under paragraph (c)(2)(ii)(B) of this section, because NRA's updated certificate is valid for the second installment period, if PRS considers a certificate for that period it must consider the updated certificate. Under paragraph (c)(1)(i)(C) of this section, PRS can only consider $3,600 ($4,000 × .90) of NRA's updated effectively connected net operating loss. Assuming PRS considers NRA's updated certificate for the second installment period, PRS must have paid a total of $245 of 1446 tax with respect to the ECTI estimated to be allocable to NRA as of the second installment due date ($1,400 ($5,000 ECTI less $3,600 net operating loss deduction) x .35 (withholding tax rate) x .50 (section 6655(e)(2)(B) percentage for the second installment period)). After considering PRS's payment of 1446 tax for the first installment period, PRS is required to pay $201.25 for the second installment period ($245 less previous payment of $43.75). See § 1.1446-3(b)(2). Further, if PRS considers NRA's updated certificate for the second installment period, when PRS files Form 8813 it must attach the updated certificate along with PRS's computation of 1446 tax due with respect to NRA.

(v) Under paragraph (d) of this section, PRS is not liable for the addition to the tax under section 6655 (as applied through § 1.1446-3) for the first installment period because PRS reasonably relied on NRA's certificate of losses for that period.

(vi) Assume that PRS's estimate of its ECTI allocable to NRA for the third and fourth installment periods is the same as for the first and second installment periods. Assume PRS may reasonably rely on NRA's updated certificate in calculating its payment of 1446 tax for the third and fourth installment periods. The third installment of 1446 tax would be $122.50 (($5,000 – $3,600) × .35 × .75 = $367.50 – $245 (total previous payments)). The fourth installment of 1446 tax would be $122.50 (($5,000- $3,600) × .35 × 1.00 = $490 – $367.50 (total previous payments)). See § 1.1446- 3(b)(2). PRS must attach to each Form 8813 a computation of the 1446 tax due with respect to NRA that takes into account the amount of effectively connected net operating loss reported on NRA's updated certificate.

(vii) Because NRA's certified net operating loss has not changed for the third and fourth installments, in lieu of attaching NRA's certificate, PRS may attach a statement containing NRA's name, TIN, and the certified net operating loss amount. However, PRS must attach NRA's certificate and a computation of the 1446 tax due with respect to NRA that takes into account NRA's certified net operating loss to the Form 8805 filed with respect to NRA. See paragraph (d)(3) of this section.

Example 5. IRS determines in subsequent taxable year that partner's certificate is defective because partner failed to timely file a U.S. income tax return. NRA and B form a partnership (PRS) in year 1 to conduct a trade or business in the United States. NRA and B provide PRS appropriate documentation under § 1.1446-1 to establish their status for purposes of section 1446. In year 4, NRA timely submits a certificate under this section (using Form 8804-C) to be considered by PRS for its first installment period. The certificate reports that NRA reasonably expects to have an effectively connected net operating loss of $5,000 available to offset its allocable share of ECTI from PRS in year 4. Further, the certificate contains all of the necessary representations required under this section. PRS estimates for each installment period that NRA's allocable share of ECTI will be $5,000 for the taxable year. PRS's actual operating results for the year result in $5,000 of ECTI allocable to NRA.

(i) PRS reasonably relies on (within the meaning of paragraph (a)(2) of this section) NRA's certificate when computing each installment payment during year 4 and the 1446 tax due on Form 8804 and appropriately considers the limitation in paragraph (c)(1)(i)(C) of this section. As a result, PRS paid $175 of 1446 tax on behalf of NRA for the taxable year ($5,000 of ECTI less $4,500 net operating loss deduction x .35 applicable percentage). As required under paragraph (d) of this section, PRS attached the certificate to the Form 8813 for the first installment period and the Form 8805 for year 4. Because NRA did not submit an updated certificate to PRS in year 4, PRS attached to the Forms 8813 for the second, third and fourth installment periods a statement containing NRA's name, TIN, and the certified net operating loss as well as the computation of 1446 tax due with respect to NRA reflecting the amount of net operating loss considered.

(ii) In year 5, NRA timely submits to PRS a certificate under this section to be considered for the first installment period. The certificate represents that NRA reasonably expects to have an effectively connected net operating loss of $5,000 available to offset its allocable share of ECTI from PRS in year 5. For the first installment period, PRS estimates that NRA's allocable share of partnership ECTI is $5,000. PRS reasonably relies on the certificate for the first installment period and determines that it is required to make a 1446 tax installment payment of $43.75 ($5,000 allocable ECTI less $4,500 (certified net operating loss as limited under paragraph (c)(1)(i)(C) of this section) x .35 (1446 tax applicable percentage) x .25 (section 6655(e)(2)(B) percentage for the first installment period)). See § 1.1446-3(b)(2). PRS makes the installment payment with the Form 8813 filed for the first installment period, and complies with paragraph (d)(3) of this section by attaching NRA's certificate and the computation of 1446 tax due with respect to NRA to the Form 8813.

(iii) The IRS provides written notification to PRS on June 1, year 5, (pursuant to paragraph (c)(3) of this section) that the certificate received from NRA in year 4 is defective because NRA failed to file a qualifying U.S. income tax return (within the meaning of paragraph (b)(2)(iii) of this section) for one of the preceding taxable years as required under paragraph (b)(1) of this section. The notice further states that PRS is not to rely on any certificate received from NRA in year 5.

(iv) Under paragraph (d)(2)(ii) of this section, because the certificate submitted by NRA in year was determined to be defective for a reason other than the amount or character of the certified deductions and losses, under section 1461 PRS is fully liable for the 1446 tax due with respect to NRA's allocable share of ECTI year 4 without regard to the certificate. The total 1446 tax due for year 4 without regard to the certificate is $1,750 ($5,000 ECTI x .35) and PRS paid $175 of 1446 tax in year 4. Therefore, PRS owes $1,575 of 1446 tax. However, PRS may be deemed to have paid the outstanding 1446 tax due if NRA paid all of its U.S. tax due in year 4. See § 1.1446-3(e).

(v) However, because PRS did not have actual knowledge or reason to know that the certificate NRA submitted in year 4 was defective, PRS reasonably relied on the certificate for purposes of paragraph (d)(2) of this section. Therefore, PRS is not liable for an addition to the tax with respect to its underpayment of 1446 tax under the principles of section 6655 (as applied through § 1.1446-3) for any installment period in year 4.

(vi) However, PRS is generally liable for interest under section 6601 and for the failure to pay addition to tax under section 6651(a)(2) on the $1,575 of 1446 tax due for year 4 for the period from April 15, year 5 (last date prescribed for payment of 1446 tax) to the date PRS pays the 1446 tax or is deemed to have paid the 1446 tax under § 1.1446-3(e).

(vii) With respect to the year 5, PRS reasonably relied on NRA's certificate when computing its first installment payment (due on April 15, year 5). Therefore, in accordance with paragraph (d)(2)(i) of this section, PRS will not be liable for an addition to the tax under the principles of section 6655 (as applied through § 1.1446-3) for the first installment period. However, because the IRS provided written notification to PRS on June 1, year 5, to disregard any certificate received from NRA for year 5, PRS may not rely on any certificate received from NRA certificate (or any new certificate provided by NRA) when it computes its second installment payment in year 5. PRS is not permitted to consider any certificate submitted by NRA until the IRS provides written notification to PRS revoking or modifying the original notice. PRS's second installment payment in year 5 must include the additional amount of 1446 tax it would have paid for the first installment period without regard to the certificate received from NRA.

Example 6. IRS determines in subsequent taxable year that partner's certificate is defective because partner's actual losses are less than amount certified and considered by the partnership. Assume the same facts as in *Example 5*, except that the IRS determines that NRA's certificate submitted in year 4 is defective because the actual effectively connected net operating loss available to NRA for year 4 was $1,000 rather than the $5,000 certified.

(i) Under paragraph (d)(2)(ii) of this section, PRS is not relieved from its liability for 1446 tax under section 1461 when it relies on a certificate of losses from a foreign partner that is later determined to be defective. However, when the IRS determines that a partner's certificate is defective because of the amount of the certified deductions and losses, the partnership is liable for the 1446 tax, interest, additions to tax, and penalties to the extent the amount of certified deductions and losses taken into account when computing 1446 tax (or, unless there was reasonable reliance on the certificate, any installment of such tax) is greater than the actual amount of available deductions and losses. Here, PRS considered the certified deductions and losses in the amount of $4,500. The IRS subsequently determined that NRA only had $1,000 of actual losses, only $900 of which were permitted to be considered under paragraph (c)(1)(i)(C) of this section. Accordingly, PRS is liable for the 1446 tax due with respect to the portion of the overstated losses that it considered when computing its 1446 tax. The remaining 1446 tax due for year 4 is $1,260 ($3,600 ($4,500 less $900) of excess losses considered x .35). However, PRS may be deemed to have paid the $1,260 of 1446 tax under § 1.1446-3(e) if NRA has paid all of NRA's U.S. income tax.

(ii) If PRS had considered only $900 (or a lesser amount) of NRA's certified net operating loss when computing and paying its 1446 tax during year 4 then, under paragraph (d)(2)(iii) of this section, PRS would not be liable for 1446 tax because it did not consider a net operating loss greater than the amount actually available to NRA.

Example 7. Partner with different taxable year than partnership. PRS partnership has two equal partners, FC, a foreign corporation, and DC, a domestic corporation. PRS conducts a trade or business in the United States and generates effectively connected income. FC maintains a June 30 fiscal taxable year end, while DC and PRS maintain a calendar taxable year end. FC and DC provide a valid Form W-8BEN and Form W-9, respectively, to PRS. FC and DC are the only persons that have ever been partners in PRS. For its year 1 through year 3 taxable years, PRS issued Forms 1065 (Schedule K-1) reporting in the aggregate $100 of net loss to each partner. For its year 4 taxable year, PRS issued Forms 1065 (Schedule K-1) to its partners reporting $150 of loss to each partner. All of the losses reported on the Forms 1065 (Schedule K-1) are effectively connected to PRS's and FC's trade or business in the United States.

(i) Assume that FC submits a valid certificate under this section certifying losses to the partnership for the partnership's year 5 taxable year. Further, assume that FC's only source of effectively connected income, gain, deduction, or loss is the activity of PRS.

(ii) For PRS's first installment period in year 5, FC may only certify deductions and losses under this section in the amount of $100 (the losses as reported on the Forms 1065 (Schedule K-1) issued for PRS's year 1 through 3 taxable years). Under section 706, the taxable income of a partner shall include the income, gain, loss, deduction, or credit of the partnership for the partnership taxable year ending within or with the taxable year of the partner. PRS's year 4 calendar taxable year ends during FC's fiscal taxable year ending June 30, year 5. Therefore, under paragraph (c)(1) of this section, as of April 15, year 5 (the last date FC may submit its first certificate under paragraph (c) of this section to have it considered for PRS's first installment due date of April 15, year 5), FC's allocable share of the PRS losses for years 1 through 3 are the only losses that FC can represent have been or will be reported on an FC U.S. income tax return filed for a taxable year ending prior to such installment due date.

(iii) The result in paragraph (ii) of this *Example 7* is the same for the year 5 second installment period, the due date of which is June 15, year 5.

(iv) FC may submit an updated certificate under this section after June 30, year 5, which includes the $150 loss for year 4. PRS may consider such an updated certificate for its third installment period (due date September 15, year 5), provided the updated certificate is received by the due date for such installment in accordance with paragraph (c) of this section.

Example 8. Failure to provide status update with respect to prior year unfiled returns. FC, a foreign corporation, and DC, a domestic corporation, form a partnership (PRS) to conduct a trade or business in the United States. FC and DC provide PRS appropriate documentation under § 1.1446-1 to establish their status for purposes of section 1446. FC and DC are equal partners in PRS, and all partnership items are allocated equally between FC and DC.

(i) In the current taxable year FC submits a certificate under this section using Form 8804-C prior to PRS's first installment due date. FC represents that it has filed or will file a qualifying U.S. income tax return (within the meaning of paragraph (b)(2)(iii) of this section) in each of the preceding three taxable years. FC specifies that it has not filed its U.S. income tax return for the immediately preceding taxable year. FC also represents that it will timely file its U.S. income tax return for the partnership taxable year during which the certificate is considered (and will timely pay all tax due with such return). Assume all other requirements under paragraph (c) of this section are met for FC's certificate to be valid.

(ii) Provided that PRS does not possess actual knowledge or reason to know that FC's certificate is defective under paragraph (a)(2) of this section, PRS may reasonably rely on FC's certificate for its first, second, and third installment payments.

(iii) If FC does not submit to PRS either an updated certificate or a status update as required by paragraph (c)(2)(ii)(B)(1) of this section by December 15th (PRS's final installment due date), PRS must disregard FC's certificate when computing its fourth installment payment of 1446 tax and when completing its Form 8804 for the taxable year. PRS's payment of 1446 tax for its fourth installment period must include the additional amount of 1446 tax it would have paid in the first, second and third installment periods had it not considered FC's certificate. Further, even if the status update is provided by December 15th, PRS may only rely on the certificate if the status update does not contradict the original certificate and such update indicates that the immediately preceding year's return will be timely filed. Finally, even if the status update is provided by December 15th, FC must also submit an updated certificate to the partnership in accordance with paragraph (c) of this section within 10 days of the date FC timely files its U.S. income tax return for the preceding taxable year.

Example 9. Partnership consideration of certified deductions and losses or de minimis certificate. For purposes of this example assume paragraph (c)(1)(ii) of this section may apply. On January 1, year 4, NRA and B form a partnership (PRS) to conduct a trade or business in the United States. NRA and B are equal partners in PRS and all partnership items are shared equally. NRA and B provide PRS appropriate documentation under § 1.1446-1 to establish their status for purposes of section 1446. During years 1 through 3, NRA's only activity generating effectively connected items was an interest in partnership XYZ. XYZ allocated NRA a loss for all three years. NRA filed qualifying U.S. income tax returns (within the meaning of paragraph (b)(2)(iii) of this section) reporting its allocable share of losses from XYZ in years 1 through 3. The XYZ partnership dissolved on December 31, year 3.

(i) In year 4, NRA's only activity giving rise to effectively connected income, gain, deduction, or loss is its interest in PRS. NRA submits to PRS a valid certificate (using Form 8804-C) certifying under paragraph (c)(1)(i) its effectively connected net operating losses from years 1 through 3 and under (c)(1)(ii) of this section that its only activity giving rise to effectively connected income, gain, deduction, or loss for the PRS taxable year that ends with or within its taxable year is (and will be) its investment in PRS.

(ii) During year 4, PRS allocates ECTI to NRA. If the 1446 tax otherwise due on the annualized amount allocated to NRA is less than $1,000, determined without regard to any deductions and losses certified by NRA under paragraph (c)(1)(i) of this section, PRS may consider the certificate received from NRA under paragraph (c)(1)(ii) of this section and not pay 1446 tax (or any installment of such tax) with respect to NRA. Alternatively, PRS may consider the deductions and losses certified by NRA under paragraph (c)(1)(i) of this section.

(iii) Regardless of whether PRS considers NRA's certification under paragraph (c)(1)(i) or (c)(1)(ii) of this section in computing its 1446 tax due with respect to NRA, PRS must file Form 8813 for all installment periods as well as a Form 8805 for NRA with its Form 8804. If PRS considers NRA's certification under paragraph (c)(1)(i) or (c)(1)(ii) of this section, PRS must attach to each Form 8813, as well as to the Form 8805, a computation of the 1446 tax with respect to NRA that takes into account its consideration of NRA's certificate. In addition, PRS must attach NRA's certificate to the Form 8813 for the first installment period it considers the certificate, as well as to the Form 8805. For all subsequent installment periods, PRS may attach a statement containing NRA's name, and TIN. If PRS is relying on NRA's certified losses under paragraph (c)(1)(i) of this section, the statement must indicate the amount of losses and deductions NRA certified. If PRS is relying on NRA's certification under paragraph (c)(ii) of this section, the statement must indicate that it is relying on NRA meeting the requirements under paragraph (c)(1)(ii) of this section and the 1446 tax on the annualized amount allocated to NRA is less than $1,000. See paragraph (d)(3)(i) of this section.

Example 10. Application of transition rule. NRA and B form a partnership (PRS) on January 1, 2004, to conduct a trade or business in the United States. NRA and B are equal partners in PRS and all partnership items are shared equally. NRA and B provide PRS appropriate documentation under § 1.1446-1 to establish their status for purposes of section 1446. For its 2004 through 2007 tax years, PRS issued Forms 1065 (Schedule K-1) to NRA and B reporting a $1,000 net loss from its U.S. trade or business to each partner for each year (for an aggregate loss of $4,000 per partner). During the 2004 through 2007 tax years, NRA's only activity generating effectively connected items was its investment in PRS.

(i) On February 10, 2008, NRA submitted a certificate to PRS, reporting its aggregate $4,000 effectively connected loss to PRS, that met the requirements of § 1.1446-6T(c) (See 26 CFR Part 1, revised as of April 1, 2007), as in effect before January 1, 2008. The certificate stated that NRA had timely filed its U.S. income tax returns for the 2004, 2005 and 2006 tax years, and that it would timely file a U.S. income tax return for its 2007 tax year. For the first and second installments period in 2008, PRS estimates that it will earn ECTI of $10,000.

(ii) Because the certificate submitted by NRA to PRS on February 10, 2008, met the requirements of § 1.1446-6T (See 26 CFR Part 1, revised as of April 1, 2007), as in effect before January 1, 2008, PRS may consider such certificate when computing its 1446 tax due for the first and second installment period even if the certificate does not meet all the requirements of paragraph (c) of this section.

(iii) NRA timely files its U.S. income tax return for the 2007 tax year on July 24, 2008. In accordance with paragraph (c)(2)(ii)(B)(1) of this section, within 10 days of filing such return NRA prepares an updated certificate to be submitted to PRS certifying that it reasonably expects to have only $3,500 of losses available to reduce its allocable share of ECTI from PRS. Because the updated certificate will be submitted after July 28, 2008, to be valid the updated certificate must meet the requirements of paragraph (c) this section.

(f) *Effective/Applicability date.*—Except as otherwise provided in this paragraph (f), the rules of this section are applicable for partnership taxable years beginning after December 31, 2007. The rules of paragraphs (b)(3)(i)(B) through (D) shall apply to partnership taxable years beginning after July 28, 2008.

(g) *Transition rule.*—A certificate that met the requirements of § 1.1446-6T(c) (See 26 CFR Part 1, revised as of April 1, 2007), as in effect before January 1, 2008, submitted on or before July 28, 2008 by a partner that met the requirements of § 1.1446-6T(b) (See 26 CFR Part 1, revised as of April 1, 2007), as in effect before January 1, 2008, shall not be considered defective because it does not meet the requirements of this section. However, any certificate (including any updated certificates and status updates) submitted, or required to be submitted, under paragraph (c) of this section after July 28, 2008, must meet the requirements of this section. See paragraph (e)(2) *Example 10* of this section. [Reg. § 1.1446-6.]

☐ [*T.D. 9394, 4-28-2008 (corrected 4-1-2009). Amended by T.D. 9926,* 11-27-2020.]

Proposed Amendments to Regulation

§ 1.1446-6. Special rules to reduce a partnership's 1446 tax with respect to a foreign partner's allocable share of effectively connected taxable income.—(a) *In general.*—(1) *Purpose and scope.*—This section provides rules regarding when a partnership required to pay withholding tax under section 1446 (1446 tax), or an installment of 1446 tax, may consider certain partner-level deductions and losses and eligibility certificates under § 1.1400Z2(a)-2(d) in computing its 1446 tax obligation under § 1.1446-3. This section also provides rules regarding when a partnership is not required to pay a de minimis amount of 1446 tax due with respect to a nonresident alien individual partner. A partnership determines the applicability of the rules of this section on a partner-by-partner basis for each installment period and when completing its Form 8804, "Annual Return for Partnership Withholding Tax (Section 1446)," and paying 1446 tax for the partnership taxable year. Except with respect to certain state and local taxes paid by the partnership on behalf of the partner, to apply the rules of this section with respect to a foreign partner, the partnership must receive a certificate described in § 1.1446-6(c)(1)(i) and (ii) from such partner for each partnership taxable year or an eligibility certificate described in § 1.1400Z2(a)-2(d) for each security-required gain (as defined in § 1.1400Z2(a)–2(c)(1)). Paragraph (b) of this section identifies the foreign partners to which this section applies. Paragraph (c) of this section identifies the deductions and losses and security-required gains that a foreign partner may certify to the partnership as well as the state and local taxes paid by the partnership on behalf of the foreign partner that can be taken into account without a certification, and establishes an exception that permits a partnership to not pay a de minimis amount of 1446 tax with respect to a nonresident alien partner. Paragraph (c) of this section also sets forth the requirements for a valid certificate. Paragraphs (a)(2) and (d) of this section establish when a partnership may rely on and consider a foreign partner's certificate in computing its 1446 tax, and the effects of relying on such a certificate. Paragraph (d) of this section also describes the effects of a partnership relying on a certificate (including an updated certificate) and the reporting requirements of a partnership with respect to a certificate. Paragraph (e) of this section sets forth examples that illustrate the rules of this section. Paragraph (f) of this section provides the Effective/Applicability date. Paragraph (g) of this section provides a transition rule.

(2) *Reasonable reliance on a certificate.*—Subject to § 1.1446-2 and the rules of this section, a partnership receiving a certificate (including an updated certificate or status update under paragraph (c)(2)(ii)(B) of this section) of deductions and losses or an eligibility certificate from a partner provided in accordance with the provisions of this section may reasonably rely on the certificate of deductions and losses (to the extent of the certified deductions and losses or other representations set forth in the certificate) or eligibility certificate (to the extent of the permitted deferral amount determined in § 1.1400Z2(a)-2(d)(7)) until such time that it has actual knowledge or reason to know that the certificate is defective or that the time for receiving an updated certificate or status update from the partner under paragraph (c)(2)(ii)(B) of this section has expired. * * *

* * *

(c) * * *

(1) * * * Under paragraph (c)(1)(iv) of this section, a partnership may take into account eligibility certificates submitted by a foreign partner with respect to security-required gains.

* * *

(iv) *Consideration of eligibility certificates.*—A partner that is a nonresident alien or foreign corporation that satisfies the requirements of § 1.1400Z2(a)-1(a)(3) may provide a copy of an eligibility certificate, as defined in § 1.1400Z2(a)–2(d)(1), for each of the partner's security-required gains, as defined in § 1.1400Z2(a)-2(c)(1).

* * *

(2) * * *

(i) * * * A partner's certification under paragraph (c)(1)(iv) of this section shall be the eligibility certificate described in § 1.1400Z2(a)-2(d)(1).

* * *

(d) * * *

(3) * * *

(i) * * * For an installment period other than the first installment period for which the partnership considers a foreign partner's certificate or updated certificate, the partnership may, instead of attaching any partner's certificate, attach to Form 8813 a list containing the name, TIN, the amount of certified deductions and losses, the amount of gain excluded resulting from an eligibility certificate, and the amount of state and local taxes the partnership may consider under paragraph (c)(1)(iii) of this section for each foreign partner whose certificate was relied upon.

* * *

(f) * * * Paragraph (c)(1)(iv) of this section and the references in paragraphs (a)(1), (a)(2), (c)(1), and (d)(3)(i) of this section to eligibility certificates, covered transfers and security-required gains, apply to any covered transfers (as defined in § 1.1400Z2(a)-2(c)(2)) occurring after [DATE OF PUBLICATION OF FINAL RULE].

* * *

[Prop. Reg. § 1.1446-6.]

[Proposed 4-14-2021.]

§ 1.1446-7. Applicability dates.—Sections 1.1446-1 through 1.1446-5 shall apply to partnership taxable years beginning after May 18, 2005. However, a partnership may elect to apply all of the provisions of §§ 1.1446-1 through 1.1446-5 to partnership taxable years beginning after December 31, 2004. A partnership shall make the election under this section by complying with the provisions of §§ 1.1446-1 through § 1.1446-5 and attaching a statement to the Form 8804 or Form 1042 annual return, filed for the taxable year in which the regulation provisions first apply, that indicates that the partnership is making the election under this section. The revisions to §§ 1.1446-3(b)(2), 1.1446-3(b)(3)(i)(A) and 1.1446-5(c)(2) contained in the final regulations published in 2008 apply to partnership taxable years beginning after December 31, 2007. See § 1.1446-6(f) and (g) for the Effective/Applicability date and Transition rule for § 1.1446-6. Section 1.1446-3 generally applies to returns filed on or after January 30, 2020 and § 1.1446-3T (as contained in 26 CFR part 1, revised as of April 1, 2019) generally applies to returns filed before January 30, 2020. The addition of § 1.1446-3(c)(4) applies to transfers of partnership interests that occur on or after January 29, 2021, except that a taxpayer may choose to apply § 1.1446-3(c)(4) to transfers of partnership interests that occur on or after January 1, 2018. Sections 1.1446-3(a)(2)(i), (d)(2)(vi), and (e)(4) and 1.1446-4(f)(1) apply to partnership taxable years beginning on or after November 30, 2020. For partnership taxable years beginning before November 30, 2020, see those sections as in effect and contained in 26 CFR part 1, revised as of April 1, 2020. Section 1.1446-4(b)(3) and (4), (c), (d), (e), and (f)(3) apply to distributions made on or after January 1, 2022. For distributions made before January 1, 2022, see §§ 1.1446-4(b)(3) and (4), (c), (d), (e) and (f)(3), as contained in 26 CFR part 1, revised as of April 1, 2020. Sections 1.1446-1(c)(2)(ii)(G) and (H) and 1.1446-2(b)(4)(iii) apply with respect to dispositions of U.S. real property interests and distributions described in section 897(h) occurring on or after December 29, 2022. For dispositions of U.S. real property interests and distributions described in section 897(h) occurring before December 29, 2022, see §§ 1.1446-1(c)(2)(ii)(G) and (H), as contained in 26 CFR part 1, revised as of April 1, 2021. [Reg. § 1.1446-7.]

☐ [*T.D. 9200, 5-13-2005. Amended by T.D. 9394, 4-28-2008, T.D. 9926, 11-27-2020 and T.D. 9971, 12-28-2022.*]

Proposed Amendments to Regulation

§ 1.1446-7. Effective/Applicability date.—* * * The references in § 1.1446-3(b)(2)(i)(B)(1) to § 1.1446-6(c)(1)(iv) apply to partnership taxable years ending after [DATE OF PUBLICATION OF FINAL RULE].

[Proposed 4-14-2021.]

§ 1.1446(f)-1. General rules.—(a) *Overview.*—This section and §§ 1.1446(f)-2 through 1.1446(f)-5 provide rules for withholding, reporting, and paying tax under section 1446(f) upon the sale, exchange, or other disposition of certain interests in partnerships. This section provides definitions and general rules that apply for purposes of section 1446(f). Section 1.1446(f)-2 provides withholding rules for the transfer of a non-publicly traded partnership interest under section

1446(f)(1). Section 1.1446(f)-3 provides rules that apply when a partnership is required to withhold under section 1446(f)(4) on distributions made to the transferee in an amount equal to the amount that the transferee failed to withhold plus interest. Section 1.1446(f)-4 provides special rules for the sale, exchange, or disposition of publicly traded partnership interests, for which the withholding obligation under section 1446(f)(1) is generally imposed on certain brokers that act on behalf of the transferor. Section 1.1446(f)-5 provides rules that address the liability for failure to withhold under section 1446(f) and rules regarding the liability of a transferor's or transferee's agent.

(b) *Definitions.*—This paragraph (b) provides definitions that apply for purposes of this section and § § 1.1446(f)-2 through 1.1446(f)-5.

(1) The term *broker* means any person, foreign or domestic, that, in the ordinary course of a trade or business during the calendar year, stands ready to effect sales made by others, and that, in connection with a transfer of a PTP interest, receives all or a portion of the amount realized on behalf of the transferor. The term broker includes a clearing organization (as defined in § 1.1471-1(b)(21)). In the case of a U.S. clearing organization clearing or settling sales of PTP interests, however, see § 1.1446(f)-4(a)(3) for an exception from the requirement to withhold on a sale of a PTP interest. The term broker does not include an escrow agent that does not effect sales other than transactions that are incidental to the purpose of escrow (such as sales to collect on collateral).

(2) The term *controlling partner* means a partner that, together with any person that bears a relationship described in section 267(b) or 707(b)(1) to the partner, owns directly or indirectly a 50 percent or greater interest in the capital, profits, deductions, or losses of the partnership at any time within the 12 months before the determination date (see paragraph (c)(4) of this section).

(3) The term *effect* has the meaning provided in § 1.6045-1(a)(10).

(4) The term *foreign person* means a person that is not a United States person, including a QI branch of a U.S. financial institution (as defined in § 1.1471-1(b)(109)).

(5) The term *PTP interest* means an interest in a publicly traded partnership if the interest is publicly traded on an established securities market or is readily tradable on a secondary market (or the substantial equivalent thereof).

(6) The term *publicly traded partnership* has the same meaning as in section 7704 and § § 1.7704-1 through 1.7704-4 but does not include a publicly traded partnership treated as a corporation under that section.

(7) The term *TIN* means the tax identifying number assigned to a person under section 6109.

(8) The term *transfer* means a sale, exchange, or other disposition, and includes a distribution from a partnership to a partner, as well as a transfer treated as a sale or exchange under section 707(a)(2)(B).

(9) The term *transferee* means any person, foreign or domestic, that acquires a partnership interest through a transfer, and includes a partnership that makes a distribution.

(10) Except as otherwise provided in this paragraph, the term *transferor* means any person, foreign or domestic, that transfers a partnership interest. In the case of a trust, to the extent all or a portion of the income of the trust is treated as owned by the grantor or another person under sections 671 through 679 (such trust, a grantor trust), the term transferor means the grantor or such other person.

(11) The term *transferor's agent* or *transferee's agent* means any person who represents the transferor or transferee (respectively) in any negotiation with another person relating to the transaction or in settling the transaction. A person will not be treated as a transferor's agent or a transferee's agent solely because it performs one or more of the activities described in § 1.1445-4(f)(3) (relating to activities of settlement officers and clerical personnel).

(12) The term *United States person* or *U.S. person* means a person described in section 7701(a)(30).

(c) *General rules of applicability.*—(1) *In general.*—This paragraph (c) provides general rules that apply for purposes of this section and § § 1.1446(f)-2 through 1.1446(f)-5.

(2) *Certifications.*—(i) *In general.*—This paragraph (c)(2) provides rules that are applicable to certifications described in this section and § § 1.1446(f)-2 through 1.1446(f)-5, except as otherwise provided therein, or as may be prescribed by the Commissioner in forms or instructions or in publications or guidance published in the Internal Revenue Bulletin (see § § 601.601(d)(2) and 601.602 of this chapter). A certification must provide the name and address of the person providing it. A certification must also be signed under penalties of perjury and, if the certification is provided by the transferor, must include a TIN if the transferor has, or is required to have, a TIN. A transferee (or other person required to withhold) may not rely on a certification if it knows that a transferor has, or is required to have, a TIN, and that TIN has not been provided with the certification. A certification includes any documents associated with the certification, such as statements from the partnership, IRS forms, withholding certificates, withholding statements, certifications, or other documentation. Documents associated with the certification form an integral part of the certification, and the penalties of perjury statement provided on the certification also applies to the associated documents. A certification (other than the certification described in § 1.1446(f)-2(d)(2)) may not be relied upon if it is obtained earlier than 30 days before the transfer or any time after the transfer.

(ii) *Penalties of perjury.*—A certification signed under penalties of perjury must provide the following: "Under penalties of perjury, I declare that I have examined the information on this document, and to the best of my knowledge and belief, it is true, correct, and complete."

(iii) *Authority to sign certifications on behalf of a business entity.*—A certification provided by a business entity must be signed by an individual who is an officer, director, general partner, or managing member of the entity, or other individual that has authority to sign for the entity under local law.

(iv) *Electronic submission.*—A certification may be sent electronically, including as text in an email, an image embedded in an email, or a Portable Document Format (.pdf) attached to an email. An electronic certification, however, may not be relied upon if the person receiving the submission knows that the certification was transmitted by a person not authorized to do so by the person required to execute the certification.

(v) *Retention period.*—Any person that relies on a certification pursuant to this section and § § 1.1446(f)-2 through 1.1446(f)-5 must retain the certification (including any documentation) for as long as it may be relevant to the determination of its withholding obligation under section 1446(f) or its withholding tax liability under section 1461.

(vi) *Submission to IRS.*—The recipient of a certification is not required to mail a copy to the IRS, except as provided in § 1.1446(f)-2(b)(7) and (c)(4)(vi) (involving certifications relating to an income tax treaty), or as may be prescribed by the Commissioner in forms or instructions or in publications or guidance published in the Internal Revenue Bulletin (see § § 601.601(d)(2) and 601.602 of this chapter).

(vii) *Grantor trusts.*—A certification provided by a transferor that is a grantor or other owner of a grantor trust must identify the portion of the amount realized that is attributable to the grantor or other owner. A certification provided by a foreign grantor trust on behalf of a transferor that is a grantor or owner must also include a Form W-8IMY, *Certificate of Foreign Intermediary, Foreign Flow-Through Entity, or Certain U.S. Branches for United States Tax Withholding and Reporting*), (or similar statement for a domestic grantor trust with a foreign grantor or owner), that includes a withholding statement that provides the percentage of the amount realized allocable to each grantor or owner of the trust, and any applicable certification for each grantor or owner. In the case of a certification so provided, a grantor or owner of the trust is treated as having provided the certification to the transferee (or broker).

(3) *Books and records.*—A partnership that relies on its books and records pursuant to this section and § § 1.1446(f)-2 through 1.1446(f)-5 (including for purposes of providing a certification or other statement) must identify in its books and records the date on which the transfer occurred, the information on which the partnership relied, and the provisions of this section and § § 1.1446(f)-2 through 1.1446(f)-5 supporting an exception from, or adjustment to, the partnership's obligation to withhold. The identification required by this paragraph (c)(3) must be made no later than 30 days after the date of the transfer. The partnership must retain the identified information in its books and records for the longer of five calendar years following the close of the last calendar year in which it relied on the information or for as long as it may be relevant to the determination of its withholding obligation under section 1446(f) or its withholding tax liability under section 1461.

(4) *Determination date.*—(i) *In general.*—This paragraph (c)(4) provides rules for the determination date. The same determination date must be used for all purposes with respect to a transfer. Any statement, certification, or books and records with regard to a transfer must state the determination date. The determination date of a transfer must be one of the following—

(A) The date of the transfer;

(B) Any date that is no more than 60 days before the date of the transfer; or

(C) The date that is the later of—

(1) The first day of the partnership's taxable year in which the transfer occurs, as determined under section 706; or

(2) The date, before the date of the transfer, of the most recent event described in § 1.704-1(b)(2)(iv)*(f)(5)* or § 1.704-1(b)(2)(iv)*(s)(1)* (revaluation event), irrespective of whether the capital accounts of the partners are adjusted in accordance with § 1.704-1(b)(2)(iv)(f).

(ii) *Controlling partner.*—The determination date for a transferor that is a controlling partner is determined without regard to paragraph (c)(4)(i)(C) of this section.

(5) *IRS forms and instructions.*—Any reference to an IRS form includes its successor form. Any form must be filed in the manner prescribed by the Commissioner in forms or instructions or in publications or guidance published in the Internal Revenue Bulletin (see §§ 601.601(d)(2) and 601.602 of this chapter).

(d) *Coordination with section 1445.*—A transferee that is otherwise required to withhold under section 1445(e)(5) or § 1.1445-11T(d)(1) with respect to the amount realized, as well as under section 1446(f)(1), will be subject to the payment and reporting requirements of section 1445 only, and not section 1446(f)(1), with respect to that amount. However, if the transferor has applied for a withholding certificate under the last sentence of § 1.1445-11T(d)(1), the transferee must withhold the greater of the amounts required under section 1445(e)(5) or 1446(f)(1). A transferee that has complied with the withholding requirements under either section 1445(e)(5) or 1446(f)(1), as applicable under this paragraph (d), will be deemed to satisfy the withholding requirement.

(e) *Applicability date.*—This section applies to transfers that occur on or after January 29, 2021. [Reg. § 1.1446(f)-1.]

□ [*T.D.* 9926, 11-27-2020.]

§ 1.1446(f)-2. Withholding on the transfer of a non-publicly traded partnership interest.—(a) *Transferee's obligation to withhold.*—Except as otherwise provided in this section, a transferee is required to withhold under section 1446(f)(1) a tax equal to 10 percent of the amount realized on any transfer of a partnership interest. This section does not apply to a transfer of a PTP interest that is effected through one or more brokers, including a distribution made with respect to a PTP interest held in an account with a broker. For rules regarding those transfers, see § 1.1446(f)-4.

(b) *Exceptions to withholding.*—(1) *In general.*—A transferee is not required to withhold under this section if it properly relies on a certification or its books and records as described in this paragraph (b). A transferee may not rely on a certification if it has actual knowledge that the certification is incorrect or unreliable. A partnership that is a transferee because it makes a distribution may not rely on its books and records if it knows, or has reason to know, that the information is incorrect or unreliable.

(2) *Certification of non-foreign status by transferor.*—A transferee may rely on a certification of non-foreign status from the transferor that states that the transferor is not a foreign person, states the transferor's name, TIN, and address, and is signed under penalties of perjury. For purposes of this paragraph (b)(2), a certification of non-foreign status includes a valid Form W-9, *Request for Taxpayer Identification Number and Certification*. For purposes of this paragraph (b)(2), a transferee may rely on a valid Form W-9 from the transferor that it already possesses if the form meets these requirements of this paragraph (b)(2).

(3) *No realized gain by transferor.*—(i) *In general.*—A transferee (other than a partnership that is a transferee because it makes a distribution) may rely on a certification from the transferor that states that the transfer of the partnership interest would not result in any realized gain (including ordinary income arising from the application of section 751 and § 1.751-1) to the transferor as of the determination date (see § 1.1446(f)-1(c)(4)). See paragraph (b)(6) of this section for rules that apply when the transferor realizes gain but is not required to recognize the gain under a provision of the Internal Revenue Code.

(ii) *No section 751 income.*—For purposes of paragraph (b)(3)(i) of this section, a transferor may rely on a certification from the partnership stating that the transfer of the partnership interest would not result in any ordinary income arising from the application of section 751 and § 1.751-1 to the transferor as of the determination date. The certification from the partnership must be attached to, and forms part of, the certification of no realized gain that the transferor provides to the transferee.

(iii) *Partnership distributions.*—A partnership that is a transferee because it makes a distribution may rely on its books and records, or on a certification from the transferor, to determine that the distribution would not result in any realized gain to the transferor as of the determination date.

(4) *Less than 10 percent effectively connected gain.*—(i) *In general.*—A transferee (other than a partnership that is a transferee because it makes a distribution) may rely on a certification from the partnership that states that—

(A) If the partnership sold all of its assets at fair market value as of the determination date in the manner described in § 1.864(c)(8)-1(c), either—

(1) The partnership would have no gain that would have been effectively connected with the conduct of a trade or business within the United States, or, if the partnership would have a net amount of such gain, the amount of the partnership's net gain that would have been effectively connected with the conduct of a trade or business within the United States would be less than 10 percent of the total net gain; or

(2) The transferor would not have a distributive share of net gain from the partnership that would have been effectively connected with the conduct of a trade or business in the United States, or, if the transferor would have a distributive share of such gain from the partnership, the transferor's distributive share of net gain from the partnership that would have been effectively connected with the conduct of a trade or business within the United States would be less than 10 percent of the transferor's distributive share of the total net gain from the partnership; or

(B) The partnership was not engaged in a trade or business within the United States at any time during the taxable year of the partnership through the date of transfer.

(ii) *Partnership distributions.*—A partnership that is a transferee because it makes a distribution may rely on its books and records to determine that paragraph (b)(4)(i)(A) of this section is satisfied as of the determination date or paragraph (b)(4)(i)(B) of this section is satisfied for the taxable year of the partnership through the date of transfer.

(5) *Less than 10 percent effectively connected income.*—(i) *In general.*—A transferee (other than a partnership that is a transferee because it makes a distribution) may rely on a certification from the transferor that states that—

(A) The transferor was a partner in the partnership throughout the look-back period described in paragraph (b)(5)(ii) of this section;

(B) The transferor's distributive share of gross effectively connected income from the partnership, as reported on a Schedule K-1 (Form 1065), *Partner's Share of Income, Deductions, Credits, etc.*, or other statement required to be furnished under § 1.6031(b)-1T, including any gross effectively connected income included in the distributive share of a partner that bears a relationship to the transferor described in section 267(b) or 707(b)(1), was less than $1 million for each of the taxable years within the look-back period described in paragraph (b)(5)(ii) of this section;

(C) The transferor's distributive share of gross effectively connected income from the partnership, as reported on a Schedule K-1 (Form 1065), or other statement required to be furnished under § 1.6031(b)-1T, for each of the taxable years within the look-back period described in paragraph (b)(5)(ii) of this section, was less than 10 percent of the transferor's total distributive share of gross income from the partnership for that year as determined under subchapter K of the Internal Revenue Code (as provided on a Schedule K-1 (Form 1065) or other statement required to be furnished under § 1.6031(b)-1T); and

(D) The transferor's distributive share of income or gain from the partnership that is effectively connected with the conduct of a trade or business within the United States or deductions or losses properly allocated and apportioned to that income in each of the taxable years within the look-back period described in paragraph (b)(5)(ii) of this section has been reported on a Federal income tax return (either filed by the transferor or, in the case of transferor that is a partnership, filed by its direct or indirect nonresident alien individual or foreign corporate partners) on or before the due date (including extensions), and all amounts due with respect to the reported amounts have been timely paid to the IRS, provided that the return was required to be filed when the transferor furnishes the certification (taking into account any extensions of time to file).

(ii) *Look-back period.*—(A) *In general.*—The transferor's look-back period is the transferor's immediately prior taxable year and the two preceding taxable years.

(B) *Immediately prior taxable year.*—The transferor's immediately prior taxable year is the transferor's most recent taxable year–

(1) With or within which a taxable year of the partnership ended; and

(2) For which a Schedule K-1 (Form 1065) was due (including extensions) or furnished (if earlier) before the transfer.

(C) *Limitation.*—A transferee may not rely on a certification that is provided before the transferor's receipt of the Schedule K-1 (Form 1065) described in paragraph (b)(5)(ii)(B) of this section.

(iii) *No distributive share of gross income.*—A transferor that did not have a distributive share of gross income in any year described in paragraph (b)(5)(ii)(A) of this section cannot provide the certification described in this paragraph (b)(5).

(iv) *Partnership distributions.*—A partnership that is a transferee by reason of making a distribution may rely on its books and records to determine that the requirements in paragraphs (b)(5)(i)(A) through (C) of this section have been satisfied (subject to the rules in paragraphs (b)(5)(ii) and (iii) of this section). The partnership must also obtain a representation from the transferor stating that the requirement in paragraph (b)(5)(i)(D) of this section has been satisfied.

(6) *Certification of nonrecognition by transferor.*—(i) *In general.*—A transferee may rely on a certification from the transferor that states that by reason of the operation of a nonrecognition provision of the Internal Revenue Code the transferor is not required to recognize any gain or loss with respect to the transfer. The certification must briefly describe the transfer and provide the relevant law and facts relating to the certification.

(ii) *Partial nonrecognition.*—Paragraph (b)(6)(i) of this section does not apply if only a portion of the gain realized on the transfer is subject to a nonrecognition provision. However, see paragraph (c)(4)(v) of this section for rules applicable to a transferor's claim for partial nonrecognition.

(7) *Income tax treaties.*—(i) *In general.*—A transferee may rely on a certification from the transferor that states that the transferor is not subject to tax on any gain from the transfer pursuant to an income tax treaty in effect between the United States and a foreign country if the requirements of this paragraph (b)(7) are met. The transferor makes the certification on a withholding certificate (on a Form W-8BEN, *Certificate of Foreign Status of Beneficial Owner for United States Tax Withholding and Reporting (Individuals)*, or Form W-8BEN-E, *Certificate of Status of Beneficial Owner for United States Tax Withholding and Reporting (Entities))* that meets the requirements for validity under § 1.1446-1(c)(2)(iv) (or an applicable substitute form that meets the requirements under § 1.1446-1(c)(5)) and that contains the information necessary to support the claim for treaty benefits. A transferee may rely on a certification of treaty benefits only if, within 30 days after the date of the transfer, the transferee mails a copy of the certification to the Internal Revenue Service, at the address provided in § 1.1445-1(g)(10), together with a cover letter providing the name, TIN, and address of the transferee and the partnership in which an interest was transferred.

(ii) *Treaty claim for less than all of the gain.*—Paragraph (b)(7)(i) of this section does not apply if treaty benefits apply to only a portion of the gain from the transfer. However, see paragraph (c)(4)(vi) of this section for rules applicable to situations in which treaty benefits apply to only a portion of the gain.

(iii) *Exclusive means to claim an exception from withholding based on treaty benefits.*—A transferor claiming treaty benefits with respect to all of the gain from the transfer must use the exception in this paragraph (b)(7) and not any other exception or determination procedure in paragraphs (b) and (c) of this section to claim an exception to withholding by reason of a claim of treaty benefits.

(c) *Determining the amount to withhold.*—(1) *In general.*—A transferee that is required to withhold under this section must withhold 10 percent of the amount realized on the transfer of the partnership interest, except as otherwise provided in this paragraph (c). Any procedures in this paragraph (c) apply solely for purposes of determining the amount to withhold under section 1446(f)(1) and this section. A transferee may not rely on a certification if it has actual knowledge that the certification is incorrect or unreliable. A partnership that is a transferee because it makes a distribution may not rely on its books and records if it knows, or has reason to know, that the information is incorrect or unreliable.

(2) *Amount realized.*—(i) *In general.*—The amount realized on the transfer of the partnership interest is determined under section 1001 (including § § 1.1001-1 through 1.1001-5) and section 752 (including § § 1.752-1 through 1.752-7). Thus, the amount realized includes the amount of cash paid (or to be paid), the fair market value of other property transferred (or to be transferred), the amount of any liabilities assumed by the transferee or to which the partnership interest is subject, and the reduction in the transferor's share of partnership liabilities. In the case of a distribution, the amount realized is the sum of the amount of cash distributed (or to be distributed), the fair market value of property distributed (or to be distributed), and the reduction in the transferor's share of partnership liabilities.

(ii) *Alternative procedures for transferee to determine share of partnership liabilities.*—(A) *In general.*—A transferee (other than a partnership that is a transferee because it makes a distribution), as an alternative to determining the share of partnership liabilities under paragraph (c)(2)(i) of this section, may use the procedures of this paragraph (c)(2)(ii) to determine the extent to which a reduction in partnership liabilities is included in the amount realized.

(B) *Certification of liabilities by transferor.*—Except as otherwise provided in this section, a transferee may rely on a certification from a transferor, other than a controlling partner, that provides the amount of the transferor's share of partnership liabilities reported on the most recent Schedule K-1 (Form 1065) issued by the partnership. If the transferor's actual share of liabilities at the time of the transfer differs from the amount reported on that Schedule K-1 (Form 1065), the certification will not be treated as incorrect or unreliable if the transferor also certifies that it does not have actual knowledge of any events occurring after receiving the Schedule K-1 (Form 1065) and before the date of the transfer that would cause the amount of the transferor's share of partnership liabilities at the time of the transfer to differ by more than 25 percent from the amount shown on the Schedule K-1 (Form 1065). A transferee may not rely on a certification if the last day of the partnership taxable year for which the Schedule K-1 (Form 1065) was provided was more than 22 months before the date of the transfer.

(C) *Certification of liabilities by partnership.*—A transferee may rely on a certification from a partnership that provides the amount of the transferor's share of partnership liabilities on the determination date. If the transferor's actual share of liabilities at the time of the transfer differs from the amount on the certification, the certification will not be treated as incorrect or unreliable if the partnership also certifies that it does not have actual knowledge of any events occurring after the determination date and before the date on which the partnership provides the certification to the transferee that would cause the amount of the transferor's share of partnership liabilities at the time of the transfer to differ by more than 25 percent from the amount shown on the certification by the partnership for the determination date.

(iii) *Partnership's determination of partnership liabilities for distributions.*—A partnership that is a transferee because it makes a distribution may rely on its books and records to determine the extent to which the transferor's share of partnership liabilities on the determination date are included in the amount realized. The information in the books and records will not be treated as incorrect or unreliable unless the partnership has actual knowledge, on or before the date of the distribution, of any events occurring after the determination date that would cause the amount of the transferor's share of partnership liabilities at the time of the transfer to differ by more than 25 percent from the amount determined by the partnership as of the determination date.

(iv) *Certification by a foreign partnership of modified amount realized.*—(A) *In general.*—When a transferor is a foreign partnership, a transferee may use the procedures of this paragraph (c)(2)(iv) to determine the amount realized. For purposes of this paragraph (c)(2)(iv)(A), the transferee may treat the modified amount realized as the amount realized to the extent that it may rely on a certification from the transferor providing the modified amount realized.

(B) *Determining modified amount realized.*—The modified amount realized is determined by multiplying the amount realized (as determined under this paragraph (c)(2), without regard to this paragraph (c)(2)(iv)) by the aggregate percentage computed as of the determination date. The aggregate percentage is the percentage of the gain (if any) arising from the transfer that would be allocated to presumed foreign taxable persons. For purposes of this paragraph (c)(2)(iv)(B), a presumed foreign taxable person is any direct or indirect partner of the transferor that has not provided either a certification of non-foreign status that meets the requirements of paragraph (b)(2) of this section or a certification of treaty benefits that states that the partner is not subject to tax on any gain from the transfer pursuant to an income tax treaty in effect between the United States and a foreign country. A valid certification of treaty benefits must meet the requirements of paragraph (b)(7) of this section (as applied to the partner claiming treaty benefits), including the requirement that the transferee mail a copy of the certification to the IRS within the time prescribed. For purposes of this paragraph (c)(2)(iv), an indirect partner is a person that owns an interest in the transferor indirectly through one or more foreign partnerships.

(C) *Certification.*—The certification is made by providing a withholding certificate (on Form W-8IMY, *Certificate of Foreign Intermediary, Foreign Flow-Through Entity, or Certain U.S. Branches for United States Tax Withholding and Reporting)* that includes a withholding statement that provides the percentage of gain allocable to each direct or indirect partner and that provides whether each such person is a United States person, a foreign partner eligible for treaty benefits, or a presumed foreign taxable person. The certification must also include the certification of non-foreign status or the certification of treaty benefits from each direct or indirect partner that is not a presumed foreign taxable person.

(3) *Lack of money or property or lack of knowledge regarding liabilities.*—The amount to withhold equals the amount realized determined without regard to any decrease in the transferor's share of partnership liabilities if—

(i) The amount otherwise required to be withheld under this paragraph (c) would exceed the amount realized determined without regard to the decrease in the transferor's share of partnership liabilities; or

(ii) The transferee is unable to determine the amount realized because it does not have actual knowledge of the transferor's share of partnership liabilities (and has not received or cannot rely on a certification described in paragraph (c)(2)(ii)(B) or (C) of this section).

(4) *Certification of maximum tax liability.*—(i) *In general.*—A transferee may use the procedures of this paragraph (c)(4) for determining the amount to withhold for purposes of section 1446(f)(1) and paragraph (a) of this section. A transferee (other than a partnership that is a transferee because it makes a distribution) may rely on a certification from a transferor that is a foreign corporation, a nonresident alien individual, a foreign partnership, or a foreign trust regarding the transferor's maximum tax liability as described in paragraph (c)(4)(ii) of this section. A partnership that is a transferee because it makes a distribution may instead rely on its books and records to determine the transferor's maximum tax liability if the books and records includes the information required by paragraphs (c)(4)(iii) and (iv) of this section. A transferor that is a foreign partnership or a foreign trust is treated as a nonresident alien individual for purposes of determining the transferor's maximum tax liability.

(ii) *Maximum tax liability.*—For purposes of this paragraph (c)(4), the term *maximum tax liability* means the amount of the transferor's effectively connected gain (as determined under paragraph (c)(4)(iii)(E) of this section) multiplied by the applicable percentage, as defined in § 1.1446-3(a)(2).

(iii) *Required information.*—The certification must include—

(A) A statement that the transferor is either a nonresident alien individual, a foreign corporation, a foreign partnership, or a foreign trust;

(B) The transferor's adjusted basis in the transferred interest on the determination date;

(C) The transferor's amount realized (determined in accordance with paragraph (c)(2) of this section) on the determination date;

(D) Whether the transferor remains a partner immediately after the transfer;

(E) The amount of outside ordinary gain and outside capital gain that would be recognized and treated as effectively connected gain under § 1.864(c)(8)-1(b) on the determination date (effectively connected gain);

(F) The transferor's maximum tax liability on the determination date;

(G) A representation from the transferor that the transferor determined the amounts described in paragraph (c)(4)(iii)(E) of this section based on the statement described in paragraph (c)(4)(iv) of this section, if applicable; and

(H) A representation from the transferor that it has provided the transferee with a copy of the statement described in paragraph (c)(4)(iv) of this section.

(iv) *Partnership statement.*—A transferor may make the representation in paragraph (c)(4)(iii)(G) of this section only if the partnership provides to the transferor a statement (that meets the requirements for a certification under the general rules for applicability in § 1.1446(f)-1(c)) that includes—

(A) The partnership's name, address, and TIN; and

(B) The transferor's aggregate deemed sale EC ordinary gain, within the meaning of § 1.864(c)(8)-1(c)(3)(ii)(A) (if any) and the transferor's aggregate deemed sale EC capital gain, within the meaning of § 1.864(c)(8)-1(c)(3)(ii)(B) (if any), in each case, on the determination date.

(v) *Partial nonrecognition.*—If a nonrecognition provision applies to only a portion of the gain realized on the transfer, a certification described in paragraph (c)(4)(i) may be relied upon only if the certification also includes the information required in paragraph (b)(6) of this section (substituting "a portion of the gain or loss" for "any gain or loss" in paragraph (b)(6)(i) of this section).

(vi) *Income tax treaties.*—If only a portion of the gain on the transfer is not subject to tax pursuant to an income tax treaty in effect between the United States and a foreign country, a certification described in paragraph (c)(4)(i) of this section may be relied upon only if the requirements of paragraph (b)(7)(i) of this section have been met, including the requirement to obtain the applicable withholding certificate indicating that the gain from the transfer is not subject to tax pursuant to an income tax treaty (substituting "a portion of the gain" for "any gain" in paragraph (b)(7)(i) of this section), and the requirement to mail a copy of the withholding certificate to the IRS.

(d) *Reporting and paying withheld amounts.*—(1) *In general.*—A transferee required to withhold under this section must report and pay any tax withheld by the 20th day after the date of the transfer using Forms 8288, *U.S. Withholding Tax Return for Dispositions by Foreign Persons of U.S. Real Property Interests,* and 8288-A, *Statement of Withholding on Dispositions by Foreign Persons of U.S. Real Property Interests,* in accordance with the instructions to those forms. The IRS will stamp Form 8288-A to show receipt and mail a stamped copy to the transferor (at the address reported on the form). See paragraph (e)(2) of this section for the procedures for the transferor to claim a credit for amounts withheld. Forms 8288 and 8288-A must include the TINs of both the transferor and the transferee. If any required TIN is not provided, the transferee must still report and pay any tax withheld on Form 8288.

(2) *Certification of withholding to partnership for purposes of section 1446(f)(4).*—A transferee (other than a partnership that is a transferee because it makes a distribution) must certify to the partnership the extent to which it has satisfied its obligation to withhold under this section no later than 10 days after the transfer. The certification must either include a copy of Form 8288-A that the transferee files with respect to the transfer, or state the amount realized and the amount withheld on the transfer. The certification must also include any certifications that the transferee relied on to apply an exception to withholding under paragraph (b) of this section or to determine the

amount to withhold under paragraph (c) of this section. A transferee that relied on a certification to apply an exception or adjustment to withholding remains liable under this section when the partnership knows, or has reason to know, that the certification is incorrect or unreliable. See § 1.1446(f)-3 for rules regarding a partnership's obligation to withhold on distributions to a transferee when this certification establishes only partial satisfaction of the required amount, is not provided, or cannot be relied upon.

(e) *Effect of withholding on transferor.*—(1) *In general.*—The withholding of tax by a transferee under this section does not relieve a foreign person from filing a U.S. tax return with respect to the transfer. See § § 1.6012-1(b)(1), 1.6012-2(g)(1), and 1.6031(a)-1. Further, the withholding of tax by a transferee does not relieve a nonresident alien individual or foreign corporation subject to tax on gain by reason of section 864(c)(8) from paying any tax due with the return that has not been fully satisfied through withholding.

(2) *Manner of obtaining credit.*—(i) *Individuals or corporations.*—Except as provided in paragraph (e)(3) of this section, an individual or corporation may claim a credit under section 33 for the amount withheld under this section by attaching to its applicable return the stamped copy of Form 8288-A provided to it under paragraph (d)(1) of this section.

(ii) *Partnerships, trusts, or estates.*—For a rule allowing a foreign partnership that is a transferor to claim a credit for the amount withheld under this section against its tax liability under section 1446(a), see § 1.1446-3(c)(4). For the rule providing the extent to which a foreign trust or estate may claim a credit for an amount withheld under this section, see § 1.1462-1. Except as provided in paragraph (e)(3) of this section, a foreign partnership, trust, or estate claiming a credit for an amount withheld must attach to its applicable return the stamped copy of Form 8288-A provided to it under paragraph (d)(1) of this section. A foreign trust or estate must also provide any other information required in forms or instructions to any beneficiary or owner that is liable for tax on any of the gain under section 864(c)(8).

(3) *Failure to receive Form 8288-A.*—If a stamped copy of Form 8288-A has not been provided to the transferor by the IRS, the transferor may establish the amount of tax withheld by the transferee by attaching to its return substantial evidence of the amount. The transferor must attach to its return a statement that includes all of the information otherwise required to be provided on Form 8288-A.

(f) *Applicability date.*—This section applies to transfers that occur on or after January 29, 2021. [Reg. § 1.1446(f)-2.]

☐ [*T.D. 9926, 11-27-2020.*]

Proposed Amendments to Regulation

§ 1.1446(f)-2. Withholding on the transfer of a non-publicly traded partnership interest.—

* * *

(b) * * *

(8) *Gain deferred under section 1400Z-2(a).*—A transferee may rely on a certification from the transferor that includes a copy of an eligibility certificate (as described in § 1.1400Z2(a)-2(d)) with respect to the transfer for an amount of security that is greater than or equal to the maximum security amount. See paragraph (c)(5) of this section for when an eligibility certificate provides an amount of security that is less than the maximum security amount.

(c) * * *

(5) *Gain deferred under section 1400Z-2(a).*—A transferee may rely on a certification from a transferor that includes a copy of an eligibility certificate (as described in § 1.1400Z2(a)-2(d)) with respect to the transfer to reduce the amount required to be withheld under this section by the amount of security provided on the eligibility certificate.

* * *

(f) *Applicability date.*—* * * Paragraphs (b)(8) and (c)(5) of this section apply to any covered transfer (as defined in § 1.1400Z2(a)-2(c)(2)) that occurs after [DATE OF PUBLICATION OF FINAL RULE]. [Prop. Reg. § 1.1446(f)-2.]

[Proposed 4-14-2021.]

§ 1.1446(f)-3. Partnership's requirement to withhold under section 1446(f)(4) on distributions to transferee.—(a) *Partnership's obligation to withhold amounts not withheld by the transferee.*—(1) *In general.*—If a transferee fails to withhold any amount required to be withheld under § 1.1446(f)-2, the partnership in which the interest was transferred must withhold from any distributions with respect to the transferred interest pursuant to this section. To determine its withholding obligation under this paragraph (a)(1), a partnership may rely on a certification received from the transferee described in § 1.1446(f)-2(d)(2) unless it knows, or has reason to know, that the certification is incorrect or unreliable. A partnership that already possesses a certification of non-foreign status (including a Form W-9) for the transferor that meets the requirements provided in § 1.1446(f)-2(b)(2) may instead rely on this certification to determine that it has no withholding obligation under this paragraph (a)(1) unless it knows, or has reason to know, that the certification is incorrect or unreliable. A partnership that receives a certification described in § 1.1446(f)-2(d)(2) that is inconsistent with the information on the certification of non-foreign status in its possession is treated as having actual knowledge, or reason to know, that the certification of non-foreign status is incorrect or unreliable.

(2) *Notification by IRS.*—A partnership that receives notification from the IRS that a transferee has provided incorrect information regarding the amount realized or amount withheld on the certification described in § 1.1446(f)-2(d)(2), or has failed to pay the IRS the amount reported as withheld on the certification, must withhold the amount prescribed in the notification on distributions with respect to the transferred interest made on or after the date that is 15 days after it receives the notification. The IRS will not issue a notification on the basis that the amount realized on the certification described in § 1.446(f)-2(d)(2) is incorrect if it determines that the transferee properly relied on a certification that included the incorrect information to compute the amount realized pursuant to § 1.1446(f)-2(c)(2).

(3) *Subsequent transferees.*—A partnership is not required to withhold under paragraph (a)(1) or (2) of this section on distributions that are made after the date on which the transferee disposes of the transferred interest, unless the partnership has actual knowledge that any person that acquires the transferee's interest in the partnership is a related person, i.e., a person that bears a relationship described in section 267(b) or 707(b)(1) with respect to the transferee or the transferor from which the transferee acquired the interest. A related person that acquires the transferee's interest is treated as liable for tax under section 1461 to the same extent that the transferee is liable for its failure to withhold under § 1.1446(f)-2.

(b) *Exceptions to withholding.*—(1) *Withholding has been satisfied by transferee.*—A partnership is not required to withhold under paragraph (a)(1) of this section if it relies on a certification described in § 1.1446(f)-2(d)(2) received from the transferee (within the time prescribed in § 1.1446(f)-2(d)(2)) that states that an exception to withholding described in § 1.1446(f)-2(b) applies or that the transferee withheld the full amount required to be withheld (taking into account any adjustments under § 1.1446(f)-2(c)) under § 1.1446(f)-2.

(2) *PTP interests.*—A partnership is not required to withhold under this section on distributions made with respect to a PTP interest.

(3) *Distributing partnerships.*—A partnership that is a transferee because it makes a distribution is not required to withhold under this section.

(c) *Withholding rules.*—(1) *Timing of withholding.*—(i) *In general.*—A partnership required to withhold under paragraph (a)(1) of this section must withhold on distributions made with respect to a transferred interest beginning on the later of—

(A) The date that is 30 days after the date of transfer; or

(B) The date that is 15 days after the date on which the partnership acquires actual knowledge that the transfer has occurred.

(ii) *Satisfaction of withholding obligation.*—A partnership is treated as satisfying its withholding obligation under paragraph (a)(1) of this section and may stop withholding on distributions with respect to a transferred interest on the earlier of—

(A) The date on which the partnership completes withholding and paying the amount required to be withheld under paragraph (c)(2) of this section; or

(B) The date on which the partnership receives and may rely on a certification from the transferee described in

§ 1.1446(f)-2(d)(2) (without regard to whether the certification is received by the time prescribed in § 1.1446(f)-2(d)(2)) that claims an exception to withholding under § 1.1446(f)-2(b).

(2) *Amount to withhold.*—(i) *In general.*—A partnership required to withhold under paragraph (a)(1) of this section must withhold the full amount of each distribution made with respect to the transferred interest until it has withheld—

(A) A tax of 10 percent of the amount realized (determined solely under § 1.1446(f)-2(c)(2)(i)) on the transfer, reduced by any amount withheld by the transferee; plus

(B) Any interest computed under paragraph (c)(2)(ii) of this section.

(ii) *Computation of interest.*—The amount of interest required to be withheld under paragraph (a)(1) of this section is the amount of interest that would be required to be paid under section 6601 and § 301.6601-1 of this chapter if the amount that should have been withheld by the transferee was considered an underpayment of tax. For purposes of this paragraph (c)(2)(ii), interest is payable between the date that is 20 days after the date of the transfer and the date on which the tax due under paragraph (a)(1) of this section is paid to the IRS.

(iii) *Certifications required.*—For purposes of paragraph (c)(2)(i)(A) of this section, a partnership must determine the amount realized on the transfer and any amount withheld by the transferee based on a certification from the transferee described in § 1.1446(f)-2(d)(2), without regard to whether the certification is received by the time prescribed in § 1.1446(f)-2(d)(2). A partnership that does not receive or cannot rely on a certification from the transferee described in § 1.1446(f)-2(d)(2) must withhold tax equal to the full amount of each distribution made with respect to a transferred interest until it receives a certification that it can rely on.

(3) *Coordination with other withholding provisions.*—Any amount required to be withheld on a distribution under any other provision of the Internal Revenue Code is not also required to be withheld under section 1446(f)(4) or this section.

(d) *Reporting and paying withheld amounts.*—The partnership must report and pay the tax withheld using Forms 8288, *U.S. Withholding Tax Return for Dispositions by Foreign Persons of U.S. Real Property Interests*, and 8288-C, *Statement of Withholding Under Section 1446(f)(4) for Withholding on Dispositions by Foreign Persons of Partnership Interests*, as provided in forms, instructions, or other guidance.

(e) *Effect of withholding on transferor and transferee.*—(1) *Transferor.*—The withholding of tax by a partnership under this section does not relieve a foreign person from filing a U.S. income tax return with respect to the transfer. See § § 1.6012-1(b)(1), 1.6012-2(g)(1), and 1.6031(a)-1. Further, the withholding of tax by a partnership does not relieve a nonresident alien individual or foreign corporation subject to tax on gain by reason of section 864(c)(8) from paying any tax due with the return that has not been fully satisfied through withholding. An individual or corporation is not allowed a credit under section 33 for amounts withheld on distributions to the transferee under this section. See, however, § § 1.1446(f)-5(a) and 1.1463-1(a), which generally provide that tax will not be recollected if paid by another person.

(2) *Transferee.*—A transferee is treated as satisfying its withholding tax liability under § 1.1446(f)-2 to the extent that a partnership withholds tax (which does not include interest) under this section. Interest computed under paragraph (c)(2)(ii) of this section that is withheld by the partnership from the transferee is treated as interest paid by the transferee with respect to its withholding tax liability under § 1.1446(f)-2. An excess amount under this section is the amount of tax and interest withheld under this section that exceeds the transferee's withholding tax liability under § 1.1446(f)-2 plus any interest owed by the transferee with respect to such liability. A transferee may claim a refund for the excess amount if payments have been made in excess of the tax which is properly due by the transferee for the tax period.

(f) *Applicability date.*—This section applies to transfers that occur on or after January 1, 2022. [Reg. § 1.1446(f)-3.]

□ [*T.D. 9926, 11-27-2020.*]

§ 1.1446(f)-4. Withholding on the transfer of a publicly traded partnership interest.—(a) *Obligation to withhold on a transfer of a PTP interest.*—(1) *In general.*—If a transfer of a PTP interest is effected through one or more brokers (as defined in § 1.1446(f)-1(b)(1)), the transferee is not required to withhold under section 1446(f)(1) and § 1.1446(f)-2. Rather, any broker required to withhold under paragraph (a)(2) of this section must withhold a tax equal to 10 percent of the amount realized (as defined in paragraph (c)(2) of this section) on the transfer of a PTP interest, except as otherwise provided in this section. For cases in which a publicly traded partnership is liable for withholding under this section, see paragraphs (b)(3)(i) and (c)(2)(iii) of this section.

(2) *Broker's requirement to withhold.*—(i) *In general.*—Except as otherwise provided in this section, a broker is required to withhold under this section if it pays an amount realized to another broker that it is required to treat as a foreign person, or if a broker pays an amount realized to a foreign transferor that is its customer.

(ii) *Payments to foreign brokers.*—A broker that pays an amount realized from the transfer of a PTP interest to another broker that it is required to treat as a foreign person must withhold under this section unless the first-mentioned broker obtains documentation on which it may rely establishing that the second-mentioned broker is described in paragraph (a)(2)(ii)(A) or (B) of this section. A broker must treat any broker to which it pays an amount realized from the transfer of a PTP interest as a foreign person unless it obtains, or already possesses, documentation (including a certification of non-foreign status) on which it may rely that establishes that the other broker is a U.S. person. A broker may rely on documentation described in this paragraph (a)(2)(ii), or in paragraph (a)(2)(ii)(A) or (B) of this section, unless it has actual knowledge that the documentation is unreliable or incorrect.

(A) A broker is described in this paragraph (a)(2)(ii)(A) if it is a qualified intermediary (as defined in § 1.1441-1(e)(5)(ii)) that provides a valid qualified intermediary withholding certificate (as described in § 1.1441-1(e)(3)(ii)) that states that it assumes primary withholding responsibility for the payment.

(B) A broker is described in this paragraph (a)(2)(ii)(B) if it is a U.S. branch of a foreign person (as described in § 1.1441-1(b)(2)(iv)) that provides a valid U.S. branch withholding certificate (as described in § 1.1441-1(e)(3)(v), but without regard to the requirement in § 1.1441-1(e)(3)(v) that the certificate state that the amount is not effectively connected with a trade or business within the United States) that states that the U.S. branch agrees to be treated as a U.S. person with respect to the payment.

(iii) *Payments to foreign transferors that are customers of the broker.*—A broker that pays an amount realized to a foreign transferor that is its customer (as defined in § 1.6045-1(a)(2)) from the transfer of a PTP interest is required to withhold under this section unless an exception under paragraph (b) of this section applies.

(3) *Exception from certain withholding by U.S. clearing organizations.*—A broker that is a U.S. clearing organization clearing or settling a sale of a PTP interest is not required to withhold on the amount realized from the sale. However, see § 1.1461-1(c)(2)(i)(R)(2) for the requirement that a U.S. clearing organization acting as a central counterparty report on Form 1042-S sales of PTP interests that it clears and settles on a net basis.

(4) *Exception when withholding already satisfied.*—A broker that receives from another broker an amount realized from the transfer of a PTP interest is required to withhold under this section unless the other broker has withheld the full amount required. A broker that receives from another broker an amount realized from the transfer of a PTP interest may treat the withholding as having been satisfied on the full amount required unless it knows or has reason to know that the withholding obligation has not already been satisfied. A broker that is a qualified intermediary determines its withholding requirement for purposes of this paragraph (a)(4) in accordance with its qualified intermediary agreement.

(5) *Documentation obtained from another person to determine a broker's status.*—A U.S. clearing organization may act as an agent for a broker receiving an amount realized from another broker that is a member of the clearing organization for purposes of furnishing valid documentation described in paragraph (a)(2) of this section of the first-mentioned broker's status to such other broker, provided the clearing organization notifies the first-mentioned broker and such broker has the ability to opt out. A broker that obtains documentation from a clearing organization under this paragraph (a)(5) for a broker to which the first-mentioned broker is paying an amount realized may rely on such documentation unless it has actual knowledge that the documentation is incorrect or unreliable.

(6) *Date of withholding with respect to a transfer other than a distribution.*—For a transfer of a PTP interest that is not a distribution, a broker is required to apply the principles of § 31.3406(a)-4(b)(1) of this chapter to determine the date on which to withhold under this section.

(7) *Payments to qualified intermediaries not assuming primary withholding responsibility.*—With respect to the transfer of a PTP interest, if a broker pays the amount realized to a foreign person that the broker may treat as a qualified intermediary (as defined in § 1.1441-1(e)(5)(ii)) that does not assume primary withholding responsibility for the payment based on a valid qualified intermediary withholding certificate described in § 1.1441-1(e)(3)(ii) upon which the broker may rely under paragraph (a)(2) of this section, the broker may withhold as provided in this paragraph (a)(7). Under this paragraph (a)(7), a broker may withhold under this section by reference to the amount of the payment that the broker can reliably determine, based on the withholding statement provided with the withholding certificate, is allocable to—

(i) Foreign transferors included in a chapter 3 withholding rate pool (as described in § 1.1441-1(e)(5)(v)(C)) that are subject to a 10 percent rate of withholding on the payment of the amount realized;

(ii) Foreign transferors included in a chapter 3 withholding rate pool (as described in § 1.1441-1(e)(5)(v)(C)) that qualify for an exception from withholding on the payment of the amount realized under paragraph (b) of this section;

(iii) Each foreign transferor for which a form acceptable under § 1.1446-1 is provided; or

(iv) U.S. transferors, based on a valid Form W-9 provided for each such transferor to the extent that the transferor is not included in a chapter 4 withholding rate pool of U.S. payees (as described in § 1.1441-1(e)(5)(v)(C), to the extent permitted for purposes of chapter 4 of the Internal Revenue Code).

(8) *Qualified intermediary or U.S. branch withholding requirement.*—A broker that is a qualified intermediary (as defined in § 1.1441-1(e)(5)(ii)) or U.S. branch must assume primary withholding responsibility under this section for a distribution from a publicly traded partnership for which the qualified intermediary or U.S. branch acts as a nominee for purposes of section 1446(a). See § 1.1446-4(b)(3).

(b) *Exceptions to withholding.*—(1) *In general.*—A broker is not required to withhold under this section if it properly relies on a certification described in paragraph (b)(2), (5), or (6) of this section, a qualified notice described in paragraph (b)(3) of this section, or if the exception described in paragraph (b)(4) of this section applies. A broker may not rely on a certification described in this paragraph (b) if it has actual knowledge that the certification is incorrect or unreliable.

(2) *Certification of non-foreign status.*—A broker may rely on a certification of non-foreign status that it obtains from the transferor. A certification of non-foreign status under this section means a Form W-9, *Request for Taxpayer Identification Number and Certification*, or valid substitute form, that meets the requirements of § 1.1441-1(d)(2). For purposes of this paragraph (b)(2), a broker may rely on a valid form that it already possesses from the transferor. A broker may instead rely on certification from a second broker (as defined in § 1.6045-1(a)(1)) that acts as an agent for the transferor when the second broker does not receive the amount realized from the transfer of the PTP interest. This certification must state that the second broker has collected a valid certification of non-foreign status (within the meaning of this paragraph (b)(2)) from the transferor, and it must include the transferor's TIN and status as a foreign or U.S. person.

(3) *Less than 10 percent effectively connected gain by partnership.*—(i) In general. A broker may rely on a qualified notice described in paragraph (b)(3)(iii) of this section that states that the 10-percent exception applies, as determined under paragraph (b)(3)(ii) of this section. In a case in which a broker properly relies on a qualified notice under paragraph (b)(1) of this section that results in underwithholding on a transfer of a PTP interest, the publicly traded partnership that issued the notice is solely liable for the underwithheld tax under section 1461. A publicly traded partnership's liability referenced in the preceding sentence, however, applies only when the publicly traded partnership fails to make a reasonable estimate of the amounts required for determining the applicability of the 10-percent exception.

(ii) *10-percent exception.*—(A) *In general.*—The 10-percent exception applies to a transfer if, on the PTP designated date described in paragraph (b)(3)(ii)(B) of this section—

(1) If the publicly traded partnership sold all of its assets at fair market value in the manner described in § 1.864(c)(8)-1(c), either—

(i) The amount of net gain that would have been effectively connected with the conduct of a trade or business within the United States would be less than 10 percent of the total net gain; or

(ii) No gain would have been effectively connected with the conduct of a trade or business in the United States; or

(2) The partnership was not engaged in a trade or business within the United States at any time during the taxable year of the partnership through the PTP designated date.

(B) *PTP designated date.*—The PTP designated date for a transfer is any date for a deemed sale determination that is designated by the publicly traded partnership in a qualified notice described in paragraph (b)(3)(iii) of this section, provided that the PTP designated date occurs on or after the date that is 92 days before the date on which the publicly traded partnership posted the qualified notice naming the PTP designated date.

(iii) *Qualified notice.*—(A) *In general.*—Except as provided in paragraphs (b)(3)(iii)(B) and (C) of this section, a qualified notice described in this paragraph (b)(3)(iii) is the most recent qualified notice (within the meaning of § 1.1446-4(b)(4)) posted by the publicly traded partnership.

(B) *Qualified notice posting date requirement.*—A qualified notice is described in this paragraph (b)(3)(iii) only if the publicly traded partnership has posted it within the 92-day period ending on the date of the transfer. For a transfer that is a distribution by the publicly traded partnership, the qualified notice is described in paragraph (b)(3)(iii) of this section only if the qualified notice is posted with respect to the distribution.

(C) *Recent posting of qualified notice.*—If the most recent qualified notice posted by the publicly traded partnership was posted during the 10-day period ending on the date of the transfer, a broker may instead rely on the immediately preceding qualified notice (within the meaning of § 1.1446-4(b)(4)) posted by the publicly traded partnership, provided that it satisfies the condition described in paragraph (b)(3)(iii)(B) of this section.

(4) *Amount subject to withholding under section 3406.*—A broker is not required to withhold under this section if the amount realized from the transfer of the PTP interest is subject to withholding under § 31.3406(b)(3)-2 of this chapter.

(5) *Income tax treaties.*—A broker may rely on a certification from the transferor that states that the transferor is not subject to tax on any gain from the transfer pursuant to an income tax treaty in effect between the United States and a foreign country if the requirements of this paragraph (b)(5) are met. The transferor makes the certification on a withholding certificate (on a Form W-8BEN, *Certificate of Foreign Status of Beneficial Owner for United States Tax Withholding and Reporting (Individuals)*, or Form W-8BEN-E, *Certificate of Status of Beneficial Owner for United States Tax Withholding and Reporting (Entities)*) that meets the requirements for validity under § 1.1446-1(c)(2)(iv) (or an applicable substitute form that meets the requirements under § 1.1446-1(c)(5)) and that contains the information necessary to support the claim for treaty benefits. For purposes of this paragraph (b)(5), a broker may rely on a withholding certificate that it already possesses from the transferor that meets the requirements of this paragraph (b)(5) unless it has actual knowledge that the information is incorrect or unreliable. The exception in this paragraph (b)(5) does not apply if treaty benefits apply to only a portion of the gain from the transfer.

(6) *Foreign dealers that provide Form W-8ECI.*—A broker may rely on a certification provided by a transferor that certifies that it is a dealer in securities (as defined in section 475(c)(1)) and that any gain from the transfer of the PTP interest is effectively connected with the conduct of a trade or business within the United States without regard to the provisions of section 864(c)(8). The certification described in the preceding sentence is made on a Form W-8ECI, *Certificate of Foreign Person's Claim That Income Is Effectively Connected With the Conduct of a Trade or Business in the United States*, that meets the requirements for validity under § 1.1446-1(c)(2)(iv) (or an applicable substitute form that meets the requirements under § 1.1446-1(c)(5))

and that contains any other information required in the instructions to the form. A broker may rely on a withholding certificate that it already possesses from the transferor that meets the requirements of this paragraph (b)(6) unless it has actual knowledge that the information is incorrect or unreliable.

(c) *Determining the amount to withhold.*—(1) *In general.*—A broker that is required to withhold under this section must withhold 10 percent of the amount realized on the transfer of the PTP interest, except as provided in this paragraph (c). Any procedures in this paragraph (c) apply solely for purposes of determining the amount to withhold under section 1446(f)(1) and this section. A broker may not rely on a certification described in this paragraph (c) if it has actual knowledge that the certification is incorrect or unreliable.

(2) *Amount realized.*—(i) *In general.*—Solely for purposes of this section, the amount realized is the amount of gross proceeds (as defined in § 1.6045-1(d)(5)) paid or credited upon the transfer to the customer or other broker (as applicable), or, in the case of a distribution, the amount determined under paragraph (c)(2)(iii) of this section.

(ii) *Certification by a foreign partnership of modified amount realized.*—(A) *In general.*—When a transferor is a foreign partnership, a broker may use the procedures of this paragraph (c)(2)(ii) to determine the amount realized. For purposes of this paragraph (c)(2)(ii)(A), the broker may treat the modified amount realized as the amount realized to the extent it may rely on a certification from the transferor providing the modified amount realized.

(B) *Determining modified amount realized.*—The modified amount realized is determined by multiplying the amount realized (as determined under this paragraph (c)(2), without regard to this paragraph (c)(2)(ii)) by the aggregate percentage computed as of the determination date (see § 1.1446(f)-1(c)(4)). The aggregate percentage is the percentage of the gain (if any) arising from the transfer that would be allocated to presumed foreign taxable persons. For purposes of this paragraph (c)(2)(ii)(B), a presumed foreign taxable person is any direct or indirect partner of the transferor that has not provided either a certification of non-foreign status that meets the requirements of paragraph (b)(2) of this section or a certification of treaty benefits that states that the partner is not subject to tax on any gain from the transfer pursuant to an income tax treaty in effect between the United States and a foreign country. A valid certification of treaty benefits must meet the requirements of paragraph (b)(5) of this section (as applied to the partner claiming treaty benefits). For purposes of this paragraph (c)(2)(ii), an indirect partner is a person that owns an interest in the transferor indirectly through one or more foreign partnerships.

(C) *Certification.*—The certification is made by providing a withholding certificate (on Form W-8IMY, *Certificate of Foreign Intermediary, Foreign Flow-Through Entity, or Certain U.S. Branches for United States Tax Withholding and Reporting)* that includes a withholding statement that provides the percentage of gain allocable to each direct or indirect partner and that provides whether each such person is a United States person, a foreign partner eligible for treaty benefits, or a presumed foreign taxable person. The certification must also include the certification of non-foreign status or the certification of treaty benefits from each direct or indirect partner that is not a presumed foreign taxable person. For purposes of this paragraph (c)(2)(ii), a broker may rely on a withholding certificate and withholding statement that it already possesses from the partnership unless it has actual knowledge that the information is incorrect or unreliable.

(iii) *Determination of amount realized on a distribution.*—The amount realized on a distribution from a publicly traded partnership is the amount of the distribution reduced by the portion of the distribution that is attributable to the cumulative net income of the partnership. The cumulative net income is the net income earned by the publicly traded partnership since its formation that has not been previously distributed by the partnership. A publicly traded partnership identifies such excess portion of the distribution as an amount in excess of cumulative net income on a qualified notice (within the meaning of § 1.1446-4(b)(4)) posted with respect to the distribution. If a broker properly withholds based on the qualified notice (applying the rules of § 1.1446-4(d)(1) to the distribution), the broker is not liable for any underwithholding on any amount attributable to an amount in excess of cumulative net income. Rather, the publicly traded partnership that issued the qualified notice is solely liable for the underwithheld tax under section 1461 on such amount that results from a broker's reliance on the notice.

(d) *Reporting and paying withheld amounts.*—A broker that is required to withhold under this section must pay the withheld tax pursuant to the deposit rules in § 1.6302-2. For rules regarding reporting on Forms 1042, *Annual Withholding Tax Return for U.S. Source Income of Foreign Persons,* and 1042-S, *Foreign Person's U.S. Source Income Subject to Withholding,* that apply to a broker that withholds under this section, see § 1.1461-1(b) and (c). For rules regarding when an amount realized on the transfer of a PTP interest is reportable on a Form 1042-S (including in certain cases in which withholding is not required), see § 1.1461-1(c)(2)(i)(Q) and (R). A broker that pays the amount realized to a foreign partnership must issue a Form 1042-S directly to the partnership rather than issuing a form to each of the partners of the partnership. *See* § 1.1461-1(c)(1)(ii)(A)(*8*) (treating the foreign partnership as a recipient for reporting purposes). A broker making a payment to a U.S. branch treated as a U.S. person must not treat the branch as a U.S. person for purposes of reporting the payment made to the branch. Therefore, a payment to that U.S. branch must be reported on Form 1042-S. *See* § 1.1461-1(c). A Form 1042-S issued directly to the transferor must include the TIN of the transferor unless the broker does not know the TIN at the time of issuance.

(e) *Effect of withholding on transferor.*—(1) *In general.*—The withholding of tax under this section does not relieve a foreign person from filing a U.S. tax return with respect to the transfer. *See* §§ 1.6012-1(b)(1), 1.6012-2(g)(1), and 1.6031(a)-1. Further, the withholding of tax by a broker does not relieve a nonresident alien individual or foreign corporation subject to tax on gain by reason of section 864(c)(8) from paying any tax due with the return that has not been fully satisfied through withholding.

(2) *Manner of obtaining credit.*—(i) *Individuals and corporations.*—An individual or corporation may claim a credit under section 33 for the amount withheld under this section by attaching to its applicable return a copy of a Form 1042-S that includes its TIN (or as otherwise provided in IRS forms or instructions).

(ii) *Partnerships, trusts, or estates.*—For a rule allowing a foreign partnership that is a transferor to claim a credit for the amount withheld under this section against its obligation to withhold under section 1446(a), see § 1.1446-3(c)(4). For the rule providing the extent to which a foreign trust or estate may claim a credit for an amount withheld under this section, see § 1.1462-1. A foreign partnership, trust, or estate claiming a credit for an amount withheld must attach to its applicable return the Form 1042-S provided to it under paragraph (d) of this section (or as otherwise provided in IRS forms or instructions). A foreign trust or estate must also provide any information required in forms or instructions to any beneficiary or owner that is liable for tax on any of the gain under section 864(c)(8).

(f) *Applicability date.*—This section applies to transfers that occur on or after January 1, 2022. [Reg. § 1.1446(f)-4.]

□ [*T.D. 9926, 11-27-2020.*]

§ 1.1446(f)-5. Liability for failure to withhold.—(a) *Liability for failure to withhold.*—Every person required to withhold and pay tax under section 1446(f), but that fails to do so, is liable for the tax under section 1461, plus any applicable interest, penalties, or additions to tax. A partnership that failed to withhold and pay tax under § 1.1446(f)-3 is liable only for the amount of tax that it failed to collect (but not any interest computed on that amount under § 1.1446(f)-3(c)(2)(ii)), plus any interest, penalties, or additions to tax with regard to the partnership's failure to withhold.

(b) *Tax liability otherwise satisfied.*—Under section 1463, if the tax required to be withheld under section 1446(f) is paid by another person required to withhold under section 1446(f), or by the nonresident alien individual or foreign corporation subject to tax on gain resulting from section 864(c)(8), the tax will not be recollected. The person required to withhold must establish proof of payment by another person required to withhold or by the nonresident alien individual or foreign corporation subject to the tax on gain resulting from section 864(c)(8). The person required to withhold may show that a reduced rate of withholding was appropriate by establishing the amount of tax due by the foreign transferor (as defined in § 1.864(c)(8)-1(g)(3)) on gain resulting from section 864(c)(8). The person required to withhold under section 1446(f) is not relieved from liability for any interest, penalties, or additions to tax that would otherwise apply. However, if the person required to withhold establishes to the satisfaction of the Commissioner that no gain on the transfer is treated as effectively connected with the conduct of a trade or business within the United States trade or business under section 864(c)(8), no interest, penalties, or additions to tax will apply.

(c) *Liability of agents.*—(1) *Duty to provide notice of false certification.*—A transferee's or transferor's agent (other than a broker required to withhold under § 1.1446(f)-4) must provide notice to a transferee (or other person required to withhold) if that person is furnished with a certification described in §§ 1.1446(f)-1 through 1.1446(f)-4 that the agent knows is false. A person required to withhold may not rely on a certification if it receives the notice described in this paragraph (c)(1).

(2) *Procedural requirements.*—Any agent who is required to provide notice under paragraph (c)(1) of this section must do so in writing (including by electronic submission) as soon as possible after learning of the false certification. If the agent first learns of the false certification before the date of transfer, notice must be given by the third day following that discovery but no later than the date of transfer (before the transferee's payment of consideration). If an agent first learns of a false certification after the date of transfer, notice must be given by the third day following that discovery. The notice must also explain the possible consequences to the recipient of a failure to withhold. The notice need not disclose the information on which the agent's statement is based. The agent must also furnish a copy of the notice to the IRS by the date on which the notice is required to be given to the recipient. The copy of the notice must be delivered to the address provided in § 1.1445-1(g)(10) and must be accompanied by a cover letter stating that the copy is being filed pursuant to the requirements of this paragraph (c)(2).

(3) *Failure to provide notice.*—Any agent who is required to provide notice under paragraph (c)(1) of this section, but fails to do so in the manner required in paragraph (c)(2) of this section, is liable for the tax that the person who should have been provided notice in accordance with paragraph (c)(2) of this section was required to withhold under section 1446(f) if the notice had been given.

(4) *Limitation on liability.*—An agent's liability under paragraph (c)(3) of this section is limited to the amount of compensation that the agent derives from the transaction. In addition, an agent that assists in the preparation of, or fails to disclose knowledge of, a false certification may be liable for civil and criminal penalties.

(d) *Applicability date.*—This section applies to transfers that occur on or after January 29, 2021. [Reg. § 1.1446(f)-5.]

□ [*T.D.* 9926, 11-27-2020.]

Application of Withholding Provisions

§ 1.1461-1. Payment and returns of tax withheld.—(a) *Payment of withheld tax.*—(1) *Deposits of tax.*—Every withholding agent who withholds tax pursuant to chapter 3 of the Internal Revenue Code (Code) and the regulations under such chapter shall deposit such amount of tax as provided in § 1.6302-2(a). If for any reason the total amount of tax required to be returned for any calendar year pursuant to paragraph (b) of this section has not been deposited pursuant to § 1.6302-2, the withholding agent shall pay the balance of tax due for such year at such place as the Internal Revenue Service (IRS) shall specify. The tax shall be paid when filing the return required under paragraph (b)(1) of this section for such year, unless the IRS specifies otherwise. With respect to withholding under section 1446, this section shall apply only to publicly traded partnerships and nominees that withhold under § 1.1446-4 and brokers and publicly traded partnerships that withhold (or are otherwise liable for underwithholding) under § 1.1446(f)-4 on transfers of publicly traded partnership interests. See § 1.1461-3 regarding withholding tax liabilities under sections 1446(a) and 1446(f) and penalties that apply for failure to withhold under either of those sections.

(2) *Penalties for failure to pay tax.*—For penalties and additions to the tax for failure to timely pay the tax required to be withheld under chapter 3 of the Code, see sections 6656, 6672, and 7202 and the regulations under those sections.

(b) *Income tax return.*—(1) *General rule.*—A withholding agent shall make an income tax return on Form 1042 (or such other form as the IRS may prescribe) for income paid during the preceding calendar year that the withholding agent is required to report on an information return on Form 1042-S (or such other form as the IRS may prescribe) under paragraph (c)(1) of this section. See section 6011 and § 1.6011-1(c). The withholding agent must file the return on or before March 15 of the calendar year following the year in which the income was paid. The return must show the aggregate amount of income paid and tax withheld required to be reported on all the Forms 1042-S for the preceding calendar year by the withholding agent, in addition to such information as is required by the form and accompanying instructions. See § 1.1474-1(c) for the requirement to show the aggregate chapter 4 reportable amounts and tax withheld on Form 1042. A single Form 1042 may be filed by a withholding agent to report amounts under chapters 3 and 4, including tax withheld. Withholding certificates or other statements or information provided to a withholding agent are not required to be attached to the return. A return must be filed under this paragraph (b)(1) even though no tax was required to be withheld during the preceding calendar year. The withholding agent must retain a copy of Form 1042 for the applicable statute of limitations on assessments and collection with respect to the amounts required to be reported on the Form 1042. See section 6501 and the regulations thereunder for the applicable statute of limitations. Adjustments to the total amount of tax withheld, as described in § 1.1461-2, shall be stated on the return as prescribed by the form and accompanying instructions.

(2) *Amended returns.*—An amended return may be filed on a Form 1042 or such other form as the IRS may prescribe. An amended return must include such information as the form or accompanying instructions shall require, including, with respect to any information that has changed from the time of the filing of the return, the information that was shown on the original return and the corrected information.

(c) *Information returns.*—(1) *Filing requirement.*—(i) *In general.*—A withholding agent (other than an individual who is not acting in the course of a trade or business with respect to a payment) must make an information return on Form 1042-S, "Foreign Person's U.S. Source Income Subject to Withholding," (or such other form as the IRS may prescribe) to report the amounts subject to reporting, as defined in paragraph (c)(2) of this section, that were paid during the preceding calendar year. Notwithstanding the preceding sentence, any person that withholds or is required to withhold an amount under section 1441, 1442, or 1443, or § 1.1446-4(a) (applicable to publicly traded partnerships required to pay tax under section 1446(a) on distributions) or § 1.1446(f)-4(a) (applicable to brokers required to withhold on transfers of publicly traded partnership interests) must file a Form 1042-S for the payment withheld upon whether or not that person is engaged in a trade or business and whether or not the payment is an amount subject to reporting. A Form 1042-S shall be prepared for each recipient of an amount subject to reporting and for each single type of income payment. The Form 1042-S shall be prepared in such manner as the form and accompanying instructions prescribe. One copy of the Form 1042-S shall be filed with the IRS on or before March 15th of the calendar year following the year in which the amount subject to reporting was paid. It shall be filed with a transmittal form as provided in the instructions to the Form 1042-S and to the transmittal form. Withholding certificates, documentary evidence, or other statements or documentation provided to a withholding agent are not required to be attached to the form. Another copy of the Form 1042-S must be furnished to the recipient for whom the form is prepared (or any other person, as required under this paragraph (c) or the instructions to the form) on or before March 15 of the calendar year following the year in which the amount subject to reporting was paid. The withholding agent must retain a copy of each Form 1042-S for the statute of limitations on assessment and collection applicable to the Form 1042 to which the Form 1042-S relates. A withholding agent required by this section to furnish a recipient copy of Form 1042-S may furnish such copy electronically by complying with the requirements provided in § 1.6050W-2(a)(2) through (5) applicable to statements required under section 6050W (substituting the phrase "Form 1042-S" for the phrases "statement required under section 6050W" or "statements required by section 6050W(f)" each place they appear). A withholding agent that meets the requirements of that section for providing electronic copies to recipients may apply these rules to payments made in calendar year 2016.

(ii) *Recipient*.—(A) *Defined*.—For purposes of this section, the term *recipient* means—

(1) A beneficial owner as defined in §1.1441-1(c)(6), including a foreign estate or a foreign complex trust, as defined in §1.1441-1(c)(25);

(2) A qualified intermediary as defined in §1.1441-1(e)(5)(ii);

(3) A withholding foreign partnership as defined in §1.1441-5(c)(2) or a withholding foreign trust under §1.1441-5(e)(5)(v);

(4) A territory financial institution treated as a U.S. person under §1.1441-1(b)(2)(iv)(A);

(5) A U.S. branch that is treated as a U.S. person under §1.1441-1(b)(2)(iv)(A);

(6) A nonwithholding foreign partnership or a foreign simple trust as defined in §1.1441-1(c)(24), but only to the extent the income is (or is treated as) effectively connected with the conduct of a trade or business in the United States by such entity, or if the nonwithholding foreign partnership or foreign simple trust is also described in paragraph (c)(1)(ii)(A)*(9)* or (c)(1)(ii)(A)*(10)* of this section;

(7) A payee, as defined in §1.1441-1(b)(2) that is presumed to be a foreign person under the presumption rules of §1.1441-1(b)(3); 1.1441-5(d) or (e)(6), or 1.6049-5(d);

(8) A partner (including a foreign partnership or a partner for which a qualified intermediary provides partner-specific documentation under §1.1446-4(e)) receiving a distribution from a publicly traded partnership subject to withholding under section 1446(a) and §1.1446-4 on distributions of effectively connected income, and a partner (including a foreign partnership or a partner for which a qualified intermediary provides partner-specific documentation under §1.1446(f)-4(a)(7)) receiving an amount realized from a transfer of a publicly traded partnership interest under section 1446(f)(1) and §1.1446(f)-4.

(9) A foreign intermediary, nonwithholding foreign partnership, or nonwithholding foreign trust that is a participating FFI or registered deemed-compliant FFI with respect to a chapter 4 reporting pool of U.S. payees;

(10) A participating FFI or a registered deemed-compliant FFI that is a recipient of a withholdable payment described in §1.1474-1(d)(1)(ii)(A)*(1)*(*iii*); and

(11) Any other person as required on Form 1042-S or the instructions to the form.

(B) *Persons that are not recipients*.—A recipient does not include—

(1) A nonqualified intermediary, except with respect to a payment (or portion of a payment) for which a nonqualified intermediary that is an FFI is a recipient reporting as described in §1.1474-1(d)(1)(ii)(A)*(1)*(*iii*), or if the nonqualified intermediary is also described in paragraph (c)(1)(ii)(A)*(9)* or (c)(1)(ii)(A)*(10)* of this section;

(2) A payee included in a chapter 3 or chapter 4 withholding rate pool;

(3) A flow-through entity, as defined in §1.1441-1(c)(23) (to the extent it is receiving amounts subject to reporting other than income effectively connected with the conduct of a trade or business in the United States), that is not a recipient described in paragraphs (c)(1)(ii)(A)*(9)* or (c)(1)(ii)(A)*(10)* of this section;

(4) A U.S. branch (including a territory financial institution) described in §1.1441-1(b)(2)(iv)(A) that is not treated as a U.S. person under that section and is not a recipient described in paragraphs (c)(1)(ii)(A)*(9)* or *(10)* of this section;

(5) A foreign broker withheld upon under §1.1446(f)-4(a)(2)(ii) by another broker paying an amount realized from the transfer of a PTP interest.

(C) *Coordination with chapter 4 reporting*.—See §1.1474-1(d)(1)(ii)(A) for persons that are defined as recipients of a withholdable payment of U.S. source FDAP income for purposes of chapter 4 in addition to the persons that are recipients under this paragraph (c)(1)(ii).

(2) *Amounts subject to reporting*.—(i) *In general*.—Subject to the exceptions described in paragraph (c)(2)(ii) of this section, amounts subject to reporting on Form 1042-S are amounts paid to a foreign payee or partner (including persons presumed to be foreign) that are amounts subject to withholding as defined in §1.1441-2(a), distributions of effectively connected income under §1.1446-4, or amounts realized from transfers of PTP interests under §1.1446(f)-4. Amounts subject to reporting include amounts subject to withholding even if no amount is deducted and withheld from the payment because of a treaty or Internal Revenue Code exception to taxation or because an amount withheld was reimbursed to the payee under the adjustment procedures of §1.1461-2. In addition, amounts subject to reporting include any amounts paid to a foreign payee on which a withholding agent withheld (including under §1.1441-2(e)(7)) an amount (either under chapter 3 of the Internal Revenue Code or section 3406) whether or not the amount is subject to withholding. Amounts subject to reporting include, but are not limited to, the following items—

(A) The entire amount of a corporate distribution (whether actual or deemed) irrespective of any estimate of the portion of the distribution that represents a taxable dividend;

(B) Interest, including the portion of a notional principal contract payment that is characterized as interest. Interest shall also be reported on Form 1042-S if it is bank deposit interest paid to nonresident alien individuals as required under §1.6049-8;

(C) Rents;

(D) Royalties;

(E) Compensation for dependent and independent personal services performed in the United States;

(F) Annuities;

(G) Pension distributions and other deferred income;

(H) Gambling winnings that are not exempt from tax under section 871(j);

(I) Income from the cancellation of indebtedness unless the withholding agent is unrelated to the debtor and does not have knowledge of the facts that give rise to the payment (see §1.1441-2(d));

(J) Amounts that are (or are presumed to be) effectively connected with the conduct of a trade or business in the United States (including deposit interest as defined in sections 871(i)(2)(A) and 881(d)) even if no withholding certificate is required to be furnished by the payee or beneficial owner. In the case of amounts paid on a notional principal contract described in §1.1441-4(a)(3) that are presumed to be effectively connected with the conduct of a trade or business in the United States, the amount required to be reported is limited to the amount of cash paid from the notional principal contract;

(K) Scholarship, fellowship, or grant income and compensation for personal services that is not excludible from gross income under section 117 (whether or not the taxable scholarship, fellowship, grant income, or compensation for personal services is exempt from tax under an income tax treaty) paid to foreign students, trainees, teachers, or researchers;

(L) Dividend equivalents as described in section 871(m) and the regulations thereunder;

(M) Any dividend or any payment that references a dividend from an underlying security pursuant to a securities lending or sale-repurchase transaction paid to a qualified derivatives dealer even when the withholding agent is not required to withhold on the payment pursuant to §1.1441-1(b)(4)(xxi), (xxii), or (xxiii);

(N) Amounts paid to foreign governments, international organizations, or the Bank for International Settlements, whether or not documentation must be provided;

(O) Original issue discount paid on the redemption of an OID obligation. The amount to be reported is the amount of OID includible in the gross income of the holder of the obligation, if known, or, if not known, the total amount of original issue discount determined as if the holder held the obligation from its original issuance. A withholding agent may determine the total amount of OID by using the most recently published "List of Original Issue Discount Instruments," (Publication 1212, available from the IRS Forms Distribution Centers);

(P) The amount of any distribution made by a publicly traded partnership that is an amount subject to withholding under §1.1446-4, or that is paid to a qualified intermediary or a U.S. branch of a foreign person that agrees to be treated as a U.S. person;

(Q) Except with respect to a broker that is a U.S. clearing organization, an amount realized on the transfer of a PTP interest under §1.1446(f)-4 (unless an exception to withholding applies under §1.1446(f)-4(b)(2) through (4)); and

(R) In the case of a broker that is a U.S. clearing organization—

(1) An amount realized (as determined under §1.1446(f)-4(c)(2)(iii)) on a distribution made by a publicly traded partnership for which withholding is required under §1.1446(f)-4(a); and

(2) An amount realized on the sale of a PTP interest cleared and settled through a net settlement system maintained by the clearing organization acting as a central counterparty in the sale (with the reporting on the non-netted amount), unless an exception to withholding would apply under § 1.1446(f)-4(b)(2) or (3).

(ii) *Exceptions to reporting.*—The amounts listed in this paragraph (c)(2)(ii) are not required to be reported on Form 1042-S—

(A) Interest (including original issue discount) that is deposit interest under sections 871(i)(2)(A) and 881(d) and that is not effectively connected with the conduct of a trade or business in the United States, unless reporting is required under § 1.6049-8 (regarding payments to certain foreign residents) or is interest that is effectively connected with the conduct of a trade or business in the United States;

(B) Interest or original issue discount on certain short-term obligations, described in section 871(g)(1)(B) or 881(a)(3);

(C) Interest paid on obligations sold between interest payment dates and the portion of the purchase price of an OID obligation that is sold or exchanged in a transaction other than a redemption, unless the sale or exchange is part of a plan, the principal purpose of which is to avoid tax and the withholding agent has actual knowledge or reason to know of such plan (see § 1.1441-2(a)(5) and (6));

(D) Any item required to be reported on a Form W-2, including an item required to be shown on Form W-2 solely by reason of § 1.6041-2 (relating to return of information for payments to employees) or § 1.6052-1 (relating to information regarding payment of wages in the form of group-term life insurance);

(E) Any item required to be reported on Form 1099, and such other forms as are prescribed pursuant to the information reporting provisions of sections 6041 through 6050W and the regulations under those sections;

(F) Amounts paid on a notional principal contract described in § 1.1441-4(a)(3)(i) that are not effectively connected with the conduct of a trade or business in the United States (or not treated as effectively connected pursuant to § 1.1441-4(a)(3)(ii));

(G) Amounts required to be reported on Form 8288 (U.S. Withholding Tax Return for Dispositions by Foreign Persons of U.S. Real Property Interests) or Form 8804 (Annual Return for Partnership Withholding Tax (section 1446)). A withholding agent that must report a distribution partly on a Form 8288 or 8804 and partly on a Form 1042-S may elect to report the entire amount on a Form 8288 or 8804;

(H) Interest (including original issue discount) paid with respect to foreign-targeted registered obligations issued before January 1, 2016, that are described in § 1.871-14(e)(2) to the extent the documentation requirements described in § 1.871-14(e)(3) and (e)(4) are required to be satisfied (taking into account the provisions of § 1.871-14(e)(4)(ii), if applicable;

(I) Interest on a foreign-targeted bearer obligation (see §§ 1.1441-1(b)(4)(i) and 1.1441-2(a)) issued before March 19, 2012;

(J) Except as provided in § 1.1461-1(c)(2)(i)(M), any payment to a qualified derivatives dealer when the withholding agent is not required to withhold on the payment pursuant to § 1.1441-1(b)(4)(xxi), (xxii), or (xxiii). This exception does not apply to withholding agents that are qualified derivatives dealers;

(K) Gain described in section 301(c)(3); and

(L) Amounts described in § 1.1441-1(b)(4)(xviii) (dealing with certain amounts paid by the U.S. government).

(iii) *Applicability date.*—Paragraph (c)(2) of this section applies beginning January 19, 2017.

(3) *Required information.*—The information required to be furnished under this paragraph (c)(3) shall be based upon the information provided by or on behalf of the recipient of an amount subject to reporting (as corrected and supplemented based on the withholding agent's actual knowledge) or the presumption rules of §§ 1.1441-1(b)(3), 1.1441-4(a); 1.1441-5(d) and (e); 1.1441-9(b)(3), 1.1446-1(c)(3) (as applied to publicly traded partnerships required to pay tax under section 1446 on distributions of effectively connected income) or 1.6049-5(d). The reference in the previous sentence to presumption rules applicable to withholding under section 1446 shall apply to partnership taxable years beginning after May 18, 2005, or such earlier time as the regulations under §§ 1.1446-1 through 1.1446-5 apply by reason of an election under § 1.1446-7. The Form 1042-S must include the following information, if applicable—

(i) The name, address, taxpayer identifying number of the withholding agent, and the withholding agent's status for chapter 3 purposes (based on the status codes applicable for chapter 3 purposes provided on the form);

(ii) A description of each category of income paid based on the income codes provided on the form (e.g., interest, dividends, royalties, etc.) and the aggregate amount in each category expressed in U.S. dollars;

(iii) For a payment not subject to withholding under chapter 4, the rate of withholding applied or the basis for exempting the payment from withholding under chapter 3, and the exemption applicable to the payment for chapter 4 purposes (based on the exemption codes provided on the form);

(iv) The name and address of the recipient;

(v) The name and address of any nonqualified intermediary, flow-through entity, or U.S. branch as described in § 1.1441-1(b)(2)(iv) (other than a branch that is treated as a U.S. person) to which the payment was made;

(vi) The taxpayer identifying number of the recipient if required under § 1.1441-1(e)(4)(vii) or if actually known to the withholding agent making the return;

(vii) The taxpayer identifying number of a nonqualified intermediary or flow-through entity (to the extent it is not a recipient) or other flow-through entity to the extent it is known to the withholding agent;

(viii) The country (based on the country codes provided on the form) of the recipient and of any nonqualified intermediary or flow-through entity the name of which appears on the form; and

(ix) Such information as the form or the instructions may require in addition to, or in lieu of, information required under this paragraph (c)(3).

(4) *Method of reporting.*—(i) *Payments by U.S. withholding agents to recipients.*—A withholding agent that is a U.S. person (other than a foreign branch of a U.S. person that is a qualified intermediary as defined in § 1.1441-1(e)(5)(ii) that makes payments of amounts subject to reporting on Form 1042-S must file a separate Form 1042-S for each recipient who receives such amount. For purposes of this paragraph (c)(4), a U.S. person includes a U.S. branch (including a territory financial institution) described in § 1.1441-1(b)(2)(iv)(A) that is treated as a U.S. person. Except as may otherwise be required on Form 1042-S or the instructions to the form, only payments for which the income code, exemption code, withholding rate, and recipient code are the same may be reported on a single Form 1042-S. See paragraph (c)(4)(ii) of this section for reporting of payments made to a person that is not a recipient. See § 1.1474-1(d)(4) for additional requirements that may apply for reporting on Form 1042-S with respect to a withholdable payment that is a chapter 4 reportable amount.

(A) *Payments to beneficial owners.*—If a U.S. withholding agent makes a payment directly to a beneficial owner it must complete Form 1042-S treating the beneficial owner as the recipient. Under the grace period rule of § 1.1441-1(b)(3)(iv), a U.S. withholding agent may, under certain circumstances, treat a payee as a foreign person while the withholding agent awaits a valid withholding certificate. A U.S. withholding agent who relies on the grace period rule to treat a payee as a foreign person must file a Form 1042-S to report all payments on Form 1042-S during the period that person was presumed to be foreign even if that person is later determined to be a U.S. person based on appropriate documentation or is presumed to be a U.S. person after the grace period ends. In the case of joint owners, a withholding agent may provide a single Form 1042-S made out to the owner whose status the U.S. withholding agent relied upon to determine the applicable rate of withholding. If, however, any one of the owners requests its own Form 1042-S, the withholding agent must furnish a Form 1042-S to the person who requests it. If more than one Form 1042-S is issued for a single payment, the aggregate amount paid and tax withheld that is reported on all Forms 1042-S cannot exceed the total amounts paid to joint owners and the tax withheld thereon.

(B) *Payments to a qualified intermediary, a withholding foreign partnership, or a withholding foreign trust.*—A U.S. withholding agent that makes payments to a qualified intermediary (whether or not the qualified intermediary assumes primary withholding responsibility for purposes of chapter 3 and chapter 4 of the Code), a withholding foreign partnership, or a withholding foreign trust shall complete Forms 1042-S treating the qualified intermediary, withholding foreign partnership, or withholding foreign trust as the recipient. The U.S. withholding agent must complete a separate Form 1042-S for each chapter 3 and chapter 4 withholding rate pool with respect to each qualified intermediary. A qualified intermediary that does not assume primary withholding responsibility on all payments it receives provides information regarding the proportions of income subject to a particular withholding rate (*i.e.*, a chapter 3 withholding rate pool) to the withholding agent on a withholding statement associated with a qualified intermediary withholding certificate. In such a case, the U.S. withholding agent must complete a separate Form 1042-S for each chapter 3 and chapter 4 withholding rate pool with respect to the qualified intermediary. To the extent a qualified intermediary is required to report a payment under chapter 61, it may provide a U.S. withholding agent with information regarding withholding rate pools for U.S. non-exempt recipients (as defined under §1.1441-1(c)(21)). Amounts paid with respect to such withholding rate pools must be reported on a Form 1099 completed for each U.S. non-exempt recipient to the extent such U.S. non-exempt recipient is subject to Form 1099 reporting and is not reported on Form 1042-S. See, however, §1.1441-1(e)(5)(v)(C) for when a qualified intermediary may provide a chapter 4 withholding rate pool of U.S payees (in lieu of reporting such payees on a withholding statement) and for the withholding rate pools (including chapter 4 withholding rate pools) otherwise reportable on a withholding statement provided by a qualified intermediary.

(C) *Amounts paid to U.S. branches treated as U.S. persons.*—A U.S. withholding agent making a payment to a U.S. branch of a foreign person (including a territory financial institution) described in §1.1441-1(b)(2)(iv)(A) shall complete Form 1042-S as follows—

(1) If the branch has provided the U.S. withholding agent with a withholding certificate that evidences its agreement with the withholding agent to be treated as a U.S. person, the U.S. withholding agent files Forms 1042-S treating the U.S. branch or territory financial institution as the recipient;

(2) If the branch has provided the U.S. withholding agent with a withholding certificate that transmits information regarding beneficial owners, qualified intermediaries, withholding foreign partnerships, or other recipients, the U.S. withholding agent must complete a separate Form 1042-S for each recipient whose documentation is associated with the U.S. branch's or territory financial institution's withholding certificate; or

(3) If the U.S. withholding agent cannot reliably associate a payment with a valid withholding certificate from the U.S. branch, it shall treat the U.S. branch as the recipient and report the income as effectively connected with the conduct of a trade or business in the United States except as otherwise provided in §1.1441-1(b)(2)(iv)(B)*(4)*.

(D) *Dual Claims.*—A U.S. withholding agent may make a payment to a foreign entity that is simultaneously claiming a reduced rate of tax on its own behalf for a portion of the payment and a reduced rate on behalf of persons in their capacity as interest holders in that entity on the remaining portion. See §1.1441-6(b)(2)(iii). If the claims are consistent and the withholding agent accepts the multiple claims, the withholding agent must file a separate Form 1042-S for those payments for which the entity is treated as the beneficial owner and Forms 1042-S for each of the interest holders in the entity for which the interest holder is treated as the recipient. For those payments for which the interest holder in an entity is treated as the recipient, the U.S. withholding agent shall prepare the Form 1042-S in the same manner as a payment made to a nonqualified intermediary or flow-through entity as set forth in paragraph (c)(4)(ii) of this section. If the claims are consistent but the withholding agent has not chosen to accept the multiple claims, or if the claims are inconsistent, the withholding agent must file a separate Form 1042-S for the person or persons it has chosen to treat as the recipients.

(ii) *Payments made by U.S. withholding agents to persons that are not recipients.*—(A) *Amounts paid to a nonqualified intermediary, a flow-through entity, and certain U.S. branches.*—If a U.S. withholding agent makes a payment to a nonqualified intermediary, a flow-through entity, or a U.S. branch (including a territory financial institution) described in §1.1441-1(b)(2)(iv) (other than a U.S. branch or territory financial institution that is treated as a U.S. person), it must complete a separate Form 1042-S for each recipient to the extent the withholding agent can reliably associate a payment with valid documentation (within the meaning of §1.1441-1(b)(2)(vii)) from the recipient which is associated with the withholding certificate provided by the nonqualified intermediary, flow-through entity, or U.S. branch or territory financial institution. See §1.1474-1(d)(4)(i) for when a withholding agent may report a chapter 4 reportable amount made to such an entity in a chapter 4 withholding rate pool. See also §1.1441-1(e)(3)(iv)(A) for when a withholding statement provided by a nonqualified intermediary may include a chapter 4 withholding rate pool of U.S. payees. If a payment is reported by the withholding agent in a chapter 4 withholding rate pool, the withholding agent must report on Form 1042-S the nonqualified intermediary or flow-through entity as a recipient associated with the applicable chapter 4 withholding rate pool. If a payment is made through tiers of nonqualified intermediaries or flow-through entities, the withholding agent must nevertheless complete Form 1042-S for the recipient to the extent it can reliably associate the payment with documentation from the recipient. A withholding agent that is completing a Form 1042-S for a recipient that receives a payment through a nonqualified intermediary, a flow-through entity, or a U.S. branch or territory financial institution must include on the Form 1042-S the name of the nonqualified intermediary, flow-through entity, U.S. branch or territory financial institution from which the recipient directly receives the payment. If a U.S. withholding agent cannot reliably associate the payment, or any portion of the payment, with valid documentation from a recipient either because no such documentation has been provided or because the nonqualified intermediary, flow-through entity, or U.S. branch or territory financial institution has failed to provide sufficient allocation information so that the withholding agent can associate the payment, or any portion thereof, with valid documentation, then the withholding agent must report the payments as made to an unknown recipient in accordance with the appropriate presumption rules for that payment. Thus, if the payment is not a withholdable payment and under the presumption rules the payment is presumed to be made to a foreign person, the withholding agent must generally withhold 30 percent of the payment and report the payment on Form 1042-S made out to an unknown recipient and shall also include the name of the nonqualified intermediary, flow-through entity, U.S. branch or territory financial institution that received the payment on behalf of the unknown recipient. If, however, the recipient is presumed to be a U.S. non-exempt recipient (as defined in §1.1441-1(c)(21)), the withholding agent must withhold on the payment as required under section 3406 and report the payment as required under chapter 61 of the Code. See §1.1474-1(d)(4) for reporting requirements that apply to payments of chapter 4 reportable amounts paid to nonqualified intermediaries and flow-through entities. If, however, the payment is a withholdable payment, the withholding agent must report the payment as made to a chapter 4 withholding rate pool of nonparticipating FFIs in accordance with the presumption rule under §1.1471-3(f)(5). For a payment to a foreign partnership on the transfer of a publicly traded partnership interest subject to §1.1446(f)-4(a), see paragraph (c)(1)(ii)(A)*(8)* of this section (treating the foreign partnership as a recipient).

(B) *Disregarded entities.*—If a U.S. withholding agent makes a payment to a disregarded entity but receives a valid withholding certificate or other documentary evidence from a foreign person that is the single owner of a disregarded entity, the withholding agent must file a Form 1042-S treating the foreign single owner as the recipient. The taxpayer identifying number on the Form 1042-S, if required, must be the foreign single owner's TIN.

(iii) *Reporting by qualified intermediaries, withholding foreign partnerships, and withholding foreign trusts.*—A qualified intermediary, a withholding foreign partnership, and a withholding foreign trust shall report payments on Form 1042-S as provided in their agreements with the IRS and the instructions to the form.

(iv) *Reporting by a nonqualified intermediary, flow-through entity, and certain U.S. branches.*—A nonqualified intermediary, flow-through entity, or U.S. branch (including a territory financial institution) described in §1.1441-1(e)(2)(iv) (other than a U.S. branch or territory financial institution that is treated as a U.S. person) is a withholding agent and must file Forms 1042-S for amounts paid to recipients in the same manner as a U.S. withholding agent. A Form 1042-S will not be required, however, if another withholding agent has reported the same amount for which the nonqualified intermediary, flow-through entity, or U.S. branch would be required to file a return and the entire amount that should be withheld from such payment has been withheld (including withholding and reporting in accordance with the applicable presumption rule for the payment). A nonqualified intermediary, flow-through entity, or U.S. branch must report payments made to recipients to the extent it has failed to provide the appropriate documentation to another withholding agent together with the information required for that withholding agent to reliably associate the payment with the recipient documentation or to the extent it knows, or has reason to know, that less than the required amount has been withheld. A nonqualified intermediary or flow-through entity that is required to report a payment on Form 1042-S must follow the same rules as apply to a U.S. withholding agent under paragraphs (c)(4)(i) and (ii) of this section.

(v) *Pro rata reporting for allocation failures.*—If a nonqualified intermediary, flow-through entity, or U.S. branch (including a territory financial institution) described in § 1.1441-1(b)(2)(iv) (other than a U.S. branch or territory financial institution treated as a U.S. person) uses the alternative procedures of § 1.1441-1(e)(3)(iv)(D) and fails to provide information sufficient to allocate the amount subject to reporting paid to a withholding rate pool to the payees identified for that pool, then the withholding agent shall report the payment in accordance with the rule provided in § 1.1441-1(e)(3)(iv)(D)(*6*).

(vi) *Other withholding agents.*—Any person that is a withholding agent not described in paragraph (c)(4)(i), (iii), or (iv) of this section (e.g., a foreign person that is not a qualified intermediary, flow-through entity, or U.S. branch) shall file Form 1042-S in the same manner as a U.S. withholding agent and in accordance with the instructions to the form.

(d) *Report of taxpayer identifying numbers.*—When so required under procedures that the IRS may prescribe in published guidance (see § 601.601(d)(2) of this chapter), a withholding agent must attach to the Form 1042 a list of all the taxpayer identifying numbers (and corresponding names) that have been furnished to the withholding agent and upon which the withholding agent has relied to grant a reduced rate of withholding and that are not otherwise required to be reported on a Form 1042-S under the provisions of this section.

(e) *Indemnification of withholding agent.*—A withholding agent is indemnified against the claims and demands of any person for the amount of any tax it deducts and withholds in accordance with the provisions of chapter 3 of the Code and the regulations under that chapter. A withholding agent that withholds based on a reasonable belief that such withholding is required under chapter 3 of the Code and the regulations under that chapter is treated for purposes of section 1461 and this paragraph (e) as having withheld tax in accordance with the provisions of chapter 3 of the Code and the regulations under that chapter. In addition, a withholding agent is indemnified against the claims and demands of any person for the amount of any payments made in accordance with the grace period provisions set forth in § 1.1441-1(b)(3)(iv). This paragraph (e) does not apply to relieve a withholding agent from tax liability under chapter 3 of the Code or the regulations under that chapter.

(f) *Amounts paid not constituting gross income.*—Any amount withheld in accordance with § 1.1441-3 shall be reported and paid in accordance with this section, even though the amount paid to the beneficial owner may not constitute gross income in whole or in part. For this purpose, a reference in this section and § 1.1461-2 to an amount shall, where appropriate, be deemed to refer to the amount subject to withholding under § 1.1441-3.

(g) *Extensions of time to file Forms 1042 and 1042-S.*—The IRS may grant an extension of time in which to file a Form 1042 or a Form 1042-S. Form 2758, Application for Extension of Time to File Certain Excise, Income, Information, and Other Returns (or such other form as the IRS may prescribe), must be used to request an extension of time for a Form 1042. Form 8809, Request for Extension of Time to File Information Returns (or such other form as the IRS may prescribe) must be used to request an extension of time for a Form 1042-S. The request must contain a statement of the reasons for requesting the extension and such other information as the forms or instructions may require. It must be mailed or delivered not later than March 15 of the year following the end of the calendar year for which the return will be filed.

(h) *Penalties.*—For penalties and additions to the tax for failure to file returns or furnish statements in accordance with this section, see sections 6651, 6662, 6663, 6721, 6722, 6723, 6724(c), 7201, 7203, and the regulations under those sections.

(i) *Reporting in electronic form.*—See §§ 301.6011-2(b) and 301.6011-15 of this chapter for the requirements of a withholding agent that is not a financial institution with respect to the filing of Forms 1042-S and 1042 in electronic form. See § 301.1474-1(a) of this chapter, which applies for purposes of this section to a withholding agent that is a financial institution with respect to the filing of Forms 1042 and 1042-S in electronic form.

(j) *Applicability date.*—The rules of this section apply to returns required to be filed for taxable years ending on or after December 31, 2023. (For returns required to be filed for taxable years ending before December 31, 2023, see this section as in effect and contained in 26 CFR part 1, as revised April 1, 2022.) [Reg. § 1.1461-1.]

☐ [*T.D.* 6187, 7-5-56. *Amended by T.D.* 6213, 11-20-56; *T.D.* 6908, 12-30-66; *T.D.* 7157, 12-29-71; *T.D.* 7977, 9-19-84; *T.D.* 8734, 10-6-97; *T.D.* 8804, 12-30-98; *T.D.* 8856, 12-29-99; *T.D.* 8881, 5-15-2000 (*corrected* 4-5-2001); *T.D.* 8952, 6-25-2001; *T.D.* 9200, 5-13-2005; *T.D.* 9507, 12-2-2010; *T.D.* 9572, 1-19-2012; *T.D.* 9648, 12-4-2013, *T.D.* 9658, 2-28-2014 (*corrected* 6-3-2014), *T.D.* 9734, 9-17-2015 (*corrected* 12-4-2015), *T.D.* 9808, 12-30-2016, *T.D.* 9815, 1-19-2017 (*corrected* 10-25-2017), *T.D.* 9926, 11-27-2020 *and T.D.* 9972, 2-21-2023.]

§ 1.1461-2. Adjustments for overwithholding or underwithholding of tax.—(a) *Adjustments of overwithheld tax.*—(1) *In general.*—Except as otherwise provided in this paragraph (a)(1), a withholding agent that has overwithheld under chapter 3 of the Internal Revenue Code, and made a deposit of the tax as provided in § 1.6302-2(a), may adjust the overwithheld amount either pursuant to the reimbursement procedure described in paragraph (a)(2) of this section or pursuant to the set-off procedure described in paragraph (a)(3) of this section. The rules in the preceding sentence do not apply to partnerships or nominees required to withhold under section 1446(a), other than on a distribution by a publicly traded partnership subject to withholding under § 1.1446-4(a) and a payment of an amount realized on the transfer of an interest in a publicly traded partnership subject to § 1.1446(f)-4.

(2) *Reimbursement of tax.*—(i) *General rule.*—Under the reimbursement procedure, the withholding agent repays the beneficial owner or payee for the amount of tax overwithheld. In such a case, the withholding agent may reimburse itself by reducing, by the amount of tax actually repaid to the beneficial owner or payee, the amount of any deposit of tax made by the withholding agent under § 1.6302-2(a)(1)(iii) for any subsequent payment period occurring before the end of the calendar year following the calendar year of overwithholding. Any such reduction that occurs for a payment period in the calendar year following the calendar year of overwithholding shall be allowed only if—

(A) The repayment to the beneficial owner or payee occurs before the earlier of the due date (not including extensions) for filing Form 1042-S for the calendar year of overwithholding or the date the Form 1042-S is actually filed with the IRS; and

(B) The withholding agent states on a timely filed (not including extensions) Form 1042 for the calendar year of overwithholding, that the filing of the Form 1042 constitutes a claim for credit in accordance with § 1.6414-1.

(ii) *Record maintenance.*—If the beneficial owner is repaid an amount of withholding tax under the provisions of this paragraph (a)(2), the withholding agent shall keep as part of its records a receipt showing the date and amount of repayment and the withholding agent must provide a copy of such receipt to the beneficial owner. For this purpose, a canceled check or an entry in a statement is sufficient provided that the check or statement contains a specific notation that it is a refund of tax overwithheld.

(3) *Set-offs.*—Under the set-off procedure, the withholding agent may repay the beneficial owner or payee by applying the amount overwithheld against any amount which otherwise would be required under chapter 3 of the Code or the regulations thereunder to be withheld from income paid by the withholding agent to such person before the earlier of the due date (without regard to extensions) for filing the Form 1042-S for the calendar year of overwithholding or the date that the Form 1042-S is actually filed with the IRS. For purposes of making a return on Form 1042 or 1042-S (or an amended form) for the calendar year of overwithholding and for purposes of making a deposit of the amount withheld, the reduced amount shall be considered the amount required to be withheld from such income under chapter 3 of the Code and the regulations thereunder.

(4) *Examples.*—The principles of this paragraph (a) are illustrated by the following examples:

Example 1. (i) N is a nonresident alien individual who is a resident of the United Kingdom. In December 2001, a domestic corporation C pays a dividend of $100 to N, at which time C withholds $30 and remits the balance of $70 to N. On February 10, 2002, prior to the time that C files its Form 1042 and Form 1042-S with respect to the payment, N furnishes a valid Form W-8 described in § 1.1441-1(e)(2)(i) upon which C may rely to reduce the rate of withholding to 15% under the provisions of the U.S.-U.K. tax treaty. Consequently, N advises C that its tax liability is only $15 and not $30 and requests reimbursement of $15. Although C has already deposited the $30 that was withheld, as required by §1.6302-2(a)(1)(iv), C repays N in the amount of $15.

(ii) During 2001, C makes no other payments upon which tax is required to be withheld under chapter 3 of the Code; accordingly, its return on Form 1042 for such year, which is filed on March 15, 2002, shows total tax withheld of $30, an adjusted total tax withheld of $15, and $30 previously paid for such year. Pursuant to §1.6414-1(b), C claims a credit for the overpayment of $15 shown on the Form 1042 for 2001. Accordingly, it is permitted to reduce by $15 any deposit required by §1.6302-2 to be made of tax withheld during the calendar year 2002. The Form 1042-S required to be filed by C with respect to the dividend of $100 paid to N in 2001 is required to show tax withheld under chapter 3 of $30 and tax repaid to N of $15.

Example 2. The facts are the same as in *Example 1*. In addition, during 2002, C makes payments to N upon which it is required to withhold $200 under chapter 3 of the Code, all of which is withheld in June 2002. Pursuant to §1.6302-2(a)(1)(iii), C deposits the amount of $185 on July 15, 2002 ($200 less the $15 for which credit is claimed on the Form 1042 for 2001). On March 15, 2003, C Corporation files its return on Form 1042 for calendar year 2002, which shows total tax withheld of $200, $185 previously deposited by C, and $15 allowable credit.

Example 3. The facts are the same as in *Example 1*. Under §1.6302-2(a)(1)(ii), C is required to deposit on a quarter-monthly basis the tax withheld under chapter 3 of the Code. C withholds tax of $100 between February 8 and February 15, 2002, and deposits $75 [($100 × 90%) less $15] of the withheld tax within 3 banking days after February 15, 2002, and by depositing $10 [($100-$15) less $75] within 3 banking days after March 15, 2002.

(b) *Withholding of additional tax when underwithholding occurs*.—A withholding agent may withhold from future payments (including distributions of effectively connected income subject to withholding under §1.1446-4 and the amount realized from the transfer of an interest in a publicly traded partnership subject to §1.1446(f)-4) made to a beneficial owner the tax that should have been withheld from previous payments to that beneficial owner under chapter 3 of the Code. In the alternative, the withholding agent may satisfy the tax from property that it holds in custody for the beneficial owner or property over which it has control. Such additional withholding or satisfaction of the tax owed may only be made before the date that the Form 1042 is required to be filed (not including extensions) for the calendar year in which the underwithholding occurred. See §1.6302-2 for making deposits of tax or §1.1461-1(a) for making payment of the balance due for a calendar year. See also §§1.1461-1, 1.1461-3, and 1.1446-1 through 1.1446-7 for rules relating to withholding under section 1446.

(c) *Definition*.—For purposes of this section, the term *payment period* means the period for which the withholding agent is required by §1.6302-2(a)(1) to make a deposit of tax withheld under chapter 3 of the Code.

(d) *Applicability date*.—This section applies to payments made on or after January 1, 2022. For payments made before January 1, 2022, see this section as in effect and contained in 26 CFR part 1, as revised April 1, 2020. [Reg. §1.1461-2.]

☐ [*T.D.* 6187, 7-5-56. *Amended by T.D.* 6213, 11-20-56, *T.D.* 6922, 6-16-67, *T.D.* 7157, 12-29-71, *T.D.* 7284, 8-2-73; *T.D.* 7977, 9-19-84; *T.D.* 8734, 10-6-97; *T.D.* 8804, 12-30-98; *T.D.* 8856, 12-29-99; *T.D.* 9200, 5-13-2005, *T.D.* 9658, 2-28-2014, *T.D.* 9808, 12-30-2016 *and T.D.* 9926, 11-27-2020.]

§1.1461-3. Withholding under section 1446.—For rules relating to the withholding tax liability of a partnership, nominee, or transferee under section 1446, see §§1.1446-1 through 1.1446-7 and 1.1446(f)-1 through 1.1446(f)-5. For interest, penalties, and additions to the tax for failure to timely pay the tax required to be paid under section 1446, see sections 6601, 6651, 6655 (in the case of publicly traded partnerships, see section 6656), 6672, and 7202 and the regulations under those sections. For additional penalties and additions to the tax for failure to comply with the regulations under section 1446, see sections 6651, 6662, 6663, 6721, 6722, 6723, 6724(c), 7201, 7203, and the regulations under those sections. The references in this section to §§1.1446-1 through 1.1446-7 apply to partnership taxable years beginning after May 18, 2005, or such earlier time as the regulations under §§1.1446-1 through 1.1446-5 apply by reason of an election under §1.1446-7, and the references in this section to §§1.1446(f)-1 through 1.1446(f)-5 shall apply with respect to returns for transfers that occur on or after January 29, 2021. [Reg. §1.1461-3.]

☐ [*T.D.* 9200, 5-13-2005. *Amended by T.D.* 9926, 11-27-2020.]

§1.1462-1. Withheld tax as credit to recipient of income.—(a) *Creditable tax*.—The entire amount of the income from which the tax is required to be withheld (including amounts calculated under the gross-up formula in §1.1441-3(f)(1)) shall be included in gross income in the return required to be made by the beneficial owner of the income, without deduction for the amount required to be or actually withheld, but the amount of tax actually withheld shall be allowed as a credit against the total income tax computed in the beneficial owner's return.

***

(c) *Effective date*.—Unless otherwise provided in this section, this section applies to payments made after December 31, 2000. [Reg. §1.1462-1.]

☐ [*T.D.* 6187, 7-5-56. *Amended by T.D.* 7977, 9-19-84; *T.D.* 8734, 10-6-97; T.D. 8804, 12-30-98; *T.D.* 8856, 12-29-99 *and T.D.* 9200, 5-13-2005.]

§1.1463-1. Tax paid by recipient of income.—(a) *Tax paid*.—If the tax required to be withheld under chapter 3 of the Internal Revenue Code is paid by the beneficial owner of the income or by the withholding agent, it shall not be re-collected from the other, regardless of the original liability therefor. However, this section does not relieve the person that did not withhold tax from liability for interest or any penalties or additions to tax otherwise applicable. See §1.1441-7(b) for additional applicable rules. See §§1.1446-3(e) and (f) and 1.1446(f)-5(a) for application of the rule of this paragraph (a), and for additional rules, in which the withholding tax was required to be paid under section 1446. The references in the previous sentence to §1.1446-3(e) and (f) apply to partnership taxable years beginning after May 18, 2005, or such earlier time as the regulations under §§1.1446-1 through 1.1446-5 apply by reason of an election under §1.1446-7, and the reference in the previous sentence to §1.1446(f)-5(a) shall apply to the tax required to be withheld under section 1446(f) for transfers that occur on or after January 29, 2021.

(b) *Effective date*.—Unless otherwise provided in this section, this section applies to failures to withhold occurring after December 31, 2000. [Reg. §1.1463-1.]

☐ [*T.D.* 6187, 7-5-56. *Amended by T.D.* 8734, 10-6-97; *T.D.* 8804, 12-30-98; *T.D.* 8856, 12-29-99, *T.D.* 9200, 5-13-2005 *and T.D.* 9926, 11-27-2020.]

§1.1464-1. Refunds or credits.—(a) *In general*.—The refund or credit under chapter 65 of the Code of an overpayment of tax which has actually been withheld at the source under chapter 3 of the Code shall be made to the taxpayer from whose income the amount of such tax was in fact withheld. To the extent that the overpayment under chapter 3 was not in fact withheld at the source, but was paid, by the withholding agent the refund or credit under chapter 65 of the overpayment shall be made to the withholding agent. Thus, where a debtor corporation assumes liability pursuant to its tax-free covenant for the tax required to be withheld under chapter 3 upon interest and pays the tax in behalf of its bondholder, and it can be shown that the bondholder is not in fact liable for any tax, the overpayment of tax shall be credited or refunded to the withholding agent in accordance with chapter 65 since the tax was not actually deducted and withheld from the interest paid to the bondholder. In further illustration, where a withholding agent who is required by chapter 3 to withhold $300 tax from rents paid to a nonresident alien individual mistakenly withholds $320 and mistakenly pays $350 as internal revenue tax, the amount of $30 shall be credited or refunded to the withholding agent in accordance with chapter 65 and the amount of $20 shall be credited or refunded in accordance with such chapter to the person from whose income such amount has been withheld. With respect to section 1446(a), this section applies only to a publicly traded partnership or nominee described in §1.1446-4 and, with respect to section 1446(f), only to a publicly traded partnership or broker described in §1.1446(f)-4.

(b) *Tax repaid to payee*.—For purposes of this section and §1.6414-1, any amount of tax withheld under chapter 3 of the Code, which, pursuant to paragraph (a)(1) of §1.1461-2, is repaid by the withholding agent to the person from whose income such amount was erroneously withheld shall be considered as tax which, within the meaning of sections 1464 and 6414, was not actually withheld by the withholding agent.

(c) *Applicability date*.—The last sentence of paragraph (a) of this section applies to nominees and publicly traded partnerships described in §1.1446-4 for partnership taxable years beginning after

6-19-2012; *T.D.* 9619, 5-10-2013 (*corrected* 8-27-2013), *T.D.* 9901, 7-9-2020, *T.D.* 9905, 9-3-2020 *and T.D.* 9921, 12-10-2020.]

§1.1502-50. Consolidated section 250.—(a) *In general.*—(1) *Scope.*—This section provides rules for applying section 250 and §§1.250-1 through 1.250(b)-6 (the *section 250 regulations*) to a member of a consolidated group (*member*). Paragraph (b) of this section provides rules for the determination of the amount of the deduction allowed to a member under section 250(a)(1). Paragraph (c) of this section provides rules governing the impact of intercompany transactions on the determination of a member's qualified business asset investment (QBAI) and the effect of intercompany transactions on the determination of a member's foreign-derived deduction eligible income (FDDEI). Paragraph (d) of this section provides rules governing basis adjustments to member stock resulting from the application of paragraph (b)(1) of this section. Paragraph (e) of this section provides definitions. Paragraph (f) of this section provides examples illustrating the rules of this section. Paragraph (g) of this section provides an applicability date.

(2) *Overview.*—The rules of this section ensure that the aggregate amount of deductions allowed under section 250 to members appropriately reflects the income, expenses, gains, losses, and property of all members. Paragraph (b) of this section allocates the consolidated group's overall deduction amount under section 250 to each member on the basis of its contribution to the consolidated foreign-derived deduction eligible income (consolidated FDDEI) and consolidated global intangible low-taxed income (consolidated GILTI). The definitions in paragraph (e) of this section provide for the aggregation of the deduction eligible income (DEI), FDDEI, deemed tangible income return, and global intangible low-taxed income (GILTI) of all members in order to calculate the consolidated group's overall deduction amount under section 250.

(b) *Allowance of deduction.*—(1) *In general.*—A member is allowed a deduction for a consolidated return year under section 250. See §1.250(a)-1(b). The amount of the deduction is equal to the sum of—

(i) The product of the consolidated FDII deduction amount and the member's FDII deduction allocation ratio; and

(ii) The product of the consolidated GILTI deduction amount and the member's GILTI deduction allocation ratio.

(2) *Consolidated taxable income limitation.*—For purposes of applying the limitation described in §1.250(a)-1(b)(2) to the determination of the consolidated FDII deduction amount and the consolidated GILTI deduction amount of a consolidated group for a consolidated return year—

(i) The consolidated foreign-derived intangible income (consolidated FDII) (if any) is reduced (but not below zero) by an amount which bears the same ratio to the consolidated section 250(a)(2) amount that such consolidated FDII bears to the sum of the consolidated FDII and the consolidated GILTI; and

(ii) The consolidated GILTI (if any) is reduced (but not below zero) by the excess of the consolidated section 250(a)(2) amount over the reduction described in paragraph (b)(2)(i) of this section.

(c) *Impact of intercompany transactions.*—(1) *Impact on qualified business asset investment determination.*—(i) *In general.*—For purposes of determining a member's QBAI, the basis of specified tangible property does not include an amount equal to any gain or loss recognized with respect to such property by another member in an intercompany transaction (as defined in §1.1502-13(b)(1)) until the time that such gain or loss is no longer deferred under §1.1502-13. Thus, for example, if a selling member owns specified tangible property with an adjusted basis (within the meaning of section 1011) of $60x and an adjusted basis (for purposes of calculating QBAI) of $80x, and sells it for $50x to the purchasing member (and the intercompany loss remains deferred), the basis of such property for purposes of computing the purchasing member's QBAI is $80x.

(ii) *Partner-specific QBAI basis.*—A member's partner-specific QBAI basis (as defined in §1.250(b)-2(g)(7)) includes a basis adjustment under section 743(b) resulting from an intercompany transaction only at the time, and to the extent, gain or loss, if any, is recognized in the transaction and no longer deferred under §1.1502-13.

(2) *Impact on foreign-derived deduction eligible income characterization.*—For purposes of redetermining attributes of members from an intercompany transaction as FDDEI, see §1.1502-13(c)(1)(i) and (c)(7)(ii)(R) (*Example 18*).

(d) *Adjustments to the basis of a member.*—For adjustments to the basis of a member related to paragraph (b)(1) of this section, see §1.1502-32(b)(3)(ii)(B).

(e) *Definitions.*—The following definitions apply for purposes of this section.

(1) *Consolidated deduction eligible income (consolidated DEI).*—With respect to a consolidated group for a consolidated return year, the term *consolidated deduction eligible income* or *consolidated DEI* means the greater of the sum of the DEI (whether positive or negative) of all members or zero.

(2) *Consolidated deemed intangible income.*—With respect to a consolidated group for a consolidated return year, the term *consolidated deemed intangible income* means the excess (if any) of the consolidated DEI, over the consolidated deemed tangible income return.

(3) *Consolidated deemed tangible income return.*—With respect to a consolidated group for a consolidated return year, the term *consolidated deemed tangible income return* means the sum of the deemed tangible income return of all members.

(4) *Consolidated FDII deduction amount.*—With respect to a consolidated group for a consolidated return year, the term *consolidated FDII deduction amount* means the product of the FDII deduction rate and the consolidated FDII, as adjusted by paragraph (b)(2) of this section.

(5) *Consolidated foreign-derived deduction eligible income (consolidated FDDEI).*—With respect to a consolidated group for a consolidated return year, the term *consolidated foreign-derived deduction eligible income* or *consolidated FDDEI* means the greater of the sum of the FDDEI (whether positive or negative) of all members or zero.

(6) *Consolidated foreign-derived intangible income (consolidated FDII).*—With respect to a consolidated group for a consolidated return year, the term *consolidated foreign-derived intangible income* or *consolidated FDII* means the product of the consolidated deemed intangible income and the consolidated foreign-derived ratio.

(7) *Consolidated foreign-derived ratio.*—With respect to a consolidated group for a consolidated return year, the term *consolidated foreign-derived ratio* means the ratio (not to exceed one) of—

(i) The consolidated FDDEI; to

(ii) The consolidated DEI.

(8) *Consolidated GILTI deduction amount.*—With respect to a consolidated group for a consolidated return year, the term *consolidated GILTI deduction amount* means the product of the GILTI deduction rate and the sum of the consolidated GILTI, as adjusted by paragraph (b)(2) of this section, and the amounts treated as dividends received by the members under section 78 which are attributable to their GILTI for the consolidated return year.

(9) *Consolidated global intangible low-taxed income (consolidated GILTI).*—With respect to a consolidated group for a consolidated return year, the term *consolidated global intangible low-taxed income* or *consolidated GILTI* means the sum of the GILTI of all members.

(10) *Consolidated section 250(a)(2) amount.*—With respect to a consolidated group for a consolidated return year, the term *consolidated section 250(a)(2) amount* means the excess (if any) of the sum of the consolidated FDII and the consolidated GILTI (determined without regard to section 250(a)(2) and paragraph (b)(2) of this section), over the consolidated taxable income of the consolidated group (within the meaning of §1.1502-11).

(11) *Deduction eligible income (DEI).*—With respect to a member for a consolidated return year, the term *deduction eligible income* or *DEI* means the member's gross DEI for the year (within the meaning of §1.250(b)-1(c)(15)) reduced (including below zero) by the deductions properly allocable to gross DEI for the year (as determined under §1.250(b)-1(d)(2)).

(12) *Deemed tangible income return.*—With respect to a member for a consolidated return year, the term *deemed tangible income return* means an amount equal to 10 percent of the member's QBAI, as adjusted by paragraph (c)(1) of this section.

(13) *FDII deduction allocation ratio.*—With respect to a member for a consolidated return year, the term *FDII deduction allocation ratio* means the ratio of—

(i) The member's positive FDDEI (if any); to

(ii) The sum of the positive FDDEI of all members.

(14) *FDII deduction rate.*—The term *FDII deduction rate* means 37.5 percent for consolidated return years beginning before January 1, 2026, and 21.875 percent for consolidated return years beginning after December 31, 2025.

(15) *Foreign-derived deduction eligible income (FDDEI).*—With respect to a member for a consolidated return year, the term *foreign-derived deduction eligible income* or *FDDEI* means the member's gross FDDEI for the year (within the meaning of § 1.250(b)-1(c)(16)) reduced (including below zero) by the deductions properly allocable to gross FDDEI for the year (as determined under § 1.250(b)-1(d)(2)).

(16) *GILTI deduction allocation ratio.*—With respect to a member for a consolidated return year, the term *GILTI deduction allocation ratio* means the ratio of—

(i) The sum of the member's GILTI and the amount treated as a dividend received by the member under section 78 which is attributable to its GILTI for the consolidated return year; to

(ii) The sum of consolidated GILTI and the amounts treated as dividends received by the members under section 78 which are attributable to their GILTI for the consolidated return year.

(17) *GILTI deduction rate.*—The term *GILTI deduction rate* means 50 percent for consolidated return years beginning before January 1, 2026, and 37.5 percent for consolidated return years beginning after December 31, 2025.

(18) *Global intangible low-taxed income (GILTI).*—With respect to a member for a consolidated return year, the term *global intangible low-taxed income* or *GILTI* means the sum of the member's GILTI inclusion amount under § 1.1502-51(b) and the member's distributive share of any domestic partnership's GILTI inclusion amount under § 1.951A-5(b)(2).

(19) *Qualified business asset investment (QBAI).*—The term *qualified business asset investment* or *QBAI* has the meaning provided in § 1.250(b)-2(b).

(20) *Specified tangible property.*—The term *specified tangible property* has the meaning provided in § 1.250(b)-2(c)(1).

(f) *Examples.*—The following examples illustrate the rules of this section.

(1) *Example 1: Calculation of deduction attributable to FDII.*—(i) *Facts.* P is the common parent of the P group and owns all of the only class of stock of subsidiaries USS1 and USS2. The consolidated return year of all persons is the calendar year. In 2018, P has DEI of $400x, FDDEI of $0, and QBAI of $0; USS1 has DEI of $200x, FDDEI of $200x, and QBAI of $600x; and USS2 has DEI of -$100x, FDDEI of $100x, and QBAI of $400x. The P group has consolidated taxable income that is sufficient to make inapplicable the limitation in paragraph (b)(2) of this section. No member of the P group has GILTI.

(ii) *Analysis*—(A) *Consolidated DEI.* Under paragraph (e)(1) of this section, the P group's consolidated DEI is $500x, the greater of the sum of the DEI (whether positive or negative) of all members ($400x + $200x - $100x) or zero.

(B) *Consolidated FDDEI.* Under paragraph (e)(5) of this section, the P group's consolidated FDDEI is $300x, the greater of the sum of the FDDEI (whether positive or negative) of all members ($0 + $200x + $100x) or zero.

(C) *Consolidated deemed tangible income return.* Under paragraph (e)(12) of this section, a member's deemed tangible income return is 10 percent of its QBAI. Therefore, P's deemed tangible income return is $0 (0.10 x $0), USS1's deemed tangible income return is $60x (0.10 x $600x), and USS2's deemed tangible income return is $40x (0.10 x $400x). Under paragraph (e)(3) of this section, the P group's consolidated deemed tangible income return is $100x, the sum of the deemed tangible income return of all members ($0 + $60x + $40x).

(D) *Consolidated deemed intangible income.* Under paragraph (e)(2) of this section, the P group's consolidated deemed intangible income is $400x, the excess of its consolidated DEI over its consolidated deemed tangible income return ($500x - $100x).

(E) *Consolidated FDII.* Under paragraph (e)(7) of this section, the P group's consolidated foreign-derived ratio is 0.60, the ratio of its consolidated FDDEI to its consolidated DEI ($300x / $500x). Under paragraph (e)(6) of this section, the P group's consolidated FDII is $240x, the product of its consolidated deemed intangible income and its consolidated foreign-derived ratio ($400x x 0.60).

(F) *Consolidated FDII deduction amount.* Under paragraph (e)(4) of this section, the P group's consolidated FDII deduction amount is $90x, the product of the FDII deduction rate and the consolidated FDII (0.375 x $240x).

(G) *Member's deduction attributable to consolidated FDII deduction amount.* Under paragraph (b)(1) of this section, a member is allowed a deduction equal, in part, to the product of the consolidated FDII deduction amount of the consolidated group to which the member belongs and the member's FDII deduction allocation ratio. Under paragraph (e)(13) of this section, a member's FDII deduction allocation ratio is the ratio of its positive FDDEI to the sum of each member's positive FDDEI for such consolidated return year. As a result, the FDII deduction allocation ratios of P, USS1, and USS2 are 0 ($0 / $300x), 2/3 ($200x / $300x), and 1/3 ($100x / $300x), respectively. Therefore, P, USS1, and USS2 are permitted deductions under paragraph (b)(1) of this section in the amount of $0 (0 x $90x), $60x (2/3 x $90x), and $30x (1/3 x $90x), respectively.

(2) *Example 2: Limitation on consolidated foreign-derived deduction eligible income.*—(i) *Facts.* The facts are the same as in paragraph (f)(1)(i) of this section (the facts in *Example 1*), except that P's FDDEI is $300x.

(ii) *Analysis*—(A) *Consolidated DEI and consolidated deemed tangible income return.* As in paragraphs (f)(1)(ii)(A) and (C) of this section (the analysis in *Example 1*), the P group's consolidated DEI is $500x and the P group's consolidated deemed tangible income return is $100x.

(B) *Consolidated FDDEI.* Under paragraph (e)(5) of this section, the P group's consolidated FDDEI is $600x, the greater of the sum of the FDDEI (whether positive or negative) of all members ($300x + $200x + $100x) or zero.

(C) *Consolidated deemed intangible income and consolidated FDII.* Under paragraph (e)(2) of this section, the P group's consolidated deemed intangible income is $400x ($500x - $100x). Under paragraph (e)(7) of this section, the P group's consolidated foreign-derived ratio is 1.00 ($600x / $500x, but not in excess of one). Under paragraph (e)(6) of this section, the P group's consolidated FDII is $400x ($400x x 1.00).

(D) *Consolidated FDII deduction amount and member's deduction attributable to consolidated FDII deduction amount.* Under paragraph (e)(4) of this section, the P group's consolidated FDII deduction amount is $150x (0.375 x $400x). Under paragraph (e)(13) of this section, the FDII deduction allocation ratios of P, USS1, and USS2 are 1/2 ($300 / $600x), 1/3 ($200x / $600x), and 1/6 ($100x / $600x), respectively. Therefore, P, USS1, and USS2 are permitted deductions under paragraph (b)(1) of this section in the amounts of $75x (1/2 x $150x), $50x (1/3 x $150x), and $25x (1/6 x $150x), respectively.

(3) *Example 3: Member with negative FDDEI.*—(i) *Facts.* The facts are the same as in paragraph (f)(1)(i) of this section (the facts in *Example 1*), except that P's FDDEI is -$100x.

(ii) *Analysis*—(A) *Consolidated DEI and consolidated deemed tangible income return.* As in paragraphs (f)(1)(ii)(A) and (C) of this section (the facts in *Example 1*), the P group's consolidated DEI is $500x and the P group's consolidated deemed tangible income return is $100x.

(B) *Consolidated FDDEI.* Under paragraph (e)(5) of this section, the P group's consolidated FDDEI is $200x, the greater of the sum of the FDDEI (whether positive or negative) of all members (-$100x + $200x + $100x) or zero.

(C) *Consolidated deemed intangible income and consolidated FDII.* Under paragraphs (e)(2) and (6) of this section, the P group's consolidated deemed intangible income is $400x ($500x - $100x), and the P group's consolidated FDII is $160x ($400x x ($200x / $500x)).

(D) *Consolidated FDII deduction amount and member's deduction attributable to consolidated FDII deduction amount.* Under paragraph (e)(4) of this section, the P group's consolidated FDII deduction amount is $60x (0.375 x $160x). Under paragraph (e)(13) of this section, the FDII deduction allocation ratios of P, USS1, and USS2 are 0 ($0 / $300x), 2/3 ($200x / $300x), and 1/3 ($100x / $300x), respectively. Therefore, P, USS1, and USS2 are permitted deductions under paragraph (b)(1) of this section in the amounts of $0 (0 x $60x), $40x (2/3 x $60x), and $20x (1/3 x $60x), respectively.

(4) *Example 4: Calculation of deduction attributable to GILTI.*—(i) *Facts.* The facts are the same as in paragraph (f)(1)(i) of this section (the facts in *Example 1*), except that USS1 owns CFC1 and USS2 owns CFC2. USS1 and USS2 have GILTI of $65x and $20x, respectively, and amounts treated as dividends received under section 78 attributable to their GILTI of $10x and $5x, respectively.

(ii) *Analysis*—(A) *Consolidated GILTI.* Under paragraph (e)(9) of this section, the P group's consolidated GILTI is $85x, the sum of the GILTI of all members ($0 + $65x + $20x).

(B) *Consolidated GILTI deduction amount.* Under paragraph (e)(8) of this section, the P group's consolidated GILTI deduction amount is $50x, the product of the GILTI deduction rate and the sum of its consolidated GILTI and the amounts treated as dividends received by the members under section 78 which are attributable to their GILTI for the consolidated return year (0.50 x ($85x + $10x + $5x)).

(C) *Member's deduction attributable to consolidated GILTI deduction amount.* Under paragraph (b)(1) of this section, a member is allowed a deduction equal, in part, to the product of the consolidated GILTI deduction amount of the consolidated group to which the member belongs and the member's GILTI deduction allocation ratio. Under paragraph (e)(16) of this section, a member's GILTI deduction allocation ratio is the ratio of the sum of its GILTI and the amount treated as a dividend received by the member under section 78 which is attributable to its GILTI for the consolidated return year to the sum of the consolidated GILTI and the amounts treated as dividends received by the members under section 78 which are attributable to their GILTI for the consolidated return year. As a result, the GILTI deduction allocation ratios of P, USS1, and USS2 are 0 ($0 / ($85x + $10x + $5x)), 3/4 (($65x + $10x) / ($85x + $10x + $5x)), and 1/4 (($20x + $5x) / ($85x + $10x + $5x)), respectively. Therefore, P, USS1, and USS2 are permitted deductions of $0 (0 x $50x), $37.50x (3/4 x $50x), and $12.50x (1/4 x $50x), respectively.

(D) *Member's deduction under section 250.* Under paragraph (b)(1) of this section, a member is allowed a deduction equal to the sum of the member's deduction attributable to the consolidated FDII deduction amount and the member's deduction attributable to the consolidated GILTI deduction amount. As a result P, USS1, and USS2 are entitled to deductions under paragraph (b)(1) of this section of $0 ($0 + $0), $97.50x ($60x + $37.50x), and $42.50x ($30x + $12.50x), respectively.

(5) *Example 5: Taxable income limitation.*—(i) *Facts.* The facts are the same as in paragraph (f)(4)(i) of this section (the facts in *Example 4*), except that the P group's consolidated taxable income (within the meaning of paragraph (e)(10) of this section) is $300x.

(ii) *Analysis*—(A) *Determination of whether the limitation described in paragraph (b)(2) of this section applies.* Under paragraph (b)(2) of this section, in the case of a consolidated group with a consolidated section 250(a)(2) amount for a consolidated year, the amount of the consolidated FDII and the consolidated GILTI otherwise taken into account in the determination of the consolidated FDII deduction amount and the consolidated GILTI deduction amount are subject to reduction. As in paragraph (f)(1)(ii)(E) of this section (the facts in *Example 1*), the P group's consolidated FDII is $240x. As in paragraph (f)(4)(ii)(A) of this section (the analysis in *Example 4*), the P group's consolidated GILTI is $85x. The P group's consolidated taxable income is $300x. Under paragraph (e)(10) of this section, the P group's consolidated section 250(a)(2) amount is $25x (($240x + $85x) - $300x), the excess of the sum of the consolidated FDII and the consolidated GILTI, over the P group's consolidated taxable income. Therefore, the limitation described in paragraph (b)(2) of this section applies.

(B) *Allocation of reduction.* Under paragraph (b)(2)(i) of this section, the P group's consolidated FDII is reduced by an amount which bears the same ratio to the consolidated section 250(a)(2) amount as the consolidated FDII bears to the sum of the consolidated FDII and consolidated GILTI, and the P group's consolidated GILTI is reduced by the excess of the consolidated section 250(a)(2) amount over the reduction described in paragraph (b)(2)(i) of this section. Therefore, for purposes of determining the P group's consolidated FDII deduction amount and consolidated GILTI deduction amount, its consolidated FDII is reduced to $221.54x ($240x - ($25x x ($240x / $325x))) and its consolidated GILTI is reduced to $78.46x ($85x - ($25x - ($25x x ($240x / $325x)))).

(C) *Calculation of consolidated FDII deduction amount and consolidated GILTI deduction amount.* Under paragraph (e)(4) of this section, the P group's consolidated FDII deduction amount is $83.08x ($221.54x x 0.375). Under paragraph (e)(8) of this section, the P group's consolidated GILTI deduction amount is $46.73x (($78.46x + 10x + 5x) x 0.50).

(D) *Member's deduction attributable to the consolidated FDII deduction amount.* As in paragraph (f)(1)(ii)(G) of this section (the analysis in *Example 1*), the FDII deduction allocation ratios of P, USS1, and USS2 are 0, 2/3, and 1/3, respectively. Therefore, P, USS1, and USS2 are permitted deductions attributable to the consolidated FDII deduction amount of $0 (0 x $83.08x), $55.39x (2/3 x $83.08x), and $27.69x (1/3 x $83.08x), respectively.

(E) *Member's deduction attributable to the consolidated GILTI deduction amount.* As in paragraph (f)(4)(ii)(C) of this section (the analysis in *Example 4*), the GILTI deduction allocation ratios of P, USS1, and USS2 are 0, 3/4, and 1/4, respectively. Therefore, P, USS1, and USS2 are permitted deductions attributable to the consolidated GILTI deduction amount of $0 (0 x $46.73x), $35.05x (3/4 x $46.73x), and $11.68x (1/4 x $46.73x), respectively.

(F) *Member's deduction pursuant section 250.* Under paragraph (b)(1) of this section, a member is allowed a deduction equal to the sum of the member's deduction attributable to the consolidated FDII deduction amount and the member's deduction attributable to the consolidated GILTI deduction amount. As a result, P, USS1, and USS2 are entitled to deductions under paragraph (b)(1) of this section of $0 ($0 + $0), $90.44x ($55.39x + $35.05x), and $39.37x ($27.69x + $11.68x), respectively.

(g) *Applicability date.*—This section applies to consolidated return years beginning on or after January 1, 2021. A taxpayer that chooses to apply the rules in § § 1.250(a)-1 and 1.250(b)-1 through 1.250(b)-6 to taxable years beginning before January 1, 2021, pursuant to § 1.250-1(b), must also apply the rules of this section in their entirety to consolidated return years beginning after December 31, 2017, and before January 1, 2021. [Reg. § 1.1502-50.]

☐ [*T.D. 9901, 7-9-2020.*]

§ 1.1502-51. Consolidated section 951A.—(a) *In general.*—This section provides rules for applying section 951A to each member of a consolidated group (each, a *member*) that is a United States shareholder of any controlled foreign corporation. Paragraph (b) of this section describes the inclusion of the GILTI inclusion amount by a member of a consolidated group. Paragraphs (c) and (d) of this section are reserved. Paragraph (e) of this section provides definitions for purposes of this section. Paragraph (f) of this section provides examples illustrating the rules of this section. Paragraph (g) of this section provides an applicability date.

(b) *Calculation of the GILTI inclusion amount for a member of a consolidated group.*—Each member who is a United States shareholder of any controlled foreign corporation includes in gross income in the U.S. shareholder inclusion year the member's GILTI inclusion amount, if any, for the U.S. shareholder inclusion year. See section 951A(a) and § 1.951A-1(b). The GILTI inclusion amount of a member for a U.S. shareholder inclusion year is the excess (if any) of the member's net CFC tested income for the U.S. shareholder inclusion year, over the member's net deemed tangible income return for the U.S. shareholder inclusion year, determined using the definitions provided in paragraph (e) of this section. In addition, see § 1.951A-1(e) (cross-referencing § 1.958-1(d)).

(c) [Reserved]

(d) [Reserved]

(e) *Definitions.*—Any term used but not defined in this section has the meaning set forth in § § 1.951A-1 through 1.951A-6. In addition, the following definitions apply for purposes of this section.

(1) *Aggregate tested income.*—With respect to a member, the term *aggregate tested income* means the aggregate of the member's pro rata share (determined under § 1.951A-1(d)(2)) of the tested income of each tested income CFC for a CFC inclusion year that ends with or within the U.S. shareholder inclusion year.

(2) *Aggregate tested loss.*—With respect to a member, the term *aggregate tested loss* means the aggregate of the member's pro rata share (determined under § 1.951A-1(d)(4)) of the tested loss of each tested loss CFC for a CFC inclusion year that ends with or within the U.S. shareholder inclusion year.

(3) *Allocable share.*—The term *allocable share* means, with respect to a member that is a United States shareholder and a U.S. shareholder inclusion year—

(i) With respect to consolidated QBAI, the product of the consolidated QBAI of the member's consolidated group and the member's GILTI allocation ratio.

(ii) With respect to consolidated specified interest expense, the product of the consolidated specified interest expense of the member's consolidated group and the member's GILTI allocation ratio.

(iii) With respect to consolidated tested loss, the product of the consolidated tested loss of the member's consolidated group and the member's GILTI allocation ratio.

(4) *Consolidated QBAI.*—With respect to a consolidated group, the term *consolidated QBAI* means the sum of each member's pro rata share (determined under § 1.951A-1(d)(3)) of the qualified business asset investment of each tested income CFC for a CFC inclusion year that ends with or within the U.S. shareholder inclusion year.

(5) *Consolidated specified interest expense.*—With respect to a consolidated group, the term *consolidated specified interest expense* means the excess (if any) of—

(i) The sum of each member's pro rata share (determined under § 1.951A-1(d)(5)) of the tested interest expense of each controlled foreign corporation for a CFC inclusion year that ends with or within the U.S. shareholder inclusion year, over

(ii) The sum of each member's pro rata share (determined under § 1.951A-1(d)(6)) of the tested interest income of each controlled foreign corporation for a CFC inclusion year that ends with or within the U.S. shareholder inclusion year.

(6) *Consolidated tested income.*—With respect to a consolidated group, the term *consolidated tested income* means the sum of each member's aggregate tested income for the U.S. shareholder inclusion year.

(7) *Consolidated tested loss.*—With respect to a consolidated group, the term *consolidated tested loss* means the sum of each member's aggregate tested loss for the U.S. shareholder inclusion year.

(8) *Controlled foreign corporation.*—The term *controlled foreign corporation* has the meaning provided in § 1.951A-1(f)(2).

(9) *Deemed tangible income return.*—With respect to a member, the term *deemed tangible income return* means 10 percent of the member's allocable share of the consolidated QBAI.

(10) *GILTI allocation ratio.*—With respect to a member, the term *GILTI allocation ratio* means the ratio of—

(i) The aggregate tested income of the member for the U.S. shareholder inclusion year, to

(ii) The consolidated tested income of the consolidated group of which the member is a member for the U.S. shareholder inclusion year.

(11) *GILTI inclusion amount.*—With respect to a member, the term *GILTI inclusion amount* has the meaning provided in paragraph (b) of this section.

(12) *Net CFC tested income.*—With respect to a member, the term *net CFC tested income* means the excess (if any) of—

(i) The member's aggregate tested income, over

(ii) The member's allocable share of the consolidated tested loss.

(13) *Net deemed tangible income return.*—With respect to a member, the term *net deemed tangible income return* means the excess (if any) of the member's deemed tangible income return over the member's allocable share of the consolidated specified interest expense.

(14) through (16) [Reserved]

(17) *Qualified business asset investment.*—The term qualified business asset investment has the meaning provided in § 1.951A-3(b).

(18) *Tested income.*—The term *tested income* has the meaning provided in § 1.951A-2(b)(1).

(19) *Tested income CFC.*—The term *tested income CFC* has the meaning provided in § 1.951A-2(b)(1).

(20) *Tested interest expense.*—The term *tested interest expense* has the meaning provided in § 1.951A-4(b)(1).

(21) *Tested interest income.*—The term *tested interest income* has the meaning provided in § 1.951A-4(b)(2).

(22) *Tested loss.*—The term *tested loss* has the meaning provided in § 1.951A-2(b)(2).

(23) *Tested loss CFC.*—The term *tested loss CFC* has the meaning provided in § 1.951A-2(b)(2).

(24) *United States shareholder.*—The term *United States shareholder* has the meaning provided in § 1.951A-1(f)(6).

(25) *U.S. shareholder inclusion year.*—The term *U.S. shareholder inclusion year* has the meaning provided in § 1.951A-1(f)(7).

(f) *Examples.*—The following examples illustrate the rules of this section. For purposes of the examples in this section, unless otherwise stated: P is the common parent of the P consolidated group; P owns all of the single class of stock of subsidiaries USS1, USS2, and USS3, all of whom are members of the P consolidated group; CFC1, CFC2, CFC3, and CFC4 are all controlled foreign corporations (within the meaning of paragraph (e)(8) of this section); and the taxable year of all persons is the calendar year.

(1) *Example 1: Calculation of net CFC tested income within a consolidated group when all CFCs are wholly owned by a member*—(i) *Facts.* USS1 owns all of the single class of stock of CFC1. USS2 owns all of the single class of stock of each of CFC2 and CFC3. USS3 owns all of the single class of stock of CFC4. In Year 1, CFC1 has tested loss of $100x, CFC2 has tested income of $200x, CFC3 has tested loss of $200x, and CFC4 has tested income of $600x. None of CFC1, CFC2, CFC3, or CFC4 has qualified business asset investment in Year 1.

(ii) *Analysis*—(A) *Consolidated tested income and GILTI allocation ratio.* USS1 has no aggregate tested income; USS2's aggregate tested income is $200x, its pro rata share (determined under § 1.951A-1(d)(2)) of CFC2's tested income; and USS3's aggregate tested income is $600x, its pro rata share (determined under § 1.951A-1(d)(2)) of CFC4's tested income. Therefore, under paragraph (e)(6) of this section, the P consolidated group's consolidated tested income is $800x ($200x + $600x). As a result, the GILTI allocation ratios of USS1, USS2, and USS3 are 0 ($0/$800x), 0.25 ($200x/$800x), and 0.75 ($600x/$800x), respectively.

(B) *Consolidated tested loss.* Under paragraph (e)(7) of this section, the P consolidated group's consolidated tested loss is $300x ($100x + $200x), the sum of USS1's aggregate tested loss, which is equal to its pro rata share (determined under § 1.951A-1(d)(4)) of CFC1's tested loss ($100x), and USS2's aggregate tested loss, which is equal to its pro rata share (determined under § 1.951A-1(d)(4)) of CFC3's tested loss ($200x). Under paragraph (e)(3)(iii) of this section, a member's allocable share of the consolidated tested loss is the product of the consolidated tested loss of the member's consolidated group and the member's GILTI allocation ratio. Therefore, the allocable shares of the consolidated tested loss of USS1, USS2, and USS3 are $0 (0 x $300x), $75x (0.25 x $300x), and $225x (0.75 x $300x), respectively.

(C) *Calculation of net CFC tested income.* Under paragraph (e)(12) of this section, a member's net CFC tested income is the excess (if any) of the member's aggregate tested income over the member's allocable share of the consolidated tested loss. As a result, the net CFC tested income of USS1, USS2, and USS3 are $0 ($0 - $0), $125x ($200x - $75x), and $375x ($600x - $225x), respectively.

(2) *Example 2: Calculation of net CFC tested income within a consolidated group when ownership of a tested loss CFC is split between members*—(i) *Facts.* The facts are the same as in paragraph (f)(1)(i) of this section (the facts in *Example 1*), except that USS2 and USS3 each own 50% of the single class of stock of CFC3.

(ii) *Analysis.* As in paragraph (f)(1)(ii)(A) of this section (paragraph (A) of the analysis in *Example 1*), USS1 has no aggregate tested income and a GILTI allocation ratio of 0, USS2 has $200x of aggregate tested income and a GILTI allocation ratio of 0.25, and USS3 has $600x of aggregate tested income and a GILTI allocation ratio of 0.75. Additionally, the P consolidated group's consolidated tested loss is $300x (the aggregate of USS1's aggregate tested loss, which is equal to its pro rata share (determined under § 1.951A-1(d)(4)) of CFC1's tested loss ($100x); USS2's aggregate tested loss, which is equal to its pro rata share (determined under § 1.951A-1(d)(4)) of CFC3's tested loss ($100x); and USS3's aggregate tested loss, which is equal to its pro rata share (determined under § 1.951A-1(d)(4)) of CFC3's tested loss ($100x)). As a result, under paragraph (e)(12) of this section, as in paragraph (f)(1)(ii)(C) of this section (paragraph (C) of the analysis in *Example 1*), the net CFC tested income of USS1, USS2, and USS3 are $0 ($0 - $0), $125x ($200x - $75x), and $375x ($600x - $225x), respectively.

(3) *Example 3: Calculation of GILTI inclusion amount*—(i) *Facts*. The facts are the same as in paragraph (f)(1)(i) of this section (the facts in *Example 1*), except that CFC2 and CFC4 have qualified business asset investment of $500x and $2,000x, respectively, for Year 1. In Year 1, CFC1 and CFC4 each have tested interest expense (within the meaning of § 1.951A-4(b)(1)) of $25x, and none of CFC1, CFC2, CFC3, and CFC4 have tested interest income (within the meaning of § 1.951A-4(b)(2)). CFC1's tested loss of $100x and CFC4's tested income of $600x take into account the tested interest expense.

(ii) *Analysis*—(A) *GILTI allocation ratio*. As in paragraph (f)(1)(ii)(A) of this section (paragraph (A) of the analysis in *Example 1*), the GILTI allocation ratios of USS1, USS2, and USS3 are 0 ($0/$800x), 0.25 ($200x/$800x), and 0.75 ($600x/$800x), respectively.

(B) *Consolidated QBAI*. Under paragraph (e)(4) of this section, the P consolidated group's consolidated QBAI is $2,500x ($500x + $2,000x), the aggregate of USS2's pro rata share (determined under § 1.951A-1(d)(3)) of the qualified business asset investment of CFC2 and USS3's pro rata share (determined under § 1.951A-1(d)(3)) of the qualified business asset investment of CFC4. Under paragraph (e)(3)(i) of this section, a member's allocable share of consolidated QBAI is the product of the consolidated QBAI of the member's consolidated group and the member's GILTI allocation ratio. Therefore, the allocable shares of the consolidated QBAI of each of USS1, USS2, and USS3 are $0 (0 x $2,500x), $625x (0.25 x $2,500x), and $1,875x (0.75 x $2,500x), respectively.

(C) *Consolidated specified interest expense*—(*1*) *Pro rata share of tested interest expense*. USS1's pro rata share (determined under § 1.951A-1(d)(5)) of the tested interest expense of CFC1 is $25x, the amount by which the tested interest expense increases USS1's pro rata share of CFC1's tested loss (from $75x to $100x) for Year 1. USS3's pro rata share (determined under § 1.951A-1(d)(5)) of the tested interest expense of CFC4 is also $25x, the amount by which the tested interest expense decreases USS3's pro rata share of CFC4's tested income (from $625x to $600x).

(*2*) *Consolidated specified interest expense*. Under paragraph (e)(5) of this section, the P consolidated group's consolidated specified interest expense is $50x, the excess of the sum of each member's pro rata share of the tested interest expense of each controlled foreign corporation ($50x, $25x from USS1 + $25x from USS3), over the sum of each member's pro rata share of tested interest income ($0). Under paragraph (e)(3)(ii) of this section, a member's allocable share of consolidated specified interest expense is the product of the consolidated specified interest expense of the member's consolidated group and the member's GILTI allocation ratio. Therefore, the allocable shares of consolidated specified interest expense of USS1, USS2, and USS3 are $0 (0 x $50x), $12.50x (0.25 x $50x), and $37.50x (0.75 x $50x), respectively.

(D) *Calculation of deemed tangible income return*. Under paragraph (e)(9) of this section, a member's deemed tangible income return means 10 percent of the member's allocable share of the consolidated QBAI. As a result, the deemed tangible income returns of USS1, USS2, and USS3 are $0 (0.1 x $0), $62.50x (0.1 x $625x), and $187.50x (0.1 x $1,875x), respectively.

(E) *Calculation of net deemed tangible income return*. Under paragraph (e)(13) of this section, a member's net deemed tangible income return means the excess (if any) of a member's deemed tangible income return over the member's allocable share of the consolidated specified interest expense. As a result, the net deemed tangible income returns of USS1, USS2, and USS3 are $0 ($0 - $0), $50x ($62.50x - $12.50x), and $150x ($187.50x - $37.50x), respectively.

(F) *Calculation of GILTI inclusion amount*. Under paragraph (b) of this section, a member's GILTI inclusion amount for a U.S. shareholder inclusion year is the excess (if any) of the member's net CFC tested income for the U.S. shareholder inclusion year, over the shareholder's net deemed tangible income return for the U.S. shareholder inclusion year. As described in paragraph (f)(1)(ii)(C) of this section (paragraph (C) of the analysis in *Example 1*), the net CFC tested income of USS1, USS2, and USS3 are $0, $125x, and $375x, respectively. As described in paragraph (f)(3)(ii)(E) of this section (paragraph (E) of the analysis in this example), the net deemed tangible income returns of USS1, USS2, and USS3 are $0, $50x, and $150x, respectively. As a result, under paragraph (b) of this section, the GILTI inclusion amounts of USS1, USS2, and USS3 are $0 ($0 - $0), $75x ($125x - $50x), and $225x ($375x - $150x), respectively.

(g) *Applicability date*.—(1) *In general*.—Except as otherwise provided in this paragraph (g), this section applies to taxable years of United States shareholders for which the due date (without extensions) of the consolidated return is after June 21, 2019. However, a consolidated group may apply the rules of this section in their entirety to all taxable years of its members that are described in § 1.951A-7(a). In such a case, the consolidated group must apply the rules of this section to all taxable years described in § 1.951A-7(a) and with respect to all members.

(2) [Reserved]

[Reg. § 1.1502-51.]

☐ [*T.D. 9866, 6-14-2019. Amended by T.D. 9902, 7-20-2020 and T.D.* 9960, 1-24-2022.]

§ 1.1502-59A. Application of section 59A to consolidated groups.—(a) *Scope*.—This section provides rules for the application of section 59A and the regulations thereunder (the *section 59A regulations*) to consolidated groups and their members (as defined in § 1.1502-1(h) and (b), respectively). Rules in the section 59A regulations apply to consolidated groups except as modified in this section. Paragraph (b) of this section provides rules treating a consolidated group (rather than each member of the group) as a single taxpayer, and a single applicable taxpayer, as relevant, for certain purposes. Paragraph (c) of this section coordinates the application of the business interest stacking rule under § 1.59A-3(c)(4) to consolidated groups. Paragraph (d) of this section addresses how the base erosion minimum tax amount is allocated among members of the consolidated group. Paragraph (e) of this section coordinates the application of this section and § 1.1502-47. Paragraph (f) of this section sets forth definitions. Paragraph (g) of this section provides examples. Paragraph (h) of this section provides the applicability date.

(b) *Consolidated group as the applicable taxpayer*.—(1) *In general*.—For purposes of determining whether the consolidated group is an applicable taxpayer (within the meaning of § 1.59A-2(b)) and the amount of tax due pursuant to section 59A(a), all members of a consolidated group are treated as a single taxpayer. Thus, for example, members' deductions are aggregated in making the required computations under section 59A. In addition, to ensure that intercompany transactions (as defined in § 1.1502-13(b)(1)(i)) do not affect the consolidated group's base erosion percentage or base erosion minimum tax amount, items resulting from intercompany transactions are not taken into account in making such computations under section 59A. For example, additional depreciation deductions resulting from intercompany asset sales are not taken into account for purposes of applying the base erosion percentage test under § 1.59A-2(e).

(2) *Consolidated group as member of the aggregate group*.—The consolidated group is treated as a single member of an aggregate group for purposes of § 1.59A-2(c).

(3) *Related party determination*.—For purposes of section 59A and the section 59A regulations, if a person is a related party with respect to any member of a consolidated group, that person is a related party of the group and of each of its members.

(c) *Coordination of section 59A(c)(3) and section 163(j) in a consolidated group*.—(1) *Overview*.—This paragraph (c) provides rules regarding the application of § 1.59A-3(c)(4) to a consolidated group's section 163(j) interest deduction. The classification rule in paragraph (c)(3) of this section addresses how to determine if, and to what extent, the group's section 163(j) interest deduction is a base erosion tax benefit. These regulations contain a single-entity classification rule with regard to the deduction of the consolidated group's aggregate current year business interest expense ("BIE"), but a separate-entity classification rule for the deduction of the consolidated group's disallowed BIE carryforwards. Paragraph (c)(3) of this section classifies the group's aggregate current year BIE deduction, in conformity with § 1.59A-3(c)(4), as constituting domestic related current year BIE deduction, foreign related current year BIE deduction, or unrelated current year BIE deduction. The allocation rules in paragraph (c)(4) of this section then allocate to specific members of the group the domestic related current year BIE deduction, foreign related current year BIE deduction, and unrelated current year BIE deduction taken in the taxable year. Any member's current year BIE that is carried forward to the succeeding taxable year as a disallowed BIE carryforward is allocated a status as domestic related BIE carryforward, foreign related BIE carryforward, or unrelated BIE carryforward under paragraph (c)(5) of this section. The status of any disallowed BIE carryforward deducted by a member in a later year is classified on a separate-entity basis by the deducting member under paragraph (c)(3) of this section, based on the status allocated to the member's disallowed BIE carryforward under paragraph (c)(5) of this section. This paragraph (c) also provides rules regarding the consequences of the deconsolidation of a corporation that has been allocated a domestic related BIE carryforward status, a foreign related BIE carryforward status, or an unrelated BIE carryforward status; and the consolidation of a corporation with a disallowed BIE carryforward classified as from payments to a domestic related party, foreign related party, or unrelated party.

(2) *Absorption rule for the group's business interest expense.*—To determine the amount of the group's section 163(j) interest deduction, and to determine the year in which the member's business interest expense giving rise to the deduction was incurred or accrued, see §§1.163(j)-4(d) and 1.163(j)-5(b)(3).

(3) *Classification of the group's section 163(j) interest deduction.*—(i) *In general.*—Consistent with §1.59A-3(c)(4)(i) and paragraph (b) of this section, the classification rule of this paragraph (c)(3) determines whether the consolidated group's section 163(j) interest deduction is a base erosion tax benefit. To the extent the consolidated group's business interest expense is permitted as a deduction under section 163(j)(1) in a taxable year, the deduction is classified first as from business interest expense paid or accrued to a foreign related party and business interest expense paid or accrued to a domestic related party (on a pro-rata basis); any remaining deduction is treated as from business interest expense paid or accrued to an unrelated party.

(ii) *Year-by-year application of the classification rule.*—If the consolidated group's section 163(j) interest deduction in any taxable year is attributable to business interest expense paid or accrued in more than one taxable year (for example, the group deducts the group's aggregate current year BIE, the group's disallowed BIE carryforward from year 1, and the group's disallowed BIE carryforward from year 2), the classification rule in paragraph (c)(3)(i) of this section applies separately to each of those years, pursuant to paragraphs (c)(3)(iii) and (iv) of this section.

(iii) *Classification of current year BIE deductions.*—Current year BIE deductions are classified under the section 59A regulations and this paragraph (c) as if the consolidated group were a single taxpayer that had paid or accrued the group's aggregate current year BIE to domestic related parties, foreign related parties, and unrelated parties. The rules of paragraph (c)(4) of this section apply for allocating current year BIE deductions among members of the consolidated group. To the extent the consolidated group's aggregate current year BIE exceeds its section 163(j) limitation, the rules of paragraph (c)(5) of this section apply.

(iv) *Classification of deductions of disallowed BIE carryforwards.*—Each member of the group applies the classification rule in this paragraph (c)(3) to its deduction of any part of a disallowed BIE carryforward from a year, after the group applies paragraph (c)(5) of this section to the consolidated group's disallowed BIE carryforward from that year. Therefore, disallowed BIE carryforward that is actually deducted by a member is classified based on the status of the components of that carryforward, assigned pursuant to paragraph (c)(5) of this section.

(4) *Allocation of domestic related current year BIE deduction status and foreign related current year BIE deduction status among members of the consolidated group.*—(i) *In general.*—This paragraph (c)(4) applies if the group has domestic related current year BIE deductions, foreign related current year BIE deductions, or both, as a result of the application of the classification rule in paragraph (c)(3) of this section. Under this paragraph (c)(4), the domestic related current year BIE, foreign related current year BIE, or both, that is treated as deducted in the current year are deemed to have been incurred pro-rata by all members that have current year BIE deduction in that year, regardless of which member or members actually incurred the current year BIE to a domestic related party or a foreign related party.

(ii) *Domestic related current year BIE deduction.*—(A) *Amount of domestic related current year BIE deduction status allocable to a member.*—The amount of domestic related current year BIE deduction status that is allocated to a member is determined by multiplying the group's domestic related current year BIE deduction (determined pursuant to paragraph (c)(3) of this section) by the percentage of current year BIE deduction allocable to such member in that year.

(B) *Percentage of current year BIE deduction allocable to a member.*—The percentage of current year BIE deduction allocable to a member is equal to the amount of the member's current year BIE deduction divided by the amount of the group's aggregate current year BIE deduction.

(iii) *Amount of foreign related current year BIE deduction status allocable to a member.*—The amount of foreign related current year BIE deduction status that is allocated to a member is determined by multiplying the group's foreign related current year BIE deduction (determined pursuant to paragraph (c)(3) of this section) by the percentage of current year BIE deduction allocable to such member (defined in paragraph (c)(4)(ii)(B) of this section).

(iv) *Treatment of amounts as having unrelated current year BIE deduction status.*—To the extent the amount of a member's current year BIE that is absorbed under paragraph (c)(2) of this section exceeds the domestic related current year BIE deduction status and foreign related current year BIE deduction status allocated to the member under paragraph (c)(4)(ii) and (iii) of this section, such excess amount is treated as from payments or accruals to an unrelated party.

(5) *Allocation of domestic related BIE carryforward status and foreign related BIE carryforward status to members of the group.*—(i) *In general.*—This paragraph (c)(5) applies in any year the consolidated group's aggregate current year BIE exceeds its section 163(j) limitation. After the application of paragraph (c)(4) of this section, any remaining domestic related current year BIE, foreign related current year BIE, and unrelated current year BIE is deemed to have been incurred pro-rata by members of the group pursuant to the rules in paragraph (c)(5)(ii), (iii), and (iv) of this section, regardless of which member or members actually incurred the business interest expense to a domestic related party, foreign related party, or unrelated party.

(ii) *Domestic related BIE carryforward.*—(A) *Amount of domestic related BIE carryforward status allocable to a member.*—The amount of domestic related BIE carryforward status that is allocated to a member equals the group's domestic related BIE carryforward from that year multiplied by the percentage of disallowed BIE carryforward allocable to the member.

(B) *Percentage of disallowed BIE carryforward allocable to a member.*—The percentage of disallowed BIE carryforward allocable to a member for a taxable year equals the member's disallowed BIE carryforward from that year divided by the consolidated group's disallowed BIE carryforwards from that year.

(iii) *Amount of foreign related BIE carryforward status allocable to a member.*—The amount of foreign related BIE carryforward status that is allocated to a member equals the group's foreign related BIE carryforward from that year multiplied by the percentage of disallowed BIE carryforward allocable to the member (as defined in paragraph (c)(5)(ii)(B) of this section).

(iv) *Treatment of amounts as having unrelated BIE carryforward status.*—If a member's disallowed BIE carryforward for a year exceeds the amount of domestic related BIE carryforward status and foreign related BIE carryforward status that is allocated to the member pursuant to paragraphs (c)(5)(ii) and (iii) of this section, respectively, the excess carryforward amount is treated as from payments or accruals to an unrelated party.

(v) *Coordination with section 381.*—If a disallowed BIE carryforward is allocated a status as a domestic related BIE carryforward, foreign related BIE carryforward, or unrelated BIE carryforward under the allocation rule of paragraph (c)(5) of this section, the acquiring corporation in a transaction described in section 381(a) will succeed to and take into account the allocated status of the carryforward for purposes of section 59A. See §1.381(c)(20)-1.

(6) *Member deconsolidates from a consolidated group.*—(i) *General rule.*—When a member deconsolidates from a group (the original group), the member's disallowed BIE carryforwards retain their allocated status, pursuant to paragraph (c)(5) of this section, as a domestic related BIE carryforward, foreign related BIE carryforward, or unrelated BIE carryforward (as applicable). Following the member's deconsolidation, the status of the disallowed BIE carryforwards of the remaining members is not redetermined.

(ii) *Gross receipts exception.*—This paragraph (c)(6)(ii) applies if the original group had insufficient gross receipts to satisfy the gross receipts test under §1.59A-2(d) and thus was not an applicable taxpayer in the year in which the deconsolidating member's disallowed BIE carryforward was incurred. If this paragraph (c)(6)(ii) applies, the deconsolidating member may determine the status of its disallowed BIE carryforward from that year by applying the classification rule of §1.59A-3(c)(4) solely to the interest payments or accruals of the deconsolidating member, rather than by applying § 1.1502-59A(c)(3).

(iii) *Failure to substantiate.*—If the deconsolidating member fails to substantiate a disallowed BIE carryforward as a domestic related BIE carryforward, foreign related BIE carryforward, or unrelated BIE carryforward, then the disallowed BIE carryforward is treated as a foreign related BIE carryforward.

(7) *Corporation joins a consolidated group.*—If a corporation joins a consolidated group (the acquiring group), and that corporation was allocated a domestic related BIE carryforward status, foreign related BIE carryforward status, or unrelated BIE carryforward status pursuant to paragraph (c)(5) of this section from another consolidated group (the original group), or separately has a disallowed BIE carryforward that is classified as from payments or accruals to a domestic related party, foreign related party, or unrelated party, the status of the carryforward is taken into account in determining the acquiring group's base erosion tax benefit when the corporation's disallowed BIE carryforward is absorbed.

(d) *Allocation of the base erosion minimum tax amount to members of the consolidated group.*—For rules regarding the allocation of the base erosion minimum tax amount, see section 1552. Allocations under section 1552 take into account the classification and allocation provisions of paragraphs (c)(3) through (5) of this section.

(e) [Reserved].

(f) *Definitions.*—The following definitions apply for purposes of this section—

(1) *Aggregate current year BIE.*—The consolidated group's *aggregate current year BIE* is the aggregate of all members' current year BIE.

(2) *Aggregate current year BIE deduction.*—The consolidated group's *aggregate current year BIE deduction* is the aggregate of all members' current year BIE deductions.

(3) *Applicable taxpayer.*—The term *applicable taxpayer* has the meaning provided in § 1.59A-2(b).

(4) *Base erosion minimum tax amount.*—The consolidated group's *base erosion minimum tax amount* is the tax imposed under section 59A.

(5) *Base erosion tax benefit.*—The term *base erosion tax benefit* has the meaning provided in § 1.59A-3(c)(1).

(6) *Business interest expense.*—The term *business interest expense*, with respect to a member and a taxable year, has the meaning provided in § 1.163(j)-1(b)(3), and with respect to a consolidated group and a taxable year, has the meaning provided in § 1.163(j)-4(d)(2)(iii).

(7) *Consolidated group's disallowed BIE carryforwards.*—The term *consolidated group's disallowed BIE carryforwards* has the meaning provided in § 1.163(j)-5(b)(3)(i).

(8) *Current year BIE.*—A member's *current year BIE* is the member's business interest expense that would be deductible in the current taxable year without regard to section 163(j) and that is not a disallowed business interest expense carryforward from a prior taxable year.

(9) *Current year BIE deduction.*—A member's *current year BIE deduction* is the member's current year BIE that is permitted as a deduction in the taxable year.

(10) *Domestic related BIE carryforward.*—The consolidated group's *domestic related BIE carryforward* for any taxable year is the excess of the group's domestic related current year BIE over the group's domestic related current year BIE deduction (if any).

(11) *Domestic related current year BIE.*—The consolidated group's *domestic related current year BIE* for any taxable year is the consolidated group's aggregate current year BIE paid or accrued to a domestic related party.

(12) *Domestic related current year BIE deduction.*—The consolidated group's *domestic related current year BIE deduction* for any taxable year is the portion of the group's aggregate current year BIE deduction classified as from interest paid or accrued to a domestic related party under paragraph (c)(3) of this section.

(13) *Domestic related party.*—A *domestic related party* is a related party that is not a foreign related party and is not a member of the same consolidated group.

(14) *Disallowed BIE carryforward.*—The term *disallowed BIE carryforward* has the meaning provided in § 1.163(j)-1(b)(11).

(15) *Foreign related BIE carryforward.*—The consolidated group's *foreign related BIE carryforward* for any taxable year, is the excess of the group's foreign related current year BIE over the group's foreign related current year BIE deduction (if any).

(16) *Foreign related current year BIE.*—The consolidated group's *foreign related current year BIE* for any taxable year is the consolidated group's aggregate current year BIE paid or accrued to a foreign related party.

(17) *Foreign related current year BIE deduction.*—The consolidated group's *foreign related current year BIE deduction* for any taxable year is the portion of the consolidated group's aggregate current year BIE deduction classified as from interest paid or accrued to a foreign related party under paragraph (c)(3) of this section.

(18) *Foreign related party.*—A *foreign related party* has the meaning provided in § 1.59A-1(b)(12).

(19) *Related party.*—The term *related party* has the meaning provided in § 1.59A-1(b)(17), but excludes members of the same consolidated group.

(20) *Section 163(j) interest deduction.*—The term *section 163(j) interest deduction* means, with respect to a taxable year, the amount of the consolidated group's business interest expense permitted as a deduction pursuant to § 1.163(j)-5(b)(3) in the taxable year.

(21) *Section 163(j) limitation.*—The term *section 163(j) limitation* has the meaning provided in § 1.163(j)-1(b)(36).

(22) *Unrelated BIE carryforward.*—The consolidated group's *unrelated BIE carryforward* for any taxable year is the excess of the group's unrelated current year BIE over the group's unrelated current year BIE deduction.

(23) *Unrelated current year BIE.*—The consolidated group's *unrelated current year BIE* for any taxable year is the consolidated group's aggregate current year BIE paid or accrued to an unrelated party.

(24) *Unrelated current year BIE deduction.*—The consolidated group's *unrelated current year BIE deduction* for any taxable year is the portion of the group's aggregate current year BIE deduction classified as from interest paid or accrued to an unrelated party under paragraph (c)(3) of this section.

(25) *Unrelated party.*—An *unrelated party* is a party that is not a related party.

(g) *Examples.*—The following examples illustrate the general application of this section. For purposes of the examples, a foreign corporation (FP) wholly owns domestic corporation (P), which in turn wholly owns S1 and S2. P, S1, and S2 are members of a consolidated group. The consolidated group is a calendar year taxpayer.

(1) *Example 1: Computation of the consolidated group's base erosion minimum tax amount.* (i) *The consolidated group is the applicable taxpayer*—(A) *Facts*. The members have never engaged in intercompany transactions. For the 2019 taxable year, P, S1, and S2 were permitted the following amounts of deductions (within the meaning of section 59A(c)(4)), $2,400x, $1,000x, and $2,600x; those deductions include base erosion tax benefits of $180x, $370x, and $230x. The group's consolidated taxable income for the year is $150x. In addition, the group satisfies the gross receipts test in § 1.59A-2(d).

(B) *Analysis*. Pursuant to paragraph (b) of this section, the receipts and deductions of P, S1, and S2 are aggregated for purposes of making the computations under section 59A. The group's base erosion percentage is 13% (($180x + $370x + $230x)/($2,400x + $1,000x + $2,600x)). The consolidated group is an applicable taxpayer under § 1.59A-2(b) because the group satisfies the gross receipts test and the group's base erosion percentage (13%) is higher than 3%. The consolidated group's modified taxable income is computed by adding back the members' base erosion tax benefits (and, when the consolidated group has consolidated net operating loss available for deduction, the consolidated net operating loss allowed multiplied by the base erosion percentage) to the consolidated taxable income, $930x ($150x + $180x + $370x + $230x). The group's base erosion minimum tax amount is then computed as 10 percent of the modified taxable income less the regular tax liability, $61.5x ($930x × 10% - $150x × 21%).

(ii) *The consolidated group engages in intercompany transactions*—(A) *Facts*. The facts are the same as in paragraph (g)(1)(i)(A) of this section (the facts in *Example* 1(i)), except that S1 sold various inventory items to S2 during 2019. Such items are depreciable in the hands of S2 (but would not have been depreciable in the hands of S1) and continued to be owned by S2 during 2019.

(B) *Analysis*. The result is the same as paragraph (g)(1)(i)(A) of this section (the facts in *Example 1*(i)). Pursuant to paragraph (b)(2) of this section, items resulting from the intercompany sale (for example, gross receipts, depreciation deductions) are not taken into account in computing the group's gross receipts under § 1.59A-2(d) and base erosion percentage under § 1.59A-2(e)(3).

(2) *Example 2: Business interest expense subject to section 163(j) and the group's domestic related current year BIE and foreign related current year BIE for the year equals its section 163(j) limitation*—(i) *Facts*. During the current year (Year 1), P incurred $150x of business interest expense to domestic related parties; S1 incurred $150x of business interest expense to foreign related parties; and S2 incurred $150x of business interest expense to unrelated parties. The group's section 163(j) limitation for the year is $300x. After applying the rules in § 1.163(j)-5(b)(3), the group deducts $150x of P's Year 1 business interest expense, and $75x each of S1 and S2's Year 1 business interest expense. Assume the group is an applicable taxpayer for purposes of section 59A.

(ii) *Analysis*—(A) *Application of the absorption rule in paragraph (c)(2) of this section*. Following the rules in section 163(j), the group's section 163(j) interest deduction for Year 1 is $300x, and the entire amount is from members' Year 1 business interest expense.

(B) *Application of the classification rule in paragraph (c)(3) of this section*. Under paragraph (c)(3) of this section, the group's aggregate current year BIE deduction of $300x is first classified as payments or accruals to related parties (pro-rata among domestic related parties and foreign related parties), and second as payments or accruals to unrelated parties. For Year 1, the group has $150x of domestic related current year BIE and $150x of foreign related current year BIE, and the group's aggregate current year BIE deduction will be classified equally among the related party expenses. Therefore, $150x of the group's deduction is classified as domestic related current year BIE deduction and $150x is classified as a foreign related current year BIE deduction.

(C) *Application of the allocation rule in paragraph (c)(4) of this section*. After the application of the classification rule in paragraph (c)(3) of this section, the group has $150x each of domestic related current year BIE deduction and foreign related current year BIE deduction from the group's aggregate current year BIE in Year 1. The domestic related current year BIE deduction and foreign related current year BIE deduction will be allocated to P, S1, and S2 based on each member's deduction of its Year 1 business interest expense.

(*1*) *Allocations to P*. The percentage of current year BIE deduction attributable to P is 50% (P's deduction of its Year 1 current year BIE, $150x, divided by the group's aggregate current year BIE deduction for Year 1, $300x). Thus, the amount of domestic related current year BIE deduction status allocated to P is $75x (the group's domestic related current year BIE deduction, $150x, multiplied by the percentage of current year BIE deduction allocable to P, 50%); and the amount of foreign related current year BIE deduction status allocated to P is $75x (the group's foreign related current year BIE deduction, $150x, multiplied by the percentage of current year BIE deduction allocable to P, 50%).

(*2*) *Allocations to S1 and S2*. The percentage of current year BIE deduction attributable to S1 is 25% (S1's deduction of its Year 1 current year BIE, $75x, divided by the group's aggregate current year BIE deduction for Year 1, $300x). Thus, the amount of domestic related current year BIE deduction status allocated to S1 is $37.5x (the group's domestic related current year BIE deduction, $150x, multiplied by the percentage of current year BIE deduction allocable to S1, 25%); and the amount of foreign related current year BIE deduction status allocated to S1 is $37.5x (the group's foreign related current year BIE deduction, $150x, multiplied by the percentage of current year BIE deduction allocable to S1, 25%). Because S2 also deducted $75 of its Year 1 current year BIE, S2's deductions are allocated the same pro-rata status as those of S1 under this paragraph (f)(2)(ii)(C)(*2*).

(D) *Application of the allocation rule in paragraph (c)(5) of this section*. Although the group will have disallowed BIE carryforwards after Year 1 (the group's aggregate current year BIE of $450x ($150x + $150x + $150x) exceeds the section 163(j) limitation of $300x), all of the domestic related current year BIE and foreign related current year BIE in Year 1 has been taken into account pursuant to the classification rule in paragraph (c)(3) of this section. Thus, under paragraph (c)(5)(iv) of this section, each member's disallowed BIE carryforward is treated as from payments or accruals to unrelated parties.

(3) *Example 3: Business interest expense subject to section 163(j)*—(i) *The group's domestic related current year BIE and foreign related current year BIE for the year exceeds its section 163(j) limitation*. (A) *Facts*. During the current year (Year 1), P incurred $60x of business interest expense to domestic related parties; S1 incurred $40x of business interest expense to foreign related parties; and S2 incurred $80x of business interest expense to unrelated parties. The group's section 163(j) limitation for the year is $60x. After applying the rules in § 1.163(j)-5(b)(3), the group deducts $20x each of P, S1, and S2's current year business interest expense. Assume the group is an applicable taxpayer for purposes of section 59A.

(B) *Analysis*—(*1*) *Application of the absorption rule in paragraph (c)(2) of this section*. Following the rules in section 163(j), the group's section 163(j) interest deduction is $60x, and the entire amount is from members' Year 1 business interest expense.

(*2*) *Application of the classification rule in paragraph (c)(3) of this section*. Under paragraph (c)(3) of this section, the group's $60x of aggregate current year BIE deduction is first classified as payments or accruals to related parties (pro-rata among domestic related parties and foreign related parties), and second as payments or accruals from unrelated parties. The group's total related party interest expense in Year 1, $100x (sum of the group's Year 1 domestic related current year BIE, $60x, and the group's Year 1 foreign related current year BIE, $40x), exceeds the group's aggregate current year BIE deduction of $60x. Thus, the group's aggregate current year BIE deduction will be classified, pro-rata, as from payments or accruals to domestic related parties and foreign related parties. Of the group's aggregate current year BIE deduction in Year 1, $36x is classified as a domestic related current year BIE deduction (the group's aggregate current year BIE deduction, $60x, multiplied by the ratio of domestic related current year BIE over the group's total Year 1 related party interest expense ($60x / ($60x+$40x))); and $24x of the group's aggregate current year BIE deduction is classified as a foreign related current year BIE deduction (the group's section 163(j) interest deduction, $60x, multiplied by the ratio of foreign related current year BIE over the group's total Year 1 related party interest expense ($40x / ($60x+$40x))).

(*3*) *Application of the allocation rule in paragraph (c)(4) of this section*. After the application of the classification rule in paragraph (c)(3) of this section, the group has $36x of domestic related current year BIE deduction and $24x of foreign related current year BIE deduction from the group's aggregate current year BIE in Year 1. The domestic related current year BIE deduction and foreign related current year BIE deduction will be allocated to P, S1, and S2 based on each member's current year BIE deduction in Year 1.

(*i*) *Allocation of the group's domestic related current year BIE deduction status*. Because each member is deducting $20x of its Year 1 business interest expense, all three members have the same percentage of current year BIE deduction attributable to them. The percentage of current year BIE deduction attributable to each of P, S1, and S2 is 33.33% (each member's current year BIE deduction in Year 1, $20x, divided by the group's aggregate current year BIE deduction for Year 1, $60x). Thus, the amount of domestic related current year BIE deduction status allocable to each member is $12x (the group's domestic related current year BIE deduction, $36x, multiplied by the percentage of current year BIE deduction allocable to each member, 33.33%).

(*ii*) *Allocations of the group's foreign related current year BIE deduction status*. The amount of foreign related current year BIE deduction status allocable to each member is $8x (the group's foreign related current year BIE deduction, $24x, multiplied by the percentage of current year BIE deduction allocable to each member, 33.33%, as computed earlier in paragraph (f)(3) of this section (*Example* 3).

(*4*) *Application of the allocation rule in paragraph (c)(5) of this section*. In Year 1 the group has $60x of domestic related current year BIE, of which $36x is deducted in the year (by operation of the classification rule). Therefore, the group has $24x of domestic related BIE carryforward. Similarly, the group has $40x of foreign related current year BIE in Year 1, of which $24x is deducted in the year. Therefore, the group has $16x of foreign related BIE carryforward. The $24x domestic related BIE carryforward status and $16x foreign related BIE carryforward status will be allocated to P, S1, and S2 in proportion to the amount of each member's disallowed BIE carryforward.

(i) *Allocation to P.* The percentage of disallowed BIE carryforward allocable to P is 33.33% (P's Year 1 disallowed BIE carryforward, $40x ($60x - $20x), divided by the group's Year 1 disallowed BIE carryforward, $120x ($60x + $40x + 80x - $60x)). Thus, the amount of domestic related BIE carryforward status allocated to P is $8x (the group's domestic related BIE carryforward, $24x, multiplied by the percentage of disallowed BIE carryforward allocable to P, 33.33%); and the amount of foreign related BIE carryforward status allocated to P is $5.33x (the group's foreign related BIE carryforward, $16x, multiplied by the percentage of disallowed BIE carryforward allocable to P, 33.33%). Under paragraph (c)(5)(iv) of this section, P's disallowed BIE carryforward that has not been allocated a status as either a domestic related BIE carryforward or a foreign related BIE carryforward will be treated as interest paid or accrued to an unrelated party. Therefore, $26.67x ($40x P's disallowed BIE carryforward - $8x domestic related BIE carryforward status allocated to P - $5.33x foreign related BIE carryforward status allocated to P) is treated as interest paid or accrued to an unrelated party.

(ii) *Allocation to S1.* The percentage of disallowed BIE carryforward allocable to S1 is 16.67% (S1's Year 1 disallowed BIE carryforward, $20x ($40x - $20x), divided by the group's Year 1 disallowed BIE carryforward, $120x ($60x + $40x + 80x - $60x). Thus, the amount of domestic related BIE carryforward status allocated to S1 is $4x (the group's domestic related BIE carryforward, $24x, multiplied by the percentage of disallowed BIE carryforward allocable to S1, 16.67%); and the amount of foreign related BIE carryforward status allocated to S1 is $2.67x (the group's foreign related BIE carryforward, $16x, multiplied by the percentage of disallowed BIE carryforward allocable to S1, 16.67%). Under paragraph (c)(5)(iv) of this section, S1's disallowed BIE that has not been allocated a status as either a domestic related BIE carryforward or a foreign related BIE carryforward will be treated as interest paid or accrued to an unrelated party. Therefore, $13.33x ($20x S1's disallowed BIE carryforward - $4x domestic related BIE carryforward status allocated to S1 - $2.67x foreign related BIE carryforward status allocated to S1) is treated as interest paid or accrued to an unrelated party.

(iii) *Allocation to S2.* The percentage of disallowed BIE carryforward allocable to S2 is 50% (S2's Year 1 disallowed BIE carryforward, $60x ($80x-$20x), divided by the group's Year 1 disallowed BIE carryforward, $120x ($60x+$40x+80x-$60x). Thus, the amount of domestic related BIE carryforward status allocated to S2 is $12x (the group's domestic related BIE carryforward, $24x, multiplied by the percentage of disallowed BIE carryforward allocable to S2, 50%); and the amount of foreign related BIE carryforward status allocated to S2 is $8x (the group's foreign related BIE carryforward, $16x, multiplied by the percentage of disallowed BIE carryforward allocable to S2, 50%). Under paragraph (c)(5)(iv) of this section, S2's disallowed BIE that has not been allocated a status as either a domestic related BIE carryforward or a foreign related BIE carryforward will be treated as interest paid or accrued to an unrelated party. Therefore, $40x ($60x S2's disallowed BIE carryforward - $12x domestic related BIE carryforward status allocated to S2 - $8x foreign related BIE carryforward status allocated to S2) is treated as interest paid or accrued to an unrelated party.

(ii) *The group deducting its disallowed BIE carryforwards*—(A) *Facts.* The facts are the same as in paragraph (g)(3)(i)(A) of this section (the facts in *Example 3*(i)), and in addition, none of the members incurs any business interest expense in Year 2. The group's section 163(j) limitation for Year 2 is $30x.

(B) *Analysis*—(*1*) *Application of the absorption rule in paragraph (c)(2) of this section.* Following the rules in section 163(j), each member of the group is deducting $10x of its disallowed BIE carryforward from Year 1. Therefore, the group's section 163(j) deduction for Year 2 is $30x.

(*2*) *Application of the classification rule in paragraph (c)(3) of this section.* Under paragraph (c)(3)(iv) of this section, to the extent members are deducting their Year 1 disallowed BIE carryforward in Year 2, the classification rule will apply to the deduction in Year 2 after the allocation rule in paragraph (c)(5) of this section has allocated the related and unrelated party status to the member's disallowed BIE carryforward in Year 1. The allocation required under paragraph (c)(5) of this section is described in paragraph (f)(3)(i)(B)(*4*) of this section.

(*i*) *Use of P's allocated domestic related BIE carryforward status and foreign related BIE carryforward status.* P has $40x of Year 1 disallowed BIE carryforward, and P was allocated $8x of domestic related BIE carryforward status and $5.33x of foreign related BIE carryforward status. In Year 2, P deducts $10x of its Year 1 disallowed BIE carryforward. Under the classification rule of paragraph (c)(3) of this section, P is treated as deducting pro-rata from its allocated status of domestic related BIE carryforward and foreign related BIE carryforward. Therefore, P is treated as deducting $6x of its allocated domestic related BIE carryforward ($10x × $8x / ($8x + $5.33x)), and $4x of its allocated foreign related BIE carryforward ($10x × $5.33x / $8x + $5.33x)). After Year 2, P has remaining $30x of Year 1 disallowed BIE carryforward, of which $2x has a status of domestic related BIE carryforward, $1.33x has the status of foreign related BIE carryforward, and $26.67x of interest treated as paid or accrued to unrelated parties.

(*ii*) *Use of S1's allocated domestic related BIE carryforward status and foreign related BIE carryforward status.* S1 has $20x of Year 1 disallowed BIE carryforward, and S1 was allocated $4x of domestic related BIE carryforward status and $2.67x of foreign related BIE carryforward status. In Year 2, S2 deducts $10x of its Year 1 disallowed BIE carryforward. Because S2's deduction of its Year 1 disallowed BIE carryforward, $10x, exceeds its allocated domestic related BIE carryforward status ($4x) and foreign related BIE carryforward status ($2.67x), all of the allocated related party status are used up. After Year 2, all of S1's Year 1 disallowed BIE carryforward, $10x, is treated as interest paid or accrued to an unrelated party.

(*iii*) *Use of S2's allocated domestic related BIE carryforward status and foreign related BIE carryforward status.* S2 has $60x of Year 1 disallowed BIE carryforward, and S2 was allocated $12x of domestic related BIE carryforward status and $8x of foreign related BIE carryforward status. In Year 2, S2 deducts $10x of its Year 1 disallowed BIE carryforward. Under the classification rule of paragraph (c)(3) of this section, S2 is treated as deducting $6x of its allocated domestic related BIE carryforward ($10x × $12x / ($12x + $8x)), and $4x of its allocated foreign related BIE carryforward ($10x × $8x / $8x + $12x)). After Year 2, P has remaining $50x of Year 1 disallowed BIE carryforward, of which $6x has a status of domestic related BIE carryforward, $4x has the status of foreign related BIE carryforward, and $40x of interest treated as paid or accrued to unrelated parties.

(h) *Applicability date.* This section applies to taxable years for which the original consolidated Federal income tax return is due (without extensions) after December 6, 2019. [Reg. § 1.1502-59A.]

☐ [*T.D. 9885, 12-2-2019. Amended by T.D. 9910, 10-8-2020.*]

§ 1.1502-80. Applicability of other provisions of law.—

* * *

(i) [Reserved]

(j) *Special rules for application of section 951(a)(2)(B) to distributions to which section 959(b) applies.*—(1) *Single United States shareholder treatment.*—In determining the amount described in section 951(a)(2)(B) that is attributable to distributions to which section 959(b) applies, members of a group are treated as a single United States shareholder (within the meaning of section 951(b) (or section 953(c)(1)(A), if applicable)) for purposes of determining the part of the year during which such shareholder did not own (within the meaning of section 958(a)) the stock described in section 951(a)(2)(A). The purpose of this paragraph (j) is to facilitate the clear reflection of income of a consolidated group by ensuring that the location of ownership of stock of a foreign corporation within the group does not affect the amount of the group's income by reason of sections 951(a)(1)(A) and 951A(a).

(2) *Examples.*—The following examples illustrate the application of paragraph (j)(1) of this section. For purposes of the examples in this paragraph (j)(2): M1 and M2 are members of a consolidated group of which P is the common parent (P group); each of CFC1, CFC2, and CFC3 is a controlled foreign corporation (within the meaning of section 957(a)) with the U.S. dollar as its functional currency (within the meaning of section 985); the taxable year of all entities is the calendar year for Federal income tax purposes; and a reference to stock owned means stock owned within the meaning of section 958(a). These examples do not address common law doctrines or other authorities that might apply to recast a transaction or to otherwise affect the tax treatment of a transaction.

(i) *Example 1: Intercompany transfer of stock of a controlled foreign corporation.*—(A) *Facts.*—Throughout Year 1, M1 directly owns all the stock of CFC1, which directly owns all the stock of CFC2. In Year 1, CFC2 has $100x of subpart F income (as defined in section 952). M1's pro rata share of CFC2's subpart F income for Year 1 is $100x, which M1 includes in its gross income under section 951(a)(1)(A). In Year 2, CFC2 has $80x of subpart F income and distributes $80x to CFC1 (the CFC2 Distribution). Section 959(b) applies to the entire CFC2 Distribution. On December 29, Year 2, M1 transfers all of its CFC1 stock to M2 in an exchange described in section 351(a). As a result, on

December 31, Year 2 (the last day of Year 2 on which CFC2 is a controlled foreign corporation), M2 owns 100% of the stock of CFC1, which owns 100% of the stock of CFC2.

(B) *Analysis*.—Under paragraph (j)(1) of this section, in determining the amount described in section 951(a)(2)(B) that is attributable to the CFC2 Distribution, all members of the P group are treated as a single United States shareholder for purposes of determining the part of Year 2 during which such shareholder did not own the stock of CFC2. Thus, the ratio of the number of days in Year 2 that such United States shareholder did not own the stock of CFC2 to the total number of days in Year 2 is 0/365. The amount described in section 951(a)(2)(B) is $0, M2's pro rata share of CFC2's subpart F income for Year 2 is $80x ($80x - $0), and M2 must include $80x in its gross income under section 951(a)(1)(A).

(ii) *Example 2: Transfer of stock of a controlled foreign corporation between controlled foreign corporations*.—(A) *Facts*.—The facts are the same as in paragraph (j)(2)(i)(A) of this section (the facts in *Example 1*), except that M1 does not transfer its CFC1 stock to M2. Additionally, throughout Year 1 and from January 1, Year 2, to December 29, Year 2, M2 directly owns all 90 shares of the only class of stock of CFC3. Further, on December 29, Year 2, CFC3 acquires all the CFC2 stock from CFC1 in exchange for 10 newly issued shares of the same class of CFC3 stock in a transaction described in section 368(a)(1)(B). As a result, on December 31, Year 2, M1 owns 10% of the stock of CFC2, and M2 owns 90% of the stock of CFC2.

(B) *Analysis*.—Under paragraph (j)(1) of this section, in determining the amount described in section 951(a)(2)(B) that is attributable to the portion of the CFC2 Distribution with respect to each of the CFC2 stock that M1 owns on December 31, Year 2, and the CFC2 stock that M2 owns on that day, all members of the P group are treated as a single United States shareholder for purposes of determining the part of Year 2 during which such shareholder did not own such stock. In each case, the ratio of the number of days in Year 2 that such United States shareholder did not own such stock to the total number of days in Year 2 is 0/365, and the amount described in section 951(a)(2)(B) is $0. M1's and M2's pro rata shares of CFC2's subpart F income for Year 2 are $8x ($8x - $0) and $72x ($72x - $0), respectively, and M1 and M2 must include $8x and $72x in gross income under section 951(a)(1)(A), respectively.

(3) *Applicability date*.—This paragraph (j) applies to taxable years for which the original consolidated Federal income tax return is due (without extensions) after February 23, 2023. [Reg. § 1.1502-80.]

☐ [*T.D.* 6894, 9-7-66. *Amended by T.D.* 8402, 3-13-92; *T.D.* 8560, 8-12-94; *T.D.* 8597, 7-12-95; *T.D.* 8677, 6-26-96; *T.D.* 9048, 3-11-2003; *T.D.* 9118, 3-17-2004 *T.D.* 9192, 3-21-2005; *T.D.* 9254, 3-9-2006; *T.D.* 9341, 7-17-2007; *T.D.* 9376, 1-14-2008, *T.D.* 9424, 9-9-2008 *and T.D.* 9973, 2-22-2023.]

§1.1503-2. Dual consolidated loss.—(a) *Purpose and scope*.—This section provides rules for the application of section 1503(d), concerning the determination and use of dual consolidated losses. Paragraph (b) of this section provides a general rule prohibiting a dual consolidated loss from offsetting the taxable income of a domestic affiliate. Paragraph (c) of this section provides definitions of the terms used in this section. Paragraph (d) of this section provides rules for calculating the amount of a dual consolidated loss and for adjusting the basis of stock of a dual resident corporation. Paragraph (e) of this section contains an anti-avoidance provision. Paragraph (f) of this section applies the rules of paragraph (d) of this section to the computation of foreign tax credit limitations. Paragraph (g) of this section provides certain exceptions to the limitation rule of paragraph (b) of this section. Finally, paragraph (h) of this section provides the effective date of the regulations and a provision for the retroactive application of the regulations to qualifying taxpayers.

(b) *In general*.—(1) *Limitation on the use of a dual consolidated loss to offset income of a domestic affiliate*.—Except as otherwise provided in this section, a dual consolidated loss of a dual resident corporation cannot offset the taxable income of any domestic affiliate in the taxable year in which the loss is recognized or in any other taxable year, regardless of whether the loss offsets income of another person under the income tax laws of a foreign country and regardless of whether the income that the loss may offset in the foreign country is, has been, or will be subject to tax in the United States. Pursuant to paragraph (c)(1) and (2) of this section, the same limitation shall apply to a dual consolidated loss of a separate unit of a domestic corporation as if the separate unit were a wholly owned subsidiary of such corporation.

(2) *Limitation on the use of a dual consolidated loss to offset income of a successor-in-interest*.—A dual consolidated loss of a dual resident corporation also cannot be used to offset the taxable income of another corporation by means of a transaction in which the other corporation succeeds to the tax attributes of the dual resident corporation under section 381 of the Code. Similarly, a dual consolidated loss of a separate unit of a domestic corporation cannot be used to offset income of the domestic corporation following the termination, liquidation, sale, or other disposition of the separate unit. However, if a dual resident corporation transfers its assets to another corporation in a transaction subject to section 381, and the acquiring corporation is a dual resident corporation of the same foreign country of which the transferor dual resident corporation is a resident, or a domestic corporation that carries on the business activities of the transferor dual resident corporation as a separate unit, then income generated by the transferee dual resident corporation, or separate unit, may be offset by the carryover losses of the transferor dual resident corporation. In addition, if a domestic corporation transfers a separate unit to another domestic corporation in a transaction subject to section 381, the income generated by the separate unit following the transfer may be offset by the carryover losses of the separate unit.

(3) *Application of rules to multiple tiers of separate units*.—If a separate unit of a domestic corporation is owned indirectly through another separate unit, the principles of paragraph (b)(1) and (2) of this section shall apply as if the upper-tier separate unit were a subsidiary of the domestic corporation and the lower-tier separate unit were a lower-tier subsidiary.

(4) *Examples*.—The following examples illustrate the application of this paragraph (b).

Example 1. P, a domestic corporation, owns all of the outstanding stock of DRC, a domestic corporation. P and DRC file a consolidated U.S. income tax return. DRC is managed and controlled in Country W, a country that determines the tax residence of corporations according to their place of management and control. Therefore, DRC is a dual resident corporation and any net operating loss it incurs is a dual consolidated loss. In Years 1 through 3, DRC incurs dual consolidated losses. Under this paragraph (b), the dual consolidated losses may not be used to offset P's income on the group's consolidated U.S. income tax return. At the end of Year 3, DRC sells all of its assets and discontinues its business operations. DRC is then liquidated into P, pursuant to the provisions of section 332. Normally, under section 381, P would succeed to, and be permitted to utilize, DRC's net operating loss carryovers. However, this paragraph (b) prohibits the dual consolidated losses of DRC from reducing P's income for U.S. tax purposes. Therefore, DRC's net operating loss carryovers will not be available to offset P's income.

Example 2. The facts are the same as in *Example 1*, except that DRC does not sell its assets and, following the liquidation of DRC, P continues to operate DRC's business as a separate unit (*e.g.*, a branch). DRC's loss carryovers are available to offset P's income generated by the assets previously owned by DRC and now held by the separate unit.

(c) *Definitions*.—The following definitions shall apply for purposes of this section.

(1) *Domestic corporation*.—The term "domestic corporation" has the meaning assigned to it by section 7701(a)(3) and (4). The term also includes any corporation otherwise treated as a domestic corporation by the Code, including, but not limited to, sections 269B, 953(d), and 1504(d). For purposes of this section, any separate unit of a domestic corporation, as defined in paragraph (c)(3) and (4) of this section, shall be treated as a separate domestic corporation.

(2) *Dual resident corporation*.—A dual resident corporation is a domestic corporation that is subject to the income tax of a foreign country on its worldwide income or on a residence basis. A corporation is taxed on a residence basis if it is taxed as a resident under the laws of the foreign country. An S corporation, as defined in section 1361, is not a dual resident corporation. For purposes of this section, any separate unit of a domestic corporation, as defined in paragraph (c)(3) and (4) of this section, shall be treated as a dual resident corporation. Unless otherwise indicated, any reference in this section to a dual resident corporation refers also to a separate unit.

(3) *Separate unit.*—(i) The term "separate unit" shall mean any of the following:

(A) A foreign branch, as defined in § 1.367(a)-6T(g) (or a successor regulation), that is owned either directly by a domestic corporation or indirectly by a domestic corporation through ownership of a partnership or trust interest (regardless of whether the partnership or trust is a United States person);

(B) an interest in a partnership; or

(C) an interest in a trust.

(ii) If two or more foreign branches located in the same foreign country are owned by a single domestic corporation and the losses of each branch are made available to offset the income of the other branches under the tax laws of the foreign country, within the meaning of paragraph (c)(15)(ii) of this section, then the branches shall be treated as one separate unit.

(4) *Hybrid entity separate unit.*—The term "separate unit" includes an interest in an entity that is not taxable as an association for U.S. income tax purposes but is subject to income tax in a foreign country as a corporation (or otherwise at the entity level) either on its worldwide income or on a residence basis.

(5) *Dual consolidated loss.*—(i) *In general.*—The term "dual consolidated loss" means the net operating loss (as defined in section 172(c) and the regulations thereunder) of a domestic corporation incurred in a year in which the corporation is a dual resident corporation. The dual consolidated loss shall be computed under paragraph (d)(1) of this section. The fact that a particular item taken into account in computing a dual resident corporation's net operating loss is not taken into account in computing income subject to a foreign country's income tax shall not cause such item to be excluded from the calculation of the dual consolidated loss.

(ii) *Exceptions.*—A dual consolidated loss shall not include the following—

(A) A net operating loss incurred by a dual resident corporation in a foreign country whose income tax laws—

(1) Do not permit the dual resident corporation to use its losses, expenses or deductions to offset the income of any other person that is recognized in the same taxable year in which the losses, expenses or deductions are incurred; and

(2) Do not permit the losses, expenses or deductions of the dual resident corporation to be carried over or back to be used, by any means, to offset the income of any other person in other taxable years; or

(B) A net operating loss incurred during that portion of the taxable year prior to the date on which the domestic corporation becomes a dual resident corporation or subsequent to the date on which the domestic corporation ceases to be a dual resident corporation. For purposes of determining the amount of the net operating loss incurred in that portion of the taxable year prior to the date on which the domestic corporation becomes a dual resident corporation or subsequent to the date on which the domestic corporation ceases to be a dual resident corporation, in no event shall more than the aggregate of the equal daily portion of the net operating loss commensurate with the portion of the taxable year during which the domestic corporation was not a dual resident corporation be allocated to that portion of the taxable year in which the domestic corporation was not a dual resident corporation.

(iii) *Dual consolidated losses of separate units that are partnership interests, including interests in hybrid entities.*—[Reserved]

(6) *Subject to tax.*—For purposes of determining whether a domestic corporation is subject to the income tax of a foreign country on its income, the fact that the corporation has no actual income tax liability to the foreign country for a particular taxable year shall not be taken into account.

(7) *Foreign country.*—For purposes of this section, possessions of the United States shall be considered foreign countries.

(8) *Consolidated group.*—The term "consolidated group" means an affiliated group, as defined in section 1504(a), with which a dual resident corporation or domestic owner files a consolidated U.S. income tax return.

(9) *Domestic owner.*—The term "domestic owner" means a domestic corporation that owns one or more separate units.

(10) *Affiliated dual resident corporation or affiliated domestic owner.*—The term "affiliated dual resident corporation" or "affiliated domestic owner" means a dual resident corporation or domestic owner that is a member of a consolidated group.

(11) *Unaffiliated dual resident corporation or unaffiliated domestic owner.*—The term "unaffiliated dual resident corporation" or "unaffiliated domestic owner" means a dual resident corporation or domestic owner that is an unaffiliated domestic corporation.

(12) *Successor-in-interest.*—The term "successor-in-interest" means an acquiring corporation that succeeds to the tax attributes of an acquired corporation by means of a transaction subject to section 381.

(13) *Domestic affiliate.*—The term "domestic affiliate" means any member of an affiliated group, without regard to the exceptions contained in section 1504(b) (other than section 1504(b)(3)) relating to includible corporations.

(14) *Unaffiliated domestic corporation.*—The term "unaffiliated domestic corporation" means a domestic corporation that is not a member of an affiliated group.

(15) *Use of loss to offset income of a domestic affiliate or another person.*—(i) A dual consolidated loss shall be deemed to offset income of a domestic affiliate in the year it is included in the computation of the consolidated taxable income of a consolidated group. The fact that no tax benefit results from the inclusion of the dual consolidated loss in the computation of the group's consolidated taxable income in the taxable year shall not be taken into account.

(ii) Except as provided in paragraph (c)(15)(iii) of this section, a loss, expense, or deduction taken into account in computing a dual consolidated loss shall be deemed to offset income of another person under the income tax laws of a foreign country in the year it is made available for such offset. The fact that the other person does not have sufficient income in that year to benefit from such an offset shall not be taken into account. However, where the laws of a foreign country provide an election that would enable a dual resident corporation or separate unit to use its losses, expenses, or deductions to offset income of another person, the losses, expenses, or deductions shall be considered to offset such income only if the election is made.

(iii) The losses, expenses, or deductions taken into account in computing a dual resident corporation's or separate unit's dual consolidated loss shall not be deemed to offset income of another person under the income tax laws of a foreign country for purposes of this section, if under the laws of the foreign country the losses, expenses, or deductions of the dual resident corporation or separate unit are used to offset the income of another dual resident corporation or separate unit within the same consolidated group (or income of another separate unit that is owned by the unaffiliated domestic owner of the first separate unit). If the losses, expenses, or deductions of a dual resident corporation or separate unit are made available under the laws of a foreign country to offset the income of other dual resident corporations or separate units within the same consolidated group (or other separate units owned by the unaffiliated domestic owner of the first separate unit), as well as the income of another person, and the laws of the foreign country do not provide applicable rules for determining which person's income is offset by the losses, expenses, or deductions, then for purposes of this section, the losses, expenses or deductions shall be deemed to offset the income of the other dual resident corporations or separate units, to the extent of such income, before being considered to offset the income of the other person.

(iv) Except to the extent paragraph (g)(1) of this section applies, where the income tax laws of a foreign country deny the use of losses, expenses, or deductions of a dual resident corporation to offset the income of another person because the dual resident corporation is also subject to income taxation by another country on its worldwide income or on a residence basis, the dual resident corporation shall be treated as if it actually had offset its dual consolidated loss against the income of another person in such foreign country.

(16) *Examples.*—The following examples illustrate this paragraph (c).

Example 1. X, a member of a consolidated group, conducts business through a branch in Country Y. Under Country Y's income tax laws, the branch is taxed as a permanent establishment and its losses may be used under the Country Y form of consolidation to offset the income of Z, a Country Y affiliate of X. In Year 1, the branch of X incurs an overall loss that would be treated as a net operating loss if the branch were a separate domestic corporation. Under paragraph (c)(3) of this section, the branch of X is treated as a separate domestic corporation and a dual resident corporation. Thus, under paragraph (c)(5), its loss constitutes a dual consolidated loss. Unless X qualifies for an exception under paragraph (g) of this section, paragraph (b) of this section precludes the use of the branch's loss to offset any income of X not derived from the branch operations or any income of a domestic affiliate of X.

Example 2. A and B are members of a consolidated group. FC is a Country X corporation that is wholly owned by B. A and B organize a partnership, P, under the laws of Country X. P conducts business in Country X and its business activity constitutes a foreign branch within the meaning of paragraph (c)(3)(i)(A) of this section. P also earns U.S. source income that is unconnected with the branch operations and, therefore, is not subject to tax by Country X. Under the laws of Country X, the branch can consolidate with FC. The interests in P held by A and B are each treated as a dual resident corporation. The branch is also treated as a separate dual resident corporation. Unless an exception under paragraph (g) of this section applies, any dual consolidated loss incurred by P's branch cannot offset the U.S. source income earned by P or any other income of A or B.

Example 3. X is classified as a partnership for U.S. income tax purposes. A, B and C are the sole partners of X. A and B are domestic corporations and C is a Country Y corporation. For U.S. income tax purposes, each partner has an equal interest in each item of partnership profit or loss. Under Country Y's law, X is classified as a corporation and its income and losses may be used under the Country Y form of consolidation to offset the income of companies that are affiliates of X. Under paragraph (c)(3) and (4) of this section, the partnership interests held by A and B are treated as separate domestic corporations and as dual resident corporations. Unless an exception under paragraph (g) of this section applies, losses allocated to A and B can only be used to offset profits of X allocated to A and B, respectively.

Example 4. P, a domestic corporation, files a consolidated U.S. income tax return with its two wholly-owned domestic subsidiaries, DRC1 and DRC2. Each subsidiary is also treated as a Country Y resident for Country Y tax purposes. Thus, DRC1 and DRC2 are dual resident corporations. DRC1 owns FC, a Country Y corporation. Country Y's tax laws permit affiliated resident corporations to file a form of consolidated return. In Year 1, DRC1 incurs a $200 net operating loss for both U.S. and Country Y tax purposes, while DRC2 recognizes $200 of income under the tax laws of each country. FC also earns $200 of income for Country Y tax purposes. DRC1, DRC2, and FC file a Country Y consolidated return. However, Country Y has no applicable rules for determining which income is offset by DRC1's $200 loss. Under paragraph (c)(15)(iii) of this section, the loss shall be treated as offsetting DRC2's $200 of income. Because DRC1 and DRC2 are members of the same consolidated group, for purposes of this section, the offset of DRC1's loss against the income of DRC2 is not considered a use of the loss against the income of another person under the laws of a foreign country.

Example 5. DRC, a domestic corporation, files a consolidated U.S. income tax return with its parent, P. DRC is also subject to tax in Country Y on its worldwide income. Therefore, DRC is a dual resident corporation and any net operating loss incurred by DRC is a dual consolidated loss. Country Y's tax laws permit corporations that are subject to tax on their worldwide income to use the Country Y form of consolidation, thus enabling eligible corporations to use their losses to offset income of affiliates. However, to prevent corporations like DRC from offsetting losses against income of affiliates in Country Y and then again offsetting the losses against income of foreign affiliates under the tax laws of another country, Country Y prevents a corporation that is also subject to the income tax of another country on its worldwide income or on a residence basis from using the Country Y form of consolidation. There is no agreement, as described in paragraph (g)(1) of this section, between the United States and Country Y. Because of Country Y's statute, DRC will be treated as having actually offset its losses against the income of affiliates in Country Y under paragraph (c)(15)(iv) of this section. Therefore, DRC will not be able to file an agreement described in paragraph (g)(2) of this section and offset its losses against the income of P or any other domestic affiliate.

(d) *Special rules for accounting for dual consolidated losses.*—(1) *Determination of amount of dual consolidated loss.*—(i) *Dual resident corporation that is a member of a consolidated group.*—For purposes of determining whether a dual resident corporation that is a member of a consolidated group has a dual consolidated loss for the taxable year, the dual resident corporation shall compute its taxable income (or loss) in accordance with the rules set forth in the regulations under section 1502 governing the computation of consolidated taxable income, taking into account only the dual resident corporation's items of income, gain, deduction, and loss for the year. However, for purposes of this computation, the following items shall not be taken into account:

(A) Any net capital loss of the dual resident corporation; and

(B) Any carryover or carryback losses.

(ii) *Dual resident corporation that is a separate unit of a domestic corporation.*—For purposes of determining whether a separate unit has a dual consolidated loss for the taxable year, the separate unit shall compute its taxable income (or loss) as if it were a separate domestic corporation and a dual resident corporation in accordance with the provisions of paragraph (d)(1)(i) of this section, using only those items of income, expense, deduction, and loss that are otherwise attributable to such separate unit.

(2) *Effect of a dual consolidated loss.*—For any taxable year in which a dual resident corporation or separate unit has a dual consolidated loss to which paragraph (b) of this section applies, the following rules shall apply.

(i) If the dual resident corporation is a member of a consolidated group, the group shall compute its consolidated taxable income without taking into account the items of income, loss, or deduction taken into account in computing the dual consolidated loss. The dual consolidated loss may be carried over or back for use in other taxable years as a separate net operating loss carryover or carryback of the dual resident corporation arising in the year incurred. It shall be treated as a loss incurred by the dual resident corporation in a separate return limitation year and (without regard to whether the dual resident corporation is a common parent) shall be subject to all of the limitations of §1.1502-21A(c) or 1.1502-21(c), as appropriate (relating to limitations on net operating loss carryovers and carrybacks from separate return limitation years).

(ii) The unaffiliated domestic owner of a separate unit, or the consolidated group of an affiliated domestic owner, shall compute its taxable income without taking into account the items of income, loss or deduction taken into account in computing the separate unit's dual consolidated loss. The dual consolidated loss shall be treated as a loss incurred by a separate corporation and its use shall be subject to all of the limitations of §1.1502-21A(c) or 1.1502-21(c), as appropriate, as if the separate unit were filing a consolidated return with the unaffiliated domestic owner or with the consolidated group of the affiliated domestic owner.

(3) *Basis adjustments for dual consolidated losses.*—(i) *Dual resident corporation that is a member of an affiliated group.*—When a dual resident corporation is a member of a consolidated group, each other member owning stock in the dual resident corporation shall adjust the basis of the stock in the following manner.

(A) *Positive adjustments.*—Positive adjustments shall be made in accordance with the principles of §1.1502-32(b)(1), except that there shall be no positive adjustment under §1.1502-32(b)(1)(ii) for any amount of the dual consolidated loss that is not absorbed as a result of the application of paragraph (b) of this section. In addition, there shall be no positive adjustment for any amount included in income pursuant to paragraph (g)(2)(vii) of this section.

(B) *Negative adjustments.*—Negative adjustments shall be made in accordance with the principles of §1.1502-32(b)(2), except that there shall be no negative adjustment under §1.1502-32(b)(2)(ii) for the amount of the dual consolidated loss subject to paragraph (b) of this section that is absorbed in a carryover year.

(ii) *Dual resident corporation that is a separate unit arising from an interest in a partnership.*—Where a separate unit is an interest in a partnership, the domestic owner shall adjust its basis in the separate unit in accordance with section 705, except that no increase in basis shall be permitted for any amount included as income pursuant to paragraph (g)(2)(vii) of this section.

(4) *Examples.*—The following examples illustrate this paragraph (d).

Example 1. (i) P, S1, S2, and T are domestic corporations. P owns all of the stock of S1 and S2. S2 owns all of the stock of T. T is a resident of Country FC for Country FC income tax purposes. Therefore, T is a dual resident corporation. P, S1, S2, and T file a consolidated U.S. income tax return. X and Y are corporations that are not members of the consolidated group.

(ii) At the beginning of Year 1, P has a basis of $1,000 in the stock of S2. S2 has a $500 basis in the stock of T.

(iii) In Year 1, T incurs interest expense in the amount of $100. In addition, T sells a noncapital asset, *u*, in which it has a basis of $10, to S1 for $50. T also sells a noncapital asset, *v*, in which it has a basis of $200, to S1 for $100. The sales of *u* and *v* are intercompany transactions described in § 1.1502-13. T also sells a capital asset, *z*, in which it has a basis of $180, to Y for $90. In Year 1, S1 earns $200 of separate taxable income, calculated in accordance with § 1.1502-12, as well as $90 of capital gain from a sale of an asset to X. P and S2 have no items of income, loss, or deduction for Year 1.

(iv) In Year 1, T has a dual consolidated loss of $100 (attributable to its interest expense). T's $90 capital loss is not included in the computation of the dual consolidated loss. Instead, T's capital loss is included in the computation of the consolidated group's capital gain net income under § 1.1502-22(c) and is used to offset S1's $90 capital gain.

(v) No elective agreement, as described in paragraph (g)(1) of this section, exists between the United States and Country FC. For Country FC tax purposes, T's $100 loss is offset against the income of a Country FC affiliate. Therefore, T is not eligible for the exception provided in paragraph (g)(2) of this section.

(vi) Because T has a dual consolidated loss for the year, the consolidated taxable income of the consolidated group is calculated without regard to T's items of income, loss or deduction taken into account in computing the dual consolidated loss. Therefore, the consolidated taxable income of the consolidated group is $200 (the sum of $200 of separate taxable income earned by S1 plus $90 of capital gain earned by S1 minus $90 of capital loss incurred by T). The $40 gain recognized by T upon the sale of item *u* to S1 and the $100 loss recognized by T upon the sale of Item *v* to S1 are deferred pursuant to § 1.1502-13(c)(1).

(vii) S2 may not make the positive adjustment provided for in § 1.1502-32(b)(1)(ii) to its basis in the stock of T for the $100 dual consolidated loss incurred by T. In addition, no positive adjustment in the basis of the stock is required for T's $90 capital loss because the loss has been absorbed by the consolidated group. S2, however, must make the negative adjustment provided for in § 1.1502-32(b)(2)(i) for its allocable part of T's deficit in earnings and profits for the taxable year attributable to both T's $100 dual consolidated loss and T's $90 capital loss. Thus, as provided in § 1.1502-32(e)(1), S2 must make a $190 net negative adjustment to its basis in the stock of T, reducing its basis to $310. As provided in § 1.1502-33(c)(4)(ii) (a), S2's earnings and profits for Year 1 will reflect S2's decrease in its basis in T stock for the taxable year. Since S2 has no other earnings and profits for the taxable year, S2 has a $190 deficit in earnings and profits for the year. As provided in § 1.1502-32(b)(2)(i), P must make a negative adjustment to its basis in the stock of S2 for its allocable part of S2's deficit in earnings and profits for the taxable year. Thus, P must make a $190 net negative adjustment to its basis in S2 stock, reducing its basis to $810.

Example 2. (i) The facts are the same as in *Example 1*, except that in Year 2, S1 sells items *u* and *v* to X for no gain or loss. The disposition of items *u* and *v* outside of the consolidated group restores the deferred loss and gain to T. T also incurs $100 of interest expense in Year 2. In addition, T sells a noncapital asset, *r*, in which it has a basis of $100, to Y for $300. P and S2 have no items of income, loss, or deduction for Year 2.

(ii) T has $40 of separate taxable income in Year 2, computed as follows:

($100)	interest expense
($100)	sale of item *v* to S1
$ 40	sale of item *u* to S1
$200	sale of item *r* to Y
$ 40	

Thus, T has no dual consolidated loss for the year.

(iii) Since T does not have a dual consolidated loss for the taxable year, the group's consolidated taxable income is calculated in accordance with the general rule of § 1.1502-11 and not in accordance with paragraph (d)(2) of this section. T is the only member of the consolidated group that has any income or loss for the taxable year. Thus, the consolidated taxable income of the group, computed without regard to T's dual consolidated loss carryover, is $40.

(iv) As provided by § 1.1502-21A(c), the amount of the dual consolidated loss arising in Year 1 that is included in the group's consolidated net operating loss deduction for Year 2 is $40 (that is, the consolidated taxable income computed without regard to the consolidated net operating loss deduction minus such consolidated taxable income recomputed by excluding the items of income and deduction of T). Thus, the group has no consolidated taxable income for the year.

(v) S2 must make the positive adjustment provided for in § 1.1502-32(b)(1)(i) to its basis in T stock for its allocable part of T's undistributed earnings and profits for the taxable year. S2 cannot make the negative adjustment provided for in § 1.1502-32(b)(2)(ii) for the dual consolidated loss of T incurred in Year 1 and absorbed in Year 2. Thus, as provided in § 1.1502-32(e)(2), S2 must make a $40 net positive adjustment to its basis in T stock, increasing its basis to $350. As provided in § 1.1502-33(c)(4)(ii)(a), S2's earnings and profits for Year 2 will reflect S2's increase in its basis in T stock for the taxable year. Since S2 has no other earnings and profits for the taxable year, S2 has $40 of earnings and profits for the year. As provided in § 1.1502-32(b)(1)(i), P must make a positive adjustment to its basis in the stock of S2 for its allocable part of the undistributed earnings and profits of S2 for the taxable year. Thus, P must make a $40 net positive adjustment to its basis in S2 stock, increasing its basis to $850.

(e) *Special rule for use of dual consolidated loss to offset tainted income.*—(1) *In general.*—The dual consolidated loss of any dual resident corporation that ceases to be a dual resident corporation shall not be used to offset income of such corporation to the extent that such income is tainted income, as defined in paragraph (e)(2) of this section.

(2) *Tainted income defined.*—Tainted income is any income derived from tainted assets, as defined in paragraph (e)(3) of this section, beginning on the date such assets are acquired by the dual resident corporation. In the absence of evidence establishing the actual amount of income that is attributable to the tainted assets, the portion of a corporation's income in a particular taxable year that is treated as tainted income shall be an amount equal to the corporation's taxable income for the year multiplied by a fraction, the numerator of which is the fair market value of the tainted asset at the end of the taxable year and the denominator of which is the fair market value of the total assets owned by the corporation at the end of the taxable year. Documentation submitted to establish the actual amount of income that is attributable to the tainted assets must be attached to the consolidated group's or unaffiliated dual resident corporation's timely filed tax return for the taxable year in which the income is recognized.

(3) *Tainted assets defined.*—Tainted assets are any assets acquired by a dual resident corporation in a nonrecognition transaction, as defined in section 7701(a)(45), or any assets otherwise transferred to the corporation as a contribution to capital, at any time during the three taxable years immediately preceding the taxable year in which the corporation ceases to be a dual resident corporation or at any time thereafter. Tainted assets shall not include assets that were acquired by such dual resident corporation on or before December 31, 1986.

(4) *Exceptions.*—Income derived from assets acquired by a dual resident corporation shall not be subject to the limitation described in paragraph (e)(1) of this section, if—

(i) For the taxable year in which the assets were acquired, the corporation did not have a dual consolidated loss (or a carry forward of a dual consolidated loss to such year); or

(ii) The assets were acquired as replacement property in the ordinary course of business.

(f) *Computation of foreign tax credit limitations.*—If a dual resident corporation or separate unit is subject to paragraph (d)(2) of this section, the consolidated group or unaffiliated domestic owner shall compute its foreign tax credit limitation by applying the limitations of paragraph (d)(2). Thus, the dual consolidated loss is not taken into account until the year in which it is absorbed.

(g) *Exception.*—(1) *Elective agreement in place between the United States and a foreign country.*—Paragraph (b) of this section shall not apply to a dual consolidated loss to the extent the dual resident corporation, or domestic owner of a separate unit, elects to deduct the loss in the United States pursuant to an agreement entered into between the United States and a foreign country that puts into place an elective procedure through which losses offset income in only one country.

(2) *Elective relief provision.*—(i) *In general.*—Paragraph (b) of this section shall not apply to a dual consolidated loss if the consolidated group, unaffiliated dual resident corporation, or unaffiliated domes-

tic owner elects to be bound by the provisions of this paragraph (g)(2). In order to elect relief under this paragraph (g)(2), the consolidated group, unaffiliated dual resident corporation, or unaffiliated domestic owner must attach to its timely filed (including extensions) U.S. income tax return for the taxable year in which the dual consolidated loss is incurred an agreement described in paragraph (g)(2)(i)(A) of this section. The agreement must be signed under penalties of perjury by the person who signs the return. For taxable years beginning after December 31, 2002, the agreement attached to the income tax return of the consolidated group, unaffiliated dual resident corporation or unaffiliated domestic owner pursuant to the preceding sentence may be an unsigned copy. If an unsigned copy is attached to the return, the consolidated group, unaffiliated dual resident corporation, or unaffiliated domestic owner must retain the original in its records in the manner specified by § 1.6001-1(e). The agreement must include the following items, in paragraphs labeled to correspond with the items set forth in paragraph (g)(2)(i)(A) through (F) of this section.

(A) A statement that the document submitted is an election and an agreement under the provisions of paragraph (g)(2) of this section.

(B) The name, address, identifying number, and place and date of incorporation of the dual resident corporation, and the country or countries that tax the dual resident corporation on its worldwide income or on a residence basis, or, in the case of a separate unit, identification of the separate unit, including the name under which it conducts business, its principal activity, and the country in which its principal place of business is located.

(C) An agreement by the consolidated group, unaffiliated dual resident corporation, or unaffiliated domestic owner to comply with all of the provisions of § 1.1503-2(g)(2)(iii)-(vii).

(D) A statement of the amount of the dual consolidated loss covered by the agreement.

(E) A certification that no portion of the dual resident corporation's or separate unit's losses, expenses, or deductions taken into account in computing the dual consolidated loss has been, or will be, used to offset the income of any other person under the income tax laws of a foreign country.

(F) A certification that arrangements have been made to ensure that no portion of the dual consolidated loss will be used to offset the income of another person under the laws of a foreign country and that the consolidated group, unaffiliated dual resident corporation, or unaffiliated domestic owner will be informed of any such foreign use of any portion of the dual consolidated loss.

(ii) *Consistency rule.*—(A) If any loss, expense, or deduction taken into account in computing the dual consolidated loss of a dual resident corporation or separate unit is used under the laws of a foreign country to offset the income of another person, then the following other dual consolidated losses (if any) shall be treated as also having been used to offset income of another person under the laws of such foreign country, but only if the income tax laws of the foreign country permit any loss, expense, or deduction taken into account in computing the other dual consolidated loss to be used to offset the income of another person in the same taxable year:

(1) Any dual consolidated loss of a dual resident corporation that is a member of the same consolidated group of which the first dual resident corporation or domestic owner is a member, if any loss, expense, or deduction taken into account in computing such dual consolidated loss is recognized under the income tax laws of such country in the same taxable year; and

(2) Any dual consolidated loss of a separate unit that is owned by the same domestic owner that owns the first separate unit, or that is owned by any member of the same consolidated group of which the first dual resident corporation or domestic owner is a member, if any loss, expense, or deduction taken into account in computing such dual consolidated loss is recognized under the income tax laws of such country in the same taxable year.

(B) The following examples illustrate the application of this paragraph (g)(2)(ii).

Example 1. P, a domestic corporation, owns A and B, which are domestic corporations, and C, a Country X corporation. A is subject to the income tax laws of Country X on a residence basis and, thus, is a dual resident corporation. B conducts business in Country X through a branch, which is a separate unit under paragraph (c)(3) of this section. The income tax laws of Country X permit branches of foreign corporations to elect to file consolidated returns with Country X affiliates. In Year 1, A incurs a dual consolidated loss, which is used to offset the income of C under the Country X form of consolidation. The branch of B also incurs a net operating loss. However, B elects not to use the loss on a Country X consolidated return to offset the income of foreign affiliates. The use of A's loss to offset the income of C in Country X will cause the separate unit of B to be treated as if it too had used its dual consolidated loss to offset the income of an affiliate in Country X. Therefore, an election and agreement under this paragraph (g)(2) cannot be made with respect to the separate unit's dual consolidated loss.

Example 2. The facts are the same as in *Example 1,* except that the income tax laws of Country X do not permit branches of foreign corporations to file consolidated income tax returns with Country X affiliates. Therefore, an election and agreement described in this paragraph (g)(2) may be made for the dual consolidated loss incurred by the separate unit of B.

(iii) *Triggering events requiring the recapture of dual consolidated losses.*—(A) The consolidated group, unaffiliated dual resident corporation, or unaffiliated domestic owner must agree that, if there is a triggering event described in this paragraph (g)(2)(iii), and no exception applies under paragraph (g)(2)(iv) of this section, the consolidated group, unaffiliated dual resident corporation, or unaffiliated domestic owner will recapture and report as income the amount of the dual consolidated loss provided in paragraph (g)(2)(vii) of this section on its tax return for the taxable year in which the triggering event occurs (or, when the triggering event is a use of the loss for foreign purposes, the taxable year that includes the last day of the foreign tax year during which such use occurs). In addition, the consolidated group, unaffiliated dual resident corporation, or unaffiliated domestic owner must pay any applicable interest charge required by paragraph (g)(2)(vii) of this section. For purposes of this section, any of the following events shall constitute a triggering event:

(1) In any taxable year up to and including the 15th taxable year following the year in which the dual consolidated loss that is the subject of the agreement filed under this paragraph (g)(2) was incurred, any portion of the losses, expenses, or deductions taken into account in computing the dual consolidated loss is used by any means to offset the income of any other person under the income tax laws of a foreign country;

(2) An affiliated dual resident corporation or affiliated domestic owner ceases to be a member of the consolidated group that filed the election. For purposes of this paragraph (g)(2)(iii)(A)(*2*), a dual resident corporation or domestic owner shall be considered to cease to be a member of the consolidated group if it is no longer a member of the group within the meaning of § 1.1502-1(b), or if the group ceases to exist because the common parent is no longer in existence or is no longer a common parent or the group no longer files on the basis of a consolidated return. Such disaffiliation, however, shall not constitute a triggering event if the taxpayer demonstrates, to the satisfaction of the Commissioner, that the dual resident corporation's or separate unit's losses, expenses, or deductions cannot be used to offset income of another person under the laws of a foreign country at any time after the affiliated dual resident corporation or affiliated domestic owner ceases to be a member of the consolidated group;

(3) An unaffiliated dual resident corporation or unaffiliated domestic owner becomes a member of a consolidated group. Such affiliation of the dual resident corporation or domestic owner, however, shall not constitute a triggering event if the taxpayer demonstrates, to the satisfaction of the Commissioner, that the losses, expenses, or deductions of the dual resident corporation or separate unit cannot be used to offset the income of another person under the laws of a foreign country at any time after the dual resident corporation or domestic owner becomes a member of the consolidated group.

(4) A dual resident corporation transfers assets in a transaction that results, under the laws of a foreign country, in a carryover of its losses, expenses, or deductions. For purposes of this paragraph (g)(2)(iii) (A)(*4*), a transfer, either in a single transaction or a series of transactions within a twelve-month period, of 50% or more of the dual resident corporation's assets (measured by the fair market value of the assets at the time of such transfer (or for multiple transactions, at the time of the first transfer)) shall be deemed a triggering event, unless the taxpayer demonstrates, to the satisfaction of the Commissioner, that the transfer of assets did not result in a carryover under foreign law of the dual resident corporation's losses, expenses, or deductions to the transferee of the assets;

(5) A domestic owner of a separate unit transfers assets of the separate unit in a transaction that results, under the laws of a foreign country, in a carryover of the separate unit's losses, expenses, or deductions. For purposes of this paragraph (g)(2)(iii)(A)(*5*), a transfer, either in a single transaction or a series of transactions over a twelve-month period, of 50% or more of the separate unit's assets

(measured by the fair market value of the assets at the time of the transfer (or for multiple transfers, at the time of the first transfer)), shall be deemed a triggering event, unless the taxpayer demonstrates, to the satisfaction of the Commissioner, that the transfer of assets did not result in a carryover under foreign law of the separate unit's losses, expenses, or deductions to the transferee of the assets;

(6) An unaffiliated dual resident corporation or unaffiliated domestic owner becomes a foreign corporation by means of a transaction (*e.g.*, a reorganization) that, for foreign tax purposes, is not treated as involving a transfer of assets (and carryover of losses) to a new entity. Such a transaction, however, shall not constitute a triggering event if the taxpayer demonstrates, to the satisfaction of the Commissioner, that the dual resident corporation's or separate unit's losses, expenses, or deductions cannot be used to offset income of another person under the laws of the foreign country at any time after the unaffiliated dual resident corporation or unaffiliated domestic owner becomes a foreign corporation.

(7) A domestic owner of a separate unit, either in a single transaction or a series of transactions within a twelve-month period, sells, or otherwise disposes of, 50% or more of the interest in the separate unit (measured by voting power or value) owned by the domestic owner on the last day of the taxable year in which the dual consolidated loss was incurred. For purposes of this paragraph (g)(2)(iii)(A)*(7)*, the domestic owner shall be deemed to have disposed of its entire interest in a hybrid entity separate unit if such hybrid entity becomes classified as a foreign corporation for U.S. tax purposes. The disposition of 50% or more of the interest in a separate unit, however, shall not constitute a triggering event if the taxpayer demonstrates, to the satisfaction of the Commissioner, that the losses, expenses, or deductions of the separate unit cannot be used to offset income of another person under the laws of the foreign country at any time after the disposition of the interest in the separate unit; or

(8) The consolidated group, unaffiliated dual resident corporation, or unaffiliated domestic owner fails to file a certification required under paragraph (g)(2)(vi)(B) of this section.

(B) A taxpayer wishing to rebut the presumption of a triggering event described in paragraphs (g)(2)(iii)(A) (2) through (7) of this section, by demonstrating that the losses, expenses, or deductions of the dual resident corporation or separate unit cannot be carried over or otherwise used under the laws of the foreign country, must attach documents demonstrating such facts to its timely filed U.S. income tax return for the year in which the presumed triggering event occurs.

(C) The following example illustrates this paragraph (g)(2)(iii).

Example. DRC, a domestic corporation, is a member of CG, a consolidated group. DRC is a resident of Country Y for Country Y income tax purposes. Therefore, DRC is a dual resident corporation. In Year 1, DRC incurs a dual consolidated loss of $100. CG files an agreement described in paragraph (g)(2) of this section and, thus, the $100 dual consolidated loss is included in the computation of CG's consolidated taxable income. In Year 6, all of the stock of DRC is sold to P, a domestic corporation that is a member of NG, another consolidated group. The sale of DRC to P is a triggering event under paragraph (g)(2)(iii)(A) of this section, requiring the recapture of the dual consolidated loss. However, the laws of Country Y provide for a five-year carryover period for losses. At the time of DRC's disaffiliation from CG, the losses, expenses and deductions that were included in the computation of the dual consolidated loss had expired for Country Y purposes. Therefore, upon adequate documentation that the losses, expenses, or deductions have expired for Country Y purposes, CG can rebut the presumption that a triggering event has occurred.

(iv) *Exceptions.*—(A) *Acquisition by a member of the consolidated group.*—The following events shall not constitute triggering events, requiring the recapture of the dual consolidated loss under paragraph (g)(2)(vii) of this section:

(1) An affiliated dual resident corporation or affiliated domestic owner ceases to be a member of a consolidated group solely by reason of a transaction in which a member of the same consolidated group succeeds to the tax attributes of the dual resident corporation or domestic owner under the provisions of section 381;

(2) Assets of an affiliated dual resident corporation or assets of a separate unit of an affiliated domestic owner are acquired by a member of its consolidated group in any other transaction; or

(3) An affiliated domestic owner of a separate unit transfers its interest in the separate unit to another member of its consolidated group.

(B) *Acquisition by an unaffiliated domestic corporation or a new consolidated group.*—*(1)* If all the requirements of paragraph (g)(2)(iv)(B)*(3)* of this section are met, the following events shall not constitute triggering events requiring the recapture of the dual consolidated loss under paragraph (g)(2)(vii) of this section:

(i) An affiliated dual resident corporation or affiliated domestic owner becomes an unaffiliated domestic corporation or a member of a new consolidated group (other than in a transaction described in paragraph (g)(2)(iv)(B)(2)*(ii)* of this section);

(ii) Assets of a dual resident corporation or a separate unit are acquired by an unaffiliated domestic corporation or a member of a new consolidated group; or

(iii) A domestic owner of a separate unit transfers its interest in the separate unit to an unaffiliated domestic corporation or to a member of a new consolidated group.

(2) If the requirements of paragraph (g)(2)(iv)(B)*(3)**(iii)* of this section are met, the following events shall not constitute triggering events requiring the recapture of the dual consolidated loss under paragraph (g)(2)(vii) of this section—

(i) An unaffiliated dual resident corporation or unaffiliated domestic owner becomes a member of a consolidated group;

(ii) A consolidated group that filed an agreement under this paragraph (g)(2) ceases to exist as a result of a transaction described in § 1.1502-13(j)(5)(i) (other than a transaction in which any member of the terminating group, or the successor-in-interest of such member, is not a member of the surviving group immediately after the terminating group ceases to exist).

(3) If the following requirements (as applicable) are satisfied, the events listed in paragraphs (g)(2)(iv)(B)*(1)* and (2) of this section shall not constitute triggering events requiring recapture under paragraph (g)(2)(vii) of this section.

(i) The consolidated group, unaffiliated dual resident corporation, or unaffiliated domestic owner that filed the agreement under this paragraph (g)(2) and the unaffiliated domestic corporation or new consolidated group must enter into a closing agreement with the Internal Revenue Service providing that the consolidated group, unaffiliated dual resident corporation, or unaffiliated domestic owner and the unaffiliated domestic corporation or new consolidated group will be jointly and severally liable for the total amount of the recapture of dual consolidated loss and interest charge required in paragraph (g)(2)(vii) of this section, if there is a triggering event described in paragraph (g)(2)(iii) of this section;

(ii) The unaffiliated domestic corporation or new consolidated group must agree to treat any potential recapture amount under paragraph (g)(2)(vii) of this section as unrealized built-in gain for purposes of section 384(a), subject to any applicable exceptions thereunder;

(iii) The unaffiliated domestic corporation or new consolidated group must file, with its timely filed (including extensions) income tax return for the taxable year in which the event described in paragraph (g)(2)(iv)(B)(1) or (2) of this section occurs, an agreement described in paragraph (g)(2)(i) of this section (new (g)(2)(i) agreement), whereby it assumes the same obligations with respect to the dual consolidated loss as the corporation or consolidated group that filed the original (g)(2)(i) agreement with respect to that loss. The new (g)(2)(i) agreement must be signed under penalties of perjury by the person who signs the return and must include a reference to this paragraph (g)(2)(iv)(B)(3)(iii). For taxable years beginning after December 31, 2002, the agreement attached to the return pursuant to the preceding sentence may be an unsigned copy. If an unsigned copy is attached to the return, the corporation or consolidated group must retain the original in its records in the manner specified by § 1.6001-1(e).

(C) *Subsequent triggering events.*—Any triggering event described in paragraph (g)(2)(iii) of this section that occurs subsequent to one of the transactions described in paragraph (g)(2)(iv)(A) or (B) of this section and does not fall within the exceptions provided in paragraph (g)(2)(iv)(A) or (B) of this section shall require recapture under paragraph (g)(2)(vii) of this section.

(D) Example. The following example illustrates the application of paragraph (g)(2)(iv)(B)(2)*(ii)* of this section:

Example. (i) Facts. C is the common parent of a consolidated group (the C Group) that includes DRC, a domestic corporation. DRC is a dual resident corporation and incurs a dual consolidated loss in its taxable year ending December 31, Year 1. The C Group elects to be bound by the provisions of this paragraph (g)(2) with respect to the Year 1 dual consolidated loss. No member of the C Group incurs a dual consolidated loss in Year 2. On December 31, Year 2, stock of C is acquired by D in a transaction described in § 1.1502-13(j)(5)(i). As a result of the acquisition, all the C Group members, including DRC, become members of a consolidated group of which D is the common parent (the D Group).

(ii) Acquisition not a triggering event. Under paragraph (g)(2)(iv)(B)(*2*)(*ii*) of this section, the acquisition by D of the C Group is not an event requiring the recapture of the Year 1 dual consolidated loss of DRC, or the payment of an interest charge, as described in paragraph (g)(2)(vii) of this section, provided that the D Group files the new (g)(2)(i) agreement described in paragraph (g)(2)(iv)(B)(*3*)(*iii*) of this section.

(iii) Subsequent event. A triggering event occurs on December 31, Year 3, that requires recapture by the D Group of the dual consolidated loss that DRC incurred in Year 1, as well as the payment of an interest charge, as provided in paragraph (g)(2)(vii) of this section. Each member of the D Group, including DRC and the other former members of the C Group, is severally liable for the additional tax (and the interest charge) due upon the recapture of the dual consolidated loss of DRC.

(v) *Ordering rules for determining the foreign use of losses.*—If the laws of a foreign country provide for the use of losses of a dual resident corporation to offset the income of another person but do not provide applicable rules for determining the order in which such losses are used to offset the income of another person in a taxable year, then for purposes of this section, the following rules shall govern:

(A) If under the laws of the foreign country the dual resident corporation has losses from different taxable years, the dual resident corporation shall be deemed to use first the losses from the earliest taxable year from which a loss may be carried forward or back for foreign law purposes.

(B) Any net loss, or income, that the dual resident corporation has in a taxable year shall first be used to offset net income, or loss, recognized by affiliates of the dual resident corporation in the same taxable year before any carryover of the dual resident corporation's losses is considered to be used to offset any income from the taxable year.

(C) Where different losses, expenses, or deductions (*e.g.*, capital losses and ordinary losses) of a dual resident corporation incurred in the same taxable year are available to offset the income of another person, the different losses shall be deemed to offset such income on a pro rata basis.

Example. DRC, a domestic corporation, is taxed as a resident under the tax laws of Country Y. Therefore, DRC is a dual resident corporation. FA is a Country Y affiliate of DRC. Country Y's tax laws permit affiliated corporations to file a form of consolidated return. In Year 1, DRC incurs a capital loss of $80 which, for Country Y purposes, offsets completely $30 of capital gain recognized by FA. Neither corporation has any other taxable income or loss for the year. In Year 1 (and in other years), DRC recognizes the same amount of income for U.S. purposes as it does for Country Y purposes. Under paragraph (d)(1)(i) of this section, however, DRC's $80 capital loss is not a dual consolidated loss. In Year 2, DRC incurs a net operating loss of $100, while FA incurs a net operating loss of $50. DRC's $100 loss is a dual consolidated loss. Since the dual consolidated loss is not used to offset the income of another person under Country Y law, DRC is permitted to file an agreement described in this paragraph (g)(2). In Year 3, DRC has a net operating loss of $10 and FA has capital gains of $60. For Country Y purposes, DRC's $10 net operating loss is used to offset $10 of FA's $60 capital gain. DRC's $10 loss is a dual consolidated loss. Because the loss is used to offset FA's income, DRC will not be able to file an agreement under this paragraph (g)(2) with respect to the loss. Country Y permits FA's remaining $50 of Year 3 income to be offset by carryover losses. However, Country Y has no applicable rules for determining which carryover losses from Years 1 and 2 are used to offset such income. Under the ordering rules of paragraph (g)(2)(v)(A) of this section, none of DRC's $100 Year 2 loss will be deemed to offset FA's remaining $50 of Year 3 income. Instead, the $50 of capital loss carryover from Year 1 will be considered to offset the income.

(vi) *Reporting requirements.*—(A) *In general.*—The consolidated group, unaffiliated dual resident corporation, or unaffiliated domestic owner must answer the applicable questions regarding dual consolidated losses on its U.S. income tax return filed for the year in which the dual consolidated loss is incurred and for each of the following fifteen taxable years.

(B) *Annual certification.*—Except as provided in §1.1503-2(g)(2)(vi)(C), until and unless Form 1120 or the Schedules thereto contain questions pertaining to dual consolidated losses, the consolidated group, unaffiliated dual resident corporation, or unaffiliated domestic owner must file with its income tax return for each of the 15 taxable years following the taxable year in which the dual consolidated loss is incurred a certification that the losses, expenses, or deductions that make up the dual consolidated loss have not been used to offset the income of another person under the tax laws of a foreign country. For taxable years beginning before January 1, 2003, the annual certification must be signed under penalties of perjury by a person authorized to sign the agreement described in §1.1503-2(g)(2)(i). For taxable years beginning after December 31, 2002, the certification is verified by signing the return with which the certification is filed. The certification for a taxable year must identify the dual consolidated loss to which it pertains by setting forth the taxpayer's year in which the loss was incurred and the amount of such loss. In addition, the certification must warrant that arrangements have been made to ensure that the loss will not be used to offset the income of another person under the laws of a foreign country and that the taxpayer will be informed of any such foreign use of any portion of the loss. If dual consolidated losses of more than one taxable year are subject to the rules of this paragraph (g)(2)(vi)(B), the certifications for those years may be combined in a single document but each dual consolidated loss must be separately identified.

(C) *Exception.*—A consolidated group or unaffiliated domestic owner is not required to file annual certifications under paragraph (g)(2)(vi)(B) of this section with respect to a dual consolidated loss of any separate unit other than a hybrid entity separate unit.

(vii) *Recapture of loss and interest charge.*—(A) *Presumptive rule.*—(*1*) *Amount of recapture.*—Except as otherwise provided in this paragraph (g)(2)(vii), upon the occurrence of a triggering event described in paragraph (g)(2)(iii) of this section, the taxpayer shall recapture and report as gross income the total amount of the dual consolidated loss to which the triggering event applies on its income tax return for the taxable year in which the triggering event occurs (or, when the triggering event is a use of the loss for foreign tax purposes, the taxable year that includes the last day of the foreign tax year during which such use occurs).

(*2*) *Interest charge.*—In connection with the recapture, the taxpayer shall pay an interest charge. Except as otherwise provided in this paragraph (g)(2)(vii), such interest shall be determined under the rules of section 6601(a) as if the additional tax owed as a result of the recapture had accrued and been due and owing for the taxable year in which the losses, expenses, or deductions taken into account in computing the dual consolidated loss gave rise to a tax benefit for U.S. income tax purposes. For purposes of this paragraph (g)(2)(vii)(A)(*2*), a tax benefit shall be considered to have arisen in a taxable year in which such losses, expenses or deductions reduced U.S. taxable income.

(B) *Rebuttal of presumptive rule.*—(*1*) *Amount of recapture.*—The amount of dual consolidated loss that must be recaptured under this paragraph (g)(2)(vii) may be reduced if the taxpayer demonstrates, to the satisfaction of the Commissioner, the offset permitted by this paragraph (g)(2)(vii)(B). The reduction in the amount of recapture is the amount by which the dual consolidated loss would have offset other taxable income reported on a timely filed U.S. income tax return for any taxable year up to and including the year of the triggering event if such loss had been subject to the restrictions of paragraph (b) of this section (and therefore had been subject to the separate return limitation year restrictions of §1.1502-21A(c) or 1.1502-21(c) (as appropriate)) commencing in the taxable year in which the loss was incurred. A taxpayer utilizing this rebuttal rule must attach to its timely filed U.S. income tax return a separate accounting showing that the income for each year that offsets the dual resident corporation's or separate unit's recapture amount is attributable only to the dual resident corporation or separate unit.

(*2*) *Interest charge.*—The interest charge imposed under this paragraph (g)(2)(vii) may be appropriately reduced if the taxpayer demonstrates, to the satisfaction of the Commissioner, that the net interest owed would have been less than that provided in paragraph (g)(2)(vii)(A)(*2*) of this section if the taxpayer had filed an amended return for the year in which the loss was incurred, and for any other affected years up to and including the year of recapture, treating the dual consolidated loss as a loss subject to the restrictions of paragraph (b) of this section (and therefore subject to the separate return limitation year restrictions of §1.1502-21A(c) or 1.1502-21(c) (as appropriate)). A taxpayer utilizing this rebuttal rule must attach to its timely filed U.S. income tax return a computation demonstrating the reduction in the net interest owed as a result of treating the dual consolidated loss as a loss subject to the restrictions of paragraph (b) of this section.

(C) *Computation of taxable income in year of recapture.—(1) Presumptive rule.*—Except as otherwise provided in paragraph (g)(2)(vii)(C)(2) of this section, for purposes of computing the taxable income for the year of recapture, no current, carryover or carryback losses of the dual resident corporation or separate unit, of other members of the consolidated group, or of the domestic owner that are not attributable to the separate unit, may offset and absorb the recapture amount.

(2) Rebuttal of presumptive rule.—The recapture amount included in gross income may be offset and absorbed by that portion of the taxpayer's (consolidated or separate) net operating loss carryover that is attributable to the dual consolidated loss being recaptured, if the taxpayer demonstrates, to the satisfaction of the Commissioner, the amount of such portion of the carryover. A taxpayer utilizing this rebuttal rule must attach to its timely filed U.S. income tax return a computation demonstrating the amount of net operating loss carryover that, under this paragraph (g)(2)(vii)(C)(2), may absorb the recapture amount included in gross income.

(D) *Character and source of recapture income.*—The amount recaptured under this paragraph (g)(2)(vii) shall be treated as ordinary income in the year of recapture. The amount recaptured shall be treated as income having the same source and falling within the same separate category for purposes of section 904 as the dual consolidated loss being recaptured.

(E) *Reconstituted net operating loss.*—Commencing in the taxable year immediately following the year in which the dual consolidated loss is recaptured, the dual resident corporation or separate unit shall be treated as having a net operating loss in an amount equal to the amount actually recaptured under paragraph (g)(2)(vii)(A) or (B) of this section. This reconstituted net operating loss shall be subject to the restrictions of paragraph (b) of this section (and therefore, the separate return limitation year restrictions of §§1.1502-21A(c) or 1.1502-21T(c) (as appropriate)). The net operating loss shall be available only for carryover, under section 172(b), to taxable years following the taxable year of recapture. For purposes of determining the remaining carryover period, the loss shall be treated as if it had been recognized in the taxable year in which the dual consolidated loss that is the basis of the recapture amount was incurred.

(F) *Consequences of failing to comply with recapture provisions.—(1) In general.*—If the taxpayer fails to comply with the recapture provisions of this paragraph (g)(2)(vii) upon the occurrence of a triggering event, then the dual resident corporation or separate unit that incurred the dual consolidated loss (or a successor-in-interest) shall not be eligible for the relief provided in paragraph (g)(2) of this section with respect to any dual consolidated losses incurred in the five taxable years beginning with the taxable year in which recapture is required.

(2) Exceptions.—In the case of a triggering event other than a use of the losses, expenses, or deductions taken into account in computing the dual consolidated loss to offset income of another person under the income tax laws of a foreign country, this rule shall not apply in the following circumstances:

(i) The failure to recapture is due to reasonable cause; or

(ii) A taxpayer seeking to rebut the presumption of a triggering event satisfies the filing requirements of paragraph (g)(2)(iii)(B) of this section.

(G) *Examples.*—The following examples illustrate this paragraph (g)(2)(vii).

Example 1. P, a domestic corporation, files a consolidated return with DRC, a dual resident corporation. In Year 1, DRC incurs a dual consolidated loss of $100 and P earns $100. P files an agreement under this paragraph (g)(2). Therefore, the consolidated group is permitted to offset P's $100 of income with DRC's $100 loss. In Year 2, DRC earns $30, which is completely offset by a $30 net operating loss incurred by P. In Year 3, DRC earns income of $25 while P recognizes no income or loss. In addition, there is a triggering event in Year 3. Therefore, under the presumptive rule of paragraph (g)(2)(vii)(A) of this section, DRC must recapture $100. However, the $100 recapture amount may be reduced by $25 (the amount by which the dual consolidated loss would have offset other taxable income if it had been subject to the separate return limitation year restrictions from Year 1) upon adequate documentation of such offset under paragraph (g)(2)(vii)(B)(*1*) of this section. Commencing in Year 4, the $100 (or $75) recapture amount is treated as a loss incurred by DRC in a separate return limitation year, subject to the restrictions of §1.1502-21A(c) or 1.1502-21(c), as appropriate. The carryover period of the loss, for purposes of section 172(b), will start from Year 1, when the dual consolidated loss was incurred.

Example 2. The facts are the same as in *Example 1,* except that in Year 2, DRC earns $75 and P earns $50. In Year 3, DRC earns $25 while P earns $30. A triggering event occurs in Year 3. The $100 presumptive amount of recapture can be reduced to zero by the $75 and $25 earned by DRC in Years 2 and 3, respectively, upon adequate documentation of such offset under paragraph (g)(2)(vii)(B)(*1*) of this section. Nevertheless, an interest charge will be owed. Under the presumptive rule of paragraph (g)(2)(vii)(A)(2) of this section, interest will be charged on the additional tax owed on the $100 of recapture income as if the tax had accrued in Year 1 (the year in which the dual consolidated loss reduced the income of P). However, the net interest will be reduced to the amount that would have been owed if the consolidated group had filed amended returns, treating the dual consolidated loss as a loss subject to the separate return limitation year restrictions of §1.1502-21A(c) or 1.1502-21(c), as appropriate, upon adequate documentation of such reduction of interest under paragraph (g)(2)(vii)(B)(2) of this section.

Example 3. P, a domestic corporation, owns DRC, a domestic corporation that is subject to the income tax laws of Country Z on a residence basis. DRC owns FE, a Country Z corporation. In Year 1, DRC incurs a net operating loss for U.S. tax purposes. Under the tax laws of Country Z, the loss is not recognized until Year 3. The Year 1 net operating loss is a dual consolidated loss under paragraph (c)(5) of this section. The consolidated group elects relief under paragraph (g)(2) of this section by filing the appropriate agreement and uses the dual consolidated loss on its U.S. income tax return. In Year 3, the dual consolidated loss is used under the laws of Country Z to offset the income of FE, which is a triggering event under paragraph (g)(2)(iii) of this section. However, the consolidated group does not recapture the dual consolidated loss. The consolidated group's failure to comply with the recapture provisions of this paragraph (g)(2)(vii) prevents DRC from being eligible for the relief provided under paragraph (g)(2) of this section for any dual consolidated losses incurred in Years 3 through 7, inclusive.

(h) *Effective date.—(1) In general.*—These regulations are effective for taxable years beginning on or after October 1, 1992. Section 1.1503-2A is effective for taxable years beginning after December 31, 1986, and before October 1, 1992. Paragraph (g)(2)(iv)(B)(2) of this section shall apply with respect to transactions otherwise constituting triggering events occurring on or after January 1, 2002.

(2) *Taxpayers that have filed for relief under §1.1503-2A.—(i) In general.*—Except as provided in paragraph (h)(ii)(b) of this section, taxpayers that have filed agreements described in §1.1503-2A(c)(3) or certifications described in §1.1503-2A(d)(3) shall continue to be subject to the provisions of such agreements or certifications, including the amended return or recapture requirements applicable in the event of a triggering event, for the remaining term of such agreements or certifications.

(ii) *Special transition rule.*—A taxpayer that has filed an agreement described in §1.1503-2A(c)(3) or a certification described in §1.1503-2A(d)(3) and that is in compliance with the provisions of §1.1503-2A may elect to replace such agreement or certification with an agreement described in paragraph (g)(2)(i) of this section. However, a taxpayer making this election must replace all agreements and certifications filed under §1.1503-2A. If the taxpayer is a consolidated group, the election must be made with respect to all dual resident corporations or separate units within the group. Likewise, if the taxpayer is an unaffiliated domestic owner, the election must be made with respect to all separate units of the domestic owner. The taxpayer must file the replacement agreement with its timely filed income tax return for its first taxable year commencing on or after October 1, 1992, stating that such agreement is a replacement for the agreement filed under §1.1503-2A(c)(3) or the certification filed under §1.1503-2A(d)(3) and identifying the taxable year for which the original agreement or certification was filed. A single agreement described in paragraph (g)(2)(i) of this section may be filed to replace more than one agreement or certification filed under §1.1503-2A; however, each dual consolidated loss must be separately identified. A taxpayer may also elect to apply §1.1503-2 for all open years, with respect to agreements filed under §1.1503-2A(c)(3) or certifications filed under § 1.1503-2A(d)(3), in cases where the agreement or certification is no longer in effect and the taxpayer has complied with the provisions of § 1.1503-2A. For example, a taxpayer may have had a triggering event under § 1.1503-2A that is not a triggering event under § 1.1503-2. If the taxpayer fully complied with the requirements of the agreement entered into under § 1.1503-2A(c)(3) and filed amended U.S. income tax returns within the time required under § 1.1503-2A(c)(3), the taxpayer may file amended U.S. income tax returns consistent with the position that the earlier triggering event is no longer a triggering event.

(3) *Taxpayers that are in compliance with § 1.1503-2A but have not filed for relief thereunder.*—A taxpayer that is in compliance with the provisions of § 1.1503-2A but has not filed an agreement described in § 1.1503-2A(c)(3) or a certification described in § 1.1503-2A(d)(3) may elect to have the provisions of § 1.1503-2 apply for any open year. In particular, a taxpayer may elect to apply the provisions of § 1.1503-2 in a case where the dual consolidated loss has been subjected to the separate return limitation year restrictions of § 1.1502-21A(c) or 1.1502-21(c) (as appropriate) but the losses, expenses, or deductions taken into account in computing the dual consolidated loss have not been used to offset the income of another person for foreign tax purposes. However, if a taxpayer is a consolidated group, the election must be made with respect to all dual resident corporations or separate units within the group. Likewise, if the taxpayer is an unaffiliated domestic owner, the election must be made with respect to all separate units of the domestic owner. [Reg. § 1.1503-2.]

☐ [*T.D. 8434, 9-4-92. Amended by T.D. 8597, 7-12-95; T.D. 8677, 6-26-96; T.D. 8823, 6-25-99; T.D. 9084, 7-29-2003; T.D. 9100, 12-18-2003 and T.D. 9300, 12-7-2006.*]

§ 1.1503(d)-1. Definitions and special rules for filings under section 1503(d).—(a) *In general.*—This section and §§ 1.1503(d)-2 through 1.1503(d)-8 provide rules concerning the determination and use of dual consolidated losses pursuant to section 1503(d). Paragraph (b) of this section provides definitions that apply for purposes of this section and §§ 1.1503(d)-2 through 1.1503(d)-8. Paragraph (c) of this section provides a reasonable cause exception and a signature requirement for filings.

(b) *Definitions.*—The following definitions apply for purposes of this section and §§ 1.1503(d)-2 through 1.1503(d)-8:

(1) Domestic corporation means an entity classified as a domestic corporation under section 7701(a)(3) and (4) or otherwise treated as a domestic corporation by the Internal Revenue Code, including, but not limited to, sections 269B, 953(d), 1504(d), and 7874. However, solely for purposes of section 1503(d), the term domestic corporation shall not include a regulated investment company as defined in section 851, a real estate investment trust as defined in section 856, or an S corporation as defined in section 1361.

(2) Dual resident corporation means—

(i) A domestic corporation that is subject to an income tax of a foreign country on its worldwide income or on a residence basis. A corporation is taxed on a residence basis if it is taxed as a resident under the laws of the foreign country;

(ii) A foreign insurance company that makes an election to be treated as a domestic corporation pursuant to section 953(d) and is treated as a member of an affiliated group for purposes of chapter 6, even if such company is not subject to an income tax of a foreign country on its worldwide income or on a residence basis. See section 953(d)(3); and

(iii) A domestic consenting corporation (as defined in § 301.7701-3(c)(3)(i) of this chapter), as provided in paragraph (c)(1) of this section. See § 1.1503(d)-7(c)(41) for an example illustrating the application of section 1503(d) to a domestic consenting corporation.

(3) Hybrid entity means an entity that is not taxable as an association for Federal tax purposes, but is subject to an income tax of a foreign country as a corporation (or otherwise at the entity level) either on its worldwide income or on a residence basis.

(4) *Separate unit.*—(i) *In general.*—The term separate unit means either of the following that is carried on or owned, as applicable, directly or indirectly, by a domestic corporation (including a dual resident corporation):

(A) Except to the extent provided in paragraph (b)(4)(iii) of this section, a business operation outside the United States that, if carried on by a U.S. person, would constitute a foreign branch as defined in § 1.367(a)-6T(g)(1) (foreign branch separate unit).

(B) An interest in a hybrid entity (hybrid entity separate unit).

(ii) *Separate unit combination rule.*.—Except as otherwise provided in this paragraph, if a domestic owner, or two or more domestic owners that are members of the same consolidated group, have two or more separate units (individual separate units), then all such individual separate units that are located (in the case of a foreign branch separate unit) or subject to an income tax either on their worldwide income or on a residence basis (in the case of a hybrid entity an interest in which is a hybrid entity separate unit) in the same foreign country shall be treated as one separate unit (combined separate unit). See § 1.1503(d)-7(c) *Example 1.* Separate units of a foreign insurance company that is a dual resident corporation under paragraph (b)(2)(ii) of this section, however, shall not be combined with separate units of any other domestic corporation. Except as specifically provided in this section or §§ 1.1503(d)-2 through 1.1503(d)-8, any individual separate unit composing a combined separate unit loses its character as an individual separate unit.

(iii) Business operations that do not constitute a permanent establishment. A business operation carried on by a domestic corporation that is not a dual resident corporation shall not constitute a foreign branch separate unit, provided the business operation:

(A) Is not carried on indirectly through a hybrid entity or a transparent entity; and

(B) Is conducted in a country with which the United States has entered into an income tax convention and is not treated as a permanent establishment pursuant to that convention, or is not otherwise subject to tax on a net basis under that convention. See § 1.1503(d)-7(c) *Example 2.*

(iv) Foreign branch separate units held by dual resident corporations or hybrid entities in the same foreign country. A foreign branch separate unit may be owned by a dual resident corporation, or through a hybrid entity (an interest in which is a separate unit), even where the foreign branch is located in the same foreign country that subjects such dual resident corporation or hybrid entity to tax on its worldwide income or on a residence basis. But see the rule under paragraph (b)(4)(ii) of this section that combines certain same-country hybrid entity separate units and foreign branch separate units. See also § 1.1503(d)-7(c) *Example 1.*

(5) Dual consolidated loss means—

(i) In the case of a dual resident corporation, and except to the extent provided in § 1.1503(d)-5(b), the net operating loss (as defined in section 172(c) and the related regulations) incurred in a year in which the corporation is a dual resident corporation; and

(ii) In the case of a separate unit, the net loss attributable to the separate unit under § 1.1503(d)-5(c) through (e).

(6) *Subject to tax.*—For purposes of determining whether a domestic corporation or another entity is subject to an income tax of a foreign country on its income, the fact that it has no actual income tax liability to the foreign country for a particular taxable year shall not be taken into account.

(7) Foreign country includes any possession of the United States.

(8) Consolidated group has the meaning provided in § 1.1502-1(h).

(9) Domestic owner means—

(i) A domestic corporation (including a dual resident corporation) that has one or more separate units or interests in a transparent entity; and

(ii) In the case of a combined separate unit, a domestic corporation (including a dual resident corporation) that has one or more individual separate units that are treated as part of the combined separate unit under paragraph (b)(4)(ii) of this section.

(10) Affiliated dual resident corporation and affiliated domestic owner mean a dual resident corporation and a domestic owner, respectively, that is a member of a consolidated group.

(11) Unaffiliated dual resident corporation, unaffiliated domestic corporation, and unaffiliated domestic owner mean a dual resident corporation, domestic corporation, and domestic owner, respectively, that is not a member of a consolidated group.

(12) Domestic affiliate means—

(i) A member of an affiliated group, without regard to the exceptions contained in section 1504(b) (other than section 1504(b)(3)) relating to includible corporations;

(ii) A domestic owner;

(iii) A separate unit; or

(iv) An interest in a transparent entity, as defined in paragraph (b)(16) of this section.

(13) *Domestic use.*—See § 1.1503(d)-2.

(14) *Foreign use.*—See § 1.1503(d)-3.

(15) Grantor trust means a trust, any portion of which is treated as being owned by the grantor or another person under subpart E of subchapter J of this chapter.

(16) *Transparent entity.*—(i) *In general.*—The term transparent entity means an entity described in this paragraph (b)(16) where all or a portion of its interests are owned, directly or indirectly, by a domestic corporation. An entity is described in this paragraph (b)(16) if the entity—

(A) Is not taxable as an association for Federal tax purposes;

(B) Is not subject to income tax in a foreign country as a corporation (or otherwise at the entity level) either on its worldwide income or on a residence basis; and

(C) Is not a pass-through entity under the laws of the applicable foreign country. For purposes of applying the preceding sentence, the applicable foreign country is the foreign country in which the relevant foreign branch separate unit is located, or the foreign country that subjects the relevant hybrid entity (an interest in which is a separate unit) or dual resident corporation to an income tax either on its worldwide income or on a residence basis.

(ii) *Example.*—A U.S. limited liability company (LLC) does not elect to be taxed as an association for Federal tax purposes and is not subject to income tax in a foreign country as a corporation (or otherwise at the entity level) either on its worldwide income or on a residence basis. The LLC is owned by a hybrid entity (an interest in which is a separate unit) that is the relevant hybrid entity. Provided the LLC is not treated as a pass-through entity by the applicable foreign country that subjects the relevant hybrid entity to an income tax either on its worldwide income or on a residence basis, the LLC would qualify as a transparent entity. See also § 1.1503(d)-7(c) *Example 26.*

(17) Disregarded entity means an entity that is disregarded as an entity separate from its owner, under § § 301.7701-1 through 301.7701-3 of this chapter, for Federal tax purposes.

(18) Partnership means an entity that is classified as a partnership, under § § 301.7701-1 through 301.7701-3 of this chapter, for Federal tax purposes.

(19) Indirectly, when used in reference to ownership, means ownership through a partnership, a disregarded entity, or a grantor trust, regardless of whether the partnership, disregarded entity, or grantor trust is a U.S. person.

(20) Certification period means the period of time up to and including the fifth taxable year following the year in which the dual consolidated loss that is the subject of a domestic use agreement (as described in § 1.1503(d)-6(d)(1)) was incurred.

(c) *Treatment of domestic consenting corporation as a dual resident corporation.*—(1) *Rule.*—A domestic consenting corporation is treated as a dual resident corporation under paragraph (b)(2)(iii) of this section for a taxable year if, on any day during the taxable year, the following requirements are satisfied:

(i) Under the tax law of a foreign country where a specified foreign tax resident is tax resident, the specified foreign tax resident derives or incurs (or would derive or incur) items of income, gain, deduction, or loss of the domestic consenting corporation (because, for example, the domestic consenting corporation is fiscally transparent under such tax law).

(ii) The specified foreign tax resident bears a relationship to the domestic consenting corporation that is described in section 267(b) or 707(b). See § 1.1503(d)-7(c)(41) for an example illustrating the application of paragraph (c) of this section.

(2) *Definitions.*—The following definitions apply for purposes of this paragraph (c).

(i) The term *fiscally transparent* means, with respect to a domestic consenting corporation or an intermediate entity, fiscally transparent as determined under the principles of § 1.894-1(d)(3)(ii) and (iii), without regard to whether a specified foreign tax resident is a resident of a country that has an income tax treaty with the United States.

(ii) The term *specified foreign tax resident* means a body corporate or other entity or body of persons liable to tax under the tax law of a foreign country as a resident.

(d) *Special rules for filings under section 1503(d).*—(1) *Reasonable cause exception.*—A person that is permitted or required to file an election, agreement, statement, rebuttal, computation, or other information pursuant to section 1503(d) and these regulations, that fails to make such filing in a timely manner, shall be considered to have satisfied the timeliness requirement with respect to such filing if the person is able to demonstrate, to the Area Director, Field Examination, Small Business/Self Employed or the Director of Field Operations, Large and Mid-Size Business (Director) having jurisdiction of the taxpayer's tax return for the taxable year, that such failure was due to reasonable cause and not willful neglect. In determining whether the taxpayer has reasonable cause, the Director shall consider whether the taxpayer acted reasonably and in good faith. In general, the taxpayer must demonstrate that it exercised ordinary care and prudence in meeting its tax obligations but nonetheless did not comply with the prescribed duty within the prescribed time. Whether the taxpayer acted reasonably and in good faith will be determined after considering all the facts and circumstances. The Director shall notify the person in writing within 120 days of the filing if it is determined that the failure to comply was not due to reasonable cause, or if additional time will be needed to make such determination. For this purpose, the 120-day period shall begin on the date the taxpayer is notified in writing that the request has been received and assigned for review. If, once such period commences, the taxpayer is not again notified within 120 days, then the taxpayer shall be deemed to have established reasonable cause. The reasonable cause exception of this paragraph (d) shall only apply if, once the person becomes aware of its failure to file the election, agreement, statement, rebuttal, computation or other information in a timely manner, the person complies with the requirements of paragraph (d)(2) of this section.

(2) *Requirements for reasonable cause relief.*—(i) *Time of submission.*—Requests for reasonable cause relief will only be considered if once the person becomes aware of the failure to file the election, agreement, statement, rebuttal, computation or other information, the person attaches all the documents that should have been filed, as well as a written statement setting forth the reasons for the failure to timely comply, to an amended return that amends the return to which the documents should have been attached pursuant to the rules of section 1503(d) and these regulations.

(ii) *Notice requirement.*—In addition to the requirements of paragraph (d)(2)(i) of this section, the taxpayer must provide a copy of the amended return and all required attachments to the Director as follows:

(A) If the taxpayer is under examination for any taxable year when the taxpayer requests relief, the taxpayer must provide a copy of the amended return and attachments to the personnel conducting the examination.

(B) If the taxpayer is not under examination for any taxable year when the taxpayer requests relief, the taxpayer must provide a copy of the amended return and attachments to the Director having jurisdiction of the taxpayer's return.

(3) *Signature requirement.*—When an election, agreement, statement, rebuttal, computation, or other information is required pursuant to section 1503(d) and these regulations to be attached to and filed by the due date (including extensions) of a U.S. tax return and signed under penalties of perjury by the person who signs the return, the attachment and filing of an unsigned copy is considered to satisfy such requirement, provided the taxpayer retains the original in its records in the manner specified by § 1.6001-1(e). [Reg. § 1.1503(d)-1.]

□ [*T.D. 9315, 3-16-2007. Amended by T.D. 9896, 4-7-2020.*]

§ 1.1503(d)-2. Domestic use.—A domestic use of a dual consolidated loss shall be deemed to occur when the dual consolidated loss is made available to offset, directly or indirectly, the income of a domestic affiliate (other than the dual resident corporation or separate unit that, in each case, incurred the dual consolidated loss) in the taxable year in which the dual consolidated loss is recognized, or in any other taxable year, regardless of whether the dual consolidated loss offsets income under the income tax laws of a foreign country and regardless of whether any income that the dual consolidated loss may offset in the foreign country is, has been, or will be subject to tax in the United States. A domestic use shall be deemed to occur in the year the dual consolidated loss is included in the computation of the taxable income of a consolidated group, unaffiliated dual resident corporation, or an unaffiliated domestic owner, as applicable, even if no tax benefit results from such inclusion in that year. See § 1.1503(d)-7(c) *Examples 2 through 4.* [Reg. § 1.1503(d)-2.]

□ [*T.D. 9315, 3-16-2007.*]

§ 1.1503(d)-3. Foreign use.—(a) *Foreign use.*—(1) *In general.*—Except as provided in paragraph (c) of this section, a foreign use of a dual consolidated loss shall be deemed to occur when any portion of a deduction or loss taken into account in computing the dual consolidated loss is made available under the income tax laws of a foreign country to offset or reduce, directly or indirectly, any item that is recognized as income or gain under such laws and that is, or would be, considered under U.S. tax principles to be an item of—

(i) A foreign corporation as defined in section 7701(a)(3) and (a)(5); or

(ii) A direct or indirect owner of an interest in a hybrid entity, provided such interest is not a separate unit. See § 1.1503(d)-7(c) *Examples 5* through *10* and *37*.

(2) *Indirect use.*—(i) *General rule.*—Except to the extent provided in paragraph (a)(2)(ii) of this section, an item of deduction or loss shall be deemed to be made available indirectly if—

(A) One or more items are taken into account as deductions or losses for foreign tax purposes, but do not give rise to corresponding items of income or gain for U.S. tax purposes; and

(B) The item or items described in paragraph (a)(2)(i)(A) of this section have the effect of making an item of deduction or loss composing the dual consolidated loss available for a foreign use as described in paragraph (a)(1) of this section.

(ii) *Exception.*—The general rule provided in paragraph (a)(2)(i) of this section shall not apply if the consolidated group, unaffiliated domestic owner, or unaffiliated dual resident corporation demonstrates, to the satisfaction of the Commissioner, that the item or items described in paragraph (a)(2)(i)(A) of this section that gave rise to the indirect foreign use—

(A) Were not incurred, or taken into account, with a principal purpose of avoiding the provisions of section 1503(d). For purposes of this paragraph (a)(2)(ii), an item incurred or taken into account as interest for foreign tax purposes, but disregarded for U.S. tax purposes, shall be deemed to have been incurred, or taken into account, with a principal purpose of avoiding the provisions of section 1503(d). Similarly, for purposes of this paragraph (a)(2)(ii), an item incurred or taken into account as the result of an instrument that is treated as debt for foreign tax purposes and equity for U.S. tax purposes, shall be deemed to have been incurred, or taken into account, with a principal purpose of avoiding the provisions of section 1503(d); and

(B) Were incurred, or taken into account, in the ordinary course of the dual resident corporation's or separate unit's trade or business.

(iii) *Examples.*—See § 1.1503(d)-7(c) *Examples 6* through *8*.

(3) *Deemed use.*—See paragraph (e) of this section for a deemed foreign use pursuant to the mirror legislation rule.

(b) *Available for use.*—A foreign use shall be deemed to occur in the year in which any portion of a deduction or loss taken into account in computing the dual consolidated loss is made available for an offset described in paragraph (a) of this section, regardless of whether it actually offsets or reduces any items of income or gain under the income tax laws of the foreign country in such year, and regardless of whether any of the items that may be so offset or reduced are regarded as income under U.S. tax principles.

(c) *Exceptions.*—(1) *In general.*—Paragraphs (c)(2) through (9) of this section provide exceptions to the general definition of foreign use set forth in paragraphs (a) and (b) of this section. These exceptions only apply to a foreign use that occurs solely as a result of the conditions or circumstances described therein, and do not apply if a foreign use occurs in any other case or by any other means. For example, the exception under paragraph (c)(4) of this section (regarding certain interests in partnerships or grantor trusts) shall not apply where the item of deduction or loss is made available through a foreign consolidation regime (or similar method). In addition, these exceptions do not apply when attempting to demonstrate that no foreign use of a dual consolidated loss can occur in any other year by any means under § 1.1503(d)-6(c), (e)(2)(i), or (j)(2). But see § 1.1503(d)-6(e)(2)(ii), which takes into account the exception under paragraph (c)(7) of this section for purposes of rebutting certain asset transfers.

(2) *Election or merger required to enable foreign use.*—Where the laws of a foreign country provide an election that would enable a foreign use, a foreign use shall be considered to occur only if the election is made. Similarly, where the laws of a foreign country would enable a foreign use through a sale, merger, or similar transaction, a foreign use shall be considered to occur only if the sale, merger, or similar transaction occurs.

(3) *Presumed use where no foreign country rule for determining use.*—This paragraph (c)(3) applies if the losses or deductions composing the dual consolidated loss are made available under the laws of a foreign country both to offset income that would constitute a foreign use and to offset income that would not constitute a foreign use, and the laws of the foreign country do not provide applicable rules for determining which income is offset by the losses or deductions. In such a case, the losses or deductions shall be deemed to be made available to offset the income that does not constitute a foreign use, to the extent of such income, before being considered to be made available to offset the income that does constitute a foreign use. See § 1.1503(d)-7(c) *Example 11*.

(4) *Certain interests in partnerships or grantor trusts.*—(i) *General rule.*—Except to the extent provided in paragraph (c)(4)(iii) of this section, this paragraph (c)(4)(i) applies to a dual consolidated loss attributable to an interest in a hybrid entity partnership or a hybrid entity grantor trust, or to a separate unit owned indirectly through a partnership or grantor trust. In such a case, a foreign use will not be considered to occur if the foreign use is solely the result of another person's ownership of an interest in the partnership or grantor trust, as applicable, and the allocation or carry forward of an item of deduction or loss composing such dual consolidated loss as a result of such ownership. See § 1.1503(d)-7(c) *Example 13*.

(ii) *Combined separate unit.*—This paragraph applies to a dual consolidated loss attributable to a combined separate unit that includes an individual separate unit to which paragraph (c)(4)(i) of this section would apply, but for the application of the separate unit combination rule provided under § 1.1503(d)-1(b)(4)(ii). In such a case, paragraph (c)(4)(i) of this section shall apply to the portion of the dual consolidated loss of such combined separate unit that is attributable, as provided under § 1.1503(d)-5(c) through (e), to the individual separate unit (otherwise described in paragraph (c)(4)(i) of this section) that is a component of the combined separate unit. See § 1.1503(d)-7(c) *Example 14*.

(iii) *Reduction in interest.*—The exception under paragraph (c)(4)(i) of this section shall not apply if, at any time following the year in which the dual consolidated loss is incurred, there is more than a de minimis reduction in the domestic owner's percentage interest in the partnership or grantor trust, as applicable, as described in paragraph (c)(5) of this section. In such a case, a foreign use shall be deemed to occur at the time the reduction in interest exceeds the de minimis amount. See § 1.1503(d)-7(c) *Example 13*.

(5) *De minimis reduction of an interest in a separate unit.*—(i) *General rule.*—This paragraph applies to a de minimis reduction of a domestic owner's interest in a separate unit (including an interest described in paragraph (c)(4)(i) of this section). Except to the extent provided in paragraph (c)(5)(ii) of this section, no foreign use shall be considered to occur with respect to a dual consolidated loss as a result of an item of deduction or loss composing such dual consolidated loss being made available solely as a result of a reduction in the domestic owner's interest in the separate unit, as provided under paragraph (c)(5)(iii) of this section. See § 1.1503(d)-7(c) *Example 5*.

(ii) *Limitations.*—The exception provided in paragraph (c)(5)(i) of this section shall not apply if—

(A) During any 12-month period the domestic owner's percentage interest in the separate unit is reduced by 10 percent or more, as determined by reference to the domestic owner's interest at the beginning of the 12-month period; or

(B) At any time the domestic owner's percentage interest in the separate unit is reduced by 30 percent or more, as determined by reference to the domestic owner's interest at the end of the taxable year in which the dual consolidated loss was incurred.

(iii) *Reduction in interest.*—The following rules apply for purposes of paragraphs (c)(4) and (5) of this section. A reduction of a domestic owner's interest in a separate unit shall include a reduction resulting from another person acquiring through sale, exchange, contribution, or other means, an interest in the foreign branch or hybrid entity, as applicable. A reduction may occur either directly or indirectly, including through an interest in a partnership, a disregarded entity, or a grantor trust through which a separate unit is carried on or owned. In the case of an interest in a hybrid entity partnership or a separate unit all or a portion of which is carried on or owned through a partnership, an interest in such separate unit (or portion of such separate unit) is determined by reference to the owner's interest in the profits or the capital in the separate unit. In the case of an interest in a hybrid entity grantor trust or a separate unit all or a portion of which is carried on or owned through a grantor trust, an interest in such separate unit (or portion of such separate unit) is determined by reference to the domestic owner's share of the assets and liabilities of the separate unit.

(iv) *Examples and coordination with exceptions to other triggering events.*—See § 1.1503(d)-7(c) *Examples 5, 13, and 14.* See also § 1.1503(d)-6(f)(3) and (f)(5) for rules that coordinate the de minimis exception to foreign use with exceptions to other triggering events described in § 1.1503(d)-6(e)(1), and provide an exception to foreign use following certain compulsory transfers.

(6) *Certain asset basis carryovers.*—No foreign use shall be considered to occur with respect to a dual consolidated loss solely as a result of items of deduction or loss composing such dual consolidated loss being made available as a result of the transfer of assets of a dual resident corporation or separate unit, provided—

(i) Such items of loss and deduction are made available solely as a result of the basis of the transferred assets being determined, under foreign law, in whole or in part by reference to the basis of the assets in the hands of the dual resident corporation or separate unit;

(ii) The aggregate adjusted basis, as determined under U.S. tax principles, of all the assets so transferred during any 12-month period is less than 10 percent of the aggregate adjusted basis, as determined under U.S. tax principles, of all the dual resident corporation's or separate unit's assets, determined by reference to the assets held at the beginning of such 12-month period; and

(iii) The aggregate adjusted basis, as determined under U.S. tax principles, of all the assets so transferred at any time is less than 30 percent of the aggregate adjusted basis, as determined under U.S. tax principles, of all the dual resident corporation's or separate unit's assets, determined by reference to the assets held at the end of the taxable year in which the dual consolidated loss was generated. See § 1.1503(d)-7(c) *Example 15.*

(7) *Assumption of certain liabilities.*—(i) *In general.*—Except to the extent provided in paragraph (c)(7)(ii) of this section, no foreign use shall be considered to occur with respect to any dual consolidated loss solely as a result of an item of deduction or loss composing such dual consolidated loss being made available following the assumption of liabilities of a dual resident corporation or separate unit, provided such availability arises solely as the result of an item of deduction or loss incurred with respect to, or as a result of, such liabilities. See § 1.1503(d)-7(c) *Example 16.*

(ii) *Ordinary course limitation.*—Paragraph (c)(7)(i) of this section shall apply only to the extent the liabilities assumed were incurred in the ordinary course of the dual resident corporation's, or separate unit's, trade or business. For purposes of this paragraph, liabilities incurred in the ordinary course of a trade or business shall include debt incurred to finance the trade or business of the dual resident corporation or separate unit.

(8) *Multiple-party events.*—This paragraph applies to a transaction that qualifies for the triggering event exception described in § 1.1503(d)-6(f)(2)(i)(B) where the acquiring unaffiliated domestic corporation or consolidated group owns, directly or indirectly, more than 90 percent, but less than 100 percent, of the transferred assets or interests immediately after the transaction. In such a case, no foreign use shall be considered to occur with respect to a dual consolidated loss of the dual resident corporation or separate unit whose assets or interests were acquired, solely as a result of the less than 10 percent direct or indirect ownership of the acquired assets or interests by persons other than the acquiring unaffiliated domestic corporation or consolidated group, as applicable, immediately after the transaction. See § 1.1503(d)-7(c) *Example 37.*

(9) *Additional guidance.*—The Commissioner may provide, by guidance published in the Internal Revenue Bulletin, that certain events or transactions do or do not result in a foreign use. Such guidance may also modify the triggering events and rebuttals described in § 1.1503(d)-6(e), and the exceptions thereto under § 1.1503(d)-6(f), as appropriate.

(d) *Ordering rules for determining the foreign use of losses.*—If the laws of a foreign country provide for the foreign use of losses of a dual resident corporation or a separate unit, but do not provide applicable rules for determining the order in which such losses are used in a taxable year, the following rules shall apply:

(1) Any net loss, or net income, that the dual resident corporation or separate unit has in a taxable year shall first be used to offset net income, or loss, recognized by its affiliates in the same taxable year before any carry over of its losses is considered to be used to offset any income from the taxable year.

(2) If under the laws of the foreign country the dual resident corporation or separate unit has losses from different taxable years, it shall be deemed to use first the losses which would not constitute a triggering event that would result in the recapture of a dual consolidated loss pursuant to § 1.1503(d)-6(h). Thereafter, it shall be deemed to use first the losses from the most recent taxable year from which a loss may be carried forward or back for foreign law purposes.

(3) Where different losses or deductions (for example, capital losses and ordinary losses) of a dual resident corporation or separate unit incurred in the same taxable year are available for foreign use, the different losses shall be deemed to be used on a pro rata basis. See § 1.1503(d)-7(c) *Example 12.*

(e) *Mirror legislation rule.*—(1) *In general.*—Except as provided in paragraph (e)(2) or (3) of this section and § 1.1503(d)-6(b) (relating to agreements entered into between the United States and a foreign country), a foreign use shall be deemed to occur if the income tax laws of a foreign country would deny any opportunity for the foreign use of the dual consolidated loss in the year in which the dual consolidated loss is incurred (mirror legislation), determined by assuming that such foreign country had recognized the dual consolidated loss in such year, for any of the following reasons:

(i) The dual resident corporation or separate unit that incurred the loss is subject to income taxation by another country (for example, the United States) on its worldwide income or on a residence basis.

(ii) The loss may be available to offset income (other than income of the dual resident corporation or separate unit) under the laws of another country (for example, the United States).

(iii) The deductibility of any portion of a deduction or loss taken into account in computing the dual consolidated loss depends on whether such amount is deductible under the laws of another country (for example, the United States). See § 1.1503(d)-7(c) *Examples 17* through *19.*

(2) *Stand-alone exception.*—(i) *In general.*—This paragraph (e)(2) applies if, in the absence of the mirror legislation described in paragraph (e)(1) of this section, no item of deduction or loss composing the dual consolidated loss of such dual resident corporation or separate unit would otherwise be available for a foreign use in the taxable year in which such dual consolidated loss is incurred. This determination is made without regard to whether such availability is limited by election (or other similar procedure). However, for purposes of this paragraph (e)(2)(i), no item of deduction or loss composing the dual consolidated loss of a dual resident corporation or separate unit is considered to be made available for foreign use solely because the laws of a foreign country would enable a foreign use through a sale, merger, or similar transaction (provided no such sale, merger, or similar transaction actually occurs). In such a case, no foreign use shall be considered to occur pursuant to paragraph (e)(1) of this section with respect to the dual consolidated loss, provided the requirements of paragraph (e)(2)(ii) of this section are satisfied. See § 1.1503(d)-7(c) *Examples 17* through *19.*

(ii) *Stand-alone domestic use agreement.*—In order to qualify for the exception under paragraph (e)(2)(i) of this section, the consolidated group, unaffiliated dual resident corporation, or unaffiliated domestic owner, as the case may be, must enter into a domestic use agreement in accordance with the provisions of § 1.1503(d)-6(d) and, in addition, must include the following items in such domestic use agreement:

(A) A statement that the document is also being submitted under the provisions of paragraph (e)(2) of this section.

(B) A certification that the conditions of paragraph (e)(2)(i) of this section are satisfied during the taxable year in which the dual consolidated loss is incurred.

(C) An agreement to include with each annual certification required under § 1.1503(d)-6(g), a certification that the conditions described in paragraph (e)(2)(i) of this section are satisfied during the taxable year of each such certification.

(iii) *Termination of stand-alone domestic use agreement.*—This paragraph (e)(2)(iii) applies to a consolidated group, unaffiliated dual resident corporation, or unaffiliated domestic owner, as the case may be, that entered into a domestic use agreement pursuant to paragraph (e)(2)(ii) of this section, with respect to a dual consolidated loss, and which subsequently makes an election pursuant to § 1.1503(d)-6(b) (relating to agreements entered into between the United States and a foreign country) with respect to such dual consolidated loss. In such a case, the dual consolidated loss shall be subject to the election under § 1.1503(d)-6(b) (and any related agreements, representations and conditions), and the domestic use agreement entered into pursuant to paragraph (e)(2)(ii) of this section shall terminate and have no further effect.

(3) *Exception for domestic consenting corporations.*—Paragraph (e)(1) of this section will not apply so as to deem a foreign use of a dual consolidated loss incurred by a domestic consenting corporation that is a dual resident corporation under § 1.1503(d)-1(b)(2)(iii). [Reg. § 1.1503(d)-3.]

☐ [*T.D. 9315, 3-16-2007. Amended by T.D. 9896, 4-7-2020.*]

§ 1.1503(d)-4. Domestic use limitation and related operating rules.—(a) *Scope.*—This section prescribes rules that apply when the general limitation on the domestic use of a dual consolidated loss under paragraph (b) of this section applies. Thus, the rules of this section do not apply when an exception to the domestic use limitation applies (for example, as a result of a domestic use election under § 1.1503(d)-6(d)). In general, when the domestic use limitation applies, the dual consolidated loss of a dual resident corporation or separate unit is subject to the separate return limitation year (SRLY) provisions of § 1.1502-21(c), as modified under this section. Paragraph (c) of this section provides rules that determine the effect of a dual consolidated loss on a consolidated group, an unaffiliated dual resident corporation, or an unaffiliated domestic owner. Paragraph (d) of this section provides rules that eliminate dual consolidated losses following certain transactions or events. Paragraph (e) of this section contains provisions that prevent dual consolidated losses from offsetting tainted income. Finally, paragraph (f) of this section provides rules for computing foreign tax credits.

(b) *Limitation on domestic use of a dual consolidated loss.*—Except as provided in § 1.1503(d)-6, the domestic use of a dual consolidated loss is not permitted. See § 1.1503(d)-2 for the definition of a domestic use. See also § 1.1503(d)-7(c) *Examples 2* through *4*.

(c) Effect of a dual consolidated loss on a consolidated group, unaffiliated dual resident corporation, or unaffiliated domestic owner. For any taxable year in which a dual resident corporation or separate unit has a dual consolidated loss that is subject to the domestic use limitation of paragraph (b) of this section, the following rules shall apply:

(1) *Dual resident corporation.*—This paragraph (c)(1) applies to a dual consolidated loss of a dual resident corporation. The unaffiliated dual resident corporation, or consolidated group that includes the dual resident corporation, shall compute its taxable income (or loss), or consolidated taxable income (or loss), respectively, without taking into account those items of deduction and loss that compose the dual resident corporation's dual consolidated loss. For this purpose, the dual consolidated loss shall be treated as composed of a pro rata portion of each item of deduction and loss of the dual resident corporation taken into account in calculating the dual consolidated loss. The dual consolidated loss is subject to the limitations on its use contained in paragraph (c)(3) of this section and, subject to such limitations, may be carried over or back for use in other taxable years as a separate net operating loss carryover or carryback of the dual resident corporation arising in the year incurred. If the dual resident corporation owns a separate unit or an interest in a transparent entity, the limitations contained in paragraph (c)(3) of this section shall apply to the dual resident corporation as if the separate unit or interest in a transparent entity were a separate domestic corporation that filed a consolidated return with the unaffiliated dual resident corporation, or with the consolidated group of the affiliated dual resident corporation, as applicable.

(2) *Separate unit.*—This paragraph (c)(2) applies to a dual consolidated loss that is attributable to a separate unit. The unaffiliated domestic owner of a separate unit, or the consolidated group of an affiliated domestic owner of a separate unit, shall compute its taxable income (or loss) or consolidated taxable income (or loss), respectively, without taking into account those items of deduction and loss that compose the separate unit's dual consolidated loss. For this purpose, the dual consolidated loss shall be treated as composed of a pro rata portion of each item of deduction and loss of the separate unit taken into account in calculating the dual consolidated loss. The dual consolidated loss is subject to the limitations contained in paragraph (c)(3) of this section as if the separate unit to which the dual consolidated loss is attributable were a separate domestic corporation that filed a consolidated return with its unaffiliated domestic owner or with the consolidated group of its affiliated domestic owner, as applicable. Subject to such limitations, the dual consolidated loss may be carried over or back for use in other taxable years as a separate net operating loss carryover or carryback of the separate unit arising in the year incurred. See § 1.1503(d)-7(c) *Examples 29 and 38.*

(3) *SRLY limitation.*—The dual consolidated loss shall be treated as a loss incurred by the dual resident corporation or separate unit in a separate return limitation year and shall be subject to all of the limitations of § 1.1502-21(c) (SRLY limitation), subject to the following modifications—

(i) Notwithstanding § 1.1502-1(f)(2)(i), the SRLY limitation is applied to any dual consolidated loss of a common parent that is a dual resident corporation, or any dual consolidated loss attributable to a separate unit of a common parent;

(ii) The SRLY limitation is applied without regard to § 1.1502-21(c)(2) (SRLY subgroup limitation) and 1.1502-21(g) (overlap with section 382);

(iii) For purposes of calculating the general SRLY limitation under § 1.1502-21(c)(1)(i), the calculation of aggregate consolidated taxable income shall only include items of income, gain, deduction, and loss generated—

(A) In the case of a hybrid entity separate unit, in years in which the hybrid entity (an interest in which is a separate unit) is taxed as a corporation (or otherwise at the entity level) either on its worldwide income or as a resident in the same foreign country in which it was so taxed during the year in which the dual consolidated loss was generated; and

(B) In the case of a foreign branch separate unit, in years in which the foreign branch qualified as a separate unit in the same foreign country in which it so qualified during the year in which the dual consolidated loss was generated;

(iv) For purposes of calculating the general SRLY limitation under § 1.1502-21(c)(1)(i), the calculation of aggregate consolidated taxable income shall not include any amount included in income pursuant to § 1.1503(d)-6(h) (relating to the recapture of a dual consolidated loss); and

(v) The SRLY limitation is applied without regard to § 1.1502-21(c)(1)(i)(E) (section 172(a) limitation applicable to a SRLY member).

(4) *Items of a dual consolidated loss used in other taxable years.*—A pro rata portion of each item of deduction or loss that composes the dual consolidated loss shall be considered to be used when the dual consolidated loss is used in other taxable years. See § 1.1503(d)-7(c) *Examples 29 and 38.*

(5) *Reconstituted net operating losses.*—For additional rules and limitations that apply to reconstituted net operating losses, see § 1.1503(d)-6(h)(6).

(d) *Elimination of a dual consolidated loss after certain transactions.*—(1) *General rule.*—In general, a dual resident corporation has a net operating loss (and, therefore, a dual consolidated loss) only if it sustains such loss, or succeeds to such loss as a result of acquiring the assets of a corporation that sustained the loss in a transaction described in section 381(a). Similarly, a net loss generally is attributable to a separate unit of a domestic owner (and therefore is a dual consolidated loss) only if the domestic owner incurs the deductions or losses, or succeeds to such deductions or losses in a transaction described in section 381(a). Except as provided in § 1.1503(d)-6(h)(6)(iii), section 1503(d) and these regulations do not alter these general rules. Thus, the provisions of §§ 1.1503(d)-1 through 1.1503(d)-8 generally do not cause a corporation to have a dual consolidated loss if it did not sustain (or inherit) the loss. Instead, these regulations either eliminate a dual consolidated loss that a corporation sustained (or inherited), or prevent the carryover of a dual consolidated loss under section 381 that would ordinarily occur, as a result of certain transactions.

(i) *Transactions described in section 381(a).*—This paragraph (d)(1)(i) applies to a dual consolidated loss of a dual resident corporation, or of a domestic owner attributable to a separate unit, that is subject to the domestic use limitation rule of paragraph (b) of this section. In such a case, and except as provided in paragraph (d)(2) of this section, the dual consolidated loss shall not carry over to another corporation in a transaction described in section 381(a) and, as a result, shall be eliminated. See § 1.1503(d)-7(c) *Example 20*.

(ii) *Cessation of separate unit status.*—This paragraph (d)(1)(ii) applies when a separate unit of an unaffiliated domestic owner ceases to be a separate unit of its domestic owner, or when a separate unit of an affiliated domestic owner ceases to be a separate unit with respect to its domestic owner and all other members of the affiliated domestic owner's consolidated group. In such a case, and except as provided in paragraph (d)(2)(iii) of this section, a dual consolidated loss of the domestic owner attributable to such separate unit, that is subject to the domestic use limitation of paragraph (b) of this section, shall be eliminated. For purposes of this paragraph (d)(1)(ii), a separate unit may cease to be a separate unit if, for example, such separate unit is terminated, dissolved, liquidated, sold, or otherwise disposed of. See § 1.1503(d)-7(c) *Example 21*.

(2) *Exceptions.*—(i) *Certain section 368(a)(1)(F) reorganizations..*—Paragraph (d)(1)(i) of this section (relating to transactions described in section 381(a)) shall not apply to a dual consolidated loss of a dual resident corporation that undergoes a reorganization described in section 368(a)(1)(F) in which the resulting corporation is a domestic corporation. In such a case, the dual consolidated loss of the resulting corporation continues to be subject to the limitations of paragraphs (b) and (c) of this section, applied as if the resulting corporation incurred the dual consolidated loss.

(ii) *Acquisition of a dual resident corporation by another dual resident corporation.*—If a dual resident corporation transfers its assets to another dual resident corporation in a transaction described in section 381(a), and the transferee corporation is a resident of (or is taxed on its worldwide income by) the same foreign country of which the transferor was a resident (or was taxed on its worldwide income), then paragraph (d)(1)(i) of this section shall not apply with respect to dual consolidated losses of the dual resident corporation, and income generated by the transferee may be offset by the carryover dual consolidated losses of the transferor, subject to the limitations of paragraphs (b) and (c) of this section applied as if the transferee incurred the dual consolidated loss. Dual consolidated losses of the transferor dual resident corporation may not, however, be used to offset income attributable to separate units or interests in transparent entities owned by the transferee because they constitute domestic affiliates under § 1.1503(d)-1(b)(12)(iii) and (iv), respectively.

(iii) *Acquisition of a separate unit by a domestic corporation.*—This paragraph (d)(2)(iii) provides exceptions to the general rules in paragraphs (d)(1)(i) and (ii) of this section that eliminate the dual consolidated loss of a domestic owner that is attributable to a separate unit following certain transactions or events. The exceptions set forth in this paragraph (d)(2)(iii) shall only apply where a domestic owner transfers its assets to a domestic corporation (transferee corporation) in a transaction described in section 381(a).

(A) *Acquisition by a corporation that is not a member of the same consolidated group.*—(*1*) *General rule.*—If a domestic owner transfers either an individual separate unit or a combined separate unit to a transferee corporation that is not a member of its consolidated group in a transaction described in section 381(a), and the transferee corporation, or a member of the transferee's consolidated group, is a domestic owner of the transferred separate unit immediately after the transaction, then paragraphs (d)(1)(i) and (ii) of this section shall not apply to such transfer. In addition, income of the transferee, or a member of the transferee's consolidated group, that is attributable to the transferred separate unit may be offset by the carryover dual consolidated losses of the transferor domestic owner that were attributable to the transferred separate unit, subject to the limitations of paragraphs (b) and (c) of this section applied as if the transferee incurred the dual consolidated losses and such losses were attributable to the separate unit. See § 1.1503(d)-7(c) *Example 21*.

(*2*) *Combination with separate units of the transferee.*—This paragraph (d)(2)(iii)(A)(*2*) applies to a transaction described in paragraph (d)(2)(iii)(A)(*1*) of this section where the transferred separate unit is combined with another separate unit of the transferee, or another member of the transferee's consolidated group, immediately after the transfer as provided under § 1.1503(d)-1(b)(4)(ii). In such a case, income generated by the transferee, or another member of the transferee's consolidated group, that is attributable to the combined separate unit may be offset by the carryover dual consolidated losses that were attributable to the transferred separate unit, subject to the limitations of paragraphs (b) and (c) of this section, applied as if the transferee incurred the dual consolidated losses and such losses were attributable to the combined separate unit.

(B) *Acquisition by a member of the same consolidated group.*—If an affiliated domestic owner transfers its assets to another member of its consolidated group in a transaction described in section 381(a), and the transferee corporation or another member of such consolidated group is a domestic owner of the separate unit to which the dual consolidated loss was attributable, then paragraphs (d)(1)(i) and (ii) of this section shall not apply. In addition, income generated by the transferee that is attributable to the transferred separate unit may be offset by the carryover dual consolidated losses that were attributable to the transferred separate unit, subject to the limitations of paragraphs (b) and (c) of this section, applied as if the transferee incurred the dual consolidated losses and such losses were attributable to the separate unit. See § 1.1503(d)-7(c) *Example 21*.

(iv) *Special rules for foreign insurance companies.*—See § 1.1503(d)-6(a) for additional limitations that apply where the transferor is a foreign insurance company that is a dual resident corporation under § 1.1503(d)-1(b)(2)(ii).

(e) *Special rule denying the use of a dual consolidated loss to offset tainted income.*—(1) *In general.*—Dual consolidated losses incurred by a dual resident corporation that are subject to the domestic use limitation rule under paragraph (b) of this section shall not be used to offset income it earns after it ceases to be a dual resident corporation to the extent that such income is tainted income.

(2) *Tainted income.*—(i) *Definition.*—For purposes of paragraph (e)(1) of this section, the term tainted income means—

(A) Income or gain recognized on the sale or other disposition of tainted assets; and

(B) Income derived as a result of holding tainted assets.

(ii) *Income presumed to be derived from holding tainted assets.*—In the absence of evidence establishing the actual amount of income that is attributable to holding tainted assets, the portion of a corporation's income in a particular taxable year that is treated as tainted income derived as a result of holding tainted assets shall be an amount equal to the corporation's taxable income for the year (other than income described in paragraph (e)(2)(i)(A) of this section) multiplied by a fraction, the numerator of which is the fair market value of all tainted assets acquired by the corporation (determined at the time such assets were so acquired) and the denominator of which is the fair market value of the total assets owned by the corporation at the end of such taxable year. To establish the actual amount of income that is attributable to holding tainted assets, documentation must be attached to, and filed by the due date (including extensions) of, the domestic corporation's tax return or the consolidated tax return of an affiliated group of which it is a member, as the case may be, for the taxable year in which the income is generated. See § 1.1503(d)-7(c) *Example 22*.

(3) *Tainted assets defined.*—For purposes of paragraph (e)(2) of this section, tainted assets are any assets acquired by a domestic corporation in a nonrecognition transaction, as defined in section 7701(a)(45), any assets otherwise transferred to the corporation as a contribution to capital, or any assets otherwise received from a separate unit or a transparent entity owned by such domestic corporation, at any time during the three taxable years immediately preceding the taxable year in which the corporation ceases to be a dual resident corporation or at any time thereafter.

(4) *Exceptions.*—Income derived from assets acquired by a domestic corporation shall not be subject to the limitation described in paragraph (e)(1) of this section, and in addition shall not be treated as tainted assets as defined in paragraph (e)(3) of this section, if—

(i) For the taxable year in which the assets were acquired, the corporation did not have a dual consolidated loss (or a carryforward of a dual consolidated loss to such year); or

(ii) The assets were acquired as replacement property in the ordinary course of business.

(f) *Computation of foreign tax credit limitation.*—If a dual consolidated loss is subject to the domestic use limitation rule under paragraph (b) of this section, the consolidated group, unaffiliated dual resident corporation, or unaffiliated domestic owner shall compute its foreign tax credit limitation by applying the limitations of paragraph (c) of this section. Thus, the items constituting the dual consolidated loss are not taken into account until the year in which such items are absorbed. [Reg. § 1.1503(d)-4.]

☐ [*T.D. 9315, 3-16-2007. Amended by T.D. 9927, 10-23-2020.*]

§ 1.1503(d)-5. Attribution of items and basis adjustments.—(a) *In general.*—This section provides rules for determining the amount of income or dual consolidated loss of a dual resident corporation. This section also provides rules for determining the income or dual consolidated loss attributable to a separate unit, as well as the income or loss attributable to an interest in a transparent entity. Paragraph (b) of this section provides rules with respect to dual resident corporations. Paragraph (c) of this section provides rules with respect to separate units and interests in transparent entities. These determinations are required for various purposes under section 1503(d). For example, it is necessary for purposes of applying the domestic use limitation rule under § 1.1503(d)-4(b) to a dual consolidated loss, and for determining the extent to which a dual consolidated loss is available to offset income as provided under § 1.1503(d)-4(c). These determinations are also necessary for purposes of determining whether the amount subject to recapture may be reduced pursuant to § 1.1503(d)-6(h)(2). Paragraph (d) of this section provides rules with respect to the foreign tax treatment of items. Paragraph (e) of this section provides rules regarding the treatment of items where a dual resident corporation, separate unit, or transparent entity only qualified as such during a portion of a taxable year. Paragraph (f) of this section provides rules for determining the assets and liabilities of a separate unit. Finally, paragraph (g) of this section provides rules for making basis adjustments to stock of certain members of a consolidated group and to certain interests in partnerships. The rules in this section apply for purposes of § § 1.1503(d)-1 through 1.1503(d)-7.

(b) *Determination of amount of income or dual consolidated loss of a dual resident corporation.*—(1) *In general.*—For purposes of determining whether a dual resident corporation has income or a dual consolidated loss for the taxable year, and except as provided in paragraph (b)(2) of this section, the dual resident corporation shall compute its income or dual consolidated loss taking into account only those items of income, gain, deduction, and loss from such year (including any items recognized by such corporation as a result of an election under section 338). In the case of an affiliated dual resident corporation, such calculation shall be made in accordance with the rules set forth in the regulations under section 1502 governing the computation of consolidated taxable income. See also paragraphs (d) and (e) of this section.

(2) *Exceptions.*—For purposes of determining the income or dual consolidated loss of a dual resident corporation, the following shall not be taken into account—

(i) Any net capital loss of the dual resident corporation;

(ii) Any carryover or carryback losses; or

(iii) Any items of income, gain, deduction, and loss that are attributable to a separate unit or an interest in a transparent entity of the dual resident corporation.

(c) *Determination of amount of income or dual consolidated loss attributable to a separate unit, and income or loss attributable to an interest in a transparent entity.*—(1) *In general.*—(i) *Scope and purpose.*—Paragraphs (c) through (e) of this section apply for purposes of determining the income or dual consolidated loss attributable to a separate unit, and the income or loss attributable to an interest in a transparent entity, for the taxable year. In the case of an affiliated domestic owner, this determination shall be made in accordance with the rules set forth in the regulations under section 1502 governing the computation of consolidated taxable income. These rules apply solely for purposes of section 1503(d).

(ii) *Only items of domestic owner taken into account.*—The computation made under paragraphs (c) through (e) of this section shall be made using only those existing items of income, gain, deduction, and loss of the separate unit's or transparent entity's domestic owner (or owners, in the case of certain combined separate units), as determined for U.S. tax purposes. These items must be translated into U.S. dollars (if necessary) at the appropriate exchange rate provided under section 989(b), as modified by regulations. The computation shall be made as if the separate unit or interest in a transparent entity were a domestic corporation, using items that are attributable to the separate unit or interest in a transparent entity. However, for purposes of making this computation, net capital losses, and carryover or carryback losses, of the domestic owner shall not be taken into account. Items of income, gain, deduction, and loss that are otherwise disregarded for U.S. tax purposes shall not be regarded or taken into account for purposes of this section. See § 1.1503(d)-7(c) *Examples 6 and 23 through 25*.

(iii) *Separate application.*—The attribution rules of this section shall apply separately to each separate unit or interest in a transparent entity. Thus, an item of income, gain, deduction, or loss shall not be considered attributable to more than one separate unit or interest in a transparent entity. In addition, for purposes of this section items of income, gain, deduction, and loss attributable to a separate unit or an interest in a transparent entity shall not offset items of income, gain, deduction, and loss of another separate unit or interest in a transparent entity. See § 1.1503(d)-7(c) *Example 24*. See also the separate unit combination rule in § 1.1503(d)-1(b)(4)(ii).

(2) *Foreign branch separate unit.*—(i) *In general.*—Except to the extent provided in paragraph (c)(4) of this section, for purposes of determining the items of income, gain, deduction (other than interest), and loss of a domestic owner that are attributable to the domestic owner's foreign branch separate unit, the principles of section 864(c)(2), (c)(4), and (c)(5), as set forth in § 1.864-4(c), and § § 1.864-5 through 1.864-7, shall apply. The principles apply without regard to limitations imposed on the effectively connected treatment of income, gain, or loss under the trade or business safe harbors in section 864(b) and the limitations for treating foreign source income as effectively connected under section 864(c)(4)(D). Except as provided in paragraph (c)(2)(iii) of this section, for purposes of determining the domestic owner's interest expense that is attributable to a foreign branch separate unit, the principles of § 1.882-5, as modified in paragraph (c)(2)(ii) of this section, shall apply. When applying the principles of section 864(c) (as modified by this paragraph) and § 1.882-5 (as modified in paragraph (c)(2)(ii) of this section), the foreign branch separate unit's domestic owner shall be treated as a foreign corporation, the foreign branch separate unit shall be treated as a trade or business within the United States, and the other assets of the domestic owner shall be treated as assets that are not U.S. assets.

(ii) *Principles of § 1.882-5.*—For purposes of paragraph (c)(2)(i) of this section, the principles of § 1.882-5 shall be applied, subject to the following modifications—

(A) Except as otherwise provided in this section, only the assets, liabilities, and interest expense of the domestic owner shall be taken into account in the § 1.882-5 formula;

(B) Except as provided under paragraph (c)(2)(ii)(C) of this section, a taxpayer may use the alternative tax book value method under § 1.861-9(i) for purposes of determining the value of its U.S. assets pursuant to § 1.882-5(b)(2) and its worldwide assets pursuant to § 1.882-5(c)(2);

(C) For purposes of determining the value of a U.S. asset pursuant to § 1.882-5(b)(2), and worldwide assets pursuant to § 1.882-5(c)(2), the taxpayer must use the same methodology under § 1.861-9T(g) (that is, tax book value, alternative tax book value, or fair market value) that the taxpayer uses for purposes of allocating and apportioning interest expense for the taxable year under section 864(e);

(D) Asset values shall be determined pursuant to § 1.861-9T(g)(2); and

(E) For purposes of determining the step-two U.S. connected liabilities, the amounts of worldwide assets and liabilities under § 1.882-5(c)(2)(iii) and (iv) must be determined in accordance with U.S. tax principles, rather than substantially in accordance with U.S. tax principles.

(iii) *Exception where foreign country attributes interest expense solely by reference to books and records.*—The principles of § 1.882-5 shall not apply if the foreign country in which the foreign branch separate unit is located determines, for purposes of computing taxable income (or loss) of a permanent establishment or branch of a nonresident corporation under the laws of the foreign country, the interest expense of the foreign branch separate unit by taking into account only the items of interest expense reflected on the foreign branch separate unit's books and records. In such a case, only those items of the domestic owner's interest expense reflected on the foreign branch separate unit's books and records (as provided in paragraph (c)(3)(i) of this section), adjusted to conform to U.S. tax principles, shall be attributable to the foreign branch separate unit. This paragraph shall not apply where the foreign country does not use a method of attributing interest based solely on the interest that is reflected on the books and records. For example, this paragraph does not apply if the foreign country uses a method for attributing interest expense similar to § 1.882-5 or that set forth in the Organization for Economic Cooperation and Development Report on the Attribution of Profits to

Permanent Establishments, Part II (Banks), December 2006. See http://www.oecd.org.

(3) *Hybrid entity separate unit and an interest in a transparent entity.*—(i) *General rule.*—This paragraph (c)(3) applies to determine the items of income, gain, deduction, and loss of a domestic owner that are attributable to a hybrid entity separate unit, or an interest in a transparent entity, of such domestic owner. Except to the extent provided in paragraph (c)(4) of this section, the domestic owner's items of income, gain, deduction, and loss are attributable to the extent they are reflected on the books and records of the hybrid entity or transparent entity, as applicable, as adjusted to conform to U.S. tax principles. See § 1.1503(d)-7(c) *Examples 23* through *26*. For purposes of this paragraph (c)(3), the term "books and records" has the meaning provided under § 1.989(a)-1(d). The treatment of items for foreign tax purposes, including under any type of foreign anti-deferral regime, is not relevant for purposes of determining whether items are reflected on the books and records of the entity, or for purposes of making adjustments to such items to conform to U.S. tax principles. The method described in the second sentence of this paragraph shall not apply to the extent that the Commissioner determines that booking practices are employed with a principal purpose of avoiding the principles of section 1503(d), including inconsistently treating the same or similar items of income, gain, deduction, and loss. In such a case, the Commissioner may reallocate the items of income, gain, deduction, and loss between or among a domestic owner, its hybrid entities, its transparent entities (and interests therein), its separate units, or any other entity, as applicable, in a manner consistent with the principles of section 1503(d) and which properly reflects income (or loss).

(ii) *Interests in certain disregarded entities, partnerships, and grantor trusts owned by a hybrid entity or transparent entity.*—This paragraph (c)(3)(ii) applies if a hybrid entity or transparent entity to which paragraph (c)(3)(i) of this section applies owns, directly or indirectly (other than through a hybrid entity or transparent entity), an interest in an entity that is treated as a disregarded entity, partnership, or grantor trust for U.S. tax purposes, but is not a hybrid entity or a transparent entity. For example, the rules of this paragraph would apply when a hybrid entity holds an interest in a limited partnership created in the United States and, for both U.S. and foreign tax purposes the entity is considered a partnership. In such a case, and except to the extent provided in paragraph (c)(4) of this section, items of income, gain, deduction, and loss that are reflected on the books and records of such disregarded entity, partnership or grantor trust, as determined under paragraph (c)(3)(i) of this section, shall be treated as being reflected on the books and records of the hybrid entity or transparent entity for purposes of applying paragraph (c)(3)(i) of this section. See § 1.1503(d)-7(c) *Example 26*.

(4) *Special rules.*—The following special rules shall apply for purposes of attributing items to separate units or interests in transparent entities under this section:

(i) *Allocation of items between certain tiered separate units and interests in transparent entities.*—(A) *Foreign branch separate unit.*—This paragraph (c)(4)(i) applies where a hybrid entity or transparent entity owns directly or indirectly (other than through a hybrid entity or a transparent entity), a foreign branch separate unit. For purposes of determining items of income, gain, deduction, and loss of the domestic owner that are attributable to the domestic owner's foreign branch separate unit described in the preceding sentence, only items of income, gain, deduction, and loss that are attributable to the domestic owner's interest in the hybrid entity, or transparent entity, as provided in paragraph (c)(3) of this section, shall be taken into account. Further, only assets, liabilities, and activities of the domestic owner's interest in the hybrid entity or the transparent entity shall be taken into account under paragraph (c)(2) of this section when applying the principles of 864(c)(2), (c)(4), (c)(5) (as set forth in § 1.864-4(c), and §§ 1.864-5 through 1.864-7), and § 1.882-5 (as modified in paragraph (c)(2)(ii) of this section). See § 1.1503(d)-7(c) *Examples 25 and 26*.

(B) *Hybrid entity separate unit or interest in a transparent entity.*.—For purposes of determining items of income, gain, deduction, and loss that are attributable to a hybrid entity separate unit or an interest in a transparent entity described in paragraph (c)(3) of this section, such items shall not be taken into account to the extent they are attributable to a foreign branch separate unit pursuant to paragraph (c)(4)(i)(A) of this section. See § 1.1503(d)-7(c) *Examples 25 and 26*.

(ii) *Combined separate unit.*—If two or more individual separate units defined in § 1.1503(d)-1(b)(4)(i) are treated as one combined separate unit pursuant to § 1.1503(d)-1(b)(4)(ii), the items of income, gain, deduction, and loss that are attributable to the combined separate unit shall be determined as follows:

(A) Items of income, gain, deduction, and loss are first attributed to each individual separate unit without regard to § 1.1503(d)-1(b)(4)(ii), pursuant to the rules of paragraphs (c) through (e) of this section.

(B) The combined separate unit then takes into account all of the items of income, gain, deduction, and loss attributable to its individual separate units pursuant to paragraph (c)(4)(ii)(A) of this section. See § 1.1503(d)-7(c) *Examples 25 and 26*.

(iii) *Gain or loss on the direct or indirect disposition of a separate unit or an interest in a transparent entity.*—(A) *In general.*—This paragraph (c)(4)(iii) applies for purposes of attributing items of income, gain, deduction, and loss that are recognized on the sale, exchange, or other disposition of a separate unit or an interest in a transparent entity (or an interest in a disregarded entity, partnership, or grantor trust that owns, directly or indirectly, a separate unit or an interest in a transparent entity). For purposes of this paragraph (c)(4)(iii), items taken into account on the sale, exchange, or other disposition include loss recapture income or gain under section 367(a)(3)(C) or 904(f)(3), and gain or loss recognized by the domestic owner as the result of an election under section 338. In cases where this paragraph (c)(4)(iii)(A) applies, items taken into account on the sale, exchange, or other disposition shall be attributable to the separate unit or the interest in the transparent entity to the extent of gain or loss that would have been recognized had the separate unit or transparent entity sold all its assets (as determined in paragraph (f) of this section) in a taxable exchange, immediately before the sale, exchange, or other disposition (deemed sale). For purposes of a deemed sale described in this paragraph (c)(4)(iii), the assets are treated as being sold for an amount equal to their fair market value, plus the assumption of the liabilities of the separate unit or interest in a transparent entity (as determined in paragraph (f) of this section). See § 1.1503(d)-7(c) *Example 27*.

(B) *Multiple separate units or interests in transparent entities.*—This paragraph (c)(4)(iii)(B) applies to a sale, exchange, or other disposition described in paragraph (c)(4)(iii)(A) of this section that results in more than one separate unit or interest in a transparent entity being, directly or indirectly, disposed of. In such a case, items of income, gain, deduction, and loss recognized on such sale, exchange, or other disposition are allocated and attributed to each separate unit or interest in a transparent entity, based on the relative gain or loss that would have been recognized by each separate unit or interest in a transparent entity pursuant to a deemed sale of their assets. See § 1.1503(d)-7(c) *Example 28*.

(iv) *Inclusions on stock.*—Any amount included in income of a domestic owner arising from ownership of stock in a foreign corporation (for example, under sections 78, 951, or 986(c)) through a separate unit, or interest in a transparent entity, shall be attributable to the separate unit or interest in a transparent entity, if an actual dividend from such foreign corporation would have been so attributed. See § 1.1503(d)-7(c) *Example 24*.

(v) *Foreign currency gain or loss recognized under section 987.*—Foreign currency gain or loss of a domestic owner recognized under section 987 as a result of a transfer or remittance shall not be attributable to a separate unit or an interest in a transparent entity.

(vi) *Recapture of dual consolidated loss.*—If all or a portion of a dual consolidated loss that was attributable to a separate unit is included in the gross income of a domestic owner under the recapture provisions of § 1.1503(d)-6(h), such amount shall be attributable to the separate unit that incurred the dual consolidated loss being recaptured. See § 1.1503(d)-7(c) *Examples 38 and 40*.

(d) *Foreign tax treatment disregarded.*—The fact that a particular item taken into account in computing the income or dual consolidated loss of a dual resident corporation or a separate unit, or the income or loss of an interest in a transparent entity, is not taken into account in computing income (or loss) subject to a foreign country's income tax shall not cause such item to be excluded from being taken into account under paragraph (b), (c), or (e) of this section.

(e) *Items generated or incurred while a dual resident corporation, a separate unit, or a transparent entity.*—For purposes of determining the amount of the dual consolidated loss of a dual resident corporation for the taxable year, only the items of income, gain, deduction, and loss generated or incurred during the period the dual resident corporation qualified as such shall be taken into account. For purposes of determining the amount of income of a dual resident corporation for the taxable year, all the items of income, gain, deduction, and loss generated or incurred during the year shall be taken into account. For purposes of determining the amount of the income or dual consolidated loss attributable to a separate unit, or the income or loss attributable to an interest in a transparent entity, for the taxable year, only the items of income, gain, deduction, and loss generated or incurred during the period the separate unit or the interest in the transparent entity qualified as such shall be taken into account. For purposes of this paragraph (e), the allocation of items to periods shall be made under the principles of § 1.1502-76(b).

(f) *Assets and liabilities of a separate unit or an interest in a transparent entity.*—A separate unit or an interest in a transparent entity shall be treated as owning assets to the extent items of income, gain, deduction, and loss from such assets would be attributable to the separate unit or interest in the transparent entity under paragraphs (c) through (e) of this section. Similarly, liabilities shall be treated as liabilities of a separate unit, or an interest in a transparent entity, to the extent interest expense incurred on such liabilities would be attributable to the separate unit, or the interest in a transparent entity, under paragraphs (c) through (e) of this section.

(g) *Basis adjustments.*—(1) *Affiliated dual resident corporation or affiliated domestic owner.*—If a member of a consolidated group owns stock in an affiliated dual resident corporation or an affiliated domestic owner that is a member of the same consolidated group, the member shall adjust the basis of the stock in accordance with the provisions of § 1.1502-32. Corresponding adjustments shall be made to the stock of other members in accordance with the provisions of § 1.1502-32. In the case where two or more individual separate units are treated as a combined separate unit pursuant to § 1.1503(d)-1(b)(4)(ii), see paragraph (g)(3) of this section.

(2) *Interests in hybrid entities that are partnerships or interests in partnerships through which a separate unit is owned indirectly.*—(i) *Scope.*—This paragraph (g)(2) applies for purposes of determining the adjusted basis of an interest in—

(A) A hybrid entity that is a partnership; and

(B) A partnership through which a domestic owner indirectly owns a separate unit.

(ii) *Determination of basis of partner's interest.*—The adjusted basis of an interest described in paragraph (g)(2)(i) of this section shall be adjusted in accordance with section 705 and this paragraph (g)(2). The adjusted basis shall not be decreased for any amount of a dual consolidated loss that is attributable to the partnership interest, or separate unit owned indirectly through the partnership interest, as applicable, that is not absorbed as a result of the application of § 1.1503(d)-4(b) and (c). The adjusted basis shall, however, be decreased for the amount of such dual consolidated loss that is absorbed in a carryover or carryback taxable year. The adjusted basis shall be increased for any amount included in income pursuant to § 1.1503(d)-6(h) as a result of the recapture of a dual consolidated loss that was attributable to the interest in the hybrid partnership, or separate unit owned indirectly through the partnership interest, as applicable.

(3) *Combined separate units.*—This paragraph (g)(3) applies where two or more individual separate units of one or more affiliated domestic owners are treated as one combined separate unit pursuant to § 1.1503(d)-1(b)(4)(ii). In such a case, a member owning stock in an affiliated domestic owner of the combined separate unit shall adjust the basis in the stock of such domestic owner as provided in paragraph (g)(1) of this section, and an affiliated domestic owner shall adjust its basis in a partnership, as provided in paragraph (g)(2) of this section, taking into account only those items of income, gain, deduction, or loss attributable to each individual separate unit, prior to combination. For purposes of this rule, if the dual consolidated loss attributable to a combined separate unit is subject to the domestic use limitation of § 1.1503(d)-4(b), then for purposes of this paragraph (g) and § 1.1502-32, the dual consolidated loss shall be allocated to an individual separate unit to the extent such individual separate unit contributed items of deduction or loss giving rise to the dual consolidated loss. In addition, if one or more affiliated domestic owners are required to recapture all or a portion of a dual consolidated loss pursuant to paragraph (h) of this section, such recapture amount shall be allocated to the affiliated domestic owner of the individual separate units composing the combined separate unit, to the extent such individual separate units contributed items of deduction or loss giving rise to the recaptured dual consolidated loss. [Reg. § 1.1503(d)-5.]

☐ [*T.D.* 9315, 3-16-2007 (*corrected* 4-24-2007).]

§ 1.1503(d)-6. Exceptions to the domestic use limitation rule.—(a) *In general.*—(1) *Scope and purpose.*—This section provides certain exceptions to the domestic use limitation rule of § 1.1503(d)-4(b). Paragraph (b) of this section provides an exception for bilateral elective agreements. Paragraph (c) of this section provides rules regarding an exception that applies when there is no possibility of a foreign use. Paragraphs (d) through (h) of this section provide rules for an exception where a domestic use election is made. Paragraph (e) of this section provides rules with respect to triggering events, and paragraph (f) of this section provides rules regarding exceptions to triggering events. Paragraph (g) of this section provides rules with respect to the annual certification reporting requirement. Paragraph (h) of this section provides rules regarding the recapture of dual consolidated losses. Finally, paragraph (j) of this section provides rules regarding the termination of domestic use agreements and the annual certification requirement.

(2) *Absence of foreign affiliate or foreign consolidation regime.*—The absence of a foreign affiliate or a foreign consolidation regime alone does not constitute an exception to the domestic use limitation rule. This is the case because it is still possible that all or a portion of the dual consolidated loss may be put to a foreign use. For example, there may be a foreign use with respect to an affiliate acquired in a year subsequent to the year in which the dual consolidated loss was incurred. In addition, a foreign use may occur in the absence of a foreign consolidation regime through a sale, merger, or similar transaction. See § 1.1503(d)-7(c) *Example* 2.

(3) *Foreign insurance companies treated as domestic corporations.*—The exceptions contained in this section shall not apply to losses of a foreign insurance company that is a dual resident corporation under § 1.1503(d)-1(b)(2)(ii), or to losses attributable to any separate unit of such foreign insurance company. In addition, these exceptions shall not apply to losses described in the preceding sentence that, subject to the rules of § 1.1503(d)-4(d), carry over to a domestic corporation pursuant to a transaction described in section 381(a).

(b) *Elective agreement in place between the United States and a foreign country.*—(1) *In general.*—The domestic use limitation rule of § 1.1503(d)-4(b) shall not apply to a dual consolidated loss to the extent the consolidated group, unaffiliated dual resident corporation, or unaffiliated domestic owner, as the case may be, elects to deduct the loss in the United States pursuant to an agreement entered into between the United States and a foreign country that puts into place an elective procedure through which losses in a particular year may be used to offset income in only one country. This exception shall apply only if all the terms and conditions required under such agreement are satisfied, including any reporting or filing requirements. See § 1.1503(d)-3(e)(2)(iii) for the effect of an agreement described in this paragraph on a stand-alone domestic use agreement.

(2) *Application to combined separate units.*—This paragraph (b)(2) applies where two or more individual separate units are treated as one combined separate unit pursuant to § 1.1503(d)-1(b)(4)(ii), and an agreement described in paragraph (b)(1) of this section would apply to at least one of the individual separate units. In such a case, and except to the extent provided in the agreement, the consolidated group, unaffiliated dual resident corporation, or unaffiliated domestic owner, as the case may be, may apply the agreement to the individual separate units, as applicable, provided the terms and conditions of the agreement are otherwise satisfied. See § 1.1503(d)-7(c) *Example 19.*

(c) *No possibility of foreign use.*—(1) *In general.*—The domestic use limitation rule of § 1.1503(d)-4(b) shall not apply to a dual consolidated loss if the consolidated group, unaffiliated dual resident corporation, or unaffiliated domestic owner, as the case may be—

(i) Demonstrates, to the satisfaction of the Commissioner, that no foreign use (as defined in § 1.1503(d)-3) of the dual consolidated loss occurred in the year in which it was incurred, and that no foreign use can occur in any other year by any means; and

(ii) Prepares a statement described in paragraph (c)(2) of this section that is attached to, and filed by the due date (including extensions) of, its U.S. income tax return for the taxable year in which the dual consolidated loss is incurred. See § 1.1503(d)-7(c) *Examples 2, 30, and 31.*

(2) *Statement.*—The statement described in this paragraph (c)(2) must be signed under penalties of perjury by the person who signs the tax return. The statement must be labeled "No Possibility of Foreign Use of Dual Consolidated Loss Statement" at the top of the page and must include the following items, in paragraphs labeled to correspond with the items set forth in paragraphs (c)(2)(i) through (iv) of this section:

(i) A statement that the document is submitted under the provisions of paragraph (c) of this section.

(ii) The name, address, taxpayer identification number, and place and date of incorporation of the dual resident corporation, and the country or countries that tax the dual resident corporation on its worldwide income or on a residence basis, or, in the case of a separate unit, identification of the separate unit, including the name under which it conducts business, its principal activity, and the country in which its principal place of business is located. In the case of a combined separate unit, such information must be provided for each individual separate unit that is treated as part of the combined separate unit under § 1.1503(d)-1(b)(4)(ii).

(iii) A statement of the amount of the dual consolidated loss at issue.

(iv) An analysis, in reasonable detail and specificity, of the treatment of the losses and deductions composing the dual consolidated loss under the relevant facts. The analysis must include the reasons supporting the conclusion that no foreign use of the dual consolidated loss can occur as described in paragraph (c)(1)(i) of this section. The analysis must be supported with official or certified English translations of the relevant provisions of foreign law. The analysis may, for example, be based on the taxpayer's interpretation of foreign law, on advice received from local tax advisers in an opinion, or on a ruling from local country tax authorities. In all cases, however, the determination must be made to the satisfaction of the Commissioner.

(d) *Domestic use election.*—(1) *In general.*—The domestic use limitation rule of § 1.1503(d)-4(b) shall not apply to a dual consolidated loss if an election to be bound by the provisions of paragraphs (d) through (j) of this section is made by the consolidated group, unaffiliated dual resident corporation, or unaffiliated domestic owner, as the case may be (elector). In order to elect such relief, an agreement described in this paragraph (d)(1) (domestic use agreement) must be attached to, and filed by the due date (including extensions) of, the U.S. income tax return of the elector for the taxable year in which the dual consolidated loss is incurred. The domestic use agreement must be signed under penalties of perjury by the person who signs the return. If dual consolidated losses of more than one dual resident corporation or separate unit requires the filing of domestic use agreements by the same elector, the agreements may be combined in a single document, but the information required by paragraphs (d)(1)(ii) and (iv) of this section must be provided separately with respect to each dual consolidated loss. The domestic use agreement must be labeled "Domestic Use Election and Agreement" at the top of the page and must include the following items, in paragraphs labeled to correspond with the following:

(i) A statement that the document submitted is an election and an agreement under the provisions of paragraph (d) of this section.

(ii) The information required by paragraph (c)(2)(ii) of this section.

(iii) An agreement by the elector to comply with all of the provisions of paragraphs (d) through (j) of this section, as applicable.

(iv) A statement of the amount of the dual consolidated loss at issue.

(v) A certification that there has not been, and will not be, a foreign use (as defined in § 1.1503(d)-3) during the certification period (as defined in § 1.1503(d)-1(b)(20)).

(vi) A certification that arrangements have been made to ensure that there will be no foreign use of the dual consolidated loss during the certification period, and that the elector will be informed of any such foreign use of the dual consolidated loss during such period.

(vii) If applicable, a notification that an excepted triggering event under paragraph (f)(2) of this section has occurred with respect to the dual consolidated loss within the taxable year in which the loss is incurred. See paragraph (g) of this section for notification of excepted triggering events occurring during the certification period.

(2) *No domestic use election available if there is a triggering event in the year the dual consolidated loss is incurred.*—Except as otherwise provided in this section, if a dual resident corporation or separate unit incurs a dual consolidated loss in a taxable year and a triggering event, as described in paragraph (e)(1) of this section, occurs (and no exception applies) with respect to the dual consolidated loss in such taxable year, then the consolidated group, unaffiliated dual resident corporation, or unaffiliated domestic owner, as the case may be, may not make a domestic use election with respect to such dual consolidated loss and the loss will be subject to the domestic use limitation rule of § 1.1503(d)-4(b). See § 1.1503(d)-7(c) *Examples 5* through *7*. See also § 1.1503(d)-4(d) for rules that eliminate a dual consolidated loss after certain transactions.

(e) *Triggering events requiring the recapture of a dual consolidated loss.*—(1) *Events.*—Except as provided under paragraphs (e)(2) (rebuttal of triggering events) and (f) (exceptions to triggering events) of this section, if there is a triggering event described in this paragraph (e)(1) with respect to a dual consolidated loss of a dual resident corporation or a separate unit during the certification period (as defined in § 1.1503(d)-1(b)(20)), the elector will recapture and report as ordinary income the amount of such dual consolidated loss as provided in paragraph (h) of this section on its tax return for the taxable year in which the triggering event occurs (or, when the triggering event is a foreign use of the dual consolidated loss, the taxable year that includes the last day of the foreign taxable year during which such use occurs). In addition, the elector must pay any applicable interest charge required by paragraph (h) of this section. For purposes of this section, any of the following events shall constitute a triggering event:

(i) *Foreign use.*—A foreign use (as defined in § 1.1503(d)-3) of the dual consolidated loss. See § 1.1503(d)-3(c) for exceptions to foreign use.

(ii) *Disaffiliation.*—An affiliated dual resident corporation or affiliated domestic owner that incurred directly or through a separate unit, respectively, a dual consolidated loss that is subject to a domestic use election, ceases to be a member of the consolidated group that made the domestic use election. For purposes of this paragraph (e)(1)(ii), an affiliated dual resident corporation or affiliated domestic owner shall be considered to cease to be a member of the consolidated group if it is no longer a member of the group within the meaning of § 1.1502-1(b), or if the group ceases to exist (for example, when the group no longer files a consolidated return). See § 1.1503(d)-7(c) *Example 34*. Any consequences resulting from this triggering event (for example, recapture of a dual consolidated loss) shall be taken into account on the tax return of the consolidated group for the taxable year that includes the date on which the affiliated dual resident corporation or affiliated domestic owner ceases to be a member of the consolidated group. This paragraph (e)(1)(ii) shall not apply to an acquisition described in § 1.1502-75(d)(3) where the consolidated group that includes the affiliated dual resident corporation or affiliated domestic owner, as applicable, is treated as remaining in existence.

(iii) *Affiliation.*—An unaffiliated dual resident corporation or unaffiliated domestic owner becomes a member of a consolidated group. Any consequences resulting from this triggering event (for example, recapture of a dual consolidated loss) shall be taken into account on the tax return of the unaffiliated dual resident corporation or unaffiliated domestic owner for the taxable year that ends at the end of the day on which such corporation becomes a member of the consolidated group.

(iv) *Transfer of assets.*—Fifty percent or more of the dual resident corporation's or separate unit's gross assets (measured by the fair market value of the assets at the time of such transaction or, for multiple transactions, at the time of the first transaction) is sold or otherwise disposed of in either a single transaction or a series of transactions within a twelve-month period. See § 1.1503(d)-7(c) *Examples 5* and *35* through *37*. In determining whether fifty percent or more of such assets is sold or otherwise disposed of, any dispositions occurring in the ordinary course of the dual resident corporation's or separate unit's trade or business shall be disregarded. In addition, for purposes of this paragraph (e)(1)(iv), an interest in another separate unit and the shares of a dual resident corporation shall not be treated as assets of a separate unit or a dual resident corporation.

(v) *Transfer of an interest in a separate unit.*—Fifty percent or more of the interest in a separate unit (measured by voting power or value at the time of such transaction, or for multiple transactions, at the time of the first transaction) of the domestic owner, as determined by reference to such domestic owner's percentage interest on the last day of the taxable year in which the dual consolidated loss was incurred, is sold or otherwise disposed of either in a single transaction or a series of transactions within a twelve-month period. See § 1.1503(d)-7(c) *Examples 5* and *35* through *37*.

(vi) *Conversion to a foreign corporation.*—An unaffiliated dual resident corporation, unaffiliated domestic owner, or hybrid entity an interest in which is a separate unit, that incurred the dual consolidated loss, becomes a foreign corporation (for example, as a result of a reorganization or an election to be classified as a corporation under § 301.7701-3(c) of this chapter).

(vii) *Conversion to a regulated investment company, a real estate investment trust, or an S corporation.*—An unaffiliated dual resident corporation or unaffiliated domestic owner elects to be a regulated investment company pursuant to section 851(b)(1), a real estate investment trust pursuant to section 856(c)(1), or an S corporation pursuant to section 1362(a).

(viii) *Failure to certify.*—The elector fails to file a certification with respect to a dual consolidated loss as required under paragraph (g) of this section.

(ix) *Cessation of stand-alone status.*—In the case of a dual consolidated loss that is subject to the stand-alone exception described in § 1.1503(d)-3(e)(2), the conditions described in § 1.1503(d)-3(e)(2)(i) are no longer satisfied. See § 1.1503(d)-7(c) *Example 18*.

(2) *Rebuttal.*—(i) *General rule.*—An event described in paragraph (e)(1) of this section shall not constitute a triggering event if the elector demonstrates, to the satisfaction of the Commissioner, that there can be no foreign use (as defined in § 1.1503(d)-3) of the dual consolidated loss during the remaining certification period by any means. See paragraph (j)(1) of this section for rules regarding the termination of domestic use agreements and annual certifications following rebuttals under this general rule.

(ii) *Certain asset transfers.*—An event described in paragraph (e)(1)(iv) of this section shall not constitute a triggering event if the elector demonstrates, to the satisfaction of the Commissioner, that the transfer of assets did not result in a carryover under foreign law of the dual resident corporation's, or separate unit's, losses, expenses, or deductions to the transferee of the assets. For purposes of this determination, the exception to foreign use in § 1.1503(d)-3(c)(7) shall be taken into account. Following rebuttal under this paragraph (e)(2)(ii), the domestic use agreement continues in effect.

(iii) *Reporting.*—In order to satisfy the requirements of paragraph (e)(2)(i) or (ii) of this section, the elector must prepare a statement, labeled "Rebuttal of Triggering Event" at the top of the page, that indicates that it is submitted under the provisions of this paragraph (e)(2). The statement must include the information described in paragraphs (c)(2)(ii) and (iii) of this section. The statement must also include the information described in paragraph (c)(2)(iv) of this section that supports the conclusions under paragraph (e)(2)(i) or (ii) of this section, as applicable. The statement must be attached to, and filed by the due date (including extensions) of, the elector's income tax return for the taxable year in which the presumed triggering event occurs.

(iv) *Examples.*—See § 1.1503(d)-7(c) *Examples 32 and 33*.

(f) *Triggering event exceptions.*—(1) *Continuing ownership of assets or interests.*—The following events shall not constitute triggering events, requiring the recapture of the dual consolidated loss under paragraph (h) of this section:

(i) *Disaffiliation as a result of a transaction described in section 381.*—An affiliated dual resident corporation or affiliated domestic owner ceases to be a member of a consolidated group solely by reason of a transaction in which a member of the same consolidated group succeeds to the tax attributes of the dual resident corporation or domestic owner under the provisions of section 381.

(ii) *Continuing ownership by consolidated group.*—This paragraph (f)(1)(ii) applies when assets of an affiliated dual resident corporation, or assets of, or interests in, a separate unit of an affiliated domestic owner are sold or otherwise disposed of. In such a case, the sale or disposition shall not be treated as a triggering event to the extent the assets or interests are acquired by one or more members of the consolidated group that includes the affiliated dual resident corporation or affiliated domestic owner, or by a partnership or a grantor trust, but only if immediately after the acquisition more than 90 percent of the partnership's or grantor trust's interests is owned, directly or indirectly, by members of such consolidated group.

(iii) *Continuing ownership by unaffiliated dual resident corporation or unaffiliated domestic owner.*—This paragraph (f)(1)(iii) applies when assets of an unaffiliated dual resident corporation, or assets of, or interests in, a separate unit of an unaffiliated domestic owner, are sold or otherwise disposed of. In such a case, the sale or disposition shall not be a triggering event to the extent such assets or interests are acquired by the unaffiliated dual resident corporation, or unaffiliated domestic owner, as applicable, or by a partnership or grantor trust, but only if immediately after the acquisition more than 90 percent of the partnership's or grantor trust's interests is owned, directly or indirectly, by the unaffiliated dual resident corporation or unaffiliated domestic owner. For example, this paragraph (f)(1)(iii) applies when an unaffiliated domestic owner acquires direct ownership of the assets of a separate unit that it had immediately before owned indirectly through a partnership.

(2) *Transactions requiring a new domestic use agreement.*—(i) *Multiple-party events.*—If all the requirements of paragraph (f)(2)(iii) of this section are satisfied, the following events shall not constitute triggering events requiring the recapture of the dual consolidated loss under paragraph (h) of this section:

(A) An affiliated dual resident corporation or affiliated domestic owner becomes an unaffiliated domestic corporation or a member of a new consolidated group (other than in a transaction described in paragraph (f)(2)(ii)(B) of this section).

(B) Assets of a dual resident corporation or assets of, or interests in, a separate unit, are sold or otherwise disposed of in a transaction in which such assets or interests are acquired by an unaffiliated domestic corporation, one or more members of a new consolidated group, or by a partnership or grantor trust, but only if immediately after the sale or disposition more than 90 percent of the partnership's or grantor trust's interests is owned, directly or indirectly, by the unaffiliated domestic owner or by members of a new consolidated group, as applicable. See the related exception to foreign use provided under § 1.1503(d)-3(c)(8). See also § 1.1503(d)-7(c) *Examples 36 and 37*.

(ii) *Events resulting in a single consolidated group.*—If the requirements of paragraph (f)(2)(iii)(A) of this section are satisfied, the following events shall not constitute triggering events requiring the recapture of the dual consolidated loss under paragraph (h) of this section:

(A) An unaffiliated dual resident corporation or unaffiliated domestic owner becomes a member of a consolidated group.

(B) A consolidated group ceases to exist as a result of a transaction described in § 1.1502-13(j)(5)(i) (relating to acquisitions of the common parent of the consolidated group), other than a transaction in which any member of the terminating group, or the successor-in-interest of such member, is not a member of the surviving group immediately after the terminating group ceases to exist. See § 1.1503(d)-7(c) *Example 34*.

(iii) *Requirements.*—(A) *New domestic use agreement.*—The unaffiliated domestic corporation or new consolidated group (subsequent elector) must file an agreement described in paragraph (d)(1) of this section (new domestic use agreement). The new domestic use agreement must be labeled "New Domestic Use Agreement" at the top of the page, and must be attached to and filed by the due date (including extensions) of, the subsequent elector's income tax return for the taxable year in which the event described in paragraph (f)(2)(i) or (f)(2)(ii) of this section occurs. The new domestic use agreement must be signed under penalties of perjury by the person who signs the return and must include the following items:

(*1*) A statement that the document submitted is an election and agreement under the provisions of paragraph (f)(2) of this section.

(*2*) An agreement to assume the same obligations with respect to the dual consolidated loss as the unaffiliated dual resident corporation, unaffiliated domestic owner, or consolidated group, as applicable, that filed the original domestic use agreement (original elector) with respect to that loss. In such a case, obligations of an elector provided under this section shall also be considered to be obligations of a subsequent elector.

(3) In the event of a transaction described in section 384(a) involving the subsequent elector, an agreement to treat any potential recapture amount under paragraph (h) of this section with respect to the dual consolidated loss as unrealized built-in gain for purposes of section 384(a), subject to any applicable exceptions (for example, the threshold requirements under section 382(h)(3)(B)). The potential recapture amount treated as unrealized built-in gain under this paragraph (f)(2)(iii)(A)(3) may be reduced to the extent permitted by paragraph (h)(2)(i) of this section.

(4) In the case of a multiple-party event described in paragraph (f)(2)(i) of this section, an agreement to be subject to the rules provided in paragraph (h)(3) of this section.

(5) The name, U.S. taxpayer identification number, and address of the original elector and prior subsequent electors, if any, with respect to the dual consolidated loss.

(B) *Statement filed by original elector.*—In the case of a multiple-party event described in paragraph (f)(2)(i) of this section, the original elector must file a statement that is attached to and filed by the due date (including extensions) of its income tax return for the taxable year in which the event occurs. The statement must be labeled "Original Elector Statement" at the top of the page, must be signed under penalties of perjury by the person who signs the tax return, and must include the following items:

(1) A statement that the document submitted is an election and agreement under the provisions of paragraph (f)(2) of this section.

(2) An agreement to be subject to the rules provided in paragraph (h)(3) of this section.

(3) The name, U.S. taxpayer identification number, and address of the subsequent elector.

(3) *Certain transfers qualifying for the de minimis exception to foreign use.*—If a transaction or event qualifies for the de minimis exception to foreign use described in § 1.1503(d)-3(c)(5), the transaction or event shall not constitute a triggering event under paragraph (e)(1)(iv) (transfers of assets) or (v) (transfers of an interest in a separate unit) of this section. For purposes of the preceding sentence, the transaction or event shall include deemed transfers that occur as a result of the transaction or event. See, for example, deemed transfers occurring pursuant to Rev. Rul. 99-5 (1999-1 CB 434), see § 601.601(d)(2)(ii)(b), and section 708 and the related regulations. See also § 1.1503(d)-7 *Example 5*. This paragraph (f)(3) only applies if the entire transaction or event qualifies for the de minimis exception to foreign use. For example, if a domestic owner sells five percent of a separate unit to a foreign corporation, which would qualify for the de minimis exception to foreign use if it were the only transfer, but pursuant to the same transaction also sells 70 percent of the same separate unit to another corporation in a manner that results in a triggering event under paragraph (e)(1)(v) of this section, this paragraph shall not apply to prevent the transaction from resulting in a triggering event.

(4) *Deemed transactions as a result of certain transfers that do not result in a foreign use.*—The rules in this paragraph (f)(4) apply where the assets of, or the interests in, a separate unit are transferred in a transaction that would not result in a foreign use and, but for resulting deemed transactions or events, would not result in a triggering event described in paragraph (e)(1) of this section. For purposes of this paragraph (f)(4), deemed transactions or events shall include transactions or events that are deemed to occur pursuant to Rev. Rul. 99-5 and section 708 and the related regulations. In such a case, the deemed transactions shall not result in a triggering event under paragraph (e)(1)(iv) (transfers of assets) or (v) (transfers of an interest in a separate unit) of this section. See also § 1.1503(d)-7 *Example 35*.

(5) *Compulsory transfers.*—Transfers of the assets or stock of a dual resident corporation, or of the assets or interests in a separate unit, shall not constitute a triggering event (including a foreign use that occurs as a result of, or following, the transfer) if such transfers are—

(i) Legally required by a government of a country as a necessary condition of doing business in the country;

(ii) Compelled by a genuine threat of immediate expropriation by a government of a country; or

(iii) The result of the expropriation of assets by a government of a country.

(6) *Subsequent triggering events.*—Any triggering event described in paragraph (e) of this section that occurs subsequent to one of the transactions described in this paragraph (f), and that itself does not meet any of the exceptions provided in this paragraph (f), shall require recapture under paragraph (h) of this section by the elector or subsequent elector, as applicable.

(g) *Annual certification reporting requirement.*—Unless and until the domestic use agreement is terminated pursuant to paragraph (j) of this section, the elector must file a certification, labeled "Certification of Dual Consolidated Loss" at the top of the page, that is attached to, and filed by the due date (including extensions) of, its income tax return for each taxable year during the certification period. The certification must provide that there has been no foreign use of the dual consolidated loss. The certification must identify the dual consolidated loss to which it pertains by setting forth the elector's year in which the loss was incurred and the amount of such loss. In addition, the certification must warrant that arrangements have been made to ensure that there will be no foreign use of the dual consolidated loss and that the elector will be informed of any such foreign use. If applicable, the certification must include a notification that an excepted triggering event under paragraph (f)(2) of this section has occurred with respect to the dual consolidated loss within the taxable year being certified. If dual consolidated losses of more than one taxable year are subject to the rules of this paragraph (g), the certification for those years may be combined in a single document, but each dual consolidated loss must be separately identified. See § 1.1503(d)-3(e)(2)(ii) for additional certifications required where taxpayers elect the stand-alone exception of § 1.1503(d)-3(e)(2).

(h) *Recapture of dual consolidated loss and interest charge.*—(1) *Presumptive rules.*—(i) *Amount of recapture.*—Except as otherwise provided in this section, upon the occurrence of a triggering event described in paragraph (e) of this section that does not meet any of the exceptions provided in paragraph (f) of this section, the dual resident corporation or domestic owner of the separate unit shall recapture as gross income the total amount of the dual consolidated loss to which the triggering event applies on its income tax return for the taxable year in which the triggering event occurs (or, when the triggering event is a foreign use of the dual consolidated loss, the taxable year that includes the last day of the foreign taxable year during which such foreign use occurs). See § 1.1503(d)-5(c)(4)(vi) for rules with respect to the attribution of recapture income to a separate unit. See also § 1.1503(d)-7 *Examples 38* through *40*.

(ii) *Interest charge.*—In connection with the recapture, the elector shall pay an interest charge. An interest charge may be due even if the amount of recapture income is reduced to zero pursuant to paragraph (h)(2)(i) of this section. See § 1.1503(d)-7(c) *Example 39*. Except as otherwise provided in this section, the amount of the interest shall be computed under the rules of section 6601(a) by treating the additional tax resulting from the recapture as though it had been due and unpaid as of the date for payment of the tax for the taxable year in which the taxpayer received a tax benefit from the dual consolidated loss. For purposes of this paragraph (h)(1)(ii), a tax benefit shall be considered to have arisen in a taxable year in which the losses or deductions taken into account in computing the dual consolidated loss reduced U.S. taxable income. For the purpose of computing the interest charge, the additional tax resulting from the recapture is determined by treating the recapture income as the last income earned in the year of recapture. The interest shall be computed to the date for payment of the tax for the year of recapture and the interest thus computed becomes a part of the tax liability for that taxable year. See section 6601 for the computation of interest on a tax liability that it is not paid timely. The recapture interest charge shall be deductible to the same extent as interest under section 6601.

(2) *Reduction of presumptive recapture amount and presumptive interest charge.*—(i) *Amount of recapture.*—The dual resident corporation or domestic owner may recapture an amount less than the total dual consolidated loss if the elector demonstrates, to the satisfaction of the Commissioner, the lesser amount described in this paragraph (h)(2)(i). The reduction in the amount of recapture is the amount by which the dual consolidated loss would have offset other taxable income reported on a timely filed U.S. income tax return for any taxable year up to and including the taxable year of the triggering event (or, when the triggering event is a foreign use of the dual consolidated loss, the taxable year that includes the last day of the foreign taxable year during which such foreign use occurs) if no domestic use election had been made for the loss such that it was subject to the domestic use limitation of § 1.1503(d)-4(b) (and therefore subject to the limitation under § 1.1503(d)-4(c)). For this purpose, the rules for attributing items of income, gain, deduction, and loss under § 1.1503(d)-5 shall apply. An elector using this rebuttal rule

must prepare a separate accounting showing the income for each year that would have offset the dual resident corporation's or separate unit's recapture amount if no domestic use election had been made for the dual consolidated loss. The separate accounting must be signed under penalties of perjury by the person who signs the elector's tax return, must be labeled "Reduction of Recapture Amount" at the top of the page, and must indicate that it is submitted under the provisions of this paragraph (h)(2)(i). The accounting must be attached to, and filed by the due date (including extensions) of, the elector's income tax return for the taxable year in which the triggering event occurs. See § 1.1503(d)-7(c) *Examples 38* through *40*.

(ii) *Interest charge.*—The interest charge imposed under this section may be reduced if the elector demonstrates, to the satisfaction of the Commissioner, that the net interest owed would have been less than that provided in paragraph (h)(1)(ii) of this section if the elector had filed an amended return for the taxable year in which the recaptured dual consolidated loss was incurred, and for any other affected taxable years up to and including the taxable year of recapture, if no domestic use election had been made for the dual consolidated loss such that it had been subject to the restrictions of § 1.1503(d)-4(b) (and therefore subject to the limitations under § 1.1503(d)-4(c)). An elector using this rebuttal rule must prepare a computation demonstrating the reduction in the net interest owed as a result of treating the dual consolidated loss as a loss subject to the restrictions of § 1.1503(d)-4(b) (and therefore subject to the limitations under § 1.1503(d)-4(c)). The computation must be labeled "Reduction of Interest Charge" at the top of the page and must indicate that it is submitted under the provisions of this paragraph (h)(2)(ii). The computation must be signed under penalties of perjury by the person who signs the elector's tax return, and must be attached to, and filed by the due date (including extensions) of, the elector's income tax return for the taxable year in which the triggering event occurs. See § 1.1503(d)-7(c) *Examples 39 and 40*.

(3) *Rules regarding multiple-party event exceptions to triggering events.*—(i) *Scope.*—The rules of this paragraph (h)(3) apply when, after a triggering event described in paragraph (e) of this section with respect to which the requirements of paragraph (f)(2)(i) of this section were met (excepted event), a triggering event under paragraph (e) of this section occurs, and no exception applies to such triggering event under paragraph (f) of this section (subsequent triggering event). See § 1.1503(d)-7(c) *Examples 36 and 37*.

(ii) *Original elector and prior subsequent electors not subject to recapture or interest charge.*—(A) Except to the extent otherwise provided in this paragraph (h)(3), neither the original elector nor any prior subsequent elector shall be subject to the rules of this paragraph (h) with respect to dual consolidated losses subject to the original domestic use agreement.

(B) In the case of a dual consolidated loss with respect to which multiple excepted events have occurred, only the subsequent elector that owns the dual resident corporation or separate unit at the time of the subsequent triggering event shall be subject to the recapture rules of this paragraph (h). For purposes of this paragraph (h), the term prior subsequent elector refers to all other subsequent electors.

(iii) *Recapture tax amount and required statement.*—(A) *In general.*—If a subsequent triggering event occurs, the subsequent elector shall take into account the recapture tax amount as determined under paragraph (h)(3)(iii)(B) of this section. The subsequent elector must prepare a statement that computes the recapture tax amount, as provided under paragraph (h)(3)(iii)(B) of this section, with respect to the dual consolidated loss subject to the new domestic use agreement. This statement must be attached to, and filed by the due date (including extensions) of, the subsequent elector's income tax return for the taxable year in which the subsequent triggering event occurs (or, when the subsequent triggering event is a foreign use of the dual consolidated loss, the taxable year that includes the last day of the foreign taxable year during which such foreign use occurs). The statement must be signed under penalties of perjury by the person who signs the return. The statement must be labeled "Statement Identifying Liability" at the top and, in addition to the calculation of the recapture tax amount, must include the following items, in paragraphs labeled to correspond with the items set forth in paragraphs (h)(3)(iii)(A)(1) through (3) of this section:

(1) A statement that the document is submitted under the provisions of § 1.1503(d)-6(h)(3)(iii).

(2) A statement identifying the amount of the dual consolidated losses at issue and the taxable years in which they were used.

(3) The name, address, and taxpayer identification number of the original elector and all prior subsequent electors.

(B) *Recapture tax amount.*—The recapture tax amount equals the excess (if any) of—

(1) The income tax liability of the subsequent elector for the taxable year that includes the amount of recapture and related interest charge with respect to the dual consolidated losses that are recaptured as a result of the subsequent triggering event, as provided under paragraphs (h)(1) and (h)(2) of this section; over

(2) The income tax liability of the subsequent elector for such taxable year, computed by excluding the amount of recapture and related interest charge described in paragraph (h)(3)(iii)(B)(1) of this section.

(iv) *Tax assessment and collection procedures.*—(A) *In general.*—(1) *Subsequent elector.*—An assessment identifying an income tax liability of the subsequent elector is considered an assessment of the recapture tax amount where the recapture tax amount is part of the income tax liability being assessed and the recapture tax amount is reflected in a statement attached to the subsequent elector's income tax return as provided under paragraph (h)(3)(iii) of this section.

(2) *Original elector and prior subsequent electors.*—The assessment of the recapture tax amount as set forth in paragraph (h)(3)(iv)(A)(1) of this section shall be considered as having been properly assessed as an income tax liability of the original elector and of each prior subsequent elector, if any. The date of such assessment shall be the date the income tax liability of the subsequent elector was properly assessed. The Commissioner may collect all or a portion of such recapture tax amount from the original elector and/or the prior subsequent electors under the circumstances set forth in paragraph (h)(3)(iv)(B) of this section.

(B) *Collection from original elector and prior subsequent electors; joint and several liability.*—(1) *In general.*—If the subsequent elector does not pay in full the income tax liability that includes a recapture tax amount, the Commissioner may collect that portion of the unpaid balance of such income tax liability attributable to the recapture tax amount in full or in part from the original elector and/or from any prior subsequent elector, provided that the following conditions are satisfied with respect to such elector:

(i) The Commissioner properly has assessed the recapture tax amount pursuant to paragraph (h)(3)(iv)(A)(1) of this section.

(ii) The Commissioner has issued a notice and demand for payment of the recapture tax amount to the subsequent elector in accordance with § 301.6303-1 of this chapter.

(iii) The subsequent elector has failed to pay all of the recapture tax amount by the date specified in such notice and demand.

(iv) The Commissioner has issued a notice and demand for payment of the unpaid portion of the recapture tax amount to the original elector, or prior subsequent elector (as the case may be), in accordance with § 301.6303-1 of this chapter.

(2) *Joint and several liability.*—The liability imposed under this paragraph (h)(3)(iv)(B) on the original elector and each prior subsequent elector shall be joint and several.

(C) *Allocation of partial payments of tax.*—If the subsequent elector's income tax liability for a taxable period includes a recapture tax amount, and if such income tax liability is satisfied in part by payment, credit, or offset, such payment, credit or offset shall be allocated first to that portion of the income tax liability that is not attributable to the recapture tax amount, and then to that portion of the income tax liability that is attributable to the recapture tax amount.

(D) *Refund.*—If the Commissioner makes a refund of any income tax liability that includes a recapture tax amount, the Commissioner shall allocate and pay the refund to each elector who paid a portion of such income tax liability as follows:

(1) The Commissioner shall first determine the total amount of recapture tax paid by and/or collected from the original elector and from any prior subsequent electors. The Commissioner shall then allocate and pay such refund to the original elector and prior subsequent electors, with each such elector receiving an amount of such refund on a pro rata basis, not to exceed the amount of recapture tax paid by and/or collected from such elector.

(2) The Commissioner shall pay the balance of such refund, if any, to the subsequent elector.

(v) *Definition of income tax liability.*—Solely for purposes of paragraph (h)(3) of this section, the term income tax liability means the income tax liability imposed on a domestic corporation under Title 26 of the United States Code for a taxable year, including additions to tax, additional amounts, penalties, and any interest charge related to such income tax liability.

(vi) *Example.*—See § 1.1503(d)-7(c) *Example 36.*

(4) *Computation of taxable income in year of recapture.*—(i) *Presumptive rule.*—Except to the extent provided in paragraph (h)(4)(ii) of this section, for purposes of computing the taxable income for the year of recapture, no current, carryover or carryback losses may offset and absorb the recapture amount.

(ii) *Exception to presumptive rule.*—The recapture amount included in gross income may be offset and absorbed by that portion of the elector's net operating loss carryover that is attributable to the dual resident corporation or separate unit that incurred the dual consolidated loss being recaptured, if the elector demonstrates, to the satisfaction of the Commissioner, the amount of such portion of the carryover. The principles of § 1.1502-21(b)(2)(iv) shall apply for purposes of determining whether any portion of a net operating loss carryover is attributable to the dual resident corporation or separate unit. In the case of a separate unit, such determination shall be made by treating the separate unit as a domestic corporation and a member of the consolidated group composing its unaffiliated domestic owner, or members of the consolidated group of which its affiliated domestic owner is a member, as appropriate. An elector utilizing this rebuttal rule must prepare a computation demonstrating the amount of net operating loss carryover that, under this paragraph (h)(4)(ii), may absorb the recapture amount included in gross income. Such computation must be signed under penalties of perjury and attached to and filed by the due date (including extensions) of, the income tax return for the taxable year in which the triggering event occurs (or, when the triggering event is a foreign use of the dual consolidated loss, the taxable year that includes the last day of the foreign taxable year during which such foreign use occurs).

(5) *Character and source of recapture income.*—The amount recaptured under this paragraph (h) shall be treated as ordinary income. Except as provided in the prior sentence, such income shall be treated, as applicable, as income from the same source, having the same character, and falling within the same separate category, for all purposes, including sections 904(d) and 907, to which the items of deduction or loss composing the dual consolidated loss were allocated and apportioned, as provided under sections 861(b), 862(b), 863(a), 864(e), 865, and the related regulations. For this determination, the pro rata computation of the items of deduction or loss composing the dual consolidated loss as described in § 1.1503(d)-4(c)(4) shall apply. See § 1.1503(d)-7(c) *Example 38.*

(6) *Reconstituted net operating loss.*—(i) *General rule.*—Except as provided in paragraphs (h)(6)(ii) and (iii) of this section, commencing in the taxable year immediately following the year in which the dual consolidated loss is recaptured, the dual resident corporation, or the domestic owner of the separate unit, that incurred the dual consolidated loss that is recaptured shall be treated as having a net operating loss (reconstituted net operating loss) in an amount equal to the amount actually recaptured under this paragraph (h). If a domestic corporation (transferee) acquires the assets of the dual resident corporation or domestic owner in a transaction described in section 381(a), the preceding sentence shall be applied by treating the transferee as the dual resident corporation or domestic owner, as applicable. In a case to which this paragraph (h)(6) applies, the transferee corporation shall be treated as having a reconstituted net operating loss in an amount equal to the amount actually recaptured under this paragraph (h). In no event, however, shall more than one corporation be treated as having a reconstituted net operating loss as a result of a single dual consolidated loss being recaptured. A reconstituted net operating loss of a domestic owner shall be attributable under § 1.1503(d)-5 to the separate unit that incurred the dual consolidated loss that was recaptured. Moreover, a reconstituted net operating loss shall be subject to the domestic use limitation of § 1.1503(d)-4(b) (and therefore subject to the limitation under § 1.1503(d)-4(c)), without regard to the exceptions contained in paragraphs (b) through (d) of this section (relating to elective agreements in place between the United States and a foreign country, the ability to demonstrate no possibility of a foreign use, and a domestic use election, respectively). The reconstituted net operating loss shall be available only for carryover, under section 172(b), to taxable years following the taxable year of recapture. For purposes of determining the remaining carryover period, the reconstituted net operating loss shall be treated as if it had been recognized in the taxable year in which the dual consolidated loss that is the basis of the recapture amount was incurred. See § 1.1503(d)-7(c) *Examples 36, 38, and 40.*

(ii) *Exception.*—Paragraph (h)(6)(i) of this section shall not apply to the extent the dual consolidated loss that is the basis of the recapture amount would have been eliminated pursuant to § 1.1503(d)-4(d) if no domestic use election had been made for such loss. See § 1.1503(d)-7(c) *Example 40.*

(iii) *Special rule for recapture following multiple-party event exception to a triggering event.*—This paragraph applies to an excepted event described in paragraph (f)(2)(i)(B) of this section that is followed by a subsequent triggering event requiring recapture as described in paragraph (f)(6) of this section. In such a case, the domestic corporation that owns, directly or indirectly, the assets of the dual resident corporation, or the assets of or the interests in a separate unit, immediately following the excepted event shall be treated as if it incurred the dual consolidated loss that is recaptured for purposes of applying paragraph (h)(6)(i) of this section. See § 1.1503(d)-7(c) *Example 36.*

(i) *[Reserved].*

(j) *Termination of domestic use agreement and annual certifications.*—(1) *Rebuttals, exceptions to triggering events, and recapture.*—The domestic use agreement filed with respect to a dual consolidated loss shall terminate prior to the end of the certification period and have no further effect if—

(i) An elector is able to rebut the presumption of a triggering event pursuant to the general rule in paragraph (e)(2)(i) of this section;

(ii) An event described in paragraph (e)(1) of this section is not a triggering event as a result of the application of paragraphs (f)(2)(i) or (ii) (relating to events requiring a new domestic use agreement) of this section; this paragraph (j)(1)(ii) does not, however, apply to terminate the new domestic use agreement filed in connection with the event pursuant to paragraph (f)(2)(iii)(A) of this section. See also paragraph (h)(3)(iv) of this section regarding collection from the original elector and prior subsequent electors in certain cases; or

(iii) A dual consolidated loss is recaptured pursuant to paragraph (h) of this section. See § 1.1503(d)-7(c) *Examples 32* through *34.*

(2) *Termination of ability for foreign use.*—(i) *In general.*—A domestic use agreement filed with respect to a dual consolidated loss shall terminate and have no further effect as of the end of a taxable year if the elector—

(A) Demonstrates, to the satisfaction of the Commissioner, that as of the end of such taxable year no foreign use (as defined in § 1.1503(d)-3) of the dual consolidated loss can occur in any other year by any means; and

(B) Prepares a statement described in paragraph (j)(2)(ii) of this section that is attached to, and filed by the due date (including extensions) of, its U.S. income tax return for such taxable year.

(ii) *Statement.*—The statement described in this paragraph (j)(2)(ii) must be signed under penalties of perjury by the person who signs the return. The statement must be labeled "Termination of Ability for Foreign Use" at the top of the page and must include the following information, in paragraphs labeled to correspond with the following:

(A) A statement that the document is submitted under the provisions of paragraph (j)(2) of this section.

(B) The information required by paragraph (c)(2)(ii) of this section.

(C) A statement of the amount of the dual consolidated loss at issue and the year in which such dual consolidated loss was incurred.

(D) The information described in paragraph (c)(2)(iv) of this section that supports the conclusion that no foreign use can occur as provided in paragraph (j)(2)(i)(A) of this section.

(3) *Agreements filed in connection with stand-alone exception.*—See § 1.1503(d)-3(e)(2)(iii) for the termination of domestic use agreements filed in connection with the stand-alone exception to the mirror legislation rule when a subsequent election is made under paragraph (b) of this section (relating to agreements entered into between the United States and a foreign country). [Reg. § 1.1503(d)-6.]

☐ *[T.D.* 9315, 3-16-2007. *Amended by T.D.* 9896, 4-7-2020.]

§1.1503(d)-7. Examples.—(a) *In general.*—This section provides examples that illustrate the application of §§1.1503(d)-1 through 1.1503(d)-6. This section also provides facts that are presumed for such examples.

(b) *Presumed facts for examples.*—For purposes of the examples in this section, unless otherwise indicated, the following facts are presumed:

(1) Each entity has only a single class of equity outstanding, all of which is held by a single owner.

(2) P, a domestic corporation and the common parent of the P consolidated group, owns S, a domestic corporation and a member of the P consolidated group.

(3) DRCX, a domestic corporation, is subject to Country X tax on its worldwide income or on a residence basis, and is a dual resident corporation.

(4) DE1X and DE2X are both Country X entities, subject to Country X tax on their worldwide income or on a residence basis, and disregarded as entities separate from their owners for U.S. tax purposes. DE3Y is a Country Y entity, subject to Country Y tax on its worldwide income or on a residence basis, and disregarded as an entity separate from its owner for U.S. tax purposes. All the interests in DE1X, DE2X, and DE3Y constitute hybrid entity separate units.

(5) FBX is a Country X business operation that, if carried on by a U.S. person, would constitute a foreign branch, as defined in §1.367(a)-6T(g)(1), and is a Country X foreign branch separate unit.

(6) Neither the assets nor the activities of an entity constitute a foreign branch separate unit.

(7) FSX is a Country X entity that is subject to Country X tax on its worldwide income or on a residence basis and is classified as a foreign corporation for U.S. tax purposes.

(8) The applicable foreign country has a consolidation regime that—

(i) Includes as members of a consolidated group any commonly controlled branches and permanent establishments in such jurisdiction, and entities that are subject to tax in such jurisdiction on their worldwide income or on a residence basis; and

(ii) Allows the losses of members of consolidated groups to offset income of other members.

(9) There is no mirror legislation, within the meaning of §1.1503(d)-3(e)(1), in the applicable foreign country.

(10) There is no elective agreement described in §1.1503(d)-6(b) between the United States and the applicable foreign country.

(11) There is no income tax convention between the United States and the applicable foreign country.

(12) If a domestic use election, within the meaning of §1.1503(d)-6(d), is made, all the necessary filings related to such election are properly completed on a timely basis.

(13) If there is a triggering event requiring recapture of a dual consolidated loss, the amount of recapture is not reduced pursuant to §1.1503(d)-6(h)(2).

(14) There are no other items of income, gain, deduction, and loss. In addition, the United States and the applicable foreign country recognize the same items of income, gain, deduction, and loss in each taxable year.

(15) All taxpayers use the calendar year as their taxable year.

(c) *Examples.*—The following examples illustrate the application of §§1.1503(d)-1 through 1.1503(d)-6:

(1) *Example 1. Separate unit combination rule.* (i) *Facts.* P owns DE3Y which, in turn, owns DE1X. DE1X owns FBX. PRS, an entity treated as a partnership for both U.S. and Country X tax purposes, is owned 50 percent by P and 50 percent by an unrelated foreign person. PRS carries on a business operation in Country X that, if carried on by a U.S. person, would constitute a foreign branch within the meaning of §1.367(a)-6T(g)(1). In addition, P owns DRCX, a member of the consolidated group of which P is the parent, which carries on business operations in Country X that constitute a foreign branch within the meaning of §1.367(a)-6T(g)(1). S owns DE2X.

(ii) *Result.* Pursuant to §1.1503(d)-1(b)(4)(ii), the interest in DE1X, the interest in DE2X, FBX, P's share of the Country X business operations carried on by PRS (which is owned by P indirectly through its interest in PRS), and DRCX's Country X business operations are combined and treated as a single separate unit of the consolidated group of which P is the parent. This is the case regardless of whether the losses of each individual separate unit are made available to offset the income of the other individual separate units under Country X tax laws. Because DRCX is a dual resident corporation, it is not combined and treated as part of this combined separate unit and, as a result, DRCx's income or dual consolidated loss is not taken into account in determining the income or dual consolidated loss of the combined separate unit. In addition, P's interest in DE3Y is not combined and is another separate unit because it is subject to tax in Country Y, rather than Country X.

(2) *Example 2. Definition of a separate unit and application of domestic use limitation—foreign branch separate unit.* (i) *Facts.* P carries on business operations in Country X that constitute a permanent establishment under the U.S.-Country X income tax convention. In year 1, a loss is attributable to P's Country X permanent establishment, as determined under §1.1503(d)-5.

(ii) *Result.* Under §§1.1503(d)-1(b)(4)(i)(A) and 1.367(a)-6T(g)(1), P's Country X permanent establishment constitutes a foreign branch separate unit. Therefore, the year 1 loss attributable to the foreign branch separate unit constitutes a dual consolidated loss pursuant to §1.1503(d)-1(b)(5)(ii). The dual consolidated loss rules apply to the dual consolidated loss even though there is no affiliate of the foreign branch separate unit in Country X, because it is still possible that all or a portion of the dual consolidated loss can be put to a foreign use. For example, there may be a foreign use with respect to a Country X affiliate acquired in a year subsequent to the year in which the dual consolidated loss was incurred. See §1.1503(d)-6(a)(2). Accordingly, unless an exception under §1.1503(d)-6 applies (such as a domestic use election), the year 1 dual consolidated loss attributable to P's Country X permanent establishment is subject to the domestic use limitation rule of §1.1503(d)-4(b). As a result, pursuant to §1.1503(d)-4(c), the year 1 dual consolidated loss cannot offset income of P that is not attributable to its Country X foreign branch separate unit, nor can it offset income of any other domestic affiliate. The loss can, however, offset income of the Country X foreign branch separate unit, subject to the application of §1.1503(d)-4(c). The result would be the same even if Country X did not have a consolidation regime that includes as members of consolidated groups Country X branches or permanent establishments of nonresident corporations. The dual consolidated loss rules apply even in the absence of a consolidation regime in the foreign country because it is possible that all or a portion of a dual consolidated loss can be put to a foreign use by other means, such as through a sale, merger, or similar transaction. See §1.1503(d)-6(a)(2).

(iii) *Alternative facts.* The facts are the same as in paragraph (c)(2)(i) of this section, except that P's Country X business operations constitute a foreign branch as defined in §1.367(a)-6T(g)(1), but do not constitute a permanent establishment under the U.S.-Country X income tax convention. Although the activities carried on by P in Country X would otherwise constitute a foreign branch separate unit as described in §1.1503(d)-1(b)(4)(i)(A), the exception under §1.1503(d)-1(b)(4)(iii) applies because the activities do not constitute a permanent establishment under the U.S.-Country X income tax convention. Thus, the Country X business operations do not constitute a foreign branch separate unit, and the year 1 loss is not subject to the dual consolidated loss rules. If P instead carried on its Country X business operations through DE1X, then the exception under §1.1503(d)-1(b)(4)(iii) would not apply because P carries on the business operations through a hybrid entity and, as a result, the business operations would constitute a foreign branch separate unit. Thus, in such a case the year 1 loss would be subject to the dual consolidated loss rules.

(3) *Example 3. Domestic use limitation—foreign branch separate unit owned through a partnership.* (i) *Facts.* P and S organize a partnership, PRSX, under the laws of Country X. PRSX is treated as a partnership for both U.S. and Country X tax purposes. PRSX owns FBX. PRSX earns U.S. source income that is unconnected with its FBX branch operations, and such income is not subject to tax by Country X. In addition, such U.S. source income is not attributable to FBX under §1.1503(d)-5.

(ii) *Result.* Under §1.1503(d)-1(b)(4)(i)(A), P's and S's shares of FBX owned indirectly through their interests in PRSX are individual foreign branch separate units. Pursuant to §1.1503(b)-1(b)(4)(ii), these individual separate units are combined and treated as a single separate unit of the consolidated group of which P is the parent. Unless an exception under §1.1503(d)-6 applies, any dual consolidated loss attributable to FBX cannot offset income of P or S (other than income attributable to FBX, subject to the application of §1.1503(d)-4(c)), including their distributive share of the U.S. source income earned through their interests in PRSX, nor can it offset income of any other domestic affiliates.

(4) *Example 4. Definition of a separate unit and domestic use limitation—interest in hybrid entity partnership and indirectly owned foreign branch separate unit.* (i) *Facts.* HPSX is a Country X entity that is subject to Country X tax on its worldwide income. HPSX is classified as a partnership for Federal tax purposes. P, S, and FSX, are the sole partners of HPSX. For U.S. tax purposes, P, S, and FSX each has an

equal interest in each item of HPSX's profit or loss. HPSX carries on operations in Country Y that, if carried on by a U.S. person, would constitute a foreign branch within the meaning of § 1.367(a)-6T(g)(1).

(ii) *Result.* Under § 1.1503(d)-1(b)(4)(i)(B), the partnership interests in HPSX held by P and S are individual hybrid entity separate units. These individual separate units are combined into a single separate unit under § 1.1503(d)-1(b)(4)(ii). In addition, P's and S's share of the Country Y operations owned indirectly through their interests in HPSX are individual foreign branch separate units under § 1.1503(d)-1(b)(4)(i)(B). These individual separate units are also combined into a single separate unit under § 1.1503(d)-1(b)(4)(ii). Unless an exception under § 1.1503(d)-6 applies, dual consolidated losses attributable to P's and S's combined interests in HPSX can only be used to offset income attributable to their combined interests in HPSX (other than income attributable to P's and S's combined interests in the Country Y foreign branch separate unit), subject to the application of § 1.1503(d)-4(c). Similarly, dual consolidated losses attributable to P's and S's combined interests in the Country Y operations of HPSX can only be used to offset income attributable to their combined interests in such Country Y operations, subject to the application of § 1.1503(d)-4(c). Neither FSX's interest in HPSX, nor its share of the Country Y operations owned by HPSX, is a separate unit because FSX is not a domestic corporation.

(5) *Example 5. Foreign use—general rule and de minimis reduction exception.* (i) *Facts.* P owns DE1X. DE1X owns FSX. In year 1, there is a $100x loss attributable to P's interest in DE1X that is a dual consolidated loss. Also in year 1, FSX earns $200x of income. DE1X and FSX file a Country X consolidated tax return. For Country X tax purposes, the year 1 $100x loss of DE1X is used to offset $100x of year 1 income generated by FSX. Under Country X tax law, unused losses are carried forward and available to offset income in subsequent taxable years.

(ii) *Result.* The $100x loss attributable to P's interest in DE1X is available to, and in fact does, offset FSX's income under the laws of Country X. In addition, under U.S. tax principles, such income is considered to be an item of FSX, a foreign corporation. As a result, under § 1.1503(d)-3(a), there has been a foreign use of the year 1 dual consolidated loss attributable to P's interest in DE1X. Therefore, P cannot make a domestic use election with respect to the loss as provided under § 1.1503(d)-6(d)(2), and such loss will be subject to the domestic use limitation rule of § 1.1503(d)-4(b). The result would be the same even if FSX, under Country X tax law, had no income against which the dual consolidated loss of DE1X could be offset (unless FSX's ability to use the loss under Country X tax law requires an election, and no such election is made).

(iii) *Alternative facts.* The facts are the same as in paragraph (c)(5)(i) of this section, except that FSX cannot use the loss of DE1X under Country X tax law without an election, and no such election is made. Pursuant to the exception in § 1.1503(d)-3(c)(2), there is no foreign use of the year 1 dual consolidated loss attributable to P's interest in DE1X. In addition, P files a domestic use election with respect to the year 1 dual consolidated loss attributable to its interest in DE1X and, at the beginning of year 3, P sells its interest in DE1X to F, a Country Y entity that is a foreign corporation. The sale of the interest in DE1X to F results in a foreign use triggering event pursuant to § 1.1503(d)-6(e)(1)(i) because, immediately after the sale, the loss attributable to the interest in DE1X carries over under Country X law and, therefore, is available under U.S. tax principles to offset income of the owner of the interest in DE1X which, in the hands of F, is not a separate unit. It is also a foreign use because the loss is available under U.S. tax principles to offset the income of F, a foreign corporation. See § 1.1503(d)-3(a)(1). Finally, the transfer is a triggering event pursuant to § 1.1503(d)-6(e)(1)(iv) and (v).

(iv) *Alternative facts.* The facts are the same as in paragraph (c)(5)(iii) of this section, except that P only sells 5 percent of its interest in DE1X to F. Pursuant to Rev. Rul. 99-5 (1999-1 CB 434), see § 601.601(d)(2)(ii)(b) of this chapter, the transaction is treated as if P sold 5 percent of its interest in each of DE1X's assets to F, and then immediately thereafter P and F transferred their interests in the assets of DE1X to a partnership in exchange for an ownership interest therein. The sale of the 5 percent interest in DE1X generally results in a foreign use triggering event because a portion of the dual consolidated loss carries over under Country X tax law and is available under U.S. tax principles to offset income of the owner of the interest in DE1X, a hybrid entity, which in the hands of F is not a separate unit. It is also a foreign use because the loss is available under U.S. tax principles to offset the income of F, a foreign corporation. See § 1.1503(d)-3(a)(1). However, pursuant to the exception under § 1.1503(d)-3(c)(5) (relating to a de minimis reduction of an interest in a separate unit), such availability does not result in a foreign use. In addition, pursuant to § 1.1503(d)-6(f)(1) and (3) , the deemed transfers pursuant to Rev. Rul. 99-5 as a result of the sale are not treated as triggering events described in § 1.1503(d)-6(e)(1)(iv) or (v).

(6) *Example 6. Foreign use and indirect foreign use—foreign reverse hybrid structure and disregarded payments.* (i) *Facts.* P owns DE1X. DE1X owns 99 percent and S owns 1 percent of FRHX, a Country X partnership that elected to be treated as a corporation for U.S. tax purposes. FRHX conducts a trade or business in Country X. In year 1, DE1X incurs interest expense on a third-party loan, which constitutes a dual consolidated loss attributable to P's interest in DE1X. In year 1, for Country X tax purposes, DE1X takes into account its distributive share of income generated by FRHX and offsets such income with its interest expense.

(ii) *Result.* In year 1, the dual consolidated loss attributable to P's interest in DE1X is available to, and in fact does, offset income recognized in Country X and, under U.S. tax principles, the income is considered to be income of FRHX, a foreign corporation. Accordingly, pursuant to § 1.1503(d)-3(a)(1), there is a foreign use of the dual consolidated loss. Therefore, P cannot make a domestic use election with respect to the year 1 dual consolidated loss attributable to its interest in DE1X, as provided under § 1.1503(d)-6(d)(2), and such loss will be subject to the domestic use limitation rule of § 1.1503(d)-4(b).

(iii) *Alternative facts.* (A) The facts are the same as in paragraph (c)(6)(i) of this section, except as follows. Instead of owning DE1X, P owns DE3Y which, in turn, owns DE1X. In addition, DE3Y, rather than DE1X, is the obligor on the third-party loan and therefore incurs the interest expense on such loan. Finally, DE3Y on-lends the loan proceeds from the third-party loan to DE1X, and DE1X pays interest to DE3Y on such loan that is generally disregarded for U.S. tax purposes.

(B) Pursuant to § 1.1503(d)-5(c)(1)(ii), for purposes of calculating income or a dual consolidated loss, DE3Y and DE1X do not take into account interest income or interest expense, respectively, with respect to amounts paid on the disregarded loan from DE3Y to DE1X. As a result, such items neither create a dual consolidated loss with respect to the interest in DE1X, nor do they reduce (or eliminate) the dual consolidated loss attributable to the interest in DE3Y. Thus, in year 1, there is a dual consolidated loss attributable to P's interest in DE3Y, but not to P's indirect interest in DE1X.

(C) In year 1, interest expense paid by DE1X to DE3Y on the disregarded loan is taken into account as a deduction in computing DE1X's taxable income for Country X tax purposes, but does not give rise to a corresponding item of income or gain for U.S. tax purposes (because it is generally disregarded). In addition, such interest has the effect of making an item of deduction or loss composing the dual consolidated loss attributable to P's interest in DE3Y available for a foreign use. This is the case because it may reduce or offset items of deduction or loss composing the dual consolidated loss for foreign tax purposes, and creates another deduction or loss that may reduce or offset income of DE1X for foreign tax purposes that, under U.S. tax principles, is treated as income of FRHX, a foreign corporation. Moreover, because the disregarded item is incurred or taken into account as interest for foreign tax purposes, it is deemed to have been incurred or taken into account with a principal purpose of avoiding the provisions of section 1503(d). Accordingly, there is an indirect foreign use of the year 1 dual consolidated loss attributable to P's interest in DE3Y, and P cannot make a domestic use election with respect to such loss as provided under § 1.1503(d)-6(d)(2). Thus, the loss will be subject to the domestic use limitation rule of § 1.1503(d)-4(b).

(7) *Example 7. Indirect foreign use—hybrid instrument.* (i) *Facts.* P owns DE1X which, in turn, owns FSX. DE1X borrows cash from an unrelated lender and transfers the cash to FSX in exchange for an instrument (hybrid instrument). The hybrid instrument is treated as equity for U.S. tax purposes and debt for Country X tax purposes. Interest expense on the loan from the unrelated lender results in a dual consolidated loss being attributable to P's interest in DE1X in year 1. DE1X does not elect under Country X law to consolidate with FSX. In year 1, FSX distributes its stock as a payment on the hybrid instrument to DE1X. For U.S. tax purposes, such payment is excluded from P's gross income under section 305. However, for Country X tax purposes, such payment is treated as interest and gives rise to a deduction taken into account in computing FSX's Country X tax liability; the payment also gives rise to interest income to DE1X for Country X tax purposes.

(ii) *Result.* The payment on the hybrid instrument does not give rise to an item of income or gain for U.S. tax purposes and therefore does not reduce (or eliminate) the dual consolidated loss attributable to P's interest in DE1X. In addition, such payment is taken into account as a deduction in computing FSX's taxable income for Country X tax purposes. Moreover, such payment has the effect of making an item of deduction or loss composing the dual consolidated loss attributable to P's interest in DE1X available for a foreign use. This is the case because it may reduce or offset items of deduction or loss composing the dual consolidated loss for foreign tax purposes, and creates a deduction that reduces or offsets income of FSX for foreign tax purposes that, under U.S. tax principles, is income of a foreign corporation. Further, because the item is incurred, or taken into account, using an instrument that is treated as equity for U.S. tax purposes and debt for foreign tax purposes, it is deemed to have been engaged in with the principal purpose of avoiding the provisions of section 1503(d). As a result, there has been an indirect foreign use of the year 1 dual consolidated loss, and P cannot make a domestic use election with respect to such loss, as provided under § 1.1503(d)-6(d)(2). Thus, the year 1 dual consolidated loss will be subject to the domestic use limitation rule of § 1.1503(d)-4(b).

(8) *Example 8. No indirect foreign use—transaction entered into in the ordinary course of business.* (i) *Facts.* P owns DE1X and FBY. FBY is a foreign branch separate unit located in Country Y. DE1X owns FBX and FSX. P's interest in DE1X and FBX are combined and treated as a single separate unit (Country X separate unit) pursuant to § 1.1503(d)-1(b)(4)(ii). Under Country X tax laws, DE1X elects to consolidate with FSX. FBY engages in the business of providing services and, in connection with its ordinary course of business, provides services to unrelated third parties and to DE1X. As compensation for services, DE1X makes a payment to FBY. Under Country X tax law, the payment is deductible. However, the payment is generally disregarded for U.S. tax purposes and, pursuant to § 1.1503(d)-5(c)(1)(ii), is not taken into account in calculating the income or dual consolidated loss attributable to the Country X separate unit or FBY. In year 1, the Country X separate unit and FBY each has a dual consolidated loss. The dual consolidated loss attributable to the Country X separate unit is subject to the domestic use limitation under § 1.1503(d)-4(b) because DE1X and FSX elect to consolidate and, as a result, the dual consolidated loss is put to a foreign use.

(ii) *Result.* The payment made by DE1X to FBY in connection with the performance of services is taken into account as a deduction in computing DE1X's taxable income for Country X tax purposes, but does not give rise to an item of income or gain for U.S. tax purposes. In addition, such payment has the effect of making an item of deduction or loss composing the dual consolidated loss attributable to FBY available for a foreign use. This is the case because it may reduce or offset items of deduction or loss composing the dual consolidated loss of FBY for foreign tax purposes, and creates another deduction that reduces or offsets income of FSX for foreign tax purposes (because DE1X and FSX elect to file a consolidated return) that, under U.S. tax principles, is income of a foreign corporation. However, the transaction between DE1X and FBY was entered into in the ordinary course of FBY's trade or business. As a result, if P can demonstrate to the satisfaction of the Commissioner that the transaction was not entered into with a principal purpose of avoiding the provisions of section 1503(d), FBY's year 1 dual consolidated loss will not be treated as having been made available for an indirect foreign use. In such a case, P would be entitled to make a domestic use election with respect to such loss.

(9) *Example 9. Foreign use—dual resident corporation with hybrid entity joint venture.* (i) *Facts.* P owns DRCX, a member of the P consolidated group. DRCX owns 80 percent of HPSX, a Country X entity that is subject to Country X tax on its worldwide income. HPSX is classified as a partnership for U.S. tax purposes. FSX owns the remaining 20 percent of HPSX. In year 1, DRCX generates a $100x net operating loss (without regard to items attributable to DRCX's interest in HPSX). Also in year 1, HPSX generates $100x of income, $80x of which is attributable to DRCX's interest in HPSX. DRCX and HPSX file a consolidated tax return for Country X tax purposes, and HPSX offsets its $100x of income with the $100x loss generated by DRCX.

(ii) *Result.* DRCX and its interest in HPSX are not combined because DRCX is a dual resident corporation and the combination rule under § 1.1503(d)-1(b)(4)(ii) only applies to separate units. The $100x year 1 net operating loss incurred by DRCX (without regard to items attributable to DRCX's interest in HPSX) is a dual consolidated loss. In addition, HPSX is a hybrid entity and DRCX's interest in HPSX is a hybrid entity separate unit; however, there is no dual consolidated loss attributable to such separate unit in year 1 (instead, there is $80x of income attributable to such separate unit). DRCX's year 1 dual consolidated loss offsets $100x of income for Country X purposes, and $20x of such income is, under U.S. tax principles, income of FSX, which owns an interest in HPSX that is not a separate unit (in addition, FSX is a foreign corporation). As a result, pursuant to § 1.1503(d)-3(a), there is a foreign use of the year 1 dual consolidated loss of DRCX, and P cannot make a domestic use election with respect to such loss pursuant to § 1.1503(d)-6(d)(2). Therefore, such loss will be subject to the domestic use limitation rule of § 1.1503(d)-4(b). The result would be the same even if HPSX, under Country X laws, had no income against which the dual consolidated loss could be offset (unless the ability to use the loss under Country X laws required an election, and no such election is made).

(10) *Example 10. Foreign use—foreign parent corporation.* (i) *Facts.* F1 and F2, nonresident alien individuals, each owns 50 percent of FPX, a Country X entity that is subject to Country X tax on its worldwide income. FPX is classified as a foreign corporation for U.S. tax purposes. FPX owns DRCX. DRCX is the parent of a consolidated group that includes as a member DS, a domestic corporation. In year 1, DRCX incurs a dual consolidated loss of $100x and, for Country X tax purposes, FPX generates $100x of income. In year 1, FPX elects to consolidate with DRCX for Country X tax purposes, and the $100x year 1 loss of DRCX is used to offset the income of FPX under the laws of Country X. For U.S. tax purposes, the items of FPX do not constitute items of income in year 1.

(ii) *Result.* The year 1 dual consolidated loss of DRCX offsets the income of FPX under the laws of Country X. Pursuant to § 1.1503(d)-3(a), the offset constitutes a foreign use because the items constituting such income are considered under U.S. tax principles to be items of a foreign corporation. This is the case even though the United States does not recognize such items as income in year 1. Therefore, DRCX cannot make a domestic use election with respect to its year 1 dual consolidated loss pursuant to § 1.1503(d)-6(d)(2). As a result, such loss will be subject to the domestic use limitation rule of § 1.1503(d)-4(b).

(iii) *Alternative facts.* The facts are the same as in paragraph (c)(10)(i) of this section, except that FPX is classified as a partnership for U.S. tax purposes. The result would be the same as in paragraph (c)(10)(ii) of this section, because the offset of the income generated by FPX is a foreign use pursuant to § 1.1503(d)-3(a). This is the case because the items constituting such income are considered under U.S. tax principles to be items of F1 and F2, the owners of interests in FPX (a hybrid entity), that are not separate units. Moreover, the result would be the same if F1 and F2 owned their interests in FPX indirectly through another partnership.

(11) *Example 11. No foreign use—absence of foreign loss allocation rules.* (i) *Facts.* P owns DE1X and DRCX. DRCX is a member of the P consolidated group and owns FSX. DE1X owns FBX. P's interest in DE1X and P's indirect interest in FBX are individual separate units that are combined into a single separate unit (Country X separate unit) pursuant to § 1.1503(d)-1(b)(4)(ii). In year 1, DRCX incurs a $200x net operating loss and $200x of income is attributable to P's Country X separate unit. The $200x net operating loss incurred by DRCX is a dual consolidated loss. FSX also earns $200x of income in year 1. DRCX, DE1X, and FSX file a Country X consolidated tax return. However, Country X has no applicable rules for determining which income is offset by DRCX's year 1 $200x loss.

(ii) *Result.* Under § 1.1503(d)-3(c)(3), DRCX's $200x loss shall be treated as having been made available to offset the $200x of income attributable to P's Country X separate unit. P's Country X separate unit is not, under U.S. tax principles, a foreign corporation, and there is no interest in DE1X (which is a hybrid entity) that is not a separate unit. As a result, DRCX's loss being made available to offset the income attributable to P's Country X separate unit is not considered a foreign use of such loss. Therefore, P can make a domestic use election with respect to DRCX's year 1 dual consolidated loss.

(iii) *Alternative facts.* The facts are the same as in paragraph (c)(11)(i) of this section, except that in year 1 only $150x of income is attributable to P's Country X separate unit. Because only $150x of income is attributed to P's Country X separate unit, $50x of DRCX's year 1 dual consolidated loss is treated as being made available to offset the income of FSX, a foreign corporation, and therefore constitutes a foreign use. As a result, DRCX cannot make a domestic use election with respect to its year 1 dual consolidated loss pursuant to § 1.1503(d)-6(d)(2), and such loss will be subject to the domestic use limitation rule of § 1.1503(d)-4(b).

(12) *Example 12. No foreign use—absence of foreign loss usage ordering rules.* (i) *Facts.* (A) P owns DRCX, a member of the P consolidated group. DRCX owns FSX. Under the Country X consolidation regime, a consolidated group may elect in any given year to use all or a portion of the losses of one consolidated group member to offset income of other consolidated group members. If no such election is made in a year in which losses are generated by a consolidated member, such losses carry forward and are available, at the election of the consolidated group, to offset income of consolidated group members in subsequent taxable years. Country X law does not provide ordering rules for determining when a loss from a particular taxable year is used because, under Country X law, losses never expire. In addition, Country X law does not provide ordering rules

for determining when a particular type of loss (for example, capital or ordinary) is used.

(B) In year 1, DRCX incurs a capital loss of $80x which, under § 1.1503(d)-5(b)(2), is not a dual consolidated loss. DRCX also incurs a net operating loss of $80x in year 1 which is a dual consolidated loss. FSX generates $60x of capital gain in year 1 which, for Country X purposes, can be offset by capital losses and net operating losses. Under the laws of Country X, DRCX elects to use $60x of its total year 1 loss of $160x to offset the $60x of capital gain generated by FSX in year 1; the remaining $100x of year 1 loss carries forward. In both year 2 and year 3, DRCX incurs a net operating loss of $100x, while FSX incurs no income or loss in years 2 and 3. DRCX's $100x losses incurred in year 2 and year 3 are dual consolidated losses. Because DRCX does not elect under the laws of Country X to use all or a portion of its year 2 or year 3 net operating losses of $100x to offset the income of other members of the Country X consolidated group, P is permitted to make (and in fact does make) a domestic use election with respect to both the year 2 and year 3 dual consolidated losses of DRCX. In year 4, DRCX has a net operating loss of $10x and FSX generates $125x of income. Country X law permits, upon an election, FSX's $125x of income generated in year 4 to be offset by losses (including carryover losses from prior years) of other group members. Accordingly, in year 4, DRCX elects to use $125x of its accumulated losses to offset the $125x of year 4 income generated by FSX.

(ii) *Result.* (A) Under the ordering rules of § 1.1503(d)-3(d)(3), a pro rata amount of DRCX's year 1 net operating loss ($30x) and capital loss ($30x) is considered to be used to offset FSX's year 1 $60x capital gain. As a result, P cannot make a domestic use election with respect to DRCX's year 1 $80x dual consolidated loss because a portion of such loss is put to a foreign use.

(B) DRCX's $10x year 4 net operating loss is also a dual consolidated loss. Under the ordering rules of § 1.1503(d)-3(d)(1), such loss is considered to be used to offset $10x of FSX's year 4 $125x of income. Consequently, P cannot make a domestic use election with respect to such loss. Under the ordering rules of § 1.1503(d)-3(d)(2), $50x of capital loss carryover and $50x of ordinary loss from year 1 will be considered to offset $100x of FSX's year 4 income because the income is first deemed to have been offset by losses the use of which would not constitute a triggering event that would result in the recapture of a dual consolidated loss. The remaining $15x of FSX's year 4 income is considered to be offset by losses from year 3 because it is the most recent taxable year from which a loss may be carried forward. Thus, a portion of the year 3 dual consolidated loss has been put to a foreign use and the entire year 3 dual consolidated loss is recaptured. However, none of DRCX's $100x year 2 net operating loss will be deemed to offset FSX's year 4 income. As a result, DRCX's year 2 dual consolidated loss will not be recaptured.

(13) *Example 13. Exception to foreign use through partnership interest.* (i) *Facts.* (A) P owns 80 percent of HPSX, a Country X entity subject to Country X tax on its worldwide income. FSZ, an unrelated foreign corporation, owns the remaining 20 percent of HPSX. HPSX is classified as a partnership for Federal tax purposes and carries on operations in Country X that, if carried on by a U.S. person, would constitute a foreign branch within the meaning of § 1.367(a)-6T(g)(1). P's interest in HPSX and P's indirect interest in the Country X branch are individual separate units that are combined into a single separate unit (Country X separate unit) pursuant to § 1.1503(d)-1(b)(4)(ii).

(B) In year 1, HPSX incurs a loss of $100x, $80x of which is attributable to P's Country X separate unit. The $80x of loss attributable to P's Country X separate unit constitutes a dual consolidated loss and P makes a domestic use election with respect to such loss. In year 2, HPSX generates $50x of income, $40x of which is attributable to P's interest in the Country X separate unit. Under Country X income tax laws, the $100x of year 1 loss incurred by HPSX is carried forward and offsets the $50x of income generated by HPSX in year 2; the remaining $50x of loss is carried forward and is available to offset income generated by HPSX in subsequent years. P and FSZ maintain their ownership interests in HPSX throughout years 1 and 2.

(ii) *Result.* In year 2, under the laws of Country X, the $100x of year 1 loss, which includes the $80x dual consolidated loss attributable to P's Country X separate unit, is made available to offset income of HPSX. Such income is attributable to P's interest in HPSX, which is a separate unit. Such income also is income of FSZ, a foreign corporation that is an owner of an interest in HPSX, which is not a separate unit. However, pursuant to § 1.1503(d)-3(c)(4), there is no foreign use of the year 1 dual consolidated loss in year 2. This is the case because P's interest in HPSX as of the end of year 1 has not been reduced by more than a de minimis amount, and the portion of the $80x dual consolidated loss was made available for a foreign use in year 2 solely as a result of FSZ's ownership in HPSX and the allocation or carry forward of the dual consolidated loss as a result of such ownership.

(iii) *Alternative facts.* The facts are the same as in paragraph (c)(13)(i) of this section, except that P also owns FSX. In addition, FSX and HPSX elect to file a consolidated return under Country X law. The exception to foreign use under § 1.1503(d)-3(c)(4) does not apply because there is a foreign use other than by reason of the dual consolidated loss being made available as a result of FSZ's ownership in HPSX and the allocation or carry forward of the dual consolidated loss as a result of such ownership. That is, the exception does not apply because there is also a foreign use of the dual consolidated loss as a result of FSX and HPSX filing a consolidated return under Country X law.

(iv) *Alternative facts.* The facts are the same as in paragraph (c)(13)(i) of this section, except that at the end of year 2, FSZ contributes cash to HPSX in exchange for additional equity of HPSX. As a result of the contribution, FSZ's interest in HPSX increases from 20 percent to 30 percent, and P's interest in HPSX decreases from 80 percent to 70 percent. P's interest in HPSX is reduced within a single 12-month period by 12.5 percent (10/80), as compared to P's interest in HPSX as of the beginning of such 12-month period. Accordingly, pursuant to § 1.1503(d)-3(c)(4)(iii), the exception to foreign use provided under § 1.1503(d)-3(c)(4)(i) does not apply. Therefore, in year 2 there is a foreign use of the $80x year 1 dual consolidated loss attributable to P's Country X separate unit. Such foreign use constitutes a triggering event in year 2 and the $80x year 1 dual consolidated loss is recaptured. Alternatively, if FSZ were a domestic corporation, there would not be a foreign use of the $80x year 1 dual consolidated loss because the loss would not be available to offset income that, under U.S. tax principles, is income of a foreign corporation or a direct or indirect owner of an interest in a hybrid entity that is not a separate unit.

(14) *Example 14. Exception to foreign use through partnership interest—combination rule.* (i) *Facts.* (A) P and FSX form PRSX. P and FSX each own 50 percent of PRSX throughout years 1 and 2. PRSX is treated as a partnership for both U.S. and Country X tax purposes. PRSX owns DEY. DEY is a Country Y entity subject to Country Y tax on its worldwide income and disregarded as an entity separate from its owner for U.S. tax purposes. DEY conducts business operations in Country Y that, if carried on by a U.S. person, would constitute a foreign branch as defined in § 1.367(a)-6T(g)(1). P's interest in the Country Y operations conducted by DEY is an individual foreign branch separate unit. P's interest in DEY, owned indirectly through PRSX, is a hybrid entity individual separate unit. P also owns FBY, a Country Y foreign branch individual separate unit. Under § 1.1503(d)-1(b)(4)(ii), FBY and P's indirect interests in DEY and DEY's Country Y business operations are treated as a combined separate unit (Country Y separate unit).

(B) In year 1, there is a $100x loss attributable to the Country Y business operations conducted by DEY. Thus, there is a $50x loss attributable to P's interest in DEY's Country Y business operations in year 1. Also in year 1, there is a $200x loss attributable to FBY. No income or loss is attributable to P's interest in DEY in year 1. Under § 1.1503(d)-5(c)(4)(ii), the dual consolidated loss attributable to P's combined Country Y separate unit is $250x ($50x loss attributable to P's indirect interest in DEY's Country Y operations, plus $200x loss attributable to FBY). In year 2, neither DEY nor DEY's Country Y operations generates income or loss. Under Country Y law, the $100x of year 1 loss incurred by DEY is carried forward and is available to offset income of DEY in year 2.

(ii) *Result.* As a result of the carryover of the year 1 $100x loss (which includes $50x of the year 1 dual consolidated loss) under Country Y law, a portion of such loss will be available to offset income of DEY that is attributable to P's interest in DEY owned indirectly through PRSX. A portion of such loss will also be available to offset income of DEY that is attributable to FSX's indirect ownership of DEY. Accordingly, under § 1.1503(d)-3(a), there would be a foreign use of a portion of P's $250x year 1 dual consolidated loss because it is available to offset an item of income of the owner of an interest in a hybrid entity, which is not a separate unit (there would also be a foreign use in this case because FSX is a foreign corporation). However, there has not been a reduction of P's interest in DEY, DEY has not consolidated under the laws of Country Y, and there has not been any other foreign use of the dual consolidated losses. As a result, no foreign use occurs as a result of the carryforward pursuant to § 1.1503(d)-3(c)(4)(i) and (ii).

(15) *Example 15. No foreign use—asset basis carryover exception.* (i) *Facts.* P owns FBX and FSX. In year 1, there is a dual consolidated loss attributable to FBX. P's items of income, gain, deduction, and loss that are taken into account in calculating FBX's dual consolidated loss include depreciation deductions attributable to FBX's as-

sets. P makes a domestic use election under § 1.1503(d)-6(d) with respect to the year 1 dual consolidated loss of FBX. At the end of year 2, P contributes a portion of FBX's assets to FSX, in exchange for stock in FSX. The aggregate adjusted basis of the assets transferred by P to FSX is less than 10 percent of the aggregate adjusted basis of all of FBX's assets held at the beginning of year 2. In addition, no other assets of FBX are transferred during the certification period. Under Country X law, FSX's basis in the transferred assets is determined by reference to P's basis in such assets. In addition, under Country X law, a portion of the depreciation deductions that were taken into account in year 1 for U.S. tax purposes, are taken into account in year 2 for Country X tax purposes.

(ii) *Result.* As a result of the transfer of assets from P to FSX, a portion of the year 1 dual consolidated loss is available for a foreign use. This is the case because a portion of the basis in FBX's assets, which gave rise to depreciation deductions that were taken into account in computing the year 1 dual consolidated loss, will give rise to a depreciation deduction under Country X laws that will be available, under U.S. tax principles, to offset the income of FSX, a foreign corporation, in year 2. However, the aggregate adjusted basis of all the assets transferred by P to FSX, within the 12-month period ending at the end of year 2, is less than 10 percent of the aggregate adjusted basis of all of FBX's assets at the beginning of such 12-month period. Moreover, the aggregate adjusted basis of the assets transferred by P to FSX at any time during the certification period is less than 30 percent of the aggregate adjusted basis of FBX's assets held at the end of year 1. In addition, the item of deduction giving rise to the foreign use is being made available solely as a result of the adjusted basis of the transferred assets being determined in whole, or in part, by reference to the adjusted basis of such transferred assets in the hands of FBX. As a result, this transfer will not result in a foreign use pursuant to § 1.1503(d)-3(c)(6).

(16) *Example 16. No foreign use—liability assumption exception.* (i) *Facts.* P owns FBX. In year 1, there is a dual consolidated loss attributable to FBX for which P makes a domestic use election under § 1.1503(d)-6(d). The dual consolidated loss includes a deduction for salary expense that was deductible for U.S. tax purposes at the end of year 1, even though it was not paid until year 2. The deduction was incurred in the ordinary course of FBX's trade or business. During year 2, and before the accrued salary expense liability was paid, P sells all the assets of FBX to FSX in exchange for cash and FSX's assumption of the liabilities of the FBX trade or business, including the obligation to pay the accrued salary expense. Under Country X law, the accrued salary expense of FBX is deductible, and is taken into account for purposes of computing the taxable income of FBX, when paid. FBX pays the accrued salary expense after the sale of FBX to FSX.

(ii) *Result.* (A) As a result of FSX's assumption of the FBX liabilities, including the accrued salary expense, a portion of the dual consolidated loss is available for a foreign use in year 2. This is the case because the deduction that was taken into account in year 1 in computing the dual consolidated loss under U.S. tax principles will, under Country X tax law, be taken into account and will be available to offset the income of FSX, a foreign corporation, in year 2. However, because this item of expense is made available solely as a result of the assumption of a liability of FBX, and such liability was incurred in the ordinary course of FBX's trade or business, there will not be a foreign use of the year 1 dual consolidated loss pursuant to § 1.1503(d)-3(c)(7).

(B) The transfer of all the assets of FBX to FSX is a triggering event under § 1.1503(d)-6(e)(1)(iv), unless P can rebut the triggering event under § 1.1503(d)-6(e)(2). For purposes of determining whether, under § 1.1503(d)-6(e)(2)(ii), the transfer of assets resulted in a carryover under foreign law of FBX's losses, expenses, or deductions, the exception to foreign use for the assumption of liabilities is taken into account. However, the other exceptions to foreign use do not apply for this purpose (or for purposes of demonstrating that no foreign use of a dual consolidated loss can occur in any other year under § 1.1503(d)-6(c), (e)(2)(i) or (j)(2)). See § 1.1503(d)-3(c)(1). Provided the other requirements of § 1.1503(d)-6(e)(2)(ii) and (iii) are satisfied, P may be able to rebut the occurrence of a triggering event upon the transfer of FBX's assets to FSX.

(17) *Example 17. Mirror legislation rule—dual resident corporation and hybrid entity separate unit.* (i) *Facts.* P owns DRCX, a member of the P consolidated group. DRCX owns FSX. In year 1, DRCX incurs a $100x net operating loss that is a dual consolidated loss. To prevent corporations like DRCX from offsetting losses both against income of affiliates in Country X and against income of foreign affiliates under the tax laws of another country, Country X mirror legislation prevents a corporation that is subject to the income tax of another country on its worldwide income or on a residence basis from using the Country X form of consolidation. Accordingly, the Country X mirror legislation prevents the loss of DRCX from being made available to offset income of FSX.

(ii) *Result.* Under § 1.1503(d)-3(e), because the losses of DRCX are subject to Country X's mirror legislation, there is a deemed foreign use of DRCX's year 1 dual consolidated loss. The stand-alone exception to the mirror rule in § 1.1503(d)-3(e)(2) does not apply because, absent the mirror legislation, DRCX's year 1 dual consolidated loss would be available for a foreign use (as defined in § 1.1503(d)-3), without regard to whether such availability is limited by election or similar procedure. That is, absent the mirror legislation, all or a portion of the dual consolidated loss would be available to offset the income of FSX under the Country X consolidation regime. This is the case even if Country X did not recognize DRCX as having a loss in year 1. Therefore, P may not make a domestic use election with respect to DRCX's year 1 dual consolidated loss pursuant to § 1.1503(d)-6(d)(2).

(iii) *Alternative facts.* The facts are the same as in paragraph (c)(17)(i) of this section, except that P owns DE1X (rather than DRCX) and, in year 1, there is a $100 dual consolidated loss attributable to P's interest in DE1X (rather than of DRCX). The Country X mirror legislation only applies to Country X dual resident corporations and, therefore, does not apply to losses attributable to P's interest in DE1X. As a result, the mirror legislation rule under § 1.1503(d)-3(e) would not deny the opportunity of such loss from being put to a foreign use (for example, by offsetting the income of FSX through the Country X consolidation regime). Therefore, a domestic use election can be made with respect to the dual consolidated loss (provided the conditions for such an election are otherwise satisfied).

(18) *Example 18. Mirror legislation rule—standalone foreign branch separate unit.* (i) *Facts.* P owns FBX. In year 1, there is a $100x dual consolidated loss attributable to FBX. Country X enacted mirror legislation to prevent Country X branches and permanent establishments of nonresident corporations from offsetting losses both against income of Country X affiliates and against other income of its owner (or foreign affiliates thereof) under the tax laws of another country. The Country X mirror legislation prevents a Country X branch or permanent establishment of a nonresident corporation from offsetting its losses against the income of Country X affiliates if such losses may be deductible against income (other than income of the Country X branch or permanent establishment) under the laws of another country.

(ii) *Result.* In general, under § 1.1503(d)-3(e), because the losses of FBX are subject to Country X's mirror legislation, there is a deemed foreign use of FBX's year 1 dual consolidated loss. However, in the absence of the Country X mirror legislation, no item of deduction or loss composing FBX's year 1 dual consolidated loss would be available in the year incurred for a foreign use (as defined in § 1.1503(d)-3), without regard to whether such availability is limited by election or otherwise. This is the case because there is no Country X entity through which the dual consolidated loss could be put to a foreign use (absent a sale, merger, or similar transaction involving FBX). As a result, the stand-alone exception in § 1.1503(d)-3(e)(2) may apply, provided P complies with the requirements of § 1.1503(d)-3(e)(2)(ii). Accordingly, P may make a domestic use election with respect to the year 1 dual consolidated loss of FBX pursuant to § 1.1503(d)-6(d). If, however, any item of the dual consolidated loss would otherwise be available for a foreign use during the certification period (for example, as a result of P acquiring a foreign corporation that is organized under the laws of Country X such that losses of FBX could be put to a foreign use through consolidation or similar means), then such loss would be recaptured pursuant to § 1.1503(d)-6(e)(1)(ix).

(iii) *Alternative facts.* The facts are the same as in paragraph (c)(18)(i) of this section, except that the Country X mirror legislation operates in a manner similar to the rules under section 1503(d). That is, it allows the taxpayer to elect to use the loss to either offset income of an affiliate in Country X, or income of an affiliate (or other income of the owner of the Country X branch or permanent establishment) in the other country, but not both. Because the Country X mirror legislation permits the taxpayer to choose to put the dual consolidated loss to a foreign use, it does not deny the opportunity to put the loss to a foreign use. Therefore, there is no deemed foreign use of the dual consolidated loss pursuant to § 1.1503(d)-4(e) and a domestic use election can be made for such loss.

(19) *Example 19. Application of mirror legislation rule to combined separate unit.* (i) *Facts.* P owns FBX, FSX, and DE1X. In year 1, there is a $50x dual consolidated loss attributable to FBX and $10x of income attributable to P's interest in DE1X. FSX has income of $100x. Pursuant to § 1.1503(d)-1(b)(4)(ii), FBX and P's interest in DE1X are combined and treated as a single separate unit (Country X separate unit) which has a year 1 dual consolidated loss of $40x. Country X enacted mirror legislation to prevent Country X branches or permanent estab-

lishments of nonresident corporations from offsetting losses both against income of Country X affiliates and against other income of its owner (or foreign affiliates thereof) under the tax laws of another country. The Country X mirror legislation prevents a Country X branch or permanent establishment of a nonresident corporation from offsetting its losses against the income of Country X affiliates if such losses may be deductible against income (other than income of the Country X branch or permanent establishment) under the laws of another country. However, the United States and Country X have entered into an agreement described in §1.1503(d)-6(b) pursuant to the U.S. -Country X income tax convention (mirror agreement). The mirror agreement applies to Country X foreign branch separate units of domestic corporations, but not to Country X hybrid entity separate units. The mirror agreement provides that neither the Country X mirror legislation nor the mirror legislation rule under §1.1503(d)-3(e) will apply to losses attributable to Country X foreign branch separate units, provided certain conditions and reporting requirements are satisfied (including a domestic use election, if the loss is to be used to offset income of a domestic affiliate). Thus, losses attributable to Country X foreign branch separate units can, subject to the requirements of the mirror agreement, be used to offset income of a domestic affiliate or a Country X affiliate (but not both).

(ii) *Result.* The Country X mirror legislation only applies to Country X foreign branch separate units and does not apply to hybrid entity separate units. In addition, if P complies with the terms and conditions of the mirror agreement, the Country X mirror legislation would not apply to FBX. As a result, the income tax laws of Country X would not deny the opportunity of a loss of either individual separate unit that composes P's combined Country X separate unit from being put to a foreign use. Therefore, notwithstanding §1.1503(d)-3(e), a domestic use election can be made with respect to the dual consolidated loss attributable to P's Country X separate unit, provided the terms and conditions of the mirror agreement are satisfied. See §1.1503(d)-6(b)(2).

(iii) *Alternative facts.* The facts are the same as in paragraph (c)(19)(i) of this section, except that the Country X mirror legislation also applies to losses attributable to DE1X, but the mirror agreement does not apply to such losses. The mirror legislation rule would apply with respect to P's interest in DE1X and, as a result, there is a deemed foreign use of the dual consolidated loss attributable to the Country X separate unit and a domestic use election cannot be made for such loss. This is the case even though, pursuant to §1.1503(d)-5(c)(4)(ii)(A), P's interest in DE1X (which is subject to the Country X mirror legislation) does not, as an individual separate unit, have a dual consolidated loss in year 1. Further, the stand-alone exception to the mirror legislation rule in §1.1503(d)-3(e)(2) does not apply because, absent the mirror legislation, the Country X combined separate unit's dual consolidated loss would be available in the year incurred for a foreign use (as defined in §1.1503(d)-3) because it could be used to offset income of FSX under the Country X consolidation regime. This is the case even if Country X requires an election to consolidate and no such election is made. The result would be the same even if Country X did not recognize DE1X as having a loss.

(20) *Example 20. Dual consolidated loss limitation after section 381 transaction—disposition of assets and subsequent liquidation of dual resident corporation.* (i) *Facts.* P owns DRCX, a member of the P consolidated group. In year 1, DRCX incurs a dual consolidated loss and P does not make a domestic use election with respect to such loss. Under §1.1503(d)-4(b), DRCX's year 1 dual consolidated loss is subject to the limitations under §1.1503(d)-4(c) and, therefore, may not be used to offset the income of P or S (or any other domestic affiliate) on the group's U.S. income tax return. At the beginning of year 2, DRCX sells all of its assets for cash and distributes the cash to P pursuant to a liquidation that qualifies under section 332.

(ii) *Result.* In general, under section 381, P would succeed to, and be permitted to use, DRCX's net operating loss carryover. However, §1.1503(d)-4(d)(1)(i) prohibits the dual consolidated loss of DRCX from carrying over to P. Therefore, DRCX's year 1 net operating loss carryover is eliminated.

(21) *Example 21. Dual consolidated loss limitation applied to a separate unit transferred in a section 381 transaction.* (i) *Facts.* S owns DE1X which, in turn, owns FBX. S's interest in DE1X and its indirect interest in FBX are combined and treated as a single separate unit (Country X separate unit) pursuant to §1.1503(d)-1(b)(4)(ii). In year 1, a dual consolidated loss is attributable to the Country X separate unit, and P does not make a domestic use election with respect to such loss. Under §1.1503(d)-4(b), the year 1 dual consolidated loss attributable to the Country X separate unit may not be used to offset the income of P or S (other than income attributable to the Country X separate unit, subject to the application of §1.1503(d)-4(c)) on the group's consolidated U.S. income tax return (nor may it be used to offset the income of any other domestic affiliates). At the beginning of year 2, S transfers its entire interest in DE1X, and thus its entire indirect interest in FBX, to FSX in a transaction described in section 381.

(ii) *Result.* Section 1.1503(d)-4(d)(1)(ii) provides that the dual consolidated loss attributable to a separate unit that is subject to the domestic use limitation under §1.1503(d)-4(b) is eliminated if the separate unit ceases to be a separate unit of its affiliated domestic owner and all other members of the affiliated domestic owner's separate group. As a result of the transfer of the Country X separate unit to FSx, the Country X separate unit ceases to be a separate unit of S, and is not a separate unit of any other member of the P consolidated group. In addition, the exceptions in §1.1503(d)-4(d)(2)(iii) do not apply because FSX is not a domestic corporation. Thus, the year 1 dual consolidated loss attributable to the Country X separate unit is eliminated.

(iii) *Alternative facts.* Assume the same facts as in paragraph (c)(21)(i) of this section, except S transfers its assets to DC, a domestic corporation that is not a member of the P consolidated group, in a transaction described in section 381(a). Immediately after the transaction, the Country X separate unit is a separate unit of DC. Under §1.1503(d)-4(d)(1)(ii), the year 1 dual consolidated loss of the Country X separate unit would be eliminated because it ceases to be a separate unit of S, and is not a separate unit of any other member of the P consolidated group. However, because the transferee is a domestic corporation and the Country X separate unit is a separate unit in the hands of DC immediately after the transaction, the exception under §1.1503(d)-4(d)(2)(iii)(A) applies. As a result, the year 1 dual consolidated loss of the Country X separate unit is not eliminated and any income generated by DC that is attributable to the Country X separate unit following the transfer may be offset by the carryover dual consolidated losses attributable to the Country X separate unit, subject to the limitations of §1.1503(d)-4(b) and (c) applied as if DC generated the dual consolidated loss and such loss was attributable to the Country X separate unit.

(iv) *Alternative facts.* Assume the same facts as in paragraph (c)(21)(iii) of this section, except that P owns DE2X and the interest in DE2X is combined with and therefore included in the Country X separate unit. In addition, a portion of the dual consolidated loss of the Country X separate unit is attributable to P's interest in DE2X. Pursuant to §1.1503(d)-4(d)(2)(iii)(A), the result would be the same as in paragraph (iii) of this *Example 21*, with respect to the portion of the dual consolidated loss attributable to the combined separate unit that is succeeded to and taken into account by DC pursuant to section 381. The portion of the dual consolidated loss attributable to P's interest in DE2X, however, does not carry over to DC but is retained by P and continues to be subject to the limitations of §1.1503(d)-4(b) and (c) with respect to P's interest in DE2X.

(v) *Alternative facts.* Assume the same facts as in paragraph (c)(21)(iv) of this section, except that DC is a member of the P consolidated group. Pursuant to §1.1503(d)-4(d)(2)(iii)(B), the dual consolidated loss of the Country X separate unit is not eliminated and income attributable to the Country X separate unit may continue to be offset by the dual consolidated loss that is succeeded to and taken into account by DC pursuant to section 381, subject to the limitations of §1.1503(d)-4(b) and (c). The result would be the same even if the interest in DE1X ceased to be a separate unit in the hands of DC (for example, because it dissolved under Country X law in connection with the transaction), provided P, or another member of the P consolidated group, continued to own a portion of the Country X separate unit.

(22) *Example 22. Tainted income.* (i) *Facts.* P owns 100 percent of DRCZ, a domestic corporation that is included as a member of the P consolidated group. DRCZ conducts a business in the United States. During year 1, DRCZ was managed and controlled in Country Z and therefore was subject to tax as a resident of Country Z and was a dual resident corporation. In year 1, DRCZ incurred a dual consolidated loss of $200x, and P did not make a domestic use election with respect to such loss. As a result, such loss is subject to the domestic use limitation rule of §1.1503(d)-4(b). At the end of year 1, DRCZ moved its management and control to the United States and, as a result, ceased being a dual resident corporation. At the beginning of year 2, P transferred asset A, a non-depreciable asset, to DRCZ in exchange for common stock in a transaction that qualified for nonrecognition under section 351. At the time of the transfer, P's tax basis in asset A equaled $50x and the fair market value of asset A equaled $100x. The tax basis of asset A in the hands of DRCZ immediately after the transfer equaled $50x pursuant to section 362. Asset A did not constitute replacement property acquired in the ordinary course of business. DRCZ did not generate income or gain during years 2, 3, or 4. On June 30, year 5, DRCZ sold asset A to a third party for $100x, its fair market value at the time of the sale, and recognized $50x of income on such sale. In addition to the $50x income generated on the

sale of asset A, DRCZ generated $100x of operating income in year 5. At the end of year 5, the fair market value of all the assets of DRCZ was $400x.

(ii) *Result.* DRCZ ceased being a dual resident corporation at the end of year 1. Therefore, its year 1 dual consolidated loss cannot be offset by tainted income. Asset A is a tainted asset because it was acquired in a nonrecognition transaction after DRCZ ceased being a dual resident corporation (and was not replacement property acquired in the ordinary course of business). As a result, the $50x of income recognized by DRCZ on the disposition of asset A is tainted income and cannot be offset by the year 1 dual consolidated loss of DRCZ. In addition, absent evidence establishing the actual amount of tainted income, $25x of the $100x year 5 operating income of DRCZ (($100x/$400x) × $100x) also is treated as tainted income and cannot be offset by the year 1 dual consolidated loss of DRCZ under § 1.1503(d)-4(e)(2)(ii). Therefore, $75x of the $150x year 5 income of DRCZ constitutes tainted income and may not be offset by the year 1 dual consolidated loss of DRCZ; however, the remaining $75x of year 5 income of DRCZ may be offset by such dual consolidated loss. The result would be the same if, instead of P transferring asset A to DRCZ, such asset was received from a separate unit or a transparent entity of DRCZ.

(23) *Example 23. Treatment of disregarded item and books and records of a hybrid entity.* (i) *Facts.* P owns DE1X which, in turn, owns FSX. In year 1, P borrows from a third party and on-lends the proceeds to DE1X. In year 1, P incurs interest expense attributable to the third-party loan. Also in year 1, DE1X incurs interest expense attributable to its loan from P, but such expense is generally disregarded for U.S. tax purposes because DE1X is disregarded as an entity separate from P. The third-party loan and related interest expense are reflected on the books and records of P (and not on the books and records of DE1X). The loan from P to DE1X and related interest expense are reflected on the books and records of DE1X. There are no other items of income, gain, deduction, or loss reflected on the books and records of DE1X in year 1.

(ii) *Result.* Because the interest expense on P's third-party loan is not reflected on the books and records of DE1X, no portion of such expense is attributable to P's interest in DE1X pursuant to § 1.1503(d)-5(c)(3) for purposes of calculating the year 1 dual consolidated loss, if any, attributable to such interest. In addition, even though P's interest in DE1X is treated as a separate domestic corporation for purposes of determining the amount of income or dual consolidated loss attributable to it pursuant to § 1.1503(d)-5(c)(1)(ii), such treatment does not cause the interest expense incurred on the loan from P to DE1X that is generally disregarded for U.S. tax purposes to be regarded for purposes of calculating the year 1 dual consolidated loss, if any, attributable to P's interest in DE1X. As a result, even though the disregarded interest expense is reflected on the books and records of DE1X, it is not taken into account for purposes of calculating income or a dual consolidated loss. Therefore, there is no dual consolidated loss attributable to P's interest in DE1X in year 1.

(24) *Example 24. Dividend income attributable to a separate unit.* (i) *Facts.* P owns DE1X which, in turn, owns FBX. P's interest in DE1X and its indirect interest in FBX are combined and treated as a single separate unit (Country X separate unit) pursuant to § 1.1503(d)-1(b)(4)(ii). DE1X owns DE3Y. DE3Y owns the stock of FSX. P's Country X separate unit would, without regard to year 1 dividend income (or related section 78 gross-up) received from FSX, have a dual consolidated loss of $75x in year 1. In year 1, FSX distributes $50x to DE3Y that is taxable as a dividend. DE3Y distributes the same amount to DE1X. P computes foreign taxes deemed paid on the dividend under section 902 of $25x and includes that amount in gross income under section 78.

(ii) *Result.* The $50x dividend is reflected on the books and records of DE3Y and, therefore, is attributable to P's interest in DE3Y pursuant to § 1.1503(d)-5(c)(3)(i). In addition, the $25x section 78 gross-up is attributable to P's interest in DE3Y pursuant to § 1.1503(d)-5(c)(4)(iv). The distribution of $50x from DE3Y to DE1X is generally disregarded for U.S. tax purposes and, therefore, does not give rise to an item that is taken into account for purposes of calculating income or a dual consolidated loss. This is the case even though the item would be reflected on the books and records of DE1X. In addition, pursuant to § 1.1503(d)-5(c)(1)(iii), each separate unit must calculate its own income or dual consolidated loss, and each item of income, gain, deduction, and loss must be taken into account only once. As a result, the dual consolidated loss of $75x attributable to P's Country X separate unit in year 1 is not reduced by the amount of dividend income attributable to P's indirect interest in DE3Y.

(25) *Example 25. Items reflected on books and records of a combined separate unit.* (i) *Facts.* P owns DE1X which, in turn, owns FBX. P's interest in DE1X and its indirect interest in FBX are combined and treated as a single separate unit (Country X separate unit) pursuant to § 1.1503(d)-1(b)(4)(ii). The following items are reflected on the books and records of DE1X in year 1: sales, depreciation expense, a political contribution, royalty expense paid to P, repairs and maintenance expense paid to a third party, and Country X income tax expense. The amount of sales under U.S. tax principles equals the amount of sales reported for accounting purposes. The depreciation expense is calculated on a straight-line basis over the useful life of the asset for accounting purposes, but is subject to accelerated depreciation for U.S. tax purposes. In addition, the repairs and maintenance expense, which is deducted when paid for accounting purposes, is properly capitalized and amortized over five years for U.S. tax purposes. Finally, P elects to claim as a credit under section 901 the Country X income tax expense that was paid in year 1.

(ii) *Result.* (A) For purposes of determining the income or dual consolidated loss attributable to P's Country X separate unit, items of income, gain, deduction, and loss must first be attributed to the individual separate units (that is, P's interest in DE1X and its indirect interest in FBX). For purposes of attributing items to P's interest in DE1X, P's items that are reflected on DE1X's books and records, as adjusted to conform to U.S. tax principles, are taken into account. See § 1.1503(d)-5(c)(3)(i). For purposes of attributing items (other than interest expense) to FBX, the principles of section 864(c)(2), (c)(4), and (c)(5) (as set forth in § 1.864-4(c) and §§ 1.864-5 through 1.864-7) must be applied and, for interest expense, the principles of § 1.882-5, as modified under § 1.1503(d)-5(c)(2)(ii), must be applied; however, for these purposes, pursuant to § 1.1503(d)-5(c)(4)(i)(A), FBX only takes into account items attributable to P's interest in DE1X and the assets, liabilities, and activities of such interest. In addition, to the extent such items are taken into account by FBX, they are not taken into account in determining the items attributable to P's interest in DE1X. § 1.1503(d)-5(c)(4)(i)(B). Because P's interest in DE1X has no assets or liabilities, and conducts no activities, other than through its ownership of FBX, all of the items that are reflected on the books and records of DE1X, as adjusted to conform to U.S. tax principles, are attributable to FBX; no items are attributable to P's interest in DE1X.

(B) The items reflected on the books and records of DE1X must be adjusted to conform to U.S. tax principles. No adjustment is required to sales because the amount of sales under U.S. tax principles equals the amount of sales for accounting purposes. The amount of straight-line depreciation expense reflected on DE1X's books and records must be adjusted to reflect the amount of depreciation on the asset that is allowable for U.S. tax purposes. The political contribution is not taken into account because it is not deductible for U.S. tax purposes. Similarly, because the royalty expense is paid to P, and therefore is generally disregarded for U.S. tax purposes, it is not taken into account. The repair and maintenance expense that is deducted in year 1 for accounting purposes also must be adjusted to conform to U.S. tax principles. Thus, the repair and maintenance expense will be taken into account in computing the income or dual consolidated loss attributable to P's Country X separate unit over five years (even though no item related to such expense would be reflected on the books and records of DE1X for years 2 through 5). Finally, because P elected to claim as a credit the Country X foreign taxes paid during year 1, no deduction is allowed for such amount pursuant to section 275(a)(4) and, therefore, the Country X tax expense is not taken into account.

(C) Pursuant to § 1.1503(d)-5(c)(4)(ii)(B), the combined Country X separate unit of P calculates its income or dual consolidated loss by taking into account all the items of income, gain, deduction, and loss that were separately attributable to P's interest in DE1X and FBX. However, in this case, there are no items attributable to P's interest in DE1X. Therefore, the items attributable to the Country X separate unit are the items attributable to FBX.

(26) *Example 26. Items attributable to a combined separate unit.* (i) *Facts.* P owns DE1X. DE1X owns a 50 percent interest in PRSZ, a Country Z entity that is classified as a partnership both for Country Z tax purposes and for U.S. tax purposes. FSX, which is unrelated to P, owns the remaining 50 percent interest in PRSZ. PRSZ carries on operations in Country X that, if carried on by a U.S. person, would constitute a foreign branch as defined in § 1.367(a)-6T(g)(1). Therefore, P's share of the Country X operations carried on by PRSZ constitutes a foreign branch separate unit. PRSZ also owns assets that do not constitute a part of its Country X branch, including all of the interests in TET, a disregarded entity. TET is an entity incorporated under the laws of Country T, a country that does not have an income tax. Under the laws of Country X, an interest holder of TET does not take into account on a current basis the interest holder's share of items of income, gain, deduction, and loss of TET.

(ii) *Result.* (A) Pursuant to § 1.1503(d)-1(b)(4)(ii), P's interest in DE1X, and P's indirect ownership of a portion of the Country X operations carried on by PRSZ, are combined and treated as a single separate unit (Country X separate unit). Pursuant to § 1.1503(d)-5(c)(4)(ii)(A), for purposes of determining P's items of income, gain, deduction, and loss attributable to the Country X separate unit, the items of P are first attributed to each separate unit that composes the Country X separate unit.

(B) Pursuant to § 1.1503(d)-5(c)(2)(i), the principles of section 864(c)(2), (c)(4), and (c)(5) (as set forth in § 1.864-4(c) and §§ 1.864-5 through 1.864-7), apply for purposes of determining P's items of income, gain, deduction (other than interest expense), and loss that are attributable to P's indirect interest in the Country X operations carried on by PRSZ. For purposes of determining P's interest expense that is attributable to P's indirect interest in the Country X operations carried on by PRSZ, the principles of § 1.882-5, as modified under § 1.1503(d)-5(c)(2)(ii), shall apply. For purposes of applying these rules, P is treated as a foreign corporation, the Country X operations carried on by PRSZ are treated as a trade or business within the United States, and the assets of P (including its share of the PRSZ assets, other than those of the Country X operations) are treated as assets that are not U.S. assets. In addition, because P carries on its share of the Country X operations through DE1X, a hybrid entity, § 1.1503(d)-5(c)(4)(i)(A) provides that only the items attributable to P's interest in DE1X, and only the assets, liabilities, and activities of P's interest in DE1X, are taken into account for purposes of this determination.

(C) TET is a transparent entity as defined in § 1.1503(d)-1(b)(16) because it is not taxable as an association for Federal tax purposes, is not subject to income tax in a foreign country as a corporation (or otherwise at the entity level) either on its worldwide income or on a residence basis, and is not treated as a pass-through entity under the laws of Country X (the applicable foreign country). TET is not a pass-through entity under the laws of Country X because a Country X holder of an interest in TET does not take into account on a current basis the interest holder's share of items of income, gain, deduction, and loss of TET. For purposes of determining P's items of income, gain, deduction, and loss that are attributable to P's interest in TET, only those items of P that are reflected on the books and records of TET, as adjusted to conform to U.S. tax principles, are taken into account. § 1.1503(d)-5(c)(3)(i). Because the interest in TET is not a separate unit, a loss attributable to such interest is not a dual consolidated loss and is not subject to section 1503(d) and these regulations. Items must nevertheless be attributed to the interests in TET. For example, such attribution is required for purposes of calculating the income or dual consolidated loss attributable to the Country X separate unit, and for purposes of applying the domestic use limitation under § 1.1503(d)-4(b) to a dual consolidated loss attributable to the Country X separate unit.

(D) For purposes of determining P's items of income, gain, deduction, and loss that are attributable to P's interest in DE1X, only those items of P that are reflected on the books and records of DE1X, as adjusted to conform to U.S. tax principles, are taken into account. § 1.1503(d)-5(c)(3)(i). For this purpose, DE1X's distributive share of the items of income, gain, deduction, and loss that are reflected on the books and records of PRSZ, as adjusted to conform to U.S. tax principles, are treated as being reflected on the books and records of DE1X, except to the extent such items are taken into account by the Country X operations of PRSZ. See § 1.1503(d)-5(c)(3)(ii) and (4)(i)(B). Because TET is a transparent entity, the items reflected on its books and records are not treated as being reflected on the books and records of DE1X.

(E) Pursuant to § 1.1503(d)-5(c)(4)(ii)(B), the combined Country X separate unit of P calculates its income or dual consolidated loss by taking into account all the items of income, gain, deduction, and loss that were separately attributable to P's interest in DE1X and the Country X operations of PRSZ owned indirectly by P.

(27) *Example 27. Sale of separate unit by another separate unit.* (i) *Facts.* P owns DE3Y which, in turn, owns DE1X. DE3Y also owns other assets that do not constitute a foreign branch separate unit. DE1X owns FBX. Pursuant to § 1.1503(d)-1(b)(4)(ii), P's indirect interests in DE1X and FBX are combined and treated as one Country X separate unit (Country X separate unit). DE3Y sells its interest in DE1X at the end of year 1 to an unrelated foreign person for cash. The sale results in an ordinary loss of $30x. Items of income, gain, deduction, and loss derived from the assets that gave rise to the $30x loss would be attributable to the Country X separate unit under § 1.1503(d)-5(c) through (e). Without regard to the sale of DE1X, no items of income, gain, deduction, and loss are attributable to P's Country X separate unit in year 1.

(ii) *Result.* Pursuant to § 1.1503(d)-5(c)(4)(iii)(A), the $30x ordinary loss recognized on the sale is attributable to the Country X separate unit, and not P's interest in DE3Y. This is the case because the Country X separate unit is treated as owning the assets that gave rise to the loss under § 1.1503(d)-5(f). Thus, the loss attributable to the sale creates a year 1 dual consolidated loss attributable to the Country X separate unit. In addition, pursuant to § 1.1503(d)-6(d)(2), P cannot make a domestic use election with respect to the dual consolidated loss because the sale of the interest in DE1X is a triggering event described in § 1.1503(d)-6(e)(1)(iv) and (v). Further, although the year 1 dual consolidated loss would otherwise be subject to the domestic use limitation rule of § 1.1503(d)-4(b), it is eliminated pursuant to § 1.1503(d)-4(d)(1)(ii). Finally, if there were a dual consolidated loss attributable to P's interest in DE3Y, the sale of the interest in DE1X would not be taken into account for purposes of determining whether there is an asset triggering event with respect to such dual consolidated loss under § 1.1503(d)-6(e)(1)(iv).

(28) *Example 28. Gain on sale of tiered separate units.* (i) *Facts.* P owns 75 percent of HPSX, a Country X entity subject to Country X tax on its worldwide income. FSX owns the remaining 25 percent of HPSX. HPSX is classified as a partnership for Federal tax purposes. HPSX carries on operations in Country Y that, if carried on by a U.S. person, would constitute a foreign branch within the meaning of § 1.367(a)-6T(g)(1). HPSX also owns assets that do not constitute a part of its Country Y operations and would not themselves constitute a foreign branch within the meaning of § 1.367(a)-6T(g)(1) if owned by a U.S. person. Neither HPSX nor the Country Y operations has liabilities. P's indirect interest in the Country Y operations carried on by HPSX, and P's interest in HPSX, are each separate units. P sells its interest in HPSX and recognizes a gain of $150x on such sale. Immediately prior to P's sale of its interest in HPSX, P's portion of the assets of the Country Y operations (that is, assets the income, gain, deduction and loss from which would be attributable to P's Country Y foreign branch separate unit) had a built-in gain of $200x, and P's portion of HPSX's other assets (that is, assets the income, gain, deduction and loss from which would be attributable to P's interest in HPSX) had a built-in gain of $100x.

(ii) *Result.* Pursuant to § 1.1503(d)-5(c)(4)(iii)(B), $100x of the total $150x of gain recognized ($200x/$300x × $150x) is attributable to P's indirect interest in its share of the Country Y operations carried on by HPSX. Similarly, $50x of such gain ($100x/$300x × $150x) is attributable to P's interest in HPSX.

(29) *Example 29. Effect on domestic affiliate.* (i) *Facts.* (A) P owns DE1X which, in turn, owns FBX. P's interest in DE1X and its indirect interest in FBX are combined and treated as a single separate unit (Country X separate unit) pursuant to § 1.1503(d)-1(b)(4)(ii). In years 1 and 2, the items of income, gain, deduction, and loss that are attributable to P's Country X separate unit pursuant to § 1.1503(d)-5 are as follows:

Table 1 to paragraph (c)(29)(i)(A)

Item	Year 1	Year 2
Sales Income	$100x	$160x
Salary expense	($75x)	($75x)
Research and experimental expense	($50x)	($50x)
Interest expense	($25x)	($25x)
Income/(dual consolidated loss)	($50x)	$10x

(B) P does not make a domestic use election with respect to the year 1 dual consolidated loss attributable to its Country X separate unit. Pursuant to § 1.1503(d)-4(b) and (c)(2), the year 1 dual consolidated loss of $50x is treated as a loss incurred by a separate domestic corporation and is subject to the limitations under § 1.1503(d)-4(c)(3). The P consolidated group has $100x of consolidated taxable income in year 2.

(ii) *Result.* (A) P must compute its taxable income for year 1 without taking into account the $50x dual consolidated loss, pursuant to § 1.1503(d)-4(c)(2). Such amount consists of a pro rata portion of the expenses that were taken into account in calculating the year 1 dual consolidated loss. Thus, the items of the dual consolidated loss that are not taken into account by P in computing its taxable income are as follows: $25x of salary expense ($75x/$150x × $50x); $16.67x of research and experimental expense ($50x/$150x × $50x); and $8.33x of interest expense ($25x/$150x × $50x). The remaining amounts of each of these items, together with the $100x of sales income, are taken into account by P in computing its taxable income for year 1 as follows: $50x of salary expense ($75x – $25x); $33.33x of research and experimental expense ($50x – $16.67x); and $16.67x of interest expense ($25x – $8.33x).

(B) Subject to the limitations provided under § 1.1503(d)-4(c), the year 1 $50x dual consolidated loss is carried forward and is available to offset the $10x of income attributable to the Country X separate unit in year 2. Pursuant to § 1.1503(d)-4(c)(4), a pro rata portion of each item of deduction or loss included in such dual consolidated loss is considered to be used to offset the $10x of income, as follows: $5x of salary expense ($25x/$50x × $10x); $3.33x of research and experimental expense ($16.67x/$50x × $10x); and $1.67x of interest expense ($8.33x/$50x × $10x). The remaining amount of each item shall continue to be subject to the limitations under § 1.1503(d)-4(c).

(30) *Example 30.* Exception to domestic use limitation—no possibility of foreign use because items are not deducted or capitalized under foreign law. (i) Facts. P owns DE1X which, in turn, owns FSX. In year 1, the sole item of income, gain, deduction, and loss attributable to P's interest in DE1X, as provided under § 1.1503(d)-5, is $100x of interest expense paid on a loan to an unrelated lender. For Country X tax purposes, the $100x interest expense attributable to P's interest in DE1X in year 1 is treated as a repayment of principal and therefore cannot be deducted (at any time) or capitalized.

(ii) *Result.* The $100x of interest expense attributable to P's interest in DE1X constitutes a dual consolidated loss. However, because the sole item constituting the dual consolidated loss cannot be deducted or capitalized (at any time) for Country X tax purposes, P can demonstrate that there can be no foreign use of the dual consolidated loss at any time. As a result, pursuant to § 1.1503(d)-6(c)(1), if P prepares a statement described in § 1.1503(d)-6(c)(2) and attaches it to its timely filed tax return, the year 1 dual consolidated loss attributable to P's interest in DE1X will not be subject to the domestic use limitation rule of § 1.1503(d)-4(b).

(31) *Example 31.* No exception to domestic use limitation—inability to demonstrate no possibility of foreign use. (i) Facts. P owns DE1X which, in turn, owns FBX. P's interest in DE1X and its indirect interest in FBX are combined and treated as a single separate unit (Country X separate unit) pursuant to § 1.1503(d)-1(b)(4)(ii). In year 1, the sole items of income, gain, deduction, and loss attributable to P's Country X separate unit, as provided under § 1.1503(d)-5, are $75x of sales income and $100x of depreciation expense. For Country X tax purposes, DE1X also generates $75x of sales income in year 1, but the $100x of depreciation expense is not deductible until year 2.

(ii) *Result.* The year 1 $25x net loss attributable to P's interest in the Country X separate unit constitutes a dual consolidated loss. In addition, even though DE1X has positive income in year 1 for Country X tax purposes, P cannot demonstrate that there is no possibility of foreign use with respect to the Country X separate unit's dual consolidated loss as provided under § 1.1503(d)-6(c)(1)(i). P cannot make such a demonstration because the depreciation expense, an item composing the year 1 dual consolidated loss, is deductible (in a later year) for Country X tax purposes and, therefore, may be available to offset or reduce income for Country X purposes that would constitute a foreign use. For example, if DE1X elected to be classified as a corporation pursuant to § 301.7701-3(c) of this chapter effective as of the end of year 1, and the deferred depreciation expense were available for Country X tax purposes to offset year 2 income of DE1X, an entity treated as a foreign corporation in year 2 for U.S. tax purposes, there would be a foreign use.

(iii) *Alternative facts.* (A) The facts are the same as in paragraph (c)(31)(i) of this section, except as follows. In year 1, the sole items of income, gain, deduction, and loss attributable to P's Country X separate unit, as provided in § 1.1503(d)-5, are $75x of sales income, $100x of interest expense, and $25x of depreciation expense. For Country X tax purposes, DE1X generates $75x of sales income in year 1; the $100x interest expense is treated as a repayment of principal and therefore cannot be deducted or capitalized (at any time); and the $25x of depreciation expense is not deductible in year 1, but is deductible in year 2.

(B) In year 1, the $50x net loss attributable to P's Country X separate unit constitutes a dual consolidated loss. Even though the $100x interest expense, a nondeductible and noncapital item for Country X tax purposes, exceeds the $50x year 1 dual consolidated loss attributable to P's Country X separate unit, P cannot demonstrate that there is no possibility of foreign use of the dual consolidated loss as provided under § 1.1503(d)-6(c)(1)(i). P cannot make such a demonstration because the $25x depreciation expense, an item of deduction or loss composing the year 1 dual consolidated loss, is deductible under Country X law (in year 2) and, therefore, may be available to offset or reduce income for Country X tax purposes that would constitute a foreign use.

(32) *Example 32. Triggering event rebuttal—expiration of losses in foreign country.* (i) *Facts.* P owns DRCX, a member of the P consolidated group. In year 1, DRCX incurs a dual consolidated loss of $100x. P makes a domestic use election with respect to DRCX's year 1 dual consolidated loss and such loss therefore is included in the computation of the P group's consolidated taxable income. DRCX has no income or loss in year 2 through year 5. In year 5, P sells the stock of DRCX to FSX. At the time of the sale of the stock of DRCX, all of the losses and deductions that were included in the computation of the year 1 dual consolidated loss of DRCX had expired for Country X tax purposes because the laws of Country X only provide for a three-year carryover period for such items.

(ii) *Result.* The sale of DRCX to FSX generally would be a triggering event under § 1.1503(d)-6(e)(1)(ii), which would require DRCX to recapture the year 1 dual consolidated loss (and pay an applicable interest charge) on the P consolidated group's tax return for the year that includes the date on which DRCX ceases to be a member of the P consolidated group. However, upon adequate documentation that the losses and deductions have expired for Country X tax purposes, P can rebut the presumption that a triggering event has occurred pursuant to § 1.1503(d)-6(e)(2)(i). If the triggering event presumption is rebutted, the domestic use agreement filed by the P consolidated group with respect to the year 1 dual consolidated loss of DRCX is terminated and has no further effect pursuant to § 1.1503(d)-6(j)(1)(i). If the presumptive triggering event is not rebutted, the domestic use agreement would terminate and have no further effect pursuant to § 1.1503(d)-6(j)(1)(iii) because the dual consolidated loss would be recaptured.

(33) *Example 33. Triggering events and rebuttals—tax basis carryover transaction.* (i) *Facts.* (A) P owns DE1X. DE1X's sole asset is A, which it acquired at the beginning of year 1 for $100x. DE1X does not have any liabilities. For U.S. tax purposes, DE1X's tax basis in A at the beginning of year 1 is $100x and DE1X's sole item of income, gain, deduction, and loss for year 1 is a $20x depreciation deduction attributable to A. As a result, the $20x depreciation deduction constitutes a dual consolidated loss attributable to P's interest in DE1X. P makes a domestic use election with respect to the year 1 dual consolidated loss.

(B) For Country X tax purposes, DE1X has a $100x tax basis in A at the beginning of year 1, but A is not a depreciable asset. As a result, DE1X does not have any items of income, gain, deduction, and loss in year 1 for Country X tax purposes.

(C) During year 2, P sells its interest in DE1X to FSX for $80x. P's disposition of its interest in DE1X constitutes a presumptive triggering event under § 1.1503(d)-6(e)(1)(iv) and (v) requiring the recapture of the year 1 $20x dual consolidated loss (plus the applicable interest charge). For Country X tax purposes, DE1X retains its tax basis of $100x in A following the sale.

(ii) *Result.* The year 1 dual consolidated loss is a result of the $20x depreciation deduction attributable to A. Although no item of deduction or loss was recognized by DE1X at the time of the sale for Country X tax purposes, the deduction composing the dual consolidated loss was retained by DE1X after the sale in the form of tax basis in A. As a result, a portion of the dual consolidated loss may be available to offset income for Country X tax purposes in a manner that would constitute a foreign use. For example, if DE1X were to dispose of A, the amount of gain recognized by DE1X would be reduced (or an amount of loss recognized by DE1X would be increased) and, therefore, an item composing the dual consolidated loss would be available, under U.S. tax principles, to reduce income of a foreign corporation (and an owner of an interest in a hybrid entity that is not a separate unit). Thus, P cannot demonstrate pursuant to § 1.1503(d)-6(e)(2)(i) that there can be no foreign use of the year 1 dual consolidated loss following the triggering event, and must recapture the year 1 dual consolidated loss. Pursuant to § 1.1503(d)-6(j)(1)(iii), the domestic use agreement filed by the P consolidated group with respect to the year 1 dual consolidated loss is terminated and has no further effect.

(iii) *Alternative facts.* The facts are the same as paragraph (c)(33)(i) of this section, except that instead of P selling its interest in DE1X to FSX, DE1X sells asset A to FSX for $80x and, for Country X tax purposes, FSX's tax basis in A immediately after the sale is $80x. P's disposition of Asset A constitutes a presumptive triggering event under § 1.1503(d)-6(e)(1)(iv) requiring the recapture of the year 1 $20x dual consolidated loss (plus the applicable interest charge). For Country X tax purposes, FSX's tax basis in A was not determined, in whole or in part, by reference to the basis of A in the hands of DE1X. As a result, the deduction composing the dual consolidated loss will not give rise to an item of deduction or loss in the form of tax basis for Country X tax purposes (for example, when FSX disposes of A). Therefore, P may be able to demonstrate (for example, by obtaining the opinion of a Country X tax advisor) pursuant to § 1.1503(d)-6(e)(2)(i) that there can be no foreign use of the year 1 dual consolidated loss and, thus, would not be required to recapture the year 1 dual consolidated loss.

(34) *Example 34. Triggering event resulting in a single consolidated group where acquirer files a new domestic use agreement.* (i) *Facts.* P owns DRCX, a member of the P consolidated group. In year 1, DRCX incurs a dual consolidated loss and P makes a domestic use election with respect to such loss. No member of the P consolidated group incurs a dual consolidated loss in year 2. At the end of year 2, T, the parent of the T consolidated group, acquires all the stock of P, and all the members of the P group, including DRCX, become members of a consolidated group of which T is the common parent.

(ii) *Result.* (A) Under § 1.1503(d)-6(f)(2)(ii)(B), the acquisition by T of the P consolidated group is not an event described in § 1.1503(d)-6(e)(1)(ii) requiring the recapture of the year 1 dual consolidated loss of DRCX (and the payment of an interest charge), provided that the T consolidated group files a new domestic use agreement described in § 1.1503(d)-6(f)(2)(iii)(A). If a new domestic use agreement is filed, then pursuant to § 1.1503(d)-6(j)(1)(ii), the domestic use agreement filed by the P consolidated group with respect to the year 1 dual consolidated loss of DRCX is terminated and has no further effect.

(B) Assume that T files a new domestic use agreement and a triggering event occurs at the end of year 3. As a result, the T consolidated group must recapture the dual consolidated loss that DRCX incurred in year 1 (and pay an interest charge), as provided in § 1.1503(d)-6(h). Each member of the T consolidated group, including DRCX and any former members of the P consolidated group, is severally liable for the additional tax (and the interest charge) due upon the recapture of the dual consolidated loss of DRCX. In addition, pursuant to § 1.1503(d)-6(j)(1)(iii), the new domestic use agreement filed by the T group with respect to the year 1 dual consolidated loss of DRCX is terminated and has no further effect.

(35) *Example 35.* Triggering event exceptions for certain deemed transfers. (i) Facts. P owns DE1X. In year 1, there is a $100x dual consolidated loss attributable to P's interest in DE1X. P files a domestic use agreement under § 1.1503(d)-6(d) with respect to such loss. During year 2, P sells 33 percent of its interest in DE1X to T, an unrelated domestic corporation.

(ii) *Result.* Pursuant to Rev. Rul. 99-5, the transaction is treated as if P sold 33 percent of its interest in each of DE1X's assets to T and then immediately thereafter P and T transferred their interests in the assets of DE1X to a partnership in exchange for an ownership interest therein. Upon the transfer of 33 percent of P's interest to T, a domestic corporation, no foreign use occurs and, therefore, there is no foreign use triggering event. However, P's deemed transfer of 67 percent of its interest in the assets of DE1X to a partnership is nominally a triggering event under § 1.1503(d)-6(e)(1)(iv). Because the initial transfer of 33 percent of DE1X's interest was to a domestic corporation and there is only a triggering event because of the deemed transfer under Rev. Rul. 99-5, the deemed asset transfer is not treated as resulting in a triggering event pursuant to § 1.1503(d)-6(f)(4).

(iii) *Alternative facts.* The facts are the same as in paragraph (c)(35)(i) of this section, except that P sells 60 percent (rather than 33 percent) of its interest in DE1X to T. The sale is a triggering event under § 1.1503(d)-6(e)(1)(iv) and (v) without regard to the occurrence of a deemed transaction. Therefore, § 1.1503(d)-6(f)(4) does not apply.

(36) *Example 36. Triggering event exception involving multiple parties.* (i) *Facts.* P owns DE1X which, in turn, owns FBX. P's interest in DE1X and its indirect interest in FBX are combined and treated as a single separate unit (Country X separate unit) pursuant to § 1.1503(d)-1(b)(4)(ii). In year 1, there is a $100x dual consolidated loss attributable to P's Country X separate unit and P makes a domestic use election with respect to such loss. No member of the P consolidated group incurs a dual consolidated loss in year 2. At the end of year 2, T, the parent of the T consolidated group, acquires all of P's interest in DE1X for cash.

(ii) *Result.* (A) Under § 1.1503(d)-6(f)(2)(i)(B), the acquisition by T of the interest in DE1X is not an event described in § 1.1503(d)-6(e)(1)(iv) or (v) requiring the recapture of the year 1 dual consolidated loss attributable to the Country X separate unit (and the payment of an interest charge), provided: (1) the T consolidated group files a new domestic use agreement described in § 1.1503(d)-6(f)(2)(iii)(A) with respect to the year 1 dual consolidated loss of the Country X separate unit; and (2) the P consolidated group files a statement described in § 1.1503(d)-6(f)(2)(iii)(B) with respect to the year 1 dual consolidated loss. If these requirements are satisfied, then pursuant to § 1.1503(d)-6(j)(1)(ii) the domestic use agreement filed by the P consolidated group with respect to the year 1 dual consolidated loss is terminated and has no further effect (if these requirements are not satisfied such that the P consolidated group recaptures the dual consolidated loss, the domestic use agreement would terminate pursuant to § 1.1503(d)-6(j)(1)(iii)).

(B) Assume a triggering event occurs at the end of year 3 that requires recapture by the T consolidated group of the year 1 dual consolidated loss, as well as the payment of an interest charge, as provided in § 1.1503(d)-6(h). T continues to own the Country X separate unit after the triggering event. In that case, each member of the T consolidated group is severally liable for the additional tax (and the interest charge) due upon the recapture of the year 1 dual consolidated loss. The T consolidated group must prepare a statement that computes the recapture tax amount as provided under § 1.1503(d)-6(h)(3)(iii). Pursuant to § 1.1503(d)-6(h)(3)(iv)(A), the recapture tax amount is assessed as an income tax liability of the T consolidated group and is considered as having been properly assessed as an income tax liability of the P consolidated group. If the T consolidated group does not pay in full the income tax liability attributable to the recapture tax amount, the unpaid balance of such recapture tax amount may be collected from the P consolidated group in accordance with the provisions of § 1.1503(d)-6(h)(3)(iv)(B). Pursuant to § 1.1503(d)-6(j)(1)(iii), the new domestic use agreement filed by the T consolidated group is terminated and has no further effect. Finally, pursuant to § 1.1503(d)-6(h)(6)(iii), T is treated as if it incurred the dual consolidated loss that is recaptured for purposes of applying § 1.1503(d)-6(h)(6)(i). Thus, T has a reconstituted net operating loss equal to the amount of the year 1 dual consolidated loss that was recaptured, and such loss is attributable to the Country X separate unit (and subject to the rules and limitations under § 1.1503(d)-6(h)(6)(i)). Because T is treated as if it incurred the year 1 dual consolidated loss, P shall not be treated as having a net operating loss under § 1.1503(d)-6(h)(6)(i).

(37) *Example 37. No foreign use following multiple-party event exception to triggering event.* (i) *Facts.* P owns DE1X which, in turn, owns FBX. P's interest in DE1X and its indirect interest in FBX are combined and treated as a single separate unit (Country X separate unit) pursuant to § 1.1503(d)-1(b)(4)(ii). In year 1, there is a $100x dual consolidated loss attributable to P's Country X separate unit and P makes a domestic use election with respect to such loss. T, a domestic corporation unrelated to P, owns 95 percent of PRS, a partnership. FSX owns the remaining 5 percent of PRS. At the beginning of year 3, PRS purchases 100 percent of the interest in DE1X from P for cash. For Country X tax purposes, the $100x loss incurred by DE1X in year 1 carries forward and is available to offset income of DE1X in subsequent years.

(ii) *Result.* P's sale of its interest in DE1X is a triggering event under § 1.1503(d)-6(e)(1)(iv) and (v). However, if P and T comply with the requirements under § 1.1503(d)-6(f)(2)(iii), the sale would qualify for the multiple-party event exception under § 1.1503(d)-6(f)(2)(i). In addition, because the $100x loss of DE1X carries forward to subsequent years for Country X purposes and is available to offset income of DE1X, there would be a foreign use of the dual consolidated loss immediately after the sale pursuant to § 1.1503(d)-3(a)(1). This is the case because the dual consolidated loss would be available to offset or reduce income that is considered, under U.S. tax principles, to be an item of FSX, a foreign corporation (it would also be a foreign use because FSX is an indirect owner of an interest in a hybrid entity that is not a separate unit). However, there is no foreign use in this case as a result of FSX's 5 percent interest in DE1X pursuant to § 1.1503(d)-3(c)(8).

(38) *Example 38. Character and source of recapture income.* (i) *Facts.* (A) P owns FBX. In year 1, the items of income, gain, deduction, and loss that are attributable to FBX for purposes of determining whether it has a dual consolidated loss are as follows:

Table 2 to paragraph (c)(38)(i)(A)

Sales Income	$100x
Salary Expense	($75x)
Interest expense	($50x)
Dual consolidated loss	($25x)

(B) P makes a domestic use election with respect to the year 1 dual consolidated loss attributable to FBX and, thus, the $25x dual consolidated loss is used to offset the P group's consolidated taxable income.

(C) Pursuant to § 1.861-8, the $75x of salary expense incurred by FBX is allocated and apportioned entirely to foreign source general limitation income. Pursuant to § 1.861-9T, $25x of the $50x interest expense attributable to FBX is allocated and apportioned to domestic source income, $15x of such interest expense is allocated and apportioned to foreign source general limitation income, and the remaining $10x of such interest expense is allocated and apportioned to foreign source passive income.

(D) During year 2, $5x of income is attributable to FBX under the rules of § 1.1503(d)-5, and the P consolidated group has $100x of consolidated taxable income. At the end of year 2, FBX undergoes a triggering event described in § 1.1503(d)-6(e)(1), and P continues to own FBX following the triggering event. Pursuant to § 1.1503(d)-6(h)(2)(i), P is able to demonstrate to the satisfaction of the Commissioner that the $25x dual consolidated loss attributable to FBX in year 1 would have offset the $5x of income attributable to FBX in year 2, if no domestic use election were made with respect to the year 1 loss such that it was subject to the limitations of § 1.1503(d)-4(b) and (c).

(ii) *Result.* P must recapture and report as ordinary income $20x ($25x - $5x) of FBX's year 1 dual consolidated loss, plus applicable interest. The $20x recapture income is attributable to FBX pursuant to § 1.1503(d)-5(c)(4)(vi). Pursuant to § 1.1503(d)-6(h)(5), the recapture income is treated as ordinary income whose source and character (including section 904 separate limitation character) is determined by reference to the manner in which the recaptured items of expense or loss taken into account in calculating the dual consolidated loss were allocated and apportioned. Further, pursuant to § 1.1503(d)-6(h)(5), the pro rata computation described in § 1.1503(d)-4(c)(4) shall apply. Thus, the character and source of the recapture income is determined in the same proportion as each item of deduction or loss that contributed to the dual consolidated loss being recaptured. Accordingly, P's $20x of recapture income is characterized and sourced as follows: $4x of domestic source income (($25x/$125x) x $20x); $14.4x of foreign source general limitation income (($75x + $15x)/$125x) x $20x); and $1.6x of foreign source passive income (($10x/$125x) x $20x). Pursuant to § 1.1503(d)-6(h)(6)(i), commencing in year 3, the $20x recapture amount is reconstituted and treated as a net operating loss incurred by FBX in a separate return limitation year, subject to the limitation under § 1.1503(d)-4(b) (and therefore subject to the restrictions of § 1.1503(d)-4(c)). Pursuant to § 1.1503(d)-6(j)(1)(iii), the domestic use agreement filed by the P consolidated group with respect to the year 1 dual consolidated loss of FBX is terminated and has no further effect.

(39) *Example 39. Interest charge without recapture.* (i) *Facts.* P owns DE1X which, in turn, owns FBX. P's interest in DE1X and its indirect interest in FBX are combined and treated as a single separate unit (Country X separate unit) pursuant to § 1.1503(d)-1(b)(4)(ii). In year 1, a dual consolidated loss of $100x is attributable to P's Country X separate unit. P makes a domestic use election with respect to such loss and uses the loss to offset the P group's consolidated taxable income. In year 2, there is $100x of income attributable to P's Country X separate unit and the P consolidated group has $200x of consolidated taxable income. At the end of year 2, the Country X separate unit undergoes a triggering event within the meaning of § 1.1503(d)-6(e)(1). P demonstrates, to the satisfaction of the Commissioner, that if no domestic use election were made with respect to the year 1 dual consolidated loss such that it was subject to the limitations of § 1.1503(d)-4(b) and (c), the year 1 $100x dual consolidated loss would have been offset by the $100x of year 2 income.

(ii) *Result.* There is no recapture of the year 1 dual consolidated loss attributable to P's Country X separate unit because it is reduced to zero under § 1.1503(d)-6(h)(2)(i). However, P is liable for one year of interest charge under § 1.1503(d)-6(h)(1)(ii), even though P's recapture amount is zero. This is the case because the P consolidated group had the benefit of the dual consolidated loss in year 1, and the income that offset the recapture income was not recognized until year 2. Pursuant to § 1.1503(d)-6(j)(1)(iii), the domestic use agreement filed by the P consolidated group with respect to the year 1 dual consolidated loss is terminated and has no further effect.

(40) *Example 40. Reduced recapture and interest charge, and reconstituted dual consolidated loss.* (i) *Facts.* S owns DE1X which, in turn, owns FBX. S's interest in DE1X and its indirect interest in FBX are combined and treated as a single separate unit (Country X separate unit) pursuant to § 1.1503(d)-1(b)(4)(ii). In year 1, there is a $100x dual consolidated loss attributable to S's Country X separate unit, and P earns $100x. P makes a domestic use election with respect to the Country X separate unit's year 1 dual consolidated loss. Therefore, the consolidated group is permitted to offset P's $100x of income with the Country X separate unit's $100x dual consolidated loss. In year 2, $30x of income is attributable to the Country X separate unit under the rules of § 1.1503(d)-5 and such income is offset by a $30x net operating loss incurred by P in such year. In year 3, $25x of income is attributable to the Country X separate unit under the rules of § 1.1503(d)-5, and P earns $15x of income. In addition, at the end of year 3 there is a foreign use of the year 1 dual consolidated loss that constitutes a triggering event. S continues to own the Country X separate unit after the triggering event.

(ii) *Result.* (A) Under the presumptive rule of § 1.1503(d)-6(h)(1)(i), S must recapture $100x (plus applicable interest). However, under § 1.1503(d)-6(h)(2)(i), S may be able to demonstrate that a lesser amount is subject to recapture. The lesser amount is the amount of the $100x dual consolidated loss that would have remained subject to § 1.1503(d)-4(c) at the time of the foreign use triggering event if a domestic use election had not been made for such loss.

(B) Although the combined separate unit earned $30x of income in year 2, there was no consolidated taxable income in such year. As a result, as of the end of year 2 the $100x dual consolidated loss would continue to be subject to § 1.1503(d)-4(c) if a domestic use election had not been made for such loss. However, the $30x earned in year 2 can be carried forward to subsequent taxable years and may reduce the recapture income to the extent of consolidated taxable income generated in subsequent years. In year 3, $25x of income was attributable to the Country X separate unit and P earns $15x of income. Thus, the P consolidated group has $40x of consolidated taxable income in year 3. As a result, the $100x of recapture income can be reduced by $40x. This is the case because if a domestic use election had not been made for the $100x year 1 dual consolidated loss such that it was subject to the limitations of § 1.1503(d)-4(b) and (c), only $60x of the loss would have remained subject to such limitations at the time of the foreign use triggering event. Accordingly, if S can adequately document the lesser amount, the amount of recapture income is $60x ($100x - $40x). The $60x recapture income is attributable to the Country X separate unit pursuant to § 1.1503(d)-5(c)(4)(vi).

(C) Pursuant to § 1.1503(d)-6(h)(6)(i), commencing in year 4, the $60x recapture amount is reconstituted and treated as a net operating loss incurred by the Country X separate unit of S in a separate return limitation year, subject to the limitation under § 1.1503(d)-4(b) (and therefore subject to the restrictions of § 1.1503(d)-4(c)). The loss is only available for carryover to taxable years after year 3 (and is not available for carryback). The carryover period of the loss, for purposes of section 172(b), will start from year 1, when the dual consolidated loss that was subject to recapture was incurred. In addition, such reconstituted net operating loss is not eligible for the exceptions contained in § 1.1503(d)-6(b) through (d). Pursuant to § 1.1503(d)-6(j)(1)(iii), the domestic use agreement filed by the P consolidated group with respect to the year 1 dual consolidated loss of the Country X separate unit is terminated and has no further effect.

(iii) *Alternative facts.* The facts are the same as in paragraph (c)(40)(i) of this section, except that the triggering event that occurs at the end of year 3 is a sale by S of its entire interest in DE1X to B, an unrelated domestic corporation. The sale does not qualify as a transaction described in section 381. The results are the same as in paragraph (c)(40)(ii) of this section, except that pursuant to § 1.1503(d)-6(h)(6)(ii) the $60x net operating loss is not reconstituted (with respect to either S or B). The loss is not reconstituted with respect to S because the Country X separate unit ceases to be a separate unit of S (or any other member of the consolidated group that includes S) and therefore would have been eliminated pursuant to § 1.1503(d)-4(d)(1)(ii) if no domestic use election had been made with respect to such loss. The loss is not reconstituted with respect to B because B was not the domestic owner of the combined separate unit when the dual consolidated loss that is recaptured was incurred, and B did not acquire the Country X separate unit in a section 381 transaction.

(41) *Example 41. Domestic consenting corporation—treated as dual resident corporation.*—(i) *Facts.* FSZ1, a Country Z entity that is subject to Country Z tax on its worldwide income or on a residence basis and is classified as a foreign corporation for U.S. tax purposes, owns all the interests in DCC, a domestic eligible entity that has filed an election to be classified as an association. Under Country Z tax law, DCC is fiscally transparent. For taxable year 1, DCC's only item of income, gain, deduction, or loss is a $100x deduction and such deduction comprises a $100x net operating loss of DCC. For Country Z tax purposes, FSZ1's only item of income, gain, deduction, or loss, other than the $100x loss attributable to DCC, is $60x of operating income.

(ii) *Result.* DCC is a domestic consenting corporation because by electing to be classified as an association, it consents to be treated as a dual resident corporation for purposes of section 1503(d). *See* § 301.7701-3(c)(3) of this chapter. For taxable year 1, DCC is treated as a dual resident corporation under § 1.1503(d)-1(b)(2)(iii) because FSZ1 (a specified foreign tax resident that bears a relationship to

DCC that is described in section 267(b) or 707(b)) derives or incurs items of income, gain, deduction, or loss of DCC. *See* § 1.1503(d)-1(c). FSZ1 derives or incurs items of income, gain, deduction, or loss of DCC because, under Country Z tax law, DCC is fiscally transparent. Thus, DCC has a $100x dual consolidated loss for taxable year 1. *See* § 1.1503(d)-1(b)(5). Because the loss is available to, and in fact does, offset income of FSZ1 under Country Z tax law, there is a foreign use of the dual consolidated loss in year 1. Accordingly, the dual consolidated loss is subject to the domestic use limitation rule of § 1.1503(d)-4(b). The result would be the same if FSZ1 were to indirectly own its DCC stock through an intermediate entity that is fiscally transparent under Country Z tax law, or if an individual were to wholly own FSZ1 and FSZ1 were a disregarded entity. In addition, the result would be the same if FSZ1 had no items of income, gain, deduction, or loss, other than the $100x loss attributable to DCC.

(iii) *Alternative facts – DCC not treated as a dual resident corporation.* The facts are the same as in paragraph (c)(41)(i) of this section, except that DCC is not fiscally transparent under Country Z tax law and thus under Country Z tax law FSZ1 does not derive or incur items of income, gain, deduction, or loss of DCC. Accordingly, DCC is not treated as a dual resident corporation under § 1.1503(d)-1(b)(2)(iii) for year 1 and, consequently, its $100x net operating loss in that year is not a dual consolidated loss.

(iv) *Alternative facts – mirror legislation.* The facts are the same as in paragraph (c)(41)(i) of this section, except that, under provisions of Country Z tax law that constitute mirror legislation under § 1.1503(d)-3(e)(1) and that are substantially similar to the recommendations in Chapter 6 of OECD/G-20, *Neutralising the Effects of Hybrid Mismatch Arrangements, Action 2: 2015 Final Report* (October 2015), Country Z tax law prohibits the $100x loss attributable to DCC from offsetting FSZ1's income that is not also subject to U.S. tax. As is the case in paragraph (c)(41)(ii) of this section, DCC is treated as a dual resident corporation under § 1.1503(d)-1(b)(2)(iii) for year 1 and its $100x net operating loss is a dual consolidated loss. Pursuant to § 1.1503(d)-3(e)(3), however, the dual consolidated loss is not deemed to be put to a foreign use by virtue of the Country Z mirror legislation. Therefore, DCC is eligible to make a domestic use election for the dual consolidated loss. [Reg. § 1.1503(d)-7.]

☐ [*T.D. 9315, 3-16-2007 (corrected 4-24-2007). Amended by T.D. 9896, 4-7-2020 (corrected 8-11-2020).*]

§ 1.1503(d)-8. Effective dates.—(a) *General rule.*—Except as provided in paragraph (b) of this section, this paragraph (a) provides the dates of applicability of §§ 1.1503(d)-1 through 1.1503(d)-7. Sections 1.1503(d)-1 through 1.1503(d)-7 shall apply to dual consolidated losses incurred in taxable years beginning on or after April 18, 2007. However, a taxpayer may apply §§ 1.1503(d)-1 through 1.1503(d)-7, in their entirety, to dual consolidated losses incurred in taxable years beginning on or after January 1, 2007, by filing its return and attaching to such return the domestic use agreements, certifications, or other information in accordance with these regulations. For purposes of this section, the term application date means either April 18, 2007, or, if the taxpayer applies these regulations pursuant to the preceding sentence, January 1, 2007. Section 1.1503-2 applies for dual consolidated losses incurred in taxable years beginning on or after October 1, 1992, and before the application date.

(b) *Special rules.*—(1) *Reduction of term of agreements filed under §§ 1.1503-2A(c)(3), 1.1503-2A(d)(3), 1.1503-2(g)(2)(i), or 1.1503-2T(g)(i).*—If an agreement is filed in accordance with §§ 1.1503-2A(c)(3), 1.1503-2A(d)(3), 1.1503-2(g)(2)(i), or 1.1503-2T(g)(2)(i) with respect to a dual consolidated loss incurred in a taxable year beginning prior to the application date and an event requiring recapture with respect to the dual consolidated loss subject to the agreement has not occurred as of the application date, then such agreement will be considered by the Internal Revenue Service to apply only for any taxable year up to and including the fifth taxable year following the year in which the dual consolidated loss that is the subject of the agreement was incurred and thereafter will have no effect.

(2) *Reduction of term of agreements filed under §§ 1.1503-2(g)(2)(iv)(B)(2)(i) (1992), 1.1503-2(g)(2)(iv)(B)(3)(i), or Rev. Proc. 2000-42.*—Taxpayers subject to the terms of a closing agreement entered into with the Internal Revenue Service pursuant to §§ 1.1503-2(g)(2)(iv)(B)(2)(*i*) (1992), 1.1503-2(g)(2)(iv)(B)(3)(*i*), or Rev. Proc. 2000-42 (2000-2 CB 394), see § 601.601(d)(2)(ii)(*b*) of this chapter, will be deemed to have satisfied the closing agreement's fifteen-year certification period requirement if the five-year certification period specified in § 1.1503(d)-1(b)(20) has elapsed, provided such closing agreement is still in effect as of the application date, and provided the dual consolidated losses have not been recaptured. For example, if a calendar year taxpayer that has a January 1, 2007, application date entered into a closing agreement with respect to a dual consolidated loss incurred in 2003 and, as of January 1, 2007, the closing agreement is still in effect and the dual consolidated loss subject to the closing agreement has not been recaptured, then the closing agreement's fifteen-year certification period will be deemed satisfied when the five-year certification period described in § 1.1503(d)-1(b)(20) has elapsed. Thus, the dual consolidated loss will be subject to the recapture and certification provisions of the closing agreement in such a case only through December 31, 2008. Alternatively, if a calendar year taxpayer that has a January 1, 2007, application date entered into a closing agreement with respect to a dual consolidated loss incurred in 2000 and, as of January 1, 2007, the closing agreement is still in effect and the dual consolidated loss subject to the closing agreement has not been recaptured, then the certification period is deemed to be satisfied.

(3) Relief for untimely filings.— Paragraphs (b)(3)(i) through (iii) of this section set forth the effective dates for rules that provide relief for the failure to make timely filings of an election, agreement, statement, rebuttal, computation, closing agreement, or other information, pursuant to section 1503(d) and these regulations.

(i) *General rule.*—Except as provided in paragraphs (b)(3)(ii) and (iii) of this section, the reasonable cause relief standard of § 1.1503(d)-1(d) applies for all untimely filings with respect to dual consolidated losses, including with respect to dual consolidated losses incurred in taxable years beginning before the application date.

(ii) *Closing agreements.*—Solely with respect to closing agreements described in § 1.1503-2(g)(2)(iv)(B)(3)(i) and Rev. Proc. 2000-42, taxpayers must request relief for untimely requests through the process provided under §§ 301.9100-1 through 301.9100-3 of this chapter. See paragraph (b)(4) of this section for rules that permit the multiple-party event exception, rather than closing agreements, for certain triggering events.

(iii) *Pending requests for relief.*—Taxpayers that have letter ruling requests under §§ 301.9100-1 through 301.9100-3 of this chapter pending as of March 19, 2007 (other than requests under paragraph (b)(3)(ii) of this section) are not required to use the reasonable cause procedure under § 1.1503(d)-1(d); however, if such taxpayers have not yet received a determination of their request, they may withdraw their request consistent with the procedures contained in Rev. Proc. 2007-1 (2007-1 IRB 1), see § 601.601(d)(2)(ii)(b) of this chapter, (or any succeeding document) and use the reasonable cause procedure set forth in § 1.1503(d)-1(d). In that event, the Internal Revenue Service will refund the taxpayer's user fee.

(4) *Multiple-party event exception to triggering events.*—This paragraph (b)(4) applies to events described in § 1.1503-2(g)(2)(iv)(B)(1)(i) through (iii) that occur after April 18, 2007 and that are with respect to dual consolidated losses that were incurred in taxable years beginning on or after October 1, 1992, and before the application date. The events described in the previous sentence are not eligible for the exception described in § 1.1503-2(g)(2)(iv)(B)(1), but instead are eligible for the multiple-party event exception described in § 1.1503(d)-6(f)(2)(i), as modified by this paragraph (b)(4). Thus, such events are not eligible for a closing agreement described in § 1.1503-2(g)(2)(iv)(B)(3)(i) and Rev. Proc. 2000-42. For purposes of applying § 1.1503(d)-6(f)(2)(i) to transactions covered by this paragraph, agreements described in § 1.1503-2(g)(2)(i) (rather than domestic use agreements) shall be filed, and subsequent triggering events and exceptions thereto have the meaning provided in § 1.1503-2(g)(2)(iii)(A) and (iv) (other than the exception provided under § 1.1503-2(g)(2)(iv)(B)(1)). For example, if a calendar year taxpayer that has a January 1, 2007, application date filed an election under § 1.1503-2(g)(2)(i) with respect to a dual consolidated loss that was incurred in 2004, and a triggering event described in § 1.1503-2(g)(2)(iv)(B)(1)(ii) occurs with respect to such dual consolidated loss after April 18, 2007, then the event is eligible for the multiple-party event exception under § 1.1503(d)-6(f)(2)(i) (and not the exception under § 1.1503-2(g)(2)(iv)(B)(1)). However, in order to comply with § 1.1503(d)-6(f)(2)(iii)(A), the subsequent elector must file a new agreement described in § 1.1503-2(g)(2)(i) (rather than a new domestic use agreement). In addition, for purposes of determining whether there is a subsequent triggering event, and exceptions thereto, pursuant to such new agreement, § 1.1503-2(g)(2)(iii)(A) and (iv) (other than the exception provided under § 1.1503-2(g)(2)(iv)(B)(1)) shall apply. Notwithstanding the general

application of this paragraph (b)(4) to events described in § 1.1503-2(g)(2)(iv)(B)(*1*)(*i*) through (*iii*) that occur after April 18, 2007, a taxpayer may choose to apply this paragraph (b)(4) to events described in § 1.1503-2(g)(2)(iv)(B)(*1*)(*i*) through (*iii*) that occur after March 19, 2007 and on or before April 18, 2007.

(5) *Basis adjustment rules.*—Taxpayers may apply the basis adjustment rules of § 1.1503(d)-5(g) for all open years in which such basis is relevant, even if the basis adjustment is attributable to a dual consolidated loss incurred (or recaptured) in a closed taxable year. Taxpayers applying the provisions of § 1.1503(d)-5(g), however, must do so consistently for all open years.

(6) *Rules regarding domestic consenting corporations.*—Section 1.1503(d)-1(b)(2)(iii) and (c), as well § 1.1503(d)-3(e)(1) and (3), apply to determinations under §§ 1.1503(d)-1 through 1.1503(d)-7 relating to taxable years ending on or after December 20, 2018. For taxable years ending before December 20, 2018, see § 1.1503(d)-3(e)(1) as contained in 26 CFR part 1 revised as of April 1, 2018.

(7) *Compulsory transfer triggering event exception.*—Section 1.1503(d)-6(f)(5)(i) through (iii) applies to transfers that occur on or after December 20, 2018. For transfers occurring before December 20, 2018, see § 1.1503(d)-6(f)(5)(i) through (iii) as contained in 26 CFR part 1 revised as of April 1, 2018. However, taxpayers may consistently apply § 1.1503(d)-6(f)(5)(i) through (iii) to transfers occurring before December 20, 2018.

(8) *Rule providing that SRLY limitation applies without regard to § 1.1502-21(c)(1)(i)(E).*—Section 1.1503(d)-4(c)(3)(v) applies to any period to which § 1.1502-21(c)(1)(i)(E) applies. [Reg. § 1.1503(d)-8.]

☐ [*T.D. 9315, 3-16-2007 (corrected 4-24-2007). Amended by T.D. 9896, 4-7-2020 and T.D. 9927, 10-23-2020.*]

Information Returns

§ 1.6031(a)-1. Return of partnership income.—(a) *Domestic partnerships.*—(1) *Return required.*—Except as provided in paragraphs (a)(3) and (c) of this section, every domestic partnership must file a return of partnership income under section 6031 (partnership return) for each taxable year on the form prescribed for the partnership return. The partnership return must be filed for the taxable year of the partnership regardless of the taxable years of the partners. For taxable years of a partnership and of a partner, see section 706 and § 1.706-1. For the rules governing partnership statements to partners and nominees, see § 1.6031(b)-1T. For the rules requiring the disclosure of certain transactions, see § 1.6011-4T.

(2) *Content of return.*—The partnership return must contain the information required by the prescribed form and the accompanying instructions.

(3) *Special rule.*—(i) A partnership that has no income, deductions, or credits for federal income tax purposes for a taxable year is not required to file a partnership return for that year.

(ii) The Commissioner may, in guidance published in the Internal Revenue Bulletin (see § 601.601(d)(2)(ii)(*b*) of this chapter), provide for an exception to partnership reporting under section 6031 and for conditions for the exception, if all or substantially all of a partnership's income is derived from the holding or disposition of tax-exempt obligations (as defined in section 1275(a)(3) and § 1.1275-1(e)) or shares in a regulated investment company (as defined in section 851(a)) that pays exempt-interest dividends (as defined in section 852(b)(5)).

(4) *Failure to file.*—For the consequences of a failure to comply with the requirements of section 6031(a) and this paragraph (a), see sections 6229(a), 6231(f), 6698, and 7203.

(b) *Foreign partnerships.*—(1) *General rule.*—(i) *Filing requirement.*—A foreign partnership is not required to file a partnership return, if the foreign partnership does not have gross income that is (or is treated as) effectively connected with the conduct of a trade or business within the United States (ECI) and does not have gross income (including gains) derived from sources within the United States (U.S.-source income). Except as provided in paragraphs (b)(2) and (3) of this section, a foreign partnership that has ECI or has U.S.-source income that is not ECI must file a partnership return for its taxable year in accordance with the rules for domestic partnerships in paragraph (a) of this section.

(ii) *Special rule.*—For purposes of this paragraph (b)(1) and paragraph (b)(3)(iii) of this section, a foreign partnership will not be considered to have derived income from sources within the United States solely because a U.S. partner marks to market his pro rata share of PFIC stock held by the foreign partnership pursuant to an election under section 1296.

(2) *Foreign partnerships with de minimis U.S.-source income and de minimis U.S. partners.*—A foreign partnership (other than a withholding foreign partnership, as defined in § 1.1441-5(c)(2)(i)) that has $20,000 or less of U.S.-source income and has no ECI during its taxable year is not required to file a partnership return if, at no time during the partnership taxable year, one percent or more of any item of partnership income, gain, loss, deduction, or credit is allocable in the aggregate to direct United States partners. The United States partners must directly report their shares of the allocable items of partnership income, gain, loss, deduction, and credit.

(3) *Filing obligations for certain other foreign partnerships with no ECI.*—(i) *General requirements for modified filing obligations.*—A foreign partnership will be subject to the modified filing obligations in paragraphs (b)(3)(ii) and (iii) of this section if, in addition to satisfying the requirements contained in paragraph 5(b)(3)(ii) and (iii) of this section—

(A) The partnership is not a withholding foreign partnership as defined in § 1.1441-5(c)(2)(i);

(B) Forms 1042 and 1042-S are filed by the partnership with respect to the amounts subject to reporting under § 1.1461-1(b) and (c), unless the partnership is not required to file such returns under § 1.1461-1(b)(2) and (c)(4), in which case Forms 1042 and 1042-S must be filed by another withholding agent or agents; and

(C) The tax liability of the partners with respect to such amounts has been fully satisfied by the withholding of tax at the source, if applicable, under chapter 3 of the Internal Revenue Code.

(ii) *Foreign partnerships with U.S.-source income but no U.S. partners.*—A foreign partnership that has U.S.-source income is not required to file a partnership return if the partnership has no ECI and no United States partners at any time during the partnership's taxable year.

(iii) *Foreign partnerships with U.S.-source income and U.S. partners.*—Except as provided in paragraph (b)(2) of this section, a foreign partnership with one or more United States partners that has U.S.-source income but no ECI must file a partnership return. However, such a foreign partnership need not file Statements of Partner's Share of Income, Credit, Deduction, Etc. (Schedules K-1) for any partners other than its direct United States partners and its passthrough partners (whether U.S. or foreign) through which United States partners hold an interest in the foreign partnership. Schedules K-1 that are not excepted from filing under this paragraph (b)(3)(iii) must contain the same information required of a domestic partnership filing under paragraph (a) of this section.

(4) *Information or returns required of partners who are United States persons.*—(i) *In general.*—If a United States person is a partner in a partnership that is not required to file a partnership return, the district director or director of the relevant service center may require that person to render the statements or provide the information necessary to verify the accuracy of the reporting by that person of any items of partnership income, gain, loss, deduction, or credit.

(ii) *Controlled foreign partnerships.*—Certain United States persons who are partners in a foreign partnership controlled (within the meaning of section 6038(e)(1)) by United States persons may be required to provide information with respect to the partnership under section 6038.

(5) *Certain partnership elections.*—For a partnership that is not otherwise required to file a partnership return, if an election that can only be made by the partnership under section 703 (affecting the computation of taxable income derived from a partnership) is to be made by or for the partnership, a return on the form prescribed for the partnership return must be filed for the partnership. Unless otherwise provided in the form or the accompanying instructions, a

return filed solely to make an election need only contain a written statement citing paragraph (b)(5)(ii) of this section, listing the name and address of the partnership making the election, and clearly identifying the specific election being made. A return filed under paragraph (b)(5)(ii) of this section solely to make an election is not a partnership return. Thus, such a return is not a return filed under section 6031(a) for purposes of sections 6501 (except regarding the specific election issue), 6231(a)(1)(A), and 6233. The return must be signed by—

(i) Each partner that is a partner in the partnership at the time the election is made; or

(ii) Any partner of the partnership who is authorized (under local law or the partnership's organizational documents) to make the election and who represents to having such authorization under penalties of perjury.

(6) *Exclusion for certain organizations.*—The return requirement of section 6031 and this section does not apply to the International Telecommunications Satellite Organization, the International Maritime Satellite Organization, or any organization that is a successor of either.

(7) *Filing obligation for certain partners of certain foreign partnerships with respect to base erosion payments.*—If a foreign partnership is not required to file a partnership return and the foreign partnership has made a payment or accrual that is treated as a base erosion payment of a partner as provided in § 1.59A-7(c), a partner in the foreign partnership who is a person required to file a Form 8991 (or successor) must include the information necessary to report those base erosion payments and base erosion tax benefits on Form 8991 (or successor) in accordance with the related instructions. A partner with a Form 8991 (or successor) filing requirement who is a partner in a foreign partnership that is not required to file a partnership return must obtain the necessary information to report any base erosion payments on Form 8991 (or successor) from the foreign partnership or from any other reliable records of these payments. This paragraph does not apply to any partner described in § 1.59A-7(d)(2).

(c) *Partnerships excluded from the application of subchapter K of the Internal Revenue Code.*—(1) *Wholly excluded.*—(i) *Year of election.*—An eligible partnership as described in § 1.761-2(a) that elects to be excluded from all the provisions of subchapter K of chapter 1 of the Internal Revenue Code in the manner specified by § 1.761-2(b)(2)(i) must timely file the form prescribed for the partnership return for the taxable year for which the election is made. In lieu of the information otherwise required, the return must contain or be accompanied by the information required by § 1.761-2(b)(2)(i).

(ii) *Subsequent years.*—Except as otherwise provided in paragraph (c)(1)(i) of this section, an eligible partnership that elects to be wholly excluded from the application of subchapter K is not required to file a partnership return.

(2) *Deemed excluded.*—An eligible partnership that is deemed to have elected exclusion from the application of subchapter K beginning with its first taxable year, as specified in § 1.761-2(b)(2)(ii), is not required to file a partnership return.

(d) *Definitions.*—(1) *Partnership.*—For the meaning of the term *partnership*, see § 1.761-1(a).

(2) *United States person.*—In applying this section, a United States person is a person described in section 7701(a)(30); the government of the United States, a State, or the District of Columbia (including an agency or instrumentality thereof); or a corporation created or organized in Guam, the Commonwealth of Northern Mariana Islands, the U.S. Virgin Islands, and American Samoa, if the requirements of section 881(b)(1)(A), (B), and (C) are met for such corporation. The term does not include an alien individual who is a resident of Puerto Rico, Guam, the Commonwealth of Northern Mariana Islands, the U.S. Virgin Islands, or American Samoa, as determined under § 301.7701(b)-1(d) of this chapter.

(3) *United States partner.*—In applying this section, a United States partner is any United States person who holds a direct or indirect interest in the partnership.

(4) *Indirect interest.*—An indirect interest is any interest held through one or more passthrough partners, as defined in section 6231(a)(9).

(e) *Procedural requirements.*—(1) *Place for filing.*—The return of a partnership must be filed with the service center prescribed in the relevant IRS revenue procedure, publication, form, or instructions to the form (see § 601.601(d)(2)).

(2) *Time for filing.*—The return of a partnership must be filed on or before the date prescribed by section 6072(b).

(3) *Magnetic media filing.*—For magnetic media filing requirements with respect to partnerships, see section 6011(e)(2) and the regulations thereunder.

(f)(1) *Applicability date.*—This section applies to returns filed on or after January 30, 2020. Section 1.6031(a)-1T (as contained in 26 CFR part 1, revised April 2019) applies to returns filed before January 30, 2020.

(2) *Applicability date.*—Paragraph (b)(7) of this section applies to taxable years ending on or after October 9, 2020. [Reg. § 1.6031(a)-1.]

☐ [*T.D. 8841, 11-10-99. Amended by T.D. 9000, 6-14-2002; T.D. 9094, 11-5-2003; T.D. 9123, 4-30-2004; T.D. 9177, 2-10-2005; T.D. 9821, 7-18-2017; T.D. 9892, 1-29-2020 and T.D. 9910, 10-8-2020.*]

§ 1.6035-1. [Reserved].

☐ [*T.D. 6364, 2-13-59. Amended by T.D. 7322, 8-23-74; T.D. 7517, 11-11-77; T.D. 7557, 8-4-78; T.D. 8028, 6-3-85 and T.D. 8573, 12-13-94. Removed and reserved by T.D. 9849, 3-11-2019.*]

§ 1.6038-2. Information returns required of United States persons with respect to annual accounting periods of certain foreign corporations.—(a) *Requirement of return.*—Every U.S. person shall make a separate annual information return with respect to each annual accounting period (described in paragraph (e) of this section) of each foreign corporation which that person controls (as defined in paragraph (b) of this section) at any time during such annual accounting period.

(1) Form 2952, "Information Return with Respect to Controlled Foreign Corporations," if such taxable year ends before December 31, 1982;

(2) Form 5471, "Information Return of U.S. Persons with Respect to Certain Foreign Corporations," if such taxable year ends on or after December 31, 1983; or

(3) Either Form 5471 or Form 2952 if such taxable year ends on or after December 31, 1982 and before December 31, 1963.

(b) *Control.*—A person shall be deemed to be in control of a foreign corporation if at any time during that person's taxable year it owns stock possessing more than 50 percent of the total combined voting power of all classes of stock entitled to vote, or more than 50 percent of the total value of shares of all classes of stock of the foreign corporation. A person in control of a corporation which, in turn, owns more than 50 percent of the combined voting power, or of the value, of all classes of stock of another corporation is also treated as being in control of such other corporation. The provisions of this paragraph may be illustrated by the following example:

Example. Corporation A owns 51 percent of the voting stock in Corporation B. Corporation B owns 51 percent of the voting stock in Corporation C. Corporation C in turn owns 51 percent of the voting stock in Corporation D. Corporation D is controlled by Corporation A.

(c) *Attribution rules.*—For the purpose of determining control of domestic or foreign corporations the constructive ownership rules of section 318(a) shall apply except that:

(1) Stock owned by or for a partner or a beneficiary of an estate or trust shall not be considered owned by the partnership, estate, or trust when the effect is to consider a United States person as owning stock owned by a person who is not a United States person;

(2) A corporation will not be considered as owning stock owned by or for a 50 percent or more shareholder when the effect is to consider a United States person as owning stock owned by a person who is not a United States person; and

(3) If 10 percent or more in value of the stock in a corporation is owned, directly or indirectly, by or for any person, section 318(a)(2)(C) shall apply.

The constructive ownership rules of section 318(a) apply only for purposes of determining control as defined in paragraph (b) of this section.

(d) *U.S. person.*—(1) *In general.*—For purposes of section 6038 and this section, the term *United States person* has the meaning assigned to it by section 7701(a)(30), except as provided in paragraphs (d)(2) and (3) of this section.

(2) *Special rule for individuals residing in certain possessions.*—(i) With respect to an individual who is a bona fide resident of Puerto Rico, the term United States person has the meaning assigned to it by § 1.957-3 except that the rules of § 1.937-2(g)(1) will apply.

(ii) With respect to an individual who is a bona fide resident of any section 931 possession, as defined in § 1.931-1(c)(1), the term United States person has the meaning assigned to it by § 1.957-3.

(3) *Special rule for certain nonresident aliens.*—An individual for whom an election under section 6013(g) or (h) is in effect will, subject to the exceptions contained in paragraph (d)(2) of this section, be considered a United States person for purposes of section 6038 and this section.

(e) *Period covered by return.*—The information required under paragraphs (f) and (g) of this section with respect to a foreign corporation shall be furnished for the annual accounting period of the foreign corporation ending with or within the United States person's taxable year. For purposes of this section, the annual accounting period of a foreign corporation is the annual period on the basis of which that corporation regularly computes its income in keeping its books. In the case of a specified foreign corporation (as defined in section 898), the taxable year of such corporation shall be treated as its annual accounting period. The term *annual accounting period* may refer to a period of less than one year, where, for example, the foreign income, war profits, and excess profits taxes are determined on the basis of an accounting period of less than one year as described in section 902(c)(5). If more than one annual accounting period ends with or within the United States person's taxable year, separate annual information returns shall be submitted for each annual accounting period.

(f) *Contents of return.*—The return on Form 5471 shall contain so much of the following information, and in such form or manner, as the form shall prescribe with respect to each foreign corporation:

(1) The name, address, and employer identification number, if any, of the corporation;

(2) The principal place of business of the corporation;

(3) The date of incorporation and the country under whose laws incorporated;

(4) The name and address of the foreign corporation's statutory or resident agent in the country of incorporation;

(5) The name, address, and identifying number of any branch office or agent of the foreign corporation located in the United States;

(6) The name and address of the person (or persons) having custody of the books of account and records of the foreign corporation, and the location of such books and records if different from such address;

(7) The nature of the corporation's business and the principal places where conducted;

(8) As regards the outstanding stock of the corporation—

(i) A description of each class of the corporation's stock, and

(ii) The number of shares of each class outstanding at the beginning and end of the annual accounting period;

(9) A list showing the name, address, and identifying number of, and the number of shares of each class of the corporation's stock held by, each United States person who is a shareholder owning at any time during the annual acounting period 5 percent or more in value of any class of the corporation's outstanding stock;

(10) For the annual accounting period, the amount of the corporation's:

(i) Current earnings and profits;

(ii) Foreign income, war profits, and excess profits taxes paid or accrued;

(iii) Distributions out of current earnings and profits for the period;

(iv) Distributions other than those described in paragraph (f)(10)(iii) of this section and the source thereof; and

(v) For Forms 5471 filed for taxable years ending after December 15, 1990, such earnings and profits information as the form shall prescribe, including post-1986 undistributed earnings described in section 902(c)(1), pre-1987 amounts, total earnings and profits, and previously taxed earnings and profits described in section 959(c); and

(11) *Transactions with certain related parties.*—(i) A summary showing the total amount of each of the following types of transactions of the corporation, which took place during the annual accounting period, with the person required to file this return, any other corporation or partnership controlled by that person, or any United States person owning at the time of the transaction 10 percent or more in value of any class of stock outstanding of the foreign corporation, or of any corporation controlling that foreign corporation—

(A) Sales and purchases of stock in trade;

(B) Sales and purchases of tangible property other than stock in trade;

(C) Sales and purchases of patents, inventions, models, or designs (whether or not patented), copyrights, trademarks, secret formulas or processes, or any other similar property rights;

(D) Compensation paid and compensation received for the rendition of technical, managerial, engineering, construction, scientific, or like services;

(E) Commissions paid and commissions received;

(F) Rents and royalties paid and rents and royalties received;

(G) Amounts loaned and amounts borrowed (except open accounts resulting from sales and purchases reported under other items listed in this paragraph (f)(11) that arise and are collected in full in the ordinary course of business);

(H) Dividends paid and dividends received;

(I) Interest paid and interest received; and

(J) Premiums paid and premiums received for insurance or reinsurance.

(ii) *Special rule for banks.*—For purposes of this paragraph (f)(11), if the United States person is a bank, as defined in section 581, or is controlled within the meaning of section 368(c) by a bank, the term transactions shall not, as to a corporation with respect to which a return is filed, include banking transactions entered into on behalf of customers; in any event, however, deposits in accounts between a foreign corporation, controlled (within the meaning of paragraph (b) of this section) by a United States person, and a person described in this paragraph (f)(11) and withdrawals from such accounts shall be summarized by reporting end-of-month balances.

(12) *Accrued payments and receipts.*—For purposes of the required summary under paragraph (f)(11) of this section, a corporation that uses an accrual method of accounting shall use accrued payments and accrued receipts for purposes of computing the total amount of each of the types of transactions listed.

(13) *Amounts involving hybrid transactions or hybrid entities under section 267A.*—If for the annual accounting period, the corporation pays or accrues interest or royalties for which a deduction is disallowed under section 267A and the regulations in this part under section 267A of the Internal Revenue Code, then Form 5471 (or successor form) must contain such information about the disallowance in the form and manner and to the extent prescribed by the form, instruction, publication, or other guidance.

(14) *Hybrid dividends under section 245A(e).*—If for the annual accounting period, the corporation pays or receives a hybrid dividend or a tiered hybrid dividend under section 245A(e) and the regulations in this part under section 245A(e) of the Internal Revenue Code, then Form 5471 (or successor form) must contain such information about the hybrid dividend or tiered hybrid dividend in the form and manner and to the extent prescribed by the form, instruction, publication, or other guidance. Form 5471 (or successor form) must also contain any other information relating to the rules of section 245A(e) and the regulations in this part under section 245A(e) of the Internal Revenue Code (including information related to a specified owner's hybrid deduction account), as prescribed by the form, instruction, publication, or other guidance.

(15) *Information reporting under section 250.*—If the person required to file Form 5471 (or any successor form) claims a deduction under section 250(a) that is determined, in whole or part, by reference to its foreign-derived intangible income, and any amount required to be reported under paragraph (f)(11) of this section is included in its computation of foreign-derived deduction eligible income, such person will provide on Form 5471 (or any successor form) such information that is prescribed by the form, instructions to the form, publication, or other guidance published in the Internal Revenue Bulletin.

(16) *Amounts related to extraordinary dispositions and extraordinary reductions.*—The corporation must report the information in the form and manner and to the extent prescribed by the form, instructions to the form, publication, or other guidance published in the Internal Revenue Bulletin if any of the following conditions are met during the corporation's annual accounting period—

(i) The corporation distributes or receives a dividend that gives rise to an ineligible amount (as defined in § 1.245A-5(i)(12)), a tiered extraordinary disposition amount (as defined in § 1.245A-5(i)(25)), or a tiered extraordinary reduction amount (as defined in § 1.245A-5(i)(26);

(ii) A section 245A shareholder with respect to the corporation has an extraordinary disposition account (as defined in § 1.245A-5(i)(6)); or

(iii) The corporation would have been deemed to have undertaken an extraordinary disposition (as defined in § 1.245A-5(i)(5)) but for the application of § 1.245A-5(c)(3)(ii)(C)(2).

(17) *Reporting of disqualified basis and disqualified payments.*—If for the annual accounting period of a corporation it holds an item of property having disqualified basis within the meaning of § 1.951A-3(h)(2)(ii) or § 1.951A-2(c)(5), or incurs an item of deduction or loss related to a disqualified payment (within the meaning of § 1.951A-2(c)(6)(ii)(A), then Form 5471 (or successor form) must contain such information about the disqualified basis, or such information relating to the disqualified payment, in the form and manner and to the extent prescribed by the form, instructions to the form, publication, or other guidance published in the Internal Revenue Bulletin.

(18) *Adjustments to extraordinary disposition accounts and disqualified basis.*—If for the annual accounting period a section 245A shareholder of the corporation reduces its extraordinary disposition account pursuant to § 1.245A-7(c) or § 1.245A-8(c), as applicable, or the corporation reduces the disqualified basis in an item of specified property pursuant to § 1.245A-7(b) or § 1.245A-8(b), as applicable, then Form 5471 (or a successor form) must contain such information about the reduction to the extraordinary disposition account or disqualified basis, as applicable, in the form and manner and to the extent prescribed by the form, instructions to the form, publication, or other guidance published in the Internal Revenue Bulletin.

(g) *Financial statements.*—The following information with respect to the foreign corporation shall be attached to and filed as part of the return required by this section. Forms 5471 filed after September 30, 1991, shall contain this information in such form or manner as the form shall prescribe with respect to each foreign corporation:

(1) A statement of the corporation's profit and loss for the annual accounting period;

(2) A balance sheet as of the end of the annual accounting period of the corporation showing—

(i) The corporation's assets;

(ii) The corporation's liabilities; and

(iii) The corporation's net worth; and

(3) An analysis of changes in the corporation's surplus accounts during the annual accounting period including both opening and closing balances.

The information listed in this paragraph (g) shall be prepared in conformity with generally accepted accounting principles, and in such detail as is customary for the corporation's accounting records.

(h) *Method of reporting.*—Except as provided in this paragraph (h), all amounts furnished under paragraphs (f) and (g) of this section shall be expressed in United States dollars with a statement of the exchange rates used. The following rules shall apply for taxable years ending after December 31, 1994, with respect to returns filed after December 31, 1995. All amounts furnished under paragraph (g) of this section shall be expressed in United States dollars computed and translated in conformity with United States generally accepted accounting principles. Amounts furnished under paragraph (g)(1) of this section shall also be furnished in the foreign corporation's functional currency as required on the form. Earnings and profits amounts furnished under paragraphs (f)(10)(i), (iii), (iv), and (v) of this section shall be expressed in the foreign corporation's functional currency except to the extent the form requires specific items to be translated into United States dollars. Tax amounts furnished under paragraph (f)(10)(ii) of this section shall be furnished in the foreign currency in which the taxes are payable and in United States dollars translated in accordance with section 986(a). All amounts furnished under paragraph (f)(11) of this section shall be expressed in U.S. dollars translated from functional currency at the weighted average exchange rate for the year as defined in § 1.989(b)-1. The foreign corporation's functional currency is determined under section 985. All statements submitted on or with the return required under this section shall be rendered in the English language.

(i) *Time and place for filing return.*—Returns on Form 5471 required under paragraph (a) of this section shall be filed with the United States person's income tax return on or before the date required by law for the filing of that person's income tax return. Directors of Field Operations and Field Directors are authorized to grant reasonable extensions of time for filing returns on Form 5471 in accordance with the applicable provisions of § 1.6081-1 of this chapter. An application for an extension of time for filing a return of income shall also be considered as an application for an extension of time for filing returns on Form 5471.

(j) *Two or more persons required to submit the same information.*—(1) *Return jointly made.*—If two or more persons are required to furnish information with respect to the same foreign corporation for the same period, such persons may, in lieu of making separate returns, jointly make one return. Such joint return shall be filed with the income tax return of any one of the persons making such joint return.

(2) *Persons excepted from furnishing information.*—(i) *Conditions.*—Any person required to furnish information under this section with respect to a foreign corporation need not furnish that information provided all of the following conditions are met:

(A) Such person does not directly own an interest in the foreign corporation;

(B) Such person is required to furnish the information solely by reason of attribution of stock ownership from a United States person under paragraph (c) of this section; and

(C) The person from whom the stock ownership is attributed furnishes all of the information required under this section of the person to whom the stock ownership is attributed. (For a rule regarding attribution from a nonresident alien, see paragraph (l) of this section).

(ii) If an individual who is a United States person required to furnish information with respect to a foreign corporation under section 6038 is entitled under a treaty to be treated as a nonresident of the United States, and if the individual claims this treaty benefit, and if there are no other United States persons that are required to furnish information under section 6038 with respect to the foreign corporation, then the individual may satisfy the requirements of paragraphs (f)(10), (f)(11), (g), and (h) of this section by filing the audited foreign financial statements of the foreign corporation with the individual's return required under section 6038.

(iii) *Illustrations.*—The rule of this paragraph (j)(2) is illustrated by the following examples:

Example (1). A, a U.S. person owns 100 percent of the stock of M, a domestic corporation. A also owns 100 percent of the stock of N, a foreign corporation organized under the laws of foreign country Y. A, in filing the information return required by this section with respect to N Corporation, in fact furnishes all of the information required of M Corporation with respect to N Corporation. M Corporation need not file the information.

Example (2). X, a domestic corporation owns 100 percent of the stock of Y, a domestic corporation, Y Corporation owns 100 percent of the stock of Z, a foreign corporation. X Corporation is not excused by this paragraph (j)(2) from filing information with respect to Z Corporation because X Corporation is deemed to control Z Corporation under the provisions of paragraph (b) of this section without recourse to the attribution rules in paragraph (c) of this section.

(3) *Statement required.*—Any United States person required to furnish information under this section with his return who does not do so by reason of the provisions of paragraph (j)(1) of this section shall file a statement with his income tax return indicating that such requirement has been (or will be) satisfied and identifying the return with which the information was or will be filed and the place of filing.

(k) *Failure to furnish information.*—(1) *Dollar amount penalty.*—(i) *In general.*—If any person required to file Form 5471 under section 6038 and this section fails to furnish any information described in paragraphs (f) and (g) of this section within the time prescribed by paragraph (i) of this section, such person shall pay a penalty of $10,000 for each annual accounting period of each foreign corporation with respect to which such failure occurs.

(ii) *Increase in penalty for continued failure after notification.*—If a failure described in paragraph (k)(1)(i) of this section continues for more than 90 days after the date on which the Director of Field Operations, Area Director, or Director of Compliance Campus Operations mails notice of such failure to the person required to file Form 5471, such person shall pay a penalty of $10,000, in addition to the penalty imposed by section 6038(b)(1) and paragraph (k)(1)(i) of this section, for each 30-day period (or a fraction of) during which such failure continues after such 90-day period has expired. The additional penalty imposed by section 6038(b)(2) and this paragraph (k)(1)(ii) shall be limited to a maximum of $50,000 for each failure.

(2) *Penalty of reducing foreign tax credit.*—(i) *Effect on foreign tax credit.*—Failure of a United States person to furnish, in accordance with the provisions of this section, any return of any information in any return, required to be filed for a taxable year under authority of section 6038 on or before the date prescribed in paragraph (i) of this section may affect the application of section 901 as provided in paragraph (k)(2)(ii) of this section and may affect the application of sections 902 and 960 as provided in paragraph (k)(2)(iii) of this section. Such failure may affect the application of sections 902 and 960 to any such United States person which is a corporation or to any person who acquires from any other person any portion (but only to the extent of such portion) of the interest of such other person in any such foreign corporation.

(ii) *Application of section 901.*—In the application of section 901 to a United States person referred to in paragraph (k)(2)(i) of this section, the amount of taxes paid or deemed paid by such person for any taxable year, with or within which the annual accounting period of a foreign corporation for which such person failed to furnish information required under this section ended, may be reduced by 10 percent. However, no tax reduced under paragraph (k)(2)(iii) of this section or deemed paid under section 904(c) shall be reduced under the provisions of this paragraph (k)(2)(ii).

(iii) *Application of sections 902 and 960.*—In the application of sections 902 and 960 to a United States person referred to in paragraph (k)(2)(i) of this section for any taxable year, the amount of taxes paid or deemed paid by each foreign corporation for the accounting period or periods for which such person was required for the taxable year of the failure to furnish information under this section may be reduced by 10 percent. The 10-percent reduction is not limited to the taxes paid or deemed paid by the foreign corporation with respect to which there is a failure to file information but may apply to the taxes paid or deemed paid by all foreign corporations controlled by that person. In applying subsections (a) and (b) of section 902, and in applying subsection (a) of section 960, the reduction provided by this paragraph (k)(2) shall not apply for purposes of determining the amount of accumulated profits in excess of income, war profits, and excess profits taxes.

(iv) *Reduction for continued failure after notice.*—(A) If the failure referred to in paragraph (k)(2)(i) of this section continues for more than 90 days after the date on which the Director of Field Operations mails notice of such failure to such United States person, then the amount of the reduction referred to in paragraph (k)(2)(ii) and (iii) of this section may be 10 percent plus an additional 5 percent for each 3-month period, or fraction thereof, during which such failure continues after the expiration of such 90-day period.

(B) No taxes shall be reduced under this paragraph (k)(2) more than once for the same failure. Taxes paid by a foreign corporation when once reduced for a failure shall not be reduced again for the same failure in their status as taxes deemed paid by a corporate shareholder. Where a failure continues, each additional periodic 5-percent reduction, referred to in paragraph (k)(2)(iv)(A) of this section, shall be considered as part of the one reduction.

(v) *Limitation on reduction of foreign tax credit.*—The amount of the reduction under this paragraph (k)(2) for each failure to furnish information with respect to a foreign corporation as required under this section shall not exceed the greater of:

(A) $10,000, or

(B) The income of the foreign corporation for its annual accounting period with respect to which the failure occurs. For purposes of this section if a person is required to furnish information with respect to more than one foreign corporation, controlled (within the meaning of paragraph (b) of this section) by that person, each failure to submit information for each such corporation constitutes a separate failure.

(vi) *Offset for dollar amount penalty imposed.*—The total amount of the reduction or reductions which, but for this paragraph (k)(2)(vi), may be made under this paragraph (k)(2) with respect to any separate failure, shall not exceed the maximum amount of such reductions which may be imposed, reduced (but not below zero) by the amount of the dollar amount penalty imposed by paragraph (k)(1) of this section with respect to such separate failure.

(3) *Reasonable cause.*—(i) For purposes of section 6038(b) and (c) and this section, the time prescribed for furnishing information under paragraph (i) of this section, and the beginning of the 90-day period after mailing of notice by the Director of Field Operations under paragraph (k)(1)(ii) and (k)(2)(iv)(A) of this section, shall be treated as being not earlier than the last day on which reasonable cause existed for failure to furnish the information.

(ii) To show that reasonable cause existed for failure to furnish information as required by section 6038 and this section, the person required to report such information must make an affirmative showing of all facts alleged as reasonable cause for such failure in a written statement containing a declaration that it is made under the penalties of perjury. The statement must be filed with the district director for the district or the director of the service center where the return is required to be filed. The district director or the director of the service center shall determine whether the failure to furnish information was due to reasonable cause, and if so, the period of time for which such reasonable cause existed. In the case of a return that has been filed as required by this section except for an omission of, or error with respect to, some of the information required, if the person who filed the return establishes to the satisfaction of the district director or the director of the service center that the person has substantially complied with this section, then the omission or error shall not constitute a failure under this section.

(4) *Other penalties.*—The information required by section 6038 and this section must be furnished even though there are no foreign taxes which would be reduced under the provisions of this section, and even though the information required may not affect the amount of any tax due under the Internal Revenue Code. For criminal penalties for failure to file a return and filing a false or fraudulent return, see sections 7203, 7206, and 7207 of the Code.

(5) *Illustrations.*—The provisions of this paragraph may be illustrated by the following examples.

Example (1). M, a domestic corporation owns 100 percent of the stock of N, a foreign corporation. Both M and N use the calendar year as a taxable year and annual accounting period, and all of the following events occur in or with respect to the 1980 taxable year. The dividend from N is the only dividend from a foreign corporation received by M during the taxable year, and the foreign taxes listed are the only foreign taxes paid or deemed paid by M and N for the taxable year. On March 15, 1981, M filed its income tax return and paid its income tax, but M did not file Form 2952 with respect to N's 1980 annual accounting period. On June 1, 1961, the district director mailed notice to M of M's failure to file Form 2952 with respect to N. On November 30, 1981, M filed a complete Form 2952 with respect to N's 1980 annual accounting period.

(a)	Gains, profits, and income of N	$100,000
(b)	Foreign tax paid by N with respect to such gains, profits, and income	40,000
(c)	Deduction of foreign tax paid by N (for purposes of M's section 902 deemed paid credit) resulting from M's failure to file information with respect to N as required under section 6038(a) and this section: failure to file within the time prescribed in paragraph (i) of this section, 10-percent reduction; continued failure for one additional 3-month period after 90-day period after notice mailed, 5-percent reduction; total reduction, 15 percent ($40,000 times 15 percent)	6,000
(d)	Foreign tax paid by N after section 6038(c)(1)(B) reduction	34,000
(e)	Dividend paid by N to M	45,000
(f)	Accumulated profits of N as defined in section 902(c)(1) (determined without regard to the section 6038(c)(1)(B) reduction)	100,000

(g)	Accumulated profits of N as described in section 902(a) (determined without regard to the section 6038(c)(1)(B) reduction)	60,000
(h)	For purposes of section 902 credit, M is deemed to have paid the same proportion of foreign taxes paid (reduced as provided under section 6038(c)) with respect to the accumulated profits described in section 902(a) (determined without regard to the reduction provided under section 6038(c)) as the amount of the dividend (determined without regard to section 78) bears to such amount of accumulated profits	25,500

$$(45{,}000 \div 60{,}000) \times 34{,}000 = 25{,}500$$

M must include $25,500 in gross income as a dividend under the provisions of section 78 of the Code. This example illustrates that the reductions in foreign taxes paid by the foreign corporation provided under section 8038(c) are taken into account in determining the amount included in gross income of the domestic corporation under section 78 of the Code as foreign taxes deemed paid, but such reductions are not taken into account in computing accumulated profits for purposes of determining the portion of foreign taxes deemed paid with respect to a particular dividend. The dollar amount penalty imposed by section 8038(b) and paragraph (k)(1) of this section does not apply with respect to information for annual accounting periods ending before September 4, 1982, and therefore does not apply to M with respect to M's failure to file Form 2952 in this example.

Example (2). The facts are the same as in example (1) except that all of the events occur in or with respect to the 1982 taxable year. On March 15, 1983, M filed its income tax return and paid its income tax, but M did not file Form 2952 or Form 5471 with respect to N's 1982 annual accounting period. On June 1, 1983, the district director mailed notice to M of M's failure to file Form 2952 or Form 5471 with respect to N. On November 30, 1983, M filed a complete Form 5471 with respect to N's 1982 annual accounting period. Under paragraph (k)(1)(i) of this section, M is subject to a penalty of $1,000. Under paragraph (k)(1)(ii) of this section, that penalty is increased by $4,000 because the failure continued for 92 days (three full 30-day periods and a fraction of a fourth 30-day period) after the end of the 90-day period following mailing of the notice by the district director, bringing M's dollar amount penalty under paragraph (k)(1) of this section to $5,000. For purpose of determining the foreign tax credit available to M, there may be imposed a reduction of foreign tax paid by N of $6,000, which would be the total of reductions under paragraph (k)(2) of this section with respect to M's failure to file under section 6038 for N's 1982 annual accounting period, before application of paragraph (k)(2)(vi) of this section. Under said paragraph (k)(2)(vi), the amount of the foreign tax reduction imposed is reduced by the amount of the dollar amount penalty, leaving a foreign tax reduction penalty of $1,000 which may be imposed in addition to the $5,000 dollar amount penalty. If imposed, the $1,000 tax reduction would then be applied in the calculation of taxes deemed paid by M under section 902 as in example (1), item (c), (d), and (h).

Example 3. A, a US person, owns 100 percent of the stock of FC. On April 15, 2008, A timely filed its 2007 income tax return but did not file Form 5471 with respect to FC's 2007 annual accounting period. On June 1, 2008, the Director of Field Operations mailed a notice to A of A's failure to file Form 5471 for 2007 with respect to FC. On August 1, 2008, A submits a written statement asserting facts for reasonable cause for failure to file the 2007 Form 5471 for FC. Based on A's statement and discussions with A, the Director of Field Operations agrees that A had reasonable cause for failure to file FC's 2007 Form 5471 and determined that it is reasonable for A to file FC's 2007 Form 5471 by September 15, 2008. The time prescribed for furnishing information under paragraph (i) of this section is September 15, 2008, and the 90-day period described under paragraphs (k)(1)(ii) and (k)(2)(iv)(A) of this section begins on that same date. Thus, if A files a completed Form 5471 by September 15, 2008, A is not subject to the penalties under paragraphs (k)(1) and (k)(2) of this section. If A does not file a completed Form 5471 by December 14, 2008, in addition to the penalties under paragraphs (k)(1) and (k)(2) of this section, A will also be subject to the penalties for continued failure under paragraphs (k)(1)(ii) and (k)(2)(iv)(A) of this section.

Example 4. The facts are the same as in Example 3 except A submits the written statement to the Director before a notice of failure to furnish information is mailed to A. The notice is mailed to A on September 7, 2008. Under these facts, the time prescribed for furnishing information under paragraph (i) of this section is September 15, 2008, and the 90-day period after mailing of notice of failure under paragraphs (k)(1)(ii) and (k)(2)(iv)(A) of this section begins on that same date.

(l) *Other persons excepted from filing.*—For tax years of foreign corporations ending on or after December 29, 1999, any person required to furnish information under this section with respect to a foreign corporation does not have to furnish that information if the following conditions are met—

(1) Such person does not own a direct or indirect interest in the foreign corporation; and

(2) Such person is required to furnish information solely by reason of attribution of stock ownership from a nonresident alien(s) under paragraph (c) of this section.

(m) *Applicability dates.*—(1) *In general.*—This section applies to taxable years of foreign corporations beginning on or after October 3, 2018. See 26 CFR 1.6038-2 (revised as of April 1, 2018) for rules applicable to taxable years of foreign corporations beginning before such date.

(2) *Special rule for paragraph (f)(16) of this section.*—Paragraph (f)(16) of this section applies with respect to information for annual accounting periods to which § 1.245A-5 applies.

(3) *Rules relating to certain hybrid arrangements.*—Paragraphs (f)(13) and (14) of this section apply with respect to information for annual accounting periods beginning on or after December 20, 2018.

(4) Paragraph (f)(15) of this section applies with respect to information for annual accounting periods beginning on or after March 4, 2019.

(5) *Special rule for paragraphs (f)(17) and (18) of this section.*—Paragraphs (f)(17) and (18) of this section apply with respect to information for annual accounting periods beginning after December 1, 2020. In addition, as provided in § 1.245A-11(b), paragraph (f)(18) of this section applies with respect to information for an annual accounting period that includes a taxable year for which a taxpayer has chosen to apply §§ 1.245A-6 through 1.245A-11 pursuant to § 1.245A-11(b). [Reg. § 1.6038-2.]

☐ [*T.D. 6621, 11-30-62. Amended by T.D. 6969, 8-22-68; T.D. 6997, 1-17-69; T.D. 8040, 7-23-85; T.D. 8573, 12-13-94; T.D. 8733, 10-6-97; T.D. 8850, 12-27-99; T.D. 9194, 4-6-2005; T.D. 9268, 6-20-2006; T.D. 9338, 7-12-2007; T.D. 9391, 4-4-2008, T.D. 9650, 12-30-2013; T.D. 9806, 12-27-2016; T.D. 9866, 6-14-2019; T.D. 9896, 4-7-2020; T.D. 9901, 7-9-2020, T.D. 9909, 8-21-2020 and T.D. 9934, 11-25-2020.*]

Proposed Amendments to Regulation

§ 1.6038-2. Information returns required of United States persons with respect to annual accounting periods of certain foreign corporations.—

* * *

(f) * * *

(16) – (18) [Reserved]

(19) *High-tax election documentation requirement.*—If for the annual accounting period of a corporation a United States shareholder makes a high-tax election under section 954(b)(4) and § 1.954-1(d)(6), then Form 5471 (or successor form) must contain such information related to the high-tax election in the form and manner and to the extent prescribed by the form, instructions to the form, publication, or other guidance published in the Internal Revenue Bulletin.

* * *

(m) * * *

(5) [Reserved]

(6) *Special rule for paragraph (f)(19) of this section.*—Paragraph (f)(19) of this section applies to taxable years of controlled foreign corporations beginning on or after [the date that final regulations are filed for public inspection], and to taxable years of United States shareholders in which or with which such taxable years of foreign corporations end. [Prop. Reg. § 1.6038-2.]

[Proposed 7-23-2020.]

§ 1.6038-3. Information returns required of certain United States persons with respect to controlled foreign partnerships (CFPs).— (a) *Persons required to make return.*—(1) *Controlling fifty-percent part-*

ners.—The term *controlling fifty-percent partner* means a United States person that controlled (as defined in paragraph (b)(1) of this section) the foreign partnership at any time during the partnership's tax year (as defined in paragraph (b)(8) of this section). Except as provided in paragraph (c), (d), or (e) of this section, for each tax year of a foreign partnership during which the partnership has one or more controlling fifty-percent partners, each controlling fifty-percent partner must complete and file Form 8865, "Return of U.S. Persons With Respect To Certain Foreign Partnerships," containing the information described in paragraph (g) of this section.

(2) *Controlling ten-percent partners.*—If at any point during a foreign partnership's tax year (as defined in paragraph (b)(8) of this section) a United States person owned a ten- percent or greater interest in the partnership while the partnership was controlled by United States persons owning ten-percent or greater interests, such United States person is a controlling ten-percent partner. See paragraph (b)(1) of this section for the definition of control. However, a United States person is not a controlling ten-percent partner with respect to a particular foreign partnership for a particular tax year of the foreign partnership if at any point during that year the partnership had a controlling fifty-percent partner, as defined in paragraph (a)(1) of this section. Except as provided in paragraph (c), (d), or (e) of this section, for each tax year of a partnership during which the partnership has controlling ten-percent partners, each controlling ten-percent partner must complete and file Form 8865 containing the information described in paragraph (g)(1) of this section.

(3) *Separate returns for each partnership.*—A United States person required to report under this paragraph (a) must file a separate Form 8865 for each foreign partnership with respect to which the person is a controlling fifty-percent partner or a controlling ten-percent partner.

(b) *Ownership determinations and definitions.*—(1) *Control.*—Control of a foreign partnership is ownership of more than a fifty-percent interest in the partnership.

(2) *Fifty-percent interest.*—A fifty-percent interest in a partnership is an interest equal to fifty percent of the capital interest in such partnership, an interest equal to fifty percent of the profits interest in such partnership, or an interest to which fifty percent of the deductions or losses of such partnership are allocated.

(3) *Ten-percent interest.*—A ten-percent interest in a partnership is an interest equal to ten percent of the capital interest in such partnership, an interest equal to ten percent of the profits interest in such partnership, or an interest to which ten percent of the deductions or losses of such partnership are allocated.

(4) *Constructive ownership rules.*—For purposes of determining an interest in a partnership, the constructive ownership rules of section 267(c) (other than section 267(c)(3)) apply, taking into account that such rules refer to corporations and not to partnerships. However, an interest will be attributed from a nonresident alien under the family attribution rules of section 267(c)(2) and (4) only if the person to whom the interest is attributed owns a direct or indirect (under the rules of 267(c)(1) or (5)) interest in the foreign partnership.

(5) *Determination of amount of interest.*—Whether a person owns a fifty-percent interest, or a ten-percent interest, as described in paragraphs (b)(2) and (3) of this section, is determined for each tax year of the foreign partnership by reference to the agreement of the partners relating to such interests during that tax year.

(6) *Definition of United States person.*—The term *United States person* is defined in section 7701(a)(30).

(7) *Definition of a foreign partnership.*—A foreign partnership is a partnership described in section 7701(a)(5).

(8) *Tax year of a foreign partnership.*—The tax year of a foreign partnership is determined under section 706.

(9) *Examples.*—The rules of paragraph (a) of this section and this paragraph (b) are illustrated by the following examples:

Example 1. Sole U.S. partner does not own more than a fifty-percent interest. No United States person owns any interest (directly or constructively) in *FPS*, a foreign partnership whose tax year under section 706 is the calendar year. On January 1, 2001, *US*, a United States person with the calendar year as its tax year, contributes property to *FPS* in exchange for a 40% interest in a section 721 transaction. No United States persons acquire directly or constructively any other interests in *FPS* during *FPS*'s 2001 tax year. *US* is not a controlling fifty-percent partner during *FPS*'s 2001 tax year. *US* did not own during that tax year, either directly or constructively, more than a 50% interest in the partnership under paragraphs (b)(2) and (4) of this section. Also, *US* is not a controlling ten-percent partner; although *US* owned a 10% or greater interest, *US* persons owning at least 10% interests did not control *FPS*. Therefore, *US* does not have to file with its 2001 income tax return a Form 8865 with respect to *FPS* under section 6038. (But see section 6038B for the reporting obligations of *US* with respect to its transfer of property to *FPS* and section 6046A for the reporting obligation of *US* with respect to its acquisition of an interest in *FPS*. See also § 1.6046A-1(f)(1) regarding the overlap between sections 6038B and 6046A).

Example 2. Controlling ten-percent partners. Assume the same facts as in *Example 1*. In addition, on January 1, 2002, *US1*, a United States person unrelated to *US* and a calendar year taxpayer, purchases a 15% interest in *FPS* from a foreign partner of *FPS*. Neither *US* nor *US1* is a controlling fifty-percent partner during *FPS*'s 2002 tax year because neither one owns more than a 50% percent interest in *FPS* during that year. However, *US* and *US1* are controlling ten-percent partners for that year because each owns at least a 10% interest (*US* owns a 40% interest and *US1* owns a 15% interest) and together they control *FPS* because collectively they own more than a 50% interest in *FPS*. As controlling ten-percent partners, under section 6038, each is required to file a Form 8865 with its 2002 income tax return. (*US1* must also report its acquisition of the 15% interest in *FPS* under section 6046A on its Form 8865 filed with its 2002 income tax return.)

Example 3. Constructive ownership rules. Assume the same facts as in *Example 2*. In addition, on January 1, 2003, *US2*, a United States person and the brother of *US*, purchases 50% of the stock of *FC*, a foreign corporation. *FC* owns a 20% interest in *FPS*. Thus, under sections 6038(e)(3) and 267(c)(1), *US2* indirectly owns a 10% interest in *FPS* (10% is *US2*'s proportionate share of *FC*'s 20% interest in *FPS*), and under sections 6038(e)(3) and 267(c)(2), *US2* is attributed *US*'s 40% interest. Additionally, *US* directly owns a 40% interest in *FPS* and is attributed *US2*'s 10% interest pursuant to section 6038(e)(3) and section 267(c)(2). Therefore, *US2* is considered to own a 50% interest (10% indirectly and 40% from *US*) in *FPS*, and *US* is considered to own a 50% interest in *FPS* (40% directly and 10% from *US2*). *FPS* has no controlling fifty-percent partners, because neither *US*, *US1*, nor *US2*, owns a greater than 50% interest. However, *US*, *US1*, and *US2* are each controlling ten-percent partners and each must file Form 8865 pursuant to section 6038 for *FPS*'s 2003 tax year ending December 31, 2003. Each must attach Form 8865 to its tax return for its 2003 tax year.

Example 4. Controlling fifty-percent partners. Assume the same facts as in *Example 3*. In addition, on June 1, 2004, *US* acquires an additional 1% direct interest in *FPS*. *US* is now a controlling fifty-percent partner of *FPS*, because *US* owns a 41% interest directly and a 10% interest constructively from *US2*. *US2* is also a controlling fifty-percent partner, because *US2* owns 10% indirectly and 41% constructively from *US*. Both *US* and *US2* are required to file Form 8865 containing all the information required to be submitted by controlling fifty-percent partners. (But see paragraph (c)(1) of this section, which contains filing exceptions when there are multiple controlling fifty-percent partners). *US1* is no longer a controlling ten-percent partner because *FPS* now has at least one controlling fifty-percent partner, and *US1* does not qualify as a controlling fifty-percent partner. Therefore, *US1* is not required to file Form 8865 under section 6038.

Example 5. Constructive ownership from a nonresident alien. *US*, a United States person, does not own directly or constructively an interest in *FPS*, a foreign partnership. The tax year of *FPS* is the calendar year. *NRA*, a nonresident alien, is the mother of *US*. In 2002, *NRA* acquires a 55% interest in *FPS*. Because *US* owns neither a direct nor a constructive interest in *FPS* under sections 6038(e)(3) and 267(c)(1) or (5), *NRA*'s interest is not attributed to *US* under sections 6038(e)(3) and 267(c)(2). If in 2003 *NRA* becomes a United States person, *NRA*'s interest will be attributed to *US*. However, *US* is excused from filing Form 8865 if *US* satisfies the requirements of the constructive owners exception in paragraph (c)(2) of this section. In 2003, *NRA* is a controlling fifty-percent partner and must file a Form 8865 under section 6038 for *FPS*'s 2003 tax year.

(c) *Exceptions when more than one United States person is required to file Form 8865 pursuant to section 6038.*—(1) *Multiple controlling fifty-percent partners.*—(i) *In general.*—If, with respect to the same foreign partnership for the same tax year, more than one United States person is a controlling fifty-percent partner, then in lieu of each controlling fifty-percent partner filing a separate Form 8865, only one

Form 8865 from one of the controlling fifty-percent partners is required, provided all of the requirements of paragraph (c)(1)(ii) of this section are satisfied. A person that is a controlling fifty-percent partner solely because of an interest to which deductions or losses are allocated may file the single return only if there is no United States person that is a controlling fifty-percent partner by reason of an interest in capital or profits.

(ii) *Requirements.*—(A) The person undertaking the filing obligation must file Form 8865 with that person's income tax return in the manner provided by Form 8865 and the accompanying instructions. The return must contain all of the information that would have been required to be reported by this section if each controlling fifty-percent partner had filed its own Form 8865.

(B) Any controlling fifty-percent partner not filing Form 8865 must file with its income tax return a statement titled "Controlled Foreign Partnership Reporting" containing the following information—

(1) A statement that the person qualified as a controlling fifty-percent partner, but is not submitting Form 8865 pursuant to the multiple controlling fifty-percent partners exception;

(2) The name, address, and taxpayer identification number (if any) of the foreign partnership of which the person qualified as a controlling fifty-percent partner;

(3) A representation that the filing requirement has been or will be satisfied;

(4) The name and address of the person filing the single return;

(5) The Internal Revenue Service Center where the single return is required to be filed; and

(6) Any additional information that Form 8865 and the accompanying instructions require.

(iii) *Penalties.*—If the requirements listed in paragraph (c)(1)(ii) of this section are not satisfied, a United States person that did not file a Form 8865 pursuant to this paragraph will be subject to the penalties in paragraph (k) of this section, unless the reasonable cause provision in paragraph (k)(4) of this section is satisfied.

(2) *Certain constructive owners excepted from furnishing information.*—(i) *In general.*—A United States person that does not own a direct interest in the foreign partnership and that is required to file Form 8865 under this section solely by reason of constructive ownership from a United States person(s) pursuant to paragraph (b)(4) of this section (an indirect partner) is not required to file Form 8865 if all of the requirements listed in paragraph (c)(2)(ii) of this section are met.

(ii) *Requirements.*—(A) The United States person(s) whose interest the indirect partner constructively owns reports all the information such person(s) is required to submit under this section, unless such person also is required to file solely by reason of constructive ownership from a United States person(s) pursuant to paragraph (b)(4) of this section, or another person reports the information pursuant to paragraph (c)(1) of this section.

(B) The indirect partner files with its income tax return a statement titled "Controlled Foreign Partnership Reporting" containing the following information—

(1) A representation that the indirect partner was required to file Form 8865, but is not doing so pursuant to the constructive owners exception;

(2) The names and addresses of the United States persons whose interests the indirect partner constructively owns;

(3) The name and address of the foreign partnership with respect to which the indirect partner would have had to have filed Form 8865 but for this exception; and

(4) Any additional information that Form 8865 and the accompanying instructions require.

(iii) *Penalties.*—A United States person that pursuant to this paragraph (c)(2) does not file a return will be subject to the penalties in paragraph (k) of this section if the requirements listed in paragraph (c)(2)(ii) of this section are not satisfied, unless such failure is due to reasonable cause, as defined in paragraph (k)(4) of this section.

(iv) *Overlap with multiple controlling fifty-percent partners exception.*—(A) If a United States person qualifies for both the exception in paragraph (c)(1) of this section and the exception in this paragraph (c)(2), such person may only utilize the multiple controlling fifty-percent partners exception in paragraph (c)(1) of this section to avoid filing Form 8865.

(B) *Example.*—The following example illustrates the operation of this paragraph (c)(2)(iv):

Example. US is a U.S. citizen. *US* owns 100% of the stock of *DC*, a domestic corporation. *DC* owns a 60% direct interest in *FPS*, a foreign partnership. *DC* and *US* are the only U.S. persons that own interests directly or constructively in *FPS*. *DC* owns directly a greater than 50% interest in *FPS*. *US* constructively owns *DC*'s interest pursuant to sections 6038(e)(3) and 267(c)(1). Therefore, both *DC* and *US* are controlling fifty-percent partners. *US* qualifies for both the exception in paragraph (c)(1) of this section (multiple controlling fifty-percent partners) and the exception in paragraph (c)(2) of this section (constructive owner exception). *US* may only utilize the paragraph (c)(1) exception to avoid its filing obligation. Accordingly, *DC* may file a single Form 8865 on behalf of *US* and itself. However, that form must contain all the information that would have been submitted had *DC* and *US* each submitted a separate Form 8865.

(3) *Members of an affiliated group of corporations filing a consolidated return.*—If one or more members of an affiliated group of corporations filing a consolidated return are required under section 6038 to file a Form 8865 for a particular foreign partnership, the common parent corporation may file one Form 8865 on behalf of all of the members of the group required to report under section 6038. Except with respect to group members who also qualify under the exception in paragraph (c)(2) of this section, the Form 8865 must contain all the information that would have been required to be submitted if each group member were required to file its own Form 8865.

(d) *Exception for certain trusts.*—Trusts relating to state and local government employee retirement plans are not required to report under this section, unless the instructions to Form 8865 provide otherwise.

(e) *Reporting under this section not required with respect to partnerships excluded from the application of subchapter K.*—The reporting requirements of this section will not apply to any United States person in respect of an eligible partnership as described in § 1.761-2(a) if such partnership has validly elected to be excluded from all of the provisions of subchapter K of chapter 1 of the Internal Revenue Code in the manner specified in § 1.761-2(b)(2)(i), or such partnership is deemed to have elected to be excluded from all of the provisions of subchapter K of chapter 1 of the Internal Revenue Code in accordance with the provisions of § 1.761-2(b)(2)(ii).

(f) *Period covered by return.*—The information required under this section must be furnished for the tax year of the foreign partnership ending with or within the United States person's tax year. See section 706 for rules regarding tax years of partnerships.

(g) *Contents of return.*—(1) *Information required to be submitted by controlling fifty-percent partners and controlling ten-percent partners.*—All controlling fifty-percent partners and all controlling ten-percent partners must submit the following information on Form 8865 in the form and manner and to the extent prescribed by Form 8865 and its instructions—

(i) The name, address, and taxpayer identification number (if any) of the foreign partnership of which the person qualified as a controlling fifty-percent partner or a controlling ten-percent partner;

(ii) A statement of the income, gain, losses, deductions and credits allocated to the direct interest in the partnership of the person reporting under section 6038;

(iii) A list of all partnerships (foreign or domestic) in which the foreign partnership owned a direct interest, or owned a constructive interest of ten percent of more under the rules of section 267(c)(1) or (5), during the partnership's tax year for which the Form 8865 is being filed;

(iv) Information about all foreign entities that were disregarded as entities separate from their owner under §§ 301.7701-2 and 301.7701-3 that were owned by the foreign partnership during the partnership's tax year for which the Form 8865 is being filed;

(v) A summary of the transactions that took place during the partnership's tax year between the partnership and the person filing the return, between the partnership and any other partnership of which the person filing the return is a controlling fifty-percent partner, and between the partnership and any corporation controlled (under section 6038(e)(2) and the regulations thereunder) by the person filing the return; and

(vi) Any other information that Form 8865 or its accompanying instructions require to be submitted.

(2) *Additional information required to be submitted by controlling fifty-percent partners.*—In addition to the information required pursuant to paragraph (g)(1) of this section, controlling fifty-percent partners must also submit the following information in the form and manner and to the extent required by Form 8865 and its instructions—

(i) A list of the names, addresses and tax identification numbers (if any) of each United States person that owned a direct interest of ten percent or more in the partnership during the partnership's tax year, and of each United States and foreign person whose interests in the partnership the controlling fifty-percent partner constructively owned under paragraph (b)(4) of this section during the partnership's tax year;

(ii) A list of transactions between the partnership and any United States person owning at the time of the transaction at least a 10-percent direct interest (as defined in paragraph (b)(3) of this section) in the foreign partnership;

(iii) A statement of the aggregate of the partners' distributive shares of items of income, gain, losses, deductions and credits;

(iv) A statement of income, gain, losses, deductions and credits allocated to each United States person holding a direct interest in the foreign partnership of ten percent or more; and

(v) Any other information Form 8865 or its accompanying instructions require controlling fifty-percent partners to submit.

(3) *Amounts involving hybrid transactions or hybrid entities under section 267A.*—In addition to the information required pursuant to paragraphs (g)(1) and (2) of this section, if, during the partnership's taxable year for which the Form 8865 is being filed, the partnership paid or accrued interest or royalties for which a deduction is disallowed under section 267A and the regulations in this part under section 267A, the controlling fifty-percent partners must provide information about the disallowance in the form and manner and to the extent prescribed by Form 8865 (or successor form), instruction, publication, or other guidance.

(4) *Additional information required to be submitted by a controlling ten-percent or a controlling fifty-percent partner that has a deduction under section 250 by reason of FDII.*—In addition to the information required pursuant to paragraphs (g)(1), (2), and (3) of this section, if, with respect to the partnership's tax year for which the Form 8865 is being filed, a controlling ten-percent partner or a controlling fifty-percent partner has a deduction under section 250 (by reason of having foreign-derived intangible income), determined, in whole or in part, by reference to the income, assets, or activities of the partnership, or transactions between the controlling-ten percent partner or controlling fifty-percent partner and the partnership, the controlling ten-percent partner or controlling fifty-percent partner must provide its share of the partnership's gross DEI, gross FDDEI, deductions that are properly allocable to the partnership's gross DEI and gross FDDEI, and partnership QBAI (as those terms are defined in the section 250 regulations) in the form and manner and to the extent prescribed by Form 8865 (or any successor form), instructions to the form, publication, or other guidance published in the Internal Revenue Bulletin. To the extent that the partnership amounts described in the previous sentence cannot be determined, the controlling ten-percent partner or controlling fifty-percent partner must provide its share of the partnership's attributes that the partner uses to determine the partner's gross DEI, gross FDDEI, deductions that are properly allocable to the partner's gross DEI and gross FDDEI, and the partner's adjusted bases in partnership specified tangible property.

(h) *Method of reporting.*—Except as otherwise provided on Form 8865 or the accompanying instructions, all amounts required to be furnished on Form 8865 must be expressed in United States dollars. All statements required on or with Form 8865 pursuant to this section must be in English.

(i) *Time and place for filing return.*—(1) *In general.*—Form 8865 must be filed with the United States person's income tax return on or before the due date (including extensions) of that return. If the United States person is not required to file an income tax return for its tax year with which or within which the foreign partnership's tax year ends, but is required to file an information return for that year (for example, Form 1065, "U.S. Partnership Return of Income," or Form 990, "Return of Organization Exempt from Income Tax"), the Form 8865 must be filed with the United States person's information return filed on or before the due date (including extensions) of that return.

(2) *Duplicate return.*—If required by the instructions to Form 8865, a duplicate Form 8865 (including attachments and schedules) must also be filed.

(j) *Overlap with section 6031.*—A partner may be required to file Form 8865 under this section and the foreign partnership in which it is a partner may also be required to file a Form 1065 or Form 1065-B under section 6031(e) for the same partnership tax year. For cases where a United States person is a controlling fifty-percent partner or a controlling ten-percent partner with respect to a foreign partnership, and that foreign partnership completes and files Form 1065 or Form 1065-B, the instructions for Form 8865 will specify the filing requirements that address this overlap in reporting obligations.

(k) *Failure to comply with reporting requirement.*—(1) *In general.*—Any United States person required to file Form 8865 under Section 6038 and this section that fails to comply (as defined in paragraph (k)(2) of this section) with the reporting requirements of this section, will be subject to the penalties described in paragraph (k)(3) of this section.

(2) *Failure to comply.*—A failure to comply is separately determined for each foreign partnership for which a United States person has a section 6038 reporting obligation. A failure to comply with the requirements of section 6038 includes the following—

(i) The failure to report at the proper time and in the proper manner any information required to be reported under the rules of this section; or

(ii) The provision of false or inaccurate information in purported compliance with the requirements of this section.

(3) *Penalties.*—A United States person that fails to comply (as defined in paragraph (k)(2) of this section) with the reporting requirements of this section must pay the following penalties, subject to the reasonable cause exception in paragraph (k)(4) of this section:

(i) *Dollar amount penalty.*—(A) *$10,000 penalty.*—A penalty of $10,000 shall be imposed for each tax year of each foreign partnership with respect to which a failure to comply occurs.

(B) *Increase in penalty.*—If a failure to comply with the applicable reporting requirements of section 6038 and this section continues for more than 90 days after the date on which the Commissioner or the Commissioner's delegate mails notice of the failure to the United States person required to file Form 8865, the person must pay an additional penalty of $10,000 for each 30-day period (or fraction thereof) during which the failure continues after the 90-day period has expired.

(C) *Limitation.*—The additional penalty imposed on any United States person by section 6038(b)(2) and paragraph (k)(3)(i)(B) of this section is limited to a maximum of $50,000 for each partnership for each tax year with respect to which the failure occurs.

(ii) *Penalty of reducing foreign tax credit.*—(A) *Effect on foreign tax credit.*—Failure to comply with the reporting requirements of section 6038 and this section may cause a reduction of foreign tax credits under section 901 (taxes of foreign countries and of possessions of the United States). In applying section 901 to a United States person for any tax year with or within which its foreign partnership's tax year ended, the amount of taxes paid (and deemed paid under sections 902 and 960) by the United States person will be reduced by 10 percent if the person fails to comply. However, no tax deemed paid under section 904(c) will be reduced under the provisions of this paragraph (k)(3)(ii).

(B) *Reduction for continued failure.*—If a failure to comply with the reporting requirements of section 6038 and this section continues for more than 90 days after the date on which the Commissioner or the Commissioner's delegate mails notice of the failure to the person required to file Form 8865, then the amount of the reduction in paragraph (k)(3)(ii)(A) of this section will be 10 percent, plus an additional 5 percent for each 3-month period (or fraction thereof) during which the failure continues after the 90-day period has expired.

(C) *Limitation on reduction.*—The amount of the reduction under paragraphs (k)(3)(ii)(A) and (B) of this section for each failure to furnish information required under this section will not exceed the greater of $10,000, or the gross income of the foreign partnership for its tax year with respect to which the failure occurred.

(D) *Offset for dollar amount penalty imposed.*—The total amount of the reduction which, but for this paragraph (k)(3)(ii)(D), may be made under this paragraph (k)(3)(ii) with respect to any separate failure, may not exceed the maximum amount of the reductions that may be imposed, reduced (but not below zero) by the dollar amount penalty imposed by paragraph (k)(3)(i) of this section with respect to the failure.

(4) *Reasonable cause limitation.*—The time prescribed for filing a complete Form 8865, and the beginning of the 90-day period after the Commissioner or the Commissioner's delegate mails notice under paragraphs (k)(3)(i)(B) and (ii)(B) of this section, will be treated as being not earlier than the last day on which reasonable cause existed for failure to furnish the information. The United States person may show reasonable cause by providing a written statement to the Commissioner's delegate having jurisdiction over the person's return to which the Form 8865 should have been attached, setting forth the reasons for the failure to comply. Whether a failure to comply was due to reasonable cause will be determined by the Commissioner, or the Commissioner's delegate, under all the facts and circumstances.

(5) *Statute of limitations.*—For exceptions to the limitations on assessment in the event of a failure to provide information under section 6038, see section 6501(c)(8).

(l) *Applicability dates.*—Except as otherwise provided, this section shall apply for tax years of a foreign partnership ending on or after December 31, 2000. For tax years of a foreign partnership ending before December 23, 2002, see §1.6038-3(j) in effect prior to the amendments made by T.D. 9033 (see 26 CFR part 1 revised April 1, 2002). Paragraph (g)(3) of this section applies for taxable years of a foreign partnership beginning on or after December 20, 2018. Paragraph (g)(4) of this section applies for tax years of a foreign partnership beginning on or after March 4, 2019. [Reg. §1.6038-3.]

□ [*T.D. 8850, 12-27-99. Amended by T.D.* 9033, 12-20-2002; *T.D.* 9065, 6-30-2003; *T.D.* 9896, 4-7-2020 *and T.D.* 9901, 7-9-2020.]

§1.6038-4. Information returns required of certain United States persons with respect to such person's U.S. multinational enterprise group.—(a) *Requirement of return.*—Except as provided in paragraph (h) of this section, every ultimate parent entity of a U.S. multinational enterprise (MNE) group must make an annual return on Form 8975, *Country-by-Country Report*, setting forth the information described in paragraph (d) of this section, and any other information required by Form 8975, with respect to the reporting period described in paragraph (c) of this section.

(b) *Definitions.*—(1) *Ultimate parent entity of a U.S. MNE group.*—An ultimate parent entity of a U.S. MNE group is a U.S. business entity that:

(i) Owns directly or indirectly a sufficient interest in one or more other business entities, at least one of which is organized or tax resident in a tax jurisdiction other than the United States, such that the U.S. business entity is required to consolidate the accounts of the other business entities with its own accounts under U.S. generally accepted accounting principles, or would be so required if equity interests in the U.S. business entity were publicly traded on a U.S. securities exchange; and

(ii) Is not owned directly or indirectly by another business entity that consolidates the accounts of such U.S. business entity with its own accounts under generally accepted accounting principles in the other business entity's tax jurisdiction of residence, or would be so required if equity interests in the other business entity were traded on a public securities exchange in its tax jurisdiction of residence.

(2) *Business entity.*—For purposes of this section, a business entity generally is any entity recognized for federal tax purposes that is not properly classified as a trust under §301.7701-4 of this chapter. However, any grantor trust within the meaning of section 671, all or a portion of which is owned by a person other an individual, is a business entity for purposes of this section. Additionally, the term business entity includes any entity with a single owner that may be disregarded as an entity separate from its owner under §301.7701-3 of this chapter and a permanent establishment, as defined in paragraph (b)(3) of this section, that prepares financial statements separate from those of its owner for financial reporting, regulatory, tax reporting, or internal management control purposes. A business entity does not include a decedent's estate or a bankruptcy estate described in section 1398.

(3) *Permanent establishment.*—For purposes of this section, the term permanent establishment includes:

(i) A branch or business establishment of a constituent entity in a tax jurisdiction that is treated as a permanent establishment under an income tax convention to which that tax jurisdiction is a party;

(ii) A branch or business establishment of a constituent entity that is liable to tax in the tax jurisdiction in which it is located pursuant to the domestic law of such tax jurisdiction; or

(iii) A branch or business establishment of a constituent entity that is treated in the same manner for tax purposes as an entity separate from its owner by the owner's tax jurisdiction of residence.

(4) *U.S. business entity.*—A U.S. business entity is a business entity that is organized or has its tax jurisdiction of residence in the United States. For purposes of this section, foreign insurance companies that elect to be treated as domestic corporations under section 953(d) are U.S. business entities that have their tax jurisdiction of residence in the United States.

(5) *U.S. MNE group.*—A U.S. MNE group comprises the ultimate parent entity of a U.S. MNE group as defined in paragraph (b)(1) of this section and all of the business entities required to consolidate their accounts with the ultimate parent entity's accounts under U.S. generally accepted accounting principles, or that would be so required if equity interests in the ultimate parent entity were publicly traded on a U.S. securities exchange, regardless of whether any such business entities could be excluded from consolidation solely on size or materiality grounds.

(6) *Constituent entity.*—With respect to a U.S. MNE group, a constituent entity is any separate business entity of such U.S. MNE group, except that the term constituent entity does not include a foreign corporation or foreign partnership for which the ultimate parent entity is not required to furnish information under section 6038(a) (determined without regard to §§1.6038-2(j) and 1.6038-3(c)) or any permanent establishment of such foreign corporation or foreign partnership.

(7) *Tax jurisdiction.*—For purposes of this section, a tax jurisdiction is a country or a jurisdiction that is not a country but that has fiscal autonomy. For purposes of this section, a U.S. territory or possession of the United States is considered to have fiscal autonomy.

(8) *Tax jurisdiction of residence.*—A business entity is considered a resident in a tax jurisdiction if, under the laws of that tax jurisdiction, the business entity is liable to tax therein based on place of management, place of organization, or another similar criterion. A business entity will not be considered a resident in a tax jurisdiction if the business entity is liable to tax in such tax jurisdiction only by reason of a tax imposed by reference to gross amounts of income without any reduction for expenses, provided such tax applies only with respect to income from sources in such tax jurisdiction or capital situated in such tax jurisdiction. If a business entity is resident in more than one tax jurisdiction, then the applicable income tax convention rules, if any, should be applied to determine the business entity's tax jurisdiction of residence. If a business entity is resident in more than one tax jurisdiction and no applicable income tax convention exists between those tax jurisdictions, or if the applicable income tax convention provides that the determination of residence is based on a determination by the competent authorities of the relevant tax jurisdictions and no such determination has been made, the business entity's tax jurisdiction of residence is the tax jurisdiction of the business entity's place of effective management determined in accordance with Article 4 of the Organisation for Economic Co-operation and Development Model Tax Convention on Income and on Capital 2014, or as provided by Form 8975. A corporation that is organized or managed in a tax jurisdiction that does not impose an income tax on corporations will be treated as resident in that tax jurisdiction, unless such corporation is treated as resident in another tax jurisdiction under another provision of this section. The tax jurisdiction of residence of a permanent establishment is the jurisdiction in which the permanent establishment is located. If a business entity does not have a tax jurisdiction of residence, then solely for purposes of paragraph (b)(1) of this section, the tax jurisdiction of residence is the business entity's country of organization.

(9) *Applicable financial statements.*—An applicable financial statement is a certified audited financial statement that is accompanied by a report of an independent certified public accountant or similarly qualified independent professional that is used for purposes of reporting to shareholders, partners, or similar persons; for purposes of reporting to creditors in connection with securing or maintaining financing; or for any other substantial non-tax purpose.

(10) *U.S. territory or possession of the United States.*—The term U.S. territory or possession of the United States means American Samoa, Guam, the Northern Mariana Islands, Puerto Rico, or the U.S. Virgin Islands.

(11) *U.S. territory ultimate parent entity.*—A U.S. territory ultimate parent entity is a business entity organized in a U.S. territory or possession of the United States that controls (as defined in section 6038(e)) a U.S. business entity and that is not owned directly or indirectly by another business entity that consolidates the accounts of the U.S. territory ultimate parent entity with its accounts under generally accepted accounting principles in the other business entity's tax jurisdiction of residence, or would be so required if equity interests in the other business entity were traded on a public securities exchange in its tax jurisdiction of residence.

(c) *Reporting period.*—The reporting period covered by Form 8975 is the period of the ultimate parent entity's applicable financial statement prepared for the 12-month period (or a 52-53 week period described in section 441(f)) that ends with or within the ultimate parent entity's taxable year. If the ultimate parent entity does not prepare an annual applicable financial statement, then the reporting period covered by Form 8975 is the 12-month period (or a 52-53 week period described in section 441(f)) that ends on the last day of the ultimate parent entity's taxable year.

(d) *Contents of return.*—(1) *Constituent entity information.*—The return on Form 8975 must contain so much of the following information with respect to each constituent entity of the U.S. MNE group, and in such form or manner, as Form 8975 prescribes:

(i) The complete legal name of the constituent entity;

(ii) The tax jurisdiction, if any, in which the constituent entity is resident for tax purposes;

(iii) The tax jurisdiction in which the constituent entity is organized or incorporated (if different from the tax jurisdiction of residence);

(iv) The tax identification number, if any, used for the constituent entity by the tax administration of the constituent entity's tax jurisdiction of residence; and

(v) The main business activity or activities of the constituent entity.

(2) *Tax jurisdiction of residence information.*—The return on Form 8975 must contain so much of the following information with respect to each tax jurisdiction in which one or more constituent entities of a U.S. MNE group is resident, presented as an aggregate of the information for the constituent entities resident in each tax jurisdiction, and in such form or manner, as Form 8975 prescribes:

(i) Revenues generated from transactions with other constituent entities;

(ii) Revenues not generated from transactions with other constituent entities;

(iii) Profit or loss before income tax;

(iv) Total income tax paid on a cash basis to all tax jurisdictions, and any taxes withheld on payments received by the constituent entities;

(v) Total accrued tax expense recorded on taxable profits or losses, reflecting only operations in the relevant annual period and excluding deferred taxes or provisions for uncertain tax liabilities;

(vi) Stated capital, except that the stated capital of a permanent establishment must be reported in the tax jurisdiction of residence of the legal entity of which it is a permanent establishment unless there is a defined capital requirement in the permanent establishment tax jurisdiction for regulatory purposes;

(vii) Total accumulated earnings, except that accumulated earnings of a permanent establishment must be reported by the legal entity of which it is a permanent establishment;

(viii) Total number of employees on a full-time equivalent basis; and

(ix) Net book value of tangible assets, which, for purposes of this section, does not include cash or cash equivalents, intangibles, or financial assets.

(3) *Special rules.*—(i) *Constituent entity with no tax jurisdiction of residence.*—The information listed in paragraph (d)(2) of this section also must be provided, in the aggregate, for any constituent entity or entities that have no tax jurisdiction of residence. In addition, if a constituent entity is an owner of a constituent entity that does not have a jurisdiction of tax residence, then the owner's share of such entity's revenues and profits will be aggregated with the information for the owner's tax jurisdiction of residence.

(ii) *Definition of revenue.*—For purposes of this section, the term revenue includes all amounts of revenue, including revenue from sales of inventory and property, services, royalties, interest, and premiums. The term revenue does not include payments received from other constituent entities that are treated as dividends in the payor's tax jurisdiction of residence. Distributions and remittances from partnerships and other fiscally transparent entities and permanent establishments that are constituent entities are not considered revenue of the recipient-owner. The term revenue also does not include imputed earnings or deemed dividends received from other constituent entities that are taken into account solely for tax purposes and that otherwise would be included as revenue by a constituent entity. With respect to a constituent entity that is an organization exempt from taxation under section 501(a) because it is an organization described in section 501(c), 501(d), or 401(a), a state college or university described in section 511(a)(2)(B), a plan described in section 403(b) or 457(b), an individual retirement plan or annuity as defined in section 7701(a)(37), a qualified tuition program described in section 529, a qualified ABLE program described in section 529A, or a Coverdell education savings account described in section 530, the term revenue includes only revenue that is reflected in unrelated business taxable income as defined in section 512.

(iii) *Number of employees.*—For purposes of this section, the number of employees on a full-time equivalent basis may be reported as of the end of the accounting period, on the basis of average employment levels for the annual accounting period, or on any other reasonable basis consistently applied across tax jurisdictions and from year to year. Independent contractors participating in the ordinary operating activities of a constituent entity may be reported as employees of such constituent entity. Reasonable rounding or approximation of the number of employees is permissible, provided that such rounding or approximation does not materially distort the relative distribution of employees across the various tax jurisdictions. Consistent approaches should be applied from year to year and across entities.

(iv) *Income tax paid and accrued tax expense of permanent establishment.*—In the case of a constituent entity that is a permanent establishment, the amount of income tax paid and the amount of accrued tax expense referred to in paragraphs (d)(2)(iv) and (v) of this section should not include the income tax paid or tax expense accrued by the business entity of which the permanent establishment would be a part, but for the third sentence of paragraph (b)(2) of this section, in that business entity's tax jurisdiction of residence on the income derived by the permanent establishment.

(v) *Certain transportation income.*—If a constituent entity of a U.S. MNE group derives income from international transportation or transportation in inland waterways that is covered by income tax convention provisions that are specific to such income and under which the taxing rights on such income are allocated exclusively to one tax jurisdiction, then the U.S. MNE group should report the information required under paragraph (d)(2) of this section with respect to such income for the tax jurisdiction to which the relevant income tax convention provisions allocate these taxing rights.

(e) *Reporting of financial amounts.*—(1) *Reporting in U.S. dollars required.*—All amounts furnished under paragraph (d)(2) of this section, other than paragraph (d)(2)(viii) of this section, must be expressed in U.S. dollars. If an exchange rate is used other than in accordance with U.S. generally accepted accounting principles for conversion to U.S. dollars, the exchange rate must be indicated.

(2) *Sources of financial amounts.*—All amounts furnished under paragraph (d)(2) of this section, other than paragraph (d)(2)(viii) of this section, should be based on applicable financial statements, books and records maintained with respect to the constituent entity, regulatory financial statements, or records used for tax reporting or internal management control purposes for an annual period of each constituent entity ending with or within the period described in paragraph (c) of this section.

(f) *Time and manner for filing.*—Returns on Form 8975 required under paragraph (a) of this section for a reporting period must be filed with the ultimate parent entity's income tax return for the taxable year, in or with which the reporting period ends, on or before the due date (including extensions) for filing that person's income tax return or as otherwise prescribed by Form 8975.

(g) *Maintenance of records.*—The U.S. person filing Form 8975 as an ultimate parent entity of a U.S. MNE group must maintain records to support the information provided on Form 8975. However, the U.S. person is not required to create and maintain records that reconcile the amounts provided on Form 8975 with the tax returns of any tax jurisdiction or applicable financial statements.

(h) *Exceptions to furnishing information.*—An ultimate parent entity of a U.S. MNE group is not required to report information under this section for the reporting period described in paragraph (c) of this section if the annual revenue of the U.S. MNE group for the immediately preceding reporting period was less than $850,000,000.

(i) [Reserved]

(j) *U.S. territories and possessions of the United States.*—A U.S. territory ultimate parent entity may designate a U.S. business entity that it controls (as defined in section 6038(e)) to file Form 8975 on the U.S. territory ultimate parent entity's behalf with respect to such U.S. territory ultimate parent entity and the business entities that would be required to consolidate their accounts with such U.S. territory ultimate parent entity under U.S. generally accepted accounting principles, or would be so required if equity interests in the U.S. territory ultimate parent entity were publicly traded on a U.S. securities exchange.

(k) *Applicability dates.*—The rules of this section apply to reporting periods of ultimate parent entities of U.S. MNE groups that begin on or after the first day of a taxable year of the ultimate parent entity that begins on or after June 30, 2016. [Reg. § 1.6038-4.]

☐ [*T.D. 9773, 6-29-2016 (corrected 9-16-2016).*]

§ 1.6038-5. Information returns required of certain United States persons to report amounts determined with respect to certain foreign corporations for global intangible low-taxed income (GILTI) purposes.—(a) *Requirement of return.*—Except as provided in paragraph (d) of this section, each United States person who is a United States shareholder (as defined in section 951(b)) of any controlled foreign corporation (as defined in section 957) must make an annual return on Form 8992, "U.S. Shareholder Calculation of Global Intangible Low-Taxed Income (GILTI)," (or successor form) for each U.S. shareholder inclusion year (as defined in § 1.951A-1(f)(7)) setting forth the information with respect to each such controlled foreign corporation, in such form and manner, as Form 8992 (or successor form) prescribes.

(b) *Time and manner for filing.*—Returns on Form 8992 (or successor form) required under paragraph (a) of this section for a taxable year must be filed with the United States person's income tax return on or before the due date (taking into account extensions) for filing that person's income tax return.

(c) *Failure to furnish information.*—(1) *Penalties.*—If any person required to file Form 8992 (or successor form) under section 6038 and this section fails to furnish the information prescribed on Form 8992 within the time prescribed by paragraph (b) of this section, the penalties imposed by section 6038(b) and (c) apply.

(2) *Increase in penalty.*—If a failure described in paragraph (c)(1) of this section continues for more than 90 days after the date on which the Director of Field Operations, Area Director, or Director of Compliance Campus Operations mails notice of such failure to the person required to file Form 8992, such person shall pay a penalty of $10,000, in addition to the penalty imposed by section 6038(b)(1), for each 30-day period (or a fraction of) during which such failure continues after such 90-day period has expired. The additional penalty imposed by section 6038(b)(2) and this paragraph (c)(2) shall be limited to a maximum of $50,000 for each failure.

(3) *Reasonable cause.*—(i) For purposes of section 6038(b) and (c) and this section, the time prescribed for furnishing information under paragraph (b) of this section, and the beginning of the 90-day period after mailing of notice by the director under paragraph (c)(2) of this section, shall be treated as being not earlier than the last day on which reasonable cause existed for failure to furnish the information.

(ii) To show that reasonable cause existed for failure to furnish information as required by section 6038 and this section, the person required to report such information must make an affirmative showing of all facts alleged as reasonable cause for such failure in a written statement containing a declaration that it is made under the penalties of perjury. The statement must be filed with the director where the return is required to be filed. The director shall determine whether the failure to furnish information was due to reasonable cause, and if so, the period of time for which such reasonable cause existed. In the case of a return that has been filed as required by this section except for an omission of, or error with respect to, some of the information required, if the person who filed the return establishes to the satisfaction of the director that the person has substantially complied with this section, then the omission or error shall not constitute a failure under this section.

(d) *Exception from filing requirement.*—Any United States person that does not own, within the meaning of section 958(a), stock of a controlled foreign corporation in which the United States person is a United States shareholder for a taxable year is not required to file Form 8992. For this purpose, whether a U.S. person owns, within the meaning of section 958(a), stock of a controlled foreign corporation is determined under § 1.951A-1(e).

(e) *Applicability date.*—This section applies to taxable years of controlled foreign corporations beginning on or after October 3, 2018. [Reg. § 1.6038-5.]

☐ [*T.D. 9866, 6-14-2019.*]

§ 1.6038A-1. General requirements and definitions.—(a) *Purpose and scope.*—This section and §§ 1.6038A-2 through 1.6038A-7 provide rules for certain foreign-owned U.S. corporations and foreign corporations engaged in trade or business within the United States (reporting corporations) relating to information that must be furnished, records that must be maintained, and the authorization of the reporting corporation to act as agent for related foreign persons for purposes of sections 7602, 7603, and 7604 that must be executed. Section 6038A(a) and this section require that a reporting corporation furnish certain information annually and maintain certain records relating to transactions between the reporting corporation and certain related parties. This section also provides definitions of terms used in section 6038A. Section 1.6038A-2 provides guidance concerning the information to be submitted and the filing of the required return. Section 1.6038A-3 provides guidance concerning the maintenance of records. Section 1.6038A-4 provides guidance concerning the application of the monetary penalty for the failure either to furnish information or to maintain records. Section 1.6038A-5 provides guidance concerning the authorization of an agent for purposes of sections 7602, 7603, and 7604. Section 1.6038A-6 provides guidance concerning the failure to furnish information requested by a summons. Finally, § 1.6038A-7 provides guidance concerning the application of the noncompliance penalty for failure by the related party to authorize an agent or by the reporting corporation to substantially comply with a summons.

(b) *In general.*—A reporting corporation must furnish the information described in § 1.6038A-2 by filing an annual information return (Form 5472 or any successor), and must maintain records as described in § 1.6038A-3.

(c) *Reporting corporation.*—(1) *In general.*—For purposes of section 6038A, a reporting corporation is either a domestic corporation that is 25-percent foreign-owned as defined in paragraph (c)(2) of this section, or a foreign corporation that is 25-percent foreign-owned and engaged in trade or business within the United States. After November 4, 1990, a foreign corporation engaged in a trade or business within the United States at any time during a taxable year is a reporting corporation. *See* section 6038C. A domestic business entity that is wholly owned by one foreign person and that is otherwise classified under § 301.7701-3(b)(1)(ii) of this chapter as disregarded as an entity separate from its owner is treated as an entity separate from its owner and classified as a domestic corporation for purposes of section 6038A. *See* § 301.7701-2(c)(2)(vi) of this chapter.

(2) *25-percent foreign-owned.*—A corporation is 25-percent foreign-owned if it has at least one direct or indirect 25-percent foreign shareholder at any time during the taxable year.

(3) *25-percent foreign shareholder.*—(i) *In general.*—A foreign person is a 25-percent foreign shareholder of a corporation if the person owns at least 25 percent of—

(A) The total voting power of all classes of stock of the corporation entitled to vote, or

(B) The total value of all classes of stock of the corporation.

(ii) *Total voting power and value.*—In determining whether one foreign person owns 25 percent of the total voting power of all classes of stock of a corporation entitled to vote or 25 percent of the total value of all classes of stock of a corporation, consideration will be given to all the facts and circumstances of each case, under principles similar to § 1.957-1(b)(2) (consideration of arrangements to shift formal voting power away from a foreign person).

(iii) *Direct 25-percent foreign shareholder.*—A foreign person is a direct 25-percent foreign shareholder if it owns directly at least 25 percent of the stock of the reporting corporation, either by vote or by value.

(iv) *Indirect 25-percent foreign shareholder.*—A foreign person is an indirect 25-percent foreign shareholder if it owns indirectly (or under the attribution rules of section 318 is considered to own indirectly) at least 25 percent of the stock of the reporting corporation, either by vote or by value.

(4) *Application to prior open years.*—For taxable years beginning before July 11, 1989, the definition of a reporting corporation under this paragraph applies in determining whether a foreign-owned corporation is a reporting corporation. An examination may be reopened if the statute of limitations period for that taxable year has not expired. A taxable year may not be reopened under section 6038A for examination purposes if the taxable year is open under section 6511 only for purposes of the carryback of net operating losses or net capital losses.

(5) *Exceptions.*—(i) *Treaty country residents having no permanent establishment.*—A foreign corporation that has no permanent establishment in the United States under an applicable income tax convention is not a reporting corporation for purposes of section 6038A and this section. Accordingly, such a foreign corporation is not subject to §§ 1.6038A-2, 1.6038A-3, and 1.6038A-5. It must timely and fully provide the required notice to the Commissioner under section 6114. See section 6114 and the regulations thereunder for the notice that such a corporation must file and the applicable penalties for failure to file such notice.

(ii) *Qualified exempt shipping income.*—A foreign corporation whose gross income is exempt from U.S. taxation under section 883 is not a reporting corporation provided that it timely and fully complies with the reporting requirements required to claim such exemption. In the event that such a corporation does not timely and fully comply with the reporting requirements under sections 887 and 883, it will be a reporting corporation subject to section 6038A, including the application of the monetary penalty for failure to file required information.

(iii) *Status as foreign related party.*—Nothing in this paragraph affects the determination of whether a person is a foreign related party as defined in paragraph (g) of this section.

(d) *Related party.*—The term "related party" means—

(1) Any direct or indirect 25-percent foreign shareholder of the reporting corporation,

(2) Any person who is related within the meaning of sections 267(b) or 707(b)(1) to the reporting corporation or to a 25-percent foreign shareholder of the reporting corporation, or

(3) Any other person who is related to the reporting corporation within the meaning of section 482 and the regulations thereunder.

However, the term "related party" does not include any corporation filing a consolidated federal income tax return with the reporting corporation.

(e) *Attribution rules.*—(1) *Attribution under section 318.*—For purposes of determining whether a corporation is 25-percent foreign-owned and whether a person is a related party under section 6038A, the constructive ownership rules of section 318 shall apply, and the attribution rules of section 267(c) also shall apply to the extent they attribute ownership to persons to whom section 318 does not attribute ownership. However, "10 percent" shall be substituted for "50 percent" in section 318(a)(2)(C), and section 318(a)(3)(A), (B), and (C) shall not be applied so as to consider a U.S. person as owning stock that is owned by a person who is not a U.S. person. Additionally, section 318(a)(3)(C) and § 1.318-1(b) shall not be applied so as to consider a U.S. corporation as being a reporting corporation if, but for the application of such sections, the U.S. corporation would not be 25-percent foreign owned.

(2) *Attribution of transactions with related parties engaged in by a partnership.*—The transactions in which a domestic or foreign partnership engages shall be attributed to any reporting corporation whose interest in the capital or profits of the partnership, either directly or indirectly, combined with the interests of all related parties of the reporting corporation partner, equals 25 percent or more of the total partnership interests. Attribution of such transactions shall be made only to the extent of the partnership interest held by that reporting corporation partner. *See* sections 875 and 702(a) and the regulations thereunder. (Attribution shall not be made, however, of transactions directly between the partnership and a reporting corporation.) Accordingly, a reporting corporation partner that is deemed to engage in transactions with related parties under this rule is subject to the information reporting requirements of § 1.6038A-2, to the record maintenance requirements of § 1.6038A-3, to the monetary penalty under § 1.6038A-4, to the requirement of authorization of agent under § 1.6038A-5, to the rules of § 1.6038A-6 relating to the requirement to produce records, and to the noncompliance penalty adjustment under § 1.6038A-7.

(f) *Foreign person.*—For purposes of section 6038A, a foreign person is—

(1) Any individual who is not a citizen or resident of the United States, but not including any individual for whom an election under section 6013(g) or (h) (relating to an election to file a joint return) is in effect;

(2) Any individual who is a citizen of any possession of the United States and who is not otherwise a citizen or resident of the United States;

(3) Any partnership, association, company, or corporation that is not created or organized in the United States or under the law of the United States or any State thereof;

(4) Any foreign trust or foreign estate, as defined in section 7701(a)(31); or

(5) Any foreign government (or agency or instrumentality thereof). To the extent that a foreign government is engaged in the conduct of commercial activity as defined under section 892 and the regulations thereunder, it will be treated as a foreign person under section 6038A and this section only for purposes of the information reporting requirements of § 1.6038A-2. A foreign government will not be treated as a foreign related party for purposes of §§ 1.6038A-3 and 1.6038A-5.

For purposes of section 6038A, a possession of the United States shall be considered to be a foreign country.

(g) *Foreign related party.*—A foreign related party is a foreign person as defined under paragraph (f) of this section that is also a related party as defined under paragraph (d) of this section.

(h) *Small corporation exception.*—A reporting corporation (other than an entity that is a reporting corporation as a result of being treated as a corporation under § 301.7701-2(c)(2)(vi) of this chapter) that has less than $10,000,000 in U.S. gross receipts for a taxable year is not subject to §§ 1.6038A-3 and 1.6038A-5 for that taxable year. Such a corporation, however, remains subject to the information reporting requirements of § 1.6038A-2 and the general record maintenance requirements of section 6001. For purposes of this paragraph, U.S. gross receipts includes all amounts received or accrued to the extent that such amounts are taken into account for the determination and computation of the gross income of the corporation. For purposes of this test, the U.S. gross receipts of all related reporting corporations shall be aggregated.

(i) *Safe harbor for reporting corporations with related party transactions of de minimis value.*—(1) *In general.*—A reporting corporation (other than an entity that is a reporting corporation as a result of being treated as a corporation under § 301.7701-2(c)(2)(vi) of this chapter) is not subject to §§ 1.6038A-3 and 1.6038A-5 for any taxable year in which the aggregate value of all gross payments it makes to and receives from foreign related parties with respect to related party transactions (including monetary consideration, nonmonetary consideration, and the value of transactions involving less than full consideration) is not more than $5,000,000 and is less than 10 percent of its U.S. gross income. Such a corporation, however, remains subject to the information reporting requirements of § 1.6038A-2 and the general record maintenance requirements of section 6001. For purposes of this paragraph, U.S. gross income means the gross income reportable by the reporting corporation (or the aggregate gross income reportable by all related reporting corporations) for U.S. income tax purposes. Gross payments made to or received from foreign related parties cannot be netted; rather, the gross payments made to and received from foreign related parties are to be aggregated. Thus, for example, if a reporting corporation receives $4,700,000 of gross payments from a related party and makes $500,000 of gross payments to the same related party, it has aggregate gross payments of $5,200,000, and, therefore, does not qualify for the safe harbor under this paragraph.

(2) *Aggregate value of gross payments made or received.*—The aggregate value of gross payments made to (or received from) a foreign related party with respect to foreign related party transactions is determined by totaling the dollar amounts of foreign related party transactions as described in § 1.6038A-2(b)(3) and (4) on all Forms 5472 filed by the reporting corporation or related reporting corporations.

(j) *Related reporting corporations.*—A reporting corporation is related to another reporting corporation if it is related to that other reporting corporation under the principles described in paragraphs (d) and (e) of this section.

(k) *Consolidated return groups.*—(1) *Required information.*—If a reporting corporation is a member of an affiliated group for which a U.S. consolidated income tax return is filed, the return requirement of § 1.6038A-2 may be satisfied by filing a consolidated Form 5472. The common parent, as identified on Form 851, must attach a schedule to the consolidated Form 5472 stating which members of the U.S. affiliated group are reporting corporations under section 6038A, and which of those are joining in the consolidated Form 5472. The schedule must provide the name, address, and taxpayer identification number of each member whose transactions are included on the consolidated Form 5472. A member is not required to join in filing a consolidated Form 5472 merely because other members of the group choose to file one or more Forms 5472 on a consolidated basis.

(2) *Maintenance of records and authorization of agent.*—Either the common parent or the principal operating company of an affiliated group filing a consolidated income tax return may be authorized under § 1.6038A-5 to act as the agent for foreign related persons engaged in transactions with members of the group solely for purposes of section 7602, 7603, and 7604 under section 6038A(e)(1) and § 1.6038A-5. Each member of the group, however, must maintain the records required under section 6038A(a) and § 1.6038A-3 relating to its related party transactions.

(3) *Monetary penalties.*—The common parent (or principal operating company) and all reporting corporations that join in the filing of a consolidated Form 5472 are liable jointly and severally for penalties for failure to file Form 5472 and for failure to maintain records under section 6038A(d) and § 1.6038A-4(e). *See* § 1.1502-77(a) regarding the scope of agency of the common parent corporation.

(l) *District Director.*—For purposes of the regulations under section 6038A, the term "District Director" means any District Director, or the Assistant Commissioner (International) when performing duties similar to those of a District Director with respect to any person over which the Assistant Commissioner (International) has appropriate jurisdiction.

(m) *Examples.*—The following examples illustrate the rules of this section.

Example 1. P, a U.S. partnership that is engaged in a U.S. trade or business, is 75 percent owned by FC1, a foreign corporation that, in turn, is wholly owned by another foreign corporation, FC2. The remaining 25 percent of P is owned by Corp, a domestic corporation, that is wholly owned by FC3. P engages in transactions solely with FC2 and FC3. These transactions are attributed to FC1 and Corp. Under section 875, FC1 is considered as being engaged in a U.S. trade or business. For purposes of section 6038A and this section, FC1 and Corp are reporting corporations and must report their pro rata shares of the value of the transactions with FC2 and FC3. Thus, Corp must report 25 percent of P's transactions with FC3 and FC1 must report 75 percent of P's transactions with FC2.

Example 2. FC2 and FC3 are both foreign corporations that are wholly owned by FC1, also a foreign corporation. FC2 engages in a trade or business in the United States through a branch. The branch engages in related party transactions with FC1. FC2 is a reporting corporation. FC3 is a foreign related party. FC1 is a direct 25-percent foreign shareholder of both FC2 and FC3. Neither FC1 nor FC3 is a reporting corporation.

Example 3. FC1 owns 25 percent of total voting power in each of FC2 and FC3. FC2 and FC3 each own 20 percent of the total voting power of Corp, a domestic corporation. The remaining stock of Corp is owned by an unrelated domestic corporation. Neither FC2 nor FC3 is engaged in a U.S. trade or business. Under section 318(a)(2)(C) and paragraph (e) of this section, FC1 constructively owns its proportionate share of the stock of Corp owned directly by FC2 and FC3. Thus, FC1 is treated as constructively owning five percent of Corp through each of FC2 and FC3 or a total of 10 percent of the Corp stock. Consequently, Corp is not a reporting corporation because no 25 percent shareholder exists.

Example 4. FP owns 100 percent of FC1 which, in turn, owns 100 percent of FC2. FC2 owns 100 percent of FC3 which owns 100 percent of RC. FP, FC1, and FC2 are indirect 25-percent foreign shareholders of RC, and FC3 is a direct 25-percent foreign shareholder.

Example 5. FP owns 100 percent of USS, a U.S. corporation, and 25 percent of FS, a foreign corporation. The remaining 75 percent of FS is publicly owned by numerous small shareholders. Sales transactions occur between USS and FS. Applying the rules of this section, USS is a reporting corporation. It is determined that USS and FS are each controlled by FP under section 482 and the regulations thereunder. Therefore, FS is related to USS within the meaning of section 482 and is a related party to USS. Accordingly, the sales transactions between USS and FS are subject to section 6038A.

Example 6. The facts are the same as in *Example 5*, except that the remaining 75 percent of FS is owned by one shareholder that is unrelated to the FP group and it is determined that FS is not controlled by FP for purposes of section 482. Under these facts, FS is not a related party of either FP or USS. Accordingly, section 6038A does not apply to the sales transactions between FS and USS.

Example 7. P, a U.S. multinational, is a holding company that wholly owns X, a U.S. operating company, which in turn wholly owns FS, a controlled foreign corporation. Applying the rule of section 318(a)(3)(C), FS is deemed to own the stock of X that is actually held by P. However, under the rules of paragraph (e) of this section, X will not be a reporting corporation by reason of section 318.

(n) *Effective dates.*—(1) *Section 1.6038A-1.*—Paragraphs (c) (relating to the definition of a reporting corporation), (d) (relating to the definition of a related party), (e)(1) (relating to the application of section 318), and (f) (relating to the definition of a foreign person) of this section are effective for taxable years beginning after July 10, 1989. The remaining paragraphs of this section are effective December 10, 1990, without regard to when the taxable year began. However, § 1.6038A-1 as it applies to entities that are reporting corporations as a result of being treated as a corporation under § 301.7701-2(c)(2)(vi) of this chapter applies to taxable years of such reporting corporations beginning after December 31, 2016, and ending on or after December 13, 2017.

(2) *Section 1.6038A-2.*—(i) *In general.*—Section 1.6038A-2 (relating to the requirement to file Form 5472) generally applies for taxable years beginning after July 10, 1989. However, § 1.6038A-2 as it applies to reporting corporations whose sole trade or business in the United States is a banking, financing, or similar business as defined in § 1.864-4(c)(5)(i) applies for taxable years beginning after December 10, 1990. Section 1.6038A-2(d) applies for taxable years ending on or after June 10, 2011. For taxable years ending on or after June 10, 2011, but before December 24, 2014, see § 1.6038A-2(e) as contained in 26 CFR part 1 revised as of April 1, 2014. Section 1.6038A-2 as it applies to entities that are reporting corporations as a result of being treated as a corporation under § 301.7701-2(c)(2)(vi) of this chapter applies to taxable years of such reporting corporations beginning after December 31, 2016, and ending on or after December 13, 2017. Section 1.6038A-2(a)(3), (b)(6), and (b)(7) apply to taxable years ending on or after December 17, 2018. However, taxpayers may apply these final regulations in their entirety for taxable years ending before December 17, 2018.

(ii) *Transition rule.*—No penalty under sections 6038A(d) or 6038C(c) will apply to a failure solely under § 1.6038A-2(a)(3), (b)(6), or (b)(7) that is corrected by March 6, 2020.

(3) *Section 1.6038A-4.*—Section 1.6038A-4 (relating to the monetary penalty) is generally effective for taxable years beginning after

July 10, 1989, for the failure to file Form 5472. For the failure to maintain records or the failure to produce documents under §1.6038A-4(f)(2), the section is effective December 10, 1990, without regard to when the taxable year to which the records relate began. For taxable years ending on or before December 31, 2017, see §1.6038A-4 as contained in 26 CFR part 1 revised as of April 1, 2018.

(4) *Section 1.6038A-5.*—Section 1.6038A-5 (relating to the authorization of agent requirement) is effective December 10, 1990, without regard to when the taxable year to which the records relate began.

(5) *Section 1.6038A-6.*—Section 1.6038A-6 (relating to the failure to furnish information under a summons) is effective November 6, 1990, without regard to when the taxable year to which the summons relates began.

(6) *Section 1.6038A-7.*—Section 1.6038A-7 (relating to the noncompliance penalty adjustment) is effective December 10, 1990, without regard to when the taxable year began. [Reg. §1.6038A-1.]

☐ [*T.D.* 8353, 6-14-91. *Amended by T.D.* 9161, 9-14-2004; *T.D.* 9456, 7-31-2009; *T.D.* 9529, 6-9-2011; *T.D.* 9667, 6-5-2014, *T.D.* 9707, 12-23-2014, *T.D.* 9796, 12-12-2016 *and T.D.* 9885, 12-2-2019.]

§1.6038A-2. Requirement of return.—(a) *Forms required.*—(1) *Form 5472.*—Each reporting corporation as defined in §1.6038A-1(c) (or members of an affiliated group filing together as described in §1.6038A-1(k)) shall make a separate annual information return on Form 5472 with respect to each related party as defined in §1.6038A-1(d) with which the reporting corporation(or any group member joining in a consolidated Form 5472) has had any reportable transaction during the taxable year. The information required by section 6038A and this section must be furnished even though it may not affect the amount of any tax due under the Code.

(2) *Reportable transaction.*—A reportable transaction is any transaction of the types listed in paragraphs (b)(3) and (4) of this section, and, in the case of a reporting corporation that is an applicable taxpayer, as defined under §1.59A-2(b), any other arrangement that, to prevent avoidance of the purposes of section 59A, is identified on Form 5472 as a reportable transaction. However, except as the Secretary may prescribe otherwise for an applicable taxpayer, the transaction is not a reportable transaction if neither party to the transaction is a United States person as defined in section 7701(a)(30) (which, for purposes of section 6038A, includes an entity that is a reporting corporation as a result of being treated as a corporation under §301.7701-2(c)(2)(vi) of this chapter) and the transaction—

(i) Will not generate in any taxable year gross income from sources within the United States or income effectively connected, or treated as effectively connected, with the conduct of a trade or business within the United States, and

(ii) Will not generate in any taxable year any expense, loss, or other deduction that is allocable or apportionable to such income.

(3) *Form 8991.*—Each reporting corporation that is an applicable taxpayer, as defined under §1.59A-2(b), must make an annual information return on Form 8991. The obligation of an applicable taxpayer to report on Form 8991 does not depend on applicability of tax under section 59A or obligation to file Form 5472.

(b) *Contents of return.*—(1) *Reporting corporation.*—Form 5472 must provide the following information in the manner the form prescribes with respect to each reporting corporation:

(i) Its name, address (including mailing code), and U.S. taxpayer identification number; each country in which the reporting corporation files an income tax return as a resident under the tax laws of that country; its country or countries of organization, and incorporation; its total assets for U.S. reporting corporation; the places where it conducts its business; and its principal business activity.

(ii) The name, address, and U.S. taxpayer identification number, if applicable, of all its direct and indirect foreign shareholders (for an indirect 25-percent foreign shareholder, explain the attribution of ownership); whether any 25-percent foreign shareholder is a surrogate foreign corporation under section 7874(a)(2)(B) or a member of an expanded affiliated group as defined in section 7874(c)(1); each country in which each 25-percent foreign shareholder files an income tax return as a resident under the tax laws of that country; the places where each 25-percent shareholder conducts its business; and the country or countries of organization, citizenship, and incorporation of each 25-percent foreign shareholder.

(iii) The number of Forms 5472 filed for the taxable year and the aggregate value in U.S. dollars of gross payments as defined in §1.6038A-1(h)(2) made with respect to all foreign related party transactions reported on all Forms 5472.

(2) *Related party.*—The reporting corporation must provide information on Form 5472, set forth in the manner the form prescribes, about each related party, whether foreign or domestic, with which the reporting corporation had a transaction of the types described in paragraphs (b) (3) and (4) of this section during its taxable year, including the following information:

(i) The name, U.S. taxpayer identification number, if applicable, and address of the related party.

(ii) The nature of the related party's business and the principal place or places where it conducts its business.

(iii) Each country in which the related party files an income tax return as a resident under the tax laws of that country.

(iv) The relationship of the reporting corporation to the related party (including, to the extent the form may prescribe, any intermediate relationships).

(3) *Foreign related party transactions for which only monetary consideration is paid or received by the reporting corporation.*—If the related party is a foreign person, the reporting corporation must set forth on Form 5472 the dollar amounts of all reportable transactions for which monetary consideration (including U.S. and foreign currency) was the sole consideration paid or received during the taxable year of the reporting corporation. The total amount of such transactions, as well as the separate amounts for each type of transaction described below, and, to the extent the form may prescribe, any further description, categorization, or listing of transactions within these types, must be reported on Form 5472, in the manner the form or its instructions may prescribe. Where actual amounts are not determinable, a reasonable estimate (as described in paragraph (b)(6) of this section) is permitted. The types of transactions described in this paragraph are:

(i) Sales and purchases of stock in trade (inventory);

(ii) Sales and purchases of tangible property other than stock in trade;

(iii) Rents and royalties paid and received (other than amounts reported under paragraph (b)(3)(iv) of this section);

(iv) Sales, purchases, and amounts paid and received as consideration for the use of all intangible property, including (but not limited to) copyrights, designs, formulas, inventions, models, patents, processes, trademarks, and other similar intangible property rights;

(v) Consideration paid and received for technical, managerial, engineering, construction, scientific, or other services;

(vi) Commissions paid and received;

(vii) Amounts loaned and borrowed (except open accounts resulting from sales and purchases reported under other items listed in this paragraph (b)(3) that arise and are collected in full in the ordinary course of business), to be reported as monthly averages or outstanding balances at the beginning and end of the taxable year, as the form shall prescribe;

(viii) Interest paid and received;

(ix) Premiums paid and received for insurance and reinsurance;

(x) Other amounts paid or received not specifically identified in this paragraph (b)(3) to the extent that such amounts are taken into account for the determination and computation of the taxable income of the reporting corporation; and

(xi) With respect to an entity that is a reporting corporation as a result of being treated as a corporation under §301.7701-2(c)(2)(vi) of this chapter, any other transaction as defined by §1.482-1(i)(7), such as amounts paid or received in connection with the formation, dissolution, acquisition and disposition of the entity, including contributions to and distributions from the entity.

(4) *Foreign related party transactions involving nonmonetary consideration or less than full consideration.*—If the related party is a foreign person, the reporting corporation must provide on Form 5472 a description of any reportable transaction, or group of reportable transactions, listed in paragraph (b)(3) of this section, for which any part of the consideration paid or received was not monetary consideration, or for which less than full consideration was paid or received. A description required under paragraph (b)(4) of this section shall include sufficient information from which to determine the nature and approximate monetary value of the transaction or group of transactions, and shall include:

(i) A description of all property (including monetary consideration), rights, or obligations transferred from the reporting corporation to the foreign related party and from the foreign related party to the reporting corporation;

(ii) A description of all services performed by the reporting corporation for the foreign related party and by the foreign related party for the reporting corporation; and

(iii) A reasonable estimate of the fair market value of all properties and services exchanged, if possible, or some other reasonable indicator of value.

If, for any transaction, the entire consideration received includes both tangible and intangible property and the consideration paid is solely monetary consideration, the transaction should be reported under paragraph (b)(3) of this section if the intangible property was related and incidental to the transfer of the tangible property (for example, a right to warranty services.)

(5) *Additional information.*—In addition to the information required under paragraphs (b)(3) and (4) of this section, a reporting corporation must provide on Form 5472, in the manner the form prescribes, the following information:

(i) If the reporting corporation imports goods from a foreign related party, whether the costs taken into account in computing the basis or inventory cost of such goods are greater than the costs taken into account in computing the valuation of the goods for customs purposes, adjusted pursuant to section 1059A and the regulations thereunder, and if so, the reasons for the difference.

(ii) If the costs taken into account in computing the basis or inventory cost of such goods are greater than the costs taken into account in computing the valuation of the goods for customs purposes, whether the documents supporting the reporting corporation's treatment of the items set forth in paragraph (b)(5)(i) of this section are in existence and available in the United States at the time Form 5472 is filed.

(iii) If, for the taxable year, a reporting corporation pays or accrues interest or royalties for which a deduction is disallowed under section 267A and the regulations in this part under section 267A, then the reporting corporation must provide such information about the disallowance in the form and manner and to the extent prescribed by Form 5472 (or successor form), instruction, publication, or other guidance.

(iv) If, for the taxable year, the reporting corporation has a deduction under section 250 (by reason of having foreign-derived intangible income) with respect to any amount required to be reported under paragraph (b)(3) or (4) of this section, the reporting corporation will provide on Form 5472 (or any successor form) such information about the deduction in the form and manner and to the extent prescribed by Form 5472 (or any successor form), instructions to the form, publication, or other guidance published in the Internal Revenue Bulletin.

(6) *Compilation of reportable transactions across multiple related parties.*—A reporting corporation must, to the extent and in the manner Form 5472 or its instructions may prescribe, include a schedule tabulating information with respect to related parties for which the reporting corporation is required to file Forms 5472. The schedule will not require information (beyond totaling) that is not required for the individual Forms 5472. The schedule may include the following:

(i) The identity and status of the related parties;

(ii) The reporting corporation's relationship to the related parties;

(iii) The reporting corporation's reportable transactions with the related parties; and

(iv) Other items required to be reported on Form 5472.

(7) *Information on Form 5472 and Form 8991 regarding base erosion payments.*—If any reporting corporation is an applicable taxpayer, as defined under § 1.59A-2(b), it must report the information required by Form 8991 and by any Form 5472 it is required to file (including the information required by their accompanying instructions), regarding:

(i) Determination of whether a taxpayer is an applicable taxpayer;

(ii) Computation of base erosion minimum tax amount, including computation of regular tax liability as adjusted for purposes of computing base erosion minimum tax amount;

(iii) Computation of modified taxable income;

(iv) Base erosion tax benefits;

(v) Base erosion percentage calculation;

(vi) Base erosion payments;

(vii) Amounts with respect to services as described in § 1.59A-3(b)(3)(i), including a breakdown of the amount of the total services cost and any mark-up component;

(viii) Arrangements or transactions described in § 1.59A-9;

(ix) Any qualified derivative payment, including:

(A) The aggregate amount of qualified derivative payments for the taxable year; and

(B) A representation that all payments satisfy the requirements of § 1.59A-6(b)(2); and

(x) Any other information necessary to carry out section 59A.

(8) *Reasonable estimate.*—(i) *Estimate within 25 percent of actual amount.*—Any amount reported under this section is considered to be a reasonable estimate if it is at least 75 percent and not more than 125 percent of the actual amount.

(ii) *Other estimates.*—If any amount reported under this paragraph (b) of this section fails to meet the reasonable estimate test of paragraph (b)(6)(i) of this section, the reporting corporation nevertheless may show that such amount is a reasonable estimate by making an affirmative showing of relevant facts and circumstances in a written statement containing a declaration that it is made under the penalties of perjury. The District Director shall determine whether the amount reported was a reasonable estimate.

(9) *Small amounts.*—If any actual amount required under this section does not exceed $50,000, the amount may be reported as "$50,000 or less."

(10) *Accrued payments and receipts.*—For purposes of this section, a reporting corporation that uses an accrual method of accounting shall use accrued payments and accrued receipts for purposes of computing the total amount of each of the types of transactions listed in this section.

(11) *Examples.*—The following examples illustrate the application of paragraph (b)(3) of this section:

Example 1. (i) In year 1, W, a foreign corporation, forms and contributes assets to X, a domestic limited liability company that does not elect to be treated as a corporation under § 301.7701-3(c) of this chapter. In year 2, W contributes funds to X. In year 3, X makes a payment to W. In year 4, X, in liquidation, distributes its assets to W.

(ii) In accordance with § 301.7701-3(b)(1)(ii) of this chapter, X is disregarded as an entity separate from W. In accordance with § 301.7701-2(c)(2)(vi) of this chapter, X is treated as an entity separate from W and classified as a domestic corporation for purposes of section 6038A. In accordance with paragraphs (a)(2) and (b)(3) of this section, each of the transactions in years 1 through 4 is a reportable transaction with respect to X. Therefore, X has a section 6038A reporting and record maintenance requirement for each of those years.

Example 2. (i) The facts are the same as in *Example 1* of this paragraph (b)(9) except that, in year 1, W also forms and contributes assets to Y, another domestic limited liability company that does not elect to be treated as a corporation under § 301.7701-3(c) of this chapter. In year 1, X and Y form and contribute assets to Z, another domestic limited liability company that does not elect to be treated as a corporation under § 301.7701-3(c) of this chapter. In year 2, X transfers funds to Z. In year 3, Z makes a payment to Y. In year 4, Z distributes its assets to X and Y in liquidation.

(ii) In accordance with § 301.7701-3(b)(1)(ii) of this chapter, Y and Z are disregarded as entities separate from each other, W, and X. In accordance with § 301.7701-2(c)(2)(vi) of this chapter, Y, Z and X are treated as entities separate from each other and W, and are classified as domestic corporations for purposes of section 6038A. In accordance with paragraph (b)(3) of this section, each of the transactions in years 1 through 4 involving Z is a reportable transaction with respect to Z. Similarly, W's contribution to Y and Y's contribution to Z in year 1, the payment to Y in year 3, and the distribution to Y in year 4 are reportable transactions with respect to Y. Moreover, X's contribution to Z in Year 1, X's funds transfer to Z in year 2, and the distribution to X in year 4 are reportable transactions with respect to X. Therefore, Z has a section 6038A reporting and record maintenance requirement for years 1 through 4; Y has a section 6038A reporting and record maintenance requirement for years 1, 3, and 4; and X has a section 6038A reporting and record maintenance requirement in years 1, 2, and 4 in addition to its section 6038A reporting and record maintenance described in *Example 1* of this paragraph (b)(9).

(c) *Method of reporting.*—All statements required on or with the Form 5472 or Form 8991 under this section and § 1.6038A-5 must be in the English language. All amounts required to be reported under paragraph (b) of this section must be expressed in United States currency, with a statement of the exchange rates used, and, to the extent the forms may require, must indicate the method by which the amount of a reportable transaction or item was determined.

(d) *Time for filing returns.*—A Form 5472 and Form 8991 required under this section must be filed with the reporting corporation's income tax return for the taxable year by the due date (including extensions) of that return. In the case of an entity that is a reporting corporation as a result of being treated as a corporation under § 301.7701-2(c)(2)(vi) of this chapter, Form 5472 must be filed at such time and in such manner as the Commissioner may prescribe in forms or instructions.

(e) *Exceptions.*—(1) *No reportable transactions.*—A reporting corporation is not required to file Form 5472 if it has no transactions of the types listed in paragraphs (b)(3) and (4) of this section during the taxable year with any related party.

(2) *Transactions solely with a domestic reporting corporation.*—If all of a foreign reporting corporation's reportable transactions are with one or more related domestic reporting corporations that are not members of the same affiliated group, the foreign reporting corporation shall furnish on Form 5472 only the information required under paragraphs (b)(1) and (2) of this section, if the domestic reporting corporations provide the information required under paragraphs (b)(3) through (5) of this section. Such a foreign reporting corporation nonetheless is subject to the record maintenance requirements of § 1.6038A-3 and the requirements of § § 1.6038A-5 and 1.6038A-6. The name, address, and taxpayer identification number of each domestic reporting corporation that provided such information must be indicated on Form 5472 in the space provided for the information under paragraphs (b)(1) and (2) of this section.

(3) *Transactions with a corporation subject to reporting under section 6038.*—A reporting corporation (other than an entity that is a reporting corporation as a result of being treated as a corporation under § 301.7701-2(c)(2)(vi) of this chapter) is not required to make a return of information on Form 5472 with respect to a related foreign corporation for a taxable year for which a U.S. person that controls the foreign related corporation makes a return of information on Form 5471 that is required under section 6038 and this section, if that return contains information required under § 1.6038-2(f)(11) with respect to the reportable transactions between the reporting corporation and the related corporation for that taxable year. Such a reporting corporation also is not subject to § § 1.6038A-3 and 1.6038A-5. It remains subject to the general record maintenance requirements of section 6001.

(4) *Transactions with a foreign sales corporation.*—A reporting corporation (other than an entity that is a reporting corporation as a result of being treated as a corporation under § 301.7701-2(c)(2)(vi) of this chapter) is not required to make a return of information on Form 5472 with respect to a related corporation that qualifies as a foreign sales corporation for a taxable year for which the foreign sales corporation files Form 1120-FSC.

(f) *Filing Form 5472 when transactions with related parties engaged in by a partnership are attributed to a reporting corporation.*—If transactions engaged in by a partnership are attributed under § 1.6038A-1(e)(2) to a reporting corporation, the reporting corporation need report on Form 5472 only the percentage of the value of the transaction or transactions equal to the percentage of its partnership interest. Thus, for example, if a partnership buys $1000 of widgets from the foreign parent of a reporting corporation whose partnership interest in the partnership equals 50 percent of the partnership interests (and the remaining 50 percent is held by unrelated parties), the reporting corporation must report $500 of purchases from a foreign related party on Form 5472.

(g) *Effective/applicability date.*—Except as otherwise provided, for applicability dates for this section for certain reporting corporations, see § 1.6038A-1(n). Paragraph (b)(10) of this section applies with respect to information for annual accounting periods beginning on or after June 21, 2006. Paragraph (b)(7)(ix) of this section applies to taxable years beginning on or after June 7, 2021. Before these final regulations are applicable, a taxpayer will be treated as satisfying the reporting requirement described in § 1.59A-6(b)(2) only to the extent that it reports the aggregate amount of qualified derivative payments on Form 8991. *See* § 1.59A-6(b)(2)(iv) (transition period for qualified derivative payment reporting). Paragraph (b)(5)(iii) of this section applies with respect to information for annual accounting periods beginning on or after December 20, 2018. Paragraph (b)(5)(iv) of this section applies with respect to information for annual accounting periods beginning on or after March 4, 2019. [Reg. § 1.6038A-2.]

☐ [*T.D.* 8353, 6-14-91. *Amended by T.D.* 9113, 2-6-2004; *T.D.* 9161, 9-14-2004; *T.D.* 9268, 6-20-2006; *T.D.* 9338, 7-12-2007; *T.D.* 9529, 6-9-2011; *T.D.* 9667, 6-5-2014; *T.D.* 9707, 12-23-2014; *T.D.* 9796, 12-12-2016; *T.D.* 9885, 12-2-2019 (*corrected* 2-18-2020); *T.D.* 9896, 4-7-2020 *and T.D.* 9901, 7-9-2020.]

§ 1.6038A-3. Record maintenance.—(a) *General maintenance requirements.*—(1) *Section 6001 and section 6038A.*—A reporting corporation must keep the permanent books of account or records as required by section 6001 that are sufficient to establish the correctness of the federal income tax return of the corporation, including information, documents, or records ("records") to the extent they may be relevant to determine the correct U.S. tax treatment of transactions with related parties. Under section 6001, the District Director may require any person to make such returns, render such statements, or keep such specific records as will enable the District Director to determine whether or not that person is liable for any of the taxes to which the regulations under Part I have application. *See* section 6001 and the regulations thereunder. Such records must be permanent, accurate, and complete, and must clearly establish income, deductions, and credits. Additionally, in appropriate cases, such records include sufficient relevant cost data from which a profit and loss statement may be prepared for products or services transferred between a reporting corporation and its foreign related parties. This requirement includes records of the reporting corporation itself, as well as to records of any foreign related party that may be relevant to determine the correct U.S. tax treatment of transactions between the reporting corporation and foreign related parties. The relevance of such records with respect to related party transactions shall be determined upon the basis of all the facts and circumstances. Section 6038A and this section provide detailed guidance regarding the required maintenance of records with respect to such transactions and specify penalties for noncompliance. Banks and other financial institutions shall follow the specific record maintenance rules described in paragraph (h) of this section.

(2) *Safe harbor.*—A safe harbor for record maintenance is provided under paragraph (c) of this section, which sets forth detailed guidance concerning the types of records to be maintained with respect to related party transactions. The safe harbor consists of an all-inclusive list of record types that could be relevant to different taxpayers under a variety of facts and circumstances. It does not constitute a checklist of records that every reporting corporation must maintain or that generally should be requested by the Service. A specific reporting corporation is required to maintain, and the Service will request, only those records enumerated in the safe harbor (including material profit and loss statements) that may be relevant to its business or industry and to the correct U.S. tax treatment of its transactions with its foreign related parties. Accordingly, not every item listed in the safe harbor must be maintained by every reporting corporation. A corporation that maintains or causes another person to maintain the records listed in paragraph (c)(2) of this section that may be relevant to its foreign related party transactions and to its business or industry will be deemed to have met the record maintenance requirements of section 6038A.

(3) *Examples.*—The following examples illustrate the rules of this paragraph.

Example 1. RC, a U.S. reporting corporation, is owned by two shareholders, F and P. F is a foreign corporation that owns 30 percent of the stock of RC. P is a domestic corporation that owns the remaining 70 percent. RC purchases tangible property from F; however, the only potential audit issue with respect to these transactions is their treatment under section 482. It is determined that F does not in fact control RC and the two corporations do not constitute a group of "controlled taxpayers" for purposes of section 482 and the regulations thereunder. There are no other reportable transactions between RC and F. Under § 1.6038A-1(g), F is a foreign related party with respect to RC. Accordingly, RC is required to report its purchases of property from F under the reporting requirements of § 1.6038A-2. Nevertheless, because section 482 is not applicable to the transactions between RC and F, the records created by F with respect to its sales to RC are not relevant for purposes of determining the correct tax treatment of these transactions. RC is required to maintain its own records of these transactions under the requirements of section 6001, but the transactions are not subject to the record maintenance requirements of this section. If, however, on audit it is determined that F does control RC, all records relevant to determining the arm's length consideration for the tangible property under section 482 will be subject to these requirements.

Example 2. FP, a foreign person, owns 30 percent of the stock of RC, a reporting corporation. The remaining 70 percent of RC stock is held by persons that are not 25-percent foreign shareholders. It is determined that FP is related to RC within the meaning of section 482 and the regulations thereunder. The only transactions between FP and RC are FP's capital contributions, dividends paid from RC to FP, and loans from FP to RC. Under section 6001, RC is required to maintain all documentation necessary to establish the U.S. tax treatment of the capital contributions, dividends, and loans. RC is not required to maintain records in other categories listed in paragraph (c)(3) of this section because they are not relevant to the transactions between FP and RC. Records of FP not related to these transactions are not subject to the record maintenance requirements under section 6038A(a) and this section.

Example 3. G, a foreign multinational group, creates Sub, a wholly-owned U.S. subsidiary, in order to purchase tangible property from unrelated parties in the United States and resell such property to G. The property purchased by Sub is either used in G's business or resold to other unrelated parties by G. Sub's sole function is to act as a buyer for G and these purchases are the only transactions that G has with any U.S. affiliates. Under all the facts and circumstances of this case, it is determined that an analysis of the group's worldwide profit attributable to the property it purchases from Sub is not relevant for purposes of determining the tax treatment of the sales from Sub to G. Therefore, the records with respect to the profitability of G are not subject to the record maintenance requirements of this section. However, all records related to the appropriate method under section 482 for determining an arm's-length consideration for the property sold by Sub to G are subject to the record maintenance requirements of this section.

Example 4. S, a U.S. reporting corporation, provides computer consulting services for its foreign parent, X. Based on the application of section 482 and the regulations, it is determined that the cost of services plus method, as described in § 1.482-9(e), will provide the most reliable measure of an arm's length result, based on the facts and circumstances of the controlled transaction between S and X. S is required to maintain records to permit verification upon audit of the comparable transactional costs (as described in § 1.482-9(e)(2)(iii)) used to calculate the arm's length price. Based on the facts and circumstances, if it is determined that X's records are relevant to determine the correct U.S. tax treatment of the controlled transaction between S and X, the record maintenance requirements under section 6038A(a) and this section will be applicable to the records of X.

(b) *Other maintenance requirements.*—(1) *Indirectly related records.*— This section applies to records that are directly or indirectly related to transactions between the reporting corporation and any foreign related parties. An example of records that are indirectly related to such transactions is records possessed by a foreign subsidiary of a foreign related party that document the raw material or component costs of a product that is manufactured or assembled by the subsidiary and sold as a finished product by the foreign related party to the reporting corporation.

(2) *Foreign related party or third-party maintenance.*—If records that are required to be maintained under this section are in the control of a foreign related party, the records may be obtained or compiled (if not already in the possession of the foreign related party or already compiled) under the direction of the reporting corporation and then maintained by the reporting corporation, the foreign related party, or a third party. Thus, for example, a foreign related party may either itself maintain such records outside the United States or permit a third party to maintain such records outside the United States, provided that the conditions described in paragraph (f) of this section are met. Upon a request for such records by the Service, a foreign related party or third party may make arrangements with the District Director to furnish the records directly, rather than through the reporting corporation.

(3) *Translation of records.*—When records are provided to the Service under a request for production, any portion of such records must be translated into the English language within 30 days of a request for translation of that portion by the District Director. To the extent that any requested documents are identical to documents that have already been translated, an explanation of how such documents are identical instead may be provided. An extension of this time period may be requested under paragraph (f)(4) of this section. Appropriate extensions will be liberally granted for translation requests where circumstances warrant. If a good faith effort is made to translate accurately the requested documents within the specified time period, the reporting corporation will not be subject to the penalties in § § 1.6038A-4 and 1.6038A-7.

(4) *Exception for foreign governments.*—A foreign government is not subject to the obligation to maintain records under this section.

(5) *Records relating to conduit financing arrangements.*—See § 1.881-4 relating to conduit financing arrangements.

(c) *Specific records to be maintained for safe harbor.*—(1) *In general.*— A reporting corporation that maintains or causes another person to maintain the records specified in this paragraph (c) that are relevant to its business or industry and to the correct U.S. tax treatment of its transactions with its foreign related parties will be deemed to have met the record maintenance requirements of this section. This paragraph provides general descriptions of the categories of records to be maintained; the particular title or label applied by a reporting corporation or related party does not control. Functional equivalents of the specified documents are acceptable. Record maintenance in accordance with this safe harbor, however, requires only the maintenance of types of documents described in paragraph (c)(2) of this section that are directly or indirectly related to transactions between the reporting corporation and any foreign related party. Additionally, to the extent the reporting corporation establishes that records in a particular category are not applicable to the industry or business of the reporting corporation and any foreign related party, maintenance of such records is not required under this paragraph. Record maintenance in accordance with this paragraph (c) generally does not require the original creation of records that are ordinarily not created by the reporting corporation or its related parties. (If, however, a document that is actually created is described in this paragraph (c), it is to be maintained even if the document is not of the type ordinarily created by the reporting corporation or its related parties.) There are two exceptions to the rule. First, basic accounting records that are sufficient to document the U.S. tax effects of transactions between related parties must be created and retained, if they do not otherwise exist. Second, records sufficient to produce material profit and loss statements as described in paragraphs (c)(2)(ii) and (3) of this section that are relevant for determining the U.S. tax treatment of transactions between the reporting corporation and foreign related parties must be created if such records are not ordinarily maintained. All internal records storage and retrieval systems used for each taxable year must be retained.

(2) *Descriptions of categories of documents to be maintained.*—The following records must be maintained in order to satisfy this paragraph (c) to the extent they may be relevant to determine the correct U.S. tax treatment of transactions between the reporting corporation and any foreign related party.

(i) *Original entry books and transaction records.*—This category includes books and records of original entry or their functional equivalents, however designated or labelled, that are relevant to transactions between any foreign related party and the reporting corporation. Examples include, but are not limited to, general ledgers, sales journals, purchase order books, cash receipts books, cash disbursement books, canceled checks and bank statements, workpapers, sales contracts, and purchase invoices. Descriptive material to explicate entries in the foregoing types of records, such as a chart of accounts or an accounting policy manual, is included in this category.

(ii) *Profit and loss statements.*—This category includes records from which the reporting corporation can compile and supply, within a reasonable time, material profit and loss statements of the reporting corporation and all related parties as defined in § 1.6038A-1(d) the "related party group") that reflect profit or loss of the related party group attributable to U.S.-connected products or services as defined in paragraph (c)(7)(i) of this section. The determination of whether a profit and loss statement is material is made under the rules provided in paragraph (c)(3) of this section. The material profit and loss statements described in this paragraph (c)(2)(ii) must reflect the consolidated revenue and expenses of all members of the related party group. Thus, records in this category include the documentation of the cost of raw materials used by a related party to manufacture finished goods that are then sold by another related party to the reporting corporation. The records should be kept under U.S. generally accepted accounting principles if they are ordinarily maintained in such manner; if not, an explanation of the material differences between the accounting principles used and U.S. generally accepted accounting principles must be made available. The statements need not reflect tracing of the actual costs borne by the group with respect to its U.S.-connected products or services; rather, any reasonable method may be used to allocate the group's worldwide costs to the revenues generated by the sales of those products or services. An explanation of the methods used to allocate specific items to a particular profit and loss statement must be made available. The explanation of material differences between accounting principles and the explanation of allocation methods must be sufficient to permit a comparison of the profitability of the group to that of the reporting corporation attributable to the provision of U.S.-connected products or services.

(iii) *Pricing documents.*—This category includes all documents relevant to establishing the appropriate price or rate for transactions between the reporting corporation and any foreign related party. Examples include, but are not limited to, documents related to transactions involving the same or similar products or services entered into by the reporting corporation or a foreign related party with related and unrelated parties; shipping and export documents; commission agreements; documents relating to production or assembly facilities; third-party and intercompany purchase invoices; manuals, specifications, and similar documents relating to or describing the performance of functions conducted at particular locations; intercompany correspondence discussing any instructions or assistance relating to such transactions provided to the reporting corporations by the related foreign person (or vice versa); intercompany and intracompany correspondence concerning the price or the negotiation of the price used in such transactions; documents related to the value and ownership of intangibles used or developed by the reporting corporation or the foreign related party; documents related to cost of goods sold and other expenses; and documents related to direct and indirect selling, and general and administrative expenses (for example, relating to advertising, sales promotions, or warranties).

(iv) *Foreign country and third party filings.*—This category includes financial and other documents relevant to transactions between a reporting corporation and any foreign related party filed with or prepared for any foreign government entity, any independent commission, or any financial institution.

(v) *Ownership and capital structure records.*—This category includes records or charts showing the relationship between the reporting corporation and the foreign related party; the location, ownership, and status (for example, joint venture, partnership, branch, or division) of all entities and offices directly or indirectly involved in the transactions between the reporting corporation and any foreign related party; a worldwide organization chart; records showing the management structure of all foreign affiliates; and loan documents, agreements, and other documents relating to any transfer of the stock of the reporting corporation that results in the change of the status of a foreign person as a foreign related party.

(vi) *Records of loans, services, and other non-sales transactions.*—This category includes relevant documents relating to loans (including all deposits by one foreign related party or reporting corporation with an unrelated party and a subsequent loan by that unrelated party to a foreign related party or reporting corporation that is in substance a direct loan between a reporting corporation and a foreign related party); guarantees of a foreign related party of debts of the reporting corporation, and vice versa; hedging arrangements or other risk shifting or currency risk shifting arrangements involving the reporting corporation and any foreign related party; security agreements between the reporting corporation and any foreign related party; research and development expense allocations between any foreign related party and the reporting corporation; service transactions between any foreign related party and the reporting corporation, including, for example, a description of the allocation of charges for management services, time or travel records, or allocation studies; import and export transactions between a reporting corporation and any foreign related party; the registration of patents and copyrights with respect to transactions between the reporting corporation and any foreign related party; and documents regarding lawsuits in foreign countries that relate to such transactions between a reporting corporation and any foreign related party (for example, product liability suits for U.S. products).

(vii) *Records relating to conduit financing arrangements.*—See § 1.881-4 relating to conduit financing arrangements.

(3) *Material profit and loss statements.*—For purposes of paragraph (c)(2)(ii) of this section, the determination of whether a profit and loss statement is material will be made according to the following rules. An agreement between the reporting corporation and the District Director as described in paragraph (e) of this section may identify material profit and loss statements of the related party group and describe the items to be included in any profit and loss statements for which records are to be maintained to satisfy the requirements of paragraph (c)(2)(ii) of this section. In the absence of such an agreement, a profit and loss statement will be material if it meets any of the following tests: the existing records test described in paragraph (c)(4) of this section, the significant industry segment test described in paragraph (c)(5) of this section, or the high profit test described in paragraph (c)(6) of this section.

(4) *Existing records test.*—A profit and loss statement is material under the existing records test described in this paragraph (c)(4) if any member of the related party group creates or compiles such statement in the course of its business operations and the statement reflects the profit or loss of the related party group attributable to the provision of U.S.-connected products or services (regardless of whether the profit and loss attributable to U.S.-connected products or services is shown separately or included within the calculation of aggregate figures on the statement). For example, a profit and loss statement is described in this paragraph if it was produced for internal accounting or management purposes, or for disclosure to shareholders, financial institutions, government agencies, or any other persons. Such existing statements and the records from which they were compiled (to the extent such records relate to profit and loss attributable to U.S.-connected products or services) are subject to the record maintenance requirements described in paragraph (c)(2)(ii) of this section.

(5) *Significant industry segment test.*—(i) *In general.*—A profit and loss statement is material under the significant industry segment test described in this paragraph (c)(5) if—

(A) The statement reflects the profit or loss of the related party group attributable to the group's provision of U.S.-connected products or services within a single industry segment (as defined in paragraph (c)(7)(ii) of this section);

(B) The worldwide gross revenue attributable to such industry segment is 10 percent or more of the worldwide gross revenue attributable to the group's combined industry segments; and

(C) The amount of gross revenue earned by the group from the provision of U.S.-connected products or services within such industry segment is $25 million or more in the taxable year.

(ii) *Form of the statements.*—Profit and loss statements compiled for the group's provision of U.S.-connected products or services in each significant industry segment must reflect revenues and expenses attributable to the operations in such segment by all members of the related party group. Statements may show each related party's revenues and expenses separately, or may be prepared in a consolidated format. Any reasonable method may be used to allocate the group's worldwide costs within the industry segment to the U.S.-connected products or services within that segment. An explanation of the methods used to prepare consolidated statements and to allocate specific items to a particular profit and loss statement must be made available, and the records from which the consolidations and allocations were prepared must be maintained.

(iii) *Special rule for component sales.*—Where the U.S.-connected products or services consist of components that are incorporated into other products or services before sale to customers, the portion of the total gross revenue derived from sales of the finished products or services attributable to the components may be determined on the basis of relative costs of production. Thus, where relevant for determining whether the $25 million threshold in paragraph (c)(5)(i)(C) of this section has been met, the amount of gross revenue derived by the related party group from the provision of the finished products or services may be reduced by multiplying it by a fraction, the numerator of which is the costs of production of the related party group attributable to the component products or services that constitute U.S.-connected products or services and the denominator of which is the costs of production of the related party group attributable to the finished products in which such components are incorporated.

(iv) *Level of specificity required.*—In applying the significant industry segment test of this paragraph (c)(5), groups of related products and services must be chosen to provide a reasonable level of specificity that results in the greatest number of separate significant industry segments in comparison to other possible classifications. This determination must be made on the basis of the particular facts presented by the operations of the related party group. The following rules, however, provide general guidelines for making such classifications. First, the related party group's operations that involve the provision of U.S.-connected products should be grouped into product lines. The rules of this paragraph (c)(5) should then be applied to determine if any such product line would, standing alone, constitute a significant industry segment when compared to the related party group's operations as a whole. Any significant industry segments determined at the level of product lines should be further segregated, and tested for significant industry segments, at the level of separate products. Finally, any significant industry segments determined at the level of separate products should be segregated, and tested for significant industry segments, at the level of separate models. Similar principles should be applied in classifying and testing types of services. A profit and loss statement reflecting the related party group's provision of any product or service (or group of products or services as classified under these rules) that constitutes a significant industry segment will be considered material for purposes of this paragraph (c)(5). For definitions of the terms "product", "related products or services", "model", and "product line", see paragraph (c)(7) of this section.

(v) *Examples.*—The rules for determining reasonable levels of specificity for significant industry segments may be illustrated by the following examples.

Example 1. A related party group is engaged in the manufacture and worldwide sales of automobiles and aftermarket parts. The group's operations within the categories of "automobiles" and "aftermarket parts" are each sufficient to constitute significant industry segments for the group under the rules of this paragraph (c)(5). No narrower classification of aftermarket parts results in any significant industry segments. Automobiles produced by the group are generally classified for marketing purposes by trade names; aggregating groups of automobiles by these trade names results in three significant industry segments, those for trade names A, B, and C. Finally, two car models sold under the trade name A ("A1" and "A2") and one car model sold under the trade name B ("B3"), produce sufficient revenue to constitute significant industry segments. Such classifications into trade names and car models are generally used in the related party group's industry; moreover, different types of classifications would produce fewer significant industry segments. Accordingly, a reasonable level of specificity for this related party group's industry segments would be eight categories of products consisting of "automobiles", "aftermarket parts", "A", "B", "C", "A1", "A2", and "B3".

Example 2. A related party group is engaged in manufacturing electronic goods that are distributed at retail in the United States by the reporting corporation. The group sells three types of products in the United States: televisions, radios, and video cassette recorders (VCRs). Each of these three broad product areas constitutes a significant industry segment for the group as a whole. VCRs can be further segregated by price into high-end and low-end models, and the provision of each constitutes a significant industry segment for the group. Revenues from only one VCR model, model number VCRX-10, are sufficiently large to make the provision of that model a significant industry segment. With respect to televisions, the group normally accounts for these products by size. Using this classification, portable televisions, medium-sized televisions, and consoles each constitute significant industry segments. Narrower classifications by television model numbers result in no additional significant industry segments. Finally, a single radio product line, those sold under the trade name R, produces sufficient revenue to constitute a significant industry segment, but no other radio models or product groups are large enough to constitute a significant industry segment. In each case, these classifications conform to normal business practices in the industry and result in the greatest possible number of significant industry segments for this related party group. Accordingly, a reasonable level of specificity for this related party group's industry segments would include the ten categories consisting of "VCRs", "high-end VCRs", "low-end VCRs", "model number VCRX-10", "televisions", "portable televisions", "medium-sized televisions", "console televisions", "radios", and "radio trade name R".

(6) *High profit test.*—(i) *In general.*—A profit and loss statement is material under the high profit test described in this paragraph (c)(6) if—

(A) The statement reflects the profit or loss of the related party group attributable to the group's provision of U.S.-connected products or services within a single industry segment (as defined in paragraph (c)(7)(ii) of this section);

(B) The amount of gross revenue earned by the group from the provision of U.S.-connected products or services within such industry segment is $100 million or more in the taxable year; and

(C) The return on assets test described in paragraph (c)(6)(ii) of this section is satisfied with respect to the products and services attributable to such segment.

Accordingly, a significant industry segment (as determined under paragraph (c)(5) of this section) must be divided into any narrower industry segments that meet the high profit test of this paragraph (c)(6), even if such narrower segments would not, standing alone, meet the significant industry segment test of paragraph (c)(5) of this section.

(ii) *Return on assets test.*—An industry segment meets the return on assets test if the rate of return on assets earned by the related party group on its worldwide operations within this industry segment exceeds 15 percent, and is at least 200 percent of the return on assets earned by the group in all industry segments combined. For purposes of this paragraph, the rate of return on assets earned by an industry segment is determined by dividing that segment's operating profit (as defined in paragraph (c)(7)(v) of this section) by its identifiable assets (as defined in paragraph (c)(7)(iv) of this section).

(iii) *Additional rules.*—The rules in paragraphs (c)(5)(ii) through (iv) of this section describing the application of the significant industry segment test shall apply in a similar manner for purposes of the high profit test.

(7) *Definitions.*—The following definitions apply for purposes of paragraphs (c)(2)(ii), (c)(5), and (c)(6) of this section.

(i) *U.S.-connected products or services.*—The term "U.S.-connected products or services" means products or services that are imported to or exported from the United States by transfers between the reporting corporation and any of its foreign related parties.

(ii) *Industry segment.*—An industry segment is a segment of the related party group's combined operations that is engaged in providing a product or service or a group of related products or services (as defined in paragraph (c)(7)(vii) of this section) primarily to customers that are not members of the related party group.

(iii) *Gross revenue of an industry segment.*—Gross revenue of an industry segment includes receipts (prior to reduction for cost of goods sold) both from sales to customers outside of the related party group and from sales or transfers to other industry segments within the related party group (but does not include sales or transfers between members of the related party group within the same industry segment). Interest from sources outside the related party group and interest earned on trade receivables between industry segments is included in gross revenue if the asset on which the interest is earned is included among the industry segment's identifiable assets, but interest earned on advances or loans to other industry segments is not included.

(iv) *Identifiable assets of an industry segment.*—The identifiable assets of an industry segment are those tangible and intangible assets of the related party group that are used by the industry segment, including assets that are used exclusively by that industry segment and an allocated portion of assets used jointly by two or more industry segments. The value of an identifiable asset may be determined using any reasonable method (such as book value or fair market value) applied consistently. Any allocation of assets among industry segments must be made on a reasonable basis, and a description of such basis must be provided. Assets of an industry segment that transfers products or services to another industry segment shall not be allocated to the receiving segment. Assets that represent part of the related party group's investment in an industry segment, such as goodwill, shall be included in the industry segment's identifiable assets. Assets maintained for general corporate purposes (that is, those not used in the operations of any industry segment) shall not be allocated to industry segments.

(v) *Operating profit of an industry segment.*—The operating profit of an industry segment is its gross revenue (as defined in paragraph (c)(7)(iii) of this section) minus all operating expenses. None of the following shall be added or deducted in computing the operating profit of an industry segment: revenue earned at the corporate level and not derived from the operations of any industry segment; general corporate expenses; interest expense; domestic and foreign income taxes; and other extraordinary items not reflecting the ongoing business operations of the industry segment.

(vi) *Product.*—The term "product" means an item of property (or combination of component parts) that is the result of a production process, is primarily sold to unrelated parties (or incorporated by the related party group into other products sold to unrelated parties), and performs a specific function.

(vii) *Related products or services.*—The term "related products or services" means groupings of products and types of services that reflect reasonable accounting, marketing, or other business practices within the industries in which the related party group operates.

(viii) *Model.*—The term "model" means a classification of products that incorporate particular components, options, styles, and any other unique features resulting in product differentiation. Examples of models are electronic products that are sold or accounted for under a single model number and automobiles sold under a single model name.

(ix) *Product line.*—The term "product line" means a group of products that are aggregated into a single classification for accounting, marketing, or other business purposes. Examples of product lines are groups of products that perform similar functions; products that are marketed under the same trade names, brand names, or trademarks; and products that are related economically (that is, having similar rates of profitability, similar degrees of risk, and similar opportunities for growth).

(8) *Example.*—The application of the rules for determining material profit and loss statements under paragraphs (c)(4) through (7) of this section is illustrated by the following example.

Example. (i) *Facts.* A multinational enterprise manufactures 50 different agricultural and chemical products that are sold through Sub1, its wholly owned U.S. subsidiary, and other subsidiaries located in foreign countries. The parent company of the enterprise, P, is a foreign corporation. The corporations participating in the enterprise form a related party group, and Sub1 is a reporting corporation for purposes of section 6038A. Under the facts and circumstances of this case, an analysis of the group's worldwide profit attributable to its products sold in the U.S. is relevant for determining an arm's length consideration under section 482 for the transfers of goods between Sub1 and its foreign affiliates.

(ii) *Existing records test.* For management purposes, the group prepares profit and loss statements that are segmented by sales in different geographic markets. One of these statements shows the combined worldwide profitability of the group. Another statement shows the profitability of the group attributable to its North American sales. Both of these profit and loss statements reflect aggregate figures that include sales to unrelated parties of products that have been transferred from P and other group members to Sub1 (that is, the group's "U.S.-connected products"). The two statements meet the existing records test described in paragraph (c)(4) of this section.

(iii) *Significant industry segments.* The group's worldwide gross revenue in all industry segments is $2 billion. An analysis of the group's 50 products demonstrates that they are reasonably grouped into eight industry segments (each of which earns roughly $250 million in worldwide gross revenue). Segments 1 through 6 relate to agricultural products and Segments 7 and 8 relate to other chemical products. More specific categories would result in groupings that generate less than 10 percent of the group's worldwide gross revenue (that is, less than $200 million each); these narrower categories would thus fail the gross revenue percentage test of paragraph (c)(5)(i)(B) of this section. The gross revenue in each of the eight segments from the sale to unrelated parties of U.S.-connected products is as follows: $180 million for Segment 1; $30 million for Segment 2; and less than $25 million for each of Segments 3 through 8. Under the $25 million threshold test of paragraph (c)(5)(i)(C) of this section, the group's significant industry segments are thus limited to Segments 1 and 2. In addition, the combined operations of the group related to agricultural products (encompassing Segments 1 through 6 on an aggregated basis), constitute a single significant industry segment.

(iv) *High profit test.* One highly profitable product line within Segment 1, HPPL, accounts for $120 million gross revenue from Sub1's domestic sales of U.S.-connected products (and thus exceeds the $100 million gross revenue threshold in paragraph (c)(6)(i)(B) of this section). The return on the identifiable assets attributable to the HPPL product line is 85 percent, which is more than 15 percent and more than twice the return on assets earned by the group from its worldwide operations in its combined industry segments. The group's industry segment for HPPL thus meets the high profit test described in paragraph (c)(6) of this section.

(v) *Material Profit and Loss Statements.* The group's material profit and loss statements consist of statements for combined worldwide sales and North American sales (under the existing records test); Segment 1, Segment 2, and aggregated Segments 1-6 (under the significant industry segment test); and HPPL (under the high profit test). Under paragraph (c) of this section, Sub1 is required to retain the combined worldwide sales and North American sales profit and loss statements and to maintain sufficient records so that it can compile and supply upon request statements of the group's profitability from sales of its U.S.-connected products within Segment 1, Segment 2, aggregated Segments 1-6, and HPPL. These records need not be in the possession of Sub1 and may be kept under the control of and produced by P or any third party. The statements for Segment 1, Segment 2, aggregated Segments 1-6, and HPPL do not require tracing of actual costs to the U.S.-connected products; rather, these statements may be prepared by using any reasonable method to allocate a portion of the industry segment's overall operating costs to the sales of U.S.-connected products within that segment.

(d) *Liability for certain partnership record maintenance.*—A reporting corporation to which transactions engaged in by a partnership are attributed under § 1.6038A-1(e)(2) is subject to the record maintenance requirements of this section to the extent of the transactions so attributed.

(e) *Agreements with the District Director.*—(1) *In general.*—The District Director who has audit jurisdiction over the reporting corporation may negotiate and enter into an agreement with a reporting corporation that establishes the records the reporting corporation must maintain or cause another to maintain, how the records must be maintained, the period of retention for the records, and by whom the records must be maintained in order to satisfy the reporting corporation's obligations under this section.

(2) *Content of agreement.*—(i) *In general.*—The agreement may include provisions relating to the authorization of agent requirement, the record maintenance requirement, and the production and translation time periods that vary the rules contained in these regulations under section 6038A. The District Director will generally require a reporting corporation to maintain only those records specified under the safe harbor provisions of paragraph (c) of this section that permit an adequate audit of the income tax return of the reporting corporation and to provide such authorizations of agent that permit adequate access to such records. In most instances, required record maintenance for a particular reporting corporation under a negotiated agreement will be less than the broad range of records described under the safe harbor provisions. Additionally, a provision specifying the effective date and the expiration date of the agreement that may vary the effective date of the regulations may be included.

(ii) *Significant industry segment test.*—A District Director may determine which industry segment profit and loss statements are material for purposes of requiring the maintenance of records (under either paragraph (a)(1) of this section or the safe harbor described in paragraph (a)(2) of this section). The industry segments that the District Director determines are material need not be the industry segments that meet the significant industry segment test under paragraph (c)(5) of this section or the high profit test under paragraph (c)(6) of this section. For this purpose, a reporting corporation will be required to maintain only those records from which profit and loss statements for the related party group may be constructed with respect to industry segments identified by the District Director. To the extent that existing profit and loss statements are similar in scope and level of detail to statements for industry segments that would otherwise be described under the tests of paragraphs (c)(5) and (6) of this section, the District Director shall accept the existing statements instead of the statements that would otherwise be required under paragraphs (c)(5) and (6) of this section.

(iii) *Example.*—The following example illustrates the rules of paragraph (e)(2)(ii) of this section.

Example. The District Director determines that RC, a reporting corporation that is a manufacturer of related chemical products, has two industry segments, Segment 1 and Segment 2. While both industry segments meet the significant industry segment test of paragraph (c)(5) of this section, Segment 1 has a relatively low volume of sales to foreign related parties. Additionally, Segment 1 consists of products that produce only a small profit margin because the product is generic and other companies also sell the product. The District Director enters into an agreement with RC that requires only records from which a profit and loss statement for the related party group can be constructed for Segment 2. Therefore, RC is not required to maintain records for Segment 1 from which a profit and loss statement for the related party group can be constructed. The other record maintenance requirements under this section apply, however.

(3) *Circumstances of agreement.*—The District Director generally will enter into an agreement under this paragraph (e) upon request by the reporting corporation when the District Director believes that the District has or can obtain sufficient knowledge of the business or industry of the reporting corporation to limit the record maintenance requirement to particular documents.

(4) *Agreement as part of APA process.*—An agreement with a reporting corporation under this paragraph (e) may be entered into as a part of the Advance Pricing Agreement (APA) process at any time during the APA process, insofar as the agreement relates to the subject matter of the APA.

(f) *U.S. maintenance.*—(1) *General rule.*—Records that must be maintained under this section must be maintained within the United States, unless the conditions described in paragraph (f)(2) of this section are met.

(2) *Non-U.S. maintenance requirements.*—A reporting corporation may maintain outside the United States records not ordinarily maintained in the United States but required to be maintained in the United States under this section. However, the reporting corporation must either:

(i) Deliver to the Service the original documents (or duplicates) requested within 60 days of the request by the Service for such records and provide translations of such documents within 30 days of a request for translations of specific documents; or

(ii) Move the original documents (or duplicates) requested to the United States within 60 days of the request of the Service for such records; provide the Service with an index to the requested records, the name and address of a custodian located within the United States having control over the records, and the address where the records are located within 60 days of the Service's request for the records; and continue to maintain the records within the United States throughout the period of retention described in paragraph (g) of this section. For summons procedures with respect to records that have been moved to the United States, see sections 6038A(e), 7602, 7603, and 7604.

With respect to any material profit and loss statements required to be created (either under paragraph (c) of this section or under an agreement with the District Director), unless otherwise specified, "120 days" shall be substituted for "60 days" in this paragraph (f)(2), and labels and text with respect to such statements must be in the English language.

(3) *Prior taxable years.*—The non-U.S. maintenance requirements described in paragraph (f)(2) of this section apply to records located outside the United States that were in existence on or after March 20, 1990, without regard to the taxable year to which such records relate.

(4) *Scheduled production for high volume or other reasons.*—Upon a written request, for good cause shown, the District Director may grant an extension of the time for the production or translation of the requested documents. Such requests should be made within 30 days of the request for records by the Service. If an extension is needed because of the volume of records requested or the amount of translation requested, the District Director may allow production or translation to be scheduled over a period of time so that not all records need be produced or translated at the same time.

(5) *Required U.S. maintenance.*—The District Director (with the concurrence of the Assistant Commissioner (International)), may require, for cause, the maintenance within the United States of any records specified in paragraph (f)(1) of this section. Such a requirement will be imposed only if there exists a clear pattern of failure to maintain or timely produce the required records. The assessment of a monetary penalty under section 6038A(d) and § 1.6038A-4 for failure to maintain records is not necessarily sufficient to require the maintenance of records within the United States.

(g) *Period of retention.*—Records required to be maintained by section 6038A(a) and this section shall be kept as long as they may be relevant or material to determining the correct tax treatment of any transaction between the reporting corporation and a related party, but in no case less than the applicable statute of limitations on assessment and collection with respect to the taxable year in which the transaction or item to which the records relate affects the U.S. tax liability of the reporting corporation. *See* section 6001 and the regulations thereunder.

(h) *Application of record maintenance rules to banks and other financial institutions.*—[Reserved].

(i) *Effective/applicability date.*—(1) *In general.*—This section is generally applicable on December 10, 1990. However, records described in this section in existence on or after March 20, 1990, must be maintained, without regard to when the taxable year to which the records relate began. Paragraph (a)(3) *Example 4* of this section is generally applicable for taxable years beginning after July 31, 2009.

(2) *Election to apply regulation to earlier taxable years.*—A person may elect to apply the provisions of paragraph (a)(3) *Example 4* of this section to earlier taxable years in accordance with the rules set forth in § 1.482-9(n)(2). [Reg. § 1.6038A-3.]

☐ [*T.D. 8353, 6-14-91. Amended by T.D. 8611, 8-10-95; T.D. 9278,* 7-31-2006 and T.D. 9456, 7-31-2009.]

§ 1.6038A-4. Monetary penalty.—(a) *Imposition of monetary penalty.*—(1) *In general.*—If a reporting corporation fails to furnish the information described in § 1.6038A-2 within the time and manner prescribed in § 1.6038A-2(d), fails to maintain or cause another to maintain records as required by § 1.6038A-3, or (in the case of records maintained outside the United States) fails to meet the non-U.S. record maintenance requirements within the applicable time prescribed in § 1.6038A-3(f), a penalty of $25,000 shall be assessed for each taxable year with respect to which such failure occurs. The filing of a substantially incomplete Form 5472 constitutes a failure to file Form 5472. Where, however, the information described in § 1.6038A-2(b)(3) through Reg. § (5) is not required to be reported, a Form 5472 filed without such information is not a substantially incomplete Form 5472.

(2) *Liability for certain partnership transactions.*—A reporting corporation to which transactions engaged in by a partnership are attributed under § 1.6038A-1(e)(2) is subject to the rules of this section to the extent failures occur with respect to the partnership transactions so attributed.

(3) *Calculation of monetary penalty.*—If a reporting corporation fails to maintain records as required by § 1.6038A-3 of transactions with multiple related parties, the monetary penalty may be assessed for each failure to maintain records with respect to each related party. The monetary penalty, however, shall be imposed on a reporting corporation only once for a taxable year with respect to each related party for a failure to furnish the information required on Form 5472, for a failure to maintain or cause another to maintain records, or for a failure to comply with the non-U.S. maintenance requirements described in § 1.6038A-3(f). An additional penalty for another failure may be imposed, however, under the rules of paragraph (d)(2) of this section. Thus, unless such failures continue after notification as described in paragraph (d) of this section, the maximum penalty under this paragraph with respect to each related party for all such failures in a taxable year is $25,000. The members of a group of corporations filing a consolidated return are jointly and severally liable for any monetary penalty that may be imposed under this section.

(b) *Reasonable cause.*—(1) *In general.*—Certain failures may be excused for reasonable cause, including not timely filing Form 5472, not maintaining or causing another to maintain records as required by § 1.6038A-3, and not complying with the non-U.S. maintenance requirements described in § 1.6038A-3(f). If an affirmative showing is made that the taxpayer acted in good faith and there is reasonable cause for a failure that results in the assessment of the monetary penalty, the period during which reasonable cause exists shall be treated as beginning on the day reasonable cause is established and ending not earlier than the last day on which reasonable cause existed for any such failure. Additionally, the beginning of the 90-day period after mailing of a notice by the District Director or the Director of an Internal Revenue Service Center of a failure described in paragraph (d) of this section shall be treated as not earlier than the last day on which reasonable cause existed.

(2) *Affirmative showing required.*—(i) *In general.*—To show that reasonable cause exists for purposes of paragraph (b)(1) of this section, the reporting corporation must make an affirmative showing of all the facts alleged as reasonable cause for the failure in a written

statement containing a declaration that it is made under penalties of perjury. The statement must be filed with the District Director (in the case of failure to maintain or furnish requested information permitted to be maintained outside the United States within the time required under § 1.6038A-3(f) or a failure to file Form 5472) or the Director of the Internal Revenue Service Center where the Form 5472 is required to be filed (in the case of failure to file Form 5472). The District Director or the Director of the Internal Revenue Service Center where the Form 5472 is required to be filed, as appropriate, shall determine whether the failure was due to reasonable cause, and if so, the period of time for which reasonable cause existed. If a return has been filed as required by § 1.6038A-2 or records have been maintained as required by § 1.6038A-3, except for an omission of, or error with respect to, some of the information required or a record to be maintained, the omission or error shall not constitute a failure for purposes of section 6038A(d) if the reporting corporation that filed the return establishes to the satisfaction of the District Director or the Director of the Internal Revenue Service Center that it has substantially complied with the filing of Form 5472 or the requirement to maintain records.

(ii) *Small corporations*.—The District Director shall apply the reasonable cause exception liberally in the case of a small corporation that had no knowledge of the requirements imposed by section 6038A; has limited presence in and contact with the United States; and promptly and fully complies with all requests by the District Director to file Form 5472, and to furnish books, records, or other materials relevant to the reportable transaction. A small corporation is a corporation whose gross receipts for a taxable year are $20,000,000 or less.

(iii) *Facts and circumstances taken into account*.—The determination of whether a taxpayer acted with reasonable cause and in good faith is made on a case-by-case basis, taking into account all pertinent facts and circumstances. Circumstances that may indicate reasonable cause and good faith include an honest misunderstanding of fact or law that is reasonable in light of the experience and knowledge of the taxpayer. Isolated computational or transcriptional errors generally are not inconsistent with reasonable cause and good faith. Reliance upon an information return or on the advice of a professional (such as an attorney or accountant) does not necessarily demonstrate reasonable cause and good faith. Similarly, reasonable cause and good faith is not necessarily indicated by reliance on facts that, unknown to the taxpayer, are incorrect. Reliance on an information return, professional advice or other facts, however, constitutes reasonable cause and good faith if, under all the circumstances, the reliance was reasonable. A taxpayer, for example, may have reasonable cause for not filing a Form 5472 or for not maintaining records under section 6038A if the taxpayer has a reasonable belief that it is not owned by a 25-percent foreign shareholder. A reasonable belief means that the taxpayer does not know or has no reason to know that it is owned by a 25-percent foreign shareholder. For example, a reporting corporation would not know or have reason to know that it is owned by a 25-percent foreign shareholder if its belief that it is not so owned is consistent with other information reported or otherwise furnished to or known by the reporting corporation. A taxpayer may have reasonable cause for not treating a foreign corporation as a related party for purposes of section 6038A where the foreign corporation is a related party solely by reason of § 1.6038A-1(d)(3) (under the principles of section 482), and the taxpayer had a reasonable belief that its relationship with the foreign corporation did not meet the standards for related parties under section 482.

(c) *Failure to maintain records or to cause another to maintain records*.—A failure to maintain records or to cause another to maintain records is determined by the District Director upon the basis of the reporting corporation's overall compliance (including compliance with the non-U.S. maintenance requirements under § 1.6038A-3(f)(2)) with the record maintenance requirements. It is not an item-by-item determination. Thus, for example, a failure to maintain a single or small number of items may not constitute a failure for purposes of section 6038A(d), unless the item or items are essential to the correct determination of transactions between the reporting corporation and any foreign related parties. The District Director shall notify the reporting corporation in writing of any determination that it has failed to comply with the record maintenance requirement.

(d) *Increase in penalty where failure continues after notification*.—(1) *In general*.—If any failure described in this section continues for more than 90 days after the day on which the District Director or the Director of the Internal Revenue Service Center where the Form 5472 is required to be filed mails notice of the failure to the reporting corporation, the reporting corporation shall pay a penalty (in addition to the penalty described in paragraph (a) of this section) of $25,000 with respect to each related party for which a failure occurs for each 30-day period during which the failure continues after the expiration of the 90-day period. Any uncompleted fraction of a 30-day period shall count as a 30-day period for purposes of this paragraph (d).

(2) *Additional penalty for another failure*.—An additional penalty for a taxable year may be imposed, however, if at a time subsequent to the time of the imposition of the monetary penalty described in paragraph (a) of this section, a second failure is determined and the second failure continues after notification under paragraph (d)(1) of this section. Thus, if a taxpayer fails to file Form 5472 and is assessed a monetary penalty and later, upon audit, is determined to have failed to maintain records, an additional penalty for the failure to maintain records may be assessed under the rules of this paragraph if the failure to maintain records continues after notification under this paragraph.

(3) *Cessation of accrual*.—The monetary penalty will cease to accrue if the reporting corporation either files Form 5472 (in the case of a failure to file Form 5472), furnishes information to substantially complete Form 5472, or demonstrates compliance with respect to the maintenance of records (in the case of a failure to maintain records) for the taxable year in which the examination occurs and subsequent years to the satisfaction of the District Director. The monetary penalty also will cease to accrue if requested information, documents, or records, kept outside the United States under the requirements of § 1.6038A-3(f) and not produced within the time specified are produced or moved to the United States under the rules of paragraph (f)(2)(ii) of this section.

(4) *Continued failures*.—If a failure under this section relating to a taxable year beginning before July 11, 1989 occurs, and if the failure continues following 90 days after the notice of failure under this paragraph is sent, the amount of the additional penalty to be assessed under this paragraph is $25,000 for each 30-day period beginning after November 5, 1990, during which the failure continues. There is no limitation on the amount of the monetary penalty that may be assessed after November 5, 1990.

(e) *Other penalties*.—For criminal penalties for failure to file a return and filing a false or fraudulent return, see sections 7203 and 7206 of the Code. For the penalty relating to an underpayment of tax, see section 6662.

(f) *Examples*.—The following examples illustrate the rules of this section.

(1) *Example 1—Failure to file Form 5472*. Corp X, a U.S. reporting corporation, engages in related party transactions with FC. Corp X does not timely file a Form 5472 or maintain records relating to the transactions with FC for Year 1 or subsequent years. The Service Center with which Corp X files its income tax return imposes a $25,000 penalty for each of Years 1, 2, and 3 under section 6038A(d) and this section for failure to provide information as required on Form 5472 and mails a notice of failure to provide information. Corp X does not file Form 5472. Ninety days following the mailing of the notice of failure to Corp X an additional penalty of $25,000 is imposed. On the 135th day following the mailing of the notice of failure, Corp X files Form 5472 for Years 1, 2, and 3. The total penalty owed by Corp X for Year 1 is $75,000 ($25,000 for not timely filing Form 5472, $25,000 for the first 30-day period following the expiration of the 90-day period, and $25,000 for the fraction of the second 30-day period). The penalty for Years 2 and 3 for the failure to file Form 5472 is also $75,000 for each year, calculated in the same manner as for Year 1. The total penalty for failure to file Form 5472 for Years 1, 2, and 3 is $225,000.

(2) *Example 2—Failure to maintain records*. Assume the same facts as in *Example 1*. In Year 5, Corp X is audited for Years 1 through 3. Corp X has not been maintaining records relating to the transactions with FC. The District Director issues a notice of failure to maintain records. Corp X has already been subject to the monetary penalty of $25,000 for each of Years 1, 2, and 3 for failure to file Form 5472 and, therefore, a monetary penalty under paragraph (a) of this section for failure to maintain records is not assessed. However, an additional penalty is assessed after the 90th day following the mailing of the notice of failure to maintain records. Corp X develops a record maintenance system as required by section 6038A and § 1.6038A-3. On the 180th day following the mailing of the notice of failure to maintain records, Corp X demonstrates to the satisfaction of the District Director that the newly developed record maintenance sys-

tem will comply with the requirements of § 1.6038A-3 and the increase in the monetary penalty after notification ceases to accrue. The additional penalty for failure to maintain records is $75,000. An additional penalty of $75,000 per year is assessed for each of years 2 and 3 for the failure to maintain records for a total of $225,000.

(g) *Effective dates.*—For effective dates for this section, see § 1.6038A-1(n). [Reg. § 1.6038A-4.]

☐ [*T.D.* 8353, 6-14-91. *Amended by T.D.* 9707, 12-23-2014 *and T.D.* 9885, 12-2-2019.]

§ 1.6038A-5. Authorization of agent.—(a) *Failure to authorize.*—The rules of § 1.6038A-7 shall apply to any transaction between a foreign related party and a reporting corporation (including any transaction engaged in by a partnership that is attributed to the reporting corporation under § 1.6038A-1(e)(2)), unless the foreign related party authorizes (in the manner described in paragraph (b) of this section) the reporting corporation to act as its limited agent solely for purposes of sections 7602, 7603, and 7604 with respect to any request by the Service to examine records or produce testimony that may be relevant to the tax treatment of such a transaction or with respect to any summons by the Service for such records or testimony.

The fact that a reporting corporation is authorized to act as an agent for a foreign related party is to be disregarded for purposes of determining whether the foreign related party either has a trade or business in the United States for purposes of the Code or a permanent establishment or fixed base in the United States for purposes of an income tax treaty.

(b) *Authorization by related party.*—(1) *In general.*—Upon request by the Service, a foreign related party shall authorize as its agent (solely for purposes of sections 7602, 7603, and 7604) the reporting corporation with which it engages in transactions. The authorization must be signed by the foreign related party or an officer of the foreign related party possessing the authority to authorize an agent for purposes of Rule 4 of the Federal Rules of Civil Procedure. The reporting corporation will accept this appointment by providing a statement to that effect, signed by an officer of the reporting corporation possessing the authority to accept such an appointment. The agency shall be effective at all times. For taxable years beginning after July 10, 1989, the authorization and acceptance must be provided to the Service within 30 days of a request by the Service to the reporting corporation for such an authorization. The authorization must contain a heading and statement as set forth below. A foreign government is not subject to the authorization of agent requirement.

AUTHORIZATION OF AGENT

"[Name of foreign related party] hereby expressly authorizes [name of reporting corporation] to act as its agent solely for purposes of sections 7602, 7603, and 7604 of the Internal Revenue Code with respect to any request to examine records or produce testimony that may be relevant to the U.S. income tax treatment of any transaction between [name of the above-named foreign related party] and [name of reporting corporation] or with respect to any summons for such records or testimony.

____________________ __________ __________

Signature of or for (Title) (Date)
[name of foreign related party]

(If signed by a corporate officer, partner, or fiduciary on behalf of a foreign related party: I certify that I have the authority to execute this authorization of agent to act on behalf of [name of foreign related party]).

____

Type or print your name below if signing for a foreign related party that is not an individual.

____

[Name of reporting corporation] accepts this appointment to act as agent for [name of foreign related party] for the above purpose.

____________________ __________ __________

Signature for (Title) (Date)
[Name of Reporting Corporation]

I certify that I have the authority to accept this appointment to act as agent on behalf of [name of foreign related party] and agree to accept service of process for the above purposes.

Type or print your name below.

____

(2) *Authorization for prior years.*—A foreign related party shall authorize a reporting corporation to act as its agent with respect to taxable years for which a Form 5472 is required to be filed prior to the date on which the final regulations under section 6038A are published by providing the above executed authorization of agent within 30 days of a request by the Service for such an authorization.

(c) *Foreign affiliated groups.*—(1) *In general.*—A foreign corporation that has effective legal authority to make the authorization of agent under paragraph (b) of this section on behalf of any group of foreign related parties may execute such an authorization for any members of the group. A single authorization may be made on a consolidated basis. In such a case, the common parent must attach a schedule to the authorization of agent stating which members of the group would otherwise be required to separately authorize the reporting corporation as agent. The schedule must provide the name, address, relationship to the reporting corporation, and U.S. taxpayer identification number, if applicable, of each member.

(2) *Application of noncompliance penalty adjustment.*—In circumstances where a consolidated authorization of agent has been executed, if the agency authorization for any member of the group is not legally effective for purposes of sections 7602, 7603, and 7604, the noncompliance penalty adjustment under section 6038A(e) and § 1.6038A-7 shall apply.

(d) *Legal effect of authorization of agent.*—The legal consequences of a foreign related party authorizing a reporting corporation to act as its agent for purposes of sections 7602, 7603, and 7604 of the Code are as follows.

(1) *Agent for purposes of commencing judicial proceedings.*—A reporting corporation that is authorized by a foreign related party to act as its agent for purposes of sections 7602, 7603, and 7604 (including service of process) is also the agent of the foreign related party for purposes of—

(i) The filing of a petition to quash under section 6038A(e)(4)(A) or a petition to review an Internal Revenue Service determination of noncompliance under section 6038A(e)(4)(B), and

(ii) The commencement of a judicial proceeding to enforce a summons under section 7604, whether commenced in conjunction with a petition to quash under section 6038A(e)(4)(A) or commenced as a separate proceeding in the federal district court for the district in which the person to whom the summons is issued resides or is found.

(2) *Foreign related party found where reporting corporation found.*—For any purposes relating to sections 7602, 7603, or 7604 (including service of process), a foreign related party that authorizes a reporting corporation to act on its behalf under section 6038A(e)(1) and this section may be found anywhere where the reporting corporation has residence or is found.

(e) *Successors in interest.*—A successor in interest to a related party must execute the authorization of agent as described in paragraph (b) of this section.

(f) *Deemed compliance.*—(1) *In general.*—In exceptional circumstances, the District Director may treat a reporting corporation as authorized to act as agent for a related party for purposes of sections 7602, 7603, and 7604 in the absence of an actual agency appointment by the foreign related party, in circumstances where the actual absence of an appointment is reasonable. Factors to be considered include—

(i) If neither the reporting corporation nor the other party to the transaction knew or had reason to know that the two parties were related at the time of the transaction, and

(ii) The extent to which the taxpayer establishes to the satisfaction of the District Director that all transactions between the reporting corporation and the related party were on arm's length terms and did not involve the participation of any known related party.

(2) *Reason to know.*—Whether the reporting corporation or other party had reason to know that the two parties were related at the time of the transaction will be determined by all the facts and circumstances.

(3) *Effect of deemed compliance.*—If a reporting corporation is deemed under this paragraph (f) to have been authorized to act as an agent for a foreign related party for purposes of section 7602, 7603, and 7604, such deemed compliance is applicable only for that particular transaction and other reportable transactions entered into prior to the time when the reporting corporation knew or had reason to know that the related party, in fact, was related. The noncompliance rule of § 1.6038A-7 shall apply to any transaction subsequent to that time with the same related party, unless the related party actually authorizes the reporting corporation to act as its agent under paragraph (a) of this section. In addition, the record maintenance requirements of § 1.6038A-3 will apply to all subsequent transactions and, with respect to prior transactions, will apply to relevant records in existence at the time the relationship was discovered.

(g) *Effective dates.*—For effective dates for this section, see § 1.6038A-1(n). [Reg. § 1.6038A-5.]

□ [*T.D.* 8353, 6-14-91.]

§ 1.6038A-6. Failure to furnish information.—(a) *In general.*—The rules of § 1.6038A-7 may be applied with respect to a transaction between a foreign related party and the reporting corporation (including any transaction engaged in by a partnership that is attributed to the reporting corporation under § 1.6038A-1(e)(2)) if a summons is issued to the reporting corporation to produce any records or testimony, either directly or as agent for such related party, to determine the correct treatment under Title 1 of the Code of such a transaction between the reporting corporation and the related party; and if—

(1)(i) The summons is not quashed in a proceeding, if any, begun under section 6038A(e)(4) and is not determined to be invalid in a proceeding, if any, begun under section 7604 to enforce such summons; and

(ii) The reporting corporation does not substantially and timely comply with the summons, and the District Director has sent by certified or registered mail a notice under section 6038A(e)(2)(C) to the reporting corporation that it has not so complied; or

(2) The reporting corporation fails to maintain or to cause another to maintain records as required by § 1.6038A-3, and by reason of that failure, the summons is quashed in a proceeding under section 6038A(e)(4) or in a proceeding begun under section 7604 to enforce the summons, or the reporting corporation is not able to provide the records requested in the summons.

(b) *Coordination with treaties.*—Where records of a related party are obtainable on a timely and efficient basis under information exchange procedures provided under a tax treaty or tax information exchange agreement (TIEA), the Service generally will make use of such procedures before issuing a summons. The absence or pendency of a treaty or TIEA request may not be asserted as grounds for refusing to comply with a summons or as a defense against the assertion of the noncompliance penalty adjustment under § 1.6038A-7. For purposes of this paragraph, information is available on a timely and efficient basis if it can be obtained within 180 days of the request.

(c) *Enforcement proceeding not required.*—The District Director is not required to begin an enforcement proceeding to enforce the summons in order to apply the rules of § 1.6038A-7.

(d) *De minimis failure.*—Where a reporting corporation's failure to comply with the requirement to furnish information under this section is *de minimis*, the District Director, in the exercise of discretion, may choose not to apply the noncompliance penalty. Thus, for example, in cases where a particular document or group of documents is not furnished upon request or summons, the District Director (in the District Director's sole discretion), may choose not to apply the noncompliance penalty if the District Director deems the document or documents not to have significant or sufficient value in the determination of the correctness of the tax treatment of the related party transaction.

(e) *Suspension of statute of limitations.*—If the reporting corporation brings an action under section 6038A(e)(4)(A) (proceeding to quash) or (e)(4)(B) (review of secretarial determination of noncompliance), the running of any period of limitation under section 6501 (relating to assessment and collection of tax) or under section 6531 (relating to criminal prosecutions) for the taxable year or years to which the summons that is the subject of such proceeding relates shall be suspended for the period during which such proceeding, and appeals therein, are pending. In no event shall any such period expire before the 90th day after the day on which there is a final determination in such proceeding.

(f) *Effective dates.*—For effective dates for this section, see § 1.6038A-1(n). [Reg. § 1.6038A-6.]

□ [*T.D.* 8353, 6-14-91.]

§ 1.6038B-1. Reporting of certain transfers to foreign corporations.—(a) *Purpose and scope.*—This section sets forth information reporting requirements under section 6038B concerning certain transfers of property to foreign corporations. Paragraph (b) of this section provides general rules explaining when and how to carry out the reporting required under section 6038B with respect to the transfers to foreign corporations. Paragraph (c) of this section and § 1.6038B-1T(d) specify the information that is required to be reported with respect to certain transfers of property that are described in section 6038B(a)(1)(A) and 367(d), respectively. Section 1.6038B-1(e) describes the filing requirements for property transfers described in section 367(e). Paragraph (f) of this section sets forth the consequences of a failure to comply with the requirements of section 6038B and this section. For effective dates, see paragraph (g) of this section. For rules regarding transfers to foreign partnerships, see section 6038B(a)(1)(B) and any regulations thereunder.

(b) *Time and manner of reporting.*—(1) *In general.*—(i) *Reporting procedure.*—Except for stock or securities qualifying under the special reporting rule of § 1.6038B-1(b)(2), and certain exchanges described in section 354 or 356 (listed below), any U.S. person that makes a transfer described in section 6038B(a)(1)(A), 367(d) or (e), is required to report pursuant to section 6038B and the rules of § 1.6038B-1 and must attach the required information to Form 926, "Return by a U.S. Transferor of Property to a Foreign Corporation." In addition, if the U.S. person files a statement under § 1.367(a)-3(d)(2)(vi)(C), a gain recognition agreement under § 1.367(a)-8, or a liquidation document under § 1.367(e)-2(b), such person must comply in all material respects with the requirements of such section pursuant to the terms of the statement, gain recognition agreement, or liquidation document, as applicable, in order to satisfy a reporting obligation under section 6038B. For special rules regarding cash transfers made in tax years beginning after February 5, 1999, see paragraphs (b)(3) and (g) of this section. For purposes of determining a U.S. transferor that is subject to section 6038B, the rules of §§ 1.367(a)-1(c) and 1.367(a)-3(d) shall apply with respect to a transfer described in section 367(a), and the rules of § 1.367(a)-1(c) shall apply with respect to a transfer described in section 367(d). Additionally, if in an exchange described in section 354 or 356, a U.S. person exchanges stock or securities of a foreign corporation in a reorganization described in section 368(a)(1)(E), or a U.S. person exchanges stock or securities of a domestic or foreign corporation pursuant to an asset reorganization described in section 368(a)(1) (involving a transfer of assets under section 361) that is not treated as an indirect stock transfer under § 1.367(a)-3(d), then the U.S. person exchanging stock or securities is not required to report under section 6038B. Notwithstanding any statement to the contrary on Form 926, the form and attachments must be attached to, and filed by the due date (including extensions) of the transferor's income tax return for the taxable year that includes the date of the transfer (as defined in § 1.6038B-1T(b)(4)). For taxable years beginning before January 1, 2003, any attachment to Form 926 required under the rules of this section is filed subject to the transferor's declaration under penalties of perjury on Form 926 that the information submitted is true, correct and complete to the best of the transferor's knowledge and belief. For taxable years beginning after December 31, 2002, Form 926 and any attachments shall be verified by signing the income tax return with which the form and attachments are filed.

(ii) *Reporting by corporate transferor.*—For transfers by corporations in taxable years beginning before January 1, 2003, Form 926 must be signed by an authorized officer of the corporation if the transferor is not a member of an affiliated group under section 1504(a)(1) that files a consolidated Federal income tax return and by an authorized officer of the common parent corporation if the transferor is a member of such an affiliated group. For transfers by corporations in taxable years beginning after December 31, 2002, Form 926 shall be verified by signing the income tax return to which the form is attached.

(iii) *Transfers of jointly-owned property.*—If two or more persons transfer jointly-owned property to a foreign corporation in a transfer with respect to which a notice is required under this section, then each person must report with respect to the particular interest transferred, specifying the nature and extent of the interest. However, a husband and wife who jointly file a single Federal income tax return may file a single Form 926 with their tax return.

(2) *Exceptions and special rules for transfers of stock or securities under section 367(a).*—(i) *Transfers on or after July 20, 1998.*—A U.S. person that transfers stock or securities on or after July 20, 1998 in a transaction described in section 6038B(a)(1)(A) will be considered to have satisfied the reporting requirement under section 6038B and paragraph (b)(1) of this section if either—

(A) The U.S. transferor owned less than 5 percent of both the total voting power and the total value of the transferee foreign corporation immediately after the transfer (taking into account the attribution rules of section 318 as modified by section 958(b)), and either:

(1) The U.S. transferor qualified for nonrecognition treatment with respect to the transfer (i.e., the transfer was not taxable under §§ 1.367(a)-3(b) or (c)); or

(2) The U.S. transferor is a tax-exempt entity and the income was not unrelated business income; or

(3) The transfer was taxable to the U.S. transferor under § 1.367(a)-3(c), and such person properly reported the income from the transfer on its timely-filed (including extensions) Federal income tax return for the taxable year that includes the date of the transfer; or

(4) The transfer is considered to be to a foreign corporation solely by reason of § 1.83-6(d)(1) and the fair market value of the property transferred did not exceed $100,000; or

(B) The U.S. transferor owned 5 percent or more of the total voting power or the total value of the transferee foreign corporation immediately after the transfer (taking into account the attribution rules of section 318 as modified by section 958(b)) and either:

(1) Except as provided in paragraph (b)(2)(iii) of this section, the U.S. transferor (or one or more successors) filed an initial gain recognition agreement under § 1.367(a)-8, and filed Form 926 in accordance with paragraph (b)(2)(iv) of this section; or

(2) The transferor is a tax-exempt entity and the income was not unrelated business income; or

(3) The transferor properly reported the income from the transfer on its timely-filed (including extensions) Federal income tax return for the taxable year that includes the date of the transfer; or

(4) The transfer is considered to be to a foreign corporation solely by reason of § 1.83-6(d)(1) and the fair market value of the property transferred did not exceed $100,000.

(ii) *Transfers before July 20, 1998.*—With respect to transfers occurring after December 16, 1987, and prior to July 20, 1998, a U.S. transferor that transferred U.S. or foreign stock or securities in a transfer described in section 367(a) is not subject to section 6038B if such person is described in paragraph (b)(2)(i)(A) of this section.

(iii) *Timely filed initial gain recognition agreement.*—Paragraph (b)(2)(i)(B)*(1)* of this section will not apply unless the initial gain recognition agreement is timely filed as determined under § 1.367(a)-8(d)(1), but for purposes of this section, determined without regard to § 1.367(a)-8(p). However, see paragraph (f)(3) of this section for certain relief that may be available.

(iv) *Satisfaction of section 6038B reporting if a gain recognition agreement is timely filed.*—If the U.S. transferor is described in paragraph (b)(2)(i)(B)*(1)* of this section and is not otherwise required to file a Form 926 with respect to a transfer of assets other than the stock or securities to the transferee foreign corporation, the requirements of this section are satisfied with respect to the transfer of the stock or securities by completing Part I and Part II of Form 926, noting on the Form 926 that a gain recognition agreement is being filed pursuant to § 1.367(a)-8; reporting on the Form 926 the fair market value, adjusted tax basis, and gain recognized with respect to the transferred stock or securities; submitting on the Form 926 any other information that Form 926, its accompanying instructions, or other applicable guidance require to be submitted with respect to the transfer of the stock or securities; and attaching a signed copy of the Form 926 to its timely filed U.S. income tax return (including extensions) for the year of the transfer. If the U.S. transferor is required to file Form 926 with respect to a transfer of assets in addition to the stock or securities, the requirements of this section are satisfied with respect to the transfer of the stock or securities by noting on the Form 926 that a gain recognition agreement is being filed pursuant to § 1.367(a)-8; reporting on the Form 926 the fair market value, adjusted tax basis, and gain recognized with respect to the transferred stock or securities; and submitting on the Form 926 any other information that Form 926, its accompanying instructions, or other applicable guidance require to be submitted with respect to the transfer of the stock or securities.

(3) *Special rule for transfers of cash.*—A U.S. person that transfers cash to a foreign corporation in a transfer described in section 6038B(a)(1)(A) must report the transfer if—

(i) Immediately after the transfer such person holds directly, indirectly, or by attribution (determined under the rules of section 318(a), as modified by section 6038(e)(2)) at least 10 percent of the total voting power or the total value of the foreign corporation; or

(ii) The amount of cash transferred by such person or any related person (determined under section 267(b)(1) through (3) and (10) through (12)) to such foreign corporation during the 12-month period ending on the date of the transfer exceeds $100,000.

(4) [Reserved]. For further guidance, see § 1.6038B-1T(b)(4).

(c) *Information required with respect to transfers described in section 6038B(a)(1)(A).*—A United States person that transfers property to a foreign corporation in an exchange described in section 6038B(a)(1)(A) (including cash transferred in taxable years beginning after February 5, 1999, and other unappreciated property) must provide the following information, in paragraphs labeled to correspond with the number or letter set forth in this paragraph (c) and § 1.6038B-1T(c)(1) through (5). If a particular item is not applicable to the subject transfer, the taxpayer must list its heading and state that it is not applicable. For special rules applicable to transfers of stock or securities, see paragraph (b)(2)(ii) of this section.

(1) through (4) introductory text [Reserved]. For further guidance, see § 1.6038B-1T(c)(1) through (4) introductory text.

(i) *Active business property.*—Describe any transferred property that qualifies under § 1.367(a)-2(a)(2). Provide here a general description of the business conducted (or to be conducted) by the transferee, including the location of the business, the number of its employees, the nature of the business, and copies of the most recently prepared balance sheet and profit and loss statement. Property listed within this category may be identified by general type. For example, upon the transfer of the assets of a manufacturing operation, a reasonable description of the property to be used in the business might include the categories of office equipment and supplies, computers and related equipment, motor vehicles, and several major categories of manufacturing equipment. However, any property that is includible in both paragraphs (c)(4)(i) and (iii) of this section (property subject to depreciation recapture under § 1.367(a)-4(a)) must be identified in the manner required in paragraph (c)(4)(iii) of this section. If property is considered to be transferred for use in the active conduct of a trade or business under a special rule in paragraph (e), (f), or (g) of § 1.367(a)-2, specify the applicable rule and provide information supporting the application of the rule.

(ii) *Stock or securities.*—Describe any transferred stock or securities, including the class or type, amount, and characteristics of the transferred stock or securities, as well as the name, address, place of incorporation, and general description of the corporation issuing the stock or securities.

(iii) *Depreciated property.*—Describe any property that is subject to depreciation recapture under § 1.367(a)-4(a). Property within this category must be separately identified to the same extent as was required for purposes of the previously claimed depreciation deduction. Specify with respect to each such asset the relevant recapture provision, the number of months that such property was in use within the United States, the total number of months the property was in use, the fair market value of the property, a schedule of the depreciation deduction taken with respect to the property, and a calculation of the amount of depreciation required to be recaptured.

(iv) *Property not transferred for use in the active conduct of a trade or business.*—Describe any property that is eligible property, as defined in § 1.367(a)-2(b) taking into account the application of § 1.367(a)-2(c), that was transferred to the foreign corporation but not for use in the active conduct of a trade or business outside the United States (and was therefore not listed under paragraph (c)(4)(i) of this section).

(v) *Property transferred under compulsion.*—If property qualifies for the exception of § 1.367(a)-2(a)(2) under the rules of paragraph (h) of that section, provide information supporting the claimed application of such exception.

(vi) *Certain ineligible property.*—Describe any property that is described in § 1.367(a)-2(c) and that therefore cannot qualify under § 1.367(a)-2(a)(2) regardless of its use in the active conduct of a trade or business outside of the United States. The description must be divided into the relevant categories, as follows:

(A) *Inventory, etc.*—Property described in § 1.367(a)-2(c)(1);

(B) *Installment obligations, etc.*—Property described in § 1.367(a)-2(c)(2);

(C) *Foreign currency, etc.*—Property described in § 1.367(a)-2(c)(3); and

(D) *Leased property.*—Property described in § 1.367(a)-2(c)(4).

(vii) *Other property that is ineligible property.*—Describe any property, other than property described in § 1.367(a)-2(c), that cannot qualify under § 1.367(a)-2(a)(2) regardless of its use in the active conduct of a trade or business outside of the United States and that is not subject to the rules of section 367(d) under § 1.367(a)-1(b)(5) (treatment of certain property as subject to section 367(d)). Each item of property must be separately identified.

(viii) [Reserved]. For further guidance, see § 1.6038B-1T(c)(4)(viii).

(5) *Transfer of foreign branch with previously deducted losses.*—If the property transferred is property of a foreign branch with previously deducted losses subject to §§ 1.367(a)-6 and -6T, provide the following information:

(i) through (iv) [Reserved]. For further information, see § 1.6038B-1T(c)(5)(i) through (iv).

(6) *Transfers subject to section 367(a)(5).*—(i) *In general.*—This paragraph (c)(6) applies to a domestic corporation (U.S. transferor) that transfers section 367(a) property (as defined in § 1.367(a)-7(f)(10)) to a foreign corporation in a section 361 exchange (as defined in § 1.367(a)-7(f)(8)) and to which the provisions of § 1.367(a)-7(c) apply. Paragraph (c)(6)(ii) of this section establishes the time and manner for the U.S. transferor to elect to apply the provisions of § 1.367(a)-7(c). Paragraph (c)(6)(iii) of this section establishes the manner for the U.S. transferor to satisfy the requirement of § 1.367(a)-7(c)(4).

(ii) *Election.*—The U.S. transferor elects to apply the provisions of § 1.367(a)-7(c) by including a statement entitled, "ELECTION TO APPLY EXCEPTION UNDER § 1.367(a)-7(c)," with its timely filed return (within the meaning of § 1.367(a)-7(f)(12)) for the taxable year during which the reorganization occurs and that includes the information described in paragraphs (c)(6)(ii)(A), (c)(6)(ii)(B), (c)(6)(ii)(C), (c)(6)(ii)(D), (c)(6)(ii)(E), (c)(6)(ii)(F), (c)(6)(ii)(G), and (c)(6)(ii)(H) of this section. See § 1.367(a)-7(c)(5)(ii) for the statement required to be filed by a control group member (as defined in § 1.367(a)-7(f)(1)) or final distributee (as defined in § 1.367(a)-7(d)).

(A) The name and taxpayer identification number (if any) of each control group member and final distributee (if any), the foreign acquiring corporation, and in the case of a triangular reorganization (within the meaning of § 1.358-6(b)(2)) the corporation that controls the foreign acquiring corporation, and the ownership interest percentage (as defined in § 1.367(a)-7(f)(7)) in the U.S. transferor of each control group member.

(B) A calculation of the gain recognized (if any) by the U.S. transferor under § 1.367(a)-7(c)(2)(i) and (c)(2)(ii), and the basis adjustments (if any) required to be made by each control group member under § 1.367(a)-7(c)(3).

(C) The date on which the U.S. transferor and each control group member or final distributee entered into the written agreement described in § 1.367(a)-7(c)(5)(iv).

(D) The amount of any deductible liability (as defined by § 1.367(a)-7(f)(2)).

(E) The fair market value (as defined by § 1.367(a)-7(f)(3)) of property transferred to the foreign acquiring corporation in the section 361 exchange.

(F) The inside basis (as defined by § 1.367(a)-7(f)(4)).

(G) The inside gain (as defined by § 1.367(a)-7(f)(5)).

(H) The section 367(a) percentage (as defined by § 1.367(a)-7(f)(9)).

(iii) *Agreement to amend U.S. transferor's tax return.*—The U.S. transferor complies with the requirement of § 1.367(a)-7(c)(4)(i) by attaching a statement to its timely filed return (within the meaning of § 1.367(a)-7(f)(12)) for the taxable year in which the reorganization occurs, entitled "STATEMENT UNDER § 1.367(a)-7(c)(4) FOR TRANSFERS OF ASSETS TO A FOREIGN CORPORATION IN A SECTION 361 EXCHANGE." The statement must certify that if a significant amount of the section 367(a) property received by the foreign acquiring corporation from the U.S. transferor in the section 361 exchange is disposed of, directly or indirectly, in one or more related transactions described in paragraph (c)(6)(iii)(B) of this section occurring within the sixty (60) month period that begins on the date of distribution or transfer (within the meaning of § 1.381(b)-1(b)), then the exception provided in § 1.367(a)-7(c) will not apply to the section 361 exchange. Accordingly, the U.S. transferor will recognize the gain realized but not recognized in the section 361 exchange, computed as if the exception provided in § 1.367(a)-7(c) had never applied. A U.S. income tax return (or amended U.S. income tax return, as the case may be) for the year in which the reorganization occurred reporting the gain must be filed. If the section 361 exchange occurs in connection with a triangular reorganization (within the meaning of § 1.358-6(b)(2)) and the corporation that controls the foreign acquiring corporation is foreign, an indirect disposition of the section 367(a) property includes the disposition by such controlling foreign corporation of the stock of the foreign acquiring corporation.

(A) *Disposition of a significant amount.*—*(1) General rule.*—Except as provided in paragraphs (c)(6)(iii)(A)(2) and (c)(6)(iii)(A)(3) of this section, for purposes of this paragraph (c)(6)(iii), a disposition of a significant amount occurs if, in one or more related transactions, the foreign acquiring corporation disposes of an amount of the section 367(a) property received from the U.S. transferor in the section 361 exchange that is greater than 40 percent of the fair market value of all of the section 367(a) property transferred in the section 361 exchange.

(2) Exception for certain nonrecognition exchanges.—Section 367(a) property that is subsequently transferred (retransferred property) pursuant to a nonrecognition provision is not treated as disposed of for purposes of paragraph (c)(6)(iii)(A)*(1)* of this section, provided such transfer satisfies, and is treated in a manner consistent with the principles underlying § 1.367(a)-8(k). Thus, for example, if section 367(a) property is subsequently transferred to a foreign corporation in exchange solely for stock in a transaction described in section 351, such retransferred property is not treated as disposed of for purposes of paragraph (c)(6)(iii)(A)*(1)* of this section; in such a case, however, a subsequent disposition of either the retransferred property by the transferee foreign corporation, or of the stock of the transferee foreign corporation received in exchange for the retransferred property, is subject to the provisions of paragraph (c)(6)(iii)(A)*(1)* of this section.

(3) *Exception for dispositions occurring in the ordinary course of business.*—Dispositions of section 367(a) property described in section 1221(a)(2) occurring in the ordinary course of business of the foreign acquiring corporation are not treated as disposed of for purposes of paragraph (c)(6)(iii)(A)(*1*) of this section.

(B) *Gain recognition transaction.*—(*1*) *General rule.*—A transaction is described in this paragraph (c)(6)(iii)(B) if the transaction is entered into with a principal purpose of avoiding the U.S. tax that would have been imposed on the U.S. transferor on the disposition of the property transferred to the foreign acquiring corporation in the section 361 exchange. A disposition may have a principal purpose of tax avoidance even if the tax avoidance purpose is outweighed by other purposes when taken together.

(*2*) *Presumptive tax avoidance.*—For purposes of this paragraph (c)(6)(iii)(B), the principal purpose of the foreign acquiring corporation's disposition of a significant amount of the section 367(a) property within the two-year period that begins on the date of distribution or transfer (within the meaning of § 1.381(b)-1(b)) (whether in a recognition or nonrecognition transaction) will be presumed to be the avoidance of the U.S. tax that would have been imposed on the U.S. transferor on the disposition of the property transferred to the foreign acquiring corporation in the section 361 exchange. However, this presumption will not apply if it is demonstrated to the satisfaction of the Director of Field Operations, Large Business & International (or any successor to the roles and responsibilities of such person (Director) that the avoidance of U.S. tax was not a principal purpose of the disposition.

(*3*) *Interest.*—If additional tax is required to be paid as a result of a transaction described in paragraph (c)(6)(iii)(B) of this section, then interest must be paid on that amount at rates determined under section 6621 with respect to the period between the date prescribed for filing the U.S. transferor's income tax return for the year in which the reorganization occurs and the date on which the additional tax for that year is paid.

(d)(1) through (1)(iii) [Reserved]. For further guidance, see § 1.6038B-1T(d)(1) through (1)(iii).

(iv) *Intangible property transferred.*—Provide a description of the intangible property transferred, including its adjusted basis. Generally, each item of intangible property must be separately identified, including intangible property described in § 1.367(d)-1(g)(2)(i). Identify all property that is subject to the rules of section 367(d) under § 1.367(a)-1(b)(5) (treatment of certain property as subject to section 367(d)). Describe any property for which the income required to be taken into account under section 367(d) and the regulations thereunder will be recognized over a 20-year period pursuant to § 1.367(d)-1(c)(3)(ii). Estimate the anticipated income or cost reductions attributable to the intangible property's use beyond the 20-year period.

(v)–(vi) [Reserved]. For further guidance, see § 1.6038B-1T(d)(1)(v) through (1)(vi).

(vii) *Coordination with loss rules.*—List any intangible property subject to section 367(d) the transfer of which also gives rise to the recognition of gain under section 904(f)(3) or §§ 1.367(a)-6 or -6T. Provide a calculation of the gain required to be recognized with respect to such property, in accordance with the provisions of § 1.367(d)-1(g)(3).

(d)(1)(viii) through (d)(2) [Reserved]. For further guidance, see § 1.6038B-1T(d)(1)(viii) through (d)(2).

(e) *Transfers subject to section 367(e).*—(1) *In general.*—If a domestic corporation (distributing corporation) makes a distribution described in section 367(e)(1) or section 367(e)(2), the distributing corporation must comply with the reporting requirements of this paragraph (e). Unless otherwise provided in this section, a distributing corporation making a distribution described in sections 367(e)(1) or 367(e)(2) must file a Form 926, "Return by a U.S. Transferor of Property to a Foreign Corporation (under section 367)," as amended and modified by this section.

(2) *Reporting requirements for section 367(e)(1) distributions of domestic controlled corporations.*—A domestic distributing corporation making a distribution of the stock or securities of a domestic corporation under section 355 is not required to file a Form 926, as described in paragraph (e)(1) of this section, and shall have no other reporting requirements under section 6038B.

(3) *Reporting requirements for section 367(e)(1) distributions of foreign controlled corporations.*—If the distributing corporation makes a section 355 distribution of the stock or securities of a foreign controlled corporation to distributee shareholders who are not qualified U.S. persons, as defined in § 1.367(e)-1(b)(1), then the distributing corporation shall complete Part 1 of the Form 926 and attach a signed copy of such form to its U.S. income tax return for the year of the distribution. The distributing corporation shall also attach to its U.S. income tax return for the year of distribution a statement signed under the penalties of perjury entitled, "Addendum to Form 926." The addendum shall contain a brief description of the transaction, state the number of shares distributed to distributees who are not qualified U.S. persons (applying the rules contained in § 1.367(e)-1(d)), and state the basis and fair market value of the distributed stock or securities (including a list stating the amounts that were distributed to distributees who were not qualified U.S. persons and distributees who were qualified U.S. persons).

(4) *Reporting rules for section 367(e)(2) distributions by domestic liquidating corporations.*—(i) *General rule.*—Except as provided in paragraph (e)(4)(ii) of this section, if the distributing corporation makes a distribution of property in complete liquidation under section 332 to a foreign distributee corporation that meets the stock ownership requirements of section 332(b) with respect to the stock of the distributing corporation, then the distributing corporation must complete a Form 926 and attach a signed copy of such form to its timely filed U.S. income tax return (including extensions) for the taxable years that include one or more liquidating distributions. The property description contained in Part III of the Form 926 must contain a description, including the adjusted tax basis and fair market value, of all property distributed by the distributing corporation (regardless of whether the distribution of the property qualifies for nonrecognition treatment). The description must also identify the items of property for which nonrecognition treatment is claimed under § 1.367(e)-2(b)(2)(ii) or (iii), as applicable.

(ii) *Special rule.*—Except as provided in paragraph (e)(4)(iii) of this section, if the distributing corporation distributes items of property that will be used by the foreign distributee corporation in the conduct of a trade or business in the United States and the distributing corporation does not recognize gain or loss on such distribution under § 1.367(e)-2(b)(2)(i) with respect to such property, then the distributing corporation may satisfy the requirements of this section by completing Part I and Part II of Form 926, noting in Part III that the information required by Form 926 is contained in a statement required by § 1.367(e)-2(b)(2)(i)(C)(*2*), and attaching a signed copy of Form 926 to its timely filed U.S. income tax return (including extensions) for each taxable year that includes one or more distributions in liquidation. In addition, if the distributing corporation distributes stock of a domestic subsidiary corporation and does not recognize gain or loss on such distribution under § 1.367(e)-2(b)(2)(iii) with respect to such stock, then the distributing corporation may satisfy the requirements of this section by completing Part I and Part II of Form 926, noting in Part III that the information required by Form 926 is contained in a statement required by § 1.367(e)-2(b)(2)(iii)(D), and attaching a signed copy of Form 926 to its timely filed U.S. income tax return (including extensions) for the taxable years that include one or more distributions of domestic subsidiary stock.

(iii) *Properly filed statement.*—Paragraph (e)(4)(ii) will not apply if there is a failure to file an initial liquidation document as determined under § 1.367(e)-2(e)(3)(i), but for purposes of this section, determined without regard to § 1.367(e)-2(f). However, see paragraph (f)(3) of this section for certain relief that may be available.

(f) *Failure to comply with reporting requirements.*—(1) *Consequences of failure.*—If a U.S. person is required to file a notice (or otherwise comply) under paragraph (b) of this section and fails to comply with the applicable requirements of section 6038B and this section, then with respect to the particular property as to which there was a failure to comply—

(i) The U.S. person shall pay a penalty under section 6038B(b)(1) equal to 10 percent of the fair market value of the transferred property at the time of the exchange, but in no event shall the penalty exceed $100,000 unless the failure with respect to such exchange was due to intentional disregard (described under paragraph (g)(4) of this section); and

(ii) The period of limitations on assessment of tax upon the transfer of that property does not expire before the date which is 3 years after the date on which the Secretary is furnished the information required to be reported under this section. See section 6501(c)(8) and any regulations thereunder.

(2) *Failure to comply.*—A failure to comply with the requirements of section 6038B is—

(i) The failure to report at the proper time and in the proper manner any material information required to be reported under the rules of this section; or

(ii) The provision of false or inaccurate information in purported compliance with the requirements of this section. Thus, a transferor that timely files Form 926 with the attachments required under the rules of this section shall, nevertheless, have failed to comply if, for example, the transferor reports therein that property will be used in the active conduct of a trade or business outside of the United States, but in fact the property continues to be used in a trade or business within the United States.

(iii) With respect to an initial gain recognition agreement filed under § 1.367(a)-8, a failure to comply as determined under § 1.367(a)-8(j)(8), but for purposes of this section, determined without regard to the application of § 1.367(a)-8(p).

(iv) With respect to an initial liquidation document filed under § 1.367(e)-2(b)(2), a failure to comply as determined under § 1.367(e)-2(e)(4)(i), but for purposes of this section, determined without regard to the application of § 1.367(e)-2(f).

(3) *Reasonable cause for failure to comply.*—(i) *Request for relief.*—If the U.S. transferor fails to comply with any requirement of section 6038B and this section, the failure shall be deemed not to have occurred if the U.S. transferor is able to demonstrate that the failure was due to reasonable cause and not willful neglect using the procedure set forth in paragraph (f)(3)(ii) of this section. Whether the failure to timely comply was due to reasonable cause and not willful neglect will be determined by the Director of Field Operations, Cross Border Activities Practice Area of Large Business & International (Director) based on all the facts and circumstances.

(ii) *Procedures for establishing that a failure to timely comply was due to reasonable cause and not willful neglect.*—(A) *Time of submission.*—A U.S. transferor's statement that the failure to timely comply was due to reasonable cause and not willful neglect will be considered only if, promptly after the U.S. transferor becomes aware of the failure, an amended return is filed for the taxable year to which the failure relates that includes the information that should have been included with the original return for such taxable year or that otherwise complies with the rules of this section, and that includes a written statement explaining the reasons for the failure to timely comply.

(B) *Notice requirement.*—In addition to the requirements of paragraph (f)(3)(ii)(A) of this section, the U.S. transferor must comply with the notice requirements of this paragraph (f)(3)(ii)(B). If any taxable year of the U.S. transferor is under examination when the amended return is filed, a copy of the amended return and any information required to be included with such return must be delivered to the Internal Revenue Service personnel conducting the examination. If no taxable year of the U.S. transferor is under examination when the amended return is filed, a copy of the amended return and any information required to be included with such return must be delivered to the Director.

(4) *Definition of intentional disregard.*—If the transferor fails to qualify for the exception under paragraph (f)(3) of this section and if the taxpayer knew of the rule or regulation that was disregarded, the failure will be considered an intentional disregard of section 6038B, and the monetary penalty under paragraph (f)(1)(ii) of this section will not be limited to $100,000. See § 1.6662-3(b)(2).

(g) *Effective/applicability dates.*—(1) This section applies to transfers occurring on or after July 20, 1998, except as provided in paragraphs (g)(2) through (g)(7) of this section, and except for transfers of cash made in tax years beginning on or before February 5, 1999 (which are not required to be reported under section 6038B), and transfers described in paragraph (e) of this section (which applies to transfers that are subject to §§ 1.367(e)-1(f) and 1.367(e)-2(e)). See § 1.6038B-1T for transfers occurring prior to July 20, 1998. See also § 1.6038B-1T(e) in effect prior to August 9, 1999, (as contained in 26 CFR part 1 revised April 1, 1999) for transfers described in section 367(e) that are not subject to §§ 1.367(e)-1(f) and 1.367(e)-2(e).

(2) The rules of paragraph (b)(1)(i) of this section as they apply to section 368(a)(1)(A) reorganizations (including reorganizations described in section 368(a)(2)(D) or (E)) apply to transfers occurring on or after January 23, 2006.

(3) The rules of paragraph (b)(1)(i) of this section that provide an exception from reporting under section 6038B for transfers of stock or securities in a section 354 or 356 exchange, pursuant to a section 368(a)(1)(G) reorganization that is not treated as an indirect stock transfer under § 1.367(a)-3(d), apply to transfers occurring on or after January 23, 2006.

(4) The rules of paragraph (b)(1)(i) of this section that provide an exception from reporting under section 6038B for transfers of stock in a section 354 or 356 exchange, pursuant to a section 368(a)(1)(E) reorganization or an asset reorganization under section 368(a)(1) that is not treated as an indirect stock transfer under § 1.367(a)-3(d), apply to transfers occurring on or after January 23, 2006. The rules of paragraph (b)(1)(i) of this section that provide an exception from reporting under section 6038B for transfers of securities in a section 354 or 356 exchange, pursuant to a section 368(a)(1)(E) reorganization or an asset reorganization under section 368(a)(1) that is not treated as an indirect stock transfer under § 1.367(a)-3(d), apply only to transfers occurring after January 5, 2005 (although taxpayers may apply such provision to transfers of securities occurring on or after July 20, 1998 and on or before January 5, 2005 if done consistently to all transactions). See § 1.6038-1T(b)(i), as contained in 26 CFR Part 1 revised as of April 1, 2005, for transfers occurring prior to the effective dates described in paragraphs (g)(2) through (4) of this section.

(5) Paragraphs (c)(6) and (f)(3) of this section apply to transfers occurring on or after April 18, 2013. For guidance with respect to paragraphs (c)(6) and (f)(3) of this section before April 18, 2013, see 26 CFR part 1 revised as of April 1, 2012.

(6) The second sentence of paragraph (b)(1)(i) and paragraphs (b)(2)(i)(B)(1), (b)(2)(iii), (b)(2)(iv), (c), (e)(4), (f)(2)(iii), and (f)(2)(iv) of this section will apply to transfers for which documents are required to be filed on or after November 19, 2014, as well as to transfers that are the subject of requests for relief submitted on or after November 19, 2014. The second sentence of paragraph (b)(1)(i) and paragraphs (b)(2)(i)(B)(1), (b)(2)(iii), (b)(2)(iv), (c), and (f)(2)(iii) of this section will also apply to any transfer that is the subject of a request for relief submitted pursuant to § 1.367(a)-8(r)(3).

(7) Paragraphs (c)(4)(i) through (vii), (c)(5), and (d)(1)(iv) and (vii) of this section apply to transfers occurring on or after September 14, 2015, and to transfers occurring before September 14, 2015, resulting from entity classification elections made under § 301.7701-3 that are filed on or after September 14, 2015. For guidance with respect to paragraphs (c)(4), (c)(5), and (d)(1) of this section before this section is applicable, see §§ 1.6038B-1 and 1.6038B-1T as contained in 26 CFR part 1 revised as of April 1, 2016. [Reg. § 1.6038B-1.]

☐ [*T.D.* 8770, 6-18-98 (*corrected* 3-31-99). *Amended by T.D.* 8817, 2-4-99 (*corrected* 3-31-99); *T.D.* 8834, 8-6-99; *T.D.* 8850, 12-27-99; *T.D.* 9100, 12-18-2003; *T.D.* 9243, 1-23-2006; *T.D.* 9300, 12-7-2006; *T.D.* 9614, 3-18-2013, T.D. 9704, 11-18-2014 (*corrected* 1-2-2015), *T.D.* 9760, 3-18-2016 *and T.D.* 9803, 12-15-2016.]

§ 1.6038B-1T. Reporting of certain transactions to foreign corporations (temporary).—(a) through (b)(3) *[Reserved].*—For further guidance, see § 1.6038B-1(a) through (b)(3).

(4) *Date of transfer.*—(i) *In general.*—For purposes of this section, the date of a transfer described in section 367 is the first date on which title to, possession of, or rights to the use of stock, securities, or other property passes pursuant to the plan for purposes of subtitle A of the Internal Revenue Code. A transfer will not be considered to begin with a decision of a board of directors or similar action unless the transaction otherwise takes effect for purposes of subtitle A of the Internal Revenue Code on that date.

(ii) *Termination of section 1504(d) election.*—A transfer deemed to occur as a result of the termination of an election under section 1504(d) will be considered to occur on the date the contiguous country corporation first fails to continue to qualify for the election under section 1504(d). The rule of this paragraph (b)(3)(ii) is illustrated by the following example.

Example. Domestic corporation W previously made a valid election under section 1504(d) to have its Mexican subsidiary S treated as a domestic corporation. On August 1, 1986, W disposes of its right, title, and interest in 10 percent of the stock of S by selling such stock to an unrelated United States person who is not a director of S. S first fails to continue to qualify for the election under section 1504(d) on August 1, 1986, since on such date it ceases to be directly or indirectly wholly owned or controlled by W. The constructive transfer of assets from "domestic" corporation S to Mexican corporation S is considered to occur on that date.

(iii) *Change in classification.*—A transfer deemed to occur as a result of a change in classification of an entity caused by a change in the governing documents, articles, or agreements of the entity (as described in § 1.367(a)-1T(c)(6)) will be considered to occur on the date that such changes take effect for purposes of subtitle A of the Internal Revenue Code.

(iv) *U.S. resident under section 6013(g) or (h).*—A transfer made by an alien individual who is considered to be a U.S resident by reason of a timely election under section 6013(g) or (h) will be considered to occur, for purposes of this section (but not for purposes of section 367), on the later of—

(A) The date on which the election under section 6013(g) or (h) is made; or

(B) The date on which the transfer would otherwise be considered to occur under the rules of this paragraph (b)(3).

The rule of this paragraph (b)(3)(iv) is illustrated by the following example.

Example. D is a nonresident alien individual who is married to a United States citizen. On March 1, 1986, D transfers property to a foreign corporation in an exchange described in section 351. On April 15, 1987, D and the spouse timely file with their tax return for the taxable year ended December 31, 1986, an election under section 6013(g) for D to be treated as a United States resident. The election is effective on January 1, 1986. For purposes of section 6038B, the transfer described in section 367(a) made by D in connection with the section 351 exchange is considered to occur on April 15, 1987, the date on which the timely election was made under section 6013(g).

(c) Introductory text [Reserved]. For further guidance, see § 1.6038B-1(c).

(1) *Transferor.*—Provide the name, U.S. taxpayer identification number, and address of the U.S. person making the transfer.

(2) *Transfer.*—Provide the following information concerning the transfer:

(i) Name, U.S. taxpayer identification number (if any), address, and country of incorporation of transferee foreign corporation;

(ii) A general description of the transfer, and any wider transaction of which it forms a part, including a chronology of the transfers involved and an identification of the other parties to the transaction to the extent known.

(3) *Consideration received.*—Provide a description of the consideration received by the U.S. person making the transfer, including its estimated fair market value and, in the case of stock or securities, the class or type, amount, and characteristics of the interest received.

(4) *Property transferred.*—Provide a description of the property transferred. The description must be divided into the following categories, and must include the estimated fair market value and adjusted basis of the property, as well as any additional information specified below.

(i) through (c)(5) introductory text [Reserved].

(i) *Branch operation.*—Describe the foreign branch the property of which is transferred, in accordance with the definition of § 1.367(a)-6T(g).

(ii) *Branch property.*—Describe the property of the foreign branch, including its adjusted basis and fair market value. For this purpose property must be identified with reasonable particularity, but may be identified by category rather than listing every asset separately. Substantially similar property may be listed together for this purpose, and property of minor value may be grouped into functional categories. For example, a reasonable description of the property of a business office might include the following categories: word processing or data processing equipment, other office equipment and furniture, and office supplies.

(iii) *Previously deducted losses.*—Set forth a detailed calculation of the sum of the losses incurred by the foreign branch before the transfer, and a detailed calculation of any reduction of such losses, in accordance with § 1.367(a)-6T(d) and (e).

(iv) *Character of gain.*—Set forth a statement of the character of the gain required to be recognized, in accordance with § 1.367(a)-6T(c)(1).

(6) [Reserved]. For further guidance, see § 1.6038B-1(c)(6).

(d) *Transfers subject to section 367(d).*—(1) *Initial transfer.*—A U.S. person that transfers intangible property to a foreign corporation in an exchange described in section 351 or 361 must provide the following information in paragraphs labelled to correspond with the number or letter set forth below. If a particular item is not applicable to the subject transfer, list its heading and state that it is not applicable. The information required by subdivisions (i) through (iii) need only be provided if such information was not otherwise provided under paragraph (c) of this section. (Note that the U.S. transferor may subsequently be required to file another return under paragraph (d)(2) of this section.)

(i) *Transferor.*—Provide the name, U.S. taxpayer identification number, and address of the U.S. person making the transfer.

(ii) *Transfer.*—Provide information concerning the transfer, including:

(A) Name, U.S. taxpayer identification number (if any), address, and country of incorporation of the transferee foreign corporation;

(B) A general description of the transfer, and any wider transaction of which it forms a part, including a chronology of the transfers involved and an identification of the other parties to the transaction to the extent known.

(iii) *Consideration received.*—Provide a description of the consideration received by the U.S. person making the transfer, including its estimated fair market value and, in the case of stock or securities, the class or type, amount, and characteristics of the interest received.

(iv) [Reserved].

(v) *Annual payment.*—Provide and explain the calculation of the annual deemed payment for the use of the intangible property required to be recognized by the transferor under the rules of section 367(d).

(vi) *Election to treat as sale.*—List any intangible with respect to which an election is being made under § 1.367(d)-1T(g)(2) to treat the transfer as a sale. Include the fair market value of the intangible on the date of the transfer and a calculation of the gain required to be recognized in the year of the transfer by reason of the election.

(vii) [Reserved].

(viii) *Other intangibles.*—Describe any intangible property sold or licensed by the transferor to the transferee foreign corporation, and set forth the general terms of each sale or license.

(2) *Subsequent transfers.*—If a U.S. person transfers intangible property to a foreign corporation in an exchange described in section 351 or 361, and at any time thereafter (within the useful life of the intangible property) either that U.S. person disposes of the stock of the transferee foreign corporation or the transferee foreign corporation disposes of the transferred intangible, then the U.S. person must provide the following information in paragraphs labelled to correspond with the number or letter set forth below. The information required by subdivisions (i) and (ii) need only be provided if such information was not otherwise provided in the same return, pursuant to paragraph (c) or (d)(1) of this section. For purposes of determining the date on which a return under this subparagraph (2) is required to be filed, the date of transfer is the date of the subsequent transfer of stock or intangible property.

(i) *Transferor.*—Provide the name, U.S. taxpayer identification number, and address of the U.S. person making the transfer.

(ii) *Initial transfer.*—Provide the following information concerning the initial transfer:

(A) The date of the transfer;

(B) The name, U.S. taxpayer identification number (if any), address, and country of incorporation of the transferee foreign corporation; and

(C) A general description of the transfer and any wider transaction of which it formed a part.

(iii) *Subsequent transfer.*—Provide the following information concerning the subsequent transfer:

(A) A general description of the subsequent transfer and any wider transaction of which it forms a part;

(B) A calculation of any gain required to be recognized by the U.S. person under the rules of § 1.367(d)-1T(d) through (f); and

(C) The name, address, and identifying number of each person that under the rules of § 1.367(d)-1T(e) or (f) will be considered to receive contingent annual payments for the use of the intangible property.

(e) [Reserved]For further guidance, see § 1.6038B-1(e).

(f)(1) through (f)(2) [Reserved].—For further guidance, see § 1.6038B-1(f)(1) through (f)(2).

(3) [Reserved.]

(f)(4) [Reserved]. For further guidance, see § 1.6038B-1T(f)(4).

(g) *Effective date.*—This section applies to transfers occurring after December 31, 1984. See § 1.6038B-1T(a) through (b)(2), (c) introductory text, and (f) (26 CFR part 1, revised April 1, 1998) for transfers occurring prior to July 20, 1998. See § 1.6038B-1 for transfers occurring on or after July 20, 1998. [Temporary Reg. § 1.6038B-1T.]

☐ [*T.D.* 8087, 5-15-86. *Amended by T.D.* 8682, 8-9-96; *T.D.* 8770, 6-18-98; *T.D.* 8834, 8-6-99; *T.D.* 9100, 12-18-2003 (*corrected* 2-2-2004); *T.D.* 9243, 1-23-2006; *T.D.* 9300, 12-7-2006, *T.D.* 9615, 3-18-2013, *T.D.* 9760, 3-18-2016 *and T.D.* 9803, 12-15-2016.]

Proposed Amendments to Regulation

§ 1.6038B-1. Reporting of certain transfers to foreign corporations.—

* * *

(d) *Transfers subject to section 367(d).*—(1) *Initial transfer.*—For further guidance, see § 1.6038B–1T(d)(1) introductory text through (d)(1)(iii).

(i) through (iii) [Reserved]

* * *

(viii) *Other intangibles.*—For further guidance, see § 1.6038B–1T(d)(1)(viii).

(2) *Subsequent transfers.*—For additional, see § 1.6038B–1T(d)(2) introductory text through (d)(2)(ii).

(i) through (ii) [Reserved]

(iii) *Subsequent transfer.*—Except for a subsequent transfer described in paragraph (d)(2)(iv) of this section, provide the following information concerning the subsequent transfer:

(A) For further guidance, see § 1.6038B–1T(d)(2)(iii)(A) through (C).

(B) through (C) [Reserved]

(iv) *Subsequent transfer of intangible property to a qualified domestic person.*—Provide the following information concerning a subsequent transfer of intangible property described in § 1.367(d)-1(f)(4)(i):

(A) A statement providing that § 1.367(d)-1(f)(4)(i)(B) applies to the subsequent transfer;

(B) A general description of the subsequent transfer and any wider transaction of which it forms a part, including the U.S. transferor's former adjusted basis in the intangible property and the transferee foreign corporation's adjusted basis in the intangible property (as determined immediately before the subsequent transfer), the amount and computation of any gain recognized by the U.S. transferor under § 1.367(d)-1(f)(4)(i)(A), and a description of whether the intangible property was, or is expected to be, subsequently transferred to one or more other persons (as described in § 1.367(d)-1(f)(4)(v));

(C) A description of the intangible property;

(D) A copy of the Form 926 with respect to the original transfer of the intangible property and any attachments identifying the intangible property as within the scope of section 367(d);

(E) The name, address, and taxpayer identification number of the qualified domestic person that receives the intangible property, including a statement describing the relationship between the U.S. transferor and the qualified domestic person, and, if applicable, such information regarding any other persons described in § 1.367(d)-1(f)(4)(v); and

(F) Any other information as may be prescribed by the Commissioner in publications, forms, instructions, or other guidance.

* * *

(g) * * *

(8) Paragraphs (d)(2)(iii) introductory text and (d)(2)(iv) of this section apply to transfers occurring on or after [date of publication of final regulations in the **Federal Register**]. [Prop. Reg. § 1.6038B-1.]

[Proposed 5-3-2023.]

§ 1.6038B-2. Reporting of certain transfers to foreign partnerships.—(a) *Reporting requirements.*—(1) *Requirement to report transfers.*—A United States person that transfers property to a foreign partnership in a contribution described in section 721 (including section 721(b)) must report that transfer on Form 8865 "Information Return of U.S. Persons With Respect To Certain Foreign Partnerships" pursuant to section 6038B and the rules of this section, if—

(i) Immediately after the transfer, the United States person owns, directly, indirectly, or by attribution, at least a 10-percent interest in the partnership, as defined in section 6038(e)(3)(C) and the regulations thereunder;

(ii) The value of the property transferred, when added to the value of any other property transferred in a section 721 contribution by such person (or any related person) to the partnership during the 12-month period ending on the date of the transfer, exceeds $100,000; or

(iii) The United States person is a U.S. transferor (as defined in § 1.721(c)-1(b)(18)) that makes a gain deferral contribution and is required to report under § 1.721(c)-6(b)(2). The reporting required under this paragraph (a) includes the annual reporting required by § 1.721(c)-6(b)(3). For purposes of applying this paragraph (a)(1)(iii) to partnerships formed on or after January 18, 2017, a domestic partnership is treated as a foreign partnership pursuant to section 7701(a)(4).

(2) *Indirect transfer through a domestic partnership.*—For purposes of this section, if a domestic partnership transfers property to a foreign partnership in a section 721 transaction, the domestic partnership's partners shall be considered to have transferred a proportionate share of the property to the foreign partnership. However, if the domestic partnership properly reports all of the information required under this section with respect to the contribution, no partner of the transferor partnership, whether direct or indirect (through tiers of partnerships), is also required to report under this section. For illustrations of this rule, see *Examples 4* and *5* of paragraph (a)(7) of this section.

(3) *Indirect transfer through a foreign partnership.*—Solely for purposes of this section, if a foreign partnership transfers section 721(c) property (as defined in § 1.721(c)-1(b)(15)) to another foreign partnership in a transfer described in § 1.721(c)-3(d) (tiered-partnership rules), then the transferor foreign partnership's partners will be considered to have transferred a proportionate share of the property to the foreign partnership.

(4) *Requirement to report dispositions.*—(i) *In general.*—If a United States person was required to report a transfer to a foreign partnership of appreciated property under paragraph (a)(1) or (2) of this section, and the foreign partnership disposes of the property while such United States person remains a direct or indirect partner, that United States person must report the disposition by filing Form 8865. The form must be attached to, and filed by the due date (including extensions) of, the United States person's income tax return for the year in which the disposition occurred.

(ii) *Disposition of contributed property in nonrecognition transaction.*—If a foreign partnership disposes of contributed appreciated property in a nonrecognition transaction and substituted basis property is received in exchange, and the substituted basis property has built-in gain under § 1.704-3(a)(8), the original transferor is not required to report the disposition. However, the transferor must report the disposition of the substituted basis property in the same manner as provided for the contributed property.

(5) *Time for filing Form 8865.*—The Form 8865 on which a transfer is reported must be attached to the transferor's timely filed (including extensions) income tax return for the tax year that includes the date of the transfer. If the person required to report under this section is not required to file an income tax return for its tax year during which the transfer occurred, but is required to file an information return for that year (for example, Form 1065, "U.S. Partnership Return of Income," or Form 990, "Return of Organization Exempt from Income Tax"), the person should attach the Form 8865 to its information return.

(6) *Returns to be made.*—(i) *Separate returns for each partnership.*—If a United States person transfers property reportable under this section to more than one foreign partnership in a taxable year, the United States person must submit a separate Form 8865 for each partnership.

(ii) *Duplicate form to be filed.*—If required by the instructions accompanying Form 8865, a duplicate Form 8865 (including attachments and schedules) must also be filed by the due date for submitting the original Form 8865 under paragraph (a)(5)(i) or (ii) of this section, as applicable.

(7) *Examples.*—The application of this paragraph (a) may be illustrated by the following examples:

Example 1. On November 1, 2001, *US*, a United States person that uses the calendar year as its taxable year, contributes $200,000 to *FP*, a foreign partnership, in a transaction subject to section 721. After the contribution, *US* owns a 5% interest in *FP*. *US* must report the contribution by filing Form 8865 for its taxable year ending December 31, 2001. On March 1, 2002, *US* makes a $40,000 section 721 contribution to *FP*, after which *US* owns a 6% interest in *FP*. *US* must report the $40,000 contribution by filing Form 8865 for its taxable year ending December 31, 2002, because the contribution, when added to the value of the other property contributed by *US* to *FP* during the 12-month period ending on the date of the transfer, exceeds $100,000.

Example 2. F, a nonresident alien, is the brother of *US*, a United States person. *F* owns a 15% interest in *FP*, a foreign partnership. *US* contributes $99,000 to *FP*, in exchange for a 1-percent partnership interest. Under sections 6038(e)(3)(C) and 267(c)(2), *US* is considered to own at least a 10-percent interest in *FP* and, therefore, *US* must report the $99,000 contribution under this section.

Example 3. US, a United States person, owns 40 percent of *FC*, a foreign corporation. *FC* owns a 20-percent interest in *FP*, a foreign partnership. Under section 267(c)(1), *US* is considered to own 8 percent of *FP* due to its ownership of *FC*. *US* contributes $50,000 to *FP* in exchange for a 5-percent partnership interest. Immediately after the contribution, *US* is considered to own at least a 10-percent interest in *FP* and, therefore, must report the $50,000 contribution under this section.

Example 4. US, a United States person, owns a 60-percent interest in *USP*, a domestic partnership. On March 1, 2001, *USP* contributes $200,000 to *FP*, a foreign partnership, in exchange for a 5-percent partnership interest. Under paragraph (a)(2) of this section, *US* is considered as having contributed $120,000 to *FP* ($200,000 × 60%). However, under paragraph (a)(2), if *USP* properly reports the contribution to *FP*, *US* is not required to report its $120,000 contribution. If *US* directly contributes $5,000 to *FP* on June 10, 2001, *US* must report the $5,000 contribution because *US* is considered to have contributed more than $100,000 to *FP* in the 12-month period ending on the date of the $5,000 contribution.

Example 5. US, a United States person, owns an 80-percent interest in *USP*, a domestic partnership. USP owns an 80-percent interest in *USP1*, a domestic partnership. On March 1, 2001, *USP1* contributes $200,000 to *FP*, a foreign partnership, in exchange for a 3-percent partnership interest. Under paragraph (a)(2) of this section, *USP* is considered to have contributed $160,000 ($200,000 × 80%) to *FP*. *US* is considered to have contributed $128,000 to *FP* ($200,000 × 80% × 80%). However, if *USP1* reports the transfer of the $200,000 to *FP*, neither *US* nor *USP* are required to report under this section the amounts they are considered to have contributed. Additionally, regardless of whether *USP1* reports the $200,000 contribution, if *USP* reports the $160,000 contribution it is considered to have made, *US* does not have to report under this section the $128,000 contribution *US* is considered to have made.

(b) *Transfers by trusts relating to state and local government employee retirement plans.*—Trusts relating to state and local government employee retirement plans are not required to report transfers under this section, unless otherwise specified in the instructions to Form 8865.

(c) *Information required with respect to transfers of property.*—With respect to transfers required to be reported under paragraph (a)(1) or (2) of this section, the return must contain information in such form or manner as Form 8865 (and its accompanying instructions) prescribes with respect to reportable events, including—

(1) The name, address, and U.S. taxpayer identification number of the United States person making the transfer;

(2) The name, U.S. taxpayer identification number (if any), and address of the transferee foreign partnership, and the type of entity and country under whose laws the partnership was created or organized;

(3) A general description of the transfer, and of any wider transaction of which it forms a part, including the date of transfer;

(4) The names and addresses of the other partners in the foreign partnership, unless the transfer is solely of cash and the transferor holds less than a ten-percent interest in the transferee foreign partnership immediately after the transfer. However, for tax years of U.S. persons beginning on or after January 1, 2000, the person reporting pursuant to section 6038B (the transferor) must provide the names and addresses of each United States person that owned a ten-percent or greater direct interest in the foreign partnership during the transferor's tax year in which the transfer occurred, and the names and addresses of any other United States or foreign persons that were direct partners in the foreign partnership during that tax year and that were related to the transferor during that tax year. See paragraph (i)(4) of this section for the definition of a related person;

(5) A description of the partnership interest received by the United States person, including a change in partnership interest;

(6) A separate description of each item of contributed property that is appreciated property subject to the allocation rules of section 704(c) (except to the extent that the property is permitted to be aggregated in making allocations under section 704(c)), or is intangible property, including its estimated fair market value and adjusted basis;

(7) A description of other contributed property, not specified in paragraph (c)(6) of this section, aggregated by the following categories (with, in each case, a brief description of the property)—

(i) Stock in trade of the transferor (inventory);

(ii) Tangible property (other than stock in trade) used in a trade or business of the transferor;

(iii) Cash;

(iv) Stock, notes receivable and payable, and other securities; and

(v) Other property;

(8) With respect to reporting required under § 1.721(c)-6(b)(2) and paragraph (a)(1)(iii) of this section with regard to a gain deferral contribution, the information required by § 1.721(c)-6(b)(2); and

(9) With respect to section 721(c) property for which reporting is required under § 1.721(c)-6(b)(3) and paragraph (a)(1)(iii) of this section, the information required by § 1.721(c)-6(b)(3).

(d) *Information required with respect to dispositions of property.*—In respect of dispositions required to be reported under paragraph (a)(4) of this section, the return must contain information in such form or manner as Form 8865 (and its accompanying instructions) prescribes with respect to reportable events, including—

(1) The date and manner of disposition;

(2) The gain and depreciation recapture amounts, if any, realized by the partnership; and

(3) Any such amounts allocated to the United States person.

(e) *Method of reporting.*—Except as otherwise provided on Form 8865, or the accompanying instructions, all amounts reported as required under this section must be expressed in United States currency, with a statement of the exchange rates used. All statements required on or with Form 8865 pursuant to this section must be in the English language.

(f) *Reporting under this section not required of partnerships excluded from the application of subchapter K.*—(1) *Election to be wholly excluded.*—The reporting requirements of this section will not apply to any United States person in respect of an eligible partnership as described in § 1.761-2(a), if such partnership has validly elected to be excluded from all of the provisions of subchapter K of chapter 1 of the Internal Revenue Code in the manner specified in § 1.761-2(b)(2)(i).

(2) *Deemed excluded.*—The reporting requirements of this section will not apply to any United States person in respect of an eligible partnership as described in § 1.761-2(a), if such partnership is validly deemed to have elected to be excluded from all of the provisions of subchapter K of chapter 1 of the Internal Revenue Code in accordance with the provisions of § 1.761-2(b)(2)(ii).

(g) *Deemed contributions.*—Deemed contributions resulting from IRS-initiated section 482 adjustments are not required to be reported under section 6038B. However, taxpayers must report deemed contributions resulting from taxpayer-initiated adjustments. Such information will be furnished timely if filed by the due date, including extensions, for filing the taxpayer's income tax return for the year in which the adjustment is made.

(h) *Failure to comply with reporting requirements.*—(1) *Consequences of a failure.*—If a United States person is required to file a return under paragraph (a) of this section and fails to comply with the reporting requirements of section 6038B and this section, or Reg. § 1.721(c)-6, then that person is subject to the following penalties:

(i) The United States person is subject to a penalty equal to 10 percent of the fair market value of the property at the time of the contribution. Such penalty with respect to a particular transfer is limited to $100,000, unless the failure to comply with respect to such transfer was due to intentional disregard.

(ii) The United States person must recognize gain (reduced by the amount of any gain recognized, with respect to that property, by the transferor after the transfer) as if the contributed property had been sold for fair market value at the time of the contribution. Adjustments to the basis of the partnership's assets and any relevant partner's interest as a result of gain being recognized under this provision will be made as though the gain was recognized in the year in which the failure to report was finally determined.

(2) *Failure to comply.*—A failure to comply with the requirements of section 6038B includes—

(i) The failure to report at the proper time and in the proper manner any information required to be reported under the rules of this section; and

(ii) The provision of false or inaccurate information in purported compliance with the requirements of this section.

(3) *Reasonable cause exception.*—Under section 6038B(c)(2) and this section, the provisions of paragraph (h)(1) of this section will not apply if the United States person shows, in a timely manner, that a failure to comply was due to reasonable cause and not willful neglect. A United States person's statement that the failure to comply was due to reasonable cause and not willful neglect will be considered timely only if, promptly after the United States person becomes aware of the failure, an amended return is filed for the taxable year to which the failure relates that includes the information that should have been included with the original return for such taxable year or that otherwise complies with the rules of this section, and that includes a written statement explaining the reasons for the failure to comply. If any taxable year of the United States person is under examination when the amended return is filed, a copy of the amended return must be delivered to the Internal Revenue Service personnel conducting the examination when the amended return is filed. If no taxable year of the United States person is under examination when the amended return is filed, a copy of the amended return must be delivered to the Director of Field Operations, Cross Border Activities Practice Area of Large Business & International (or any successor to the roles and responsibilities of such position, as appropriate) (Director). Whether a failure to comply was due to reasonable cause and not willful neglect will be determined by the Director under all the facts and circumstances.

(4) *Statute of limitations.*—For exceptions to the limitations on assessment in the event of a failure to provide information under section 6038B, see section 6501(c)(8).

(i) *Definitions.*—(1) *Appreciated property.*—Appreciated property is property that has a fair market value in excess of basis.

(2) *Domestic partnership.*—A domestic partnership is a partnership described in section 7701(a)(4).

(3) *Foreign partnership.*—A foreign partnership is a partnership described in section 7701(a)(5).

(4) *Related person.*—Persons are related persons if they bear a relationship described in section 267(b)(1) through (3) or (10) through (12), after application of section 267(c) (except for (c)(3)), or in section 707(b)(1)(B).

(5) *Substituted basis property.*—Substituted basis property is property described in section 7701(a)(42).

(6) *Taxpayer-initiated adjustment.*—A taxpayer-initiated adjustment is a section 482 adjustment that is made by the taxpayer pursuant to § 1.482-1(a)(3).

(7) *United States person.*—A United States person is a person described in section 7701(a)(30).

(j) *Effective dates.*—(1) *In general.*—Except as otherwise provided in this section, this section applies to transfers made on or after January 1, 1998. However, for a transfer made on or after January 1, 1998, but before January 1, 1999, the filing requirements of this section may be satisfied by—

(i) Filing a Form 8865 with the taxpayer's income tax return (including a partnership return of income) for the first taxable year beginning on or after January 1, 1999; or

(ii) Filing a Form 926 (modified to reflect that the transferee is a partnership, not a corporation) with the taxpayer's income tax return (including a partnership return of income) for the taxable year in which the transfer occurred.

(2) *Transfers made between August 5, 1997 and January 1, 1998.*—A United States person that made a transfer of property between August 5, 1997, and January 1, 1998, that is required to be reported under section 6038B may satisfy its reporting requirement by reporting in accordance with the provisions of this section or in accordance with the provisions of Notice 98-17 (1998-11 IRB 6) (see § 601.601(d)(2) of this chapter).

(3) *Special rule for transfers made before January 1, 2000.*—Even if not reported in accordance with the rules provided in paragraph (a)(5) of this section, or paragraph (j)(1) or (2) of this section, a transfer that occurred before January 1, 2000 will nevertheless be considered timely reported if the transferor reports it on a Form 8865 attached to an amended tax return for the transferor's tax year in which the transfer occurred, provided such amended return is filed no later than September 15, 2000.

(4) *Transfers of section 721(c) property.*—Paragraph (c)(8) of this section applies to transfers occurring on or after August 6, 2015, and to transfers that occurred before August 6, 2015 resulting from an entity classification election made under § 301.7701-3 of this chapter that was effective on or before August 6, 2015 but was filed on or after August 6, 2015. Paragraphs (a)(1)(iii), (a)(3), and (c)(9) of this section apply to transfers occurring on or after January 18, 2017, and to transfers that occurred before January 18, 2017 resulting from entity classification elections made under § 301.7701-3 of this chapter that were effective on or before January 18, 2017 but were filed on or after January 18, 2017.

(5) *Reasonable cause exception.*—Paragraph (h)(3) of this section applies to all requests for relief for transfers of property to partnerships filed on or after January 18, 2017. [Reg. § 1.6038B-2.]

☐ [*T.D.* 8817, 2-4-99 (*corrected* 3-31-99). *Amended by T.D.* 8850, 12-27-99, *T.D.* 9814, 1-18-2017 *and T.D.* 9891, 1-17-2020.]

§ 1.6038D-1. Reporting with respect to specified foreign financial assets, definition of terms.—(a) *In general.*—The following definitions apply for purposes of section 6038D and the regulations—

(1) *Specified person.*—The term *specified person* means a specified individual or a specified domestic entity.

(2) *Specified individual.*—The term *specified individual* means an individual who is a—

(i) U.S. citizen;

(ii) Resident alien of the United States for any portion of the taxable year;

(iii) Nonresident alien for whom an election under section 6013(g) or (h) is in effect; or

(iv) Nonresident alien who is a bona fide resident of Puerto Rico or a section 931 possession (as defined in § 1.931-1(c)(1)).

(3) *Resident alien.*—The term *resident alien* has the meaning set forth in section 7701(b) and §§ 301.7701(b)-1 through 301.7701(b)-9 of this chapter.

(4) *Bona fide resident of a U.S. possession.*—The term *bona fide resident of a U.S. possession* means an individual who is a "bona fide resident" under section 937(a) and § 1.937-1.

(5) *U.S. possession.*—The term *U.S. possession* means American Samoa, Guam, the Northern Mariana Islands, Puerto Rico, or the U.S. Virgin Islands.

(6) *Specified foreign financial asset.*—The term *specified foreign financial asset* has the meaning set forth in § 1.6038D-3.

(7) *Financial account.*—The term *financial account* has the meaning set forth in § 1.1471-5(b), provided, however, that the exclusions of retirement and pension accounts and non-retirement savings ac-

counts under § 1.1471-5(b)(2)(i) and retirement and pension accounts, non-retirement savings accounts, and accounts satisfying similar conditions in an applicable Model 1 IGA or Model 2 IGA under § 1.1471-5(b)(2)(vi) shall not apply (see the section 6038D coordination rule in § 1.1471-5(b)(2)(i)(D)). See § 1.6038D-3(a)(2) relating to financial accounts maintained by a financial institution that is organized under the laws of a U.S. possession.

(8) *Financial institution.*—The term *financial institution* has the meaning set forth in section 1471(d)(5) and the regulations thereunder.

(9) *Foreign financial institution.*—The term *foreign financial institution* has the meaning set forth in § 1.1471-5(d).

(10) *Foreign entity.*—The term *foreign entity* has the meaning set forth in § 1.1473-1(e).

(11) *Annual return.*—The term *annual return* means an annual federal income tax return of a specified individual or an annual federal income tax return or information return of a specified domestic entity filed with the Internal Revenue Service under section 876, 6011, 6012, 6013, 6031, or 6037, and the regulations.

(12) *Specified domestic entity.*—The term *specified domestic entity* has the meaning set forth in § 1.6038D-6.

(13) *Model 1 IGA* and *Model 2 IGA.*—The terms *Model 1 IGA* and *Model 2 IGA* have the meanings set forth in § 1.1471-1(b)(78) and (79), respectively.

(b) *Effective/applicability dates.*—(1) *In general.*—Except as otherwise provided in this paragraph (b), this section applies to taxable years ending after December 19, 2011. Taxpayers may elect to apply the rules of this section to taxable years ending prior to December 19, 2011.

(2) *Financial accounts.*—For purposes of applying the financial account definition in § 1.6038D-1(a)(7), the treatment under § 1.1471-5(b)(2)(vi) of retirement and pension accounts, non-retirement savings accounts, and accounts satisfying similar conditions in an applicable Model 1 IGA or Model 2 IGA (see § 1.1471-1(b)(78) and (79)) as financial accounts for purposes of the reporting required under section 6038D and § 1.6038D-2(a) shall apply to taxable years beginning after December 12, 2014. [Reg. § 1.6038D-1.]

□ [*T.D. 9706, 12-11-2014. Amended by T.D. 9752, 2-22-2016.*]

§ 1.6038D-2. Requirement to report specified foreign financial assets.—(a) *Reporting requirement.*—(1) *In general.*—Except as otherwise provided, a specified person that has any interest in a specified foreign financial asset during the taxable year must attach Form 8938, "Statement of Specified Foreign Financial Assets," to that specified person's annual return for the taxable year to report the information required by section 6038D and § 1.6038D-4 if the aggregate value of all such assets exceeds—

(i) $50,000 on the last day of the taxable year; or

(ii) $75,000 at any time during the taxable year.

(2) *Special rule for married specified individuals filing a joint annual return.*—Except as provided in paragraph (a)(4) of this section, married specified individuals who file a joint annual return for the taxable year must attach a single Form 8938 to their joint annual return for the taxable year to report the information required by section 6038D and § 1.6038D-4 if the aggregate value of all of the specified foreign financial assets in which either married specified individual has an interest exceeds—

(i) $100,000 on the last day of the taxable year; or

(ii) $150,000 at any time during the taxable year.

(3) *Special rule for certain specified individuals living abroad.*—Except as provided in paragraph (a)(4) of this section, a specified individual who is a qualified individual under section 911(d)(1) for the taxable year must attach a Form 8938 to his or her annual return for the taxable year to report the information required by section 6038D and § 1.6038D-4 if the aggregate value of the specified foreign financial assets in which the specified individual has an interest exceeds—

(i) $200,000 on the last day of the taxable year; or

(ii) $300,000 at any time during the taxable year.

(4) *Special rule for married specified individuals filing a joint annual return and living abroad.*—A specified individual who is a qualified individual under section 911(d)(1) for the taxable year and the qualified individual's spouse who file a joint annual return for the taxable year must attach a single Form 8938 to their return for the taxable year to report the information required by section 6038D and § 1.6038D-4 if the aggregate value of the all of the specified foreign financial assets in which either married individual has an interest exceeds—

(i) $400,000 on the last day of the taxable year; or

(ii) $600,000 at any time during the taxable year.

(5) *Assets with no positive value.*—A specified foreign financial asset is subject to reporting even if the specified foreign financial asset does not have a positive value. See § 1.6038D-5(b)(3) to determine the maximum value of a specified foreign financial asset that does not have a positive value during the taxable year.

(6) *Aggregate value calculation in case of specified foreign financial asset excluded from reporting.*—(i) *Specified individual.*—The value of any specified foreign financial asset in which a specified individual has an interest and that is excluded from reporting on Form 8938 pursuant to § 1.6038D-7(a) (concerning certain assets reported on another form) is included for purposes of determining the aggregate value of specified foreign financial assets. The value of any specified foreign financial asset in which a specified individual has an interest and that is excluded from reporting under § 1.6038D-7(b) (concerning assets held by certain domestic trusts) or § 1.6038D-7(c) (concerning certain assets owned by a bona fide resident of a U.S. possession) is excluded for purposes of determining the aggregate value of specified foreign financial assets.

(ii) *Specified domestic entity.*—The value of any specified foreign financial asset in which a specified domestic entity has an interest and that is excluded from reporting on Form 8938 pursuant to § 1.6038D-7(a) (concerning certain assets reported on another form) is excluded for purposes of determining the aggregate value of specified foreign financial assets. For purposes of determining the aggregate value of specified foreign financial assets, a specified domestic entity that is a corporation or partnership and that has an interest in any specified foreign financial asset is treated as owning all the specified foreign financial assets (excluding specified foreign financial assets excluded from reporting on Form 8938 pursuant to § 1.6038D-7(a)) held by all domestic corporations and domestic partnerships that are closely held by the same specified individual as determined under § 1.6038D-6(b)(2).

(7) *Form 8938 filed with annual return.*—(i) *General rule.*—A specified person, including a specified individual who is a bona fide resident of a U.S. possession, is not required to file Form 8938 with respect to a taxable year if the specified person is not required to file an annual return with the Internal Revenue Service with respect to such taxable year.

(ii) *Consolidated returns.*—If a specified domestic entity is a member of an affiliated group of corporations that files a consolidated income tax return, the Form 8938 of the specified domestic entity must be filed with the affiliated group's annual return.

(8) *Reporting required regardless of tax result.*—The Form 8938 required by section 6038D and this section must be furnished by a specified person even if none of the specified foreign financial assets that must be reported affect the specified person's tax liability under the Internal Revenue Code for the taxable year.

(9) *Reporting period.*—The reporting period covered by Form 8938 is the specified person's taxable year, except the reporting period for a specified person that is a specified individual for less than an entire taxable year is the portion of the taxable year that the specified person is a specified individual.

(10) *Successor forms.*—References to Form 8938 include any successor form.

(b) *Interest in a specified foreign financial asset.*—(1) *In general.*—A specified person has an interest in a specified foreign financial asset if any income, gains, losses, deductions, credits, gross proceeds, or distributions attributable to the holding or disposition of the specified foreign financial asset are or would be required to be reported, included, or otherwise reflected by the specified person on an annual return. A specified person has an interest in a specified foreign financial asset even if no income, gains, losses, deductions, credits, gross proceeds, or distributions are attributable to the holding or disposition of the specified foreign financial asset for the taxable year.

(2) *Property transferred in connection with the performance of services.*—A specified person that is transferred property in connection with the performance of personal services is first considered to have an interest in the property for purposes of section 6038D on the first date that the property is substantially vested (within the meaning of § 1.83-3(b)) or, in the case of property with respect to which a specified person makes a valid election under section 83(b), on the date of transfer of the property.

(3) *Special rule for parent making election under section 1(g)(7).*—A parent who makes an election under section 1(g)(7) to include certain unearned income of a child in the parent's gross income has an interest in any specified foreign financial asset held by the child for the purposes of section 6038D and the regulations.

(4) *Entities.*—(i) *In general.*—Except as provided in this paragraph (b)(4), a specified person is not treated as having an interest in any specified foreign financial assets held by a corporation, partnership, trust, or estate solely as a result of the specified person's status as a shareholder, partner, or beneficiary of such entity.

(ii) *Specified foreign financial assets held by certain trusts.*—A specified person that is treated as the owner of a trust or any portion of a trust under sections 671 through 679, other than a domestic liquidating trust under § 301.7701-4(d) of this chapter created pursuant to a court order issued in a bankruptcy under Chapter 7 (11 U.S.C. 701 *et seq.*) or a confirmed plan under Chapter 11 (11 U.S.C. 1101 *et seq.*) of the Bankruptcy Code, or a domestic widely held fixed investment trust under § 1.671-5, is treated as having an interest in any specified foreign financial assets held by the trust or the portion of the trust.

(iii) *Specified foreign financial assets held by a disregarded entity.*—A specified person that owns a foreign or domestic entity that is disregarded as an entity separate from its owner as described in § 301.7701-2 of this chapter (a disregarded entity) is treated as having an interest in any specified foreign financial assets held by the disregarded entity.

(iv) *Interest in a foreign trust or foreign estate.*—See § 1.6038D-3(c) to determine whether an interest in a foreign trust or foreign estate is a specified foreign financial asset. See § 1.6038D-5(f) to determine the maximum value of an interest in a foreign trust or foreign estate.

(c) *Special rules for joint interests.*—(1) *In general.*—(i) *Determining aggregate value of assets.*—Except as otherwise provided in this paragraph (c), each specified person that is a joint owner of a specified foreign financial asset (whether with a spouse or other person) must include the entire value of the specified foreign financial asset (and not the value of the specified person's interest) for purposes of determining whether the aggregate value of the specified person's specified foreign financial assets exceeds the reporting thresholds set forth in § 1.6038D-2(a).

(ii) *Reporting maximum value.*—Except as provided in paragraph (d) of this section, a specified person that is a joint owner of a specified foreign financial asset must report the entire value of each jointly owned specified foreign financial asset on Form 8938.

(2) *Aggregate asset value for married specified individuals filing a joint annual return.*—Married specified individuals who file a joint annual return must include the value of each specified foreign financial asset that they jointly own or in which both have an interest under paragraph (b)(1) of this section only once in determining whether the aggregate value of all of the specified foreign financial assets in which either married specified individual has an interest exceeds the reporting thresholds set forth in § 1.6038D-2(a).

(3) *Aggregate asset value for married specified individual filing a separate annual return.*—(i) *Both spouses are specified individuals.*—If a married specified individual files a separate annual return and his or her spouse is a specified individual, the married specified individual must include one-half of the value of a specified foreign financial asset that the married specified individual jointly owns with his or her spouse in determining whether the married specified individual has an interest in specified foreign financial assets the aggregate value of which exceeds the reporting thresholds set forth in § 1.6038D-2(a).

(ii) *One spouse is not a specified individual.*—If a married specified individual files a separate annual return and his or her spouse is not a specified individual, the married specified individual must include the entire value of a specified foreign financial asset that the married specified individual jointly owns with his or her spouse in determining whether the married specified individual has an interest in specified foreign financial assets the aggregate value of which exceeds the reporting thresholds set forth in § 1.6038D-2(a).

(d) *Annual return filed by a married specified individual.*—(1) *Joint annual return.*—Married specified individuals who file a joint annual return must file a single Form 8938 to fulfill their reporting requirements under section 6038D and § 1.6038D-2(a). The single Form 8938 must report all of the specified foreign financial assets in which either married specified individual has an interest. If both married specified individuals jointly own a specified foreign financial asset or if they have an interest in a specified foreign financial asset under paragraph (b)(1) of this section, the asset must be reported only once on the single Form 8938 filed for the taxable year.

(2) *Separate annual return.*—A married specified individual who files a separate annual return for the taxable year must fulfill the reporting requirements under section 6038D and § 1.6038D-2(a) by filing a separate Form 8938 with his or her return that reports all of the specified foreign financial assets in which the married specified individual has an interest, including each of the assets jointly owned with the married specified individual's spouse or with another person. If both of the spouses are specified individuals, each specified individual must report the entire value of each specified foreign financial asset that the spouses jointly own on Form 8938, not the value taken into account under paragraph (c)(3)(i) of this section for purposes of applying the applicable reporting thresholds.

(e) *Special rules for dual resident taxpayers.*—(1) *In general.*—Subject to the provisions of paragraphs (e)(2) and (3) of this section, a specified individual is not required to report specified foreign financial assets on Form 8938 for a taxable year or any portion of a taxable year that the individual is a dual resident taxpayer (within the meaning of § 301.7701(b)-7(a)(1) of this chapter) who is treated as a nonresident alien pursuant to § 301.7701(b)-7 of this chapter for purposes of computing his or her U.S. tax liability with respect to the portion of the taxable year the individual is considered a dual resident taxpayer.

(2) *Dual resident taxpayer filing as a nonresident alien at end of taxable year.*—If a specified individual to whom this paragraph (e) applies computes his or her U.S. income tax liability as a nonresident alien on the last day of the taxable year and complies with the filing requirements of § 301.7701(b)-7(b) and (c) of this chapter and, in particular, such individual timely files with the Internal Revenue Service Form 1040NR, "U.S. Nonresident Alien Income Tax Return," or Form 1040NR-EZ, "U.S. Income Tax Return for Certain Nonresident Aliens With No Dependents," as applicable, and attaches thereto Form 8833, "Treaty-Based Return Position Disclosure Under Section 6114 or 7701(b)," such individual will not be required to report specified foreign financial assets on Form 8938 with respect to the portion of the taxable year covered by Form 1040NR (or Form 1040NR-EZ).

(3) *Dual resident taxpayer filing as resident alien at end of taxable year.*—If a specified individual to whom this paragraph (e) applies computes his or her U.S. income tax liability as a resident alien on the last day of the taxable year and complies with the filing requirements of § 1.6012-1(b)(2)(ii)(*a*) and, in particular, such individual timely files with the Internal Revenue Service Form 1040, "U.S. Individual Income Tax Return," or Form 1040EZ, "Income Tax Return for Single and Joint Filers With No Dependents," as applicable, and attaches a properly completed Form 8833 to the schedule required by § 1.6012-1(b)(2)(ii)(*a*), such individual will not be required to report specified foreign financial assets on Form 8938 with respect to the portion of the individual's taxable year reflected on the schedule to such Form 1040 or Form 1040EZ required by § 1.6012-1(b)(2)(ii)(*a*).

(f) *Example.*—The following example illustrates the application of paragraph (c) of this section:

Example. (1) *Facts.* Two married specified individuals, H and W, jointly own a specified foreign financial asset with a value of $90,000 at all times during the taxable year. H separately has an interest in a specified foreign financial asset with a value of $10,000 at all times during the taxable year. W separately has an interest in a specified foreign financial asset with a value of $1,000 at all times during the taxable year.

(2) *Filing requirement.*—(i) *Married specified individuals filing separate annual returns.* If H and W file separate annual returns, the aggregate value of the specified foreign financial assets in which H has an interest at the end of the taxable year is $55,000, comprising one-half of the value of the jointly owned asset, $45,000, and the value of H's separately owned specified foreign financial asset, $10,000. The aggregate value of the specified foreign financial assets in which W has an interest at the end of the taxable year is $46,000, comprising one-half of the value of the jointly owned asset, $45,000, and the value of W's separately owned specified foreign financial asset, $1,000. H must file Form 8938 with his annual return for the taxable year because the aggregate value of the specified foreign financial assets in which H has an interest exceeds the applicable reporting threshold ($50,000) set forth in § 1.6038D-2(a)(1). H must report the maximum value of the entire jointly owned asset, $90,000, and the maximum value of the separately owned asset, $10,000. See § 1.6038D-5(b) regarding the maximum value of a jointly owned specified foreign financial asset to be reported by a specified person, including a married specified individual, that is a joint owner of an asset. The aggregate value of the specified foreign financial assets in which W has an interest, $46,000, does not exceed the applicable reporting threshold set forth in § 1.6038D-2(a)(1). W is not required to file Form 8938 with her separate annual return.

(ii) *Married specified individuals filing a joint annual return.* If H and W file a joint annual return, they must file a single Form 8938 with their joint annual return for the taxable year because the aggregate value of all of the specified foreign financial assets in which either H or W have an interest ($90,000 (included only once), $10,000, and $1000, or $101,000) exceeds the applicable reporting threshold ($100,000) set forth in § 1.6038D-2(a)(2). The single Form 8938 must report the maximum value of the jointly owned specified foreign financial asset, $90,000, and the maximum value of the specified foreign financial assets separately owned by H and W, $10,000 and $1,000, respectively.

(g) *Effective/applicability dates.*—This section, with the exception of § 1.6038D-2(a)(6)(ii), applies to taxable years ending after December 19, 2011. Section 1.6038D-2(a)(6)(ii) applies to taxable years beginning after December 31, 2015. Taxpayers may elect to apply the rules of this section, with the exception of § 1.6038D-2(a)(6)(ii), to taxable years ending on or prior to December 19, 2011. [Reg. § 1.6038D-2.]

☐ [*T.D. 9706, 12-11-2014. Amended by T.D. 9752, 2-22-2016.*]

§ 1.6038D-3. Specified foreign financial assets.—(a) *Financial accounts.*—(1) *In general.*—Except as otherwise provided in this section, a specified foreign financial asset includes any financial account maintained by a foreign financial institution. An asset held in a financial account maintained by a foreign financial institution is not required to be separately reported on Form 8938, "Statement of Specified Foreign Financial Assets."

(2) *Financial account in a U.S. possession.*—A specified foreign financial asset includes a financial account maintained by a financial institution that is organized under the laws of a U.S. possession.

(3) *Excepted financial accounts.*—(i) *Accounts maintained by U.S. payors.*—A financial account maintained by a U.S. payor as defined in § 1.6049-5(c)(5)(i) (including assets held in such an account) is not a specified foreign financial asset for purposes of section 6038D and the regulations.

(ii) *Mark-to-market election under section 475.*—A financial account is not a specified foreign financial asset if the rules of section 475(a) apply to all of the holdings in the account or an election under section 475(e) or (f) is made with respect to all of the holdings in the account.

(b) *Other specified foreign financial assets.*—(1) *In general.*—Except as otherwise provided in this section, a specified foreign financial asset includes any of the following assets that are not financial accounts and that are held for investment and not held in an account maintained by a financial institution—

(i) Stock or securities issued by a person other than a United States person (including stock or securities issued by a person organized under the laws of a U.S. possession);

(ii) A financial instrument or contract that has an issuer or counterparty which is other than a United States person (including a financial instrument or contract issued by a person organized under the laws of a U.S. possession); and

(iii) An interest in a foreign entity.

(2) *Mark-to-market election under section 475.*—An asset is not a specified foreign financial asset if the rules of section 475(a) apply to the asset or an election under section 475(e) or (f) is made with respect to the asset.

(3) *Held for investment.*—An asset is held for investment for purposes of section 6038D and the regulations if that asset is not used in, or held for use in, the conduct of a trade or business of a specified person.

(4) *Trade-or-business test.*—For purposes of section 6038D and the regulations, an asset is used in, or held for use in, the conduct of a trade or business and not held for investment if the asset is—

(i) Held for the principal purpose of promoting the present conduct of the trade or business;

(ii) Acquired and held in the ordinary course of the trade or business, as, for example, in the case of an account or note receivable arising from that trade or business; or

(iii) Otherwise held in a direct relationship to the trade or business as determined under paragraph (b)(5) of this section.

(5) *Direct relationship between holding an asset and a trade or business.*—(i) *In general.*—In determining whether an asset is held in a direct relationship to the conduct of a trade or business by a specified person, principal consideration will be given to whether the asset is needed in the trade or business of the specified person. An asset shall be considered needed in the trade or business, for this purpose, only if the asset is held to meet the present needs of that trade or business and not its anticipated future needs. An asset shall be considered as needed in the trade or business if, for example, the asset is held to meet the operating expenses of the trade or business. Conversely, an asset shall be considered as not needed in the trade or business if, for example, the asset is held for the purpose of providing for future diversification into a new trade or business, future plant replacement, or future business contingencies. Stock is never considered used or held for use in a trade or business for purposes of applying this test.

(ii) *Presumption of direct relationship.*—An asset will be treated as held in a direct relationship to the conduct of a trade or business of a specified person if—

(A) The asset was acquired with funds generated by the trade or business of the specified person or the affiliated group of the specified person, if any;

(B) The income from the asset is retained or reinvested in the trade or business; and

(C) Personnel who are actively involved in the conduct of the trade or business exercise significant management and control over the investment of such asset.

(c) *Special rule for interests in foreign trusts and foreign estates.*—An interest in a foreign trust or a foreign estate is not a specified foreign financial asset of a specified person unless the person knows, or has reason to know based on readily accessible information, of the interest. Receipt of a distribution from the foreign trust or foreign estate constitutes actual knowledge for this purpose.

(d) *Examples.*—Examples of assets other than financial accounts that may be considered other specified foreign financial assets include, but are not limited to—

(1) Stock issued by a foreign corporation;

(2) A capital or profits interest in a foreign partnership;

(3) A note, bond, debenture, or other form of indebtedness issued by a foreign person;

(4) An interest in a foreign trust;

(5) An interest rate swap, currency swap, basis swap, interest rate cap, interest rate floor, commodity swap, equity swap, equity index swap, credit default swap, or similar agreement with a foreign counterparty; and

(6) Any option or other derivative instrument with respect to any of the items listed as examples in this paragraph or with respect to any currency or commodity that is entered into with a foreign counterparty or issuer.

(e) *Effective/applicability dates.*—This section applies to taxable years ending after December 19, 2011. Taxpayers may elect to apply the rules of this section to taxable years ending prior to December 19, 2011. [Reg. § 1.6038D-3.]

☐ [*T.D.* 9706, 12-11-2014.]

§ 1.6038D-4. Information required to be reported.—(a) *Required information.*—The following information must be reported on Form 8938, "Statement of Specified Foreign Financial Assets," with respect to each specified foreign financial asset:

(1) In the case of a financial account, the name and address of the foreign financial institution with which the account is maintained and the account number of the financial account;

(2) In the case of stock or securities, the name and address of the issuer, and information that identifies the class or issue of which the stock or security is a part;

(3) In the case of a financial instrument or contract, information that identifies the financial instrument or contract, including the names and addresses of all issuers and counterparties;

(4) In the case of an interest in a foreign entity, information that identifies the interest, including the name and address of the foreign entity in which the interest is held;

(5) The maximum value of the specified foreign financial asset during the portion of the taxable year in which the specified person has an interest in the asset;

(6) In the case of a financial account that is a depository account as defined in § 1.1471-5(b)(3)(i) or a custodial account as defined in § 1.1471-5(b)(3)(ii), whether the account was opened or closed during the taxable year;

(7) The date, if any, on which the specified foreign financial asset, other than a financial account that is a depository account as defined in § 1.1471-5(b)(3)(i) or a custodial account as defined in § 1.1471-5(b)(3)(ii), was either acquired or disposed of (or both) during the taxable year;

(8) The amount of any income, gain, loss, deduction, or credit recognized for the taxable year with respect to the reported specified foreign financial asset, and the schedule, form, or return filed with the Internal Revenue Service on which the income, gain, loss, deduction, or credit, if any, is reported or included by the specified person;

(9) The foreign currency in which the account is maintained or the asset is denominated, the foreign currency exchange rate and, if the source of such rate is other than as described in § 1.6038D-5(c)(1), the source of the rate used to determine the specified foreign financial asset's U.S. dollar value, including maximum value;

(10) For any specified foreign financial asset excepted from reporting on Form 8938 under § 1.6038D-7(a), the specified person must report the number of Forms 3520, "Annual Return To Report Transactions With Foreign Trusts and Receipt of Certain Foreign Gifts," Forms 3520-A, "Annual Information Return of Foreign Trust With a U.S. Owner," Forms 5471, "Information Return of U.S. Persons With Respect To Certain Foreign Corporations," Forms 8621, "Return by a Shareholder of a Passive Foreign Investment Company or a Qualified Electing Fund," Forms 8865, "Return of U.S. Persons With Respect To Certain Foreign Partnerships," and, solely for taxable years beginning after March 18, 2010, and ending on or before December 31, 2013, Forms 8891, "U.S. Information Return for Beneficiaries of Certain Canadian Registered Retirement Plans," or such other form under Title 26 of the United States Code identified by the Secretary under § 1.6038D-7(a), timely filed with the Internal Revenue Service on which excepted foreign financial assets are reported or reflected for the taxable year; and

(11) Such other information as may be required by Form 8938 or its instructions or other guidance.

(b) *Effective/applicability dates.*—This section applies to taxable years ending after December 19, 2011. Taxpayers may elect to apply the rules of this section to taxable years ending prior to December 19, 2011. [Reg. § 1.6038D-4.]

☐ [*T.D.* 9706, 12-11-2014.]

§ 1.6038D-5. Valuation guidelines.—(a) *Fair market value.*—Except as provided in paragraphs (c) and (e) of this section, the value of a specified foreign financial asset for purposes of determining the aggregate value of specified foreign financial assets held by a specified person and the maximum value of a specified foreign financial asset required to be reported on Form 8938, "Statement of Specified Foreign Financial Assets," is the asset's fair market value.

(b) *Valuation of assets.*—(1) *Maximum value.*—Except as provided in this section, the maximum value of a specified foreign financial asset means a reasonable estimate of the asset's maximum fair market value during the taxable year.

(2) *U.S. dollars.*—For purposes of determining the aggregate value of specified foreign financial assets in which a specified person has an interest and determining the maximum value of a specified foreign financial asset, the value of a specified foreign financial asset denominated in a foreign currency during the taxable year must be determined in the foreign currency and then converted to U.S. dollars.

(3) *Asset with no positive value.*—If the maximum fair market value of a specified foreign financial asset is zero or less than zero, then the asset's value is treated as zero for purposes of determining the aggregate value of specified foreign financial assets in which a specified person has an interest, and the maximum value of the specified foreign financial asset is zero for purposes of reporting under § 1.6038D-4(a)(5).

(c) *Foreign currency conversion.*—(1) *In general.*—Except as provided in paragraphs (c)(2) and (d) of this section, the U.S. Treasury Department's Bureau of the Fiscal Service foreign currency exchange rate is to be used to convert the value of a specified foreign financial asset into U.S. dollars for purposes of determining the aggregate value of specified foreign financial assets in which a specified person has an interest and determining the maximum value of a specified foreign financial asset.

(2) *Other publicly available exchange rate.*—If no U.S. Treasury Department Bureau of the Fiscal Service foreign currency exchange rate is available for a particular currency, another publicly available foreign currency exchange rate may be used to convert the value of a specified foreign financial asset into U.S. dollars. In such case, the source of the foreign currency exchange rate must be disclosed on Form 8938.

(3) *Currency exchange rate.*—In converting the currency of a foreign country, the foreign currency exchange rate applicable for converting the currency into U.S. dollars (that is, to purchase U.S. dollars) must be used.

(4) *Determination date.*—In converting the currency of a foreign country into U.S. dollars for purposes of determining the maximum value of a specified foreign financial asset and determining the aggregate value of specified foreign financial assets in which a specified person has an interest, the applicable foreign currency exchange rate is the rate on the last day of the taxable year of the specified person, even if the specified person sold or otherwise disposed of a specified foreign financial asset prior to the last day of such year.

(d) *Financial accounts.*—A specified person may rely upon periodic account statements that are provided at least annually by or on behalf of a financial institution maintaining an account, including the foreign currency conversion reflected in those statements, to determine the financial account's maximum value unless the specified person has actual knowledge, or reason to know based on readily accessible information, that the statements do not reflect a reasonable estimate of the maximum account value during the taxable year.

(e) *Asset held in a financial account.*—The value of an asset held in a financial account maintained by a foreign financial institution is included in determining the value of that financial account for purposes of § 1.6038D-5(a).

(f) *Other specified foreign financial assets.*—(1) *General rule.*—Except as provided in paragraphs (f)(2) and (3) of this section, for specified foreign financial assets that are not financial accounts and that are held for investment and not held in an account maintained by a financial institution, a specified person may use the value of the asset as of the last day of the taxable year on which the specified person has an interest in the asset as the maximum value of that asset, unless the specified person has actual knowledge, or reason to know based on readily accessible information, that the value does not reflect a reasonable estimate of the maximum value of the asset during the taxable year.

(2) *Interests in trusts that are specified foreign financial assets.*—(i) *Maximum value.*—If a specified person is a beneficiary of a foreign trust, the maximum value of the specified person's interest in the trust is the sum of-

(A) The fair market value, determined as of the last day of the taxable year, of all of the currency or other property distributed from the foreign trust during the taxable year to the specified person as a beneficiary; and

(B) The value, determined as of the last day of the taxable year, of the specified person's right as a beneficiary to receive mandatory distributions from the foreign trust as determined under section 7520.

(ii) *Reporting threshold.*—For purposes of determining the aggregate value of specified foreign financial assets in which a specified person has an interest, if the specified person does not know, or have reason to know based on readily accessible information, the fair market value of the person's interest in a foreign trust during the taxable year, the value to be included in determining the aggregate value of the specified foreign financial assets is the maximum value of the specified person's interest in the foreign trust under paragraph (f)(2)(i) of this section.

(3) *Interests in estates, pension plans, and deferred compensation plans.*—(i) *Maximum value.*—The maximum value of a specified person's interest in a foreign estate, foreign pension plan, or foreign deferred compensation plan is the fair market value, determined as of the last day of the taxable year, of the specified person's beneficial interest in the assets of the foreign estate, foreign pension plan, or foreign deferred compensation plan. If the specified person does not know, or have reason to know based on readily accessible information, such fair market value, the maximum value to be reported is the fair market value, determined as of the last day of the taxable year, of the currency and other property distributed during the taxable year to the specified person as a beneficiary or participant.

(ii) *Reporting threshold.*—For purposes of determining the aggregate value of specified foreign financial assets in which a specified person has an interest, if the specified person does not know, or have reason to know based on readily accessible information, the fair market value of the person's interest in a foreign estate, foreign pension plan, or foreign deferred compensation plan during the taxable year, the value to be included in determining the aggregate value of the specified foreign financial assets is the fair market value, determined as of the last day of the taxable year, of the currency and other property distributed during the taxable year to the specified person as a beneficiary or participant.

(g) *Effective/applicability dates.*—This section applies to taxable years ending after December 19, 2011. Taxpayers may elect to apply the rules of this section to taxable years ending prior to December 19, 2011. [Reg. § 1.6038D-5.]

☐ [*T.D. 9706, 12-11-2014.*]

§ 1.6038D-6. Specified domestic entities.—(a) *Specified domestic entity.*—A specified domestic entity is a domestic corporation, a domestic partnership, or a trust described in section 7701(a)(30)(E), if such corporation, partnership, or trust is formed or availed of for purposes of holding, directly or indirectly, specified foreign financial assets. Whether a domestic corporation, a domestic partnership, or a trust described in section 7701(a)(30)(E) is a specified domestic entity is determined annually.

(b) *Corporations and partnerships.*—(1) *Formed or availed of.*—Except as otherwise provided in paragraph (d) of this section, a domestic corporation or a domestic partnership is formed or availed of for purposes of holding, directly or indirectly, specified foreign financial assets if and only if—

(i) The corporation or partnership is closely held by a specified individual as determined under paragraph (b)(2) of this section; and

(ii) At least 50 percent of the corporation's or partnership's gross income for the taxable year is passive income or at least 50 percent of the assets held by the corporation or partnership for the taxable year are assets that produce or are held for the production of passive income as determined under paragraph (b)(3) of this section (passive assets). For purposes of this paragraph (b)(1)(ii), the percentage of passive assets held by a corporation or partnership for a taxable year is the weighted average percentage of passive assets (weighted by total assets and measured quarterly), and the value of assets of a corporation or partnership is the fair market value of the assets or the book value of the assets that is reflected on the corporation's or partnership's balance sheet (as determined under either a U.S. or an international financial accounting standard).

(2) *Closely held.*—(i) *Domestic corporation.*—A domestic corporation is closely held by a specified individual if at least 80 percent of the total combined voting power of all classes of stock of the corporation entitled to vote, or at least 80 percent of the total value of the stock of the corporation, is owned, directly, indirectly, or constructively, by a specified individual on the last day of the corporation's taxable year.

(ii) *Domestic partnership.*—A partnership is closely held by a specified individual if at least 80 percent of the capital or profits interest in the partnership is held, directly, indirectly, or constructively, by a specified individual on the last day of the partnership's taxable year.

(iii) *Constructive ownership.*—For purposes of this paragraph (b)(2), sections 267(c) and (e)(3) apply for the purpose of determining the constructive ownership of a specified individual in a corporation or partnership, except that section 267(c)(4) is applied as if the family of an individual includes the spouses of the individual's family members.

(3) *Determination of passive income and assets.*—(i) *Definition of passive income.*—Except as provided in paragraph (b)(3)(ii) of this section, for purposes of paragraph (b)(1)(ii) of this section, passive income means the portion of gross income that consists of—

(A) Dividends, including substitute dividends;

(B) Interest;

(C) Income equivalent to interest, including substitute interest;

(D) Rents and royalties, other than rents and royalties derived in the active conduct of a trade or business conducted, at least in part, by employees of the corporation or partnership;

(E) Annuities;

(F) The excess of gains over losses from the sale or exchange of property that gives rise to passive income described in paragraphs (b)(3)(i)(A) through (b)(3)(i)(E) of this section;

(G) The excess of gains over losses from transactions (including futures, forwards, and similar transactions) in any commodity, but not including—

(1) Any commodity hedging transaction described in section 954(c)(5)(A), determined by treating the corporation or partnership as a controlled foreign corporation; or

(2) Active business gains or losses from the sale of commodities, but only if substantially all the corporation or partnership's commodities are property described in paragraph (1), (2), or (8) of section 1221(a);

(H) The excess of foreign currency gains over foreign currency losses (as defined in section 988(b)) attributable to any section 988 transaction; and

(I) Net income from notional principal contracts as defined in § 1.446-3(c)(1).

(ii) *Exception from passive income treatment for dealers.*—Notwithstanding paragraph (b)(3)(i) of this section, in the case of a corporation or partnership that regularly acts as a dealer in property described in paragraph (b)(3)(i)(F) of this section (referring to the sale or exchange of property that gives rise to passive income), forward contracts, option contracts, or similar financial instruments (including notional principal contracts and all instruments referenced to commodities), the term passive income does not include—

(A) Any item of income or gain (other than any dividends or interest) from any transaction (including hedging transactions and transactions involving physical settlement) entered into in the ordinary course of such dealer's trade or business as such a dealer; and

(B) If such dealer is a dealer in securities (within the meaning of section 475(c)(2)), any income from any transaction entered into in the ordinary course of such trade or business as a dealer in securities.

(iii) *Related entities.*—For purposes of applying the passive income and asset thresholds of paragraph (b)(1)(ii) of this section, all domestic corporations and domestic partnerships that are closely held by the same specified individual as determined under paragraph (b)(2) of this section and that are connected through stock or partnership interest ownership with a common parent corporation or partnership are treated as owning the combined assets and receiving the combined income of all members of that group. For purposes of the preceding sentence, assets relating to any contract, equity, or debt existing between members of such a group, as well as any items of gross income arising under or from such contract, equity, or debt, are eliminated. A domestic corporation or a domestic partnership is considered connected through stock or partnership interest ownership with a common parent corporation or partnership if stock representing at least 80 percent of the total combined voting power of all classes of stock of the corporation entitled to vote or of the value of such corporation, or partnership interests representing at least 80 percent of the profits interests or capital interests of such partnership, in each case other than stock of or partnership interests in the common parent, is owned by one or more of the other connected corporations, connected partnerships, or the common parent.

(4) *Examples.*—The following examples illustrate the application of this section:

Example 1. Closely held and constructive ownership. (i) *Facts.* DC1 is a domestic corporation the total value of the stock of which is owned 60% by A, a specified individual, 30% by B, a member of A's family for purposes of section 267(c)(2) who is not a specified individual, and 10% by FC1, a foreign corporation. DC1 owns 90% of the total value of the stock of DC2, a domestic corporation. FC2, a foreign corporation, owns 10% of DC2. Neither A nor B owns, directly, indirectly, or constructively, any stock in FC1 or FC2.

(ii) *Closely held ownership determination.* A is considered to own 90% and 81% of the total value of DC1 and DC2, respectively, by application of the rules of section 267(c) and this section. DC1 and DC2 are closely held by A within the meaning of paragraph (b)(2) of this section because A, a specified individual, is considered to own more than 80% of their total value.

Example 2. Application of aggregation rule and reporting threshold. (i) *Facts.* L is a specified individual. In Year X, L wholly owns DC1, a domestic corporation, and also owns a 90% capital interest in DP, a domestic partnership. DC1 owns 80% of the sole class of stock of DC2, a domestic corporation. DC1 has no assets other than its interest in DC2. DC2's only assets are assets that produce passive income, with a maximum value in Year X of $40,000 on October 12. DC2's assets are comprised in relevant part of specified foreign financial assets with a maximum value in Year X of $15,000 on October 12. DP's only assets are assets that produce passive income and that are specified foreign financial assets with a maximum value of $90,000 in Year X on October 12.

(ii) *Specified domestic entity status*—(A) *DC1 and DC2.* DC1 and DC2 are closely held by a specified individual for purposes of paragraph (b)(2) of this section. DC1 and DC2 are considered related entities that are connected through stock ownership with a common parent corporation under paragraph (b)(3)(iii) of this section, because DC1 and DC2 are closely held by L, and DC2 is connected with DC1 through DC1's ownership of stock of DC2 representing at least 80% of the voting power or value of DC2. As a result, for purposes of applying paragraph (b)(1)(ii) of this section, each of DC1 and DC2 is considered as owning the combined assets, and receiving the combined income, of both DC1 and DC2; however, DC1's equity interest in DC2 is disregarded for this purpose under paragraph (b)(3)(iii) of this section. Therefore, DC1 and DC2 each satisfies the passive asset threshold of paragraph (b)(1)(ii) of this section, because 100 percent of each company's assets is passive. DC1 and DC2 are specified domestic entities for Year X.

(B) *DP.* DP is closely held by a specified individual for purposes of paragraph (b)(2) of this section. DP is not considered a related entity with DC1 and DC2 under paragraph (b)(3)(iii) of this section, because DC1 and DP are not owned by a common parent corporation or partnership. As a result, whether the passive income or passive asset threshold of paragraph (b)(1)(ii) of this section is met with respect to DP is determined solely by reference to DP's separately earned passive income and separately held passive assets. DP holds only passive assets during Year X and therefore satisfies paragraph (b)(1)(ii) of this section. DP is a specified domestic entity for Year X.

(iii) *Reporting requirements*—(A) *DC1.* Under § 1.6038D-2(a)(6)(ii), DC1 is not treated as owning the specified foreign financial assets held by DC2 and DP for purposes of applying the reporting threshold of § 1.6038D-2(a)(1), because DC1 does not have an interest in any specified foreign financial assets. DC1 is not required to file Form 8938 because DC1 does not satisfy the reporting threshold of § 1.6038D-2(a)(1).

(B) *DC2 and DP.* Under § 1.6038D-3, DC2 and DP each has an interest in specified foreign financial assets. For purposes of applying the reporting threshold of § 1.6038D-2(a)(1), § 1.6038D-2(a)(6)(ii) provides that DC2 is treated as owning in addition to its own assets the assets of DP, and DP is treated as owning in addition to its own assets the assets of DC2. As a result, DC2 and DP each satisfies the reporting threshold of § 1.6038D-2(a)(1), because the value of the specified foreign financial assets each is considered as owning for purposes of § 1.6038D-2(a)(1) is $105,000 on October 12, Year X, which exceeds DC2's and DP's $75,000 reporting threshold. DC2 and DP must each file Form 8938 for Year X to report their respective specified foreign financial assets in which they have an interest and disclose their maximum values as provided in § 1.6038D-4 ($15,000 in the case of DC2 and $90,000 in the case of DP).

Example 3. Application of aggregation rule and entity with an active trade or business. (i) *Facts.* The facts are the same as in *Example 2*, except that DC2 also owns an active business. The assets attributable to the business are not passive assets and constitute at least 60% of the value of DC2's assets at all times during Year X. The income from the business is not passive income and constitutes at least 60% of the gross income generated by DC2 in Year X.

(ii) *Specified domestic entity status*—(A) *DC1 and DC2.* DC1 and DC2 are considered related entities that are connected through stock ownership with a common parent corporation under paragraph (b)(3)(iii) of this section because DC1 and DC2 are closely held by L, and DC2 is connected with DC1 though DC1's ownership of stock of DC2 representing at least 80% of the voting power or value of DC2. As a result, for purposes of applying paragraph (b)(1)(ii) of this section, each of DC1 and DC2 is treated as owning the combined assets, and receiving the combined income, of both DC1 and DC2; however, DC1's equity interest in DC2 is disregarded for this purpose under paragraph (b)(3)(iii) of this section. As a result, no more than 40 percent of the value of DC1's and DC2's assets at all times during Year X are passive and no more than 40 percent of DC1's and DC2's gross income for Year X is passive. DC1 and DC2 do not satisfy the passive income or passive asset threshold in paragraph (b)(1)(ii) of this section for Year X. DC1 and DC2 are not specified domestic entities for Year X.

(B) *DP.* For the reasons described in paragraph (ii)(B) of *Example 2*, DP is a specified domestic entity for Year X.

(iii) *Reporting requirements*—(A) *DC1 and DC2.* DC1 and DC2 are not specified domestic entities for Year X, and are not required to file Form 8938.

(B) *DP.* Under § 1.6038D-3, DP has an interest in specified foreign financial assets. Under § 1.6038D-2(a)(6)(ii), DP is treated as owning in addition to its own assets the assets of DC2. As a result, DP satisfies the reporting threshold of § 1.6038D-2(a)(1) because the value of the specified foreign financial assets it is considered to own for purposes of § 1.6038D-2(a)(1) is $105,000 on October 12, Year X, which exceeds DP's $75,000 reporting threshold. DP must file Form 8938 for Year X to report the specified foreign financial assets in which it has an interest and disclose their maximum values as provided in § 1.6038D-4, which is $90,000.

(c) *Domestic trusts.*—Except as otherwise provided in paragraph (d) of this section, a trust described in section 7701(a)(30)(E) is formed or availed of for purposes of holding, directly or indirectly, specified foreign financial assets if and only if the trust has one or more specified persons as a current beneficiary. The term current beneficiary means, with respect to the taxable year, any person who at any time during such taxable year is entitled to, or at the discretion of any person may receive, a distribution from the principal or income of the trust (determined without regard to any power of appointment to the extent that such power remains unexercised at the end of the taxable year). The term current beneficiary also includes any holder of a general power of appointment, whether or not exercised, that was exercisable at any time during the taxable year, but does not include any holder of a general power of appointment that is exercisable only on the death of the holder.

(d) *Excepted domestic entities.*—An entity is not considered to be a specified domestic entity if the entity is—

(1) *Certain persons described in section 1473(3).*—An entity, except for a trust that is exempt from tax under section 664(c), that is excepted from the definition of the term "specified United States person" under section 1473(3) and the regulations issued under that section;

(2) *Certain domestic trusts.*—A trust described in section 7701(a)(30)(E) provided that the trustee of the trust—

(i) Has supervisory authority over or fiduciary obligations with regard to the specified foreign financial assets held by the trust;

(ii) Timely files (including any applicable extensions) annual returns and information returns on behalf of the trust; and

(iii) Is—

(A) A bank that is examined by the Office of the Comptroller of the Currency, the Board of Governors of the Federal Reserve System, the Federal Deposit Insurance Corporation, or the National Credit Union Administration;

(B) A financial institution that is registered with and regulated or examined by the Securities and Exchange Commission; or

(C) A domestic corporation described in section 1473(3)(A) or (B), and the regulations issued with respect to those provisions.

(3) *Domestic trusts owned by one or more specified persons.*—A trust described in section 7701(a)(30)(E) to the extent such trust or any portion thereof is treated as owned by one or more specified persons under sections 671 through 678 and the regulations issued under those sections.

(e) *Effective/applicability dates.*—This section applies to taxable years beginning after December 31, 2015. [Reg. § 1.6038D-6.]

☐ [*T.D. 9706, 12-11-2014. Amended by T.D. 9752, 2-22-2016.*]

§ 1.6038D-7. Exceptions from the reporting of certain assets under Section 6038D.—(a) *Elimination of duplicative reporting of assets.*—(1) *In general.*—A specified person is not required to report a specified foreign financial asset on Form 8938, "Statement of Specified Foreign Financial Assets," if the specified person—

(i) Reports the asset on at least one of the following forms timely filed with the Internal Revenue Service for the taxable year—

(A) Form 3520, "Annual Return To Report Transactions With Foreign Trusts and Receipt of Certain Foreign Gifts" (in the case of a specified person that is the beneficiary of a foreign trust);

(B) Form 5471, "Information Return of U.S. Persons With Respect To Certain Foreign Corporations";

(C) Form 8621, "Return by a Shareholder of a Passive Foreign Investment Company or Qualified Electing Fund";

(D) Form 8865, "Return of U.S. Persons With Respect To Certain Foreign Partnerships";

(E) For taxable years beginning after March 18, 2010, and ending on or before December 31, 2013, Form 8891, "U.S. Information Return for Beneficiaries of Certain Canadian Registered Retirement Plans"; or

(F) Any other form under Title 26 of the United States Code timely filed with the Internal Revenue Service and identified for this purpose by the Secretary in regulations or other guidance; and

(ii) Reports on Form 8938 the filing of the form on which the asset is reported.

(2) *Foreign grantor trusts.*—A specified person that is treated as an owner of a foreign trust or any portion of a foreign trust under sections 671 through 679 is not required to report any specified foreign financial assets held by the foreign trust on Form 8938, provided—

(i) The specified person reports the trust on a Form 3520 timely filed with the Internal Revenue Service for the taxable year;

(ii) The trust timely files Form 3520-A, "Annual Information Return of Foreign Trust With a U.S. Owner," with the Internal Revenue Service for the taxable year; and

(iii) The Form 8938 filed by the specified person for the taxable year reports the filing of the Form 3520 and Form 3520-A.

(3) *Joint Form 5471 or Form 8865 filing.*—A specified person that is included as part of a joint Form 5471 filing pursuant to § 1.6038-2(j) or a joint Form 8865 filing pursuant to § 1.6038-3(c) and who notifies the Internal Revenue Service as required by § 1.6038-2(i) or § 1.6038D-(3)(c) will be considered to have filed a Form 5471 or Form 8865 for purposes of paragraph (a)(1) of this section.

(b) *Owner of certain trusts.*—A specified person that is treated as an owner of any portion of a domestic trust under sections 671 through 678 is not required to file Form 8938 to report any specified foreign financial asset held by the trust if the trust is—

(1) A widely-held fixed investment trust under § 1.671-5; or

(2) A liquidating trust within the meaning of § 301.7701-4(d) of this chapter that is created pursuant to a court order issued in a bankruptcy under Chapter 7 (11 U.S.C. 701 *et seq.*) or a confirmed plan under Chapter 11 (11 U.S.C. 1101 *et seq.*) of the Bankruptcy Code.

(c) *Special rules for bona fide residents of a U.S. possession.*—A specified individual who is a bona fide resident of a U.S. possession is not required to include the following specified foreign financial assets in the determination of the aggregate value of his or her specified foreign financial assets and, if required to file Form 8938 with the Internal Revenue Service, is not required to report the following specified foreign financial assets:

(1) A financial account maintained by a financial institution organized under the laws of the U.S. possession of which the specified individual is a bona fide resident;

(2) A financial account maintained by a branch of a financial institution not organized under the laws of the U.S. possession of which the specified individual is a bona fide resident, if the branch is subject to the same tax and information reporting requirements applicable to a financial institution organized under the laws of the U.S. possession;

(3) Stock or securities issued by an entity organized under the laws of the U.S. possession of which the specified individual is a bona fide resident;

(4) An interest in an entity organized under the laws of the U.S. possession of which the specified individual is a bona fide resident; and

(5) A financial instrument or contract held for investment, provided each issuer or counterparty that is not a United States person is—

(i) An entity organized under the laws of the U.S. possession of which the specified individual is a bona fide resident; or

(ii) A bona fide resident of the U.S. possession of which the specified individual is a bona fide resident.

(d) *Effective/applicability dates.*—This section applies to taxable years ending after December 19, 2011. Taxpayers may elect to apply the rules of this section to taxable years ending prior to December 19, 2011. [Reg. § 1.6038D-7.]

☐ [*T.D. 9706, 12-11-2014.*]

§ 1.6038D-8. Specified domestic entities.—(a) *In general.*—If a specified person fails to file a Form 8938, "Statement of Specified Foreign Financial Assets," that includes the information required by section 6038D(c) and § 1.6038D-4 with respect to any taxable year at the time and in the manner described in section 6038D(a) and § 1.6038D-2, a penalty of $10,000 will apply to that specified person.

(b) *Married specified individuals filing a joint annual return.*—Married specified individuals who file a joint annual return and fail to file a required Form 8938 that includes the information required by section 6038D(c) and § 1.6038D-4 with respect to any taxable year at the time and in the manner described in section 6038D(a) and § 1.6038D-2 are subject to penalties under this section as if the married specified individuals are a single specified individual. The liability of married specified individuals who file a joint annual return with respect to any penalties under this section is joint and several.

(c) *Increase in penalty.*—If any failure to comply with the applicable reporting requirement of section 6038D and the regulations continues for more than 90 days after the day on which the Commissioner or his delegate mails a notice of the failure to the specified person required to file the Form 8938, the specified person is required to pay an additional penalty of $10,000 for each 30-day period (or fraction thereof) during which the failure continues after the 90-day period has expired. The additional penalty imposed by section 6038D(d)(2) and this paragraph (c) is limited to a maximum of $50,000 for each such failure.

(d) *Presumption of aggregate value.*—For the purpose of assessing penalties imposed under section 6038D(d), if the Commissioner or his delegate determines that a specified person has an interest in one or more specified foreign financial assets and the specified person does not provide sufficient information to demonstrate the aggregate value of the assets upon request by the Commissioner or his delegate, then the aggregate value of the assets is treated as being in excess of the applicable reporting threshold set forth in § 1.6038D-2(a).

(e) *Reasonable cause exception.*—(1) *In general.*—If the failure to report the information required in section 6038D(c) and § 1.6038D-4 is shown to be due to reasonable cause and not due to willful neglect, no penalty will be imposed under section 6038D(d) or this section.

(2) *Affirmative showing required.*—In order to show that the failure to report the information required in section 6038D(c) and § 1.6038D-4 is due to reasonable cause and not due to willful neglect for purposes of section 6038D(g) and this section, the specified person must make an affirmative showing of all the facts alleged as reasonable cause for the failure to disclose.

(3) *Facts and circumstances taken into account.*—The determination of whether a failure to disclose a specified foreign financial asset on Form 8938 was due to reasonable cause and not due to willful neglect is made on a case-by-case basis, taking into account all pertinent facts and circumstances. The fact that a foreign jurisdiction would impose

a civil or criminal penalty on the specified person (or any other person) for disclosing the required information is not reasonable cause.

(f) *Penalties for underpayments attributable to undisclosed foreign financial assets.*—(1) *Accuracy-related penalty.*—For application of the accuracy-related penalty in the case of any portion of an underpayment attributable to any undisclosed foreign financial asset understatement, see section 6662(j).

(2) *Criminal penalties.*—In addition to other penalties, failure to comply with the reporting requirements of section 6038D and the regulations, or any underpayment related to such failure, may result in criminal penalties under sections 7201, 7203, 7206, et seq., or other provisions of Federal law.

(g) *Effective/applicability dates.*—This section applies to taxable years ending after December 19, 2011. Taxpayers may elect to apply the rules of this section to taxable years ending prior to December 19, 2011. [Reg. § 1.6038D-8.]

☐ [*T.D.* 9706, 12-11-2014.]

§ 301.6039E-1. Information reporting by passport applicants.—(a) *In general.*—Every individual who applies for a U.S. passport or the renewal of a passport (passport applicant), other than a passport for use in diplomatic, military, or other official U.S. government business, shall include with his or her passport application the information described in paragraph (b)(1) of this section in the time and manner described in paragraph (b)(2) of this section.

(b) *Required information.*—(1) *In general.*—The information required under paragraph (a) of this section shall include the following information:

(i) The passport applicant's full name and, if applicable, previous name;

(ii) The passport applicant's permanent address and, if different, mailing address;

(iii) The passport applicant's taxpayer identifying number (TIN), if such a number has been issued to the passport applicant. A TIN means the individual's social security number (SSN) issued by the Social Security Administration. A passport applicant who does not have an SSN must enter zeros in the appropriate space on the passport application; and

(iv) The passport applicant's date of birth.

(2) *Time and manner for furnishing information.*—A passport applicant must provide the information required by this section with his or her passport application, whether by personal appearance or mail, to the Department of State (including United States Embassies and Consular posts abroad).

(c) *Penalties.*—(1) *In general.*—If the information required by paragraph (b)(1) of this section is incomplete or incorrect, or the information is not filed in the time and manner described in paragraph (b)(2) of this section, then the passport applicant may be subject to a penalty equal to $500 per application. Before assessing a penalty under this section, the IRS will provide to the passport applicant written notice of the potential assessment of the $500 penalty, requesting the information being sought, and offering the applicant an opportunity to explain why the information was not provided with the passport application. A passport applicant has 60 days from the date of the notice of the potential assessment of the penalty (90 days from such date if the notice is addressed to an applicant outside the United States) to respond to the notice. If the passport applicant demonstrates to the satisfaction of the Commissioner (or the Commissioner's delegate) that the failure is due to reasonable cause and not due to willful neglect, after considering all the surrounding circumstances, then the IRS will not assess the penalty.

(2) *Example.*—The following example illustrates the provisions of paragraph (c) of this section.

Example. C, a citizen of the United States, makes an error in supplying information on his passport application. Based on the nature of the error and C's timely response to correct the error after being contacted by the IRS, the Commissioner concludes that the mistake is due to reasonable cause and not due to willful neglect. Accordingly, no penalty is assessed.

(d) *Effective/applicability date.*—This section applies to passport applications submitted after July 18, 2014. [Reg. § 301.6039E-1.]

☐ [*T.D.* 9679, 7-17-2014.]

§ 1.6046-1. Returns as to organization or reorganization of foreign corporations and as to acquisitions of their stock.—(a) *Officers or directors.*—(1) *When liability arises on January 1, 1963.*—Each United States citizen or resident who is on January 1, 1963, an officer or director of a foreign corporation shall make a return on Form 5471 (or subsequent form) showing the name, address, and identifying number of each United States person who, on January 1, 1963, owns 5 percent or more in value of the outstanding stock of such foreign corporation.

(2) *When liability arises after January 1, 1963.*—(i) *Requirement of return.*—Each United States citizen or resident who is at any time after January 1, 1963, an officer or director of a foreign corporation shall make a return on Form 5471 setting forth the information described in paragraph (a)(2)(ii) of this section with respect to each United States person who, during the time such citizen or resident is such an officer or director —

(*a*) Acquires (whether in one or more transactions) outstanding stock of such corporation which equals, or which when added to any such stock then owned by him equals, 10 percent or more of the total combined voting power of all classes of stock of the foreign corporation entitled to vote or the total value of the stock of the foreign corporation;

(*b*) Acquires (whether in one or more transactions) an additional 10 percent or more of the total combined voting power of all classes of stock of the foreign corporation entitled to vote or the total value of the stock of the foreign corporation; or

(*c*) Is not described in paragraph (a)(2)(i)(*a*) or (*b*) of this section, and who, at any time after January 1, 1987, is treated as a United States shareholder under section 953(c) with respect to such foreign corporation.

(ii) *Information required to be shown on return.*—The return required under subdivision (i) of this subparagraph shall contain the following information:

(*a*) Name, address, and identifying number of each shareholder with respect to whom the return is filed;

(*b*) A statement showing that the shareholder is either described in subdivision (i)(*a*) or (i)(*b*) of this subparagraph; and

(*c*) The date on which the shareholder became a person described in subdivision (i)(*a*) or (i)(*b*) of this subparagraph.

(3) *Application of rules.*—The provisions of this paragraph may be illustrated by the following examples:

Example (1). A, a United States citizen, is, on January 1, 1963, a director of M, a foreign corporation. X, on January 1, 1963, is a United States person owning 5 percent in value of the outstanding stock of M Corporation. A must file a return under the provisions of subparagraph (1) of this paragraph.

Example 2. (i) *Facts.* A, a United States citizen, is, on January 1, 2014, a director of M Corporation, a foreign corporation. X, on January 1, 2014, is a United States person owning 4% of the outstanding stock of M Corporation. On July 1, 2014, X acquires 4% of the outstanding stock of M Corporation and on September 1, 2014, he acquires an additional 4% of such stock.

(ii) *Results.* The July 1, 2014, transaction does not give rise to liability for A to file a return; however, A must file a return as a result of the September 1, 2014, transaction because X's holdings now exceed 10%.

Example 3. (i) *Facts.* The facts are the same as in *Example 2* and, on September 15, 2014, X acquires an additional 8% of the outstanding stock of M Corporation. (X's total holdings are now 20%.) On November 1, 2014, X acquires an additional 4% of the outstanding stock of M Corporation.

(ii) *Results.* The September 15, 2014, transaction does not give rise to liability to file a return since X has not acquired 10% of the outstanding stock of M Corporation since A last became liable to file a return. However, A must file a return as a result of the November 1, 2014, transaction because X has now acquired an additional 10% of the outstanding stock of M Corporation.

Example 4. (i) *Facts.* The facts are the same as in *Examples* 2 and 3 and, in addition, B, a United States citizen, becomes an officer of M Corporation on September 10, 2014.

(ii) *Results.* B is not required to file a return either as a result of the facts set forth in *Example 2* or as a result of the September 15, 2014, transaction described in *Example 3*. However, B is required to file a return as a result of the November 1, 2014, transaction described in *Example 3* because X has acquired an additional 10% in value of the outstanding stock of M Corporation while B is an officer or director.

(b) *Returns required of United States persons when liability to file arises on January 1, 1963.*—Each United States person who, on January 1, 1963, owns 5 percent or more in value of the outstanding stock of a foreign corporation, shall make a return on Form 959 with respect to such foreign corporation setting forth the following information:

(1) The name, address, and identifying number of the shareholder (or shareholders) filing the return, and the internal revenue district in which such shareholder filed his most recent United States income tax return;

(2) The name, business address, and employer identification number, if any, of the foreign corporation, the name of the country under the laws of which it is incorporated, and the name of the country in which is located its principal place of business;

(3) The date of organization and, if any, of each reorganization of the foreign corporation if such reorganization occurred on or after January 1, 1960, while the shareholder owned 5 percent or more in value of the outstanding stock of such corporation;

(4) The name and address of the foreign corporation's statutory or resident agent in the country of incorporation;

(5) The name, address, and identifying number of any branch office or agent of the foreign corporation located in the United States;

(6) If the foreign corporation has filed a United States income tax return, or participated in the filing of a consolidated return, for any of its last three calendar or fiscal years immediately preceding January 1, 1963, state each year for which a return was filed (including, in the case of a consolidated return, the name of the corporation filing such return), the type of form used, the internal revenue office to which it was sent, and the amount of tax, if any, paid;

(7) The name and address of the person (or persons) having custody of the books of account and records of the foreign corporation, and the location of such books and records if different from such address;

(8) The names, addresses, and identifying numbers of all United States persons who are principal officers (for example, president, vice president, secretary, treasurer, and comptroller) or members of the board of directors of the foreign corporation as of January 1, 1963;

(9) A complete description of the principal business activities in which the foreign corporation is actually engaged and, if the foreign corporation is a member of a group constituting a chain of ownership with respect to each unit of which the shareholder owns 5 percent or more in value of the outstanding stock, a chart showing the foreign corporation's position in the chain of ownership and the percentages of ownership;

(10) The following information prepared in accordance with generally accepted accounting principles and in such detail as is customary for the corporation's accounting records.

(i) The corporation's profit and loss statement for the most recent complete annual accounting period; and

(ii) The corporation's balance sheet as of the end of the most recent complete annual accounting period;

(11) A statement showing as of January 1, 1963, the amount and type of any indebtedness of the foreign corporation—

(i) To any United States person owning 5 percent or more in value of its stock, or

(ii) To any other foreign corporation owning 5 percent or more in value of the outstanding stock of the foreign corporation with respect to which the return is filed provided that the shareholder filing the return owns 5 percent or more in value of the outstanding stock of such other foreign corporation,

together with the name, address, and identifying number, if any, of each such shareholder or entity;

(12) A statement, as of January 1, 1963, showing the name, address, and identifying number, if any, of each person who is, on January 1, 1963, a subscriber to the stock of the foreign corporation, and the number of shares subscribed to by each;

(13) A statement showing the number of shares of each class of stock of the foreign corporation owned by each shareholder filing the return and—

(i) If such stock was acquired after December 31, 1953, the dates of acquisition, the amounts paid or value given therefor, the method of acquisition, i.e., by original issue, purchase on open market, direct purchase, gift, inheritance, etc., and from whom acquired; or

(ii) If such stock was acquired before January 1, 1954, a statement that such stock was acquired before such date, and the value at which such stock is carried on the books of such shareholder;

(14) A statement showing as of January 1, 1963, the name, address, and identifying number of each United States person who owns 5 percent or more in value of the outstanding stock of the foreign corporation, the classes of stock held, the number of shares of each class held, including the name, address, and identifying number, if any, of each actual owner if such person is different from the shareholder of record and a statement of the nature and amount of the interests of each such actual owner; and

(15) The total number of shares of each class of outstanding stock of the foreign corporation (or other data indicating the shareholder's percentage of ownership).

(c) *Returns required of United States persons when liability to file arises after January 1, 1963.*—(1) *United States persons required to file.*—A return on Form 5471, containing the information required by paragraph (c)(4) of this section, shall be made by each United States person when at any time after January 1, 1963:

(i) Such person acquires (whether in one or more transactions) outstanding stock of such foreign corporation which equals, or which when added to any such stock then owned by him equals, 10 percent or more of the total combined voting power of all classes of stock of the foreign corporation entitled to vote or the total value of the stock of the foreign corporation;

(ii) Such person, having already acquired the interest referred to in paragraph (b) of this section or in paragraph (c)(1)(i) of this section —

(a) Acquires (whether in one or more transactions) an additional 10 percent or more of the total combined voting power of all classes of stock of the foreign corporation entitled to vote or the total value of the stock of the foreign corporation;

(b) Owns 10 percent or more of the total combined voting power of all classes of stock of the foreign corporation entitled to vote or the total value of the stock of the foreign corporation when such foreign corporation is reorganized (as defined in paragraph (f)); or

(c) Disposes of sufficient stock in such foreign corporation to reduce his interest to less than 10 percent of the total combined voting power of all classes of stock of the foreign corporation entitled to vote or the total value of the stock of the foreign corporation; or

(iii) Such person is, at any time after January 1, 1987, treated as a United States shareholder under *section 953(c)* with respect to a foreign corporation.

(2) *Examples.*—The provisions of paragraph (c)(1) of this section may be illustrated by the following examples:

Example 1. (i) *Facts.* On January 15, 2014, A, a United States person, acquires 10% of the outstanding stock of M, a foreign corporation.

(ii) *Results.* A must file a return under the provisions of paragraph (c)(1) of this section.

Example 2. (i) *Facts.* On January 1, 2014, B, a United States person, owns 4% of the outstanding stock of M, a foreign corporation. On February 1, 2015, B acquires an additional 6% of the outstanding stock of M Corporation.

(ii) *Results.* B is not required to file a return for 2014 under the provisions of this section because he does not own 10% or more of the outstanding stock of M Corporation. B must file a return for 2015 under the provisions of paragraph (c)(1) of this section.

Example 3. (i) *Facts.* On January 1, 2014, C, a United States person, owns 12% of the outstanding stock of M Corporation, a foreign corporation. On February 1, 2014, C acquires an additional 4% of the outstanding stock of M Corporation in a transaction not involving a reorganization.

(ii) *Results.* C is not required to file a return under the provisions of paragraph (c)(1) of this section with respect to the acquisition of the additional 4% of M Corporation.

Example 4. (i) *Facts.* The facts are the same as in *Example 3* except that, in addition, on April 1, 2014, C acquires 4% of the outstanding stock of M Corporation in a transaction not involving a reorganization. (C's total holdings are now 20%.) On May 1, 2014, C acquires 2% of the outstanding stock of M Corporation.

(ii) *Results.* C is not required to file a return under the provisions of paragraph (c)(1) of this section as a result of the April 1, 2014, acquisition because he has not acquired 10% or more of the outstanding stock of M Corporation since he last became liable to file a return. C must file a return under the provisions of paragraph (c)(1) of this section as a result of the May 1, 2014, acquisition because C acquired 10% of the outstanding stock of M Corporation during 2014.

Example 5. (i) *Facts.* On June 1, 2014, D, a United States person, owns 24% of the outstanding stock of M Corporation, a foreign corporation. Also, on June 1, 2014, M Corporation is reorganized and, as a result of such reorganization, D owns only 12% of the outstanding stock of such foreign corporation.

(ii) *Results.* D must file a return under the provisions of paragraph (c)(1) of this section.

Example 6. (i) *Facts.* The facts are the same as in *Example 5* except that, in addition, on November 1, 2015, D donates 4% of the outstanding stock of M Corporation to a charity.

(ii) *Results.* Since D has disposed of sufficient stock to reduce his interest in M Corporation to less than 10% of the outstanding stock of such corporation, D must file a return under the provisions of paragraph (c)(1) of this section.

(3) *Shareholders who become United States persons.*—A return on Form 5471, containing the information required by paragraph (c)(4) of this section, shall be made by each person who at any time after January 1, 1963, becomes a United States person while owning 10 percent or more of the total combined voting power of all classes of stock of the foreign corporation entitled to vote or the total value of the stock of the foreign corporation.

(4) *Information required to be shown on return.*—(i) *In general.*—The return on Form 5471, required to be filed by persons described in paragraph (c)(1) or (3) of this section, shall set forth the same information as is required by the provisions of paragraph (b) of this section except that where such provisions require information with respect to January 1, 1963, such information shall be furnished with respect to the date on which liability arises to file the return required under this paragraph.

(ii) *Additional information.*—In addition to the information required under paragraph (c)(4)(i) of this section, the following information shall also be furnished in the return required under this paragraph:

(a) The date on or after January 1, 1963, if any, on which such shareholder (or shareholders) last filed a return under this section with respect to the corporation;

(b) If a return is filed by reason of becoming a United States person, the date the shareholder became a United States person;

(c) If a return is filed by reason of the disposition of stock, the date and method of such disposition and the person to whom such disposition was made; and

(d) If a return is filed by reason of the organization or reorganization of the foreign corporation on or after January 1, 1963, the following information with respect to such organization or reorganization:

(1) A statement showing a detailed list of the classes and kinds of assets transferred to the foreign corporation including a description of the assets (such as a list of patents, copyrights, stock, securities, etc.), the fair market value of each asset transferred (and, if such asset is transferred by a United States person, its adjusted basis), the date of transfer, the name, address, and identifying number, if any, of the owner immediately prior to the transfer, and the consideration paid by the foreign corporation for such transfer;

(2) A statement showing the assets transferred and the notes or securities issued by the foreign corporation, the name, address, and identifying number, if any, of each person to whom such transfer or issue was made, and the consideration paid to the foreign corporation for such transfer or issue; and

(3) An analysis of the changes in the corporation's surplus accounts occurring on or after January 1, 1963.

(iii) *Exclusion of information previously furnished.*—In any case where any identical item of information required to be filed under this paragraph by a shareholder with respect to a foreign corporation has previously been furnished by such shareholder in any return made in accordance with the provisions of this section, such shareholder may satisfy the requirements of this paragraph by filing Form 5471, identifying such item of information, the date furnished, and stating that it is unchanged.

(d) *Associations, etc.*—Returns are required to be filed in accordance with the provisions of this section with respect to any foreign association, foreign joint-stock company, or foreign insurance company, etc., which would be considered to be a corporation under § 301.7701-2 of this chapter (Regulations on Procedure and Administration). Persons who would qualify by the nature of their functions and ownership in such associations, etc., as officers, directors, or shareholders thereof will be treated as such for purposes of this section without regard to their designations under local law.

(e) *Special provisions.*—(1) *Return jointly made.*—Any two or more persons required under paragraph (a) of this section to make a return with respect to one or more shareholders of the same corporation, or under paragraph (b) or (c) of this section to make a return with respect to the same corporation, may in lieu of making several returns, jointly make one return.

(2) *Separate return for each corporation.*—When returns are required with respect to more than one foreign corporation, a separate return must be made for each corporation.

(3) *Use of power of attorney by officers or directors.*—(i) *In general.*—Any two or more persons required under paragraph (a) of this section to make a return with respect to one or more shareholders of the same corporation may, by means of one or more duly executed powers of attorney, constitute one of their number as attorney in fact for the purpose of making such returns or for the purpose of making a joint return under subparagraph (1) of this paragraph.

(ii) *Nature of power of attorney.*—The power of attorney referred to in subdivision (i) of this subparagraph shall be limited to the making of returns required under paragraph (a) of this section and shall be limited to a single calendar year with respect to which such returns are required.

(iii) *Manner of execution of power of attorney.*—The use of technical language in the preparation of the power of attorney referred to in subdivision (i) of this subparagraph is not necessary. Such power of attorney shall be signed by the individual United States citizen or resident required to file a return or returns under paragraph (a) of this section. Such power of attorney must be acknowledged before a notary public or, in lieu thereof, witnessed by two disinterested persons. The notarial seal must be affixed unless such seal is not required under the laws of the state or country wherein such power of attorney is executed.

(iv) *Manner of execution of return under authority of power of attorney.*—A return made under authority of one or more powers of attorney referred to in subdivision (i) of this subparagraph shall be signed by the attorney in fact for each principal for which such attorney in fact is acting. A copy of such one or more powers of attorney shall be kept at a convenient and safe location accessible to internal revenue officers, and shall at all times be available for inspection by such officers.

(v) *Effect on penalties.*—The fact that a return is made under authority of a power of attorney referred to in subdivision (i) of this subparagraph shall not affect the principal's liability for penalties provided for failure to file a return required under paragraph (a) of this section or for filing a false or fraudulent return.

(4) *Persons excepted from filing returns.*—(i) *Return required of officer or director under paragraph (a)(1).*—Notwithstanding paragraph (a)(1) of this section, any United States citizen or resident required to make a return under such paragraph with respect to shareholders of a foreign corporation, need not make such return if, on January 1, 1963, three or fewer United States persons own 95 percent or more in value of the outstanding stock of such foreign corporation and file a return or returns with respect to such corporation under paragraph (b) of this section.

(ii) *Return required of officer or director under paragraph (a)(2).*—Notwithstanding paragraph (a)(2) of this section, any United States citizen or resident required to make a return under such paragraph with respect to a person acquiring stock of a foreign corporation in an acquisition described in subdivision (i)*(a)* or *(b)* of such paragraph need not make such return, if—

(a) As a result of such acquisition of stock of such foreign corporation, a United States person files a return as a shareholder under paragraph (c)(1) of this section, and

(b) Immediately after such acquisition of stock, three or fewer United States persons own 95 percent or more in value of the outstanding stock of such foreign corporation.

(iii) *Return required by reason of attribution rules.*—Notwithstanding paragraph (b) or (c) of this section, any person required to make a return under such paragraph with respect to a foreign corporation need not make such return, if—

(a) Such person does not directly own an interest in the foreign corporation,

(b) Such person is required to furnish the information solely by reason of attribution of stock ownership from a United States person under paragraph (i) of this section, and

(c) The person from whom the stock ownership is attributed furnishes all of the information required under paragraph (b) or (c) of this section of the person to whom such stock ownership is attributed.

(iv) *Return required of officer or director with respect to person described in subdivision (iii).*—Notwithstanding paragraph (a) of this section, any United States citizen or resident required to make a return under such paragraph with respect to a person exempted under subdivision (iii) of this subparagraph from making a return need not make a return with respect to such person.

(5) *Persons excepted from furnishing items of information.*—Any person required to furnish any item of information under paragraph (b) or (c) of this section with respect to a foreign corporation may, if such item of information is furnished by another person having an equal or greater stock interest (measured in terms of either the total combined voting power of all classes of stock of the foreign corporation entitled to vote or the total value of the stock of the foreign corporation) in such foreign corporation, satisfy such requirement by filing a statement with his return on Form 5471 indicating that such requirement has been satisfied and identifying the return in which such item of information was included. This paragraph (e)(5) does not apply to persons excepted from filing a return by reason of the provisions of paragraph (e)(4) of this section.

(f) *Meaning of terms.*—For purposes of this section—

(1) *Acquisition.*—Stock in a foreign corporation shall be considered acquired when a person has an unqualified right to receive such stock, even though such stock is not actually issued. For example, when under the law of a foreign country, all the necessary steps for incorporation are completed but stock in the corporation will not be issued within 30 days, every United States citizen or resident who is an officer or a director of such corporation, provided a United States person has an interest of 10 percent or more in such corporation, and every such United States person shall, within 90 days of the date of incorporation, file the returns required under section 6046 and this section. In the case of a reorganization, new stock may be acquired, depending on the type of reorganization, whether or not any stock certificates are surrendered or exchanged or the designation of such stock is altered.

(2) *Reorganization.*—With respect to a foreign corporation, the term "reorganization" shall mean not only a transaction described in section 368(a)(1) and the regulations thereunder but also any other transaction or series of transactions which has the same effect.

(3) *U.S. person.*—(i) *In general.*—For purposes of section 6046 and this section, the term *United States person* has the meaning assigned to it by section 7701(a)(30), except as provided in paragraphs (f)(3)(ii) and (iii) of this section.

(ii) *Special rule for individuals residing in certain possessions.*—(A) With respect to an individual who is a bona fide resident of Puerto Rico, the term United States person has the meaning assigned to it by § 1.957-3 except that the rules of § 1.937-2(g)(1) will apply.

(B) With respect to individuals who are bona fide residents of any section 931 possession, as defined in § 1.931-1(c)(1), the term United States person has the meaning assigned to it by § 1.957-3.

(iii) *Special rule for certain nonresident aliens.*—An individual for whom an election under section 6013(g) or (h) is in effect will, subject to the exceptions contained in paragraph (f)(3)(ii) of this section, be considered a United States person for purposes of section 6046 and this section.

(4) [Reserved].

(5) *Accounting period and taxable year.*—In the case of a specified foreign corporation (as defined in section 898), the taxable year of such corporation shall be treated as its annual accounting period.

(g) *Method of reporting.*—All amounts furnished in returns prescribed under this section shall be expressed in United States currency with a statement of the exchange rates used. All statements required to be submitted on or with returns under this section shall be rendered in the English language. For taxable years ending after December 31, 1994, with respect to returns filed after December 31, 1995, all amounts furnished under paragraph (c) of this section shall be expressed in United States dollars computed and translated in conformity with United States generally accepted accounting principles. Amounts furnished under paragraph (c)(3)(i) of this section shall also be furnished in the foreign corporation's functional currency as required on the form. Information described in paragraphs (b)(10) and (c)(3) of this section shall be submitted in such form or manner as the form shall prescribe. If an individual who is a United States person required to make a return with respect to a foreign corporation under section 6046 is entitled under a treaty to be treated as a nonresident of the United States, and if the individual claims this treaty benefit, and if there are no other United States persons that are required to furnish information under section 6046 with respect to the foreign corporation, then the individual may satisfy the requirements of paragraphs (b)(10), (11) and (12), (c)(3)(ii)(d), and (g) of this section by filing the audited foreign financial statements of the foreign corporation with the individual's return required under section 6046.

(h) *Actual ownership of stock.*—If any shareholder, referred to in this section, is not the actual owner of the stock of the foreign corporation, the information required under this section shall be furnished in the name of and by such actual owner. For example, in the case of stock held by a nominee, the information required under this section shall be furnished by the actual owner of such stock.

(i) *Constructive ownership of stock.*—(1) *In general.*—Stock owned directly or indirectly by or for a foreign corporation or a foreign partnership shall be considered as being owned proportionately by its shareholders or partners. Thus, any United States person who is a member of a nonresident foreign partnership which becomes a shareholder in a foreign corporation shall be considered to be a shareholder in such foreign corporation to the extent of his proportionate share in such partnership.

(2) *Members of family.*—An individual shall be considered as owning the stock owned directly or indirectly by or for his brothers and sisters (whether by the whole or half blood), his spouse, his ancestors, and his lineal descendants. However, when stock is treated as owned by an individual under the rule provided in this subparagraph, it shall not be treated as owned by him for the purpose of again applying such rule in order to make another the constructive owner of such stock. The provisions of this subparagraph may be illustrated by the following example:

Example. H, W, and HF are United States citizens. W, wife of H, owns 20 percent of the value of the outstanding stock of X, a foreign corporation. X Corporation owns 90 percent of the value of the outstanding stock of Y Corporation, a foreign corporation. Y Corporation becomes the owner of 50 percent of the value of the outstanding stock of each of two newly organized foreign corporations, M and N. In applying the "members of family" rule, H is considered to own 20 percent of the value of the outstanding stock of X Corporation, and 18 percent of the value of the outstanding stock of Y Corporation, and 9 percent of M Corporation and N Corporation. However, HF, the father of H, is not considered to own stock of X, Y, M, or N since his son, H, is not treated as the owner of such stock for purposes of again applying the "members of family" rule.

(j) *Time and place for filing return.*—(1) *Time for filing.*—Any return required by section 6046 and this section shall be filed on or before the 90th day after the date on which a United States citizen, resident, or person becomes liable to file such return under any provision of section 6046(a) and of paragraph (a), (b), or (c) of this section. With respect to returns filed after September 3, 1982, such return shall be filed on or before such later date (if any) as may be authorized by the return form. The Director of the Internal Revenue Service Center where the return is required to be filed is authorized to grant reasonable extensions of time for filing returns under section 6046 and this section in accordance with the applicable provisions of section 6081(a) and § 1.6081-1.

(2) *Place for filing.*—Returns required by section 6046 and this section shall be filed with the Internal Revenue Service Center designated in the instructions of the applicable form.

(k) *Penalties.*—(1) For criminal penalties for failure to file a return and filing a false or fraudulent return, see sections 7203, 7206, and 7207.

(2) For civil penalty for failure to file return, or failure to show information required on a return, under this section, see section 6679.

(l) *Effective/applicability date.*—(1) Paragraph (f)(3) of this section applies to taxable years ending after April 9, 2008.

(2) Paragraph (c)(1)(iii) of this section applies to taxable years ending on or after December 31, 2013.

(3) Paragraph (e)(5) of this section applies to returns filed on or after December 31, 2013. See paragraph (e)(5) of § 1.6046-1, as contained in 26 CFR part 1 revised as of April 1, 2012, for returns filed before December 31, 2013. [Reg. § 1.6046-1.]

☐ [*T.D. 6623, 11-30-62. Amended by T.D. 6997, 1-17-69; T.D. 7322, 8-23-74; T.D. 7925, 12-12-83; T.D. 8573, 12-13-94; T.D. 8733, 10-6-97; T.D. 9194, 4-6-2005; T.D. 9391, 4-4-2008, T.D. 9650, 12-30-2013 (corrected 5-9-2014) and T.D. 9806, 12-27-2016.*]

§ 1.6046A-1. Return requirement for United States persons who acquire or dispose of an interest in a foreign partnership, or whose proportional interest in a foreign partnership changes substantially.—(a) *Return requirement.*—(1) *General rule.*—If a United States person has a reportable event (as defined in paragraph (b)(1) of this section) during the person's tax year, then, except as provided in paragraph (f) of this section, the United States person is required to complete and file Form 8865, "Return of U.S. Persons With Respect To Certain Foreign Partnerships," containing the information described in paragraph (c) of this section.

(2) *Separate return for each partnership.*—If a United States person has a reportable event with respect to an interest in more than one foreign partnership, the United States person must file a separate Form 8865 for each foreign partnership.

(b) *Definitions.*—(1) *Reportable event.*—There are three categories of reportable events under section 6046A: acquisitions, dispositions, and changes in proportional interests.

(i) *Acquisitions.*—A United States person that acquires a foreign partnership interest has a reportable event if—

(A) The person did not own a ten-percent or greater direct interest in the partnership and as a result of the acquisition the person owns a ten-percent or greater direct interest in the partnership. For purposes of this paragraph (b)(1)(i)(A), an acquisition includes an increase in a person's direct proportional interest; or

(B) Subject to paragraph (b)(2) of this section, compared to the person's direct interest when the person last had a reportable event, after the acquisition the person's direct interest has increased by at least a ten-percent interest.

(ii) *Dispositions.*—A United States person that disposes of a foreign partnership interest has a reportable event if—

(A) The person owned a ten-percent or greater direct interest in the partnership before the disposition and as a result of the disposition the person owns less than a ten-percent direct interest. For purposes of this paragraph (b)(1)(ii)(A), a disposition includes a decrease in a person's direct proportional interest; or

(B) Subject to paragraph (b)(2) of this section, compared to the person's direct interest when the person last had a reportable event, after the disposition the person's direct interest has decreased by at least a ten-percent interest.

(iii) *Changes in proportional interests not otherwise reportable as acquisitions or dispositions under paragraph (b)(1)(i)(A) or (b)(1)(ii)(A) of this section.*—A United States person has a reportable event if, subject to paragraph (b)(2) of this section, compared to the person's direct proportional interest the last time the person had a reportable event, the person's direct proportional interest has increased or decreased by at least the equivalent of a ten-percent interest.

(2) *Special rule for foreign partnership interests owned on December 31, 1999.*—If a United States person owned a ten-percent or greater direct interest in a foreign partnership on December 31, 1999, then to determine whether the person has a reportable event under paragraph (b)(1)(i)(B), (b)(1)(ii)(B), or (b)(1)(iii) of this section, the comparison should be made to the person's direct interest on December 31, 1999. Once the person has a reportable event after December 31, 1999, future comparisons should be made by reference to the last reportable event.

(3) *Change in a proportional interest.*—A partner's proportional interest in a foreign partnership may change for a number of reasons, for example, the change may be caused by changes in other partners' interests resulting from a partner withdrawing from the partnership. A proportional change may also occur by operation of the partnership agreement, for example, if the partnership agreement provides that a partner's interest in profits will change on a set date or when the partnership has earned a specified amount of profits and one of those events occurs.

(4) *Ten-percent interest.*—Under section 6046A(d) and this section, a *ten-percent interest* in a foreign partnership, as described in section 6038(e)(3)(C) and the regulations thereunder, means an interest equal to ten percent of the capital interest in such partnership, an interest equal to ten percent of the profits interest in such partnership, or an interest to which ten percent of the deductions or losses of such partnership are allocated.

(5) *United States person.*— *United States person* means a person described in section 7701(a)(30).

(6) *Foreign partnership.*— *Foreign partnership* means any partnership that is a foreign partnership under sections 7701(a)(2) and (5).

(7) *Examples.*—The rules of paragraph (a) of this section and this paragraph (b) are illustrated by the following examples:

Example 1. Acquisition of an indirect interest. FP, a foreign partnership, has two partners, *FC1* and *FC2*, both foreign corporations. *FC1* owns a 40% interest in *FP*, and *FC2* owns a 60% interest in *FP*. No United States person owns an interest in *FP*, either directly, or constructively under section 6038(e)(3)(C) and section 267(c). On January 1, 2001, *US*, a United States person and calendar year taxpayer, acquires by purchase 100% of *FC2*'s stock. *US* has acquired an indirect interest of 60% in *FP*. See sections 6038(e)(3)(C) and 267(c)(1). However, *US* is not required to report the January 1, 2001 indirect acquisition under section 6046A. *US* did not own a 10% or greater direct interest in *FP* before the acquisition, and *US* does not own a 10% or greater direct interest as a result of the acquisition. (*US* must, however, comply with the reporting requirements under section 6038 (controlled foreign corporation and controlled foreign partnership reporting) with respect to *FC2* and *FP*.)

Example 2. Acquisition of direct interests. (i) Assume the same facts as *Example 1*. In addition, on June 1, 2001, *US* purchases a 5% direct interest in *FP* from *FC1*. *US* did not own a 10% or greater direct interest in *FP* before the acquisition. After the acquisition, *US* does not own a direct interest of 10% or more. *US* owns a 10% or greater total interest (direct and indirect), but only a 5% direct interest. Therefore, *US* is not required to report the June 1, 2001, acquisition under section 6046A.

(ii) On September 1, 2001, *US* purchases a 7% direct interest in *FP* from *FC1*. The September 1, 2001 acquisition constitutes a reportable event under paragraph (b)(1)(i)(A) of this section. Before the September 1 acquisition, *US* did not own a 10% or greater direct interest in *FP*. After the September 1 acquisition, *US* owns a 12% direct interest, and therefore, as a result of the September 1 acquisition, *US* now owns a 10% or greater direct interest in *FP*. Consequently, *US* must report its September 1 acquisition under section 6046A on Form 8865 filed with *US*'s 2001 income tax return.

(iii) On December 1, 2001, *US* acquires an additional 4% direct interest in *FP* from *FC1*, so that *US*'s total direct interest has increased from 12% to 16%. This acquisition does not constitute a reportable event. Compared to *US*'s direct interest when *US* last had a reportable event (12% on September 1, 2001), after acquiring the 4% interest *US*'s direct interest has not increased by at least a 10% direct interest (i.e., its direct interest increased by only 4%). Therefore, *US* does not have to report the December 1, 2001, acquisition under section 6046A. On April 1, 2002, *FC2* distributes a 6% direct interest in *FP* to *US*. *US* now owns a 22% direct interest in *FP*. Compared to *US*'s direct interest when *US* last had a reportable event (12% on September 1, 2001), after the April 1 acquisition *US*'s direct interest has increased by at least a 10% interest (12% to 22%). *US* must report the April 1, 2002 acquisition on a Form 8865 attached to *US*'s 2002 income tax return.

Example 3. Change in proportional interest resulting from withdrawal of a partner. Assume the same facts as *Example 3*. In addition, on January 5, 2003, *FC2* withdraws entirely from *FP*. As a result, the direct interests of *US* and *FC1* in *FP* each increase by at least the equivalent of 10% interests. Compared to *US*'s direct interest the last time *US* had a reportable event (22% on April 1, 2002), *US*'s direct interest has increased by at least the equivalent of a ten percent interest. Therefore, *US* has had a reportable event pursuant to paragraph (b)(1)(iii) of this section, and *US* must report the change in its interest resulting from *FC2*'s withdrawal from the partnership on *US*'s Form 8865 filed with *US*'s 2003 tax year income tax return.

Example 4. Change in proportional interest constituting an acquisition. FP is a foreign partnership that has no United States persons as direct or constructive partners. *US* is a United States person and a calendar year taxpayer. On January 1, 2001, *US* purchases an 8% direct interest in *FP*. *US* is not required to report this acquisition. *US* did not own a 10% or greater direct interest in *FP*, and *US* does not own a 10% or greater direct interest as a result of the acquisition. On March 1, 2001, *FC*, a foreign partner of *FP*, withdraws from *FP*, and as result, *US*'s direct interest in *FP* increases by a 7% interest. The increase in *US*'s direct interest is considered an acquisition of an interest under paragraph (b)(1)(i)(A) of this section. *US* did not own a 10% or greater direct interest in *FP* before *FC* withdrew, and as a result of the increase in *US*'s direct interest because of *FC*'s withdrawal from *FP*, *US* now owns a 10% or greater direct interest in *FP*. Therefore, *US* must report under section 6046A the increase in *US*'s direct interest resulting from the withdrawal of *FC* from *FP* on Form 8865 filed with *US*'s tax return for *US*'s 2001 tax year.

(c) *Content of return.*—The Form 8865 that must be filed under paragraph (a)(1) of this section must contain the following information in such form and manner and to the extent that Form 8865 and its instructions prescribe—

(1) The name, address, and taxpayer identification number of the United States person required to file the return;

(2) Information about other persons (foreign or domestic) whose interests in the foreign partnership the person reporting under section 6046A is considered to own under section 6038(e)(3)(C) and section 267(c);

(3) Information about all foreign entities that were disregarded as entities separate from their owners under "301.7701-2 and 301.7701-3 of this chapter that were owned by the foreign partnership during the partnership's tax year ending with or within the tax year of the person filing Form 8865 pursuant to section 6046A;

(4) For each reportable event, the date of the event, the type of event (acquisition, disposition, or change in proportional interest), and the United States person's direct percentage interest in the foreign partnership immediately before and immediately after the event;

(5) The fair market value of the interest acquired or disposed of;

(6) Information about partnerships (foreign and domestic) in which the foreign partnership owned a direct interest, or a constructive interest of ten percent or more under sections section 267(c)(1) and (5) and the regulations thereunder, during the partnership's tax year ending with or within the tax year of the person filing Form 8865 pursuant to section 6046A; and

(7) Any other information required to be submitted by Form 8865 and its instructions.

(d) *Time and manner for filing returns.*—The Form 8865 must be filed with the timely filed (including extensions) income tax return of the United States person for the tax year in which the reportable event occurs. If the United States person is not required to file an income tax return for its tax year in which the reportable event occurs, but is required to file an information return for that year (for example, Form 1065, "U.S. Partnership Return of Income," or Form 990, "Return of Organization Exempt from Income Tax"), the United States person should attach the Form 8865 to its information return filed for that tax year.

(e) *Duplicate returns.*—If required by the instructions to Form 8865, a duplicate Form 8865 (including attachments and schedules) must also be filed.

(f) *Persons excepted from filing return.*—(1) *Section 6038B overlap.*—If a United States person acquires an interest in a foreign partnership as a result of a section 721 contribution required to be reported under section 6038B, and the person properly reports the contribution under section 6038B, then the United States person is not required to report the acquisition of the partnership interest under section 6046A(a) should it constitute a reportable event under paragraph (b)(1) of this section. The acquisition will still constitute a reportable event for purposes of making future comparisons pursuant to paragraphs (b)(1)(i)(B), (b)(1)(ii)(B) and (b)(1)(iii) of this section. A person that fails to properly report the section 721 contribution under section 6038B and the regulations thereunder and that fails to properly report the acquisition of the partnership interest under section 6046A may be subject to the penalties applicable to a failure to comply with the requirements of section 6038B, as well as the penalties applicable for a failure to comply with the requirements of section 6046A. See paragraph (h) of this section for more information about the penalties for failure to comply with the requirements of section 6046A.

(2) *Trusts relating to state and local government employee retirement plans.*—The return requirement of section 6046A does not apply to trusts relating to state and local government employee retirement plans, unless the instructions to Form 8865 provide otherwise.

(3) *Reporting under this section not required of partnerships excluded from the application of subchapter K.*—The reporting requirements of this section will not apply to any United States person in respect of an eligible partnership as described in §1.761-2(a) in which that United States person is a partner, if such partnership has validly elected to be excluded from all of the provisions of subchapter K of chapter 1 of the Internal Revenue Code in the manner specified in §1.761-2(b)(2)(i), or is deemed to have elected to be excluded from all of the provisions of subchapter K of chapter 1 of the Internal Revenue Code in accordance with the provisions of §1.761-2(b)(2)(ii).

(4) *Exclusion for satellite organizations.*—The return requirement of section 6046A does not apply to the International Telecommunications Satellite Organization (or a successor organization) or the International Maritime Satellite Organization (or a successor organization).

(g) *Method of reporting.*—Except as otherwise provided on Form 8865, or the accompanying instructions, any amounts required to be reported under section 6046A and this section must be expressed in United States dollars, with a statement of the exchange rates used. All statements required on or with Form 8865 pursuant to this section must be in English.

(h) *Penalties for violating section 6046A.*—For penalties for violating section 6046A, see sections 6679 and 7203.

(i) *Statute of limitations.*—For exceptions to the limitations on assessment in the event of a failure to provide information under section 6046A, see section 6501(c)(8).

(j) *Effective date.*—This section applies to reportable events occurring after December 31, 1999. No reporting under section 6046A is required for reportable events occurring on or before December 31, 1999. [Reg. §1.6046A-1.]

☐ [*T.D.* 8851, 12-27-99.]

§1.6049-4. Return of information as to interest paid and original issue discount includible in gross income after December 31, 1982.—(a) *Requirement of reporting.*—(1) *In general.*—Except as provided in paragraph (c) of this section, an information return shall be made by a payor, as defined in paragraph (a)(2) of this section, of amounts of interest and original issue discount paid after December 31, 1982. Such return shall contain the information described in paragraph (b) of this section.

(2) *Payor.*—For payments made after December 31, 2002, a payor is a person described in paragraph (a)(2)(i) or (ii) of this section.

(i) Every person who makes a payment of the type and of the amount subject to reporting under this section (or under an applicable section under this chapter) to any other person during a calendar year.

(ii) Every person who collects on behalf of another person payments of the type and of the amount subject to reporting under this section (or under an applicable section under this chapter), or who otherwise acts as a middleman (as defined in paragraph (f)(4) of this section) with respect to such payment.

(b) *Information to be reported.*—(1) *Interest payments.*—Except as provided in paragraphs (b)(3) and (5) of this section, in the case of interest other than original issue discount treated as interest under §1.6049-5(f), an information return on Form 1099 shall be made for the calendar year showing the aggregate amount of the payments, the name, address, and taxpayer identification number of the person to whom paid, the amount of tax deducted and withheld under section 3406 from the payments, if any, and such other information as required by the forms. An information return is generally not required if the amount of interest paid to a person aggregates less than $10 or if the payment is made to a person who is an exempt recipient described in paragraph (c)(1)(ii) of this section, unless the payor backup withholds under section 3406 on such payment (because, for example, the payee (*i.e.*, exempt recipient) has failed to furnish a Form W-9 on request), in which case the payor must make a return under this section, unless the payor refunds the amount withheld pursuant to §31.6413(a)-3 (Employment Tax Regulations). For reporting interest paid to certain nonresident alien individuals, see §1.6049-8.

(2) *Original issue discount*.—Except as provided in paragraph (b)(3) and (b)(5) of this section, in the case of original issue discount, an information return on Forms 1096 and 1099 shall be made for each calendar year of any holder of an obligation as to which there is original issue discount includible in gross income aggregating $10 or more. For calendar years before 1992, semiannual record date reporting under §1.6049-1(a)(1)(ii)(*b*)(*1*) may be used, and if it is used, the original issue discount includible in gross income is determined by treating each holder as holding the obligation on every day it was outstanding during the calendar year. An information return shall be made, however, in any case in which an amount of tax is required to be deducted and withheld under section 3406. In such case, the amount required to be reported is the amount subject to withholding even if the amount of original issue discount includible in gross income is less than $10. With respect to an obligation described in §1.1232-3A(e) or (f) (relating respectively to deposits in banks and similar financial institutions and to face-amount certificates), §1.6049-1(a)(1)(ii)(*d*) and the last sentence of §1.6049-1(a)(1)(ii)(*a*)(*2*) shall apply. The information return shall show—

(i) The name, address, and taxpayer identification number of each record holder for whom an amount of original issue discount is includible in gross income;

(ii) The account, serial, or other identifying number of each obligation with respect to which a return is being made;

(iii) The aggregate amount of original issue discount includible in the gross income of each holder for the period during the calendar year for which the return is made (or, if the aggregation rules of §1.6049-1(a)(1)(ii)*(b)(2)* are being used, the aggregate amount or original issue discount for the period such holder held the obligations). For calendar years before 1992, semiannual record date reporting under §1.6049-1(a)(1)(ii)(*b*)(*1*) may be used, and if it is used, the original issue discount includible in gross income is determined by treating each holder as holding the obligation on every day it was outstanding during the calendar year. For purposes of this section, an obligation shall be considered to be outstanding from the date of original issue (as defined in §1.1232-3(b)(3));

(iv) The amount of tax withheld under section 3406, if any;

(v) The name and address of the person filing the return; and

(vi) Such other information as is required by the forms. Section 1.6049-1(a)(1)(ii)(*b*)(2) and, for calendar years before 1992, §1.6049-1(a)(1)(ii)(*b*)(*1*), and (c), apply for purposes of this paragraph.

(3) *Returns made by middleman*.—(i) *In general*.—Except as provided in paragraph (b)(5) of this section, every person acting as a middleman (as defined in paragraph (f)(4) of this section) shall make an information return for the calendar year. In the case of interest payments (other than original issue discount and other than interest described in §1.6049-8), the information return shall be made on Form 1099 and shall show the aggregate amount of the interest, the name, address, and taxpayer identification number of the person on whose behalf received, the amount of tax withheld under section 3406, if any, and such other information as required by the forms. In the case of original issue discount, the information return shall show the information required to be shown for the person on whose behalf received, as described in paragraph (b)(2) of this section. See §1.6049-5(f) to determine whether a middleman is required to make an information return with respect to original issue discount. A middleman shall make an information return regardless of whether the middleman receives a Form 1099. A middleman shall not be required to make an information return if the payment of interest aggregates less than $10 or if the payment is made to an exempt recipient described in paragraph (c)(1)(ii) of this section, unless the payor backup withholds under section 3406 on such payment (because, for example, the payee has failed to furnish a Form W-9 on request), in which case the payor must make a return under this section, unless the payor refunds the amount withheld pursuant to §31.6413(a)-3 of this chapter (Employment Tax Regulations).

(ii) *Forwarding of interest coupons and original issue discount obligations*.—In the case of a middleman who, from within the United States, forwards an interest coupon or discount obligation on behalf of a payee for presentation, collection or payment outside the United States, the middleman shall make an information return on Form 1099 for the calendar year showing, in the case of an interest coupon, the information required under paragraph (b)(3)(i) of this section and, in the case of a discount obligation, information required under paragraph (b)(2) of this section. For purposes of this paragraph (b)(3)(ii), a middleman is considered to forward an interest coupon or discount obligation on behalf of a payee for presentation, collection or payment outside the United States if the middleman forwards the coupon or obligations outside the United States on or after the date when the payee is entitled to be paid or at an earlier date that is within 90 days of such date or if the middleman has actual knowledge that the coupon or obligation is being forwarded outside the United States for presentation, collection, or payment outside the United States. However, the transfer, although subject to information reporting under this section, is not subject to backup withholding under section 3406.

(iii) *Example*.—The following example illustrates the provisions of paragraph (b)(3)(ii) of this section:

Example. Individual F, who is entitled to payment on an interest coupon, instructs an office of Bank M in the United States to forward the coupon to Bank N for collection by Bank N outside the United States. Bank M in the United States forwards the interest coupon to Bank N outside the United States. Bank M is required to make an information return for the calendar year under paragraph (b)(3)(ii) of this section showing the aggregate amount of the interest coupon forwarded, the name, address of the permanent residence, and the taxpayer identification number, if any, of Individual F and such other information as the form requires.

(4) *Returns made with respect to payments on certificates of deposit issued in bearer form*.—Except as provided in paragraph (b)(5) of this section, every person carrying on the banking business who makes payments of interest to another person (whether or not aggregating $10 or more) during a calendar year with respect to a certificate of deposit issued in bearer form shall make an information return on Forms 1096 and 1099. The information return shall show the information required in §1.6049-1(a)(1)(vi)*(a)* through *(e)* inclusive and a statement as to amount of tax withheld under section 3406, if any.

(5) *Interest payments to certain nonresident alien individuals*.—(i) *General rule*.—In the case of interest aggregating $10 or more paid to a nonresident alien individual (as defined in section 7701(b)(1)(B)) that is reportable under §1.6049-8(a), the payor shall make an information return on Form 1042-S, "Foreign Person's U.S. Source Income Subject to Withholding," for the calendar year in which the interest is paid. The payor or middleman shall prepare and file Form 1042-S at the time and in the manner prescribed by section 1461 and the regulations under that section and by the form and its accompanying instructions. See §§1.1461-1(b) (rules regarding the preparation of a Form 1042) and §§1.6049-6(e)(4) (rules for furnishing a copy of the Form 1042-S to the recipient). To determine whether an information return is required for original issue discount, see §§1.6049-5(f) and §§1.6049-8(a).

(ii) *Effective/applicability date*.—Paragraph (b)(5)(i) of this section shall be applicable for payments made on or after January 1, 2013. (For interest paid to a Canadian nonresident alien individual on or before December 31, 2012, see paragraph (b)(5) of this section as in effect and contained in 26 CFR part 1 revised April 1, 2000.)

(c) *Information returns not required*.—(1) *Payment to exempt recipient*.—(i) *In general*.—No information return is required with respect to any payment made to an exempt recipient described in paragraph (c)(1)(ii) of this section, except to the extent otherwise provided in §1.6049-5(d)(3)(ii) and (iii). However, if the payor backup withholds under section 3406 on such payment (because, for example, the payee has failed to furnish a Form W-9 on request), then the payor is required to make a return under this section, unless the payor refunds the amount withheld in accordance with §31.6413(a)-3 of this chapter (Employment Tax Regulations).

(ii) *Exempt recipient defined*.—The term *exempt recipient* means any person described in paragraphs (c)(1)(ii)(A) through (Q) of this section. An exempt recipient is generally exempt from information reporting without filing a certificate claiming exempt status unless the provisions of this paragraph (c)(1)(ii) require a payee to file a certificate. A payor may, in any case, require a payee that is a U.S. person not otherwise required to file a certificate under this paragraph (c)(1)(ii) to file a certificate in order to qualify as an exempt recipient. See §31.3406(h)-3(a)(1)(iii) and (c)(2) of this chapter for the certificate that a payee that is a U.S. person must provide when a payor requires the certificate to treat the payee as an exempt recipient under this paragraph (c)(1)(ii). A payor may treat a payee as an exempt recipient based upon a properly completed form as described in §31.3406(h)-3(e)(2) of this chapter, its actual knowledge that the payee is a person described in this paragraph (c)(1)(ii), or the indicators described in this paragraph (c)(1)(ii).

(A) *Corporation*.—A corporation, as defined in section 7701(a)(3), whether domestic or foreign, is an exempt recipient. In addition, for purposes of this paragraph (c)(1), the term *corporation* includes a partnership all of whose members are corporations described in this paragraph (c)(1), but only if the partnership files with the payor a certificate stating that each member of the partnership meets one of the requirements of paragraphs (c)(1)(ii)(A)(*1*) through (*4*) of this section. Absent actual knowledge otherwise, a payor may treat a payee as a corporation (and, therefore, as an exempt recipient) if one of the requirements of paragraph (c)(1)(ii)(A)(*1*), (*2*), (*3*), or (*4*), of this section are met before a payment is made.

(*1*) The name of the payee contains an unambiguous expression of corporate status that is Incorporated, Inc., Corporation, Corp., P.C., (but not Company or Co.) or contains the term *insurance company, indemnity company, reinsurance company*, or *assurance company*, or its name indicates that it is an entity listed as a per se corporation under § 301.7701-2(b)(8)(i) of this chapter.

(*2*) The payor has on file a corporate resolution or similar document clearly indicating corporate status. For this purpose, a similar document includes a copy of Form 8832, filed by the entity to elect classification as an association under § 301.7701-3(b) of this chapter.

(*3*) The payor receives a Form W-9 which includes an EIN and a statement from the payee that it is a domestic corporation.

(*4*) The payor receives a withholding certificate described in § 1.1441-1(e)(2)(i), that includes a certification that the person whose name is on the certificate is a foreign corporation.

(B) *Tax exempt organization*.—(*1*) *In general*.—Any organization that is exempt from taxation under section 501(a) is an exempt recipient. A custodial account under section 403(b)(7) shall be considered an exempt recipient under this paragraph. A payor may treat an organization as an exempt recipient under this paragraph (c)(1)(ii)(B) without requiring a certificate if the organization's name is listed in the compilation by the Commissioner of organizations for which a deduction for charitable contributions is allowed, if the name of the organization contains an unambiguous indication that it is a tax-exempt organization, or if the organization is known to the payor to be a tax-exempt organization.

(*2*) *Examples*.—The application of the provisions of this paragraph (c)(1)(ii)(B) may be illustrated by the following examples:

Example 1. The following persons maintain accounts at M Bank: N College, O University, and P Church. M may treat N, O, and P as exempt recipients even though such persons have not filed an exemption certificate with M because the names of the organizations contain an unambiguous indication that they are tax exempt organizations.

Example 2. Q is listed in the current edition of Internal Revenue Service Publication 78 as an organization for which deductions are permitted for charitable contributions under section 170(c). Such listing has not been revoked by an announcement published in the Internal Revenue Bulletin (see § 601.601(d)(2) of this chapter). A payor may treat Q as an exempt recipient even though Q has not filed an exemption certificate with the payor.

Example 3. Employer R maintains a section 403(b)(7) custodial account with Regulated Investment Company S on behalf of R's employees. S may treat the account as an exempt recipient even though R or its employees have not filed an exemption certificate with S.

(C) *Individual retirement plan*.—An individual retirement plan as defined in section 7701(a)(37) is an exempt recipient. A payor may treat any such plan of which it is the trustee or custodian as an exempt recipient under this paragraph (c)(1) without requiring a certificate.

(D) *United States*.—The United States Government and any wholly-owned agency or instrumentality thereof are exempt recipients. A payor may treat a person as an exempt recipient under this paragraph (c)(1) without requiring a certificate if the name of such person reasonably indicates it is described in this paragraph (c)(1).

(E) *State*.—A State, the District of Columbia, a possession of the United States, a political subdivision of any of the foregoing, wholly-owned agency or instrumentality of any one or more of the foregoing, and a pool or partnership composed exclusively of any of the foregoing are exempt recipients. A payor may treat a person as an exempt recipient under this paragraph (c)(1) without requiring a certificate if the name of such person reasonably indicates it is described in this paragraph (c)(1) or if such person is known generally in the community to be a State, the District of Columbia, a possession of the United States or a political subdivision or a wholly-owned agency or instrumentality of any one or more of the foregoing (for example, an account held in the name of "Town of S" or "County of T" may be treated as held by an exempt recipient under this paragraph (c)(1)(ii)(E)).

(F) *Foreign government*.—A foreign government, a political subdivision of a foreign government, and any wholly-owned agency or instrumentality of either of the foregoing are exempt recipients. A payor may treat a foreign government or a political subdivisions thereof as an exempt recipient under this paragraph (c)(1) without requiring a certificate provided that its name reasonably indicates that it is a foreign government or provided that it is known to the payor to be a foreign government or a political subdivision thereof (for example, an account held in the name of the "Government of V" may be treated as held by a foreign government).

(G) *International organization*.—An international organization and any wholly owned agency or instrumentality thereof are exempt recipients. The term *international organization* shall have the meaning ascribed to it in section 7701(a)(18). A payor may treat a payee as an international organization without requiring a certificate if the payee is designated as an international organization by executive order (pursuant to 22 U.S.C. 288 through 288(f)).

(H) *Foreign central bank of issue*.—A foreign central bank of issue is an exempt recipient. A foreign central bank of issue is a bank which is by law or government sanction the principal authority, other than the government itself, issuing instruments intended to circulate as currency. See § 1.895-1(b)(1). A payor may treat a person as a foreign central bank of issue (and, therefore, as an exempt recipient) without requiring a certificate provided that such person is known generally in the financial community as a foreign central bank of issue or if its name reasonably indicates that it is a foreign central bank of issue.

(I) *Securities or commodities dealer*.—A dealer in securities, commodities, or notional principal contracts, that is registered as such under the laws of the United States or a State or under the laws of a foreign country is an exempt recipient. A payor may treat a dealer as an exempt recipient under this paragraph (c)(1) without requiring a certificate if the person is known generally in the investment community to be a dealer meeting the requirements set forth in this paragraph (c)(1) (for example, a registered broker-dealer or a person listed as a member firm in the most recent publication of members of the National Association of Securities Dealers, Inc.).

(J) *Real estate investment trust*.—A real estate investment trust, as defined in section 856 and § 1.856-1, is an exempt recipient. A payor may treat a person as a real estate investment trust (and, therefore, as an exempt recipient) without requiring a certificate if the person is known generally in the investment community as a real estate investment trust.

(K) *Entity registered under the Investment Company Act of 1940*.—An entity registered at all times during the taxable year under the Investment Company Act of 1940, as amended (15 U.S.C. 80a-1), (or during such portion of the taxable year that it is in existence), is an exempt recipient. An entity that is created during the taxable year will be treated as meeting the registration requirement of the preceding sentence provided that such entity is so registered at all times during the taxable year for which such entity is in existence. A payor may treat such an entity as an exempt recipient under this paragraph (c)(1) without requiring a certificate if the entity is known generally in the investment community to meet the requirements of the preceding sentence.

(L) *Common trust fund*.—A common trust fund, as defined in section 584(a), is an exempt recipient. A payor may treat the fund as an exempt recipient without requiring a certificate provided that its name reasonably indicates that it is a common trust fund or provided that it is known to the payor to be a common trust fund.

(M) *Financial institution*.—A financial institution such as a bank, mutual savings bank, savings and loan association, building and loan association, cooperative bank, homestead association, credit union, industrial loan association or bank, or other similar organization, whether organized in the United States or under the laws of a foreign country is an exempt recipient. A financial institution also includes a clearing organization defined in § 1.163-5(c)(2)(i)(D)(*8*) and the Bank for International Settlements. A payor may treat any person described in the preceding sentence as an exempt recipient without requiring a certificate if the person's name (including a foreign name, such as "Banco" or "Banque") reasonably indicates the payee is a financial institution described in the preceding sentence. In the case of a foreign person, a payor may also treat a person on such list as the Internal Revenue Service may publish or approve (such as in the Thomson Bank Directory or a list approved by the Federal Reserve Board).

(N) *Trust.*—A trust which is exempt from tax under section 664(c) (i.e., a charitable remainder annuity trust or a charitable remainder unitrust) or is described in section 4947(a)(1) (relating to certain charitable trusts) is an exempt recipient. A payor which is a trustee of the trust may treat the trust as an exempt recipient without requiring a certificate.

(O) *Nominees or custodians.*—A nominee or custodian.

(P) *Brokers.*—A broker as defined in section 6045(c) and § 1.6045-1(a)(1).

(Q) *Swap dealers.*—A dealer in notional principal contracts as defined in § 1.446-3(c)(4)(iii).

(iii) *Exempt recipient no longer exempt.*—Any person who ceases to be an exempt recipient shall, no later than 10 days after such cessation, notify the payor in writing when it ceases to be an exempt recipient unless it reasonably appears that the person formerly qualifying as an exempt recipient will not thereafter receive a reportable payment from the payor. If a payor treats a person as an exempt recipient by requiring the exempt recipient to file a certificate claiming exempt status, that person shall revoke the certificate as provided in the preceding sentence. If the exempt recipient terminates its relationship with the payor prior to the time that the notice of change in status is otherwise required, the exempt recipient is not required to notify the payor. If, however, the person who formerly qualified as an exempt recipient later reinstates the relationship with the payor, the person must, prior to receiving a reportable payment from such relationship, notify the payor that it no longer qualifies as an exempt recipient in case the payor relies upon the previous treatment.

(2) *Payments by certain middlemen.*—An information return shall not be required if—

(i) The record owner is required to file a fiduciary return on Form 1041 disclosing the name, address, and taxpayer identification number of the actual owner, and furnishes Form K-1 to each actual owner containing the information required to be shown on the form, including amounts withheld under section 3406;

(ii) The record owner is a nominee of a banking institution or trust company exercising trust powers, and such banking institution or trust company is required to file a fiduciary return on Form 1041 disclosing the name, address, and identifying number of the actual owner, and furnishes Form K-1 to each actual owner containing the information required to be shown on the form, including amounts withheld under section 3406;

(iii) The record owner is a banking institution or trust company exercising trust powers, or a nominee thereof, and the actual owner is an organization exempt from taxation under section 501(a) for which such banking institution or trust company files an annual return, but only if the name, address, and taxpayer identification number of the record owner is included on or with the Form 1041 fiduciary return filed for the estate or trust or the annual return filed for the tax exempt organization.

(3) *Coordination with reporting rules for widely held fixed investment trusts under § 1.671-5 of this chapter.*—See § 1.671-5 for the reporting rules for widely held fixed investment trusts (as defined under that section).

(4) *Coordination of reporting with chapter 4 reporting or an applicable IGA.*—(i) *U.S. accounts reported by FFIs that are non-U.S. payors.*—An information return shall not be required with respect to an interest payment made by a participating FFI (including a reporting Model 2 FFI), or registered deemed-compliant FFI (including a reporting Model 1 FFI), that is a non-U.S. payor (as defined in § 1.6049-5(c)(5)) to an account holder of an account maintained by the FFI, when the payment is not subject to withholding under chapter 4 or to backup withholding under section 3406, and the conditions of paragraphs (c)(4)(i)(A), (B), or (C) of this section, as applicable, are met. See paragraph (c)(4)(iii) of this section for circumstances in which an FFI may allocate a payment described in this paragraph (c)(4)(i) to a chapter 4 withholding rate pool of U.S. payees.

(A) The FFI is a participating FFI (including a reporting Model 2 FFI) reporting the account holder of the U.S. account (as defined in § 1.1471-1(b)(133)) pursuant to either § 1.1471-4(d)(3) or (5) for the year in which the payment is made (including reporting of the account holder's TIN).

(B) The FFI is a registered deemed-compliant FFI (other than a reporting Model 1 FFI) reporting the account holder of the U.S. account pursuant to the conditions of its applicable deemed-compliant status under § 1.1471-5(f)(1) for the year in which the payment is made (including reporting of the account holder's TIN).

(C) The FFI is a reporting Model 1 FFI reporting the account holder of the reportable U.S. account pursuant to an applicable Model 1 IGA for the year in which the payment is made (including reporting of the account holder's TIN).

(ii) *Other accounts reported by FFIs under chapter 4.*—An information return shall not be required under this section with respect to a payment that is not subject to withholding under chapter 3 (as defined in § 1.1441-2(a)) or backup withholding under § 31.3406(g)-1(e) and that is made to a recalcitrant account holder of a participating FFI or registered deemed-compliant FFI (or non-consenting U.S. account of a reporting Model 2 FFI), provided that the FFI reports such account holder in accordance with the classes of account holders described in § 1.1471-4(d)(6) for the year in which the payment is made. See paragraph (c)(4)(iii) of this section for circumstances in which an FFI may allocate a payment described in this paragraph (c)(4)(ii) to a chapter 4 withholding rate pool of U.S. payees. In the case of a payment made by an FFI that is a reporting Model 1 FFI, an information return shall not be required with respect to a payment that is not subject to withholding under chapter 3 or backup withholding under § 31.3406(g)-1(e) and that is made to an account holder of the FFI if the account—

(A) Has U.S. indicia for which appropriate documentation sufficient to treat the account as held by other than a specified U.S. person has not been provided pursuant to the due diligence requirements described in an applicable Model 1 IGA, and

(B) Is therefore treated as a U.S. reportable account that the FFI is required to report pursuant to the applicable Model 1 IGA.

(iii) *Coordination of reporting exceptions with reporting of chapter 4 withholding rate pools.*—For purposes of paragraphs (c)(4)(i) and (ii) of this section, a participating FFI (including a reporting Model 2 FFI) or registered deemed-compliant FFI (including a reporting Model 1 FFI) receiving a payment from another payor may provide a withholding statement to the payor allocating the payment to a chapter 4 withholding rate of pool of U.S. payees only if the payment is excepted from reporting under paragraph (c)(4)(i) of this section or if the payment is both excepted from reporting under paragraph (c)(4)(ii) of this section and not subject to withholding under chapter 4. See § 1.6049-5(b)(14) (providing an exception from reporting under section 6049 to a payor that has been furnished a withholding statement from an participating FFI (including a reporting Model 2 FFI) or registered deemed-compliant FFI (including a reporting Model 1 FFI) and that allocates the payment to a chapter 4 withholding rate pool). Thus, for example, a U.S. payor that is a participating FFI may not allocate a payment to a chapter 4 withholding rate pool of U.S. payees on a withholding statement described in § 1.6049-5(b)(14) when the payment is made to a U.S. account maintained by the FFI, regardless of whether the FFI reports the account in accordance with § 1.1471-4(d)(3) because the U.S. payor is not excepted from reporting under this section pursuant to paragraph (c)(4)(i) of this section.

(iv) *Example.*—The application of the provisions of paragraphs (c)(4)(ii) and (iii) of this section may be illustrated by the following example:

Example. USP is a payor that makes an interest payment that is not a withholdable payment (as defined in paragraph (f)(15) of this section) to RM2, a U.S. payor and reporting Model 2 FFI. The payment is paid and received outside of the United States and is not an amount subject to withholding under chapter 3. RM2 receives the payment as an intermediary with respect to a preexisting account held by A. RM2 has account information with respect to A which includes U.S. indicia as described in § 1.1441-7(b)(5) or (8). A does not provide consent for RM2 to report A's account. Under the presumption rules described in § 1.6049-5(d)(2)(i), RM2 is required to treat A as a U.S. non-exempt recipient. Despite this presumption rule, and because backup withholding does not apply under § 31.3406(g)-1(e), no information return shall be required with respect to the payment under paragraph (c)(4)(ii) of this section if A is reported by RM2 consistent with § 1.1471-4(d)(6) as a non-consenting account holder. Additionally, RM2 may include A in the chapter 4 withholding rate pool of U.S. payees on the withholding statement provided to USP consistent with the requirements of paragraph (c)(4)(iii) of this section.

(d) *Special rules.*—(1) *Aggregation of payments.*—For purposes of paragraph (b) of this section, until such time as the Commissioner determines that it is feasible to require aggregation of payments on two or more accounts, insurance contracts, or investment certificates, and, until this section is amended accordingly to provide for reporting on an aggregate basis, the requirement for filing Form 1099 under this section will be met if a person making payments of interest subject to reporting files a separate Form 1099 with respect to each account, insurance contract, or investment certificate. In the case of obligations described in section 6049(b)(1)(A), separate Forms 1099 may be filed as provided in the preceding sentence with respect to holdings in different issues.

(2) *Treatment of original issue discount.*—The amount of original issue discount subject to reporting under section 6049 shall be the amount of original issue discount includible in the gross income of any holder that is treated as paid under § 1.6049-5(f).

(3) *Conversion into United States dollars of amounts paid in foreign currency.*—(i) *Conversion rules.*—When a payment is made in foreign currency, the U.S. dollar amount of the payment shall be determined by converting such foreign currency into U.S. dollars on the date of payment at the spot rate (as defined in § 1.988-1(d)(1)) or pursuant to a reasonable spot rate convention. For example, a withholding agent may use a month-end spot rate or a monthly average spot rate. A spot rate convention must be used consistently with respect to all non-dollar amounts withheld and from year to year. Such convention cannot be changed without the consent of the Commissioner or the Commissioner's delegate.

(ii) *Special rule for § 1.988-5(a) transactions where the payor on both components of a qualified hedging transaction is the same person.*—(A) *In general.*—Interest or original issue discount on a qualified debt instrument that is part of a qualified hedging transaction under § 1.988-5(a) shall be computed for section 6049 reporting purposes under the rules described in § 1.988-5(a)(9)(ii) if—

(1) The payor on the qualified debt instrument and the counterparty to the § 1.988-5(a) hedge are the same person; and

(2) The payee complies with the requirements of § 1.988-5(a) and so notifies its payor prior to the date required for filing Form 1099 as required by this section.

(B) *Effective date.*—The provisions of this paragraph (d)(3)(ii) apply to transactions entered into after December 31, 2000.

(4) *Determination of person to whom interest or original issue discount is paid or for whom it is received.*—Section 1.6049-1(a)(3) and (4) shall apply with respect to payments of interest and original issue discount after December 31, 1982.

(5) *Payments by governmental units.*—In the case of payments made by any governmental unit or any agency or instrumentality thereof, the officer or employee having control of the payment of interest or original issue discount (or the person appropriately designated for purposes of this section) shall make the returns and statements required under section 6049.

(6) *When payment deemed made.*—(i) *In general.*—Except as provided in paragraph (d)(6)(ii) of this section, for purposes of section 6049, interest is deemed to have been paid when it is credited or set apart to a person without any substantial limitation or restriction as to the time or manner of payment or condition upon which payment is to be made, and is made available to him so that it may be drawn at any time, and its receipt brought within his own control and disposition.

(ii) *Instruments paid on presentment or demand.*—In the case of a payment made on an obligation described in paragraph (e)(2) of this section (relating to transactional reporting), interest is deemed to have been paid at the time the obligation is presented for payment. For example, interest represented by a coupon detached from a bond is considered paid for purposes of section 6049 when the coupon is presented for payment.

(7) *Magnetic media requirement.*—For rules relating to permission to submit the information required by Form 1099 on magnetic tape or other media, see § 1.9101-1. For the requirement to submit the information required by Form 1099 on magnetic media for payments after December 31, 1983, see section 6011(e) and § 301.6011-2 of this chapter (Regulations on Procedure and Administration).

(8) *Obligations that are not exempt from taxation.*—When an issuer of an obligation that is not exempt from taxation receives an envelope or "shell", signed by the payee, stating that interest on the obligation is exempt from taxation under section 103(a) (as described in § 1.6049-5(b)(2)), the issuer shall make an information return under section 6049. The information return shall show the name, address, and taxpayer identification number of the person who signed the statement claiming that interest on the obligation is exempt from taxation, the amount of interest paid, and such other information as is required by the form. An information return is required regardless of the amount of interest. The issuer shall also furnish a written statement to such person showing the information required by § 1.6049-6(b).

(9) *Savings bonds.*—(i) *In general.*—A person who makes payment on a United States savings bond when the bond is presented for payment shall report the difference between the amount to be paid and the amount paid for the bond. The amount subject to reporting shall not be reduced to take into account—

(A) Amounts previously included in the income of a holder as a result of an election under 454 to include annually the increase in the redemption price of the bond; or

(B) Amounts accrued prior to transfer of the bond where the bond has been reissued in the name of the person presenting the bond for payment. With respect to a savings bond that is reissued in another person's name, the amount subject to reporting when the bond is reissued is the amount of interest that has accrued. With respect to a savings bond that is exchanged in a tax-deferred transaction (as described in section 1037), the amount subject o reporting is the amount of cash paid to the holder at the time of the transaction.

(ii) *Examples.*—The application of the provisions of paragraph (d)(9)(i) of this section may be illustrated by the following examples:

Example (1). On June 10, 1943, A purchases a $50 Series E savings bond. The amount paid for the savings bond is $37.50. A elects under section 454 to include the increase in the redemption price of the bond annually in income. A presents the bond to Bank M to be cashed on July 1, 1983. The amount to be paid on the bond on that date is $204.96. Bank M is required to make an information return under section 6049 showing that it paid $167.46 (the difference between $204.96 and $37.50) of interest, without regard to A's election to include annually the increase in the redemption price of the bond.

Example (2). On December 1, 1970, B purchases a $500 Series E savings bond. The amount paid for the bond is $375. On August 1, 1984, the bond is reissued by the Bureau of Public Debt by deleting B's name and inserting the name of B's child. At the time of reissue, the redemption value of the bond is $1,015.80. The accrued interest is $640.80 (the difference between $1,015.80 and $375). The reissue is a taxable transaction, and B must include in income the accrued interest at the time of reissue. The Bureau of Public Debt is required to make an information return under section 6049 showing that it paid $640.80 of interest to B.

Example (3). Assume the same facts as in example (2) except that B exchanges the bond for a Series HH savings bond in the amount of $1,000 issued in B's name. The exchange is tax-deferred under section 1037. The Bureau of Public Debt stamps a legend on the bond stating that interest of $625 has been deferred. The amount of $15.80 is paid to B. The Bureau of the Public Debt must make an information return showing that it paid $15.80 of interest to B.

Example (4). Assume the same facts as in example (3) except that the exchange is not a tax-deferred exchange. The Bureau of the Public Debt must make an information return showing that it paid $640.80 of interest to B.

(e) *Transactional reporting.*—(1) *In general.*—An information return required to be made under paragraph (b) of this section may be made on a transaction-by-transaction basis, rather than on an annual aggregation basis, if payment described in paragraph (e)(2) of this section is made by a person described in paragraph (e)(3) of this section.

(2) *Payments subject to transactional reporting.*—An information return may be made on a transactional basis if payment is made on—

(i) A United States savings bond,

(ii) An interest coupon (but see § 1.6049-5(b) which provides that no information return is required to be made with respect to an interest coupon that is exempt from taxation),

(iii) A discount obligation having a maturity at issue of 1 year or less, including commercial paper and short-term government obligations defined in section 1232(a)(3), and

(iv) Any obligation similar to those described in subdivisions (i) through (iii). The information return with respect to payments on the types of obligations described in this paragraph shall be made on Form 1099-INT. A payor may include all interest paid in one transaction on one information return, irrespective of whether obligations of different issuers are paid as part of the transaction.

(3) *Persons subject to transactional reporting.*—A person may make a return on a transactional basis if the person is—

(i) A middleman (as defined in paragraph (f)(4) of this section) who is required to make an information return under paragraph (b)(3) of this section with respect to any payment described in paragraph (e)(2) of this section, or

(ii) A federal agency making payments on a United States savings bond.

(4) *Transaction defined.*—For purposes of this paragraph (e), a transaction means a payment at one time on one or more obligations. For example, if an individual who is exempt from withholding under section 3406 presents at one time five Series EE bonds on each of which $3 of interest has accrued, $15 of interest will be paid as part of the transaction. Accordingly, an information return is required under § 1.6049-4(a)(2)(iii) because the interest paid in the transaction exceeds $10. If only three of the savings bonds were presented, however, no return would be required even if the remaining two bonds were redeemed the following day. See paragraph (a)(2)(i) of this section for the requirement that an information return be made if any amount of tax is withheld under section 3406.

(5) *Information required.*—The information return for any transaction under paragraph (e) of this section shall show the following:

(i) The name, address, and taxpayer identification number of the person to whom the interest is paid;

(ii) The name and address of the person filing the form;

(iii) The amount of interest paid;

(iv) The amount of tax withheld under section 3406 if any; and

(v) Such other information as is required by the form.

(f) *Definitions.*—For purposes of section 6049, this section, and §§ 1.6049-5 and 1.6049-6—

(1) *Person.*—The term "person" includes any governmental unit, international organization, and any agency or instrumentality thereof. Therefore, interest paid by one of these entities must be reported unless one of the exceptions under section 6049 applies.

(2) *Natural person.*—The term "natural person" means any individual, but shall not include a partnership (whether or not composed entirely of individuals), a trust, or an estate.

(3) *Obligation.*—The term *obligation* includes bonds, debentures, notes, certificates, and other evidences of indebtedness regardless of how denominated. For the definition of the term *offshore obligation*, see paragraph (f)(9) of this section.

(4) *Middleman.*—(i) *In general.*—The term "middleman" means any person, including a financial institution as described in paragraph (c)(1)(ii)(M) of this section, a broker as defined in section 6045(c), or a nominee, who makes payment of interest for, or collects interest on behalf of, another person, or otherwise acts in a capacity as intermediary between a payor and a payee. For example, a person (other than an issuer of an obligation) who makes payment on an interest coupon of the obligation to another person is a middleman, irrespective of whether such person purchases the coupon for his own account, accepts the coupon as agent for the payee, or otherwise deals with the coupon. The term "middleman" also includes a trustee, including a corporate trustee of a trust where the trust is the payee. See § 1.6049-4(c)(2) providing that the trustee does not have to make an information return on Form 1099 to a beneficiary if the trustee is required to file Form 1041 and furnishes Form K-1 to the beneficiary showing the information required to be shown on the form, including amounts withheld under section 3406. A person shall be considered to be a middleman as to any portion of an interest payment made to such person which portion is actually owned by another person, whether or not the other person's name is also shown on the information return filed with respect to such interest payment, except that a husband or wife will not be considered as acting in the capacity of a middleman with respect to his or her spouse. A person who, from within the United States, forwards an interest coupon or discount obligation on behalf of a payee for presentation, collection or payment outside the United States is also a middleman for purposes of this section (but the transfer, although subject to information reporting under this section, does not make the payment subject to backup withholding under section 3406).

(ii) *Example.*—The application of the provisions of paragraph (f)(4) of this section may be illustrated by the following example:

Example. In January 1984, Broker B, a U.S. payor, purchases on behalf of its customer, Individual A, an obligation issued by partnership in a public offering on that date. Broker B holds the obligation for A throughout 1984. Broker B is required to make an information return showing the amount of original issue discount treated as paid to A under § 1.6049-5(f).

(5) *Chapter 4 withholding rate pool.*—The term *chapter 4 withholding rate pool* has the meaning set forth in § 1.1471-1(b)(20). However, for determining the U.S. payees included in a chapter 4 withholding rate pool for purposes of section 6049, see paragraph (c)(4)(iii) of this section.

(6) *Foreign financial institution (or FFI).*—The term *foreign financial institution* or *FFI* means an entity described in § 1.1471-1(b)(47).

(7) *Intergovernmental agreement (or IGA).*—The term *intergovernmental agreement* or *IGA* has the meaning set forth in § 1.1471-1(b)(67) (*i.e.*, either a *Model 1 IGA* described in § 1.1471-1(b)(78) or a *Model 2 IGA* described in § 1.1471-1(b)(79)).

(8) *Non-consenting U.S. accounts.*—The term *non-consenting U.S. accounts* has the meaning set forth in an applicable Model 2 IGA.

(9) *Offshore obligation.*—The term offshore obligation means an offshore obligation defined in § 1.6049-5(c)(1). For the definition of the term *obligation*, see paragraph (f)(3) of this section.

(10) *Participating FFI.*—The term *participating FFI* means an FFI that is described in § 1.1471-1(b)(91).

(11) *Recalcitrant account holder.*—The term *recalcitrant account holder* has the same meaning set forth in § 1.1471-1(b)(110).

(12) *Registered deemed-compliant FFI.*—The term *registered deemed-compliant FFI* means an FFI that is described in § 1.1471-1(b)(111).

(13) *Reporting Model 1 FFI.*—The term *reporting Model 1 FFI* means an FFI that is described in § 1.1471-1(b)(114).

(14) *Reporting Model 2 FFI.*—The term *reporting Model 2 FFI* means a participating FFI that is described in § 1.1471-1(b)(91).

(15) *Withholdable payment.*—The term *withholdable payment* means a payment described in § 1.1471-1(b)(145).

(16) *Paid and received outside the United States.*—(i) *In general.*—Except as otherwise provided in paragraphs (f)(16)(ii) and (iii) of this section, the term *paid and received outside the United States* means an amount that is paid by a payor or middleman outside the United States as described in § 1.6049-5(e).

(ii) *Transfers to the United States.*—Without regard to the location of the account from which the amount is drawn, an amount that is described in paragraph (f)(16)(ii)(A) or (B) of this section and paid by transfer to an account maintained by the payee in the United States or by mail to a United States address (including an amount paid with respect to a bond or a discount obligation described in § 1.6049-5(e)(4)) is not considered to be paid and received outside the United States.

(A) An amount is described in this paragraph (f)(16)(ii)(A) if it is paid by an issuer or the paying agent of the issuer with respect to an obligation that is—

(1) Issued by a U.S. payor, as defined in § 1.6049-5(c)(5);

(2) Registered under the Securities Act of 1933 (15 U.S.C. 77a); or

(3) Listed on an exchange that is registered as a national securities exchange in the United States or included in an interdealer quotation system in the United States.

(B) An amount is described in this paragraph (f)(16)(ii)(B) if it is paid by a U.S. middleman (as defined in § 1.6049-5(c)(5)) that, as a custodian, nominee, or other agent of a payee, collects the amount for or on behalf of the payee.

(iii) *Deposits or accounts with banks and other financial institutions.*—In the case of an amount paid by a bank or other financial institution with respect to a deposit or an account that is considered paid at a branch or office outside the United States as described in § 1.6049-5(e)(2), the amount is not considered paid and received outside the United States if the institution has knowledge that the customer has transmitted instructions to an agent, branch, or office of the institution from inside the United States by mail, telephone, electronic transmission, or otherwise concerning the deposit or account (unless the transmission from the United States has taken place in isolated and infrequent circumstances).

(iv) *Examples.*—The application of the provisions of paragraph (f)(16) of this section may be illustrated by the following examples:

Example 1. FC is a foreign corporation that is not a U.S. payor or U.S. middleman, as defined in § 1.6049-5(c)(5). A holds FC coupon bonds that are not in registered form under section 163(f) and the regulations. FB, a foreign branch of DC, a domestic corporation, is the designated paying agent with respect to the bonds issued by FC. A does not have an account with FB. A presents a coupon to FB at its office outside the United States with instructions to transfer funds to a bank account maintained by A in the United States. FB transfers the funds in accordance with A's instructions. Even though the amount is credited to an account in the United States, the interest on the FC bonds is paid and received outside the United States under paragraph (f)(16)(ii) of this section and § 1.6049-5(e)(3) because the coupon is presented for payment outside the United States; because FC is a foreign person that is not a U.S. payor or U.S. middleman, as defined in § 1.6049-5(d)(1); because FB is not acting as A's agent; and because the obligation is not registered under the Securities Act of 1933 (15 U.S.C. 77a), listed on a securities exchange that is registered as a national securities exchange in the United States, or included in an interdealer quotation system.

Example 2. FC is a foreign corporation that is not a U.S. payor or U.S. middleman, as defined in § 1.6049-5(d)(1). B, a United States citizen, holds a bond issued by FC in registered form under section 163(f) and the regulations thereunder and registered under the Securities Act of 1933 (15 U.S.C. 77a). The bond is not a foreign-targeted registered obligation as defined in § 1.871-14(e)(2). DB, a United States branch of a foreign corporation engaged in the commercial banking business, is the registrar of the bonds issued by FC. DB supplies FC with a list of the holders of the FC bonds. Interest on the FC bonds is paid to B and other bondholders by checks prepared by FC at its principal office outside the United States, and B's check is mailed from there to his designated address in the United States. The bond is described in paragraph (f)(16)(ii)(A)(2) of this section. The interest on the FC bonds paid to B by FC is not paid and received outside the United States under paragraph (f)(16) of this section.

Example 3. The facts are the same as in *Example 2* except that the checks are prepared and mailed in the United States by DC, a U.S. corporation engaged in the commercial banking business that is the designated paying agent with respect to the bonds issued by FC, and B's check is mailed to his designated address outside the United States. For purposes of section 6049, the interest on the FC bonds paid by DC is not paid and received outside the United States under paragraph (f)(16)(i) of this section.

(g) *Time and place for filing a return for the payment of interest.*—(1) *Annual return.*—Except as provided in paragraph (g)(2) of this section, the returns required under this section for any calendar year for the payment of interest shall be filed after September 30 of such year, but not before the payor's final payment to the payee for the year, and on or before February 28 (March 31 if filed electronically) of the following year. Such returns shall be filed with the appropriate Internal Revenue Service Center, the address of which is listed in the instructions for Form 1096. For extensions of time for filing returns under this section, see § 1.6081-1.

(2) *Transactional return.*—In the case of a return under paragraph (e) of this section, relating to returns on a transactional basis, such return shall be filed at any time but in no event later than February 28 (March 31 if filed electronically) of the year following the calendar year in which the interest was paid. The return shall be filed with the appropriate Internal Revenue Service Center, the address of which is listed in the instructions for Form 1096. For extensions of time for filing returns under this section, see § 1.6081-1.

(3) *Cross-reference to penalty.*—For provisions relating to the penalty provided for failure to file timely a correct information return required under section 6049(a) and § 1.6049-4(a)(1), see § 301.6721-1 of this chapter (Procedure and Administration Regulations). See § 301.6724-1 of this chapter for the waiver of a penalty if the failure is due to reasonable cause and is not due to willful neglect.

(h) *Effective/applicability dates.*—Except as otherwise provided in paragraphs (b)(5)(ii) and (d)(3)(ii)(B) of this section, this section applies to payments made on or after January 6, 2017. (For payments made after June 30, 2014, and before January 6, 2017, see this section as in effect and contained in 26 CFR part 1, as revised April 1, 2016.) [Reg. § 1.6049-4.]

☐ [*T.D.* 7881, 3-22-83. *Amended by T.D.* 8366, 9-27-91; *T.D.* 8664, 4-15-96; *T.D.* 8734, 10-6-97; *T.D.* 8804, 12-30-98; *T.D.* 8856, 12-29-99; *T.D.* 8881, 5-15-2000; *T.D.* 8895, 8-17-2000; *T.D.* 9010, 7-25-2002 *T.D.* 9241, 1-23-2006; *T.D.* 9584, 4-17-2012, *T.D.* 9658, 2-28-2014 *and T.D.* 9808, 12-30-2016.]

§ 1.6049-5. Interest and original issue discount subject to reporting after December 31, 1982.—(a) *Interest subject to reporting requirement.*—For purposes of §§ 1.6049-4, 1.6049-6 and this section, except as provided in paragraph (b) of this section, the term "interest" means—

(1) Interest on an obligation—

(i) In registered form (as defined in § 5f.103-1(c)), or

(ii) Of a type offered to the public. Principles consistent with § 5f.163-1 shall be applied to determine whether an obligation is of a type offered to the public.

(2) Interest on deposits with persons carrying on the banking business. Such term shall include deposits evidenced by time certificates of deposit issued in any amount whether negotiable or nonnegotiable. The term "interest" includes payments to a mortgage escrow account and amounts paid with respect to repurchase agreements and banker's acceptances. Property which the payee receives from the payor as interest (or in lieu of a cash payment of interest) shall be interest for purposes of section 6049. The amount subject to reporting is the fair market value of such property.

(3) Amounts, whether or not designated as interest, paid or credited by mutual savings banks, savings and loan associations, building and loan associations, cooperative banks, homestead associations, credit unions, industrial loan associations or banks, or similar organizations, in respect of deposits, face amount certificates, investment certificates, or withdrawable or repurchasable shares. Thus, even though amounts paid or credited by such organizations with respect to deposits are designated as "dividends", such amounts are included in the definition of interest for purposes of section 6049. The term "interest" includes payments to a mortgage escrow account and amounts paid with respect to repurchase agreements. Property which the payee receives from the payor as interest (or in lieu of a cash payment of interest) is "interest" for purposes of section 6049. The fair market value of such property is the amount subject to reporting.

(4) Interest on amounts held by insurance companies under an agreement to pay interest thereon. Any increment in value of "advance premiums", "prepaid premiums", or "premium deposit funds" which is applied to the payment of premiums due on insurance policies, or made available for withdrawal by the policyholder, shall be considered interest subject to reporting. Interest that an insurance company pays pursuant to an agreement with the policyholder to a beneficiary because the payment due has been delayed is interest subject to reporting. Interest subject to reporting also includes interest paid by insurance companies with respect to policy "dividend" accumulations (see sections 61 and 451 and the regulations thereunder for rules as to when such interest is considered paid), and interest paid with respect to the proceeds of insurance policies left with the insurer. The so-called "interest element" in the case of annuity or installment payments under life insurance or endowment contracts does not constitute interest for purposes of section 6049.

(5) Interest on deposits with brokers as defined in section 6045(c) and the regulations thereunder. Any payment made in lieu of interest to a person whose obligation has been borrowed in connection with a short sale or other similar transaction is subject to reporting under section 6049. See § 1.6045-2 for reporting requirements with respect to payments in lieu of tax-exempt interest.

(6) Interest paid on amounts held by investment companies as defined in section 3 of the Investment Company Act (15 U.S.C.

section 80-a) and on amounts paid on pooled funds or trusts. The interest to be reported with respect to a widely held fixed investment trust, as defined in § 1.671-5(b)(22), shall be the interest earned on the assets held by the trust. See § 1.671-5 for the reporting rules for widely held fixed investment trusts (as defined under that section).

(b) *Interest excluded from reporting requirement.*—The term *interest* or *original issue discount* (OID) does not include—

(1) Interest on any obligation issued by a natural person as defined in § 1.6049-4(f)(2), irrespective of whether such interest is collected on behalf of the holder of the obligation by a middleman.

(2) Interest on any obligation if such interest is exempt from taxation under section 103(a), relating to certain governmental obligations, or interest which is exempt from taxation under any other provision of law without regard to the identity of the holder. The holder of a tax exempt obligation that is not in registered form must provide written certification to the payor (other than the issuer of the obligation) that the obligation is exempt from taxation. A statement that interest coupons are tax exempt on the envelope or shell commonly used by financial institutions to process such coupons, signed by the payee, will be sufficient for this purpose if the envelope is properly completed (i.e., shows the name, address, and taxpayer identification number of the payee). A payor may rely on such written certification in treating such interest as tax exempt for purposes of section 6049. See § 1.6049-4(d)(8) with respect to the requirement that the issuer of a taxable obligation shall make an information return if such issuer receives an envelope which improperly claims that the interest coupons contained therein are tax exempt.

(3) Interest on amounts held in escrow to guarantee performance on a contract or to provide security. However, interest on amounts held in escrow with a person described in paragraph (a)(2) or (3) of this section is interest subject to reporting under section 6049.

(4) Interest that a governmental unit pays with respect to tax refunds.

(5) Interest on deposits for security, such as deposits posted with a public utility company. However, interest on deposits posted for security with a person described in paragraph (a)(2) or (3) of this section is interest subject to reporting under section 6049.

(6) Amounts from sources outside the United States (determined under the provisions of part I, subchapter N, chapter 1 of the Internal Revenue Code (Code) and the regulations under those provisions) paid by a non-U.S. payor or a non-U.S. middleman (as defined in paragraph (c)(5) of this section) and paid and received outside the United States. See § 1.6049-4(f)(16) for circumstances in which a payment is considered to be paid and received outside the United States.

(7) Portfolio interest, as defined in § 1.871-14(b)(1), paid with respect to obligations in bearer form described in section 871(h)(2)(A), as in effect prior to the amendment by section 502 of the Hiring Incentives to Restore Employment Act of 2010 (HIRE Act), Public Law 111-147, or section 881(c)(2)(A), as in effect prior to the amendment by section 502 of the HIRE Act, that were issued prior to March 19, 2012, or with respect to a foreign-targeted registered obligation described in § 1.871-14(e)(2) that was issued prior to January 1, 2016, and for which the documentation requirements described in § 1.871-14(e)(3) and (4) have been satisfied (other than by a U.S. middleman (as defined in paragraph (c)(5) of this section) that, as a custodian or nominee of the payee, collects the amount for, or on behalf of, the payee, regardless of whether the middleman is also acting as agent of the payor).

(8) Portfolio interest described in § 1.871-14(c)(1)(ii), paid with respect to obligations in registered form described in section 871(h)(2) or 881(c)(2) that is not described in paragraph (b)(7) of this section.

(9) Any amount paid by an international organization described in § 1.6049-4(c)(1)(ii)(G) (or its paying, transfer, or other agent that is not also a payee's agent) with respect to an obligation of which the international organization is the issuer.

(10)(i) Amounts paid and received outside the United States under § 1.6049-4(f)(16) (other than by a U.S. middleman (as defined in paragraph (c)(5) of this section) that are paid by a custodian or nominee or other agent of the payee, of amounts that that it receives for, or on behalf of, the payee, regardless of whether the middleman is also acting as agent of the payor) with respect to an obligation that: Has a face amount or principal amount of not less than $500,000 (as determined based on the spot rate on the date of issuance if in foreign currency); has a maturity (at issue) of 183 days or less; satisfies the requirements of sections 163(f)(2)(B)(i) and (ii)(I), as in effect prior to the amendment by section 502 of the HIRE Act, and the regulations thereunder (as if the obligation would otherwise be a registration-required obligation within the meaning of section 163(f)(2)(A)) (however, an original issue discount obligation with a maturity of 183 days or less from the date of issuance is not required to satisfy the certification requirement of § 1.163-5(c)(2)(i)(D)(3)) and is issued in accordance with the procedures of § 1.163-5(c)(2)(i)(D); and has on its face the following statement (or a similar statement having the same effect):

> By accepting this obligation, the holder represents and warrants that it is not a United States person (other than an exempt recipient described in section 6049(b)(4) of the Internal Revenue Code and regulations thereunder) and that it is not acting for or on behalf of a United States person (other than an exempt recipient described in section 6049(b)(4) of the Internal Revenue Code and the regulations thereunder).

(ii) If the obligation is in registered form, it must be registered in the name of an exempt recipient described in § 1.6049-4(c)(1)(ii). For purposes of this paragraph (b)(10), a middleman may treat an obligation as described in section 163(f)(2)(B)(i) and (f)(2)(B)(ii)(I), as in effect prior to the amendment by section 502 of the HIRE Act, and the regulations under that section if the obligation, or coupons detached therefrom, whichever is presented for payment, contains the statement described in this paragraph (b)(10). The exemption from reporting described in this paragraph (b)(10) shall not apply if the payor has actual knowledge that the payee is a U.S. person who is not an exempt recipient.

(11) Amounts paid with respect to an account or deposit with a U.S. or foreign branch of a domestic or foreign corporation or partnership that is paid with respect to an obligation described in either paragraph (b)(11)(i) or (ii) of this section, if the branch is engaged in the commercial banking business; and the interest or OID is paid and received outside the United States as defined in § 1.6049-4(f)(16) (other than by a U.S. middleman (as defined in paragraph (c)(5) of this section) that acts as a custodian, nominee, or other agent of the payee, and collects the amount for, or on behalf of, the payee, regardless of whether the middleman is also acting as agent of the payor). The exemption from reporting described in this paragraph (b)(11) shall not apply if the payor has actual knowledge that the payee is a U.S. person who is not an exempt recipient.

(i) An obligation is described in this paragraph (b)(11)(i) if it is not in registered form (within the meaning of section 163(f) and the regulations under that section), is described in section 163(f)(2)(B), as in effect prior to the amendment by section 502 of the HIRE Act, and issued in accordance with the procedures of § 1.163-5(c)(2)(i)(C) or (D), and, in the case of a U.S. branch, is part of a larger single public offering of securities. For purposes of this paragraph (b)(11)(i), a middleman may treat an obligation as described in section 163(f)(2)(B), as in effect prior to the amendment by section 502 of the HIRE Act, if the obligation, and any detachable coupons, contains the statement described in section 163(f)(2)(B)(ii)(II), as in effect prior to the amendment by section 502 of the HIRE Act, and the regulations under that section.

(ii)(A) An obligation is described in this paragraph (b)(11)(ii) if it produces income described in section 871(i)(2)(A); has a face amount or principal amount of not less than $500,000 (as determined based on the spot rate on the date of issuance if in foreign currency); satisfies the requirements of sections 163(f)(2)(B)(i) and (ii)(I), as in effect prior to the amendment by section 502 of the HIRE Act, and the regulations thereunder (as if the obligation would otherwise be a registration-required obligation within the meaning of section 163(f)(2)(A)) and is issued in accordance with the procedures of § 1.163-5(c)(2)(i)(C) or (D) (however, an original issue discount obligation with a maturity of 183 days or less from the date of issuance is not required to satisfy the certification requirement of § 1.163-5(c)(2)(i)(D)(3)). For purposes of this paragraph (b)(11)(ii), a middleman may treat an obligation as described in sections 163(f)(2)(B)(i) and (ii), as in effect prior to the amendment by section 502 of the HIRE Act, and the regulations under that section if the obligation, or any detachable coupon, contains the statement described in paragraph (b)(11)(ii)(B) of this section.

(B) The obligation must have on its face, and on any detachable coupons, the following statement (or a similar statement having the same effect):

> By accepting this obligation, the holder represents and warrants that it is not a United States person (other than an exempt recipient described in section 6049(b)(4) and regulations under that section) and that it is not acting for or on behalf of a United States person (other than an exempt recipient described in section 6049(b)(4) and the regulations under that section).

(C) If the obligation is in registered form, it must be registered in the name of an exempt recipient described in § 1.6049-4(c)(1)(ii).

(12) Payments that a payor can, prior to payment, reliably associate with documentation upon which it may rely to treat the payment as made to a foreign beneficial owner in accordance with § 1.1441-1(e)(1)(ii) or as made to a foreign payee in accordance with paragraph (d)(1) of this section or presumed to be made to a foreign payee under paragraph (d)(2) or (3) of this section. However, such payments may be reportable under § 1.1461-1(b) and (c) or under § 1.1474-1(d)(2) (for a chapter 4 reportable amount (as described in § 1.1471-1(b)(18)). The provisions of § 1.1441-1 shall apply by substituting the term "payor" for the term "withholding agent" and without regard to the fact that the provisions apply only to amounts subject to withholding under chapter 3 of the Code. In the event of a conflict between the provisions of § 1.1441-1 and paragraph (d) of this section in determining the foreign status of the payee, the provisions of § 1.1441-1 shall govern for payments of amounts subject to withholding under chapter 3 of the Code and the provisions of paragraph (d) of this section shall govern in other cases. This paragraph (b)(12) does not apply to interest paid on or after January 1, 2013, to a nonresident alien individual to the extent provided in § 1.6049-8.

(13) Amounts for the period that the debt obligation with respect to which the interest arises represents an asset blocked as described in § 1.1441-2(e)(3). Payment of such amounts, including interest that is past due and OID on obligations that mature on or before the date that the assets are no longer blocked, is deemed to occur in accordance with the rules of § 1.1441-2(e)(3).

(14) Payments that a payor or middleman can, prior to payment, reliably associate with documentation upon which it may rely to treat as made to a foreign intermediary or flow-through entity in accordance with § 1.1441-1(b) if it obtains from the foreign intermediary or flow-through entity a withholding statement under § 1.1471-3(c)(3)(iii)(B)(*2*) (describing an FFI withholding statement), § 1.1471-3(c)(3)(iii)(B)(*3*) (describing a chapter 4 withholding statement), § 1.1441-1(e)(3)(iv) (describing a withholding statement provided by a non-qualified intermediary), § 1.1441-1(e)(5)(v) (describing a withholding statement provided by a qualified intermediary), or under § 1.1441-5 (describing a withholding statement provided by a foreign partnership, foreign simple trust, or foreign grantor trust), that allocates the payment (or portion of a payment) to a chapter 4 withholding rate pool or specific payees to which withholding applies under chapter 4. The provisions of each of the foregoing sections shall apply by substituting the term "payor" for the term "withholding agent." A payor or middleman may rely on a withholding statement provided by a foreign intermediary or flow-through entity that identifies a chapter 4 withholding rate pool of U.S. payees (as described in § 1.6049-4(c)(4)) or, with respect to a withholdable payment, a chapter 4 withholding rate pool of recalcitrant account holders (as described in § 1.1471-4(d)(6)) provided that the payor or middleman identifies the foreign intermediary or flow-through entity that maintains the accounts (as described in § 1.1471-5(b)(5)) included in the chapter 4 withholding rate pool as a participating FFI (including a reporting Model 2 FFI) or registered deemed-compliant FFI (including a reporting Model 1 FFI) by applying the rules in § 1.1471-3(d)(4) or in § 1.1471-3(e)(4)(vi)(B), as applicable, for identifying the payee of a payment (by substituting the term "payor" for the term "withholding agent"). See, however, § 1.1441-1(e)(5)(v)(C)(*2*)(*i*) for when a qualified intermediary may provide a single pool of recalcitrant account holders (without the need to subdivide into the pools described in § 1.1471-4(d)(6)). Additionally, when a foreign intermediary or flow through entity provides to a payor or middleman a withholding statement that allocates the payment (or portion of a payment) to a chapter 4 withholding rate pool of U.S. payees, the payor or middleman may also rely on the withholding statement if the payor or middleman identifies the intermediary or flow-through entity as a qualified intermediary (as defined in § 1.1441-1(c)(15) by applying the rules described in § 1.1441-1(b)(2)(vii)) that provides the certification described in § 1.1441-1(e)(3)(ii)(D) with respect to U.S. payees that hold accounts with a foreign intermediary or flow-through entity other than the qualified intermediary providing the certification.

(15) If a foreign intermediary, as described in § 1.1441-1(c)(13), or a U.S. branch that is not treated as a U.S. person receives a payment from a payor, which payment the payor can reliably associate with a valid withholding certificate described in § 1.1441-1(e)(3)(ii) or (iii), or § 1.1441-1(e)(3)(v), respectively, furnished by such intermediary or branch, then the intermediary or branch is not required to report such payment when it, in turn, pays the amount, unless, and to the extent, the intermediary or branch knows that the payment is required to be reported under this section and was not so reported. For example, if a U.S. branch described in § 1.1441-1(b)(2)(iv) fails to provide information regarding U.S. persons that are not exempt from reporting under § 1.6049-4(c)(1)(ii) to the person from whom the U.S. branch receives the payment, the amount paid by the U.S. branch to such person is interest or original issue discount. See, however, § 1.6049-4(c)(4) for when reporting under section 6049 is coordinated with reporting under chapter 4 or an applicable IGA (as defined in § 1.6049-4(f)(7)). The exception for payments described in this paragraph (b)(15) shall not apply to a qualified intermediary that assumes reporting responsibility under chapter 61 of the Code for the payment under the agreement described in § 1.1441-1(e)(5)(iii).

(16) Amounts of interest as determined under the provisions of § 1.446-3(g)(4) (dealing with interest in the case of a significant nonperiodic payment with respect to a notional principal contract). Such amounts are governed by the provisions of section 6041. See § 1.6041-1(d)(5).

(c) *Applicable rules.*—(1) *Documentary evidence for offshore obligations and certain other obligations.*—(i) A payor may rely on documentary evidence described in § 1.1471-3(c)(5)(i) instead of a beneficial owner withholding certificate described in § 1.1441-1(e)(2)(i) in the case of an amount paid outside the United States (as described in paragraph (e) of this section) with respect to an offshore obligation, or, in the case of broker proceeds described in § 1.6045-1(c)(2), to the extent provided in § 1.6045-1(g)(1)(i). For purposes of this section, the term *offshore obligation* means—

(A) An account maintained at an office or branch of a bank or other financial institution located outside the United States; or

(B) An obligation as defined in § 1.6049-4(f)(3) (other than an account described in paragraph (c)(1)(i)(A) of this section), contract, or other instrument with respect to which the payor is either engaged in business as a broker or dealer in securities or a financial institution (as defined in § 1.1471-5(e)) that engages in significant activities at an office or branch located outside the United States. For purposes of the preceding sentence, an office or branch of such payor shall be considered to engage in significant activities with respect to an obligation when it participates materially and actively in negotiating the obligation under the principles described in § 1.864-4(c)(5)(iii) (substituting the term "obligation" for the term "stock or security").

(ii) A payor may rely on documentary evidence if the payor has established procedures to obtain, review, and maintain documentary evidence sufficient to establish the identity of the payee and the status of that person as a foreign person; and the payor obtains, reviews, and maintains such documentary evidence in accordance with those procedures. A payor maintains the documents reviewed for purposes of this paragraph (c)(1) by retaining an original, certified copy, or photocopy (including a microfiche, electronic scan, or similar means of electronic storage) of the documents reviewed for as long as it may be relevant to the determination of the payor's obligation to report under § 1.6049-4 and this section and noting in its records the date on which the document was received and reviewed. Documentary evidence furnished for a payment of an amount subject to withholding under chapter 3 of the Code or that is a chapter 4 reportable amount under § 1.1474-1(d)(2) must contain all of the information that is necessary to complete a Form 1042-S for that payment. See §§ 1.1471-3(c) and 1.1471-4(c) for additional documentation requirements to identify a payee or account holder for chapter 4 purposes that may apply in addition to the requirements under paragraph (c) of this section.

(iii) Even if an account or obligation (as defined in § 1.6049-4(f)(3)) is not maintained outside the United States (maintained in the United States), a payor may rely on documentary evidence associated with a withholding certificate described in § 1.1441-1(e)(3)(iii) with respect to the persons for whom an entity acting as an intermediary collects the payment. A payor may also rely on documentary evidence associated with a flow-through withholding certificate for payments treated as made to foreign partners of a nonwithholding foreign partnership, as defined in § 1.1441-1(c)(28), the foreign beneficiaries of a foreign simple trust, as defined in § 1.1441-1(c)(24), or foreign owners of a foreign grantor trust, as defined in § 1.1441-1(c)(26), even though the partnership or trust account is an obligation maintained in the United States.

(iv) For accounts opened on or after July 1, 2014, and before January 1, 2015, and for obligations entered into on or after July 1, 2014, and before January 1, 2015, a payor may continue to apply the rules of § 1.6049-5(c)(1) and (c)(4) as in effect and contained in 26 CFR part 1 revised April 1, 2013, rather than this paragraph (c)(1) and paragraph (c)(4) of this section. A payor that applies the rules of § 1.6049-5(c)(1) and (c)(4) as in effect and contained in 26 CFR part 1 revised April 1, 2013, to an account or obligation must also apply

§ 1.1441-6(c)(2) (to the extent applicable) and § 1.6049-5(e) both as in effect and contained in 26 CFR part 1 revised April, 2013, with respect to the account or obligation.

(2) *Other applicable rules.*—The provisions of § 1.1441-1(e)(4)(i) through (xii) (regarding who may sign a certificate, validity period of certificates and documentary evidence, retention of certificates, reliance rules, etc.) shall apply (by substituting the term "payor" for the term "withholding agent" and disregarding the fact that the provisions under § 1.1441-1(e)(4) only apply to amounts subject to withholding under chapter 3 of the Code) to withholding certificates and documentary evidence furnished for purposes of this section. See § 1.1441-1(b)(2)(vii) for provisions dealing with reliable association of a payment with documentation.

(3) *Standards of knowledge.*—A payor may not rely on a withholding certificate or documentary evidence described in paragraph (c)(1) or (4) of this section if it has actual knowledge or reason to know that any information or certification stated in the certificate or documentary evidence is unreliable. A payor has reason to know that information or certifications are unreliable only if the payor would have reason to know under the provisions of § 1.1441-7(b)(2) and (3) that the information and certifications provided on the certificate or in the documentary evidence are unreliable or, in the case of a Form W-9 (or an acceptable substitute), it cannot reasonably rely on the documentation as set forth in § 31.3406(h)-3(e) of this chapter (see the information and certification described in § 31.3406(h)-3(e)(2)(i) through (iv) of this chapter that are required in order for a payor reasonably to rely on a Form W-9). The provisions of § 1.1441-7(b)(2) and (3) shall apply for purposes of this paragraph (c)(3) irrespective of the type of income to which § 1.1441-7(b)(2) is otherwise limited. The exemptions from reporting described in paragraphs (b)(10) and (11) of this section shall not apply if the payor has actual knowledge that the payee is a U.S. person who is not an exempt recipient.

(4) *Special documentation rules for certain payments.*—This paragraph (c)(4) modifies the provisions of paragraph (c)(1) of this section for payments of amounts that are not subject to withholding under chapter 3 of the Code, other than amounts described in paragraph (d)(3)(iii) of this section (dealing with U.S. short-term OID and U.S. source deposit interest described in section 871(i)(2)(A) or 881(d)(3)). Amounts are not subject to withholding under chapter 3 of the Code if they are not included in the definition of amounts subject to withholding under § 1.1441-2(a) (*e.g.*, deposit interest with foreign branches of U.S. banks, foreign source income, or broker proceeds). A payor may rely upon documentation in lieu of documentary evidence (as described in paragraph (c)(1) of this section) or a written statement (as defined in § 1.1471-1(b)(150)) or another statement to the extent permitted in paragraphs (c)(4)(i) through (iii) of this section, until the payor knows or has reason to know of a change in circumstance that makes the documentation unreliable or incorrect (as defined in § 1.1441-1(e)) when the payor does not have customer information for the payee that includes any of the U.S. indicia described in § 1.1471-3(c)(6)(ii)(C)(*1*). Further, a payor may maintain such documentation or documentary evidence as required in paragraph (c)(4)(iv) of this section.

(i) *Statement in lieu of documentary evidence with respect to accounts.*—If under the local laws, regulations, or practices of a country in which an account is maintained, it is not customary to obtain documentary evidence described in paragraph (c)(1) of this section with respect to the type of account, the payor may, instead of obtaining a beneficial owner withholding certificate described in § 1.1441-1(e)(2)(i) or documentary evidence described in paragraph (c)(1) of this section, establish a payee's foreign status based on the statement described in this paragraph (c)(4)(i) (or such substitute statement as the Internal Revenue Service may prescribe) made on an account opening form. However, see, also § 1.1471-4(c) or an applicable IGA for additional documentation requirements that may apply to a participating FFI (including a reporting Model 2 FFI) for determining the status of its account holders for chapter 4 purposes. The statement referred to in this paragraph (c)(4)(i) must appear near the signature line and must state, "By opening this account and signing below, the account owner represents and warrants that he/she/it is not a U.S. person for purposes of U.S. Federal income tax and that he/she/it is not acting for, or on behalf of, a U.S. person. A false statement or misrepresentation of tax status by a U.S. person could lead to penalties under U.S. law. If your tax status changes and you become a U.S. citizen or a resident, you must notify us within 30 days." Additionally, a payor may, instead of obtaining a beneficial owner withholding certificate described in § 1.1441-1(e)(2)(i) or § 1.1471-3(c)(3)(ii) or documentary evidence described in paragraph (c)(1) of this section, establish a payee's foreign status based on a written statement described in paragraph § 1.1471-1(b)(150) to the extent a payor uses such written statement to establish a payee's chapter 4 status and is permitted to use the written statement under § 1.1471-3(d) (by substituting the term "payor" for the term "withholding agent") without any other documentary evidence.

(ii) *Documentation under IGA.*—A payor that is a reporting Model 1 FFI or reporting Model 2 FFI may rely upon documentation or information establishing a payee's status that is permitted under an applicable IGA for determining whether the account of the payee is other than a U.S. account and regardless of whether such documentation or certification is described in paragraph (c)(1) of this section or § 1.1441-1(e)(2).

(iii) *Maintenance of documentation and written statement.*—A payor maintains documentation if it either maintains the documentary evidence as described in paragraph (c)(1) of this section or retains a record of the documentary evidence reviewed if the payor is not required to retain copies of the documentation pursuant to the payor's AML due diligence (as defined in § 1.1471-1(b)(4)). A payor retains a record of documentary evidence reviewed by noting in its records the type of documentation reviewed, the date the document was reviewed, the document's identification number (if any), and whether such documentation contained any U.S. indicia described in § 1.1441-7(b)(8). Any statement described in paragraph (c)(4)(i) of this section, must be retained in accordance with § 1.1471-3(c)(6)(iii).

(5) *U.S. payor, U.S. middleman, non-U.S. payor, and non-U.S. middleman.*—The terms *payor* and *middleman* have the meanings ascribed to them under § 1.6049-4(a). A *non-U.S. payor* or *non-U.S. middleman* means a payor or middleman other than a U.S. payor or U.S. middleman. The term *U.S. payor* or *U.S. middleman* means—

(i) *Definition.*—(A) A person described in section 7701(a)(30) (including a foreign branch or office of such person);

(B) The government of the United States or the government of any State or political subdivision thereof (or any agency or instrumentality of any of the foregoing);

(C) A controlled foreign corporation within the meaning of section 957, determined without applying section 318(a)(3)(A), (B), and (C) so as to consider a United States person as owning stock which is owned by a person who is not a United States person.

(D) A foreign partnership, if at any time during its tax year, one or more of its partners are U.S. persons (as defined in § 1.1441-1(c)(2)) who, in the aggregate hold more than 50 percent of the income or capital interest in the partnership or if, at any time during its tax year, it is engaged in the conduct of a trade or business in the United States;

(E) A foreign person 50 percent or more of the gross income of which, from all sources for the three-year period ending with the close of its taxable year preceding the collection or payment (or such part of such period as the person has been in existence), was effectively connected with the conduct of trade or business within the United States; or

(F) A U.S. branch or territory financial institution described in § 1.1441-1(b)(2)(iv) that is treated as a U.S. person.

(ii) *Reporting by U.S. payors in U.S. possessions.*—U.S. payors are not required to report on Form 1099 income that is from sources within a possession of the United States and that is exempt from taxation under section 931, 932, or 933, each of which sections exempts certain income from sources within a possession of the United States paid to a bona fide resident of that possession. For purposes of this paragraph (c)(5)(ii), a U.S. payor may treat the beneficial owner as a bona fide resident of the possession of the United States from which the income is sourced if, prior to payment of the income, the U.S. payor can reliably associate the payment with valid documentation that supports the claim of residence in the possession of the United States from which the income is sourced. This paragraph (c)(5)(ii) shall not apply if the U.S. payor has actual knowledge or reason to know that the documentation is unreliable or incorrect or that the income does not satisfy the requirements for exemption under section 931, 932, or 933. For the rules determining whether income is from sources within a possession of the United States, see section 937(b) and the regulations thereunder.

(6) *Examples.*—The following examples illustrate the provisions of paragraphs (b) and (c) of this section:

Example 1. FC is a foreign corporation that is not engaged in a trade or business in the United States during the current calendar year. D, an individual who is a resident and citizen of the United States, holds a registered obligation issued by FC in a public offering. Interest is paid on the obligation within the United States by DC, a U.S. corporation that is the designated paying agent of FC. D does not have an account with DC. Although interest paid on the obligation issued by FC is foreign source, the interest paid by DC to D is considered to be interest under paragraph (b)(6) of this section for purposes of information reporting under section 6049 because it is not paid and received outside the United States within the meaning of § 1.6049-4(f)(16).

Example 2. The facts are the same as in *Example 1* except that D is a nonresident alien individual who has furnished DC with a Form W-8 in accordance with the provisions of § 1.1441-1(e)(1)(ii). By reason of paragraph (b)(12) of this section, the payment of interest by DC to D is not considered to be a payment of interest for purposes of information reporting under section 6049. Therefore, DC is not required to make an information return under section 6049.

Example 3. The facts are the same as in *Example 2* except that the obligation of FC is held in a custodial account for D by FB, a foreign branch of a U.S. financial institution. By reason of paragraph (c)(5) of this section, FB is considered to be a U.S. middleman. Therefore, FB is required to make an information return unless FB may treat D as a beneficial owner that is a foreign person in accordance with the provisions of § 1.1441-1(e)(1)(ii).

Example 4. The facts are the same as in *Example 3* except that the FC obligation is held for D by NC, in a custodial account at NC's foreign branch. NC is a foreign corporation that is a non-U.S. middleman described in paragraph (c)(5) of this section. The payment by NC to D is paid and received outside of the United States under § 1.6049-4(f)(16) and therefore is not considered to be a payment of interest for purposes of section 6049 pursuant to paragraph (b)(6) of this section. Therefore, NC is not required to make an information return under section 6049 with respect to the payment.

(d) *Determination of status as U.S. or foreign payee and applicable presumptions in the absence of documentation.*—(1) *Identifying the payee.*—The provisions of §§ 1.1441-1(b)(2), 1.1441-5(c)(1) and (e)(2) and (3) shall apply (by substituting the term "payor" for the term "withholding agent") to identify the payee (other than a payee included in a chapter 4 withholding rate pool described in paragraph (b)(14) of this section) for purposes of this section (and other sections of the regulations under this chapter to which this paragraph (d)(1) applies), except to the extent provided in this paragraph (d)(1) in the case of a payment of an amount that is not subject to withholding under chapter 3 of the Code and that is not a withholdable payment (as defined in § 1.6049-4(f)(15)). Amounts are not subject to withholding under chapter 3 of the Code if they are not included in the definition of amounts subject to withholding under § 1.1441-2(a) (*e.g.*, deposit interest with foreign branches of U.S. banks, foreign source income, or broker proceeds). The exceptions to the application of § 1.1441-1(b)(2) to amounts that are not subject to withholding under chapter 3 of the Code and that are not withholdable payments are as follows:

(i) The provisions of § 1.1441-1(b)(2)(ii), dealing with payments to a U.S. agent or intermediary of a foreign person, shall not apply. Thus, a payment to a U.S. agent or intermediary of a foreign person is treated as a payment to a U.S. payee.

(ii) Payments to U.S. branches or territory financial institution described in § 1.1441-1(b)(2)(iv) shall be treated as payments to a foreign payee, irrespective of the fact that the U.S. branch or territory financial institution is otherwise treated as a U.S. person for payments of amounts subject to withholding under chapter 3 and withholdable payments, and irrespective of the fact that the branch or territory financial institution is treated as a U.S. payor for purposes of paragraph (c)(5) of this section.

(2) *Presumptions of U.S. or foreign status in the absence of documentation.*—(i) *In general.*—Except as otherwise provided in this paragraph (d)(2)(i), for purposes of this section (and other sections of regulations under this chapter 61 to which this paragraph (d)(2) applies), the provisions of § 1.1441-1(b)(3)(i) through (ix) and § 1.1441-5(d) and (e)(6) shall apply (by substituting the term "payor" for the term "withholding agent") to determine the classification (*e.g.*, individual, corporation, partnership, trust), status (*i.e.*, a U.S. or a foreign person), and other relevant characteristics (*e.g.*, beneficial owner or intermediary) of a payee if a payment cannot be reliably associated with valid documentation under § 1.1441-1(b)(2)(vii) irrespective of whether the payments are subject to withholding under chapter 3 of the Code or are withholdable payments. The provisions of § 1.1441-1(b)(3)(iii)(D) and (vii)(B) (referencing presumption rules for payments with respect to offshore obligations) shall not apply to a payment of an amount not subject to withholding under chapter 3, unless it is an amount that is a withholdable payment made to a payee that is an entity. Thus, in the case of a withholdable payment made to an entity, the presumption rules of § 1.1441-1(b)(3)(iii)(D) and (vii)(B) shall apply regardless of whether the payment is an amount subject to withholding under chapter 3. Additionally, in the case of an amount paid outside the United States with respect to an offshore obligation described in § 1.1441-1(b)(3)(iii)(D) or (vii)(B) of an amount not subject to withholding under chapter 3 and that is treated as made to a payee that is an individual, the presumption rules of § 1.1441-1(b)(3)(iii) shall not apply, and the payee shall be presumed a U.S. person only when the payee has any of the indicia of U.S. status that are described in § 1.1441-7(b)(5) or (8). In a case in which a withholding agent makes a withholdable payment that cannot reliably be associated with documentation, see § 1.1471-3(f)(4) and (5) for determining the status of the payee for chapter 4 purposes when the payment is treated as made to a foreign entity (by substituting the term "payor" for the term "withholding agent"). The rules of § 1.1441-1(b)(2)(vii) shall apply for purposes of determining when a payment can reliably be associated with documentation, by substituting the term "payor" for the term "withholding agent." For this purpose, the information, documentary evidence, statement, or other documentation described in paragraph (c)(4) of this section can be treated as documentation with which a payment can be associated.

(ii) *Grace period in the case of indicia of a foreign payee.*—When the conditions of this paragraph (d)(2)(ii) are satisfied, the 30-day grace period provisions under section 3406(e) shall not apply and the provisions of this paragraph (d)(2)(ii) shall apply instead. A payor that, at any time during the grace period described in this paragraph (d)(2)(ii), credits an account with payments described in § 1.1441-6(c)(2) (or credits an account with broker proceeds from securities described in § 1.1441-6(c)(2)), that are reportable under section 6042, 6045, 6049, or 6050N may, instead of treating the account as owned by a U.S. person and applying backup withholding under section 3406, if applicable, choose to treat the account as owned by a foreign person (and apply the grace period described in § 1.1441-1(b)(3)(iv)) if, at the beginning of the grace period, the address that the payor has in its records for the account holder is in a foreign country, the payor has been furnished the information contained in a withholding certificate described in § 1.1441-1(e)(2), or the payor holds a withholding certificate that is no longer reliable other than because the validity period as described in § 1.1441-1(e)(4)(ii)(A) has expired. In the case of a newly opened account, the grace period begins on the date that the payor first credits the account. In the case of an existing account for which the payor holds a Form W-8 or documentary evidence of foreign status, the payor may apply the provisions of the grace period described in § 1.1441-1(b)(3)(iv), beginning on the date that the payor first credits the account after the existing documentation held with regard to the account can no longer be relied upon (other than because the validity period described in § 1.1441-1(e)(4)(ii)(A) has expired). A new account shall be treated as an existing account for purposes of this paragraph (d)(2)(ii) if the account holder already holds an account at the branch location at which the new account is opened, or if the account is treated as a consolidated obligation as defined in § 1.1471-(1)(b)(23) for purpose of chapter 4 to the extent the account does not receive any amounts subject to withholding under chapter 3. A new account shall also be treated as an existing account for purposes of this paragraph (d)(2)(ii) if an account is held at another branch location if the institution maintains an account information system described in § 1.1441-1(e)(4)(ix). The grace period terminates on the earlier of the close of the 90th day from the date on which the grace period begins or the date that valid documentation is provided. The grace period also terminates when the remaining balance in the account (due to withdrawals or otherwise) is equal to or less than 28 percent (or other statutory tax rate that is applicable to backup withholding) of the total amounts credited since the beginning of the grace period that would be subject to backup withholding if the provisions of this paragraph (d)(2)(ii) did not apply. At the end of the grace period, the payor shall treat the amounts credited to the account, or paid with respect to an account, during the grace period as paid to a U.S. or foreign payee depending upon whether documentation has been furnished and the nature of any such documentation furnished upon which the payor may rely to treat the account as owned by a U.S. or foreign payee. If the documentation has not been received on or before the date of expiration of the grace period, the payor may also apply the presumptions described in this paragraph (d) to amounts credited to the account after the date on which the grace period expires (until such time as the payor can reliably associate the documentation with amounts credited). See § 31.6413(a)-3(a)(1)(iv) of this chapter for treating backup withheld amounts under section 3406 as erroneously withheld when the documentation establishing foreign status is furnished prior to the end of the calendar year in which backup withholding occurs. If the provisions of this paragraph (d)(2)(ii) apply, the provisions of § 31.3406(d)-3 of this chapter shall not apply. For purposes of this paragraph (d)(2)(ii), an account holder's reinvestment of gross proceeds of a sale into other instruments constitutes a withdrawal and a non-qualified electronic transmission of information on a withholding certificate is a transmission that is not in accordance with the provisions of § 1.1441-1(e)(4)(iv). See § 1.1092(d)-1 for a definition of the term actively traded for purposes of this paragraph (d)(2)(ii).

(iii) *Joint owners.*—Amounts paid to accounts held jointly for which a certificate or documentation is required as a condition for being exempt from reporting under paragraph (b) of this section are presumed made to U.S. payees who are not exempt recipients if, prior to payment, the payor cannot reliably associate the payment either with a Form W-9 furnished by one of the joint owners in the manner required in § § 31.3406(d)-1 through 31.3406(d)-5 of this chapter, or with documentation described in paragraph (b)(12) of this section furnished by each joint owner upon which it can rely to treat each joint owner as a foreign payee or foreign beneficial owner. In the case of an amount that is a withholdable payment made to a joint account, however, see § 1.1471-3(f)(7) for when the payment is treated as made to a foreign payee that is a nonparticipating FFI (as defined in § 1.1471-1(b)(82)). For purposes of applying this paragraph (d)(2)(iii), the grace period described in paragraph (d)(2)(ii) of this section shall apply only if each payee qualifies for such grace period.

(3) *Payments to foreign intermediaries or flow-through entities.*—(i) *Payments of amounts subject to withholding under chapter 3 of the Code or withholdable payments.*—In the case of payments of amounts that the payor may treat as made to a foreign intermediary or flow-through entity in accordance with § § 1.1441-1(b)(3)(ii)(C) and (b)(3)(v)(A) and 1.1441-5(c) or (e) and that are subject to withholding under § 1.1441-2(a), the provisions of § § 1.1441-1(b)(2)(v) and 1.1441-5(c)(1), (e)(2), and (3) shall apply (by substituting the term "payor" for the term "withholding agent") to identify the payee. If a payment of an amount subject to withholding cannot be reliably associated with valid documentation from a payee in accordance with § 1.1441-1(b)(2)(vii), the presumption rules of § § 1.1441-1(b)(3)(v) and 1.1441-5(d) and (e)(6) shall apply to determine the payee's status for purposes of this section (and other sections of regulations under this chapter to which this paragraph (d)(3) applies). In the case of an amount that is a withholdable payment, see § 1.1471-3(c)(3) for rules to identify the payee and see § 1.1471-3(f)(5) for the presumption rule that shall apply to amounts treated as made to a foreign intermediary or flow-through entity (by substituting the term "payor" for the term "withholding agent"). For example, where a withholdable payment is made to an intermediary under § 1.1471-3 that is treated as a nonparticipating FFI under § 1.1471-3(f)(5), the nonparticipating FFI shall be treated as the payee under § 1.1471-3(c)(3) and for purposes of this paragraph (d)(3)(i), therefore, no information return shall be required under this section.

(ii) *Payments of amounts not subject to withholding under chapter 3 of the Code and that are not withholdable payments.*—Except as provided in paragraph (d)(3)(iii) of this section, amounts that are not subject to withholding under chapter 3 of the Code and that are not withholdable payments that the payor may treat as paid to a foreign intermediary or flow-through entity shall be treated as made to an exempt recipient described in § 1.6049-4(c) except to the extent that the payor has actual knowledge that any person for whom the intermediary or flow-through entity is collecting the payment is a U.S. person who is not an exempt recipient. In the case of such actual knowledge, the payor shall treat the payment that it knows is allocable to such U.S. person as a payment to a U.S. payee who is not an exempt recipient and has actual knowledge of the amount allocable to such a person.

(iii) *Special rule for payments of certain short-term original issue discount.*—(A) *General rule.*—A payment of U.S. source bank deposit interest not subject to chapter 4 withholding or U.S. source interest or original issue discount on the redemption of an obligation with a maturity from the date of issue of 183 days or less (short-term OID) described in section 871(g)(1)(B) or 881(e) that the payor may treat as paid to a foreign intermediary or flow-through entity in accordance with the provisions of § 1.1441-1(b)(3)(ii)(C), (b)(3)(v)(A), § 1.1441-5(d) or (e) (by substituting the term "payor" for the term "withholding agent"), shall be treated as paid to an undocumented U.S. payee that is not an exempt recipient under paragraph § 1.6049-4(c) unless the payor has documentation from the payees of the payment and the payment is allocated to foreign payees, as a group, and to each U.S. non-exempt recipient payee. See § 1.1441-1(e)(3)(iv)(C)(2). However, a payor may rely on a withholding statement provided by an intermediary described in § 1.1441-1(e)(3)(iv) (or similar withholding statement for a flow-through entity) that identifies a chapter 4 withholding rate pool of U.S. payees (as described in § 1.6049-4(c)(4)(iii)) only if it identifies the foreign intermediary or flow-through entity as a participating FFI (including a reporting Model 2 FFI) or registered deemed-compliant FFI (including a reporting Model 1 FFI) under § 1.1471-3(d)(4) (by substituting the term "payor" for the term "withholding agent"). See also § 1.6049-4(c)(4)(iii) for when an FFI may provide a chapter 4 withholding rate pool of U.S. payees on a withholding statement.

(B) *Payee may be an intermediary.*—If a payment is made to a person described in § 1.6049-4(c)(1)(ii) that has not provided an intermediary withholding certificate under § 1.1441-1(e)(3)(i) but the payor knows or has reason to know that the payee may be an intermediary, the payor must apply the rules of paragraph (d)(3)(iii)(A) of this section. A payor has reason to know that such a person may be an intermediary if that person has provided documentation as an intermediary for another account with the same payor.

(iv) *Short-term deposits and repurchase transactions.*—The provisions of paragraph (d)(3)(ii) of this section and not paragraph (d)(3)(iii) of this section shall apply to deposits with banks and other financial institutions that remain on deposit for a period of two weeks or less, to amounts of original issue discount arising from a sale and repurchase transaction that is completed within a period of two weeks or less, or to amounts described in paragraphs (b)(7), (10) and (11) of this section (relating to certain obligations issued in bearer form).

(4) *Examples.*—The rules of paragraphs (d)(1) through (3) of this section are illustrated by the examples in this paragraph (d)(4). Unless otherwise specified in an example, the following facts apply: all FFIs, such as a nonqualified intermediary that is an FFI, are treated as participating FFIs; all payees have been identified with chapter 4 statuses that do not require withholding under chapter 4; and none of the payments are withholdable payments.

Example 1. (i) *Facts.* USP is a U.S. payor as defined in paragraph (c)(5) of this section. USP pays interest from sources within the United States that is a withholdable payment to an account maintained in the United States by X. The interest is not deposit interest described in sections 871(i)(2)(A) or 881(d). USP does not have a Form W-9, or withholding certificate from X as defined in § 1.1441-1(c)(16). Moreover, USP cannot treat X as an exempt recipient, as defined in § 1.6049-4(c)(1)(ii), without documentation and there is no indication that X is an individual, trust, or estate.

(ii) *Analysis.* The U.S. source interest is an amount subject to withholding as defined in § 1.1441-2(a). Under paragraph (d)(1) of this section, USP must apply the provisions of § § 1.1441-1(b)(2) and 1.1441-5(c) and (e) to determine the payee of the interest. Under § 1.1441-1(b)(2)(i), X, the person to whom the payment is made, is considered to be the payee, unless X is determined to be a flow-through entity, in which case the rules of § 1.1441-5 apply to determine the payee. Under paragraph (d)(2)(i) of this section, the rules of § 1.1441-1(b)(3)(ii) apply to determine the classification of a payee as an individual, trust, estate, corporation, or partnership. Under § 1.1441-1(b)(3)(ii)(B), X is presumed to be a partnership, since X does not appear to be an individual, trust or estate, and X cannot be presumed to be an exempt recipient in the absence of documentation. Paragraph (d)(2)(i) of this section requires USP to apply the provisions of § § 1.1441-1(b)(3)(iii) and 1.1441-5(d) to determine whether X is presumed to be a U.S. or foreign partnership. Under § § 1.1441-1(b)(3)(iii) and 1.1441-5(d)(2), X is presumed to be a U.S. partnership in absence of any indicia of foreign partnership status. The presumption of U.S. status applies even though the payment is a withholdable payment (see paragraph (d)(2) of this section and § 1.1471-3(f)(2) cross referencing the presumption rules of § 1.1441-1(b)(3)). The U.S. source interest paid to X is reportable under section 6049 on Form 1099 and the interest is subject to backup withholding under section 3406 because X has not provided its TIN on a valid Form W-9. No withholding or reporting applies to the payment under chapter 3 or 4 of the Code.

Example 2. (i) *Facts.* The facts are the same as in *Example 1*, except that the interest paid by USP is from sources outside the United States.

(ii) *Analysis.* Interest from sources outside the United States is not an amount subject to withholding, as defined in § 1.1441-2(a) or a withholdable payment. Under paragraph (d)(1) of this section, USP must apply the provisions of §§1.1441-1(b)(2) and 1.1441-5(c) and (e) to determine the payee. Under §1.1441-1(b)(2)(i), X, the person to whom the payment is made, is considered to be the payee, unless X is determined to be a flow-through entity, in which case the rules of §1.1441-5(c) or (e) apply to determine the payee. Under paragraph (d)(2)(i) of this section, the rules of §1.1441-1(b)(3)(ii) apply to determine the classification of a payee as an individual, trust, estate, corporation, or partnership. These rules apply irrespective of whether the payment is an amount subject to withholding. Under §1.1441-1(b)(3)(ii)(B), X is presumed to be a partnership, since X does not appear to be an individual, trust or estate, and X cannot be presumed to be an exempt recipient in the absence of documentation. Paragraph (d)(2)(i) of this section requires USP to apply the provisions of §§1.1441-1(b)(3)(iii) and 1.1441-5(d) to determine whether, X is presumed to be a U.S. or foreign partnership. Under §§1.1441-1(b)(3)(iii) and 1.1441-5(d)(2), X is presumed to be a U.S. partnership in absence of any indicia of foreign partnership status. The foreign source interest is a payment subject to reporting on Form 1099 under §1.6049-5(a). Further, because X is a non-exempt recipient that has failed to provide its TIN on a valid Form W-9, the foreign source interest is subject to backup withholding under section 3406.

Example 3. (i) *Facts.* USP is a U.S. payor as defined in paragraph (c)(5) of this section. USP makes a payment of U.S. source interest outside the United States to an offshore account of X. See paragraphs (c)(1) for a definition of offshore account and (e) for a payment outside the United States. USP does not have a withholding certificate from X as defined in §1.1441-1(c)(16) nor does it have documentary evidence as described in §1.1441-1(e)(1)(ii)(A)(2) and §1.6049-5(c)(1).

(ii) *Analysis.* The interest is an amount subject to withholding as defined in §1.1441-2(a). Under paragraph (d)(1) of this section, USP must apply the provisions of §1.1441-1(b)(2) and §1.1441-5(c) and (e) to determine the payee. Under §1.1441-1(b)(2)(i), X, the person to whom the payment is made, is considered to be the payee, unless X is determined to be a flow-through entity, in which case the rules of §1.1441-5(c) or (e) apply to determine the payee. Under paragraph (d)(2)(i) of this section, the rules of §1.1441-1(b)(3)(ii) apply to determine the classification of a payee as an individual, trust, estate, corporation, or partnership. Under §1.1441-1(b)(3)(ii)(B), X is presumed to be a partnership, since X does not appear to be an individual, trust or estate, and X cannot be presumed to be an exempt recipient in the absence of documentation. Paragraph (d)(2)(i) of this section requires USP to apply the provisions of §§1.1441-1(b)(3)(iii) and 1.1441-5(d) to determine whether, X is presumed to be a U.S. or foreign partnership. Under §§1.1441-1(b)(3)(iii)(D) and 1.1441-5(d)(2), X is presumed to be a foreign partnership. Therefore, under paragraph (d)(1) of this section and §1.1441-5(c)(1)(i)(E), the payees of the interest are presumed to be the partners of X. Under §1.1441-5(d)(3), the partners are presumed to be undocumented foreign persons. Therefore, USP must withhold 30% of the interest payment under §1.1441-1(b)(1) and report the payment on Form 1042-S in accordance with §1.1461-1(c).

Example 4. (i) *Facts.* The facts are the same as in *Example 3*, except that the interest is paid by F, a non-U.S. payor.

(ii) *Analysis.* The analysis and result are the same as in *Example 3*. F is a withholding agent under §1.1441-7 and its status as a non-U.S. payor under paragraph (c)(5) of this section is irrelevant.

Example 5. (i) *Facts.* USP is a U.S. payor as defined in paragraph (c)(5) of this section that is not an FFI. USP makes a payment outside the United States of interest from sources outside the United States with respect to an offshore obligation held by X. USP does not have a withholding certificate from X as defined in §1.1441-1(c)(16) nor does it have documentary evidence as described in §§1.1471-3(c)(5)(i) and 1.6049-5(c)(1). USP does not have actual knowledge of an employer identification number for X. X does not appear to be an individual, trust, or estate and cannot be treated as an exempt recipient, as defined in §1.6049-4(c)(1)(ii) in the absence of documentation.

(ii) *Analysis.* The interest is not an amount subject to withholding as defined in §1.1441-2(a) and is not a withholdable payment. Under paragraph (d)(1) of this section, USP must apply the rules of §§1.1441-1(b)(2) and 1.1441-5(c) and (e) to determine the payee of the interest. Under §1.1441-1(b)(2)(i), X, the person to whom the payment is made, is considered to be the payee, unless X is determined to be a flow-through entity, in which case the rules of §1.1441-5(c) or (e) apply to determine the payee. Under paragraph (d)(2)(i) of this section, §1.1441-1(b)(3)(ii) applies to determine X's classification as an individual, trust, estate, corporation or partnership. Under §1.1441-1(b)(3)(ii)(B), X is treated as a partnership, since it does not appear to be an individual, trust, or estate and cannot be treated as an exempt recipient without documentation. Paragraph (d)(2)(i) of this section requires USP to apply the provisions of §§1.1441-1(b)(3)(iii) and 1.1441-5(d) to determine whether, X is presumed to be a U.S. or foreign partnership. Paragraph (d)(2)(i) of this section also states that the presumptions of foreign status for payments made with respect to offshore obligations contained in §§1.1441-1(b)(3)(iii)(D) and 1.1441-5(d)(2) do not apply to amounts that are not subject to withholding and that are not withholdable payments described in paragraph (d)(2)(i). Therefore, under §§1.1441-1(b)(3)(iii) and 1.1441-5(d)(2), X is presumed to be a U.S. partnership because it does not have actual knowledge that X's employer identification number begins with the digits "98." Therefore, USP must treat X as a U.S. person that is not an exempt recipient and report the payment on Form 1099 under section 6049. Under §31.3406(g)-1(e) of this chapter, however, USP is not required to backup withhold on the payment unless it has actual knowledge that X is a U.S. person that is not an exempt recipient.

Example 6. (i) *Facts.* The facts are the same as in *Example 5*, except that the interest is paid by F, a non-U.S. payor, as defined under paragraph (c)(5) of this section.

(ii) *Analysis.* The analysis is the same as under *Example 5*. However, F is a non-U.S. payor paying foreign source interest outside the United States, and there is no indication that the amount is received in the United States under §1.6049-4(f)(16). Thus, paragraph (b)(6) of this section exempts the payment from reporting under section 6049.

Example 7. (i) *Facts.* USP, a U.S. payor as defined in paragraph (c)(5) of this section that is not an FFI, makes a payment of U.S. source interest that is a withholdable payment to NQI, a nonqualified intermediary as defined in §1.1441-1(c)(14), that is a certified deemed-compliant FFI under §1.1471-5(f)(2). The interest is paid inside the United States to an account of a bank or other financial institution maintained in the United States. NQI has provided USP with a nonqualified intermediary withholding certificate, as described in §1.1441-1(e)(3)(iii) that includes its chapter 4 status, but has not attached any documentation from the persons on whose behalf it acts or a withholding statement as described in §1.1441-1(e)(3)(iv).

(ii) *Analysis.* U.S. source interest is an amount subject to withholding under §1.1441-2(a). USP may treat the payment as made to a foreign intermediary under §1.1441-1(b)(3)(v)(A) because USP has received a nonqualified intermediary withholding certificate from NQI and may except NQI from withholding under chapter 4 of the Code given NQI's status for chapter 4 purposes as a deemed-compliant FFI. Under paragraph (d)(3)(i) of this section, USP must then apply §1.1471-3(c)(3) to treat the persons on whose behalf NQI is acting as the payees. Paragraph (d)(3)(i) of this section also requires USP to apply the presumption rules of §1.1441-1(b)(3)(v) if it cannot reliably associate the payment with valid documentation from a payee. See §1.1441-1(b)(2)(vii). As the payment is a withholdable payment, the interest is treated as paid to a nonparticipating FFI under §1.1471-3(f)(4). Therefore, the payment is not subject to reporting on Form 1099 under paragraph (b)(12) of this section. See §1.1471-2(a) for the withholding requirement with respect to the payment and §1.1474-1(d)(2) for the requirement to report the payment on Form 1042-S.

Example 8. (i) *Facts.* The facts are the same as in *Example 7*, except that the interest is paid outside the United States, as defined in paragraph (e) of this section to an offshore account, as defined in paragraph (c)(1) of this section and is not a withholdable payment.

(ii) *Analysis.* Under §1.1441-1(b)(3)(v)(B), the interest is treated as paid to an unknown foreign payee because it cannot be reliably associated with documentation under §1.1441-1(b)(2)(vii). Therefore, the payment is not subject to reporting on Form 1099 under paragraph (b)(12) of this section because the payment is presumed made to a foreign person. The payment is subject to withholding, however, under §1.1441-1(b) at a rate of 30% and is subject to reporting on Form 1042-S under §1.1461-1(c).

Example 9. (i) *Facts.* The facts are the same as in *Example 8*, except that the interest is paid by F, a non-U.S. payor, as defined in paragraph (c)(5) of this section.

(ii) *Analysis.* The analysis and results are the same as in *Example 8*.

Example 10. (i) *Facts.* USP, a U.S. payor as defined in paragraph (c)(5) of this section, makes a payment of foreign source interest (other than deposit interest) to NQI, a foreign corporation and a nonqualified intermediary as defined in §1.1441-1(c)(14). NQI has provided USP with a nonqualified intermediary withholding certificate, as described in §1.1441-1(e)(3)(iii), but has not attached any documentation from the persons on whose behalf it acts or a withholding statement as described in §1.1441-1(e)(3)(iv).

(ii) *Analysis.* Foreign source interest is not an amount subject to withholding under chapter 3 of the Code and is not a withholdable payment. See §§1.1441-2(a) and 1.1473-1(a). Under paragraph (d)(3)(ii) of this section, amounts that are not subject to withholding under chapter 3 of the Code and that are not withholdable payments described in paragraph (d)(2)(i) of this section that a payor may treat as paid to a foreign intermediary are treated as made to an exempt recipient described in §1.6049-4(c) absent actual knowledge that the payee is a U.S. person who is not an exempt recipient. Therefore, the foreign source interest is not subject to reporting on Form 1099.

Example 11. (i) *Facts.* USP is a U.S. payor as defined in paragraph (c)(5) of this section that is a bank. USP pays U.S. source original issue discount from the redemption of an obligation described in section 871(g)(1)(B) to NQI, a foreign corporation that is a nonqualified intermediary as defined in §1.1441-1(c)(14). The redemption proceeds are not paid outside of the United States as they are paid with respect to an account NQI has with a branch of a bank in the United States. See §1.6049-5(e)(2). NQI provides a nonqualified intermediary withholding certificate as described in §1.1441-1(e)(3)(iii) that includes a certification of its status as a registered deemed-compliant FFI but does not attach any payee documentation or a withholding statement described in §1.1441-1(e)(3)(iv).

(ii) *Analysis.* Under paragraph (d)(3)(ii)(A) of this section, USP must treat the payment as made to an undocumented U.S. payee that is not an exempt recipient and report the payment on Form 1099. Further, because the payment is made inside the United States, the exception to backup withholding with respect to offshore obligations contained in §31.3406(g)-1(e) of this chapter does not apply, and the payment is subject to backup withholding.

Example 12. (i) *Facts.* P, a payor, makes a payment to NQI of U.S. source interest on debt obligations issued prior to July 18, 1984, that mature 30 years from their issuance dates. Therefore, the interest does not qualify as portfolio interest under section 871(h) or 881(d). Additionally, the interest is not a withholdable payment under §1.1471-2(b) as the interest is a payment with respect to a grandfathered obligation for purposes of chapter 4 of the Code. NQI, a U.S. payor, is a nonqualified foreign intermediary, as defined in §1.1441-1(c)(14), and has furnished P a valid nonqualified intermediary withholding certificate described in §1.1441-1(e)(3)(iii) to which it has attached a valid Form W-9 for A, and two valid beneficial owner Forms W-8, one for B and one for C. A is not an exempt recipient under §1.6049-4(c). NQI furnishes a withholding statement, described in §1.1441-1(e)(3)(iv), in which it allocates 20% of the U.S. source interest to A, but does not allocate the remaining 80% of the interest between B and C. B's withholding certificate indicates that B is a foreign pension fund, exempt from U.S. tax under the U.S. income tax treaty with Country T. C's withholding certificate indicates that C is a foreign corporation not entitled to a reduced rate of withholding.

(ii) *Analysis.* As the interest is not a withholdable payment under paragraph (d)(3)(i) of this section, P applies the rules of §1.1441-1(b)(2)(v) to determine the payees of the interest even though NQI has not certified its status for purposes of chapter 4 of the Code. Under that section, the payees are the persons on whose behalf NQI acts—A, B and C. Because P can reliably associate 20% of the payment with valid documentation provided by A, P must treat 20% of the interest as paid to A, a U.S. person not exempt from reporting, and report the payment on Form 1099. P cannot reliably associate the remaining 80% of the payment with valid documentation under §1.1441-1(b)(2)(vii) and, therefore, under paragraph (d)(3)(i) of this section must apply the presumption rules of §1.1441-1(b)(3)(v). Under that section, the interest is presumed paid to an unknown foreign payee. Under paragraph (b)(12) of this section, P is not required to report the interest presumed paid to a foreign person on Form 1099. Under §1.1441-1(b), 80% of the interest is subject to 30% withholding, however, and the interest is reportable on Form 1042-S under §1.1461-1(c).

Example 13. (i) *Facts.* The facts are the same as in *Example 12*, except that P can reliably associate 30% of the payment of interest to B, but cannot reliably associate the remaining 70 percent with A or C.

(ii) *Analysis.* Under paragraph (d)(3)(i) of this section, P applies the rules of §1.1441-1(b)(2)(v) to determine the payees of the interest. Under that section, the payees are the persons on whose behalf NQI acts—A, B and C. Because P can reliably associate 30% of the payment with B, a foreign pensions fund exempt from withholding under an income tax treaty, P may treat that payment as paid to B and not subject to reporting on Form 1099 under paragraph (b)(12) of this section. P cannot reliably associate the remaining 70% of the payment with valid documentation under §1.1441-1(b)(2)(vii) and, therefore, under paragraph (d)(3)(i) of this section must apply the presumption rules of §1.1441-1(b)(3)(v). Under that section, the interest is presumed paid to an unknown foreign payee. Under paragraph (b)(12) of this section, P is not required to report the interest presumed paid to a foreign person on Form 1099. Under §1.1441-1(b), 80% of the interest is subject to 30% withholding, however, and the interest is reportable on Form 1042-S under §1.1461-1(c).

Example 14. (i) *Facts.* The facts are the same as in *Example 12*, except that P also makes a payment of foreign source interest to NQI.

(ii) *Analysis.* Under paragraph (d)(3)(ii), P may treat the foreign source interest as paid to an exempt recipient as defined in §1.6049-4(c) and not subject to reporting on Form 1099 even though some or all of the foreign source interest may in fact be owned by A, the U.S. person that is not exempt from reporting.

Example 15. (i) *Facts.* The facts are the same as in *Example 12*, except that NQI is a non-U.S. payor.

(ii) *Analysis.* The analysis is the same as under *Example 12* with respect to B and C. However, because NQI is a non-U.S. payor, it may under §1.6049-4(c)(4)(iii) allocate the portion of the payment to A to a chapter 4 withholding rate pool of U.S. payees on a withholding statement provided to P in lieu of furnishing the Form W-9 to P when NQI reports the payments in accordance with §1.6049-4(c)(4)(i). In such a case, provided that P obtains a certification form confirming NQI's status as a participating FFI, P is excepted from reporting the payment under paragraph (b)(14) of this section because P can reliably associate the payment with the documentation provided by NQI.

(e) *Determination of whether amounts are considered paid outside the United States.*—(1) *In general.*—For purposes of section 6049 and this section, an amount is considered to be paid by a payor or middleman outside the United States if the payor or middleman completes the acts necessary to effect payment outside the United States. See paragraphs (e)(2) through (5) of this section for further clarification of where amounts are considered paid. A payment shall not be considered to be made within the United States for purposes of section 6049 merely by reason of the fact that it is made on a draft drawn on a United States bank account or by a wire or other electronic transfer from a United States account.

(2) *Amounts paid with respect to deposits or accounts with banks and other financial institutions.*—Notwithstanding paragraph (e)(1) of this section, an amount paid by a bank or other financial institution with respect to a deposit or with respect to an account with the institution is considered paid at the branch or office at which the amount is credited unless the amount is collected by the financial institution as the agent of the payee. However, an amount will not be considered to be paid at the branch or office where the amount is considered to be credited unless the branch or office is a permanent place of business that is regularly maintained, occupied, and used to carry on a banking or similar financial business; the business is conducted by at least one employee of the branch or office who is regularly in attendance at such place of business during normal business hours; and the branch or office receives deposits and engages in one or more of the other activities described in §1.864-4(c)(5)(i).

(3) *Coupon bonds and discount obligations in bearer form.*—Notwithstanding paragraph (e)(1) of this section, an amount paid with respect to a bond with coupons attached (including a certificate of deposit with detachable interest coupons) or a discount obligation that is not in registered form (within the meaning of section 163(f) and the regulations thereunder) is considered to be paid where the coupon or the discount obligation is presented to the payor or its paying agent for payment.

(4) *Foreign-targeted registered obligations.*—Notwithstanding paragraph (e)(1) of this section, where the payor is the issuer or the issuer's agent, an amount is considered paid outside the United States with respect to a foreign-targeted registered obligation issued before January 1, 2016, as described in §1.871-14(e)(2), if either the amount is paid by transfer to an account maintained by the registered owner outside the United States, or by mail to an address of the registered owner outside the United States, or by credit to an international account. For purposes of this paragraph (e)(4), the term *international account* means the book-entry account of a financial institution (within the meaning of section 871(h)(4)(B)) or of an international financial organization with the Federal Reserve Bank of New York for which the Federal Reserve Bank of New York maintains records that specifically identify an international financial organization or a financial institution (within the meaning of section 871(h)(4)(B)) as either a non-United States person or a foreign branch of a United States person as registered owner. An international financial organization is a central bank or monetary authority of a foreign government or a public international organization of which the United States is a member to the extent that such central bank, authority, or organiza-

tion holds obligations solely for its own account and is exempt from tax under section 892 or 895.

(5) *Examples.*—The application of the provisions of this paragraph (e) is illustrated by the following examples:

Example 1. FC is a foreign corporation that is not a U.S. payor or U.S. middleman, as defined in paragraph (c)(5) of this section. A holds FC coupon bonds that are not in registered form under section 163(f) and the regulations thereunder. FB, a foreign branch of DC, is the designated paying agent with respect to the bonds issued by FC. A does not have an account with FB. A presents a coupon from a FC bond for payment to FB at its office outside the United States. FB pays A with a check drawn against a bank account maintained in the United States. For purposes of section 6049, the place of payment of interest on the FC bond by FB to A is considered to be outside the United States under paragraph (e)(3) of this section.

Example 2. Individual C deposits funds in an account with FB, a foreign country X branch of DB, a U.S. corporation engaged in the commercial banking business. FB maintains an office and employees in foreign country X, accepts deposits, and conducts one or more of the other activities listed in § 1.864-4(c)(5)(i). The terms of C's deposit provide that it will be payable with accrued interest. Under paragraph (e)(2) of this section, FB is considered to pay the interest on C's deposit outside the United States.

Example 3. DC, a U.S. corporation engaged in the commercial banking business, maintains FB, a branch in foreign country X. FB has an office and employees in foreign country X, accepts deposits, and engages in one or more of the other activities listed in § 1.864-4(c)(5)(i). D, a United States citizen, purchases a certificate of deposit issued in 1980 by FB. The certificate of deposit has a maturity of 20 years and has detachable interest coupons payable at six-month intervals. D presents some of the coupons at the U.S. office of DC and receives payment in cash. Because the coupon is presented to DC for payment within the United States, DC is considered to have made the payment within the United States under paragraph (e)(3) of this section.

Example 4. FB is recognized by both foreign country X and by the Federal Reserve Bank as a foreign country X branch of DC, a U.S. corporation engaged in the commercial banking business. A local foreign country X bank serves as FB's resident agent in Country X. FB maintains no physical office or employees in foreign country X. All the records, accounts, and transactions of FB are handled at the United States office of DC. E deposits funds in an amount maintained with FB. Interest earned on the deposit is periodically credited to E's account with FB by employees of DC. For purposes of section 6049, the place of payment of the interest on E's deposit with FB is considered to be within the United States by reason of paragraphs (e)(1) and (e)(2) of this section.

Example 5. DC is a U.S. corporation. A holds bonds that were issued by DC in registered form under section 163(f), as in effect prior to the amendment by section 502 of the HIRE Act of 2010, and the regulations thereunder and that are foreign-targeted registered obligations as defined in § 1.871-14(e)(2). DB, a commercial banking business, is the registrar of bonds issued by DC. Interest on the DC bonds is paid to A and other bondholders by check prepared by DB at its principal office inside the United States and mailed from there to A's address outside the United States. The check is drawn on a United States account maintained by DC with DB within the United States. The place of payment to A by DB of the interest on the DC bonds is considered to be outside the United States under paragraph (e)(4) of this section.

(f) *Original issue discount treated as payment of interest.*—In determining whether an obligation is one which was issued at a discount and the amount of discount which is includible in income of the holder, a payor (other than the issuer of the obligation) may rely on the Internal Revenue Service's publication of publicly traded original issue discount obligations. In the case of an obligation as to which there is during any calendar year an amount of original issue discount includible in the gross income of any holder (as determined under sections 1232 and 1232A and the regulations thereunder), the issuer of the obligation or a middleman (as defined in § 1.6049-4(f)(4)) shall be treated as having paid to such holder during such calendar year an amount of interest equal to the amount of original issue discount so includible without regard to any reduction by reason of a purchase allowance under section 1232(a)(2)(C)(ii), 1232A(a)(6) or (b)(4) or a purchase at a premium under 1232A(c)(4)(A) or paragraph (d)(2) of § 1.1232-3. Thus, the determination of the amount of original issue discount includible in the gross income of any holder with respect to any obligation shall be determined as if any holder of the obligation were the original holder. However, see § 1.6049-9 for the reporting of premium for a debt instrument acquired on or after January 1, 2014. In the case of (1) an obligation to which section 1232A does not apply (for example, a short-term government obligation as defined in section 1232(a)(3)) and (2) and obligation issued on or before December 31, 1982, in bearer form, the amount of original issue discount includible in gross income shall be treated as if paid in the calendar year in which the date of maturity occurs or in which the date of redemption occurs if redemption occurs before maturity. The amount subject to reporting on an obligation issued in bearer form with a maturity at the date of issue of more than 1 year (a long term obligation) is the amount of original issue discount includible in the gross income of the holder during the calendar year of maturity or redemption if redemption occurs before maturity. The amount of original issue discount subject to reporting on a long term obligation shall not be reduced to reflect any purchase allowance. Discount on short term government obligations as defined in section 1232(a)(3), such as Treasury bills, and discount on other obligations with a maturity at the date of issue of not more than 1 year (a short term obligation), including commercial paper, when paid at maturity or redemption if redemption occurs before maturity, shall constitute a payment of interest for purposes of section 6049. In general, the amount subject to reporting on short term obligations is the difference between the stated redemption price at maturity and the original issue price. The procedure set forth in section 3455(b)(2)(B) and § 31.3455(b)-1(b)(3) for establishing the price at which a holder purchased an obligation subsequent to the date of original issue shall apply for purposes of section 6049. Original issue discount on an obligation (including an obligation with a maturity of not more than six months from the date of original issue) held by a nonresident alien individual or foreign corporation is interest described in paragraph (b)(1)(vi)(A) or (B) of this section and, therefore is not interest subject to reporting under section 6049 unless it is described in § 1.6049-8(a) (relating to deposit interest paid on or after January 1, 2013, to certain nonresident alien individuals).

(g) *Applicability dates.*—Except as otherwise provided in this paragraph (g), this section applies to payments made on or after January 6, 2017. For payments made after June 30, 2014, and before January 6, 2017, see this section as in effect and contained in 26 CFR part 1, as revised April 1, 2016. For payments made after December 31, 2000, and before July 1, 2014, see this section as in effect and contained in 26 CFR part 1, as revised April 1, 2013. Paragraph (c)(5)(i)(C) of this section applies to payments made on or after October 1, 2019. For payments made before October 1, 2019, a taxpayer may apply paragraph (c)(5)(i)(C) of this section for payments during the last taxable year of a foreign corporation beginning before January 1, 2018, and each subsequent taxable year of the foreign corporation, provided that the taxpayer and United States persons that are related (within the meaning of section 267 or 707) to the taxpayer consistently apply such paragraph with respect to all foreign corporations. For payments made before October 1, 2019, where the taxpayer does not apply the provisions of paragraph (c)(5)(i)(C) of this section, see paragraph (c)(5)(i)(C) of this section as in effect and contained in 26 CFR part 1, as revised April 1, 2020. [Reg. § 1.6049-5.]

☐ [*T.D.* 7881, 3-22-83. *Amended by T.D.* 7987, 10-23-84; *T.D.* 8029, 6-4-85; *T.D.* 8664, 4-15-96; *T.D.* 8734, 10-6-97; *T.D.* 8804, 12-30-98; *T.D.* 8856, 12-29-99; *T.D.* 8881, 5-15-2000 (*corrected* 4-5-2001); *T.D.* 9241, 1-23-2006 *T.D.* 9253, 3-13-2006; *T.D.* 9584, 4-17-2012, *T.D.* 9658, 2-28-2014, *T.D.* 9713, 3-12-2015, *T.D.* 9808, 12-30-2016 (*corrected* 6-29-2017) *and T.D.* 9908, 9-21-2020.]

§ 1.6049-6. Statements to recipients of interest payments and holders of obligations for attributed original issue discount.—(a) *Requirement of furnishing statement to recipient.*—Every person filing a Form 1099 under section 6049(a) and § 1.6049-4(e) shall furnish to the person whose identifying number is required to be shown on the form a written statement showing the information required by paragraph (b) of this section. With respect to interest other than interest reported on a transactional basis under § 1.6049-4(e), no statement is required to be furnished under section 6049(c) and this section if the aggregate of the payments for the calendar year is less than $10, unless such payment is subject to the tax imposed under section 3406. In the case of any payment that is subject to withholding under section 3406, a statement shall be furnished irrespective of the amount of the payment. With respect to payments which are reported on a transactional basis, no statement is required to be furnished under section 6049(c) and this section to a person if the payment of interest to (or received on behalf of) such person for the transaction is less than $10 unless the payment is subject to withholding under section 3406. Again, in the case of any payment that is subject to withholding under section 3406, a statement shall be furnished irrespective of the amount of the payment.

(b) *Form of statement.*—The written statement required to be furnished to a person under paragraph (a) of this section shall show the following information:

(1) With respect to payments of interest (other than original issue discount) to any person during a calendar year, the statement shall show—

(i) The aggregate amount of payments shown on Form 1099 as having been made to (or received on behalf of) such person;

(ii) The amount of tax withheld under section 3406, if any;

(iii) The name and address of the person filing the form; and

(iv) A legend stating that such amount is being reported to the Internal Revenue Service.

(2) With respect to original issue discount includible in the gross income of a holder of an obligation during a calendar year, the statement shall show—

(i) The aggregate amount of original issue discount includible in the gross income by (or on behalf of) such person for the calendar year with respect to the obligation (determined by applying the rules of paragraph (b)(2) of § 1.6049-4);

(ii) The amount of tax withheld under section 3406, if any;

(iii) The account, serial, or other identifying number of each obligation with respect to which a return is being made;

(iv) All other items shown on Form 1099 for such calendar year, and

(v) A legend stating that such amount and such items are being reported to the Internal Revenue Service.

(3) With respect to both statements to persons receiving payments of interest and persons holding obligations, the statement shall include the name, address, and taxpayer identifying number of such person. An IRS truncated taxpayer identifying number (TTIN) may be used as the identifying number for the person. For provisions relating to the use of TTINs, see § 301.6109-4 of this chapter (Procedure and Administration Regulations).

(c) *Time for furnishing statements.*—Each statement required by this section to be furnished to any person for a calendar year with respect to a payment of interest (other than interest where a middleman or a Federal agency makes a return on a transactional basis (as described in paragraph (e) of § 1.6049-4)) shall be furnished to such person after April 30 of the year of payment and on or before January 31 of the following year, but no statement may be furnished before the final interest payment for the calendar year. If a middleman or a Federal agency makes a return on a transactional basis, the statement shall be furnished at, or any time subsequent to, the time of payment, but in no event later than January 31 of the year following the calendar year of payment. However, for a statement required to be furnished after December 31, 2008, the February 15 due date under section 6045 applies to the statement if the statement is furnished in a consolidated reporting statement under section 6045. *See* § § 1.6045-1(k)(3), 1.6045-2(d)(2), 1.6045-3(e)(2), 1.6045-4(m)(3), and 1.6045-5(a)(3)(ii).

(d) *Special rule.*—The requirements of this section for the furnishing of a statement to any person, including the legend requirement of paragraph (b)(1)(iv) and (2)(v) of this section, may be met by the furnishing to such person a copy of the Form 1099 filed pursuant to § 1.6049-4, or an acceptable substitute, in respect of such person. However, in the case of Form 1099 with respect to original issue discount on obligations subject to section 1232A, a copy of the instructions must also be sent to such person. A statement shall be considered to be furnished to a person within the meaning of this section if it is mailed to such person at his last known address.

(e) *Statements to recipients.*—(1) *Requirement.*—A person required to make an information return under section 6049(a) and § 1.6049-4 must furnish a statement to each recipient whose identifying number is required to be shown on the related information return for interest or original issue discount paid or accrued.

(2) *Form, manner, and time for providing statements to recipients.*—The statement required by paragraph (e)(1) of this section must be either the official Form 1099 prescribed by the Internal Revenue Service for the respective calendar year or an acceptable substitute statement. The rules under § 1.6042-4 (relating to statements with respect to dividends) apply comparably in determining the form of an acceptable substitute statement permitted by this paragraph (e). Those rules also apply for purposes of determining the manner of and time for providing the Form 1099 or its acceptable substitute to a recipient under paragraph (e)(1) of this section. However, with respect to original issue discount, the Form 1099 or acceptable substitute statement required by paragraph (e)(1) of this section must show the aggregate amount of original issue discount includible in the gross income by the recipient for the calendar year with respect to the obligation (determined by applying the rules of § 1.6049-4(b)(2)), and the amount, serial number, or other identifying number of each obligation with respect to which a return is being made. With respect to interest or original issue discount, the Form 1099 or acceptable substitute statement required by paragraph (e)(1) of this section must be furnished to the recipient on or before January 31 of the year following the calendar year for which the return under section 6049(a)(1) was required to be made. However, for a statement required to be furnished after December 31, 2008, the February 15 due date under section 6045 applies to the statement if the statement is furnished in a consolidated reporting statement under section 6045. *See* § § 1.6045-1(k)(3), 1.6045-2(d)(2), 1.6045-3(e)(2), 1.6045-4(m)(3), and 1.6045-5(a)(3)(ii).

(3) *Cross-reference to penalty.*—For provisions relating to the penalty provided for failure to furnish timely a correct payee statement required under section 6049(c) and § 1.6049-6(a), see § 301.6722-1 of this chapter (Procedure and Administration Regulations). See § 301.6724-1 of this chapter for the waiver of a penalty if the failure is due to reasonable cause and is not due to willful neglect.

(4) *Special rule for amounts described in § 1.6049-8(a).*—In the case of amounts described in § 1.6049-8(a) (relating to payments of deposit interest to certain nonresident alien individuals) paid on or after January 1, 2013, any person who makes a Form 1042-S, "Foreign Person's U.S. Source Income Subject to Withholding," under section 6049(a) and § 1.6049-4(b)(5) shall furnish a statement to the recipient either in person or by first class mail to the recipient's last known address. The statement shall include a copy of the Form 1042-S required to be prepared pursuant to § 1.6049-4(b)(5) and a statement to the effect that the information on the form is being furnished to the United States Internal Revenue Service. A person required by this paragraph (e)(4) to furnish a recipient copy of Form 1042-S may furnish such copy electronically by complying with the requirements provided in § 1.6050W-2(a)(2) through (5) applicable to statements required under section 6050W (substituting the phrase "Form 1042-S" for the phrases "statement required under section 6050W" or "statements required by section 6050W(f)" each place they appear).

(5) *Effective/applicability date.*—Paragraph (b)(3) applies to payee statements due after December 31, 2014. Paragraph (e)(4) of this section applies to payee statements reporting payments of deposit interest to nonresident alien individuals paid on or after January 2, 2020, but it may be applied to payments made on or after January 1, 2016. For payee statements reporting payments of deposit interest to nonresident alien individuals paid on or after January 1, 2013 and before January 2, 2020, see paragraph (e)(4) of this section as in effect and contained in 26 CFR part 1 revised April 1, 2019. For the substantially similar statement mailing requirements that apply with respect to forms required to be filed after October 22, 1986, and before January 1, 1996, see Rev. Proc. 84-70 (1984-2 C.B. 716)(or successor revenue procedures). See § 601.601(d)(2) of this chapter. (For interest paid to a Canadian nonresident alien individual on or before December 31, 2012, see paragraph (e)(4) of this section as in effect and contained in 26 CFR part 1 revised April 1, 2000.) [Reg. § 1.6049-6.]

☐ [*T.D.* 7881, 3-22-83. *Amended by T.D.* 8637, 12-20-95; *T.D.* 8664, 4-15-96; *T.D.* 8734, 10-6-97 (T.D. 8804 delayed the effective date of T.D. 8734 from January 1, 1999, to January 1, 2000; T.D. 8856 further delayed the effective date of T.D. 8734 until January 1, 2001) *T.D.* 9504, 10-12-2010; *T.D.* 9584, 4-17-2012, *T.D.* 9675, 7-14-2014 *and T.D.* 9890, 12-27-2019.]

§ 1.6049-8. Interest and original issue discount paid to certain nonresident aliens.—(a) *Interest subject to reporting requirement.*—For purposes of § § 1.6049-4, 1.6049-6, and this section, and except as provided in paragraph (b) of this section, the term *interest* means interest described in section 871(i)(2)(A) that relates to a deposit maintained at an office within the United States, and that is paid to a nonresident alien individual who is a resident of a country that is identified, in an applicable revenue procedure (see § 601.601(d)(2) of this chapter) as of December 31 prior to the calendar year in which the interest is paid, as a country with which the United States has in effect an income tax or other convention or bilateral agreement relating to the exchange of tax information within the meaning of section 6103(k)(4), under which the competent authority is the Secretary of the Treasury or his delegate and the United States agrees to provide, as well as receive, information. Notwithstanding the foregoing, for purposes of § § 1.6049-4, 1.6049-6, and this section, for any year for which the information return under § 1.6049-4(b)(5) is required, a payor may elect to treat interest as including all interest described in section 871(i)(2)(A) that relates to a deposit maintained at an office within the United States and that is paid to any nonresident alien individual. A payor shall make this election by reporting all such interest. For purposes of the regulations under section 6049 (§§1.6049-1 through 1.6049-8), a nonresident alien individual is a person described in section 7701(b)(1)(B). A payor or middleman may rely upon the permanent residence address provided on a valid Form W-8BEN, "Beneficial Owners Certificate of Foreign Status for U.S. Tax Withholding", to determine the country in which a nonresident alien individual is resident unless such payor or middleman knows or has reason to know that such documentation of the country of residence is unreliable or incorrect. Amounts described in this paragraph (a) are not subject to backup withholding under section 3406 if the payor may treat the payee as a foreign beneficial owner or foreign payee under the rules of §1.6049-5(b)(12). See §31.3406(g)-1(d) of this chapter. However, if the payor or middleman does not have either a valid Form W-8BEN or valid Form W-9, "Request for Taxpayer Identification Number and Certification", the payor or middleman must report the payment as made to a U.S. non-exempt recipient if it must so treat the payee under the presumption rules of §1.6049-5(d)(2) and §1.1441-1(b)(3)(iii), and the payor must also backup withhold under section 3406. (For interest paid to a Canadian nonresident alien individual on or before December 31, 2012, see paragraph (a) of this section as in effect and contained in 26 CFR part 1 revised April 1, 2000).

(b) *Interest excluded from reporting requirement.*—The term *interest* does not include an amount that is paid by the issuer or its agent outside the United States with respect to an obligation that is described in paragraph (b)(1) or (2) of this section.

(1)(i) The obligation is not in registered form (within the meaning of section 163(f) and the regulations thereunder); is part of a larger single public offering of securities; and is described in section 163(f)(2)(B).

(ii) Unless it has actual knowledge to the contrary, a middleman may treat an obligation as if it is described in section 163(f)(2)(B) if the obligation or coupon therefrom, whichever is presented for payment, contains the statement described in section 163(f)(2)(B)(ii)(II) and the regulations thereunder.

(2)(i) The obligation has a face or principal amount of not less than $500,000, and satisfies the requirements described in paragraphs (b)(2)(i)(A), (B), and (C) of this section.

(A) The obligation satisfies the requirements of sections 163(f)(2)(B)(i) and (ii)(I) and the regulations thereunder (as if it were a registration-required obligation within the meaning of section 163(f)(2)(A)) and is issued in accordance with the procedures of §1.163-5(c)(2)(i)(D)).

(B) If the obligation is in registered form, it is registered in the name of an exempt recipient described in §1.6049-4(c)(1)(ii).

(C) The obligation has on its face and on any detachable coupons the following statement (or a similar statement having the same effect):"By accepting this obligation or coupon, the holder represents and warrants that it is not a United States person (other than an exempt recipient described in the regulations under section 6049(b)(4) of the Internal Revenue Code and the regulations thereunder) and that it is not acting for or on behalf of a United States person (other than an exempt recipient described in the regulations under section 6049(b)(4) of the Internal Revenue Code and the regulations thereunder)."

(ii) Unless the middleman has actual knowledge to the contrary, it may treat an obligation as satisfying the requirements of sections 163(f)(2)(B)(i) and (ii)(I) and the regulations thereunder if the obligation or a coupon therefrom, whichever is presented for payment, contains the statement in paragraph (b)(2)(i)(C) of this section. [Reg. §1.6049-8.]

☐ [*T.D. 8664, 4-15-96. Amended by T.D. 8734, 10-6-97* (T.D. 8804 delayed the effective date of T.D. 8734 from January 1, 1999, to January 1, 2000; T.D. 8856 further delayed the effective date of T.D. 8734 until January 1, 2001) *and T.D. 9584, 4-17-2012.*]

§301.6114-1. Treaty-based return positions.—(a) *Reporting requirement.*—(1) *General rule.*—(i) Except as provided in paragraph (c) of this section, if a taxpayer takes a return position that any treaty of the United States (including, but not limited to, an income tax treaty, estate and gift tax treaty, or friendship, commerce and navigation treaty) overrules or modifies any provision of the Internal Revenue Code and thereby effects (or potentially effects) a reduction of any tax incurred at any time, the taxpayer shall disclose such return position on a statement (in the form required in paragraph (d) of this section) attached to such return.

(ii) If a return of tax would not otherwise be required to be filed, a return must nevertheless be filed for purposes of making the disclosure required by this section. For this purpose, such return need include only the taxpayer's name, address, taxpayer identifying number, and be signed under penalties of perjury (as well as the subject disclosure). Also, the taxpayer's taxable year shall be deemed to be the calendar year (unless the taxpayer has previously established, or timely chooses for this purpose to establish, a different taxable year). In the case of a disclosable return position relating solely to income subject to withholding (as defined in §1.1441-2(a) of this chapter), however, the statement required to be filed in paragraph (d) of this section must instead be filed at times and in accordance with procedures published by the Internal Revenue Service.

(2) *Application.*—(i) A taxpayer is considered to adopt a return position when the taxpayer determines its tax liability with respect to a particular item of income, deduction or credit. A taxpayer may be considered to adopt a return position whether or not a return is actually filed. To determine whether a return position is a "treaty-based return position" so that reporting is required under this paragraph (a), the taxpayer must compare:

(A) The tax liability (including credits, carrybacks, carryovers, and other tax consequences or attributes for the current year as well as for any other affected tax years) to be reported on a return of the taxpayer, and

(B) The tax liability (including such credits, carrybacks, carryovers, and other tax consequences or attributes) that would be reported if the relevant treaty provision did not exist.

If there is a difference (or potential difference) in these two amounts, the position taken on a return is a treaty-based return position that must be reported.

(ii) In the event a taxpayer's return position is based on a conclusion that a treaty provision is consistent with a Code provision, but the effect of the treaty provision is to alter the scope of the Code provision from the scope that it would have in the absence of the treaty, then the return position is a treaty-based return position that must be reported.

(iii) A return position is a treaty-based return position unless the taxpayer's conclusion that no reporting is required under paragraphs (a)(2)(i) and (ii) of this section has a substantial probability of successful defense if challenged.

(3) *Examples.*—The application of section 6114 and paragraph (a)(2) of this section may be illustrated by the following examples:

Example (1). X, a Country A corporation, claims the benefit of a provision of the income tax treaty between the United States and Country A that modifies a provision of the Code. This position does not result in a change of X's U.S. tax liability for the current tax year but does give rise to, or increases, a net operating loss which may be carried back (or forward) such that X's tax liability in the carryback (or forward) year may be affected by the position taken by X in the current year. X must disclose this treaty-based return position with its tax return for the current tax year.

Example (2). Z, a domestic corporation, is engaged in a trade or business in Country B. Country B imposes a tax on the income from certain of Z's petroleum activities at a rate significantly greater than the rate applicable to income from other activities. Z claims a foreign tax credit for this tax on its tax return. The tax imposed on Z is specifically listed as a creditable tax in the income tax treaty between the United States and Country B; however, there is no specific authority that such tax would otherwise be a creditable tax for U.S. purposes under sections 901 or 903 of the Code. Therefore, in the absence of the treaty, the creditability of this petroleum tax would lack a substantial probability of successful defense if challenged, and Z must disclose this treaty-based return position (see also paragraph (b)(7) of this section).

(b) *Reporting specifically required.*—Reporting is required under this section except as expressly waived under paragraph (c) of this section. The following list is not a list of all positions for which reporting is required under this section but is a list of particular positions for which reporting is specifically required. These positions are as follows:

(1) That a nondiscrimination provision of a treaty precludes the application of any otherwise applicable Code provision, other than with respect to the making of or the effect of an election under section 897(i);

(2) That a treaty reduces or modifies the taxation of gain or loss from the disposition of a United States real property interest;

(3) That a treaty exempts a foreign corporation from (or reduces the amount of tax with respect to) the branch profits tax (section 884(a)) or the tax on excess interest (section 884(f)(1)(B));

(4) That, notwithstanding paragraph (c)(1)(i) of this section,

(i) A treaty exempts from tax, or reduces the rate of tax on, interest or dividends paid by a foreign corporation that are from sources within the United States by reason of section 861(a)(2)(B) or section 884(f)(1)(A); or

(ii) A treaty exempts from tax, or reduces the rate of tax on, fixed or determinable annual or periodical income subject to withholding under section 1441 or 1442 that a foreign person receives from a U.S. person, but only if described in paragraphs (b)(4)(ii)(A) and (B) of this section, or in paragraph (b)(4)(ii)(C) or (D) of this section as follows—

(A) The payment is not properly reported to the Service on a Form 1042S; and

(B) The foreign person is any of the following:

(1) A controlled foreign corporation (as defined in section 957) in which the U.S. person is a U.S. shareholder within the meaning of section 951(b);

(2) A foreign corporation that is controlled within the meaning of section 6038 by the U.S. person;

(3) A foreign shareholder of the U.S. person that, in the case of tax years beginning on or before July 10, 1989, is controlled within the meaning of section 6038A by the foreign shareholder, or, in the case of tax years beginning after July 10, 1989, is 25-percent owned within the meaning of section 6038A by the foreign shareholder; or

(4) With respect to payments made after October 10, 1990, a foreign related party, as defined in section 6038A(c)(2)(B), to the U.S. person; or

(C) For payments made after December 31, 2000, with respect to a treaty that contains a limitation on benefits article, that—

(1) The treaty exempts from tax, or reduces the rate of tax on income subject to withholding (as defined in § 1.1441-2(a) of this chapter) that is received by a foreign person (other than a State, including a political subdivision or local authority) that is the beneficial owner of the income and the beneficial owner is related to the person obligated to pay the income within the meaning of sections 267(b) and 707(b), and the income exceeds $500,000; and

(2) A foreign person (other than an individual or a State, including a political subdivision or local authority) meets the requirements of the limitation on benefits article of the treaty; or

(D) For payments made after December 31, 2000, with respect to a treaty that imposes any other conditions for the entitlement of treaty benefits, for example as a part of the interest, dividends, or royalty article, that such conditions are met;

(5) That, notwithstanding paragraph (c)(1)(i) of this section, under a treaty—

(i) Income that is effectively connected with a U.S. trade or business of a foreign corporation or a nonresident alien is not attributable to a permanent establishment or a fixed base of operations in the United States and, thus, is not subject to taxation on a net basis, or that

(ii) Expenses are allowable in determining net business income so attributable, notwithstanding an inconsistent provision of the Code;

(6) Except as provided in paragraph (c)(1)(iv) of this section, that a treaty alters the source of any item of income or deduction;

(7) That a treaty grants a credit for a specific foreign tax for which a foreign tax credit would not be allowed by the Code; or

(8) For returns relating to taxable years for which the due date for filing returns (without extensions) is after December 15, 1997, that residency of an individual is determined under a treaty and apart from the Internal Revenue Code.

(c) *Reporting requirement waived.*—(1) Pursuant to the authority contained in section 6114(b), reporting is waived under this section with respect to any of the following return positions taken by the taxpayer:

(i) For amounts received on or after January 1, 2001, reporting under paragraph (b)(4)(ii) is waived, unless reporting is specifically required under paragraphs (b)(4)(ii)(A) and (B) of this section, paragraph (b)(4)(ii)(C) of this section, or paragraph (b)(4)(ii)(D) of this section;

(ii) Notwithstanding paragraph (b)(4) or (5) of this section, that a treaty has reduced the rate of withholding tax otherwise applicable to a particular type of fixed or determinable annual or periodical income subject to withholding under section 1441 or 1442, such as dividends, interest, rents, or royalties to the extent such income is beneficially owned by an individual or a State (including a political subdivision or local authority);

(iii) For returns relating to taxable years for which the due date for filing returns (without extensions) is on or before December 15, 1997, that residency of an individual is determined under a treaty and apart from the Internal Revenue Code.

(iv) That a treaty reduces or modifies the taxation of income derived from dependent personal services, pensions, annuities, social security and other public pensions, or income derived by artistes, athletes, students, trainees or teachers;

(v) That income of an individual is resourced (for purposes of applying the foreign tax credit limitation) under a treaty provision relating to elimination of double taxation;

(vi) That a nondiscrimination provision of a treaty allows the making of an election under section 897(i);

(vii) That a Social Security Totalization Agreement or a Diplomatic or Consular Agreement reduces or modifies the taxation of income derived by the taxpayer; or

(viii) That a treaty exempts the taxpayer from the excise tax imposed by section 4371, but only if:

(A) The person claiming such treaty-based return position is an insured, as defined in section 4372(d) (without the limitation therein referring to section 4371(1)), or a U.S. or foreign broker of insurance risks,

(B) Reporting under this section that would otherwise be required to be made by foreign insurers or reinsurers on a Form 720 on a quarterly basis is made on an annual basis on a Form 720 by a date no later than the date on which the return is due for the first quarter after the end of the calendar year, or

(C) A closing agreement relating to entitlement to the exemption from the excise tax has been entered into with the Service by the foreign insurance company that is the beneficial recipient of the premium that is subject to the excise tax.

(ix) Notwithstanding paragraph (b)(1) of this section, that a nondiscrimination provision of a qualified income tax treaty, as defined in Treas. Reg. § 1.5000C-1(c)(13), exempts a payment from tax under section 5000C, but only if the foreign person claiming such relief has provided a Section 5000C Certificate (such as Form W-14, "Certificate of Foreign Contracting Party Receiving Federal Procurement Payments") to the acquiring agency in accordance with section 5000C and the regulations thereunder.

(2) Reporting is waived for an individual if payments or income items otherwise reportable under this section (other than by reason of paragraph (b)(8) of this section), received by the individual during the course of the taxable year do not exceed $10,000 in the aggregate or, in the case of payments or income items reportable only by reason of paragraph (b)(8) of this section, do not exceed $100,000 in the aggregate.

(3) Reporting with respect to payments or income items the treatment of which is mandated by the terms of a closing agreement with the Internal Revenue Service, and that would otherwise be subject to the reporting requirements of this section, is also waived.

(4) If a partnership, trust, or estate that has the taxpayer as a partner or beneficiary discloses on its information return a position for which reporting is otherwise required by the taxpayer, the taxpayer (partner or beneficiary) is then excused from disclosing that position on a return.

(5) This section does not apply to a withholding agent with respect to the performance of its withholding functions.

(6)(i) For taxable years ending after December 31, 2004, except as provided in paragraph (c)(6)(ii) of this section, reporting under paragraph (b)(4)(ii) of this section is waived for amounts received by a related party, within the meaning of section 6038A(c)(2), from a withholding agent that is a reporting corporation, within the meaning of section 6038A(a), and that are properly reported on Form 1042-S.

(ii) Paragraph (c)(6)(i) of this section does not apply to any amounts for which reporting is specifically required under the instructions to Form 8833.

(7)(i) For taxable years ending after December 31, 2004, except as provided in paragraph (c)(7)(iv) of this section, reporting under paragraph (b)(4)(ii) of this section is waived for amounts properly reported on Form 1042-S (on either a specific payee or pooled basis) by a withholding agent described in paragraph (c)(7)(ii) of this section if the beneficial owner is described in paragraph (c)(7)(iii) of this section.

(ii) A withholding agent described in this paragraph (c)(7)(ii) is a U.S. financial institution, as defined in § 1.1441-1(c)(5) of this chapter, a qualified intermediary, as defined in § 1.1441-1(e)(5)(ii) of this chapter, a withholding foreign partnership, as defined

§ 1.1441-5(c)(2)(i) of this chapter, or a withholding foreign trust, as defined in § 1.1441-5(e)(5)(v) of this chapter.

(iii) A beneficial owner described in this paragraph (c)(7)(iii) of this section is a direct account holder of a U.S. financial institution or qualified intermediary, a direct partner of a withholding foreign partnership, or a direct beneficiary or owner of a simple or grantor trust that is a withholding foreign trust. A beneficial owner described in this paragraph (c)(7)(iii) also includes an account holder to which a qualified intermediary has applied section 4A.01 or 4A.02 of the qualified intermediary agreement, contained in Revenue Procedure 2000-12 (2000-1 C.B. 387), (as amended by Revenue Procedure 2003-64, (2003-2 C.B. 306); Revenue Procedure 2004-21 (2004-1 C.B. 702); Revenue Procedure 2005-77 (2005-51 I.R.B. 1176) (see § 601.601(b)(2) of this chapter) a partner to which a withholding foreign partnership has applied section 10.01 or 10.02 of the withholding foreign partnership agreement, and a beneficiary or owner to which a withholding foreign trust has applied section 10.01 or 10.02 of the withholding foreign trust agreement, contained in Revenue Procedure 2003-64, (2003-2 C.B. 306), (as amended by Revenue Procedure 2004-21 (2004-1 C.B. 702); Revenue Procedure 2005-77 (2005-51 I.R.B. 1176); (see § 601.601(b)(2) of this chapter).

(iv) Paragraph (c)(7)(i) of this section does not apply to any amounts for which reporting is specifically required under the instructions to Form 8833.

(8)(i) For taxable years ending after December 31, 2004, except as provided in paragraph (c)(8)(ii) of this section, reporting under paragraph (b)(4)(ii) of this section is waived for taxpayers that are not individuals or States and that receive amounts of income that have been properly reported on Form 1042-S, that do not exceed $500,000 in the aggregate for the taxable year and that are not received through an account with an intermediary, as defined in § 1.1441-1(c)(13), or with respect to interest in a flow-through entity, as defined in § 1.1441-1(c)(23),

(ii) The exception contained in paragraph (c)(8)(i) of this section does not apply to any amounts for which reporting is specifically required under the instructions to Form 8833.

(d) *Information to be reported.*—(1) *Returns due after December 15, 1997.*—When reporting is required under this section for a return relating to a taxable year for which the due date (without extensions) is after December 15, 1997, the taxpayer must furnish, in accordance with paragraph (a) of this section, as an attachment to the return, a fully completed Form 8833 (Treaty-Based Return Position Disclosure Under Section 6114 or 7701(b)) or appropriate successor form.

(2) *Earlier returns.*—For returns relating to taxable years for which the due date for filing returns (without extensions) is on or before December 15, 1997, the taxpayer must furnish information in accordance with paragraph (d) of this section in effect prior to December 15, 1997 (see § 301.6114-1(d) as contained in 26 CFR part 301, revised April 1, 1997).

(3) *In general.*—(i) *Permanent establishment.*—For purposes of determining the nature and amount (or reasonable estimate thereof) of gross receipts, if a taxpayer takes a position that it does not have a permanent establishment or a fixed base in the United States and properly discloses that position, it need not separately report its payment of actual or deemed dividends or interest exempt from tax by reason of a treaty (or any liability for tax imposed by reason of section 884).

(ii) *Single income item.*—For purposes of the statement of facts relied upon to support each separate Treaty-Based Return Position taken, a taxpayer may treat payments or income items of the same type (e.g., interest items) received from the same ultimate payor (e.g., the obligor on a note) as a single separate payment or income item.

(iii) *Foreign source effectively connected income.*—If a taxpayer takes the return position that, under the treaty, income that would be income effectively connected with a U.S. trade or business is not subject to U.S. taxation because it is income treated as derived from sources outside the United States, the taxpayer may treat payments or income items of the same type (e.g., interest items) as a single separate payment or income item.

(iv) *Sales or services income.*—Income from separate sales or services, whether or not made or preformed by an agent (independent or dependent), to different U.S. customers on behalf of a foreign corporation not having a permanent establishment in the United States may be treated as a single payment or income item.

(v) *Foreign insurers or reinsurers.*—For purposes of reporting by foreign insurers or reinsurers, as described in paragraph (c)(1)(vii)(B) of this section, such reporting must separately set forth premiums paid with respect to casualty insurance and indemnity bonds (subject to section 4371(1)); life insurance, sickness and accident policies, and annuity contracts (subject to section 4371(2)); and reinsurance (subject to section 4371(3)). All premiums paid with respect to each of these three categories may be treated as a single payment or income item within that category. For reports first due before May 1, 1991, the report may disclose, for each of the three categories, the total amount of premiums derived by the foreign insurer or reinsurer in U.S. dollars (even if a portion of these premiums relate to risks that are not U.S. situs). Reasonable estimates of the amounts required to be disclosed will satisfy these reporting requirements.

(e) *Effective/applicability date.*—(1) *In general.*—This section is effective for taxable years of the taxpayer for which the due date for filing returns (without extensions) occurs after December 31, 1988. However, if—

(i) A taxpayer has filed a return for such a taxable year, without complying with the reporting requirement of this section, before November 13, 1989, or

(ii) A taxpayer is not otherwise than by paragraph (a) of this section required to file a return for a taxable year before November 13, 1989, such taxpayer must file (apart from any earlier filed return) the statement required by paragraph (d) of this section before June 12, 1990, by mailing the required statement to the Internal Revenue Service, P.O. Box 21086, Philadelphia, PA 19114. Any such statement filed apart from a return must be dated, signed and sworn to by the taxpayer under the penalties of perjury. In addition, with respect to any return due (without extensions) on or before March 10, 1990, the reporting required by paragraph (a) of this section must be made no later than June 12, 1990. If a taxpayer files or has filed a return on or before November 13, 1989, that provides substantially the same information required by paragraph (d) of this section, no additional submission will be required. Foreign insurers and reinsurers subject to reporting described in paragraph (c)(7)(ii) of this section must so report for calendar years 1988 and 1989 no later than August 15, 1990.

(2) *Section 5000C.*—Paragraph (c)(1)(ix) of this section applies to payments made on and after November 16, 2016 pursuant to contracts entered into on and after January 2, 2011. However, a taxpayer that receives payments exempt from tax under section 5000C by reason of a qualified income tax treaty before November 16, 2016 is not required to disclose this position on Form 8833, provided it has properly relied on Notice 2015-35, I.R.B. 2016-14, 533, in claiming the exemption.

(f) *Cross reference.*—For the provisions concerning penalties for failure to disclose a treaty-based return position, see section 6712 and § 301.6712-1. [Reg. § 301.6114-1.]

☐ [*T.D.* 8292, 3-13-90. *Amended by T.D.* 8305, 7-11-90; *T.D.* 8733, 10-6-97; *T.D.* 8734, 10-6-97; *T.D.* 8804, 12-30-98; *T.D.* 8856, 12-29-99, *T.D.* 9253, 3-13-2006 *and T.D.* 9782, 8-17-2016.]

Accuracy-Related and Fraud Penalties

§ 1.6662-1. Overview of the accuracy-related penalty.—Section 6662 imposes an accuracy-related penalty on any portion of an underpayment of tax required to be shown on a return that is attributable to one or more of the following:

(a) Negligence or disregard of rules or regulations;

(b) Any substantial understatement of income tax;

(c) Any substantial valuation misstatement under chapter 1;

(d) Any substantial overstatement of pension liabilities; or

(e) Any substantial estate or gift tax valuation understatement.

Sections 1.6662-1 through 1.6662-5 address only the first three components of the accuracy-related penalty, *i.e.*, the penalties for negligence or disregard of rules or regulations, substantial understatements of income tax, and substantial (or gross) valuation misstatements under chapter 1. The penalties for disregard of rules or regulations and for a substantial understatement of income tax may be avoided by adequately disclosing certain information as provided in § 1.6662-3(c) and §§1.6662-4(e) and (f), respectively. The penalties for negligence and for a substantial (or gross) valuation misstatement under chapter 1 may not be avoided by disclosure. No accuracy-related penalty may be imposed on any portion of an underpayment if there was reasonable cause for, and the taxpayer acted in good faith with respect to, such portion. The reasonable cause and good faith exception to the accuracy-related penalty is set forth in §1.6664-4. [Reg. §1.6662-1.]

☐ [*T.D.* 8381, 12-30-91. *Amended by T.D.* 8617, 8-31-95.]

§1.6662-2. Accuracy-related penalty.—(a) *In general.*—Section 6662(a) imposes an accuracy-related penalty on any portion of an underpayment of tax (as defined in section 6664(a) and §1.6664-2) required to be shown on a return if such portion is attributable to one or more of the following types of misconduct:

(1) Negligence or disregard of rules or regulations (see §1.6662-3);

(2) Any substantial understatement of income tax (see §1.6662-4); or

(3) Any substantial (or gross) valuation misstatement under chapter 1 ("substantial valuation misstatement" or "gross valuation misstatement"), provided the applicable dollar limitation set forth in section 6662(e)(2) is satisfied (see §1.6662-5).

The accuracy-related penalty applies only in cases in which a return of tax is filed, except that the penalty does not apply in the case of a return prepared by the Secretary under the authority of section 6020(b). The accuracy-related penalty under section 6662 and the penalty under section 6651 for failure to timely file a return of tax may both be imposed on the same portion of an underpayment if a return is filed, but is filed late. The fact that a return is filed late, however, is not taken into account in determining whether an accuracy-related penalty should be imposed. No accuracy-related penalty may be imposed on any portion of an underpayment of tax on which the fraud penalty set forth in section 6663 is imposed.

(b) *Amount of penalty.*—(1) *In general.*—The amount of the accuracy-related penalty is 20 percent of the portion of an underpayment of tax required to be shown on a return that is attributable to any of the types of misconduct listed in paragraphs (a)(1) through (a)(3) of this section, except as provided in paragraph (b)(2) of this section.

(2) *Increase in penalty for gross valuation misstatement.*—In the case of a gross valuation misstatement, as defined in section 6662(h)(2) and §1.6662-5(e)(2), the amount of the accuracy-related penalty is 40 percent of the portion of an underpayment of tax required to be shown on a return that is attributable to the gross valuation misstatement, provided the applicable dollar limitation set forth in section 6662(e)(2) is satisfied.

(c) *No stacking of accuracy-related penalty components.*—The maximum accuracy-related penalty imposed on a portion of an underpayment may not exceed 20 percent of such portion (40 percent of the portion attributable to a gross valuation misstatement), notwithstanding that such portion is attributable to more than one of the types of misconduct described in paragraph (a) of this section. For example, if a portion of an underpayment of tax required to be shown on a return is attributable both to negligence and a substantial understatement of income tax, the maximum accuracy-related penalty is 20 percent of such portion. Similarly, the maximum accuracy-related penalty imposed on any portion of an underpayment that is attributable both to negligence and a gross valuation misstatement is 40 percent of such portion.

(d) *Effective dates.*—(1) *Returns due before January 1, 1994.* Section 1.6662-3(c) and §§1.6662-4(e) and (f) (relating to methods of making adequate disclosure) (as contained in 26 CFR part 1 revised April 1, 1995) apply to returns the due date of which (determined without regard to extensions of time for filing) is after December 31, 1991, but before January 1, 1994. Except as provided in the preceding sentence and in paragraphs (d)(2), (3), and (4) of this section, §§1.6662-1 through 1.6662-5 apply to returns the due date of which (determined without regard to extensions of time for filing) is after December 31, 1989, but before January 1, 1994. To the extent the provisions of these regulations were not reflected in the statute as amended by the Omnibus Budget Reconciliation Act of 1989 (OBRA 1989), in Notice 90-20, 1990-1 C.B. 328, or in rules and regulations in effect prior to March 4, 1991 (to the extent not inconsistent with the statute as amended by OBRA 1989), these regulations will not be adversely applied to a taxpayer who took a position based upon such prior rules on a return filed before January 1, 1992.

(2) *Returns due after December 31, 1993.*—Except as provided in paragraphs (d)(3), (4) and (5) of this section and the last sentence of this paragraph (d)(2), the provisions of §§1.6662-1 through 1.6662-4 and §1.6662-7 (as revised to reflect the changes made to the accuracy-related penalty by the Omnibus Budget Reconciliation Act of 1993) and of §1.6662-5 apply to returns the due date of which (determined without regard to extensions of time for filing) is after December 31, 1993. These changes include raising the disclosure standard for the penalties for disregarding rules or regulations and for a substantial understatement of income tax from not frivolous to reasonable basis, eliminating the disclosure exception for the negligence penalty, and providing guidance on the meaning of reasonable basis. The Omnibus Budget Reconciliation Act of 1993 changes relating to the penalties for negligence or disregard of rules or regulations will not apply to returns (including qualified amended returns) that are filed on or before March 14, 1994, but the provisions of §§1.6662-1 through 1.6662-3 (as contained in 26 CFR part 1 revised April 1, 1995) relating to those penalties will apply to such returns.

(3) *Special rules for tax shelter items.*—Sections 1.6662-4(g)(1) and 1.6662-4(g)(4) apply to returns the due date of which (determined without regard to extensions of time for filing) is after September 1, 1995. Except as provided in the last sentence of this paragraph (d)(3), §§1.6662-4(g)(1) and 1.6662-4(g)(4) (as contained in 26 CFR part 1 revised April 1, 1995) apply to returns the due date of which (determined without regard to extensions of time for filing) is on or before September 1, 1995, and after December 31, 1989. For transactions occurring after December 8, 1994, §§1.6662-4(g)(1) and 1.6662-4(g)(2) (as contained in 26 CFR part 1 revised April 1, 1995) are applied taking into account the changes made to section 6662(d)(2)(C) (relating to the substantial understatement penalty for tax shelter items of corporations) by section 744 of Title VII of the Uruguay Round Agreements Act, Pub. L. 103-465 (108 Stat. 4809).

(4) *Special rules for reasonable basis.*—Section 1.6662-3(b)(3) applies to returns filed on or after December 2, 1998.

(5) *For returns filed after December 31, 2002.*—Sections 1.6662-3(a), 1.6662-3(b)(2) and 1.6662-3(c)(1) (relating to adequate disclosure) apply to returns filed after December 31, 2002, with respect to transactions entered into on or after January 1, 2003. Except as provided in paragraph (d)(1) of this section, §§1.6662-3(a), 1.6662-3(b)(2) and 1.6662-3(c)(1) (as contained in 26 CFR part 1 revised April 1, 2003) apply to returns filed with respect to transactions entered into prior to January 1, 2003. [Reg. §1.6662-2.]

☐ [*T.D.* 8381, 12-30-91. *Amended by T.D.* 8617, 8-31-95; *T.D.* 8790, 12-1-98 *and T.D.* 9109, 12-29-2003.]

§1.6662-3. Negligence or disregard of rules or regulations.—(a) *In general.*—If any portion of an underpayment, as defined in section 6664(a) and §1.6664-2, of any income tax imposed under subtitle A of the Internal Revenue Code that is required to be shown on a return is attributable to negligence or disregard of rules or regulations, there is added to the tax an amount equal to 20 percent of such portion. The penalty for disregarding rules or regulations does not apply, however, if the requirements of paragraph (c)(1) of this section are satisfied and the position in question is adequately disclosed as provided in paragraph (c)(2) of this section (and, if the position relates to a reportable transaction as defined in §1.6011-4(b) (or §1.6011-4T(b), as applicable), the transaction is disclosed in accordance with §1.6011-4 (or §1.6011-4T, as applicable)), or to the extent that the reasonable cause and good faith exception to this penalty set forth in §1.6664-4 applies. In addition, if a position with respect to an item (other than with respect to a reportable transaction, as defined in §1.6011-4(b) or §1.6011-4T(b), as applicable) is contrary to a revenue ruling or notice (other than a notice of proposed rulemaking) issued by the Internal Revenue Service and published in the Internal Revenue Bulletin (see §601.601(d)(2) of this chapter), this penalty does not apply if the position has a realistic possibility of being sustained on its merits. See §1.6694-2(b) of the income tax return preparer penalty regulations for a description of the realistic possibility standard.

(b) *Definitions and rules.*—(1) *Negligence.*—The term "negligence" includes any failure to make a reasonable attempt to comply with the provisions of the internal revenue laws or to exercise ordinary and reasonable care in the preparation of a tax return. "Negligence" also includes any failure by the taxpayer to keep adequate books and records or to substantiate items properly. A return position that has a reasonable basis as defined in paragraph (b)(3) of this section is not attributable to negligence. Negligence is strongly indicated where—

(i) A taxpayer fails to include on an income tax return an amount of income shown on an information return, as defined in section 6724(d)(1);

(ii) A taxpayer fails to make a reasonable attempt to ascertain the correctness of a deduction, credit or exclusion on a return which would seem to a reasonable and prudent person to be "too good to be true" under the circumstances;

(iii) A partner fails to comply with the requirements of section 6222, which requires that a partner treat partnership items on its return in a manner that is consistent with the treatment of such items on the partnership return (or notify the Secretary of the inconsistency); or

(iv) A shareholder fails to comply with the requirements of section 6242, which requires that an S corporation shareholder treat subchapter S items on its return in a manner that is consistent with the treatment of such items on the corporation's return (or notify the Secretary of the inconsistency).

(2) *Disregard of rules or regulations.*—The term "disregard" includes any careless, reckless or intentional disregard of rules or regulations. The term "rules or regulations" includes the provisions of the Internal Revenue Code, temporary or final Treasury regulations issued under the Code, and revenue rulings or notices (other than notices of proposed rulemaking) issued by the Internal Revenue Service and published in the Internal Revenue Bulletin. A disregard of rules or regulations is "careless" if the taxpayer does not exercise reasonable diligence to determine the correctness of a return position that is contrary to the rule or regulation. A disregard is "reckless" if the taxpayer makes little or no effort to determine whether a rule or regulation exists, under circumstances which demonstrate a substantial deviation from the standard of conduct that a reasonable person would observe. A disregard is "intentional" if the taxpayer knows of the rule or regulation that is disregarded. Nevertheless, a taxpayer who takes a position (other than with respect to a reportable transaction, as defined in § 1.6011-4(b) or § 1.6011-4T(b), as applicable) contrary to a revenue ruling or notice has not disregarded the ruling or notice if the contrary position has a realistic possibility of being sustained on its merits.

(3) *Reasonable basis.*—Reasonable basis is a relatively high standard of tax reporting, that is, significantly higher than not frivolous or not patently improper. The reasonable basis standard is not satisfied by a return position that is merely arguable or that is merely a colorable claim. If a return position is reasonably based on one or more of the authorities set forth in § 1.6662-4(d)(3)(iii) (taking into account the relevance and persuasiveness of the authorities, and subsequent developments), the return position will generally satisfy the reasonable basis standard even though it may not satisfy the substantial authority standard as defined in § 1.6662-4(d)(2). (See § 1.6662-4(d)(3)(ii) for rules with respect to relevance, persuasiveness, subsequent developments, and use of a well-reasoned construction of an applicable statutory provision for purposes of the substantial understatement penalty.) In addition, the reasonable cause and good faith exception in § 1.6664-4 may provide relief from the penalty for negligence or disregard of rules or regulations, even if a return position does not satisfy the reasonable basis standard.

(c) *Exception for adequate disclosure.*—(1) *In general.*—No penalty under section 6662(b)(1) may be imposed on any portion of an underpayment that is attributable to a position contrary to a rule or regulation if the position is disclosed in accordance with the rules of paragraph (c)(2) of this section (and, if the position relates to a reportable transaction as defined in § 1.6011-4(b) (or § 1.6011-4T(b), as applicable), the transaction is disclosed in accordance with § 1.6011-4 (or § 1.6011-4T, as applicable)) and, in case of a position contrary to a regulation, the position represents a good faith challenge to the validity of the regulation. This disclosure exception does not apply, however, in the case of a position that does not have a reasonable basis or where the taxpayer fails to keep adequate books and records or to substantiate items properly.

(2) *Method of disclosure.*—Disclosure is adequate for purposes of the penalty for disregarding rules or regulations if made in accordance with the provisions of §§ 1.6662-4(f)(1), (3), (4) and (5), which permit disclosure on a properly completed and filed Form 8275 or 8275-R, as appropriate. In addition, the statutory or regulatory provision or ruling in question must be adequately identified on the Form 8275 or 8275-R, as appropriate. The provisions of § 1.6662-4(f)(2), which permit disclosure in accordance with an annual revenue procedure for purposes of the substantial understatement penalty, do not apply for purposes of this section.

(d) *Special rules in the case of carrybacks and carryovers.*—(1) *In general.*—The penalty for negligence or disregard of rules or regulations applies to any portion of an underpayment for a year to which a loss, deduction or credit is carried, which portion is attributable to negligence or disregard of rules or regulations in the year in which the carryback or carryover of the loss, deduction or credit arises (the "loss or credit year").

(2) *Transition rule for carrybacks to pre-1990 years.*—A 20 percent penalty under section 6662(b)(1) is imposed on any portion of an underpayment for a carryback year, the return for which is due (without regard to extensions) before January 1, 1990, if—

(i) That portion is attributable to negligence or disregard of rules or regulations in a loss or credit year; and

(ii) The return for the loss or credit year is due (without regard to extensions) after December 31, 1989.

(3) *Example.*—The following example illustrates the provisions of paragraph (d) of this section. This example does not take into account the reasonable cause exception under § 1.6664-4.

Example. Corporation M is a C corporation. In 1990, M had a loss of $200,000 before taking into account a deduction of $350,000 that M claimed as an expense in careless disregard of the capitalization requirements of section 263 of the Code. M failed to make adequate disclosure of the item for 1990. M reported a $550,000 loss for 1990 and carried back the loss to 1987 and 1988. M had reported taxable income of $400,000 for 1987 and $200,000 for 1988, before application of the carryback. The carryback eliminated all of M's taxable income for 1987 and $150,000 of taxable income for 1988. After disallowance of the $350,000 expense deduction and allowance of a $35,000 depreciation deduction with respect to the capitalized amount, the correct loss for 1990 was determined to be $235,000. Because there is no underpayment for 1990, the penalty for negligence or disregard of rules or regulations does not apply for 1990. However, as a result of the 1990 adjustments, the loss carried back to 1987 is reduced from $550,000 to $235,000. After application of the $235,000 carryback, M has taxable income of $165,000 for 1987 and $200,000 for 1988. This adjustment results in underpayments for 1987 and 1988 that are attributable to the disregard of rules or regulations on the 1990 return. Therefore, the 20 percent penalty rate applies to the 1987 and 1988 underpayments attributable to the disallowed carryback. [Reg. § 1.6662-3.]

☐ [*T.D. 8381, 12-30-91. Amended by T.D. 8617, 8-31-95; T.D. 8790, 12-1-98 and T.D. 9109, 12-29-2003.*]

§ 1.6662-4. Substantial understatement of income tax.—(a) *In general.*—If any portion of an underpayment, as defined in section 6664(a) and § 1.6664-2, of any income tax imposed under subtitle A of the Code that is required to be shown on a return is attributable to a substantial understatement of such income tax, there is added to the tax an amount equal to 20 percent of such portion. Except in the case of any item attributable to a tax shelter (as defined in paragraph (g)(2) of this section), an understatement is reduced by the portion of the understatement that is attributable to the tax treatment of an item for which there is substantial authority, or with respect to which there is adequate disclosure. General rules for determining the amount of an understatement are set forth in paragraph (b) of this section and more specific rules in the case of carrybacks and carryovers are set forth in paragraph (c) of this section. The rules for determining when substantial authority exists are set forth in § 1.6662-4(d). The rules for determining when there is adequate disclosure are set forth in § 1.6662-4(e) and (f). This penalty does not apply to the extent that the reasonable cause and good faith exception to this penalty set forth in § 1.6664-4 applies.

(b) *Definitions and computational rules.*—(1) *Substantial.*—An understatement (as defined in paragraph (b)(2) of this section) is "substantial" if it exceeds the greater of—

(i) 10 percent of the tax required to be shown on the return for the taxable year (as defined in paragraph (b)(3) of this section); or

(ii) $5,000 ($10,000 in the case of a corporation other than an S corporation (as defined in section 1361(a)(1)) or a personal holding company (as defined in section 542)).

(2) *Understatement.*—Except as provided in paragraph (c)(2) of this section (relating to special rules for carrybacks), the term "understatement" means the excess of—

(i) The amount of the tax required to be shown on the return for the taxable year (as defined in paragraph (b)(3) of this section), over

(ii) The amount of the tax imposed which is shown on the return for the taxable year (as defined in paragraph (b)(4) of this section), reduced by any rebate (as defined in paragraph (b)(5) of this section).

The definition of understatement also may be expressed as—

Understatement = X – (Y – Z)

where X = the amount of the tax required to be shown on the return; Y = the amount of the tax imposed which is shown on the return; and Z = any rebate.

(3) *Amount of the tax required to be shown on the return.*—The "amount of the tax required to be shown on the return" for the taxable year has the same meaning as the "amount of income tax imposed" as defined in § 1.6664-2(b).

(4) *Amount of the tax imposed which is shown on the return.*—The "amount of the tax imposed which is shown on the return" for the taxable year has the same meaning as the "amount shown as the tax by the taxpayer on his return," as defined in § 1.6664-2(c), except that—

(i) There is no reduction for the excess of the amount described in § 1.6664-2(c)(1)(i) over the amount described in § 1.6664-2(c)(1)(ii), and

(ii) The tax liability shown by the taxpayer on his return is recomputed as if the following items had been reported properly:

(A) Items (other than tax shelter items as defined in § 1.6662-4(g)(3)) for which there is substantial authority for the treatment claimed (as provided in § 1.6662-4(d)).

(B) Items (other than tax shelter items as defined in § 1.6662-4(g)(3)) with respect to which there is adequate disclosure (as provided in § 1.6662-4(e) and (f)).

(C) Tax shelter items (as defined in § 1.6662-4(g)(3)) for which there is substantial authority for the treatment claimed (as provided in § 1.6662-4(d)), and with respect to which the taxpayer reasonably believed that the tax treatment of the items was more likely than not the proper tax treatment (as provided in § 1.6662-4(g)(4)).

(5) *Rebate.*—The term "rebate" has the meaning set forth in § 1.6664-2(e), except that—

(i) "Amounts not so shown previously assessed (or collected without assessment)" includes only amounts not so shown previously assessed (or collected without assessment) as a deficiency, and

(ii) The amount of the rebate is determined as if any items to which the rebate is attributable that are described in paragraph (b)(4) of this section had received the proper tax treatment.

(6) *Examples.*—The following examples illustrate the provisions of paragraph (b) of this section. These examples do not take into account the reasonable cause exception under § 1.6664-4:

Example 1. In 1990, Individual A, a calendar year taxpayer, files a return for 1989, which shows taxable income of $18,200 and tax liability of $2,734. Subsequent adjustments on audit for 1989 increase taxable income to $51,500 and tax liability to $12,339. There was substantial authority for an item resulting in an adjustment that increases taxable income by $5,300. The item is not a tax shelter item. In computing the amount of the understatement, the amount of tax shown on A's return is determined as if the item for which there was substantial authority had been given the proper tax treatment. Thus, the amount of tax that is treated as shown on A's return is $4,176, i.e., the tax on $23,500 ($18,200 taxable income actually shown on A's return plus $5,300, the amount of the adjustment for which there was substantial authority). The amount of the understatement is $8,163, i.e., $12,339 (the amount of tax required to be shown) less $4,176 (the amount of tax treated as shown on A's return after adjustment for the item for which there was substantial authority). Because the $8,163 understatement exceeds the greater of 10 percent of the tax required to be shown on the return for the year, i.e., $1,234 ($12,339 × .10) or $5,000, A has a substantial understatement of income tax for the year.

Example 2. Individual B, a calendar year taxpayer, files a return for 1990 that fails to include income reported on an information return, Form 1099, that was furnished to B. The Service detects this omission through its document matching program and assesses $3,000 in unreported tax liability. B's return is later examined and as a result of the examination the Service makes an adjustment to B's return of $4,000 in additional tax liability. Assuming there was neither substantial authority nor adequate disclosure with respect to the items adjusted, there is an understatement of $7,000 with respect to B's return. There is also an underpayment of $7,000. (See § 1.6664-2.) The amount of the understatement is not reduced by imposition of a negligence penalty on the $3,000 portion of the underpayment that is attributable to the unreported income. However, if the Service does impose the negligence penalty on this $3,000 portion, the Service may only impose the substantial understatement penalty on the remaining $4,000 portion of the underpayment. (See § 1.6662-2(c), which prohibits stacking of accuracy-related penalty components.)

(c) *Special rules in the case of carrybacks and carryovers.*—(1) *In general.*—The penalty for a substantial understatement of income tax applies to any portion of an underpayment for a year to which a loss, deduction or credit is carried that is attributable to a "tainted item" for the year in which the carryback or carryover of the loss, deduction or credit arises (the "loss or credit year"). The determination of whether an understatement is substantial for a carryback or carryover year is made with respect to the return of the carryback or carryover year. "Tainted items" are taken into account with items arising in a carryback or carryover year to determine whether the understatement is substantial for that year.

(2) *Understatements for carryback years not reduced by amount of carrybacks.*—The amount of an understatement for a carryback year is not reduced on account of a carryback of a loss, deduction or credit to that year.

(3) *Tainted items defined.*—(i) *In general.*—Except in the case of a tax shelter item (as defined in paragraph (g)(3) of this section), a "tainted item" is any item for which there is neither substantial authority nor adequate disclosure with respect to the loss or credit year.

(ii) *Tax shelter items.*—In the case of a tax shelter item (as defined in paragraph (g)(3) of this section), a "tainted item" is any item for which there is not, with respect to the loss or credit year, both substantial authority and a reasonable belief that the tax treatment is more likely than not the proper treatment.

(4) *Transition rule for carrybacks to pre-1990 years.*—A 20 percent penalty under section 6662(b)(2) is imposed on any portion of an underpayment for a carryback year, the return for which is due (without regard to extensions) before January 1, 1990, if—

(i) That portion is attributable to one or more "tainted items" (as defined in paragraph (c)(3) of this section) arising in a loss or credit year; and

(ii) The return for the loss or credit year is due (without regard to extensions) after December 31, 1989.

The preceding sentence applies only if the understatement in the carryback year is substantial. See *Example 2* in paragraph (c)(5) of this section.

(5) *Examples.*—The following examples illustrate the rules of paragraph (c) of this section regarding carrybacks and carryovers. These examples do not take into account the reasonable cause exception under § 1.6664-4.

Example 1. (i) Corporation N, a calendar year taxpayer, is a C corporation. N was formed on January 1, 1987, and timely filed the following income tax returns:

Tax Year	*1987*	*1988*	*1989*	*1990*
Taxable Income	$30,000	$100,000	($300,000)	$50,000 (Before NOLCO)
Tax Liability	$4,575	$22,250	-0-	$ 7,500 (Before NOLCO)

(ii) During 1990, N files Form 1139, Corporation Application for Tentative Refund, to carry back the NOL generated in 1989 (NOLCB). N received refunds of $4,575 for 1987 and $22,250 for 1988.

(iii) For tax year 1990, N carries over $50,000 of the 1989 loss to offset $50,000 of income earned in 1990 and reduce taxable income to zero. N would have reported $7,500 of tax liability for 1990 if it were not for use of the net operating loss carryover (NOLCO). N assumes there is a remaining NOLCO of $120,000 to be applied for tax year 1991.

(iv) In June 1991, the Service completes its examination of the 1989 loss year return and makes the following adjustment:

Taxable income per 1989 return	($300,000)
Adjustment: Unreported income	310,000
Corrected taxable income	$ 10,000
Corrected tax liability	$1,500

(v) There was not substantial authority for N's treatment of the items comprising the 1989 adjustment and N did not make adequate disclosure.

(vi) As a result of the adjustment to the 1989 return, N had an understatement of $4,575 for tax year 1987; an understatement of $22,250 for tax year 1988; an understatement of $1,500 for tax year 1989; and an understatement of $7,500 for tax year 1990. Only the $22,250 understatement for 1988 is a substantial understatement, i.e., it exceeds the greater of (a) $2,225 (10 percent of the tax required to be shown on the return for the taxable year (.10 × $22,250)) or (b) $10,000. The underpayment for 1988 is subject to a penalty rate of 20 percent.

Example 2. The facts are the same as in *Example 1*, except that in addition to examining the 1989 return, the Service also examines the 1987 return and makes an adjustment that results in an understatement. (This adjustment is unrelated to the adjustment on the 1987 return for the disallowance of the NOLCB from 1989.) If the understatement resulting from the adjustment to the 1987 return, when combined with the understatement resulting from the disallowance of the NOLCB from 1989, exceeds the greater of (a) 10 percent of the tax required to be shown on the return for 1987 or (b) $10,000, the underpayment for 1987 will also be subject to a substantial understatement penalty. The portion of the underpayment attributable to the adjustment unrelated to the disallowance of the NOLCB will be subject to a penalty rate of 25 percent under former section 6661. The portion of the underpayment attributable to the disallowance of the NOLCB will be subject to a penalty rate of 20 percent under section 6662.

Example 3. Individual P, a calendar year single taxpayer, files his 1990 return reporting taxable income of $10,000 and a tax liability of $1,504. An examination of the 1990 return results in an adjustment for unreported income of $25,000. There was not substantial authority for P's failure to report the income, and P did not make adequate disclosure with respect to the unreported income. P's correct tax liability for 1990 is determined to be $7,279, resulting in an understatement of $5,775 (the difference between the amount of tax required to be shown on the return ($7,279) and the tax shown on the return ($1,504)). Because the understatement exceeds the greater of (a) $728 (10 percent of the tax required to be shown on the return (.10 × $7,279)) or (b) $5,000, the understatement is substantial. Subsequently, P files his 1993 return showing a net operating loss. The loss is carried back to his 1990 return, reducing his taxable income for 1990 to zero. However, the amount of the understatement for 1990 is not reduced on account of the NOLCB to that year. P is subject to the 20 percent penalty rate under section 6662 on the underpayment attributable to the substantial understatement for 1990, notwithstanding that the tax required to be shown on the return for that year, after application of the NOLCB, is zero.

(d) *Substantial authority.*—(1) *Effect of having substantial authority.*—If there is substantial authority for the tax treatment of an item, the item is treated as if it were shown properly on the return for the taxable year in computing the amount of the tax shown on the return. Thus, for purposes of section 6662(d), the tax attributable to the item is not included in the understatement for that year. (For special rules relating to tax shelter items see § 1.6662-4(g).)

(2) *Substantial authority standard.*—The substantial authority standard is an objective standard involving an analysis of the law and application of the law to relevant facts. The substantial authority standard is less stringent than the more likely than not standard (the standard that is met when there is a greater than 50-percent likelihood of the position being upheld), but more stringent than the reasonable basis standard as defined in § 1.6662-3(b)(3). The possibility that a return will not be audited or, if audited, that an item will not be raised on audit, is not relevant in determining whether the substantial authority standard (or the reasonable basis standard) is satisfied.

(3) *Determination of whether substantial authority is present.*—(i) *Evaluation of authorities.*—There is substantial authority for the tax treatment of an item only if the weight of the authorities supporting the treatment is substantial in relation to the weight of authorities supporting contrary treatment. All authorities relevant to the tax treatment of an item, including the authorities contrary to the treatment, are taken into account in determining whether substantial authority exists. The weight of authorities is determined in light of the pertinent facts and circumstances in the manner prescribed by paragraph (d)(3)(ii) of this section. There may be substantial authority for more than one position with respect to the same item. Because the substantial authority standard is an objective standard, the taxpayer's belief that there is substantial authority for the tax treatment of an item is not relevant in determining whether there is substantial authority for that treatment.

(ii) *Nature of analysis.*—The weight accorded an authority depends on its relevance and persuasiveness, and the type of document providing the authority. For example, a case or revenue ruling having some facts in common with the tax treatment at issue is not particularly relevant if the authority is materially distinguishable on its facts, or is otherwise inapplicable to the tax treatment at issue. An authority that merely states a conclusion ordinarily is less persuasive than one that reaches its conclusion by cogently relating the applicable law to pertinent facts. The weight of an authority from which information has been deleted, such as a private letter ruling, is diminished to the extent that the deleted information may have affected the authority's conclusions. The type of document also must be considered. For example, a revenue ruling is accorded greater weight than a private letter ruling addressing the same issue. An older private letter ruling, technical advice memorandum, general counsel memorandum or action on decision generally must be accorded less weight than a more recent one. Any document described in the preceding sentence that is more than 10 years old generally is accorded very little weight. However, the persuasiveness and relevance of a document, viewed in light of subsequent developments, should be taken into account along with the age of the document. There may be substantial authority for the tax treatment of an item despite the absence of certain types of authority. Thus, a taxpayer may have substantial authority for a position that is supported only by a well-reasoned construction of the applicable statutory provision.

(iii) *Types of authority.*—Except in cases described in paragraph (d)(3)(iv) of this section concerning written determinations, only the following are authority for purposes of determining whether there is substantial authority for the tax treatment of an item: applicable provisions of the Internal Revenue Code and other statutory provisions; proposed, temporary and final regulations construing such statutes; revenue rulings and revenue procedures; tax treaties and regulations thereunder, and Treasury Department and other official explanations of such treaties; court cases; congressional intent as reflected in committee reports, joint explanatory statements of managers included in conference committee reports, and floor statements made prior to enactment by one of a bill's managers; General Explanations of tax legislation prepared by the Joint Committee on Taxation (the Blue Book); private letter rulings and technical advice memoranda issued after October 31, 1976; actions on decisions and general counsel memoranda issued after March 12, 1981 (as well as general counsel memoranda published in pre-1955 volumes of the Cumulative Bulletin); Internal Revenue Service information or press releases; and notices, announcements and other administrative pronouncements published by the Service in the Internal Revenue Bulletin. Conclusions reached in treatises, legal periodicals, legal opinions or opinions rendered by tax professionals are not authority. The authorities underlying such expressions of opinion where applicable to the facts of a particular case, however, may give rise to substantial authority for the tax treatment of an item. Notwithstanding the preceding list of authorities, an authority does not continue to be an authority to the extent it is overruled or modified, implicitly or explicitly, by a body with the power to overrule or modify the earlier authority. In the case of court decisions, for example, a district court opinion on an issue is not an authority if overruled or reversed by the United States Court of Appeals for such district. However, a Tax Court opinion is not considered to be overruled or modified by a court of appeals to which a taxpayer does not have a right of appeal, unless the Tax Court adopts the holding of the court of appeals. Similarly, a private letter ruling is not authority if revoked or if inconsistent with a subsequent proposed regulation, revenue ruling or other administrative pronouncement published in the Internal Revenue Bulletin.

(iv) *Special rules.*—(A) *Written determinations.*—There is substantial authority for the tax treatment of an item by a taxpayer if the treatment is supported by the conclusion of a ruling or a determination letter (as defined in § 301.6110-2(d) and (e)) issued to the taxpayer, by the conclusion of a technical advice memorandum in which the taxpayer is named, or by an affirmative statement in a revenue agent's report with respect to a prior taxable year of the taxpayer ("written determinations"). The preceding sentence does not apply, however, if—

(1) There was a misstatement or omission of a material fact or the facts that subsequently develop are materially different from the facts on which the written determination was based, or

(2) The written determination was modified or revoked after the date of issuance by—

(i) A notice to the taxpayer to whom the written determination was issued,

(ii) The enactment of legislation or ratification of a tax treaty,

(iii) A decision of the United States Supreme Court,

(iv) The issuance of temporary or final regulations, or

(v) The issuance of a revenue ruling, revenue procedure, or other statement published in the Internal Revenue Bulletin.

Except in the case of a written determination that is modified or revoked on account of § 1.6662-4(d)(3)(iv)(A)*(1)*, a written determination that is modified or revoked as described in § 1.6662-4(d)(3)(iv)(A)(2) ceases to be authority on the date, and to the extent, it is so modified or revoked. See section 6404(f) for rules which require the Secretary to abate a penalty that is attributable to erroneous written advice furnished to a taxpayer by an officer or employee of the Internal Revenue Service.

(B) *Taxpayer's jurisdiction.*—The applicability of court cases to the taxpayer by reason of the taxpayer's residence in a particular jurisdiction is not taken into account in determining whether there is substantial authority for the tax treatment of an item. Notwithstanding the preceding sentence, there is substantial authority for the tax treatment of an item if the treatment is supported by controlling precedent of a United States Court of Appeals to which the taxpayer has a right of appeal with respect to the item.

(C) *When substantial authority determined.*—There is substantial authority for the tax treatment of an item if there is substantial authority at the time the return containing the item is filed or there was substantial authority on the last day of the taxable year to which the return relates.

(v) *Substantial authority for tax returns due before January 1, 1990.*—There is substantial authority for the tax treatment of an item on a return that is due (without regard to extensions) after December 31, 1982 and before January 1, 1990, if there is substantial authority for such treatment under either the provisions of paragraph (d)(3)(iii) of this section (which set forth an expanded list of authorities) or of § 1.6661-3(b)(2) (which set forth a narrower list of authorities). Under either list of authorities, authorities both for and against the position must be taken into account.

(e) *Disclosure of certain information.*—(1) *Effect of adequate disclosure.*—Items for which there is adequate disclosure as provided in this paragraph (e) and in paragraph (f) of this section are treated as if such items were shown properly on the return for the taxable year in computing the amount of the tax shown on the return. Thus, for purposes of section 6662(d), the tax attributable to such items is not included in the understatement for that year.

(2) *Circumstances where disclosure will not have an effect.*—The rules of paragraph (e)(1) of this section do not apply where the item or position on the return—

(i) Does not have a reasonable basis (as defined in § 1.6662-3(b)(3));

(ii) Is attributable to a tax shelter (as defined in section 6662(d)(2)(C)(iii) and paragraph (g)(2) of this section); or

(iii) Is not properly substantiated, or the taxpayer failed to keep adequate books and records with respect to the item or position.

(3) *Restriction for corporations.*—For purposes of paragraph (e)(2)(i) of this section, a corporation will not be treated as having a reasonable basis for its tax treatment of an item attributable to a multi-party financing transaction entered into after August 5, 1997, if the treatment does not clearly reflect the income of the corporation.

(f) *Method of making adequate disclosure.*—(1) *Disclosure statement.*—Disclosure is adequate with respect to an item (or group of similar items, such as amounts paid or incurred for supplies by a taxpayer engaged in business) or a position on a return if the disclosure is made on a properly completed form attached to the return or to a qualified amended return (as defined in § 1.6664-2(c)(3)) for the taxable year. In the case of an item or position other than one that is contrary to a regulation, disclosure must be made on Form 8275 (Disclosure Statement); in the case of a position contrary to a regulation, disclosure must be made on Form 8275-R (Regulation Disclosure Statement).

(2) *Disclosure on return.*—The Commissioner may by annual revenue procedure (or otherwise) prescribe the circumstances under which disclosure of information on a return (or qualified amended return) in accordance with applicable forms and instructions is adequate. If the revenue procedure does not include an item, disclosure is adequate with respect to that item only if made on a properly completed Form 8275 or 8275-R, as appropriate, attached to the return for the year or to a qualified amended return.

(3) *Recurring item.*—Disclosure with respect to a recurring item, such as the basis of recovery property, must be made for each taxable year in which the item is taken into account.

(4) *Carrybacks and carryovers.*—Disclosure is adequate with respect to an item which is included in any loss, deduction or credit that is carried to another year only if made in connection with the return (or qualified amended return) for the taxable year in which the carryback or carryover arises (the "loss or credit year"). Disclosure is not also required in connection with the return for the taxable year in which the carryback or carryover is taken into account.

(5) *Pass-through entities.*—Disclosure in the case of items attributable to a pass-through entity (pass-through items) is made with respect to the return of the entity, except as provided in this paragraph (f)(5). Thus, disclosure in the case of pass-through items must be made on a Form 8275 or 8275-R, as appropriate, attached to the return (or qualified amended return) of the entity, or on the entity's return in accordance with the revenue procedure described in paragraph (f)(2) of this section, if applicable. A taxpayer (i.e., partner, shareholder, beneficiary, or holder of a residual interest in a REMIC) also may make adequate disclosure with respect to a pass-through item, however, if the taxpayer files a properly completed Form 8275 or 8275-R, as appropriate, in duplicate, one copy attached to the taxpayer's return (or qualified amended return) and the other copy filed with the Internal Revenue Service Center with which the return of the entity is required to be filed. Each Form 8275 or 8275-R, as appropriate, filed by the taxpayer should relate to the pass-through items of only one entity. For purposes of this paragraph (f)(5), a pass-through entity is a partnership, S corporation (as defined in section 1361(a)(1)), estate, trust, regulated investment company (as defined in section 851(a)), real estate investment trust (as defined in section 856(a)), or real estate mortgage investment conduit ("REMIC") (as defined in section 860D(a)).

(g) *Items relating to tax shelters.*—(1) *In general.*—(i) *Noncorporate taxpayers.*—Tax shelter items (as defined in paragraph (g)(3) of this section) of a taxpayer other than a corporation are treated for purposes of this section as if such items were shown properly on the return for a taxable year in computing the amount of the tax shown on the return, and thus the tax attributable to such items is not included in the understatement for the year, if—

(A) There is substantial authority (as provided in paragraph (d) of this section) for the tax treatment of that item; and

(B) The taxpayer reasonably believed at the time the return was filed that the tax treatment of that item was more likely than not the proper treatment.

(ii) *Corporate taxpayers.*—(A) *In general.*—Except as provided in paragraph (g)(1)(ii)(B) of this section, all tax shelter items (as defined in paragraph (g)(3) of this section) of a corporation are taken into account in computing the amount of any understatement.

(B) *Special rule for transactions occurring prior to December 9, 1994.*—The tax shelter items of a corporation arising in connection with transactions occurring prior to December 9, 1994 are treated for purposes of this section as if such items were shown properly on the return if the requirements of paragraph (g)(1)(i) are satisfied with respect to such items.

(iii) *Disclosure irrelevant.*—Disclosure made with respect to a tax shelter item of either a corporate or noncorporate taxpayer does not affect the amount of an understatement.

(iv) *Cross-reference.*—See § 1.6664-4(f) for certain rules regarding the availability of the reasonable cause and good faith exception to the substantial understatement penalty with respect to tax shelter items of corporations.

(2) *Tax shelter.*—(i) *In general.*—For purposes of section 6662(d), the term "tax shelter" means—

(A) A partnership or other entity (such as a corporation or trust),

(B) An investment plan or arrangement, or

(C) Any other plan or arrangement,

if the principal purpose of the entity, plan or arrangement, based on objective evidence, is to avoid or evade Federal income tax. The principal purpose of an entity, plan or arrangement is to avoid or evade Federal income tax if that purpose exceeds any other purpose. Typical of tax shelters are transactions structured with little or no motive for the realization of economic gain, and transactions that utilize the mismatching of income and deductions, overvalued assets or assets with values subject to substantial uncertainty, certain nonrecourse financing, financing techniques that do not conform to standard commercial business practices, or the mischaracterization of the substance of the transaction. The existence of economic substance does not of itself establish that a transaction is not a tax shelter if the transaction includes other characteristics that indicate it is a tax shelter.

(ii) *Principal purpose.*—The principal purpose of an entity, plan or arrangement is not to avoid or evade Federal income tax if the entity, plan or arrangement has as its purpose the claiming of exclusions from income, accelerated deductions or other tax benefits in a manner consistent with the statute and Congressional purpose. For example, an entity, plan or arrangement does not have as its principal purpose the avoidance or evasion of Federal income tax solely as a result of the following uses of tax benefits provided by the Internal Revenue Code: the purchasing or holding of an obligation bearing interest that is excluded from gross income under section 103; taking an accelerated depreciation allowance under section 168; taking the percentage depletion allowance under section 613 or section 613A; deducting intangible drilling and development costs as expenses under section 263(c); establishing a qualified retirement plan under sections 401-409; claiming the possession tax credit under section 936; or claiming tax benefits available by reason of an election under section 992 to be taxed as a domestic international sales corporation ("DISC"), under section 927(f)(1) to be taxed as a foreign sales corporation ("FSC"), or under section 1362 to be taxed as an S corporation.

(3) *Tax shelter item.*—An item of income, gain, loss, deduction or credit is a "tax shelter item" if the item is directly or indirectly attributable to the principal purpose of a tax shelter to avoid or evade Federal income tax. Thus, if a partnership is established for the principal purpose of avoiding or evading Federal income tax by acquiring and overstating the basis of property for purposes of claiming accelerated depreciation, the depreciation with respect to the property is a tax shelter item. However, a deduction claimed in connection with a separate transaction carried on by the same partnership is not a tax shelter item if the transaction does not constitute a plan or arrangement the principal purpose of which is to avoid or evade tax.

(4) *Reasonable belief.*—(i) *In general.*—For purposes of section 6662(d) and paragraph (g)(1)(i)(B) of this section (pertaining to tax shelter items of noncorporate taxpayers), a taxpayer is considered reasonably to believe that the tax treatment of an item is more likely than not the proper tax treatment if (without taking into account the possibility that a return will not be audited, that an issue will not be raised on audit, or that an issue will be settled)—

(A) The taxpayer analyzes the pertinent facts and authorities in the manner described in paragraph (d)(3)(ii) of this section, and in reliance upon that analysis, reasonably concludes in good faith that there is a greater than 50-percent likelihood that the tax treatment of the item will be upheld if challenged by the Internal Revenue Service; or

(B) The taxpayer reasonably relies in good faith on the opinion of a professional tax advisor, if the opinion is based on the tax advisor's analysis of the pertinent facts and authorities in the manner described in paragraph (d)(3)(ii) of this section and unambiguously states that the tax advisor concludes that there is a greater than 50-percent likelihood that the tax treatment of the item will be upheld if challenged by the Internal Revenue Service.

(ii) *Facts and circumstances; reliance on professional tax advisor.*—All facts and circumstances must be taken into account in determining whether a taxpayer satisfies the requirements of paragraph (g)(4)(i) of this section. However, in no event will a taxpayer be considered to have reasonably relied in good faith on the opinion of a professional tax advisor for purposes of paragraph (g)(4)(i)(B) of this section unless the requirements of § 1.6664-4(c)(1) are met. The fact that the requirements of § 1.6664-4(c)(1) are satisfied will not necessarily establish that the taxpayer reasonably relied on the opinion in good faith. For example, reliance may not be reasonable or in good faith if the taxpayer knew, or should have known, that the advisor lacked knowledge in the relevant aspects of Federal tax law.

(5) *Pass-through entities.*—In the case of tax shelter items attributable to a pass-through entity, the actions described in paragraphs (g)(4)(i)(A) and (B) of this section, if taken by the entity, are deemed to have been taken by the taxpayer and are considered in determining whether the taxpayer reasonably believed that the tax treatment of an item was more likely than not the proper tax treatment. [Reg. § 1.6662-4.]

☐ [*T.D.* 8381, 12-30-91. *Amended by T.D.* 8617, 8-31-95; *T.D.* 8790, 12-1-98 *and T.D.* 9109, 12-29-2003.]

§ 1.6662-5. Substantial and gross valuation misstatements under chapter 1.—(a) *In general.*—If any portion of an underpayment, as defined in section 6664(a) and § 1.6664-2, of any income tax imposed under chapter 1 of subtitle A of the Code that is required to be shown on a return is attributable to a substantial valuation misstatement under chapter 1 ("substantial valuation misstatement"), there is added to the tax an amount equal to 20 percent of such portion. Section 6662(h) increases the penalty to 40 percent in the case of a gross valuation misstatement under chapter 1 ("gross valuation misstatement"). No penalty under section 6662(b)(3) is imposed, however, on a portion of an underpayment that is attributable to a substantial or gross valuation misstatement unless the aggregate of all portions of the underpayment attributable to substantial or gross valuation misstatements exceeds the applicable dollar limitation ($5,000 or $10,000), as provided in section 6662(e)(2) and paragraphs (b) and (f)(2) of this section. This penalty also does not apply to the extent that the reasonable cause and good faith exception to this penalty set forth in § 1.6664-4 applies. There is no disclosure exception to this penalty.

(b) *Dollar limitation.*—No penalty may be imposed under section 6662(b)(3) for a taxable year unless the portion of the underpayment for that year that is attributable to substantial or gross valuation misstatements exceeds $5,000 ($10,000 in the case of a corporation other than an S corporation (as defined in section 1361(a)(1)) or a personal holding company (as defined in section 542)). This limitation is applied separately to each taxable year for which there is a substantial or gross valuation misstatement.

(c) *Special rules in the case of carrybacks and carryovers.*—(1) *In general.*—The penalty for a substantial or gross valuation misstatement applies to any portion of an underpayment for a year to which a loss, deduction or credit is carried that is attributable to a substantial or gross valuation misstatement for the year in which the carryback or carryover of the loss, deduction or credit arises (the "loss or credit year"), provided that the applicable dollar limitation set forth in section 6662(e)(2) is satisfied in the carryback or carryover year.

(2) *Transition rule for carrybacks to pre-1990 years.*—The penalty under section 6662(b)(3) is imposed on any portion of an underpayment for a carryback year, the return for which is due (without regard to extensions) before January 1, 1990, if—

(i) That portion is attributable to a substantial or gross valuation misstatement for a loss or credit year; and

(ii) The return for the loss or credit year is due (without regard to extensions) after December 31, 1989.

The preceding sentence applies only if the underpayment for the carryback year exceeds the applicable dollar limitation ($5,000, or $10,000 for most corporations). See *Example 3* in paragraph (d) of this section.

(d) *Examples.*—The following examples illustrate the provisions of paragraphs (b) and (c) of this section. These examples do not take into account the reasonable cause exception under § 1.6664-4.

Example 1. Corporation Q is a C corporation. In 1990, the first year of its existence, Q had taxable income of $200,000 without considering depreciation of a particular asset. On its calendar year 1990 return, Q overstated its basis in this asset by an amount that caused a substantial valuation misstatement. The overstated basis resulted in depreciation claimed of $350,000, which was $250,000 more than the $100,000 allowable. Thus, on its 1990 return, Q showed a loss of $150,000. In 1991, Q had taxable income of $450,000 before application of the loss carryover, and Q claimed a carryover loss deduction under section 172 of $150,000, resulting in taxable income of $300,000 for 1991. Upon audit of the 1990 return, the basis of the asset was corrected, resulting in an adjustment of $250,000. For 1990, the underpayment resulting from the $100,000 taxable income (–$150,000 + $250,000) is attributable to the valuation misstatement. Assuming the underpayment resulting from the $100,000 taxable income exceeds the $10,000 limitation, the penalty will be imposed in 1990. For 1991, the elimination of the loss carryover results in additional taxable income of $150,000. The underpayment for 1991 resulting from that adjustment is also attributable to the substantial valuation misstatement on the 1990 return. Assuming the underpayment resulting from the $150,000 additional taxable income for 1991 exceeds the $10,000 limitation, the substantial valuation misstatement penalty also will be imposed for that year.

Example 2. (i) Corporation T is a C corporation. In 1990, the first year of its existence, T had a loss of $3,000,000 without considering depreciation of its major asset. On its calendar year 1990 return, T overstated its basis in this asset in an amount that caused a substantial valuation misstatement. This overstatement resulted in depreciation claimed of $3,500,000, which was $2,500,000 more than the $1,000,000 allowable. Thus, on its 1990 return, T showed a loss of $6,500,000. In 1991, T had taxable income of $4,500,000 before application of the carryover loss, but claimed a carryover loss deduction under section 172 in the amount of $4,500,000, resulting in taxable income of zero for that year and leaving a $2,000,000 carryover available. Upon audit of the 1990 return, the basis of the asset was corrected, resulting in an adjustment of $2,500,000.

(ii) For 1990, the underpayment is still zero (–$6,500,000 + $2,500,000 = –$4,000,000). Thus, the penalty does not apply in 1990. The loss for 1990 is reduced to $4,000,000.

(iii) For 1991, there is additional taxable income of $500,000 as a result of the reduction of the carryover loss ($4,500,000 reported income before carryover loss minus corrected carryover loss of $4,000,000 = $500,000). The underpayment for 1991 resulting from reduction of the carryover loss is attributable to the valuation misstatement on the 1990 return. Assuming the underpayment resulting from the $500,000 additional taxable income exceeds the $10,000 limitation, the substantial valuation misstatement penalty will be imposed in 1991.

Example 3. Corporation V is a C corporation. In 1990, V had a loss of $100,000 without considering depreciation of a particular asset which it had fully depreciated in earlier years. V had a depreciable basis in the asset of zero, but on its 1990 calendar year return erroneously claimed a basis in the asset of $1,250,000 and depreciation of $250,000. V reported a $350,000 loss for the year 1990, and carried back the loss to the 1987 and 1988 tax years. V had reported taxable income of $300,000 in 1987 and $200,000 in 1988, before application of the carryback. The $350,000 carryback eliminated all taxable income for 1987, and $50,000 of the taxable income for 1988. After disallowance of the $250,000 depreciation deduction for 1990, V still had a loss of $100,000. Because there is no underpayment for 1990, no valuation misstatement penalty is imposed for 1990. However, as a result of the 1990 depreciation adjustment, the carryback to 1987 is reduced from $350,000 to $100,000. After absorption of the $100,000 carryback, V has taxable income of $200,000 for 1987. This adjustment results in an underpayment for 1987 that is attributable to the valuation misstatement on the 1990 return. The valuation misstatement for 1990 is a gross valuation misstatement because the correct adjusted basis of the depreciated asset was zero. (See paragraph (e)(2) of this section.) Therefore, the 40 percent penalty rate applies to the 1987 underpayment attributable to the 1990 misstatement, provided that this underpayment exceeds $10,000. The adjustment also results in the elimination of any loss carryback to 1988 resulting in an increase in taxable income for 1988 of $50,000. Assuming the underpayment resulting from this additional $50,000 of income exceeds $10,000, the gross valuation misstatement penalty is imposed on the underpayment for 1988.

(e) *Definitions.*—(1) *Substantial valuation misstatement.*—There is a substantial valuation misstatement if the value or adjusted basis of any property claimed on a return of tax imposed under chapter 1 is 200 percent or more of the correct amount.

(2) *Gross valuation misstatement.*—There is a gross valuation misstatement if the value or adjusted basis of any property claimed on a return of tax imposed under chapter 1 is 400 percent or more of the correct amount.

(3) *Property.*—For purposes of this section, the term "property" refers to both tangible and intangible property. Tangible property includes property such as land, buildings, fixtures and inventory. Intangible property includes property such as goodwill, covenants not to compete, leaseholds, patents, contract rights, debts and choses in action.

(f) *Multiple valuation misstatements on a return.*—(1) *Determination of whether valuation misstatements are substantial or gross.*—The determination of whether there is a substantial or gross valuation misstatement on a return is made on a property-by-property basis. Assume, for example, that property A has a value of 60 but a taxpayer claims a value of 110, and that property B has a value of 40 but the taxpayer claims a value of 100. Because the claimed and correct values are compared on a property-by-property basis, there is a substantial valuation misstatement with respect to property B, but not with respect to property A, even though the claimed values (210) are 200 percent or more of the correct values (100) when compared on an aggregate basis.

(2) *Application of dollar limitation.*—For purposes of applying the dollar limitation set forth in section 6662(e)(2), the determination of the portion of an underpayment that is attributable to a substantial or gross valuation misstatement is made by aggregating all portions of the underpayment attributable to substantial or gross valuation misstatements. Assume, for example, that the value claimed for property C on a return is 250 percent of the correct value, and that the value claimed for property D on the return is 400 percent of the correct value. Because the portions of an underpayment that are attributable to a substantial or gross valuation misstatement on a return are aggregated in applying the dollar limitation, the dollar limitation is satisfied if the portion of the underpayment that is attributable to the misstatement of the value of property C, when aggregated with the portion of the underpayment that is attributable to the misstatement of the value of property D, exceeds $5,000 ($10,000 in the case of most corporations).

(g) *Property with a value or adjusted basis of zero.*—The value or adjusted basis claimed on a return of any property with a correct value or adjusted basis of zero is considered to be 400 percent or more of the correct amount. There is a gross valuation misstatement with respect to such property, therefore, and the applicable penalty rate is 40 percent.

(h) *Pass-through entities.*—(1) *In general.*—The determination of whether there is a substantial or gross valuation misstatement in the case of a return of a pass-through entity (as defined in § 1.6662-4(f)(5)) is made at the entity level. However, the dollar limitation ($5,000 or $10,000, as the case may be) is applied at the taxpayer level (*i.e.*, with respect to the return of the shareholder, partner, beneficiary, or holder of a residual interest in a REMIC).

(2) *Example.*—The rules of paragraph (h)(1) of this section may be illustrated by the following example.

Example. Partnership P has two partners, individuals A and B. P claims a $40,000 basis in a depreciable asset which, in fact, has a basis of $15,000. The determination that there is a substantial valuation misstatement is made solely with reference to P by comparing the $40,000 basis claimed by P with P's correct basis of $15,000. However, the determination of whether the $5,000 threshold for application of the penalty has been reached is made separately for each partner. With respect to partner A, the penalty will apply if the portion of A's underpayment attributable to the passthrough of the depreciation deduction, when aggregated with any other portions of A's underpayment also attributable to substantial or gross valuation misstatements, exceeds $5,000 (assuming there is not reasonable cause for the misstatements (*see* § 1.6664-4(c)).

(i) [Reserved]

(j) *Transactions between persons described in section 482 and net section 482 transfer price adjustments.*—[Reserved]

(k) *Returns affected.*—Except in the case of rules relating to transactions between persons described in section 482 and net section 482 transfer price adjustments, the provisions of section 6662(b)(3) apply to returns due (without regard to extensions of time to file) after December 31, 1989, notwithstanding that the original substantial or gross valuation misstatement occurred on a return that was due (without regard to extensions) before January 1, 1990. Assume, for example, that a calendar year corporation claimed a deduction on its 1990 return for depreciation of an asset with a basis of X. Also assume that it had reported the same basis for computing depreciation on its returns for the preceding 5 years and that the basis shown on the return each year was 200 percent or more of the correct basis. The corporation may be subject to a penalty for substantial valuation misstatements on its 1989 and 1990 returns, even though the original misstatement occurred prior to the effective date of sections 6662(b)(3) and (e). [Reg. § 1.6662-5.]

☐ [*T.D. 8381, 12-30-91.*]

§ 1.6662-5T. Substantial and gross valuation misstatements under chapter 1 (Temporary).—(a) through (e)(3) [Reserved]. For further information, see § 1.6662-5(a) through (e)(3).

(e)(4) *Tests related to section 482.*—(i) *Substantial valuation misstatement.*—There is a substantial valuation misstatement if there is a misstatement described in § 1.6662-6(b)(1) or (c)(1) (concerning substantial valuation misstatements pertaining to transactions between related persons).

(ii) *Gross valuation misstatement.*—There is a gross valuation misstatement if there is a misstatement described in § 1.6662-6(b)(2) or (c)(2) (concerning gross valuation misstatements pertaining to transactions between related persons).

(iii) *Property.*—For purposes of this section, the term *property* refers to both tangible and intangible property. Tangible property includes property such as money, land, buildings, fixtures and inventory. Intangible property includes property such as goodwill. covenants not to compete, leaseholds, patents, contract rights, debts, choses in action, and any other item of intangible property described in § 1.482-4(b).

(f) through (h) [Reserved] For further information, see § 1.6662-5(f) through (h).

(i) [Reserved].

(j) *Transactions between persons described in section 482 and net section 482 transfer price adjustments.*—For rules relating to the penalty imposed with respect to a substantial or gross valuation misstatement arising from a section 482 allocation, see § 1.6662-6. [Temporary Reg. § 1.6662-5T.]

☐ [*T.D. 8519, 1-27-94. Amended by T.D. 8656, 2-8-96.*]

§ 1.6662-6. Transactions between persons described in section 482 and net section 482 transfer price adjustments.—(a) *In general.*—(1) *Purpose and scope.*—Pursuant to section 6662(e) a penalty is imposed on any underpayment attributable to a substantial valuation misstatement pertaining to either a transaction between persons described in section 482 (the transactional penalty) or a net section 482 transfer price adjustment (the net adjustment penalty). The penalty is equal to 20 percent of the underpayment of tax attributable to that substantial valuation misstatement. Pursuant to section 6662(h) the penalty is increased to 40 percent of the underpayment in the case of a gross valuation misstatement with respect to either penalty. Paragraph(b) of this section provides specific rules related to the transactional penalty. Paragraph (c) of this section provides specific rules related to the net adjustment penalty, and paragraph (d) of this section describes amounts that will be excluded for purposes of calculating the net adjustment penalty. Paragraph (e) of this section sets forth special rules in the case of carrybacks and carryovers. Paragraph (f) of this section provides coordination rules between penalties. Paragraph (g) of this section provides the effective date of this section.

(2) *Reported results.*—Whether an underpayment is attributable to a substantial or gross valuation misstatement must be determined from the results of controlled transactions that are reported on an income tax return, regardless of whether the amount reported differs from the transaction price initially reflected in the taxpayer's books and records. The results of controlled transactions that are reported on an amended return will be used only if the amended return is filed before the Internal Revenue Service has contacted the taxpayer regarding the corresponding original return. A written statement furnished by a taxpayer subject to the Coordinated Examination Program or a written statement furnished by the taxpayer when electing Accelerated Issue Resolution or similar procedures will be considered an amended return for purposes of this section if it satisfies either the requirements of a qualified amended return for purposes of § 1.6664-2(c)(3) or such requirements as the Commissioner may prescribe by revenue procedure. In the case of a taxpayer that is a member of a consolidated group, the rules of this paragraph (a)(2) apply to the consolidated income tax return of the group.

(3) *Identical terms used in the section 482 regulations.*—For purposes of this section, the terms used in this section shall have the same meaning as identical terms used in regulations under section 482.

(b) *The transactional penalty.*—(1) *Substantial valuation misstatement.*—In the case of any transaction between related persons, there is a substantial valuation misstatement if the price for any property or services (or for the use of property) claimed on any return is 200 percent or more (or 50 percent or less) of the amount determined under section 482 to be the correct price.

(2) *Gross valuation misstatement.*—In the case of any transaction between related persons, there is a gross valuation misstatement if the price for any property or services (or for the use of property) claimed on any return is 400 percent or more (or 25 percent or less) of the amount determined under section 482 to be the correct price.

(3) *Reasonable cause and good faith.*—Pursuant to section 6664(c), the transactional penalty will not be imposed on any portion of an underpayment with respect to which the requirements of § 1.6664-4 are met. In applying the provisions of § 1.6664-4 in a case in which the taxpayer has relied on professional analysis in determining its transfer pricing, whether the professional is an employee of, or related to, the taxpayer is not determinative in evaluating whether the taxpayer reasonably relied in good faith on advice. A taxpayer that meets the requirements of paragraph (d) of this section with respect to an allocation under section 482 will be treated as having established that there was reasonable cause and good faith with respect to that item for purposes of § 1.6664-4. If a substantial or gross valuation misstatement under the transactional penalty also constitutes (or is part of) a substantial or gross valuation misstatement under the net adjustment penalty, then the rules of paragraph (d) of this section (and not the rules of § 1.6664-4) will be applied to determine whether the adjustment is excluded from calculation of the net section 482 adjustment.

(c) *Net adjustment penalty.*—(1) *Net section 482 adjustment.*—For purposes of this section, the term *net section 482 adjustment* means the sum of all increases in the taxable income of a taxpayer for a taxable year resulting from allocations under section 482 (determined without regard to any amount carried to such taxable year from another taxable year) less any decreases in taxable income attributable to collateral adjustments as described in § 1.482-1(g). For purposes of this section, amounts that meet the requirements of paragraph (d) of this section will be excluded from the calculation of the net section 482 adjustment. Substantial and gross valuation misstatements that are subject to the transactional penalty under paragraph (b)(1) or (2) of this section are included in determining the amount of the net section 482 adjustment. See paragraph (f) of this section for coordination rules between penalties.

(2) *Substantial valuation misstatement.*—There is a substantial valuation misstatement if a net section 482 adjustment is greater than the lesser of 5 million dollars or ten percent of gross receipts.

(3) *Gross valuation misstatement.*—There is a gross valuation misstatement if a net section 482 adjustment is greater than the lesser of 20 million dollars or twenty percent of gross receipts.

(4) *Setoff allocation rule.*—If a taxpayer meets the requirements of paragraph (d) of this section with respect to some, but not all of the allocations made under section 482, then for purposes of determining the net section 482 adjustment, setoffs, as taken into account under § 1.482-1(g)(4), must be applied ratably against all such allocations. The following example illustrates the principle of this paragraph (c)(4):

Example. (i) The Internal Revenue Service makes the following section 482 adjustments for the taxable year:

(1)	Attributable to an increase in gross income because of an increase in royalty payments	$9,000,000
(2)	Attributable to an increase in sales proceeds due to a decrease in the profit margin of a related buyer	6,000,000
(3)	Because of a setoff under § 1.482-1(g)(4)	(5,000,000)
	Total section 482 adjustments	10,000,000

(ii) The taxpayer meets the requirements of paragraph (d) with respect to adjustment number one, but not with respect to adjustment number two. The five million dollar setoff will be allocated ratably against the nine million dollar adjustment ($9,000,000/$15,000,000 x $5,000,000 = $3,000,000) and the six million dollar adjustment ($6,000,000/$15,000,000 x $5,000,000 = $2,000,000). Accordingly, in determining the net section 482 adjustment, the nine million dollar adjustment is reduced to six million dollars ($9,000,000 - $3,000,000) and the six million dollar adjustment is reduced to four million dollars ($6,000,000 - $2,000,000). Therefore, the net section 482 adjustment equals four million dollars.

(5) *Gross receipts.*—For purposes of this section, gross receipts must be computed pursuant to the rules contained in § 1.448-1T(f)(2)(iv), as adjusted to reflect allocations under section 482.

(6) *Coordination with reasonable cause exception under section 6664(c).*—Pursuant to section 6662(e)(3)(D), a taxpayer will be treated as having reasonable cause under section 6664(c) for any portion of an underpayment attributable to a net section 482 adjustment only if the taxpayer meets the requirements of paragraph (d) of this section with respect to that portion.

(7) *Examples.*—The principles of this paragraph (c) are illustrated by the following examples:

Example 1. (i) The Internal Revenue Service makes the following section 482 adjustments for the taxable year:

(1)	Attributable to an increase in gross income because of an increase in royalty payments	$2,000,000
(2)	Attributable to an increase in sales proceeds due to a decrease in the profit margin of a related buyer	2,500,000
(3)	Attributable to a decrease in the cost of goods sold because of a decrease in the cost plus mark-up of a related seller	2,000,000
	Total section 482 adjustments	6,500,000

(ii) None of the adjustments are excluded under paragraph (d) of this section. The net section 482 adjustment ($6.5 million) is greater than five million dollars. Therefore, there is a substantial valuation misstatement.

Example 2. (i) The Internal Revenue Service makes the following section 482 adjustments for the taxable year:

(1)	Attributable to an increase in gross income because of an increase in royalty payments	$11,000,000
(2)	Attributable to an increase in sales proceeds due to a decrease in the profit margin of a related buyer	2,000,000
(3)	Because of a setoff under § 1.482-1(g)(4)	(9,000,000)
	Total section 482 adjustments	4,000,000

(ii) The taxpayer has gross receipts of sixty million dollars after taking into account all section 482 adjustments. None of the adjustments are excluded under paragraph (d) of this section. The net section 482 adjustment ($4 million) is less than the lesser of five million dollars or ten percent of gross receipts ($60 million × 10% = $6 million). Therefore, there is no substantial valuation misstatement.

Example 3. (i) The Internal Revenue Service makes the following section 482 adjustments to the income of an affiliated group that files a consolidated return for the taxable year:

(1)	Attributable to Member A	$1,500,000
(2)	Attributable to Member B	1,000,000
(3)	Attributable to Member C	2,000,000
	Total section 482 adjustments	4,500,000

(ii) Members A, B, and C have gross receipts of 20 million dollars, 12 million dollars, and 11 million dollars, respectively. Thus, the total gross receipts are 43 million dollars. None of the adjustments are excluded under paragraph (d) of this section. The net section 482 adjustment ($4.5 million) is greater than the lesser of five million dollars or ten percent of gross receipts ($43 million x 10% = $4.3 million). Therefore, there is a substantial valuation misstatement.

Example 4. (i) The Internal Revenue Service makes the following section 482 adjustments to the income of an affiliated group that files a consolidated return for the taxable year:

(1)	Attributable to Member A	$1,500,000
(2)	Attributable to Member B	3,000,000
(3)	Attributable to Member C	2,500,000
	Total section 482 adjustments	7,000,000

(ii) Members A, B, and C have gross receipts of 20 million dollars, 35 million dollars, and 40 million dollars, respectively. Thus, the total gross receipts are 95 million dollars. None of the adjustments are excluded under paragraph (d) of this section. The net section 482 adjustment (7 million dollars) is greater than the lesser of five million dollars or ten percent of gross receipts ($95 million × 10% = $9.5 million). Therefore, there is a substantial valuation misstatement.

Example 5. (i) The Internal Revenue Service makes the following section 482 adjustments to the income of an affiliated group that files a consolidated return for the taxable year:

(1)	Attributable to Member A	$2,000,000
(2)	Attributable to Member B	1,000,000
(3)	Attributable to Member C	1,500,000
	Total section 482 adjustments	4,500,000

(ii) Members A, B, and C have gross receipts of 10 million dollars, 35 million dollars, and 40 million dollars, respectively. Thus, the total gross receipts are 85 million dollars. None of the adjustments are excluded under paragraph (d) of this section. The net section 482 adjustment ($4.5 million) is less than the lesser of five million dollars or ten percent of gross receipts ($85 million x 10% = $8.5 million). Therefore, there is no substantial valuation misstatement even though individual member A's adjustment ($2 million) is greater than ten percent of its individual gross receipts ($10 million x 10% = $1 million).

(d) *Amounts excluded from net section 482 adjustments.*—(1) *In general.*—An amount is excluded from the calculation of a net section 482 adjustment if the requirements of paragraph (d)(2), (3), or (4) of this section are met with respect to that amount.

(2) *Application of a specified section 482 method.*—(i) *In general.*—An amount is excluded from the calculation of a net section 482 adjustment if the taxpayer establishes that both the specified method and documentation requirements of this paragraph (d)(2) are met with respect to that amount. For purposes of this paragraph (d), a method will be considered a specified method if it is described in the regulations under section 482 and the method applies to transactions of the type under review. An unspecified method is not considered a specified method. See §§ 1.482–3(e) and 1.482–4(d).

(ii) *Specified method requirement.*—(A) The specified method requirement is met if the taxpayer selects and applies a specified method in a reasonable manner. The taxpayer's selection and application of a specified method is reasonable only if, given the available data and the applicable pricing methods, the taxpayer reasonably concluded that the method (and its application of that method) provided the most reliable measure of an arm's length result under the principles of the best method rule of § 1.482-1(c). A taxpayer can reasonably conclude that a specified method provided the most reliable measure of an arm's length result only if it has made a reasonable effort to evaluate the potential applicability of the other specified methods in a manner consistent with the principles of the best method rule. The extent of this evaluation generally will depend on the nature of the available data, and it may vary from case to case and from method to method. This evaluation may not entail an exhaustive analysis or detailed application of each method. Rather, after a reasonably thorough search for relevant data, the taxpayer should consider which method would provide the most reliable measure of an arm's length result given that data. The nature of the available data may enable the taxpayer to conclude reasonably that a particular specified method provides a more reliable measure of an arm's length result than one or more of the other specified methods, and accordingly no further consideration of such other specified methods is needed. Further, it is not necessary for a taxpayer to conclude that the selected specified method provides a more reliable measure of an arm's length result than any unspecified method. For examples illustrating the selection of a specified method consistent with this paragraph (d)(2)(ii), see § 1.482-8. Whether the taxpayer's conclusion was reasonable must be determined from all the facts and circumstances. The factors relevant to this determination include the following:

(1) The experience and knowledge of the taxpayer, including all members of the taxpayer's controlled group.

(2) The extent to which reliable data was available and the data was analyzed in a reasonable manner. A taxpayer must engage in a reasonably thorough search for the data necessary to

determine which method should be selected and how it should be applied. In determining the scope of a reasonably thorough search for data, the expense of additional efforts to locate new data may be weighed against the likelihood of finding additional data that would improve the reliability of the results and the amount by which any new data would change the taxpayer's taxable income. Furthermore, a taxpayer must use the most current reliable data that is available before the end of the taxable year in question. Although the taxpayer is not required to search for relevant data after the end of the taxable year, the taxpayer must maintain as a principal document described in paragraph (d)(2)(iii)(B)(*9*) of this section any relevant data it obtains after the end of the taxable year but before the return is filed, if that data would help determine whether the taxpayer has reported its true taxable income.

(*3*) The extent to which the taxpayer followed the relevant requirements set forth in regulations under section 482 with respect to the application of the method.

(*4*) The extent to which the taxpayer reasonably relied on a study or other analysis performed by a professional qualified to conduct such a study or analysis, including an attorney, accountant, or economist. Whether the professional is an employee of, or related to, the taxpayer is not determinative in evaluating the reliability of that study or analysis, as long as the study or analysis is objective, thorough, and well reasoned. Such reliance is reasonable only if the taxpayer disclosed to the professional all relevant information regarding the controlled transactions at issue. A study or analysis that was reasonably relied upon in a prior year may reasonably be relied upon in the current year if the relevant facts and circumstances have not changed or if the study or analysis has been appropriately modified to reflect any change in facts and circumstances.

(*5*) If the taxpayer attempted to determine an arm's length result by using more than one uncontrolled comparable, whether the taxpayer arbitrarily selected a result that corresponds to an extreme point in the range of results derived from the uncontrolled comparables. Such a result generally would not likely be closest to an arm's length result. If the uncontrolled comparables that the taxpayer uses to determine an arm's length result are described in § 1.482-1(e)(2)(iii)(B), one reasonable method of selecting a point in the range would be that provided in § 1.482-1(e)(3).

(*6*) The extent to which the taxpayer relied on a transfer pricing methodology developed and applied pursuant to an Advance Pricing Agreement for a prior taxable year, or specifically approved by the Internal Revenue Service pursuant to a transfer pricing audit of the transactions at issue for a prior taxable year, provided that the taxpayer applied the approved method reasonably and consistently with its prior application, and the facts and circumstances surrounding the use of the method have not materially changed since the time of the IRS's action, or if the facts and circumstances have changed in a way that materially affects the reliability of the results, the taxpayer makes appropriate adjustments to reflect such changes.

(*7*) The size of a net transfer pricing adjustment in relation to the size of the controlled transaction out of which the adjustment arose.

(B) *Services cost method.*—A taxpayer's selection of the services cost method for certain services, described in § 1.482-9(b), and its application of that method to a controlled services transaction will be considered reasonable for purposes of the specified method requirement only if the taxpayer reasonably allocated and apportioned costs in accordance with § 1.482-9(k), and reasonably concluded that the controlled services transaction satisfies the requirements described in § 1.482-9(b)(2). Whether the taxpayer's conclusion was reasonable must be determined from all the facts and circumstances. The factors relevant to this determination include those described in paragraph (d)(2)(ii)(A) of this section, to the extent applicable.

(iii) *Documentation requirement.*—(A) *In general.*—The documentation requirement of this paragraph (d)(2)(iii) is met if the taxpayer maintains sufficient documentation to establish that the taxpayer reasonably concluded that, given the available data and the applicable pricing methods, the method (and its application of that method) provided the most reliable measure of an arm's length result under the principles of the best method rule in § 1.482-1(c), and provides that documentation to the Internal Revenue Service within 30 days of a request for it in connection with an examination of the taxable year to which the documentation relates. With the exception of the documentation described in paragraphs (d)(2)(iii)(B)(*9*) and (*10*) of this section, that documentation must be in existence when the return is filed. The district director may, in his discretion, excuse a minor or inadvertent failure to provide required documents, but only if the taxpayer has made a good faith effort to comply, and the taxpayer promptly remedies the failure when it becomes known. The required documentation is divided into two categories, principal documents and background documents as described in paragraphs (d)(2)(iii)(B) and (C) of this section.

(B) *Principal documents.*—The principal documents should accurately and completely describe the basic transfer pricing analysis conducted by the taxpayer. The documentation must include the following—

(*1*) An overview of the taxpayer's business, including an analysis of the economic and legal factors that affect the pricing of its property or services;

(*2*) A description of the taxpayer's organizational structure (including an organization chart) covering all related parties engaged in transactions potentially relevant under section 482, including foreign affiliates whose transactions directly or indirectly affect the pricing of property or services in the United States;

(*3*) Any documentation explicitly required by the regulations under section 482;

(*4*) A description of the method selected and an explanation of why that method was selected, including an evaluation of whether the regulatory conditions and requirements for application of that method, if any, were met;

(*5*) A description of the alternative methods that were considered and an explanation of why they were not selected;

(*6*) A description of the controlled transactions (including the terms of sale) and any internal data used to analyze those transactions. For example, if a profit split method is applied, the documentation must include a schedule providing the total income, costs, and assets (with adjustments for different accounting practices and currencies) for each controlled taxpayer participating in the relevant business activity and detailing the allocations of such items to that activity. Similarly, if a cost-based method (such as the cost plus method, the services cost method for certain services, or a comparable profits method with a cost-based profit level indicator) is applied, the documentation must include a description of the manner in which relevant costs are determined and are allocated and apportioned to the relevant controlled transaction.

(*7*) A description of the comparables that were used, how comparability was evaluated, and what (if any) adjustments were made;

(*8*) An explanation of the economic analysis and projections relied upon in developing the method. For example, if a profit split method is applied, the taxpayer must provide an explanation of the analysis undertaken to determine how the profits would be split;

(*9*) A description or summary of any relevant data that the taxpayer obtains after the end of the tax year and before filing a tax return, which would help determine if a taxpayer selected and applied a specified method in a reasonable manner; and

(*10*) A general index of the principal and background documents and a description of the recordkeeping system used for cataloging and accessing those documents.

(C) *Background documents.*—The assumptions, conclusions, and positions contained in principal documents ordinarily will be based on, and supported by, additional background documents. Documents that support the principal documentation may include the documents listed in § 1.6038A-3(c) that are not otherwise described in paragraph (d)(2)(iii)(B) of this section. Every document listed in those regulations may not be relevant to pricing determinations under the taxpayer's specific facts and circumstances and, therefore, each of those documents need not be maintained in all circumstances. Moreover, other documents not listed in those regulations may be necessary to establish that the taxpayer's method was selected and applied in the way that provided the most reliable measure of an arm's length result under the principles of the best method rule in § 1.482-1(c). Background documents need not be provided to the Internal Revenue Service in response to a request for principal documents. If the Internal Revenue Service subsequently requests background documents, a taxpayer must provide that documentation to the Internal Revenue Service within 30 days of the request. However, the district director may, in his discretion, extend the period for producing the background documentation.

(D) Satisfaction of the documentation requirements described in § 1.482-7(k)(2) for the purpose of complying with the rules for CSAs under § 1.482-7 also satisfies all of the documentation requirements listed in paragraph (d)(2)(iii)(B) of this section, except the requirements listed in paragraphs (d)(2)(iii)(B)(2) and (10) of this section, with respect to CSTs and PCTs described in § 1.482-7(b)(1)(i) and (ii), provided that the documentation also satisfies the requirements of paragraph (d)(2)(iii)(A) of this section.

(3) *Application of an unspecified method.*—(i) *In general.*—An adjustment is excluded from the calculation of a net section 482 adjustment if the taxpayer establishes that both the unspecified method and documentation requirements of this paragraph (d)(3) are met with respect to that amount.

(ii) *Unspecified method requirement.*—(A) *In general.*—If a method other than a specified method was applied, the unspecified method requirement is met if the requirements of paragraph (d)(3)(ii)(B) or (C) of this section, as appropriate, are met.

(B) *Specified method potentially applicable.*—If the transaction is of a type for which methods are specified in the regulations under section 482, then a taxpayer will be considered to have met the unspecified method requirement if the taxpayer reasonably concludes, given the available data, that none of the specified methods was likely to provide a reliable measure of an arm's length result, and that it selected and applied an unspecified method in a way that would likely provide a reliable measure of an arm's length result. A taxpayer can reasonably conclude that no specified method was likely to provide a reliable measure of an arm's length result only if it has made a reasonable effort to evaluate the potential applicability of the specified methods in a manner consistent with the principles of the best method rule. However, it is not necessary for a taxpayer to conclude that the selected method provides a more reliable measure of an arm's length result than any other unspecified method. Whether the taxpayer's conclusion was reasonable must be determined from all the facts and circumstances. The factors relevant to this conclusion include those set forth in paragraph (d)(2)(ii) of this section.

(C) *No specified method applicable.*—If the transaction is of a type for which no methods are specified in the regulations under section 482, then a taxpayer will be considered to have met the unspecified method requirement if it selected and applied an unspecified method in a reasonable manner. For purposes of this paragraph (d)(3)(ii)(C), a taxpayer's selection and application is reasonable if the taxpayer reasonably concludes that the method (and its application of that method) provided the most reliable measure of an arm's length result under the principles of the best method rule in §1.482-1(c). However, it is not necessary for a taxpayer to conclude that the selected method provides a more reliable measure of an arm's length result than any other unspecified method. Whether the taxpayer's conclusion was reasonable must be determined from all the facts and circumstances. The factors relevant to this conclusion include those set forth in paragraph (d)(2)(ii) of this section.

(iii) *Documentation requirement.*—(A) *In general.*—The documentation requirement of this paragraph (d)(3) is met if the taxpayer maintains sufficient documentation to establish that the unspecified method requirement of paragraph (d)(3)(ii) of this section is met and provides that documentation to the Internal Revenue Service within 30 days of a request for it. That documentation must be in existence when the return is filed. The district director may, in his discretion, excuse a minor or inadvertent failure to provide required documents, but only if the taxpayer has made a good faith effort to comply, and the taxpayer promptly remedies the failure when it becomes known.

(B) *Principal and background documents.*—See paragraphs (d)(2)(iii)(B) and (C) of this section for rules regarding these two categories of required documentation.

(4) *Certain foreign to foreign transactions.*—For purposes of calculating a net section 482 adjustment, any increase in taxable income resulting from an allocation under section 482 that is attributable to any controlled transaction solely between foreign corporations will be excluded unless the treatment of that transaction affects the determination of either corporation's income from sources within the United States or taxable income effectively connected with the conduct of a trade or business within the United States.

(5) *Special rule.*—If the regular tax (as defined in section 55(c)) imposed on the taxpayer is determined by reference to an amount other than taxable income, that amount shall be treated as the taxable income of the taxpayer for purposes of section 6662(e)(3). Accordingly, for taxpayers whose regular tax is determined by reference to an amount other than taxable income, the increase in that amount resulting from section 482 allocations is the taxpayer's net section 482 adjustment.

(6) *Examples.*—The principles of this paragraph (d) are illustrated by the following examples:

Example 1. (i) The Internal Revenue Service makes the following section 482 adjustments for the taxable year:

(1)	Attributable to an increase in gross income because of an increase in royalty payments .	$9,000,000
(2)	Not a 200 percent or 400 percent adjustment	2,000,000
(3)	Attributable to a decrease in the cost of goods sold because of a decrease in the cost plus mark-up of a realted seller	9,000,000
	Total section 482 adjustments	20,000,000

(ii) The taxpayer has gross receipts of 75 million dollars after all section 482 adjustments. The taxpayer establishes that for adjustments number one and three, it applied a transfer pricing method specified in section 482, the selection and application of the method was reasonable, it documented the pricing analysis, and turned that documentation over to the IRS within 30 days of a request. Accordingly, eighteen million dollars is excluded from the calculation of the net section 482 adjustment. Because the net section 482 adjustment is two million dollars, there is no substantial valuation misstatement.

Example 2. (i) The Internal Revenue Service makes the following section 482 adjustments for the taxable year:

(1)	Attributable to an increase in gross income because of an increase in royalty payments .	$9,000,000
(2)	Attributable to an adjustment that is 200 percent or more of the correct section 482 price	2,000,000
(3)	Attributable to a decrease in the cost of goods sold because of a decrease in the cost plus mark-up of a related seller	9,000,000
	Total section 482 adjustments	20,000,000

(ii) The taxpayer has gross receipts of 75 million dollars after all section 482 adjustments. The taxpayer establishes that for adjustments number one and three it applied a transfer pricing method specified in section 482, the selection and application of the method was reasonable, it documented that analysis, and turned the documentation over to the IRS within 30 days. Accordingly, eighteen million dollars is excluded from the calculation of the section 482 transfer pricing adjustments for purposes of applying the five million dollar or 10% of gross receipts test. Because the net section 482 adjustment is only two million dollars, the taxpayer is not subject to the net adjustment penalty. However, the taxpayer may be subject to the transactional penalty on the underpayment of tax attributable to the two million dollar adjustment.

Example 3. CFC1 and CFC2 are controlled foreign corporations within the meaning of section 957. Applying section 482, the IRS disallows a deduction for 25 million dollars of the interest that CFC1 paid to CFC2, which results in CFC1's U.S. shareholder having a subpart F inclusion in excess of five million dollars. No other adjustments under section 482 are made with respect to the controlled taxpayers. However, the increase has no effect upon the determination of CFC1's or CFC2's income from sources within the United States or taxable income effectively connected with the conduct of a trade or business within the United States. Accordingly, there is no substantial valuation misstatement.

(e) *Special rules in the case of carrybacks and carryovers.*—If there is a substantial or gross valuation misstatement for a taxable year that gives rise to a loss, deduction or credit that is carried to another taxable year, the transactional penalty and the net adjustment penalty will be imposed on any resulting underpayment of tax in that other taxable year. In determining whether there is a substantial or gross valuation misstatement for a taxable year, no amount carried from another taxable year shall be included. The following example illustrates the principle of this paragraph (e):

Example. The Internal Revenue Service makes a section 482 adjustment of six million dollars in taxable year 1, no portion of which is excluded under paragraph (d) of this section. The taxpayer's income tax return for year 1 reported a loss of three million dollars, which was carried to taxpayer's year 2 income tax return and used to reduce income taxes otherwise due with respect to year 2. A determination is made that the six million dollar allocation constitutes a substantial valuation misstatement, and a penalty is imposed on the underpayment of tax in year 1 attributable to the substantial valuation misstatement and on the underpayment of tax in year 2 attributable to the disallowance of the net operating loss in year 2. For purposes of determining whether there is a substantial or gross valuation misstatement for year 2, the three million dollar reduction of the net operating loss will not be added to any section 482 adjustments made with respect to year 2.

(f) *Rules for coordinating between the transactional penalty and the net adjustment penalty.*—(1) *Coordination of a net section 482 adjustment subject to the net adjustment penalty and a gross valuation misstatement subject to the transactional penalty.*—In determining whether a net section 482 adjustment exceeds five million dollars or 10 percent of gross receipts, an adjustment attributable to a substantial or gross valuation misstatement that is subject to the transactional penalty will be taken into account. If the net section 482 adjustment exceeds five million dollars or ten percent of gross receipts, any portion of such amount that is attributable to a gross valuation misstatement will be subject to the transactional penalty at the forty percent rate, but will not also be subject to net adjustment penalty at a twenty percent rate. The remaining amount is subject to the net adjustment penalty at the twenty percent rate, even if such amount is less than the lesser of five million dollars or ten percent of gross receipts.

(2) *Coordination of net section 482 adjustment subject to the net adjustment penalty and substantial valuation misstatements subject to the transactional penalty.*—If the net section 482 adjustment exceeds twenty million dollars or 20 percent of gross receipts, the entire amount of the adjustment is subject to the net adjustment penalty at a forty percent rate. No portion of the adjustment is subject to the transactional penalty at a twenty percent rate.

(3) *Examples.*—The following examples illustrate the principles of this paragraph (f):

Example 1. (i) Applying section 482, the Internal Revenue Service makes the following adjustments for the taxable year:

(1) Attributable to an adjustment that is 400 percent or more of the correct section 482 arm's length result	$2,000,000
(2) Not a 200 or 400 percent adjustment	2,500,000
Total	4,500,000

(ii) The taxpayer has gross receipts of 75 million dollars after all section 482 adjustments. None of the adjustments is excluded under paragraph (d) (Amounts excluded from net section 482 adjustments) of this section, in determining the five million dollar or 10% of gross receipts test under section 6662(e)(1)(B)(ii). The net section 482 adjustment (4.5 million dollars) is less than the lesser of five million dollars or ten percent of gross receipts ($75 million × 10% = $7.5 million). Thus, there is no substantial valuation misstatement. However, the two million dollar adjustment is attributable to a gross valuation misstatement. Accordingly, the taxpayer may be subject to a penalty, under section 6662(h), equal to 40 percent of the underpayment of tax attributable to the gross valuation misstatement of two million dollars. The 2.5 million dollar adjustment is not subject to a penalty under section 6662(b)(3).

Example 2. The facts are the same as in *Example 1*, except the taxpayer has gross receipts of 40 million dollars. The net section 482 adjustment ($4.5 million) is greater than the lesser of five million dollars or ten percent of gross receipts ($40 million × 10% = $4 million). Thus, the five million dollar or 10% of gross receipts test has been met. The two million dollar adjustment is attributable to a gross valuation misstatement. Accordingly, the taxpayer is subject to a penalty, under section 6662(h), equal to 40 percent of the underpayment of tax attributable to the gross valuation misstatement of two million dollars. The 2.5 million dollar adjustment is subject to a penalty under sections 6662(a) and 6662(b)(3), equal to 20 percent of the underpayment of tax attributable to the substantial valuation misstatement.

Example 3. (i) Applying section 482, the Internal Revenue Service makes the following transfer pricing adjustments for the taxable year:

(1) Attributable to an adjustment that is 400 percent or more of the correct section 482 arm's length result	$6,000,000
(2) Not a 200 or 400 percent adjustment	15,000,000
Total	21,000,000

(ii) None of the adjustments are excluded under paragraph (d) (Amounts excluded from net section 482 adjustments) in determining the twenty million dollar or 20% of gross receipts test under section 6662(h). The net section 482 adjustment (21 million dollars) is greater than twenty million dollars and thus constitutes a gross valuation misstatement. Accordingly, the total adjustment is subject to the net adjustment penalty equal to 40 percent of the underpayment of tax attributable to the 21 million dollar gross valuation misstatement. The six million dollar adjustment will not be separately included for purposes of any additional penalty under section 6662.

(g) *Effective/applicability date.*—(1) *In general.*—This section is generally applicable on February 9, 1996. However, taxpayers may elect to apply this section to all open taxable years beginning after December 31, 1993.

(2) *Special rules.*—The provisions of paragraphs (d)(2)(ii)(B), (d)(2)(iii)(B)(*4*) and (d)(2)(iii)(B)(*6*) of this section are applicable for taxable years beginning after July 31, 2009. However, taxpayers may elect to apply the provisions of paragraphs (d)(2)(ii)(B), (d)(2)(iii)(B)(*4*) and (d)(2)(iii)(B)(*6*) of this section to earlier taxable years in accordance with the rules set forth in § 1.482-9(n)(2). [Reg. § 1.6662-6.]

☐ [*T.D.* 8656, 2-8-96. *Amended by T.D.* 9278, 7-31-2006; *T.D.* 9441, 12-31-2008; *T.D.* 9456, 7-31-2009 *and T.D.* 9568, 12-16-2011.]

§ 1.6662-7. Omnibus Budget Reconciliation Act of 1993 changes to the accuracy-related penalty.—(a) *Scope.*—The Omnibus Budget Reconciliation Act of 1993 made certain changes to the accuracy-related penalty in section 6662. This section provides rules reflecting those changes.

(b) *No disclosure exception for negligence penalty.*—The penalty for negligence in section 6662(b)(1) may not be avoided by disclosure of a return position.

(c) *Disclosure standard for other penalties is reasonable basis.*—The penalties for disregarding rules or regulations in section 6662(b)(1) and for a substantial understatement of income tax in section 6662(b)(2) may be avoided by adequate disclosure of a return position only if the position has at least a reasonable basis. See § 1.6662-3(c) and §§ 1.6662-4(e) and (f) for other applicable disclosure rules.

(d) *Reasonable basis.*—For purposes of §§ 1.6662-3(c) and 1.6662-4(e) and (f) (relating to methods of making adequate disclosure), the provisions of § 1.6662-3(b)(3) apply in determining whether a return position has a reasonable basis. [Reg. § 1.6662-7.]

☐ [*T.D.* 8617, 8-31-95. *Amended by T.D.* 8790, 12-1-98.]

§ 1.6664-4T. Reasonable cause and good faith exception to section 6662 penalties.—(a) through (e) [Reserved].

(f) *Transactions between persons described in section 482 and net section 482 transfer price adjustments.*—For purposes of applying the reasonable cause and good faith exception of section 6664(c) to net section 482 adjustments, the rules of § 1.6662-6(d) apply. A taxpayer that does not satisfy the rules of § 1.6662-6(d) for a net section 482 adjustment cannot satisfy the reasonable cause and good faith exception under section 6664(c). The rules of this section apply to underpayments subject to the transactional penalty in § 1.6662-6(b). If the standards of the net section 482 penalty exclusion provisions under § 1.6662-6(d) are met with respect to such underpayments, then the taxpayer will be considered to have acted with reasonable cause and good faith for purposes of this section. [Temporary Reg. § 1.6664-4T.]

☐ [*T.D.* 8519, 1-27-94. *Amended by T.D.* 8656, 2-8-96.]

§ 301.6689-1. Failure to file notice of redetermination of foreign income taxes.—(a) *Application of civil penalty.*—If a foreign tax redetermination occurs, and the taxpayer failed to notify the Internal Revenue Service (IRS) on or before the date and in the manner prescribed in § 1.905-4 of this chapter, or as required under section 404A(g)(2), for giving notice of a foreign tax redetermination, then, unless paragraph (d) of this section applies, there is added to the deficiency (or the imputed underpayment as determined under section 6225) attributable to such redetermination an amount determined under paragraph (b) of this section. Subchapter B of chapter 63 of the Internal Revenue Code (relating to deficiency proceedings) does not apply with respect to the assessment of the amount of the penalty.

(b) *Amount of the penalty.*—The amount of the penalty shall be equal to—

(1) Five percent of the deficiency (or imputed underpayment) if the failure is for not more than one month; plus

(2) An additional five percent of the deficiency (or imputed underpayment) for each month (or fraction thereof) during which the failure continues, but not to exceed in the aggregate twenty-five percent of the deficiency (or imputed underpayment).

(c) *Foreign tax redetermination defined.*—For purposes of this section, a foreign tax redetermination is any redetermination for which a notice is required under sections 905(c) or 404A(g)(2). See §§ 1.905-3 through 1.905-5 of this chapter for rules relating to the notice requirement under section 905(c).

(d) *Reasonable cause.*—The penalty set forth in this section shall not apply if it is established to the satisfaction of the IRS that the failure to file the notification within the prescribed time was due to reasonable cause and not due to willful neglect. An affirmative showing of reasonable cause must be made in the form of a written statement that sets forth all the facts alleged as reasonable cause for the failure to file the notification on time and that contains a declaration by the taxpayer that the statement is made under the penalties of perjury. This statement must be filed with the Internal Revenue Service Center in which the notification was required to be filed. The taxpayer must file this statement with the notice required under section 905(c) or 404A(g)(2). If the taxpayer exercised ordinary business care and prudence and was nevertheless unable to file the notification within the prescribed time, then the delay will be considered to be due to reasonable cause and not willful neglect.

(e) *Applicability date.*—This section applies to foreign tax redeterminations occurring in taxable years ending on or after December 16, 2019, and to foreign tax redeterminations of foreign corporations occurring in taxable years that end with or within a taxable year of a United States shareholder ending on or after December 16, 2019. [Reg. § 301.6689-1.]

☐ [*T.D.* 9922, 11-2-2020.]

Departing Aliens

§1.6851-2. Certificates of compliance with income tax laws by departing aliens.—(a) *In general.*—(1) *Requirement.*—The rules of this section are applicable, except as otherwise expressly provided, to any alien who departs from the United States or any of its possessions after January 20, 1961. Except as provided in subparagraph (2) of this paragraph, no such alien, whether resident or nonresident, may depart from the United States unless he first procures a certificate that he has complied with all of the obligations imposed upon him by the income tax laws. In order to procure such a certificate, an alien who intends to depart from the United States (i) must file with the district director for the internal revenue district in which he is located the statements or returns required by paragraph (b) of this section to be filed before obtaining such certificate, (ii) must appear before such district director if the district director deems it necessary, and (iii) must pay any taxes required under paragraph (b) of this section to be paid before obtaining the certificate. Either such certificate of compliance, properly executed, or evidence that the alien is excepted under subparagraph (2) of this paragraph from obtaining the certificate must be presented at the point of departure. An alien who presents himself at the point of departure without a certificate of compliance, or evidence establishing that such a certificate is not required, will be subject at such departure point to examination by an internal revenue officer or employee and to the completion of returns and statements and payment of taxes as required by paragraph (b) of this section.

(2) *Exceptions.*—(i) *Employees of foreign governments or international organizations.*—*(a) Diplomatic representatives, their families and servants.*—*(1)* Representatives of foreign governments bearing diplomatic passports, whether accredited to the United States or other countries, and members of their households shall not, upon departure from the United States or any of its possessions, be examined as to their liability for United States income tax or be required to obtain a certificate of compliance. If a foreign government does not issue diplomatic passports but merely indicates on passports issued to members of its diplomatic service the status of the bearer as a member of such service, such passports are considered as diplomatic passports for income tax purposes.

(2) Likewise, the servant of a diplomatic representative who accompanies any individual bearing a diplomatic passport upon departure from the United States or any of its possessions shall not be required, upon such departure, to obtain a certificate of compliance or to submit to examination as to his liability for United States income tax. If the departure of such a servant from the United States or any of its possessions is not made in the company of an individual bearing a diplomatic passport, the servant is required to obtain a certificate of compliance. However, such certificate will be issued to him on Form 2063 without examination as to his income tax liability upon presentation to the district director for the internal revenue district in which the servant is located of a letter from the chief of the diplomatic mission to which the servant is attached certifying *(i)* that the name of the servant appears on the "White List," a list of employees of diplomatic missions, and *(ii)* that the servant is not obligated to the United States for any income tax, and will not be so obligated up to and including the intended date of departure.

(b) Other employees.—Any employee of an international organization or of a foreign government (other than a diplomatic representative to whom *(a)* of this subdivision applies) whose compensation for official services rendered to such organization or government is excluded from gross income under section 893 and who has received no gross income from sources within the United States, and any member of his household who has received no gross income from sources within the United States, shall not, upon departure from the United States or any of its possessions after November 30, 1962 be examined as to his liability for United States income tax or be required to obtain a certificate of compliance.

(c) Effect of waiver.—An alien who has filed with the Attorney General the waiver provided for under section 247(b) of the Immigration and Nationality Act (8 U.S.C. 1257(b)) is not entitled to the exception provided by this subdivision.

(ii) *Alien students, industrial trainees, and exchange visitors.*—A certificate of compliance shall not be required, and examination as to United States income tax liability shall not be made, upon the departure from the United States or any of its possessions of—

(A) An alien student, industrial trainee, or exchange visitor, and any spouse and children of that alien, admitted solely on an F-1, F-2, H-3, H-4, J-1 or J-2 visa, who has received no gross income from sources inside the United States other than—

(1) Allowances to cover expenses incident to study or training in the United States (including expenses for travel, maintenance, and tuition);

(2) The value of any services or accommodations furnished incident to such study or training;

(3) Income derived in accordance with the employment authorizations in 8 CFR 274a.12(b) and (c) that apply to the alien's visa; or

(4) Interest on deposits described in section 871(i)(2)(A); or

(B) An alien student, and any spouse or children of that alien admitted solely on an M-1 or M-2 visa, who has received no gross income from sources inside the United States other than income derived in accordance with the employment authorization in 8 CFR 274a.12(c)(6) or interest on deposits described in section 871(i)(2)(A).

(b) *Issuance of certificate of compliance.*—(1) *In general.*—(i) Upon the departure of an alien required to secure a certificate of compliance under paragraph (a) of this section, the district director shall determine whether the departure of such alien jeopardizes the collection of any income tax for the current or the preceding taxable year, but the district director may determine that jeopardy does not exist in some cases. If the district director finds that the departure of such an alien results in jeopardy, the taxable period of the alien will be terminated, and the alien will be required to file returns and make payment of tax in accordance with subparagraph (3)(iii) of this paragraph. On the other hand, if the district director finds that the departure of the alien does not result in jeopardy, the alien will be required to file the statement on returns required by subparagraph (2) or (3)(ii) of this paragraph, but will not be required to pay income tax before the usual time for payment.

(ii) The departure of an alien who is a resident of the United States or a possession thereof (or treated as a resident under section 6013(g) or (h)) and who intends to continue such residence (or treatment as a resident) shall be treated as not resulting in jeopardy, and thus not requiring termination of his taxable period, except when the district director has information indicating that the alien intends by such departure to avoid the payment of his income tax. In the case of a nonresident alien (including a resident alien discontinuing residence), the fact that the alien intends to depart from the United States will justify termination of his taxable period unless the alien establishes to the satisfaction of the district director that he intends to return to the United States and that his departure will not jeopardize collection of the tax. The determination of whether the departure of the alien results in jeopardy will be made on examination of all the facts in the case. Evidence tending to establish that jeopardy does not result from the departure of the alien may be provided, for example, by information showing that the alien is engaged in trade or business in the United States or that he leaves sufficient property in the United States to secure payment of his income tax for the taxable year and of any income tax for the preceding year which remains unpaid.

(2) *Alien having no taxable income and resident alien whose taxable period is not terminated.*—A statement on Form 2063 shall be filed with the district director by every alien required to obtain a certificate of compliance—

(i) Who is a resident of the United States and whose taxable period is not terminated either because he has had no taxable income for the taxable year up to and including the date of his departure (and for the preceding taxable year where the period for making the income tax return for such year has not expired) or because, although he has had taxable income for such period or periods, the district director has not found that his departure jeopardizes collection of the tax on such income; or

(ii) Who is not a resident of the United States and who has had no taxable income for the taxable year up to and including the date of his departure (and for the preceding taxable year where the period for making the income tax return for such year has not expired).

Any alien described in subdivision (i) or (ii) of this subparagraph who is in default in making return of, or paying, income tax for any taxable year shall, in addition, file with the district director any returns which have not been made as required and pay to the district director the amount of any tax for which he is in default. Upon compliance by an alien with the foregoing requirements of this subparagraph, the district director shall execute and issue to the alien the certificate of compliance attached to Form 2063. The certificate of compliance so issued shall be effective for all departures of the alien during his current taxable year, subject to revocation upon any subsequent departure should the district director have reason to believe that such subsequent departure would result in jeopardy. The statement required of a resident alien under this subparagraph, if made before January 21, 1961, with respect to a departure after January 20, 1961, may be made on a Form 1040C in lieu of a Form 2063.

(3) *Nonresident alien having taxable income and resident alien whose taxable period is terminated.*—(i) *Nonresident alien having taxable income.*—Every nonresident alien required to obtain a certificate of compliance (but not described in subparagraph (2) of this paragraph) who wishes to establish that his departure does not result in jeopardy shall furnish to the district director such information as may be required for the purpose of determining whether the departure of the alien jeopardizes collection of the income tax and thus requires termination of his taxable period.

(ii) *Nonresident alien whose taxable period is not terminated.*—Every nonresident alien described in subdivision (i) of this subparagraph whose taxable period is not terminated upon departure shall file with the district director—

(*a*) A return in duplicate on Form 1040C for the taxable year of his intended departure, showing income received, and reasonably expected to be received, during the entire taxable year within which the departure occurs; and

(*b*) Any income tax returns which have not been filed as required.

Upon compliance by the alien with the foregoing requirements of this subdivision, and the payment of any income tax for which he is in default, the district director shall execute and issue to the alien the certificate of compliance on the duplicate copy of Form 1040C. The certificate of compliance so issued shall be effective for all departures of the alien during his current taxable year, subject to revocation by the district director upon any subsequent departure if the taxable period of the alien is terminated on such subsequent departure.

(iii) *Alien (whether resident or nonresident) whose taxable period is terminated.*—Every alien required to obtain a certificate of compliance, whether resident or nonresident, whose taxable period is terminated upon departure shall file with the district director—

(*a*) A return in duplicate on Form 1040C for the short taxable period resulting from such termination, showing income received, and reasonably expected to be received, during the taxable year up to and including the date of departure;

(*b*) Where the period for filing has not expired, the return required under section 6012 and § 1.6012-1 for the preceding taxable years; and

(*c*) Any other income tax returns which have not been filed as required.

Upon compliance with the foregoing requirements of this subdivision, and payment of the income tax required to be shown on the returns filed pursuant to (*a*) and (*b*) of this subdivision and of any income tax due and owing for prior years, the departing alien will be issued the certificate of compliance on the duplicate copy of Form 1040C. The certificate of compliance so issued shall be effective only for the specific departure with respect to which it is issued. A departing alien may postpone payment of the tax required to be shown on the returns filed in accordance with (*a*) and (*b*) of this subdivision until the usual time of payment by furnishing a bond as provided in § 301.6863-1 of this chapter (regulations on procedure and administration).

(4) *Joint return on Form 1040C.*—A departing alien may not file a joint return on Form 1040C unless—

(i) Such alien and his spouse may reasonably be expected to be eligible to file a joint return at the normal close of their taxable periods for which the return is made; and

(ii) If the taxable period of such alien is terminated, the taxable periods of both spouses are so terminated as to end at the same time.

(5) *Annual return.*—Notwithstanding that Form 1040C has been filed for either the entire taxable year of departure or for a terminated period, the return required under section 6012 and § 1.6012-1 for such taxable year shall be filed. Any income tax paid on income shown on the return on Form 1040C shall be applied against the tax determined to be due on the income required to be shown on the subsequent return under section 6012 and § 1.6012-1. [Reg. § 1.6851-2.]

☐ [*T.D.* 6426, 11-30-59. *Amended by T.D.* 6537, 1-19-61; *T.D.* 6620, 11-29-62; *T.D.* 7575, 12-15-78; *T.D.* 7670, 1-30-80; *T.D.* 8332, 1-25-91 *and T.D.* 8526, 3-2-94.]

Definitions

§ 301.7701-1. Classification of organizations for federal tax purposes.—(a) *Organizations for federal tax purposes.*—(1) *In general.*—The Internal Revenue Code prescribes the classification of various organizations for federal tax purposes. Whether an organization is an entity separate from its owners for federal tax purposes is a matter of federal tax law and does not depend on whether the organization is recognized as an entity under local law.

(2) *Certain joint undertakings give rise to entities for federal tax purposes.*—A joint venture or other contractual arrangement may create a separate entity for federal tax purposes if the participants carry on a trade, business, financial operation, or venture and divide the profits therefrom. For example, a separate entity exists for federal tax purposes if co-owners of an apartment building lease space and in addition provide services to the occupants either directly or through an agent. Nevertheless, a joint undertaking merely to share expenses does not create a separate entity for federal tax purposes. For example, if two or more persons jointly construct a ditch merely to drain surface water from their properties, they have not created a separate entity for federal tax purposes. Similarly, mere co-ownership of property that is maintained, kept in repair, and rented or leased does not constitute a separate entity for federal tax purposes. For example, if an individual owner, or tenants in common, of farm property lease it to a farmer for a cash rental or a share of the crops, they do not necessarily create a separate entity for federal tax purposes.

(3) *Certain local law entities not recognized.*—An entity formed under local law is not always recognized as a separate entity for federal tax purposes. For example, an organization wholly owned by a State is not recognized as a separate entity for federal tax purposes if it is an integral part of the State. Similarly, tribes incorporated under section 17 of the Indian Reorganization Act of 1934, as amended, 25 U.S.C. 477, or under section 3 of the Oklahoma Indian Welfare Act, as amended, 25 U.S.C. 503, are not recognized as separate entities for federal tax purposes.

(4) *Single owner organizations.*—Under §§ 301.7701-2 and 301.7701-3, certain organizations that have a single owner can choose to be recognized or disregarded as entities separate from their owners.

(b) *Classification of organizations.*—The classification of organizations that are recognized as separate entities is determined under §§301.7701-2, 301.7701-3, and 301.7701-4 unless a provision of the Internal Revenue Code (such as section 860A addressing Real Estate Mortgage Investment Conduits (REMICs)) provides for special treatment of that organization. For the classification of organizations as trusts, see §301.7701-4. That section provides that trusts generally do not have associates or an objective to carry on business for profit. Sections 301.7701-2 and 301.7701-3 provide rules for classifying organizations that are not classified as trusts.

(c) *Cost sharing arrangements.*—A cost sharing arrangement that is described in §1.482-7 of this chapter, including any arrangement that the Commissioner treats as a CSA under §1.482-7(b)(5) of this chapter, is not recognized as a separate entity for purposes of the Internal Revenue Code. See §1.482-7 of this chapter for the rules regarding CSAs.

(d) *Domestic and foreign business entities.*—See §301.7701-5 for the rules that determine whether a business entity is domestic or foreign.

(e) *State.*—For purposes of this section and §301.7701-2, the term *State* includes the District of Columbia.

(f) *Effective/applicability dates.*—Except as provided in the following sentence, the rules of this section are applicable as of January 1, 1997. The rules of paragraph (c) of this section are applicable on January 5, 2009. [Reg. §301.7701-1.]

☐ [*T.D.* 6503, 11-15-80. *Amended by T.D.* 6797, 2-2-65; *T.D.* 7515, 10-17-77; *T.D.* 8697, 12-17-96; *T.D.* 9153, 8-11-2004; *T.D.* 9246, 1-27-2006; *T.D.* 9441, 12-31-2008 *and T.D.* 9568, 12-16-2011.]

Proposed Amendments to Regulation

§301.7701-1. Classification of organizations for Federal tax purposes.—(a) * * *

(5) *Series and series organizations.*—(i) *Entity status of a domestic series.*—For Federal tax purposes, except as provided in paragraph (a)(5)(ix) of this section, a series (as defined in paragraph (a)(5)(viii)(C) of this section) organized or established under the laws of the United States or of any State, whether or not a juridical person for local law purposes, is treated as an entity formed under local law.

(ii) *Certain foreign series conducting an insurance business.*—For Federal tax purposes, except as provided in paragraph (a)(5)(ix) of this section, a series organized or established under the laws of a foreign jurisdiction is treated as an entity formed under local law if the arrangements and other activities of the series, if conducted by a domestic company, would result in classification as an insurance company within the meaning of section 816(a) or section 831(c).

(iii) *Recognition of entity status.*—Whether a series that is treated as a local law entity under paragraph (a)(5)(i) or (ii) of this section is recognized as a separate entity for Federal tax purposes is determined under this section and general tax principles.

(iv) *Classification of series.*—The classification of a series that is recognized as a separate entity for Federal tax purposes is determined under paragraph (b) of this section.

(v) *Jurisdiction in which series is organized or established.*—A series is treated as created or organized under the laws of a State or foreign jurisdiction if the series is established under the laws of such jurisdiction. See §301.7701-5 for rules that determine whether a business entity is domestic or foreign.

(vi) *Ownership of series and the assets of series.*—For Federal tax purposes, the ownership of interests in a series and of the assets associated with a series is determined under general tax principles. A series organization is not treated as the owner for Federal tax purposes of a series or of the assets associated with a series merely because the series organization holds legal title to the assets associated with the series.

(vii) *Effect of Federal and local law treatment.*—To the extent that, pursuant to the provisions of this paragraph (a)(5), a series is a taxpayer against whom tax may be assessed under Chapter 63 of Title 26, then any tax assessed against the series may be collected by the Internal Revenue Service from the series in the same manner the assessment could be collected by the Internal Revenue Service from any other taxpayer. In addition, to the extent Federal or local law permits a debt attributable to the series to be collected from the series organization or other series of the series organization, then, notwithstanding any other provision of this paragraph (a)(5), and consistent with the provisions of Federal or local law, the series organization and other series of the series organization may also be considered the taxpayer from whom the tax assessed against the series may be administratively or judicially collected. Further, when a creditor is permitted to collect a liability attributable to a series organization from any series of the series organization, a tax liability assessed against the series organization may be collected directly from a series of the series organization by administrative or judicial means.

(viii) *Definitions.*—(A) *Series organization.*—A *series organization* is a juridical entity that establishes and maintains, or under which is established and maintained, a series (as defined in paragraph (a)(5)(viii)(C) of this section). A series organization includes a series limited liability company, series partnership, series trust, protected cell company, segregated cell company, segregated portfolio company, or segregated account company.

(B) *Series statute.*—A *series statute* is a statute of a State or foreign jurisdiction that explicitly provides for the organization or establishment of a series of a juridical person and explicitly permits—

(1) Members or participants of a series organization to have rights, powers, or duties with respect to the series;

(2) A series to have separate rights, powers, or duties with respect to specified property or obligations; and

(3) The segregation of assets and liabilities such that none of the debts and liabilities of the series organization (other than liabilities to the State or foreign jurisdiction related to the organization or operation of the series organization, such as franchise fees or administrative costs) or of any other series of the series organization are enforceable against the assets of a particular series of the series organization.

(C) *Series.*—A *series* is a segregated group of assets and liabilities that is established pursuant to a series statute (as defined in paragraph (a)(5)(viii)(B) of this section) by agreement of a series organization (as defined in paragraph (a)(5)(viii)(A) of this section). A series includes a series, cell, segregated account, or segregated portfolio, including a cell, segregated account, or segregated portfolio that is formed under the insurance code of a jurisdiction or is engaged in an insurance business. However, the term *series* does not include a segregated asset account of a life insurance company. See section 817(d)(1); §1.817-5(e). An election, agreement, or other arrangement that permits debts and liabilities of other series or the series organization to be enforceable against the assets of a particular series, or a failure to comply with the record keeping requirements for the limitation on liability available under the relevant series statute, will be disregarded for purposes of this paragraph (a)(5)(viii)(C).

(ix) *Treatment of series and series organizations under Subtitle C - Employment Taxes and Collection of Income Tax (Chapters 21, 22, 23, 23A, 24 and 25 of the Internal Revenue Code).*—[Reserved.]

(x) *Examples.*—The following examples illustrate the principles of this paragraph (a)(5):

Example 1. Domestic Series LLC. (i) *Facts.* Series LLC is a series organization (within the meaning of paragraph (a)(5)(viii)(A) of this section). Series LLC has three members (1, 2, and 3). Series LLC establishes two series (A and B) pursuant to the LLC statute of state Y, a series statute within the meaning of paragraph (a)(5)(viii)(B) of this section. Under general tax principles, Members 1 and 2 are the owners of Series A, and Member 3 is the owner of Series B. Series A and B are not described in §301.7701-2(b) or paragraph (a)(3) of this section and are not trusts within the meaning of §301.7701-4.

(ii) *Analysis.* Under paragraph (a)(5)(i) of this section, Series A and Series B are each treated as an entity formed under local law. The classification of Series A and Series B is determined under paragraph (b) of this section. The default classification under §301.7701-3 of Series A is a partnership and of Series B is a disregarded entity.

Example 2. Foreign Insurance Cell. (i) *Facts.* Insurance CellCo is a series organization (within the meaning of paragraph (a)(5)(viii)(A) of this section) organized under the laws of foreign Country X. Insurance CellCo has established one cell, Cell A, pursuant to a Country X law that is a series statute (within the meaning of paragraph (a)(5)(viii)(B) of this section). More than half the business of Cell A during the taxable year is the issuing of insurance or annuity contracts or the reinsuring of risks underwritten by insurance companies. If the activities of Cell A were conducted by a domestic company, that company would qualify as an insurance company within the meaning of sections 816(a) and 831(c).

(ii) *Analysis.* Under paragraph (a)(5)(ii) of this section, Cell A is treated as an entity formed under local law. Because Cell A is an insurance company, it is classified as a corporation under § 301.7701-2(b)(4).

* * *

(e) *State.*—For purposes of this section and §§ 301.7701-2 and 301.7701-4, the term *State* includes the District of Columbia.

(f) *Effective/applicability dates.*—(1) *In general.*—Except as provided in paragraphs (f)(2) and (f)(3) of this section, the rules of this section are applicable as of January 1, 1997.

(2) *Cost sharing arrangements.*—The rules of paragraph (c) of this section are applicable on January 5, 2009.

(3) *Series and series organizations.*—(i) *In general.*—Except as otherwise provided in this paragraph (f)(3), paragraph (a)(5) of this section applies on and after the date final regulations are published in the **Federal Register**.

(ii) *Transition rule.*—(A) *In general.*—Except as provided in paragraph (f)(3)(ii)(B) of this section, a taxpayer's treatment of a series in a manner inconsistent with the final regulations will be respected on and after the date final regulations are published in the **Federal Register**, provided that—

(1) The series was established prior to September 14, 2010;

(2) The series (independent of the series organization or other series of the series organization) conducted business or investment activity, or, in the case of a series established pursuant to a foreign statute, more than half the business of the series was the issuing of insurance or annuity contracts or the reinsuring of risks underwritten by insurance companies, on and prior to September 14, 2010;

(3) If the series was established pursuant to a foreign statute, the series' classification was relevant (as defined in § 301.7701-3(d)), and more than half the business of the series was the issuing of insurance or annuity contracts or the reinsuring of risks underwritten by insurance companies for all taxable years beginning with the taxable year that includes September 14, 2010;

(4) No owner of the series treats the series as an entity separate from any other series of the series organization or from the series organization for purposes of filing any Federal income tax returns, information returns, or withholding documents in any taxable year;

(5) The series and series organization had a reasonable basis (within the meaning of section 6662) for their claimed classification; and

(6) Neither the series nor any owner of the series nor the series organization was notified in writing on or before the date final regulations are published in the **Federal Register** that classification of the series was under examination (in which case the series' classification will be determined in the examination).

(B) *Exception to transition rule.*—Paragraph (f)(3)(ii)(A) of this section will not apply on and after the date any person or persons who were not owners of the series organization (or series) prior to September 14, 2010 own, in the aggregate, a fifty percent or greater interest in the series organization (or series). For purposes of the preceding sentence, the term *interest* means—

(1) In the case of a partnership, a capital or profits interest; and

(2) In the case of a corporation, an equity interest measured by vote or value.

Prop. Reg. § 301.7701-1.]

[Proposed 9-14-2010.]

§ 301.7701-2. Business entities; definitions.—(a) *Business entities.*—For purposes of this section and § 301.7701-3, a *business entity* is any entity recognized for federal tax purposes (including an entity with a single owner that may be disregarded as an entity separate from its owner under § 301.7701-3) that is not properly classified as a trust under § 301.7701-4 or otherwise subject to special treatment under the Internal Revenue Code. A business entity with two or more members is classified for federal tax purposes as either a corporation or a partnership. A business entity with only one owner is classified as a corporation or is disregarded; if the entity is disregarded, its activities are treated in the same manner as a sole proprietorship, branch, or division of the owner. But see paragraphs (c)(2)(iii) through (vi) of this section for special rules that apply to an eligible entity that is otherwise disregarded as an entity separate from its owner.

(b) *Corporations.*—For federal tax purposes, the term *corporation* means—

(1) A business entity organized under a Federal or State statute, or under a statute of a federally recognized Indian tribe, if the statute describes or refers to the entity as incorporated or as a corporation, body corporate, or body politic;

(2) An association (as determined under § 301.7701-3);

(3) A business entity organized under a State statute, if the statute describes or refers to the entity as a joint-stock company or joint-stock association;

(4) An insurance company;

(5) A State-chartered business entity conducting banking activities, if any of its deposits are insured under the Federal Deposit Insurance Act, as amended, 12 U.S.C. 1811 et seq., or a similar federal statute;

(6) A business entity wholly owned by a State or any political subdivision thereof, or a business entity wholly owned by a foreign government or any other entity described in § 1.892-2T;

(7) A business entity that is taxable as a corporation under a provision of the Internal Revenue Code other than section 7701(a)(3); and

(8) *Certain foreign entities.*—(i) *In general.*—Except as provided in paragraphs (b)(8)(ii) and (d) of this section, the following business entities formed in the following jurisdictions:

American Samoa, Corporation
Argentina, Sociedad Anonima
Australia, Public Limited Company
Austria, Aktiengesellschaft
Barbados, Limited Company
Belgium, Societe Anonyme
Belize, Public Limited Company
Bolivia, Sociedad Anonima
Brazil, Sociedade Anonima
Bulgaria, Aktsionerno Druzhestvo
Canada, Corporation and Company
Chile, Sociedad Anonima
People's Republic of China, Gufen Youxian Gongsi
Republic of China (Taiwan), Ku-fen Yu-hsien Kung-szu
Colombia, Sociedad Anonima
Costa Rica, Sociedad Anonima
Cyprus, Public Limited Company
Czech Republic, Akciova Spolecnost
Denmark, Aktieselskab
Ecuador, Sociedad Anonima or Compania Anonima
Egypt, Sharikat Al-Mossahamah
El Salvador, Sociedad Anonima
Estonia, Aktsiaselts
European Economic Area/European Union, Societas Europaea
Finland, Julkinen Osakeyhtio/Publikt Aktiebolag
France, Societe Anonyme
Germany, Aktiengesellschaft
Greece, Anonymos Etairia
Guam, Corporation
Guatemala, Sociedad Anonima
Guyana, Public Limited Company
Honduras, Sociedad Anonima
Hong Kong, Public Limited Company
Hungary, Reszvenytarsasag
Iceland, Hlutafelag
India, Public Limited Company
Indonesia, Perseroan Terbuka
Ireland, Public Limited Company
Israel, Public Limited Company
Italy, Societa per Azioni
Jamaica, Public Limited Company
Japan, Kabushiki Kaisha
Kazakstan, Ashyk Aktsionerlik Kogham

Republic of Korea, Chusik Hoesa
Latvia, Akciju Sabiedriba
Liberia, Corporation
Liechtenstein, Aktiengesellschaft
Lithuania, Akcine Bendroves
Luxembourg, Societe Anonyme
Malaysia, Berhad
Malta, Public Limited Company
Mexico, Sociedad Anonima
Morocco, Societe Anonyme
Netherlands, Naamloze Vennootschap
New Zealand, Limited Company
Nicaragua, Compania Anonima
Nigeria, Public Limited Company
Northern Mariana Islands, Corporation
Norway, Allment Aksjeselskap
Pakistan, Public Limited Company
Panama, Sociedad Anonima
Paraguay, Sociedad Anonima
Peru, Sociedad Anonima
Philippines, Stock Corporation
Poland, Spolka Akcyjna
Portugal, Sociedade Anonima
Puerto Rico, Corporation
Romania, Societate pe Actiuni
Russia, Otkrytoye Aktsionernoy Obshchestvo
Saudi Arabia, Sharikat Al-Mossahamah
Singapore, Public Limited Company
Slovak Republic, Akciova Spolocnost
Slovenia, Delniska Druzba
South Africa, Public Limited Company
Spain, Sociedad Anonima
Surinam, Naamloze Vennootschap
Sweden, Publika Aktiebolag
Switzerland, Aktiengesellschaft
Thailand, Borisat Chamkad (Mahachon)
Trinidad and Tobago, Limited Company
Tunisia, Societe Anonyme
Turkey, Anonim Sirket
Ukraine, Aktsionerne Tovaristvo Vidkritogo Tipu
United Kingdom, Public Limited Company
United States Virgin Islands, Corporation
Uruguay, Sociedad Anonima
Venezuela, Sociedad Anonima or Compania Anonima

(ii) *Clarification of list of corporations in paragraph (b)(8)(i) of this section.*—(A) *Exceptions in certain cases.*—The following entities will not be treated as corporations under paragraph (b)(8)(i) of this section:

(1) With regard to Canada, a Nova Scotia Unlimited Liability Company (or any other company or corporation all of whose owners have unlimited liability pursuant to federal or provincial law).

(2) With regard to India, a company deemed to be a public limited company solely by operation of Section 43A(1) (relating to corporate ownership of the company), section 43A(1A) (relating to annual average turnover), or section 43A(1B) (relating to ownership interests in other companies) of the Companies Act, 1956 (or any combination of these), provided that the organizational documents of such deemed public limited company continue to meet the requirements of section 3(1)(iii) of the Companies Act, 1956.

(3) With regard to Malaysia, a Sendirian Berhad.

(B) *Inclusions in certain cases.*—With regard to Mexico, the term Sociedad Anonima includes a Sociedad Anonima that chooses to apply the variable capital provision of Mexican corporate law (Sociedad Anonima de Capital Variable).

(iii) *Public companies.*—For purposes of paragraph (b)(8)(i) of this section, with regard to Cyprus, Hong Kong, and Jamaica, the term Public Limited Company includes any Limited Company that is not defined as a private company under the corporate laws of those jurisdictions. In all other cases, where the term Public Limited Company is not defined, that term shall include any Limited Company defined as a public company under the corporate laws of the relevant jurisdiction.

(iv) *Limited companies.*—For purposes of this paragraph (b)(8), any reference to a Limited Company includes, as the case may be, companies limited by shares and companies limited by guarantee.

(v) *Multilingual countries.*—Different linguistic renderings of the name of an entity listed in paragraph (b)(8)(i) of this section shall be disregarded. For example, an entity formed under the laws of Switzerland as a Societe Anonyme will be a corporation and treated in the same manner as an Aktiengesellschaft.

(9) *Business entities with multiple charters.*—(i) An entity created or organized under the laws of more than one jurisdiction if the rules of this section would treat it as a corporation with reference to any one of the jurisdictions in which it is created or organized. Such an entity may elect its classification under § 301.7701-3, subject to the limitations of those provisions, only if it is created or organized in each jurisdiction in a manner that meets the definition of an eligible entity in § 301.7701-3(a). The determination of a business entity's corporate or non-corporate classification is made independently from the determination of whether the entity is domestic or foreign. See § 301.7701-5 for the rules that determine whether a business entity is domestic or foreign.

(ii) *Examples.*—The following examples illustrate the rule of this paragraph (b)(9):

Example 1. (i) *Facts.* X is an entity with a single owner organized under the laws of Country A as an entity that is listed in paragraph (b)(8)(i) of this section. Under the rules of this section, such an entity is a corporation for Federal tax purposes and under § 301.7701-3(a) is unable to elect its classification. Several years after its formation, X files a certificate of domestication in State B as a limited liability company (LLC). Under the laws of State B, X is considered to be created or organized in State B as an LLC upon the filing of the certificate of domestication and is therefore subject to the laws of State B. Under the rules of this section and § 301.7701-3, an LLC with a single owner organized only in State B is disregarded as an entity separate from its owner for Federal tax purposes (absent an election to be treated as an association). Neither Country A nor State B law requires X to terminate its charter in Country A as a result of the domestication, and in fact X does not terminate its Country A charter. Consequently, X is now organized in more than one jurisdiction.

(ii) *Result.* X remains organized under the laws of Country A as an entity that is listed in paragraph (b)(8)(i) of this section, and as such, it is an entity that is treated as a corporation under the rules of this section. Therefore, X is a corporation for Federal tax purposes because the rules of this section would treat X as a corporation with reference to one of the jurisdictions in which it is created or organized. Because X is organized in Country A in a manner that does not meet the definition of an eligible entity in § 301.7701-3(a), it is unable to elect its classification.

Example 2. (i) *Facts.* Y is an entity that is incorporated under the laws of State A and has two shareholders. Under the rules of this section, an entity incorporated under the laws of State A is a corporation for Federal tax purposes and under § 301.7701-3(a) is unable to elect its classification. Several years after its formation, Y files a certificate of continuance in Country B as an unlimited company. Under the laws of Country B, upon filing a certificate of continuance, Y is treated as organized in Country B. Under the rules of this section and § 301.7701-3, an unlimited company organized only in Country B that has more than one owner is treated as a partnership for Federal tax purposes (absent an election to be treated as an association). Neither State A nor Country B law requires Y to terminate its charter in State A as a result of the continuance, and in fact Y does not terminate its State A charter. Consequently, Y is now organized in more than one jurisdiction.

(ii) *Result.* Y remains organized in State A as a corporation, an entity that is treated as a corporation under the rules of this section. Therefore, Y is a corporation for Federal tax purposes because the rules of this section would treat Y as a corporation with reference to one of the jurisdictions in which it is created or organized. Because Y is organized in State A in a manner that does not meet the definition of an eligible entity in § 301.7701-3(a), it is unable to elect its classification.

Example 3. (i) *Facts.* Z is an entity that has more than one owner and that is recognized under the laws of Country A as an unlimited company organized in Country A. Z is organized in Country A in a manner that meets the definition of an eligible entity in § 301.7701-3(a). Under the rules of this section and § 301.7701-3, an unlimited company organized only in Country A with more than one owner is treated as a partnership for Federal tax purposes (absent an election to be treated as an association). At the time Z was formed, it was also organized as a private limited company under the laws of Country B. Z is organized in Country B in a manner that meets the definition of an eligible entity in § 301.7701-3(a). Under the rules of this section and § 301.7701-3, a private limited company organized only in Country B is treated as a corporation for Federal tax purposes (absent an election to be treated as a partnership). Thus, Z is organized in more than one jurisdiction. Z has not made any entity classification elections under § 301.7701-3.

(ii) *Result*. Z is organized in Country B as a private limited company, an entity that is treated (absent an election to the contrary) as a corporation under the rules of this section. However, because Z is organized in each jurisdiction in a manner that meets the definition of an eligible entity in § 301.7701-3(a), it may elect its classification under § 301.7701-3, subject to the limitations of those provisions.

Example 4. (i) *Facts*. P is an entity with more than one owner organized in Country A as a general partnership. Under the rules of this section and § 301.7701-3, an eligible entity with more than one owner in Country A is treated as a partnership for federal tax purposes (absent an election to be treated as an association). P files a certificate of continuance in Country B as an unlimited company. Under the rules of this section and § 301.7701-3, an unlimited company in Country B with more than one owner is treated as a partnership for federal tax purposes (absent an election to be treated as an association). P is not required under either the laws of Country A or Country B to terminate the general partnership in Country A, and in fact P does not terminate its Country A partnership. P is now organized in more than one jurisdiction. P has not made any entity classification elections under § 301.7701-3.

(ii) *Result*. P's organization in both Country A and Country B would result in P being classified as a partnership. Therefore, since the rules of this section would not treat P as a corporation with reference to any jurisdiction in which it is created or organized, it is not a corporation for federal tax purposes.

(c) *Other business entities*.—For federal tax purposes—

(1) The term *partnership* means a business entity that is not a corporation under paragraph (b) of this section and that has at least two members.

(2) *Wholly owned entities*.—(i) *In general*.—Except as otherwise provided in this paragraph (c), a business entity that has a single owner and is not a corporation under paragraph (b) of this section is disregarded as an entity separate from its owner.

(ii) *Special rule for certain business entities*.—If the single owner of a business entity is a bank (as defined in section 581, or, in the case of a foreign bank, as defined in section 585(a)(2)(B) without regard to the second sentence thereof), then the special rules applicable to banks under the Internal Revenue Code will continue to apply to the single owner as if the wholly owned entity were a separate entity. For this purpose, the special rules applicable to banks under the Internal Revenue Code do not include the rules under sections 864(c), 882(c), and 884.

(iii) *Tax liabilities of certain disregarded entities*.—(A) *In general*.—An entity that is disregarded as separate from its owner for any purpose under this section is treated as an entity separate from its owner for purposes of—

(1) Federal tax liabilities of the entity with respect to any taxable period for which the entity was not disregarded;

(2) Federal tax liabilities of any other entity for which the entity is liable; and

(3) Refunds or credits of Federal tax.

(B) *Examples*.—The following examples illustrate the application of paragraph (c)(2)(iii)(A) of this section:

Example 1. In 2006, X, a domestic corporation that reports its taxes on a calendar year basis, merges into Z, a domestic LLC wholly owned by Y that is disregarded as an entity separate from Y, in a state law merger. X was not a member of a consolidated group at any time during its taxable year ending in December 2005. Under the applicable state law, Z is the successor to X and is liable for all of X's debts. In 2009, the Internal Revenue Service (IRS) seeks to extend the period of limitations on assessment for X's 2005 taxable year. Because Z is the successor to X and is liable for X's 2005 taxes that remain unpaid, Z is the proper party to sign the consent to extend the period of limitations.

Example 2. The facts are the same as in *Example 1*, except that in 2007, the IRS determines that X miscalculated and underreported its income tax liability for 2005. Because Z is the successor to X and is liable for X's 2005 taxes that remain unpaid, the deficiency may be assessed against Z and, in the event that Z fails to pay the liability after notice and demand, a general tax lien will arise against all of Z's property and rights to property.

(iv) *Special rule for employment tax purposes*.—(A) *In general*.—Except as provided in paragraph (c)(2)(iv)(C) of this section, paragraph (c)(2)(i) of this section (relating to certain wholly owned entities) does not apply to taxes imposed under Subtitle C—Employment Taxes and Collection of Income Tax (Chapters 21, 22, 23, 23A, 24, and 25 of the Internal Revenue Code).

(B) *Treatment of entity*.—Except as provided in paragraph (c)(2)(iv)(C) of this section, an entity that is disregarded as an entity separate from its owner for any purpose under this section is treated as a corporation with respect to taxes imposed under Subtitle C—Employment Taxes and Collection of Income Tax (Chapters 21, 22, 23, 23A, 24, and 25 of the Internal Revenue Code). For special rules regarding the application of certain employment tax exceptions, see §§ 31.3121(b)(3)-1(d), 31.3127-1(b), and 31.3306(c)(5)-1(d) of this chapter.

(C) *Special rules*.—*(1)* Paragraphs (c)(2)(iv)(A) and (B) of this section do not apply to withholding requirements imposed by section 3406 (backup withholding). Thus, in the case of an entity that is disregarded as an entity separate from its owner for any purpose under this section, the owner is subject to the withholding requirements imposed by section 3406 (backup withholding).

(2) Paragraph (c)(2)(i) of this section applies to taxes imposed under subtitle A of the Code, including Chapter 2—Tax on Self-Employment Income. Thus, an entity that is treated in the same manner as a sole proprietorship under paragraph (a) of this section is not treated as a corporation for purposes of employing its owner; instead, the entity is disregarded as an entity separate from its owner for this purpose and is not the employer of its owner. The owner will be subject to self-employment tax on self-employment income with respect to the entity's activities. Also, if a partnership is the owner of an entity that is disregarded as an entity separate from its owner for any purpose under this section, the entity is not treated as a corporation for purposes of employing a partner of the partnership that owns the entity; instead, the entity is disregarded as an entity separate from the partnership for this purpose and is not the employer of any partner of the partnership that owns the entity. A partner of a partnership that owns an entity that is disregarded as an entity separate from its owner for any purpose under this section is subject to the same self-employment tax rules as a partner of a partnership that does not own an entity that is disregarded as an entity separate from its owner for any purpose under this section.

(D) *Example*.—The following example illustrates the application of paragraph (c)(2)(iv) of this section:

Example. (i) LLCA is an eligible entity owned by individual A and is generally disregarded as an entity separate from its owner for Federal tax purposes. However, LLCA is treated as an entity separate from its owner for purposes of subtitle C of the Internal Revenue Code. LLCA has employees and pays wages as defined in sections 3121(a), 3306(b), and 3401(a).

(ii) LLCA is subject to the provisions of subtitle C of the Internal Revenue Code and related provisions under 26 CFR subchapter C, Employment Taxes and Collection of Income Tax at Source, parts 31 through 39. Accordingly, LLCA is required to perform such acts as are required of an employer under those provisions of the Internal Revenue Code and regulations thereunder that apply. All provisions of law (including penalties) and the regulations prescribed in pursuance of law applicable to employers in respect of such acts are applicable to LLCA. Thus, for example, LLCA is liable for income tax withholding, Federal Insurance Contributions Act (FICA) taxes, and Federal Unemployment Tax Act (FUTA) taxes. See sections 3402 and 3403 (relating to income tax withholding); 3102(b) and 3111 (relating to FICA taxes), and 3301 (relating to FUTA taxes). In addition, LLCA must file under its name and EIN the applicable Forms in the 94X series, for example, Form 941, "Employer's Quarterly Employment Tax Return," Form 940, "Employer's Annual Federal Unemployment Tax Return;" file with the Social Security Administration and furnish to LLCA's employees statements on Forms W-2, "Wage and Tax Statement;" and make timely employment tax deposits. See §§ 31.6011(a)-1, 31.6011(a)-3, 31.6051-1, 31.6051-2, and 31.6302-1 of this chapter.

(iii) A is self-employed for purposes of subtitle A, chapter 2, Tax on Self-Employment Income, of the Internal Revenue Code. Thus, A is subject to tax under section 1401 on A's net earnings from self-employment with respect to LLCA's activities. A is not an employee of LLCA for purposes of subtitle C of the Internal Revenue Code. Because LLCA is treated as a sole proprietorship of A for income tax purposes, A is entitled to deduct trade or business expenses paid or incurred with respect to activities carried on through LLCA, including the employer's share of employment taxes imposed under sections 3111 and 3301, on A's Form 1040, Schedule C, "Profit or Loss for Business (Sole Proprietorship)."

(v) *Special rule for certain excise tax purposes.*—(A) *In general.*—Paragraph (c)(2)(i) of this section (relating to certain wholly owned entities) does not apply for purposes of—

(*1*) Federal tax liabilities imposed by Chapters 31, 32 (other than section 4181), 33, 34, 35, 36 (other than section 4461), 38, and 49 of the Internal Revenue Code, or any floor stocks tax imposed on articles subject to any of these taxes;

(*2*) Collection of tax imposed by Chapters 33 and 49 of the Internal Revenue Code;

(*3*) Registration under sections 4101, 4222, and 4412;

(*4*) Claims of a credit (other than a credit under section 34), refund, or payment related to a tax described in paragraph (c)(2)(v)(A)(*1*) of this section or under section 6426 or 6427; and

(*5*) Assessment and collection of an assessable payment imposed by section 4980H and reporting required by section 6056.

(B) *Treatment of entity.*—An entity that is disregarded as an entity separate from its owner for any purpose under this section is treated as a corporation with respect to items described in paragraph (c)(2)(v)(A) of this section.

(C) *Example.*—The following example illustrates the provisions of this paragraph (c)(2)(v):

Example. (i) LLCB is an eligible entity that has a single owner, B. LLCB is generally disregarded as an entity separate from its owner. However, under paragraph (c)(2)(v) of this section, LLCB is treated as an entity separate from its owner for certain purposes relating to excise taxes.

(ii) LLCB mines coal from a coal mine located in the United States. Section 4121 of chapter 32 of the Internal Revenue Code imposes a tax on the producer's sale of such coal. Section 48.4121-1(a) of this chapter defines a "producer" generally as the person in whom is vested ownership of the coal under state law immediately after the coal is severed from the ground. LLCB is the person that owns the coal under state law immediately after it is severed from the ground. Under paragraph (c)(2)(v)(A)(*1*) of this section, LLCB is the producer of the coal and is liable for tax on its sale of such coal under chapter 32 of the Internal Revenue Code. LLCB must report and pay tax on Form 720, "Quarterly Federal Excise Tax Return," under its own name and taxpayer identification number.

(iii) LLCB uses undyed diesel fuel in an earthmover that is not registered or required to be registered for highway use. Such use is an off-highway business use of the fuel. Under section 6427(l), the ultimate purchaser is allowed to claim an income tax credit or payment related to the tax imposed on diesel fuel used in an off-highway business use. Under paragraph (c)(2)(v) of this section, for purposes of the credit or payment allowed under section 6427(l), LLCB is the person that could claim the amount on its Form 720 or on a Form 8849, "Claim for Refund of Excise Taxes." Alternatively, if LLCB did not claim a payment during the time prescribed in section 6427(i)(2) for making a claim under section 6427, § 1.34-1 of this chapter provides that B, the owner of LLCB, could claim the income tax credit allowed under section 34 for the nontaxable use of diesel fuel by LLCB.

(iv) Assume the same facts as in paragraph (c)(2)(v)(C) *Example* (i) and (ii) of this section. If LLCB does not pay the tax on its sale of coal under chapter 32 of the Internal Revenue Code, any notice of lien the Internal Revenue Service files will be filed as if LLCB were a corporation.

(vi) *Special rule for reporting under section 6038A.*—(A) *In general.*—An entity that is disregarded as an entity separate from its owner for any purpose under this section is treated as an entity separate from its owner and classified as a corporation for purposes of section 6038A if—

(*1*) The entity is a domestic entity; and

(*2*) One foreign person has direct or indirect sole ownership of the entity.

(B) *Definitions.*—(*1*) *Indirect sole ownership.*—For purposes of paragraph (c)(2)(vi)(A)(*2*) of this section, indirect sole ownership means ownership by one person entirely through one or more other entities disregarded as entities separate from their owners or through one or more grantor trusts, regardless of whether any such disregarded entity or grantor trust is domestic or foreign.

(*2*) *Entity disregarded as separate from its owner.*—For purposes of paragraph (c)(2)(vi)(B)(*1*) of this section, an entity disregarded as an entity separate from its owner is an entity described in paragraph (c)(2)(i) of this section.

(*3*) *Grantor trust.*—For purposes of paragraph (c)(2)(vi)(B)(*1*) of this section, a grantor trust is any portion of a trust that is treated as owned by the grantor or another person under subpart E of subchapter J of chapter 1 of the Code.

(C) *Taxable year.*—The taxable year of an entity classified as a corporation for section 6038A purposes pursuant to paragraph (c)(2)(vi)(A) of this section is—

(*1*) The same as the taxable year of the foreign person described in paragraph (c)(2)(vi)(A)(2) of this section, if that foreign person has a U.S. income tax or information return filing obligation for its taxable year; or

(*2*) The calendar year, if paragraph (c)(2)(vi)(C)(*1*) of this section does not apply, unless otherwise provided in forms, instructions, or published guidance.

(d) *Special rule for certain foreign business entities.*—(1) *In general.*—Except as provided in paragraph (d)(3) of this section, a foreign business entity described in paragraph (b)(8)(i) of this section will not be treated as a corporation under paragraph (b)(8)(i) of this section if—

(i) The entity was in existence on May 8, 1996;

(ii) The entity's classification was relevant (as defined in § 301.7701-3(d)) on May 8, 1996;

(iii) No person (including the entity) for whom the entity's classification was relevant on May 8, 1996, treats the entity as a corporation for purposes of filing such person's federal income tax returns, information returns, and withholding documents for the taxable year including May 8, 1996;

(iv) Any change in the entity's claimed classification within the sixty months prior to May 8, 1996, occurred solely as a result of a change in the organizational documents of the entity, and the entity and all members of the entity recognized the federal tax consequences of any change in the entity's classification within the sixty months prior to May 8, 1996;

(v) A reasonable basis (within the meaning of section 6662) existed on May 8, 1996, for treating the entity as other than a corporation; and

(vi) Neither the entity nor any member was notified in writing on or before May 8, 1996, that the classification of the entity was under examination (in which case the entity's classification will be determined in the examination).

(2) *Binding contract rule.*—If a foreign business entity described in paragraph (b)(8)(i) of this section is formed after May 8, 1996, pursuant to a written binding contract (including an accepted bid to develop a project) in effect on May 8, 1996, and all times thereafter, in which the parties agreed to engage (directly or indirectly) in an active and substantial business operation in the jurisdiction in which the entity is formed, paragraph (d)(1) of this section will be applied to that entity by substituting the date of the entity's formation for May 8, 1996.

(3) *Termination of grandfather status.*—(i) *In general.*—An entity that is not treated as a corporation under paragraph (b)(8)(i) of this section by reason of paragraph (d)(1) or (d)(2) of this section will be treated permanently as a corporation under paragraph (b)(8)(i) of this section from the earliest of:

(A) The effective date of an election to be treated as an association under § 301.7701-3;

(B) A termination of the partnership under section 708(b)(1)(B) (regarding sale or exchange of 50 percent or more of the total interest in an entity's capital or profits within a twelve month period);

(C) A division of the partnership under section 708(b)(2)(B); or

(D) The date any person or persons, who were not owners of the entity as of November 29, 1999, own in the aggregate a 50 percent or greater interest in the entity.

(ii) *Special rule for certain entities.*—For purposes of paragraph (d)(2) of this section, paragraph (d)(3)(i)(B) of this section shall not apply if the sale or exchange of interests in the entity is to a related person (within the meaning of sections 267(b) and 707(b)) and occurs no later than twelve months after the date of the formation of the entity.

(e) *Effective/applicability date.*—(1) Except as otherwise provided in this paragraph (e), the rules of this section apply as of January 1, 1997, except that paragraph (b)(6) of this section applies on or after January 14, 2002, to a business entity wholly owned by a foreign government regardless of any prior entity classification, and paragraph (c)(2)(ii) of this section applies to taxable years beginning after January 12, 2001. The reference to the Finnish, Maltese, and Norwegian entities in paragraph (b)(8)(i) of this section is applicable on November 29, 1999. The reference to the Trinidadian entity in paragraph (b)(8)(i) of this section applies to entities formed on or after November 29, 1999. Any Maltese or Norwegian entity that becomes an eligible entity as a result of paragraph (b)(8)(i) of this section in effect on November 29, 1999, may elect by February 14, 2000, to be classified for Federal tax purposes as an entity other than a corporation retroactive to any period from and including January 1, 1997. Any Finnish entity that becomes an eligible entity as a result of paragraph (b)(8)(i) of this section in effect on November 29, 1999, may elect by February 14, 2000, to be classified for Federal tax purposes as an entity other than a corporation retroactive to any period from and including September 1, 1997. However, paragraph (d)(3)(i)(D) of this section applies on or after October 22, 2003.

(2) Paragraph (c)(2)(iii) of this section applies on and after September 14, 2009. For rules that apply before September 14, 2009, see 26 CFR part 301, revised as of April 1, 2009.

(3)(i) *General rule.*—Except as provided in paragraph (e)(3)(ii) of this section, the rules of paragraph (b)(9) of this section apply as of August 12, 2004, to all business entities existing on or after that date.

(ii) *Transition rule.*—For business entities created or organized under the laws of more than one jurisdiction as of August 12, 2004, the rules of paragraph (b)(9) of this section apply as of May 1, 2006. These entities, however, may rely on the rules of paragraph (b)(9) of this section as of August 12, 2004.

(4) The reference to the Estonian, Latvian, Liechtenstein, Lithuanian, and Slovenian entities in paragraph (b)(8)(i) of this section applies to such entities formed on or after October 7, 2004, and to any such entity formed before such date from the date any person or persons, who were not owners of the entity as of October 7, 2004, own in the aggregate a 50 percent or greater interest in the entity. The reference to the European Economic Area/European Union entity in paragraph (b)(8)(i) of this section applies to such entities formed on or after October 8, 2004.

(5)(i) Except as provided in this paragraph (e)(5), paragraph (c)(2)(iv) of this section applies with respect to wages paid on or after January 1, 2009.

(ii) Paragraph (c)(2)(iv)(B) applies with respect to wages paid on or after September 14, 2009. For rules that apply before September 14, 2009, see 26 CFR part 301 revised as of April 1, 2009.

(iii) Paragraph (c)(2)(iv)(C)(*1*) of this section applies with respect to wages paid on or after November 1, 2011. For rules that apply before November 1, 2011, see 26 CFR part 301, revised as of April 1, 2011. However, taxpayers may apply paragraph (c)(2)(iv)(C)(*1*) of this section with respect to wages paid on or after January 1, 2009.

(6)(i) Except as provided in this paragraph (e)(6), paragraph (c)(2)(v) of this section applies to liabilities imposed and actions first required or permitted in periods beginning on or after January 1, 2008.

(ii) Paragraphs (c)(2)(v)(B) and (c)(2)(v)(C) *Example* (iv) of this section apply on and after September 14, 2009.

(iii) Paragraph (c)(2)(v)(A)(*5*) of this section applies for periods after December 31, 2014.

(iv) References to Chapter 49 in paragraph (c)(2)(v) of this section apply to taxes imposed on amounts paid on or after July 1, 2012.

(7) The reference to the Bulgarian entity in paragraph (b)(8)(i) of this section applies to such entities formed on or after January 1, 2007, and to any such entity formed before such date from the date that, in the aggregate, a 50 percent or more interest in such entity is owned by any person or persons who were not owners of the entity as of January 1, 2007. For purposes of the preceding sentence, the term *interest* means—

(i) In the case of a partnership, a capital or profits interest; and

(ii) In the case of a corporation, an equity interest measured by vote or value.

(8) Paragraph (c)(2)(iv)(C)(*2*) of this section applies on the later of—

(i) August 1, 2016; or

(ii) The first day of the latest-starting plan year beginning after May 4, 2016, and on or before May 4, 2017, of an affected plan (based on the plans adopted before, and the plan years in effect as of, May 4, 2016) sponsored by an entity that is disregarded as an entity separate from its owner for any purpose under this section. For rules that apply before the applicability date of paragraph (c)(2)(iv)(C)(*2*) of this section, see 26 CFR part 301 revised as of April 1, 2016. For the purposes of this paragraph (e)(8)—

(A) An affected plan includes any qualified plan, health plan, or section 125 cafeteria plan if the plan benefits participants whose employment status is affected by paragraph (c)(2)(iv)(C)(*2*) of this section;

(B) A qualified plan means a plan, contract, pension, or trust described in paragraph (A) or (B) of section 219(g)(5) (other than paragraph (A)(iii)); and

(C) A health plan means an arrangement described under § 1.105-5 of this chapter.

(9) *Reporting required under section 6038A.*—Paragraph (c)(2)(vi) of this section applies to taxable years of entities beginning after December 31, 2016, and ending on or after December 13, 2017. [Reg. § 301.7701-2.]

☐ [*T.D. 6503, 11-15-60. Amended by T.D. 6797, 2-2-65; T.D. 7515, 10-17-77; T.D. 7889, 4-25-83; T.D. 8475, 5-13-93; T.D. 8697, 12-17-96 (corrected 4-3-2008); T.D. 8844, 11-26-99; T.D. 9012, 7-31-2002; T.D. 9093, 10-21-2003; T.D. 9153, 8-11-2004; T.D. 9183, 2-24-2005 T.D. 9197, 4-13-2005; T.D. 9235, 12-15-2005; T.D. 9246, 1-27-2006; T.D. 9356, 8-15-2007; T.D. 9388, 3-20-2008; T.D. 9433, 11-26-2008; T.D. 9462, 9-11-2009; T.D. 9553, 10-25-2011; T.D. 9554, 10-31-2011; T.D. 9596, 6-22-2012, T.D. 9655, 2-10-2014, T.D. 9670, 6-25-2014, T.D. 9766, 5-3-2016, T.D. 9796, 12-12-2016 and T.D. 9869, 6-28-2019.*]

§ 301.7701-3. Classification of certain business entities.—(a) *In general.*—A business entity that is not classified as a corporation under § 301.7701-2(b)(1), (3), (4), (5), (6), (7), or (8) (an *eligible entity*) can elect its classification for federal tax purposes as provided in this section. An eligible entity with at least two members can elect to be classified as either an association (and thus a corporation under § 301.7701-2(b)(2)) or a partnership, and an eligible entity with a single owner can elect to be classified as an association or to be disregarded as an entity separate from its owner. Paragraph (b) of this section provides a default classification for an eligible entity that does not make an election. Thus, elections are necessary only when an eligible entity chooses to be classified initially as other than the default classification or when an eligible entity chooses to change its classification. An entity whose classification is determined under the default classification retains that classification (regardless of any changes in the members' liability that occurs at any time during the time that the entity's classification is relevant as defined in paragraph (d) of this section) until the entity makes an election to change that classification under paragraph (c)(1) of this section. Paragraph (c) of this section provides rules for making express elections, including a rule under which a domestic eligible entity that elects to be classified as an association consents to be subject to the dual consolidated loss rules of section 1503(d). Paragraph (e) of this section provides special rules for classifying entities resulting from partnership terminations and divisions under section 708(b). Paragraph (f) of this section sets forth the effective date of this section and a special rule relating to prior periods.

(b) *Classification of eligible entities that do not file an election.*—(1) *Domestic eligible entities.*—Except as provided in paragraph (b)(3) of this section, unless the entity elects otherwise, a domestic eligible entity is—

(i) A partnership if it has two or more members; or

(ii) Disregarded as an entity separate from its owner if it has a single owner.

(2) *Foreign eligible entities.*—(i) *In general.*—Except as provided in paragraph (b)(3) of this section, unless the entity elects otherwise, a foreign eligible entity is—

(A) A partnership if it has two or more members and at least one member does not have limited liability;

(B) An association if all members have limited liability; or

(C) Disregarded as an entity separate from its owner if it has a single owner that does not have limited liability.

(ii) *Definition of limited liability.*—For purposes of paragraph (b)(2)(i) of this section, a member of a foreign eligible entity has limited liability if the member has no personal liability for the debts of or claims against the entity by reason of being a member. This determination is based solely on the statute or law pursuant to which the entity is organized, except that if the underlying statute or law allows the entity to specify in its organizational documents whether the members will have limited liability, the organizational documents may also be relevant. For purposes of this section, a member has personal liability if the creditors of the entity may seek satisfaction of all or any portion of the debts or claims against the entity from the member as such. A member has personal liability for purposes of this paragraph even if the member makes an agreement under which another person (whether or not a member of the entity) assumes such liability or agrees to indemnify that member for any such liability.

(3) *Existing eligible entities.*—(i) *In general.*—Unless the entity elects otherwise, an eligible entity in existence prior to the effective date of this section will have the same classification that the entity claimed under §§301.7701-1 through 301.7701-3 as in effect on the date prior to the effective date of this section; except that if an eligible entity with a single owner claimed to be a partnership under those regulations, the entity will be disregarded as an entity separate from its owner under this paragraph (b)(3)(i). For special rules regarding the classification of such entities prior to the effective date of this section, see paragraph (h)(2) of this section.

(ii) *Special rules.*—For purposes of paragraph (b)(3)(i) of this section, a foreign eligible entity is treated as being in existence prior to the effective date of this section only if the entity's classification was relevant (as defined in paragraph (d) of this section) at any time during the sixty months prior to the effective date of this section. If an entity claimed different classifications prior to the effective date of this section, the entity's classification for purposes of paragraph (b)(3)(i) of this section is the last classification claimed by the entity. If a foreign eligible entity's classification is relevant prior to the effective date of this section, but no federal tax or information return is filed or the federal tax or information return does not indicate the classification of the entity, the entity's classification for the period prior to the effective date of this section is determined under the regulations in effect on the date prior to the effective date of this section.

(c) *Elections.*—(1) *Time and place for filing.*—(i) *In general.*—Except as provided in paragraphs (c)(1)(iv) and (v) of this section, an eligible entity may elect to be classified other than as provided under paragraph (b) of this section, or to change its classification, by filing Form 8832, Entity Classification Election, with the service center designated on Form 8832. An election will not be accepted unless all of the information required by the form and instructions, including the taxpayer identifying number of the entity, is provided on Form 8832. See §301.6109-1 for rules on applying for and displaying Employer Identification Numbers.

(ii) *Further notification of elections.*—An eligible entity required to file a Federal tax or information return for the taxable year for which an election is made under §301.7701-3(c)(1)(i) must attach a copy of its Form 8832 to its Federal tax or information return for that year. If the entity is not required to file a return for that year, a copy of its Form 8832 ("Entity Classification Election") must be attached to the Federal income tax or information return of any direct or indirect owner of the entity for the taxable year of the owner that includes the date on which the election was effective. An indirect owner of the entity does not have to attach a copy of the Form 8832 to its return if an entity in which it has an interest is already filing a copy of the Form 8832 with its return. If an entity, or one of its direct or indirect owners, fails to attach a copy of a Form 8832 to its return as directed in this section, an otherwise valid election under §301.7701-3(c)(1)(i) will not be invalidated, but the non-filing party may be subject to penalties, including any applicable penalties if the Federal tax or information returns are inconsistent with the entity's election under §301.7701-3(c)(1)(i). In the case of returns for taxable years beginning after December 31, 2002, the copy of Form 8832 attached to a return pursuant to this paragraph (c)(1)(ii) is not required to be a signed copy.

(iii) *Effective date of election.*—An election made under paragraph (c)(1)(i) of this section will be effective on the date specified by the entity on Form 8832 or on the date filed if no such date is specified on the election form. The effective date specified on Form 8832 can not be more than 75 days prior to the date on which the election is filed and can not be more than 12 months after the date on which the election is filed. If an election specifies an effective date more than 75 days prior to the date on which the election is filed, it will be effective 75 days prior to the date it was filed. If an election specifies an effective date more than 12 months from the date on which the election is filed, it will be effective 12 months after the date it was filed. If an election specifies an effective date before January 1, 1997, it will be effective as of January 1, 1997. If a purchasing corporation makes an election under section 338 regarding an acquired subsidiary, an election under paragraph (c)(1)(i) of this section for the acquired subsidiary can be effective no earlier than the day after the acquisition date (within the meaning of section 338(h)(2)).

(iv) *Limitation.*—If an eligible entity makes an election under paragraph (c)(1)(i) of this section to change its classification (other than an election made by an existing entity to change its classification as of the effective date of this section), the entity cannot change its classification by election again during the sixty months succeeding the effective date of the election. However, the Commissioner may permit the entity to change its classification by election within the sixty months if more than fifty percent of the ownership interests in the entity as of the effective date of the subsequent election are owned by persons that did not own any interests in the entity on the filing date or on the effective date of the entity's prior election. An election by a newly formed eligible entity that is effective on the date of formation is not considered a change for purposes of this paragraph (c)(1)(iv).

(v) *Deemed elections.*—(A) *Exempt organizations.*—An eligible entity that has been determined to be, or claims to be, exempt from taxation under section 501(a) is treated as having made an election under this section to be classified as an association. Such election will be effective as of the first day for which exemption is claimed or determined to apply, regardless of when the claim or determination is made, and will remain in effect unless an election is made under paragraph (c)(1)(i) of this section after the date the claim for exempt status is withdrawn or rejected or the date the determination of exempt status is revoked.

(B) *Real estate investment trusts.*—An eligible entity that files an election under section 856(c)(1) to be treated as a real estate investment trust is treated as having made an election under this section to be classified as an association. Such election will be effective as of the first day the entity is treated as a real estate investment trust.

(C) *S corporations.*—An eligible entity that timely elects to be an S corporation under section 1362(a)(1) is treated as having made an election under this section to be classified as an association, provided that (as of the effective date of the election under section 1362(a)(1)) the entity meets all other requirements to qualify as a small business corporation under section 1361(b). Subject to §301.7701-3(c)(1)(iv), the deemed election to be classified as an association will apply as of the effective date of the S corporation election and will remain in effect until the entity makes a valid election, under §301.7701-3(c)(1)(i), to be classified as other than an association.

(vi) *Examples.*—The following examples illustrate the rules of this paragraph (c)(1):

Example 1. On July 1, 1998, X, a domestic corporation, purchases a 10% interest in Y, an eligible entity formed under Country A law in 1990. The entity's classification was not relevant to any person for federal tax or information purposes prior to X's acquisition of an interest in Y. Thus, Y is not considered to be in existence on the effective date of this section for purposes of paragraph (b)(3) of this section. Under the applicable Country A statute, all members of Y have limited liability as defined in paragraph (b)(2)(ii) of this section. Accordingly, Y is classified as an association under paragraph (b)(2)(i)(B) of this section unless it elects under this paragraph (c) to be classified as a partnership. To be classified as a partnership as of July 1, 1998, Y must file a Form 8832 by September 14, 1998. See paragraph (c)(1)(i) of this section. Because an election cannot be effective more than 75 days prior to the date on which it is filed, if Y files its Form 8832 after September 14, 1998, it will be classified as an association from July 1, 1998, until the effective date of the election. In that case, it could not change its classification by election under this paragraph (c) during the sixty months succeeding the effective date of the election.

Example 2. (i) Z is an eligible entity formed under Country B v and is in existence on the effective date of this section within the aning of paragraph (b)(3) of this section. Prior to the effective date this section, Z claimed to be classified as an association. Unless Z es an election under this paragraph (c), it will continue to be ssified as an association under paragraph (b)(3) of this section.

(ii) Z files a Form 8832 pursuant to this paragraph (c) to be ssified as a partnership, effective as of the effective date of this ction. Z can file an election to be classified as an association at any ne thereafter, but then would not be permitted to change its ssification by election during the sixty months succeeding the ective date of that subsequent election.

(2) *Authorized signatures.*—(i) *In general.*—An election made der paragraph (c)(1)(i) of this section must be signed by—

(A) Each member of the electing entity who is an owner at e time the election is filed; or

(B) Any officer, manager, or member of the electing entity no is authorized (under local law or the entity's organizational cuments) to make the election and who represents to having such thorization under penalties of perjury.

(ii) *Retroactive elections.*—For purposes of paragraph (c)(2)(i) of s section, if an election under paragraph (c)(1)(i) of this section is be effective for any period prior to the time that it is filed, each rson who was an owner between the date the election is to be ective and the date the election is filed, and who is not an owner at e time the election is filed, must also sign the election.

(iii) *Changes in classification.*—For paragraph (c)(2)(i) of this ction, if an election under paragraph (c)(1)(i) of this section is made change the classification of an entity, each person who was an vner on the date that any transactions under paragraph (g) of this ction are deemed to occur, and who is not an owner at the time the ection is filed, must also sign the election. This paragraph (c)(2)(iii) plies to elections filed on or after November 29, 1999.

(3) *Consent to be subject to section 1503(d).*—(i) *Rule.*—A domestic gible entity that elects to be classified as an association consents to treated as a dual resident corporation for purposes of section 03(d) (such an entity, a *domestic consenting corporation*), for any xable year for which it is classified as an association and the ndition set forth in § 1.1503(d)-1(c)(1) of this chapter is satisfied.

(ii) *Transition rule — deemed consent.*—If, as a result of the plicability date (see paragraph (c)(3)(iii) of this section) relating to ragraph (c)(3)(i) of this section, a domestic eligible entity that is assified as an association has not consented to be treated as a omestic consenting corporation pursuant to paragraph (c)(3)(i) of is section, then the domestic eligible entity is deemed to consent to so treated as of its first taxable year beginning on or after Decem-r 20, 2019. The first sentence of this paragraph (c)(3)(ii) does not ply if the domestic eligible entity elects, on or after December 20, 18 and effective before its first taxable year beginning on or after ecember 20, 2019, to be classified as a partnership or disregarded tity such that it ceases to be a domestic eligible entity that is assified as an association. For purposes of the election described in e second sentence of this paragraph (c)(3)(ii), the sixty month nitation under paragraph (c)(1)(iv) of this section is waived.

(iii) *Applicability date.*—The sixth sentence of paragraph (a) of is section and paragraph (c)(3)(i) of this section apply to a domestic igible entity that on or after December 20, 2018 files an election to classified as an association (regardless of whether the election is fective before December 20, 2018). Paragraph (c)(3)(ii) of this sec-on applies as of December 20, 2018.

(d) *Special rules for foreign eligible entities.*—(1) *Definition of rele-nce.*—(i) *General rule.*—For purposes of this section, a foreign eligi-e entity's classification is relevant when its classification affects the ability of any person for federal tax or information purposes. For ample, a foreign entity's classification would be relevant if U.S. come was paid to the entity and the determination by the with-olding agent of the amount to be withheld under chapter 3 of the ternal Revenue Code (if any) would vary depending upon whether e entity is classified as a partnership or as an association. Thus, the assification might affect the documentation that the withholding gent must receive from the entity, the type of tax or information turn to file, or how the return must be prepared. The date that the assification of a foreign eligible entity is relevant is the date an vent occurs that creates an obligation to file a federal tax return, information return, or statement for which the classification of the entity must be determined. Thus, the classification of a foreign entity is relevant, for example, on the date that an interest in the entity is acquired which will require a U.S. person to file an information return on Form 5471.

(ii) *Deemed relevance.*—(A) *General rule.*—For purposes of this section, except as provided in paragraph (d)(1)(ii)(B) of this section, the classification for Federal tax purposes of a foreign eligible entity that files Form 8832, "Entity Classification Election", shall be deemed to be relevant only on the date the entity classification election is effective.

(B) *Exception.*—If the classification of a foreign eligible entity is relevant within the meaning of paragraph (d)(1)(i) of this section, then the rule in paragraph (d)(1)(ii)(A) of this section shall not apply.

(2) *Entities the classification of which has never been relevant.*—If the classification of a foreign eligible entity has never been relevant (as defined in paragraph (d)(1) of this section), then the entity's classification will initially be determined pursuant to the provisions of paragraph (b)(2) of this section when the classification of the entity first becomes relevant (as defined in paragraph (d)(1)(i) of this section).

(3) *Special rule when classification is no longer relevant.*—If the classification of a foreign eligible entity is not relevant (as defined in paragraph (d)(1) of this section) for 60 consecutive months, then the entity's classification will initially be determined pursuant to the provisions of paragraph (b)(2) of this section when the classification of the foreign eligible entity becomes relevant (as defined in paragraph (d)(1)(i) of this section). The date that the classification of a foreign entity is not relevant is the date an event occurs that causes the classification to no longer be relevant, or, if no event occurs in a taxable year that causes the classification to be relevant, then the date is the first day of that taxable year.

(4) *Effective date.*—Paragraphs (d)(1)(ii), (d)(2), and (d)(3) of this section apply on or after October 22, 2003.

(e) *Coordination with section 708(b).*—Except as provided in § 301.7701-2(d)(3) (regarding termination of grandfather status for certain foreign business entities), an entity resulting from a transaction described in section 708(b)(1)(B) (partnership termination due to sales or exchanges) or section 708(b)(2)(B) (partnership division) is a partnership.

(f) *Changes in number of members of an entity.*—(1) *Associations.*—The classification of an eligible entity as an association is not affected by any change in the number of members of the entity.

(2) *Partnerships and single member entities.*—An eligible entity classified as a partnership becomes disregarded as an entity separate from its owner when the entity's membership is reduced to one member. A single member entity disregarded as an entity separate from its owner is classified as a partnership when the entity has more than one member. If an elective classification change under paragraph (c) of this section is effective at the same time as a membership change described in this paragraph (f)(2), the deemed transactions in paragraph (g) of this section resulting from the elective change preempt the transactions that would result from the change in membership.

(3) *Effect on sixty month limitation.*—A change in the number of members of an entity does not result in the creation of a new entity for purposes of the sixty month limitation on elections under paragraph (c)(1)(iv) of this section.

(4) *Examples.*—The following examples illustrate the application of this paragraph (f):

Example 1. A, a U.S. person, owns a domestic eligible entity that is disregarded as an entity separate from its owner. On January 1, 1998, *B*, a U.S. person, buys a 50 percent interest in the entity from *A*. Under this paragraph (f), the entity is classified as a partnership when *B* acquires an interest in the entity. However, *A* and *B* elect to have the entity classified as an association effective on January 1, 1998. Thus, *B* is treated as buying shares of stock on January 1, 1998. (Under paragraph (c)(1)(iv) of this section, this election is treated as a change in classification so that the entity generally cannot change its classification by election again during the sixty months succeeding the effective date of the election.) Under paragraph (g)(1) of this section, *A* is treated as contributing the assets and liabilities of the entity to the newly formed association immediately before the close of December 31, 1997. Because *A* does not retain control of the association as required by section 351, *A*'s contribution will be a taxable event. Therefore, under section 1012, the association will take a fair market value basis in the assets contributed by *A*, and *A* will have a fair market value basis in the stock received. *A* will have no additional gain upon the sale of stock to *B*, and *B* will have a cost basis in the stock purchased from *A*.

Example 2. (i) On April 1, 1998, *A* and *B*, U.S. persons, form *X*, a foreign eligible entity. *X* is treated as an association under the default provisions of paragraph (b)(2)(i) of this section, and *X* does not make an election to be classified as a partnership. *A* subsequently purchases all of *B*'s interest in *X*.

(ii) Under paragraph (f)(1) of this section, *X* continues to be classified as an association. *X*, however, can subsequently elect to be disregarded as an entity separate from *A*. The sixty month limitation of paragraph (c)(1)(iv) of this section does not prevent *X* from making an election because *X* has not made a prior election under paragraph (c)(1)(i) of this section.

Example 3. (i) On April 1, 1998, *A* and *B*, U.S. persons, form *X*, a foreign eligible entity. *X* is treated as an association under the default provisions of paragraph (b)(2)(i) of this section, and *X* does not make an election to be classified as a partnership. On January 1, 1999, *X* elects to be classified as a partnership effective on that date. Under the sixty month limitation of paragraph (c)(1)(iv) of this section, *X* cannot elect to be classified as an association until January 1, 2004 (i.e., sixty months after the effective date of the election to be classified as a partnership).

(ii) On June 1, 2000, *A* purchases all of *B*'s interest in X. After *A*'s purchase of *B*'s interest, X can no longer be classified as a partnership because X has only one member. Under paragraph (f)(2) of this section, X is disregarded as an entity separate from *A* when *A* becomes the only member of X. X, however, is not treated as a new entity for purposes of paragraph (c)(1)(iv) of this section. As a result, the sixty month limitation of paragraph (c)(1)(iv) of this section continues to apply to X, and *X* cannot elect to be classified as an association until January 1, 2004 (i.e., sixty months after January 1, 1999, the effective date of the election by X to be classified as a partnership).

(5) *Effective date.*—This paragraph (f) applies as of November 29, 1999.

(g) *Elective changes in classification.*—(1) *Deemed treatment of elective change.*—(i) *Partnership to association.*—If an eligible entity classified as a partnership elects under paragraph (c)(1)(i) of this section to be classified as an association, the following is deemed to occur: The partnership contributes all of its assets and liabilities to the association in exchange for stock in the association, and immediately thereafter, the partnership liquidates by distributing the stock of the association to its partners.

(ii) *Association to partnership.*—If an eligible entity classified as an association elects under paragraph (c)(1)(i) of this section to be classified as a partnership, the following is deemed to occur: The association distributes all of its assets and liabilities to its shareholders in liquidation of the association, and immediately thereafter, the shareholders contribute all of the distributed assets and liabilities to a newly formed partnership.

(iii) *Association to disregarded entity.*—If an eligible entity classified as an association elects under paragraph (c)(1)(i) of this section to be disregarded as an entity separate from its owner, the following is deemed to occur: The association distributes all of its assets and liabilities to its single owner in liquidation of the association.

(iv) *Disregarded entity to an association.*—If an eligible entity that is disregarded as an entity separate from its owner elects under paragraph (c)(1)(i) of this section to be classified as an association, the following is deemed to occur: The owner of the eligible entity contributes all of the assets and liabilities of the entity to the association in exchange for stock of the association.

(2) *Effect of elective changes.*—(i) *In general.*—The tax treatment of a change in the classification of an entity for federal tax purposes by election under paragraph (c)(1)(i) of this section is determined under all relevant provisions of the Internal Revenue Code and general principles of tax law, including the step transaction doctrine.

(ii) *Adoption of plan of liquidation.*—For purposes of satisfying the requirement of adoption of a plan of liquidation under section 332, unless a formal plan of liquidation that contemplates the election to be classified as a partnership or to be disregarded as an entity separate from its owner is adopted on an earlier date, the making, by an association, of an election under paragraph (c)(1)(i) of this section to be classified as a partnership or to be disregarded as an entity separate from its owner is considered to be the adoption of a plan of liquidation immediately before the deemed liquidation described in paragraph (g)(1)(ii) or (iii) of this section. This paragraph (g)(2)(ii) applies to elections filed on or after December 17, 2001. Taxpayers may apply this paragraph (g)(2)(ii) retroactively to elections filed before December 17, 2001, if the corporate owner claiming treatment under section 332 and its subsidiary making the election take consistent positions with respect to the federal tax consequences of the election.

(3) *Timing of election.*—(i) *In general.*—An election under paragraph (c)(1)(i) of this section that changes the classification of an eligible entity for federal tax purposes is treated as occurring at the start of the day for which the election is effective. Any transactions that are deemed to occur under this paragraph (g) as a result of a change in classification are treated as occurring immediately before the close of the day before the election is effective. For example, if an election is made to change the classification of an entity from an association to a partnership effective on January 1, the deemed transactions specified in paragraph (g)(1)(ii) of this section (including the liquidation of the association) are treated as occurring immediately before the close of December 31 and must be reported by the owners of the entity on December 31. Thus, the last day of the association's taxable year will be December 31 and the first day of the partnership's taxable year will be January 1.

(ii) *Coordination with section 338 election.*—A purchasing corporation that makes a qualified stock purchase of an eligible entity taxed as a corporation may make an election under section 338 regarding the acquisition if it satisfies the requirements for the election, and may also make an election to change the classification of the target corporation. If a taxpayer makes an election under section 338 regarding its acquisition of another entity taxable as a corporation and makes an election under paragraph (c) of this section for the acquired corporation (effective at the earliest possible date as provided by paragraph (c)(1)(iii) of this section), the transactions under paragraph (g) of this section are deemed to occur immediately after the deemed asset purchase by the new target corporation under section 338.

(iii) *Application to successive elections in tiered situations.*—When elections under paragraph (c)(1)(i) of this section for a series of tiered entities are effective on the same date, the eligible entities may specify the order of the elections on Form 8832. If no order is specified for the elections, any transactions that are deemed to occur in this paragraph (g) as a result of the classification change will be treated as occurring first for the highest tier entity's classification change, then for the next highest tier entity's classification change, and so forth down the chain of entities until all the transactions under this paragraph (g) have occurred. For example, Parent, a corporation, wholly owns all of the interest of an eligible entity classified as an association (S1), which wholly owns another eligible entity classified as an association (S2), which wholly owns another eligible entity classified as an association (S3). Elections under paragraph (c)(1)(i) of this section are filed to classify S1, S2, and S3 each as disregarded as an entity separate from its owner effective on the same day. If no order is specified for the elections, the following transactions are deemed to occur under this paragraph (g) as a result of the elections, with each successive transaction occurring on the same day immediately after the preceding transaction: S1 is treated as liquidating into Parent, then S2 is treated as liquidating into Parent, and finally S3 is treated as liquidating into Parent.

(4) *Effective date.*—Except as otherwise provided in paragraph (g)(2)(ii) of this section, this paragraph (g) applies to elections that are filed on or after November 29, 1999. Taxpayers may apply this paragraph (g) retroactively to elections filed before November 29, 1999 if all taxpayers affected by the deemed transactions file consistently with this paragraph (g).

(h) *Effective date.*—(1) *In general.*—Except as otherwise provided in this section, the rules of this section are applicable as of January 1, 1997.

(2) *Prior treatment of existing entities.*—In the case of a business entity that is not described in § 301.7701-2(b)(1), (3), (4), (5), (6), or (7), and that was in existence prior to January 1, 1997, the entity's claimed classification(s) will be respected for all periods prior to January 1, 1997, if—

(i) The entity had a reasonable basis (within the meaning of section 6662) for its claimed classification;

(ii) The entity and all members of the entity recognized the federal tax consequences of any change in the entity's classification within the sixty months prior to January 1, 1997; and

(iii) Neither the entity nor any member was notified in writing on or before May 8, 1996, that the classification of the entity was under examination (in which case the entity's classification will be determined in the examination).

(3) *Deemed elections for S corporations.*—Paragraph (c)(1)(v)(C) of this section applies to timely S corporation elections under section 1362(a) filed on or after July 20, 2004. Eligible entities that filed timely S elections before July 20, 2004 may also rely on the provisions of the regulation. [Reg. § 301.7701-3.]

☐ [*T.D.* 6503, 11-15-60. *Amended by T.D.* 8632, 12-19-95; *T.D.* 8697, 12-17-96; *T.D.* 8767, 3-23-98; *T.D.* 8827, 7-12-99 (*corrected* 10-29-99); *T.D.* 8844, 11-26-99; *T.D.* 8970, 12-14-2001; *T.D.* 9093, 10-21-2003; *T.D.* 9100, 12-18-2003; *T.D.* 9139, 7-19-2004; *T.D.* 9153, 8-11-2004; *T.D.* 9203, 5-20-2005 *T.D.* 9300, 12-7-2006 *and T.D.* 9896, 4-7-2020.]

§ 301.7701-5. Domestic and foreign business entities.—(a) *Domestic and foreign business entities.*—A business entity (including an entity that is disregarded as separate from its owner under § 301.7701-2(c)) is domestic if it is created or organized as any type of entity (including, but not limited to, a corporation, unincorporated association, general partnership, limited partnership, and limited liability company) in the United States, or under the law of the United States or of any State. Accordingly, a business entity that is created or organized both in the United States and in a foreign jurisdiction is a domestic entity. A business entity (including an entity that is disregarded as separate from its owner under § 301.7701-2(c)) is foreign if it is not domestic. The determination of whether an entity is domestic or foreign is made independently from the determination of its corporate or noncorporate classification. See §§ 301.7701-2 and 301.7701-3 for the rules governing the classification of entities.

(b) *Examples.*—The following examples illustrate the rules of this section:

Example 1. (i) *Facts.* Y is an entity that is created or organized under the laws of Country A as a public limited company. It is also an entity that is organized as a limited liability company (LLC) under the laws of State B. Y is classified as a corporation for Federal tax purposes under the rules of §§ 301.7701-2, and 301.7701-3.

(ii) *Result.* Y is a domestic corporation because it is an entity that is classified as a corporation and it is organized as an entity under the laws of State B.

Example 2. (i) *Facts.* P is an entity with more than one owner organized under the laws of Country A as an unlimited company. It is also an entity that is organized as a general partnership under the laws of State B. P is classified as a partnership for Federal tax purposes under the rules of §§ 301.7701-2, and 301.7701-3.

(ii) *Result.* P is a domestic partnership because it is an entity that is classified as a partnership and it is organized as an entity under the laws of State B.

(c) *Effective date.*—(1) *General rule.*—Except as provided in paragraph (c)(2) of this section, the rules of this section apply as of August 12, 2004, to all business entities existing on or after that date.

(2) *Transition rule.*—For business entities created or organized under the laws of more than one jurisdiction as of August 12, 2004, the rules of this section apply as of May 1, 2006. These entities, however, may rely on the rules of this section as of August 12, 2004. [Reg. § 301.7701-5.]

☐ [*T.D.* 6503, 11-15-60. *Amended by T.D.* 8813, 2-1-99; *T.D.* 9153, 8-11-2004 *and T.D.* 9246, 1-27-2006.]

§ 301.7701(b)-1. Resident alien.—(a) *Scope.*—Section 301.7701(b)-1(b) provides rules for determining whether an alien individual is a lawful permanent resident of the United States. Section 301.7701(b)-1(c) provides rules for determining if an alien individual satisfies the substantial presence test. Section 301.7701(b)-2 provides rules for determining when an alien individual will be considered to maintain a tax home in a foreign country and to have a closer connection to that foreign country. Section 301.7701(b)-3 provides rules for determining if an individual is an exempt individual because of his or her status as a foreign government-related individual, teacher, trainee, student, or professional athlete. Section 301.7701(b)-3 also provides rules for determining whether an individual may exclude days of presence in the United States because the individual was unable to leave the United States because of a medical condition. Section 301.7701(b)-4 provides rules for determining an individual's residency starting and termination dates. Section 301.7701(b)-5 provides rules for applying section 877 to a nonresident alien individual. Section 301.7701(b)-6 provides rules for determining the taxable year of an alien. Section 301.7701(b)-7 provides rules for determining the effect of these regulations on rules in tax conventions to which the United States is a party. Section 301.7701(b)-8 provides procedural rules for establishing that an individual is a nonresident alien. Section 301.7701(b)-9 provides the effective dates of section 7701(b) and the regulations under that section. Unless the context indicates otherwise, the regulations under §§ 301.7701(b)-1 through 301.7701(b)-9 apply for purposes of determining whether a United States citizen is also a resident of the United States. (This determination may be relevant, for example, to the application of section 861(a)(1) which treats income from interest-bearing obligations of residents as income from sources within the United States.) The regulations do not apply and §§ 1.871-2 and 1.871-5 of this chapter continue to apply for purposes of the bona fide residence test of section 911. See § 1.911-2(c) of this chapter. For purposes of determining whether an individual is a resident of the United States for estate and gift tax purposes, see § 20.0-1(b)(1) and (2) and § 25.2501-1(b) of this chapter, respectively.

(b) *Lawful permanent resident.*—(1) *Green card test.*—An alien is a resident alien with respect to a calendar year if the individual is a lawful permanent resident at any time during the calendar year. A lawful permanent resident is an individual who has been lawfully granted the privilege of residing permanently in the United States as an immigrant in accordance with the immigration laws. Resident status is deemed to continue unless it is rescinded or administratively or judicially determined to have been abandoned.

(2) *Rescission of resident status.*—Resident status is considered to be rescinded if a final administrative or judicial order of exclusion or deportation is issued regarding the alien individual. For purposes of this paragraph, the term "final judicial order" means an order that is no longer subject to appeal to a higher court of competent jurisdiction.

(3) *Administrative or judicial determination of abandonment of resident status.*—An administrative or judicial determination of abandonment of resident status may be initiated by the alien individual, the Immigration and Naturalization Service (INS), or a consular officer. If the alien initiates this determination, resident status is considered to be abandoned when the individual's application for abandonment (INS Form I-407) or a letter stating the alien's intent to abandon his or her resident status, with the Alien Registration Receipt Card (INS Form I-151 or Form I-551) enclosed, is filed with the INS or a consular officer. If INS replaces any of the form numbers referred to in this paragraph or § 301.7701(b)-2(f), refer to the comparable INS replacement form number. For purposes of this paragraph, an alien individual shall be considered to have filed a letter stating the intent to abandon resident status with the INS or a consular office if such letter is sent by certified mail, return receipt requested (or a foreign country's equivalent thereof). A copy of the letter, along with proof that the letter was mailed and received, should be retained by the alien individual. If the INS or a consular officer initiates this determination, resident status will be considered to be abandoned upon the issuance of a final administrative order of abandonment. If an individual is granted an appeal to a federal court of competent jurisdiction, a final judicial order is required.

(c) *Substantial presence test.*—(1) *In general.*—An alien individual is a resident alien if the individual meets the substantial presence test. An individual satisfies this test if he or she has been present in the United States on at least 183 days during a three year period that includes the current year. For purposes of this test, each day of presence in the current year is counted as a full day. Each day of presence in the first preceding year is counted as one-third of a day and each day of presence in the second preceding year is counted as one-sixth of a day. For purposes of this paragraph, any fractional days resulting from the above calculations will not be rounded to the nearest whole number. (See § 301.7701(b)-9(b)(2) for transitional rules for calendar years 1985 and 1986.)

(2) *Determination of presence.*—(i) *Physical presence.*—For purposes of the substantial presence test, an individual shall be treated as present in the United States on any day that he or she is physically present in the United States at any time during the day. (But see § 301.7701(b)-3 relating to days of presence that may be excluded.)

(ii) *United States.*—For purposes of section 7701(b) and the regulations thereunder, the term "United States" when used in a geographical sense includes the states and the District of Columbia. It also includes the territorial waters of the United States and the seabed and subsoil of those submarine areas which are adjacent to the territorial waters of the United States and over which the United States has exclusive rights, in accordance with international law, with respect to the exploration and exploitation of natural resources. It does not include the possessions and territories of the United States or the air space over the United States.

(3) *Current year.*—The term "current year" means any calendar year for which an alien individual is determining his or her resident status.

(4) *Thirty-one day minimum.*—If an individual is not physically present for more than 30 days during the current year, the substantial presence test will not be applied for that year even if the three-year total is 183 or more days. For purposes of the substantial presence test, it is irrelevant that an individual was not present for more than 30 days in the first or second year preceding the current year.

(d) *Application of section 7701(b) to the possessions and territories.*—(1) *Application to aliens for purposes of mirror systems.*—Section 7701(b) provides the basis for determining whether an alien individual is a resident of a United States possession or territory that administers income tax laws that are identical (except for the substitution of the name of the possession or territory for the term "United States" where appropriate) to those in force in the United States, for purposes of applying such laws with respect to income tax liability incurred to such possession or territory.

(2) *Non-application for bona fide resident determination.*—Section 7701(b) does not provide the basis for determining whether an individual (including an alien individual) is a bona fide resident of a United States possession or territory for Federal income tax purposes. For the applicable rules for making this determination, see section 937(a) and § 1.937-1 of this chapter.

(e) *Examples.*—This section may be illustrated by the following examples:

Example 1. B, an alien individual, is present in the United States for 122 days in the current year. He was present in the United States for 122 days in the first preceding calendar year and for 122 days in the second preceding calendar year. In determining his status for the current year, B counts all 122 days in the United States in the current year plus $^1/_3$ of the 122 days in the United States in the first preceding calendar year (40 $^2/_3$ days) and $^1/_6$ of the 122 days in the United States during the second preceding calendar year (20 $^1/_3$ days). The total of 122 + 40 $^2/_3$ + 20 $^1/_3$ equals 183 days. B meets the substantial presence test and is a resident alien for the current year.

Example 2. C, an alien individual, is present in the United States for 25 days during the current year. She was present in the United States for 365 days during the first preceding year and 365 days during the second preceding year. The substantial presence test does not apply because C is present in the United States for fewer than 31 days during the current year.

Example 3. D, an alien individual, is present in the United States for 170 days during the current year. He was present in the United States for 30 days during the first preceding year and 30 days during the second preceding year. In determining his status for the current year, D counts all 170 days in the United States in the current year plus $^1/_3$ of the 30 days in the United States in the first preceding calendar year (10 days) and $^1/_6$ of the 30 days in the United States during the second preceding calendar year (5 days). The total of 170 + 10 + 5 equals 185 days. D meets the substantial presence test and is a resident alien for the current year notwithstanding the fact that he was present in the United States for fewer than 31 days in each of the two preceding years. [Reg. § 301.7701(b)-1.]

□ [*T.D.* 8411, 4-24-92. *Amended by T.D.* 9194, 4-6-2005 *and T.D.* 9391, 4-4-2008.]

§ 301.7701(b)-2. Closer connection exception.—(a) *In general.*—An alien individual who meets the substantial presence test may nevertheless be considered a nonresident alien for the current year if the following conditions are satisfied—

(1) The individual is present in the United States for fewer than 183 days in the current year;

(2) The individual maintains a tax home in a foreign country during the current year; and

(3) Except as provided in paragraph (e) of this section, the individual has a closer connection during the current year to a single foreign country in which he or she maintains a tax home than to the United States.

(b) *Foreign country.*—For purposes of section 7701(b) and the regulations thereunder, the term "foreign country" when used in a geographical sense includes any territory under the sovereignty of the United Nations or a government other than that of the United States. It includes the territorial waters of the foreign country (determined in accordance with the laws of the United States), and the seabed and subsoil of those submarine areas which are adjacent to the territorial waters of the foreign country and over which the foreign country has exclusive rights, in accordance with international law, with respect to the exploration and exploitation of natural resources. It also includes the possessions and territories of the United States.

(c) *Tax home.*—(1) *Definition.*—For purposes of section 7701(b) and the regulations under that section, the term "tax home" has the same meaning that it has for purposes of section 162(a)(2) (relating to travel expenses while away from home). Thus, an individual's tax home is considered to be located at the individual's regular or principal (if more than one regular) place of business. If the individual has no regular or principal place of business because of the nature of the business, or because the individual is not engaged in carrying on any trade or business within the meaning of section 162(a), then the individual's tax home is the individual's regular place of abode in a real and substantial sense.

(2) *Duration and nature of tax home.*—The tax home maintained by the alien individual must be in existence for the entire current year. The tax home must be located in the same foreign country for which the individual is claiming to have the closer connection described in paragraph (d) of this section.

(d) *Closer connection to a foreign country.*—(1) *In general.*—For purposes of section 7701(b) and the regulations under that section, an alien individual will be considered to have a closer connection to a foreign country than the United States if the individual or the Commissioner establishes that the individual has maintained more significant contacts with the foreign country than with the United States. In determining whether an individual has maintained more significant contacts with a foreign country than the United States, the facts and circumstances to be considered include, but are not limited to, the following—

(i) The location of the individual's permanent home;

(ii) The location of the individual's family;

(iii) The location of personal belongings, such as automobiles, furniture, clothing and jewelry owned by the individual and his or her family;

(iv) The location of social, political, cultural or religious organizations with which the individual has a current relationship;

(v) The location where the individual conducts his or her routine personal banking activities;

(vi) The location where the individual conducts business activities (other than those that constitute the individual's tax home);

(vii) The location of the jurisdiction in which the individual holds a driver's license;

(viii) The location of the jurisdiction in which the individual votes;

(ix) The country of residence designated by the individual on forms and documents; and

(x) The types of official forms and documents filed by the individual, such as Form 1078 (Certificate of Alien Claiming Residence in the United States), Form W-8 (Certificate of Foreign Status) or Form W-9 (Payee's Request for Taxpayer Identification Number).

(2) *Permanent home.*—For purposes of paragraph (d)(1)(i) of this section, it is immaterial whether a permanent home is a house, an apartment, or a furnished room. It is also immaterial whether the home is owned or rented by the alien individual. It is material, however, that the dwelling be available at all times, continuously, and not solely for stays of short duration.

(e) *Special rule.*—An alien individual may demonstrate in one year that he or she has a closer connection to two foreign countries (but no more than two) if he or she satisfies all of the following conditions—

(1) The individual maintains a tax home beginning on the first day of the current year in one foreign country;

(2) The individual changes his or her tax home during the current year to a second foreign country;

(3) The individual continues to maintain his or her tax home in the second foreign country for the remainder of the current year;

(4) The individual has a closer connection to each foreign country than to the United States for the period during which the individual maintains a tax home in that foreign country; and

(5) The individual is subject to taxation as a resident pursuant to the internal laws of either foreign country for the entire year or subject to taxation as a resident in both foreign countries for the period during which the individual maintains a tax home in each foreign country.

(f) *Closer connection exception unavailable.*—An alien individual who has personally applied, or taken other affirmative steps, to change his or her status to that of a permanent resident during the current year or has an application pending for adjustment of status during the current year will not be eligible for the closer connection exception. Affirmative steps to change status to that of a permanent resident include, but are not limited to, the following—

(1) The filing of Immigration and Naturalization Form I-508 (Waiver of Immunities) by the alien;

(2) The filing of Immigration and Naturalization Form I-485 (Application for Status as Permanent Resident) by the alien;

(3) The filing of Immigration and Naturalization Form I-130 (Petition for Alien Relative) on behalf of the alien;

(4) The filing of Immigration and Naturalization Form I-140 (Petition for Prospective Immigrant Employee) on behalf of the alien;

(5) The filing of Department of Labor Form ETA-750 (Application for Alien Employment Certification) on behalf of the alien; or

(6) The filing of Department of State Form OF-230 (Application for Immigrant Visa and Alien Registration) by the alien.

(g) *Filing requirements.*—See §301.7701(b)-8 with regard to the statement that must be filed by an alien individual claiming the closer connection exception. [Reg. §301.7701(b)-2.]

☐ [*T.D.* 8411, 4-24-92.]

§301.7701(b)-3. Days of presence in the United States that are excluded for purposes of section 7701(b).—(a) *In general.*—In computing days of presence in the United States, an alien is considered to be present if the individual is physically present in the United States at any time during the day (see §301.7701(b)-1(c)(2)(i)). However, for purposes of section 7701(b) and the regulations under that section, the following days shall be excluded and will not count as days of presence in the United States—

(1) Any day that an individual is present in the United States as an exempt individual;

(2) Any day that an individual is prevented from leaving the United States because of a medical condition that arose while the individual was present in the United States—

(3) Any day that an individual is in transit between two points outside the United States; and

(4) Any day on which a regular commuter residing in Canada or Mexico commutes to and from employment in the United States.

(b) *Exempt individuals.*—(1) *In general.*—An exempt individual is an individual who is either a—

(i) Foreign government-related individual as defined in paragraph (b)(2) of this section;

(ii) Teacher or trainee as defined in paragraph (b)(3) of this section;

(iii) Student as defined in paragraph (b)(4) of this section; or

(iv) Professional athlete as defined in paragraph (b)(5) of this section.

(2) *Foreign government-related individual.*—(i) *In general.*—A foreign government-related individual is an individual (and that individual's immediate family) who is temporarily present in the United States—

(A) as a full-time employee of an international organization;

(B) by reason of diplomatic status; or

(C) by reason of a visa that the Secretary of the Treasury or his or her delegate (after consultation with the Secretary of State when appropriate) determines represents full-time diplomatic or consular status. An individual described in this paragraph shall be considered to be temporarily present in the United States if the individual is not a lawful permanent resident as described in §301.7701(b)-1(b)(1), regardless of the actual amount of time that the individual is present in the United States.

(ii) *Definition of international organization.*—The term "international organization" means any public international organization that has been designated by the President by Executive Order as being entitled to enjoy the privileges, exemptions, and immunities provided for in the International Organizations Act (22 U.S.C. 288). An individual described in paragraph (b)(2)(i) of this section will be a full-time employee of an international organization if that individual's employment with the organization is consistent with an employment schedule of a person with a standard full-time work schedule with the organization.

(iii) *Full-time diplomatic or consular status.*—An individual is considered to have full-time diplomatic or consular status if—

(A) The individual has been accredited by a foreign government recognized de jure or de facto by the United States;

(B) The individual intends to engage primarily in official activities for that foreign government while in the United States; and

(C) The individual has been recognized by the President, or by the Secretary of State, or by a consular officer acting on behalf of the Secretary of State, as being entitled to such status.

(3) *Teacher or trainee.*—A teacher or trainee includes any individual (and that individual's immediate family), other than a student, who is admitted temporarily to the United States as a nonimmigrant under section 101(a)(15)(J) (relating to the admission of teachers and trainees into the United States) or section 101(a)(15)(Q) (relating to the admission of participants in international cultural exchange programs) of the Immigration and Nationality Act (8 U.S.C. 1101(a)(15)(J), (Q)) and who substantially complies with the requirements of being admitted.

(4) *Student.*—A student is any individual (and that individual's immediate family) who is admitted temporarily to the United States as a nonimmigrant under section 101(a)(15)(F) or (M) (relating to the admission of students into the United States) or as a student under section 101(a)(15)(J) (relating to the admission of teachers and trainees into the United States) or section 101(a)(15)(Q) (relating to the admission of participants in international cultural exchange programs) of the Immigration and Nationality Act (8 U.S.C. 1101(a)(15)(F), (J), (M), (Q)) who substantially complies with the requirements of being admitted. For rules concerning taxation of certain nonresident students or trainees, see section 871(c) and §1.871-9(a) of this chapter.

(5) *Professional athlete.*—A professional athlete is an individual who is temporarily present in the United States to compete in a charitable sports event described in section 274(l)(1)(B). For purposes of computing the days of presence in the United States, only days on which the athlete actually competes in a charitable sports event described in section 274(l)(1)(B) shall be excluded. Thus, days on which the individual is present to practice for the event, to perform promotional or other activities related to the event, or to travel between events shall be included for purposes of the substantial presence test.

(6) *Substantial compliance.*—An individual described in paragraph (b)(3) or (4) of this section will be deemed to comply substantially with the visa requirements relevant to residence for tax purposes if the individual has not engaged in activities that are prohibited by the Immigration and Nationality Act and the regulations thereunder and could result in the loss of F, J or M visa status. An individual will not be deemed to comply substantially with the visa requirements relevant to residence for tax purposes merely by showing that the individual's visa has not been revoked. An independent determination of substantial compliance may be made by the Internal Revenue Service for any individual claiming to be an exempt individual under paragraph (b)(3) or (4) of this section. For example, if an individual with an F visa (student visa) is found to have accepted unauthorized employment or to have maintained a course of study that is not considered by the Internal Revenue Service to be full-time, the individual will not be considered to

comply substantially with the individual's visa requirements regardless of whether the individual's visa has been revoked.

(7) *Limitation on teacher or trainee and student exemptions.*—(i) *Teacher or trainee limitation in general.*—Except as otherwise provided, an individual shall not exclude days of presence as a teacher or trainee if the individual has been exempt as a teacher, trainee, or student for any part of two of the six preceding calendar years.

(ii) *Special teacher or trainee limitation for section 872 (b)(3) compensation.*—If—

(A) A teacher or trainee receives compensation in the current year and all of that compensation is described in section 872(b)(3);

(B) That individual was present in the United States as a teacher or trainee in any prior year within the last 6 years; and

(C) During each prior year (within the 6 year period) in which the individual was present as a teacher or trainee, the individual received compensation all of which was described in section 872(b)(3);

then that individual shall include days of presence as a teacher or trainee in the current year only if the individual has been exempt as a teacher, trainee, or student for any part of four of the six preceding calendar years.

(iii) *Limitation on student exemption.*—An individual will not be able to exclude days of presence as a student if the individual has been exempt as a teacher, trainee, or student for any part of more than five calendar years, unless it is established to the satisfaction of the district director that the individual does not intend to reside permanently in the United States and has substantially complied with the requirements of the student visa providing for the individual's temporary presence in the United States. For purposes of this paragraph (b)(7), the facts and circumstances to be considered in determining if an individual has demonstrated an intent to reside permanently in the United States include (but are not limited to)—

(A) Whether the individual has maintained a closer connection with a foreign country as described in § 301.7701(b)-2; and

(B) Whether the individual has taken affirmative steps within the meaning of paragraph (f) of § 301.7701(b)-2 to adjust the individual's status from nonimmigrant to lawful permanent resident.

(iv) *Transition rule.*—The rules in this paragraph (b)(7) relating to stated periods of exempt status apply only for those stated periods that occur after 1984. Thus, for example, an alien who is present as a student during the calendar years 1982-1990 will not be subject to the five year rule for students until 1990.

(v) *Examples.*—The following examples illustrate the application of paragraphs (b)(7)(i) and (ii) of this section:

Example 1. B is temporarily present in the United States during the current year as a teacher, within the meaning of section 101(a)(15)(J) of the Immigration and Nationality Act. B does not receive compensation described in section 872(b)(3) in the current year. B has been treated as an exempt student for the past three years. Although this is the first year that B is seeking to be exempt as a teacher, he will not be considered an exempt individual for the year because he has been exempt as a student for at least two of the past six years.

Example 2. C is temporarily present in the United States during the current year as a teacher and receives compensation described in section 872(b)(3) in the current year. C has been treated as an exempt teacher for the past two years but C's compensation for those years was not described in section 872(b)(3). C will not be considered an exempt individual for the current year because she has been exempt as a teacher for at least two of the past six years.

Example 3. The facts are the same as in *Example 2*, except that all of C's compensation for the two preceding years was described in section 872(b)(3). C will be considered to be an exempt individual for the current year because she has not been exempt as a student, teacher or trainee for four of the six preceding calendar years.

Example 4. D is temporarily present in the United States during the current year as a teacher, within the meaning of section 101(a)(15)(J) of the Immigration and Nationality Act. D does not receive compensation described in section 872(b)(3) in the current year. D entered the United States in December of the second preceding year and intends to remain in the United States until June of the current year. D will not be considered an exempt individual for the current year because he has been exempt as a teacher for at least two of the past six years.

(8) *Immediate family.*—The immediate family of an exempt individual includes the individual's spouse and unmarried children (whether by blood or adoption) but only if the spouse's or unmarried children's visa status are derived from and dependent on the visa classification of the exempt individual. For the purposes of this paragraph, the term "unmarried children" means those children who are under 21 years of age, who reside regularly in the household of the exempt individual, and who are not members of some other household. The immediate family of an exempt individual does not include the attendants, servants, and personal employees of that individual.

(c) *Medical condition.*—(1) *In general.*—An individual will not be considered present on any day that the individual intends to leave and is unable to leave the United States because of a medical condition or medical problem that arose while the individual was present in the United States. A day of presence will not be excluded if the individual, who was initially prevented from leaving, is subsequently able to leave the United States and then remains in the United States beyond a reasonable period for making arrangements to leave the United States. A day will also not be excluded if the medical condition arose during a prior stay in the United States (whether or not days of presence during the prior stay were excluded) and the alien returns to the United States for treatment of the medical condition or medical problem that arose during the prior stay.

(2) *Intent to leave the United States.*—For purposes of paragraph (c)(1) of this section, whether an individual intends to leave the United States on a particular day will be determined based on all the facts and circumstances. Thus, if at the time an individual's medical condition or medical problem arose, the individual was present in the United States for a definite purpose which by its nature could be accomplished within the United States during a period of time that would not cause the individual to be a resident under the substantial presence test, the individual may be able to establish that he or she intended to leave the United States. However, if the individual's purpose is of such a nature that an extended period of time would be required for its accomplishment (sufficient to cause the individual to be a resident under the substantial presence test), the individual would not be able to establish the requisite intent to leave the United States. If the individual is present in the United States for no particular purpose or a purpose by its nature that does not require a specific period of time to accomplish, the determination of whether the individual has the requisite intent to leave the United States will depend on all the surrounding facts and circumstances. In the case of an individual adjudicated mentally incompetent, proof of intent to leave the United States may be determined by analyzing the incompetent's pattern of behavior prior to the adjudication of incompetence. Generally, an individual will be presumed to have intended to leave during a period of illness if the individual leaves the United States within a reasonable period of time (time to make arrangements to leave) after becoming physically able to leave.

(3) *Pre-existing medical condition.*—A medical condition or problem will not be considered to arise while the individual is present in the United States, if the condition or problem existed prior to the individual's arrival in the United States, and the individual was aware of the condition or problem, regardless of whether the individual required treatment for the condition or problem when the individual entered the United States.

(4) *Examples.*—The following examples illustrate the application of this paragraph (c):

Example 1. B is in a serious automobile accident in the United States on March 25. B intended to leave the United States on March 31 (as evidenced by an airline ticket), but was unable to leave on that date as a result of the injuries suffered in the accident. B recovered from the injuries and was able to leave and did leave the United States on May 31. B's presence in the United States during the period from April 1 through May 31 will not be counted as days of presence in the United States.

Example 2. The facts are the same as in *Example 1*, except that B's return flight (as evidenced by an airline ticket) was scheduled for May 31. Because B did not intend to leave the United States until May 31, B may not exclude any days of presence in the United States.

(d) *Days in transit.*—An alien individual may exclude days of presence in the United States if the individual is in transit between two foreign points, and is physically present in the United States for fewer than 24 hours. For purposes of this paragraph, an individual will be considered to be in transit if the individual pursues activities that are substantially related to completing his or her travel to a foreign point of destination. For example, an alien who travels between airports in the United States in order to change planes en route to the individual's destination will be considered to be in transit. However, if the individual attends a business meeting while he or she is present in the United States, whether or not that meeting is within the confines of the airport, the individual will not be considered to be in transit. For purposes of this paragraph, the term "foreign point" means any areas that are not included within the definition of the term "United States" provided in § 301.7701(b)-1(c)(2)(ii).

(e) *Regular commuters from Mexico or Canada.*—(1) *General rule.*—An alien individual will not be considered to be present in the United States on days that the individual commutes to the United States from the individual's residence in Mexico or Canada if the individual regularly commutes from Mexico or Canada. An alien individual will be considered to commute regularly if the individual commutes to the individual's location of employment or self-employment in the United States from his or her residence in Mexico or Canada on more than 75% of the workdays during the working period.

(2) *Definitions.*—(i) The term "commutes" means to travel to employment or self-employment and to return to one's residence within a 24-hour period.

(ii) The term "workdays" means days on which the individual works in the United States or Canada or Mexico.

(iii) The term "working period" means the period beginning with the first day in the current year on which the individual is physically present in the United States for purposes of engaging in employment or self-employment and ending on the last day in the current year on which the individual is physically present in the United States for purposes of engaging in that employment or self-employment. If the nature of the employment or self-employment is such that it requires the individual to be present in the United States only on a seasonal or cyclical basis, the working period will begin with the first day of the season or cycle on which the individual is present in the United States for purposes of engaging in that employment or self-employment and end on the last day of the season or cycle on which the individual is present in the United States for the purpose of engaging in that employment or self-employment. Thus, there may be more than one working period in a calendar year and a working period may begin in one calendar year and end in the following calendar year.

(3) *Examples.*—The following examples illustrate the operation of this paragraph (e):

Example 1. B lives in Mexico and is employed by Corporation X in its office in Mexico. B was temporarily assigned to X's office in the United States. B's employment in the United States office began on February 1, 1988, and continued through June 1, 1988. On June 2, B resumed his employment in Mexico. On 59 days in the period beginning on February 1, 1988, and ending on June 1, 1988, B travelled each morning from his residence in Mexico to X Corporation's United States office for the purpose of engaging in his employment with X Corporation. B returned to his residence in Mexico on each of those evenings. On seven days in the period from February 1, 1988, through June 1, 1988, B worked in X's Mexico office. B is not considered to have been present in the United States on any of the days that he travelled to X's United States office for the purpose of engaging in employment with Corporation X because he commuted to his place of employment within the United States on more than 75% of the workdays during the working period (59 workdays in the United States/66 workdays in the working period = 89.4%).

Example 2. C, who lives in Canada, contracted with a resort located in the United States to provide snow-skiing instructions for the resort's customers for two skiing seasons, the first beginning on November 15, 1987, and ending on March 15, 1988, and the second beginning on November 15, 1988, and ending on March 15, 1989. On 90 days in each of the two skiing seasons, C travelled in the morning from Canada to the resort to provide skiing instructions pursuant to the contract. C returned to Canada on each of those evenings. On 20 days during each of the two skiing seasons, C worked in Canada. C is not considered to have been present in the United States on any of the days that she travelled to the United States to provide ski instructions in either the first working period beginning on November 15, 1987, and ending on March 15, 1988, or the second working period beginning on November 15, 1988, and ending on March 15, 1989, because she commuted to her employment within the United States on more than 75% of the workdays during each of the working periods (90 workdays in the United States / 110 workdays in the working period = 81.8%).

Example 3. D, who lives in Canada, is the sole proprietor of a wholesale lumber business with offices in both the United States and Canada. Beginning on January 4, 1988, and ending on February 12, 1988, D commuted to work in his United States office on 30 days. Beginning on February 15, 1988, and ending on March 25, 1988, D commuted to work in his Canadian office on 30 days. Beginning on March 28, 1988, and ending on May 27, 1988, D commuted to work in his United States office on 45 days. Subsequent to May 27, D did not commute to the United States on any other days in 1988. D is considered to have been present in the United States on each day that he travelled to his office in the United States because D did not commute to the United States office on more than 75% of the workdays during the working period beginning on January 4, 1988, and ending on May 27, 1988 (75 workdays in the United States / 105 workdays in the working period = 71.4%).

(f) *Determination of excluded days applies beyond year of determination.*—If a day of presence is excluded under this section, then that day shall not be taken into account in the current year or the first or second preceding year. [Reg. § 301.7701(b)-3.]

□ [*T.D. 8411, 4-24-92. Amended by T.D. 8733, 10-6-97.*]

§ 301.7701(b)-4. Residency time periods.—(a) *First year of residency.*—An alien individual who was not a United States resident during the preceding calendar year and who is a United States resident for the current year will begin to be a resident for tax purposes on the alien's residency starting date. The residency starting date for an alien who meets the substantial presence test is the first day during the calendar year on which the individual is present in the United States. The residency starting date for an alien who meets the lawful permanent resident test (green card test), described in paragraph (b)(1) of § 301.7701(b)-1, is the first day during the calendar year in which the individual is physically present in the United States as a lawful permanent resident. The residency starting date for an alien who satisfies both the substantial presence test and the green card test will be the earlier of the first day the individual is physically present in the United States as a lawful permanent resident of the United States or the first day during the year that the individual is present for purposes of the substantial presence test. (See § 301.7701(b)-9(b)(1) for the transitional rule relating to the residency starting date of an alien individual who was a lawful permanent resident in 1984. See also § 301.7701(b)-3 for days that may be excluded.)

(b) *Last year of residency.*—(1) *General rule.*—An alien individual who is a United States resident during the current year but who is not a United States resident at any time during the following calendar year will cease to be a resident for tax purposes on the individual's residency termination date. Generally, the residency termination date will be the last day of the calendar year.

(2) *Exceptions.*—Notwithstanding paragraph (b)(1) of this section, the residency termination date for an alien individual who meets the substantial presence test is the last day during the calendar year that the individual is physically present in the United States if the individual establishes that, for the remainder of the calendar year, the individual's tax home was in a foreign country and he or she maintained a closer connection (within the meaning of § 301.7701(b)-2(d)) to that foreign country than to the United States. Similarly, the residency termination date for an alien who meets the green card test is the first day during the calendar year that the alien is no longer a lawful permanent resident if the individual establishes that, for the remainder of the calendar year, his or her tax home was in a foreign country and he or she maintained a closer connection to that foreign country than to the United States. The residency termination date for an alien who satisfies both the substantial presence test and the green card test for the current year, will be the later of the first day the individual is no longer a lawful permanent resident of the United States or the last day the individual was physically present in the United States if the alien establishes that, for the remainder of the calendar year, his or her tax home was in a foreign country and he or she maintained a closer connection to that foreign country than to the United States. It is immaterial whether the individual's tax home was in the United States, or that the individual had a closer connection to the United States than to the foreign country, prior to the date of his or her departure from the United States or the date on which the individual was no longer a lawful permanent resident, whichever is applicable.

(c) *Rules relating to residency starting date and residency termination date.*—(1) *De minimis presence.*—An alien individual may be present in the United States for up to 10 days without triggering the residency starting date (for purposes of the substantial presence test) or extending the residency termination date (for purposes of the substantial presence test) if the individual is able to establish that, during that period, the individual's tax home was in a foreign country and he or she maintained a closer connection to that foreign country than to the United States. Days from more than one period of presence may be disregarded for purposes of determining an individual's residency starting date or termination date so long as the total is not more than 10 days. However, an individual may not disregard any days that occur in a period of consecutive days of presence, if all the days that occur during that period cannot be excluded. An individual must include days of presence for purposes of determining whether the individual meets the substantial presence test even though the days may be disregarded for purposes of determining the individual's residency starting date or residency termination date.

(2) *Proration.*—If an individual's residency starting date does not fall on the first day of the tax year, or the individual's residency termination date does not fall on the last day of the tax year, the individual's income tax liability should be calculated in accordance with § 1.871-13 of this chapter dealing with the taxation of individuals who change residence status during the taxable year.

(3) *Residency starting date for certain individuals.*—(i) *In general.*—If an alien individual (who otherwise does not meet the substantial presence test or the green card test for the current year) is physically present in the United States for at least 31 consecutive days during the current year, and also for a period of continuous presence beginning with the first day of that thirty-one day period (see paragraph (c)(3)(iii) of this section), then the individual may elect to be treated as a resident during the current year. The individual's residency starting date shall be the first day of that thirty-one day period, if—

(A) The individual was not a resident of the United States under the substantial presence test or the green card test in the year preceding the current year; and

(B) The individual is a resident of the United States in the subsequent year under the substantial presence test (whether or not the individual is also a resident of the United States under the green card test).

(ii) *Determination of presence.*—Except as otherwise provided in paragraph (c)(3)(iii) of this section, an individual shall be treated as present in the United States on any day that the individual is physically present in the United States at any time during the day.

(iii) *Thirty-one day period.*—For purposes of this paragraph (c)(3), the term "thirty-one day period" means any period of 31 consecutive days during which an individual is physically present in the United States during each day of the period.

(iv) *Period of continuous presence.*—For purposes of this paragraph (c)(3), the term "continuous presence" means a period of presence in the United States that includes 75 percent of the days in the current year beginning with (and including) the first day of the individual's thirty-one day period of presence. Only for purposes of the continuous presence requirement, an individual will be deemed to be present in the United States for up to 5 days on which the individual is absent from the United States. These days will not be deemed to be days of presence for purposes of the thirty-one day period of presence requirement. If an individual is present for more than one thirty-one day period of presence and satisfies the continuous presence requirement with regard to each period, the individual's residency starting date shall be the first day of the first thirty-one day period of presence. If an individual is present for more than one thirty-one day period of presence but satisfies the continuous presence requirement only for a later thirty-one day period, the individual's residency starting date shall be the first day of the later thirty-one day period of presence. For purposes of this paragraph (c)(3), days of presence that are otherwise excluded under section 7701(b)(3)(D)(i) and § 301.7701(b)-3(a)(1) (exempt individual), (a)(2) (medical condition), (a)(3) (in transit between two foreign points), and (a)(4) (regular commuter) shall not be counted as days of presence for purposes of either the thirty-one day period or continuous presence requirement.

(v) *Election procedure.*—(A) *Filing requirements.*—An alien individual shall make an election to be treated as a resident under paragraph (c)(3) of this section by attaching a statement (described in paragraph (c)(3)(v)(C) of this section) to the individual's income tax return (Form 1040) for the taxable year for which the election is to be in effect (the election year). The alien individual may not make this election until such time as he has satisfied the substantial presence test for the year following the election year. If an alien individual has not satisfied the substantial presence test for the year following the election year as of the due date (not including extensions) of the tax return for the election year, the alien individual may request an extension of time for filing the return until a reasonable period after he or she has satisfied such test, provided that the individual pays with his or her extension application the amount of tax he or she expects to owe for the election year computed as if he or she were a nonresident alien throughout the election year. An election made under paragraph (c)(3) of this section may not be revoked without the approval of the Commissioner or his delegate.

(B) *Election on behalf of a dependent child.*—An individual may make an election on behalf of a dependent child (as defined in paragraphs (1) and (2) of section 152(a), without regard to section 152(b)(3)) if the individual is qualified to make an election on his or her own behalf, the child qualifies to make an election under this paragraph (c)(3), and the child is not required by section 6012 to file a United States income tax return for the year for which the election is to be effective.

(C) *Statement.*—The statement required by paragraph (c)(3)(v)(A) of this section shall include the name and address of the alien individual and contain a signed declaration that the election is being made. If the individual is also making an election on behalf of any dependent children, then the statement must include the required information with respect to those children. The statement must specify—

(1) That the alien individual was not a resident in the year immediately preceding the election year;

(2) That the alien individual is a resident under the substantial presence test in the year following the election year;

(3) The individual's number of days of presence in the United States during the year following the election year;

(4) The date or dates of the alien individual's thirty-one day period of presence and period of continuous presence in the United States during the election year; and

(5) The date or dates of absence from the United States during the election year that are deemed to be days of presence.

(vi) *Penalty for failure to comply with filing requirements.*—(A) *General rule.*—If an individual fails to comply with the election procedure of paragraph (c)(3)(v) of this section, the individual must file his or her income tax return for the current year as a nonresident alien.

(B) *Exception.*—The penalty described in paragraph (c)(3)(vi)(A) of this section shall not apply if the individual can show by clear and convincing evidence that he or she took reasonable actions to become aware of the filing requirements and significant affirmative steps to comply with the requirements. An individual who requests an extension of time to file his or her income tax return pursuant to paragraph (c)(3)(v) of this section will be considered to have taken significant affirmative steps to comply with the requirement that the individual pay his or her tax determined as if the individual were a nonresident alien if the individual paid with his or her extension application at least 90 percent of the amount of the tax the individual actually owed for the election year computed as if he or she were a nonresident alien throughout the election year.

(d) *Examples.*—The following examples illustrate the operation of this section:

Example 1. B, a citizen of foreign country X, is an alien who has never before been a United States resident for tax purposes. B comes to the United States on January 6, 1985, to attend a business meeting and returns to country X on January 10, 1985. B is able to establish a closer connection to country X for the period January 6-10. On March 1, 1985, B moves to the United States and resides here until August 20, 1985, when he returns to country X. On December 12, 1985, B comes to the United States for pleasure and stays here until December 16, 1985 when he returns to country X. B is able to establish a closer connection to country X for the period December 12-16. B is not a United States resident for tax purposes during the following year and can establish a closer connection to country X for the remainder of calendar year 1985. B is a resident of the United States under the substantial presence test because B is present in the United States for 183 days (5 days in January plus 173 days for the period March 1-August 20 plus 5 days in December). B's residency starting date is March 1, 1985, and his residency termination date is August 20, 1985.

Example 2. The facts are the same as in *Example 1,* except that B remains in the United States until December 17, 1985, and is able to establish a closer connection to country X for the period December 18 through 31. B's residency termination date is December 17, 1985.

Example 3. C, a citizen of foreign country Y, is an alien who has never before been a United States resident for tax purposes. C comes to the United States for the first time on February 10, 1985, and attends a business conference until February 24, 1985, when she returns to country Y. On April 20, 1985, C enters the United States as a lawful permanent resident. On November 10, 1985, C ceases to be a lawful permanent resident but stays on in the United States until November 20, 1985 when she returns to country Y. On December 8, 1985, C comes to the United States and stays here until December 17, 1985 when she returns to country Y. She can establish a closer connection to country Y for that period. C is not a resident of the United States during the following calendar year and can establish a closer connection to country Y for the remainder of calendar year 1985. C qualifies as a United States resident under both the green card test and the substantial presence test. C's residency starting date under the green card test is April 20, 1985. Under the substantial presence test, C's residency starting date is February 10, 1985, because she is present for more than ten days in February and cannot take advantage of the de minimis presence rule. Therefore, C's residency starting date is February 10, 1985. C's residency termination date under the green card test is November 10, 1985. Her residency termination date under the substantial presence test is November 20, because B can disregard ten days of presence in December. Thus, her residency termination date is November 20, 1985, the later of her residency termination date under the substantial presence test or the green card test.

Example 4. The facts are the same as in *Example 3,* except that C is initially present in the United States on business from February 5 to February 9, 1985. C is able to establish a closer connection to country Y for that period. C may take advantage of only ten days of de minimis presence and may exclude days from a continuous period of presence only if she can exclude all the days that occur during that period. Thus, C may choose either of the following periods of residency: residency starting date February 5, 1985, and residency termination date November 20, 1985, or residency starting date April 20, 1985, and residency termination date December 17, 1985.

Example 5. D, a citizen of foreign country Z, is an alien who has never before been a United States resident for tax purposes. D comes to the United States on November 1, 1985 and is present in the United States on 31 consecutive days (from November 1 through December 1, 1985). D returns to country Z on December 1 and does not come back to the United States until December 17, 1985. He remains in the United States for the rest of the year. During 1986, D is a resident of the United States under the substantial presence test. D may elect to be treated as a resident of the United States for 1985 because he was present in the United States in 1985 for a 31 consecutive day period of presence (November 1 through December 1, 1985) and for at least 75 percent of the days following (and including) the first day of D's 31 consecutive day period of presence (46 total days of presence in the United States/61 days in the period from November 1 through December 31 = 75.4%). If D makes the election to be treated as a resident, his residency starting date will be November 1, 1985.

Example 6. The facts are the same as in *Example 5,* except that D is absent from the United States on December 24, 25, 29, 30 and 31. D may make the election to be treated as a resident for 1985 because up to five days of absence will be deemed to be days of presence for purposes of the continuous presence requirement.

Example 7. F, a citizen of foreign country M, is an alien individual who has never before been a United States resident for tax purposes. F comes to the United States on January 1, 1985 and remains in the United States through January 31, 1985, when she returns to country M. F comes back to the United States on October 1, 1985 and is present in the United States through November 1, 1985. From November 1, 1985 through December 31, 1985, F is present in the United States for 38 days. Although F satisfies two 31 consecutive day periods of presence, (January 1 through January 31 and October 1 through November 1), she satisfies the continuous presence requirement only with regard to the later period of presence (69 total days of presence/92 days in the period from October 1 through December 31 = 75%). Thus, if F makes the election to be treated as a resident, his residency starting date is October 1, 1985.

(e) *No lapse.*—(1) *Residency in prior year.*—An alien individual who was a United States resident during any part of the preceding calendar year and who is a United States resident for any part of the current year will be considered to be taxable as a resident at the beginning of the current year. For purposes of this paragraph (e)(1), it is immaterial whether an individual is considered to be a resident under the substantial presence test or the green card test.

(2) *Residency in following year.*—An alien individual who is a United States resident for any part of the current year and who is also a United States resident for any part of the following year (regardless of whether the individual has a closer connection to a foreign country than the United States during the current year) will be taxable as a resident through the end of the current year. For purposes of this paragraph (e)(2), it is immaterial whether an individual is considered to be a resident under the substantial presence test or the green card test.

(3) *Special rule.*—If an individual meets the green card test for the current year but is not physically present in the United States during the current year, then the individual's residency starting date shall be the first day of the following year.

(4) *Example.*—The following example illustrates the application of this paragraph (e).

Example. B, an alien individual who is a citizen of foreign country M, comes to the United States for the first time on May 1, 1985, and remains in the United States until November 5, 1985, when he returns to country M. B comes back to the United States on March 5, 1986 as a lawful permanent resident and remains in the United States until September 10, 1986, when he ceases to be a lawful permanent resident and returns to country M. B is not a resident in calendar year 1987. B's United States residency in calendar year 1985 continues through December 31, 1985, because he is a United States resident in the following calendar year. In calendar year 1986, B's United States residency is deemed to begin on January 1, 1986 because B qualified as a resident in the preceding calendar year. Thus, B's residency period in the United States begins on May 1, 1985, and ends on September 10, 1986. [Reg. § 301.7701(b)-4.]

☐ [*T.D.* 8411, 4-24-92.]

§ 301.7701(b)-5. Coordination with section 877.—(a) *General rule.*—An alien individual will be subject to United States income tax in the manner provided by section 877, regardless of whether the individual has a tax avoidance motive, if—

(1) The alien individual is a resident alien of the United States for at least three consecutive calendar years (the initial residency period) beginning after December 31, 1984;

(2) The period of residence for each of the three consecutive calendar years includes at least 183 days;

(3) The alien is once again taxed as a nonresident (including an individual taxed as a nonresident under § 301.7701(b)-7(a)(1); and

(4) The alien then becomes a resident of the United States before the close of the third calendar year beginning after the individual's residency termination date in the initial residency period.

(b) *Tax imposed.*—The tax provided for under paragraph (a) of this section will be imposed for the intervening period of nonresidency only if the amount of tax would exceed the amount of tax that would be imposed under section 871, relating to the taxation of nonresident aliens.

(c) *Example.*—The following example illustrates the application of this section.

Example. B, a citizen of foreign country F, enters the United States on April 1, 1985, as a lawful permanent resident. On August 1, 1987, B ceases to be a lawful permanent resident and returns to country F. B meets the initial residency period requirement because he is a resident of the United States for at least 183 days in each of three consecutive years (1985, 1986 and 1987). B returns to the United States on October 5, 1990, as a lawful permanent resident. Because B became a resident of the United States before the close of the third calendar year (1990) beginning after the close of the initial residency period (August 1, 1987), he is subject to tax under section 877(b) for the intervening period of nonresidency, August 2, 1987 through October 4, 1990, if the amount of the tax imposed under section 877 is more than the tax imposed under section 871. [Reg. § 301.7701(b)-5.]

☐ [*T.D.* 8411, 4-24-92.]

§ 301.7701(b)-6. Taxable year.—(a) *In general.*—An alien individual who has not established a fiscal year as his or her taxable year prior to the period that the individual is subject to United States income tax as a resident or a nonresident shall adopt the calendar year as his or her taxable year. An alien who has established a fiscal year in a foreign country prior to the period that the individual is subject to United States income tax may adopt the calendar year as his or her taxable year for United States income tax purposes without requesting a change in accounting period. An individual will be considered to have established a fiscal year (whether in the United States or a foreign country) if the annual accounting period on which the individual computes his or her income is a fiscal year, the individual keeps his or her books in accordance with that fiscal year, and the requirements of section 441 and § 1.441-1(b) of this chapter are otherwise satisfied. An alien who has established a fiscal year and is a resident alien during the calendar year will be treated as a resident alien with respect to any portion of his or her taxable year (beginning with the individual's residency starting date and ending with the individual's residency termination date) that falls within such calendar year. Once the individual has established either a fiscal or calendar year taxable year for any period for which the individual is subject to United States income tax, the individual may not change that taxable year without the approval of the Secretary. See section 442.

(b) *Examples.*—The following examples illustrate the operation of this section:

Example 1. B, a citizen and resident of foreign country F, was engaged in a United States business during 1982 and filed a return on a fiscal year basis. B's fiscal year runs from October 1 to September 30. B comes to the United States on March 8, 1985 and remains in the United States until October 10, 1985, when he returns to country F. B maintains a closer connection to and his tax home in Country F for the remainder of calendar year 1985. B, who is not a United States resident at any time in 1986, is a United States resident for the period that begins on March 8, 1985, and ends on October 10, 1985. B has adopted a fiscal year taxable year for purposes of computing his United States income tax liability. For his fiscal year that ends on September 30, 1985, B will be taxed as a United States resident for the period that begins on March 8, 1985 and ends on September 30, 1985. For his fiscal year that ends on September 30, 1986, B will only be taxed as a United States resident for the period that begins on October 1, 1985 and ends on October 10, 1985.

Example 2. The facts are the same as in *Example 1,* except that B's 1982 business was a country F business established on a fiscal year basis and at no time prior to 1985 was B subject to United States income tax. B may adopt a calendar year as his taxable year for United States income tax purposes without requesting a change of accounting period. B continues to use a fiscal year as his taxable year. For his fiscal year that ends on September 30, 1985, B will be taxed as a United States resident for the period that begins on March 8, 1985 and ends September 30, 1985. For his fiscal year that ends on September 30, 1986, B will be taxed as a United States resident for the period that begins on October 1, 1985 and ends on October 10, 1985.

Example 3. The facts are the same as in *Example 1,* except that B's 1982 business was a country F business established on a fiscal year basis and at no time prior to 1985 was B subject to United States income tax. B may adopt a calendar year as his taxable year for United States income tax purposes without requesting a change of accounting period. B adopts a calendar year as his taxable year for 1985. For his calendar year taxable year ending on December 31, 1985, B will be taxed as a United States resident for the period that begins on March 8, 1985, and ends on October 10, 1985. [Reg. § 301.7701(b)-6.]

□ [*T.D.* 8411, 4-24-92. *Amended by T.D.* 8996, 5-16-2002.]

§ 301.7701(b)-7. Coordination with income tax treaties.—(a) *Consistency requirement.*—(1) *Application.*—The application of this section shall be limited to an alien individual who is a dual resident taxpayer pursuant to a provision of a treaty that provides for resolution of conflicting claims of residence by the United States and its treaty partner. A "dual resident taxpayer" is an individual who is considered a resident of the United States pursuant to the internal laws of the United States and also a resident of a treaty country pursuant to the treaty partner's internal laws. If the alien individual determines that he or she is a resident of the foreign country for treaty purposes, and the alien individual claims a treaty benefit (as a nonresident of the United States) so as to reduce the individual's United States income tax liability with respect to any item of income covered by an applicable tax convention during a taxable year in which the individual was considered a dual resident taxpayer, then that individual shall be treated as a nonresident alien of the United States for purposes of computing that individual's United States income tax liability under the provisions of the Internal Revenue Code and the regulations thereunder (including the withholding provisions of section 1441 and the regulations under that section in cases in which the dual resident taxpayer is the recipient of income subject to withholding) with respect to that portion of the taxable year the individual was considered a dual resident taxpayer.

(2) *Computation of tax liability.*—If an alien individual is a dual resident taxpayer, then the rules on residency provided in the convention shall apply for purposes of determining the individual's residence for all purposes of that treaty.

(3) *Other Code purposes.*—Generally, for purposes of the Internal Revenue Code other than the computation of the individual's United States income tax liability, the individual shall be treated as a United States resident. Therefore, for example, the individual shall be treated as a United States resident for purposes of determining whether a foreign corporation is a controlled foreign corporation under section 957 or whether a foreign corporation is a foreign personal holding company under section 552. In addition, the application of paragraph (a)(2) of this section does not affect the determination of the individual's residency time periods under § 301.7701(b)-4.

(4) *Special rules for S corporations.*—[Reserved]

(b) *Filing requirements.*—An alien individual described in paragraph (a) of this section who determines his or her U.S. tax liability as if he or she were a nonresident alien shall make a return on Form 1040NR on or before the date prescribed by law (including extensions) for making an income tax return as a nonresident. The individual shall prepare a return and compute his or her tax liability as a nonresident alien. The individual shall attach a statement (in the form required in paragraph (c) of this section) to the Form 1040NR. The Form 1040NR and the attached statement, shall be filed with the Internal Revenue Service Center, Philadelphia, PA 19255. The filing of a Form 1040NR by an individual described in paragraph (a) of this section may affect the determination by the Immigration and Naturalization Service as to whether the individual qualifies to maintain a residency permit.

(c) *Contents of statement.*—(1) *In general.*—(i) *Returns due after December 15, 1997.*—The statement filed by an individual described in paragraph (a)(1) of this section, for a return relating to a taxable year for which the due date (without extensions) is after December 15, 1997, must be in the form of a fully completed Form 8833 (Treaty-Based Return Position Disclosure Under Section 6114 or 7701(b)) or appropriate successor form. See section 6114 and § 301.6114-1 for rules relating to other treaty-based return positions taken by the same taxpayer.

(ii) *Earlier returns.*—For returns relating to taxable years for which the due date for filing returns (without extensions) is on or before December 15, 1997, the statement filed by the individual described in paragraph (a)(1) of this section must contain the information in accordance with paragraph (c)(1) of this section in effect prior to December 15, 1997 (see § 301.7701(b)(-7(c)(1) as contained in 26 CFR part 301, revised April 1, 1997).

(2) *Controlled foreign corporation shareholders.*—If the taxpayer who claims a treaty benefit as a nonresident of the United States is a United States shareholder in a controlled foreign corporation (CFC), as defined in section 957 or section 953(c), and there are no other United States shareholders in that CFC, then for purposes of paragraph (c)(1) of this section, the approximate amount of subpart F income (as defined in section 952) that would have been included in the taxpayer's income may be determined based on the audited foreign financial statements of the CFC.

(3) *S corporation shareholders.*—[Reserved]

(d) *Relationship to section 6114(a) treaty-based return positions.*—The statement required by paragraph (b) of this section will be considered disclosure for purposes of section 6114 and § 301.6114-1(a), but only if the statement is in the form required by paragraph (c) of this section. If the taxpayer fails to file the statement required by paragraph (b) of this section on or before the date prescribed in paragraph (b) of this section, the taxpayer will be subject to the penalties imposed by section 6712. See section 6712 and § 301.6712-1.

(e) *Examples.*—The following examples illustrate the application of this section:

Example 1. B, an alien individual, is a resident of foreign country X, under X's internal law. Country X is a party to an income tax convention with the United States. B is also a resident of the United States under the Internal Revenue Code. B is considered to be a resident of country X under the convention. The convention does not specifically deal with characterization of foreign corporations as controlled foreign corporations or the taxability of United States shareholders on inclusions of subpart F income, but it provides, in an "Other Income" article similar to Article 21 of the 1981 draft of the United States Model Income Tax Convention (U.S. Model), that items of income of a resident of country X that are not specifically dealt with in the convention shall be taxable only in country X. B owns 80% of the one class of stock of foreign corporation R. The remaining 20% is owned by C, a United States citizen who is unrelated to B. In 1985, corporation R's only income is interest that is foreign personal holding company income under § 1.954A-2 of this chapter. Because the United States-X income tax convention does not deal with characterization of foreign corporations as controlled foreign corporations, United States internal income tax law applies. Therefore, B and C are United States shareholders within the meaning of § 1.951-1(g) of this chapter, corporation R is a controlled foreign corporation within the meaning of § 1.957-1 of this chapter, and corporation R's income is included in C's income as subpart F income under § 1.951-1 of this chapter. B may avoid current taxation on his share of the subpart F inclusion by filing as a nonresident (*i.e.,* by following the procedure in § 301.7701 (b)-7(b)).

Example 2. The facts are the same as in *Example 1,* except that B also earns United States source dividend income. The United States-X income tax convention provides that the rate of United States tax on United States source dividends paid to residents of country X shall not exceed 15 percent of the gross amount of the dividends. B's United States tax liability with respect to the dividends would be smaller if he were treated as a resident alien, subject to tax on a net basis (*i.e.,* after the allowance of deductions) than if he were treated as a nonresident alien. If, however, B chooses to file as a nonresident in order to claim treaty benefits with respect to his share of R's subpart F income, his overall United States tax liability, including the portion attributable to the dividends, must be determined as if he were a nonresident alien.

Example 3. C, a married alien individual with three children, is a resident of foreign country Y, under Y's internal law. Country Y is a party to an income tax convention with the United States. C is also a resident of the United States under the Internal Revenue Code. C is considered to be a resident of country Y under the convention. The convention specifically covers, among other items of income, personal services income, dividends and interest. C is sent by her country Y employer to work in the United States from January 1, 1985 until December 31, 1985. During 1985, C also earns United States source dividends and interest and incurs mortgage interest expenses on her personal residence. The United States-Y treaty provides that remuneration for personal services performed in the United States by a country Y resident is exempt from United States tax if, among other things, the individual performing such services is present in the United States for a period that is not in excess of 183 days. The treaty provides that the rate of United States tax on United States source dividends paid to residents of Y shall not exceed 15 percent of the gross amount of the dividends and it exempts residents of Y from United States tax on United States source interest. In filing her 1985 tax return, C may choose to file either as a resident alien without claiming any treaty benefits or as a nonresident alien if she desires to claim any treaty benefit. C files as a nonresident (*i.e.,* by following the procedure described in § 301.7701(b)-7(b)). Because C does not satisfy the requirements of the United States-Y treaty with regard to exempting personal services income from United States tax, C will be taxed on her personal services income at graduated rates under section 1 of the Code pursuant to section 871(b) of the Code. She will not be entitled to deduct her mortgage interest expenses or to claim more than one personal exemption because she is taxed as a nonresident alien under the Code by virtue of her decision to claim treaty benefits, and section 873 of the Code denies nonresidents the deduction for personal residence mortgage interest expense and generally limits them to only one personal exemption. C will be subject to a tax of 15 percent of the gross amount of her dividend income under section 871(a) of the Code as modified by the treaty, and she will be exempt from tax on her interest income. C is not entitled to file a joint return with her spouse even if he is a resident alien under the Code for 1985.

Example 4. The facts are the same as in *Example 3,* except that C does not choose to claim treaty benefits with respect to any items of income covered by the treaty (*i.e.,* she files as a resident). Therefore, she is taxed as a resident under the Code and pays tax at graduated rates on her personal services income, dividends, and interest. In addition, she is entitled to deduct her mortgage interest expenses and to take personal exemptions for her spouse and three children. C will be entitled to file a joint return with her spouse if he is a resident alien for 1985 or, if he is a nonresident alien, C and her spouse may elect to file a joint return pursuant to section 6013. [Reg. § 301.7701(b)-7.]

☐ [*T.D. 8411, 4-24-92. Amended by T.D. 8733, 10-6-97.*]

§ 301.7701(b)-8. Procedural rules.—(a) *Who must file.*—(1) *Closer connection exception.*—An alien individual who otherwise meets the substantial presence test must file a statement to explain the basis of the individual's claim that he or she is able to satisfy the closer connection exception described in § 301.7701(b)-2.

(2) *Exempt individuals and individuals with a medical condition.*—An alien individual must file a statement to explain the basis of the individual's claim that he or she is able to exclude days of presence in the United States because the individual—

(i) Is an exempt individual as described in § 301.7701(b)-3(b)(3) (teacher/trainee) or (b)(4) (student);

(ii) Is an exempt individual described in § 301.7701(b)-3(b)(5) (professional athlete); or

(iii) Has a medical condition or problem as described in § 301.7701(b)-3(c).

(3) *De minimis presence and residency starting and termination dates.*—A statement must be filed by an individual who is seeking to establish—

(i) That a period of de minimis presence of ten or fewer days should be disregarded for purposes of the individual's residency starting or termination date; or

(ii) A residency termination date.

(b) *Contents of statement.*—(1) *Closer connection exception.*—(i) *Returns due after December 15, 1997.*—The statement filed by an individual described in paragraph (a)(1) of this section, for a return relating to a taxable year for which the due date (without extensions) is after December 15, 1997, must be in the form of a fully completed Form 8840 (Closer Connection Exception Statement) or appropriate successor form.

(ii) *Earlier returns.*—For returns relating to taxable years for which the due date for filing returns (without extensions) is on or before December 15, 1997, the statement filed by the individual described in paragraph (a)(1) of this section must contain the information in accordance with paragraph (b)(1) of this section in effect prior to December 15, 1997 (see § 301.7701(b)-8(b)(1) as contained in 26 CFR Part 301, revised April 1, 1997).

(2) *Exempt individuals and individuals with a medical condition.*—(i) *Returns due after December 15, 1997.*—The statement filed by an individual described in paragraph (a)(2) of this section, for a return relating to a taxable year for which the due date (without extensions) is after December 15, 1997, must be in the form of a fully completed Form 8843 (Statement for Exempt Individuals and Individuals with a Medical Condition) or appropriate successor form.

(ii) *Earlier returns.*—For returns relating to taxable years for which the due date for filing returns (without extensions) is on or before December 15, 1997, the statement filed by the individual described in paragraph (a)(2) of this section must contain the information in accordance with paragraph (b)(2) of this section in effect prior to December 15, 1997 (see § 301.7701(b)-8(b)(2) as contained in 26 CFR Part 301, revised April 1, 1997).

(3) *De minimis presence and residency starting and termination dates.*—The statement filed by an individual described in paragraph (a)(3) of this section shall be dated, signed by the individual seeking to exclude de minimis presence for purposes of the individual's residency starting or termination date or to establish a residency termination date, and verified by a declaration that the statement is made under the penalty of perjury. The statement shall contain the information described in paragraphs (b)(1)(i), (ii) and (iii) of this section and the following information (as applicable)—

(i) The first day that the individual was present in the United States during the current year;

(ii) The last day that the individual was present in the United States during the current year;

(iii) Dates of de minimis presence that the individual is seeking to exclude from his or her residency starting or termination dates;

(iv) Sufficient facts to establish that the individual has maintained his or her tax home in and a closer connection to a foreign country during a period of de minimis presence;

(v) Sufficient facts to establish that the individual has maintained his or her tax home in and a closer connection to a foreign country following the individual's last day of presence in the United States during the current year or following the abandonment or rescission of the individual's status as a lawful permanent resident during the current year;

(vi) Date that the individual's status as a lawful permanent resident was abandoned or rescinded; and

(vii) Sufficient facts (including copies of relevant documents) to establish that the individual's status as lawful permanent resident has been abandoned or rescinded.

(c) *How to file.*—Individuals described in paragraph (a) of this section who are required to make a return on Form 1040 or 1040NR pursuant to paragraph (a) or (b) of § 1.6012-1 of this chapter must attach the statement described in paragraph (b) of this section to their return for the taxable year for which the statement is relevant. An individual who is not required to file either Form 1040 or 1040NR must file the statement with the Internal Revenue Service Center, Philadelphia, PA 19255 on or before the date prescribed by law (including extensions) for making an income tax return as a nonresident for the calendar year for which the statement applies. The statement may be signed and filed for the taxpayer by the taxpayer's agent in accordance with § 1.6061-1 of this chapter.

(d) *Penalty for failure to file statement.*—(1) *General rule.*—If an individual is required to file a statement pursuant to paragraph (a)(1), (a)(2)(ii), (a)(2)(iii) or (a)(3) of this section and fails to file such statement on or before the date prescribed by paragraph (c) of this section, the individual will not be eligible for the closer connection exception described in § 301.7701(b)-2 and will be required to include all days of presence in the United States (calculated without the benefit of §§ 301.7701(b)-3(b)(5), 301.7701(b)-3(c), and 301.7701(b)-4(c)(1)) for purposes of the substantial presence test and for determining the individual's residency starting and termination dates. If an individual is considered to be a resident because of this paragraph and the individual is also a resident of a country with which the United States has an income tax convention pursuant to that convention, the individual shall be treated in the manner provided in § 301.7701(b)-7(a) (relating to the treatment of individuals who are dual residents).

(2) *Exception.*—The penalty described in paragraph (d)(1) of this section shall not apply if the individual can show by clear and convincing evidence that he or she took reasonable actions to become aware of the filing requirements and significant affirmative steps to comply with those requirements.

(e) *Filing requirement disregarded.*—Notwithstanding paragraph (d) of this section, the Secretary or his or her delegate may in their sole discretion, when it is in the best interest of the government to do so and based on all of the facts and circumstances, disregard the individual's failure to file timely the statement described in paragraph (a) of this section in determining the individual's days of presence in the United States. [Reg. § 301.7701(b)-8.]

☐ [*T.D.* 8411, 4-24-92. *Amended by T.D.* 8733, 10-6-97.]

§ 301.7701(b)-9. Effective/applicability dates of §§ 301.7701(b)-1 through 301.7701(b)-7.—(a) *In general.*—Except as indicated in paragraph (b) of this section, §§ 301.7701(b)-1 through 301.7701(b)-7 apply to taxable years beginning after December 31, 1984. For the rules applicable to earlier taxable years, see §§ 1.871-2 through 1.871-5 of this chapter.

(b) *Special rules.*—(1) *Green card test-residency starting date.*—If an alien was a lawful permanent resident throughout 1984 (regardless of whether the individual was physically present in the United States), or was physically present in the United States at any time during 1984 while a lawful permanent resident, the individual will be considered to have been a resident of the United States during 1984 for purposes of applying the provisions of section 7701(b)(2)(A) and § 301.7701(b)-4 such that the individual will, if he meets the substantial presence or green card test in 1985, be considered a resident of the United States as of January 1, 1985, regardless of when the individual was first present in the United States in 1985.

(2) *Substantial presence test-years included.*—For purposes of applying the substantial presence test for calendar years 1985 and 1986, days of presence in 1984 will only be counted for aliens who had been residents under prior law (§§ 1.871-2 through 1.871-5 of this chapter) at the end of calendar year 1984. Days of presence in 1983 will only be counted for aliens who had been residents under prior law at the end of both calendar year 1983 and 1984.

(3) *Professional athletes.*—For purposes of applying the substantial presence test, only days of presence in the United States after October 22, 1986, shall be excluded for individuals described in § 301.7701(b)-3(b)(5) (professional athletes).

(4) *Procedural rules and filing requirements.*—The procedural rules and filing requirements described in §§ 301.7701(b)-7(b) and 301.7701(b)-8 shall apply to taxable years beginning after December 31, 1991.

(5) *Possessions and territories.*—For purposes of applying section 7701(b) and the regulations under that section, § 301.7701(b)-1(d) applies to taxable years ending after April 9, 2008. [Reg. § 301.7701(b)-9.]

☐ [*T.D.* 8411, 4-24-92. *Amended by T.D.* 9391, 4-4-2008.]

§ 1.7701(l)-1. Conduit financing arrangements.—Section 7701(l) authorizes the issuance of regulations that recharacterize any multiple-party financing transaction as a transaction directly among any two or more of such parties where the Secretary determines that such recharacterization is appropriate to prevent avoidance of any tax imposed by title 26 of the United States Code. [Reg. § 1.7701(l)-1.]

☐ [*T.D.* 8611, 8-10-95. *Amended by T.D.* 8735, 10-6-97.]

§ 1.7701(l)-4. Rules regarding inversion transactions.—(a) *Overview.*—This section provides rules applicable to United States shareholders of controlled foreign corporations after certain inversion transactions. Paragraph (b) of this section defines specified transactions and provides the scope of the rules in this section. Paragraph (c) of this section provides rules recharacterizing certain specified transactions. Paragraph (d) of this section sets forth rules governing transactions that affect the stock of an expatriated foreign subsidiary following a recharacterized specified transaction. Paragraph (e) of this section sets forth a rule concerning the treatment of amounts included in income as a result of a specified transaction as foreign personal holding company income. Paragraph (f) of this section sets forth definitions that apply for purposes of this section. Paragraph (g) of this section sets forth examples illustrating these rules. Paragraph (h) of this section provides applicability dates. See § 1.367(b)-4(e) and (f) for rules concerning certain other exchanges after an inversion transaction. See also § 1.956-2(a)(4), (c)(5), and (d)(2) for additional rules applicable to United States property held by controlled foreign corporations after an inversion transaction.

(b) *Specified transaction.*—(1) *In general.*—Except as provided in paragraph (b)(2) of this section, paragraph (c) of this section applies to specified transactions. For purposes of this section, a *specified transaction* is, with respect to an expatriated foreign subsidiary, a transaction in which stock of the expatriated foreign subsidiary is issued or transferred to a person that immediately before the issuance or transfer is a specified related person, provided the transaction occurs during the applicable period. However, a specified transaction does not include a transaction in which stock of the expatriated foreign subsidiary is deemed issued pursuant to section 304.

(2) *Exceptions.*—Paragraph (c) of this section does not apply to a specified transaction—

(i) That is a fast-pay arrangement that is recharacterized under § 1.7701(l)-3(c)(2);

(ii) In which the specified stock was transferred by a shareholder of the expatriated foreign subsidiary, and the shareholder either—

(A) Pursuant to § 1.367(b)-4(e)(1), both—

(1) Included in gross income as a deemed dividend the section 1248 amount attributable to the specified stock; and

(2) After taking into account the increase in basis provided in § 1.367(b)-2(e)(3)(ii) resulting from the deemed dividend (if any), recognized all realized gain with respect to the stock that otherwise would not have been recognized; or

(B) Included in gross income all of the gain recognized on the transfer of the specified stock (including gain included in gross income as a dividend pursuant to section 964(e), section 1248(a), or section 356(a)(2)); or

(iii) In which—

(A) Immediately after the specified transaction and any related transaction, the expatriated foreign subsidiary is a controlled foreign corporation;

(B) The post-transaction ownership percentage with respect to the expatriated foreign subsidiary is at least 90 percent of the pre-transaction ownership percentage with respect to the expatriated foreign subsidiary; and

(C) The post-transaction ownership percentage with respect to any lower-tier expatriated foreign subsidiary is at least 90 percent of the pre-transaction ownership percentage with respect to the lower-tier expatriated foreign subsidiary. See *Example 3* and *Example 4* of paragraph (g) of this section.

(c) *Recharacterization of specified transactions.*—(1) *In general.*—Except as otherwise provided, a specified transaction that is recharacterized under this paragraph (c) is recharacterized for all purposes of the Internal Revenue Code as of the date on which the specified transaction occurs, unless and until the rules of paragraph (d) of this section apply to alter or terminate the recharacterization. For purposes of paragraphs (c)(2) and (3) and (d) of this section, stock is considered owned by a section 958(a) U.S. shareholder if it is owned within the meaning of section 958(a) by the section 958(a) U.S. shareholder.

(2) *Specified transactions through stock issuance.*—A specified transaction in which the specified stock is issued by an expatriated foreign subsidiary to a specified related person is recharacterized as follows—

(i) The transferred property is treated as having been transferred by the specified related person to the persons that were section 958(a) U.S. shareholders of the expatriated foreign subsidiary immediately before the specified transaction, in proportion to the stock of the expatriated foreign subsidiary owned by each section 958(a) U.S. shareholder, in exchange for deemed instruments in the section 958(a) U.S. shareholders; and

(ii) The transferred property treated as transferred to the section 958(a) U.S. shareholders pursuant to paragraph (c)(2)(i) of this section is treated as having been contributed by the section 958(a) U.S. shareholders (through intermediate entities, if any, in exchange for equity in the intermediate entities) to the expatriated foreign subsidiary in exchange for deemed issued stock in the expatriated foreign subsidiary. See *Example 1, Example 2,* and *Example 6* of paragraph (g) of this section.

(3) *Specified transactions through shareholder transfer.*—A specified transaction in which specified stock is transferred by shareholders of the expatriated foreign subsidiary to a specified related person is recharacterized as follows—

(i) The transferred property is treated as having been transferred by the specified related person to the persons that were section 958(a) U.S. shareholders of the expatriated foreign subsidiary immediately before the specified transaction, in proportion to the specified stock owned by each section 958(a) U.S. shareholder, in exchange for deemed instruments in the section 958(a) U.S. shareholders; and

(ii) To the extent the section 958(a) U.S. shareholders are not the transferring shareholders, the transferred property treated as transferred to the section 958(a) U.S. shareholders pursuant to paragraph (c)(3)(i) of this section is treated as having been contributed by the section 958(a) U.S. shareholders (through intermediate entities, if any, in exchange for equity in the intermediate entities) to the transferring shareholder in exchange for equity in the transferring shareholder. See *Example 5* of paragraph (g) of this section.

(4) *Treatment of deemed instruments following a recharacterized specified transaction.*—(i) *Deemed instruments.*—The deemed instruments described in paragraphs (c)(2) and (3) of this section have the same terms as the specified stock issued or transferred pursuant to the specified transaction (that is, the disregarded specified stock), other than the issuer. When a distribution is made with respect to the disregarded specified stock, matching seriatim distributions with respect to the deemed issued stock are treated as made by the expatriated foreign subsidiary, through intermediate entities, if any, to the section 958(a) U.S. shareholders, which, in turn, then are treated as making corresponding payments with respect to the deemed instruments to the specified related person.

(ii) *Paying agent.*—The expatriated foreign subsidiary is treated as the paying agent of the section 958(a) U.S. shareholder with respect to the deemed instruments treated as issued by the section 958(a) U.S. shareholder to the specified related person.

(d) *Transactions affecting ownership of stock of an expatriated foreign subsidiary following a recharacterized specified transaction.*—(1) *Transfers of stock other than specified stock.*—When, after a specified transaction with respect to an expatriated foreign subsidiary that is recharacterized under paragraph (c)(2) or (3) of this section, stock of the expatriated foreign subsidiary, other than disregarded specified stock, that is owned by a section 958(a) U.S. shareholder is transferred, the deemed issued stock treated as owned by the section 958(a) U.S. shareholder as a result of the specified transaction continues to be treated as directly owned by the holder, as are the deemed instruments treated as issued to the specified related person as a result of the specified transaction.

(2) *Transactions in which the expatriated foreign subsidiary ceases to be a foreign related person.*—When, after a specified transaction with respect to an expatriated foreign subsidiary that is recharacterized under paragraph (c)(2) or (3) of this section, there is a transaction that affects the ownership of the stock (including disregarded specified stock) of the expatriated foreign subsidiary, and, immediately after the transaction, the expatriated foreign subsidiary is not a foreign related person (determined without taking into account the recharacterization under paragraph (c)(2) or (3) of this section), then, immediately before the transaction—

(i) Each section 958(a) U.S. shareholder that is treated as owning deemed issued stock in the expatriated foreign subsidiary under paragraph (c)(2) or (3) of this section is treated as transferring the deemed issued stock (after the deemed issued stock is deemed to be transferred to the section 958(a) U.S. shareholder through intermediate entities, if any, in redemption of equity deemed issued by the intermediate entities pursuant to paragraph (c)(2) or (3) of this section) to the specified related person that is treated as holding the deemed instruments issued by the section 958(a) U.S. shareholder under paragraph (c)(2) or (3) of this section, in redemption of the deemed instruments; and

(ii) The deemed issued stock that is treated as transferred pursuant to paragraph (d)(2)(i) of this section is treated as recapitalized into the disregarded specified stock actually held by the specified related person, which immediately thereafter is treated as specified stock owned by the specified related person for all purposes of the Internal Revenue Code. See *Example 8, Example 9,* and *Example 12* of paragraph (g) of this section.

(3) *Transfers in which disregarded specified stock ceases to be held by a foreign related person, specified related person, or expatriated entity.*—When, after a specified transaction with respect to an expatriated foreign subsidiary that is recharacterized under paragraph (c)(2) or (3) of this section, there is a direct or indirect transfer of the disregarded specified stock in the expatriated foreign subsidiary, and immediately after the transfer, the expatriated foreign subsidiary is a foreign related person, then, to the extent that, as a result of the transfer, the disregarded specified stock is actually held (determined without taking into account the recharacterization under paragraph (c)(2) or (3) of this section) by a person that is not a foreign related person, a specified related person, or an expatriated entity, immediately before the transfer—

(i) Each section 958(a) U.S. shareholder that is treated as owning all or a portion of the deemed issued stock in the expatriated foreign subsidiary is treated as transferring the deemed issued stock that is allocable to the transferred disregarded specified stock that is out-of-group transferred disregarded specified stock (after the deemed issued stock is deemed to be transferred to the section 958(a) U.S. shareholder through intermediate entities, if any, in redemption of equity deemed issued by the intermediate entities pursuant to paragraph (c)(2) or (3) of this section) to the specified related person that is treated as holding the deemed instruments allocable to the out-of-group transferred disregarded specified stock, in redemption of the deemed instruments that are allocable to the out-of-group transferred disregarded specified stock; and

(ii) The deemed issued stock that is treated as transferred pursuant to paragraph (d)(3)(i) of this section is treated as recapitalized into the disregarded specified stock actually held by the specified related person, which immediately thereafter is treated as specified stock owned by the specified related person for all purposes of the Internal Revenue Code. See *Example 7* and *Example 11* of paragraph (g) of this section.

(4) *Certain direct transfers of disregarded specified stock to which unwind rules do not apply.*—When a specified related person directly transfers the disregarded specified stock of the expatriated foreign subsidiary and paragraphs (d)(2) and (3) of this section do not apply with respect to the transfer, the specified related person is deemed to

transfer the deemed instruments allocable to the transferred disregarded specified stock, whether it is in-group transferred disregarded specified stock or out-of-group transferred disregarded specified stock, to the transferee of the specified stock, in lieu of the disregarded specified stock, in exchange for the consideration provided by the transferee for the disregarded specified stock. See *Example 10* of paragraph (g) of this section.

(5) *Determination of deemed issued stock and deemed instruments allocable to transferred disregarded specified stock.*—(i) *Out-of-group transfers of disregarded specified stock.*—For purposes of paragraphs (d)(3) and (4) of this section, the portion of the deemed issued stock treated as owned, and of the deemed instruments treated as issued, by each section 958(a) U.S. shareholder as a result of the specified transaction that is allocable to out-of-group transferred disregarded specified stock is the amount that is proportionate to the ratio of the amount of the out-of-group transferred disregarded specified stock to the amount of disregarded specified stock of the expatriated foreign subsidiary that is actually held by the specified related person immediately before the transfer referred to in paragraph (d)(3) or (4) of this section as a result of the specified transaction.

(ii) *In-group direct transfers of disregarded specified stock.*—For purposes of paragraph (d)(4) of this section, the portion of the deemed issued stock treated as owned by each section 958(a) U.S. shareholder as a result of the specified transaction that is allocable to in-group transferred disregarded specified stock is the amount that is proportionate to the ratio of the amount of the in-group transferred disregarded specified stock to the amount of disregarded specified stock of the expatriated foreign subsidiary that is actually held by the specified related person immediately before the transfer described in paragraph (d)(4) of this section as a result of the specified transaction.

(e) *Certain exception from foreign personal holding company income not available.*—An amount included in the gross income of a controlled foreign corporation as a dividend with respect to stock transferred in a specified transaction does not qualify for the exception from foreign personal holding company income provided by section 954(c)(6) (to the extent in effect).

(f) *Definitions.*—In addition to the definitions in § 1.7874-12, the following definitions and special rules apply for purposes of this section:

(1) *Deemed instruments* mean, with respect to a specified transaction, instruments deemed issued by a section 958(a) U.S. shareholder in exchange for transferred property in the specified transaction.

(2) *Deemed issued stock* means, with respect to a specified transaction, stock of an expatriated foreign subsidiary deemed issued to a section 958(a) U.S. shareholder (or an intermediate entity) in the specified transaction.

(3) *Disregarded specified stock* means, with respect to a specified transaction, specified stock that is actually held by a specified related person but that is disregarded for all purposes of the Internal Revenue Code pursuant to paragraph (c)(2) or (3) of this section.

(4) *Indirect ownership.*—To determine indirect ownership of the stock of a corporation for purposes of calculating a pre-transaction ownership percentage or post-transaction ownership percentage with respect to that corporation, the principles of section 958(a) apply without regard to whether an intermediate entity is foreign or domestic. For this purpose, stock of the corporation that is directly or indirectly (applying the principles of section 958(a) without regard to whether an intermediate entity is foreign or domestic) owned by a domestic corporation that is an expatriated entity is not treated as indirectly owned by a non-EFS foreign related person.

(5) *In-group transferred disregarded specified stock* means disregarded specified stock that is directly transferred to a foreign related person, a specified related person, or an expatriated entity.

(6) A *lower-tier expatriated foreign subsidiary* means an expatriated foreign subsidiary, stock of which is directly or indirectly owned by an expatriated foreign subsidiary.

(7) *Out-of-group transferred disregarded specified stock* means disregarded specified stock that, as a result of a transfer of disregarded specified stock, is actually held by a person that is not a foreign related person, a specified related person, or an expatriated entity.

(8) *Pre-transaction ownership percentage* means, with respect to a corporation, 100 percent less the percentage of stock (by value) in the corporation that, immediately before a specified transaction and any related transaction, is owned, in the aggregate, directly or indirectly by non-EFS foreign related persons.

(9) *Post-transaction ownership percentage* means, with respect to a corporation, 100 percent less the percentage of stock (by value) in the corporation that, immediately after the specified transaction and any related transaction, is owned, in the aggregate, directly or indirectly by non-EFS foreign related persons.

(10) A *section 958(a) U.S. shareholder* means, with respect to an expatriated foreign subsidiary, a United States shareholder with respect to the expatriated foreign subsidiary that owns (within the meaning of section 958(a)) stock of the expatriated foreign subsidiary and that is an expatriated entity.

(11) *Specified stock* means the stock of the expatriated foreign subsidiary that is issued or transferred to a specified related person in a specified transaction.

(12) *Transferred property* means the property transferred by the specified related person in exchange for specified stock in a specified transaction.

(g) *Examples.*—The following examples illustrate the regulations described in this section. Except as otherwise provided, FA, a foreign corporation, wholly owns DT, a domestic corporation, which, in turn, wholly owns FT, a foreign corporation that is a controlled foreign corporation. FA also wholly owns FS, a foreign corporation that is a controlled foreign corporation for its taxable year beginning January 1, 2017, but not for prior taxable years. FA acquired DT in an inversion transaction that was completed on January 1, 2015. Accordingly, DT is the domestic entity and a section 958(a) U.S. shareholder with respect to FT, FT is an expatriated foreign subsidiary, and FA and FS are non-EFS foreign related persons and specified related persons. All entities have a calendar year tax year for U.S. tax purposes.

Example 1. (i) *Facts.* On February 1, 2015, FA acquires $6x of FT stock, representing 60% of the total voting power and value of the stock of FT, from FT in a stock issuance, in exchange for $6x of cash.

(ii) *Analysis.* (A) Under paragraph (b) of this section, FA's acquisition of the FT specified stock from FT is a specified transaction because stock of an expatriated foreign subsidiary was issued to a specified related person (FA) during the applicable period. Furthermore, the exceptions to recharacterization in paragraph (b)(2) of this section do not apply to the transaction.

(B) FA's acquisition of the FT specified stock is recharacterized under paragraphs (c)(1) and (2) of this section as follows, with the result that FT continues to be a CFC even before its taxable year beginning January 1, 2017:

(*1*) DT is treated as having issued deemed instruments to FA in exchange for $6x of cash.

(*2*) DT is treated as having contributed the $6x of cash to FT in exchange for deemed issued stock of FT.

(C) Under paragraph (c)(4)(i) of this section, any distribution with respect to the FT specified stock issued to FA will be treated as a distribution to DT, which, in turn, will be treated as making a matching distribution with respect to the deemed instruments that DT is treated as having issued to FA. Under paragraph (c)(4)(ii) of this section, FT is treated as the paying agent of DT with respect to the deemed instruments issued by DT to FA.

Example 2. (i) *Facts.* DT owns stock of FT representing 60% of the total voting power and value of the stock of FT, and the remaining stock of FT, representing 40% of the total voting power and value, is owned by USP, a domestic corporation that is not an expatriated entity. On February 1, 2015, FA acquires $6x of FT stock, representing 60% of the total voting power and value of the stock of FT, from FT in a stock issuance, in exchange for $6x of cash.

(ii) *Analysis.* (A) Under paragraph (b) of this section, FA's acquisition of the FT specified stock from FT is a specified transaction because stock of an expatriated foreign subsidiary was issued to a specified related person (FA) during the applicable period. Furthermore, the exceptions to recharacterization in paragraph (b)(2) of this section do not apply to the transaction.

(B) FA's acquisition of the FT specified stock is recharacterized under paragraphs (c)(1) and (2) of this section as follows, with the result that FT continues to be a CFC even before its taxable year beginning January 1, 2017:

(*1*) DT is treated as having issued deemed instruments to FA in exchange for $6x of cash.

(*2*) DT is treated as having contributed the $6x of cash to FT in exchange for deemed issued stock of FT.

(*3*) DT is treated as owning $8.40x of the stock of FT, representing 84% of the total voting power and value of the stock of FT. USP owns $1.60x of the stock of FT, representing 16% of the total voting power and value of the stock of FT.

(C) Under paragraph (c)(4)(i) of this section, any distribution with respect to the FT specified stock issued to FA will be treated as a distribution to DT, which, in turn, will be treated as making a matching distribution with respect to the deemed instruments that DT is treated as having issued to FA. Under paragraph (c)(4)(ii) of this section, FT is treated as the paying agent of DT with respect to the deemed instruments issued by DT to FA.

Example 3. (i) *Facts.* DT owns stock of FT representing 50% of the total voting power and value of the $8x of stock of FT outstanding, and the remaining stock of FT, representing 50% of the total voting power and value, is owned by USP, a domestic corporation that is not an expatriated entity. On April 30, 2016, FA and USP each simultaneously acquire $1x of FT stock from FT in a stock issuance, in exchange for $1x of cash each.

(ii) *Analysis.* (A) Under paragraph (b) of this section, FA's acquisition of the FT specified stock from FT is a specified transaction because stock of an expatriated foreign subsidiary was issued to a specified related person (FA) during the applicable period.

(B) However, the specified transaction is not recharacterized under paragraphs (c)(1) and (2) of this section because the exception in paragraph (b)(2)(iii) of this section applies. The exception applies because FT remains a controlled foreign corporation immediately after the specified transaction and any related transaction, and the post-transaction ownership percentage with respect to FT is 90% (90%/100%), or at least 90%, of the pre-transaction ownership percentage with respect to FT. The rule in paragraph (b)(2)(iii)(C) of this section does not apply because there is no lower-tier expatriated foreign subsidiary. Although FA (a non-EFS foreign related person) indirectly owns $4x of FT stock both immediately before and after the specified transaction and any related transaction, all of that stock is directly owned by DT (a domestic corporation), and as a result, under paragraph (f)(4) of this section, none of that stock is treated as directly or indirectly owned by FA for purposes of calculating the pre-transaction ownership percentage and the post-transaction ownership percentage with respect to FT. Accordingly, under paragraph (f)(8) of this section, the pre-transaction ownership percentage with respect to FT (100% less the percentage of stock (by value) in FT that, immediately before the specified transaction with respect to FT and any related transaction, is owned by non-EFS foreign related persons) is 100 (100% - 0%). Under paragraph (f)(9) of this section, the post-transaction ownership percentage with respect to FT (100% less the percentage of stock (by value) in FT that, immediately after the specified transaction with respect to FT and any related transaction, is owned by non-EFS foreign related persons) is 90 (100% - 10% ($1x/$10x)).

Example 4. (i) *Facts.* On February 1, 2015, FA acquires 60% of the FT stock owned by DT in exchange for $2.40x of cash in a fully taxable transaction. DT recognizes and includes in income all of the gain (including any gain treated as a deemed dividend pursuant to section 1248(a)) with respect to the FT stock transferred to FA.

(ii) *Analysis.* (A) Under paragraph (b) of this section, FA's acquisition of the FT specified stock is a specified transaction because stock of an expatriated foreign subsidiary was transferred to a specified related person (FA) during the applicable period.

(B) However, the specified transaction is not recharacterized under paragraphs (c)(1) and (c)(3) of this section because the exception in paragraph (b)(2)(ii) of this section applies. The exception applies because DT recognizes and includes in income all of the gain (including any gain treated as a deemed dividend pursuant to section 1248(a)) with respect to the FT specified stock transferred to FA.

Example 5. (i) *Facts.* On February 1, 2015, DT and FA organize FPRS, a foreign partnership, with nominal capital. DT transfers all of the stock of FT to FPRS in exchange for 40% of the capital and profits interests in the partnership. Furthermore, FA contributes property to FPRS in exchange for the other 60% of the capital and profits interests.

(ii) *Analysis.* (A) Under paragraph (b) of this section, DT's transfer of the FT specified stock is a specified transaction, because stock of an expatriated foreign subsidiary was transferred to a specified related person (FPRS) during the applicable period. The exceptions to recharacterization in paragraph (b)(2) of this section do not apply to the transaction.

(B) DT's transfer of the FT specified stock is recharacterized under paragraphs (c)(1) and (c)(3) of this section as follows, with the result that FT continues to be a CFC even before its taxable year beginning January 1, 2017:

(*1*) FPRS is treated as having issued 40% of its capital and profits interests to DT in exchange for deemed instruments treated as having been issued by DT.

(*2*) DT is treated as continuing to own all of the stock of FT, as well as the FPRS interests.

(C) Under paragraph (c)(4)(i) of this section, any distribution with respect to the FT specified stock transferred to FPRS will be treated as a distribution to DT, which, in turn, will be treated as making a matching distribution with respect to the deemed instruments that DT is treated as having issued to FPRS. Under paragraph (c)(4)(ii) of this section, FT is treated as the paying agent of DT with respect to the deemed instruments issued by DT to FPRS.

Example 6. (i) *Facts.* DT wholly owns FT2, a foreign corporation that is a controlled foreign corporation. FT and FT2 each own 50% of the capital and profits interests in DPRS, a domestic partnership. DPRS wholly owns FT3, a foreign corporation that is a controlled foreign corporation. FT2 and FT3 are expatriated foreign subsidiaries. On April 30, 2016, FS acquires $9x of the stock of each of FT and FT2, representing 9% of the total voting power and value of the stock of FT and FT2, from FT and FT2, respectively, in a stock issuance, in exchange for cash of $9x each. Also on April 30, 2016, in a related transaction, FS acquires $9x of the stock of FT3, representing 9% of the total voting power and value of the stock of FT3, from FT3 in a stock issuance, in exchange for cash of $9x.

(ii) *Analysis.* (A) Under paragraph (b) of this section, the acquisitions by FS of the specified stock of each of FT, FT2, and FT3 from FT, FT2, and FT3 are specified transactions with respect to each of FT, FT2, and FT3, respectively, because stock of an expatriated foreign subsidiary was issued to a specified related person (FS) during the applicable period.

(B) If FS had acquired only stock of FT and FT2, and had not acquired stock of FT3 in a related transaction, the specified transactions resulting from the acquisitions with respect to FT and FT2 would not have been recharacterized under paragraphs (c)(1) and (2) of this section, because the exception from recharacterization in paragraph (b)(2)(iii) of this section would have applied. FT and FT2 remain controlled foreign corporations immediately after each specified transaction and any related transaction. Under paragraph (f)(9) of this section, the post-transaction ownership percentage with respect to each of FT, FT2, and FT3 (a lower-tier expatriated foreign subsidiary of FT and FT2) would have been 91% ((100% - 9%)/(100% - 0%)), or at least 90%, of the pre-transaction ownership percentage determined under paragraph (f)(8) of this section with respect to each of FT, FT2, and FT3 (100%).

(C) However, for the specified transactions with respect to FT, FT2, and FT3, the post-transaction ownership percentage determined under paragraph (f)(9) of this section with respect to FT3 (the lower-tier expatriated foreign subsidiary of FT and FT2), 100% less the percentage of stock (by value) in FT3 that, immediately after each of the specified transactions with respect to each of FT and FT2 and any related transaction, is owned by the non-EFS foreign related persons, is 82.81 (100%-(9%x50%x91%)-(9%x50%x91%)-9%). Accordingly, the post-transaction ownership percentage with respect to FT3 is 82.81% (82.81/(100%-0%)), which is less than 90%, of the pre-transaction ownership percentage determined under paragraph (f)(8) of this section with respect to FT3. Thus, the exception from recharacterization in paragraph (b)(2)(iii) of this section does not apply with respect to the specified transactions with respect to FT, FT2, or FT3.

(D) The specified transactions with respect to FT and FT2 are recharacterized under paragraphs (c)(1) and (2) of this section as follows:

(*1*) DT is treated as having issued 2 deemed instruments worth $9x each to FA in exchange for $18x ($9x + $9x) of cash.

(*2*) DT is treated as having contributed $9x of cash to each of FT and FT2 in exchange for deemed issued stock of FT and FT2.

(*3*) DT is treated as continuing to own all of the stock of FT and FT2.

(E) Under paragraph (c)(4)(i) of this section, any distribution with respect to the FT and FT2 specified stock issued to FS will be treated as a distribution to DT, which, in turn, will be treated as making a matching distribution with respect to the deemed instruments that DT is treated as having issued to FS. Under paragraph (c)(4)(ii) of this section, FT and FT2 are treated as the paying agents of DT with respect to the deemed instruments issued by DT to FS.

(F) The specified transaction with respect to FT3 is recharacterized under paragraphs (c)(1) and (2) of this section as follows:

(*1*) DPRS is treated as having issued a deemed instrument worth $9x to FA in exchange for $9x of cash.

(*2*) DPRS is treated as having contributed $9x of cash to FT3 in exchange for deemed issued stock of FT3.

(*3*) DPRS is treated as continuing to own all of the stock of FT3.

(G) Under paragraph (c)(4)(i) of this section, any distribution with respect to the FT3 specified stock issued to FS will be treated as a distribution to DPRS, which, in turn, will be treated as making a matching distribution with respect to the deemed instruments that

DPRS is treated as having issued to FS. Under paragraph (c)(4)(ii) of this section, FT3 is treated as the paying agent of DPRS with respect to the deemed instrument issued by DPRS to FS.

Example 7. (i) *Facts.* The facts are the same as in *Example 1* of this paragraph (g). On April 30, 2016, FA transfers $4x of the FT disregarded specified stock that it acquired on February 1, 2015 to USP, a domestic corporation that is not an expatriated entity, in exchange for $4x of cash.

(ii) *Results.* After the transfer, FT remains a foreign related person. Therefore, paragraph (d)(2) of this section does not apply. However, the $4x of FT disregarded specified stock transferred to USP ceases to be held by a foreign related person, a specified related person, or an expatriated entity (determined without taking into account paragraph (c)(2) or (3) of this section). Therefore, under paragraph (d)(3) of this section, immediately before the transfer of the disregarded specified stock, DT is deemed to transfer $4x ($6x x ($4x/$6x)) of the FT deemed issued stock that it is treated as owning to FA, the specified related person, in redemption of $4x ($6x x ($4x/$6x)) of the DT deemed instruments that FA is treated as owning, and the $4x of FT deemed issued stock deemed transferred to FA is deemed recapitalized into disregarded specified stock actually held by FA, which is thereafter treated as owned by FA for all purposes of the Code until the transfer to USP.

Example 8. (i) *Facts.* The facts are the same as in *Example 7* of this paragraph (g), except that on April 30, 2016, FA transfers all $6x of the FT disregarded specified stock to USP in exchange for $6x of cash.

(ii) *Results.* After the transfer, FT ceases to be a foreign related person (determined without taking into account paragraph (c)(2) or (3) of this section). Therefore, under paragraph (d)(2) of this section, immediately before the transfer of the disregarded specified stock, DT is deemed to transfer the $6x of FT deemed issued stock that it is treated as owning to FA, the specified related person, in redemption of the $6x of DT deemed instruments that FA is treated as owning, and the $6x of FT deemed issued stock deemed transferred to FA is deemed recapitalized into disregarded specified stock actually held by FA, which is thereafter treated as owned by FA for all purposes of the Code until the transfer to USP.

Example 9. (i) *Facts.* The facts are the same as in *Example 7* of this paragraph (g), except that on April 30, 2016, FA transfers $5.5x of the FT disregarded specified stock to USP in exchange for $5.5x of cash.

(ii) *Results.* After the transfer, FT ceases to be a foreign related person (determined without taking into account paragraph (c)(2) or (3) of this section). Therefore, under paragraph (d)(2) of this section, immediately before the transfer of the disregarded specified stock, DT is deemed to transfer the $6x of FT deemed issued stock that it is treated as owning to FA, the specified related person, in redemption of the $6x of DT deemed instruments that FA is treated as owning, and the $6x of FT deemed issued stock deemed transferred to FA is deemed recapitalized into disregarded specified stock actually held by FA, which is thereafter treated as owned by FA for all purposes of the Code and $5.5x of which is transferred to USP. The remaining $0.5x of the specified stock continues to be treated as owned by FA for all purposes of the Code.

Example 10. (i) *Facts.* The facts are the same as in *Example 1* of this paragraph (g). On April 30, 2016, FA transfers $5x of the FT disregarded specified stock that it acquired on February 1, 2015 to DS, a domestic corporation wholly owned by DT, in exchange for $5x of cash.

(ii) *Results.* After the transfer, FT remains a foreign related person because DS is wholly owned by DT. Therefore, paragraph (d)(2) of this section does not apply. Furthermore, the $5x of FT disregarded specified stock is not, as a result of the transfer, held by a person that is not a foreign related person, a specified related person, or an expatriated entity. Therefore, paragraph (d)(3) of this section does not apply. Because FA, a specified related person, directly transferred disregarded specified stock of FT in a transaction to which paragraphs (d)(2) and (3) of this section do not apply, under paragraph (d)(4) of this section, FA is treated as transferring the $5x of deemed instruments of DT allocable to the $5x of in-group transferred disregarded specified stock ($6x x ($5x/$6x)) to DS.

Example 11. (i) *Facts.* On February 1, 2015, FS acquires $6x of FT stock, representing 60% of the total voting power and value of the stock of FT, from FT in a stock issuance, in exchange for $6x of cash. The $6x of FT stock is specified stock, and the transaction is recharacterized under paragraph (c)(2) of this section. See *Example 1* of this paragraph (g). On April 30, 2016, FA transfers stock of FS representing 60% of the total voting power and value of the stock of FS to USP, a domestic corporation that is not an expatriated entity. As a result of the transfer, FS ceases to be a foreign related person.

(ii) *Results.* After the February 1, 2015 transfer, FT remains a foreign related person because the FT stock is acquired by FS, a foreign related person with respect to DT at that time. Therefore, paragraph (d)(2) of this section does not apply. However, after the April 30, 2016 transfer, because FS ceases to be a foreign related person, it ceases to be a specified related person. Furthermore, the $6x of disregarded specified stock held before the transaction continues to be held by FS after the transaction, and therefore is not held by a foreign related person, a specified related person, or an expatriated entity after the transaction. Accordingly, under paragraph (d)(3) of this section, immediately before the transfer of FS disregarded specified stock, DT is deemed to transfer $6x ($6x x ($6x/$6x)) of the FT deemed issued stock that it is treated as owning to FS, the specified related person, in redemption of $6x ($6x x ($6x/$6x)) of the DT deemed instruments that FS is treated as owning, and the $6x of FT deemed issued stock deemed transferred to FS is deemed recapitalized into disregarded specified stock actually held by FS, which thereafter is treated as owned by FS for all purposes of the Code, including after the transfer of 60% of the FS stock to USP.

Example 12. (i) *Facts.* The facts are the same as in *Example 1* of this paragraph (g). On April 30, 2016, FP, a foreign corporation that is not a foreign related person acquires $15x of FT stock, representing 60% of the total voting power and value of the stock of FT, from FT in a stock issuance, in exchange for $15x of cash.

(ii) *Results.* After the transaction, FT ceases to be a foreign related person. Therefore, under paragraph (d)(2) of this section, immediately before the issuance of FT stock to FP, DT is deemed to transfer the $6x of FT deemed issued stock that it is treated as owning to FA, the specified related person, in redemption of the $6x of DT deemed instruments that FA is treated as owning, and the $6x of FT deemed issued stock deemed transferred to FA is deemed recapitalized into disregarded specified stock actually held by FA, which thereafter is treated as owned by FA for all purposes of the Code.

Example 13. (i) *Facts.* The facts are the same as in *Example 1* of this paragraph (g). On April 30, 2016, FS acquires $4x of the FT stock owned by DT in exchange for $4x of cash in a fully taxable transaction. DT recognizes and includes in income all of the gain (including any gain treated as a deemed dividend pursuant to section 1248(a)) with respect to the FT stock transferred to FS.

(ii) *Results.* (A) The transfer of FT stock by DT to FS is a specified transaction, but it is not recharacterized under paragraphs (c)(1) and (3) of this section because the exception in paragraph (b)(2)(ii) of this section applies. See *Example 4* of this paragraph (g).

(B) After the transfer, FT remains a foreign related person. Therefore, paragraph (d)(2) of this section does not apply. The disregarded specified stock of FT is not, as a result of the transfer, held by a person that is not a foreign related person, a specified related person, or an expatriated entity. Therefore, paragraph (d)(3) of this section does not apply. There has been no direct transfer of specified stock. Therefore, paragraph (d)(4) of this section also does not apply.

(C) Under paragraph (d)(1) of this section, the $6x of deemed issued stock treated as owned by DT as a result of the specified transaction in which FA acquired FT stock continues to be treated as owned by DT, and the $6x of deemed instruments treated as issued by DT to FA continue to be treated as owned by FA.

(h) *Applicability date.*—Except as otherwise provided in this paragraph (h), this section applies to specified transactions completed on or after September 22, 2014, but only if the inversion transaction was completed on or after September 22, 2014. Paragraph (b)(2)(ii)(A)(2) of this section applies to specified transactions completed on or after November 19, 2015, but only if the inversion transaction was completed on or after September 22, 2014. Paragraphs (d) and (f)(5), (7), and (10) of this section apply to specified transactions completed on or after April 4, 2016, but only if the inversion transaction was completed on or after September 22, 2014. For inversion transactions completed on or after September 22, 2014, however, taxpayers may elect to apply paragraphs (d) and (f)(5), (7), and (10) of this section to specified transactions completed before April 4, 2016. In addition, for inversion transactions completed on or after September 22, 2014, in lieu of applying paragraphs (d) and (f)(5) and (7) of this section to specified transactions completed on or after September 22, 2014, and before April 4, 2016, taxpayers may elect to apply the principles of § 1.7701(l)-3(c)(3)(iii). Furthermore, for inversion transactions completed on or after September 22, 2014, in lieu of applying paragraph (f)(10) of this section to specified transactions completed on or after September 22, 2014, and before April 4, 2016, taxpayers may elect to define a section 958(a) U.S. shareholder as a United States shareholder with respect to the expatriated foreign subsidiary that owns (within the meaning of section 958(a)) stock in the expatriated foreign subsidiary, but only if such United States shareholder is related (within the meaning of section 267(b) or 707(b)(1)) to the specified related person or is under the same common control (within the meaning of section 482) as the specified related person. [Reg. § 1.7701(l)-4.]

☐ [*T.D.* 9834, 7-11-2018.]

Provisions Affecting More Than One Subtitle

§ 1.7874-1. Disregard of affiliate-owned stock.—(a) *Scope.*—Section 7874(c)(2)(A) provides that stock of the foreign acquiring corporation held by members of the expanded affiliated group shall not be taken into account in determining ownership for purposes of section 7874(a)(2)(B)(ii). This section provides rules under section 7874(c)(2)(A). The rules provided in this section are also subject to section 7874(c)(4). For definitions that apply for purposes of this section, see 1.7874-12.

(b) *General rule.*—Except as provided in paragraph (c) of this section, for purposes of determining the ownership percentage described in section 7874(a)(2)(B)(ii), stock held by one or more members of the EAG is not included in either the numerator or the denominator of the ownership fraction.

(c) *Exceptions to general rule.*—(1) *Overview.*—Stock held by one or more members of the EAG shall be included in the denominator, but not in the numerator, of the ownership fraction, if the domestic entity acquisition qualifies as an *internal group restructuring* or results in a *loss of control*, as described in paragraph (c)(2) and (c)(3) of this section. For rules addressing the interaction of this section and other rules, see paragraph (d) of this section.

(2) *Internal group restructuring.*—For purposes of paragraph (c)(1) of this section, a domestic entity acquisition qualifies as an internal group restructuring if:

(i) Before the domestic entity acquisition, 80 percent or more of the stock (by vote and value) or the capital and profits interest, as applicable, of the domestic entity was held directly or indirectly by the corporation that is the common parent of the EAG after the acquisition; and

(ii) After the domestic entity acquisition, 80 percent or more of the stock (by vote and value) of the foreign acquiring corporation is held directly or indirectly by such common parent.

(iii) *Special rule.*—If § 1.7874-6(c)(2) applies for purposes of applying section 7874(c)(2)(A) and this section, then, for purposes of paragraph (c)(2) of this section (and so much of paragraph (c)(1) of this section as relates to paragraph (c)(2) of this section), the determination of the EAG after the domestic entity acquisition, as well as the determination of stock held by one or more members of the EAG after the domestic entity acquisition, is made without regard to one or more transfers (other than by issuance), in a transaction (or series of transactions) after and related to the acquisition, of stock of the acquiring foreign corporation by one or more members of the foreign-parented group described in § 1.7874-6(c)(2)(i).

(3) *Loss of control.*—For purposes of paragraph (c)(1) of this section, the domestic entity acquisition results in a loss of control if after the acquisition, the former domestic entity shareholders or former domestic entity partners do not hold, in the aggregate, directly or indirectly, more than 50 percent of the stock (by vote or value) of any member of the EAG.

(d) *Interaction of expanded affiliated group rules with other rules.*—(1) *Exclusion rules.*—Stock that is excluded from the denominator of the ownership fraction pursuant to § 1.7874-4(b), 1.7874-7(b), 1.7874-8(b), 1.7874-9(b), or section 7874(c)(4) is taken into account for purposes of determining whether an entity is a member of the expanded affiliated group for purposes of applying section 7874(c)(2)(A) and paragraph (b) of this section and determining whether a domestic entity acquisition qualifies as an internal group restructuring or results in a loss of control, as described in paragraphs (c)(2) and (3) of this section, respectively. However, such stock is excluded from the denominator of the ownership fraction regardless of whether it otherwise would be included in the denominator of the ownership fraction as a result of the application of paragraph (c) of this section. See *Example 8* and *Example 9* of § 1.7874-4(i) for illustrations of the application of this paragraph (d)(1).

(2) *NOCD rule.*—Stock of the foreign acquiring corporation treated as received by former domestic entity shareholders or former domestic entity partners, as applicable, under § 1.7874-10(b) is not taken into account for purposes of determining whether an entity is a member of the expanded affiliated group for purposes of applying section 7874(c)(2)(A) and paragraph (b) of this section and determining whether a domestic entity acquisition qualifies as an internal group restructuring or results in a loss of control, as described in paragraphs (c)(2) and (3) of this section, respectively. However, such stock is included in the numerator and denominator of the ownership fraction, except to the extent that it is treated as held by a member of the EAG and is excluded from the numerator or both the numerator and the denominator, as applicable, under section 7874(c)(2)(A) or paragraphs (b) or (c) of this section.

(e) *Treatment of certain hook stock.*—This paragraph applies to stock of a corporation that is held by an entity in which at least 50 percent of the stock (by vote or value) or at least 50 percent of the capital or profits interest, as applicable, in such entity, is held directly or indirectly by the corporation. The stock to which this paragraph applies shall not be included in either the numerator or denominator of any fraction for the following purposes:

(1) For applying paragraph (c)(1) of this section; and

(2) For determining whether the domestic entity acquisition qualifies as an internal group restructuring (described in paragraph (c)(2) of this section) or results in a loss of control (described in paragraph (c)(3) of this section).

(f) *Stock held by a partnership.*—For purposes of this section, each partner in a partnership shall be treated as holding its proportionate share of stock held by the partnership, as determined under the rules and principles of sections 701 through 777.

(g) *Treatment of transactions related to the acquisition.*—Except as provided in paragraph (c)(2)(iii) of this section, all transactions that are related to an acquisition are taken into account in applying this section.

(h) *Examples.*—The application of this section is illustrated by the following examples. It is assumed that all transactions in the examples occur after March 4, 2003. In all the examples, if an entity or other person is not described as either domestic or foreign, it may be either domestic or foreign. In addition, each entity has only a single class of equity outstanding. Finally, the analysis of the following examples is limited to a discussion of issues under section 7874, even though the examples may raise other issues (for example, under section 367).

Example 1. Disregard of hook stock—(i) *Facts.* USS, a domestic corporation, has 100 shares of stock outstanding. USS's stock is held by a group of individuals. Pursuant to a plan, USS forms FS, a foreign corporation, and transfers to FS the stock of several wholly owned foreign corporations, in exchange for 90 shares of FS stock. FS then forms Merger Sub, a domestic corporation. Under a merger agreement and state law, Merger Sub merges into USS, with USS surviving the merger. In exchange for their USS stock, the former shareholders of USS receive, in the aggregate, 100 shares of newly issued FS stock. As a result of the merger FS holds 100 percent of the USS stock. USS continues to hold 90 shares of FS stock.

(ii) *Analysis.* FS has indirectly acquired substantially all the properties held directly or indirectly by USS pursuant to a plan. After the acquisition, the former shareholders of USS hold 100 shares of FS stock by reason of holding stock in USS, and USS holds 90 shares of FS stock. Under paragraph (b) of this section, the 90 shares of FS stock held by USS, a member of the EAG, are not included in either the numerator or the denominator of the ownership fraction. Accordingly, the ownership fraction is 100/100. If the condition in section 7874(a)(2)(B)(iii) is satisfied, FS is a surrogate foreign corporation which is treated as a domestic corporation under section 7874(b).

Example 2. Internal group restructuring; wholly owned corporation—(i) *Facts.* P, a corporation, owns all 100 outstanding shares of USS, a domestic corporation. USS forms FS, a foreign corporation, and transfers all its assets to FS in exchange for all 100 shares of the stock of FS, in a reorganization described in section 368(a)(1). P exchanges its USS stock for FS stock under section 354.

(ii) *Analysis.* FS has directly acquired substantially all the properties held directly or indirectly by USS pursuant to a plan. The acquisition is an internal group restructuring described in paragraph (c)(2) of this section because P, the common parent of the EAG after the acquisition, held directly or indirectly 80 percent or more of the stock (by vote and value) of USS before the acquisition, and after the acquisition, P holds directly or indirectly 80 percent or more of the stock (by vote and value) of FS. Accordingly, under paragraph (c)(1) of this section, the FS stock held by P is included in the denominator, but not in the numerator of the ownership fraction. Therefore, the ownership fraction is 0/100. FS is not a surrogate foreign corporation.

Example 3. Internal group restructuring; wholly owned corporation—(i) *Facts*. The facts are the same as in *Example 2*, except that USS does not transfer any of its assets to FS. Instead, P transfers all 100 shares of USS stock to FS in exchange for all 100 shares of FS stock.

(ii) *Analysis*. FS has indirectly acquired substantially all the properties held directly or indirectly by USS pursuant to a plan. The acquisition is an internal group restructuring described in paragraph (c)(2) of this section because P, the common parent of the EAG after the acquisition, held directly or indirectly 80 percent or more of the stock (by vote and value) of USS before the acquisition, and after the acquisition, P holds directly or indirectly 80 percent or more of the stock (by vote and value) of FS. Accordingly, under paragraph (c)(1) of this section, the FS stock held by P is included in the denominator, but not in the numerator of the ownership fraction. Accordingly, the ownership fraction is 0/100. FS is not a surrogate foreign corporation.

Example 4. Internal group restructuring; less than wholly owned corporation—(i) *Facts*. The facts are the same as in *Example 3*, except that P holds 85 shares of USS stock. The remaining 15 shares of USS stock are held by A, a person unrelated to P. P and A transfer their shares of USS stock to FS in exchange for 85 and 15 shares of FS stock, respectively.

(ii) *Analysis*. FS has indirectly acquired substantially all the properties held directly or indirectly by USS pursuant to a plan. The acquisition is an internal group restructuring described in paragraph (c)(2) of this section because P, the common parent of the EAG after the acquisition, held directly or indirectly 80 percent or more of the stock (by vote and value) of USS before the acquisition, and after the acquisition P holds directly or indirectly 80 percent or more of the stock (by vote and value) of FS. Therefore, under paragraph (c)(1) of this section, the FS stock held by P is included in the denominator, but not in the numerator of the ownership fraction. Accordingly, the ownership fraction is 15/100. FS is not a surrogate foreign corporation.

Example 5. Internal group restructuring exception not applicable; less than 80 percent owned corporation—(i) *Facts*. The facts are the same as in *Example 2*, except that P owns 55 shares of USS stock, and A, a person unrelated to P, holds 45 shares of USS stock. P and A exchange their shares of USS stock for 55 shares and 45 shares of FS stock, respectively.

(ii) *Analysis*. FS has acquired substantially all the properties held directly or indirectly by USS pursuant to a plan. P, the common parent of the EAG after the acquisition, did not hold directly or indirectly 80 percent or more of the stock (by vote and value) of USS before the acquisition, and after the acquisition P does not hold directly or indirectly 80 percent or more of the stock (by vote and value) of FS. Thus, the acquisition is not an internal group restructuring described in paragraph (c)(1) of this section, and the general rule of paragraph (b) of this section applies. Under paragraph (b) of this section, the FS stock held by P, a member of the EAG, is not included in either the numerator or the denominator of the ownership fraction. Accordingly, the ownership fraction is 45/45. If the condition in section 7874(a)(2)(B)(iii) is satisfied, FS is a surrogate foreign corporation which is treated as a domestic corporation under section 7874(b).

Example 6. Internal group restructuring; hook stock—(i) *Facts*. USS, a domestic corporation, has 100 shares of stock outstanding. P, a corporation, holds 80 shares of USS stock. The remaining 20 shares of USS stock are held by A, a person unrelated to P. USS owns all 30 outstanding shares of FS, a foreign corporation. Pursuant to a plan, FS forms Merger Sub, a domestic corporation. Under a merger agreement and state law, Merger Sub merges into USS, with USS surviving the merger as a subsidiary of FS. In exchange for their USS stock, P and A, the former shareholders of USS, respectively receive 56 and 14 shares of FS stock. USS continues to hold 30 shares of FS stock.

(ii) *Analysis*. FS has indirectly acquired substantially all the properties held directly or indirectly by USS pursuant to a plan. Under paragraph (b) of this section, the shares of FS stock held by P and USS, both of which are members of the EAG, are not included in either the numerator or denominator of the ownership fraction, unless the acquisition results in an internal group restructuring or loss of control of USS such that the exception of paragraph (c)(1) of this section applies. In determining whether the acquisition of USS is an internal group restructuring, under paragraph (e)(2) of this section, the FS stock held by USS is disregarded. Because P held directly or indirectly 80 percent or more of the stock (by vote and value) of USS before the acquisition, and after the acquisition P holds directly or indirectly 80 percent or more of the stock (by vote and value) of FS (when disregarding the FS stock held by USS), the acquisition is an internal group restructuring and the exception of paragraph (c)(1) of this section applies. Accordingly, when determining whether FS is a surrogate foreign corporation, the FS stock held by P is included in the denominator, but not the numerator of the ownership fraction. However, under paragraph (b) of this section, the FS stock held by USS is not included in either the numerator or denominator of the ownership fraction. Accordingly, the ownership fraction is 14/70, or 20 percent, since only the stock held by A is included in the numerator, and the stock held by both P and A is included in the denominator. Accordingly, FS is not a surrogate foreign corporation.

Example 7. Loss of control—(i) *Facts*. P, a corporation, holds all the outstanding stock of USS, a domestic corporation. B, a corporation unrelated to P, holds all 60 outstanding shares of FS, a foreign corporation. P transfers to FS all the outstanding stock of USS in exchange for 40 newly issued shares of FS.

(ii) *Analysis*. FS has indirectly acquired substantially all the properties held directly or indirectly by USS pursuant to a plan. After the acquisition, B holds 60 percent of the outstanding shares of the FS stock. Accordingly, B, FS and USS are members of an EAG. After the acquisition, P does not hold directly or indirectly more than 50 percent of the stock (by vote or value) of any member of the EAG and, thus, the acquisition results in a loss of control described in paragraph (c)(3) of this section. Accordingly, under paragraph (c)(1) of this section, the FS stock owned by B is included in the denominator, but not in the numerator, of the ownership fraction. Therefore, the ownership fraction is 40/100. FS is not a surrogate foreign corporation.

Example 8. Internal group restructuring; partnership—(i) *Facts*. LLC, a Delaware limited liability company, is engaged in the conduct of a trade or business. P, a corporation, holds 90 percent of the interests of LLC. A, a person unrelated to P, holds 10 percent of the interests of LLC. LLC has not elected to be treated as an association taxable as a corporation. P and A transfer their interests in LLC to FS, a newly formed foreign corporation, in exchange for 90 shares and 10 shares, respectively, of FS's stock, which are all of the outstanding shares of FS. Accordingly, LLC becomes a disregarded entity.

(ii) *Analysis*. Prior to the FS's acquisition of the interests of LLC, LLC was a domestic partnership for Federal income tax purposes. FS has acquired substantially all the properties constituting a trade or business of LLC pursuant to a plan. After the acquisition, P holds 90 percent of FS's stock (by vote and value) by reason of holding a capital and profits interest in LLC, and A holds 10 percent of FS's stock (by vote and value) by reason of holding a capital and profits interest in LLC. The internal group restructuring exception under paragraph (c)(2) of this section applies, because before the acquisition, P held 80 percent or more of the capital and profits interest in LLC, and after the acquisition, P holds 80 percent or more of the stock (by vote and value) of FS. Under paragraph (c)(1) of this section, the FS stock held by P is included in the denominator, but not the numerator, of the ownership fraction. Accordingly, the ownership fraction is 10/100. FS is not a surrogate foreign corporation.

(i) *Applicability dates*.—(1) *In general*.—Except as otherwise provided, this section shall apply to domestic entity acquisitions completed on or after May 20, 2008. This section shall not, however, apply to a domestic entity acquisition that was completed on or after May 20, 2008, provided such acquisition was entered into pursuant to a written agreement which was (subject to customary conditions) binding prior to May 20, 2008, and at all times thereafter (binding commitment). For purposes of the preceding sentence, a binding commitment shall include entering into options and similar interests in connection with one or more written agreements described in the preceding sentence. Notwithstanding the general application of this paragraph, taxpayers may elect to apply this section to domestic entity acquisitions completed before May 20, 2008, but must apply it consistently to all acquisitions within its scope. Paragraph (f) of this section shall apply to acquisitions completed on or after June 7, 2012. See § 1.7874-1T(f), as contained in 26 CFR part 1 revised as of April 1, 2012, for domestic entity acquisitions completed before June 7, 2012.

(2) *Applicability date of certain provisions of this section*.—Except as provided in this paragraph (i)(2), paragraph (c)(2)(iii) of this section applies to domestic entity acquisitions completed on or after April 4, 2016. Except as provided in this paragraph (i)(2), paragraph (d) of this section (interaction of EAG rules with other rules) applies to domestic entity acquisitions completed on or after July 12, 2018. See

§§1.7874-4(h) and 1.7874-7T(e), as contained in 26 CFR part 1 revised as of April 1, 2017, for certain coordination rules for domestic entity acquisitions completed before July 12, 2018. Except as provided in this paragraph (i)(2), paragraph (g) of this section applies to domestic entity acquisitions completed on or after September 22, 2014. For domestic entity acquisitions completed before April 4, 2016, however, taxpayers may elect to consistently apply paragraphs (c)(2)(iii) and (g) of this section, and §1.7874-6(c)(2), (d)(2), and (f)(2)(ii). In addition, for domestic entity acquisitions completed before July 12, 2018, taxpayers may elect to consistently apply paragraph (d) of this section. [Reg. §1.7874-1.]

☐ [*T.D. 9399, 5-19-2008. Amended by T.D. 9453, 6-9-2009; T.D. 9591, 6-7-2012, T.D. 9654, 1-16-2014, T.D. 9761, 4-4-2016; T.D. 9812, 1-13-2017 and T.D. 9834, 7-11-2018.*]

§1.7874-2. Surrogate foreign corporation.—(a) *Scope.*—This section provides rules for determining whether a foreign corporation is treated as a surrogate foreign corporation under section 7874(a)(2)(B). Paragraph (b) of this section provides definitions and special rules. Paragraph (c) of this section provides rules to determine whether a foreign corporation has acquired properties held by a domestic corporation (or a partnership). Paragraph (d) of this section provides rules that apply when two or more foreign corporations complete, in the aggregate, a domestic entity acquisition. Paragraph (e) of this section provides rules that apply when, pursuant to a plan, a single foreign corporation completes more than one domestic entity acquisition. Paragraph (f) of this section provides rules to identify the stock of a foreign corporation that is held by reason of holding stock in a domestic corporation (or an interest in a domestic partnership). Paragraph (g) of this section provides rules that treat certain publicly traded foreign partnerships as foreign corporations for purposes of section 7874. Paragraph (h) of this section provides rules concerning the treatment of certain options (or similar interests) for purposes of section 7874. Paragraph (i) of this section provides rules that treat certain interests (including debt, stock, or a partnership interest) as stock of a foreign corporation for purposes of section 7874. Paragraph (j) of this section provides rules concerning the conversion of a foreign corporation to a domestic corporation by reason of section 7874(b). Paragraph (k) of this section provides examples that illustrate the rules of this section. Paragraph (l) of this section provides the applicability dates of this section. For additional definitions that apply for purposes of this section, see §1.7874-12.

(b) *Definitions and special rules.*—In addition to the definitions in §1.7874-12, the following definitions and special rules apply for purposes of this section.

(1) The rules of this section are subject to section 7874(c)(4).

(2) References to *properties held* by a domestic corporation include properties held directly or indirectly by the domestic corporation.

(3) The rules and principles of sections 701 through 777 shall be applied for purposes of determining a proportionate amount (or share) of properties held by a partnership (such as stock).

(4) Any reference to the acquisition of properties held by a domestic corporation (or a partnership) includes a direct or indirect acquisition of such properties.

(5) In the case of an acquisition of stock of a domestic corporation or an interest in a partnership, the proportionate amount of properties held by the domestic corporation (or the partnership) that is treated as indirectly acquired shall, as applicable, be determined at the time of the acquisition based on the relative value of—

(i) The stock acquired compared to all outstanding stock of the domestic corporation; or

(ii) The interest acquired compared to all interests in the partnership.

(6) The determination of whether a foreign corporation is a surrogate foreign corporation is made after the domestic entity acquisition. A foreign corporation that is treated as a surrogate foreign corporation (including a surrogate foreign corporation treated as a domestic corporation described in section 7874(b)) shall continue to be treated as a surrogate foreign corporation (or a domestic corporation), even if the conditions of section 7874(a)(2)(B)(ii) and (iii) are not satisfied at a later date.

(7) A *former initial acquiring corporation shareholder* of an initial acquiring corporation means any person that held stock in the initial acquiring corporation before the subsequent acquisition, including any person that holds stock in the initial acquiring corporation both before and after the subsequent acquisition.

(8) An *initial acquisition* means, with respect to a subsequent acquisition, a domestic entity acquisition occurring, pursuant to a plan that includes the subsequent acquisition (or a series of related transactions), before the subsequent acquisition.

(9) An *initial acquiring corporation* means, with respect to an initial acquisition, the foreign acquiring corporation.

(10) A *subsequent acquisition* means, with respect to an initial acquisition, a transaction occurring, pursuant to a plan that includes the initial acquisition (or a series of related transactions), after the initial acquisition in which a foreign corporation directly or indirectly acquires (within the meaning of paragraph (c)(4)(ii) of this section) substantially all of the properties held directly or indirectly by the initial acquiring corporation.

(11) A *subsequent acquiring corporation* means, with respect to a subsequent acquisition, the foreign corporation that directly or indirectly acquires substantially all of the properties held directly or indirectly by the initial acquiring corporation.

(12) *Special rule regarding initial acquisitions.*—With respect to an initial acquisition, the determination of the ownership percentage described in section 7874(a)(2)(B)(ii) is made without regard to the subsequent acquisition and all related transactions occurring after the subsequent acquisition.

(13) *Special rule regarding subsequent acquisitions.*—With respect to a subsequent acquisition (or a similar acquisition under the principles of paragraph (c)(4)(i) of this section) that is an inversion transaction, the applicable period begins on the first date that properties are acquired as part of the initial acquisition.

(c) *Acquisition of properties.*—(1) *Indirect acquisition of properties.*—For purposes of section 7874(a)(2)(B)(i), an indirect acquisition of properties held by a domestic corporation (or a partnership) includes, but is not limited to, the acquisitions described in paragraphs (c)(1)(i) through (iv) of this section. An acquisition of less than all of the stock of a domestic corporation (or interests in a partnership) shall constitute an indirect acquisition of a proportionate amount of the properties held by the domestic corporation or the partnership. See paragraph (b)(8) of this section for rules determining the proportionate amount of properties indirectly acquired.

(i) An acquisition of stock of a domestic corporation. See *Example 1* of paragraph (k) of this section for an illustration of the rules of this paragraph (c)(1)(i).

(ii) An acquisition of an interest in a partnership. See *Example 2* of paragraph (k) of this section for an illustration of the rules of this paragraph (c)(1)(ii).

(iii) An acquisition by a corporation (acquiring corporation) of properties held by a domestic corporation (or a partnership) in exchange for stock of a foreign corporation (foreign issuing corporation) that is part of the expanded affiliated group that includes the acquiring corporation after the acquisition shall be treated as an acquisition by the foreign issuing corporation. See *Example 3* of paragraph (k) of this section for an illustration of the rules of this paragraph (c)(1)(iii).

(iv) An acquisition by a partnership (acquiring partnership) of properties held by a domestic corporation (or a partnership) in exchange for stock of a foreign corporation that is part of the expanded affiliated group that would include the acquiring partnership after the acquisition (if the partnership were a corporation) shall be treated as an acquisition by the foreign issuing corporation.

(2) *Acquisition of stock of a foreign corporation.*—Except as provided in paragraph (c)(4) of this section, an acquisition of stock of a foreign corporation that owns directly or indirectly stock of a domestic corporation (or an interest in a partnership) shall not constitute an indirect acquisition of any properties held by the domestic corporation (or the partnership). See *Example 4* of paragraph (k) of this section for an illustration of the rules of this paragraph (c)(2).

(3) *Downstream transactions.*—An acquisition by a corporation of its stock from another corporation or a partnership (for example, as a result of a downstream merger) is an acquisition of the other corporation's or partnership's properties for purposes of section 7874(a)(2)(B)(i).

(4) *Multiple-step acquisitions.*—(i) *Rule.*—A subsequent acquisition is treated as a domestic entity acquisition, and the subsequent acquiring corporation is treated as a foreign acquiring corporation. See *Example 21* of paragraph (k) of this section for an illustration of this rule. See also paragraph (f)(1)(iv) of this section (treating certain stock of the subsequent acquiring corporation as stock of a foreign corporation that is held by reason of holding stock of, or a partnership interest in, the domestic entity).

(ii) *Acquisition of property pursuant to a subsequent acquisition.*—In determining whether a foreign corporation directly or indirectly acquires substantially all of the properties held directly or indirectly by an initial acquiring corporation, the principles of section 7874(a)(2)(B)(i) apply, including paragraph (c) of this section other than paragraph (c)(2) of this section. For this purpose, the principles of paragraph (c)(1) of this section, including paragraph (b)(5) of this section, apply by substituting the term "foreign" for "domestic" wherever it appears.

(iii) *Additional related transactions.*—If, pursuant to the same plan (or a series of related transactions), a foreign corporation directly or indirectly acquires (under the principles of paragraph (c)(4)(ii) of this section) substantially all of the properties directly or indirectly held by a subsequent acquiring corporation in a transaction occurring after the subsequent acquisition, then the principles of paragraph (c)(4)(i) of this section apply to such transaction (and any subsequent transaction or transactions occurring pursuant to the plan (or the series of related transactions)).

(d) *Acquisitions by multiple foreign corporations.*—If, pursuant to a plan (or a series of related transactions), two or more foreign corporations complete, in the aggregate, a domestic entity acquisition, then each foreign corporation shall be treated as completing the acquisition for purposes of determining whether such foreign corporation is treated as a surrogate foreign corporation. See *Examples 5* and *6* of paragraph (k) of this section for illustrations of the rules of this paragraph (d).

(e) *Acquisitions of multiple domestic entities.*—If, pursuant to a plan (or a series of related transactions), a foreign corporation completes two or more domestic entity acquisitions involving domestic corporations and/or domestic partnerships (domestic entities), then, for purposes of section 7874(a)(2)(B)(ii), the acquisitions shall be treated as a single acquisition and the domestic entities shall be treated as a single domestic entity. If the transaction involves one or more domestic corporations and one or more domestic partnerships, the stock of the foreign corporation held by former domestic entity shareholders and former domestic entity partners by reason of holding stock or a partnership interest in the domestic entities shall be aggregated for purposes of determining whether the ownership condition of section 7874(a)(2)(B)(ii) is satisfied. See *Example 7* of paragraph (k) of this section for an illustration of the rules of this paragraph (e).

(f) *Stock held by reason of holding stock in a domestic corporation or an interest in a domestic partnership.*—(1) *Certain transactions.*—For purposes of section 7874(a)(2)(B)(ii), stock of a foreign corporation that is held by reason of holding stock in a domestic corporation (or an interest in a domestic partnership) includes, but is not limited to, the stock described in paragraphs (f)(1)(i) through (iv) of this section.

(i) Stock of a foreign corporation received in exchange for, or with respect to, stock of a domestic corporation.

(ii) Stock of a foreign corporation received in exchange for, or with respect to, an interest in a domestic partnership.

(iii) To the extent that paragraph (f)(1)(ii) of this section does not apply, stock of a foreign corporation received by a domestic partnership in exchange for all or part of its properties. In such a case, each partner in the domestic partnership shall be treated as holding its proportionate share of the stock of the foreign corporation by reason of holding an interest in the domestic partnership.

(iv) Stock of a subsequent acquiring corporation received by a former initial acquiring corporation shareholder pursuant to a subsequent acquisition in exchange for, or with respect to, stock of an initial acquiring corporation that is held by reason of holding stock of, or a partnership interest in, a domestic entity.

(2) *Transactions involving other property.*—(i) *Stock of a domestic corporation.*—If, pursuant to the same transaction, stock of a foreign corporation is received in exchange for, or with respect to, stock of a domestic corporation and other property, the stock of the foreign corporation that was received in exchange for, or with respect to, the stock of the domestic corporation shall be determined based on the relative value of the stock of the domestic corporation compared to the aggregate value of such stock and the other property.

(ii) *Interest in a domestic partnership.*—If, pursuant to the same transaction, stock of a foreign corporation is received in exchange for, or with respect to, an interest in a domestic partnership and other property, the stock of the foreign corporation that was received in exchange for, or with respect to, the interest in the domestic partnership shall be determined based on the relative value of the interest in the domestic partnership compared to the aggregate value of such interest and the other property.

(3) See *Examples 8* through *10* of paragraph (k) of this section for illustrations of the rules of this paragraph (f).

(g) *Publicly traded foreign partnerships.*—(1) *Treatment as a foreign corporation.*—For purposes of section 7874, a publicly traded foreign partnership described in paragraph (g)(2) of this section shall be treated as a foreign corporation that is organized in the foreign country in which, or under the law of which, the publicly traded foreign partnership was created or organized, and the partnership interests in the publicly traded foreign partnership shall be treated as stock of the foreign corporation. For purposes of determining whether the foreign corporation shall be treated as a surrogate foreign corporation, a deemed acquisition of assets and liabilities by reason of § 1.708-1(b)(4) shall not constitute an acquisition described in section 7874(a)(2)(B)(i).

(2) *Publicly traded foreign partnership.*—A publicly traded foreign partnership described in this paragraph (g)(2) is any foreign partnership that would, but for section 7704(c), be treated as a corporation under section 7704(a)—

(i) At the time of the domestic entity acquisition; or

(ii) At any time after the domestic entity acquisition pursuant to a plan that existed at the time of the domestic entity acquisition. For this purpose, a plan shall be deemed to exist at the time of the domestic entity acquisition if the foreign partnership would, but for section 7704(c), be treated as a corporation under section 7704(a) at any time during the two-year period following the completion of the domestic entity acquisition.

(3) *Surrogate foreign corporation to which section 7874(b) applies.*—If paragraph (g)(1) of this section applies to a publicly traded foreign partnership and the foreign corporation is a surrogate foreign corporation to which section 7874(b) applies, the publicly traded foreign partnership shall be treated as a domestic corporation for purposes of the Internal Revenue Code (Code). See paragraph (g)(6) of this section for the timing and treatment of the conversion of the publicly traded foreign partnership to a domestic corporation. See *Example 11* of paragraph (k) of this section for an illustration of the rules of this paragraph (g)(3).

(4) *Surrogate foreign corporation to which section 7874(b) does not apply.*—If paragraph (g)(1) of this section applies to a publicly traded foreign partnership and the foreign corporation is a surrogate foreign corporation to which section 7874(b) does not apply, the publicly traded foreign partnership shall continue to be treated as a foreign partnership for purposes of the Code, but section 7874(a)(1) shall apply to any expatriated entity (as defined in section 7874(a)(2)(A)). See *Example 13* of paragraph (k) of this section for an illustration of the rules of this paragraph (g)(4).

(5) *Foreign corporation not treated as a surrogate foreign corporation.*—If paragraph (g)(1) of this section applies to a publicly traded foreign partnership and the foreign corporation is not treated as a surrogate foreign corporation, the status of the publicly traded foreign partnership as a foreign partnership shall not be affected by section 7874. See *Example 12* of paragraph (k) of this section for an illustration of the rules of this paragraph (g)(5).

(6) *Conversion to a domestic corporation.*—Except for purposes of determining whether the publicly traded foreign partnership is a surrogate foreign corporation, if paragraph (g)(1) of this section applies to a publicly traded foreign partnership and the foreign corporation is a surrogate foreign corporation to which section 7874(b) applies, then at the later of the end of the day immediately preceding the first date properties are acquired as part of the domestic entity acquisition or immediately after the formation of the publicly traded foreign partnership, the publicly traded foreign partnership shall be treated as transferring all of its assets and liabilities to a newly formed domestic corporation in exchange solely for stock of the domestic corporation, and then distributing such stock to its partners in proportion to their partnership interests in liquidation of the partnership. The treatment of the transfer of assets and liabilities to the domestic corporation and the distribution of the stock of the domestic corporation to the partners in liquidation of the partnership shall be determined under all relevant provisions of the Code and general tax principles.

(h) *Options.*—(1) *Value.*—Except to the extent otherwise provided in this paragraph (h), for purposes of section 7874, including for purposes of determining the membership of an expanded affiliated group under section 7874(c)(1), an option with respect to a corporation or partnership will be treated as stock in the corporation, or an interest in the partnership, as applicable, with a value equal to the holder's claim on the equity of the corporation or partnership. For this purpose, claim on the equity equals the value of the stock or partnership interest that may be acquired pursuant to the option, less the exercise price (but in no case is a claim on the equity less than zero). Also for this purpose, the equity of the corporation or partnership shall not include the amount of any property the holder of the option would be required to provide to the corporation or partnership under the terms of the option if such option were exercised. See *Example 14* and *Example 16* of paragraph (k) of this section for illustrations of the rules of this paragraph (h)(1).

(2) *Voting power.*—Except to the extent otherwise provided in this paragraph (h), for purposes of determining the voting power of a foreign corporation under section 7874, including for purposes of determining the membership of an expanded affiliated group under section 7874(c)(1), an option will be treated as exercised only if a principal purpose of the issuance or transfer of the option is to avoid the foreign corporation being treated as a surrogate foreign corporation.

(3) *Timing.*—For purposes of this paragraph (h), the value of the holder's claim on the equity is determined—

(i) In the case of a domestic corporation or a domestic partnership, immediately before the domestic entity acquisition.

(ii) In the case of a foreign corporation or foreign partnership, immediately after the domestic entity acquisition.

(4) *Certain options disregarded.*—The rules of paragraph (h)(1) of this section shall not apply to an option if—

(i) A principal purpose of the issuance or acquisition of the option is to avoid the foreign corporation being treated as a surrogate foreign corporation, or

(ii) At the time of the domestic entity acquisition, the probability of the option being exercised is remote.

(5) *Options and interests similar to an option.*—For purposes of this paragraph (h), an option includes an interest similar to an option. Examples of options (including interests similar to options) include, but are not limited to, a warrant, a convertible debt instrument, an instrument other than debt that is convertible into stock or a partnership interest, a put, stock or a partnership interest subject to risk of forfeiture, a contract to acquire or sell stock or a partnership interest, and an exchangeable share or exchangeable partnership interest.

(6) *Multiple claims on equity.*—Paragraph (h)(1) of this section shall not apply to an option to the extent treating the option as stock or a partnership interest would duplicate a shareholder's or partner's claim on the equity of the corporation or partnership by reason of holding stock in the corporation or an interest in the partnership. See *Example 15* of paragraph (k) of this section for an illustration of the rules of this paragraph (h)(6).

(i) *Interests treated as stock of a foreign corporation.*—(1) *Stock or other interests.*—If the conditions of paragraphs (i)(1)(i) and (ii) of this section are satisfied, then, for purposes of section 7874, any interest (including stock or a partnership interest) that is not otherwise treated as stock of a foreign corporation (including under paragraph (h) of this section) shall be treated as stock of the foreign corporation. See *Examples 17* and *18* of paragraph (k) of this section for illustrations of the rules of this paragraph (i)(1).

(i) The interest provides the holder distribution rights that are substantially similar in all material respects to the distribution rights provided by stock in the foreign corporation. For this purpose, distribution rights include rights to dividends (or partnership distributions), distributions in redemption of the interest (in whole or in part), distributions in liquidation, or other similar distributions that represent a return on, or of, the holder's investment in the interest.

(ii) Treating the interest as stock of the foreign corporation has the effect of treating the foreign corporation as a surrogate foreign corporation under section 7874(a)(2)(B).

(2) *Creditor claims.*—(i) *Domestic corporation.*—For purposes of section 7874, if, immediately prior to the first date properties are acquired as part of a domestic entity acquisition, a domestic corporation is in a title 11 or similar case (as defined in section 368(a)(3)), or the liabilities of the domestic corporation exceed the value of its assets, then each creditor of the domestic corporation shall be treated as a shareholder of the domestic corporation and any claim of the creditor against the domestic corporation shall be treated as stock of the domestic corporation. See *Example 19* of paragraph (k) of this section for an illustration of the rules of this paragraph (i)(2)(i).

(ii) *Domestic or foreign partnership.*—For purposes of section 7874, if, immediately prior to the first date properties are acquired as part of a domestic entity acquisition, a partnership (foreign or domestic) is in a title 11 or similar case (as defined in section 368(a)(3)), or the liabilities of the partnership exceed the value of its assets, then each creditor of the partnership shall be treated as a partner in the partnership and any claim of the creditor against the partnership shall be treated as an interest in the partnership.

(iii) *Treatment of creditor as shareholder or partner.*—A creditor that is treated as a shareholder or partner under paragraph (i)(2)(i) or (ii) of this section shall be treated as a shareholder or partner for all purposes of section 7874. See, for example, § 1.7874-1(c) and paragraph (f) of this section. See *Example 19* of paragraph (k) of this section for an illustration of the rules of this paragraph (i)(2)(iii).

(j) *Application of section 7874(b).*—(1) *Conversion to a domestic corporation.*—Except for purposes of determining whether a foreign corporation is treated as a surrogate foreign corporation, the conversion of a foreign corporation to a domestic corporation by reason of section 7874(b) shall constitute a reorganization described in section 368(a)(1)(F) that occurs at the later of the end of the day immediately preceding the first date properties are acquired as part of the domestic entity acquisition or immediately after the formation of the foreign corporation. See, for example, §§ 1.367(b)-2 and 1.367(b)-3 for certain consequences of the reorganization. The treatment of all other aspects of the conversion shall be determined under the relevant provisions of the Code and general tax principles. See *Example 20* of paragraph (k) of this section for an illustration of the rules of this paragraph (j)(1).

(2) *Entity classification.*—A foreign corporation that is treated as a domestic corporation under section 7874(b) is not an eligible entity as defined in § 301.7701-3(a), and therefore may not elect to be classified as other than an association (and thus cannot be treated as other than a corporation) for Federal tax purposes.

(3) *Application of section 367.*—If a foreign corporation is treated as a domestic corporation under section 7874(b), section 367 shall not apply to any transfer of property by a United States person to such foreign corporation as part of the domestic entity acquisition. However, section 367 shall apply to the conversion of the foreign corporation to a domestic corporation. See paragraph (j)(1) of this section. See *Example 20* of paragraph (k) of this section for an illustration of the rules of this paragraph (j)(3).

(k) *Examples.*—(1) *Assumed facts.*—Except as otherwise stated, assume the following for purposes of the examples included in paragraph (k)(2) of this section.

(i) DC1 and DC2 are domestic corporations.

(ii) FA, FP, F1, F2, F3, and F4 are foreign corporations organized in Country A.

(iii) DPS is a domestic partnership that conducts a trade or business.

(iv) FPS is a foreign partnership that is not publicly traded.

(v) Under the terms of the partnership agreements of DPS and FPS, each partner's share in the partnership's items of income, gain, deduction, and loss is determined in accordance with the partner's partnership interest percentage in the partnership, as stated in the examples.

(vi) A, B, and C are unrelated individuals.

(vii) Each entity has a single class of equity outstanding and is unrelated to all other entities.

(viii) All transactions are completed pursuant to a plan.

(ix) All acquisitions of properties are completed after March 4, 2003.

(x) Section 7874(c)(4) does not apply, and no option is issued or acquired with a principal purpose to avoid a foreign corporation being treated as a surrogate foreign corporation.

(2) *Examples.*—The following examples illustrate the rules of this section.

Example 1. Acquisition of stock of a domestic corporation. (i) *Facts.* FA acquires 25% of the outstanding stock of DC1.

(ii) *Analysis.* Under paragraph (c)(1)(i) of this section, for purposes of section 7874(a)(2)(B)(i), FA is treated as acquiring 25% of the properties held by DC1 on the date of the stock acquisition.

Example 2. Acquisition of a partnership interest. (i) *Facts.* DPS wholly owns DC1. FA acquires a 40% interest in DPS.

(ii) *Analysis.* Under paragraph (c)(1)(ii) of this section, for purposes of section 7874(a)(2)(B)(i), FA is treated as acquiring 40 percent of the DC1 stock held by DPS on the date of the acquisition of the partnership interest. Further, under paragraph (c)(1)(i) of this section, for purposes of section 7874(a)(2)(B)(i), FA is treated as acquiring 40% of the properties held by DC1 on the date of the acquisition of the partnership interest.

Example 3. Acquisition of stock by a subsidiary. (i) *Facts.* FP wholly owns FA. FA acquires all the outstanding stock of DC1 in exchange solely for FP stock. FP and FA are members of the same expanded affiliated group after the acquisition.

(ii) *Analysis.* Under paragraph (c)(1)(i) of this section, for purposes of section 7874(a)(2)(B)(i), FA is treated as acquiring 100% of the properties held by DC1 on the date of the stock acquisition. Further, under paragraph (c)(1)(iii) of this section, for purposes of section 7874(a)(2)(B)(i), FP is also treated as acquiring 100% of the properties held by DC1 on the date of the stock acquisition. The result would be the same if instead FA had directly acquired all the properties held by DC1 in exchange for FP stock.

Example 4. Acquisition of stock of a foreign corporation. (i) *Facts.* FP wholly owns DC1. FA acquires all of the outstanding stock of FP.

(ii) *Analysis.* Under paragraph (c)(2) of this section, for purposes of section 7874(a)(2)(B)(i), FA is not treated as acquiring any properties held by DC1 on the date of the acquisition of the FP stock.

Example 5. Acquisition of stock by multiple foreign corporations. (i) *Facts.* Pursuant to the same plan, the shareholders of DC1 transfer all of their DC1 stock equally to F1, F2, F3, and F4 in exchange solely for stock of each foreign corporation.

(ii) *Analysis.* Under paragraph (c)(1)(i) of this section, in the aggregate F1, F2, F3, and F4 are treated as acquiring substantially all of the properties held by DC1. Because the acquisition was pursuant to the same plan, under paragraph (d) of this section, F1, F2, F3, and F4 are each treated as acquiring substantially all of the properties held by DC1 for purposes of determining whether each foreign corporation shall be treated as a surrogate foreign corporation.

Example 6. Acquisition of assets by multiple foreign corporations. (i) *Facts.* Individual A wholly owns DC1. DC1 forms F1, F2, F3, and F4, and transfers an equal portion of its properties to each corporation in exchange solely for stock of the corporation. Pursuant to the same plan DC1 then distributes the stock of each foreign corporation to individual A.

(ii) *Analysis.* Because pursuant to the same plan F1, F2, F3, and F4 acquired, in the aggregate, substantially all of the properties held by DC1, under paragraph (d) of this section, F1, F2, F3, and F4 are each treated as acquiring substantially all of the properties held by DC1 for purposes of determining whether each foreign corporation shall be treated as a surrogate foreign corporation.

Example 7. Acquisition of multiple domestic corporations. (i) *Facts.* Individual A wholly owns DC1, and individual B wholly owns DC2. Pursuant to the same plan, individuals A and B transfer all of their DC1 stock and DC2 stock to FA, a newly formed corporation, in exchange solely for all 100 shares of FA stock outstanding.

(ii) *Analysis.* Under paragraph (c)(1)(i) of this section, for purposes of section 7874(a)(2)(B)(i), FA is treated as acquiring all of the properties held by DC1 and DC2 on the date of the stock acquisition. Under paragraph (e) of this section, because pursuant to the same plan FA acquired substantially all of the properties held by DC1 and DC2, for purposes of determining whether FA shall be treated as a surrogate foreign corporation, DC1 and DC2 shall be treated as a single domestic corporation, of which individuals A and B are former domestic entity shareholders. Thus, individuals A and B are treated as holding all 100 shares of the FA stock by reason of holding stock of such domestic corporation, and the ownership fraction under section 7874(a)(2)(B)(ii) is 100/100, or 100%.

Example 8. Exchange of stock and other property. (i) *Facts.* Individual A wholly owns DC1 and F1. DC1 has a $40x value and F1 has a $60x value. Individual A transfers all of the DC1 stock and F1 stock to FA, a newly formed corporation, in exchange solely for FA stock.

(ii) *Analysis.* Under paragraphs (f)(1)(i) and (f)(2)(i) of this section, for purposes of section 7874(a)(2)(B)(ii), individual A is considered to hold 40% of the FA stock by reason of holding stock in DC1 ($100x FA stock multiplied by $40x/$100x, the relative value of the DC1 stock to all the property transferred by A to FA).

Example 9. Stock received as a distribution. (i) *Facts.* Pursuant to a divisive reorganization described in section 368(a)(1)(D), DC1 contributes substantially all of its properties to FA, a newly formed corporation, in exchange solely for FA stock and then distributes the FA stock to its shareholders in a transaction qualifying under section 355.

(ii) *Analysis.* Under paragraph (f)(1)(i) of this section, for purposes of section 7874(a)(2)(B)(ii), the FA stock received by the DC1 shareholders as a distribution with respect to the DC1 stock is considered held by reason of holding stock in DC1. The result would be the same if the transaction did not qualify as a reorganization (for example, if the distribution were subject to sections 301 and 311(b)).

Example 10. Incorporation of a partnership trade or business. (i) *Facts.* Individuals A and B equally own DPS. DPS transfers substantially all of its properties constituting a trade or business to FA, a newly formed corporation, solely in exchange for FA stock. DPS retains the FA stock after the transaction.

(ii) *Analysis.* Under paragraph (f)(1)(iii) of this section, for purposes of section 7874(a)(2)(B)(ii), individuals A and B are treated as holding a proportionate amount (that is, an equal amount) of the FA stock held by DPS by reason of holding an interest in DPS.

Example 11. Publicly traded foreign partnership treated as domestic corporation. (i) *Facts.* Pursuant to a plan, DC1 and individual B organize a limited liability company (HPS) under the law of Country A. DC1 owns 90% of the membership interests in HPS, and B owns 10% of the membership interests in HPS. HPS is a foreign eligible entity under § 301.7701-2, and DC1 and B make an election under § 301.7701-3 to treat HPS as a partnership for Federal tax purposes as of the date of the formation of HPS. HPS forms DC2. One day after the formation of HPS, DC2 merges with and into DC1. Pursuant to the merger agreement, the DC1 shareholders exchange their DC1 stock solely for membership interests in HPS. After the merger HPS wholly owns DC1, and the former domestic entity shareholders of DC1 own a greater than 80% interest in HPS by reason of holding stock of DC1. Public trading of the HPS ownership interests begins the day after the date on which the merger is completed. HPS is not treated as a corporation under section 7704(a) by reason of section 7704(c). If HPS were a corporation, the condition of section 7874(a)(2)(B)(iii) would be satisfied.

(ii) *Analysis.* HPS is a publicly traded foreign partnership that is described in paragraph (g)(2) of this section. Therefore, under paragraph (g)(1) of this section, for purposes of section 7874, HPS is treated as a foreign corporation organized under the law of Country A and the membership interests in HPS are treated as stock of the foreign corporation. The foreign corporation is treated as a surrogate foreign corporation under section 7874(a)(2)(B) because, pursuant to the merger, HPS acquired substantially all of the properties held by DC1, the former domestic entity shareholders of DC1 hold at least 60% of the stock of the foreign corporation by reason of holding stock of DC1, and the expanded affiliated group that includes the foreign corporation does not have substantial business activities in Country A when compared to the total business activities of the expanded affiliated group. Further, because the former domestic entity shareholders of DC1 hold at least 80% of the stock of the foreign corporation by reason of holding stock of DC1, section 7874(b) applies to the surrogate foreign corporation, and therefore HPS is treated as a domestic corporation for purposes of the Code. Under paragraph (g)(6) of this section, except for purposes of determining whether HPS is a surrogate foreign corporation, at the end of the day immediately preceding the date of the merger of DC2 with and into DC1, HPS is treated as transferring all of its assets and liabilities to a new domestic corporation in exchange solely for stock of the domestic corporation. HPS is then treated as proportionately distributing such stock to its membership interest holders in liquidation of the partnership. In addition, as a result of the merger of DC2 with and into DC1, the former domestic entity shareholders of DC1 shall be treated as receiving stock of a domestic corporation in exchange for their DC1 stock.

Example 12. Publicly traded foreign partnership not treated as a surrogate foreign corporation. (i) *Facts.* The facts are the same as in *Example 11* of this section, except that, after the domestic entity acquisition, the expanded affiliated group that includes HPS (treated as a foreign corporation for this purpose) has substantial business activities in Country A when compared to the total business activities of the expanded affiliated group.

(ii) *Analysis.* Under paragraph (g)(1) of this section, for purposes of section 7874, HPS is treated as a foreign corporation and the membership interests in HPS are treated as stock of the foreign corporation. However, the foreign corporation is not treated as a surrogate foreign corporation under section 7874(a)(2)(B) because, after the domestic entity acquisition, the expanded affiliated group that includes HPS has substantial business activities in Country A when compared to the total business activities of the expanded affiliated group. Therefore, under paragraph (g)(5) of this section, section 7874 does not apply and the status of HPS as a foreign partnership is not affected. In addition, DC1 is not treated as an expatriated entity under section 7874(a) by reason of the domestic entity acquisition.

Example 13. Publicly traded foreign partnership treated as a surrogate foreign corporation but not as a domestic corporation. (i) *Facts.* FPS is a publicly traded foreign partnership organized in Country A that, by reason of section 7704(c), is not treated as a corporation under section 7704(a). FPS acquires all the stock of DC1 in exchange for partnership interests in FPS. After the acquisition, the former domestic entity shareholders of DC1 hold a 75%-interest in FPS by reason of holding DC1 stock. After the acquisition, the expanded affiliated group that includes FPS (treated as a foreign corporation for this purpose) does not have substantial business activities in Country A when compared to the total business activities of the expanded affiliated group.

(ii) *Analysis.* Under paragraph (g)(1) of this section, for purposes of section 7874, FPS is treated as a foreign corporation and the partnership interests in FPS are treated as stock of the foreign corporation. FPS is treated as a surrogate foreign corporation because the conditions of section 7874(a)(2)(B) are satisfied. However, because the former domestic entity shareholders of DC1 hold less than an 80%-interest in FPS by reason of holding DC1 stock, section 7874(b) does not apply to FPS. Therefore, under paragraph (g)(4) of this section FPS continues to be treated as a foreign partnership for purposes of the Code, but section 7874(a)(1) applies to DC1 and any other expatriated entity.

Example 14. Warrant to acquire stock from the foreign corporation. (i) *Facts.* Individual A wholly owns DC1. DC1 has a $200x value. Individual B wholly owns FA. The value of B's FA stock is $400x. Individual C holds a warrant to acquire FA stock from FA at an exercise price of $20x. Individual A transfers all of its DC1 stock to FA in exchange solely for FA stock with a value of $200x. At the time of the transfer, the FA stock that individual C can acquire pursuant to the warrant has a $70x value.

(ii) *Analysis.* Under paragraphs (h)(1) of this section, for purposes of section 7874, individual C is treated as owning FA stock with a $50x value. This amount represents individual C's claim on the equity of FA after the domestic entity acquisition ($70x value of FA stock that may be acquired pursuant to the warrant, less the $20x exercise price), without taking into account the $20x individual C would be required to provide to FA upon the exercise of the warrant. Thus, for purposes of section 7874, the value of the stock of FA immediately after the transaction is $650x ($600x of FA stock, plus C's $50x claim on the equity of FA). C's warrant is not taken into account for purposes of determining the voting power of FA under section 7874.

Example 15. Option to acquire stock from another shareholder. (i) *Facts.* The facts are the same as in *Example 14* except that, instead of holding a warrant issued by FA, individual C holds an option to acquire FA stock from individual B for an exercise price of $20x. At the time of the domestic entity acquisition, the FA stock that individual C can acquire under the option has a $70x value.

(ii) *Analysis.* Under paragraph (h)(6) of this section, for purposes of section 7874, individual C is not treated as owning FA stock by reason of holding the option because treating the option as FA stock would have the effect of partially duplicating individual B's claim on the equity of FA at the time of the domestic entity acquisition by reason of holding FA stock. However, all of the FA stock owned by individual B will be taken into account for purposes of section 7874. C's warrant is not taken into account for purposes of determining voting power of FA under section 7874.

Example 16. Warrant to acquire stock from the domestic corporation. (i) *Facts.* A DC1 employee holds a warrant to acquire DC1 stock from DC1. In connection with the domestic entity acquisition by FA of substantially all of the properties held by DC1, the DC1 employee receives a warrant from FA to acquire 15 shares of FA stock in exchange for the warrant to acquire DC1 stock.

(ii) *Analysis.* Under paragraphs (h)(1) of this section, for purposes of section 7874, the warrant held by the DC1 employee is treated as DC1 stock with a value equal to the employee's claim on the equity of DC1 immediately before the domestic entity acquisition. Further, for purposes of section 7874, the DC1 employee is treated as holding FA stock with a value equal to the employee's claim on the equity of FA after the domestic entity acquisition by reason of holding the warrant to acquire DC1 stock (treated as DC1 stock for this purpose). The option held by the DC1 employee is not taken into account for purposes of determining the voting power of FA under section 7874.

Example 17. Stock in a subsidiary treated as stock of a foreign parent corporation. (i) *Facts.* (A) Individuals A and B equally own DC1. FA, a newly formed corporation, issues stock in a public offering for cash. FA contributes part of the cash from the public offering to DC2, a newly formed corporation, in exchange for all the stock of DC2. DC2 merges with and into DC1 with DC1 surviving. Pursuant to the merger agreement, individuals A and B exchange their DC1 stock for cash and shares of class B stock of DC1. Following the merger FA owns all the class A stock of DC1. FA does not hold significant assets other than the class A stock of DC1. Individuals A and B own all the class B stock of DC1. DC1 has no other class of stock outstanding.

(B) The class B stock entitles individuals A and B to dividend distributions approximately equal to any dividend distributions made by FA with respect to its publicly traded stock. In certain circumstances, the class B stock also permits individuals A and B to require DC1 to redeem the stock at fair market value. The class B stock does not provide individuals A and B voting rights with respect to FA.

(ii) *Analysis.* The dividend rights provided by the class B stock are substantially similar in all material respects to the dividend rights provided by the FA stock. In addition, because FA does not hold significant assets other than the class A stock, the value of the class B stock held by individuals A and B is approximately equal to the value of a corresponding amount of publicly traded FA stock. The distribution rights on liquidation (or redemption) provided by the class B stock, therefore, are substantially similar in all material respects to the distribution rights on liquidation (or redemption) provided by the FA stock. As a result, the distribution rights provided by the class B stock are substantially similar in all material respects to the distribution rights provided by the publicly traded FA stock. Thus, if treating the class B stock as FA stock would have the effect of treating FA as a surrogate foreign corporation, under paragraph (i)(1) of this section the class B stock will be treated as FA stock for purposes of section 7874.

Example 18. Partnership interest treated as stock of foreign acquiring corporation. (i) *Facts.* (A) Individuals A and B equally own DC1. FA, a newly formed corporation, issues stock in a public offering for cash. Individuals A and B and FA organize FPS. FA transfers part of the cash from the public offering to FPS in exchange for a class A partnership interest. FA does not hold any significant assets other than the class A partnership interest. Individuals A and B transfer their DC1 stock to FPS in exchange for class B partnership interests.

(B) The class B partnership interests entitle individuals A and B to cash distributions from FPS approximately equal to any dividend distributions made by FA with respect to its publicly traded stock. In certain circumstances, the class B partnership interests also permit individuals A and B to require FPS to redeem the interests in exchange for cash equal to the value of an amount of FA stock as determined on the redemption date. The class B partnership interests do not provide individuals A or B voting rights with respect to FA.

(ii) *Analysis.* The non-liquidating distribution rights provided by the class B partnership interests are substantially similar in all material respects to the dividend rights provided by the FA stock. Because FA does not hold any significant assets other than the class A partnership interest, the value of the class B partnership interests held by individuals A and B is approximately equal to a corresponding amount of FA stock. The distribution rights on liquidation (or redemption) provided by the class B partnership interests, therefore, are substantially similar in all material respects to distribution rights on liquidation (or redemption) provided by the FA stock. Thus, the distribution rights provided by the class B partnership interests are substantially similar in all material respects to the distribution rights provided by the publicly traded FA stock. As a result, if treating the class B partnership interests as FA stock would have the effect of treating FA as a surrogate foreign corporation, under paragraph (i)(1) of this section the class B partnership interests will be treated as FA stock for purposes of section 7874.

Example 19. Creditor treated as a shareholder. (i) *Facts.* Individuals A and B equally own DC1. The liabilities of DC1 exceed the value of its assets. Pursuant to a plan, FA, a newly formed corporation, acquires substantially all of the properties held by DC1 in exchange solely for FA stock. Pursuant to the plan, the DC1 stock held by individuals A and B is cancelled, and the creditors of DC1 receive all the FA stock in exchange for their claims against DC1.

(ii) *Analysis.* Because immediately before the first date on which properties are acquired as part of the domestic entity acquisition the liabilities of DC1 exceed the value of its assets, under paragraph (i)(2)(i) of this section, for purposes of section 7874, the creditors of DC1 are treated as shareholders of DC1 and the creditors' claims against DC1 are treated as DC1 stock. Therefore, for purposes of section 7874(a)(2)(B)(ii), the FA stock received by the creditors of DC1 by reason of their claims against DC1 is considered held by former domestic entity shareholders of DC1 by reason of holding DC1 stock.

Example 20. Conversion to a domestic corporation and application of section 367. (i) *Facts.* Individuals A and B are United States persons and equally own DC1. Pursuant to a plan, individuals A and B transfer their DC1 stock to FA in exchange solely for 80% of the outstanding FA stock. After the acquisition, the expanded affiliated group that includes FA does not have substantial business activities in Country A when compared to the total business activities of the expanded affiliated group.

(ii) *Analysis.* Under paragraph (c)(1)(i) of this section, for purposes of section 7874(a)(2)(B)(i), FA is treated as acquiring all of the properties held by DC1 on the date of the stock acquisition. After the acquisition, the former domestic entity shareholders of DC1 own 80% of the stock of FA by reason of holding DC1 stock. Therefore, FA is a surrogate foreign corporation that is treated as a domestic corporation under section 7874(b). Under paragraph (j)(1) of this section, except for purposes of determining whether FA is treated as a surrogate foreign corporation, the conversion of FA to a domestic corporation constitutes a reorganization described in section 368(a)(1)(F) that occurs at the end of the day immediately preceding the date of the stock acquisition. Section 367 applies to the conversion of FA to a domestic corporation. See, for example, §§1.367(b)-2 and 1.367(b)-3 for the consequences of the conversion. Under paragraph (j)(3) of this section, section 367 does not apply to the transfers of DC1 stock by individuals A and B to FA.

Example 21. Application of multiple-step acquisition rule—(i) *Facts.* Individual A owns all 70 shares of stock of DC1, a domestic corporation. Individual B owns all 30 shares of stock of F1, a foreign corporation that is a tax resident (as described in §1.7874-3(d)(11)) of Country X. Pursuant to a reorganization described in section 368(a)(1)(D), DC1 transfers all of its properties to F1 solely in exchange for 70 newly issued voting shares of F1 stock (DC1 acquisition) and distributes the F1 stock to Individual A in liquidation pursuant to section 361(c)(1). Pursuant to a plan that includes the DC1 acquisition, F2, a newly formed foreign corporation that is also a tax resident of Country X, acquires 100 percent of the stock of F1 solely in exchange for 100 newly issued shares of F2 stock (F1 acquisition). After the F1 acquisition, Individual A owns 70 shares of F2 stock, Individual B owns 30 shares of F2 stock, F2 owns all 100 shares of F1 stock, and F1 owns all the properties held by DC1 immediately before the DC1 acquisition. In addition, the form of the transaction is respected for U.S. federal income tax purposes.

(ii) *Analysis*—(A) The DC1 acquisition is a domestic entity acquisition, and F1 is a foreign acquiring corporation, because F1 directly acquires 100 percent of the properties of DC1. In addition, the 70 shares of F1 stock received by A pursuant to the DC1 acquisition in exchange for Individual A's DC1 stock are stock of a foreign corporation that is held by reason of holding stock in DC1. As a result, those 70 shares are included in both the numerator and the denominator of the ownership fraction when applying section 7874 to the DC1 acquisition.

(B) The DC1 acquisition is also an initial acquisition because it is a domestic entity acquisition that, pursuant to a plan that includes the F1 acquisition, occurs before the F1 acquisition (which, as described in paragraph (ii)(C) of this *Example 21*, is a subsequent acquisition). Thus, F1 is the initial acquiring corporation.

(C) The F1 acquisition is a subsequent acquisition because it occurs, pursuant to a plan that includes the DC1 acquisition, after the DC1 acquisition and, pursuant to the F1 acquisition, F2 acquires 100 percent of the stock of F1 and therefore is treated under paragraph (c)(4)(ii) of this section (which applies the principles of section 7874(a)(2)(B)(i) with certain modifications) as indirectly acquiring substantially all of the properties held directly or indirectly by F1. Thus, F2 is the subsequent acquiring corporation.

(D) Under paragraph (c)(4)(i) of this section, the F1 acquisition is treated as a domestic entity acquisition, and F2 is treated as a foreign acquiring corporation. In addition, under paragraph (f)(1)(iv) of this section, the 70 shares of F2 stock received by Individual A (a former initial acquiring corporation shareholder) pursuant to the F1 acquisition in exchange for Individual A's F1 stock are stock of a foreign corporation that is held by reason of holding stock in DC1. As a result, those 70 shares are included in both the numerator and the denominator of the ownership fraction when applying section 7874 to the F1 acquisition.

(l) *Applicability date.*—(1) *In general.*—This section applies to domestic entity acquisitions completed on or after June 7, 2012. For domestic entity acquisitions completed prior to June 7, 2012, see §1.7874-2T(o), as contained in 26 CFR part 1, revised as of April 1, 2012.

(2) *Applicability date of certain provisions of this section.*—Paragraphs (a), (b)(7) through (13), (c)(2) and (4), and (f)(1)(iv) of this section, as well as the introductory text of paragraph (f)(1) and *Example 21* of paragraph (k)(2), apply to domestic entity acquisitions completed on or after April 4, 2016. [Reg. §1.7874-2.]

☐ [*T.D. 9591, 6-7-2012. Amended by T.D. 9761, 4-4-2016 and T.D. 9834, 7-11-2018.*]

§1.7874-3. Substantial business activities.—(a) *Scope.*—This section provides rules regarding when an expanded affiliated group will be considered to have substantial business activities in the relevant foreign country when compared to the total business activities of the expanded affiliated group for purposes of section 7874(a)(2)(B)(iii). Paragraph (b) of this section describes the general rule for determining whether the expanded affiliated group has substantial business activities in the relevant foreign country when compared to its total business activities. Paragraph (c) of this section describes certain items that are not taken into account as located or derived in the relevant foreign country. Paragraph (d) of this section provides definitions and certain rules of application. Paragraph (e) of this section provides rules regarding the treatment of partnerships for purposes of this section. Paragraph (f) of this section provides the effective/applicability dates.

(b) *General rule.*—The expanded affiliated group will be considered to have substantial business activities in the relevant foreign country on the completion date when compared to the total business activities of the expanded affiliated group only if, subject to paragraph (c) of this section, each of the requirements of this paragraph (b) are satisfied.

(1) *Group employees.*—(i) *Number of employees.*—The number of group employees based in the relevant foreign country is at least 25 percent of the total number of group employees on the applicable date.

(ii) *Employee compensation.*—The employee compensation incurred with respect to group employees based in the relevant foreign country is at least 25 percent of the total employee compensation incurred with respect to all group employees during the testing period.

(2) *Group assets.*—The value of the group assets located in the relevant foreign country is at least 25 percent of the total value of all group assets on the applicable date.

(3) *Group income.*—The group income derived in the relevant foreign country is at least 25 percent of the total group income during the testing period.

(4) *Tax residence of foreign acquiring corporation.*—The foreign acquiring corporation is a tax resident of the relevant foreign country. However, this paragraph (b)(4) does not apply if the relevant foreign country does not impose corporate income tax.

(c) *Items not to be considered.*—(1) *General rule.*—Except to the extent provided in paragraph (c)(2) of this section, the following items are not taken into account in the numerator, but are taken into account in the denominator, for each of the tests described in paragraphs (b)(1) through (3) of this section:

(i) Any group assets, group employees, or group income attributable to business activities that are associated with properties or liabilities the transfer of which is disregarded under section 7874(c)(4).

(ii) Any group assets or group employees located in, or group income derived in, the relevant foreign country as part of a plan with a principal purpose of avoiding the purposes of section 7874.

(iii) Any group assets or group employees located in, or group income derived in, the relevant foreign country if such group assets or group employees, or the business activities to which such group income is attributable, are subsequently transferred to another country in connection with a plan that existed at the time of the domestic entity acquisition.

(2) *Transfers of properties to the expanded affiliated group.*—Any group assets, group employees, or group income attributable to business activities that are associated with property that is transferred to the expanded affiliated group in a transfer that is disregarded under section 7874(c)(4) are not taken into account in the numerator or the denominator for each of the tests described in paragraphs (b)(1) through (3) of this section.

(d) *Definitions and special rules*.—In addition to the definitions in § 1.7874-12, the following definitions and special rules apply for purposes of this section.

(1) The term *applicable date* means either of the following dates, applied consistently for all purposes of this section:

(i) The completion date; or

(ii) The last day of the month immediately preceding the month that includes the completion date.

(2) The term *employee compensation* means all amounts incurred by members of the expanded affiliated group that directly relate to services performed by group employees (including, for example, wages, salaries, deferred compensation, employee benefits, and employer payroll taxes). Employee compensation with respect to a particular group employee is treated as incurred when it would be deductible by the employer as compensation, and the amount of employee compensation equals the amount that would be deductible by the employer as compensation. Both the timing and the amount of the deduction for employee compensation must be determined for all group employees under U.S. federal income tax principles or for all group employees based on the relevant tax laws. Employee compensation is determined in U.S. dollars, translated, if necessary, using the weighted average exchange rate (as defined in § 1.989(b)-1) for the testing period.

(3) The term *group assets* means tangible personal property or real property used or held for use in the active conduct of a trade or business by members of the expanded affiliated group, provided such property is either owned or, in the circumstances described below, rented by members of the expanded affiliated group at the close of the completion date. A group asset is considered to be located in the relevant foreign country only if the asset was physically present in such country at the close of the completion date and the asset was physically present in such country for more time than in any other country during the testing period. Notwithstanding the foregoing, a group asset that is mobile in nature and is used in a transportation activity, such as a vessel, an aircraft, or a motor vehicle, is considered to be located in the relevant foreign country if the asset was physically present in such country for more time than in any other country during the testing period, regardless of whether the asset was physically present in such country at the close of the completion date. Group assets must be valued on a gross basis (that is, not reduced by liabilities) by consistently using for all group assets of the expanded affiliated group either the adjusted tax basis or fair market value determined in U.S. dollars, translated, if necessary, at the spot rate determined under the principles of § 1.988-1(d)(1), (2), and (4). Tangible personal property or real property that is rented by members of the expanded affiliated group from a person other than a member of the expanded affiliated group is also treated as a group asset, provided such property is used in the active conduct of a trade or business and is being rented by members of the expanded affiliated group at the close of the completion date. For purposes of this section, a group asset that is rented is valued at eight times the net annual rent paid or accrued with respect to the property by members of the expanded affiliated group.

(4) The term *group employees* means all individuals who are employees of members of the expanded affiliated group. Whether individuals are employees must be determined for all members of the expanded affiliated group under U.S. federal tax principles or for all members of the expanded affiliated group based on the relevant tax laws. A group employee is considered to be based in the relevant foreign country only if the employee spent more time providing services in such country than in any other single country during the testing period.

(5) The term *group income* means gross income of members of the expanded affiliated group from transactions occurring in the ordinary course of business with customers that are not related persons. Group income must be determined consistently for all members of the expanded affiliated group either under U.S. federal income tax principles or as reflected in the relevant financial statements. Group income is translated into U.S. dollars, if necessary, using the weighted average exchange rate (as defined in § 1.989(b)-1) for the testing period. Group income is considered derived in the relevant foreign country only if it is derived from a transaction with a customer located in such country.

(6) The term *net annual rent* means the annual rent paid or accrued with respect to property, less any payments received or accrued from subleasing such property (or other similar arrangement).

(7) The term *related person* has the meaning specified in section 954(d)(3), except that section 954(d)(3) is applied by substituting "one or more members of the expanded affiliated group" for "a controlled foreign corporation" and "the controlled foreign corporation" each place they appear.

(8) The term *relevant financial statements* means financial statements prepared consistently for all members of the expanded affiliated group in accordance with either U.S. Generally Accepted Accounting Principles (U.S. GAAP) or the International Financial Reporting Standards (IFRS) used for the expanded affiliated group's consolidated financial statements, but, if, after the domestic entity acquisition, financial statements will not be prepared consistently for all members of the expanded affiliated group in accordance with either U.S. GAAP or IFRS, then, for each member, financial statements prepared in accordance with either U.S. GAAP or IFRS. The relevant financial statements must take into account all items of income generated by all members of the expanded affiliated group for the entire testing period.

(9) The term *relevant foreign country* means the foreign country in which, or under the law of which, the foreign acquiring corporation was created or organized.

(10) The term *relevant tax law* means, for purposes of determining whether a particular individual who performs services for a member of the expanded affiliated group is an employee for purposes of paragraph (d)(6) of this section and the timing and amount of employee compensation for a particular employee of a member of the expanded affiliated group for purposes of paragraph (d)(3) of this section, the tax law to which the member is subject. Notwithstanding the foregoing, if the tax law to which a member is subject does not distinguish between whether an individual is an employee, or, for example, an independent contractor, then for this purpose the relevant tax law is considered to be U.S. federal tax law.

(11) The term *tax resident* means, with respect to a foreign country, a body corporate liable to tax under the laws of the country as a resident.

(12) The term *testing period* means the one-year period ending on the applicable date.

(e) *Treatment of partnerships*.—(1) *Stock held by a partnership*.—In determining the members of the expanded affiliated group for purposes of this section, each partner in a partnership, as determined without regard to the application of paragraph (e)(2) of this section, shall be treated as holding its proportionate share of the stock held by the partnership, as determined under the rules and principles of sections 701 through 777.

(2) *Business activities of a partnership*.—For purposes of this section, if one or more members of the expanded affiliated group, as determined after the application of paragraph (e)(1) of this section, own, in the aggregate, more than 50 percent (by value) of the interests in a partnership, the partnership will be treated as a corporation that is a member of the expanded affiliated group. Thus, all items of such a partnership are taken into account for purposes of this section. No items of a partnership are taken into account for purposes of this section unless the partnership is treated as a member of the expanded affiliated group pursuant to this paragraph (e)(2).

(f) *Applicability dates*.—(1) *General rule*.—Except as otherwise provided in paragraph (f)(2) of this section, this section applies to domestic entity acquisitions that are completed on or after June 3, 2015. For domestic entity acquisitions completed before June 3, 2015, see § 1.7874-3T as contained in 26 CFR part 1 revised as of April 1, 2016.

(2) *Paragraphs (b)(4), (d)(8), and (d)(11) of this section*.—The first sentence of paragraph (b)(4) of this section applies to domestic entity acquisitions completed on or after November 19, 2015, and the second sentence applies to domestic entity acquisitions completed on or after July 12, 2018. Paragraph (d)(8) of this section applies to domestic entity acquisitions completed on or after April 4, 2016. Paragraph (d)(11) of this section applies to domestic entity acquisitions completed on or after July 12, 2018. For domestic entity acquisitions completed on or after June 3, 2015, and before April 4, 2016, however, taxpayers may elect to apply paragraph (d)(8) of this section. For domestic entity acquisitions completed on or after November 19, 2015, and before July 12, 2018, taxpayers may elect to apply the second sentence of paragraph (b)(4) and paragraph (d)(11) of this section. [Reg. § 1.7874-3.]

□ [*T.D. 9720, 6-3-2015. Amended by T.D. 9761, 4-4-2016 and T.D.* 9834, 7-11-2018.]

§ 1.7874-4. Disregard of certain stock related to the domestic entity acquisition.—(a) *Scope*.—This section identifies certain stock of the foreign acquiring corporation that is disregarded in determining the ownership fraction and modifies the scope of section 7874(c)(2)(B). Paragraph (b) of this section sets forth the general rule that certain stock of the foreign acquiring corporation, and only such stock, is treated as stock described in section 7874(c)(2)(B) and therefore is excluded from the denominator of the ownership fraction. Paragraph (c) of this section identifies the stock of the foreign acquiring corporation that is subject to paragraph (b) of this section. Paragraph (d) of this section provides a de minimis exception to the application of the general exclusion rule of paragraph (b) of this section. Paragraph (e) of this section provides rules for transfers of stock of the foreign acquiring corporation in satisfaction of, or in exchange for the assumption of, one or more obligations of the transferor. Paragraph (f) of this section provides rules for certain transfers of stock of the foreign acquiring corporation involving multiple properties or obligations. Paragraph (g) of this section provides rules for the treatment of partnerships, and paragraph (h) of this section provides definitions. Paragraph (h) of this section provides definitions. Paragraph (i) of this section provides examples illustrating the application of the rules of this section. Paragraph (j) of this section provides dates of applicability. See § 1.7874-1(d)(1) for rules addressing the interaction of this section with the expanded affiliated group rules of section 7874(c)(2)(A) and § 1.7874-1.

(b) *Exclusion of disqualified stock under section 7874(c)(2)(B)*.—Except as provided in paragraph (d) of this section, disqualified stock (as determined under paragraph (c) of this section) is treated as stock described in section 7874(c)(2)(B) and therefore is not included in the denominator of the ownership fraction. Section 7874(c)(2)(B) shall not apply to exclude stock from the denominator of the ownership fraction that is not disqualified stock.

(c) *Disqualified stock*.—(1) *General rule*.—Except as provided in paragraph (c)(2) of this section, disqualified stock is stock of the foreign acquiring corporation (other than stock described in § 1.7874-2(f)) that is transferred in an exchange described in paragraph (c)(1)(i) or (ii) of this section that is related to the domestic entity acquisition. This paragraph (c) applies without regard to whether the stock of the foreign acquiring corporation is publicly traded at the time of the transfer or at any other time.

(i) *Exchanged for nonqualified property*.—The stock is transferred to a person other than the domestic entity in exchange for nonqualified property. See *Example 1, Example 2, Example 6, Example 8*, and *Example 9* of paragraph (i) of this section for illustrations of the application of this paragraph (c)(1)(i).

(ii) *Exchanged for property with associated obligations*.—(A) *General rule*.—Subject to the limitation provided in in paragraph (c)(1)(ii)(B) of this section, the stock is transferred by a person (transferor) to another person (transferee) in exchange for property (exchanged property) and, pursuant to the same plan (or series of related transactions), the transferee subsequently transfers such stock (or, if the transferee exchanges such stock for other property, such other property) in satisfaction of, or in exchange for the assumption of, one or more obligations of the transferee or a person related (within the meaning of section 267 or 707(b)) to the transferee. See *Example 6* and *Example 10* of paragraph (i) of this section for illustrations of the application of paragraph (c)(1)(ii) of this section.

(B) *Limitation*.—The amount of stock treated as transferred in an exchange described in paragraph (c)(2)(ii)(A) of this section shall not exceed—

(1) With respect to a transferee that is the domestic entity, the proportionate share of obligations associated with the exchanged property (determined based on the fair market value of the exchanged property relative to the fair market value of all properties with which the obligations are associated) that, pursuant to the same plan (or series of related transactions), is not assumed by the transferor.

(2) With respect to any other transferee, the proportionate share of obligations associated with the exchanged property (determined based on the fair market value of the exchanged property relative to the fair market value of all properties with which the obligations are associated) that, pursuant to the same plan (or series of related transactions), is not assumed by the transferor, multiplied by a fraction, the numerator of which is the amount of exchanged property that is qualified property, and the denominator of which is the total amount of exchanged property.

(C) *Associated obligations*.—For purposes of paragraph (c)(1)(ii) of this section, an obligation is associated with property if, for example, the obligation arose from the conduct of a trade or business in which the property has been used, regardless of whether the obligation is a non-recourse obligation.

(2) *Stock transferred in an exchange that does not increase the fair market value of the assets or decrease the amount of liabilities of the foreign acquiring corporation*.—Stock is disqualified stock only to the extent that the transfer of the stock in the exchange increases the fair market value of the assets of the foreign acquiring corporation or decreases the amount of its liabilities. This paragraph (c)(2) is applied to an exchange without regard to any other exchange described in paragraph (c)(1)(i) or (ii) of this section or any other transaction related to the domestic entity acquisition. See *Example 4* and *Example 7* of paragraph (i) of this section for illustrations of the application of this paragraph (c)(2).

(d) *Exception to exclusion of disqualified stock*.—(1) *De minimis ownership*.—Except as provided in paragraph (d)(2) of this section, paragraph (b) of this section does not apply if both:

(i) The ownership percentage described in section 7874(a)(2)(B)(ii), determined without regard to the application of paragraph (b) of this section and §§ 1.7874-7(b) and 1.7874-10(b), is less than five (by vote and value); and

(ii) On the completion date, each five percent former domestic entity shareholder or five percent former domestic entity partner, as applicable, owns (applying the attribution rules of section 318(a) with the modifications described in section 304(c)(3)(B)) less than five percent (by vote and value) of the stock of (or a partnership interest in) each member of the expanded affiliated group. For this purpose, a five percent former domestic entity shareholder (or five percent former domestic entity partner) is a former domestic entity shareholder (or former domestic entity partner) that, before the domestic entity acquisition, owned (applying the attribution rules of section 318(a) with the modifications described in section 304(c)(3)(B)) at least five percent (by vote and value) of the stock of (or a partnership interest in) the domestic entity. See *Example 5* of this paragraph (i) for an illustration of this paragraph (d).

(2) *Stock issued to avoid the purposes of section 7874*.—The exception in paragraph (d)(1) of this section does not apply to disqualified stock that is transferred in a transaction (or series of transactions) related to the domestic entity acquisition with a principal purpose of avoiding the purposes of section 7874.

(e) *Satisfaction or assumption of obligations*.—Except to the extent stock is treated as disqualified stock as a result of being described in paragraph (c)(1)(ii) of this section, this paragraph (e) applies if, in a transaction related to the domestic entity acquisition, stock of the foreign acquiring corporation is transferred to a person other than the domestic entity in exchange for the satisfaction or the assumption of one or more obligations of the transferor. In such a case, solely for purposes of this section, the stock of the foreign acquiring corporation is treated as if it is transferred in exchange for an amount of cash equal to the fair market value of such stock.

(f) *Transactions involving multiple properties*.—For purposes of this section, if stock and other property are exchanged for qualified property and nonqualified property, the stock is treated as transferred in exchange for the qualified property or nonqualified property, respectively, based on the relative fair market value of the property. See also § 1.7874-2(f)(2) (allocating stock of a foreign acquiring corporation between an interest in the domestic entity and other property).

(g) *Treatment of partnerships*.—For purposes of this section, if one or more members of the expanded affiliated group own, in the aggregate, more than 50 percent (by value) of the interests in a partnership, such partnership is treated as a corporation that is a member of the expanded affiliated group.

(h) *Definitions*.—In addition to the definitions in § 1.7874-12, the following definitions apply for purposes of this section:

(1) *Marketable securities* has the meaning set forth in section 453(f)(2), except that the term marketable securities does not include stock of a corporation or an interest in a partnership that becomes a member of the expanded affiliated group in a transaction (or series of transactions) related to the domestic entity acquisition. See *Example 4* of paragraph (i) of this section for an illustration of this paragraph (h)(1).

(2) *Nonqualified property* is property described in paragraphs (h)(2)(i) through (iv) of this section. Thus, stock in a corporation or an interest in a partnership is nonqualified property to the extent pro-

vided in paragraph (h)(2)(ii) or (iv) of this section. Qualified property is property other than nonqualified property.

(i) Cash or cash equivalents.

(ii) Marketable securities, within the meaning of paragraph (h)(1) of this section.

(iii) An obligation owed by any of the following:

(A) A member of the expanded affiliated group, unless the holder of the obligation immediately before the domestic entity acquisition and any related transaction (or its successor) is a member of the expanded affiliated group after the domestic entity acquisition and all related transactions. See *Example 6* of paragraph (i) of this section for an illustration of this paragraph (h)(2)(iii)(A).

(B) A former domestic entity shareholder or former domestic entity partner of the domestic entity that owns (applying the attribution rules of section 318(a) with the modifications described in section 304(c)(3)(B)) at least five percent (by vote or value) of the stock of, or partnership interests in, the domestic entity before the domestic entity acquisition.

(C) A person, other than a member of the expanded affiliated group, that, before or after the domestic entity acquisition, either owns (applying the attribution rules of section 318(a) with the modifications described in section 304(c)(3)(B)) at least five percent (by vote or value) of the stock of (or partnership interests in) or is related (within the meaning of section 267 or 707(b)) to—

(1) A member of the expanded affiliated group; or

(2) A person described in paragraph (h)(2)(iii)(B) of this section.

(iv) Any other property acquired with a principal purpose of avoiding the purposes of section 7874, regardless of whether the transaction involves an indirect transfer of property described in paragraph (h)(2)(i), (ii), or (iii) of this section. See *Example 2* and *Example 3* of paragraph (i) of this section for illustrations of the application of this paragraph (h)(2)(iv).

(3) An *obligation* means any fixed or contingent obligation to make a payment or provide value without regard to whether the obligation is otherwise taken into account for purposes of the Internal Revenue Code. An obligation includes, but is not limited to, a debt obligation, an environmental obligation, a tort obligation, a contract obligation (including an obligation to provide goods or services), a pension obligation, an obligation under a short sale, and an obligation under derivative financial instruments such as options, forward contracts, futures contracts, and swaps. An obligation does not include any obligation treated as stock for purposes of section 7874 (see, for example, § 1.7874-2(i), which treats certain interests, including certain creditor claims, as stock).

(4) A *transfer* is, with respect to stock of the foreign acquiring corporation, an issuance, sale, distribution, exchange, or any other disposition of such stock.

(i) *Examples.*—The following examples illustrate the application of the rules of this section. For purposes of the examples, unless otherwise indicated, assume the following facts in addition to the facts stated in the examples:

(1) FA, FMS, FS, and FT are foreign corporations, all of which have only one class of stock issued and outstanding;

(2) DMS and DT are domestic corporations;

(3) P and R are corporations that may be either domestic or foreign;

(4) PRS is a partnership with individual partners;

(5) The de minimis ownership exception in paragraph (d)(1) of this section does not apply;

(6) None of the shareholders or partners in the entities described in the examples are related persons with respect to each other;

(7) All transactions described in each example occur pursuant to the same plan;

(8) No property is acquired with a principal purpose of avoiding the purposes of section 7874;

(9) FA, FMS, FS, and FT are tax residents in the same foreign country;

(10) For purposes of determining the ownership fraction, no shares of FA stock are excluded from the denominator pursuant to § 1.7874-7(b) (which disregards stock attributable to passive assets); and

(11) For purposes of determining the ownership fraction, no shares of FA stock are treated as received by former shareholders of DT pursuant to § 1.7874-10(b) (which disregards certain distributions).

Example 1. Stock transferred in exchange for marketable securities—(i) *Facts.* Individual A wholly owns DT. PRS transfers marketable securities (within the meaning of paragraph (h)(1) of this section) to FA, a newly formed corporation, in exchange solely for 25 shares of FA stock. Then Individual A transfers all the DT stock to FA in exchange solely for 75 shares of FA stock.

(ii) *Analysis.* Under paragraph (h)(2)(ii) of this section, the marketable securities constitute nonqualified property. Accordingly, the 25 shares of FA stock transferred by FA to PRS in exchange for the marketable securities constitute disqualified stock described in paragraph (c)(1) of this section by reason of paragraph (c)(1)(i) of this section. Paragraph (c)(2) of this section does not reduce the amount of disqualified stock described in paragraph (c)(1)(i) of this section because the transfer of FA stock in exchange for the marketable securities increases the fair market value of the assets of FA by the fair market value of the marketable securities transferred. Under paragraph (b) of this section, the 25 shares of FA stock transferred to PRS are not included in the denominator of the ownership fraction. See also section 7874(c)(4). Accordingly, the only FA stock included in the ownership fraction is the FA stock transferred to Individual A in exchange for the DT stock, and that FA stock is included in both the numerator and the denominator of the ownership fraction. Thus, the ownership fraction is 75/75.

Example 2. Stock transferred in exchange for property acquired with a principal purpose of avoiding the purposes of section 7874—(i) *Facts.* Individual A wholly owns DT. PRS transfers marketable securities (within the meaning of paragraph (h)(1) of this section) to FT, a newly formed corporation, in exchange solely for all the FT stock. Then PRS transfers the FT stock to FA, a newly formed corporation, in exchange solely for 25 shares of FA stock. Finally, Individual A transfers all the DT stock to FA in exchange solely for 75 shares of FA stock. FA acquires the FT stock with a principal purpose of avoiding the purposes of section 7874.

(ii) *Analysis.* Under paragraph (h)(2)(iv) of this section, the FT stock constitutes nonqualified property because a principal purpose of FA acquiring the FT stock is to avoid the purposes of section 7874. Accordingly, the 25 shares of FA stock transferred by FA to PRS in exchange for the FT stock constitute disqualified stock described in paragraph (c)(1) of this section by reason of paragraph (c)(1)(i) of this section. Paragraph (c)(2) of this section does not reduce the amount of disqualified stock described in paragraph (c)(1)(i) of this section because the transfer of FA stock in exchange for the FT stock increases the fair market value of FA's assets by the fair market value of the FT stock. Under paragraph (b) of this section, the 25 shares of FA stock transferred to PRS are not included in the denominator of the ownership fraction. Furthermore, even in the absence of paragraph (h)(2)(iv) of this section, the transfer of marketable securities to FT would be disregarded pursuant to section 7874(c)(4). Accordingly, the only FA stock included in the ownership fraction is the FA stock transferred to Individual A in exchange for the DT stock, and that FA stock is included in both the numerator and the denominator of the ownership fraction. Thus, the ownership fraction is 75/75.

Example 3. Stock transferred in exchange for property acquired with a principal purpose of avoiding the purposes of section 7874—(i) *Facts.* DT is a publicly traded corporation. PRS is a foreign partnership that is unrelated to DT. PRS transfers certain business assets (PRS properties) to FA, a newly formed foreign corporation, in exchange solely for 25 shares of FA stock. The shareholders of DT transfer all of their DT stock to FA in exchange solely for the remaining 75 shares of FA stock (DT acquisition). None of the PRS properties is property described in paragraph (h)(2)(i) through (iii) of this section, but FA acquires the PRS properties with a principal purpose of avoiding the purposes of section 7874.

(ii) *Analysis.* Under paragraph (h)(2)(iv) of this section, the PRS properties transferred to FA constitute nonqualified property, because FA acquires the PRS properties in a transaction related to the DT acquisition with a principal purpose of avoiding the purposes of section 7874. Accordingly, the 25 shares of FA stock transferred by FA to PRS in exchange for the PRS properties constitute disqualified stock described in paragraph (c)(1) of this section by reason of paragraph (c)(1)(i) of this section. Paragraph (c)(2) of this section does not apply to reduce the amount of disqualified stock described in paragraph (c)(1)(i) of this section because the transfer of FA stock in exchange for the PRS properties increases the fair market value of FA's assets by the fair market value of the PRS properties. Accordingly, pursuant to paragraph (b) of this section, the 25 shares of FA stock transferred to PRS in exchange for the PRS properties are not included in the denominator of the ownership fraction. Furthermore, even in the absence of paragraph (h)(2)(iv) of this section, the transfer of the PRS properties to FA would be disregarded pursuant to section 7874(c)(4). Therefore, the only FA stock included in the ownership fraction is the FA stock transferred to the former domestic entity shareholders of DT in exchange for their DT stock, and that FA stock is included in both the numerator and the denominator of the ownership fraction. Thus, the ownership fraction is 75/75.

Example 4. Stock transferred in exchange for stock of a foreign corporation that becomes a member of the expanded affiliated group—(i) *Facts.* FT, a publicly traded corporation, forms FA, and then FA forms DMS and FMS. FMS merges with and into FT, with FT surviving the merger (FMS-FT merger). Pursuant to the FMS-FT merger, the FT shareholders exchange their FT stock solely for 100 shares of FA stock and FT becomes a wholly owned subsidiary of FA. Following the FMS-FT merger, DMS merges with and into DT, also a publicly traded corporation, with DT surviving the merger (DT acquisition). Pursuant to the DT acquisition, the DT shareholders exchange their DT stock solely for the remaining 100 shares of FA stock, and DT becomes a wholly owned subsidiary of FA. After the completion of the plan, FA wholly owns FT and DT, DMS and FMS cease to exist, and the stock of FA is publicly traded.

(ii) *Analysis.* Because FT becomes a member of the expanded affiliated group that includes FA in a transaction related to the DT acquisition, the FT stock does not constitute marketable securities (within the meaning of paragraph (h)(1) of this section) and therefore does not constitute nonqualified property pursuant to paragraph (h)(2)(ii) of this section. Accordingly, no FA stock is disqualified stock described in paragraph (c)(1) of this section and therefore the FA stock transferred in exchange for the FT stock and DT stock is included in the denominator of the ownership fraction. Thus, the ownership fraction is 100/200.

(iii) *Alternative facts.* The facts are the same as in paragraph (i) of this *Example 4*, except that, instead of undertaking the FMS-FT merger, FT merges with and into FA with FA surviving the merger (FT-FA merger). Pursuant to the FT-FA merger, the FT shareholders exchange their FT stock solely for 100 shares of FA stock. At the time of the FT-FA merger, FT does not hold nonqualified property and has no obligations. Accordingly, FA stock transferred by FA to FT in exchange for the property of FT is not disqualified stock described in paragraph (c)(1) of this section. Furthermore, pursuant to paragraph (c)(2) of this section, the 100 shares of FA stock transferred by FT to the shareholders of FT in exchange for their FT stock do not constitute disqualified stock described in paragraph (c)(1) of this section. Although the FT stock is nonqualified property (the FT stock constitutes marketable securities within the meaning of paragraph (h)(2)(ii) of this section because the stock of FT is publicly traded and FT is not a member of the expanded affiliated group that includes FA after the DT acquisition), under paragraph (c)(2) of this section, the transfer of FA stock by FT to the shareholders of FT neither increases the fair market value of the assets of FA nor decreases the liabilities of FA. Accordingly, no FA stock is disqualified stock described in paragraph (c)(1) of this section and, therefore, the FA stock transferred in exchange for the assets of FT and the DT stock is included in the denominator of the ownership fraction. Thus, the ownership fraction is 100/200.

Example 5. De minimis exception—(i) *Facts.* Individual A wholly owns DT. The fair market value of the DT stock is $100x. PRS transfers $96x of cash to FA, a newly formed corporation, in exchange solely for 96 shares of FA stock. Then Individual A transfers the DT stock to FA in exchange for $96x of cash and 4 shares of FA stock (DT acquisition).

(ii) *Analysis.* Under paragraph (h)(2)(i) of this section, cash constitutes nonqualified property. Accordingly, the 96 shares of FA stock transferred by FA to PRS in exchange for $96x of cash constitute disqualified stock described in paragraph (c)(1) of this section by reason of paragraph (c)(1)(i) of this section. Furthermore, paragraph (c)(2) of this section does not reduce the amount of disqualified stock described in paragraph (c)(1)(i) of this section because the transfer of FA stock in exchange for $96x of cash increases the fair market value of the assets of FA by $96x. However, without regard to the application of paragraph (b) of this section and §§1.7874-7(b) and 1.7874-10T(b), the ownership percentage described in section 7874(a)(2)(B)(ii) would be less than 5 (by vote and value), or 4 (4/100, or 4 shares of FA stock held by Individual A by reason of owning the DT stock, determined under §1.7874-2(f)(2), over 100 shares of FA stock outstanding after the DT acquisition). Furthermore, after the DT acquisition and all related transactions, Individual A owns less than 5% (by vote and value, applying the attribution rules of section 318(a) with the modifications described in section 304(c)(3)(B)) of the stock of FA and DT (the members of the expanded affiliated group that includes FA). Accordingly, the de minimis exception in paragraph (d)(1) of this section applies and therefore paragraph (b) of this section does not apply to exclude the FA stock transferred to PRS from the denominator of the ownership fraction. Therefore, the FA stock transferred to Individual A and PRS is included in the denominator of the ownership fraction. Thus, the ownership fraction is 4/100.

Example 6. Obligation of the expanded affiliated group satisfied with stock—(i) *Facts.* Individual A wholly owns DT. The stock of DT held by Individual A has a fair market value of $75x. Individual A also holds an obligation of DT with a value and face amount of $25x. DT holds property with a value of $100x, and the $25x obligation is associated with the property. FA, a newly formed corporation, transfers 100 shares of FA stock to Individual A in exchange for all the DT stock and the $25x obligation of DT.

(ii) *Analysis.* Under paragraph (h)(2)(iii)(A) of this section, the $25x obligation of DT constitutes nonqualified property because DT is a member of the expanded affiliated group that includes FA, and Individual A (the holder of the obligation immediately before the domestic entity acquisition and any related transaction) is not a member of the EAG after the domestic entity acquisition and all related transactions. Thus, the shares of FA stock transferred by FA to Individual A in exchange for the obligation of DT constitute disqualified stock described in paragraph (c)(1) of this section by reason of paragraph (c)(1)(i) of this section. Under §1.7874-2(f)(2), Individual A is treated as receiving 75 shares of FA stock in exchange for the DT stock (100 x $75x/$100x) and 25 shares of FA stock in exchange for the obligation of DT (100 x $25x/$100x). Thus, 25 shares of FA stock constitute disqualified stock described in paragraph (c)(1) of this section by reason of paragraph (c)(1)(i) of this section. Paragraph (c)(2) of this section does not reduce the amount of disqualified stock described in paragraph (c)(1)(i) of this section because the transfer of FA stock for the $25x obligation increases the fair market value of FA's assets by $25x. Therefore, under paragraph (b) of this section, the 25 shares of FA stock transferred to Individual A in exchange for the obligation of DT are not included in the denominator of the ownership fraction. Accordingly, the only FA stock included in the ownership fraction is the 75 shares of FA stock transferred to Individual A in exchange for the DT stock, and that FA stock is included in both the numerator and the denominator of the ownership fraction. Thus, the ownership fraction is 75/75.

(iii) *Alternative facts.* The facts are the same as in paragraph (i) of this *Example 6*, except that instead of acquiring the stock of DT and the $25x obligation of DT, FA acquires the $100x of property from DT in exchange solely for 100 shares of FA stock. DT distributes 75 shares of FA stock to Individual A in exchange for Individual A's DT stock and transfers 25 shares of FA stock to Individual A in satisfaction of DT's obligation to Individual A, and liquidates. The 25 shares of FA stock transferred by FA to DT in exchange for the property of DT and then transferred by DT in satisfaction of DT's obligation to Individual A constitute disqualified stock described in paragraph (c)(1) of this section by reason of paragraph (c)(1)(ii) of this section. Paragraph (c)(2) of this section does not reduce the amount of disqualified stock described in paragraph (c)(1)(ii) of this section because the transfer of FA stock in exchange for the property of DT increases the fair market value of FA's assets by $100x (although the amount of disqualified stock is limited to 25 shares of FA stock in this case). Therefore, under paragraph (b) of this section, the 25 shares of FA stock that constitute disqualified stock are not included in the denominator of the ownership fraction. Accordingly, only 75 shares of FA stock are included in the ownership fraction, and that FA stock is included in both the numerator and the denominator of the ownership fraction. Thus, the ownership fraction is 75/75.

Example 7. "Over-the-top" stock transfer—(i) *Facts.* Individual A wholly owns DT. Individual B holds all 100 outstanding shares of FA stock. Individual C acquires 20 shares of FA stock from Individual B for cash, and then FA acquires all of the stock of DT from Individual A in exchange solely for 100 shares of FA stock.

(ii) *Analysis.* Under paragraph (h)(2)(i) of this section, cash constitutes nonqualified property. Accordingly, absent the application of paragraph (c)(2) of this section, the 20 shares of FA stock transferred by Individual B to Individual C in exchange for cash would constitute disqualified stock described in paragraph (c)(1) of this section by reason of paragraph (c)(1)(i) of this section. Nevertheless, because Individual B's sale of FA stock neither increases the assets of FA nor decreases the liabilities of FA, such FA stock is not disqualified stock by reason of paragraph (c)(2) of this section. Accordingly, paragraph (b) of this section does not apply to exclude the 20 shares of FA stock sold by Individual B to Individual C, and that FA stock is included in the denominator of the ownership fraction. The 100 shares of FA stock received by Individual A are the only shares included in the numerator of the ownership fraction. Thus, the ownership fraction is 100/200.

Example 8. Interaction with internal group restructuring rule—(i) *Facts.* P holds 85 shares of DT stock. The remaining 15 shares of DT stock are held by Individual A. P and Individual A transfer their shares of DT stock to FA, a newly formed corporation, in exchange for 85 and 15 shares of FA stock, respectively (DT acquisition), and

PRS transfers $75x of cash to FA in exchange for the remaining 75 shares of FA stock.

(ii) *Analysis.* Under paragraph (h)(2)(i) of this section, cash constitutes nonqualified property. Accordingly, the 75 shares of FA stock transferred by FA to PRS in exchange for $75x of cash constitute disqualified stock described in paragraph (c)(1) of this section by reason of paragraph (c)(1)(i) of this section. Furthermore, paragraph (c)(2) of this section does not reduce the amount of disqualified stock described in paragraph (c)(1)(i) of this section because the transfer of FA stock in exchange for $75x of cash increases the fair market value of the assets of FA by $75x. Therefore, under paragraph (b) of this section, the 75 shares of FA stock transferred to PRS are not included in the denominator of the ownership fraction. Although PRS's shares of FA stock are excluded from the denominator of the ownership fraction under paragraph (b) of this section, under § 1.7874-1(d)(1), such shares of FA stock nonetheless are taken into account for purposes of determining whether P is a member of the expanded affiliated group that includes FA and for purposes of determining whether the DT acquisition qualifies as an internal group restructuring. Because P holds 48.6% of the FA stock (85/175) after the DT acquisition and all transactions related to the DT acquisition, it is not a member of the expanded affiliated group that includes FA. In addition, the DT acquisition does not qualify as an internal group restructuring described in § 1.7874-1(c)(2) because P does not hold, directly or indirectly, 80% or more of the shares of FA stock (by vote and value) after the DT acquisition and all transactions related to the DT acquisition. Therefore, the FA stock held by P (along with the FA stock held by Individual A) is included in the numerator and the denominator of the ownership fraction. Thus, the ownership fraction is 100/100.

Example 9. Interaction with loss of control rule—(i) *Facts.* P wholly owns DT. P transfers all of its shares of DT stock to FA, a newly formed corporation, in exchange for 49 shares of FA stock (DT acquisition), and R transfers marketable securities (within the meaning of paragraph (h)(1) of this section) to FA in exchange for the remaining 51 shares of FA stock.

(ii) *Analysis.* Under paragraph (h)(2)(ii) of this section, the marketable securities constitute nonqualified property. Accordingly, the shares of FA stock transferred by FA to R in exchange for the marketable securities constitute disqualified stock described in paragraph (c)(1) of this section by reason of paragraph (c)(1)(i) of this section. Paragraph (c)(2) of this section does not reduce the amount of disqualified stock described in paragraph (c)(1)(i) of this section because the transfer of FA stock in exchange for the marketable securities increases the fair market value of the assets of FA by the fair market value of the marketable securities transferred. Therefore, under paragraph (b) of this section, the shares of FA stock transferred to R are not included in the denominator of the ownership fraction. Although under paragraph (b) of this section R's shares of FA stock are excluded from the denominator of the ownership fraction, under § 1.7874-1(d)(1), such stock is taken into account for purposes of determining whether P or R is a member of the expanded affiliated group that includes FA. Because P holds 49% of the shares of FA stock (49/100), P is not a member of the expanded affiliated group that includes FA, and P's FA stock is included in both the numerator and the denominator of the ownership fraction. Because R holds 51% of the shares of FA stock (51/100), R is a member of the expanded affiliated group that includes FA and, before taking into account § 1.7874-1(c), R's FA stock would be excluded from the numerator and denominator of the ownership fraction under section 7874(c)(2)(A) and § 1.7874-1(b). However, the DT acquisition results in a loss of control described in § 1.7874-1(c)(3) because P does not hold, in the aggregate, directly or indirectly, more than 50% of the shares of stock (by vote or value) of R, FA, or DT after the acquisition. Accordingly, the FA stock held by R would be included in the denominator of the ownership fraction under § 1.7874-1(c)(1). Nevertheless, the FA stock held by R is excluded from the denominator of the ownership fraction under paragraph (b) of this section and § 1.7874-1(d)(1). Thus, the ownership fraction is 49/49.

(iii) *Alternative facts.* The facts are the same as in paragraph (i) of this *Example 9*, except that, in exchange for 51 shares of FA stock, R transfers marketable securities (within the meaning of paragraph (h)(1) of this section) with a value equal to that of 16 shares of FA stock and qualified property (within the meaning of paragraph (h)(2) of this section) with a value equal to that of 35 shares of FA stock. Accordingly, 16 of the 51 shares of FA stock transferred to R constitute disqualified stock described in paragraph (c)(1) of this section by reason of paragraph (c)(1)(i) of this section, and 35 of such shares do not constitute disqualified stock. Paragraph (c)(2) of this section does not reduce the amount of disqualified stock described in paragraph (c)(1)(i) of this section because the transfer of FA stock in exchange for the marketable securities increases the fair market value of the assets of FA by the fair market value of the marketable securities transferred. Therefore, under paragraph (b) of this section, 16 of the 51 shares of FA stock transferred to R are not included in the denominator of the ownership fraction. Although 16 of the 51 shares of FA stock that are transferred to R are excluded from the denominator of the ownership fraction, under § 1.7874-1(d)(1), all 51 of R's shares of FA stock are taken into account for purposes of determining whether P or R is a member of the expanded affiliated group that includes FA. Because P holds 49% of the shares of FA stock (49/100), it is not a member of the expanded affiliated group that includes FA, and its FA stock is included in both the numerator and the denominator of the ownership fraction. Because R holds 51% of the shares of FA stock (51/100), it is a member of the expanded affiliated group that includes FA and, before taking into account § 1.7874-1(c), its FA stock is excluded from the numerator and denominator of the ownership fraction under section 7874(c)(2)(A) and § 1.7874-1(b). However, the DT acquisition results in a loss of control described in § 1.7874-1(c)(3) because P does not hold, in the aggregate, directly or indirectly, more than 50% of the shares of stock (by vote or value) of R, FA, or DT after the acquisition. Accordingly, the 51 shares of FA stock held by R would be included in the denominator of the ownership fraction under § 1.7874-1(c)(1). Nevertheless, the 16 shares of FA stock that constitute disqualified stock are excluded from the denominator of the ownership fraction under paragraph (b) of this section and § 1.7874-1(d)(1). In addition, the 35 shares of FA stock received by R that do not constitute disqualified stock are included in the denominator. Thus, the ownership fraction is 49/84.

Example 10. Stock issued in lieu of assuming associated obligation—(i) *Facts.* Individual A wholly owns DT. The stock of DT has a fair market value of $100x. Individual B wholly owns FT, a foreign corporation, which conducts two businesses, Business C and Business D. Business C comprises property with a gross fair market value of $70x and $20x of associated obligations. Business D comprises property with a gross fair market value of $45x and $35x of associated obligations. Individual A transfers all of the shares of DT stock to FA, a newly formed corporation, in exchange for $100x of FA stock (DT acquisition). In transactions related to the DT acquisition, FA acquires all of the Business C property from FT in exchange for $70x of FA stock and then FT transfers $30x of the FA stock to its creditors in satisfaction of $30x of its obligations. None of the Business C property is nonqualified property.

(ii) *Analysis.* Under paragraph (c)(1) of this section by reason of paragraph (c)(1)(ii) of this section, the $30x of FA stock transferred to FT (the transferee) in exchange for the Business C property (the exchanged property) and then transferred by FT in satisfaction of $30x of its obligations is disqualified stock, except to the extent limited by paragraph (c)(1)(ii)(B) of this section. Under paragraph (c)(1)(ii)(B)(*1*) of this section, the proportionate share of obligations associated with the exchanged property that is not assumed by FA must be determined. The proportionate share of obligations associated with the exchanged property is $20x, calculated as $20x (the obligations associated with the Business C properties) multiplied by $70x/$70x (the fair market value of the exchanged property, $70x, relative to the fair market value of all the Business C property, $70x). The proportionate share of obligations associated with the exchanged property that is not assumed by FA is $20x, calculated as the proportionate share of obligations associated with the exchanged property ($20x) less the obligations assumed by FA ($0x). Under paragraph (c)(1)(ii)(B)(2) of this section, the amount of disqualified stock is limited to the proportionate share of obligations associated with the exchanged property that is not assumed ($20x) multiplied by a fraction, which in this case is $70x/$70x (the amount of exchanged property that is qualified property, $70x, divided by the total amount of exchanged property, $70x). Accordingly, $20x of FA stock is disqualified stock under paragraph (c)(1) of this section by reason of paragraph (c)(1)(ii) of this section. Paragraph (c)(2) of this section does not reduce the amount of disqualified stock described in paragraph (c)(1)(ii) of this section because the transfer of the FA stock in exchange for the exchanged property increases the fair market value of FA's assets by $70x (although the amount of disqualified stock is limited to $20x of FA stock in this case). Therefore, under paragraph (b) of this section, the $20x of FA stock that constitutes disqualified stock is not included in the denominator of the ownership fraction. Accordingly, only $150x of FA stock is included in the denominator of the ownership fraction, calculated as the $100x of FA stock received by Individual A plus the $70x of FA stock received by FT less the $20x of FA stock that is disqualified stock. Thus, the ownership fraction is $100x/$150x. The result would be the same if, in transactions related to the DT acquisition, FT instead sold the $30x of FA stock for $30x cash and then transferred the cash in satisfaction of $30x of its obligations.

(iii) *Alternative facts*. The facts are the same as in paragraph (i) of this *Example 10*, except that FA acquires only $42x of the Business C property in exchange for $30x of FA stock and the assumption of $12x of the obligations associated with the Business C property. Under paragraph (c)(1) of this section by reason of paragraph (c)(1)(ii) of this section, the $30x of FA stock transferred to FT (the transferee) in exchange for the Business C property (the exchanged property) and then transferred by FT in satisfaction of $30x of its obligations is disqualified stock, except to the extent limited by paragraph (c)(1)(ii)(B) of this section. Under paragraph (c)(1)(ii)(B)(*1*) of this section, the proportionate share of obligations associated with the exchanged property that is not assumed by FA must be determined. The proportionate share of obligations associated with the exchanged property is $12x, calculated as $20x (the obligations associated with the Business C property) multiplied by $42x/$70x (the fair market value of the exchanged property, $42x, relative to the fair market value of all the Business C property, $70x). The proportionate share of obligations associated with the exchanged property that is not assumed by FA is $0, calculated as the proportionate share of obligations associated with the exchanged property ($12x) less the obligations assumed by FA ($12x). Accordingly, as a result of the application of paragraph (c)(1)(ii)(B)(2) of this section, no FA stock is disqualified stock under paragraph (c)(1) of this section by reason of paragraph (c)(1)(ii) of this section. As a result, $130x of FA stock is included in the denominator of the ownership fraction, calculated as the $100x of FA stock received by Individual A plus the $30x of FA stock received by FT. Thus, the ownership fraction is $100x/$130x.

(j) *Applicability dates*.—(1) *General rule*.—Except to the extent otherwise provided in paragraph (j) of this section, this section applies to domestic entity acquisitions completed on or after September 17, 2009. Paragraphs (h)(1) and (h)(2)(iv) of this section apply to domestic entity acquisitions completed on or after November 19, 2015. Paragraph (d)(1)(i) of this section applies to domestic entity acquisitions completed on or after April 4, 2016. Paragraphs (c)(1)(ii), (h)(2)(iii), and (h)(3) of this section apply to domestic entity acquisitions completed on or after January 13, 2017. For domestic entity acquisitions completed before November 19, 2015, see § 1.7874-4T(i)(6) and (i)(7)(iv) (the predecessors of paragraphs (h)(1) and (h)(2)(iv) of this section) as contained in 26 CFR part 1 revised as of April 1, 2016. For domestic entity acquisitions completed on or after September 22, 2014, and before April 4, 2016, see § 1.7874-4T(d)(1)(i) as contained in 26 CFR part 1 revised as of April 1, 2016. For domestic entity acquisitions completed before January 13, 2017, see § 1.7874-4T(c)(1)(ii), (i)(7)(iii) (the predecessor of paragraph (h)(2)(iii) of this section), and (i)(8) (the predecessor of paragraph (h)(3) of this section) as contained in 26 CFR part 1 revised as of April 1, 2016. Paragraph (d)(1)(ii) of this section applies to domestic entity acquisitions completed on or after July 12, 2018, though taxpayers may elect to consistently apply paragraph (d)(1)(ii) of this section to domestic entity acquisitions completed before July 12, 2018. For domestic entity acquisitions completed before July 12, 2018, see § 1.7874-4(d)(1)(ii) as contained in 26 CFR part 1 revised as of April 1, 2017.

(2) *Transitional rules for domestic entity acquisitions completed on or after September 17, 2009, but before January 16, 2014*.—For domestic entity acquisitions completed on or after September 17, 2009, but before January 16, 2014, except as provided in paragraph (j)(3) of this section, this section shall be applied with the following modifications:

(i) Nonqualified property does not include property described in paragraph (h)(2)(iii) of this section.

(ii) A transfer is limited to an issuance of stock of the foreign acquiring corporation.

(iii) The determination of whether stock of the foreign acquiring corporation is described in paragraph (c)(1) of this section is made without regard to paragraphs (c)(1)(ii), (c)(2), and (e) of this section.

(iv) Paragraph (d) of this section and § 1.7874-1(d)(1) do not apply.

(3) *Election for domestic entity acquisitions completed on or after September 17, 2009, and before January 13, 2017*.—If, pursuant to paragraph (j)(1) or (2) of this section, a paragraph of this section would not otherwise apply to a domestic entity acquisition completed on or after September 17, 2009, and before January 13, 2017 (transition period), a taxpayer may elect to apply the paragraph if the taxpayer applies the paragraph consistently to all acquisitions completed during the transition period. The election is made by applying the paragraph to all such acquisitions on a timely filed original return (including extensions) or an amended return filed no later than six months after January 13, 2017. A separate statement or form evidencing the election need not be filed. [Reg. § 1.7874-4.]

☐ [*T.D. 9812, 1-13-2017 (corrected 9-6-2017). Amended by T.D. 9834, 7-11-2018.*]

§ 1.7874-5. Effect of certain transfers of stock related to the acquisition.—(a) *General rule*.—Stock of a foreign acquiring corporation that is described in section 7874(a)(2)(B)(ii) shall not cease to be so described as a result of any subsequent transfer of the stock by the former domestic entity shareholder or former domestic entity partner that received such stock, even if the subsequent transfer is related to the domestic entity acquisition.

(b) *Example*.—The rule of this section is illustrated by the following example:

Example. (i) *Facts*. Individual A wholly owns DT, a domestic corporation. FA, a newly formed foreign corporation, acquires all of the stock of DT from Individual A in exchange solely for 100 shares of FA stock. Pursuant to a binding commitment that was entered into in connection with FA's acquisition of the DT stock, Individual A sells 25 shares of FA stock to B, an unrelated person, in exchange for cash. For federal income tax purposes, the form of the steps of the transaction is respected.

(ii) *Analysis*. Under § 1.7874-2(f)(1), the 100 shares of FA stock received by Individual A are stock of a foreign corporation (FA) that is held by reason of holding stock in a domestic corporation (DT). Accordingly, such stock is described in section 7874(a)(2)(B)(ii). Under paragraph (a) of this section, all 100 shares of FA stock retain their status as being described in section 7874(a)(2)(B)(ii), even though Individual A sells 25 of the 100 shares in connection with the acquisition described in section 7874(a)(2)(B)(i) pursuant to the binding commitment. Therefore, all 100 of the shares of FA stock are included in both the numerator and denominator of the ownership fraction.

(c) *Certain transfers involving expanded affiliated group members*.—For rules addressing whether certain stock is treated as held by members of the expanded affiliated group for purposes of applying section 7874(c)(2)(A) and § 1.7874-1, see § 1.7874-6.

(d) *Definitions*.—The definitions provided in § 1.7874-12 apply for purposes of this section.

(e) *Applicability dates*.—This section applies to domestic entity acquisitions that are completed on or after January 16, 2014. [Reg. § 1.7874-5.]

☐ [*T.D. 9812, 1-13-2017. Amended by T.D. 9834, 7-11-2018.*]

§ 1.7874-6. Stock transferred by members of the EAG.—(a) *Scope*.—This section provides rules regarding whether transferred stock is treated as held by members of the EAG for purposes of applying section 7874(c)(2)(A) and § 1.7874-1. Paragraph (b) of this section sets forth the general rule under which transferred stock is not treated as held by members of the EAG for purposes of applying section 7874(c)(2)(A) and § 1.7874-1. Paragraph (c) of this section provides exceptions to the general rule. Paragraph (d) of this section provides rules regarding the treatment of partnerships, and paragraph (e) of this section provides rules regarding transactions related to the acquisition. Paragraph (f) of this section provides definitions. Paragraph (g) of this section provides examples illustrating the application of the rules of this section. Paragraph (h) of this section provides dates of applicability.

(b) *General rule*.—Except as provided in paragraph (c) of this section, transferred stock is not treated as held by members of the EAG for purposes of applying section 7874(c)(2)(A) and § 1.7874-1. Transferred stock that is not treated as held by members of the EAG for purposes of applying section 7874(c)(2)(A) and § 1.7874-1 is included in the numerator and the denominator of the ownership fraction. See § 1.7874-5(a).

(c) *Exceptions*.—Transferred stock is treated as held by members of the EAG for purposes of applying section 7874(c)(2)(A) and § 1.7874-1 if paragraph (c)(1) or (2) of this section applies. Transferred stock that is treated as held by members of the EAG for purposes of applying section 7874(c)(2)(A) and § 1.7874-1 is excluded from the numerator of the ownership fraction and, depending upon the application of § 1.7874-1(c), may be excluded from the denominator of the ownership fraction. See §§ 1.7874-1(b) and (c).

(1) *Transfers involving a U.S.-parented group.*—This paragraph (c)(1) applies if the following conditions are satisfied:

(i) Before the domestic entity acquisition, the transferring corporation is a member of a U.S.-parented group.

(ii) After the domestic entity acquisition, each of the transferring corporation (or its successor), any person that holds transferred stock, and the foreign acquiring corporation are members of a U.S.-parented group the common parent of which—

(A) Before the domestic entity acquisition, was a member of the U.S.-parented group described in paragraph (c)(1)(i) of this section; or

(B) Is a corporation that was formed in a transaction related to the domestic entity acquisition, provided that, immediately after the corporation was formed (and without regard to any related transactions), the corporation was a member of the U.S.-parented group described in paragraph (c)(1)(i) of this section.

(2) *Transfers involving a foreign-parented group.*—This paragraph (c)(2) applies if the following conditions are satisfied:

(i) Before the domestic entity acquisition, the transferring corporation and the domestic entity are members of the same foreign-parented group.

(ii) After the domestic entity acquisition, the transferring corporation—

(A) Is a member of the EAG; or

(B) Would be a member of the EAG absent one or more transfers (other than by issuance), in a transaction (or series of transactions) after and related to the domestic entity acquisition, of stock of the foreign acquiring corporation by one or more members of the foreign-parented group described in paragraph (c)(2)(i) of this section.

(d) *Treatment of partnerships.*—(1) *Stock held by a partnership.*—For purposes of this section, each partner in a partnership, as determined without regard to the application of paragraph (d)(2) of this section, is treated as holding its proportionate share of the stock held by the partnership, as determined under the rules and principles of sections 701 through 777.

(2) *Partnership treated as corporation.*—For purposes of this section, if one or more members of an affiliated group, as determined after the application of paragraph (d)(1) of this section, own, in the aggregate, more than 50 percent (by value) of the interests in a partnership, the partnership will be treated as a corporation that is a member of the affiliated group.

(e) *Treatment of transactions related to the acquisition.*—Except as provided in paragraphs (c)(1)(ii)(B) and (c)(2)(ii)(B) of this section, all transactions that are related to a domestic entity acquisition are taken into account in applying this section.

(f) *Definitions.*—In addition to the definitions provided in §1.7874-12, the following definitions apply for purposes of this section.

(1) A *foreign-parented group* means an affiliated group that has a foreign corporation as the common parent corporation. A *member of the foreign-parented group* is an entity included in the foreign-parented group.

(2) *Transferred stock.*—(i) *In general.*—Transferred stock means stock of the foreign acquiring corporation described in section 7874(a)(2)(B)(ii) that is received by a transferring corporation and, in a transaction (or series of transactions) related to the domestic entity acquisition, is subsequently transferred.

(ii) *Special rule.*—This paragraph (f)(2)(ii) applies in certain cases in which a transferring corporation receives stock of the foreign acquiring corporation described in section 7874(a)(2)(B)(ii) that has the same terms as other stock of the foreign acquiring corporation that is received by the transferring corporation in a transaction (or series of transactions) related to the domestic entity acquisition or that is owned by the transferring corporation prior to the domestic entity acquisition (the stock described in this sentence, collectively, *fungible stock*). Pursuant to this paragraph (f)(2)(ii), if, in a transaction (or series of transactions) related to the domestic entity acquisition, the transferring corporation subsequently transfers less than all of the fungible stock, a pro rata portion of the stock subsequently transferred is treated as consisting of stock of the foreign acquiring corporation described in section 7874(a)(2)(B)(ii). The pro rata portion is based, at the time of the subsequent transfer, on the relative fair market value of the fungible stock that is stock of the foreign acquiring corporation described in section 7874(a)(2)(B)(ii) to the fair market value of all the fungible stock.

(3) A *transferring corporation* means a corporation that is a former domestic entity shareholder or former domestic entity partner.

(4) A *U.S.-parented group* means an affiliated group that has a domestic corporation as the common parent corporation. A *member of the U.S.-parented group* is an entity included in the U.S.-parented group, including the common parent corporation.

(g) *Examples.*—The following examples illustrate the application of this section.

Example 1. U.S.-parented group exception not available—(i) *Facts.* USP, a domestic corporation wholly owned by Individual A, owns all the stock of DT, a domestic corporation, as well as other property. The DT stock does not represent substantially all of the property of USP for purposes of section 7874. Pursuant to a reorganization described in section 368(a)(1)(D), USP transfers all the DT stock to FA, a newly formed foreign corporation, in exchange for 100 shares of FA stock (DT acquisition) and distributes the FA stock to Individual A pursuant to section 361(c)(1).

(ii) *Analysis.* The 100 FA shares received by USP are stock of a foreign acquiring corporation described in section 7874(a)(2)(B)(ii) and, under §1.7874-5(a), the shares retain their status as such even though USP subsequently distributes the shares to Individual A pursuant to section 361(c)(1). Thus, the 100 FA shares are included in the ownership fraction, unless the shares are treated as held by members of the EAG for purposes of applying section 7874(c)(2)(A) and §1.7874-1 and are excluded from the ownership fraction under those rules. For purposes of applying section 7874(c)(2)(A) and §1.7874-1, the 100 FA shares, which constitute transferred stock under paragraph (f)(2) of this section, are treated as held by members of the EAG only if an exception in paragraph (c) of this section applies. See paragraph (b) of this section. The U.S.-parented group exception described in paragraph (c)(1) of this section does not apply. Although before the DT acquisition, USP (the transferring corporation) is a member of a U.S.-parented group of which USP is the common parent, after the DT acquisition, and taking into account all transactions related to the acquisition, each of USP, Individual A (the person that holds the transferred stock), and FA (the foreign acquiring corporation) are not members of a U.S.-parented group described in paragraph (c)(1)(ii)(A) or (B) of this section. Accordingly, because the 100 FA shares are not treated as held by members of the EAG, those shares are included in the numerator and the denominator of the ownership fraction. Therefore, the ownership fraction is 100/100.

Example 2. U.S.-parented group exception available—(i) *Facts.* USP, a domestic corporation wholly owned by Individual A, owns all the stock of USS, a domestic corporation, and USS owns all the stock of FT, a foreign corporation. FT owns all the stock of DT, a domestic corporation. FT does not own any other property and has no liabilities. Pursuant to a reorganization described in section 368(a)(1)(F), FT transfers all of its DT stock to FA, a newly formed foreign corporation, in exchange for 100 shares of FA stock (DT acquisition) and distributes the FA stock to USS in liquidation pursuant to section 361(c)(1). In a transaction after and related to the DT acquisition, USP sells 60 percent of the stock of USS (by vote and value) to Individual B.

(ii) *Analysis.* The 100 FA shares received by FT are stock of a foreign acquiring corporation described in section 7874(a)(2)(B)(ii) and, under §1.7874-5(a), the shares retain their status as such even though FT subsequently distributes the shares to USS pursuant to section 361(c)(1). Thus, the 100 FA shares are included in the ownership fraction, unless the shares are treated as held by members of the EAG for purposes of applying section 7874(c)(2)(A) and §1.7874-1 and are excluded from the ownership fraction under those rules. For purposes of applying section 7874(c)(2)(A) and §1.7874-1, the 100 FA shares, which constitute transferred stock under paragraph (f)(2) of this section, are treated as held by members of the EAG only if an exception in paragraph (c) of this section applies. See paragraph (b) of this section. The U.S.-parented group exception described in paragraph (c)(1) of this section applies. The requirement set forth in paragraph (c)(1)(i) of this section is satisfied because before the DT acquisition, FT (the transferring corporation) is a member of a U.S.-parented group of which USP is the common parent (the USP group). The requirement set forth in paragraph (c)(1)(ii) of this section is satisfied because after the DT acquisition, and taking into account all transactions related to the acquisition, each of FA (which is both the successor to FT, the transferring corporation, and the foreign acquiring corporation) and USS (the person that holds the transferred stock) are members of a U.S.-parented group of which USS (a member of the USP group before the DT acquisition) is the common parent. Moreover, the DT acquisition qualifies as an internal group restructuring under § 1.7874-1(c)(2). The requirement set forth in § 1.7874-1(c)(2)(i) is satisfied because before the DT acquisition, 80 percent or more of the stock (by vote and value) of DT was held directly or indirectly by USS (the corporation that after the acquisition, and taking into account all transactions related to the acquisition, is the common parent of the EAG). The requirement set forth in § 1.7874-1(c)(2)(ii) is satisfied because after the acquisition, and taking into account all transactions related to the acquisition, 80 percent or more of the stock (by vote and value) of FA (the foreign acquiring corporation) is held directly or indirectly by USS. Therefore, the 100 FA shares are excluded from the numerator, but included in the denominator, of the ownership fraction. Accordingly, the ownership fraction is 0/100.

Example 3. U.S.-parented group exception available—(i) *Facts*. USP, a domestic corporation wholly owned by Individual A, owns all the stock of USS, a domestic corporation, and USS owns all the stock of DT, also a domestic corporation. DT owns all the stock of FT, a foreign corporation. The FT stock represents substantially all of the property of DT for purposes of section 7874. Pursuant to a reorganization described in section 368(a)(1)(D), DT transfers all the FT stock to FA, a newly formed foreign corporation, in exchange for 100 shares of FA stock (DT acquisition) and distributes the FA stock to USS pursuant to section 361(c)(1). In a related transaction, USS distributes all the FA stock to USP under section 355(c)(1). Lastly, in another related transaction and pursuant to a divisive reorganization described in section 368(a)(1)(D), USP transfers all the stock of USS and FA to DP, a newly formed domestic corporation, in exchange for all the stock of DP and distributes the DP stock to Individual A pursuant to section 361(c)(1).

(ii) *Analysis*. The 100 FA shares received by USS are stock of a foreign acquiring corporation described in section 7874(a)(2)(B)(ii) and, under § 1.7874-5(a), the shares retain their status as such even though USS subsequently transfers the shares to USP. Thus, the 100 FA shares are included in the ownership fraction, unless the shares are treated as held by members of the EAG for purposes of applying section 7874(c)(2)(A) and § 1.7874-1 and are excluded from the ownership fraction under those rules. For purposes of applying section 7874(c)(2)(A) and § 1.7874-1, the 100 FA shares, which constitute transferred stock under paragraph (f)(2) of this section, are treated as held by members of the EAG only if an exception in paragraph (c) of this section applies. See paragraph (b) of this section. The U.S.-parented group exception described in paragraph (c)(1) of this section applies. The requirement set forth in paragraph (c)(1)(i) of this section is satisfied because before the DT acquisition, USS (the transferring corporation) is a member of a U.S.-parented group of which USP is the common parent (the USP group). The requirement set forth in paragraph (c)(1)(ii) of this section is satisfied because after the DT acquisition, and taking into account all transactions related to the acquisition, each of USS, DP (the person that holds the transferred stock), and FA (the foreign acquiring corporation) are members of a U.S.-parented group of which DP (a corporation that was formed in a transaction related to the DT acquisition and that, immediately after it was formed (but without regard to any related transactions) was a member of the USP group) is the common parent. Therefore, the 100 FA shares are excluded from the numerator and the denominator of the ownership fraction. Accordingly, the ownership fraction is 0/0.

Example 4. Foreign-parented group exception—(i) *Facts*. Individual A owns all the stock of FT, a foreign corporation, and FT owns all the stock of DT, a domestic corporation. FT does not own any other property and has no liabilities. Pursuant to a reorganization described in section 368(a)(1)(F), FT transfers all the stock of DT to FA, a newly formed foreign corporation, in exchange for 100 shares of FA stock (DT acquisition) and distributes the FA stock to Individual A in liquidation pursuant to section 361(c)(1).

(ii) *Analysis*. The 100 FA shares received by FT are stock of a foreign acquiring corporation described in section 7874(a)(2)(B)(ii) and, under § 1.7874-5(a), the shares retain their status as such even though FT subsequently distributes the shares to Individual A pursuant to section 361(c)(1). Thus, the 100 FA shares are included in the ownership fraction, unless the shares are treated as held by members of the EAG of purposes of applying section 7874(a)(2)(A) and § 1.7874-1 and are excluded from the ownership fraction under those rules. For purposes of applying section 7874(c)(2)(A) and § 1.7874-1, the 100 FA shares, which constitute transferred stock under paragraph (f)(2) of this section, are treated as held by members of the EAG only if an exception in paragraph (c) of this section applies. See paragraph (b) of this section. The foreign-parented group exception described in paragraph (c)(2) of this section applies. The requirement set forth in paragraph (c)(2)(i) of this section is satisfied because before the DT acquisition, FT (the transferring corporation) and DT are members of the foreign-parented group of which FT is the common parent. The requirement set forth in paragraph (c)(2)(ii) of this section is satisfied because after the acquisition, and taking into account all transactions related to the acquisition, FT would be a member of the EAG absent the distribution of the FA shares pursuant to section 361(c)(1). Moreover, the DT acquisition qualifies as an internal group restructuring under § 1.7874-1(c)(2). The requirement set forth in § 1.7874-1(c)(2)(i) is satisfied because before the acquisition, 80 percent or more of the stock (by vote and value) of DT was held directly or indirectly by FT, the corporation that, without regard to the distribution of the FA shares pursuant to section 361(c)(1), would be common parent of the EAG after the acquisition. See § 1.7874-1(c)(2)(iii). The requirement set forth in § 1.7874-1(c)(2)(ii) is satisfied because after the acquisition, but without regard to the distribution of the FA shares pursuant to the section 361(c)(1) distribution, FT would directly or indirectly hold 80 percent or more of the stock (by vote and value) of FA (the foreign acquiring corporation). See § 1.7874-1(c)(2)(iii). Therefore, the 100 FA shares are excluded from the numerator, but included in the denominator, of the ownership fraction. Accordingly, the ownership fraction is 0/100.

(iii) *Alternative facts*. The facts are the same as in paragraph (i) of this *Example 4*, except that in a transaction after and related to the DT acquisition, FA issues 200 shares of FA stock to Individual B in exchange for qualified property (within the meaning of § 1.7874-4(h)(2)). The foreign-parented group exception does not apply because after the acquisition, and taking into account FA's issuance of the 200 FA shares to Individual B, FT would not be a member of the EAG absent FT's distribution of the 100 FA shares pursuant to section 361(c)(1). Accordingly, the 100 FA shares received by FT are not treated as held by a member of the EAG for purposes of applying section 7874(c)(2)(A) and § 1.7874-1. As a result, the ownership fraction is 100/300.

(h) *Applicability dates*.—Except as otherwise provided in this paragraph (h), this section applies to domestic entity acquisitions completed on or after September 22, 2014. Paragraphs (d)(2) and (f)(2)(ii) of this section apply to domestic entity acquisitions completed on or after April 4, 2016. Taxpayers, however, may elect either to apply paragraph (c)(2) of this section to domestic entity acquisitions completed before September 22, 2014, or to consistently apply paragraphs (c)(2), (d)(2), and (f)(2)(ii) of this section and §§ 1.7874-1(c)(2)(iii) and (g) to domestic entity acquisitions completed before April 4, 2016. [Reg. § 1.7874-6.]

☐ [*T.D.* 9834, 7-11-2018.]

§ 1.7874-7. Disregard of certain stock attributable to passive assets.—(a) *Scope*.—This section identifies certain stock of a foreign acquiring corporation that is attributable to passive assets and that is disregarded in determining the ownership fraction by value. Paragraph (b) of this section sets forth the general rule regarding when stock of a foreign acquiring corporation is excluded from the denominator of the ownership fraction under this section. Paragraph (c) of this section provides a de minimis exception to the application of the general rule of paragraph (b) of this section. Paragraph (d) of this section provides rules for the treatment of partnerships, and paragraph (e) of this section provides definitions. Paragraph (f) of this section provides examples illustrating the application of the rules of this section. Paragraph (g) of this section provides dates of applicability. The rules provided in this section are also subject to section 7874(c)(4). See § 1.7874-1(d)(1) for rules addressing the interaction of this section with the expanded affiliated group rules of section 7874(c)(2)(A) and § 1.7874-1.

(b) *General rule*.—If, on the completion date, more than fifty percent of the gross value of all foreign group property constitutes foreign group nonqualified property, then, for purposes of determining the ownership percentage by value (but not vote) described in section 7874(a)(2)(B)(ii), stock of the foreign acquiring corporation is excluded from the denominator of the ownership fraction in an amount equal to the product of—

(1) The value of the stock of the foreign acquiring corporation, other than stock that is described in section 7874(a)(2)(B)(ii) and stock that is excluded from the denominator of the ownership fraction under § 1.7874-1(b), § 1.7874-4(b), § 1.7874-8(b), § 1.7874-9(b), or section 7874(c)(4); and

(2) The foreign group nonqualified property fraction.

(c) *De minimis ownership*.—Paragraph (b) of this section does not apply if—

(1) The ownership percentage described in section 7874(a)(2)(B)(ii), determined without regard to the application of

paragraph (b) of this section and §§1.7874-4(b) and 1.7874-10(b), is less than five (by vote and value); and

(2) On the completion date, each five percent former domestic entity shareholder or five percent former domestic entity partner, as applicable, owns (applying the attribution rules of section 318(a) with the modifications described in section 304(c)(3)(B)) less than five percent (by vote and value) of the stock of (or a partnership interest in) each member of the expanded affiliated group. For this purpose, a five percent former domestic entity shareholder (or five percent former domestic entity partner) is a former domestic entity shareholder (or former domestic entity partner) that, before the domestic entity acquisition, owned (applying the attribution rules of section 318(a) with the modifications described in section 304(c)(3)(B)) at least five percent (by vote and value) of the stock of (or a partnership interest in) the domestic entity.

(d) *Treatment of partnerships.*—For purposes of this section, if one or more members of the modified expanded affiliated group own, in the aggregate, more than 50 percent (by value) of the interests in a partnership, the partnership is treated as a corporation that is a member of the modified expanded affiliated group.

(e) *Definitions.*—In addition to the definitions provided in §1.7874-12, the following definitions apply for purposes of this section.

(1) *Foreign group nonqualified property.*—(i) *General rule.*—Foreign group nonqualified property means foreign group property described in §1.7874-4(h)(2), other than the following:

(A) Property that gives rise to income described in section 954(h), determined—

(1) In the case of property held by a foreign corporation, by substituting the term "foreign corporation" for the term "controlled foreign corporation;" and

(2) In the case of property held by a domestic corporation, by substituting the term "domestic corporation" for the term "controlled foreign corporation," without regard to the phrase "other than the United States" in section 954(h)(3)(A)(ii)(I), and without regard to any inference that the tests in section 954(h) should be calculated or determined without taking transactions with customers located in the United States into account.

(B) Property that gives rise to income described in section 954(i), determined by substituting the term "foreign corporation" for the term "controlled foreign corporation."

(C) Property that gives rise to income described in section 1297(b)(2)(A) or (B) (determined without regard to other passive foreign investment company rules).

(D) Property held by a domestic corporation that is subject to tax as an insurance company under subchapter L of chapter 1 of subtitle A of the Internal Revenue Code, provided that the property is required to support, or is substantially related to, the active conduct of an insurance business.

(ii) *Special rule.*—Foreign group nonqualified property also means any foreign group property that, in a transaction related to the domestic entity acquisition, is acquired in exchange for other property, including cash, if such other property would be described in paragraph (e)(1)(i) of this section had the transaction not occurred.

(2) *Foreign group property* means any property (including excluded property, as described in paragraph (e)(3)(ii) of this section)) held on the completion date by the modified expanded affiliated group, other than—

(i) Property that is directly or indirectly acquired in the domestic entity acquisition;

(ii) Stock or a partnership interest in a member of the modified expanded affiliated group; and

(iii) An obligation of a member of the modified expanded affiliated group.

(3) *Foreign group nonqualified property fraction.*—(i) *In general.*—Foreign group nonqualified property fraction means a fraction calculated with the following numerator and denominator:

(A) The numerator of the fraction is the gross value of all foreign group nonqualified property, other than excluded property (as described in paragraph (e)(3)(ii) of this section).

(B) The denominator of the fraction is the gross value of all foreign group property, other than excluded property (as described in paragraph (e)(3)(ii) of this section)

(ii) *Excluded property.*—For purposes of paragraph (e)(3) of this section, excluded property means property that gives rise to stock that is excluded from the ownership fraction with respect to the domestic entity acquisition under §1.7874-4(b), §1.7874-8(b), §1.7874-9(b), or section 7874(c)(4). For this purpose, only property that was directly or indirectly acquired in a prior domestic entity acquisition (as described in §1.7874-8(g)(4)) or covered foreign acquisition (as described in §1.7874-9(d)(4)) with respect to the domestic entity acquisition may be considered to give rise to stock that is excluded from the ownership fraction with respect to the domestic entity acquisition under §1.7874-8(b) or §1.7874-9(b). If only a portion of the consideration provided in a prior domestic entity acquisition or covered foreign acquisition consisted of stock of the foreign acquiring corporation, then only a pro rata portion of a property directly or indirectly acquired in the prior domestic entity acquisition or covered foreign acquisition may be considered excluded property, based on a fraction the numerator of which is the amount of the consideration that consisted of stock of the foreign acquiring corporation and the denominator of which is the total amount of consideration.

(4) *Modified expanded affiliated group* means, with respect to a domestic entity acquisition, the group described in either paragraph (e)(4)(i) of this section or paragraph (e)(4)(ii) of this section. A *member of the modified expanded affiliated group* is an entity included in the modified expanded affiliated group.

(i) When the foreign acquiring corporation is not the common parent corporation of the expanded affiliated group, the expanded affiliated group determined as if the foreign acquiring corporation was the common parent corporation.

(ii) When the foreign acquiring corporation is the common parent corporation of the expanded affiliated group, the expanded affiliated group.

(f) *Examples.*—The following examples illustrate the rules of this section.

Example 1. Application of general rule—(i) *Facts.* Individual A owns all 20 shares of the sole class of stock of FA, a foreign corporation. FA acquires all the stock of DT, a domestic corporation, solely in exchange for 76 shares of newly issued FA stock (DT acquisition). In a transaction related to the DT acquisition, FA issues 4 shares of stock to Individual A in exchange for Asset A, which has a gross value of $50x. On the completion date, in addition to the DT stock and Asset A, FA holds Asset B, which has a gross value of $150x, and Asset C, which has a gross value of $100x. Assets A and B, but not Asset C, are nonqualified property (within the meaning of §1.7874-4(h)(2)). Further, Asset C was not acquired in a transaction related to the DT acquisition.

(ii) *Analysis.* The 4 shares of FA stock issued to Individual A in exchange for Asset A are disqualified stock under §1.7874-4(c) and are excluded from the denominator of the ownership fraction pursuant to §1.7874-4(b). Furthermore, additional shares of FA stock are excluded from the denominator of the ownership fraction pursuant to paragraph (b) of this section. This is because on the completion date, the gross value of all foreign group property is $300x (the sum of the gross values of Assets A, B, and C), the gross value of all foreign group nonqualified property is $200x (the sum of the gross values of Assets A and B), and thus 66.67% of the gross value of all foreign group property constitutes foreign group nonqualified property ($200x/$300x). Because FA has only one class of stock outstanding, the shares of FA stock that are excluded from the denominator of the ownership fraction pursuant to paragraph (b) of this section are calculated by multiplying 20 shares of FA stock (100 shares less the 76 shares described in section 7874(a)(2)(B)(ii) and the 4 shares of disqualified stock) by the foreign group nonqualified property fraction. The numerator of the foreign group nonqualified property fraction is $150x (the gross value of Asset B) and the denominator is $250x (the sum of the gross values of Assets B and C). Asset A is not taken into account for purposes of the foreign group nonqualified property fraction because it gives rise to FA stock that is excluded under §1.7874-4(b) (4 shares) and, as a result, is excluded property. Accordingly, 12 shares of FA stock are excluded from the denominator of the ownership fraction pursuant to paragraph (b) of this section (20 shares multiplied by $150x/$250x). Thus, a total of 16 shares are excluded from the denominator of the ownership fraction (4 + 12). As a result, the ownership fraction by value is 76/84.

Example 2. Application of de minimis exception—(i) *Facts.* Individual A owns all 96 shares of the sole class of stock of FA, a foreign corporation. Individual B wholly owns DT, a domestic corporation. Individuals A and B are not related. FA acquires all the stock of DT solely in exchange for 4 shares of newly issued FA stock (DT acquisition). On the completion date, in addition to all of the stock of DT, FA holds Asset A, which is nonqualified property (within the meaning of § 1.7874-4(h)(2)).

(ii) *Analysis.* Without regard to the application of §§ 1.7874-4(b) and 1.7874-10(b) as well as paragraph (b) of this section, the ownership percentage described in section 7874(a)(2)(B)(ii) would be less than 5 (by vote and value), or 4 (4/100, or 4 shares of FA stock held by Individual B by reason of owning the DT stock, determined under § 1.7874-2(f)(2), over 100 shares of FA stock outstanding after the DT acquisition). Furthermore, on the completion date, Individual B owns less than 5% (by vote and value) of the stock of FA and DT (the members of the expanded affiliated group). Accordingly, the de minimis exception in paragraph (c) of this section applies. Therefore, paragraph (b) of this section does not apply and the ownership fraction is 4/100.

Example 3. Foreign acquiring corporation not common parent of EAG—(i) *Facts.* FP, a foreign corporation, owns all 85 shares of the sole class of stock of FA, a foreign corporation. FA acquires all the stock of DT, a domestic corporation, solely in exchange for 65 shares of newly issued FA stock (DT acquisition). On the completion date, FA, in addition to all of the stock of DT, owns Asset A, which has a gross value of $40x, and Asset B, which has a gross value of $45x. Moreover, on the completion date, in addition to the 85 shares of FA stock, FP owns Asset C, which has a gross value of $10x. Assets A and C, but not Asset B, are nonqualified property (within the meaning of § 1.7874-4(h)(2)). Further, Asset B was not acquired in a transaction related to the DT acquisition in exchange for nonqualified property.

(ii) *Analysis.* Under paragraph (e)(2) of this section, Assets A and B, but not Asset C, are foreign group property. Although Asset C is held on the completion date by FP, a member of the expanded affiliated group, Asset C is not foreign group property because FP is not a member of the modified expanded affiliated group. This is the case because if the expanded affiliated group were determined based on FA as the common parent corporation, FP would not be a member of such expanded affiliated group (see paragraph (e)(4)(i) of this section). Under paragraph (e)(1) of this section, Asset A, but not Asset B, is foreign group nonqualified property. Therefore, on the completion date, the gross value of all foreign group property is $85x (the sum of the gross values of Assets A and B), and the gross value of all foreign group nonqualified property is $40x (the gross value of Asset A). Accordingly, on the completion date, only 47.06% of the gross value of all foreign group property constitutes foreign group nonqualified property ($40x/$85x). Consequently, paragraph (b) of this section does not apply to exclude any FA stock from the denominator of the ownership fraction.

Example 4. Coordination with serial acquisition rule—(i) *Facts.* Individual A owns all 30 shares of the sole class of stock of FA, a foreign corporation. In Year 1, FA acquires all the stock of DT1, a domestic corporation, solely in exchange for 40 shares of newly issued FA stock (DT1 acquisition). In Year 2, FA acquires all the stock of DT2, a domestic corporation, solely in exchange for 50 shares of newly issued FA stock (DT2 acquisition). On the completion date for the DT2 acquisition, in addition to the DT2 stock, FA holds Asset A, which has a gross value of $15x, Asset B, which has a gross value of $15x, and all the stock of DT1, which has a gross value of $40x. At all times, DT1 holds only Asset C, which has a gross value of $30x, and Asset D, which has a gross value of $10x. Assets A and C, but not Assets B and D, are nonqualified property (within the meaning of § 1.7874-4(h)(2)). In addition, at all times, the fair market value of each share of FA stock is $1x. Further, there have been no redemptions of FA stock subsequent to the DT1 acquisition. Lastly, under § 1.7874-8, the DT1 acquisition is a prior domestic entity acquisition with respect to the DT2 acquisition and $40x of FA stock is excluded from the denominator of the ownership fraction with respect to the DT2 acquisition.

(ii) *Analysis.* Shares of FA stock are excluded from the denominator of the ownership fraction pursuant to paragraph (b) of this section. This is because on the completion date, the gross value of all foreign group property is $70x (the sum of the gross values of Assets A, B, C, and D), the gross value of all foreign group nonqualified property is $45x (the sum of the gross values of Assets A and C), and thus 64.29% of the gross value of all foreign group property constitutes foreign group nonqualified property ($45x/$70x). The shares of FA stock that are excluded from the denominator of the ownership fraction pursuant to paragraph (b) of this section are calculated by multiplying $30x ($120x, the value of all the shares of FA stock, less $50x, the value of the stock described in section 7874(a)(2)(B)(ii), less $40x, the value of the stock excluded under § 1.7874-8(b)) by the foreign group nonqualified property fraction. The property taken into account for purposes of determining the foreign group nonqualified property fraction is Asset A and Asset B. Asset C and Asset D are not taken into account for purposes of the foreign group nonqualified property fraction because they are excluded property. This is because FA indirectly acquired the Assets in the DT1 acquisition (a prior domestic entity acquisition with respect to the DT2 acquisition) and, as a result of that acquisition, $40x of FA stock is excluded from the denominator of the ownership fraction with respect to the DT2 acquisition under § 1.7874-8(b). Thus, the numerator of the foreign group nonqualified property fraction is $15x (the gross value of Asset A) and the denominator is $30x (the sum of the gross values of Asset A, $15x, and Asset B, $15x). Accordingly, $15x of FA stock is excluded from the denominator of the ownership fraction pursuant to paragraph (b) of this section ($30x multiplied by $15x/$30x). Thus, a total of $55x of FA stock is excluded from the denominator of the ownership fraction ($40x + $15x), making the denominator $65x ($120x - $55x). As a result, the ownership percentage with respect to the DT2 acquisition by value is 76.92 ($50x/$65x).

(iii) *Alternative facts.* The facts are the same as in paragraph (i) of this *Example 4*, except as follows. Initially, there are 40 shares of FA stock outstanding, all of which are owned by Individual A. At all times, the gross value of asset D is $20x. In the DT1 acquisition, FA acquires all the stock of DT1 ($50x fair market value) solely in exchange for 40 shares of newly issued FA stock and $10x of other property. As in paragraph (i) of this Example 4, shares of FA stock are excluded from the denominator of the ownership fraction pursuant to paragraph (b) of this section. This is because on the completion date, the gross value of all foreign group property is $80x (the sum of the gross values of Assets A, B, C, and D), the gross value of all foreign group nonqualified property is $45x (the sum of the gross values of Assets A and C), and thus 56.25% of the gross value of all foreign group property constitutes foreign group nonqualified property ($45x/$80x). The shares of FA stock that are excluded from the denominator of the ownership fraction pursuant to paragraph (b) of this section are calculated by multiplying $40x ($130x, the value of all the shares of FA stock, less $50x, the value of the stock described in section 7874(a)(2)(B)(ii), less $40x, the value of the stock excluded under § 1.7874-8(b)) by the foreign group nonqualified property fraction. The property taken into account for purposes of determining the foreign group nonqualified property fraction is Asset A, Asset B, and the portion of Asset C and Asset D that is not excluded property. Eighty percent of each of Asset C and Asset D are considered excluded property because FA indirectly acquired Asset C and Asset D in the DT1 acquisition (a prior domestic entity acquisition with respect to the DT2 acquisition); as a result of that acquisition, $40x of FA stock is excluded from the denominator of the ownership fraction with respect to the DT2 acquisition under § 1.7874-8(b); and 80% of the consideration provided in the DT1 acquisition consisted of stock of FA ($40x/$50x). Thus, the numerator of the foreign group nonqualified property fraction is $21x (the sum of the gross values of Asset A, $15x, and the portion of Asset C that is not excluded property, $6x) and the denominator is $40x (the sum of the gross values of Asset A, $15x, Asset B, $15x, and the portion of Asset C and Asset D that is not excluded property, $6x and $4x, respectively). Accordingly, $21x of FA stock is excluded from the denominator of the ownership fraction pursuant to paragraph (b) of this section ($40x multiplied by $21x/$40x). Thus, a total of $61x of FA stock is excluded from the denominator of the ownership fraction pursuant to paragraph (b) of this section ($40x + $21x), making the denominator $69x ($130x - $61x). As a result, the ownership percentage with respect to D2 acquisition by value is 72.46 ($50x/$69x).

(g) *Applicability dates.*—This section applies to domestic entity acquisitions completed on or after July 12, 2018. For domestic entity acquisitions completed before July 12, 2018, see § 1.7874-7T, as contained in 26 CFR part 1 revised as of April 1, 2017. However, to the extent this section differs from § 1.7874-7T, as contained in 26 CFR part 1 revised as of April 1, 2017, taxpayers may elect to consistently apply the differences to domestic entity acquisitions completed before July 12, 2018. [Reg. § 1.7874-7.]

☐ [*T.D.* 9834, 7-11-2018.]

§ 1.7874-8. Disregard of certain stock attributable to serial acquisitions.—(a) *Scope.*—This section identifies stock of a foreign acquiring corporation that is disregarded in determining an ownership fraction by value because it is attributable to certain prior domestic entity acquisitions. Paragraph (b) of this section sets forth the general rule regarding the amount of stock of a foreign acquiring corporation that is excluded from the denominator of the ownership fraction by value under this section, and paragraphs (c) through (f) of this section provide rules for determining this amount. Paragraph (g) provides definitions. Paragraph (h) of this section provides examples illustrating the application of the rules of this section. Paragraph (i) of this section provides dates of applicability. This section applies after taking into account § 1.7874-2(e). See § 1.7874-1(d)(1) for rules addressing the interaction of this section with the expanded affiliated group rules of section 7874(c)(2)(A) and § 1.7874-1.

(b) *General rule.*—This paragraph (b) applies to a domestic entity acquisition (relevant domestic entity acquisition) when the foreign acquiring corporation (including a predecessor, as defined in § 1.7874-10(f)(1)) has completed one or more prior domestic entity acquisitions. When this paragraph (b) applies, then, for purposes of determining the ownership percentage by value (but not vote) described in section 7874(a)(2)(B)(ii), stock of the foreign acquiring corporation is excluded from the denominator of the ownership fraction in an amount equal to the sum of the excluded amounts computed separately with respect to each prior domestic entity acquisition and each relevant share class.

(c) *Computation of excluded amounts.*—With respect to each prior domestic entity acquisition and each relevant share class, the excluded amount is the product of—

(1) The total number of prior acquisition shares, reduced by the sum of the number of allocable redeemed shares for all redemption testing periods; and

(2) The fair market value of a single share of stock of the relevant share class on the completion date of the relevant domestic entity acquisition.

(d) *Computation of allocable redeemed shares.*—(1) *In general.*—With respect to each prior domestic entity acquisition and each relevant share class, the allocable redeemed shares, determined separately for each redemption testing period, is the product of the number of redeemed shares during the redemption testing period and the redemption fraction.

(2) *Redemption fraction.*—The redemption fraction is determined separately with respect to each prior domestic entity acquisition, each relevant share class, and each redemption testing period, as follows:

(i) The numerator is the total number of prior acquisition shares, reduced by the sum of the number of allocable redeemed shares for all prior redemption testing periods.

(ii) The denominator is the sum of—

(A) The number of outstanding shares of the foreign acquiring corporation stock as of the end of the last day of the redemption testing period; and

(B) The number of redeemed shares during the redemption testing period.

(e) *Rules for determining redemption testing periods.*—(1) *In general.*—Except as provided in paragraph (e)(2) of this section, a redemption testing period with respect to a prior domestic entity acquisition is the period beginning on the day after the completion date of the prior domestic entity acquisition and ending on the day prior to the completion date of the relevant domestic entity acquisition.

(2) *Election to use multiple redemption testing periods.*—A foreign acquiring corporation may establish a reasonable method for dividing the period described in paragraph (e)(1) of this section into shorter periods (each such shorter period, a redemption testing period). A reasonable method would include a method based on a calendar convention (for example, daily, monthly, quarterly, or yearly), or on a convention that triggers the start of a new redemption testing period whenever a share issuance occurs that exceeds a certain threshold. In order to be reasonable, the method must be consistently applied with respect to all prior domestic entity acquisitions and all relevant share classes.

(f) *Appropriate adjustments required to take into account share splits and similar transactions.*—For purposes of this section, appropriate adjustments must be made to take into account changes in a foreign acquiring corporation's capital structure, including, for example, stock splits, reverse stock splits, stock distributions, recapitalizations, and similar transactions. Thus, for example, in determining the total number of prior acquisition shares with respect to a relevant share class, appropriate adjustments must be made to take into account a stock split with respect to that relevant share class that occurs after the completion date with respect to a prior domestic entity acquisition.

(g) *Definitions.*—In addition to the definitions provided in § 1.7874-12, the following definitions apply for purposes of this section.

(1) A *binding contract* means an instrument enforceable under applicable law against the parties to the instrument. The presence of a condition outside the control of the parties (including, for example, regulatory agency approval) does not prevent an instrument from being a binding contract. Further, the fact that insubstantial terms remain to be negotiated by the parties to the contract, or that customary conditions remain to be satisfied, does not prevent an instrument from being a binding contract. A tender offer that is subject to section 14(d) of the Securities and Exchange Act of 1934, (15 U.S.C. 78n(d)(1)), and Regulation 14D (17 CFR 240.14d-1 through 240.14d-103) and that is not pursuant to a binding contract, is treated as a binding contract made on the date of its announcement, notwithstanding that it may be modified by the offeror or that it is not enforceable against the offerees.

(2) A *relevant share class* means, with respect to a prior domestic entity acquisition, each separate legal class of shares in the foreign acquiring corporation from which prior acquisition shares were issued. See also paragraph (f) of this section (requiring appropriate adjustments in certain cases).

(3) *Total number of prior acquisition shares* means, with respect to a prior domestic entity acquisition and each relevant share class, the total number of shares of stock of the foreign acquiring corporation that were described in section 7874(a)(2)(B)(ii) as a result of that acquisition (without regard to whether the 60 percent test of section 7874(a)(2)(B)(ii) was satisfied), other than stock treated as received by former domestic entity shareholders or former domestic entity partners under § 1.7874-10(b) or section 7874(c)(4), adjusted as appropriate under paragraph (f) of this section.

(4) *A prior domestic entity acquisition.*—(i) *General rule.*—Except as provided in this paragraph (g)(4), a prior domestic entity acquisition means, with respect to a relevant domestic entity acquisition, a domestic entity acquisition that occurred within the 36-month period ending on the signing date of the relevant domestic entity acquisition.

(ii) *Exception.*—A domestic entity acquisition is not a prior domestic entity acquisition if it is described in paragraph (g)(4)(ii)(A) or (B) of this section.

(A) *De minimis.*—A domestic entity acquisition is described in this paragraph (g)(4)(ii)(A) if—

(1) The ownership percentage described in section 7874(a)(2)(B)(ii) with respect to the domestic entity acquisition was less than five (by vote and value); and

(2) The fair market value of the stock of the foreign acquiring corporation described in section 7874(a)(2)(B)(ii) as a result of the domestic entity acquisition (without regard to whether the 60 percent test of section 7874(a)(2)(B)(ii) was satisfied) did not exceed $50 million, as determined on the completion date with respect to the domestic entity acquisition.

(B) *Foreign-parented group.*—A domestic entity acquisition is described in this paragraph (g)(4)(ii)(B) if—

(1) Before the domestic entity acquisition and any related transaction, the domestic entity was a member of a foreign-parented group (as described in § 1.7874-6(f)(1)); and

(2) The domestic entity acquisition qualified for the internal group restructuring exception under § 1.7874-1(c)(2).

(5) A *redeemed share* means a share of stock in a relevant share class that was redeemed (within the meaning of section 317(b)).

(6) A *signing date* means the first date on which the contract to effect the relevant domestic entity acquisition is a binding contract, or if another binding contract to effect a substantially similar acquisition was terminated with a principal purpose of avoiding section 7874, the first date on which such other contract was a binding contract.

(h) *Examples.*—The following examples illustrate the rules of this section.

Example 1. Application of general rule—(i) *Facts.* Individual A wholly owns DT1, a domestic corporation. Individual B owns all 100 shares of the sole class of stock of FA, a foreign corporation. In Year 1, FA acquires all the stock of DT1 solely in exchange for 100 shares of newly issued FA stock (DT1 acquisition). On the completion date with respect to the DT1 acquisition, the fair market value of each share of FA stock is $1x. In Year 3, FA enters into a binding contract to acquire all the stock of DT2, a domestic corporation wholly owned by Individual C. Thereafter, FA acquires all the stock of DT2 solely in exchange for 150 shares of newly issued FA stock (DT2 acquisition). On the completion date with respect to the DT2 acquisition, the fair market value of each share of FA stock is $1.50x. FA did not complete the DT1 acquisition and DT2 acquisition pursuant to a plan (or series of related transactions) for purposes of applying § 1.7874-2(e). In addition, there have been no redemptions of FA stock subsequent to the DT1 acquisition.

(ii) *Analysis.* The DT1 acquisition is a prior domestic entity acquisition with respect to the DT2 acquisition (the relevant domestic entity acquisition) because the DT1 acquisition occurred within the 36-month period ending on the signing date with respect to the DT2 acquisition. Accordingly, paragraph (b) of this section applies to the DT2 acquisition. As a result, and because there were no redemptions of FA stock, the excluded amount is $150x, calculated as 100 (the total number of prior acquisition shares) multiplied by $1.50x (the fair market value of a single share of FA stock on the completion date with respect to the DT2 acquisition). Accordingly, the numerator of the ownership fraction by value is $225x (the fair market value of the stock of FA that, with respect to the DT2 acquisition, is described in section 7874(a)(2)(B)(ii)) (150 shares x $1.50x per share). In addition, the denominator of the ownership fraction is $375x (calculated as $525x, the fair market value of all 350 shares of FA stock as of the completion date with respect to the DT2 acquisition, less $150x, the excluded amount). Therefore, the ownership percentage by value is 60 ($225x divided by $375x).

Example 2. Effect of certain redemptions—(i) *Facts.* The facts are the same as in paragraph (i) of *Example 1* of this paragraph (h), except that in Year 2 FA redeems 50 shares of its stock (the Year 2 redemption).

(ii) *Analysis.* As is the case in paragraph (ii) of *Example 1* of this paragraph (h), the DT1 acquisition is a prior domestic entity acquisition with respect to the DT2 acquisition (the relevant domestic entity acquisition), and paragraph (b) of this section thus applies to the DT2 acquisition. Because of the Year 2 redemption, the allocable redeemed shares, and thus the redemption fraction, must be calculated. For this purpose, the redemption testing period is the period beginning on the day after the completion date with respect to the DT1 acquisition and ending on the day prior to the completion date with respect to the DT2 acquisition. The redemption fraction for the redemption testing period is thus 100/200, calculated as 100 (the total number of prior acquisition shares) divided by 200 (150, the number of outstanding shares of FA stock on the last day of the redemption testing period, plus 50, the number of redeemed shares during the redemption testing period), and the allocable redeemed shares for the redemption testing period is 25, calculated as 50 (the number of redeemed shares during the redemption testing period) multiplied by 100/200 (the redemption fraction for the redemption testing period). As a result, the excluded amount is $112.50x, calculated as 75 (100, the total number of prior acquisition shares, less 25, the allocable redeemed shares) multiplied by $1.50x (the fair market value of a single share of FA stock on the completion date with respect to the DT2 acquisition). Accordingly, the numerator of the ownership fraction by value is $225x (the fair market value of the stock of FA that, with respect to the DT2 acquisition, is described in section 7874(a)(2)(B)(ii)) (150 shares x $1.50x per share), and the denominator of the ownership fraction is $337.50x (calculated as $450x, the fair market value of all 300 shares of FA stock as of the completion date with respect to the DT2 acquisition, less $112.50x, the excluded amount). Therefore, the ownership percentage by value is 66.67 ($225x divided by $337.50x).

Example 3. Stock split—(i) *Facts.* The facts are the same as in paragraph (i) of *Example 2* of this paragraph (h), except as follows. After the Year 2 redemption, but before the DT2 acquisition, FA undergoes a stock split and, as a result, each of the 150 shares of FA stock outstanding are converted into two shares (Year 2 stock split). Further, pursuant to the DT2 acquisition, FA acquires all the stock of DT2 solely in exchange for 300 shares of newly issued FA stock. Moreover, on the completion date with respect to the DT2 acquisition, the fair market value of each share of FA stock is $0.75x.

(ii) *Analysis.* As is the case in paragraph (ii) of *Example 1* of this paragraph (h), the DT1 acquisition is a prior domestic entity acquisition with respect to the DT2 acquisition (the relevant domestic entity acquisition), and paragraph (b) of this section thus applies to the DT2 acquisition. In addition, as is the case in paragraph (ii) of *Example 2* of this paragraph (h), the redemption testing period is the period beginning on the day after the completion date with respect to the DT1 acquisition and ending on the day prior to the completion date with respect to the DT2 acquisition. To calculate the redemption fraction, the total number of prior acquisition shares and the number of redeemed shares during the redemption testing period must be appropriately adjusted to take into account the Year 2 stock split. See paragraph (f) of this section. In this case, the appropriate adjustment is to increase the total number of prior acquisition shares from 100 to 200 and to increase the number of redeemed shares during the redemption testing period from 50 to 100. Thus, the redemption fraction for the redemption testing period is 200/400, calculated as 200 (the total number of prior acquisition shares) divided by 400 (300, the number of outstanding shares of FA stock on the last day of the redemption testing period, plus 100, the number of redeemed shares during the redemption testing period), and the allocable redeemed shares for the redemption testing period is 50, calculated as 100 (the number of redeemed shares during the redemption testing period) multiplied by 200/400 (the redemption fraction for the redemption testing period). In addition, for purposes of calculating the excluded amount, the total number of prior acquisition shares must be adjusted from 100 to 200. See paragraph (f) of this section. Accordingly, the excluded amount is $112.50x, calculated as 150 (200, the total number of prior acquisition shares, less 50, the allocable redeemed shares) multiplied by $0.75x (the fair market value of a single share of FA stock on the completion date with respect to the DT2 acquisition). Consequently, the numerator of the ownership fraction by value is $225x (the fair market value of the stock of FA that, with respect to the DT2 acquisition, is described in section 7874(a)(2)(B)(ii)) (300 shares x $0.75x per share), and the denominator of the ownership fraction is $337.50x (calculated as $450x, the fair market value of all 600 shares of FA stock as of the completion date with respect to the DT2 acquisition, less $112.50x, the excluded amount). Therefore, the ownership percentage by value is 66.67 ($225 divided by $337.50x).

(i) *Applicability dates.*—Except as provided in this paragraph (i), this section applies to domestic entity acquisitions completed on or after April 4, 2016, regardless of when a prior domestic entity acquisition was completed. Paragraphs (g)(3) and (g)(4)(ii) of this section apply to domestic entity acquisitions completed on or after July 12, 2018. However, taxpayers may elect to consistently apply paragraphs (g)(3) and (g)(4)(ii) of this section to domestic entity acquisitions completed on or after April 4, 2016, and before July 12, 2018. For domestic entity acquisitions completed on or after April 4, 2016, and before July 12, 2018, see § 1.7874-8T(g)(3) and (g)(4)(ii) as contained in 26 CFR part 1 revised as of April 1, 2017. [Reg. § 1.7874-8.]

□ [*T.D.* 9834, 7-11-2018.]

§ 1.7874-9. Disregard of certain stock in third-country transactions.—(a) *Scope.*—This section identifies certain stock of a foreign acquiring corporation that is disregarded in determining the ownership fraction. Paragraph (b) of this section provides a rule that, in a third-country transaction, excludes from the denominator of the ownership fraction stock in the foreign acquiring corporation held by former shareholders of an acquired foreign corporation by reason of holding certain stock in that foreign corporation. Paragraph (c) of this section defines a third-country transaction, and paragraph (d) of this section provides other definitions. Paragraph (e) of this section provides operating rules. Paragraph (f) of this section provides an example illustrating the application of the rules of this section. Paragraph (g) of this section provides the dates of applicability. See § 1.7874-1(d)(1) for rules addressing the interaction of this section with the expanded affiliated group rules of section 7874(c)(2)(A) and § 1.7874-1.

(b) *Exclusion of certain stock of a foreign acquiring corporation from the ownership fraction.*—When a domestic entity acquisition is a third-country transaction, stock of the foreign acquiring corporation held by reason of holding stock in the acquired foreign corporation (within the meaning of paragraph (e)(4) of this section) is, to the extent the stock otherwise would be included in the denominator of the ownership fraction, excluded from the denominator of the ownership fraction pursuant to this paragraph.

(c) *Third-country transaction.*—A domestic entity acquisition is a third-country transaction if the following requirements are satisfied:

(1) The foreign acquiring corporation completes a covered foreign acquisition pursuant to a plan (or series of related transactions) that includes the domestic entity acquisition.

(2) After the covered foreign acquisition and all related transactions are complete, the foreign acquiring corporation is not a tax resident of the foreign country in which the acquired foreign corporation was a tax resident before the covered foreign acquisition and all related transactions.

(3) The ownership percentage described in section 7874(a)(2)(B)(ii), determined without regard to the application of paragraph (b) of this section, is at least 60.

(d) *Definitions.*—In addition to the definitions provided in § 1.7874-12, the following definitions apply for purposes of this section.

(1) A *foreign acquisition* means a transaction in which a foreign acquiring corporation directly or indirectly acquires substantially all

of the properties held directly or indirectly by an acquired foreign corporation (within the meaning of paragraph (e)(2) of this section).

(2) An *acquired foreign corporation* means a foreign corporation whose properties are acquired in a foreign acquisition.

(3) *Foreign ownership percentage* means, with respect to a foreign acquisition, the percentage of stock (by vote or value) of the foreign acquiring corporation held by reason of holding stock in the acquired foreign corporation (within the meaning of paragraph (e)(3) of this section).

(4) *Covered foreign acquisition.*—(i) *In general.*—Except as provided in paragraphs (d)(4)(ii) and (iii) of this section, a covered foreign acquisition means a foreign acquisition in which, after the acquisition and all related transactions are complete, the foreign ownership percentage is at least 60.

(ii) *Substantial business activities exception.*—A foreign acquisition is not a covered foreign acquisition if, on the completion date, the following requirements are satisfied:

(A) The foreign acquiring corporation is a tax resident of a foreign country.

(B) The expanded affiliated group has substantial business activities in the country in which the foreign acquiring corporation is a tax resident when compared to the total business activities of the expanded affiliated group. For this purpose, the principles of § 1.7874-3 apply and the determination of whether there are substantial business activities is made without regard to the domestic entity acquisition.

(iii) *No income tax exception.*—A foreign acquisition is not a covered foreign acquisition if—

(A) Before the acquisition and all related transactions, the acquired foreign corporation was created or organized in, or under the law of, a foreign country that does not impose corporate income tax and was not a tax resident of any other foreign country; and

(B) After the acquisition and all related transactions are complete, the foreign acquiring corporation is created or organized in, or under the law of, a foreign country that does not impose corporate income tax and is not a tax resident of any other foreign country.

(5) A *tax resident* of a foreign country has the meaning set forth in § 1.7874-3(d)(11).

(e) *Operating rules.*—The following rules apply for purposes of this section.

(1) *Acquisition of multiple foreign corporations that are tax residents of the same foreign country.*—When multiple foreign acquisitions occur pursuant to the same plan (or a series of related transactions) and two or more of the acquired foreign corporations were tax residents of the same foreign country before the foreign acquisitions and all related transactions, then those foreign acquisitions are treated as a single foreign acquisition and those acquired foreign corporations are treated as a single acquired foreign corporation for purposes of this section.

(2) *Acquisition of properties of an acquired foreign corporation.*—For purposes of determining whether a foreign acquisition occurs, the principles of section 7874(a)(2)(B)(i) and § 1.7874-2(c) and (d) (regarding acquisitions of properties of a domestic entity and acquisitions by multiple foreign corporations) apply with the following modifications:

(i) The principles of § 1.7874-2(c)(1) (providing rules for determining whether there is an indirect acquisition of properties of a domestic entity), including § 1.7874-2(b)(5) (providing rules for determining the proportionate amount of properties indirectly acquired), apply by substituting the term "foreign" for "domestic" wherever it appears.

(ii) The principles of § 1.7874-2(c)(2) (regarding acquisitions of stock of a foreign corporation that owns a domestic entity) apply by substituting the term "domestic" for "foreign" wherever it appears.

(3) *Computation of foreign ownership percentage.*—For purposes of determining a foreign ownership percentage, the principles of all rules applicable to calculating an ownership percentage apply (including §§ 1.7874-2, 1.7874-4, 1.7874-5, 1.7874-7, and section 7874(c)(4)) with the following modifications:

(i) Stock of a foreign acquiring corporation described in section 7874(a)(2)(B)(ii) is not taken into account.

(ii) The principles of this section, section 7874(c)(2)(A), and §§ 1.7874-1, 1.7874-6, 1.7874-8, and 1.7874-10 do not apply.

(iii) The principles of § 1.7874-7 apply by, in addition to the exclusions listed in § 1.7874-7(e)(2)(i) through (iii), also excluding from the definition of foreign group property any property held directly or indirectly by the acquired foreign corporation immediately before the foreign acquisition and directly or indirectly acquired in the foreign acquisition.

(4) *Stock held by reason of holding stock in an acquired foreign corporation.*—For purposes of determining stock of a foreign acquiring corporation held by reason of holding stock in an acquired foreign corporation, the principles of section 7874(a)(2)(B)(ii) and §§ 1.7874-2(f) and 1.7874-5 apply.

(5) *Change in the tax residency of a foreign corporation.*—For purposes of this section, a change in a country in which a foreign corporation is a tax resident is treated as a transaction. Further, for purposes of this section, if a foreign acquiring corporation changes the country in which it is a tax resident in a manner that would not otherwise be considered to result in a foreign acquisition (for example, by changing where it is managed and controlled), then the foreign acquiring corporation is treated as—

(i) Both an acquired foreign corporation and a foreign acquiring corporation; and

(ii) Directly or indirectly acquiring all of the properties held directly or indirectly by the acquired foreign corporation solely in exchange for stock of the foreign acquiring corporation.

(f) *Example.*—The following example illustrates the rules of this section.

Example. Third-country transaction—(i) *Facts.* FA, a newly formed foreign corporation that is a tax resident of Country Y, acquires all the stock of DT, a domestic corporation that is wholly owned by Individual A, solely in exchange for 65 shares of newly issued FA stock (DT acquisition). Pursuant to a plan that includes the DT acquisition, FA acquires all the stock of FT, a foreign corporation that is a tax resident of Country X and wholly owned by Individual B, solely in exchange for the remaining 35 shares of newly issued FA stock (FT acquisition). After the FT acquisition and all related transactions, the expanded affiliated group does not have substantial business activities in Country Y when compared to the total business activities of the expanded affiliated group, as determined under the principles of § 1.7874-3 and without regard to the DT acquisition.

(ii) *Analysis.* As described in paragraphs (A) through (C) of this *Example*, the requirements set forth in paragraphs (c)(1) through (3) of this section are satisfied and, as result, the DT acquisition is a third-country transaction.

(A) The FT acquisition is a foreign acquisition because, pursuant to the FT acquisition, FA (a foreign acquiring corporation) acquires 100 percent of the stock of FT and is thus treated as indirectly acquiring 100 percent of the properties held by FT (an acquired foreign corporation). See § 1.7874-2(c)(1) and paragraph (e)(2) of this section. Moreover, Individual B is treated as receiving 35 shares of FA stock by reason of holding stock in FT. See § 1.7874-2(f)(1)(i) and paragraph (e)(4) of this section. As a result, not taking into account the 65 shares of FA stock held by Individual A (a former domestic entity shareholder), 100 percent (35/35) of the stock of FA is held by reason of holding stock in FT and, thus, the foreign ownership percentage is 100. See paragraph (e)(3) of this section. Accordingly, the FT acquisition is a covered foreign acquisition. Therefore, because the FT acquisition occurs pursuant to a plan that includes the DT acquisition, the requirement set forth in paragraph (c)(1) of this section is satisfied.

(B) The requirement set forth in paragraph (c)(2) of this section is satisfied because, after the FT acquisition and all related transactions, the foreign country in which FA is a tax resident (Country Y) is different than the foreign country in which FT was a resident (Country X) before the FT acquisition and all related transactions.

(C) The requirement set forth in paragraph (c)(3) of this section is satisfied because, not taking into account paragraph (b) of this section, the ownership fraction is 65/100 and the ownership percentage is 65.

(D) Because the DT acquisition is a third-country transaction, the 35 shares of FA stock held by reason of holding stock in FT are excluded from the denominator of the ownership fraction. See paragraph (b) of this section. As a result, the ownership fraction is 65/65 and the ownership percentage is 100. The result would be the same if instead FA had directly acquired all of the properties held by FT in exchange for FA stock, for example, in a transaction that would qualify for U.S. federal income tax purposes as an asset reorganization under section 368.

(iii) *Alternative facts.* The facts are the same as in paragraph (i) of this example, except that before the FT acquisition, but in a transaction related to the FT acquisition, FT becomes a tax resident of Country Y by reincorporating in Country Y. As is the case in paragraph (ii) of this *Example*, the requirements set forth in paragraphs (c)(1) and (3) of this section are satisfied. The requirement set forth in paragraph (c)(2) of this section is satisfied because, after the FT acquisition and any related transactions, the foreign country of which FA is a tax resident (Country Y) is different than the foreign country of which FT was a tax resident (Country X) before the FT acquisition and the reincorporation. See paragraph (e)(5) of this section. Accordingly, the DT acquisition is a third-country transaction and the consequences are the same as in paragraph (ii)(D) of this *Example*.

(iv) *Alternative facts.* The facts are the same as in paragraph (i) of this *Example*, except that, instead of FA acquiring all of the stock of FT, FS, a newly formed foreign corporation that is wholly owned by FA and that is a tax resident of Country X, acquires all the stock of FT solely in exchange for 35 shares of newly issued FA stock (FT acquisition). As a result of the FT acquisition, FS and FA are each treated as indirectly acquiring 100 percent of the properties held by FT. See § 1.7874-2(c)(1)(i) and (iii) and paragraph (e)(2) of this section. Accordingly, each of FS's and FA's indirect acquisition of properties of FT (an acquired foreign corporation) is a foreign acquisition. However, FS's indirect acquisition of FT's properties is not a covered foreign acquisition because no shares of FS stock are held by reason of holding stock in FT; thus, with respect to this foreign acquisition, the foreign ownership percentage is zero. See § 1.7874-2(f) and paragraphs (e)(3) and (4) of this section. FA's indirect acquisition of FT's properties is a covered foreign acquisition because 35 shares of FA stock (the shares received by Individual B) are held by reason of holding stock in FT; thus, the foreign ownership percentage is 100 percent (35/35). See § 1.7874-2(f)(1)(i) and paragraphs (e)(3) and (4) of this section. Accordingly, because the FT acquisition occurs pursuant to a plan that includes the DT acquisition, the requirement set forth in paragraph (c)(1) of this section is satisfied. Further, as is the case in paragraphs (ii)(B) through (C) of this *Example*, the requirements set forth in paragraphs (c)(2) and (3) of this section are satisfied. Therefore, the DT acquisition is a third-country transaction and the consequences are the same as in paragraph (ii)(D) of this *Example*.

(g) *Applicability dates.*—This section applies to domestic entity acquisitions completed on or after July 12, 2018. For domestic entity acquisitions completed before July 12, 2018, see § 1.7874-9T, as contained in 26 CFR part 1 revised as of April 1, 2017. However, to the extent this section differs from § 1.7874-9T, as contained in 26 CFR part 1 revised as of April 1, 2017, taxpayers may elect to consistently apply the differences to domestic entity acquisitions completed before July 12, 2018. [Reg. § 1.7874-9.]

□ [*T.D.* 9834, 7-11-2018.]

§ 1.7874-10. Disregard of certain distributions.—(a) *Scope.*—This section identifies distributions made by a domestic entity that are disregarded in determining an ownership fraction. Paragraph (b) of this section provides the general rule that former domestic entity shareholders or former domestic entity partners are treated as receiving additional stock of the foreign acquiring corporation when the domestic entity has made non-ordinary course distributions (NOCDs). Paragraph (c) of this section identifies distributions that, in whole or in part, are outside the scope of this section. Paragraph (d) of this section provides a de minimis exception to the application of the general rule in paragraph (b) of this section. Paragraph (e) of this section provides rules concerning the treatment of distributions made by a predecessor, and paragraph (f) of this section provides rules for identifying a predecessor. Paragraph (g) of this section provides a special rule for certain distributions described in section 355. Paragraph (h) of this section provides rules regarding the allocation of NOCD stock. Paragraph (i) of this section addresses cases in which there are multiple foreign acquiring corporations, and paragraph (j) of this section addresses cases in which multiple domestic entities are treated as a single domestic entity. Paragraph (k) of this section provides definitions. Paragraph (l) of this section provides dates of applicability. See § 1.7874-1(d)(2) for rules addressing the interaction of this section with the expanded affiliated group rules of section 7874(c)(2)(A) and § 1.7874-1.

(b) *General rule regarding NOCDs.*—Except as provided in paragraph (d) of this section, for purposes of determining the ownership percentage by value (but not vote) described in section 7874(a)(2)(B)(ii), former domestic entity shareholders or former domestic entity partners, as applicable, are treated as receiving, by reason of holding stock or partnership interests in a domestic entity, stock of the foreign acquiring corporation with a fair market value equal to the amount of the non-ordinary course distributions (NOCDs), determined as of the date of the distributions, made by the domestic entity during the look-back period. The stock of the foreign acquiring corporation treated as received under this paragraph (b) (NOCD stock) is in addition to stock of the foreign acquiring corporation otherwise treated as received by the former domestic entity shareholders or former domestic entity partners by reason of holding stock or partnership interests in the domestic entity.

(c) *Distributions that are not NOCDs.*—If only a portion of a distribution is an NOCD, section 7874(c)(4) may apply to the remainder of the distribution. This section does not, however, create a presumption that section 7874(c)(4) applies to the remainder of the distribution.

(d) *De minimis exception to the general rule.*—Paragraph (b) of this section does not apply if—

(1) The ownership percentage described in section 7874(a)(2)(B)(ii), determined without regard to the application of paragraph (b) of this section and §§ 1.7874-4(b) and 1.7874-7(b), is less than five (by vote and value); and

(2) On the completion date, each five percent former domestic entity shareholder or five percent former domestic entity partner, as applicable, owns (applying the attribution rules of section 318(a) with the modifications described in section 304(c)(3)(B)) less than five percent (by vote and value) of the stock of (or a partnership interest in) each member of the expanded affiliated group. For this purpose, a five percent former domestic entity shareholder (or five percent former domestic entity partner) is a former domestic entity shareholder (or former domestic entity partner) that, before the domestic entity acquisition, owned (applying the attribution rules of section 318(a) with the modifications described in section 304(c)(3)(B)) at least five percent (by vote and value) of the stock of (or a partnership interest in) the domestic entity.

(e) *Treatment of distributions made by a predecessor.*—For purposes of this section, a corporation or a partnership (relevant entity), including a domestic entity, is treated as making the following distributions made by a predecessor with respect to the relevant entity:

(1) A distribution made before the predecessor acquisition with respect to the predecessor; and

(2) A distribution made in connection with the predecessor acquisition to the extent the property distributed is directly or indirectly provided by the predecessor. See paragraph (k)(1)(iv) of this section.

(f) *Rules for identifying a predecessor.*—(1) *Definition of predecessor.*—A corporation or a partnership (tentative predecessor) is a predecessor with respect to a relevant entity if—

(i) The relevant entity completes a predecessor acquisition; and

(ii) After the predecessor acquisition and all related transactions are complete, the tentative predecessor ownership percentage is at least 10.

(2) *Definition of predecessor acquisition.*—(i) *In general.*—Predecessor acquisition means a transaction in which a relevant entity directly or indirectly acquires substantially all of the properties held directly or indirectly by a tentative predecessor.

(ii) *Acquisition of properties of a tentative predecessor.*—For purposes of determining whether a predecessor acquisition occurs, the principles of section 7874(a)(2)(B)(i) apply, including § 1.7874-2(c) other than § 1.7874-2(c)(2) and (4) (regarding acquisitions of properties of a domestic entity), without regard to whether the tentative predecessor is domestic or foreign.

(iii) *Lower-tier entities of a predecessor.*—If, before a predecessor acquisition and all related transactions, the predecessor held directly or indirectly stock in a corporation or an interest in a partnership, then, for purposes of this section, the relevant entity is not considered to directly or indirectly acquire the properties held directly or indirectly by the corporation or partnership.

(3) *Definition of tentative predecessor ownership percentage.*—Tentative predecessor ownership percentage means, with respect to a predecessor acquisition, the percentage of stock or partnership interests (by value) in a relevant entity held by reason of holding stock or partnership interests in the tentative predecessor. For purposes of

computing the tentative predecessor ownership percentage, the following rules apply:

(i) For purposes of determining the stock or partnership interests in a relevant entity held by reason of holding stock or partnership interests in the tentative predecessor, the principles of section 7874(a)(2)(B)(ii) and §§1.7874-2(f)(1)(i) through (iii) and 1.7874-5 apply.

(ii) For purposes of determining the stock or partnership interests in a relevant entity included in the numerator of the fraction used to compute the tentative predecessor ownership percentage, the rules of paragraph (f)(3)(i) of this section apply, and all the rules applicable to calculating the numerator of an ownership fraction with respect to a domestic entity acquisition apply, except that—

(A) The principles of section 7874(c)(2)(A) and §§1.7874-1 and 1.7874-6 do not apply; and

(B) The principles of paragraph (b) of this section do not apply.

(iii) For purposes of determining stock or partnership interests in a relevant entity included in the denominator of the fraction used to compute the tentative predecessor ownership percentage, the principles of section 7874(a)(2)(B)(ii) and all rules applicable to calculating the denominator of an ownership fraction with respect to a domestic entity acquisition apply, except that—

(A) The principles of section 7874(c)(2)(A) and §§1.7874-1 and 1.7874-6 do not apply; and

(B) The principles of §§1.7874-4 and 1.7874-7 through 1.7874-9 do not apply.

(g) *Rule regarding direction of a section 355 distribution.*—For purposes of this section, if a domestic corporation (distributing corporation) distributes the stock of another domestic corporation (controlled corporation) pursuant to a transaction described in section 355, and, immediately before the distribution, the fair market value of the stock of the controlled corporation owned by the distributing corporation and any related person (determined under section 7874(d)(3), without regard to whether the person is foreign) represents more than 50 percent of the fair market value of the stock of the distributing corporation, then, the controlled corporation is deemed, on the date of the distribution, to have distributed the stock of the distributing corporation. The deemed distribution is equal to the fair market value of the stock of the distributing corporation (but not taking into account the fair market value of the stock of the controlled corporation) on the date of the distribution.

(h) *Allocation of NOCD stock.*—NOCD stock is allocated among the former domestic entity shareholders or former domestic entity partners, as applicable, based on the amount of NOCDs that the former domestic entity shareholders or former domestic entity partners, as applicable, are treated as having received under this paragraph (h). Under this paragraph (h), a pro rata portion of each distribution during a look-back year is treated as comprising an NOCD with respect to the look-back year, based on a fraction the numerator of which is the amount of NOCDs during the look-back year and the denominator of which is the amount of distributions during the look-back year. Thus, each former domestic entity shareholder or former domestic entity partner, as applicable, is treated as receiving an amount of NOCD stock equal to the amount of NOCDs treated as received by the former domestic entity shareholder or former domestic entity partner, as applicable.

(i) *Multiple foreign acquiring corporations.*—If there are multiple foreign acquiring corporations with respect to a domestic entity acquisition, then the foreign acquiring corporation or corporations as to which NOCD stock is considered comprised is based on the proportion of consideration directly or indirectly provided by a foreign acquiring corporation in the domestic entity acquisition relative to the total amount of consideration directly or indirectly provided by the foreign acquiring corporations in the domestic entity acquisition. For purposes of this paragraph (i), consideration is not considered directly provided by a foreign acquiring corporation if it was indirectly provided by another foreign acquiring corporation. In addition, for purposes of this paragraph (i), consideration provided in the domestic entity acquisition does not include money or other property described in paragraph (k)(1)(iii) of this section.

(j) *Multiple domestic entities.*—If pursuant to §1.7874-2(e) two or more domestic entities are treated as a single domestic entity, then the determination of the amount of NOCDs made by the single domestic entity is made by—

(1) Applying the rules of this section to each domestic entity on a separate basis, with the result that the amount of NOCDs made by each domestic entity is separately computed; and

(2) Treating the amount of NOCDs made by the single domestic entity as the sum of the separately computed NOCDs made by each domestic entity.

(k) *Definitions.*—In addition to the definitions provided in §1.7874-12, the following definitions apply for purposes of this section.

(1) A *distribution* means the following:

(i) Any distribution made by a corporation with respect to its stock other than—

(A) A distribution to which section 305 applies;

(B) A distribution to which section 304(a)(1) applies; and

(C) Except as provided in paragraphs (k)(1)(iii) and (iv) of this section, a distribution pursuant to section 361(c)(1) (other than a distribution to which section 355 applies).

(ii) Any distribution by a partnership (other than a distribution pursuant to section 752(b) to the extent that the transaction giving rise to such distribution does not reduce the partnership's value).

(iii) In the case of a domestic entity, a transfer of money or other property to the former domestic entity shareholders or former domestic entity partners that is made in connection with the domestic entity acquisition to the extent the money or other property is directly or indirectly provided by the domestic entity.

(iv) In the case of a predecessor, a transfer of money or other property to the former owners of the predecessor that is made in connection with the predecessor acquisition to the extent the money or other property is directly or indirectly provided by the predecessor.

(2) *Distribution history period.*—(i) *In general.*—Except as provided in paragraph (k)(2)(ii) or (iii) of this section, a distribution history period means, with respect to a look-back year, the 36-month period preceding the start of the look-back year.

(ii) *Formation date less than 36 months but at least 12 months before look-back year.*—If the formation date is less than 36 months, but at least 12 months, before the start of a look-back year, then the distribution history period with respect to that look-back year means the entire period, starting with the formation date, that precedes the start of the look-back year.

(iii) *Formation date less than 12 months before look-back year.*—If the formation date is less than 12 months before the start of a look-back year, then there is no distribution history period with respect to that look-back year.

(3) *Formation date* means, with respect to a domestic entity, the date that the domestic entity was created or organized, or, if earlier, the earliest date that any predecessor of the domestic entity was created or organized.

(4) *Look-back period* means, with respect to a domestic acquisition, the 36-month period ending on the completion date or, if shorter, the entire period, starting with the formation date, that ends on the completion date.

(5) *Look-back year* means, with respect to a look-back period, the following:

(i) If the look-back period is 36 months, the three consecutive 12-month periods that comprise the look-back period.

(ii) If the look-back period is less than 36 months, but at least 24 months-

(A) The 12-month period that ends on the completion date;

(B) The 12-month period that immediately precedes the period described in paragraph (k)(5)(ii)(A) of this section; and

(C) The period, if any, that immediately precedes the period described in paragraph (k)(5)(ii)(B) of this section.

(iii) If the look-back period is less than 24 months, but at least 12 months—

(A) The 12-month period that ends on the completion date; and

(B) The period, if any, that immediately precedes the period described in paragraph (k)(5)(iii)(A) of this section.

(iv) If the look-back period is less than 12 months, the entire period, starting with the formation date, that ends on the completion date.

(6) *NOCDs* mean, with respect to a look-back year, the excess of all distributions made during the look-back year over the NOCD threshold for the look-back year.

(7) *NOCD threshold* means, with respect to a look-back year, the following:

(i) If the look-back year has at least a 12-month distribution history period, 110 percent of the sum of all distributions made during the distribution history period multiplied by a fraction. The numerator of the fraction is the number of days in the look-back year and the denominator is the number of days in the distribution history period with respect to the look-back year.

(ii) If the look-back year has no distribution history period, zero.

(l) *Applicability date.*—This section applies to domestic entity acquisitions completed on or after July 12, 2018. For domestic entity acquisitions completed before July 12, 2018, see § 1.7874-10T, as contained in 26 CFR part 1 revised as of April 1, 2017. However, to the extent this section differs from § 1.7874-10T, as contained in 26 CFR part 1 revised as of April 1, 2017, taxpayers may elect to consistently apply the differences to domestic entity acquisitions completed before July 12, 2018. [Reg. § 1.7874-10.]

□ [*T.D.* 9834, 7-11-2018.]

§ 1.7874-11. Rules regarding inversion gain.—(a) *Scope.*—This section provides rules for determining the inversion gain of an expatriated entity for purposes of section 7874. Paragraph (b) of this section provides rules for determining the inversion gain of an expatriated entity. Paragraph (c) of this section provides special rules with respect to certain foreign partnerships in which an expatriated entity owns an interest. Paragraph (d) of this section provides additional definitions. Paragraph (e) of this section provides an example that illustrates the rules of this section. Paragraph (f) of this section provides the applicability dates.

(b) *Inversion gain.*—(1) *General rule.*—Except as provided in paragraphs (b)(2) and (3) of this section, inversion gain includes income (including an amount treated as a dividend under section 78) or gain recognized by an expatriated entity for any taxable year that includes any portion of the applicable period by reason of a direct or indirect transfer of stock or other properties or license of any property either as part of the domestic entity acquisition, or after such acquisition if the transfer or license is to a specified related person.

(2) *Exception for property described in section 1221(a)(1).*—Inversion gain does not include income or gain recognized by reason of the transfer or license, after the domestic entity acquisition, of property that is described in section 1221(a)(1) in the hands of the transferor or licensor.

(3) *Treatment of partnerships.*—Except to the extent provided in paragraph (c) of this section and section 7874(e)(2), inversion gain does not include income or gain recognized by reason of the transfer or license of property by a partnership.

(c) *Transfers and licenses by partnerships.*—If a partnership that is a foreign related person transfers or licenses property, a partner of the partnership shall be treated as having transferred or licensed its proportionate share of that property, as determined under the rules and principles of sections 701 through 777, for purposes of determining the inversion gain of an expatriated entity. See section 7874(e)(2) for rules regarding the treatment of transfers and licenses by domestic partnerships and transfers of interests in certain domestic partnerships.

(d) *Definitions.*—The definitions provided in § 1.7874-12 apply for purposes of this section.

(e) *Example.*—The following example illustrates the rules of this section.

Example—(i) *Facts.* On July 1, 2016, FA, a foreign corporation, acquires all the stock of DT, a domestic corporation, in an inversion transaction. When the inversion transaction occurred, DT wholly owned FS, a foreign corporation that is a controlled foreign corporation (within the meaning of section 957(a)). During the applicable period, FS sells to FA property that is not described in section 1221(a)(1) in the hands of FS. Under section 951(a)(1)(A), DT has a $80x gross income inclusion that is attributable to FS's gain from the sale of the property. Under section 960(a)(1), DT is deemed to have paid $20x of the post-1986 foreign income taxes of FS by reason of this income inclusion and includes $20x in gross income as a deemed dividend under section 78. Accordingly, DT recognizes $100x ($80x + $20x) of gross income because of FS's sale of property to FA.

(ii) *Analysis.* Pursuant to section 7874(a)(2)(A), DT is an expatriated entity. Under paragraph (b)(1) of this section, DT's $100x gross income recognized under sections 951(a)(1)(A) and 78 is inversion gain, because it is income recognized by an expatriated entity during the applicable period by reason of an indirect transfer of property by DT (through its wholly-owned CFC, FS) after the inversion transaction to a specified related person (FA). Sections 7874(a)(1) and (e) therefore prevent the use of certain tax attributes (such as net operating losses) to reduce the U.S. tax owed with respect to DT's $100x gross income recognized under sections 951(a)(1)(A) and 78.

(f) *Applicability dates.*—Except as otherwise provided in this paragraph (f), this section applies to transfers and licenses of property completed on or after November 19, 2015, but only if the inversion transaction was completed on or after September 22, 2014. For inversion transactions completed on or after September 22, 2014, however, taxpayers may elect to apply paragraph (b) of this section by excluding the phrase "(including an amount treated as a dividend under section 78)" for transfers and licenses of property completed on or after November 19, 2015, and before April 4, 2016. [Reg. § 1.7874-11.]

□ [*T.D.* 9834, 7-11-2018.]

§ 1.7874-12. Definitions.—(a) *Definitions.*—Except as otherwise provided, the following definitions apply for purposes of this section and § § 1.367(b)-4, 1.956-2, 1.7701(l)-4, and 1.7874-1 through 1.7874-11.

(1) An *affiliated group* has the meaning set forth in section 1504(a) but without regard to section 1504(b)(3), except that section 1504(a) is applied by substituting "more than 50 percent" for "at least 80 percent" each place it appears. A *member of the affiliated group* is an entity included in the affiliated group.

(2) The *applicable period* means, with respect to an inversion transaction, the period described in section 7874(d)(1). However, see also § 1.7874-2(b)(13) in the case of a subsequent acquisition (or a similar acquisition under the principles of § 1.7874-2(c)(4)(i)) that is an inversion transaction.

(3) The *completion date* means, with respect to a domestic entity acquisition, the date that the domestic entity acquisition and all transactions related to the domestic entity acquisition are complete.

(4) A *controlled foreign corporation* (or *CFC*) has the meaning provided in section 957.

(5) A *domestic entity acquisition* means an acquisition described in section 7874(a)(2)(B)(i).

(6) A *domestic entity* means, with respect to a domestic entity acquisition, a domestic corporation or domestic partnership described in section 7874(a)(2)(B)(i). A reference to a domestic entity includes a successor to such domestic corporation or domestic partnership, including a corporation that succeeds to and takes into account amounts with respect to the domestic entity pursuant to section 381.

(7) An *expanded affiliated group* (or *EAG*) means, with respect to a domestic entity acquisition, an affiliated group that includes the foreign acquiring corporation, determined as of the completion date. A *member of the EAG* is an entity included in the EAG, and a reference to a member of the EAG includes a predecessor with respect to such member.

(8) An *expatriated entity* means, with respect to an inversion transaction—

(i) The domestic entity; and

(ii) A United States person that, on any date on or after the completion date, is or was related (within the meaning of section 267(b) or 707(b)(1)) to the domestic entity.

(9) *Expatriated foreign subsidiary.*—(i) *General rule.*—Except as provided in paragraph (a)(9)(ii) of this section, an expatriated foreign subsidiary means a foreign corporation that is a CFC (determined without applying subparagraphs (A), (B), and (C) of section 318(a)(3) so as to consider a United States person as owning stock which is owned by a person who is not a United States person) and in which an expatriated entity is a United States shareholder (determined without applying subparagraphs (A), (B), and (C) of section 318(a)(3) so as to consider a United States person as owning stock which is owned by a person who is not a United States person).

(ii) *Exception to the general rule.*—A foreign corporation is not an expatriated foreign subsidiary if, with respect to the inversion transaction as a result of which the foreign corporation otherwise would be an expatriated foreign subsidiary—

(A) On the completion date, the foreign corporation was both a CFC (determined without applying subparagraphs (A), (B), and (C) of section 318(a)(3) so as to consider a United States person as owning stock which is owned by a person who is not a United States person) and a member of the EAG; and

(B) On or before the completion date, the domestic entity was not a United States shareholder (determined without applying subparagraphs (A), (B), and (C) of section 318(a)(3) so as to consider a United States person as owning stock which is owned by a person who is not a United States person) with respect to the foreign corporation.

(10) A *foreign acquiring corporation* means, with respect to a domestic entity acquisition, the foreign corporation described in section 7874(a)(2)(B). A reference to a foreign acquiring corporation includes a successor to the foreign acquiring corporation, including a corporation that succeeds to and takes into account amounts with respect to the foreign acquiring corporation pursuant to section 381.

(11) A *foreign related person* means, with respect to an inversion transaction, a foreign person that is related (within the meaning of section 267(b) or 707(b)(1)) to, or under the same common control as (within the meaning of section 482), a person that is an expatriated entity with respect to the inversion transaction.

(12) A *former domestic entity partner* of a domestic entity that is a domestic partnership is any person that held an interest in the partnership before the domestic entity acquisition, including any person that holds an interest in the partnership both before and after the domestic entity acquisition.

(13) A *former domestic entity shareholder* of a domestic entity that is a domestic corporation is any person that held stock in the domestic corporation before the domestic entity acquisition, including any person that holds stock in the domestic corporation both before and after the domestic entity acquisition.

(14) An *interest in a partnership* includes a capital or profits interest.

(15) An *inversion transaction* means a domestic entity acquisition in which the foreign acquiring corporation is treated as a surrogate foreign corporation under section 7874(a)(2)(B), taking into account section 7874(a)(3).

(16) A *non-EFS foreign related person* means, with respect to an inversion transaction, a foreign related person that is not an expatriated foreign subsidiary.

(17) The *ownership fraction* means, with respect to a domestic entity acquisition, the ownership percentage described in section 7874(a)(2)(B)(ii), expressed as a fraction.

(18) A *specified related person* means, with respect to an inversion transaction—

(i) A non-EFS foreign related person;

(ii) A domestic partnership in which a non-EFS foreign related person is a partner; and

(iii) A domestic trust of which a non-EFS foreign related person is a beneficiary.

(19) A *United States person* means a person described in section 7701(a)(30).

(20) A *United States shareholder* has the meaning provided in section 951(b).

(b) *Applicability dates.*—Except as otherwise provided in this paragraph (b), this section applies to domestic entity acquisitions completed on or after September 22, 2014. The following apply to domestic entity acquisitions completed on or after April 4, 2016: paragraph (a)(8) of this section; in paragraph (a)(6) of this section, the phrase ", including a corporation that succeeds to and takes into account amounts with respect to the domestic entity pursuant to section 381"; and the second sentence of paragraph (a)(10) of this section. For domestic entity acquisitions completed on or after September 22, 2014, and before April 4, 2016, however, taxpayers, may elect to apply the provisions in the immediately prior sentence. [Reg. § 1.7874-12.]

☐ [*T.D.* 9834, 7-11-2018.]

INDEX TO CODE

References are to Code Section numbers.

INDEX TO REGULATIONS

References are to Reg. § numbers; boldface references are to proposed Reg. § numbers.

A

B

C